A Reader's Guide to
DEVON ISLAND

Making Special Note of those Locations Mentioned in the Graphic Novel

CRATER XV

N

BJORNE PENINSULA

YDKAP ICE CAP

ESMERE ISLAND

HELM PENINSULA

South Cape Fiord

ESMERE ISLAND

Todd Bay

South Cape
CAPE WILDGRAVE

SOUTH CAPE

Pilir & Vijjuk Bay

Tern Cove

Beckham Fiord

MASON ICEFIELD

Smith Bay

CAPE NORTON SHAW

Glacier Strait

es Sound

Smith

r Bay

E SVARTEN

Sverdrup
Inlet

CAPE SPARBO
CAPE HARDY

Brae
Bay

CAPE SKOGN

CAPE
NEWMAN
SMITH

TRUELOVE
LOWLANDS

WARD
POINT

TREUTER MOUNTAINS

BELCHER
POINT

Lady Ann Strait

CAPE
CALEDON

CAPE
FITZ ROY

JOHNSON
POINT

Bowden
Bay

CAPE
PARKER

HODGSON HEAD

Coburg
Island
Prison

CAPE
SPENCE

PHILLIPS
POINT

MARINA
PENINSULA

CAMBRIDGE
POINT

COBURG
ISLAND

ISLAND

DEVON ICE CAP

CUNNINGHAM MOUNTAINS

Dundas Harbour
(Abandoned)

Monty
Peak

Hyde Inlet

PHILPOTS
ISLAND

Bethune
Point

BEATRICE
POINT

CAPE
SHERARD

CAPE HORSBURGH

CAPE COCKBURN

Croker
Bay

CAPE ROSAMOND
CAPE RIBEN

CAPE RUBEN

CARDSON BAY
WARREN POINT
DUNDAS HARBOUR
LEMIEUX POINT

CAPE WARRENDER

acy
e

Burnett Inlet

Powell Inlet

Cuming Inlet

Elephant
Cape
CAPE PENHORN

Strathona Inlet

Baffin Bay

Lancaster Sound
(Parry Channel)

2012 Kevin Cannon

CRATER XV

by Kevin Cannon

TOP SHELF PRODUCTIONS

ATLANTA / PORTLAND

ISBN 978-1-60309-100-8

1. NAUTICAL FICTION
2. SPACE TRAVEL
3. GRAPHIC NOVELS

PUBLISHED BY TOP SHELF PRODUCTIONS,
P.O. BOX 1282, MARIETTA, GEORGIA
30061-1282, UNITED STATES OF AMERICA.

PUBLISHERS: BRETT WARNOCK AND CHRIS STAROS.

TOP SHELF PRODUCTIONS® AND THE TOP SHELF LOGO ARE
REGISTERED TRADEMARKS OF TOP SHELF PRODUCTIONS, INC.
VISIT OUR ONLINE CATALOG AT WWW.TOPSHELFCOMIX.COM.

FIRST PRINTING, MAY 2013

PRINTED IN CHINA

DISCARD

OLD AGE DIVINES WITH GLASSES ON
AND SEES THE GRAVE BEFORE IT YAWN,
ALL THOUGHTS OF TIME RETURNING -- GROUNDLESS;
NO MATTER: CHILDISH HOPE APPEARS
TO MURMUR LIES IN AGED EARS.

-- ALEXANDER PUSHKIN, EUGENE ONEGIN

PROLOGUE

"While no one blames Mr. Shanks for mourning the loss of his nephew, Alistair...

"...or the other lives lost (which can be read about at great length in our previous articles on the subject)...

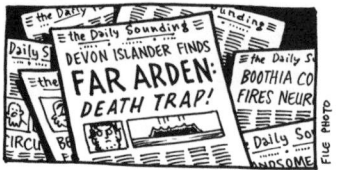

"...the Devon Island public simply cannot stand the depraved acts he has engineered since the Far Arden tragedy. *Scotch raids,* *meat looting,* and even *newsstand break-ins* are now near nightly occurrences.

[ARTIST'S INTERPRETATION]

"And while critics point out that the man himself has never been caught in the act, it is clear to this writer that a ship as aimless and dented as Army Shanks -- whether guilty of these offenses or not -- is a ship we don't want in our fair arctic port.

"Which is why this writer does not hesitate to say to our community's fallen hero: ..."

8

9

I

In an abandoned whaling station on the Northwest Peninsula of DEVON ISLAND lives a man as cold and unforgiving as the arctic itself...

ARMY SHANKS
ARCTIC PIRATE

"Crater XV"

23

24

DON'T LIGHT THAT OUT **HERE**, MY LOVE!

WE WANT TO REMAIN **UNNOTICED** BY THE CANADIANS...

27

28

29

ALRIGHT, WHO'S NEXT?

GIMME A TICKET FOR THE BAY OF WHALES.

YOU KNOW THAT'S BAY OF WHALES, **ANTARCTICA**, DON'T YOU?

THAT SIGN IS JUST THE **LAST STOP** IN THE SERVICE -- YOU DON'T ACTUALLY HAVE TO **GO** THERE.

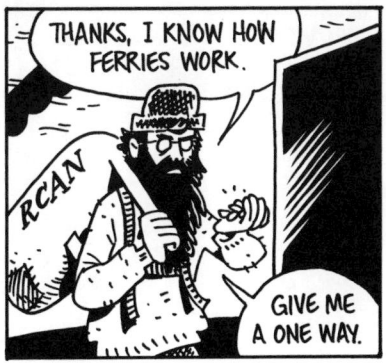

THANKS, I KNOW HOW FERRIES WORK.

GIVE ME A ONE WAY.

...WANT TO MAKE A **DONATION**?

?

MY NAME IS **WENDY BYRD**, AND I'M TRYING TO RAISE--

OH GOOD, THERE ARE MORE OF YOU! MY NAME IS...

I S'POSE YOU THINK SHE'S **CUTE**, HUH?

EH?

SHE'S A SOUTHERN GIRL-- NEWFOUNDLAND.

SPIT!

THE **WHOLE TRIP** HERE, SHE WOULDN'T SHUT UP ABOUT HOW SHE'S GOING TO BECOME A **WORLD TRAVELER**.

TRYING TO RAISE MONEY TO GO TO **EUROPE**.

YOU KNOW WHAT I TOLD HER...

FROM PICKING UP GARBAGE...
...TO MONITORING WEATHER...
...TO FEEDING NEWS TO
THE PRESS...

...IT ALL HAPPENS **HERE**, UNDER THIS ROOF!

SEE, DEVON ISLAND -- AND **MANY** OF THE GREAT CANADIAN ARCTIC ISLANDS -- ARE RUN BY THE **BUREAUCRACY**.

THAT'S A **CAPITAL "B"** IF YOU'RE TAKING NOTES.

SEE, THINGS RUN SO SMOOTHLY HERE BECAUSE IN A BUREAUCRACY, OFFICIALS LIKE ME ARE **APPOINTED**.

THAT GUARANTEES WE KNOW WHAT WE'RE DOING, AND CUTS DOWN ON EXPENSIVE AND NEEDLESS **ELECTIONS**.

ADJUST

DO YOU WANT A BUNCH OF **KNOW-NOTHINGS** CHOOSING YOUR REPRESENTATIVES?

OF COURSE YOU DON'T!

YAWN!

LOSING INTEREST

UH... LET'S SWITCH GEARS... WHAT PART OF GOVERNMENT ARE **YOU** INTERESTED IN?

UM...

PIRATES!

AH! YOU MUST MEAN **RCAN**, OR "ROYAL CANADIAN ARCTIC NAVY."

RCAN

LET'S SNEAK A PEEK AT THE MEN WHO CONTROL OUR WATERS!

OH.

YOU LIKE SWORD FIGHTING? JUST THINK, ONE DAY YOU COULD BE PROCESSING SWORD-RELATED WORKERS' COMP CLAIMS... RIGHT FROM THIS VERY ROOM!

NO, WE WANT TO BE PIRATES! LIKE ARMY SHANKS!

the Daily Sounding

THIS MAN SHANKS IS A MENACE!

NO OFFENSE, KID, BUT THIS "ARCTIC PIRATE" PERSONA DOESN'T EXIST.

I ACTUALLY KNOW ARMY SHANKS...

39

...WHICH IS WHY THE **HIGH ARCTIC LEAGUE (HAL)** WAS FORMED.

HAL
HIGH ARCTIC LEAGUE

"**CANADA** IS A MEMBER, AS ARE THE OTHER SIX NATIONS THAT INHABIT ARCTIC WATERS.

"**HAL** HANDLES WHAT **RCAN** CANNOT: INTERNATIONAL BOUNDARY DISPUTES, CLIMATE ISSUES, MAPPING PROJECTS..."

...AND **I** AM AT THE CENTER OF IT, AS THE ASSISTANT TO **KEN ARLUK**, CANADA'S AMBASSADOR!

UH... EXCUSE ME FOR A SEC...

HELLO?

41

43

...SEEMS THEY'VE FINALLY COME TO THEIR **SENSES!**

NET

II

WHAT **ARE** THOSE THINGS??

MORE THAN I BARGAINED FOR.

...NOW START SWINGING!

OKAY, LET ME EXPLAIN WHAT'S GOING TO HAPPEN. IT'S A LITTLE **CLICHÉD**, SO BEAR WITH ME.

CRANE

YOU'RE GONNA **CRAB** 'EM!!

RIGHT. I'M GOING TO LOWER THE NET INTO THE CRABS. ...BUT **VERY SLOWLY!**

SLOW

CRANE

THAT WILL HEIGHTEN THE **TENSION** -- AND ULTIMATE **ENJOYMENT** OF--

LOOK!!

SWING WILDLY!

SCREW IT.

I'LL JUST THROW 'EM IN THE DRINK.

BARTY, I DON'T KNOW WHAT THE HELL YOU SAID TO THAT TOUR GROUP, BUT **KEEP IT UP!**

THANK YOU, MR. ARLUK!

IT'S GOOD TO SEE YOUNG PEOPLE SO MOTIVATED TO BE **PUBLIC SERVANTS!**

KEN ARLUK

I'D BUY YOU A BEER IF WE WEREN'T SO DAMN BUSY WITH THIS **HAL SUMMIT** HAPPENING TOMORROW.

ACTUALLY, I DON'T DRIN--

MAYBE I'M PUTTING TOO MUCH PRESSURE ON MYSELF TO MAKE THIS YEAR'S SUMMIT **FLAWLESS.**

BUT IT'S THE **FIRST TIME** IT'S ON DEVON ISLAND...

...AND I'LL BE DAMNED IF **BARROW** HOSTS FIVE YEARS IN A ROW!

OH, I ALMOST FORGOT, THERE'S A **MESSAGE**...

...FROM **RCAN!**

AND SO...

IT'S A **HUGE** SHIP, MR. ARLUK. MAYBE AN **OIL TANKER** OR A **CRUISE LINER**.

WE'RE TRACKING IT CLOSELY, BUT HAVEN'T MADE CONTACT.

FRANKLY, SIR, I'M WONDERING IF THIS ISN'T SOME **GRAND, UNANNOUNCED ENTRANCE** BY ONE OF THE **HAL AMBASSADORS**?

GOOD THOUGHT, SAILOR... BUT I'M CERTAIN THAT EVERY AMBASSADOR HAS ALREADY ARRIVED.

GATHER ALL AVAILABLE CUTTERS, SAILOR, BUT DON'T MAKE CONTACT UNTIL I GET THERE.

YES, SIR!

GRAB YOUR COAT, BARTY--WE'RE GOING TO MEET OUR INTRUDER...

...FACE TO FACE!

LATER...

SO THEN, WHAT ARE YOU DOING **HERE**? ON **DEVON**, I MEAN.

FUNDRAISING, UNFORTUNATELY... TRYING TO RAISE MONEY TO JOIN THE **NEWFOUNDLAND EUROPA PROJECT (NEP)**.

THEY'RE A PRIVATE SPACE PROGRAM TRAINING YOUTH ASTRONAUTS TO GO TO EUROPA.

THEY'RE ACTUALLY TESTING THEIR **MOON BASE** OUT HERE, ON DEVON ISLAND'S **HAUGHTON CRATER**.

NEWFOUNDLAND EUROPA PROJECT

HAUGHTON CRATER

DEVON ISLAND

NEP

SEE, DEVON ISLAND IS THE BEST PLACE IN THE **WORLD** TO SIMULATE LIVING ON ANOTHER PLANET.

THE CLIMATE, THE TERRAIN, THE ISOLATION--

--IT'S JUST PERFECT!

57

58

MEANWHILE, ON ANOTHER SIDE OF DEVON ISLAND...

IT'S CLEARLY HERE FOR **OIL**, MR. ARLUK.

I MEAN, IT STOPPED RIGHT ON TOP OF THE **LEACOCK OIL FIELD!**

NO, THAT'S TOO OBVIOUS. IT MUST BE CONNECTED SOMEHOW TO TOMORROW'S **HIGH ARCTIC LEAGUE SUMMIT.**

WE NEED SOMEONE TO **INFILTRATE** THAT TANKER, MR. ARLUK.

BUT HE CAN'T BE ON THE GOVERNMENT'S **PAYROLL**-- THAT'LL GIVE US **PLAUSIBLE DENIABILITY** IF HE'S CAUGHT.

WE NEED SOMEONE ON THE **FRINGE** OF SOCIETY, WITH NOTHING LEFT TO LIVE FOR, BUT WHO'S ALSO GOT TOP-LEVEL **RCAN TRAINING.**

the Daily Sounding

THIS MAN SHANKS IS A MENACE !!!

by LARKIN TIPE

FILE PHOTO

EYEBROW RAISE!

64

WHAT A WEIRD GUY.

SAY, MISS?

IT'S **WENDY**, RIGHT?

IT'S NONE OF MY BUSINESS, I REALIZE, BUT...

...I DON'T KNOW HOW LONG YOU'RE PLANNING ON STAYING IN DEVON, BUT I WOULDN'T GET TOO ATTACHED TO OLD **ARMY SHANKS.**

LOOK A' **THIS.**

ANTARCTICA-- OH, WHAT A NICE VACATION!

IT'S **SIMPLE**. YOU SNEAK ABOARD A **FREIGHT ROCKET** (THE SALT SHAKER)...

...WAIT UNTIL YOU GET INTO **SPACE**...

...THEN **COMMANDEER** THE SHIP, THROW THE CREW OVERBOARD, AND YOU'RE **HOME FREE** TO EUROPA!

THAT'S HOW I GOT TO **HANS ISLAND** ONCE-- WORKED LIKE A CHARM!

UH, YOU DON'T KNOW MUCH ABOUT **SPACE TRAVEL**, DO YOU?

HEY!

EVERYONE PAY ATTENTION TO WHAT I'M SAYING!

WE'RE ABOUT TO GET A VISIT FROM--

III

GOOD TO SEE YOU TOO, ARMY! LOOKS LIKE **LORD BEARDMORE'S** BEEN TREATING YOU WELL!

HEY!

STROKE

MR. SHANKS -- IF I MAY INTERRUPT--

-- I JUST WANT TO SAY HOW SORRY I AM ABOUT YOUR **NEPHEW**. LAST YEAR'S **FAR ARDEN** TRAGEDY MUST WEIGH HEAVILY ON YOU.

PLEASE KNOW THAT THE HIGH ARCTIC LEAGUE CONSIDERS YOU A **HERO**. YOUR WORK IN FINDING THAT **DEADLY ISLAND** WILL NO DOUBT SAVE **TENS** OF LIVES.

HRMPH.

YOU TWO'RE BUTTERING ME UP PRETTY **GOOD**.

WHICH MEANS WHATEVER YOU'RE ABOUT TO ASK ME TO DO...

"...MUST BE PRETTY **BAD**."

YOU'RE **WASTING** YOUR TIME.

I **KNOW** THE *LUNAYEV*.

SHE'S AN **OIL** TANKER. THIS "MOON ROCKET" STUFF IS CLEARLY A **BLUFF**.

TRANSCRIPT

"KOHLER AND I USED TO RUN 'ERRANDS' IN THE **FAROES**, AND I SAW THE *LUNAYEV* THERE.

"SHE'S ONE OF **HANDSOME JACK'S** SHIPS, I THINK ... ALTHOUGH THAT WAS A PRETTY LONG TIME AGO."

LUNAYEV

ANYWAY, THAT **EXTRA SILO** YOU TALKED ABOUT IS PROBABLY CARRYING **CONTRABAND**...

TRANS

79

83

AND WHO IS THIS **WENDY**, IF YOU DON'T MIND ME ASKING?

AN OLD FLAME YOU WANT TO SEND INTO OUTER SPACE?

OH, SOMEONE I MET THIS MORNING, ACTUALLY.

I DON'T REALLY KNOW HER...

SHRUG

"...BUT SHE REMINDS ME OF A GIRL I KNEW GROWING UP.

BEECHEY ORPHANAGE

"SHE WAS CALLED **PRAVDA**. NOT HER REAL NAME, OBVIOUSLY, BUT THAT'S WHAT WAS WRITTEN ON HER COLLAR WHEN SHE SHOWED UP AT THE ORPHANAGE.

"PRAVDA WAS A WILD KID, AND SHE BROUGHT A LOT OF COLOR TO A PRETTY GRAY EXISTENCE."

BUT I HAVEN'T SEEN HER SINCE--

WE'RE HERE!

AND SO...

RCAN BRIEFING ROOM

BENDRIX? ARE YOU READY FOR US?

AH, YES! COME IN!

HELLO, I'M **MORRIS BENDRIX**. AND LET ME JUST SAY, MR. SHANKS...

...HOW **DELIGHTED** I AM THAT YOU'RE COMING OUT OF **RETIREMENT** TO HELP THE NAVY ONCE AGAIN!

!

"RETIREMENT"??
THE LAST TIME I WORE AN RCAN UNIFORM WAS WHEN YOU GUYS **EXILED** ME TO **EGLINTON ISLAND**...

...PRESUMABLY TO MY **DEATH**!

...OH, ER...

FOR CHRISSAKE, BENDRIX, HE'S JUST HELPING US OUT WITH THIS **ONE** JOB...

...AS A **FREELANCER**.

RIGHT, THEN-- ON TO THE PRESENTATION!

CLAP!

YOUR ASSIGN-MENT, OF COURSE, IS TO **BOARD** THE **LUNAYEV** TO FIND EVIDENCE OF A **ROCKET**.

IF YOU **FIND** ONE, THEN RCAN MUST ABIDE BY **HAL STATUTE 106-41** AND BACK OFF.

CAN ?&D

BUT IF THERE'S **NO EVIDENCE** OF SPACE FLIGHT, THEN WE HAVE **REA-SONABLE CAUSE** TO ATTACK.

WHICH IS WHAT WE WANT!

HOWEVER, MR. SHANKS, SPACE FLIGHT HAS CHANGED A LOT SINCE THE GOOD OL' DAYS OF THE **CANADIAN ARCTIC SPACE AGENCY (CASA)**.

THE **ROCKET** YOU'RE LOOKING FOR MAY NOT ACTUALLY LOOK LIKE ANY ROCKET YOU'VE SEEN BEFORE. LET ME EXPLAIN:

CLICK

FOCUS -- AND CENTER

BEEP! HERE'S THE SOVIET R7 --

R7

-- THE ROCKET THAT PUT THE FIRST MAN IN SPACE.

BEEP! CUT TO MODERN DAY. THIS **PROTON** ROCKET LAUNCHES MOST OF THE WORLD'S SATELLITES.

PROTON

BEEP! AND HERE ARE SOME OF THE ROCKETS THAT LAUNCHED THE AMERICANS. NOTE THE VARIATIONS.

TITAN

SATURN V

RED-STONE

BEEP! AND THIS IS A **RAILGUN**.

RAILGUN

HERE, HIGH VOLTAGE RAILS **SHOOT** A ROCKET INTO SPACE -- WITHOUT USING COMBUSTIBLE FUEL.

PFFT! IS THAT EVEN **POSSIBLE**?

YES, IT'S **VERY** POSSIBLE!

WHAT I DON'T UNDERSTAND IS, IF THEY'VE GOT A ROCKET, WHY NOT LAUNCH IT FROM **SIBERIA**?

WHY **HERE**?

ACTUALLY, THERE ARE A **NUMBER** OF SOUND REASONS WHY THE LAUNCH LOCATION MATTERS.

FLIP!

HOPEFULLY, WHAT YOU FIND ONBOARD...

... EVEN A SMALL CHARGE PACKS A **WALLOP**!

USE SOME IF YOU COME TO A **LOCKED DOOR**, AS A LITTLE BIT OF THIS'LL BLOW IT **WIDE OPEN**!

ALSO, THIS SHOE HAS **GARROTE WIRE** FOR LACES...

... AND THIS INNOCENT-LOOKING FOUNTAIN PEN EMITS A **POTENT GAS** IF YOU TWIST THE CAP 45°!!

YOU'LL SOON HOP ABOARD A COMPLETELY **UNDETECTABLE** **SUBMERSIBLE**...

...WHICH WILL SHUTTLE YOU **UNDERWATER**...

...**ATTACH** TO THE TANKER'S **HULL** LIKE A BARNACLE...

...AND **DRILL** AN **ENTRY HOLE** FOR YOU TO SQUEEZE INTO!

SHANKS

LUNAYEV

POSIBLE ROCKET?

?

SUBMERSIBLE VEHICLE

92

IV

WAKE UP SUDDENLY

STRUGGLE

WELCOME ABOARD, SHANKS! I ALMOST DIDN'T **RE-COGNIZE** YOU!

YOU'VE HAD A VISIT FROM **LORD BEARDMORE** SINCE I LAST SAW YOU!

SZTAB?!

?!?

SZTAB, IS THAT **YOU**?!

BUT I THOUGHT YOU **PLUMMETED** TO YOUR **DEATH** DURING HANDSOME JACK'S INFAMOUS "PICNIC ON THE VESTMANNA BIRD CLIFFS"!!

AH YES, THE **VESTMANNA** AFFAIR...

...THANKS FOR **REMINDING** ME.

100

I'M **SUR-PRISED** AT YOU, SHANKS! WORKING AS A **SPY** FOR RCAN!

BACK ON THE FAROES, YOU HAD NOTHING BUT **VENOM** FOR THAT BLOATED INSTITUTION.

BUT **NOW** LOOK AT YOU. A WITHERED OLD MAN, SNEAKING ONBOARD TO SNEAK A **GLIMPSE** AT OUR **ROCKET**.

YOU KNOW... ...THAT SEEMS ALMOST **SEXUAL** IF YOU LOOK AT IT FROM A **SYMBOLIC** STANDPOINT.

THAT'S A DEFT INTERPRETATION, DMITRI, BUT IGNORES THE FACT THAT OUR MAN SHANKS IS COMPLETELY LACKING IN SUBTEXT.

HAR HAR HAR HAR

LET ME GO! I KNOW THERE'S **NO ROCKET**...

...AND THAT THIS WHOLE CHARADE IS ABOUT **STEALING OIL.**

SHRUG

BUT I DON'T CARE ABOUT ANY OF THAT.

I'M HERE FOR **PRAVDA.**

SO I'M OFFERING YOU A **DEAL:** CUT ME LOOSE, LET ME LEAVE WITH PRAVDA...

...AND I'LL TELL **RCAN** YOU'VE GOT A WHOLE **SPACE PROGRAM** ON BOARD.

NO OFFENSE, SHANKS...

105

109

110

111

IN HERE!

"CARGO"

DAMN--LOCKED!

"CARGO"

OH, ARMY...

V

125

...THE R7.

FASCINATING!

SO YEAH, THEY'VE TURNED THE *LUNAYEV* INTO A FLOATING **LAUNCH PAD**...

...BUT ISN'T ANYONE INTERESTED IN HOW I SINGLE-HANDEDLY RESCUED MY LONG LOST CHILDHOOD SWEETHEART FROM THE CLUTCHES OF HUNDREDS OF **BLOOD-THIRSTY SIBERIANS**?

beat.

UH, KEN, COULD I SEE YOU OUTSIDE FOR A MINUTE?

126

NOT TO UNDERMINE YOUR **JUDGMENT**, KEN...

...BUT TRUSTING **SHANKS** IS LIKE TRUSTING A CRACKED **THEODOLITE**!

LOOK, I REALIZE THAT ARMY SHANKS ISN'T THE MOST **TRUSTWORTHY** --

--OR **STABLE**, OR **COHERENT**, OR **EVEN-KEELED** MAN RCAN'S EVER WORKED WITH...

...BUT HIS **EYEWITNESS ACCOUNT** IS ALL WE'VE GOT TO WORK WITH RIGHT NOW.

I HAVE NO CHOICE BUT TO TRUST THAT HE SAW AN R7 ROCKET ON BOARD THE *LUNAYEV.*

OH, I BELIEVE HIM ABOUT THE **ROCKET**, KEN--

-- IT'S THE STUFF ABOUT THIS **WOMAN** I DON'T BELIEVE!

I MEAN, "LONG LOST CHILDHOOD SWEETHEART"?? WHAT IS THIS, AN EPISODE OF *STRUGGLE FOR HAPPINESS*?

HA HA

GOOD ONE!

THIS "PRAVDA" IS CLEARLY A **SPY**, SENT BY CAPTAIN SZTAB TO PREY ON SHANKS' MAJOR WEAKNESS...

...THE **LADIES**!

YEAH, IT IS A PRETTY **PREPOSTEROUS** STORY...

"...AND CONSIDERING SHANKS' TRAUMATIC LOSS OF HIS NEPHEW, ALISTAIR, A YEAR AGO..."

...IT'S LIKELY THAT THE POOR MAN IS GRASPING AT STRAWS... SEEING IN THIS SIBERIAN WOMAN SOMETHING THAT IS SIMPLY **NOT THERE.**

LIEUTENANT STWALLEY, YOU CHECK THE BUREAUCRACY'S RECORDS TO FIND ANYTHING YOU CAN ON THIS WOMAN.

YES, SIR!

AND BARTY, YOU MAKE SURE THAT RCAN IS WATCHING THAT WOMAN AT **ALL TIMES.**

LIKE WHITE ON ICE!

MEANWHILE, I'M GOING TO CALL A MEETING WITH THE BRASS...

"...TO FIGURE OUT HOW TO GET MORE TRUSTWORTHY EYES ON THAT SHIP!"

LOOK, PRAVDA, I'M NOT **BLIND.** I REALIZE YOU DON'T RECOGNIZE ME.

SO LET'S JUST GIVE IT SOME TIME TO COME BACK TO YOU. NO PRESSURE.

BUT WHEN WE GET OUT OF HERE, I'D LIKE US TO VISIT THE **ORPHANAGE.** ...MAYBE THAT'LL HELP JOG YOUR MEMORY.

WHAT DO YOU THINK?

LEAN IN

RECOIL!

?

DON'T WORRY -- I'M NOT TRYING TO **KISS YOU ON THE MOUTH** OR ANYTHING...

... I MEAN -- CHRIST, YOU'RE STILL A **KID** IN MY EYES!

LOOK, AS I WAS **TRYING** TO TELL YOU WHEN YOU WERE BEATING UP ALL THE HENCHMEN --

--AND WHAT I **ATTEMPTED** TO EXPLAIN WHILE YOU WERE BUILDING A MAKESHIFT ZIP LINE WITH A HARPOON CABLE AND AN OLD COAT HANGER --

--IS THAT I'M NOT THIS "**PRAVDA**" PERSON YOU'RE OBSESSED WITH. I'VE NEVER SEEN YOU BEFORE IN MY **LIFE**!

SO PLEASE, IF YOU HAVE **ANY** HEART AT ALL, LET ME GO BACK TO THE **LUNAYEV**...

132

133

THIS IS **ESPEN FRAM**, NORWAY'S AMBASSADOR.

AND ESPEN, THIS IS MY ASSISTANT, **BARTHIZOD REDGRAVE**.

BARTY, ESPEN WAS PART OF THE **SVALBARD SPACE PROGRAM** BACK IN THE DAY.

YES...

...BUT IT WAS SHUT DOWN AT THE SAME TIME AS YOUR **CASA**, I'M AFRAID.

PLEASURE TO MEET YOU, MR. FRAM.

SO GOOD TO FINALLY VISIT YOU ON **CANADIAN** SOIL, KEN!

AND YOU'RE STILL USING THE OLD **BLOCKHOUSE**! RESOURCEFUL!

FOR **TODAY**, ANYWAY.

HAL

HOLD ON... ...DOES ANYONE ELSE FEEL A **CHILL** IN THE AIR?

141

142

143

WALK WITH ME, SHANKS.

ARMY, LISTEN. I ASKED THEM TO TAKE PRAVDA TO A **MAKESHIFT CLINIC** IN THE BASEMENT OF THE BLOCKHOUSE.

I WANT TO HAVE HER CHECKED OUT.

ABSOLUTELY... NOT!!

HEY!

SHANKS, IF SHE SUFFERED ANY SORT OF ABUSE ON THE *LUNAYEV*, SHE NEEDS PROPER TREATMENT. PLUS, WITH THE DOCTOR'S HELP...

...SHE MAY BE ABLE TO REGAIN HER **MEMORY**.

145

LATER...

SO AM I YOUR... YOUR **PRISONER**?

ha ha

NO! SORRY ABOUT THE **GUNS**, WENDY -- THEY'RE A NECESSARY EVIL WHEN LIVING AMONG **POLAR BEARS**.

I BET.

THANKS FOR **SAVING MY LIFE**, BY THE WAY.

I GOT SO TURNED AROUND --

NO PROBLEM! WE'RE HAPPY YOU'RE OKAY...

...AND HAPPY TO HAVE SOME **COMPANY**!

NOW, WENDY, SIT BACK...

FLIP LIGHTS OFF

146

...AND LET ME EXPLAIN WHAT WE'RE **ALL ABOUT!**

C ANADIAN
A RCTIC
S PACE
A GENCY

"CASA WAS CREATED IN THE 1960s WHEN IT BECAME CLEAR THAT SOON **MAN** WOULD BE LIVING ON THE **MOON.**

[ARTIST'S INTERPRETATION]

"OWING TO ITS UNIQUE GEOGRAPHY, **DEVON ISLAND** WAS CHOSEN TO HOST A SERIES OF SIMULATED **MOON BASES.**

DEVON ISLAND

N

"ASTRONAUTS LIVE **YEAR-ROUND** IN THESE BASES, TESTING EQUIPMENT AND COLLECTING VITAL STATISTICS.

"THIS DATA IS SENT ELECTRONICALLY TO THE CASA BLOCKHOUSE...

CASA

"...WHERE IT IS BEING USED TO GUIDE FUTURE **MOON DWELLERS.'** "

147

148

"... SO YOU CAN SEE HOW **REAL** WE REALLY ARE!"

DON'T BE AFRAID-- IT'S JUST A CHECK-UP!

WOW, DO YOU REALLY THINK THAT WOMAN COULD BE ARMY SHANKS' LONG-LOST CHILDHOOD FRIEND?

OF COURSE NOT. SHE'S A SIBERIAN SPY NAMED **MOLNIYA SEMYORKA**.

SHE HAS A LIST OF **PIRACY CHARGES** GOING ALL THE WAY BACK TO HER **CHILDHOOD**.

MOLNIYA SEMYORKA

AGE:

SIBERIA

NO DOUBT HIRED BY CAPTAIN SZTAB TO BE A **MOLE**.

THEN WHY LET HER IN THE BLOCK-HOUSE?!

BECAUSE SHE'S USEFUL.

SHE'S KEEPING OUR EYEWITNESS CALM...

VI

HELP!!

PANT

PANT

?

TOILET...
... HURRY!...

PANT

PANT

haha DON'T BUST A GUT, FRIEND. THERE'S A PUBLIC RESTROOM RIGHT OVER--

NO! IN THE TOILET... JUST NOW...

PANT
PANT

...I FOUND THREE RCAN SAILORS GAGGED & BOUND!

"YOU'VE GOTTA HELP HER OUT, DOC! ... THESE SIBERIANS HAVE **STRIPPED** PRAVDA OF HER **IDENTITY!**"

155

I DON'T KNOW WHAT TO TELL YOU, MR. SHANKS.

CLINIC

I'M A **MEDICAL** DOCTOR. RCAN IS PAYING ME TO GIVE **PHYSICALS**, NOT **PSYCH EXAMS**.

AND BESIDES, **MEMORIES** ARE COMPLICATED THINGS.

EXAMINE

THEY'RE JUST CONNECTIONS OF NEURAL PATHWAYS...

...SUBJECT TO **ERODE** WITH DISUSE...

...OR EVEN TO **CHANGE COMPLETELY** WITH OUTSIDE INFLUENCES.

C'MON, PRAVDA, YOU MUST REMEMBER THE NIGHT THEY BROUGHT ME INTO THE **ORPHANAGE**...

"...MY BROTHER AND I HAD BEEN TRAVELING FOR THREE DAYS IN THE BELLY OF A **HERRING BOAT**, AND **SMELLED** LIKE IT.

"EVERYONE AVOIDED ME, BUT YOU GAVE ME A GIFT--A **NECKLACE** YOU HAD MADE.

"THE NECKLACE MADE MY BORROWED SHIRT LOOK LIKE A **DRESS**.

HAR HAR

"SOME KID LAUGHED AT ME, AND YOU WRUNG HIS NECK."

157

159

MEANWHILE, UPSTAIRS...

WE ALL HERE? GOOD. THANK YOU, EVERYONE, FOR ASSEMBLING A DAY EARLY FOR THIS ADDENDUM TO TOMORROW'S **HIGH ARCTIC LEAGUE** SUMMIT.

I'M SORRY THAT THINGS ARE STARTING OUT THIS WAY, BUT IF ANYTHING, THIS EMERGENCY REINFORCES THE **RELEVANCE** AND **IMPORTANCE** OF WHAT WE DO.

TO START OFF -- FOR FORMALITY'S SAKE-- LET'S DO SOME BRIEF INTRODUCTIONS.

I'M **KEN ARLUK**, AS YOU ALL KNOW, AND I REPRESENT **CANADA**.

160

AND OF COURSE WE HAVE **ESPEN FRAM** OF **NORWAY**...

... **SALAMINA KOCH** OF **GREENLAND**...

.. **ULRIK NORDENSKIÖLD** OF **FINLAND**...

... **GRETA LUST** OF **SWEDEN**...

... **UUL FENN** OF **SIBERIA**...

...AND LAST BUT NOT LEAST, MISS **LEDA BASCOM** OF **THE U.S.**

162

"...I GUESS I LOST TRACK OF THE TIME."

SO, KEN...

...DO YOU HAVE A **FLAME** FOR ME?

EH?

OH, RIGHT.

LIGHT

SO, THE WILD MISS BASCOM HAS FINALLY BEEN **TIED DOWN**. I ASSUME IT'S TO THE COWBOY YOU WERE DATING AT THE **LAST** SUMMIT?

PENSIVE DRAG

NO, I MET SOMEONE MORE **STABLE**, KEN, AND MORE SUPPORTIVE OF MY **WHIMS**.

OF WHICH THERE ARE MANY.

163

BE **NICE**, KEN, YOU'D LIKE HIM. DONOVAN IS A **FREELANCE PILOT**. HE'S ACTUALLY DOING SOME WORK UP HERE IN CANADA, MOVING SOME OLD PLANES AROUND.

UH-HUH.

...SPECIFICALLY, DECOMMISSIONED **HARRIER JETS**. IN FACT, HE DISCOVERED YESTERDAY THAT ONE OF THEM STILL HAS A **MISSILE** LEFT IN ITS CASING THAT YOUR CANADIAN BOYS FORGOT TO TAKE OUT!

ALRIGHT, LEDA, **ENOUGH**. I GET IT-- YOU'VE MARRIED THE MAN OF THE YEAR.

WALK AWAY

AND HOW ABOUT **YOU**, KEN? SEEING ANYONE?

"...OR ARE YOU STILL WORKING OUT YOUR **TRUST ISSUES**?"

BENDRIX! HOW'S THAT **PROJECTOR** COMING ALONG?

ALMOST READY, KEN!

YEP, JUST A FEW MORE TURNS OF THE SCREW...

"...AND WE'LL BE READY TO LAUNCH."

HOLY SMOKES!

YOU GUYS SURE LIKE BATTERIES!

SHE SHOULDN'T BE HERE, DRAKE.

SHE'S RUINING THE SIMULATION!

WE'RE ON THE MOON, SUPPOSEDLY... WE CAN'T HAVE GUESTS!

I COULDN'T--

--I COULDN'T JUST LET HER FREEZE TO DEATH, RICHTER.

BUT DRAKE--

ALRIGHT! ... I'LL TALK TO HER.

166

BEFORE YOU THROW ME BACK TO EARTH, PLEASE JUST HEAR ME OUT.

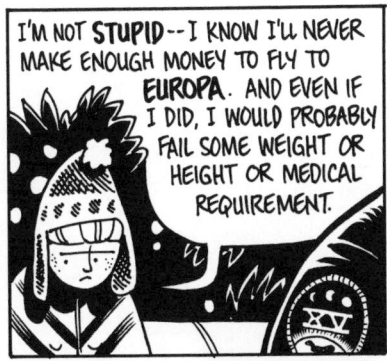

I'M NOT **STUPID** -- I KNOW I'LL NEVER MAKE ENOUGH MONEY TO FLY TO **EUROPA**. AND EVEN IF I DID, I WOULD PROBABLY FAIL SOME WEIGHT OR HEIGHT OR MEDICAL REQUIREMENT.

SO THIS LITTLE **BASE** YOU'VE GOT HERE MIGHT BE THE CLOSEST I EVER GET TO LIVING ON A **LUNAR SURFACE**.

SO **PLEASE** LET ME STAY, DRAKE -- I'M **BEGGING** YOU!

I'LL DO **ANYTHING**: SCRUB THERMAL TANKS, DE-ICE WAIN DRIVERS, PLUG UP SPARKING T-8's -- **ANYTHING**!

UM...

...CAN YOU **COOK**?

A GYNE-COLOGICAL EXAM?!

YES. THERE ARE SOME PEOPLE AT THE DOOR WHO WANT TO TAKE YOU TO A CLINIC NEARBY.

YOU'LL BE MORE COMFORTABLE THERE-- AND THEY SAY YOU'LL BE CHECKED OUT BY A **FEMALE** DOCTOR.

HOP OFF

HUFF

IF THAT'S WHAT IT TAKES TO **RELEASE** ME, THEN I'LL DO IT.

BUT I PRAY THAT SOMEDAY YOU WILL BOTH FEEL AS **HUMILIATED** AS I DO RIGHT NOW.

STORM OFF

168

YOU'RE NOT GOING WITH HER?

WHAT IF YOU'RE RIGHT, DOC, AND I'M JUST **IMAGINING** THIS WHOLE THING?

SLUMP

IT MIGHT BE BEST IF I STEP BACK FROM PRAVDA -- OR **WHOEVER** SHE IS...

"...AND GET A LITTLE **GROUNDED**."

≥SIGH≤

OKAY, GENTLEMEN. TAKE ME AWAY.

"OKAY, EVERYONE, SETTLE DOWN."

...A LOT HAS BEEN HAPPENING, AND I'D LIKE TO GET US ALL UP TO SPEED.

A DAY AGO, THE RETROFITTED OIL TANKER **LUNAYEV** ENTERED CANADIAN WATERS.

LUNAYEV

THE SHIP IS **SIBERIAN**, AND MASTERED BY A **CAPTAIN SZTAB.**

OUR INTERNAL FILE ON MR. SZTAB IS QUITE THIN, BUT WE BELIEVE HE HAS A BASE OF OPERATIONS SOMEWHERE IN THE LENA DELTA.

NORMALLY, RCAN WOULD **BOARD** A TRESPASSING SHIP AND GUIDE IT BACK TO INTERNATIONAL WATERS.

TAP TAP TAP

THIS, HOWEVER, IS A **UNIQUE** CIRCUMSTANCE.

170

CAPTAIN SZTAB HAS INVOKED HAL STATUTE 106-41...

...WHICH PROHIBITS US FROM GOING NEAR AN **ACTIVE LAUNCH SITE**, WHICH THEY CLAIM THEIR SHIP IS.

HAL STATUTES 100-10-119-90

GENERAL CONFUSION

WELL PLAYED, UUL... BUT JUST **WHAT** EXACTLY ARE YOU SIBERIAN DOGS TRYING TO **ACCOMPLISH**?

I ASSURE YOU, I KNOW **NOTHING** ABOUT THIS!

THE *LUNAYEV* IS A ROGUE SHIP!

171

172

174

...AND SHE KNOWS AS MUCH ABOUT MODERN SPACE TECHNOLOGY AS **WE** DO. SHE MIGHT BE ABLE TO HELP OUT WITH *PROJECT MAURICE*!

SO JUST GIVE HER A **CHANCE**, OKAY?

ALRIGHT, YOU GUYS...

...DIG IN!

LATER

SEE WHAT YOU'VE BEEN MISSING?

I DON'T KNOW HOW YOU GUYS SURVIVED SO LONG WITHOUT A **WOMAN!**

AND FOR **TWENTY YEARS**! *SHEESH!*

STAND UP ABRUPTLY

?

WAS IT SOMETHING I **SAID**?

YOU SHOULD KNOW, WENDY, THAT RICHTER AND I BOTH MADE CERTAIN **SACRIFICES** WHEN WE AGREED TO LIVE ON THIS BASE...

176

VII

THERE, THAT SHOULD DO IT.

HAVE YOUR MEN KEEP A **CLOSE WATCH** ON THIS DYNAMITE, LIEUTENANT STWALLEY.

IF THESE EXPLOSIVES FALL INTO THE HANDS OF A **PSYCHOPATH**, THEN WE'RE ALL IN A LOT OF TROUBLE.

NOW I'M OFF TO CHECK IN ON THIS **HAL VOTE**. THE SOONER THE STATUTE IS REPEALED, THE SOONER WE CAN BOARD THE **LUNAYEV**...

"...AND FIND OUT WHAT'S **REALLY** GOING ON!"

MAY I PRESENT TO YOU...

LUNTONIUM:
THE FUTURE OF ENERGY!

COLORLESS, ODORLESS, CLEAN-BURNING...AND **POWERFUL!**

A FEW DROPS FROM THIS VIAL COULD RUN YOUR BLOCKHOUSE FOR A **WEEK**.

WHAT YOU SEE HERE IS ALL THAT CURRENTLY EXISTS OF **LUNTONIUM**; EXTRACTED FROM SOVIET LUNAR SOIL SAMPLES OVER THE LAST TWENTY YEARS.

BUT ALL OF THAT WILL CHANGE IN ONE WEEK, WHEN WE LAND ON THE MOON AND BEGIN PROCESSING LUNTONIUM FOR OURSELVES.

WITHIN **ONE YEAR**, ALL OF YOUR FOSSIL FUEL RESERVES WILL BE **WORTHLESS!!**

GENERAL COMMOTIO...

CAPTAIN SZTAB, YOU CAN'T BE SERIOUS. IF THIS HIGHLY DUBIOUS CLAIM **IS** TRUE -- THAT YOU HAVE THE POWER TO PRODUCE **CHEAP, CLEAN** ENERGY--

--WHY NOT SHARE IT WITH THE **WORLD**?

EUROPE, INDIA, JAPAN -- THEY ALL HAVE SPACE PROGRAMS. I'M SURE THEY'D BE **THRILLED** TO HELP YOU SET UP LUNAR MINING FACILITIES.

WHY SEND UP A **PRIVATE ROCKET** LIKE THIS IN THE DEAD OF NIGHT?

*BECAUSE I'M A **BUSINESS-MAN**, MR. ARLUK...*

183

185

RIGHT. UH... **HOCKEY?**

I WAS A BIG **DEVON WHALERS** FAN BACK IN THE DAY.

GOOD! WHAT ELSE?

I LIKE **SAILING.**

CATCHING A PERFECT WIND AND SEEING THE BOW CUT THROUGH THE SURF LIKE AN ULU THROUGH BLUBBER.

BUT MOSTLY, I LIKE BEING RIGHT NEXT TO A **POLAR BEAR.**

GOOD, THAT'S--

MY HANDS AGAINST ITS THROAT. EVERY MUSCLE IN MY BODY TRYING TO KEEP ITS CLAWS FROM SINKING INTO MY FLESH.

SIT UP

THAT LAST GROAN BEFORE ITS BREATH GOES QUIET AND ITS EYES GO COLD AND ITS LIMBS FALL LIMP AGAINST THE RED SNOW.

SEE? LOOK AT EVERYTHING YOU'VE GOT TO **LIVE** FOR!

SEETHE!

187

BUT THERE'S ALSO SOMETHING TO BE SAID FOR **COSMETIC SURGERY**.

"LOOKING GOOD LEADS TO FEELING GOOD" AND ALL THAT.

LIKE A **MAKEOVER**?

WIPE

SOMETHING LIKE THAT.

DON'T TAKE THIS THE WRONG WAY, SHANKS...

SWITCH!

...BUT IT'S TIME FOR YOU TO DO THE RIGHT THING.

"AM I TOO LATE?"

189

FLIP LIGHTS BACK ON

ha ha NOW CLEARLY THIS IS A **HOAX**, SO LET'S GET THIS VOTE UNDERWAY TO REPEAL THE STATUTE.

NOW HOLD ON A MINUTE, ARLUK-- WE NEED TO **DISCUSS** THIS!

JA! VAT IF DIS IZ FUR **REAL**?

ARE YOU **SERIOUS**?

THINK OF WHAT THIS **CLEAN, CHEAP** ENERGY COULD MEAN TO THE **ARCTIC**... TO THE **WORLD**!

NO MORE REGULATIONS. NO MORE FILTHY YELLOW SKY.

YOU CAN'T REALLY BE CONSIDERING THIS! "MOON ENERGY" IS JUST A... A **SCI-FI CONCEIT**!

AND NOT A VERY ORIGINAL ONE!

LEDA, YOUR PEOPLE WERE ACTUALLY **ON** THE MOON, AND YOU SAW HOW **WORTHLESS** IT IS!

I DON'T KNOW, KEN. I MEAN, **WATER'S** BEEN FOUND ON THE SURFACE ... SO MAYBE ANYTHING'S POSSIBLE.

UH... I VOTE FOR A SMOKE BREAK.

I **SEKUND.**

IF WE NEED A THIRD, I'LL BE THAT THIRD.

Mere paces away...

C'MON, LET'S GET OUT OF HERE BEFORE THE CANADIANS FIGURE OUT SHE'S GONE.

MOLNIYA?

MOLNIYA!

SNAP OUT OF IT

RIGHT. COMING!

SNEAK PAST BAILY

MADE IT!

NOT SO FAST, MEDVEDKIN. WE CAN'T LET OUR GUARD DOWN YET-- THERE WILL CERTAINLY BE OTHER SAILORS SNOOPING ABOUT. STAY SHARP.

SLUMP OVER!

MOLNIYA!

ARE YOU OKAY, MRS. SZTAB? DID THEY **HURT** YOU IN THERE?

NO, NO, I'M FINE.

IT'S JUST-- SEEING MY HUSBAND'S FACE SO **LARGE** MADE ME FEEL SO **STRANGE**!

IT SOUNDS FUNNY, BUT...

194

"...AND **SLICE**."

PULL INTO DARK HALLWAY

LIES, KEN! CAPTAIN SZTAB IS FULL OF **LIES**!!

I'M **CERTAIN** THE SIBERIANS WANT TO LAUNCH A **MISSILE**!

MY HANDS ARE TIED, BARTY.

REVOKING THE STATUTE IS OUR ONLY WAY TO LEGALLY BOARD THAT SHIP.

UNFORTUNATELY, THE AMBASSADORS' **REASONING CAPABILITIES** HAVE BEEN ECLIPSED BY CAPTAIN SZTAB'S "LUNTONIUM" HORSESHIT.

IF ONLY THE SIBERIANS WOULD **STRIKE** AT US SOMEHOW! THAT WOULD GIVE US **JUST CAUSE** FOR **RETALIATION**...

196

YOU'RE A CIGAR WOMAN, AREN'T YOU, LEDA? CARE FOR A PUFF?

NO, I -- I HAVE TO GO.

WHO **MAKES** THESE THINGS? I'D LIKE TO READ A BOOK ABOUT **THAT**!

DUCK INSIDE

AMBASSADOR LEDA BASCOM HERE.

GET ME THE **TREASURY** SECRETARY IMMEDIATELY...

"... I NEED TO MAKE A **WITHDRAWAL**."

EVERYTHING'S SET, BARTY.

AND ADMIRAL OUTLINE LEFT A WHILE AGO, SO HE'LL HAVE AN ALIBI.

GOOD WORK, STWALLEY. NOW SET THE TIMER AND GET YOUR MEN THE **HELL OUT** OF HERE.

I'LL SEE YOU ON THE OTHER SIDE.

?!

WAIT-- YOU'RE GOING BACK **INSIDE**?

I HAVE NO CHOICE. ...I CAN'T LET THE HIGH ARCTIC LEAGUE SUSPECT ME.

THIS HAS TO LOOK LIKE THE **SIBERIANS'** DOING.

SMOOTH AS A HERRING'S BELLY, DOC!

RING! RING! RIN--

MAKESHIFT CLINIC, HELLO?

WHOA, WHOA-- SLOW DOWN, SAILOR...

"...TELL ME WHAT YOU SEE."

BARTY?

EVERYTHING OKAY? YOU SEEM KIND OF... DISTRACTED.

NOTHING! JUST CAUGHT OFF GUARD BY THIS **LUNTONIUM** ANNOUNCEMENT, I GUESS.

WELL, LET'S NOT WORRY ABOUT THE **VOTE**. ONCE THE AMBASSADORS LOOK AT THIS SITUATION RATIONALLY...

OKAY, I'LL BE RIGHT THERE!

DOC, WHAT IS IT?

HANG UP

APPARENTLY, THREE RCAN SAILORS ARE GAGGED AND BOUND IN THE OUTDOOR RESTROOM!

THE **STRANGEST** THING IS THAT THEIR **UNIFORMS** HAVE DISAPPEARED.

WAIT-- THE MEN WHO TOOK YOUR PRAVDA-- THEY MAY HAVE BEEN **IMPOSTERS!**

I SHOULD HAVE KNOWN... ...THERE'S NO "WOMAN'S CLINIC" NEAR HERE!

SNAP!

OUTSIDE...

Huff! Huff!

HMMM...

...THERE GO **TWO MORE** SAILORS RUNNING AWAY FROM THE BLOCKHOUSE, AND--

-- WAIT A SECOND--

--ARE THEY CLOSING THE **BLAST DOOR**?!

CASA BLOCKHOUSE

I DON'T LIKE THIS.

I DON'T LIKE THIS EITHER.

SOMETHING'S WRONG HERE!

I SAY WE MAKE A RUN FOR THE ZODIAC AS QUICKLY AS POSSIBLE, AND GET THE HELL OFF THIS CANADIAN **ROCK**.

RCAN

AGREED.

OKAY, ON MY MARK...

CASA

tick tick tick...

"SKREE! SKREE!..."

NEARBY...

SKREE! SKREE! SKRE SK

LUNA

SKREE SK-- RIP!

DOT MATRIXTRON - 80

"...moneys have been transferred to the Tiksi Regional Bank in the amount of--" **HOLY SMOKES!**

CAPTAIN SZTAB! CAPTAIN SZTAB!

YOU WON'T BELIEVE THIS-- THE AMERICANS HAVE PURCHASED A **CONTROLLING SHARE** IN OUR **LUNTONIUM** COMPANY!

EXCELLENT...

"...THAT'S ONE LESS THING TO WORRY ABOUT."

RACE UP STAIRS

SHUTTING...

10... 9... 8...

...7... 6...

...STILL SHUTTING...

...5... 4...

SLO-MO LEAP!

VIII

213

215

216

217

LEDA, I, UH--

BANG! BANG!

ARMY! ARMY! CAN YOU HEAR ME?

?

H-HELLO?

ARMY, IT'S ME-- PRAVDA!

YOU MEAN THE WOMAN I **THOUGHT** WAS PRAVDA.

NO-- I DON'T KNOW WHAT HAPPENED, ARMY, BUT... IT'S **ME**. ...THE **REAL** ME!

ARMY, I'M STARTING TO **REMEMBER**!

VELL, I'M GLAD **SOME-VUN'S** HAPPY.

WHO **IS** THAT WRETCHED MAN?

219

NOW, DOES ANYONE HAVE A **RADIO**?

ANYONE?

ALRIGHT, THEN.

I'LL HAVE TO MANUALLY BOOT UP THE ORIGINAL **CASA** ELECTRICAL GRID TO GET THAT DOOR OPEN.

DETERMINED WALK

YOU CAN **DO** THAT?

FORTUNATELY FOR ALL OF US, I USED TO WORK HERE AT CASA.

IN FACT, I HELPED DESIGN A LOT OF THESE SYSTEMS...

...SO I SHOULD BE ABLE TO PULL THIS OFF IN NO TIME.

221

WHO'S THAT **THIRD** GUY?

KEN ARLUK. GOOD GUY. FROM RANKIN INLET, I THINK.

HE'S...HE'S **DEAD**?

OH-- ha ha -- NO. HE WAS **FIRED**.

WELL, PULLED FROM THIS BASE, ANYWAY.

HE DIDN'T PLAY BY THE CASA HANDBOOK -- HAD SOME RADICAL IDEAS ON HOW WE SHOULD GO TO THE MOON. ONE HE CALLED **PROJECT MAURICE** --

ha ha SORRY, I'M **RAMBLING**. SO ANYWAY, THEY SENT ARLUK TO WORK IN THE NEW **BLOCKHOUSE**...

"...WHERE THEY COULD KEEP AN EYE ON HIM."

OKAY...

...PLEASE HAND ME A.. LET'S SEE... A D-CLAMP WITH A 5/16 TRIPMOUNT.

DIG DIG DIG

?

CASA

FOUND IT!

CASA

HERE YOU GO, KEN!

THANKS, ESPEN!

IS THIS EVEN GOING TO **WORK**? ALL THIS STUFF IS SO **OLD**!

CASA

ARE YOU **KIDDING**? THIS EQUIPMENT WAS BUILT TO **LAST**!

AND I SHOULD KNOW...

"...I DESIGNED MOST OF IT!"

DULL THUD!

DULL THUD!

DULL THUD!

C'MON, YOU SON OF A BITCH, GIVE ME A **HOLLOW THUD.**

IF **I'D** BUILT THIS THING, THERE'D BE AT LEAST **TEN** ESCAPE TUNNELS.

AH, PRAVDA, WHO AM I KIDDING?

MAYBE THIS IS JUST A SIGN THAT I DON'T DESERVE YO--

SMASH!!

OH.

HEY, DOC.

How many **dead**, Shanks? Whatever it is, don't ⋮HIC!⋮ tell me. ⋮HIC!⋮

I can't ⋮HIC!⋮ **handle** this, Shanks...

...I was supposed to be a **podiatrist**! ⋮HIC!⋮

⋮HIC!⋮

But then I followed the herd... became a generalist... ⋮HIC!⋮

Oh, what happens to a dream deferred... ♫

"**FOLLOW!**" THAT'S IT!

HEY, WENDY!

WELD!!

SMOKE BREAK!

I'M AFRAID IT'S A ROLL-YOUR-OWN PROGRAM. WE'RE VERY DIY HERE AT CRATER XV.

I THINK I CAN HANDLE IT.

RICHTER? YOU WANT ONE?

SEEING AS HOW WE WON'T BE ABLE TO SMOKE ON THE ACTUAL MOON...

...NO.

THAT'S EXACTLY WHY YOU SHOULD GET YOUR KICKS **NOW**!

HA HA HA HA HA HA HA HA HA

WHAT'S SO FUNNY?

OH, I WAS JUST THINKING...

...ABOUT HOW GOOD YOU GUYS ARE AT **KEEPING SECRETS**.

UH... WHAT DO YOU MEAN, WENDY?

OH, JUST THAT I'VE READ ALL THE LITERATURE ON CANADIAN SPACE TRAVEL I COULD GET MY HANDS ON--

--TO HELP MY CHANCES OF BEING ACCEPTED INTO THE NEWFOUNDLAND EUROPA PROJECT, I MEAN--

--AND I HAVEN'T HEARD A **SINGLE THING** ABOUT CASA OR THIS MOON-BASE PROGRAM! DON'T YOU THINK THAT'S **WEIRD**?

YES, **VERY** WEIRD, ACTUALLY.

WE'RE JUST **HIGHLY CLASSIFIED** IS ALL.

FORCED LAUGHTER

LEAN IN

WAIT, DRAKE, SHE'S GOT A **POINT**.

WE'RE **NOT** CLASSIFIED -- OUR FINDINGS ARE SUPPOSED TO BE **PUBLIC**.

WHY THE HELL HAVE I BEEN CHARTING MY **BOWEL MOVEMENTS** FOR TWENTY YEARS IF NOT TO HELP FUTURE ASTRONAUTS LIKE WENDY?

OKAY, CALM DOWN, RICH--

NO! I WANT TO TALK TO **KEN ARLUK** ABOUT THIS!

FLIP
FLIP
FLIP

History of
CANADI

OH
MY!

story o

234

WENDY!!

COME BACK, WENDY...

...IT'S **DANGEROUS** OUT HERE!

IX

KEN, C'MERE-- I THINK YOU SHOULD HEAR THIS!

TARA **WHO**?

NO-- **TERRA NULLIUS**.

IT'S A TERM USED FOR A PIECE OF LAND THAT HAS NO LEGAL OWNER.

IN **THIS** DAY AND AGE? I FIND THAT HARD TO BELIEVE.

I'M BARTHIZOD REDGRAVE, BY THE WAY. KEN ARLUK'S ASSISTANT. ... I WASN'T AROUND FOR THE INTRODUCTIONS.

EQUIVALENT of CRICKETS CHIRPING

MOVING ON...

THE **MOON** IS ALSO *TERRA NULLIUS*-- NOT OWNED BY ANYONE.

WELL, SURE... IT'S THE **MOON**. IT BELONGS TO **EVERYONE**.

BUT THEN WHY DOESN'T **DEVON ISLAND** BELONG TO EVERYONE?

BECAUSE PEOPLE LIVE HERE-- THEY MAKE THEIR LIVELIHOOD HERE.

EXACTLY: **THIS** LAND IS **USEFUL**.

HISTORICALLY, LANDS CONSIDERED USE**LESS** WERE LABELED *TERRA NULLIUS*-- NO ONE OWNED THEM BECAUSE NO ONE **WANTED** THEM.

BUT NOW THAT CAPTAIN SZTAB CAN **EXTRACT** SOMETHING FROM THE MOON, HE MAY BE ABLE TO **CLAIM** IT.

YOU MEAN **OWN** IT?

245

248

257

261

MEANWHILE, IN THE BLOCKHOUSE...

WHAT DO YOU THINK, KEN? CAN WE DO IT?

DO **WHAT**, ESPEN?

YOU KNOW...

...BEAT THE **SIBERIANS** TO THE **MOON!**

SEEING AS HOW YOUR MAN **BENDRIX** IS SO **TECH-SAVVY**, MAYBE HE COULD WHIP UP SOME KIND OF **CANADIAN** ROCKET!

I LIKE YOUR ENTHUSIASM, ESPEN. IT REMINDS ME OF OUR OLD TRAINING CAMPS ON HALVMÅNEØYA.

BUT LEDA WAS RIGHT. WE HAVE TO KNOW WHEN WE'RE BEAT.

AT THIS POINT, WE SHOULD BE **CELEBRATING** THE FACT THAT SZTAB HAS DEVELOPED CLEAN FUEL...

...AND HOPE THAT HE CAN PULL IT OFF.

BUT AS FOR **CANADIANS** ON THE MOON...

"...**THAT** DREAM DIED A LONG TIME AGO."

BEAR

YOU CAN'T GO RUNNING OFF LIKE THAT, WENDY.

PANT
PANT

LOOK, I'M SORRY FOR CHASING AFTER YOU. BUT YOU DON'T KNOW HOW HARD IT IS JUST TO **STAY ALIVE** OUT HERE.

CASE IN POINT--

RIGHT... RAMPAGING POLAR BEAR.

SPEAKING OF STAYING ALIVE...

...IS THE CANADIAN ARCTIC SPACE AGENCY--?

NO.

CASA NO LONGER EXISTS...

...AND I HAVEN'T BEEN IN CONTACT WITH **KEN ARLUK** OR ANY OF THE OTHERS FOR NEARLY **TWO DECADES.**

SO YOU AND RICHTER HAVE BEEN RUNNING THE CRATER XV BASE BY **YOURSELVES**! IN **SECRET**! COMPLETELY **UNSUPPORTED**!

YOU TWO HAVE **GONE ROGUE**!

YES, BUT WITH ONE CAVEAT...

...RICHTER DOESN'T KNOW IT.

WHAAAA

"...HE'S DOOMED!!"

SAIL STRAIGHT TOWARDS IMPENETRABLE WALL OF ICE!

AND SO...

I...

...I DON'T KNOW HOW IT HAPPENED, ARMY...

...IT'S LIKE WAKING UP FROM A **DREAM**!

MEMORIES OF MY CHILDHOOD ARE SLOWLY COMING BACK TO ME!

ARE YOU **SO** HAPPY?

I AM.

LISTEN, PRAVDA, THERE'S SOME-PLACE I'D LIKE TO **TAKE** YOU--

LEAN IN

ANYWHERE! JUST PLEASE PROMISE TO DO **ONE THING**...

"...ALL WE CAN DO NOW IS CONTINUE OUR **MISSION**."

SO LET ME GET THIS STRAIGHT--

--YOU'VE BEEN **LYING** TO RICHTER FOR TWENTY YEARS ABOUT CASA'S VERY **EXISTENCE**?!

I DON'T **BELIEVE** YOU!

HOW CAN HE NOT HAVE **KNOWN**?

AND HOW DO I KNOW YOU'RE NOT LYING TO **ME**?!

WENDY, IT'S... IT'S **COMPLICATED**. AND VERY **SENSITIVE**.

WHAT IS? YOUR **MISSION**? YOU DON'T **HAVE A MISSION**!

NOT ONE FROM **CASA**, ANYWAY.

LOOK, IF I TELL YOU WHAT'S GOING ON-- TELL YOU **EVERYTHING**, I MEAN -- YOU'VE GOT TO PROMISE NOT TO TELL RICHTER ABOUT CASA'S **DEMISE**.

THE TRUTH WOULD...

...THE TRUTH WOULD **CRUSH** HIM.

DEAL?

DEAL.

SKEPTICAL ACCEPTANCE

ALRIGHT THEN, GET COMFORTABLE...

"...THIS MIGHT TAKE A WHILE."

I SAY, KEN, WHEN IS THE **POWER** COMING BACK ON?

JA, I VANT TO **LEEVE**!

ALMOST THERE, GRETA.

ESPEN, I NEED YOU TO GO PULL DOWN THE SECOND CURTAIN FROM THE RIGHT.

SURE!

C001...............135k

≥GASP!≥

WHAT DOES **THAT** MEAN?

IT'S GOOD-- IT MEANS WE'RE ON THE RIGHT TRACK.

THE COMPUTER NEEDS TO GO THROUGH A **SELF-DIAGNOSIS** BEFORE IT'LL LET US OPEN THE BLAST DOOR.

BUT WHAT DOES "C001" MEAN?

OH, THAT'S "CRATER I" -- THE FIRST OF SEVERAL TEST MOON BASES CASA BUILT BACK IN THE DAY.

C001...............135k

THE OTHER NUMBER MEANS THERE MUST BE 135 KILO-BYTES OF ELECTRONIC MESSAGES FROM CRATER I STILL WAITING IN THE QUEUE.

≥GASP!≥ "**E**"-MESSAGES?

YOU MEAN DOZE BASES ARE STEELE **OPERATING**?

ha ha NO. THOSE BASES ARE **LONG GONE**.

IT JUST MEANS THAT SOME DATA FROM THE BASE WERE SENT **AFTER** THE BLOCKHOUSE MAINFRAME WAS SHUT DOWN FOR GOOD.

KIND OF LIKE POSTCARDS STUFFED UNDER THE DOOR OF AN ABANDONED HOUSE -- NEVER BEEN READ!

CAN WE **READ** ONE OF THESE MESSAGES?

I SUPPOSE, BUT UNFORTUNATELY THEY'RE NOT VERY INTERESTING.

JUST DAILY REPORTS OF THINGS LIKE ASTRONAUTS' WEIGHT, MOOD, DIET... THAT SORT OF THING.

BLIP

C001 .... 135k
C002 .... 98k

LOOK, THERE'S ANOTHER ONE!

I SAY, ARLUK...

279

"...HOW MANY OF THESE BASES DID YOU **MAKE**?"

CRATER
IX

AS YOU KNOW, THERE WERE **THREE** OF US INITIALLY ASSIGNED TO CRATER XV...

"...MYSELF, RICHTER, AND KEN ARLUK.

CRATER
XV

"WHEN KEN'S CONTROVERSIAL ROCKET DESIGNS WERE DISCOVERED AND HE WAS PULLED FROM THE BASE, RICHTER TOOK IT ALL PRETTY HARD.

CASA

REASSIGNMENT ORDERS
(see other side for details)

ARLUK

"SEE, FOR RICHTER, STAYING IN CHARACTER -- PRETENDING WE WERE **ACTUALLY** ON THE MOON -- WAS CRUCIAL.

"SO IN RICHTER'S MIND, KEN WASN'T **TRANSFERRED**... HE HAD **DIED**."

K. ARLUK

SET UP A **CAIRN** FOR HIM AND EVERYTHING.

THAT'S SO **WEIRD!**

I THOUGHT SO TOO, INITIALLY.

BUT OVER TIME, I GREW TO SEE IT AS **ADMIRABLE.**

"SEE, AT THE END OF THE DAY -- IF WE EVER **DO** MAKE IT TO THE MOON--

MAURICE

DESIGNED BY KEN ARLUK

"--I WOULD WANT A MAN LIKE RICHTER UP THERE BY MY SIDE."

ANYWAY, BACK TO KEN'S "DEATH"...

"KEN WAS NOW AT THE BLOCKHOUSE, AND WOULD SOMETIMES TALK TO US OVER THE RADIO.

"BUT HEARING KEN'S VOICE **RUINED** THE SIMULATION IN RICHTER'S HEAD...

"...SO RICHTER STAYED **FAR** AWAY FROM THE RADIO ROOM. LEFT ALL COMMUNICATION UP TO **ME**.

"THEN THE HAMMER FELL. ONE YEAR INTO CASA, KEN CALLED TO TELL ME OUR SPACE AGENCY WAS **DISSOLVING**.

"FROM THE APOLLO LANDINGS IT WAS CLEAR THAT THERE WAS NO NEED FOR **REAL** MOON BASES, NOT TO MENTION **FAKE** ONES.

"IMMEDIATELY THE FUNDING FELL OUT FROM UNDERNEATH CASA...

flip off

"...AND ALL OF THE BASES WERE ORDERED TO VACATE."

BUT YOU NEVER TOLD RICHTER!

WHY? BECAUSE YOU DIDN'T THINK HE COULD **TAKE** IT?

WELL, IT'S NOT THAT SIMPLE...

"BOTH KEN AND I BELIEVED STRONGLY THAT THERE WOULD BE PUBLIC UPROAR, AND PEOPLE WOULD DEMAND THAT CASA BE REINSTATED.

"SO UNTIL THAT HAPPENED, I WAS GOING TO KEEP RUNNING CRATER XV LIKE NORMAL. WHEN CASA CAME BACK ONLINE, OUR DATA WOULD BE SEAMLESS, LIKE NOTHING HAPPENED. NO NEED TO TELL RICHTER.

"...BUT OF COURSE, THAT DAY NEVER CAME."

"EVENTUALLY, KEN MOVED TO AMERICA, AND RICHTER AND I WERE ALONE IN CRATER XV.

"AFTER CASA DISSOLVED, THE FOOD DROPS STOPPED, AS DID THE RESUPPLY SHIPMENTS.

"I BENT THE TRUTH AND TOLD RICHTER THAT FUNDING WAS DOWN, SO WE'D HAVE TO SUPPLEMENT OUR CASA FOOD DROPS WITH **WILD GAME**.

"RICHTER TOOK THE NEWS IN STRIDE, PRETENDING THE GAME WERE **ALIENS**, EVEN THOUGH HE KNEW IT WAS RIDICULOUS.

"I SNUCK OUT AT NIGHT AND STOLE SUPPLIES FROM SURROUNDING ABANDONED CRATER BASES.

"FORTUNATELY, THERE ARE A LOT OF THEM, AND MOST WERE WELL-STOCKED WHEN ABANDONED."

"...I HAVEN'T TOLD YOU THE **BOMBSHELL** YET!"

SO, KEN, HOW DID YOU GO FROM **ASTRONAUT-IN-TRAINING** TO **HIGH ARCTIC LEAGUE AMBASSADOR**?

ha ha

IT'S ACTUALLY A MORE **CONVOLUTED** ROAD THAN YOU MIGHT EXPECT.

AFTER **CASA** DISSOLVED, I WANTED TO DO SOMETHING **COMPLETELY DIFFERENT**. SO I MOVED TO AMERICA AND TRAINED TO BE A **MAGICIAN**.

BLIP

TURNS OUT THE **SLEIGHT OF HAND** I LEARNED IS ACTUALLY A USE-FUL SKILL AS A **POLITICIAN**!

POLITE LAUGHTER

KEN, **LOOK!**

C009	...... 69 k
C010	...... 101 k
C011	...... 22 k
C012	...... 83 k
C013	...... 61 k
C014	...... 102 k
C015	...... 608141 k

DAMMIT, RICHTER, WHAT HAVE YOU--

CRK-CLICK

EASY THERE, RICH--

WHAT THE HELL IS GOING ON, DRAKE??

I CAN'T GET AHOLD OF **CASA**-- I CAN'T GET AHOLD OF **ANYBODY**!

HOLD STEADY, RICHTER. WE'VE CHANGED FREQUENCIES OVER THE LAST TWENTY YEARS.

CALMLY SET DOWN GU

JUST GIVE ME A MINUTE TO GET THINGS SQUARE.

AND SO...

PUSH

TOGGLE

UH... THIS IS **CRATER XV** CALLING **CASA HQ**, CAN YOU HEAR ME?

beat.

HMM... I GUESS THEY MUST BE OUT TO LUNCH, OR--

DAMN YOU, DRAKE...

MIC INPUT

...THE **MIC CORD** ISN'T EVEN PLUGGED IN!

WHY DOES HE SOUND SO **SURPRISED**? DON'T YOU GUYS TALK, LIKE, **EVERY DAY**?

UH, **KEN**, YES...

...YES, IT IS **VERY STRANGE** FOR US TO BE TALKING RIGHT NOW...

...SINCE WE NORMALLY DON'T CHECK IN UNTIL **1400** HOURS.

???

I HOPE THAT CASA IS STILL RUNNING SMOOTH, LIKE **NORMAL**. OVER.

MUTUAL SHRUG

UH...

LIE

YES, UH... WE BRIEFLY LOST COM-MUNICATION WITH SOME OF THE BASES...

...AND WE'RE TRYING TO FIGURE OUT WHAT'S GOING ON. OVER.

LEAN IN

HMM... MAYBE INTERFERENCE CAUSED BY A SOLAR FLARE?

IS THAT **RICHTER FRONT**? I'LL BE DAMNED!

294

SWITCH OFF

KEN, WHAT WAS **THAT** ALL ABOUT?

JA! VUT DOES ZIS **MEAN**?

IT MEANS THERE'S BEEN A CHANGE OF PLANS.

WE'RE NOT GOING TO **STOP** THE SIBERIANS... WE'RE GOING TO **BEAT THEM.**

WHA-- **HOW?**

TURNS OUT WE'VE GOT SOME **CANADIAN** BOYS IN THE FIELD WHO ARE NEARLY **LAUNCH-READY.** WHICH MEANS THAT IN LESS THAN A WEEK...

...**CANADA** IS GOING TO THE **MOON!**

296

XI

SOON...

...I HAVE DIRECT ORDERS FROM THE **HIGH ARCTIC LEAGUE** TO DELIVER YOUR CARGO TO A **TOP SECRET LOCATION**!

I THINK YOU MADE A **MISTAKE**, BUDDY, THIS AIN'T **CARGO** --

-- IT'S JUST A BUNCH OF **MECHANICAL JUNK** WE'RE GOING TO DUMP ON EGLINTON ISLAND.

JUNK **NOW**, MAYBE, BUT IN A WEEK, IT'LL BE A **MOON ROCKET**!

WHATEVER YOU SAY, MAN...

SCRA
SC

...AS LONG AS **SOMEONE'S** PAYING, I'LL DROP THIS CRAP ANYWHERE YOU WANT.

"YOU'RE **MAD**, ARLUK!"

I DON'T CARE HOW WELL-EQUIPPED THIS LITTLE **MOON BASE** IS...

...YOU CAN'T BUILD A **ROCKET** IN A **WEEK**!

THAT'S A **BREATHTAKING** PACE!

LOOK, YOU DON'T KNOW **BENDRIX**. WITH HIS MECHANICAL EXPERTISE, WE **WILL** PLANT A CANADIAN FLAG IN LUNAR SOIL BEFORE THE **SIBERIANS** DO!

FLAG.

MOON.

WEEK.

302

303

306

INSIDE...

BLOOD & SWASH by D. Gregg

PARENTS!!

WELL DON'T JUST **STAND** THERE-- PUT YOUR **NICE** CLOTHES ON!

YELP!!

QUIET, BENJI! NO ONE WANTS TO TAKE HOME A **CRIER**!

YOU BOYS GET DOWN HERE--

--THIS COULD BE IT!!

pfft.

yeah right.

NO WAY!

YOU GUYS, LOOK WHO IT IS!!

FRANTICALLY PUT ON LIPSTICK

♫ Hello ♫

WELCOME TO THE BEECHEY ORPHANAGE!

RIGHT THIS WAY...

WATCH YOUR STEP...

NOW, I'M NOT SUPPOSED TO DO THIS--

--BUT BECAUSE YOU SEEM LIKE SUCH A NICE COUPLE...

... I WANT TO TELL YOU ABOUT OUR TWO-FOR-ONE DEAL--

WE'RE NOT HERE FOR A KID, LADY...

"...WE JUST CAME TO SEE WHERE WE GREW UP."

I'M SORRY, I HAVEN'T BEEN WORKING HERE VERY LONG.

THE AGENCY CYCLES THROUGH US PRETTY QUICKLY.

"Out of whose womb came the ice?"
JOB 38:29

FRANKLY, BEECHEY IS KIND OF A **TRAINING GROUND**. YOU KNOW, SOMETHING TO CUT YOUR **TEETH** ON.

UNFORTUNATELY, MY PREDECESSORS HAVE BEEN PRETTY **SPOTTY** ABOUT KEEPING **RECORDS**.

HOPEFULLY, THEY--

AH, HERE WE GO!

I'M GOING TO LOOK AROUND UPSTAIRS.

OKAY, ARMY.

311

"...THAT'S ODD."

YOU'RE ARMY SHANKS.

YOU'RE ALISTAIR'S UNCLE.

YEP.

WHERE DID HE SLEEP?

ARE YOU HERE TO VISIT HIM?

I--I DON'T UNDERSTAND. WHAT DO YOU MEAN "**VISIT**" HIM?

YOU KNOW HE'S **BURIED** HERE.

OUT BACK.

OH.

NO, I'VE NEVER STEPPED FOOT IN THAT GRAVEYARD...

...AND I DON'T INTEND TO START **NOW**.

ARE YOU **SCARED**?

DO YOU THINK IT'S **HAUNTED**?

WHAT? NO, I JUST--

CHANGE SUBJECT

HEY, UH...

SO WHERE ARE ALL THE **GIRLS**? IT WAS ABOUT **HALF AND HALF** WHEN I LIVED HERE.

THEY ALL GOT PICKED.

HAVE FAMILIES NOW.

TAKE A KNEE

C'MERE.

TELL ME...

WHAT DO GIRLS DO WHEN THEY'RE **SAD**?

315

UH...
THEY **CRY**?

THAT'S RIGHT. THEY LET IT ALL OUT FOR THE WORLD TO SEE. BUT WE DON'T GET TO DO THAT, DO WE?

YOU WANT TO KNOW WHAT I DO WHEN I'M SAD? WHEN I FEEL LIKE NO ONE WANTS ME?

I TAKE THAT FEELING, AND I **SQUEEZE** IT INTO A LITTLE **BRICK**.

AND I ADD THAT BRICK TO MY **WALL**.

AND PRETTY SOON I'VE GOT A **HUGE** WALL AROUND ME, TEN BRICKS THICK, AND **NOTHING** CAN GET INSIDE IT.

THIS IS IT.

THAT'S INTERESTING. USUALLY WHEN KIDS GET **ADOPTED** THEY TAKE ALL THEIR BELONGINGS **WITH** THEM.

WERE YOU--

KIDNAPPED.

I **THINK**, ANYWAY. BY **SIBERIAN PIRATES.**

≷SIGH≷ I WISH THAT KIDNAPPINGS WERE A THING OF THE PAST.

320

...BEHIND ALL THESE VINTAGE MARITIME-THEMED **PORNO MAGS**.

FO'C'LE FOLLIES!
ALL ICE QUEENS
SEXY STOWAWAYS
Real Siren
Aces of the THIGHS
SHE-PIRATES
Salty Mama
INTERVIEW:
POOPDECK
CROW'S NEST
TABOO TATTOO

THERE YOU ARE.

P.R.A.V.D.

Army...

EH?

ELSEWHERE... WHAT GOOD IS HAVING A **LEAGUE** IF WE DON'T STICK TOGETHER IN TIMES LIKE THIS?!

W-WAIT!!

THIS IS A **ONCE IN A LIFETIME** OPPORTUNITY!

WE'RE TALKING ABOUT THE **MOON**, DAMMIT!

WHY--WHY ARE THEY ALL **LEAVING**?

LET IT GO, KEN...

...WE DON'T NEED THEM.

324

XII

327

328

SOMETHING **HAPPENED** TO ME BACK THERE, PRAVDA. LIKE A WEIGHT BEING LIFTED.

MAYBE IT'S BECAUSE I WAS **YANKED AWAY** FROM THE ORPHANAGE SO SUDDENLY AS A CHILD...

AND **ALISTAIR**. SEEING WHERE ALISTAIR SPENT THE SEVEN YEARS OF HIS LIFE. MEETING HIS FRIENDS...

PLUS THE TWO OF US RETURNING TO WHERE WE **FIRST MET**...

ALL I KNOW IS THAT I FEEL LIKE I'VE FINALLY GOT SOME **CLOSURE** -- A **FRESH START** -- AND I'VE GOT **YOU** TO THANK FOR IT.

YES, ARMY...

329

"...IT'S A FRESH START FOR BOTH OF US."

LET'S SEE...

TO PULL THIS OFF, WE'LL NEED RCAN'S **BEST ENGINEERS** TO MAN THE CONTROLS HERE, AND THEY'LL NEED A **CRASH COURSE** IN--

KEN?

BUT ALL OUR ENGINEERS WENT TO **CRATER XV** TO FINISH THE ROCKET--

--DAMMIT!

KEN--

BE RIGHT BACK. I JUST HAD A **SVERDRUP** OF AN IDEA!

-- I REALIZE THAT YOU'RE FULFILLING YOUR LIFE'S DREAM OF LAUNCHING A **MOON ROCKET**, ETC., ETC...

...BUT WE CAN'T LOSE SIGHT OF THE **LUNAYEV**! I THOUGHT WE AGREED THAT THIS "LUNTONIUM" THING IS ONE BIG **HOAX**, AND THE "ROCKET" MIGHT ACTUALLY BE A **MISSILE**!

STAND

YOU SAID SO **YOUR-SELF**!

330

BARTY. YOU'VE BEEN A VALUABLE ASSET TO MY OFFICE OVER THE PAST YEAR...

PICK UP CLIPBOARD

...BUT YOU'RE ONLY WELCOME IN THIS BLOCKHOUSE IF YOU'RE **100% COMMITTED** TO GETTING OUR BOYS TO THE MOON.

SET IT BACK DOWN AGAIN

UH, **KEN**?...

EMPLOYEE PHONEBOOK

"...I THINK I KNOW WHERE WE CAN FIND SOME **ENGINEERS**!"

YOU WANT TO TALK TO **WHOM**? THE **JANITOR**?!?

DMS DMS

DEVON MONTAGE SUPPLIES

KEEP IT SHORT, SIEVERT. THIS IS THE **RED** PHONE!

HELLO? KEN **ARLUK**? BUT IT'S BEEN **TWENTY YEARS** SINCE--

MS DMS

YOU WANT ME TO COME BACK FOR A **WHAT** MISSION?!

DMS

CLATTER

331

335

337

IT'S JUST...

...THIS **ACCELERATED FLIGHT PLAN** HAS GOT ME ON EDGE.

NOT TO MENTION HAVING ENGINEERS **CRAWLING** ALL OVER THE PLACE, INSPECTING OUR WORK.

HAVE YOU... UH... **TALKED** TO A LOT OF THEM?

THE ENGINEERS?

NO.

I THINK DRAKE IS TRYING TO **SHIELD** ME FROM THEM.

I THINK HE THINKS I'M GOING TO START **RESENTING** THEM, DUE TO THE FACT THAT THEY'VE ALSO BEEN WORKING AT **CASA** FOR TWENTY YEARS...

...BUT HAVE BEEN ABLE TO HAVE **FAMILIES**.

YEAH, I BET THAT'S IT.

HERE, LET ME HELP YOU.

NO REASON FOR ME TO BE KEEPING PILES OF BOOKS ON THE FLOOR IN THE FIRST PLACE.

THESE ARE YOURS?

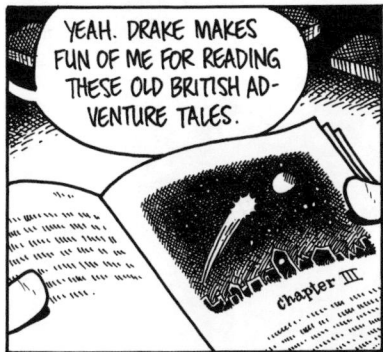

YEAH. DRAKE MAKES FUN OF ME FOR READING THESE OLD BRITISH ADVENTURE TALES.

Chapter III

THINKS IT'S **CHILD-ISH.**

WELL, WHEN YOU GET BACK FROM THE MOON, YOU'LL HAVE YOUR **OWN** ADVENTURE TALE!

... WENDY, I DON'T THINK YOU FULLY UNDERSTAND WHAT'S ABOUT TO HAPPEN.

THIS IS GOING TO BE A **ONE-WAY** TRIP.

DRAKE AND I, ... WELL...

341

LOOK, I KNOW WHAT YOU'RE ALL THINKING:

"THAT AIN'T SHANKS. WHAT KINDA **SCHEME** IS HE RUNNIN'?"

REMOVES CAP FOR THE FIRST TIME IN SERIES

NO SCHEME.

PRAVDA AND I ARE IN **LOVE**. A LOVE WE'VE SHARED SINCE CHILDHOOD.

AND WHEN YOU'RE IN LOVE, NOTHING CAN DISTRACT YOU FROM--

WHAT THE--?

343

THANK YOU AGAIN FOR YOUR HOSPITALITY. I REALIZE THIS IS AN INCONVEN- IENCE.

BOW

WELL **HECK**, ANYTHING I CAN DO TO HELP TURN THAT RUSSKIE TANKER INTO A **SMOKING HULL**, EH?

RCAN

I'LL BE IN MY QUARTERS. YOU NEED ANYTHING, JUST USE THE INTERCOM.

BUT BE CAREFUL YOU DON'T SWITCH IT TO "LOUD- SPEAKER" MODE. IT'S FRICKIN' **LOUD**!

CUT OUT PHOTO

RCAN

SHUT

WHAT HAPPENS **NOW**, BARTY?

NOW, STWALLEY...

347

SLUMP

C'MON.

NO--I'M **TIRED**, ARMY! WE'VE BEEN OUT HERE A **WEEK**! (AS YOU KNOW.)

TAKE ME BACK!

YOU KNOW I CAN'T.

NOT UNTIL I KNOW SHE'S ALIVE -- OR DEAD.

ONE WAY OR THE OTHER.

I...I MAY BE ABLE TO HELP WITH THAT.

EH?

I--I'VE NEVER TOLD ANYONE THIS, BECAUSE I'VE ALWAYS BEEN **ASHAMED** OF IT--

--FRIGHTENED OF IT, EVEN.

OF **WHAT**?

I HAVE A **GIFT**, ARMY. SOMETHING THAT MIGHT HELP US FIND WENDY.

A **GIFT**? YOU COULDN'T HAVE MENTIONED THIS A **WEEK** AGO? I DON'T WANT TO BE OUT HERE ANY MORE THAN **YOU** DO.

FLUMP

SO?... ...LET'S SEE IT!

349

350

SHE **KNEW** SHE WAS LEAVING ME. THAT'S THE ONLY EXPLANATION.

AS SOON AS WE HIT CANADIAN WATERS, SHE BECAME AS COLD AS **PACK ICE** AND AS DISTANT AS A **POLYNYA**.

HAD SHE PLANNED THIS WHOLE THING WITH SHANKS FROM THE **BEGINNING**?

...KNOWING THAT BEING "KIDNAPPED" WAS THE ONLY WAY TO GET OFF OF THE LUNAYEV?

BUT **WHY**?

I'VE BEEN A... A...

SLUG

...A MODEL HUSBAND!

"GATHER 'ROUND, BOYS."

XIII

359

KNOCK!
KNOCK!

COME IN.

LIEUTENANT STWALLEY! WHAT'VE YOU BROUGHT ME?

MORE OLD SIBERIAN NEWSPAPERS. TRIED TO FIND ANY MENTION OF CAPTAIN SZTAB.

YAY!

THANK GOD THESE ARE ALL IN ENGLISH. I COULD DO WITHOUT THE BACKWARDS "N" THOUGH.

HOW GOES THE RESEARCH, SIR?

SADLY, STWALLEY, I HAVEN'T YET FOUND ANYTHING THAT GIVES SZTAB **MOTIVE** TO WANT TO **BOMB CANADA.**

"JUST A BUNCH OF ARTICLES ABOUT HOW SZTAB WAS A **FAILED COSMONAUT**...

"...HOW HE MOVED TO THE **LENA DELTA** WITH **MOLNIYA SEMYORKA**...

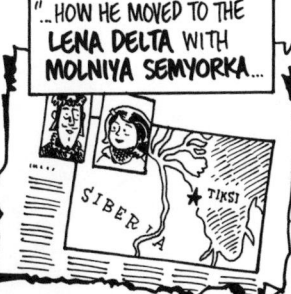

"...AND HOW THE **LENA DELTA** WILL SOON **RUN OUT OF OIL**."

NYET OIL

SO LIKE I SAID, NOTHING HELPFUL.

BUT ANY DAY NOW THIS CASE AGAINST SZTAB WILL **CRACK**, STWALLEY.

AND WHEN IT DOES...

361

MEANWHILE...

sniff
sniff

ARE YOU STILL SMELLING IT? THE THING YOU WERE SMELLING EARLIER?

ALMOST THERE. IT'S GETTING STRONGER.

SHOULD BE JUST OVER THAT RIDGE.

GASP!

IT LOOKS LIKE SOME KIND OF **MOON BASE!**

LATER... HMMM...

SOMEONE'S BEEN HERE RECENTLY, BUT I'M NOT SURE IF IT WAS **WENDY**.

LOOK, PRAVDA... I'M SORRY THAT I FREAKED OUT EARLIER ABOUT YOUR... UH...

chew chew

...YOUR "GIFT."

IT'S JUST THAT I DON'T LIKE TO THINK ABOUT "THE OTHER SIDE" SINCE...

...SINCE...WELL, YOU KNOW.

NO-- WHAT?

365

... YOU KNOW, OUR OLD **HEAD-MISTRESS**?

HER STORIES ABOUT THE **DEAD CHILDREN**?

LEA IN

YOUR NIGHT IN THE **GRAVEYARD**?

REMIND ME!

PREPARE for FLASHBACK

MISS PUTNIK. OUR HEAD-MISTRESS.

"SHE RAN THAT PLACE LIKE A COBURG ISLAND PRISON.

"NOT A SINGLE DIRTY NAIL, NOT A HAIR OUT OF PLACE. (I CAN'T BELIEVE YOU DON'T REMEMBER THIS!)

"SHE WAS A BIG BELIEVER IN **PREVENTATIVE** DISCIPLINE, THROUGH **THREATS**.

"HER **FAVORITE** THREAT, OF COURSE, INVOLVED THE **GRAVEYARD** OUT BACK.

"EVEN BACK THEN, THE GRAVEYARD WAS OVERRUN WITH LITTLE CAIRNS.

"DECADES OF CHILDREN LOST TO NEGLIGENCE, LONELINESS, OR WORSE."

367

"ANYWAY, PUTNIK OFTEN THREATENED TO MAKE KIDS **SLEEP** IN THE GRAVEYARD IF THEY MISBEHAVED.

"THAT USUALLY DID THE TRICK."

HAR HAR HAR

BUT YOU -- YOU WERE **COCKY**. COCKIER THAN I EVER WAS.

YOU THOUGHT SHE WAS BLUFFING, AND ONE DAY YOU CALLED HER ON IT.

"OF COURSE, SHE WASN'T BLUFFING. PUTNIK GOT SO ENRAGED...

SLOWLY RAISE MIDDLE FINGER

"...THAT SHE LOCKED YOU INSIDE THE GATE THAT VERY NIGHT AFTER SUPPER."

"WE HEARD YOU SCREAMING ALL NIGHT. NO ONE SLEPT A WINK.

"I WAS TOO YOUNG THEN TO KNOW THAT I COULD HAVE HELPED YOU.

"THE NEXT MORNING, PUTNIK WALKED YOU IN QUIETLY LIKE NOTHING HAD HAPPENED."

"BUT YOU HAD **CHANGED**.

"FROM THEN ON, NO ONE EVER HEARD YOU SPEAK A SINGLE WORD.

"WE HAD BEEN FRIENDS BEFORE THAT... BUT NOW YOU WOULDN'T LEAVE MY SIDE.

"I WAS YOUR PROTECTOR OR SOMETHING.

"YOU STAYED IN A TIGHT, SILENT ORBIT AROUND ME, DAY AND NIGHT...UNTIL..."

UNTIL **WHAT**?

UNTIL NOTHING. I WAS SCOOPED UP AND SHIPPED OFF TO THE ARCTIC ACADEMY.

"NO WARNING. NO REAL CHANCE TO SAY GOODBYE.

"THOSE BASTARDS JUST WALKED IN, TOLD ME TO PACK UP MY THINGS, AND THAT WAS IT."

I HAD ALWAYS ASSUMED THE **WORST**-- THAT WITHOUT ME AT YOUR SIDE, YOU HAD **WITHERED UP** AND **DIED.**

EGOTISTICAL, RIGHT? BECAUSE **LOOK**...

...HERE YOU ARE!

SURPRISE HUG!

ALRIGHT, NOW SHOW ME THIS **GIFT** OF YOURS.

IS THIS HOW MY HANDS SHOULD GO, OR--

ARMY, WE DON'T HAVE TO DO THIS.

C'MON! IF **YOU** OF ALL PEOPLE ARE OKAY WITH TALKING WITH DEAD FOLKS, THEN I THINK **I** CAN BE, TOO.

SO, ASSUMING THAT POOR WENDY HAS CROSSED TO THE OTHER SIDE...

373

374

378

376

375

LET ME **EXPLAIN**, CAPTAIN!

"DEEP INSIDE YOU HAVE ONLY **ONE** LOVE: **SPACE TRAVEL**.

"WHEN THE **SIBERIAN ROCKET PROGRAM** LEFT YOU STANDING ON THE LAUNCH PAD, YOU WERE **CRUSHED**.

"AFTER THAT, YOU USED WOMEN -- INCLUDING MOLNIYA -- TO FILL THE VOID LEFT BY THE SRP'S COLLAPSE.

"BUT CAPTAIN, THE FEELING YOU GET FROM A BEAUTIFUL WOMAN...

"...IS NO SUBSTITUTE FOR THE FEELING OF BREAKING THROUGH THE EQUIGRAVISPHERE."

381

DAMN THE **SRP**! THEY LET **DOGS** FLY IN SPACE BEFORE ME!

SO PERHAPS, CAPTAIN, WE COULD TAKE THE PROFITS FROM THIS OIL -- AND THE AMERICAN'S C$51 MILLION -- AND START OUR **OWN** SPACE PROGRAM!

WOULDN'T THAT BE NICE, SIR?

AH, BY THE TIME A ROCKET -- A **REAL** ROCKET, NOT THIS MUSEUM PIECE -- WAS READY, I'D BE TOO OLD TO FLY IT.

LET'S FACE IT: I HAD **ONE SHOT** TO GO INTO SPACE...

"...AND I MISSED IT."

газета

LAUNCHUS INTERRUPTUS

MAN, CAPTAIN SZTAB MUST HAVE BEEN **PISSED**.

382

383

384

XIV

390

GOODNIGHT, GUYS. AND REMEMBER, GET A GOOD NIGHT'S SLEEP...

...BECAUSE TOMORROW'S THE **BIG DAY**!

A LITTLE LATER...

SO WHAT DO YOU THINK, ESPEN? ARE WE CRAZY FOR DOING THIS?

IRRATIONAL IS MORE LIKE IT.

LEDA!

WHAT'RE YOU DOING, CREEPING AROUND HERE AT NIGHT?

JUST WANTED TO SEE WHAT THE **COMPETITION'S** UP TO.

BY NOW, IT'S NO SECRET THAT I'VE INVESTED HEAVILY IN THE SIBERIANS' LUNTONIUM CLEAN ENERGY PROJECT.

UNLIKE YOU, I'M LOOKING **FORWARD**, KEN, NOT **BACKWARD**.

ALSO SIT

LOOK, RICHTER, I'M SORRY THAT I --

DON'T.

I MAY BE **REELING** FROM THE SHOCK OF IT ALL...

...BUT I'M NOT **MAD** AT YOU.

I WOULD HAVE DONE THE SAME THING.

WOW...

...YOU'RE BEING **VERY** OPEN-MINDED ABOUT ALL THIS.

WELL, DESPITE TWENTY YEARS OF LIES, **TOMORROW** IS **REAL**.

WE'VE BOTH SPENT **HALF OUR LIVES** PREPARING FOR THIS, DRAKE.

MAURICE IS GOING TO **FLY**!

396

399

"...DECADES IN THE MAKING!"

CA/A

Dear Astronaut RICHTER FRONT,

CONGRATULATIONS!

If you're reading this, then you have made it to the moon-- the REAL moon! Inside this time capsule are things you thought you... to have with you on... lunar surface to remind you of home.

Sincerely,
THE CANADIAN ARCTIC SPACE AGENCY

♥ Becky

PULL OUT SOME STATIONERY AND A ZERO-GRAVITY PEN

Dear Drake

NOW, I DON'T EXPECT YOU TO REMEMBER ME WORKING ON THIS BACK IN THE ORPHANAGE.

YOU WERE AROUND ME SO OFTEN THAT I COULD ONLY CARVE THE LETTERS WHEN YOU WERE ASLEEP.

WELL-- HERE.

THEY SHIPPED ME OFF TO THE ACADEMY SO FAST I COULDN'T GIVE IT TO YOU BACK THEN.

IT WASN'T EVEN DONE. I HAD TO SNEAK IN THE LAST "A" OVER THE PAST WEEK WHILE YOU WERE SLEEPING.

JUST LIKE OLD TIMES, EH?

HERE, LET ME PUT IT ON YOU!

LEAN IN

SHANKS, NO. I COULDN'T.

C'MON --

NO.

I MEAN... THIS NECKLACE WAS MEANT FOR THE **GIRL** PRAVDA, NOT THE **ADULT**.

??

WHAT THE HELL'S THE **DIFFERENCE**? IT'S MEANT FOR **YOU**!

NOW LEMME SEE THAT NECK, OKAY?

OH... OKAY.

407

408

409

410

CRATER
FIFTEEN?

XV

419

421

425

THE ROCKET IS IN **THERE**, I IMAGINE?

YES, BUT IT'S OFF-LIMITS TO --

SHOULDN'T THERE BE MORE **ENGINEERS** RUNNING AROUND?

CHECKING WIRES AND THAT SORT OF THING?

UH...

AND WHERE IS CAPTAIN SZTAB?

I WANT TO SPEAK WITH **CAPTAIN SZTAB!**

SLOWLY REMOVE CAP

I'M SORRY, MRS. BASCOM, THE CAPTAIN HAS STEPPED OFF THE SHIP FOR A WHILE...

THIS IS **EXACTLY** WHAT I WAS TRY-ING TO **AVOID**! THE SECOND RICHTER HEARD ABOUT **CASA DISSOLVING**, HE WOULD HAVE RUN HOME TO THAT **GIRLFRIEND** OF HIS.

THRO

"BECKY THIS" AND "BECKY THAT"-- THAT'S ALL I HEARD NONSTOP FOR **YEARS**!

WAIT A SECOND ... MY **MOM'S** NAME WAS BECKY!

Beat.

YOU MEAN **BECKY ELAINE GREENE** FROM MAXWELL BAY?

NO, **BECKY ANNABELLE PEWTERSCHMIDT** FROM GRAND BRUIT.

OH. OH.

428

429

"...I THINK I JUST FOUND OUR **SMOKING GUN!**"

I'M GOING TO BE HONEST WITH YOU: I'M NOT EXCITED ABOUT YOU BEING MY CO-PILOT.

I THINK YOU'RE TOO YOUNG TO COMPREHEND THE GRAVE REPERCUSSIONS THIS DECISION WILL HAVE ON YOU AND YOUR FAMILY.

BUT I'M NO LONGER IN THE BUSINESS OF TRYING TO THINK FOR OTHER PEOPLE, SO I'M JUST GOING TO TREAT YOU LIKE AN ADULT AND NOT TRY TO TALK YOU OUT OF IT.

JUST TELL ME YOU UNDERSTAND THAT THIS IS A **ONE-WAY TRIP**, AND WHEN THAT FACT **SINKS IN**--AND IT **WILL**-- YOU KNOW THERE'S NO TURNING BACK.

I **KNOW**. RICHTER AND I HAD A SUPER-LONG TALK ABOUT IT.

DRAKE, THIS IS MY **DREAM**. AND IF I DIDN'T GO NOW...

...WITH YOU...

"...I'D SPEND THE REST OF MY LIFE REGRETTING IT."

LOOK! SEE THE **DISPLACEMENT MARKERS**?

THE LUNAYEV HASN'T SPENT THE LAST WEEK PREPPING THEIR **ROCKET**--

--THEY'VE BEEN SUCKING UP **OIL**!

HA-HA! I **KNEW** IT!

"LUNTONIUM" IS A **HOAX**!

doof!

"BARTY WAS RIGHT ALL ALONG!"

435

BREAK on THROUGH...

...and RECOVER!

AND SO... CALLING ALL CASA MOON BASES, CALLING ALL CASA MOON BASES...

FIDDLE WITH KNOBS

...I'M LOOKING FOR A **LOST GIRL** NAMED **WENDY.** I REPEAT, A **LOST GIRL** NAMED--

ARMY?

YES, MA'AM, I'M CALLING FROM THE NINTH CRATER, AND I'M TRYING TO TRACK DOWN A--

ARMY, SLOW DOWN, IT'S **ME**...

...IT'S **WENDY.**

WENDY? IS THAT REALLY **YOU**? WHERE **ARE** YOU?

I'M FINE, ARMY, BUT I CAN'T TALK LONG -- I'VE ALLOWED MYSELF TO BE **TIED DOWN AND TRAPPED** IN A TINY METAL ROOM SURROUNDED BY WIRES AND BUTTONS. ha ha WHAT I MEAN TO SAY IS THAT I'M DOING IT, ARMY! I'M GOING TO THE MOON! NOT JUPITER'S MOON, GRANTED, BUT IT'S BETTER THAN NOTHING, RIGHT?

I KNOW THIS ALL SEEMS OUT OF THE BLUE, BUT I GUESS WE'RE TRYING TO BEAT SOME **CRAZY SIBERIAN NAMED SZTAB** WHO'S TRYING TO BLOW UP THE MOON OR SOMETHING. ANYWAY, IF YOU'RE NEARBY, YOU SHOULD COME TO A POST-LAUNCH PARTY **HELD IN CRATER FIFTEEN**.

OOP-- GOTTA GO! BYE-BYE!

...TIED DOWN AND TRAPPED... : STATIC! : ...CRAZY SIBERIAN NAMED SZTAB...

: STATIC! :

...HELD IN CRATER FIFTEEN...

WENDY?? **HELLO??**

WHAT DID YOU SAY? **FIFTEEN**??

DEVON ISLAND

FIFTEEN, FIFTEEN, FIFTEEN, FIFTEEN, FIFTEEN, FIF--

CRATER XV

BINGO.

443

"... AND PREPARE TO **STORM THE SHIP!**"

XVI

448

449

450

451

HOWDY, BOYS!...

...MY WIFE ASKED ME TO DELIVER A **PRESENT**...

...COURTESY OF **UNCLE SAM**!

BASCOM

GRAB MY HAND!

HURRY!!

457

462

COUGH UP BLOOD!

WHY, MOLNIYA? WHY DID YOU LEAVE ME FOR THAT TWO-BIT FISH-STICK EATER **SHANKS**?

OH, MY HUSBAND, IT'S ALL SO SIMPLE AND SO HORRIBLE! A LITTLE OVER A WEEK AGO...

STRAIN to HEAR

MRGH.

BUT... BUT WHY DIDN'T YOU JUST **TELL** ME RIGHT AWAY? WE COULD HAVE FIGURED THIS WHOLE THING OUT...
...TOGETHER!

BECAUSE, MY LOVE...

465

PRAVDA, ER-- MOLNIYA, ER--

--WHAT THE **HELL'S** GOING ON??

:SIGH:

IT ALL STARTED AS THE *LUNAYEV* NEARED DEVON ISLAND...

OOP--HANG ON, HANG ON... I CAN'T HEAR A WORD YOU'RE SAYING. CAN YOU COME CLOSER, OR--

NEVERMIND, DON'T MOVE. I GOT IT.

DRAG

OKAY, PLEASE START OVER.

RIGHT. IT ALL STARTED AS THE *LUNAYEV* NEARED DEVON ISLAND...

"SZTABYA AND I HAD A WHOLE **PLAN** WORKED OUT. USING AN OLD **R7 ROCKET** AS A **DIVERSION**...

"...WE WERE GOING TO SAVE OUR CASH-STRAPPED **LENA DELTA** BY STEALING YOUR COUNTRY'S **UNTAPPED OIL**.

LEACOCK OIL FIELD

"BUT SUDDENLY I HAD A **VISION**--A **HORRIBLE** VISION--OF THE FUTURE!

"IN MY VISION, I SAW MY HUSBAND **DYING** IN MY ARMS, A DESTROYED ROCKET SMOLDERING BEHIND US.

"I DIDN'T KNOW WHAT TO DO."

"BUT AFTER THE EXPLOSION AT THE BLOCKHOUSE, I HAD AN **EPIPHANY**."

OH MY GOD.

I REALIZED THAT THE ONLY WAY TO **SAVE** MY HUSBAND WAS TO **STAY AWAY** FROM HIM...

...SINCE IN THE **VISION** WE WERE **TOGETHER**.

"AND SO, RELUCTANTLY, I PLAYED ALONG WITH YOUR BELIEF THAT I WAS THE ADULT VERSION OF THIS **PRAVDA** GIRL...

"...BECAUSE I KNEW IF YOU BELIEVED **THAT**, THEN YOU'D NEVER LET SZTAB **NEAR** ME, AND MAYBE I COULD STOP MY VISION FROM COMING TRUE!"

BUT... BUT WHAT ABOUT **US**? WHAT ABOUT **ROME**?...

469

"...WAS THAT ALL A **LIE**?"

KEN? ANYONE? CAN YOU HEAR ME?

LOUD AND CLEAR, DRAKE.

HOW ARE YOU BOTH DOING?

FINE, KEN. WE FELT SOME RUMBLING, BUT WE WERE FAR ENOUGH AWAY FROM THE EXPLOSION TO AVOID ANY STRUCTURAL DAMAGE TO **OUR** ROCKET.

AND **WENDY**? IS SHE--

I'M OKAY, TOO!

WIDESPREAD CONFUSION

BUT THE **BOGEY**... ...THE **EXPLOSION**... I THOUGHT...

KEN, WHAT'S GOING **ON**?

:SIGH:

THERE'S NO EASY WAY TO SAY THIS:

I **LIED** TO YOU. TO **ALL** OF YOU.

BENDRIX'S "MOON ROCKET" WAS A **FAKE**.

MOOOOAANNN...

I **KNEW** THIS ALL SEEMED TOO GOOD TO BE TRUE. NOW WE'LL **NEVER** GET TO THE MOON.

NOT SO FAST, ESPEN. I HAD BENDRIX BUILD THAT FAKE ROCKET AS A **TRAP** FOR LEDA BASCOM.

TO DISTRACT HER FROM THE **REAL** ROCKET.

ALLOW ME TO EXPLAIN:

SEE, I KNOW LEDA WELL ENOUGH TO HAVE PREDICTED THAT SHE WOULD TRY TO **SABOTAGE** OUR MISSION... SO I HAD BENDRIX BUILD A **FAKE ROCKET**.

THE **REAL** ROCKET IS AN UNDERGROUND **RAILGUN** DESIGN. RICHTER AND DRAKE HAVE BEEN WORKING ON IT **PIECE BY PIECE** FOR NEARLY TWENTY YEARS.

I LIED TO YOU IN THE NAME OF **SAFETY**. I FELT IT WAS NECESSARY TO KEEP YOU IN THE DARK TO PREVENT **LEDA** FROM FINDING OUT.

SO... ARE WE COOL?

EH? ESPEN?

YEAH, WE'RE COOL.

OKAY, THEN...

START the CLOCK!

TEN...

"...NINE...

ROME **WAS** REAL, ARMY. I FELL IN **LOVE** WITH YOU.

"...EIGHT...

OR, AT LEAST...

...I FELL IN LOVE WITH BEING YOUR **PRAVDA.**

"...SEVEN...

THE WAY YOU **LOOKED** AT ME...

"...SIX...

...IT FELT LIKE YOU REALLY **HAD** KNOWN ME ALL MY LIFE.

473

KEN! I'VE GOT **BARTY** CALLING FROM THE DECK OF THE **LUNAYEV!** SOUNDS **URGENT!**

KEN ARLUK HERE.

I WAS **RIGHT**, KEN! "LUNTONIUM" IS A **SHAM!** THE "ROCKET" IS AN **ANTIQUE!**

THIS WAS ALWAYS ABOUT STEALING **OIL!**

I KNOW, BARTY.

THEN WHY DO YOU SOUND SO **CALM?**

YOU JUST SENT TWO CANADIANS-- ONE OF THEM A **MINOR** -- TO THEIR **DEATHS!!**

478

479

481

EPILOGUE

FOUR DAYS LATER...

"WHY, WITHIN **HOURS** OF THE LAUNCH, WE WITNESSED THE RESIGNATION OF **KEN ARLUK**...

"...WHO HAD **RESTARTED CASA** ILLEGALLY, AND WHO, BY SOME ACCOUNTS, EVEN KEPT **HAL** AMBASSADORS **HOSTAGE** IN THE BLOCKHOUSE!

"NO WORD ON WHERE MR. ARLUK IS **NOW**... HE SEEMS TO HAVE DROPPED OFF THE FACE OF THE EARTH!"

"FINE BY ME, DALE, BECAUSE IN MY HUMBLE OPINION THE **REAL** HERO ON THE GROUND IS **BARTHIZOD REDGRAVE.**

"THAT'S RIGHT, MICHAEL. MR. REDGRAVE **VALIANTLY** FOUGHT OFF THE **SIBERIAN** OIL THIEVES...

"...AND NOW TAKES KEN ARLUK'S SPOT AS THE CANADIAN AMBASSADOR TO THE **HIGH ARCTIC LEAGUE!**"

488

BUT MAYBE THE MOST **BIZARRE** ASPECT OF THIS STORY IS THAT ONE-TIME HEADLINE MAKER **ARMY SHANKS** WAS FOUND WOUNDED AT THE LAUNCH SITE.

"GOVERNMENT OFFICIALS EITHER **CAN'T** OR **WON'T** SAY WHAT SHANKS WAS **DOING** THERE...

"...BUT **MY** SOURCES TELL ME THAT SHANKS AND OIL THIEF **CAPTAIN SZTAB** WERE SEEN TRYING TO STORM A **DECOY ROCKET** NEAR THE SITE."

"I GUESS THE JOKE'S ON SHANKS, BECAUSE THE **REAL** ROCKET WAS ACTUALLY BUILT **UNDERGROUND**."

"ha ha... SO TRUE, DALE -- I'D SAY THE JOKE'S **DEFINITELY** ON OLD ARMY SHANKS."

≡CLICK≡

489

ALRIGHT...

491

Much of **CRATER XV** was inspired by my time working as an artist on Jim Ottaviani's nonfiction graphic novel **T-MINUS: THE RACE TO THE MOON**. I highly encourage everyone to check it out to see what a **REAL** space race looks like.

A warm and heartfelt thanks go out to Chris Staros, Brett Warnock, Leigh Walton, Robert Venditti, and Chris Ross at Top Shelf for the enthusiasm and critical eye they have given this book, and for their patience and support in getting **CRATER XV** in front of fans a year early via **DOUBLE BARREL**.

Thanks to my mom and Zander Cannon who, as early readers, provided lots of great feedback and encouragement.

Special thanks to Lea Brovedani who sent me numerous newspapers and documents during her travels in Nunavut, and thanks to Espen Jorgensen for mailing me cool arctic-themed stuff from Oslo, including copies of Norwegian newspapers on the 100th anniversary of Roald Amundsen's discovery of the last place on Earth. These documents are rich sources of inspiration for the Shanks stories.

Finally, thanks to the outspoken fans of **FAR ARDEN**. This sequel wouldn't exist without your enthusiasm.

Kevin Cannon is a cartoonist and illustrator from Minneapolis. His most recent graphic novels include **UNDERSTANDING RHETORIC** and **EVOLUTION: THE STORY OF LIFE ON EARTH**. He has also illustrated a handful of children's books, most notably **BEN AND LUCY PLAY POND HOCKEY** and **THE GLUTEN GLITCH**.

www.kevincannon.org

interrogative	interrog	interrogativo
invariable	invar	invariable
Ireland	Ir	Irlanda
ironic	iro	irónico
irregular	irr	irregular
	Law	Derecho
Linguistics	Ling	Lingüística
Literature	Lit	Literatura
literary	lit	literario
masculine	m	masculino
Mathematics	Math	Matemáticas
Mechanics	Mech	Mecánica
Medicine	Med	Medicina
Metallurgy	Metal	Metalurgia
Meteorology	Meteorol	Meteorología
Mexico	Mex	Méjico, México
masculine and feminine	mf	masculino y femenino
Military	Mil	Militar
Mining	Min	Minería
masculine plural	mpl	masculino plural
Music	Mus	Música
Mythology	Myth	Mitología
noun	n	nombre, sustantivo
Nautical	Naut	Náutica
negative	neg	negativo
noun feminine	nf	nombre femenino
Nicaragua	Nic	
noun masculine	nm	nombre masculino
noun masculine and feminine	nmf	nombre masculino y femenino
Optics	Opt	Óptica
Ornithology	Orn	Ornitología
Panama	Pan	Panamá
Paraguay	Par	
Parliament	Parl	Parlamento
pejorative	pej	peyorativo, despectivo
Peru	Per	Perú
personal	pers	personal
Pharmacy	Pharm	Farmacia
Philosophy	Philos	Filosofía
Phonetics	Phon	Fonética
Photography	Phot	Fotografía
Physics	Phys	Física
Physiology	Physiol	Fisiología
plural	pl	plural
Poetry	Poet	Poesía
poetic	poet	poético
Politics	Pol	Política
possessive	poss	posesivo
	Post	Correos
Puerto Rico	PR	
preposition	prep	preposición
pronoun	pron	pronombre
provincial	prov	provincial
Psychology	Psych	Psicología
past participle	ptp	participio del pasado
	Radio	
Railways	Rail	Ferrocarriles
Religion	Rel	Religión
relative	rel	relativo
River Plate Region	RPl	Región de la Plata
El Salvador	Salv	
Spanish America	SAm	Hispanoamérica
	School	Escuela
Scotland	Scot	Escocia
Santo Domingo, Dominican Republic	SD	República Dominicana
	see	véase
Sewing	Sew	Costura
singular	sing	singular
slang	sl	argot, vulgarismo
	Sport	Deportes
subjunctive	subj	subjuntivo
superlative	superl	superlativo
	Surveying	Agrimensura
taboo, not in decent use	tabu	tabú
Bullfighting	Taur	Tauromaquia
Technical	Tech	Técnica
Telephone	Tel	Teléfono
	Tennis	Tenis
Theatre	Theat	Teatro
Television	TV	Televisión
Typography	Typ	Tipografía
University	Univ	Universidad
Uruguay	Urug	
United States	US	Estados Unidos
auxiliary verb	v aux	verbo auxiliar
Venezuela	Ven	
Veterinary Medicine	Vet	Veterinaria
intransitive verb	vi	verbo intransitivo (o neutro)
impersonal verb	v impers	verbo impersonal
reflexive verb	vr	verbo reflexivo
transitive verb	vt	verbo transitivo (o activo)
transitive and intransitive verb	vti	verbo transitivo e intransitivo
Zoology	Zool	Zoología

This book is given to our library
in honor of the Past Presidents
of Morrill PTA.

February 8, 1983

COLLINS
SPANISH - ENGLISH
ENGLISH - SPANISH
DICTIONARY

DICCIONARIO
ESPAÑOL - INGLÉS
INGLÉS - ESPAÑOL

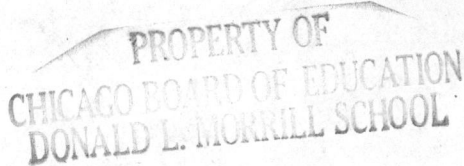

COLLINS
DICCIONARIO
ESPAÑOL-INGLÉS
INGLÉS-ESPAÑOL

por Colin Smith
en colaboración con
Manuel Bermejo Marcos
y Eugenio Chang-Rodríguez

Collins · London & Glasgow

COLLINS
SPANISH-ENGLISH
ENGLISH-SPANISH
DICTIONARY

by Colin Smith
in collaboration with
Manuel Bermejo Marcos
and Eugenio Chang-Rodríguez

Collins · London & Glasgow

COLIN SMITH IS PROFESSOR OF SPANISH, UNIVERSITY OF
CAMBRIDGE, AND FELLOW OF ST. CATHARINE'S COLLEGE
MANUEL BERMEJO MARCOS IS SENIOR LECTURER IN SPANISH,
UNIVERSITY OF LEEDS
EUGENIO CHANG-RODRÍGUEZ IS CHAIRMAN, LATIN AMERICAN
AREA STUDIES,
QUEENS COLLEGE OF THE CITY UNIVERSITY OF NEW YORK

ISBN 0 00 433471 X
Thumb Index ISBN 0 00 433472 8

*Manufactured in the United States
of America by Rand McNally & Company*

Contents

Materias

Preface

Given the rapidity of change in language and in its social and theoretical aspects, a new dictionary hardly needs an apology. This dictionary would be justified even if it were of the traditional type; in fact it incorporates new principles (discussed in the Introduction) which may be of interest to linguists, and whose practical application should ease the task of users at every level.

The lexicographer who attempts to equate and harmonize two great world languages must honestly recognize that both in theory and in practice his task cannot be perfectly fulfilled. The simplest word often has such a range, such semantic potentiality and such nuances that it cannot be fully defined within a single-language dictionary; it is more difficult still to translate it in a two-language dictionary of modest size.

This is, however, an optimistic undertaking. It presupposes that the two linguistic areas are in contact for reasons of trade, diplomacy, and tourism; for cultural, literary, scientific and sporting exchanges; that each has something to learn from the other and the will to do so. It presupposes free intercommunication across the frontiers and the oceans. The dictionary is a tool of understanding and it speaks for peace, tolerance and mutual respect.

I am greatly indebted to the following: Dr M. Bermejo Marcos, who read all the drafts; Prof. E. Chang-Rodríguez, who read the first part to check information about American Spanish; Mr H. B. Hall, who advised on principles at the start and read sections of the second part; and for a variety of contributions, to Mr T. C. Bookless, Prof. R. F. Brown, Dr G. A. Davies, Miss A. Johnson, Mr A. Madigan, Mr A. McCallum, Miss G. Weston, Sr J. and Sra M. del Río, Sra A. Espinosa de Walker and Sra M. J. Fernández de Wangermann. My wife helped in all the ways that wives do. To them all, my warmest thanks.

Cambridge

CCS
March 1971

Prefacio

El rápido desarrollo de las lenguas y de sus aspectos sociales y teóricos eximen al autor de la necesidad de disculparse al publicar un nuevo diccionario. Este libro se justificaría aun cuando fuera del tipo tradicional; se justifica más incorporando varios principios nuevos que pueden tener interés para los lingüistas, y cuya aplicación práctica podrá ayudar a los usuarios de todo tipo.

El lexicógrafo que se esfuerza por juntar y armonizar dos grandes idiomas mundiales tiene que reconocer honradamente que tanto en la teoría como en la práctica es imposible llevar perfectamente a cabo su cometido. La palabra más sencilla puede tener tal extensión, tanta potencialidad semántica y tantos matices que resulta imposible definirla en un libro monolingüe; es más difícil todavía traducirla en un diccionario bilingüe de tamaño modesto.

Con todo, esta empresa se funda en el optimismo. Ello supone que las dos áreas lingüísticas están en contacto por razones comerciales, diplomáticas y turísticas; para el intercambio cultural, literario, científico y deportivo; porque cada una tiene interés en aprender de la otra, y la voluntad de hacerlo. Ello supone que existe la libre comunicación a través de las fronteras y de los océanos. El diccionario sirve para la comprensión mutua y habla en pro de la paz.

Agradezco la ayuda de: Dr M. Bermejo Marcos, que leyó todos los borradores; Prof. E. Chang-Rodríguez, que leyó la 1ª parte para mejorar lo referente al español de América; Sr H. B. Hall, que me aconsejó al principio y leyó varias letras de la 2ª parte. Han contribuido también: Sr T. C. Bookless, Prof. R. F. Brown, Dr G. A. Davies, Srta A. Johnson, Sr A. Madigan, Sr A. McCallum, Srta G. Weston, Sr J. y Sra M. del Río, Sra A. Espinosa de Walker y Sra M. J. Fernández de Wangermann. Mi mujer ha prestado su ayuda en las maneras en que suelen prestarla las mujeres. Para todos, mis gracias.

Introduction

I *GENERAL PRINCIPLES AND AIMS*

MY PRINCIPLES IN COMPILING THIS dictionary have been carefully thought out and applied. Since they differ somewhat from those obtaining in comparable works, and in order that the user should profit fully from the book and appreciate the reasons why things are done as they are, it is worth stating these principles and explaining their application in detail.

1 Modern usage

My aim was to make a dictionary of modern current English and Spanish which, rather than taking the abstraction of one national *langue* (as it is represented, for example, in the Oxford English and Spanish Academy dictionaries) and translating it into the other, should embrace no more than the typical *parole* or personal language of the average educated English speaker of 1970, and that of the corresponding speaker of Spanish. This average educated speaker uses a relatively few dozens of absolutely basic words — verbs, nouns and prepositions — which come to his lips many times a day; he further possesses an active vocabulary of a few thousand words which he speaks on occasion, reads in novels and newspapers, hears on TV and radio, uses at his work (if not too technical) and in business correspondence, and so on. This average speaker has a family and a car, an interest in a variety of mildly scholarly subjects, an active or passive interest in a number of sports; he watches his health, follows space exploration and scientific progress in general terms, travels abroad, grows flowers, eats with some variety, prays, votes, makes love and occasionally war. It is likely that he has some slightly specialized technical competence and the vocabulary that goes with it because of his work or his hobbies; and since the personal *parole* of one man — the compiler — may be untypical in this respect,

Introducción

PRINCIPIOS Y PROPÓSITOS EN GENERAL

LOS PRINCIPIOS EN QUE SE BASA EL diccionario han sido pensados con cierto cuidado. Son algo distintos de los que se observan en otros trabajos de este tipo; para ayudar al lector a sacar el máximo provecho de la obra, y para que comprenda su sistema y sus métodos, he creído tener la obligación de explicar estos principios y su aplicación en forma detallada.

El uso moderno

Mi propósito ha sido el de hacer un diccionario de las formas modernas y corrientes de los dos idiomas, tomando no la abstracción de una *langue* (lengua) nacional (tal como ésta se encuentra representada, por ejemplo, en los diccionarios de Oxford y de la Academia Española) y traduciéndola a la otra, sino abarcando tan sólo la *parole* (habla) típica o lenguaje personal del inglés (y norteamericano) culto medio de 1970, y del hispanohablante correspondiente. Este hablante típico dentro de su relativa cultura emplea algunas docenas de palabras verdaderamente básicas — verbos, sustantivos y preposiciones — que se le vienen a los labios muchísimas veces cada día; posee además un vocabulario activo de varios miles de palabras que emplea de vez en cuando, que lee en novelas y periódicos, que escucha por TV y por radio, que emplea en su trabajo (no siendo éste de tipo demasiado técnico) y en la correspondencia comercial, etc. Este hablante medio tiene familia y coche, tiene interés en varios temas ligeramente eruditos, y un interés activo o pasivo en los deportes; cuida su salud, presta atención en términos generales a la exploración espacial y al progreso científico, viaja por el extranjero, cultiva algunas flores, come con cierta variedad, reza, vota, hace el amor y alguna vez la guerra. Es probable que tenga conocimientos de alguna técnica especializada y del vocabulario que la acompaña, gracias a su for dictionary purposes we put together a number of these technical *paroles*, none of them at all abstruse.

The dictionary does not claim, then, as others produced on different principles no doubt rightly do, that it contains so many tens of thousands of main entries, takes in most of *la langue*, and has almost all the words however abstruse which the user is likely to want to look up perhaps only once in a lifetime, perhaps never. I have borne our average educated man constantly in mind and freed these pages of lexicographical lumber; what remains is, I hope, fairly typical usage in the two languages.

2 Treatment of basic words

Attention has been concentrated on the relatively few basic words which are always in frequent use, each of them a small semantic world of its own and each of them constantly entering into idioms, figurative expressions, comparisons and the like. The reader may satisfy himself about this point by a glance at such English entries as *do, give, go, have, put, on, up, hand, life, time, way,* and on the Spanish side *dar, hacer, poner, a, en, mano*. Also special attention has been given to those words, mainly verbs, which in the experience of the compiler give students some difficulty in translation: *enjoy, like, fail, miss*. Since a verb is often a lifeless thing in isolation, the policy has been regularly to give the construction which it requires, sometimes by a sort of formula and sometimes by practical example early in the entry; these matters seem to me to belong in the dictionary and not to deserve relegation to a grammar book. The usual idioms and set phrases, even clichés, are included in great numbers, and there are often separate sections in which the figurative senses are explored. The major innovation in this regard is, however, the provision of abundant usage examples. Words hardly have an existence in isolation but come to life in meaningful continuous discourse, and I have provided these live contexts wherever possible; such examples have the further purpose of demonstrating the use of constructions, word-order differences in the two languages, the replacement of English passive by Spanish

trabajo o a algún pasatiempo; y puesto que la *parole* personal de un solo hombre — esto es, del autor — puede distar de ser típico en este aspecto, juntamos para los propósitos lexicográficos cierta cantidad de estas *paroles* técnicas, sin que ninguna de ellas llegue a ser realmente recóndita.

El diccionario no pretende, pues, como pretenden otros — sin duda con razón, pues están hechos sobre otros principios — abarcar tantas decenas de miles de palabras, ni incluir la mayor parte de *la langue*, ni contener casi todas las palabras por más oscuras que sean que el usuario pudiera buscar una vez en la vida, quizá nunca. He tenido siempre en cuenta nuestro hablante culto típico, y he procurado que estas páginas queden libres de palabras-trastos; confío en que lo que queda represente el verdadero uso típico de los dos idiomas.

Tratamiento de las palabras básicas

Se ha cifrado la atención en las palabras básicas — en número relativamente pequeño — que están en uso constantemente, siendo cada una de ellas un pequeño mundo semántico en sí, y entrando cada una a formar frases hechas, modismos, expresiones figuradas, comparaciones, etc. El lector se satisfará sobre este particular consultando p.ej. los artículos ingleses *do, give, go, have, put, on, up, hand, life, time, way,* y los españoles *dar, hacer, poner, a, en, mano*. Se ha prestado también atención especial a las palabras (sobre todo verbos) que mayor dificultad presentan en la traducción; p.ej. *enjoy, like, fail, miss*. Como el verbo casi no tiene vida cuando se cita aislado, cito de modo regular el régimen que cada uno pide, algunas veces mediante una especie de fórmula y otras mediante un ejemplo casi al principio del artículo; esta información me ha parecido ser propia del diccionario y no pertenecer únicamente al libro de gramática. Se incluyen en grandes cantidades los modismos y frases hechas, hasta los clichés, y a menudo se dedica un apartado especial a los sentidos figurados de las palabras. Pero en este aspecto la mayor innovación consiste en la provisión de copiosos ejemplos del uso. Las palabras apenas tienen verdadera existencia en el aislamiento, pero cobran vida en el discurso continuo que comunica algo; siempre cuando ha sido posible les he dado este contexto vivo. Los ejemplos del uso tienen también el propósito de demostrar las construcciones, las

reflexive, and so on. These usage examples have been made as lively, human and authentic as the compiler's imagination allowed.

A further point in the argument for expanding the treatment of the basic words and excluding abstruse terminology is that the former often go on presenting difficulties even to those who know the other language well. The correct use of modest monosyllabic prepositions can cause intense anxiety, whereas anyone possessing a slight acquaintance with English or Spanish can predict that the word *intramolecular* in English will be *intramolecular* in Spanish, or that the new state of *Pogolandia* in Spanish must be *Pogoland* in English.

3 Organization of the entry

Since many of the basic word entries are lengthy, much thought has been given to the problem of planning them (before anything was translated), and to their clear division into sections and subsections. This is explained in detail below. Here we may remark that although this is not unique it is at least unusual in English-Spanish lexicography, in which the tradition seems to be of a headword followed by a jumble of translations and phrases vaguely separated by commas and semicolons but not offering much guidance to the user. In addition to the subdivision of the longer entries, there is in this dictionary a constant provision of abbreviations and semantic and other indicators which should lead the user to the correct translation; the process of tracking down takes place within the one entry, and the ancient cry of "Keep checking back in the other half of the dictionary until you find the right word" need no longer be heard. Further details of this system are given below.

4 Technical terminology

In breadth of technical terminology, as explained, this dictionary does not stretch very far; basic medicine is included but not virology, automobile maintenance but not the parts of the nuclear breeder-reactor, elementary typography but not the arcane terms known only to typographers. To aid users who seek further information in such fields

diferencias en el orden de palabras en los dos idiomas, la sustitución de la voz pasiva inglesa por el verbo reflexivo español, etc. He procurado dar a estos ejemplos toda la viveza, humanidad y autenticidad que la imaginación ha permitido.

Hay otra razón para excluir las palabras recónditas y aumentar el espacio dedicado a las palabras básicas: es que éstas siguen planteando problemas aun para aquéllos que dominan bastante bien el otro idioma. El uso correcto de las preposiciones monosílabas, tan modestas, puede motivar la mayor incertidumbre, mientras el que tenga el más superficial conocimiento del inglés y del español podrá predecir que la palabra inglesa *intramolecular* será en español *intramolecular*, o bien que el nuevo estado de *Pogolandia* en español habrá forzosamente de llamarse en inglés *Pogoland*.

Organización del artículo

Debido a la gran extensión de muchos artículos sobre las palabras básicas, se ha estudiado con cuidado el problema de organizarlos (antes de empezar la traducción) y el problema de dividirlos claramente. El sistema se explica detalladamente más abajo. Aquí conviene apuntar que tal sistema aunque no es único es poco corriente en la lexicografía anglo-española, pues parece haber casi una tradición de que a la palabra cabeza de artículo le siga una masa de traducciones y de frases vagamente divididas por comas o por comas y puntos, donde apenas tiene guía el lector. En este diccionario no sólo se dividen y subdividen los artículos extensos sino también se ofrecen a cada paso abreviaturas y aclaraciones semánticas y de otros tipos cuya finalidad es guiar al lector hasta que encuentre la traducción apropiada; esta búsqueda se lleva a cabo dentro del mismo artículo, para que nadie tenga que volver a escuchar aquello tan repetido de "Siga comprobando en la otra parte del diccionario hasta dar con la palabra exacta".

Términos técnicos

Según hemos dicho, este diccionario no tiene gran alcance en lo referente a terminología técnica; se incluye la medicina elemental pero la virología no, la manutención del automóvil pero no los componentes del reactor-generador nuclear, algunas nociones de tipografía pero no las palabras raras que conocen únicamente los tipógrafos. Para a list of bilingual technical dictionaries is given in an appendix. Two special fields call for comment: that of sport and spectacle, and that of natural history. In sport the policy has been to include a good deal of vocabulary for games which are international and therefore translatable; so there is plenty of football but not much cricket. Spaniards and Americans have, to the compiler's regretful but certain knowledge, the faintest possible interest in the latter subject; to tell them that an *over* consists of six throwings (?) of a ball from one end of the wicket would be pointless if brief, space-consuming if long, and would in any case probably never be read. Bullfighting (not a sport, of course) at first seemed to be in the same category of the non-translatable — though not by any means non-interesting — but a certain amount of vocabulary from it has been included under pressure from others. I remain doubtful whether the typical translation "a certain pass with the cape" is of very much help to the user who had already deduced as much from the context in which he heard or read the word. Obviously the person who really wants to know will turn to a full technical description by a specialist in the art. In natural history the problem is different but equally insoluble for the present. No doubt a *seagull* is a *gaviota* and this is all that some need to know, but it is not a specific term in scientific usage; if one divides up the vaguely generic notion of *seagull* one finds that there are agreed and quite widely known English terms, but that Spaniards — who are poor on such subjects — do not have a word at all, or have an official term which is simply a vulgarization of the Latin generic and specific names but has no real currency; one finds also that the dictionaries are cluttered with contradictory information. (On this and cognate problems, see K. Whinnom, *A Glossary of Spanish Bird-names*, London, Támesis, 1966.) The names of fish seem to change every 50 kilometres along the Spanish coasts, and British species may not correspond exactly to Spanish ones, let alone to those of the Americas. The same problems arise with insect names and botanical terms. Clearly the general lexicographer can do little until those who are qualified scientifically and in the two languages have produced reliable lists; such persons are rare in Britain and the US and very rare indeed on Hispanic territory. Even when such lists are available large parts of them would consist of Latin names and vernacular names

ayudar a los lectores que busquen más información sobre tales cosas doy en un apéndice una lista de diccionarios técnicos. Necesitan comentario especial dos esferas del vocabulario: la de los deportes y del espectáculo, y la de la historia natural. En cuanto al deporte, se ha incluido el vocabulario para los juegos que tienen carácter internacional, así que está bien representado el fútbol pero escasamente el críquet. El interés que muestran los hispanohablantes por el críquet es casi nulo; decirles que el *over* consiste en seis echadas (?) de una pelota desde un extremo del *wicket* (intraducible) sería inútil en forma escueta y ocuparía mucho espacio si se explicara adecuadamente, y en todo caso es probable que nadie lo vaya a leer. A primera vista me pareció que el toreo (que no es ningún deporte, desde luego) pertenecía a la misma categoría de lo intraducible, pero accediendo a los ruegos de otros he incluido cierta cantidad del léxico taurino. Sigo sin embargo dudando que la típica traducción "cierto pase con la capa" le vaya a ayudar al lector, pues éste ya lo habrá adivinado por el contexto en que ha oído o leído la palabra. El lector que realmente quiera saber irá naturalmente a una descripción técnica y completa por un especialista en el arte. En la historia natural el problema es distinto pero igualmente insoluble. Sin duda un *seagull* es una *gaviota* y con decirlo les basta a algunos lectores; pero *seagull* no es nombre específico que valga en el uso científico. Si se divide la vaga noción genérica de *seagull* nos encontramos con que en inglés existen nombres convenidos y extensamente conocidos, pero que los españoles — que no son muy fuertes en este campo — o no tienen palabra, o tienen un término oficial que no es más que una forma vulgarizada de los nombres latinos genérico y específico, y que deja de tener verdadera aceptación. También nos encontramos con que los diccionarios están llenos de información contradictoria. (Para este problema y afines, véase K. Whinnom, *A Glossary of Spanish Bird-names*, Londres, Támesis, 1966.) Los nombres de los peces parecen cambiar cada cierta distancia en la costa española, y las especies británicas pueden no cuadrar exactamente con las españolas, ni mucho menos con las de América. Surgen los mismos problemas con los nombres de insectos y con la botánica. Es evidente que el lexicógrafo general puede hacer muy poco hasta que aquellas personas in one language only, without any possible correspondence in the other vernacular.

que estén capacitadas en cada ciencia y en los dos idiomas hayan publicado un estudio para cada especialidad; son escasas tales personas en el Reino Unido y en EE.UU., y escasísimas en territorio hispánico. Aun cuando dispongamos de tales listas, gran parte de ellas consistirán en nombres latinos y nombres vernáculos en un idioma nada más, no habiendo correspondencia posible en el otro.

5 Time scale and social register

"Modern" and "current" perhaps require elucidation. The time scale has been stretched to take in some words which appear in the standard literature of the two countries likely to be read by foreigners, and which are widely known even if no longer in current use. This does not of course include words from as far back as Shakespeare and the *Celestina*. Other well-known archaisms are included and marked as such, for they occasionally appear in period plays and films, and in jocular use.

The range of social tone, of "register", represented in the two languages, is wide. High-class words proper to poetry and to literature are included and labelled accordingly. At the lower end of the scale a very great number of familiar or colloquial words and phrases are included on the grounds that they are an essential part of "usage" as defined above, and because in the general relaxation of the social formalities in our time such words are heard in ministerial broadcasts and read in newspaper leaders from which they were absent 20 years ago; the labelling of such items is rather arbitrary, and depends on the compiler's instinct rather than on any printed authority. As for slang, while it is picturesque, expressive, and close to the compiler's heart, it is by definition restricted in scope, and also transitory and unestablished, so that although it can often be translated only the more widely known words merit inclusion. Wherever possible the social tone of a word has been translated accurately, familiar by familiar and so on, sometimes with the addition of a more standard term for those who prefer safety first. Clichés of conversation, correspondence, news reports, political speeches and the like are also well represented; inclusion does not imply approval.

No great originality is claimed for the supplementary information given in preliminaries and appendices, but thought has been given to its presentation.

La palabra en el tiempo y su tono social

El concepto de lo "moderno" y "corriente" en la lengua pide alguna aclaración. Se ha extendido la noción para abarcar las palabras que aparecen en la literatura clásica de los dos idiomas y que son bastante conocidas aunque no están todavía en uso. No se abarcan, desde luego, palabras de época tan remota como son la de Shakespeare o de la *Celestina*. Se incluyen (con la abreviatura correspondiente) los arcaísmos más conocidos, pues éstos aparecen alguna vez en dramas históricos y en películas, y en el uso humorístico.

Es muy ancha la gama de tono social, de "registro", que abarca el diccionario. Se incluyen las palabras aristocráticas propias de la poesía y de la literatura. En el otro extremo se incluyen muchísimas voces y frases familiares o coloquiales, siendo éstas parte tan esencial del "uso" tal como lo hemos definido, y también porque con la relajación progresiva de la etiqueta social en nuestros tiempos, tales palabras (desconocidas en estos contextos hace unos 20 años) se escuchan cuando los ministros hablan por radio y se leen en los artículos de fondo. En muchos casos es discutible la clasificación de estas palabras como *fam* (familiares); ello depende del instinto del autor y no de autoridad impresa. En cuanto al argot (*slang*), por más pintoresco y expresivo que sea, tiene por definición una aplicación restringida, es pasajero y carece de base fija, así que solamente las palabras más conocidas merecen ser incluidas. Siempre donde ha sido posible se ha traducido exactamente el tono social de la palabra, familiar por familiar, etc, a veces añadiéndose una voz más clásica para el uso de quien prefiera sentirse más seguro. Hay buen número de los clichés de la conversación, de la correspondencia, de los reportajes periodísticos, de los discursos políticos, etc; la mención en el diccionario no presupone la aprobación del autor.

No hay grandes novedades en las materias

preliminares ni en los apéndices, pero se ha estudiado con cuidado el problema de su redacción.

II WHAT KIND OF ENGLISH AND WHAT KIND OF SPANISH?

1 European and American

THE PROBLEM POSED BY THE GEOGRAPHICAL spread and the cultural breadth of these two great world languages has been mentioned in the Preface; it has greatly preoccupied the author and the publishers. At first the idea was to produce a rather severely limited dictionary by Europeans and for Europeans, concerned, that is, with British English and European Spanish; the corollary being that English and Spanish in the New World could be better handled by natives of the Americas. Two factors, one theoretical and the other very practical, led to the scope of the work being widened so as to take in American usage, though not without misgivings on the author's part. The first factor was the realization that contacts run not merely north and south but in all directions; North Americans have a great interest in Spain, trade and cultural contacts between Britain and Latin America are far from negligible. Moreover the standards of usage, pronunciation etc set by the mother countries (in the purely linguistic sense) of Britain and Spain are not without influence in the Americas. The second factor was the association of the British publishers for the purposes of this dictionary series with a United States house, which naturally meant that American speech and lexical preferences had to be taken into account. Considerable help was given by the United States house with details of American English, and the services of Professor E. Chang-Rodríguez were secured so that Latin American usage in Spanish could be properly covered. In the result the dictionary has a much more comprehensive look about it than was originally intended, and it is hoped that this consideration outweighs any mid-Atlantic anomalies.

2 "Oxford" English and "Academy" Spanish

The problem of authority in matters of language exists for English but is distressingly

INGLÉS Y ESPAÑOL: ¿DE QUÉ TIPO?

Lo europeo y lo americano

SE HA ALUDIDO EN EL PREFACIO AL problema planteado por la extensión geográfica y la amplitud cultural de estos dos grandes idiomas mundiales; tal problema ha preocupado mucho al autor y a la casa editorial. En un principio pensamos hacer un diccionario de carácter muy limitado, por europeos y para europeos; esto es, tendría que ver con el inglés británico y el español europeo, entendiéndose como consecuencia que el inglés y el español de América podrían ser manejados mejor por americanos. Dos factores, teórico uno y muy práctico el otro, nos llevaron a extender el campo para abarcar lo americano, pero no sin alguna duda de parte del autor. Primero nos dimos cuenta de que los contactos no se limitan a seguir la línea norte-sur, sino que van en todas las direcciones; los norteamericanos se interesan vivamente por España, y no son de despreciar los contactos comerciales y culturales entre Gran Bretaña y la América Latina. Además no dejan de tener influencia las normas del uso, de la pronunciación, etc, establecidas por las dos madres patrias (en sentido lingüístico, nada más) de Gran Bretaña y España. Vino en segundo lugar la asociación — en lo referente a la serie de diccionarios — de la casa editorial británica con la compañía norteamericana, con la consecuencia lógica de que había que tomar en cuenta el habla norteamericana y sus preferencias léxicas. La compañía norteamericana nos prestó una ayuda eficaz en el asunto del inglés americano, y el Profesor E. Chang-Rodríguez ha mejorado mucho toda la materia hispanoamericana. Resulta así que el libro sale con aspecto mucho más completo del que en un principio se pensaba, y se espera que este hecho compense sobradamente cualquier anomalía que se pueda observar en alguna palabra a la deriva en el Atlántico.

El inglés de Oxford y el español de la Academia

Existe para el inglés el problema de la autoridad lingüística, pero es mucho más grave acute for Spanish. In Britain the Oxford dictionaries, the works on usage of the Fowlers, Gowers, Partridge and others have always enjoyed (although they have scrupulously never claimed to possess) an enormous authority; in the United States the same may be said of Webster, Random House and others. But in all varieties of English it may be said that there is in fact no conception of a linguistic authority, at any rate not in the sense in which it exists in Hispanic countries with their ancient Academies. Words flow into English from other languages; they have no gender, their plurals are always very simply formed with -s or -es, and the English organs of speech seem to be able to get around almost any awkward consonant group or modify it to the general satisfaction; moreover in the general chaos of English spelling a few new anomalies are neither here nor there. In Spanish the scene is very different. Ancient and highly prestigious Academies attempt (indeed, are obliged by their mottoes: *Limpia, fija y da esplendor*) to apply to language a policy which we may in general call conservative and purist; they take a view of language which has never been current in Britain or the US and which, it must be said, is difficult to maintain in current linguistic theory. Quite apart from this, Spanish by its very nature is less able to accommodate loanwords and other innovations which have been pouring into it in the 1950s and 60s. It has fewer phonemes than English; it has a gender problem and much more uncertainty about plurals and spellings of foreign words than does English. Spanish informants, questioned about the pronunciation of (for example) *corner* or the plural of *club*, may emerge covered in confusion; the printed sources often disagree, and in this particular Latin American usage often differs again from that of Spain. The current very strong influence of English and French on Spanish is not of course confined to individual items of vocabulary; it extends to phrasing, to word order, to the use of the passive voice and to many other aspects of language. (Sections of the book of Emilio Lorenzo, *El español de hoy, lengua en ebullición*, Madrid, Gredos, 1966, illustrate these matters admirably.)

para el español. Esta autoridad la poseen (sin haberla reclamado nunca) en Gran Bretaña los diccionarios de Oxford y las obras de los Fowler, de Gowers y Partridge y otros, sobre el uso; y en Estados Unidos lo mismo se puede decir de Webster, de Random House etc. Sin embargo, respecto al inglés hay que reconocer que realmente no existe la autoridad lingüística, por lo menos en el sentido en que tal autoridad existe en los países hispánicos, cada uno con su venerable Academia. Las voces extranjeras entran libremente en el inglés; no tienen género, su plural se forma muy sencillamente con -s o con -es, y los órganos articulatorios ingleses parecen ser capaces de dominar cualquier grupo consonántico o bien de modificarlo para contentar a todos; además, dentro de la total confusión de la ortografía inglesa, no tienen gran importancia unas cuantas rarezas más. Todo es muy distinto en español. Las Academias viejas y prestigiosas se esfuerzan por aplicar al lenguaje unas normas que podemos en general calificar de conservadoras y casticistas; de hecho, su lema les obliga a ello (*Limpia, fija y da esplendor*). Su concepto del lenguaje no ha tenido nunca aceptación en Gran Bretaña ni en Estados Unidos, y hay que reconocer que dentro de las teorías lingüísticas actuales resulta difícil sostenerlo. Aparte de esto, el español por su misma naturaleza es menos capaz para recibir los préstamos y otras innovaciones que lo han invadido en los años 50 y 60 de este siglo. Tiene menos fonemas que el inglés; tiene el problema del género y vacila mucho en lo tocante a los plurales y a la ortografía de los extranjerismos. Rogamos a nuestros amigos españoles que nos ayuden pronunciando, p.ej., la palabra *corner* o que nos digan el plural de *club* y no logran ponerse de acuerdo; alguna autoridad impresa nos da una solución pero otra la contradice, y en este respecto el uso de Hispanoamérica a menudo difiere del de España. Hoy día la influencia del inglés y del francés sobre el español — influencia poderosísima — no se limita, desde luego, a los elementos del léxico; se extiende a la fraseología, al orden de palabras, al uso de la voz pasiva y a otros muchos aspectos del lenguaje. (Todo esto lo ilustran muy bien varios capítulos del libro de Emilio Lorenzo, *El español de hoy, lengua en ebullición*, Madrid, Gredos, 1966.)

3 Usage and authority

The consequence of all this for our purpose is that doubts arise and the need to give several alternative forms is felt. In English, since it is my native language, I can usually resolve these doubts in a friendly confrontation between my instinct and the authorities. In Spanish, even with the help of Spaniards, this is not the case. My own criterion is extremely liberal and in no way purist: if the word exists and is widely used it belongs in the dictionary in at least one of its forms; if it has various plurals and pronunciations these should be included; if for most Spaniards the English *slogan* is *un slogan* (rather than *un lema*) and the English *camping ground* or *campsite* is (via French) *un camping*, the fact must be honestly stated. To apply traditional and purist criteria to such cases and to neglect usage — that of the educated classes, not that of the least cultured in a society — would be to mislead the user; it would be to offer him a bookish fiction, a word which although "correct" has little currency, a word which might cause jocularity or eyebrow-raising. The authority which this dictionary hopes to have is that of accurate translation in terms of everyday usage, not that of acting as arbiter about what is "good English" or (still less) "good Spanish".

None the less it would be improper to disclaim all responsibility in this matter. The Spanish Academy is on the move, if rather slowly; it is admitting numerous neologisms and new senses and deciding questions of gender, spelling and definition, with skill and good sense. The results of many of its deliberations were published by the late Julio Casares in *Novedades en el Diccionario Académico*, Madrid, Aguilar, 1963, and others have continued to publish the Academy's decisions in numbers of the *Boletín de la Real Academia Española* since that year. I have taken account of these decisions by marking words with the abbreviation *Acad* in both parts of the dictionary; the entry in Part II "**film** = film *m*, filme *m* (*Acad*)" implies that the Academy has accepted the anglicism but only in the form *filme* (for excellent reasons), while from the order in which the two translations are given it may be assumed that as observed in conversation and in the press most Spaniards go on using the first form and obstinately pay little attention to the Academy's decision. Logically those neologisms and very numerous Spanish American words which do not have the Academy's sanction should have been

El uso y la autoridad

Las consecuencias de todo esto para nosotros son que surgen dudas y se siente la necesidad de ofrecer varias formas alternativas. Yo en inglés (lengua materna) puedo resolver estas dudas por lo general confrontando mi instinto con las autoridades. En español, aun contando con la ayuda de españoles, no ocurre esto. Mi propio criterio es de lo más liberal y de ningún modo casticista; si la palabra existe y tiene un uso extenso, ha de figurar en el diccionario bajo una de sus formas a lo menos; si tiene varias formas en plural y diversas maneras de pronunciarse éstas merecen ser incluidas; si para la mayor parte de los hispanohablantes el *slogan* inglés es *un slogan* (y no *un lema*) y el *camping ground* o *campsite* inglés es — a través del francés — *un camping*, hay que reconocer honradamente tal hecho. Seguir las normas tradicionales y casticistas y desatender el uso en tales casos — esto es, el uso de las personas cultas, no el de la clase menos culta de la sociedad — sería despistar al lector; sería ofrecerle una ficción libresca, una palabra que por más "correcta" que sea tiene poca aceptación, una palabra que pudiera motivar la risa o la extrañeza. Esperamos que el diccionario pueda reclamar cierta autoridad a base de ofrecer buenas traducciones dentro del uso diario, y rechazamos la idea de que pueda servir de árbitro en lo referente a cuestiones de "buen inglés" y (más todavía) de "castellano correcto".

A pesar de todo, sería cobarde desentenderse completamente de cierta responsabilidad en esta materia. La Real Academia Española trabaja, si bien con lentitud; admite muchos neologismos y significados nuevos y resuelve problemas de género, de ortografía y de definición, atinada y sensatamente. El fallecido Julio Casares publicó los resultados de sus discusiones en su libro *Novedades en el Diccionario Académico*, Madrid, Aguilar, 1963, y otros continúan esta labor en los números del *Boletín de la Real Academia Española*. He tomado en cuenta estas decisiones mediante la abreviatura *Acad*; así el artículo de la segunda parte, "**film** = film *m*, filme *m* (*Acad*)" quiere decir que la Academia ha dado paso al anglicismo pero (por razones muy sólidas) únicamente bajo la forma *filme*; por otra parte se supone, dado el orden en que se imprimen las dos traducciones, que según lo observado en la conversación y en la marked *non-Acad*, but this would have been a vast undertaking and would also have conceded more importance to the purists' views than I feel it is proper to give.

4 What is a word?

One of the very few problems which arises on the English side is the large one of what constitutes a word and, for dictionary listing purposes, a main entry or headword. My instinct was to use the hyphen freely and in many cases to run two words completely together without hyphen, since I felt that usage was tending in this direction. It followed that there could be no main entries which consisted of two or more separate words, these being placed as no more than sub-entries under the main noun. This policy had to be revised when collaboration with American colleagues began, for their practice differs from that of Britain; there are now fewer hyphens and a large number of main entries which consist of two or more words, and doubtless some anomalies have resulted in this process of achieving mid-Atlantic harmony. The numerous differences in spelling and pronunciation between Britain and the US have been more easily resolved by summarizing US habits in introductory notes and by constant statement of the differences within the entries, sometimes with cross-references.

prensa los españoles en general emplean la primera forma y se obstinan en no hacer caso de la decisión de su Academia. Sería lógico poner la tacha *non-Acad* a los numerosos neologismos y sudamericanismos que no han merecido la aprobación de la Academia, pero hacerlo así hubiera exigido un enorme esfuerzo y también hubiera concedido más importancia a la opinión casticista de la que ésta merece.

¿Qué es una palabra?

Uno de los pocos problemas que se plantea para el inglés es el de determinar lo que constituye *una* palabra, y, para el diccionario, lo que constituye una palabra cabeza de artículo. En un principio empleé extensamente el guión y en muchos casos uní dos palabras para formar otra sin guión, pues me parecía que tal era la tendencia del uso. La consecuencia de esto era que no podía haber palabra cabeza de artículo que constara de dos palabras separadas o de más, colocándose éstas en cambio dentro del artículo. Pero al iniciarse la colaboración con los colegas norteamericanos hubo que suprimir esta norma, pues la práctica norteamericana es distinta de la británica; por tanto hay ahora menos palabras con guión y muchas palabras que encabezan artículo aun constando de dos elementos o más; sin duda el cambio habrá creado algunas anomalías. Ha sido más fácil conciliar las diferencias en cuanto a la ortografía y pronunciación entre lo británico y lo norteamericano resumiendo las costumbres de Estados Unidos en una nota preliminar y mencionando constantemente las diferencias en cada artículo.

III EXPLANATORY NOTES

1 Alphabetical order is followed throughout. It must be remembered that *CH, LL* and *Ñ* are separate letters of the alphabet in Spanish; thus **achacar** comes after **acústico** and not after **acezar**.

2 Cross-references include alternative spellings, parts of irregular verbs, contracted forms, many prefixes and some suffixes, and parts of compound words.

3 Superior numbers are used to separate words of like spelling and pronunciation, eg **port¹, port²**.

4 Noun plurals in Spanish are indicated after the headword only when irregular (eg **crisis**, *pl* **crisis**). In all other cases the basic rules apply: if a noun ends in a vowel it takes -s in the plural (eg **casa-s, tribu-s**); if it ends in a consonant (including for this purpose **y**) it takes **-es** in the plural (eg **pared-es, árbol-es**). Note the following, however:

  (i) Nouns that end in stressed **-í** take **-es** in the plural (eg **rubí, rubíes**). Exception: **esquí, esquís.**

  (ii) Nouns that end in **-z** change this to **c** and add **-es** in the plural (eg **luz, luces; paz, paces**). The pronunciation is not affected.

  (iii) The accent which is written on a number of endings of singular nouns is not needed in the plural (eg **nación-naciones, patán-patanes, inglés-ingleses**). Some words having no written accent in the singular need one in the plural (eg **crimen-crímenes, joven-jóvenes**).

  (iv) There is little agreement about the plural of recent anglicisms and gallicisms, and some latinisms. Each case is treated separately in the dictionary; see eg **barman, chófer, club.**

5 Noun plurals in English are indicated after the headword only when they are truly irregular (eg **ox, oxen**), and in the few cases where a word in **-o** takes a plural in **-oes** (eg **potato-es**). In all other cases the basic rules apply:

  (i) Most English nouns take **-s** in the plural: **bed-s, site-s, photo-s.**

  (ii) Nouns that end in **-s, -x, -z, -sh** and some in **-ch** [tʃ] take **-es** in the plural: **boss-es, box-es, dish-es, patch-es.**

NOTAS EXPLICATIVAS

1 El orden alfabético queda rigurosamente establecido. Se mantiene la costumbre de considerar la *CH*, la *LL* y la *Ñ* como letras independientes.

2 Con referencias a otros artículos figuran las variantes ortográficas, las formas de los verbos irregulares, las formas contractas, muchos prefijos y algunos sufijos, y elementos de palabras compuestas.

3 Los números altos sirven para distinguir las palabras que se escriben y se pronuncian iguales, p.ej. **port¹, port²**.

4 Forma plural del sustantivo en español. Estas formas se hacen constar después de la voz cabeza de artículo sólo cuando son irregulares (p.ej. **crisis**, *pl* **crisis**). En los demás casos se aplican las siguientes reglas: si el sustantivo termina en vocal se añade **-s** para formar el plural (p.ej. **casa-s, tribu-s**); si termina en consonante (la **y** se considera como consonante en esta posición) se añade **-es** para formar el plural (p.ej. **pared-es, árbol-es**). Hay algunas excepciones:

  (i) Los sustantivos que terminan en **-í** acentuada forman el plural añadiendo **-es** (p.ej. **rubí, rubíes**). Excepción: **esquí, esquís.**

  (ii) Los sustantivos que terminan en **-z** la cambian en **c** al formarse el plural (p.ej. **luz, luces; paz, paces**). Esto no cambia la pronunciación.

  (iii) El acento que se escribe en varias desinencias de los sustantivos en singular se suprime en el plural (p.ej. **nación-naciones, patán-patanes**). Algunas palabras que no llevan acento escrito en singular lo tienen en plural (p.ej. **crimen-crímenes**).

  (iv) Reina bastante confusión acerca de la forma plural de los anglicismos y galicismos, y de algún latinismo, de reciente acuñación. Se trata separadamente cada caso; véase p.ej. **barman, chófer, club.**

5 Forma plural del sustantivo en inglés. Estas formas se hacen constar después de la voz cabeza de artículo sólo cuando son irregulares (p.ej. **ox, oxen**), y en los pocos casos donde una palabra terminada en **-o** forma el plural en **-oes** (p.ej. **potato-es**). En los demás casos se aplican las siguientes reglas:

  (i) La mayor parte de los sustantivos en inglés forman el plural añadiendo **-s**: **bed-s, site-s, photo-s.**

  (ii) Los sustantivos terminados en **-s, -x, -z,**

(iii) Nouns that end in **-y** not preceded by a vowel change the **-y** to **-ies** in the plural: **lady-ladies**, **berry-berries** (but **tray-s**, **key-s**).

6 Spanish and English verbs. All Spanish verb headwords are referred by number and letter (eg [1a], [2e]) to the table of verb paradigms on pp. 624–30. In a few cases in which verbs have slight irregularities or are defective, the fact is noted after the headword. English irregular or strong verbs have their principal parts noted in bold face after the headword; these are also listed on pp. 633–4. Minor variations of spelling are listed on p. 634.

7 Proper names occupy their alphabetical places in the main text. Current abbreviations are listed in the appendices, but a few which have assumed the character of words in their own right are included in the main text (eg **O.K.**).

8 Grammatical functions are distinguished by bold face numerals and abbreviations, eg **arder 1** *vt* . . . **2** *vi* . . . **3 arderse** *vr* . . . A separate division has been provided for *vr* in the English–Spanish, on the grounds that even though English has no strictly reflexive verbs this represents a convenience in translation and for the user.

9 The diverse meanings of the headword within each entry or grammatical function are separated by letters in bold face, **(a)** . . . **(b)** . . . Sometimes the distinctions made are rather fine but necessary both for the compiler and the user; they are practical rather than scientific in terms of semantics. A certain order is normally followed: basic and concrete senses first, figurative and familiar ones later; *SAm* and *US* senses and highly specialized applications come last.

10 Field and style labels in italics: some are abbreviations (eg *Bio*, *Mus*, *fam*), others complete words (eg *Art*, *Sport*); both types are in English but readily intelligible in Spanish.

11 Indicators are complete words in italics placed before the translation; they aid in meaning discrimination and help the user find

-sh y algunos en **-ch** [tʃ] forman el plural añadiendo **-es**: **boss-es**, **box-es**, **dish-es**, **patch-es**.

(iii) Los sustantivos terminados en **-y** no precedida por vocal forman el plural cambiando la **-y** en **-ies**: **lady-ladies**, **berry-berries** (pero **tray-s**, **key-s**).

6 Verbo español y verbo inglés. Los verbos españoles que encabezan artículo llevan una referencia por número y letra (p.ej. [1a], [2e]) al cuadro de conjugaciones en las págs. 624–30. En los casos donde el verbo es ligeramente irregular o defectivo, se nota tal hecho en el artículo. Se imprimen en negrilla inmediatamente después de la palabra cabeza de artículo el pretérito y participio de pasado de los verbos irregulares ingleses, y hay además lista de ellos en las págs. 633–4. Las ligeras variantes ortográficas de los verbos ingleses constan en las pág. 634.

7 Los nombres propios ocupan su lugar apropiado en el orden alfabético del diccionario. Las abreviaturas pasan sin embargo al apéndice, figurando entre los artículos del diccionario algunas que han adquirido carácter de palabras con derecho propio (p.ej. **O.K.**).

8 Las funciones gramaticales se señalan mediante números en negrilla y abreviaturas, p.ej. **arder 1** *vt* . . . **2** *vi* . . . **3 arderse** *vr* . . . En la Parte 2ª hay división especial para el *vr*, por el motivo de que (aunque el verbo inglés no tiene en rigor formas reflexivas) tal sistema es muy útil en la traducción y para el usuario.

9 Los diversos significados de la palabra cabeza de artículo quedan separados por letras en negrilla, **(a)** . . . **(b)** . . . Alguna vez la distinción puede parecer nimia, pero es necesaria para el autor y más para el lector; esto tiene una finalidad práctica y no pretende tener validez científica. Se ha establecido cierto orden para estas subdivisiones: primero los significados básicos y concretos, después los figurados y familiares; las acepciones *SAm* y *US* y las aplicaciones técnicas vienen en último lugar.

10 Las indicaciones de campo semántico y de tono se imprimen en cursiva. Algunas son abreviaturas (p.ej. *Bio*, *Mus*, *fam*), y otras palabras completas (p.ej. *Art*, *Sport*); ambas están en inglés pero serán fácilmente inteligibles en español.

11 Contribuyen a hacer las distinciones semánticas las indicaciones de palabras enteras en cursiva, colocadas delante de la traducción;

that part of the headword's range which he is seeking. They have been made as brief and typical as possible, but they cannot be comprehensive and must not be taken to constitute full definitions or exact limitations. The main types of indicator are:

(i) For a noun headword: a variety of near-synonyms, part-definitions and hints (in parentheses), eg **poke** (*push*) . . . (*with elbow*) . . . (*jab*) . . . (*with poker*) . . .

(ii) For an adjective headword: nouns (without parentheses) with which the adjective in its various applications might typically agree, eg **soft** (**b**) (*fig*) *air, sound . . . voice . . . step . . . water . . .*

(iii) For a transitive verb headword: nouns (without parentheses) which might typically be the objects of the verb in its various applications, eg **pluck** *fruit, flower . . . bird . . . guitar . . .*

(iv) For an intransitive or reflexive verb headword: nouns (in parentheses) which might be typical subjects of the verb, eg **rise 2** (**c**) (*of sun, moon*) . . . (*smoke etc*) . . . (*building, mountain*) . . .

Indicators are not repeated in derivatives but can be transferred by the user, eg adjective to adverb, adjective to abstract noun (*fair-fairness*).

12 The order of material within the entry or subdivision has been planned for convenience and does not follow a rigid pattern. However, a typical order for a lengthy noun entry is: (i) basic translations of the headword; (ii) phrases consisting of noun + adjective; (iii) the noun preceded by a preposition (often with verb as well); (iv) the noun with a verb. Alphabetical order is followed within each of these categories. No attempt is made to separate idioms from usage examples. In long verb entries in the English–Spanish all cases of verb + adverb and verb + preposition are collected into one subdivision placed towards the end of the entry, eg **do 1** (**e**), **play 2** (**j**) and **3** (**h**).

13 The placing of phrases in entries raises many problems. The principles generally followed are:

(i) Phrases consisting of noun + noun, verb + verb, adjective + adjective are entered under the first component, eg

se proponen llamar la atención del lector hacia la parte de la extensión de la palabra con que tiene que ver. Hemos ideado estas aclaraciones para que sean breves y típicas; pero ellas no pueden ser universales, e importa mucho que no se las considere como definiciones completas ni como limitaciones exactas. Las indicaciones son de varias clases:

(i) Para sustantivo que encabeza artículo: sinónimos aproximativos, definiciones parciales, consejos (en paréntesis), p.ej. **poke** (*push*) . . . (*with elbow*) . . . (*jab*) . . . (*with poker*) . . .

(ii) Para adjetivo que encabeza artículo: sustantivos (sin paréntesis) con los que el adjetivo en sus diversas aplicaciones pudiera concordar, p.ej. **soft** (**b**) (*fig*) *air, sound . . . voice . . . step . . . water . . .*

(iii) Para verbo transitivo que encabeza artículo: sustantivos (sin paréntesis) que típicamente pudieran ser los objetos del verbo, p.ej. **pluck** *fruit, flower . . . bird . . . guitar . . .*

(iv) Para verbo intransitivo o reflexivo que encabeza artículo: sustantivos (entre paréntesis) que típicamente pudieran ser los sujetos del verbo, p.ej. **rise 2** (**c**) (*of sun, moon*) . . . (*smoke etc*) . . . (*building, mountain*) . . .

Estas aclaraciones no se repiten para las palabras derivadas, pero las podrá trasladar el lector, p.ej. del adjetivo al adverbio, o del adjetivo al sustantivo abstracto (*fair-fairness*).

12 El orden de material dentro del artículo o subdivisión ha sido pensado para ayudar al lector y no sigue un sistema rígido. Sin embargo, el orden normal para un artículo sobre sustantivo es: (i) las traducciones básicas de la palabra cabeza de artículo; (ii) las frases que consisten en sustantivo con adjetivo; (iii) el sustantivo precedido por preposición (muchas veces con verbo también); (iv) el sustantivo con verbo. Dentro de cada categoría se mantiene el orden alfabético. No se separan los modismos de los ejemplos que ilustran el uso. En los artículos extensos sobre verbos en la Parte 2ª, se juntan en una subdivisión todos los casos de verbo + adverbio y de verbo + preposición, hacia el fin del artículo, p.ej. **do 1** (**e**), **play 2** (**j**) y **3** (**h**).

13 La colocación de las frases en los artículos suscita muchos problemas. En general los principios son:

(i) Las frases que consisten en sustantivo + sustantivo, verbo + verbo etc figuran en el artículo del primer elemento, p.ej.

"casa y comida" under **casa**, "black and blue" under **black**.

(ii) Phrases consisting of noun + adjective (Spanish) or adjective + noun (English) are entered under the noun component, eg "cabina electoral" under **cabina**, "black coffee" under **coffee**. It should be noted however that many such combinations in English now have a sufficiently independent existence to figure as main entries; thus **black box** and **black lead** are main entries in their alphabetical place, not sub-entries under **box** and **lead** respectively.

(iii) Phrases consisting of verb + noun are entered under the noun component, eg "abrir carrera" under **carrera**, "to show cause" under **cause**; but many phrases will be found in the verb entries as usage examples also.

(iv) Verb + adverb, verb + preposition (English) are normally entered under the verb, eg "to go in, go over, go up" under **go**; in the case of less common adverbs and prepositions the phrase may well appear under the adverb or preposition, eg "to go astern" under **astern**, the adverb hardly existing except in such phrases.

There is, however, intentional duplication of phrases. Thus "año bisiesto" belongs, by rule (ii) above, under **año**; but it is also the sole phrase under the headword **bisiesto**. In many other cases phrases are duplicated because they illustrate something about both headwords.

14 Translation by single word is obviously sufficient in many cases. Often a liberal policy has been followed in offering a number of near-synonyms separated by commas; this is especially true of the more emotive and less precise adjectives. The abbreviation (*approx*) is used where no full translation exists. Explanations in italics are given where a word has no correspondence in the other language, eg **cachetero (b)**, **cante**. For greater precision explanations in italics and in parentheses are occasionally added after the translation, eg **caló, camayo**.

15 The gender of every Spanish noun is given immediately after it in both parts of the dictionary.

16 Spanish feminine forms. In the English–Spanish the typical entry "**teacher** = profesor

"casa y comida" en **casa**, "black and blue" en **black**.

(ii) Las frases que consisten en sustantivo + adjetivo (español) o adjetivo + sustantivo (inglés) figuran en el artículo del elemento sustantivo, p.ej. "cabina electoral" en **cabina**, "black coffee" en **coffee**. Pero son muchas las combinaciones inglesas de adjetivo + sustantivo que han adquirido ya una existencia bastante independiente para que figuren como palabras cabezas de artículo; así encabezan artículos en su lugar alfabético correspondiente **black box** y **black lead**, y no están respectivamente en **box** y **lead**.

(iii) Las frases que consisten en verbo + sustantivo figuran en el artículo del sustantivo, p.ej. "to show cause" en **cause**, "abrir carrera" en **carrera**; pero se citan muchas frases de este tipo en los verbos, como ejemplos del uso.

(iv) Las frases de verbo + adverbio, verbo + preposición (inglés) están normalmente en el artículo del verbo, p.ej. "to go in, go over, go up" en **go**; pero en el caso de los adverbios y preposiciones menos frecuentes la frase bien puede estar en el artículo del adverbio o preposición, p.ej. "to go astern" en **astern**, pues el adverbio apenas tiene existencia fuera de tales frases.

Hay, sin embargo, muchos casos donde se duplica de propósito la frase. Así "año bisiesto" pertenece, según la regla (ii) arriba, a **año**; pero también es la única frase en **bisiesto**. En otros casos se duplican las frases por el motivo de que en ambos lugares ilustran algo.

14 La traducción por una sola palabra basta en muchos casos. Pero a menudo hemos seguido una norma liberal ofreciendo varios sinónimos o casi sinónimos, separados por comas, sobre todo para los adjetivos emotivos y por lo tanto menos precisos. Donde no existe traducción adecuada se emplea la abreviatura (*approx*). Cuando la palabra no tiene correspondencia en el otro idioma damos una explicación en cursiva, p.ej. para **cachetero (b)**, **cante**. Alguna vez se añade a la traducción, en cursiva y en paréntesis, una aclaración o precisión, p.ej. para **caló, camayo**.

15 El género de todo sustantivo español consta inmediatamente después de la palabra en las dos partes del diccionario.

16 Desinencias femeninas en español. En la Parte 2ª el artículo típico "**teacher** = profesor *m*, ora *f*" is to be read as "= profesor *m*, profesora *f*". Often a written accent on the masculine form is not needed in the feminine, eg "**Dane** = danés *m*, esa *f*" (to be read as "= danés *m*, danesa *f*"). The endings affected are: **-án, -ana; -és, -esa; -ón, -ona.** Where one vowel is given as the feminine ending, it replaces the **-e** or **-o** of the masculine; thus "**cook** = cocinero *m*, a *f*" is read as "= cocinero *m*, cocinera *f*".

m, ora *f*" ha de leerse "= profesor *m*, profesora *f*". A menudo el acento que lleva el masculino se suprime en el femenino, p.ej. "**Dane** = danés *m*, esa *f*" (ha de leerse "= danés *m*, danesa *f*"). Tales desinencias son: **-án, -ana; -és, esa; -ón, -ona.** Donde se cita una sola vocal de la forma femenina, esta vocal sustituye la **-e** o la **-o** del masculino; así "**cook** = cocinero *m*, a *f*" ha de leerse "= cocinero *m*, cocinera *f*".

Pronunciation and orthography

Pronunciación y ortografía

I. *LA PRONUNCIACIÓN DEL INGLÉS (BRITÁNICO)*

COMO ES SABIDO, LA ORTOGRAFÍA DEL inglés se ajusta a criterios históricos y etimológicos y en muchos puntos apenas ofrece indicaciones ciertas de cómo ha de pronunciarse cada palabra. Por ello nos ha parecido aconsejable y de utilidad para los hispanohablantes dar para cada palabra inglesa una pronunciación figurada o transcripción. Al tratar de explicar en estas notas los sonidos del inglés mediante comparaciones con los sonidos del español en un espacio reducido nos damos cuenta de que realizamos una labor que no pasa de ser aproximativa. Tales comparaciones tienen una finalidad práctica y carecen del rigor científico que exigen los fonetistas especializados.

1 Sistema de signos

Se emplean los signos de la IPA (International Phonetic Association). Hemos seguido en general las transcripciones de Daniel Jones, *English Pronouncing Dictionary*, London, Dent, 13th ed., 1967. En el prólogo de esta obra el autor explica los principios que le han guiado en su trabajo.

2 Acentuación

En las transcripciones el signo ['] se coloca delante de la sílaba acentuada. El signo [ˌ] se pone delante de la sílaba que lleva el acento secundario o más ligero en las palabras largas, p.ej. *acceleration* [ækˌseləˈreiʃən]. Dos signos de acento principal [ˈ ˈ] indican que las dos sílabas, o bien dos de las sílabas, se acentúan igualmente, p.ej. *A 1* [ˈeiˈwʌn], *able-bodied* [ˈeiblˈbɔdid]. Las palabras compuestas que encabezan artículo, estando sus elementos separados o unidos con guión, se tratan para nuestros propósitos como unidades: p.ej. *anti-roll device* [ˈæntiˈrəuldiˈvais].

3 Signos impresos en cursiva

En la palabra *annexation* [ˌænekˈseiʃən], la [ə] en cursiva indica que este sonido puede o no pronunciarse; o porque muchos hablantes la pronuncian pero que otros muchos no la pronuncian, o bien porque es un sonido que se oye en el habla lenta y cuidada pero que no se oye en el habla corriente y en el ritmo de la frase entera.

4 Transcripciones alternativas

En los casos donde se dan dos transcripciones, ello indica que ambas pronunciaciones son igualmente aceptables en el uso de las personas cultas, p.ej. *medicine* [ˈmedsin, ˈmedisin], o bien que la pronunciación varía bastante según la posición de la palabra en la frase y el contexto fonético, p.ej. *an* [æn, ən, n].

5 Véase también la nota sobre la pronunciación del inglés norteamericano.

6 El orden en que se explican los signos abajo es más o menos ortográfico y no el estrictamente fonético.

Vocales

[æ]	sonido breve, bastante abierto, parecido al de *a* en *carro*	bat	[bæt]
		apple	[ˈæpl]
[ɑː]	sonido largo parecido al de *a* en *caro*	farm	[fɑːm]
		calm	[kɑːm]
[e]	sonido breve, bastante abierto, parecido al de *e* en *perro*	set	[set]
		less	[les]

[xxi]

[ə]	"vocal neutra", siempre átona; parecida a la *e* del artículo francés *le* y a la *a* final del catalán (p.ej. *casa, porta*)	above porter convey	[ə'bʌv] ['pɔːtə*] [kən'vei]
[əː]	forma larga del anterior, en sílaba acentuada; algo parecido al sonido de *eu* en la palabra francesa *leur*	fern work murmur	[fəːn] [wəːk] ['məːmə*]
[i]	sonido breve, abierto, parecido al de *i* en *esbirro, irreal*	tip pity	[tip] ['piti]
[iː]	sonido largo parecido al de *i* en *vino*	see bean ceiling	[siː] [biːn] ['siːliŋ]
[ɔ]	sonido breve, bastante abierto, parecido al de *o* en *corra, torre*	rot wash	[rɔt] [wɔʃ]
[ɔː]	sonido largo, bastante cerrado, algo parecido al de *o* en *por*	ball board	[bɔːl] [bɔːd]
[u]	sonido muy breve, más cerrado que la *u* en *burro*	soot full	[sut] [ful]
[uː]	sonido largo, parecido al de *u* en *uno, supe*	root fool	[ruːt] [fuːl]
[ʌ]	sonido abierto, breve y algo oscuro, sin correspondencia en español; se pronuncia en la parte anterior de la boca sin redondear los labios	come rum blood nourish	[kʌm] [rʌm] [blʌd] ['nʌriʃ]

Diptongos

[ai]	sonido parecido al de *ai* en *fraile, vais*	lie fry	[lai] [frai]
[au]	sonido parecido al de *au* en *pausa, sauce*	sow plough	[sau] [plau]
[ei]	sonido medio abierto, pero más cerrado que la *e* de *casé*; suena como si le siguiese una [i] débil, especialmente en sílaba acentuada	fate say waiter straight	[feit] [sei] ['weitə*] [streit]
[əu]	sonido que es una especie de *o* larga, sin redondear los labios ni levantar la lengua; suena como si le siguiese una [u] débil	ago also atrocious note	[ə'gəu] ['ɔːlsəu] [ə'trəuʃəs] [nəut]
[ɛə]	sonido que se encuentra únicamente delante de la *r*; el primer elemento se parece a la *e* de *perro*, pero es más abierto y breve; el segundo elemento es una forma débil de la "vocal neutra" [ə]	there rare fair ne'er	[ðɛə*] [rɛə*] [fɛə*] [nɛə*]
[iə]	sonido cuyo primer elemento es una *i* medio abierta; el segundo elemento es una forma débil de la "vocal neutra" [ə]	here interior fear beer	[hiə*] [in'tiəriə*] [fiə*] [biə*]
[ɔi]	sonido cuyo primer elemento es una *o* abierta, seguido de una *i* abierta pero débil; parecido al sonido de *oy* en *voy* o de *oi* en *coime*	toy destroy voice	[tɔi] [dis'trɔi] [vɔis]
[uə]	sonido cuyo primer elemento es una *u* medio larga; el segundo elemento es una forma débil de la "vocal neutra" [ə]	allure sewer pure	[ə'ljuə*] [sjuə*] [pjuə*]

Consonantes

[b]	como la *b* de *tumbar, umbrío*	bet able	[bet] ['eibl]
[d]	como la *d* de *conde, andar*	dime mended	[daim] ['mendid]

[f]	como la *f* de *fofo, inflar*	face	[feis]
		snaffle	['snæfl]
[g]	como la *g* de *grande, rango*	go	[gəu]
		agog	[ə'gɔg]
[h]	es una aspiración fuerte, algo así como la jota castellana [x] pero sin la aspereza gutural de aquélla	hit	[hit]
		reheat	['riː'hiːt]
[j]	como la *y* de *cuyo, reyes*	you	[juː]
		pure	[pjuə*]
		million	['miljən]
[k]	como la *c* de *cama* o la *k* de *kilómetro*, pero acompañada por una ligera aspiración inexistente en español	catch	[kætʃ]
		kiss	[kis]
		chord	[kɔːd]
		box	[bɔks]
[l]	como la *l* de *leer, pala*	lick	[lik]
		place	[pleis]
[m]	como la *m* de *mes, comer*	mummy	['mʌmi]
		roam	[rəum]
[n]	como la *n* de *nada, hablan*	nut	[nʌt]
		sunny	['sʌni]
[ŋ]	como el sonido que tiene la *n* en *banco, rango*	bank	[bæŋk]
		sinker	['siŋkə*]
		singer	['siŋə*]
[p]	como la *p* de *palo, ropa*, pero acompañada por una ligera aspiración inexistente en español	pope	[pəup]
		pepper	['pepə*]
[r]	Es un sonido muy débil, casi semivocal, que no tiene la vibración fuerte que caracteriza la *r* española. Se articula elevando la punta de la lengua hacia el paladar duro. (NB—En el inglés de Inglaterra la *r* escrita se pronuncia únicamente delante de vocal; en las demás posiciones es muda. Véase la nota sobre la pronunciación del inglés norteamericano, y el asterisco * abajo)	rate	[reit]
		pear	[pɛə*]
		fair	[fɛə*]
		blurred	[bləːd]
		sorrow	['sɔrəu]
[s]	como la *s* (sorda) de *casa, sesión*	sit	[sit]
		scent	[sent]
		cents	[sents]
		pox	[pɔks]
[t]	como la *t* de *tela, rata*, pero acompañada por una ligera aspiración inexistente en español	tell	[tel]
		strut	[strʌt]
		matter	['mætə*]
[v]	Inexistente en español (aunque se encuentra en catalán y valenciano). En inglés es sonido labiodental, y se produce juntando el labio inferior con los dientes superiores	vine	[vain]
		river	['rivə*]
		cove	[kəuv]
[w]	como la *u* de *huevo, puede*	wine	[wain]
		bewail	[bi'weil]
[z]	como la *s* (sonora) de *desde, mismo*	zero	['ziərəu]
		roses	['rəuziz]
		buzzer	['bʌzə*]
[ʒ]	Inexistente en español, pero como la *j* de las palabras francesas *jour, nager*, o como la *g* de las palabras portuguesas *gente, geral*	rouge	[ruːʒ]
		leisure	['leʒə*]
		azure	['eiʒə*]
	Este sonido aparece a menudo en el grupo [dʒ], parecido al grupo *dj* de la palabra francesa *adjacent*	page	[peidʒ]
		edge	[edʒ]
		jail	[dʒeil]
[ʃ]	Inexistente en español, pero como la *ch* de las palabras francesas *chambre, fiche*, o como la *x* de la palabra portuguesa *roxo*	shame	[ʃeim]
		ocean	['əuʃən]
		ration	['ræʃən]
		sugar	['ʃugə*]

Este sonido aparece a menudo en el grupo [tʃ], parecido al grupo *ch* del español *mucho, chocho*

much	[mʌtʃ]
chuck	[tʃʌk]
natural	['nætʃrəl]

[θ]   como la *z* de *zumbar* o la *c* de *ciento*

thin	[θin]
maths	[mæθs]

[ð]   forma sonorizada del anterior, algo parecido a la *d* de *todo*, *hablado*

this	[ðis]
other	['ʌðə*]
breathe	[briːð]

[x]   sonido que en rigor no pertenece al inglés de Inglaterra, pero que se encuentra en el inglés de Escocia y en palabras escocesas usadas en Inglaterra etc; es como la *j* de *joven, rojo*

loch	[lɔx]

[*]   El asterisco en las transcripciones indica que la *r* escrita en posición final de palabra se pronuncia en el inglés británico en muchos casos cuando la palabra siguiente empieza con vocal. En algún dialecto inglés y sobre todo en los Estados Unidos esta *r* se pronuncia siempre, así cuando la palabra se pronuncia aislada como cuando la siguen otras (empezando con vocal o sin ella)

bear	[bɛə*]
humour	['hjuːmə*]
after	['ɑːftə*]

Sonidos extranjeros

El grado de corrección con que el inglés pronuncia las palabras extranjeras que acaban de incorporarse al idioma depende — como en español — del nivel cultural del hablante y de los conocimientos que pueda tener del idioma de donde se ha tomado la palabra. Las transcripciones que damos de tales palabras representan una pronunciación más bien culta. En las transcripciones la tilde [˜] indica que la vocal tiene timbre nasal (en muchas palabras de origen francés). En las pocas palabras tomadas del alemán aparece a veces la [x], para cuya explicación véase el cuadro de las consonantes.

Las letras del alfabeto inglés

Cuando se citan una a una, o cuando se deletrea una palabra para mayor claridad, o cuando se identifica un avión etc por una letra y su nombre, las letras suenan así:

a	[ei]	j	[dʒei]	s	[es]
b	[biː]	k	[kei]	t	[tiː]
c	[siː]	l	[el]	u	[juː]
d	[diː]	m	[em]	v	[viː]
e	[iː]	n	[en]	w	['dʌbljuː]
f	[ef]	o	[əu]	x	[eks]
g	[dʒiː]	p	[piː]	y	[wai]
h	[eitʃ]	q	[kjuː]	z	[zed] *(en*
i	[ai]	r	[ɑː*]		*US* [ziː])

II. *LA PRONUNCIACIÓN DEL INGLÉS NORTEAMERICANO*

Sería sin duda deseable dar aquí un resumen de las diferencias más notables que existen entre el inglés de Inglaterra y el de las regiones del Reino Unido — Escocia, Gales, Irlanda del Norte — y el de los principales países extranjeros y continentes donde se ha arraigado este idioma: Irlanda, Estados Unidos y el Canadá, las Antillas, Australia y Nueva Zelanda, Sudáfrica y los países sucesores de las antiguas colonias en el Este y Oeste de África, la India, etc. Para tal labor no disponemos ni del espacio ni mucho menos de los conocimientos necesarios. Siendo este diccionario un trabajo angloamericano, sin embargo, y considerando el predominio actual de los Estados Unidos en tantas esferas (entre ellas la lingüística), es de todos modos imprescindible apuntar algunas de las múltiples diferencias que existen entre el inglés de Inglaterra y el hablado en Estados Unidos.

Empleamos las abreviaturas *Brit* (British) y *US* (United States).

1 Acentuación

Las palabras que tienen dos sílabas o más después del acento principal llevan en *US* un acento secundario que no tienen en *Brit*, p.ej. *dictionary* [*US* 'dikʃəˌneri = *Brit* 'dikʃənri], *secretary* [*US* 'sekrəˌteri = *Brit* 'sekrətri]. En algunos casos se acentúa en *US* una sílaba distinta de la que lleva el acento en *Brit*: p.ej. *primarily* [*US* prai'mærili = *Brit* 'praimərili]. Este cambio de acento se percibe ahora también, por influencia norteamericana, en el inglés de Inglaterra.

2 Entonación

El inglés de *US* se habla con un ritmo más lento y en un tono más monótono que en Inglaterra, debido en parte al alargamiento de las vocales que se apunta abajo.

3 Sonidos

Muchas de las vocales breves acentuadas en *Brit* se alargan mucho en *US*, y alguna vocal inacentuada en *Brit* se oye con más claridad en *US*, p.ej. *rapid* [*US* ˈræːpid = *Brit* ˈræpid], *capital* [*US* ˈkæːbidəl = *Brit* ˈkæpitl].

Peculiaridad muy notable del inglés en *US* es la nasalización de las vocales antes y después de las consonantes nasales [m, n, ŋ].

En las vocales individuales también hay diferencias. El sonido [ɑː] en *Brit* en muchas palabras se pronuncia en *US* como [æ] o bien [æː], p.ej. *grass* [*US* græs o græːs = *Brit* grɑːs], *answer* [*US* ˈænsər o ˈæːnsər = *Brit* ˈɑːnsə*]. El sonido [ə] en *Brit* se pronuncia en *US* casi como una [ɑ] oscura, p.ej. *dollar* [*US* ˈdɑlər = *Brit* ˈdələ*], *hot* [*US* hɑt = *Brit* hət], *topic* [*US* ˈtɑpik = *Brit* ˈtəpik]. El diptongo que se pronuncia en *Brit* [juː] en sílaba acentuada se pronuncia en la mayor parte de *US* sin [j], p.ej. *Tuesday* [*US* ˈtuːzdi = *Brit* ˈtjuːzdi], *student* [*US* ˈstuːdənt = *Brit* ˈstjuːdənt]; pero muchas palabras de este tipo se pronuncian en *US* igual que en *Brit*, p.ej. *music, pure, fuel*. En último lugar entre las vocales, se nota que la sílaba final -*ile* que se pronuncia en *Brit* [ail] es a menudo en *US* [əl] o bien [il], p.ej. *missile* [*US* ˈmisəl, ˈmisil = *Brit* ˈmisail]. Existen otras diferencias en la pronunciación de las vocales de palabras individuales, p.ej. *tomato*, pero éstas se tratan individualmente en el texto del diccionario.

En cuanto a las consonantes, destacamos dos diferencias. La consonante sorda [t] entre vocales suele sonorizarse bastante en *US*, p.ej. *united* [*US* juˈnaidid = *Brit* juːˈnaitid], o sufre lenición [t̬]. La *r* escrita en posición final después de vocal o entre vocal y consonante es por la mayor parte muda en *Brit*, pero se pronuncia a menudo en *US*, p.ej. *where* [*US* wɛər = *Brit* wɛə*], *sister* [*US* ˈsistər = *Brit* ˈsistə*]. Hemos tomado esto en cuenta en las transcripciones en el texto del diccionario. También en posición final de sílaba (no sólo de palabra) se nota esta pronunciación de la *r* escrita: *burden* [*US* ˈbəːrdn = *Brit* ˈbəːdn], *jersey* [*US* ˈdʒəːrzi = *Brit* ˈdʒəːzi].

Conviene advertir que aun dentro del inglés de Estados Unidos hay notables diferencias regionales; la lengua de Nueva Inglaterra difiere bastante de la del Sur, la del Mediooeste no es la de California, etc. Los datos que constan arriba no son más que indicaciones muy someras.

III. THE PRONUNCIATION OF EUROPEAN SPANISH

1 Except for a very few anomalies such as the writing of silent *h* and the existence of the two symbols *b* and *v* for the same sound, the pronunciation of Spanish is so well represented by normal orthography that it would be a waste of space to give a phonetic transcription for every Spanish word in Part I as is done for English in Part II. The general introduction given below should suffice. However, a transcription in IPA (International Phonetic Association) symbols is given for those few Spanish words in which spelling and pronunciation are not in accord, such as *reloj* [reˈlo], and for those numerous anglicisms and gallicisms which retain an un-Spanish spelling or which have unexpected and unpredictable pronunciations even for those acquainted with the original languages. In some cases alternative pronunciations are given, an indication that cultured Spanish usage has not yet fixed firmly on one.

In this section the pronunciation described is that of educated Castilian, and little account is taken of that of the Spanish regions, even though some (notably Andalusia) have considerable cultural strength and a pronunciation which is socially acceptable throughout Spain. The pronunciation of Spanish in America is treated in a separate section.

It must be noted that in this attempt to describe the sounds of Spanish in terms of English, and in a limited space, one is conscious of making no more than approximations. Such comparisons have a practical end and inevitably lack the scientific exactness which trained phoneticians require.

2 Accentuation of Spanish words

For Spanish, unlike English, simple rules can be devised and stated which will enable the stress to be placed correctly on each word at sight:

(a) If the word ends in a vowel, or in *n* or *s*

(often the signs of the plural of verbs and nouns respectively), the penultimate syllable is stressed: *zapato, zapatos, divide, dividen, dividieron, antiviviseccionista, telefonea, historia, diluviaba* (such words are called *palabras llanas* or *graves*).

(b) If the word ends in a consonant other than *n* or *s*, the last syllable is stressed: *verdad, practicar, decibel, virrey, coñac, pesadez* (such words are called *palabras agudas*).

(c) If the word is to be stressed in some way contrary to rules (a) and (b), an acute accent is written over the vowel to be stressed: *hablará, guaraní, rubí, esté, rococó; máquina, métodos, viéndolo, paralítico, húngaro* (words of this latter type are called *palabras esdrújulas*). With only two exceptions, the same syllable is stressed in the singular and plural forms of each word, but an accent may have to be added or suppressed in the plural: *crimen, crímenes; nación, naciones*. The two exceptions are *carácter, caracteres*, and *régimen, regímenes*. Only in a few verbal forms can the stress fall further back than on the antepenultimate syllable: *cántamelo, prohíbaselo*.

3 Diphthongs, hiatus and syllable division

It will have been noted in **2 (a)** above, in cases like *telefonea* and *historia*, that not all vowels count equally for the purposes of syllable division and stress. The convention is that *a, e* and *o* are "strong" vowels, and *i, u* "weak". Four rules then apply:

(a) A combination of weak + strong forms a diphthong (one syllable), the stress falling on the stronger element: *baila, cierra, puesto, peine, causa*.

(b) A combination of weak + weak forms a diphthong (one syllable), the stress falling on the second element: *ruido, fuimos, viuda*.

(c) Two strong vowels remain in hiatus as two distinct syllables, the stress falling according to rules (a) and (b) in section 2; *ma/es/tro* (three syllables in all), *con/tra/er* (three syllables in all), *cre/er* (two syllables).

(d) Any word having a vowel combination whose parts are not stressed according to rules (a) to (c) bears an acute accent on the stressed part: *creído, período, baúl, ríe, tío*.

Note — in those cases where IPA transcriptions are given for Spanish words, the stress mark ['] is inserted in the same way as explained for English, above, section 2.

The Spanish letters and their sounds

Note — the order in which the explanations are set out is that of the alphabet and not that of the phonetic system. The system of transcription adopted is a fairly "broad" one; a more exact or "narrow" system would involve, for example, division of the vowel [e] according to quality and length, and the use of two symbols instead of one [e, ɛ].

Vowels

Spanish vowels are clearly and rather sharply pronounced, and single vowels are free from the tendency to diphthongize which is noticeable in English (eg *side* [said], *know* [nəu]). Moreover when they are in unstressed positions they are relaxed only slightly, again in striking contrast to English (compare English *natural* ['nætʃrəl] with Spanish *natural* [natu'ral]). Stressed vowels are somewhat more open and short before *rr* (compare *carro* with *caro*, *perro* with *pero*).

(NOTE: Examples are pronounced as in British English.)

a	[a]	Not so short as *a* in English *pat, patter*, nor so long as in English *rather, bar*	pata amara
e	[e]	In an open syllable (one which ends in the vowel) like *e* in English *they*, but without the sound of the *y*. In a closed syllable (one which ends in a consonant) is a shorter sound, like the *e* in English *set, wet*	me pelo sangre peldaño
i	[i]	Not so short as *i* in English *bit, tip*, nor so long as in English *machine*	iris filo
o	[o]	In an open syllable (one which ends in the vowel) like *o* in English *note*, but without the sound of [u] which ends the vowel in this word. In a closed syllable (one which ends in a consonant) is a shorter sound, though not quite so short as in English *pot, cot*	poco cosa bomba conté

u	[u]	Like *u* in English *rule* or *oo* in *food*. Silent after *q* and in the groups *gue, gui*, unless marked by a diaeresis (*argüir, fragüe, antigüedad*)	luna pula
y	[i]	As a vowel — that is in the conjunction *y* "and", and at the end of a word such as *ley, voy* — is pronounced like *i*.	

Diphthongs
(See also section 3 above)

ai, ay	[ai]	like *i* in English *side*	baile estay
au	[au]	like *ou* in English *sound*	áureo causa
ei, ey	[ei]	like *ey* in English *they*	reina rey
eu	[eu]	like the vowel sounds in English *may-you*, without the sound of the *y*	deuda feudo
oi, oy	[oi]	like *oy* in English *boy*	oiga soy

Semiconsonants

These are two, and appear in a variety of combinations as the first element; not all the combinations are listed here.

i, y	[j]	like *y* in English *yes, yacht* (See also the note under *y* in the list of consonants)	bien hielo yunta apoyo
u	[w]	like *w* in English *well*	huevo fuente agua guardar

Consonants

b, v		These two letters have the same value in Spanish. There are two distinct pronunciations depending on position and context:	
	[b]	At the start of the breath-group and after written *m* and *n* (pronounced [m]) the sound is plosive like English *b*	bomba boda enviar
	[β]	In all other positions the sound is a bilabial fricative (unknown in English) in which the lips do not quite meet	haba severo yo voy de Vigo
c		There are two different values:	
	[k]	*c* before *a, o, u* or a consonant is like English *k* in *keep*, but without the slight aspiration which accompanies it	calco acto cuco
	[θ]	*c* before *e, i* is like English *th* in *thin*. In parts of Andalusia and in *SAm* this is pronounced like English voiceless *s* in *same*, a phenomenon known as *seseo*	celda hacer cinco cecear
		Note — in words like *acción, sección* both types of *c*-sound are heard [kθ]	
ch	[tʃ]	like English *ch* in *church*	mucho chocho
d		There are three different values depending on position and context:	

[xxvii]

	[d]	At the start of the breath-group and after *l, n* the sound is plosive like English *d*	dama
			aldea
			andar
	[ð]	Between vowels and after consonants other than *l, n* the sound is relaxed and approaches English voiced *th* [ð] in *this*; in parts of Spain and in uneducated speech it is further relaxed and even disappears, particularly in the *-ado* ending	pide
			cada
			pardo
			sidra
		In the final position, the second type of [ð] is further relaxed or altogether omitted (though purists condemn this as a vulgar error). In eastern parts of Spain, however, this final *-d* may be heard as a [t]	verdad
			usted
			Madrid
			callad
f	[f]	like English *f* in *for*	fama
			fofo
g		There are three different values depending on position and context:	
	[x]	Before *e, i* it is the same as the Spanish *j* (below)	Gijón
			general
	[g]	At the start of the breath-group and after *n*, the sound is that of the English *g* in *get*	gloria
			rango
			pingüe
	[ɣ]	In other positions the sound is as in the second type above, but is fricative not plosive, there being no more than a close approximation of the vocal organs	haga
			agosto
			la guerra
		Note — in the group *gue, gui* the *u* is silent (*guerra, guindar*) except when marked by a diaeresis (*antigüedad, argüir*). In the group *gua* all the letters are sounded (*guardia, guapo*)	
h		always silent, a written convention only	honor
			hombre
			rehacer
j	[x]	a strong guttural sound not found in the English of England, but like the *ch* of Scots *loch*, Welsh *bach*, or German *Aachen, Achtung*; it is silent at the end of a word (*reloj*)	jota
			jején
			baraja
k	[k]	like English *k* in *kick*, but without the slight aspiration which accompanies it	kilogramo
l	[l]	like English *l* in *love*	lelo
			panal
ll	[ʎ]	approximating to English *lli* in *million*; in parts of Spain and most of *SAm* is pronounced as [j] and in other parts as [ʒ]; the pronunciation as [j] is condemned in Spain as a vulgar error but is extending rapidly even in Castile	calle
			ella
			lluvia
			millón
m	[m]	like English *m* in *made*	mano
			mamar
n	[n]	like English *n* in *none*; but before written *v* is pronounced as *m*, the group making [mb] (eg *enviar, sin valor*)	nadie
			pan
			pino
ñ	[ɲ]	approximating to English *ni* [nj] in *onion*	uña
			ñoño
p	[p]	like English *p* in *put*, but without the slight aspiration which accompanies it; it is often silent in *septiembre, séptimo*	padre
			papa
q	[k]	like English *k* in *kick*, but without the slight aspiration which accompanies it; it is always written in combination with *u*, which is silent	que
			quinqué
			busqué
			quiosco
r	[r]	a single trill or vibration stronger than any *r* in the English of England, but like the *r* in Scots; it is more relaxed in the final	coro
			quiere

		position and is indeed silent in parts of Spain and *SAm*; pronounced like *rr* at the start of a word and also after *l, n, s*	rápido real
rr	[rr]	strongly trilled in a way that does not exist in English (except in parodies of Scots)	torre arre burra irreal
s		Two pronunciations:	
	[s]	Except in the instances mentioned next, is a voiceless *s* like *s* in English *same*	casa Isabel soso
	[z]	Before a voiced consonant (*b, d, g, l, m, n*) is in most speakers a voiced *s* like *s* in English *rose, phase*	desde asgo mismo asno
t	[t]	like English *t* in *tame*, but without the slight aspiration which accompanies it	título patata
v		(*see* b)	
w		found in a few recent loanwords only; usually pronounced like Spanish *b, v* or like an English *v*, or kept as English *w*	wáter week-end wolframio
x		There are several possible pronunciations:	
	[ks]	Between vowels, *x* is pronounced like English *x* in box [ks], or	máximo
	[gs]	like *gs* in *big stick* [gs]	examen
	[s]	In a few words the *x* is pronounced between vowels like English *s* by many (but not all) speakers	exacto auxilio
	[s]	Before a consonant *x* is pronounced like English *s* in *same* by many (but not all) speakers	extra sexto
y	[j]	as a consonant or semiconsonant, is pronounced like *y* in English *yes, youth*; in emphatic speech in Spain and *SAm* this is heard as a voiced palatal plosive rather like the *j* in English *jam* [dʒ]; in *RPl, Chi etc* this *y* is pronounced like the *s* in English *leisure* [ʒ]	mayo yo mayor ya
z	[θ]	like English *th* in *thin*; in parts of Andalusia and in *SAm* this is pronounced like English voiceless *s* in *same*, a phenomenon known as *seseo*	zapato zopenco zumbar luz

Additional notes on pronunciation

1 The letter *b* is usually not pronounced in groups with *s* such as *obscuro, substituir*, and such words are now often written (with the Academy's sanction) *oscuro, sustituir etc*; they are so printed in this dictionary. A tendency to drop the *b* in pronouncing other similar groups is also noticeable, for example in *subjuntivo*, but in these cases the *b* is still always written.

2 With one exception there are no real double consonants in Spanish speech; *cc* in words like *acción* is two separate sounds [kθ], while *ll* and *rr* have their own values (see the table above).

The exception is the -*nn*- group found in learned words having the Latin prefix *in-*, eg *innato*, or occasionally *con-, sin-*, as in *connatural, sinnúmero*. In these cases the *n* is pronounced double [nn].

3 Final -*s* of the definite and indefinite articles, plural, and of plural adjectives, is usually silent when the following noun starts with *r-*: eg *unos rábanos* [uno'rraβanos], *los romanos, varias razones, dos ratas* [do'rratas].

4 Foreign sounds in Spanish hardly warrant separate treatment for our purposes; whereas the cultured Briton makes some attempt to maintain at least a vaguely French sound when he pronounces English loanwords from

French, with nasal vowels and so on, the cultured Spaniard for the most part and certainly his less cultured compatriot adapts the sounds (but often not the spelling) of loanwords taken from French or English to suit his native speech habits. This is best studied in the transcriptions of individual items in the main text of the dictionary; see for example *chalet, gag, jazz, shock*.

5 No old-established Spanish word begins with what is called "impure *s*", that is, *s* plus a consonant as an initial group. When Spaniards have to pronounce a foreign name having such a group they inevitably precede it with an *e-* sound, so that *Smith* is [ez'miθ] or [ez'mis]. Very recent anglicisms tend to be written in Spanish as *slip, slogan* and so on, but must be pronounced [ez'lip], [ez'loɣan]; those that are slightly better established are written *esnob, esprínter* etc, and then present no problem in pronunciation.

6 See also section VI of this Introduction, on "Spanish orthography and the *Nuevas Normas*".

The letters of the Spanish alphabet

When the letters are cited one by one, or when a word is spelled out for greater clarity, or when an aircraft is identified by a letter and a name, and so on, the names of the letters used are:

a	[a]	j	['xota]	r	['ere]
b	[be]	k	[ka]	rr	['erre]
c	[θe]	l	['ele]	s	['ese]
ch	[tʃe]	ll	['eʎe]	t	[te]
d	[de]	m	['eme]	u	[u]
e	[e]	n	['ene]	v	['uβe]
f	['efe]	ñ	['eɲe]	x	['ekis]
g	[xe]	o	[o]	y	[i'ɣrjeɣa]
h	['atʃe]	p	[pe]	z	['θeta] or
i	[i]	q	[ku]		['θeða]

The letters are of the feminine gender: "mayo se escribe con una *m* minúscula", "¿esto es una *c* o una *t*?". One says "una *a*" and "la *a*", "una *h*" and "la *h*" (not applying the rule as in *un ave, el agua*).

IV. THE PRONUNCIATION OF SPANISH IN AMERICA

To generalize briefly about the vast area over which Spanish ranges in the New World is difficult; the following notes are very tentative. The upland regions (settled by Castilians from the *meseta*) tend to be linguistically conserva-

tive and to have more Castilian features; the lowland and coastal regions share many of the features of Andalusian speech. Among the vowels there is little to note. Among the consonants:

1 The Castilian [θ] sound — in writing *c* or *z* — is pronounced as various kinds of *s* [s] throughout America, a phenomenon known as *seseo*.

2 At the end of a syllable and a word, *s* is a slight aspiration, eg *las dos* [lah'doh], *mosca* ['mohka]; but in parts of the Andean region, in upland Mexico and in Peru the [s] is maintained as in Castilian.

3 Castilian written *ll* [ʎ] is pronounced in three different ways in regions of America. It survives as [ʎ] in part of Colombia, all Peru, Bolivia, N. Chile and Paraguay; in Argentina, Uruguay, upland Ecuador and part of Mexico it is pronounced [ʒ]; and in the remaining areas it is pronounced [j]. When this last kind [j] is in contact with the vowels *e* and *i* it disappears altogether and one finds in uneducated writing such forms as *gaína* (for *gallina*) and *biete* (for *billete*).

4 In vulgar speech in all parts there is much confusion of *l* and *r*: *clin* (for *crin*), *carma* (for *calma*) etc.

5 Written *h* is silent in Castilian, but in parts of Mexico and Peru this *h* is aspirated at the start of a word (when it derives from Latin initial *f-*), so that in uneducated writing one finds such forms as *jarto* (for *harto*) and *jablar* (for *hablar*). Compare *halar/jalar* and other cases in the text of the dictionary.

V. *LA ORTOGRAFÍA DEL INGLÉS*

El extranjero, mientras lucha con las muchas confusiones y rarezas de la ortografía inglesa, se consuela recordando que los propios niños ingleses, y muchas personas mayores, sostienen la misma lucha. El inglés ha de ser el único idioma para el que ha valido la pena — la cosa estuvo de moda hacia unos 20 años — organizar certámenes ortográficos, en los que se pedía que los concursantes deletreasen palabras como *parallel, precede* y *proceed* y *supersede, sylph* y *Ralph*. Ha habido muchas tentativas de reforma — siendo quizá la más conocida la de G. B. Shaw — pero ninguna se ha llevado a la práctica; las reformas norteamericanas (véase abajo) son útiles pero afectan sólo una pequeña parte del problema.

1 En general se aplica el sistema en todo su rigor y las dudas y desviaciones permitidas son escasísimas. Es lícito escribir algunas palabras con o sin *e* muda, como *blond(e)*, *judg(e)ment*; varía la vocal en *enquiry-inquiry*, *encrust-incrust*, y la consonante en muchas palabras terminadas en *-ise*, *-ize* (pero siempre *advertise, chastise*). En casos como *spirt–spurt* se hace generalmente una distinción de sentido. Son toleradas *grandad* y *granddad*, *mummie* y *mummy*, *nappie* y *nappy*. Las variantes más importantes constan en el texto del diccionario.

2 En las novelas en que se presenta la vida de la clase baja urbana (p.ej. de los *Cockneys* de Londres) o de gente del campo, el autor puede representar su habla — con sus incorrecciones y barbarismos, según el criterio casticista — con formas como las siguientes:

'e	= he		Oim	= I'm
'ere	= here		roit	= right
'ope	= hope		Lunnun	= London
'ed	= head		bruvver	= brother
et	= ate		Fursday	= Thursday
'arf	= half		dook	= duke
yer	= your		dunno	= don't know

La *-d* final tras *n* se suprime a menudo en este lenguaje, p.ej. *an'* = *and*, y la *-g* final se suprime en la desinencia *-ing*, p.ej. *boozin'* = *boozing*. Como curiosidad apuntamos que este último fenómeno se da también en representaciones del habla de las familias aristocráticas, de los militares viejos etc: *huntin'*, *shootin'* and *fishin'*. Nótese el modo de emplear la comilla (') para indicar la supresión de una letra. Tales cambios en la escritura pueden representar una diferencia no de clase sino de región, p.ej. en escocés *awa'* = away, y en el inglés de las Antillas *dis* = this.

3 Se observan a veces deformaciones hechas con intención humorística (*luv* = *love*, *Injun* = *Indian*) o con afán de ultramodernidad (*nite* = *night*) o como truco publicitario en el comercio (*sox* = *socks*) o como parte de la jerga de un grupo social (*showbiz* = *show business*).

4 Son mucho más importantes las diferencias ortográficas entre el inglés británico (*Brit*) y el norteamericano (*US*):
(a) La *u* que se escribe en *Brit* en las palabras terminadas en *-our* y derivadas del latín, se suprime en *US*: *US* color = *Brit* colour, *US* labor = *Brit* labour. (Esto no afecta los monosílabos como *dour, flour, sour*, donde no hay diferencia). También en *US* se suprime la *u* del grupo *ou* [əu] en el interior de la palabra: *US* mold = *Brit* mould, *US* smolder = *Brit* smoulder.
(b) Muchas palabras que en *Brit* terminan en *-re* se escriben en *US* *-er*: *US* center = *Brit* centre, *US* meter = *Brit* metre, *US* theater = *Brit* theatre. (Pero no existe diferencia en *acre, lucre, massacre*).
(c) Ciertas vocales finales, que no tienen valor en la pronunciación, se escriben en *Brit* pero se suprimen en *US*: *US* catalog = *Brit* catalogue, *US* prolog = *Brit* prologue, *US* program = *Brit* programme, *US* kilogram = *Brit* kilogramme.
(d) En *US* se suele simplificar los diptongos de origen griego y latino *ae*, *oe*, escribiendo sencillamente *e*: *US* anemia = *Brit* anaemia, *US* anesthesia = *Brit* anaesthesia. En *US* se duda entre *subpoena* y *subpena*; en *Brit* se mantiene siempre el primero.
(e) En algunos casos las palabras que en *Brit* terminan en *-ence* se escriben *-ense* en *US*: *US* defense = *Brit* defence, *US* offense = *Brit* offence.
(f) Algunas consonantes que en *Brit* se escriben dobles se escriben en *US* sencillas: *US* wagon = *Brit* waggon (pero *wagon* se admite también en Inglaterra), y sobre todo en formas verbales: *US* kidnaped = *Brit* kidnapped, *US* worshiped = *Brit* worshipped. El caso de *l*, *ll* intervocálicas ofrece más complejidades. Alguna vez lo que se escribe con *ll* en Brit se encuentra con una *l* en *US*: así *US* councilor = *Brit* councillor, *US* traveler = *Brit* traveller. Por el contrario, en posición final de sílaba o de palabra la *l* en *Brit* es a menudo *ll* en *US*: así *US* enroll, enrolls = *Brit* enrol, enrols, *US* skillful = *Brit* skilful.
(g) En *US* se modifica algún otro grupo ortográfico del inglés, pero sólo en la escritura de tono familiar: *US* tho = *Brit* though, *US* thru = *Brit* through. También son más corrientes en *US* las formas como *Peterboro* (o bien *Peterboro'*), aunque éstas no son desconocidas en *Brit*.
(h) Viene luego una serie de palabras aisladas que se escriben de modo diferente:

US	Brit	US	Brit
ax	axe	mustache	moustache
check	cheque	pajamas	pyjamas
cozy	cosy	plow	plough
gray	grey	skeptic	sceptic
gypsy	gipsy	tire	tyre
hello	hullo		

En otros casos se duda bastante; en *US* hay lucha entre *rime, rhyme,* mientras en *Brit* se escribe únicamente el segundo; en *US* hay lucha entre *tiro, tyro,* mientras en *Brit* se escribe siempre el segundo.

Conviene notar que mientras la influencia del inglés norteamericano se percibe a cada paso en el inglés británico en cuanto al léxico, a la fraseología y a la sintaxis, ésta parece no haber afectado para nada la ortografía del inglés en el Reino Unido.

5 Las mayúsculas se emplean más en inglés que en español. Se emplean como en español al principio de la palabra en los siguientes casos: en la primera palabra de la frase; en los nombres propios de toda clase; en los nombres, sobrenombres y pronombres posesivos de Dios, Cristo, Nuestra Señora etc; en las graduaciones y títulos de las autoridades del estado, del ejército, de la iglesia, de las profesiones etc.

Las mayúsculas se emplean en inglés en los siguientes casos donde se escribe minúscula en español:

(a) Los nombres de los días y meses: *Monday, Tuesday, April, May.*

(b) El pronombre personal de sujeto, primera persona: *I* (*yo*). Pero el pronombre de segunda persona se escribe en inglés con minúscula: *you* (*Vd, Vds*).

(c) Los nombres de los habitantes de los países y provincias, los adjetivos derivados de éstos y los nombres de los idiomas: *I like the French, two Frenchwomen, French cheese, to talk French, a text in old Aragonese.* Se emplea la mayúscula también en los nombres y adjetivos derivados de otras clases de nombres propios: *a Darwinian explanation, the Bevanites, two well-known Gongorists, a Beatle haircut, the Alphonsine school.* Sin embargo el adjetivo de nacionalidad puede escribirse con minúscula en algún caso cuando se refiere a una cosa corriente u objeto conocido de todos, p.ej. *a french window, french beans, german measles* (en este diccionario hemos preferido escribir algunas de estas palabras con mayúscula).

(d) En los sustantivos y adjetivos principales en los títulos de libros, artículos, películas etc: *The Third Man, Gone with the Wind, The Potato in Hungarian Folklore.*

6 La puntuación en inglés. Los signos y el modo de emplearlos son como en español con las siguientes excepciones:

(a) Los signos de admiración y de interrogación (¡¿) no se emplean en inglés en principio de frase.

(b) En inglés se emplea menos la doble raya (— . . . —) con función parentética; se prefiere en muchos casos el paréntesis (. . .).

(c) La raya (—) que sirve a menudo en español para introducir el diálogo y la oración directa, y a veces también para cerrarlos, se sustituye en inglés por las comillas (" . . ."). Conviene apuntar que éstas se emplean obligatoriamente al terminar la cita u oración directa y no sólo para introducirla. Los signos « » del español se escriben siempre como comillas (". . .") en inglés.

7 La división de la palabra en inglés. Las reglas para dividir una palabra en final de renglón son menos estrictas en inglés que en español. En general se prefiere cortar la palabra tras vocal, *hori-zontal, vindi-cation,* pero se prefiere mantener como unidades ciertos sufijos comunes, *vindica-tion, glamorous.* De acuerdo con esto se divide la palabra dejando separada la desinencia *-ing,* p.ej. *sicken-ing,* pero si ésta está precedida por un grupo de consonantes, una de ellas va unida al *-ing,* p.ej. *tick-ling, ramb-ling.* Se divide el grupo de dos consonantes iguales: *pat-ter, yel-low, disap-pear,* y los demás grupos consonánticos de acuerdo con los elementos separables que forman la palabra: *dis-count, per-turb;* son admisibles *be-tween, bet-ween* y *atmo-sphere, atmos-phere.*

VI. SPANISH ORTHOGRAPHY AND THE NUEVAS NORMAS

The system of spelling in Spanish is extremely logical and apart from a few small anomalies it presents no problems. The more important of the Academy's *Nuevas Normas* of 1959 are appended for information and to help maintain the unity of the system. An excellent book for those in doubt is Manuel Seco's *Diccionario de dudas y dificultades de la lengua española,* Madrid, Aguilar, 2nd ed., 1964.

1 Spelling reform in Spanish to correct the few remaining anomalies is rarely attempted. Some favour always writing *j* (not a mixture of *g* and *j*) for the [x] sound: *jeneral, Jibraltar* — quite logically, since *jirafa, jícara* and *jirón,* and many others, are so spelled by everybody. Poetic texts of Juan Ramón Jiménez are always printed with such spellings.

cachete nm (a) (fat) cheek; (Med) swollen cheek. (b) punch in the face, slap. (c) dagger. (d) (CR, Guat) favour.

cacheteada nf (Arg) slap, box on the ear.

cachetear [1a] vt (Arg, Per) to slap, box on the ear.

cachetero nm (a) dagger. (b) (Taur) bullfighter who finishes the bull off with a dagger.

cachetina nf fist fight, punch-up (fam).

cachetón adj (a) plump-cheeked, fat-faced. (b) (Mex) impudent, barefaced; (Chi) proud. (c) (CR) attractive, congenial.

cachicán 1 adj sly, crafty. 2 nm (a) (Agr) foreman, gaffer. (b) (pej) sly sort.

cachicano nm (Col, Ven) armadillo.

cachicuerno adj weapon with a horn handle.

cachiflén nm squib, cracker.

cachifo nm (Col, CR, Ven) boy, young schoolboy.

cachigordo adj squat, chunky (fam.

cachimba nf (a) (SAm) pipe. (b) (SAm) empty cartridge. (c) (RPl) shallow well, hole dug in the beach for drinking water. (d) (Cu) loose woman.

cachimbo nm (a) (SAm) pipe; **chupar** — (PR, Ven) to smoke a pipe; (hum: of child) to suck its thumb. (b) (Cu) small sugar mill. (c) (Cu) poor man. (d) (Per: Univ) freshman.

cachipolla nf mayfly.

cachiporra nf truncheon; club, big stick, cosh.

cachiporrazo nm blow with a truncheon (etc).

cachirula nf (Col) lace mantilla.

cachivache nm (a) pot, utensil. (b) worthless person, useless fellow. (c) —s pots and pans, kitchen utensils; (fig) trash, junk, lumber.

cacho[1] 1 adj bent, crooked.
2 nm (a) crumb; bit, small piece, slice; ¡— de gloria! my precious!; ¡— de ladrón! you thief! (b) (SAm) horn; —s (fig) (number of) cattle; **hombre de muchos —s** man of great wealth in cattle. (c) (Ec, Per, RPl) dice box, dice, set of dice; **jugar al —** to play dice. (d) (Chi) drinking vessel (made of horn); **empinar el —** to drink a lot. (e) (RPl) bunch of bananas. (f) (Chi) unsaleable goods, unsold merchandise. (g) (Col, CR, Ec, Par, Ven) anecdote, joke; prank; hoax; (Ven) mockery, derision. (h) (phrases) **echar — a uno** (Col) to excel someone; **estar fuera de —** to be in safe keeping; **raspar el — a uno** (Chi) to tell someone off; ¡—s **para arriba!** (Chi) that's marvellous!, splendid!

cacho[2] nm (Fish) chub.

cachón[1] adj (Mex) long-horned.

cachón[2] nm wave, breaker; small waterfall.

cachondearse [1a] vr (fam) to take things as a joke; — **de uno** to mock at someone, tease someone, ridicule someone.

cachondeo nm (fam) farce, poor show (fam), mess; ¡esto es un —! what a mess!, what a farce this is!

cachondez nf (a) heat, rut, readiness to mate. (b) sexiness; randiness.

cachondo adj (a) (Zool) on heat, in rut. (b) (of human) **ser —** to be sexy; **estar —** to feel randy, be in the mood.

cachorro nm, **cachorra** nf (a) pup, puppy; cub. (b) (Cu, PR, Ven) uncouth person; ¡—! you brute!

cachudo 1 adj (a) (Ec, Mex) horned, with horns. (b) (Col) wealthy. (c) (Chi) suspicious, distrustful; cunning. (d) (Mex) grim-faced.
2 nm: **el —** the devil, the horned one.

cachuela nf (a) stew, fricassee. (b) (Bol, Per) rapids.

cachupín nm, **cachupina** nf (SAm: pej) Spanish settler (in America).

cada adj invar each; (followed by numeral) every; — **día** each day, every day; — **uno** each one, every one; — **3 meses** every 3 months; — **y cuando** every now and then; — **y cuando que ...** whenever ...; as soon as ...; — **y siempre que ...** as soon as ...; — **cierta distancia por la carretera** every so often along the road, at intervals along the road; — **cierto tiempo** every so often; ¿— **cuánto?** how often?

cadalso nm scaffold; (Tech) stand, platform.

cadarzo nm floss, floss silk.

cadáver nm body, dead body, corpse, cadaver (US); (of animal) body, carcass; **ingresó —** he was dead on arrival (at hospital).

cadavérico adj cadaverous; ghastly, deathly pale.

cadena nf (a) (in most senses) chain; (fig) bond, link; series, sequence; — **antideslizante** tyre chain; — **de fabricación** production line; — **de hoteles** chain

of hotels; — **de montaje** assembly line; — **de montañas** range of mountains; — **de oruga** caterpillar track; — **de reloj** watch chain; — **sin fin** endless chain; **reacción en —** chain reaction. (b) (Law: Hist) chain gang. (c) (Law) — **perpetua** life imprisonment. (d) (Archit) pier, buttress.

cadencia nf cadence, rhythm; measure; (Mus: piece) cadenza.

cadencioso adj rhythmic(al), cadenced.

cadeneta nf (Sew) chain stitch; — **de papel** paper chain.

cadenilla nf, **cadenita** nf small chain; necklace.

cadera nf hip.

cadetada nf thoughtless action, irresponsible act.

cadete nm cadet.

cadi nm (angl: Golf) caddie.

Cádiz Cadiz.

cadmio nm cadmium.

caducar [1g] vi (a) (person) to become senile; to dodder, be in one's dotage. (b) to get out of date; to fall into disuse; (Comm, Law) to expire, lapse; **el abono ha caducado** the season ticket has expired.

caducidad nf lapse, lapsing, expiry.

caduco adj (a) person senile, very old, decrepit; worn out. (b) (Bot) deciduous. (c) pleasure etc fleeting, perishable. (d) (Comm, Law) lapsed, expired, invalid; **quedar — to lapse.

caduquez nf senility, decrepitude.

caedizo 1 adj about to fall; weak; (Bot) deciduous.
2 nm (Col) shed; sloping roof.

caer [2o] 1 vt (fam) to drop, let fall; liquid to spill; house etc to knock down; (of horse etc) to throw.
2 vi and (in some senses) **caerse** vr (a) (general sense) to fall; to fall down; to tumble (down), collapse; to fall off, fall out; (Aer) to crash, come down; (of curtain etc) to hang; (of hair, branch) to hang down; — **al suelo** to fall to the ground; **el edificio se está cayendo** the building is falling down; — **sobre** (fig) to fall on, pounce on; to descend upon; **cayó un rayo en la torre** the tower was struck by lightning; **estar al —** to be about to fall, (fig) be about to happen, be due to happen; **dejar —** to drop, let fall; **dejarse —** to let oneself go, let oneself fall; **hacer —** to knock down, knock off, cause to fall; **se me cayó el guante** I dropped my glove, my glove fell off; **Eslobodia nunca cayó tan bajo** Slobodia never fell so low; — **en cama**, — **enfermo** to fall ill; — **en un error** to fall into error; — **redondo** to fall in a heap; —**se de miedo** to be terrified; —**se de tonto** (etc) to be very silly (etc); **se cae de viejo** he's so old he can hardly walk; **eso cae de suyo** that's obvious, that goes without saying. (b) to fall (in battle); (Mil: of town) to fall, be captured; **ha caído el gobierno** the government has fallen; — **como chinches**, — **como moscas** to die like flies. (c) (of level, price, temperature etc) to fall, go down; to diminish; (of conversation) to flag; (of custom etc) to lapse. (d) (of sun, wind) to go down. (e) (of day) to decline, draw to its close; (of night) to fall, close in; **al — de la noche** at nightfall. (f) (of colour) to fade. (g) (of place) to fall, lie, be located; **cae en el segundo tomo** it comes in the second volume; **eso cae más hacia el este** that lies further to the east. (h) (of windows etc) — **a**, — **hacia** to look over, look out on, look towards. (i) (of date, event) to fall; **el aniversario cae en martes** the anniversary falls on a Tuesday. (j) (Comm, Fin) to fall due. (k) (of inheritance) — **a** to fall to, come to, fall to the lot of; see **suerte**. (l) to realize; **no caigo** I don't get it; **ya caigo** I see, now I understand; — **en que ...** to realize that ...; see **cuenta**. (m) (of dress) — **bien a uno** (of clothes) to suit someone, look well on someone; **el traje le caía mal** the suit did not fit him, the suit was not right for him. (n) (of impression) **A no le cayó bien a B** A did not make a good impression on B; A was not well received by B; **no les caí** (CAm) I didn't hit it off with them, I didn't get on well with them, they didn't take to me. (o) (RPl) to come, arrive, drop in; **él suele — por aquí** he usually comes here.

café nm (a) (drink, berry, plant) coffee; — **helado** iced coffee; — **instantáneo** instant coffee; — **con leche** white coffee, coffee with milk; — **molido** ground coffee; — **negro** (SAm), — **solo** black coffee; — **tostado** roasted coffee; **estar de mal** — (CAm) to be out of sorts.
(b) café; coffee house; restaurant, bar; — **cantante** low night club.
(c) (RPl) ticking-off.

cafeína nf caffein(e).

cafetal nm (a) coffee plantation. (b) (Guat) coffee tree.

cafetalero (SAm) 1 adj coffee (attr), coffee-growing (attr); **industria cafetalera** coffee industry. 2 nm coffee grower.

cafetalista nm (SAm) coffee grower.

cafetear [1a] vt (RPl) to tick off.

cafetera nf (a) coffee pot; — **automática** electric kettle; — **filtradora** percolator. (b) (fam) old car, old crock, jalop(p)y.

cafetería nf café, coffee house; (Rail) buffet, refreshment room; (Ant, Col, Chi) retail coffee shop.

cafetero (SAm) 1 adj coffee (attr); **industria cafetera** coffee industry. 2 nm café proprietor, café owner; coffee grower; coffee merchant.

cafetín nm low-class bar, small café.

cafeto nm (SAm) coffee tree.

cafetucho nm seedy little café.

caficultor nm (CAm) coffee grower.

caficultura nf (CAm) coffee growing.

cáfila nf group, flock, large number; **una** — **de disparates** a string of inanities.

cafre 1 adj (a) Kaffir. (b) (fig) cruel, savage; uncouth. 2 nmf Kaffir; **como** —s (fig) like savages, like beasts.

caga(a)ceite nm missel thrush.

cagada nf (a) (tabu) shit (tabu); **ser como** —s **de hormiga** (or **ratones** etc: hum) to be wholly unimportant; to be chicken feed.
(b) (fig) shocking blunder, stupid thing (to do).

cagadero nm (tabu) bog (sl), lavatory.

cagado adj (tabu) yellow, funky (fam).

cagajón nm horse dung, mule dung.

cagalera nf (tabu) runs (fam), diarrhoea; **¡brava —!** (iro) what a mess!

cagar [1h] (tabu) 1 vt (a) to shit (tabu).
(b) clothing to dirty, to soil.
(c) (fig) to bungle, make a mess of, mess up. 2 vi to shit (tabu), have a shit (tabu).
3 **cagarse** vr (a) = vi.
(b) **¡me cago!, me cago en la mar!** (etc) well I'm damned!; damn it!

cagarruta nf sheep dirt, goat dirt.

cagatintas nm, pl **cagatintas** penpusher, quill driver; (Col) miser.

cagón adj (tabu) = **cagado**.

cahuin nm (Chi) (a) drunkenness, drunken state. (b) rowdy gathering.

caída nf (a) fall; tumble, spill; falling, falling-out; (fig) fall, collapse, downfall; (Theat) flop, failure; **la C—** (Rel) the Fall; **la — del gobierno** the fall of the government; **la — del imperio** the collapse of the empire; **la — de los dientes** the falling-out of one's teeth, the loss of one's teeth; — **de agua** waterfall; — **de cabeza** fall headfirst, header; **a la — del sol** at sunset; **a la — de la tarde** in the evening; **sufrir una —** to have a fall, have a tumble.
(b) (of level, price etc) fall, drop (de 5 grados of 5 degrees; de la temperatura in temperature); decline, diminution.
(c) (of ground) drop, fall, slope; (Geol) dip; (of shoulders) slope.
(d) (of curtain etc) fold(s); (of dress) set, hang.
(e) — **radiactiva** radioactive fallout.
(f) —s (Tech) shoddy.
(g) —s (fam) witty remarks; **¡qué —s tiene!** isn't he witty?

caído 1 adj (a) fallen; head etc drooping; collar turndown; flower etc languid, limp, drooping.
(b) (fig) crestfallen, dejected.
(c) — **de color** pale.
2 —s nmpl: **los** —s the fallen; **los** —s **por España** those who fell for Spain; **monumento a los** —s war memorial.

caigo etc see **caer**.

caimacán nm (Col) important person, big shot (fam); ace, star, expert.

caimán nm (SAm) alligator, caiman; (Bol) iguana.
(b) (Mex: Mech) wrench. (c) (Ec) lazy fellow.

caimanear [1a] (SAm) 1 vt to swindle. 2 vi to hunt alligators.

caimiento nm (a) fall, falling; (Med) decline. (b) dejection; limpness.

Caín m Cain; **pasar las de** — to have a ghastly time (fam); **venir con las de** — to have evil intentions.

cairel nm wig; fringe.

cairelear [1a] vt to trim, fringe.

Cairo: el — Cairo.

caita 1 adj invar (Chi) wild, shy; unsociable. 2 nm (Chi) migratory agricultural worker.

caite nm (CAm) rough leather sandal.

caitearse [1a] vr (CAm): —**las** to run away, beat it (fam).

caja nf (a) box; chest; case, crate; coffin, casket (US); — **de colores** paintbox; — **del cuerpo** chest, thorax; — **de herramientas** toolbox, tool chest; — **de música** musical box; — **de sorpresa** jack-in-the-box; — **del tambor**, — **del tímpano** (Anat) eardrum; **un cuarto como** — **de muerto** a poky little room; **no entrar en** — to be of no advantage, (person) to be a square peg in a round hole, fail to adapt oneself.
(b) (Mech) case, casing, housing; (of vehicle) body; — **de cambios** gearbox; — **del cigüeñal** crankcase; — **de eje** axle box; — **de engranajes** gearbox; — **de fuego** (Rail) fire box; — **de sebo** grease cup; — **de velocidades** gearbox.
(c) (Elec) box; — **de empalmes** junction box; — **de fusibles** fuse box.
(d) (Archit: of staircase) well; (of lift) well, shaft; — **de registro** manhole.
(e) — (**de fusil**) stock.
(f) (Bot) seed case, capsule.
(g) (Comm, Fin) cashbox, safe; cashier's desk, cashdesk; cashier's office; — **de alquiler** safe-deposit box; — **de caudales** strongbox, safe; — **fuerte** strongroom, bank vault; strongbox; — **de** (**gastos**) **menores** petty cash; — **registradora** cash register, till; **metálico en** — cash in hand; **hacer** — to make up the accounts for the day; **ingresar en** — (person) to pay in, (cash) be paid in.
(h) (Fin) fund; — **de ahorros** savings bank; — **postal de ahorros** post office savings bank; — **de construcciones** building society; — **de jubilaciones** pension fund; — **de reclutamiento** recruiting office; — **de resistencia** (Pol) strike fund.
(i) (Mus) drum; **despedir** (or **echar**) **a uno con** —s **destempladas** to send someone packing, send someone away with a flea in his ear.
(j) (Mus) (of piano etc) case; (o violin etc) body, case; (Radio) cabinet; — **de resonancia** soundbox; (fig) sounding board.
(k) (Typ) case; — **alta** upper case; — **baja** lower case.
(l) (Chi) (dry) riverbed.

cajero nm, **cajera** nf cashier; (bank) teller.

cajeta nf (a) small box; (CAm, Chi, Ec, Mex, Ven) small round box of jelly (or of candy etc); (CAm, Chi, Ec, Mex, Ven) jelly, candy, sweet; (Cu, PR) tobacco pouch, cigar case.
(b) (CR, Ec, Per) lip (of animal).
(c) **de** — (CAm, Mex: iro) first-rate, marvellous.

cajete nm (Mex) pan, casserole.

cajetilla 1 nf small box; — **de cigarrillos** packet of cigarettes, pack of cigarettes (US).
2 nm (RPl) toff (fam), dude (US); city slicker (US); effeminate person.

cajista nm compositor, typesetter.

cajita nf small box; — **de cerillas** box of matches, matchbox.

cajón nm (a) big box, case; crate; chest; — **de embalaje** packing case.
(b) (Chi, Per, RPl) coffin, casket (US).
(c) drawer; locker; (Comm) till; — **de sastre** (fig) odds and ends; ragbag; (person) muddle-headed sort; **estar como** — **de sastre** to be in utter disorder, be in a terrible mess.
(d) (Comm) stall, booth; (Mex) grocer's shop; — **de ropa** (Mex) dry-goods store.
(e) (Tech) — **hidráulico**, — **de suspensión** caisson.
(f) (Chi, Guat, RPl, Ven) ravine.
(g) **eso es de** — that's a matter of course, that goes without saying; that's the usual thing.

cal nf lime; — **apagada**, — **muerta** slaked lime; — **viva** quicklime; **cerrar algo a** — **y canto** to shut something firmly (or securely); **de** — **y canto** firm, strong, tough.

cala[1] nf (Geog) cove; creek, inlet; fishing ground; (Naut) hold; — **de construcción** slipway.

cala[2] nf (of fruit) sample slice; (Med) suppository; (Surg) probe; **hacer** — **y cata** to test for quality.

calabacear [1a] vt (Univ) candidate to fail, plough (sl); subject to fail in, plough in (sl); lover to jilt.

calabacera nf pumpkin (plant), gourd.

calabacín *nm* (**a**) (*Bot*) marrow. (**b**) (*fig*) dolt.

calabaza *nf* (**a**) (*Bot*) pumpkin; gourd, calabash. (**b**) (*fig*) dolt. (**c**) **dar** —s a *candidate* to fail, plough (*sl*); *lover* to jilt; to snub, offend; **llevarse** —s, **recibir** —s (*Univ*) to fail, plough (*sl*); (*lover*) to be jilted; **salir** — to be a flop (*fam*), prove a miserable failure.

calabazada *nf* butt, knock (with the head); blow on the head.

calabazazo *nm* bump on the head.

calabazo *nm* (**a**) pumpkin, gourd. (**b**) (*Ant*) drum.

calabobos *nm* drizzle.

calabozo *nm* prison; prison cell; (*esp Hist*) dungeon; (*Mil sl*) glasshouse (*sl*).

calabrote *nm* (*Naut*) cable, hawser.

calache *nm* (*CAm*) thing, thingummyjig (*fam*).

calada *nf* (**a**) soaking. (**b**) (*of net*) lowering. (**c**) (*fam*) ticking-off; **dar una** — **a** uno to tick someone off, haul someone over the coals.

calado 1 *adj*: **estar** — (**hasta los huesos**) to be soaked (to the skin). **2** *nm* (**a**) (*Tech*) fretwork; (*Sew*) openwork. (**b**) (*Naut*) depth of water; (*of ship*) draught; **en iguales** —s on an even keel.

calafate *nm* caulker; shipwright.

calafatear [1a] *vt* (*Naut*) to caulk; to plug (up).

calaguritano 1 *adj* of Calahorra. **2** *nm*, **calaguritana** *nf* native (*or* inhabitant) of Calahorra; **los** —s the people of Calahorra.

calamaco *adj* (*Arg*) *poncho* red; (*Arg, PR*) *poncho* old, faded; poor-quality.

calamar *nm* squid.

calambre *nm* (*also* —s) cramp; — **de los escribientes** writer's cramp.

calambur *nm* (*SAm*) pun.

calamidad *nf* calamity, disaster; **es una** — (*fam*: *event etc*) it's a great pity; it's a nuisance; (*person*) he's utterly useless, he's a dead loss; **estar hecho una** — to be in a very bad way; **¡vaya** —! what bad luck!

calamina *nf* calamine.

calamitosamente *adv* calamitously, disastrously.

calamitoso *adj* calamitous, disastrous.

cálamo *nm* (*Bot*) stem, stalk; (*Mus*) reed; (*Mus*: *Hist*) flute; (*poet*) pen; **empuñar el** — to take up one's pen; **menear** — to wield a pen.

calamocano *adj* (*fam*) merry (*fam*), tipsy.

calamoco *nm* icicle.

calamorra *nf* (*sl*) nut (*sl*), head.

calamorrada *nf* (*fam*) butt; bump on the head.

calandraco *adj* (*Arg, Col*) annoying, tedious; scatterbrained.

calandria¹ *nf* (*Orn*) calandra lark.

calandria² *nf* mangle; (*Tech*) calender.

calaña *nf* model, pattern; (*fig*) nature, kind, stamp.

calañés *nm* (*Andalusia*) *hat with a turned-up brim*.

calar¹ 1 *adj* calcareous, lime (*attr*). **2** *nm* limestone quarry.

calar² [1a] 1 *vt* (**a**) *person* to soak, drench; *material* to soak, drench; *material* to soak into, saturate, permeate. (**b**) to penetrate, perforate, pierce, go through. (**c**) (*Tech*) *metal* to do fretwork on; (*Sew*) to do openwork on. (**d**) *person* to size up; *intention* to see through; *secret* to penetrate; **¡nos ha calado!** he's rumbled us! (*fam*); **a ésos los tengo muy calados** I've got them thoroughly weighed up (*or* sized up). (**e**) *bayonet* to fix; *mast* to fix, step. (**f**) *bridge* to lower, let down; *net, sail* to lower. (**g**) *fruit* to cut a sample slice of; (*Arg, Mex, PR*) *corn* to take a sample of. (**h**) (*Col*) to crush, flatten, sit on.

2 *vi* (**a**) (*of liquid*) to sink in, soak in; (*of shoe*) to leak, let in the water. (**b**) (*Naut*) to draw; **el buque cala 12 metros** the ship draws 12 metres, the ship has a draught of 12 metres. (**c**) (*Mech*) to stop, stall.

3 calarse *vr* (**a**) to get soaked, get drenched (*hasta los huesos* to the skin). (**b**) to get in, squeeze in; to sneak in. (**c**) (*Orn*) to swoop (down) (*sobre* on). (**d**) — **el sombrero** to pull one's hat down; to put one's hat on firmly; — **las gafas** to stick one's glasses on; to push one's glasses back.

calatear [1a] *vt* (*Per*) to undress.

calato *adj* (*Per*) naked; (*fig*) penniless, broke (*fam*).

calavera 1 *nf* (**a**) (*Anat*) skull; **estar como** — **de muerto** to be as bald as a coot. (**b**) (*Mex*: *Aut*) rear light.

2 *nm* gay dog; madcap; (*pej*) rake, roué; (*pej*) rotter, cad, heel (*sl*).

calaverada *nf* madcap escapade, foolhardy act.

calaverear [1a] *vi* to be a gay dog, live it up; to have one's fling; (*pej*) to lead a wild life, live recklessly.

calca *nf* (*Per*) barn, granary.

calcado *nm* tracing.

calcañal *nm*, **calcañar** *nm*, **calcaño** *nm* heel.

calcar [1g] *vt* (**a**) to trace, make a tracing of. (**b**) — **A en B** to model A on B, base A on B; (*pej*) to copy A slavishly from B.

calcáreo *adj* calcareous, lime (*attr*).

calce *nm* (**a**) (*steel*) tyre; wedge, shim; iron tip; (*Ec*) filling (*of a tooth*). (**b**) (*CAm, Mex, PR*) foot, lower margin (of a document). (**c**) (*Arg*) chance, opportunity.

calcés *nm* masthead.

calceta *nf* (**a**) (knee-length) stocking. (**b**) fetter, shackle. (**c**) **hacer** — to knit.

calcetería *nf* (**a**) hosiery. (**b**) hosier's (shop).

calcetero *nm*, **calcetera** *nf* hosier.

calcetín *nm* sock.

calcificar [1g] **1** *vt* to calcify. **2 calcificarse** *vr* to calcify.

calcina *nf* concrete.

calcinación *nf* calcination.

calcinar [1a] **1** *vt* (**a**) to calcine; to burn, reduce to ashes, blacken; **las ruinas calcinadas del edificio** the blackened ruins of the building. (**b**) (*fam*) to bother, annoy. **2 calcinarse** *vr* to calcine.

calcio *nm* calcium.

calco *nm* (**a**) tracing. (**b**) (*Ling*) calque (*de* on), semantic borrowing (*de* from); **la palabra es** — **del inglés** the word is a calque on English, the (sense of the) word is borrowed from English.

calcomanía *nf* transfer.

calculable *adj* calculable.

calculador *adj* (**a**) calculating. (**b**) (*Chi, PR*) selfish, mercenary.

calculadora *nf* calculating machine, computer.

calcular [1a] *vt* (**a**) to calculate, compute; to add up, work out. (**b**) — **que . . .** to reckon that . . .; to anticipate that . . ., expect that . . .

cálculo *nm* (**a**) calculation; reckoning; estimate; conjecture; (*Math*) calculus; — **de costo** costing; — **diferencial** differential calculus; **libro de** —s **hechos** ready reckoner; — **mental** mental arithmetic; **según mis** —s according to my calculations, by my reckoning; **obrar con mucho** — to act cautiously. (**b**) (*Med*) stone, gallstone.

Calcuta Calcutta.

calcha *nf* (**a**) (*Arg*) clothing, bedding; harness. (**b**) (*Chi*) fetlock; fringe (of hair); tatters, strands.

calchona *nf* (*Chi*) ghost, bogey; (*fig*) hag.

calchudo *adj* (*Chi*) shrewd, cunning.

caldas *nfpl* hot springs, hot mineral baths.

caldeamiento *nm* warming, heating.

caldear [1a] **1** *vt* to warm (up), heat (up); (*Tech*) to weld; **estar caldeado** to be very hot. **2 caldearse** *vr* to get very hot, get overheated.

caldeo *nm* warming, heating; (*Tech*) welding.

caldera *nf* (*Tech*) boiler; boiling-pan; (*RPl*) pot; kettle, teapot; (*Ec*) crater; **las** —s **de Pedro Botero** hell.

calderero *nm* boilermaker; coppersmith; — **remendón** tinker.

caldereta *nf* (**a**) small boiler. (**b**) (*Eccl*) holy-water vessel. (**c**) (*Cook*) fish stew; lamb stew.

calderilla *nf* (**a**) (*Eccl*) holy-water vessel. (**b**) (*Fin*) small change, coppers; **en** — in coppers.

caldero *nm* small boiler, copper; (*Tech*) drum, boiler.

calderón *nm* (**a**) large boiler, cauldron. (**b**) (*Naut*) hold. (**c**) (*Typ*) paragraph sign, section mark; (*Mus*) pause (sign).

caldo *nm* (**a**) broth, bouillon; gravy; consommé, clear soup; dressing; — **de carne** beef tea; — **de cultivo** (*Bio*) culture medium; — **de pollo** chicken broth; **hacer el** — **gordo** to take advantage of a situation; **hacer el** — **gordo a uno** to play into someone's hands, make it easy for someone. (**b**) —s (*Comm*) oil, wine, cider (and other vegetable juices); **los** —s **jerezanos** the wines of Jerez, sherries.

cale *nm* slap, smack.

calefacción *nf* heating; — **central** central heating; **sistema de** — heating (system).

calefaccionar [1a] *vt* to heat.

calefón *nm* (*Arg*) coal-fired boiler.

cale(i)doscopio *nm* kaleidoscope.

calembé nm (Cu, Ven) loincloth; underpants; (Ven) ragged clothes, shabby clothing.

calendario nm calendar; **— de pared** wall calendar; **— de taco** tear-off calendar; **hacer —s** to muse, dream.

caléndula nf marigold.

calentador nm heater; **— de cama** (Hist) warming pan; **— eléctrico** electric fire; **— a gas** gas heater, (for bath) geyser, water heater; **— de inmersión** immersion heater.

calentamiento nm heating, warming.

calentar [1k] **1** vt (a) furnace, water etc to heat (up); body, chair, food, room etc to warm (up); **— al blanco** to make white-hot; **— al rojo** to make red-hot.
(b) business etc to hurry on, speed up, get moving.
(c) (Arg, Mex, Ven) to provoke, irritate.
(d) (fam) to warm (fam), tan (fam).
2 calentarse vr (a) to heat up, warm up, get hot, get warm; (at fire) to warm oneself.
(b) (fig: of argument) to get heated; (of person) to get heated, get het up, get excited (por about).
(c) (Zool) to be on heat; (Arg, Mex, Ven) to get randy, feel in the mood.
(d) (Arg, Mex, Per, Ven) to get cross.

calentón nm (a) (Mex) water heater. (b) (Arg, Per) randy person. (c) (Arg, Per) **tener un —** to feel randy, be in the mood.

calentura nf (a) (Med) fever, (high) temperature; **estar con —, tener —** to be feverish, have a temperature.
(b) (Chi) tuberculosis.
(c) (Per, RPl) randiness, sexual desire.
(d) (Col) fit of anger, tantrum.

calenturiento adj (a) (Med) feverish. (b) (Chi) consumptive, tubercular.

calenturón nm high fever.

calenturoso adj (Med) feverish.

calera nf limestone quarry; lime kiln.

calero 1 adj lime (attr). **2** nm lime kiln.

calesa nf chaise, buggy.

calesera nf Andalusian jacket.

calesín nm gig, fly.

calesita nf (Arg, Per) merry-go-round.

caleta nf (a) (Geog) cove, small bay, inlet. (b) (Col, Ec) coasting vessel.

caletero nm (Ven) docker, port worker.

caletre nm (fam) gumption (fam), brains.

calibrador nm gauge; calliper(s); **— de alambre** wire gauge.

calibrar [1a] vt to calibrate; to gauge, measure.

calibre nm (a) calibre; (Mil) calibre, bore; (Rail) gauge; (of wire, pipe etc) diameter; (fig) calibre; **de grueso —** large-bore. (b) **= calibrador**.

calicanto nm (Arg, PR) stone wall; jetty.

calicó nm calico.

caliche nm (a) (Bol, Chi, Per) saltpetre; ground rich in saltpetre. (b) (Arg) crust of whitewash which flakes from a wall.

calidad nf (a) quality; grade; **de — of** quality; **de mala —** of bad quality, bad-quality, low-quality.
(b) position, capacity; **en — de** in the capacity of.
(c) (in contract) stipulation, term; **a — de que . . .** provided that . . .
(d) rank, importance, quality.
(e) **—es** (moral) qualities; gifts.

cálido adj climate, country hot; (fig) blanket, applause, colour etc warm.

calidoscópico adj kaleidoscopic.

calidoscopio nm kaleidoscope.

calienta-camas nm, pl **calienta-camas** electric blanket.

calientapiés nm, pl **calientapiés** hot-water bottle; foot warmer.

calienta-platos nm, pl **calienta-platos** hotplate.

caliente adj (a) warm, hot.
(b) (fig) fiery, spirited; argument heated; battle raging.
(c) **estar —** (Zool) to be on heat; (SAm) to feel randy, be in the mood.
(d) **en —** at once, immediately; (Tech) hot; **montar algo en —** (Tech) to assemble something while it is hot, shrink something on.

califa nm caliph.

califato nm caliphate.

calificación nf (a) qualification; assessment; decription, label. (b) rating, standing; grade, mark; **— de sobresaliente** first-class mark.

calificado adj (a) qualified, competent; worker skilled. (b) well-known, eminent; proof etc undisputed; theft proven, manifest.

calificar [1g] **1** vt (a) to qualify (also Gram).
(b) to assess; to rate; exam to grade, mark; script to correct.
(c) **— a uno** to distinguish someone, give someone his standing (or fame); to ennoble someone.
(d) **— a uno de tonto** to call someone silly, describe someone as silly, label someone silly.
2 calificarse vr (SAm: Pol) to register as a voter.

calificativo 1 adj qualifying. **2** nm qualifier, epithet.

California f California.

california nf (a) (Arg) horse race. (b) (Arg) wire-stretcher. (c) (PR) 20-dollar gold coin.

californiano, californio 1 adj Californian. **2** nm, **californiana, california** nf Californian.

caligine nf (poet) mist, darkness.

caliginoso adj (poet) misty, dark.

caligrafía nf calligraphy, penmanship.

caligráfico adj calligraphic.

calilla nf (CAm, Mex) (a) bore, tedious person. (b) nuisance. (c) hoax.

calina nf haze, mist.

calinoso adj hazy, misty.

calipso nm calypso.

calistenia nf cal(l)isthenics.

cáliz nm (a) (Bot) calyx. (b) (Eccl) chalice, communion cup; (poet) cup, goblet; **— de amargura, — de dolor** cup of sorrow, cup of bitterness.

caliza nf limestone.

calizo adj lime (attr); ground limy.

calma nf (a) (Meteorol, Naut) calm, calm weather; **— chicha** dead calm; **estar en —** to be calm.
(b) (Comm, Fin) calm, inactivity, lull (de in); cessation, suspension (de of); **estar en —** (market) to be steady.
(c) (of temperament) calm, calmness; (pej) slowness, phlegm, laziness; ¡—!, ¡con —! calm down!, don't get so worked up!, take your time!; **hacer algo con —** to do something calmly; **tomarlo con —** to take things gently; **perder la —** to get ruffled, lose one's composure.

calmante 1 adj soothing, sedative. **2** nm sedative, tranquillizer.

calmar [1a] **1** vt to calm; person to calm (down), quieten (down), soothe; nerves to soothe, steady; pain to relieve.
2 vi (of mind etc) to abate, fall calm.
3 calmarse vr to calm down, calm oneself; ¡cálmese! calm down!, don't get so worked up!

calmazo nm dead calm.

calmoso adj (a) calm, quiet. (b) (pej) slow, sluggish; lazy.

caló nm gipsy slang; underworld slang; low-class speech of Madrid (equivalent to Cockney).

calofriarse [1c] vr see **escalofriarse**.

calofrío nm see **escalofrío**.

calor nm (a) heat (also Phys, Tech etc); warmth; **un — agradable** a pleasant warmth; **un — excesivo** an excessive heat; **— blanco** white heat; **— rojo** red heat; ¡qué —! isn't it hot!, how hot it is!; **entrar en —** to get warm, begin to feel warm; (before game, with exercises) to warm up; **hace —** it's hot; **hace mucho —** it's very hot; **tener —** to be hot, feel hot.
(b) (fig: of argument) warmth, heat; (of battle) heat; (of welcome etc) warmth; (of feelings) ardour, fervour; excitement, passion.

caloría nf calorie.

calórico adj caloric.

calorífero 1 adj heat-producing, heat-giving. **2** nm heating system; furnace, stove; heater, radiator; **— mural** wall radiator.

calorífico adj calorific.

calorifugar [1h] vt boiler, pipe to lag.

calorífugo adj heat-resistant, non-conducting; fireproof.

calote nm (RPl) fraud, swindle.

calotear [1a] (RPl) to swindle, cheat.

calta nf marsh marigold (also **— palustre**).

caluma nf (Per) gap, pass (in the Andes).

calumnia nf calumny; (Law) slander (de of), (written) libel (de on).

calumniador nm, **calumniadora** nf slanderer, libeller.

calumniar [1b] vt to slander, libel.

calumnioso adj slanderous, libellous.

calurosamente adv (fig) warmly, enthusiastically, heartily.

caluroso adj (a) warm, hot. (b) (fig) warm, enthusiastic, hearty.

calva nf (on head) bald patch; (on dress) bare spot, worn place; (in wood etc) clearing.

Calvario *nm* (a) (*Eccl*) Calvary; Stations of the Cross. (b) c— (*fig*) cross, heavy burden; series of disasters; string of debts.

calvatrueno *nm* (*fam*) (a) bald pate. (b) wild fellow, madcap.

calvero *nm* (a) glade, clearing. (b) chalkpit, marlpit.

calvicie *nf* baldness; — **precoz** premature baldness.

calvinismo *nm* Calvinism.

calvinista 1 *adj* Calvinistic. 2 *nmf* Calvinist.

calvo 1 *adj* (a) *head, man* bald; *patch* bald, hairless; **quedarse** — to go bald. (b) *ground* bare, barren; *garment* threadbare. 2 *nm* bald man.

calza *nf* (a) wedge; scotch, chock; **poner** — **a** to wedge, scotch.
(b) (*fam*) stocking; —**s** hose; breeches; tights; **estar en** —**s prietas** to be in a fix.
(c) (*Ec, Col, Pan, Nic: of tooth*) filling.

calzada *nf* roadway, highway; causeway; (*up to house*) drive; (*SD*) pavement, sidewalk (*US*); — **romana** Roman road.

calzado 1 *adj* shod, wearing shoes; — **de** shod with, wearing; **conviene ir** — it's better to wear shoes, one has to wear something on one's feet. 2 *nm* footwear.

calzador *nm* shoehorn.

calzar [1f] 1 *vt* (a) *shoes, spurs etc* to put on; to wear; **calzaba zapatos verdes** she was wearing green shoes, she had green shoes on; **¿qué número calza Vd?** what size do you wear (*or* take)?; **el que primero llega, ése la calza** first come first served.
(b) *person* to put shoes on; to provide with footwear, supply with shoes; **me ayudó a** —**me las botas** he helped me to put my boots on.
(c) (*of firearm*) to carry, take.
(d) *wheel etc* to wedge, scotch, chock; to put a wedge in (*or* under *etc*), put chocks under; to block; to secure.
(e) (*Ec, Col, Pan, Nic*) *tooth* to fill.
(f) to tip, put an iron tip on.
2 *vi* (a) **calza bien** he wears good shoes.
(b) (*fig*) **calza poco, no calza mucho** he's pretty dim.
3 **calzarse** *vr* (a) — **los zapatos** to put on one's shoes; **¿qué zapatos calzaba?** what shoes was he wearing?
(b) — **un empleo** to get a job; — **a uno** to keep someone under one's thumb.

calzo *nm* wedge, scotch, chock; shim; (*Mech*) shoe; (*Naut*) skid, chock.

calzón *nm* (*also* —**es**) (a) (*man's*) breeches; shorts; (*SAm*) trousers, pants (*US*); — **de baño** bathing trunks; **amarrarse los** —**es** (*SAm*) to act resolutely, button down to the job; **hablar a** — **quitado** to speak with excessive frankness; to ride roughshod over people; (*Mex*) to talk energetically, talk without stopping; **ponerse los** —**es** (*of woman: fig*) to wear the trousers.
(b) (*woman's*) shorts; (*Arg*) pants, drawers, knickers; —**es blancos** pants; — **de baño** pants part of two-piece swimsuit.

calzonario *nm* (*SAm*) pants, knickers.

calzonazos *nm, pl* **calzonazos** (*fam*) stupid fellow, weak-willed fellow; henpecked husband.

calzoncillos *nmpl* pants, underpants (*US*), shorts (*US*).

calzoneras *nfpl* (*Mex, PR*) trousers buttoned down the sides.

calzonudo 1 *adj* (*CAm, Per, RPl*) stupid, weak-willed; henpecked; (*Mex*) energetic; bold, brave. 2 *nm* (*Mex*) Indian.

callada: **a la** —, **de** — on the quiet, secretly; **dar la** — **por respuesta** to say nothing.

calladamente *adv* quietly, silently; secretly.

callado *adj* (a) (*by temperament*) quiet, reserved, reticent.
(b) quiet, silent; **todo estaba muy** — everything was very quiet; **tener algo** — to keep quiet about something, keep something secret; **¡qué** — **se lo tenía Vd!** you kept pretty quiet about it!; **pagar para tener** — **a uno** to pay to keep someone quiet.

callampa *nf* (*Chi*) mushroom; (*fam*) umbrella; —**s** (*fam*) big ears.

callana *nf* (*SAm*) flat earthenware pan; (*Chi: hum*) pocket watch.

callandico *adv*, **callandito** *adv* softly, very quietly; stealthily.

callar [1a] 1 *vt secret* to keep; *fact, passage etc* to pass over in silence, say nothing about, not mention; to keep back, keep to oneself, keep secret; *shameful matter* to keep quiet about, hush up; *see* **pico**.
2 *vi and* **callarse** *vr* to keep quiet, be silent, remain silent; (*of noise*) to stop; to stop talking (*or*

playing *etc*); to become quiet; (*of sea, wind*) to become still, be hushed; **¡calla!, ¡cállate!, ¡cállese!** (*order*) shut up!, be quiet!, hold your tongue!; **calla, calle** (*giving agreement*) say no more, enough said; **¡calla!** (*fig*) you don't mean to say!, well!; **hacer** — **a uno** to make someone be quiet, make someone stop talking (*etc*); (*energetically*) to shut someone up; **¿quieres** —**?** you've said enough, that's enough now; **sería mejor** —**se** it would be best to say nothing.

calle *nf* (a) street, road; — **abajo** down the street; — **arriba** up the street; — **de la amargura** (*fig*) difficult situation, jam; — **de dirección**, — **de un sentido** (*Mex*) one-way street; — **mayor** high street, main street; —**s exclusivas para el tránsito de peatones** pedestrian precinct; **dejar a uno en la** — to put someone out of a job; **echar por la** — **de en medio** to push on, press on regardless (*fam*); **echarse a la** — to go out into the street; (*of mob*) to turn out, riot, demonstrate; **poner a uno (de patitas) en la** — to kick someone out, chuck someone out; to put someone out of a job; **quedarse en la** — not to have a penny to one's name; *see* **aplanar, rondar** *etc*.
(b) passage, way; room; **¡—!** make way!; **abrir** —, **hacer** — to make way, clear the way.
(c) (*Sport*) lane; (*Golf*) fairway.

calleja *nf* = **callejuela**.

callejear [1a] *vi* to wander about the streets, stroll around; (*pej*) to loaf, hang about idly.

callejero *adj* (a) street (*attr*); **accidente** — street accident; **disturbios** —**s** trouble in the streets, rioting in the streets.
(b) *person* fond of walking about the streets, fond of gadding about.

callejón *nm* alley, alleyway, passage; (*Col*) main street; (*Taur*) space between inner and outer barriers; — **sin salida** cul-de-sac; blind alley (*also fig*); **las negociaciones están en un** — **sin salida** the negotiations are at an impasse, the negotiations are deadlocked.

callejuela *nf* (a) narrow street, side street; alley, passage. (b) (*fig*) subterfuge; way out (*of the difficulty*).

callicida *nm* corn cure.

callista *nmf* chiropodist.

callo *nm* (a) corn; callus, callosity; **criar** —**s** to be callous, have no feelings. (b) —**s** (*Cook*) tripe; —**s al ajo** tripe with garlic.

callosidad *nf* callosity, hard patch (*on hand etc*), rough place.

calloso *adj* horny, hard, rough.

cama *nf* (a) bed; bedstead; couch; — **de campaña** campbed; — **de columnas**, — **imperial** fourposter bed; —**s gemelas** twin beds; — **de matrimonio** double bed; — **media** —, — **de monja**, — **de soltero** single bed; — **en petaca** apple-pie bed; — **plegable**, — **de tijera** folding bed, campbed; — **turca** divan bed, day bed; — **de viento** (*Col, Hond*) cot; **caer en (la)** — to fall ill; **estar en** — (*Med*), **guardar** — to be ill in bed, be confined to bed; **hacer la** — to make the bed; **hacer** (*or* **poner**) **la** — **a uno** (*fig*) to work harm for someone behind his back; **quien mala** — **hace en ella se yace** having made your bed you must lie on it; **ir a la** — to go to bed; **levantarse por los pies de la** — to get out of bed on the wrong side.
(b) (*for animal*) bed, bedding, litter.
(c) (*Zool*) den, lair.
(d) (*of cart*) floor.
(e) (*Geol*) layer, stratum; (*Cook*) layer.

camachuelo *nm* bullfinch.

camada *nf* (a) (*Zool*) litter, brood; (*persons*) gang, band; *see* **lobo**. (b) (*Geol*) layer; (*Archit*) course.

camafeo *nm* cameo.

camagua *nf* (*CAm*) ripening maize, ripening corn (*US*); (*Mex*) unripened maize.

camal *nm* (a) halter. (b) meat hook; (*Bol, Per*) slaughterhouse.

camaleón *nm* chameleon.

camalote *nm* (*SAm*) an aquatic plant (*which forms floating islands*).

camamila *nf* camomile.

camándula *nf* rosary; **tener muchas** —**s** (*fam*) to be full of tricks, be a sly sort.

camandulear [1a] *vi* to be a hypocrite, be falsely devout; (*SAm*) to intrigue; to bumble, avoid taking decisions.

camandulería *nf* prudery, priggishness; hypocrisy, false devotion.

camandulero 1 *adj* prudish, priggish; hypocritical, falsely devout; sly, tricky; (*SAm*) intriguing; bumbling.
2 *nm* prude, prig; hypocrite; sly sort, tricky person; (*SAm*) intriguer; bumbler.
cámara 1 *nf* (**a**) room, hall; — **acorazada** strongroom, vault; — **ardiente**, — **mortuoria** funeral chamber; — **frigorífica** cold-storage room; **música de —** chamber music.
(**b**) royal chamber; **médico de —** royal doctor; **gentilhombre de —** gentleman-in-waiting.
(**c**) (*Naut*) stateroom, cabin; saloon; wardroom; — **de cartas** chartroom; — **de motores** engine room.
(**d**) (*Agr*) granary.
(**e**) (*Pol etc*) chamber, house; — **alta** upper house; — **baja** lower house; — **de comercio** chamber of commerce; — **de compensación** (*Fin*) clearing house; **C—** **de los Comunes** House of Commons; **C—** **de los Lores** House of Lords; **C—** **de Representantes** House of Representatives.
(**f**) (*Mech*, *Phys*) chamber; — **de aire** air chamber; — **de combustión** combustion chamber; — **de compresión** compression chamber; — **de gas** (*airship*) gasbag, (*Nazi etc*) gas chamber; — **de oxígeno** oxygen tent; — **de vacío** vacuum chamber.
(**g**) (*Aut etc: also* — **de aire**, — **neumática**) tyre, inner tube; **sin —** tyre solid.
(**h**) (*Mil*) breech, chamber.
(**i**) (*Anat*) cavity.
(**j**) (*Phot: also* — **fotográfica**) camera; — **de cine**, — **cinematográfica**, — **filmadora** cine-camera, film camera; **a — lenta** in slow motion; — **oscura** camera obscura; — **de televisión**, — **televisora** television camera.
(**k**) —**s** (*Med*) diarrhoea; stool; **tener** —**s en la lengua** (*fam*) to gossip a lot, tell tales (out of school).
2 *nm* cameraman.
camarada *nm* comrade, companion; chum, pal, mate; (*Pol*) comrade.
camaradería *nf* comradeship; companionship; matiness; (*Sport*) team spirit.
camarera *nf* (*in restaurant*) waitress; (*in hotel*) maid, chambermaid; (*in house*) parlourmaid; lady's maid; (*Naut*) stewardess.
camarero *nm* (*in restaurant*) waiter; (*Naut*) steward; — **mayor** (*Hist*) royal chamberlain; — **principal** head waiter.
camareta *nf* (*Naut*) cabin; messroom; — **alta** deck-house.
camarico *nm* (*Chi*) (**a**) favourite place. (**b**) love affair.
camarilla *nf* (**a**) small room. (**b**) clique, coterie; (*Pol*) lobby; (*Pol*) caucus (*of party*).
camarín *nm* (**a**) (*Theat*) dressing room; boudoir; side room; lift car, elevator car (*US*).
(**b**) (*Eccl*) niche for an image; small room where images are dressed (*behind the altar*).
camarón *nm* (**a**) (*Zool*) shrimp, prawn. (**b**) (*CR*) tip, gratuity. (**c**) (*Per*) turncoat; **hacer —** to change sides.
camaronear [1a] *vi* (**a**) (*Mex*) to go shrimping. (**b**) (*Per: Pol*) to change sides.
camaronero *nm* (*Per*) kingfisher.
camarote *nm* (*Naut*) cabin, stateroom; — **de lujo** first-class cabin.
camarotero *nm* (*SAm*) steward, cabin servant.
camastro *nm* rickety old bed; (*Naut*) bunk.
camastrón *adj* (*fam*) sly, untrustworthy.
camayo *nm* (*Per*) foreman (*of a country estate*).
cambado *adj* (*Arg*, *Col*, *Ven*) bow-legged.
cambalache *nm* (**a**) swap, exchange. (**b**) (*SAm*) secondhand shop.
cambalach(e)ar [1a] *vt* to swap, exchange.
cambar [1a] *vt* (*Arg*, *Ven*) = **combar**.
cámbaro *nm* crab.
cambiable *adj* (**a**) changeable; variable. (**b**) ex-changeable.
cambiadiscos *nm*, *pl* **cambiadiscos** record changer.
cambiador *nm* (**a**) barterer; moneychanger; (*Chi*, *Mex*, *Per: Rail*) switchman. (**b**) — **de discos** record changer.
cambiante 1 *adj* (**a**) changing; variable.
(**b**) (*pej*) fickle, temperamental.
2 *nm* (**a**) moneychanger.
(**b**) iridescent fabric.
(**c**) —**s** changing colours, iridescence.
cambiar [1b] **1** *vt* (**a**) to change, alter, convert, turn (*en* into).
(**b**) to change, exchange (*con*, *por* for); — **libras en francos**, — **libras por francos** to change pounds

into francs; — **saludos** to exchange greetings; — **sellos** to exchange stamps, swap stamps.
(**c**) (*of place*) to shift, move; **¿lo cambiamos a otro sitio?** shall we move it somewhere else?
2 *vi* (**a**) to change, alter; — **a un nuevo sistema** to change (*or* switch) to a new system; **no ha cambiado nada** nothing has changed; **entonces, la cosa cambia** that alters matters; **está muy cambiado** he's changed a lot, he has greatly altered.
(**b**) — **de** to change; — **de dueño** to change hands; — **de idea** to change one's mind; — **de ropa** to change one's clothes; — **de color** to change colour; — **de sitio** to shift, move; — **de sitio con uno** to change places with someone; **cambiamos de sombrero** we exchanged hats.
(**c**) (*of wind*) to veer, change round.
3 cambiarse *vr* (**a**) to change; (*of wind*) to veer, change round.
(**b**) — **en** to change into, be changed into.
cambiavía *nm* (*Cu*, *Mex*, *PR: Rail*) (**a**) switchman.
(**b**) switch, points.
cambiazo *nm* (*Comm: fam*) switch; **dar el —** to switch the goods.
cambio *nm* (**a**) change, alteration; changeover; substitution; (*in policy etc*) change, switch, shift; (*of tide*) turn; (*of place*) shift, move (*a* to); **ha habido muchos —s** there have been many changes; **el — se efectuó en 1970** the changeover took place in 1970; — **de decoración** (*Theat*) change of scenery; — **de domicilio** change of address; — **de guardia** changing of the guard; — **de marchas**, — **de velocidades** gear-change, gear-lever, gearshift (*US*); **con — de marchas automático** with automatic gearbox; — **de la marea** turn of the tide; — **de tiempo** change in the weather; — **de vía** (*Rail*) points.
(**b**) (*Fin*) change, small change; **¿tienes — encima?** have you any change on you?
(**c**) exchange; barter; **libre —** free trade; "**admitimos su coche usado a —**" "we take your old car in part exchange"; **a — de** in exchange for, in return for; **a las primeras de —** (*fig*) at the very start; at first sight; **en —** in exchange; on the other hand; instead.
(**d**) (*Fin*) rate of exchange; **al — de** at the rate of.
cambista *nm* moneychanger.
Camboya *f* Cambodia.
camboyano 1 *adj* Cambodian. **2** *nm*, **camboyana** *nf* Cambodian.
cambrona *nf* (*Arg*) tough cotton cloth.
cambucho *nm* (*Chi*) paper cone; paper basket for dirty clothes; straw wrapping of a bottle; poky little room, hovel.
cambujo *adj* (*CAm*, *Mex*) *animal* black; *person* dark, swarthy.
cambullón *nm* (*Col*, *Chi*, *Per*) swindle; plot, intrigue; swap, exchange.
cambur *nm* (*Ven*) banana; (*hum*) public office, sinecure.
cambuto *adj* (*Per*) small, squat; chubby.
camelar [1a] *vt* (**a**) *woman* to flirt with. (**b**) to cajole, blarney. (**c**) (*Mex*) to look into, look towards (*etc*); to spy on.
camelia *nf* camellia.
camelo *nm* (**a**) flirtation.
(**b**) joke, hoax; cock-and-bull story; humbug; blarney; **dar — a uno** to make fun of someone; **me huele a —** it smells fishy (*fam*), there's something funny going on here.
camello *nm* camel.
camellón *nm* drinking trough; (*Agr*) ridge (*between furrows*).
cameraman *nm*, *pl* **cameramans** *or* **cameramen** (*angl*) cameraman.
camerino *nm* (*Theat*) dressing room.
camero *adj* (**a**) bed (*attr*); for a big bed, for a double bed. (**b**) (*Cu: fam*) big.
Camerón *nm* Cameroon.
camilucho *nm* (*Arg*, *Mex*) Indian day labourer.
camilla *nf* sofa, couch; cot; table with a heater under-neath; (*Med*) stretcher.
camillero *nm* stretcher-bearer.
caminante *nm* traveller, wayfarer; walker.
caminar [1a] **1** *vt* *distance* to cover, travel, do.
2 *vi* (**a**) to walk, go; to travel, journey; (*of river etc*) to go, move, flow; (*fig*) to act, move, go; — **derecho** to behave properly; — **con pena** to trudge along, move with difficulty.
caminata *nf* long walk; hike, ramble; excursion, outing, jaunt.

caminero 1 *adj* road (*attr*); *see* **peón. 2** *nm* (*SAm*) road builder.
caminito *nm*: **— de rosas** (*fig*) primrose path.
camino *nm* (a) road; track, path; trail; **— de acceso, — de entrada** approach road; **— forestal** forest track; **— francés** (*Hist*) **— de Santiago** pilgrims' road to Santiago de Compostela; **C— de Santiago** (*Astron*) Milky Way; **— de herradura** bridle path; **— real** highroad (*also fig*); **— de sirga** towpath; **— trillado** well-trodden path, (*fig*) beaten track; **tener el — trillado** (*fig*) to have the ground prepared for one; **— vecinal** country road, lane, by-road; **C—s, Canales y Puertos** (*Univ course*) Civil Engineering.
(b) (*of direction, distance etc: also fig*) way, road (*de* to), route; journey; (*fig*) way, path, course; **el — a seguir** the route to follow; **el — de La Paz** the way to La Paz; the La Paz road; **es el — del desastre** that is the road to disaster, that way lies disaster; **el — de en medio** (*fig*) the middle way, the way of compromise; **— de Lima** on the way to Lima; **vamos — de la muerte** death awaits us all; **a medio —** halfway (there); **de —** on the way, (*fig*) in passing; **en el —** on the way, en route; **está en — de desaparecer** it's on its way out; **después de 3 horas de —** after travelling for 3 hours; **nos quedan 20 kms de —** we still have 20 kms to go; **es mucho —** it's a long way; **¿cuánto — hay de aquí a San José?** how far is it from here to San José?; **por buen —** along the right road; **ir por buen —** (*fig*) to be on the right track; **¿vamos por buen —?** are we on the right road?; **traer a uno por buen —** (*fig*) to put someone on the right road; to disabuse someone; **allanar el —** to smooth the way (*a uno* for someone); **echar — adelante** to strike out; **errar el —** to lose one's way; **llevar a uno por mal —** (*fig*) to lead someone astray; **partir el — con uno** to meet someone halfway; **ponerse en —** to set out, set forth, start.
(c) (*Arg, Per, Urug*) runner, strip of carpet (*or* matting etc); **— de mesa** table runner.
camión *nm* (*Aut*) lorry, truck (*esp US*); van; heavy wagon, dray; (*Mex*) bus; **— y acoplado** lorry and trailer; **— de agua** water cart, water wagon; **— de la basura** dustcart, refuse lorry; **— blindado** troop carrier; **— de bomberos** fire engine; **— frigorífico** refrigerator lorry; **— ganadero** cattle truck; **— de mudanzas** removal van; **— de riego** water cart, water wagon.
camionaje *nm* haulage, cartage.
camionero *nm* lorry driver, truckdriver (*US*), teamster (*US*).
camioneta *nf* van, light truck.
camionista *nm* = **camionero.**
camión-tanque *nm*, *pl* **camiones-tanque** (*Aut*) tanker.
camisa *nf* (a) (*man's*) shirt; **— (de mujer, de señora)** chemise, slip; (*SAm*) garment, article of clothing; **¡—!** not on your life! **— de deporte** sports shirt, vest; **— de dormir** nightdress; **— de fuerza** straitjacket; **—T** T-shirt; **estar en — (mangas de)** to be in one's shirt-sleeves; **dejar a una en —** (*fig*) to leave a girl without a dowry; **dejar a uno sin —** to leave someone destitute; **no le llegaba la — al cuerpo** he was simply terrified; **meterse en — de once varas** to interfere in other people's affairs.
(b) (*Bot*) skin; (*Zool: of snake*) slough.
(c) (*Mech*) jacket; case, casing; sleeve; **— de agua** water jacket; **— de gas** gas mantle.
(d) folder (*for papers*); (*Typ*) jacket, dust jacket, wrapper.
camisería *nf* outfitter's (shop).
camisero *nm* shirt maker; outfitter.
camiseta *nf* vest, undershirt (*US*); (*Sport*) singlet, vest.
camisilla *nf* (*Par, PR*) = **camiseta.**
camisolín *nm* stiff shirt front, dickey.
camisón *nm* (*also* **— de noche**) nightdress, night-gown; (*man's*) nightgown.
camítico *adj* Hamitic.
camomila *nf* camomile.
camita *nf* small bed, cot.
camón *nm* big bed; (*Archit*) oriel window; **— de vidrios** glass partition.
camorra *nf* (*fam*) row, set-to (*fam*); **armar — to** kick up a row; **buscar — to** go looking for trouble.
camorrear [1a] *vi* (*Guat, RPl*) to start a row, brawl.
camorrero *nm* = **camorrista.**
camorrista 1 *adj* quarrelsome, rowdy, brawling. **2** *nmf* quarrelsome person, rowdy element, hooligan.

camote *nm* (a) (*SAm: Bot*) sweet potato; (*Mex*) tuber, bulb.
(b) (*CAm, Chi*) bump, swelling, weal.
(c) (*Chi*) large stone.
(d) (*Chi*) bore, tedious person.
(e) (*Guat*) calf of the leg.
(f) (*Guat*) nuisance, bother.
(g) (*SAm*) love; passionate friendship, crush (*fam*); lovesickness; **tener un —** to be in love.
(h) (*Chi, Per*) lover, sweetheart.
(i) (*Chi*) fib.
(j) (*Mex*) rascal.
(k) (*Arg, Ec*) fool.
camotear [1a] **1** *vt* (a) (*Arg*) to rob, fleece; to take for a ride (*fam*).
(b) (*Guat*) to annoy.
2 *vi* (a) (*Mex*) to wander about aimlessly.
(b) (*Guat*) to be trying, cause trouble.
campal *adj*: **batalla —** pitched battle.
campamento *nm* camp; encampment; **— para prisioneros** prison camp; **— de trabajo** labour camp; **— de veraneo** holiday camp.
campana *nf* (a) bell; **a — herida, a — tañida, a toque de —** to the sound of bells; **echar las —s a vuelo** to peal the bells; (*fig*) to rejoice, celebrate (prematurely); **oír —s y no saber dónde** to get hold of the wrong end of the stick; **tañer las —s, tocar las —s** to peal the bells.
(b) bell-shaped object; **— de bucear, — de buzo** diving bell; **— de cristal** bell glass, glass cover.
(c) (*Col, Per, RPl*) thieves' look-out man.
campanada *nf* (a) stroke, peal (of a bell); (sound of) ringing.
(b) (*fig*) scandal, sensation, commotion; **dar una —** to make a big stir, cause a great surprise.
campanario *nm* (a) belfry, bell tower, church tower.
(b) **de —** (*pej*) mean, narrow-minded; **espíritu de —** parochial spirit, parish-pump attitude.
campanazo *nm* (a) = **campanada.** (b) (*Col*) warning.
campaneado *adj* (*fig*) much talked-of.
campanear [1a] *vi* (a) to ring the bells. (b) (*Col, Per, RPl: of thief*) to keep watch.
campaneo *nm* bell ringing, pealing, chimes.
campanero *nm* (*Tech*) bell founder; (*Mus*) bell ringer.
campanilla *nf* (a) small bell, handbell, electric bell; **de muchas —s** (*fam*) big, grand; high-class.
(b) bubble.
(c) (*Anat*) uvula.
(d) (*Sew*) tassel.
(e) (*Bot*) bell flower; **— azul** harebell; **— blanca, — de febrero** snowdrop.
campanillazo *nm* loud ring, sudden ring.
campanillear [1a] *vi* to ring, tinkle.
campanilleo *nm* ringing, tinkling.
campante *adj* (a) outstanding.
(b) (*pej*) self-satisfied, smug; **siguió tan —** he went on cheerfully, he went on as if nothing had happened; **allí estaba tan —** there he was as large as life, there he sat (*etc*) as cool as a cucumber.
campanudo *adj* (a) bell-shaped; *skirt* wide, spreading.
(b) *style* high-flown, bombastic, sonorous; *speaker* pompous, windy; **dijo —** he said pompously.
campánula *nf* bell flower, campanula; **— azul** blue-bell.
campaña *nf* (a) countryside; level country, plain; **batir la —, correr la —** to reconnoitre.
(b) (*Mil, Pol and fig*) campaign; (*Comm*) sales drive; **de —** (*Mil*) field (*attr*), campaign (*attr*); **hacer — to** campaign; **hacer — en contra de** to campaign against; **hacer — a favor de** (*or* **en pro de**) to campaign for.
(c) (*Naut*) cruise, expedition, trip.
(d) (*Agr etc*) season.
campañol *nm* vole.
campar [1a] *vi* (a) (*Mil etc*) to camp. (b) to stand out, excel; *see* **campear.**
campear [1a] *vi* (a) (*Agr: of animals*) to go to graze, go out to pasture; (*of man*) to work in the fields.
(b) (*Bot*) to show green.
(c) (*Mil*) to reconnoitre; (*SAm*) to scour the countryside.
(d) (*Col*) to make one's way through.
(e) (*Col*) to bluster.
campechana *nf* (a) (*Ven*) hammock. (b) (*Cu, Mex*) cocktail. (c) (*Ven*) whore.
campechanería *nf*, **campechanía** *nf* frankness, openness; heartiness, cheerfulness, geniality; fellow feeling; generosity.
campechano *adj* frank, open; good-hearted, hearty, cheerful, genial; comradely; generous.

campeón nm, **campeona** nf champion; **— de venta** bestseller, bestselling article.

campeonato nm championship; **de —** (fig) absolute, out-and-out.

campera nf (Arg) windjammer (jacket).

campero 1 adj (a) unsheltered, (out) in the open; open-air (attr); **ganado —** stock that sleeps out in the open. (b) (RPl) knowledgeable about the countryside; expert in farming matters; animal trained to travel in difficult country. **2** nm (Col) jeep, land rover.

camperuso (Ven) **1** adj rural, rustic. **2** nm peasant.

campesina nf peasant (woman).

campesinado nm (CAm) peasantry, peasants.

campesino 1 adj (a) country (attr), rural; peasant (attr); (pej) rustic. (b) (Zool) field (attr). **2** nm peasant; countryman; farmer; (pej) peasant.

campestre adj (a) country (attr), rural; **en lo más — del campo** deep in the countryside, in the heart of the country. (b) (Bot) wild.

camping ['kampin] nm, pl **campings** ['kampin] (angl) (a) camping; **hacer —** to go camping. (b) camping site, camping ground.

campiña nf countryside, open country; flat stretch of farmland, large area of cultivated land.

campirano nm (SAm) (a) peasant; (pej) rustic, country bumpkin. (b) expert in farming matters; guide, pathfinder; skilled horseman; stockbreeding expert.

campiruso (Ven) = **camperuso**.

campista[1] nmf camper.

campista[2] **1** adj (CAm, PR, Ven) rural, country (attr). **2** nm (a) (CAm) herdsman. (b) (Mex, PR) countryman.

campisto 1 adj (CAm, PR, Ven) rural, country (attr). **2** nm (CR) peasant.

campo nm (a) country, countryside; **— abierto, — raso** open country; **a — raso** in the open; **ir a — traviesa, ir — travieso** to go across country, take a cross-country route; **ir al —** to go into the country; **¿te gusta el —?** do you like the country(side)?; **el — está espléndido** the countryside looks lovely. (b) (Agr; also Mil, Phys, etc) field; (Sport) field, ground, pitch; **— de aterrizaje** landing field; **— aurífero** goldfield; **— de aviación** airfield; **— de batalla** battlefield; **— de deportes** sports ground, playing field; recreation ground; **— de ejercicios** (Mil) drilling ground; **C—s Elíseos** Elysian Fields; **— de fútbol** football ground, football pitch; **— de golf** golf course, golf links; **— de instrucción** (Mil) drilling ground; **— de juego** playground; **— magnético** magnetic field; **— de minas** minefield; **— petrolífero** oilfield; **— santo** cemetery, churchyard; **— de tiro** firing range; **— visual** field of vision; **trabajo de —, trabajo en el propio —** fieldwork; **abandonar el —** to give something up as a bad job, chuck it up; **batir el —, reconocer el —** to reconnoitre; **dejar el — libre** to leave the field open (para for); **se le halló el — orégano** (Arg) it all turned out nicely for him; **quedar en el —** to fall in battle; to be killed in a duel. (c) (Col) farm, ranch; farmhouse; (Arg) land too poor to support stock; (Chi, Per) mining concession. (d) (Art) ground, background; (Her) field. (e) (Mil) camp; **— de concentración** concentration camp; **— de internamiento** internment camp; **— de trabajo** labour camp; **levantar el —** to strike camp; (fig) to give up. (f) (in games) side. (g) (fig) scope; range, sphere; **el — de aplicación del invento** the scope of the invention, the range of application of the invention; **hay — para más** there is scope for more; **dar — a** to give free range to, allow ample scope for.

camposanto nm cemetery, churchyard.

campus nm, pl **campus** (SAm Univ) campus.

campusano nm, **campus(i)o** nm (CR etc) peasant.

camuesa nf pippin.

camueso nm (a) pippin tree. (b) (fam) dolt, blockhead.

camuflado adj camouflaged.

camuflaje nm camouflage.

camuflar [1a] vt to camouflage; (SAm: fig) to hide, disguise, cover up.

can nm (a) (Zool) arch or hum) dog, hound (hum). (b) (Mil) trigger. (c) (Archit) corbel.

cana[1] nf (also **—s**) white hair, grey hair; **echar una — al aire** to let one's hair down, cut loose; **faltar a las —s** to show a lack of respect for one's elders; **peina —s** he's getting on.

cana[2] nf (SAm) jail; police, policeman.

canaca nmf (a) (Chi, Ec, Per) Chinese. (b) (Chi) brothel keeper; brothel.

canaco adj (Chi, Ec) pale, yellow.

Canadá: el — Canada.

canadiense 1 adj Canadian. **2** nmf Canadian.

canal[1] nm (a) (Naut) canal; waterway; **C— de Panamá** Panama Canal; **C— de Suez** Suez Canal; **— de navegación** ship canal; **— de riego** irrigation channel. (b) (Naut: within river etc) deep channel; navigation channel. (c) (Geog) channel, straight; **C— de la Mancha** English Channel. (d) (Anat) canal, duct, tract. (e) (TV) channel.

canal[2] nf (a) conduit, pipe; underground watercourse; **— de desagüe** (Per) sewer; **— de humo** (Mex) flue. (b) (Archit) gutter, guttering; spout; drainpipe. (c) (Archit) groove. (d) (Geog) narrow valley. (e) dressed carcass; **abrir en —** to cut down the middle, slit open.

canaladura nf = **acanaladura**.

canalera nf (Archit) guttering.

canaleta nf (Arg) pipe, conduit.

canalete nm paddle.

canalización nf (a) canalization, channelling. (b) (Tech) piping; (Elec) wiring; (of gas etc) mains; (SAm) sewerage system, drainage.

canalizar [1f] vt river etc to canalize; to confine between banks, rebuild the banks (or course) of; waters to harness; to pipe; irrigation water to channel; (fig) interests etc to channel, direct.

canalizo nm navigable channel.

canalón nm (a) (Archit) gutter, guttering; spout; drainpipe. (b) shovel hat. (c) **—es** (Cook) ravioli.

canalla 1 nf rabble, mob, riffraff. **2** nm swine, rotter, blackguard; **¡—!** you swine!

canallada nf, **canallería** nf (PR, SD) dirty trick, mean thing (to do), despicable act; nasty remark, vile thing (to say).

canallesco adj mean, rotten (fam), despicable; **diversión canallesca** low form of amusement .

canana nf (a) cartridge belt. (b) (SAm) goitre. (c) (SD) mean trick, low prank. (d) **—s** (Col) handcuffs.

canapé nm (a) sofa, settee, couch. (b) (Cook) canapé.

canaquear [1a] vi (Chi) to go whoring.

canar [1a] vi (Col) to go grey.

Canarias fpl, also **Islas** fpl **Canarias** Canaries, Canary Isles.

canario[1] **1** adj of the Canary Isles. **2** nm, **canaria** nf native (or inhabitant) of the Canary Isles; **los —s** the people of the Canary Isles.

canario[2] nm (a) (Orn) canary. (b) (SAm) yellow.

canario[3] interj well I'm blowed!

canasta nf (a) (round) basket; hamper; crate; **— para desperdicios** wastepaper basket. (b) (Cards) canasta.

canastero nm basket maker.

canastilla nf small basket; (baby's) layette; (Per, PR, RPl: bride's) trousseau, (hum) bottom drawer, hope chest (US); (Mex) bucket; **— de la costura** sewing basket.

canastillo nm wicker tray, small basket.

canasto nm (a) large basket; hamper; crate. (b) (Col) servant. (c) (interj) good heavens!

cáncamo nm (Naut) eyebolt; **— de argolla** ringbolt.

cancamurria nf (fam) blues, gloom.

cancamusa nf (fam) trick; **armar una — a uno** to throw sand in someone's eyes.

cancán nm cancan.

cáncana nf (Chi) spit, jack; (Chi) candlestick; (Col) thin person.

cancanear [1a] vi (a) to loiter, loaf about. (b) (RPl) to dance the cancan. (c) (CAm, Col, Mex) to express oneself with difficulty; to stammer; to read haltingly, read without understanding.

cancaneo nm (CAm, Col, Mex) faltering, stammering.

cáncano nm (fam) louse; **andar como — loco** to go round in circles.

cancel nm windproof door, storm door; (SAm) folding screen; (SAm) partition, thin wall.

cancela nf lattice gate, wrought-iron gate; outer door, outer gate.

cancelación nf cancellation.

cancelar [1a] vt to cancel; debt to write off, wipe out; decision to cancel, annul; (fig) to dispel, banish (from one's mind); to do away with.

cancelaría nf papal chancery.

cáncer *nm* (a) (*Med*) cancer; — **de pulmón** lung cancer. (b) **C**— (*Astron*) Cancer.

cancerado *adj* cancerous; (*fig*) corrupt.

cancerarse [1a] *vr* (a) (*Med*) to become cancerous; (*person*) to get cancer, have cancer. (b) (*fig*) to become corrupt.

canceroso *adj* cancerous.

canciller *nm* chancellor.

cancilleresco *adj* (a) *style etc* of the chancellery. (b) (*fig*) formal, ceremonious; ruled by protocol.

canción *nf* song; (*Lit*) lyric, song; — **amatoria** love song; — **cuartelera** barrack-room ballad; — **de cuna** lullaby, cradle song; — **infantil** nursery rhyme; **¡siempre la misma** —! the same old story!; **volvemos a la misma** — here we go again, you're harping on the same old theme.

cancionero *nm* (*Mus*) song book, collection of songs; (*Lit*) anthology, collection of verse.

cancionista *nmf* (a) songwriter. (b) ballad singer; singer, vocalist, crooner.

canco *nm* (a) (*Chi*) earthen jug; flowerpot; chamberpot. (b) —**s** (*Bol, Chi*) buttocks; hips.

cancro *nm* (*Bot*) canker; (*Med*) cancer.

cancha[1] *nf* (*in senses, esp SAm*) field, ground; open space, tract of level ground; cockpit; (*Bol, Urug*) wide part of a river; (*Urug*) path, road; ¡—! gangway! — **de aterrizaje** landing ground; — **de carreras** racecourse; racetrack; — **de fútbol** football ground; — **de pelota** pelota court; — **de tenis** tennis court; **abrir** —, **hacer** — to make way, make room; **estar en su** — (*Chi, RPl*) to be in one's element; **en la** — **se ven los pingos** deeds speak louder than words; **tener** — (*Arg*) to be experienced.

cancha[2] *nf* (*Col, Per*) toasted maize, popcorn; toasted beans.

canchar [1a] *vt* (*Arg, Per*) to toast.

canche *adj* (a) (*Guat*) blond(e). (b) (*Col*) poorly seasoned, tasteless.

canchero *nm*, **canchera** *nf* (a) experienced person; (*Sport*) experienced player. (b) (*Chi*) layabout, loafer; (*Per*) grasping priest.

candado *nm* (a) padlock; (*of book*) clasp; **poner algo bajo siete** —**s** to lock something safely away. (b) (*Col*) goatee beard.

candanga *nm*: **el** — (*Mex*) the devil.

candar [1a] *vt* to lock; to lock up, put away.

cande *adj*: **azúcar** — sugar candy, rock candy.

candeal 1 *adj*: **pan** — white bread. 2 *nm* (*Arg, Per*) egg flip.

candela *nf* (a) candle; candlestick; (*Phys*) candle power; **en** — (*Naut*) vertical; **arrimar** — **a uno** (*fam*) to give someone a tanning (*fam*); **estar con la** — **en la mano** (*fig*) to be at death's door.
(b) (*esp SAm*) fire; (*for cigarette*) light; **dar** — to be a nuisance, be trying; **echar** — (*of eyes etc*) to sparkle; **pegar** — **a**, **prender** — **a** to set fire to, set alight.

candelabro *nm* candelabra; candlestick.

Candelaria *nf* Candlemas.

candelaria *nf* (*Bot*) mullein.

candelero *nm* (a) candlestick; oil lamp; **estar en (el)** — (*of person*) to be high up, be in a position of authority; (*of event*) to be under way, be in progress; **poner a uno en (el)** — to give someone a high post. (b) (*Naut*) stanchion.

candelilla *nf* (a) small candle.
(b) (*Bot*) catkin.
(c) (*SAm*) glow-worm; (*Arg, Chi*) will-o'-the-wisp; (*Ec*) lively child.
(d) (*Arg, Cu: Sew*) hem, border.

candelizo *nm* icicle.

candelo *adj* (*Col*) reddish-blond(e).

candente *adj* (a) red-hot, white-hot; glowing, burning. (b) (*fig*) *question* burning; *atmosphere etc* charged, electric.

candi *adj*: **azúcar** — sugar candy, rock candy.

candidato *nm* (a) candidate (*a* for); applicant (*a* for).
(b) (*Arg: sl*) sucker (*sl*).

candidatura *nf* candidature.

candidez *nf* (a) simplicity, ingenousness, innocence; naïveté; stupidity. (b) (*una* —) silly remark.

cándido *adj* (a) simple, ingenuous, innocent; naïve; (*pej*) stupid. (b) (*poet*) snow-white.

candil *nm* (a) oil lamp, kitchen lamp, (*Mex*) chandelier; **arder en un** — (*fig: of wine*) to be very strong; (*of subject etc*) to be pretty strong stuff.
(b) (*Zool*) tine, point, small horn.

candileja *nf* oil reservoir of a lamp; small oil lamp; —**s** (*Theat*) footlights.

candinga[1] *nf* (*Chi*) impertinence, insistence.

candinga[2] *nm*: **el** — (*Mex*) the devil.

candiota *nf* wine cask.

candiotero *nm* cooper.

candonga *nf* (*fam*) blarney, flattery; trick; playful trick, hoax, practical joke; teasing; **dar** — **a uno** to tease someone, kid someone (*fam*).

candongas *nfpl* (*Col, Ec*) earrings.

candongo (*fam*) *adj* 1 smooth, oily; sly, crafty; lazy. 2 *nm* creep (*sl*), toady, flatterer, sly sort; shirker, idler, lazy blighter (*sl*).

candonguear [1a] (*fam*) 1 *vt* to tease, kid (*fam*). 2 *vi* to shirk, dodge work.

candonguero *adj* (*fam*) = **candongo** 1.

candor *nm* (a) innocence, guilelessness, simplicity; frankness, candidness. (b) (*poet*) pure whiteness.

candorosamente *adv* innocently, guilelessly, simply; frankly, candidly.

candoroso *adj* innocent, guileless, simple; *confession etc* frank, candid.

candungo *nm* (*Per*) idiot.

caneca *nf* (a) (*Arg*) wooden vessel, bucket; (*Cu*) hot-water bottle; wine bottle (with a spout); (*Mex*) glazed earthenware bottle.
(b) (*Cu, Ec, Mex*) *liquid measure* = 24.42 litres.

caneco *adj* (*Bol, Ven*) tipsy.

canela *nf* (a) (*Bot, Cook*) cinnamon; — **de la China** cassia. (b) (*fig*) lovely thing, exquisite object; *see* **flor**. (c) (*Ant*) mulatto girl. (d) *interj* (*euph*) good gracious!

canelero *nm* cinnamon tree.

canelo 1 *adj* cinnamon, cinnamon-coloured. 2 *nm* cinnamon tree.

canelón *nm* (a) = **canalón**. (b) icicle. (c) rolled fringe (*of hair*); (*Guat, Ven*) corkscrew curl.

canesú *nm* (a) (*Sew*) yoke. (b) underbodice, camisole.

caney *nm* (a) (*Col, Cu, Ven*) log cabin, hut; (*Ant: Hist*) chief's house; (*Col, Ven*) large shed. (b) (*Cu*) river bend.

canfín *nm* (*SAm*) petroleum.

cangallar [1a] *vt* (*Bol, Chi*) to steal.

cangilón *nm* (a) pitcher; metal tankard; (*of water-wheel*) bucket, scoop; (*Col*) drum. (b) (*SAm*) cart track, rut; (*Ec*) mudhole, miry place.

cangrejo *nm* (a) — (**de mar**) crab; — (**de río**) crayfish. (b) (*Naut*) gaff. (c) (*Ec*) idiot; (*Per*) rogue, crafty person.

cangro *nm* (*SAm*) cancer.

canguelo *nm* (*fam*) funk (*fam*).

canguro *nm* kangaroo.

caníbal 1 *adj* cannibal; cannibalistic, man-eating; (*fig*) fierce, savage. 2 *nm* cannibal.

canibalismo *nm* cannibalism; (*fig*) fierceness, savageness.

canica *nf* marble; (*game*) marbles.

canicie *nf* (*of hair*) greyness, whiteness.

canícula *nf* dog days, midsummer heat; **C**— Dog Star, Sirius.

canicular 1 *adj*: **calores** —**es** midsummer heat. 2 —**es** *nmpl* dog days.

caniche *nm* poodle.

canijo *adj* weak, frail, sickly.

canilla *nf* (a) (*Anat*) long bone (*of arm or leg*); shin, shinbone; (*esp SAm*) shank, thin leg; — **de la pierna** shinbone, tibia; — **del brazo** armbone, ulna.
(b) (*Tech*) bobbin, reel, spool.
(c) tap; (*of cask*) spout, cock, tap.
(d) (*of cloth*) rib.
(e) (*PR*) cowardice.
(f) (*Mex*) strength; **a** — by force; against all opposition, against the odds; **tener** — to have great physical strength.

canillento *adj* (*Per*) long-legged.

canillera *nf* (*SAm*) fear, cowardice.

canillita *nm* (*SAm*) newsvendor, newspaper boy.

canillón *adj* (*SAm*), **canilludo** *adj* (*SAm*) long-legged.

canina *nf* dog dirt.

caninez *nf* ravenous hunger.

canino 1 *adj* (a) canine; dog (*attr*). (b) **hambre canina** ravenous hunger. 2 *nm* canine (tooth).

canje *nm* exchange.

canjear [1a] *vt* to exchange; to swap; to change over, interchange.

cano *adj* (a) grey-haired, white-haired, white-headed; **quedar** — to go grey. (b) (*poet*) snow-white. (c) (*fig*) venerable; (*pej*) hoary, ancient.

canoa *nf* (a) canoe; boat, launch; — **automóvil** motor boat, launch. (b) (*SAm*) conduit, pipe; feeding trough; chicken coop, dovecot.

canódromo *nm* dog track.

canoero *nm* (*SAm*), **canoísta** *nmf* canoeist.

canon *nm* (a) (*Eccl, Mus, Art*) canon; (*Fin*) tax, levy; (*Agr*) rent; — **de tránsito** (*Aut etc*) toll. (b) —**es** (*Eccl*) canon law.

canonical *adj* canonical; (*fig*) *life* easy.
canonicato *nm* (*Eccl*) canonry; (*fam*) sinecure, cushy job (*sl*).
canónico *adj* canonical; **derecho** — canon law.
canóniga *nf* (*fam*) nap before lunch; **coger una —** (*fam*) to have one over the eight.
canónigo *nm* canon.
canonista *nm* canon lawyer, expert in canon law.
canonización *nf* canonization.
canonizar [1f] **1** *vt* to canonize; (*fig*) to consecrate; to applaud, extol, show approval of.
canonjía *nf* (*Eccl*) canonry; (*fam*) sinecure, cushy job.
canoro *adj* melodious, sweet, tuneful; **ave canora** songbird.
canoso *adj* grey-haired, white-haired; *beard* grizzled, hoary.
canotaje *nm* boating.
cansadamente *adv* (a) wearily, in a tired way. (b) tediously, boringly; tiresomely.
cansado *adj* (a) tired, weary (*de* of); *eyes* tired, strained; *pen etc* well-worn, no longer new; **con voz cansada** in a weary voice; **estar —** to be tired; **estoy — de hacerlo** I'm tired of doing it, I'm sick of doing it.
  (b) tedious, boring; tiresome, trying.
  (c) **a las cansadas** (*PR, RPl*) after much delay, after a long wait.
cansador *adj* (*Arg*) tiring, wearisome.
cansancio *nm* tiredness, weariness; (*Med*) fatigue, exhaustion; **estar muerto de —** to be dead tired, be dog-tired.
cansar [1a] **1** *vt* to tire, tire out, weary; (*Med*) to fatigue, exhaust; *eyes* to tire, strain, try; *patience* to try, wear out; (*Agr*) *soil* to exhaust; *appetite* to jade; (*fig*) to bore; to badger, bother (*con* with).
  2 *vi* (a) to tire. (b) to be trying, be tiresome.
  3 cansarse *vr* (a) to tire, get tired, grow weary (*con, de* of); to get bored (*con, de* with); to tire oneself out; **— de hacer algo** to get tired of doing something, get bored with doing something.
cansera *nf* (*fam*) bother.
cantable *adj* suitable for singing, to be sung, cantabile; melodious.
Cantabria *f* Cantabria.
cantábrico *adj* Cantabrian; **Mar C—** Bay of Biscay.
cantadera *nf* (*SAm*) loud singing, prolonged singing.
cantador *nm*, **cantadora** *nf* folksinger, singer of popular songs.
cantal *nm* (a) boulder; stone block. (b) stony ground.
cantaletear [1a] *vt* (*SAm*) (a) to repeat ad nauseam, say over and over. (b) to laugh at, make fun of.
cantalupa *nf* (*CAm*), **cantalupo** *nm* cantaloupe.
cantante **1** *adj* singing. **2** *nmf* (professional) singer, vocalist; **— de ópera** opera singer.
cantar [1a] **1** *vt* to sing; to chant; to sing about, sing of, sing the praises of; *mass* to sing, say; **—las claras** to speak out, speak frankly, (*pej*) be cheeky.
  2 *vi* (a) (*Mus*) to sing; to chant; (*of insect etc*) to chirp; (*of machine, wheel, etc*) to creak, squeak, grind; **— a dos voces** to sing a duet.
  (b) (*fam*) to squeal (*sl*), blab, spill the beans (*sl*); **— de plano** (*fam*) to tell all one knows, make a full confession.
  (c) (*Arg, PR, Urug*) to ask a high price, overcharge.
  (d) (*Cu*) to smell bad.
  3 *nm* (a) singing; chanting.
  (b) song; poem (set to music); epic poem; **C— de los C—es** Song of Songs; **— de gesta** epic poem; **C— de mio Cid** Poem of the Cid; **eso es otro —** that's another story.
cántara *nf* (a) large pitcher. (b) *liquid measure* = 16.13 *litres*.
cantarería *nf* (a) pottery shop, earthenware shop. (b) pottery.
cantarero *nm* potter, dealer in earthenware.
cantárida *nf* (*also* **polvo de —**) Spanish fly, (*Pharm*) cantharides.
cantarín **1** *adj person* fond of singing; *stream* tinkling, musical; *tone* singsong, lilting. **2** *nm*, **cantarina** *nf* singer.
cántaro *nm* pitcher, jug; jugful; **a —s** in plenty; **llover a —s** to rain cats and dogs, rain in torrents.
cantata *nf* cantata.
cante *nm*: **— flamenco**, **— jondo** Andalusian gipsy singing.
cantera *nf* (a) quarry, pit; **— de arena** sandpit; **— de piedra** stone quarry. (b) (*fig*) talent, genius.
cantería *nf* (a) quarrying, stone cutting. (b) masonry, stonework. (c) piece of masonry, stone.

cantero *nm* (a) quarryman; stonemason.
  (b) end, extremity; **— de pan** crust of bread.
  (c) (*RPl*) bed, plot (*of vegetables*); flower bed; (*Mex, Per*) plot of sugar cane.
cántico *nm* (*Eccl*) canticle; (*fig*) song.
cantidad *nf* quantity; amount, number; (*of money*) amount, sum; **— alzada** lump sum; **— de movimiento** (*Phys*) momentum; **en —** in quantity; **—, (una) gran —** de a great quantity of, lots of; **tengo una — de cosas que hacer** I've lots of things to do, I've masses of things to do.
cantil *nm* shelf, ledge (*on rock*); coastal shelf; cliff.
cantilena *nf* ballad, song, chant; **la misma —** (*fig*) the same old stuff.
cantimplora *nf* water bottle, canteen; decanter; (*Tech*) syphon; (*Col*) powder flask; **¡—!** (*Cu, Per*) not on your life!
cantina *nf* (a) (*Rail*) buffet, refreshment room; (*Mil etc*) canteen; snack bar; (*SAm*) bar, saloon; (*Arg*) cheap restaurant.
  (b) wine cellar.
  (c) lunch box; (*Col*) milk churn; **—s** (*Mex*) saddlebags.
cantinela *nf* = **cantilena**.
cantinero *nm* barman, publican.
cantinflismo *nm* (*Mex*) unintelligible chatter.
cantío *nm* (*Cu, PR*) folksong, popular song.
cantiral *nm* stony ground, stony place.
canto[1] *nm* (*Mus*) (a) (*art and in general*) singing; chanting.
  (b) (*act in general*) singing; **el — de los pájaros** the singing of the birds.
  (c) (*piece*) song; **— llano** plainsong; **al — del gallo** at cockcrow, at daybreak.
  (d) (*Poet*) song, lyric; (*section of epic etc*) canto.
canto[2] *nm* (a) edge; rim, border; (*of knife*) back; end, point; corner; (*of bread*) crust; **ni un — de uña** absolutely nothing; **estar de —** to be on edge, be edgeways; to be on end; **le faltó el — de un duro** he had a narrow shave; **tener 3 cm de —** to be 3 cm thick.
  (b) stone, pebble; rock; (*also* **— rodado**) boulder.
cantón[1] *nm* corner; (*Her, Pol*) canton; (*Mil*) cantonment.
cantón[2] *nm* (*Sew*) cotton material.
cantonada *nf*: **dar — a uno** to dodge someone, shake someone off.
cantonal *adj* cantonal.
cantonear [1a] *vi* to loaf around.
cantonera *nf* (a) corner shelf; corner bracket, angle iron; corner table; corner cupboard; (*of book etc*) corner band.
  (b) (*fam*) streetwalker.
cantonero *nm* loafer, idler, good-for-nothing.
cantonés **1** *adj* Cantonese. **2** *nm*, **cantonesa** *nf* Cantonese. **3** *nm* (*dialect*) Cantonese.
cantor **1** *adj* singing, that sings; **ave cantora** songbird.
  2 *nm*, **cantora** *nf* singer; (*Orn*) songbird.
Cantorberi, Cantórbery Canterbury.
cantorral *nm* stony ground, stony place.
cantuja *nf* (*Per*) underworld slang.
canturía *nf* singing, vocal music; singing exercise; (*pej*) monotonous singing, droning.
canturrear [1a] *vti* to hum, croon, sing softly; to drone.
canturreo *nm* humming, crooning, soft singing; droning.
canutero *nm* (*SAm*) barrel (*of pen*).
canuto *nm* = **cañuto**.
canzonetista *nf* singer, vocalist.
caña *nf* (a) (*Bot: species*) reed.
  (b) (*Bot: part*) stem, stalk, cane; **— de azúcar**, **— dulce**, **— melar** sugar cane; **— de pescar** fishing rod; (*tabu, hum*) prick (*tabu*); **— del timón** tiller, helm; **las —s se vuelven lanzas** a joke can easily turn into something unpleasant.
  (c) (*Anat*) long bone (*of arm or leg*), (*esp*) shinbone; (*of boot, stocking*) leg; (*of anchor, column, horse*) shank.
  (d) tall wineglass, long glass; **— de cerveza** glass of beer; beer glass; **"¡dos —s!"** (*in bar*) "two beers please".
  (e) (*SAm*) sugar cane; rum, brandy.
  (f) (*Min*) gallery.
  (g) (*Ven*) swig (*fam*), drink.
  (h) (*Col, Ec, Ven*) false piece of news; (*Col, Ven*) piece of bluff, piece of bluster.
cañada *nf* (a) gully, ravine; glen. (b) cattle track, drover's road. (c) (*SAm*) stream.
cañadón *nm* (*Arg*) low-lying part of a field.
cañamar *nm* hemp field.

cañamargal nm (SAm) sugar-cane plantation.
cañamazo nm (coarse) canvas; burlap.
cañamelar nm sugar-cane plantation.
cañameno adj hempen.
cañamero adj hemp (attr).
cañamiel nf sugar cane.
cáñamo nm (Bot) hemp; hempen cloth; (CAm, Chi, SD) hempen cord; **— agranado** dressed hemp; **— indio** (CAm) Indian hemp, marijuana.
cañamón nm hemp seed; **—es** birdseed.
cañavera nf reed grass.
cañaveral nm reedbed; (Agr) sugar-cane plantation.
cañengo adj, **cañengue** adj (Col, Cu) weak, sickly; skinny.
cañería nf pipe, piece of piping, length of piping; pipeline, conduit; drain; (Mus) organ pipes; **—** pipes, piping; **— maestra (de gas)** (gas) main.
cañero 1 adj (a) (SAm) sugar-cane (attr); **machete — ** sugar-cane knife.
　(b) (Col, Ec, Ven) lying, boastful.
　2 nm (a) (Tech) plumber.
　(b) (SAm: Agr) owner (or manager) of a sugar-cane plantation.
　(c) (Col, Ec, Ven) liar, bluffer, boaster.
cañete nm small pipe.
cañista nm plumber.
cañiza nf coarse linen.
cañizal nm, **cañizar** nm reedbed.
cañizo nm (Agr) hurdle (for drying fruit etc).
caño nm (a) tube, pipe; (Mus) pipe; (of fountain) jet, spout; (Archit) gutter; drain, (open) sewer.
　(b) gallery.
　(c) wine cellar.
　(d) (Naut) navigation channel, deep channel; (Col, Ven) deep navigable river.
cañón 1 nm (a) tube, pipe; (Mus) pipe, organ pipe; (of chimney) flue; shaft, stack; (of column, lift, elevator) shaft; (of staircase) well; (of gun, pen) barrel; (of pipe) stem; (Mountaineering) chimney; **escopeta de dos —es** double-barrelled gun; **— rayado** rifled barrel; **ni a — rayado** (Chi, Per, PR) by no means, not at all.
　(b) (Mil) gun; (esp Hist) cannon; **— de agua** water cannon; **— antiaéreo** anti-aircraft gun; **— antitanque** anti-tank gun; **— de avancarga** muzzle loader; **— de campaña** field gun.
　(c) (of feather) quill.
　(d) (Geog) canyon, gorge.
　(e) (Col: Bot) trunk.
　(f) (Mex, Per) path (in mountain country).
　2 as adj (fam) fabulous (fam), marvellous; **¡el hombre está —!** he's fabulous!; **¡la función estaba —!** the show was great! (fam); **una noticia —** a stunning piece of news.
cañonazo nm (a) gunshot; (Hist) cannon shot; **—s** gunfire, shellfire; **salva de 21 —s** 21-gun salute; **— de advertencia** (Naut) warning shot, shot across the bows.
　(b) (fig) bolt from the blue, unexpected piece of news.
cañonear [1a] vt to shell, bombard.
cañoneo nm shelling, shellfire, gunfire; bombardment, cannonade.
cañonera nf (a) (Mil: Hist) embrasure. (b) (Naut: also **lancha —**) gunboat. (c) (SAm) holster.
cañonero nm gunboat.
cañoso adj reedy.
cañusero nm (Col) owner of a sugar-cane plantation.
cañutero nm pincushion.
cañuto nm (a) small tube, small container. (b) (Bot) internode. (c) (fam) telltale.
caoba nf mahogany.
caolín nm kaolin.
caos nm chaos.
caótico adj chaotic.
capa nf (a) cloak, cape; (Eccl: also **— pluvial**) cope; **— aguadera** waterproof cloak; **— del cielo** canopy of heaven; **— de ladrones** (fig) fence; **— rota** (fig) secret emissary; **— torera** bullfighter's cape; **abrirse de —** to pluck up courage; **andar de — caída** to be in a bad way, be on the decline; **echar una — a uno** to cover up for someone; **echar la — al toro** to make a final desperate effort; **hacer de su — un sayo** to do what one likes with one's own things, act freely; **de — y espada** cloak-and-dagger (attr).
　(b) (fig) cloak, pretence; mask, disguise; **so — de** under the pretext of, in the guise of.
　(c) (Geol) layer, bed, stratum; (Meteorol, Anat etc) layer; (of smoke) pall; (of dust) layer, film; (of snow) layer, covering, mantle; (Cook) coating; (of paint) coat; **primera —** undercoat, first coat; **—s sociales** social layers, social levels; **madera de tres —s** three-ply wood.
　(d) (Naut) **estar a la —, ponerse a la —** to lie to.
capacidad nf (a) capacity (also Comm, Phys, Tech etc); capaciousness, size; **una sala con — para 900** a hall with room for 900, a hall that can hold 900; **un avión con — para 20 plazas** a 20-seater plane; **— adquisitiva, — de compra** purchasing power; **— de arrastre** (of speaker etc) drawing power, power of attraction; **— de carga** carrying capacity; **— financiera** financial standing; **— de ganancia** earning power; **— de repercusión** resilience; **— útil** effective capacity.
　(b) (fig) (mental) capacity, ability, capability; talent; competence, efficiency; **tener — para** to have an aptitude for, have talent for; **no tiene — para los negocios** he has no business sense.
　(c) (SAm) able person, talented person.
capacitación nf capacitation; (Tech etc) training.
capacitado adj qualified; **estar — para + infin** to be qualified to + infin.
capacitar [1a] **1** vt (a) **— a uno para algo** to fit someone for something, qualify someone for something; (Tech) to train someone for something; **— a uno para + infin** to enable someone to + infin.
　(b) (Chi) **— a uno para hacer algo** to empower (or authorize) someone to do something.
　2 capacitarse vr: **— para algo** to fit oneself for something, qualify for something.
capacha nf (a) basket, frail. (b) (Arg, Bol, Chi) jail; **caer en la —** (Arg) to fall into the trap.
capacheca nf (Chi, Per) street-vendor's barrow (or stall).
capacho nm (a) wicker basket, big basket; (Tech) hod; (Per) saddlebag. (b) (Bol, Ec, RPl) old hat. (c) (Ec) jail.
capadura nf castration.
capar [1a] vt (a) to castrate, geld.
　(b) (fig) to reduce, cut down, curtail.
　(c) (Ant, Mex: Agr) to cut back, prune.
　(d) (Bol, Ven) food to start on, begin to eat.
caparazón nm (a) (Hist) caparison; horse blanket; nosebag. (b) (Zool) shell.
caparrón nm bud.
caparrosa nf vitriol; **— azul** copper sulphate, blue vitriol.
capataz nm foreman, overseer.
capaz adj (a) (of size) capacious, roomy, large; **— de, — para** with a capacity of, with room for, that holds; **un coche — para 4 personas** a car with room for 4 people.
　(b) (of ability) able, capable; efficient, competent; fit; (Law) competent; **ser — de algo** to be capable of something; **ser — de hacer algo** to be capable of doing something, be up to doing something; to be competent to do something; **es — de cualquier tontería** he is capable of any stupidity, one might expect any idiocy from him; **¡sería —!** one could well believe it of him, I'm not surprised; **— de funcionar** (Tech) operational, in working order; **ser — para un trabajo** to be qualified for a job, be up to a job.
　(c) (Mex) **es — que venga** he'll probably come.
capazo nm large basket; (child's) carrycot.
capcioso adj wily, deceitful.
capeador nm bullfighter who uses the cape.
capear [1a] **1** vt (a) (Taur) to play with the cape, wave the cape at; (fig) to take in, deceive.
　(b) (Naut and fig) storm to ride out, weather.
　2 vi (Naut) to ride out the storm; to lie to.
capelo nm (a) (Eccl) cardinal's hat; (fig) cardinalate. (b) (Arg, Mex) bell glass, glass cover. (c) (SAm: Univ) **— de doctor** doctor's short cape.
capellada nf toecap; patch (on shoe).
capellán nm chaplain; priest, clergyman; **— castrense, — de ejército** army chaplain.
capellanía nf chaplaincy.
capellina nf (Med) head bandage.
capero nm hallstand, hatstand.
Caperucita Roja f (Little) Red Riding Hood.
caperuza nf (pointed) hood; (Mech) hood, cowling; **— de chimenea** chimney cowl.
capi[1] nm (fam) = **capitán**.
capi[2] nf (Bol) white maize flower; (Chi) unripe pod.
capia nf (Arg, Bol) white maize flower; (Arg, Col) variety of maize bearing soft sweet grain.
capiango nm (Arg) clever thief.
capicúa nf reversible number, symmetrical number (eg 12321); palindrome.
capigorra nm, **capigorrista** nm, **capigorrón** nm idler, loafer.

capilar 1 *adj* capillary; hair (*attr*); **tubo** — capillary. **2** *nm* capillary.

capilaridad *nf* capillarity.

capilla *nf* (a) (*Eccl*) chapel; — **ardiente** funeral chapel; — **mayor** choir, chancel; — **de la Virgen** Lady Chapel; **estar en** (**la**) — (*fig*) to be awaiting execution; to be in great danger; to be in suspense, be on tenterhooks.
  (b) (*Mus*) choir.
  (c) (*Typ*) proof sheet; **estar en** —**s** to be in proof.
  (d) cowl; (*Tech*) hood, cowl.

capiller(o) *nm* churchwarden; sexton.

capillo *nm* (a) baby's bonnet; (*falcon's*) hood. (b) (*Bot, Zool*) = **capullo**.

capirotazo *nm* flip, flick.

capirote *nm* (a) (*Hist, Univ*, also *falcon's*) hood. (b) flip, flick. (c) **tonto de** — prize idiot, utter fool.

capirucho *nm* hood.

capisayo *nm* (*Col*) vest, undershirt (*US*).

capitación *nf* poll tax, capitation.

capital 1 *adj* (*in many senses*) capital; *city, crime,* capital; *enemy, sin* mortal; *feature* main, chief, principal; *point* essential, fundamental; *importance* capital, supreme, paramount; *letter* (*SAm*) capital; **lo** — the main thing, the essential point.
  2 *nm* (*Fin*) capital; capital sum; — **activo** working capital, (*Col, Chi*) capital assets; — **de explotación** working capital; — **físico** (*Chi*) capital assets; — **social** share capital; **inversión de** —**es** capital investment.
  3 *nf* (*Pol: of country*) capital, capital city; (*of region*) chief town, centre; — **de provincia** provincial capital, administrative centre of the province.

capitalino (*SAm*) **1** *adj* of the capital. **2** *nm*, **capitalina** *nf* native (*or* inhabitant) of the capital; **los** —**s** the people of the capital.

capitalismo *nm* capitalism.

capitalista 1 *adj* capitalist(ic). **2** *nmf* capitalist.

capitalización *nf* capitalization; compounding.

capitalizar [1f] *vt* to capitalize; *interest* to compound.

capitán *nm* (*Mil, Naut, Sport etc*) captain; leader, chief, commander; — **de corbeta** lieutenant-commander; — **de fragata** commander; — **general** (**de ejército**) (*approx*) field marshal; — **general** (**de armada**) chief of naval operations; — **de navío** captain; — **del puerto** harbour master.

capitana *nf* flagship.

capitanear [1a] *vt team* to captain; *expedition, rising etc* to lead, head, command.

capitanía *nf* (a) captaincy; rank of captain. (b) — **del puerto** harbour master's office. (c) harbour dues.

capitel *nm* (*Archit*) capital.

capitolio *nm* capitol; large edifice, imposing building; statehouse, parliament building; **C—** Capitol; **subir al** — (*fam*) to get to the top.

capitoné *nm* (a) removal van, furniture van. (b) (*Arg*) quilt, quilted blanket.

capitonear [1a] *vt* (*Arg*) to quilt.

capitoste *nm* (*pej*) chief, boss; petty tyrant.

capitulación *nf* (a) (*Mil*) capitulation, surrender; — **sin condiciones** unconditional surrender.
  (b) agreement, pact; —**es** (**de boda, matrimoniales**) marriage settlement.

capitular[1] *adj* (*Eccl*) chapter (*attr*); **sala** — chapter house, meeting room.

capitular[2] **1** *vt* (a) *terms* to agree to, agree on.
  (b) (*Law*) to charge (*de* with), impeach.
  2 *vi* (a) to come to terms, make an agreement (*con* with); — **con** (*pej*) to compound with.
  (b) (*Mil*) to capitulate, surrender.

capitulear [1a] *vi* (*Chi, Per: Parl*) to lobby.

capituleo *nm* (*Chi, Per: Parl*) lobbying.

capítulo *nm* (a) (*Lit, Typ*) chapter.
  (b) reproof, reprimand; — **de culpas** charge.
  (c) subject, matter; point; **ganar** — to make one's point.
  (d) —**s matrimoniales** marriage contract, marriage settlement.
  (e) meeting (*of a council*); (*Eccl*) chapter; **llamar a uno a** — to call someone to task, call comeone to account.
  (f) (*Eccl*) chapter house.

capó *nm* (*Aut*) bonnet, hood (*US*).

capoc *nm* kapok.

capón[1] *nm* rap on the head.

capón[2] **1** *adj* castrated. **2** *nm* capon; eunuch; (*RPl*) (*any*) castrated animal.

caponera *nf* (*Agr*) chicken coop, fattening pen; (*fig*) place of easy living, open house; (*sl*) clink (*sl*).

caporal *nm* chief, leader, (*Mex*) foreman, head man.

capot [ka'po] *nm* (*Aut*) = **capó**.

capota *nf* (a) (*woman's*) bonnet. (b) (*of carriage, pram*) hood; (*Aer*) cowling; (*Aut*) hood, top (*US*); — **plegable** folding hood, folding top (*US*).

capotaje *nm* somersault; overturning; (*Aer*) loop; (*Aer*) nose dive.

capotar [1a] *vi* (*Aut etc*) to turn over, turn turtle; to somersault; (*Aer*) to nose-dive.

capote *nm* (a) long cloak, cloak with sleeves; (*also* — **de brega**) bullfighter's cloak; (*Mil*) greatcoat; — **de monte** poncho; **a mi** —, **para mi** — to my way of thinking; **de** — (*Mex*) on the sly, in an underhand way; **darse** — (*Mex*) to give up one's job; to acknowledge defeat; **decir para su** — to say to oneself; **echar un** — **a uno** to give someone a helping hand.
  (b) frown, scowl; (*Meteorol*) mass of dark clouds.
  (c) (*Cards*) slam.
  (d) (*Arg: Cards*) **quedar** — not to win a single point, be whitewashed.
  (e) (*Chi, Mex*) beating.

capotear [1a] *vt* (a) *person* to deceive, bamboozle.
  (b) *difficulty etc* to shirk, duck, dodge. (c) (*Arg: Cards*) to win all the tricks against, whitewash.

capotera *nf* (a) (*CAm, Chi, Mex*) clothes rack. (b) (*Col, Cu, Ven: of horseman*) canvas bag.

capotudo *adj* frowning, scowling.

Capricornio *m* Capricorn.

capricho *nm* (a) whim, caprice, (*passing*) fancy; keen desire, sudden urge (*de* for); (*pej*) craze, fad, silly notion; **por puro** — just to please oneself, out of sheer cussedness; **es un** — **nada más** it's just a passing whim; **fue un** — **suyo** it was one of his silly notions; **tiene sus** —**s** he has his little whims, he has his moods.
  (b) (*in general*) whimsicality, fancifulness.
  (c) (*Anat*) birthmark.
  (d) (*Mus*) caprice, capriccio.

caprichosamente *adv* capriciously.

caprichoso *adj* capricious; full of whims, having odd fancies; full of one's own pet notions; *idea, novel, etc* fanciful, whimsical; (*pej*) wilful; moody, temperamental; wayward.

caprichudo *adj* stubborn, obstinate, unyielding (about one's odd ideas).

cápsula *nf* (*Aer, Anat, Bot, Pharm etc*) capsule; (*of bottle*) cap; (*of cartridge*) case; (*SD*) cartridge; — **espacial** space capsule; — **fulminante** percussion cap.

capsular *adj* capsular; **en forma** — in capsule form.

captafaros *nm*, *pl* **captafaros** (*also* **placa de** —) reflector.

captar [1a] *vt* (a) to captivate; *support* to win, gain, attract; *confidence etc* to win, get; *will* to gain control over; *attention etc* to get, secure; *person* to win over.
  (b) *waters* to collect; to dam, harness.
  (c) (*Radio*) *station* to tune in to; *signal* to get, pick up.

captura *nf* capture; seizure; arrest.

capturar [1a] *vt* to capture; to seize; to arrest.

capucha *nf* (a) hood; (*Eccl*) hood, cowl. (b) (*Ling*) circumflex accent.

capuchina *nf* (a) (*Eccl*) Capuchin sister. (b) (*Bot*) nasturtium.

capuchino *nm* (a) (*Eccl*) Capuchin. (b) (*SAm*) Capuchin monkey. (c) coffee with a little milk.

capucho *nm* cowl, hood.

capuchón *nm* (a) lady's hooded cloak. (b) (*Phot*) hood. (c) (*Aut etc*) valve cap. (d) (*of pen*) top, cap.

capujar [1a] *vt* (*Arg*) to catch in the air; to snatch; to say what someone else was about to say.

capullo *nm* (a) (*Zool*) cocoon. (b) (*Bot*) bud, flower bud; (*of acorn*) cup; — **de rosa** rosebud. (c) (*Anat*) prepuce.

caqui[1] *nm* khaki.

caqui[2] *nm* (*Chi*) date plum; (*fig*) red.

caquino *nm*: **reírse a** —**s**, **reírse a** — **suelto** (*Mex*) to laugh uproariously.

cara *nf* (a) (*Anat*) face; — **cortada** (*as nickname*) scarface; — **de cuchillo** hatchet face; — **a** — face to face; **a** — **descubierta** openly; **de** — opposite, facing; **de** — **al norte** facing north; **mirar a uno a la** — to look someone in the face; **los banqueros sin** — the faceless bankers; **asomar la** — to show one's face (*also fig*); **se le caía la** — **de vergüenza** he blushed with shame; **cruzar la** — **a uno** to slash someone across the face; **dar la** — to face the consequences of what one has done; **dar la** — **por otro** to answer for someone else; **dar** — **a** to face up to; **decir algo en** (*or* **por**) **la** — **de uno** to say something to someone's face; **echar algo en** — **a uno** to reproach someone for something, cast something in someone's teeth; **to allude to** something; **entrar** (or **pasar**) **por la** — to gatecrash; **hacer a dos** —s to engage in double-dealing; **hacer** — **a** to face; enemy etc to face up to, stand up to; **huir la** — **a uno** to avoid meeting someone; **lavar la** — **a uno** to lick someone's boots; **no mirar la** — **a uno** (fig) to be at daggers drawn with someone; **sacar la** — **por uno** to stick up for someone; **nos veremos las** —s (as threat) we'll meet again, we'll see; **no volver la** — **atrás** not to flinch.

(b) (as adv) — **adelante** forwards; facing forwards; — **atrás** backwards; facing backwards; — **al sol** facing the sun.

(c) look, appearance; **tener** — **de** to look like; **tener** — **de querer** + infin to look as if one would like to + infin; **tener** — **de aburrirse** to look bored; **tener buena** — to look nice, (Med) look well; **tener mala** — to look bad, (Med) look ill; — **de acelga** pale look; — **de aleluya** cheerful look; **tener** — **de pocos amigos** to look black, have a hangdog look; — **de corcho** cheeky look; — **dura** shamelessness; cheek, nerve; ¡qué — **más dura!** what a nerve!; — **de hereje** ugly face; hangdog look; — **de (justo) juez** stern face, grim-looking face; **mala** — wry face, grimace; **poner mala** — to pout, grimace, make a (wry) face; **tener** — **de monja boba** to look all innocent; **tener** — **de palo** to have a wooden expression; — **de pascua(s)** smiling face; **tener** — **de pascua(s)** to look pretty pleased; **tener** — **de roñoso** to look mean; — **de viernes** sad look; — **de vinagre** sour expression.

(d) boldness, nerve; **tener** — **para** + infin to have the nerve to + infin.

(e) (of object) face; outside, surface; (Archit) face, façade, front; (Geom) face; (of cloth etc) face, right side, finished side; (of slice, record etc) side; (of coin) face, obverse, (in tossing up) heads; — **o cruz** heads or tails; **echar** (or **jugar, sortear**) **algo a** — **o cruz** to toss up for something; —, **yo gano; cruz, Vd pierde** heads I win, tails you lose.

cárabe nm amber.

carabela nf caravel.

carabina nf (a) (Mil) carbine, rifle; **ser la** — **de Ambrosio** (fam) to be a dead loss.

(b) (fam) chaperon; **hacer de** —, **ir de** — to go as chaperon; to play gooseberry.

carabinero nm carabineer, rifleman; revenue guard.

cárabo nm tawny owl.

caracol nm (a) (Zool) snail; snail shell, sea shell.

(b) (of hair) curl.

(c) (in shape) spiral; **escalera de** — spiral staircase, winding staircase; **subir en** — (of smoke etc) to spiral up, corkscrew up; **hacer** —es (person) to weave about, zigzag; (pej) to reel, stagger; (horse) to prance about.

(d) ¡—es! (euph) good heavens!

caracolear [1a] vi (of horse) to prance about.

carácter nm, pl **caracteres** (a) character; nature, kind, condition; **de medio** — of an ill-defined nature; **de** — **totalmente distinto** of quite a different kind.

(b) (of person) character; **una persona de** — a person of character; **de** — **duro** hard-natured; **no tiene** — he lacks firmness, he's a weak character.

(c) (SAm: Lit, Theat) character, personage.

(d) (Bio) character; feature, characteristic; — **adquirido** acquired characteristic; — **hereditario** inherited characteristic.

(e) (Typ) character; — **de letra** handwriting; —es **de imprenta** type, typeface; **escribir en** —es **de imprenta** to write in block letters.

característica nf (a) characteristic; trait, quality, attribute. (b) (Theat) character actress.

característicamente adv characteristically.

característico 1 adj characteristic, typical (de of). **2** nm (Theat) character actor.

caracterizado adj distinguished, of note; special, peculiar, having special characteristics, typical.

caracterizar [1f] **1** vt (a) to characterize; to typify; to distinguish, set apart.

(b) to confer (a) distinction on, confer an honour on.

(c) (Theat) role to play with great effect.

2 caracterizarse vr (Theat) to make up, dress for the part.

caracú nm (SAm) bone marrow.

caracha nf (SAm) mange, itch; scab.

carachento adj, **carachoso** adj (SAm) mangy, scabby.

caracho adj violet-coloured.

caradura 1 nmf rotter, cad, shameless person; ¡—! you swine! **2** nf see **cara** (c).

carajear [1a] vt (Arg) to insult, swear at.

carajiento adj (Ec) foul-mouthed.

carajo nm (tabu) prick (tabu); ¡—! hell!, damn it all!; ¡vete al —! go to hell!

caramba interj (fam) well!, good gracious!; very odd!, how strange!; hang it all!; ¡—con...! to hell with...!

carámbano nm icicle.

carambola nf (Billiards) cannon; (fig) trick, ruse; **por** — by a lucky chance; indirectly, in a roundabout way.

caramelear [1a] vt (Col) to pull the wool over the eyes of, deceive.

caramelo nm sweet, toffee; caramel; — **americano** candyfloss, cotton candy (US).

caramillo nm (a) (Mus) flageolet; recorder; rustic pipe.

(b) untidy heap.

(c) piece of gossip; intrigue; **armar un** — to make mischief, start a gossiping campaign.

caramilloso adj fussy.

caranchear [1a] vt (Arg) to provoke.

carancho nm (Per) owl; (RPI) vulture.

caranga nf (Ec, Guat, Hond), **carángano** nm (Col, CR, Cu, Ec, Per) louse.

carantamaula nf (fam) ugly mug (sl), ugly person.

carantoña nf (fam) (a) ugly mug (sl).

(b) **ella es una** — she's mutton dressed up as lamb, she's tarted herself up to look younger.

(c) —s caresses; petting, fondling; **hacer** —s **a uno** to make faces at someone; to make sheep's eyes at someone.

carapacho nm shell, carapace; **meterse en su** — to go into one's shell.

caraqueño 1 adj of Caracas. **2** nm, **caraqueña** nf native (or inhabitant) of Caracas; **los** —s the people of Caracas.

carátula nf (a) mask; **la** — (fig: Theat) the stage, the theatre. (b) (Guat, Mex) face, dial. (c) (SAm: Typ) title page.

caravana nf (a) (Hist) caravan; (fig) group, band; (fig) crowd of trippers, group of picnickers; (of cars) stream, long succession, queue.

(b) (Aut: angl) caravan, trailer.

(c) (Cu) bird trap.

(d) (SAm) exaggerated bow; courtesy, compliment; **bailar** (or **correr, hacer**) **la** — **a uno** to overdo the courtesies; to pay exaggerated compliments to someone.

(e) —s (SAm) long earrings.

caravan(s)era nf, **caravasar** nm caravanserai.

caray interj (sl) gosh! (sl), good heavens!; well I'm blowed!

carbohidrato nm carbohydrate.

carbólico adj carbolic.

carbón nm (a) (Min) coal; — **bituminoso** soft coal; — **de leña**, — **vegetal** charcoal; — **menudo** small coal, slack; — **de piedra** coal.

(b) (Typ: also **papel** —) carbon paper, carbon; **copia al** — carbon copy.

(c) (Elec) carbon.

(d) (Agr) smut.

carbonada nf (Chi, Per, RPI) meat stew.

carbonato nm carbonate; — **de calcio** calcium carbonate; — **sódico** sodium carbonate.

carboncillo nm (Art) charcoal; (Min) small coal, slack; (Aut) carbon.

carbonear [1a] vt (a) to make charcoal of. (b) (Chi) to spur on, encourage.

carbonera nf (a) coalmine. (b) coal tip, coal heap. (c) coal bin, coal bunker. (d) charcoal kiln.

carbonería nf coalyard.

carbonero 1 adj coal (attr); charcoal (attr); **barco** — collier; **estación carbonera** coaling station.

2 nm (a) coal merchant; charcoal burner.

(b) (Naut) collier, coal ship.

(c) (Orn) coal tit.

carbónico 1 adj carbonic. **2** nm (Arg) carbon paper, carbon.

carbonífero adj carboniferous.

carbonilla nf (a) small coal, coaldust; cinder. (b) (Aut) carbon.

carbonización nf (Chem) carbonization; charring.

carbonizar [1f] **1** vt (Chem) to carbonize; to char; wood to make charcoal of; **quedar carbonizado** to be charred, be burnt to a cinder; (Elec) to be electrocuted; (of building) to be burnt down, be reduced to ashes.

2 carbonizarse vr (Chem) to carbonize; = **quedar carbonizado**.

carbono nm (Chem) carbon.

carbonoso adj carbonaceous.

carborundo nm carborundum.

carbunclo nm (Min), **carbunco** nm (Med) carbuncle.
carburador nm carburettor.
carburante nm fuel.
carburo nm carbide.
carca adj invar (sl) square (fam).
carcaj nm quiver; (Mex) rifle case, pistol holster.
carcajada nf (loud) laugh, peal of laughter, guffaw; **hubo —s** there was loud laughter; **reírse a —s** to laugh heartily, roar with laughter; **soltar la —** to burst out laughing.
carcajear [1a] vi and **carcajearse** vr to roar with laughter, have a good laugh (de at).
carcamal nm (fam) old crock, wreck; **es un —** he's a wreck.
carcamán nm (a) (Naut) tub, hulk; (Per, PR) old crock, wreck. (b) (Cu, Per, RPl) low-class foreign immigrant. (c) (Arg: Pol) diehard, reactionary.
carcancha nf (Mex) bus.
carcasa nf (Aut etc) chassis, grid; (of tyre) carcass.
carcayú nm wolverine.
cárcel nf (a) prison, jail; **— modelo** model prison; **poner en la —** to jail, send to jail, put in prison. (b) (Tech) clamp.
carcelario adj prison (attr).
carcelería nf imprisonment, detention.
carcelero 1 adj prison (attr). 2 nm warder, jailer.
carcinogénico adj carcinogenic.
carcinoma nm carcinoma.
carcoma nf (a) (Ent) deathwatch beetle; woodworm. (b) (fig) anxiety, perpetual worry; (person) spendthrift.
carcomer [2a] 1 vt (a) to bore into, eat into, eat away. (b) (fig) health etc to undermine; fortune to eat into, eat away.
    2 **carcomerse** vr (a) to get worm-eaten. (b) (fig) to decay, waste away; to be eaten away.
carcomido adj worm-eaten, wormy, infested with woodworm; rotten; (fig) rotten, decayed.
carcoso adj (Ec) dirty.
carda nf (a) (Bot) teasel; (Tech) teasel, card (for combing wool). (b) (act) carding. (c) (fam) reprimand; **dar una —** a uno to rap someone over the knuckles.
cardamomo nm cardamom.
cardar [1a] vt (a) (Tech) to card, comb. (b) (fam; also **— la lana** a) to tell off, rap over the knuckles.
cardenal nm (a) (Eccl) cardinal. (b) (Med) bruise, mark, weal. (c) (Chi) geranium.
cardenalato nm cardinalate.
cardencha nf (Bot, Tech) teasel.
cardenillo nm verdigris.
cárdeno adj purple, violet; livid; water opalescent.
cardíaco 1 adj cardiac, heart (attr). 2 nm, **cardíaca** nf heart case, sufferer from a heart complaint.
cardinal adj (all senses) cardinal.
cardiología nf cardiology.
cardiológico adj cardiological.
cardiólogo nm cardiologist.
cardo nm thistle.
cardume(n) nm (a) (Fish) shoal. (b) (Chi, Per, RPl) great number, mass; **un — de gente** a lot of people, a crowd of people.
carear [1a] 1 vt persons to bring face to face; texts to compare, collate, check against each other.
    2 vi: **— a** to face towards, look on to.
    3 **carearse** vr (a) to come face to face, come together, meet.
    (b) **— con** to face, face up to.
carecer [2d] vi (a) **— de** to lack, be in need of, be without, want for; **carece de talento** he lacks talent, he has no talent; **no carecemos de dinero** we don't lack money, we're not short of money; **eso carece de sentido** that doesn't make sense; **aquí se carece de todo** here there is a great need of everything. (b) (Urug) **carece hacerlo** it is necessary to do it; **carece no dejarla** we must not allow her to.
carecimiento nm lack, need.
carena nf (a) careening; **dar — a** to careen. (b) (fam) ragging; **dar — a uno** to rag someone, tease someone.
carenar [1a] vt to careen.
carencia nf lack (de of), shortage (de of), need (de for); scarcity; (Med etc) deficiency.
carencial adj: **mal —** deficiency disease.
carente adj: **— de** lacking (in), devoid of.
carentón adj (Arg) large-faced.
careo nm confrontation, meeting (face to face); comparison, collation.
carero adj expensive, dear, pricey (fam).
carestía nf scarcity, shortage, dearth; famine; (Comm) high price(s), high cost; **— de la vida** high cost of living; **época de —** period of shortage, lean period, bad time.

careta nf mask; (Min etc) breathing apparatus, respirator; **— antigás** gasmask; **— de esgrima** fencing mask; **quitar la — a uno** to unmask someone.
carey nm tortoiseshell; (Zool) turtle.
carga nf (a) load; cargo, freight; burden, weight; **la — fiscal** the tax burden; **a —s** in plenty, in abundance, galore; **en plena —** under full load; **bestia de —** beast of burden; **buque de —** freighter; **tomar —** to load up, (Naut) take on cargo.
    (b) (Elec) charge; load; **— máxima** peak load; **hilo con —** live wire.
    (c) (Mech) load; **— fija, — muerta** dead load; **— de fractura, — de rotura** breaking load; **— de pago, — útil** payload.
    (d) (Mil; also of shell, furnace, etc) charge; **— explosiva** explosive charge; **— de pólvora** (Min) blasting powder; **— de profundidad** depth charge.
    (e) (Fin) tax, charge, duty.
    (f) duty, obligation, charge; onus, responsibility; **— de familia** dependent relative; **— personal** personal commitments; **echar la — a uno** to put the blame on someone, put the onus on someone; **echarse con la —** (fam) to throw up the sponge; **llevar la —** (fam) to carry the can (sl).
    (g) (Mil) charge, attack; (Sport) charge, tackle; **— a la bayoneta** bayonet charge; **— de caballería** cavalry charge; **tocar a —** to sound the charge; **volver a la —** (fig) to return to the charge, return to the attack.
    (h) (act) loading; (Elec, Mil) loading; charging; **andén de —** loading platform; **"permitido — y descarga"** (sign) "loading and unloading".
cargada nf (a) (Arg) unpleasant practical joke.
    (b) (Mex) = **carga** (h).
    (c) (Mex) **ir a la —** to bet on the most heavily-backed card; (fig) to jump on the bandwagon.
cargaderas nfpl (Col) braces, suspenders (US).
cargadero nm (a) loading point; (Rail) goods platform, loading bay. (b) (Archit) lintel.
cargado adj and ptp (a) loaded, with a load, under load; dice loaded; (esp fig) laden, burdened, weighed down (de with); **estar — (de vino)** to be drunk; **estar — de años** to be very old, be weighed down with age; **estar cargada** (fam) to be in the family way; **ser — de espaldas** to be round-shouldered, have a stoop; **un árbol — de fruto** a tree laden with fruit.
    (b) (Elec) live, charged, hot.
    (c) (Mil) **— (con bala)** live.
    (d) coffee, tea strong.
    (e) sky overcast; atmosphere heavy, sultry, close.
cargador nm (a) (person) loader; (Naut) docker, stevedore; (of furnace) stoker.
    (b) (Tech: of gun) chamber; (of pen) filler; (Mil: Hist) ramrod; **— de acumuladores, — de baterías** battery charger.
    (c) **—es** (Col) braces, suspenders (US).
cargadora nf (Col, Ven) nursemaid.
cargamento nm (a) (act) loading. (b) load; (Naut) cargo; shipment; **— de retorno** return cargo.
cargante adj boring, tiresome, annoying; task irksome, tedious; child trying.
cargar [1h] 1 vt (a) to load (de with; a, en on); to overload, burden, weigh down (de with); dice to load; imagination, mind etc to fill (de with); **— a uno de deudas** to encumber someone with debts; **— a uno de nuevas obligaciones** to burden someone with new duties.
    (b) (Elec) to charge.
    (c) furnace to stoke, charge.
    (d) to increase the weight of, cause to bear down more heavily; see **mano**.
    (e) tax to impose, lay (sobre on); to increase.
    (f) (Comm, Fin) to charge, debit (en cuenta a to, to the account of); **— de menos a uno** to undercharge someone.
    (g) to impute, ascribe (a to); blame to lay (a on); responsibility to entrust (a to), place (a on).
    (h) (Law) to charge, accuse; **— a uno de poco escrupuloso** to accuse someone of being unscrupulous, charge someone with being unscrupulous.
    (i) (Mil) to charge, attack.
    (j) (Mil) gun to load.
    (k) (Naut) sail to take in.
    (l) (Univ: sl) to plough (sl), fail.
    (m) (SAm) to carry, have, use; **— anteojos** to wear glasses; **— revólver** to pack a gun (sl); **carga siempre mucho dinero** he always carries a lot of money, he always has a lot of money on him.
    (n) (Chi, Per: of dog etc) to attack, go for.

(o) (*fam*) to bore; to annoy, vex; **esto me carga** this annoys me, I find this annoying.

2 *vi* **(a)** to load, load up; to take on a load; (*Naut*) to take on (a) cargo; — **(demasiado, mucho)** to overeat, drink too much.

(b) — **con** *object*, *weight* to pick up, carry away, take away; *burden* (*fig*) to shoulder, take upon oneself; *responsibility* to assume, take on; *blame* to bear.

(c) (*Ling*: *of accent*) to fall (**en**, **sobre** on).

(d) to lean, tip, incline.

(e) — **en**, — **sobre** to lean on, lean against; (*Archit etc*) to rest on, be supported by.

(f) — **sobre uno** to urge someone, press someone; to importune someone.

(g) to pester, be annoying.

(h) (*Meteorol*) to turn, veer (*a* to, *hacia* towards).

(i) (*of people*) to crowd together.

3 cargarse *vr* **(a)** — **algo** to take something on oneself; — **de algo** to be full of something, be loaded with something; to fill oneself up with something, (*fig*) get one's fill of something; — **de hijos** to overburden oneself with children; — **de años** to get very old; **el árbol se carga de manzanas** the tree produces apples in abundance.

(b) = *vi* **(d)** *and* **(e)**.

(c) (*Elec*) to become charged, become live.

(d) (*Meteorol*: *of sky*) to become overcast; (*of atmosphere*) to become heavy, become oppressive.

(e) (*fam*) to get cross; to get bored.

(f) —**la** (*fam*) to get into hot water.

(g) — **a uno** (*fam*) to bump someone off (*sl*), do someone in (*sl*); **¡algún día me lo cargaré!** I'll get him one day!

cargazón *nf* **(a)** load; (*Naut*) cargo, shipment; (*fig*) dead weight, useless mass.

(b) (*Med*) heaviness (*of stomach etc*).

(c) (*Meteorol*) mass of heavy cloud.

(d) — **de espaldas** stoop.

(e) (*Arg, Chi*) abundance of fruit (*on tree*).

cargo *nm* **(a)** load, weight, burden.

(b) (*fig*) burden; — **de conciencia** burden on one's conscience; remorse, guilty feeling.

(c) (*Comm*) charge, debit; **una cantidad en** — **a uno** a sum to be charged to someone; **ser en** — **a uno** to be indebted to someone; **girar a** — **de**, **librar a** — **de** to draw on.

(d) (*Theat and fig*) role, part; — **estelar** star role; **un** — **casi sin responsabilidades** a post almost without duties; **desempeñar un** — to fill an office; **vestir el** — to look the part, dress the part.

(e) duty, obligation, responsibility; charge, care; **a** — **de** in the charge of; **tener algo a su** — to have something in one's charge, be in charge of something; **hacerse** — **de** to take charge of; to see about; to realize, understand; **el ejército se hizo** — **del poder** the army took over power; **apenas si pude hacerme** — **de ello** I could scarcely grasp what was going on; **parecía no hacerse** — **de la dificultad** he seemed not to understand the difficulty.

(f) (*Law*) charge; reproach, accusation; **hacer a uno** — **de algo** to charge somebody with something.

cargosear [1a] *vt* (*Chi, Per, RPl*) to pester, keep on at, annoy.

cargoso *adj* (*Chi, RPl*) troublesome, annoying; burdensome.

carguera *nf* (*Col, Ven*) nursemaid.

carguero *nm* **(a)** (*Naut*) freighter, cargo boat; (*Aer*) freight plane, transport plane; — **militar** air-force transport plane.

(b) (*Arg, Col, Per*) beast of burden.

carguío *nm* load; cargo, freight.

cariacontecido *adj* crestfallen, down in the mouth, woebegone.

cariado *adj* *tooth* bad, rotten, decayed, carious.

cariadura *nf* (*Med*) caries, decay.

cariancho *adj* broad-faced.

cariar [1h] **1** *vt* to cause to decay, cause decay in. **2 cariarse** *vr* to decay, become decayed.

cariátide *nf* caryatid.

caribe 1 *adj* **(a)** (*Geog etc*) Caribbean; **Mar C—** Caribbean Sea.

(b) (*SAm*) cannibalistic; (*fig*) savage, cruel; (*Ant*) furious, bad-tempered; **ponerse** — to get furious.

(c) (*Ant*) *flavour* hot, strong.

2 *nmf* Carib, inhabitant of the Caribbean area.

3 *nm* (*SAm*) cannibal; (*Ant*: *fig*) savage, brute.

caribú *nm* caribou.

caricato *nm* (*Mex*) = **caricatura**.

caricatura *nf* caricature (*also fig*); cartoon.

caricaturista *nmf* caricaturist; cartoonist.

caricaturesco *adj* absurd, ridiculous.

caricaturizar [1f] *vt* to caricature.

caricia *nf* **(a)** caress; pat, stroke; **hacer** —**s** to caress, fondle, stroke.

(b) (*fig*) endearment.

caricioso *adj* caressing, affectionate.

caridad *nf* charity; charitableness; **la** — **empieza en uno mismo** charity begins at home; **hacer** — **a uno** to give alms to someone.

caries *nf*, *pl* **caries (a)** (*Med*) dental decay, caries.

(b) (*Agr*) blight.

carigordo *adj* fat-faced.

carilampiño *adj* clean-shaven; smooth-faced, beardless.

carilargo *adj* long-faced.

carilla *nf* **(a)**. mask. **(b)** (*Typ*) page.

carillero *adj* round-faced, full-faced.

carillón *nm* carillon.

carimbo *nm* (*SAm*: *Hist*) branding iron (*also Bol*: *Agr*).

cariño *nm* **(a)** affection, love (*a*, *por* for); fondness, liking (*a*, *por* for); tenderness; **sentir** — **por**, **tener** — **a** to like, be fond of; **por el** — **que te tengo** because I'm fond of you; **tomar** — **a** to take a liking to, get fond of.

(b) (*SAm*) caress, stroke; gift, token (*of affection*).

(c) —**s** endearments; show of affection.

cariñosamente *adv* affectionately, lovingly, fondly; tenderly.

cariñoso *adj* affectionate, loving, fond; tender.

carioca *adj* (*SAm*) of Rio de Janeiro.

cariparejo *adj* poker-faced.

carirraído *adj* brazen, shameless.

carirredondo *adj* round-faced.

carisellazo *nm* (*Col*) toss of a coin; **echar un** — to toss up.

carisma *nm* charisma.

carita *nf* little face; **de** — (*Col*) first-class; jolly good (*fam*); **dar** (*or* **hacer**) — (*Mex*: *of a woman*) to smile back, accept a man's advances; **hacer** —**s** (*Col*) to make faces.

caritativamente *adv* charitably.

caritativo *adj* charitable (*con*, *para* to).

cariz *nm* look, aspect; outlook; (*Meteorol*) look of the sky; **mal** — scowl; **poner mal** — to scowl; **esto va tomando mal** — this business is beginning to look bad, I don't like the look of this.

carlanca *nf* **(a)** (*Col, CR*) shackle, fetter.

(b) (*Chi, Hond*) tedious person; boredom; annoyance, vexation.

(c) —**s** tricks, cunning; **tener muchas** —**s** to be full of tricks.

carlinga *nf* (*Aer*) cockpit, cabin.

carlismo *nm* Carlism.

carlista 1 *adj* Carlist. **2** *nmf* Carlist.

Carlitos *m* (*pet name for* **Carlos**) Charlie.

Carlomagno *m* Charlemagne.

Carlos *m* Charles.

Carlota *f* Charlotte.

carlota *nf* (*Cook*) charlotte.

carmelita¹ (*Eccl*) **1** *adj* Carmelite. **2** *nmf* Carmelite; — **descalzo** discalced Carmelite.

carmelita² *adj*, **carmelito** *adj* (*esp SAm*) light brown, tan.

carmelitano *adj* Carmelite.

carmen¹ *nm* (*Granada*) country house, villa.

carmen² *nm* (*Lit*) song, poem.

Carmen *nm* (*Eccl*) Carmelite Order.

carmenar [1a] *vt* **(a)** (*Tech*) *wool* to card, teasel; *silk etc* to unravel; *hair* to disentangle; — **el pelo a uno** (*fam*) to pull someone's hair.

(b) (*fam*) to fleece, swindle.

carmesí 1 *adj* crimson. **2** *nm* crimson.

carmín *nm* **(a)** carmine; rouge. **(b)** (*Bot*) dog rose.

carminativo 1 *adj* carminative. **2** *nm* carminative.

carmíneo *adj* carmine, crimson.

carnada *nf* bait, live bait.

carnal *adj* **(a)** carnal, of the flesh. **(b)** (*of relation*) full, blood; **hermano** — full brother; **primo** — first cousin; **tío** — real uncle.

carnalidad *nf* lust, carnality.

carnaval *nm* carnival (*also fig*); (*Eccl*) Shrovetide; **martes de** — Shrove Tuesday.

carne *nf* **(a)** (*Anat*) flesh; — **de gallina** (*fig*) gooseflesh; **me pone la** — **de gallina** it gives me gooseflesh, (*fig*) it gives me the creeps; **de** — **y hueso** of flesh and blood; **de abundantes** —**s**, **de muchas** —**s** fat; **de pocas** —**s** thin; **en** — **viva** on the raw; **en** —**s** naked, with nothing on; **se me abrieron las** —**s** I was terrified; **cobrar** (*or* **criar**, **echar**) —**s** to put on weight; **perder** —**s** to lose weight.

(b) (*Cook*) meat; — **adobada** salt meat; — **asada** roast meat; — **de cañón** cannon fodder; — **de carnero** mutton; — **de cerdo** pork; — **concentrada** meat extract; — **congelada** frozen meat, chilled meat; — **de cordero** lamb, mutton; — **fiambre** cold meat; — **de horca** good-for-nothing, gallows bird; — **magra**, — **mollar** lean meat; — **de oveja**, — **ovina** mutton, lamb; — **picada** mince, minced meat; — **porcina** pork; — **de res** (*SAm*) beef; — **de ternera** veal; — **de vaca** beef; — **de venado** venison; **no ser ni** — **ni pescado** to be neither one thing nor the other, be nondescript; **poner toda la** — **en el asador** to go the whole hog, stake one's all.

(c) (*Bot*) flesh, fleshy part, pulp; (*SAm*) heart, hardest part (*of timber*); — **de membrillo** quince jelly.

(d) (*Eccl etc*) flesh, carnality.

carné *nm* (*Acad*) = **carnet**.

carneada *nf* (*Arg*) slaughter(ing).

carnear [1a] *vt* **(a)** (*Chi, RPl*) *animal* to slaughter (and dress); (*fig*) to murder, butcher.
(b) (*Chi*) *to* deceive, take in (*fam*).

carnerada *nf* flock of sheep.

carnerear [1a] *vi* (*RPl*) to blackleg, be a strike-breaker.

carnerero *nm* shepherd.

carnero *nm* (*Zool*) sheep, ram; — **marino** seal; — **de la tierra** (*SAm*) llama, alpaca; — **de simiente** breeding ram; **no hay tales** —**s** there's no such thing; it's nothing of the sort; **cantar para el** — (*Arg*) to kick the bucket (*sl*).
(b) (*Cook*) mutton.
(c) sheepskin.
(d) (*Chi, RPl*) weak-willed person; blackleg, strikebreaker.
(e) (*Chi*) **botarse** (*or* **echarse**) **al** — to chuck it all up, do nothing.

carnestolendas *nfpl* Shrovetide.

carnet [kar'ne] *nm, pl* **carnets** [kar'ne] (*gall*) note-book; bank book; (tourist's) travel voucher; — **de conducir**, — **de conductor**, — **de chófer** driving licence; — **de identidad** identity card; — **de socio** membership card.

carnicería *nf* **(a)** butcher's (shop); meat market; slaughterhouse.
(b) (*fig*) slaughter, carnage; — **en las carreteras** slaughter on the roads; **hacer una** — **de** to massacre, slaughter.

carnicero 1 *adj* **(a)** (*Zool*) carnivorous, flesh-eating; (*Orn*) of prey; *person* (*fam*) fond of meat.
(b) (*fig*) savage, cruel, bloodthirsty.
2 *nm* **(a)** butcher (*also fig*).
(b) (*Zool*) carnivore.

cárnico *adj* meat (*attr*); **industria cárnica** meat industry.

carnívoro 1 *adj* carnivorous, flesh-eating. **2** *nm* carnivore.

carnosidad *nf* **(a)** fleshiness; corpulence, obesity. **(b)** (*Med*) proud flesh.

carnoso *adj* beefy, fat.

carnudo *adj* fleshy.

caro 1 *adj* **(a)** dear, beloved; **las cosas que nos son tan caras** the things which are so dear to us.
(b) (*Comm*) dear, expensive; **un coche carísimo** a terribly expensive car.
2 *adv* dear, dearly; **le costó muy** — it cost him dear; **eso sale bastante** — that comes rather expensive; **vender** — to sell at a high price.

carocas *nfpl* wheedling, cajolery; **hacer** —**s** to put it on, give oneself airs.

caroleno *nm* (*Mex*) back slang.

Carolina[1] *f* Caroline.

Carolina[2] *f* (*Geog*): — **del Norte** North Carolina. — **del Sur** South Carolina.

carolingio *adj* Carolingian.

carón *adj* (*SAm*) broad-faced.

carona *nf* **(a)** saddle padding; *part of horse's back where the saddle rests.* **(b)** (*Arg*) bed.

caroso *adj* (*Per*) blond, fair; faded.

carótida *nf* carotid (artery).

carozo *nm* **(a)** cob of maize, corncob (*US*). **(b)** (*SAm*) stone, core (*of fruit*).

carpa[1] *nf* (*Fish*) carp; — **dorada** goldfish.

carpa[2] *nf* (*SAm*) tent; awning; market stall, open-air shop.

carpanta *nf* (*fam*) ravenous hunger.

Cárpatos: Montes *mpl* — Carpathians.

carpeta *nf* **(a)** folder, file; portfolio; briefcase; **cerrar la** — to close the file (*in an investigation*).
(b) table cover (*also* — **de mesa**).
(c) (*Ant, Arg, Per*) table, desk.

carpetazo *nm*: **dar** — **a** to shelve, put on one side, do nothing about.

carpetero *nm* filing cabinet.

carpetovetónico *adj* terribly Spanish, Spanish to the core.

carpidor *nm, also* **carpidora** *nf* (*SAm*) weeding hoe.

carpintear [1a] *vi* **(a)** to carpenter; to do woodwork (*as a hobby*).
(b) (*Col, RPl*) to insist; to make disagreeable noises.

carpintería *nf* **(a)** carpentry, joinery, woodwork.
(b) carpenter's shop.

carpintero *nm* **(a)** (*Tech*) carpenter; woodworker; — **de blanco** joiner; — **de carretas**, — **de prieto** cartwright, wheelwright; — **de buque**, — **de ribera** ship's carpenter, shipwright.
(b) (*Orn*) woodpecker.
(c) (*SAm*) annoying person.

carpir [3a] *vt* (*SAm*) to weed, hoe.

carraca *nf* **(a)** (*Naut: Hist*) carrack; (*pej*) tub, old hulk.
(b) (*Mus, Sport*) rattle.
(c) (*Tech*) ratchet brace.
(d) (*PR, Ven: Aut*) old crock.

carraco 1 *adj* feeble, decrepit. **2** *nm* (*Aut etc*) old crock.

carrada *nf* (*RPl*) = **carretada**.

carral *nm* barrel, vat.

carralero *nm* cooper.

carrasca *nf* kermes oak.

carraspear [1a] *vi* to be hoarse, have a frog in one's throat; to clear one's throat, hawk.

carraspera *nf* hoarseness, frog in the throat.

carrasposo *adj* **(a)** hoarse, having a sore throat. **(b)** (*SAm*) rough, harsh.

carrera *nf* **(a)** (*act*) run; running; chase, rush; **a** — (**abierta**), **a** — **tendida** at full speed, all out; **a la** — at full speed; hastily; **de** — hastily; rashly, without thinking; easily; **partir de** — to proceed rashly; **dar** — **libre a** to give free rein to; **no poder hacer** — **con uno** to make no headway with some-one, be unable to get someone to see reason; — **de aterrizaje** (*Aer*) landing run; — **del oro** goldrush.
(b) (*Sport: Baseball etc*) run.
(c) (*Sport: contest*) race; —**s** races, racing; **de** —(**s**) racing (*attr*), race (*attr*); **caballo de** —(**s**) racehorse; **coche de** —**s** racing car; — **de armamentos** arms race; — **de carretas**, — **de carrettas** horse race; — **por carretera** road race; — **contra el reloj** (*fig*) race against the clock; — **corta** dash, short run, sprint; — **de fondo** long-distance race; — **lisa** flat race; — **hacia la luna** race for the moon, race to get to the moon; — **de Maratón** marathon; — **de obstáculos** obstacle race; — **pedestre** walking race; — **de relevos** relay race; — **de resistencia** endurance race, long-distance race; — **de sacos** sackrace; — **de vallas** hurdle race, hurdles, (*horses*) steeplechase; **abrir** — to set the pace, be the pacemaker.
(d) row, line; (*Archit: of bricks etc*) course; track; avenue, boulevard; (*in hair*) parting; (*in stocking*) run, ladder; (*Astron*) course; **la** — **del sol** the course of the sun.
(e) (*Archit*) beam, girder, joist.
(f) (*Mus*) run.
(g) (*Naut*) run, route.
(h) (*Mech: of piston*) stroke; (*of valve*) lift; — **ascendente** upstroke; — **descendente** downstroke.
(i) (*fig*) career; profession; **diplomático de** — career diplomat; **dar** — **a uno** to give someone his education, pay for someone's professional studies; to put someone to a career; **hacer** — to get on in one's career; to get on in the world, make headway; **no tiene** — he has no profession, he doesn't do anything serious in life.
(j) (*Univ*) course, studies; **cuando termine la** — when he finishes his course, when he qualifies.
(k) course of human life.

carrerista 1 *adj* fond of racing; (*pej*) horsy. **2** *nmf* racing man, racing woman, racegoer; (*professional*) punter. **3** *nf* (*fam*) streetwalker.

carrero *nm* carter, cart driver.

carreta *nf* **(a)** (long narrow) wagon, low cart; — **de mano** = **carretilla**; — **de bueyes** oxcart.
(b) (*Col*) wheel.
(c) **hacer la** — to purr.

carretada *nf* cart load; (*fig*) cart load, great quality; **a** —**s** in loads, galore.

carretaje *nm* cartage, haulage.

carrete *nm* reel, spool; (*Sew*) reel, bobbin; (*Elec*) coil, (*Phot*) spool; (*Fish*) reel; (*of cycle*) hub; — **de encendido** (*Aut*) ignition coil; — **de inducción** (*Elec*) induction coil.

carretear [1a] **1** vt (a) load to cart, haul. (b) cart to drive; (Aer) to taxi. **2** vi (Aer) to taxi.

carretel nm reel, spool, bobbin.

carretela nf (Hist) coach, carriage; calash; (CAm, Mex) cart.

carretera nf (main) road, highway; **de —** road (attr); **por —** by road; **— de acceso** approach road; **— de circunvalación** bypass, ring road; **— nacional** motorway, major route; **— de primer orden** first-class road.

carretero 1 adj vehicle (attr), for vehicles. **2** nm carter; cartwright, wheelwright; **jurar como un —** to swear like a trooper.

carretilla nf (a) truck, trolley; (also **— de mano**) handcart, barrow; (Agr, Hort) wheelbarrow; (child's) go-cart; (shopper's) trolley; **— eléctrica** electric truck; **— de horquilla** fork-lift truck.
(b) squib, cracker.
(c) (Chi, RPl) jaw, jawbone.
(d) (Col) lot, series.
(e) **aprender algo de —** to learn something mechanically; **saber algo de —** to know something by heart.

carretón nm small cart; wagon, dray; **— de remolque** trailer.

carricoche nm covered wagon, (gipsy) caravan; (fam) crock.

carricuba nf water cart.

carriel nm (CAm, Ec, Ven) briefcase, attaché case.

carril nm (a) rut, track; cart track, lane; (of motorway) lane; (Agr) furrow; **entrar en (el) —** (fig) to get on the right track.
(b) (Rail) rail; (Chi, PR) train; **— de toma** third rail.

carrilano nm (Chi) (a) robber, holdup man. (b) (Rail) railwayman.

carrilera nf (a) rut, track. (b) (Cu: Rail) siding.

carrilero nm (Per) railwayman.

carrillera nf (a) (Zool) jaw. (b) chinstrap.

carrillo nm (a) cheek; jowl; **comer a dos —s** to eat greedily, stuff oneself; (fig) to have the best of both worlds.
(b) (Tech) pulley.

carrindanga nf (RPl) old car, broken-down cart (etc).

carriola nf truckle bed.

carrito nm tea trolley, serving-trolley.

carrizal nm reedbed.

carrizo nm (a) reed. (b) **—s** (Ec, Mex) thin legs; **hacer —** (Col) to cross one's legs.

carro nm (a) cart, wagon; (Hist: also **— de guerra**) chariot; (SAm) (any) vehicle, (esp) car, automobile; (Mil) tank; (SAm: Rail) car, truck, coach; **— alegórico** float (in a procession); **— aljibe** water cart; **— blindado** armoured car; **— de combate** tank; **— correo** (SAm: Rail) mail van; **— cuba** tank truck; **— fuerte** heavy trolley; **— fúnebre** hearse; **— de mudanzas** removal van; **— de riego** water cart; **— tranvía, — urbano** (SAm) tramcar, streetcar (US); **aguantar —s y carretas** to put up with anything, remain undismayed; **arrimarse al — del que manda** to climb on the bandwagon; **enganchar el — a los bueyes** to put the cart before the horse; **¡pare Vd el —!** hold your horses!; **tirar del —** (fig) to do all the donkey work; **untar el — a uno** to grease someone's palm.
(b) (quantity) cartload.
(c) (of typewriter) carriage.

carrocería nf (a) coachbuilder's; carriage repair shop. (b) (Aut etc) bodywork, coachwork.

carrocero nm coachbuilder, carriage builder.

carrocha nf (Ent) eggs.

carromato nm covered wagon, (gipsy) caravan.

carroña nf carrion.

carroño adj (a) rotten, putrid, foul. (b) (Col) cowardly.

carroza nf (a) (state) coach, carriage; (in procession) float; **— fúnebre** hearse. (b) (Naut) awning.

carruaje nm carriage; vehicle.

carrusel nm (gall) merry-go-round, roundabout.

carta nf (a) (Post etc) letter; **— abierta** open letter; **— adjunta** covering letter; **— aérea** air letter; **— de ajuste** (TV) test card; **— de amor, — amorosa** love letter; **— certificada** registered letter; **— 'de crédito** letter of credit; **— de emplazamiento** (Law) summons; **— particular, — privada** private letter, personal letter; **— pastoral** pastoral letter; **— de pedido** (Comm) order; **— de pésame** letter of condolence; **— de porte** bill of lading; **— postal** (SAm) postcard; **— de recomendación** letter of introduction (para to); **— de solicitud** application;

— urgente special-delivery letter; **echar una — al correo** to post a letter.
(b) (Law) document, deed; (Hist: of town etc) charter; **— blanca** carte blanche; **dar — blanca a uno** to give someone carte blanche; **tener — blanca** to have a free hand; **— de ciudadanía, — de naturaleza** naturalization papers; **adquirir — de naturaleza** (fig) to come to seem native, be thoroughly accepted; **— ejecutoria, — de hidalguía** (Hist) letters patent (of nobility); **C— Magna** (Brit) Magna Carta; **— de pago** receipt, discharge in full; **— partida por abc** indenture; **— de privilegio** charter; **— de venta** bill of sale; **a — cabal** thoroughly, in every respect; loyally; **¡— canta!** there it is in black and white!
(c) (Geog) map (also **— geográfica**); **— de marear, — marítima** chart; **— meteorológica** weather map.
(d) (Cards) card, playing card; **— de figura** court card, picture card; **a —s vistas** openly, honestly; with inside information; **echar las —s** to tell someone's fortune (with cards); **enseñar las —s** (fig) to show one's hand; **poner las —s boca arriba, poner las —s sobre la mesa** to put one's cards on the table; **no saber a qué — quedarse** not to know what to think, be undecided; **tener —s en un asunto** to intervene in a matter, come in on an affair.
(e) (Cook) menu; **— de vinos** wine list; **a la — à** la carte.

cartabón nm (carpenter's) square, bevel; (draughtsman's) triangle; (Mil, surveyor's) quadrant.

cartagenero 1 adj of Cartagena. **2** nm, **cartagenera** nf native (or inhabitant) of Cartagena; **los —s** the people of Cartagena.

cartaginés 1 adj Carthaginian. **2** nm, **cartaginesa** nf Carthaginian.

Cartago f Carthage.

cartapacio nm notebook; folder, briefcase; (School) satchel.

carta-tarjeta nf, pl **cartas-tarjeta** letter-card.

cartear [1a] **1** vi (Cards) to play low. **2 cartearse** vr to correspond (con with); **se cartearon durante 2 años** they wrote to each other for 2 years.

cartel nm (a) poster, placard; (Theat etc) bill; (School) wall chart; **— de escaparate** window card; **torero de —** star bullfighter; **tener —** (fam) to be a hit, be all the rage; **"se prohibe fijar —es"** "post no bills".
(b) (Comm, Fin: angl) cartel, trust.

cartela nf (a) slip of paper, bit of card. (b) (Archit) console; corbel; tablet.

cartelera nf hoarding, billboard; notice board; (in newspaper) list of plays, theatre section; **mantenerse en la —, seguir en la —** to run; **se mantuvo en la — durante 3 años** it ran for 3 years.

cartelero nm billsticker, billposter.

cartelón nm large notice; sign; banner.

carteo nm correspondence, exchange of letters.

cárter nm (Mech) housing, case; **— del cigüeñal** crankcase.

cartera nf (a) wallet, pocketbook; letterfile, portfolio, briefcase; (Sew) pocket flap; (SAm) handbag, purse (US); (on motorcycle) pannier bag; **— de bolsillo** wallet; **— de herramientas** toolbag; **— de mano** briefcase.
(b) (Pol) portfolio, ministerial post; **ministro sin —** minister without portfolio.
(c) (Fin) portfolio, holdings; **efectos en —** holdings, stocks.

carterero nm (Chi) pickpocket; bagsnatcher.

carterista nm pickpocket.

carterita nf: **— de fósforos** folder of matches.

cartero nm postman, mailman (US).

cartesiano 1 adj Cartesian. **2** nm Cartesian.

cartilaginoso adj cartilaginous.

cartílago nm cartilage.

cartilla nf (a) (School) primer, first reader; spelling book; **cantar (or leer) la — a uno** to give someone a severe ticking off; **no saber la —** not to know a single thing.
(b) **— de ahorros** savings bank book, deposit book; **— de identidad** identity card; **— de racionamiento** ration book.
(c) (Eccl) certificate of ordination; liturgical calendar.

cartografía nf cartography, mapmaking.

cartógrafo nm cartographer, mapmaker.

cartomancia nf fortunetelling (with cards).

cartón nm (a) (material) cardboard, pasteboard; (of book) board; **— alquitranado** tar paper; **— de**

encuadernar millboard; **— ondulado** corrugated cardboard; **— piedra** papier mâché.
(b) (*Art*) cartoon.
(c) (*container*) (cardboard) box, carton.
(d) (*SAm: Typ: angl*) cartoon; comic strip, strip cartoon.
cartoné *nm* (*Typ*): **en —** (bound) in boards.
cartuchera *nf* cartridge belt.
cartucho *nm* **(a)** (*Mil*) cartridge; cartridge case; **— sin bala, — en blanco** blank cartridge; **luchar hasta quemar el último —** to fight on to the last ditch.
(b) paper cone, paper cornet; (*of coins*) roll; (*SAm*) cornucopia.
Cartuja *nf* (*Eccl*) Carthusian order.
cartuja *nf* Carthusian monastery.
cartujano 1 *adj* Carthusian. **2** *nm* Carthusian.
cartujo *nm* Carthusian.
cartulario *nm* cartulary.
cartulina *nf* fine cardboard, pasteboard.
carura *nf* (*CAm, Ec, RPl*) **(a)** high price, expensiveness. **(b)** expensive thing.
casa *nf* **(a)** house; flat, apartment; building; **— de alquiler** block of flats, apartment block; **— de asistencia** (*Col, Mex*) boarding house; **— de azotea** penthouse; **— de baños** bathhouse; **—s baratas** low-cost housing; **— de bebidas** bar, saloon; **— de bombas** pumphouse; **— de campo** country house; **— de citas, — pública, — de putas** (*fam*), **— de tolerancia, — de vicio** brothel; **— consistorial** town hall; civic centre; **— de corrección** reformatory, remand home; **— de correos** post office; **— de departamentos** (*SAm*) apartment house (*US*); **— embrujada, — de fantasmas** haunted house; **— de fieras** zoo, menagerie; **— de guarda** lodge; **— de huéspedes** boarding house; **— de juego** gambling house; **— de labor, — de labranza** farm, farmhouse; **— de locos, — de orates** asylum; **— de maternidad** maternity hospital; **— de muñecas** doll's house; **— de pisos** block of flats; **— religiosa** monastery; convent; **— de salud** sanatorium, private hospital; **— de socorro** first-aid post; **— de vecindad** block of tenements, apartment house (*US*).
(b) (*with personal connotations*) home; residence, house; household; **— y comida** board and lodging; **¿dónde tiene Vd su —?** where is your home?; **— mortuoria** house of mourning, home of the deceased; **— paterna** parents' home; **— solariega** family seat, ancestral home; **es una — alegre** it's a happy home, it's a happy household; **ir a —** to go home; **ir hacia —** to head for home, go homewards; **ir a — de Juan** to go to John's house, go to John's place, go to John's; **salir de —** to leave home; **ir de — en —** to go from house to house; **estar en —** to be at home, be in; **¿está la señora en —?** is the lady in?, is the lady at home?; **están en — de los abuelos** they're at their grandparents'; **estar fuera de —** to be out, be away from home; **voy para —** I'm off home; **estar por la —** to be about the house; **de —** home (*attr*), household (*attr*); **sport, clothing** indoor; **animal** pet, family (*attr*); **estar de —** to be in one's ordinary clothes.
(c) (*home: phrases with verb*) **abandonar la —** to leave home, move out; **echar la — por la ventana** to go to enormous expense; to roll out the red carpet for someone; **franquear la — a uno** to open one's house to someone; **hacer —** to get rich; **llevar la —** to keep house, run the house; (*fam*) **to wear the trousers**; **cada uno manda en su —** one's home is one's castle; **poner —** to set up house; **sentirse como en su —** to feel at home; **no tener — ni hogar** to be homeless.
(d) (*courtesy formulae*) **Vd está en su —, aquí tiene Vd su —** you're always very welcome.
(e) (*Comm, Fin*) firm, business house (*also — de comercio*); **— armadora** shipbuilding company; **— de banca, — bancaria** banking house; **— central** head office; **— editorial** publishing house; **— de empeños** pawnshop; **— matriz** head office; parent company; **— de (la) moneda** mint.
(f) house, line, family; **— real** royal house; **la — de Borbón** the house of Bourbon.
(g) (*in games*) square.
casabe *nm* (*SAm*) cassava.
Casa *nf* **Blanca** White House.
casaca *nf* **(a)** dress coat; **— de montar** riding coat; **cambiar de —, volver la —** to turn one's coat, be a turncoat.
(b) (*fam*) wedding, marriage.
casación *nf* cessation, annulment.
casacón *nm* greatcoat.

casa-cuna *nf*, *pl* **casas-cuna** day nursery, crèche.
casada *nf* married woman.
casadero *adj* marriageable, of an age to be married.
casado 1 *adj* married; **mal —** unhappily married; **— y arrepentido** if you marry in haste you repent at leisure; **estar —** to be married (*con* to); **estar — a media carta** to live in sin.
2 *nm* **(a)** married man; **los —s** married men; married people; **los recién —s** the newlyweds.
(b) (*Typ*) imposition.
(c) (*SAm*) *two separate varieties of food eaten together*.
casal *nm* **(a)** country house; farmhouse; ancestral home. **(b)** (*RPl*) married couple; (*Zool*) pair.
casamata *nf* casemate.
casamentero *nm*, **casamentera** *nf* matchmaker.
casamiento *nm* marriage, wedding (ceremony); **— por amor** love match; **— de conveniencia** marriage of convenience; **— a la fuerza** forced marriage, shotgun marriage; **prometer a una joven en —** to betroth a girl (*con* to).
Casandra *f* Cassandra.
casapuerta *nf* entrance hall, vestibule.
casar[1] *nm* hamlet.
casar[2] [1a] **1** *vt* **(a)** (*subject: priest*) to marry, join in marriage, join in wedlock.
(b) (*subject: father*) to marry (off), give in marriage (*con* to).
(c) (*fig*) to pair, couple; to match; (*Typ*) to impose.
(d) (*Law*) to quash, annul.
2 *vi* **(a)** = *vr*.
(b) (*fig*) to match, harmonize.
3 casarse *vr* **(a)** to marry, get married; **A se casó con B** A married B; **¿cuándo tc vas a casar?** when are you getting married?; **volver a —, — en segundas nupcias** to marry again (*and see* nupcias).
(b) (*fig*) to match, harmonize.
casatienda *nf* shop with dwelling accommodation, shop with flat over.
casca *nf* **(a)** bark (for tanning). **(b)** grape skins.
cascabel *nm* (little) bell; **de — gordo** pretentious; **ser un —** (*fam*) to be a scatterbrain; **echar (or soltar) el —** to drop a hint; **poner el — al gato** to bell the cat.
cascabela *nf* (*CAm*) rattlesnake.
cascabelear [1a] **1** *vt* to take in (*fam*), raise the hopes of, beguile.
2 *vi* **(a)** (*SAm*) to jingle, tinkle.
(b) (*fig*) to act recklessly, behave frivolously, be inconsiderate.
(c) (*Chi*) to growl, grumble.
cascabeleo *nm* jingle, jingling, tinkling.
cascabelero 1 *adj* (*fam*) scatterbrained. **2** *nm*, **cascabelera** *nf* (*fam*) scatterbrain.
cascabillo *nm* **(a)** little bell. **(b)** (*Bot: of grain*) husk, chaff; (*of acorn*) cup.
cascada *nf* waterfall; cascade.
cascado *adj* **(a)** broken (down); *person* infirm, decrepit, worn out. **(b)** *voice* weak, unmelodious, cracked; *piano etc* tinny.
cascajo *nm* **(a)** (piece of) gravel; (*Archit etc*) rubble; (*of pots etc*) fragments, sherds.
(b) junk, rubbish, lumber; **estar hecho un —** (*fam*) to be a wreck.
cascajoso *adj* gritty, gravelly.
cascanueces *nm*, *pl* **cascanueces** nutcracker; **un —** a pair of nutcrackers.
cascar [1g] **1** *vt* **(a)** to crack, split, break (open); to crunch; *nut* to crack.
(b) (*fig*) *health* to shatter, undermine.
(c) (*fam*) to bash (*fam*), slosh (*fam*); (*Sport*) to beat hollow, wipe the floor with (*fam*).
2 *vi* **(a)** to chatter, talk too much.
(b) (*sl*) to kick the bucket (*sl*).
3 cascarse *vr* **(a)** to crack, split, break (open).
(b) (*of health*) to crack up; (*of voice*) to break, crack.
cáscara *nf* **(a)** (*of egg, nut, ruined building*) shell; (*of grain*) husk; (*of fruit*) rind, peel, skin; (*of tree*) bark; **— de huevo** eggshell; **— de limón** lemon peel; **— sagrada** (*Pharm*) cascara; **patatas cocidas con —** potatoes in their jackets; **ser de la — amarga** to be wild, be mischievous, (*Pol*) have radical ideas; **dar —s de novillo a** (*SAm*) to thrash.
(b) **¡—!** (*euph*) well I'm blowed!
(c) **—s** (*Col, Per: sl*) clothes.
cascarazo *nm* **(a)** (*Col, PR*) punch; (*Col*) lash. **(b)** (*PR*) swig of liquor (*fam*).
cascarear [1a] *vt* (*CAm, Col*) to bash (*fam*), slosh (*fam*).

cascarilla 1 *adj* (Arg, Cu, PR) touchy, peppery.
2 *nf* **(a)** (Arg, Cu, PR) quick-tempered person.
(b) (Per, RPl) medicinal herb; dried cacao leaves (*used as tea*).
cascarón *nm* (broken) eggshell; (Mex, PR) eggshell filled with confetti.
cascarrabias *nmf*, *pl* **cascarrabias** (*fam*) quick-tempered person, irritable sort.
cascarria *nf* (Arg) filth, grease; (Agr) sheep droppings.
cascarriento *adj* (Arg) filthy, greasy.
cascarrón *adj* (*fam*) gruff, abrupt, rough.
cascarudo 1 *adj* thick-shelled, thickskinned. **2** *nm* (Arg) beetles (*collectively*).
casco (a) (Mil *etc*) helmet; (*part of hat*) crown; **— de acero** steel helmet; **— de corcho** sun helmet; **— protector** crash helmet; **— sideral** space helmet.
(b) (Anat) skull; (*fam*) brains, head, nut (*sl*); **alegre de —s, ligero de —s** scatterbrained, frivolous; **romper los —s a uno** to bash someone's head in (*fam*); **romperse los —s** to rack one's brains; **sentar los —s** to quieten down, settle down, learn to behave oneself; **tener los —s a la jineta** to be scatterbrained.
(c) (*of pot*) fragment, sherd; (Mex) returnable soft drink bottle.
(d) (*of onion*) skin, coat.
(e) cask, barrel.
(f) (Naut) hull; (*pej*) old hulk.
(g) (Zool) hoof.
(h) (Mech) casing.
(i) (*of city*) inner part, central area; (Mex: Agr) compound, main buildings and surrounding land; (Arg: *of estate*) part, section.
(j) (Per) chest, breast.
(k) (Arg, Cu, Mex: *of fruit*) quarter, segment.
cascote *nm* (piece of) rubble, (piece of) debris.
cascundear [1a] *vt* (CAm) to beat, thrash.
cáseo 1 *adj* cheesy. **2** *nm* curd.
caseoso *adj* cheesy.
casera *nf* landlady (*owner*); housekeeper; *see also* **casero 2.**
casería (a) country house. **(b)** (SAm) customers, clientèle.
caserío (a) country house. **(b)** hamlet, settlement, group of dwellings.
casero 1 *adj* **(a)** domestic, household (*attr*); *bread etc* home-made; *cloth* homespun; *remedy* household; *dress* house (*attr*), indoor, ordinary; *gathering, party* family (*attr*).
(b) *person* home-loving.
2 *nm* **(a)** landlord (*owner*); caretaker; porter, concierge, janitor (US); tenant, occupier; (Comm) house agent.
(b) (*also* **casera** *nf*) stay-at-home, home-lover.
(c) (SAm: *also* **casera** *nf*) customer, client; (Cu, Chi, Ec, Per) hawker, huckster.
caserón *nm* large (ramshackle) house, barracks (of a place).
caseta *nf* (*in market*) stall, stand, booth; (*at exhibition*) stand; (*at fair*) sideshow, booth; (Sport) pavilion; (*at swimming pool*) cubicle, changing room; (*on beach*) bathing hut; (*in country*) cottage; **— de perro** kennel, doghouse (US); **— del timón** (Naut) wheelhouse.
casi *adv* almost, nearly; **— —** very nearly, as near as makes no difference; **está —terminado** it's almost finished, it's well-nigh finished; **— nada** next to nothing; **— nunca** almost never, hardly ever; **300 o —** some 300, 300 or thereabouts.
casilla *nf* **(a)** (Archit) hut, cabin, shed; keeper's lodge; (*in market etc*) booth, stall; (Rail) platelayer's hut, guard's hut.
(b) (Aut, Rail: *of engine*) cab.
(c) (Theat) box office.
(d) pigeonhole; (*of box etc*) compartment; (*of paper*) ruled column, section; (Chess *etc*) square; (Bol, Chi, Per, Urug) post office box (number).
(e) (Ec) lavatory.
(f) (Cu) bird trap.
(g) sacar a uno de sus —s to shake someone up, shake someone out of his complacency; to make someone cross, get someone worked up; **salir de sus —s** to fly off the handle (*fam*).
casillero *nm* (set of) pigeonholes.
casimba *nf* (SAm) = **cacimba.**
casimir *nm* cashmere.
casimiro *adj* (SAm) cross-eyed.
casinista *nm* clubman.
casino *nm* club; social club, political club; casino.
Casio *m* Cassius.
casita *nf* small house; cottage.

caso *nm* **(a)** (Gram) case.
(b) (Med) case; **es un — perdido** (*hum*) he's a dead loss, he's a disaster.
(c) (*in experiment etc*) case, subject; **soy un — difícil** I'm a difficult subject.
(d) case, instance; event, happening; circumstances; **— de autos** (Law) case in hand; **— fortuito** (Law) act of God; unforeseen circumstance; **el — Hess** the Hess affair, the Hess case; **el — Romeo-Julieta** the Romeo and Juliet affair; the trouble between Romeo and Juliet; **en el — de Eslobodia** in the case of Slobodia; **en — de** in the event of; **— que venga, en (el) — de que venga** in case he should come, should he come, in the event of his coming; **y en el — contrario** and if not, and if it should not be so; **en el mejor de los —s** at best; **en tal —** in such a case; **en todo —** in any case, at all events; **en último —** as a last resort, in the last resort; **y en su — también otros** and where appropriate, others also; **según el —** as the case may be; **según lo requiera el —** as the case may require; **dado el — que . . .** supposing (that) . . .; **el — es que . . .** the fact is that . . .; **creerse en el — de + *infin*** to think fit to + *infin*; **hablar al —** to speak to the point; **hacer al —, venir al —** to be relevant; to be appropriate; **no hacer al —, no venir al —** to be beside the point; **pongamos por — que . . .** let us suppose that . . .; **pongamos por — a X** let us take X as an example; **servir para el —** to serve one's purpose; **¡vamos al —!** let's get to the point!; let's get down to business!; **verse en el — de + *infin*** to be compelled to + *infin*.
(e) notice; **hacer — a** to heed, notice; **no me hacen —** they don't pay me any attention; **¡no haga Vd —!** take no notice!, don't worry!; **maldito el — que me hace** a fat lot of notice he takes of me; **hacer — de** to pay attention to; to take into account; **sin hacer — de eso** regardless of that; **hacer — omiso de** to ignore, fail to mention, deliberately pass over.
casorio *nm* (*fam*) hasty marriage, unwise marriage.
caspa *nf* dandruff, scurf.
Caspio: Mar *m* **—** Caspian Sea.
caspiroleta *nf* (Col, Cu, Chi, Ec, Per) eggnog.
cáspita *interj* my goodness!; come off it!
casquete *nm* skullcap; (Mil) helmet; (Mech) cap; **— de hielo** icecap; **— polar** polar cap.
casquijo *nm* gravel.
casquillo *nm* **(a)** tip, cap; (*of stick*) ferrule, tip; (Mech) sleeve, bushing; (Mil) cartridge case. **(b)** (SAm) horseshoe.
casquinona *nf* (Col) beer bottle; beer.
casquivano *adj* scatterbrained.
casta *nf* **(a)** caste; breed, race; (*fig*) class; quality; **de —** of quality, of breeding; **carecer de —** to lack breeding, have no class; **eso le viene de —** that comes naturally to him.
(b) (Mex: Typ) fount.
castamente *adv* chastely, purely.
castaña *nf* **(a)** chestnut; **— del Brasil, — de Pará** Brazil nut; **— de Indias** horse chestnut; **dar (*or* meter) la — a uno** to swindle someone, make a fool out of someone; **pelar la —** (*of lovers*) to do their courting; to chat, talk sweet nothings; **sacar a uno las —s del fuego** to pull someone's chestnuts out of the fire for him.
(b) (*of hair*) bun, chignon.
castañar *nm* chestnut grove.
castañazo *nm* (RPl) bash (*fam*), punch.
castañero *nm*, **castañera** *nf* chestnut seller.
castañeta *nf* **(a)** snap (of the fingers). **(b)** **—s** (Mus) castanets.
castañetazo *nm* snap, crack, click.
castañetear [1a] **1** *vt* **(a)** *fingers* to snap. **(b)** (Mus) to play on the castanets.
2 *vi* **(a)** (*of fingers*) to snap; to click; (*of plates etc*) to clatter; (*of teeth*) to chatter, rattle; (*of bones*) to crack; (*of knees*) to knock together; **— con los dedos** to snap one's fingers.
(b) (Mus) to play the castanets.
castañeteo *nm* **(a)** snap(ping); click(ing); clatter(ing); chatter(ing); rattling; crack(ing); knocking. **(b)** (Mus) sound of the castanets.
castaño 1 *adj* chestnut(-coloured), brown.
2 *nm* chestnut tree; **— de Indias** horse chestnut tree; **esto pasa de — oscuro** this is really too much, this is beyond a joke.
castañuelas *nfpl* castanets; **estar como unas —s** to be very merry, be in high spirits.
castañuelo *adj* chestnut(-coloured), brown.

castellanizar [1f] *vt* to hispanicize, give a Spanish form to.
castellano 1 *adj* Castilian; Spanish. **2** *nm*, **castellana** *nf* Castilian; Spaniard. **3** *nm* (*language*) Castilian, Spanish.
castellonense 1 *adj* of Castellón de la Plana. **2** *nmf* native (*or* inhabitant) of Castellón de la Plana; los —s the people of Castellón de la Plana.
castellonés *adj*, *n* = **castellonense**.
casticidad *nf* (**a**) (*Ling*) purity, correctness. (**b**) (*Bio*) purity of breed(ing); racial purity. (**c**) traditional character; authenticity, genuineness.
casticismo *nm* (**a**) (*Ling*) purity, correctness. (**b**) traditionalism; = **casticidad** (c).
casticista 1 *adj* purist. **2** *nmf* purist.
castidad *nf* chastity, purity.
castigador *nm* (**a**) punisher. (**b**) ladykiller; (*pej*) seducer, libertine.
castigar [1h] *vt* (**a**) to punish (*de*, *por* for); (*Sport*) to penalize (*por* for).
 (**b**) (*fig*) to castigate; *flesh* to mortify; (*of disease etc*) to afflict, affect; (*emotionally*) to afflict, grieve; (*physically*) to strain, use hard; — **mucho a un caballo** to ride a horse hard.
 (**c**) (*fig*) *style etc* to refine; *text* to correct, revise.
 (**d**) (*Comm*) to write down.
 (**e**) (*Mex: Mech*) to tighten up.
castigo *nm* (**a**) punishment; (*Sport etc*) penalty; fine. (**b**) (*fig*) castigation; mortification, affliction. (**c**) (*fig*) refinement; correction, revision.
Castilla *nf* Castile; — **la Nueva** New Castile; — **la Vieja** Old Castile; ¡**ancha es** —! it takes all sorts!
castilla *nf* (*Arg*, *Par*, *Mex*) (**a**) (*language*) Castilian, Spanish; **hablar la** — to speak Spanish. (**b**) (*Hist*) **de** — from Castile, from Spain, from the home country.
castillejo *nm* (**a**) (*Archit*) scaffolding. (**b**) (*child's*) go-cart; playpen.
castillo *nm* castle; (*of elephant*) howdah; —**s en el aire** castles in the air; — **de fuego** firework set piece; — **de naipes** house of cards; — **de proa** forecastle.
castizo *adj* (**a**) (*Ling*) pure, correct.
 (**b**) (*Bio*) purebred, pedigree; racially pure; pure-blooded; untainted.
 (**c**) (*fig*) traditional; pure, authentic; genuine; **es un tipo** — (*fam*) he's one of the best.
casto *adj* chaste, pure.
castor *nm* beaver.
castoreño *nm* beaver (*hat*); (*Taur*) picador's hat.
castoreo *nm* (*Pharm*) castor.
castra *nf* (*Bot*) pruning; pruning season.
castración *nf* (**a**) castration, gelding. (**b**) (*Bot*) pruning. (**c**) extraction of honeycombs.
castrado 1 *adj* castrated. **2** *nm* eunuch.
castrar [1a] *vt* (**a**) to castrate, geld; *cat etc* to doctor (*euph*).
 (**b**) (*Bot*) to prune, cut back.
 (**c**) *hives* to extract honeycombs from.
 (**d**) (*fig*) to mutilate, impair, weaken.
castrense *adj* army (*attr*), military; **las glorias** —**s** military glories.
casual *adj* (**a**) fortuitous, accidental, chance. (**b**) incidental. (**c**) (*Gram*) case (*attr*); **desinencia** — case ending.
casualidad *nf* (**a**) chance, accident; coincidence; **fue una pura** — it was sheer coincidence, it was entirely a matter of chance; **por** — by chance; ¿**tienes por** — **una pluma?** do you have a pen, by any chance?, do you happen to have a pen? **me encontraba allí por** — I happened to be there, I chanced to be there; **un día entró por** — one day he dropped in; **da la** — **que** . . . it (so) happens that . . .; **dio la** — **que** . . . it happened that . . ., luck had it that . . .; ¡**qué** —! what a coincidence!; ¡**qué** — **verle aquí!** what a coincidence meeting you here!, fancy meeting you here!
 (**b**) —**es** (*CAm: angl*) casualties.
casualmente *adv* by chance, by accident, for-tuitously; — **le vi ayer** I happened to see him yesterday, as it happens I saw him yesterday.
casuario *nm* cassowary.
casuca *nf*, **casucha** *nf* hovel, shack; slum.
casuista *nmf* casuist.
casuística *nf* casuistry.
casulla *nf* chasuble.
cata[1] *nf* (**a**) (*in general*) tasting, testing, sampling; blending.
 (**b**) taste, sample.
 (**c**) (*SAm*) trial excavation, test bore; prospecting.
 (**d**) **ir en** — **de algo** (*fam*) to go looking for something.

cata[2] *nf* (*Bol*, *Chi*, *Mex*, *RPl*) parrot.
catabre *nm* (*Col*, *Ven*) gourd; basket.
catacaldos *nm*, *pl* **catacaldos** (**a**) rolling stone; quitter, person who starts things but gives up easily; (*Art etc*) dilettante.
 (**b**) busybody, meddler.
cataclismo *nm* cataclysm.
catacumbas *nfpl* catacombs.
catador *nm* (*of tea*, *wine etc*) taster, blender, sampler; (*fig*) connoisseur.
catadura[1] *nf* tasting, sampling, blending.
catadura[2] *nf* (*fam*) mug (*sl*), looks, face.
catafalco *nm* catafalque.
catajarria *nf* (*Ven*) string, line, series.
catalán 1 *adj* Catalan, Catalonian. **2** *nm*, **catalana** *nf* Catalan, Catalonian. **3** *nm* (*language*) Catalan.
catalanismo *nm* (**a**) (*Pol*) *movement for Catalan autonomy*. (**b**) (*Ling*) catalanism, word (*or* phrase *etc*) borrowed from Catalan.
catalanista 1 *adj* that supports (*etc*) Catalan auto-nomy; **el movimiento** — the movement for Catalan autonomy; **la familia es muy** — the family strongly supports Catalan autonomy.
 2 *nmf* supporter (*etc*) of Catalan autonomy, Catalan nationalist, Catalan separatist.
catalejo *nm* spyglass, telescope.
catalepsia *nf* catalepsy.
cataléptico 1 *adj* cataleptic. **2** *nm*, **cataléptica** *nf* cataleptic.
Catalina *f* Catherine.
catalinaria *nf* cabal, conspiracy.
catalizador *nm* catalyst.
catalogación *nf* cataloguing.
catalogar [1h] *vt* to catalogue.
catálogo *nm* catalogue.
Cataluña *f* Catalonia.
catamarán *nm* catamaran.
cataplasma *nf* (**a**) (*Med*) poultice. (**b**) (*fam*) bore.
cataplum *interj* bang!, crash!
catapulta *nf* catapult.
catapún *adj*: **una cosa del año** — an antiquated thing, a totally obsolete thing.
catar [1a] *vt* (**a**) to taste, sample, try; (*fig*) to examine, inspect, have a look at; (*fig*) to esteem.
 (**b**) to look at; to look out for; ¡**cata!**, ¡**cátale!** just look at him!; ¡**cátate eso!** you just think!
 (**c**) *hives* to extract honeycombs from.
catarata *nf* (**a**) (*Geog*) waterfall, falls; cataract; **C**—**s de Niágara** Niagara Falls; **C**—**s de Victoria** Victoria Falls.
 (**b**) (*Med*) cataract.
catarral *adj* catarrhal.
catarriento *adj* (*SAm*) = **catarroso**.
catarro *nm* cold; catarrh; — **crónico del pecho** chest trouble; **coger un** — to catch a cold.
catarroso *adj* subject to colds; having catarrh, suffering from catarrh.
catarsis *nf* catharsis.
catártico *adj* cathartic.
catasalsas *nm*, *pl* **catasalsas** = **catacaldos**.
catástrofe *nf* catastrophe.
catastrófico *adj* catastrophic.
catatán *nm* (*Chi*) punishment.
catauro *nm* (*Cu*) basket.
catavinos *nm*, *pl* **catavinos** wine taster, wine sampler; (*fam*) boozer.
cate *nm* (*sl*) punch, bash (*fam*); **dar** — **a uno** (*Univ*) to plough someone (*sl*).
catear [1a] *vt* (**a**) to investigate; to try, sample.
 (**b**) (*Univ: sl*) to plough (*sl*).
 (**c**) (*Arg*, *Chi*, *Mex: Min*) *land* to make test borings in, explore, prospect.
 (**d**) (*Mex: of police*) to search, make a search in.
catecismo *nm* catechism.
catecúmeno *nm*, **catecúmena** *nf* catechumen; (*fig*) convent.
cátedra 1 *nf* (**a**) (*Univ*) chair, professorship; lecture-ship; (*School*) senior teaching post (*in a grammar school*); — **del Espíritu Santo** (*Eccl*) pulpit; **explicar una** — to hold a chair (*de* of); **hacer oposiciones para una** —, **opositar a una** — to try to win a chair (*etc*) by public competitive examina-tion; **sentar** — **sobre un argumento** to take one's stand on an argument.
 (**b**) (*Univ*, *School*) subject.
 (**c**) lecture room.
 (**d**) group of students, class.
 (**e**) (*Cu*, *Ven*) wonder, marvel; **es** —, **está la** — it's marvellous.
 2 *adj* (*Cu*, *Ven*) wonderful, marvellous, excellent.
catedral *nf* cathedral.

catedrática nf (a) (Univ) woman professor, woman lecturer; professor's wife. (b) — **de instituto** grammar-school teacher.

catedrático nm (a) (Univ) professor, lecturer. (b) — **de instituto** grammar-school teacher.

categoría nf category; class, group; rank, standing; quality; prestige; **de** — important; distinguished, high-ranking, prominent; **es hombre de cierta** — he is a man of some standing; **de baja** — of low quality; of low rank; **de segunda** — (pej) second-rate; **no tiene** — he has no standing; **tiene** — **de ministro** he has the rank of minister.

categóricamente adv categorically.

categórico adj categorical; lie downright, outright; order strict, express.

catenaria nf (Rail, Elec) overhead power cable.

catequizar [1f] vt (a) (Eccl) to catechize, instruct in Christian doctrine. (b) (fam) to win over, talk round.

caterva nf host, throng, crowd; **venir en** — to come in a throng, come thronging.

catéter nm catheter.

catimbao nm (a) (Chi, Per) clown, carnival clown. (b) (Per) short fat man.

catinga nf (a) (Bol, RPl) body odour; (of animals etc) strong smell. (b) (Chi: in sailors' parlance) soldier.

catingoso adj (Arg, Bol), **catingudo** adj (Bol, RPl) smelly, having a nasty smell.

catire adj (SAm), **catiro** adj (SAm) blond, fair; reddish, red-haired.

catita nf (SAm) parrot.

catitear [1a] vi (Arg) to dodder, shake with old age.

catisumba(da) nf (CAm) lot, great number; **una** — **de** a lot of.

catoche nm (Mex) bad mood, bad temper.

catódico adj cathodic, cathode (attr).

cátodo nm cathode.

catolicismo nm (Roman) Catholicism.

católico 1 adj (a) (Eccl) (Roman) Catholic; **no** — non-Catholic.
    (b) (fig) doctrine true, infallible; certain; (fam) right, as it should be; **no estar muy** — not to be quite right, be none too good, have something up (with it); (Med) to be under the weather.
    2 nm, **católica** nf Catholic; **no** — non-Catholic.

Catón m Cato.

catorce adj fourteen.

catorceno adj fourteenth.

catorro nm (Mex) punch, blow.

catre nm (a) cot; (Chi, Per) bedstead; — **de tijera**, — **de viento** (Mex, Per, Ven) campbed, folding bed. (b) (Arg) — **de balsa** raft.

catrecillo nm campstool, folding seat.

catrera nf (Arg) bunk, bed.

catrín nm (CAm, Mex) toff (fam), dude (US).

Catulo m Catullus.

caucasiano (Geog), **caucásico** (by race) 1 adj Caucasian. 2 nm, **caucasiana** nf, **caucásica** nf Caucasian.

Cáucaso m Caucasus.

cauce nm riverbed; (Agr) irrigation channel.

caución nf (a) caution, wariness. (b) (Law) pledge, security, bond; bail; **admitir a uno a** — to grant someone bail.

caucionar [1a] vt (a) to prevent, guard against. (b) (Law) to bail, go bail for.

cauch nm (CAm, PR: angl) couch.

cauchal nm rubber plantation.

cauchar 1 nm (Col, Ec) rubber plantation. 2 vi (Col, Ec) to extract rubber from trees.

cauchera nf (a) rubber plant, rubber tree. (b) (Col, Ec, Per) rubber plantation.

cauchero 1 adj rubber (attr); **industria cauchera** rubber industry. 2 nm (SAm) worker in a rubber plantation, rubber worker.

caucho[1] nm (a) rubber; — **esponjoso** foam rubber; — **natural** natural rubber; — **sintético** synthetic rubber.
    (b) raincoat, mac; (Col) waterproof blanket; (Col) rubber shoe; (Ven) tyre.

caucho[2] nm (PR: angl) couch.

caudal[1] nm (a) (of river) volume, flow.
    (b) plenty, abundance, wealth; (of person etc) fortune, wealth; property; — **social** assets of a partnership.

caudal[2] adj caudal.

caudaloso adj (a) river large, carrying much water. (b) copious, abundant; person etc wealthy, rich.

caudillaje nm (a) leadership; **bajo el** — **de** under the leadership of. (b) (SAm: pej) tyranny, rule by political bosses.

caudillo nm (a) leader, chief; head of state; **el C—** (Spain) the Leader, the Head of State. (b) (SAm: pej) tyrant, political boss.

caula nf (CAm, Chi) plot, intrigue, cabal.

cauri nm cowrie.

causa[1] nf (a) cause; reason, motive; (for complaint) grounds; **veamos qué** — **tiene esto** let us see what is the reason for this; — **final** final cause; — **primera** first cause; **a** — **de**, **por** — **de** on account of, because of, owing to; **por mi** — for my sake; **por poca** —, **sin** — for no good reason.
    (b) (Pol etc) cause; **hacer** — **común con** to make common cause with.
    (c) (Law) lawsuit; case, trial; prosecution; **instruir** — to take legal proceedings.

causa[2] nf (a) (Chi) snack, bite between meals; light meal, picnic lunch. (b) (Per) potato salad.

causal 1 adj causal. 2 nf reason, grounds.

causalidad nf causality; causation.

causante 1 adj causing, originating; **el coche** — **del accidente** the car which caused the accident, the car responsible for the accident.
    2 nmf (a) causer, originator.
    (b) (Mex) taxpayer.
    3 nf (SAm) cause.

causar [1a] vt to cause; expense, work to create, entail, make; impression to create, make; anger, protest to provoke; — **risa a uno** to make someone laugh.

causear [1a] vi (Chi) to have a snack, have a bite between meals; to have a light meal, have a picnic lunch.

causeo nm (Chi) = **causa**[2].

causativo adj causative.

cáustico adj caustic (also fig).

cautamente adv cautiously, warily, carefully.

cautela nf (a) caution, cautiousness, wariness; **con mucha** — very cautiously; **tener la** — **de** + infin to take the precaution of + ger. (b) (pej) cunning.

cautelar [1a] 1 vt to prevent, guard against. 2 **cautelarse** vr to be on one's guard (de against).

cautelosamente adv (a) cautiously, warily, carefully. (b) (pej) cunningly, craftily.

cauteloso adj (a) cautious, wary, careful. (b) (pej) cunning, crafty.

cauterio nm (a) cautery, cauterization. (b) (fig) eradication.

cauterizar [1f] vt (a) to cauterize. (b) (fig) to eradicate.

cautivar [1a] vt (a) (Mil etc) to capture, take prisoner. (b) (fig) to charm, captivate, win over; to enthrall; heart to steal, captivate.

cautiverio nm, **cautividad** nf captivity; (fig) bondage, serfdom.

cautivo 1 adj captive. 2 nm, **cautiva** nf captive.

cauto adj cautious, wary, careful.

cava nf cultivation, digging and hoeing.

cavador nm digger; excavator; — **de oro** gold digger.

cavadura nf digging, excavation.

cavar [1a] 1 vt hole to dig; well to sink; (Agr) to dig over, hoe, fork over.
    2 vi (a) to dig; (of wound) to go deep.
    (b) (fig) to delve (en into), go deeply (en into); to meditate profoundly (en on).

cavazón nf digging, excavation.

caverna nf cave, cavern.

cavernícola 1 adj (a) cave-dwelling, cave (attr); **hombre** — caveman.
    (b) (Pol: fam) reactionary.
    2 nmf (a) cave dweller.
    (b) (Pol: fam) reactionary, backwoodsman.

cavernoso adj (a) cavernous; cave (attr); mountain full of caves, honeycombed with caves. (b) sound, voice hollow.

caviar nm caviar(e).

cavidad nf cavity; hollow, space; — **nasal** nasal cavity.

cavilación nf (a) deep thought, rumination. (b) (unfounded) suspicion, apprehension.

cavilar [1a] vt to ponder, consider closely; to brood over, be obsessed with.

cavilosear [1a] vi (PR) to harbour illusions; (PR) to cavil; (CAm) to gossip.

cavilosidad nf (unfounded) suspicion, apprehension.

caviloso adj (a) brooding, obsessed; suspicious, mistrustful.
    (b) (CAm) gossipy, backbiting.
    (c) (Col) quarrelsome, touchy, belligerent.

cayado nm staff, stick; (Agr) crook; (Eccl) crozier.

cayo nm (Ant) islet, reef, key; **C— Hueso** Key West.

cayubro adj (Col) reddish-blond, red-haired.

cayuca nf (Cu, PR) head, bean (sl).

cayuco nm (Cu, PR, Ven) dugout canoe.

caz nm millrace.

caza 1 nf (a) (in general) hunting; shooting, sport; (una —) hunt; shoot; chase, pursuit; — **furtiva** poaching, illegal hunting; — **de grillos** fool's errand, wild-goose chase; — **del hombre** manhunt; — **con hurón** ferreting; — **del jabalí** boar hunt(ing); — **con papelillos** paper chase; — **de patos** duck shoot(ing); — **submarina** underwater fishing; — **del tesoro** treasure hunt; — **del zorro** fox-hunt(ing); **andar a (la)** — **de** to go hunting for; **dar** — to give chase, go in pursuit; **dar** — **a** to hunt, chase, go after; to hunt down; **dar** — **a un empleo** to hunt for a job; **ir a la** —, **ir de** — to go hunting, go (out) shooting.
(b) game; — **mayor** big game; — **menor** small game; **levantar la** — to put up the game, (fig) start the ball rolling.
2 nm (Aer) fighter, fighter-plane; — **de escolta** escort fighter; — **nocturno** night-fighter.

cazabe nm (Ant) = **casabe**.

caza-bombardero nm fighter-bomber.

cazaclavos nm, pl **cazaclavos** claw-hammer, nail-puller.

cazadero nm hunting ground.

cazador nm (a) hunter; huntsman; — **de alforja**, — **de pieles** trapper; — **de cabezas** headhunter; — **furtivo** poacher; — **de zorros** foxhunter, huntsman.
(b) (Mil) chasseur.

cazadora nf (a) huntress. (b) hunting jacket; — **de piel** leather jacket.

cazagenios nm, pl **cazagenios** talent scout, talent spotter.

cazamoscas nm, pl **cazamoscas** (Orn) flycatcher.

cazar [1f] vt (a) to hunt; to chase, pursue; to go after; (esp fig) to hunt down, track down, run to earth; **le cacé por fin en la tienda** I eventually ran him down in the shop.
(b) to catch; total, game etc to bag; job etc to land, get; (pej) to get hold of by trickery, wangle (fam); person to win over (by flattery); (pej) to take in (fam); —**las al vuelo** to be pretty sharp.
(c) to catch out.

cazasubmarinos nm, pl **cazasubmarinos** submarine chaser.

cazatalentos nm, pl **cazatalentos** talent scout, talent spotter.

cazcalear [1a] vi (fam) to fuss around, buzz about.

cazcarrias nfpl splashes of mud on one's clothes.

cazcarriento adj splashed with mud, mud-stained.

cazo nm (a) saucepan; — **de cola** gluepot; — **eléctrico** electric kettle. (b) ladle, dipper.

cazolero nm = **cominero**.

cazoleta nf (a) (small) pan; (of pipe) bowl; (of shield) boss. (b) (of sword) guard. (c) (Mech) housing.

cazón nm dogfish.

cazonete nm (Naut) toggle.

cazuela nf (a) (Cook) pan, casserole; (meal) casserole; (SAm) chicken stew. (b) (Theat) gallery, gods.

cazumbrón nm cooper.

cazurro adj surly, sullen.

cazuz nm ivy.

ce¹ interj hey!

ce² nf name of the letter c; — **por** be down to the tiniest detail, leaving nothing whatsoever out; **por** — **o por be** somehow or other.

ceba nf (a) (Agr) fattening. (b) (of gun) charge, priming. (c) (of furnace) stoking.

cebada nf barley; — **perlada** pearl barley.

cebadal nm barley field.

cebadera nf (a) nosebag. (b) (Tech) hopper.

cebadero nm (a) barley dealer.
(b) leading mule (of a team).
(c) feeding place.
(d) (Tech) mouth for charging a furnace.

cebado adj (SAm) animal man-eating.

cebadura nf (a) (Agr) fattening.
(b) (of gun) priming; (of furnace) stoking.
(c) (Arg) brewing, making (of maté).
(d) (Arg: of coffee, maté) grounds, dregs.

cebar [1a] **1** vt (a) (Agr) to fatten (up), feed (up) (con on).
(b) fire, furnace to feed, stoke (up); gun, lamp, pump to prime; firework to light, set off.
(c) hook, line, trap to bait.
(d) passions etc to feed, nourish; anger to inflame; hope to stimulate.
(e) (SAm) maté to make, brew, prepare and serve.
2 vi (a) of nut etc) to grip, catch, go on; (of nail) to go in.

3 cebarse vr (a) (CR, Mex: of shot, firework) to fail to go off.
(b) — **en** to vent one's fury on; to batten on, prey upon; (of plague etc) to rage among; (of fire) to devour, rage in.
(c) — **en un estudio** to devote oneself to a study, become absorbed in a study.
(d) — **en la sangre** to gloat over the blood(shed), revel in the blood(shed).

cebellina nf (Zool) sable.

cebiche nm (Per) fish marinaded with lime juice.

cebo nm (a) (Agr) feed, food.
(b) (of gun) charge, priming; (Tech) fuel, oven load.
(c) (Fish) bait; (fig) bait, lure, incentive; — **vivo** live bait.

cebolla nf (a) onion; (of tulip etc) bulb; — **escalonia** shallot. (b) (SAm: hum) watch.

cebollana nf chive.

cebollino nm young onion, spring onion, onion for transplanting; onion seed; chive.

cebollita 1 nf: — **perla** small onion, cocktail onion.
2 nm (Arg) young boy, lad.

cebollón nm (Chi, RPl) old bachelor.

cebollona nf (Chi, RPl) old maid.

cebón 1 adj fat, fattened. **2** nm fattened animal.

ceboruco nm (Cu) reef; (Mex) rough rocky place; (PR) brush, scrub(land).

cebra nf zebra.

cebú nm zebu.

ceca nf: **andar (or ir) de la** — **a la Meca** to go hither and thither, chase about all over the place.

cecear [1a] vi to lisp; to pronounce [s] as [θ].

ceceo nm lisp; pronunciation of [s] as [θ].

ceceoso adj lisping, having a lisp.

Cecilia f Cecily.

Cecilio m Cecil.

cecina nf dried meat, smoked meat; corned beef; **estar como una** — to be terribly thin.

cedazo nm sieve.

ceder [2a] **1** vt to hand over, give up; to yield (up); to part with; territory to cede; property to transfer, make over; (Sport) ball to pass; see **paso** etc.
2 vi (a) to give in, yield (a to); **no ceden fácilmente a las innovaciones** they do not give in (or give way) easily to innovations; **no cede a nadie en experiencia** he is inferior to none in experience; — **de una pretensión** to give up a claim, renounce a claim.
(b) to diminish, decline, go down; (of fever, wind etc) to abate.
(c) (of floor, rope etc) to give, give way, sag.

cedilla nf cedilla.

cedizo adj meat high, tainted.

cedro nm cedar.

cédula nf certificate, document; form, blank, (slip of) paper; (official) order, decree; (Comm) warrant; — **de aduana** customs permit; — **en blanco** blank cheque; — **de cambio** bill of exchange; — **personal**, — **de vecindad** identity card; — **real** royal letter patent; **dar** — **a uno** to license someone.

cefalea nf severe headache, migraine.

cefálico adj cephalic.

céfiro nm zephyr.

cegador adj blinding; **brillo** — blinding glare.

cegajoso adj weepy, bleary-eyed.

cegar [1h and 1k] **1** vt (a) person to blind, make blind.
(b) (fig) passage, pipe to block up, stop up; hole to fill up; door, window to wall up.
2 vi to go blind, become blind(ed).
3 cegarse vr (fig) to become blinded (de by).

cegato adj short-sighted.

cegatón adj (SAm) short-sighted.

cegatoso adj = **cegajoso**.

ceguedad nf, **ceguera** nf blindness (also fig); — **para los colores** colour blindness; — **nocturna** night blindness.

Ceilán m Ceylon.

ceilanés 1 adj Ceylonese. **2** nm, **celanesa** nf Ceylonese.

ceja nf (a) (Anat) eyebrow; **arquear las** —**s** to raise one's eyebrows; **fruncir las** —**s** to knit one's brows, frown; **meterse algo entre** — **y** — to get something firmly into one's head; **quemarse las** —**s** to burn the midnight oil; **tener a uno entre** — **y** — to look askance at someone; to have a grudge against someone; **tomar a uno entre** — **y** — to take a dislike to someone.
(b) (fig: Tech) rim, flange; (Sew) edging; (Archit) projection; (of hill) brow, crown; (Meteorol) cloud-cap; (Mus) bridge; (SAm) edge of a wood; belt of trees, copse.

cejar [1a] *vi* to move back, go back; (*fig*) to give way, back down; (*in argument etc*) to climb down; (*in effort*) to relax, slacken, weaken; **no** — to keep it up, keep going, hold out; **sin** — unflinchingly, undaunted; **no** — **en sus esfuerzos** to keep up one's efforts; **no** — **en su trabajo** to keep on with one's work.

cejijunto *adj* with bushy eyebrows; having brows that meet; (*fig*) scowling, frowning.

cejudo *adj* black-browed, with bushy eyebrows.

celada *nf* (a) ambush, trap; (*fig*) trick, ruse; **caer en la** — to fall into the trap. (b) (*Mil: Hist*) helmet; (*Her*) helmet, sallet.

celador *nm* (*of building etc*) watchman, guard; (*of library, museum*) attendant; (*at exam*) invigilator; (*Tech*) maintenance man; (*Elec*) linesman; (*Aut*) parking attendant; (*CAm, Mex*) prison warder.

celadora *nf* (*of library, museum*) attendant.

celaje *nm* (a) sky with clouds of varied hue; (*Naut*) clouds; —s sunset clouds, sky with scudding clouds. (b) (*CAm*) cloud painting; cloud effect. (c) (*Archit*) skylight. (d) (*fig*) (promising) sign, token. (e) (*Per, PR, SD*) ghost; **como un** — like lightning, in a flash.

celar[1] [1a] **1** *vt* to watch over, keep a watchful eye on, keep a check on; — **las leyes** to see that the laws are kept; — **la justicia** to see that justice is done.
2 *vi*: — **por**, — **sobre** to watch over.

celar[2] [1a] *vt* to conceal, cover, hide.

celda *nf* cell; — **de aislamiento** (**para furiosos**) padded cell; — **de castigo** solitary confinement cell.

celdilla *nf* (*of beehive*) cell; cavity, hollow; pigeonhole; (*Archit*) niche.

cele *adj* (*CAm*) light green.

celebérrimo *adj superl* of **célebre**.

celebración *nf* (a) celebration; holding; conclusion; solemnization. (b) praise; applause; welcome; preaching.

celebrante *nm* (*Eccl*) celebrant, officiating priest.

celebrar [1a] **1** *vt* (a) *anniversary, happy event etc* to celebrate; *meeting* to hold; *interview, talks* to have, hold (*con* with); *treaty* to conclude (*con* with); *feast, festivity* to keep, celebrate; *marriage* to perform, solemnize; *mass* to say. (b) to praise; to applaud, welcome; *advantages* to preach, dwell on; *joke* to laugh at, find amusing; — + *infin* to be glad to + *infin*, be delighted to + *infin*; **lo celebro** I'm very glad; **lo celebro mucho por él** I'm very glad for his sake.
2 *vi* (a) (*Eccl*) to say mass. (b) to be glad, be delighted. (c) (*Cu*) to fall in love.
3 celebrarse *vr* (*of feast day etc*) to fall, occur, be celebrated; (*of meeting*) to be held, take place.

célebre *adj* (a) famous, celebrated, noted (*por* for); remarkable. (b) *person* witty, facetious; *event* funny, amusing; **es** — ¿**no?** he's a scream, isn't he? ¡**fue** —! it was killing! (c) (*CAm, Col, Ven*) charming, pretty, lovely.

celebridad *nf* (a) (*in general*) celebrity, fame. (b) (*person*) celebrity. (c) celebration(s); festivity; pageant.

célere *adj* rapid, swift.

celeridad *nf* speed, swiftness; **con** — quickly, speedily, promptly.

celeste *adj* celestial, heavenly; (*Astron*) heavenly; (*colour*) sky blue.

celestial *adj* (a) celestial, heavenly. (b) (*fig*) heavenly, delightful. (c) (*fam*) silly.

celestina *nf* bawd, procuress; (*of brothel*) madame.

celibato *nm* (a) celibacy. (b) (*fam*) bachelor.

célibe **1** *adj* single, unmarried; celibate. **2** *nmf* unmarried person, bachelor, spinster; celibate.

célico *adj* heavenly, celestial.

celidonia *nf* celandine.

celo *nm* (a) zeal, fervour, ardour; conscientiousness; (*Rel*) religious fervour, piety; (*pej*) envy, mistrust. (b) (*Zool*) rut, heat; **caer en** — to come into rut, come into season; **estar en** — to be on heat, be in rut, be in season; *see* **época**. (c) —s jealousy; **dar** —s to give grounds for jealousy; **dar** —s **a uno**, **infundir** —s **a uno** to make someone jealous; **tener** —s **de uno** to be jealous of someone.

celofán *nm* cellophane.

celosamente *adv* (a) zealously; eagerly; fervently; (b) (*pej*) suspiciously, distrustfully. (c) jealously.

celosía *nf* (a) lattice (window); blind, shutter. (b) jealousy.

celoso *adj* (a) zealous (*de* for), keen (*de* about, on); eager; fervent. (b) (*pej*) suspicious, distrustful. (c) jealous (*de* of). (d) (*Mech etc*) highly sensitive; *firearm* (*SAm*) delicate, liable to go off; *boat* (*Ec*) unsteady, easily upset.

celta **1** *adj* Celtic. **2** *nmf* Celt. **3** *nm* (*language*) Celtic.

Celtiberia *f* Celtiberia.

celtibérico, celtíbero **1** *adj* Celtiberian. **2** *nm*, **celtibérica** *nf*, **celtíbera** *nf* Celtiberian.

céltico *adj* Celtic.

célula *nf* cell; — **fotoeléctrica** photoelectric cell; — **germen** germ cell; — **nerviosa** nerve cell; — **sanguínea** blood cell.

celular *adj* cellular; cell (*attr*); *see* **coche** *etc*.

celuloide *nm* celluloid.

celulosa *nf* celulose.

cellisca *nf* sleet; sleet storm.

cellisquear [1a] *vi* to sleet.

cementación *nf* (*Tech*) case-hardening, cementation.

cementar [1a] *vt* (*Tech*) to case-harden, cement.

cementerio *nm* cemetery, graveyard; — **de coches** used-car dump.

cementista *nm* cement worker.

cemento *nm* (*Anat, Tech*) cement; concrete; — **armado**, — **reforzado** (*Col*) reinforced concrete.

cemita *nf* (*SAm*) white bread roll.

cena *nf* supper; evening meal; (*formal etc*) dinner; **la C—, la Última C—** the Last Supper; **C— de Baltasar** Belshazzar's Feast.

cenáculo *nm* group, coterie; literary group, cenacle.

cenador *nm* arbour; pavilion; summerhouse.

cenaduría *nf* (*Mex*) eating house, restaurant.

cenagal *nm* bog, quagmire, morass; (*fig*) nasty affair, sticky business.

cenagoso *adj* muddy, boggy.

cena-homenaje *nf*, *pl* **cenas-homenaje** formal dinner, celebratory dinner; **ofrecer una** — **a uno** to hold a dinner for someone.

cenancle *nm* (*Mex*) maize cob, corncob (*US*).

cenar [1a] **1** *vt* to have for supper (*etc*), sup on, sup off.
2 *vi* to have one's supper, have dinner, dine; **invitar a uno a** — to invite someone to dinner; **vengo cenado** I've had dinner (*etc*).

cenceño *adj* thin, skinny.

cencerrada *nf* tin-pan serenade (*given to a widow or widower who remarries*); rowdy music, noise, din.

cencerrear [1a] *vi* to jangle; (*of machine etc*) to rattle, clatter; (*of door, wagon etc*) to creak; (*Mus*) to play terribly, make a dreadful noise.

cencerreo *nm* jangle; rattle, clatter; creak; (*Mus*) dreadful noise.

cencerro *nm* cowbell; **a —s tapados** stealthily, on the sly; **llevar el** — to be the leader.

cendal *nm* gauze; fine silk stuff, sendal.

cenefa *nf* (*Sew*) edging, trimming, border; (*Archit*) border.

cenicero *nm* ashtray; ash pan; ash pit, ash tip.

Cenicienta: la — Cinderella.

ceniciento *adj* ashen, ash-coloured.

cenit *nm* zenith.

ceniza *nf* ash, ashes; cinder; —s (*of person*) ashes, mortal remains; **huir de las —s y dar en las brasas** to jump out of the frying pan into the fire; **reducir algo a —s** to reduce something to ashes.

cenizo **1** *adj* ashen, ash-coloured.
2 *nm* (a) (*Bot*) goosefoot. (b) jinx (*fam*), hoodoo; **es un avión** — it's a plane with a jinx on it; **entrar el** — **en casa** to have a spell of bad luck. (c) (*person*) bringer of bad luck; wet blanket.

cenojil *nm* garter.

cenotafio *nm* cenotaph.

cenote *nm* (*CAm, Mex*) freshwater deposit deep in a cave; cavern where an underground river appears at the surface.

censal *adj* = **censual**.

censar [1a] *vt* (*Arg*) to take a census of.

censo *nm* (a) (*of population*) census; — **de tráfico** traffic census, traffic count; **levantar el** — **de** to take a census of. (b) (*Fin*) tax; (annual) ground rent; mortgage; leasehold. (c) (*Pol*) — **electoral** electoral roll, (*fig*) electorate. (d) **ser un** — (*fam*) to be a constant source of trouble.

censor nm (a) (Pol) censor.
(b) (Univ) proctor.
(c) (Comm, Fin) — **de cuentas** auditor; — **jurado de cuentas** chartered accountant.
(d) (fig) critic.
censual adj (a) census (attr), relating to a census.
(b) tax (attr), mortage (attr) etc. (c) electoral, relating to the electoral roll.
censura nf (a) (Pol) censorship; censoring; **someter a la** — to censor.
(b) censor's office.
(c) censure, stricture, criticism; blame, reproach; (Lit etc) criticism, judgement; —**s** (fam) gossip, idle talk; **digno de** — censurable, blameworthy.
(d) (Comm, Fin) — **de cuentas** auditing.
censurable adj censurable, reprehensible, blameworthy.
censurar [1a] vt (a) (Pol) to censor. (b) to censure, condemn, criticize, blame, reproach; to find fault with; (Lit etc) to criticize, judge, review.
censurista 1 adj censorious. 2 nmf critic, faultfinder.
centaura nf centaury.
centauro nm centaur.
centavo 1 adj hundredth. 2 nm (a) hundredth (part).
(b) (Fin) cent.
centella nf spark (also fig); flash of lightning.
centelleante adj (a) sparkling; gleaming, glinting, twinkling; flashing. (b) (fig) sparkling.
centell(e)ar [1a] vi (a) to sparkle; to gleam, glint, glitter; (of star) to twinkle; (of lightning) to flash.
(b) (fig) to sparkle.
centelleo nm sparkle, sparkling; gleam(ing); glinting; flashing.
centena nf hundred.
centenada nf hundred.
centenal[1] nm, **centenar**[1] nm hundred; **a** —**es** by the hundred, by hundreds.
centenal[2] nm, **centenar**[2] nm (Agr) rye field.
centenario 1 adj centenary, centennial. 2 nm centenary, centennial. 3 nm, **centenaria** nf (person) centenarian.
centeno nm rye.
centésima nf hundredth (part).
centesimal adj centesimal.
centésimo 1 adj hundredth. 2 nm hundredth (part).
centígrado adj centigrade.
centigramo nm centigram.
centilitro nm centilitre.
centímetro nm centimetre.
céntimo 1 adj hundredth.
2 nm hundredth part (esp of a peseta), cent; **no tiene un** — he hasn't a penny, he hasn't a bean (fam); **no vale un** — it's worthless.
centinela nmf sentry, guard, sentinel; look-out man; **estar de** — to be on guard, do sentry duty; **hacer** — (fig) to keep watch, be on the look-out.
centiplicado adj hundredfold.
centolla nf (large) crab.
centón nm (a) (Sew) patchwork quilt, crazy quilt.
(b) (Lit) cento. (c) (fam) — **de conocimientos** walking encyclopaedia.
central 1 adj central; middle.
2 nf (Comm) head office, headquarters; (Tech) plant, station; (Tel) exchange; — **azucarera** (Cu, PR) sugar mill; — **de correos** head post office, main post office; — **depuradora** waterworks; — **eléctrica**, — **de energía** power station; — **telefónica**, — **de teléfonos** telephone exchange; — **de teléfonos automática** automatic telephone exchange; — **de teléfonos manual** (or **con servicio a mano**) manual telephone exchange.
centralismo nm centralism, tendency to concentrate power in the centre.
centralista 1 adj centralist, centralizing, tending to concentrate power in the centre.
2 nmf centralist, believer in the concentration of power in the centre.
3 nm (Cu, PR) sugarmill owner.
centralita nf (Tel) switchboard.
centralización nf centralization.
centralizar [1f] vt to centralize.
centrar [1a] vt to centre.
céntrico adj central, middle; **es muy** — it's very central, it's very convenient; **ocupar una situación céntrica** to occupy a central position (also fig).
centrífuga nf centrifuge.
centrifugar [1h] vt to centrifuge.
centrífugo adj centrifugal.
centrípeto adj centripetal.
centro nm (a) centre, middle; (Math) centre; (of activity) centre, hub; (of fire) seat; — **de atracción** centre of attraction, main attraction; — **demo-**

gráfico, — **de población** centre of population; — **docente** teaching institution; — **de fricción** trouble spot; — **de gravedad** centre of gravity; — **de interés** centre of interest, main point of interest; — **de intrigas** centre of intrigue; — **de mesa** centrepiece; — **neurálgico** nerve centre (also fig); — **de rastreo** (Astron) tracking centre; — **social** community centre; **estar en su** — (fig) to be in one's element; **ir al** — (of town) to go into the centre, go up to the centre, to go up to town.
(b) (fig) goal, purpose, objective.
(c) (Sport) centre; **delantero** — centre-forward; **medio** — centre-half.
(d) (CAm) trousers and waistcoat; (Cu) suit (trousers, waistcoat and shirt); (Bol, Cu, Mex) underskirt; (Ec) thick flannel skirt.
Centroamérica f Central America.
centroamericano 1 adj Central American. 2 nm, **centroamericana** nf Central American.
Centroeuropa nf Central Europe.
centuplicar [1g] vt to multiply a hundredfold, centuple.
centuplo 1 adj hundredfold, centuple. 2 nm centuple.
centuria nf century.
centurión nm centurion.
cénzalo nm mosquito; daddy-long-legs.
ceñido adj (a) dress tight, tight-fitting, close-fitting, clinging; narrow-waisted; curve tight.
(b) (fig) sparing, frugal, thrifty; moderate; — **y corto** straight to the point.
ceñidor nm sash, girdle.
ceñiglo nm goosefoot.
ceñir [3h and 3l] 1 vt (a) to girdle, encircle, surround; (Mil) to besiege; **la muralla ciñe la ciudad** the wall surrounds the city; — **una ciudad con una muralla** to encircle a city with a wall, throw a wall round a city.
(b) to fasten round one's waist; sword to gird on; belt etc to put on.
(c) brow to bind, encircle, wreathe (con, de with).
(d) to wear, carry; — **espada** to wear a sword.
(e) to fit tight; to tighten (up), draw in; **el vestido ciñe bien el cuerpo** the dress fits well; **habrá que ceñirlo más** we shall have to draw it in.
(f) (fig) to shorten, cut down, condense.
2 **ceñirse** vr (a) — **algo** to put something on; **se ciñó la espada** he put his sword on; — **la corona** to take the crown.
(b) to reduce expenditure, tighten one's belt; (in speaking) to limit oneself, be brief; — **a un tema** to limit oneself to a subject, concentrate on a subject; — **al asunto** to stick to the matter in hand.
ceño nm (a) frown, scowl; **arrugar el** —, **fruncir el** — to frown, knit one's brows; **mirar con** — (vt) to frown at, scowl at, give black looks to, (vi) to frown, scowl, look black.
(b) (Meteorol) threatening appearance.
ceñudo adj person frowning, grim; look black, grim.
cepa nf (a) (Bot) stump; (of vine) stock; vine; (Zool: of horn, tail) root; (Archit) pier.
(b) (fig) stock; **de buena** — (person) of good stock, (thing) of high quality; **de buena** — **castellana** of good Castilian stock.
(c) (Mex) large pit, ditch, foundation trench.
cepillado nm brush (act); **se elimina con un suave** — it goes away with a gentle brush.
cepillar [1a] vt (a) to brush; (Tech) to plane (down).
(b) (Univ: sl) to plough (sl). (c) (SAm) to flatter, butter up (fam).
cepillo nm (a) brush; — **de dientes** toothbrush; — **para el pelo** hairbrush; — **de** (or **para**) **la ropa** clothesbrush; — **para las uñas** nailbrush; — **para el suelo** scrubbing brush.
(b) (Tech) plane.
(c) (Eccl) poorbox, alms box.
(d) (SAm) flatterer, creep (sl).
cepo nm (a) (Bot) branch, bough.
(b) (Hunting) trap, snare; (Mil) mantrap; stocks.
(c) (Mech) reel; (of anvil, anchor) stock.
(d) (Eccl) poorbox, alms box.
cequión nm (Chi) large irrigation channel.
cera nf (a) wax; — **de abejas** beeswax; — **de lustrar** wax polish; — **de los oídos** earwax; — **para suelos** floor polish.
(b) —**s** honeycomb.
(c) (Col, Ec, Mex) candle.
cerafolio nm chervil.
cerámica nf (a) (Art) ceramics, pottery. (b) (objects) pottery (also —**s**).
cerámico adj ceramic.

ceramista *nmf* potter.
cerbatana *nf* (*Mil etc*) blowpipe; (*toy*) peashooter; (*Med*) ear trumpet.
cerca[1] *nf* fence, wall; — **viva** hedge.
cerca[2] **1** *adv* near, nearby, close; **de** — closely; (*Mil*) at close range; **examinar algo de** — to examine something closely; **aquí** — near here; **por aquí** — nearby, hereabouts, somewhere round here.
2 — **de** *prep* (**a**) (*of place*) near, close to; in the neighbourhood of; **estar** — **de** + *infin* to be near + *ger*, be on the point of + *ger*.
(**b**) (*of quantity*) nearly, about; (*of time*) nearly; **hay** — **de 8 toneladas** there are about 8 tons; **son** — **de las 6** it's nearly 6 o'clock.
(**c**) (*Pol*) to; **embajador** — **de la corte de Ruritania** ambassador to the court of Ruritania.
3 *nm* (**a**) **tiene buen** — it looks all right close up.
(**b**) (*Art*) —**s** objects in the foreground.
cercado *nm* (**a**) enclosure; enclosed garden, fenced field, orchard; — **de reunión** (*Racing*) paddock.
(**b**) fence, wall.
(**c**) (*Bol*) village common land.
(**d**) (*Per*) *territorial division consisting of a state capital and surrounding towns*.
cercanía *nf* (**a**) nearness, closeness, proximity.
(**b**) —**s** neighbourhood, vicinity; surroundings.
(**c**) —**s** (*of town*) outskirts, outer suburbs, outlying areas; **tren de** —**s** suburban train.
cercano *adj* near, close; nearby, neighbouring, next; *relative* close; *death, doom* approaching; — **a** near to, close to.
Cercano Oriente *m* Near East.
cercar [1g] *vt* (**a**) to fence in, wall in, hedge; to enclose; to encircle, surround, ring (**de** with); (*of mountains, enemy etc*) to hem in.
(**b**) (*Mil*) *town* to surround, besiege; *troops* to surround, cut off, encircle.
cercén: a — *adv* (**a**) (*Bot*) close to the root; **cortar algo a** — (*fig*) to nip something in the bud. (**b**) entirely, completely.
cercenar [1a] *vt* (**a**) to clip; to cut the edge off, trim the edges of; *end* to cut off, slice off; *limb* to cut off, amputate; *coin* to clip.
(**b**) (*fig*) *expenses* to cut down, reduce; *passage etc* to shorten, cut down; to delete, cut out.
cerceta *nf* teal.
cerciorar [1a] **1** *vt* to inform, assure. **2 cerciorarse** *vr* to find out; to make sure; — **de** to find out about, ascertain; to make sure of.
cerco *nm* (**a**) (*Agr etc*) enclosure; (*SAm*) fence, hedge; (*Per*) small walled property; **saltar el** — (*Arg: Pol*) to change sides, jump on the bandwagon.
(**b**) (*Tech: of wheel*) rim; (*of barrel*) hoop; (*Archit*) casing, frame.
(**c**) (*Astron, Meteorol*) halo.
(**d**) social group, circle.
(**e**) (*Mil*) siege; **alzar** (*or* **levantar**) **el** — to raise the siege; **poner** — **a** to lay siege to.
cercón *adv* (*SAm*) rather close.
cerda *nf* (**a**) (*Zool*) pig, sow. (**b**) bristle; horsehair; (*Hunting*) snare, noose.
cerdear [1a] *vi* (**a**) (*Mus*) to scratch, rasp, grate. (**b**) (*fam*) to hedge, jib, hold back.
Cerdeña *f* Sardinia.
cerdito *nm*, **cerdita** *nf* piglet.
cerdo *nm* (**a**) (*Zool*) pig; — **padre** boar; — **salvaje** wild pig.
(**b**) (*Zool*) — **marino** porpoise.
(**c**) (*Cook*) pork.
(**d**) (*fig*) dirty person, slovenly fellow.
cerdoso *adj animal* shaggy, hairy, bristly; *chin* bristly, stubbly.
cereal **1** *adj* cereal; grain (*attr*). **2** *nm* cereal; —**es** cereals, grain; —**es** (*Cook*) cereals, cornflakes.
cerebelo *nm* cerebellum.
cerebral *adj* cerebral, brain (*attr*).
cerebro *nm* brain; cerebrum; (*fig*) brains, intelligence; — **electrónico** electronic brain; **estrujar el** — to rack one's brains.
ceremonia *nf* (**a**) (*act*) ceremony; (*Eccl*) ceremony, service; **hacer** —**s** to stand on ceremony.
(**b**) (*quality*) ceremony, ceremoniousness; formality; pomp; **falta de** — informality; **reunión de** — formal meeting, ceremonial meeting; **reunirse de** — to meet with all due ceremony; **por** — as a matter of form; **hablar sin** — to speak informally; **hacer algo sin** — to do something without fuss.
ceremonial **1** *adj* ceremonial. **2** *nm* ceremonial.
ceremoniosamente *adv* ceremoniously; formally; stiffly, with an excess of politeness.

ceremonioso *adj* ceremonious; *person, dress, greeting, visit etc* formal; (*pej*) stiff, over-polite.
céreo *adj* wax (*attr*), waxen.
cerería *nf* wax-chandler's shop.
cerero *nm* wax chandler.
cereza *nf* cherry; **un suéter rojo** — a cherry-red jumper; — **silvestre** wild cherry.
cerezal *nm* cherry orchard.
cerezo *nm* cherry tree; cherry wood.
cerilla *nf* (**a**) match; wax taper. (**b**) (*Anat*) earwax.
cerillera *nf*, **cerillero** *nm* (*SAm*) matchbox.
cerillo *nm* (*Mex*) match.
cernedor *nm* sieve.
cernejas *nfpl* fetlock.
cerner [2g] **1** *vt* (**a**) to sift, sieve.
(**b**) (*fig*) to scan, watch.
2 *vi* (**a**) (*Bot*) to bud, blossom.
(**b**) (*Meteorol*) to drizzle.
3 cernerse *vr* (**a**) to hover; to soar; — **sobre** to be poised over, hang over; — **sobre** (*fig*) to threaten, hang over.
(**b**) (*of person*) to waddle.
cernícalo *nm* (**a**) (*Orn*) kestrel. (**b**) (*fam*) lout, dolt. (**c**) **coger un** — (*fam*) to get tight.
cernidillo *nm* (**a**) waddle, rolling gait. (**b**) (*Meteorol*) drizzle.
cernido *nm* (**a**) sifting; sifted flour. (**b**) (*Col*) drizzle.
cernidor *nm* sieve.
cernidura *nf* sifting.
cero *nm* nothing; nought; (*Phys etc*) zero; (*Sport*) **por 3 goles a** — by 3 goals to nil, by 3 goals to nought; (*Tennis*) **estamos a 40 contra** — the game stands at 40-love; — **absoluto** absolute zero; **8 grados bajo** — 8 degrees below zero, 8 degrees below freezing, 8 degrees of frost; **es un** — **a la izquierda** he's a nonentity, he's a nobody; **tendremos que partir nuevamente de** — (*fig*) we shall have to start from scratch again.
ceroso *adj* (**a**) waxen; waxy, waxlike. (**b**) (*Mex*) *egg* lightly boiled.
cerote *nm* (**a**) (shoemaker's) wax.
(**b**) (*fam*) panic, funk (*fam*).
(**c**) (*CR, Mex*) piece of human excrement; **estar hecho un** — (*Col, Per*), **tener** — (*Arg, Mex*) to have got one's clothes dirty.
cerotear [1a] **1** *vt thread* to wax. **2** *vi* (*Chi: of candle*) to drip.
cerquillo *nm* (**a**) fringe of hair round the tonsure; (*Arg, Mex*) fringe, curls. (**b**) (*Tech*) seam, welt.
cerquita *adv* quite near, close by.
cerradero **1** *adj device* locking, fastening; **caja f cerradera** box that can be locked, box with a lock.
2 *nm* locking device; clasp, fastener; (*of lock*) strike, keeper; (*of purse*) purse strings.
cerrado *adj* (**a**) closed, shut; locked; *fist* clenched; "**— por obras**" "closed for repairs (*or* alterations)"; **aquí huele a** — it smells stuffy in here, it's thick in here.
(**b**) *subject* obscure, incomprehensible.
(**c**) (*Meteorol*) *sky* cloudy, overcast; *atmosphere* heavy; *night* dark, black.
(**d**) *curve* sharp, tight.
(**e**) *beard* thick, full.
(**f**) *person* quiet, reserved, uncommunicative; (*pej*) secretive; — **de mollera** dense, dim; pigheaded.
(**g**) *person* (*pej*) typical, all-too-typical; **es un eslobodio** — he's a typical Slobodian, he has all the worst features of the Slobodian.
(**h**) (*Ling*) *vowel* close.
(**i**) (*Ling*) *person* with a broad accent; *accent* broad, marked, strong; *speech* thick, broad; **habló con** — **acento gallego** he spoke with a strong Galician accent.
(**j**) (*Arg, Per*) pigheaded.
cerradura *nf* (**a**) (*act*) closing, shutting; locking.
(**b**) lock; — **de combinación** combination lock; — **de golpe**, — **de muelle** spring lock; — **de seguridad** safety lock.
cerraja *nf* (**a**) lock. (**b**) (*Bot*) sow-thistle.
cerrajería *nf* (**a**) locksmith's craft (*or* trade). (**b**) locksmith's (shop).
cerrajero *nm* locksmith.
cerrar [1k] **1** *vt* (**a**) *box, eyes, mouth etc* to close, shut; *door* to lock (up); to bolt; *fist* to clench, close; *letter* to seal; *ranks* to close; — **algo con llave** to lock something.
(**b**) *hole, opening, pipe etc* to block (up), stop (up), close, obstruct; *harbour, pass* to close; **han cerrado la frontera** they have closed the frontier;

la carretera está cerrada por la nieve the road is blocked by snow.

(c) *ground, area* to enclose, close off, fence (in), wall (in).

(d) *tap, gas, water etc* to turn off.

(e) (*Elec*) *circuit* to make, close, complete.

(f) *shop, business* to shut, close; (*permanently*) to shut up; *factory* to close (down).

(g) *procession* to bring up the rear of; **— la marcha** to come last, bring up the rear.

(h) *account, debate, story* to close; *programme* to end, be the final item in.

(i) *bargain* to seal, strike.

2 *vi* **(a)** to close, shut; **la puerta cierra mal** the door doesn't close properly; **cerramos a las 9** we close at 9; **dejar una puerta sin —** to leave a door open.

(b) (*of night*) to come down, set in; (*of winter*) to close in.

(c) **— con uno** to close with someone, grapple with someone; **— con el enemigo** to come to close quarters with the enemy.

3 cerrarse *vr* **(a)** to close, shut; (*of wound*) to close up, heal; (*Mil*) to close ranks.

(b) (*Meteorol*) to cloud over, become overcast.

(c) **— en + infin** to persist in + *ger*, go on stubbornly + *ger*.

cerrazón *nf* **(a)** (*Meteorol*) threatening sky, storm clouds. **(b)** (*RPl*) fog, mist. **(c)** (*Col: of mountain range*) spur.

cerrero *adj* **(a)** *animal* wild; untamed, unbroken; *person* rough, uncouth. **(b)** (*Col, Cu, Ven*) unsweetened; bitter; *bread etc* ordinary.

cerril *adj* **(a)** *ground* rough; mountainous. **(b)** = **cerrero** (a).

cerrillar [1a] *vt coin* to mill.

cerro *nm* **(a)** hill; **andar** (*or* **echarse, ir**) **por los —s de Úbeda** to wander from the point, get off the track; to talk a lot of rubbish.

(b) (*Zool*) neck; backbone, back; **en —** bareback.

(c) (*Tech*) bunch of cleaned hemp (*or* flax).

(d) (*Col*) lot, heap; **un —** **de** a lot of.

cerrojazo *nm* bolting; **dar —** to slam the bolt; (*fig*) to come to an end unexpectedly; **dar — a uno** (*sl*) to give someone the mitten (*sl*).

cerrojo *nm* bolt, latch; (*Sport: also* **táctica de —**) stonewalling, negative play; **echar el —** to bolt the door.

certamen *nm* competition, contest; **— de belleza** beauty contest.

certeramente *adv* accurately, unerringly.

certero *adj* **(a)** accurate, sure, certain.

(b) *shot* accurate, well-aimed; telling; *aim* excellent; *marksman* sure, good, crack.

(c) well-informed.

certeza *nf* certainty; **tener la — de que . . .** to know for certain that . . ., have the certain knowledge that . . .

certidumbre *nf* certainty; conviction.

certificable *adj* certifiable.

certificación *nf* certification; (*Post*) registration; (*Law*) affidavit.

certificado 1 *adj* certified; (*Post*) registered.

2 *nm* **(a)** certificate; **— de aptitud** testimonial; **— de ciudadanía** naturalization papers; **— médico** medical certificate; **— de vacuna** vaccination certificate.

(b) (*Post*) registered packet, registered item.

certificar [1g] *vt* **(a)** to certify; to guarantee, vouch for; **— que . . .** to certify that . . . **(b)** (*Post*) to register.

certitud *nf* certainty, certitude.

cerúleo *adj* sky blue.

cerumen *nm* earwax.

cerval *adj* deer (*attr*), deer-like.

cervantino *adj* Cervantine; of Cervantes; peculiar to Cervantes; like (that of) Cervantes; **los estudios —s** Cervantes studies, studies of Cervantes; **el estilo —** the Cervantine style.

cervantista *nmf* Cervantes scholar, specialist in Cervantes.

cervato *nm* fawn.

cervecería *nf* **(a)** brewery. **(b)** bar, public house.

cervecero *nm* brewer.

cerveza *nf* beer; **— de barril, —** (**servida**) **al grifo** draught beer, beer on draught; **— de botella, — en botellas, — embotellada** bottled beer; **— clara** light beer; **— estilo Pilsen** lager; **— negra** dark beer.

cervical *adj* neck (*attr*), cervical; (*relating to part of the womb*) cervical.

cerviz *nf* **(a)** neck, nape of the neck; **de dura —** stubborn, headstrong, wild; **bajar** (*or* **doblar**) **la**

— to submit, bow down; levantar la — to lift one's head up (again).

(b) (*part of the womb*) cervix.

cervuno *adj* deer-like; deer-coloured.

cesación *nf* cessation; suspension, stoppage; **— del fuego** ceasefire.

cesante 1 *adj* out of a job, out of office; discharged; retired; on half-pay.

2 *nm* civil servant *who has been compulsorily retired, dismissed public employee.*

cesantía *nf* **(a)** state of being a *cesante*. **(b)** retirement pension, half-pay, redundancy compensation.

César *m* Caesar.

cesar [1a] **1** *vt* **(a)** to cease, stop; *payment, work* to stop, suspend.

(b) (*SAm*) to sack (*fam*), fire (*fam*); **le cesaron en el trabajo** they sacked him from his work.

2 *vi* **(a)** to cease, stop; to desist; **— de hacer algo** to stop doing something, leave off doing something; **no cesa de hablar** she never stops talking; **sin —** ceaselessly, incessantly.

(b) (*of employee*) to leave, quit; to retire; **— en el trabajo** to give up one's work, retire from work.

cesáreo *adj* **(a)** Caesarean; imperial. **(b)** (*Med*) **operación cesárea** Caesarean operation.

cese *nm* **(a)** cessation; suspension, stoppage; **— de alarma** (*Mil*) all-clear signal; **— de fuego, — de hostilidades** ceasefire; **— de pagos** suspension of payments, stoppage of payments; **— temporal de los bombardeos** temporary halt to the bombing.

(b) (*of civil servant*) dismissal, compulsory retirement; (*of worker*) sacking (*fam*), firing (*fam*); **dar el — a uno** to sack someone (*fam*).

cesión *nf* **(a)** (*Pol etc*) cession. **(b)** (*Law*) cession, granting, transfer; **— de bienes** surrender of property.

cesionario *nm*, **cesionaria** *nf* grantee, assign.

cesionista *nmf* grantor, assignor.

césped *nm* **(a)** grass, lawn, (stretch of) turf; (*for games*) pitch; (*for bowls*) green. **(b)** turf, sod.

cesta *nf* basket; (*pelota*) long wicker racquet; **— para compras** shopping basket; **— de costura** sewing basket; **— para papeles, — de los papeles** (**rotos**) wastepaper basket; **llevar la —** (*fam*) to go along as chaperon; to play gooseberry.

cestada *nf* basketful.

cestería *nf* **(a)** basketmaking. **(b)** wickerwork, basketwork; **silla de —** wicker(work) chair. **(c)** basket shop.

cestero *nm*, **cestera** *nf* basketmaker; basket seller.

cestillo *nm* small basket; (*of balloon*) basket; **— del polen** (*of bee*) pollen sac.

cesto *nm* **(a)** (large) basket; hamper; **— de la colada** clothes basket; **— para papeles, — de los papeles** (**rotos**) wastepaper basket.

(b) **estar hecho un —** to be very drowsy; to be fuddled with drink; **estar metido en un —** to be a spoiled child.

(c) (*fam*) idiot.

cesura *nf* caesura.

cetáceo 1 *adj* cetacean. **2** *nm* cetacean.

cetorrino *nm* basking shark.

cetrería *nf* falconry, hawking.

cetrero *nm* **(a)** falconer. **(b)** (*Eccl*) verger.

cetrino *adj* greenish-yellow; *face, complexion* sallow; (*fig*) melancholy, jaundiced.

cetro *nm* sceptre; (*fig*) sway, power, dominion; **empuñar el —** to ascend the throne, begin to reign.

cía *nf* hip bone.

cianhídrico *adj* hydrocyanic.

cianotipia *nf*, **cianotipo** *nm* blueprint.

cianuro *nm* cyanide; **— potásico, — de potasio** potassium cyanide.

ciar [1c] *vi* **(a)** to go backwards; (*Naut*) to go astern, back water. **(b)** (*fig*) to back down, back out.

ciática *nf* sciatica.

ciático *adj* sciatic.

cibernética *nf* cybernetics.

cicatear [1a] *vi* to be stingy, be mean.

cicatería *nf* stinginess, meanness.

cicatero 1 *adj* stingy, mean. **2** *nm*, **cicatera** *nf* miser, skinflint; (*fam*) pickpocket.

cicatriz *nf* scar (*also fig*).

cicatrización *nf* healing.

cicatrizar [1f] **1** *vt* to heal. **2 cicatrizarse** *vr* to heal (up), form a scar.

Cicerón *m* Cicero.

cicerone *nm* guide, cicerone.

ciceroniano *adj* ciceronian.

ciclamen *nm*, **ciclamino** cyclamen.

cíclico *adj* cyclic(al).

ciclismo *nm* cycling; (*Sport*) cycle racing.
ciclista *nmf* cyclist.
ciclo *nm* cycle; (*Lit*) cycle; (*of lectures etc*) course, series, programme; (*School*) term; (*SAm: Univ*) year, course.
ciclo-cross *nm* cyclo-cross.
ciclomoto(r) *nm* moped, autocycle.
ciclón *nm* cyclone.
cíclope m Cyclops.
ciclorama *nm* cyclorama.
ciclotrón *nm* cyclotron.
—cico, —cica (*in some combinations* **—ecico, —ecica**) *suffix: see* **—ito**.
cicuta *nf* hemlock.
cidra *nf* citron.
cidracayote *nm* (*SAm*) gourd, calabash.
cidro *nm* citron (tree).
ciega *nf* blind woman.
ciego 1 *adj* (a) blind; blinded; **a ciegas** blindly; **andar a ciegas, caminar a ciegas** to grope one's way; **volar a ciegas** to fly blind; **jugar a la ciega** (*Chess*) to play blindfold; **quedar —** to go blind; **quedó — después de la explosión** he was blinded in the accident; **más — que un topo** as blind as a bat; **tan — el uno como el otro** it's a case of the blind leading the blind.
  (b) (*fig*) blind; **— a, — para** blind to; **— de ira** blind with rage; **con una fe ciega** with a blind faith, with an unquestioning faith; **a ciegas** blindly; heedlessly, thoughtlessly.
  (c) (*Archit*) blind; *pipe etc* blocked, stopped up, choked.
  2 *nm* (a) blind man, blind person; **los —s** the blind, blind people.
  (b) (*RPl: Cards*) player who holds bad cards.
  (c) (*Cu*) meadow enclosed by forest.
cielo *nm* (a) sky; (*Astron*) sky, heavens, firmament; **— aborregado** mackerel sky; **— encopetado** overcast sky; **— máximo** (*Aer*) ceiling; **a — abierto, a — raso** in the open air; **mina a — abierto** opencast mine; **a — descubierto** in the open; **se le juntaron el — con la tierra** he had terrible trouble, he was in an awful mess; (*SAm*) he lost his nerve; **mover — y tierra** to move heaven and earth; **querer tapar el — con las manos** (*SAm*) to try to hide something obvious; **se vino el — abajo** it rained cats and dogs, the heavens opened.
  (b) (*Archit: also* **— raso**) ceiling; (*of mouth*) roof; (*of bed*) canopy; (*CAm: Aut*) roof.
  (c) (*Rel*) heaven; **¡—!** good heavens!; **esto clama al —** this cries out to heaven (to be reformed *etc*); **ganar el —** to win salvation; **ganar el — con rosario ajeno** to use other people's efforts to one's own advantage; **ir al —** to go to heaven; **poner a uno en el —** (*or* **en los cielos,** *SAm* **por los cielos**) to praise someone to the skies; **tomar el — con las manos** to be asking for trouble, be over-optimistic; **ver el — abierto** to see one's way out of a difficulty; *see* **llover**.
  (d) (*term of endearment*) my love, sweetheart.
ciempiés *nm, pl* **ciempiés** centipede.
cien¹ *adj* (*apocopated form of* **ciento,** *before n*) (a) a hundred; **— mil** a hundred thousand; **las últimas — páginas** the last hundred pages.
  (b) **10 por —** ten per cent; **por —** (*fig*) a hundred per cent (*also fig*); **es español — por —** he's Spanish through and through, he's Spanish to the core; **lo apoyo — por —** I support it a hundred per cent, I support it wholeheartedly.
cien² *nm* (*RPl*) lavatory.
ciénaga *nf* marsh, bog, swamp.
ciencia *nf* science; (*older sense*) knowledge, learning, scholarship, erudition; **hombre de —** scientist; **— del hogar** domestic science, home economics (*US*); **—s naturales** natural sciences; **—s ocultas** occult sciences; **a — y paciencia de uno** with someone's knowledge and agreement, with someone's connivance; **saber algo a — cierta** to know something for certain (*or* for a fact).
ciencia-ficción *nf* science fiction.
cieno *nm* mud, mire, silt, ooze; slime.
cienoso *adj* muddy, miry; slimy.
científicamente *adv* scientifically.
científico 1 *adj* scientific. **2** *nm* scientist.
cientista *nmf* (*SAm*) scientist.
ciento *adj and nm* hundred, (one) hundred; **— veinte** a hundred and twenty; **en su año —** its hundredth year; **15 por —** 15 per cent; **hay un 5 por — de descuento** there is a 5 per cent discount; **por —s** in hundreds, by the hundred; **de — en boca** tiny, insignificant; **dar — y raya al más pintado** to be a match for anyone; **había — y la**

madre there were far too many; and even that was still too many; **pero por allí pasan de — a viento** but hardly anybody comes that way.
cierne *nm* blossoming, budding; **en —(s)** (*Bot*) in blossom; (*fig*) in its infancy; **es un ajedrecista en —s** he's a budding chessplayer, he's a future chess champion.
cierre *nm* (a) (*act*) closing, shutting; locking; (*Radio, TV*) close-down; (*of factory*) shutdown; **— de los dueños, — patronal** lockout.
  (b) closing device, locking device; snap fastener; (*of dress*) fastener; (*of belt*) buckle, clasp; (*of book*) clasp; (*of door*) catch; (*of shop*) shutter, blind; (*Aut*) choke; **— de cremallera, — relámpago** (*Per, RPl*) zip fastener, zipper; **— hidráulico** water seal; **— metálico** roll shutter, metal blind.
  (c) **de —** closing; **precios de —** (*Fin*) closing prices.
cierro *nm* (a) = **cierre.** (b) (*Chi*) wall; envelope.
ciertamente *adv* certainly, surely; **no era — de los más inteligentes** he was certainly not one of the brightest.
cierto *adj* (a) sure, certain; *promise etc* positive, definite; **¡—!** certainly!; **por —** certainly; by the way; **por — que no era el único** and moreover he was not the only one, and what is more he wasn't the only one; **no, por —** certainly not; **¡sí, por —!** yes of course!; **es —** it is true; that's it; **¿es — eso?** it that really so?; **es — que** . . . it is certain that . . . , it is true that . . . ; **lo — es que** . . . the fact is that . . . ; **lo único — es que** . . . the only sure thing is that . . . ; **estar —** to be sure; **¿estás —?** are you sure?; **estar — de + infin** to be certain to + *infin*; **estar en lo —** to be right; **saber algo de —** to know something for certain.
  (b) a certain; **—s** some, certain; **— día de mayo** one day in May; **cierta persona que yo conozco** a certain person I know; *see* **cada** *etc*.
cierva *nf* hind.
ciervo *nm* deer; stag; **— común** red deer; **— volante** stag beetle.
cierzo *nm* north wind.
cifra *nf* (a) number, numeral; **— arábiga** Arabic numeral; **— romana** Roman numeral; **escribirlo en —s y palabras** to write it down in figures and in words.
  (b) number, quantity, amount; sum; **— global** lump sum; **la — de este año es elevada** the quantity this year is large; **la — de los muertos** the number of dead.
  (c) code, cipher; **en —** in code; (*fig*) mysteriously, enigmatically.
  (d) abbreviation; monogram; abridgement, summary; **en —** in brief, briefly, concisely; in a shortened form.
cifradamente *adv* (a) in code. (b) in brief, in a shortened form.
cifrado *adj* coded, in code.
cifrar [1a] *vt* (a) *message* to code, write in code; (*fig*) to abridge, summarize; to abbreviate. (b) *hope* to place, concentrate (*en* on).
cigarra *nf* cicada.
cigarral *nm* (*Toledo*) country house on the banks of the Tagus.
cigarrera *nf* (a) cigar case. (b) cigar maker; cigar seller.
cigarrería *nf* (*SAm*) tobacconist's (shop); tobacco factory.
cigarrero *nm* cigar maker; cigar seller.
cigarrillo *nm* cigarette.
cigarro *nm* cigar (*also* **— puro**); cigarette (*also* **— de papel**); **— habano** Havana cigar.
cigoto *nm* zygote.
ciguato *adj* (a) (*Ant, Mex*) simple, stupid. (b) (*Mex, Ven*) pale, anaemic.
cigüeña *nf* (a) (*Orn*) stork. (b) (*Mech*) crank, handle; winch, capstan. (c) (*CAm*) barrel organ. (d) (*Ant*) railway barrow.
cigüeñal *nm* crankshaft.
cija *nf* barn; hayloft.
cilampa *nf* (*CAm*) drizzle.
cilampear [1a] *vi* (*CAm*) to drizzle.
cilantro *nm* (*Bot, Cook*) coriander.
cilicio *nm* hair shirt.
cilindrada *nf* cylinder capacity.
cilindradora *nf* steamroller, road roller.
cilindrar [1a] *vt* to roll, roll flat.
cilíndrico *adj* cylindrical.
cilindro *nm* (*Math, Tech*) cylinder; (*of typewriter*) roller; (*Mex*) barrel organ; **— de caminos, — compresor** steamroller, road roller.
cilla *nf* (a) tithe barn, granary. (b) tithe.

cima nf (of tree) top; (of mountain) top, peak, summit; (fig) summit, height; (fig) completion; **dar — a** to complete, crown with success, carry out successfully.

cimarra nf: **hacer —** (Arg, Chi) to play truant.

cimarrón 1 adj (a) (SAm: Bot, Zool) wild; (fig) rough, uncouth; lazy; **negro —** (Hist) runaway slave, fugitive slave.
(b) (RPl) maté bitter, unsweetened.
2 nm (RPl) (a) unsweetened maté.
(b) wild dog; prairie dog.

cimarronear [1a] vi (a) (SAm: of slave) to run away.
(b) (RPl) to drink unsweetened maté.

cimba nf (Bol) plaited rope of hard leather; (Per) pigtail; (Per) hairband; (Per) rope ladder.

címbalo nm cymbal.

cimbel nm decoy (also fig).

cimbor(r)io nm (Archit) dome; base of a dome; (Min) roof.

cimbrear [1a] **1** vt (a) to brandish; to shake, swish, swing; to bend.
(b) **— a uno** to thrash someone; **le cimbreó de un porrazo** he clouted him with his stick.
2 vi to swerve, change direction unexpectedly.
3 cimbrearse vr to sway, swing, to shake; to bend; **— al viento** to sway in the wind.

cimbreño adj pliant, flexible; figure willowy, lithe.

cimbreo nm swaying, swinging; shaking; bending.

cimbrón nm (Arg, Col, CR) shudder of pain; strong nervous convulsion; (Ec) stab of pain; (Chi, Mex) blow with the flat of a sword; (Arg, Col, CR, Mex) swish (of lasso etc); (Arg, Col, CR, Mex) violent jerk, strong tug; (Arg) vibration.

cimbronada nf (Arg, Col, Mex), **cimbronazo** nm (Arg, Col, Mex) = **cimbrón**; (Ven) earthquake.

cimentación nf (a) foundation. (b) laying of foundations.

cimentar [1k] vt (a) (Archit) to lay the foundations of (or for); (fig) to found, establish. (b) (fig) to strengthen, cement.

cimera nf crest (also Her).

cimero adj top, topmost, uppermost.

cimiento nm foundation, groundwork; (fig) basis, source; **—s** (Archit) foundations; **abrir los —s** to dig the foundations; **echar los —s de** to lay the foundations for.

cimitarra nf scimitar.

cimpa nf (Bol, Per) = **cimba**.

cinabrio nm cinnabar.

cinc nm zinc.

cincel nm chisel.

cincelador nm (a) sculptor; engraver; stone cutter. (b) (chipping) chisel.

cincelar [1a] vt to chisel; to carve, engrave, cut.

cinco 1 adj five; (date) fifth; **las — five** o'clock; **estar sin — (**fam) to be broke (fam); **no estar en sus — (**fam) to be off one's rocker (sl); **le dije cuántas son —** I told him a thing or two; **saber cuántas son —** to know what's what, know a thing or two; **tener los — muy listos** (fam) to be light-fingered; **¡vengan esos —!** shake (on it)!
2 nm (a) five.
(b) (CAm, Col, Ven) 5-stringed guitar.
(c) (Mex) bottom, backside (fam).

cincoenrama nf cinquefoil.

cincuenta adj fifty; fiftieth.

cincuentavo 1 adj fiftieth. **2** nm fiftieth.

cincuentena nf fifty, group of about fifty.

cincuenteno adj fiftieth.

cincuentón 1 adj fifty-year old, fiftyish. **2** nm, **cincuentona** nf person of about fifty.

cincha nf (a) girth, saddle strap; **a revienta —s** at breakneck speed; hurriedly; (SAm) reluctantly.
(b) (Sew: for chairs etc) webbing.
(c) (Col) **tener —** to have a strain of Negro (or Indian) blood.

cinchada nf (Mex, RPl) tug-of-war.

cinchar [1a] vt to girth, secure the girth of; (Tech) to band, hoop, secure with hoops.

cincho nm sash, belt, girdle; iron hoop, metal band; (CAm, Mex, PR) = **cincha**.

cinchona nf (SAm) quinine bark.

cine nm (a) (in general, as art) cinema; film(s), movies (US); **el — español actual** the present-day Spanish cinema; **— en colores** colour films; **— hablado, — sonoro** talkies; **— mudo** silent films; **hacer —** to make films, be engaged in film work, be working for the cinema.
(b) (building) cinema, movie theatre (US), picture house (US); **ir al —** to go to the cinema, go to the pictures, go to the movies (US).

cine-club nm, pl **cine-clubs** [pronunciation: see **club**] cine club, film club.

cinema nm cinema.

cinemateca nf film library, film archive.

cinematografía nf films, film-making, cinematography.

cinematografiar [1a] vt to film.

cinematográfico adj cine- . . ., film (attr); cinematographic.

cinematógrafo nm (a) cinema. (b) cine projector, film projector.

cinematurgo nm scriptwriter, scenarist.

cineración nf incineration.

cinerama nm cinerama.

cinerario adj (a) cinerary. (b) = **ceniciento**.

cinéreo adj ashy; ash-grey, ashen.

cinética nf kinetics.

cinético adj kinetic.

cingalés 1 adj Singhalese. **2** nm, **cingalesa** nf Singhalese.

cíngaro 1 adj gipsy. **2** nm gipsy.

cinguería nf (Arg) sheet-metal work; sheet-metal shop.

cinguero nm (Arg) sheet-metal worker.

cínicamente adv (a) cynically. (b) brazenly, shamelessly, impudently; in an unprincipled way.

cínico 1 adj (a) cynical. (b) brazen, shameless, impudent; unprincipled. **2** nm (a) cynic. (b) brazen individual; unprincipled person, humbug.

cinismo nm (a) cynicism. (b) brazenness, shamelessness, effrontery, impudence; lack of principle, humbug; **¡qué —!** what humbug!

cinta nf (a) band, strip; tape; (Sew) ribbon, tape; (Cine) film; reel; **— adhesiva** adhesive tape; **— aisladora, — aislante** insulating tape; **— de cotizaciones, — de teleimpresor** ticker tape; **— de freno** brake lining; **— de goma** rubber band; **— de llegada** (Sport) (finishing) tape; **— para máquina de escribir** typewriter ribbon; **— magnética, — magnetofónica** magnetic tape, recording tape; **— de corto metraje** short (film); **— de largo metraje** full-length film; **— métrica** tape measure; **— de pelo** hairband; **— simbólica** ceremonial tape; **— transportadora, — de transporte** conveyor belt.
(b) (Archit) fillet, scroll.
(c) (of pavement) kerb.
(d) (SAm) tin, can.
(e) (Mex) **—s** shoelaces.

cinteado adj beribboned.

cintero nm (a) (woman's) girdle. (b) rope.

cintillo nm (a) hatband. (b) small ring with jewels. (c) (PR) kerb.

cinto nm (Mil) belt, girdle, sash; **armas de —** side arms.

cintura nf (a) (Anat) waist; waistline; **— de avispa** wasp waist; **de la — (para) arriba** from the waist up; **tener poca —** to have a slim waist.
(b) girdle; **meter a uno en —** to bring (or keep) someone under control, keep someone under; to make someone see reason.

cinturilla nf waistband.

cinturón nm (a) belt; girdle; **— de salvamento, — salvavidas** lifebelt; **— de seguridad** safety belt; **apretarse el —** (fig) to tighten one's belt.
(b) (fig) belt, zone; **el — industrial de Madrid** the Madrid industrial belt; **— verde** green belt.

cipayo nm (a) sepoy. (b) (Arg) politician in the service of foreign commerce.

cipe nm sickly child.

cipo nm memorial stone; milestone, signpost.

cipote 1 adj (a) (Col, Ven) stupid.
(b) (Guat) plump, chubby.
2 nm (a) (CAm, Ven) lad, youngster; urchin.
(b) (Nic) Indian club.
(c) (CAm) chump (fam), blockhead.
(d) (Col) **— de chica** smashing girl (sl); **— de película** splendid film.
(e) (esp RPl, Ven: tabu) prick (tabu).

ciprés nm cypress (tree).

cipresal nm cypress grove.

circo nm (a) circus, amphitheatre. (b) (show) circus. (c) (Mex) acrobatic troupe.

circuir [3g] vt to encircle, surround.

circuito nm circuit; circumference, distance round (the outside); (Elec etc) circuit; (Sport) lap; **— en bucle** loop; **— cerrado** closed circuit, loop; **— cerrado de TV, — interno de TV, TV por — cerrado** closed-circuit TV; **— corto** short circuit.

circulación nf (a) circulation (also Fin, Med); (fig) circulation; propagation; **— fiduciaria** paper money, paper currency; **— sanguínea, — de la sangre**

circulation of the blood; **estar fuera de** — to be out of circulation, be no longer current; **poner algo en** — to issue something, put something into circulation.

(**b**) (*Aut*) traffic; movement of traffic; — **rodada** vehicular traffic, wheeled traffic; "**cerrado a la** — **rodada**" "closed to vehicles"; **la** — **es por la derecha** they drive on the right; **calle de gran** — busy street, street much used by traffic.

circulante *adj library* lending, circulating.

circular 1 *adj* circular, round; *ticket* return, round-trip (*US: attr*); *trip* round; *letter* circular.
2 *nf* circular.
3 *vt* to circulate; to pass round, send round; to put into circulation.
4 *vi* (**a**) to circulate (*also Fin, Med*); (*Fin*) to be in circulation; **hacer** — **una carta** to circulate a letter, send round a letter.

(**b**) (*of persons*) to move about, walk around (*por* in); **¡circulen!** move along!; **hacer** — **a la gente** to move people along.

(**c**) (*Aut*) to drive; — **por la izquierda** (*in nation*) to drive on the left, (*in street etc*) to keep to the left; **hacer** — **los coches** to keep the cars moving.

(**d**) (*of transport*) to run; **no circula los domingos** it does not run on Sundays; **circula entre A y B** it runs between A and B, it operates between A and B.

circulatorio *adj* circulatory.

círculo *nm* (**a**) (*Math etc*) circle; — **máximo** great circle; **C—** **Polar Antártico** Antarctic Circle; **C—** **Polar Ártico** Arctic Circle; — **vicioso** vicious circle (*also fig*).

(**b**) circle, ring, band.

(**c**) (*of people*) circle, club, group; clubhouse; (*Per, RPl*) social gathering; (*Pol*) political group, faction.

(**d**) (*fig*) scope, compass, extent.

circun . . . circum . . .

circuncidar [1a] *vt* (**a**) to circumcise. (**b**) (*fig*) to curtail; to moderate.

circuncisión *nf* circumcision.

circunciso *adj* circumcised.

circundante *adj* surrounding.

circundar [1a] *vt* to surround.

circunferencia *nf* circumference.

circunflejo *nm* circumflex.

circunlocución *nf*, **circunloquio** *nm* circumlocution, roundabout expression.

circunnavegación *nf* circumnavigation.

circunnavegar [1a] *vt* to sail round, circumnavigate.

circunscribir [3a: *ptp* **circunscrito**] **1** *vt* to circumscribe; (*fig*) to circumscribe, limit, restrict (*a* to).
2 **circunscribirse** *vr* (*fig*) to be limited, be confined (*a* to).

circunscripción *nf* (*of territory*) division, subdivision; (*Parl*) constituency, electoral district.

circunspección *nf* circumspection, caution, prudence.

circunspecto *adj* circumspect, cautious, prudent; deliberate; *words* carefully chosen, guarded.

circunstancia *nf* circumstance; —**s agravantes** aggravating circumstances; —**s atenuantes** extenuating circumstances; **en las** —**s in** (*or* under) the circumstances; **en las** —**s actuales** in the present state of things, under present conditions; **las** —**s cambian los casos** circumstances alter cases; *see* **altura**.

circunstanciado *adj* detailed, circumstantial.

circunstancial *adj* (**a**) circumstantial. (**b**) *arrangement etc* makeshift, emergency (*attr*).

circunstante 1 *adj* (**a**) surrounding. (**b**) *person* present. **2** *nmf* onlooker, bystander; **los** —**s those present.

circunvalación *nf*: **carretera de** — bypass, ring road.

circunvecino *adj* adjacent, neighbouring, surrounding.

cirial *nm* (*Eccl*) processional candlestick.

cirio *nm* (*Eccl*) (wax) candle.

cirquero *nm* (*Mex*) circus performer, acrobat; circus impresario.

cirro *nm* cirrus.

cirrosis *nf* cirrhosis.

ciruela *nf* plum; — **claudia**, — **verdal** greengage; — **damascena** damson; — **pasa** prune.

ciruelo *nm* (**a**) (*Bot*) plum tree. (**b**) (*fam*) dolt, idiot.

cirugía *nf* surgery; — **estética**, — **plástica** plastic surgery.

cirujano *nm* surgeon.

ciscar [1g] **1** *vt* (**a**) to dirty, soil, mess up.
(**b**) (*Cu, Mex*) to put to shame.
(**c**) (*Cu, Mex*) to upset, needle (*fam*).

2 ciscarse *vr* (**a**) to soil oneself; **¡me cisco en todo!** (*euph*) blast it!
(**b**) (*Cu, Mex*) to feel ashamed.
(**c**) (*Cu, Mex*) to get upset, take offence, get needled (*fam*).

cisco *nm* (**a**) coaldust, slack; **estar hecho** — (*fam*) to be a wreck, be all in.
(**b**) (*fam*) row, shindy; **armar un** —, **meter** — to kick up a row, make trouble.

ciscón *adj* (*Cu, Mex*) easily offended.

cisma *nm* (**a**) (*Eccl*) schism; (*Pol etc*) split; (*fig*) discord, disagreement. (**b**) (*Col*) prudery, overniceness. (**c**) (*Col*) gossip.

cismático *adj* (**a**) (*Eccl*) schismatic(al); (*fig*) troublemaking, fractious, dissident. (**b**) (*Col*) prudish, overnice; finicky. (**c**) (*Col*) gossipy.

cisne *nm* (**a**) (*Orn*) swan. (**b**) (*RPl*) powder puff.

Cister *nm* Cistercian Order.

cisterciense 1 *adj* Cistercian. **2** *nm* Cistercian.

cisterna *nf* cistern; tank; reservoir.

cistitis *nf* cystitis.

cita *nf* (**a**) appointment, engagement; meeting; place of meeting, rendez-vous; (*of lovers*) meeting, (*with girlfriend*) date; — **espacial** rendez-vous in space, space link-up; **acudir a una** — to keep an appointment, turn up for an appointment; **se dieron (una) cita para las 8** they agreed to meet at 8; **faltar a una** — to miss an appointment, break an appointment, not turn up for a date; **tener una** — **con uno** to have an appointment with someone, have a date with someone.

(**b**) (*Lit etc*) quotation (*de* from); reference; (*act*) citation; **con largas** —**s probatorias** with long quotations in support.

citable *adj* quotable.

citación *nf* (**a**) (*Lit etc*) quotation. (**b**) (*Law*) summons, citation; — **a licitadores** invitation to bidders, invitation of tenders.

citado *adj* aforementioned; **en el** — **país** in the aforementioned country, in this country; in the country in question.

citar [1a] **1** *vt* (**a**) to make an appointment with; to make a date with; **la cité para las 9** I arranged to meet her at 9; **la cité para delante de Correos** I arranged to meet her in front of the post office.

(**b**) (*Law*) to call, summon; **tiene facultades para** — **testigos** he has the power to call witnesses.

(**c**) (*Taur*) to incite, provoke, stir up; to call out to.

(**d**) (*Lit etc*) to quote, cite (*de* from).

2 citarse *vr*: — **con uno** to arrange to meet someone (*para las 7 at 7*); **citémonos para delante del estadio** let's meet outside the stadium.

cítara *nf* zither.

-cito, -cita *suffix* (*in some combinations* **-ecito, -ecita**): see **-ito**.

citrato *nm* citrate.

cítrico *adj* citric.

citrón *nm* lemon.

ciudad *nf* city, town; **C—** **del Cabo** Cape Town; **C—** **Eterna** Eternal City (*Rome*); **C—** **Imperial** (*Spanish Hist*) Toledo; **C—** **del Vaticano** Vatican City; **es el mejor café de la** — it's the best café in town; **hoy vamos a la** — we're going to (*or* into, up to) town today.

ciudadanía *nf* (**a**) citizens, citizenry.

(**b**) citizenship; — **de honor** freedom of a city; **derechos de** — citizen's rights, rights of citizenship.

ciudadano 1 *adj* civic, city (*attr*); **el orgullo** — civic pride.

2 *nm*, **ciudadana** *nf* (**a**) city dweller, townsman.

(**b**) (*Pol etc*) citizen; —**s** townsfolk, townspeople; inhabitants; — **de honor** freeman of city; — **del mundo** citizen of the world; —**s de segunda clase** second-class citizens, under-privileged persons.

ciudadela *nf* (**a**) citadel, fortress. (**b**) (*SAm*) tenement block.

civeta *nf* civet cat.

civeto *nm* civet.

cívico 1 *adj* civic; domestic; (*fig*) public-spirited, patriotic. **2** *nm* (*SAm*) policeman.

civil 1 *adj* (**a**) (*Pol etc*) civil; **derechos** —**es** civil rights; **guerra** — civil war; **casarse por lo** — to have a civil wedding, get married in a registry office (*or equivalent*).

(**b**) (*Mil*) **población** — civil population, civilian population.

(**c**) (*fig*) civil, courteous, polite.

2 *nm* (**a**) policeman.

(**b**) (*in Mil parlance*) civilian.

civilidad *nf* civility, courtesy, politeness.

civilización nf civilization.
civilizador adj influence etc civilizing.
civilizar [1f] **1** vt to civilize. **2 civilizarse** vr to become civilized.
civilmente adv civilly, courteously, politely.
civismo nm public spirit; community spirit; patriotism.
cizalla nf **(a)** (also —s) wire cutters, metal shears. **(b)** —s shavings, metal clippings.
cizaña nf **(a)** (Bot) darnel; (Bib) tares.
(b) (fig) discord; **sembrar** — to sow discord (entre among).
(c) (fig) vice, corruption, harmful influence.
cizañar [1a] vt to sow discord among.
cizañero nm, **cizañera** nf troublemaker, mischief-maker.
clac nm, pl **claques** (gall) **(a)** collapsible opera hat; cocked hat. **(b)** = **claque**.
clamar [1a] **1** vt to clamour for, cry out for; to appeal earnestly for.
2 vi to cry out, clamour; — **contra** to cry out against, protest vociferously against; — **por** to clamour for, demand vociferously; **esto clama al cielo** this cries out to heaven (to be reformed etc).
clamor nm **(a)** cry, shout; noise, clamour. **(b)** (of bell) tolling, knell. **(c)** (fig) clamour, outcry, protest.
clamorear [1a] **1** vt = **clamar 1. 2** vi (of bell) to toll.
clamoreo nm **(a)** clamour(ing), (prolonged) shouting. **(b)** (fig) sustained outcry, vociferous protests; —s **de protesta** vigorous protests.
clamorosamente adv noisily, loudly, clamorously.
clamoroso adj **(a)** noisy, loud, clamorous; screaming, shrieking. **(b)** (fig) success resounding, enormous.
clan nm clan; (fig) faction, group.
clandestinamente adv secretly, clandestinely; by stealth, stealthily.
clandestinidad nf secrecy; secret nature; **en la** — in secrecy.
clandestinista nm (SAm) bootlegger.
clandestino adj secret, clandestine; stealthy; (Pol) activity etc clandestine, underground; agent secret, undercover; marriage secret; runaway.
claque nf (gall) claque.
clara nf **(a)** white of an egg. **(b)** bald spot; (in cloth) bare patch, thin place. **(c)** (Meteorol) bright interval.
claraboya nf skylight.
claramente adv **(a)** brightly; clearly. **(b)** (fig) clearly, plainly.
clarea nf mulled wine.
clarear [1a] **1** vt **(a)** to brighten; to light up; colour to make lighter.
(b) (fig) to clarify, make clear(er).
(c) (Mex) — **a uno** to shoot someone through.
2 vi **(a)** (Meteorol) to clear up, brighten up.
(b) (of day) to dawn, break; to grow light.
3 clarearse vr **(a)** (cloth) to be transparent, let the light through.
(b) (fam) to give the game away.
clarete nm claret; rosé, light red wine.
claridad nf **(a)** brightness; light.
(b) clearness, clarity; **lo explicó todo con mucha** — he explained it all very clearly.
(c) —es sharp remarks, unpleasant remarks; home truths.
claridoso adj (CAm, Mex) blunt, plain-spoken.
clarificación nf **(a)** illumination, lighting (up). **(b)** (fig) clarification.
clarificar [1g] vt **(a)** to illuminate, light (up); to brighten.
(b) liquid to clarify; to refine, purify.
(c) wood to clear, thin out.
(d) (fig) to clarify.
clarín nm bugle, trumpet; (esp fig) clarion.
clarinada nf (fam) uncalled-for remark.
clarinazo nm (fig) trumpet call.
clarinete nm clarinet.
clarión nm chalk, white crayon.
clarividencia nf **(a)** clairvoyance. **(b)** (fig) far-sightedness; discernment; intuition.
clarividente 1 adj far-sighted, far-seeing; discerning; gifted with intuition. **2** nmf clairvoyant(e).
claro 1 adj **(a)** day, light, eyes etc bright; room light, bright, well-lit.
(b) water clear, transparent; glass clear.
(c) beer, colour light; **verde** — light green; **una tela verde** — a light-green cloth.
(d) outline, writing etc clear, distinct; bold; **tan** — **como la luz del día** as plain as a pikestaff; **más** — **que el sol** as clear as daylight.
(e) (in consistency) liquid thin; tea etc weak; hair thin, sparse.
(f) sound, voice clear.

(g) explanation, language, proof etc clear; plain, evident; **todo queda muy** — it's all very clear; **¡—! naturally!,** of course!; **¡pues —!** I quite agree with you!; **¡— que sí!** yes of course!; **¡— que no!** of course not!; — **que no es verdad** of course it isn't true; **está** — **que . . .** it is plain that . . ., it is obvious that . . .; **a las claras** clearly, plainly; openly.
(h) (fig) famous, illustrious; noble.
2 adv clearly; **hablar** — (fig) to speak plainly, speak bluntly.
3 nm **(a)** **poner algo en** — to explain something, clear up something, clarify something; (SAm) to copy something out; **no sacamos nada en** — we couldn't get anything definite; there were no concrete decisions.
(b) **pasar la noche en** — to have a sleepless night.
(c) **de** — **en** — obviously, plainly; from dusk to dawn.
(d) opening; gap, break, space; (in wood) opening, clearing, glade; (in traffic etc) gap, break.
(e) (Archit) light, window; skylight.
(f) (Art) highlight; light tone.
(g) (Naut) break in the clouds; (CAm) bright interval.
(h) (Cu) guava jelly; (Ven) sugar-cane brandy.
claroscuro nm chiaroscuro.
clase 1 nf **(a)** (in general) class; kind, sort; **con toda** — **de** with all kinds of, with every sort of, with all manner of; **gente de toda** — people of every kind, all sorts of people; **de esta** — of this kind; **de otra** — of another sort; **de una misma** — of the same kind; **de primera** — first-class; **os deseo toda** — **de felicidades** I wish you every kind of happiness.
(b) (transport, vehicles) class; **primera** — first class; — **de cámara,** — **intermedia** (Naut) cabin class; — **turista** tourist class.
(c) (School) class; (Univ) lecture, class; — **de geografía** geography class, geography lesson; — **de conducción** driving lesson; **dar** —s to teach; **ella da** —s **de italiano** she gives Italian lessons; **faltar a** — to miss class, not go to class; **fumarse la —,** **soplarse la** — to play truant.
(d) (School) classroom, (Univ) lecture room.
(e) (Pol) class; — **alta** upper class; — **baja** lower class(es); — **media** middle class(es); — **obrera** working class; **de la** — **obrera** working-class (attr); **las** —s **poseyentes** the property-owning classes; **las** —s **pudientes** the well-to-do, the moneyed classes; **ser de la** — (Ant: euph) to belong to the black race, be a half-breed.
(f) (Mil) —s **de tropa** non-commissioned officers.
2 adj (Col, Per) first-rate, classy (fam); handsome.
clasicismo nm classicism.
clásico 1 adj **(a)** classical.
(b) (fig) classic; outstanding, remarkable; car etc vintage; institution traditional, typical; custom time-honoured; **le dio el** — **saludo** he gave him the time-honoured salute; **es la clásica plazuela española** it is a typical Spanish square.
2 nm **(a)** classic.
(b) (person) classicist.
clasificable adj classifiable.
clasificación nf classification; (Sport) table, league; (Naut) rating; — **nacional del disco** (equivalent to) top twenty, record hit parade.
clasificador nm **(a)** classifier. **(b)** filing cabinet; — **de cartas** letter file.
clasificar [1g] **1** vt to classify (en la B under B); to grade, rate, class; letters to sort.
2 clasificarse vr **(a)** (Sport) to win a place; to occupy a position; **Meca se clasificó después de la Ceca** Meca came after Ceca, Meca finished after Ceca; **¿dónde se clasificó el equipo local?** where did the home team come?
(b) (Sport) to qualify; **no se clasificó el equipo para la final** the team did not qualify for the final.
clasista adj (Pol) class (attr).
claudia nf greengage.
claudicar [1g] vi **(a)** to limp. **(b)** (fig) to act deceitfully; to bungle it; to waver, stall. **(c)** (fig) to give way, abandon one's principles, back down.
claustro nm **(a)** (Eccl etc) cloister. **(b)** (Univ) staff, faculty (US); (as assembly) senate. **(c)** (Anat) — **materno** womb.
claustrofobia nf claustrophobia.
cláusula nf clause.
clausura nf **(a)** closing, closure; formal closing, closing ceremony. **(b)** (Eccl) monastic life; **convento de** — enclosed convent.

clausurar [1a] vt (a) to close, bring to a close; (Parl etc) to adjourn. (b) (SAm) house etc to close (up).
clava nf club, cudgel.
clavado adj (a) nailed; stuck fast, firmly fixed; **quedó — en la pared** it stuck in the wall, it remained fixed in the wall; **el reloj estaba — en las 7** the watch was stopped at 7.
(b) studded with nails.
(c) dress just right, exactly fitting.
(d) **dejar a uno —** to leave someone speechless; **quedó —** he was dumbfounded.
(e) **a las 5 clavadas** at 5 sharp, at 5 on the dot.
(f) **es Domingo —** he's the living image of Domingo.
(g) ¡—! exactly!, precisely!
clavar [1a] **1** vt (a) nail to knock in, drive in, bang in; to fasten, fix; to pin; boards etc to nail together, nail up; dagger, knife etc to stick, thrust (en into), bury (en in); gun to spike; **— un anuncio a** (or **en**) **la puerta** to nail an announcement to the door.
(b) jewel to set, mount.
(c) eyes, gaze to fix (en on), rivet (en to).
(d) (fam) to cheat, twist (fam); **me clavaron 50 dólares** they stung me for 50 dollars (fam).
2 clavarse vr (a) (of nail etc) to penetrate, go in.
(b) **— una astilla en el dedo** to get a splinter in one's finger; **— una espina** to prick oneself on a thorn; **se clavó el cuchillo en el pecho** he thrust the knife into his chest.
(c) (fig) to be mistaken.
(d) **—la** (CAm) to get drunk.
(e) (Mex) **— algo** to steal something, pinch something (fam).
clave 1 nf (a) (to code, classification etc) key; **la — del problema** the key to the problem.
(b) (Chess) key move.
(c) (Mus) clef; **— de fa** bass clef; **— de sol** treble clef.
(d) (Archit) keystone.
2 nm (Mus) harpsichord.
3 adj, attr key (attr); **cuestión — key** question; **posición —** key position.
clavecín nm spinet.
clavel nm carnation; **— de poeta, — de ramillete, — de San Isidro** sweet william.
clavelón nm marigold.
clavellina nf pink.
clavero[1] nm (Bot) clove tree.
clavero[2] nm keeper of the keys; treasurer, cashier.
claveteado nm studs, studding.
clavetear [1a] vt (a) door etc to stud, decorate with studs. (b) shoelace etc to put a metal tip on. (c) (fig) deal etc to clinch, close, wind up.
clavicémbalo nm, **clavicordio** nm clavichord.
clavícula nf collar bone, clavicle.
clavija nf peg, dowel, pin; (Mus) peg; (Elec) plug; **— hendida, — de dos patas** cotter pin; **apretar las —s a uno** to put the screws on someone (fam).
clavijero nm set of pegs, row of pegs; clothes rack.
clavillo nm (also **clavito** nm) small nail, brad, tack, pin. (b) (Bot) clove.
clavo nm (a) (Tech) nail; tack; stud; spike; **— romano** brass-headed nail; **— de rosca** screw; **de — pasado** obvious, undeniable; easy; outworn, out-of-date; **verdad de — pasado** platitude, truism; **dar en el —** (fig) to hit the nail on the head; **remachar el —** (fig) to make matters worse; ¡to add completely superfluous reasons.
(b) (Bot) clove.
(c) (Med) corn.
(d) (Med) sharp pain; (fig) anguish, acute distress.
(e) (Hond, Mex) rich vein of ore.
(f) (Arg, Bol) unpleasant thing; nasty situation; (Comm) unsaleable article, drug on the market.
claxon nm, pl **claxons** ['klakson] (Aut) horn, hooter; **tocar el —** to sound one's horn, hoot.
claxonar [1a] vi (Aut) to sound one's horn, hoot.
claxonazo nm (Aut) hoot, toot (on the horn).
clemátide nf clematis.
clemencia nf mercy, clemency; leniency.
clemente adj merciful, clement; lenient.
cleptomanía nf kleptomania.
cleptómano nm, **cleptómana** nf kleptomaniac.
clerecía nf (a) priesthood. (b) (persons) clergy.
clergyman [klerxi'man] adj invar: **traje —** (Eccl) modernized form of priest's attire (adopted in Spain 1966).
clerical 1 adj clerical. **2** nm (CAm, Pan, PR) clergyman.
clericalismo nm clericalism.
clericato nm, **clericatura** nf priesthood.
clericó nm (RPl: angl) fruit cup.

clérigo nm (Catholic) priest; (Anglican) clergyman, priest; (other) minister.
clero nm clergy.
cliché nm (a) (Typ) stencil. (b) (Lit) cliché; see **clisé**.
cliente nmf (Comm) client, customer; (Law) client; (Med) patient.
clientela nf (Comm) clients, clientèle, customers; (Med) practice; patients.
clima nm climate.
climatérico adj climacteric.
climático adj climatic.
climatología nf climatology.
clímax ['klimas] nm, pl **clímax** (all senses) climax.
clinch [klinʃ] nm (SAm: angl), **clincha** nf (angl) clinch.
clínica nf (a) clinic; private hospital, nursing home; teaching hospital; **— de reposo** convalescent home.
(b) clinical training.
clínico adj clinical.
clip nm, pl **clips** [klis] (angl) paper clip; trouser clip; (jewel) clip; (SAm) earring.
clíper nm (Naut: angl) clipper.
clisar [1a] vt to stereotype, stencil.
clisé nm (Typ) cliché, stereotype plate; stencil, skin; (Phot) plate.
clisos nmpl (sl) eyes, peepers (sl).
clo nm cluck; **hacer —** to cluck.
cloaca nf sewer (also fig); drain.
cloquear [1a] vi to cluck.
cloqueo nm clucking.
cloral nm chloral.
clorhídrico adj hydrochloric.
clorinar [1a] vt to chlorinate.
cloro nm chlorine.
clorofila nf chlorophyl(l).
cloroformar [1a] vt (Arg, Chi, Mex, PR), **cloroformizar** [1f] vt to chloroform.
cloroformo nm chloroform.
cloruro nm chloride; **— de cal** chloride of lime.
clown [klawn] nm, pl **clowns** [klawn] (angl) clown.
club [klu or kluβ] nm, pl **clubs** [klus or kluβs] and **clubes** (SAm) (a) club; **— campestre** country club; **— nocturno** night club. (b) (Aut) saloon car, sedan (US).
clueca nf broody hen.
clueco adj (a) hen broody. (b) (Arg) sickly, unwell. (c) (Ant) stuck-up (fam).
cluniacense 1 adj Cluniac. **2** nm Cluniac.
co . . . co . . .
coa nf (a) (Cu, Mex, Pan, Ven) pointed stick used in digging (or sowing). (b) (Chi) underworld slang.
coacción nf coercion, compulsion; duress.
coaccionar [1a] vt to coerce, compel, put great pressure on.
coactivo adj coercive; compelling.
coadjutor nm, **coadjutora** nf assistant, coadjutor.
coadjuvar [1a] vt to help, assist; to help in, contribute to.
coagulación nf coagulation; clotting; curdling.
coagulante nm coagulant.
coagular [1a] **1** vt to coagulate; to clot, congeal; milk to curdle. **2 coagularse** vr to coagulate; to clot, congeal; to curdle.
coágulo nm coagulated mass; clot; congealed lump.
coalición nf coalition; **gobierno de —** coalition government.
coartada nf alibi.
coartar [1a] vt to limit, restrict.
coautor nm, **coautora** nf co-author.
coba nf (fam) (a) fib; neat trick. (b) soft soap (sl); cajolery; **dar — a uno** to soap someone up (sl), soft-soap someone (sl), play up to someone; to bamboozle someone (fam).
cobalto nm cobalt.
cobarde 1 adj cowardly; fainthearted, timid. **2** nmf coward.
cobardear [1a] vi to be a coward, show cowardice, act in a cowardly way.
cobardía nf cowardliness; faintheartedness, timidity.
cobardón nm shameful coward, great coward.
cobaya nf, **cobayo** nm guinea pig.
cobertera nf (a) lid, cover; watchcase. (b) (Bot) white water lily. (c) procuress.
cobertizo nm shed, outhouse, lean-to; shelter; covered passage; **— de aviación** hangar; **— de coche** carport.
cobertor nm bedspread, coverlet.
cobertura nf (a) cover, covering. (b) bedspread. (c) **— del seguro** insurance cover.
cobija nf (a) (Archit) coping tile, imbrex. (b) (SAm) poncho, blanket; **—s** bedclothes. (c) (Cu, PR) roof (of palm leaves).

cobijar [1a] **1** vt (a) to cover (up), close in.
(b) to protect, shelter; to take in, give shelter to, (pej) harbour.
(c) (Ant, Ec) to thatch, roof.
2 cobijarse vr to take shelter.

cobijo nm (a) shelter, lodging. (b) (fig) cover.

cobista (fam) **1** adj soapy, smarmy (fam). **2** nm soapy individual, smarmy sort (fam).

cobo nm (Ant) (a) (Zool) sea snail. (b) unsociable person, shy person.

cobra¹ nf (Zool) cobra.

cobra² nf (Hunting) retrieval.

cobrable adj, **cobradero** adj (a) retrievable. (b) (Comm) price chargeable; sum recoverable.

cobrador nm (a) (Comm) collector. (b) (of bus etc) conductor. (c) (dog) retriever.

cobradora nf conductress, clippie (fam).

cobranza nf (a) = cobro. (b) (Hunting) retrieval.

cobrar [1a] **1** vt (a) lost object to recover; (Hunting) to retrieve, fetch, bring back; rope to take in, pull in; blow to get, receive.
(b) price to charge; **cobran 200 dólares por componerlo** they charge 200 dollars to repair it; **¿cuánto me va Vd a —?** what are you doing to charge me?; **me han cobrado demasiado** they've charged me too much, they've overcharged me.
(c) sum to collect, receive; cheque to cash; salary, wages to earn; to draw, get, collect; **¿cuánto cobras al año?** how much do you get a year?, how much do they pay you a year?; **fue a la oficina a — el sueldo** he went to the office to get his wages; **cantidades por —** sums payable, sums due; **cuenta por —** unpaid bill.
(d) (SAm) **— a uno** to press someone for payment.
(e) flesh to put on.
(f) credit, fame etc to get, acquire, gain; courage to summon up, muster; strength to gather; **— cariño a uno** to take a liking to someone, grow fond of someone; **— fama de** to acquire a reputation as (or for being).
2 vi (a) (Fin) to draw one's pay, get one's wages; to collect one's salary; **cobra los viernes** he gets paid on Fridays; **te pagaré en cuanto cobre** I'll pay you when I get my wages.
(b) **— al número llamado** (Tel) to reverse the charges.
(c) (fam) **¡vas a —!** you'll cop it! (sl).
3 cobrarse vr (a) (Med) to recover, get well; to come to.
(b) **— de una pérdida** to make up for a loss.

cobre nm (a) copper.
(b) (Cook) copper pans, kitchen utensils.
(c) (Mus) brass (also **—s**); **batir(se) el — to** work hard, work with a will; to hustle; (in argument) to get worked up; **batirse el — por + infin** to go all out to + infin.
(d) (SAm) cent, small copper coin; **enseñar el —** (Col, Mex) to show one's nasty side.

cobreado adj copperplated.

cobreño adj copper (attr), coppery.

cobrero nm coppersmith.

cobrizo adj coppery.

cobro nm (a) recovery, retrieval.
(b) (Fin) collection; payment; **cargo por —** collection charge; **deuda de — difícil** debt that is hard to collect; **— a la entrega** collect on delivery; **poner al** (or **en**) **—** to make payable; bill to send out.
(c) safe place; **poner algo en —** to put something in a safe place, put something out of harm's way; **ponerse en —** to take refuge, get to safety.

coca¹ nf (fam) (a) head, nut (sl). (b) rap on the nut. (c) (of hair) bun, coil. (d) (in rope) kink.

coca² nf (a) (SAm: Bot) coca; coca tea. (b) (Mex) **de —** free, gratis; vainly.

coca³ nf (SD, Ven) bogeyman.

cocacolo nm, **cocacola** nf (Col) frivolous teenager, idle young person.

cocacho nm (Arg, Bol) tap on the head.

cocaína nf cocaine.

cocal nm (Per, PR, Ven) coca plantation.

cocción nf (Cook) cooking; (Tech) baking, firing.

cocear [1a] vti to kick (also fig).

cocer [2b and 2h] **1** vt (a) (Cook) to cook; to boil; to bake.
(b) (Tech) bricks etc to bake, fire.
2 vi to cook; to boil; to bubble, seethe; (of wine) to ferment.
3 cocerse vr (fig) to suffer intensely, be in great pain.

cocido 1 adj (a) boiled, cooked; **bien —** well done.

(b) skilled, experienced; **estar — en** to be skilled at, be expert at.
2 nm stew (in Spain: of meat, bacon, chickpeas etc); **— irlandés** Irish stew; **ganarse el —** to earn one's living; to eke out a living.

cociente nm quotient; **— intelectual** intelligence quotient, IQ.

cocina nf (a) (room) kitchen; **de —** kitchen (attr).
(b) stove, cooker; **— económica** cooker, range, boiler; **— eléctrica** electric cooker; **— a gas, — de gas** gas stove, gas cooker; **— de petróleo** oil stove.
(c) (art) cooking, cookery; cuisine; **— casera** plain cooking, homely cooking; **la — valenciana** Valencian cooking, the Valencian cuisine; **libro de —** cookery book, cookbook (US).

cocinar [1a] **1** vt to cook. **2** vi (a) to cook, do the cooking. (b) (fig) to meddle.

cocinero nm, **cocinera** nf cook.

cocinilla nf (a) small kitchen, kitchenette. (b) small cooker; spirit stove; chafing dish.

cocker ['kokeɪ] nm (angl) cocker (spaniel).

cocktel nm, pl **cockteis** or **cócteles** (angl) = **cóctel.**

coco¹ nm (Med) coccus; (Ent) grub, maggot.

coco² nm (a) bogeyman; **parece un —** he's an ugly devil.
(b) face, grimace; **hacer —s a uno** to make faces at someone, (lovers) make eyes at someone; to coax someone, wheedle someone.

coco³ **1** nm (a) (Bot) coconut; coconut palm.
(b) (hum) nut (sl), noddle (fam).
(c) (SAm) cup (etc) made from a coconut shell.
(d) (Col, Ec) derby hat.
(e) (Per, Urug) percale.
2 adj (Ant) (a) hard, strong.
(b) obstinate.

cococha nf (of cod etc) barbel.

cocodrilo nm crocodile.

cocoliche nm (RPl) macaronic slang of Italiaɪ immigrants; Italian.

cocoliste nm (Mex) infectious disease; sunstroke.

cócona nf (Cu) tip.

coconote nm (Mex) child; chubby child; squat person.

cócora nmf (a) (fam) bore. (b) (Arg) conceited person.

cocoroco adj (Chi) vain, stuck-up (fam); brazen.

cocoso adj maggoty, worm-eaten.

cocotal nm coconut grove, coconut plantation.

cocotero nm coconut palm.

coctel nm, **cóctel** ['koktel or 'kotel] nm, pl **coctels** or **cócteles** (angl) (a) cocktail.
(b) cocktail party; **ofrecer un — en honor de uno** to hold a cocktail party in someone's honour.

coctelera nf cocktail shaker.

cocuyo nm (SAm) firefly.

cocha nf (Chi, Ec) pool; swamp; lagoon.

cochambre nm muck, filth; litter; filthy thing, disgusting object; (fig) muck, rubbish.

cochambroso adj muck, nauseating, stinking; (fig) vile.

cochayuyo nm (Bol, Chi, Per) seaweed.

coche¹ nm (a) (Aut) car, motorcar, automobile (US); **— ambulancia** ambulance; **— de alquiler** taxi, cab; hire car; **— blindado** armoured car; **— de bomberos** fire engine; **— de carreras** racing car; **— celular** Black Maria, prison van; **—s de choque** dodgem cars; **— deportivo** sports car; **— de época** vintage car; **— fúnebre** hearse; **— de punto** taxi; **— de turismo** saloon car, sedan (US); tourer; **ir en — to** go by car; to drive, motor; **ir en el — de San Fernando** to go on Shank's pony, ride Shank's mare.
(b) (Rail) coach, car, carriage; **— directo** through carriage; **— de equipajes** luggage van, baggage car (US); **— de viajeros** passenger coach.
(c) (Hist) coach, carriage.

coche² nm (CAm, Mex) pig, hog; **— de monte** wild pig.

coche-cabina nm, pl **coches-cabina** bubble car.

coche-cama nm, pl **coches-cama** sleeping car, sleeper.

cochecillo nm small carriage (etc); **— de inválido** invalid carriage.

cochecito nm (a) pram, perambulator, baby carriage (US); **— de niño** go-cart. (b) (Aut) bubble car.

coche-comedor nm, pl **coches-comedor** dining car, restaurant car.

coche-correo nm, pl **coches-correo** (Rail) mail van, mobile sorting office.

coche-cuba nm, pl **coches-cuba** tank lorry, water wagon.

coche-habitación nm, pl **coches-habitación** caravan, trailer.

coche-patrulla nm, pl **coches-patrulla** patrol car.

cochera *nf* (a) coach house; — **de alquiler** livery stable. (b) (*Aut*) garage, carport. (c) — **de tranvías** tram shed, tram depot.

cocherada *nf* (*Mex*) coarse expression.

coche-restaurante *nm*, *pl* **coches-restaurante** dining car, restaurant car.

cochero 1 *adj*: **puerta cochera** carriage entrance. **2** *nm* coachman; — **de punto** cabman, cabby (*fam*); **hablar (en)** — (*Mex*) to use coarse language.

cocherón *nm* (*Rail*) engine shed, locomotive depot.

coche-salón *nm*, *pl* **coches-salón** (*Rail*) saloon coach.

coches-tope *nmpl* dodgem cars.

coche-vivienda *nm*, *pl* **coches-vivienda** caravan, trailer.

cochina *nf* sow.

cochinada *nf* (a) filth, filthiness. (b) filthy object, dirty thing. (c) (*fig*) beastly thing (to do); filthy act, filthy word; dirty trick; **eso fue una** — that was a beastly thing to do; **hacer una** — **a uno** to play a dirty trick on someone.

cochinear [1a] *vi* (*fam*) to talk smut, tell dirty stories, wallow in filth.

cochinería *nf* = **cochinada**.

cochinilla *nf* (a) (*Zool*) woodlouse. (b) (*Ent, colouring*) cochineal. (c) **de** — (*Cu, Mex*) trivial.

cochinillo *nm* piglet, sucking-pig.

cochino 1 *adj* (a) filthy, dirty. (b) (*fig*) filthy, rotten, measly (*fam*); **esta vida cochina** this wretched life. **2** *nm* (a) pig; — **de leche** sucking-pig; — **montés** wild pig. (b) (*fig*) hog; swine; filthy person; **realmente es un** — he really is a swine.

cochiquera *nf*, **cochitril** *nm* pigsty (*also fig*).

cochoso *adj* (*Col, Ec*) filthy.

cochura *nf* (a) (*act*) = **cocción**. (b) batch of loaves (*or cakes, bricks etc*).

codal *nm* (a) (*Bot*) vine shoot. (b) (*Archit*) strut, prop.

codaste *nm* stern post.

codazo *nm* (a) jab, poke, nudge (with one's elbow). (b) (*Mex*) tip, hint.

codeador *adj* (*Chi, Ec, Per*) bothersome, demanding.

codear [1a] **1** *vt* (a) to elbow, nudge, jostle. (b) (*Chi, Ec, Per*) — **a uno** to make insistent requests to someone, keep dropping hints to someone. **2** *vi* (a) to elbow, jostle; **abrirse paso codeando** to elbow one's way through. (b) (*Chi, Ec, Per*) to beg persistently, sponge. **3 codearse** *vr*: — **con** to hobnob with, rub shoulders with.

codeína *nf* codeine.

codeo *nm* (*Chi, Ec, Per*) sponging (*fam*).

codeso *nm* laburnum.

códice *nm* manuscript, codex.

codicia *nf* greed, covetousness; — **de** greed for, lust for.

codiciable *adj* covetable, desirable; enviable.

codiciado *adj* widely desired; much in demand; sought-after, coveted; **obtuvo el** — **título** he won the coveted title.

codiciar [1b] *vt* to covet.

codicilo *nm* codicil.

codiciosamente *adv* greedily, covetously.

codicioso *adj* greedy, covetous; **ser** — **de** to be greedy for, covet; **estoy** — **de verte** I am very eager to see you.

codificación *nf* codification.

codificar [1g] *vt* to codify.

código *nm* (a) (*Law etc*) code; law, statute; rules, set of rules; — **de (la) circulación** highway code; — **de leyes** law code, statute book; — **militar** articles of war; — **penal** penal code. (b) (*Tel etc*) code; **mensaje en** — message in code, coded message; — **de señales** signal code.

codillo *nm* (*Zool*) knee; (*Bot*) stump; (*Tech*) elbow (joint), bend; angle iron.

codo *nm* (a) (*Anat*) elbow, (*Zool*) knee; **comerse los** —**s de hambre** to be utterly destitute; **dar con el** — **a uno, dar de(l)** — **a uno** to nudge someone; **empinar el** — to booze, drink; **hablar por los** —**s** to talk too much, talk 19 to the dozen; **llevar a uno** — **con** — to frogmarch someone along, drag someone along with his hands tied behind his back; (*fig*) to arrest someone; **mentir por los** —**s** to tell huge lies; **morderse el** — (*Mex, RPl*) to restrain oneself; **ser del** —, **ser duro de** — (*CAm*) to be mean. (b) (*Tech*) elbow (joint), bend; angle iron. (c) (*fig*) elbow grease; **hacer más** —**s** to put more

elbow grease into it; **sacó la oposición a base de** —**s** he won the post by sheer hard work.

codorniz *nf* quail.

coeducación *nf* coeducation.

coeducacional *adj* coeducational.

coeficiente *nm* coefficient; — **de inteligencia** intelligence quotient, IQ.

coercer [2b] *vt* to coerce, constrain; to restrain.

coerción *nf* coercion, constraint; restraint.

coercitivo *adj* coercive.

coetáneo 1 *adj* contemporary (**con** with). **2** *nm*, **coetánea** *nf* contemporary.

coevo *adj* coeval.

coexistencia *nf* coexistence; — **pacífica** peaceful coexistence.

coexistente *adj* coexistent.

coexistir [3a] *vi* to coexist (**con** with).

cofa *nf* (*Naut*) top; — **mayor** maintop.

cofia *nf* (*of nurse, servant etc*) cap, white cap; (*arch*) coif; bonnet.

cofrade *nm* member (of a brotherhood), brother.

cofradía *nf* brotherhood, fraternity; guild, association; (*of thieves etc*) gang.

cofre *nm* chest; case (for jewels *etc*).

cofrecito *nm* casket.

cogedero 1 *adj* fruit ripe, ready to be picked. **2** *nm* handle.

cogedor *nm* small shovel, ash shovel; dustpan.

coger [2c] **1** *vt* (a) *handle, object etc* to take hold of, catch hold of; to seize, grasp; to hold on to; *ball etc* to catch; *fallen object* to pick up; *dress etc* to gather up, hold up; *book etc* to pick up, take up; *tool* (*fig*) to hold, use; — **a uno de la mano** to take someone by the hand; **ir cogidos de la mano** to go hand-in-hand, (*lovers*) to go along holding hands; **no ha cogido un fusil en la vida** he's never held a gun in his life.

(b) to take, pinch (*fam*); **me coge siempre las cerillas** he always takes my matches; **en la aduana le cogieron una radio** they found a radio on him in the customs, they confiscated a radio from him in the customs.

(c) *flower, fruit etc* to pick, pluck; to harvest; to gather, collect.

(d) *person etc* to catch; (*Law*) to arrest; (*Mil*) to take prisoner; *prisoner* to take, capture; *animal* to catch, capture, trap; *fish* to catch; *runner etc* to catch (up with); **¡por fin te he cogido!** caught you at last!; — **un buen marido** to catch oneself (*or get, acquire*) a good husband; — **a uno en una mentira** to catch someone in a lie; **la noche nos cogió todavía en el mar** the night caught us still at sea; **la guerra nos cogió en Francia** the war caught us in France; **antes que nos coja la noche** before night overtakes us (*or comes down on us*); — **a uno en la hora tonta,** — **a uno detrás de la puerta** to catch someone at a disadvantage; *see also* **desprevenido** *etc*.

(e) (*of bull*) to gore; to toss; (*of car*) to knock down, run over.

(f) — **los dedos en la puerta** to catch one's fingers in the door.

(g) *tip etc* to take, accept; *work* to take on; *news etc* to take, receive; **cogió la noticia sin interés** he received the news without interest.

(h) *course, period, work etc* to begin on; **cogí la conferencia a mitad** I joined the discussion halfway through.

(i) to get, obtain, acquire; **he cogido el billete del avión** I've got my air ticket; **cógeme un puesto en la cola** get me a place in the queue; **acabo de** — **una cocinera nueva** I've got a new cook.

(j) *disease, cold etc* to catch; *dust* to gather, collect; *habit* to get, get into, catch, acquire; **el niño cogió sarampión** the child got (*or caught*) measles; **los perros cogen pulgas** dogs get fleas; **ha cogido la manía de las quinielas** he's caught the pools craze.

(k) (*of emotion*) to take; — **cariño a** to take a liking to; — **celos a** to become jealous of; — **aversión a** to take a strong dislike to.

(l) *sense, meaning* to get, understand; *spoken words* to catch; *radio* to pick up, get; *expression* to pick up; *accent* to catch, acquire; *technique* to pick up, learn; **con esta radio cogemos Praga** with this set we can get Prague.

(m) *notes etc* to take down; **le cogieron el discurso taquigráficamente** they took his speech down in shorthand.

(n) to choose, pick; **has cogido un mal momento** you've picked a bad time.

(o) *means of transport* to take, catch, go by; **vamos a** — **el tren** let's take the train.

(p) (*of container*) to hold, take; *area* to cover, extend over, take up.

(q) (*Arg, Bol, Cu, Mex, Par, Urug*: *tabu*) to lay (*tabu*), screw (*tabu*).

2 *vi* **(a)** (*Bot*) to take, strike.

(b) to fit, go, have room; **aquí no coge** it doesn't fit in here, there's no room for it here.

3 cogerse *vr* **(a)** to catch; **— los dedos en la puerta** to catch one's fingers in the door; **— a uno** to cling tight to someone, press close against someone.

(b) **— algo** to steal something, pinch something (*fam*).

(c) **— con uno** (PR, SD) to get on (well) with someone; **— en algo** to get involved in something; to get used to something.

cogestión *nf* co-partnership (*in industry etc*).

cogida *nf* **(a)** (*Agr*) gathering, picking; harvesting; (*of fish*) catch. **(b)** (*Taur*) goring, tossing; **tener una — to be gored, be tossed.

cogido *nm* (*Sew*) fold, gather, tuck.

cogienda *nf* **(a)** (*Col, Ven*)=**cogida** **(a)**; (*Mil*) forced enlistment. **(b)** (*Arg, Mex*: *tabu*) screwing (*tabu*).

cognado 1 *adj* cognate. **2** *nm* cognate.

cognición *nf* cognition.

cogollo *nm* **(a)** (*of plant*) shoot, sprout; (*of lettuce, cabbage*) heart; (*of tree*) top; (*SAm*) top of sugar cane.

(b) (*fig*) best part, cream; **el — de la sociedad** the cream of society.

(c) (*fig*) centre, core, nucleus.

cogotazo *nm* blow on the back of the neck; (*Boxing etc*) rabbit punch.

cogote *nm* back of the neck, nape; **de —** (*RPl*) *animal* fat; **carne de —** (*Chi, RPl*) trash; **ponérselas en el —** (*CAm*) to beat it (*fam*).

cogotudo *adj* (*Chi, Per, RPl*) well heeled (*sl*), moneyed; (*SD*) powerful in politics.

cogulla *nf* cowl.

cohabitación *nf* cohabitation.

cohabitar [1a] *vi* to live together, cohabit (*also pej*).

cohechar [1a] *vt* to bribe, offer a bribe to.

cohecho *nm* bribe, bribery.

coheredera *nf* coheiress.

coheredero *nm* coheir, joint heir.

coherencia *nf* coherence; (*Phys etc*) cohesion.

coherente *adj* coherent.

cohesión *nf* cohesion.

cohesivo *adj* cohesive.

cohete *nm* **(a)** rocket; **— espacial** (space) rocket; **— luminoso**, **— de señales** flare, star shell, distress signal.

(b) (*CAm, Mex*) pistol; (*Mex*) blasting fuse; (*Mex*) blast hole; **—s** (*Mex*) fireworks (*in general*).

(c) (*Bol, RPl*) **al —** in vain; without rhyme or reason.

cohetería *nf* rocketry.

cohibición *nf* restraint; inhibition.

cohibido *adj* restrained, restricted; (*in temperament*) inhibited, full of inhibitions; shy, timid, self-conscious; ill at ease; **sentirse —** to feel shy, feel embarrassed.

cohibir [3a] **1** *vt* to restrain, check, restrict; to inhibit; to make uneasy, make shy, embarrass.

2 cohibirse *vr* to feel inhibited; to get uneasy, to become shy, feel embarrassed.

cohombro *nm* cucumber.

cohonestar [1a] *vt* **(a)** to explain away, whitewash, make appear reasonable. **(b)** *two qualities etc* to blend, harmonize.

cohorte *nf* cohort.

coima *nf* **(a)** concubine. **(b)** (*of gambling operator*) rake-off (*fam*). **(c)** (*Chi, Per, RPl*) bribe.

coime *nm* **(a)** pimp, ponce. **(b)** gambling operator. **(c)** (*Col*) waiter.

coimero *adj* (*Chi, Per, RPl*) easily bribed, given to taking bribes.

coincidencia *nf* **(a)** coincidence. **(b)** agreement; **en — con** in agreement with.

coincidente *adj* coincidental.

coincidir [3a] *vi* **(a)** to coincide (*con* with). **(b)** to coincide, agree; **todos coinciden en que ...** everybody agrees that ...

coito *nm* intercourse, coitus.

cojear [1a] *vi* **(a)** (*person*) to limp, hobble (along); to be lame (*de* in); (*furniture*) to wobble, rock, be rocky; **cojean del mismo pie** they both have the same faults; **sabemos de qué pie cojea** we know his weak spots (*or* weaknesses).

(b) (*fig*) to slip up, be at fault (*de* in); to deviate from virtue.

cojera *nf* lameness; limp.

cojijo *nm* **(a)** bug, small insect. **(b)** (*fig*) peeve (*fam*), grudge, grumble.

cojijoso *adj* peevish, cross, grumpy.

cojín *nm* cushion.

cojinete *nm* **(a)** small cushion, pad.

(b) (*Mech*) **— a bolas**, **— de bolas** ball bearing; **— de rodillos** roller bearing.

(c) (*Rail etc*) chair.

(d) **—s** (*Col, Mex, Ven*) saddlebags.

cojinillos *nmpl* (*CAm, Mex*) saddlebags.

cojo 1 *adj* **(a)** *person* lame; crippled; limping; *furniture* wobbly, rocky; **— de un pie** lame in one foot.

(b) (*fig*) lame, weak, shaky; **así el verso queda —** so the line is defective; **la frase está coja** the sentence is incomplete.

2 *nm*, **coja** *nf* lame person, cripple.

cojón *nm* (*tabu*) ball (*tabu*), testicle; **¡—es!** balls!; **¡hace falta tener —es!** you've got to have guts; **es un tipo sin —es** he's a gutless individual.

cojonudo *adj* **(a)** marvellous, splendid; **¡qué —!** great stuff! (*fam*). **(b)** (*SAm*) brave, bold. **(c)** (*SAm*) lazy, slow, stupid.

cojudo *adj* **(a)** (*Agr*) *animal* entire, not castrated; used for stud purposes. **(b)** (*Bol, Chi, Ec, Urug*) simple-minded, gullible; **hacerse el —** to act dumb.

cok [kok] *nm*, **coke** ['koke] *nm* (*SAm*: *angl*) coke.

col *nf* cabbage; **— de bruselas** (Brussels) sprouts; **— rizada** kale; **— roja** red cabbage; **— de Saboya** savoy; **entre — y —**, **lechuga** a change is a good thing, variety is the spice of life.

cola¹ *nf* **(a)** (*Aer, Astron, Orn, Zool*) tail.

(b) (*of coat*) tail; (*of dress*) train.

(c) (*position*) end, last place, bottom; tail end; end seat; **estar a la — de la clase** to be (at the) bottom of the class; **venir a la —** to come last, come at the back; **estar arrimado a la —** (*Pol*) to be a reactionary; **vagón de —** last truck, rear coach.

(d) (*of cars, people etc*) queue, line; **hacer —** to queue (up), line up; **¡a la —!**, **¡haga Vd —!** get in the queue!

(e) (*Tech*) **— de milano**, **— de pato** dovetail.

(f) (*fig*) **tener —**, **traer —** to have grave consequences.

cola² *nf* glue, gum; (*for painting*) size; **— de pescado** fish glue; isinglass; **— de retal** size; **pintura a la —** distemper, (*Art*) tempera; **comer —** (*RPl*) to have a setback; **eso no pega ni con —** that has nothing whatsoever to do with it; that's utter rubbish.

colaboración *nf* **(a)** collaboration; **escrito en —** written in collaboration.

(b) (*to journal etc*) contribution (*a, en* to); (*to conference*) paper, communication.

colaboracionismo *nm* (*Pol*: *pej*) collaboration.

colaboracionista *nmf* (*Pol*: *pej*) collaborator, collaborationist.

colaborador *nm*, **colaboradora** *nf* collaborator, helper, co-worker; (*Lit etc*) contributor.

colaborar [1a] *vi* **(a)** to collaborate; to help, assist; **— con uno en un trabajo** to collaborate with someone on a piece of work.

(b) (*Lit etc*) **— a**, **— en** to contribute (articles) to, write for.

colación *nf* **(a)** collation, comparison; **sacar a —** to mention, bring up; to air; (*pej*) to drag in, drag up; **traer algo a —** to adduce something as proof.

(b) (*Cook*) collation (*also Eccl*); light meal, snack; buffet meal; reception, wedding breakfast; (*SAm*) sweet.

colacionar [1a] *vt* to collate, compare.

colada *nf* **(a)** wash, washing; **día de —** washing day; **tender la —** to hang out the washing. **(b)** bleach, lye. **(c)** (*Agr*) sheep run, cattle run; (*Geog*) defile.

coladera *nf* **(a)** strainer; colander. **(b)** (*Mex*) sewer.

coladero *nm*, **colador** *nm* strainer; colander.

colado *adj* **(a)** *metal* cast. **(b)** **aire —** draught. **(c)** (*fam*) **estar —** to be in love.

coladura *nf* **(a)** (*act*) straining. **(b)** **—s** grounds, dregs. **(c)** (*fam*) absurdity, piece of nonsense; blunder.

colapso *nm* **(a)** (*Med*) collapse; breakdown; **— nervioso** nervous breakdown. **(b)** (*fig*) collapse; breakdown; stoppage; ruin, destruction.

colar [1m] **1** *vt* **(a)** *coffee, vegetables etc* to strain (off); to filter; *metal* to cast, pour.

(b) *clothes* to bleach.

(c) **— algo por un sitio** to slip something through a place, squeeze something past a place; **— unos géneros por la aduana** to slip goods through the customs.

(d) **— algo a uno** to foist something off on someone, palm something off on someone; **— una moneda** to pass a (false) coin; **— una noticia a uno**

to make someone believe a (false) piece of news; **¡a mí no me la cuelas!** I'm not going to swallow that!, don't give me that stuff!

(e) (*Mex*) to drive, bore; *shaft* to sink.

2 *vi* **(a)** (*of liquid*) to ooze, seep (through), filter (through), percolate; (*of air*) to get in (*por* through).

(b) to pass; **esa noticia es demasiado sospechosa para —** that news item is too suspect to pass.

(c) (*fam*) to booze, tipple.

3 colarse *vr* **(a)** to slip in, slip past, squeeze in; (*at meeting etc*) to slip in, sneak in, get in unobserved; (*at party*) to gatecrash; **la moto se cuela por entre la circulación** the motorcycle slips through the traffic; **se ha colado algún indeseable** some undeseable has slipped in.

(b) to blunder, slip up; to put one's foot in it.

colateral *adj* collateral.

colca *nf* (*Per*) barn, granary; cotton store; attic food store.

colcrén *nm* (*angl*) cold cream.

colcha *nf* bedspread, counterpane.

colchón *nm* mattress; **— de aire** airbed; (*Tech*) air cushion; **— de muelles** spring mattress, interior sprung mattress; **— neumático** airbed; **— de plumas** feather bed.

cole *nm* (*a*) **=colegio**.

colear [1a] **1** *vt* **(a)** (*Taur*) *bull* to grab by the tail, hold on to the tail of; (*Arg, Col, Mex, Ven*) to throw by twisting its tail.

(b) (*Col, Ven*) to vex, nag, harass; (*Guat*) to tail, follow.

2 *vi* **(a)** **el perro colea** the dog wags its tail.

(b) (*fig*) **el asunto todavía colea** the affair is still not settled; **estar vivito y coleando** to be still hale and hearty.

(c) (*CAm, PR*) **colea en los 50** he's close on 50, he's knocking on 50 (*fam*).

colección *nf* collection.

coleccionador *nm*, **coleccionadora** *nf* collector.

coleccionar [1a] *vti* to collect.

coleccionista *nmf* collector.

colecta *nf* **(a)** collection (for charity). **(b)** (*Eccl*) collect.

colectar [1a] *vt taxes etc* to collect.

colecticio *adj* **(a)** (*Mil*) raw, untrained. **(b) tomo —** omnibus edition, collected works.

colectivamente *adv* collectively.

colectivero *nm* (*Arg*) bus driver.

colectividad *nf* **(a)** sum total, whole; unit, group, community; **la —** social society, the whole community. **(b)** (*Pol*) collective ownership.

colectivizar [1f] *vt* to collectivize.

colectivo 1 *adj* collective (*also Gram*); **acción colectiva** joint action, group action, communal action. **2** *nm* (*Bol, RPl*) (small) bus.

colector *nm* **(a)** (*person*) collector. **(b)** (*Elec*) collector; (*Mech*) sump; trap, container; sewer.

colega *nm* colleague.

colegial 1 *adj* **(a)** school (*attr*), college (*attr*). **(b)** (*Eccl*) collegiate. **(c)** (*Mex*) raw, inexperienced. **2** *nm* schoolboy; (*fig*) inexperienced person, callow youth.

colegiala *nf* schoolgirl.

colegiata *nf* collegiate church.

colegio *nm* **(a)** independent secondary school, private (*or* fee-paying) high school; **— (de párvulos)** kindergarten, primary school; **— integrado** comprehensive school; **— de internos** boarding school; **— de pago** fee-paying school; **ir al —** to go to school.

(b) (*Univ*) college; **— mayor** (*Hist*) college (*eg of Salamanca or Oxford*), (*modern*) hall of residence.

(c) (*other*) **— de abogados** bar association; **C— de cardenales** College of Cardinals; **— electoral** electoral college.

colegir [3c *and* 3l] *vt* **(a)** to collect, gather. **(b)** to infer, gather, conclude (*de* from); **de lo cual colijo que . . .** from which I gather that . . .

coleóptero *nm* beetle.

cólera 1 *nf* **(a)** anger, rage; **descargar la — en** to vent one's anger on; **montar en —** to get angry. **(b)** (*Anat*) bile. **2** *nm* (*Med*) cholera.

colérico *adj* angry, furious, irate; (*by nature*) irascible, bad-tempered.

coleta *nf* **(a)** pigtail; **gente de —** bullfighters, bullfighting people; **cortarse la —** to quit the ring, give up bullfighting; (*fig*) to quit, give it all up, retire.

(b) (*fam*) postscript, afterthought.

coletazo *nm* **(a)** (*Zool etc*) lash, blow with the tail. **(b)** (*of vehicle*) sway, swaying movement; **dar —s** to sway about.

(c) (*fig*) sting in the tail; unexpected after-effect.

coletero *nm* wren.

coleto *nm* **(a)** (*Hist*) doublet, jerkin.

(b) (*fam*) body; oneself; **decir para su —** to say to oneself; **echarse algo al —** to eat something right up; to drink something down; **echarse un libro al —** to read a book right through, devour a book.

colgadero *nm* hook, hanger, peg.

colgadizo 1 *adj* hanging, loose. **2** *nm* lean-to shed; (*Ant*) flat roof.

colgado *adj and ptp* **(a)** uncertain, doubtful.

(b) dejar — a uno to let someone down, fail someone; **quedarse —** to be disappointed; **antes le veré — que . . .** I'll see him damned before . . .

colgadura *nf* (*also* **—s**) hangings, drapery; tapestry; **—s de cama** bed hangings, bed curtains.

colgajo *nm* **(a)** rag, tatter, shred. **(b)** (*Bot*) bunch. **(c)** (*Med*) flap of flesh.

colgante 1 *adj* hanging; droopy, floppy; dangling; **puente —** suspension bridge; **con la lengua —** with his tongue hanging out.

2 *nm* **(a)** drop, pendant, earring; (*Arg, Par, PR*) watch chain.

(b) (*Archit*) festoon.

(c) —s fringe.

(d) —s (*tabu*) balls (*tabu*).

colgar [1h *and* 1m] **1** *vt* **(a)** *picture etc* to hang (up) (*de* from, *en* on); *person* to hang; *flag, washing etc* to hang out.

(b) *wall* to decorate with hangings, drape (*de* with).

(c) to attribute, impute (*a* to); **— la culpa a uno** to pin the blame on someone.

(d) (*Univ sl*) to plough (*sl*).

2 *vi* **(a)** to hang, be suspended (*de* on, from); (*of ears etc*) to hang down, droop, dangle; (*Tel*) to hang up, ring off.

colibrí *nm* hummingbird.

cólico *nm* colic.

colicuar [1d] **1** *vt* to melt, dissolve; to fuse. **2 colicuarse** *vr* to melt, dissolve, liquefy.

coliflor *nf* cauliflower.

coligado 1 *adj*: **estar coligados** to be allied, be in league. **2** *nm* ally, confederate.

coligarse [1h] *vr* to unite, join together, make common cause (*con* with).

colilla *nf* fag end; butt, stub.

colimbo *nm* grebe.

colín *nm* (*Ant*) machete, cane knife.

colina *nf* hill.

colindante *adj* adjacent, adjoining, neighbouring.

colindar [1a] *vi* to adjoin, be adjacent; **— con** to adjoin, be adjacent to, border on.

colirrojo *nm* redstart.

colís *nm* (*Col*) machete, cane knife.

Coliseo *nm* Coliseum.

colisión *nf* **(a)** (*Aut etc*) collision; crash, smash; **— de frente** head-on collision. **(b)** (*fig*) clash.

colitis *nf* colitis.

colmado 1 *adj* abundant, copious; full (*de* of), overflowing (*de* with); heaped (*de* with); **una cucharada colmada** one heaped spoonful; **una tarde colmada de incidentes** an afternoon (more than) full of incident.

2 *nm* cheap seafood restaurant; (*Catalonia*) grocer's shop; (*Andalusia*) retail wine shop.

colmar [1a] *vt* **(a)** to fill to the brim, fill right up, fill to overflowing (*with* de); to heap (*de* with).

(b) (*fig*) *hopes etc* to fulfill, more than satisfy, realize completely.

(c) (*fig*) **— a uno de honores** to shower honours upon someone; **— a uno de alabanzas** to heap praises on someone; **— a uno de favores** to lavish favours on someone, overwhelm someone with favours.

colmena *nf* **(a)** beehive; (*fig*) hive. **(b)** (*Mex*) bee; bees.

colmenar *nm* apiary.

colmenero *nm* beekeeper.

colmillo *nm* **(a)** (*Anat*) eye tooth, canine (tooth); (*Zool*) fang; (*of walrus, elephant etc*) tusk.

(b) (*fig*) **enseñar los —s** to show one's teeth; **escupir por el —** to talk big, brag; **tener el — torcido** to be an old fox; **¡ya tengo —s!** (*Mex*) you can't fool me!

colmillón *nm* (*SAm*) greed.

colmilludo *adj* **(a)** having big teeth (*or* fangs *etc*). **(b)** (*fig*) sharp, alert.

colmo *nm* (*fig*) height, summit, extreme; **el — de la elegancia** the height of elegance; **el — de lo absurdo** the height of absurdity; **a — en** plenty, in abundance; **con —** heaped, to overflowing; **para — de desgracias** to make matters worse, to cap it all;

¡es el —! it's the limit!, it's the last straw!; **sería el —
si** . . . it would be the end if . . .
colocación nf **(a)** (act) placing; positioning; (Comm)
investment. **(b)** job, place, situation; **no encuentro
—** I can't find a job. **(c)** place, position.
colocado adj: **apostar para —** to back (a horse) for
a place.
colocar [1g] **1** vt **(a)** to place, put, position; to arrange;
troops etc to position, station; **— la quilla de un
buque** to lay down a ship's keel; **— un satélite en
órbita** to put (or place) a satellite in orbit.
 (b) person to place (in a job), find a post for.
 (c) (Comm, Fin) goods, order to place; money to
place, invest; loan to float.
 (d) — una historia a uno to bore someone with
the same old story; **— una responsabilidad a uno**
to saddle someone with a responsibility.
 2 colocarse vr **(a)** to place oneself, station oneself.
 (b) (Sport) to be placed, get a place; **el equipo se
ha colocado en quinto lugar** the team has climbed
to fifth position.
 (c) (person) to get a job.
colocho (CAm) **1** adj curly(-haired). **2 —s** nmpl
curls; wood shavings.
colodrillo nm back of the neck.
colofón nm colophon.
colofonia nf rosin, colophony.
colombianismo nm colombianism, word (or phrase
etc) peculiar to Colombia.
colombiano 1 adj Colombian. **2** nm, **colombiana** nf
Colombian.
colombino adj of Columbus, relating to Columbus.
Colón m Columbus.
colon nm (Anat) colon.
Colonia Cologne.
colonia¹ nf **(a)** (Bio, Pol etc) colony; (of town) suburb,
estate; **— escolar** summer camp for schoolchildren;
— obrera working-class housing settlement; **— penal**
penal settlement; **— veraniega** holiday camp; **las
antiguas —s españolas** the former Spanish colonies.
 (b) silk ribbon.
 (c) (PR, SD) sugar-cane plantation.
colonia² nf eau-de-Cologne.
coloniaje nm (SAm) colonial period; system of
colonial government; (pej) slavery, slave status.
colonial adj colonial; food, product overseas (attr),
imported.
colonialismo nm colonialism.
colonialista 1 adj colonialist. **2** nmf colonialist.
colonización nf colonization; settlement.
colonizador 1 adj colonizing. **2** nm colonist, colonizer,
settler; pioneer.
colonizar [1f] vt to colonize; to settle.
colono nm **(a)** (Pol) colonist, settler; colonial. **(b)** (Agr)
tenant farmer. **(c)** (PR, SD) sugar planter.
coloquial adj colloquial, familiar.
coloquio nm conversation, talk; conference;
(scientific etc) colloquium; (Lit) dialogue.
color nm **(a)** (in general) colour; hue, shade; (fig)
colour, colouring; **a —, en —es** film in colour, colour
(attr); **a todo —** in full colour; **gente de —** (euph)
coloured people (euph); **zapatos de —** brown shoes;
subido de — blue, rude, scabrous; **so — de** under
pretext of; **el suceso tuvo —es trágicos** the event
had its tragic aspect, the event had a sad side to it;
— base basic colour; **— local** local colour; **—
muerto, — quebrado** dull colour; **— sólido** fast
colour; **un vestido de — malva** a mauve(-coloured)
dress; **un vino — fresa** a strawberry-coloured wine;
verlo todo — de rosa to see everything through
rose-coloured spectacles, be ridiculously optimistic;
cambiar de —, mudar de — to change colour;
ponerse de mil —es to colour up; **sacar los —es a
uno** to make someone blush; **le salieron los —es**
she blushed.
 (b) (Art) colour, paint; (Tech) dye, colouring
matter; rouge.
 (c) —es (Mil) colours; **los —es nacionales** the
national colours, the national flag.
coloración nf coloration, colouring; (Zool etc)
coloration, markings.
colorado 1 adj **(a)** coloured, (esp) red; complexion
rosy, ruddy; **poner — a uno** to make someone
blush; **ponerse —** to blush.
 (b) (fig) joke blue, rude, scabrous; argument
plausible.
 2 nm (Cu) scarlet fever.
coloradote adj red-faced, ruddy.
colorante 1 adj colouring. **2** nm colouring (matter).
colorar [1a] vt to colour; to dye, tint, stain; **— algo de
amarillo** to colour (or dye etc) something yellow.

colorear [1a] **1** vt **(a)** = **colorar. (b)** (fig) to excuse;
to put in a favourable light; to gloss over, white-
wash. **2** vi to redden, show red.
colorete nm rouge.
colorido nm colour(ing).
colorín 1 adj (Chi) reddish blond(e).
 2 nm **(a)** bright colour; **tener muchos —es** to
have vivid colours; **¡qué —es tiene el niño!** what rosy
cheeks the little fellow has!
 (b) (Orn) linnet.
 (c) (Med) measles.
colorir [3a; defective] **1** vt **(a)** to colour. **(b)** (fig) =
colorear (b). 2 vi to take on a colour, colour up.
colosal adj colossal.
coloso nm colossus.
coludo adj (Chi, RPl) long-tailed.
Columbina f Columbine.
columbrar [1a] vt **(a)** to glimpse, spy, make out.
 (b) (fig) to guess.
columna nf **(a)** (Archit) column; pillar.
 (b) (Mil) column; **— blindada** armoured column;
quinta — fifth column; **— volante** flying column.
 (c) (Anat) **— vertebral** spine, spinal column.
 (d) (Mech) column; **— de dirección** steering
column.
 (e) (Typ) column.
 (f) (fig) pillar, support; **una — de la religión** a
pillar of religion.
columnata nf colonnade.
columnista nmf columnist.
columpiar [1b] **1** vt to swing. **2 columpiarse** vr **(a)**
to swing; (body etc) to sway; to waddle; to swagger
(along). **(b)** (fig) to swing to and fro, seesaw.
columpio nm swing; (SAm) rocking chair; **—
basculante, — de tabla** seesaw.
colusión nf collusion.
colza nf (Bot) rape, colza.
collado nm **(a)** hill, height; hillock. **(b)** mountain pass.
collage [ko'la:3] nm (Art) collage.
collalba nf (Orn) wheatear.
collar nm **(a)** necklace; chain (of office); (dog)
collar; (Orn, Zool etc) collar, ruff; **— de perlas** pearl
necklace.
 (b) (Mech) collar, ring.
 (c) — de fuerza stranglehold.
colleja nf dandelion.
collera nf **(a)** horse collar. **(b)** (SAm) **—s** cufflinks.
collín nm (CAm), **collines** nm (Ec) cane knife,
machete.
coma¹ nm (Med) coma.
coma² nf (Typ) comma; **sin faltar una —** right down
to the last detail, with complete accuracy.
comadre nf **(a)** godmother or mother (with respect to
each other).
 (b) neighbour; friend, crony; village woman,
peasant woman; gossip; **un grupo de —s** a group of
gossips, a gathering of gossipy women.
 (c) (Med) midwife.
 (d) (pej) go-between, procuress.
 (e) (fam) pansy (fam).
 (f) (prov) in direct address between women, not
translated.
comadrear [1a] vi to gossip.
comadreja nf weasel.
comadreo nm, **comadrería** nf gossip; gossiping,
chattering.
comadrona nf midwife.
comal nm (CAm, Mex) flat earthenware pan, frying
pan.
comandancia nf **(a)** command. **(b)** rank of major.
 (c) commander's headquarters (or office). **(d)** area
under a commander's jurisdiction.
comandante nm **(a)** commandant, commander; **—
en jefe** commander-in-chief. **(b)** (rank) major.
comandar [1a] vt to command, lead.
comandita nf sleeping partnership, silent partnership (US).
comanditario adj: **socio —** sleeping partner, silent
partner (US).
comando nm **(a)** (Mil) command; (Tech) control; **— a
distancia** remote control. **(b)** (angl) commando
(group and individual). **(c)** duffel coat.
comarca nf region, area, part.
comarcal adj road local; radio station local, regional.
comarcano adj neighbouring, bordering.
comarcar [1g] vi to border (con on), be adjacent
(con to).
comatoso adj comatose.
comba nf **(a)** bend; bulge, warp, sag. **(b)** skipping
rope; **dar a la —** to turn the skipping rope; **saltar a
la —** to skip. **(c)** (game) skipping.
combadura nf (on road) curve, camber; = **comba (a).**

combar [1a] **1** *vt* to bend, curve. **2 combarse** *vr* to bend, curve; to bulge, warp; to sag.

combate *nm* fight, combat, engagement; (*fig*) battle, struggle; — **naval** naval battle, sea fight; — **singular** single combat; **estar fuera de** — to be out of action (*also fig*); (*Boxing*) to be knocked out; **poner a uno fuera de** — to put someone out of action, (*Boxing*) to knock someone out; **ganar por fuera de** — to win by a knockout.

combatiente *nm* combatant; **no** — non-combatant.

combatir [1a] **1** *vt* (**a**) (*Mil*) to attack; (*fig*) *tendency, proposal etc* to combat, fight, oppose; *mind* to assail, harass.

(**b**) (*of waves, wind*) to beat upon.

2 *vi and* **combatirse** *vr* to fight, struggle (**con**, *contra* against).

combatividad *nf* fighting spirit, fight; (*pej*) aggressiveness.

combativo *adj* full of fight, spirited; (*pej*) aggressive.

combés *nm* (*Naut*) waist.

combi *nf* (*fam*), **combinable** *nf* multi-purpose van.

combinación *nf* (**a**) (*act etc*) combination.

(**b**) (*Chem*) compound; (*drink*) cocktail.

(**c**) (*Rail etc*) connection; **hacer** — **con** to connect with.

(**d**) (*Math, Pools etc*) permutation; — **métrica** (*Lit*) stanza form, rhyme scheme.

(**e**) arrangement, setup, scheme; plan; (*pej*) cunning scheme, deep-laid plan.

(**f**) (*Sew*) slip.

combinado *nm* cocktail.

combinar [1a] **1** *vt* to combine; to join, unite, put together; *colours etc* to blend, mix, match; *scheme* to devise, work out.

2 combinarse *vr* to combine; (*persons*) to get together, join together (**para** + *infin* to + *infin*); (*pej*) to form a ring, gang up, conspire.

combo 1 *adj* bent; bulging; warped. **2** *nm* (**a**) (*SAm*) sledgehammer. (**b**) (*Chi, Per*) slap, punch.

combustible 1 *adj* combustible. **2** *nm* fuel, combustible.

combustión *nf* combustion; — **espontánea** spontaneous combustion.

comebolas *nm*, *pl* **comebolas** (*Cu*) simple soul, gullible individual.

comedero 1 *adj* eatable, edible.

2 *nm* (**a**) (*Agr*) trough, manger.

(**b**) dining room.

(**c**) (*fam*) food, grub (*sl*); **limpiar a uno el** — to deprive someone of his bread and butter.

(**d**) (*Ant*) brothel.

(**e**) (*Col*) haunt, hangout (*fam*).

comedia *nf* (**a**) (*modern*) comedy; (*Hist*) play, drama, *comedia*; **alta** — high comedy; — **en un acto** one-act play; — **de costumbres** comedy of manners; — **de capa y espada** cloak-and-dagger play; — **de enredos** comedy of intrigue.

(**b**) (*fig*) farce; pretence; **hacer la** — to make believe, pretend.

comedianta *nf* (**a**) (comic) actress, comedienne. (**b**) (*pej*) hypocrite.

comediante *nm* (**a**) (comic) actor. (**b**) (*pej*) hypocrite.

comedidamente *adv* moderately; courteously; (*SAm*) obligingly.

comedido *adj* moderate, restrained; courteous; (*SAm*) obliging.

comedimiento *nm* moderation, restraint; courtesy; (*SAm*) helpfulness.

comedirse [3l] *vr* (**a**) to behave moderately, be restrained, restrain oneself; to be courteous, answer (*etc*) politely; — **en las palabras** to choose one's words carefully.

(**b**) (*SAm*) — **a** + *infin* to offer to + *infin*, volunteer to + *infin*.

comedón *nm* blackhead.

comedor 1 *adj* greedy, gluttonous.

2 *nm* (**a**) dining room; restaurant; — **de beneficencia** soup kitchen.

(**b**) dining-room suite.

3 *nm*, **comedora** *nf* glutton; **ser buen** — to have a good appetite; **ser mal** — to have a poor appetite, not eat much.

comefuego *nm* (*Circus*) fire eater.

comegente *nm* (*Ec, PR*) glutton.

comején *nm* (**a**) (*Ent*) termite, white ant. (**b**) (*Col*) glutton. (**c**) (*Ec, Per*) worry, gnawing anxiety.

comelitona *nf* (*Mex*) = **comilona.**

comelón *adj* (*SAm*) = **comilón.**

comelona *nf* (*SAm*) = **comilona.**

comendador *nm* knight commander (*of a military order*).

comendatorio *adj*: **carta comendatoria** letter of recommendation.

comensal *nmf* (**a**) companion at table; fellow diner; **habrá 13** —**es** there will be 13 to dinner; **me lo dijo mi** — the man sitting next to me at dinner told me so.

(**b**) (*Col*) (*at hotel*) guest.

comentador *nm* commentator.

comentar [1a] *vt* to comment on; *theory etc* to expound; (*fam*) to discuss; to criticize, gossip about.

comentario *nm* (**a**) comment, remark, observation; **y ahora sin más** — ... and now without further ado ...

(**b**) (*Lit*) commentary.

(**c**) —**s** gossip, (nasty) talk, tittle-tattle; **dar lugar a** —**s** to cause gossip; **hacer** —**s** to gossip, pass (nasty) remarks.

comentarista *nm* commentator (*also Radio*); — **deportivo** sports commentator.

comento *nm* comment; (*Lit*) commentary; (*fig*) lie, pretence.

comenzar [1f *and* 1k] *vti* to begin, start, commence; — **protestando** to begin by protesting; — **a hacer algo** to begin to do something, start to do something, start doing something; — **con** to begin with; — **por** to begin with; — **por** + *infin* to begin by + *ger*.

comer [2a] **1** *vt* (**a**) to eat; **sin** —**lo ni beberlo** (*fig*) without having (had) anything to do with it.

(**b**) to eat (*or* have) for lunch; **hoy comimos truchas** today we had trout for lunch.

(**c**) (*Chem*) to eat away, eat into, corrode; (*of sea etc*) to swallow up, erode; **me come la pierna** my leg itches; **esto come las existencias** this devours (*or* uses up) the stocks.

(**d**) *colour* to fade; — **los colores a uno** to take away someone's colours.

(**e**) (*fig*) **le come la envidia** she is eaten up with envy.

(**f**) (*Chess etc*) to take, capture.

2 *vi* (**a**) to eat; — **de** to eat, partake of, have some of; — **como una vaca** to eat like a horse; **no** — **ni dejar** — to be a dog in the manger; *see* **dar.**

(**b**) to have a meal, eat; (*esp*) to have lunch, (*in some regions*) to dine, to have supper.

(**c**) (*fig*) **¡pero** — **y callar!** but I'd better say no more!; **el mismo que come y viste** the very same; **este pescado es de buen** — this fish is good eating; **Juan es de buen** — John eats anything, John has a hearty appetite; **no tienen qué** — they don't have enough to live on.

3 comerse *vr* (**a**) to eat up; **se lo comió todo** he ate it all up.

(**b**) (*fig*) *resources etc* to consume, devour, eat up.

(**c**) (*fig*) *passage etc* to skip; *consonant* to swallow, slur.

(**d**) (*idioms*) — **a uno por pies** to take someone in completely; **se comen unos a otros** they're at daggers drawn; *see* **vista** *etc.*

comerciable *adj* (**a**) (*Comm*) marketable, saleable.

(**b**) (*fig*) sociable.

comercial 1 *adj* commercial; business (*attr*), trading (*attr*); **barrio** — business quarter, shopping district; **centro** — business centre. **2** *nm* (*TV: angl*) commercial.

comercialización *nf* (**a**) commercialization. (**b**) marketing.

comercializar [1f] *vt* (**a**) (*in general*) to commercialize. (**b**) *product* to market.

comerciante *nm* trader, dealer, merchant; — **al por mayor** wholesaler; — **al por menor** retailer.

comerciar [1b] *vi* (*of two persons*) to have dealings; (*of two countries*) to trade; — **con** (*also* — **en**) *goods* to deal in, handle; *person* to do business with, have dealings with, *country* trade with.

comercio *nm* (**a**) (*in general*) commerce; trade; business; — **de**, — **en** trade in, traffic in; **dealings in; el** — **español** Spanish trade; — **de esclavos** slave trade; — **de exportación** export trade; — **exterior** foreign trade, overseas trade; — **de importación** import trade; — **interior** home trade.

(**b**) (*persons collectively*) business interests, business world; big business.

(**c**) shop, store (*US*).

(**d**) (*fig*) intercourse; dealings, contacts (**con** with); — **sexual** sexual intercourse; — **social** social intercourse, social contacts.

comestible 1 *adj* eatable; *fungus etc* edible.

2 *nm* (**a**) foodstuff, comestible; —**s** foods, foodstuffs.

(**b**) (*Comm*) —**s** groceries, provisions; **tienda de** —**s** grocer's (shop), grocery (*US*).

cometa[1] *nm* (*Astron*) comet.

cometa[2] *nf* kite.

cometer [2a] *vt* (a) *crime etc* to commit; *error* to make, commit. (b) *task etc* to entrust, commit (*a* to). (c) (*Ling*) to use, employ.

cometido *nm* task, assignment; commitment.

comezón *nf* (a) itch, itching; (*of heat etc*) tingle, tingling sensation; **siento — en el brazo** my arm itches; my arm tingles, (b) (*fig*) itch (*por* for); **sentir — de + *infin*** to feel an itch to + *infin*.

comi *nf* (*fam*) =**comisaría** (a).

comible *adj* eatable, fit to eat.

cómica *nf* (comic) actress; comedienne.

comicastro *nm* ham (actor) (*sl*).

comicidad *nf* humour, comedy, comicalness.

comicios *nmpl* elections, voting.

cómico 1 *adj* (a) comic(al), funny, amusing. (b) (*Theat*) comedy (*attr*); **autor —** playwright. **2** *nm* (comic) actor; comedian.

comida *nf* (a) (*in general*) food.
(b) (*act*) eating; meal, (*esp*) lunch, dinner; **bendecir la —** to say grace.
(c) (*in lodging etc*) board, keep; **— y casa** board and lodging.

comidilla *nf* (a) hobby, special interest. (b) **ser la — de la ciudad** (*etc*) to be the talk of the town.

comido *adj and ptp* (a) **estar —** to have had lunch (*etc*); **venir —** to come after lunch (*etc*). (b) **es — por servido** it doesn't pay, it's not worth while.

comience *nm* (*Col*) =**comienzo**.

comienzo *nm* beginning, start; (*of plan etc*) birth, inception; (*Med etc*) onset; **al —** at the start, at first; **en los —s de este siglo** at the beginning of this century; **dar — a un acto** to begin a ceremony; **dar — a una carrera** to start a race (off).

comilón 1 *adj* fond of one's food, having a good appetite; (*pej*) greedy. **2** *nm* big eater, person with a good appetite; (*pej*) glutton, pig.

comilona *nf* (*fam*) spread (*fam*), blow-out (*sl*), feast.

comillas *nfpl* quotation marks, inverted commas; **en —, entre —** in inverted commas.

cominero 1 *adj* fussy. **2** *nm* fusspot (*fam*), fussy person.

comino *nm* cumin, cumin seed; **no vale un —** it's not worth tuppence; **no se me da un —, (no) me importa un —** I don't care two hoots (*de* about).

comisaría *nf* (a) police station. (b) (*Mil*) commissariat.

comisariato *nm* commissariat.

comisario *nm* commissary (*also Mil*); (*Pol*) commissar; **— de policía** police superintendent, commissioner of police.

comiscar [1g] *vt* to nibble from time to time (at).

comisión *nf* (a) assignment, task, commission; mission.
(b) (*Parl etc*) committee; board, commission; (*Comm, Fin*) board; **— mixta** joint committee; **— permanente** standing committee; **— planificadora** planning board.
(c) (*Comm*) commission; **— porcentual** percentage commission (*sobre* on); **— sobre las ventas** sales commission; **a —** on a commission basis.
(d) (*act*) commission; **pecado de —** sin of commission.

comisionado *nm* commissioner; (*Parl etc*) committee member; (*Comm, Fin*) board member.

comisionar [1a] *vt* to commission.

comisionista *nm* commission agent, man working on a commission basis.

comiso *nm* (*Law*) (a) seizure, confiscation. (b) confiscated goods.

comisquear [1a] *vt* =**comiscar**.

comistrajo *nm* bad meal, awful food; (*fig*) mess, hotchpotch.

comisura *nf* join; corner, angle; **— de los labios** corner of the mouth.

comité *nm* committee; **C— de No Intervención** Non-Intervention Committee.

comitiva *nf* suite, retinue; train; procession; **— fúnebre** cortège, funeral procession.

como 1 *adv* as, like; such as; as it were; about, approximately; **es —** un pez it's like a fish; **hay peces, — truchas y salmones** there are fish, such as trout and salmon; **juega —** yo he plays like I do; **toca — canta** she plays in much the same way as she sings, her singing is like her playing; **asistió — espectador** he attended as a spectator; **lo dice — juez** he says it (in his capacity) as a judge; **éste hay pocos** there are few like this; **vale más — poeta** he is better as a poet; **libre — estaba** free as he was; **la manera — sucedió** the way (in which) it happened; **había — cincuenta** there were about fifty; **sentía una — tristeza** she felt a sort of sadness; **fue así —**

comenzó la cosa it was thus that the thing began, the thing started in that way; **tuvo resultados — no se habían conocido antes** it had results such as had never been known before; **pues tocar, — tocar, no sabe** if you mean really play, well, she doesn't; she doesn't actually play.

2 *conj* (a) (+ *indic*) as, since; **— no tenía dinero** as (*or* since, because) I had no money; **— que . . .** because . . ., since . . .
(b) (+ *indic*) as soon as; **— nos vio lanzó un grito** as soon as he saw us he shouted.
(c) (+ *subj*) **— si** . . . as if . . .
(d) (+ *subj*) if, unless; provided that; **— no lo haga en seguida** unless he does it at once; **— sea** as the case may be; **— no sea para + *infin*** unless it be to + *infin*, except to + *infin*; *see* **así, pronto, querer** *etc*.

cómo 1 *adv interrog* how?; why?, how is it that . . .?; **¿— lo hace?** how does he do it?; **¿— son?** what are they like?, what do they look like?; **¿— están mis nietos?** how are my grandchildren?; **¿— está Vd?** how are you?; **¿— es de alto?** how tall is it?, what height is it?; **¿a — son las peras?** how much are the pears?; **¿— así?, ¿— eso?** how can that be?, how come?; **¿— no?** why not?; what do you mean?; **no sé — hacerlo** I don't know how to do it; **no veo — I** don't see how; **no había — alcanzarlo** there was no way of reaching it.

2 *interj etc*: **¿—?** I beg your pardon?, what?, eh?; (*surprise*) what was that?; (*anger*) how dare you!; **¡—!, ¡— no!** of course!

3 *nm*: **el por qué y el — de** the whys and wherefores of.

cómoda *nf* chest of drawers; bureau.

cómodamente *adv* comfortably; conveniently.

comodidad *nf* (a) comfort; comfortableness; convenience; **pensar en su propia —** to consider one's own convenience; **venga a su —** come at your convenience.
(b) **—es** comforts, amenities, pleasant things; **—es de la vida** good things of life; **vivir con —es** to live in easy circumstances.
(c) **—es** (*CAm: angl, Comm*) commodities, goods.

comodín 1 *adj* (*Col, Mex, Per, PR*) =**comodón**. **2** *nm* (a) (*Cards*) joker. (b) (*Mech etc*) useful gadget. (c) useful lever, standby.

cómodo *adj* (a) *chair etc* comfortable; *room* comfortable; cosy, snug, comfy (*fam*); *object* convenient, handy; *arrangement* convenient; *job, task* agreeable. (b) *person* comfortable; **así estarás más —** you'll be more comfortable this way; **ponerse —** to make oneself comfortable.

comodón *adj* comfort-loving; easy-going, liking a quiet life; **es muy —** he'll do anything for a quiet life.

comodonería *nf* love of comfort; liking for a quiet life.

comodoro *nm* commodore.

comoquiera *conj* (*lit*): **— que** (a) (+ *indic*) since, in view of the fact that. (b) (+ *subj*) in whatever way; **— que sea so** however that may be, in whatever way that may be.

compacidad *nf* compactness.

compactación *nf* compacting, compression.

compactar [1a] *vt* to compact, press together (*or* down *etc*), compress.

compacto *adj* compact; dense; *lines, threads, type etc* close.

compadecer [2d] **1** *vt* to pity, be sorry for; to sympathize with. **2 compadecerse** *vr*: **— con** to harmonize with, blend with; to agree with, fit, square with; **— de** =*vt*.

compadrada *nf* (*RPl*) brag, boast; threat; piece of effrontery.

compadrazgo *nm* status of the godfather.

compadre *nm* (a) godfather *or* father (*with respect to each other*). (b) (*fam*) friend, pal (*fam*), buddy (*esp US*); (*prov: in direct address*) friend. (c) (*RPl*) braggart; swank (*fam*), show-off (*fam*); bully.

compadrear [1a] *vi* (a) (*fam*) to be pals (*fam*). (b) (*RPl*) to brag; to swank (*fam*), show off; to adopt a bullying attitude.

compadrito *nm* (*SAm*) =**compadre** (c).

compaginar [1a] **1** *vt* (a) to arrange, put in order.
(b) (*Typ*) to make up.
(c) **— A con B** to reconcile A with B, bring A into line with B, adjust A and B.
2 compaginarse *vr* to agree, tally; **— con** to agree with, tally with, square with; (*colours*) to blend with; **no se compagina esa conducta con su carácter** such conduct does not fit in with (*or* square with) his character.

compañerismo nm comradeship, fellowship; companionship; (Sport etc) team spirit.

compañero nm, **compañera** nf (a) companion; partner (also Cards); mate; **— de armas** comrade-in-arms; **— de baile** dancing partner; **— de cama** bedfellow; **— de clase** schoolmate, classmate; **— de cuarto** roommate; **— de infortunio** companion in misfortune; **— de juego** playmate; **— de rancho** messmate; **— de viaje** fellow traveller (also fig); **es un —** divertido he's good company.

(b) **dos calcetines que no son —s** two socks which do not match, two socks which do not make up a pair; **¿dónde está el — de éste?** where is the one that goes with this?, where is the other one (of the pair)?

compañía nf (a) (in general) company; **hacer — a uno** to keep someone company; **andar en malas —s, frecuentar malas —s** to keep bad company, have unsavoury companions.

(b) (Comm, Eccl, Theat etc) company; **C— de Jesús** Society of Jesus; **Pérez y C—** Perez and Company (abbr: and Co.); **— inversionista** investment trust; **— naviera** shipping company; **— de seguros** insurance company; **— tenedora** holding company.

comparable adj comparable (a, con to, with).

comparación nf (a) comparison; **en — con** in comparison with, beside; **es superior a toda —, no tiene —** it is beyond compare, it is incomparable.

(b) (Lit) simile.

comparado adj (a) **— con** compared with, in comparison with, beside. (b) study etc comparative.

comparar [1a] vt to compare (a, con to, with); to liken (con to).

comparativo 1 adj comparative. 2 nm (Gram) comparative.

comparecencia nf (Law) appearance (in court); **su no —** his non-appearance.

comparecer [2d] vi (Law) to appear (in court); **— ante un juez** to appear before a judge.

comparecencia nf (Chi, RPl) = comparecencia.

comparendo nm (Law) summons; subpoena.

comparsa 1 nf group, procession; masquerade. 2 nmf (Theat) extra, supernumerary.

comparsería nf (Theat) extras, supernumeraries.

compartimiento nm (a) (act) division, sharing; distribution.

(b) (Naut, Rail etc) compartment; **— de bombas** (Aer) bomb bay; **— estanco** watertight compartment.

compartir [3a] vi to divide (up), share (out); opinion, responsibility etc to share (con with); **no comparto ese criterio** I do not share that view.

compás nm (a) (Mus) measure, time; beat, rhythm; bar; **— de 2 por 4** 2/4 time; **— de vals** waltz time; **a —** in time; **al — de la música** in time to the music; **martillar a —** to hammer rhythmically; **fuera de —** off beat; **llevar el —** to beat time, keep time; **perder el —** to lose the beat; **entraron a los —es de un vals** they came in to the strains of a waltz.

(b) (Math etc) compasses, pair of compasses.

(c) (Naut etc) compass.

compasado adj measured, moderate.

compasar [1a] = acompasar.

compasión nf pity, compassion; sympathy; **¡por —!** for pity's sake!; **mover a uno a —** to move someone to pity; **tener — de** to feel sorry for, take pity on; **tener pronta —** to be quick to pity, be easily moved to pity.

compasivamente adv compassionately; pityingly; sympathetically, understandingly.

compasivo adj compassionate, full of pity; sympathetic, understanding.

compatibilidad nf compatibility.

compatible adj compatible (con with).

compatriota nmf compatriot, fellow countryman, fellow countrywoman.

compeler [2a] vt to compel; **— a uno a + infin** to compel someone to + infin.

compendiar [1b] vt to abridge, condense, summarize.

compendio nm abridgement, condensed version; summary, abstract; compendium; **en —** briefly, in brief.

compendiosamente adv briefly, succinctly.

compendioso adj condensed, abridged; brief, succinct.

compenetración nf (fig) mutual understanding, fellow feeling, natural sympathy; mutual influence.

compenetrarse [1a] vr (a) (Chem etc) to interpenetrate, fuse.

(b) (fig) to (come to) share each other's feelings; to undergo mutual influence; **— de** to share the feeling of; to enter into the spirit of; to absorb, take

in, become permeated by, undergo the pervasive influence of.

compensación nf (a) compensation; (Law) redress, compensation; **en —** in exchange, as compensation. (b) (Fin) clearing; **cámara de —** clearing house.

compensador adj compensating, compensatory.

compensar [1a] vt person to compensate (de for); loss to compensate for, make up (for); mistake etc to redeem, make amends for; (Mech etc) to balance, adjust, equalize; **le compensaron con 10 dólares por los cristales rotos** they gave him 10 dollars' compensation for the broken windows.

compensatorio adj compensatory.

competencia nf (a) competition (also Comm); rivalry; competitiveness; **— desleal** unfair competition; **a —** vying with each other, as rivals; **en — con** in competition with; **estar en — to be in** competition; **hacer — con** to compete against.

(b) competence (also Law); aptitude; adequacy; suitability.

(c) domain, field, province; **y otras cosas de su —** and other things which concern him, and other things for which he is responsible; **no es de mi —** that is not my responsibility; that is not (in) my field.

competente adj (a) (Law) competent; proper, appropriate; **esto se elevará al ministerio —** this will be sent to the appropriate ministry.

(b) competent; fit, adequate, suitable; **ser — para un cargo** to be suitable for a post.

(c) sum etc adequate, proper.

competentemente adv (a) appropriately. (b) competently; adequately, suitably.

competer [2a] vi: **— a** to be the responsibility of, fall to; **le compete castigarlos** it is his job to punish them, it is up to him to punish them.

competición nf competition (also Sport); contest.

competidor 1 adj competing, rival. 2 nm, **competidora** nf competitor (also Comm); rival (a for); opponent.

competir [3l] vi (a) to compete (also Comm, Sport; con against, with; en in; para for).

(b) **— con** (fig) to rival, vie with; **los dos cuadros compiten en belleza** the two pictures vie with each other in beauty; **en cuanto a resistencia A no compite con B** A cannot compete with B for stamina.

competitivo adj (Comm etc) competitive.

compilación nf compilation.

compilador nm, **compiladora** nf compiler.

compilar [1a] vt to compile.

compinche nm pal (fam), chum, buddy (esp US).

complacencia nf (a) pleasure, satisfaction.

(b) willingness; **lo hizo con —** he did it gladly.

(c) indulgence, indulgent attitude; **tiene excesivas —s con los empleados** he is too indulgent towards his employees.

(d) (SAm: angl) complacency.

complacer [2x] 1 vt person to please; client etc to help, oblige; despot to humour; wish etc to gratify, indulge; **nos complace que sea así** we are glad it is so; **¿en qué puedo —le?** (Comm etc) can I help you?, what can I do for you?

2 **complacerse** vr: **— en + infin** to be pleased (or glad) to + infin; to take pleasure in + ger; **el Banco se complace en comunicar a su clientela que ...** the Bank is glad to tell its clients that ...

complacido adj pleased, satisfied; **me miró complacida** she gave me a grateful look; **quedamos —s de la visita** we were pleased with our visit.

complaciente adj (a) person kind, obliging, helpful; look etc cheerful; **ser — con** to be helpful to, be well-disposed towards. (b) husband complaisant.

complejidad nf complexity.

complejo 1 adj complex. 2 nm (a) (Psych) complex; **— de Edipo** Oedipus complex; **— de inferioridad** inferiority complex. (b) (Tech) complex; **— industrial** industrial complex.

complementar [1a] vt to complement; to complete, make up, round off.

complementario adj complementary.

complemento nm (a) (Math etc) complement.

(b) (Gram) complement, object; **— directo** direct object; **— indirecto** indirect object.

(c) essential part, natural concomitant; **el vino es un — de la buena comida** wine is an essential concomitant to good food.

(d) culmination; rounding-off, perfection; **sería el — de su felicidad** it would complete her happiness, it would be a crowning happiness to her.

(e) **—s** (Aut etc) accessories.

completamente adv completely.

completar [1a] vt to complete; to round off, make up; to perfect; *loss* to make good; (*angl*) to complete, finish.

completas nfpl (Eccl) compline.

completo 1 adj (a) complete; perfect, rounded, finished; *search etc* thorough; *board, charge* inclusive, all-in; **por —** completely, utterly; **fue un — fracaso** it was a complete (or total, utter) failure.
(b) (*vehicle etc*) full.
2 nm: **en la sesión estuvo el —** all members were present at the meeting.

complexión nf (a) constitution, make-up; temperament. (b) (*SAm: angl*) complexion.

complexionado adj: **bien —** strong, tough, robust; **mal —** weak, frail.

complexional adj constitutional; temperamental.

complicación nf complication, complexity; **una persona sin —** an uncomplicated person; **han surgido —es** complications have arisen.

complicado adj complicated, complex; *fracture etc* complex; *decoration etc* elaborate; *method* complicated, involved, intricate.

complicar [1g] **1** vt (a) to complicate.
(b) *person* to involve (en in).
2 complicarse vr (a) to get complicated.
(b) **— en un asunto** to get involved (or entangled) in a matter.

cómplice nmf accomplice.

complicidad nf complicity, involvement (en in).

complot [kom'plo] nm, pl **complots** [kom'plo] plot; conspiracy; intrigue.

complutense adj of Alcalá de Henares.

componenda nf (a) compromise; (provisional) settlement, (temporary) arrangement. (b) (*pej*) shady deal.

componente 1 adj component, constituent. **2** nm (*Chem etc*) component; (*of drink etc*) ingredient.

componer [2r] **1** vt (a) *collection etc* to make up, put together, compose.
(b) (*of elements*) to compose, constitute, make up; *number* to make up; **componen el jurado 12 personas** 12 persons make up the jury, the jury consists of 12 persons.
(c) (*Lit, Mus etc*) to compose, write.
(d) (*Typ*) to make up, set up (in type), compose.
(e) (*Cook*) to prepare; *salad etc* to garnish, season; *wine* to strengthen.
(f) *broken object* to mend, repair, fix; to overhaul; (*SAm*) *bones* to set; (*Med*) *stomach etc* to settle; to strengthen; *spirit* to quieten, soothe; *abuse* to set to rights, correct.
(g) *quarrel* to settle, compose, resolve; *differences* to reconcile; *persons* to reconcile.
(h) to arrange; to tidy up, polish up, adorn; *person* to dress up, deck out.
(i) (*Chi, Mex, RPl*) to castrate.
(j) (*Col*) to bewitch.
2 componerse vr (a) **— de** to consist of, be composed of, be made up of; **se compone de 6 partes** it consists of 6 parts.
(b) (*woman etc*) to dress up; to tidy oneself up; to make up.
(c) **— con uno** to come to terms with someone, reach an agreement with someone.
(d) **—las** to manage, get along; to find a way; **—las para** + *infin* to manage to + *infin*, contrive to + *infin*.

componible adj (a) repairable; worth mending. (b) reconcilable; capable of settlement.

comportable adj bearable.

comportamentista adj (Bio etc) behavioural.

comportamiento nm behaviour, conduct; (*Mech etc*) performance.

comportar [1a] **1** vt (a) to bear, endure, put up with.
(b) to involve, carry with it; **ello no comporta obligación alguna** it carries no obligation.
(c) (*Col, RPl*) to entail, cause, be the cause of.
2 comportarse vr to behave; to comport oneself, conduct oneself; **— como es debido** to behave properly.

comporte nm (a) = **comportamiento**. (b) bearing, carriage.

composición nf (a) (in several senses, also Lit, Mus) composition.
(b) (*of quarrel*) settlement; (*of persons*) reconciliation.
(c) arrangement.
(d) agreement.
(e) (*quality*) composure.

compositor nm, **compositora** nf (Mus) composer.

compostelano 1 adj of Santiago de Compostela.
2 nm, **compostelana** nf native (or inhabitant) of Santiago de Compostela; **los —s** the people of Santiago de Compostela.

compostura nf (a) composition; structure; make-up.
(b) (*Mech etc*) mending, repair, repairing; overhauling; **estar en —** to be undergoing repairs.
(c) (*Cook*) condiment, seasoning.
(d) arrangement; tidying, polishing, adornment.
(e) arrangement, agreement; settlement.
(f) (*quality*) composure; discretion, good sense; sedateness, modesty.

compota nf compote, preserve; (*with meat etc*) sauce; **— de frutas** stewed fruit.

compra nf (a) (*act*) purchase, buying; **— al contado** cash purchase; **— a plazos** hire purchase; **ir de —s** to go shopping, shop.
(b) (*article*) purchase; **—s** purchases, shopping.

comprador nm, **compradora** nf buyer, purchaser; (*in shop*) shopper, customer.

comprar [1a] vt (a) to buy, purchase (a, de from); **— al contado** to pay cash for; **— al fiado** to buy on credit; **— a plazos** to buy on hire purchase, pay for in instalments.
(b) (*fig*) to buy off, bribe; to win over, secure the allegiance of.

compraventa nf (a) buying and selling, dealing. (b) (*Law*) contract of sale.

comprender [2a] vti (a) to comprise, include; to take in; to extend to; to consist of; **servicio no comprendido** service not included; **todo comprendido** everything included, all in.
(b) to understand; to see; **— que ...** to understand that ..., see that ...; to realize that ...; **¿comprendes?** see?, understand?; **¡comprendido!** all right!, sure!; agreed!; **¡ya comprendo!** I see!, now I get it!; **no comprendo cómo** I don't see how; **comprendo su actitud** I understand his attitude; **cuando comprendió que no iba a ayudarle** when he realized (or saw) I was not going to help him; **compréndase bien que ...** let it be clearly understood that ...; **compréndanme Vds** let's be clear about this; **hacerse —** to make oneself understood.

comprensible adj understandable, comprehensible (*para* to); **no es — que ...** it is incomprehensible that ..., I (*etc*) cannot understand how ...

comprensión nf (a) comprehensiveness, inclusiveness; inclusion.
(b) (*act, faculty*) understanding, comprehension; grasp.
(c) (*emotion*) understanding (attitude); sympathy, tolerance, kindness.

comprensivo adj (a) comprehensive, inclusive; all-embracing; **un bloque — de 50 viviendas** a block containing 50 flats.
(b) *person, attitude* understanding; sympathetic, tolerant, kindly.

compresa nf compress; **— higiénica** sanitary towel, sanitary napkin (US).

compresibilidad nf compressibility.

compresible adj compressible.

compresión nf compression.

compresor nm compressor.

comprimible adj compressible.

comprimido 1 adj compressed. **2** nm (Med) pill, tablet; **— para dormir** sleeping pill.

comprimir [3a] **1** vt (a) to compress (*also Tech; en* into); to squeeze (down etc), press (down etc); to condense.
(b) (*fig*) to control, restrain; *tears* to keep back.
2 comprimirse vr (*fig*) to control oneself, contain oneself; **tuve que comprimirme para no reír** I had to keep myself from laughing; **tendremos que comprimirnos** (*Fin*) we shall have to restrict ourselves.

comprobable adj provable, demonstrable; **un alegato fácilmente —** an allegation which is easy to check.

comprobación nf checking, verification; proof; **en — de ello** in proof whereof, as proof of what I (*etc*) say; **de difícil —** hard to check, difficult to prove.

comprobador nm: **— de lámparas** valve tester.

comprobante 1 adj: **documento —** supporting document; **documentos —s de ello** documents in proof thereof.
2 nm proof; (*Comm*) receipt, voucher.

comprobar [1m] vt (a) to check, verify; to prove; to confirm, show; **— que ...** to check that ...; to show that ..., establish that ...; **— si ...** to check whether ...
(b) (*Mech etc*) to check, test, overhaul.

comprometedor adj compromising.

comprometer [2a] **1** vt (a) *person* to compromise; to embarrass, put in an awkward situation; *suspect etc* to involve, implicate; **aquellas cartas le comprometieron** those letters compromised him.

(**b**) to risk; to endanger, imperil, jeopardize; — **la reputación** to risk one's reputation; — **la neutralidad del país** to imperil one's country's neutrality.

(**c**) — **a uno a algo** to hold someone to something, pin someone down to something; — **a uno a** + *infin* to force someone to + *infin*, make someone feel obliged to + *infin*.

(**d**) (*Comm, Law*) to agree formally to; *room, seats etc* to book, reserve.

2 comprometerse *vr* (**a**) to compromise oneself; to get involved (**en** in).

(**b**) — **a** + *infin* to undertake to + *infin*, promise to + *infin*, engage to + *infin*; **se compromete a todo** he'll say yes to anything.

comprometido *adj* (**a**) *situation etc* awkward, embarrassing.

(**b**) *writer etc* engaged; committed; **no** — uncommitted; *country* non-aligned.

(**c**) **estar** — to be engaged; to be involved; to be at stake; **estar** — **para** + *infin* to be engaged to + *infin*.

compromiso *nm* (**a**) obligation; commitment; undertaking, pledge, promise; engagement, date; **por** — out of a sense of duty; **libre de** —, **sin** — (*Comm*) without obligation; **adquirir un** — **de** + *infin* to commit oneself to + *infin*, take on an obligation for + *ger*; **atender** (*or* **cumplir**) **sus** —**s** to meet one's obligations; **hacer honor a sus** —**s** to honour one's pledges; **tener muchos** —**s** to have many commitments; **¿tienes** — **para esta noche?** have you anything on this evening?, are you booked up tonight?

(**b**) agreement; — **matrimonial** engagement (to marry); — **verbal** verbal agreement, gentlemen's agreement.

(**c**) awkward situation, jam, fix; predicament; **estar en un fuerte** — to be in a real jam; **poner a uno en un** — to place someone in an embarrassing situation; **poner a uno en el** — **de** + *infin* to put someone in the position of + *ger*; **salir de un** — to get out of a jam.

compuerta *nf* sluice, floodgate; (*in door etc*) hatch.

compuesto 1 *ptp of* **componer**; **estar** — **de** to be composed of, consist of, be made up of.

2 *adj* (**a**) (*Chem, Ling, Math, interest etc*) compound; *flower, material* composite.

(**b**) *person etc* elegant, dressed up; tidy, neat.

(**c**) (*fig*) composed, calm.

3 *nm* compound (*also Chem*); preparation; composite material; — **químico** chemical compound.

compulsa *nf* (**a**) (*act*) checking, comparison. (**b**) (*Law*) attested copy, certified true copy.

compulsar [1a] *vt* (**a**) to collate, compare. (**b**) (*Law*) to make an attested copy of.

compulsión *nf* compulsion.

compulsivo *adj* compulsory; compulsive.

compulsorio *adj* (*S Am: angl*) compulsory.

compunción *nf* compunction, regret; pity; sorrow.

compungido *adj* remorseful, contrite, sorry.

compungimiento *nm* remorse, contrition.

compungir [3c] **1** *vt* to make remorseful, arouse feelings of contrition in.

2 compungirse *vr* to feel remorseful (*por* about, because of), feel sorry (*por* for).

compurgar [1h] *vt* (*Mex, Per, RPl*) *offence* to purge.

computación *nf* = **cómputo**.

computador *nm*, **computadora** *nf* computer; — **digital** digital computer.

computar [1a] *vt* to calculate, compute, reckon (*en* at).

cómputo *nm* calculation, computation, reckoning; **según nuestros** —**s** according to our calculations.

comulgante *nmf* communicant.

comulgar [1h] **1** *vt* to administer communion to.

2 *vi* to take communion, receive communion.

comulgatorio *nm* communion rail, altar rail.

común 1 *adj* (**a**) common (*a* to); joint; public, belonging to all, held in common; *gender, grave etc* common; **los intereses** —**es** common interests; **de** — **con** in common with; **A no tiene nada de** — **con B** A has nothing in common with B; **en** — in common; joint (*attr*), mutual; **hacer algo en** — to do something jointly (*or* together).

(**b**) *distribution etc* common; *custom, opinion* common, widespread, general; **es costumbre muy** — it is a very widespread custom; **la planta es** — **en la provincia** the plant is common in the province.

(**c**) *quality* common, ordinary; **fuera de lo** — out of the ordinary; **por lo** — generally.

2 *nm* (**a**) **el** — the community, the people (at large); **bienes del** — communal property, public property.

(**b**) **el** — **de las gentes** most people, the common run of people.

(**c**) toilet.

(**d**) **los C**—**s** (*Brit: Pol*) the Commons.

comuna *nf* (**a**) commune. (**b**) (*Arg, Chi, Guat, Per*) municipality.

comunal *adj* communal; community (*attr*).

comunalmente *adv* communally; as a community.

comunicable *adj* (**a**) communicable, that can be communicated. (**b**) *person* approachable; sociable.

comunicación *nf* (**a**) communication; contact; **las** —**es están rotas** communications are broken; **no hemos tenido más** — **con él** we have had no further contact with him, we have heard nothing further from him.

(**b**) message; report; (*to conference etc*) paper.

(**c**) (*Tel*) connection, contact; **póngame en** — **con el Sr Q** please give me Mr Q's number.

comunicado *nm* communiqué.

comunicar [1g] **1** *vt* (**a**) *information* to communicate, tell, pass on (*a* to); *news* to convey, tell (*a* to); *message* to give, pass (*a* to); *disease etc* to carry; to give (*a* to); *custom* to transmit, pass on; *bequest etc* to pass on (*a* to), bestow (*a* on); *fear etc* to communicate (*a* to); **nos comunicó su miedo** he affected us with his fear, his fear infected us.

(**b**) *two rooms etc* to connect, join, open a way between.

2 *vi* (**a**) to send a report (*de* from); **comunican desde Lisboa que . . .** it is reported from Lisbon that . . .

(**b**) (*Tel*) **estar comunicando** to be engaged.

(**c**) (*Archit*) — **con** to connect with; to open into.

3 comunicarse *vr* (**a**) (*persons*) to communicate (with each other); to be in touch, correspond; **nos comunicamos nuestras impresiones** we exchanged impressions.

(**b**) to pass, be transmitted; **el miedo se comunicó a todos** the fear affected everybody.

(**c**) (*Archit*) to be connected, lead into each other, intercommunicate.

comunicativo *adj* (**a**) communicative; approachable, sociable. (**b**) *laughter etc* infectious.

comunidad *nf* community; society, corporation; (*Eccl*) community; **C— Europea del Carbón y del Acero** European Coal and Steel Community (*or* Pool); **C— Británica de Naciones** British Commonwealth; **de** — (*Law*) jointly.

comunión *nf* communion.

comunismo *nm* communism.

comunista 1 *adj* communist(ic). **2** *nmf* communist.

comunizar [1f] *vt* to communize.

comúnmente *adv* commonly; usually, generally; frequently.

con 1 *prep* (**a**) (*general sense*) with; **atado** — **cuerda** tied with string; — **su ayuda** with his help; **andar** — **muletas** to walk on (*or* with) crutches; **me escribo** — **ella** I write to her; **¡**— **lo difícil que es todo esto!** what with all this being so difficult!

(**b**) in spite of; — **tantas dificultades, no se descorazonó** in spite of all the difficulties he was not discouraged; — **ser su madre, le odia** even though she is his mother she hates him.

(**c**) (*also* **para** —) to, towards; **amable** — **todos** kind to everybody; **ser insolente** — **el jefe** to be disrespectful to the boss.

(**d**) (+ *infin*) — **llegar tan tarde** (by) arriving so late; — **confesarlo se libró del castigo** by owning up he escaped punishment; — **decirle que no voy** when I tell you I'm not going; — **llegar a las 6 estará bien** if you come at 6 it will be all right.

2 — **que** *conj* and so, so then; whereupon; **¿**— **que Vd es el jefe?** so you're the boss?; — **que fuimos a la cama** and so we went to bed.

conato *nm* attempt; endeavour; effort (*de* + *infin* to + *infin*); — **de robo** attempted robbery; **hacer un** — **de** + *infin* to make an attempt to + *infin*; **poner** — **en algo** to put everything into a task.

concatenación *nf* concatenation, linking; — **de circunstancias** chain of circumstances.

concatenar [1a] *vt* to link together, concatenate.

concavidad *nf* concavity, hollow, cavity.

cóncavo 1 *adj* concave; hollow. **2** *nm* hollow, cavity.

concebible *adj* conceivable, thinkable; **no es** — **que . . .** it is unthinkable that . . .

concebir [3l] *vt* to conceive; to imagine; to understand; — **esperanzas** to nourish hopes; to become hopeful; — **una antipatía hacia** (*or* **por**) to take a dislike to; **no concibo que . . .** I cannot understand how (or why) . . .

2 vi (Bio) to conceive, become pregnant.

conceder [2a] vt to concede, grant; to confer, bestow (a on); attention etc to pay; discount to allow; prize to award (a to); honour to confer (a on); **— que . . .** to concede that . . ., admit that . . .

concejal nm town councillor.

concejil adj relating to a town council; municipal, public.

concejo nm council; **— municipal** town council.

concentración nf (all senses) concentration.

concentrado 1 adj concentrated. **2** nm extract, concentrate; **— de carne** meat extract.

concentrar [1a] **1** vt (all senses) to concentrate (**en un lugar** in a place, **en una escena** on a scene).

2 concentrarse vr (a) (Mil etc) to concentrate, be concentrated.

(b) (fig) **— a** + infin to concentrate on + ger; **el interés se concentra en esta lucha** the interest is centred on this fight.

concéntrico adj concentric.

concepción nf (a) (Bio etc) conception; **la Purísima C—** the Immaculate Conception. (b) (faculty) understanding. (c) conception, idea.

conceptismo nm witty, allusive and involved style (esp 17th century).

conceptista 1 adj witty, allusive and involved. **2** nmf writer in the style of conceptismo.

concepto nm (a) concept, conception; idea, notion; thought; **un — grandioso** a bold conception, a bold plan; **formarse un — de algo** to get an idea of something.

(b) view, opinion; judgement; **en mi —** in my view; **formarse un — de uno** to form an opinion of someone; **¿qué — has formado de él?** what do you think of him?; **tener buen — de uno, tener en buen — a uno** to think highly of someone.

(c) (of account etc) heading, section; **bajo todos (los) —s, por todos —s** from every point of view; in every way, in every respect; **en — de, por — de** as, by way of; under the heading of; **se le pagó esa cantidad por — de derechos** he was paid that amount as royalties; **por ningún —** in no way.

(d) (Lit) conceit.

conceptual adj conceptual.

conceptuar [1e] vt to think, judge, deem; **le conceptúo poco apto para eso** I think him unsuited for that; **— a uno de** (or **como, por**) to regard someone as, deem someone to be . . .; **no está bien conceptuado actualmente** he is not well thought of at present.

conceptuosamente adv wittily; (pej) over-elaborately, in a mannered way.

conceptuoso adj witty, full of conceits; (pej) over-elaborate, mannered.

concerniente adj: **— a** concerning, relating to; **en lo — a** with regard to, as for.

concertadamente adv methodically, systematically; in an orderly fashion; harmoniously.

concertado 1 adj methodical, systematic; orderly; harmonious. **2** nm, **concertada** nf (CR, Cu, Ven) servant.

concertar [1k] **1** vt (a) (Mus) to harmonize, bring into harmony; to tune (up).

(b) efforts to coordinate; differences to adjust, bring into line, reconcile; persons to achieve agreement between; to reconcile; **— a varias personas para que . . .** to get various people to agree to + infin.

(c) to agree to; agreement, treaty to conclude (**con** with); deal to arrange, fix up; price to agree, fix (**en** at); **— una venta en 20 dólares** to agree to sell something for 20 dollars, agree to a sale price of 20 dollars; **hemos concertado el piso en mil pesetas** we have agreed to rent the flat for 1000 pesetas; **— hacer algo** to agree to do something.

2 vi (a) (Mus) to harmonize, be in tune.

(b) (fig) to agree (also Gram).

3 concertarse vr (a) (Mus etc) to harmonize.

(b) (persons) to reach agreement, come to terms; **— para** + infin (pej) to conspire together to + infin.

concertina nf concertina.

concertino nm first violin, leader (of the orchestra), concertmaster (US).

concertista nmf soloist, solo performer.

concesión nf concession; grant(ing); allowance; award; (Comm) concession.

concesionario nm concessionaire, licensee.

concesivo adj concessive.

conciencia nf (a) conscience; moral sense; conscientiousness; **a —** conscientiously; **hecho a —** solidly built, well built; **en —** with a clear conscience; honestly, in truth; **con — limpia** with a clear conscience; **ancho de —** not overscrupulous; **anchura de —** lack of scruple; **libertad de —** freedom of worship; **hombre sin —** unscrupulous person; **empezó a acusarle la —** his conscience began to prick him; **tener la — tranquila** to have a clear conscience.

(b) knowledge, awareness, consciousness; **a — de que . . .** fully aware that . . ., in the certain knowledge that . . .; **tener plena — de** to be fully aware of; **tomar — de** to become aware of.

concienzudamente adv conscientiously, painstakingly, thoroughly.

concienzudo adj conscientious, painstaking, thorough.

concierto nm (a) concert, agreement; order; harmony; **de — con** in concert with; **quedar de — acerca de** to be in agreement with regard to.

(b) (Mus) concert; **— sinfónico** symphony concert.

(c) (Mus) concerto.

conciliable adj reconcilable; **dos opiniones no fácilmente —s** two opinions which it is not easy to reconcile.

conciliación nf (a) conciliation; reconciliation. (b) affinity, similarity.

conciliador 1 adj conciliatory. **2** nm conciliator.

conciliar[1] [1b] **1** vt (a) enemies etc to reconcile; attitudes etc to harmonize, bring into line, blend.

(b) respect etc to win, gain; **— el sueño** to get to sleep.

2 conciliarse vr: **— algo** to win something, gain something.

conciliar[2] **1** adj (Eccl) of a council, council (attr). **2** nm council member.

conciliatorio adj conciliatory; propitiatory.

concilio n (Eccl) council; **el Segundo C— Vaticano** the Second Vatican Council.

concisamente adv concisely, briefly, tersely.

concisión nf concision, conciseness, brevity.

conciso adj concise, brief, terse.

concitar [1a] vt to stir up, incite (contra against).

conciudadano nm, **conciudadana** nf fellow citizen.

cónclave nm conclave.

concluir [3g] **1** vt (a) to conclude, finish.

(b) to infer, deduce; consequence etc to reach, arrive at.

(c) person to convince; to crush, silence.

(d) **— a uno de ignorante** to judge someone to be ignorant.

2 vi to end, conclude, finish; **— de** + infin to finish + ger; **— por** + infin to end up by + ger; **— con, — en, — por** (of word etc) to end in; **todo ha concluido** it's all over; **¡vamos a — de una vez!** let's get it over!

3 concluirse vr to end, conclude.

conclusión nf (all senses) conclusion; **en —** in conclusion, lastly, finally; **llegar a la — de que . . .** to come to the conclusion that . . .

concluyente adj conclusive; decisive; unanswerable.

concluyentemente adv conclusively; decisively; unanswerably.

concomitante adj concomitant.

concordancia nf (a) concordance; harmony. (b) (Gram) concord, agreement. (c) (Mus) harmony. (d) **—s** (Lit) concordance.

concordante adj concordant.

concordar [1m] **1** vt to reconcile; to bring into line; (Gram) to make agree.

2 vi to agree (**con** with), tally (**con** with), correspond (**con** to); (Gram) to agree; **esto no concuerda con los hechos** this does not square with (or fit in with) the facts; **los dos concuerdan en sus gustos** the two agree in their tastes, the two have the same tastes.

concordato nm concordat.

concorde adj: **estar —s** to be agreed, be in agreement; **estar — en** + infin to agree to + infin; **poner a dos personas —s** to bring about agreement between two people.

concordia nf (a) concord, harmony, agreement; conformity. (b) double finger-ring.

concreción nf concretion; (Med) stone.

concretamente adv particularly, specifically; exactly; to be exact; **se refirió — a dos** he referred specifically to two; **no es — una fiesta** it's not exactly a party; **— eran 39** to be exact there were 39.

concretar [1a] **1** vt to make concrete, make (more) specific; to express in concrete terms; to pinpoint, put one's finger on; to reduce to essentials, boil down; **concreta sus esperanzas a ganar el premio** he is concentrating all his hopes on winning the prize; **concretemos, para** — let us be more specific, let's come down to details.

2 concretarse *vr* (a) to become (more) definite; — a to come down specifically to.

(b) — **a** + *infin* to limit oneself to + *ger*, confine oneself to + *ger*; to concentrate on + *ger*.

concreto 1 *adj* (a) concrete; definite, actual, particular, specific; **en este caso** — in this particular instance; **no me dijo ninguna hora concreta** he didn't tell me any definite (*or* particular) time; **en** — to sum up; exactly, specifically, to be exact; **en** — **había 7** there were 7 to be exact; **no hay nada en** — there's nothing you can put your finger on, there's nothing definite.

2 *nm* (a) concretion.

(b) (*SAm: angl*) concrete.

concubina *nf* concubine.

concubinato *nm* concubinage.

concúbito *nm* copulation.

concupiscencia *nf* (a) greed, acquisitiveness. (b) lustfulness, concupiscence.

concupiscente *adj* (a) greedy, acquisitive. (b) lewd, lustful, concupiscent.

concurrencia *nf* (a) (*of events etc*) concurrence.

(b) crowd, gathering, assembly; spectators, public, audience; attendance, turnout; **había una numerosa** — there was a big attendance, there was a large crowd (present).

(c) (*Comm*) competition.

concurrente 1 *adj* (a) *event etc* concurrent.

(b) (*Comm etc*) competing.

2 *nm* (a) person present, person attending; — **al cine** cinemagoer, moviegoer (*US*); **los** —**s** those present, those in the audience (*etc*).

(b) competitor.

concurrido *adj place* crowded; much frequented; *street* busy, crowded; *show* popular, well-attended, full (of people).

concurrir [3a] *vi* (a) (*of roads etc*) to meet, come together (**en** at).

(b) (*of people*) to meet, gather, assemble (**a** at, **en** in); — **a un baile** to go to a dance, attend a dance; — **a las urnas** to go to the polls; **concurren a la misma tertulia** they go to the same group.

(c) (*of people: pej*) to conspire, come together (*para* + *infin* to + *infin*).

(d) to contribute; — **a la derrota** to contribute to the defeat; — **al éxito de una empresa** to contribute to the success of an enterprise; — **con su dinero** to contribute one's money; — **en una empresa** to cooperate in an undertaking.

(e) (*of qualities etc*) to be found, be present; **concurren en ella muchas buenas cualidades** she has many good qualities.

(f) — **en una opinión** to concur in an opinion, agree with an opinion.

(g) (*of events*) to coincide (**con** with).

(h) (*Comm*) to compete; — **a un mercado to** compete in a market.

(i) (*Sport etc*) to compete (**a** in), take part (**a** in).

concursado *nm* (*Law*) insolvent debtor, bankrupt.

concursante *nmf* competitor, contestant, participant.

concursar [1a] **1** *vt* (a) (*Law*) to declare insolvent, declare bankrupt.

(b) to compete in, compete for; **va a** — **la vacante** he is going to compete for (*or* apply for) the vacancy.

2 *vi* to compete, participate.

concurso *nm* (a) = **concurrencia**.

(b) — **de acreedores** (*Law*) meeting of creditors.

(c) (*of events*) coincidence, concurrence.

(d) help, collaboration; cooperation; **con el** — **de** with the help of; **prestar su** — to help, collaborate.

(e) (*Sport etc*) competition, contest; meeting, match, tournament; show; (*for post*) examination, open competition; — **de belleza** beauty contest; — **hípico** horse show, show-jumping contest; — **de pastoreo** sheepdog trials; — **radiofónico** radio quiz (show); **precios sin** —**s** competitive prices; unbeatable prices; **ganar un puesto por** — to win a post in open competition.

concusión *nf* (a) (*Med*) concussion. (b) (*Fin*) extortion.

concusionario *nm* extortioner.

Concha *f* pet name for **María de la Concepción.**

concha *nf* (a) (*Zool*) shell; shellfish; tortoiseshell; **meterse en su** — to retire into one's shell; **tener muchas** —**s** to be very sharp, be a sly one.

(b) (*of china*) flake, chip.

(c) (*Theat*) prompt box.

(d) (*Col, Ec, Per, PR*) nerve, cheek.

(e) (*Col*) sloth, sluggishness.

(f) (*Anat: euph*) = **coño.**

conchabado *nm,* **conchabada** *nf* (*SAm*) servant.

conchabar [1a] **1** *vt* (a) to mix, blend.

(b) (*SAm*) *servant* to hire, engage, employ.

(c) (*Chi, Ec*) to barter.

2 conchabarse *vr* (a) to gang up (*contra* on), plot, conspire (*para* + *infin* to + *infin*).

(b) (*SAm*) to hire oneself out, get a job (as a servant).

conchabo *nm* (a) (*SAm*) hiring, engagement; **oficina de** — (*Arg*) domestic employment agency. (b) (*Chi*) barter(ing).

Conchita *f* = **Concha.**

conchito *nm* (*Chi, Per*) youngest child (of a family).

concho[1] *nm* (*SD*) taxi.

concho[2] *nm* (*CR*) peasant; (*pej*) rustic, country bumpkin.

concho[3] **1** *adj* (*Ec, Per*) dark reddish-brown.

2 *nm* (*SAm: also* —**s**) dregs, sediment; residue; left-overs; **hasta el** — to the very end; **irse al** — (*Chi*) to sink.

concho[4] *nm* (*Chi, Per*) = **conchito.**

concho[5] *nm* (*Anat: euph*) = **coño.**

conchudo 1 *adj* (*Arg, Col, SD*) sluggish.

2 *nm,* **conchuda** *nf* (a) (*Ec, Mex, Per*) shameless person.

(b) (*PR*) stubborn individual; fearless person.

condado *nm* county; (*Hist*) earldom.

conde *nm* earl, count; **el C— Fernán González** Count Fernán González.

condecoración *nf* decoration, medal; badge; insignia.

condecorar [1a] *vt* to decorate (*con* with).

condena *nf* (*Law*) sentence; conviction; term (*of imprisonment*); — **a perpetuidad,** — **de reclusión perpetua** life sentence, sentence of life imprisonment; **el año pasado hubo X** —**s por embriaguez** last year there were X convictions for drunkenness; **cumplir una** — to serve a sentence.

condenable *adj* condemnable; blameworthy.

condenación *nf* (a) condemnation; (*Eccl*) damnation; (*Law*) = **condena.** (b) ¡—! damnation!, damnation!

condenadamente *adv* (*fam*): **una mujer** — **lista** a darned clever woman (*fam*); **es un trabajo** — **duro** it's darned hard work (*fam*).

condenado 1 *adj* (a) condemned; (*Law*) condemned, convicted; (*Eccl*) damned.

(b) (*fig*) doomed; **el buque** — the doomed vessel; **una especie condenada a la extinción** a species doomed to extinction; **instituciones condenadas a desaparecer** institutions doomed to disappear.

(c) (*fam*) *child* mischievous, naughty.

(d) (*fam*) damned, flaming (*fam*), ruddy (*euph*); **aquel** — **teléfono** that ruddy telephone.

(e) (*Chi*) clever; sharp.

2 *nm,* **condenada** *nf* (a) (*Law*) convicted person, criminal; **el** — **a muerte** the condemned man.

(b) (*Eccl*) damned soul.

(c) (*fam*) **el** — **de mi tío** that ruddy uncle of mine (*euph*).

condenar [1a] **1** *vt* (a) to condemn.

(b) (*Law*) to condemn, convict, sentence; to find guilty; — **a uno a 3 meses de cárcel** to sentence someone to 3 months in jail, give someone a 3-month prison sentence; — **a uno a una multa** to sentence someone to pay a fine; — **a uno a presidio** to sentence someone to hard labour; **le condenaron por ladrón** they found him guilty of robbery.

(c) (*Eccl*) to damn.

(d) (*Archit*) to block up, wall up.

(e) (*fam*) to vex, annoy.

2 condenarse *vr* (a) to confess (one's guilt), own up; to blame oneself.

(b) (*Eccl*) to be damned.

(c) (*fam*) to get cross, get worked up.

condensación *nf* condensation.

condensado *adj* condensed.

condensador *nm* condenser.

condensar [1a] **1** *vt* to condense. **2 condensarse** *vr* to condense, become condensed.

condesa *nf* countess.

condescendencia *nf* helpfulness, willingness (to help); affability; acquiescence (*a* in); **aceptar algo por** — to accept something so as not to hurt feelings.

condescender [2g] *vi* to acquiesce, comply, agree, say yes; — **a algo** to consent to, say yes to; — **a los ruegos de uno** to agree to someone's requests; — **en** + *infin* to agree to + *infin*.

condescendiente *adj* helpful, willing (to help); kind; affable; acquiescent.

condición nf **(a)** nature, condition; temperament, character; **la — humana** the human condition; **de — perversa** of a perverse nature; **de — cruel** cruel-natured.
(b) social class, rank; status, position; **persona de — person** of rank; **de humilde —** of lowly origin; **una boda de personas de distinta —** a wedding between people of different social scale.
(c) —es qualities; **de excelentes —es** of splendid qualities; **ella no tiene —es para pintora** she is not cut out to be a painter.
(d) —es condition, state; **—es de trabajo** working conditions; **— de vida, —es vitales** living conditions; **nuestras —es económicas** our economic circumstances; **el coche está en malas —es** the car is in a bad state; **no está en (buenas) —es** it's not in a fit state; **no está en —es para** + infin it is not fit to + infin; **no estamos en —es para** + infin we are not in a position to + infin.
(e) condition; term, provision, stipulation; **las —es del contrato** the terms of the contract; **— sine qua non** essential condition; **a — de que . . .** on condition that . . ., provided that . . .; **con esta —** on this condition; **ayuda sin —es** help with no strings attached; **rendición sin —es** unconditional surrender; **rendirse sin —es** to surrender unconditionally.
condicionado adj conditioned.
condicional adj conditional (also Gram).
condicionalmente adv conditionally.
condicionar [1a] vt to condition; to determine; to prepare.
condigno adj proper, corresponding.
condimentar [1a] to flavour, season; to spice.
condimento nm seasoning, flavouring; dressing.
condiscípulo nm, **condiscípula** nf fellow pupil, fellow student.
condolencia nf condolence, sympathy.
condolerse [2h] vr: **— de, — por** to sympathize with, feel sorry for.
condominio nm **(a)** (Law) joint ownership; (Pol) condominium. **(b)** (Mex) flat, apartment (US) (owned by the occupant).
condonar [1a] vt act to condone; punishment to remit; debt to cancel, forgive; criminal to reprieve.
cóndor nm condor.
conducción nf **(a)** (act) leading; guiding; management; transport(ation); conveyance; piping; (Phys) conduction.
(b) (Aut) drive; driving; **— a derecha** right-hand drive; **coche de — interior** saloon car; **— descuidada** reckless driving.
(c) (Tech) pipe; intake; outlet; **— de agua** water pipe; **— principal de agua** water main; **— principal de gas** gas main.
(d) (Comm) agreement (on transport charges).
conducente adj: **— a** conducive to, leading to.
conducir [3o] **1** vt **(a)** liquid etc to take, convey; to pass; load to take, transport, convey; **los cables conducen la electricidad** the cables carry the electricity.
(b) (Aut etc) to drive; to steer; **— por la derecha** to drive on the right.
(c) person to take, lead (a to); to guide, conduct (a to); **me condujeron por un pasillo** they led me along a passage.
(d) business, matter to direct, manage, conduct; army, group, revolt etc to lead.
2 vi **(a)** (Aut) to drive; **aprender a —** to learn to drive.
(b) — a (fig) to lead to; **esto ha de — al desastre** this is bound to lead to disaster; **¿a qué conduce?** what's the point?; **no conduce a ninguna parte** this is getting us nowhere.
3 conducirse vr to behave, conduct oneself.
conducta nf **(a)** (of person) conduct, behaviour; **mala —** misconduct, misbehaviour; **cambiar de —** to mend one's ways.
(b) (of business etc) direction, management.
conductibilidad nf (Phys) conductivity.
conducto nm **(a)** (for water etc) pipe, tube, conduit; (Anat) duct, canal; (Elec) lead, cable, flex; **—s** (Aut) leads; **— alimenticio** alimentary canal; **— biliar** bile duct; **— de desagüe** drain; **— de humo** flue; **— lacrimal** tear duct.
(b) (fig) agency; channel; (person) agent, intermediary; **por —** de through, by means of.
conductor 1 adj **(a)** leading, guiding.
(b) (Phys) conductive.
2 nm (Phys) conductor; (Elec) lead; **no — non-conductor.**

3 nm, **conductora** nf **(a)** leader; guide; (Sport) leader.
(b) (Aut) driver; motorist; **aprendiz de —, — novato** learner, learner-driver.
(c) (SAm: Mus: angl) conductor; (of bus etc) conductor, conductress.
condueño nm, **condueña** nf joint owner, part owner, co-owner.
condumio nm (fam) food, grub (sl).
conectado adj (Elec etc) connected; **estar — to** be on, (of wire etc) to be live.
conectar [1a] **1** vt **(a)** (Tech) to connect (up); (Elec, TV etc) to connect (up); to switch on, plug in; **— un aparato a tierra** (or **con masa**) to earth a piece of apparatus, ground a piece of apparatus (US).
(b) (SAm) **— a uno con otra persona** to put someone in touch with somebody else; **yo les puedo — I** can put you in touch (with each other).
2 vi (SAm: angl): **este asunto conecta con lo otro** this business links up with the other.
conectivo adj connective.
coneja nf doe rabbit.
conejar nm warren, burrow; (fig) warren.
conejera nf **(a)** warren, burrow; rabbit hutch. **(b)** (fam) den, dive (fam).
conejillo nm young rabbit; bunny; **— de Indias** guinea-pig.
conejo 1 adj (CAm) flat, unsweetened; bitter, sour.
2 nm **(a)** (Zool) rabbit; **— casero** tame rabbit; **— de Noruega** lemming.
(b) (RPl) biceps.
(c) (Guat) detective.
(d) (Anat: euph) = **coño**.
conejuna nf rabbit fur, coney.
conexión nf **(a)** (Tech) connection; plug; coupling; joint. **(b)** (fig) connection; relationship.
conexionarse [1a] vr to get in touch; to make connections, establish contacts.
conexo adj connected, related.
confabulación nf plot; intrigue; dubious scheme; (Comm) ring.
confabularse [1a] vr to plot, conspire, scheme (para + infin to + infin); (Comm) to form a ring.
confección nf **(a)** (act) making; making-up, preparation; **— de vestidos** dressmaking.
(b) (art) workmanship, work; **traje de alta — ready-to-wear** suit.
(c) manufactured article, made-up article; (Pharm) concoction, preparation; (Sew) ready-made garment (or suit etc); **es una — Pérez** it's a Pérez creation, it's a Pérez product.
confeccionado adj (Sew) ready-made, ready-to-wear; **— a la medida** made to measure.
confeccionar [1a] vt list etc to make out; account to prepare, write up; (Sew) to make (up); (Pharm) to concoct, make up.
confederación nf confederation, confederacy, league.
confederado 1 adj confederate. **2** nm confederate.
confederarse [1a] vr to confederate, form a confederation.
conferencia nf **(a)** (Pol etc) conference, meeting; **— (en la) cumbre** summit conference; **— de desarme** disarmament conference; **— de prensa** press conference.
(b) lecture, address; **dar una —** to give a lecture.
(c) (Tel) call; **— de cobro revertido** reversed-charge call; **— interurbana, — de larga distancia** long-distance call, trunk call; **— de persona a persona** personal call.
conferenciante nmf lecturer.
conferenciar [1b] vti to confer (con with); to be in conference.
conferencista nmf (SAm) lecturer.
conferir [3i] vt **(a)** prize to award (a to); honour to grant (a to), confer (a on), bestow (a on).
(b) (fig) quality to lend, give (a to); **los cuadros confieren dignidad al cuarto** the pictures give the room dignity.
(c) documents etc to compare (con with).
confesante nm (Hist) penitent.
confesar [1k] **1** vt **(a)** to confess, admit, acknowledge, own up to; (Eccl) sin to confess.
(b) (Eccl) sinner to confess, hear the confession of.
2 vi and **confesarse** vr to confess, own up; (Eccl) to confess (a, con to), make one's confession; **— de sus pecados** to confess one's sins.
confesión nf (all senses) confession.
confesional adj confessional.
confes(i)onario nm confessional.

confeso 1 adj (a) confessed. (b) (Hist) Jew converted.
2 nm (Hist) converted Jew; (Eccl) lay-brother.
confesor nm confessor.
confeti nm (also —s) confetti.
confiabilidad nf reliability, trustworthiness.
confiable adj reliable, trustworthy.
confiadamente adv (a) trustingly. (b) confidently; self-confidently; hopefully. (c) conceitedly.
confiado adj (a) trusting; unsuspecting, gullible.
(b) confident; — **en sí mismo** self-confident, self-reliant; **estar muy** — to be excessively hopeful, nourish false hopes.
(c) (pej) vain, conceited, presumptuous.
confianza nf (a) trust (en in), reliance (en on); trustfulness; **margen de** — credibility gap; **persona de (toda)** — reliable person, trustworthy person; **puesto de** — responsible post, post of responsibility; **decir algo en** — to say something in confidence; **dicho sea en** — let it be said in confidence (or strictly between ourselves); **defraudar la** — **de uno** to let someone down; **poner su** — **en** to put one's trust in.
(b) confidence; — **en sí mismo** self-confidence; **con toda** — with complete confidence; **estar lleno de** — to be full of confidence; **infundir** — **a uno** to give someone confidence.
(c) (pej) vanity, conceit; presumption.
(d) intimacy, familiarity (con with); **amigo de** — close friend, intimate friend; **reunión de** — intimate gathering, informal gathering; **en tono de** — in a confidential tone; **tener** — **con uno** to be on close terms with someone; **tratar a uno con** — to treat someone without formality, not stand on ceremony with someone; **os ruego tratarme con toda** — I ask you to treat me as one of yourselves.
(e) —s confidences; (pej) familiarities; **se toma demasiadas** —s he is too familiar, he's too fresh, he takes too many liberties.
confianzudo adj (a) overfamiliar, fresh. (b) (SAm) meddlesome.
confiar [1c] **1** vt: — **algo a uno**, — **algo en uno** to entrust something to someone, commit something to the care of someone; — **algo al azar** to leave something to chance.
2 vi to trust, be trusting; — **en** to trust in; to rely on, count on; — **en el éxito de algo** to feel confident about the success of something; **confiemos en Dios** let us trust in God; — **en que . . .** to trust that . . .; to expect that . . .
3 confiarse vr (a) — **a algo** to entrust oneself to something.
(b) — **a uno** (fig) to open one's heart to someone.
confidencia nf confidence, secret; confidential remark; (to police) tip-off; **hacer** —s **a uno** to tell secrets to someone, confide in someone.
confidencial adj confidential.
confidencialmente adv confidentially.
confidente nm, **confidenta** nf (a) confidant(e); intimate friend. (b) informer; secret agent.
configuración nf shape, configuration; **la** — **del futuro** the shape of things to come; **la** — **del terreno** the lie of the land.
configurar [1a] vt to shape, form, fashion.
confín nm limit, boundary; horizon; —es confines, limits (also fig); remote part, outermost parts, edges.
confinado adj air thick.
confinar [1a] **1** vt to confine (a, en in); to banish, exile (a to); to arrest; to shut away.
2 vi: — **con** to border on (also fig).
3 confinarse vr to shut oneself away.
confirmación nf confirmation (also Eccl).
confirmar [1a] vt to confirm (also Eccl); to corroborate; to endorse, bear out, prove; — **a uno de** (or **como**, **por**) to confirm someone as; **la excepción confirma la regla** the exception proves the rule.
confirmatorio adj confirmatory.
confiscación nf confiscation.
confiscar [1g] vt to confiscate.
confisgado adj (CAm) rascally.
confitar [1a] vt to preserve (in syrup); to candy; to sweeten (also fig).
confite nm sweet, candy (US).
confitería nf (a) confectionery, sweets, candies (US). (b) confectioner's (shop), sweetshop, candy store (US).
confitero nm, **confitera** nf confectioner.
confitura nf preserve; crystallized fruit; jam.
conflagración nf conflagration; (fig) flare-up, outbreak; — **bélica** outbreak of war.
conflictivo adj: **la edad conflictiva** the age of conflict.

conflicto nm (a) (Mil) conflict; struggle; (fig) clash; — **de intereses** clash of interests; — **laboral** labour dispute.
(b) (fig) difficulty, fix, jam; **estar en un** — to be in a jam.
confluencia nf confluence.
confluente adj confluent.
confluir [3g] vi (of rivers etc) to meet, join, come together; (of people etc) to gather, come together; to mass.
conformación nf shape, form, structure.
conformado adj (a) **bien** — well-made, well-shaped. (b) patient, resigned, long-suffering.
conformar [1a] **1** vt to shape, fashion; to adjust (a to), adapt (a to), bring into line (a with); **enemies to reconcile**.
2 vi to agree (con with).
3 conformarse vr to conform; to resign oneself; — **con** original to conform to, agree with; rule to comply with, abide by, observe; policy etc to adjust to, conform to, fall into line with; unpleasant situation to resign oneself to, accept; **se conforma con cualquier cosa** he agrees to anything; he puts up with anything; **no me conformo con hacerlo así** I do not agree to doing it your way.
conforme 1 adj (a) alike, similar; **son muy** —s **en todo** they are very similar in every respect, they agree well enough.
(b) consistent (a with); **un premio** — **a sus méritos** a prize consistent with his merits, a reward in accordance with his merits.
(c) (of persons etc) agreed, in agreement; ¡—(s)! agreed!, all right!; **estar** —s to be agreed; **estamos** —s **en el precio** we are agreed about the price; **estamos** —s **en que . . .** we agree that . . .; **declararse** — **con algo** to consent to something, acquiesce in something; **por fin se mostró** — finally he agreed.
(d) (of persons etc) satisfied, content (con with); resigned (con to); **no se quedó** — **con la propina** he was not satisfied with the tip.
2 prep: — **a** in conformity with, in accordance with; in keeping with; — **a la muestra** as per sample; **lo hicieron** — **a sus instrucciones** they acted according to their instructions.
3 conj as; in proportion as; **todo sigue** — **estaba** everything is as it was; — **lo iban sacando** (in proportion) as they were taking it out; —**. . . así . . .** as . . . so . . .
4 nm agreement; **dar el** — to agree, give one's agreement.
conformidad nf (a) similarity; correspondence; uniformity (entre between).
(b) agreement; approval, consent; **de** — by common consent; **de** — **con** in accordance with; **en** — accordingly; **en** — **con** in compliance with; **no** — nonconformity; disagreement; **dar su** — to consent, give one's approval.
(c) resignation (con to); forbearance; **soportar algo con** — to bear something with resignation, resign oneself to putting up with something.
confort [kon'foɾ(t)] nm, pl **conforts** [kon'foɾ(t)] (gall) comfort; "**todo** —" (adverts) "all mod cons".
confortable adj comfortable.
confortablemente adv comfortably.
confortante adj (a) comforting. (b) (Med) invigorating, tonic.
confortar [1a] vt (a) to comfort, console; to encourage. (b) (Med etc) to strengthen, invigorate, act as a tonic to.
confortativo 1 adj (a) comforting, consoling; encouraging.
(b) (Med etc) invigorating, tonic.
2 nm (a) comfort, consolation; encouragement. (b) (Med etc) tonic, restorative.
confraternidad nf fraternity, brotherhood.
confraternizar [1f] vi (SAm) to fraternize (con with).
confrontación nf (a) confrontation; — **nuclear** nuclear confrontation. (b) comparison.
confrontar [1a] **1** vt (a) danger etc to confront, face; to face up to.
(b) two persons to bring face to face; — **a uno con otro** to confront somebody with someone else.
(c) texts to compare, collate.
2 vi to border (con on).
3 confrontarse vr: — **con** to confront, face.
Confucio m Confucius.
confundible adj: **fácilmente** — easily mistaken (con for), easily confused (con with).
confundir [3a] **1** vt (a) outline etc to blur, confuse.
(b) to mistake (con for), confuse (con with), mix up (con with); person to confuse, muddle; **confundimos el camino** we mistook our way, we got

our route wrong; **ha confundido todos los sellos** he has mixed up (or jumbled up) all the stamps.
    (**c**) *substances* to mix, mingle (**con** with).
    (**d**) *opponent* to confound; to confuse, put off; to bewilder, perplex; — **a uno con atenciones** to bewilder (or overwhelm) someone with kindness.
    (**e**) *accuser* to put to shame, humble.
    (**f**) to lose; **me has confundido ese libro otra vez** you've lost that book of mine again.
    2 confundirse *vr* (**a**) (*outline etc*) to become blurred, become confused.
    (**b**) to get confused, get in a muddle; to get bewildered; to make a mistake; **Vd se ha confundido de número** (*Tel*) you have the wrong number.
    (**c**) to feel humbled, feel ashamed.
    (**d**) to mix; to blend, fuse; **se confundió con la multitud** he became lost in the crowd, he disappeared in the crowd; **los policías se confundieron con los manifestantes** the police mingled with the demonstrators.
confusamente *adv* *remember etc* confusedly; vaguely, hazily; *retreat* in confusion, in disorder.
confusión *nf* (*all senses*) confusion; **no hagamos —es** let's be clear about this, let's get this straight.
confusionismo *nf* confusion; uncertainty; confused state; **sembrar el — y desconcierto** to spread alarm and despondency.
confuso *adj* (*in most senses*) confused; mixed up, jumbled up, in disorder; *memory* confused, vague, hazy; *image* blurred, cloudy; **estar —** (*person*) to be confused, be bewildered; to be embarrassed.
confutar [1a] *vt* to confute.
conga *nf* (*SAm: Mus*) conga.
congal *nm* (*Mex*) brothel.
congelación *nf* (**a**) freezing; congealing. (**b**) (*Med*) frostbite. (**c**) (*Fin etc*) freeze, freezing; **— de créditos** credit freeze; **— de salarios** wage freeze.
congelado *adj* (**a**) *meat etc* frozen, chilled; *fat* congealed. (**b**) (*Med*) frostbitten. (**c**) (*Fin etc*) frozen, blocked.
congelador *nm* freezer; freezing unit.
congeladora *nf* deep freeze.
congelar [1a] **1** *vt* (**a**) *meat, water etc* to freeze; *blood, fat* to congeal.
    (**b**) (*Med*) to freeze, affect with frostbite.
    (**c**) (*Fin etc*) to freeze, block.
    2 congelarse *vr* (**a**) to freeze, become frozen; to congeal.
    (**b**) (*Med*) to get frostbitten.
congénere *nm* fellow, person (*etc*) of the same sort; **el criminal y sus —es** the criminal and others like him, the criminal and people of that sort.
congeniar [1b] *vi* to get on (well; **con** with).
congenital *adj* (*SAm: angl*), **congénito** *adj* congenital.
congestión *nf* (*all senses*) congestion.
congestionado *adj* (**a**) congested. (**b**) (*Med*) congested, (*esp*) chesty; *face* flushed, red.
congestionar [1a] **1** *vt* to congest, produce congestion in.
    2 congestionarse *vr* to become congested; **se le congestionó la cara** his face became flushed, he got red in the face.
conglomeración *nf* conglomeration.
conglomerado *nm* (*Geol, Tech*) conglomerate; (*fig*) conglomeration.
conglomerar [1a] **1** *vt* to conglomerate. **2 conglomerarse** *vr* to conglomerate.
Congo: el — the Congo; **¡vete al —!** (*fam*) get lost! (*fam*).
congo *nm* (*SAm*) Negro.
congoja *nf* anguish, distress, grief.
congola *nf* (*Col, Ec*) pipe.
congoleño 1 *adj* Congolese. **2** *nm*, **congoleña** *nf* Congolese.
congolés = **congoleño.**
congosto *nm* narrow pass, canyon.
congraciador *adj* ingratiating.
congraciamiento *nm* ingratiation; winning over.
congraciante *adj* ingratiating.
congraciar [1b] **1** *vt* to win over. **2 congraciarse** *vr* to ingratiate oneself (**con** with).
congratulaciones *nfpl* congratulations.
congratular [1a] **1** *vt* to congratulate (*por* on).
    2 congratularse *vr* to congratulate oneself, be pleased; **de eso nos congratulamos** on that we congratulate ourselves, we are glad about that.
congregación *nf* gathering, assembly; brotherhood, guild; (*Eccl*) congregation; **— de los fieles** Christendom.
congregacionalista *adj* congregational.
congresal *nmf* (*SAm*) = **congresista.**
congresional *adj* congressional

congresista *nmf* delegate, member (of a congress).
congreso *nm* congress; assembly, convention; conference; **C—** (*Pol*) Congress (*US*).
congrio *nm* conger (eel).
congruencia *nf* (**a**) congruence (*also Math*), congruity. (**b**) suitability.
congruente *adj*, **congruo** *adj* (**a**) congruent (*also Math*), congruous (*con* with); in keeping (*con* with); related (*con* to). (**b**) suitable, fitting.
cónico *adj* conical; *section etc* (*Math*) conic.
conífera *nf* conifer.
conífero *adj* coniferous.
conjetura *nf* guess, conjecture, surmise; **por —** by guesswork; **son meras —s** it's just guesswork.
conjeturable *adj* that can be guessed at; **es — que . . .** one may conjecture that . . .
conjetural *adj* conjectural.
conjeturar [1a] *vt* to guess (at), conjecture, surmise (*de, por* from; *que* that).
conjugación *nf* conjugation.
conjugar [1h] **1** *vt* (**a**) (*Gram*) to conjugate.
    (**b**) to combine, bring together, fit together, blend; **la obra conjuga cualidades y defectos** the work has both qualities and defects; **es difícil — los deseos de los dos** it is difficult to fit their two wishes together.
    2 conjugarse *vr* (**a**) (*Gram*) to be conjugated.
    (**b**) to fit together, blend; to be as one, become indistinguishable.
conjunción *nf* (*all senses*) conjunction.
conjuntivitis *nf* conjunctivitis.
conjuntivo *adj* conjunctive.
conjuntamente *adv* jointly, together; **— con** together with.
conjunto 1 *adj* (**a**) *effort etc* joint; united.
    (**b**) *subject etc* allied, related.
    2 *nm* (**a**) as a whole, altogether; **en su —** in its entirety; **foto de —** group photo; **impresión de —** overall impression; **vista de —** all-embracing view; **formar un —** to form a whole.
    (**b**) (*Sew*) ensemble; costume.
    (**c**) (*Mus: chamber etc*) ensemble; (*pop*) group; **los Beatles formaron su —** the Beatles formed their group.
    (**d**) (*Theat*) chorus.
    (**e**) (*Mech*) unit, assembly.
conjura *nf*, **conjuración** *nf* plot, conspiracy.
conjurado *nm*, **conjurada** *nf* plotter, conspirator.
conjurar [1a] **1** *vt* (**a**) *devil* to exorcise.
    (**b**) *danger* to stave off, ward off.
    (**c**) *thought etc* to rid oneself of, get rid of.
    (**d**) *person* to entreat, beseech.
    2 *vi* and **conjurarse** *vr* to plot, conspire (together).
conjuro *nm* (**a**) incantation, conjuration, exorcism; spell; **al — de sus palabras** under the magical effect of his words. (**b**) entreaty.
conllevar [1a] *vt* (**a**) *infirmity etc* to bear, suffer (patiently), live with.
    (**b**) *person* to bear, put up with.
    (**c**) **— las penas de otro** to help someone else to bear his troubles.
    (**d**) (*fig*) **— a uno** to hedge with someone, jolly someone along with empty promises.
conmemoración *nf* commemoration.
conmemorar [1a] *vt* to commemorate.
conmemorativo 1 *adj* commemorative; memorial (*attr*). **2** *nm* (*Post*) commemorative.
conmigo *pron* with me; with myself.
conmilitón *nm* fellow soldier.
conminar [1a] *vt* (**a**) to threaten (*con* with). (**b**) **— a uno a hacer algo** to warn someone (officially) to do something, instruct someone to do something.
conminatorio *adj* threatening, warning.
conmiseración *nf* pity, sympathy; commiseration.
conmoción *nf* (**a**) (*Geol*) shock; tremor, earthquake. (**b**) (*Med*) **— cerebral** concussion.
    (**c**) (*fig*) shock; commotion, disturbance; upheaval; **una — social** a social upheaval; **producir una — desagradable a uno** to give someone a nasty shock.
conmovedor *adj* touching, moving; poignant; exciting, stirring; disturbing.
conmover [2h] **1** *vt* (**a**) *building etc* to shake, disturb.
    (**b**) (*fig*) to move, touch, stir, affect; to disturb, upset.
    2 conmoverse *vr* (**a**) to shake, be shaken.
    (**b**) (*fig*) to be moved, be stirred.
conmuta *nf* (*Chi, Ec, Per*) change, alteration.
conmutador *nm* (*Elec*) switch.
conmutar [1a] *vt* (**a**) to exchange (*con, por* for); to convert (*en* into). (**b**) (*Law*) to commute (*en, por* to).
connatural *adj* innate, inherent.

connaturalizarse [1f] *vr* to become accustomed (*con* to); to become acclimatized, become acclimated (*US*) (*con* to).

connivencia *nf* collusion; connivance; **estar en — con** to be in collusion with.

connotación *nf* (**a**) connotation. (**b**) distant relationship.

connotado *adj* (*SAm*) notable, famous; outstanding.

connotar [1a] *vt* to connote.

cono *nm* (*all senses*) cone.

conocedor 1 *adj* expert, knowledgeable; **muy — de** very knowledgeable about.

2 *nm*, **conocedora** *nf* expert (*de* in), judge (*de* of); connoisseur (*de* of); **es buen — de ganado** he's a good judge of cattle.

conocencia *nf* (*esp SAm*) girlfriend, sweetheart.

conocer [2d] **1** *vt* (**a**) to know; to know about, understand; (*for first time*) to meet, get to know; **— a uno de vista** to know someone by sight; **le conozco ligeramente** I know him slightly; **conozco las dificultades** I know the difficulties; **la conocí en Sevilla** I met her in Seville; **vengo a — Portugal** I have come to get to know Portugal; **conoce su oficio** he knows his job; **no conoce gran cosa de ciencias** he doesn't know much about science; **le conozco de haber trabajado juntos** I know him from having worked with him; **dar a — to introduce, present; *report etc* to release** (*to the press etc*), (*improperly*) leak; **darse a — to make a name for oneself; to make one's debut; **darse a — a uno** to make oneself known to someone.

(**b**) to know, tell, recognize, distinguish (**en**, *por* by); **— a uno por su modo de andar** to know someone by (*or* from) his walk; **él conoce cuáles son buenos** he knows (*or* can tell) which ones are good; **conocieron el peligro** they recognized the danger; **¿de qué le conoces?** how do you recognize him?; **no me conoce de nada** he doesn't know me from Adam.

2 *vi* (**a**) **— de** to know about.

(**b**) (*Law*) **— de** (*or* **en**) **una causa** to try a case.

3 conocerse *vr* (**a**) (*person*) to know oneself; to attain self-knowledge.

(**b**) (*2 persons*) to know each other; to get to know each other, meet, get acquainted; **se conocieron en un baile** they met at a dance.

(**c**) **se conoce que . . .** it is clear that . . .; it is known that . . .; it is established that . . .; it is recognized that . . .

conocible *adj* knowable.

conocido 1 *adj* known; well-known, (*pej*) notorious; famous, noted (*por* for); **un médico — a well-known** doctor, a prominent doctor; **un hecho conocidísimo** a very well-known fact.

2 *nm*, **conocida** *nf* acquaintance.

conocimiento *nm* (**a**) knowledge; **hablar con — de causa** to know what one is talking about; **obrar con — de causa** to know what one is up to; **hacer — de un hecho** to learn a fact; **hacer — de un tema** to learn about a subject, become acquainted with a subject; **ha llegado a mi — que . . .** it has come to my notice that . . .; **poner algo en — a uno** to inform someone of something; to bring something to someone's attention; **tener — de** to know about, have knowledge of; **al tenerse — del suceso** as soon as the event became known; **venir en — de** to learn of, hear about.

(**b**) **—s** knowledge (*de* of); information (*de* about); **—s elementales** basic knowledge; **mis pocos —s de filosofía** my small knowledge of philosophy.

(**c**) **—s** (*persons*) acquaintances.

(**d**) good sense, understanding; **los niños no tienen — children have no sense.

(**e**) (*Med*) consciousness; **estar sin — to be unconscious; **perder el — to lose consciousness; **recobrar el — to regain consciousness.

(**f**) (*Naut*) bill of lading.

conorte *nm* (*SAm*) comfort.

conque 1 *conj see* **con 2**. **2** *nm* (**a**) (*fam*) condition, reservation; **—s ifs and buts. (**b**) (*also* **conqué** *SAm*) wherewithal, money, means.

conquense 1 *adj* of Cuenca. **2** *nmf* native (*or* inhabitant) of Cuenca; **los —s** the people of Cuenca.

conquibus *nm* (*fam*) wherewithal, money, means.

conquista *nf* conquest (*also fig*); **ir de — (*fig*) to be** dressed up to kill.

conquistador 1 *adj* conquering. **2** *nm* (**a**) conqueror; (*16th century*) conquistador. (**b**) (*fam*) wolf (*fam*), ladykiller.

conquistar [1a] *vt* (**a**) to conquer (*a* from); to overcome.

(**b**) (*fig*) *post etc* to win; *market* to win, open up;

person to win round, win over; *woman* to win, succeed in attracting.

consabido *adj* (**a**) well-known, familiar; usual; old, oft-repeated, timeworn. (**b**) above-mentioned.

consagración *nf* consecration, dedication.

consagrado *adj* (**a**) consecrated (*a* to); dedicated (*a* to).

(**b**) (*fig*) time-honoured, hallowed, ritual, traditional; **según la expresión consagrada** in the time-honoured phrase.

consagrar [1a] **1** *vt* (**a**) (*Rel*) to consecrate, hallow; to dedicate (*a* to); *emperor* to deify.

(**b**) (*fig*) *life, time, effort etc* to devote, dedicate (*a* to); put in (*a* at); *monument, plaque* to put up, dedicate (*a* to).

(**c**) to confirm; **este triunfo le consagra como un cirujano excepcional** this success confirms him as (*or* shows him to be) a really exceptional surgeon.

2 consagrarse *vr*: **— a** to devote oneself to.

consanguíneo *adj* related by blood, consanguineous.

consanguinidad *nf* blood relationship, consanguinity.

consciente 1 *adj* (**a**) conscious; **estar — de** to be conscious of, be aware of.

(**b**) (*Med*) **estar — to be conscious.

(**c**) (*Law*) fully responsible for one's actions, aware of what one is doing.

2 *nm* conscious, conscious mind.

conscientemente *adv* consciously.

conscripción *nf* (*SAm*) conscription.

conscripto *nm* (*SAm*) conscript.

consecución *nf* obtaining, acquisition; attainment; **de difícil — hard to obtain, difficult to get hold of; **les ayudó en la — de trabajo** he helped them in obtaining work; **para la — de estos objetos** for the attainment of these aims.

consecuencia *nf* (**a**) consequence; outcome, result; conclusion; **a — de eso, en — de eso** as a result of that, as a consequence of that; **como —, en — in consequence, accordingly; **aceptar las —s** to take the consequences; **¡pues aténgase a las —s!** then you'd better watch out!; **saqué la — de que . . .** I gathered that . . .; I drew the conclusion that . . .; **no tuvo —s** it had no ill effects, nothing bad happened as a result; **traer algo a — to bring something up.

(**b**) importance; **de — of importance, of some weight; **ser de — to be important.

(**c**) consistency; **obrar con — to act consistently.

consecuente *adj* (**a**) consistent (*con* with). (**b**) (*Philos*) consequent.

consecuentemente *adv* consistently.

consecutivo *adj* (*Gram etc*) consecutive.

conseguible *adj* obtainable; attainable.

conseguir [3d *and* 3l] *vt* (**a**) to get, obtain, secure; to bring about; **— + infin** to succeed in + *ger*, manage to + *infin*; **que uno haga algo** to manage to make someone do something, get someone to do something.

(**b**) *aim etc* to attain, achieve.

conseja *nf* story, tale, legend; old wives' tale.

consejero *nm*, **consejera** *nf* adviser; consultant; member (of a board *etc*); (*Pol*) councillor; **— de publicidad** advertising consultant.

consejo *nm* (**a**) **un — a piece of advice; a hint; **su — his advice, his counsel; **agradezco el — I am grateful** for your advice; **pedir — a uno** to ask someone for advice, ask someone's advice; **— pericial** expert advice; **—s** advice.

(**b**) (*Pol etc*) council; (*Comm*) board; (*Law*) tribunal; court; **— de administración** board of directors; **— de disciplina** disciplinary board; **— de ministros** cabinet; cabinet meeting; **— privado** privy council; **— de guerra** court-martial; **— de guerra sumarísimo** drumhead court-martial.

consenso *nm* accord; assent; consensus.

consentido *adj* (**a**) *child* spoiled, pampered. (**b**) *husband* complaisant.

consentidor *adj* *mother etc* indulgent; weak, compliant; *husband* complaisant.

consentimiento *nm* consent.

consentir [3i] **1** *vt* (**a**) to consent to; to allow, permit; to tolerate; **— a uno + infin, — que uno + subj** to allow someone to + *infin*; **aquí no consienten hablar** they don't let you speak here; **¡eso no se puede —!** we can't have (*or* allow) that!

(**b**) to admit; to bear, put up with, wear (*fam*); **la plataforma no consiente más peso** the platform will not bear any more weight; **el abrigo consiente un arreglo más** the overcoat will bear repairing once more.

(**c**) *child* to pamper, spoil.

2 *vi* (**a**) to agree, consent, say yes (*en* to); to give in; — **en hacer algo** to agree to + *infin*, consent to + *infin*.

(**b**) — **con** to pamper, spoil.

3 consentirse *vr* to break, give (way); to split, crack (up etc).

conserje *nm* porter; doorman; caretaker.

conserjería *nf* porter's office.

conserva *nf* (**a**) (*act*) preserving.

(**b**) preserved foods; preserve(s); jam; pickle; **—s alimenticias** tinned foods, canned goods; **—s de carne** canned meat; potted meat; **en** — preserved; pickled; tinned, canned.

(**c**) (*Naut*) convoy; **navegar en (la)** — to sail in convoy.

conservación *nf* conservation; preservation; (*Archit etc*) maintenance, upkeep; — **refrigerada** cold storage; — **de suelos** soil conservation; **gastos de** — upkeep costs, maintenance expenses; **instinto de** — instinct of self-preservation.

conservador 1 *adj* (**a**) preservative.

(**b**) (*Pol*) conservative.

2 *nm*, **conservadora** *nf* (**a**) (*Pol*) conservative.

(**b**) (*of museum*) curator, keeper; — **adjunto** assistant keeper.

conservadurismo *nm* (*Pol etc*) conservatism.

conservar [1a] **1** *vt* (**a**) *food etc* to preserve; *meat* to tin, can; *resources* to conserve; (*Archit etc*) to preserve.

(**b**) *person, life* to preserve, save.

(**c**) *custom* to keep up, maintain, retain; *estate etc* to keep up; *colour, secret, friends etc* to keep; **"conserve su derecha"** "keep to the right"; **conservo varias cartas suyas** I have a few letters of his; **conserva todavía la señal** he still has (*or* bears) the mark.

2 conservarse *vr* (**a**) to survive, remain, still exist; to be retained, be kept; to last out.

(**b**) (*person*) to keep (well); to take good care of oneself; — **con** (*or* **en**) **salud** to keep well; **¡consérvese bien!** look after yourself!, I hope you keep well!

conservatismo *nm* conservatism.

conservativo *adj* preservative.

conservatorio *nm* (**a**) (*Mus*) conservatoire. (**b**) (*Chi*) greenhouse. (**c**) (*Arg*) private school.

conservero *adj* canning (*attr*); **la industria conservera** the canning industry.

considerable *adj* considerable; substantial; sizeable.

consideración *nf* (**a**) (*act*) consideration; thought; reflexion; **está en** — it is under consideration; **tomar en** — to take into account, take into consideration.

(**b**) consideration; respect, regard; **en** — **a** considering, in consideration of; **por** — **a** out of regard for; **sin** — **a** irrespective of; without regard to; **hablar sin** — to speak disrespectfully; **tratar a uno sin** — to treat someone without consideration; **no le tengan Vds ninguna** — don't give him any special treatment.

(**c**) respect, esteem; **tengo una gran** — **por él** I hold him in high esteem.

(**d**) **—es** kindness; **tener —es con uno** to be kind to someone.

(**e**) importance; **una casa de cierta** — a sizeable house; **una herida de** — a serious wound; **de poca** — unimportant, of no account.

consideradamente *adv* considerately, kindly, thoughtfully.

considerado *adj* (**a**) respected, esteemed; **mal** — unworthy. (**b**) considerate, kind (*con* to), thoughtful.

considerar [1a] *vt* (**a**) to consider; to think about, reflect on; — **que** ... to consider that ..., think that ...

(**b**) to take into account; **considera que** ... bear in mind that ..., don't forget that ...

(**c**) to think, deem; **lo considero imposible** I consider it (to be) impossible; **le consideran como loco** they think him mad; **le consideran como futuro rey** they consider him to be a future king.

(**d**) to esteem, respect; **poco a** to scorn, despise.

(**e**) to be kind to, show consideration for.

consigna *nf* (**a**) order, instruction; (*Mil*) watchword; (*of campaign etc*) watchword, slogan, motto; catchword; **—s de un vuelo** (*Mil etc*) operating instructions for a flight, operational orders for a flight.

(**b**) (*Rail etc*) cloakroom, left-luggage office, checkroom (US).

consignación *nf* (**a**) consignment, shipment. (**b**) (*Fin*) appropriation; earmarked sum.

consignador *nm* consignor.

consignar [1a] *vt* (**a**) (*Comm*) to send, dispatch, remit (*a* to); to consign (*a* to); to deposit (*a* with).

(**b**) (*Fin*) to assign (*para* to, for).

(**c**) *detail, fact* to record, register; to put, set down, state; **olvidé** — **mi nombre** I forgot to write my name in, I forgot to state my name; **el hecho no quedó consignado en ningún libro** the fact was not recorded (*or* set down) in any book.

consignatario *nm* (*Comm*) consignee; (*Comm*) agent; (*Law*) assign(ee); (*of letter etc*) recipient, addressee.

consigo *pron* with him, with her; with you; with one(self) etc; **no lleva nada** — he wasn't taking anything with him; **hablaba** — she was talking to herself; see **dar** etc.

consiguiente *adj* consequent (*a* upon); resulting; **por** — and so, therefore, consequently.

consistencia *nf* consistence, consistency.

consistente *adj* (**a**) *conduct, theory etc* consistent; *person* (*SAm: angl*) consistent; *reason etc* sound, valid.

(**b**) *material* solid, firm, tough, durable; *paste etc* stiff, thick; substantial.

(**c**) — **en** consisting of.

consistir [3a] *vi*: — **en** (*SAm:* — **de**, *angl*) (**a**) to consist of; to be made of, be composed of; **¿en qué consiste?** what does it consist of?

(**b**) (*of cause etc*) to lie in, be due to; **no consiste en eso la dificultad** the difficulty does not lie in that; **su atractivo consiste en su naturalidad** her charm lies in her naturalness; **si en mí solo consistiese** if it lay with me alone, if it depended entirely on me.

consistorial *adj* (*Eccl*) consistorial; see **casa**.

consistorio *nm* (*Eccl*) consistory; (*Pol*) town council.

consocio *nm* fellow member; (*Comm*) co-partner, associate.

consola *nf* console table; (*Archit, Mus*) console.

consolación *nf* consolation.

consolador 1 *adj* consoling, comforting. **2** *nm*, **consoladora** *nf* consoler, comforter.

consolar [1m] **1** *vt* to console, comfort; **me consuela de no haber ido** it consoles me for not having gone.

2 consolarse *vr* to console oneself; to find consolation (*con* in), take comfort (*con* from).

consolatorio *adj* consolatory.

consolidación *nf* consolidation.

consolidados *nmpl* (*Fin*) consols.

consolidar [1a] *vt* to consolidate, strengthen; *wall etc* to shore up; *debt* to fund.

consomé *nm* consommé, clear soup.

consonancia *nf* (**a**) consonance, harmony; **en** — **con** in accordance with, in harmony with. (**b**) (*Lit*) consonance, rhyme.

consonante 1 *adj* (**a**) consonant, harmonious; consistent.

(**b**) (*Ling*) consonantal.

(**c**) (*Lit*) rhyming.

2 *nm* (*Lit*) rhyme, rhyming word.

3 *nf* (*Ling*) consonant.

consonántico *adj* consonantal.

consonar [1m] *vi* (**a**) (*Mus and fig*) to be in harmony, harmonize. (**b**) (*Lit*) to rhyme (*con* with).

consorcio *nm* (**a**) (*Comm*) consortium; association, partnership; syndicate. (**b**) (*of circumstances etc*) conjunction.

consorte *nmf* (**a**) consort, spouse; **príncipe** — prince consort. (**b**) (*fig*) partner, companion. (**c**) (*Law*) **—s** colitigants; (*pej*) partners in crime, accomplices.

conspicuo *adj* eminent, famous.

conspiración *nf* conspiracy.

conspirador *nm*, **conspiradora** *nf* conspirator.

conspirar [1a] *vi* to conspire, plot (*con* with, *contra* against); — **a** + *infin* to conspire to + *infin* (*also fig*).

constancia *nf* (**a**) constancy; steadiness; firmness, steadfastness; loyalty.

(**b**) certainty; proof, evidence; **no hay** — **de ello** there is no certainty of it; there is no record of it, it is not recorded; **dejar** — **de algo** to place something on record; to show evidence of something.

(**c**) (*SAm*) documentary proof, written evidence.

constante 1 *adj* (**a**) *wind, effort etc* constant; *unchanging*; steady; *person* firm, steadfast; *friend* loyal, faithful, staunch.

(**b**) constant; continual; unending.

2 *nf* (*Math and fig*) constant.

constantemente *adv* constantly.

Constantinopla Constantinople.

Constanza *f* Constance.

constar [1a] *vi* (**a**) — **de** to be clear from, be evident from; **consta que** ... it is clear that ..., it is a fact that ...; it is known that ...; **me consta que** ... I know for sure that ..., I have evidence that ...;

conste que yo no lo aprobé let it be clearly understood that I did not approve it; **consta por . . .** as is shown by . . .

(b) to be on record, exist in recorded form; **"no consta"** (*of book*) "not available"; **no consta en el catálogo** it is not listed in the catalogue, it does not figure in the catalogue; **en el carnet no consta su edad** his age is not stated on the licence; **hacer —** to record; to certify; **hacer — que . . .** to reveal that . . .

(c) **— de** to consist of, be composed of.

constatar [1a] *vt* (*gall*) to confirm; to show, prove, check (*que* that).

constelación *nf* constellation.

constelado *adj* starry, full of stars; (*fig*) bespangled (*de* with).

consternación *nf* consternation, dismay.

consternado *adj*: **estar —, quedarse —** to be dismayed, be shattered; to be aghast; **dejar — =consternar**.

consternar [1a] **1** *vt* to dismay, shatter, shock. **2 consternarse** *vr* to be dismayed, be shattered; to be aghast.

constipación *nf*=**constipado** 2.

constipado **1** *adj*: **estar —** to have a cold. **2** *nm* (*Med*) cold, catarrh; **coger un —** to catch a cold.

constiparse [1a] *vr* to catch a cold.

constitución *nf* (*all senses*) constitution.

constitucional **1** *adj* constitutional. **2** *nmf* constitutionalist.

constitucionalmente *adv* constitutionally.

constituir [3g] **1** *vt* (a) *family, whole etc* to constitute, form, make up; **lo constituyen 12 miembros** it consists of 12 members, it is made up of 12 members; **esa industria constituye su principal riqueza** that industry constitutes (*or* is, forms) its chief wealth.

(b) (*equivalence*) to be; **eso no constituye estorbo** that isn't an obstacle; that doesn't amount to an obstacle; **para mí constituye un placer** for me it is a pleasure.

(c) *body, committee etc* to constitute, create, set up, establish; *school etc* to found; *scholarship etc* to institute, endow.

(d) **— una nación en república** to make a country into a republic; **— una ciudad en capital** to make a city the capital; **— a uno en árbitro** to set someone up as arbiter; **— heredero a uno** to make someone one's heir; **— algo en principio** to erect something into a principle, set something up as a principle.

(e) **— a uno en una obligación** to force someone into an obligation.

2 constituirse *vr* (a) **— en** (*or por*) **algo** to set oneself up as something, make oneself into something.

(b) **— en un lugar** to present oneself at a place, appear in person in a place, (*in orders*) report at a place.

constitutivo **1** *adj* constitutive; (*Parl, Pol etc*) constituent. **2** *nm* constituent.

constituyente *adj* (*Pol*) constituent.

constreñir [3h *and* 3l] *vt* (a) *initiative, movement etc* to restrict.

(b) **— a uno a hacer algo** to compel (*or* force, constrain) someone to do something.

(c) (*Med*) *artery* to constrict; *person, bowels* to constipate.

constricción *nf* constriction.

construcción *nf* (a) construction; building; structure; **— de buques,** **— naval** shipbuilding; **— de carreteras** road building; **en —, en vía de —** under construction, in course of construction.

(b) (*Gram*) construction.

constructivamente *adv* constructively.

constructivo *adj* constructive.

constructor **1** *adj* building, construction (*attr*).

2 *nm* builder (*also fig*); **— de buques,** **— naval** shipbuilder; **— cinematográfico** designer of film sets.

construir [3g] *vt* (a) to construct; to build, erect, put up. (b) (*Gram*) to construe.

consuelda *nf* comfrey.

consuelo *nm* consolation, solace, comfort; **llorar sin —** to weep inconsolably; **premio de —** consolation prize.

consuetudinario *adj* (a) habitual, customary; *drunkard* hardened, confirmed. (b) **derecho —** common law.

cónsul *nm* consul.

consulado *nm* (*post*) consulship; (*office*) consulate.

consular *adj* consular.

consulta *nf* (a) (*act*) consultation.

(b) (*Med*) consulting room.

(c) (*Med*) examination; **horas de —** surgery hours;

la — es de 5 a 8 the surgery is from 5 to 8; **el doctor no pasa — a domicilio** the doctor does not make home visits.

(d) (*Hist*) opinion.

(e) **libro de —, obra de —** reference book, work of reference.

consultación *nf* consultation.

consultar [1a] *vt* (a) *person* to consult (*acerca de, sobre* about, on); **— a un médico** to consult a doctor, see a doctor.

(b) *matter* to discuss, raise, take up (*con* with); **lo consultaré con mi abogado** I will take the matter up with my lawyer.

(c) *book* to consult, look up; *reference, word* to look up; to hunt up, chase up.

consultivo *adj* consultative.

consultor *nm* consultant.

consultorio *nm* information bureau; (*Med*) surgery, consulting room; (*of magazine*) problem page.

consumación *nf* consummation; end; extinction.

consumado *adj* consummate, perfect; accomplished (*en* in); *rogue etc* thorough, out-and-out.

consumar [1a] *vt* (a) to complete, accomplish, carry out; *crime* to commit; *raid, robbery* to carry out; *deal* to close, complete; *marriage* to consummate; (*Law*) *sentence* to carry out.

(b) (*CAm, Col*) to submerge.

consumición *nf* (a) consumption. (b) (*in restaurant etc*) meal.

consumido *adj* (a) *person* skinny, wasted; *fruit etc* shrunken. (b) (*fig*) timid; fretful, easily upset; **tener — a uno** to keep someone in a nervous state.

consumidor *nm* consumer.

consumir [3a] **1** *vt* (a) *food* to consume, eat; *product* to use, consume; *fuel* to burn, use, consume; (*in restaurant etc*) to take, have.

(b) *material* to wear away; *patience* to wear down; *liquid content* to dry up; *person* to waste away, exhaust the energies of, wear out.

(c) (*fig*) **le consumen los celos** he is eaten up with jealousy; **ese deseo le consume** that desire is burning him up; **me consume· su terquedad** his obstinacy is getting on my nerves.

2 consumirse *vr* (a) (*fruit etc*) to shrink, shrivel (up), lose its substance; (*person*) to waste away; (*soup etc*) to boil down.

(b) (*by fire*) to burn out, be consumed, be devoured.

(c) (*person: fig*) to burn oneself out; to pine away, mope (*de* because of); **— de envidia** to be eaten up with jealousy; **— de rabia** to fume with rage; **me consumo de verle así** it vexes me to see him like that.

consumo *nm*, **consunción** *nf* (*all senses*) consumption.

consuno: de — *adv* with one accord.

consustancial *adj* consubstantial; **ser — con** to be inseparable from, be all of a piece with.

contabilidad *nf* accounting, book-keeping; (*as profession*) accountancy.

contabilizadora *nf* accounting machine, adding machine.

contabilizar [1f] *vt* to enter in the accounts.

contable **1** *adj* countable. **2** *nm* accountant, book-keeper; **— automático** adding machine.

contacto *nm* (a) contact (*also fig*); touch; **estar en — con** to be in touch with; **entrar en — con** to come into contact with; **poner a A en — con B** to put A in touch with B; **ponerse en — con** to get into touch with, contact; **lo hizo el municipio en — con el gobierno** the city did it in collaboration with the government.

(b) (*SAm*) switch, contact breaker.

contado **1** *adj* (a) **tiene los días —s** his days are numbered.

(b) **—s** few, scarce; rare; **en contadas ocasiones** on rare occasions; **contadas veces** seldom, rarely; **son —s los que . . .** there are few who . . .; **pero son contadísimos los que pueden** but those who can are very few and far between.

2 *nm* (a) (*Comm*) **al —, de —** (*SAm*) for cash, cash down; **pago al —** cash payment.

(b) **por de —** naturally, of course; **tomar algo por de —** to take something for granted.

(c) (*Col*) instalment.

contador *nm* (a) (*Math*) abacus, counting frame.

(b) (*of café*) counter.

(c) (*Comm*) accountant, book-keeper; cashier; (*Law*) receiver, official auditor; (*Ec*) pawnbroker, moneylender; **— de navío** purser.

(d) (*Tech*) meter; **— de aparcamiento** parking meter; **— de electricidad** electricity meter; **— de gas** gas meter; **— Geiger** Geiger counter; **— de revoluciones** tachometer; **— de taxi** taximeter.

contaduría nf (a) (as profession) accountancy. (b) accountant's office; cashier's office; (Theat) box office; (Ec) pawnbroker's, pawnshop.

contagiar [1b] 1 vt (a) disease to pass on, transmit, give (a to); to spread; person to infect (con with). (b) (fig) to infect, contaminate (con with); to corrupt. 2 **contagiarse** vr (a) to become infected; — **de** to become infected with, catch. (b) (fig) — **de** to become infected with, be tainted with.

contagio nm infection, contagion; (fig) contagion, corruption; taint.

contagioso adj disease contagious, infectious, catching; person infected, infectious; (fig) catching; corrupting.

contaminación nf (a) contamination; (of text) corruption; (lit) influence; — **del aire** air pollution. (b) (fig) taint, infection; defilement.

contaminar [1a] 1 vt (a) to contaminate; air, water to pollute; dress to soil; text to corrupt; (lit) to influence. (b) (fig) to taint, infect; to defile; (Eccl) to profane. 2 **contaminarse** vr to be(come) contaminated (con, de with, by).

contante adj: **dinero** — (y **sonante**) cash, ready money.

contar [1m] 1 vt (a) (Math) to count; to number off; money etc to count (up); to include, count in; **cuenta 18 años** she is 18; — **con los dedos** to count on one's fingers; **hay 9 kms a** — **desde aquí** it's 9 kms starting from here. (b) to count, reckon, consider; **al niño le cuentan por medio** they count the child as half; **le cuento entre mis amigos** I reckon him among my friends; **sin** — not counting, not including; except for; not to mention; **sin** — **con que** . . . leaving aside the fact that . . . (c) to remember, bear in mind; **cuenta que es más fuerte que tú** don't forget he's stronger than you are. (d) story etc to tell; **es muy largo de** — it's a long story; **¡cuéntaselo a tu abuela!** (etc) go tell that to the marines!; **¡a quien se lo cuentas!** you're telling me! 2 vi (a) (Math) to count, count up; **hay que** — **mucho para llegar al final del mes** we have to go carefully (or watch it) in order to get to the end of the month; **cuenta por dos** he counts for (or as) two. (b) (fig) to count; **esos puntos no cuentan** those points don't count; **no cuenta para nada** he doesn't count at all. (c) — **con** to rely on, count on, depend on; to have; **cuenta conmigo** trust me, you can rely on me; **contaban por segura su ayuda** they were relying absolutely on his help, they thought he was sure to help them; **cuenta con varias ventajas** it has a number of advantages; **no contábamos con eso** we had not bargained for that, that was unexpected. 3 **contarse** vr (a) to be counted; to be included, to figure (entre among); **se le cuenta entre los más famosos** he is reckoned among the most famous; **me cuento entre sus admiradores** I count myself among his admirers. (b) (story) to be told; **cuéntase que** . . . it is said that . . . , it is related that . . . ; **¿qué te cuentas?** (fam) how's things? (fam).

contemplación nf (a) contemplation; meditation, reflexion. (b) —**es** indulgence; leniency, gentle treatment; **no andarse con** —**es** not to stand on ceremony; **tener demasiadas** —**es con uno** to be too indulgent towards someone, be too soft on someone; **tratar a uno con** —**es** to treat someone leniently; to handle someone with kid gloves; **no me vengas con** —**es** don't come to me with excuses; **sin** —**es** without ceremony; without any explanation.

contemplar [1a] 1 vt (a) to look at, gaze at, watch, contemplate; (fig) to contemplate. (b) person to show (extra) consideration for, treat (too) indulgently, be (too) lenient with. 2 vi (Rel) to meditate.

contemplativo adj contemplative.

contemporáneo 1 adj contemporary; contemporaneous. 2 nm, **contemporánea** nf contemporary.

contemporizador 1 adj excessively compliant; lacking firm principles. 2 nm timeserver, compromiser; person who lacks firm principles.

contemporizar [1f] vi to be compliant, show oneself ready to compromise; (pej) to lack firm principles; to temporize; — **con uno** to hedge with someone.

contención nf (a) (Mil etc) containing, containment. (b) contention; rivalry. (c) (Law) suit.

contencioso adj (a) contentious; person argumentative, captious. (b) (Law) litigious.

contender [2g] vi to contend (con with, sobre over); to compete, be rivals (en in); (Mil etc) to fight; — **en unas oposiciones** to take part in a competitive examination.

contendiente nm contestant, contender.

contener [2l] 1 vt (a) contents to hold, contain. (b) (Mil etc) to contain; mob to hold back; rebels to keep down, hold down; horse to hold back, restrain; breath to hold; emotion to keep back, choke back, bottle up; anger to contain; yawn, laughter to smother; tendency to check, restrain, curb. (c) (Chi) to mean. 2 **contenerse** vr to control oneself, restrain oneself, hold oneself in check.

contenido 1 adj (a) person restrained, controlled; moderate; equable. (b) emotion suppressed. 2 nm contents; content.

contenta nf (Comm) endorsement; (Mil) good-conduct certificate; (Law) release, acknowledgement.

contentadizo adj (also **bien** —) easy to please; **mal** — hard to please.

contentamente adv contentedly.

contentamiento nm contentment, satisfaction.

contentar [1a] 1 vt (a) to satisfy, content; to please, make happy. (b) (Comm) to endorse. (c) (SAm) to reconcile. 2 **contentarse** vr (a) — **con** to be contented with, be satisfied with; — **con** + infin to content oneself with + ger; **se contenta con cualquier cosita** he's satisfied with anything, any little thing keeps him happy. (b) (SAm) to be reconciled (con with).

contento 1 adj contented, satisfied; pleased; glad, happy; **estar** — **con** (or **de**) to be satisfied with, be happy about, be content with; **están** —**s con el coche** they are pleased with the car; **no está** — **en su trabajo** he's not happy in his work; **viven muy** —**s** they live very happily; **¿estás** —? are you happy?; **estar tan** — **como unas castañuelas** to be as happy as a lark; **para dejar** (or **poner**, **tener**) **a uno** — in order to keep someone happy; **estar** (or **quedar**) — **de** + infin to be content to + infin; **estaría tan** — **de** + infin I would as soon + infin. 2 nm contentment; joy, happiness; **a** — to one's satisfaction; **no caber en sí de** — to be overjoyed, be overwhelmed with joy.

contentura nf (Ant, Pan) = **contento 2**.

contera nf (a) (metal) tip, end; ferrule. (b) (fig) small extra, small addition. (c) **por** — to crown it all, as a final blow.

contertuliano nm, **contertuliana** nf, **contertulio** nm, **contertulia** nf fellow member (of a social set); patron, regular guest (of hotel); —**s de café** café companions, people who regularly meet in a café, members of the same coffee set.

contesta nf (a) (SAm) answer. (b) (Mex, Pan) talk, chat. (c) (Mex) declaration of love.

contestable adj questionable, debatable.

contestación nf answer, reply; — **a la demanda** (Law) defence plea; **mala** — sharp retort, piece of backchat; **dejar una carta sin** — to leave a letter unanswered.

contestador adj (SAm) cheeky, saucy.

contestar [1a] 1 vti (a) to answer, reply; (pej) to answer back; — **una pregunta** (Univ etc) to answer a question; — **una carta** to reply to a letter; — **el teléfono** to answer the telephone; — **a un saludo** to return a greeting, respond to a greeting; **contestó que sí** he replied that it was (or he would etc); **abstenerse de** — to make no reply; **un 7 por 100 se abstuvo de** — (in poll) there were 7% "don't knows". (b) (Law) to corroborate, confirm. 2 vi (Mex) to chat, talk; to argue.

contesto nm (Mex, Per, RPl) answer, reply.

contexto nm (a) (Lit etc) context. (b) (Tech) web, tangle.

contextura nf (a) contexture. (b) (Anat) build, physique; constitution; make-up.

contienda nf contest; struggle, fight.

contigo pron with you; (arch, to God) with thee.

contigüidad nf nearness, closeness, contiguity.

contiguo adj next; adjacent (a to); contiguous (a to), adjoining; **en un cuarto** — in an adjoining room.

continencia nf continence.

continental adj continental.

continente 1 *adj* continent.
2 *nm* **(a)** (*Geog*) continent; **el — norteamericano** the North-American continent.
(b) container.
(c) (*fig*) air, mien, bearing; **de — distinguido** with an air of distinction; **de — duro** harsh-looking.
contingencia *nf* contingency; risk; hazard, danger.
contingente 1 *adj* contingent. **2** *nm* **(a)** (*Mil etc*) contingent. **(b)** = **contingencia**. **(c)** (*Comm etc*) quota; **— de importación** import quota.
continuación *nf* continuation; sequel; **a —** then, next; immediately after; later (on), subsequently; **según lo expuesto a —** as set out below, as follows; **a — de** after, following.
continuamente *adv* continuously; continually, constantly.
continuar [1e] **1** *vt* to continue, go on with; to resume; to carry on (with); *road etc* to continue, prolong, extend.
2 *vi* **(a)** to continue; to go on, carry on; **"continuará"** (*serial*) "to be continued"; **— hablando** to continue talking, continue to talk, go on talking; **continúa lloviendo** it's still raining; **la puerta continúa cerrada** the door is still shut; **continuaba en Noruega** he was still in Norway; he remained in Norway; **— con su trabajo** to continue (or go on) with one's work; **— con salud** to keep in good health; **— en su puesto** to stay at one's job, carry on with one's work.
(b) (*of route etc*) to continue; **la carretera continúa más allá de la frontera** the road continues (on) beyond the frontier; **— con** (*also* **—se con**) to adjoin; to link up with, connect with.
continuidad *nf* continuity.
continuo 1 *adj* **(a)** (*in space, time; of series*) continuous; (*Tech*) *belt etc* endless; *see* **acto, sesión.**
(b) (*of action*) continual, constant; **sus continuas quejas** his continual complaints.
(c) a la continua, (de) — continually.
2 *nm* continuum.
contonearse [1a] *vr* (*man*) to swagger, strut; (*woman*) to swing one's hips, walk with a waggle; to walk affectedly, show off as one walks.
contoneo *nm* swagger, strut; hip-swinging, waggle; affected gait.
contorcerse [2b *and* 2h] *vr* to writhe, twist.
contorno *nm* **(a)** outline (*also Art*); (*Geog*) contour; perimeter; form, shape; **en —** round about, all around.
(b) measurement round, distance round; **— de un árbol** girth of a tree, distance round a tree's trunk; **el — de cintura es de 22 pulgadas** her waist measurement is 22 inches.
(c) —s environs, neighbourhood, surrounding area; **Caracas y sus —s** Caracas and its environs.
contorsión *nf* contortion.
contorsionarse [1a] *vr* to contort oneself.
contorsionista *nmf* contortionist.
contra 1 *adv* **(a)** against; **puntos en —** points against; **hablar en —** to speak against; **votar en —** to vote against; **opinar en —** to disagree, take the contrary view.
(b) de — (*SAm*) extra, over and above.
2 *prep* against; (*of view etc*) opposite, facing; (*Comm: of draft*) on; **apoyar algo — la pared** to lean something against the wall; **en — de** against; **hablar en — de un proyecto** to speak against a plan; **en — de lo que habíamos pensado** contrary to what we had thought; **ir en — de algo** to go against something, run counter to something.
3 *nm* con; *see* **pro.**
4 *nf* **(a)** (*Fencing*) counter.
(b) trouble, snag; inconvenience.
(c) hacer la — to be consistently obstructive, persist in taking an opposite view; **llevar la — a uno** to oppose someone, contradict someone.
(d) (*SAm*) antidote.
(e) (*Cu, Mex, PR*) extra, bonus.
contra . . . counter-. . ., contra . . .; cross- . . .; *eg* **contramanifestación** counter-demonstration; **contrapropaganda** counter-propaganda.
contraalmirante *nm* rear admiral.
contraatacar [1g] *vti* to counter-attack.
contraataque *nm* counter-attack.
contrabajo *nm* double bass.
contrabalancear [1a] *vt* to counterbalance.
contrabalanza *nf* counterbalance.
contrabandear [1a] *vi* to smuggle, live by smuggling.
contrabandista *nmf* smuggler; **— de armas** gun-runner.
contrabando *nm* **(a)** (*act*) smuggling; **— de armas** gun-running.
(b) contraband, smuggled goods; prohibited article, banned item; **géneros de —** smuggled goods; **amores de —** (*fig*) clandestine love affair; **pasar** (*or* **introducir**) **algo de —** to smuggle something in, get something in illegally.
contrabordo *nm* (*Mex*) kerb.
contracción *nf* **(a)** contraction; shrinkage; wasting. **(b)** (*Col*) diligence, industry.
contracifra *nf* key (to a code).
contracorriente 1 *nf* cross-current; undercurrent.
2 *adv*: **estar —, ir —** to go against the tide (*fig*), go against current tendencies.
contráctil *adj* contractile.
contractual *adj* contractual.
contrachapado 1 *adj*: **madera** *f* **contrachapada** = **2** *nm* plywood.
contradecir [3p] *vt* to contradict.
contradicción *nf* contradiction; (*fig*) incompatibility; **espíritu de —** contrariness; **A y B están en —** A and B stand in contradiction to each other.
contradictorio *adj* contradictory.
contraempuje *nm* counter-thrust.
contraer [2p] **1** *vt* **(a)** *material, substance etc* to contract; to shrink; to make smaller (*or* tighter *etc*); *script, speech* to condense, shorten; **— la frente** to wrinkle one's brow; **la humedad contrae las cuerdas** the damp makes the ropes tauten.
(b) *debt, obligation etc* to contract; *habit* to acquire, pick up, get into; *disease* to contract, catch; **— matrimonio** to marry (*con una* someone); **— parentesco con** to become related to.
(c) to restrict, limit (*a* to); **contrae su teoría a ciertos puntos** he limits his theory to certain points.
2 contraerse *vr* **(a)** to contract; to shrink; to get smaller; to tighten, tauten.
(b) — a to limit oneself to.
contraespionaje *nm* counter-espionage.
contraexplosión *nf* (*Aut etc*) backfire.
contrafallar [1a] *vt* to overtrump.
contrafuerte *nm* (*Archit*) buttress; (*Mil*) outwork; (*Geog*) spur; foothill; (*of shoe*) stiffener.
contragambito *nm* counter-gambit.
contragolpe *nm* counter-blow; (*fig*) backlash, reaction, kickback.
contrahacer [2s] *vt* to copy, imitate; *coin* to counterfeit; *document, proof* to forge, fake; *book* to pirate; *person* to mimic, impersonate, do an impression of.
contrahaz *nm* (*of cloth*) wrong side.
contrahecho *adj* **(a)** counterfeit; fake, faked, forged; spurious, pirated. **(b)** (*Anat*) hunchbacked, deformed.
contrahechura *nf* counterfeit; forgery, fake; pirated edition, spurious edition.
contraído *adj* **(a)** contracted; shrunken, wasted. **(b)** (*Col*) diligent, industrious.
contrainteligencia *nf* counter-intelligence.
contrainterrogatorio *nm* (*Law*) cross-examination, cross-questioning.
contrairritante *nm* counterirritant.
contralto 1 *adj* contralto. **2** *nm* counter tenor. **3** *nf* contralto.
contraluz *nf* view against the light; **a —** against the light.
contramaestre *nm* (*Naut*) warrant officer; boatswain; (*Tech*) foreman.
contramandar [1a] *vt* to countermand.
contramandato *nm* counter-order.
contramarcha *nf* **(a)** (*Mil*) countermarch. **(b)** (*Aut etc*) reverse; **dar —** **(a)** to reverse, (*fig*) go into reverse.
contramarchar [1a] *vi* to countermarch.
contramatar [1a] **1** *vt* (*SAm*): **— a uno** to hurt someone by banging him into something.
2 contramatarse *vr* **(a)** (*SAm*) to crash into something, collide with something.
(b) (*Mex*) **— de** + *infin* to repent of + *ger*.
contramedia *nf* counter-measure.
contranatural *adj* unnatural.
contraofensiva *nf* counter-offensive.
contraoferta *nf* counter-offer.
contraorden *nf* counter-order.
contrapartida *nf* **(a)** (*Comm, Fin: in account*) balancing entry. **(b)** (*fig*) compensation; counter-weight; **como — de** as compensation for; as a counterweight to.
contrapelo: a — ** *adv* **(a) acariciar un gato a — to stroke a cat up the wrong way.
(b) a — the wrong way; against the grain; **a — de** against, counter to; **todo lo hace a —** he does everything the wrong way round; **intervino muy a —** he spoke up in a most unfortunate way, he chose quite the wrong way in which to intervene.
contrapesar [1a] *vt* to counterbalance (*con* with); (*fig*) to offset; balance, compensate for.

contrapeso *nm* (a) counterpoise, counterweight; (*Comm*) makeweight; (*Circus*) balancing pole. (b) (*fig*) counterweight. (c) (*Chi*) anxiety, worry.

contraponer [2r] *vt* (a) *two colours etc* to compare, set against each other.
(b) — **A a B** to set up A against B, put up A as a barrier against B; **a esta idea ellos contraponen su teoría de que** ... against this idea they set up their theory that ...

contraposición *nf* comparison; contrast, clash; **en — a** in contrast to.

contraproducente *adj* self-defeating; counter-productive; **tener un resultado —** to have a boomerang effect, boomerang.

contrapuerta *nf* storm door; double door; protective door.

contrapuntear [1a] *vi* (*SAm*) to sing improvised verses in competition; (*fig*) to compete.

contrapunteo *nm* (*Cu, Per, PR, RPl*) argument; abuse, angry words; **en —** (*Per*) in competition.

contrapuntístico *adj* contrapuntal.

contrapunto *nm* (a) counterpoint. (b) (*SAm*) poetic competition with improvised verses; **de —** in competition.

contrariar [1c] *vt* (a) to oppose, be opposed to, go against; to impede, thwart. (b) to vex, upset, annoy.

contrariedad *nf* (a) obstacle; setback, misfortune; snag, trouble.
(b) vexation, annoyance; **producir — a uno** to upset someone, cause annoyance to someone.
(c) contrary nature; opposition.

contrario 1 *adj* (a) (*of person*) opposed, different; **son —s en sus aficiones** they have opposing tastes, they differ widely in tastes.
(b) *direction, side etc* opposite; **en sentido —** the other way, in the other direction.
(c) *sense* opposite (*de* to); **se ha interpretado en sentido — del que realmente tiene** it has been interpreted in the opposite sense to its true one.
(d) contrary (*a* to); harmful, damaging, hostile (*a* to); **— a los intereses del país** contrary to the nation's interests.
(e) *wind etc* contrary; *fortune* adverse.
(f) (*of opinion*) opposed; **él es — a las reformas** he is opposed to the reforms, he is against the changes.
(g) (*idioms*) **al —, por el —** on the contrary; **al — de** unlike; **al — de lo que habíamos pensado** against what we had thought; **todo salió al — de lo que habíamos previsto** it all turned out differently from what we had expected; **hablar al —** to speak to the contrary, speak against; **lo — the** opposite, the reverse; **de lo —** otherwise; were it not so; **todo lo —** quite the reverse; **llevar la contraria** to maintain an opposite point of view; **llevar la contraria a uno** to oppose someone, contradict someone.
2 *nm*, **contraria** *nf* enemy, adversary; (*Law, Sport etc*) opponent.
3 *nm* obstacle, snag.

contrarreclamación *nf* counterclaim.
contrarreferencia *nf* cross-reference.
Contrarreforma *nf* Counter-Reformation.
contrarrestar [1a] *vt* (a) to counteract, offset, balance; *effects* to counter, counteract. (b) *ball* to return.
contrarrevolución *nf* counter-revolution.
contrasentido *nm* (a) contradiction; piece of nonsense; **aquí hay un —** there is a contradiction here; **pero esto hace un —** but this is a contradiction (in terms).
(b) misinterpretation; mistranslation.

contraseña *nf* (a) countersign, secret mark; (*Mil etc*) watchword, password. (b) (*Theat*) pass-out ticket.
(c) (*Arg*) countersignature.

contrastar [1a] **1** *vt* (a) to resist.
(b) *metal* to assay; to hallmark; *weights and measures* to check; *radio* to monitor.
2 *vi* (a) to contrast, form a contrast (*con* with).
(b) **— a, — con, — contra** to resist; to face up to.

contraste *nm* (a) contrast (*also TV*); **en — con** in contrast to; **por —** in contrast; **hacer — con** to contrast with.
(b) assay; check; (**marca del**) **—** hallmark.
(c) inspector of weights and measures.

contratante *nmf* (*Comm*) contractor; (*Law*) contracting party.

contratar [1a] **1** *vt goods etc* to contract for; to negotiate for; to sign a contract for; *work* to put out to contract; *lease etc* to take on; *person* to hire, engage; *player etc* to sign up.

2 contratarse *vr* (*player etc*) to sign on; **— para hacer algo** to contract to do something.

contratiempo *nm* (a) setback, reverse; mishap, accident. (b) (*Mus*) **a —** offbeat.

contratista *nmf* contractor; **— de edificación** building contractor, builder.

contrato *nm* contract (*de* for).

contratuerca *nf* locknut.

contravención *nf* contravention, infringement, violation.

contraveneno *nm* antidote (*de* to).

contravenir [3s] *vi*: **— a** to contravene, infringe, violate.

contraventana *nf* shutter.

contribución *nf* (a) contribution; **poner a —** to make use of, put to use.
(b) (*Fin*) tax; **—es** taxes, taxation; **— directa** direct tax; **— municipal** rates; **exento de —es** free of tax, tax-free, tax-exempt (*US*); **pagar las —es** to pay one's taxes (*or* rates).

contribuir [3g] *vti* (a) to contribute (*a, para* to, towards); **— una cantidad** to contribute a sum; **— al éxito de algo** to contribute to (*or* help towards) the success of something; **— a + infin** to help to + *infin*.
(b) (*Fin*) to pay (in taxes).

contribuyente *nm* contributor; (*Fin*) taxpayer.

contrición *nf* contrition.

contrincante *nm* opponent, rival.

contristar [1a] **1** *vt* to sadden. **2 contristarse** *vr* to grow sad, grieve.

contrito *adj* contrite.

control *nm* (a) (*in general*) control; **bajo —** under control; **fuera de —** out of control; **perder el —** to lose control (of oneself); **perder — de** to lose control of; **— de alquileres** rent control; **— de cambio** exchange control; **— de la circulación** traffic control; point duty; **— a distancia, — remoto** remote control; **— de (la) natalidad** birth control; **— de precios** price control; **— de sí mismo** self-control; **— de tonalidad** tone control; **— de volumen** volume control.
(b) inspection, check, checking; (*Comm, Fin*) audit(ing); (*Aut: in rally*) checkpoint; **— de frontera** frontier checkpoint; **— nuclear** nuclear inspection; **— de pasaportes** passport inspection.

controlar [1a] *vt* (a) to control. (b) to inspect, check; (*Comm, Fin*) to audit.

controversia *nf* controversy.

controvertible *adj* controversial; debatable, disputable.

controvertir [3i] **1** *vt* to dispute, question; to argue about. **2** *vi* to argue.

contubernio *nm* (a) ring, conspiracy; collusion. (b) cohabitation (*also pej*).

contumacia *nf* obstinacy, stubborn disobedience; perversity; (*Law*) contempt (of court); contumacy.

contumaz *adj* (a) obstinate, stubbornly disobedient; wayward, perverse; *drinker etc* inveterate, hardened, incorrigible; (*Law*) guilty of contempt (of court); contumacious.
(b) (*Med*) disease-carrying, germ-laden.

contumazmente *adv* obstinately; perversely; contumaciously.

contumelia *nf* contumely.

contumerioso *adj* (*CAm*) finicky; prudish.

contundente *adj* (a) *weapon* offensive, for striking a blow with; **instrumento —** blunt instrument.
(b) (*fig*) *argument etc* forceful, convincing, impressive; *proof* conclusive; *tone* forceful; *defeat etc* crushing, overwhelming.

contundir [3a] *vt* to bruise, contuse.

conturbar [1a] **1** *vt* to trouble, dismay, perturb. **2 conturbarse** *vr* to be troubled, be dismayed, become perturbed.

contusión *nf* bruise, bruising, contusion.

contusionar [1a] *vt* to bruise; to hurt, damage.

contuso *adj* bruised.

conuco *nm* (*Ant, Col, Ven*) smallholding, small farm.

conuquero *nm* (*Ant, Col, Ven*) smallholder, farmer.

convalecencia *nf* convalescence.

convalecer [2d] *vi* to convalesce, get better (*de* after), recover (*de* from).

convaleciente 1 *adj* convalescent. **2** *nmf* convalescent.

convección *nf* convection.

convecino *nm*, **convecina** *nf* (close) neighbour.

convencer [2b] *vti* to convince; to persuade; **¡convéncete!** believe you me!, I tell you it is so!; you'll have to get used to the idea!; **— a uno de que algo es mejor** to convince someone something is better; **— a uno para que haga algo** to persuade someone to do something; **no me convence del todo** I'm not fully convinced; **el argumento no convence** the argument does not convince (*or* is not convincing); **no me convence ese tío** I don't really trust that chap; **dejarse —** to allow oneself to be persuaded.

convencimiento *nm* (a) (*act*) convincing; persuasion.
(b) conviction, certainty; **llegar al — de** to become convinced of; **llevar algo al — de uno** to convince someone of something; **tener el — de que ...** to be convinced that ...

convención *nf* (*all senses*) convention.

convencional *adj* conventional.

convencionalismo *nm* conventionalism.

convencionero *adj* (*Mex, Per*) compliant, accommodating.

convenible *adj* (a) suitable; fitting; *price* fair, reasonable. (b) *person* accommodating.

conveniencia *nf* (a) suitability, fitness; usefulness, advantageousness; expediency; advisability; **a la primera —** at one's earliest opportunity, when convenient; **ser de la — de uno** to suit someone; **atender a la propia —** to think of how something will affect one.
(b) **—s** conventions (*also* **—s sociales**); proprieties, decencies.
(c) agreement.
(d) domestic post, job as a servant.
(e) **—s** (*Fin*) property; income; perquisites.

conveniente *adj* suitable; fit, fitting, proper; useful, profitable, advantageous; expedient; advisable; **nada —** *person* unsuitable; **no es — que ...** it is not advisable that ...; it is not desirable that ...; **creer** (*or* **estimar, juzgar**) **—** to think fit, see fit; **juzgar —** + *infin* to see fit to + *infin*, deem it wise to + *infin*.

convenio *nm* agreement, treaty, covenant; **— comercial** trade agreement; **— de préstamos y arriendos** lend-lease agreement.

convenir [3s] **1** *vi* (a) to agree (**con** with, **en** about); **— (en) hacer algo** to agree to do something; **— (en) que ...** to agree that ...; **"sueldo a —"** (*advert*) "salary to be agreed".
(b) to suit, be suited for; to be suitable for; to be good for; **si le conviene** if it suits you; **me convince quedarme aquí** it is best for me to stay here; **él no te conviene para marido** he's not the husband for you; **lo que más le conviene es un reposo completo** the best thing for him is complete rest.
(c) (*impersonal*) **conviene** + *infin* it is as well to + *infin*; it is important to + *infin*; **conviene recordar que ...** it is as well to remember that ..., it is to be remembered that ...; **no conviene que se publique eso** it is not desirable that that should be published; **conviene a saber** namely, that is.
2 convenirse *vr* to agree, come to an agreement (**en** on, about).

conventillo *nm* (*Bol, Chi, Per, RPl*) tenement house.

convento *nm* monastery; **— (de monjas)** convent, nunnery; (*Ec, Per*) priest's house.

conventual *adj* conventual.

convergencia *nf* (a) convergence. (b) (*fig*) common tendency, common direction; concurrence.

convergente *adj* (a) convergent, converging. (b) (*fig*) having a common tendency, tending in the same direction.

converger [2c] *vi*, **convergir** [3c] *vi* (a) to converge (**en** on).
(b) (*fig*) to have a common tendency, tend in the same direction (**con** as); to concur, be in accord (**con** with); **sus esfuerzos convergen a un fin común** their efforts have a common purpose, their efforts are directed towards the same objective.

conversa *nf* (*esp SAm*) talk, chat.

conversación *nf* conversation, talk; **cambiar de —** to change the subject; **trabar — con uno** to get into conversation with someone.

conversador 1 *adj* (*SAm*) talkative, garrulous. **2** *nm*, **conversadora** *nf* (a) conversationalist. (b) (*SAm*) talkative person, gossip.

conversar [1a] **1** *vt* (a) (*Chi, Ec*) to tell, relate; to report. (b) (*SD*) to chat up (*sl*). **2** *vi* (a) to talk, converse. (b) (*Mil*) to wheel.

conversata *nf* (*Chi*) talk, chat.

conversión *nf* (a) conversion. (b) (*Mil*) wheel.

converso 1 *adj* converted. **2** *nm*, **conversa** *nf* convert; (*Hist: esp*) converted Jew(ess).

conversón (*Ec, Col*) **1** *adj* talkative, gossiping. **2** *nm*, **conversona** *nf* talkative person, gossip.

conversor *nm* (*Radio*) converter.

convertibilidad *nf* convertibility.

convertible *adj* convertible.

convertidor *nm* (*Elec, Metal*) converter.

convertir [3i] **1** *vt* (a) to convert (*also Eccl*); to transform, turn (**en** into); (*Comm, Elec, Tech*) to convert; **— a uno al catolicismo** to convert someone to Catholicism.
(b) *eyes etc* to turn (**a** on).
2 convertirse *vr* to be converted, be transformed, be changed (**en** into); (*Eccl*) to be converted, convert (**a** to).

convexidad *nf* convexity.

convexo *adj* convex.

convicción *nf* conviction.

convicto 1 *adj* convicted, found guilty; condemned. **2** *nm* (*SAm: angl*) convict.

convidada *nf* round (*esp* of drinks); **dar una —, pagar una —** to stand a round.

convidado *nm*, **convidada** *nf* guest.

convidar [1a] **1** *vt* (a) to invite; **— a uno a hacer algo** to invite someone to do something; **— a uno a una cerveza** to stand someone a beer, treat someone to a beer, invite someone to have a beer; **— a uno con un café** to offer someone a cup of coffee.
(b) (*fig*) **— a** to stir to, move to; **el ambiente convida a la meditación** the setting invites one to indulge in meditation, the atmosphere is conducive to meditation.
2 convidarse *vr* (a) (*fam*) to invite oneself along.
(b) to volunteer, offer one's services.

convincente *adj* convincing.

convincentemente *adv* convincingly.

convite *nm* (a) invitation. (b) banquet, feast; treat; party; **— a escote** Dutch treat.

convivencia *nf* living together, life together, co-existence.

convivir [3a] *vi* to live together (*esp* amicably, in harmony); to share the same life, coexist; (*fig*) to exist side by side (**con** with).

convocación *nf* summoning, calling, convoking.

convocar [1g] *vt* to summon, call (together), convoke.

convocatoria *nf* (a) summons, call (to a meeting); notice of a meeting; **"C—s para hoy"** (*in press*) "Today's Meetings". (b) **=convocación**.

convólvulo *nm* convolvulus.

convoy *nm* (a) (*Naut*) convoy; (*Rail*) train; (*fam*) procession; retinue. (b) cruet, cruet stand.

convoyar [1a] **1** *vt* (a) to convoy; to guard, escort. (b) (*Chi*) to give financial backing to. **2 convoyarse** *vr* (*PR, Ven*) to connive together, plot.

convulsión *nf* convulsion.

convulsionar [1a] *vt* to convulse.

convulsivo *adj* convulsive.

convulso *adj* convulsed (**de** with).

conyugal *adj* conjugal; married.

cónyuge *nmf* spouse; partner; husband *or* wife; *see next entry*.

cónyuges *nmfpl* spouses; married couple, husband and wife.

coña *nf* (*tabu*) humour, humorous tone, joking way.

coñac [ko'na] *nm*, *pl* **coñacs** [ko'nas] brandy, cognac.

coñearse [1a] *vr* to speak in a joking way, adopt a humorous tone.

coñete *adj* (*Chi, Per*) mean.

coño *nm* (a) (*Anat: tabu*) cunt (*tabu*).
(b) (*fam: to person*) you idiot!; (*interj: also* ¡qué **—**!) hell!, damn it all!; well I'm damned!; (*more mildly*) well!, good heavens!
(c) (*Chi, Mex*) *pej* term applied to Spaniards.

cooperación *nf* cooperation.

cooperador 1 *adj* cooperative; collaborating, participating. **2** *nm*, **cooperadora** *nf* collaborator, co-worker.

cooperar [1a] *vi* to cooperate (*a, en* in; *con* with); **— a** + *infin* to cooperate in + *ger*; **— a un mismo fin** to work for a common aim, work together in a common cause; **— en** to collaborate in, work together on, take part (together) in; **los factores que cooperaron al fracaso** the factors which together led to failure, the factors which contributed to the failure.

cooperativa *nf* cooperative, mutual association; **— agrícola** agricultural cooperative.

cooperativo *adj* cooperative.

coordenada *nf* (*Math*) coordinate.

coordinación *nf* coordination.

coordinado *adj* coordinated; (*Mil*) *operation* combined.

coordinador *nm* coordinator.

coordinar [1a] *vt* to coordinate.

copa *nf* (a) glass; (*poet*) goblet; (*Sport etc*) cup, trophy; **llevar una — de más** to have (had) one over the eight; **tomarse unas —s** to have a drink or two.

(b) (*fig*) — **de la amargura** cup of sorrow; **apurar la** — to know the utmost depths of suffering. **(c)** (*of hat*) crown; (*of tree*) top. **(d)** —**s** (*Cards*) hearts; **la** — the ace of hearts. **(e)** (*Col*) connoisseur, judge of wine.

copado *adj tree* thick, with dense foliage.

copal *nm* (*CAm, Mex*) resin.

copante *nm* (*Guat, Hond, Mex*) stepping stone.

copar [1a] *vt* **(a)** (*Mil*) to surround, cut off; (*fig*) to corner; **quedar copado en un trabajo** to get bogged down in a piece of work.
(b) (*Cards etc*) to win (all the tricks), sweep the board; (*Pol and fig*) to sweep the board, win hands down; *prize, cup* to walk off with, collar (*fam*).

copartícipe *nmf* partner; fellow participant, fellow competitor; joint owner; collaborator (*en in*).

copear [1a] *vi* **(a)** (*fam*) to booze, tipple; to go on a pub crawl (*fam*). **(b)** to sell wine (*etc*) by the glass.

Copenhague Copenhagen.

Copérnico *m* Copernicus.

copete *nm* **(a)** (*of person*) tuft (*of hair*), quiff; (*of horse*) forelock; (*Orn*) tuft, crest; **estar hasta el** — (*Mex, PR*) to be utterly fed up.
(b) (*fig*) pride, haughtiness; **de alto** — aristocratic; important, socially prominent; **tener mucho** — to be haughty, be stuck-up (*fam*).

copetín *nm* (*Arg, Per, Urug*) glass of spirits; cocktail, aperitif.

copetón *adj* **(a)** (*SAm*) =**copetudo (a)**. **(b)** (*Col*) **estar** — to be tight. **(c)** (*Ven*) cowardly.

copetudo *adj* **(a)** tufted; crested. **(b)** highborn, of noble birth, blue-blooded; haughty, stuck-up (*fam*).

copia *nf* **(a)** copy; (*Art*) copy; replica, reproduction; duplicate; — **de calco**, — **al carbón**, — **carbónica** (*Arg*) carbon copy; — **fotostática** photostat; **en limpio** fair copy; **sacar una** — **de** to make a copy of.
(b) abundance, plenty; **con gran** — **de** with an abundance of, with a great deal of.

copiador *nm* **(a)** copier, copyist. **(b)** copybook. **(c)** copying machine.

copiante *nmf* copyist.

copiar [1b] *vt* to copy (*de* from); *style etc* to imitate; *dictation* to take down.

copiloto *nm* (*Aut*) co-driver; (*Aer*) co-pilot.

copiosamente *adv* copiously, abundantly, plentifully.

copioso *adj* copious, abundant, plentiful.

copista *nmf* copyist.

copita *nf* (small) glass; (*Golf*) tee; **una** — **de jerez** a glass of sherry; **tomarse unas** —**s** to have a drink or two.

copla *nf* **(a)** (*Lit*) verse (*esp* of 4 lines); couplet; (*Mus*) popular song, folksong, ballad; —**s** verses, poetry; —**s de Calaínos** *silly story* (*etc*) *with which someone irrelevantly interrupts*; —**s de ciego** doggerel; **hacer** —**s** (*fam*) to write verse.
(b) (*Chi, Guat, RPl*) pipe joint.

copo *nm* **(a)** (*of flax etc*) tuft, small bundle; — **de algodón** cotton ball; —**s de avena** oatmeal, rolled oats; — **de nieve** snowflake.
(b) (*Col, Ven*) tree top.
(c) (*RPl*) piled-up clouds.

coproducción *nf* (*Cine etc*) joint production.

copropietario *nm*, **copropietaria** *nf* co-owner, joint owner.

copucha *nf* (*Chi*) lie, fib.

copuchar [1a] *vi* (*Chi*) to tell lies, fib.

copuchento *adj* (*Chi*) lying, untrustworthy.

copudo *adj tree* bushy, thick.

cópula *nf* **(a)** (*Bio*) copulation; — **carnal** copulation, sexual intercourse. **(b)** (*Ling*) conjunction.

copularse [1a] *vr* to copulate (*con* with).

copulativo *adj* (*Ling*) copulative.

coque *nm* (*angl*) coke.

coqueluche *nf* (*gall*) whooping cough.

coqueta **1** *adj* flirtatious, flighty, coquettish. **2** *nf* **(a)** flirt, coquette. **(b)** roll, small loaf. **(c)** dressing table (with a full-length mirror).

coquetear [1a] *vi* to flirt (*con* with; *also fig*).

coqueteo *nm*, **coquetería** *nf* **(a)** (*quality*) flirtatiousness, flightiness, coquetry; (*fig*) affection. **(b)** (*act*) flirtation.

coquetón **1** *adj* **(a)** *object* smart, natty, attractive. **(b)** *man* flirtatious; attractive (*to women*). **(c)** = **coqueta 1. 2** *nm* ladykiller, wolf (*fam*).

coquitos *nmpl*: **hacer** — to make faces (*a* at).

coracha *nf* leather bag.

coraje *nm* **(a)** fighting spirit; toughness; courage; fortitude. **(b)** anger; **dar** — **a** to make angry, enrage.

corajina *nf* fit of temper, explosion of rage.

corajudo *adj* **(a)** spirited; tough; bold; (*Arg*) brave.
(b) quick-tempered, peppery.

coral[1] (*Mus*) **1** *adj* choral. **2** *nm* chorale. **3** *nf* choir, choral group.

coral[2] *nm* (*Zool*) coral.

coralino *adj* coral (*attr*), coralline.

corambre *nf* hides, skins.

Corán *m* Koran.

corana *nf* (*Chi, Per*) sickle.

coránico *adj* Koranic.

coraza *nf* **(a)** (*Mil, Hist*) cuirass; (*fig*) breastplate, protection. **(b)** (*Naut*) armour-plating. **(c)** (*Zool*) shell. **(d)** (*Aut*) grille (*of the radiator*).

corazón *nm* **(a)** (*Anat and fig*) heart; **de** — willingly; **de todo** — from the heart; **de buen** — kind-hearted; **¡hijo de mi** —**!** my precious child!; **duro de** — hard-hearted; **sin** — heartless; **con el** — **en la mano** frankly; sincerely; **estar enfermo del** — to have heart trouble; **arrancar** (*or* **partir, romper**) **el** — **a uno** to break someone's heart; **no caber a uno el** — **en el pecho** to be bursting with joy; **le dio en el** — she had a premonition; **encoger a uno el** — to fill someone with fear (*or* dismay, pity); **llevar el** — **en la mano** to wear one's heart on one's sleeve; **meter a uno el** — **en un puño** (*or* **en la boca**) to put the wind up someone; **morir con el** — **destrozado** to die of a broken heart; **poner el** — **en algo** to set one's heart on something; **no tener** — to have no heart, be heartless; **tener el** — **para** + *infin* to have the heart to + *infin*; **no tener el** — **para algo** not to feel up to something; *see* **íntimo** *etc.*
(b) (*Bot*) core.
(c) (*Cards*) —**es** hearts.

corazonada *nf* **(a)** presentiment, hunch. **(b)** rash impulse, sudden impulse; impulsive act.

corbata *nf* tie, necktie; cravat(e); — **de lazo** bow tie.

corbatín *nm* bow tie.

corbeta *nf* corvette.

Córcega *f* Corsica.

corcel *nm* steed, charger.

corcor *nm* (*CAm, PR*) gurgle; **beber** — to swig (*fam*).

corcova *nf* **(a)** hump, hunchback. **(b)** (*Bol, Chi, Ec, Per*) prolongation of a party (*into the following day or days*).

corcovado **1** *adj* hunchbacked. **2** *nm*, **corcovada** *nf* hunchback.

corcovar [1a] *vt* to bend (over); to crook.

corcovear [1a] *vi* **(a)** to prance about, cut capers; to buck, plunge. **(b)** (*Arg, Chi, Per, PR, Urug*) to grumble, grouse (*fam*). **(c)** (*Mex*) to be scared.

corcovo *nm* **(a)** prance, caper; buck, plunge. **(b)** crookedness.

corcha *nf* (piece of) cork bark.

corchea *nf* (*Mus*) quaver.

corchero *adj* cork (*attr*); **industria corchera** cork industry.

corcheta *nf* (*Sew*) eye.

corchete *nm* **(a)** (*Sew*) snap fastener; catch, clasp; hook and eye. **(b)** (*Typ*) —**s** square brackets.

corcho *nm* cork; cork bark; cork mat; cork-soled clog; (*Fish*) float; — **bornizo**, — **virgen** virgin cork; **sacar el** — to draw the cork, uncork.

corchoso *adj* corklike, corky.

cordada *nf* (*Mountaineering*) team, roped team.

cordaje *nm* cordage; (*of racquet*) strings; (*Naut*) rigging.

cordel *nm* cord, line; **a** — in a straight line.

cordelería *nf* **(a)** cordage, ropes; (*Naut etc*) ropewalk; (*Naut*) rigging. **(b)** cordmaking, ropemaking.

cordelero *nm* cordmaker, ropemaker.

cordería *nf* cordage, cords, ropes.

corderillo *nm*, **corderina** *nf* lambskin.

cordero *nm*, **cordera** *nf* **(a)** lamb; — **asado** roast lamb; **C— de Dios** Lamb of God; **¡no hay tales** —**s!** it's nothing of the sort!
(b) lambskin.
(c) (*fig*) meek and mild person.

corderuna *nf* lambskin.

cordial **1** *adj* **(a)** cordial; heartfelt, hearty. **(b)** (*Pharm*) tonic, invigorating. **2** *nm* cordial; tonic.

cordialidad *nf* warmth, cordiality.

cordialmente *adv* cordially; heartily; (*ending letter*) sincerely.

cordillera *nf* range, chain (*of mountains*).

cordillerano *adj* (*Chi, RPl*) from the Andes, of the Andes.

Córdoba Cordova.

cordobán *nm* cordovan (leather).

cordobana: **andar a la** — to go around stark naked.

cordobés **1** *adj* Cordovan. **2** *nm*, **cordobesa** *nf* Cordovan.

cordón *nm* (**a**) cord, string; (*Naut*) strand; (*of shoe*) lace; (*Mil*) braid, lace; (*Elec*) flex, extension wire (*US*); **lana de 3 —es** 3-ply wool.
  (**b**) (*Anat*) cord; **— umbilical** umbilical cord.
  (**c**) (*Archit*) cordon.
  (**d**) (*Mil, of police etc*) cordon; **— sanitario** sanitary cordon, cordon sanitaire.
  (**e**) (*RPl*) kerb.
  (**f**) (*Chi, Per, PR*) **— de cerros** chain of hills.
  (**g**) (*Per, Cu*) liquor, brandy.

cordoncillo *nm* (*of cloth*) rib; (*Sew*) braid, piping; (*of coin*) milling, milled edge.

cordura *nf* good sense, prudence, wisdom; **con —** sensibly, prudently, wisely.

Corea *f* Korea; **— del Norte** North Korea; **— del Sur** South Korea.

coreano 1 *adj* Korean. **2** *nm*, **coreana** *nf* Korean.

corear [1a] **1** *vt* to say in a chorus; (*Mus*) to sing the chorus of, join in the chorus of. **2** *vi* to speak all together; (*Mus*) to sing all together, join in.

coreografía *nf* choreography.

coreógrafo *nm* choreographer.

coriana *nf* (*Col*) blanket.

corifeo *nm* (**a**) (*Hist*) coryphaeus. (**b**) (*fig*) leader, spokesman.

corindón *nm* corundum.

corintio *adj* Corinthian.

Corinto Corinth.

corista 1 *nmf* (*Eccl*) chorister. **2** *nf* (*Theat etc*) chorus girl.

cormorán *nm*: **— (grande)** cormorant.

cornada *nf* butt, thrust (with the horns), goring; **dar una — a** to gore.

cornadura *nf* horns; (*of deer*) antlers.

cornalina *nf* cornelian, carnelian.

cornamenta *nf* horns; (*of deer*) antlers.

cornamusa *nf* bagpipe; hunting horn.

córnea *nf* cornea.

cornear [1a] *vt* to butt, gore.

corneja *nf* crow; **— negra** carrion crow; **— calva** rook.

córneo *adj* horny, corneous.

córner ['korne] *nm*, *pl* **córners** ['korne *or* 'kornes] (*Sport: angl*) corner kick; **¡—!** (*interj*) corner!; (*SAm: Sport, Boxing*) corner.

cornerina *nf* cornelian, carnelian.

corneta 1 *nf* bugle; **— acústica** ear trumpet; **— de llaves** cornet; **— de monte** hunting horn. **2** *nm* bugler; cornet player.

cornetín *nm* (**a**) cornet. (**b**) cornet player.

corneto *adj* (**a**) (*CAm*) bow-legged. (**b**) (*Arg, Mex, Ven*) cow with a bent horn.

cornezuelo *nm* (*Bot*) ergot.

cornflaques *nmpl*, **cornflés** *nmpl* (*SAm: angl*) cornflakes.

cornial *adj* horn-shaped.

córnico 1 *adj* Cornish. **2** *nm* (*language*) Cornish.

corniforme *adj* horn-shaped.

cornisa *nf* cornice.

cornisamento *nm* entablature.

corno *nm* (*Mus*) horn; **— de caza** hunting horn; **— inglés** cor anglais.

Cornualles *m* Cornwall.

cornucopia *nf* cornucopia, horn of plenty.

cornudo 1 *adj* (**a**) horned; antlered. (**b**) *husband* cuckolded. **2** *nm* cuckold.

cornúpeta *nm* (*Taur*) bull.

coro *nm* (**a**) (*Mus, Theat*) chorus; **una chica del —** a girl from the chorus, a chorus girl; **cantar el —** de to sing the chorus of; **cantar las partes a —s** to sing the parts alternately; **decir algo a —** to say something in a chorus, say something in unison; **aprender algo de —** to learn something by heart; to learn something by rote; **hacer — de** (*or* **a**) **las palabras de uno** to echo someone's words.
  (**b**) (*Mus, Eccl*) choir; **— celestial** celestial choir, heavenly choir; **niño de —** choirboy.
  (**c**) (*Archit*) choir.

corola *nf* corolla.

corolario *nm* corollary.

corona *nf* (**a**) crown; **— de espinas** crown of thorns; **ceñirse la —** to take the crown; **perder la —** (*euph*) to lose one's virginity; **rey sin — de Eslobodia** uncrowned king of Slobodia.
  (**b**) (*Astron*) corona; (*Meteorol*) halo.
  (**c**) (*of flowers*) garland; chaplet; **— funeraria** wreath.
  (**d**) (*Anat*) crown (of the head), top of the head; (*Eccl*) tonsure.
  (**e**) (*Fin*) crown; **media —** half-a-crown, half-crown.

coronación *nf* (**a**) coronation. (**b**) (*fig*) crowning, completion. (**c**) = **coronamiento** (**b**). (**d**) (*Chess*) queening.

coronamiento *nm* (**a**) (*fig*) crowning, completion. (**b**) (*Archit*) crown, coping stone; top, ornamental finish.

coronar [1a] *vt* (**a**) to crown; **— a uno (por) rey** to crown someone king.
  (**b**) *building etc* to crown (**con**, **de** with); to top, cap.
  (**c**) (*fig*) to crown; to complete, round off; **— algo con éxito** to crown something with success; **para —lo** to crown it all.
  (**d**) (*Chess*) to queen.
  (**e**) (*Ant, Per, RPl*) to cuckold, make a cuckold of.

coronario *adj* coronary.

coronel *nm* colonel; **— de aviación** group captain, colonel (*US*).

coronilla *nf* crown, top of the head; **andar** (*or* **bailar, ir**) **de —** to slog away, do one's utmost (to please someone); **dar de —** to bump one's head; **estar hasta la —** to be utterly fed up (**de** with).

coronta *nf* (*Bol, Chi, Per*) corncob.

coroto *nm* (*Ant, Col, Ec, Pan, Ven*) (**a**) gourd, vessel. (**b**) thing, affair; **—s** gear (*fam*), things; junk.

corpacho *nm*, **corpanchón** *nm*, **corpazo** *nm* (*fam*) carcass (*fam*).

corpiño *nm* bodice.

corporación *nf* corporation; association; (*Comm, Fin: angl*) corporation, company.

corporal *adj* corporal, bodily; **ejercicio —** physical exercise; **higiene —** personal hygiene.

corporativo *adj* corporate.

corpóreo *adj* corporeal, bodily.

corpulencia *nf* burliness, heavy build; stoutness, massiveness; **cayó con toda su —** he fell with his full weight.

corpulento *adj* *person* well-built, burly, heavily-built; *tree etc* stout, solid, massive.

Corpus *m* Corpus Christi.

corpúsculo *nm* corpuscle.

corral *nm* (*Agr*) yard, farmyard; stockyard, cattlepen, corral (*US*); (*child's*) playpen; (*Cu*) small farm; **— de abasto** (*RPl*) slaughterhouse; **— de carbonera** coal dump, coalyard; **— de madera** timberyard; **— de vacas** (*fam*) slum; **— de vecindad** tenement; **hacer —es** to play truant.

corralillo *nm* playpen.

corralón *nm* large yard; (*RPl*) timberyard; (*Per*) vacant lot.

correa *nf* (**a**) strap; leather strap, thong; belt (*also Tech*); leash, tether; **— para pasar navaja** razor strop; **— de seguridad** safety belt; **— sin fin** endless belt; **— transportadora**, **— de transporte** conveyor belt; **— de ventilador** (*Aut etc*) fan belt; **besar la —** to eat humble pie.
  (**b**) (*quality*) give, stretch, elasticity; leatheriness; **tener —** to be able to put up with a lot, know how to take it, be long-suffering.

correaje *nm* belts, straps; (*Tech*) belting.

corrección *nf* (**a**) (*act*) correction; adjustment.
  (**b**) rebuke, reprimand; punishment.
  (**c**) (*quality*) correctness; courtesy, politeness; good manners; properness.

correccional *nm* reformatory.

correcorre *nm* (*Cu, PR*) headlong rush.

correctamente *adv* (**a**) correctly; accurately; aright. (**b**) regularly. (**c**) correctly, politely; properly, fittingly.

correctivo 1 *adj* corrective. **2** *nm* corrective.

correcto *adj* (**a**) correct; accurate; right; **¡—!** right!, O.K.! (*fam*).
  (**b**) *features etc* regular, well-formed.
  (**c**) *person* correct; courteous, polite, well-mannered; *conduct* courteous, correct; *dress* proper, fitting; **estuvo muy — conmigo** he was very polite to me.

corrector *nm*, **correctora** *nf* (*Typ*) proofreader.

corredera *nf* (**a**) (*Tech*) slide; track, rail, runner; slide valve; (*of fastener*) zip, zipper; **puerta de —** sliding door.
  (**b**) (*Naut*) log.
  (**c**) (*Tech*) upper millstone.
  (**d**) (*Ent*) cockroach.
  (**e**) (*Sport*) racetrack.
  (**f**) (*Arg*) rapids.

corredero *nm* (**a**) (*Mex*) racetrack. (**b**) (*Col*) old riverbed. (**c**) (*Mex*) haunt, favourite spot.

corredizo *adj* sliding; *crane* travelling; *knot* running; slip (*attr*).

corredor 1 *nm* (**a**) (*Sport*) runner; athlete; **— automovilista** racing driver, racing motorist; **— ciclista** racing cyclist; **— de cortas distancias**

sprinter; — **de fondo**, — **de larga distancia** long-distance runner; — **de pista** track athlete.

(b) (*Comm*) agent, broker; (*pej*) procurer, pimp; — **de bienes raíces**, — **de propiedades** (*Chi*) real-estate broker; — **de bodas** matchmaker; — **de bolsa** stockbroker; — **de casas** house agent; — **de comercio** business agent; — **de fincas rurales** land agent; — **de noticias** gossip.

2 *nm* corridor, passage; — **de popa** (*Naut*) stern gallery.

corredía *nf* brokerage.

corregible *adj* which can be corrected.

corregidor *nm* (*Hist*) chief magistrate.

corregidora *nf* (*Hist*) wife of the chief magistrate.

corregir [3c *and* 3l] **1** *vt* **(a)** to correct; to put right, adjust; to revise, look over; *proofs* to correct, read.

(b) to rebuke, reprimand; to punish.

2 corregirse *vr* (*person*) to reform, mend one's ways; — **de su terquedad** to stop being obstinate.

correísta *nmf* (*Arg*) post-office employee.

correlación *nf* correlation.

correlacionar [1a] *vt* to correlate.

correlativo 1 *adj* correlative. **2** *nm* correlative.

correligionario *nm*, **correligionaria** *nf* (*Eccl*) co-religionist, person of the same faith; (*Pol*) fellow supporter, sympathizer, like-minded person.

correlón *adj* **(a)** (*Col, Guat, Ven*) running; fast, good at running. **(b)** (*Guat, Mex, Ven*) cowardly.

correntada *nf* (*Arg*) rapids, strong current.

correntilíneo *adj* (*Mex*) streamlined.

correntón 1 *adj* **(a)** busy, active; gadabout. **(b)** jokey, jolly, fond of a lark. **2** *nm* (*Col, PR*) strong current.

correntoso *adj* (*SAm*) *river* strong-flowing, rapid; in flood, in spate; *water* torrential.

correo *nm* **(a)** (*person*) courier; postman, mailman (*US*); (*Mil*) dispatch rider; (*Pol*) diplomatic courier.

(b) (*Post*) post, mail; — **aéreo** airmail; — **certificado** registered post; — **de primera clase** first-class mail; — **urgente** special delivery; **echar al** —, **poner en el** — to post, mail (*esp US*); **llevar algo al** — to take something to the post; **¿ha llegado el** —? has the post come?; **a vuelta de** — by return (of post); **por** — by post, through the post.

(c) — **s** post office; **Administración General de C—s** General Post Office; **ir a** —**s**, **pasar por** —**s** to go to the post office.

correosidad *nf* toughness, leatheriness; flexibility.

correoso *adj* tough, leathery; flexible.

correr [2a] **1** *vt* **(a)** *ground, distance* to traverse, cover, travel over; to pass over; **ha corrido medio mundo** he's been over half the world.

(b) (*Mil: Hist*) to overrun; to raid, invade; to lay waste.

(c) *object* to push along; *chair* to pull up, draw up; *bolt* to shoot, slide, draw; *key* to turn; *curtain, veil* to draw; *buttons etc* to move; *sail* to unfurl; *knot* to undo, untie.

(d) *horse* to race, run; *bull* to fight; *quarry* to chase, hunt, pursue.

(e) *risk* to run; *adventure* to have; *fate* to suffer, undergo.

(f) *colours* to make run.

(g) (*Comm*) to auction.

(h) *person* (*also* **dejar corrido**) to embarrass, put to shame, cover with confusion.

(i) — **la clase** (*fam*) to cut class, play hooky.

(j) —**la** (*fam*) to live it up (*fam*); to have one's fling; to go on a spree (*fam*).

(k) (*CAm, Mex, Ven*) — **a uno** to chuck someone out.

2 *vi* **(a)** to run; **corrió a decírselo** he ran to tell him, he hastened to tell him; — **a la perdición** to rush headlong to disaster; **¡no corras tanto!** don't run so hard!, not so fast!; — **a todo** — to run as hard as one can; **echar a** — to start to run, break into a run; to run off; **dejar** — **las cosas** to let things run on, let matters ride, let things take their course.

(b) (*of water, electricity etc*) to run, flow; (*of air*) to flow, go, pass; (*of tap*) to run; (*of fountain*) to play; (*of wind*) to pass; **el río corre muy crecido** the river is running very high; **corre mucho viento** it's very windy, there's a strong wind blowing; **dejar** — **la sangre** to let the blood flow.

(c) (*of time*) to pass (quickly), elapse; (*of period*) to run, extend, stretch; **el tiempo corre** time is passing, time presses; **el mes que corre** the present month, the current month; **durante lo que corre del año** during the rest of the year, for the remainder of the year.

(d) (*of money etc*) to pass, be valid, be acceptable; (*of rumour*) to circulate, go round; (*of belief*) to be commonly held.

(e) (*Geog etc*) to run; **las montañas corren del este al oeste** the mountains run from east to west.

(f) (*of salary etc*) to be payable; **su sueldo correrá desde el primer día del mes** his salary will be payable from the first of the month.

(g) — **con la casa** to run the house, manage the house; — **con los gastos** to pay (*or* meet, bear) the expenses; **él corre con eso** he is responsible for that, that is in his charge.

(h) (*Comm*) — **a**, — **por** to sell at.

3 correrse *vr* **(a)** (*object*) to slide, move along; (*ballast, cargo*) to shift; (*person*) to move (up); **se ha corrido unos centímetros el tablero** the board has moved a few centimetres; **córrete un poco hacia este lado** move a bit this way.

(b) (*person: fig*) to go too far, let oneself go; **no te vayas a** — **en la propina** don't overdo it on the tip.

(c) (*colours*) to run; (*ice etc*) to melt; (*ink*) to spread, make a blot.

(d) (*person: fig*) to get embarrassed; to become confused.

(e) — **una juerga** *etc: see* **juerga**.

(f) (*Cu, Guat, Mex, Ven*) to get scared, run away.

correría *nf* (*Mil*) raid, foray; (*fig*) trip, excursion; —**s** (*fig*) trips, travels.

correspondencia *nf* **(a)** (*in general*) correspondence.

(b) correspondence, letters; post, mail; — **entrante** incoming mail; — **particular** private correspondence; **curso por** — correspondence course; **entrar en** — **con uno** to enter into correspondence with someone; **estar en** — **con uno** to be in correspondence with someone.

(c) (*between places*) communications, contact; (*Rail etc*) connection (*con* with).

(d) agreement; harmony; gratitude; (*of affection etc*) return; **mis ofertas no tuvieron** — my offers met with no response; **yo esperaba más** — I had expected a greater response.

corresponder [2a] **1** *vi* **(a)** to correspond (*a* to, *con* with); to tally (*con* with).

(b) to be suitable, be fitting, be right; to belong; — **a** (*of colour, furniture etc*) to match; to fit, fit in with, go with; **ese libro no corresponde aquí** that book doesn't belong here; **la llave corresponde a esta cerradura** the key fits this lock; **todavía no corresponde hacerlo** it is still not the right time to do it; **el resultado no ha correspondido a nuestras esperanzas** the result did not come up to our hopes; **con una gravedad que corresponde a su importancia** with a gravity which befits its importance.

(c) — **a** to fall to the lot of, be the share of; **le dieron lo que le correspondía** they gave him his share; **correspondieron 100 ptas a cada uno** everyone got 100 ptas (as his share), each one's share amounted to 100 ptas.

(d) — **a** (*of duty etc*) to concern; to rest with, devolve upon; **"a quien corresponda"** "to whom it may concern"; **me corresponde hacerlo** it is my job to do it, it is my business to do it; **no me corresponde criticarle** it is not for me to criticize him; **me corresponde jugar a mí** it's my turn to play.

(e) to respond, reply; — **a** *affection* to return, reciprocate; *favour* to repay; — **dignamente a to** make a fitting reply etc; **ella le correspondió con una corbata** she gave him a tie in return; **pero ella le correspondió con desprecio** but she responded scornfully, but all she gave in return was disdain; **nunca podré** — **a tanta generosidad** I can never adequately repay such generosity; **un amor no correspondido** an unrequited love, a love which was never returned.

(f) (*Rail etc*) to connect (*con* with).

(g) (*Archit*) to communicate (*con* with).

2 corresponderse *vr* **(a)** to correspond; to agree, be in harmony (*con* with); to have mutual affection (*etc*), have regard for one another.

(b) (*Post*) to correspond (*con* with).

correspondiente 1 *adj* corresponding (*a* to); respective. **2** *nm* (*of academy etc*) correspondent.

corresponsal *nm* (newspaper) correspondent; — **extraordinario** special correspondent; — **de guerra** war correspondent.

corretaje *nm* brokerage.

corretear [1a] **1** *vt* **(a)** (*SAm*) to pursue relentlessly, harass.

(b) (*CAm*) to scare off, get rid of.

(c) (*Arg*) to sell on someone else's behalf; to act as agent for.

(d) (*Chi*) *task* to hurry along.

2 *vi* (a) to run about, rush around.

(b) to loiter, hang about the streets.

corretero *nm*, **corretera** *nf* busy person, gadabout.

correve(i)dile *nm* (a) gossip. (b) pimp.

corrida *nf* (a) run, dash, sprint; **dar una —** to make a dash; **decir algo de —** to rattle off something from memory; **en una —** in an instant.

(b) **— de toros** bullfight.

(c) (*Mex*) **calle de una —** one-way street.

(d) (*Chi, PR, SD*) revelry, celebration.

(e) (*Chi*) row, line, file; (*Geol*) outcrop.

corrido 1 *adj* (a) **tres noches corridas** three nights running; **hasta muy corrida la noche** far into the night.

(b) *weight etc* extra (large); **un kilo —** a good kilo, a kilo and a bit more.

(c) (*Archit etc*) continuous.

(d) (*fig*) *person* abashed, sheepish; confused; embarrassed; **— de vergüenza** covered with shame.

(e) (*fig*) *person* experienced (in the wicked ways of the world), wise, sharp, knowing; **es una mujer corrida** she's a woman who has been around.

(f) *style* fluent, confident; **decir algo de —** to rattle something off; **lo sabía de —** he knew it all right through, he could say it all from memory.

(g) (*SAm*) *party* excellent, splendid.

2 *nm* (a) (*Andalusia, Col, Mex*) ballad.

(b) (*Per*) fugitive from justice.

corriente 1 *adj* (a) *water* running; *style* flowing, fluent, easy, smooth; *money etc* current, valid, accepted; *account, publication, year etc* current; *interest, news* topical; **el año —** the current year, the present year.

(b) ordinary, normal, common, everyday; standard; **— y moliente** ordinary, run-of-the-mill; **lo — es no pintarlo** the usual thing is not to paint it; **aquí es — ver eso** it's common to see that here, that is a common sight here; **es una chica —** she's an ordinary sort of girl.

(c) in order; **tiene — la documentación** his papers are in order; **todo está — para la partida** everything is fixed up for your departure.

(d) **ir** (*or* **estar**) **— en los pagos** to be up to date in one's payments.

2 *nm* (a) current month; **el 9 del corriente** the 9th of the current month, the 9th inst.

(b) **al —** punctually, on time; up-to-date.

(c) **estar al — de** to be informed about, be aware of, be well up with; **mantenerse al —** to keep up to date (*de* with); **tener a uno al — de** to keep someone informed about, keep someone in touch with; **téngame al —** keep me informed.

3 *nf* (a) (*of water*) current; stream, flow; **C— del Golfo** Gulf Stream; **— de lava** stream of lava; **— sanguínea** bloodstream; **— submarina** undercurrent.

(b) **— de aire** draught; **— de aire caliente** flow of warm air.

(c) (*Elec*) current; **— alterna** alternating current; **— directa** direct current; **el hilo está con —** the wire is live.

(d) (*of events etc*) course; tendency; drift; **dejarse llevar de la —** to drift along, follow the crowd; **las —s modernas del arte** modern trends in art; **una fuerte — innovadora** a strong innovating tendency.

corrillero *nm*, **corrillera** *nf* idler, person with time to gossip.

corrillo *nm* huddle, knot of people, small group; (*fig*) clique, coterie.

corrimiento *nm* (a) slipping, sliding; **— de tierras** landslide.

(b) (*Med*) discharge; (*Chi, PR, SD*) rheumatism; (*Per*) tooth abscess.

(c) (*fig*) embarrassment; shyness, sheepishness.

corrincho *nm* (a) mob. (b) (*Col*) uproar, row. (c) (*Ec*) excitement; haste.

corro *nm* (a) ring, circle; huddle, knot (of people); **la gente hizo —** the people formed a ring.

(b) (*children's game*) ring-a-ring-a-roses; **los niños cantan esto en —** the children sing this in a ring.

(c) circular space; **hacer —** to make room, leave a circular space.

(d) small area, part, piece (of a surface); (*Agr*) plot, small field, patch.

corroboración *nf* corroboration.

corroborar [1a] *vt* to corroborate.

corroborativo *adj* corroborative.

corroer [2a] **1** *vt* to corrode; (*Geol*) to erode; (*fig*) to

corrode, eat away, eat up; **le corroen los celos** he is eaten up with jealousy.

2 corroerse *vr* to corrode, become corroded.

corromper [2a] **1** *vt* (a) *wood etc* to rot; *food* to turn bad; to spoil, ruin, cause damage to.

(b) (*fig*) *customs, language, youth etc* to corrupt, pervert; *pleasures* to spoil; *judge, official* to bribe.

(c) *woman* to seduce, debauch, dishonour.

(d) (*fam*) to vex, annoy.

2 *vi* (*fam*) to smell bad.

3 corromperse *vr* (a) to rot; to go bad, deteriorate; to be spoiled.

(b) (*fig*) to become corrupted, become perverted.

corrompido *adj* (a) rotten, putrid. (b) (*fig*) corrupted, corrupt; depraved, degenerate, perverted.

corroncha *nf* (*CAm, Col, Ec*) crust, scale.

corroncho *adj* (a) (*Ven*) slow, sluggish. (b) (*Col*) *person* difficult, prickly.

corronchoso *adj* (*CAm, Col, Ven*) rough, coarse; scaly.

corrongo *adj* (*CR, Cu*) first-rate, splendid; charming, attractive.

corrosión *nf* corrosion; rust; (*Geol*) erosion.

corrosivo *adj* corrosive.

corrugación *nf* contraction, shrinkage.

corrupción *nf* (a) rot, decay; stink, stench.

(b) (*fig*) corruption; perversion; (*of text*) corruption; (*Law*) corruption; graft, bribery; (*Law*) seduction; **en el gobierno existe mucha —** there is a lot of corruption in the government.

corruptela *nf* (a) (*in general*) corruption. (b) (*una —*) corrupt practice, abuse.

corruptible *adj* (a) *person* corruptible, bribable.

(b) *foods etc* perishable.

corrupto *adj* corrupt.

corruptor 1 *adj* corrupting. **2** *nm*, **corruptora** *nf* corrupter, perverter.

corsario *nm* privateer, corsair.

corsé *nm* corset.

corso 1 *adj* Corsican. **2** *nm*, **corsa** *nf* Corsican.

corta *nf* felling, cutting.

cortaalambres *nm*, *pl* **cortaalambres** wire cutters.

cortabolsas *nm*, *pl* **cortabolsas** pickpocket.

cortacésped *nm* lawnmower.

cortacircuitos *nm*, *pl* **cortacircuitos** circuit breaker.

cortacorriente *nm* switch.

cortada *nf* (a) (*SAm*) cut, slash; trench. (b) (*of bread etc*) slice.

cortadillo *nm* (a) small glass. (b) lump of sugar.

cortado 1 *adj* (a) cut; clipped; **— a pico** steep, sheer, precipitous.

(b) *milk* sour.

(c) *style* abrupt; disjointed.

(d) shamed, shamefaced; confused; embarrassed.

(e) **estar —** (*Chi, RPl*) to be broke (*fam*).

2 *nm* white coffee, coffee with a little milk.

cortador 1 *adj* cutting.

2 *nm* (a) cutter (*also Tech*); **— de cristal** glass cutter.

(b) (*Sew*) cutter-out.

cortadora *nf* cutter, cutting machine; slicer; **— de césped** lawnmower.

cortadura *nf* (a) (*act*) cut, cutting.

(b) cut; slash, slit; cut edge.

(c) (*Geog*) narrow pass, defile.

(d) **—s** cuttings, clippings; (*from newspaper*) cuttings.

cortafrío *nm* cold chisel.

cortahuevos *nm*, *pl* **cortahuevos** egg slicer.

cortalápices *nm*, *pl* **cortalápices** pencil sharpener.

cortante 1 *adj* (a) cutting, sharp. (b) *wind* cutting, biting; *cold* bitter. **2** *nm* cleaver, chopper; (*Arg*) scissors.

cortapapeles *nm*, *pl* **cortapapeles** paper knife; (*Tech*) paper cutter, guillotine.

cortapicos *nm*, *pl* **cortapicos** earwig.

cortapisa *nf* (a) restriction, limitation (attached to a concession), condition (attached to a gift); **sin —s** without strings attached.

(b) snag, obstacle; **se pone —s para sí mismo** he makes obstacles for himself; **hablar sin —s** to talk freely.

(c) charm, wit.

cortaplumas *nm*, *pl* **cortaplumas** penknife.

cortapuros *nm*, *pl* **cortapuros** cigar cutter.

cortar [1a] **1** *vt* (a) (*general sense*) to cut; to hack, chop, slash; *hair* to cut, clip, trim; *branch, limb etc* to cut off; *throat* to cut, slit; *tree* to cut down, fell; *meat* to carve, cut up; *cutting, drawing, dress* to cut out; **— por la mitad** to cut down the middle.

(b) (*Math*) to cut; (*Geog*) to cut, cut across; **esa**

línea corta la provincia en dos that line cuts the province in two.
 (c) *ball (Sport)* to cut, slice, spin.
 (d) *air, water etc* to cut through.
 (e) *skin (of cold)* to chap, crack, split.
 (f) *cards* to cut.
 (g) *enemy, region, retreat, supply, town etc* to cut off; *bridge, road* to cut; *water etc* to cut off, turn off, shut off; *(Elec)* to switch off; *fire etc* to prevent the spread of; **la carretera está cortada** the road is cut; **quedaron cortados por la nieve** they were cut off by snow.
 (h) *letter, speech etc* to cut short, stop, bring to a close; *person* to interrupt; *conversation* to interrupt, cut into, break into.
 (i) *passage, detail etc* to cut out, remove, suppress.
 (j) *language* to pronounce, speak; *verse* to read; **no corta bien el idioma** he does not speak the language well.
 2 *vi* **(a)** to cut; **este cuchillo no corta** this knife doesn't cut; *see* **sano** *etc.*
 (b) *(Cards)* to cut.
 (c) *(of wind)* to be biting; **hace un viento que corta** there's a bitter wind.
 (d) — **con el pasado** to (make a) break with the past.
 3 cortarse *vr* **(a)** — **el pelo** to have one's hair cut.
 (b) *(hands)* to get chapped; *(material)* to split, come apart.
 (c) *(milk)* to curdle, turn, turn sour.
 (d) *(fig)* to become embarrassed, get confused, become tongue-tied; to be daunted.
 (e) *(Arg)* to become separated, get left behind; *(in deal etc)* to get left out.
 (f) *(RPl)* to die.
 (g) *(Mex, Per, PR)* to catch a chill, get feverish.
 (h) *(Chi: horse)* to be out of breath.
cortavidrios *nm, pl* **cortavidrios** glass cutter.
corte[1] *nm* **(a)** *(act)* cut, cutting; *(Sew)* cutting out; *(of trees)* cutting, felling; *(Cine)* cutting; — **de pelo** haircut; — **a lo garçon** Eton crop, shingle.
 (b) *(mark)* cut.
 (c) *(in text)* cut, deletion; **el censor lo dejó sin** —**s** the censor did not cut it, the censor did not delete anything.
 (d) *(Elec etc)* cut; failure; — **de corriente** power cut, power failure.
 (e) *(Tech)* section; — **transversal** cross section.
 (f) *(Min)* stint.
 (g) *(Sew)* piece, length; — **de vestido** dress length.
 (h) *(Sew)* tailoring; cut, style; **un traje de** — **muy moderno** a suit of very modern cut; **academia de** — **(y confección)** dressmaking establishment.
 (i) edge *(also Typ)*; **con** —**s dorados** with gilt edges; **dar** — **a** to sharpen, put an edge on.
 (j) darse —**s** *(RPl)* to put on airs.
corte[2] *nf* **(a)** *(royal)* court.
 (b) capital (city); **La C**— Madrid.
 (c) suite, retinue.
 (d) C—**s** *(Spain: Hist)* Spanish parliament; **C**—**s Constituyentes** constituent assembly, constitution-making body.
 (e) hacer la — **a una** to woo someone, pay court to someone.
 (f) *(SAm)* law court; **C**— **Suprema** Supreme Court.
cortedad *nf* **(a)** shortness, smallness; — **de vista** shortsightedness.
 (b) bashfulness, timidity, shyness; diffidence.
 (c) *(also* — **de alcances)** stupidity.
cortejar [1a] *vt* to court, woo *(also fig)*.
cortejo *nm* **(a)** entourage, suite, retinue.
 (b) procession; solemn gathering; — **fúnebre** funeral procession; — **nupcial** wedding procession, wedding party.
 (c) wooing, courting; courtship.
 (d) *(person)* lover, beau.
cortés *adj* **(a)** courteous, polite; gracious. **(b) amor** — courtly love.
cortesana *nf* courtesan.
cortesanía *nf* politeness; good manners.
cortesano 1 *adj* of the court; courtly; court *(attr)*; **ceremonias cortesanas** court ceremony. **2** *nm* courtier.
cortesía *nf* **(a)** courtesy, politeness; graciousness; **visita de** — formal visit, courtesy call; **entrada de** — free ticket, complimentary ticket; **días de** — *(Comm)* days of grace; **por** — as a courtesy.

 (b) social etiquette; **la** — **pide que . . .** etiquette demands that . . .
 (c) present, gift.
 (d) title.
 (e) bow; curtsy; **hacer una** — **a** to bow to; to curtsy to.
cortésmente *adv* courteously, politely; graciously.
corteza *nf* **(a)** *(of tree)* bark; *(of fruit)* peel, skin, rind; *(Bot)* cortex; *(of bread)* crust; **añadir una** — **de limón** to add a bit of lemon peel.
 (b) *(fig)* outside, outward appearance; hide, exterior.
 (c) *(fig)* roughness, coarseness.
cortijo *nm* farm, farmhouse.
cortina *nf* curtain; screen, flap; — **de fuego** *(Mil)* barrage; — **de hierro** *(esp SAm)* iron curtain; — **de humo** smoke screen; — **de tienda** tent flap; **correr la** — *(fig)* to draw a veil over something; **descorrer la** — *(fig)* to draw back the veil.
cortinilla *nf* lace curtain; thin curtain.
cortisona *nf* cortisone.
corto *adj* **(a)** *(in space)* short, *(in time)* brief, short; *(Comm, Radio)* short; **a la corta o a la larga** sooner or later; **el vestido le ha quedado corto** the dress has got too short for her; **el niño va todavía de** — the child is still wearing short trousers *(etc)*.
 (b) *supply etc* scant, scanty; inadequate; defective; *ration etc* small; — **de oído** hard of hearing; — **de resuello** short of breath, short-winded; — **de vista** shortsighted; **pongamos 50 ptas y me quedo** — let's say 50 ptas and that's an underestimation; **se quedó** — **en la comida** she did not provide enough food, she underestimated the food that would be needed.
 (c) bashful, timid, shy; socially backward; tongue-tied; **quedarse** — to say less than one should say, not say nearly enough.
 (d) *(also* — **de alcances)** of limited intelligence, not very bright.
cortocircuito *nm* short-circuit; **poner(se) en** — **to** short-circuit.
cortometraje *nm* *(Cine)* short.
cortón *nm* *(Ent)* mole cricket.
Coruña: La — Corunna.
coruñés 1 *adj* of Corunna. **2** *nm,* **coruñesa** *nf* native *(or* inhabitant*)* of Corunna; **los** —**es** the people of Corunna.
corva *nf* back of the knee.
corvadura *nf* curve, curvature; bend.
corvejón *nm* *(of horse)* hock; *(of cock)* spur.
corveta 1 *adj* *(CAm)* bow-legged. **2** *nf* curvet, prance.
corvetear [1a] *vi* to curvet, prance.
corvo *adj* curved; bent.
corza *nf* doe.
corzo *nm* roe deer, roebuck.
cosa *nf* **(a)** thing; matter; **hay una** — **que no me gusta** there is something I don't like; **alguna** — something; **¿alguna** — **más?** anything else?; **20 kilos o** — **así** 20 kilos or thereabouts; **ni** — **que le parezca** nor anything else of the kind; **otra** — anything else, something else; **ésa es otra** — that's another matter (altogether); **no me queda otra** — I have no alternative; **poca** — nothing much; **es poca** —, **no es gran** — it's not important; it isn't up to much; **como si tal** — as if nothing (out of the ordinary) had happened; as cool as you please; **así las** —**s . . .** at this point . . .; **la** — **es que . . .** the trouble is that . . .; **no es** — **que no dejes todo** there's no reason for you to give it all up; **no sea** — **que . . .** lest . . ., in case. . .; **lo que son las** —**s** in spite of everything; **tal como están las** —**s** as things stand; **¡no hay tal** —**!** nothing of the sort!; **¡vaya una** —**!** well!; **las** —**s van mejor** things are going better; **pasa cada** — anything can happen; **como el que no quiere la** — tentatively; unobtrusively, surreptitiously; **decir una** — **por otra** *(euph)* to lie; **decir cuatro** —**s a uno** to give someone a piece of one's mind.
 (b) *(with adj etc)* **es** — **de nunca acabar** there's no end to it; **no es** — **de broma** *(or* risa*)* it's no laughing matter; —**(s) de comer** eatables, food; **es** — **distinta** that's another matter; — **dura,** — **fuerte** tough business, hard thing to bear; —**s de escribir** writing things, writing materials; **es** — **fácil** it's easy; **¿has visto** — **igual?** did you ever see the like?; **es** — **perdida** he's a dead loss; — **rara** strange thing; **¡(qué** — **más rara!** how strange!, most odd!; **y,** — **rara, nadie lo vio** and, oddly enough, nobody saw it; **es** — **de ver** it's worth seeing, one must see it; **ésa es** — **vieja** that's stale, that's old history.

(c) affair, business; **ésa es — tuya** that's your affair, that's up to you.

(d) **—s** (fig) odd ideas, wild notions; **¡—s de España!** that's typical of Spain!, what else can you expect in Spain!; **¡—s de muchachos!** boys will be boys!; **¡son —s de Juan!** that's typical of John!, that's John all over!; **¡qué —s dices!** (hum) what dreadful things you say!; **¡tienes unas —s!** the things you say!

(e) **— de 8 días** about a week; **en — de 10 minutos** in about 10 minutes; **es — de unas 4 horas** it takes about 4 hours.

(f) **— que . . .** (SAm: as conj) so that . . ., in order that . . .; in such a way that . . .

cosaco 1 adj Cossack. **2** nm, **cosaca** nf **(a)** Cossack. **(b)** (Arg) mounted policeman.

coscacho nm (Chi, Ec) rap on the head.

coscarana nf cracknel.

coscoja nf kermes oak.

coscolino adj **(a)** (Mex) peevish, touchy; child naughty. **(b)** of loose morals.

coscorrón nm **(a)** bump on the head. **(b)** (fig) setback, disappointment, knock.

coscurro nm hard crust.

cosecha nf crop, harvest (also fig); (act) harvesting, gathering; (season) harvest, harvest time; **la — de 1972** (wine) the 1972 vintage; **de — propia** vegetables etc home-grown, home-produced; **cosas de su propia —** (fig) things of one's own invention, things out of one's own head; **no añadas nada de tu —** don't add anything that you've made up.

cosechadora nf combine-harvester.

cosechar [1a] vt **(a)** to harvest, gather (in); to pick; to grow, cultivate; **aquí no cosechan sino patatas** the only thing they grow here is potatoes.

(b) (fig) to reap, reap the reward of; admiration etc to win.

cosechero nm, **cosechera** nf harvester, reaper; picker.

cosechón nm bumper crop.

coseno nm cosine.

coser [2a] **1** vt **(a)** to sew (up); to stitch (up); button etc to sew on, stitch on; (Med) to stitch (up); (Naut) to lash.

(b) (fig) to unite, join closely (con to).

(c) **es cosa de — y cantar** it's straightforward; it's plain sailing; it's a cinch (sl).

(d) **— a uno a balazos** to riddle someone with bullets; **— a uno a puñaladas** to stab someone repeatedly, carve someone up; **le encontraron cosido a puñaladas** they found him covered with stab wounds.

2 vi to sew.

3 coserse vr: **— con uno** to become closely attached to someone.

cosiaca nf (SAm) small thing, trifle.

cosido nm sewing, needlework.

cosignatario nm, **cosignataria** nf cosignatory.

cosijoso adj **(a)** (CAm, Mex) bothersome, annoying. **(b)** (CAm, Mex) peevish, irritable.

cosmético 1 adj cosmetic. **2** nm cosmetic.

cósmico adj cosmic.

cosmogonía nf cosmogony.

cosmografía nf cosmography.

cosmógrafo nm cosmographer.

cosmología nf cosmology.

cosmonauta nmf cosmonaut, spaceman, spacewoman.

cosmopolita 1 adj cosmopolitan. **2** nmf cosmopolitan.

cosmos nm cosmos.

coso[1] nm arena, enclosure, (esp) bullring.

coso[2] nm (Ent) deathwatch beetle, woodworm.

coso[3] nm (hum) = **cosa**.

cospel nm blank (for a coin).

cosquillar [1a] vt to tickle.

cosquillas nfpl tickling (sensation); ticklishness; **buscar las — a uno** to tease someone, try to stir someone up; **me hace —** it tickles; **hacer — a uno** to tickle someone; (fig) to tickle someone's curiosity; **siento — en el pie** my foot tickles; **tener — to be** ticklish; **no sufre —, tiene malas —** he's touchy, he can't take a joke.

cosquillear [1a] vt to tickle (also fig).

cosquilleo nm tickling (sensation).

cosquilloso adj **(a)** ticklish. **(b)** (fig) touchy, easily offended.

costa[1] nf (Fin) cost, price; **—s** (Law) costs; **a —** (Comm) at cost; **a — de** at the expense of; **a toda —** at any price; **a — de lo que sea** cost what it may; **condenar a uno en —s** (Law) to order someone to pay the costs.

costa[2] nf **(a)** (Geog) coast; coastline; shore, seashore; (RPl) riverbank, lake-side.

(b) **C— Azul** Côte d'Azur; **C— de Marfil** Ivory Coast; **C— de Oro** Gold Coast.

(c) (Spain: tourist areas) **C— Blanca** coast near Almería; **C— Brava** coast north of Barcelona; **C— Clara** coast near Valencia; **C— Dorada** coast near Tarragona; **C— del Sol** coast west of Málaga.

costado nm **(a)** (Anat, Naut, of object) side; (Mil) flank; **de — pass** sideways, lie on one's side; **neumáticos de — blanco** white-walled tyres.

(b) (Mex: Rail) platform.

(c) **—s** ancestors; genealogy; **español por los 4 —s** Spanish on both sides of the family, (fig) thoroughly Spanish, wholly Spanish, Spanish through and through; **es un gandul por los 4 —s** he's an absolute idler.

costal nm sack, bag; **— de huesos** (fig) bag of bones.

costalada nf violent blow.

costalar [1a] vi (RPl) to roll over; to fall on one's side (or back).

costalazo nm violent blow.

costanera nf **(a)** side, flank. **(b)** slope. **(c)** (Arg) jetty; paved area beside the sea (or river); (Cu) firm ground (surrounding a swamp). **(d)** **—s** (Tech) rafters.

costanero adj **(a)** sloping; steep. **(b)** (Naut) coastal.

costar [1m] vti (Comm, Fin) **(a)** to cost; **¿cuánto cuesta?** how much does it cost?, (in shop) how much is it?

(b) (fig) to cost (dear, dearly); **cueste lo que cueste** cost what it may; **le ha costado caro** it has cost him dear; **eso me ha costado reñir con él** doing that has meant my falling out with him, I did that only at the cost of quarrelling with him; **es un trabajo que cuesta unos minutos** it's a job which takes a few minutes; see **trabajo** etc.

(c) **— + infin** to find it hard to + infin, have a job to + infin; **me cuesta hablar alemán** I find it difficult to speak German, I have trouble speaking German; **me cuesta creerlo** I find that hard to believe.

Costa f Rica Costa Rica.

costarricense = costarriqueño.

costarriqueñismo nm word (or phrase etc) peculiar to Costa Rica.

costarriqueño 1 adj Costa Rican. **2** nm, **costarriqueña** nf Costa Rican.

coste nm cost, price; expense; see also **costo**.

costear[1] [1a] vt (Fin) to pay for, defray the cost of; to endow; (Radio, TV etc) to back, sponsor; **costea los estudios a su sobrino** he is paying for his nephew's education; **no lo podemos —** we can't afford it.

costear[2] [1a] **1** vt (Naut) to sail along the coast of; (fig) to skirt, go along the edge of; to pass close to. **2 costearse** vr (Chi, RPl) to have to go from place to place.

costear[3] [1a] vt (Arg) cattle to pasture.

costeño adj coastal.

costera nf **(a)** (of packet etc) side. **(b)** (Geog) slope. **(c)** (Naut) coast; fishing season.

costero adj coastal; vessel, trade coasting.

costilla nf **(a)** (Naut, Anat) rib; **— flotante** floating rib.

(b) (as meat) chop; **— de cerdo** pork chop, pork cutlet.

(c) **—s** (fam) back, shoulders; **todo carga sobre mis —s** I get all the burdens; **medir las —s a uno** to give someone a hiding.

(d) (hum) wife, better half.

costilludo adj broad-shouldered, strapping.

costo nm cost; **— efectivo** actual cost; **— de expedición** shipping charges; **—, seguro y flete** (csf) cost, insurance and freight (cif); **— de (la) vida** cost of living; **el — de salarios de la industria** the industry's wages bill.

(b) (SAm) trouble, effort.

costosamente adv expensively.

costoso adj costly, expensive.

costra nf crust; (Med) scab.

costroso adj crusty, incrusted; (Med) scabby.

costumbre nf custom, habit; **—s** customs, ways, (fig) morals; **las —s de esta provincia** the customs of this province; **persona de buenas —s** respectable person, decent person; **de —** (adj) usual, (adv) usually; **como de —** as usual; **más que de —** more than usual; **he perdido la —** I have got out of the habit, (Sport etc) I'm out of practice; **tener la — de + infin, tener por — + infin** to be in the habit of + ger; **novela de —s** novel of (local) customs and manners.

costumbrismo nm literary genre of (local) customs and manners.

costumbrista 1 adj novel etc of (local) customs and manners. **2** nmf writer about (local) customs and manners, author with a strong regional flavour.

costura nf (a) (Sew, Naut) seam; **medias de — francesa** fully-fashioned stockings; **sentar las —s** to press the seams; **sentar las — a uno** (hum) to give someone a hiding.
(b) sewing; needlework; dressmaking; **alta —** haute couture, high fashion, fashion designing; **la — italiana** Italian fashions, the Italian fashion trade.

costur(e)ar [1a] vti (SAm) = **coser**.

costurera nf dressmaker, seamstress.

costurero nm (a) sewing box, sewing case; sewing room. (b) couturier, fashion designer.

cota[1] nf (Hist): **— de malla** coat of mail.

cota[2] nf (a) = **cuota**. (b) (Geog) height above sea level.

cotarro nm (Hist) night shelter for tramps etc; **alborotar el —** to stir up trouble; **andar** (or **ir**) **de — en —** to wander about, gad about; **dirigir el —** to be the boss.

coteja nf (Bol, Ec, Pan) equal, match.

cotejar [1a] vt (a) to compare, collate; to check. (b) (Ant, Ec) to arrange.

cotejo 1 adj (SAm) similar, same. **2** nm comparison, collation; check.

cotense nm (Bol, Chi, Mex), **cotensia** nf (Arg, Bol), **cotensio** nm (Chi) coarse hemp fabric.

coterna nf (Col) broad hat.

cotí nm ticking.

cotidiano adj daily.

cotiledón nm cotyledon.

cotilla nmf busybody, gossip.

cotillear [1a] vi to gossip.

cotilleo nm gossip(ing).

cotillero nm, **cotillera** nf = **cotilla**.

cotín nm (Sport) backhand shot.

cotiza nf (Col, Ven) sandal.

cotización nf (a) (Fin) quotation, price; **— de apertura** opening price; **— de cierre, — de clausura** closing price. (b) quota. (c) (of membership) dues.

cotizado adj in demand, popular, sought-after; (fig) valued, esteemed.

cotizar [1f] **1** vt (a) (Fin) share to quote, price (en at).
(b) quota to fix; subscription, contribution to pay.
(c) (Arg, PR) to value (en at).
(d) (Chi) to share out proportionally.
(e) (Per, PR) to sell.
2 cotizarse vr (a) (Comm, Fin) **— a** to sell at, sell for, fetch, stand at; (Stock Exchange) to stand at, be quoted at; **estos tomates son los que más se cotizan** these tomatoes are the ones which fetch the highest price.
(b) (fig) to be valued, be esteemed; **tales conocimientos se cotizan mucho** such knowledge is highly valued.

coto[1] nm (a) (Agr) enclosure, enclosed pasture; (Hunting) preserve; reserve; **— cerrado** (fig) closed shop; **— redondo** large estate.
(b) boundary stone; (fig) limit; **poner — a** to put a stop to.
(c) (Comm) price-fixing agreement.

coto[2] nm (SAm) goitre.

cotón nm (a) cotton fabric. (b) (SAm) shirt; (Mex) vest, undervest (US); (Mex) blouse.

cotona nf (SAm) strongly-made shirt; (Chi) camisole; vest, undervest (US); (CR, Ec, PR) blouse; (Mex) leather jacket; (PR) child's nightdress.

cotorra nf (a) (Orn) parrot, cockatoo; magpie. (b) (fam) garrulous woman, chatterbox. (c) (Mex) chamberpot. (d) (Mex) taxi.

cotorrear [1a] vi to chatter, gabble.

cotorreo nm chatter, gabble.

cotorrera nf = **cotorra** (a) and (b).

cototo nm (Chi) bump, bruise (on the head).

cotudo adj (a) hairy, cottony. (b) (Med) suffering from goitre. (c) (Ec) stupid.

coturno nm buskin; **de alto —** (fig) lofty, elevated.

covacha nf (a) small cave. (b) (Per, PR, RPl) lumber room; (Ant, Guat) hut; (Ec) vegetable stall; (PR) kennel.

covadera nf (Bol, Chi, Per) guano deposit.

covín nm, **covín** nm (Chi) popcorn.

coxcojilla nf hopscotch.

coy nm (Naut) hammock; (Col, PR) cradle, cot.

coyote nm (a) (Zool) coyote, prairie wolf.
(b) (Mex) white person.
(c) (Mex) astute person; (Comm, Fin) speculator, dealer in shares (etc).
(d) (Mex) youngest child.

coyotear [1a] vi (CAm, Mex) (a) to be smart, be clever. (b) (Comm, Fin) to deal (or speculate) in shares.

coyunda nf (a) (CAm) strap; tether, halter; lash. (b) (hum) yoke (of marriage).

coyuntura nf (a) (Anat) joint.
(b) (fig) moment, juncture, occasion; opportunity; **— crítica** critical moment; turning point; **esperar una — favorable** to await a favourable moment.

coz nf (a) kick; **dar coces, dar de coces a** to kick; **dar coces contra el aguijón** to kick against the pricks; **tirar coces** to lash out (also fig).
(b) (of gun: movement) kick; (of water) ebb, backward flow.
(c) (of gun: part) butt.
(d) (fig) insult, rude remark; **tratar a uno a coces** to be rude to someone, treat someone like dirt.

crac[1] nm (a) (Comm, Fin) failure, crash; bankruptcy; **— financiero** financial crash. (b) (fig) crack-up.

crac[2] interj snap!, crack!; **hizo ¡—! y se abrió** it went crack! and it opened out.

crampón nm crampon.

cranearse [1a] vr (Chi) to swot (fam), cram.

cráneo nm skull, cranium.

crápula nf drunkenness; (fig) dissipation.

crapuloso adj drunken; (fig) dissipated.

craque nm = **crac**[1].

craquear [1a] vt (Tech) to crack.

craqueo nm (Tech) cracking.

crasitud nf fatness.

craso adj (a) person fat. (b) liquid greasy, thick. (c) (fig) error gross, crass, stupid. (d) (Arg, Ec) person coarse.

cráter nm crater.

crayón nm crayon, chalk.

creación nf (all senses) creation.

creador 1 adj creative. **2** nm, **creadora** nf creator; inventor, originator; **el C—** the Creator.

crear [1a] vt to create; to make; to invent, originate; to found, establish, institute.

crece nm or f (Arg, Chi) = **crecida**.

crecer [2d] **1** vi (general sense) to grow; to increase; (of price, river) to rise; (of days) to get longer; (of moon) to wax; **dejar — la barba** to grow a beard, let one's beard grow.
2 crecerse vr (a) (Sew) "se crece un punto" "increase by one stitch".
(b) to grow bolder, acquire greater confidence; (pej) to get conceited, have an exaggerated sense of one's importance.

creces nfpl (a) increase.
(b) (Sew) room to let out.
(c) **con —** amply, fully; (fig) with a vengeance; **pagar a uno con —** to more than repay one's debt; **devolver algo con —** to return something with interest; **había cumplido su obligación con —** he had amply carried out his obligation.

crecida nf (of river) rise; spate, flood.

crecido adj (a) person, plant etc full-grown; grown up; **ya eres — para eso** you're too big for that now.
(b) number, proportion large.
(c) **estar —** (river) to be in flood.
(d) (fig) vain, conceited.

creciente 1 adj growing; increasing; rising; **luna —** crescent moon, waxing moon.
2 nm crescent.
3 nf (a) (of river) flood; **— del mar** high tide, flood tide.
(b) crescent moon.

crecimiento nm growth; increase; rise; (Fin) rise in value.

credenciales nfpl credentials.

credibilidad nf credibility.

crediticio adj (Fin) credit (attr).

crédito nm (a) credit; belief; credence; **dar — a** to believe (in), credit; **apenas daba — a sus oídos** he could scarcely believe his ears.
(b) (of person) credit; authority, standing, reputation; **persona (digna) de —** reliable person; **tiene — de muy escrupuloso** he has the reputation of being thoroughly honest.
(c) (Comm, Fin) credit; **a —** on credit; **abrir — a** to give credit to.

credo nm creed; credo; **en un —, en menos que se canta un —** in a jiffy.

credulidad nf credulity.

crédulo adj credulous.

creederas nfpl: **tiene buenas —** he's terribly gullible, he'll swallow anything.

creencia nf belief (en in); **en la — de que . . .** in the belief that . . .

creer [2e] **1** vti (a) to think, believe; **— que . . .** to think that . . ., believe that . . .; **creo que sí, lo creo** I think so; **creo que no, no creo** I don't think so; **¡ya lo creo!** I should think so!, rather!; of course!;

¡ya lo creo que está roto! I should jolly well say it's broken!; **créame** believe me, take my word for it; **no se vaya Vd a — que** . . . don't go thinking that . . .; **es difícil, no creas** it's hard enough, I'm telling you.

(b) **— en** to believe in.

(c) to think, deem, consider; **no le creo tan culpable** I don't think him so much to blame; **creo de él que es sincero** I consider him to be sincere; **lo creo de mi deber** I consider it (to be) my duty.

2 **creerse** vr to believe oneself (to be), consider oneself (to be); **se cree muy astuto** he thinks he's pretty clever; **¿quién se cree que es?** who do you think you are?

creíble adj believable, credible; **¿es — que** . . .? is it conceivable that . . .?

creído adj (a) (SAm) credulous, trusting. (b) (Col, Chi, Ec, RPl) vain, conceited.

crema nf (a) (of milk) cream; (Cook) cream; custard; **— batida** whipped cream; **un coche color —** a cream-coloured car.

(b) (cosmetic) cold cream, face cream; **— de afeitar** shaving cream; **— base** foundation cream; **— de belleza** beauty cream; **— dental** toothpaste; **— hidratante** moisturizing cream; **— de limpiar** cleansing cream.

(c) **— para el calzado** shoe polish.

(d) (fig) cream, best; **la — de la sociedad** the cream of society.

cremación nf cremation.

cremallera nf (a) (also **cierre de —**) zip fastener, zipper. (b) (Tech) rack; **— y piñón** rack and pinion.

crematorio 1 adj: **horno —** =2 nm crematorium.

crémor nm (also **— tártaro**) cream of tartar.

cremoso adj creamy.

crencha nf (of hair) parting.

creosota nf creosote.

crepitación nf crackling; sizzling.

crepitar [1a] vi (log etc) to crackle; (bacon) to sizzle.

crepuscular adj twilight, crepuscular; **luz —** twilight.

crepúsculo nm twilight, dusk.

cresa nf maggot.

Creso m Croesus.

crespo 1 adj (a) hair curly; kinky; leaf etc curled.

(b) style involved, tortuous.

(c) person cross, angry.

2 nm hair, head of hair; (esp Arg, Chi, Cu) curl, ringlet.

crespón nm crape, crêpe.

cresta nf (a) (Orn) crest, comb; tuft. (b) wig, toupée.

(c) (of wave) crest. (d) (Geog) crest, ridge; summit.

crestomatía nf anthology, collection of texts.

crestón nm (Her) crest.

Creta f Crete.

creta nf chalk.

cretáceo adj cretaceous.

cretense 1 adj Cretan. 2 nmf Cretan.

cretinez nf utter stupidity.

cretino 1 adj cretinous (also fig). 2 nm, **cretina** nf cretin (also fig).

cretona nf cretonne.

cretoso adj chalky.

creyente nmf believer.

creyón nm crayon, chalk.

cría nf (a) rearing, keeping, breeding; **— caballar** horse breeding; **— de ganado** cattle breeding, stock raising; **hembra de —** breeding female.

(b) baby animal, young creature; (collectively) young; litter, brood.

criada nf servant, maid; **— por horas** charwoman, cleaner; **— para todo** maid of all work, servant with general duties.

criadero nm (a) (Bot) nursery.

(b) (Zool) breeding ground, breeding place; **— de ostras** oyster bed; **— de peces** fish hatchery.

(c) (Geol) vein, seam.

criadilla nf (a) potato, tuber; **—s de tierra** truffles. (b) small loaf, roll.

criado 1 adj bred, reared, brought up; **bien —** well-bred; **mal —** see **malcriado**. 2 nm servant.

criador nm breeder.

criandera nf (SAm) nursemaid, wet-nurse.

crianza nf (a) (Agr etc) rearing, keeping, breeding.

(b) (Med) lactation. (c) (fig) breeding; **mala —** bad breeding, lack of breeding; **sin —** ill-bred.

criar [1c] 1 vt (a) young to suckle, feed; **— a los pechos** to breast-feed, nurse.

(b) plants to grow; to tend, cultivate.

(c) animals to rear, raise; to keep, breed; to fatten.

(d) (of land etc) to bear, grow, produce; **esta tierra no cría hierba** this land does not grow grass, this soil is not suitable for grass; **los perros crían pulgas** dogs have (or get) fleas; **— carnes** to put on weight; **está criando pelo** he's getting some hair, his hair is growing.

(e) children to bring up, raise; to educate.

(f) (fig) hopes etc to foster, nourish, nurture.

2 vi (of animal) to have young, produce.

3 **criarse** vr to grow (up); **se criaron juntos** they were brought up together, they grew up together; **— en buena cuna** (or **en buenos pañales**) to be born with a silver spoon in one's mouth.

criatura nf (a) creature (also fig); being.

(b) infant, baby, small child; **¡—!** look out!; I say, do be careful!; **todavía es una —** she's still very young, she's only a child still; **¡no seas —!** be your age!; **hacer una — a una** to get a girl in the family way.

criba nf sieve, screen.

cribar [1a] vt to sieve, sift, screen.

cric nm (Mech) jack.

Crimea f Crimea.

crimen nm crime; **— de guerra** war crime.

criminal 1 adj criminal. 2 nmf criminal; **— de carretera** dangerous driver, roadhog; **— de guerra** war criminal.

criminalidad nf (a) criminality; guilt. (b) crime rate.

criminalista nm (a) criminologist. (b) criminal lawyer.

criminología nf criminology.

crin nm horsehair; (also **—es**) mane.

crinolina nf crinoline.

crinudo adj (SAm) horse long-maned.

crío nm (fam) kid (fam), child; (pej) brat.

criollaje nm (SAm) Creoles (collectively); peasantry.

criollo 1 adj (a) Creole.

(b) (SAm) native (to America), indigenous; national.

2 nm, **criolla** nf (a) Creole.

(b) (SAm) native (of America), native American.

(c) (Col) coward.

cripta nf crypt.

cripto . . . crypto . . .

criptocomunista nmf crypto-communist.

criptografía nf cryptography.

criptográfico adj cryptographic(al).

criptógrafo nm cryptographer.

criptograma nm cryptogram.

crisálida nf chrysalis.

crisalidar [1a] vi to pupate.

crisantemo nm chrysanthemum.

crisis nf, pl **crisis** crisis; **— económica** economic crisis; **— nerviosa** nervous breakdown; **— de la vivienda** housing shortage; **llegar a la —** to reach crisis point, come to a head.

crisma[1] nf (a) (Eccl) chrism, holy oil. (b) (sl) **romper la — a uno** to knock someone's block off (sl).

crisma[2] nf (Mex) Christmas present; see also **christma(s)**.

crisol nm crucible; (fig) melting pot.

crispar [1a] 1 vt (a) muscle to cause to twitch (or contract); nerves to set on edge; **con el rostro crispado por la ira** with his face contorted with anger; **eso me crispa los nervios** that gets on my nerves; that jars (or grates) on me.

(b) (fam) **— a uno** to annoy someone intensely, get on someone's nerves.

2 **crisparse** vr to twitch, contract; (nerves) to get all on edge.

crispetas nfpl (Col) popcorn.

cristal nm (a) (Chem) crystal (also fig); **— de roca** rock crystal.

(b) glass; **un —** a pane of glass, a sheet of glass; **—es** (freq) window(s); **— ahumado** smoked glass; **— de aumento** lens, magnifying glass; **— cilindrado** plate glass; **—es emplomados** leaded lights; **— hilado** fibreglass; **— inastillable** splinterproof glass; **— de patente** (Naut) bull's-eye; **— de seguridad** safety glass; **— tallado** cut glass; **de — glass** (attr); **puerta de —es** glass door.

(c) glass, mirror.

cristalería nf (a) (art) glasswork; glass making. (b) (factory) glassworks; glassware shop. (c) glasses (collectively); glassware.

cristalero nm (RPl) cupboard for glassware.

cristalino adj (Phys) crystalline; (fig) clear, limpid, translucent.

cristalizar [1f] 1 vti to crystallize. 2 **cristalizarse** vr to crystallize.

cristalografía nf crystallography.

cristianamente adv in a Christian way; **morir —** to die as a Christian, to die like a good Christian.
cristianar [1a] vt to christen, baptize; see **trapo**.
cristiandad nf Christendom.
cristianismo nm Christianity.
cristianizar [1f] vt to Christianize.
cristiano 1 adj (a) (Rel) Christian.
  (b) vino — pure wine, unwatered wine.
  (c) (SAm) simple-minded.
  2 nm, **cristiana** nf Christian.
  3 nm (a) person, (living) soul; **eso lo sabe cualquier —** any idiot knows that.
  (b) ordinary language, (esp) Spanish; **hablar en — to** speak straightforwardly, make sense with what one says; (equivalent to) to speak the King's English.
Cristo m Christ; **el año 41 antes de —** 41 BC; **el año 80 después de —** 80 AD; **donde — dio las tres voces** at the back of beyond; in the middle of nowhere; **¡ni — que lo fundó!** don't you believe it!; **poner a uno como un —** to give someone a dressing-down; to heap abuse on someone.
cristo nm crucifix.
Cristóbal m Christopher.
criterio nm (a) criterion; yardstick, standard of judgement.
  (b) viewpoint, attitude, approach; **depende del — de cada uno** it depends on the individual viewpoint; **lo mira con otro —** he looks at it from a different point of view; **hace falta tener un — más maduro** one needs a more mature approach.
  (c) discernment, discrimination; **lo dejo a su —** I leave it to your discretion; **tiene buen —** his taste is admirable.
  (d) view, opinion; **en mi —** in my opinion; **cambiar de —** to change one's mind; **no comparto ese —** I do not share that view; **formar un — sobre** to form an opinion of.
crítica nf (a) (in general) criticism; **— literaria** literary criticism; **— teatral** dramatic criticism.
  (b) (una —) criticism; review, notice, critique; (pej) criticism; (pej) slander, gossip.
criticador 1 adj critical. **2** nm, **criticadora** nf critic.
criticar [1g] vt to criticize.
criticastro nm hack critic, ignorant critic.
crítico 1 adj critical. **2** nm critic.
criticón 1 adj hypercritical, overcritical, faultfinding. **2** nm, **criticona** nf carping critic, faultfinder.
critiquizar [1f] vt to be overcritical of, indulge in petty criticism of.
Croacia f Croatia.
croar [1a] vi to croak.
croasán nm (gall) croissant, breakfast roll.
croata 1 adj Croat(ian). **2** nmf Croatian.
crocitar [1a] vi to crow, caw.
croché nm (Sew) crochet(work); **hacer —** to crochet.
crochet [kro'tʃe] nm (gall) (a) (Sew) = **croché**.
  (b) (Boxing) hook.
crol nm (Swimming: angl) crawl.
cromado 1 adj chromium-plated; chrome. **2** nm chromium plating, chrome.
cromático adj chromatic.
cromo nm (a) (Chem) chromium; chrome. (b) (also — recortado) transfer.
cromosoma nm chromosome.
crónica nf (a) (Hist) chronicle; **C—s** (Bible) Chronicles; (fig) chronicle, account.
  (b) (newspaper) news report; feature, article; **— deportiva** sports page; **— literaria** literary page; **— de sociedad** society column, gossip column; **"C— de sucesos"** "News in Brief".
crónico adj (Med and fig) chronic; vice ingrained.
cronista nmf (a) (Hist) chronicler. (b) (newspaper) reporter, feature writer, columnist; **— de radio** radio commentator.
cronología nf chronology.
cronológicamente adv chronologically, in chronological order.
cronológico adj chronological.
cronometrador nm timekeeper.
cronometraje nm timing.
cronometrar [1a] vt to time.
cronómetro nm (Tech etc) chronometer; (Sport) stopwatch.
croquet [kro'ke] nm (angl) croquet.
croqueta nf croquette, (approx) rissole.
croquis nm, pl **croquis** sketch.
cross [kros] nm, pl **cross** (angl) cross-country race.
crótalo nm (a) (Zool) rattlesnake. (b) (Mus) **—s** castanets.
crotchet nm see **crochet**.
cruce nm (a) (act) crossing.
  (b) (Math etc) (point of) intersection.

(c) (Aut etc) crossing, intersection; **— de carreteras** crossroads; **— giratorio** roundabout, traffic circle (US); **— a nivel** level crossing, grade crossing (US); **— de peatones** pedestrian crossing.
  (d) (Tel) crossing of lines; **hay un — en las líneas** the wires are crossed.
  (e) (Bio) cross, crossing.
  (f) (Ling) cross, mutual interference.
crucero nm (a) (Mil) cruiser; **— de batalla** battle cruiser; **— pesado** heavy cruiser.
  (b) (Naut) cruise; **— de recreo** pleasure cruise.
  (c) (Eccl) transept.
  (d) (Carp) crosspiece.
  (e) (Aut etc) crossroads; crossing; (Rail) crossing.
  (f) (Eccl: person) crossbearer.
  (g) (Astron) **C— (Austral)** Southern Cross.
cruceta nf (a) (Carp etc) crosspiece; (Naut) crosstree.
  (b) (Mech) universal joint, crosshead. (c) (Chi) turnstile.
crucial adj crucial.
crucificar [1g] vt to crucify; (fig) to torment, torture; to mortify.
crucifijo nm crucifix.
crucifixión nf crucifixion.
cruciforme adj cruciform.
crucigrama nm crossword.
crudelísimo adj (lit: superl of **cruel**) most cruel, terribly cruel.
crudeza nf (a) rawness; unripeness. (b) indigestibility. (c) hardness. (d) bleakness, harshness. (e) crudity, crudeness, coarseness. (f) **—s** indigestible foods.
crudo 1 adj (a) meat raw; (Cook) half-cooked, underdone, raw; vegetables green, uncooked; fruit etc unripe.
  (b) foodstuffs hard to digest.
  (c) water hard.
  (d) (Tech) untreated; silk raw; linen unbleached.
  (e) weather raw, bleak, harsh.
  (f) (lit) cruel, merciless.
  (g) expression, subject etc crude, coarse; over-realistic.
  (h) (Arg, Mex) yellowish, creamy.
  2 nm (SAm) coarse cloth, sackcloth.
cruel adj cruel (con, para to).
crueldad nf cruelty.
cruelmente adv cruelly.
cruento adj (lit) bloody, gory.
crujía nf corridor, gallery; bay; (Med) ward; **pasar —** to have a tough time of it.
crujido nm rustle; creak; crack; crunch; grinding, gnashing; chattering; crackle.
crujiente adj rustling; creaking; crunchy; grinding; crackling.
crujir [3a] vi (of leaves, silk, paper) to rustle; (of wood, furniture, branch) to creak; (of joint, bone) to crack; (of gravel etc) to crunch; (of teeth) to grind, gnash; to chatter; (of burning object) to crackle; **hacer — los nudillos** to crack one's knuckles.
crustáceo nm crustacean.
cruz nf (a) (general sense) cross; **— gamada** swastika; **— de hierro** iron cross; **— de Malta** Maltese Cross; **— de mayo** (SAm), **C— del Sur** Southern Cross; **C— Roja** Red Cross; **¡— y raya!** that's quite enough!, no more!; **en —** cross-shaped; crosswise; **con los brazos en —** with arms crossed; **por éstas que son cruces** by all that is holy; **firmar con una —** to make one's mark; **hacerse cruces** to cross oneself; (fig) to show one's surprise; **hacerse cruces de que . . .** to be astonished that . . .; **quedar en —** to be in an agonizing situation.
  (b) (of sword) hilt; (of anchor) crown; (side of coin) tails; (Typ) dagger; (Zool) withers.
  (c) (fig) cross, burden; **cada uno lleva su —** each of us has his cross to bear.
cruza nf (Chi, RPl) (a) (Agr) second ploughing. (b) (Bio) cross.
cruzada nf crusade; **La C—** (in official Spanish usage) the Civil War of 1936-39.
cruzadilla nf (CAm) level crossing, grade crossing (US).
cruzado 1 adj (a) arms, cheque etc crossed; (placed) crosswise. (b) (Sew) double-breasted. (c) (Zool) crossbred, hybrid. **2** nm (Hist) crusader.
cruzamiento nm (a) (Bio) crossing. (b) (Rail) crossover.
cruzar [1f] **1** vt (a) (in most senses) to cross; to cut across, intersect; **— un palo sobre otro** to place a stick across another; **— el lago a nado** to swim across the lake.
  (b) (Naut) to cruise.
  (c) (Bio) to cross.
  (d) swords to cross; words to have, exchange.
  (e) (gambling) money to put, stake.

(f) (*Agr, esp SAm*) to plough a second time.

(g) (*Chi, Ec, Per*) to fight, attack.

2 cruzarse *vr* **(a)** (*roads, lines etc*) to cross, cross each other; to intersect.

(b) — **de brazos** *see* **brazo**.

(c) (*persons*) to pass each other; — **con uno en la calle** to pass someone in the street.

(d) (*Chi, Ec, Per*) — **con uno** to fight someone, attack someone.

cuacar [1g] *vt* (*Col, Chi, PR*) = **cuajar**; **no me cuaca** I don't want to; I don't like it; it doesn't suit me.

cuácara *nf* (*Col, Ven*) frock coat; (*Chi*) workman's blouse.

cuaco *nm* (*Arg, Mex, SD*) horse.

cuacho (*CAm*) = **cuate**.

cuaderna *nf* (*Naut*) timber; rib, frame.

cuadernillo *nm* booklet; — **de sellos** book of stamps.

cuaderno *nm* notebook; (*School etc*) exercise book; folder; (*fam*) pack of cards; — **de bitácora** (*Naut*), — **de trabajo** logbook; **C— de Cortes** (*Hist*) official parliamentary record.

cuadra *nf* (a) (*Agr*) stable; — **de carreras** racing stable.

(b) (*of hospital etc*) ward.

(c) (*Mil*) hut.

(d) hall, large room.

(e) (*SAm*) block (of houses), city block.

(f) (*Per*) reception room.

(g) (*Ec, Ven*) small rural property (*near a town*).

(h) (*measure*): *Arg, Bol, Chi* = 125.50 *metres*, (*CAm, Col, Par, Urug, Ven*) = 83.5 *metres*.

cuadrada *nf* (*Mus*) breve.

cuadrado 1 *adj* **(a)** (*Math etc*) square (*also fig*).

(b) *design* with squares, chequered.

(c) *person* broad, square-shouldered.

(d) (*Cu, RPl*) coarse, rude.

(e) (*Col*) graceful, elegant; generous.

2 *nm* **(a)** (*shape, also Math*) square.

(b) (*Math*) ruler.

(c) (*Tech*) die.

(d) (*Sew*) gusset.

(e) (*Typ*) quadrat.

(f) (*Cu, RPl*) coarse fellow, uncouth person.

Cuadragésima *nf* Quadragesima.

cuadragésimo *adj* fortieth.

cuadrangular 1 *adj* quadrangular. **2** *nm* (*Baseball*) home run.

cuadrángulo *adj* quadrangular.

cuadrante *nm* **(a)** (*Math, Naut*) quadrant. **(b)** (*of instrument, radio*) dial; (*of clock*) face; — **solar** sundial.

cuadrar [1a] **1** *vt* **(a)** (*Math*) to square.

(b) (*Carp etc*) to square (off), make square.

(c) *paper* = **cuadricular**.

(d) (*fig*) to please; to suit; **si le cuadra** if it suits you.

2 *vi* **(a)** — **con** to square with, tally with, fit, correspond to; to match; to suit, go with.

(b) (*Chi*) — + *infin* to be ready to + *infin*.

3 cuadrarse *vr* **(a)** to square up, square one's shoulders; (*Mil*) to stand to attention.

(b) (*fig*) to dig one's heels in, refuse to budge.

(c) — **con uno** to become very solemn towards someone, adopt a coldly official attitude towards someone.

(d) (*PR, SD*) to make one's pile (*fam*).

(e) (*Ven*) to come off well, be successful.

cuadratura *nf* quadrature.

cuadrícula *nf* squares (ruled on paper *etc*); criss-cross pattern; (*Chess*) square.

cuadriculado *adj* = **cuadricular 1**; **papel** — squared paper.

cuadricular 1 *adj* *paper* ruled in squares, divided into squares; squared; *fabric* chequered. **2** [1a] *vt* to rule squares on, divide into squares.

cuadrilátero 1 *adj* quadrilateral, four-sided. **2** *nm* (*Math, Archit*) quadrilateral; (*Boxing*) ring.

cuadrilongo 1 *adj* oblong. **2** *nm* oblong.

cuadrilla *nf* party, group; band; gang; (*Mil*) squad; (*of workmen*) gang, squad, team; shift; (*Taur*) quadrille; (*pej*) gang; — **de demolición** demolition squad; — **de noche** night shift.

cuadrillazo *nm* (*Arg, Chi, Ec, Per*) gang attack.

cuadrillero *nm* group leader; chief; gang leader; (*Tech*) foreman; (*pej, esp Chi, Ec*) gang member.

cuadripartido *adj* quadripartite.

cuadrito *nm* (*Cook etc*) cube; **cortar en** —s to dice.

cuadrivio *nm* quadrivium.

cuadro *nm* **(a)** square; — **de vidrio** pane of glass; **2 metros en** — 2 metres square; **diseño a** —s chequered pattern, check (pattern).

(b) (*Archit, Tech*) frame; — **de bicicleta** bicycle frame; — **de ventana** window frame.

(c) (*Art*) picture, painting; **dos** —s **de Velázquez** two Velazquez paintings.

(d) (*Theat*) scene (*also fig*); (*TV*) picture; —s **vivos** tableau; **fue un** — **desgarrador** it was a heartbreaking scene (*or* picture).

(e) (*Lit*) description, picture; — **de costumbres** description of (regional) customs, scene of local colour.

(f) (*Agr, Hort*) bed; patch; plot; — **alpino** rock garden.

(g) (*Elec etc*) panel; — **de conexión manual** (*Tel*), — **de conmutadores** (*Elec*), — **de distribución** (*Elec*) switchboard; — **de instrumentos** instrument panel; (*Aut*) dashboard; — **de mandos** control panel.

(h) (*Mil*) square (formation); **formar el** — (*fig*) to resolve to stand together.

(i) table, chart, diagram (*also* — **sinóptico**).

(j) (*persons*) cadre; staff, establishment of officials (*etc*).

(k) (*Chi*) slaughterhouse.

(l) (*Col*) blackboard.

cuadrúpedo *nm* quadruped; four-footed animal.

cuádruple *adj* quadruple; fourfold.

cuadruplicado *adj* quadruplicate; **por** — in quadruplicate.

cuadruplicar [1g] **1** *vt* to quadruple. **2 cuadruplicarse** *vr* to quadruple.

cuádruplo 1 *adj* quadruple. **2** *nm* quadruple.

cuajada *nf* curd; cottage cheese.

cuajado *adj* **(a)** curdled, set, coagulated, congealed.

(b) — **de** (*fig*) full of, filled with; covered with; **una situación cuajada de peligros** a situation fraught with dangers; **un texto** — **de problemas** a text bristling with problems; **una corona cuajada de joyas** a crown covered with jewels.

(c) **estar** — (*fig*) to be dumbfounded.

(d) **quedarse** — (*fig*) to fall asleep.

cuajaleche *nm* bedstraw.

cuajar [1a] **1** *vt* **(a)** to thicken; *milk* to curdle; *blood etc* to congeal, coagulate, clot; *fat* to congeal; *jelly etc* to set.

(b) to cover, adorn (excessively; *de* with); to fill (*de* with); **una música que cuaja el ambiente de alegría** music which fills the air with joy.

2 *vi* **(a)** (*of seed etc*) to set; (*of snow*) to lie; *see* **3**.

(b) (*fig*) to become set, become established; to jell; (*of plan etc*) to take shape; to come off, work; (*of result*) to materialize; (*of proposal, motion*) to be received, be acceptable; **el noviazgo no cuajó** the engagement did not work, the engagement was not a success.

(c) (*Mex*) to chatter.

3 cuajarse *vr* **(a)** to thicken; to curdle; to congeal, coagulate; to set.

(b) — **de** (*fig*) to fill with, fill up with; to become crowded with.

(c) (*fig*) to go fast asleep.

cuajarón *nm* clot.

cuajo *nm* **(a)** rennet.

(b) (*fig*) phlegm, calmness; **tiene mucho** — he's very phlegmatic.

(c) *see* **llorar**.

(d) **arrancar algo de** — to tear something out by its roots; **arrancar una puerta de** — to wrench a door out of its frame; **extirpar un vicio de** — to eradicate a vice completely.

(e) (*Mex*) chat; chatter.

(f) (*Mex*) harmless fib.

(g) (*Mex*) impossible plan.

(h) (*Mex: School*) playtime.

cual 1 *adj* (*lit*) such as, of the kind (that); (*Law*) said, aforementioned; **los cuales bienes** the said property, which property; **las ceremonias fueron** —**es convenían a su importancia** the ceremonies were such as befitted his importance.

2 *pron* **(a)** **cada** — each one; **allá cada** — every man to his own taste; **son a** — **más gandul** each is as idle as the other; **gritar a** — **más** to see who can shout the loudest; — **más**, — **menos** some more, some less.

(b) (*relative*) **el** — (*etc*) which; who; whom; **ese edificio, el** — **se construyó en el siglo XV** that building, which was built in the 15th century; **un policía, el** — **me puso una multa** a policeman, who gave me a fine.

(c) **lo** — (*relative*) which; a fact which; **se rieron mucho, lo** — **me disgustó** they laughed a lot, which upset me; **con lo** — at which, whereupon; **por lo** — (and) so, and because of this, on account of which; whereby.

3 *adv and conj*: + *noun* like, as; + *verb* (just) as;

brillaba — **estrella** it shone like a star; **cual** . . . **tal** (or **así**) . . . like . . . like . . .; (verb) just as . . ., so . . .; — **el padre, tal el hijo** like father like son; — **el otro, tal éste** this one is just like the other, this one is as bad (etc) as the other; — **llega la noche** just as day follows night; — **si** . . . as if; see **tal.**

cuál interrog pron which (one)?; ¿— **quieres?** which (one) do you want?; ¿— **es el que dices?** which one are you talking about?; **si es tan malo A,** ¿— **debe ser B?** if A is so bad, what must B be like?; **ignora** — **será el resultado** he does not know what the outcome will be.

cualidad nf quality; attribute, trait, characteristic; (Philos, Phys etc) property; **tiene buenas** —**es** he has good qualities.

cualificado adj (a) worker skilled, qualified; **obrero no** — unskilled worker. (b) **estar** — **para** + infin to be entitled to + infin. (c) see **calificado.**

cualitativo adj qualitative.

cualquier(a), pl **cualesquier(a) 1** adj (a) any; any . . . you care to name (or like to mention etc); — **hombre de los de aquí** any man from these parts; **en** — **momento** at any time; **en** — **sitio donde lo busques** in whatever place you look for it, whichever place you look for it in; **con** —**resultado que sea** with whatever result it may be.
(b) (after noun) any; **ella no es una mujer** — she's not just any woman, she's not just an ordinary woman.
2 pron (a) anybody; whoever; whichever; **te lo diría** — anyone would tell you the same; — **puede hacer eso** anybody can do that; **yo me contento con** — I am happy with any (or either); I don't mind either (of the two).
(b) — **que sea** whoever he is; whichever it is.
(c) **es un** — he's a nobody; **yo no me caso con un** — I'm not marrying just anybody.

cuan adv (lit): **tan estúpidos** — **criminales** as much criminal as they are stupid.

cuán adv how; ¡— **agradable fue todo eso!** how delightful it all was!

cuando 1 adv and conj (a) (time) when; — **nos veamos** when we meet again; — **iba allí le veía** whenever I went there I saw him; **ven** — **quieras** come when(ever) you like; **me acuerdo de** — . . . I remember the time when . . .; **lo dejaremos para** — **estés mejor** we'll leave it until you're better.
(b) (concessive) if, even if, although; — **lo dice él, será verdad** if he says so, it must be true; — **no sea así** even if it is not so; — **más** at (the) most; — **menos** at least; — **no** if not, otherwise; ¡— **no!** (SAm) of course!, I should jolly well think so! (fam).
(c) (causal) since, when; see also **aun, cada** etc.
2 prep at the time of; **eso fue** — **la guerra** that was during the war; **ocurrió** — **la boda** it happened at the same time as the wedding; — **niño** as a child, when I (etc) was a child.

cuándo interrog adv and conj when; ¿— **lo perdiste?** when did you lose it?; **no sé** — **será** I don't know when it will be; ¿**de** — **acá?** since when?; (fig) how come?; ¿**desde** — **es esto así?** how long has it been like this?; — **con A,** — **con B** sometimes with A, sometimes with B.

cuantía nf quantity, amount; extent; importance; **de mayor** — first-rate; important; **de menor** —, **de poca** — second-rate; unimportant, of little account; **se ignora la** — **de las pérdidas** the extent of the losses is not known.

cuántico adj: **teoría cuántica** quantum theory.

cuantioso adj large, substantial; abundant; numerous.

cuantitativo adj quantitative.

cuanto 1 adj all that, as much as, whatever; **tiene todo** — **desea** he has all he wishes for; **daremos** —**s créditos se precisen** we will give all the credits that may be necessary, we will give whatever credits are needed; —**s hombres la ven la quieren** all the men that see her fall in love with her; **unos** —**s libros** a few books, some books; —**s más haya tantas más comidas habrá que preparar** the more there are the more meals will have to be cooked.
2 pron all that (which), as much as; —**s** all those that, as many as; **tiene** — **desea** he has all (that) he wants; **tome** — **quiera** take all you want, take as much as you want; —**s más, mejor** the more the merrier.
3 adv and conj (a) **en** — inasmuch as; **él, en** — **erudito,** . . . he, as a scholar, . . .; **en** — (conj) as soon as, immediately, directly; **en** — **lo supe me fui** as soon as I heard it I left; **en** — **a** as for, as to, with regard to; **por** — and so, hence.
(b) — **más** at least; — **más difícil parezca**

the more difficult it may seem, however difficult it seems; — **más trabaja menos gana** the more he works the less he earns; — **más que resultó ser mujer** all the more so because it turned out to be a woman; see **antes** etc.

cuánto adj, pron and adv **1** excl (a) (+ verb) ¡— **has crecido!** how you've grown!; ¡— **trabajas!** how hard you work!; ¡— **has gastado!** what a lot you've spent!; ¡— **me alegro!** I'm so glad!
(b) (+ noun) ¡**cuánta gente!** what a lot of people!; ¡— **tiempo perdido!** what a lot of time wasted!, the time you've wasted!; see **bueno.**
2 interrog (a) (sing) how much? ¿— **has gastado?** how much have you spent?; ¿— (**tiempo**)? how long?; ¿— **durará esto?** how long will this last?; ¿— **hay de aquí a Bilbao?** how far is it from here to Bilbao?; ¿**a** — **están las peras?** how much are (the) pears?; **le dije** — **la quería** I told her how much I loved her; see **cada, cinco.**
(b) ¿—**s?** how many?; ¿**cuántas personas había?** how many people were there?; ¿**a** —**s estamos?** what's the date?
(c) **el señor no sé** —**s** Mr So-and-So; **el señor Anastasio no sé** —**s** Mr Anastasius Something.

cuaquerismo nm Quakerism.

cuáquero 1 adj Quaker. **2** nm, **cuáquera** nf Quaker.

cuarcita nf quartzite.

cuarenta adj forty; **ésas son otras** — (Arg, Per, Urug) that's a different story; **cantar las** — **a uno** to tell someone a few home truths.

cuarentena nf (Med etc) quarantine.

cuarentón 1 adj forty-year old, fortyish. **2** nm, **cuarentona** nf person of about forty.

cuaresma nf Lent.

cuaresmal adj Lenten.

cuarta nf (a) (Math) quarter, fourth, fourth part.
(b) (of hand) span.
(c) (Naut) point (of the compass).
(d) (SAm) whip, riding crop.
(e) (RPl) extra pair of oxen.
(f) **andar de la** — **al pértigo** (RPl), **vivir la** — (Chi, Mex) to live in poverty.

cuartago nm pony.

cuartazos nm, pl **cuartazos** (fam) fat person, lump.

cuartear [1a] **1** vt (a) to quarter; to divide up, cut up.
(b) steep road to zigzag up.
(c) (Naut) compass to box.
(d) (Mex, PR) to whip, beat.
2 vi (a) (Cards) to make a fourth (player), make up a four.
(b) (Taur) to dodge, step aside.
3 cuartearse vr (a) (surface) to crack, split.
(b) (Taur) to dodge, step aside.
(c) (Mex) to go back on one's word, behave badly; to get scared.
(d) (Ven) to hedge; to change one's mind.

cuartel nm (a) quarter; (of city) quarter, district.
(b) (Her) quarter.
(c) (Hort) bed.
(d) (Mil) barracks; —**es** quarters; — **de bomberos** fire station; — **general** headquarters; —**es de invierno** winter quarters; **vida de** — army life, service life.
(e) **guerra sin** — war without mercy; **no dar** — to give no quarter, show no mercy; **no hubo** — **para los revoltosos** no mercy was shown to the rioters.

cuartelada nf (pej) military uprising, mutiny, putsch.

cuartelero nm (Ec, Per) waiter, hotel servant.

cuartería nf (Cu, Chi, SD) labourers' living quarters (on a ranch).

cuarterón nm (a) quarter pound. (b) (Archit) door panel. (c) (SAm) quadroon.

cuarteta nf quatrain.

cuarteto nm (a) (Mus) quartet(te). (b) (Lit) quatrain.

cuartilla nf (a) sheet (of paper); —**s** (Typ) manuscript, copy; notes, jottings. (b) (of horse) pastern. (c) fourth part (of a measure).

cuarto 1 adj fourth.
2 nm (a) quarter, fourth, fourth part; **abrigo tres** —**s** three-quarter length coat; —**s de final** quarter finals; — **de hora** quarter of an hour; **las 6 y** — a quarter past 6; **las 7 menos** — a quarter to seven; **tardó tres** —**s de hora** he took three-quarters of an hour; — **de luna** quarter of the moon; — **creciente** first quarter; — **menguante** last quarter; **de tres al** — insignificant, worthless.
(b) (of meat) joint; —**s** (of animal) legs, limbs; — **trasero** hindquarters, (as meat) rump.
(c) (Typ) quarto; **libro en** — quarto volume.
(d) (Fin) an ancient coin; —**s** (fam) money, brass (sl); **por 5** —**s** for a song; **es hombre de**

muchos —**s** he's a man with dough (*sl*); **estar sin un —, no tener un —** to be broke (*fam*); **dar un — al pregonero** to tell everyone one's private business.

(**e**) (*Archit*) room; rooms; small flat; **— de aseo,** **— de baño** bathroom; **— de desahogo, — trastero** lumber room; **— de descanso** rest room; **— de estar** living room; **— de juego** playroom; **— de los niños** nursery; **— oscuro** (*Phot*) darkroom; **poner —** to set up house; **poner — a la querida** to set one's mistress up in a little place.

(**f**) household, establishment of servants.

cuarzo *nm* quartz.

cuartones *nmpl* dressed timber, beams, planks.

cuás *nm* (*Mex*) bosom pal (*fam*).

cuasi *adv* (*lit*) = **casi.**

cuate (*CAm, Ec, Mex*) **1** *adj* twin. **2** *nm* (**a**) twin. (**b**) pal (*fam*), buddy (*esp US*). (**c**) double-barrelled gun.

cuaternario 1 *adj* quaternary. **2** *nm* quaternary.

cuatre(re)ar [1a] **1** *vt* (*RPl*) *cattle* to rustle, steal. **2** *vi* (*RPl*) to act treacherously.

cuatrero 1 *adj* (*CAm*) treacherous, disloyal. **2** *nm* (*RPl*) cattle rustler, horse thief.

cuatrillizos *nmpl*, **cuatrillizas** *nfpl* quadruplets.

cuatrimotor 1 *adj* four-engined. **2** *nm* four-engined plane.

cuatro 1 *adj* four; (*date*) fourth; **las —** four o'clock; **más de —** (*fig*) quite a few, rather a lot. **2** *nm* (**a**) four. (**b**) (*Col, PR, SD, Ven*) four-stringed guitar. (**c**) (*Mex*) trick, fraud; blunder.

cuatrocientos *adj* four hundred.

Cuba *f* Cuba.

cuba[1] *nf* (**a**) cask, barrel; tub; vat; (*Rail*) tank car; **— para el agua de lluvia** rainwater butt; **— de riego** water wagon, street sprinkler. (**b**) (*fam*) pot-bellied person. (**c**) (*fam*) drunkard, boozer; **estar hecho una —** to be as drunk as a lord.

cuba[2] *nm* (*Col*) youngest child.

cubaje *nm* (*SAm*) volume, contents.

cubanismo *nm* cubanism, word (*or* phrase *etc*) peculiar to Cuba.

cubano 1 *adj* Cuban. **2** *nm*, **cubana** *nf* Cuban.

cubero *nm* cooper.

cubertería *nf* cutlery.

cubeta *nf* keg, small cask; pail; (*Chem, Phot*) tray; (*of thermometer*) bulb; **— de siembra** seed box.

cubicar [1g] *vt* (**a**) (*Math*) to cube. (**b**) (*Phys*) to determine the volume of.

cúbico *adj* cubic; **metro —** cubic metre; **raíz cúbica** cube root.

cubículo *nm* cubicle.

cubierta *nf* (**a**) cover, covering; (*Typ*) cover, jacket; (*Archit*) roof; (*Tech*) casing; (*Aut*) bonnet, hood (*US*); (*Aut etc*) tyre, outer cover; (*Post*) envelope; **— de cama** coverlet; **— de lona** tarpaulin, canvas; **bajo esta —** (*Post*) under the same cover, enclosed herewith; **bajo — separada** (*Post*) under separate cover.

(**b**) (*Naut*) deck; **— de aterrizaje, — de vuelo** flight deck; **— de botes** boat deck; **— de paseo** promenade deck; **— de sol** sun deck.

(**c**) (*Col, Ec, Mex*) sheath.

(**d**) (*fig*) cover, pretext.

cubierto 1 *ptp* of **cubrir** and *adj*: (**a**) covered; *sky* overcast; **no — cheque** bad, unbacked; **poco — tyre** threadbare, worn.

(**b**) **la vacante está ya cubierta** the place has already been filled.

2 *nm* (**a**) **a —, bajo—** under cover; **a — de** safe from, out of the way of; **ponerse a —** to take cover, shelter (*de* from).

(**b**) place (at table); knife, fork and spoon, set of cutlery; (*Cook*) meal; meal at a fixed charge; **—s** cutlery; **— de 80 pesetas** 80-peseta meal; **precio del — cover** charge.

cubil *nm* den, lair.

cubilete *nm* (**a**) (*Cook*) mug, tumbler; small copper pan. (**b**) (*in games*) cup; dicebox. (**c**) (*SAm*) intrigue. (**d**) (*SAm*) top hat; bowler hat.

cubiletear [1a] *vi* (**a**) to shake the dicebox. (**b**) (*fig*) to intrigue, scheme.

cubiletero *nm* conjurer.

cubismo *nm* cubism.

cubista 1 *adj* cubist. **2** *nmf* cubist.

cubito *nm* (**a**) (*child's*) bucket, beach pail. (**b**) **— de hielo** ice cube.

cúbito *nm* ulna.

cubo *nm* (**a**) (*Math*) cube.

(**b**) bucket, pail; tub; **— de (la) basura** dustbin, ashcan (*US*); **— para el carbón** coal scuttle; **llover a —s** to rain cats and dogs, rain in torrents.

(**c**) (*Mech*) barrel, drum.

(**d**) (*of wheel*) hub.

(**e**) millpond.

(**f**) (*Archit*) round turret.

cubrebocas *nm*, *pl* **cubrebocas** (*Med*) mask.

cubrecama *nf* coverlet, bedspread.

cubrecorsé *nm* camisole.

cubremesa *nf* (*SAm*) table cover.

cubreobjetos *nm*, *pl* **cubreobjetos** (*Bio etc*) slide cover.

cubrerrueda *nf* mudguard, fender (*US*).

cubretetera *nf* tea cosy.

cubrir [3a; *ptp* **cubierto**] **1** *vt* (**a**) (*general sense*) to cover (in, over, up; *con, de* with); (*Archit*) to roof, put a roof over; *fire* to make up, bank up; **lo cubrieron los aguas** the waters closed over it; **el agua casi me cubría** the water almost covered me, I was almost out of my depth; **no te metas donde te cubra el agua** don't go out of your depth.

(**b**) (*Mil*) to cover; **— a uno con un revólver** to cover someone with a revolver.

(**c**) (*of emotion etc*) to cover; to hide, conceal, cloak; **cubre su tristeza con una falsa alegría** she covers up her sadness with a false cheerfulness.

(**d**) **— a uno de improperios** to shower insults on someone, shower someone with insults; **— a uno de alabanzas** to heap praises on someone; **— a uno de atenciones** to overwhelm someone with kindnesses; **— a uno de oprobio** to cover someone in shame; **— a uno de besos** to smother someone with kisses.

(**e**) *friend etc* to cover, protect; to cover up for.

(**f**) *distance* to cover, travel, do; **— 80 kms en una hora** to cover 80 kms in an hour.

(**g**) *post* to fill.

(**h**) (*Bio*) to cover, mate with.

(**i**) (*Fin etc*) *expenses, needs* to meet, cover; *deficit, overdraft etc* to cover; *debt* to repay; **esto cubre todas nuestras necesidades** this meets all our needs; **ello apenas cubre los gastos** this scarcely covers the expenses.

2 cubrirse *vr* (**a**) to cover oneself; to put on one's hat.

(**b**) (*fig*) **— de gloria** to cover oneself with glory.

(**c**) **— contra un riesgo** to cover (*or* protect) oneself against a risk; **— contra una posibilidad** to take precautions against an eventuality.

(**d**) (*of sky*) to become overcast.

cuca *nf* (**a**) (*fam*) tart (*sl*), whore. (**b**) **—s** sweets, candy (*US*); titbits; confectionery.

cucambé *nm* (*Col, Ven*) hide-and-seek.

cucaña *nf* (**a**) plum, soft job; bargain; cinch (*sl*), easy thing. (**b**) (*at fair etc*) greasy pole.

cucañero *nm*, **cucañera** *nf* (*fam*) shrewd person, fly sort; hanger-on; social climber.

cucar [1g] *vt* (**a**) to wink. (**b**) to deride, poke fun at. (**c**) (*SAm*) to urge on, incite, provoke.

cucaracha *nf* (**a**) (*Ent*) cockroach. (**b**) (*Arg, Mex: Aut*) old crock.

cucarachero *nm* (*Col, PR*) parasite, hanger-on; (*Ec*) flatterer, creep (*sl*).

cuclillas: en — squatting, crouching; **sentarse en —** to squat, sit on one's heels.

cuclillo *nm* (**a**) (*Orn*) cuckoo. (**b**) (*Bot*) ragged robin. (**c**) (*fam*) cuckold.

cuco 1 *adj* (**a**) shrewd; sly, crafty. (**b**) pretty; cute; dainty.

2 *nm* (**a**) (*Orn*) cuckoo. (**b**) (*Ent*) grub, caterpillar. (**c**) (*fam*) gambler. (**d**) (*Mex*) **hacer — a uno** to poke fun at someone.

cucú *nm* (*sound*) cuckoo.

cucuche (*CAm*): **ir a —** to ride astride.

cucufato *nm* (*Arg, Bol, Per*) hypocrite, sanctimonious person.

cucurucho *nm* (**a**) paper cone, cornet; (*fig*) cornucopia. (**b**) (*Eccl etc*) hooded garment; pointed hat. (**c**) (*Ant, CAm, Col, Pan*) top, summit, apex.

cuchara *nf* (**a**) spoon; scoop; ladle; (*Tech*) scoop; bucket; dipper; **— de café** coffee spoon, (*equivalent to*) teaspoon; **— de sopa, — sopera** soup spoon, (*as measure*) tablespoon; **militar de —** officer who has risen from the ranks; **meter su —** (*in conversation*) to butt in, (*in matter*) to meddle, shove one's oar in; **meter algo a uno con —** to have a hard job getting someone to understand something; **despacharse (or**

cucharada 156 **cuento**

servirse) con la — grande (*esp SAm*) to give oneself a big helping, (*fig*) to look after number one. **(b)** (*SAm*) flat trowel; **albañil de —** skilled bricklayer. **(c)** (*CAm, Chi, PR*) pout; **hacer —** to pout. **(d)** (*Mex*) pickpocket.

cucharada *nf* spoonful; **— de café** teaspoonful; **— de sopa** tablespoonful.

cucharadita *nf* teaspoonful.

cucharear [1a] *vt* to spoon out, ladle out; (*Agr*) to pitch.

cucharetear [1a] *vi* **(a)** to stir (with a spoon). **(b)** (*fig*) to meddle.

cucharilla *nf*, **cucharita** *nf* small spoon, teaspoon (*also* **— de café, — de té**).

cucharón *nm* ladle; (*Tech*) scoop, bucket; **tener el — por el mango** (*fig*) to have the situation well in hand.

cuchí *nm* (*Per*) pig.

cuchichear [1a] *vi* to whisper (*a* to).

cuchicheo *nm* whispering.

cuchilla *nf* **(a)** (large, kitchen) knife; chopper, cleaver; (*Tech, also of weapon*) blade; (*of skate*) runner; scraper; (*SAm*) penknife; **— de afeitar** razor blade. **(b)** (*Geog*) ridge, crest; (*SAm*) line of low hills; (*PR*) mountain top.

cuchillada *nf* **(a)** slash, cut, gash, knife wound; **— de cien reales** long gash, severe wound; **dar —** (*fig*) to make a hit, get talked about. **(b)** (*Sew*) slash, slit. **(c)** **—s** (*fig*) fight, brawl.

cuchillazo *nm* (*SAm*) = **cuchillada** (a).

cuchillería *nf* **(a)** cutlery. **(b)** cutler's (shop).

cuchillero 1 *adj* (*SAm*) quarrelsome, brawling; clever with a knife. **2** *nm* cutler.

cuchillo *nm* **(a)** knife; **— de caza, — de monte** hunting knife; **— de cocina** kitchen knife; **— del pan** breadknife; **— de trinchar** carving knife; **pasar a — to** put to the sword. **(b)** (*Archit: also* **— de armadura**) upright, support. **(c)** **— de aire** sharp draught, cold draught. **(d)** (*Mex*) surgeon.

cuchipanda *nf* (*fam*) feed (*fam*), beano (*fam*).

cuchitril *nm* **(a)** (*Agr*) pigsty. **(b)** (*fig*) hovel; pigsty; den, hole.

cucho (a) (*CAm*) hunchback. **(b)** (*Chi*) puss. **(c)** (*Col, Ec, Per*) = **cuchitril** (b).

cuchuflé *nm* (*Cu*) = **cuchuflí**.

cuchufleta *nf* (*fam*) joke, crack (*fam*).

cuchuflí *nm* (*Cu*) uncomfortable place; jail.

cuchugos *nmpl* (*Col, Ec, Ven*) saddlebags.

cuchumbo *nm* (*CAm*) funnel; bucket, pail; dicebox.

cuelga *nf* **(a)** hanging (of fruit *etc* to dry); bunch (of drying fruit *etc*). **(b)** birthday present. **(c)** (*Col, Chi*) fall (in the level of a stream *etc*).

cuelgacapas *nm*, *pl* **cuelgacapas** coat hanger; hallstand.

cuellicorto *adj* short-necked.

cuellilargo *adj* long-necked.

cuello *nm* **(a)** (*Anat*) neck; **cortar el — a uno** to cut someone's throat; **erguir el —** to be haughty; **levantar el —** to get on one's feet again (*fig*). **(b)** collar; **— alto** high collar; **— blando** soft collar; **— postizo** detachable collar; **— de recambio** spare collar.

cuenca *nf* **(a)** hollow; (*Anat*) eye socket. **(b)** (*Hist*) wooden bowl. **(c)** (*Geog*) bowl, deep valley; (*of river*) basin, catchment area; **la — del Ebro** the Ebro basin; **— hullera, — minera** coalfield.

cuenco *nm* **(a)** hollow; (*of spoon*) bowl; **— de la mano** hollow of the hand. **(b)** earthenware bowl, wooden bowl.

cuenta *nf* **(a)** (*Math*) count, counting; calculation; (*esp fig*) reckoning; (*Boxing*) count; **— de la vieja** counting on one's fingers; **— (hacia) atrás, — al revés** (*rocket launch etc*) countdown; **a esa —** at that rate; **por la —** apparently, as far as one can tell; **beber más de la —** to have too much to drink, have one over the eight; **caer en la —** to catch on (*de* to), see the point (*de* of); **habida — de eso** bearing that in mind; **hacer algo con su — y razón** to be fully aware of what one is doing; **perder la — de** to lose count of; **tener** (*or* **tomar**) **en —** to bear in mind, take into account; **es otra cosa a tener en —** that's another thing to be borne in mind. **(b)** (*Comm, Fin: at bank*) account; **— de ahorros, — a plazo (fijo)** deposit account; **— bancaria, — de banco** bank account; **— corriente** current account; **— indistinta, — en participación** joint account; **abrir una —** to open an account; **a — on** account;

tomar un coche a — to take a car in part payment; **abonar una cantidad a —** a uno to credit a sum to someone's account; **cargar una cantidad en — a uno** to charge a sum to someone's account. **(c)** (*Comm, Fin: sent out*) account, bill; (*in restaurant etc*) bill; (*fig*) check, tally; **la — del sastre** the tailor's bill; **— de diversos** sundries account; **— de gastos** expense account; **— pendiente** unpaid bill, outstanding account; **la — es la —** business is business; **ajustar** (*or* **liquidar**) **una —** to settle an account; **echar las —s** to reckon up; **hacer las —s de la lechera** to indulge in wishful thinking, count one's chickens before they are hatched; **llevar la — de** to keep an account of; **pasar la — to** send the bill; **vivir a — de** to live at the expense of. **(d)** (*fig*) account; **ajustar —s** to settle up (*con* with); **ajustar —s viejas con uno** to settle old scores with someone; **le ajusté las —s** (*fam*) I told him where to get off; **voy a ajustar —s con él** I'm going to have it out with him; **¡vamos a —s!** let's get down to business!; **tener —s pendientes con uno** to have a matter to settle with someone. **(e)** (*fig*) account; report, statement; **en resumidas —s** in short, in a nutshell; all in all; **dar — de** to give an account of, report on; **dar — a uno de sus actos** to account to someone for one's actions; **no tiene que dar —s a nadie** he's not answerable to anyone; **dar — de una botella** to finish off a bottle, put paid to a bottle; **dar buena — de sí** to give a good account of oneself; to give as good as one gets; **darse — de** to realize (*que* that); **sin darse —** without realizing it, without noticing; **exigir** (*or* **pedir**) **—s a uno** to call someone to account, bring someone to book; **rendir —s a uno** to report to someone. **(f)** (*fig*) affair, business; **ésa es — mía** that's my affair, that's up to me; **de — y riesgo de uno** at one's own risk; **por — propia, por su propia —** on one's own account, for oneself; **por mi —** in my opinion; as for me; **eso corre de** (*or* **por**) **mi —** that's my affair; **éste corre por mi —** (*drinks etc*) this one's on me; **no querer —s con uno** to want nothing to do with someone; to want no trouble with someone; *see* **apañar** *etc*. **(g)** **—s** plans; **echar —s** to reflect, take stock; **echar — de + infin** to plan to + *infin*; **le salieron fallidas las —s** his plans went wrong. **(h)** (*fig*) importance; **de (mucha) —** important; **no tiene — + infin** there is no point in + *ger*. **(i)** (*of necklace etc, also Eccl*) bead.

cuentacorrentista *nmf* depositor.

cuentagotas *nm*, *pl* **cuentagotas** (*Med*) dropper.

cuentakilómetros *nm*, *pl* **cuentakilómetros** *equivalent to* milometer; speedometer.

cuentarrevoluciones *nm*, *pl* **cuentarrevoluciones** tachometer.

cuentear [1a] **1** *vt* (*Col*) to court; to compliment. **2** *vi* (*CAm*) to gossip.

cuenterete *nm* (*CAm*) piece of gossip; tall story, tale.

cuentero *nm* (*RPl*) confidence trickster, con(fidence) man (*US*).

cuentista *nmf* **(a)** storyteller; (*Lit*) short-story writer. **(b)** gossip; talebearer. **(c)** affected person, person with a theatrical manner; conceited person, swank (*fam*). **(d)** (*RPl*) confidence trickster.

cuento[1] *nm* **(a)** story, tale; (*Lit*) short story; funny story, joke; **— de hadas** fairy tale; **— del tío** (*Chi, Per, RPl*) confidence trick, confidence game (*US*); **— de viejas** old wives' tale; **es un — largo** it's a long story; **esto es mucho —** this is terribly tedious; **es el — de nunca acabar** it's an endless business; **estar en el —** to be in the know; **ir a uno con el —** to go off and tell someone; **va de —** the story goes that . . . , it is said that . . .; **traer algo a —** to mention something, bring something up; (*pej*) to drag something in; **eso no viene a —** that's off the point, that's irrelevant; **vivir del —** to live by one's wits. **(b)** sin **—** countless. **(c)** (*pej*) story, tale, fib; pretext; **¡puro —!** a likely story!; **— chino** tall story; **¡déjese de —s!** stop beating about the bush!, get on with it!; **se me hace — (RPl)** I don't believe it. **(d)** **—s** (*fig*) trouble, difficulties; upsets; **han tenido no se qué —s entre ellos** they've had some upset among themselves; **no quiero —s con él** I don't want to have anything to do with him. **(e)** (*fam*) fuss; exaggeration; hot air, mere words; **tiene mucho —** he makes a lot of fuss (about nothing), he exaggerates everything so.

cuento[2] *nm* point, tip; ferrule.

cuera nf (a) (SAm) hide; leather strap. (b) (Mex) leather jacket. (c) (CAm) —s leggings. (d) (Bol, Pan, PR) flogging.

cuerazo nm (SAm) lash.

cuerda nf (a) rope; string, cord; (for dog) lead; (Fish) fishing line; (Surveying) measuring tape; — arrojadiza lasso; — floja tightrope; — de plomada plumbline; — de salvamento, — salvavidas lifeline; — para tender la ropa clothesline; aflojar la — (fig) to ease up; apretar la — (fig) to tighten up; bailar en la — floja to keep in with both parties; estirar la — (fig) to go too far, overdo it; son de la misma — they're all as bad as each other; bajo —, por debajo de — in an underhand way, by stealth, on the side.
   (b) (of watch) spring; (Mech) clockwork mechanism; dar — al reloj to wind up one's watch; dar — a uno to encourage someone (to talk); un coche de — a clockwork car.
   (c) (Mus) string, cord; — de arco bowstring; — de tripa catgut; estar en su — (SAm) to be in one's element; to be witty; estar con — (SAm) to be in a merry mood.
   (d) (Mus: fig) vocal range.
   (e) (Anat) cord; tendon; — espinal spinal cord; —s vocales vocal chords.
   (f) (Math) chord.

cuerdamente adv (a) sanely. (b) wisely, sensibly, prudently.

cuerdo adj (a) person sane. (b) act etc wise, sensible, prudent.

cuereada nf (SAm) beating, tanning (fam).

cuerear [1a] vt (a) (SAm) to skin, flay. (b) (SAm) to whip, beat. (c) (Cu, RPl) to criticize mercilessly; to malign.

cuerito: de — a — adv (SAm) from end to end.

cueriza nf (SAm) beating, tanning (fam).

cuerna nf (a) (Zool) horns; antlers. (b) drinking horn. (c) (Mus) horn.

cuerno nm (a) (in most cases) horn; antler; — de la abundancia horn of plenty; estar en los —s (del toro) to be in danger; to be in a jam; poner a uno en los —s (del toro) to place someone at risk; to get someone into a fix; poner los —s a uno to cuckold someone; ir al — (business) to fall through; (person) to go to the dogs; ¡vete al —! go to hell!; oler (or saber) a — quemado to be suspicious; to leave a nasty taste; esto me sabe a — quemado this upsets me, this makes my blood boil.
   (b) (Cook) roll, croissant.
   (c) (Mil) horn.

cuero nm (a) (Zool) skin, hide; (of rabbit etc) pelt; (Tech, as substance etc) leather; — adobado tanned skin; — cabelludo scalp; — charolado patent leather; andar en —s to go about stark naked; dejar a uno en —s (fig) to rob someone of everything.
   (b) wineskin; (fam) toper, old soak (fam); estar hecho un — to be as drunk as a lord.
   (c) (of tap) washer.
   (d) (SAm) whip; arrimar (or dar etc) el — a uno to give someone a beating.
   (e) (Col, Ec, PR, Ven) whore; (Col) old maid; (Cu) old woman; (Ec, Mex) mistress.
   (f) (Cu, Guat) impudence, effrontery.

cuerpear [1a] vi (RPl) to dodge.

cuerpo nm (a) (Anat etc) body; figure; build; corpse; (Sport) length; combate — a — hand-to-hand fight; luchar — a — to fight hand-to-hand; de — entero mirror, picture full-length; rogue etc thoroughgoing, out-and-out; true, real; de medio — half-length; en — y alma fully; dar con el — en tierra to fall down; echar el — atrás to lean suddenly backwards; estar de — presente to lie in state; ganar por 4 —s to win by 4 lengths; ganar por medio — to win by half a length; hacer del — to relieve oneself; hurtar el — to dodge, move (one's body) out of the way; ir a —, ir en — to go without a coat; vivir a — de rey to live like a king.
   (b) (of state etc) body; corporation; — estatal public body.
   (c) — de doctrina body of teaching; — de leyes body of laws.
   (d) (persons) body; brigade; force; (Mil) corps; — de baile corps de ballet; — de bomberos fire brigade, fire department (US); — diplomático diplomatic corps; — de ejército army corps; — de intendencia service corps; — de sanidad medical corps.
   (e) (Chem) body, substance; — compuesto compound; — simple element; — extraño foreign body.
   (f) (Astron) body.
   (g) (Anat: special sense) trunk; (fig) main part; mass, bulk; el — de un libro the main part of a book,
the book proper; un vino de mucho — a full-bodied wine; dar — a un líquido to thicken a liquid; tomar — to swell, get bigger; (of plan etc) to take shape.
   (h) (of building) wing; part; (of furniture) part, section.
   (i) (Sew) bodice.
   (j) (Typ: of letter) size; (of paper etc) thickness.
   (k) (Lit) volume; una biblioteca de 50 mil —s a library of 50,000 books.

cucrudo adj (a) (SAm) horse slow, sluggish; lazy. (b) (SAm) person annoying. (c) (Arg) brave, tough. (d) (CAm, Cu, PR) impudent, shameless.

cuervo nm raven; — marino cormorant.

cuesco nm (a) (Bot) stone. (b) millstone (of oil mill). (c) (fam) punch, bash (fam). (d) (tabu) fart (tabu).

cuesta nf (a) slope; (on road etc) hill; — abajo downhill; ir — abajo (fig) to decline, go downhill; — arriba uphill; se me hace — arriba + infin I find it hard to + infin; — de enero period of financial stringency following Christmas spending; hemos vencido la — ya we're over the hump now; we're more than halfway.
   (b) a —s on one's back; echar algo a —s to put something on one's back, (fig) to take on the burden of something; lleva también eso a —s he has the additional burden of that.

cuestación nf charity collection.

cuestión nf (a) matter, question, issue; (Math etc) problem; — batallona vexed question; — clave key question; — madre really big question; — candente, — palpitante burning question; la cosa en — the matter at issue, the thing in question; en — de about, concerning; es — de it is a matter of; eso es otra — that's another matter; otra — sería si . . . it would be different if . . .
   (b) quarrel, dispute; trouble; complication; hay — sobre si . . . there's an argument about whether . . .; la — es que . . . the trouble is that . . .; no quiero —es con los empleados I don't want trouble with the staff; no tengamos — let's not have an argument about it, let's not have a fuss about it.

cuestionable adj questionable.

cuestionar [1a] 1 vt to question, dispute, argue about. 2 vi to argue.

cuestionario nm questionnaire; (School, Univ etc) question paper.

cuestor nm quaestor.

cuete 1 adj (Mex) drunk. 2 nm (a) (Guat, Mex, Per) pistol; =cohete. (b) (Mex) drunkenness.

cuetearse [1a] vr (Col) (a) to go off, explode. (b) (sl) to kick the bucket (sl).

cueva nf cave; (for wine, in house etc) cellar, vault; — de ladrones den of thieves.

cuévano nm pannier.

cui nm (SAm) guinea-pig.

cuica nf (Ec) earthworm.

cuico 1 adj (Ec) thin; (Cu) rachitic, feeble. 2 nm (a) (Arg, Chi) foreigner, outsider; (Chi, Per, RPl: pej) Bolivian; (Cu) Mexican. (b) (Mex) policeman.

cuidado nm (a) care, worry, concern; solicitude; dar — to cause concern; estar con — to be anxious, be worried; estar de — to be gravely ill, be in a bad way; enfermar de — to fall seriously ill; ¡no haya —!, ¡pierda Vd —! don't worry!; eso me trae (or tiene) sin — I'm not worried about that; I couldn't care less.
   (b) care, carefulness; ¡—! careful!, look out!, watch out!; ¡ — con el paquete! careful with the parcel!; ¡ — con el perro! beware of the dog!; ¡ — con los rateros! watch out for pickpockets!; ¡ — con perderlo! mind you don't lose it!; andarse con — to go carefully, watch out; poner mucho — en algo to take great care over something; tener — to be careful, take care; tener — con to be careful of, watch out for, beware of; hay que tener — con él you have to handle him carefully; ¡ten —! careful!
   (c) care; affair; business, concern; ¡allá —s! let others worry about that!, that's their funeral! (fam); "al — del Sr A" (Post) "care of Mr A"; eso no es — mío, eso no corre de mi — that's not my concern; lo dejo a su — I leave it to you; está al — de la computadora he's in charge of the computer; los niños están al — de la abuela the children are in their grandmother's charge.

cuidador nm (Boxing) second; (Racing) trainer.

cuidadora nf (Mex) nursemaid, nanny.

cuidadosamente adv (a) carefully. (b) anxiously; solicitously.

cuidadoso adj (a) careful (con about, with). (b) anxious, concerned (de, por about); solicitous (de for).

cuidar [1a] **1** vt (a) to take care of, look after; to pay attention to; **ella cuida a los niños** she looks after the children, she minds the children; **no cuidan la casa** they don't look after the house.

(b) (Med) to care for.

2 vi (a) — de to take care of, look after; — **de una obligación** to attend to a duty; — **de que . . .** to take care that . . ., see (to it) that . . .; **cuidó de que todo saliera bien** he ensured that everything should go smoothly; **cuide de que no pase nadie** see that nobody gets in; **que cuide que no le pase lo mismo** let him beware lest the same thing happens to him; **cuide de no caer** take care not to fail.

(b) **cuida con esa gente** to be wary of those people.

3 cuidarse vr (a) to look after oneself (also Med); (pej) to look after number one; **ella ha dejado de —** she's let herself go.

(b) — **de algo** to worry about something; — **de + infin** to be careful to + infin; **no se cuida del qué dirán** she doesn't worry about what people will think.

(c) — **muy bien de + infin** to take good care not to + infin.

cuita nf (a) worry, trouble; grief, affliction; **contar sus —s a uno** to tell someone one's troubles. (b) (CAm) excrement; birdlime.

cuitado adj (a) worried, troubled; wretched. (b) timid.

cuja nf (a) bedstead. (b) (Hond, Mex) envelope.

cujinillos nmpl (Guat, Mex) saddlebags.

culantro nm coriander.

culata nf (a) (of gun) butt; (of cannon) breech; (of cylinder) head.

(b) (Zool) haunch, hindquarters.

(c) (SAm: of a house) side; rear, back.

(d) (RPl) hut, temporary shelter.

culatazo nm kick, recoil.

culebra nf (a) snake; — **de anteojos** cobra; — **de cascabel** rattlesnake; **hacer —** to zigzag, stagger along.

(b) (Col, Ec, Per) debt, bill.

(c) (Mex) waterspout.

culebrear [1a] vi (a) to wriggle (along); to zigzag; (river etc) to wind, meander. (b) (Ant) to stall, hedge.

culebreo nm wriggling; zigzag; winding, meandering.

culebrina nf (a) (Hist) culverin. (b) (Meteorol) forked lightning.

culeco adj (a) (SAm) hen broody.

(b) (SAm) person home-loving.

(c) (Per, PR, RPl) **estar —** to be very much in love.

(d) (Ant, CAm, Mex, Per) **estar — con algo** to be very pleased about something; to be very proud of something.

culero 1 adj lazy. **2** nm nappy, diaper (US).

culí nm coolie.

culibajo adj short, dumpy.

culigordo adj big-bottomed, broad in the beam (fam).

culillo nm (a) (Ant, Col, Pan) fear, fright. (b) (Cu) haste, impatience.

culinario adj culinary, cooking (attr).

culipandear [1a] vi and **culipandearse** vr (Cu, Mex, PR) to stall, hedge, make false promises.

culminación nf culmination.

culminante adj point etc highest, topmost, culminating; moment culminating; (fig) outstanding.

culminar [1a] vi to reach its highest point, reach a peak; to culminate (en in).

culo nm (a) (tabu in parts of SAm) bottom, backside, arse (tabu), ass (US sl); anus, arsehole (tabu); **dar a uno un puntapié en el —** to kick someone's backside, (fig) to boot someone out; **ser un — de mal asiento** to be restless, be fidgety; to chop and change, keep changing one's job (etc); **ir con el — a rastras** to be in a jam; to be broke (fam); **la ciudad va de —** the city is going downhill.

(b) (of jar etc) bottom.

culón adj = **culigordo**.

culpa nf (a) fault; blame; (Law etc) guilt; **por — de** through the fault of; through the negligence of; **no le alcanza —** no blame attaches to him; **echar la — a uno** to blame someone (de for); **tener la —** to be to blame (de for); **nadie tiene la —** nobody is to blame; **Vd tiene la —** it's your fault; **la — fue de los frenos** the brakes were to blame; **es — suya** it's his fault.

(b) sin, offence; **pagar las —s ajenas** to pay for someone else's sins.

culpabilidad nf guilt.

culpable 1 adj (a) **la persona —** the person to blame, the person at fault; (Law) the guilty person, the

culprit; **confesarse —** to plead guilty; **declarar — a uno** to find someone guilty.

(b) act to be condemned, blameworthy; **es — no hacerlo** it is criminal not to do it; **con descuido —** with culpable negligence.

2 nmf culprit; (Law etc) offender, guilty party.

culpado 1 adj guilty. **2** nm, **culpada** nf culprit; (Law) the accused.

culpar [1a] vt to blame, accuse; to condemn; — **a uno de algo** to blame someone for something; — **a uno de descuidado** to blame someone for being careless, accuse someone of carelessness.

cultamente adv in a cultured way, in a refined tone (etc); elegantly.

culteranismo nm (Lit) latinized, precious and highly metaphorical style (esp 17th century).

culterano (Lit) **1** adj latinized, precious and highly metaphorical. **2** nm writer in the style of culteranismo.

cultismo nm (Ling) learned word.

cultivable adj cultivable.

cultivador nm farmer, grower; (of specific crop) cultivator, grower; — **de vino** winegrower; — **de café** coffee grower, coffee planter.

cultivadora nf (Tech) cultivator.

cultivar [1a] vt (a) land to cultivate, work, till; crop etc to grow.

(b) (fig) study, art etc to cultivate; aptitude etc to develop; memory to develop, improve; friendship to cultivate.

cultivo nm (a) (act) cultivation, growing.

(b) crop; **el — principal de la región** the chief crop of the area; **rotación de —s** rotation of crops.

(c) (Bio) culture.

culto 1 adj (a) cultivated, cultured, refined; educated; elegant.

(b) (Ling) learned; **palabra culta** learned word.

2 nm worship; cult (a of); (Eccl) divine service, worship; — **a la personalidad** personality cult; **rendir — a** to worship; (fig) to pay homage to, pay tribute to.

cultura nf culture; refinement; education; elegance; — **física** physical culture; **la — popular** popular culture; **persona de —** cultured person; educated person.

cultural adj cultural.

cuma nf (a) (CAm) long knife, curved machete. (b) (Per, RPl) crone, gossip.

cumbancha nf (Ant) spree (fam), drinking bout.

cúmbila nm (Cu) pal (fam), buddy (esp US).

cumbo nm (a) (CAm) top hat, bowler hat. (b) (Guat, Hond) narrow-mouthed cup.

cumbre nf summit, top; (fig) top, height, pinnacle; **conferencia (en la) —** summit conference; **está en la — de su empresa** he is at the top of his company; **está en la — de su poderío** he is at the height of his power.

cume nm, **cumiche** nm (CAm) baby of the family.

cumpa nm (SAm) pal (fam), buddy (esp US).

cumpleañero nm, **cumpleañera** nf (SAm) person celebrating a birthday, person whose birthday it is.

cumpleaños nm, pl **cumpleaños** birthday; — **del matrimonio** (SAm) wedding anniversary.

cumplido 1 adj (a) complete, perfect; full; **un — caballero** a perfect gentleman, a real gentleman.

(b) (Sew etc) full, extra large.

(c) meal etc large, plentiful.

(d) courteous, correct; formal (in manner); (pej) stiff, ceremonious.

(e) **tiene 60 años —s** he is all of 60, he is at least 60.

2 nm compliment; courtesy; **visita de —** formal visit, courtesy call; **por —** as a compliment; out of politeness, as a matter of courtesy; **¡sin —s!** no ceremony, please!; make yourself at home!; **andarse con —s, estar de —, usar —s** to stand on ceremony, be formal; **cambiar los —s de etiqueta** to exchange formal courtesies; **he venido por —** I came out of a sense of duty.

cumplidor adj reliable, trustworthy.

cumplimentar [1a] vt (a) to pay one's respects to, pay a courtesy call on; to congratulate (por on). (b) order etc to carry out; duty to perform, do.

cumplimentero adj formal, ceremonious; effusive.

cumplimiento nm (a) (act) fulfilment; completion; performance; **falta de —** non-fulfilment, non-compliance; **dar — a** to fulfill. (b) = **cumplido 2**.

cumplir [3a] **1** vt (a) promise, wish, contract, threat etc to carry out, fulfil; stipulation to comply with; (Cards) contract to make; law etc to observe, obey; ambition to fulfil, realize.

(b) sentence to serve.

(c) *years etc* to reach, attain, complete; **hoy cumple 8 años** she's 8 today; **cuando cumpla los 21 años** when you're 21, when you reach the age of 21; **¿cuándo cumple Vd años?** when is your birthday?; **¡que los cumplas muy felices!** many happy returns (of the day).

2 *vi* **(a)** *(of period)* to end, expire; *(of payment)* to fall due.

(b) *(Mil)* to finish one's military service.

(c) to do one's duty, carry out one's task, do what is required of one; **sólo por —** as a matter of form, as a mere formality.

(d) — con = 1(a); — con uno to do one's duty by someone; **— con la iglesia** to fulfil one's religious obligations; **— por uno** to act on someone's behalf.

(e) le cumple hacerlo it behoves him to do it, it is up to him to do it; **no le cumple** + *infin* it is not his place to + *infin.*

3 cumplirse *vr* **(a)** *(plan etc)* to be fulfilled, come true.

(b) *(period)* to expire, end, be up.

cumucho *nm* (*Chi*) **(a)** gathering, mob, crowd. **(b)** hut, hovel.

cumulativo *adj* cumulative.

cúmulo *nm* **(a)** pile, heap; accumulation; *(fig)* pile, lot. **(b)** *(Meteorol)* cumulus.

cumulonimbo *nm* cumulonimbus.

cuna *nf* **(a)** cradle; cot; **— portátil** carrycot.

(b) home, foundling hospital.

(c) *(fig)* family, stock, birth; **de — humilde** of humble origin; **criarse en buena —** to be born with a silver spoon in one's mouth.

(d) *(fig)* birthplace; **— del famoso poeta** the birthplace of the famous poet.

(e) —s *(fig)* cat's-cradle.

cundir [3a] *vi* **(a)** *(fig)* to spread; *(fig)* to spread, expand, increase; *(fig and pej)* to be rampant, be rife.

(b) *(of rice etc)* to swell, expand; to produce a good *(etc)* quantity, give good *(etc)* results; **hoy no me ha cundido el trabajo** work did not go well for me today.

cunear [1a] **1** *vt* to rock, cradle. **2 cunearse** *vr* **(a)** to rock, sway. **(b)** *(in walking)* to walk with a swing, walk with a roll.

cuneco *nm* (*Ven*) baby of the family.

cuneiforme *adj* cuneiform.

cuneta *nf* **(a)** ditch, gutter. **(b)** *(Aut)* verge, hard shoulder.

cuña *nf* **(a)** wedge; *(of wheel)* chock.

(b) meter — to sow discord.

(c) *(SAm)* big shot *(fam)*, influential person.

(d) *(SAm)* lever (to obtain something), influence; **tener —s** (*Chi, RPl*) to have pull, have influence.

(e) *(CAm, Cu, SD)* two-seater car.

(f) *(Col: Radio)* plug *(sl)*, spot, advert.

cuñada *nf* sister-in-law.

cuñado *nm* brother-in-law.

cuñete *nm* keg.

cuño *nm* **(a)** *(Tech)* stamp, die-stamp; **de nuevo —** *(fig)* newly-coined. **(b)** *(fig)* stamp, mark.

cuota *nf* **(a)** quota; share. **(b)** fee, dues; **— de enseñanza** school fees; **— de entrada** admission fee; **— del gremio** union dues; **— de socio** membership fee.

cuotidiano *adj* = **cotidiano.**

cupe *etc see* **caber.**

cupé *nm* *(Aut)* coupé.

Cupido *m* Cupid.

cuplé *nm* pop song, light lyric.

cupo *nm* **(a)** quota; share; **— de azúcar** sugar quota. **(b)** *(Mex)* space, room, capacity; contents.

cupón *nm* coupon; *(Comm)* trading stamp; **— de dividendos** dividend voucher; **— de respuestas internacional** international reply coupon.

cúpula *nf* **(a)** *(Archit)* dome, cupola. **(b)** *(Naut)* turret. **(c)** *(Bot)* husk, shell.

cuquería *nf* craftiness.

cura¹ *nm* *(Eccl)* priest; father; **— párroco** parish priest; **sí, señor —** yes, father.

cura² *nf* **(a)** *(Med)* cure, healing; treatment; remedy; **primera —** first aid; **— de reposo** rest cure; **— de urgencia** emergency treatment, first aid; **tiene —** it can be cured, it is curable; **no tiene —** *(fam)* there's no remedy, it's quite hopeless.

(b) *(Eccl)* **— de almas** cure of souls.

curable *adj* curable.

curaca *nf* **(a)** *(Bol, Per)* priest's housekeeper. **(b)** *(Bol, Ec, Per)* Indian chief, Indian native authority.

curación *nf* cure, healing; treatment; **primera —** first aid.

curadillo *nm* **(a)** *(Cook)* dried cod. **(b)** *(Tech)* bleached linen.

curado *adj* **(a)** *(Tech)* cured; hardened; tanned, prepared. **(b)** *(Chi, Per, Urug)* drunk.

curandero *nm* quack; bonesetter.

curar [1a] **1** *vt* **(a)** *(Med)* *person, illness* to cure *(de* of); *wound* to treat, dress; *(with a drug etc)* to treat *(con* with).

(b) *(fig) wrong* to remedy, put right.

(c) *meat, fish* to cure, salt; *skin* to tan; *cloth* to bleach; *wood* to season.

2 *vi* *(Med)* to get well *(de* after), recover *(de* from).

3 curarse *vr* **(a)** *(Med)* to recover, get better; *(wound etc)* to heal up; to be on a cure, go for a cure.

(b) — de to take notice of, heed; to look after.

(c) *(Bol, Chi, Per, RPl)* to get drunk; *(Mex)* to sober up.

curativo *adj* curative.

curato *nm* curacy, parish.

curazao *nm* curaçao.

curca *nf* *(Chi, Per)* hump.

curco *adj* *(Chi, Ec, Per)* hunchbacked.

curcuncho 1 *adj* **(a)** *(SAm)* hunchbacked. **(b)** *(Bol, Ec, Per)* depressed; annoyed. **2** *nm* *(SAm)* hunchback.

curda *(fam)*: **estar —, estar con la —** to be sozzled *(fam)*.

cureña *nf* gun carriage; **a — rasa** out in the open.

curia *nf* **(a)** *(Eccl: also* **— romana)** Curia, papal Curia. **(b)** *(Law)* the Bar.

curiana *nf* cockroach.

curiche *nm* *(Chi)* Negro.

curiosamente *adv* **(a)** curiously; oddly. **(b)** neatly, cleanly.

curiosear [1a] **1** *vt* to glance at, look over; to look round; to nose out.

2 *vi* to look round, wander round; to poke about, nose about; *(pej)* to snoop, pry; **— por las tiendas** to wander round the shops; **— por los escaparates** to go window-shopping.

curiosidad *nf* **(a)** *(in general)* curiosity; *(pej)* inquisitiveness; **despertar la — de uno** to arouse someone's curiosity; **la — de noticias me llevó allí** the quest for news took me there; **tenemos — de saber si . . .** we are curious to know if . . .; **estar muerto de —** to be dying of curiosity.

(b) *(object)* curiosity; curio; **—es** sights, attractions; **visitar las —es** to see the sights.

(c) neatness, cleanliness.

(d) care(fulness), conscientiousness.

curioso 1 *adj* **(a)** *(of person)* curious; eager; *(pej)* inquisitive; **— de** eager for; **estar — por** + *infin* to be curious to + *infin*, be eager to + *infin*.

(b) *object, act etc* curious, odd; quaint; **¡qué —!** how curious!, how odd!

(c) neat, clean, tidy.

(d) careful, conscientious.

(e) *(fam)* queer *(fam)*.

2 *nm*, **curiosa** *nf* **(a)** bystander, spectator, onlooker; *(pej)* busybody; **los —s de la literatura** those interested in literature.

(b) *(fam)* queer *(fam)*.

curriculum m vitae curriculum vitae, personal and professional record.

currinche *nm* **(a)** *(Typ)* apprentice journalist, cub reporter. **(b)** *(fam)* little man, nonentity.

curro *adj* *(fam)* **(a)** smart; showy, flashy. **(b)** cocky *(fam)*, brashly confident.

currutaco 1 *adj* **(a)** loud, showy, flashy.

(b) *(SAm)* short, squat.

2 *nm* **(a)** toff *(fam)*, masher *(fam)*, dude *(US)*.

(b) insignificant little man.

(c) —s *(CAm)* diarrhoea.

cursante *nmf* *(SAm)* student.

cursar [1a] **1** *vt* **(a)** *message* to send, dispatch; *order* to send out; *application* to pass on, dispatch, deal with.

(b) *subject* to study; *course* to take, attend.

(c) *place* to frequent.

2 *vi*: **el mes que cursa** the present month.

cursi 1 *adj* in bad taste, vulgar; pretentious; loud, showy, flashy; posh, genteel, pseudo-refined; affected. **2** *nmf* = **cursilón.**

cursilería *nf* bad taste, vulgarity; pretentiousness; loudness, showiness, flashiness; poshness *(fam)*, gentility, pseudo-refinement; affectation.

cursilón *nm*, **cursilona** *nf* common but pretentious person; flashy type; posh sort *(fam)*, genteel individual; affected person.

cursillista *nmf* member (of a course).

cursillo *nm* short course; short series (of lectures).

cursiva *nf* *(Typ)* italics.

cursivo *adj* cursive; *(Typ)* italic.

curso nm (a) (of river etc) course; direction; flow; — **de agua** watercourse.

(b) (Astron) course.

(c) (fig) course; **el — de la enfermedad** the course of the disease, the progress of the disease; **dejar que las cosas sigan su —** to let matters take their course; **en el — de la vida** in the course of a lifetime; **en el — de la semana** in the course of the week; **el proceso está en —** the process is going on, the process is under way; **el año en —** the current year, the present year.

(d) (Law) **moneda de — legal** legal tender.

(e) **dar — a una solicitud** to deal with an application; **dar — a su indignación** to express one's indignation; **dar — al llanto** to let one's tears flow.

(f) (School, Univ: of students) year; **los del segundo —** those in the second year, the second years.

(g) (School, Univ: subject) course; subject; **he perdido 2 —s** I failed 2 subjects, I have to repeat 2 subjects; **— acelerado** crash course; **— por correspondencia** correspondence course; **— de secretaria** secretarial course.

(h) (Fin) price; **primer — de la bolsa** opening price on the stock exchange.

cursor nm (Tech) slide.

curtido 1 adj (a) leather tanned; skin hardened, leathery; face tanned, weather-beaten (also **— a la intemperie**).

(b) (fig) **estar — en** to be expert at, be skilled in; hardships to be inured to.

2 nm (a) tanning.

(b) tanned hide.

curtidor nm tanner.

curtiduría nf, **curtiembre** nf (SAm) tannery.

curtir [3a] **1** vt (a) hide to tan.

(b) face etc to tan, bronze.

(c) to harden, inure.

2 curtirse vr (a) to become tanned, become bronzed; to get weather-beaten.

(b) to become inured.

(c) (CAm, Col, Mex, SD) to get oneself dirty, dirty one's clothes.

curva nf curve; (Aut etc) curve, bend; **— en herradura** hairpin bend; **— de nivel** contour line.

curvatura nf curvature.

curvilíneo adj curved, curvilinear.

curvo adj (a) curved; crooked, bent. (b) (Col) bow-legged. (c) (PR) left-handed.

cusca nf (a) **hacer la — a uno** to play a dirty trick on someone; to harm someone, damage someone's interests. (b) (CAm) flirt. (c) (Mex) whore, slut.

cuscurro nm crouton.

cuscha nf (CAm) liquor, rum.

cusma nf (Col, Ec, Per) sleeveless shirt, tunic.

cúspide nf (a) (Anat) cusp. (b) (Geog) summit, peak; tip, apex. (c) (Math) apex.

custodia nf (a) care, safekeeping, custody (also Law); **— preventiva** protective custody; **bajo la — de** in the care (or custody) of. (b) (Eccl) monstrance.

custodiar [1b] vt to keep, take care of, look after; to guard, watch over.

custodio nm guardian, keeper, custodian; (of house etc) caretaker; see **ángel.**

cususa nf (CAm) liquor, rum.

cutacha nf = **cuma.**

cutama nf (a) (Arg) blanket. (b) (Chi) bag, sack.

cutáneo adj cutaneous, skin (attr).

cutaras nfpl (CR, Cu, Mex), **cutarras** nfpl (CAm, Pan) sandals, rough shoes.

cúter nm (Naut) cutter.

cutí nm ticking.

cutícula nf cuticle.

cutis nm skin, complexion.

cuto adj (a) (Bol, CAm) person maimed, crippled; toothless; object damaged, spoiled. (b) (Ec) short.

cuy nm (SAm) guinea-pig.

cuya nf (Chi, Ven) gourd, drinking vessel.

cuyano nm (Chi: pej) Argentinian.

cuyo rel adj (a) whose; of whom, of which; **la señora en cuya casa nos hospedábamos** the lady in whose house we were staying; **el asunto —s detalles conoces** the matter of which you know the details, the matter whose details you know about.

(b) **en — caso** in which case; **por cuya razón** for which reason, and for this reason.

cuz: ¡ — —! interj (to dog) here boy!

CH

chabacanear [1a] *vi* (*SAm*) to say (*or* do) coarse things.

chabacanería *nf* (a) (*quality*) vulgarity, bad taste; commonness; shoddiness.
(b) (*una* —) coarse thing (to say), vulgar remark (*etc*); platitude; shoddy piece of work.

chabacano[1] *adj* joke, *play etc* vulgar, coarse, in bad taste; *article* cheap, common; *workmanship etc* shoddy, crude.

chabacano[2] *nm* (*Mex*) apricot.

chabola *nf* shack.

chacal *nm* jackal.

chacalín *nm*, **chacalina** *nf* (*CAm*) kid (*fam*), child.

chacanear [1a] *vt* (a) (*Chi*) to spur violently. (b) (*Chi*) to pester, annoy. (c) (*Bol*, *RPl*) to use daily.

chacaneo *nm* (*Bol*, *RPl*): **para el** — for daily use, ordinary.

chácara[1] *nf* (a) (*CAm*, *Col*, *Chi*) sore, ulcer. (b) (*Col*, *Pan*, *Ven*) large leather bag; (*Col*) case.

chácara[2] *nf* (*SAm*) = **chacra**.

chacarería *nf* (a) group of *chacras*. (b) (*Chi*, *Ec*, *Per*) horticulture, market gardening, truck farming (*US*); farm work.

chacarero *nm* (*SAm*) farmer, grower; market gardener, truck farmer (*US*); farm overseer; farm labourer.

chacó *nm* shako.

chacolotear [1a] *vi* to clatter.

chacoloteo *nm* clatter(ing).

chacón *nm* salamander.

chacota *nf* noisy merriment, fun (and games), high jinks; **estar de** — to be in a joking mood; **echar algo a** —, **hacer** — **de algo** to make fun of something, take something as a joke.

chacotear [1a] **1** *vi* to have fun, make merry. **2 chacotearse** *vr*: — **de algo** to make fun of something, take something as a joke.

chacotería *nf* (*RPl*) = **chacota**.

chacotero *adj*, **chacotón** *adj* (*RPl*) fond of a laugh, merry.

chacra *nf* (*SAm*) (a) small farm, smallholding, market garden, truck farm (*US*); country estate; cultivated land. (b) farmhouse. (c) farm produce.

chacuaco 1 *adj* (*SD*, *Urug*) coarse, rough; (*PR*) clumsy. **2** *nm* (*CAm*) roughly-made cigar; (*CAm*, *Mex*) cigar stub.

chacha *nf* maid, nursemaid.

chachacaste *nm* (*CAm*) liquor, brandy.

chachalaca *nf* (*CAm*, *Mex*) chatterbox.

chachar [1a] *vt* (*Bol*, *Ec*, *Per*) coca leaves to chew.

cháchara *nf* (a) chatter, idle talk, small talk; —**amorosa** sweet nothings. (b) (*Ec*) joke. (c) —**s** (*Chi*, *Mex*) things, bits and pieces; junk.

chacharachas *nfpl* (*Chi*) useless ornaments; trinkets.

chacharear [1a] **1** *vt* (*Mex*) to deal in, sell. **2** *vi* to chatter, jaw (*fam*).

chacharería *nf* (*Chi*, *Mex*) trinkets.

chacharero 1 *adj* chattering, garrulous. **2** *nm*, **chacharera** *nf* chatterbox.

chacho *nm* (a) boy, lad. (b) (*CAm*) twin. (c) (*Mex*) servant.

chafalonía *nf* (*Bol*, *Per*) worn-out gold jewellery.

chafalote 1 *adj* (*RPl*) common, vulgar. **2** *nm* = **chafarote**.

chafallar [1a] *vt* to botch, mend clumsily, make a mess of.

chafallo *nm* botched job.

chafar [1a] *vt* (a) to flatten; to crumple; to ruffle, muss up; to crease; *potatoes* (*Cook*) to mash.
(b) — **a uno, dejar chafado a uno** to crush someone; to cut someone short, shut someone up; to take someone down a peg.
(c) *deal etc* to mess up, make a hash of, spoil; **le**

chafaron el negocio they messed up the deal for him.
(d) (*Chi*) *employee* to fire (*fam*).
(e) (*Arg*) to hoax, deceive.

chafarote *nm* (*Hist*) cutlass; (*fam*) sword; (*SAm*) broadsword, big flat knife.

chafarrinada *nf* spot, stain.

chafarrinar [1a] *vt* to blot, stain.

chafarrinón *nm* spot, stain; **echar un** — **a** (*fig*) to smear, slander.

chafir(r)o *nm* (*CAm*, *Mex*: *angl*) knife.

chaflán *nm* bevel, chamfer.

chaflanar [1a] *vt* to bevel, chamfer.

chagra[1] **1** *nf* (*Col*, *Ec*) = **chacra**. **2** *nm* (*Ec*) peasant farmer.

chagra[2] *nf* (*Cu*) = **chaira**.

chagrén *nm* shagreen.

chagua *nf* (*Col*) gang; system of gang labour.

chaguar [1i] *vt* (*Arg*) *cow* to milk; *washing* to squeeze (dry).

cháguar *nm* (*Arg*, *Bol*, *Per*) agave fibre, hemp; rope of agave fibre.

cháguara *nf* (*Arg*, *Urug*) = **cháguar**.

chagüe *nm* (*CAm*) swamp, bog.

chagüite *nm* (*CAm*, *Mex*) swamp, flooded place; damp field; banana plantation.

chai(ne) *nm* (*Col*, *Mex*, *Pan*: *angl*) shoeshine.

chaira *nf* steel (*for sharpening*); shoemaker's knife; (*fam*) knife, razor, dagger.

chairar [1a] *vt* (*RPl*) to sharpen.

chal *nm* shawl.

chala *nf* (a) (*Bol*, *Chi*, *Per*, *RPl*) tender leaf of maize. (b) (*Arg*, *Bol*) money, dough (*sl*); **pelar la** — **a uno** to fleece someone.

chalado *adj* (*fam*) dotty (*fam*); cranky; ¡**estás** —! are you mad?; **estar** — **por una** to be crazy about someone.

chalán *nm* (a) dealer, huckster, (*esp*) horse dealer; (*pej*) shady businessman, shark (*fam*). (b) (*SAm*) horse breaker.

chalana *nf* barge, lighter, wherry.

chalanear [1a] **1** *vt* (a) *person* to haggle successfully with, beat down; *deal* to handle cleverly, bring off.
(b) (*SAm*) *horse* to break in, tame.
(c) (*Arg*) to pester.
(d) (*CAm*) to make fun of.
2 *vi* to bargain shrewdly.

chalar [1a] (*fam*) **1** *vt* to drive crazy, drive round the bend (*sl*). **2 chalarse** *vr* to go crazy, go off one's rocker (*sl*); — **por** to be crazy about.

chalé *nm* (*Acad*) *see* **chalet**.

chaleco *nm* waistcoat, vest (*US*); — **salvavidas** life jacket.

chalecón *adj* (*Mex*) tricky, deceitful.

chalequear [1a] *vt* (*Mex*) to steal; (*Guat*) to get by a trick.

chalet [tʃa'le] *nm*, *pl* **chalets** [tʃa'les] (*angl*, *gall*) (*rural*) villa, cottage; (*seaside*) bungalow; (*mountain*) chalet; (*town*) semi-detached house, detached house (with a garden); (*Golf etc*) clubhouse.

chalina *nf* cravat(e), floppy bow tie; (*SAm*) small shawl.

chalón *nm* (*SAm*) shawl, wrap.

chalona *nf* (*SAm*) dried meat, dried mutton.

chalote *nm* shallot.

chalupa[1] *nf* launch, boat; lifeboat; (*Ec*, *Mex*, *Per*, *PR*) narrow canoe.

chalupa[2] *nf* (*Mex*) small maize cake (with chopped meat *etc*).

chalupa[3] (*sl*) **1** *adj* crazy; **volver** — **a uno** to drive someone crazy. **2** *nm* madman, crackpot.

chamaca *nf* (*Mex etc*) girl; girlfriend, sweetheart.

chamaco *nm* (*Mex etc*) boy, child; lad, young man.

chamagoso *adj* (*Mex*) filthy; vile, loathsome.

chamarasca *nf* kindling, brushwood; brush fire.

chamaril(l)ero *nm* secondhand dealer, junk dealer.
chamarra *nf* (a) sheepskin jacket; (*CAm, Ven*) blanket, cloak. (b) (*CAm*: *fig*) fraud, trick.
chamarrear [1a] *vt* (*CAm*) to trick, swindle.
chamarrero *nm* (*Ven*) quack doctor.
chamarro *nm* (*CAm, Chi, Mex*) coarse woollen blanket.
chamba[1] *nf* (a) (*Arg, Ec*) turf, sod.
(b) (*Col, Ec*) pond, pool; (*Col, Ven*) ditch. (c) (*Guat, Mex*) work; business; occupation; (*Mex*) unproductive work; (*CAm, Mex*) cinch (*sl*); plum, sinecure, soft job.
chamba[2] *nf* fluke, lucky break; **por —** by a fluke.
chambear [1a] (*Mex*) **1** *vt* to exchange, swap, barter. **2** *vi* to work (unproductively).
chambelán *nm* chamberlain.
chambergo *nm* broad-brimmed soft hat.
chambón 1 *adj* (a) awkward, clumsy. (b) lucky. (c) slovenly. **2** *nm* clumsy but lucky player, fluky player.
chambonada *nf* (a) awkwardness, clumsiness. (b) fluke, stroke of luck, lucky shot. (c) blunder.
chambonear [1a] *vi* (*esp SAm*) to have a stroke of luck, win (*etc*) by a fluke.
chamborote *adj* (*Ec, Guat*) long-nosed.
chambra[1] *nf* housecoat; blouse; loose jacket.
chambra[2] *nf* (*Ven*) din, hubbub.
chambra[3] *nf* (*SD*) *machete*, broad knife.
chambrana *nf* (*Col, Ven*) row, uproar; brawl.
chamburgo *nm* (*Col*) pool, stagnant water.
chamelicos *nmpl* (*Chi, Per*) lumber, junk, old clothes; (*Col*) adornments.
chamizo *nm* (a) half-burned tree (*or* log *etc*). (b) thatched hut; shack, slum; (*fam*) den, joint (*sl*).
chamorro *adj* head shorn, close-cropped.
champa[1] *nf* (*SAm*) (a) sod, turf; ball of earth (*left round roots*). (b) mass of dishevelled hair, long unkempt hair. (c) (*fig*) tangled mass.
champa[2] *nf* (*CAm, Mex*) roughly-built hut.
champán *nm* champagne.
Champaña *f* Champagne.
champaña *nm* champagne.
champañazo *nm* (*Chi etc*) champagne party.
champiñón *nm* mushroom.
champú *nm* shampoo.
champudo *adj* (*SAm*) *hair* dishevelled, messy; *person* long-haired.
champurrado *nm* mixture of liquors, cocktail; (*Cu, Mex*) mixed drink (*of various ingredients*); (*fig*) mixture, mess.
champurrar [1a] *vt drinks* to mix, make a cocktail of.
champurreado *nm* (a) (*Chi, RPl*) hastily-prepared dish, hash; (*fig*) hash, botch. (b) = **champurrado**.
champurrear [1a] *vt* (*Chi, PR, RPl*) = **champurrar**; = **chapurr(e)ar**.
chamuchina *nf* (a) (*SAm*) rabble, mob; crowd of small children, mob of kids (*fam*). (b) (*Ec, Ven*) row, shindy.
chamullar [1a] *vti* (*sl*) to speak, talk; **yo también chamullo el caló** I can talk slang too; **chamullaban en árabe** they were jabbering away in Arabic.
chamuscar [1g] **1** *vt* (a) to scorch, sear, singe. (b) (*Mex*) to sell cheap. **2 chamuscarse** *vr* (a) to get scorched, singe. (b) (*Col*) to get cross, take offence.
chamusquina *nf* (a) singeing, scorching.
(b) row, quarrel, shindy; **esto huele a —** I can see there's trouble brewing, there's something nasty coming.
(c) (*Col, CR*) mob of kids.
chanada *nf* (*fam*) trick, swindle.
chanca *nf* (a) (*Arg, Chi, Ec, Per*) grinding, crushing. (b) (*Chi, Per*) beating.
chancaca *nf* (a) (*CAm*) maize cake, wheat cake. (b) (*Ec*) sore, ulcer. (c) (*SAm*) brown sugar, honey mass (*used in the preparation of chicha*).
chancadora *nf* (*SAm*) grinder, crusher.
chancar [1g] *vt* (a) (*SAm*) to grind, crush, triturate; (*fig*) to beat; to beat up; to ill-treat. (b) (*Chi, Ec*) to botch, bungle.
chance *nm* (*sometimes f*) (*SAm*: *angl*) chance; (*gall*) good luck.
chancear [1a] *vi* and **chancearse** *vr* to joke, make jokes (*de* about); to fool about, play around (*con* with); **— se de uno** to make fun of someone.
chancero *adj* joking, merry, facetious; fond of a joke.
chancillería *nf* chancery.
chancla *nf* old shoe, broken shoe; = **chancleta**.
chancleta 1 *nf* (a) slipper. (b) (*SAm*) baby girl. (c) (*Ven: Aut*) accelerator. **2** *nmf* (*fam*) good-for-nothing.
chancletero *adj* (*Ant, Col, Mex*), **chancletudo** *adj* (*Chi, Ec, Per, Ven*) common, low-class.
chanclo *nm* clog; rubber overshoe, galosh.
chancro *nm* chancre.

chancha *nf* (a) (*SAm*) sow. (b) (*Chi*) small wooden cart. (c) (*Col*: *hum*) mouth; (*Bol, Col, Chi*) **hacer la —** to play truant.
chanchería *nf* (*SAm*) pork-butcher's shop.
chanchero *nm* (*SAm*) pork butcher.
chanchi (*sl*) **1** *adj* marvellous, smashing (*sl*), jolly good (*fam*); **¡estás —!** I think you're marvellous!
2 *adv* marvellously, jolly well (*fam*); **me fue —** I had a smashing time (*sl*), it went like a bomb (*fam*).
chancho 1 *adj* (*SAm*) dirty, filthy.
2 *nm* (a) (*SAm*) pig, hog; **— salvaje** wild boar. (b) (*SAm*: *Chess etc*) blocked piece. (c) (*Chi*) = **chancadora**. (d) (*SAm*: *fig*) **son como —s** they're very thick; **hacerse el — rengo** to pretend not to notice; **quedar como —** to come off badly.
chanchullero (*fam*) **1** *adj* crooked, bent (*fam*). **2** *nm* crook, twister (*fam*).
chanchullo *nm* (*fam*) fiddle (*fam*), wangle (*fam*); crooked deal; piece of graft, dirty business; **andar en —s** to be on the fiddle, be engaged in something shady.
chanfaina *nf* (*Bol, Col, Hond, Per*) entanglement; complication; mess.
chanfle[1] *nm* (*Arg, Urug*) policeman, bobby (*sl*), cop (*sl*).
chanfle[2] *nm* (*Mex*) = **chaflán**.
chanflón *adj* misshapen; (*fig*) crude, coarse.
changa[1] *nf* (a) (*Bol, RPl*) (portering) job; odd job, occasional job. (b) (*Bol, RPl*) tip, payment (to a porter).
changa[2] *nf* (*Ant*) joke.
changador *nm* (*Bol, RPl*) porter; odd-job man.
changango *nm* (*RPl*) (a) small guitar. (b) low-class party. (c) merriment.
changarro[1] *nm* (*fam*) old car, jalopy.
changarro[2] *nm* (*Mex*) small shop.
chango 1 *adj* (a) (*Mex*) quick, sharp; alert; **¡ponte —!** wake up!, get wise! (*fam*); watch out!
(b) (*Ant, Mex*) mischievous, playful. (c) (*Mex, PR*) silly, brainless; stupidly affected. (d) (*Chi*) annoying. (e) (*Mex etc*) **la gente está changa** there are lots of people.
2 *nm*, **changa** *nf* (a) (*Mex*) small monkey. (b) (*Arg, Mex*) child; young servant.
changear [1a] *vi* (*Ant, Col, Mex*) = **chancear**.
changüí *nm* (*fam*) (a) joke. (b) trick, swindle; **dar — a** to trick, swindle.
chantaje *nm* blackmail(ing).
chantajista *nmf* blackmailer.
chantar [1a] *vt* (a) *dress etc* to put on.
(b) *object* to thrust, stick; to put. (c) **— algo a uno** to tell someone something to his face. (d) (*Per, RPl*) *object* to throw, chuck. (e) (*Chi, Per, RPl*) *person* to put, throw; **— a uno en la calle** to throw someone out; **— a uno en la cárcel** to put someone in jail. (f) (*Chi, Per, RPl*) *blow* to give. (g) (*Urug*) to leave in the lurch; to deceive, trick.
chantre *nm* (*Eccl*) precentor.
chanza *nf* joke; piece of tomfoolery, lark; **—s** jokes, banter; tomfoolery; **de —**, **en —** in fun, as a joke; **estar de —** to be joking.
chañaca *nf* (*Chi*) (a) itch, rash. (b) (*fig*) bad reputation.
chao *nm* chow.
chapa *nf* (a) (*metal*) plate, sheet; **— acanalada**, **— ondulada** (sheet of) corrugated iron.
(b) (*wood*) board, panel, sheet; veneer; **madera de 3 —s** 3-ply wood. (c) small metal plate, disc, tally; counter; check; **— de matrícula**, **— de patente** (*SAm*) licence plate. (d) (*SAm*) lock. (e) rouge; flush (on the cheeks). (f) good sense, prudence; **hombre de —** sensible man.
chapado *adj* (a) covered (*or* lined) with sheet metal (*or* veneer); **— de roble** with an oak veneer, with an oak finish; **— de oro** gold-plated.
(b) (*fig*) **— a la antigua** old-fashioned, of the old school.
chapalear [1a] *vi* (a) (*person*) to splash (about); (*water*) to lap. (b) (*hooves etc*) to clatter.
chapaleo *nm* (a) splash(ing); lap(ping). (b) clatter(ing).
chapar[1] [1a] *vt* (a) to plate, cover (*or* line) with sheet metal (*or* veneer); *wall* to tile. (b) *remark etc* to throw out, come out with.

chapar[2] [1a] vt (a) (*Col, Ec, Per*) to spy on. (b) (*Per*) to catch; to catch up with, overtake; *object* to seize, grasp.

chaparra nf kermes oak.

chaparrada nf = **chaparrón**.

chaparral nm thicket (of kermes oaks).

chaparrear [1a] vi to pour in torrents.

chaparreras nfpl (*Mex*) leather overalls.

chaparro 1 adj squat, short and chubby. 2 nm (a) kermes oak, dwarf oak. (b) (*fig*) short chubby person; (*Mex*) child, kid (*fam*).

chaparrón nm downpour, cloudburst.

chapatal nm muddy place.

chape nm (*Col, Chi*) tress, pigtail.

chapear [1a] vt (a) = **chapar**[1]. (b) (*SAm: Agr*) to weed. (c) (*Cu*) — a uno to cut someone's throat.

chapeta nf = **chapa** (e).

chapetón (*SAm*) 1 adj new (in a job); awkward, unhandy. 2 nm (a) Spaniard newly arrived in America. (b) (*Mex*) horse brass.

chapetonada nf (a) (*Chi, Per*) illness caused by a change of climate.
(b) (*Bol, Chi, Ec, RPl*) awkwardness, clumsiness; inexperience.
(c) (*SD*) sudden downpour.

chapín 1 adj (*SAm*) with crooked legs (*or* feet). 2 nm (a) clog. (b) (*CAm: hum*) Guatemalan.

chapinada nf (*CAm: hum*) action typical of a Guatemalan, dirty trick.

chapisca nf (*CAm*) maize harvest.

chapita nf (*Ec: pej*) cop (*sl*).

chapitel nm capital; (*of tower*) spire.

chapo adj (*Mex*) stunted, dwarfed.

chapodar [1a] vt (a) *tree* to prune, trim. (b) (*fig*) to cut down, reduce.

chapola nf (*Col*) butterfly.

chapote nm (*Ant, Guat, Mex*) pitch, asphalt.

chapotear [1a] 1 vt to sponge (down); to wet, moisten. 2 vi to splash about; to paddle; to dabble (one's hands).

chapoteo nm (a) sponging; moistening. (b) splashing; paddling; dabbling.

chapucear [1a] vt (a) to botch, bungle, make a mess of. (b) (*Mex*) to swindle.

chapuceramente adv roughly, crudely, shoddily; amateurishly; clumsily.

chapucería nf (a) shoddiness. (b) (una —) botched job, shoddy piece of work, mess.

chapucero 1 adj *object* rough, crude, shoddy; *work* bungling, slapdash; amateurish; *person* clumsy, bungling.
2 nm bungler, clumsy workman (*etc*); bungling amateur.

chapulú nm (*CAm*) (a) locust. (b) (*fam*) child, kid (*fam*).

chapuro nm (*CAm*) asphalt.

chapurr(e)ar [1a] vt (a) *drinks* to mix. (b) *language* to speak badly; **chapurrea el italiano** he speaks broken (*or* bad) Italian.

chapuz nm (a) ducking; plunge, dive, dip. (b) = **chapuza**.

chapuza nf (a) botched job, shoddy piece of work, mess; odd job, spare-time job. (b) (*Mex*) trick, swindle.

chapuzar [1f] 1 vt to duck, dip, plunge. 2 vi *and* **chapuzarse** vr to duck, dive.

chapuzón nm (a) dip, swim; ducking; **darse un** — to go for a dip. (b) (*of capsule*) splashdown.

chaqué nm morning coat.

chaquet [tʃa'ke] nm, pl **chaquets** [tʃa'kes] = **chaqué**.

chaqueta nf jacket; — **de cuero** leather jacket; — **de smoking** dinner jacket; **cambiar la** — = **chaquetear**.

chaquetar [1a] vi (*Mex*), **chaquetear** [1a] vi to change sides, be a turncoat, turn traitor; to go back on one's word, rat (*fam*).

chaquete nm backgammon.

chaquetero nm (*Mex, SD*) turncoat.

chaquetón nm long jacket, reefer, shooting jacket.

chaquira nf small pearl; glass bead.

charada nf charade.

charaludo adj (*Mex*) thin.

charamusca nf (a) (*SAm: also* —s) firewood, kindling. (b) (*Mex*) candy twist. (c) (*Cu, PR*) noise, row.

charanga nf (a) hullabaloo (*fam*), merry din. (b) (*Mus*) brass band; band of street musicians; (*Arg, Per*) cavalry band. (c) (*CR, Mex, Per, PR*) informal dance.

charango nm (*Bol, Chi, Per*) a small five-stringed guitar.

charanguero adj = **chapucero** 1.

charca nf pond, pool.

charco nm pool, puddle; **cruzar el —, pasar el —** to cross the water, (*esp*) to cross the herring-pond (*ie* the Atlantic).

charcón adj (*Bol, RPl*) thin, skinny.

charla nf talk, chat; (*pej*) chatter; (*pej*) talk, gossip; — **radiofónica** radio talk; — **literaria** literary talk, informal literary lecture.

charlador 1 adj talkative; gossipy. 2 nm, **charladora** nf chatterbox; gossip.

charladuría nf (*also* —s) small talk, chatter, gossip.

charlar [1a] vi to chat, talk (*de* about); (*pej*) to chatter, gossip.

charlatán 1 adj talkative; gossipy.
2 nm, **charlatana** nf (a) chatterbox; gossip; big-mouth (*sl*), indiscreet talker.
(b) (confidence) trickster; smooth-tongued salesman, clever (but untrustworthy) salesman, showman; (*Med*) quack, charlatan.

charlatanear [1a] vi to chatter away, babble on; (*pej*) to shoot one's mouth off.

charlatanería nf (a) talkativeness, garrulity. (b) (clever) salesmanship; showmanship; quackery, charlatanism. (c) sales talk, patter; hot air.

charlatanismo nm = **charlatanería** (a).

charleta nmf (*Arg*) chatterbox; gossip.

charnela nf hinge.

charol nm (a) varnish; patent leather; **calzarse las de** — (*RPl*) to do oneself a good turn, make a packet (*fam*); **darse** — to swank (*fam*), brag. (b) (*SAm*) tray.

charola nf (a) (*SAm*) tray. (b) (*CAm*) —s eyes, shiners (*sl*).

charolado adj polished, shiny.

charolar [1a] vt to varnish, japan.

charpa nf (*CAm: Mil*) pistol belt, sword belt; (*Med*) sling.

charquear [1a] vt (*SAm*) (a) *beef* to dry, jerk. (b) *person* to carve up, slash, wound severely; to beat (up).

charqui nm (*SAm*) dried beef, jerked meat; (*Chi, RPl*) dried fruit, dried vegetables; **hacer** — a uno (*fig*) = **charquear** (b).

charra nf (a) (*prov: Salamanca*) peasant woman; (*fig*) low-class woman, coarse woman. (b) (*Guat, Hond*) broad-brimmed hat. (c) (*Ec*) itch, pimple.

charrada nf (a) coarse thing, piece of bad breeding; example of bad taste.
(b) flashy ornament, vulgar adornment; tastelessly decorated object.
(c) (quality) coarseness, bad breeding; bad taste; tawdriness, gaudiness.
(d) (*Mus*) country dance.

charral nm (*CAm*) scrub, scrubland.

charramasca nf (*CAm*) firewood, kindling.

charrán[1] nm (*Orn*) tern.

charrán[2] nm rascal, villain.

charranada nf dirty trick.

charrasca nf (*Bol, Mex, RPl*) knife, sharp weapon.

charrasquear [1a] vt (a) (*Mex*) to knife, stab. (b) (*Ec, Pan, Ven*) to strum.

charretera nf epaulette; shoulder flash.

charro 1 adj (a) *person* rustic; coarse, vulgar, ill-bred.
(b) *dress etc* loud, gaudy; *object* flashy, showy; over-ornamented, decorated in bad taste.
(c) (*Mex*) picturesque, quaint.
(d) (*Mex*) skilled in horsemanship.
2 nm (a) (*prov: Salamanca*) peasant.
(b) (*pej*) rustic, boor, coarse individual; flashy sort, overdressed individual.
(c) (*Mex*) horseman, cowboy; typical Mexican.
(d) (*Mex*) wide-brimmed hat.

charrúa (*SAm*) 1 adj Uruguayan. 2 nmf Uruguayan.

chasca nf (*SAm*) mop of hair, tangled hair; tangle.

chascar [1g] 1 vt (a) *tongue etc* to click; *fingers* to snap; *whip* to crack; *gravel etc* to crunch. (b) *food* to swallow. 2 vi to click, snap; to crack; to crunch.

chascarrillo nm funny story.

chasco[1] adj (*Arg, Bol*) *hair etc* thick and crinkly, coarse.

chasco[2] nm (a) disappointment; failure, let-down; **dar un** — a uno to disappoint someone; **llevarse (un)** — to be disappointed; suffer a let-down; **¡vaya que me llevé!** I just was sick about that!
(b) trick, joke; prank; **dar** — a uno to pull someone's leg; **dar un** — a uno to play a trick on someone.

chascón adj (*Bol, Chi*) (a) *hair* dishevelled, matted, entangled. (b) (*fig*) slow, clumsy.

chasis nm, pl **chasis** (*Aut etc*) chassis; (*Phot*) plateholder.

chasque nm (*SAm*) see **chasqui**.

chasquear[1] vt (a) to disappoint, let down (*also* **dejar chasqueado**). (b) to play a trick on, make a fool of. (c) *promise* to break.

chasquear² **1** *vt* =chascar 1; (*Col, Pan*) *bit* to champ. **2** *vi* =chascar 2; (*of wood etc*) to creak; to crack, crackle; — **con la lengua** to click one's tongue.

chasqui *nm* (*SAm*) messenger, courier.

chasquido *nm* click; snap; crack; crunch; creak, crackle.

chata *nf* (a) bedpan. (b) (*Naut*) lighter, barge, transport. (c) (*RPl: Rail*) flatcar. (d) (*RPl: Aut*) transporter.

chatarra *nf* scrap iron, junk; (*Mil: hum*) medals; **vender para** — to sell for scrap.

chatarrero *nm* scrap dealer, scrap merchant.

chateo *nm* (*fam*) pub crawl (*fam*), drinking expedition; **ir de** — to go on a pub crawl.

chati *nf* (*sl*) girl, bird (*sl*); **¡oye** —**!** hey, beautiful! (*fam*).

chato **1** *adj* (a) nose flat, snub; *person* snub-nosed; **¡oye, chata!** (*fam*) hey, beautiful! (*fam*). (b) *object* flattened, blunt; *boat etc* flat; *tower etc* low, squat. (c) (*PR, RPl*) ordinary, commonplace. (d) **dejar** — **a uno** (*SAm*) to crush someone; to embarrass someone; (*Mex*) to swindle someone; **quedarse** — **con algo** to appropriate something. **2** *nm* wine glass; glass (of wine); **tomarse unos** —**s** to have a glass or two.

chatre *nm* (*Chi, Ec*) smartly-dressed.

chatungo *adj* (*sl*) =chato; **¡eh,** —**!** (*to child*) hey, lad!; **¡oye, chatunga!** (*to girl*) hey, beautiful! (*fam*).

chau *interj* (*RPl*) so long!

chaucha **1** *adj invar* (a) (*Chi, Ec: Agr etc*) ripening early; unripe, not fully grown; *birth* premature; *woman* who gives birth prematurely. (b) (*RPl*) poor-quality; insipid, tasteless, characterless; in poor taste. **2** *nf* (a) (*SAm*) early potato, small potato; (*Bol, RPl*) string bean; (*Per*) food (*in general*); **pelar la** — (*Bol, Per, RPl*) to brandish (*or use*) one's knife. (b) (*Bol, Chi*) 20-cent coin; (*Bol, Chi, Per*) money (*in general*).

chauchau *nm* (*Chi, Per*) food, chow (*sl*).

chauchera *nf* (*Chi, Ec, Per*) purse, pocketbook.

chauchero *nm* (*Chi*) errand boy; odd-job man; poorly-paid worker.

chauvinismo *nm* chauvinism.

chauvinista **1** *adj* chauvinist(ic). **2** *nmf* chauvinist.

chaval *nm* (*fam*) lad, boy, kid (*fam*); **estar hecho un** — to feel (*or look*) very young again; **es un** — he's only a kid (still).

chavala *nf* (*fam*) girl, kid (*fam*).

chavalo *nm* (*CAm, Mex, Ven*) street urchin.

chavalongo *nm* (*Arg, Chi*) fever; sunstroke; drowsiness, drowsy feeling.

chaveta *nf* cotter, cotter pin; (*Mex*) broad-bladed knife; **perder la** — (*fam*) to go off one's rocker (*sl*); to go through the roof (*fam*); **perder la** — **por una** to be crazy about a girl.

chavetear [1a] *vt* (*Cu, Per*) to knife.

chavo *nm* (*fam*): **no tener un** —, **estar sin un** — to be stony-broke (*fam*), be stone-broke (*US*).

chavó *interj* (*sl*) jolly good! (*fam*); well I'm blowed!

che *interj* (*Bol, RPl*) hey!, hi!, I say!; (*Hond, Ven*) who cares!, so what?

checar [1g] *vt* (*Mex etc*) =chequear.

checo **1** *adj* Czech. **2** *nm*, **checa** *nf* Czech. **3** *nm* (*language*) Czech.

checoslovaco **1** *adj* Czechoslovak. **2** *nm*, **checoslovaca** Czechoslovak.

Checoslovaquia *f* Czechoslovakia.

cheche *nm* (*Cu, PR*) bully, braggart.

chécheres *nmpl* (*CAm, Col, Pan*) things, gear (*fam*); junk, lumber.

chechón *adj* (*Mex*) *child* spoilt, pampered.

cheikh [tʃeik] *nm* sheik(h).

cheira *nf* =chaira.

chelear [1a] *vt* (*CAm*) to whiten, whitewash.

chelín *nm* (*Fin*) shilling.

chelo¹ *nm* (*Mus: fam*) 'cellist.

chelo² *adj* (*Mex*) fair, blond(e).

chepa **1** *nf* hump. **2** *nm* hunchback.

cheque *nm* (*angl*) cheque, check (*US*); — **abierto** open cheque; — **en blanco** blank cheque; — **cruzado** crossed cheque; — **sin fondos**, — **sin provisión** bad cheque; — **al portador** cheque payable to bearer; — **de viajero** traveller's cheque; **pagar mediante** — to pay by cheque.

chequear [1a] *vt* (*esp SAm: angl*) *document, account, health etc* to check; *person* to check (up) on; (*CAm, PR, SD*) *cheque* to issue, write; to issue a cheque for; (*CAm, Col, PR*) *luggage* to register; (*Col*) to note down, record, register; (*Mex: Aut*) to service, overhaul, check.

chequeo *nm* (*esp SAm: angl*) check; checking-up; (*Med*) check-up; (*Aut*) servicing, overhaul(ing), checking.

chequera *nf* (*SAm*) cheque book.

cherife *nm* (*SAm: angl*) sheriff (*US*).

cheruto *nm* cheroot.

cheurón *nm* (*Her*) chevron.

chévere **1** *adj* (*Ant, Col, Mex*) smashing (*sl*), super (*fam*). **2** *nm* (*Cu, PR*) bully, braggart.

chibato *nm* (*etc*) see **chivato** (*etc*).

chibola *nf* (*CAm*), **chibolo** *nm* (*Col, Ec, Hond, Per*) bump, swelling; wen.

chic **1** *adj invar* chic, smart, elegant. **2** *nm* elegance; composure.

chica¹ *nf* girl; maid, servant.

chica² *nf* (*RPl*) plug of chewing tobacco.

chicana *nf* (*SAm: gall*) chicanery.

chicanear [1a] *vi* (*SAm: gall*) to use trickery, be cunning.

chicanero *adj* (a) (*SAm*) tricky, crafty. (b) (*Ec*) mean.

chicle *nm* chewing gum; — **de burbuja**, — **de globo** bubble gum.

chiclear [1a] *vi* (*CAm, Mex*) (a) to extract gum (*for chewing*). (b) to chew gum.

chico **1** *adj* (a) small, little, tiny; **dejar** — **a uno** to put someone in the shade. (b) (*Mex: iro*) big, huge. **2** *nm* (a) boy; child, youngster, lad; (*in direct address*) my boy, old boy, old man; **es un buen** — he's a good lad (*or chap, fellow*); **los** —**s del equipo** the chaps in the team; **los** —**s de la oficina** the fellows at the office; — **de la calle** street urchin; — **de oficina**, — **para los recados** office boy; **como** — **con zapatos nuevos** as happy as a sandboy; **me han tomado por el** — **del portero** they think I must know everything. (b) (*SAm: Billiards, Cards etc*) game, round; first game.

chicolear [1a] **1** *vi* (a) (*fam*) to flirt, murmur sweet nothings, say nice things. (b) (*Arg*) to amuse oneself, have a good time; to do childish things. **2 chicolearse** *vr* (*Per*) to amuse oneself.

chicoleo *nm* (a) (*fam*) compliment, flirtatious remark; **decir** —**s** to say nice things. (b) (*fam*) flirting; **estar de** — to be in a flirtatious mood. (c) (*Arg*) childish thing; **no andemos con** —**s** let's be serious.

chicolero *adj* flirtatious.

chicoría *nf* chicory.

chicota *nf* fine girl; (*pej*) big girl, hefty wench.

chicotazo *nm* (*SAm*) lash, swipe.

chicote *nm* (a) big chap, fine lad. (b) (*Naut*) piece of rope, rope end; (*SAm*) whip, lash. (c) (*fam*) cigar; (*Arg, Col, Mex, Ven*) cigar stub. (d) knotted handkerchief.

chicotear [1a] **1** *vt* (*SAm*) to whip, lash; (*SAm*) to beat up; (*Col*) to kill. **2** *vi* (*SAm: of tail etc*) to lash about.

chicha¹ *nf* (a) (*SAm*) chicha, maize liquor, corn liquor (*US*); — **de uva** (*Arg, Per*) unfermented grape juice; **como** — (*Col*) in plenty, in abundance; **no es ni** — **ni limonada** it's neither one thing nor the other; it's useless; it's dull, it's uninteresting; **sacar la** — **a uno** (*RPl*) to make the utmost use of someone; to make someone sweat. (b) (*RPl*) blood. (c) (*CAm, Ec*) rage, bad temper; **estar de** — to be in a bad mood.

chicha² *nf* (*Per*) thick-soled shoe.

chicha³ *nf* (*fam*) meat; **tener poca(s)** —**(s)** to be thin, be weak.

chícharo *nm* pea, chickpea.

chicharra *nf* (a) harvest bug, cicada; **es como** — **en verano** it's nasty, it's unpleasant; **canta la** — it's terribly hot. (b) (*fig*) chatterbox. (c) (*Elec*) bell, buzzer. (d) (*Guat, Hond, SD, Ven*) crackling (*of pork*).

chicharrero *nm* oven, hothouse; (*fig*) suffocating heat.

chicharrón *nm* (a) crackling (*of pork*); piece of burnt meat; **estar hecho un** — (*Cook*) to be burnt to a cinder; (*person*) to be as red as a lobster. (b) (*fig*) sunburnt person. (c) (*Cu*) flatterer.

chiche **1** *adj and adv* (*CAm*) easy, simple; easily; **está** — it's a cinch (*sl*). **2** *nm* (a) (*SAm*) breast, teat.

(b) (*SAm: fig*) precious thing, delightful object; fancy jewel, trinket; small toy; trustworthy person, clever person; well-dressed person; elegant place, nice room (*etc*). **3** *nf* (*Mex*) nursemaid.

chichear [1a] *vti* to hiss.

chicheo *nm* hiss, hissing.

chichera *nf* (*CAm*) jail.

chichería *nf chicha* tavern; *chicha* factory.

chichero *nm chicha* vendor (*or* maker).

chichi *nf* (*Mex*) **(a)** teat. **(b)** nursemaid.

chichigua *nf* **(a)** (*CAm, Mex*) nursemaid. **(b)** (*Ant*) kite. **(c)** (*Mex*) tree that gives shade.

chicho *nm* **(a)** curl, ringlet. **(b)** curler, curling iron.

chichón¹ *adj* **(a)** (*RPl*) merry, jovial. **(b)** (*CAm*) easy, straightforward.

chichón² *nm* bump, lump, swelling.

chichonear [1a] *vi* (*RPl*) to joke.

chifa *nf* (*Per*) Chinese restaurant.

chifla *nf* hiss, hissing, whistling.

chiflado (*fam*) *adj* **1** daft, barmy (*sl*); cranky, crackpot; **estar — con, estar — por** to be crazy about.
2 *nm* crazy man, crank, crackpot.

chifladura *nf* **(a)** =**chifla**.
(b) (*fam: in general*) daftness, craziness.
(c) (*fam: una —*) whim, fad, mania; crazy idea, wild scheme; **su — es el ajedrez** his mania is chess, he is crazy about chess; **ese amor no es más que una —** what he calls love is just a stupid infatuation.

chiflar [1a] **1** *vt* **(a)** (*Theat*) to hiss, boo, whistle at; **whistle to blow**.
(b) (*fam*) to drink, knock back (*sl*).
(c) (*fam*) to entrance, captivate; to drive crazy; **me chifla ese conjunto** I rave about that group, I think that group is smashing (*sl*); **me chiflan los helados** I just adore ice cream; **a mí no me chiflan los eslobodios** I don't exactly go overboard for the Slobodians (*fam*); **esa chica le chifla** (*or* **tiene chiflado**) he's crazy about that girl.
2 *vi* to whistle, hiss; (*Guat, Mex: of birds*) to sing.
3 chiflarse *vr* **(a)** (*fam*) to go barmy (*sl*), go crazy; **— con, — por** to be (*or* go) crazy about.
(b) **—las** (*CAm*) to die.

chifle *nm* **(a)** whistle; call, bird call. **(b)** (*Hist, also Ant, Guat*) powder horn, powder flask.

chiflido *nm* whistle, shrill sound; hiss.

chiflón *nm* **(a)** (*Arg, Col, Per, Urug*) draught, blast (of air); (*CAm, Mex*) gale.
(b) (*Chi, Guat, Ven*) rapids, violent current; (*CAm*) waterfall; (*Mex*) flume, race; (*Mex*) nozzle.

chifonía *nf* (*Mus*) organistrum.

Chile *m* Chile.

chile *nm* **(a)** (*Bot, Cook*) chili, red pepper. **(b)** (*CAm: fig*) lie.

chilenismo *nm* chilenism, word (*or* phrase *etc*) peculiar to Chile.

chileno, chileño 1 *adj* Chilean. **2** *nm*, **chilena** *nf*, **chileña** *nf* Chilean.

chilicote *nm* (*Arg, Bol*) cricket.

chilpayate, chilpayata *nmf* (*Mex*) child.

chilla¹ *nf* thin board; weatherboard, clapboard (*US*).

chilla² *nf* (*Arg, Chi*) fox.

chilla³ *nf* (*Mex*) **(a)** (*Theat*) gods, gallery. **(b)** poverty; **estar en la —** to be very poor.

chilla³ *nf* (*Hunting*) call.

chillador *adj* howling, screeching, screaming; blaring; squealing; creaking.

chillante *adj* **(a)** =**chillador**. **(b)** (*fig*) =**chillón (b)**.

chillar [1a] **1** *vi* **(a)** (*of wild animal, cat etc*) to howl; (*of mouse*) to squeak; (*of pig*) to squeal; (*of bird*) to screech, squawk; (*of person*) to yell; to shriek, scream; (*of radio*) to blare; (*of brakes*) to screech, squeal; (*of door*) to creak; (*of frying*) to sizzle; **— a uno** to yell at someone, scream at someone.
(b) (*of colours*) to scream, jar, be loud.
(c) (*SAm: fig*) to shout, protest; **no —** (*Arg, PR*) to keep one's mouth shut, not say a word; (*Hond, PR*) to squeal, turn informer.
2 chillarse *vr* **(a)** (*SAm*) to complain (*con* to), protest (*con* to).
(b) (*Col, Ec, Mex, Per, PR*) to get cross; to take offence.
(c) (*CAm*) to get embarrassed.

chillería *nf* row, hubbub.

chillido *nm* howl; squeak; squeal; screech; squawk; yell, shriek, scream; blare; creak; sizzling.

chillo *nm* **(a)** (*CAm*) debt. **(b)** (*PR*) rabble, mob. **(c)** (*Ec*) anger; loud protest.

chillón¹ *adj* **(a)** *person* loud, shrill, noisy; *sound, voice* shrill, strident; harsh; piercing. **(b)** *colour* loud, gaudy, lurid.

chillón² *nm* (*Tech*) small nail, panel pin, finishing nail (*US*).

chimal *nm* (*Mex*) dishevelled hair, mop of hair.

chimar [1a] *vt* **(a)** (*CAm*) to scratch. **(b)** (*Mex, Nic*) to annoy, bother.

chimba¹ *nf* (*Chi, Per*) opposite bank (of a river); (*Chi*) poor quarter (*on other side of river*); (*Per*) ford.

chimba² *nf* (*Col, Ec*) pigtail.

chimbar [1a] *vt* (*Ec, Per*) river to ford.

chimbero *adj* (*Chi*) =**arrabalero**.

chimbo 1 *adj* **(a)** (*Col, Ven*) worn-out, wasted, old. **(b)** (*Col*) *cheque* bad. **2** *nm* (*Col*) piece of meat.

chimenea *nf* **(a)** chimney; (*Naut etc*) funnel; smokestack; (*Min*) shaft; (*Mountaineering*) chimney; **— de aire** air shaft; **— refrigeradora** cooling tower.
(b) (*in room*) hearth, fireplace; **— (francesa)** fireplace, mantelpiece; chimney piece.

chimiscolear [1a] *vi* (*Mex*) to gossip; to gad about.

chimiscolero *nm*, **chimiscolera** *nf* (*Mex*) gossip; gadabout.

chimpancé *nm* chimpanzee.

chimpín *nm* (*Ec*) brandy, liquor.

chimuelo *adj* (*SAm*) toothless.

China *f* China.

china¹ *nf* (*Cook etc*) china; chinaware; porcelain.

china² *nf* **(a)** (*Geol*) pebble; guessing game played with pebbles; **le tocó la —** he had bad luck; he carried the can (*sl*). **(b)** (*Col*) spinning top.

china³ *nf* **(a)** (*SAm*) (Indian) woman, (half-breed) girl; (*Bol, CAm, RPl*) nursemaid; (*Chi, Ec, Per*) servant, girl; (*SAm: pej*) mistress, concubine; (*Col*) elegant young lady.
(b) (*Tech: SAm*) fan, blower.

china⁴ *nf* (*Ant, Mex, Ven*) orange.

chinarro *nm* large pebble, stone.

chinazo *nm* blow from a stone; **le tocó el —** he had bad luck; he carried the can (*sl*).

chinchada *nf* (*RPl*) tug-of-war.

chinchal *nm* (*Ant*) tobacco stall; small shop.

chinchar [1a] (*fam*) **1** *vt* to pester, bother, annoy; **me chincha tener que** + *infin* it upsets me to have to + *infin*.
2 chincharse *vr* to get cross, get upset; **¡chínchate!** get stuffed! (*sl*); **¡para que te chinches!** so there!; and you can lump it!; **¡y que se chinchen los demás!** and the rest can go chase themselves! (*fam*).

chincharrero *nm* (*Col, Ec, Per*) fishing boat.

chinche *m or f* (*Acad: f*) **(a)** (*Ent*) bug, (*esp*) bedbug; **caer** (*or* **morir**) **como —s** to die like flies.
(b) drawing pin, thumbtack (*US*).
(c) (*fig*) nuisance; annoying person, pest, bore; (*Col, Pan*) naughty child.

chincheta *nf* drawing pin, thumbtack (*US*).

chinchibí *nm* (*Bol, CAm, Chi: angl*), **chinchibirra** *nf* (*Arg: angl*) ginger beer.

chinchilla *nf* chinchilla.

chinchín¹ *nm* **(a)** street music, tinny music. **(b)** (*RPl*) baby's rattle.

chinchín² *nm* (*Ant, Ven*) drizzle.

chinchona *nf* quinine.

chinchorrería *nf* **(a)** fussiness; critical nature, disrespectful manner; impertinence. **(b)** piece of gossip; malicious tale.

chinchorrero *adj* **(a)** fussy (about details); critical, disrespectful; impertinent. **(b)** gossipy; malicious.

chinchorro *nm* **(a)** net, dragnet, trawl. **(b)** rowing boat, dinghy. **(c)** (*Ant, Col, Pan, Ven*) hammock; poor tenement; (*Ant*) little shop.

chinchoso *adj* **(a)** full of bugs. **(b)** =**chinchorrero**. **(c)** tiresome, annoying; boring. **(d)** (*Col, Ec, Per, PR*) touchy, irritable.

chinear [1a] **1** *vt* (*CAm*) *child* to carry in one's arms; to care for; (*pej*) to spoil. **2** *vi* (*Chi, RPl*) to have an affair with a half-breed girl.

chinela *nf* slipper, mule; clog.

chinero¹ *nm* china cupboard.

chinero² *adj* (*Chi, Ec*) fond of the (half-breed) girls.

chinesco *adj* Chinese.

chinetero *adj* (*Arg*) =**chinero²**.

chinga *nf* **(a)** (*CAm, Ven*) fag end, cigar stub; (*fig*) drop, small amount; **una — de agua** a drop of water. **(b)** (*Ven*) drunkenness. **(c)** (*Mex*) thrashing.

chingadura *nf* (*Chi*) failure.

chingana *nf* **(a)** (*Bol, Chi, Ec, Per, RPl*) dive (*fam*), tavern, cheap dance hall. **(b)** (*Chi, RPl*) wild party.

chinganear [1a] *vi* (*Bol, Chi, Ec, Per, RPl*) to go on the town, live it up (*fam*).

chinganero (*Bol, Chi, Ec, Per, RPl*) **1** *adj* fond of living it up, wildly social. **2** *nm* owner of a *chingana*.

chingar [1h] **1** vt (a) (CAm) to dock, cut off the tail of.
(b) (Mex, Salv) to annoy.
(c) (Arg) shot to aim badly, miss with; attempt to fail in.
(d) (Ven) to carry on one's shoulder.
2 vi (a) to drink too much.
(b) (CAm) to joke.
3 chingarse vr (a) (fam) to get sozzled (fam).
(b) (SAm) to fail, fall through, come to nothing; la fiesta se chingó the party was a failure; el cohete se chingó the rocket failed to go off, the rocket was a dud.

chingo 1 adj (a) (CAm, Pan) dress short; knife blunt; animal docked, tailless; person in one's underclothes, bare.
(b) (Ven) small, tiny; nose flat, snub.
(c) (Ven) estar — por algo to be crazy about something.
2 nm (a) (Col, Ec) colt.
(b) (Col, Pan) small boat.
(c) (CAm) —s underclothes.

chingue 1 adj (Chi) stinking, repulsive. **2** nm (Chi) skunk.

chinguear [1a] vt etc (CAm) = **chingar.**

chinguirito nm (Cu, Mex) rough liquor, firewater; (Cu, Per) swig (of liquor: fam).

chinita[1] nf small stone, pebble; **poner** —s en el camino to lay a trail of pebbles; **poner** —s a uno (fig) to make trouble for someone.

chinito nm, **chinita**[2] nf (a) (RPl) servant. (b) (SAm: in direct address) dear, dearest.

chino[1] **1** adj Chinese.
2 nm, **china** nf Chinese; (m also) Chinaman.
3 nm (language) Chinese; (fig) Greek, double Dutch; **ni que hablara en** — ... I couldn't have understood less even if he'd been talking Chinese.

chino[2] nm (Geol) pebble, stone.

chino[3] **1** adj (a) (CAm) bald, hairless.
(b) (Mex) curly, kinky.
(c) (CAm, Cu) angry, furious; **estar** — to be angry; **estar** — por algo to be crazy about something.
2 nm (a) (SAm) half-breed; (Arg, Chi, Par, Ven) Indian; (Per: also — cholo) offspring of Indian and Negress; (Cu) offspring of mulatto and Negress; (Col, Chi, Ec, Ven) servant; (Col) street urchin; (SAm: in direct address) dear, dearest; **quedar como un** — (Chi, PR, RPl) to come off badly; **trabajar como un** — (Chi, PR, RPl) to work like a slave.
(b) (Andalusia, CR, Mex) pig.
(c) —s (Mex) curls.
(d) (Arg, CAm, Cu) anger; **le salió el** — he got angry; **tener un** — to be angry.

chinorri nf (sl) dame (sl), wench, bint (sl).

chipe 1 adj (CAm) (a) weak, sickly. (b) whining, snivelling. **2** nmf (CAm, Col, Mex) baby, child.

chipear [1a] vt (CAm) to bother, pester.

chipi adj etc = **chipe.**

chipichipi nm (prov, SAm) continuous drizzle, mist.

chipión nm (CAm) telling off.

chipirón nm squid.

chipotear [1a] vt (CAm) to slap.

Chipre f Cyprus.

chipriota, chipriote 1 adj Cyprian, Cypriot. **2** nmf Cypriot.

chiquear [1a] **1** vt (Cu, Mex) to spoil, indulge; to flatter, suck up to (fam).
2 chiquearse vr (a) (Mex) to demand flattery, expect to be flattered.
(b) (CAm) to swagger along.

chiqueo nm (a) (Cu, Mex) piece of flattery; —s flattery, toadying. (b) (CAm) swagger.

chiquero nm pigsty; (Taur) bull pen; (RPl) hen run.

chiquilicuatro nm (fam) young rascal, whippersnapper; schemer.

chiquilín nm (CAm, Mex, RPl) tiny tot, small boy.

chiquillada nf childish prank; childish thing (to do); eso son —s that's kid's stuff, that's for children.

chiquillería nf: una — a crowd of youngsters, a mob of kids (fam); llevar la — to take the kids.

chiquillo nm, **chiquilla** nf kid (fam), youngster, child.

chiquitín 1 adj very small, tiny. **2** nm, **chiquitina** nf small child, tiny tot.

chiquito 1 adj very small, tiny.
2 nm, **chiquita** nf kid (fam), youngster; **andarse en chiquitas** to beat about the bush, fuss about details.
3 nm (RPl): un — a bit, a little; ¡espera un —! wait a moment!

chiquitura nf (a) (CAm, RPl) small thing; insignificant detail. (b) (CAm) = **chiquillada.**

chira nf (Col) rag, tatter; (CAm) wound, sore.

chirajos nmpl (CAm) lumber, junk; (Col) rags, tatters.

chirajoso adj (CAm) ragged, tattered.

chircal nm (Col) brickworks, tileworks.

chiribita nf (a) spark; **echar** —s, estar que echa —s to be furious, blow one's top (fam); le hacían —s los ojos her eyes sparkled, her eyes lit up.
(b) —s (fam) spots before the eyes.
(c) (Bot) daisy.

chiribitil nm attic, garret; den; cubbyhole; (pej) slum, hole.

chirigota nf joke; (person) laughing stock; **hacer de uno una** — to make a laughing stock out of someone.

chirigotero adj full of jokes, facetious.

chirimbolo nm thingummyjig (fam); strange object, oddlooking implement; —s things, gear, equipment; lumber, junk; (Cook) kitchen things.

chirimía nf hornpipe.

chirimoya nf custard apple.

chirinada nf (a) (RPl) failure, disaster. (b) = **chirinola.**

chirinola nf (a) fuss, row; heated discussion; lengthy conversation, lively talk; **pasar la tarde de** — to spend the afternoon deep in conversation.
(b) trifle, triviality, unimportant thing.

chiripa nf (Billiards) lucky break; (fig) lucky event, fluke, stroke of luck; de — (SAm), por — by a fluke, by chance.

chiripá nm (Bol, Chi, RPl) kind of blanket worn as trousers; **gente de** — country people, peasants.

chiripero 1 adj lucky, fluky. **2** nm lucky sort.

chirivía nf (a) (Bot) parsnip. (b) (Orn) wagtail.

chirivisco nm (CAm) firewood, kindling.

chirle adj (a) soup etc watery, wishy-washy (fam).
(b) (fig) flat, dull, wishy-washy (fam); **poeta** — mere versifier, uninspired poet.

chirlo nm gash, slash (in the face); long scar.

chirola nf (CAm, PR, SD), **chirona** nf (fam) jug (sl), jail; **estar en** — to be in jug.

chiros nmpl (Col) rags, tatters.

chiroso adj (CAm, Col) ragged, tattered.

chirota nf (CAm) mannish woman; shameless woman.

chirriado adj (Col) witty; merry, jovial.

chirriar [1b] vi (a) (of cricket etc) to chirp, sing; (of bird) to chirp; to screech, squawk; (of wheel, hinge, door) to creak, squeak; (of brakes) to screech, squeal; (of frying) to hiss, sizzle; (of person) to sing (or play) out of tune.
(b) (Col) to shiver (with cold etc).
(c) (Col) to go on a spree (fam).

chirrido nm shrill sound, high-pitched unpleasant sound; chirp(ing); screech(ing), squawk(ing); creak(ing), squeak(ing); squeal(ing); sizzle, sizzling.

chirrión nm (a) tumbrel. (b) (CAm, Col, Mex, Pan) whip. (c) (CAm) string, line. (d) (CAm) chat, conversation (esp between lovers).

chirrionar [1a] vt (Col, Mex) to whip, lash.

chirrisco adj (a) (CAm, Ven) very small, tiny. (b) (Mex) rude, obscene; **viejo** — dirty old man.

chirusa nf (RPl) girl, child; low-class woman.

chis interj sh!

chiscón nm shack, hovel, slum.

chischís nm (Col, Hond, Pan, PR) drizzle.

chisgarabís nm (fam) meddler, nosey parker; good-for-nothing.

chisme nm (a) (Tech) gadget, contrivance, jigger (sl); —s things, gear, tackle.
(b) (fig) thing, whatnot (fam), thingummyjig (fam); **dáme el** — ese give me that whatsit, please (fam); —s (fig) paraphernalia, things, odds and ends.
(c) (fig) piece of gossip, tale; —s gossip, tittle-tattle, tales; **no me vengas con esos** —s don't bring those tales to me, I don't want to hear your tittle-tattle.
(d) es un — he's worthless, he's a dead loss.

chismear [1a] vi to gossip, tell tales, spread scandal.

chismería nf, **chismerío** nm (PR, RPl) gossip, tittle-tattle, scandal.

chismero adj and n = **chismería.**

chismorrear [1a] vi = **chismear.**

chismorreo nm = **chismería.**

chismoso 1 adj gossiping, scandalmongering. **2** nm, **chismosa** nf talebearer, scandalmonger.

chispa 1 nf (a) spark (also Elec); (fig) sparkle, gleam; **echar** —s (fig), **estar que echa** —s (fig) to be hopping mad.
(b) drop (esp of rain); —s sprinkling (of rain); **caen** —s it's damping, there are a few drops falling.
(c) flake; small particle, (esp) small diamond.
(d) (fig) bit, tiny amount; **ni** — not the least bit, nothing at all; **eso no tiene (ni)** — de gracia that's not in the least bit funny; **si tuviera una** — de inteligencia if he had an atom of intelligence.

(e) (*fig*) sparkle, wit; life; **el cuento tiene —** the story has some wit; **dar —s** to show oneself to be bright (*or* lively, efficient); **no da —** it's awfully dreary; he's utterly dull; **ser una —, tener (mucha) —** to be a lively sort.

(f) (*fam*) drunkenness; drunk (*fam*); **coger** (*or* **pillar**) **una —** to get tight; **estar con la —, tener la —** to be tight.

(g) (*Mex*) light two-wheeled carriage.

(h) (*Guat, Mex*) **dar —** to work, be successful, yield results.

(i) (*Col*) rumour.

2 *adj invar* (*fam*) **(a) estar —** to be tight.

(b) (*Mex*) funny, amusing.

chisparse [1a] *vr* **(a)** (*Col, PR*) =**achisparse. (b)** (*Guat, Mex*) to run away, slip off.

chispazo *nm* **(a)** spark (*also fig*); **primeros —s** (*fig*) first signs, opening shots, intimations. **(b)** (*fig*) = **chisme (c).**

chispeante *adj* (*fig*) sparkling, scintillating.

chispear [1a] **1** *vi* **(a)** to spark (*also Elec*).

(b) (*fig*) to sparkle, scintillate.

(c) (*Meteorol*) to drizzle, spot with rain.

(d) (*Col*) to gossip, spread scandal.

2 chispearse *vr* (*Arg, SD*) =**achisparse.**

chispero 1 *adj* (*Col, SD*) gossiping, scandalmongering. **2** *nm* underworld Madrid character.

chispita *f* (*fam*): **una — de vino** a drop of wine.

chisporrotear [1a] *vi* to throw out sparks; (*esp Cook*: *of oil etc*) to hiss, splutter; (*of bacon etc*) to sizzle; (*of burning wood*) to crackle.

chistar [1a] *vi*: **no —** not to say a word; **lo aceptó sin —** he took it without a word; **nadie chistó** nobody spoke up, nobody answered back.

chiste *nm* joke, funny story; **— goma** shaggy-dog story; **— verde** dirty story; **caer en el —** to get the point of the story, get it; **dar en el —** to guess right; **hacer — de algo, tomar algo a —** to take something as a joke; **¡aquello tiene —!** (*iro*) I suppose you think that's funny?; **no veo el —** I don't get it; what's funny about that?

chistera *nf* **(a)** fish basket; (*Sport*) long curved variety of pelota racquet. **(b)** (*fam*) top hat, topper (*fam*).

chistosamente *adv* funnily, amusingly; wittily.

chistoso 1 *adj* funny, amusing; witty. **2** *nm*, **chistosa** *nf* wit, amusing person.

chistu *nm* (*Basque*) flute.

chistulari *nm* (*Basque*) flute player, flautist.

chita[1]: **a la — callando** quietly; unobtrusively; (*pej*) on the quiet, on the sly.

chita[2] *nf* **(a)** anklebone; *boys' game played with an ankle bone;* **dar en la —** to hit the nail on the head; **no se me da una —, (no) me importa una —** I don't care two hoots (*de* about).

(b) (*Mex*) net bag; money; small savings.

chiticalla *nmf* (*fam*) quiet sort, clam.

chiticallando *see* **chita**[1].

chito, chitón *interj* sh!

chiva *nf* **(a)** (*Agr, Zool*) kid; (*SAm*) goat, nanny-goat; sheep.

(b) (*SAm*) goatee (beard).

(c) (*Col, Pan*) bus; car.

(d) (*CAm*) blanket, bedcover.

(e) (*PR, RPl*) naughty little girl; (*Chi, Hond*) mannish woman; (*Col, Ec, PR, SD, Urug*) immoral woman.

(f) (*Hond, RPl*) rage, tantrum (*fam*).

(g) (*Ven*) knapsack.

chivar [1a] (*prov, SAm*) **1** *vt* to annoy, upset; to swindle. **2 chivarse** *vr* **(a)** to get annoyed. **(b)** = **chivatear (a).**

chivatazo *nm* (*fam*) tip-off; **dar —** to inform, give a tip-off.

chivatear [1a] **1** *vi* **(a)** (*fam*) to split (*fam*; *contra* on), inform (*contra* on), squeal (*sl*).

(b) (*Chi, Ec, Per*) to shout, make a hullabaloo (*fam*); to jump about; (*Ec, Per, RPl*) to indulge in horse-play, have a noisy free-for-all.

(c) (*Ven*) to create a big impression.

2 chivatearse *vr* (*Cu*) to get scared.

chivato *nm* **(a)** (*Agr, Zool*) kid.

(b) (*fam*) stool pigeon), informer.

(c) (*SAm*) child, kid (*fam*).

(d) (*Col*) rascal, villain.

(e) (*Bol*) apprentice, mate.

(f) (*Ven*) outstanding individual.

(g) (*Chi*) cheap liquor, firewater.

chivearse [1a] *vr* (*Mex*) to get scared.

chivera *nf* (*CAm, Col*) goatee (beard).

chivero *nm* **(a)** (*Col*) busdriver. **(b)** (*Ec*) brawler. **(c)** (*Cu, PR*) intriguer.

chivo *nm* **(a)** (*Agr, Zool*) kid; goat; billy goat; **esto huele a —** (*PR, RPl*) this smells suspicious.

(b) (*CAm*) dice; game of dice.

(c) (*Ant*) fraud; plot, intrigue; (*Comm*) smuggling; illegal trading; contraband, smuggled goods.

(d) (*Col, Ec, Hond, RPl, Ven*) rage, fit of anger; **comer —** (*Col, Ven*), **ponerse como —** (*Ant, CAm*) to get furious.

(e) (*Mex*) day's wages.

(f) (*Cu*) punch, blow.

(g) (*Ec, Guat*) naughty boy.

chivón (*Cu*) **1** *adj* annoying, tedious. **2** *nm*, **chivona** *nf* bore.

chocante *adj* **(a)** startling, striking; odd, strange; noteworthy; **es — que . . .** it is odd that . . ., it is surprising that . . .; it is noteworthy that . . .; **lo — es que . . .** the odd thing about it is that . . .

(b) shocking, scandalous.

(c) (*esp SAm*) tiresome, tedious, annoying; impertinent; (*Arg*) offensive; (*Mex*) unpleasant.

chocantería *nf* (*SAm*) **(a)** impertinence. **(b)** coarse joke.

chocar [1g] **1** *vt* **(a)** to shock; to startle, surprise; **me choca que no lo hayan hecho** I am surprised that they haven't done it; **ello me chocó bastante** it gave me rather a jolt; it did surprise me rather.

(b) (*Elec*) to give a shock to.

(c) *glasses* to clink; *hand* to shake; **¡chócala!** (*fam*) put it there! (*fam*), shake (on it)!; **— la mano con uno** to shake hands with someone.

2 *vi* **(a)** to shock; to be surprising, be startling, be odd; **no es de —** it's not all that surprising.

(b) (*Aut etc*) to collide, crash; (*of glasses*) to clink; (*of plates*) to clatter; (*Mil*) to clash; **— con** to collide with, crash into, smash against; to hit, strike; **el buque chocó con una mina** the ship struck a mine; **el balón chocó con el poste** the ball crashed into the post; **por fin chocó con el jefe** finally he fell out with (*or* clashed with) the boss; **esta teoría choca con dificultades** this theory runs into (*or* up against) difficulties.

chocarrear [1a] *vi* **(a)** to clown, act the fool. **(b)** to tell rude jokes.

chocarrería *nf* **(a)** (*quality*) coarseness, vulgarity; scurrility; clownishness. **(b)** (*una —*) coarse joke, dirty story; clownish act.

chocarrero *adj* coarse, vulgar, rude; scurrilous; clownish.

choclo[1] *nm* clog; sandal; overshoe; (*Mex*) low-heeled shoe; **meter el —** (*Mex*) to put one's foot in it.

choclo[2] *nm* **(a)** (*SAm*) ear of (tender) maize, cob of sweet corn; Indian maize stew.

(b) (*Chi*) **—s** children's arms, children's legs.

(c) (*Per*) bunch; group; **un — de** (*fig*) a group of, a lot of.

(d) (*Arg*) difficulty, trouble; annoyance; burden, task.

choco[1] (*Chi, Ec*) **1** *adj* curly, curly-haired. **2** *nm* poodle.

choco[2] *adj* (*Bol, Col, Ec, RPl*) dark red; chocolate-coloured; swarthy, dark.

choco[3] **1** *adj* (*CAm, Chi, Mex*) one-armed, one-legged; one-eyed; (*Chi*) tailless. **2** *nm* **(a)** (*Chi*) stump. **(b)** (*Bol*) top hat.

choco[4] *nm* (*Zool*) cuttlefish.

chocolate 1 *adj* (*SAm*) chocolate-coloured; dark red. **2** *nm* **(a)** chocolate; drinking chocolate, cocoa.

(b) (*SAm*: *hum*) blood; **sacar el — a uno** to make someone's nose bleed.

chocolatera *nf* **(a)** chocolate pot. **(b)** (*fam*) old thing, piece of junk; (*Aut*) old crock; (*Naut*) hulk.

chocolatería *nf* chocolate factory; *café specializing in serving drinking chocolate.*

chocolatero 1 *adj* fond of chocolate. **2** *nm* **(a)** (*Andalusia*) chocolate pot. **(b)** (*Cu, Mex*) strong northerly wind.

chocolear [1a] **1** *vt* (*Col*) to dock, cut off the tail of. **2** *vi* to get depressed.

chocha *nf* (*also* **— perdiz**) woodcock.

chochear [1a] *vi* **(a)** to dodder, be doddery, be senile; to be in one's dotage. **(b)** (*fig*) to be soft, go all sentimental.

chochera *nf*, **chochez** *nf* **(a)** dotage; senility; second childhood.

(b) (*una —*) silly thing; sentimental act.

(c) (*Per, RPl*) favourite, thing (*or* person) on which one dotes; **tener — por una** to dote on someone, be crazy about someone.

chochín *nm*, **chochita** *nf* wren.

chocho[1] *adj* **(a)** doddering, doddery, senile. **(b)** (*fig*) soft, doting, sentimental; **estar — por** to dote on, be soft about.

chocho[2] nm candy stick; —s sweets, candies (US).
chocholear [1a] vt (Col) to spoil, pamper.
chófer nm, **chofer** nm (SAm), pl **chóferes, chofers** (SAm) driver; motorist; chauffeur.
cholada nf (Ec, Per) action typical of a cholo.
cholería nf (Per), **cholerío** nm (Per) group of cholos.
cholo 1 adj (a) (SAm) half-breed, mestizo (and see 2).
    (b) (Chi) cowardly.
    2 nm, **chola** nf (a) (SAm) half-breed, mestizo; (any) dark-skinned person; (Pan) half-civilized Indian; (Chi) pure Indian from the South.
    (b) (SAm: hum) Peruvian.
    (c) (Chi) coward.
    (d) (Ec, Per, Ven: in direct address) darling, honey (US).
cholla nf (a) (fam) nut (sl), head; (fig) brains. (b) (CAm) wound, sore. (c) (CAm, Col) laziness, slowness.
chollo nm (fam) bargain, snip (sl); plum, soft job.
cholludo adj (CAm, Col) lazy, slow.
chamba nf (Chi) = **chompa.**
chompa nf (SAm: angl) jumper, sweater.
chonco (CAm) **1** adj = **choco**[3]. **2** nm stump.
chongo nm (a) (Chi) blunt knife, worn-out knife. (b) (PR, SD) old horse. (c) (Guat, Mex) —s pigtails, tresses; bun (of hair).
chontal adj (a) (CAm) Indian wild, uncivilized; rebellious; unruly. (b) (CAm, Col, Ven) uncivilized; rough, coarse; (Ven) rough-spoken.
chopa nf (sl) jacket.
chopera nf poplar grove.
chopo nm (a) (Bot) black poplar; — de Italia, — lombardo Lombardy poplar.
    (b) (Mil: fam) gun; **cargar con el** — (fig) to join up, do one's military service.
choque nm (a) impact; (of vehicle in movement) jolt, jar; (of explosion) blast, shock wave.
    (b) (noise) crash; (of plates etc) clatter; (of glasses) clink.
    (c) (Aut, Rail etc) crash, smash; collision; — de frente head-on collision; — de trenes rail smash, rail accident.
    (d) (Elec) shock.
    (e) (Med) shock.
    (f) (Mil and fig) clash; conflict; **entrar en** — to clash; **estar en abierto** — **con** to conflict openly with.
choquezuela nf kneecap.
chorcha nf (a) (Mex) group of merry people, light-hearted gathering; noisy party; **una** — **de amigos** a group of friends (out for a good time).
    (b) (CAm: Orn) crest, comb.
    (c) (CAm) goitre.
chorchero adj (Mex) merry.
chorear [1a] vi (Chi) to grumble, complain.
choreo nm (Chi) grouse (fam), complaint.
chorizo nm (a) (Cook) hard pork sausage, salami.
    (b) (Circus) balancing pole.
    (c) (tabu) prick (tabu).
    (d) (Bol, RPl) rump steak.
    (e) (Bol, RPl) mixture of clay and straw used in plastering.
    (f) (Col, Ec) idiot.
    (g) (Cu: pej) mulatto, Negro.
chorlitejo nm, **chorlito** nm plover.
chorlo nm, **chorla** nf (CAm, Col, PR) great-great-grandchild.
chorote nm (a) (Mex, Ven) drinking chocolate (with brown sugar); (Col) thick drinking chocolate; (Cu) (any) thick drink; (Cu, PR, Ven) watery drink; (PR) coffee.
    (b) (Col) unglazed chocolate pot.
chorra nf (a) (sl) luck, jam; ¡**qué** — **tiene!** look at that for jam! (b) (Chi) underworld slang.
chorrada nf (a) (of milk etc) extra drop; bonus; **dar algo con** — to give something and a bit extra. (b) unnecessary adornment; superfluous detail.
chorrear [1a] **1** vt (a) (Mil sl, also Cu) to tick off, dress down.
    (b) (Ec) to soak.
    (c) (RPl: sl) to pinch (fam).
    2 vi (a) to gush (forth), spout (out), spirt; to drip, trickle; — **de sudor** to run with sweat; **la ropa chorrea todavía** his clothes are still wringing wet.
    (b) (fig) to trickle (in, away etc); **chorrean todavía las solicitudes** the applications are still trickling in.
    3 chorrearse vr (Col): — **algo** to pinch something (fam).
chorreo nm (a) gushing, spouting; dripping; trickling.
    (b) (fig) constant drain (on resources etc).
chorrera nf (a) spout; channel, runlet.
    (b) mark (left by dripping water etc).
    (c) (of river) rapids.

    (d) —s (Sew) frill, lace adornment.
    (e) (SAm: fig) string, stream, lot; **una** — **de a** whole string of, a lot of.
    (f) (Cu) ticking off.
    (g) see **jamón.**
chorretada nf (a) spirt, squirt, jet. (b) = **chorrada** (a).
chorrillo nm (fig) constant stream, steady trickle.
chorro nm (a) jet; spirt, squirt, stream; dribble, trickle; **beber a** — to drink a jet of wine (from a wineskin); **llover a** —s to pour; **salir a** —s to gush forth, come spirting out.
    (b) (Tech) jet, blast; (Aer) jet; — **de arena** sandblast; — **de vapor** steam jet; **avión a** — jet plane; **motor a** — jet engine; **con propulsión a** — jet-propelled.
    (c) (fig) stream; **un** — **de palabras** a stream of words, a torrent of words; **un** — **de voz** a verbal blast, an awfully loud voice; **a** —s in plenty, in abundance; **hablar a** —s to talk nineteen to the dozen; **soltar el** — to burst out laughing; to produce a torrent of insults (etc).
    (d) (Bol) strand (of a whip).
    (e) (CAm) tap, faucet.
    (f) (Cu, PR) ticking off.
    (g) (RPl: sl) thief, pickpocket.
chotacabras nm, pl **chotacabras** nightjar.
chotear [1a] **1** vt (a) (Ant, CAm, Mex, Per) to make fun of.
    (b) (Col) to spoil, pamper.
    (c) (Guat) suspect to shadow, tail.
    2 **chotearse** vr to joke, take things as a joke.
chotis nm, pl **chotis** schottische.
choto 1 adj (CAm) abundant, plentiful; **estar** — **de** to be full of, be loaded with; **de** — free, for nothing.
    2 nm kid; calf.
chotuno adj kid, calf sucking, very young; lamb weakly; **oler a** — to smell of goat.
chova nf crow, rook; — **piquirroja** chough.
choza nf hut, shack; — **de nieve** igloo, ice house.
chozno nm, **chozna** nf great-great-grandchild.
chrisma ['krisma] nf, **christma(s)** ['krisma] nm, pl **christmas** ['krismas] (angl) Christmas card.
chubasco nm (a) (Meteorol) shower, squall; — **de nieve** (brief) snowstorm.
    (b) (fig) setback; series of reverses (or troubles etc); **aguantar el** — (fig) to weather the storm.
chubascoso adj squally, stormy.
chubasquero nm oilskins.
chucán adj (CAm) buffoonish; coarse, rude.
chúcaro adj (SAm) animal wild, untamed; person shy.
chucear [1a] vt (SAm) to prick, goad.
chuco adj (CAm, Ec, Mex) fish etc high, off.
chucruta nf sauerkraut.
chucha nf (a) (Zool) dog, bitch. (b) (fam) sweetheart.
    (c) (Col) opossum. (d) (Col) body odour. (e) (Col) hide-and-seek. (f) (Bol, Per: tabu) cunt (tabu).
chuchada nf (CAm) trick, swindle.
chuchear[1] [1a] vt to hunt, trap.
chuchear[2] [1a] vi = **cuchichear.**
chuchería nf (a) trinket, bit of jewellery, knick-knack. (b) titbit, dainty morsel; sweet.
chucho 1 adj (a) (Col) fruit soft, watery; person wrinkled.
    (b) (CAm) mean.
    2 nm (a) (Zool: pej) dog, hound, mongrel; ¡—! down boy!
    (b) (fam) sweetheart.
    (c) (Ant: Rail) switch; (Cu: Rail) siding.
    (d) (Ant, Ven) rawhide whip.
    (e) (Chi) jail.
    (f) (SAm: Med) chill, fever; (esp) malaria.
chuchumeca nf (Chi, Per) whore.
chuchumeco nm (a) mean person, skinflint.
    (b) (Chi) sickly person; dwarf, runt; wastrel; (Col) old dodderer.
    (c) (Cu, Per) toff (fam), dude (US).
    (d) (PR) idiot.
chueca nf (a) (Bot) stump.
    (b) (Anat) rounded bone; round head of a bone.
    (c) (fig) practical joke, hoax, prank; **gastar una** — **a uno** to play a joke on someone.
chueco adj (SAm) knock-kneed; (Arg, Per) pigeon-toed; (Col) lame; (Mex) one-armed, one-legged; (CAm, Mex, Ven) crooked, twisted, bent.
chufa nf chufa, earth almond.
chufeta nf = **chufleta.**
chufla nf joke, merry quip; **tomar algo a** — to take something as a joke.
chuflarse [1a] vr to joke, make jokes; to take things as a joke.
chufleta nf joke, merry quip; taunt.

chufletear [1a] *vi* to joke, make jokes; to jeer, make taunting remarks.

chula *nf* (a) woman from the back streets (of Madrid), low-class woman, coarse woman. (b) loud wench, flashy female, brassy girl. (c) (*SAm*) girlfriend.

chulada *nf* (a) coarse thing; funny thing; mean trick. (b) = **chulería** (a).

chulear [1a] *vt* (*fam*) (a) to make fun of. (b) to pinch (*fam*), swipe (*sl*).

chulería *nf* (a) (*quality*) natural charm, winning ways; (*pej*) commonness, vulgarity; (*pej*) flashiness; flamboyant manner.
(b) (*la* —) the *chulos* (*collectively, as a group*).
(c) (*una* —) = **chulada** (a).

chulesco *adj* = **chulo 1**.

chuleta *nf* (a) chop, cutlet; — **de puerco** pork chop; — **de ternera** veal chop.
(b) (*Sew*) insert, piece let in; (*Carp*) filling.
(c) (*fam*) punch, bash (*fam*).
(d) (*Univ: fam*) crib (*fam*), trot (*US*).
(e) —**s** (*fam*) side-whiskers.

chulillo *nm* (*Per*) tradesman's assistant.

chulo 1 *adj* (a) amusing; charming, attractive, winning.
(b) (*in appearance*) smart, showy, attractive; (*pej*) flashy, vulgar, gaudy.
(c) (*of walk, air*) proud; jaunty, swaggering; **con el sombrero a lo** — with his hat at a rakish angle; **iba muy** — he walked with a swagger, he swaggered along.
(d) (*of manner*) bold, free from servility, outspoken; (*pej*) overbold, fresh; pert, saucy; brassy; **no te pongas** — **conmigo** don't get fresh with me.
(e) (*of character*) slick; rascally, villainous.
(f) (*CAm, Col, Mex*) pretty; attractive, elegant, graceful.
2 *adv* (*CAm, Mex*) well; **jugar** — to play well.
3 *nm* (a) *typical working-class Madrilenian* (*equivalent to Cockney*); common but likeable chap; easy-going sort, free-and-easy person.
(b) (*pej*) spiv (*sl*), layabout, ne'er-do-well; villain, rascal; — **de putas** pimp, pander.
(c) (*Taur*) bullfighter's assistant.
(d) (*Col*) turkey buzzard.

chulón *adj* (*CAm*) naked.

chulleco *adj* (*Chi*) twisted, crooked.

chuma *nf* (*Ec, RPl*) drunkenness.

chumacera *nf* (*Mech*) ball bearing, journal bearing; (*Naut*) rowlock, oarlock (*US*).

chumarse [1a] *vr* (*Ec, RPl*) to get drunk.

chumbar [1a] *vt* (a) (*RPl: of dog*) to attack, go for; **¡chúmbale!** at him, boy! (b) (*Bol*) to shoot. (c) (*Col*) *baby* to swaddle.

chumbe *nm* (*SAm*) sash.

chumbera *nf*, **chumbimba** *nf* (*SAm*) prickly pear.

chumbo[1] *nm* prickly pear (*fruit*); see **higo**.

chumbo[2] *nm* (*RPl*) shot, pellet.

chumeco *nm* (*CAm*) apprentice; helper, mate.

chunco *adj* (*CAm, Col*) = **choco**[3].

chuncho (*Per*) 1 *adj* savage; rustic. 2 *nm*, **chuncha** *nf* savage Indian.

chunga *nf* (*fam*) joke; fun, banter; **contar** —**s** to crack jokes (*fam*); **estar de** — to be in a merry mood; **decir algo de** — to say something banteringly; **tomar las cosas en** — to take things as a joke.

chungar [1h], **chunguear** [1a] *vi and* **chungarse**, **chunguearse** *vr* (*fam*) to gag, crack jokes (*fam*), be in a merry mood; to banter; — **de uno** to have a bit of fun with someone, make fun of someone.

chuño *nm* (*SAm*) (dish made with) potato starch.

chupa[1] *nf*: **poner a uno como** — **de dómine** to give someone a tremendous ticking off; to shower insults on someone; **en la prensa le pusieron como** — **de dómine** they gave him a tremendous pasting in the press (*sl*).

chupa[2] *nf* (a) (*SAm*) drunkenness. (b) (*Pan*) bag.

chupada *nf* suck; (*at pipe etc*) pull, puff; —**s** sucking, suction; **dar** —**s a la pipa** to puff away at one's pipe.

chupado *adj* (a) *person* skinny, gaunt; emaciated; — **de cara** with a gaunt face, lantern-jawed.
(b) *skirt* tight.
(c) **estar** — **de frío** to be pinched with cold.
(d) (*SAm*) **estar** — to be drunk.

chupador *nm* (a) teething ring; teat (*of bottle*). (b) (*SAm*) drunkard. (c) (*SAm*) smoker.

chupaflor *nm* (*CR, PR, Ven*) hummingbird.

chupalla *nf* (*Chi, Mex*) straw hat.

chupamirto *nm* (*Mex, PR*) hummingbird.

chupantina *nf* (*RPl*) boozy party.

chupar [1a] 1 *vt* (a) to suck; to suck out, suck up; to absorb, take in, take up; *drink* to sip; *essence etc* to extract; *breast, toffee etc* to suck; *pipe etc* to suck, smoke, puff at; *stamp etc* to lick, moisten (with one's tongue).
(b) (*SAm*) to smoke.
(c) (*SAm*) to drink (*esp* to excess).
(d) (*fig*) to milk; to sap; **le chupan el dinero** they are milking him (of his money); **el trabajo le chupa la salud** his work is undermining his health.
2 *vi* to suck.
3 **chuparse** *vr* (a) (*fam*) **¡chúpate eso!** put that in your pipe and smoke it! (*fam*).
(b) — **el dedo** to suck one's finger; see also **dedo**.
(c) (*SAm*) — **un insulto** to put up with an insult, swallow an affront.
(d) (*Med*) to waste away, decline, get thin.
(e) (*Ven*) to get scared.

chupatintas *nm, pl* **chupatintas** (*pej*) penpusher, scribe.

chupe *nm* (*SAm*) *a typical spicy soup*.

chupeta *nf* (*Naut*) roundhouse.

chupete *nm* (a) dummy, pacifier (*US*); teat (*of bottle*); (*SAm*) lollipop. (b) (*SAm*) suck. (c) **de** — see **rechupete**.

chupo *nm* (a) (*SAm: Med*) boil. (b) (*Col*) baby's bottle.

chupón *nm* (a) (*Bot*) sucker.
(b) (*fam*) sponger (*fam*), hanger-on, parasite; swindler.
(c) lollipop, sucking sweet; — **de caramelo** toffee apple.
(d) (*SAm*) dummy, pacifier (*US*); teething ring; baby's bottle.
(e) (*Col, PR*) puff, pull (*at pipe etc*).
(f) (*Col: Med*) boil.

churdón *nm* raspberry; raspberry cane; raspberry jam.

chureca *nf* sweet pea.

churo[1] *adj* (*Arg, Bol*) handsome, attractive.

churo[2] *nm* (a) (*Bol, Ec, Per*) coiled wind instrument. (b) (*Ec*) spiral staircase. (c) (*Ec*) curl.

churrasco *nm* (*Bol, Chi, RPl*) barbecue, barbecued meat; (*Arg*) steak, choice piece of meat.

churrasquear [1a] *vt* (*RPl*) *meat* to barbecue, roast; to prepare; *barbecued meat* to eat.

churre *nf* thick grease; filth.

churrería *nf* fritter stall.

churrero *nm*, **churrera** *nf* fritter maker, fritter seller.

churrete *nm* grease spot, dirty mark.

churretear [1a] *vt* (*SAm*) to spot, stain, dirty.

churrias *nfpl* (*Col, Guat, SD*) diarrhoea.

churriento *adj* (a) greasy; filthy. (b) (*SAm: Med*) loose.

churrigueresco *adj* (a) (*Archit*) baroque. (b) (*fig*) excessively ornate, flowery; flashy.

churro 1 *adj wool* coarse; *sheep* coarse-wooled.
2 *nm* (a) (*Cook*) fritter.
(b) (*fam*) botch, mess; **el dibujo ha salido un** — the sketch came out all wrong, he messed up the drawing.
(c) (*fam*) fluke.

churrullero *adj* talkative, gossipy.

churruscar [1g] 1 *vt* to fry crisp; to burn, overdo. 2 *vi* to sizzle. 3 **churruscarse** *vr* to burn, do too much, get scorched.

churrusco[1] *nm* burnt toast.

churrusco[2] *adj* (*Col, Pan*) *hair* kinky, curly.

churumbela *nf* (a) (*Mus*) flageolet. (b) (*SAm*) maté cup; (*Col, Ec*) short-stemmed pipe. (c) (*Col*) worry, care.

chus: no decir — **ni mus** not to say a word.

chuscada *nf* funny remark, joke; coarse joke.

chusco *adj* (a) funny, droll; *person* coarse but amusing; *event* oddly amusing. (b) (*Per*) *dog* mongrel; *horse etc* ordinary; *person* coarse, ill-mannered.

chuse *nm* (*Arg*) coarse woollen cloth; (*Per*) blanket.

chusma *nf* rabble, mob, riffraff.

chusmaje *nm* (*SAm*) = **chusma**.

chuspa *nf* (*SAm*) bag, pouch.

chut *nm* (*Sport: angl*) shot (at goal).

chutar [1a] *vi* (*Sport: angl*) to shoot (at goal).

chuzar [1f] *vt* (*Col*) to prick; to sting, hurt.

chuzo *nm* (a) (*Mil, Hist*) pike; spiked stick, pointed stick; prick, goad; (*Chi*) pickaxe; (*Cu, Chi, PR*) whip; (*CAm: Orn*) beak; (*CAm: of scorpion*) sting; **aunque caigan** —**s** whatever the weather, (*fig*) come what may; **echar** —**s** (*fam*) to brag; **llover a** —**s** to rain cats and dogs, rain in torrents. (b) (*Per*) shoe.

chuzón *adj* (a) wily, sharp, cunning. (b) witty, amusing.

chuzonada *nf* piece of tomfoolery, piece of buffoonery.

D

dable *adj* possible, feasible, practicable; **no es —
hacerlo** it is not possible to do it; **en lo que sea —** as
far as possible, as far as is feasible.

daca *interj* hand it over!; **en — las pajas** in a jiffy;
andar al — y toma to be at cross-purposes.

dacrón *nm* dacron.

dactilar *adj* finger (*attr*); **huella —, impresión —**
fingerprint.

dactílico *adj* dactylic.

dáctilo *nm* dactyl.

dactilografía *nf* typing.

dactilógrafo *nm*, **dactilógrafa** *nf* typist.

dadaísmo *nm* dadaism.

dadista *nm* (*Mex*) gambler.

dádiva *nf* gift, present; (*fig*) sop.

dadivosidad *nf* generosity, lavishness with gifts.

dadivoso *adj* generous, open-handed, lavish with gifts.

dado[1] *nm* (a) (*in games*) die; **—s** dice; **el — está
tirado** the die is cast. (b) (*Archit*) dado. (c) (*Mech*)
block.

dado[2] *ptp of* **dar**: (a) **en un caso —** in a given case;
dada su corta edad in view of his youth; **dadas estas
circunstancias** since these circumstances exist, in
view of these circumstances.
(b) **ser — a** to be given to; **es muy — a** + *infin*
he is much given to + *ger*.
(c) **— que** ... (*as conj*) provided that ..., so long
as ...; given that ..., granted that ...

dador *nm*, **dadora** *nf* giver, donor; (*of letter*) bearer;
(*Comm*) drawer; **— de sangre** blood donor.

Dafne *f* Daphne.

dafodelo *nm* (*angl*) daffodil.

daga *nf* dagger, stiletto; (*Mex, PR*) machete.

dagazo *nm* (*Mex, PR*) stab wound.

daifa *nf* mistress, concubine; prostitute.

dalia *nf* dahlia.

Dalmacia *f* Dalmatia.

daltoniano *adj* colour-blind.

daltonismo *nm* colour blindness.

dallar [1a] *vt* to scythe, mow with a scythe.

dalle *nm* scythe.

dama *nf* (a) (*in general*) lady; (*noble*) lady, gentle-
woman; (*pej*) mistress, lover, concubine; **el poeta y
su —** the poet and his lady, the poet and his
mistress; **primera —** (*Theat*) leading lady, (*Pol*)
first lady (*US*), president's wife; **— de honor** (*royal*)
lady-in-waiting; (*at wedding*) bridesmaid, maid of
honour; **— joven** (*Theat*) ingénue; **— regidora**
carnival queen.
(b) (*Cards, Chess*) queen; (*Draughts*) king.
(c) **—s** (*game*) draughts, checkers (*US*).

damajuana *nf*, **damasana** *nf* (*SAm*) demijohn.

Damasco Damascus.

damasco *nm* (a) damask. (b) (*Bot*) damson; (*SAm*)
apricot.

damasquinado *adj*, **damasquino** *adj* (*Tech*)
damask; damascene.

damasquinar [1a] *vt* (*Tech*) to damask.

damesana *nf* (*SAm*) demijohn.

damisela *nf* (*Hist*) damsel; (*pej*) courtesan, prostitute.

damita *nf* (*CAm*) young lady.

damnificar [1g] *vt* to injure, harm; to disable; to
harm the interests of; **los damnificados** (*in accident
etc*) the victims, those affected, those who have
suffered loss.

Dámocles *m* Damocles.

dancing ['dansin] *nm* (*esp SAm: angl-gall*) dance hall;
night club.

dandi *nm* (*angl: Acad*), **dandy** *nm* (*angl*) dandy, fop.

danés 1 *adj* Danish. **2** *nm*, **danesa** *nf* Dane. **3** *nm*
(*language*) Danish.

Daniel *m* Daniel.

danta *nf* (*CAm, Col, Mex*) tapir.

dantesco *adj* (a) of Dante, relating to Dante. (b) (*fig*)
Dantesque; horrific, weird, macabre.

Danubio *nm* Danube.

danza *nf* (a) (*in general*) dancing; (*una —*) dance; **—
de espadas** sword dance; **— de figuras** square-
dance; **— guerrera** war dance; **— de la muerte**
dance of death.
(b) (*fam*) shady affair, suspect deal; mess; **meterse
en la —** to get caught up in a shady affair.
(c) (*fam*) row, rumpus (*fam*); **armar una —** to
kick up a row.

danzante *nm*, **danzanta** *nf* (a) dancer. (b) (*fam*)
hustler, live wire, person who is always on the go;
(*pej*) busybody. (c) (*fam*) scatterbrain.

danzar [1f] **1** *vt* to dance. **2** *vi* (a) to dance (*also fig*).
(b) (*fam*) to meddle; to butt in, shove one's oar in.

danzarín *nm*, **danzarina** *nf* (a) dancer; artistic
dancer, professional dancer. (b) **=danzante** (b) *and*
(c).

dañado *adj* (a) damaged; spoiled; bad. (b) (*fig*) bad,
wicked, evil.

dañar [1a] **1** *vt* to damage, harm, hurt; to spoil. **2
dañarse** *vr* to get damaged, get hurt; to spoil; to
rot, go bad; (*Med*) to hurt oneself, do oneself harm.

dañinear [1a] *vt* (a) (*Chi*) **=dañar**. (b) (*Arg*) to steal.

dañino 1 *adj* harmful; damaging; injurious; **animales
—s** vermin, pests, injurious creatures. **2** *nm* (*Arg*)
thief.

daño *nm* (a) damage; hurt, harm, injury; **en — de** to
the detriment of; **por mi —** to my cost; **hacer — a**
to damage, harm; (*Med*) to hurt, injure; *stomach* to
upset; **no hace —** it doesn't hurt; **el ajo me hace —**
garlic disagrees with me; **hacerse —** to hurt oneself,
do oneself an injury; **se hizo — en el pie** he hurt his
foot.
(b) (*Med*) trouble; **los médicos no saben dónde
está el —** the doctors cannot tell where the trouble
is.
(c) (*Law*) **—s y perjuicios** damages.
(d) (*SAm*) witchcraft.

dañoso *adj* harmful, bad, injurious; **— para** harmful
to, bad for.

dar [1r] **1** *vt* (a) (*general sense*) to give; *object* to give,
hand, pass (*a* to); *message* to give, deliver; *notice,
warning* to give; *permission* to give, grant, concede;
example to set; *step* to take; *ride, walk* to take, go for;
blow to give, deal, fetch, strike; *beating* to give; *cry*
to give, utter; *sigh* to fetch, heave; *battle* to fight; *ir
dando cuerda* to pay out a rope, let out a rope; **—
los buenos días a uno** to wish (*or* bid) someone
good-day; **— de comer a uno** to give someone
something to eat; **nos daban garbanzos** they gave
us chickpeas (to eat); **ahí me las den todas** that
won't bother me, I can cope with everything; **por si
vienen mal dadas** in case of emergency, (*save etc*)
for a rainy day.
(b) *crop, profit etc* to yield, bear, produce, give;
dan un 7 por 100 de interés they yield 7% interest,
they bear interest at 7%.
(c) (*Cards*) to deal.
(d) *feeling* to give, cause, produce; *pleasure* to
give; *pity* to cause, excite, arouse; **le dio un fuerte
dolor de costado** he felt a sharp pain in his side.
(e) (*Theat etc*) to do, perform, put on.
(f) (*time*) to strike; **el reloj dio las 3** the clock
struck 3; **han dado las 4, son las 4 dadas** it's past
4 o'clock.
(g) **— como, — por** to consider, regard, assume;
lo dio como cierto he regarded it as certain, he
considered it definite; **lo daba por bien empleado** he
considered it well spent; **lo podremos — por
terminado** we shall be able to consider it finished.
(h) **— de barniz a** to varnish; **— de jalbegue a**
to whitewash.

(i) — **a uno de puñetazos** to punch someone.

(j) —**la de** to brag of being; to set oneself up as; **la da de poeta** he tries to make out he's a poet.

(k) ¡**dale!** (*Boxing etc*) hit him!; (*in chase*) after him!; (*Sport etc*) come on!; get on with it!; (*iro*) just look at him!, what an idiot!; ¡**y dale!** there he goes again!; ¡**dale que dale!** you do carry one so!, stop harping on it!

(l) lo mismo da it's all the same, it makes no difference; **lo mismo me da** it's all the same to me; ¡**qué más da!** what does it matter!; never mind!; ¡**qué más da un sitio que otro!** surely one place is as good as another!

(m) *for very many phrases and idioms, see the noun entry etc*; *eg* **caza, grito, paseo, conocer, entender** *etc*.

2 *vi* **(a)** — **a** (*of window*) to look out on, look on to, overlook; (*of house*) to face, face towards; — **sobre** to overlook.

(b) — **a la bomba** to pump, work the pump.

(c) — **con** *person etc* to meet, run into, find; *idea, solution etc* to hit on; to run across; — **con algo en el suelo** to knock something to the ground, drop something; **dio con la cabeza contra la pared** he banged his head on the wall; **no doy con el nombre** I can't think of the name.

(d) — **consigo en** to end up in, land in; **dio consigo en la cárcel** he ended up in jail.

(e) — **contra** to hit (against), knock against, bang into; **el barco dio con el puente** the ship crashed into the bridge, the ship struck the bridge.

(f) — **de cabeza** to fall on one's head; — **de narices** to fall flat on one's face; — **de narices contra la puerta** to bang one's face on the door.

(g) — **en** + *infin* to take to + *ger*, get into the habit of + *ger*.

(h) — **en** *floor etc* to hit, strike; *target* to hit, land on; *solution* to hit on; *error* to fall into; *joke* to catch on to, see, get the point of; — **en ello** to see the point, get it; **el sol le daba en la cara** the sun was shining straight into her face.

(i) le da por + *infin* he takes it into his head to + *infin*, he decides to + *infin*; he persists in + *ger*; **le ha dado por no venir a clase** he has begun to cut classes; **al chico le daba por dormirse en clase** the boy was apt to go to sleep in class; **les dio por venir a vernos** they took it into their heads to come and see us.

(j) — **tras uno** to pursue someone vigorously, set off after someone.

(k) — **de sí** (*of cloth etc*) to give, stretch; (*Agr etc*) to bear heavily, yield well, produce a lot.

3 darse *vr* **(a)** to surrender, give in; to give oneself up (*a* to).

(b) — **a** to take to; to devote oneself to; (*pej*) to abandon oneself to; — **a la bebida** to take to drink; — **a creer que . . .** to take to thinking that . . .

(c) (*event*) to happen; **si se da el caso** if that happens.

(d) (*Bio etc*) to exist, occur, be found; **la planta no se da en el sur** the plant is not found in the south.

(e) (*Agr*) to grow, come up; **el cultivo se da bien este año** the crop is coming on well this year.

(f) — **por** to consider oneself (as); — **por ofendido** to take offence; — **por perdido** to give oneself up for lost; — **por vencido** to give up, acknowledge defeat.

(g) —**las de** to pose as, fancy oneself as; **nunca me las di de experto** I never claimed to be an expert.

(h) no se me da mal I'm not doing too badly.

(i) no se me da un bledo (or **higo, rábano** *etc*) I don't care two hoots (*de* about).

(j) *for many phrases and idioms, see the noun entry, eg* **prisa, tono**.

Dardanelos *mpl* Dardanelles.

dardo *nm* dart, shaft.

dares *nmpl*: — **y tomares** (*fam*) arguments, bickering; **andar en** — **y tomares con uno** to bicker with someone, squabble with someone.

Darío *m* Darius.

dársena *nf* dock; basin, inner harbour; — **de marea** tidal basin.

darviniano, darwiniano *adj* Darwinian.

darvinismo, darwinismo *nm* Darwinism.

data *nf* **(a)** date. **(b)** (*Comm*) item.

datar [1a] **1** *vt* to date, put a date on. **2** *vi*: — **de** to date from, date back to; **esto data de muy atrás** this dates back a long time, this goes a long way back.

dátil *nm* (*Bot*) date.

datilera *nf* date palm.

dativo *nm* dative.

dato *nm* fact, datum, piece of information; **un — interesante** an interesting fact; —**s** data, facts, information; **no tenemos todos los** —**s** we do not have all the facts; —**s estadísticos** statistical information, statistical data, statistics; —**s personales** personal particulars, details about oneself.

David *m* David.

de *prep* **(a)** (*possession*) of; **el coche** — **mi amigo** the car of my friend, my friend's car; **los coches** — **mis amigos** my friends' cars; **es** — **ellos** it's theirs; **la señora** — **Pérez** Mrs Pérez; **el interés del préstamo** the interest on the loan.

(b) (*superlative*) in; **el peor alumno** — **la clase** the worst pupil in the class; **es el coche más caro del mercado** it's the dearest car on the market.

(c) (*value*) **una moneda** — **a 5 pesos** a 5-peso coin; **un pan** — **a libra** a pound loaf.

(d) (*origin, distance*) from; **es** — **Calatayud** she's from Calatayud; **Dolores no es** — **aquí** Dolores is not from these parts; **los** — **Madrid son los mejores** those from Madrid are the best, the Madrid ones are the best; — **A a B hay 5 kms** it is 5 kms from A to B; **ir** — **A a Z** to go from A to Z; **altura del suelo** height above ground; — **puerta en puerta** from door to door; **bajar la escalera** — **4 en 4** to go down 4 stairs at a time; — **esto se deduce que . . .** from this one deduces that . . .; **tiene 3 hijos** — **su primera mujer** he has 3 children by his first wife; **el camino** — **Elche** the Elche road, the road to Elche.

(e) (*apposition*) of; **la ciudad** — **Caracas** the city of Caracas.

(f) (*partitive*) of; **uno** — **nosotros** one of us.

(g) (*numerals*) **3** — **cada 4** 3 in every 4, 3 out of every 4.

(h) (*subject*) **una clase** — **francés** a French class; **un libro** — **biología** a biology book, a book about (or on) biology; **no sé nada** — **él** I don't know anything about (or of, concerning) him; **hablaba** — **política** he was talking about politics.

(i) (*material*) of; **una cadena** — **oro** a chain of gold, a gold(en) chain.

(j) (*content*) of; **una tacita** — **café** a cup of coffee.

(k) (*age*) of; **un chico** — **15 años** a boy of 15, a 15-year old boy.

(l) (*profession*) by; **es abogado** — **profesión** he's a lawyer by profession.

(m) (*authorship*) by, of; **un libro** — **Cela** a book by Cela, a book of Cela's.

(n) (*purpose*) **goma** — **mascar** chewing gum; **máquina** — **coser** sewing machine.

(o) (*powered by*) **cocina** — **gas** gas stove; **este modelo es** — **electricidad** this model works on electricity, this is an electric model.

(p) (*manner, style*) in; **amueblado** — **roble** furnished in oak; **vestido** — **azul** dressed in blue; **pintado** — **negro** painted (in) black.

(q) (*means*) at, in, with; — **un salto** at one bound, with one jump; — **un trago** at a gulp.

(r) (*cause*) with; **estar loco** — **contento** to be crazy with joy; **saltar** — **alegría** to jump for joy; **morir** — **hambre** to die of (or from) starvation, starve to death; **estar enfermo** — **gripe** to be ill with flu; **no poder moverse** — **miedo** to be unable to move for (or with) fright; — **puro cansado** out of sheer tiredness.

(s) (*with respect to*) in; **mejor** — **salud** better in health; **paralizado** — **las dos piernas** paralysed in both legs.

(t) (*descriptive*) with; **la niña** — **pelo largo** the girl with long hair; **ese tío del sombrero** that chap with (or in) a hat.

(u) (*in the quality of*) as; — **niño** as a child; when a child; **"el gran actor,** — **Segismundo"** (*caption*) "the great actor as Segismundo".

(v) (*passive agent*) by; **una persona amada** — **todos** a person loved by all, a person beloved of all.

(w) (*time*) in, by; **a las 7** — **la mañana** at 7 o'clock, at 7 a.m.; **muy** — **mañana** very early in the morning; — **día** by day, during the day(time); — **noche** at night, by night, in the night time.

(x) (*conditional*) if; — **no poder encontrarlo** if we can't find it; — **no ser así** if it were not so, were it not so.

(y) (*after* más, menos) than; **más** — **7** more than 7.

(z) (*idioms*) **aquel burro** — **ministro** that ass of a minister; **el pobre** — **Pedro** poor old Peter; **el bueno** — **Juan** good old John; *for many other phrases, see noun entry etc, eg* **pie, prisa**.

dé *see* **dar**.

deambular [1a] *vi* to saunter, stroll, wander (*por* along, about in, through).

deambulatorio *nm* (*Eccl*) ambulatory.

deán nm (*Eccl*) dean.
debacle nf (*gall: hum*) débâcle, disaster.
debajo 1 adv (*also* **por —**) underneath, below; on the underside.
  2 — de prep under; below, beneath; **— de la mesa** under the table, underneath the table; **por — de** under; below.
debate nm debate (*also Parl*); discussion, argument.
debatir[1] [3a] vt to debate (*also Parl*); to discuss, argue about.
debatir[2] [3a] vi *and* **debatirse** vr (*gall*) to struggle; to writhe; to flail about.
debe nm debit, debit side (*of account*); **— y haber** debit and credit; **asentar algo al — de uno** to debit something to someone.
debelador nm conqueror.
deber [2a] **1** vt to owe; **me debes 5 dólares** you owe me 5 dollars; **el respeto que todos deben a la patria** the respect which everybody owes to his country; **esto lo debe a influencia francesa** he owes this to French influence.
  2 vi (a) **debo hacerlo** I must do it, I have to do it; I ought to do it; **no debes comer tanto** you shouldn't eat so much; **debiera ir** he ought to go, he should go; **deberá cambiarse cada mes** (*instruction*) it should be changed every month; **debíamos partir ayer** we were to have left yesterday; **he debido perderlo** I must have lost it; **hubieras debido traerlo** you ought to have brought it, you should have brought it.
  (b) **debe de ser así** it must be like that; that must be it; **debe de hacer mucho frío allí** it must be pretty cold there; **debe de ser brasileño** he must be a Brazilian; **no debe de ser muy caro** it can't be very dear; **debe de haber ido** he must have gone; **debió de perderlo** he must have lost it.
  3 deberse vr: **— a** to be owing to, be due to, be on account of; **se debe al mal tiempo** it's on account of the bad weather; **se debe a que no hay carbón** it is because (of the fact that) there's no coal; **puede — a que . . .** it may be because . . .; **¿a qué se debe esto?** what is the explanation of this?, why is this?
  4 nm (a) duty, obligation; **últimos —es** last rites; **cumplir con un —** to perform a duty, carry out a duty.
  (b) (*Fin*) debt.
  (c) **—es** (*School*) homework; task, assignment.
debidamente adv properly, as one should (*or* as it should be *etc*); in due form, duly; **si te conduces —** if you behave properly; **un documento — redactado** a properly drawn document.
debido adj (a) proper, due, just; right, correct; **en debida forma** duly, in due form; **con el — respeto** with due respect; **como es —**, **según es —** as is (only) proper, as is right; **un padre como es — no haría eso** a true father would not do that.
  (b) **— a** owing to, due to, because of; **— a ello** because of this; **— a la falta de agua** because of the water shortage; **— a que no hay plátanos** because (of the fact that) there are no bananas.
débil adj (*in most senses*) weak; (*in body*) weak, feeble, frail; *health* poor; *character* weak; *effort etc* feeble; half-hearted; *cry* faint, feeble, weak; *light* dim, wan, weak.
debilidad nf (a) weakness; feebleness; faintness; dimness; **— senil** senility, senile decay.
  (b) (*una*) **—** weakness; **tener una — por el chocolate** to have a weakness for chocolate; **tener una — por uno** to have a soft spot for someone.
debilitación nf weakening, debilitation, enfeeblement.
debilitar [1a] **1** vt to weaken, debilitate; *resistance etc* to weaken, impair, lower. **2 debilitarse** vr to grow weak(er), weaken.
débilmente adv weakly; feebly; half-heartedly; faintly; dimly, wanly.
debitar [1a] vt (*Comm: angl*) to debit.
débito nm (*Comm: angl*) debit; debt.
debocar [1g] vti (*SAm*) to vomit.
Deborá f Deborah.
debut [de'βu] nm, **debuts** [de'βus] (*gall*) début.
debutanta nf, **debutante** nf (*gall*) débutante.
debutar [1a] vi (*gall*) to make one's début.
década nf decade; set of ten, series of ten.
decadencia nf decadence, decline, decay; **estar en franca —** to be in full decline.
decadente adj decadent; effete.
decaer [2o] vi to decay, decline; (*of effort*) to flag, weaken; (*of fashion*) to wane; (*of business*) to fall off; (*in health*) to decline, sink, fail; **— de ánimo** to lose heart; **ella ha decaído en belleza** her beauty is not what it was; **decayó de poderío** his power declined.
decagramo nm decagramme, decagram (*US*).

decaimiento nm decay; decline; weakening, weakness; warning; falling-off; **— de ánimo** discouragement, depression.
decalitro nm decalitre, decaliter (*US*).
decálogo nm decalogue.
decámetro nm decametre, decameter (*US*).
decanato nm deanship; deanery.
decano nm (a) (*Univ etc*) dean. (b) (*in group, of press etc*) doyen, senior member.
decantar[1] [1a] vt (*lit*) to praise, laud; **el tan decantado edificio** (*iro*) this building which has been so effusively praised.
decantar[2] [1a] vt *wine etc* to decant; to pour off; *sediment* to leave behind, form, deposit.
decapitar [1a] vt to behead, decapitate.
decasílabo 1 adj decasyllabic, ten-syllable. **2** nm decasyllable.
decena nf (about) ten; **—s** (*Math*) tens; **una — de barcos** about ten ships, some ten ships; **—s de miles de españoles** tens of thousands of Spaniards; **contar por —s** to count in tens; **vender por —s** to sell in tens.
decenal adj decennial.
decencia nf (a) decency; seemliness, decorum; respectability; modesty; **faltar a la —** to offend against decency. (b) cleanness, tidiness.
decenio nm decade.
decente adj (a) decent; seemly, proper; respectable; modest. (b) clean, tidy. (c) (*Per*) respectable, middle-class, white, non-Indian.
decentemente adv (a) decently; properly; respectably; modestly. (b) tidily.
decepción nf disappointment.
decepcionante adj disappointing.
decepcionar [1a] vt to disappoint.
deceso nm (*SAm*) decease, passing.
decibel nm, **decibelio** nm decibel.
decible adj expressible; communicable; **eso no es —** that cannot be told; that cannot be expressed.
decididamente adv decidedly.
decidido adj decided, determined; resolute; emphatic.
decidir [3a] **1** vt (a) *person* to decide, persuade, convince; **esto le decidió a dejarlo** this decided him to give it up; **esto por fin le decidió** this finally made his mind up (for him).
  (b) *outcome, question* to decide, settle, resolve.
  2 vi to decide (*de, en* about); **— + infin** to decide to **+** infin; **— en favor de uno** to decide in someone's favour; **— sobre cuál conviene más** to decide which is more suitable.
  3 decidirse vr to decide, make up one's mind (*a + infin* to **+** infin).
decidor 1 adj (a) witty, amusing, racy. (b) fluent, eloquent. **2** nm (a) wit, witty talker. (b) fluent speaker, eloquent speaker.
décima nf (a) (*Math*) tenth; tenth part (*esp of a* lottery ticket). (b) (*Eccl*) tithe. (c) (*Lit: Hist*) a ten-line stanza.
decimación nf decimation.
decimal 1 adj decimal. **2** nm decimal. **3** nf: **— periódica pura** recurring decimal.
décimo 1 adj tenth. **2** nm tenth.
decimoctavo adj eighteenth.
decimocuarto adj fourteenth.
decimonónico adj (*hum or pej*) nineteenth-century (*attr*); Victorian; (*fig*) outdated, antiquated.
decimonono adj, **decimonoveno** adj nineteenth.
decimoquinto adj fifteenth.
decimoséptimo adj seventeenth.
decimosexto adj sixteenth.
decimotercio adj, **decimotercero** adj thirteenth.
decir 1 [3p] vti (a) (*general senses*) to say; to tell; (*SAm*) to speak; (*of text*) to say, read; *fortune* to tell; *lie* to tell; *truth* to speak, tell; *mass* to say; *nonsense etc* to talk; **no dijo nada** he said nothing; **¿quién te lo dijo?** who told you?; **dicen que . . .** they say that . . ., people say that . . .; **— a uno que se calle** to tell someone to be quiet; **nos dijo que fuéramos** he told us to go.
  (b) (*idioms: general*) **¿digo algo?** have I said something?; **eso digo** that's what I say; that's just what I'm saying; **¡digo, digo!** hey!, say!; just listen to this!; now wait a minute!; **pero digo mal "decadent"** but I am wrong to say (*or* to call them *etc*) "decadent"; **pero dice mal** but he is wrong; **y dice bien** and he is right; **no lo digo por ti** I'm not referring to you, I'm not getting at you; **— que no** to say no; **— que sí** to say yes; **— para sí**, **— entre sí** to say to oneself; **como quien dice**, **como si dijéramos** so to speak; in a way, more or less; **como quien no dice nada** quite casually; as though it wasn't important; **¿cómo ha dicho Vd?** what did you say?,

pardon?; **¿decía Vd?** you were saying?; **¿cómo diríamos?** how shall I put it?; **¡lo que he dicho!** I stand by what I said!; **¡quién lo diría!** would you believe it!; did you ever? (*fam*).

(c) (*idioms with infin*) **es —** that is to say; **ya es —** that's saying a lot, that's a big claim to make; **me permito — que . . .** I submit that . . ., I venture to say that . . .; **querer —** to mean; **¿qué quiere — "spatha"?** what does "spatha" mean?; **¿qué quiere Vd — con eso?** what do you mean by that?; **dar que — (a la gente)** to make people talk, set the tongues wagging; **no sé qué —** I don't know what to say; **no hay más que — que . . .** there's no more to be said about it; **no hay que — que . . ., ni que — tiene que . . .** it goes without saying that . . .; **no hay para qué —** of course . . .; **— por —** to talk for talking's sake; **o por mejor —** or rather; **por —lo así** so to speak.

(d) (*idioms with future*) **dirá Vd aquel otro** you must mean that other one; **Vd dirá** it's for you to say; (*pouring drink*) how much do you like?, say when (*fam*); **ello dirá** the event will show; **el qué dirán** public opinion, what people will say; **pero no quiso por el qué dirán** but she didn't want to because of what people might say; **el maldito "qué dirán"** the curse of concern for what people will think.

(e) (*idioms with subjunctive*) **¡diga!, ¡dígame!** (*Tel*) hullo?; **digan lo que digan** whatever they (may) say; let them say what they please; **digámoslo así** so to speak; for want of a better word; **¡no me digas!** you don't say!; well I'm blowed!; come off it!; **¡y que lo digas!** you can say that again!; **y no digamos de . . .** not to mention . . .; **no estuvo muy cortés, que digamos** actually he wasn't all that polite, he wasn't what you could call polite; **no es un pintor, que digamos** he's not what you could really call a painter; **es, digamos, un comerciante** he's a sort of dealer, he's a dealer . . . for want of a better word.

(f) (*idioms with ptp*) **mejor dicho** rather; **no es para dicho** it's not fit to be told; **¡lo dicho dicho!** I stand by what I said!; **¡dicho y hecho!** no sooner said than done!; **¡haberlo dicho!** you might have told me!

(g) to show, indicate, reveal; **su cara dice lo que es** his face shows him up for what he is; **una situación que tan mal dice de nuestro gobierno** a situation which shows our government up in such a bad light.

(h) (*fam*) to call; **al niño le dicen Anastasio** they call the child Anastasius.

(i) to suit; **— con** to go with, match; **el vestido le dice bien** the dress suits her (nicely); **el color dice bien con su cutis** the colour goes with (*or* suits, harmonizes with) her complexion.

2 decirse *vr* **(a)** **yo sé lo que me digo** I know what I'm talking about; I know what I'm up to.

(b) to be called, be named; **esta plaza se dice de la Revolución** this is called Revolution Square; **¿cómo se dice en inglés "cursi"?** what's the English for "cursi", how do you say "cursi" in English?

(c) **se dice** it is said, they say, people say; the story goes . . .; **se me ha dicho que . . .** I have been told that . . .; **no se diría eso ahora** that could not be said nowadays.

(d) **hablar portugués, lo que se dice hablar, no sé** I can't really talk Portuguese, I don't speak Portuguese at all well; **esto es lo que se dice un queso** this is a real cheese, this is what you really call a cheese.

3 *nm* saying; witty remark; **es un —** it's just a phrase; **if I may use the expression . . .;** I was only thinking aloud; **a — de todos** by all accounts; **al — de X** according to X; as X has it, as X would have it.

decisión *nf* **(a)** (*una —*) decision; (*Law*) judgement; **forzar una —** to force the issue; **tomar una —** to make (*or* take) a decision.

(b) (*quality*) decisiveness; determination, resolution.

decisivo *adj* decisive; *argument, consideration* overriding; *vote* casting.

declamación *nf* **(a)** declamation; recital, recitation; (*quality*) delivery. **(b)** (*pej*) ranting.

declamador *nm* **(a)** orator; reciter. **(b)** (*pej*) ranter.

declamar [1a] **1** *vt* to declaim; *verse etc* to recite. **2** *vi* **(a)** to speak out, hold forth (*contra* against). **(b)** (*pej*) to rant, carry on.

declamatorio *adj* declamatory; (*pej*) ranting.

declaración *nf* **(a)** declaration; pronouncement, statement; explanation; (*to girl*) proposal (of marriage); **— de derechos** (*Pol*) bill of rights; **— de ingresos, — de renta, — fiscal** (*Mex*) income tax return.

(b) (*Cards*) bid.

(c) (*Law*) statement; evidence; **— de culpabilidad** confession of guilt; **— jurada** sworn statement, affidavit; **prestar —** to make a statement; to give evidence; **tomar la — a uno** to take a statement from someone.

declaradamente *adv* confessedly, declaredly.

declarado *adj* confessed, declared.

declarante *nmf* **(a)** (*Law*) person making a statement, person giving evidence. **(b)** (*Cards*) bidder, declarer.

declarar [1a] **1** *vt* **(a)** to declare, state (*que* that); to explain, expound; (*at customs*) to declare; *war* to declare (*a* on).

(b) (*Cards*) to bid; **— 2 picos** to bid 2 spades.

(c) (*Law*) to find; **— culpable a uno** to find someone guilty.

2 *vi* **(a)** to declare; **según él mismo declara** as he himself declares.

(b) (*Cards*) to bid, declare; **declaró menos de lo que tenía** he underbid.

(c) (*Law*) to make a statement; to testify, give evidence.

3 declararse *vr* **(a)** to declare oneself; to make one's opinion (*or* position *etc*) known; (*to girl*) to propose (*a* to); **— por** to come out in favour of, declare one's support for, side with.

(b) (*Law*) **— culpable** to plead guilty; **— inocente** to plead not guilty.

(c) (*epidemic, fire, war etc*) to break out.

declinable *adj* declinable.

declinación *nf* **(a)** decline, falling-off; decay. **(b)** (*Astron, Naut*) declination. **(c)** (*Gram*) declension.

declinar [1a] **1** *vt* **(a)** to decline, refuse; (*Law*) to reject.

(b) (*Gram*) to decline; to inflect.

2 *vi* **(a)** to decline, fall off, fall away; to decay; to deteriorate; (*of day*) to draw to a close.

(b) (*of ground*) to slope (away, down).

(c) (*Gram*) to decline.

declive *nm* **(a)** slope, incline, declivity; pitch; (*Rail*) gradient; **tierra en —** sloping ground, land on a slope; **estar en —** to slope.

(b) (*fig: Fin etc*) slump (also **— económico**).

decocción *nf* decoction.

decolorar [1a] **1** *vt* to discolour, affect the colour of. **2 decolorarse** *vr* to get discoloured, lose colour.

decomisar [1a] *vt* to seize, confiscate.

decoración *nf* **(a)** decoration; **— de escaparate** window display; **— de escaparates** window dressing; **— del hogar, — de interiores** interior decorating. **(b)** (*also* **—es**: *Theat*) scenery, set.

decorado *nm* (*Cine, Theat*) scenery, set.

decorador *nm*, **decoradora** *nf* decorator.

decorar[1] [1a] *vt* to decorate, adorn (*de* with).

decorar[2] [1a] *vt* to learn, memorize.

decorativo *adj* decorative, ornamental.

decoro *nm* **(a)** decorum, propriety, decency; proprieties; **— virginal** maidenly modesty. **(b)** honour, respect.

decorosamente *adv* decorously.

decoroso *adj* decorous, proper, decent; seemly; modest.

decrecer [2d] *vi* to decrease, diminish; (*of flood, water*) to go down; (*of days*) to get shorter, draw in.

decreciente *adj* decreasing, diminishing.

decrecimiento *nm*, **decremento** *nm* decrease, diminution; fall; shortening.

decrépito *adj* decrepit.

decrepitud *nf* decrepitude.

decretar [1a] *vt* **(a)** to decree, order, ordain; **— que . . .** to decree that . . . **(b)** *prize* to award (*a* to). **(c)** (*Mex*) *dividend* to declare.

decreto *nm* decree, order; (*Parl*) act.

decreto-ley *nm*, *pl* **decretos-leyes** bill, law.

decúbito *nm* (*Med*): **— prono** prone position; **— supino** supine position; **úlcera de —** bedsore.

decuplar [1a] *vt*, **decuplicar** [1g] *vt* to multiply tenfold, increase tenfold.

décuplo 1 *adj* tenfold. **2** *nm*: **es el — de lo que era** it is ten times what it was, it has increased tenfold.

decurso *nm* (*lit*): **en el — de los años** over the years; **en el — del tiempo** in the course of time.

dedada *nf* thimbleful; (*fig*) very small quantity, very modest amount; (*of jam etc*) spot, dab, drop; (*of snuff*) pinch; **dar una — de miel a uno** (*fig*) to give someone a slight hope.

dedal *nm* **(a)** thimble. **(b)** (*fig*) thimbleful.

dedalera *nf* foxglove.

dédalo *nm* **(a)** labyrinth. **(b)** (*fig*) tangle, mess.

dedicación *nf* **(a)** dedication; (*fig*) dedication, devotion (*a* to).

(b) (*Eccl*) consecration.

(c) estar en (régimen de) — exclusiva (*or* **plena**), **trabajar con — plena** to work full-time; **"— plena"** (*advert*) "full-time".

dedicar [1g] **1** *vt* **(a)** to dedicate (*a* to); (*Eccl*) to consecrate; *book* to dedicate (*a* to), *copy* to autograph, inscribe, write in.

(b) *effort, time* to devote, give (*a* to); **dedico un día a la semana a pescar** I spend one day a week fishing; **tengo que — mucho tiempo a eso** I have to give up a lot of time to that.

2 dedicarse *vr*: **— a** to devote oneself to; to go in for, take up; **— a** + *infin* to devote oneself to + *ger*; **se dedicó a la cerámica** he devoted himself to pottery, he took up pottery; **¿a qué se dedica Vd?** what do you do?; what's your line?, what business are you in?

dedicatoria *nf* inscription, dedication.
dedicatorio *adj* dedicatory.
dedil *nm* fingerstall.
dedillo *nm*: **saber algo al —** to have something at one's fingertips; **saber una lección al —** to have a lesson off pat; **dijo la lista al —** he rattled off the list with complete accuracy.
dedo *nm* **(a)** finger; **— (del pie)** toe; **— anular** ring finger; **— auricular, — meñique** little finger; **— del corazón, — cordial** middle finger; **— chico** little toe; **— gordo** big toe; **— índice** index finger, forefinger; **— pulgar** thumb; **ligero de —s** light-fingered; **comerse** (*or* **morderse**) **los —s** to get very impatient; **contar con los —s** to count on one's fingers; **chuparse los —s** to eat with relish; (*fig*) to smack one's lips; to rub one's hands; **dale un — y se toma hasta el codo** give him an inch and he'll take a yard; **entrar a —** to get in (*or* get a job) by pulling strings; **se le escapó de entre los —s** it slipped through his fingers; **hacer —s** (*Mus*) to practise, do scales; **no se mama el —** he's pretty smart; **meterse los —s en la nariz** to put one's fingers to one's nose; **meter el — en la boca a uno** to try to get someone to talk; **poner el — en** to put one's finger on, pinpoint, identify precisely; **poner el — en la llaga** to put one's finger on the spot; **señalar algo con el —** to point something out; **no se ven los —s de la mano** it's pitch-dark.

(b) (*fig*) spot, bit, drop; (*as measure*) finger; finger's breadth; **¡dos —s nada más!** (*drink*) just a tiny drop!; **estar a dos —s de** to be within an inch of, be within an ace of; to be on the verge of; **no tiene dos —s de frente** he's pretty dim; he's a lout.

deducción *nf* **(a)** deduction; inference. **(b)** (*sum etc*) deduction.
deducible (a) deducible, inferable (*de* from); **según es fácilmente —** as may readily be deduced. **(b)** (*Fin etc*) deductible; (*for tax purposes*) allowable.
deducir [3o] *vt* **(a)** to deduce, infer (*de* from); *formula* to deduce, derive. **(b)** *sum etc* to deduct; **deducidos los gastos** less charges. **(c)** (*Arg*) to produce.
deductivo *adj* deductive.
deescalación *nf* de-escalation.
defalcar [1g] *vt* = **desfalcar**.
defecación *nf* defecation.
defecar [1g] *vi* to defecate.
defección *nf* defection, desertion.
defectible *adj* fallible, imperfect; faulty.
defectivo *adj* defective (*also Gram*).
defecto *nm* fault, defect, flaw; (*Elec, Tech*) fault; (*in manufacture, argument*) flaw; (*moral*) shortcoming; failure; **— físico** physical defect; **— de fonación, — de la palabra** speech defect, impediment; **en — de** for lack of, for want of.
defectuosamente *adv* defectively, faultily.
defectuoso *adj* defective, faulty.
defender [2g] **1** *vt* to defend (*contra* against, *de* from); to protect; (*Law*) to defend; *cause* to champion, uphold; **para —los contra el frío** in order to protect them from the cold.

2 defenderse *vr* **(a)** to defend oneself (*contra* against, *de* from); **— bien** to resist firmly; to give a good account of oneself.

(b) (*fig*) **me defiendo en inglés** I can manage in English, I can get along in English, I can keep going in English; **"¿qué tal?" . . . "hombre, nos defendemos"** "how are things?" . . . "we're managing"; **— como un gato, — panza arriba** to get by but only just; to scrape through.
defendible *adj* defensible; that can be defended.
defensa 1 *nf* **(a)** defence (*also Chess, Law, Sport*); protection, shelter; **— contra, — de** defence against; **— pasiva** civil defence; **— en profundidad** defence in depth; **en — propia** in self-defence.

(b) (*Naut*) fender; (*Sport*) shinpad, leg pad; **— marítima** (*Arg*) sea wall.

(c) —s (*Mil*) defences, defensive works; **—s costeras** coastal defences.

2 *nm* (*Sport*) back, fullback.
defensiva *nf* defensive; **estar a la —** to be on the defensive.
defensivo 1 *adj* defensive. **2** *nm* defence, safeguard.
defensor *nm*, **defensora** *nf* defender; protector; (*of cause*) champion, upholder; (*Law: also* **abogado —**) defending counsel.
deferencia *nf* deference.
deferente *adj* deferential.
deferir [3l] **1** *vt* (*Law*) to refer, relegate (*a* to). **2** *vi*: **— a** to defer to.
deficiencia *nf* deficiency, shortcoming, defect (*de* in, of).
deficiente *adj* deficient, wanting (*en* in); defective.
déficit *nm* *or* **defícit** *nm*, *pl* **déficits** *or* **defícits** (*Comm, Fin*) deficit; (*fig*) lack, shortage; shortfall.
definible *adj* definable, that can be defined.
definición *nf* definition; **por —** by definition.
definido *adj* definite (*also Gram*); **bien —** well defined, clearly defined.
definir [3a] *vt* to define; to clarify, explain; to determine, establish.
definitivo *adj* definitive; final, ultimate; **en definitiva** definitively; finally, once and for all; in short.
deflación *nf* deflation.
deflacionar [1a] *vt* to deflate.
deflacionario *adj*, **deflacionista** *adj* deflationary.
deflector *nm* (*Tech*) baffle, baffle plate.
deformación *nf* deformation; (*Radio etc*) distortion; (*Mech*) strain; (*of wood etc*) warping.
deformar [1a] **1** *vt* to deform; to disfigure; (*Radio etc*) to distort; (*Mech*) to strain; *wood etc* to warp, push out of shape.

2 deformarse *vr* to become deformed; to get distorted; to warp, get out of shape, lose shape.
deforme *adj* deformed, misshapen; ugly; abnormal.
deformidad *nf* **(a)** deformity, malformation; abnormality. **(b)** (*fig*) (moral) shortcoming.
defraudación *nf* **(a)** defrauding; deceit; **— fiscal, — de impuestos** tax evasion. **(b)** dashing, disappointment.
defraudar [1a] *vt* **(a)** to cheat, defraud; to deceive; **— impuestos** to evade taxes, fiddle one's income tax (*fam*). **(b)** *hopes* to dash, disappoint, frustrate. **(c)** (*Phys*) *light* to intercept, cut off.
defuera *adv* (*also* **por —**) outwardly, on the outside.
defunción *nf* decease, demise.
degeneración *nf* **(a)** degeneration (*en* into). **(b)** (moral) degeneracy.
degenerado 1 *adj* degenerate. **2** *nm* degenerate, degenerate type.
degenerar [1a] *vi* to degenerate (*en* into); to decline, decay; to get worse, get more serious; **la manifestación degeneró en una sangrienta revuelta** the demonstration degenerated into a bloody disturbance.
deglución *nf* swallowing.
deglutir [3a] *vti* to swallow.
degollación *nf* throat cutting; (*Law*) beheading, execution; (*wider sense*) massacre, slaughter; **D— de los Inocentes** Massacre of the Innocents.
degolladero *nm* (*Anat*) throat, neck, throttle.

(b) (*Hist*) scaffold, block (for executions); **ir al —** (*fig*) to expose oneself to mortal danger, (*hum*) put one's head in the lion's mouth, go to the chopping block.

(c) slaughterhouse.
degollador *nm* (*Hist*) executioner.
degollar [1n] *vt* **(a)** to cut (*or* slit) the throat of; (*Law*) to behead, decapitate; (*fig*) to massacre, slaughter.

(b) (*fig*) to destroy; *play etc* to murder, make nonsense of; *part* to make a dreadful hash of.

(c) (*Sew*) to cut low in the neck.
degradación *nf* **(a)** degradation; humiliation. **(b)** (*Mil etc*) demotion, reduction in rank.
degradante *adj* degrading.
degradar [1a] **1** *vt* **(a)** to degrade, debase; to humiliate. **(b)** (*Mil etc*) to demote, reduce in rank. **2 degradarse** *vr* to demean oneself.
degüello *nm* **(a)** = **degollación**; **entrar a — en una ciudad** to put the people of a city to the sword, give no quarter to the inhabitants of a town.

(b) (*of weapon*) shaft, neck, narrow part.
degustación *nf* tasting, sampling.
degustar [1a] *vt* to taste, sample.
dehesa *nf* pasture, meadow; pastureland, range.
deidad *nf* deity; divinity; **— pagana** pagan god, pagan deity.
deificación *nf* deification; apotheosis (*also fig*).

deificar [1g] *vt* (**a**) to deify; to apotheosize (*also fig*). (**b**) (*fig*) to exalt, over-praise, put on a pedestal.

deísmo *nm* deism.

deísta 1 *adj* deistic(al). **2** *nmf* deist.

dejación *nf* (**a**) (*Law*) abandonment, relinquishment. (**b**) (*CAm, Col*) carelessness.

dejadez *nf* (**a**) untidiness, slovenliness; abandon. (**b**) carelessness, negligence, neglect, slackness; laziness; supineness, lack of willpower.

dejado *adj* (**a**) untidy, slovenly; abandoned; unkempt. (**b**) careless, negligent, slack; lazy. (**c**) dejected. (**d**) — **de la mano de Dios** (*fig*) godforsaken; beyond all hope of redemption.

dejamiento *nm* = **dejación** (a); = **dejadez**.

dejar [1a] **1** *vt* (**a**) to leave; to forget, leave out; to leave, abandon, desert, forsake; *book etc* to lend; *effort, work etc* to give up, stop, abandon; *passenger* to put down, set down; to drop; (*Comm*) *balance etc* to show, leave; *profit* to produce, yield; — **aparte** to leave aside; — **atrás** to leave behind, outstrip, outdistance; (*fig*) to surpass; — **a uno muy atrás** to leave someone far behind; — **algo para mañana** to leave something till tomorrow, postpone (*or* put off) something till tomorrow; — **algo para después** to leave something till later; **lo dejamos por muy difícil** we gave it up because it was too hard; **lo dejamos por imposible** we gave it up as (being) impossible; **así que lo dejamos** so we gave it up; **¡— eso!** stop that, drop that!, chuck it!; **se lo dejo en la conserjería** I'll leave it for you at the porter's office; — **así las cosas** to leave things as they are; **dejémoslo así** let's leave it at that; **como dejo dicho** as I have said; **deja escritas 3 novelas** he left 3 novels which he had written; he left 3 finished novels; **deja mucho que desear** it leaves a lot to be desired.

(**b**) to let, allow; **quiero pero no me dejan** I want to but they won't let me; — **a uno** + *infin* to let someone + *infin*, allow someone to + *infin*; — **a uno entrar** to let someone in; **dejar a uno pasar** to let someone in (*or* through, past *etc*); — **a uno salir** to let someone out; — **que las cosas vayan de mal en peor** to let things go from bad to worse; — **que se enfríe** (*instruction*) let it get cold; *see* **caer, mano** *etc*.

2 *vi*: — **de** + *infin* (**a**) to stop + *ger*, leave off + *ger*, give up + *ger*; **dejó de cantar** she stopped singing; **cuando deje de llover** when it stops raining, when the rain stops; **no puedo** — **de fumar** I can't give up smoking; *see* **existir** *etc*.

(**b**) to fail to + *infin*, neglect to + *infin*; **no dejes de visitarles** don't fail to visit them, on no account neglect to pay them a visit.

(**c**) **no puedo** — **de asombrarme** I cannot but be amazed, I cannot help being astonished; **no puedo** — **de pensar que . . .** I can't help thinking that . . .; **no deja de ser algo raro** all the same it's rather odd; **yo había dejado de oírle tocar desde hacía 5 años** I had not heard him play for 5 years.

3 dejarse *vr* (**a**) to neglect oneself, let oneself go, get slovenly.

(**b**) — **de** + *infin* to allow oneself to be + *ptp*, let oneself be + *ptp*; — **persuadir** to allow oneself to be persuaded; **no se dejó engañar** he was not to be deceived; **se dejó decir que . . .** he let it slip that . . .; **se dejó oír una débil voz** a weak voice made itself heard (*or* could be heard); *see* **vencer** *etc*.

(**c**) — **de** + *infin* to stop + *ger*; **¡déjese de eso!** stop that!, cut it out!; *see* **broma**.

dejo *nm* (**a**) aftertaste, tang; **tiene un** — **raro** it leaves an odd taste.

(**b**) (*fig*) touch, smack, tang, flavour.

(**c**) (*Ling*) accent, trace of accent, special inflection.

del = **de** + **el**.

delación *nf* accusation; denunciation; information.

delantal *nm* apron; — **de cuero** leather apron; — **de niña** pinafore.

delante 1 *adv* (*also* **por** —) in front; ahead; opposite; **la parte de** — the front part; **la casa no tiene nada** — the house has nothing opposite; **estando otros** — with others present; in the presence of others; **abierto por** — open in front; **¡las damas por —!** ladies first!; **entrar al puerto (con) la popa** — to enter harbour stern first; **tenemos todavía 4 horas por** — we still have 4 hours in front of us.

2 — *prep* in front of, before; ahead of.

delantera *nf* (**a**) front, front part; (*Theat*) front row; (*Sport*) forward line.

(**b**) (*fig*) advantage, lead; **llevar la** — to lead, be in the lead; **llevar la** — **a uno** to be ahead of someone; **coger la** — **a uno** to get ahead of someone; to

get a start on someone; **sacar la** — **a uno** to steal a march on someone; **tomar la** — to take the lead.

(**c**) —**s** overalls.

delantero 1 *adj* *part, row, wheel etc* front; *leg* front, fore; *line, position* (*Sport*) forward; (*in progress etc*) first, foremost.

2 *nm* (*Sport*) forward; — **centro** centre-forward; — **extremo** outside-forward, wing-forward; — **interior** inside-forward.

delatar [1a] *vt* (**a**) to denounce, inform against, accuse; to betray; **éste los delató a la policía** this man reported them to the police, (*pej*) this man gave them away to the police.

(**b**) (*fig*) to reveal, betray.

delator *nm*, **delatora** *nf* informer, accuser; betrayer.

delectación *nf* delight, delectation.

delegación *nf* (**a**) (*act*) delegation; — **de poderes** (*Parl*) devolution.

(**b**) (*body*) delegation; **la** — **fue a cumplimentar al Ministro** the delegation went to pay its respects to the minister.

(**c**) (*Comm etc*) local office, branch; office of a government department; police station; — **de Hacienda** local Treasury office.

delegado *nm*, **delegada** *nf* delegate; (*Comm*) agent, representative.

delegar [1h] *vt* to delegate (*a* to).

deleitable *adj* enjoyable, delightful, delectable.

deleitación *nf*, **deleitamiento** *nm* delectation.

deleitar [1a] **1** *vt* to delight, charm. **2 deleitarse** *vr*: — **con**, — **en** to delight in, take pleasure in; — **en** + *infin* to delight in + *ger*.

deleite *nm* delight, pleasure; joy; —**s** delights.

deleitosamente *adv* delightfully; deliciously.

deleitoso *adj* delightful, pleasing; delicious.

deletéreo *adj* deleterious.

deletrear [1a] *vt* (**a**) to spell (out). (**b**) (*fig*) to decipher, interpret. (**c**) (*Chi*) to observe in great detail, look minutely at.

deletreo *nm* (**a**) spelling. (**b**) decipherment, interpretation.

deleznable *adj* (**a**) fragile, brittle; crumbly; unstable; *surface etc* slippery. (**b**) (*fig*) frail; *argument etc* weak; fleeting, ephemeral; insubstantial.

délfico *adj* Delphic.

delfín *nm* (*Zool*) dolphin.

Delfos Delphi.

delgadez *nf* (**a**) thinness; slimness. (**b**) delicateness; tenuousness. (**c**) sharpness.

delgado 1 *adj* (**a**) thin; *person, figure* thin; slim, slender; slight.

(**b**) (*fig*) delicate; light, tenuous.

(**c**) (*fig*) *soil* poor, exhausted.

(**d**) (*fig*) sharp, clever.

2 *adv*: **hilar** (**muy**) — to draw it fine, (*pej*) to split hairs.

deliberación *nf* deliberation.

deliberadamente *adv* deliberately.

deliberado *adj* deliberate.

deliberar [1a] **1** *vt* to debate, discuss; — + *infin* to decide to + *infin*. **2** *vi* to deliberate (*sobre* on), discuss (*si* whether).

deliberativo *adj* deliberative.

delicadamente *adv* delicately.

delicadez *nf* (**a**) = **delicadeza**. (**b**) weakness. (**c**) hypersensitiveness, touchiness, susceptibility.

delicadeza *nf* (**a**) delicacy; daintiness; thinness; frailness; refinement.

(**b**) touchiness, hypersensitiveness; fastidiousness; squeamishness; tactfulness; subtlety; **falta de** — tactlessness; **¡qué** —**!** how charming of you!

delicado *adj* (**a**) delicate; dainty; *machine etc* delicate, sensitive; *material* thin; slender, frail; *health* delicate; *colour* soft, delicate; *dish* dainty; *taste* refined, exquisite; *distinction* nice, delicate, subtle; *situation* delicate, tricky; embarrassing; *point* tender, sensitive; sore; **está** — **del estómago** he has a delicate stomach.

(**b**) (*of person's character*) demanding; hard to please; touchy, hypersensitive; fastidious; squeamish; (over)scrupulous; tactful; considerate; *mind* subtle; keen; **es muy** — **en el comer** he's very choosy about food (*fam*); **es muy** — **para la limpieza** he's very particular about cleanliness.

delicia *nf* delight; delightfulness; **el país es una** — the country is delightful; **tiene un jardín que es una** — he has a delightful garden; **un libro que ha hecho las** —**s de muchos niños** a book which has been the delight of many children.

delictivo *adj* act *etc* criminal.

delimitación *nf* delimitation.

delimitar [1a] *vt* to delimit.

delincuencia *nf* delinquency, criminality; — **juvenil**, — **de menores** juvenile delinquency; **cifras de la** — figures of crimes committed, incidence of criminality.
delincuente 1 *adj* delinquent; criminal; guilty.
2 *nmf* delinquent, criminal, offender; guilty person; — **sin antecedente penal** first offender; — **habitual** hardened criminal; — **juvenil** juvenile delinquent.
delineación *nf*, **delineamiento** *nm* delineation.
delineante *nm* draughtsman.
delinear [1a] *vt* to delineate; to outline; to draw.
delinquimiento *nm* delinquency; guilt.
delinquir [3e] *vi* to commit an offence; to offend, transgress.
deliquio *nm* swoon, fainting fit.
delirante *adj* delirious; light-headed; raving.
delirar [1a] *vi* to be delirious, rave; (*fig*) to rave, rant, talk nonsense.
delirio *nm* (**a**) (*Med and fig*) delirium; ravings, wanderings; nonsense, nonsensical talk.
(**b**) frenzy; mania; — **de grandezas** megalomania; — **de persecución** persecution mania.
(**c**) (*fam*) **con** — madly; **me gusta con** — I'm crazy about it; **¡fue el** —! it was great! (*fam*) **cuando acabó de hablar fue el** — when he finished speaking there were scenes of wild enthusiasm.
delírium *nm* **tremens** delirium tremens.
delito *nm* (**a**) crime, offence; — **de mayor cuantía** felony; — **de menor cuantía** misdemeanour. (**b**) (*fig*) misdeed, wicked act, offence.
delta 1 *nm* (*Geog*) delta. **2** *nf* (*letter*) delta.
deludir [3a] *vt* to delude.
delusorio *adj* delusive.
demacración *nf* emaciation.
demacrado *adj* emaciated, wasted away.
demacrarse [1a] *vr* to become emaciated, waste away.
demagogia *nf* demagogy, demagoguery.
demagógico *adj* demagogic.
demagogismo *nm* demagogy, demagoguery.
demagogo *nm* demagogue.
demanda *nf* (**a**) demand, request (**de** for); inquiry; claim; petition; — **de pago** demand for payment; — **del Santo Grial** quest for the Holy Grail; **escribir en** — **de ayuda** to write asking for help; **ir en** — **de** to go in search of, go looking for; **partir en** — **de** to go off in search of.
(**b**) (*Theat*) call.
(**c**) (*Comm*) demand; **hay mucha** — **de cerillas** matches are in great demand; **tener** — to be in demand; **ese producto no tiene** — there is no demand for that product.
(**d**) (*Elec*) load; — **máxima** peak load.
(**e**) (*Law*) action, lawsuit; **entablar** — to bring an action, take legal proceedings, sue; **presentar** — **de divorcio** to sue for divorce, take divorce proceedings.
demandado *nm*, **demandada** *nf* defendant; (*in divorce*) respondent.
demandante *nmf* claimant; (*Law*) plaintiff.
demandar [1a] *vt* (**a**) to demand, ask for, request; to claim; to petition.
(**b**) (*Law*) to sue, file a suit against, start proceedings against; **demandó al periódico por calumnia** he sued the paper for libel; — **a uno por daños y perjuicios** to sue someone for damages; **ser demandado por libelo** to be sued for libel.
demaquillante *nm* make-up remover.
demarcación *nf* demarcation; **línea de** — demarcation line.
demarcar [1g] *vt* to demarcate.
demás 1 *adj*: **los** — **libros** the other books, the rest of the books, the remaining books; **y** — **gente de ese tipo** and other people of that sort.
2 *pron*: **lo** — the rest (of it); **los** —, **las** — the others, the rest (of them); **por lo** — for the rest, as to the rest; otherwise; furthermore, moreover.
3 *adv* = **además**; **por** — moreover; in vain; **y** — **etcétera**, and so on; *see* **más (estar de más)**.
demasía *nf* (**a**) excess, surplus; superfluity; **en** — too much, excessively. (**b**) (*fig*) excess, outrage, wicked thing; wrong; affront. (**c**) (*fig*) boldness; insolence.
demasiado 1 *adj* (**a**) too much; overmuch, excessive; **eso es** — that's too much; **con** — **cuidado** with excessive care; **hace** — **calor** it's too hot; **¡esto es** —! this is too much!, that's the limit!
(**b**) —**s** too many.
2 *adv* too; too much, excessively; (*SAm*) a lot, a great deal; **comer** — to eat too much; **es** — **pesado para levantar** it is too heavy to lift; — **lo sé** I know it only too well.
demediar [1b] **1** *vt* to divide in half. **2** *vi* to be divided in half.

demencia *nf* madness, insanity, dementia.
dementar [1a] **1** *vt* to drive mad. **2 dementarse** *vr* to go mad, become demented.
demente 1 *adj* mad, insane, demented. **2** *nmf* mad person, lunatic.
demérito *nm* (**a**) demerit, fault; disadvantage. (**b**) unworthiness. (**c**) (*SAm*) depreciation.
demeritorio *adj* undeserving, unworthy.
democracia *nf* democracy.
demócrata *nf* democrat.
democráticamente *adv* democratically.
democrático *adj* democratic.
democratizar [1f] *vt* to democratize.
demografía *nf* demography.
demográfico *adj* demographic; population (*attr*); **la explosión demográfica** the population explosion.
demoledor *adj* (*fig*) argument *etc* powerful, overwhelming; *attack* shattering.
demoler [2h] *vt* (**a**) to demolish; pull down. (**b**) (*fig*) to demolish.
demolición *nf* demolition.
demonche *nm* (*euph*) = **demonio**.
demoníaco *adj* demoniacal, demonic.
demonio *nm* (**a**) devil; demon; evil spirit.
(**b**) **ese** — **de sereno** that devil of a night watchman; **como el** — like the devil; **ir como el** — to go like the devil, go hell for leather; **esto pesa como el** — this is devilish heavy; **¡vete al** —! go to the devil!; **¡vaya con mil** —**s!** go to blazes!; **¡que se lo lleve el** —! to hell with it!; the devil take it!; **tener el** — **en el cuerpo** to be always on the go, have the devil in one; **esto sabe a** —(**s**) this tastes awful (*fam*); **un ruido de todos los** —**s** a devil of a noise.
(**c**) (*exclamatory etc*) **¡**—**!**, **¡qué** —! (*rage*) hell!, confound it!; (*exasperation*) hang it all!; (*surprise*) good heavens!; what the devil . . .?; the devil it is!; **¿qué** —**s será?** what the devil can that be?; **¡qué príncipe ni qué** —**s!** prince my foot!; **¿dónde** — **lo habré dejado?** where the devil can I have left it?
demontre *nm* (*euph*) = **demonio**.
demora *nf* (**a**) delay; **sin** — without delay. (**b**) (*Naut*) bearing.
demorado *adj* effect *etc* delayed.
demorar [1a] **1** *vt* to delay; to hold up, hold back.
2 *vi* to stay on, linger on, delay, waste time.
3 demorarse *vr* = **2**; — **en** + *infin* (*esp SAm*) to take a long time to + *infin*, be slow in + *ger*.
demorón *adj* (Arg, Chi, Per) = **demoroso**.
demoroso *adj* (Chi) slow, lazy; late, overdue; **ser** — **en** + *infin* to take a long time to + *infin*, be slow in + *ger*.
Demóstenes *m* Demosthenes.
demostrable *adj* demonstrable, that can be demonstrated.
demostración *nf* demonstration, show, display; gesture; — **de cariño** show of affection; — **de cólera** display of anger; — **comercial** commercial display, trade exhibition.
demostrar [1m] *vt* to demonstrate, show; to show off; to prove; — **cómo se hace algo** to demonstrate how something is done; — **que . . .** to show that . . ., prove that . . .; **Vd no puede** —**me nada** you can't prove anything against me.
demostrativo 1 *adj* demonstrative. **2** *nm* demonstrative.
demótico *adj* demotic.
demudación *nf* change, alteration.
demudado *adj* (*fig*) upset, distraught.
demudar [1a] **1** *vt* to change, alter.
2 demudarse *vr* (**a**) to change, alter.
(**b**) (*fig*) to change colour, change countenance; to look upset, show one's distress; **sin** — without a flicker of emotion; **continuó sin** — he went on quite unaffected (*or* unabashed).
denegación *nf* refusal; rejection; denial.
denegar [1h *and* 1k] *vt* to refuse; to reject; to deny; (*Law*) *appeal* to reject, refuse to allow.
dengoso *adj* affected; prudish; dainty, finicky.
dengue *nm* (**a**) affectation; coyness; prudery; daintiness, finickiness; **hacer** —**s** to act coyly, simper; to be finicky; **no me vengas con esos** —**s** I don't want to hear your silly complaints.
(**b**) (*Med*) influenza, flu (*fam*).
denguero *adj* = **dengoso**.
denier *nm* denier.
denigrante *adj* insulting; degrading.
denigrar [1a] *vt* to denigrate, revile, run down; to insult.
denodadamente *adv* boldly, dauntlessly, intrepidly; **luchar** — to fight bravely.
denodado *adj* bold, dauntless, intrepid, brave.

denominación nf (a) (act) naming. (b) name, designation; denomination; — **social** (Mex) firm's official name.

denominado adj named, called; so-called.

denominador nm denominator; — **común** common denominator.

denominar [1a] vt to name, call, designate.

denostar [1m] vt to insult, revile, abuse; to condemn.

denotar [1a] vt to denote; to indicate, show; to express.

densamente adv densely; compactly; thickly; drily; solidly.

densidad nf density; compactness; thickness; heaviness, dryness; solidity; — **de población** density of population.

denso adj (in most senses) dense; compact; smoke, liquid etc thick; book, reading, speech heavy, dry; solid.

dentado adj having teeth; wheel cogged, toothed; edge jagged; stamp perforated; (Bot) dentate.

dentadura nf set of teeth, teeth (collectively); denture; — **artificial**, — **postiza** false teeth, denture(s); **tener mala** — to have bad teeth.

dental 1 adj dental. **2** nf dental.

dentar [1k] **1** vt to put teeth on, furnish with teeth; edge to make jagged; (Tech) to indent; stamp to perforate; **sello sin** — imperforate stamp. **2** vi to teethe, cut one's teeth.

dentellada nf (a) bite, nip; **partir algo a** —s to sever something with one's teeth. (b) tooth mark.

dentellar [1a] vi (of teeth) to chatter; **estaba dentellando** his teeth were chattering; **el susto le hizo** — the fright made his teeth chatter.

dentellear [1a] vt to bite, nibble (at), sink one's teeth into.

dentera nf (a) the shivers, the shudders; **dar** — **a uno** to set someone's teeth on edge, give someone the shivers.
(b) (fig) envy, jealousy; great desire; **dar** — **a uno** to make someone jealous; to make one's mouth water; **le da** — **que hagan fiestas al niño** it makes him jealous when they make a fuss of the baby.

dentición nf (a) (act) teething; **estar con la** — to be teething. (b) (Anat) dentition.

dentífrico 1 adj tooth (attr); **pasta dentífrica** toothpaste. **2** nm dentifrice, toothpaste.

dentina nf (of tooth) ivory.

dentista nmf dentist.

dentón adj large-toothed, buck-toothed, toothy.

dentrera nf (Col) servant.

dentro 1 adv (a) (estar) inside; indoors; feel etc inwardly, inside; **allí** — in there; **de** —, **desde** — from inside; **por** — inside, on the inside, in the interior.
(b) (ir) in, inside; indoors; **meter algo para** — to push something in; **vamos** — let's go in(side).
2 **de** prep (a) (estar) in, inside, within; — **de la casa** inside the house.
(b) (meter) **del** — into, inside; **lo metió** — **del cajón** he put it into the drawer.
(c) (time) within, inside; — **de 3 meses** inside 3 months, within 3 months; — **de poco** shortly; soon after.
(d) — **de lo posible** as far as one (etc) can, as far as is possible; **eso no cabe** — **de lo posible** that does not come within the bounds of possibility.

dentrodera nf (Col) servant.

denudación nf denudation.

denudar [1a] vt to denude (de of); to lay bare.

denuedo nm boldness, daring; bravery.

denuesto nm insult; **llenar a uno de** —s to heap insults on someone.

denuncia nf report; denunciation; (Law etc) accusation; — **de accidente** report of an accident; — **falsa** false accusation.

denunciable adj crime indictable, punishable.

denunciación nf denunciation; accusation.

denunciador nm, **denunciadora** nf, **denunciante** nmf accuser; informer; **el** — **del accidente** the person who reported the accident.

denunciar [1b] vt to report (a to); to proclaim, announce; to foretell; (Law etc) to denounce (a to), accuse (a before), inform against; (pej) to betray, give away (a to); **denunciaron los precios abusivos a las autoridades** they reported the exorbitant prices to the authorities; **el accidente fue denunciado a la policía** the accident was reported to the police; **esto denunciaba la presencia del gas** this betrayed the presence of gas, this indicated the presence of gas; **lo hemos denunciado muchas veces** we have denounced this many times.

denuncio nm (SAm) = **denuncia**.

deparar [1a] vt to provide, furnish with; to present, offer; **nos deparó la ocasión para . . .** it gave us a chance to . . .; **los placeres que el viaje nos deparó** the pleasures which the trip afforded us; **pero también nos deparó la solución** but it also furnished us with the solution.

departamental adj departmental.

departamento nm (a) (in general) department, section; office; bureau; — **jurídico** legal department; — **de visados** visa section.
(b) (of box etc) compartment.
(c) (Rail etc) compartment; — **de fumadores** smoking compartment; — **de no fumadores** nonsmoking compartment; — **de primera** first-class compartment.
(d) (Naut) — **de máquinas** engine room.
(e) (SAm) flat, apartment.
(f) (SAm) department, administrative district, province.

departir [1a] vi to talk, converse (con with, de about).

depauperación nf (a) impoverishment. (b) (Med) weakening, exhaustion.

depauperar [1a] vt (a) to impoverish. (b) (Med) to weaken, deplete, exhaust.

dependencia nf (a) (in general) dependence (de on); reliance (de on).
(b) relationship, kinship.
(c) (Pol etc) dependency.
(d) (Comm) section, office; branch office.
(e) (Archit) room; outbuilding, outhouse.
(f) (Comm etc) personnel, sales staff, employees.
(g) —s accessories.

dependienta nf salesgirl, saleswoman, shop assistant.

dependiente 1 adj dependent (de on). **2** nm employee; clerk; salesman. nf shop assistant.

depender [2a] vi to depend; — **de** to depend on; to rely on; **depende** it (all) depends; **depende de lo que haga él** it depends on what he does; **todo depende de que él esté listo** it all turns on his being ready; **no depende de mí** it does not rest with me; **todos dependemos de ti** we are all relying on you.

depilar [1a] vt to depilate, remove the hair from; eyebrows to pluck.

depilatorio 1 adj depilatory. **2** nm depilatory.

deplorable adj deplorable; lamentable, regrettable.

deplorar [1a] vt to deplore, regret; to condemn; **lo deploro mucho** I greatly deplore it, I'm extremely sorry.

deponente 1 adj (a) (Ling) deponent. (b) (Law) **la persona** — the person giving evidence. **2** nmf (Law) person giving evidence, person making a statement.

deponer [2r] **1** vt (a) to lay down; to lay aside; to remove, take down; arms to lay down.
(b) king to depose; ruler to oust, overthrow; minister to remove from office.
2 vi (a) (Law) to give evidence, make a statement.
(b) (CAm, Mex) to vomit.

deportación nf deportation.

deportar [1a] vt to deport.

deporte nm sport; game; outdoor recreation; — **acuáticos** water sports; — **de bucear** skin diving; — **hípico** horse-riding; — **de invierno** winter sports; — **del remo** rowing; — **de la vela** sailing; **el fútbol es un** — football is a game; **es muy aficionado a los** —s he is very fond of sport.

deportista 1 adj sports (attr); sporting; **el público** — the sporting public. **2** nm sportsman; sporting man, sports fan (fam). **3** nf sportswoman.

deportividad nf sportsmanship.

deportivo 1 adj (a) club, paper etc sports (attr). (b) outlook, conduct etc sporting, sportsmanlike. **2** nm (Aut) sports car.

deposición nf (a) (act) deposition, removal. (b) assertion, affirmation; (Law) deposition, evidence, statement.

depositador nm, **depositadora** nf, **depositante** nmf (Comm, Fin) depositor.

depositar [1a] **1** vt to deposit; to place; to lay aside; to put away, store, put into store; to entrust (en to), confide (en to). **2 depositarse** vr (liquid) to settle.

depositaría nf depository; (Fin etc) trust.

depositario nm, **depositaria** nf depository, trustee; receiver; (of secret etc) repository.

depósito nm (a) (Chem etc) deposit; sediment; (Geol, Min) deposit.
(b) (Comm, Fin) deposit; — **bancario** bank deposit; **dejar una cantidad en** — to leave a sum as a deposit.
(c) (Comm etc) store, storehouse, warehouse; depot; (for lost objects, cars etc) pound; (Mil) depot; dump; — **de aduana** customs warehouse; —

afianzado bonded warehouse; **— de basura** rubbish dump, tip; **— de cadáveres** mortuary, morgue; **— de carbón** coal tip; **— de equipajes** cloakroom; **— de libros** book stack; **— de locomotoras** engine shed; **— de maderas** timber yard; **— de municiones** ammunition dump.

(d) (for liquids) tank; cistern; reservoir; **— de agua** water tank, cistern; **— de gasolina** petrol tank; **— de combustible** fuel tank.

depravación nf depravity, depravation, corruption.

depravado adj depraved, corrupt.

depravar [1a] **1** vt to deprave, corrupt. **2 depravarse** vr to become depraved.

depreciación nf depreciation.

depreciar [1b] **1** vt to depreciate, reduce the value of. **2 depreciarse** vr to depreciate, lose value.

depredación nf depredation; outrage, excess; pillage.

depredar [1a] vt to pillage; to commit outrages against.

depresión nf (a) (Geog etc) depression; hollow; (in horizon etc) dip; (in wall) recess, niche.

(b) (act) lowering; drop, fall (de in); **— del mercurio** fall in temperature (or pressure).

(c) (Meteorol) depression.

(d) (Econ) depression, slump, recession.

(e) (mental) depression.

depresivo adj, **deprimente** adj depressing; depressive.

deprimido adj (all senses) depressed.

deprimir [3a] **1** vt (a) (physically) to depress, press down; to flatten.

(b) (mentally etc) to depress.

(c) level etc to lower, reduce.

(d) (fig) to humiliate; to belittle, disparage. **2 deprimirse** vr to get depressed.

depuración nf (a) purification; cleansing. (b) (Pol etc) purge.

depurador nm purifier.

depurar [1a] vt (a) to purify; to cleanse, purge. (b) (Pol etc) to purge.

depurativo nm blood tonic.

derecha nf (a) right hand; right side, right-hand side; **estar a la —** to be on the right of; **torcer a la —** to turn (to the) right; **conducción a —** (Aut) right-hand drive; **el poste de la —** the post on the right; **seguir por la —** to keep (to the) right.

(b) (Pol) right.

(c) **a —s** rightly, aright; justly; **si le entiendo a —s** if I understand you aright.

derechamente adv (a) straight, directly. (b) (fig) properly, rightly.

derechazo nm (Boxing) right; (Tennis) forehand drive; (Taur) a pass with the cape.

derechista **1** adj rightist, right-wing. **2** nmf rightist, right-winger.

derecho 1 adj (a) right; right-hand.

(b) right-handed.

(c) straight; upright, erect, standing; **más — que una vela** as straight as a die; **poner algo —** to stand something upright.

(d) (CAm, Col, SD, Ven) lucky.

2 adv (a) straight, directly; upright.

(b) straight, directly; **ir — a** to go straight to.

3 nm (a) right side.

(b) right; claim, title; privilege, exemption; **—s cinematográficos** film rights; **—s civiles** civil rights; **— divino** divine right; **— de paso**, **— de tránsito** right of way; **— de propiedad literaria** copyright; **— de visita** right of search; **— de votar** right to vote, franchise; **con —** rightly, justly; **con — a** with a right to, with entitlement to; **por — propio** in his own right; **según —** by right(s); **"reservados todos los —s"** "all rights reserved", "copyright"; **¡no hay —!** it's not fair!; **tener — a** to have a right to, be entitled to; **tener — a + infin** to have a right to + infin.

(c) (Law) law; justice; **Facultad de D—** Faculty of Law; **estudiante de —** law student; **lo que manda el — en este caso** what justice demands in this case.

(d) (Fin) due(s); fee(s); tax(es); (on book, oil etc) royalties; (professional) fee(s); **franco de —s** duty-free; **sujeto a —s** subject to duty, dutiable; **—s de aduana**, **—s arancelarios** customs duty; **—s de autor** royalties; **—s de entrada** import duties; **—s de peaje** (Aut) toll; **— preferente** prefential duty; **—s de puerto** harbour dues.

derechura nf (a) straightness; directness; **hablar en —** to speak plainly, talk straight; **hacer algo en —** to do something right away.

(b) rightness, justice.

(c) (CAm, Per) (good) luck.

deriva nf (Naut) drift; leeway; (from course) deviation; **buque a la —** ship adrift, drifting ship; **ir a la —** to drift, be adrift.

derivación nf (a) derivation (also Ling); origin, source. (b) (Elec) shunt; **en —** shunt (attr); **hacer una —** en un alambre to tap a wire.

derivado 1 adj derived; derivative (also Ling). **2** nm (a) derivative (also Ling). (b) (Chem etc) by-product.

derivar¹ [1a] **1** vt to derive (de from; also Ling). **2** vi and **derivarse** vr to derive, be derived (de from).

derivar² [1a] vi (Naut) to drift.

derivativo 1 adj derivative. **2** nm derivative.

dermatología nf dermatology.

dermatólogo nm dermatologist.

dérmico adj skin (attr); **enfermedad dérmica** skin disease.

derogación nf repeal, abolition.

derogar [1h] vt to repeal, abolish.

derrabar [1a] vt to dock, cut off the tail of.

derramadero nm spillway.

derramamiento nm (a) spilling; shedding; overflowing; **— de sangre** bloodshed. (b) scattering, spreading. (c) (fig) squandering, wasting, lavishing.

derramar [1a] **1** vt (a) liquid to spill; to pour out, pour away; tears to weep, shed; blood to shed; light to shed, cast; **— una taza de café** to spill a cup of coffee.

(b) to scatter, spread (about); gossip, news to spread.

(c) taxes to apportion.

(d) (fig) to squander, waste; gifts etc to lavish (en on).

2 derramarse vr (a) to spill; to pour out, overflow, run over, flow out; (of pen, vessel) to leak; **llenar una taza hasta —** to fill a cup to overflowing.

(b) to spread, scatter, be scattered; **la multitud se derramó por todos lados** the crowd scattered in all directions.

derrame nm (a) (act) = **derramamiento**.

(b) (quantity) loss; overflow; outflow; leakage; waste.

(c) (Med) discharge; excess of liquid present in the body; **— sinovial** water on the knee.

derrapar [1a] vi (Aut) to skid; (Naut) to yaw.

derrape nm (Aut) skid; (Naut) yaw.

derredor: al — (de), **en — (de)** adv and prep around, about; **en su —** round about him.

derrelicto nm (Naut) derelict.

derrengado adj (a) bent, twisted, crooked. (b) crippled, lame; **estar —** (fig) to ache all over; to be footsore; **dejar — a uno** (fig) to wear someone out.

derrengar [1h] vt (a) to bend, twist, make crooked.

(b) **— a uno** to break someone's back, cripple someone; (fig) to wear someone out.

derrepente nm (CAm): **en un —** = **de repente**.

derretido adj (a) metal melted; molten; snow thawed.

(b) **estar — por una** to be crazy about someone.

derretimiento nm (a) melting; thawing. (b) (fig) squandering. (c) (fig) mad passion, burning love.

derretir [3l] **1** vt (a) metal to melt; to liquefy; ice cream etc to melt; snow to thaw.

(b) (fig) to squander, throw away.

(c) (fam) to bore to tears; to exasperate.

2 derretirse vr (a) to melt; to run, liquefy.

(b) (fig) to be very susceptible to love, fall in love easily; **— por una** to be crazy about someone.

(c) (fam) to get worked up, fret and fume.

derribar [1a] **1** vt (a) building to knock down, pull down, demolish; barrier to tear down; door to batter down.

(b) person to knock down; to floor, lay out; wrestler to floor, throw.

(c) (Aer) to shoot down, bring down; **fue derribado sobre el Canal** he was shot down over the Channel.

(d) (Hunting) to shoot, bag, bring down.

(e) government etc to bring down, overthrow, overturn.

(f) (fig) to humiliate.

2 derribarse vr (a) to fall down, collapse.

(b) (person) to throw oneself down, hurl oneself to the ground; to prostrate oneself.

derribo nm (a) knocking down, demolition. (b) (Wrestling) throw. (c) (Aer) shooting down; destruction. (d) overthrow. (e) **—s** rubble, debris.

derrisco nm (Cu) gorge, ravine.

derrocadero nm cliff, precipice, steep place.

derrocamiento nm (a) flinging down, throwing down. (b) demolition. (c) overthrow, toppling; ousting. (d) humbling.

derrocar [1g] **1** vt (a) object, person to fling down, hurl down.

(b) building etc to knock down, demolish.

(c) *government* to overthrow, topple; *minister etc* to oust (*de* from). **(d)** (*fig*) to humble.

2 derrocarse *vr:* — **por un precipicio** to throw oneself over a cliff.

derrochador 1 *adj* spendthrift. **2** *nm* spendthrift, wastrel.

derrochar [1a] *vt* **(a)** *money etc* to squander, waste; to lavish, pour out. **(b)** — **salud** to be bursting with health; — **mal genio** to be excessively bad-tempered.

derroche *nm* **(a)** squandering, waste; lavish expenditure; extravagance; **con un formidable** — **de recursos** with a lavish use of resources; **no se puede tolerar tal** — such extravagance is not to be tolerated.

(b) abundance, excess; **con un** — **de buen gusto** with an excess of good taste.

derrota[1] *nf* **(a)** road, route, track. **(b)** (*Naut*) course.

derrota[2] *nf* defeat; rout; débâcle, disaster; **sufrir una grave** — to suffer a serious defeat, (*in plan etc*) to suffer a grave setback.

derrotado *adj* **(a)** defeated; *team* defeated, beaten, losing. **(b)** *dress, person* shabby; **un actor** — a shabby old actor, a down-and-out actor.

derrotar [1a] *vt* **(a)** (*Mil*) to defeat; to rout, put to flight; *team etc* to defeat, beat. **(b)** *clothing* to tear, ruin; (*fig*) *health* to ruin.

derrotero *nm* **(a)** (*Naut*) course; (*fig*) course, plan of action; **tomar otro** — (*fig*) to adopt a different course. **(b)** (*Cu*) hidden treasure.

derrotismo *nm* defeatism.

derrotista 1 *adj* defeatist. **2** *nmf* defeatist.

derruir [3g] *vt* to demolish, tear down.

derrumbadero *nm* **(a)** cliff, precipice, steep place. **(b)** (*fig*) danger, hazard; pitfall.

derrumbamiento *nm* **(a)** plunge, headlong fall. **(b)** demolition; collapse; fall, cave-in; — **de piedras** fall of rocks; — **de tierra** landslide. **(c)** (*fig*) collapse, ruin, destruction; (*of price*) sharp fall, collapse.

derrumbar [1a] **1** *vt* **(a)** *object, person* to fling down, hurl down; to throw headlong. **(b)** *building etc* to knock down, demolish. **(c)** *balanced object* to upset, overturn.

2 derrumbarse *vr* **(a)** (*person etc*) to fling oneself, hurl oneself (headlong; *por* down, over); to fall headlong. **(b)** (*building etc*) to collapse, fall down, tumble down; (*roof*) to fall in, cave in. **(c)** (*fig: hopes etc*) to collapse, be ruined; **se han derrumbado los precios** prices have tumbled; the bottom has fallen out of the market.

derrumbe *nm* **(a)** = derrumbadero. **(b)** = derrumbamiento.

derviche *nm* dervish.

des — **de . . .**, **des . . .**; **un . . .**; *eg* **descolonización** decolonization; **desmilitarizado** demilitarized; **desempleo** unemployment; **desfavorable** unfavourable; **desgana** unwillingness.

desabastecido *adj:* **estar** — **de** to be out of (supplies of); **nos cogió** — **s de gasolina** it caught us without petrol.

desabillé *nm* deshabille.

desabollar [1a] *vt* to knock the dents out of, straighten.

desabonarse [1a] *vr* to stop subscribing.

desabono *nm* (*fig*) discredit; **hablar en** — **de uno** to say damaging things about someone, speak ill of someone.

desaborido *adj* **(a)** insipid, tasteless; *person* dull. **(b)** flimsy, unsubstantial.

desabotonar [1a] **1** *vt* to unbutton, undo. **2** *vi* (*Bot*) to open, blossom. **3 desabotonarse** *vr* to come undone.

desabrido *adj* **(a)** tasteless, insipid, flat. **(b)** *weather* unpleasant. **(c)** *person* surly, rude, disagreeable; *manner* harsh, rough; *answer etc* sharp; *debate* bitter, acrimonious.

desabrigado *adj* (*fig*) unprotected, exposed; defenceless.

desabrigar [1h] **1** *vt* **(a)** to remove the clothing of; to leave bare, uncover. **(b)** (*fig*) to leave without shelter, deprive of protection.

2 desabrigarse *vr* to take off one's (outer) clothing; to leave oneself bare, uncover oneself; — **en la cama** to throw off one's bedcovers.

desabrigo *nm* **(a)** (*act*) uncovering. **(b)** (*state*) bareness; exposure; lack of clothing (*or* covers). **(c)** (*fig*) unprotectedness; poverty, destitution.

desabrimiento *nm* **(a)** tastelessness, insipidness. **(b)** unpleasantness.

(c) surliness, rudeness; harshness; sharpness; acrimony; **contestar con** — to answer sharply. **(d)** (*fig*) depression, lowness of spirits; uneasy feeling.

desabrir [3a] *vt* **(a)** to give a nasty taste to. **(b)** (*fig*) to embitter; to torment.

desabrochar [1a] **1** *vt* **(a)** to undo, unfasten, unbutton; *person* to loosen the clothing of. **(b)** (*fig*) to penetrate, expose.

2 desabrocharse *vr* (*fig*) to unbosom oneself (*con* to).

desacatador *adj* disrespectful, insulting.

desacatar [1a] *vt* to be disrespectful to, behave insultingly towards.

desacato *nm* disrespect; insulting behaviour; (*Law etc*) contempt, act of contempt; — **a la justicia** contempt of court.

desacertadamente *adv* mistakenly, erroneously, wrongly; unwisely, injudiciously.

desacertado *adj* mistaken, erroneous, wrong; unwise, injudicious.

desacertar [1k] *vi* to be mistaken, be wrong; to get it wrong; to act unwisely.

desacierto *nm* mistake, miscalculation, error; miss; unfortunate remark (*etc*); **fue uno de muchos** — **s suyos** it was one of his many errors; **ha sido un** — **elegir tal sitio** it was a mistake to choose such a place.

desacomodado *adj* **(a)** unemployed, out of a job. **(b)** badly off. **(c)** awkward, troublesome, inconvenient.

desacomodar [1a] **1** *vt* **(a)** *servant* to discharge. **(b)** to put out, inconvenience. **2 desacomodarse** *vr* to lose one's post.

desaconsejable *adj* inadvisable.

desaconsejado *adj* ill-advised.

desaconsejar [1a] *vt person* to dissuade, advise against; **los rigores del viaje desaconsejaron esa decisión** the rigours of the journey made that decision seem inadvisable (*or* made that decision seem wrong).

desacoplar [1a] *vt* (*Elec*) to disconnect; (*Mech*) to take apart, uncouple.

desacordar [1m] **1** *vt* to put out of tune. **2 desacordarse** *vr* **(a)** (*Mus*) to get out of tune. **(b)** to be forgetful; — **de algo** to forget something.

desacorde *adj* **(a)** (*Mus*) discordant. **(b)** (*fig*) discordant, incongruous.

desacostumbrado *adj* unusual, unaccustomed.

desacostumbrar [1a] **1** *vt:* — **a uno de** to break someone of the habit of, wean someone away from. **2 desacostumbrarse** *vr:* — **de** to break oneself of the habit of.

desacreditar [1a] **1** *vt* **(a)** to discredit, damage the reputation of, bring into disrepute. **(b)** to cry down, disparage, run down. **2 desacreditarse** *vr* to become discredited.

desacuerdo *nm* **(a)** discord, disagreement; — **amistoso** agreement to differ; **estar en** — to be out of keeping (*con* with), be at variance (*con* with); **la corbata está en** — **con la camisa** the tie does not go with the shirt. **(b)** error, blunder. **(c)** forgetfulness.

desadeudarse [1a] *vr* to get out of debt.

desadorno *nm* bareness, lack of ornamentation.

desadvertido *adj* careless.

desadvertir [3i] *vt* to fail to notice; to disregard.

desafecto 1 *adj* disaffected; hostile; **elementos** — **s al régimen** those hostile to the régime, those out of sympathy with the régime. **2** *nm* disaffection; ill-will, dislike; hostility.

desaferrar [1k] *vt* **(a)** to loosen, unfasten. **(b)** — **a uno** to make someone change his mind, dissuade someone (from a strongly held opinion *etc*). **(c)** (*Naut*) *anchor* to weigh.

desafiador 1 *adj* defiant; challenging. **2** *nm*, **desafiadora** *nf* challenger.

desafiante *adj* challenging; *attitude etc* defiant.

desafiar [1a] *vt* **(a)** to challenge; — **a uno a** + *infin* to challenge someone to + *infin*, dare someone to + *infin*.

(b) to defy; to face, face up to; **han desafiado todos los peligros** they have defied all the dangers. **(c)** (*fig*) to challenge, compete with, measure up to. **(d)** (*Mex*) to fight.

desaficionarse [1a] *vr:* — **de** to come to dislike, take a dislike to.

desafilar [1a] **1** *vt* to blunt, dull. **2 desafilarse** *vr* to get blunt.

desafinadamente *adv sing etc* out of tune, off key.

desafinado adj: **estar —** to be out of tune.
desafinar [1a] vi (a) to be (or play, sing) out of tune; to go out of tune. (b) (fig) to speak out of turn.
desafío nm (a) challenge; duel. (b) (fig) challenge; defiance; competition, rivalry; **es un — a todos nosotros** it is a challenge to us all.
desaforadamente adv (a) behave etc outrageously. (b) shout at the top of one's voice.
desaforado adj (a) lawless, violent, disorderly; behaviour outrageous; **es un —** he's a violent sort, he's dangerously excitable.
(b) great, huge; shout mighty, ear-splitting.
desaforarse [1m] vr to behave in an outrageous way, act violently; to get worked up, lose control.
desafortunado adj unfortunate, unlucky.
desafuero nm outrage, excess.
desagraciado adj graceless, unattractive; unsightly.
desagradable adj disagreeable, unpleasant; **ser — con uno** to be rude to someone.
desagradablemente adj unpleasantly.
desagradar [1a] 1 vt to displease; to bother, upset; **me desagrada ese olor** I don't like that smell; **me desagrada tener que hacerlo** I dislike having to do it.
2 vi to be unpleasant.
desagradecido adj ungrateful.
desagradecimiento nm ingratitude.
desagrado nm displeasure; dislike; dissatisfaction; **hacer algo con —** to do something with distaste, do something unwillingly.
desagraviar [1b] 1 vt (a) person to make amends to; to indemnify; to apologize to.
(b) offence etc to make amends for, put right.
2 **desagraviarse** vr to get one's own back; to exact an apology; to restore one's honour.
desagravio nm amends; compensation, indemnification, satisfaction; **en — de** as amends for.
desagregación nf disintegration.
desagregar [1h] 1 vt to disintegrate. 2 **desagregarse** vr to disintegrate.
desaguadero nm drain (also fig; de on).
desaguar [1i] 1 vt (a) to drain, empty, run off. (b) (fig) to squander. 2 vi (a) to drain away, drain off. (b) (of river) **— en** to drain into, flow into.
desagüe nm (a) (act) drainage, draining. (b) drainage channel; drainpipe; outlet, drain; **tubo de —** drainpipe, waste pipe.
desaguisado 1 adj illegal. 2 nm offence, outrage.
desahogado 1 adj (a) dress, house etc roomy, large.
(b) space clear, free, unencumbered.
(c) life, situation comfortable; person comfortably off, in easy circumstances.
(d) brazen, impudent, fresh; **el tan — se lo comió todo** he was brazen enough to eat it all up.
2 nm brazen person, shameless individual.
desahogar [1h] 1 vt (a) pain etc to ease, relieve; anger to vent (en on).
(b) person to console.
2 **desahogarse** vr (a) to recover; to make things more comfortable for oneself; to take it easy, relax.
(b) to get out of a difficulty (or debt etc).
(c) (emotionally) to relieve one's feelings; to let off steam, let oneself go; to speak one's mind frankly; to confess; to get something off one's chest (fam); **— con uno** to unbosom oneself to someone.
desahogo nm (a) comfort, ease; comfortable circumstances; **vivir con —** to be comfortably off.
(b) relief; recovery; **es un — de tantas cosas malas** it's an outlet for so many unpleasant things, it's a way of getting rid of so many bad things.
(c) freedom; (pej) excessive freedom, brazenness, impudence; **expresarse con cierto —** to express oneself with a certain freedom, feel free to say what one really thinks.
desahuciado adj case hopeless.
desahuciar [1b] 1 vt (a) tenant to evict, eject; occupant of post to oust, remove, get out; (Chi) to dismiss.
(b) to deprive of hope, kill the hopes of; sick person to give up hope for, declare past recovery; **con esa decisión le desahuciaron definitivamente** by that decision they finally put an end to his hopes.
2 **desahuciarse** vr to lose all hope.
desahucio nm eviction, ejection; (Chi) dismissal.
desairado adj (a) disregarded. (b) unsuccessful; **quedar —** to be unsuccessful, come off badly. (c) unattractive; graceless; shabby.
desairar [1a] vt (a) to slight, snub; to disregard; to rebuff; **lo haré por no —** I'll do it rather than cause offence. (b) (Comm) to dishonour; to default on.
desaire nm (a) slight, snub; act of disrespect; rebuff; **fue un — sin precedentes** it was an unprecedented

snub; **dar** (or **hacer**) **un — a uno** to rebuff someone, offend someone; **¿me va Vd a hacer ese —?** (concerning invitation) I won't take no for an answer!; **sufrir un —** to suffer a rebuff; **no lo tome Vd a —** don't be offended.
(b) unattractiveness, gracelessness, lack of charm.
desajustar [1a] 1 vt to disarrange, disturb the order of. 2 **desajustarse** vr (a) to get out of order. (b) to disagree, fall out.
desajuste nm (a) disorder, disarrangement. (b) (in person) imbalance, lack of balance. (c) disagreement.
desalación nf desalination.
desalado adj hasty; impatient; eager; anxious.
desalar[1] [1a] vt to remove the salt from; sea water to desalinate.
desalar[2] [1a] 1 vt to clip the wings of. 2 **desalarse** vr (a) to rush, hasten along. (b) to long, yearn; **— por + infin** to long to + infin; to be keen to + infin.
desalentar [1k] 1 vt (a) **— a uno** to make someone breathless, make someone gasp for breath.
(b) (fig) to discourage.
2 **desalentarse** vr to get discouraged, lose heart.
desaliento nm (fig) discouragement; depression, dejection; dismay.
desalinar [1a] vt, **desalinizar** [1f] vt to desalinate.
desalinización nf desalination.
desaliñado adj (a) slovenly, dirty, down-at-heel; shabby; untidy, unkempt, dishevelled. (b) careless, slipshod, slovenly.
desaliño nm (a) slovenliness, dirtiness; shabbiness; untidiness; dishevelled state. (b) carelessness.
desalmado adj cruel, heartless.
desalmarse [1a] vr: **— por** to long for, crave (for).
desalojamiento nm (a) ejection, ousting, removal; dislodging. (b) evacuation; abandonment; clearing.
desalojar [1a] 1 vt (a) occupant to eject, oust, remove (from de); to dislodge (also Mil; de from); to clear out.
(b) contents, gas etc to dislodge, remove, expel.
(c) place to evacuate; to abandon, move out of, move away from; **— un tribunal de público** to clear a court, to clear the public from a court; **las tropas han desalojado el pueblo** the troops have moved out of the village; **la policía desalojó el local** the police cleared people out of the place.
2 vi to move out.
desalquilado adj vacant, untenanted.
desalquilar [1a] 1 vt to vacate, move out of. 2 **desalquilarse** vr to become vacant.
desalterar [1a] 1 vt to assuage, calm; to quieten down. 2 **desalterarse** vr to calm down, quieten down.
desamar [1a] vt to cease to love; to dislike, detest.
desamarrar [1a] vt to untie; (Naut) to cast off.
desamor nm coldness, indifference; dislike; enmity.
desamorado adj cold-hearted.
desamparado adj (a) child etc helpless, defenceless; abandoned; **los niños —s de la ciudad** the city's waifs and strays; **sentirse —** to feel helpless.
(b) place exposed.
(c) place lonely, deserted.
desamparar [1a] vt (a) person to desert, abandon, leave helpless; to forsake. (b) place to leave, abandon; to leave defenceless.
desamparo nm (a) (act) desertion, abandonment. (b) (state) helplessness; defencelessness, lack of protection.
desamueblado adj unfurnished.
desamueblar [1a] vt to remove the furniture from, clear the furniture out of.
desandar [1q] vt: **— lo andado, — el camino** to retrace one's steps, go back the way one has come; **no se puede — lo andado** one cannot undo what has been done.
desangramiento nm bleeding; **morir de —** to bleed to death.
desangrar [1a] 1 vt (a) person to bleed; lake to drain. (b) (fig) to impoverish, bleed white. 2 **desangrarse** vr to lose a lot of blood; to bleed to death.
desangre nm (SAm) bleeding, loss of blood.
desanidar [1a] 1 vt to oust, dislodge. 2 vi to fly, begin to fly.
desanimado adj (a) downhearted, dispirited, dejected. (b) dull, lifeless, flat; **fue una fiesta de lo más —** it was a terribly dull party.
desanimar [1a] 1 vt to discourage; to depress, sadden. 2 **desanimarse** vr to get discouraged, lose heart.
desánimo nm (a) despondency, depression, dejection. (b) dullness, lifelessness.
desanudar [1a] vt to untie; to disentangle; **— la voz to** manage to speak again, find one's voice.
desapacible adj unpleasant, disagreeable; sound sharp, jangling; nasty; discordant; tone harsh,

rough; *taste* unpleasant, sharp; *discussion* bitter, bad-tempered.

desaparecer [2d] **1** *vt* to hide; to remove, take away; to cause to vanish. **2** *vi* to disappear, vanish; to drop out of sight; (*of effects*) to wear off.

desaparecido *adj* missing; extinct; **el libro** — the missing book; **número de muertos, heridos y** —s number of dead, wounded and missing; **uno de los animales** —s one of the extinct animals.

desaparejar [1a] *vt* **(a)** to unharness, unhitch. **(b)** (*Naut*) to unrig.

desaparición *nf* disappearance; extinction.

desapasionadamente *adv* dispassionately, impartially.

desapasionado *adj* dispassionate, impartial.

desapego *nm* **(a)** coolness, indifference (*a* towards); alienation, detachment (*a* from). **(b)** detachment, impartiality.

desapercibido *adj* **(a)** unnoticed; **marcharse** — to slip away (unseen); **pasar** — to go unnoticed. **(b)** unprepared.

desaplicación *nf* slackness, laziness.

desaplicado *adj* slack, lazy.

desapoderado *adj action, movement* headlong, precipitate; *passion etc* wild, violent, uncontrollable; *greed etc* excessive; *pride* overweening.

desapoderar [1a] *vt* to deprive of authority; to dispossess (*de* of).

desaprender [2a] *vt* to forget; to unlearn.

desaprensión *nf* unscrupulousness, lack of scruple.

desaprensivamente *adv* unscrupulously.

desaprensivo *adj* unscrupulous.

desapretar [1k] *vt* to loosen, slacken, undo.

desaprobación *nf* disapproval; condemnation; rejection.

desaprobar [1m] *vt* to disapprove of; to frown on, condemn; *request etc* to reject, dismiss.

desapropiarse [1b] *vr:* — **de** to divest oneself of, surrender, give up.

desaprovechado *adj* **(a)** unproductive, unprofitable; below expectations. **(b)** *student etc* slow, backward; slack.

desaprovechar [1a] **1** *vt* to fail to take advantage of, not use, waste; *opportunity* to waste, miss. **2** *vi* to lose ground, slip back.

desarbolar [1a] *vt* to dismast.

desarmador *nm* (*of gun*) hammer; (*Mex*) screwdriver.

desarmar [1a] **1** *vt* **(a)** (*Mil*) to disarm. **(b)** (*Mech*) to take apart, take to pieces, dismantle; to strip down; *oars* to ship. **(c)** (*fig*) *person* to disarm; *anger* to calm, appease. **2** *vi* to disarm.

desarme *nm* disarmament.

desarraigado *adj person* rootless, without roots.

desarraigar [1h] *vt* **(a)** to uproot, root out, dig up. **(b)** (*fig*) to root out, eradicate; to extirpate; *person* to uproot; to banish, expel.

desarraigo *nm* (*fig*) eradication; extirpation; uprooting; banishment, expulsion.

desarrajar [1a] *vt* (*SAm*) to break open, force the lock of.

desarrapado *adj* = **desharrapado**.

desarrebujar [1a] *vt* **(a)** to untangle; to uncover. **(b)** (*fig*) to clarify, elucidate.

desarreglado *adj* **(a)** (*Mech etc*) out of order; *stomach etc* upset; *room etc* untidy, in disorder. **(b)** *conduct* disorderly; *appearance* slovenly, untidy; (*in habits*) irregular; unsystematic; (*pej*) immoderate.

desarreglar [1a] **1** *vt* to disarrange; to disturb, mess up, upset; (*Mech*) to put out of order; **el viento le desarregló el peinado** the wind made a mess of her hairdo; **no desarregles la cama** don't mess up your bed. **2 desarreglarse** *vr* to get disarranged, get untidy; (*Mech*) to get out of order.

desarreglo *nm* disorder, confusion, chaos; untidiness; irregularity; (*Mech*) trouble; (*Med*) upset; **para evitar los** —s **estomacales** in order to avoid stomach upsets; **viven en el mayor** — they live in complete chaos.

desarrimado *nm* (*fam*) loner (*fam*), lone wolf.

desarrollado *adj* (*also* **bien** —) well-developed.

desarrollar [1a] **1** *vt* **(a)** *object* to unroll, unwind; to unfold, open (out). **(b)** *abbreviation, equation* to expand. **(c)** (*fig*) to develop; to evolve; *theory etc* to explain, expound. **(d)** (*Mech*) **el motor desarrolla 30 caballos** the engine develops 30 hp. **2 desarrollarse** *vr* **(a)** to unroll, unwind; to open (out).

(b) (*fig*) to develop; to evolve; to unfold; (*of event, meeting etc*) to take place; **la industria se desarrolla rápidamente** the industry is developing rapidly; **la acción se desarrolla en Roma** (*Cine etc*) the scene is set in Rome, the action takes place in Rome.

desarrollo *nm* development; evolution; unfolding; expansion; growth; ((*of game, play*) run; — **en línea** ribbon development; **durante el** — **de** in the course of; during the development of; **un país en vías de** — a developing country; **la industria está en pleno** — the industry is making rapid growth, the industry is expanding steadily; **el niño tiene mucho** — **para su edad** the child is overdeveloped for his age.

desarroparse [1a] *vr* to undress; to uncover oneself.

desarrugar [1h] *vt* to smooth (out), remove the wrinkles from.

desarticulado *adj* disjointed.

desarticular [1a] *vt* to take apart, take to pieces; to separate; *bones* to put out.

desarzonar [1a] *vt rider* to throw, unsaddle.

desaseado *adj* slovenly, dirty; untidy, unkempt; messy; shabby.

desasear [1a] *vt* to dirty, soil; to mess up.

desaseo *nm* slovenliness, dirtiness; untidiness; messiness; shabbiness.

desasimiento *nm* **(a)** loosening, undoing; release. **(b)** (*fig*) detachment (*de* from), disinterest; (*pej*) indifference (*de* to), remoteness (*de* from).

desasir [3a, *but present like* **salir**] **1** *vt* to loosen, undo, let go. **2 desasirse** *vr* **(a)** to extricate oneself (*de* from), get clear (*de* of). **(b)** — **de** to let go, give up; to rid oneself of, free oneself of; to get rid of.

desasnar [1a] *vt* to civilize, improve, knock the corners off; to make less stupid.

desasosegado *adj* uneasy, anxious; restless.

desasosegar [1h *and* 1k] **1** *vt* to disturb, perturb, make uneasy; to make restless. **2 desasosegarse** *vr* to become uneasy, get perturbed; to become restless.

desasosiego *nm* disquiet, uneasiness, anxiety; restlessness; (*Pol etc*) unrest.

desastrado *adj* **(a)** dirty, shabby, ragged. **(b)** unlucky; wretched.

desastre *nm* disaster; **¡un** —! (*hum*) what a calamity!; how awful! (*fam*); **la boda fue un** — the wedding was a disaster; **la función fue un** — the show was a shambles.

desastroso *adj* disastrous, calamitous.

desatado *adj* (*fig*) wild, violent, uncontrolled.

desatar [1a] **1** *vt* **(a)** to untie, undo, unfasten; to loosen, slacken; to detach, separate; *dog* to unleash; (*Chem*) to dissolve. **(b)** (*fig*) *repression etc* to unleash. **(c)** (*fig*) *mystery* to solve, clear up, unravel. **2 desatarse** *vr* **(a)** to come untied, come undone, unfasten itself; to work loose; (*dog etc*) to break away, break loose. **(b)** — **de un compromiso** to get out of an agreement. **(c)** (*fig: storm etc*) to break, burst; (*riot*) to break out; (*enthusiasm*) to break all bounds; (*disaster*) to fall (*sobre* on); — **en injurias** to begin to pour out a stream of insults. **(d)** (*fig: person*) to get worked up, lose self-control; to talk wildly; to go too far, forget oneself.

desatascar [1g] *vt* **(a)** *cart etc* to pull out of the mud; — **a uno** (*fig*) to get someone out of a jam. **(b)** *pipe etc* to clear, free, unblock.

desatención *nf* **(a)** inattention; absent-mindedness. **(b)** discourtesy.

desatender [2g] *vt* to disregard, pay no attention to; to ignore; *duty* to neglect; *person* to slight, offend.

desatentado *adj* **(a)** thoughtless, rash, ill-advised; unwise, foolish. **(b)** excessive, extreme, out of all proportion.

desatento *adj* **(a)** heedless, careless; inattentive. **(b)** discourteous, unmannerly (*con* to).

desatierre *nm* (*SAm*) slag heap, rubbish tip.

desatinadamente *adv* foolishly; wildly, recklessly.

desatinado *adj* silly, foolish; wild, reckless.

desatinar [1a] **1** *vt* to perplex, bewilder. **2** *vi* to act foolishly; to talk nonsense, rave; to get rattled, begin to act wildly.

desatino *nm* **(a)** foolishness, folly, silliness; tactlessness. **(b)** (*act etc*) silly thing, foolish act; blunder, mistake; —s nonsense; **¡qué** —! how silly!, what rubbish!; **un libro lleno de** —s a book stuffed with nonsense; **cometer un** — to make a blunder.

desatornillar [1a] *vt* to unscrew.

desatracar [1g] *vi* (*Naut*) to cast off.

desatraillar [1a] *vt* to unleash, let off the lead.

desatrancar [1g] *vt* (a) *door* to unbar, unbolt. (b) *pipe etc* to clear, unblock; *well* to clean out.

desatufarse [1a] *vr* (a) to get some fresh air, go out for a breather. (b) (*fig*) to calm down.

desautorizado *adj* unauthorized; unwarranted.

desautorizar [1f] *vt* (a) *person* to deprive of authority; to declare without authority. (b) *report etc* to deny, issue a denial of.

desavenencia *nf* disagreement; friction, unpleasantness; rift, quarrel.

desavenido *adj* incompatible; contrary, opposing; in disagreement; **ellos están —s** they are at odds, they disagree.

desavenir [3s] **1** *vt* to cause a rift between, make trouble between; to split, break the unity of.
2 desavenirse *vr* to disagree (*con* with), fall out (*con* with).

desaventajado *adj* inferior; unfavourable, disadvantageous.

desayunado *ptp*: **estar —** to have had breakfast; **venir —** to come after breakfast.

desayunar [1a] *vi and* **desayunarse** *vr* to breakfast, have breakfast; **— con** to have for breakfast, breakfast on; **— de un acontecimiento** to receive the first news of an event.

desayuno *nm* breakfast.

desazón *nf* (a) tastelessness, lack of flavour.
(b) (*of soil*) poorness.
(c) (*Med*) discomfort, indisposition, slight trouble.
(d) (*fig*) annoyance, displeasure; frustration; uneasiness.

desazonar [1a] **1** *vt* (a) *food* to make tasteless, take the flavour out of.
(b) (*fig*) to annoy, upset, displease; to worry, cause anxiety to.
2 desazonarse *vr* (a) (*Med*) to feel off-colour, be out of sorts.
(b) (*fig*) to be annoyed; to worry, be anxious.

desbancar [1g] **1** *vt* (a) *banker* (*Cards*) to bust (*fam*), take the bank from.
(b) (*fig*) to displace, oust; to cut out, supplant (in someone's affections).
2 *vi* (*Cards*) to bust (*fam*).

desbandada *nf* rush (to get away); **hubo una — general de turistas** there was a mass exodus of tourists, masses of tourists suddenly left; **cuando empezó a llover hubo una — general** when it started to rain everyone rushed for shelter; **a la —** in disorder; helter-skelter; **retirarse a la —** to retreat in disorder, make a disorderly retreat.

desbandarse [1a] *vr* (a) (*Mil*) to disband. (b) (*fig*) to flee in disorder; to go off in all directions, disperse in confusion.

desbarajustar [1a] *vt* to throw into confusion.

desbarajuste *nm* confusion, chaos, disorder.

desbaratar [1a] **1** *vt* (a) to ruin, spoil, destroy; to mess up; *plan etc* to foil, thwart, frustrate; *system* to disrupt, cause chaos in; *theory* to make nonsense of, debunk.
(b) (*Mil*) to throw into confusion.
(c) *fortune* to squander.
(d) (*Mech*) to take to pieces.
2 *vi* to rave, talk nonsense.
3 desbaratarse *vr* (a) (*Mech*) to get out of order, develop a defect.
(b) (*person*) to fly off the handle (*fam*), go off the deep end; to become unbalanced.

desbaratamiento *nm*, **desbarate** *nm*, **desbarato** *nm* (a) ruin, destruction, foiling, thwarting; disruption; debunking.
(b) (*Mil*) rout.
(c) (*Med*: *also* **— de vientre**) bowel upset.
(d) squandering.

desbarbar [1a] *vt* *person* to shave; *paper* to trim the edges of; *plants* to cut back, trim (off).
2 desbarbarse *vr* to shave.

desbarrancadero *nm* (*Col, Guat, Mex, Ven*) precipice.

desbarrancar [1g] **1** *vt* (a) *ground* to level. (b) (*SAm*) to fling over a precipice. (c) (*Col, Per, PR*) to ruin.
2 desbarrancarse *vr* (*SAm*) to fall over a precipice.

desbarrar [1a] *vi* to talk rubbish; to be very wide of the mark.

desbastar [1a] **1** *vt* (a) (*Tech*) to rough-hew; to plane (down), smooth (down).
(b) (*fig*) to take the rough edges off; to refine, polish; *recruit etc* to knock the corners off, lick into shape.
2 desbastarse *vr* (*fig*) to acquire some polish.

desbaste *nm* (a) (*Tech*) planing, smoothing. (b) (*fig*) polishing, refinement; licking into shape.

desbeber [2a] *vi* (*tabu*) to piss (*tabu*).

desbloquear [1a] *vt* (a) to break the blockade of. (b) (*Comm, Fin*) to unfreeze, unblock.

desbocado *adj* (a) *vessel* with a broken rim.
(b) *gun* wide-mouthed.
(c) *horse* runaway; *animal* escaped, stray.
(d) *tool* worn, defective, damaged.
(e) *person* foul-mouthed, foul-spoken.
(f) *liquid* (*SAm*) overflowing.

desbocar [1g] **1** *vt* *vessel* to break the rim (*or* mouth) of.
2 *vi*: **— en** (*of river*) to run into, flow into; (*of street*) to open into, come out into.
3 desbocarse *vr* (a) (*horse*) to bolt, run away.
(b) (*person*) to start to swear, let out a stream of insults.

desbordamiento *nm* (a) overflowing, flooding; spilling. (b) (*fig*) eruption, outburst; **un tremendo — de entusiasmo** a great upsurge of enthusiasm.

desbordar [1a] **1** *vt* to pass, go beyond; to exceed, surpass; **desbordaron las líneas enemigas** they burst through the enemy lines; **el proyecto desborda los límites señalados** the plan goes well beyond the limits which were set; **esto desborda mi tolerancia** this exceeds my capacity for tolerance.
2 *vi and* **desbordarse** *vr* (a) (*of river*) to overflow, flood, burst its banks; (*of liquid*) to overflow, spill (over).
(b) (*of enthusiasm etc*) to erupt, burst forth.
(c) (*of person*) to give free rein to one's feelings; (*pej*) to fly off the handle (*fam*), lose one's self-control; **—(se) de alegría** to be bursting with happiness.

desborde *nm* (*Arg*) = **desbordamiento**.

desbravador *nm* horse-breaker.

desbravar [1a] **1** *vt* to break in, tame.
2 *vi and* **desbravarse** *vr* (a) (*of animal*) to get less wild, grow less fierce.
(b) (*of current etc*) to lose its strength, diminish in force.
(c) (*of liquor*) to lose its strength.

desbrozar [1f] *vt* *passage etc* to clear (of rubbish); *land* to clear of scrub, clear the undergrowth from.

descabalgar [1h] *vi* to dismount.

descabellado *adj* (*fig*) wild, crazy, preposterous.

descabellar [1a] *vt* (a) *person* to dishevel; to ruffle, rumple. (b) *bull* to kill with a thrust in the neck, administer the coup de grâce to.

descabello *nm* (*Taur*) final thrust, coup de grâce.

descabezado *adj* (a) headless. (b) (*fig*) wild, crazy, light-headed.

descabezar [1f] **1** *vt* (a) *person etc* to behead, cut head off; *tree* to lop, poll, cut the top off; *plant* to top.
(b) (*fig*) *difficulty* to begin to get over, get over the worst part of, surmount.
2 descabezarse *vr* (a) (*Bot*) to shed the grain.
(b) (*person*) to rack one's brains.

descachalambrarse [1a] *vr* (*Col, Ec, Per*) to dress carelessly.

descachar [1a] *vt* (*Col, Chi, Ven*) to de-horn.

descacharrado *adj* (*CAm*) dirty, slovenly.

descalabrado *adj*: **salir —** to come out the loser (*de* in), come off badly.

descalabrar [1a] **1** *vt* (a) to smash, damage; *person* to hit, hurt, (*esp*) to hit on the head; (*Naut*) to cripple, disable.
(b) (*fig*) to harm, damage, injure; to attack the character of.
2 descalabrarse *vr* to hurt one's head, give oneself a bang on the head.

descalabro *nm* blow, setback; disaster, misfortune; damage; (*Mil*) defeat; **— electoral** electoral setback, disaster at the polls.

descalificación *nf* disqualification.

descalificar [1g] *vt* to disqualify.

descalzar [1f] **1** *vt* (a) *shoe* to take off.
(b) **— a uno** to take off someone's shoes (*etc*); **A no vale para — a B** A can't hold a candle to B.
(c) *wheel* to remove the chocks from.
(d) (*fig*) to dig under, undermine.
2 descalzarse *vr* (a) to take off one's shoes (*etc*); **— los guantes** to take off one's gloves.
(b) (*of horse*) to cast a shoe.

descalzo *adj* (a) barefoot(ed); shoeless, stockingless; **estar —, estar con los pies —s** to be barefooted, have one's shoes off, have no shoes (*etc*) on; **ir — to** go barefooted.
(b) (*Eccl*) discalced.
(c) (*fig*) destitute.

descamarse [1a] *vr* to flake off, scale off.

descaminado adj (a) andar —, ir — to be on the wrong road.
(b) (fig) mistaken; misguided; ill-advised; ir — to be on the wrong track; andar — en to be mistaken in (or about); en eso no anda Vd muy — you're not far wrong there.

descaminar [1a] 1 vt (a) to misdirect, give wrong directions to, put on the wrong road; (fig) to mislead, lead astray.
(b) goods to seize as contraband.
(c) (SAm) to hold up.
2 **descaminarse** vr (a) to get lost, go the wrong way; (fig) to go astray.
(b) to run off the road.

descamisado 1 adj (fig) ragged, shabby; wretched. 2 nm ragamuffin; down-and-out; poor devil, wretch.

descamisar [1a] vt (a) to strip the shirt off. (b) (Col, Guat, Per) fruit etc to remove the outer covering of; (fig) to ruin; (at cards etc) to fleece.

descampado nm open space, piece of empty ground; comer al — to eat in the open air; vivir en — to live in open country; se fue a vivir en — he went off to live in the wilds.

descansadero nm stopping place, resting place.

descansado adj (a) rested, refreshed. (b) restful; life etc tranquil, unworried, free from care.

descansapié nm pedal, footrest.

descansar [1a] 1 vt (a) to rest, support, lean (sobre on).
(b) to rest; esto descansa la vista más this rests one's eyes better.
(c) to help, give a hand to.
(d) — sus penas en uno to tell one's troubles to someone, confide in someone about one's troubles.
2 vi (a) (of person) to rest; to take a rest, have a break (de from); to sleep, lie down; (of corpse) to lie, rest; necesito — un rato I need to rest a bit; podemos — aquí we can rest here; — en paz to rest in peace; no descansé en todo el día I didn't have a moment's rest all day; ¡descanse Vd! don't worry!; ¡que Vd descanse!, ¡descanse bien! sleep well!
(b) (Agr) to lie fallow.
(c) — en (Archit) to rest on, be supported by.
(d) — en (fig) to rely on; to trust in; el argumento descansa sobre los siguientes hechos the argument is based on the following facts.
3 **descansarse** vr: — en uno to rely on someone, count on someone; to confide in someone.

descansillo nm (Archit) landing.

descanso nm (a) (in general) rest; repose; (from pain etc) relief; (period) rest, break; tomarse unos días de — to take a few days' rest; trabajar sin — to work without a break; es un — saber que no estás solo it's a relief to know you are not alone.
(b) (Sport) interval, half-time; (Theat) interval.
(c) (Tech) rest, support; bench; bracket; — de cabeza headrest.
(d) (Archit) landing.

descañonar [1a] vt (a) fowl to pluck. (b) face to shave against the grain. (c) (Cards: fam) to fleece, clean out (sl).

descapachar [1a] vt (Col) maize to husk.

descapiruzar [1f] vt (Col) to rumple the hair of.

descapotable (Aut) 1 adj convertible. 2 nm convertible.

descapsulador nm bottle opener.

descaradamente adv shamelessly, brazenly; cheekily, saucily; blatantly.

descarado adj shameless, brazen, barefaced; cheeky, saucy; blatant.

descararse [1a] vr to behave impudently, be insolent, be cheeky (con to); — a pedir algo to have the nerve to ask for something.

descarbonizar [1f] vt, **descarburar** [1a] vt to decarbonize.

descarga nf (a) (Naut etc) unloading; clearing; — de aduana customs clearance.
(b) (Mil) firing, discharge; — (cerrada) volley; como una — suddenly, unexpectedly.
(c) (Elec) discharge.

descargadero nm wharf.

descargado adj empty, unloaded; battery flat.

descargador nm docker.

descargar [1h] 1 vt (a) boat, cart etc to unload; to empty.
(b) gun to fire, discharge, shoot; to unload; — un golpe en uno to let fly a blow at someone, deal someone a blow; — golpes sobre la mesa to beat the table, rain blows on the table; — un golpe contra la censura to strike a blow against the censorship.

(c) (Elec) to discharge; battery to flatten, exhaust.
(d) bowels to evacuate.
(e) (of cloud) hail etc to send down, let fall.
(f) anger etc to vent (en, sobre on).
(g) conscience to ease, relieve; heart to unburden.
(h) (Comm) draft to take up.
(i) person to relieve, release (de una obligación from an obligation); to free (de una deuda from a debt); (Law etc) to clear, acquit (de of).
2 vi (a) — en (of river) to run into, flow into; (of street) to open into, come out into.
(b) (Elec) to discharge.
(c) (of storm) to burst, break.
3 **descargarse** vr (a) to unburden oneself, disburden oneself; — de algo to get rid of something; — con (or en) uno de algo to unload something on to someone.
(b) (Law etc) to clear oneself, vindicate oneself (de of).
(c) to resign.

descargo nm (a) unloading; emptying.
(b) (of debt) discharge.
(c) (Comm) receipt, voucher.
(d) — de una obligación release from an obligation; — de una acusación acquittal on a charge.
(e) (Law: also —s, pliego de —s) evidence, depositions (in favour of the defendant); (fig) excuses, piece of special pleading; testigo de — witness for the defence.

descargue nm unloading; emptying.

descarnado adj thin, lean, scrawny; emaciated; cadaverous; (fig) bare.

descarnador nm dental scraper; cuticle remover.

descarnar [1a] 1 vt (a) bone to remove the flesh from; hide to scrape the flesh from.
(b) (fig) to eat away, corrode, wear down.
2 **descarnarse** vr to lose flesh, get thin.

descaro nm shamelessness, brazenness; cheek, sauce, nerve; blatancy; tuvo 'el — de decirme que . . . he had the nerve to tell me that . . .; ¡qué —! what cheek!, what a nerve!

descarriar [1c] 1 vt (a) to misdirect, put on the wrong road.
(b) (fig) to lead astray.
(c) animal to separate from the herd, single out.
2 **descarriarse** vr (a) to lose one's way; (animal) to stray, get separated (from the herd).
(b) (fig) to err, go astray.

descarrilamiento nm derailment.

descarrilar [1a] vi (also **descarrilarse** vr (SAm)) (a) (Rail) to be derailed, run off the rails, jump the track.
(b) (fig) to get off the track, wander from the point.

descarrilo nm derailment.

descartar [1a] 1 vt to discard (also Cards); to put aside, lay aside; to reject; possibility etc to rule out.
2 **descartarse** vr (a) (Cards) to discard.
(b) — de to excuse oneself from; to shun, shirk, evade.

descarte nm (a) (Cards) discard. (b) discarding, rejection, ruling out. (c) (fig) excuse; shirking, evasion.

descasar [1a] vt (a) to annul the marriage of. (b) (fig) to disarrange, upset the arrangement of.

descascar [1g] 1 vt (a) to peel; to shell; to remove the bark from. 2 **descascarse** vr (a) to smash to pieces, come apart. (b) (fam) to chatter.

descascarar [1a] 1 vt (a) to peel; to shell, take the shell off.
(b) (Col) to flay, skin.
(c) (Col) to dishonour.
2 **descascararse** vr to peel (off), scale (off); to chip off.

descastado adj (a) that has lost caste, untouchable; word etc improper. (b) alienated from one's family; cold, indifferent (to affection).

descaudalado adj penniless.

descendedero nm ramp.

descendencia nf (a) descent, origin. (b) offspring, descendants; morir sin dejar — to die without issue, leave no children.

descendente adj descending, downward; downward-sloping; quantity diminishing; tren — down train.

descender [2g] 1 vt (a) to lower, let down; luggage etc to get down, lift down, take down.
(b) stairs etc to go down, descend.
2 vi (a) to descend, come down, go down.
(b) (of fever, temperature, water level etc) to drop, fall, go down (en un 5 por cien by 5%).
(c) (of liquid) to run, flow.

(d) (*of curtain etc*) to hang.

(e) (*of person, strength*) to fail, get weak, decay; **— de** (*or* **en**) **energía** to suffer a loss of energy.

(f) **— a** (*fig*) to stoop to, lower oneself to.

(g) **— de** to descend from, be descended from; **to be derived from; — de linaje de reyes** to come from a line of kings; **la tribu desciende de la región central** the tribe comes from the central region; the tribe originated in the central region; **de esa palabra descienden otras muchas** many other words derive from that one.

descendiente *nmf* descendant.

descendimiento *nm* descent; lowering; **el D— de la Cruz** the Descent from the Cross.

descenso *nm* **(a)** (*act*) descent; going down; (*of fever, temperature etc*) drop, fall; (*of production*) downturn; (*Sport*) relegation; (*in quality*) decline, falling-off; **las cifras han experimentado un brusco — the figures show a sharp fall; **hay un — de calidad** there is a falling-off in quality.

(b) (*Min etc*) collapse, subsidence.

(c) (*Med*) rupture; **— del útero** prolapse, fallen womb.

(d) (*place*) slope, drop, descent; **el — hacia el río** the descent to the river, the slope down to the river.

descentrado *adj* **(a)** off centre.

(b) (*fig*) out of focus; wrongly adjusted; **parece que el problema está —** the problem seems to be out of focus, it seems that the question has not been properly stated; **todavía está algo —** he is still somewhat out of touch, he is still not properly adjusted (to the situation).

descentralización *nf* decentralization.

descentralizar [1f] *vt* to decentralize.

desceñir [3h *and* 3l] *vt* to loosen; to undo, unfasten.

descepar [1a] *vt* **(a)** (*Agr*) to uproot, pull up by the roots. **(b)** (*fig*) to extirpate, eradicate.

descercar [1g] *vt* **(a)** to remove the fence round. **(b)** (*Mil*) *city* to relieve, raise the siege of.

descerco *nm* (*Mil*) relief.

descerrajado *adj* (*fam*) **(a)** raving mad, unhinged. **(b)** wicked.

descerrajar [1a] *vt* **(a)** to force the lock of; to break open, force. **(b)** *shot* to let off, fire (*a* at).

descervigar [1h] *vt* **(a)** to break the neck of. **(b)** (*fig*) to humiliate.

descifrable *adj* decipherable.

descifrador *nm* decipherer; decoder; **el — del misterio** the man who solved the mystery.

descifrar [1a] *vt writing* to decipher, (manage to) read; *message* to decode; *problem* to puzzle out, figure out; *mystery* to solve, crack.

descinchar [1a] *vt horse* to loosen the girths of.

desclasificación *nf* disqualification.

desclasificar [1g] *vt* (*Sport*) to disqualify.

desclavar [1a] *vt* to pull out the nails from, unnail.

descobijar [1a] *vt* to uncover, leave exposed.

descocado *adj* (*fam*) **=descarado**; *girl* brazen, forward.

descocarse [1g] *vr* (*fam*) **=descararse**.

descoco *nm* **=descaro**.

descochollado *adj* (*Chi*) **(a)** ragged, shabby. **(b)** wicked. **(c)** ill-tempered.

descoger [2c] *vt* to spread out, unfold.

descolada *nf* (*Mex*) snub, rebuff.

descolar [1a] *vt* **(a)** to dock, cut the tail off. **(b)** (*CAm*) to fire, sack. **(c)** (*Mex*) to snub, slight.

descolgar [1h *and* 1m] **1** *vt* **(a)** to take down, get down; to unhook; to lower, let down; *telephone* to pick up.

2 descolgarse *vr* **(a)** to let oneself down (*con* by, *de* from); to come down, descend, climb down; **— por una pared** to climb down a wall.

(b) (*fig: person*) to turn up unexpectedly; (*Meteorol*) to come on suddenly, set in unexpectedly.

(c) — con una estupidez to come out with a silly remark, blurt out something silly.

descolocado *adj servant* out of work, unplaced.

descolón *nm* (*Mex*) snub, rebuff.

descolonización *nf* decolonization.

descoloramiento *nm* discolo(u)ration.

descolorar [1a] *vt* **=decolorar**.

descolorido *adj* **(a)** discoloured, faded, pale. **(b)** (*fig*) colourless.

descollante *adj* outstanding.

descollar [1m] *vi* to stand out, be outstanding; **descuella entre los demás** he stands out among the others; **la obra que más descuella de las suyas** his most outstanding work; **la iglesia descuella sobre los demás edificios** the church stands out above (*or* towers over) the other buildings.

descombrar [1a] *vt* to clear (of obstacles), disencumber.

descomedidamente *adv* **(a)** excessively. **(b)** rudely, insolently, disrespectfully.

descomedido *adj* **(a)** excessive, immoderate. **(b)** *person* rude, insolent, disrespectful (*con* to, towards).

descomedimiento *nm* rudeness, insolence, disrespect.

descomedirse [3l] *vr* to be rude, be disrespectful (*con* to, towards).

descompaginar [1a] *vt* to disarrange, disorganize, mess up.

descompasado *adj* excessive, out of all proportion; **a una hora descompasada** at an unearthly hour; **de tamaño —** of disproportionate size, extra big.

descompasarse [1a] *vr* **=descomedirse**.

descompletar [1a] *vt* (*SAm*) to make incomplete, impair the completeness of; *set* to break, ruin.

descomponer [2r] **1** *vt* **(a)** to separate into its constituent parts; (*Chem*) to separate into its elements; *unit, mass etc* to split up, break down; *argument* to break down, analyse, reduce to a series of points; (*Math*) to break down.

(b) *decaying matter* to rot, decompose.

(c) (*Mech*) to break; to put out of order; to tamper with, mess up; *features* to distort; *stomach etc* to upset; **— el peinado a una** to disarrange someone's hair.

(d) *order etc* to disarrange, disturb, upset; *calm* to ruffle, disturb; **— los planes de uno** to upset someone's plans, mess up someone's plans.

(e) *person* to shake up, give a jolt to; to put out; to anger, provoke.

(f) *two persons* to cause a rift between, set at odds.

2 descomponerse *vr* **(a)** to rot, decompose.

(b) (*Mech*) to break down, get out of order, develop a fault; (*stomach*) to get upset; (*weather*) to break up, change for the worse; **— el brazo** (*Col*) to put one's arm out of joint.

(c) to lose one's temper, get worked up; **— con uno** to fall out with someone.

descomposición *nf* **(a)** splitting up, breakdown; (*Chem*) decomposition; **— estadística** statistical breakdown.

(b) rotting, decomposition.

(c) (*Med*) **— de vientre** stomach upset, diarrhoea.

(d) (*fig*) discomposure.

descompostura *nf* **(a)** (*Mech etc*) breakdown, fault, trouble; bad working order; disorder; disorganization; untidiness, slovenliness.

(b) (*fig*) discomposure.

(c) (*fig*) brazenness, forwardness.

(d) (*Col*) dislocation.

descompresión *nf* decompression.

descompuesto *adj* **(a)** (*Mech etc*) broken, out of order, faulty; *face, features* twisted, distorted; *system etc* disordered, disorganized, chaotic; *room* untidy; *appearance* slovenly.

(b) (*fig*) angry; **ponerse —** to get angry, get worked up, lose one's composure.

(c) (*fig*) brazen, forward; rude.

(d) (*SAm*) **estar —** to be tipsy.

descomunal *adj* huge, enormous, colossal.

desconcentración *nf* decentralization, breaking-up.

desconcentrar [1a] *vt industry etc* to decentralize, break up, distribute over a wider area.

desconceptuado *adj* discredited; not well thought-of, ill-reputed.

desconcertado *adj* (*fig*): **estar —, quedar —** to be disconcerted, be taken aback; to be bewildered.

desconcertador *adj*, **desconcertante** *adj* disconcerting, upsetting; embarrassing; baffling, bewildering, puzzling.

desconcertar [1k] **1** *vt* **(a)** (*Mech etc*) to put out of order, damage; (*Anat*) to dislocate; *order* to disarrange, disturb; *plan* to upset, dislocate, throw out of gear.

(b) *person* to disconcert, upset, put out; to embarrass; (*of problem etc*) to baffle, bewilder, puzzle; **le desconcertó encontrarme allí** it disconcerted him to find me there; **la noticia desconcertó a todos** the news upset everybody.

2 desconcertarse *vr* **(a)** (*Mech etc*) to get out of order, develop a fault; (*Anat*) to get out of joint, be dislocated.

(b) (*person*) to be disconcerted, be upset, be put out; to get embarrassed; to be bewildered; **siguió sin —** he went on quite unruffled; **esto basta para que se desconcierte el más sosegado** this would get even the calmest of men worked up.

desconcierto *nm* **(a)** (*Mech etc*) disorder, trouble; damage; disarrangement, disturbance, chaos.

(b) (*fig*) uneasiness, uncertainty; embarrassment;

bewilderment; **contribuye al — de la juventud** it increases young people's bewilderment; **sembrar el — en el partido** to sow confusion in the party, create discord in the party; **hay un — fundamental** there is a basic disagreement.

desconchabar [1a] *vt* (*SAm*) to dislocate.

desconchar [1a] **1** *vt* to strip off, peel off; to chip off. **2 desconcharse** *vr* to peel off, flake off; to chip.

desconectar [1a] *vt* (*Mech*) to disconnect; to uncouple; (*Elec*) to disconnect; to switch off, turn off.

desconfiado *adj* distrustful, suspicious (*de* of).

desconfianza *nf* distrust, mistrust, lack of confidence; **voto de —** vote of no confidence.

desconfiar [1c] *vi* to be distrustful; to lack confidence; **— de** to distrust, mistrust, suspect; to have no confidence in; **desconfío de ello** I doubt it; **desconfíe de las imitaciones** (*Comm*) beware of imitations; **desconfía de sus posibilidades** he has no faith in his potentiality; **desconfío de que llegue a tiempo** I doubt if he will get here in time, I cannot be sure that he will arrive in time.

desconformar [1a] *vi* and **desconformarse** *vr* (**a**) to disagree, dissent. **(b) se desconforman** they do not get on well together; they are not suited to each other.

desconforme *adj* =**disconforme.**

descongelar [1a] *vt* *refrigerator* to defrost.

descongestión *nf* (*of city overcrowding, traffic pressure etc*) relief, relieving; **una política de —** a policy of relieving population pressure in the cities.

descongestionar [1a] *vt* *head* to clear; *town etc* to make less crowded, relieve the population pressure in; *street* to relieve the traffic problems of, make less crowded.

desconocer [2d] *vt* (**a**) not to know, be ignorant of, be unfamiliar with; to be unaware of; to fail to remember; **desconocen los principios fundamentales** they are ignorant of the basic principles; **no desconozco que . . .** I am not unaware that . . .
(b) not to recognize; to pretend not to know; to ignore, disregard.
(c) to disown, repudiate; **pero el poeta desconoció la obra** but the poet disowned the work.

desconocido 1 *adj* (**a**) unknown, not known (*de, para* to); strange, unfamiliar; unrecognized; **lo —** the unknown; **por razones desconocidas** for reasons which are not known (to us *etc*); **el triunfo de un atleta —** the success of an unknown athlete. **(b)** much changed; **está —** he is much altered, he is hardly recognizable.
(c) ungrateful.
2 *nm*, **desconocida** *nf* stranger; unknown person.

desconocimiento *nm* (**a**) ignorance. **(b)** disregard, repudiation. **(c)** ingratitude.

desconsideración *nf* inconsiderateness, thoughtlessness.

desconsideradamente *adv* inconsiderately, thoughtlessly.

desconsiderado *adj* inconsiderate, thoughtless.

desconsoladamente *adv* disconsolately.

desconsolado *adj* disconsolate; *face* sad, woebegone.

desconsolador *adj* distressing, grievous.

desconsolar [1m] **1** *vt* to distress, grieve. **2 desconsolarse** *vr* to be grieved; to despair, lose hope.

desconsuelo *nm* affliction, distress, grief; sadness; despair; **con —** sadly, despairingly.

descontado *adj*: **por —** of course, naturally; **eso lo podemos dar por —** we can take that for granted, we can assume that; we can rely on that.

descontaminación *nf* decontamination.

descontaminar [1a] *vt* to decontaminate.

descontar [1m] *vt* (**a**) to take away; (*Comm*) to discount, deduct. **(b)** to discount; to assume, take for granted.

descontentadizo *adj* hard to please; restless, unsettled.

descontentar [1a] *vt* to displease.

descontento 1 *adj* dissatisfied, discontented (*de* with); disgruntled (*de* about, at); **estar — de** to be dissatisfied with, be unhappy about.
2 *nm* (**a**) dissatisfaction, displeasure; disgruntlement.
(b) (*Pol etc*) discontent, unrest; **hay mucho —** there is a lot of unrest.

descontinuación *nf* discontinuation.

descontinuar [1e] *vt* to discontinue.

descontrolado *adj* (*SAm*) upset, irritated; uncontrolled.

desconvenir [3s] *vi* (**a**) (*persons*) to disagree (*con* with).
(b) to be incongruous; not to fit, not match; to differ (*con* from).

(c) to be inconvenient; to be unsuitable.

descorazonador *adj* discouraging, disheartening.

descorazonamiento *nm* discouragement; dejection, depression.

descorazonar [1a] **1** *vt* to discourage, dishearten. **2 descorazonarse** *vr* to get discouraged, lose heart.

descorchador *nm* corkscrew.

descorchar [1a] *vt* (**a**) *tree* to remove the bark from; to strip. **(b)** *bottle* to uncork, draw the cork of, open. **(c)** *chest etc* to force, break open.

descornar [1m] **1** *vt* to de-horn, poll. **2 descornarse** *vr* (*fig*) to slog away, work like a slave; to rack one's brains.

descorrer [2a] *vt* *curtain, bolt* to draw back.

descortés *adj* discourteous, rude, impolite.

descortesía *nf* discourtesy, rudeness, impoliteness.

descortésmente *adv* discourteously, rudely, impolitely.

descortezar [1f] *vt* (**a**) *tree* to strip the bark from, remove the bark of; *bread* to cut the crust off; *fruit etc* to peel.
(b) (*fig*) to polish up a bit, knock the corners off.

descoser [2a] **1** *vt* (**a**) (*Sew*) to unstitch, unpick; to rip, tear.
(b) to separate, part; see **labio.**
2 descoserse *vr* (**a**) to come apart (at the seam), burst, tear.
(b) (*fam*) to blurt out a secret, let the cat out of the bag.
(c) (*tabu*) to fart (*tabu*).
(d) — de risa to split one's sides with laughing, die of laughing.

descosido 1 *adj* (**a**) (*Sew*) unstitched, torn; shabby.
(b) (*fig*) *narrative etc* disconnected, disjointed, chaotic.
(c) *person, speech etc* wild, immoderate; talkative; big-mouthed (*sl*), indiscreet, blabbing.
2 *nm* (**a**) (*Sew*) open seam; rip, tear.
(b) obrar como un — to act wildly; **beber como un —** to drink an awful lot; **comer como un —** to eat to excess, stuff oneself; **gastar como un —** to spend money wildly; **estudiar** (*etc*) **como un —** to study (*etc*) like mad.

descoyuntado *adj* (**a**) (*Anat*) dislocated, out of joint. **(b)** *narrative etc* incoherent, disjointed, chaotic.

descoyuntar [1a] **1** *vt* (**a**) (*Anat*) to dislocate, put out of joint.
(b) *person* (*fig*) to tire out; to bother; to weary, annoy.
(c) *facts etc* to twist, force the sense of, adapt improperly.
2 descoyuntarse *vr* (**a**) (*Anat*) **— un hueso** to put a bone out of joint; **los huesos se descoyuntaron** the bones became dislocated.
(b) — de risa to split one's sides with laughing, die of laughing; **— a cortesías** to overdo the courtesies, be exaggeratedly polite.

descrecer [2d] *vi* to decrease.

descrédito *nm* discredit; disrepute; **caer en —** to fall into disrepute; **ir en — de** to be to the discredit of, damage the reputation of.

descreencia *nf* (*esp SAm*) unbelief.

descreer [2e] **1** *vt* (**a**) to disbelieve; to place no faith in. **(b)** to deny due credit to. **2** *vi* (*Rel*) to lose one's faith.

descreído 1 *adj* unbelieving; (*pej*) godless. **2** *nm*, **descreída** *nf* unbeliever.

descreimiento *nm* unbelief.

descremar [1a] *vt* (*SAm*) *milk* to skim.

descrestar [1a] *vt* (**a**) to cut the comb of. **(b)** (*fam*) to swindle, cheat.

describir [3a; *ptp* **descrito**] *vt* (*all senses*) to describe.

descripción *nf* description; **supera a toda —** it is beyond description, it is indescribable.

descriptible *adj* describable.

descriptivo *adj* descriptive.

descrismar [1a] **1** *vt*: **— a uno** to bash someone on the head (*fam*); **¡o eso o te descrismo!** either that or I'll bash you! (*fam*).
2 descrismarse *vr* (**a**) to slave away; to rack one's brains.
(b) (*fam*) to blow one's top (*fam*).

descrito *ptp* of **describir**; **no es para —** it is indescribable, it beggars description.

descuajar [1a] *vt* (**a**) *solid mass* to melt, dissolve.
(b) (*Bot*) to uproot, pull up by the root; *object* to pull out, tear from its place.
(c) (*fig*) to eradicate.
(d) (*fig*) to dishearten.

descuajaringarse [1h] *vr* (**a**) (*Anat*) to come apart; to do oneself an injury; **— de risa** to split one's sides

with laughing, die of laughing; **es para** — it's enough to make you die of laughing.
(**b**) (SAm) to fall to bits.

descuartizar [1f] *vt* (**a**) *animal* to carve up, cut up. (**b**) *person* (Hist) to quarter; (*fig*) to tear apart; **ni que me descuarticen** not even if they tear me apart.

descubierta 1 *nm* (Mil) scout. 2 *nf* (**a**) (Mil) reconnoitring, patrolling. (**b**) **a la** — openly; in the open.

descubierto 1 *ptp of* **descubrir**.
2 *adj* (**a**) *situation* open, exposed; (Mil) under fire; *body* bare, uncovered; *head* bare; *person* bareheaded, hatless; *car* open; *field* open, bare, treeless.
(**b**) **al** — in the open; exposed; in full view; **poner algo al** — to lay something bare, expose something to view; **quedar al** — to be exposed; to be manifest, be obvious.
3 *nm* (Comm: *in account*) deficit, shortage; (*on loan*) overdraft; **a** — short; *loan etc* unbacked; **vender al** — to sell short; **estar en** — to be overdrawn; **girar en** — to overdraw.

descubridero *nm* look-out post.
descubridor *nm* (**a**) discoverer. (**b**) (Mil) scout.
descubrimiento *nm* discovery; detection; disclosure, revelation; unveiling.

descubrir [3a; *ptp* **descubierto**] 1 *vt* (**a**) to discover; to find, detect, spot; to bring to light; to unearth, uncover; *oil etc* to find, strike; *answer etc* to discover, ascertain, learn.
(**b**) to see, make out, glimpse; **apenas lo descubría entre las nubes** I could just see it among the clouds.
(**c**) *statue, plaque etc* to unveil.
(**d**) to expose to view; to show, reveal, disclose; — **el estómago** to uncover one's stomach, bare one's stomach; — **la cabeza** to bare one's head; — **sus intenciones** to reveal one's intentions; — **su pecho a uno** to unbosom oneself to someone; **le descubrió su escritura** his writing gave him away, his writing betrayed him; **fue la criada la que les descubrió a la policía** it was the servant who gave them away to the police.
2 descubrirse *vr* (**a**) to reveal oneself, show oneself; to disclose one's whereabouts.
(**b**) to take off one's hat; to raise one's hat (in greeting).
(**c**) — **a uno**, — **con uno** to confess to someone, unbosom oneself to someone.

descuento *nm* discount; rebate, reduction; **a** — below par; **al** —, **con** — at a discount; — **por pago al contado** discount for cash payment.

descuerar [1a] *vt* (Chi) (**a**) to flay, skin. (**b**) (*fig*) to defame.

descuernar [1a] *vt* (Col, Cu, Guat, PR) to de-horn.

descuidadamente *adv* (**a**) carelessly; slackly, negligently; forgetfully. (**b**) untidily; in a slovenly way.

descuidado *adj* (**a**) careless; slack, negligent; forgetful.
(**b**) *appearance etc* untidy, slovenly; unkempt.
(**c**) unprepared; off guard; **coger** (*or* **pillar** *etc*) **a uno** — to catch someone off his guard, catch someone at a careless moment.
(**d**) easy in one's mind, without worries; **puedes estar** — you needn't worry.
(**e**) neglected; **con aspecto de niños** —**s** with the look of neglected children.

descuidar [1a] 1 *vt* to neglect; to disregard; to overlook; **ha descuidado mucho su negocio** he has neglected his business a lot.
2 *vi and* **descuidarse** *vr* (**a**) to be careless, be negligent; to get careless; to feel safe, drop one's guard; **en cuanto me descuide él me lo roba** the moment I drop my guard (*or* cease to watch out) he'll steal it from me; **a poco que uno se descuide le cobran el doble** you've got to watch them all the time or they'll charge you double.
(**b**) not to worry; **¡descuida!** don't worry!, it's all right!, you can forget about that!; —**se de algo** not to bother about something; —**se de hacer algo** not to bother to do something.
(**c**) to let oneself go, stop taking care of oneself.

descuidero *nm* sneak thief.
descuido *nm* (**a**) (*in general*) carelessness; slackness; negligence; forgetfulness; **al** — nonchalantly; **con** — thoughtlessly, without thinking.
(**b**) (*of appearance*) untidiness, slovenliness.
(**c**) (*un* —) oversight; mistake, slip; **en un** — (SAm) when least expected; **por** — by an oversight, inadvertently.

deschachar [1a] *vt* (CAm) to sack (*fam*), fire (*fam*).
deschalar [1a] *vt* (Arg, Per) *maize* to husk.
deschapar [1a] *vt* (SAm) *lock* to break.

desde 1 *prep* (**a**) (*place etc*) from; — **Burgos hay 30 km** it's 30 km from Burgos; — **abajo** from below; — **arriba** from (up) above; — **lejos** from afar, from a long way off; — **A hasta M** from A to M.
(**b**) (*time*) from; since; — **ahora** from now on; — **entonces** since then; — **el siglo XV para acá** from the 15th century onward; — **1960 no existe** it ceased to exist in 1960, it went out of existence in 1960; — **el martes** since Tuesday, after Tuesday; — **el 4 hasta el 16** from the 4th to the 16th; **llueve** — **hace 3 días** it's been raining for 3 days; — **hace 2 años no le vemos** we haven't seen him for 2 years, we haven't seen him these last 2 years; **¿— cuándo es esto así?** how long has it been like this?
(**c**) — **niño** since childhood, since I (*etc*) was a child.
2 — **que** *conj* since; — **que llovió** since it rained; — **que puedo recordar** ever since I can remember, (for) as long as I can remember.

desdecir [3p] 1 *vi*: — **de** (**a**) to be unworthy of, be below the standard set by; to be unbecoming to; **desdice de su patria** he is unworthy of his country; **esta novela no desdice de las otras** this novel is well up to the standard of the others, this novel is not inferior to the others.
(**b**) to clash with, not match, not suit; **la corbata desdice del traje** the tie does not go with the suit.
2 desdecirse *vr* to retract, withdraw; to go back on what one has said; — **de algo** to go back on something, take back something one has said; — **de una promesa** to go back on a promise.

desdén *nm* scorn, disdain; **al** — carelessly, nonchalantly.
desdentado *adj* toothless.
desdeñable *adj* contemptible; **una cantidad nada** — a far from negligible amount.
desdeñar [1a] 1 *vt* to scorn, disdain; to turn up one's nose at; to despise. 2 **desdeñarse** *vr*: — **de** + *infin* to scorn to + *infin*, not deign to + *infin*.
desdeñosamente *adv* scornfully, disdainfully; contemptuously.
desdeñoso *adj* scornful, disdainful; contemptuous.
desdibujado *adj* blurred; unclear; faded.
desdibujar [1a] 1 *vt* to blur (the outlines of).
2 desdibujarse *vr* to blur, get blurred, fade (away); **el recuerdo se ha desdibujado** the memory has become blurred.
desdicha *nf* (**a**) (*in general*) unhappiness, wretchedness; misfortune; misery. (**b**) (*una* —) misfortune, calamity.
desdichadamente *adv* unhappily; unluckily, unfortunately.
desdichado 1 *adj* (**a**) unhappy; unlucky; unfortunate; wretched; **¡qué** — **soy!** how wretched I am!
(**b**) unlucky, ill-fated; **fue un día** — it was an unlucky day.
2 *nm* poor devil, wretch.
desdinerar [1a] 1 *vt* to impoverish. 2 **desdinerarse** *vr* (*fam*) to cough up (*sl*), fork out (*fam*).
desdoblado *adj* (*fig*) *personality* split.
desdoblar [1a] *vt* (**a**) to unfold, spread out; *wire etc* to untwist, straighten; to take apart.
(**b**) (Chem) to break down (*en* into).
(**c**) (*fig*) to double, make two of; to split; — **un cargo** to split the functions of a post.
desdorar [1a] *vt* to tarnish (*also fig*).
desdoro *nm* (*fig*) blot, blemish, stigma, dishonour; **consideran un** — **trabajar** they think it dishonourable to work; **es un** — **para todos** it is a blot on us all; **hablar en** — **de uno** to speak disparagingly of someone, discredit someone by what one says.
deseable *adj* desirable.
desear [1a] *vt* to want, desire, wish (for); **os deseo toda clase de éxito** I wish you every success; **¿qué desea la señora?** (Comm *etc*) what can I do for you, madam?; **desearía más tiempo** I should like more time; **estoy deseando que esto termine** I wish this would end; — + *infin* to want to + *infin*, wish to + *infin*; see **dejar**.
desecación *nf* desiccation.
desecar [1g] 1 *vt* to dry up, desiccate; *land* to drain. 2 **desecarse** *vr* to dry up.
desecha *nf* (Col) = **desecho**.
desechar [1a] *vt* (**a**) *rubbish* to throw out; *useless object* to scrap, get rid of, jettison; *clothing* to cast off.
(**b**) *advice, fear, scruple* to cast aside; *claim, offer* to reject; *idea, plan* to drop, discard.
(**c**) to underrate, underestimate; to think little of.
(**d**) to censure, reprove.
(**e**) *key* to turn.
desecho *nm* (**a**) (*also* —**s**) residue; waste, rubbish; scrap, junk; (*of butcher*) offal; (*of corn*) chaff; — **de**

desellar

187

desengañar

hierro, hierro de — scrap iron; **producto de** — waste product; **vestidos de** — cast-off clothing.

(b) **el** — **de la sociedad** the scum of society, the dregs of society.

(c) **ese tío es un** — that fellow is a disaster, that chap is a dead loss.

(d) contempt, scorn; low opinion.

(e) (Cu) superior-quality tobacco.

(f) (SAm) short cut; detour; path, temporary road.

desellar [1a] vt to unseal, open.

desembalaje nm unpacking.

desembalar [1a] vt to unpack.

desembanastar [1a] **1** vt (a) to unpack; to take out (of a basket); (fam) sword to draw. (b) (fig) secret to blurt out.

2 desembanastarse vt (a) (animal) to break out. (b) to alight.

desembarazado adj (a) way etc clear, free, open; unburdened, light. (b) (fig) free and easy, free of commitments; — **de trabas** free, unrestrained.

desembarazar [1f] **1** vt (a) road etc to clear, free (de of); — **un cuarto de trastos** to clear a room of furniture.

(b) place to vacate, leave free, leave empty.

(c) — **a uno de algo** to rid someone of something.

(d) (Chi, Ec, Per, PR) to give birth to.

2 desembarazarse vr: — **de algo** to get rid of something, free oneself of something.

desembarazo nm (a) (act) clearing, freeing; disencumbrance; unburdening.

(b) (Chi, Ec, Per, PR) birth, delivery.

(c) (state) freedom; ease, naturalness; lack of restraint; **hablar con** — to talk easily, talk freely.

desembarcadero nm quay, landing stage, pier.

desembarcar [1g] **1** vt persons to land, put ashore; goods to land, unload.

2 vi and **desembarcarse** vr (a) to land, go ashore, disembark.

(b) (esp SAm) to alight (de from), get out (de of).

(c) **estar para** — (fam) to be about to give birth.

desembarco nm (Archit, Naut) landing.

desembargar [1h] vt to free; to remove the embargo on, remove the impediments from.

desembarque nm landing; unloading.

desembarrancar [1g] vt boat to refloat, get off.

desembarrar [1a] vt to clear of mud, remove the silt from.

desembaular [1a] vt (a) to unpack; to take out, get out (of a trunk); (fig) to empty. (b) (fig) to unburden oneself of.

desembocadero nm, **desembocadura** nf outlet, exit; (of river) mouth; (of drain) outfall; (of street) opening, end.

desembocar [1a] vi: — **en** (a) (of river) to flow into, run into, empty into; (of street) to meet, join, run into, lead into.

(b) (fig) to end in, result in, produce; **esto desembocó en una tragedia** this ended in tragedy, this led to tragedy.

desembolsar [1a] vt to pay out.

desembolso nm payment; disbursement; outlay, expenditure; — **inicial** deposit, down payment; **cubrir** —**s** to cover expenses.

desembozar [1f] vt to unmask (also fig), uncover.

desembragar [1h] **1** vt (Mech) to disengage, disconnect; clutch to release, let out. **2** vi (Aut) to declutch, let out the clutch.

desembrague nm disengagement; (Aut: act) declutching; (part) clutch release.

desembravecer [2d] vt to tame; (fig) to calm, pacify.

desembriagar [1h] **1** vt to sober up. **2 desembriagarse** vr to sober up.

desembrollar [1a] vt to unravel, disentangle.

desembuchar [1a] **1** vt to disgorge; (fig) to tell, reveal, let out.

2 vi (fig) to reveal a secret, spill the beans (sl); **¡desembucha!** out with it!

3 desembucharse vr (Chi) to be sick.

desemejante adj dissimilar, unlike; **A es** — **de B** A is unlike B, A is different from B.

desemejanza nf dissimilarity.

desemejar [1a] **1** vt to alter (the appearance of), change (for the worse); to disfigure. **2** vi to be dissimilar, look different, not look alike.

desempacar [1g] vt to unpack.

desempacharse [1a] vr (a) **se desempachó** he got over his sick feeling; his stomach settled down (after its upset).

(b) (fig) to cease to feel shy, stop feeling awkward.

desempacho nm ease, confidence; unconcern; (pej) forwardness.

desempañar [1a] vt glass to clean, de-mist.

desempapelar [1a] vt parcel to unwrap; wall to remove the paper from.

desempaquetar [1a] vt to unpack, unwrap.

desempatar [1a] vi: **volvieron a jugar para** — they held a play-off (to resolve the earlier tie).

desempate nm play-off (to resolve an earlier tie).

desempedrar [1k] vt street to take up the paving stones of; **ir desempedrando la calle** (fig) to dash along the street.

desempeñar [1a] **1** vt (a) pawned property to redeem, recover, get out of pawn.

(b) — **a uno** to get someone out of debt, pay someone's debts; (fig) to get someone out of a jam.

(c) post to hold, fill, occupy; duty to perform, discharge; (Theat and fig) role to play.

2 desempeñarse vr to get out of debt; (fig) to get oneself out of a jam.

desempeño nm (a) redeeming, redemption.

(b) payment.

(c) occupation; performance, discharge; (Theat and fig) performance, acting, showing; **un** — **meritorio** a worthy performance.

desempleado 1 adj unemployed, out of work. **2** nm unemployed man.

desempleo nm unemployment.

desempolvar [1a] vt to dust, remove the dust from.

desencadenar [1a] **1** vt (a) to unchain; to unleash, let loose.

(b) (fig) to unleash; to cause, start, set off.

2 desencadenarse vr (a) to break loose, free oneself.

(b) (fig: storm etc) to burst; (war) to break out; **se desencadenaron los aplausos** a storm of clapping broke out; **se desencadenó una violenta reacción** a violent reaction was produced.

desencajado adj face twisted, contorted; eyes wild.

desencajar [1a] **1** vt (a) to throw out of joint; (Anat) to dislocate.

(b) (Mech) to disconnect, disengage, put out of gear.

2 desencajarse vr (face) to become distorted (with fear); (eyes) to look wild.

desencajonar [1a] vt to unpack.

desencallar [1a] vt boat to refloat, get off.

desencantar [1a] vt to disillusion, disenchant.

desencanto nm disillusion(ment), disenchantment.

desencoger [2c] **1** vt to spread out; to smooth out, straighten out. **2 desencogerse** vr to lose one's timidity.

desenconar [1a] **1** vt (a) inflammation to reduce.

(b) (fig) to calm down, soothe.

2 desenconarse vr (a) to grow less.

(b) (fig: hatred) to die down, abate; (person) to calm down.

desencorvar [1a] vt to unbend, straighten (out).

desenchufar [1a] vt to disconnect, unplug.

desendeudar [1a] vi (SAm) to pay one's debts, get out of the red.

desenfadaderas nfpl: **tener buenas** — to be unflappable, be slow to anger; to be good at getting out of jams.

desenfadado adj (a) character, manner etc free, uninhibited; free-and-easy; carefree; unabashed; (pej) forward, disrespectful; dress etc casual, unconventional.

(b) space free, unencumbered; ample.

desenfadar [1a] **1** vt to pacify, calm down. **2 desenfadarse** vr to calm down.

desenfado nm freedom, lack of inhibition; free-and-easy manner; (pej) forwardness, disrespect.

desenfocado adj out of focus.

desenfrenadamente adv wildly, in an uncontrolled way; immoderately; licentiously.

desenfrenado adj wild, uncontrolled; immoderate; unbridled, licentious.

desenfrenarse [1a] vr (a) (person etc) to give free rein to one's passions, let one's feelings run wild, lose all self-control; (crowd) to run riot, rampage.

(b) (storm etc) to burst; to rage.

desenfreno nm wildness; lack of self-control; lack of moderation; licentiousness.

desenganchar [1a] vt to unhook, undo, unfasten; (Rail) to uncouple; (Mech) to disengage; horse to unhitch.

desengañado adj (a) disillusioned. (b) (Chi, Ec) terribly ugly.

desengañar [1a] **1** vt to disillusion; to disabuse (de about, of); **es mejor no** —**la** it is best not to disillusion her; it is best not to destroy her hopes.

I.S.D.—8

2 desengañarse *vr* (**a**) to become disillusioned (*de* about).

(**b**) to see the light, come down to earth, see things as they really are; ¡**desengáñate**! don't you believe it!, don't go deceiving yourself!

desengaño *nm* (**a**) disillusion(ment); disappointment; **sufrir un — amoroso** to be disappointed in love, have an unhappy love affair; **le enseñarán los —s** the disillusioning experiences (of life) will teach you. (**b**) admonition, reproof; home truth.

desengranar [1a] *vt* to disengage.

desengrasar [1a] *vt* to degrease, remove the grease from; to scour.

desenjaular [1a] *vt* (**a**) to take out of a cage; to release from a cage. (**b**) (*fam*) to let out of jail.

desenlace *nm* outcome; (*Lit*) ending; dénouement; **— fatal**, **— trágico** tragic ending; **el libro tiene un — feliz** the book has a happy ending.

desenlatar [1a] *vt* (*SAm*) *canned goods* to open.

desenlazar [1f] **1** *vt* (**a**) to untie, unlace, undo. (**b**) (*fig*) *problem* to solve; *plot* to unravel.

2 desenlazarse *vr* (**a**) to come undone. (**b**) (*Lit*) to end, turn out.

desenmarañar [1a] *vt* to disentangle, unravel (*also fig*).

desenmascarar [1a] *vt* (*fig*) to unmask, expose.

desenojar [1a] *vt* to soothe, appease, calm down.

desenredar [1a] **1** *vt* to unravel; to straighten out; to resolve, clear up.

2 desenredarse *vr* (*fig*) to get out of a jam; **— de** to get out of, extricate oneself from.

desenredo *nm* (**a**) unravelling, disentanglement. (**b**) (*Lit*) dénouement.

desenrollar [1a] **1** *vt* to unroll, unwind. **2 desenrollarse** *vr* to unroll, unwind; to get unrolled.

desenroscar [1g] *vt* (*SAm*) to unscrew.

desensibilizar [1f] *vt* to desensitize.

desensillar [1a] *vt* to unsaddle.

desentenderse [2g] *vr*: **— de** (**a**) to affect ignorance of, pretend not to know about.

(**b**) to wash one's hands of; to repudiate; to have nothing to do with; **se ha desentendido de todo eso** he has ceased to take any part in that, he has withdrawn completely from that.

desentendido *adj*: **hacerse el —** to pay no attention; to pretend not to be interested (*or* to hear *etc*); **no te hagas el —** don't pretend you haven't heard.

desenterrar [1k] *vt* (**a**) *corpse* to exhume, disinter. (**b**) (*fig*) to unearth, dig up, rake up.

desentonado *adj* (**a**) (*Mus*) out of tune. (**b**) *colour* clashing, not matching.

desentonar [1a] **1** *vi* (**a**) (*Mus*) to be out of tune. (**b**) (*fig*) to be out of tune (*con* with); (*of colours*) to clash (*con* with), not match.

2 desentonarse *vr* (*fig*) to behave rudely, speak disrespectfully, raise one's voice angrily.

desentono *nm* (*fig*) rudeness, disrespect; rude (*or* angry) tone of voice.

desentorpecer [2d] *vt* (**a**) *limb etc* to stretch, loosen up. (**b**) *person* (*fam*) to polish up.

desentramparse [1a] *vr* to get out of the red.

desentrañar [1a] *vt* (**a**) to disembowel; to eviscerate. (**b**) (*fig*) *mystery* to puzzle out, get to the bottom of, unravel; *meaning* to puzzle out, work out.

desentrenado *adj* out of practice; off form.

desentumecer [2d] *vt* to free from numbness, restore the feeling to, get the feeling back into; *limb* to stretch; *muscles* (*Sport*) to loosen up.

desenvainar [1a] *vt* (**a**) *sword* to draw, unsheathe; *peas* to shell; *claws* to show, put out. (**b**) (*fig*) to show, reveal, expose.

desenvoltura *nf* ease, naturalness; confidence; free-and-easy manner; (*of speech*) fluency, facility; (*pej*) forwardness, brazenness.

desenvolver [2h; *ptp* **desenvuelto**] *vt* *packet etc* to unwrap; *roll* to unwind, unroll; *wool etc* to disentangle, unravel.

(**b**) *theory etc* to develop; to expound, explain, set out.

desenvolvimiento *nm* development; exposition.

desenvuelto *adj* easy, natural; confident; free-and-easy; *speech* fluent, easy; (*pej*) forward, brazen.

desenyugar [1h] *vt* (*SAm*), **desenyuntar** [1a] *vt* (*SAm*) to unyoke.

deseo *nm* wish, desire; **el — de** the desire for; **el — de + infin** the desire to + *infin*; **— de saber** thirst for knowledge; **buen —** good intentions; **arder en —s de algo** to yearn for something; **se cumplieron sus —s** his wishes were fulfilled; **tener — de**, **venir en — de** to want, yearn for.

deseoso *adj*: **ser — de + infin** to be anxious to + *infin*, be eager to + *infin*.

desequilibrado *adj* (**a**) unbalanced; badly balanced, out of true; one-sided, lop-sided. (**b**) (*Med*) (mentally) unbalanced.

desequilibrar [1a] *vt* to unbalance; to overbalance, throw off balance.

desequilibrio *nm* (**a**) disequilibrium; unbalance, lack of balance; (*fig*) imbalance. (**b**) (*Med*) unbalanced mental condition, instability, psychological disorder.

deserción *nf* desertion; defection.

desertar [1a] **1** *vt* (**a**) to desert; *home* to desert, abandon, quit.

(**b**) (*Law*) *right of appeal* to forfeit, give up.

2 *vi*: **— de** (*Mil etc*) to desert; **— del hogar** to abandon one's home, leave home; **— de sus deberes** to neglect one's duties; **— de una tertulia** to stop going to a gathering.

desertor *nm* deserter.

deservicio *nm* disservice.

desescalada *nf* de-escalation.

desescalar [1a] *vti* to de-escalate.

desescarchador *nm* (*Mech*) defroster.

desescombrar [1a] *vt* to clear up, clear of rubbish (*or* debris *etc*).

desescombro *nm* clearing-up.

desespañolizar [1f] *vt* to weaken the Spanish nature of; *person* to cause to become less Spanish, wean away from Spanish habits (*etc*).

desesperación *nf* (**a**) despair, desperation; **con —** despairingly.

(**b**) fury; **nadar con —** to swim furiously.

(**c**) infuriating thing; **es una —** it's maddening; it's unbearable; **es una — tener que . . .** it's infuriating to have to . . .

desesperadamente *adv* desperately, despairingly; hopelessly.

desesperado **1** *adj* (**a**) desperate, despairing; in despair; hopeless; **estar — de** to have despaired of, have no hope of.

(**b**) *effort etc* furious, frenzied.

2 *nm*: **como un —** like mad.

3 *nf*: **hacer algo a la desesperada** to do something as a last hope, try a final desperate solution.

desesperante *adj* maddening, infuriating.

desesperanzar [1f] **1** *vt* to deprive of hope. **2 desesperanzarse** *vr* to lose hope, despair.

desesperar [1a] **1** *vt* to deprive of hope, drive to despair; (*fam*) to drive to distraction, drive crazy.

2 *vi* to despair (*de* of), lose hope; **— de + infin** to give up all hope of + *ger*.

3 desesperarse *vr* to despair, lose hope; to get desperate.

desespero *nm* (*esp SAm*) despair, desperation.

desestancar [1g] *vt* *product* to remove the state monopoly from, allow a free market in.

desestimar [1a] *vt* (**a**) to have a low opinion of; to scorn, belittle, disparage. (**b**) *claim, motion etc* to reject.

desfachatado *adj* brazen, impudent, barefaced; cheeky.

desfachatez *nf* brazenness, impudence; cheek, nerve.

desfalcador *nm* embezzler.

desfalcar [1g] *vt* to embezzle.

desfalco *nm* embezzlement.

desfallecer [2d] **1** *vt* to weaken. **2** *vi* to get weak, weaken; to faint; (*of voice*) to fail, falter; **— de ánimo** to lose heart.

desfallecido *adj* weak; faint.

desfallecimiento *nm* weakness; faintness.

desfasado *adj*: **estar —** to be out of step (*fig*; *de* with); (*Mech*) to be out of phase, be badly adjusted.

desfasar [1a] *vt* to phase out.

desfavorable *adj* unfavourable.

desfavorablemente *adv* unfavourably.

desfavorecer [2d] *vt* (**a**) to cease to favour, withdraw support from. (**b**) (*of clothes*) to be unbecoming to, not suit, not look well on.

desfiguración *nf*, **desfiguramiento** *nm* disfigurement, disfiguration; defacement; alteration; distortion, misrepresentation; (*Phot etc*) blurring; (*Radio*) distortion.

desfigurado *adj* disfigured; deformed; *meaning etc* distorted, twisted; *outline* (*also Phot*) blurred; (*Radio*) distorted.

desfigurar [1a] *vt* *face* to disfigure; *body* to deform; *picture etc* to deface; *outline* (*also Phot*) to blur; *voice* to alter, disguise; *meaning* to distort, twist; to cloud; *event* to misrepresent, distort the truth of, alter the details of; **una cicatriz le desfigura la cara** a scar disfigures his face; **la niebla lo desfigura todo** everything, the fog makes everything look strange.

desfiladero *nm* defile, pass; gorge.

desfilar [1a] *vi* to parade; to march past; to file by, file out (*etc*), file past; **desfilaron ante el general** they paraded before the general, they marched past the general.

desfile *nm* procession; (*Mil*) parade, march-past; — **de modelos** fashion show, fashion parade; — **naval** naval review; — **de la victoria** victory parade.

desfloración *nf* (a) deflowering, defloration. (b) tarnishing, messing-up, destruction of the fine appearance of.

desflorar [1a] *vt* (a) *woman* to deflower.
(b) to tarnish, mess up, destroy the fine appearance of.
(c) — **un asunto** to touch briefly on a matter, treat a matter no more than superficially.

desfogar [1h] **1** *vt* (*fig*) to vent (con, en on).
2 *vi* (*Naut: of storm*) to burst.
3 desfogarse *vr* (*fig*) to vent one's anger; to let oneself go, let off steam.

desfogue *nm* (*fig*) venting.

desfondar [1a] *vt* (a) to knock the bottom out of, stave in (*also Naut*). (b) (*Agr*) to plough deeply.

desfortalecer [2d] *vt* to dismantle (the fortifications of).

desgaire *nm* (a) (*of dress etc*) slovenliness, carelessness.
(b) (*of manner*) nonchalance, affected carelessness; scornful attitude, disdain.
(c) **vestido al** — dressed in a slovenly way; **hacer algo al** — to do something with a scornful air; **mirar a uno al** — to sneer at someone, look scornfully at someone.

desgajar [1a] **1** *vt* (a) to tear off, break off, split off.
(b) — **a uno de** to tear someone away from.
2 desgajarse *vr* (a) to come off, break off, split away.
(b) — **de** (*person*) to tear oneself away from.

desgalichado *adj* *movement etc* clumsy, awkward; *dress* shabby, slovenly, sloppy; *person* down-at-heel, unprepossessing.

desgana *nf* (a) lack of appetite, loss of appetite.
(b) (*fig*) unwillingness, disinclination, reluctance; **su — para hacerlo** his unwillingness to do it; **hacer algo a** — to do something reluctantly.
(c) (*Med*) weakness, faintness.

desganado *adj:* **estar —, sentirse** — to have no appetite, not be hungry.

desganarse [1a] *vr* (a) to lose one's appetite. (b) (*fig*) to lose interest, get bored, get fed up.

desgañitarse [1a] *vr* to bawl, shout; to scream oneself hoarse.

desgarbado *adj* (*in movement*) clumsy, ungainly, gawky; graceless; (*in appearance*) slovenly, uncouth.

desgarrado *adj* (a) torn; tattered, in tatters. (b) (*fig*) shameless, barefaced, brazen. (c) (*fig*) vicious, licentious.

desgarrador *adj* heartbreaking, heartrending; uncontrollable; cry piercing.

desgarrar [1a] *vt* (a) to tear, rip (up), rend. (b) (*fig*) to shatter, crush; *heart* to break. (c) (*SAm*) *phlegm* to cough up.

desgarro *nm* (a) tear, rip, rent. (b) (*fig*) impudence, brazenness, effrontery; (*woman's*) forwardness. (c) (*fig*) boastfulness. (d) (*SAm*) phlegm.

desgastar [1a] **1** *vt* (a) to wear away, wear down; (*Geol*) to erode, weather; *rope etc* to chafe, fray; *metal* to corrode, eat away, eat into; — **la ropa** to wear one's clothes out.
(b) (*fig*) to spoil, ruin.
2 desgastarse *vr* (a) to wear away; to erode; to chafe, fray; to corrode; to get worn out.
(b) (*Med*) to get weak, decline; to wear oneself out.

desgaste *nm* (a) wear; wear and tear; erosion; chafing; fraying; corrosion; **aumenta el — del motor** it increases wear on the engine; **debido al — de su ropa** because his clothes were so worn.
(b) waste, loss; slow wasting; (*Mil*) attrition; (*Med*) weakening, decline; — **económico** drain on one's resources; **guerra de** — war of attrition.

desglobar [1a] *vt* *figures etc* to break down, analyse, split up.

desglosar [1a] *vt* to separate, remove, detach.

desgobernado *adj* uncontrollable, undisciplined; *child* wild.

desgobernar [1k] *vt* (a) (*Pol*) to misgovern, misrule; *affair* to mismanage, handle badly, make a mess of. (b) (*Anat*) to dislocate.

desgobierno *nm* (a) misgovernment, misrule; mismanagement, bad handling. (b) dislocation.

desgolletar [1a] *vt* *bottle* to knock the neck off.

desgoznar [1a] **1** *vt* (a) to take off its hinges, unhinge.
(b) to take the hinges off.
2 desgoznarse *vr* (a) (*person*) to get wild, lose control; to go off the rails.
(b) (*of plan etc*) to be thrown out of gear.

desgracia *nf* (a) misfortune; mishap; accident; (*piece of*) bad luck; setback; **por** — unfortunately; **¡qué** —! what a misfortune!; what bad luck!; **estar en** — to be unfortunate, suffer constant setbacks; **en el accidente no hay que lamentar —s personales** there were no casualties in the accident; **la familia ha tenido una serie de** —s the family has had a series of misfortunes.
(b) disgrace; disfavour; **caer en (la)** — to fall into disgrace.

desgraciadamente *adv* unfortunately, unluckily; **¡**—**!** more's the pity!, alas!

desgraciado 1 *adj* (a) unlucky, unfortunate; luckless, hapless; wretched; unhappy, miserable; **una elección desgraciada** an unfortunate choice; — **en sus amores** unlucky in love; — **en el juego** unlucky at cards; **era — en su matrimonio** he was unhappy in his marriage; **una vida desgraciada** a wretched life, a life of misery; **¡qué — estoy!** how wretched I am!
(b) ill-fated, unlucky; **ese día** — that ill-fated day.
(c) *appearance* graceless, ugly, lacking charm.
(d) unpleasant.
2 *nm*, **desgraciada** *nf* wretch, poor devil, unfortunate; **lo tiene aquel** — that wretched creature has got it.

desgraciar [1b] **1** *vt* (a) to spoil, ruin (the appearance of).
(b) to displease.
2 desgraciarse *vr* (a) to spoil, be ruined, suffer damage; (*plan etc*) to fall through, collapse, fail to mature.
(b) — **con uno** to fall out with someone; to lose someone's favour.

desgranar [1a] **1** *vt* (a) to remove the grain (*or pips etc*) from; *corn* to thresh; *peas* to shell; — **un racimo** to pick the grapes from a bunch.
(b) — **las cuentas del rosario** to tell one's beads.
(c) — **imprecaciones** to produce a rapid series of imprecations; — **mentiras** to come out with a string of lies.
2 desgranarse *vr* (a) (*Bot*) to fall; (*corn*) to shed its grain, (*other plant*) to drop its seeds.
(b) (*of beads*) to come apart.

desgrasar [1a] *vt* = **desengrasar**.

desgravar [1a] *vt* *product* to reduce the tax (*or duty etc*) on.

desgreñado *adj* dishevelled, tousled.

desgreñar [1a] *vt* to dishevel, rumple, tousle.

desgreño *nm* (*Col, Chi, RPl*) dishevelment; (*fig*) disorder, disarray; (*fig*) carelessness.

desguarnecer [2d] *vt* (a) (*Tech*) to strip down; to remove the accessories (*or trimmings etc*) from; — **un barco de velas** to remove the sails from a boat.
(b) *horse* to unharness.
(c) (*Mil*) *town* to abandon, remove the garrison from; *fortress* to dismantle (the fortifications of).

desguarnecido *adj* (a) bare, shorn of trimmings (*etc*). (b) *city* undefended, unprotected; *flank* exposed.

desguazar [1f] *vt* (a) *timber* to dress, rough-hew. (b) *ship* to break up.

deshabitado *adj* uninhabited; deserted; empty, vacant.

deshabitar [1a] *vt* to move out of, leave empty; to desert, quit.

deshabituarse [1e] *vr* to lose the habit, get out of the habit.

deshacer [2s] **1** *vt* to undo, unmake; to spoil, ruin, damage, destroy; (*Mech etc*) to take apart; to pull to pieces; *carcass, joint* to cut up, carve up; *ship* to break up; *bed* to unmake, pull to pieces; *parcel* to undo, unpack, unwrap; *trunk* to unpack; *knot* to undo, untie; *seam* to unpick; *metal etc* to wear down; *ice etc* to melt, dissolve; *eyesight* to harm, damage; *person, economy etc* to shatter; *enemy* to shatter, rout, put to flight; *opponent* to defeat; *treaty etc* to break, violate; *wrong* to right; — **algo en agua** to dissolve something in water; **la lluvia deshizo el techo** the rain damaged the roof; — **un brazo contra algo** to hurt one's arm on something.
2 deshacerse *vr* (a) to come undone; to be spoiled, get damaged; to come apart; to fall to pieces; to break up; to come untied; to melt, dissolve; to be shattered, disintegrate; to vanish; **se deshizo la pierna al caer** he hurt his leg when he

fell; **se deshizo como el humo** it vanished into thin air, it vanished like smoke; **cuando se deshizo la reunión** when the meeting broke up.

(**b**) (*Med*) to get weak, grow feeble; to waste away.

(**c**) (*emotionally*) to grieve; to pine; to get impatient, get worked up.

(**d**) — **de algo** to get rid of something; (*Comm etc*) to dump something, unload something; **no quiero deshacerme de eso** I don't want to part with that; **logramos deshacernos de él** we managed to get rid of him.

(**e**) — **en lágrimas** to burst into tears; — **en elogios de uno** to shower praises on someone; — **en cumplidos** to pay lavish compliments, come out with extravagant courtesies; to overdo the politeness.

(**f**) — **por los melocotones** to be crazy about peaches, adore peaches; — **por hacer algo** to strive to do something, struggle to do something; — **por complacer a uno** to do one's utmost to please someone.

desharrapado adj ragged, tattered, shabby.
deshebillar [1a] vt to unbuckle.
deshebrar [1a] vt to unthread.
deshechizar [1f] vt to remove the spell from, disenchant.
deshecho 1 adj (**a**) undone; untied; broken, smashed, in pieces; shattered; **tener un brazo** — to have a badly injured arm; **estar** — (*fam*) to be worn out.
(**b**) (*Med*) *person* weak, emaciated; *health* broken.
(**c**) (*fig*) *storm* violent.
(**d**) (*Arg*) untidy.
2 nm (*Col, Chi, Ven*) short cut.
deshelador nm (*Aer*) de-icer.
deshelar [1k] **1** vt to thaw, melt; (*Tech*) to defrost; (*Aer*) to de-ice. **2** vi and **deshelarse** vr to thaw, melt; (*Meteorol*) to thaw.
desherbaje nm weeding.
desherbar [1k] vt to weed.
desheredar [1a] vt to disinherit.
desherrarse [1k] vr (*horse*) to cast a shoe.
deshidratación nf dehydration.
deshidratado adj dehydrated.
deshidratar [1a] vt to dehydrate.
deshielo nm thaw.
deshilachado adj shabby; worn, frayed.
deshilachar [1a] **1** vt to pull threads out of; to wear, fray. **2 deshilacharse** vr to wear, fray.
deshilada nf: **a la** — (**a**) (*Mil*) in single file. (**b**) (*fig*) secretly, stealthily.
deshilado nm (*Sew*) openwork.
deshilar [1a] **1** vt (*Sew*) to unravel; *meat* to shred. **2** vi to get thin. **3 deshilarse** vr to get worn, fray, come apart.
deshilvanado adj (*fig*) disjointed, disconnected, incoherent.
deshilvanar [1a] vt (*Sew*) to untack, take the stitches out of.
deshinchar [1a] **1** vt (**a**) *tyre* to deflate, let down; *swelling* to reduce (the swelling of).
(**b**) (*fig*) *anger* to give vent to.
2 deshincharse vr (**a**) (*tyre*) to go flat; (*swelling*) to go down.
(**b**) (*fig*) to get down off one's high horse.
deshipotecar [1g] vt *property* to pay off the mortgage on.
deshojado adj *branch etc* leafless; *flower* stripped of its petals.
deshojar [1a] **1** vt *tree* to strip the leaves off, (*Chem*) to defoliate; *flower* to pull the petals off; (*SAm*) *maize* to husk; *fruit* to peel; *book* to tear the pages out of.
2 deshojarse vr to lose its leaves (*etc*).
deshollejar [1a] vt *grapes etc* to peel, skin.
deshollinador nm (chimney) sweep.
deshollinar [1a] vt (**a**) to sweep. (**b**) (*fig*) to take a close look at.
deshonestamente adv indecently, lewdly.
deshonestidad nf indecency, impropriety, lewdness.
deshonesto adj indecent, improper, lewd.
deshonor nm (**a**) dishonour, disgrace. (**b**) (*un* —) insult, affront (*de* to); **no es un** — **trabajar** it is no disgrace to work.
deshonorar [1a] vt (**a**) to dishonour, disgrace; to be unworthy of. (**b**) to spoil, disfigure. (**c**) to dismiss, deprive of office (*or* title *etc*).
deshonra nf (**a**) dishonour, disgrace; shame; **lo tiene a** — he thinks it shameful, he considers it beneath him; **tienen a** — **trabajar** they think it beneath them to work.
(**b**) shameful act.

deshonrabuenos nmf, pl **deshonrabuenos** (**a**) slanderer. (**b**) black sheep (of the family).
deshonrar [1a] vt (**a**) to dishonour, disgrace, bring disgrace on. (**b**) to insult. (**c**) *woman* to seduce, ruin.
deshonroso adj dishonourable, disgraceful, ignominious.
deshora: a — adv at the wrong time; at an inconvenient time; **llegar a** — to come unexpectedly; **acostarse a** — to go to bed at some unearthly hour; **hacer algo a** — to do something at the wrong moment, mistime something.
deshuesar [1a] vt *meat* to bone; *fruit* to stone.
deshumanizar [1f] vt to dehumanize.
deshumedecerse [2d] vr to dry up, lose its moisture.
desiderátum nm, pl **desiderátums** desideratum.
desidia nf (**a**) laziness, idleness. (**b**) neglect; slovenliness, carelessness.
desidioso adj (**a**) lazy, idle. (**b**) neglected; slovenly, careless.
desierto 1 adj (**a**) *island, region etc* desert; *landscape* empty, bleak, desolate; *house etc* empty, deserted; **la calle estaba desierta** the street was deserted.
(**b**) **declarar** — **un premio** to declare that a prize will not be awarded (for lack of good candidates *etc*); **declarar desiertas unas oposiciones** to declare a competition void.
2 nm desert; wilderness; **clamar en el** — to cry in the wilderness.
designación nf (**a**) (*act*) designation, appointment. (**b**) designation, name.
designar [1a] vt to designate, appoint, name; to select; *date, place etc* to name, fix, decide on.
designio nm plan, design.
desigual adj (**a**) unequal, different; *struggle etc* unequal; *treatment* unfair, inequitable.
(**b**) *weather etc* variable, changeable; *character* unpredictable.
(**c**) *ground, writing etc* uneven; irregular; *edge* rough.
desigualdad nf (**a**) inequality. (**b**) variableness, changeableness; unpredictability. (**c**) unevenness; irregularity; roughness.
desilusión nf disillusion(ment), disappointment; **caer en la** — to get disillusioned; **sufrir una** — to suffer a disappointment.
desilusionante adj disillusioning, disappointing.
desilusionar [1a] **1** vt to disillusion; to disappoint, let down.
2 desilusionarse vr to get disillusioned, lose one's illusions; to be disappointed; to have one's hopes destroyed.
desinencia nf (*Ling*) ending.
desinfección nf disinfection.
desinfectante nm disinfectant.
desinfectar [1a] vt to disinfect.
desinfestar [1a] vt to decontaminate.
desinflación nf disinflation, deflation.
desinflacionar [1a] vt (*Comm, Fin*) to deflate.
desinflacionista adj disinflationary, deflationary.
desinflar [1a] vt to deflate, let the air out of.
desinsectación nf protection against insect pests; **la** — **de un jardín** the campaign to free a garden of insect pests.
desintegración nf disintegration; — **nuclear** nuclear fission; **la** — **del átomo** the smashing of the atom.
desintegrar [1a] **1** vt to disintegrate; *atom* to split, smash. **2 desintegrarse** vr to disintegrate; to split, be smashed.
desinterés nm disinterestedness, impartiality; unselfishness.
desinteresado adj disinterested, impartial; unselfish.
desintoxicar [1g] **1** vt to sober up. **2 desintoxicarse** vr to sober up.
desistimiento nm (**a**) desisting. (**b**) (*Law*) waiving of a right.
desistir [3a] vi (**a**) to stop, desist; — **de algo** to desist from something; — **de** + *infin* to desist from + *ger*, stop + *ger*.
(**b**) (*Law*) to waive a right; — **de un derecho** to waive a right.
desjarretar [1a] vt *animal* to hamstring; (*Med*) to weaken, debilitate.
desjuntar [1a] vt to separate, take apart; to divide.
deslavado adj (**a**) half-washed. (**b**) (*fig*) brazen, barefaced. (**c**) = **deslavazado**.
deslavar [1a] vt (**a**) to half-wash, wash superficially; to wash away. (**b**) to weaken; to fade.
deslavazado adj (**a**) soft, weak, limp; drooping; *person* limp. (**b**) faded, washed-out, pale; (*fig*) colourless. (**c**) (*fig*) *speech etc* disjointed, incoherent.

desleal adj disloyal (a, con to); competition (Comm) unfair.

deslealmente adv disloyally; unfairly.

deslealtad nf disloyalty; unfairness.

deslechar [1a] vt to milk.

desleído adj (a) dissolved; diluted. (b) (fig) idea etc weak, woolly.

desleír [3m] 1 vt to dissolve; to dilute, thin; to make weaker. 2 **desleírse** vr to dissolve; to become diluted; to get weaker.

deslenguado adj foul-mouthed.

deslenguarse [1i] vr to shoot one's mouth off, talk too much, be too free in what one says; to speak insolently; to pour out obscenities.

desliar [1c] 1 vt to untie, undo. 2 **desliarse** vr to come undone.

desligado adj (a) loose, free; unfastened. (b) (fig) separate, detached; **vive — de todo** he lives detached from everything, he lives in a world of his own.

desligamiento nm (fig) detachment (de from).

desligar [1h] 1 vt (a) to untie, undo, unfasten; to unbind; to extricate (de from).
(b) (fig) to separate, detach; to consider separately; — **el primer aspecto del segundo** to separate the first aspect from the second.
(c) (fig) matter to unravel, disentangle, clarify.
(d) person to absolve, free (de from); to excuse, exempt (de from); — **a uno de una promesa** to release someone from a promise.
2 **desligarse** vr to come undone, get unfastened; (person) to extricate oneself (de from).

deslindar [1a] vt (a) to mark out, fix the limits (or boundaries) of. (b) (fig) to define.

deslinde nm (a) demarcation, fixing of limits (or boundaries). (b) definition.

desliz nm (a) slip, slide; (Aut) skid.
(b) (fig) slip; lapse; indiscretion; — **de lengua** slip of the tongue; **los deslices de la juventud** the indiscretions of youth, the minor sins of youth.

deslizadero nm (a) slide; slippery spot. (b) (Tech) chute, slide.

deslizadizo adj slippery.

deslizador nm (a) (child's) scooter. (b) (Naut) small speedboat. (c) (Aer) glider; — **acuático** hovercraft. (d) (of skate etc) runner, skid.

deslizamiento nm slide, sliding, slipping; (Aut) skid; — (suave) glide; — **de tierra** landslide.

deslizar [1f] 1 vt (a) to slide, slip (en into, por along, through); — **una mesa por el suelo** to slide a table along the floor.
(b) — **una propina a uno** to slip someone a tip; — **una observación** to slip a remark in; to let slip a remark.
2 **deslizarse** vr (a) (accidentally) to slip (en on, up on), slide (por along); (Aut) to skid.
(b) (secret) to slip out; (error) to slip in, creep in; **aquí se ha deslizado un error** an error has crept in here.
(c) (of movement, snake etc) to slide, glide, slither; (boat) to glide; (water) to go (gently), pass, flow gently; (time) to pass, glide past; (person) to slip away, slip off; to slip in; — **en un cuarto** to slip into a room; — **en una fiesta** to slip unnoticed into a party; — **fuera de un agujero** to wriggle out of a hole; **el agua se desliza mansamente** the water flows along gently; **la anguila se deslizaba entre mis manos** the eel slipped away between my fingers.
(d) (person: fig) to slip up, blunder; to go wrong morally, get into bad ways, backslide.

deslomar [1a] 1 vt to break the back of; (fig) to wear out, exhaust utterly; — **a uno a garrotazos** to beat someone mercilessly.
2 **deslomarse** vr (fig) to get worn out; to work one's guts out.

deslucido adj (a) tarnished; worn out, old and useless.
(b) flat, dull, lifeless; undistinguished, characterless; **hizo un papel —** he was dull in the part; **el jugador estuvo muy —** the player was far from his best form, he played in a very lifeless way.
(c) graceless, inelegant, awkward.
(d) fruitless, unsuccessful; **quedar —** to be unsuccessful.

deslucimiento nm (a) tarnished state; useless condition.
(b) flatness, dullness, lifelessness; lack of character.
(c) gracelessness, inelegance.
(d) failure, lack of success.

deslucir [3f] 1 vt (a) to tarnish; to damage, spoil, ruin; to impair the splendour of, diminish the attractiveness of, dull; **la lluvia deslució el acto** the rain ruined the ceremony.
(b) to discredit, damage the standing of.

2 **deslucirse** vr (fig) to fail, be unsuccessful; to do badly.

deslumbrador adj (a) dazzling, brilliant; glaring. (b) (fig) dazzling; puzzling, confusing, bewildering.

deslumbramiento nm (a) glare, dazzle; brilliance. (b) (fig) confusion; bewilderment.

deslumbrante adj dazzling.

deslumbrar [1a] vt (a) to dazzle; to blind.
(b) (fig) to dazzle; to puzzle, confuse, bewilder; to daze; **deslumbró a todos con su oratoria** he captivated everyone with his oratory, he gave a dazzling oratorical display.

deslustrado adj (a) glass frosted, ground; pottery unglazed. (b) (esp fig) dull, lustreless; tarnished.

deslustrar [1a] vt (a) glass to frost. (b) (esp fig) to dull, tarnish (the brilliance of), dim (the lustre of). (c) (fig) reputation etc to sully, stain, tarnish.

deslustre nm (a) frosting. (b) tarnishing; dullness, dimness. (c) (fig) stigma, stain; disgrace.

deslustroso adj (a) unbecoming, unsuitable. (b) (fig) disgraceful.

desmadejamiento nm enervation, weakness.

desmadejar [1a] vt to enervate, weaken, take it out of.

desmalezar [1f] vt (SAm) to weed.

desmallar [1a] 1 vt stitches to pull out; stocking to make a ladder (or run) in. 2 **desmallarse** vr (stocking) to ladder.

desmamar [1a] vt to wean.

desmán[1] nm excess, outrage; piece of bad behaviour; abuse (of authority); **cometer un —** to commit an outrage (contra on).

desmán[2] nm (Zool) muskrat.

desmanchar [1a] 1 vt (SAm) to clean, remove the spots (or stains etc) from.
2 **desmancharse** vr (CAm, Col, Ec, Per) (a) to hurry out; to withdraw.
(b) (Agr) to stray from the herd.

desmandado adj (a) unruly, unbridled; wild; uncontrollable, out of hand; obstreperous. (b) animal stray; horse runaway.

desmandarse [1a] vr (a) to get out of hand, run wild, go out of control; to be obstreperous, behave badly; to be insolent.
(b) (animal) to stray (from the herd); (horse) to bolt, run away.

desmanotado adj clumsy, awkward.

desmantelamiento nm (a) (act) dismantling; abandonment. (b) (state) dilapidation.

desmantelar [1a] 1 vt (Mil etc) to dismantle, raze; scaffold etc to take down; walls to strip; house etc to strip of its contents, leave bare; (Naut) to unmast, unrig; (fig) to abandon, forsake.
2 **desmantelarse** vr (house etc) to fall into disrepair, become dilapidated.

desmaña nf clumsiness, awkwardness; slowness, helplessness; unpractical nature.

desmañado adj clumsy, awkward; slow, helpless; unpractical.

desmarcado adj (Sport) unmarked.

desmayado adj (a) (Med) unconscious. (b) (fig) weak, faint; languid; character etc dull, lacklustre, colourless. (c) colour pale, dull.

desmayar [1a] 1 vi (of person) to lose heart, get discouraged, get depressed; (of effort etc) to falter, flag.
2 **desmayarse** vr (a) (Med) to faint (away), swoon. (b) (plant etc) to droop low, trail.

desmayo nm (a) (Med: act) faint, fainting fit, swoon; (state) unconsciousness; **sufrir un —** to have a fainting fit, faint.
(b) (of voice) faltering, flagging; (of spirit) dejection, depression; (of body in general) languidness, limpness, limp feeling, listlessness; **tenía un — 'en todo el cuerpo** he felt limp all over; **las ramas caen con —** the branches droop low, the branches trail; **hablar con —** to talk in a small voice, speak falteringly.

desmedido adj excessive, disproportionate, out of all proportion; ambition, pride boundless, overweening; grief etc exaggerated.

desmedirse [3l] vr to forget oneself, go too far.

desmedrado adj (a) impaired; reduced; in decline. (b) (Med) run down; weak, emaciated; ill-looking.

desmedrar [1a] 1 vt (a) to impair; to reduce; to spoil, ruin, affect badly.
(b) (fig) to disparage, belittle.
2 vi and **desmedrarse** vr (a) to fall off, decline; to go downhill; to deteriorate.
(b) (Med) to get weak; to get thin; (child) to be sickly, waste away; (Bot) to grow poorly, do badly.

desmedro nm (a) impairment; reduction; decline, deterioration.. (b) (Med) weakness, emaciation, thinness. (c) disparagement, belittling.

desmejora nf, **desmejoramiento** nm = **desmedro** (a) and (b).

desmejorado adj: **queda muy desmejorada** she's lost her looks, she's not as attractive as she used to be; (Med) she's not looking at all well.

desmejorar [1a] **1** vt (a) to impair, spoil, damage; to cause to deteriorate.
   (b) (Med) to weaken, affect the health of.
   2 desmejorarse vr (a) to be impaired, be spoiled; to decline, deteriorate, go downhill.
   (b) (person) to lose one's looks, look less attractive; (Med) to lose one's health, suffer, waste away.

desmelenado adj dishevelled, tousled.

desmelenar [1a] vt to dishevel, tousle the hair of.

desmembración nf dismemberment, break-up.

desmembrar [1k] vt to dismember, separate, break up.

desmemoria nf poor memory, forgetfulness.

desmemoriado adj forgetful, absent-minded.

desmemoriarse [1b] vr to grow forgetful, become absent-minded.

desmentida nf denial; **dar una — a** to deny, give the lie to.

desmentimiento nm denial; refutation.

desmentir [3i] **1** vt accusation to deny, refute, give the lie to; rumour to deny, scotch, scout; theory etc to refute, explode; to contradict; character, origins etc to belie, not fit in with, be unworthy of; — **rotundamente una acusación** to deny a charge flatly.
   2 vi to be out of line, not fit; — **de** to belie, clash with, be unworthy of.
   3 desmentirse vr to contradict oneself; to go back on one's word.

desmenuzable adj crumbly, crumbling; flaky; friable.

desmenuzar [1f] **1** vt (a) bread etc to crumble (up), break into small pieces; meat to chop, shred, mince; cheese to shred.
   (b) (fig) to examine minutely, take a close look at.
   2 desmenuzarse vr to crumble (up), break up.

desmerecer [2d] **1** vt to be unworthy of.
   2 vi (a) to deteriorate, go off, be less good; to lose value.
   (b) — **de** to compare unfavourably with, not be comparable to, not live up to; **ésta no desmerece de sus otras películas** this is in no way inferior to his other films, this is every bit as good as his earlier films.

desmesura nf (a) excess, enormity; disproportion; extra size. (b) lack of moderation.

desmesuradamente adv disproportionately, excessively; enormously; **abrir — la boca** to open one's mouth extra wide.

desmesurado adj (a) disproportionate, excessive, inordinate; enormous; ambition etc boundless; (in measurement) extra big, unduly large, much too big.
   (b) insolent, impudent.

desmesurarse [1a] vr to become insolent, forget oneself, lose all restraint.

desmigajar [1a] vt, **desmigar** [1h] vt to crumble.

desmilitarización nf demilitarization.

desmilitarizado adj demilitarized.

desmilitarizar [1f] vt to demilitarize.

desmirriado adj weak, sickly; thin, weedy.

desmochar [1a] vt tree to lop, cut off the top of; to pollard; horns to cut off the points of; text etc to cut, hack about, mutilate.

desmoche nm (a) lopping, pollarding.
   (b) (fig) general slaughter, mowing down, mass removal; **hubo un — en el primer examen** there was a mass slaughter of candidates in the first exam.

desmocho nm lopped branches, cuttings.

desmolado adj toothless.

desmonetizar [1f] vt (a) to demonetize; to convert into gold. (b) (Arg) to devalue.

desmontable **1** adj detachable; sectional, in sections, which takes apart; collapsible; that takes down. **2** nm tyre lever.

desmontaje nm dismantling, stripping down; demolition.

desmontar [1a] **1** vt (a) (Mech) to dismantle, strip down; to take apart, take to pieces; (Archit) to knock down, demolish; shotgun to uncock; enemy guns to silence, knock out; sail to take down.
   (b) ground to level; to clear of trees (etc); trees to fell; rubbish to clear away.
   (c) rider to throw, unseat, unhorse; — **a uno de un vehículo** to help someone down from a vehicle.
   2 vi and **desmontarse** vr to dismount, alight (de from).

desmonte nm (a) (act) levelling; clearing; clearing away, removal; **los trabajos exigirán el — de X metros cúbicos** the work will necessitate the removal of X cubic metres.
   (b) levelled ground; heap of soil extracted.
   (c) (Rail) cutting, cut (US).
   (d) felled timber.

desmoralizador adj demoralizing.

desmoralizar [1f] vt army etc to demoralize; customs etc to corrupt.

desmoronadizo adj crumbling; rickety; dilapidated.

desmoronado adj tumbledown, ruinous, dilapidated.

desmoronamiento nm crumbling, dilapidation, decay; collapse (also fig).

desmoronar [1a] **1** vt to wear away, destroy little by little; (fig) to erode, affect, make inroads into.
   2 desmoronarse vr (Geol etc) to crumble, fall apart; (house etc) to get dilapidated, become ruinous, fall into disrepair; (part of masonry) to fall, come down, collapse; (fig) to decline, decay.

desmovilización nf demobilization.

desmovilizar [1f] vt to demobilize.

desmultiplicar [1g] vt (Mech) to gear down.

desnacionalización nf denationalization.

desnacionalizado adj (a) industry etc denationalized.
   (b) person stateless.

desnacionalizar [1f] vt to denationalize.

desnarigada nf (hum): **la —** the skull.

desnatar [1a] vt milk to skim, take the cream off; other liquid to remove the top of, remove the scum from; (fig) to take the cream off; **leche sin —** whole milk.

desnaturalizado adj (a) (Chem) denatured. (b) person etc unnatural; cruel, inhuman.

desnaturalizar [1f] **1** vt (a) (Chem) to denature.
   (b) (fig) to denaturalize, alter the fundamental nature of; to pervert, corrupt; text etc to distort; sense to misrepresent, twist.
   2 desnaturalizarse vr to give up one's nationality; to become stateless.

desnivel nm (a) unevenness; high ground, low ground.
   (b) (fig) inequality, difference, gap; lack of adjustment (entre between).

desnivelado adj (a) uneven. (b) (fig) unbalanced, badly adjusted, unequal.

desnivelar [1a] vt (a) to make uneven. (b) (fig) to unbalance, upset the balance of, create imbalance in.

desnucar [1g] **1** vt to break the neck of; to fell, poleaxe. **2 desnucarse** vr to break one's neck.

desnuclearizado adj: **región desnuclearizada** nuclear-free area.

desnudar [1a] **1** vt (a) to strip (also Bot and fig; de of); person to strip, undress; arm etc to bare; sword to draw; (Geol) to denude; object, statue etc to lay bare, uncover, remove the coverings from.
   (b) (fig) to ruin, break; gambler to fleece.
   2 desnudarse vr (a) (person) to undress, get undressed; to strip (off); — **hasta la cintura** to strip to the waist.
   (b) — **de algo** to get rid of something, cast something aside; **el árbol se está desnudando de sus hojas** the tree is shedding (or losing) its leaves.

desnudez nf (a) nudity, nakedness. (b) (fig) bareness.

desnudismo nm nudism.

desnudista nmf nudist.

desnudo **1** adj (a) body naked, nude; unclothed, bare; arm, tree etc bare; landscape bare, flat, featureless; **en las paredes desnudas** on the bare walls; **la ciudad quedó desnuda como la palma de la mano** the town was left as flat as a pancake (after bombing etc); **cavar con las manos desnudas** to dig with one's bare hands.
   (b) (fig) bare, unadorned; truth naked, plain, unvarnished; **estar — de** to be devoid of, be bereft of, be without.
   (c) (fig) penniless; **y ahora están —s** and now all they've got is what they stand up in; **quedarse — to** be ruined, be bankrupt.
   2 nm (a) (Art etc) nude; **la retrató al —** he painted her in the nude.
   (b) **poner algo al —** (fig) to lay something bare.

desnutrición nf malnutrition, undernourishment.

desnutrido adj undernourished.

desobedecer [2d] vti to disobey.

desobediencia nf disobedience.

desobediente adj disobedient.

desobstruir [3g] vt to unblock, unstop, clear.

desocupación nf (a) leisure; (pej) idleness. (b) (Econ) unemployment.

desocupado adj (a) space, seat etc empty, vacant, unoccupied.
   (b) time spare, free; leisure (attr).

(c) *person* free, not busy; at leisure; (*pej*) idle; (*Econ*) unemployed.

desocupar [1a] **1** *vt* (a) *house etc* to vacate, move out of; to leave empty; *container* to empty.

(b) *contents* to remove, take out.

2 *vi* (*tabu*) to shit (*tabu*).

3 desocuparse *vr* (a) — **de un puesto** to give up one's job.

(b) (*Arg, Chi, Ven*) to give birth.

desodorante *nm* deodorant.

desodorizar [1f] *vt* to deodorize.

desoír [3q] *vt* to ignore, disregard; to turn a deaf ear to.

desojarse [1a] *vr* to strain one's eyes.

desolación *nf* (a) desolation. (b) (*fig*) grief, distress.

desolado *adj* (a) desolate. (b) (*fig*) sad, distressed, disconsolate; **estoy** — **por aquello** I'm terribly grieved about that.

desolador *adj* distressing, grievous.

desolar [1a] **1** *vt* to lay waste, ruin, desolate. **2 desolarse** *vr* to grieve, be distressed, be disconsolate.

desolladero *nm* (a) slaughterhouse. (b) (*fam*) talking-shop, place for gossip; gambling joint (*sl*).

desollado *adj* (*fam*) brazen, barefaced.

desollador *nm* (*fig*) extortioner, robber.

desolladura *nf* (a) skinning, flaying. (b) (*Med*) graze, abrasion; bruise. (c) (*fig*) extortion, piece of robbery.

desollar [1m] *vt* (a) to skin, flay.

(b) — **vivo a uno** (*fig*) to fleece someone, make someone pay through the nose; to flay someone verbally, criticize someone unmercifully.

desopinar [1a] *vt* to denigrate.

desorbitado *adj* (a) disproportionate, excessive; *claim etc* exaggerated. (b) **con los ojos** —**s** wide-eyed, pop-eyed, with bulging eyes.

desorbitar [1a] **1** *vt* (a) to carry to extremes; to exaggerate.

(b) — **un asunto** to misinterpret a matter, get a matter out of perspective, take an unbalanced view of a matter.

2 desorbitarse *vr* (*person*) to go to extremes, lose one's sense of proportion; (*matter etc*) to get out of hand.

desorden *nm* (a) disorder; confusion; turmoil; disarray; (*Pol*) disorder; **en** — in confusion, in disorder; **poner las cosas en** — to upset things, confuse things.

(b) (*un* —) mess, litter, confusion.

(c) (*fig*) irregular life; loose living.

(d) —**es** (*of youth etc*) excesses.

desordenadamente *adv* (a) untidily; in disorder, in a mess. (b) in a disorderly fashion; irregularly; unmethodically; wildly; lawlessly.

desordenado *adj* (a) *room etc* untidy, in disorder; *objects* disordered, confused, in a mess.

(b) *behaviour* disorderly; *life* irregular; *character* unmethodical; *child etc* wild, unruly; *country* lawless.

desordenar [1a] *vt* (a) to disarrange, mess up; to throw into confusion. (b) (*Mech etc*) to put out of order.

desorejado *adj* (a) (*Col, Chi, PR*) without handles.

(b) (*Bol, Per*) hard of hearing.

(c) (*fig*) abject, degraded; dissolute.

(d) (*Cu*) lavish; wasteful.

(e) (*Guat*) silly.

desorganización *nf* disorganization, disruption.

desorganizar [1f] *vt* to disorganize, disrupt.

desorientar [1a] **1** *vt*: — **a uno** (a) to make someone lose his way.

(b) (*fig*) to lead someone astray; to confuse someone, bewilder someone, put someone off.

2 desorientarse *vr* (a) to lose one's way, lose one's bearings.

(b) (*fig*) to go wrong, go astray, get off the track; to get confused.

desovar [1m] *vi* (*Fish*) to spawn; (*insect, amphibian etc*) to lay eggs.

desove *nm* spawning; egg-laying.

desovillar [1a] *vt* (a) *wool* to unravel, unwind; to disentangle. (b) (*fig*) to unravel, clarify.

desoxidar [1a] *vt* to deoxidize.

despabiladeras *nfpl* snuffers; **unas** — a pair of snuffers.

despabilado *adj* (a) wide-awake. (b) (*fig*) wide-awake; alert, watchful; quick, sharp.

despabilar [1a] **1** *vt* (a) *candle* to snuff; *lamp, wick* to trim.

(b) (*fig*) *wits* to sharpen; *person* to wake up; to sharpen the wits of, liven up, brighten up.

(c) (*fig*) *fortune* to squander rapidly; *meal* to dispatch; *business* to get through quickly.

(d) (*fam*) to pinch (*fam*).

(e) (*sl*) — **a uno** to do someone in (*sl*).

2 *vi* and **despabilarse** *vr* (a) to wake up; (*fig*) to look lively, get a move on; ¡**despabílate**! get a move on!, jump to it!

(b) (*Cu, Chi, Guat*) to vanish, disappear suddenly.

despacio 1 *adv* (a) slowly; gently; gradually; ¡—! gently!, not so fast!, easy there!

(b) (*SAm*) softly, in a low voice.

2 *nm* (*SAm*) (a) delay; slowness.

(b) delaying tactic.

despaciosamente *adv* (*SAm*) slowly.

despacioso *adj* slow, deliberate; sluggish; phlegmatic.

despacito *adv* (a) very slowly, very gently. (b) softly.

despachaderas *nfpl* (a) surly retort, unfriendly answer.

(b) resourcefulness, quickness of mind; business sense, practical know-how; **tener buenas** — to be practical, be on the ball; to be good at getting rid of fools.

(c) brazenness, insolence.

despachado *adj* (a) resourceful, quick; businesslike; practical; **ir bien** — **de** to be well off for, be well provided with. (b) brazen, insolent.

despachador *nm*, **despachadora** *nf* dispatcher, sender.

despachante *nm* (*Arg*) clerk; =**despachador**.

despachar [1a] **1** *vt* (a) *task* to complete; *business* to do, complete, dispatch, settle, transact; *correspondence* to deal with, attend to; *theme etc* to deal with; to polish off, knock off; — **asuntos con el gerente** to do business with the manager, settle matters with the manager; **medio capítulo llevo despachado ya** I've already knocked off half a chapter.

(b) (*fam*) *food etc* to dispatch, put away, knock off (*fam*); *drink* to knock back (*sl*).

(c) *ticket etc* to issue.

(d) *goods, person* to send, dispatch (*a* to).

(e) to expedite, hurry along.

(f) *person* to send away, send off; to send packing; *employee* to fire (*fam*), sack (*fam*).

(g) (*fam*) to kill, do in (*sl*).

(h) (*Comm*) *goods* to sell, deal in; *customer* to attend to; **en seguida le despacho** I'll attend to you at once.

2 *vi* (a) (*Comm*) to do business; to serve; **no despacha los domingos** he doesn't do business on Sundays, he's not in on Sundays; ¿**quién despacha**? is anybody serving?

(b) to finish things off, get things settled, come to a decision; ¡**despacha de una vez**! settle it once and for all!, make up your mind!

(c) to hurry up, get on with it; ¡**despacha**! get on with it!

3 despacharse *vr* (a) to finish off; **me despacho a las 5** I finish at 5, I knock off at 5; — **de algo** to finish something off; to get rid of something, get clear of something.

(b) to hurry (up).

(c) — **a su gusto con uno** to say what one really thinks to someone, speak very plainly to someone.

(d) — **con el cucharón** (*fam*) to help oneself to the biggest (*or* best) portion.

despachero *nm* (*Chi*) shopkeeper.

despacho *nm* (a) (*act*) dispatch; sending (out); (*of business*) dispatch, handling, settling.

(b) (*quality*) resourcefulness, quickness of mind; business sense; promptness, energy, efficiency; **tener buen** — to be very efficient, be on top of one's job.

(c) (*Comm*) sale (*of goods*); **géneros sin** — unsaleable goods; **tener buen** — to find a ready sale, be in good demand.

(d) message; (*Mil, diplomatic*) dispatch; — **telegráfico** telegram.

(e) (*Comm, Pol etc*) office; (*in house*) study; — **de billetes**, — **de boletos** (*SAm*) booking office; — **de localidades** box office; — **de telégrafos** telegraph office.

(f) (*Comm*) shop; depot; (*Chi*) general stores; small village shop.

(g) set of office furniture.

(h) (*Mil*) — **de oficial** commission.

despachurrar [1a] *vt* (a) *material* to squash, crush; to squelch; (*Cook*) to mash.

(b) *account, story* to mangle, make a dreadful mess of.

(c) *person* (*in argument etc*) to crush, flatten, floor.

despampanante *adj* (*fam*) stunning, shattering.

despampanar [1a] **1** *vt* (a) *vine* to prune, trim.

(b) (*fam*) to shatter, stun, bowl over.

2 *vi* (*fam*) to blow one's top (*fam*), give vent to one's feelings; to speak out freely.

3 despampanarse *vr* (*fam*) to give oneself a nasty knock.

despancar [1g] *vt* (Bol, Per) *maize* to husk.

desparejado *adj*, **desparejo** *adj*: **son —s** they're odd, they don't match.

desparpajar [1a] **1** *vt* (a) to take apart carelessly; to botch, bungle, spoil, mess up.

　(b) (CAm, Mex) to scatter, disperse.

2 *vi* to talk wildly, rant, rave.

3 desparpajarse *vr* (a) =*vi*.

　(b) (Hond, PR) to wake up.

desparpajo *nm* (a) ease of manner, self-confidence; naturalness; charm; (*pej*) glibness; (*pej*) nerve, pertness, impudence.

　(b) savoir-faire, practical know-how; sharpness, quickness of mind; presence of mind.

　(c) (CAm) disorder, muddle.

　(d) (Col) flippant remark.

desparramado *adj* scattered; wide, open.

desparramar [1a] **1** *vt* (a) to scatter, spread (*por* over); *liquid etc* to spill; *parts* to separate.

　(b) *fortune* to squander; *attention* to spread too widely, fail to concentrate.

2 desparramarse *vr* (a) to scatter, spread out; to spill, be spilt; (*of animals*) to bolt, stampede.

　(b) (*fam*) to have a whale of a time.

desparramo *nm* (a) (Cu, Chi, RPl) scattering, spreading; spilling; disorderly flight, rush, stampede. (b) (Chi) confusion, disorder.

despatarrado *adj*: **quedar —** (a) to have one's legs wide apart.|(b) (*fig*) to be dumbfounded; to be scared to death.

despatarrar [1a] **1** *vt* (*fig*) to amaze, dumbfound; to scare to death.

2 despatarrarse *vr* (a) to open one's legs wide; (*on floor etc*) to do the splits; to fall with one's legs spread wide.

　(b) (*fig*) to be amazed, be dumbfounded; to be scared to death.

despatriar [1b] *vt* (Col, Per, PR) to exile.

despavorido *adj*: **estar —** to be utterly terrified.

despe *nf* (*fam*) tag, "he"; **dar la —** to play tag.

despeado *adj* footsore, weary.

despearse [1a] *vr* to get footsore, get utterly weary.

despectivamente *adv* contemptuously, scornfully; in derogatory terms; (Ling) pejoratively.

despectivo *adj* contemptuous, scornful; derogatory; (Ling) pejorative.

despechado *adj* angry, indignant; spiteful.

despechar [1a] **1** *vt* (a) to anger, enrage; to spite; to drive to despair.

　(b) (Chi, Hond, PR) to wean.

2 despecharse *vr* to get angry; to fret; to despair.

despecho *nm* (a) spite, rancour; despair; **de puro —**, **por —** out of (sheer) spite.

　(b) **a — de** in spite of, despite; in defiance of.

　(c) (Chi, Hond, PR) weaning.

despechugado *adj person* with one's collar open, with one's shirt front undone; *shirt* open-necked, open at the neck.

despechugarse [1h] *vr* to open one's collar, unbutton one's shirt at the neck; to unbutton one's shirt down the front.

despedazar [1f] *vt* (a) to tear apart, tear to pieces; to cut into bits; to lacerate, mangle, cut to shreds. (b) (*fig*) *heart* to break; *honour* to ruin.

despedida *nf* (a) farewell; leave-taking; send-off; (*from job*) dismissal, sacking (*fam*); **cena de —** farewell dinner; **función de —** (Theat) farewell performance; **regalo de —** parting gift.

　(b) farewell ceremony.

　(c) (Lit etc) closing couplet; (*in letter*) closing formula, closing phrases.

despedir [3l] **1** *vt* (a) *guest, friend* to see off; to see out; to say goodbye to; *client etc* to show out; **fuimos a —le a la estación** we went to see him off at the station.

　(b) *workman etc* to dismiss, sack (*fam*), discharge; *bore* to get rid of, send away; *tenant* to evict; to give notice to.

　(c) **— algo de sí** to get rid of something; **— un pensamiento de sí** to put a thought out of one's mind, banish a thought from one's mind.

　(d) *object* to hurl, fling; to project; *arrow etc* to fire; *missile* to launch; *jet etc* to send up; *rider* to throw; *smell etc* to give off, give out, emit, throw off; *heat* to give out; *juice etc* to release, allow to come out; **— el espíritu** to give up the ghost.

2 despedirse *vr* to say goodbye, take one's leave; to give up one's job, leave (one's work); **se despi-**

dieron they said goodbye to each other; **— de uno** to say goodbye to someone, take one's leave of someone; (*at station etc*) to see someone off; **¡ya puedes despedirte de ese dinero!** you can say goodbye to that money!

despegado 1 *adj* (a) detached, loose. (b) *person* cold, indifferent, unconcerned. **2** *nm*: **es un —** he has cut himself off from his family, he has kept no roots.

despegar [1h] **1** *vt* (a) to unglue, unstick; to detach, loosen; *envelope* to open; **sin — los labios** without uttering a word.

2 *vi* (Aer) to take off.

3 despegarse *vr* (a) to come loose, come unstuck; to come apart.

　(b) (*person*) to become alienated, become detached (*de* from); **— de los amigos** to break with one's friends; **— del mundo** to withdraw from the world, renounce worldly things.

　(c) (*fam*) **— con** not to go well with.

despego *nm* =**desapego**.

despegue *nm* (Aer) takeoff; **— corto** short takeoff; **— vertical** vertical takeoff.

despeinado *adj* dishevelled, tousled; unkempt.

despeinar [1a] *vt hair, person* to tousle, ruffle; *hairdo* to mess up, muss.

despejado *adj* (a) *way, space* clear, free, unobstructed, open; *brow* clear; *room etc* unencumbered, spacious.

　(b) *sky* cloudless, clear.

　(c) (*person: estar*) wide-awake; (Med) free of fever; lucid.

　(d) (*person: ser*) sharp, bright, smart.

despejar [1a] **1** *vt* (a) *space etc* to clear, disencumber, free from obstructions; **los bomberos despejaron el teatro** the firemen cleared the theatre (of people); **los guardias obligaron a — el tribunal** the police ordered the court to be cleared, the police ordered people to leave the court; **¡despejen!** move along!; everybody out!

　(b) (Sport) *ball* to clear.

　(c) *mystery* to clear up, clarify, resolve; (Math) *unknown quantity* to find.

2 *vi* (a) (Sport) to clear (the ball).

　(b) (Meteorol) to clear.

3 despejarse *vr* (a) (Meteorol) to clear, clear up; (*of mystery etc*) to become clearer.

　(b) (*person*) to liven oneself up; to feel better, feel brighter; to clear one's head.

　(c) (*person*) to relax, amuse oneself.

　(d) (*person: in temperament*) to become more free and easy.

despeje *nm* (Sport) clearance.

despejo *nm* brightness; self-confidence, ease of manner; fluency.

despeluchado *adj* dishevelled, tousled.

despeluchar [1a] *vt* to dishevel, tousle.

despeluzar [1f] **1** *vt* (a) *hair* to dishevel, tousle, rumple.

　(b) **— a uno** (*fig*) to horrify someone, make someone's hair stand on end.

　(c) (Cu) to ruin, leave penniless.

2 despeluzarse *vr* (a) (*hair*) to stand on end.

　(b) (*person*) to be horrified.

despellejar [1a] *vt* (a) to skin, flay. (b) (*fig*) to flay, criticize unmercifully. (c) (*fam*) **— a uno** to fleece someone.

despenar [1a] *vt* (*sl*) to bump off (*sl*).

despendedor *adj* extravagant.

despensa *nf* (a) pantry, larder; food store; (Naut) storeroom. (b) stock of food.

despensero *nm* butler, steward; (Naut) storekeeper.

despeñadero *nm* (a) (Geog) cliff, precipice. (b) (*fig*) risky enterprise.

despeñadizo *adj* dangerously steep, sheer, precipitous.

despeñar [1a] **1** *vt* to fling down, hurl from a height, throw over a cliff.

2 despeñarse *vr* (a) to hurl oneself down, throw oneself over a cliff; to fall headlong.

　(b) **— en el vicio** to plunge into vice.

despeño *nm* (*fig*) failure, collapse.

despepitar [1a] **1** *vt* to remove the pips (*etc*) from.

2 despepitarse *vr* (a) to bawl, shriek (one's head off), shout oneself hoarse; to rave, act wildly.

　(b) **— por algo** to long for something, be crazy about something; **— por + infin** to long to + *infin*.

despercudir [3a] *vt* (a) to clean, wash. (b) (SAm: *fig*) *person* to liven up, wake up, ginger up.

desperdiciado *adj* wasteful.

desperdiciador 1 *adj* spendthrift. **2** *nm* spendthrift.

desperdiciar [1b] *vt* to waste, squander, fritter away; *time* to waste; *chance* to throw away.

desperdicio nm (a) waste; wasting; squandering.
(b) —s rubbish, refuse; scraps, left-overs; (Bio, Tech) waste products; —s de algodón cotton waste; —s de cocina kitchen scraps; —s de hierro scrap iron, junk.
(c) el cerdo es un animal que no tiene — nothing from a pig is wasted, everything from a pig can be used; el muchacho no tiene — he's a fine lad.

desperdigar [1h] 1 vt to scatter, separate, disperse; energy to spread too widely, dissipate. 2 desperdigarse vr to scatter, separate.

desperezarse [1f] vr to stretch (oneself).

desperfecto nm flaw, blemish, imperfection; slight damage; sufrió algunos —s en el accidente it suffered slight damage in the accident.

despernado adj footsore, weary.

despersonalizar [1f] vt to depersonalize.

despertador nm (a) alarm clock; — de viaje travelling clock. (b) (person) knocker-up. (c) (fig) warning.

despertamiento nm awakening; (fig) awakening, revival, rebirth.

despertar [1k] 1 vt (a) person etc to wake (up), awaken.
(b) (fig) hopes etc to awaken, raise, arouse; memory to awaken, revive, recall; feeling to arouse, stir up.
2 vi and **despertarse** vr to wake up, awaken; —a la realidad to wake up to reality.
3 nm: el — religioso the religious awakening; el — de la primavera the awakening of spring.

despestañarse [1a] vr (a) to strain one's eyes. (b) (fig) to burn the midnight oil.

despiadadamente adv cruelly; mercilessly, relentlessly; heartlessly.

despiadado adj cruel; merciless, relentless; heartless.

despicarse [1g] vr to get even, get one's revenge.

despichar [1a] 1 vt (Col, Chi, Ven) to crush, smash. 2 vi (sl) to kick the bucket (sl).

despido nm dismissal, sacking (fam).

despiece nm (of carcass) quartering, carving-up.

despierto adj (a) awake. (b) (fig) wide-awake; sharp; alert, watchful.

despilfarrado adj (a) extravagant, wasteful, spendthrift. (b) ragged, shabby.

despilfarrador 1 adj = despilfarrado. 2 nm spendthrift.

despilfarrar [1a] vt to waste, squander.

despilfarro nm (a) (act) wasting, squandering. (b) (quality) extravagance, wastefulness. (c) shabbiness, slovenliness, ragged state.

despintar [1a] 1 vt (a) to take the paint off.
(b) (fig) story etc to alter, distort; to spoil.
(c) (Col, Chi, PR) no —a uno not to let someone out of one's sight.
2 vi: A no despinta de B A is not unworthy of B, A is in no way inferior to B.
3 **despintarse** vr (a) to wash off; to fade, lose its colour.
(b) no se me despinta que . . . I never forget that . . .; I remember vividly that . . .

despiojar [1a] vt (a) to delouse. (b) — a uno (fig) to rescue someone from the gutter.

despique nm satisfaction, revenge.

despistado 1 adj (a) (ser) vague, absent-minded; unpractical; hopeless.
(b) (estar) confused, out of touch, all at sea; off the beam (fam); ando muy — con todo esto I'm terribly muddled about all this.
2 nm, **despistada** nf absent-minded person, vague individual; unpractical type; es un — he's hopeless, he's a dream.

despistar [1a] 1 vt (a) (Hunting) to throw off the track (or scent).
(b) (fig) to put off the scent; to mislead, muddle; esa pregunta está hecha para — that question is designed to put people off.
2 **despistarse** vr (fig) to go wrong, take the wrong route (or turning etc); to get confused.

despiste nm (a) (Aut etc) swerve.
(b) mistake, slip.
(c) absent-mindedness; muddle, confusion, bewilderment; ¡qué — tienes! you're a bright one!, what a clot you are!; tiene un terrible — he's terribly absent-minded; he's hopelessly unpractical; he's hopeless, he's a dream.

desplacer 1 [2x] vt to displease. 2 nm displeasure.

desplantador nm trowel.

desplantar [1a] vt (a) plant to pull up, uproot, take up. (b) object to move out of vertical, tilt.

desplante nm (a) incorrect position (of the body); irregular posture.
(b) bold statement, outspoken remark; (pej)

impudent remark (etc); dar un — to interrupt someone rudely.

desplazado 1 adj (a) displaced, wrongly placed, off-centre.
(b) person badly adjusted; out of one's depth, out of one's element; (Pol) displaced; sentirse un poco — to feel rather out of place.
2 nm, **desplazada** nf misfit; ill-adjusted person, outsider; (Pol) displaced person.

desplazamiento nm (a) displacement, movement; — de tierras landslip.
(b) (Naut) displacement.
(c) journey, trip.
(d) (of opinion, votes etc) shift, swing.

desplazar [1f] 1 vt (a) object to displace, move.
(b) (Naut, Phys) to displace.
(c) person etc to displace, supplant, take the place of.
2 **desplazarse** vr (a) (object) to move, shift.
(b) (person, vehicle) to go, travel; tiene que — todos los días 25 kms he has to travel 25 kms every day; el avión se desplaza a más de 1500 mph the aircraft travels at more than 1500 mph.
(c) (opinion, votes etc) to shift, swing; se ha desplazado un 4 por 100 de los votos there has been a swing of 4% in the voting.

desplegar [1h and 1k] 1 vt (a) to unfold, open (out), spread (out); wings to spread, open; sails to unfurl; (Mil) to deploy; sin — los labios without uttering a word.
(b) (fig) energy etc to put forth, use, display; resources to deploy.
(c) (fig) mystery to clarify, elucidate.
2 **desplegarse** vr (flower etc) to open (out), unfold; to spread (out); (Mil) to deploy.

despliegue nm (a) unfolding, opening; (Mil) deployment. (b) (fig) display, manifestation, show, exhibition.

desplomarse [1a] vr (a) to lean, tilt, get out of vertical; to bulge, warp.
(b) to collapse, tumble down, come crashing down; to topple over; (prices etc) to slump, tumble; (government, system) to collapse; (Aer) to make a pancake landing; (person) to collapse, crumple up; se ha desplomado el techo the ceiling has fallen in, the ceiling has collapsed; ¡se desploma el cielo! it's incredible!

desplome nm (a) (act) leaning, tilting; fall, collapse; slump; (Aer) pancake landing.
(b) (Archit, Geol etc) overhang, projecting part; (Mountaineering) overhang.

desplomo nm = desplome (b).

desplumar [1a] 1 vt (a) to pluck. (b) (fig) to fleece, skin. 2 **desplumarse** vr to moult.

despoblación nf depopulation; — rural, — del campo rural depopulation, drift from the land.

despoblado 1 adj unpopulated, deserted; (fig) desolate. 2 nm deserted spot, uninhabited place; wilderness.

despoblar [1m] vt to depopulate; to reduce the population of, clear people out of; to lay waste; — una zona de árboles to clear an area of trees.

despojar [1a] 1 vt: — de to strip of, clear of, leave bare of; (fig) to divest of, denude of; (Law) to dispossess of, deprive of; habían despojado la casa de muebles they had stripped the house of furniture, they had cleared all the furniture out of the house; verse despojado de su autoridad to find oneself stripped of one's authority.
2 **despojarse** vr to undress; — de to take off, remove, strip off; leaves etc to shed; powers etc to divest oneself of, relinquish, give up; prejudice to get rid of, free oneself from.

despojo nm (a) (act) spoliation, despoilment; plundering.
(b) (Mil etc) plunder, loot, spoils.
(c) —s waste, left-overs, scraps; (of animal) offal; (Archit) rubble; secondhand building materials, usable waste; (Geol) debris; —s de hierro scrap iron; —s mortales mortal remains.

despolvorear [1a] vt to dust.

desportilladura nf chip; nick.

desportillar [1a] 1 vt to chip, nick. 2 **desportillarse** vr to chip, chip off.

desposado adj newly-wed, recently married; los —s the bridal couple, the newly-weds.

desposar [1a] 1 vt (of priest) couple to marry.
2 **desposarse** vr (one person) to become engaged (con to); to get married (con to).
(b) (two persons) to get engaged; to marry, get married.

desposeer [2e] **1** vt to dispossess (de of); to oust (de un puesto from a post); — **a uno de su autoridad** to remove someone's authority, strip someone of his authority.
2 desposeerse vr: — **de algo** to give something up, relinquish something, divest oneself of something.
desposeído nm, **desposeída** nf: **los** —**s** the deprived, those in want, the have-nots.
desposeimiento nm dispossession; ousting.
desposorios nmpl engagement, betrothal; marriage (ceremony).
déspota nm despot.
despóticamente adv despotically.
despótico adj despotic.
despotismo nm despotism.
despotricar [1g] vi to rave, rant, carry on (contra about).
despreciable adj (morally) despicable, contemptible; (in quality) worthless, trashy, valueless; (in quantity) negligible; **una suma nada** — a far from negligible amount.
despreciar [1b] **1** vt to scorn, despise, look down on; to spurn, reject; to slight; to underestimate, underrate; — **los peligros** to scorn the dangers; — **una oferta** to reject an offer; **no hay que** — **tal posibilidad** one should not underestimate such a possibility.
2 despreciarse vr: — **de** + infin to think it beneath oneself to + infin, not deign to + infin.
despreciativamente adv scornfully, contemptuously; in a derogatory way; cynically.
despreciativo adj scornful, contemptuous; remark etc derogatory; cynical.
desprecio nm (a) scorn, contempt, disdain; disparaging attitude; cynicism; **lo miró con** — he looked at it contemptuously.
(b) slight, snub; **le hicieron el** — **de no acudir** they snubbed him by not coming.
desprender [2a] **1** vt (a) to unfasten, loosen, detach, separate.
(b) gas etc to give off; skin etc to shed.
2 desprenderse vr (a) (part) to become detached, work loose, fall off; to fly off.
(b) — **de un estorbo** to extricate oneself from a difficulty, get free of a difficulty; **la serpiente se desprende de la piel** the snake sheds its skin.
(c) — **de algo** to give something up, part with something; to get rid of something; to deprive oneself of something; **se desprendió de sus joyas** she parted with her jewels; **tendremos que desprendernos del coche** we shall have to get rid of the car; **se desprendió de su autoridad** he relinquished his authority.
(d) (gas etc) to be given off, issue; **de la pared se desprende humedad** there is damp coming from the wall.
(e) (meaning etc) — **de** to follow from; to be implied by; to be clear from; **se desprende que . . .** one gathers that . . .; **se desprende de esta declaración que . . .** it is clear from this statement that . . .; **por fin se desprendió que . . .** finally it transpired that . . .
desprendido adj (a) part loose, detached; unfastened.
(b) (fig) disinterested; generous.
desprendimiento nm (a) loosening, detachment; unfastening; — **de tierras** landslide.
(b) (of gas etc) release, emission; (of skin etc) shedding.
(c) (fig) disinterestedness; generosity.
despreocupación nf (a) unconcern; carefree nature; nonchalance, casualness.
(b) unconventional outlook (or style etc); (pej) sloppiness, slovenliness.
(c) impartiality.
(d) indifference, apathy; broad-mindedness.
(e) looseness.
despreocupado adj (a) unworried, unconcerned; carefree; nonchalant, casual; free-and-easy.
(b) (in dress etc) unconventional, casual; (pej) careless, sloppy, slovenly.
(c) (in judgement) unbiassed, impartial.
(d) (Rel) indifferent, apathetic; broad-minded.
(e) woman loose.
despreocupamiento nm lack of interest, apathy.
desprestigiar [1b] **1** vt to disparage, run down; to discredit; to cheapen. **2 desprestigiarse** vr to lose (one's) prestige; to lose caste; to cheapen oneself.
desprestigio nm disparagement; discredit; loss of prestige (or caste, standing); unpopularity; **esas cosas que van en** — **nuestro** those things which are to our discredit, those things which harm our reputation.

desprevención nf unreadiness, unpreparedness; lack of foresight.
desprevenido adj unready, unprepared; **coger a uno** — to catch someone unawares, catch someone off his guard, take someone by surprise.
desproporción nf disproportion, lack of proportion.
desproporcionadamente adv disproportionately.
desproporcionado adj disproportionate, out of proportion.
despropósito nm absurdity, silly thing (to say), piece of nonsense; —**s** nonsense.
desprovisto adj: — **de** devoid of, bereft of, without; **estar** — **de** to lack, be lacking in, be devoid of; **estar** — **de medios** to be without means; **un libro no** — **de méritos** a book not without merit.
después 1 adv (a) (time) afterwards, later; since, since then; next; **un año** — a year later; **años** — years later; **¿qué pasó** —? what happened then?; **poco** — soon after, shortly after.
(b) (order) next, after; **¿y** —? and what comes next?; **nuestra casa viene** — and then our house is next.
2 — **de** prep (a) (time) after; since; — **de esa fecha** (past) since that date, (future) from that date, after that date; — **de verlo** after seeing it; **no** — **de 1980** not later than 1980; — **de descubierta la isla** after the discovery of the island, after the island had been discovered.
(b) (order) next (to); **mi nombre está** — **del tuyo** my name comes next to yours; my name comes after yours; **es el primero** — **de éste** it's the next one after this.
3 — (**de**) **que** conj after; — (**de**) **que lo escribí** after (or since) I wrote it, after writing it.
despuntado adj blunt.
despuntar [1a] **1** vt to blunt, dull (the point or edge of).
2 vi (a) (Bot) to sprout, bud, begin to show.
(b) (of dawn) to break, appear; (of day) to dawn.
(c) (of person etc) to excel, stand out; to shine, sparkle; to show intelligence; — **de agudo** to have a sparkling wit; **despunta en matemáticas** he shines at maths; **despunta por su talento** her talent shines out, her talent is outstanding.
desquiciar [1b] vt (a) door to unhinge, take off its hinges.
(b) (fig) to upset, disturb, turn upside down, make a mess of.
(c) person (mentally) to disturb, upset; to unhinge, affect seriously, unbalance; to anger, provoke.
(d) person (from post) to oust, lever out.
desquicio nm (Arg, Guat) confusion, disorder.
desquitarse [1a] vr to obtain satisfaction; (Comm, Fin) to recover a debt, get one's money back; (fig) to get even (con with), get one's own back (con on); — **de una pérdida** to make up for a loss, compensate oneself for a loss; — **de una mala pasada** to get one's own back for a dirty trick (played on one).
desquite nm satisfaction; compensation for a loss, recovery of a debt; revenge, retaliation; (Sport, also **partido de** —) return match; **tomar el** — to have one's revenge, get one's own back; **tomar el** — **de algo** to make up for something.
desratizar [1f] vt to clear of rats.
desrazonable adj unreasonable.
desrielar [1a] vt (SAm) to derail.
destacable adj, **destacado** adj notable, outstanding, distinguished.
destacamento nm (Mil) detachment.
destacar [1g] **1** vt (a) (Art etc) to make stand out; (fig) to emphasize, show up, point up, bring out; to throw into relief; **quiero** — **que . . .** I wish to emphasize that . . .; **sirve para** — **su belleza** it serves to enhance her beauty, it serves to show up her beauty.
(b) (Mil) to detach, detail.
2 vi and **destacarse** vr (a) to stand out; —**se contra**, —**se en**, —**se sobre** to stand out against, be outlined against, be silhouetted against.
(b) (fig) to stand out, be outstanding, be exceptional.
destajar [1a] vt (a) (Cards) to cut. (b) (Col, Ec, Guat, Mex) carcass to cut up. (c) work etc to contract for, make arrangements about; to do as piecework.
destajero nm, **destajista** nm pieceworker.
destajo nm (in general) piecework; contract work; (**un** —) job; stint; **a** — by the job; (fig) eagerly, keenly; energetically; (Chi) by guesswork; **trabajar a** — to do piecework, be on piecework; **trabajo a** — piecework; **hablar a** — (fam) to talk nineteen to the dozen.

destapar [1a] **1** *vt* to uncover; *bottle* to open, uncork; *box* to open, take the lid off; *vessel* to take the lid off, raise the lid of; (*fig*) to reveal, uncover.
2 destaparse *vr* **(a)** to get uncovered.
(b) (*fig*) to cause surprise, do something unexpected; to show oneself in one's true character; **se destapó metiéndose monja** she astounded everyone by becoming a nun.
(c) (*fig*) — **con uno** to unbosom oneself to someone.
destaponar [1a] *vt* to uncork.
destartalado *adj room etc* untidy, in disorder; *house etc* large and rambling; ruinous, tumbledown, dilapidated; *vehicle etc* rickety, shaky.
destazar [1f] *vt* to cut up.
destechar [1a] *vt* to unroof.
destejar [1a] *vt* **(a)** to remove the tiles from. **(b)** (*fig*) to leave unprotected.
destejer [2d] *vt* **(a)** to undo, unravel; to take the stitches out of. **(b)** (*fig*) to upset; to interfere with the progress of; *see* **tejer.**
destellante *nm* (*Aut*) indicator, winking light.
destellar [1a] *vi* to sparkle, flash; to glint, gleam; (*Aut: of light*) to wink.
destello *nm* **(a)** sparkle; flash; glint, gleam; wink(ing). **(b)** (*Tech*) signal light, winking light. **(c)** (*fig*) atom, particle; **no tiene un — de verdad** there's not an atom of truth in it. **(d)** —**s** (*fig*) glimmer; **tiene a veces —s de inteligencia** he sometimes shows a glimmer (*or* glimmerings) of intelligence.
destemplado *adj* **(a)** (*Mus*) *instrument* out of tune; *voice* harsh, unpleasant. **(b)** (*Art*) inharmonious, badly blended, ill-matched. **(c)** *pulse* irregular. **(d)** (*Med*) indisposed, out of sorts; feverish. **(e)** *character, gesture etc* ill-tempered; *attitude* ill-judged, intemperate, harsh. **(f)** (*Meteorol*) unpleasant.
destemplanza *nf* **(a)** (*Mus*) tunelessness; harshness, unpleasantness. **(b)** lack of harmony. **(c)** irregularity. **(d)** (*Med*) indisposition; feverish condition. **(e)** intemperance, harshness. **(f)** (*Meteorol*) unpleasantness, inclemency. **(g)** (*una* —) sharp remark, harsh comment.
destemplar [1a] **1** *vt* **(a)** (*Mus*) to untune, put out of tune, upset the pitch of. **(b)** (*fig*) to upset, disturb (the order of); to disconcert.
2 destemplarse *vr* **(a)** (*Mus*) to get out of tune, lose its pitch. **(b)** (*fig*) to get out of order; (*person*) to get upset, get worked up; (*pulse*) to become irregular; (*Med*) to become indisposed, get out of sorts. **(c)** (*SAm*) **con eso me destemplo** that sets my teeth on edge, that gives me the shivers.
destemple *nm* (*in most senses*) = **destemplanza**; (*of metal*) lack of temper, poorly-tempered nature.
desteñido *adj* faded, discoloured.
desteñir [3l] **1** *vt* to fade, discolour, take the colour out of.
2 *vi* and **desteñirse** *vr* **(a)** to fade, lose colour, discolour. **(b)** (*of colours in fabric*) to run; **"esta tela no destiñe"** "this fabric will not run".
desternillarse [1a] *vr*: — **de risa** to split one's sides with laughing, die of laughing.
desterrado *nm*, **desterrada** *nf* exile; outlaw; (*esp fig*) outcast.
desterrar [1k] *vt* **(a)** to exile, banish. **(b)** (*fig*) to banish; to dismiss, put aside; — **una sospecha** to banish a suspicion from one's mind; — **el uso de las armas de fuego** to banish firearms, prohibit the use of firearms. **(c)** (*Agr, Min*) to remove the soil from.
destetar [1a] **1** *vt* to wean. **2 destetarse** *vr* **(a)** to be weaned; — **con el vino** (*fig*) to have been brought up on wine. **(b)** to break oneself of a (bad) habit.
destete *nm* weaning.
destiempo *nm*: **a** — at the wrong time, at an inopportune moment.
destierro *nm* **(a)** exile; banishment; **vivir en el** — to live in exile. **(b)** (*fig*) wilderness; remote spot.
destilación *nf* distillation.
destiladera *nf* still, distilling vessel; (*SAm*) filter.
destilador *nm* **(a)** still. **(b)** (*person*) distiller.
destilar [1a] **1** *vt* **(a)** *alcohol* to distil; *blood etc* to exude, ooze. **(b)** (*fig*) to exude, ooze; to reveal; **la carta**

destilaba odio the letter exuded hatred; **es una orden que destila crueldad** it is an order which is steeped in cruelty.
2 *vi* to drip, fall (drop by drop); to ooze (out); to filter through.
destilatorio *nm* still.
destilería *nf* distillery; — **de petróleo** oil refinery.
destinar [1a] *vt* **(a)** to destine (*a, para* for, to); to assign (*a* to); to design (*a* for); to intend, mean (*a, para* for); *funds etc* to set aside, earmark (*a* for); **me habían destinado una habitación elegante** they had assigned me an elegant room; **le destinan al sacerdocio** they intend him for the priesthood; **fabricantes de aviones destinados a Eslobodia** makers of aircraft destined for (*or* for use in) Slobodia; **una carta que viene destinada a Vd** a letter for you, a letter addressed to you; **ir destinado a** (*Naut etc*) to be bound for; **estar destinado a + infin** to be destined to + *infin*.
(b) *person* to appoint, assign (*a* to); (*Mil etc*) to post (*a* to); **le han destinado a Lima** they have appointed him to Lima.
destinatario *nm*, **destinataria** *nf* addressee.
destino *nm* **(a)** destiny, fate; **es mi — no encontrarlo** I am fated not to find it; **el — lo quiso así** it was destiny, fate willed it thus. **(b)** (*of traveller, ship etc*) destination; **van con — a Londres** they are going to London, (*Naut*) they are bound for London; **salir con — a** to leave for; **¿cuál es el — de este cuadro?** what is the destination of this picture?, where is this picture for? **(c)** job, post, position; — **público** public appointment; **buscarse un — de sereno** to look for a job as night watchman. **(d)** use, utility; **dar — a algo** to put something to good use, find a use for something.
destitución *nf* dismissal, removal.
destituido *adj*: — **de** devoid of, bereft of, lacking (in).
destituir [3g] *vt* **(a)** *person* to dismiss, remove, sack (*fam; de* from); to remove from office; **le destituyeron por inmoral** they sacked him for immorality. **(b)** — **a uno de algo** to deprive someone of something.
destorcer [2b *and* 2h] **1** *vt string etc* to untwist, take the twists out of; *rod etc* to straighten. **2 destorcerse** *vr* (*Naut*) to get off course.
destornillado *adj* (*fam*) crazy, potty (*fam*).
destornillador *nm* screwdriver.
destornillar [1a] **1** *vt* to unscrew. **2 destornillarse** *vr* **(a)** (*fig*) to behave wildly; (*fam*) to go crazy. **(b)** (*SAm*) = **desternillarse.**
destrabar [1a] *vt* to loosen, detach; *prisoner etc* to unfetter, take the shackles off.
destraillar [1a] *vt* to let off the leash, unleash.
destral *nm* hatchet.
destreza *nf* skill, dexterity; cleverness; handiness.
destripacuentos *nm*, *pl* **destripacuentos** interrupter, person who butts in.
destripador *nm*: **Juanito el D—** Jack the Ripper.
destripar [1a] *vt* **(a)** *animal* to gut, draw, paunch; *person* to disembowel; to cut open the belly of, slash the stomach of. **(b)** (*fig*) to mangle, crush; *story* to spoil (by interrupting and telling its ending).
destripaterrones *nm*, *pl* **destripaterrones** poor labourer; (*fig*) clodhopper.
destronamiento *nm* dethronement; (*fig*) overthrow.
destronar [1a] *vt* to dethrone; (*fig*) to overthrow.
destroncar [1g] *vt* **(a)** *tree* to chop off, lop (the top off); (*Chi, Mex*) *plant* to cut off at ground level; to uproot. **(b)** *person* to maim; (*fig*) to tire out, exhaust; *steed* to wear out. **(c)** (*fig*) *plans etc* to ruin; *development* to harm, damage, dislocate; *speech etc* to interrupt.
destrozado *adj* smashed, shattered, ruined.
destrozar [1f] *vt* **(a)** to smash, shatter, ruin; to break up, break to pieces; to destroy; *clothing, shoes* to ruin; (*Mil*) *army, enemy* to smash; *flesh* to mangle, lacerate, tear; *nerves* to shatter; *resources etc* to squander, dissipate. **(b)** (*fig*) *person* to ruin; to shatter; *life etc* to ruin; *heart* to break; — **la armonía** to ruin the harmony; — **a uno en una discusión** to crush someone in an argument; **le ha destrozado el que no quisiera casarse con él** he was shattered when she wouldn't marry him, her refusal to marry him broke him up.
destrozo *nm* destruction; (*of army*) smashing, annihilation, rout; (*of persons*) massacre; —**s** damage, havoc, ravages; **causar —s en** to create havoc in, cause great damage to, ravage.

destrozón *adj:* **un niño —** a child who is hard on his clothes; **la criada es muy destrozona** the servant is a terrible one for breaking things.

destrucción *nf* destruction.

destructible *adj* destructible.

destructivo *adj* destructive.

destructor 1 *adj* destructive. 2 *nm (Naut)* destroyer.

destruible *adj* destructible.

destruir [3g] 1 *vt* to destroy; to ruin, wreck; to damage; *balance etc* to destroy, upset; *resources* to squander; *plans* to ruin.

2 **destruirse** *vr (Math)* to cancel (each other) out.

desudar [1a] *vt* to wipe the sweat off.

desuellacaras *nm, pl* **desuellacaras** *(fam)* (a) clumsy barber. (b) rogue, villain.

desuello *nm* (a) skinning, flaying. (b) brazenness, insolence. (c) *(fam)* extortion; **¡es un —!** it's daylight robbery!

desuncir [3b] *vt* to unyoke.

desunión *nf* (a) separation; disconnection. (b) disunity; rift.

desunir [3a] *vt* (a) to separate, sever, detach; *(Tech)* to disconnect, disengage, uncouple. (b) *(fig)* to cause a rift between.

desuñarse [1a] *vr* (a) to work one's fingers to the bone *(por + infin* to + *infin)*. (b) *(fig)* to be constantly involved in wicked things.

desurbanización *nf* relief of city overcrowding, dispersal of city population(s) (to satellite towns).

desusado *adj* (a) obsolete, antiquated, out of date.
(b) **esa palabra está desusada de los buenos escritores** that word is no longer in use among good writers.
(c) *(fig)* unwonted, unusual.

desusar [1a] 1 *vt* to stop using, discontinue the use of, give up. 2 **desusarse** *vr* to go out of use, become obsolete.

desuso *nm* disuse; desuetude; **caer en —** to fall into disuse, become obsolete; **una expresión caída en —** an obsolete expression; **dejar algo en —** to cease to use something, discontinue the use of something.

desvaído *adj* (a) *colour* pale, dull, washed-out.
(b) *outline* ill-defined, vague, blurred.
(c) *person (in character)* weak, characterless; *personality* flat, dull.
(d) *(in stature)* gaunt.

desvainar [1a] *vt peas etc* to shell.

desvalido *adj* helpless; destitute; *(Pol)* under-privileged; **los —s** the helpless, *(Pol)* the under-privileged; **niños —s** waifs and strays, abandoned children.

desvalijamiento *nm* robbing, robbery; rifling; burgling.

desvalijar [1a] *vt* to rob, plunder; *drawer, case etc* to rifle; *shop* to burgle, burglarize *(US)*, break into, rob.

desvalorar [1a] *vt* to devaluate; *currency* to devalue.

desvalorización *nf* devaluation.

desvalorizar [1f] *vt* to devalue.

desván *nm* loft, attic; garret.

desvanecer [2d] 1 *vt* (a) to cause to vanish, make disappear.
(b) *doubt etc* to dispel; *thought, memory* to banish, dismiss.
(c) *colours* to tone down; *outline* to blur; *(Phot)* to mask.

2 **desvanecerse** *vr* (a) to vanish, disappear.
(b) *(doubt etc)* to vanish, be dispelled.
(c) *(Chem etc)* to evaporate; to dissolve, melt away, disappear.
(d) *(Med)* to faint (away).
(e) *(sound, also Radio)* to fade (away), fade out.

desvanecido *adj* (a) *(Med)* faint; giddy, dizzy; **caer —** to fall in a faint. (b) *(fig)* vain; proud, haughty.

desvanecimiento *nm* (a) vanishing, disappearance; dissipation, dispelling.
(b) blurring; *(Phot)* masking.
(c) evaporation; melting.
(d) *(Med)* fainting fit, swoon; dizzy spell, attack of giddiness.
(e) *(Radio etc)* fading.
(f) *(fig)* vanity; pride, haughtiness.

desvarar [1a] *vt* to refloat.

desvariar [1c] *vi* (a) *(Med)* to be delirious. (b) *(fig)* to rave, talk nonsense.

desvarío *nm (Med)* (a) delirium; raving. (b) *(fig)* absurdity; extravagant notion, strange notion; whim; **—s** ravings, ramblings.

desvelado *adj* (a) sleepless, wakeful; **estar —** to be awake, be unable to get to sleep. (b) *(fig)* watchful, vigilant.

desvelar [1a] 1 *vt* to keep awake; **el café me desvela** coffee keeps me awake.

2 **desvelarse** *vr* (a) to stay awake, keep awake; to go without sleep, have a sleepless night.
(b) *(fig)* to be watchful, be vigilant, keep one's eyes open; **— por algo** to be anxious about something, be much concerned about something; to take great care over something; **— por +** *infin* to do everything possible to + *infin*; **se desvela porque no nos falte nada** she works hard so that we should not go short of anything.

desvelo *nm* (a) lack of sleep; sleeplessness, insomnia.
(b) *(fig)* watchfulness, vigilance.
(c) **—s** *pl (fig)* anxiety, care, concern; effort, hard work; **gracias a sus —s** thanks to his efforts.

desvencijado *adj* ramshackle, rickety, broken-down.

desvencijar [1a] 1 *vt* (a) to break; to loosen, weaken.
(b) *person* to weaken, exhaust.

2 **desvencijarse** *vr* (a) to come apart, fall to pieces, break; to become disjointed.
(b) *(Med)* to rupture oneself.

desventaja *nf* disadvantage; handicap, liability; **estar en — con respecto a otros** to be in a disadvantageous position compared with others.

desventajosamente *adv* disadvantageously, unfavourably.

desventajoso *adj* disadvantageous, unfavourable.

desventura *nf* misfortune.

desventuradamente *adv* unfortunately.

desventurado 1 *adj* (a) unfortunate, unlucky; ill-fated.
(b) miserable, wretched; unhappy; **¡qué — estoy!** how wretched I am!
(c) timid, shy.
(d) mean.

2 *nm,* **desventurada** *nf* wretch, unfortunate; **algún —** some poor devil.

desvergonzado 1 *adj* shameless; impudent, brazen; unblushing. 2 *nm,* **desvergonzada** *nf* shameless person.

desvergonzarse [1f *and* 1m] *vr* (a) to lose all sense of shame.
(b) to be impudent, be insolent *(con* to); to behave in a shameless way *(con* to).
(c) **— a pedir algo** to have the nerve to ask for something, dare to ask for something.

desvergüenza *nf* shamelessness; brazenness, effrontery, impudence; **esto es una —** this is shameful, this is shameful; **¡qué —!** how shocking!; what a nerve!, the effrontery of it!; **tener la — de +** *infin* to have the impudence *(or* nerve) to + *infin*.

desvestir [3l] 1 *vt* to undress. 2 **desvestirse** *vr* to undress.

desviación *nf* (a) *(act)* deviation *(from* de); deflection *(de* from), departure *(de* from); *(Mech, Phys, of compass)* deviation; **— normal** standard deviation; **es una — de sus principios** it is a deviation *(or* departure) from his principles.
(b) *(Pol, Psych)* deviation.
(c) *(Aut etc)* detour; diversion; bypass, ring road; **— de la circulación** traffic diversion.

desviacionismo *nm* deviationism.

desviacionista 1 *adj* deviationist. 2 *nmf* deviationist.

desviadero *nm (Rail)* siding.

desviado *adj* (a) oblique; deflected. (b) *place* remote, off the beaten track; **— de** remote from, away from.

desviar [1c] 1 *vt* (a) *(in physical sense)* to turn aside; to deflect, divert *(de* from); *arrow etc* to deflect; *ball* to deflect, glance; *blow, thrust* to parry, ward off, deflect; *question* to parry; *eyes* to avert, turn away; *(Aut)* to divert, re-route *(por* through); *(Rail)* to switch (into a siding), shunt aside; **— el cauce de un río** to alter the course of a river.
(b) *(fig)* to turn aside *(de* from); **le desviaron de su propósito** they dissuaded him from his intention; **— a uno de su vocación** to turn someone from his (true) vocation; **— a uno de su pensamiento** to side-track someone from his theme; **— a uno de las malas compañías** to wean someone away from evil company; **— a uno del buen camino** *(fig)* to lead someone astray.

2 **desviarse** *vr (person etc)* to turn aside, turn away, deviate *(de* from); *(road)* to branch off, leave; *(Naut)* to sheer off; *(Naut)* to go off course; *(Aut)* to turn off; to swerve; **— de un tema** to digress from a theme; to wander from the point.

desvincularse [1a] *vr:* **— con** to break one's links with, sever one's connections with; to get free of.

desvío *nm* (a) *(act)* deflection, deviation *(de* from); *(Aut etc)* swerve.
(b) *(Aut etc)* detour, diversion; bypass; *(Rail)* siding.
(c) *(fig)* coldness, indifference; dislike.

desvirgar [1h] *vt* to deflower.

desvirtuar [1e] **1** *vt* to impair, spoil; to detract from, adversely affect the quality of; to counteract, cancel, nullify the effect of.
2 desvirtuarse *vr* to spoil, go off, decline in quality.

desvivirse [3a] *vr:* — **por algo** to crave something, yearn for something, long for something; to be crazy about something; — **por los amigos** to do one's utmost for one's friends, live only to help one's friends; — **por** + *infin* to be very eager to + *infin*; to do one's best to + *infin*, go out of one's way to + *infin*; **se desvivió por ayudarme** he leant over backwards to help me.

desyerbar [1a] *vt* = **desherbar**.

desyerba *nf*, **desyerbo** *nm* (*SAm*) weeding.

detalladamente *adv* in detail, with full particulars; at great length.

detallado *adj* detailed; circumstantial; *knowledge* detailed, intimate.

detallar [1a] *vt* **(a)** to detail, list in detail, specify, itemize. **(b)** *story etc* to tell in detail. **(c)** (*Comm*) to sell retail.

detalle *nm* **(a)** detail, particular; item; **al** — in detail; **con todo** —, **con todos los** —**s** in detail, with full details; with full particulars; **en** — in detail; **hasta en sus menores** —**es** down to the last detail; **para más** —**s vea** . . . for further details see . . .; **no pierde** — he misses nothing, he doesn't miss a trick; **me observaba sin perder** — he was watching me very closely, he watched my every move.
(b) (*fig*) token (of appreciation), gesture; **¡qué** —! how sweet of you!, what a nice gesture!; **tiene muchos** —**s** he is very considerate; **es el primer** — **que te veo en mucho tiempo** it's the first sign of consideration I've had from you for a long time.
(c) (*Comm*) **al** — retail (*adj, adv*); **vender al** — to sell retail; **comercio al** — retail trade.

detallista 1 *adj* retail; **comercio** — retail trade. **2** *nmf* retailer, retail trader.

detección *nf* detection.

detectar [1a] *vt* to detect.

detective *nm* (*angl*) detective; — **de la casa** house detective; — **privado** private detective.

detectivesco *adj* detective (*attr*); **dotes detectivescas** gifts as a detective.

detector *nm* (*Naut, Tech etc*) detector; — **de mentiras** lie detector; — **de minas** mine detector.

detención *nf* **(a)** stopping; stoppage, holdup; delay; — **de juego** (*Sport*) stoppage of play; **una** — **de 15 minutos** a 15-minute delay.
(b) (*Law*) arrest, detention; — **ilegal** unlawful detention; — **en masa** mass arrest.
(c) = **detenimiento**.

detener [2l] **1** *vt* **(a)** *person, ball, vehicle, charge, epidemic etc* to stop; to hold up, check, delay; — **el progreso de** to hold up the progress of; **no quiero** —**le** I don't want to delay you; **me detuvo en la calle** he stopped me in the street, he accosted me in the street.
(b) to keep, hold back, retain; *breath* to hold.
(c) (*Law*) to arrest, detain.
2 detenerse *vr* to stop; to pause; to delay, linger; **se detuvo a mirarlo** he stopped to look at it; **¡no te detengas!** don't hang about!, don't delay!; **se detiene mucho en eso** he's taking a long time over that.

detenidamente *adv* carefully, thoroughly; at great length.

detenido 1 *adj* **(a)** (*Law*) arrested, under arrest.
(b) *story etc* detailed; *examination* lengthy, thorough; careful; (*pej*) slow, dilatory.
(c) (*fig*) timid.
(d) (*fig*) mean, niggardly.
2 *nm*, **detenida** *nf* person under arrest.

detenimiento *nm* care, thoroughness; **con** — carefully, thoroughly.

detentar [1a] *vt* **(a)** (*Sport etc*) *record, title* to hold. **(b)** (*pej*) *title* to hold unlawfully; *post etc* to occupy unlawfully.

detentor *nm* (*Sport*) holder; — **de marca** record holder; — **de trofeo** cup holder, champion.

detergente 1 *adj* detergent. **2** *nm* detergent.

deterger [2c] *vt* to clean, clean of grease; *wound* to clean; (*Cook etc*) to clean with detergent.

deteriorado *adj* spoiled, damaged; worn; *goods* shop-soiled, damaged.

deteriorar [1a] **1** *vt* to spoil, damage; to impair; (*Mech etc*) to cause wear on, cause wear and tear to.
2 deteriorarse *vr* to deteriorate, spoil; to get damaged; (*Mech etc*) to wear, get worn.

deterioro *nm* deterioration; impairment; damage; (*Mech etc*) wear, wear and tear; **en caso de** — **de las**

mercancías should the goods be imperfect in any way; **sin** — **de sus derechos** without any loss of rights, without any impairment of his rights.

determinable *adj* determinable; **fácilmente** — easy to determine.

determinación *nf* **(a)** (*act*) determination; decision; **tomar una** — to take a decision. **(b)** (*quality*) determination, resolution.

determinado *adj* **(a)** fixed, set, certain; **un día** — on a certain day; **on a given day; hay** —**s límites** there are fixed limits; **no hay ningún tema** — there is no particular theme, there is no set subject.
(b) (*Math*) determinate; (*Ling*) *article* definite.
(c) *person* determined, resolute; purposeful.

determinante 1 *adj* determinant. **2** *nm* determinant.

determinar [1a] **1** *vt* **(a)** to determine, fix, settle; *date, price etc* to fix; *damages, tax etc* to determine, assess; *course* to fix, decide, shape; — **el peso de algo** to determine (*or* calculate, work out, fix) the weight of something; **el reglamento determina que** . . . **the** rule lays it down that . . ., the rule states that . . .
(b) to cause, bring about; **aquello determinó la caída del gobierno** that brought about the fall of the government.
(c) *person* to decide, make up the mind of; **esto le determinó** this decided him; — **a uno a hacer algo** to determine someone to do something, lead someone to do something.
2 determinarse *vr* to decide, make up one's mind; **¿te has determinado?** have you made up your mind?; — **a hacer algo** to decide to do something, determine to do something; **no se determina a marcharse** he can't make up his mind to go.

determinismo *nm* determinism.

detersión *nf* cleaning (of grease); cleansing.

detestable *adj* detestable; odious, hateful; damnable.

detestablemente *adv* detestably.

detestación *nf* detestation, hatred, loathing.

detestar [1a] *vt* to detest, hate, loathe.

detonación *nf* detonation; report, explosion, bang.

detonador *nm* detonator.

detonante *adj* (*fig*) stunning, shattering.

detonar [1a] *vi* to detonate, explode, go off.

detracción *nf* disparagement; knocking (*sl*); slander; vilification.

detractor 1 *adj* disparaging; slanderous. **2** *nm*, **detractora** *nf* detractor, (*Pol etc*) knocker (*sl*); slanderer.

detraer [2p] *vt* **(a)** to remove, separate, take away. **(b)** to turn aside. **(c)** to disparage, (*Pol etc*) knock (*sl*); to slander; to vilify.

detrás 1 *adv* behind; at the back, in the rear; — **la foto lleva una dedicatoria** the photo has a dedication on the back; **salir de** — to come out from behind; **por** — behind; **atacar a uno por** — to attack someone from behind; **los coches de** — the cars at the back, the cars in the rear.
2 — **de** *prep* behind, back of (*US*); **por** — **de uno** (*fig*) behind someone's back; **salir de** — **de un árbol** to come out from behind a tree.

detrimento *nm* (*to object*) harm, damage; (*to interests etc*) detriment; **en** — **de** to the detriment of; **lo hizo sin** — **de su dignidad** he did it without detriment to (*or* loss of) his dignity.

detrito *nm*, **detritus** *nm* (*Geol etc*) detritus; debris.

deuda *nf* **(a)** (*in general*) indebtedness, debt; **estar en** — to be in debt, owe (*por* for); **estar en** — **con uno** to be in debt to someone, (*fig*) to be indebted to someone.
(b) (*una* —) debt; — **a largo plazo** long-term debt; —**s activas** (*Fin*) assets; —**s pasivas** liabilities; — **exterior** foreign debt; — **incobrable** bad debt; — **pública** national debt; **una** — **de gratitud** a debt of gratitude; **contraer** —**s** to contract debts, get into debt; **estar lleno de** —**s** to be heavily in debt, be burdened with debts.
(c) (*Eccl*) sin; **perdónanos nuestras** —**s** forgive us our trespasses.

deudo *nm* relative.

deudor 1 *adj* **(a)** **saldo** — debit balance, adverse balance.
(b) **le soy muy** — I am greatly indebted to you.
2 *nm*, **deudora** *nf* debtor; — **moroso** slow payer, defaulter.

deuterio *nm* deuterium.

devalar [1a] *vi* (*Naut*) to drift off course.

devaluación *nf* (*Fin*) devaluation.

devaluar [1e] *vt* (*Fin*) to devalue.

devanadera *nf* (*Sew*) reel, spool; winding frame.

devanado *nm* (*Elec*) winding.

devanador *nm* (*Sew*) reel, spool, bobbin.

devanar [1a] **1** *vt* to wind; (*of insect, spider*) to spin. **2 devanarse** *vr* (a) — los sesos to rack one's brains.
(b) (*Cu, Guat, Mex*) — de dolor to double up with pain; — de risa to double up with laughter.

devanear [1a] *vi* to rave, talk nonsense.

devaneo *nm* (a) (*Med*) delirium; (*fig*) ravings, nonsense, absurd talk. (b) time-wasting pastime, idle pursuit. (c) affair, flirtation.

devastación *nf* devastation.

devastador *adj* devastating (*also fig*).

devastar [1a] *vt* to devastate.

devengar [1h] *vt* wages to earn; to draw, receive; *interest* to earn, bear; **interés devengado** accrued interest, earned interest.

devenir 1 [3s] *vi* to become, evolve into; — **en** to become, turn into, change into.
2 *nm* evolution, process of development, (slow) change, transformation; **una nación en perpetuo** — a nation in a constant process of development, a nation which is changing all the time.

devoción *nf* (a) (*Rel etc*) devotion; devoutness, piety; **con** — devoutly; piously; **la** — **a esta imagen** the cult of this image, the veneration for this image.
(b) (*in general*) devotion (*a* to); attachment (*a* to); liking, affection (*a* for); **sienten** — **por su general** they feel devotion to their general, they are devoted to their general; **estar a la** — **de uno** to be completely under someone's thumb; **tener gran** — **a uno** to be wholly devoted to someone; **tener por** — **+** *infin* to be in the habit of + *ger*.
(c) (*Eccl*) devotion, prayer; religious observance; *see* **santo**.

devocionario *nm* prayer book.

devolución *nf* return; (*Sport*) return; (*Comm*) repayment, refund; (*Fin*) drawback; **pidió la** — **de los libros** he asked for the books to be given back, he asked for the return of the books.

devolver [2h; *ptp* **devuelto**] **1** *vt* (a) to return; to give back, send back; to hand back; *ball, blow* to return; (*Comm*) to repay, refund; (*fam*) to throw up, vomit; *favour etc* to return; **una carta al remitente** to return a letter to the sender; — **un florero a su sitio** to put a vase back in its place; — **mal por bien** to return ill for good; **el espejo devuelve la imagen the** mirror sends back (*or* reflects) the image; — **la salud a uno** to give someone back his health, restore someone to health.
(b) to restore; **han devuelto el castillo a su antiguo esplendor** they have restored the castle to its former glory.
2 devolverse *vr* (*SAm*) to return, come back, go back.

devorador *adj* devouring; **fuego** — all-consuming fire; **hambre devoradora** ravenous hunger.

devorar [1a] *vt* (a) to devour; to eat up, gobble up.
(b) (*fig*) to devour; to consume, use up; **todo lo devoró el fuego** the fire consumed everything; **devora las novelas de amores** she laps up love stories, she devours love stories; **le devoran los celos** he is consumed with jealousy; **los chicos devoran el calzado** the kids are terribly hard on their shoes.

devotamente *adv* devoutly.

devoto 1 *adj* (a) (*Rel*) devout; pious; **ser muy** — **de un santo** to have a special devotion to a saint; **ser** — **de la Virgen del puño** to be tight-fisted.
(b) (*Rel*) **obra devota** devotional work, work of devotion.
(c) devout; devoted; **su** — **amigo** your devoted friend; **es** — **de ese café** he is much attached to that café.
2 *nm*, **devota** *nf* (a) (*Rel*) devout person; (*in church*) worshipper; **los** —**s the faithful**, (*in church*) the worshippers, the congregation.
(b) (*fig*) devotee, votary, admirer; **la estrella y sus** —**s** the star and her admirers (*or* fans: *fam*); **los** —**s del ajedrez** devotees of chess.

deyección *nf* (*also* —**es**) excrement, (*Med*) motion; (*Geol*) debris.

dextrosa *nf* dextrose.

di *etc see* **dar.**

día *nm* (a) day; **el** — **2 de mayo** (on) the second of May; **ocho** —**s** week; **quince** —**s** fortnight; **cuatro** —**s** (*fig*) a couple of days; **¿qué** — **es?** what's the date today?; **hace buen** — it's a fine day, it's fine today; **¡buenos** —**s!** good morning!, good day!; **dar los buenos** —**s a uno** to wish (*or* bid) someone good day; **dar los** —**s a uno** to wish someone many happy returns of the day (*birthday or saint's day*); — **y noche** night and day; **no tener más que el** — **y la noche** to be utterly poor.
(b) (*expressions with article, adj etc*) **el** — **de hoy** today; **el** — **de mañana** tomorrow; (*fig*) at some future date; **el mejor** — some fine day; **el** — **menos pensado** when you least expect it; **un** — **de éstos** one of these days; **un** — **sí y otro no,** — **(de) por medio** (*SAm*) every other day; on alternate days; — **tras** — day after day; **algún** — some day, sometime; **cada** — each day, every day; **¡cualquier** —! (*iro*) not on your life!; **cualquier** — **viene** (*iro*) some fine day he'll turn up; **otro** — some other day, some other time; **dejémoslo para otro** — let's leave it for the moment; **¡tal** — **hará un año!** a fat lot I care!; **todos los** —**s** every day, daily; **no es cosa de todos los** —**s** it's not an everyday thing; **todo el santo** — the whole livelong day; the whole blessed day; *see* **hoy.**
(c) (*expressions with prep*) **a** —**s** at times, once in a while; **a los pocos** —**s** within a few days, after a few days, a few days later; **al otro** — (on) the following day; **al** — **siguiente** on the following day; **7 veces al** — 7 times a day, 7 times daily; **estar al** — to be up to date; (*in fashion etc*) to be with it (*fam*); **quien quiera estar al** — **en estos estudios, lea . . .** if anybody wants to keep up to date in these matters, he should read . . .; **poner al** — *diary* to enter up, write up; *ledger* to write up; **vivir al** — to live from hand to mouth; **de** — **en** — from day to day; **ese problema es ya de** —**s** that's an old problem; **pollitos de un** — day-old chicks; **los estilos del** — fashionable styles, up-to-date styles, with-it styles (*fam*); **en** —**s de Dios** (*or* **del mundo, de la vida**) never; **en los** —**s de Victoria** in Victoria's day, in Victoria's times; **en su** — in due time; **¡hasta otro** —! so long!
(d) (*forms with adj etc*) — **de asueto** day off; — **de ayuno** fast day; — **de la banderita** flag day; — **de boda** wedding day; — **feriado** holiday, day off; — **festivo,** — **de fiesta** holiday; —**s de gracia** (*Comm*) days of grace, days (allowed) to pay; — **hábil** working day; — **inhábil** non-working day; — **de inocentes** equivalent to All Fools' Day (*in Britain and US, 1 April; in Spain, 28 December*); — **del Juicio (Final)** Judgement Day; **estaremos aquí hasta el** — **del Juicio** we'll be here till Kingdom come; — **laborable** working day, weekday; — **lectivo** (*School*) working day, class day, teaching day; — **libre** free day, day off; — **malo,** — **nulo** of day; — **de paga** payday; **D**— **de la Raza** Columbus Day (*12 October*); **D**— **de Reyes** Epiphany (*6 January, on which the Magi bring presents to Spanish children*); — **señalado** special day, red-letter day; — **de trabajo,** — **útil** working day, weekday; — **de tribunales** court day; — **de vigilia** day of abstinence; *see* **anunciación, año** *etc*.
(e) daytime; daylight; **antes del** — before dawn; **de** — by day, during the day(time); **en pleno** — in broad daylight.

diabetes *nf* diabetes.

diabético 1 *adj* diabetic. **2** *nm*, **diabética** *nf* diabetic.

diabla *nf*, **diablesa** *nf* she-devil; **a la diabla** carelessly, any old how.

diablillo *nm* (*fam*) imp, monkey.

diablo *nm* (a) devil; fiend; **ése es el** — that's the devil of it; **ahí será el** — there'll be the devil to pay; **donde el** — **perdió el poncho** (*Arg, Chi*) in some godforsaken spot.
(b) (*fig*) devil; fiend; **pobre** — poor devil; **algún pobre** — **de cartero** some poor devil of a postman; *for numerous fig phrases, see* **demonio.**
(c) —**s azules** (*SAm: angl*) blue devils, delirium tremens.
(d) (*Chi*) heavy oxcart.

diablura *nf* devilry, devilment; prank; —**s** mischief, monkey tricks.

diabólicamente *adv* diabolically, fiendishly.

diabólico *adj* diabolical, devilish, fiendish.

diaconato *nm* (*post*) deaconry.

diaconía *nf* (*area, house*) deaconry.

diaconisa *nf* deaconess.

diácono *nm* deacon.

diacrítico *adj* diacritic(al); **signo** — diacritic, diacritical mark.

diacrónico *adj* diachronic.

diacho *nm* (*fam: euph*) = **diablo.**

diadema *nf* diadem; crown; (*jewel*) tiara.

diafanidad *nf* transparency; filminess; sheerness; limpidity.

diáfano *adj* diaphanous, transparent; filmy; sheer; *water* limpid, crystal-clear.

diafragma *nm* diaphragm.

diagnosis *nf, pl* **diagnosis** diagnosis.

diagnosticar [1g] *vt* to diagnose.

diagnóstico 1 *adj* diagnostic. **2** *nm* diagnosis.

diagonal 1 adj diagonal. **2** nf diagonal.
diagonalmente adv diagonally.
diagrama nm diagram.
dialectal adj dialectal, dialect (attr); **es palabra —** it's a dialect word.
dialectalismo nm (a) dialectal nature, dialectalism; **un texto lleno de —** a text of a strongly dialectal character.
(b) dialectalism, dialect word (or phrase etc).
dialéctico adj dialectical.
dialecto nm dialect.
dialogar [1h] **1** vt to set down (or compose etc) as a dialogue, write in dialogue form. **2** vi to talk, converse; **— con** (Pol etc) to engage in a dialogue with.
diálogo nm dialogue.
diamante nm (a) diamond; **— en bruto** uncut diamond; **— falso** paste; **— de imitación** imitation diamond. (b) **—s** (Cards) diamonds.
diamantífero adj diamond-bearing.
diamantino adj diamond-like, adamantine; glittering.
diamantista nm diamond cutter; diamond merchant.
diametral adj diametrical.
diametralmente adv diametrically; **— opuesto a** diametrically opposed to.
diámetro nm diameter; **— de giro** (Aut) turning circle; **faros de gran —** wide-angle headlights.
Diana f Diana.
diana nf (a) (Mil) reveille. (b) (of target) centre, bull's-eye; **dar en la —, hacer —** to get a bull's-eye.
diantre nm (fam: euph) =diablo; **¡—!** oh hell!; **los había como un —** (Chi) there were a devil of a lot of them.
diapasón nm (a) (Mus) diapason; range, scale.
(b) (of violin etc) finger board.
(c) **— normal** tuning-fork.
(d) (fig: of voice) tone; **bajar el —** to lower one's voice; **subir el —** to raise one's voice.
diapositiva nf (Phot) slide, transparency; (of glass) lantern slide.
diariamente adv daily, every day.
diario 1 adj daily; everyday; day-to-day.
2 adv (SAm) daily, every day.
3 nm (a) newspaper, daily; diary; (Comm) daybook; **— de a bordo, — de navegación** (Naut) logbook; **— hablado** (Radio etc) news, news bulletin; **— dominical** Sunday paper; **— matinal, — de la mañana** morning paper; **— de la noche, — vespertino** evening paper; **— de sesiones** (Parl) parliamentary report, report of proceedings in Parliament.
(b) (Fin) daily expenses.
(c) **a —** daily; **de —, para —** for everyday use; **nuestro mantel de —** our tablecloth for everyday (use), our ordinary tablecloth.
diarismo nm (SAm) journalism.
diarista nmf (a) diarist. (b) (SAm) newspaper owner (or publisher).
diarrea nf diarrhoea.
diarrucho nm (SAm: fam) rag (fam).
diatónico adj diatonic.
diatriba nf diatribe, tirade.
dibujante nm (a) (Art) sketcher; cartoonist. (b) (Tech) draughtsman; designer.
dibujar [1a] **1** vt (a) (Art) to draw, sketch.
(b) (Tech) to design.
(c) (fig) to sketch (in words), describe, depict.
2 dibujarse vr (a) to be outlined (contra against); to loom, show up.
(b) (of emotion etc) to show, appear; **el sufrimiento se dibujaba en su cara** suffering showed in his face.
dibujo nm (a) (art in general) drawing; sketching; art of design.
(b) (un —) drawing, sketch; (Tech) design; pattern; (in newspaper etc) cartoon; caricature; **— animado, —s animados** (Cine) cartoon (film); **— al carbón** charcoal drawing; **— del natural** drawing from life; **— (hecho) a pulso** freehand drawing; **un papel con — a rayas** a wallpaper with a striped pattern; **sedas con —s de última novedad** silks with the latest patterns (or designs).
(c) (fig) description, depiction.
dicción nf (a) (in general) diction; style. (b) (una —) word; expression.
diccionario nm dictionary; **— de bolsillo** pocket dictionary; **— bilingüe** bilingual dictionary; **— geográfico** gazetteer.
diccionarista nmf lexicographer, dictionary maker.
diciembre nm December.
dicotomía nf dichotomy.
dictado nm (a) dictation; **escribir al —** to take

dictation; **escribir algo al —** to take something down (as it is dictated).
(b) **—s** (fig) dictates; **los —s de la conciencia** the dictates of conscience.
(c) honorific title, title of honour.
dictador nm dictator.
dictadura nf dictatorship.
dictáfono nm Dictaphone.
dictamen nm opinion, dictum; judgement; report; (Law) legal opinion; **— contable** (Mex) auditor's report; **— facultativo** (Med) medical report; **emitir un —** to issue a report; **tomar — de** to consult with.
dictaminar [1a] **1** vt judgement to pass. **2** vi to pass judgement, give an opinion (en on).
dictar [1a] **1** vt (a) letter etc to dictate (a to).
(b) judgement to pass, pronounce; decree etc to issue.
(c) to suggest, say, dictate; **lo que dicta el sentido común** what common sense suggests.
(d) (SAm) class to give; lecture to deliver.
2 vi: **— a su secretaria** to dictate to one's secretary.
dictatorial adj, **dictatorio** adj dictatorial.
dicterio nm insult, taunt.
dicha nf (a) happiness; **para completar su —** to complete her happiness.
(b) (una —) happy thing, happy event; **es una — poder ...** it is a happy thing to be able to ...
(c) luck, good luck; **por —** by chance, fortunately.
dicharachero 1 adj witty, racy, sparkling; slangy; (pej) coarse.
2 nm witty person, racy talker, sparkling conversationalist; slangy sort; (pej) coarse individual.
dicharacho nm coarse remark, rude thing (to say).
dicho 1 ptp of **decir.**
2 adj said; above-mentioned, aforementioned; **—s animales** the said animals; **en — país** in this country, in this same country; **las avispas propiamente dichas** true wasps, wasps in the strict sense; see also **decir 2** (f).
3 nm saying, proverb; tag; bright remark, witty observation; insult; **— gordo** rude remark; **del — al hecho hay gran trecho** talking is not the same as actually doing; there's many a slip 'twixt cup and lip; **es un —** it's just a saying; **tomarse los —s** to exchange promises of marriage.
dichosamente adv luckily, fortunately.
dichoso adj (a) happy; **hacer — a uno** to make someone happy; **me siento — de + infin** I feel privileged to + infin.
(b) lucky, fortunate.
(c) (fam) blessed; **¡aquel — coche!** that blessed car!
didáctico adj didactic.
diecinueve adj nineteen; (date) nineteenth.
diecinueveavo adj ninteenth.
dieciochavo adj, **dieciocheno** adj eighteenth.
dieciochesco adj eighteenth-century (attr).
dieciocho adj eighteen; (date) eighteenth.
dieciséis adj sixteen; (date) sixteenth.
dieciseisavo 1 adj sixteenth. **2** nm sixteenth (part).
diecisiete adj seventeen; (date) seventeenth.
diecisieteavo adj seventeenth.
Diego m James.
diente nm (a) (Anat) tooth; (Zool) tusk; fang; **— canino** canine (tooth); **— cariado** decayed tooth, bad tooth; **— incisivo** incisor; **— de leche** milk tooth; **— molar** molar; **—s postizos** false teeth; **de —s afuera** (fig) as mere lip service, without meaning it; **más cerca están mis —s que mis parientes** charity begins at home; **daba — con —** his teeth were chattering; he was trembling like a leaf, he was all of a shiver; **enseñar los —s** (fig) to show one's claws, turn nasty; **estar a — to** be ravenous; **hablar entre —s** to mumble, mutter; **hincar el — en** to sink one's teeth into, bite into; **hincar el — en uno** (fig) to get one's knife into someone; **nunca pude hincar el — a ese libro** I could never get my teeth into that book; **pelar el —** (SAm) to smile affectedly; to flirt; (CAm) to laugh a lot; **tener buen — to** be a hearty eater.
(b) (Mech) cog; (of buckle) tongue; (of comb, saw etc) tooth.
(c) (Bot) **— de ajo** clove of garlic; **— de león** dandelion.
diéresis nf diaeresis.
Diesel: motor m — Diesel engine.
dieseléctrico adj diesel-electric.
diestra nf right hand.
diestramente adv (a) skilfully; dexterously; deftly.
(b) shrewdly; (pej) cunningly.

diestro 1 *adj* (a) (*not left*) right; (*Her*) dexter; **a — y siniestro** wildly, at random, all over the place; **repartir golpes a — y siniestro** to lash out wildly, throw out punches right and left.
(b) skilful; dexterous; handy, deft.
(c) shrewd, clever; (*pej*) cunning.
2 *nm* (a) (*Taur*) matador, bullfighter.
(b) expert swordsman; expert fencer.
(c) bridle.
dieta *nf* (a) (*Med*) diet; **— láctea** milk diet; **estar a —** to diet, be on a diet. (b) (*Pol*) diet, assembly. (c) **—s** subsistence allowance, expense allowance.
dietética *nf* dietetics.
dietético 1 *adj* dietetic, dietary. **2** *nm* dietician.
dietista *nmf* dietician.
diez[1] **1** *adj* ten; (*date*) tenth; **las — ten o'clock; hacer las — de últimas** to scoop the pool, sweep the board; (*fig*) to queer one's own pitch, damage one's own cause.
2 *nm* ten.
diez[2] *nm euph for* **Dios,** *in many fam phrases.*
diezmar [1a] *vt* to decimate (*also fig*).
diezmillo *nm* (*Mex*) = **solomillo.**
diezmo *nm* tithe.
difamación *nf* slander, defamation (*de* of); libel (*de* on).
difamador 1 *adj* slanderous, defamatory, libellous. **2** *nm,* **difamadora** *nf* slanderer, defamer; scandalmonger.
difamar [1a] *vt* (*Law*) to slander, defame; (*in writing esp*) to libel; (*fig*) to slander, malign.
difamatorio *adj* slanderous, defamatory, libellous.
diferencia *nf* (*all senses*) difference; **— de edades** difference in ages; **a — de** unlike; in contrast to; as distinguished from; **con corta —, con poca —** more or less; **hacer — entre** to make a distinction between; **partir la —** to split the difference; **partir la — con uno** (*fig*) to meet someone halfway, agree to compromise; **— va de A a Z** there's a big difference between A and Z; **no veo — de A a Z** I see no difference between A and Z; I see nothing to choose between A and Z.
diferencial 1 *adj* differential (*also Math*); distinctive; *duty etc* discriminatory. **2** *nm* (*Math*) differential. **3** *nm* (*also sometimes f*) (*Aut*) differential.
diferenciar [1b] **1** *vt* (a) to differentiate between; to make a difference between; **— A de B** to separate A from B, distinguish between A and B.
(b) (*Math*) to differentiate.
(c) to vary (the use of), alter the function of.
2 *vi* to differ (*de* from), be in disagreement (*de* with; *en* about, over).
3 diferenciarse *vr* (a) to differ, be different (*de* from); to be distinctive, be distinguished; **no se diferencian en nada** they do not differ at all; **se diferencian en que . . .** they differ in that . . .
(b) to distinguish oneself.
diferente *adj* (a) different; **— de algo** different from something, unlike something. (b) **—s** several, various; **por —s razones** for various reasons.
diferentemente *adv* differently.
diferir [3i] **1** *vt* (a) to defer, postpone, put off; to hold over; (*Law*) *judgement* to reserve.
(b) *period, turn* to prolong, extend.
2 *vi* to differ, be different (*de* from, *en* in).
difícil *adj* (a) difficult, hard; awkward; **— de vencer** hard to beat, difficult to overcome; **es — que . . .** it is unlikely that . . ., it is doubtful whether . . .; **encuentro — decidir** I find it hard to decide, I find difficulty in deciding; **se hizo un silencio —** there was an awkward (*or* embarrassing) silence.
(b) (*in character*) difficult; **es un hombre —** he's a difficult man.
(c) (*fam*) *face* odd, ugly.
difícilmente *adv* with difficulty; hardly; **— se podrá hacer** it can hardly be done; **aquí — va a haber para todos** there's hardly going to be enough of this for everybody.
dificultad *nf* difficulty; trouble; objection; **sin — alguna** without the least difficulty; **la — es que . . .;** the difficulty is that . . ., the trouble is that . . .; **no hay — para aceptar que . . .** there is no difficulty about accepting that . . .; **ha tenido —es con la policía** he's been in trouble with the police; **tuvieron algunas —es para llegar a casa** they had some trouble getting home; **poner —es** to raise objections; to create obstacles; **me pusieron —es para darme el pasaporte** they created obstacles to giving me a passport, they made it awkward for me to get a passport.
dificultar [1a] *vt* (a) *way etc* to obstruct, impede, hinder; to put obstacles in the way of; to interfere

with, hold up; to render difficult; **las restricciones dificultan el comercio** the restrictions hinder trade, the restrictions make trade difficult.
(b) **— que +** *subj* to make it unlikely that . . .; (*person*) to think it unlikely that . . .
dificultoso *adj* (a) difficult, hard; awkward, troublesome. (b) (*fam*) *face* odd, ugly. (c) *person* difficult, awkward, full of silly objections.
difracción *nf* diffraction.
difractar [1a] *vt* to diffract.
difteria *nf* diphtheria.
difundir [3a] **1** *vt* to diffuse; to spread, disseminate; to divulge, circulate; *gas etc* to give off, give out, emit; **— una noticia** to spread a piece of news, divulge a piece of news; **— la alegría** to spread happiness, radiate happiness.
2 difundirse *vr* to spread (out); to become diffused.
difunto 1 *adj* dead, deceased; **el — ministro** the late minister.
2 *nm,* **difunta** *nf* (a) deceased person; **la familia del —** the family of the deceased; **Día de D—s** All Souls' Day.
(b) corpse.
difusión *nf* (a) (*act*) diffusion; spread(ing), dissemination; divulging, circulation. (b) (*quality*) diffuseness.
difuso *adj* (a) *light* diffused; *knowledge etc* widespread, widely extended. (b) *style etc* diffuse, wordy, discursive.
digerible *adj* digestible.
digerir [3i] *vt* (a) *food* to digest; to swallow.
(b) (*Chem*) to digest, absorb, dissolve.
(c) (*fig*) *opinions etc* to digest, absorb, assimilate; to ponder, think over; (*in negative phrases*) to swallow, stomach; **no puedo — a ese tío** I can't stand that chap.
digestible *adj* digestible.
digestión *nf* digestion.
digestivo *adj* digestive.
digesto *m* (*Law etc*) digest.
digitación *nf* (*Mus*) fingering.
digital 1 *adj* digital; finger (*attr*); **impresión — fingerprint. 2** *nf* (*Bot*) foxglove; (*drug*) digitalis.
dígito *nm* (*Math etc*) digit.
dignación *nf* condescension.
dignamente *adv* (a) worthily; fittingly, properly, appropriately. (b) honourably. (c) with dignity, in a dignified way. (d) decently.
dignarse [1a] *vr:* **— +** *infin* (a) to deign to + *infin,* condescend to + *infin.*
(b) (*formulae*) please . . ., *eg* **dígnese venir a esta oficina** please (be so good as to) come to this office.
dignatario *nm* dignitary.
dignidad *nf* (a) (*quality*) dignity; honour; self-respect; **herir la — de uno** to offend someone's self-respect.
(b) post, office; rank; **tiene — de ministro** he has the rank of a minister.
(c) (*person*) dignitary, worthy.
dignificar [1g] *vt* to dignify.
digno *adj* (a) worthy; fitting; proper, appropriate; **— de** worthy of, deserving; **— de elogio** praiseworthy; **— de toda alabanza** thoroughly praiseworthy, highly commendable; **— de mención** worth a mention, worth mentioning; **un — castigo** a fitting punishment; **es — de nuestra admiración** it deserves our admiration; **es — de verse** it is worth seeing.
(b) *person etc* worthy, upright, honourable.
(c) (*in manner, appearance*) dignified.
(d) decent; **viviendas dignas para los obreros** decent homes for the workers.
digresión *nf* digression.
dije[1] *etc see* **decir.**
dije[2] *nm* (a) medallion, locket; amulet, charm; (*pej*) trinket. (b) (*fig*) gem, treasure, person of sterling qualities.
dilación *nf* delay; **sin —** without delay, forthwith; **esto no admite —** this must suffer no delay, this is most urgent.
dilapidación *nf* squandering, waste.
dilapidar [1a] *vt* to squander, waste.
dilatación *nf* (a) dilation; expansion (*also Phys*), enlargement, widening, stretching; protraction, prolongation. (b) (*fig*) calm, calm dignity.
dilatado *adj* dilated; vast, extensive, spacious; numerous; long drawn-out; long-winded, discursive.
dilatar [1a] **1** *vt* (a) (*in space*) to dilate; to expand (*also Phys*), enlarge, widen; to stretch, extend; *fame etc* to spread.
(b) (*in time*) to protract, prolong, stretch out.
(c) to delay, put off.

2 dilatarse vr **(a)** to dilate; to expand (also Phys); to stretch, extend; to spread; **la llanura se dilata hasta el horizonte** the plain spreads (or extends, rolls) right to the horizon; **el valle se dilata en aquella parte** the valley widens (or spreads out) at that point.

  (b) to be long-winded, be discursive; **— en**, **— sobre** to expatiate on; to linger over, take one's time over.

  (c) (SAm) to delay, be slow; (train etc) to be late; **— en + infin** to take a long time to + infin, be slow to + infin.

dilativo adj dilatory.

dilatorias nfpl procrastination; delaying tactics; **andar en — con uno, traer a uno en —** to use delaying tactics with someone, hedge with someone; **no me venga Vd con —** don't hedge with me.

dilección nf affection.

dilema nm dilemma; **estar en un —** to be in a dilemma.

diletante nmf dilettante.

diligencia nf **(a)** (quality) diligence, care; assiduity; speed, dispatch.

  (b) piece of business; errand, job, mission; **hacer —s** to do business; **hacer una —** to run an errand, go on an errand; (fam: tabu) to do one's business (fam); **hacer las —s de costumbre** to take the usual steps; **practicar sus —s** to make every possible effort, do one's utmost (para + infin to + infin).

  (c) (Law) **—s** formalities; inquiries; steps (of an investigation etc); **—s judiciales** judicial proceedings; **—s previas** inquest.

  (d) (Hist) stagecoach.

diligenciar [1b] vt matter to see about, deal with; to further, get moving.

diligente adj diligent; industrious, assiduous; quick, speedy, prompt; **un alumno poco —** a slack pupil, a lazy pupil.

diligentemente adv diligently; industriously; assiduously; speedily.

dilucidar [1a] vt to elucidate, explain, clarify; case, mystery etc to solve, clear up.

dilución nf dilution.

diluido adj dilute; diluted, weak; watered down.

diluir [3g] vt to dilute; to water down, weaken; (fig) to water down.

diluviar [1b] vi to pour with rain, rain in torrents.

diluvio nm deluge, flood (also fig); **el D—** the Flood; **un — de cartas** a deluge of letters; **¡fue el —!** it was chaos!; **¡esto es el —!** what a mess!

dimanar [1a] vi: **— de** to arise from, spring from, stem from.

dimensión nf **(a)** dimension (also fig); **de grandes —es** of great size, of large dimensions.

  (b) (fig: of personal quality) stature, standing; **un matemático de — universal** a mathematician of world stature.

dimes nmpl: **— y diretes** bickering, squabbling; gossip; petty intrigue; **andar en — y diretes con uno** to bicker (or squabble) with someone.

diminuendo nm (Mus) diminuendo.

diminutivo 1 adj diminutive. **2** nm diminutive.

diminuto adj **(a)** tiny, minute, exceedingly small; miniature. **(b)** defective, imperfect.

dimisión nf resignation; **presentar la —** to send in (or tender, submit) one's resignation.

dimitente 1 adj resigning, outgoing, retiring; **el presidente —** the outgoing chairman, the retiring chairman. **2** nmf person resigning.

dimitir [3a] **1** vt to resign; to give up, relinquish; **— la jefatura del partido** to resign (from) the party leadership. **2** vi to resign (de from).

din nm (sl) dough (sl); **el — y el don** money and rank, dough and dukedom.

Dinamarca f Denmark.

dinamarqués = danés.

dinámica nf (la —) dynamics; (una —) dynamic.

dinámico adj dynamic.

dinamita nf dynamite.

dinamitar [1a] vt to dynamite.

dinamitazo nm dynamite explosion; dynamiting.

dinamo, **dínamo** nf (often m in SAm) dynamo.

dinastía nf dynasty.

dinástico adj dynastic.

dinerada nf, **dineral** nm fortune, mint of money; **habrá costado un —** it must have cost a fortune.

dinerario adj money (attr), financial.

dinerillos nmpl (fam): **tiene sus —** she's got a bit of money (put by).

dinero nm money; (of country, period etc) currency, coinage, money; **persona de —** moneyed person, wealthy person; **es hombre de —** he is a man of means; **¿cuánto es en — americano?** how much is

that in American money?; **— contante** cash; **— contante y sonante** cash, ready money; **— de curso legal** legal tender; **— en caja** cash in hand; **— por callar** hush money; **los —s del sacristán cantando se vienen y cantando se van** easy come easy go; **el — malo echa fuera al bueno** bad money drives out good; **el — lo puede todo, el — puede mucho** money can do anything, money talks; **andar mal de —** to be badly off, be in financial difficulties; **el negocio no da —** the business does not pay, the business is not profitable, the business is not a paying proposition; **ganar — a espuertas** (or **a porrillo**) to make money hand over fist.

dinosaurio nm dinosaur.

dintel nm lintel; (SAm) threshold.

diñar [1a] vt (fam) to give; **—la** to kick the bucket (sl); **—sela a uno** to swindle someone.

diocesano adj diocesan.

diócesi(s) nf, pl **diócesis** diocese.

Dionisio m Denis; (classical) Dionysius.

Dios m **(a)** God; **— delante** with God's help; **— mediante** God willing, D.V.; **a — gracias** thank heaven; **a la buena de —** at random; thoughtlessly, without preparation; trusting to luck; any old how; **a la de — (es Cristo)** rashly; **una de — es Cristo** an almighty row; **armar la de — es Cristo** to raise hell, cause a tremendous fuss; **esto clama a —** this cries out to heaven (to be reformed etc); **— los cría y ellos se juntan** birds of a feather flock together; **dar a — lo que es de — y al César lo que es del César** render unto Caesar that which is Caesar's and unto God that which is God's; **lo hace como — le da a entender** he does it as best he can, he does it according to his lights; **como — manda** as is proper; properly; well; **donde — pasó de largo** a godforsaken spot; **cuando — quiera** all in God's good time; **a — rogando y con el mazo dando** God helps those who help themselves; **sabe — knows; sólo — sabe** God alone knows; **sabe — que no quería ofender** God knows I did not intend to cause offence; **vaya con —** good-bye, (formally) may God be with you, (iro) and good riddance, and the best of luck; **le vino a ver —** he struck lucky, he had a stroke of luck.

  (b) (exclamatory) **¡— mío!** good gracious!, good heavens!; well!; **¡por —!** for God's sake!; **¡— le ampare!**, **¡— le asista!**, **¡— te la depare buena!** (iro) I hope it keeps fine for you!, and the best of luck!; **¡— le ayude!** (on sneezing) bless you!; **¡— te bendiga!** God bless you!; **¡— me libre!** Heaven forbid!; **¡líbreme — de...!** Heaven forbid that I...!; **¡plegue a —!** please God!; **¡no lo quiera —!** God forbid!; **¡válgame —!** bless my soul!; **¡vive —!** good God!

dios nm god; idol; **los —es paganos** the pagan gods.

diosa nf goddess.

diploma nm diploma.

diplomacia nf diplomacy.

diplomado 1 adj qualified, trained, having a diploma. **2** nm, **diplomada** nf qualified person, holder of a diploma.

diplomarse [1a] vr (SAm) to graduate (from college etc).

diplomática nf **(a)** (Hist, Law) diplomatic. **(b)** (Pol) diplomatic corps; diplomatic career, (career in the) foreign service.

diplomáticamente adv diplomatically.

diplomático 1 adj diplomatic. **2** nm diplomat; (fig) diplomatist.

dipsomanía nf dipsomania.

dipsomaníaco nm, **dipsomaníaca** nf, **dipsómano** nm, **dipsómana** nf dipsomaniac.

díptero nm fly.

diptongar [1h] vti to diphthongize.

diptongo nm diphthong.

diputación nf deputation, delegation; committee; **— permanente** (Parl) standing committee.

  (b) **—** provincial equivalent to county council; county council offices.

diputado nmf delegate, representative; (Parl) deputy, member of parliament, representative (US); **— a Cortes** (Spain) parliamentary deputy, member of the Spanish Cortes; **el — por Guadalajara** the member for Guadalajara; **— provincial** equivalent to member of a county council.

diputar [1a] vt to delegate, depute; to empower.

dique nm **(a)** dike, sea wall; jetty, mole; breakwater; dam; dock; **— de contención** dam; **— flotante** floating dock; **— seco** dry dock; **entrar en —, hacer —** to dock.

  (b) (fig) check; barrier; **es un — contra la expansión** it is a barrier to expansion; **poner un — a** to check, restrain.

diré *etc see* **decir.**

dirección *nf* (a) (*general sense*) direction; way; (*fig*) course, trend; — **del viento** wind direction; **con — norte** in a northerly direction; **con — a, en — a, en la —** de in the direction of; towards; "**— prohibida**" (*Aut*) "no entry", "no thoroughfare"; **calle de — obligatoria, calle de — única** one-way street; **calle de 2 —es** street with two-way traffic; **conmutador de 2 —es** two-way switch; **cambiar de —** to change direction; **¿podría Vd indicarme la — de . . .?** could you please direct me to . . .?; **salir con — a** to leave for, depart for; to go off in the direction of; **salir con — desconocida** to leave for an unknown destination.

(b) (*act*) direction; guidance; control; (*Comm etc*) management; (*Pol*) leadership; **bajo la — de** under the direction of; **asumir la —, tomar la —** to take (over) control.

(c) (*persons*) management; board of directors; (*Pol*) leadership; **habrá cambios en la — del partido** there will be changes in the party leadership, there will be changes among the party's top men.

(d) (*post*) directorship; post of manager; (*of newspaper*) editorship; (*Mus*) conductorship.

(e) (*Aut etc*) steering; **— asistida** power steering; **de —** steering (*attr*).

(f) (*head*) office, administrative office; **D— General de Turismo** State Tourist Office; **D— General de Seguridad** State Security Office (*or* Service).

(g) (*Post*) address; **— del remitente** return address; **ponga claramente su —** write your address clearly.

direccional *adj* directional.

directa *nf* (*Aut*) top gear.

directamente *adv* (*all senses*) directly.

directiva *nf* board of directors; governing body.

directivo 1 *adj board etc* managing, governing; *function* managerial, administrative; *class* managerial, executive.

2 *nm* (*Comm etc*) manager, executive; **un congreso de los —s de la industria** a conference of executives from the industry.

directo 1 *adj* (a) direct; straight; immediate; *action, manner, translation etc* direct.

(b) (*Rail etc*) through, non-stop.

(c) (*TV*) *programme, shot* live; **transmitir en —** to broadcast live.

2 *nm* (*Boxing*) straight punch; (*Tennis*) forehand shot (*or drive etc*).

director 1 *adj* leading; controlling; guiding; **= directivo.**

2 *nm* director; (*Comm etc*) director; manager, executive; (*Mus*) conductor; (*School*) headmaster; principal; (*of training college etc*) principal; (*Univ: of college*) master, (*of residence*) warden; (*of prison*) governor; (*of newspaper*) editor; **— de escena** stage manager; producer; **— espiritual** father confessor; **— de funeraria** undertaker, funeral director, mortician (*US*); **— gerente** managing director; **— de hotel** hotel manager; **— de orquesta** conductor; **— de personal** personnel manager.

directora *nf* manageress (*see also* **director**); (*School*) headmistress; principal; (*Univ: of college*) mistress, (*of residence*) warden.

directorial *adj* (*Comm etc*) managing, executive; *clase* **—** managers, management, executive class.

directorio *nm* (a) directive, instructions.

(b) (*persons*) directors, board of directors, directorate.

(c) (*book*) directory; **— de teléfonos** (*Mex*) telephone directory.

dirigencia *nf* (*Pol etc*) leadership.

dirigente 1 *adj* leading. **2** *nm* (*Pol etc*) leader; **— de la oposición** leader of the opposition; **los —s del partido** the party leaders.

dirigible 1 *adj* (*Aer*) dirigible; (*Naut*) navigable. **2** *nm* dirigible.

dirigido *adj missile* guided.

dirigir [3c] **1** *vt* (a) (*general sense*) to direct (*a, hacia* at, to, towards); *accusation* to level (*a* at), make (*a* against); *letter, protest, question, remark* to address (*a* to); *order* to place (*a* with); *book* to dedicate (*a* to); *look* to direct (*a* towards), turn (*a* on); *hose* to play, turn (*a* on); *gun, telescope etc* to aim, point (*a* at).

(b) (*Comm etc*) *business* to manage; to run, operate; *expedition, party, revolt* to lead, head; *newspaper, series etc* to edit; *thesis, work etc* to direct, supervise.

(c) *person* to direct; to guide, advise (*en* about,

in); *course of action* to direct, shape; *efforts* to direct (*a* towards), concentrate (*a* on).

(d) (*Aut, Naut*) to steer; (*Aut*) to drive.

(e) (*Mus*) to conduct.

(f) (*Cine, Theat*) to produce, direct.

2 dirigirse *vr*: **— a** (a) to go to, make one's way to; to head for; to turn towards; (*Naut etc*) to steer for, head for; **— hacia** to head for.

(b) (*fig*) to speak to, address; to approach; **— a uno solicitando algo** to apply to someone for something; **se dirigió a mí en la calle** he spoke to me in the street; he accosted me in the street; "**diríjase a . . .**" (*adverts*) "apply to . . .", "write to . . ."

dirigismo *nm* management, control; **— estatal** state control.

dirimente *adj argument etc* decisive; *vote* casting; *opinion, decision* (*in competition etc*) final.

dirimir [3a] *vt* (a) *contract, marriage etc* to dissolve, annul, declare void. (b) *dispute* to settle.

discernidor *adj* discerning, discriminating.

discernimiento *nm* discernment, discrimination; judgement; **edad de —** years of discretion.

discernir [3i] **1** *vt* (a) to discern, distinguish; **— A de B** to distinguish A from B.

(b) (*Law*) *guardian* to appoint.

(c) (*esp SAm: gall*) *prize etc* to award (*a* to); confer (*a* on).

2 *vi*: **— entre** to distinguish between, discriminate between.

disciplina *nf* (a) (*in most senses*) discipline. (b) whip; **—s** lashes.

disciplinar [1a] *vt* (a) to discipline. (b) to school, train; (*Mil*) to drill, train. (c) to whip, scourge.

disciplinario *adj* disciplinary.

discipulado *nm* (a) (*Rel*) discipleship. (b) group of pupils, body of students.

discípulo *nm*, **discípula** *nf* (a) (*Eccl, Philos etc*) disciple; follower. (b) (*School*) pupil, student.

disco *nm* (a) disk, disc; (*Sport*) discus; (*Rail*) signal; (*Tel*) dial; (*Mus etc*) gramophone record, phonograph record (*US*); **— de duración extendida** extended-play record (*EP*); **— de larga duración, — microsurco** long-playing record (*LP*); **— giratorio** (*gramophone*) turntable; **— de marcar** (*Tel*) dial; **— volante** flying saucer.

(b) (*fam*) boring affair; boring speech; tedious tale; **es un —** it's a bore, it's so boring; **nos soltó el — una vez más** he told us the whole dreary tale again.

discóbolo *nm* discus thrower.

discográfico *adj* record (*attr*); **el momento — actual** the present state of the record industry.

díscolo *adj* uncontrollable, unruly; rebellious; *child* mischievous.

disconforme *adj* differing; **estar —** to be in disagreement (*con* with), not agree.

disconformidad *nf* disagreement.

discontinuidad *nf* lack of continuity.

discontinuo *adj* discontinuous.

discordancia *nf* discord (*also fig*).

discordante *adj* discordant (*also fig*).

discordar [1m] *vi* (a) (*Mus*) to be out of tune. (b) (*persons etc*) to disagree (*de* with), differ (*from*); (*of opinions, colours etc*) to clash.

discorde *adj* (a) (*Mus*) *sound* discordant, unharmonious; *instrument* out of tune.

(b) (*fig*) discordant, differing; clashing; **estar —s** (*persons*) to disagree, be in disagreement (*de* with).

discordia *nf* discord, disagreement.

discoteca *nf* record library, record collection; discothèque.

discreción *nf* (a) discretion, tact, good sense; discrimination; prudence; wisdom, sagacity, shrewdness.

(b) secrecy.

(c) wit; witticism.

(d) **a —** at one's discretion; **añadir azúcar a —** (*Cook*) add sugar to taste; **comer a —** to eat as much as one likes; **con vino a —** with as much wine as one wants; **¡a —!** (*Mil*) stand easy!; **rendirse a —** (*Mil*) to surrender unconditionally.

discrecional *adj* discretionary; optional, not prescribed, within one's judgement; **parada —** request stop.

discrepancia *nf* discrepancy; divergence; (*between persons etc*) disagreement.

discrepante *adj* divergent; dissenting; **hubo varias voces —s** there were some dissenting voices, some were not in agreement.

discrepar [1a] *vi* to differ (*de* from), disagree (*de* with); **discrepamos en varios puntos** we disagree on a number of points; **discrepo de esa opinión** I disagree with that view.

discretamente *adv* (a) discreetly, tactfully, sensibly; with discrimination; prudently, shrewdly. (b) soberly; quietly; unobtrusively.

discretear [1a] *vi* to try to be clever, be frightfully witty.

discreto *adj* (a) (*of person, character etc*) discreet, tactful, sensible; discriminating; prudent, wise, sagacious, shrewd.
(b) *dress etc* sober, sensible; *colour* quiet, sober; *position etc* unobtrusive; *hint, reminder* discreet, gentle, tactful.
(c) fair, middling, reasonable; **de inteligencia discreta** of reasonable intelligence, reasonably intelligent; ¡**le daremos un plazo** — we'll allow him a reasonable time.
(d) (*Phys etc*) discreet.

discriminación *nf* discrimination (*contra* against); — **racial** racial discrimination.

discriminar [1a] *vi* to discriminate (*contra* against).

discriminatorio *adj* discriminatory.

disculpa *nf* excuse; plea; apology.

disculpable *adj* excusable, pardonable.

disculpar [1a] **1** *vt* to excuse, pardon, forgive; to exonerate (*de culpa* from blame); **disculpa el que venga tarde** forgive me for coming late; **le disculpan sus pocos años** his youth is an excuse, his youth provides an excuse; **te ruego —me con el anfitrión** please make my apologies to the. host.
2 disculparse *vr* to excuse oneself (*de* from); to apologize (*por* + *infin* for + *ger*); — **con uno por haber hecho algo** to apologize to someone for having done something.

discurrir [3a] **1** *vt* to invent, think up, contrive; **esos chicos no discurren nada bueno** these lads must be cooking up something nasty, these lads are up to no good.
2 *vi* (a) to roam, wander (*por* about, along).
(b) (*river*) to flow.
(c) (*time*) to pass, flow by; (*life, period, meeting*) to go, pass, be spent; **la sesión discurrió sin novedad** the meeting went off quietly; **el verano discurrió sin grandes calores** the summer passed without great heat.
(d) to think, reason, meditate (*en* about, on); to speak, discourse (*sobre* about, on).
(e) — **poco** to do little, produce little, be inactive; **discurre menos que un mosquito** he doesn't do a stroke.

discursear [1a] *vi* to speechify.

discurso *nm* (a) speech, address, discourse; — **de clausura** closing speech; — **político** political speech; **pronunciar un —, dictar un —** (*SAm*) to make (*or* deliver) a speech.
(b) (*written*) treatise.
(c) (*in general*) speech, faculty of speech.
(d) (*mental*) reasoning power, mental powers.
(e) (*of time*) period; passing, passage; **en el — del tiempo** with the passage of time; **en el — de 4 generaciones** in the space of 4 generations.

discusión *nf* discussion; argument; **eso no admite —** there can be no argument about that; **estar en —** to be under discussion.

discutible *adj* debatable, arguable; **es — si . . .** it is debatable whether . . .; **de mérito algo —** of somewhat dubious worth.

discutido *adj* much-discussed; controversial.

discutidor *adj* argumentative, disputatious.

discutir [3a] **1** *vt* to discuss, debate, talk over; to argue about; to contradict, argue against, object to; — **a uno lo que uno está diciendo** to contradict what someone is saying.
2 *vi* to discuss, talk; to argue (*de, sobre* about, over); — **de política** to argue about politics, talk politics; ¡**no discutas!** don't argue!

disecar [1g] *vt* (a) (*Med and fig*) to dissect. (b) (*for museum etc*) *animal* to stuff; *plant* to preserve, mount.

disección *nf* (a) dissection. (b) stuffing; preservation, mounting.

diseminación *nf* dissemination, spread(ing), scattering; — **nuclear** spread of nuclear weapons.

diseminar [1a] *vt* to disseminate, spread, scatter.

disensión *nf* dissension.

disentería *nf* dysentery.

disentimiento *nm* dissent, disagreement.

disentir [3I] *vi* to dissent (*de* from), disagree (*de* with).

diseñador *nm* (*Tech etc*) designer.

diseñar [1a] *vt* (*Tech etc*) to design; (*Art*) to draw, sketch; to outline.

diseño *nm* (*Tech etc*) design; (*Art*) drawing, sketch; (*Sew etc*) pattern, design; (*in words*) sketch, outline.

disertación *nf* dissertation, disquisition, discourse.

disertar [1a] *vi* to speak, discourse; — **acerca de, — sobre** to discourse upon, expound on, speak about; — **largamente** to speak at length.

disfavor *nm* disfavour.

disforme *adj* ill-proportioned, badly-proportioned; monstrous, huge; ugly.

disfraz *nm* (a) disguise; mask; fancy dress; (*Mil*) camouflage; (*fig*) pretext, blind (*de* for); **baile de disfraces** fancy dress ball; **bajo el — de** in the guise of; under the cloak of.
(b) (*fam*) **ser un —** to be out of place; to look all wrong.

disfrazado *adj:* — **de** disguised as; in the guise of; **ir — de duque** to be made up like a duke; to masquerade as a duke.

disfrazar [1f] **1** *vt* to disguise; to cover up, mask, conceal, cloak; (*Mil*) to camouflage; — **a uno de lavandera** to disguise someone as a washerwoman, make someone up as a washerwoman.
2 disfrazarse *vr:* — **de** to disguise oneself as, make oneself up as.

disfrutar [1a] **1** *vt* to enjoy; to make use of, have the benefit of.
2 *vi* (a) to enjoy oneself, have a good time; ¡**cómo disfruto!** I'm enjoying this!, this is the life!; — **con algo** to enjoy something, benefit from something; **siempre disfruto con los libros así** I always enjoy books of that sort.
(b) — **de** to enjoy; to have, possess; — **de buena salud** to enjoy good health; **disfruta de las rentas de su finca** he enjoys (*or* has) the income from his estate.

disfrute *nm* enjoyment; use; possession.

disfuerzo *nm* (*Per*) (a) impudence, effrontery. (b) prudishness. (c) **—s** threats, bravado.

disgregación *nf* disintegration; break(ing)-up; separation; severance.

disgregar [1h] **1** *vt* to disintegrate; to break up; to separate (*de* from); to sever (*de* from). **2 disgregarse** *vr* to disintegrate; to break up (*en* into).

disgustar [1a] **1** *vt* to annoy, upset, displease; to offend; **es un olor que me disgusta** it's a smell which upsets me; **me disgusta tener que repetirlo** it annoys me to have to repeat it, I don't like having to repeat it; **comprendí que le disgustaba mi presencia** I realized that my presence annoyed him; **estaba muy disgustado con el asunto** he was very upset about the affair.
2 disgustarse *vr* (a) to be annoyed, get upset (*con, de* about); to be displeased, be offended, feel hurt (*con, de* about); — **de algo** to get bored with something, get fed up with something.
(b) (*2 persons*) to fall out; — **con uno** to fall out with someone.

disgusto *nm* (a) (*feeling*) annoyance, displeasure; vexation; grief, chagrin, sorrow; repugnance; boredom; **a —** unwillingly, against one's will.
(b) (*act*) trouble, bother, difficulty; unpleasant experience; misfortune; blow, shock; **reírse de los —s del prójimo** to laugh at a fellow man's troubles (*or* misfortunes); **me causó un gran —** it was a great blow to me; it upset me very much; **han de sobrevenir —s** there's trouble ahead; **matar a uno a —s** to wear someone out with burdens, heap troubles on someone.
(c) quarrel, upset; **tener un — con uno** to have a quarrel with someone, fall out with someone.

disidencia *nf* dissidence, disagreement; (*Eccl*) dissent.

disidente 1 *adj* dissident; dissenting. **2** *nmf* dissident person (*or* element *etc*); (*Eccl*) dissenter, nonconformist.

disidir [3a] *vi* to dissent.

disílabo 1 *adj* disyllabic. **2** *nm* disyllable.

disimulación *nf* dissimulation; furtiveness; cunning.

disimuladamente *adv* furtively; cunningly, slyly; covertly.

disimulado *adj* furtive; underhand; cunning, sly; covert; **hacerse el —** to dissemble; to pretend not to notice (*etc*); **hacer la disimulada** to feign ignorance.

disimular [1a] **1** *vt* (a) to hide; (*fig*) to hide, cloak, disguise; *emotion, intention etc* to conceal.
(b) to excuse; to condone, overlook; to tolerate; *offence etc* to pass off; *person etc* to be lenient to, behave tolerantly towards; **le ruego — la indiscreción** please pardon the liberty; **disimule mi atrevimiento** forgive me if I have been too bold.
2 *vi* to dissemble, pretend.

disimulo *nm* (a) dissimulation; furtiveness; craftiness; **con —** cunningly, craftily. (b) indulgence, tolerance.

disipación *nf* (*all senses*) dissipation.

disipado *adj* (a) dissipated; rakish, raffish. (b) extravagant, spendthrift.

disipador nm spendthrift.
disipar [1a] **1** vt (a) *mist etc* to drive away, cause to disappear, dispel.
  (b) *doubt etc* to dispel, remove; *hope* to destroy.
  (c) *money* to squander, fritter away (*en* on).
  2 disiparse vr (a) (*smoke etc*) to vanish; to evaporate.
  (b) (*doubt etc*) to be dispelled, vanish.
dislate nm absurdity, silly thing; **—s** nonsense.
dislocación nf dislocation; (*Med*) dislocation, sprain; (*Geol*) slip, fault.
dislocar [1g] vt to dislocate; to sprain.
disloque nm (*fam*): **es el —** it's the limit, it's the last straw; **fue el —** (*of humour etc*) it was the great moment, it was the crowning touch.
disminución nf diminution, decrease (*de* of), fall (*de* in); **proceso de — de réditos** law of diminishing returns; **continuar sin —** to continue unchecked, continue unabated; **ir en —** to diminish, be on the decrease.
disminuir [3g] vti to diminish, decrease, lessen.
disociación nf dissociation.
disociar [1b] **1** vt to dissociate, separate (*de* from).
  2 disociarse vr to dissociate oneself (*de* from).
disoluble adj dissoluble, dissolvable.
disolución nf (a) (*act*) dissolution (*also Parl*). (b) (*Chem*) solution. (c) (*Comm*) liquidation. (d) (*moral*) dissoluteness, dissipation.
disoluto adj dissolute, dissipated.
disolvente nm solvent.
disolver [2h; *ptp* **disuelto**] **1** vt (a) to dissolve; to melt (down).
  (b) *contract, marriage* to dissolve; (*Parl*) to dissolve; *meeting, riot etc* to break up.
  2 disolverse vr (a) to dissolve, melt.
  (b) (*Comm*) to be dissolved, go into liquidation; (*Parl*) to dissolve.
disonancia nf (a) (*Mus*) dissonance. (b) (*fig*) discord, disharmony; **hacer — con** to be out of harmony with.
disonante adj (a) (*Mus*) dissonant, discordant. (b) (*fig*) discordant.
disonar [1m] vi (a) (*Mus*) to be discordant, be out of harmony, be out of tune; to sound wrong.
  (b) (*fig*) to lack harmony; to disagree; **— con** to be out of keeping with, clash with.
dísono adj discordant.
dispar adj unlike, different, disparate.
disparada nf (*SAm*) sudden flight, stampede, wild rush; **ir a la —** to go at full speed; **irse a la —** to be off like a shot; **de una —** (*Arg*) in a trice, instantly; **tomar la —** (*Arg*) to beat it (*fam*).
disparadero nm trigger, trigger mechanism; **poner a uno en el —** to drive someone to distraction, make someone resort to violence.
disparado adj: **entrar —** to shoot in; **salir —** to shoot out, be off like a shot; **ir —** to go like mad, go hell for leather.
disparador 1 adj (*Mex*) lavish. **2** nm (*Mil etc*) trigger; (*Phot, Tech*) release; (*of watch*) escapement; **— atómico** aerosol, spray; **— de bombas** bomb release.
disparar [1a] **1** vt gun, rocket etc to shoot, fire; stone to throw, hurl, let fly (*contra* at); (*Sport*) ball to shoot (*a* at, *en* into).
  2 vi (a) to shoot, fire; **¡disparad!** fire!; **— a una distancia de 5 metros** to fire at a range of 5 metres.
  (b) =**disparatar.**
  (c) (*Mex*) to spend lavishly.
  3 dispararse vr (a) (*gun etc*) to go off; (*catch etc*) to be released.
  (b) (*person*) to rush off, dash away; see **disparado.**
  (c) (*horse etc*) to bolt.
  (d) (*emotionally*) to lose control, blow one's top (*fam*).
disparatadamente adv absurdly, nonsensically.
disparatado adj absurd, crazy, nonsensical.
disparatar [1a] vi to talk nonsense; to do something silly, blunder.
disparate nm (a) foolish remark, silly idea; absurd thing (to do); blunder, crass mistake; **—s** nonsense; **¡qué —!** what rubbish!, how absurd!; **hiciste un — protestando** it was silly of you to complain.
  (b) **reírse un —** to laugh a lot; **costar un —** to cost a fortune.
disparidad nf disparity.
disparo nm (a) shot; report; (*of rocket*) firing; (*Sport*) shot; **—s** shots, shooting, exchange of shots; **— inicial** (*of rocket*) blast-off.
  (b) (*Mech*) release, trip.
  (c) (*fig*) =**disparate.**
dispendio nm waste; extravagance.
dispendioso adj expensive.

dispensa nf exemption, excusal (*de* from); (*Eccl*) dispensation.
dispensable adj dispensable.
dispensación nf dispensation.
dispensador nm dispenser.
dispensar [1a] **1** vt (a) to dispense; to give out, distribute; *honour* to give, grant; *attention* to pay; *aid* to give; *welcome etc* to give, accord.
  (b) to excuse, exempt (*de* from); *person, fault etc* to excuse, pardon; **¡Vd dispense!, ¡dispénseme Vd!** I beg your pardon!, do forgive me!; **— a uno de una obligación** to excuse someone (from) an obligation; **me dispensaron la multa, me dispensaron del pago de la multa** they excused me (from payment of) the fine; **— a uno de + infin** to excuse someone from + *ger*, relieve someone of the need to + *infin*; **— que uno + subj** to excuse someone for + *ger*; **así el cuerpo queda dispensado de ese esfuerzo** thus the body is freed from that effort (*or* relieved of that effort).
  2 dispensarse vr: **no puedo dispensarme de + infin** I cannot help + *ger*, I cannot refrain from + *ger*.
dispensario nm dispensary; clinic; **— de alimentos** soup kitchen.
dispepsia nf dyspepsia.
dispéptico adj dyspeptic.
dispersar [1a] **1** vt to disperse, scatter; (*Mil*) to rout; *riot etc* to break up, disperse. **2 dispersarse** vr to disperse, scatter; to break up.
dispersión nf dispersion, dispersal; (*Phys*) dispersion.
disperso adj scattered; dispersed; sparse; (*Mil*) separated, straggling.
displicencia nf (a) peevishness, bad temper. (b) lack of enthusiasm; indifference.
displicente adj (a) disagreeable, peevish, bad-tempered; fretful. (b) unenthusiastic, lukewarm; indifferent.
disponer [2r] **1** vt (a) to arrange, dispose; to lay out; to put in order; to line up.
  (b) to prepare, get ready.
  (c) to order, decide; (*Med*) to order; **— que ... to** order that ..., arrange that ..., provide that ...; **la ley dispone que ...** the law provides that ...
  2 vi **— de** (a) to have, own; to have available, have at one's disposal; to make use of, avail oneself of; **dispone de 2 coches** he has 2 cars; **disponemos de poco tiempo** we have very little time (at our disposal).
  (b) to dispose of (as one wishes); **no puede — de esos bienes** she cannot dispose of those properties.
  3 disponerse vr: **— a + infin, — para + infin** to prepare to + *infin*, get ready to + *infin*.
disponibilidad nf (a) availability. (b) **—es** resources, means.
disponible adj available; on hand, spare.
disposición nf (a) arrangement, disposition; order; layout (*also Archit*).
  (b) order; provision, disposition; stipulation; **según las —es del código** according to the provisions of the statute; **última —** last will and testament.
  (c) **—es** preparations (*para* for); steps, measures; **tomar sus —es** to make one's preparations, take steps.
  (d) disposal; **a la — de** at the disposal of; **a la — de Vd, a su —** at your service; **tener algo a su —** to have something at one's disposal, have something available; **poner algo a la — de uno** to put something at someone's disposal.
  (e) position; **estar en — de + infin** to be in a position to + *infin*.
  (f) disposition, temperament; aptitude (*para* for); turn of mind; **— de ánimo** attitude of mind; **no tener — para** to have no aptitude for.
dispositivo nm device, mechanism; appliance; contrivance; gadget; **— de arranque** starting mechanism; **— de seguridad** safety catch, safety device.
dispuesto adj and ptp (a) arranged, disposed; **— según ciertos principios** arranged according to certain principles; **bien —** (*Archit*) well designed, well laid out.
  (b) (*person*) **bien —** well-disposed (*hacia* towards); **mal —** ill-disposed; (*Med*) ill, indisposed.
  (c) **estar — a + infin**, to be prepared to + *infin*; **estar poco — a + infin** to be reluctant to + *infin*.
  (d) bright, clever, go-ahead.
  (e) **bien —** handsome.
disputa nf dispute; argument; controversy; **los asuntos en —** the matters in dispute, the matters at issue; **sin —** undoubted(ly), beyond dispute.
disputable adj disputable, debatable.

disputador 1 *adj* disputatious. **2** *nm* disputant.
disputar [1a] **1** *vt* **(a)** *matter* to dispute, question, challenge; to debate.
    (b) *possession* to fight for, contend for.
    2 *vi* **(a)** to debate, argue (*con* with; *de, sobre* about).
    (b) — con uno por un premio to contend with someone for a prize.
    3 disputarse *vr*: **— un premio** to contend for a prize; **— la posesión de** to fight over (*or* for) the possession of.
disquero *adj* record (*attr*).
disquisición *nf* **(a)** disquisition. **(b) —es** comments on the side, marginal reflections.
distancia *nf* distance; (*of time etc*) interval; gap, difference, disparity; **— de despegue** (*Aer*) length of takeoff; **— focal** focal distance; **— de parada** braking distance; **— del suelo, — sobre el suelo** (*Aut etc*) height off the ground, clearance; **a — at** a distance; **a gran —, a larga —** long-distance (*attr*); **mantener a uno a —** to keep someone at a distance, keep someone at arm's length; **mantenerse a —** to keep one's distance, (*fig*) to hold back, remain aloof; **cada cierta —** every so often, at intervals; **guardar las —s** to keep one's distance, maintain proper (social) distinctions.
distanciado *adj* **(a)** remote (*de* from); widely separated, isolated.
    (b) (*fig*) far apart; **estamos algo —s** we are not particularly close; **ella está distanciada de su familia** she has grown apart from her family, she has no close ties with her family; **estamos —s en ideas** our ideas are poles apart.
distanciamiento *nm* **(a)** (*act*) spacing out. **(b)** (*state*) remoteness, isolation; (*fig*) distance, lack of close links (*entre* between).
distanciar [1b] **1** *vt* **(a)** *objects* to space out, separate; to put further apart.
    (b) *rival* to outdistance.
    (c) *persons* to cause a rift between.
    2 distanciarse *vr* **(a) — de un rival** to get ahead of a rival.
    (b) (*two persons*) to fall out, become estranged; to become (more) remote from each other.
distante *adj* **(a)** distant; far-off, remote; **— de 10 kms** 10 kms away. **(b)** (*fig*) distant.
distar [1a] *vi* **(a) dista 5 kms de aquí** it is 5 kms from here; **dista mucho** it's a long way away; **¿dista mucho?** is it far?, how far is it?
    (b) dista mucho de la verdad it's very far from the truth, it's a long way off the truth; **disto mucho de aprobarlo** I am far from approving of it.
distender [2g] *vt* to distend; to stretch.
distensión *nf* distension; stretching; (*Med*) strain; **— muscular** muscular strain.
dístico *nm* distich.
distinción *nf* **(a)** distinction, difference; distinctness, differentness; **a — de** unlike, in contrast to; **sin —** indiscriminately; all together, mixed; **obrar sin —** to act arbitrarily, act blindly; **sin — de personas** without respect to persons, without regard for the differences (of rank *etc*) between people; **sin — de edades** irrespective of differences of age; **hacer una — entre** to make a distinction between, differentiate between; **hacer — con uno** to show someone special consideration.
    (b) clarity, distinctness.
    (c) distinction, honour; **— honorífica** honour.
    (d) elegance, refinement.
distingo *nm* reservation; subtle distinction; (petty) objection; **aquí hago un —** here I must make a reservation.
distinguible *adj* distinguishable.
distinguido *adj* **(a)** distinguished; prominent, well-known. **(b)** elegant, refined; gentlemanly, ladylike, cultured.
distinguir [3d] **1** *vt* **(a)** to distinguish, discern, make out; to recognize.
    (b) to distinguish (*de* from, *entre* between), tell (*de* from); **no distingo cuál es el mío** I can't tell which is mine; **lo sabría — entre cien iguales** I would know mine among a hundred similar ones.
    (c) to distinguish, separate, single out; **aquí distingo dos aspectos** here I distinguish two aspects.
    (d) to mark, stamp, distinguish; **lo distinguen con una señal especial** they mark it with a special sign.
    (e) to single out, mark out (for special treatment); to honour, bestow an honour on; *friend etc* to have a special regard for; **me distingue con su amistad** he honours me with his friendship.
    2 *vi*: **no —** to have no critical sense, be undis-

criminating; **es un hombre que sabe —** he is a discerning (*or* discriminating) person.
    3 distinguirse *vr* **(a)** (*fig*) to be distinguished (*de* from), differ (*de* from).
    (b) (*fig*) to distinguish oneself.
distintivo 1 *adj* distinctive; *mark etc* distinguishing. **2** *nm* badge, emblem; (*fig*) distinguishing mark, characteristic, typical feature.
distinto *adj* **(a)** *outline etc* clear, distinct, plain; well-defined.
    (b) different, distinct (*a, de* from); **son muy —s** they are very different.
    (c) —s several, various; **hay distintas opiniones sobre eso** there are various opinions about that.
distorsión *nf* **(a)** (*Anat*) torsion, twisting. **(b)** (*Radio etc*) distortion.
distracción *nf* **(a)** distraction; amusement, relaxation; hobby, pastime; **es mi — favorita** it's my favourite amusement; **lo hace como — nada más** he only does it as a hobby.
    (b) absence of mind, forgetfulness; heedlessness; **por —** through sheer forgetfulness, absent-mindedly.
    (c) slip, blunder, oversight; **fue una — mía** it was an oversight on my part.
    (d) (*Fin*) embezzlement.
distraer [2p] **1** *vt* **(a)** to distract, divert, lead away (*de* from); (*morally*) to lead astray; **— a uno para robarle algo** to distract someone's attention so as to steal something from him; **— a uno de su dolor** to take someone's mind off his grief; **— a uno de su pensamiento** to divert someone from his train of thought.
    (b) to amuse, relax, entertain; **la música me distrae** music relaxes me, I find music relaxing.
    (c) (*Fin*) to embezzle, divert to one's own use.
    2 *vi* to be relaxing; **el pescar distrae** fishing is a relaxation.
    3 distraerse *vr* **(a)** to amuse oneself, entertain oneself; to relax; **me distraigo pescando** I relax when I fish, I find fishing relaxing; **no me opongo a que se distraiga honestamente** I don't mind her having a little innocent amusement.
    (b) to be (*or* get) absent-minded; to cease to pay attention; **me distraje un momento** I allowed my attention to wander for a moment; **— de** to forget about, be inattentive to.
distraídamente *adv* **(a)** absent-mindedly; unobservantly; (*pej*) inattentively; slackly. **(b)** idly, casually.
distraído 1 *adj* **(a)** *person's character* absent-minded; vague, dreamy, unpractical; unobservant; (*pej*) inattentive; slack, lackadaisical; **iba yo algo —** I was rather absorbed in other things, I was not taking much notice.
    (b) *look, manner etc* absent-minded; idle, casual; **con aire —** idly, casually, in a casual manner; **me miró distraída** she gave me a casual glance.
    (c) *game etc* amusing, entertaining.
    (d) *life* dissolute.
    (e) (*Chi, Mex*) slovenly, untidy, shabby.
    2 *nm*: **hacerse el —** to pretend not to notice; to pretend not to be interested.
distribución *nf* **(a)** (*act*) distribution; giving-out; sending out; (*Post*) sorting; delivery; **— de premios** prize giving.
    (b) (*statistical etc*) distribution; incidence; **la — de los impuestos** the incidence of taxes.
    (c) (*state*) distribution, arrangement; (*Archit*) layout, ground plan.
    (d) (*Pol*) deal; **Nueva D—** New Deal; **D— Equitativa** Fair Deal (*esp US Pol*).
    (e) (*Mech*) timing gears.
distribuido *adj*: **una casa bien distribuida** a well-designed house.
distribuidor *nm* **(a)** (*person*) distributor; (*Post*) sorter; (*Comm*) dealer, agent, stockist; **su — habitual** your regular dealer.
    (b) — automático (automatic) vending machine, slot machine.
    (c) (*Aut*) distributor.
distribuidora *nf* (*Tech*) spreader.
distribuir [3g] *vt* **(a)** to distribute; to hand out; to give out; to send out, send round; *letters* to sort; *letters, milk etc* to deliver; *duties etc* to allocate; *prizes* to give out, award; (*Tech*) to spread; *cargo etc* to stow, arrange; *weight* to distribute (equally *etc*).
    (b) (*Archit*) to design, plan, lay out.
distributivo *adj* distributive.
distrito *nm* district, region, zone; administrative area; (*Law*) circuit; **— electoral** constituency, ward, electoral area; precinct (*US*); **— postal** postal district.

distrofia *nf:* — **muscular** (progressive) muscular dystrophy.

disturbio *nm* (a) disturbance; riot, commotion; los —s the disturbances, the troubles. (b) (*Tech*) disturbance; — **aerodinámico** (*Aer*) wash, slipstream.

disuadir [3a] *vt* to dissuade, deter, discourage (*de* from); — **a uno de** + *infin* to dissuade someone from + *ger*.

disuasión *nf* dissuasion; (*Mil etc*) deterrent.

disuasivo *adj* discouraging; dissuasive; (*Mil*) deterrent.

disuasorio *adj* (*Mil*) deterrent; *see* **fuerza**.

disyuntiva *nf* dilemma; crisis.

disyuntivo *adj* disjunctive.

disyuntor *nm* (*Elec*) circuit breaker.

dita[1] *nf* (a) surety; security, bond. (b) (*Andalusia*) loan at a high rate of interest; (*SAm*) small debt.

dita[2] *nf* (PR) dish, cup, pot.

ditirambo *nm* dithyramb.

diurético 1 *adj* diuretic. **2** *nm* diuretic.

diurno *adj* diurnal, day (*attr*).

diva *nf* prima donna.

divagación *nf* digression; —es wanderings, ramblings.

divagador *adj* rambling, discursive.

divagar [1h] *vi* to digress; to wander, ramble; ¡no —! get on with it!, come to the point!

diván *nm* divan.

divergencia *nf* divergence.

divergente *adj* divergent; contrary, opposite.

divergir [3c] *vi* (a) to diverge. (b) (*of views etc*) to differ, be opposed, clash; (*of persons*) to differ, disagree.

diversidad *nf* diversity, variety.

diversificación *nf* diversification.

diversificar [1g] *vt* to diversify.

diversión *nf* (a) amusement, entertainment; recreation; hobby, pastime; —es de salón parlour games, indoor games. (b) (*Mil*) diversion.

diverso *adj* **1** (a) diverse. (b) different (*de* from); other; **se trata de — asunto** it's about a different (*or* another) matter. (c) —s several, various; some; sundry; **está en —s libros** it figures in several books. **2** —s *nmpl* (*Comm*) sundries, miscellaneous items.

divertido *adj* (a) entertaining, amusing; funny; enjoyable; *party etc* gay, merry; *joke* funny; *person* funny, amusing, witty. (b) (*iro*) **estar** — to be in for a good time; ¡**estamos** —s! how terribly amusing! (I don't think); **la que se case con él estará divertida** the girl who marries him is much to be pitied. (c) (*SAm*) **estar** — to be tight.

divertimiento *nm* (a) amusement, entertainment. (b) diversion (*also Mil*).

divertir [3i] **1** *vt* (a) to amuse, entertain. (b) to divert, distract (the attention of). **2 divertirse** *vr* to amuse oneself; to have a good time; **la juventud moderna no quiere más que** — all modern youth wants to do is have a good time; — **haciendo algo** to amuse oneself doing something; — **con el amor de una** to toy with someone's affections; ¡**que se diviertan!** have a good time!

dividendo *nm* dividend.

dividir [3a] *vt* to divide (up); to split (up), separate; to share out, distribute; — **12 entre 4** to divide 12 among 4; — **12 por 4** (*Math*) to divide 12 by 4; — **algo en 5 partes** to divide something into 5 parts; — **algo por mitad** to divide something into two, halve something; — **algo por la mitad** to divide something down the middle.

divieso *nm* (*Med*) boil.

divinamente *adv* divinely (*also fig*).

divinidad *nf* (a) divinity. (b) divinity; godhead; deity; — **marina** sea god; — **pagana** pagan god(dess), pagan divinity; **la D**— the Deity. (c) (*fig*) goddess, beauty, beautiful woman; precious thing, lovely object.

divinizar [1f] *vt* to deify; (*fig*) to exalt, extol.

divino *adj* divine (*also fig*).

divisa *nf* (a) emblem, badge; (*Her*) device, motto. (b) —s (*Fin*) foreign exchange; **control de —s** exchange control.

divisar [1a] *vt* to make out, spy, descry.

divisible *adj* divisible.

división *nf* (*Math, Mil etc*) division; (*Pol: of party*) split; (*of country*) partition.

divisional *adj* (*Mil*) divisional.

divisivo *adj* divisive.

divisor *nm* (*Math*) divisor; **máximo común** — highest common factor.

divisoria *nf* dividing line; (*Geog*) divide; — **de aguas** watershed; — **continental** continental divide.

divisorio *adj* dividing; divisive; **línea divisoria de las aguas** watershed.

divorciado 1 *adj* (a) divorced. (b) (*fig*) **las opiniones están divorciadas** opinions are divided. **2** *nm*, **divorciada** *nf* divorcee.

divorciar [1b] **1** *vt* (a) to divorce. (b) (*fig*) to divorce, separate (*de* from). **2 divorciarse** to get divorced, get a divorce (*de* from).

divorcio *nm* (a) divorce. (b) (*fig*) separation; division, split; **existe un — entre A y B** there is a wide division between A and B.

divulgación *nf* spreading, circulation; popularizing; (*pej*) disclosure.

divulgar [1h] **1** *vt* to spread, circulate, publish; to popularize; (*pej*) to divulge, disclose, let out. **2 divulgarse** (*secret*) to leak out; (*rumour etc*) to get about, become known.

diz (*arch form of* **dice**; *SAm*): — **que**... they say that ..., it is said that ...

dobladillar [1a] *vt* to hem.

dobladillo *nm* hem; (*of trousers*) turn-up(s), cuff(s) (US).

doblado *adj* (a) (*Sew etc*) double; doubled over, folded. (b) (*Anat*) stocky, thickset. (c) *surface* rough. (d) (*fig*) sly, deceitful.

dobladura *nf* fold, crease.

doblaje *nm* (*Cine*) dubbing.

doblamiento *nm* folding, creasing.

doblar [1a] **1** *vt* (a) (*general sense*) to double; — **el sueldo a uno** to double someone's salary; **te doblo la edad** I'm twice your age. (b) *material, paper etc* to fold (up, over), crease; *hem* to turn up; *page* to turn down; *head, knee, pipe etc* to bend; (*Mex*) to shoot down; — **a uno a palos** to give someone a beating. (c) *corner* to turn, round, go round; *cape* (*Naut*) to round; (*Aut: gall*) to overtake. (d) *film* to dub. (e) (*Theat*) **dos papeles** to take two parts; — **a uno** to understudy (for) someone. (f) (*Bridge*) to double; *stake, money* (*in quiz game*) to double. **2** *vi* (a) to turn (*a la izquierda* to the left). (b) (*of bell*) to toll (*a muerto, por uno* for a death). (c) (*Theat etc*) to stand in (*a* for). **3 doblarse** *vr* (a) (*in quantity etc*) to double. (b) to fold (up), crease; to bend, buckle. (c) (*fig*) to give in, yield (*a* to).

doble 1 *adj* (a) double; *door, flower, meaning etc* double; *control, nationality etc* dual; *bottom* false; *material* double, extra thick; *string* thick, stout; — **o nada** double or quits. (b) (*fig*) insincere; two-faced, deceitful. **2** *nm* (a) double (quantity); **el** — twice the quantity, twice the amount; twice as much; **hoy gana el** — today he earns double, todays he earns twice as much; **su sueldo es el — del mío** his salary is twice mine; **un — de whiskey** a double whisky; **un — de cerveza** a big glass of beer. (b) (*Sew etc*) fold, crease. (c) (*of bell*) toll, tolling; knell. (d) —s (*Tennis*) doubles; —s (de) **damas** ladies' doubles; —s de **caballeros**, —s **masculinos** men's doubles; —s **mixtos** mixed doubles. (e) (*Bridge*) double; — **de castigo** penalty double; — **de llamada** asking double. **3** *nmf* (*Cine*) double, stand-in; **ser el — de uno** (*fig*) to be someone's double.

doblegar [1h] **1** *vt* (a) to fold, crease; to bend. (b) *weapon* to brandish. (c) (*fig*) to persuade, sway; — **a uno** to force someone to abandon his course (*or* change his ways etc), make someone give in. **2 doblegarse** *vr* (*fig*) to yield, give in.

doblemente *adv* (a) doubly. (b) insincerely; deceitfully.

doblez 1 *nm* fold, crease; hem; (*of trousers*) turn-up(s), cuff(s) (US). **2** *nf* insincerity; double-dealing, deceitfulness, duplicity.

doblón *nm* (*Hist*) doubloon; — **de a ocho** piece of eight.

dócar *nm* dogcart.

doce 1 *adj* twelve; (*date*) twelfth; **las** — twelve o'clock. **2** *nm* twelve.

docena *nf* dozen; — **del fraile** baker's dozen; **a —s** by the dozen, in great numbers; **por —(s)** by the dozen, in dozens.

doceno *adj* twelfth.

docente adj educational; teaching (attr); **centro —** teaching institution; **personal —** teaching staff.

dócil adj docile; obedient; gentle, mild.

docilidad nf docility; obedience; gentleness; mildness.

dócilmente adv in a docile way; obediently; gently, mildly.

doctamente adv learnedly.

docto 1 adj learned, erudite; scholarly. **2** nm scholar; learned person.

doctor nm (Med, Univ) doctor; (Eccl) father, saint; **— en derecho** doctor of laws; **—es tiene la Iglesia** there are plenty of people well able to pass an opinion (on that).

doctora nf (Med) woman doctor; (Univ) doctor; (fam) bluestocking.

doctorado nm doctorate.

doctoral adj doctoral.

doctorar [1a] **1** vt to confer a doctor's degree on. **2 doctorarse** vr to take one's doctor's degree (or doctorate).

doctrina nf doctrine; learning; teaching; (School) catechism, religious instruction; **no saber la —** to know nothing at all.

doctrinal adj doctrinal.

doctrinar [1a] vt to teach.

doctrinario 1 adj doctrinaire. **2** nm, **doctrinaria** nf doctrinaire.

doctrinero nm (SAm) parish priest (among Indians).

documentación nf (a) documentation. (b) papers, documents; **— del barco** ship's papers; **la —, por favor** your papers, please.

documental 1 adj documentary. **2** nm (Cine etc) documentary.

documentar [1a] vt to document, establish with documentary evidence.

documento nm document; paper; record; certificate; (Law) exhibit; **—s del coche** papers relating to a car; **— justificativo** voucher, certificate; supporting document; **— nacional de identidad** identity card; **— secretísimo** top-secret document; **los —s, por favor** your papers, please.

dodo nm, **dodó** nm dodo.

dogal nm halter; hangman's noose; **estar con el — al cuello** (or **a la garganta**) to be in an awful jam.

dogma nm dogma.

dogmáticamente adv dogmatically.

dogmático adj dogmatic.

dogmatismo nm dogmatism.

dogmatizador nm dogmatist.

dogmatizar [1f] vi to dogmatize.

dogo nm (angl) bulldog.

doguillo nm, **doguino** nm small bulldog.

dola nf (fam)=**pídola**.

dolamas nfpl, **dolames** nfpl (Vet) hidden defects (of a horse); (SAm) chronic complaint, constant indisposition.

dólar nm dollar.

dolencia nf ailment, complaint, affliction; ache; (fig) ailment, ill; **la — de la economía** the ills of the economy.

doler [2i] **1** vti (a) (Med) to hurt, pain; to ache; **me duele el brazo** my arm hurts, my arm aches; **me duele el estómago** I have a pain in my stomach, my stomach aches, I've got stomach ache; **¿dónde te duele?** where does it hurt (you)?; **¿duele mucho?** does it hurt much?; **no me ha dolido nada** it didn't hurt at all.

(b) (fig) to grieve, distress; **le duele aún la pérdida** the loss still grieves him, he still feels the loss; **no me duele el dinero** I don't mind about the money, the money doesn't bother me; **a cualquiera le dolería verlo** it would grieve anyone to see it; **¡ahí (le) duele!** that's the whole point!, you've put your finger on it!

2 dolerse vr (a) to grieve (de about, for), feel sorry (de about, for); **— de** to regret (of); **— person** to feel sorry for, pity; **¡duélete de mí!** pity me!; show some sympathy for me!; **se duele de que no le visitéis** he resents the fact that you don't go to see him; **— de los pecados** to repent (of) one's sins.

(b) to complain; to moan, groan; **lo sufre todo sin —** he puts up with everything without complaining.

doliente 1 adj (a) (Med) suffering, ill; aching.

(b) sad, sorrowful; (in bereavement) grieving, mourning; **la familia —** the bereaved family, the sorrowing relatives.

2 nmf (a) (Med) sufferer, sick person; patient.

(b) bereaved person; (at funeral) mourner.

dolo nm fraud, deceit; **sin —** openly, honestly.

dolomita nf dolomite.

dolor nm (a) pain; ache; pang; **— de cabeza** headache; **con — de mi corazón** with an ache in my heart; **— de estómago** stomach ache; **— de muelas** toothache; **— de oídos** earache; **—es del parto** labour pains; **sordo** dull ache; **estar con mucho —, tener mucho —** to be in great pain; **estar con —es** (woman) to feel the labour pains beginning.

(b) (fig) grief, sorrow; affliction, distress; regret; **le causa mucho —** it causes him great distress, it is a great grief to him; **con — te lo digo** it grieves me to say it to you; **es un —** it's a shame, it's a pity.

dolorido adj (a) (Med) sore, tender, aching; **la parte dolorida** the part which hurts, the part where the pain is.

(b) (fig) person distressed; grieving, grief-stricken.

(c) tone plaintive, sad, pained.

dolorosa nf (hum) bill, check (US) (in a restaurant).

dolorosamente adv (a) (Med) painfully. (b) (fig) painfully, grievously, distressingly.

doloroso adj (a) (Med) painful. (b) (fig) painful, grievous, distressing.

doloso adj fraudulent, deceitful.

doma nf=**domadura**.

domable adj tamable; controllable.

domador nm, **domadora** nf trainer; tamer; **— de caballos** horse-breaker.

domadura nf (a) taming; training; breaking-in. (b) (fig) mastering, controlling.

domar [1a] vt (a) to tame; to train; horse etc to break in. (b) (fig) to master, control; to repress.

domeñar [1a] vt=**domar**.

domesticación nf domestication; taming.

domesticado adj tame; pet; **un tejón —** a tame badger, a pet badger.

domesticar [1g] **1** vt to tame, domesticate; to make a pet of. **2 domesticarse** vr to become tame, become domesticated.

domesticidad nf (a) domesticity, homeliness; homely atmosphere.

(b) (of animal) (state of being in) captivity; **el lobo no vive bien en —** the wolf does not live happily in captivity, the wolf does not take to captivity.

doméstico 1 adj (a) life etc domestic; home (attr), family (attr); **economía doméstica** home economy, housekeeping, home economics (US); **gastos —s** household expenses, housekeeping expenditure; **faenas domésticas** household jobs.

(b) animal tame, pet.

2 nm, **doméstica** nf servant, domestic.

Domiciano m Dcmitian.

domiciliar [1b] **1** vt (a) to domicile, establish; to house. (b) (Mex) letter to address. **2 domiciliarse** vr to establish oneself, take up (one's) residence.

domiciliario adj domiciliary; house (attr); **arresto —** house arrest.

domicilio nm home; (in official parlance) domicile, residence, abode; **— particular** private residence; **— social** (Comm) head office; **a —** (Sport) at home; **servicio a —** delivery service; **sin — fijo** of no fixed abode.

dominación nf (a) domination; dominance; rule, sway. (b) (Mil) high ground, commanding position.

dominador adj (a) dominating, controlling. (b) character domineering.

dominante adj (a) dominant (also Mus); predominant; **la tendencia —** the dominant tendency, the ruling tendency; **el viento —** the prevailing wind; **la consideración —** the overriding consideration.

(b) character domineering; masterful; love etc possessive.

dominar [1a] **1** vt (a) to dominate; to rule (over), hold sway over; person to overpower; boat, horse etc to control, bring under control; epidemic, fire to check, bring under control; revolt to put down, suppress, subdue; passion to control, master; grief etc to get over; **le domina la envidia** he is ruled by envy, his ruling passion is envy.

(b) language to know well, be fluent in, have a good command of; **domina 7 idiomas** he knows 7 languages well.

(c) (of building etc) to dominate, tower above (or over), look down on.

2 vi (of building etc) to dominate; (of colour, feature etc) to stand out; (of opinion, wind, tendency etc) to predominate, prevail.

3 dominarse vr to control oneself.

dómine nm (Hist) schoolmaster; (hum) pedant.

domingo nm Sunday; **D— de Cuasimodo** Low Sunday; **D— de Ramos** Palm Sunday; **D— de Resurrección** Easter Sunday; **hacer —** to take a day off, make a day into a holiday.

dominguejo nm (a) (Chi, Per) scarecrow. (b) (Ven) poor devil.

dominguero adj Sunday (attr).

Dominica f Dominica.

dominical adj Sunday (attr); **periódico —** Sunday newspaper.

dominicanismo nm word (or phrase etc) peculiar to the Dominican Republic.

dominicano 1 adj (Eccl and Pol) Dominican. **2** nm (Eccl) Dominican. **3** nm, **dominicana** nf (Pol) Dominican.

dominico nm (Eccl), **domínico** nm (SAm) Dominican.

dominio nm (a) (dominion; power, sway, authority (sobre over); ascendancy, supremacy; hold, grip (de on); (of language) command (de of), fluency (de in); **— público** public property, national property; **ser del — público** (of news etc) to be widely known, be common knowledge; **— de** (or **sobre**) **sí mismo** self-control.

(b) (land) domain; (Pol) dominion.

dominó nm domino; **un —** a domino; a set of dominoes; **juego de —** dominoes.

don[1] nm courtesy title equivalent to Mr, used before Christian name: on envelopes = Esquire; in other cases not directly translated, eg **soy alumno de don Ramón** I am one of Menéndez Pidal's students; **el rey don Pedro** King Peter; see also **Juan.**

don[2] nm (a) gift; present.

(b) (in fairy tale) wish; **el hada le concedió 3 —es** the fairy gave him 3 wishes.

(c) (fig) gift; knack; aptitude, talent (de for); **tiene un — especial** he has a special gift; **— de acierto** happy knack (of doing things well); intuition; **— de gentes** personal charm, human touch; **tener — de gentes** to have a way with people, have the human touch, know how to handle people; **— de lenguas** gift for languages; **— de mando** (qualities of) leadership, (Mil) generalship; **— de palabra** gift of the gab (fam).

dona nf (Chi) gift; legacy; **—s** (Mex) trousseau.

donación nf donation; (Law) gift.

donada nf lay sister.

donado nm lay brother.

donador nm, **donadora** nf donor; **— de sangre** blood donor.

donaire nm (a) charm, wit, cleverness. (b) grace(fulness); elegance. (c) (un —) witticism; **tiene muchos —s** he's terribly witty.

donante nmf donor; **— de sangre** blood donor.

donar [1a] vt to donate; to grant, bestow.

donativo nm donation, contribution.

doncel nm (Hist) page; young nobleman, young squire.

doncella nf (a) maid, lady's maid, maidservant. (b) virgin; (Hist and lit) maid, maiden.

doncellez nf (a) (state) virginity, maidenhood. (b) (Anat) maidenhead.

donde 1 rel adv (a) where; (fig) wherein; in which; **el sitio — lo encontré** the place where I found it; **a — to where,** to which; **fue a — estaban** he went to (the place) where they were; **es a — vamos nosotros** that's where we're going; **de — from where;** from which, out of which; **el país de — vienen the** country they come from; **la caja de — lo sacó** the box from which he took it, the box he took it out of; **en — where;** in which; **por — through which;** (fig) whereby; **no hay por — cogerle** there's no way to catch him, he has no weak spots.

(b) (Chi) as, since.

2 prep (a) **es allí — el farol** it's where the lamppost is, it's over there by the lamppost.

(b) (SAm) at the house (etc) of; **están cenando — mi madre** they are dining at my mother's (house).

dónde interrog adv (a) where?; **¿ — lo dejaste?** where did you leave it?; **¿a — vás?** where are you going (to)?; **¿de — vienes?** where have you come from?; **¿en —?** where?; **¿por —?** where?, whereabouts?; **which way?;** why?, for what reason?; **¿por — se va al estadio?** which way to the stadium?, how do I get to the stadium?

(b) (indirect) where; **no sé — lo puse** I don't know where I put it.

(c) (SAm) how?

dondequiera 1 adv anywhere; **por — everywhere,** all over the place. **2** conj anywhere, wherever; **— que lo busques** wherever you look for it.

donosamente adv (lit) wittily, amusingly.

donoso adj (lit) witty, amusing; (iro) fine; **¡donosa idea!** (iro) highly amusing I'm sure!

donostiarra 1 adj of San Sebastián. **2** nmf native (or inhabitant) of San Sebastián; **los —s** the people of San Sebastián.

Don Quijote m Don Quixote.

doña nf courtesy title, used before Christian names; not translated.

dopar [1a] vt (angl) to dope, drug.

doping ['dopin] nm (angl) doping, drugging.

dopingar [1h] vt (angl) to dope, drug.

doquier adv (arch or lit) = **dondequiera; por — all** over, everywhere; all over the place.

dorado 1 adj golden; (Tech) gilt, gilded; gold-plated. **2** nm (a) (Tech) gilding, gilt. (b) (Fish) dorado; goldfish.

doradura nf gilding.

dorar [1a] vt (a) (Tech) to gild; (Cook) to brown, cook lightly. (b) (fig) to gild; to palliate, make more palatable, put a gloss on; **— la píldora** to gild the pill.

dormida nf (SAm) sleep.

dormidera nf (a) (opium) poppy. (b) **tener buenas —s** to get off to sleep easily.

dormidero nm (SAm: of cattle) sleeping place; (of hens) roost.

dormilón 1 adj sleepy; much given to sleeping. **2** nm, **dormilona** nf sleepyhead; (pej) sleepy sort, lazy sort, lie-a-bed. **3 dormilona** nf deckchair, reclining chair.

dormir [3k] **1** vt (a) **— la siesta** to have one's afternoon nap, have a doze.

(b) **—la** (fam) to sleep it off; **— la mona** (fam) to sleep off a hangover.

(c) **— a uno** to send someone to sleep, make someone go to sleep; **Delius me duerme de maravilla** Delius is marvellous for sending me to sleep.

2 vi to sleep; to stay overnight, spend the night; **— como un lirón** (or **tronco, poste** etc) to sleep like a log; **— como un santo** (or **bendito**) to sleep peacefully, be fast asleep; **— a pierna suelta** (or **tendida**) to sleep soundly, sleep the sleep of the just; **— con una** to sleep with someone; **quedarse dormido** to go to sleep, drop off; **durmiendo se me pasó la hora** the time went by while I slept, I overslept.

3 dormirse vr (a) to go to sleep, fall asleep.

(b) (limb) to go to sleep, get numb.

dormirela nf (fam) nap, snooze.

dormirlas nm hide-and-seek.

dormitar [1a] vi to doze, snooze.

dormitorio nm bedroom; (of school etc) dormitory.

dornillo nm wooden bowl; (Agr) small trough.

Dorotea f Dorothy.

dorsal adj dorsal; back (attr).

dorso nm back (also fig); **escribir algo al — to** write something on the back; **"véase al —"** "see other side"; **"please turn over"** (PTO).

dos 1 adj (a) two; (date) second; **las — two** o'clock; **a — two against two;** **— por — son 4** two times two makes 4; **a cada — por tres** in rapid succession, continually; intermittently; **de — en — in** twos, two by two; **cortar algo en — to** cut something in(to) two; **como ése no hay —** they don't come any better than that.

(b) **los — the** two of them, both (of them); **es para los — it's** for both of you; **para entre los — (strictly)** between you and me.

2 nm two; **estamos a — (Tennis)** the score is deuce; **en un — por tres** in no time at all.

doscientos adj two hundred.

dosel nm canopy.

doselera nf valance.

dosificación nf dosage.

dosificar [1g] vt medicine to measure out, put up in doses; ingredients to measure out, mix in proportion.

dosis nf, pl **dosis** (a) dose; dosage, amount, quantity; injection, shot. (b) (fig) dose; admixture; **con buena — de vanidad** with a good proportion of vanity.

dos piezas nm, pl **dos piezas** two-piece.

dotación nf (a) (act, money) endowment.

(b) staff, establishment, personnel; (Naut) crew, complement; **una — del parque de bomberos** a squad of firemen; **la — es insuficiente** the staff is inadequate, we are under-staffed.

dotado adj (a) person gifted; **los niños excepcionalmente —s** exceptionally gifted children; **bien — highly** talented, well-equipped for life.

(b) **— de** person endowed with; machine etc equipped with, fitted with, possessing.

dotar [1a] vt (a) woman to endow (con with), give a dowry to; **la dotó muy bien** he gave her a good dowry; **la dotó con** (or **en**) **un millón** he gave her a million as a dowry.

(b) (fig) to endow (con, de with); **la naturaleza le dotó de buenas cualidades** nature endowed him with good qualities.

(c) foundation etc to endow; to provide funds for, assign money to; to fix a salary for; to provide staff (etc) for; **son necesarias X pesetas para — estos**

puestos de enseñanza X pesetas are needed to pay for these teaching posts; **la Academia ha dotado 2 premios** the Academy has established (or set aside funds for) 2 prizes.

(d) (*Mech etc*) to supply, fit, provide (*de* with); **un avión de todos los adelantos modernos** to equip a plane with all the latest devices.

(e) *ship etc* to man (*de* with); *laboratory, office etc* to staff (*de* with).

dote *n gen f* (a) dowry, marriage portion; **con un millón de —** with a dowry of a million.

(b) (*fig*) **—s** gifts, talents, aptitude; **tiene excelentes —s** she has great gifts; **—s de adherencia** (*Aut*) road-holding qualities; **—s de mando** (qualities of) leadership.

doy *see* **dar**.

dozavo 1 *adj* twelfth. **2** *nm* twelfth (part); **en —** (*Typ*) in duodecimo.

dracma *nf* (a) (*Pharm*) drachm, dram. (b) (*coin*) drachma.

draconiano *adj* draconian.

draga *nf* dredge; (*boat*) dredger.

dragado *nm* dredging.

dragaminas *nm, pl* **dragaminas** minesweeper.

dragar [1h] *vt* to dredge; *mines* to sweep.

dragomán *nm* dragoman.

dragón *nm* (a) dragon. (b) (*Mil*) dragoon. (c) (*Bot*) snapdragon.

dragona *nf* (a) (*Mil*) shoulder knot. (b) (*Chi, Mex, Per*) guard (*of sword*). (c) (*Mex*) hooded cloak.

dragoncillo *nm* (*Bot*) tarragon.

dragonear [1a] **1** *vt* (*RPl*) to court, woo. **2** *vi* (*SAm*) to boast, brag; **— de** to boast of being; (*Chi*) to pretend to be, pass oneself off as.

drama *nm* drama (*also fig*).

dramática *nf* drama, dramatic art.

dramáticamente *adv* dramatically.

dramático *adj* **1** dramatic (*also fig*). **2** *nm* dramatist; (tragic) actor.

dramatizar [1f] *vt* to dramatize.

dramaturgo *nm* dramatist, playwright.

drásticamente *adv* drastically.

drasticidad *nf* drastic nature, drastic character.

drástico *adj* drastic.

drenaje *nm* (*esp Agr, Med*) drainage.

drenar [1a] *vt* to drain.

Dresde Dresden.

dribl(e)ar [1a] *vti* (*Sport: angl*) to dribble; **— a uno** to dribble past someone.

drible *nm* (*Sport: angl*) dribble.

dril *nm* duck, drill.

driza *nf* halyard.

droga *nf* (a) (*Med, Pharm*) drug; medicine; (*pej*) drug; (*Horseracing etc*) dope; **— milagrosa** wonder drug; **el peligro de las —s** the drug menace.

(b) (*fam*) trick, hoax; stratagem; fib.

(c) (*fam*) nuisance; **es (mucha) —** it's a dreadful nuisance.

(d) (*Arg, Chi, Mex, Per*) debt; bad debt; **hacer —** to refuse to pay up.

(e) (*Cu*) drug on the market, unsaleable article.

(f) (*CAm, Cu*) **mandar a uno a la —** to tell someone to go to hell.

drogadicto *nm*, **drogadicta** *nf* (*CAm, Mex*) drug addict.

drogado *nm* (*Sport*) doping.

drogar [1h] **1** *vt* to drug; (*Sport*) to dope. **2 drogarse** *vr* to drug oneself, take drugs.

droguería *nf* druggist's (shop).

droguero *nm* (a) druggist. (b) (*fam*) cheat, crook; (*Arg, Chi, Mex, Per*) slow payer, defaulter.

droguista *nm* = **droguero**.

drogui *nm* (*RPl*) (a) liquor, alcohol. (b) drunkard.

dromedario *nm* dromedary.

dromeo *nm* emu.

druida *nm* druid.

dual *adj* dual (*also Gram*).

dualidad *nf* (a) duality. (b) (*Chi*) tied vote, indecisive election.

dualismo *nm* dualism.

dubletón *nm* (*Bridge: angl*) doubleton.

Dublín Dublin.

ducado *nm* (a) duchy, dukedom. (b) (*Fin*) ducat.

ducal *adj* ducal.

duco *nm* thick paint, lacquer; **pintar al —** to lacquer, spray (with paint).

ducentésimo *adj* two hundredth.

dúctil *adj* (a) ductile, soft. (b) (*fig*) flexible, yielding; easy to handle.

ductilidad *nf* ductility, softness.

ducha *nf* shower, shower bath; (*Med*) douche; **tomarse una —** to have a shower, shower oneself;

dar una — de agua fría a un proyecto (*fig*) to pour cold water on a plan.

duchar [1a] **1** *vt* (*Med*) to douche. **2 ducharse** *vr* to have a shower, shower oneself.

ducho *adj*: **— en** well versed in, experienced in; skilled at, adept at.

duda *nf* doubt; misgiving; indecision; suspense; **fuera de toda —** beyond all doubt; **sin —** no doubt, doubtless; undoubtedly; **¡sin —!** of course!; **le acometieron —s** he was assailed by doubts, he began to have doubts; **ello constituye una — importante** this is a big question mark, it's a big if; **no cabe —** there is no doubt about it; **no cabe — de que . . .** there can be no doubt that . . .; **¿qué cabe** (or **coge**)? is something bothering you?; **no le quepa —** make no mistake about it, get this straight; **para desvanecer toda —** in order to dispel all uncertainty; **queda la — en pie** the doubt remains; **surge una —** a question arises; **estar en —** to be in doubt; **poner algo en —** to cast doubt on something, call something in question.

dudar [1a] **1** *vt* to doubt; **no lo dudo** I don't doubt it.

2 *vi* to doubt, be in doubt; **— acerca de** to be uncertain about; **— de** to doubt; to question; to mistrust; **no dudo de su talento** I don't question his talent; **— en + infin** to hesitate to + *infin*; **— entre A y B** to hesitate between A and B; **— que . . ., — si . . .** to doubt whether; **dudo que sea capaz de hacerlo** I doubt whether he will be capable of doing it.

dudosamente *adv* doubtfully, uncertainly; **— eficaz** of doubtful efficacy.

dudoso *adj* (a) doubtful, dubious, uncertain; *point* debatable; *result* unclear, indecisive.

(b) hesitant, undecided.

(c) (*of moral quality*) dubious, suspect.

duela *nf* stave.

duelista *nm* duellist.

duelo¹ *nm* (*Mil*) duel; **batirse en —** to fight a duel.

duelo² *nm* (a) grief, sorrow; bereavement; **—s** sufferings, hardships; **sin —** unrestrainedly; **gastar sin —** to spend lavishly; **pegar a uno sin —** to beat someone mercilessly.

(b) (*period, dress etc*) mourning; (*persons*) mourners, party of mourners.

duende *nm* (a) imp, goblin, elf; ghost; mischievous child; prankster. (b) **tener —** to have it, to have magic, be out of this world.

duendecillo *nm* (*Aer etc*) gremlin (*sl*), jinx (*US fam*).

dueña *nf* (a) owner, proprietress; landlady; **— de la casa** mistress of the house, lady of the house.

(b) (*Hist*) lady; matron; duenna, companion, governess.

(c) (*fig*) mistress; **la marina era — de los mares** the navy was mistress of the seas.

dueño *nm* owner, proprietor; landlord; master; employer; **organismo de los —s** (*Comm etc*) employers' organization; **ser — de** to own, be the owner of, possess; **ser — del baile, ser — de la situación** to be the master of the situation, have the situation in hand; **ser — de sí mismo** to be self-possessed, have self-control; **ser muy — de sí** to be very much in control of oneself; **es Vd muy —, es Vd — de mi casa** you're very welcome; **ser — de + infin** to be free to + *infin*; **cambiar de —** to change hands; **hacerse — de** to take over, take possession of; to acquire.

duermevela *nf* (*fam*) nap, snooze.

Duero *m* Douro.

dula *nf* common land, common pasture.

dulcamara *nf* nightshade.

dulce 1 *adj* (in most senses) sweet; *water* fresh; *metal* soft; *voice, sound* soft; *character* gentle, sweet, mild; *climate* mild; **un instrumento —** a sweet-sounding instrument; a mellow instrument; **con el acento — del país** with the soft accent of the region; **más — que el almíbar** (or *azúcar etc*) sweeter than honey.

2 *adv* gently, softly; **habla muy —** she speaks very softly.

3 *nm* (a) sweet, candy (*US*); **—s** sweets; **— de almíbar** preserved fruit; **melocotón en —** preserved peaches; **a nadie le amarga un —** nobody says no to a bit of luck.

(b) (*CAm, Col, Ven*) brown sugar.

dulcémele *nm* dulcimer.

dulcemente *adv* sweetly; softly; gently, mildly.

dulcería *nf* confectioner's, sweetshop, candy store (*US*).

dulcificar [1g] **1** *vt* (a) to sweeten.

(b) (*fig*) to soften, make more gentle; to make more pleasant, make more tolerable.

2 dulcificarse *vr* (*weather*) to turn mild.

dulzarrón *adj* (**a**) sickly-sweet, too sugary. (**b**) (*fig*) cloying, sickening.

dulzura *nf* sweetness; softness; gentleness; mildness; **con —** sweetly, softly.

dumping ['dumpin] *nm* (*Comm: angl*) dumping; **hacer —** to dump goods.

dunas *nfpl* dunes.

dundeco *adj* (*CAm, Col*) silly, stupid.

dundera *nf* (*CAm, Col*) silliness, stupidity.

dundo *adj* (*CAm, Col*)=**dundeco.**

Dunquerque Dunkirk.

dúo *nm* duet, duo.

duodecimal *adj* duodecimal.

duodécimo *adj* twelfth.

duodeno *nm* duodenum.

duplicación *nf* duplication.

duplicado 1 *adj* duplicate; **número 14 —** (*abbr* **dpdo**) No. 14ᴬ. **2** *nm* duplicate; **por —** in duplicate.

duplicar [1g] **1** *vt* to duplicate; to repeat; *number, quantity* to double.

   2 duplicarse *vr* to double; **la cifra antigua se ha duplicado** the old number has doubled.

duplicidad *nf* duplicity, deceitfulness.

duplo *adj* double; **12 es — de 6** 12 is twice 6.

duque *nm* duke.

duquesa *nf* duchess.

durabilidad *nf* durability.

durable *adj* durable, lasting.

duración *nf* duration; period, length of time; (*Aut, Mech etc*) life; **— media de la vida** average life span; **de larga —** *illness etc* long-lasting, lengthy; *record* long-playing.

duradero *adj* (**a**) *cloth, dress etc* hard-wearing, tough, durable. (**b**) *effects etc* lasting, permanent.

duramente *adv* (*fig*) harshly; cruelly, callously.

durante *prep* during; **— todo el reinado** during the whole reign, right through the reign; **— muchos años**

for many years; **habló — una hora** he spoke for an hour.

durar [1a] *vi* (*of period etc*) to last, go on for, continue; (*of effect, memory etc*) to survive, endure, remain; to survive; (*of clothing etc*) to last, wear (well).

duraznero *nm* peach tree.

durazno *nm* peach; peach tree.

Durero *m* Dürer.

dureza *nf* (**a**) hardness, toughness; stiffness.

   (**b**) harshness; callousness; roughness.

   (**c**) **— de oído** hardness of hearing; **— de vientre** constipation.

   (**d**) (*Med*) hard patch, callosity.

durmiente 1 *adj* sleeping. **2** *nmf* (**a**) sleeper; **la bella D— (del Bosque)** Sleeping Beauty. **3** *nm* (*Rail*) sleeper, tie (*US*).

duro 1 *adj* (**a**) (*general sense*) hard; tough; *bread* stale, old; *meat, vegetables etc* tough; *collar* stiff; *door, joint, mechanism* stiff; *punch* hard, heavy; *light, sound, water* hard; **más — que una piedra** (*etc*) as hard as nails; **más — que un mendrugo** as tough as old boots; **tomar las duras con las maduras** to take the rough with the smooth.

   (**b**) *character, climate, test etc* tough; *attitude, policy* tough, harsh, hard; cruel, callous; *play* rough; *style etc* harsh; **ser — con uno** to be tough with (*or* on) someone, adopt a tough attitude to someone.

   (**c**) **— de mollera** dense, dim; pigheaded; **— de oído** hard of hearing, (*Mus*) tone-deaf; **es muy — de pelar** (*or* **roer**) it's a tough job, it's a hard nut to crack.

   (**d**) (*Mex, Urug*) **estar —** to be drunk.

   2 *adv* (*SAm*) hard.

   3 *nm* Spanish coin, =5 pesetas; **estar sin un —** to be broke (*fam*).

dux *nm* doge.

E

e *conj* (*before words beginning with* **i**— *and* **hi**—, *but not* **hie**—) *and; see also* **y**.

ea *interj* hey!; come on!; ¡— **pues!** well then!; let's see!

ebanista *nm* cabinetmaker, carpenter.

ebanistería *nf* (**a**) cabinetmaking; woodwork, carpentry. (**b**) cabinetmaker's (shop), carpenter's (shop).

ébano *nm* ebony.

ebonita *nf* ebonite.

ebriedad *nf* intoxication.

ebrio *adj* (**a**) intoxicated, drunk. (**b**) (*fig*) blind (*de* with); — **de algería** drunk with happiness, beside oneself with joy.

ebullición *nf* (**a**) boiling; **punto de** — boiling point; **entrar en** — to begin to boil, come to the boil. (**b**) (*fig*) movement, activity; state of flux; ferment; **la juventud está en** — youth is in a state of ferment.

eclecticismo *nm* eclecticism.

ecléctico 1 *adj* eclectic. **2** *nm,* **ecléctica** *nf* eclectic.

eclesiástico 1 *adj* ecclesiastic(al); church (*attr*). **2** *nm* clergyman, priest, ecclesiastic.

eclipsar [1a] *vt* to eclipse; (*fig*) to eclipse, outshine, overshadow.

eclipse *nm* eclipse *nm* (*also fig*).

eclisa *nf* (*Rail*) fishplate.

eclosión *nf* bloom, blooming; **hacer** — (*fig*) to bloom, blossom (forth).

eco *nm* (**a**) echo; **hacer** — to echo, awaken an echo. (**b**) (*fig*) echo; response; **despertar un** —, **encontrar un** — to produce a response (*en from*), awaken an echo (*en in*); **la llamada no encontró** — the call produced no response, the call had no effect; **hacer** — to fit, correspond; to make an impression; **hacerse** — **de una opinión** to echo an opinion; **tener** — to catch on, arouse interest.

ecología *nf* ecology.

ecológico *adj* ecological.

ecólogo *nm* ecologist.

economato *nm* cooperative store; cut-price store; company store; (*Mil: equivalent to*) NAAFI shop, PX (*US*).

econometría *nf* econometrics.

economía *nf* (**a**) economy; **la** — **ruritana** the Ruritanian economy; — **dirigida** planned economy; — **de pleno empleo,** — **de empleo completo** full-employment economy; — **doméstica** home economy, housekeeping, home economics (*US*); — **política** political economy; economics. (**b**) (*una* —) economy, saving; **hacer** —**s** to make economies, economize, save. (**c**) (*quality*) economy, thrift, thriftiness.

económicamente *adv* economically.

económico *adj* (**a**) economic; *year etc* fiscal, financial; **la situación económica** the economic position; the state of the economy; **estudio** — economic study. (**b**) *person* economical, thrifty; (*pej*) miserly. (**c**) (*Comm, Fin*) economical, inexpensive; cheap; **edición económica** cheap edition, popular edition.

economista *nmf* economist.

economizar [1f] **1** *vt* to economize (on), save; — **tiempo** to save time. **2** *vi* to economize, save; to save up; (*pej*) to be miserly, skimp, pinch.

ecónomo *nm* trustee, guardian; ecclesiastical administrator.

ectoplasma *nm* ectoplasm.

ecuación *nf* equation; — **cuadrática,** — **de segundo grado** quadratic equation.

ecuador *nm* equator.

Ecuador: el — Ecuador.

ecuánime *adj character* level-headed, equable; *mood, state* calm, composed; *judgement etc* impartial.

ecuanimidad *nf* level-headedness; calmness, composure; impartiality.

ecuatoreñismo *nm* word (*or* phrase *etc*) peculiar to Ecuador.

ecuatorial *adj* equatorial.

ecuatoriano 1 *adj* Ecuador(i)an. **2** *nm,* **ecuatoriana** *nf* Ecuador(i)an.

ecuestre *adj* equestrian.

ecuménico *adj* (o)ecumenical.

eczema *nm* (*Acad: f*) eczema.

echacuervos *nm, pl* **echacuervos** (**a**) pimp. (**b**) cheat, impostor.

echada *nf* (**a**) throw, cast; pitch, shy; (*of coin etc*) toss. (**b**) (*Mex*) boast; bluff.

echadizo 1 *adj* (**a**) *person* spying, sent to spy. (**b**) *propaganda* secretly spread; *letter* circulated in a clandestine way. (**c**) *material* waste. **2** *nm* spy.

echado *adj and ptp* (**a**) **estar** — to lie, be lying (down). (**b**) thrown; thrown away. (**c**) (*CAm, PR*) well-placed, in a good position. (**d**) (*CR*) lazy. (**e**) (*Arg, Per*) — **para atrás** boastful; swanky (*fam*).

echador (*Cu, Mex, SD*) **1** *adj* boastful, bragging. **2** *nm* boaster, braggart.

echadora *nf:* — **de cartas** fortuneteller.

echamiento *nm* throwing *etc* (*see* **echada**).

echar [1a] **1** *vt* (**a**) to throw; to cast, fling, pitch, toss; *anchor, hook* to cast; *coin* to toss; *look* to cast, give; *lots* to cast, draw; *dice* to throw. (**b**) (*Cook etc*) to put in, add; — **un poco de azúcar al líquido** add a little sugar to the liquid; — **carbón a la lumbre** to put coal on the fire. (**c**) *wine etc* to pour out; *food* to serve (out); **échame agua** give me some water, pour me some water. (**d**) to emit, send forth, discharge; *gas* to give off, give out; *blood* to lose, shed; *cards* to deal; *curses* to mutter. (**e**) *person* to eject, throw out, chuck out; to turn out; *employee* to dismiss, fire (*fam*); (*from club etc*) to expel; *rubbish* to throw away, throw out; (*Naut*) to jettison; *skin* to slough; — **algo de sí** to throw something off, get rid of something; **cuando protesté me echaron** when I protested they threw me out; **¡que le echen fuera!** chuck him out! (**f**) *hair etc* to grow, begin to grow, begin to have; *teeth* to cut; (*Bot*) *leaves etc* to put forth, sprout. (**g**) *key* to turn; *bolt* to shoot; *catch* to slide, work. (**h**) to move, push; — **a uno a un lado** to push someone aside; — **atrás a la multitud** to push the crowd back; — **el cuerpo atrás** to lean suddenly backwards. (**i**) — **abajo** to demolish, pull down; (*fig*) to overthrow. (**j**) *speech* to give, make, deliver; *reprimand* to give; *decree* to issue. (**k**) *letter* to post, put in the post, mail. (**l**) *tax* to levy, impose (*a on*). (**m**) to attribute, ascribe (*a to*); (*pej*) to impute (*a to*); *blame* to lay (*a on*). (**n**) (*Arg, PR*) *animal* to urge on. (**o**) (*other idiomatic uses*) *account* to make up, balance; *brake* to apply, put on; *cigarette* to have, smoke; *fortune* to tell; *foundations* to lay; *root* to strike; *game* to have, play; *play* to put on, perform. (**p**) —**la de** to pose as, give oneself the airs of, claim to be. (**q**) (*Chi*) —**las** to run away; *for many phrases, see the noun entry.*

2 *vi* (**a**) — **por una dirección** to go in a direction, turn in a direction; — **por una calle** to go down a street; **echemos por aquí** let's go this way. (**b**) — **a** + *infin* to begin to + *infin*, start to

+ ger; — **a reír** to start laughing, burst out laughing; — **a correr** to start to run, break into a run; to run off; *see* **ver** *etc.*

3 echarse *vr* **(a)** — **un pitillo** to have a smoke; — **una novia** to get oneself a girlfriend; — **una siestecita** to have a doze.

(b) to throw oneself, fling oneself; — **atrás** to throw oneself back(wards); — **en brazos de uno** to throw oneself into someone's arms; — **por un precipicio** to throw oneself over a cliff; — **sobre uno** to hurl oneself at someone, rush at someone; to fall on someone.

(c) to lie down; to stretch out; **se echó en el suelo** he lay down on the floor.

(d) — **a** + *infin* = 2 **(b)**.

(e) —**las** = 1 **(p)**.

echarpe *nm* (*gall*) scarf, sash.

echazón *nf* **(a)** (*act*) throwing. **(b)** (*Naut*) jettison, jetsam.

echón *nm* (*Mex, Ven*) braggart, swank (*fam*), poseur.

echona *nf* (*Arg, Chi*) small sickle, reaping hook.

edad *nf* **(a)** (*of person*) age; **¿qué — tiene?** what age is he?, how old is he?; **a la — de 8 años, en — de 8 años** at the age of 8; **de —** elderly; **de corta —** young, of tender years; **de — madura, de mediana —** middle-aged; **avanzado de —, de — avanzada** advanced in years; **a una — avanzada** at an advanced age, late in life; **mayor —** majority; **ser mayor de —** to be of age, be adult; **llegar a mayor —, cumplir la mayoría de —** to come of age; **menor —** minority; **ser menor de —** to be under age; **el instrumento es como una guitarra menor de —** the instrument is like a young (*or* undersized, underdeveloped) guitar; — **adulta** adult age; manhood, womanhood; **llegar a la — adulta** to reach manhood (*etc*); **la — ingrata** the awkward age (13–16); **la — del pavo, la — del chivateo** (*SAm*) the tender years, the green years; the awkward age; — **tierna** tender years; — **viril** manhood; prime of life; — **crítica** change of life; — **escolar** school age; **ella no aparenta la — que tiene** she doesn't look her age; **¿qué — le das?** how old do you think she is?

(b) (*Hist*) age, period; **E—es Bárbaras** Dark Ages; **E— de Bronce** Bronze Age; **E— de Hierro** Iron Age; **E— Media** Middle Ages; **E— de Piedra** Stone Age.

edecán *nm* aide-de-camp.

Edén *m* Eden, Paradise; **es un e—** it's a garden of Eden, it's an earthly paradise.

edible *adj* (*SAm*) edible.

edición *nf* **(a)** (*act*) publication, issue; publishing.

(b) edition; — **aérea** airmail edition; — **de bolsillo** pocket edition; — **económica** cheap edition, popular edition; — **extraordinaria** special edition; **late-night final**; — **de la mañana** morning edition; — **príncipe** first edition; — **semanal** weekly edition; **en — de** edited by; **"al cerrar la —"** (*Typ*) "stop-press"; **ser la segunda — de uno** to be the very image of someone.

(c) (*Comm*) **E—es Ramírez** Ramirez Publications.

edicto *nm* edict, proclamation.

edificación *nf* **(a)** (*Archit*) construction, building. **(b)** (*fig*) edification.

edificante *adj* **(a)** edifying; improving; uplifting, ennobling; **una escena poco —** an unedifying spectacle. **(b)** (*Chi*) scandalous; dishonest.

edificar [1g] *vt* **(a)** (*Archit*) to build, construct. **(b)** (*fig*) to edify; to improve; to uplift, ennoble.

edificio *nm* building; edifice; (*fig*) edifice, structure.

Edimburgo Edinburgh.

Edipo *m* Oedipus.

editar [1a] *vt* **(a)** to publish. **(b)** to edit, correct.

editor 1 *adj* publishing (*attr*); **casa editora** publishing house. **2** *nm* **(a)** publisher. **(b)** editor, corrector. **(c)** (*SAm: angl*) newspaper editor.

editorial 1 *adj* **(a)** publishing (*attr*); **casa —** publishing house. **(b)** *function, policy etc* editorial. **2** *nm* leading article, editorial. **3** *nf* publishing house.

editorialista *nm* leader-writer.

edredón *nm* eiderdown; feather pillow.

eduardiano *adj* Edwardian.

Eduardo *m* Edward.

educable *adj* educable, teachable.

educación *nf* **(a)** education; training; upbringing; — **física** physical education; — **de la voz** elocution lessons; **Ministro de E— Nacional** Minister of Education.

(b) (good) manners, (good) breeding; politeness, civility; **mala —** bad manners, incivility; **es de mala — escupir** it's bad manners to spit, it's ill-mannered to spit; **es de mala — comportarse así** it's rude to behave like that; **es una persona sin —** he's a badly-bred person, he's an ill-mannered

individual; **¡qué falta de —!** how rude!; **¡habla con más —!** don't be so rude!, be more civil!; **no tener —** to lack breeding, lack good manners.

educacional *adj* educational.

educacionista *nmf* education(al)ist.

educado *adj* well-mannered, polite; nicely behaved; cultivated, cultured; **mal —** ill-mannered, unmannerly; rude.

educador *nm*, **educadora** *nf* educator, teacher.

educando *nm*, **educanda** *nf* pupil.

educar [1g] *vt* to educate; to train; to raise, bring up; *voice* to train.

educativo *adj* educative.

educción *nf* **(a)** deduction, inference. **(b)** (*Tech*) exhaust.

edulcoración *nf* (*Pharm*) sweetening.

edulcorado *adj* (*fig*) *person* sweet, charming.

edulcorar [1a] *vt* (*Pharm*) to sweeten.

efectismo *nm* straining after effect; sensationalism.

efectista 1 *adj* strained; sensational. **2** *nmf* strainer after effect; sensationalist.

efectivamente *adv* really; in fact; (*as reply*) exactly, precisely, just so; sure enough.

efectivo 1 *adj* **(a)** effective; **hacer algo —** to make something effective, carry something out; to put something into effect; **hacer — un cheque** to cash a cheque.

(b) actual, real; **el poder — está en manos de X** the real power is in X's hands.

(c) *employment* regular, permanent.

2 *nm* **(a)** cash; specie; **con 50 libras en —** with £50 in cash; **y 3 premios en — and 3 cash prizes**; — **en caja, — en existencia** cash in hand.

(b) —**s** (*Mil etc*) forces, troops; establishment.

efecto *nm* **(a)** effect; —**s sonoros** sound effects; — **útil** (*Mech*) efficiency, output; **hacer —** (*of medicine*) to take effect; **hacer —, surtir —** to have the desired effect; to work; to tell (*en on*); (*of idea etc*) to get across, have an impact; **poner en —** to put into effect, carry out; **tener —** to take effect; (*of event etc*) to take place; **en —** in effect; in fact, really; (*as reply*) yes indeed, precisely.

(b) result; **tener por —** to have as a result (*or* consequence).

(c) purpose, end; **a este —, a tal —** to this end; **a cuyo —** to which end; —**s de** + *infin* with a view to + *ger*, with the object of + *ger*; **construido al —** (specially) built for the purpose.

(d) effect, impression, impact; **hacer —** to make an impression.

(e) (*on ball*) spin; **dar — a una pelota** to put some spin on a ball; **lanzar una pelota con —** to throw a ball so that it spins (*or* swerves).

(f) —**s** (*Fin*) securities; —**s a cobrar** bills receivable; —**s a pagar** bills payable.

(g) —**s** effects, goods; things; (*Fin*) assets; (*Comm*) goods, articles, merchandise; —**s de consumo** consumer goods; —**s de escritorio** writing materials.

efectuación *nf* accomplishment; bringing about.

efectuar [1e] *vt* to effect, carry out, bring about; *plan, repair* to carry out; *recovery, tour, visit, stop, trick* (*Cards*) *etc* to make; *census* to take.

efervescencia *nf* **(a)** effervescence; fizziness; **entrar en —, estar en —** to effervesce. **(b)** (*fig*) commotion, agitation; high spirits, effervescence.

efervescente *adj* **(a)** effervescent; fizzy, bubbly. **(b)** (*fig*) effervescent; high-spirited, bubbling.

eficacia *nf* **(a)** efficacy, effectiveness. **(b)** efficiency.

eficaz *adj* **(a)** efficacious, effective; telling. **(b)** efficient.

eficazmente *adv* **(a)** efficaciously, effectively; tellingly. **(b)** efficiently.

eficiencia *nf* efficiency.

eficiente *adj* efficient.

eficientemente *adv* efficiently.

efigie *nf* effigy; **quemar a uno en —** to burn someone in effigy.

efímera *nf* mayfly.

efímero *adj* ephemeral, fleeting, short-lived.

eflorescente *adj* efflorescent.

efluente *adj* effluent.

efugio *nm* subterfuge, evasion.

efusión *nf* **(a)** outpouring; shedding; — **de sangre** bloodshed, shedding of blood.

(b) (*fig*) effusion, outpouring; warmth, effusiveness; (*pej*) gush, gushing manner; **con —** effusively.

efusivo *adj* effusive; *thanks* effusive, warm; *manner* effusive, (*pej*) gushing; **mis más efusivas gracias** my warmest thanks.

Egeo: Mar *m* **—** Aegean Sea.

égida *nf* **(a)** aegis, protection; **bajo la — de** under the aegis of. **(b)** rule, domination; **bajo la — de Stalin** under Stalin's rule.

egipcio 1 *adj* Egyptian. **2** *nm*, **egipcia** *nf* Egyptian. **Egipto** *m* Egypt.

egiptología *nf* Egyptology.

eglantina *nf* eglantine.

eglefino *nm* haddock.

égloga *nf* eclogue.

egocéntrico *adj* egocentric(al), self-centred.

egoísmo *nm* egoism; selfishness.

egoísta 1 *adj* egoistical; selfish. **2** *nmf* egoist, selfish person.

egolatría *nf* self-worship.

egotismo *nm* egotism.

egotista 1 *adj* egotistic(al). **2** *nmf* egotist.

egregio *adj* eminent, distinguished.

egresado *nm*, **egresada** *nf* (*SAm*) graduate.

egresar [1a] *vi* (*SAm*) **(a)** to go out, go away, leave; **— de** to go away from, leave; to emerge from. **(b)** (*Univ*) to graduate, take one's degree.

egreso *nm* (*SAm*) **(a)** departure, leaving, going away. **(b)** (*Univ*) graduation.

eh *interj* hey!, hi!; I say!

eider *nm* eider, eider duck.

Eire *m* Eire.

eje *nm* **(a)** (*Geog, Math*) axis; **partir a uno por el —** (*fam*) to muck up someone's plans; to do someone a mischief.
(b) (*Mech: of wheel*) axle; **— delantero** front axle; **— trasero** rear axle; **untar el —** (*fam*) to grease someone's palm.
(c) (*Mech: of machine*) shaft, spindle; **— de balancín** rocker shaft; **— del cigüeñal** crankshaft; **— de la hélice** propeller shaft; **— de impulsión**, **— motor** drive shaft.
(d) (*Pol*) axis; **las fuerzas del E—** the Axis forces.
(e) (*fig*) hinge, hub; essential part, crux, core; central idea, main idea.

ejecución *nf* **(a)** execution, performance, carrying out; fulfilment; enforcement; **poner en —** to carry out, carry into effect.
(b) (*Law*) attachment, distraint.
(c) (*Mus*) performance, rendition.
(d) (*killing*) execution.

ejecutable *adj* feasible, practicable.

ejecutante *nmf* (*Mus*) performer.

ejecutar [1a] *vt* **(a)** *order etc* to execute, carry out; *wishes* to perform, fulfil; *deed* to execute.
(b) (*Law*) to attach, distrain on.
(c) (*Mus*) to perform, render, play.
(d) (*kill*) to execute.

ejecutivo 1 *adj* **(a)** *function, power* executive.
(b) *demand etc* pressing, insistent; *response* prompt.
2 *nm* **(a)** (*Pol*) executive.
(b) (*SAm: Comm*) board member, executive (*US*).

ejecutor *nm* (*also* **— testamentario**) executor.

ejecutoria *nf* **(a)** letters patent of nobility; (*fig*) pedigree. **(b)** (*Law*) final judgement.

ejem *interj* hem!

ejemplar 1 *adj* exemplary; model.
2 *nm* **(a)** example; (*Zool etc*) specimen, example; (*of book*) copy; (*of journal*) number, issue; **— gratuito** free copy; **— de regalo** complimentary copy.
(b) example, model, precedent; **sin —** unprecedented.

ejemplaridad *nf* exemplariness.

ejemplarizador *adj* (*SAm*) exemplary.

ejemplarizar [1f] *vt* (*esp SAm*) to set an example to; to exemplify, demonstrate by example, set an example of.

ejemplificar [1g] *vt* to exemplify, illustrate, be illustrative of.

ejemplo *nm* example, instance; object lesson; precedent, parallel; **por —** for example, for instance; **sin —** unprecedented, unparalleled; **dar —** to set an example; **tomar algo por —** to take something as an example.

ejercer [2b] **1** *vt* to exercise; *influence* to exert, use, bring to bear; *power* to exercise, wield; *profession* to practise; *business etc* to manage, conduct, run; *functions* to perform.
2 *vi* to practise (*de as*); to be in office, hold office.

ejercicio *nm* **(a)** exercise; practice; drill; (*Mil*) exercise, drill, training; **— acrobático** (*Aer*) stunt; **— antiaéreo** air-raid drill; **— de castigo** (*School*) imposition; **— de defensa contra incendios** fire drill; **—s gimnásticos** gymnastic exercises; **hacer —s** to do exercises; to take exercise; (*Mil*) to drill, train.
(b) (*of office*) tenure.
(c) (*Comm, Fin*) fiscal year; financial year;

business year; **durante el — actual** during the current financial year.

ejercitar [1a] **1** *vt* to exercise; *profession* to practise; *troops* to drill, train. **2 ejercitarse** *vr* to exercise; to practise; (*Mil*) to drill, train.

ejército *nm* army; **— de ocupación** army of occupation; **— permanente** standing army; **E— de Salvación** Salvation Army; **estar en el —** to be in the army.

ejido *nm* common.

—ejo, —eja *n and adj suffix* (*pej*), *eg* **animalejo** odd-looking creature, nasty animal; **caballejo** old horse, poor horse, nag; **discursejo** tedious speech, rotten speech; **palabreja** strange word; nasty-sounding word.

ejote *nm* (*CAm, Mex*) string bean.

el[1] *def art m*, **la** *f* the; *not translated in such cases as* **La India** India; **en el México de hoy** in present-day Mexico; **me gusta el fútbol** I like football; **está en la cárcel** he's in jail; **el General Prim** General Prim; **¿qué manda la señora?** what would madam like?; **a las ocho** at eight o'clock; **a los quince días** after a fortnight.

el[2] *dem pron*; **mi libro y — de Vd** my book and yours; **este jugador y — de la camisa azul** this player and the one in the blue shirt; **— de Pepe es mejor** Joe's is better; **y — de todos los demás** and that of everybody else, and everybody else's.

el[3]: **— que** *rel pron* (*also* **la que, los que, las que**) he who, whoever; the one(s) that; **el que haga** whoever wants to can get on with it; **los que hacen eso son tontos** those who do so are foolish; **el que compramos no vale** the one we bought is no good; **a los que mencionamos añádase éste** add this one to the ones we mentioned.

él *pers pron m* **(a)** (*subject: person*) he, (*thing*) it.
(b) (*after prep: person*) him, (*thing*) it; **esto es para —** this is for him; **vamos sin —** let's go without him.
(c) (*after de: person*) his, (*thing*) its; **mis libros y los de —** my books and his; **todo eso es de él** all that is his, all that belongs to him.

elaboración *nf* elaboration; manufacture, production; working; working-out.

elaborar [1a] *vt* to elaborate; to make, manufacture, produce; to prepare; *metal, wood etc* to work; *plan etc* to work on, work out.

elación *nf* **(a)** haughtiness, pride. **(b)** generosity. **(c)** (*of style*) pomposity. **(d)** (*SAm: angl*) elation.

elasticidad *nf* **(a)** elasticity; spring, sponginess; give. **(b)** (*fig*) elasticity; (*moral*) resilience.

elástico 1 *adj* **(a)** elastic; flexible; *surface etc* springy. **(b)** (*fig*) elastic; (*morally*) resilient. **2** *nm* elastic.

elección *nf* **(a)** choice, selection; option; **una — acertada** a sensible choice; **su patria de —** his chosen country.
(b) (*Pol etc*) election (*a for*); **— complementaria, —es parciales** by-election; **—es generales** general election.

eleccionario *adj* (*SAm*) electoral, election (*attr*).

electivo *adj* elective.

electo *adj* elect; **el presidente —** the president-elect.

elector *nm*, **electora** *nf* elector; voter.

electorado *nm* electorate; voters.

electoral *adj* electoral; **potencia —** voting power, power in terms of votes.

electricidad *nf* electricity; **— estática** static electricity.

electricista *nm* electrician.

eléctrico *adj* electric(al).

electrificación *nf* electrification.

electrificar [1g] *vt* to electrify.

electrizante *adj* (*fig*) electrifying.

electrizar [1f] *vt* to electrify (*also fig*).

electro . . . electro . . .

electrocardiograma *nm* electrocardiogram.

electrocución *nf* electrocution.

electrocutar [1a] *vt* to electrocute.

electrochapado *adj* electroplated.

electrodinámica *nf* electrodynamics.

electrodo *nm* electrode.

electroimán *nm* electromagnet.

electrólisis *nf* electrolysis.

electromagnético *adj* electromagnetic.

electromotor *nm* electric motor.

electrón *nm* electron.

electrónica *nf* electronics.

electrónico *adj* electronic; electron (*attr*).

electrotecnia *nf* electrical engineering.

electrotermo *nm* immersion heater.

elefante *nm*, **elefanta** *nf* elephant; **— blanco** (*SAm: angl*) white elephant.

elefantino *adj* elephantine.

elegancia *nf* elegance; gracefulness; stylishness, smartness; tastefulness; polish.

elegante *adj* elegant; graceful; *dress, party, shop etc* stylish, fashionable, smart; *society* fashionable, elegant; *decoration etc* tasteful; *phrase etc* elegant, well-turned, polished; **no es — escupir** it's rude to spit, it's not nice to spit.

elegantemente *adv* elegantly; gracefully; stylishly, fashionably, smartly; tastefully; in a polished way.

elegantoso *adj* (*SAm*) = **elegante**.

elegía *nf* elegy.

elegíaco *adj* elegiac.

elegibilidad *nf* eligibility.

elegible *adj* eligible.

elegido *adj* (a) chosen, selected. (b) (*Pol etc*) elect, elected.

elegir [3c *and* 3l] *vt* (a) to choose, select; to opt for; **café con bizcochos a —** coffee with a choice of cakes; **a — entre 5 tipos** there are 5 sorts to choose from; **hablará en francés o italiano, a —** he will talk in French or Italian, as you (*etc*) prefer; **le toca a Vd —** the choice is yours, it's up to you to choose. (b) (*Pol etc*) to elect.

elementado *adj* (*Col, Chi*) bewildered; silly, stupid.

elemental *adj* elementary; elemental; **eso es —** that's elementary.

elementarse [1a] *vr* (*Chi*) to get bewildered.

elemento *nm* (a) element; **los cuatro —s** the four elements; **estar en su —** to be in one's element. (b) (*Chem etc*) element; (*fig*) ingredient, constituent (part); (*in situation*) element, factor; **—s** material, ingredients. (c) (*Elec*) element; (*of battery*) cell. (d) (*SAm*) person, individual; **vino a verle un —** someone came to see you; **dos —s distinguidos** two distinguished individuals. (e) (*Chi, Per, PR, SD*) dimwit (*fam*), ass. (f) (*PR, SD*) odd person, eccentric. (g) (*Spain: pej*) undesirable person, suspicious individual. (h) **—s** (*of a subject*) elements, rudiments, first principles.

Elena *f* Helen.

elenco *nm* catalogue, list; (*Theat: esp SAm*) cast.

elevación *nf* (a) (*act*) elevation (*a* to), raising, lifting; (*Eccl*) elevation; (*in price, rate etc*) rise. (b) (*Geog etc*) elevation, height, altitude. (c) (*of mind, style etc*) elevation; (*of person*) exaltation, loftiness; (*pej*) conceit, pride. (d) rapture.

elevadamente *adv* loftily, sublimely.

elevado 1 *adj* (a) elevated, raised; high, lofty; *building* high, tall; *price, rate etc* high; *post* exalted, high; **a precios elevadísimos** at terribly high prices. (b) *thought, style etc* elevated, lofty, noble; grand, sublime; **de pensamientos —s** of noble thoughts, high-minded.
2 *nm* (*Cu*) overhead railway.

elevador *nm* elevator, hoist; (*SAm*) lift, elevator (*US*); **— de granos** (grain) elevator.

elevar [1a] *vt* (a) to raise, lift (up), elevate; *price, rate* to raise, put up; *production* to step up; (*Elec*) to boost; (*Math*) to raise (*a una potencia* to a power); *person* to promote; to exalt; *style* to raise the tone of; **— los pensamientos a Dios** to raise one's thoughts to God. (b) *report etc* to present, submit (*a* to); **el comité elevará un informe al ministro** the committee will report to the minister.
2 elevarse *vr* (a) to rise, go up; (*of building etc*) to rise, soar, tower; **la cantidad se eleva a . . .** the quantity amounts to . . .; **los precios se han elevado mucho** prices have risen a lot. (b) to be transported, go into a rapture. (c) (*pej*) to get conceited, become overbearing.

elidir [3a] **1** *vt* to elide. **2 elidirse** *vr* to elide, be elided.

eliminación *nf* elimination; removal; **— progresiva** (*Sport*) knockout.

eliminar [1a] **1** *vt* to eliminate; to remove; *need etc* to remove, obviate; *waste products* to get rid of; (*Sport*) to eliminate, knock out.
2 eliminarse *vr* (*Mex*) to go away.

eliminatoria *nf* (*Sport*) heat, preliminary round, qualifying round; knockout competition.

elipse *nf* ellipse.

elipsis *nf, pl elipsis* ellipsis.

elíptico *adj* elliptic(al).

Eliseo *m* Elysium.

elisión *nf* elision.

elite [e'lite] *nf* (*gall*) élite.

elixir *nm* elixir.

elocución *nf* elocution.

elocuencia *nf* eloquence.

elocuente *adj* eloquent; (*fig*) telling; significant; **un dato —** a significant fact, a fact which speaks for itself.

elocuentemente *adv* eloquently.

elogiable *adj* praiseworthy.

elogiar [1b] *vt* to praise, eulogize.

elogio *nm* praise, eulogy; tribute; **queda por encima de todo —** it's beyond praise; **hacer — de** to praise, extol; to pay (a) tribute to; **hizo un caluroso — del héroe** he paid a warm tribute to the hero, he was warm in his praise of the hero.

elogiosamente *adv* eulogistically; very favourably, with warm approval; **comentó — sus cualidades** he spoke very favourably of his qualities.

elogioso *adj* eulogistic; highly favourable, warmly approving; **en términos —s** in highly favourable terms.

elotada *nf* (*CAm, Mex*) (a) ears of green maize (*collectively*). (b) *meal at which elotes are eaten*.

elote *nm* (*CAm, Mex*) ear of green maize; sweet corn; **coger a uno asando —s** to catch someone red-handed.

elotear [1a] *vi* (*CAm, Mex: of maize*) to come into ear.

elucidación *nf* elucidation.

elucidar [1a] *vt* to elucidate.

eludible *adj* avoidable.

eludir [3a] *vt* to elude, evade, avoid, escape.

elusivo *adj* (*SAm*) evasive, tricky.

ella *pers pron f* (a) (*subject: person*) she, (*thing*) it. (b) (*after prep: person*) she, (*thing*) it; **estuve con —** I was with her; **no podemos sin —** without her we can't. (c) (*after de: person*) hers, (*thing*) its; **mi sombrero y el de —** my hat and hers; **nada de esto es de —** none of this is hers, none of this belongs to her.

ellas *see* **ellos**.

ello "*neuter*" *pron* (a) it; this business, that whole affair; **— es difícil** it's awkward; **— no me gusta** I don't like it; **todo — se acabó** the whole thing is over and done with; **no tiene fuerzas para —** he is not strong enough for it. (b) (*idioms*) **— es que . . .** the fact is that . . .; **por — no quiero** that's why I don't want to; **es por que . . .** (*SAm*) that is why . . .; **luego será —** there'll be trouble later; **— dirá** the event will show; **¡a por —!** here goes!; **¡aquí fue —!** and then it started, and that was it.

ellos *pers pron mpl*, **ellas** *pers pron fpl* (a) (*subject*) they. (b) (*after prep*) them. (c) (*after de*) theirs; *see* **él, ella** *for usage examples*.

emanación *nf* emanation; smell, effluvium.

emanar [1a] *vi* **— de** to emanate from, come from, originate in.

emancipación *nf* emancipation; freeing.

emancipado *adj* emancipated; independent, free.

emancipar [1a] **1** *vt* to emancipate; to free.
2 emanciparse *vr* to become emancipated (*de* from); to become independent (*de* of); to free oneself (*de* from).

emascular [1a] *vt* to castrate; (*fig*) to emasculate.

embadurnar [1a] *vt* to daub, bedaub, smear (*de* with).

embaidor *nm* cheat, swindler.

embaimiento *nm* imposture, trick, swindle; deceit.

embaír [3a: *defective*] *vt* to swindle, cheat.

embajada *nf* (a) embassy. (b) ambassadorship. (c) (*fig*) errand, message.

embajador *nm* ambassador (*en* in, *cerca de* to); **— itinerante** roving ambassador, ambassador at large.

embajadora *nf* (woman) ambassador; ambassador's wife.

embalador *nm*, **embaladora** *nf* packer.

embaladura *nf* (*SAm*), **embalaje** *nm* packing.

embalar [1a] **1** *vt* to pack, parcel up, wrap; *heavy goods* to crate, bale.
2 *vi* (a) (*Sport*) to sprint, make a dash; (*Aut*) to step on it. (b) (*PR, SD*) to run off, escape.
3 embalarse *vr* (*SAm: Aut*) to coast at high speed.

embaldosado *nm* tiled floor.

embaldosar [1a] *vt* to tile, pave with tiles.

embalsadero *nm* boggy place.

embalsado *nm* (*Arg*) mass of floating water weeds.

embalsamar [1a] *vt* to embalm.

embalsar [1a] **1** *vt* (a) *water* to dam, dam up; to retain, collect; **este mes se han embalsado X m³** this month reservoir stocks have gone up by X cubic metres. (b) (*Naut*) to sling, hoist.
2 *vi* (*Col*) to cross a river (*etc*).

embalse nm dam; reservoir.

embanastar [1a] vt to put into a basket; (fig) to jam in, overcrowd.

embancarse [1g] vr (Chi, Ec) to silt up, become blocked by silt.

embanderar [1a] vt to deck with flags; **embanderado** beflagged, decked with flags.

embarazada 1 adj pregnant; **dejar — a una** to get a girl pregnant, put a girl in the family way. **2** nf pregnant woman, expectant mother.

embarazar [1f] vt (a) to obstruct, hamper, hinder. (b) woman to make pregnant, get with child, put in the family way.

embarazo nm (a) obstacle, obstruction, hindrance. (b) pregnancy; **durante el —** during pregnancy.

embarazosamente adv awkwardly, inconveniently; embarrassingly.

embarazoso adj awkward, inconvenient, troublesome; embarrassing.

embarcación nf (a) boat, craft, (small) vessel; **— de arrastre** trawler; **— de cabotaje** coasting vessel; **— pesquera** fishing boat; **— de recreo** pleasure boat; **— de vela** sailing boat. (b) (act) embarkation.

embarcadero nm (a) pier, landing stage, jetty. (b) (SAm: Rail) goods station; loading platform; (Arg) cattle pen (attached to a railway station).

embarcar [1g] **1** vt (a) persons to embark, put on board; cargo to ship, get on board, stow. (b) (fig) **— a uno en una empresa** to launch someone on an enterprise. (c) (Arg, Mex, Per, PR) **— a uno** to persuade someone dishonestly to undertake a dubious enterprise.

2 embarcarse vr (a) to embark, go on board; (of sailor) to sign on; **— para** to sail for. (b) (SAm: Rail etc) to get on, get in; **se embarcó en el autobús** he got on the bus, he boarded the bus. (c) (fig) **— en un asunto** to get involved in a matter.

embarco nm embarcation.

embargar [1h] vt (a) to impede, hinder; to restrain, put a check on. (b) senses to blunt, confuse, paralyse, overpower. (c) (Law) to seize, impound, distrain upon.

embargo nm (a) (Law) seizure, distraint; (Comm etc) embargo; **sin —** still, however, none the less; **sin — de** notwithstanding, in spite of. (b) (Med) indigestion.

embarnizar [1f] vt to varnish.

embarque nm shipment, loading.

embarrada nf (SAm) blunder.

embarradura nf smear, daub.

embarrancar [1g] **1** vti (a) (Naut) to run aground. (b) (Aut etc) to run into a ditch. **2 embarrancarse** vr (a) to run aground. (b) to run into a ditch; to get stuck.

embarrar [1a] **1** vt (a) to smear, bedaub (de with); to splash with mud. (b) (SAm) wall to cover with mud; to plaster. (c) (CAm, Mex) **— a uno** to involve someone in a shady affair. (d) (Cu, Chi, PR, RPl) **— a uno** to smear someone, damage someone's standing. **2 embarrarse** vr (Ven: of child) to dirty oneself.

embarrialarse [1a] vr (a) (CAm, Ven) to get covered with mud. (b) (CAm: Aut) to get stuck.

embarullador adj bungling.

embarullar [1a] vt to bungle, mess up.

embastar [1a] vt to stitch, tack.

embaste nm stitching, tacking.

embate nm (a) (Mil etc) sudden attack; brunt of the attack. (b) (of waves) dashing, breaking, beating; violence. (c) (fig) **—s de la fortuna** blows of fate.

embaucador nm, **embaucadora** nf trickster, swindler; impostor; humbug.

embaucamiento nm swindle, swindling; humbug.

embaucar [1g] vt to trick, swindle; to fool, lead up the garden path.

embaular vt (a) to pack (into a trunk). (b) (fam) food to tuck away (fam), stuff oneself with.

embazar [1f] **1** vt (a) to dye brown. (b) (fig) to astound, amaze. (c) (fig) to hinder. **2** vi to be dumbfounded, stand amazed. **3 embazarse** vr to get tired, get bored; to have had enough.

embebecer [2d] **1** vt to entertain, amuse; to fascinate. **2 embebecerse** vr to be fascinated, be lost in wonder; to be dumbfounded.

embebecimiento nm (a) absorption, fascination; enchantment. (b) astonishment, wonderment.

embeber [2a] **1** vt (a) to absorb, soak up; to saturate. (b) (Sew) to take in, gather in. (c) (fig) to imbibe; to insert, introduce (en into); to contain, incorporate, comprise. **2** vi (of cloth) to shrink. **3 embeberse** vr (a) to be absorbed, become engrossed (en in), to be enraptured, be enchanted (en with). (b) **— de** to imbibe, soak oneself in, become well versed in.

embelecar [1g] vt to deceive, cheat.

embeleco nm, **embelequería** nf (Col, Chi, PR) deceit, fraud.

embelequero adj (a) (SAm) given to making a great fuss, highly emotional. (b) (Col, Cu, PR) shifty.

embelesado adj spellbound, enraptured.

embelesador adj enchanting, entrancing.

embelesar [1a] **1** vt to enchant, entrance, enrapture. **2 embelesarse** vr to be enchanted, be enraptured.

embeleso nm (a) enchantment, rapture, delight. (b) (endearment) sweetheart, my love.

embellecedor nm (Aut) hub cap.

embellecer [2d] vt to embellish, beautify.

embellecimiento nm embellishment.

embestida nf (a) assault, onslaught; (of bull etc) charge, rush. (b) (fig) importunate demand.

embestir [3l] **1** vt (a) to assault, attack, assail; to rush at (or upon); (of bull etc) to charge. (b) (fig) **— a uno** to pester someone for a loan. **2** vi (a) to attack; to rush, charge; **— con, — contra** to rush upon; (of bull etc) to charge down on.

embetunar [1a] vt to impregnate with pitch; shoes to black.

embicar [1g] vt (a) (Chi, RPl) boat to head straight for land. (b) (Cu) to insert. (c) (Mex) to turn upside down, upturn.

embicharse [1a] vr (Arg) to become wormy; (Bot) to get maggoty.

embiste nm (Ven) =**embestida**.

emblandecer [2d] **1** vt to soften; (fig) to mollify. **2 emblandecerse** vr to soften, get soft; (fig) to relent.

emblanquecer [2d] **1** vt to whiten; to bleach. **2 emblanquecerse** vr to whiten, turn white; to bleach.

emblema nm emblem.

emblemático adj emblematic.

embobamiento nm amazement; fascination.

embobar [1a] **1** vt to amuse, entertain; to amaze; to fascinate; **esa niña me emboba** that girl is driving me crazy. **2 embobarse** vr to be amazed, stand agape (con, de, en at); to be fascinated (con, de, en by); **reírse embobado** to laugh like mad.

embobecer [2d] **1** vt to make silly. **2 embobecerse** vr to get silly.

embocadura nf (a) narrow entrance; (of river) mouth; (Naut) passage, narrows. (b) (Mus) mouthpiece; (of cigarette etc) tip; (of bridle) bit. (c) (of wine) taste, flavour. (d) (Theat) proscenium arch.

embocar [1g] vt (a) **— algo** to put something into someone's mouth; **— una cosa en un agujero** to insert something into a hole; **— la comida** to cram one's food, wolf one's food. (b) **— un negocio** to undertake a piece of business. (c) **— algo a uno** (fig) to put one over on someone, hoax someone with something.

embochinchar [1a] vt (SAm) to throw into confusion, create chaos in.

embolado nm (a) bull with wooden balls on its horns. (b) (Theat) bit part, minor role. (c) (fam) trick.

embolador nm (SAm) bootblack.

embolar [1a] **1** vt (a) bull's horns to tip with wooden balls. (b) (SAm) shoes to black, shine. (c) (CAm, Mex) to make drunk.

embolia nf (Med) clot; embolism; **— cerebral** clot on the brain.

embolismar [1a] vt to gossip about; to make mischief for.

embolismo nm (a) muddle, mess, confusion. (b) gossip. (c) hoax, trick.

émbolo nm plunger; (Mech) piston.

embolsar [1a] vt, **embolsicar** [1g] vt (SAm) to pocket, put into one's pocket; money, proceeds etc to pocket, collect, take in.

embonar [1a] vt (a) (Cu, Chi, Mex) land to manure. (b) (fig) to improve. (c) (Naut) to sheathe; (Ec, Mex) to join (the ends of). (d) (Cu, Ec, Mex) **le embona el sombrero** the hat suits him, the hat looks well on him.

emboque nm (fam) trick, hoax.
emboquillado adj cigarette tipped.
emboquillar [1a] vt (a) cigarette to tip. (b) (Arg, Chi: Archit) to point, repoint.
emborrachar [1a] 1 vt to intoxicate, make drunk; to get drunk. 2 **emborracharse** vr to get drunk (con, de on).
emborrar [1a] vt (a) to stuff, pad, wad (de with). (b) (fam) food to cram, wolf.
emborrascarse [1g] vr (a) to get stormy. (b) (fig) to get cross, get worked up. (c) (Comm: of business) to fail. (d) (Arg, Hond, Mex: of lode) to peter out.
emborronar [1a] 1 vt to blot, make blots on; to scribble on. 2 vi to make blots; to scribble.
emboscada nf ambush; **tender una —** a to lay an ambush for.
emboscarse [1g] vr to lie in ambush; to hide away (in the woods); **estaban emboscados cerca del camino** they were in ambush near the road.
embotado adj dull, blunt (also fig).
embotamiento nm (a) (act) dulling, blunting (also fig). (b) (state) dullness, bluntness (also fig).
embotar [1a] vt (a) to dull, blunt. (b) (fig) to dull, blunt; to weaken, enervate.
embotellado 1 adj bottled; speech etc prepared (beforehand). 2 nm bottling.
embotellador nm bottler.
embotellamiento nm (a) (Aut) traffic jam. (b) (place) bottleneck (also fig).
embotellar [1a] 1 vt (a) to bottle.
  (b) (Mil etc) to bottle up.
  (c) (Ant) speech to prepare beforehand, memorize. 2 **embotellarse** vr (a) (Aut) to get into a jam, get jammed.
  (b) (Ant) to learn a speech off by heart.
emboticarse [1g] vr (Chi, Mex) to stuff oneself with medicines.
embotijar [1a] 1 vt to put into jars; to keep in jars. 2 **embotijarse** vr (fig) to fly into a passion.
embovedar [1a] vt to arch, vault.
embozadamente adv covertly, stealthily.
embozado adj (a) muffled up (to the eyes). (b) (fig) covert, stealthy.
embozalar [1a] vt (Arg) to muzzle.
embozar [1f] 1 vt (a) to muffle (up), wrap (up). (b) (fig) to cloak, disguise, conceal. 2 **embozarse** vr to muffle oneself up (con, de in).
embozo nm (a) muffler; mask, covering of the face; **quitarse el —** (fig) to drop the mask, end the play-acting.
  (b) turned-down bedclothes.
  (c) (fig) cunning; concealment; **sin —** frankly, openly.
embragar [1h] 1 vt (Aut, Mech) to engage; parts to connect, couple; (Naut) to sling. 2 vi (Aut etc) to put the clutch in.
embrague nm (Aut, Mech) clutch.
embravecer [2d] 1 vt to enrage, infuriate.
  2 vi (Bot) to flourish, grow strongly.
  3 **embravecerse** vr (a) (of sea) to get rough.
  (b) (of person) to get furious.
embravecido adj (a) sea rough; wind etc wild. (b) person furious, enraged.
embravecimiento nm rage, fury.
embrear [1a] vt to tar, cover with tar; to cover with pitch; **— y emplumar a uno** to tar and feather someone.
embretar [1a] vt (SAm) animals to pen, corral.
embriagador adj intoxicating; wine etc heady, strong.
embriagar [1h] 1 vt (a) to make drunk, intoxicate; to get drunk. (b) (fig) to enrapture, delight. 2 **embriagarse** to get drunk.
embriaguez nf (a) drunkenness, intoxication. (b) (fig) rapture, delight.
embridar [1a] vt (a) to bridle, put a bridle on. (b) (fig) to check, restrain.
embrión nm embryo; **en —** in embryo.
embrionario adj embryonic.
embrocación nf embrocation.
embrocar [1g] 1 vt (a) (Sew) thread to wind (on to a bobbin); shoes to tack.
  (b) liquid to pour from one container into another.
  (c) to turn upside down, invert.
  2 **embrocarse** vr (Mex): **— un vestido** to put a dress on over one's head.
embrollar [1a] 1 vt matter to muddle, confuse, complicate; to mess up; persons to involve, embroil (en in.)
  2 **embrollarse** vr to get into a muddle, get into a mess; **— en un asunto** to get involved in a matter.

embrollista nm (Chi, Guat, Per) = **embrollón**.
embrollo nm muddle, tangle, confusion; fix, jam, entanglement; (pej) fraud, trick.
embrollón nm, **embrollona** nf troublemaker, mischief-maker.
embromado adj (SAm): **estar —** to be in a fix; to be having a tough time; (Med) to be in a bad way; (Fin) to be in financial trouble.
embromar [1a] 1 vt (a) to tease, make fun of, rag.
  (b) to wheedle, cajole.
  (c) to hoodwink.
  (d) (SAm) to annoy, vex; to harm, set back (in health etc), affect badly.
  2 **embromarse** vr (SAm) to get cross; to get bored.
embrujado adj person bewitched; house, place haunted; **una casa embrujada** a haunted house.
embrujar [1a] vt person to bewitch, put a spell on; house, place to haunt; **la casa está embrujada** the house is haunted.
embrutecer [2d] 1 vt to brutalize, deprave; to coarsen. 2 **embrutecerse** vr to become brutalized, get depraved; to coarsen.
embuchacarse [1g] vr (CAm, Mex): **— algo** to pocket something; (fig) to pocket something, appropriate something.
embuchado nm (a) (Cook) sausage. (b) (fam) pretext, blind.
embuchar [1a] vt (a) (Cook) to stuff with minced meat. (b) (fam) food to wolf, bolt.
embudar [1a] vt (a) (Tech) to fit with a funnel, put a funnel into. (b) (fig) to trick.
embudo nm (a) funnel; (Col, Mex) hopper. (b) (fig) trick, fraud.
embullar [1a] (CAm, Col, Cu, PR, Ven) 1 vt (a) to excite, disturb.
  (b) enemy to put to flight.
  2 **embullarse** vr (a) to get excited, get worked up; to become tense.
  (b) to revel, have a good time.
embullo nm (Ant, CAm) noise, excitement, bustle; revelry.
emburujar [1a] 1 vt (a) to jumble together, jumble up; to pile up; thread etc to tangle up.
  (b) (Col) to bewilder.
  2 **emburujarse** vr (Col, Mex, PR, Ven) to wrap oneself up.
emburujo nm (Ant) ruse, trick.
embuste nm (a) trick, fraud, imposture; lie, (hum) fib, story. (b) **—s** trinkets.
embustería nf trickery, deceit; lying.
embustero 1 adj (a) deceitful, rascally.
  (b) (Chi) **persona embustera** person who cannot spell properly.
  (c) (Guat) haughty.
  2 nm, **embustera** nf cheat; impostor; liar, (hum) fibber, storyteller; hypocrite; **¡—!** (affectionately) you rascal!
embutido nm (a) (Cook) sausage. (b) (Tech) inlay, inlaid work, marquetry. (c) (Mex, RPl, Ven) strip of lace.
embutir [3a] 1 vt (a) to insert (en into); to pack tight, stuff, cram (de with, en into); (fam) food to cram, scoff (fam); **— algo a uno** to make someone swallow something; **ella estuvo embutida en un vestido apretadísimo** she had been poured into a terribly close-fitting dress.
  (b) (Tech) to inlay; metal to hammer, work.
  2 **embutirse** vr (fam) to stuff oneself (de with).
emergencia nf (a) emergence; appearance. (b) emergency; **de —** emergency (attr).
emergente adj (a) resultant, consequent. (b) nation emergent.
emerger [2c] vi to emerge; to appear; (of submarine) to surface.
emeritense 1 adj of Mérida. 2 nmf native (or inhabitant) of Mérida; **los —s** the people of Mérida.
emérito adj emeritus, retired.
emético 1 adj emetic. 2 nm emetic.
emigración nf emigration; migration.
emigrado nm, **emigrada** nf emigrant; (Pol etc) emigré(e).
emigrante 1 adj emigrant. 2 nmf emigrant.
emigrar [1a] vi to emigrate; to migrate.
Emilia f Emily.
emilianense adj of San Millán de la Cogolla (Riojan monastery).
eminencia nf (a) (Geog) height, eminence; loftiness. (b) (fig) eminence; prominence. (c) (in titles) **Su E—** His Eminence; **Vuestra E—** Your Eminence.
eminente adj (a) high, lofty. (b) (fig) eminent, distinguished; prominent.

eminentemente *adv* eminently, especially.

emir *nm* emir.

emisario *nm* emissary.

emisión *nf* (**a**) emission; (*Fin etc*) issue.
(**b**) (*Radio, TV*) broadcasting; broadcast, programme; — **deportiva** sports programme; — **publicitaria** commercial, advertising spot.

emisor *nm* transmitter; — **de radar** radar station.

emisora *nf* radio station; broadcasting station; — **de onda corta** shortwave radio station.

emisor-receptor *nm* walkie-talkie, transmitting and receiving set, transceiver.

emitir [3a] *vt* (**a**) sound, *smell etc* to emit, give off, give out.
(**b**) *money, stamps, bonds etc* to issue; *forged money* to utter; *loan* to float, launch.
(**c**) *opinion* to express; *vote* to give, cast.
(**d**) (*Radio, TV*) to broadcast; *signal* to send out.

emoción *nf* (**a**) emotion; feeling; **sentir una honda** — to feel a deep emotion; **nos comunica una** — **de nostalgia** it gives us a nostalgic feeling.
(**b**) excitement; thrill; tension, suspense; **¡qué** —! how exciting!; **al abrirlo sentí gran** — I felt very excited on opening it; **la** — **de la película no disminuye** the excitement (*or* tension) of the film does not flag.

emocionado *adj* deeply moved, deeply stirred.

emocional *adj* emotional.

emocionante *adj* exciting, thrilling; touching, moving; stirring.

emocionar [1a] **1** *vt* to excite, thrill; to touch, move; to stir.
2 emocionarse *vr* to get excited, be thrilled; to be moved; to be stirred; **¡no te emociones tanto!** don't get so excited!, don't get so worked up!

emolumento *nm* emolument.

emotivo *adj* emotive.

empacada *nf* (*SAm*) (**a**) balk, shy. (**b**) (*fig*) obstinacy.

empacadizo *adj* (*Arg*) easily packed.

empacadora *nf* (*Agr*) baler, baling machine.

empacar [1g] **1** *vt* (**a**) to bale, crate, pack up; (*Agr*) to bale. (**b**) (*Mex, Per*) to package.
2 empacarse *vr* (**a**) to get rattled, get confused. (**b**) (*SAm: horse*) to balk, shy; (*fig*) to be obstinate, get stubborn.

empachado *adj* (**a**) clogged; (*Naut*) overloaded; *stomach* upset, uncomfortable. (**b**) embarrassed. (**c**) awkward, clumsy.

empachar [1a] **1** *vt* (**a**) to stop up, clog; (*Naut*) to overload; (*Med*) *stomach* to upset, make uncomfortable; *person* to give indigestion to.
(**b**) to impede, hinder; to embarrass.
2 empacharse *vr* (**a**) to get stopped up, get clogged; (*Med*) to get indigestion, have indigestion.
(**b**) to get embarrassed, feel awkward; to become bashful.

empacho *nm* (**a**) hindrance, obstacle.
(**b**) (*Med*) surfeited feeling, indigestion.
(**c**) (*fig*) embarrassment; awkwardness, awkward feeling; bashfulness; **sin** — without ceremony; unconcernedly; **no tener** — **en** + *infin* to have no objection to + *ger*.

empachoso *adj* (**a**) *food* cloying, indigestible. (**b**) (*fig*) embarrassing.

empadronamiento *nm* (**a**) census; register. (**b**) (*act*) census-taking; registration.

empadronar [1a] *vt* to take a census of; to register, enter on a register.

empajar [1a] *vt* to cover (*or* fill *etc*) with straw; (*Col, Chi*) to thatch.

empalagar [1h] **1** *vt* (**a**) to pall on, surfeit, cloy. (**b**) (*fig*) to pall on, bore; to sicken. **2** *vi* to pall. **3 empalagarse** *vr* to get surfeited (*de* with).

empalago *nm* (**a**) cloying, palling. (**b**) boredom; disgust.

empalagoso *adj* (**a**) cloying; sickeningly sweet, over-rich. (**b**) (*fig*) boring, wearisome; trying.

empalar [1a] **1** *vt* to impale. **2 empalarse** *vr* (*Chi, Per*) to dig one's heels in.

empalizada *nf* fence (of palings); (*Mil etc*) palisade, stockade.

empalmar [1a] **1** *vt* (**a**) to join, connect; *ropes* to splice. (**b**) (*fig*) to combine, put together.
2 *vi* (*Rail etc: of lines*) to join, meet, come together; (*of trains*) to connect (*con* with).

empalme *nm* (**a**) (*Tech*) joint, connection, union; splice. (**b**) combination. (**c**) (*of lines, roads*) junction; (*of trains*) connection.

empamparse [1a] *vr* (*SAm*) (**a**) to get lost on the pampas; to get disorientated, lose one's way. (**b**) to be amazed, stand agape.

empanada *nf* (**a**) (meat) pie, patty; (kind of) shepherd's pie. (**b**) fraud, piece of shady business.

empanado *adj* (*Cook*) done (*or* rolled *etc*) in breadcrumbs.

empanar [1a] *vt* (**a**) (*Cook*) to do (*or* roll *etc*) in breadcrumbs; to roll in pastry. (**b**) (*Arg*) to sow with wheat.

empantanado *adj* flooded, swampy.

empantanar [1a] **1** *vt* (**a**) to flood, swamp.
(**b**) (*fig*) to obstruct; to bog down.
2 empantanarse *vr* (**a**) to be flooded, get swamped.
(**b**) (*fig*) to be obstructed, be held up; — **en un asunto** to get bogged down in a matter.

empañado *adj* *window etc* misty, steamy, steamed-up; *outline* dim, blurred; *surface* tarnished; *voice* faint, unsteady; *honour* tarnished.

empañar [1a] **1** *vt* (**a**) *baby* to swaddle, wrap up.
(**b**) *window etc* to mist, steam up; *outline* to dim, blur; *surface, honour* to tarnish.
2 empañarse *vr* to film over, get misty; to cloud over; (*voice*) to falter.
(**b**) (*fig*) to become sad, get gloomy.

empañetar [1a] *vt* (*SAm*) to plaster; to whitewash.

empapar [1a] **1** *vt* (**a**) to soak, saturate, drench; to steep (*also fig; de, en* in).
(**b**) to soak up, absorb.
2 empaparse *vr* (**a**) to soak.
(**b**) — **de** to soak up, soak in.
(**c**) — **de**, — **en** (*fig*) to steep oneself in; to become imbued with.

empapelado *nm* papering, paperhanging.

empapelador *nm* paperhanger.

empapelar [1a] *vt* *object* to wrap in paper; *box* to paper, line with paper; *room, wall* to paper.

empaque *nm* (**a**) packing. (**b**) (*fam*) look, appearance; manner. (**c**) (*fig*) solemnness, pomposity. (**d**) (*SAm*) nerve, effrontery.

empaquetador *nm*, **empaquetadora** *nf* packer.

empaquetadura *nf* packing; filling; (*Mech*) gasket.

empaquetar [1a] *vt* to pack; to pack up, parcel up; (*Comm*) to package.

emparamarse [1a] *vr* (*Bol, Ec, Col, Ven*) to get soaked; to get numb with cold, die of cold.

emparedado *nm* sandwich.

emparedar [1a] *vt* to immure, confine.

emparejar [1a] **1** *vt* (**a**) to pair, match. (**b**) to level, make level; to make flush; to even up. **2** *vi* (**a**) to catch up (*con* with), come abreast (*con* of). (**b**) to be even (*con* with). **3 emparejarse** *vr* to match.

emparentado *adj* related by marriage (*con* to).

emparentar [1k] *vi* to become related by marriage (*con* to); — **con una familia** to marry into a family.

emparrado *nm* trained vine; vine arbour.

emparrandarse [1a] *vr* (*SAm*) to go on a binge (*sl*).

empastado *adj* (**a**) (*Typ*) clothbound, bound. (**b**) *tooth* filled.

empastar [1a] **1** *vt* (**a**) to paste.
(**b**) (*Typ*) to bind in stiff covers, bind in cloth.
(**c**) *tooth* to fill, stop.
(**d**) (*SAm*) to convert into pasture land.
2 empastarse *vr* (*Arg, Chi: of cattle*) to get blown.

empaste *nm* filling.

empatar [1a] **1** *vt* (**a**) (*SAm*) to join, connect, tie firmly together.
(**b**) (*Ven*) to bother, harass.
(**c**) (*Chi*) *time* to waste.
2 *vi* (*games*) to draw, tie; (*races*) to tie, have a dead heat; (*voting*) to tie; **los equipos empataron a 2** the teams drew 2-all.

empate *nm* (**a**) draw, tie; dead heat; **un** — **a 0** a 0-0 draw, a goalless draw. (**b**) (*SAm*) joint, connection.

emparar [1a] **1** *vt* (**a**) (*Ec*) to anger. (**b**) (*Per*) to make fun of. **2 empararse** *vr* (*Per*) to blush.

empavesado *nm* bunting.

empavesar [1a] *vt* to deck, adorn; *ship* to dress.

empavonar [1a] **1** *vt* (**a**) (*Tech*) *steel* to blue. (**b**) (*SAm*) to grease, cover with grease. **2 empavonarse** *vr* (*CAm*) to dress up.

empecatado *adj* (**a**) incorrigible; wily, fiendish. (**b**) ill-fated.

empecinado *adj* (*SAm*) stubborn, pigheaded.

empecinamiento *nm* (*SAm*) stubbornness, pigheadedness.

empecinarse [1a] *vr* (*SAm*) to be stubborn; — **en algo** to be stubborn about something; — **en** + *infin* to persist wilfully in + *ger*.

empedarse [1a] *vr* (*Mex, RPl*) to get drunk.

empedernido *adj* (**a**) *person* heartless; obdurate; *heart* flinty, stony.
(**b**) (*in a bad habit*) hardened, inveterate; **un fumador** — a strongly addicted smoker, a smoker

firmly set in the habit; **un pecador** — an unregenerate sinner.

empedernir [3a: *defective*] **1** *vt* to harden. **2 empedernirse** *vr* (a) to harden; to petrify. (b) (*fig*) to harden one's heart, resolve to be tough.

empedrado 1 *adj surface* paved; (*fig*) pitted (*de* with); *face* pockmarked; *colouring* dappled, flecked; *sky* cloud-flecked. **2** *nm* paving.

empedrar [1k] *vt* to pave.

empegado *nm* tarpaulin.

empeine *nm* (a) (*Anat*) groin; instep. (b) (*Bot*) cotton flower. (c) —s (*Med*) ringworm.

empelotado *adj* (a) (*Col, Cu, Chi, Mex*) naked, stripped. (b) (*Mex*) in love.

empelotar [1a] **1** *vt* (a) (*SAm*) to undress, strip to the skin.
(b) (*SAm*) to strip down, dismantle, take to pieces.
2 empelotarse *vr* (a) (*fam*) to get muddled.
(b) (*fam*) to get into a row.
(c) (*Col, Cu, Chi, Mex*) to strip naked.
(d) (*Cu, Mex*) to fall in love (*con* with).

empelucado *adj* bewigged.

empella *nf* (a) (*shoemaker's*) vamp; uppers. (b) (*SAm*) lard.

empellar [1a] *vt* to push, shove, jostle.

empellón *nm* push, shove; **mover a** —**es** to shove, move by pushing; **abrirse paso a** —**es** to get through by shoving, push one's way rudely through, push roughly past; **dar** —**es** to shove, jostle.

empenachar [1a] *vt* to adorn with plumes.

empeñado *adj* (a) *valuable* pawned.
(b) **estar** — **hasta los ojos** to be deeply in debt.
(c) *person* determined; **estar** — **en** + *infin* to be determined to + *infin*, be completely set on + *ger*.
(d) *argument* bitter, heated.

empeñar [1a] **1** *vt* (a) *valuable* to pawn, pledge.
(b) *word* to pledge, give; *person* to engage, compel.
(c) *battle* to join; *argument* to start.
2 empeñarse *vr* (a) to bind oneself, pledge oneself.
(b) to get into debt.
(c) — **en algo** to insist on something; to persist in something; — **en** + *infin* to be determined to + *infin*, be set on + *ger*; to insist on + *ger*; **se empeña en que es así** he insists that it is so.
(d) — **en una lucha** to engage in a fight; — **en una discusión** to get involved in a heated argument.
(e) — **por uno** to intercede for someone, intervene on someone's behalf.

empeñero *nm* (*Mex*) pawnbroker, moneylender.

empeño *nm* (a) pledge.
(b) obligation, undertaking.
(c) determination; insistence; **su** — **en hacerlo** his determination to do it; his insistence on doing it; **con** — with determination; insistently; eagerly, keenly; **tener** — **en** + *infin* to be bent on + *ger*, be eager to + *infin*.
(d) pawnshop; moneylender's.

empeñoso *adj* (*SAm*) persevering, diligent.

empeoramiento *nm* deterioration, worsening.

empeorar [1a] **1** *vt* to make worse, worsen; to impair.
2 *vi and* **empeorarse** *vr* to get worse, worsen, deteriorate.

empequeñecer [2d] *vt* (a) to dwarf, make (seem) smaller. (b) (*fig*) to minimize; to belittle.

emperador *nm* (a) emperor. (b) (*Cu*) swordfish.

emperatriz *nf* empress.

emperejilarse [1a] *vr* to dress up, doll oneself up.

empericarse [1g] *vr* (a) (*Col, Ec*) to get drunk. (b) (*Cu, Mex*) to blush.

emperifollar [1a] **1** *vt* to adorn, deck; *person* to doll up. **2 emperifollarse** *vr* to dress up, doll oneself up.

empernar [1k] *vt* to bolt, secure with a bolt; to fit a bolt to.

empero *conj* (*arch and lit*) but; yet, however.

emperramiento *nm* stubbornness.

emperrarse [1a] *vr* to get stubborn, be obstinate; — **en algo** to be stubborn about something; to persist in something.

emperro *nm* (*prov, Ec*) stubbornness; fit of temper.

empertigar [1h] *vt* (*Chi*) *horse* to hitch up.

empezar [1f *and* 1k] *vti* to begin, start; — **a** + *infin* to start to + *infin*; — **por** + *inf*, — + *ger* to begin by + *ger*, start by + *ger*; **empezó diciendo que . . .** he began by saying that . . .; **bueno, para** — well, to start with.

empicotar [1a] *vt* to pillory.

empiezo *nm* (*Arg, Col, Ec, Guat*) = **comienzo**.

empilchar [1a] *vt* (*RPl*) *horse* to saddle; *person* to provide with clothing.

empilonar [1a] *vt* (*Col, Cu, PR*) to pile up.

empinada *nf* (*Aer*) steep climb, zoom upward.

empinado *adj* (a) steep; high, lofty. (b) (*fig*) proud; stiff.

empinar [1a] **1** *vt* (a) to raise, lift; to tip up; *see* **codo**.
(b) to straighten.
2 *vi* (*fam*) to drink, booze.
3 empinarse *vr* (a) (*person*) to stand on tiptoe; (*horse*) to rear up; (*building*) to tower, soar; (*Aer*) to climb steeply, zoom upwards.
(b) (*Chi, Ec*) to overeat.

empingorotado *adj* (*fam*) stuck-up (*fam*).

empipada *nf* (*Chi, Ec*) blow-out (*sl*).

empiparse *vr* (*Chi, Ec*): — **algo** to eat something right up, drink something down.

empírico 1 *adj* empiric(al). **2** *nm* empiricist.

empirismo *nm* empiricism.

empizarrado *nm* slate roof.

empizarrar [1a] *vt* to roof with slates.

emplantillar [1a] *vt* (a) (*Chi, Per, SD*) *shoes* to put insoles into. (b) (*Chi, Per*) *wall* to fill with rubble.

emplastar [1a] *vt* (a) (*Med*) to put a plaster on, poultice. (b) *face* to make up, paint. (c) *deal* to block.

emplaste *nm* (a) (*Med*) plaster, poultice. (b) (*fig*) makeshift arrangement. (c) weakling; misfit, useless individual. (d) (*SAm*) bore, tedious person.

emplazamiento *nm* (a) (*Law*) summons; summoning. (b) site, location; (*Mil*) (gun) emplacement.

emplazar [1f] *vt* (a) to summon, convene; (*Law*) to summons; to subpoena. (b) to site, locate, place; *statue etc* to set up, erect.

empleado *nm* employee; (*esp*) clerk, office worker, clerical worker; — **bancario**, — **de banco** bank clerk; — **de confianza** confidential clerk; — **de correos** post-office worker; — **de pompas fúnebres** undertaker's assistant, mortician's assistant (*US*); — **público** civil servant; — **de ventanilla** booking office clerk, counter clerk.

emplear [1a] **1** *vt* *tool, word etc* to use, employ; *person* to employ; to give a job to, engage, hire; *time* to occupy, spend; to put in; *money* to invest; — **mal** to misuse; -- **mal el tiempo** to waste time.
2 emplearse *vr* to be used, be employed; — **haciendo algo** to occupy oneself doing something; **¡bien se te emplea!** it serves you right!

empleo *nm* (a) (*in general*) use, employment; occupation, spending; (*Comm*) investment; **modo de** —" (*on label*) "instructions for use"; **el** — **de esa palabra es censurable** the use of that word is to be condemned.
(b) employment, work; **pleno** — full employment.
(c) job, employment, post; **buscar un** — to look for a job; **estar sin** — to be unemployed, be out of a job; "**solicitan** —" (*heading*) "situations wanted".

emplomadura *nf* leading; lead covering, lead lining; (*Arg: of tooth*) filling.

emplomar [1a] *vt* to lead; to cover (*or* line, weight *etc*) with lead; to seal with lead; (*Arg*) *tooth* to fill.

emplumar [1a] **1** *vt* (a) to adorn with feathers; (*punishment*) to tar and feather; **¡que te cmplumen!** (*fam*) get lost! (*fam*).
(b) (*CAm, Cu*) to swindle.
(c) (*CAm*) to beat up; to thrash.
(d) (*Cu*) *employee* to fire (*fam*).
(e) (*Col, Chi*) —**las** to run away.
2 *vi* (a) to grow feathers.
(b) (*SAm*) to run away, take to one's heels.

emplumecer [2d] *vi* to grow feathers.

empobrecer [2d] **1** *vt* to impoverish. **2 empobrecerse** *vr* to become poor, become impoverished.

empobrecimiento *nm* impoverishment.

empolvado *adj substance* powdery; *surface* dusty.

empolvar [1a] **1** *vt* *face* to powder; *surface* to cover with dust, make dusty.
2 empolvarse *vr* (a) (*person*) to powder oneself, powder one's face, put powder on; (*surface*) to get dusty, gather dust.
(b) (*Mex*) to get rusty, get out of practice.
(c) (*SD*) to run away.

empollar [1a] **1** *vt* (a) to incubate, sit on; to hatch. (b) (*Univ etc: fam*) *subject* to swot up (*fam*).
2 *vi* (a) (*of hen*) to sit, brood.
(b) (*of insects*) to breed.
(c) (*Univ etc: fam*) *subject* to swot (*fam*), cram.

empollón *nm*, **empollona** *nf* (*Univ etc: fam*) swot (*fam*).

emponchado *adj* (a) (*SAm*) wearing a poncho, covered with a poncho. (b) (*Arg, Per, Urug*) suspicious; crafty, hypocritical.

emponcharse [1a] *vr* (*SAm*) to put on one's poncho, wrap oneself up in one's poncho.

emponzoñamiento *nm* poisoning.

emponzoñar [1a] *vt* to poison; (*fig*) to poison; to taint, corrupt.

emporcar [1g *and* 1m] *vt* to soil, dirty, foul.

emporio *nm* emporium, mart, trading centre; (*SAm*) large department stores.

emporroso *adj* (*CAm*, *Ven*) annoying; wearisome.

empotrado *adj* cupboard *etc* built-in; (*Mech*) fixed, integral.

empotrar [1a] **1** *vt* to embed, fix; *cupboard etc* to build in.

2 empotrarse *vr*: **el coche se empotró en la tienda** the car embedded itself in the shop; **los vagones se empotraron uno en otro** the carriages telescoped together.

empotrerar [1a] *vt* (a) (*SAm*) *cattle* to pasture, put out to pasture. (b) (*Arg*, *Cu*) *land* to convert into fenced pasture.

empozarse [1f] *vr* (*Arg*, *Per*) to form pools.

emprendedor 1 *adj* enterprising; go-ahead, pushful. **2** *nm* (*Fin*) entrepreneur.

emprender [1a] *vt* (a) to undertake; to take on, tackle; to begin on, embark on; — **marcha a** to set out for; — **el regreso** to go back, return; to begin the homeward journey; — **la retirada** to retreat.

(b) —**la** to start, set out; —**la con uno** to tackle someone about a matter, have it out with someone; to have a row with someone; **la emprendieron con el árbitro a botellazos** they attacked the referee by throwing bottles at him.

empreñar [1a] **1** *vt* *woman* to make pregnant, get with child; *animal* to impregnate, mate with. **2 empreñarse** *vr* to become pregnant.

empresa *nf* (a) (*spirit etc*) enterprise; — **libre**, **libre** — free enterprise; — **privada** private enterprise.

(b) (*Comm*, *Fin*) enterprise, undertaking, venture; company, concern; — **colectiva** joint venture; — **funeraria** undertaker's; — **particular** private company; — **de servicios públicos** public utility company.

(c) (*esp Theat*) management; **la — lamenta que ...** the management regrets that ...

empresarial *adj* owners', managers'; *function*, *class etc* managerial.

empresario *nm* (*Tech*) manager; (*Mus*, *of opera etc*) impresario; (*Boxing*) promoter; (*Comm*) contractor; — **de pompas fúnebres** undertaker, mortician (*US*); — **de transporte** (*Arg*) shipping agent.

emprestar [1a] *vt* (*SAm*) to lend; to borrow.

empréstito *nm* (public) loan; — **de guerra** war loan.

empujada *nf* (*Arg*, *Guat*, *Urug*, *Ven*) push, shove.

empujadora-niveladora *nf* bulldozer.

empujar [1a] *vt* (a) to push, shove; to push, thrust (*en* into); (*Mech*) to drive, move, propel; *bicycle* to push, wheel; *button* to press; **"empujad"** (*on doors etc*) "push"; — **el botón a fondo** to press the button down hard; **¡no empujen!** stop pushing!, don't shove!

(b) (*fam*) *person* to sack (*fam*), give the push to (*fam*).

(c) — **algo** (*fam*) to work behind the scenes for something, intrigue to get something.

empujatierra *nf* bulldozer.

empuje *nm* (a) (*in general*) pressure; (*Mech*, *Phys*) thrust.

(b) (*un* —) push, shove.

(c) (*fig*) push, pushfulness, drive, thrustfulness; **le falta** — he hasn't got any go to him, he lacks drive; **en un espíritu de** — in a thrustful spirit.

empujón *nm* push, shove; dig, poke, jab; **abrirse paso a** —**es** to shove one's way through, get through by pushing; **avanzar a** —**es** to go forward by fits and starts, go jerkily forward; **trabajar a** —**es** to work intermittently.

empulgueras *nfpl* thumbscrew.

empuntar [1a] *vt* (a) to put a point on. (b) (*Col*, *Ec*) —**las** to run away. **2 empuntarse** *vr* (*Ven*) to dig one's heels in.

empuñadura *nf* (a) (*of sword*) hilt; (*of tool etc*) grip, handle. (b) (*of story*) start, opening.

empuñar [1a] *vt* (a) to grasp, clutch, grip, take (firm) hold of; (*Chi*) *fist* to clench. (b) (*fig*) — **las armas** to take up arms; — **el bastón** to take command. (c) (*Bol*) to punch, hit with one's fist.

empupar [1a] *vt* (*SAm*) to pupate.

empurrarse [1a] *vr* (*CAm*) to get angry.

emú *nm* emu.

emulación *nf* emulation.

emulador 1 *adj* emulous (*de* of). **2** *nm*, **emuladora** *nf* rival.

emular [1a] **1** *vt* to emulate, rival. **2** *vi*: — **con** = *vt*.

émulo 1 *adj* emulous. **2** *nm*, **emula** *nf* rival, competitor.

emulsión *nf* emulsion.

emulsionar [1a] *vt* to emulsify.

en *prep* (a) (*place*) in; into; on, upon; at; **está** — **el cajón** it's in the drawer; **meter algo** — **el bolsillo** to put something in (*or* into) one's pocket; **no entra** — **el agujero** it won't go into the hole; **está** — **el suelo** it's on the floor; **está** — **Argentina** he's in Argentina; **está** — **Santiago** he's in Santiago; **está** — **algún lugar de la Mancha** he's at some place in la Mancha; — **casa** at home; **te esperé** — **la estación** I waited for you at the station; **trabaja** — **la tienda** she works in the shop; **ir de puerta** — **puerta** to go from door to door.

(b) (*time*) in; on; — **1605** in 1605; — **el siglo X** in the 10th century; — **aquella ocasión** on that occasion; **lo terminaron** — **3 semanas** they finished it in 3 weeks.

(c) (*price*) at, for; **lo vendió** — **5 dólares** he sold it at (*or* for) 5 dollars.

(d) (*rate*) by; **reducir algo** — **una tercera parte** to reduce something by a third; **ha aumentado** — **un 20 por cien** it has increased by 20%.

(e) (*means*) **le conocí** — **el andar** I recognized him by his walk; **ir** — **avión** to go by plane, go by air; **vine** — **el autobús** I came by bus, I came in the bus.

(f) (*with verb*) — **viéndole se lo dije** the moment I saw him I told him; — **viéndole se lo diré** the moment I see him I'll tell him, as soon as I see him I'll tell him.

enaceitar [1a] *vt* (*RPl*) to oil.

enagua *nf* (*SAm*), **enaguas** *nfpl* petticoat; underskirt.

enaguazar [1f] *vt* to flood.

enajenación *nf*, **enajenamiento** *nm* (a) (*Law etc*) alienation; transfer; **enajenación forzosa** expropriation.

(b) estrangement.

(c) absentmindedness; rapture, trance; — **mental** mental derangement.

enajenar [1a] **1** *vt* (a) (*Law etc*) *property* to alienate, transfer; *rights* to dispose of.

(b) *person* to alienate, estrange.

(c) (*fig*) to enrapture, carry away; to drive mad.

2 enajenarse *vr* (a) — **algo** to deprive oneself of something; — **las simpatías** to alienate people, make oneself disliked.

(b) (*of friends*) to become estranged.

(c) to be enraptured, get carried away.

enaltecer [2d] *vt* to exalt; to praise, extol.

enamoradizo *adj* susceptible (to women), of an amorous disposition.

enamorado *adj* (a) in love, lovesick. (b) **estar** — **to** be in love (*de* with). (c) (*Arg*, *Chi*, *PR*) = **enamoradizo**.

enamoramiento *nm* falling in love; infatuation.

enamorar [1a] **1** *vt* to inspire love in, win the love of; **por fin la enamoró** eventually he got her to fall in love with him.

2 enamorarse *vr* to fall in love (*de* with).

enamoricarse [1g] *vr*, **enamoriscarse** [1g] *vr* (*SAm*) to be just a bit in love (*de* with); to become mildly infatuated (*de* with).

enancar [1g] **1** *vt* (*SAm*) to put someone on the crupper (of one's horse).

2 *vi* (*Arg*) to follow, be a consequence (*a* of).

3 enancarse *vr* (a) (*SAm*) to get up on the crupper, ride behind.

(b) (*Mex*: *of horse*) to rear up.

enangostar [1a] **1** *vt* to narrow. **2 enangostarse** *vr* to narrow, get narrower.

enano 1 *adj* dwarf, small, tiny; stunted. **2** *nm* dwarf; midget; (*pej*) runt.

enarbolar [1a] **1** *vt* *flag etc* to hoist, raise; to hang up, hang out; *sword etc* to flourish.

2 enarbolarse *vr* (a) (*person*) to get angry.

(b) (*horse*) to rear up.

enarcar [1g] *vt* (a) (*Tech*) to hoop, put a hoop on.

(b) *eyebrows* to raise, arch; *back* (*of cat*) to arch; *chest* to throw out.

enardecer [2d] **1** *vt* to fire, inflame; to fill with enthusiasm.

2 enardecerse *vr* (a) (*Med*) to become inflamed.

(b) (*fig*) to get excited, get enthusiastic (*por* about); to blaze, be afire (*de* with).

enarenar [1a] **1** *vt* to sand, cover with sand. **2 enarenarse** *vr* (*Naut*) to run aground.

enastado *adj* horned; antlered, with antlers.

encabalgamiento *nm* (*Lit*) enjambement.

encabestrar [1a] **1** *vt* (a) to put a halter on; to lead by a halter. (b) (*fig*) to overcome, dominate. **2 encabestrarse** *vr* (*SAm*) to dig one's heels in.

encabezado 1 *adj wine* fortified. **2** *nm* **(a)** *(Mex)* heading; headline. **(b)** *(PR)* foreman.

encabezamiento *nm* **(a)** heading; headline; rubric; caption; opening words, preamble; *(Comm)* bill head, letterhead. **(b)** roll, register.

encabezar [1f] *vt* **(a)** *movement, revolution etc* to lead, head.
(b) *list, league etc* to head, be at the top of, come first in.
(c) *paper, document* to put a heading to; *article* to head, entitle; *sketch etc* to caption.
(d) *population etc* to register (for tax purposes etc).
(e) *wine* to fortify.

encabrestarse *vr* *(SAm)*=**emperrarse**.

encabritarse [1a] *vr* *(of horse)* to rear up.

encabronar [1a] *vt* *(Col, Cu)* to make angry.

encabuyar [1a] *vt* *(Ant, Col, Ven)* to tie up (with sisal cord).

encachar [1a] **1** *vt* *(Chi)* head to lower. **2** *vi* *(Mex)* to get oneself a sweetheart. **3 encacharse** *vr* *(Ven)* to refuse to give way.

encachilarse [1a] *vr* *(Arg)* to get furious.

encachorrarse [1a] *vr* *(Col)* to get angry; *(Chi, PR, Ven)* to turn obstinate.

encadenación *nf*, **encadenamiento** *nm* **(a)** chaining (together). **(b)** *(fig)* linking, connection, concatenation.

encadenar [1a] *vt* **(a)** to chain (together); to put chains on, fetter, shackle. **(b)** *(fig)* to shackle, paralyse, immobilize. **(c)** *(fig)* to connect, link.

encajadura *nf* **(a)** *(act)* insertion, filling. **(b)** socket; groove; frame.

encajar [1a] **1** *vt* **(a)** to insert, fit *(en* into); to push in, thrust in, force in; *machine etc* to house, encase; *parts* to join, fit together, fit into each other.
(b) *remark etc* to get in, put in, intrude; *story (fam)* to come out with, choose the wrong moment to tell; *hint* to drop.
(c) — *algo a uno* to palm something off on someone, foist something off on someone; — *una historia a uno* to force someone to listen to a (disagreeable) story.
(d) *blow (fam)* to give, deal; **le encajó un bofetón** he gave him a punch.
(e) *(fam)* to chuck *(a* at).
2 *vi* **(a)** to fit; to fit well (*or* properly); **esto no encaja bien** this doesn't fit properly.
(b) *(fig)* to fit, match, correspond; to be appropriate; **esto no encaja con lo que dijo antes** this does not square with what he said before.
3 encajarse *vr* **(a)** *(fam)* to squeeze (oneself) in; *(fig)* to intrude, gatecrash; — **en una reunión** to intrude upon a meeting; — **en una fiesta** to crash a party *(fam)*.
(b) *(fam)* to butt in.
(c) — *una chaqueta* to put on a jacket.

encaje *nm* **(a)** *(act)* insertion, fitting; fitting together, joining.
(b) socket, cavity; groove; frame; *(Mech)* housing.
(c) inlay, inlaid work, mosaic; *(Sew)* lace; — **de aplicación** appliqué (work).
(d) *(Fin)* reserve, stock; — **de oro** gold reserve.

encajera *nf* lacemaker.

encajetillar [1a] *vt* *(Mex)* to pack in boxes, box.

encajonado *nm* cofferdam.

encajonar [1a] **1** *vt* **(a)** to box (up), put in a box, crate, pack (in a box); *(Mech)* to box in, encase.
(b) *river* to confine (between banks), canalize.
(c) to squeeze in, squeeze through.
2 encajonarse *vr* *(SAm: of river)* to run through a narrow place, run between steep banks.

encalabrinar [1a] **1** *vt* **(a)** *(Med)* to make dizzy, make giddy.
(b) — **a uno** to get someone worked up; to fluster someone.
(c) *(fam)* — **a una** to attract a girl, click with a girl *(fam)*, get a girl to show an interest.
2 encalabrinarse *vr* *(fam)* **(a)** to get an obsession, get the bit between one's teeth; to dig one's heels in.
(b) — **de una** to get infatuated with a girl; **X anda encalabrinado con Z** X is mad keen on Z *(fam)*.

encaladura *nf* **(a)** whitewash(ing). **(b)** *(Agr)* liming.

encalambrarse [1a] *vr* *(SAm)* to get cramp; to get stiff with cold.

encalamocar [1g] **1** *vt* *(Col, Ven)* **(a)** to make drunk.
(b) to confuse, bewilder.
2 encalamocarse *vr* *(Col, Ven)* **(a)** to get drunk.
(b) to get confused, get bewildered.

encalar [1a] *vt* **(a)** *wall* to whitewash. **(b)** *(Agr)* to lime.

encalatarse [1a] *vr* *(Per)* **(a)** to strip naked. **(b)** to be ruined.

encalmado *adj* **(a)** *(Naut)* becalmed. **(b)** *(Comm, Fin)* quiet, slack, dull.

encalmarse [1a] *vr* to be becalmed.

encalvecer [2d] *vi* to go bald.

encalladero *nm* shoal, sandbank.

encalladura *nf* stranding, running aground.

encallar [1a] *vi* **(a)** *(Naut)* to run aground, run ashore, get stranded *(en* on). **(b)** *(fig)* to fail; *(in negotiation etc)* to get stuck, get bogged down.

encallecido *adj* hardened.

encamar [1a] **1** *vt* **(a)** *(CAm, Mex)* to take to hospital, hospitalize.
(b) *(Cu) animals* to litter, bed down.
2 encamarse *vr* **(a)** to take to one's bed; — **con una** *(Arg, Per)* to go to bed with someone; **estar encamado** to be confined to bed.
(b) *(corn etc)* to be laid, be flattened.
(c) *(animal)* to crouch, hide.

encamillado *nm*, **encamillada** *nf* *(CAm, Mex)* stretcher case.

encaminar [1a] **1** *vt* **(a)** to guide, direct, set on the right road *(a* to); **pude —le** I was able to tell him the way to go.
(b) *vehicle, expedition etc* to route *(por* via).
(c) *attention, energies etc* to direct *(a* towards); **medidas encaminadas a corregir esto** measures designed to correct this; **el proyecto está encaminado a + infin** the plan is directed towards + ger, the plan is designed to + infin.
2 encaminarse *vr* **(a)** — **a** to set out for, make for, take the road to.
(b) *(fig)* — **a** to be directed towards, be intended for.

encamotado *adj* *(SAm)*: **estar —** to be in love *(de* with).

encamotarse [1a] *vr* *(SAm)* to fall in love *(de* with); to become very affectionate *(de* towards).

encampanado *adj* bell-shaped.

encampanar [1a] **1** *vt* **(a)** *(Col, PR, SD, Ven)* to raise, raise on high.
(b) *(Mex, Per, PR)* to leave in the lurch, leave in a jam.
(c) *(PR, Ven)* — **a uno a** to send someone to.
2 encampanarse *vr* **(a)** *(SAm)* to boast, brag.
(b) *(Col)* to fall in love.
(c) *(Mex)* to get into a jam.
(d) *(Ven)* to go off to a remote spot.

encanalar [1a] *vt*, **encanalizar** [1f] *vt* to pipe; to channel, canalize.

encanallarse [1a] *vr* to degrade oneself; to become coarse, acquire coarse habits.

encanar [1a] *vt* *(Arg, Col, Chi)* to nick *(sl)*, arrest.

encandecer [2d] *vt* to make white-hot.

encandelar [1a] *vt* *(Cu)* to annoy, irritate.

encandelillar [1a] *vt* *(SAm)* to dazzle; to bewilder.

encandellar [1a] *vt* *(Col, Per)* to kindle, light.

encandiladera *nf* procuress; madame.

encandilado *adj* high, erect.

encandiladora *nf* procuress; madame.

encandilar [1a] **1** *vt* **(a)** to dazzle.
(b) *fire* to stir, poke.
(c) *(fig) person* to daze, bewilder.
(d) *(fig) emotion* to kindle, stimulate.
(e) *(Per, PR)* to deprive of sleep.
2 encandilarse *vr* **(a)** *(eyes)* to glitter, sparkle, look unnaturally bright.
(b) *(Col, Per, PR)* to get scared; *(Mex, PR)* to get angry.

encanecer [2d] *vi* and **encanecerse** *vr* **(a)** *(of hair)* to go grey; *(of person)* to go grey, look old. **(b)** *(fig)* to go mouldy.

encanijado *adj* weak, puny.

encanijarse [1a] *vr* to grow weak, become emaciated, begin to look ill.

encanillar [1a] *vt* to wind (on to a spool).

encantado *adj* **(a)** bewitched; haunted; *spot* romantic, bewitching; *house (fig)* rambling.
(b) delighted, pleased, charmed; **¡—!** *(at introduction)* how do you do!, pleased to meet you; **estoy — de conocerle** I'm delighted to meet you; **yo, —** it's all right with me.
(c) absent-minded, daydreaming; **parecer estar —** to seem to be in a trance.

encantador 1 *adj* charming, delightful, lovely, enchanting. **2** *nm*, **encantadora** *nf* magician, enchanter; — **de serpientes** snake charmer.

encantamiento *nm* enchantment.

encantar [1a] *vt* **(a)** to bewitch, cast a spell on (*or* over).
(b) to charm, delight, enchant, captivate,

fascinate; **nos encanta la casa** we are delighted with the house, we are charmed with the house; **pero pronto dejó de —nos** but we soon stopped liking it.

encanto *nm* **(a)** charm, spell, enchantment; **como por — ** as if by magic; *(fig)* in a flash, instantly.

(b) *(fig)* charm; enchantment, delight; **la playa es un —** the beach is delightful, the beach is marvellous; **el niño es un —** the child is a little treasure; **¡qué — de jardín!** what a lovely garden!

(c) *(as endearment)* sweetheart, my love; **¡oye, —!** hullo gorgeous! *(fam)*.

encantoso *adj* *(Mex)* =**encantador.**

encañada *nf* ravine.

encañado *nm* conduit, pipe.

encañar [1a] **1** *vt* **(a)** *water* to pipe. **(b)** *plant* to stake, prop up. **(c)** *land* to drain. **(d)** *silk* to wind (on to a spool). **2** *vi* *(of plant)* to form a stalk.

encañizado *nm* wire netting, protective fence.

encañonar [1a] **1** *vt* **(a)** to pipe. **(b)** *(fam)* to stick up *(sl)*, hold up; to cover (with a gun). **2** *vi* *(of bird)* to grow feathers.

encapado *adj* cloaked, wearing a cloak.

encapotado *adj* **(a)** cloaked, wearing a cloak. **(b)** *sky* cloudy, overcast.

encapotar [1a] **1** *vt* to cover with a cloak.

2 encapotarse *vr* **(a)** to put on one's cloak; to wrap up.

(b) *(fig)* to frown.

(c) *(Meteorol)* to become cloudy, cloud over, become overcast.

encapricharse [1a] *vr* to persist in one's foolishness; to dig one's heels in, insist on having one's way; **— por** to take a fancy to, get infatuated with.

encapuchado *adj* hooded.

encarado *adj*: **bien —** good-looking, with nice features; **mal —** ill-favoured, plain; *(SAm)* wicked-looking, with criminal features.

encaramar [1a] **1** *vt* **(a)** to raise, lift up.

(b) to praise, extol.

(c) *(Col, CR)* to embarrass, cause to blush.

2 encaramarse *vr* **(a)** to perch, sit up high; **— a** to climb (up, on to), get to the top of.

(b) *(Col, CR)* to get embarrassed, blush.

encarapitarse [1a] *vr* *(Col, Ec, SD)* =**encaramarse (a).**

encarar [1a] **1** *vt* **(a)** *gun* to aim, point.

(b) to face; *(SAm)* to face up to, begin to study.

(c) *(Par)* to sicken.

2 encararse *vr*: **— a, — con** to face, confront, come face to face with; **tendrá que — con los electores** he will have to face the electorate; **se encaró en seguida con el problema** he immediately faced up to the problem.

encarcelación *nf*, **encarcelamiento** *nm* imprisonment.

encarcelar [1a] *vt* to imprison, jail.

encarecer [2d] **1** *vt* **(a)** *(Comm)* to put up the price of, make more expensive.

(b) to praise, extol; *person* to recommend; *policy etc* to recommend (*a* to), urge (*a* on); *difficulty etc* to stress, emphasize; to exaggerate; **le encarezco que . . .** I urge you to + *infin*.

2 *vi* and **encarecerse** *vr* *(Comm)* to get dearer, rise in price.

encarecidamente *adv* insistently, earnestly, strongly.

encarecimiento *nm* **(a)** rise in price, price increase.

(b) extolling; stressing, emphasizing; exaggeration, overrating; **con —** insistently, earnestly, strongly.

encargado **1** *adj*: **el empleado — de estos géneros** the employee in charge of these stocks.

2 *nm*, **encargada** *nf* agent, representative; person in charge; **— de curso** lecturer in charge; **— de mostrador** counter clerk; **— de negocios** *(Pol)* chargé d'affaires; *(Col, Mex)* agent; **— de la recepción** receptionist; **— de relaciones públicas** public relations officer; **encargada de vestuario** *(Theat)* wardrobe mistress.

encargar [1h] **1** *vt* to entrust; to charge, commission; to urge, recommend, advise; to ask for; *(Comm)* to order; **— algo a uno** to entrust something to someone; to put someone in charge of something; **— un deber a uno** to charge someone with a duty.

2 encargarse *vr* **(a)** **— de algo** to take charge of something; to take something over; to look after something, see about something, attend to something; **no había queso, pues las ratas se habían encargado de ello** there was no cheese, because the rats had seen to that (or had made sure of that).

(b) **— de** + *infin* to see about + *ger*, attend to the matter of + *ger*; to undertake to + *infin*.

encargo *nm* **(a)** assignment, job; post; charge, commission; responsibility; **tener — de** + *infin* to have

the job of + *ger*, have the responsibility of + *ger*.

(b) order, request; *(Comm)* order (*de* for); **cancelar el —** to cancel the order for, stop the delivery of.

(c) **estar de —** *(Arg, SD, Urug)* to be pregnant.

encargue *nm* *(Arg, Par)* =**encargo.**

encariñado *adj*: **estar — con** to be fond of, be attached to.

encariñarse [1a] *vr*: **— con** to grow fond of, get attached to.

encarnación *nf* incarnation; embodiment.

encarnadino *adj* incarnadine, blood-red.

encarnado *adj* **(a)** incarnate. **(b)** red, blood-red; flesh-coloured; *complexion* ruddy, *(pej)* florid; **ponerse —** to blush red.

encarnar [1a] **1** *vt* **(a)** to embody, personify; *(Theat)* *role* to play, bring to life.

(b) *fish hook* to bait.

2 *vi* **(a)** *(Rel etc)* to become incarnate.

(b) *(Med)* to heal (up).

(c) *(of weapon)* to enter the flesh, penetrate the body.

encarnecer [2d] *vi* to put on flesh.

encarnizadamente *adv* *(fig)* bloodily, bitterly, fiercely.

encarnizado *adj* **(a)** *wound etc* red, inflamed; *eye* bloodshot. **(b)** bloody; bitter, fierce.

encarnizamiento *nm* rage, fury; bitterness, ferocity.

encarnizar [1f] **1** *vt* *(fig)* to enrage, infuriate; to make cruel.

2 encarnizarse *vr* **(a)** **— en** to gorge on; to become greedy for.

(b) *(fig)* to get furious; to fight fiercely; **— con, — en** to be cruel to, treat cruelly.

encaro *nm* **(a)** stare, staring gaze. **(b)** aim(ing). **(c)** *(Hist)* blunderbuss.

encarpetar [1a] *vt* **(a)** to file away; to pigeonhole; *(fig)* *plan etc* to shelve, bury. **(b)** *(SAm)* *motion* to table, propose.

encarrilar [1a] *vt* **(a)** to put back on the rails.

(b) *(fig)* to put on the right track, start off again on the right lines; to correct; to direct, guide.

(c) **ir encarrilado** *(fig)* to be on the right lines, be doing nicely; *(pej)* to be in a rut.

encarrujar [1a] *vt* *(RPl: Sew)* to ruffle, frill.

encartuchar [1a] *vt* *paper* to make a cone of, roll up into a cone.

encartar [1a] *vt* **(a)** to enroll, register, enter (on a list); *(Law)* to summon. **(b)** *criminal* to outlaw.

encartonar [1a] *vt* to cover with cardboard; *(Typ)* to bind in boards.

encasar [1a] *vt* *bone* to set.

encasillado **1** *adj* *actor* type-cast. **2** *nm* (set of) pigeonholes.

encasillar [1a] *vt* **(a)** to pigeonhole; to sort out, classify; to file. **(b)** *(Theat etc)* to type-cast.

encasquetar [1a] *vt* **(a)** *hat* to pull on, pull down tight, jam on. **(b)** **— una idea a uno** to get an idea firmly fixed in someone's mind. **2 encasquetarse** *vr* see *vt*.

encasquillador *nm* *(SAm)* blacksmith, horse-shoer.

encasquillar [1a] **1** *vt* **(a)** to put a tip on.

(b) *(SAm)* *horse* to shoe.

2 encasquillarse *vr* **(a)** *(Cu, Ec: of bullet)* to stick in the barrel.

(b) *(Ec: in speech etc)* to get stuck, dry up *(fam)*.

(c) *(Cu)* to get scared.

encastillado *adj* **(a)** *(Archit)* castellated. **(b)** *(fig)* haughty; stubborn.

encastillar [1a] *vt* to fortify, defend with castles. **2 encastillarse** *vr* **(a)** *(Mil)* to take to the hills; *(Hist)* to shut oneself up in a castle. **(b)** *(fig)* to refuse to yield; **— en un principio** to stick to a principle, refuse to give up a principle.

encatrado *nm* *(Arg, Chi)* hurdle.

encatrinarse [1a] *vr* *(Mex)* to dress up.

encauchado *nm* *(Col, Ven)* rubberized cloth; waterproof blanket.

encauchar [1a] *vt* to rubberize, waterproof.

encausar [1a] *vt* to prosecute, sue; to put on trial.

encauzar [1f] *vt* **(a)** to channel.

(b) *(fig)* to channel, direct, guide; **las protestas se pueden — a fines buenos** the protests can be directed towards good objectives, the protests can be guided into useful channels.

encefalitis *nf* encephalitis; **— (letárgica)** sleeping sickness.

enceguecer [2d] *(SAm)* **1** *vt* to blind. **2** *vi* and **enceguecerse** *vr* to go blind.

encelar [1a] **1** *vt* to make jealous. **2 encelarse** *vr* to become jealous.

encenagado *adj* **(a)** muddy, mud-stained. **(b)** *(fig)* sunk in vice, depraved.

encenagarse [1h] *vr* (**a**) to get muddy. (**b**) (*fig*) to wallow in vice, get depraved.

encendedor *nm* (**a**) lighter; — **de cigarrillos** cigarette lighter; — **a gas** gas lighter; — **del gas** gas poker. (**b**) lamplighter.

encender [2g] **1** *vt* (**a**) to light; to set fire to, ignite; to kindle; *match* to strike, light; (*Elec*) *light* to turn on, switch on, put on; *gas* to light, turn on; *radio* to switch on, turn on.
　(**b**) (*fig*) to kindle, inflame; to stir up, provoke.
　(**c**) (*Cu*) to beat.
　2 encenderse *vr* (**a**) (*fire*) to catch, catch fire, ignite; (*flame*) to burn up, flare up.
　(**b**) (*fig*) to get excited; to flare up.
　(**c**) (*face*) to blush, get red.

encendida *nf* (*Cu*) beating.

encendidamente *adv* passionately, ardently.

encendido 1 *adj* (**a**) **estar** — to be alight, be on fire, be burning; (*light*) to be on; (*wire*) to be live.
　(**b**) *colour* glowing (*de* with); fiery.
　(**c**) *face* red (*de* with); inflamed (*de* with). **2** *nm* (*Aut*) ignition.

encendimiento *nm* (**a**) burning; kindling. (**b**) (*fig*) passion, ardour; eagerness; intensity.

encenizar [1f] *vt* to cover with ashes.

encentar [1k] *vt* to begin to use; *loaf etc* to cut the first slice from.

encerado 1 *adj* waxed; waxy, wax-coloured. **2** *nm* (**a**) oilcloth; (*Naut*) tarpaulin. (**b**) (*Med*) sticking plaster. (**c**) (*School etc*) blackboard.

encerador *nm*, **enceradora** *nf* polisher, polishing machine.

encerar [1a] *vt* to wax; *floor* to wax, polish.

encercamiento *nm* (*SAm*) encirclement.

encercar [1g] *vt* (*SAm: angl*) to encircle; = **cercar**.

encerotar [1a] *vt* thread to wax.

encerradero *nm* fold, pen.

encerrar [1k] **1** *vt* (**a**) to shut in, shut up; to lock in, lock up; to enclose; to confine, hem in.
　(**b**) to include, contain, comprise; **el libro encierra profundas verdades** the book contains deep truths.
　(**c**) to involve, imply.
　2 encerrarse *vr* to shut oneself up, lock oneself in; to go into seclusion; **se encerró en su cuarto** she shut herself in her room; — **en el silencio** to maintain a total silence.

encespedar [1a] *vt* to turf.

encía *nf* (*Anat*) gum.

encíclica *nf* encyclical.

enciclopédico *adj* encyclopaedic.

enciclopedia *nf* encyclopaedia.

encielar [1a] *vt* (*Chi, Guat*) to roof, put a roof on.

encierra *nf* (*Chi*) (**a**) penning (of cattle, for slaughter). (**b**) winter pasture.

encierre *nm* (*Ven*) penning (of cattle, for slaughter).

encierro *nm* (**a**) shutting-in. shutting-up, locking, closing; confinement.
　(**b**) enclosure; prison, lock-up; (*Agr*) pen; (*Taur*) bull pen.
　(**c**) (*Taur*) penning (of bulls), corralling.

encima 1 *adj* (**a**) (*place*) above, over; overhead; at the top; on top; **por** — over, overhead; **muy por** — (*fig*) very superficially, very hastily; **póngalo** — **y no debajo** put it over and not under, put it on top and not underneath; **el avión pasó** — the plane passed over.
　(**b**) (*fig*) **echarse algo** — to take something upon oneself, **quitarse algo de** — to get rid of something; to cast something off, shake something off; **la guerra está** — war is upon us, war is imminent; **no llevo tabaco** — I haven't any tobacco on me, I don't carry tobacco; **¿tienes un duro** —? do you have a *duro* about you?; **¿tienes cambio** —? have you any change on you?; **tienes bastante** — you've got enough to worry about.
　(**c**) (*fig*) besides; **y otras muchas cosas** — and a lot else besides, and much else in addition; **de** — (*SAm*) into the bargain; **y** — **no me dio las gracias** and on top of all that he didn't even thank me.
　2 — **de** *prep* (**a**) (*place*) above, over; on; on top of; **por** — **de** over; **pasó** — **de nuestras cabezas** it passed over our heads.
　(**b**) (*fig*) besides, in addition to; **y luego** — **de todo eso** and then in addition to all that, and then on top of all that.

encimar [1a] (*Col, Chi, Per*) **1** *vt* to give as a bonus, put in as an extra. **2** *vi* (*Cards*) to add a new stake.

encime *nm* (*Col*) bonus, extra.

encina *nf* ilex, holm oak, evergreen oak.

encinar *nm* holm-oak wood.

encinta *adj* pregnant; (*Zool*) with young; **mujer** —

pregnant woman, expectant mother; **dejar a una** — to get a girl with a child, put a girl in the family way.

encintado *nm* kerb, kerbstone.

encizañar [1a] **1** *vt* to sow discord among, create trouble among. **2** *vi* to sow discord, cause trouble.

enclaustrar [1a] *vt* to cloister; (*fig*) to hide away.

enclavar [1a] **1** *vt* (**a**) to nail; to pierce, transfix.
　(**b**) to embed, set; *building etc* to set, place; **las ruinas están enclavadas en un valle** the ruins are set in a valley, the ruins have a valley as their setting.
　(**c**) (*fam*) to swindle.
　2 enclavarse *vr* to interlock.

enclave *nm* (*Pol etc*) enclave; small area, isolated area; — **regional de gobierno** regional seat of government.

enclavijar [1a] *vt* to peg, pin; to join.

enclencle *adj* (*SAm*) terribly thin.

enclenco *adj* (*Col, PR*), **enclenque** *adj* weak, weakly, sickly.

enclítico *adj* enclitic.

enclocar [1g and 1m] *vi*, **encloquecer** [2d] *vi* to go broody.

encobar [1a] *vi and* **encobarse** *vr* (*of hen*) to sit, brood.

encocorante *adj* annoying, maddening.

encocorar [1a] (*fam*) **1** *vt* to annoy, enrage, madden. **2 encocorarse** *vr* (**a**) to get cross, get mad. (**b**) (*Cu*) to get suspicious.

encofrado *nm* (*Tech: for concrete etc*) form, plank mould.

encoger [2c] **1** *vt* (**a**) to shrink, contract, shorten.
　(**b**) (*fig*) to intimidate, scare, discourage.
　2 encogerse *vr* (**a**) to shrink, contract; to shrivel up.
　(**b**) — **de hombros** to shrug one's shoulders.
　(**c**) (*fig*) to cringe; to get discouraged, get disheartened; to be shy, be timid.

encogidamente *adv* (*fig*) shyly, timidly, bashfully.

encogido *adj* (**a**) shrunken; shrivelled. (**b**) (*fig*) shy, timid, bashful.

encogimiento *nm* (**a**) shrinking, contraction; shrinkage. (**b**) — **de hombros** shrug (of the shoulders). (**c**) (*fig*) shyness, timidity, bashfulness.

encogollado *adj* (*Chi*) stiff, haughty.

encogollarse [1a] *vr* (*Chi*) to get conceited, be haughty.

encohetarse [1a] *vr* (*Bol, CR*) to get furious.

encojar [1a] **1** *vt* to lame, cripple. **2 encojarse** *vr* to go lame; (*fam*) to pretend to be ill.

encolar [1a] *vt* to glue, gum, paste; to size; to stick down, stick together.

encolerizar [1f] **1** *vt* to anger, provoke. **2 encolerizarse** *vr* to get angry.

encomendar [1k] **1** *vt* to entrust, commend (*a* to, to the charge of). **2 encomendarse** *vr*: — **a** to entrust oneself to, put one's trust in; to send greetings to.

encomendería *nf* (*Per*) grocery store.

encomendero *nm* (*Per*) grocer; (*Cu*) wholesale meat supplier.

encomiar [1b] *vt* to praise, extol, pay tribute to.

encomienda *nf* (**a**) (*Hist*) concession, holding (*land and inhabitants granted to a conquistador*).
　(**b**) charge, commission.
　(**c**) protection; patronage.
　(**d**) praise, tribute, commendation.
　(**e**) (*SAm: Post*) parcel; parcel post; — **contra reembolso** parcel sent cash on delivery.
　(**f**) —**s** regards, respects.

encomio *nm* praise, eulogy, tribute.

encomioso *adj* (*SAm*) laudatory, eulogistic.

enconado *adj* (**a**) (*Med*) inflamed, angry; sore. (**b**) (*fig*) angry, bitter.

enconar [1a] **1** *vt* (**a**) (*Med*) to inflame; to make sore.
　(**b**) (*fig*) to anger, irritate, provoke.
　(**c**) (*Cu, Mex*) to pilfer.
　2 enconarse *vr* (**a**) (*Med*) to become inflamed; to fester.
　(**b**) (*fig*) to get angry, get irritated; (*of grievance*) to fester, rankle.

enconcharse [1a] *vr* (*SAm*) to go into one's shell; to retire into seclusion.

encono *nm* (**a**) rancour, spite(fulness); ill-feeling, bad blood. (**b**) (*Col, Chi*) inflammation, soreness.

enconoso *adj* (**a**) (*Med*) sensitive, subject to inflammation. (**b**) (*fig*) resentful, rancorous, malevolent. (**c**) (*SAm*) *plant* noxious, poisonous.

encontradizo *adj* met by chance; **hacerse el** — to contrive an apparently chance meeting, manage to bump into someone.

encontrado *adj* contrary, conflicting, hostile.

encontrar [1m] **1** *vt* (**a**) to find; **lo encontró bastante fácil** he found it pretty easy; **¿qué tal lo encuentras?**

how do you find it?; **no lo encuentro en ninguna parte** I can't find it anywhere; **no sé lo que le encuentran** I don't know what they see in her.

(b) to meet, encounter, run into; **— dificultades** to encounter difficulties, run into trouble.

2 encontrarse vr **(a)** to meet, meet each other; **— con uno** to meet someone, run across someone, encounter someone; **— con un obstáculo** to run into an obstacle, encounter an obstacle; **me encontré con que no tenía gasolina** I found I was out of petrol; I was faced with the fact that I had no petrol.

(b) (vehicles etc) to crash, collide; (opinions etc) to clash, conflict, come into collision.

(c) to be, be situated, be located, stand; **se encuentra en la plaza principal** it is in the main square; **¿dónde se encuentra el cine?** where is the cinema?

(d) to find oneself, be; **se encuentra enferma** she is ill; **¿cómo te encuentras ahora?** how are you now?, how do you feel now?, how do you find yourself now?; **me encontré sin coche** I found myself without a car.

(e) **si lo haces te la encuentras** (fam) if you do that you'll have it coming to you (fam).

encontrón nm, **encontronazo** nm collision, crash, smash.

encopetado adj **(a)** of noble birth; blue-blooded. **(b)** haughty, high and mighty; conceited; important, prominent; of high social position.

encopetarse [1a] vr to get conceited, give oneself airs.

encorajar [1a] **1** vt **(a)** to encourage, put heart into. **(b)** to inflame. **2 encorajarse** vr to fly into a rage.

encorajinar [1a] **1** vt (SAm) = encorajar; (Mex) to anger, irritate. **2 encorajinarse** vr (Chi: of deal) to fail, go awry.

encorar [1m] vt to cover with leather.

encorchar [1a] vt **(a)** bottle to cork. **(b)** bees to hive.

encordado (a) nm (Arg: Mus) strings; guitar. **(b)** (Boxing) ring.

encordar [1m] **1** vt **(a)** (Mus etc) to string, fit strings to. **(b)** to bind, tie, lash (with ropes); to rope together. **(c)** space, area to rope off. **2 encordarse** vr (mountaineers) to rope themselves together.

encordelar [1a] vt to tie (with string).

encornado adj: **un toro bien —** a bull with good horns.

encornadura nf horns.

encornar [1m] vt to gore.

encornudar [1a] vt to cuckold.

encorralar [1a] vt to pen, corral.

encorvada nf stoop, bend; **hacer la —** (fam) to malinger, pretend to be ill.

encorvado adj curved, bent; stooping; crooked.

encorvadura nf curve, curving, curvature; bend; crookedness.

encorvar [1a] **1** vt to bend, curve; to bend (down, over); stoop; to hook; to make crooked. **2 encorvarse** vr **(a)** to bend (down, over), stoop. **(b)** to sag, warp; to buckle.

encrespado adj curly.

encrespador nm curling tongs.

encrespar [1a] **1** vt **(a)** hair to curl, frizzle; feathers to ruffle; water to ripple; to make rough, produce waves on. **(b)** (fig) to anger, irritate. **2 encresparse** vr **(a)** to curl; to ripple; to get rough. **(b)** (fig) to get cross, get irritated.

encrestado adj haughty.

encrucijada nf crossroads; intersection, junction.

encuadernación nf **(a)** binding; **— en cuero, — en piel** leather binding; **— en tela** cloth binding. **(b)** bindery, binder's.

encuadernador nm bookbinder.

encuadernar [1a] vt to bind (en in); to cover; **libro sin —** unbound book.

encuadrar [1a] **1** vt **(a)** to frame, put in a frame, make a frame for. **(b)** to fit, insert (en into). **(c)** (fig) to contain, comprise. **(c)** (SAm) to summarize, give a synthesis of. **2** vi (Arg) to fit, square (con with).

encuadre nm (Phot etc) setting, background, frame.

encuartar [1a] (Mex) **1** vt to join, put together. **2 encuartarse** vr **(a)** (animal) to shy, balk; to get caught in its straps (etc). **(b)** (fig) to get involved, get bogged down (en in). **(c)** to butt in.

encuartelar [1a] vt (SAm) = acuartelar.

encubierta nf fraud.

encubierto adj hidden, concealed; underhand; undercover.

encubridor 1 adj concealing. **2** nm, **encubridora** nf harbourer; receiver of stolen goods; (Law) accessory after the fact, abettor.

encubrimiento nm concealment, hiding; receiving of stolen goods; (Law) complicity, abetment.

encubrir [3a; ptp **encubierto**] vt to conceal, hide, cover (up), cloak; criminal, suspect to harbour, shelter; crime to conceal; to abet, be an accomplice in.

encucurucharse [1a] vr (CAm, Col) to get up on top, reach the top.

encuentro nm **(a)** meeting, encounter; **un — fortuito** a chance meeting; **su primer — con la policía** his first encounter with the police; **ir al — de uno** to go to meet someone; **ir al — de lo desconocido** to go out to face the unknown.

(b) (Mil) encounter; skirmish, action, fight.

(c) (Sport) meeting, match, game.

(d) (Aut etc) collision, smash, crash; (of opinions etc) clash; **llevarse a uno de —** (Mex, PR) to knock someone down, (fig) to drag someone down to disaster.

encuerada nf (Cu, Mex) naked woman, nude.

encuerado adj (Cu, Mex) ragged; nude, naked.

encuerar [1a] **1** vt (Cu, Chi, Mex) **(a)** to strip (naked). **(b)** (fig) to skin, fleece. **2 encuerarse** vr **(a)** (Cu, Chi, Mex) to strip off, get undressed. **(b)** (Ven) to live in sin.

encuerista nf (Cu, Mex) striptease artiste.

encuesta nf **(a)** (Law) inquiry, investigation; probe (de into); inquest (fig); **— judicial** post-mortem, coroner's inquest. **(b)** public-opinion poll; **E— Gallup** Gallup Poll.

encuestador nm, **encuestadora** nf pollster.

encuitarse [1a] vr **(a)** to grieve. **(b)** (Col) to get into debt.

encujado nm (Cu, PR, Ven) framework, lattice.

enculecarse [1g] vr (SAm) to go broody.

encumbrado adj **(a)** building etc lofty, towering, high. **(b)** person exalted, eminent. **(c)** (pej) high and mighty, haughty.

encumbramiento nm **(a)** (act) raising, elevation. **(b)** height, loftiness; exaltation, eminence. **(c)** (fig) haughtiness.

encumbrar [1a] **1** vt **(a)** to raise, elevate. **(b)** person to elevate, exalt (a to); (fig) to extol. **2 encumbrarse** vr **(a)** (of building) to rise, soar, tower. **(b)** (fig) **— sobre** to tower over, be far superior to. **(c)** (fig: pej) to be proud, be haughty.

encurrucarse [1g] vr (SAm) = acurrucarse.

encurtido nm pickle.

encurtir [3a] vt to pickle.

enchapado nm plating; veneer.

enchapar [1a] vt **(a)** to plate, overlay (with metal); to veneer. **(b)** (Mex) to fit locks to.

enchaquetarse [1a] vr **(a)** (Col, Per, PR) to put one's jacket on. **(b)** (Col) to dress up.

encharcada nf pool, puddle.

encharcado adj still, stagnant.

encharcar [1g] **1** vt to swamp, flood; to cover with puddles, turn into pools. **2 encharcarse** vr **(a)** (land) to swamp, get flooded, get covered with puddles. **(b)** (water) to form puddles, form a pool; to become stagnant. **(c)** (SAm) to get muddy. **(d)** (Arg) to get stuck in a puddle. **(e)** (fig) **— en los vicios** to wallow in vice.

encharralarse [1a] vr (CAm) to make an ambush, lie in ambush.

enchauchado adj (Chi) well heeled (sl).

enchicharse [1a] vr **(a)** (SAm) to get drunk on chicha. **(b)** (CAm, Col, Ec) to get angry, boil up.

enchilada nf (Guat, Mex) rolled omelette seasoned with chili.

enchilado 1 cdj **(a)** (CAm, Mex: Cook) seasoned with chili. **(b)** (Mex) bright red. **2** nm (Cu, Mex) stew with chili sauce.

enchilar [1a] **1** vt **(a)** (CAm, Mex: Cook) to season with chili. **(b)** (CR, Mex) to annoy, vex; (CR) to disappoint. **2** vi (CR, Mex) to sting, burn.

enchiloso adj (CAm, Mex) taste hot.

enchilotarse [1a] vr (Arg) to get cross.

enchinar [1a] **1** vt (Mex) to curl, frizzle. **2 enchinarse** vr: **— el cuerpo** to get gooseflesh; to get scared.

enchinchar [1a] **1** vt **(a)** (Guat, Mex, SD) to put out, bother. **(b)** (Mex) to cause to waste time; matter to delay. **2 enchincharse** vr **(a)** (Guat, Mex, Per, PR) to get infested with bugs. **(b)** (Arg) to get bad-tempered.

enchiquerar [1a] *vt* (*SAm*) to pen, corral.

enchisparse [1a] *vr* (*SAm*) to get tight.

enchisterado *adj* top-hatted, with a top hat on.

enchivarse [1a] *vr* (*Col, Ec*) to fly into a rage.

enchufable *adj* which plugs in, plug-in (*attr*).

enchufar [1a] *vt* (a) (*Tech etc*) to join, connect, fit together, fit in; to telescope together; (*Elec*) to plug in. (b) (*Comm, Fin*) to merge.

enchufe *nm* (a) (*Tech etc*) joint, connection; sleeve; socket.
  (b) (*Elec*) plug; point, socket.
  (c) (*fam*) connection, useful contact; **tiene un — en el ministerio** he's got a contact in the ministry, he can pull wires at the ministry; **hay que tener —s** you've got to have contacts.
  (d) (*fam*) soft job, cushy job (*sl*).

enchufismo *nm* (*fam*) (system of getting things done by) wirepulling (*fam*), use of contacts to obtain favours; old-boy network.

enchufista *nm* (*fam*) wirepuller (*fam*), contact man, man who uses the old-boy network.

ende *adv* (*arch or lit*): **por —** hence, therefore.

endeble *adj* (*Med*) feeble, weak, frail; (*fig*) feeble, flimsy.

endeblez *nf* feebleness, weakness, frailty; flimsiness.

endecasílabo 1 *adj* hendecasyllabic. 2 *nm* hendecasyllable.

endecha *nf* dirge.

endecharse [1a] *vr* to grieve, mourn.

endémico *adj* endemic; (*fig*) rife, chronic.

endemoniado *adj* (a) possessed of the devil. (b) (*fig*) devilish, fiendish; perverse; furious, wild.

endemoniar [1b] 1 *vt* (a) to bedevil. (b) (*fam*) to provoke, anger. 2 **endemoniarse** *vr* (*fam*) to get angry.

endenantes *adv* (*SAm*) a short time back.

endentadura *nf* serration, teeth.

endentar [1k] *vti* (*Mech*) to engage, mesh (*con* with).

endentecer [2d] *vi* to teethe, cut one's teeth.

enderezado *adj* appropriate; favourable, opportune.

enderezar [1f] 1 *vt* (a) to straighten, straighten out (*or* up); to unbend.
  (b) to set upright, stand vertically; (*Naut*) to right; *vehicle etc* to stand the right way up, put back on its wheels (*etc*).
  (c) (*fig*) to put in order, set to rights.
  (d) (*fig*) to direct; to manage; to address, dedicate (*a* to); **las medidas están enderezadas a** (*or* **para**) **corregirlo** the measures are designed to correct it.
  2 **enderezarse** *vr* (a) to straighten up, stand up straight, draw oneself up; (*Naut*) to right itself; (*Aer*) to flatten out.
  (b) **— a un lugar** to set out for a place.
  (c) **— a + *infin*** to take steps to + *infin*, prepare to + *infin*; (*of measure etc*) to be designed to + *infin*.

endespués *adv* (*Col, PR*) = **después**.

endeudarse [1a] *vr* to get into debt (*con* with), contract a debt (*con* to).

endeveras *adv* (*SAm*) = **de veras**.

endiablado *adj* (a) devilish, diabolical, fiendish.
  (b) (*hum*) impish, mischievous, wicked.
  (c) ugly.
  (d) furious, angry.
  (c) (*SAm*) *road etc* difficult, dangerous; *affair* complicated, tricky.

endiablar [1a] 1 *vt* (a) to bedevil, bewitch. (b) (*fam*) to pervert, corrupt. 2 **endiablarse** *vr* to get furious.

endibia *nf* endive.

endija *nf* (*SAm*) = **rendija**.

endilgar [1a] *vr* (*fam*) (a) to send, direct; to guide.
  (b) *blow* to fetch.
  (c) **— algo a uno** to spring something on someone; to unload something on to someone; **— un sermón a uno** to give someone a lecture, ram a sermon down someone's throat.

endiñar [1a] *vt* (*fam*) *blow* to fetch.

endiosado *adj* stuck-up (*fam*), conceited; stand-offish.

endiosamiento *nm* (a) vanity, conceit; haughtiness.
  (b) absorption.

endiosar [1a] 1 *vt* to deify; (*fig*) to make a god out of. 2 **endiosarse** *vr* (a) to get conceited, give oneself airs; to be stand-offish.
  (b) **— en algo** to be(come) absorbed in something.

enditarse [1a] *vr* (*Guat, Per*) to get into debt.

endocrina *nf* endocrine.

endocrino *adj* endocrine.

endogamia *nf* inbreeding; **engendrado por —** inbred.

endomingado *adj* all dressed up, in one's Sunday best.

endomingarse [1h] *vr* to dress up, put on one's Sunday best.

endorsar [1a] *vt* (*CAm, Mex, PR: angl*) = **endosar**; (*fig*) to endorse, support, back; to confirm.

endosante *nmf* endorser.

endosar [1a] *vt* (a) *cheque etc* to endorse.
  (b) (*fam*) **— algo a uno** to lumber someone with something, make someone put up with something; to unload something on to someone.

endosatario *nm*, **endosataria** *nf* endorsee.

endoso *nm* endorsement; **sin —** unendorsed.

endriago *nm* fabulous monster, dragon.

endrogarse [1h] *vr* (*Mex, Per*) to get into debt.

endulzante *nm* (*Arg*) sweetening, sugar.

endulzar [1f] *vt* (a) to sweeten. (b) (*fig*) to sweeten; to soften, mitigate.

endurecer [2d] 1 *vt* (a) to harden, make hard; to toughen; to stiffen; *mud etc* to harden, cake, set.
  (b) (*fig*) to toughen, inure; **— a uno a los peligros** to inure someone to dangers.
  2 **endurecerse** *vr* (a) to harden, get hard; to stiffen; to cake, set, set firm; (*Fin: of price*) to harden.
  (b) (*fig*) to become cruel, become hard-hearted.
  (c) **— a los peligros** to become inured to danger, inure oneself to danger.

endurecido *adj* (a) hard; tough; stiff; *mud etc* hardened, caked, set.
  (b) (*fig*) hardy, tough; **— a** inured to, used to.
  (c) (*fig: pej*) cruel, callous, hard-hearted; obdurate.

endurecimiento *nm* (a) (*act*) hardening; stiffening; setting; **— de las arterias** hardening of the arteries.
  (b) (*state*) hardness; toughness; stiffness; firmness.
  (c) (*fig*) cruelty, callousness, hard-heartedness; obduracy.

enea *nf* = **anea**.

Eneas *m* Aeneas.

enebro *nm* juniper.

Eneida *f* Aeneid.

enema *nf* enema.

enemiga *nf* enmity, hostility.

enemigo 1 *adj* enemy, hostile; unfriendly; **ser — de** (*fig*) to dislike, be hostile to; (*of tendency etc*) to be inimical to; **una actitud enemiga de todo progreso** an attitude inimical to all progress.
  2 *nm*, **enemiga** *nf* enemy; foe, adversary, opponent; **el E—, el — malo** the devil; **pasarse al — to** go over to the enemy.

enemistad *nf* enmity.

enemistar [1a] 1 *vt* to make enemies of, cause a rift between, set at odds.
  2 **enemistarse** *vr* to become enemies; **— con uno** to become an enemy of someone; to fall out with someone, become estranged from someone.

energético *adj* (*SAm: angl*) = **enérgico**.

energía *nf* (a) energy; vigour, drive, push, go; **obrar con —** to act energetically; **reaccionar con —** to react vigorously.
  (b) (*Tech*) power; energy; (*Elec*) power, energy, current; **— atómica** atomic energy; **— hidráulica** water power; **— nuclear** nuclear power.

enérgicamente *adv* energetically; vigorously; forcefully; emphatically; strenuously; boldly, drastically.

enérgico *adj* energetic; *person* energetic, vigorous; (*in manner*) forceful, forthright; vital; pushful; *gesture*, *speech*, *tone etc* emphatic, forceful; *effort* determined, vigorous; *exercise* strenuous; *campaign* vigorous, forceful, high-pressure; *stroke* bold; *measure* bold, drastic; *attack etc* vigorous, strong; **ponerse — con uno** to get tough with someone.

energúmeno *nm*, **energúmena** *nf* person possessed of the devil; (*fig*) demon, wild person, madman.

enero *nm* January.

enervador *adj* enervating.

enervar [1a] *vt* to enervate.

enésimo *adj* (a) (*Math*) nth; **elevado a la enésima potencia** raised to the nth power, (*fig*) to the nth degree. (b) (*fig*) umpteenth (*fam*); **por enésima vez** for the umpteenth time.

enfadadizo *adj* irritable, crotchety.

enfadar [1a] 1 *vt* (a) to anger, irritate, annoy; to offend.
  (b) (*SAm*) to bore.
  2 **enfadarse** *vr* (a) to get angry, get cross, get annoyed (*con* with, *de* about, *at*); **no te enfades** don't be cross; don't be offended; **de nada sirve enfadarte** it's no good getting cross.
  (b) (*SAm*) to be bored, get bored.

enfado *nm* (a) annoyance, irritation, anger. (b) trouble, bother.

enfadoso *adj* annoying, vexatious; irksome, tedious.

enfajillar [1a] *vt* (*CAm*, *Mex*: *Post*) to put a wrapper on.

enfangar [1h] **1** *vt* to cover with mud.
 2 enfangarse *vr* (**a**) to get muddy, get covered in mud; to sink into the mud.
 (**b**) (*fig*) to dirty one's hands, get involved in dirty work; — **en los vicios** to wallow in vice.

enfardadora *nf* (*Agr etc*) baler, baling machine.

enfardar [1a] *vt* to bale.

énfasis *nm* (**a**) emphasis; stress; **hablar con** — to speak emphatically; to speak ponderously.
 (**b**) (*fig*) emphasis; **poner el** — **en** to put the emphasis on, stress.

enfático *adj* emphatic; positive; *speech* heavy, ponderous; **dijo** — he said emphatically.

enfatizar [1f] *vt* (*SAm*: *angl*) to emphasize, stress.

enfermar [1a] **1** *vt* to make ill, cause illness in. **2** *vi* to fall ill, be taken ill (**de** with); — **del corazón** to develop heart trouble.

enfermedad *nf* (**a**) illness; sickness; **durante esta** — during this illness; **una** — **que duró 6 meses** an illness which lasted 6 months; **ausentarse por** — to be away ill, be away sick.
 (**b**) illness, disease; complaint; (*fig*) disease, malady, ill; **una** — **muy peligrosa** a very dangerous disease; — **contagiosa** contagious disease; — **de la piel** skin disease, skin infection; — **profesional** occupational disease; — **del sueño** sleeping sickness; — **venérea** venereal disease; — **por virus** virus disease; **contagiar a uno con una** —, **pegar una** — **a uno** to give someone a disease.

enfermera *nf* nurse; — **ambulante** visiting nurse; — **jefa** matron.

enfermería *nf* infirmary; sanatorium; (*of school etc*) sick bay; (*Taur*) hospital, medical section.

enfermero *nm* male nurse; (*Mil*) medical orderly.

enfermizo *adj* sickly, weak, unhealthy; infirm; *mind* morbid, unhealthy.

enfermo 1 *adj* ill, sick, unwell; sickly; — **de amor** lovesick; **caer** —, **ponerse** — to fall ill (**de** with); **estar** — **de gravedad**, **estar** — **de peligro** to be seriously ill, be dangerously ill.
 2 *nm*, **enferma** *nf* patient; invalid, sick person.

enfermoso *adj* (*SAm*) =**enfermizo**.

enfiestarse [1a] *vr* (*SAm*) to have a good time, make merry.

enfilada *nf* enfilade.

enfilar [1a] *vt* (**a**) (*Mil*) to enfilade.
 (**b**) to line up, put in a row; *beads* to thread.
 (**c**) *course* to direct, bear.
 (**d**) *street etc* to go straight along (*or* down *etc*).

enflaquecer [2d] **1** *vt* to make thin; to weaken, sap the strength of.
 2 *vi* and **enflaquecerse** *vr* (**a**) to get thin, lose weight.
 (**b**) (*fig*: *effort etc*) to flag, weaken; (*person*) to lose heart.

enflaquecido *adj* thin, extenuated.

enflaquecimiento *nm* (**a**) loss of weight; emaciation.
 (**b**) (*fig*) weakening.

enflatarse [1a] *vr* (**a**) (*CAm*, *Ven*) to grow sad. (**b**) (*Cu*, *Mex*) to fly into a rage.

enflautada *nf* (*Guat*, *Hond*, *Per*) blunder.

enflautado *adj* pompous.

enflautar [1a] *vt* (*Col*, *Guat*, *Mex*): — **algo a uno** to unload something on to someone.

enfocar [1g] **1** *vt* (**a**) (*Phot etc*) to focus (**a**, **sobre** on).
 (**b**) *problem etc* to approach, consider, look at; to size up; **podemos** —' **este problema de tres maneras** we can approach this problem in three ways; **no me gusta su modo de** — **la cuestión** I do not like his approach to the question.
 2 *vi* and **enfocarse** *vr* to focus (**a**, **sobre** on).

enfoque *nm* (**a**) (*Phot etc*) focus; focusing. (**b**) magnification; **potencia de** — magnifying power, magnification. (**c**) (*fig*) grasp; approach.

enfoscar [1g] **1** *vt* to fill with mortar.
 2 enfoscarse *vr* (**a**) to sulk, be sullen.
 (**b**) — **en un negocio** to plunge into a deal, rush into a deal.
 (**c**) (*of sky*) to cloud over.

enfrascar [1g] **1** *vt* to bottle.
 2 enfrascarse *vr* (**a**) — **en un libro** to bury oneself in a book, become absorbed in a book.
 (**b**) — **en un problema** to get tangled up in a problem, get deeply involved in a problem.

enfrenar [1a] *vt* (**a**) *horse* to bridle; (*Mech*) to brake, slow, halt. (**b**) (*fig*) to curb, restrain.

enfrentar [1a] **1** *vt* (**a**) to put face to face.
 (**b**) to face, confront.
 2 *vi* to face.
 3 enfrentarse *vr*: — **con** to face, face up to, con-

front; to stand up to; (*Sport*) to meet, play against; **hay que** — **con el peligro** one must face up to the danger, one must face the danger squarely.

enfrente 1 *adv* opposite; in front, facing; (*fig*) in opposition; **la casa de** — the house opposite, the house across the street.
 2 — **de** *prep* opposite (to), facing; (*fig*) opposed to, against.

enfriadera *nf* cooling jar; bottle cooler.

enfriadero *nm* cold storage; refrigerator.

enfriador *nm* cooler, cooling plant.

enfriamiento *nm* (**a**) cooling; refrigeration. (**b**) (*Med*) cold, chill.

enfriar [1c] **1** *vt* (**a**) to cool, chill; (*fig*) to cool down, take the heat out of.
 (**b**) (*SAm*) to kill.
 2 enfriarse *vr* (**a**) to cool, cool down, cool off; **déjelo hasta que se enfríe** leave it till it gets cool, leave it to cool down.
 (**b**) (*fig*) to cool off, grow cold.

enfrijolarse [1a] *vr* (*Mex*: *of a deal*) to get messed up.

enfullinarse [1a] *vr* (*Chi*) to get angry.

enfundar [1a] *vt* (**a**) to sheathe; to put away, put in its case. (**b**) to fill, stuff (*de* with).

enfurecer [2d] **1** *vt* to enrage, madden. **2 enfurecerse** *vr* (**a**) to get furious, fly into a rage. (**b**) (*of sea*) to get rough.

enfurruñarse [1a] *vr* (*fam*) (**a**) to get angry. (**b**) to sulk; to get disgruntled.

engaitar [1a] *vt* (*fam*): — **a uno** to wheedle someone, talk someone round.

engajado *adj* (*Col*) curly.

engalanar [1a] **1** *vt* to adorn, deck (*de* with). **2 engalanarse** *vr* to adorn oneself; to dress up, deck oneself out.

enganchar [1a] **1** *vt* (**a**) to hook; to hitch; to hang up; *horse* to harness; *horse*, *wagon*, *trailer* to hitch up; (*Mech*) to couple, connect; (*Rail*) to couple (up).
 (**b**) (*fig*) to inveigle, ensnare; to rope in.
 (**c**) (*Mil*) to recruit; to persuade to join up, lure into military service.
 2 engancharse *vr* (**a**) to get hooked up, catch (**en** on); (*Mech*) to engage (**en** with).
 (**b**) (*Mil*) to enlist, join up, sign on.

enganche *nm* (**a**) (*act*) hooking (up); hitching; coupling, connection.
 (**b**) (*Mech*) coupling, connection; (*Rail*) coupling.
 (**c**) (*Mil*) recruitment, enlistment; (*payment*) bounty.

engañabobos *nm*, *pl* **engañabobos** (**a**) trickster. (**b**) trick, trap.

engañadizo *adj* gullible.

engañador 1 *adj* deceiving, cheating; deceptive. **2** *nm*, **engañadora** *nf* cheat, deceiver, impostor.

engañapichanga *nf* (*Bol*, *Chi*, *RPl*) trick, fraud, hoax.

engañar [1a] **1** *vt* to deceive; to cheat, trick, swindle, fool; to mislead; to beguile, delude; *hunger* to stay; *time* to kill, while away; **a mí no me engaña nadie** you can't fool me; **logró** — **al inspector** he managed to trick the inspector.
 2 *vi* to be deceptive; **las apariencias engañan** appearances are deceptive.
 3 engañarse *vr* to deceive oneself; to be wrong, be mistaken; to delude oneself; **en eso te engañas** you're wrong there; **se engaña con falsas esperanzas** she deludes herself with false hopes.

engañifa *nf* (*fam*) trick, swindle.

engañito *nm* (*Chi*) small gift, token.

engaño *nm* (**a**) deceit; deception; fraud, trick, swindle; sham; delusion; — **sentimental** (*Philos*, *Poet*) pathetic fallacy; **todo es** — it's all a sham; **aquí no hay** — there is no attempt to deceive anybody here, it's all on the level (*fam*).
 (**b**) mistake, misunderstanding; **no haya** — let there be no mistake about it; **padecer** — to labour under a misunderstanding.
 (**c**) —**s** wiles, tricks.
 (**d**) (*Chi*) small gift, token.

engañosamente *adv* deceitfully, dishonestly; deceptively; misleadingly, wrongly.

engañoso *adj* *person etc* deceitful, dishonest; *appearance* deceptive; *advice etc* misleading, wrong.

engarabitarse [1a] *vr* (**a**) to climb, shin up. (**b**) to get stiff with cold. (**c**) (*Col*) to grow weak, get thin.

engaratusar [1a] *vt* (*CAm*, *Col*, *Mex*) =**engatusar**.

engarce *nm* (**a**) setting, mount. (**b**) (*fig*) linking, connection. (**c**) (*Col*) row, shindy.

engaripolarse [1a] *vr* (*Ven*) to doll oneself up.

engarrotarse [1a] *vr* (*SAm*: *of limbs*) to get stiff, go numb.

engarruñarse [1a] *vr* (*Col*, *Hond*, *Mex*) =**engurruñarse**.

engarzar [1f] **1** *vt* **(a)** *jewel* to set, mount; *beads* to thread; *hair* to curl.
  (b) *(fig)* to link, connect.
  (c) *(Col)* to hook (up).
  2 engarzarse *vr* (*Chi, RPl*) to get tangled, get stuck.

engastar [1a] *vt* to set, mount.

engaste *nm* setting, mount.

engatado *adj* thievish.

engatusar [1a] *vt* to coax, wheedle, inveigle; **— a uno para que haga algo** to coax someone into doing something.

engendrar [1a] *vt* **(a)** *(Bio)* to beget, breed; to have as offspring. **(b)** *(Math)* to generate. **(c)** *(fig)* to breed, cause, engender.

engendro *nm* **(a)** *(Bio)* foetus; *(pej)* runt.
  (b) *(fig)* abortion, monstrosity; bungled job; idiotic scheme, impossible plan; brain-child; **el proyecto es el — del ministro** the plan is some brain-child of the minister.
  (c) mal —, — del diablo bad lot, no-good lout (*US fam*).

engerido *adj* (*Col, Ven*) weak, sickly; wretched; timid.

engerirse [3l] *vr* (*Col, Ven*) to grow sad.

engestado *adj* ugly.

engestarse [1a] *vr* (*Mex*) to make a wry face.

englobar [1a] *vt* **(a)** to include, comprise. **(b)** to lump together, put all together.

engodo *nm* (*Cu*) bait.

engolfarse [1a] *vr* **(a)** *(Naut)* to sail out to sea, lose sight of land.
  (b) — en *(fig)* to get deeply involved in; to plunge into, become deeply absorbed in; to launch out into.

engolondrinarse [1a] *vr* **(a)** to get conceited. **(b)** to have a flirtation.

engolosinar [1a] **1** *vt* to tempt, entice. **2 engolosinarse** *vr*: **— con** to grow fond of; to grow accustomed to.

engolletarse [1a] *vr* to give oneself airs.

engorda *nf* **(a)** (*Col, Chi, Mex: Agr*) fattening (up).
  (b) (*Chi, Mex*) fattened animals (*collectively*).

engomar [1a] *vt* to gum, glue, stick.

engordar [1a] **1** *vt* to fatten (up). **2** *vi* **(a)** to get fat; to fill out, put on weight; (*Agr*) to fatten. **(b)** (*fam*) to get rich.

engorde *nm* fattening (up).

engorrar [1a] *vt* (*Mex, PR, Ven*) to annoy.

engorro *nm* bother, nuisance.

engorroso *adj* bothersome, vexatious, trying; cumbersome, awkward.

engrampar [1a] *vt* (*SAm*) to clip together, staple.

engranaje *nm* gear; gears, gearing; mesh; gear teeth; **— de distribución** timing gear.

engranar [1a] **1** *vt* to gear; to put into gear; **— con** to gear into, engage.
  2 *vi* to interlock; (*Mech*) to engage (*con una rueda* a wheel), mesh (*con* with); **A engrana con B** A is in gear with B; **A y B están engranados** A and B are in mesh.
  3 engranarse *vr* **(a)** (*Arg, Mex: Mech*) to seize up, get locked, jam.
  (b) (*Arg*) to get angry.

engrandecer [2d] *vt* **(a)** to enlarge, magnify. **(b)** *(fig)* to extol, magnify; to exalt; to exaggerate.

engrandecimiento *nm* **(a)** enlargement. **(b)** exaltation; exaggeration.

engrane *nm* **(a)** mesh, meshing. **(b)** (*Arg, Mex: Mech*) seizing, jamming.

engrasación *nf* greasing, lubrication.

engrasado *nm* greasing, lubrication.

engrasador *nm* greaser, lubricator; grease point; grease cup; **— de compresión, — de pistón** grease gun.

engrasamiento *nm* greasing, lubrication.

engrasar [1a] *vt* **(a)** (*Mech*) to grease, lubricate, oil.
  (b) to make greasy, stain with grease. **(c)** (*Agr*) to manure.

engrase *nm* greasing, lubrication.

engreído *adj* **(a)** vain, conceited, stuck-up (*fam*).
  (b) (*SAm*) affectionate; spoiled.

engreimiento *nm* vanity, conceit.

engreír [3l] **1** *vt* **(a)** to make vain, make conceited.
  (b) (*SAm*) *child* to spoil, pamper.
  2 engreírse *vr* **(a)** to get conceited.
  (b) (*SAm*) to get spoiled, be pampered.
  (c) (*SAm*) **— a, — con** to grow fond of.

engrescar [1g] *vt* **(a)** to goad into fighting. **(b)** to rouse to merriment.

engrifarse [1a] *vr* (*Col*) to get haughty. **(b)** (*Mex*) to get cross; (*Mex: fam*) to get high on drugs.

engrillar [1a] **1** *vt* **(a)** to shackle.
  (b) (*Col, PR*) to trick.
  2 engrillarse *vr* **(a)** (*PR, Ven: of horse*) to lower its head.
  (b) (*PR, Ven*) to get conceited.
  (c) (*Col, Pan*) to get into debt.

engringolarse [1a] *vr* **(a)** (*Col*) to get excited; to become insolent. **(b)** (*Ec, Nic*) to get awry. **(c)** (*Ven*) to doll oneself up.

engrosar [1m] **1** *vt* to enlarge; *quantity* to increase, swell; to thicken. **2** *vi* to get fat. **3 engrosarse** *vr* to increase, swell, expand.

engrudar [1a] *vt* to paste.

engrudo *nm* paste.

enguacharse [1a] *vr* (*Col*) to coarsen, get coarse.

enguadar [1a] *vt* (*Cu*) =**engatusar.**

engualichar [1a] *vt* (*Arg*) **(a)** to bewitch; **— a uno** to give someone a potion. **(b)** *lover* to rule, tyrannize.

enguandos *nmpl* (*Col*) **(a)** useless things. **(b)** wiles, dodges.

enguandujar [1a] *vt* (*Col*) to cover with useless adornments.

enguantado *adj* gloved, wearing a glove.

enguantarse [1a] *vr* to put one's gloves on.

enguaracarse [1g] *vr* (*CAm*) to hide oneself away.

enguaraparse [1a] *vr* (*CAm: of sugar cane*) to ferment.

enguasimar [1a] *vt* (*Cu*) to hang.

enguijarrado *nm* cobbles.

enguijarrar [1a] *vt* to cobble.

enguirnaldar [1a] *vt* to garland, wreathe (*de, con* with); *(fig)* to wreathe.

engullir [3a *and* 3h] *vt* to gobble, bolt, gulp (down); to devour.

engurruñarse [1a] *vr* to get sad, grow gloomy.

enhebrar [1a] *vt* to thread.

enhestar [1k] **1** *vt* **(a)** to erect; to set upright.
  (b) to hoist (up), raise (on high).
  2 enhestarse *vr* **(a)** to straighten up, stand up straight.
  (b) to rise high.

enhiesto *adj* **(a)** erect, straight, upright. **(b)** raised; lofty, towering.

enhilar [1a] *vt* **(a)** *needle* to thread. **(b)** *(fig)* to arrange, put in order.

enhorabuena 1 *nf* congratulations; **¡—!** congratulations!, and the best of luck!; **dar la — a uno** to congratulate someone, wish someone well.
  2 *adv*: **¡—!** all right!; well and good; **— que . . .** thank heavens that . . .

enhoramala *interj*: **¡—!** good riddance!; **¡vete —!** go to the devil!

enhorquetarse [1a] *vr* (*Ant, Arg, Mex, Urug*) to sit astride.

enhuerar [1a] *vt* to addle.

enigma *nm* enigma; puzzle; mystery.

enigmáticamente *adv* enigmatically.

enigmático *adj* enigmatic; puzzling; mysterious.

enjabonar [1a] *vt* **(a)** to soap; to lather. **(b)** *(fam)* to soap up (*sl*), soft-soap (*sl*). **(c)** *(fam)* to abuse.

enjaezar [1f] *vt* to harness, saddle up.

enjalbegado *nm*, **enjalbegadura** *nf* whitewashing.

enjalbegar [1h] *vt* to whitewash; *face* to paint, make up.

enjambrar [1a] **1** *vt* to hive. **2** *vi* to swarm.

enjambre *nm* swarm (*also fig*).

enjaranarse [1a] *vr* (*CAm*) to get into debt.

enjarciar [1b] *vt* (*Naut*) to rig.

enjaretado *nm* grating, grille.

enjaretar [1a] *vt* (*Arg, Mex*): **— algo a uno** to lumber someone with something.

enjaular [1a] *vt* **(a)** to cage, put in a cage; to coop up, pen in; (*fam*) to jail, lock up.

enjertar [1a] *vt* =**injertar.**

enjetado *adj* (*Arg*) cross-looking.

enjetarse [1a] *vr* (*Arg, Mex*) to get cross.

enjoyado *adj* bejewelled, set with jewels.

enjoyar [1a] *vt* to adorn with jewels, set with precious stones; to set precious stones in; (*fig*) to bejewel, adorn, embellish.

enjuagadientes *nm*, *pl* **enjuagadientes** mouthwash.

enjuagar [1h] *vt* to rinse, rinse out; to wash out, swill out.

enjuague *nm* **(a)** mouthwash. **(b)** (*act*) rinse, rinsing; washing, swilling. **(c)** *(fig)* scheme, intrigue.

enjuagamanos *nm*, *pl* **enjuagamanos** towel.

enjugar [1h] *vt* **(a)** to wipe (off), wipe the moisture from; to dry; **—se la frente** to wipe one's brow, mop one's brow. **(b)** *debt, deficit* to wipe out.

enjuiciamiento *nm* **(a)** judgement. **(b)** (*Law*) **—** civil lawsuit, civil suit; **—** criminal trial, criminal prosecution.

enjuiciar [1b] *vt* **(a)** to judge, pass judgement on; to examine. **(b)** (*Law*) to indict; to prosecute, try; to sentence.

enjuncado *adj* rush-covered.

enjundia *nf* **(a)** animal fat, grease. **(b)** (*fig*) substance; strength, drive, vigour; essence, character.

enjundioso *adj* **(a)** fat. **(b)** (*fig*) substantial, solid, meaty.

enjuto *adj* **(a)** dry; dried; *see* **pie**. **(b)** shrivelled up; wizened. **(c)** lean, skinny, spare.

enlabiar [1b] *vt* to blarney, bamboozle (*fam*), take in.

enlabio *nm* blarney, honeyed words, plausible talk.

enlace *nm* **(a)** link, tie-up, connection; bond; relationship; (*Chem, Elec*) linkage; (*Mil etc*) liaison; (*Rail*) connection; marriage, union; meeting, rendez-vous; **el — de A con B** the marriage of A and B; **el — de las dos familias** the linking of the two families by marriage; **los buques no lograron efectuar el — en el punto indicado** the ships did not manage to rendez-vous at the spot indicated. **(b)** — **sindical** shop steward.

enladrillado *nm* brick paving.

enladrillar [1a] *vt* to pave with bricks.

enlardar [1a] *vt* (*Cook*) to baste.

enlatado *nm* canning, tinning.

enlatar [1a] *vt* to can, tin.

enlazar [1f] **1** *vt* **(a)** to link, connect; to tie (together), bind (together); to knit together.
(b) (*SAm*) to lasso.
2 *vi* (*Rail etc*) to connect (con with).
3 enlazarse *vr* to link (up), be linked; to be connected; to join; to interlock; to entwine; to marry, get married; (*of families*) to become linked by marriage (con to).

enlistar [1a] *vt* (*Guat, Mex, PR, SD*) =**alistar**.

enlodar [1a], **enlodazar** [1f] **1** *vt* **(a)** to muddy, cover in mud. **(b)** (*fig*) to besmirch, stain; to smear, defame. **2 enlodarse** *vr*, **enlodazarse** *vr* to get muddy.

enloquecedor *adj* maddening; *headache* splitting; *pain* excruciating.

enloquecer [2d] **1** *vt* to drive mad; (*fig*) to madden, drive crazy. **2** *vi and* **enloquecerse** *vr* to go mad, go out of one's mind.

enloquecimiento *nm* madness.

enlosado *nm* flagstone pavement.

enlosar [1a] *vt* to pave (with flagstones).

enlozado *adj* (*SAm*) enamelled, glazed.

enlozar [1f] *vt* (*SAm*) to enamel, glaze.

enlucido *nm* plaster.

enlucidor *nm* plasterer.

enlucir [3f] *vt* to plaster; *metal* to polish.

enlutado *adj* in mourning, wearing mourning; *city etc* stricken.

enlutar [1a] **1** *vt* **(a)** *person* to put into mourning; to dress in mourning.
(b) *dress etc* to put crêpe on; to put a symbol of mourning on.
(c) *city, country etc* to plunge into mourning; (*fig*) to sadden, grieve; **el accidente enlutó a la ciudad entera** the accident plunged the whole town into mourning.
(d) (*fig*) to darken.
2 enlutarse *vr* to go into mourning, dress in mourning.

enmaderado *adj* timbered; boarded.

enmaderamiento *nm* timbering; boarding.

enmaderar [1a] *vt* to timber; to board (up).

enmalezarse [1f] *vr* (*Chi, Per, PR*) to get overgrown, get covered in scrub.

enmaniguarse [1i] *vr* (*Cu, PR*) **(a)** to get overgrown with trees, turn into jungle. **(b)** (*person*) to revert to rustic ways.

enmarañar [1a] **1** *vt* **(a)** to tangle (up), entangle.
(b) (*fig*) to complicate, make more involved; to make a mess of; to confuse, perplex; **sólo logró — más el asunto** he only managed to make a still worse mess of the matter, he only succeeded in complicating things further.
2 enmarañarse *vr* **(a)** to get tangled (up), become entangled.
(b) (*fig*) to get more involved; to get into a mess; to get confused; — **en un asunto** to get entangled in an affair.
(c) (*of sky*) to darken, cloud over.

enmarcar [1g] *vt* (*fig*) to provide the setting for, act as a background to.

enmarillecerse [2d] *vr* to turn yellow; to turn pale.

enmascarar [1a] **1** *vt* **(a)** to mask. **(b)** (*fig*) to mask, disguise. **2 enmascararse** *vr* to put on a mask.
(b) (*fig*) — **de** to masquerade as.

enmendación *nf* emendation, correction.

enmendar [1k] **1** *vt* **(a)** to emend, correct; *law, constitution etc* to amend.
(b) (*morally*) to reform.
(c) *loss* to make good, compensate for.
2 enmendarse *vr* to reform, mend one's ways.

enmienda *nf* **(a)** emendation; correction; (*Law, Pol etc*) amendment; **la quinta** — the fifth amendment. **(b)** reform. **(c)** compensation, indemnity.

enmohecer [2d] **1** *vt* **(a)** *metal* to rust. **(b)** (*Bot etc*) to make mouldy. **2 enmohecerse** *vr* **(a)** to rust, get rusty. **(b)** (*Bot etc*) to get mouldy.

enmohecido *adj* **(a)** rusty, rust-covered. **(b)** mouldy, mildewed.

enmonarse [1a] *vr* (*SAm*) to get tight.

enmontarse [1a] *vr* (*CAm, Col, Ven*) to get overgrown, revert to scrub.

enmudecer [2d] **1** *vt* to silence. **2 enmudecerse** *vr* to be silent; to remain silent, say nothing; to become dumb; to lose one's voice.

enmugrar [1a] *vt* (*Col, Chi, Mex*), **enmugrecer** [2d] *vt*, **enmugrentar** [1a] *vt* (*Chi*) to begrime, soil, dirty.

ennegrecer [2d] **1** *vt* to blacken; to dye black; to darken, obscure. **2** *vi and* **ennegrecerse** *vr* to turn black; to get dark, darken.

ennoblecer [2d] *vt* **(a)** to ennoble. **(b)** (*fig*) to embellish, adorn; to dignify.

ennoblecimiento *nm* ennoblement.

enojada *nf* (*Mex, PR*) (fit of) anger.

enojadizo *adj* irritable, peevish, short-tempered.

enojado *adj* angry, cross; **dijo** — he said angrily.

enojar [1a] **1** *vt* to anger; to upset, annoy, vex.
2 enojarse *vr* to get angry, lose one's temper; to get annoyed, get cross (con, contra with; de at, about); **¡no te enojes!** don't bother!, don't trouble yourself!

enojo *nm* **(a)** anger; annoyance, vexation; **decir con** — to say angrily.
(b) de prontos —**s, de repentinos** —**s** quick-tempered; **tener prontos** (or **repentinos**) —**s** to be quick to anger, be easily upset.
(c) —**s** troubles, trials.

enojón *adj* (*Chi, Ec, Mex*) =**enojadizo**.

enojoso *adj* irritating, annoying.

enorgullecer [2d] **1** *vt* to fill with pride. **2 enorgullecerse** *vr* to be proud, swell with pride; — **de** to be proud of, pride oneself on.

enorme *adj* **(a)** enormous, huge, vast; tremendous. **(b)** (*fig*) heinous, monstrous.

enormemente *adv* enormously, vastly; tremendously.

enormidad *nf* **(a)** enormousness; hugeness.
(b) (*fig: quality*) heinousness, monstrousness, enormity.
(c) (*act etc*) wicked thing, monstrous thing.
(d) (*fam*) **me gustó una** — I liked it enormously.

enqué *nm* (*Col, Ec, Ven*) container, bag.

enrabiar [1b] **1** *vt* to enrage. **2 enrabiarse** *vr* to get enraged.

enraizar [1f] *vi* to take root.

enramada *nf* **1** **(a)** arbour, bower. **(b)** (*RPl*) cover (*etc*) made of branches. **2** *vi* (*RPl: Bot*) to come into leaf.

enranciarse [1b] *vr* to go rancid, get stale.

enrarecer [2d] **1** *vt* **(a)** *air etc* to rarefy.
(b) to make scarce, cause to become rare.
2 enrarecerse *vr* **(a)** to become rarefied, get thin.
(b) to become scarce, grow rare.

enrarecido *adj* rarefied.

enrarecimiento *nm* **(a)** rarefaction; thinness. **(b)** scarceness, rareness.

enrastrojarse [1a] *vr* (*SAm*) to get covered in scrub.

enrazado *adj* (*Col*) half-breed; crossbred.

enrazar [1f] *vt* (*Col*) to mix (racially); *animals* to crossbreed.

enredadera *nf* (*Bot*) climbing plant, creeper; — **(de campo)** bindweed.

enredador **1** *adj* trouble-making, mischief-making.
2 *nm*, **enredadora** *nf* gossip; busybody, meddler; troublemaker, mischief-maker.

enredar [1a] **1** *vt* **(a)** *animal etc* to net, catch in a net.
(b) *trap* to set.
(c) to intertwine, interweave; (*pej*) to entangle, tangle (up).
(d) *affair* to confuse, complicate; to make a mess of.
(e) *person* to embroil, involve, implicate (en in).
(f) *persons* to sow discord among (or between); — **a A con B** to sow discord between A and B, embroil A with B.
2 enredarse *vr* **(a)** to get entangled, get tangled (up); — **en** (*rope etc*) to catch on, (*Naut*) foul.

(b) (*affair*) to get complicated; to get into a mess.
(c) (*person*) to get entangled (*con* with), get involved (*con* with); **no se enrede Vd** don't you get mixed up in this, keep out of this mess; **se enredó con una estudiante** he got involved with a student, he had an affair with a student; **— de** (*or* **en**) **palabras** to get involved in an argument.

enredista *nmf* (*SAm*) =**enredador 2**.

enredo *nm* **(a)** tangle.
(b) (*fig*) tangle, entanglement; love affair; mess, confusion, mix-up; (*of details etc*) maze, tangle.
(c) jam, difficult situation.
(d) embroilment, involvement.
(e) (*Theat*) plot.
(f) **—s** intrigues; mischief, mischievous lies; **comedia de —s** comedy of intrigue.

enredoso *adj* **(a)** tangled, complicated; tricky. **(b)** (*Mex*) =**enredador 1**.

enrejado *nm* grating, grille; (*of window*) lattice; (*in garden*) trellis; (*Sew*) openwork; fence, railings; (*of cage*) bars; **— de alambre** wire netting (fence).

enrejar [1a] *vt* **(a)** to fix a grating to, put a grating on; to fence, put railings round.
(b) (*SAm*) to put a halter on.
(c) (*Mex*) to darn, patch.

enrevesado *adj* =**revesado**.

enriciar [1a] *vt* **(a)** (*Tech*) to make into ingots.
(b) (*SAm*) to lay rails on.
(c) (*SAm*) to put on the tracks, set on the rails; (*fig*) to put on the right track.

Enrique *m* Henry.

enriquecer [2d] **1** *vt* to make rich, enrich.
2 enriquecerse *vr* to get rich; to prosper; (*pej*) to enrich oneself; **— a costa ajena** to do well at other people's expense.

enriquecimiento *nm* enrichment.

enriscado *adj* craggy, rocky.

enristrar [1a] *vt* **(a)** to string, make a string of, put on a string. **(b)** (*fig*) difficulty to straighten out, iron out. **(c)** *place* to go straight to.

enrizar [1f] **1** *vt* to curl. **2 enrizarse** *vr* to curl.

enrocar [1g] *vi* (*Chess*) to castle.

enrojecer [2d] **1** *vt* to redden, turn red; *person* to make blush; *metal* to make red-hot.
2 *vi* and **enrojecerse** *vr* to blush, redden; to go red (with anger); to get red-hot.

enrojecimiento *nm* reddening; blushing, blush.

enrolar [1a] (*SAm*) **1** *vt* to enrol, sign on, sign up; (*Mil*) to enlist. **2 enrolarse** *vr* to enrol, sign on; (*Mil*) to enlist, join up.

enrollable *adj* that rolls up, roll-up (*attr*); **persiana —** slatted shutter.

enrollamiento *nm* roll; (*Elec etc*) coil.

enrollar [1a] *vt* to roll (up), wind (up); to coil.

enronquecer [2d] **1** *vt* to make hoarse. **2** *vi* and **enronquecerse** *vr* to get hoarse, grow hoarse.

enronquecido *adj* hoarse.

enroque *nm* (*Chess*) castling.

enroscado *adj* **(a)** coiled; twisted; kinky. **(b)** (*Col*) angry.

enroscadura *nf* coil; twist; kink.

enroscar [1g] **1** *vt* **(a)** to coil (round), wind; to twist, twine; to curl (up).
(b) to screw in.
(c) to wreathe (*de* in).
2 enroscarse *vr* to coil, wind; to twist, twine; to curl (up); **— alrededor de un árbol** to twine round a tree.

enrulado *adj* (*RPl*) curly; set in curls.

enrular [1a] *vt* (*Bol, RPl*) to curl.

enrumbar *vi* (*SAm*) to decide on a direction, go, set off.

ensacar [1g] *vt* to sack, bag, put into bags.

ensalada *nf* **(a)** (*Cook*) salad; **— de col** cabbage salad; **— de patatas** potato salad. **(b)** (*fig*) hotchpotch, unholy mixture; mix-up; medley; (*Aut*) traffic jam.

ensaladera *nf* salad bowl, salad dish.

ensaladilla *nf* **(a)** (*Russian-type*) salad. **(b)** (*Col, Ven*) lampoon, satirical verse.

ensalmado *adj* (*SAm*) magic.

ensalmador *nm* quack, bonesetter.

ensalmar [1a] *vt* bone to set; *complaint* to cure by spells, treat by quack remedies.

ensalme *nm* (*Ec*) spell, incantation.

ensalmo *nm* spell, charm, incantation; (*Med*) quack remedy, quack treatment; (**como** **por —** as if by magic.

ensalzamiento *nm* exaltation; extolling.

ensalzar [1f] *vt* to exalt; to praise, extol.

ensamblador *nm* joiner; fitter.

ensambladura *nf* **(a)** (*in general*) joinery; assembling.
(b) (*Tech*) joint; **— de inglete** mitre joint.

ensamblaje *nm* (*Tech*) assembly; **planta de —** assembly plant.

ensamblar [1a] *vt* to join; to assemble.

ensanchador *nm* (*Tech*) stretcher.

ensanchar [1a] **1** *vt* to enlarge, widen, extend; to stretch; to expand; (*Sew*) to enlarge, let out.
2 ensancharse *vr* **(a)** to get wider, spread, expand; to stretch.
(b) (*fig*) to give oneself airs.

ensanche *nm* enlargement, widening, extension; expansion; stretch(ing); (*of town*) extension, new suburb, suburban development; (*Sew*) extra piece, room to let out.

ensangrentado *adj* bloodstained; bloody, gory.

ensangrentar [1k] **1** *vt* to stain with blood, cover in blood.
2 ensangrentarse *vr* (*fig*) to get angry; **— con,** **— contra** to be cruel to, treat cruelly, be vindictive towards.

ensañado *adj* furious; cruel, merciless.

ensañamiento *nm* rage; fury; cruelty, barbarity.

ensañar [1a] **1** *vt* to enrage. **2 ensañarse** *vr*: **— con,** **— en** to vent one's anger on; to delight in tormenting, take a sadistic pleasure in the sufferings of.

ensarnarse [1a] *vr* (*CAm, Chi, Mex*) to get mangy.

ensartador *nm* (*Arg*) roasting spit.

ensartar [1a] **1** *vt* **(a)** *beads etc* to string; *needle* to thread; *meat* to spit, broach.
(b) (*fig*) to string together; to link; *excuses etc* to reel off, trot out, rattle off.
2 ensartarse *vr* **(a)** (*Col, PR*) to get into a jam.
(b) (*Arg*) to come badly out of a deal.

ensayar [1a] *vt* **(a)** to test, try, try out.
(b) *metal* to assay.
(c) (*Mus, Theat*) to rehearse.
2 ensayarse *vr* to practise; to rehearse; **— a +** *infin* to practise + *ger*.

ensaye *nm* assay.

ensayista *nmf* essayist.

ensayo *nm* **(a)** test, trial; experiment; attempt; practice, exercise; **de —** tentative; practice (*attr*); experimental; **pedido de —** (*Comm*) trial order; **viaje de —** trial run; **vuelo de —** test flight; **hacer algo a modo de —** to do something as an experiment, do something to try it out; **hacer —s to** practise (*en* on), train.
(b) (*of metal*) assay.
(c) (*Lit, School etc*) essay.
(d) (*Mus, Theat*) rehearsal; **— general** dress rehearsal.
(e) (*Rugby*) try.

ensebado *adj* greased, greasy.

enselvado *adj* wooded.

ensenada *nf* **(a)** inlet, cove; creek. **(b)** (*Arg*) small fenced pasture.

enseña *nf* ensign, standard; **la E— Blanca** (*Brit*) the White Ensign.

enseñado *adj* trained; informed; educated; **bien —** dog house-trained.

enseñanza *nf* **(a)** education; teaching; instruction, training; schooling; tuition; **primera —, — primaria** elementary education; **segunda —,** **— secundaria** secondary education; **— superior** higher education; **— universitaria** university education; **—** **de los niños atrasados** remedial teaching, teaching of backward children; **— para ambos sexos** co-education; **la — es gratuita** the training is free.
(b) teaching, doctrine; **la — de la Iglesia** the teaching of the Church.

enseñar [1a] **1** *vt* **(a)** to teach, instruct, train; to educate; **— a uno a hacer algo** to teach someone (how) to do something, train someone to do something; to show someone how to do something.
(b) to show; to point out; **nos enseñó el museo** he showed us (over) the museum; **te enseñaré mis aguafuertes** I'll show you my etchings; **esto nos enseña las dificultades** this reveals the difficulties to us.
2 enseñarse *vr* **(a)** (*SAm*) to learn; **— a hacer algo** to learn (how) to do something.
(b) (*esp SAm*) to accustom oneself, become inured (*a* to); **no me enseño aquí** I can't get used to it here, I can't settle down here.

enseñorearse [1a] *vr* **(a)** to control oneself. **(b)** **— de** to take possession of, take over; (*fig*) to overlook, dominate.

enseres *nmpl* goods and chattels; things, gear, tackle, equipment; **— domésticos** household goods.

enseriarse [1b] *vr* (*Ant, Col, Guat, Per, Ven*) to become serious.

ensilado *nm*: **— de patatas** potato clamp.

ensiladora *nf* silo.

ensilar [1a] *vt* to store in a silo.
ensillar [1a] *vt* to saddle (up), put a saddle on.
ensimismamiento *nm* absorption; reverie, brown study.
ensimismarse [1a] *vr* (a) to be(come) lost in thought, go into a reverie, go into a brown study. (b) (*SAm*) to get conceited.
ensoberbecer [2d] **1** *vt* to make proud. **2 ensoberbecerse** *vr* (a) to become proud, become arrogant. (b) (*sea*) to get rough.
ensombrecer [2d] **1** *vt* (a) to darken, cast a shadow over. (b) (*fig*) to overshadow, put in the shade. **2 ensombrecerse** *vr* (a) to darken, get dark. (b) (*fig*) to get gloomy.
ensoñación *nf* (a) (*SAm*) fantasy, fancy, dream. (b) ¡ni por —! not a bit of it!, never!
ensoñador **1** *adj* dreamy. **2** *nm* dreamer.
ensopar [1a] (*SAm*) **1** *vt* to soak, drench, saturate; *biscuit etc* to dip, dunk. **2 ensoparse** *vr* to get soaked.
ensordecedor *adj* deafening.
ensordecer [2d] **1** *vt* to deafen; *noise* to muffle. **2** *vi* to go deaf; (*fig*) to pretend not to hear, pretend to be deaf.
ensortijar [1a] **1** *vt* (a) *hair* to curl, put curls into. (b) *nose* to ring, fix a ring in. **2 ensortijarse** *vr* to curl.
ensuciamiento *nm* soiling, dirtying.
ensuciar [1b] **1** *vt* (a) to soil, dirty; to foul; to mess up, make a mess of. (b) (*fig*) to defile, pollute. **2 ensuciarse** *vr* to get dirty; (*child*) to soil oneself; to wet the bed.
ensueño *nm* (a) dream, fantasy, illusion; reverie; **de —** dream-like; other-wordly; **una cocina de —** a dream kitchen, a kitchen of one's dreams; **mundo de —** dream world, world of fantasy. (b) **—s** visions, fantasies; ¡ni por **—s!** not a bit of it!, never!
entabicar [1g] *vt* (*SAm*) to partition off.
entablado *nm* boarding, planking; floorboard.
entabladura *nf* boarding, planking.
entablar [1a] **1** *vt* (a) to board (in, up), plank, cover with boards. (b) *chessmen* to set up; *game* to draw. (c) (*Med*) to splint, put in a splint. (d) *conversation etc* to start, strike up; *deal* to enter into; *lawsuit* to begin, file, bring; *claim* to file, put in. **2** *vi* (a) (*Chess*) to draw. (b) (*Per*) to boast. **3 entablarse** *vr* (*wind*) to settle.
entable *nm* (a) boarding, planking. (b) (*Chess*) position. (c) (*SAm*) order, arrangement, disposition. (d) (*Col*) (start of an) enterprise; (*Ec*) breaking, opening up (*of new land*).
entablillar [1a] *vt* (*Med*) to splint, put in a splint.
entablonada *nf* (*Ec, Per*) boast.
entalegar [1h] *vt* (a) to bag, put in a bag. (b) (*fig*) to hoard, stash away (*fam*).
entallador *nm* sculptor; engraver.
entalladura *nf* (a) sculpture, carving; engraving. (b) slot, notch, cut, groove.
entallar [1a] **1** *vt* (a) to sculpt, carve; to engrave; — **el nombre en un árbol** to carve one's name on a tree. (b) to notch, cut a slot in, cut a groove in. (c) (*Sew*) to cut, tailor. **2** *vi* to fit (well); **traje que entalla bien** a suit that fits well, a well-cut suit.
entallecer [2d] *vi and* **entallecerse** *vr* to shoot, sprout.
entapizado **1** *adj* (a) upholstered (*de* with); hung (*de* with); covered (*de* with). (b) (*Bot*) overgrown (*de* with). **2** *nm* (*Chi, RPl*) carpets, carpeting; (*Mex*) wall-coverings, tapestries.
entapizar [1f] *vt* (a) to upholster (*de* with, in); *wall* to hang with tapestries; *chair etc* to cover with fabric; (*RPl*) *floor* to carpet. (b) (*Bot*) to grow over, cover, spread over.
entarascar [1g] **1** *vt* to dress up, doll up. **2 entarascarse** *vr* to dress up, doll up.
entarimado *nm* floorboarding, roof boarding; inlaid floor; — (**de hojas quebradas**) parquet.
entarimar [1a] *vt* to board, plank; to put an inlaid floor on (*or* over).
entarugado *nm* block flooring, block paving.
ente *nm* (a) entity, being; — **oficial** official entity, official body. (b) (*fam*) fellow, chap (*fam*); odd sort.
entecarse [1g] *vr* (*Chi*) to be stubborn.
enteco *adj* weak, sickly, frail.
entechar [1a] *vt* (*SAm*) to roof.

entejar [1a] *vt* (*SAm*) to tile.
enteje *nm* (*SAm*) tiling.
entelerido *adj* (a) shivering with cold; shaking with fright. (b) (*SAm*) weak, sickly, frail. (c) (*SAm*) distressed, upset.
entenada *nf* stepdaughter.
entenado *nm* stepson; stepchild.
entendederas *nfpl* (*fam*) brains; **ser corto de —, tener malas —** to be pretty dim, be slow on the uptake.
entendedor *nm*, **entendedora** *nf* understanding person; **al buen —, pocas palabras (le bastan)** a word to the wise is sufficient; enough said!
entender [2g] **1** *vti* (a) to understand; to realize, grasp; to comprehend; **¿entiendes?** (do you) understand?, do you get me?; **no le entiendo** I don't understand you; **lo que es —, entiendo** I understand it as far as anybody can understand it; **no entiendo palabra** it's Greek to me; **no entendió jota** (*or* **una patata** *etc*) he didn't understand a word of it; **a mi —** to my way of thinking, in my opinion; **— mal** to misunderstand; **dar a — que ...** to give to understand that ..., imply that ...; **según él da a —** according to what he says, as he implies; **hacer — algo a uno** to make someone understand something, put something across to someone; **hacerse —** to make oneself understood, get across (*por* to); **lograr —** to manage to grasp; to get the hang of. (b) to intend, mean; **¿qué entiendes con eso?** what do you mean by that? (c) to think, believe; to infer.
2 *vi* (a) **— de** to be an expert on, be good at, know all about; **— de carpintería** to know all about carpentry, be an expert carpenter; **yo no entiendo de vinos** I'm no judge of wines; **ella no entiende de coches** she's hopeless with cars. (b) **— en** to deal with, be concerned with, have to do with; to be familiar with; **— en un asunto** to have the authority to handle a matter, be in charge of an affair. (c) **— por** (*of dog*) to answer to the name of.
3 entenderse *vr* (a) to be understood; to be meant; **¿qué se entiende por estas palabras?** what is meant by these words?; **¿cómo se entiende que ...?** how can one understand that ...?, how can one grasp that ...?; **se entiende que ...** it is understood that ...; **eso se entiende** that is understood. (b) to know what one is about; **yo me entiendo** I know what I'm up to; I have my reasons; **— con algo** to know how to deal with something. (c) (*of 2 persons*) to understand each other; to get along (well) together; to have a (secret) understanding; **— con uno** to come to an arrangement with someone, fix things with someone; **— con una mujer** to have an affair with a woman. (d) **eso no se entiende conmigo** that doesn't concern me, that has nothing to do with me.
entendido 1 *adj* (a) understood; agreed; ¡—! agreed!; **bien — que ...** on the understanding that ...; **no darse por —** to pretend not to understand; **tenemos — que ...** we understand that ...; **según tenemos —** as far as we can gather. (b) *person* expert; skilled, trained; wise; knowing; well-informed; **ser — en** to be versed in, be skilled at.
2 *nm*, **entendida** *nf* knowledgeable person; expert; connoisseur; **según el juicio de los —s** in the opinion of those who know, according to the experts; **el whisk(e)y de los —s** the connoisseur's whisky.
entendimiento *nm* (a) understanding; grasp, comprehension. (b) mind, intellect, understanding; **de — poco lucido** of limited understanding. (c) judgement.
entenebrecer [2d] **1** *vt* (a) to darken, obscure. (b) (*fig*) to fog, cloud, obscure; **esto entenebrece más el asunto** this fogs the issue still more. **2 entenebrecerse** *vr* to get dark.
enterado *adj* (a) knowledgeable; well-informed; **lo sabe cualquier persona enterada** any well-informed person knows it; **estar —** to be informed, be in the know; **estar — de** to know about, be aware of; **estar — de que ...** to know that ..., be aware that ...; **no darse por —** to pretend not to understand, not take the hint. (b) (*Chi*) conceited, stuck-up (*fam*).
enteramente *adv* entirely, completely; quite.
enterar [1a] **1** *vt* (a) to inform (*de* about, of), acquaint (*de* with), tell (*de* about). (b) (*SAm*) *money* to pay, hand over; (*Arg, Chi,*

Mex, Per) quantity to make up, complete, round off.
2 *vi* **(a)** (*SAm*) to get better, get well.
(b) (*Chi*) to let the days go by.
3 enterarse *vr* **(a)** to find out, get to know; — **de**
to find out about, learn of, hear of, get to know
about; **¿se entera?** do you hear?; do you understand?, do you get it?; **¡entérate!, ¡entérese!** listen!,
get this!
(b) (*SAm*) to recoup one's losses.
entereza *nf* **(a)** entirety; completeness; perfection.
(b) (*fig*) integrity; decency, honesty; strength of
mind; fortitude; firmness.
(c) (*fig*) strictness, severity.
entérico *adj* enteric.
enteritis *nf* enteritis.
enterizo *adj* in one piece, one-piece (*attr*).
enternecedor *adj* affecting, touching, moving.
enternecer [2d] **1** *vt* to soften; to affect, touch, move
(to pity). **2 enternecerse** *vr* to relent; to be
affected, be touched, be moved (to pity).
entero 1 *adj* **(a)** entire, complete; whole; **la cantidad
entera** the whole sum, the complete sum; **por el
mundo** — over the whole world; **con entera satisfacción** with complete satisfaction; **por** — wholly,
completely, fully.
(b) (*Math*) whole, integral.
(c) (*Bio*) not castrated.
(d) (*fig*) upright, honest; resolute, firm.
(e) sound; robust; *cloth etc* strong, thick.
(f) (*Guat, Per, SD, Ven*) identical, similar.
2 *nm* **(a)** (*Math*) integer.
(b) (*Comm, Fin*) point; **las acciones han subido
dos** —**s** the shares have gone up two points.
(c) (*SAm*) payment.
(d) (*Chi*) balance.
enterradero *nm* (*Arg*) burial ground.
enterrado *adj* buried; *nail* ingrowing.
enterrador *nm* gravedigger.
enterramiento *nm* burial, interment.
enterrar [1a] *vt* **(a)** to bury, inter. **(b)** (*SAm*) *weapon*
to bury (*en* in), thrust (*en* into). **(c)** (*fig*) to bury,
forget.
enterratorio *nm* (*Chi, RPl*) Indian burial ground;
archaeological remains, site of archaeological
interest.
entesar [1k] *vt* to stretch, tauten.
entibiar [1b] **1** *vt* **(a)** to cool; to take the chill off. **(b)**
(*fig*) to cool (down). **2 entibiarse** *vr* **(a)** to become
lukewarm, cool down. **(b)** (*fig*) to cool off.
entibo *nm* (*Min*) prop.
entidad *nf* **(a)** entity; (*Pol etc*) body, organization;
(*Comm, Fin*) firm, concern, company. **(b) de** — of
importance, of consequence.
entierro *nm* **(a)** burial, interment. **(b)** funeral;
asistir al — to go to the funeral. **(c)** grave. **(d)** (*SAm*)
(buried) treasure; treasure-trove.
entintar [1a] *vt* to ink; to ink in; to stain with ink.
entizar [1f] *vt* (*SAm: Billiards*) cue to chalk.
entoldado *nm* awning; marquee, large tent.
entoldar [1a] **1** *vt* **(a)** to put an awning over, fit with
an awning.
(b) to decorate (with hangings).
2 entoldarse *vr* **(a)** (*Meteorol*) to cloud over,
become overcast.
(b) (*emotion, joy*) to be dimmed.
(c) (*person*) to give oneself airs.
entomología *nf* entomology.
entomólogo *nm* entomologist.
entonación *nf* **(a)** (*Ling*) intonation. **(b)** (*fig*) conceit.
entonado *adj* **(a)** (*Mus*) toned; harmonious; in tune.
(b) (*fig*) conceited; haughty, arrogant, stiff.
entonar [1a] **1** *vt* **(a)** (*Mus*) *song etc* to intone; *voice* to
modulate; to sing in tune; *note* to give, pitch, set;
organ to blow.
(b) (*fig*) *praises* to sound.
(c) (*Art, Phot*) to tone.
(d) (*Med*) to tone up.
2 *vi* **(a)** (*Mus*) to intone; to be in tune (*con* with).
(b) (*fig*) to be in tune (*con* with), harmonize
(*con* with).
3 entonarse *vr* to give oneself airs.
entonces *adv* **(a)** (*time*) then; at that time; **desde** —
since then; **en aquel** — at that time; **hasta** —
up till then; **las costumbres de** — the customs
of the time; **el** — **embajador de Eslobodia** the
then ambassador of Slobodia; **fue** — **que . . .** it was
then that . . .
(b) (*concessive*) and so; then; **pues** — well then;
¿cómo no viniste? then why didn't you come?;
¡y —**!** (*Arg, PR*) why of course!
entonelar [1a] *vt* to put into barrels (*or* casks).
entongado *adj* (*Col*) cross.

entongar [1h] *vt* **(a)** (*Cu, Mex*) to pile up, make a pile
of. **(b)** (*Col*) to stun; to anger.
entono *nm* **(a)** (*Mus*) intoning; being in tune, singing
in tune. **(b)** (*fig*) conceit; haughtiness.
entontecer [2d] **1** *vt* to make silly. **2** *vi and* **entonte-
cerse** *vr* to get silly.
entorchado *nm* gold braid, silver braid; lace.
entorchar [1a] *vt* **(a)** to twist (up). **(b)** to braid.
entornado *adj* half-closed; ajar.
entornar [1a] *vt* **(a)** *eyes* to half-close; to screw up;
door to half-close, leave ajar. **(b)** to upset, tip over.
entorpecer [2d] *vt* **(a)** to dull, benumb, stupefy; to
make torpid, make lethargic.
(b) to obstruct, hinder; *plans etc* to set back;
traffic, movement to slow down, slow up; *work* to
hinder, delay.
entorpecimiento *nm* **(a)** stupefaction; numbness;
torpor, lethargy.
(b) obstruction; obstacle, drawback; delay,
slowing-up.
entrada *nf* **(a)** (*place*) entrance (*de* to), way in (*de*
to); gate, gateway; access; (*Min*) entrance, adit;
(*part of house*) porch, doorway; entrance hall.
(b) (*Mech*) inlet, intake; — **de aire** air intake.
(c) (*act*) entry, entrance (*en* into); admission (*en*
into); right of entry; **la** — **de las tropas en 1940** the
entry of the troops in 1940; **la** — **de turistas este
año** this year's influx of tourists; — **en escena** (*Theat*)
entrance; — **a viva fuerza** forced entry; "— **gratis**"
"admission free"; "**prohibida la** —" "no entry",
"no admission", "keep out"; **su** — **en la Academia**
his admission to the Academy; **la** — **de la palabra
en el diccionario** the admission of the word into the
dictionary, the acceptance of the word for the
dictionary; **dar** — **a** to admit; **hacer su** — to make
one's entry, make a formal entry.
(d) (*Theat etc*) ticket; — **de favor,** — **de regalo**
complimentary ticket.
(e) (*Theat etc*) house, audience; (*Sport*) gate,
crowd; — **floja** thin audience; **gran** —, — **llena** full
house; **hubo poca** — there was a small audience.
(f) (*Theat, Fin*) receipts, takings; (*Sport*) gate
money.
(g) (*of book, speech, year etc*) beginning; **la** — **de la
primavera** the start of spring; **de** — right away,
from the start.
(h) (*Cook*) entrée.
(i) (*Sport*) innings.
(j) (*Comm*) entry.
(k) (*Arg, Cu, Mex*) attack, onslaught; assault.
(l) (*Arg, Cu, Mex*) beating.
(m) (*Col*) down payment, deposit.
(n) —**s** (*Fin*) receipts, takings; income; —**s
familiares** family income; —**s brutas** gross receipts;
—**s y salidas** income and expenditure.
entrado *adj* **(a)** — **en años** elderly, advanced in years.
(b) hasta muy entrada la noche until late at
night; on into the small hours.
(c) (*Chi*) meddling, officious.
entrador *adj* **(a)** (*SAm*) brave; spirited; energetic;
enterprising.
(b) (*Chi*) meddling, officious.
(c) (*SAm*) charming, likeable, attractive.
(d) (*Col, Ec, Mex, Per, Ven*) amorously inclined.
(e) entradora (*Guat, Ven*) coquettish; fast, loose.
entramado *nm* (*Archit*) truss; timber framework; (*of
bridge*) framework; span.
entrambos *adj pl* (*lit*) both.
entrampar [1a] **1** *vt* **(a)** to trap, catch, snare; (*fig*) to
snare, trick.
(b) (*fig*) to mess up, make a mess of.
(c) (*Comm*) to burden with debts.
2 entramparse *vr* (*fig*) **(a)** to get into a mess, get
tangled up.
(b) (*Comm*) to get into debt.
entrante 1 *adj* **(a)** next, coming; **la semana** — next
week.
(b) *person* new, incoming.
2 *nm* **(a)** (*Geog*) inlet.
(b) ser — **en una casa** to have the run of a
house, have free entry to a house.
entraña *nf* **(a)** (*fig*) core, root, essential part; **ésta es
la verdadera** — **del problema** this is the real core of
the problem.
(b) de mala — malicious; evil-minded.
(c) —**s** (*Anat*) entrails; insides; bowels; (*fig*)
core, innermost parts; (*fig*) heart, feelings; disposition; **¡hijo de mis** —**s!** my precious child!;
arrancar las —**s a uno** (*fig*) to break someone's
heart; **dar hasta las** —**s** to give one's all; **echar las**
—**s** (*fam*) to puke; **no tener** —**s** (*fig*) to be heartless,
lack all feelings.

entrañable *adj* **(a)** close, intimate. **(b)** beloved, dearly loved. **(c)** affectionate.

entrañablemente *adv* love etc dearly, deeply.

entrañar [1a] **1** *vt* **(a)** to bury deep.
(b) (*fig*) to contain, carry within; to entail.
2 entrañarse *vr* **(a)** to become deeply attached.
(b) — **en** to reach to the bottom of, reach to the very heart of.

entrañudo *adj* (*Arg*) **(a)** brave, daring. **(b)** cruel, heartless.

entrar [1a] **1** *vt* **(a)** to introduce; to bring in, show in.
(b) to influence, get at.
(c) (*Mil*) to attack; to invade; to capture, enter.
2 *vi* **(a)** to go in, come in, enter; — **a** (*SAm*), — **en** to go into, come into, enter; (*fig*) to enter into; — **bien** to be fitting, be appropriate; to be relevant; — **a puerto** to enter port, come into port; **el enchufe entra en esa toma** the plug goes into (*or* fits into) that point; **el paquete no entra en el saco** the parcel won't go into the bag; — **en una profesión** to adopt a profession, take up a profession; — **en una sociedad** to join a society, become a member of a society, be admitted to a society; **el río entra en el lago** the river flows into the lake; — **en el número de** to be one of, count among, be reckoned among; — **en detalles** to go into details; **eso no entra en nuestros planes** that does not enter into our plans; **entra por una sexta parte** he gets a sixth, his share is one sixth; **le entraron deseos de** + *infin* he felt a sudden urge to + *infin*.
(b) (*of year etc*) to begin; (*of wind, tide*) to rise; **el año que entra** next year.
(c) **ese tío no me entra** I can't bear that fellow, I can't get on with that chap; **no me entra la lógica** I can't get the hang of logic.
(d) — **a** + *infin* to begin to + *infin*.

entrazado *adj* (*Arg*) **(a)** ragged, shabby; **mal** — shabby. **(b)** nasty-looking.

entre *prep* between; among, amongst; in the midst of; — **tú y yo** between the two of us; — **esto y lo otro** what with this and that; — **azul y verde** midway between blue and green, of some colour between blue and green; **había** — **todos 12 personas** there were 12 people in all (*or* all told); **de** — out of, from among; **por** — through; between; **decir** — **sí** to say to oneself.

entre . . . inter . . .

entreabierto *adj* half-open; ajar.

entreabrir [3a; *ptp* **entreabierto**] *vt* to half-open, open halfway; to leave ajar.

entreacto *nm* interval, entr'acte.

entreayudarse [1a] *vr* to help one another, be of mutual assistance.

entrecano *adj* greyish, greying.

entrecarril *nm* (*Ven: Rail*) gauge.

entrecejo *nm* space between the eyebrows; frown; **arrugar el** —, **fruncir el** — to frown, wrinkle one's brow.

entrecerrar [1k] *vt* (*CAm, Mex*) to half-close, close halfway; to leave ajar.

entrecoger [2c] *vt* **(a)** to catch, intercept; to seize. **(b)** (*fig*) to press, compel; to silence.

entrecomillado *nm* inverted commas.

entrecoro *nm* chancel.

entrecortado *adj* intermittent; *speech* faltering, hesitant, confused; **en voz entrecortada** in a faltering voice, in a voice choked with emotion.

entrecortar [1a] *vt* **(a)** to cut into, partially cut, cut halfway through.
(b) to cut off, interrupt (from time to time); *voice* to cause to falter, choke from time to time.

entrecruzar [1f] **1** *vt* **(a)** to interlace, interweave. **(b)** (*Bio*) to cross, interbreed. **2 entrecruzarse** *vr* (*Bio*) to interbreed.

entrecubiertas *nfpl* between-decks.

entrechocarse [1g] *vr* to collide, crash; to clash.

entredicho *nm* **(a)** prohibition, ban, interdict; (*Law*) injunction; **estar en** — to be under a ban, be banned; **levantar el** — **a** to raise the ban on.
(b) (*Arg*) disagreement, split; breaking-off of relations.
(c) (*Bol*) alarm bell.

entredós *nm* (*Sew*) insertion, panel.

entrefino *adj* medium, medium-quality.

entrefuerte *adj* (*SAm*) *tobacco* medium strong.

entrega *nf* **(a)** (*act*) delivery; handing over, surrender; (*Post*) post, delivery; — **contra pago**, — **contra reembolso** cash on delivery; — **en fecha futura** forward delivery; **pagadero a la** — payable on delivery; **hacer** — **de** to hand over (formally), present.

(b) (*of novel etc*) part, instalment; (*of journal etc*) part, number, fascicule.

entregar [1h] **1** *vt* to deliver; to hand, hand over, hand in; to surrender; to give up, part with; — **algo a un abogado** to refer something to a lawyer, place a matter in a lawyer's hands; —**la** (*sl*) to kick the bucket (*sl*); **no quiso** —**melo** he refused to hand it over to me.
2 entregarse *vr* **(a)** to surrender, give in, submit.
(b) — **a** to devote oneself to; (*pej*) to give oneself up to, abandon oneself to, indulge in; — **a estudiar** to devote oneself to studying.
(c) — **de** to take possession of.

entreguerras: el período de — the inter-war period, the period between the wars (*ie* 1918-39).

entrelazado *adj* entwined, interlaced; criss-crossed (*de* with); interlocking.

entrelazar [1f] **1** *vt* to entwine, interlace, interweave; to interlock. **2 entrelazarse** *vr* to entwine, interlace; to interlock.

entrelistado *adj* striped.

entrelucir [3f] *vi* **(a)** to show through. **(b)** to gleam, shine dimly.

entremás *adv* (*Arg, Col, Mex, Per*) moreover; especially.

entremedias 1 *adv* in between, halfway; in the meantime. **2** — **de** *prep* between; among.

entremés *nm* **(a)** (*Theat: Hist*) interlude, short farce.
(b) (*Cook*) side dish; — **salado** savoury; —**es** hors d'oeuvres.

entremeter [2a] *vt* to insert, put in; to put between.

entremeterse *etc see* **entrometerse** *etc*.

entremezclar [1a] **1** *vt* to intermingle; **entremezclado de** interspersed with. **2 entremezclarse** *vr* to intermingle.

entrenador *nm* **(a)** (*Sport*) trainer, coach. **(b)** (*Aer*) trainer, training plane.

entrenamiento *nm* training; coaching.

entrenar [1a] **1** *vt* (*Sport*) to train, coach; *horse* to exercise; **estar entrenado** (*footballer etc*) to be in training, be fit. **2 entrenarse** *vr* to train.

entreoír [3q] *vt* to half-hear, hear indistinctly.

entrepaño *nm* door panel; shelf.

entrepierna *nf* (*also* —**s**) crotch, crutch.

entrepuente *nm* between-decks; steerage.

entrerrenglonar [1a] *vt* to interline, write between the lines of.

entresacar [1g] *vt* to pick out, select; to sift; *hair, plants etc* to thin out.

entresemana *nf* midweek; (*SAm*) working days of the week; **de** — midweek (*attr*); **cualquier día de** — any day in midweek.

entresijo *nm* **(a)** (*Anat*) mesentery.
(b) (*fig*) secret, mystery; hidden aspect; difficulty, snag; **esto tiene muchos** —**s** this is very complicated, this has its ins and outs; **él tiene sus** —**s** he's a deep one.

entresuelo *nm* mezzanine, entresol.

entretanto 1 *adj* meanwhile, meantime. **2** *nm* meantime; **en el** — in the meantime.

entretecho *nm* (*Chi, RPl*) attic, garret.

entretejer [2a] *vt* to interweave; to intertwine, entwine; (*fig*) to interweave, insert, put in.

entretela *nf* **(a)** (*Sew*) interlining. **(b)** —**s** inmost being; heartstrings; **¡te voy a sacar las** —**s!** (*fam*) I'll tear your guts out! (*fam*).

entretelar [1a] *vt* to interline.

entretelones *nmpl* (*fig*) inner workings, secret goings-on.

entretención *nf* (*SAm*) entertainment, amusement.

entretener [2l] **1** *vt* **(a)** to entertain, amuse; to distract.
(b) to delay; to hold up, detain, keep waiting; to keep occupied; to keep in suspense; **nos entretuvo en conversación** he engaged us in conversation; he kept us talking; — **a los acreedores** to keep one's creditors at bay, hold off one's creditors; **pues no le entretengo más** then I won't keep you any longer.
(c) *hunger* to kill, stave off; *pain* to allay; *time* to while away.
(d) (*Mech etc*) to maintain.
2 entretenerse *vr* **(a)** to amuse oneself; to while away the time.
(b) to delay; to loiter (on the way); **¡no te entretengas!** don't hang about!, don't loiter on the way!

entretenida *nf* **(a)** mistress; kept woman.
(b) **dar (con) la** — **a uno** to hold someone off with vague promises, hedge with someone, stall someone; to keep someone talking.

entretenido *adj* entertaining, amusing.

entretenimiento nm (a) entertainment, amusement; diversion, distraction; recreation; **es un — nada más** it's just an amusement.

(b) (Mech etc) upkeep, maintenance; **sólo necesita un — mínimo** it only needs minimum maintenance.

entretiempo nm period between seasons; spring, autumn.

entrever [2v] vt (a) to glimpse, catch a glimpse of; to see indistinctly, make out something of. (b) (fig) to guess, suspect (something of).

entreverado adj mixed; patchy; bacon streaky.

entreverar [1a] 1 vt to mix, intermingle; to mix up.

2 **entreverarse** vr (a) to intermix, be intermingled.

(b) (Arg) to mix in a confused mass, mingle in confusion.

entrevero nm (a) mix-up; jumble. (b) (Bol, Chi, Per, RPl) confusion, disorder; brawl; (Mil) confused cavalry skirmish.

entrevía nf (Rail) gauge; **— angosta** narrow gauge; **de — angosta** narrow-gauge (attr); **— normal** standard gauge.

entrevista nf interview; meeting, conference; **celebrar una — con** to have an interview with, hold a meeting with.

entrevistar [1a] 1 vt to interview.

2 **entrevistarse** vr to have an interview, meet; **— con** to interview, meet, have an interview with; **el ministro se entrevistó con la reina ayer** the minister saw the queen yesterday.

entripado nm (Arg) ghastly secret; concealed anger, secret rage.

entripar [1a] 1 vt (a) (Arg, Col, Ec) to anger, upset.

(b) (Ant, Mex) to soak.

2 **entriparse** vr (a) (Arg, Col, Ec) to get cross, get upset.

(b) (Ant, Mex) to get soaked.

entristecer [2d] 1 vt to sadden, grieve. 2 **entristecerse** vr to grow sad, grieve.

entrometerse [2a] vr to meddle, interfere (en in, with), intrude.

entrometido 1 adj meddlesome, interfering. 2 nm, **entrometida** nf busybody, meddler; intruder.

entromparse [1a] vr (SAm) to get cross.

entrón adj (a) (Col) meddlesome. (b) (Mex) spirited, daring. (c) **entrona** (Mex) coquettish; fast, loose.

entroncar [1g] 1 vt to connect, establish a relationship between. 2 vi (a) to be related, be connected (con to, with). (b) (SAm) to connect (con with).

entronización nf (a) enthronement. (b) (fig) exaltation.

entronizar [1f] vt (a) to enthrone. (b) (fig) to exalt.

entronque nm (a) relationship, connection, link. (b) (SAm) connection; junction.

entruchada nf (a) (fam) trap, trick. (b) (Chi) violent interview, shouting match; friendly talk.

entruchar [1a] 1 vt (fam) to lure, decoy, lead by the nose. 2 **entrucharse** vr (Mex) (a) to stick one's nose into other people's affairs. (b) to get besotted with love.

entuerto nm (a) wrong, injustice. (b) **—s** (Med) afterpains.

entumecer [2d] 1 vt to numb, benumb. 2 **entumecerse** vr (a) (limb) to get numb, go to sleep. (b) (river) to swell, rise; (sea) to surge.

entumecido adj numb, stiff.

entumecimiento nm numbness, stiffness.

entumido adj (a) (SAm) numb, stiff. (b) (Col, Mex) timid.

enturbiar [1b] 1 vt (a) water to muddy; to disturb, make cloudy.

(b) issue to fog, confuse; mind, person to derange, unhinge.

2 **enturbiarse** vr (a) to get muddy; to become cloudy.

(b) to get confused, become obscured; to become deranged.

entusiasmar [1a] 1 vt to fill with enthusiasm; to fire, excite; to delight, please a great deal.

2 **entusiasmarse** vr to get enthusiastic, get excited (con, por about); **— con, — por** to be keen on, rave about, be delighted with; **se ha quedado entusiasmada con el vestido** she was delighted with the dress, she raved about the dress.

entusiasmo nm enthusiasm (por for); excitement; keenness, zeal, zest; delight, pleasure; **con — en**thusiastically; keenly.

entusiasta 1 adj enthusiastic; keen (de on); zealous (de for). 2 nmf enthusiast; fan (fam), follower, supporter; admirer.

entusiástico adj enthusiastic.

enumeración nf enumeration; count, reckoning.

enumerar [1a] vt to enumerate; to count, reckon up.

enunciación nf enunciation; statement, declaration.

enunciar [1b] vt to enunciate; to state, declare.

enuresis nf enuresis, bedwetting.

envagonar vt (SAm) goods to load into a railway truck.

envainar [1a] 1 vt (a) to sheathe, put in a sheath; **¡enváinala!** (sl) shut your trap! (sl). (b) (Col) to vex, annoy. 2 vi (Col) to succumb. 3 **envainarse** vr (Col) to get into trouble.

envalentonamiento nm boldness; (pej) Dutch courage; bravado.

envalentonar [1a] 1 vt to embolden; (pej) to fill with Dutch courage.

2 **envalentonarse** vr to take courage, become bolder; (pej) to strut, brag; to put on a bold front.

envanecer [2d] 1 vt to make conceited. 2 **envanecerse** vr to grow vain, get conceited, give oneself airs; to swell with pride (con, de at).

envanecido adj conceited, stuck-up (fam).

envanecimiento nm conceit, vanity.

envarar [1a] 1 vt (Col: Agr) to stake. 2 **envararse** vr (Mex) to be numb, become stiff.

envasar [1a] 1 vt (a) to pack, wrap; to package; to bottle; to can, tin; to barrel; to sack, bag.

(b) wine (fam) to knock back (sl), put away.

(c) (esp SAm) **— un puñal en uno** to plunge a dagger into someone, bury a dagger in someone.

2 vi (fam) to tipple, knock it back (sl).

envase nm (a) (act) packing, wrapping; packaging; bottling; canning.

(b) container; package, wrapping; bottle; can, tin; barrel; bag; **— de hojalata** tin can; **precio con —** price including packing; **géneros sin —** loose goods, unwrapped goods; **—s a devolver** returnable empties.

envasijar [1a] vt (SAm) = envasar.

envedijarse [1a] vr to get tangled (up).

envegarse [1h] vr (Chi) to get swampy, turn into a swamp.

envejecer [2d] 1 vt to age, make (seem) old.

2 vi and **envejecerse** vr (a) to age, get old, grow old; to look old; **en 2 años ha envejecido mucho** he's got very old these last two years.

(b) to become old-fashioned, become antiquated, get out-of-date.

envejecido adj old, aged; old-looking; **está muy —** he looks terribly old.

envelar [1a] vi (Chi) to hoist the sails; (fig: also **—las**) to run away.

envenenador nm, **envenenadora** nf poisoner.

envenenamiento nm poisoning.

envenenar [1a] 1 vt to poison; (fig) to poison, embitter. 2 **envenenarse** vr to poison oneself, take poison.

enverdecer [2s] vi to turn green.

envergadura nf (a) expanse, spread, extent; (Naut) breadth, beam; (Aer: also **— de alas**) wingspan; (Ent, Orn) span, wingspan; (of boxer) reach.

(b) (fig) scope, compass; magnitude; **un programa de gran —** a programme of considerable scope, a far-reaching programme; **una operación de cierta —** an operation of some magnitude; an operation of some size; **la obra es de —** the plan is ambitious.

envés nm (of cloth) back, wrong side; (of sword) back, flat; (Anat: fam) back.

enviado nm envoy.

enviar [1b] vt to send; **— a uno a hacer algo** to send someone to do something; **— a uno a una misión** to send someone on a mission; **— por el médico** to send for the doctor, fetch the doctor.

enviciar [1b] 1 vt to corrupt; (fig) to vitiate.

2 **enviciarse** vr to get corrupted; **— con, — en** to become (unhealthily) addicted to, acquire an excessive fondness for.

envidar [1a] vti (Cards) to bid.

envidia nf envy, jealousy; desire; bad feeling; **es pura —** it's sheer envy; **tener — a** to envy.

envidiable adj enviable.

envidiar [1b] vt to envy; to desire, covet; **— algo a uno** to envy someone something, begrudge someone something.

envidioso adj envious, jealous; covetous.

envilecer [2d] 1 vt to debase, degrade. 2 **envilecerse** vr to degrade oneself, lower oneself; to grovel, crawl.

envilecimiento nm degradation, debasement.

envinado adj (a) (Arg) drunk. (b) (Mex) wine-coloured.

envinarse [1a] vr (Mex) (a) to get drunk (on wine). (b) to become satiated with wine.

envío nm (a) (act) sending, dispatch; shipment; **gastos de —** (cost of) postage and packing, transport charges.
(b) (of goods) consignment, lot, (Naut) shipment; (of money) remittance.
envión nm push, shove.
envite nm (a) stake; side bet. (b) offer, bid; invitation. (c) push, shove; **al primer —** right away, from the very start.
enviudar [1a] vi to become a widow(er), be widowed; **— de su primera mujer** to lose one's first wife; **enviudó 3 veces** she lost three husbands.
envoltijo nm, **envoltorio** nm bundle, package.
envoltura nf cover; wrapper, wrapping; case, casing; sheath; (Aer, Bot etc) envelope; **—s swaddling** clothes.
envolvedero nm, **envolvedor** nm cover; wrapper, wrapping; envelope.
envolvente adj surrounding; movement (Mil) encircling, enveloping.
envolver [2h; ptp **envuelto**] 1 vt (a) (with paper etc) to wrap (up), pack (up), tie up, do up; (with clothes) to wrap, swathe, cover; to envelop, enfold; to muffle (up); **envuelto en una capa** wrapped in a cloak, muffled up in a cloak; **dos paquetes envueltos en papel** two parcels wrapped in paper; **¿quiere que se lo envuelva?** shall I wrap it (up) for you?
(b) (Mil) to encircle, surround.
(c) (fig) to imply, involve, mean; **person** to involve, implicate (en in).
2 **envolverse** vr (a) to wrap oneself up (en in).
(b) (fig) to become involved (en in).
envolvimiento nm (a) wrapping; envelopment. (b) (Mil) encirclement. (c) (fig) involvement.
enyerbar [1a] 1 vt (Col, Chi, Mex) to bewitch.
2 **enyerbarse** vr (a) (SAm) to get covered with grass.
(b) (Cu: of deal) to fail.
(c) (Guat, Mex) to poison oneself.
(d) (Mex) to fall madly in love.
enyesado nm, **enyesadura** nf plastering.
enyesar [1a] vt (a) to plaster. (b) (Med) to put in a plaster cast.
enyugar [1h] vt to yoke.
enyuntar [1a] vt (SAm) to put together, join.
enzacatarse [1a] vr (CAm, Mex) to get covered with grass.
enzarzar [1f] 1 vt (fig) to involve (in a dispute), entangle, embroil.
2 **enzarzarse** vr to get involved in a dispute; to get oneself into trouble; **— en una discusión** to get involved in an argument.
enzima nf enzyme.
enzocar [1g] vt (Chi) to insert, put in, fit in.
enzolvar [1a] vt (Mex) to clog, stop up.
eón nm aeon.
épica nf epic.
epicentro nm epicentre.
épico adj epic.
epicúreo 1 adj epicurean. 2 nm epicurean.
epicureísmo nm, **epicurismo** nm epicureanism.
epidemia nf epidemic.
epidémico adj epidemic.
epidermis nf epidermis.
Epifanía nf Epiphany.
epiglotis nf epiglottis.
epígrafe nm epigraph; inscription; title, headline; caption; motto.
epigrama nm epigram.
epigramático adj epigrammatic(al).
epilepsia nf epilepsy.
epiléptico 1 adj epileptic. 2 nm, **epiléptica** nf epileptic.
epilogar [1h] vt to sum up; to round off, provide a conclusion to.
epílogo nm epilogue.
episcopado nm (a) (office) bishopric. (b) (period) episcopate. (c) bishops (collectively), episcopacy.
episcopal adj episcopal.
episcopaliano 1 adj episcopalian. 2 nm, **episcopaliana** nf episcopalian.
episcopalista adj and nmf = **episcopaliano**.
episódico adj episodic.
episodio nm episode; incident; (of story etc) episode, instalment, part.
epístola nf epistle.
epistolar adj epistolary.
epistolario nm collected letters.
epitafio nm epitaph.
epíteto nm epithet.
epitomar [1a] vt to condense, abridge; to summarize.

epítome nm summary, abstract, résumé; compendium.
época nf period, time; age, epoch; spell; **la — de Carlos III** the age of Charles III; **en la — de Carlos III** in Charles III's time; **en aquella —** at that time, in that period; **— de celo** (Zool) mating season, rutting season; **— de la serpiente de mar** (hum) silly season; **muebles de —** period furniture; **coche de —** vintage car; **una puerta victoriana de primera —** an early Victorian door; **con decoraciones de —** with period set; **anticiparse** (or **adelantarse**) **a su —** to be ahead of one's time; **formar —, hacer —** to be epoch-making, be a landmark; **el invento hace —** it's an epoch-making discovery; **eso hizo — en nuestra historia** that was a landmark in our history; **todos tenemos —s así** we all go through spells like that.
epopeya nf epic (also fig).
equidad nf equity; justice, fairness, impartiality; (of price etc) reasonableness.
equidistante adj equidistant.
equilátero adj equilateral.
equilibrar [1a] 1 vt (a) to balance; to poise. (b) (fig) to balance; to adjust, redress; budget to balance.
2 **equilibrarse** vr to balance (oneself; en on).
equilibrio nm (a) balance, equilibrium; **perder el —** to lose one's balance. (b) (fig) balance; (social etc) poise; **— político** balance of power.
equilibrista nmf (a) tightrope walker; acrobat. (b) (SAm) politician of shifting allegiance.
equino 1 adj equine, horse (attr). 2 nm sea urchin.
equinoccio nm equinox; **— otoñal** autumnal equinox; **— vernal** vernal equinox.
equipaje nm (a) (el —) luggage, baggage (US); (un —) piece of luggage, piece of baggage (US); equipment, outfit, kit; **— de mano** hand luggage; **facturar el —** to register one's luggage; **hacer el —** to pack, do the packing.
(b) (Naut) crew.
equipal nm (Mex) leather chair.
equipar [1a] vt to equip, furnish, fit up (con, de with); (Naut) to fit out.
equiparable adj comparable (con to, with); applicable (con to); **esa experiencia con animales no es — con la del hombre** that experience with animals is not applicable to man's; **los dos no son —s** the two are not comparable.
equiparación nf comparison.
equiparar [1a] 1 vt to put on the same level, consider equal; to compare (con with).
2 **equipararse** vr: **— con** to be on a level with, rank equally with.
equipo nm (a) equipment; outfit, kit; gear, tackle; (industrial) plant; (of turbines etc) set; **el — de la fábrica está bastante anticuado** the factory plant is pretty antiquated; **— de alpinismo** climbing kit; **— de caza** hunting gear; **— cinematográfico móvil** mobile film unit; **— de fumador** smoker's outfit, smoker's accessories; **— de novia** trousseau; **— de primeros auxilios** first-aid kit; **— de reparaciones** repair kit; **— rodante** (Rail) rolling stock.
(b) (of men) team; gang; (of workers) shift; (hum) outfit; **— de día** day shift; **— médico** medical team, medical unit; **no tuve nada que ver con ese —** I had nothing to do with that outfit.
(c) (Sport) team; side; **— de fuera** away team; **— de fútbol** football team; **los —s formaron así . . .** the teams lined up as follows . . .
equis nf (a) name of the letter X; **pongamos que cuesta — dólares** let us suppose it costs X dollars; **averiguar la —** to find the value of X.
(b) (CAm, Col, Ec) **estar en la —** to be all skin and bones; to be broke (fam).
equitación nf (a) riding; **escuela de —** riding school. (b) horsemanship.
equitativamente adv equitably, fairly; reasonably.
equitativo adj equitable, fair; reasonable; **trato —** fair deal, square deal.
equivalencia nf equivalence.
equivalente 1 adj equivalent (a to). 2 nm equivalent.
equivaler [2a] vi to be equivalent, be equal; **— a** to be equivalent to, be equal to; to rank as, rank with, be on a level with.
equivocación nf mistake, error; oversight; misunderstanding; **por —** by mistake, in error; mistakenly; **ha sido por —** it was a mistake.
equivocado adj wrong, mistaken; affection, trust etc misplaced; **Vd está —** you are mistaken.
equivocar [1g] 1 vt to mistake; **— A con B** to mistake A for B; **— el camino** to take the wrong road, go the wrong way.
2 **equivocarse** vr to be wrong, be mistaken; to

make a mistake; **pero se equivocó** but he was wrong; **A puede — con B** A can be mistaken for B; **— de casa** to go to the wrong house; **— de camino** to take the wrong road; **— en una elección** to make a wrong choice, choose wrongly.

equívoco 1 *adj* equivocal, ambiguous. **2** *nm* (a) equivocation, ambiguity; quibble. (b) pun, wordplay, play on words. (c) ambiguous word.

equivoquista *nmf* quibbler; punster.

era[1] *etc see* **ser**.

era[2] *nf* era, age; **— atómica** atomic age; **— cristiana,** **— de Cristo** Christian era.

era[3] *nf* (Agr) threshing floor; (*Hort*) bed, plot, patch.

erario *nm* exchequer, treasury; public funds, public finance.

erasmismo *nm* Erasmism.

erasmista 1 *adj* Eramist. **2** *nmf* Erasmist.

Erasmo *m* Erasmus.

erección *nf* erection, raising; (*fig*) establishment, foundation.

eremita *nm* hermit; recluse.

ergio *nm* erg.

ergonómica *nf* ergonomics.

erguido *adj* (a) erect, straight. (b) (*fig*) proud.

erguir [3n] **1** *vt* (a) to raise, lift.
(b) to straighten.
2 erguirse *vr* (a) to straighten up, stand up straight, sit up straight.
(b) (*fig*) to swell with pride.

erial 1 *adj* uncultivated, untilled. **2** *nm* common; uncultivated land.

Erico *m* Eric.

erigir [3c] **1** *vt* (a) to erect, raise, build.
(b) (*fig*) to establish, found.
(c) **— a uno en algo** to set someone up as something.
2 erigirse *vr:* **— en algo** to set oneself up as something.

erisipela *nf* erysipelas.

erizado *adj* (a) bristly; **— de espinas** covered with thorns, with prickles all over. (b) **— de problemas** bristling with problems.

erizarse [1f] *vr* to bristle; to stand on end.

erizo *nm* (a) (*Zool*) hedgehog; **— de mar, — marino** sea urchin. (b) (*Bot*) burr; prickly husk. (c) (*fam*) surly individual, grumpy sort.

ermita *nf* hermitage.

ermitaño *nm* (a) hermit. (b) (*Zool*) hermit crab.

ermitía *nf* hermitage.

Ernesto *m* Ernest.

erogación *nf* (a) distribution. (b) (*Arg, Mex, Par*) expenditure, payment; (*Per, Ven*) contribution.

erogar [1h] *vt* (a) *property* to distribute. (b) (*Arg*) to pay; *debt* to settle; (*Chi, Ec*) to contribute; (*Mex*) to spend, lay out.

erosión *nf* (Geol etc) erosion; (*Med*) graze; **causar — en** to erode.

erosionar [1a] **1** *vt* to erode. **2 erosionarse** *vr* to erode, be eroded.

erosivo *adj* erosive.

erótico *adj* erotic; *verse etc* love (*attr*); **el género —** the genre of love poetry.

erotismo *nm* eroticism.

erotomanía *nf* (pathological) eroticism.

erotómano *adj* (pathologically) erotic.

errabundeo *nm* wanderings.

errabundo *adj* wandering, roving.

erradamente *adv* mistakenly.

erradicación *nf* eradication.

erradicar [1g] *vt* to eradicate.

erradizo *adj* wandering, roving.

errado *adj* mistaken, wrong; wide of the mark; unwise.

errante *adj* (a) wandering, roving; itinerant; nomadic; *animal* lost, stray. (b) (*fig*) errant; **el marido —** the errant husband.

errar [1l] **1** *vt* (a) *shot* to miss with, aim badly; *target* to miss; *vocation etc* to miss, mistake; **— el camino** to lose one's way.
(b) *person* to fail, fail in one's duty to.
2 *vi* (a) to wander, rove; to roam about.
(b) = **3 errarse** *vr* to err, go astray, be mistaken; **— es cosa humana** to err is human.

errata *nf* misprint, erratum, printer's error; **es — por "poder"** it's a misprint for "poder".

errático *adj* erratic.

erre *nf name of the letter* R; **— que —** stubbornly, pigheadedly.

erróneamente *adv* mistakenly, erroneously; falsely.

erróneo *adj* mistaken, erroneous; false, untrue.

error *nm* error, mistake; fault; fallacy; **— de copia** clerical error; **— de imprenta, — tipográfico** misprint, printer's error; **— judicial** miscarriage of justice; **— de pluma** clerical error; **— de tecla** typing error; **por —** by mistake, in error; **caer en un —** to fall into error; **salvo — u omisión** errors and omissions excepted.

eructación *nf* belch.

eructar [1a] *vi* to belch.

eructo *nm* belch.

erudición *nf* erudition, learning, scholarship.

eruditamente *adv* learnedly.

erudito 1 *adj* erudite, learned, scholarly.
2 *nm*, **erudita** *nf* scholar; savant; learned person; **los —s en esta materia** those who are expert in this subject, those who really know about this subject; **— a la violeta** (*pej*) pseudo-intellectual, soi-disant expert.

erupción *nf* (a) (Geol) eruption; **— solar** solar flare; **estar en —** to be erupting; **entrar en —** to erupt. (b) (*Med: also* **— cutánea**) rash, eruption. (c) (*fig*) eruption; outbreak, explosion; outburst.

eruptivo *adj* eruptive.

esa, ésa *etc see* **ese, ése.**

Esaú *m* Esau.

esbeltez *nf* slimness, slenderness; litheness, willowyness; gracefulness.

esbelto *adj* slim, slender; lithe, willowy; graceful.

esbirro *nm* henchman; (*Hist*) bailiff, constable.

esbozar [1f] *vt* to sketch, outline; **— una sonrisa** to smile wanly, force a smile.

esbozo *nm* sketch, outline.

escabechar [1a] *vt* (a) (Cook) to pickle, souse. (b) *hair* to dye. (c) (*fam*) to do in (*sl*), carve up. (d) (*Univ: sl*) to plough (*sl*).

escabeche *nm* (a) (liquid) pickle, brine. (b) soused fish; **estar como el — (of meal)** to be stone-cold.

escabel *nm* low stool, footstool.

escabiosa *nf* scabious.

escabioso *adj* scabby; mangy.

escabro *nm* (Vet) sheep scab, scabs; (*Bot*) scaly bark.

escabrosamente *adv* (*fig*) riskily, scabrously, salaciously.

escabrosidad *nf* (a) roughness, ruggedness; unevenness. (b) harshness. (c) toughness, difficulty. (d) riskiness, scabrous nature, salaciousness.

escabroso *adj* (a) *ground* rough, rugged; *surface* uneven. (b) (*fig*) *sound etc* harsh. (c) *problem etc* tough, difficult, thorny. (d) *joke etc* risky, risqué, blue, scabrous.

escabuche *nm* weeding hoe.

escabullarse [1a] *vr* (SAm), **escabullirse** [3a] *vr* to slip away, slip off, clear out; to make oneself scarce; to scamper; **— por** to slip through.

escachalandrado *adj* (CAm, Col) slovenly.

escafandra *nf* diving suit.

escafandrismo *nm* underwater fishing.

escala *nf* (a) ladder; **— de cuerda, — de viento** (*Naut*) rope ladder.
(b) (*Math, Mus and fig*) scale; (*of colours, speeds etc*) range; **— móvil** sliding scale; **— de la popularidad** popularity chart, (*Mus*) hit parade; **— de sueldos** salary scale; **a (or en) — nacional** on a national scale; **una investigación a — nacional** a nation-wide inquiry, a countrywide investigation; **en gran(de)** — on a large scale, in a big way; **un plan en gran —** a large-scale plan; **a (or en) pequeña —** on a small scale; **reproducir según —** to reproduce to scale.
(c) stopping place; (*Naut*) port of call; intermediate stop, stopover; **vuelo sin —s** non-stop flight; **hacer — en** to stop at, make an intermediate stop at, (*Naut*) to call at, put in at.

escalación *nf* (Mil, Pol) escalation.

escalada *nf* (a) climb; climbing, scaling; **— en rocas** rock climbing. (b) (Mil, Pol) escalation.

escalador *nm* (a) climber; mountaineer; **— en rocas** rock climber. (b) burglar, housebreaker.

escalafón *nm* (a) roll, list, register; list of officials, establishment.
(b) salary scale, wage scale.
(c) (*fig*) table, chart; **en esta industria España ocupa el tercer lugar en el — mundial** Spain occupies third place in the world table for this industry.

escalamera *nf* rowlock, oarlock (US).

escalamiento *nm* (a) climbing, scaling. (b) (Mil, Pol) escalation.

escálamo *nm* thole, tholepin.

escalante *adj* (Mil, Pol) escalating; **la crisis —** the escalating crisis.

escalar [1a] **1** *vt* **(a)** *mountain etc* to climb, scale. **(b)** *house* to burgle, burglarize (*US*), break into, force an entry into. **2** *vi* **(a)** to climb. **(b)** (*Naut*) to call, put in (*en* at). **(c)** (*Mil, Pol*) to escalate.

Escalda *m* Scheldt.

escaldado *adj* **(a)** wary, fly, cautious. **(b)** *woman* loose.

escaldadura *nf* **(a)** scald, scalding. **(b)** chafing.

escaldar [1a] **1** *vt* **(a)** *person* to scald. **(b)** *skin* to chafe, rub. **(c)** *metal* to make red-hot. **2 escaldarse** *vr* **(a)** to get scalded, scald oneself. **(b)** to chafe.

escalera *nf* **(a)** stairs, staircase, stairway; ladder; steps, flight of steps; (*of cart, lorry*) tailboard; **— de caracol** spiral staircase, winding staircase; **— doble**, **— de mano**, **— de tijera** steps, stepladder; **— de incendios** fire escape; **— mecánica**, **— móvil**, **— rodante** escalator, moving staircase; **— de servicio** service stairs, backstairs. **(b)** (*Cards*) run, sequence.

escalerilla *nf* small ladder; low step; (*Naut*) gangway.

escalfador *nm* chafing dish.

escalfar [1a] *vt* *egg* to poach.

escalinata *nf* steps, flight of steps; outside staircase.

escalofriado *adj*: **estar —** to feel chilly, feel shivery, feel hot-and-cold.

escalofriante *adj* bloodcurdling, hair-raising; chilling, frightening.

escalofriarse [1c] *vr* **(a)** to feel chilly, get the shivers, feel hot-and-cold by turns. **(b)** to shiver with fright, get a cold shiver of fright.

escalofrío *nm* **(a)** (*Med*) chill, feverish chill. **(b)** **—s** (*fig*) shivers; shivery fright.

escalón *nm* **(a)** (*of stairway*) step, stair; (*of ladder*) rung; (*part of stair*) tread; (*of rocket*) stage; **— de hielo** ice step. **(b)** (*fig*) stage, grade; (*towards success etc*) ladder; rung, stepping stone. **(c)** (*Mil*) echelon.

escalonar [1a] *vt* to spread out at intervals; (*Mil etc*) to echelon; *land* to terrace, cut in a series of steps; *hours, production etc* to stagger.

escalope *nm* (*Cook*) escalope; **— de ternera** escalope of veal.

escalpar [1a] *vt* to scalp.

escalpelo *nm* scalpel.

escama *nf* **(a)** (*Bot, Fish etc*) scale; (*of soap etc*) flake; **—s de jabón, jabón en —s** soapflakes. **(b)** (*fig*) resentment, grudge; suspicion.

escamado *adj* **(a)** wary, fly, cautious. **(b)** (*Arg*) wearied, cloyed.

escamar [1a] **1** *vt* **(a)** to scale, remove the scales from. **(b)** (*fig*) to make wary, create distrust in, shake the confidence of; **eso me escama** that makes me suspicious, that sounds ominous to me. **2 escamarse** *vr* **(a)** to scale (off), flake off. **(b)** (*fig*) to get wary, become suspicious; **y luego se escamó** and after that it was a case of once bitten twice shy.

escamocha *nf* (*Mex*) left-overs.

escamón *adj* wary, distrustful; apprehensive.

escamondar [1a] *vt* to prune; (*fig*) to prune, trim.

escamoso *adj* *fish* scaly; *substance* flaky.

escamoteador *nm* **(a)** conjurer, juggler. **(b)** (*pej*) swindler.

escamot(e)ar [1a] *vt* **(a)** to whisk away, whisk out of sight, snatch away, make vanish; *card* to palm. **(b)** (*fam*) to lift (*fam*), swipe (*sl*). **(c)** (*fig*) *difficulty etc* to shirk, disregard.

escamoteo *nm* **(a)** sleight of hand; conjuring; palming. **(b)** (*un —*) conjuring trick. **(c)** (*fam*) lifting (*fam*), swiping (*sl*); swindling; (*un —*) swindle. **(d)** shirking.

escampar [1a] **1** *vt* to clear out. **2** *vi* **(a)** (*of sky*) to clear; (*of rain*) to stop; (*of weather*) to clear up, stop raining. **(b)** (*CAm, Col, Chi, Mex, PR*) to shelter from the rain. **(c)** (*SAm: fam*) to clear off, beat it (*fam*).

escampavía *nf* revenue cutter.

escanciador *nm* wine waiter; (*Hist*) cupbearer.

escanciar [1b] **1** *vt* *wine* to pour (out), serve; *glass* to drain. **2** *vi* to drink a lot of wine, make merry on wine.

escandalizar [1f] **1** *vt* to scandalize, shock. **2** *vi* to make a fuss, kick up a row. **3 escandalizarse** *vr* to be shocked (*de* at, by), be scandalized; to be offended (*de* at, by); **se escandalizó ante la pintura** he threw up his hands in horror at the picture.

escándalo *nm* **(a)** scandal; outrage; **¡qué —!** what a scandal!; **el — de los autobuses municipales** the scandal of the town's buses. **(b)** row, uproar, commotion; **armar un —** to make a scene, cause an uproar. **(c)** sense of shock; astonishment.

escandalosa *nf* **(a)** (*Naut*) topsail. **(b)** (*Col*) tulip.

escandalosamente *adv* scandalously, shockingly, outrageously; flagrantly; licentiously.

escandaloso *adj* scandalous, shocking, outrageous; *crime etc* flagrant; *life* scandalous; disorderly, licentious; *laughter* uproarious, hearty; *child* noisy; uncontrollable, undisciplined; *colours* (*Col*) loud.

escandallo *nm* (*Naut*) lead.

Escandinavia *f* Scandinavia.

escandinavo **1** *adj* Scandinavian. **2** *nm*, **escandinava** *nf* Scandinavian.

escandir *vt* *verse* to scan.

escansión *nf* scansion.

escantillón *nm* pattern, template.

escaño *nm* bench; settle; (*Parl*) seat.

escapada *nf* **(a)** escape, flight; **— en una tabla** narrow squeak, near thing; **en una —** in a jiffy. **(b)** (*Racing, Sport*) breakaway. **(c)** flying visit, quick trip; **hice una — a la capital** I made a flying visit to the capital. **(d)** (*pej*) escapade.

escapado *adj*, *adv* at top speed, in a rush; **irse —** to rush off, be off like a shot; **se volvió —** he rushed back; **tengo que volverme — a la tienda** I must get back double-quick to the shop; **lo harán —s** they'll do it like a shot.

escapar [1a] **1** *vt* *horse* to ride hard, drive hard. **2** *vi* **(a)** to escape, flee, run away; **— a uno** to escape from someone; **— de la cárcel** to escape from prison; **escapó de mis manos** it escaped from my hands, it eluded my grasp. **(b)** (*Racing, Sport*) to break away. **3 escaparse** *vr* **(a)** (*person*) to escape, flee, run away, get away; **— con algo** to make off with something; **— de morir** to miss death narrowly; **— por un pelo, — en una tabla** to have a narrow escape, have a close shave. **(b)** (*gas etc*) to leak, leak out, escape. **(c)** (*detail, news etc*) **se me escapa** it eludes me, it escapes me; **se me escapa su nombre** his name escapes me; **se le escapó la fecha de la reunión** he let the date of the meeting slip out, he unintentionally revealed the date of the meeting; **ese detalle se me había escapado** that detail had escaped my notice.

escaparate *nm* **(a)** shop window; showcase, display case. **(b)** (*SAm*) wardrobe.

escaparatista *nmf* window dresser.

escapatoria *nf* **(a)** escape, flight; getaway; (*fam*) secret trip; **— del trabajo** escape from work. **(b)** (*fig*) way out, loophole; excuse, pretext.

escape *nm* **(a)** escape, flight, getaway; **a — at full speed; in a great hurry; salir a — to rush out. **(b)** (*of gas etc*) leak, leakage, escape. **(c)** (*Tech*) exhaust; **gases de —** exhaust (fumes); **tubo de —** exhaust (pipe). **(d)** (*Mech*) escapement.

escapismo *nm* escapism.

escapista **1** *adj* escapist. **2** *nmf* escapist.

escápula *nf* scapula, shoulder blade.

escapulario *nm* scapular(y).

escaque *nm* (*of chessboard*) square; **—s** (*Hist*) chess.

escaquearse [1a] *vr* (*fam*) to shirk.

escara *nf* (*Med*) crust, slough.

escarabajas *nfpl* firewood, kindling.

escarabajear [1a] **1** *vt* (*fam*) to bother, worry. **2** *vi* **(a)** to crawl; to wriggle, squirm. **(b)** to scrawl, scribble.

escarabajo *nm* **(a)** (*Ent*) beetle; **— del Colorado, — de la patata** Colorado beetle. **(b)** (*Tech*) flaw. **(c)** (*fam*) dwarf, runt. **(d)** **—s** (*fam*) scrawl, scribble.

escaramujo *nm* **(a)** (*Bot*) wild rose, dog rose, briar; hip. **(b)** (*Zool*) goose barnacle. **(c)** (*Cu*) bewitchment.

escaramuza *nf* **(a)** (*Mil*) skirmish, brush. **(b)** (*fig*) brush; squabble.

escaramuzar [1f] *vi* to skirmish.

escarapela *nf* **(a)** cockade, rosette. **(b)** (*fam*) brawl, shindy.

escarapelar [1a] **1** *vt* **(a)** (*Col, CR, Mex, Ven*) to scrape off, scale off, chip off. **(b)** (*Col*) to crumple, rumple, muss. **2** *vi* **(a)** to wrangle, quarrel. **(b)**=**3 escarapelarse** *vr* **(a)** (*Col, CR, Mex, Ven*) to peel off, flake off. **(b)** (*Mex, Per*) to get gooseflesh, tremble all over.

escarbadientes *nm*, *pl* **escarbadientes** toothpick.

escarbador *nm* scraper.

escarbar [1a] **1** vt (a) ground (of chicken) to scratch; fire to poke; ears, teeth to pick, clean.
(b) (fig) to inquire into, investigate, delve into; (pej) to pry into; to rake around in (or among).
2 vi (a) to scratch.
(b) — en = **1** (b).
escarcear [1a] vi (Chi, RPl, Ven) to prance.
escarcela nf (a) (Hunting) pouch, bag. (b) — **para limosnas** collecting tin.
escarceo nm (a) (of horse) nervous movement; prance.
(b) —s small waves.
(c) —s (fig): —s **amorosos** amorous posturings, amorous attitudinizing.
escarcha nf frost, hoarfrost.
escarchado adj (a) covered in hoarfrost, frosted. (b) fruit crystallized.
escarchar [1a] **1** vt (a) to frost, cover in hoarfrost.
(b) (Cook) cake to ice.
(c) (Sew) to embroider with silver (or gold).
2 vi: **escarcha** there is a frost, it's frosty, it's freezing.
escarchilla nf (Col, Ec, Ven) small ice particles.
escarcho nm roach.
escarda nf (a) weeding, hoeing. (b) weeding hoe.
escardador nm weeding hoe.
escardadura nf weeding, hoeing.
escardar [1a] vt (a) to weed, weed out. (b) (fig) to weed out.
escardillo nm weeding hoe.
escariador nm reamer.
escariar [1b] vt to ream.
escarificación nf (Agr, Med) scarification.
escarificador nm scarifier.
escarificar [1g] vt to scarify.
escarlata **1** adj invar scarlet. **2** nf (a) scarlet. (b) scarlet cloth.
escarlatina nf scarlet fever.
escarmenar [1a] vt (a) wool to comb. (b) (fig) to punish; — **algo a uno** (fam) to do someone out of something bit by bit.
escarmentado adj wary, cautious.
escarmentar [1k] **1** vt to punish severely, teach a lesson to.
2 vi to learn one's lesson; **yo escarmenté y no lo volví a hacer** I learned my lesson and never did it again; **¡para que escarmientes!** that'll teach you!; — **en cabeza ajena** to learn by someone else's mistakes.
escarmiento nm punishment; lesson, warning, example; **para — de los malhechores** as a lesson to wrongdoers; **que esto te sirva de —** let this be a lesson (or warning) to you.
escarnecedor **1** adj mocking. **2** nm scoffer, mocker.
escarnecer [2d] vt to scoff at, mock, ridicule.
escarnio nm jibe, taunt; derision, ridicule.
escarola nf (a) (Bot) endive. (b) (Mex: Sew) ruff, flounce.
escarolar [1a] vt (Sew) to frill, flounce; to curl.
escarpa nf (a) slope; (Geog, Mil) scarp, escarpment. (b) (Mex) pavement.
escarpado adj steep, sheer; craggy.
escarpadura nf = **escarpa** (a).
escarpar [1a] vt (a) (Geog etc) to escarp. (b) (Tech) to rasp.
escarpia nf spike; meat hook; (Tech) tenterhook.
escarpín nm pump, slipper; extra sock, outer sock; ankle sock.
escarrancharse [1a] vr (fam) to do the splits.
escasamente adv (a) scantily, sparingly; meagrely. (b) scarcely, hardly, barely.
escasear [1a] **1** vt to be sparing with, give out in small amounts, skimp. **2** vi to be scarce, get scarce; to fall short; to diminish.
escasez nf (a) scarcity, shortage, lack; poverty, want; — **de dinero** lack of money, shortage of funds; **vivir con —** to live in poverty. (b) meanness, stinginess.
escaso adj (a) scarce; scant, scanty; limited; slight; allowance meagre, skimpy; audience, crop thin, sparse; chance slim, slender, small; resources slender; money scarce, tight; supply small, short, insufficient; visibility poor; — **de población** thinly populated; — **de recursos naturales** poor in natural resources; **andar — de dinero** to be short of money, be in need of money; **con escasa compasión** with scant pity; **su inteligencia es escasa** his intelligence is slight, his intelligence is limited.
(b) bare; **hay 2 toneladas escasas** there are barely 2 tons; **tiene 15 años —s** he's barely 15, he's hardly 15; **ganar por una cabeza escasa** to win by a short head.
(c) mean, stingy; sparing.

escatimar [1a] vt to curtail, cut down; to give grudgingly, skimp, stint; to be sparing of; **no — esfuerzo para** + infin to spare no effort to + infin; **no escatimaba sus alabanzas de . . .** he was unstinting in his praise of . . ., he did not stint his praise of . . .
escatimoso adj (a) sparing, scrimpy, mean. (b) malicious.
escatología nf eschatology.
escayola nf (Med etc) plaster.
escayolar [1a] vt to put in plaster; **con la pierna escayolada** with his leg in plaster; **tener el cuello escayolado** to have one's neck in plaster.
escena nf (a) (in general) scene; **una — conmovedora** a touching scene; **con —s de la revolución** with scenes from the revolution; — **muda** by-play; — (Cine) **retrospectiva** flashback.
(b) stage; **entrar en —** to enter, come on; **poner en —** to stage, put on, perform.
(c) scenery.
escenario nm (a) (Theat) stage; setting; scenery; **en el —** on (the) stage.
(b) (Cine) scenario; continuity.
(c) (fig) scene; setting; **el — del crimen** the scene of the crime; **fue — de un motín** it was the scene of a riot; **desapareció del — político** he disappeared from the political scene; **la ceremonia tuvo por — X** the ceremony was set in X, the ceremony had X as its setting.
escénico adj scenic.
escenografía nf scenography.
escenógrafo nm theatrical designer, designer of sets; scene painter.
escepticismo nm scepticism.
escéptico **1** adj sceptical. **2** nm, **escéptica** nf sceptic; doubter.
Escila f Scylla; — **y Caribdis** Scylla and Charybdis.
escindible adj fissionable.
escindir [3a] **1** vt to split; **el partido está escindido** the party is split. **2 escindirse** vr to split (en into); (of faction) to split off.
Escipión m Scipio.
escisión nf (a) scission; fission; split; (Med) excision; — **nuclear** nuclear fission. (b) (fig) split, division; **la — del partido** the split in the party.
esclarecer [2d] **1** vt (a) to light up, illuminate. (b) (fig) to explain, elucidate, shed light on. (c) (fig) to enlighten. (d) (fig) to ennoble. **2** vi to dawn.
esclarecido adj illustrious, distinguished.
esclarecimiento nm (a) illumination. (b) explanation, elucidation, clarification. (c) enlightenment. (d) ennoblement.
esclava nf (a) slave; (fig) slave, drudge; — **blanca** white slave. (b) slave bangle, bracelet.
esclavatura nf (SAm: Hist) (a) slaves (collectively). (b) period of slavery. (c) slavery.
esclavina nf short cloak, cape, tippet.
esclavitud nf slavery, servitude, bondage.
esclavizar [1f] vt to enslave.
esclavo nm slave; **ser — del tabaco** to be a slave to tobacco; **vender a uno como —** to sell someone into slavery.
esclerosis nf sclerosis.
esclusa nf lock, sluice; floodgate; — **de aire** airlock.
esclusero nm lock keeper.
escoba nf (a) broom; brush. (b) (Bot) broom.
escobada nf brush, sweep.
escobar [1a] vt to sweep, sweep out.
escobazo nm (a) blow with a broom. (b) quick sweep; **dar un —** to have a quick sweep-up; **echar a uno a —s** to kick someone out.
escobilla nf (a) small broom, brush; whisk. (b) (Aut, Elec) brush. (c) (Bot) teasel.
escobillar [1a] vi (SAm) to dance with quick steps.
escobillón nm (Mech, Med) swab.
escobón nm large broom, long-handled broom; scrubbing brush; (Mech, Med) swab.
escocedor adj (fig) painful, hurtful.
escocer [2b and 2h] **1** vt to annoy, upset.
2 vi to smart, sting; to feel a burning pain; **esto escuece en la lengua, esto me escuece la lengua** it makes my tongue smart.
3 escocerse vr to chafe, get chafed.
escocés **1** adj Scotch, Scots, Scottish. **2** nm Scot, Scotsman. **3** nm (dialect) Scots.
escocesa nf Scot, Scotswoman.
Escocia f Scotland.
escoda nf stonecutter's hammer.
escofina nf rasp, file.
escofinar [1a] vt to rasp, file.
escogedor nm (Agr etc) riddle.

escoger [2c] *vti* to choose, select, pick (out); (*Pol etc*) to elect.

escogido *adj* chosen, selected; (*in quality*) choice, select; *works* selected.

escogimiento *nm* (a) (*act*) choosing, selecting, picking. (b) selection; choice, pick.

escolar 1 *adj* scholastic; school (*attr*); **año —** school year. **2** *nm* schoolboy, pupil.

escolaridad *nf* schooling; **— obligatoria** compulsory schooling, compulsory attendance at school; **el porcentaje de — es elevado** the school population is high, the proportion of those in school is high.

escolástica *nf*, **escolasticismo** *nm* scholasticism.

escolástico 1 *adj* scholastic. **2** *nm* scholastic, schoolman.

escoleta *nf* (*Mex*) (a) amateur band. (b) rehearsal, practice (of an amateur band). (c) dancing lesson.

escoliar [1b] *vt text* to gloss, furnish with explanations.

escolopendra *nf* (*Zool*) centipede.

escolta *nf* escort; **dar — a** to escort, accompany.

escoltar [1a] *vt* to escort; to guard, protect; to attend, accompany; (*Naut*) to escort, convoy.

escollar [1a] *vi* (a) (*Arg, Per*) to hit a reef, strike a rock. (b) (*Arg, Chi: of enterprise*) to fail, come unstuck.

escollera *nf* breakwater, jetty.

escollo *nm* (a) reef, rock. (b) (*fig*) pitfall; stumbling block; hidden danger.

escombrar [1a] *vt* to clear out, clean out, clear of rubbish.

escombrera *nf* tip, dump, rubbish heap; (*Min*) slag heap.

escombro *nm* (*Fish*) mackerel.

escombros *nmpl* rubbish; debris, wreckage, rubble; (*Min*) waste, slag.

escondedero *nm* hiding place.

esconder [2a] **1** *vt* to hide, conceal (*de* from). **2 esconderse** *vr* to hide (*de* from); to hide oneself, conceal oneself; to be hidden; to lurk.

escondida(s) *nf(pl)* (*SAm*) hide-and-seek; **hacer algo a —s** to do something secretly, do something by stealth; **hacer algo a —s de uno** to do something behind someone's back.

escondite *nm* (a) hiding place. (b) hide-and-seek; **jugar al — con** (*fig*) to play hide-and-seek with.

escondido(s) *nm(pl)* (*SAm*) hide-and-seek.

escondrijo *nm* hiding place, hideout; (*fig*) nook.

escopeta *nf* shotgun; **— de aire comprimido** popgun; airgun; **— de dos cañones, — de tiro doble** double-barrelled gun; **— de viento** airgun.

escopetazo *nm* (a) gunshot; gunshot wound. (b) (*fig*) bad news; blow; bombshell.

escopetear [1a] **1** *vt* (a) to shoot at (with a shotgun). (b) (*Mex*) to get at, allude offensively to. **2** *vi* (*Ven*) to answer irritably. **3 escopetearse** *vr*: **se escopetearon en el bosque** they shot at each other in the wood; **se escopetean a injurias** they shower one another with insults, they heap insults upon each other.

escopeteo *nm* (a) shooting, volley of shots. (b) (*of insults etc*) shower, lively exchange.

escopetero *nm* gunsmith.

escoplear [1a] *vt* to chisel.

escoplo *nm* chisel.

escor *nm* (*SAm: angl*) score.

escora *nf* (*Naut*) (a) level line, load line. (b) prop, shore. (c) list; **con una — de 30 grados** with a thirty-degree list.

escorar [1a] *vi* (*Naut*) to list, heel (over); **— a babor** to list to port.

escorbútico *adj* scorbutic.

escorbuto *nm* scurvy.

escorchar [1a] *vt* (a) to flay, skin. (b) (*Arg*) to bother, annoy.

escoria *nf* (a) (*Metal*) slag, dross; **— básica** basic slag. (b) (*fig*) scum, dregs; **la — de la humanidad** the scum of humanity.

escorial *nm* dump, slag heap, tip; bed of lava, deposit of volcanic ash.

escorpión *nm* scorpion; **E—** Scorpio.

escorzar [1f] *vt* to foreshorten.

escorzo *nm* foreshortening.

escota *nf* (*Naut*) sheet.

escotado 1 *adj dress* low-cut, low-necked, cut low, décolleté. **2** *nm* = **escotadura**.

escotadura *nf* (a) (*Sew*) low neck(line). (b) (*Theat*) large trap door. (c) recess; notch.

escotar [1a] **1** *vt* (a) (*Sew*) to cut out, cut to fit; to cut low in front. (b) *river etc* to draw water from. **2** *vi* to pay one's share.

escote *nm* (a) (*Sew*) low neck; décolletage. (b) (*Fin*) share; **ir a —, pagar a —** to share the expenses, go fifty-fifty, (*on outing*) to go Dutch.

escotilla *nf* (*Naut etc*) hatch, hatchway.

escotillón *nm* trap door.

escozor *nm* (a) smart, sting; burning pain. (b) (*fig*) grief, heartache.

escriba *nm* scribe.

escribanía *nf* (a) writing desk; writing case. (b) writing materials; inkstand. (c) (*Law*) clerkship; clerk's office, (*Hist*) notary's office.

escribano *nm* (a) court clerk; lawyer's clerk; (*Hist*) notary; **— municipal** town clerk. (b) (*Orn*) bunting; **— cerillo** yellowhammer.

escribiente *nm* copyist, amanuensis; clerk; **— en jefe** chief clerk, head clerk.

escribir [3a; *ptp* **escrito**] **1** *vti* (a) to write; **— a mano** to write in longhand; to write out; **— a máquina** to type; **el que esto escribe** the present writer, (*to press etc*) this correspondent. (b) to spell; **"voy" se escribe con "v" "voy"** is spelled with a "v"; **¿cómo se escribe eso?** how is that spelled?, how do you spell that? **2 escribirse** *vr* to write to each other.

escrito 1 *ptp of* **escribir**. **2** *adj* written; said, stated; **lo arriba —** what has been said above. **3** *nm* writing, document; text; manuscript; (*Law*) brief; **—s** (*Lit etc*) writings, works; **por —** in writing; in black and white; **acuerdo por —** written agreement, agreement in writing; **poner algo por —** to commit something to paper; to write something down, get something down in writing; **tomar algo por —** to write something down.

escritor *nm*, **escritora** *nf* writer; **— de material publicitario** copywriter; **— satírico** satirist, satirical writer.

escritorio *nm* (a) desk, bureau; writing case. (b) office.

escritorzuelo *nm* hack (writer), scribbler.

escrituario *adj* scriptural.

escritura *nf* (a) (*act, art*) writing. (b) (*of nation etc*) writing, script; alphabet; (*of person*) writing, handwriting; **tiene malísima —** her writing is terrible; **no acierto a leer su —** I can't read his writing; **— aérea** skywriting; **— corrida, — normal** longhand; **— china** Chinese writing, Chinese script; **— fonética** phonetic script; **— a máquina** typing. (c) **Sagrada E—** (Holy) Scripture. (d) (*Law*) deed; document, instrument; **— de aprendizaje** indenture; **— de propiedad** title deed; **— de seguro** insurance certificate; **— de traspaso** conveyance.

escriturar [1a] *vt* (a) (*Law*) to execute by deed, formalize legally; *apprentice* to indenture. (b) (*Theat etc*) to book, engage, sign up.

escriturístico *adj* Scriptural.

escrófula *nf* scrofula.

escrofuloso *adj* scrofulous.

escroto *nm* scrotum.

escrupulizar [1f] *vt* to scruple, hesitate; **no — en +** *infin* not to scruple to + *infin*.

escrúpulo *nm* (a) scruple; doubt, hesitation; **falta de —s** unscrupulousness; **sin —** unscrupulous; **no hizo — de +** *infin* he did not scruple to + *infin*, he did not hesitate to + *infin*. (b) scrupulousness. (c) (*Pharm*) scruple.

escrupulosamente *adv* scrupulously; exactly, precisely.

escrupulosidad *nf* scrupulousness; exactness, preciseness.

escrupuloso *adj* scrupulous; exact, particular, precise.

escrutador 1 *adj look etc* searching, penetrating. **2** *nm* (*Pol*) returning officer, scrutineer; inspector of election returns; (*Parl*) teller.

escrutar [1a] *vt* (a) to scrutinize, examine. (b) *votes* to count.

escrutinio *nm* (a) scrutiny, examination, inspection. (b) (*Pol*) count, counting (of votes); voting, ballot.

escuadra *nf* (a) (*Tech*) carpenter's square, draughtsman's square; bracket; angle iron; **— de delineante** set square; **a —** square, at right angles; **fuera de —** out of true. (b) (*Mil*) squad; (*Naut*) squadron; (*of cars etc*) fleet; **— de demolición** demolition squad; **— de fusilamiento** firing squad. (c) (*Col*) pistol.

escuadrar [1a] *vt* (*Tech*) to square.

escuadrilla *nf* (*Aer*) wing, squadron.

escuadrón *nm* (*Aer*) squadron; (*Mil*) squadron, troop.

escualidez *nf* paleness, weakness, emaciation; skinniness, scragginess.

escuálido *adj* pale, weak, emaciated; skinny, scraggy.

escualo *nm* shark, dogfish.

escucha 1 *nf* (a) (*act*) listening; listening-in; **estar a la —** to listen in; **estar de —** to spy, eavesdrop.
 (b) (*Eccl*) chaperon.
 2 *nm* (*Mil*) scout; (*Radio*) monitor (*person*); listener.

escuchar [1a] **1** *vt* to listen to; (*SAm*) to hear; *advice etc* to listen to, heed, pay attention to; *applause, ovation, warning etc* to receive. **2** *vi* to listen.

escucho *nm* (*Col*) whispered secret.

escuchón *adj* (*Ec*) prying, inquisitive.

escudar [1a] **1** *vt* to shield, protect, defend. **2 escudarse** *vr* to shield oneself, protect oneself.

escudero *nm* (*Hist*) squire; page.

escudete *nm* (a) (*Her, Hist*) escutcheon. (b) (*Sew*) gusset. (c) (*Bot*) white water lily.

escudilla *nf* bowl, basin.

escudo *nm* shield (*also fig*); **— de armas** (*Her*) coat of arms.

escudriñar [1a] *vt* to inquire into, investigate; to examine, scan, scrutinize.

escuela *nf* (a) school; **— de artes y oficios** technical school, trade school; **— automovilista** driving school; **— de baile** school of dancing; ballet school; **— de comercio** business school, school of business studies; **— elemental, — primaria, — de primera enseñanza** primary school; **— de equitación** riding school; **— de formación profesional** polytechnic; **— de hogar** domestic science college; **— laboral** technical school; trade school; **— nocturna** night school; **— normal** training college, college of education; **— particular, — privada** private school; **— de párvulos** infant(s') school, kindergarten; **estar en la —** to be at school; **ir a la —** to go to school; **soplarse la —** to play truant.
 (b) (*of thought etc*) school; **la — catalana** the Catalan school; **gente de la vieja —** people of the old school; **formarse en una — dura** to learn in a tough school.

escuelante *nm* (a) (*Mex*) schoolmaster. (b) (*Col, Ven*) schoolboy.

escuelero 1 *adj* (*SAm*) school (*attr*). **2** *nm* (a) (*CAm, Cu, Chi, Mex, Per, Urug, Ven: pej*) schoolmaster. (b) (*Col, Guat, Par, Ven*) schoolboy, pupil.

escuelista *nmf* (*Urug*) schoolboy, schoolgirl, pupil.

escuerzo *nm* toad.

escuetamente *adv* plainly; baldly, without frills.

escueto *adj* plain, unadorned, bare; bald.

escuincle *nm* (*Mex*) child.

esculcar [1g] *vt* (*Ant, CAm, Col, Mex*) to search.

esculpir [3a] *vt* to sculpture; to carve, engrave; *inscription* to cut.

escultor *nm* sculptor.

escultora *nf* sculptress.

escultura *nf* sculpture, carving; **— en madera** wood carving.

escultural *adj* sculptural; (*fig*) *figure etc* statuesque.

escupidera *nf* (a) spittoon. (b) (*SAm: euph*) chamberpot; **pedir la —** to get scared; to give in, give oneself up.

escupidor *nm* (a) spitter. (b) (*Ec, PR*) spittoon. (c) (*Col*) round mat, doormat.

escupir [3a] *vti* (a) to spit; *food etc* to spit out; **— a uno** to spit at someone; **— a la cara a uno** to spit in someone's face; **— en el suelo** to spit on the ground.
 (b) (*fig*) *word* to spit, spit out, fling (*a* at); *flames etc* to spit, belch, give out; to throw off, fling off, cast aside; **— a** to scoff at.

escurana *nf* (*SAm*) darkness; overcast sky, threatening sky.

escurialense *adj* of (*or* from) El Escorial.

escurreplatos *nm, pl* **escurreplatos** plate rack.

escurribanda *nf* (*fam*) (a) (*Med*) looseness, diarrhoea. (b) (*Med: of sore*) running. (c) escape; (*fig*) loophole, way out. (d) thrashing.

escurridero *nm* draining board, drainboard (*US*).

escurridizo *adj* (a) slippery; difficult to hold; *knot* running; **hacerse —** to slip away, vanish. (b) *character* slippery.

escurrido *adj* (a) narrow-hipped, slightly built; wearing a tight-fitting skirt. (b) (*Cu, Mex, Per, PR*) abashed, ashamed.

escurridor *nm* wringer; **— (de loza)** plate rack; (*Cook*) colander, strainer; (*Phot*) drying rack.

escurriduras *nfpl* dregs.

escurrir [3a] **1** *vt clothes* to wring (out); *plates, liquid* to drain; *substance* to press dry, squeeze dry.
 2 *vi* (a) (*of liquid*) to drip, trickle; to ooze; (*of object*) to slip, slide.
 (b) (*of surface*) to be slippery.
 3 escurrirse *vr* (a) (*liquid*) to drip, trickle; to ooze; (*object*) to slip, slide; **se me escurrió de entre las manos** it slipped out of my hands.
 (b) (*dishes etc*) to drain; (*Cook*) to drain, strain; **"se escurre bien"** (*recipe*) "drain well".
 (c) (*remark etc*) to slip out.
 (d) (*person etc*) to slip away, sneak off; to glide away.

escúter *nm* (*angl*) (motor) scooter.

esdrújula 1 *adj* having dactylic stress, accented on the antepenult.
 2 *nm* word having dactylic stress, word accented on the antepenult (*eg* **mísero**, miserly).

ese¹ *nf* (a) *name of the letter* S. (b) S-shaped part (*or* link *etc*); **hacer —s** to zigzag, twist and turn; (*of drunk*) to reel about, stagger along.

ese² *dem adj m*, **esa** *f* that; **esos** *dem adj mpl*, **esas** *fpl* those.

ése *dem pron m*, **ésa** *f* that; that one; the former; **ésos** *dem pron mpl*, **ésas** *fpl* those; the former; **en ésa** in your town; **ni por ésas** on no account, under no circumstances; **¡no me salgas ahora con ésas!** don't bring all that up again!; **no es una chica de ésas** she's not one of those, she's not that kind of a girl.

esencia *nf* essence; (*of problem etc*) heart, core; **en —** in essence.

esencial 1 *adj* essential; chief, main; **lo —** the essential thing, the main thing; **cosa no —** non-essential thing, inessential. **2** *nm* essential.

esfágnea *nf* sphagnum.

esfera *nf* (a) (*Geog, Math etc*) sphere; globe; **— celeste** celestial sphere; **en forma de —** spherical, globular.
 (b) (*Tech*) dial; (*of watch*) face.
 (c) (*fig*) sphere; plane, field; **— de acción** scope, range; **— de actividad** sphere of activity; **— de influencia** sphere of influence.

esférico *adj* spherical.

esferográfica *nf* (*Cu*) ballpoint pen.

esferoide *nm* spheroid.

esfinge *nf* (a) sphinx. (b) (*Ent*) hawk moth.

esfínter *nm* sphincter.

esforzado *adj* vigorous, energetic, strong; tough; enterprising; brave, valiant.

esforzar [1f *and* 1m] **1** *vt* (a) to strengthen; to invigorate.
 (b) to encourage, raise the spirits of.
 2 esforzarse *vr* to exert oneself, make an effort; to strain; **hay que — más** you must try harder, you must put more effort into it; **— en + infin, — por + infin** to struggle to + *infin*, strive to + *infin*.

esfuerzo *nm* (a) effort, endeavour; exertion; (*of imagination*) effort, stretch; **sin —** effortlessly, without strain; **no perdonar —s para + infin** to spare no effort to + *infin*; **bien vale el —** it's well worth the effort.
 (b) (*Mech*) stress.
 (c) courage, spirit; vigour; **con —** with spirit.

esfumar [1a] **1** *vt* (*Art*) to shade (in); to tone down, soften.
 2 esfumarse *vr* (a) to fade away, melt away.
 (b) (*person*) to vanish, make oneself scarce.

esfumino *nm* (*Art*) stump.

esgrima *nf* (*Sport*) fencing; (*Mil: art*) swordsmanship.

esgrimidor *nm* (*Sport*) fencer; (*Mil*) swordsman.

esgrimir [3a] **1** *vt sword* to wield; to brandish; (*fig*) *argument etc* to use; to brandish, flourish, fling about. **2** *vi* to fence.

esgrimista *nmf* (*SAm*) fencer.

esguazar [1f] *vt* to ford.

esguince *nm* (a) swerve, dodge, avoiding action; **dar un —** to swerve, duck, dodge.
 (b) (*Med*) sprain.
 (c) scowl, frown; scornful look.
 (d) (*of plot, story*) twist; **un — ingenioso** an ingenious twist.

eslabón *nm* link (*also fig*); steel; (*Naut, Tech*) shackle; **— giratorio** swivel; **— hipotético, — perdido** (*Bio and fig*) missing link.

eslabonar [1a] *vt* to link (together, up), join; (*fig*) to link, interlink, connect, knit together.

eslavo 1 *adj* Slav, Slavonic. **2** *nm*, **eslava** *nf* Slav. **3** *nm* (language) Slavonic.

eslinga *nf* (*Naut: angl*) sling.

eslingar [1h] *vt* (*Naut*) to sling.

eslip *nm, pl* **eslips** (*angl*) *see* **slip**.

eslogan *nm, pl* **eslogans** (*angl*) *see* **slogan**.

eslora nf (Naut) length; **tiene 250 m de —** she is 250 m in length.

eslovaco 1 adj Slovak(ian). **2** nm, **eslovaca** nf Slovak.

esloveno 1 adj Slovene. **2** nm, **eslovena** nf Slovene.

esmaltar [1a] vt (a) to enamel; nails to varnish, paint. (b) (fig) to embellish, beautify, adorn (with a variety of colours).

esmalte nm (a) (Anat, Tech) enamel; enamelwork, smalt; **— de uñas** nail varnish, nail polish. (b) (fig) lustre.

esmeradamente adv carefully, neatly; elegantly.

esmerado adj (a) work careful, neat; polished, elegant. (b) person careful, painstaking, conscientious.

esmeralda nf emerald.

esmerar [1a] **1** vt to polish, brighten up.
2 esmerarse vr to take great pains (en over), exercise great care (en in), do one's best; to shine, do well; **— en** + infin to take great pains to + infin, go to great trouble to + infin.

esmerejón nm merlin.

esmeril nm emery.

esmerilar [1a] vt to polish with emery.

esmero nm care, carefulness; neatness; polish, elegance; refinement; **con el mayor —** with the greatest care; **poner — en algo** to take great care over something.

Esmirna Smyrna.

esmirriado adj = desmirriado.

esmoladera nf grindstone.

esmoquin nm (Acad) dinner jacket, tuxedo (US).

esnob (angl) **1** adj invar person snobbish; car, restaurant etc posh (fam), de luxe, swish (sl). **2** nmf, pl **esnobs** [ez'noβ] snob.

esnobismo nm snobbery, snobbishness.

eso dem pron "neuter" that; that thing, that affair, that matter; **— no me gusta** I don't like that; **¿qué es —?** what's that?; **— de su coche** that business about his car; **— de no tener dinero el colegio** that story about the college having no money; **— de que los cerdos volarán algún día** the idea that pigs will fly one day; **¿qué es — de que . . .?** what's all this about . . .?; **¡— a ellos!** that's their look-out!; **— es** that's it, that's right; that's just it; **no es —** that's not the reason; **¡no es —!** hardly!; **nada de —** nothing of the kind, far from it; **¡nada de —!** not a bit of it!; **¿no es —?** isn't that so?; **— sí** yes; naturally, of course; **el coche es viejo, — sí** the car is certainly old, to be sure the car is old; **a — de las 2** at about 2 o'clock, round about 2; **antes de —** before that; **después de —** after that; **en —** thereupon, at that point; **por —** therefore, and so; **por — no vine** that's why I didn't come; **y — que llovía** in spite of the fact that it was raining; bearing in mind that it was raining.

esófago nm oesophagus, gullet.

Esopo m Aesop.

esotérico adj esoteric.

espabilada nf (Col) blink; **en una —** in a jiffy.

espabilar [1a] **1** vt candle to snuff; see **despabilar**. **2** vi (Col) to blink.
3 espabilarse vr to wake up; (fig) to look lively, get a move on; **¡espabílate!** get a move on!; jump to it!; **¡espabilado!** (iro) wake up!, you're a bright one!

espaciador nm spacing key, spacing bar.

espacial adj (a) (Math etc) spatial. (b) space (attr); **programa —** space programme; **viajes —es** space travel.

espaciar [1b] **1** vt to space (out; also Typ); to spread, expand; news to spread.
2 espaciarse vr (a) to expatiate, spread oneself; **— en un tema** to enlarge on a subject, expatiate on a subject. (b) to relax, take one's ease; to make merry.

espacio nm (a) (in general) space, room; distance; period, interval; **— libre** room, clear space; **— muerto** clearance; **— vital** living space, (Pol) lebensraum; **en el — de una hora** in the space of one hour; **en el — de 3 generaciones** in the space of 3 generations, over 3 generations; **por — de** during, for. (b) (Aer, Geog) space; **exploración del —** space exploration; **— estelar, — exterior, — extraterrestre** outer space. (c) delay, slowness. (d) (Typ) space; spacing; **a dos —s, a doble —** double-spaced. (e) (Mus) interval. (f) (Radio, TV) short programme, item; spot; **— publicitario** advertising spot, commercial.

espacioso adj (a) spacious, roomy, big; capacious. (b) movement slow, deliberate.

espada 1 nf (a) sword; **estar entre la — y la pared** to be between the devil and the deep blue sea; **estar hecho una —** to be as thin as a rake; **poner a —** to put to the sword. (b) **—s** (Cards) spades. **2** nm (a) swordsman; (Taur) matador. (b) (pej) bully; swashbuckler.

espadachín nm skilled swordsman; (pej) bully, thug.

espadaña nf bullrush.

espadarte nm swordfish.

espadazo nm sword thrust, slash with a sword.

espadero nm swordsmith.

espadín nm dress sword, ceremonial sword.

espadón nm (a) broadsword. (b) (hum) big shot (fam), top person; (Mil) brass hat (sl).

espaguetis nmpl spaghetti.

espalda nf (a) (also —s) back, shoulder(s); **a —s de uno** behind someone's back; **a —s (vueltas)** treacherously; **eso ha quedado ya a la —** that's all behind us now; **echar algo a las —s** to forget about something; **— con —** back to back; **de —s** from behind; **dar de —s** to fall on one's back; **estar de —s** to be on one's back; **de —s a la marcha** (in vehicle) facing backwards; **volverse de —s a** to turn one's back on (also fig); **fue muerto por la —** he was killed from behind; **echar algo sobre las —s** to take something on, take charge of something; **tener guardadas las —s** to have influential friends; **volver la —** to turn away; (pej) to turn tail; **volver las —s a uno** to give someone the cold shoulder, cold-shoulder someone. (b) (Ec) fate, destiny; star.

espaldar nm (a) (of chair) back. (b) (Hort) trellis, espalier. (c) **—es** wall hangings.

espaldarazo nm slap on the back; (Hist) accolade.

espaldera nf trellis, espalier.

espaldero nm (Ven) bodyguard, henchman.

espaldilla nf shoulder blade.

espantable adj = espantoso.

espantada nf (a) sudden scare, sudden fear; **dar la — a uno** to scare the wits out of someone. (b) stampede, panic.

espantadizo adj shy, timid, easily scared (off).

espantado adj frightened, scared, terrified; (SAm) ill from fright.

espantador adj (a) frightening. (b) (Arg, Col, Guat) = espantadizo.

espantajo nm (a) scarecrow. (b) (fig) scarecrow; sight, fright; bogey, bogeyman.

espantapájaros nm, pl **espantapájaros** scarecrow.

espantar [1a] **1** vt to frighten, scare; to frighten off, scare away; to appal, horrify.
2 espantarse vr (a) to get frightened, get scared (de at, of); to be appalled; to be amazed, be astonished (de at).
(b) (SD) to get suspicious.

espanto nm (a) fright, terror; consternation, dismay; amazement, astonishment. (b) threat, menace. (c) (SAm) ghost. (d) (fam) **¡qué —!** how awful! (fam); goodness!; **es un coche de —** it's a smashing car (sl), it's a tremendous car (fam).

espantosamente adv frightfully; terrifyingly; shockingly; amazingly.

espantosidad nf (CAm, Col, PR) horror.

espantoso adj frightful, dreadful; terrifying; shocking; appalling; amazing.

España f Spain; **Nueva —** (Hist) New Spain (ie Mexico); **la — de pandereta** (pej) touristy Spain, pseudo-romantic Spain, picturesque Spain.

español 1 adj Spanish.
2 nm, **española** nf Spaniard; **los —es** the Spaniards, the Spanish.
3 nm (language) Spanish; **— antiguo** Old Spanish; **— medieval** Medieval Spanish; **— moderno** Modern Spanish.

españolidad nf Spanishness.

españolísimo adj superl typically Spanish, unmistakably Spanish, Spanish to the core; terribly Spanish.

españolismo nm (a) love of Spain, love of things Spanish; tendency to adopt Spanish ways (etc). (b) Spanishness; Spanish nature, essentially Spanish character. (c) (Ling) hispanicism, word (or phrase etc) borrowed from Spanish.

españolizar [1f] **1** vt to make Spanish, hispanicize; to give a Spanish flavour (or colouring etc) to.
2 españolizarse vr to adopt Spanish ways (etc);

to acquire a Spanish flavour (*etc*); (*pej*) to affect Spanish ways; **se españolizó por completo** he became completely Spanish.

esparadrapo *nm* sticking plaster; adhesive tape.

esparaván *nm* **(a)** (*Orn*) sparrowhawk. **(b)** (*Vet*) spavin.

esparavel *nm* (fishing) net.

esparceta *nf* sainfoin.

esparcido *adj* **(a)** scattered. **(b)** (*fig*) merry, jolly, cheerful; open, frank.

esparcimiento *nm* **(a)** spreading, scattering. **(b)** (*fig*) relaxation; amusement, diversion; recreation. **(c)** (*fig*) cheerfulness; openness, frankness.

esparcir [3b] **1** *vt* **(a)** to spread, scatter; to sow; to disseminate.
(b) (*fig*) to amuse, divert.
2 esparcirse *vr* **(a)** to spread (out), scatter, be scattered.
(b) (*fig*) to relax; to amuse oneself.

espárrago *nm* asparagus; **estar hecho un — to be as thin as a rake; ¡vaya a freír —s!** (*fam*) go to hell!; **mandar a uno a freír —s** (*fam*) to tell someone to go to hell.

esparrancado *adj* (with legs) wide apart, (with legs) spread far apart.

esparrancarse [1g] *vr* to spread one's legs (wide apart); to do the splits; **— sobre algo** to straddle something.

Esparta Sparta.

espartal *nm* esparto field.

espartano 1 *adj* Spartan (*also fig*). **2** *nm*, **espartana** *nf* Spartan.

esparteña *nf* = **alpargata**.

espartillo *nm* (*SAm*) esparto (grass).

espartizal *nm* esparto field.

esparto *nm* esparto (grass); **estar como el — to be all dried up.**

espasmo *nm* spasm; jerk, sudden movement, fitful movement.

espasmódico *adj* spasmodic; jerky, fitful.

espasticidad *nf* spasticity.

espástico 1 *adj* spastic. **2** *nm*, **espástica** *nf* spastic.

espato *nm* (*Geol*) spar.

espátula *nf* **(a)** (*Med*) spatula; (*Art*) palette knife; (*Archit*) putty knife; **estar hecho una — to be as thin as a rake. (b)** (*Orn*) spoonbill.

especia *nf* spice.

especiado *adj* spiced, spicy.

especial *adj* special, especial; **en — especially, particularly.**

especialidad *nf* speciality, specialty; special branch, special field (of study *etc*), line; **no es de mi — it's not in my line.**

especialista *nmf* specialist.

especializado *adj* specialized; *worker* skilled, trained; **mano de obra especializada** skilled labour.

especializarse [1f] *vr* to specialize (**en** in).

especialmente *adv* (e)specially, particularly.

especiar [1b] *vt* to spice.

especie *nf* **(a)** (*Bio*) species.
(b) kind, sort; **de otra — of another kind.**
(c) matter; idea, notion; piece of news; remark; pretext; **con la — de que ...** on the pretext that ...; **corre la — de que ...** there is a rumour about that ...; **soltar la — to mention a matter, drop a remark.**
(d) en — in kind; pagar en — to pay in kind.

especificación *nf* specification.

específicamente *adv* specifically.

especificar [1g] *vt* to specify; to particularize; to list, itemize.

específico 1 *adj* specific. **2** *nm* (*Med*) specific; patent medicine.

espécimen *nm*, *pl* **especímenes** *or* **especimens** specimen.

especioso *adj* specious, plausible; deceitful.

espectacular *adj* spectacular.

espectacularidad *nf* spectacular nature; showiness.

espectáculo *nm* spectacle; sight; (*Theat etc*) show; function, performance; **— de variedades** variety show; **— de luz y sonido** son et lumière show; **dar un — to make a scene; to create a stir.**

espectador *nm*, **espectadora** *nf* spectator; onlooker, looker-on; **los —es** the spectators; (*Theat etc*) the audience.

espectral *adj* **(a)** (*Phys*) spectral. **(b)** (*fig*) ghostly; unearthly.

espectro *nm* **(a)** (*Phys*) spectrum. **(b)** spectre, ghost; (*fig*) spectre; **el — del hambre** the spectre of famine.

espectroscopio *nm* spectroscope.

especulación *nf* **(a)** speculation; contemplation, meditation. **(b)** (*Comm, Fin*) speculation; venture; **— bursátil** speculation on the stock exchange.

especulador *nm*, **especuladora** *nf* speculator.

especular[1] [1a] **1** *vt* to examine, inspect; to speculate about, reflect on, contemplate.
2 *vi* **(a)** to speculate, meditate.
(b) (*Comm, Fin*) to speculate (**en**, **sobre** in, on).

especular[2] [1a] *vt* (*SAm*) to ruffle the hair of.

especulativo *adj* speculative.

espéculo *nm* (*Med*) speculum.

espejado *adj* glossy, bright, shining, mirror-like.

espejeante *adj* shining.

espejear [1a] *vi* to shine (like a mirror), gleam, glimmer, glint.

espejeras *nfpl* (*Cu*) chafing, chafed patch.

espejismo *nm* **(a)** mirage. **(b)** (*fig*) mirage, illusion; (piece of) wishful thinking.

espejo *nm* **(a)** mirror, looking-glass; **— de cuerpo entero** full-length mirror, pier glass; **— retrovisor, — de retrovisión** driving mirror, rear-view mirror; **mirarse al — to look at oneself in the mirror.**
(b) (*Zool*) white patch.
(c) (*fig*) model; **un — de caballería** a model of chivalry.

espejuelo *nm* small looking-glass; **—s** lenses, spectacles.

espeleología *nf* spelaeology, potholing.

espeleólogo *nm* spelaeologist, potholer.

espelta *nf* (*Bot*) spelt.

espeluznante *adj* hair-raising, horrifying, blood-curdling; lurid.

espeluzno *nm* (*Mex*) = **escalofrío**.

espera *nf* **(a)** wait, period of waiting; waiting; delay; **en — de** waiting for; expecting; **la cosa no tiene — the matter brooks no delay, the affair is most urgent.**
(b) (*Law*) stay, respite.
(c) (*quality*) restraint.

esperable *adj* to be hoped for; to be expected; **unos adelantos que hace 10 años no eran —s** certain advances which were not to be hoped for 10 years ago.

esperanto *nm* Esperanto.

esperanza *nf* hope; expectation; prospect; **un jugador de —s** a promising player, a player of promise; **¡qué —!** (*SAm*) some hope!; not on your life!; **hay pocas —s de que venga** there is little prospect of his coming; **no daba —s de permitirlo** he held out no prospect of allowing it, he gave no hope of allowing it; **tener —s de** to have hopes of; **tener la — puesta en** to pin one's faith to; to set one's heart on.

esperanzador *adj* hopeful, encouraging.

esperanzar [1f] *vt* to give hope to, buoy up with hope.

esperar [1a] **1** *vt* **(a)** to hope for; to expect (**de** of); **no esperaba yo menos, no se podía — menos** it was the least that could be expected; **no esperaba menos de Vd** I expected nothing less of you, I hoped for nothing less from you; **— que + *subj*** to hope that ...; **espero que sea así** I hope it is so, I hope it will be so; **espero que te haya gustado** I hope you liked it; **espero que vengas** I hope you'll come.
(b) to wait for, await; *baby, visitors etc* to expect; **— el avión** to wait for the plane; **espero la llamada en cualquier momento** I expect his call at any moment; **ir a — a uno** to go and meet someone; **no me esperes después de las 7** don't wait for me after 7.
2 *vi* **(a)** to hope; to expect; **— + *infin*** to hope to + infin; **— a que + *subj*** to expect that ..., anticipate that ...; **— en uno** to put one's hopes (*or* trust) in someone; **— en Dios** to trust in God; **desesperando** to hope against hope.
(b) to wait; to stay; **esperaré aquí** I'll wait here; **¡espera un momento!** wait a moment!, just a minute!; **— que salga uno** to wait for someone to come out; **— a (*or* hasta) que uno haga algo** to wait for someone to do something, wait until someone does something; **hacer — a uno** to make someone wait, keep someone waiting; **espera y verás** wait and see.
3 esperarse *vr*: **como podía — as might have been expected, as was to be expected; no fue tan bueno como se esperaba** it was not so good as was hoped, it did not come up to expectations; **se espera que todo esté listo** it is hoped that all will be ready.

esperma *nf* **(a)** sperm; **— de ballena** spermaceti. **(b)** (*SAm*) candle.

espermaceti *nm* spermaceti.

espermatozoo *nm* spermatozoon.

espernancarse [1g] *vr* = **esparrancarse**.

esperón *nm* (*Cu*) long wait.

esperpento nm (a) fright, sight; scarecrow. (b) (fig) absurdity, (piece of) nonsense. (c) macabre story, grostesque tale.

espesamente adv thickly; densely.

espesar [1a] 1 vt (a) to thicken; to make dense(r). (b) fabric to weave tighter.
2 **espesarse** vr to thicken, get thicker, get denser; to coagulate, solidify.

espeso adj (a) thick; dense; paste etc stiff; liquid thick, heavy. (b) dirty, untidy.

espesor nm thickness; density; (of snow) depth; **tiene medio metro de** — it is half a metre thick.

espesura nf (a) thickness; density.
(b) (Bot) thicket, overgrown place; **se refugiaron en las —s serranas** they took refuge in the mountain fastnesses.
(c) dirtiness, untidiness.

espetar [1a] 1 vt (a) to transfix, pierce, run through; meat to skewer, spit; person to run through.
(b) (fig) order to rap out; lecture, sermon to read; question to pop; — **algo a uno** to broach a subject (unexpectedly) with someone, spring something on someone.
2 **espetarse** vr (a) to steady oneself, settle oneself.
(b) to get on one's high horse.

espetón nm (a) skewer, spit; large pin, iron pin; poker. (b) jab, poke.

espía nmf spy.

espiantar [1a] 1 vt (Arg, Urug) to pinch (fam). 2 vi and **espiantarse** vr (Arg, Chi) to scram (sl), beat it (fam).

espiar [1c] 1 vt (a) to spy on; to watch out for. (b) (Arg, CAm) to look at, see, watch. 2 vi to spy.

espichar[1] [1a] 1 vt (a) to prick.
(b) (Chi) to hand over reluctantly, relinquish.
(c) (Chi, Per) to put a tap on.
2 vi (sl) to peg out (sl).
3 **espicharse** vr (a) (Col: tyre) to go flat.
(b) (Cu, Mex) to get thin.
(c) (Mex) to feel ashamed.
(d) (Guat) to get scared.

espichar[2] [1a] vi (SAm) to make a speech; to speechify.

espiche[1] nm spike; peg.

espiche[2] nm (SAm: angl) speech.

espidómetro nm (SAm: angl) speedometer.

espiga nf (a) (Bot: of grain) ear; (of flowers) spike.
(b) (Tech) spigot; tenon, dowel, peg; (of bolt etc) shaft; (of knife) tang.
(c) (of bell) clapper.
(d) (Mil) fuse.
(e) (Naut) masthead.

espigadera nf gleaner.

espigado adj (a) (Bot) ripe; ready to seed. (b) tall, lanky; grown-up.

espigador nm, **espigadora** nf gleaner.

espigar [1h] 1 vt (a) (Agr) to glean (also fig).
(b) (Tech) to pin, peg, dowel.
2 vi (a) (of wheat) to form ears, come into ear; to run to seed.
(b) = 3 **espigarse** vr to get very tall, shoot up.

espigón nm (a) (Bot) ear; spike. (b) (Zool) sting. (c) (of tool) sharp point, spike. (d) (Naut) breakwater.

espigueo nm gleaning.

espiguero nm (Mex) granary.

espina nf (a) (Bot) thorn, prickle; splinter; **estar en —s** to be on tenterhooks, be all on edge; **me da mala — it worries me, it makes me suspicious; it gives me a bad impression; **sacarse la — (fig) to pay off an old score, get even.
(b) (fig) bone.
(c) (Anat: also — **dorsal**) spine.
(d) (fig) doubt, worry, suspicion.

espinaca nf, **espinacas** nfpl (as food) spinach.

espinal adj spinal.

espinar 1 [1a] vt (a) to prick. (b) (fig) to sting, hurt, nettle. 2 nm (a) thicket, thornbrake, thorny place. (b) (fig) difficulty.

espinazo nm spine, backbone.

espineta nf (Mus) spinet.

espinilla nf (a) (Anat) shin, shinbone. (b) (Med) blackhead.

espinillera nf shinpad, shin guard (US).

espino nm hawthorn (also — **albar**, — **blanco**); — **negro** blackthorn, sloe.

espinoso 1 adj (a) plant thorny, prickly; fish bony, spiny. (b) (fig) thorny, knotty, difficult. 2 nm stickleback.

espinudo adj (SAm) = **espinoso** 1.

espión nm spy.

espionaje nm spying, espionage; **novela de — spy story.

espira nf (Math etc) spiral; (Zool) whorl, ring; (Elec etc) turn.

espiráculo nm blow-hole; spiracle.

espiral 1 adj spiral; winding; (Tech) helical; corkscrew (attr), corkscrew-shaped.
2 nm (of watch) hairspring.
3 nf spiral; corkscrew (shape); (Tech) whorl; (of smoke etc) spiral, wreath; **la — inflacionista** the inflationary spiral; **dar vueltas en — to spiral (up etc); **el humo subía en —** the smoke went spiralling up.

espirar [1a] 1 vt to breathe out, exhale; to give off, give out. 2 vi to breathe; to breathe out, exhale.

espiritado adj (fig) like a wraith, ghost-like.

espiritifláutico adj (hum) thin, weedy.

espiritismo nm spiritualism.

espiritista 1 adj spiritualist(ic). 2 nmf spiritualist.

espiritoso adj (a) liquor spirituous. (b) person spirited, lively.

espíritu nm (a) spirit; — **de cuerpo** esprit de corps; — **de equipo** team spirit; — **guerrero, — de lucha** fighting spirit; **en la letra y en el — in the letter and in the spirit; **pobre de — poor in spirit; **levantar el — de uno** to raise someone's spirits.
(b) mind; intelligence; turn of mind; **con — amplio** with an open mind; in a generous spirit; **de — crítico** of a critical turn of mind; **edificar el — de uno** to improve someone's mind.
(c) (Rel) spirit, soul; **E— Santo** Holy Ghost; **dar el —, rendir el — to give up the ghost.
(d) spirit, ghost; "**Un — burlón**" "Blithe Spirit".
(e) spirits, liquor; — **de vino** spirits of wine.

espiritual adj (a) spiritual. (b) unworldly; ghostly. (c) (Col, Chi: gall) gay, witty.

espiritualidad nf spirituality.

espiritualizar [1f] vt to spiritualize.

espiritualmente adv spiritually.

espita nf (a) tap, faucet (US), cock, spigot; **abrir la — de las lágrimas** (hum) to weep buckets. (b) (fam) drunkard, soak (fam).

espitar [1a] vt to tap, broach.

espleen nm (angl) = **esplín**.

espléndidamente adv (a) splendidly, magnificently, grandly. (b) lavishly; generously; "**gratificaré —**" (advert) "there will be a generous reward".

esplendidez nf (a) splendour; magnificence, grandeur; pomp. (b) lavishness; generosity.

espléndido adj (a) splendid; magnificent, grand. (b) lavish; liberal, generous.

esplendor nm splendour; magnificence, grandeur; brilliance.

esplendoroso adj magnificent; brilliant, radiant.

esplénico adj splenetic.

espliego nm lavender.

esplín nm (angl) melancholy, depression, the blues.

espolada nf (a) prick with a spur. (b) — **de vino** swig of wine.

espolazo nm prick with a spur.

espolear [1a] vt (a) horse to spur (on). (b) (fig) to spur on, stimulate; to stir up, enliven, keep on one's toes.

espoleta nf (a) (Mil) fuse. (b) (Anat) wishbone.

espolín nm fixed spur, small spur.

espolón 1 nm (a) (Zool: of cock) spur; (of horse) fetlock.
(b) (Geog) spur (of a mountain range).
(c) (Naut: of bow) stem; (as weapon) ram.
(d) (Naut) sea wall, dike; jetty; (of bridge) cutwater; (Archit) buttress.
(e) promenade.
(f) (Med: fam) chilblain.
2 adj (Col) sharp, astute.

espolvorear [1a] vt to dust, sprinkle (de with): **espolvoree X sobre la superficie** dust X on the surface, dust the surface with X.

espondeo nm spondee.

esponja nf (a) sponge; — **de baño** bath sponge; **beber como una —** to drink like a fish; **pasar la — (fam)** to scrub round it (fam), forget about it.
(b) (fam) sponger (fam).
(c) (Arg, Mex, Par) old soak (fam), toper.

esponjado adj (a) spongy; fluffy. (b) (fig) puffed up, pompous.

esponjar [1a] 1 vt to make spongy; wool etc to fluff up, make fluffy.
2 **esponjarse** vr (a) to become spongy; to fluff up, become fluffy.
(b) (fig) to glow with health; to look prosperous.
(c) (fig) to be puffed up, swell with conceit.

esponjosidad nf sponginess; sogginess.

esponjoso adj spongy; porous; soggy, waterlogged.

esponsales nmpl betrothal.

espontáneamente adv spontaneously.

espontanearse [1a] *vr* to own up; to speak frankly; to unbosom oneself.

espontaneidad *nf* spontaneity.

espontáneo 1 *adj* spontaneous; impromptu, unprepared. **2** *nm* (*Taur*) intruder, spectator who rushes into the ring and attempts to take part.

espora *nf* spore.

esporádicamente *adv* sporadically.

esporádico *adj* sporadic.

esportillo *nm* basket, pannier.

esportivo *adj* (*SAm*: *angl*) sporty.

esportón *nm* large basket; **a —es** in vast quantities, by the ton.

esposa *nf* (**a**) wife. (**b**) **—s** handcuffs; manacles; **poner las —s a uno** to handcuff someone.

esposar [1a] *vt* to handcuff.

esposo *nm* husband; **los —s** husband and wife, the couple.

esprín *nm* (*CAm*: *angl*) spring; spring mattress.

esprint *nm*, *pl* **esprints** (*angl*) sprint; sudden dash, burst of speed.

esprintar [1a] *vi* (*angl*) to sprint.

esprínter *nm* (*angl*) sprinter.

espuela *nf* (**a**) spur (*also fig*); **— de caballero** larkspur.
   (**b**) (*Col*) feminine charm; coquettishness.
   (**c**) (*Col*) skill in business, acumen.
   (**d**) (*fam*) last drink, one for the road.

espueleado *adj* (*Col, PR*) tested, tried.

espuelear [1a] *vt* (**a**) (*SAm*) to spur, spur on. (**b**) (*Col, PR*) to test, try out.

espuelón *adj* (*Col*) sharp, astute.

espuerta *nf* basket, pannier; **a —s** in vast quantities, by the ton.

espulgar [1h] *vt* (**a**) to delouse, rid of fleas, get the lice (*or* fleas) out of. (**b**) (*fig*) to scrutinize.

espuma *nf* (*of water*) foam, spray; surf; (*on beer*) froth, head; (*of soap*) lather; floating waste, surface scum; **— de caucho**, **— de látex** foam rubber; **— de mar** (*fig*) meerschaum; **crecer como la —** to flourish like the green bay tree; **echar —** to foam, froth.

espumadera *nf*, **espumador** *nm* (*SAm*: *Cook etc*) skimmer, skimming ladle; (*of spray*) nozzle.

espumajear [1a] *vi* to foam at the mouth.

espumajo *nm* froth, foam (*at the mouth*).

espumajoso *adj* frothy, foamy.

espumar [1a] **1** *vt* to skim off. **2** *vi* to froth, foam; (*of wine*) to sparkle.

espumarajo *nm* froth, foam (*at the mouth*); **echar —s (de rabia)** to foam with rage, splutter with rage.

espumilla *nf* (*CAm, Ec*) meringue.

espumoso *adj* frothy, foamy; foaming; *wine* sparkling.

espurio *adj* spurious; adulterated; *child* bastard.

esputar [1a] *vti* to spit (out), hawk (up).

esputo *nm* spit, spittle, (*Med*) sputum.

esqueje *nm* (*Hort*) slip, cutting.

esquela *nf* (**a**) note; **— amorosa** love letter, billet doux. (**b**) notice, announcement; **— de defunción**, **— mortuoria** death notice, announcement of death.

esquelético *adj* skeletal.

esqueleto *nm* (**a**) (*Anat*) skeleton.
   (**b**) (*fig*) skeleton; bare bones (of a matter); framework; (*SAm*) rough draft, outline, preliminary plan; **en —** unfinished, incomplete.
   (**c**) (*CAm, Col, Mex*) blank, form.

esquema *nm* (**a**) diagram, plan; scheme; sketch, outline. (**b**) (*Eccl*) schema.

esquemático *adj* schematic; diagrammatic.

esquí *nm*, *pl* **esquís** (**a**) (*object*) ski. (**b**) (*sport*) skiing; **— acuático** water-skiing; surfriding; **hacer —** to go skiing.

esquiador *nm*, **esquiadora** *nf* skier.

esquiar [1c] *vi* to ski.

esquife *nm* skiff.

esquila[1] *nf* small bell, handbell; cowbell.

esquila[2] *nf* (*Agr*) shearing.

esquilador *nm* shearer.

esquilar [1a] *vt* to shear; to clip, crop.

esquileo *nm* shearing.

esquilimoso *adj* fastidious, finicky.

esquilmar [1a] *vt* (**a**) *crop* to harvest. (**b**) *soil* (*also fig*) to exhaust, impoverish. (**c**) (*fam*) *gambler* to skin (*fam*), fleece.

esquilmo *nm* harvest, crop; yield.

Esquilo m Aeschylus.

esquimal 1 *adj* Eskimo. **2** *nmf* Eskimo. **3** *nm* (*language*) Eskimo.

esquina *nf* (**a**) corner (*also Sport*); **doblar la —** to turn the corner; (*Chi*) to die. (**b**) (*SAm*) corner shop, village store.

esquinado *adj* (**a**) having corners; sharp-cornered.

(**b**) (*SAm*) furniture standing in a corner, corner (*attr*). (**c**) (*fig*) prickly; unsociable.

esquinar [1a] **1** *vt* (**a**) to form a corner with; to be on the corner of.
   (**b**) *timber etc* to square (off).
   (**c**) (*SAm*) to put in a corner.
   2 *vi*: **— con** to form a corner with; to be on the corner of.
   3 esquinarse *vr* (**a**) to quarrel (*con* with), fall out (*con* with).
   (**b**) to sulk.

esquinazo *nm* (**a**) (*fam*) corner. (**b**) (*Arg, Chi*) serenade. (**c**) **dar — a uno** to dodge someone, give someone the slip, shake someone off.

esquirla *nf* splinter.

esquirol *nm* blackleg, scab (*fam*), strikebreaker, fink (*US*).

esquisto *nm* schist.

esquite *nm* (*CAm, Mex*) popcorn.

esquivada *nf* (*SAm*) dodge, evasion.

esquivar [1a] **1** *vt* to avoid, shun; to elude, dodge, side-step; **— el contacto con uno** to avoid meeting someone; **— un golpe** to dodge a blow; **— + infin** to avoid + *ger*, be chary of + *ger*, be shy of + *ger*.
   2 esquivarse *vr* to withdraw, stand back, shy away; to dodge.

esquivez *nf* (**a**) shyness, reserve, aloofness; unsociability; evasiveness. (**b**) scorn, disdain.

esquivo *adj* (**a**) shy, reserved, aloof; unsociable; evasive. (**b**) scornful, disdainful.

esquizofrenia *nf* schizophrenia.

esquizofrénico 1 *adj* schizophrenic. **2** *nm*, **esquizofrénica** *nf* schizophrenic.

esquizoide 1 *adj* schizoid. **2** *nmf* schizoid.

esta, ésta *etc see* **este, éste**.

estabilidad *nf* stability.

estabilización *nf* stabilization.

estabilizador *nm* stabilizer.

estabilizar [1f] **1** *vt* to stabilize; to make stable, steady; *prices* to stabilize, peg. **2 estabilizarse** *vr* to become stable, become stabilized.

estable *adj* stable, steady; firm; regular.

establecer [2d] **1** *vt* to establish; set up, found, institute; *people* to settle; *allegation* to justify, substantiate; *record* to set (up); *residence* to take up, establish.
   2 establecerse *vr* to establish oneself, settle; (*Comm*) to set up in business, start a business; to open an office, open a branch.

establecimiento *nm* (**a**) (*act*) establishment, setting-up, founding; institution; settlement.
   (**b**) establishment; (*RPl*) plant, works; **— central** head office; **— comercial** commercial establishment, business house.
   (**c**) (*Law*) statute, ordinance.

establero *nm* stableboy, groom.

establo *nm* cowshed, stall; (*esp SAm*) barn; **—s de Augias** Augean stables.

estaca *nf* (**a**) stake, post, paling; (*for croquet, tent*) peg; cudgel, stick.
   (**b**) (*Agr*) cutting.
   (**c**) (*Chi, Ec, Per*) spur.
   (**d**) (*Arg, Col, Chi, Per*) mining claim, mining property.
   (**e**) (*Mex*) wish to obtain something.
   (**f**) (*Ven*) hint, taunt.

estacada *nf* (**a**) fence, fencing; (*Mil*) palisade, stockade; (*SAm*) dike; **dejar a uno en la —** (*fig*) to leave someone in the lurch; **estar** (*or* **quedar**) **en la —** to be in a jam, be left in the lurch; to fail disastrously.
   (**b**) (*SAm*) wound, prick.

estacar [1g] **1** *vt* (**a**) *land, claim etc* to stake (out, off), mark with stakes; to fence with stakes; (*SAm*) to stretch by fastening to stakes.
   (**b**) *animal* to tie to a post.
   (**c**) (*Ven*) to wound, prick.
   (**d**) (*Col, Ven*) to deceive.
   2 estacarse *vr* (**a**) to stand rooted to the spot, stand stiff as a pole.
   (**b**) (*CAm, Col, Cu. Ven*) **— un pie** to prick oneself in the foot, hurt one's foot.

estación *nf* (**a**) station; **— balnearia** spa; **— ballenera** whaling station; **— de bombeo** pumping station; **— cabecera** (*Arg*), **— de cabeza**, **— terminal** terminus; **— carbonera** coaling station; **— cósmica**, **— espacial** space station; **— depuradora**, **— purificadora de aguas residuales** sewage works, sewage farm; **— emisora** broadcasting station; **— de empalme**, **— de enlace** junction; **— de ferrocarril** railway station; **— de fuerza** power station; **— de gasolina** petrol station; **— de mercancías** goods station; **— meteorológica** weather station; **— de**

rastreo, — **de seguimiento** tracking station; — **de servicio** service station; — **transformadora** substation; — **transmisora** transmitter; — **veraniega** summer resort.

(**b**) (*Eccl*) **E**—**es del vía Crucis** Stations of the Cross; **correr las** —**es** (*fam*) to go on a pub crawl (*fam*).

(**c**) season; — **de las lluvias** rainy season; — **muerta** off season, dead season.

estacional *adj* seasonal.

estacionamiento *nm* stationing, placing; (*Aut*) parking.

estacionar [1a] **1** *vt* to station, place; (*Aut*) to park. **2 estacionarse** *vr* to station oneself; (*Aut*) to park; to remain stationary.

estacionario *adj* stationary; motionless; (*Comm, Fin*) slack.

estacionómetro *nm* (*Mex*) parking meter.

estacón *nm* (*Col, Cu, Guat, Mex*) prick, jab.

estadía *nf* (**a**) (*Comm*) demurrage. (**b**) (*Naut*) stay in port; (*SAm*) stay.

estadígrafo *nm* statistician.

estadio *nm* (**a**) stage, phase. (**b**) (*Math*) furlong. (**c**) (*Sport*) stadium.

estadista *nm* (**a**) (*Pol*) statesman. (**b**) (*Math*) statistician.

estadística *nf* (**a**) statistics; official return(s). (**b**) (*una* —) figure, statistic.

estadístico 1 *adj* statistical. **2** *nm* statistician.

estado *nm* (**a**) (*in general*) state, condition; — **de ánimo** state of mind; — **de emergencia** state of emergency; — **de guerra** state of war; — **de sitio** state of siege; **estar en** — **(interesante)**, **estar en** — **de buena esperanza** to be pregnant, be expecting, be in the family way; **estar en buen** — to be in good condition; to be in good order, be in working order; **estar en malísimo** — to be in a terrible condition.

(**b**) status, rank, class; — **civil** marital status.

(**c**) (*Pol: Hist*) estate; **el cuarto** — the fourth estate; — **llano** third estate, commoners.

(**d**) — **mayor** (*Mil*) staff; — **mayor general** general staff.

(**e**) (*Pol*) state; **las fuerzas del E**— the forces of the state; — **benefactor**, — **de bienestar**, — **de previsión** welfare state; — **policía** police state; — **tapón** buffer state; **hombre de** — statesman.

(**f**) list (*of employees*).

(**g**) summary; report, statement; — **de contabilidad** (*Mex*) balance sheet; — **de cuenta(s)** statement of account.

Estados *mpl* **Unidos** United States.

estadounidense 1 *adj* United States (*attr*), American. **2** *nmf* United States citizen (*etc*), American.

estafa *nf* swindle, trick; (*Comm, Fin*) racket, ramp (*fam*), fraud.

estafador *nm* swindler, trickster; (*Comm, Fin*) swindler; racketeer.

estafar [1a] *vt* to swindle, defraud, twist (*fam*); — **algo a uno** to swindle something out of someone, defraud someone of something.

estafeta *nf* (**a**) post; — **diplomática** diplomatic bag. (**b**) (sub) post office. (**c**) (*person*) courier (*also nm*).

estafetero *nm* postmaster, post-office clerk.

estafilococo *nm* staphylococcus.

estagnación *nf* (*CAm, PR: angl*) = **estancamiento**.

estaje *nm* (*CAm*) piecework.

estajear [1a] *vt* (*CAm*) to do as piecework; to discuss rates and conditions for.

estajero *nm* (*CAm*) pieceworker.

estalactita *nf* stalactite.

estalagmita *nf* stalagmite.

estalladura *nf* bursting, explosion; eruption; shattering; crack; breaking-out, outbreak; (*Aut*) burst, blow-out.

estallar [1a] *vi* (*of shell etc*) to burst, explode, go off; (*like volcano*) to erupt; (*of tyre*) to burst; (*of glass etc*) to shatter; (*of whip*) to crack; (*of epidemic*) to break out; (*of revolt*) to break out, flare up; — **en llanto** to burst into tears; **el parabrisas estalló en pedazos** the windscreen shattered; **cuando estalló la guerra** when the war broke out; **hacer** — to set off; (*fig*) to spark off, start.

estallido *nm* explosion, report; crash, crack; (*fig*) outbreak.

estambre *nm* (**a**) worsted, woollen yarn. (**b**) (*Bot*) stamen.

Estambul Istanbul.

estamento *nm* (*Pol*) state.

estameña *nf* serge.

estampa *nf* (**a**) imprint; footprint, track; (*Typ*) print, engraving; (*fig*) stamp; appearance, aspect; **de** — **poco agradable** of disagreeable appearance, un-

pleasant-looking; **ser la propia** — **de uno** to be the very image of someone; **romper la** — **a uno** (*fam*) to do someone in (*sl*).

(**b**) printing; printing press; **dar un libro a la** — to publish a book.

estampación *nf* printing; engraving; (*Typ*) tooling.

estampado 1 *adj fabric* printed; *dress* print. **2** *nm* (**a**) printing; stamping. (**b**) print (dress), cotton print.

estampar [1a] *vt* to print, stamp; to engrave; (*Typ*) *cover* to tool; *kiss* to plant, place (*en on*); (*fig*) to stamp, imprint (*en on*); **quedaba estampado en la memoria** it was stamped on one's memory.

estampía: de — *adv* suddenly, without warning, unexpectedly.

estampida *nf* (**a**) (*Agr, Zool: esp SAm*) stampede. (**b**) **de** — *see* **estampía**. (**c**) = **estampido**.

estampido *nm* report; detonation; bang, boom, crash; — **sónico** sonic boom.

estampilla *nf* (**a**) stamp, seal; rubber stamp. (**b**) (*SAm: Post*) stamp.

estampillado *nm* (*SAm*) stamp duty.

estampillar [1a] *vt* to stamp, put a stamp on; to rubber-stamp.

estancado *adj* (**a**) *water* stagnant. (**b**) (*fig*) static; **estar** — to be held up, be blocked, be at a standstill; to be deadlocked.

estancamiento *nm* (**a**) stagnancy, stagnation. (**b**) (*fig*) stagnation; blockage, stoppage, suspension; deadlock.

estancar [1g] **1** *vt* (**a**) *water* to hold up, hold back, stem.

(**b**) (*fig*) *progress* to stem, block, check, hold up; *business* to stop, suspend; *negotiation* to bring to a standstill; to deadlock; (*Comm: officially*) to monopolize, establish a monopoly in; (*pej*) to corner.

2 estancarse *vr* (**a**) (*of water*) to stagnate, become stagnant; to be held back.

(**b**) (*fig*) to stagnate.

estancia *nf* (**a**) stay. (**b**) dwelling, abode; living room. (**c**) (*SAm*) farm, cattle ranch; (*Cu, PR*) small farm, smallholding. (**d**) (*Poet*) stanza.

estanciero *nm* (*SAm*) farmer, rancher.

estanco 1 *adj* watertight.

2 *nm* state monopoly; government store where monopoly goods are sold, (*esp*) tobacconist's (shop), cigar store (*US*); (*Ec*) liquor store.

estándar (*angl*) **1** *adj* standard. **2** *nm* standard.

estandar(d)ización *nf* standardization.

estandar(d)izado *adj* standardized.

estandar(d)izar [1f] *vt* to standardize.

estandarte *nm* banner, standard; — **real** royal standard.

estánnico *adj* stannic.

estanque *nm* pool, pond, small lake; (*Agr etc*) tank, reservoir; — **de juegos**, — **para chapotear** paddling pool.

estanquero *nm* tobacconist.

estanquillo *nm* (*Mex*) booth, kiosk, stall; = **estanco**.

estante *nm* (**a**) shelf. (**b**) rack, stand; — **(para libros)** bookcase. (**c**) (*SAm*) prop.

estantería *nf* shelving, shelves.

estantigua *nf* apparition; (*fam*) fright, sight, scarecrow.

estantillo *nm* (*Col, Ven*) prop, support.

estañar [1a] *vt* (**a**) (*Tech*) to tin; to solder. (**b**) (*Ven*) to wound. (**c**) (*Ven*) *employee* to fire (*fam*).

estaño *nm* tin.

estaquear [1a] *vt* (*SAm*) *hides* to spread, stretch (with stakes).

estaquilla *nf* peg; pin; spike, long nail; tent peg.

estaquillar [1a] *vt* to pin, peg (down, out), fasten with pegs.

estar [1p] **1** *vi* (**a**) to be; to stand, be found; to be in, be at home; to stay, remain, keep; to be present (*en* at); **el monumento está en el mercado** the monument is (or stands) in the market; **¿está?** is he in?; **la señora no está** the lady is not in, the lady is not at home; **está fuera** she's away; she's out of town, she's on a trip; **¿cómo está?** how is he?; **está mucho mejor** he's much better; **"nunca habéis estado mejor"** (*slogan*) "you never had it so good"; **¿cómo estamos?** how do we stand?; (*Sport*) what's the score?; **el día que estuve a verlo** the day I went to see it.

(**b**) (+ *adj*) to be; **está enfermo** he is ill; **ahora está vacío** now it's empty; **¡qué elegante estás!** how smart you're looking!; **está más viejo** he looks older, he seems older.

(**c**) (*idiom*) **¿está Vd?** do you get it?, understand?; **¿estamos?** are we agreed?

(**d**) (*idiom*) to be ready; **en seguida está** it'll be ready in a moment; **dos vueltas más y ya está** two more turns and that's it, two more turns and it's done; **¡ya estamos!** that's it!; _(angrily)_ that's enough!, I'll not listen to any more!

(e) _(+ ger)_ to be; **estaba corriendo** he was running; **me está molestando** he's annoying me; **está siendo preparado** it is being prepared; **nos estamos engañando** we are deceiving ourselves.

(f) _(+ ptp)_ to be; **está envasado en papel** it is wrapped in paper; **para las 5 estará terminado** it will be finished for 5 o'clock.

(g) _(date)_ **estamos a 5 de mayo** it is the 5th of May, today is the 5th of May; **¿a cuántos estamos?** what's the date?

(h) _(price)_ — **a** to be, sell at, stand at; _(record)_ to stand at; **las uvas están a 5 pesetas** grapes are at 5 pesetas; **el récord anterior estaba a** (or **en**) **33 minutos** the previous record stood at 33 minutes.

(i) — **a lo que resulte** to stand by the result.

(j) — **con la gripe** to have flu, be down with flu; **estuvo con la enfermedad durante 2 años** she suffered from the disease for 2 years.

(k) — **de vacaciones** to be (away) on holiday; — **de paseo** to be out for a walk; — **de viaje** to be travelling, be on a trip.

(l) — **de embajador** to be acting as ambassador, be acting ambassador.

(m) **estoy así de nervioso** I'm so nervous, I'm that nervous.

(n) — **en** to be the cause of; **en eso está** that's the reason, that must be the motive.

(o) — **en algo** to be involved in something, be mixed up in something.

(p) **no está en él hacerlo** it is not in his power to do it.

(q) — **en que...** to believe that..., understand that...; to be sure that...

(r) — **para** + _infin_ to be about to + _infin_, be on the point of + _ger_.

(s) — **para** + _n_ to be in the mood for + _n_.

(t) — **por** _policy_ to be in favour of; _person to_ back, support, side with.

(u) — **por** + _infin_ to be half inclined to + _infin_, have half a mind to + _infin_.

(v) **está todavía por hacer** it remains to be done, it is still to be done; **la historia de aquello está por escribir** the history of that is still to be written.

(w) **está que rabia** he's hopping mad, he's furious.

(x) — **sobre sí** to be on one's guard; to be puffed up with conceit; _see_ **bien, mal, más,** _and many noun entries._

2 estarse _vr_ (a) _reinforces sense of vi:_ **se estaba muriendo** he was (gradually, at that moment) dying.

(b) to stay, remain; — **tranquilamente en casa** to stay quietly at home.

(c) **¡estáte quieto!** keep still!, stop fidgeting!; behave yourself!

estarcido _nm_ stencil.
estarcir [3b] _vt_ to stencil.
estatal _adj_ state _(attr)._
estática _nf_ statics.
estático _adj_ static.
estatificación _nf_ nationalization.
estatificado _adj_ nationalized.
estatificar [1g] _vt_ to nationalize.
estatización _nf (CAm, Chi)_ nationalization.
estatizar [1f] _vt (CAm, Chi)_ to nationalize.
estator _nm (Elec, Math)_ stator.
estatua _nf_ statue.
estatuaria _nf_ statuary _(art)._
estatuario _adj_ statuesque.
estatuilla _nf_ statuette, figure.
estatuir [3g] _vt_ (a) to establish, enact, ordain. (b) to prove. (c) to arrange.
estatura _nf_ stature, height; **de regular** — of average height; **un hombre de 1,80m de** — a man 1.80m in height.
estatutario _adj_ statutory.
estatuto _nm (Law)_ statute; _(of city etc)_ by-law; _(of committee)_ rule, standing rule.
estay _nm (Naut)_ stay.
este[1] _(Geog)_ **1** _adj part_ east, eastern; _direction_ easterly; _wind_ east, easterly.
2 _nm_ (a) east; **en la parte del** — in the eastern part; **al** — **de Toledo** to the east of Toledo, on the east side of Toledo; **eso cae más hacia el** — that lies further (to the) east.
(b) east wind.
este[2] _dem adj m,_ **esta** _f_ this; **estos** _dem adj mpl,_ **estas** _fpl_ these.
éste _dem pron m,_ **ésta** _f_ this; this one; the latter; **éstos** _dem pron mpl,_ **éstas** _fpl_ these; the latter; en

ésta in this town (from where I am writing); **jurar por éstas** to swear by all that is holy.
estearina _nf (Chem)_ stearin; _(SAm)_ candle.
esteatita _nf_ soapstone.
Esteban _m_ Stephen.
estela _nf_ (a) _(Naut)_ wake, wash; _(Aer)_ trail; — **de condensación** vapour trail.
(b) _(fig)_ trail; **el discurso dejó larga** — **de comentarios** the speech left a long trail of criticism.
(c) _(Archit)_ stele, stela.
estelar _adj_ (a) _(Astron)_ stellar, sidereal. (b) _(Theat etc)_ star _(attr);_ **cargo** — star role; **combate** — _(Boxing)_ star bout, star contest.
estemple _nm_ pit prop.
esténcil _nm (SAm: angl)_ stencil.
estenografía _nf_ shorthand, stenography.
estenografiar [1c] _vt_ to take down in shorthand.
estenográfico _adj_ shorthand _(attr)._
estenógrafo _nm,_ **estenógrafa** _nf_ shorthand writer, stenographer.
estentóreo _adj_ stentorian.
estepa _nf_ (a) _(Geog)_ steppe. (b) _(Bot)_ rockrose.
estera _nf_ mat, matting; — **de baño** bathmat.
esteral _nm (Arg, Urug)_ swamp, marsh.
esterar [1a] **1** _vt_ to cover with a mat, put a mat on (or over). **2** _vi (fam)_ to put on one's winter clothes (ahead of time).
estercoladura _nf,_ **estercolamiento** _nm_ manuring; muck spreading.
estercolar [1a] _vt_ to manure.
estercolero _nm_ manure heap, dunghill.
estereo... stereo...
estereofonía _nf_ stereophony.
estereofónico _adj_ stereophonic.
estereoscópico _adj_ stereoscopic.
estereoscopio _nm_ stereoscope.
estereotipado _adj_ stereotyped.
estereotipar [1a] _vt_ to stereotype.
estereotipo _nm_ stereotype.
estéril _adj_ (a) sterile, barren. (b) _(fig)_ _effort etc_ vain, futile, unproductive.
esterilidad _nf_ (a) sterility, barrenness. (b) _(fig)_ futility, uselessness.
esterilización _nf_ sterilization.
esterilizar [1f] _vt_ to sterilize.
estérilmente _adv (fig)_ vainly, uselessly, fruitlessly.
esterilla _nf_ (a) small mat; straw mat.
(b) matting; _(SAm)_ wickerwork, rush matting; **silla de** — rush chair, wicker chair; — **de alambre** wire mesh.
(c) _(Sew)_ gold (or silver) braid.
esterlina _adj:_ **libra** — pound sterling.
esternón _nm_ breastbone, sternum.
estero[1] _nm_ matting.
estero[2] _nm_ estuary; tideland; inlet; _(RPl)_ swamp, marsh; _(Chi, Ec)_ brook; _(Ven)_ puddle, pool; **estar en el** — _(Ven)_ to be in a fix.
estertor _nm_ death rattle.
estertoroso _adj_ stertorous.
esteta **1** _nmf_ aesthete. **2** _nm (fam)_ pansy _(fam),_ queer _(fam)._
estética _nf_ aesthetics; aesthetic doctrine, aesthetic outlook.
esteticismo _nm_ aestheticism.
estético _adj_ aesthetic.
estetoscopio _nm_ stethoscope.
esteva _nf_ plough handle.
estevado _adj_ bow-legged, bandy-legged.
estiaje _nm_ low water.
estiba _nf_ (a) _(Mil: Hist)_ rammer. (b) _(Naut)_ stowage; **mudar la** — to shift the cargo about.
estibador _nm_ stevedore.
estibar [1a] _vt_ (a) _(Naut)_ to stow, put; to house, store. (b) _wool etc_ to pack tight, compress.
estiércol _nm_ dung, manure; — **de caballo** horse manure.
Estigio _m_ Styx.
estigio _adj_ Stygian.
estigma _m_ (a) stigma; mark, brand; birthmark; **—s** _(Eccl)_ stigmata. (b) _(Bot)_ stigma.
estigmatizar [1f] _vt_ to stigmatize.
estilar [1a] **1** _vt_ (a) _document_ to draw up (in due form).
(b) to use, be in the habit of using; to wear, adopt.
2 _vi and_ **estilarse** _vr_ to be in fashion, be used, be worn; **ya no se estila la chistera** top hats aren't in fashion anymore; — + _infin_ to be customary to + _infin._
estilete _nm_ stiletto; _(of gramophone etc)_ stylus.
estilista _nmf (Lit etc)_ stylist; _(Tech)_ designer.
estilística _nf_ stylistics.

estilístico adj stylistic.
estilización nf (Tech) styling.
estilizado adj stylized.
estilizar [1f] vt to stylize; (Tech) to design, style.
estilo nm (a) (in general) style; manner; fashion; **el —
oscuro del escritor** the writer's obscure style; **—
directo** (Gram) direct speech; **el — de vida británico**
the British way of life; **un comedor — Luis XV** a
dining-room suite in Louis XV style; **al — de** in the
style of; after the manner of; **al — antiguo** in the old
style; **algo por el —** something of the sort, that sort
of thing; something along these lines; **los dictadores
y otros por el —** dictators and others of that sort,
dictators and suchlike; **no tenemos nada por ese —**
we have nothing in that line.
   (b) (Swimming) stroke; **— libre** freestyle; **— (de)
pecho** breast-stroke.
   (c) (pen: Tech) stylus.
   (d) (Bot) style.
estilográfica nf fountain pen.
estima nf (a) esteem, respect; **tener a uno en gran —**
to hold someone in high esteem. (b) (Naut) dead
reckoning.
estimable adj (a) estimable, esteemed; reputable; **su
— carta** (Comm) your esteemed letter. (b) quantity
etc considerable.
estimación nf (a) (act) estimation; valuation. (b)
estimate, estimation; valuation. (c) esteem, regard;
— propia self-esteem.
estimar [1a] **1** vt (a) to estimate; to appraise; to gauge,
reckon, compute; **algo en mil pesetas** to value
something at a thousand pesetas.
   (b) **— que ...** to think that ..., reckon that ...
   (c) (morally) to esteem, respect; **— a uno en
mucho** to have a high regard for someone; **— a uno
en poco** to have a low opinion of someone; **se lo
estimo mucho** I am much indebted to you for it.
   2 estimarse vr (a) to be estimated (en at), be
valued (en at).
   (b) **¡se estima!** thanks very much!, I appreciate it!
   (c) to have a good opinion of oneself.
estimulante **1** adj stimulating. **2** nm stimulant.
estimular [1a] vt to stimulate; to encourage, excite,
incite, prompt; appetite to stimulate; discussion etc
to promote; effort, industry to encourage, boost.
estímulo nm stimulus, stimulation; encouragement;
inducement, incentive.
estío nm summer.
estipendiar [1b] vt to pay a stipend to.
estipendiario **1** adj stipendiary. **2** nm stipendiary.
estipendio nm stipend; salary; fee.
estíptico **1** adj (a) styptic. (b) constipated. (c) (fig)
mean, miserly. **2** nm styptic.
estipulación nf stipulation, condition, proviso.
estipular [1a] vt to stipulate.
estirado adj (a) stretched, extended; stretched tight;
(Tech) drawn. (b) (fig) stiff, starchy; pompous;
(RPl) vain, stuck-up (fam). (c) (fig) tight-fisted.
estirador nm (Tech) stretcher.
estiraje nm stretching.
estirajar [1a] (fam) = **estirar.**
estirar [1a] **1** vt (a) to stretch, pull out, draw out; to
extend; (Tech) wire etc to draw; ears to prick up;
neck to stretch, crane; clothes to iron lightly, run the
iron over.
   (b) to overstretch, strain.
   (c) (fig) money, speech etc to spin out, stretch out.
   (d) (Arg, Bol, Chi, Per) to kill, shoot.
   (e) (Per) to flog.
   (f) (Mex, Par) to pull, tug at.
   2 estirarse vr to stretch.
estirón nm (a) pull, tug, jerk. (b) spurt, sudden
growth; **dar un —** (child) to shoot up.
estironear [1a] vt (Chi, RPl) to pull hard at, tug
sharply at.
estirpe nf stock, lineage; race; **de la — regia** of royal
stock, of the blood royal.
estítico = **estíptico.**
estitiquez nf (SAm) constipation.
estival adj summer (attr); summery.
esto dem pron "neuter" this; this thing, this affair, this
matter; **— es difícil** this is difficult; **todo — es
inútil** all this is useless; **— es, ...** that is (to say),
...; **— de la boda** this business about the wedding;
antes de — before this; **con —** herewith; hereupon;
durante — in the meantime, while this was going
on; **en —** at this point; **por —** for this reason;
¿qué es —? what's all this?; **y esto ¿qué es?** whatever
is this?
estocada nf (a) stab, thrust; lunge; stab wound;
(Taur etc) death blow, (final) thrust. (b) (fig) sharp
retort.

Estocolmo Stockholm.
estofa nf (a) quilting, quilted material. (b) (fig)
quality, class; **de baja —** poor-quality, person
low-class.
estofado **1** adj (a) (Cook) stewed. (b) (Sew) quilted.
2 nm stew, hotpot.
estofar [1a] vt (a) (Cook) to stew. (b) (Sew) to quilt.
estoicismo nm stoicism.
estoico **1** adj stoic(al). **2** nm stoic.
estola nf stole.
estolidez nf stupidity.
estólido adj stupid.
estomacal **1** adj stomachic; stomach (attr); **trastorno
—** stomach upset. **2** nm stomachic.
estomagante adj (fam) upsetting, annoying.
estomagar [1h] vt (a) to give indigestion to, upset.
(b) (fig) to upset, annoy.
estómago nm stomach; **dolor de —** stomach ache;
revolver el — a uno to revolt someone, make someone's stomach turn over; to upset someone, annoy
someone; **tener buen —** (fig) to be thick-skinned;
to have an elastic conscience, be none too scrupulous.
Estonia f Esthonia.
estonio **1** adj Esthonian. **2** nm, **estonia** nf Esthonian.
3 nm (language) Esthonian.
estopa nf tow; burlap; (Naut) oakum; (Cu) cotton
waste; **— de acero** steel wool.
estoperol nm (a) tow wick. (b) (Col, Chi) brass tack.
(c) (Col) frying pan.
estopilla nf cheesecloth.
estoque nm (a) rapier, sword; **estar hecho un —** to be
as thin as a rake. (b) (Bot) gladiolus.
estoquear [1a] vt to stab, run through.
estorbar [1a] **1** vt to hinder, obstruct, impede, be (or
get) in the way of; to interfere with; to bother,
disturb, upset. **2** vi to be in the way.
estorbo nm hindrance, obstruction, impediment,
obstacle; drag; nuisance; **no hay — para que se haga**
there is no obstacle (or bar, impediment) to its
being done; **el mayor — es el director** the biggest
obstacle is the headmaster.
estornino nm starling.
estornudar [1a] vi to sneeze.
estornudo nm sneeze.
estoy etc see **estar.**
estrabismo nm squint, strabismus.
estrada nf (a) road, highway; **batir la —** (Mil) to
reconnoitre. (b) (Bol, Per) section of a rubber plantation (150 trees).
estrado nm stage, platform; dais; (Mus) bandstand;
(Hist) drawing room; **—s** law courts; **— del testigo**
witness stand; **citar a uno para —s** to subpoena
someone.
estrafalario adj (a) odd, outlandish, eccentric. (b)
dress slovenly, sloppy.
estragado adj ruined; corrupted, spoiled, perverted;
depraved; slovenly, careless, disorderly.
estragar [1h] vt to ruin; taste etc to corrupt, spoil,
pervert; to deprave.
estrago nm ruin, destruction; corruption, perversion;
—s havoc, destruction, ravages; **los —s del tiempo**
the ravages of time; **hacer —s en** (or **entre**) to play
havoc with, wreak havoc among.
estragón nm (Bot, Cook) tarragon.
estramador nm (Mex) comb.
estrambólico adj (SAm), **estrambótico** adj odd,
outlandish, eccentric.
estrangul nm (Mus) mouthpiece.
estrangulación nf strangulation.
estrangulador nm (a) (person) strangler. (b) (Mech)
throttle; (Aut etc) choke.
estrangulamiento nm (Aut) narrow stretch of road,
bottleneck.
estrangular [1a] vt (a) person to strangle. (b) (Med)
to strangulate. (c) (Mech) to throttle; to choke.
estraperlista **1** adj black-market (attr). **2** nm
blackmarketeer.
estraperlo nm black market; **comprar algo en el —,
comprar algo de —** to buy something on the black
market.
estrapontín nm back seat; side seat, extra seat.
Estrasburgo Strasbourg.
estratagema nf stratagem.
estratega nm strategist.
estrategia nf strategy; generalship.
estratégico adj strategic(al).
estratificación nf stratification.
estratificado adj stratified.
estratificar [1g] **1** vt to stratify. **2 estratificarse** vr
to stratify, be stratified.

estrato nm stratum, layer; **los —s sociales** the social strata, the social levels.

estratosfera nf stratosphere.

estratosférico adj stratospheric; **avión —** strato-cruiser.

estraza nf rag; **papel de —** brown paper, wrapping paper.

estrechamente adv (a) narrowly; tightly. (b) austerely. (c) closely, intimately. (d) strictly, rigidly; meanly; narrow-mindedly.

estrechar [1a] **1** vt (a) to narrow; *dress* to make smaller, reduce, take in; *link etc* to tighten (up), draw tighter.
   (b) to squeeze; *person* to hug, embrace, enfold in one's arms; *hand* to grasp, clasp; to shake.
   (c) (*fig*) *enemy* to press hard.
   (d) (*fig*) to compel, constrain, bring pressure to bear on.
   2 estrecharse vr (a) to narrow, get narrow; to tighten, get tighter; **— en** to squeeze into.
   (b) (*of two persons*) to embrace (one another), hug.
   (c) **se estrecharon la mano** they shook hands.
   (d) (*of link etc*) to become closer, become more intimate; **— con uno** to get very friendly with someone.
   (e) **— (en los gastos)** to stint oneself, economize, cut down on expenditure.

estrechez nf (a) narrowness, tightness; cramped nature, smallness, lack of room.
   (b) (*Fin*) want; financial stringency; **— del dinero** tightness of money, shortage of money; **estrecheces** financial difficulties, financial straits; **vivir con —** to live in straitened circumstances.
   (c) closeness, intimacy.
   (d) strictness, rigidity; austerity; **— de conciencia** small-mindedness; **— de miras** narrow-mindedness.

estrecho 1 adj (a) narrow; tight; *room* cramped, small; *skirt etc* tight; *trousers* tight, narrow, close-fitting; **estos zapatos me están muy —s** these shoes are too small for me, these shoes pinch my feet.
   (b) *money etc* tight; short; *living* austere.
   (c) *relationship etc* close, intimate; *link* close.
   (d) *attitude, prohibition* strict, rigid; *character* austere; (*pej*) mean, mean-spirited; (*also* **— de conciencia**) small-minded; (*also* **— de miras**) narrow-minded; insular, parochial.
   2 nm (a) (*Geog*) strait(s); narrows, channel; **E— de Gibraltar** Straits of Gibraltar.
   (b) fix (*fam*), jam, predicament; **al —** by force, under compulsion; **poner a uno en el — de + infin** to force someone into a position of having to + *infin*.

estrechura nf (a) =**estrechez**. (b) =**estrecho 2**.

estregadera nf (a) scrubbing brush; floor mop. (b) door scraper, boot scraper.

estregar [1h *and* 1k] vt to rub; to scrape; to scrub, scour.

estrella nf (a) (*Astron and fig*) star; **— de Belén** star of Bethlehem; **— fija** fixed star; **— fugaz** shooting star; **— de guía** guiding star; **— de mar** starfish; **del norte** north star; **— polar** polar star; **— de rabo** comet; **— vespertina** evening star; **(la bandera de las) —s y bandas, —s y listas** the Stars and Stripes; **creer en su buena —** to believe in one's lucky star; **nacer con —** to be born under a lucky star, be born lucky; **poner a uno sobre las —s** to praise someone to the skies; **tener (buena) —** to be lucky; **tener mala —** to be unlucky; **ver las —s** (*fig*) to see stars.
   (b) (*Typ*) asterisk, star.
   (c) (*Zool*) blaze, white patch.
   (d) (*Mil*) star, pip.
   (e) (*Cine, Theat etc*) star; **— del cine** movie star, film star; **ser la —** to star, be the star.

estrelladera nf (*Cook etc*) slice.

estrelladero nm egg pan.

estrellado adj (a) starred; star-shaped; *sky* starry, full of stars; *dress* spangled. (b) smashed, shattered. (c) (*Cook*) egg fried.

estrellamar nf starfish.

estrellar [1a] **1** vt (a) to star, spangle, cover with stars.
   (b) to smash, shatter; to dash to pieces, smash to pieces; **lo estrelló contra la pared** he smashed it against the wall; **estrelló el balón en el poste** he crashed the ball into the goal-post; **la corriente amenazaba con — el barco contra las rocas** the current threatened to dash the boat on to the rocks.
   (c) egg to fry.
   2 estrellarse vr to smash, shatter, crash (*contra* against); to be dashed to pieces; **— contra** (*Aer, Aut etc*) to crash into; **— con una dificultad** to come right up against a difficulty.

estrellato nm stardom.

estrellón nm (a) (*fig*) star, large star; star firework. (b) (*fam*) stroke of luck. (c) (*esp SAm: Aer*) crash; (*Aut*) crash, smash, collision.

estremecer [2d] **1** vt to shake (*also fig*).
   2 estremecerse vr (*building etc*) to shake, vibrate, tremble; (*person: with fear*) to tremble (*ante* at, *de* with); (*with horror*) to shiver, shudder (*de* with); (*with excitement*) to tingle, tremble, thrill (*de* with); (*with cold*) to shiver (*de* with).

estremecido adj shaking, trembling (*de* with).

estremecimiento nm, **estremezón** nm (*Col, Ven*) tremor, vibration; shiver, shudder; shaking, trembling; tingling.

estrena nf (a) good-luck gift, token. (b) =**estreno**.

estrenar [1a] **1** vt (a) (*fig*) to use for the first time; to wear (*or* put on *etc*) for the first time, show off for the first time.
   (b) (*Cine*) film to give its première, show for the first time; to release, put on release; (*Theat*) play to perform for the first time, give a first performance to.
   2 vi (a) (*Theat*) **aquí estrenan mucho** they stage a lot of premières here, they put on a lot of new plays here.
   (b) (*Cu*) to make a down payment.
   3 estrenarse vr (a) (*person*) to make one's début, appear for the first time.
   (b) (*film*) to have its première, be shown for the first time; (*play*) to open, have its first night; to be performed for the first time.
   (c) (*Comm*) to make the first sale of the day.

estrenista nmf (*Theat*) first-nighter.

estreno nm (a) first use; first appearance; **fue cuando el — del coche nuevo** it was when we went out in the new car for the first time.
   (b) (*of person*) début, first appearance; **¡mal —!** what a wretched start!
   (c) (*Cine*) première; release; (*Theat*) first night, first performance; **general** general release; **riguroso —** world première.
   (d) (*Cu*) down payment, deposit.

estrenque nm stout esparto rope.

estrenuo adj vigorous, energetic; enterprising.

estreñido adj constipated, costive.

estreñimiento nm constipation.

estreñir [3h *and* 3l] **1** vt to constipate, bind. **2 estreñirse** vr to get constipated.

estrepitarse [1a] vr (*Cu*) to kick up a fuss, make a scene.

estrépito nm noise, racket, row; tremendous din; fuss; **reírse con —** to laugh uproariously.

estrepitosamente adv noisily; loudly, deafeningly; rowdily, boisterously.

estrepitoso adj noisy; loud, deafening; *person, party etc* rowdy, boisterous; **con aplausos —s** with loud applause.

estreptococo nm streptococcus.

estreptomicina nf streptomycin.

estría nf groove; (*Archit*) flute, fluting; (*Bio etc*) striation.

estriado adj grooved; (*Archit*) fluted; (*Bio etc*) striate, striated.

estriar [1c] vt to groove, make a groove in; to flute; to striate.

estribación nf (*Geog etc*) spur; **—es** spurs, foothills.

estribar [1a] vi: **— en** to rest on, be supported by; (*fig*) to rest on, be based on; **la dificultad estriba en el texto** the difficulty lies in the text, the difficulty stems from the text; **su prosperidad estriba en esta industria** their prosperity is based on (*or* derives from) this industry.

estribera nf (a) stirrup. (b) (*SAm*) girth, saddle strap.

estribillo nm (*Lit*) refrain; (*Mus*) chorus; (*fig*) pet word, pet phrase; **¡siempre (con) el mismo —!** same old story!

estribo nm (a) (*rider's*) stirrup; (*Aut etc*) running board, step, footboard; footrest; **perder los —s** (*fig*) to fly off the handle, lose one's temper; to get hot under the collar; to lose one's head.
   (b) (*Tech*) brace, bracket, stay.
   (c) (*Archit*) buttress; (*of bridge*) pier, support.
   (d) (*Geog*) spur.
   (e) (*fig*) basis, foundation.
   (f) (*Bol, Ec, RPl*) **tomar algo para el —** to drink a stirrup cup; to have one for the road.

estribor nm starboard.

estricnina nf strychnine.

estricote nm (*Ven*) (a) disorderly life, licentious conduct. (b) **andar al —** to go hither and thither; to live in a disorderly way; to get mixed up in a brawl.

estrictamente adv strictly; severely.

estrictez *nf* (*SAm*) strictness; severity.

estricto *adj* strict; severe.

estridente *adj* strident, raucous, unpleasant-sounding; jangling.

estridor *nm* stridency; raucousness; screech; jangling sound.

estrillar [1a] *vi* (*Per, RPl*) to get cross.

estrillo *nm* (*Per, RPl*) bad temper, annoyance.

estro *nm* inspiration.

estrofa *nf* verse, stanza, strophe.

estrófico *adj* strophic; composed in stanzas.

estroncio *nm* strontium; — 90 strontium 90.

estropajo *nm* (a) scourer, scrubber; dishcloth; swab, mop; **poner a uno como un** — to shower insults on someone; to make someone feel a heel; **servir de** — to be exploited, be used to do the dirty work.
 (**b**) dirt, rubbish; worthless object.

estropajoso *adj* (a) *meat etc* tough, leathery, gristly. (**b**) *speech* stammering; indistinct. (**c**) *person* slovenly; mean, despicable.

estropeado *adj* damaged, spoiled; ruined; crumpled, torn; *person* maimed, crippled.

estropear [1a] **1** *vt* to damage, spoil; to ruin; to mess up, make a mess of; to crumple, tear; *person* to maim, cripple, hurt; *text etc* to mangle; *meaning* to pervert, destroy.
 2 estropearse *vr* to get damaged; to spoil, go bad; to deteriorate; (*plan etc*) to fail.

estropicio *nm* (*fam*) (a) breakage, smashing, smash-up.
 (**b**) harmful effects, damaging results; **ese alimento es responsable de muchos** —s that foodstuff can have very harmful effects.
 (**c**) (*fig*) rumpus (*fam*), row, fuss; turmoil.

estructura *nf* structure; frame, framework; arrangement.

estructural *adj* structural.

estructuralmente *adv* structurally.

estructurar [1a] *vt* to construct; to arrange, organize.

estruendo *nm* (a) noise, clamour, din; crash, clatter, racket; thunder. (**b**) (*fig*) uproar, turmoil, confusion. (**c**) (*fig*) pomp, ostentation.

estruendosamente *adv* noisily, uproariously; loudly, obstreperously.

estruendoso *adj* noisy; uproarious; *person* loud, obstreperous.

estrujadura *nf* squeeze, press(ing).

estrujar [1a] *vt* to squeeze, press, crush; to bruise, mash; (*fig*) to drain, bleed white.

estrujón *nm* squeeze, press; pressing, crushing; (*Agr*) final pressing of grapes; (*fam*) crush, jam.

Estuardo *m* Stuart.

estuario *nm* estuary.

estucar [1g] *vt* to stucco, plaster.

estuco *nm* stucco, plaster.

estuche *nm* (a) box, case, container; sheath; — **de afeites** vanity case; — **de aseo** toilet case; — **de cigarros** cigar case; — **de joyas** jewel box.
 (**b**) **ser un** — (*fam*) to be a real expert, be a useful chap (*fam*).

estudiado *adj* (*fig*) studied, elaborate; (*pej*) recherché.

estudiantado *nm* (a) (*SAm*) students (*collectively*), student body. (**b**) (*Chi*) college.

estudiante *nmf* student; — **de derecho** law student; — **de medicina** medical student; — **de ruso** student of Russian.

estudiantil *adj* student (*attr*); **vida** — student life; **los problemas** —es student problems, problems of students, problems relating to students.

estudiantina *nf* student music group, student band.

estudiantino *adj* student (*attr*); **a la estudiantina** like a student, in the manner of students.

estudiar [1b] *vti* to study; to work; to think about, think over, ponder; — **para abogado** to study to become a lawyer, study law; **tengo que ir a** — I must go and work; **estudia todo el día en la biblioteca** he works all day in the library; **lo estudiaré** I'll think about it.

estudio *nm* (a) (*in general*) study; research; survey; investigation; plan, design (*de for*); planning; —**s** schooling, education; —**s** work, studies, researches; **le pagaron los** —**s** they paid for his schooling, they paid for his education; **hizo sus** —**s en París** he studied in Paris; **se fue a Suiza para completar sus** —**s** she went to Switzerland to finish her education; **los** —**s de Menéndez Pidal sobre la épica española** Menéndez Pidal's work on Spanish epic; **los últimos** —**s de lingüística** the latest work in linguistics, recent research in linguistics; **publicó un** — **sobre Bécquer** he published a study of Bécquer; —**s del mercado**, — **de mercados** market research;

—**s de tiempo y movimiento** time and motion study; **estar en** — to be under consideration.
 (**b**) (*room in house*) study.
 (**c**) (*Art, Cine, Radio etc*) studio; — **de cine**, — **cinematográfico** film studio; — **radiofónico** broadcasting studio; — **de registro de sonidos** sound-recording studio; — **de televisión** television studio.
 (**d**) (*Art*) study.
 (**e**) (*Mus*) study, étude.
 (**f**) (*Arg: lawyer's etc*) office.
 (**g**) studiousness, diligence.
 (**h**) learning; **un hombre de mucho** — a man of great learning.

estudiosamente *adv* studiously.

estudioso **1** *adj* studious; bookish. **2** *nm* student, scholar.

estufa *nf* (a) stove, heater; — **eléctrica** electric fire; — **de gas** gas fire; — **de petróleo** oil stove. (**b**) (*Agr*) hothouse; **criar a uno en** — (*fig*) to pamper someone.

estufilla *nf* (a) small stove, brazier. (**b**) muff.

estulticia *nf* stupidity, foolishness.

estultificar [1g] *vt* (*CAm*): — **a uno** to make someone look stupid, make someone out to be a fool.

estulto *adj* stupid, foolish.

estupefacción *nf* stupefaction.

estupefaciente **1** *adj* stupifying; narcotic; **sustancia** — =**2** *nm* narcotic, drug.

estupefacto *adj* astonished, speechless, thunderstruck; **me miró** — he looked at me in amazement; **dejar a uno** — to leave someone speechless.

estupendamente *adv* stupendously; (*fam*) marvellously, wonderfully, terrifically (*fam*).

estupendo *adj* stupendous; (*fam*) marvellous, wonderful, terrific (*fam*), great (*fam*); ¡—! that's great!, splendid!; **tiene un coche** — he's got a marvellous car; **hay chicas estupendas** there are some smashing girls (*sl*); **es** — **para tocar la trompeta** he's great on the trumpet.

estúpidamente *adv* stupidly.

estupidez *nf* (a) stupidity, silliness. (**b**) stupid thing, piece of stupidity; **fue una** — **mía** it was a silly mistake of mine; **cometer una** — to do something silly.

estúpido *adj* stupid, silly.

estupor *nm* (a) (*Med etc*) stupor. (**b**) (*fig*) astonishment, amazement.

estuprar [1a] *vt* to rape.

estupro *nm* rape.

estuque *nm* stucco.

estuquería *nf* stuccoing, stucco work.

esturión *nm* sturgeon.

estuve *etc see* **estar**.

—eta *n suffix diminutive*: *eg* **avioneta** light aircraft; **camioneta** van, light truck; *see* **caseta** *etc*.

etapa *nf* (a) (*of journey etc*) stage; (*Sport*) stage, leg; lap; (*Mil*) stopping place; **a cortas** —**s, a pequeñas** —**s** in easy stages.
 (**b**) (*of rocket*) stage; **cohete de 3** —**s** 3-stage rocket.
 (**c**) (*Mil*) food ration (*for stage of a march*).
 (**d**) (*fig*) stage, phase; **en la segunda** — **del plan** in the second phase of the plan; **una adquisición proyectada por** —**s** a phased takeover; **lo haremos por** —**s** we'll do it in stages, we'll do it gradually.

etcétera *adv* etcetera; **gatos y perros** —, — **cats and** dogs and so on, cats and dogs and what have you.

éter *nm* ether.

etéreo *adj* ethereal (*also fig*).

eternamente *adv* eternally, everlastingly.

eternidad *nf* eternity.

eternizar [1f] **1** *vt* to etern(al)ize, perpetuate; to make everlasting; (*pej*) to drag out, prolong endlessly. **2 eternizarse** *vr* (*pej*) to be interminable.

eterno *adj* eternal, everlasting.

ética *nf* ethics; — **profesional** (*Med etc*) professional ethics.

ético[1] *adj* ethical.

ético[2] *adj* (*Med*) consumptive; (*fig*) frail.

etilo *nm* ethyl.

etimología *nf* etymology; — **doble** doublet.

etimológico *adj* etymological.

etíope **1** *adj* Ethiopian. **2** *nmf* Ethiopian.

Etiopía *f* Ethiopia.

etiquencia *nf* (*Cu, Mex, PR: Med*) consumption.

etiqueta *nf* (a) etiquette; formality; —**s** refinements, formalities, ceremony; **de** — formal, full-dress (*attr*); **baile de** — ball, dress ball, formal dance; "**vestir de** —" (*on invitation*) "dress: formal".
 (**b**) ticket, label, tag.

etiquetero *adj* formal, ceremonious, punctilious; stiff, prim.

étnico *adj* ethnic.

etnografía *nf* ethnography.

etnología *nf* ethnology.

etrusco 1 adj Etruscan. **2** nm, **etrusca** nf Etruscan. **3** nm (language) Etruscan.
eucalipto nm eucalyptus, gum tree.
Eucaristía nf Eucharist.
eucarístico adj eucharistic.
Euclides m Euclid.
eufemismo nm euphemism.
eufemístico adj euphemistic.
eufonía nf euphony.
eufónico adj euphonic, euphonious.
euforia nf euphoria; exuberance.
eufórico adj euphoric; exuberant.
Eufrates m Euphrates.
eugenesia nf eugenics.
Eugenio m Eugene.
eugenismo nm eugenics.
eunuco nm eunuch.
eurasiano 1 adj Eurasian. **2** nm, **eurasiana** nf Eurasian.
eureka excl eureka!
Eurídice f Eurydice.
Eurípedes m Euripides.
eurítmica nf eurhythmics.
euro nm (lit) east wind.
Europa f Europe.
europeidad nf Europeanness; Europe-mindedness; European character.
europeísta 1 adj pro-European; European-minded; **la tendencia — actual en Inglaterra** the present tendency in England to favour close links with Europe. **2** nmf pro-European; European-minded person.
europeización nf Europeanization.
europeizante adj (SAm) = **europeísta**.
europeizar [1f] **1** vt to Europeanize. **2 europeizarse** vr to become Europeanized.
europeo 1 adj European. **2** nm, **europea** nf European.
Eurovisión f Eurovision.
éuscaro 1 adj Basque. **2** nm (language) Basque.
eutanasia nf euthanasia, mercy killing.
Eva f Eve.
evacuación nf (a) evacuation. (b) (Tech) waste; exhaust.
evacuado nm, **evacuada** nf evacuee.
evacuar [1d] vt (a) to evacuate; to move out of, leave empty, vacate; city, population to evacuate; vessel to empty; sore (Med) to drain.
(b) **— el vientre** to have a movement of the bowels.
(c) duty to fulfil; consultation to carry out, undertake; business to transact; deal to conclude.
evacuatorio nm public lavatory.
evadido nm fugitive, escaped prisoner.
evadir [3a] **1** vt to evade, avoid. **2 evadirse** vr to escape; to break out, slip away.
evaluación nf evaluation.
evaluar [1e] vt to evaluate.
evanescente adj evanescent.
evangélico adj evangelic(al).
evangelio nm gospel; **el E— según San Juan** the Gospel according to St John; **ser como el** — to be certain, be infallible; **dice como el** — he speaks the gospel truth.
Evangelista adj: **San Juan** — St John the Evangelist.
evangelista nm (a) gospeller; **los cuatro —s** the four evangelists. (b) (Mex) public writer, scribe.
evangelizador nm evangelist.
evangelizar [1f] vt to evangelize.
evaporación nf evaporation.
evaporar [1a] **1** vt to evaporate. **2 evaporarse** vr to evaporate; (fig) to vanish.
evaporizar [1f] **1** vt to vapourize. **2 evaporizarse** vr to vapourize.
evasión nf escape, flight; (fig) evasion; **— de capitales** (Fin) flight of capital; **— fiscal, — tributaria** tax evasion.
evasiva nf evasion; loophole, way out; excuse.
evasivo adj evasive, non-committal, ambiguous.
evento nm (a) unforeseen happening; contingency; eventuality; **a cualquier** — whatever happens, in any event.
(b) (SAm: angl) event; sporting fixture; social event.
eventual adj (a) fortuitous; possible; conditional upon circumstances. (b) work, worker temporary, casual; official etc acting; solution stopgap, temporary.
eventualidad nf eventuality; contingency; **en esa —** in that eventuality.
eventualmente adv (a) by chance, fortuitously. (b) possibly, depending upon circumstances.
evidencia nf (a) evidence, proof; **poner en** — to make clear; to show, demonstrate; **ponerse en** — to put oneself forward. (b) obviousness.

evidenciar [1b] vt to prove, show, demonstrate; to make evident; **— de modo inconfundible** to give clear proof of, prove unmistakably.
evidente adj obvious, clear, evident.
evidentemente adv obviously, clearly, evidently.
evitable adj avoidable, preventable; **un accidente fácilmente** — an accident which could easily be avoided.
evitación nf avoidance, prevention; **— de accidentes** accident prevention.
evitar [1a] vt to avoid; to prevent; danger etc to avoid, escape; trouble to save, spare; temptation etc to shun; **para** — **tales dificultades** in order to avoid such difficulties; **para —se trabajo** in order to save oneself trouble; **no lo lograrán si puedo —lo** they won't get away with that if I can help it; **— hacer algo** to avoid doing something; to be chary of doing something.
evocación nf evocation; invocation.
evocador adj evocative; reminiscent (de of).
evocar [1g] vt to evoke, call forth, conjure up; spirits etc to invoke, call up.
evocativo adj (SAm) evocative.
evolución nf (a) (Bio) evolution. (b) (fig) evolution, change, development. (c) (Mil etc) manoeuvre.
evolucionar [1a] vi (a) (Bio) to evolve. (b) (fig) to evolve, change, develop. (c) (Mil) to manoeuvre, wheel; (Aer) to manoeuvre, circle, wheel.
evolutivo adj evolutionary.
ex . . . ex; former, late; **ex secretario** ex-secretary, former secretary; **la ex querida de** the former mistress of, the ex-mistress of, the one-time mistress of.
exabrupto nm (hum) broadside; sudden attack.
exacción nf (a) (act) exaction, extortion. (b) (sum etc) demand; levy.
exacerbante adj (SAm) irritating, provoking; (fig) aggravating.
exacerbar [1a] vt to irritate, provoke; (fig) to aggravate, exacerbate.
exactamente adv exactly; accurately; precisely; punctually; correctly.
exactitud nf exactness; accuracy; precision; punctuality; correctness.
exacto adj exact; accurate; precise; punctual; right, correct; **¡—! exactly!, quite right!; that's just what I say!; **eso no es del todo** — that's not quite right.
exageración nf exaggeration.
exageradamente adv in an exaggerated way; excessively, exorbitantly; over-demonstratively, theatrically; intensely; fulsomely; oddly.
exagerado adj account, claim etc exaggerated; highly-coloured; price etc excessive, exorbitant, steep; person over-demonstrative, theatrical, given to extravagant gestures; intense; fulsome; peculiar, odd.
exageradura nf (Ven) exaggeration.
exagerar [1a] **1** vt to exaggerate; to overdo, over-state, make too much of; to enlarge upon. **2** vi to exaggerate; (pej) to overdo it, overdo things.
exaltación nf (a) exaltation. (b) overexcitement; elation; excitability, intenseness; hotheadedness; passion, impassioned nature. (c) (Pol) extremism.
exaltado 1 adj (a) exalted.
(b) state, mood over-excited, worked up; elated; (in character) excitable, intense; hot-headed; speech etc impassioned.
(c) (Pol) extreme, far out.
2 nm (Pol) extremist, far-out person.
exaltar [1a] **1** vt (a) to exalt; to elevate, raise (a to).
(b) (fig) to extol, praise.
(c) to excite, carry away, work up; emotion to intensify; imagination to fire.
2 exaltarse vr (person) to get excited, get worked up; to get carried away (con by); (in argument) to get heated; (emotion) to run high, become very intense; **¡no te exaltes!** don't get so worked up!
exalumno nm, **exalumna** nf (SAm: Univ) graduate; former student; alumnus, alumna (US).
examen nm examination; exam (fam); inquiry (de into); inspection; **— de admisión, — de ingreso** entrance examination; **— de conductor** driving test; **— eliminatorio** qualifying examination; **— de fin de curso** final examination, finals; **— oral** oral examination; **presentarse a un** — to enter (or go in for, sit) an examination.
examinado nm, **examinada** nf examinee, candidate.
examinador nm, **examinadora** nf examiner.
examinando nm, **examinanda** nf examinee, candidate.
examinar [1a] **1** vt to examine (also Med, School, Univ etc); to test; to inspect, look through, go over; to inquire into, investigate, look into.

2 examinarse *vr* to take an examination, be examined (*en* in; *de* for the degree of); **— de doctor** to take one's doctoral examination.

exangüe *adj* bloodless; anaemic; (*fig*) weak.

exánime *adj* lifeless; (*fig*) weak, exhausted, lifeless; **caer —** to fall in a faint.

exasperación *nf* exasperation.

exasperador *adj*, **exasperante** *adj* exasperating, infuriating.

exasperar [1a] **1** *vt* to exasperate, infuriate. **2 exasperarse** *vr* to get exasperated, lose patience.

excarcelación *nf* release (from prison).

excarcelar [1a] *vt* to release (from prison).

excavación *nf* excavation.

excavador *nm* excavator, digger.

excavar [1a] *vt* to excavate, dig (out); to hollow out.

excedente 1 *adj* excess, surplus; excessive. **2** *nm* excess, surplus.

exceder [2a] **1** *vt* to exceed, surpass; to pass, outdo, excel; (*in importance etc*) to transcend.

   2 *vi:* **— de** to exceed, surpass.

   3 excederse *vr* (**a**) to excel oneself.

   (**b**) (*pej*) to overreach oneself; to go too far, go to extremes; **— en sus funciones** to exceed one's duty.

   (**c**) **— de** to exceed, surpass; **no — de lo corriente** to be no more than average.

excelencia *nf* (**a**) excellence; superiority, superior quality; **por — par** excellence. (**b**) **su E—** his Excellency; **sí, E—** yes, your Excellency.

excelente *adj* excellent; superior.

excelentemente *adv* excellently.

excelso *adj* lofty, exalted, sublime.

excentricidad *nf* eccentricity.

excéntrico 1 *adj* eccentric; erratic. **2** *nm* eccentric.

excepción *nf* exception; **— de la regla** exception to the rule; **la — confirma la regla** the exception proves the rule; **a — de** with the exception of, except for; **hacer una —** to make an exception.

excepcional *adj* exceptional.

excepcionalmente *adv* exceptionally; as an exception.

excepto *prep* except (for), excepting.

exceptuar [1e] *vt* to except, exclude, leave out of account; (*Law etc*) to exempt.

excesivamente *adv* excessively; unreasonably, unduly.

excesivo *adj* excessive; unreasonable, undue; over-, *eg* **con generosidad excesiva** over-generously, with excessive generosity.

exceso *nm* (**a**) excess; (*of food*) surfeit; (*Comm, Fin*) surplus; **— de equipaje** excess luggage, excess baggage (*US*); **— de peso** excess weight; **debido al — de peso** because of the extra weight; **me detuvieron por — de velocidad** they arrested me for speeding, they booked me for exceeding the speed limit; **en —, por —** excessively, to excess; **cuidado en —** excessively careful, too careful; **una cantidad en — de X toneladas** a quantity in excess of (*or* over) X tons; **generoso hasta el —** generous to a fault; **beber en —** to drink to excess; **llevar algo al —** to carry something to excess, overdo something.

   (**b**) (*fig*) excess; **los —s de la revolución** the excesses of the revolution.

excisión *nf* excision.

excitabilidad *nf* excitability.

excitable *adj* excitable; highly-strung, high-strung (*US*), nervy; temperamental.

excitación *nf* (**a**) excitement; **— loca** hysteria. (**b**) excitation.

excitante 1 *adj* (**a**) exciting. (**b**) (*Med*) stimulating. **2** *nm* stimulant.

excitar [1a] **1** *vt* (**a**) to excite; *feeling* to excite, arouse, stir up; *doubts, hopes* to raise.

   (**b**) to incite, urge on; **— al pueblo a la rebelión** to incite the populace to rebellion; **— a uno a hacer algo** to urge someone to do something.

   (**c**) (*Elec*) to excite, energize.

   2 excitarse *vr* to get excited, get worked up.

exclamación *nf* exclamation; cry.

exclamar [1a] **1** *vi* to exclaim; to cry out. **2 exclamarse** *vr* to complain (*contra* about), protest (*contra* against).

exclamativo *adj*, **exclamatorio** *adj* exclamatory.

exclaustración *nf* (*Eccl*) secularization; expulsion (*of monks or nuns*).

exclaustrada *nf* secularized nun; expelled nun; ex-nun.

exclaustrado (*Eccl*) **1** *adj* secularized; expelled (from the order). **2** *nm* secularized monk, expelled monk; ex-monk.

excluir [3g] *vt* to exclude (*from* de); to shut out; *solution* to reject; *possibility etc* to exclude, rule out, preclude.

exclusión *nf* exclusion; **con — de** excluding, to the exclusion of; **por —** as an exception.

exclusiva *nf* (**a**) (*Comm*) sole right, sole agency; **tener la — de un producto** to have the sole right to sell a product, be the sole agents for a product.

   (**b**) (*Journalism*) exclusive interview; exclusive news release.

   (**c**) refusal, rejection (*for a post etc*).

exclusivamente *adv* exclusively.

exclusive 1 *adv* exclusively. **2** *prep* exclusive of, not counting.

exclusividad *nf* (**a**) exclusiveness; clannishness; snobbery. (**b**) (*Comm*) **=exclusiva** (a).

exclusivista *adj club etc* exclusive, select; *group* clannish; *attitude* snobbish.

exclusivo *adj* exclusive; sole; (*of working hours*) full-time.

excluyente *adj* (*SAm*) class, club etc exclusive.

excombatiente *nm* exserviceman, veteran (*US*).

excomulgado 1 *adj* (**a**) (*Eccl*) excommunicated. (**b**) (*fam*) blessed, cursed. **2** *nm*, **excomulgada** *nf* excommunicated person.

excomulgar [1h] *vt* (**a**) (*Eccl*) to excommunicate. (**b**) (*fig*) to ban, banish; (*fam*) to curse.

excomunión *nf* excommunication.

excoriar [1b] **1** *vt* to skin, flay; to graze, take the skin off. **2 excoriarse** *vr* to graze oneself, skin oneself.

excrecencia *nf* excrescence.

excreción *nf* excretion.

excremento *nm* excrement.

excretar [1a] *vt* to excrete.

exculpación *nf* exoneration; (*Law*) acquittal.

exculpar [1a] **1** *vt* to exonerate, exculpate; (*Law*) to acquit (*de* of). **2 exculparse** *vr* to exonerate oneself.

excursión *nf* excursion, outing, trip; (*Mil*) raid, incursion; **— campestre** picnic; **— de caza** hunting trip; **— a pie** walk, hike, ramble; **ir de —** to go (off) on a trip, go on an outing.

excursionar [1a] *vi* (*SAm*) to go on a trip, have an outing.

excursionismo *nm* going on trips; sightseeing; walking, hiking, rambling.

excursionista *nmf* tourist; tripper; sightseer; hiker, rambler.

excusa *nf* excuse; apology; **buscar —** to look for an excuse; **presentar sus —s** to make one's excuses, excuse oneself; **presentar —s de su país** to make excuses for one's country.

excusabaraja *nf* hamper, basket with a lid.

excusable *adj* excusable, pardonable.

excusado 1 *adj* (**a**) unnecessary, superfluous; **— es decir que...** needless to say..., I (*etc*) need scarcely say that...; **pensar en lo —** to think of something which is quite out of the question.

   (**b**) **estar — de** to be exempt from.

   (**c**) reserved, private.

   2 *nm* lavatory, toilet.

excusar [1a] **1** *vt* (**a**) to excuse; **— a A con B** to tell B that A begs to be excused, to present A's apologies to B.

   (**b**) to exempt (*de* from).

   (**c**) to avoid, prevent; **así excusamos disgustos** this way we avoid difficulties; **podemos — lo otro** we can forget about the rest of it, we don't have to bother with the rest.

   (**d**) **— + infin** not to have to **+ infin**; to save the trouble of **+ ger**; **excusamos decirle que...** we don't have to tell you that...; **por eso excuso escribirte más largo** I can save myself the trouble of writing at greater length.

   2 excusarse *vr* to excuse oneself; to apologize (*de* for); **— de + infin** to decline to **+ infin**; to apologize for not being able to **+ infin**; **— de haber hecho algo** to apologize for having done something.

execrable *adj* execrable.

execración *nf* execration.

execrar [1a] *vt* to execrate, loathe, abominate.

exégesis *nf* exegesis.

exención *nf* exemption (*de* from); immunity, freedom (*de* from).

exencionar [1a] *vt* to exempt (*de* from).

exentar [1a] *vt* to exempt (*de* from); to excuse (*de* from).

exento *adj* (**a**) exempt (*de* from); free (*de* from, of); **— de alquileres** rent-free; **— de derechos** duty-free; **— de impuestos** tax-free, tax-exempt (*US*), free of tax; **estar — de cuidados** to be free of worries; **una expedición no exenta de peligros** an expedition not without (its) dangers.

   (**b**) *passage, place etc* clear, unobstructed, open.

   (**c**) (*Archit*) free-standing.

exequias *nfpl* funeral rites, obsequies.

éxeunt *vi* exeunt.

exfoliador *nm* (*Chi, Mex*) tear-off pad, loose-leaf notebook.

exhalación *nf* (a) exhalation; fumes, vapour. (b) (*Astron*) shooting star; **como una —** at top speed, like lightning.

exhalar [1a] **1** *vt* to exhale, breathe out; *fumes etc* to emit, give off, give out; *sigh* to breathe, heave; *moan* to utter.
  2 exhalarse *vr* to breathe hard; to hurry, run.

exhaustivo *adj* exhaustive.

exhausto *adj* exhausted.

exheredar [1a] *vt* to disinherit.

exhibición *nf* exhibition, display, show; **— de escaparate** window display; **la pobre — del equipo** the team's poor showing; **una impresionante — de fuerza** an impressive show of strength.

exhibicionismo *nm* exhibitionism.

exhibicionista 1 *adj* exhibitionist. **2** *nmf* exhibitionist.

exhibir [3a] **1** *vt* (a) to exhibit, display, show. (b) (*Mex*) *sum* to pay in cash. **2 exhibirse** *vr* to show oneself.

exhortación *nf* exhortation.

exhortar [1a] *vt* to exhort (*a* + *infin* to + *infin*).

exhorto *nm* (*Eccl, Law*) charge.

exhumar [1a] *vt* to exhume, disinter.

exigencia *nf* (a) demand, requirement; exigency; **según las —s de la situación** as the situation requires; **tener muchas —s** to be very demanding.
  (b) (*Ven*) request.

exigente *adj* demanding, exacting, exigent; particular; **ser — con uno** to be hard on someone; **es muy — en la limpieza** she is very particular about cleanliness.

exigir [3c] *vt* (a) *contribution etc* to exact, levy (*a* from).
  (b) to demand, require (*a* of, from); to call for (*a* from); **— el pago** to demand payment; **esto exige mucho cuidado** this needs a lot of care; **exigirá mucho dinero** it will require (*or* need, take) a lot of money; **ello no exige comentario** it does not call for any comment, comment on it would be superfluous; **exige mucho** he's very demanding.
  (c) (*Ven*) *thing* to ask for, request; *person* to beg, plead with, entreat.

exiguo *adj* meagre, small, scanty, exiguous.

exilado 1 *adj* exiled, in exile. **2** *nm,* **exilada** *nf* exile.

exilar [1a], **exiliar** [1b] (*Acad*) **1** *vt* to exile. **2 exilarse** *vr*, **exiliarse** *vr* to go into exile; to exile oneself.

exiliado (*SAm*) **=exilado**.

exilio *nm* exile; **estar en el —, vivir en el —** to be in exile; **gobierno en el —** government in exile.

eximio *adj* (a) *person* distinguished, eminent. (b) *goods* choice, select.

eximir [3a] **1** *vt* to exempt (*de* from); to free, excuse (*de* from); **esto me exime de toda obligación con él** this frees me from any obligation to him.
  2 eximirse *vr:* **— de** + *infin* to excuse oneself from + *ger*; to free oneself from having to + *infin*.

existencia *nf* (a) existence; being; life; **lucha por la —** struggle for survival; **amargar la — a uno** to make someone's life a misery; **quitarse la —** (*euph*) to do away with oneself, commit suicide.
  (b) (*also* **—s**: *Comm*) stock; goods; **nuestras —s de carbón** our coal stocks, our stock(s) of coal; **estar en —** to be in stock; **tener en —** to have in stock.

existencial *adj* existential.

existencialismo *nm* existentialism.

existencialista 1 *adj* existentialist. **2** *nmf* existentialist.

existente *adj* (a) existing; in being, in existence; *text etc* extant; surviving; **la situación —** the existing (*or* present) situation. (b) (*Comm*) in stock.

existir [3a] *vi* to exist, be; **dejar de —** to pass out of existence, come to an end; (*of person: euph*) to pass away (*euph*); **esta sociedad existe desde hace 90 años** the company has been in existence for 90 years, the company was founded 90 years ago; **no existe tal cosa** there's no such thing.

éxito *nm* (a) result, outcome; **buen —** happy outcome, success; **con buen —** successfully; **tener buen —** to succeed, be successful; **tener mal —** to have an unfortunate outcome, fail, be unsuccessful.
  (b) success; **con —** successfully; **tener — en** to be successful in; to make a success of; **el hombre de —** the successful man; **es una chica de mucho —** she's a girl who has lots of success (with the men).
  (c) (*Mus, Theat and fig*) success, hit; **— editorial, — de librería** bestseller; **— de taquilla** box-office

success, successful play; **— clamoroso, — fulminante, — rotundo** huge success, overwhelming success; (*Mus etc*) hit song, smash hit.

exitosamente *adv* (*SAm*) successfully.

exitoso *adj* (*SAm*) successful.

éxodo *nm* exodus; **el — rural** the depopulation of the countryside, the drift from the land.

exoneración *nf* (a) exoneration; freeing, relief. (b) dismissal.

exonerar [1a] *vt* (a) to exonerate; **— a uno de un deber** to free someone from a duty, relieve someone of a duty.
  (b) *employee* to dismiss.
  (c) **— el vientre** to have a movement of the bowels.

exorbitancia *nf* exorbitance.

exorbitante *adj* exorbitant.

exorcismo *nm* exorcism.

exorcizar [1f] *vt* to exorcise.

exornar [1a] *vt* to adorn, embellish (*de* with).

exótico *adj* exotic.

exotismo *nm* exoticism; taste for the exotic.

expandir [3a] **1** *vt* (*Anat*) to expand; (*Comm etc*) to expand, enlarge; (*fig*) to expand, extend, spread; **— el mercado de un producto** to expand the market for a product; **— la afición a la lectura** to spread a love of reading.
  2 expandirse *vr* to expand; to extend, spread; **Madrid se expande** Madrid is expanding, Madrid is spreading.

expansible *adj* expansible; that can be expanded (*or* extended etc).

expansión *nf* (a) expansion; enlargement; extension, spread(ing); **la — económica** economic growth; **la — industrial** industrial expansion.
  (b) (*fig*) relaxation.
  (c) (*fig*) expansiveness.

expansionar [1a] **1** *vt market etc* to expand.
  2 expansionarse *vr* (a) to expand.
  (b) (*fig*) to relax.
  (c) (*fig*) to unbosom oneself, open one's heart (*con* to).

expansionismo *nm* (*Pol etc*) expansionism.

expansionista *adj* (*Pol etc*) expansionist.

expansivo *adj* (a) expansive. (b) (*fig*) expansive, affable; communicative.

expatriación *nf* expatriation; exile.

expatriado *nm,* **expatriada** *nf* expatriate; exile.

expatriarse [1b] *vr* to emigrate, leave one's country; (*Pol etc*) to go into exile.

expectación *nf* (a) expectation; **— de vida** expectation of life.
  (b) expectation, expectancy, anticipation; eagerness; excitement; **la — crece de un momento a otro** the excitement is growing every moment.

expectante *adj* expectant; eager; excited.

expectativa *nf* expectation; hope, prospect; **— de vida** expectation of life; **estar a la —** to wait and see (what will happen); **estar a la — de algo** to look out for something, be on the watch for something.

expectorar [1a] *vti* to expectorate.

expedición *nf* (a) expedition (*also Geog, Mil etc*); **— de salvamento** rescue expedition; **— militar** military expedition.
  (b) (*Comm etc*) shipment, shipping; **gastos de —** shipping charges.
  (c) (*fig*) speed, dispatch.

expedicionario *adj* expeditionary.

expedidor *nm* shipper, shipping agent.

expedientar [1a] *vt* to make a file on, draw up a dossier on; (*fig*) to expel.

expediente *nm* (a) expedient; means; device, makeshift; **recurrir al — de** + *infin* to resort to the device of + *ger*.
  (b) (*Law*) action, proceedings; records of a case; **— judicial** legal proceedings; **incoar —** to start proceedings; **instruir un —** to collect all the documents.
  (c) record; dossier; file; **— policíaco** police dossier; **— académico** (*School etc*) student's record, pupil's record card.
  (d) **cubrir el —** to do just enough to keep out of trouble.

expedienteo *nm* (*pej*) bureaucracy, red tape.

expedir [3l] *vt goods etc* to send, ship off, forward; *document* to draw up; to make out, issue; *order, ticket etc* to issue; *business* to deal with, dispatch.

expeditar [1a] *vt* (*SAm*) to expedite, hurry along; to conclude.

expeditivo *adj* expeditious.

expedito *adj* (a) expeditious, prompt, speedy. (b) *road, way* clear, unobstructed, free; **dejar — el camino para** to clear the way for. (c) (*SAm*) easy.

expeler [2a] *vt* to expel, eject.

expendedor *nm* (a) (*person*) dealer, retailer; agent; tobacconist; (*Theat*) ticket agent; — **de billetes** ticket clerk, booking clerk; — **de moneda falsa** distributor of counterfeit money.
(b) — **automático** vending machine; — **automático de bebidas** drink vending machine.

expendeduría *nf* retail shop, (*esp*) tobacconist's (shop), cigar store (*US*).

expender [2a] *vt* (a) *money* to expend, spend.
(b) *counterfeit money* to utter; to pass, circulate.
(c) *goods* to sell (retail); to be an agent for, sell on commission; to deal in.

expendición *nf*: — **de moneda falsa** uttering counterfeit money, passing false coin.

expendio *nm* (a) expense, outlay.
(b) (*SAm*) retail store, (*esp*) tobacconist's (shop), cigar store (*US*), liquor store; — **de boletos** (*Mex*) ticket office.
(c) (*act*) retailing, retail selling.

expensar [1a] *vt* (*SAm*) to defray the costs of.

expensas *nfpl* expenses; (*Law*) costs; **a** — **de** at the expense of (*also fig*); **a mis** — at my expense.

experiencia *nf* (a) experience; **una triste** — a sad experience; **aprender por la** — to learn by experience; **saber algo por** — to know something from experience.
(b) (*scientific etc*) experiment (**en** on).

experimentación *nf* experimentation.

experimentado *adj* experienced.

experimental *adj* experimental.

experimentalmente *adv* experimentally.

experimentar [1a] *vt* (a) (*Tech etc*) to test, try out; to experiment with; **el nuevo fármaco está siendo experimentado** the new drug is being tested, experiments with the new drug are going on; **están experimentando un nuevo helicóptero** they are testing a new helicopter.
(b) *change etc* to experience, undergo, go through; *loss, decline* to suffer; *rise, increase* to show; *emotion* to feel; **las cifras han experimentado un aumento de un 5 por 100** the figures show an increase of 5%; **no experimenté ninguna sensación nueva** I felt no new sensation.
2 *vi* to experiment (**con** with, **en** on).

experimento *nm* experiment (**con** with, **en** on); **como** — as an experiment, by way of experiment; **hacer** —**s** to experiment (**con** with, **en** on).

experticia *nf* expertise.

experto 1 *adj* expert; skilled, experienced; seasoned; knowledgeable. 2 *nm* expert.

expiación *nf* expiation, atonement.

expiar [1c] *vt* to expiate, atone for.

expiatorio *adj* expiatory.

expiración *nf* expiration.

expirar [1a] *vi* to expire.

explanación *nf* (a) (*Tech*) levelling. (b) (*fig*) explanation, elucidation.

explanada *nf* raised area, terrace, platform; levelled area; esplanade; (*Mil*) glacis; — **de ensillado** saddling enclosure.

explanar [1a] *vt* (a) (*Rail, Tech etc*) to level, grade. (b) (*fig*) to unfold; to explain, elucidate.

explayar [1a] 1 *vt* to extend, expand, enlarge.
2 **explayarse** *vr* (a) to extend, spread; to open out, unfold.
(b) (*fig*) to relax, take it easy; to take an outing.
(c) (*in speech etc*) to speak at length; to spread oneself; — **a su gusto** to talk one's head off, talk to one's heart's content; — **con uno** to unbosom oneself to someone, confide in someone.

explicable *adj* explicable, explainable; **cosas no fácilmente** —**s** things not easily explained, things not easy to explain.

explicación *nf* explanation; reason (**de** for); **sin dar** —**es** without giving any reason.

explicaderas *nfpl*: **tener buenas** — to be good at explaining things (away); (*pej*) to be plausible.

explicar [1g] 1 *vt* to explain; *theory etc* to expound; *course* to lecture on, teach; *subject* to lecture in; *lecture* to give, deliver.
2 **explicarse** *vr* (a) to explain (oneself); **se explica con claridad** he states things clearly; **¡explíquese Vd!** explain yourself!; **explíquese con la mayor brevedad** please be as brief as possible.
(b) — **algo** to understand something; **no me lo explico** I can't understand it, I can't make it out.
(c) to be explained; **esto no se explica fácilmente** this cannot be explained (away) easily.

explicativo *adj*, **explicatorio** *adj* explanatory.

explícitamente *adv* explicitly.

explícito *adj* explicit.

exploración *nf* exploration; (*Mil*) reconnaissance, scouting; (*Radar etc*) scanning; — **submarina** underwater exploration, (*as sport*) skin diving.

explorador *nm* (a) (*Geog etc*) explorer; pioneer; (*Mil*) scout; (**niño**) — (boy) scout. (b) (*Med*) probe; (*Radar etc*) scanner.

exploradora *nf* girl guide, girl scout (*US*).

explorar [1a] 1 *vt* (*Geog etc*) to explore; to pioneer, open up; (*Med*) to probe; (*Radar etc*) to scan. 2 *vi* to explore; (*Mil*) to scout, reconnoitre.

exploratorio *adj* exploratory.

explosión *nf* (a) explosion; blast; **motor de** — internal combustion engine; **hacer** — to explode.
(b) (*fig*) explosion, outburst; **una** — **de cólera** an explosion of anger.

explosionar [1a] *vti* to explode.

explosiva *nf* (*Ling*) plosive (consonant).

explosivo 1 *adj* explosive (*also fig*). 2 *nm* explosive; **alto** —, — **detonante**, — **de gran potencia**, — **rompedor** high explosive.

explotación *nf* exploitation; running, operation; (*Min etc*) working; — **a cielo abierto** opencast working, opencast mining; — **forestal** forestry; **en** — in operation; **gastos de** — operating costs, operating expenses.

explotar [1a] 1 *vt* (a) to exploit; *plant etc* to run, operate; *mine, seam* to work; *resources* to exploit, tap; to harness.
(b) (*pej*) *workers* to exploit; *situation* to exploit, make capital out of.
(c) (*Mil etc*) to explode.
2 *vi* (*Mil etc*) to explode; to go off; **explotaron 2 bombas** 2 bombs exploded; **cayó sin** — it fell but did not go off, it landed without going off.

exponente 1 *nmf* exponent.
2 *nm* (a) (*Math*) index, exponent.
(b) (*SAm*) model, (prime) example; **el tabaco cubano es** — **de calidad** Cuban tobacco is the best of its kind.

exponer [2r] 1 *vt* (a) to expose (*also Eccl, Phot*); *picture etc* to show, exhibit, put on show; *notice* to display, put up.
(b) *life* to risk.
(c) *child* to abandon.
(d) *argument* to expound; *idea* to explain, unfold; *facts* to set out, set forth, state; (*Law*) *charge* to bring.
2 **exponerse** *vr*: — **a** to expose oneself to, lay oneself open to; — **a** + *infin* to run the risk of + *ger*.

exportable *adj* exportable.

exportación *nf* (a) (*act*) export, exportation.
(b) export, exported article; exports; **géneros de** — exports, exported goods; **comercio de** — export trade.

exportador *nm*, **exportadora** *nf* exporter; shipper.

exportar [1a] *vt* to export.

exposición *nf* (a) (*act*) exposing, exposure; (*Phot*) exposure; (*of picture etc*) showing; **debido a una** — **excesiva al sol** because of undue exposure to sunlight; **no se puede permitir la** — **de tal cuadro** the showing of such a picture cannot be allowed.
(b) (*of facts etc*) statement, exposition; (*to authorities*) petition, claim.
(c) (*Art etc*) show, exhibition; (*Comm*) show, fair; — **canina** dog show; — **de modas** fashion show; — **universal** world fair.

exposímetro *nm* (*Phot*) exposure meter.

expósito 1 *adj*: **niño** — = 2 *nm*, **expósita** *nf* foundling.

expositor *nm*, **expositora** *nf* (*Art etc*) exhibitor; (*of theory*) exponent.

exprés *nm* (*SAm*) express train.

expresado *adj* above-mentioned; **según las cifras expresadas** according to these figures, according to the figures I (*etc*) have already quoted, according to the figures given earlier.

expresamente *adv* expressly; on purpose, deliberately; clearly, plainly; **no lo dijo** — he didn't say so in so many words.

expresar [1a] 1 *vt* to express; to voice, to word, phrase, put; to state, set forth; to quote; **expresa las opiniones de todos** he is voicing the opinions of us all; **estaba expresado de otro modo** it was worded differently; **el papel no lo expresa** the paper doesn't say so; **Vd deberá** — **el número del giro postal** you should quote (*or* give, state) the number of the postal order.
2 **expresarse** *vr* (a) to express oneself; **no se expresa bien** he doesn't express himself well.
(b) to be stated; **el número no se expresa** the number is not given, the number is not stated; **como abajo se expresa** as is stated below.

expresión *nf* (a) expression; **esta — de nuestro agradecimiento** this expression of our gratitude.
(b) (*Ling*) expression; — **familiar** colloquialism, conversational expression; **la — es poco clara** the expression is not very clear.
(c) —**es** greetings, regards; **¡mis —es a los amigos!** give my regards to everybody!, remember me to them!

expresionismo *nm* expressionism.

expresivamente *adv* (a) expressively. (b) tenderly, affectionately, warmly.

expresivo *adj* (a) expressive. (b) tender, affectionate, warm.

expreso 1 *adj* (a) express; specific, clear, exact.
(b) *train etc* fast.
2 *nm* (a) special messenger; **empresa de —** express company; **mandar algo por —** to send something by express (delivery).
(b) (*Rail etc*) fast train.

exprimelimones *nm, pl* **exprimelimones** lemon squeezer.

exprimidera *nf* squeezer.

exprimidor *nm* (a) squeezer; — **de limones** lemon squeezer. (b) (*for clothing*) wringer.

exprimir [3a] *vt* (a) to squeeze; to squeeze out, press out, express; *clothes* to wring out, squeeze dry; *lemon etc* to squeeze.
(b) — **a uno** (*fig*) to pick someone's brains.

exprofeso *adv* on purpose.

expropiación *nf* expropriation; commandeering.

expropiar [1b] *vt* to expropriate; to commandeer.

expuesto 1 *ptp of* **exponer; según lo arriba —** according to what has been stated (*or* set out, said) above.
2 *adj* (a) *place etc* exposed; dangerous.
(b) *picture etc* on show, on display, on view; **los artículos —s en el escaparate** the goods displayed in the window.
(c) **estar — a** to be exposed to, be open to; to be liable to.

expugnar [1a] *vt* to take by storm.

expulsanieves *nm, pl* **expulsanieves** snowplough.

expulsar [1a] *vt* to expel (*de* from), eject (*de* from), turn out (*de* of); *player* to send off; — **a uno a puntapiés** to kick someone out.

expulsión *nf* expulsion, ejection; (*Sport*) sending-off.

expulsor 1 *adj:* **asiento —** (*Aer*) ejector seat. **2** *nm* (*Tech*) ejector.

expurgar [1h] *vt* to expurgate.

expurgatorio *adj* expurgatory; **índice —** (*Eccl*) Index.

exquisitamente *adv* (a) exquisitely; deliciously, delightfully; excellently. (b) (*pej*) affectedly.

exquisitez *nf* (a) exquisiteness; excellence. (b) (*pej*) affectation.

exquisito *adj* (a) exquisite; delicious, delightful; excellent. (b) (*pej*) affected.

extasiar [1c] **1** *vt* to entrance, enrapture, captivate.
2 extasiarse *vr* to become entranced; to go into ecstasies, rhapsodize (*ante* over, about).

éxtasis *nm, pl* **éxtasis** ecstasy; rapture; (*of medium etc*) trance; **estar en el —** to be in ecstasy.

extático *adj* ecstatic, rapturous; **lo miró —** he looked at it ecstatically.

extender [2g] **1** *vt* (a) to extend; to enlarge, make bigger; to prolong; to stretch (out), expand; *cloth, map etc* to spread (out), open (out); to lay out; *cards* to lay down; *butter, face cream* to spread; *pile* to spread out; *war* to extend, widen, escalate; *knowledge* to extend, spread (*a* to).
(b) *document* to draw up; to write out; *cheque* to draw, make out; *receipt* to make out; *certificate* to issue.
2 extenderse *vr* (a) (*in space*) to extend; to stretch (out); to spread (out); to be, lie; **delante de nosotros se extendía la mar** before us the sea stretched away, the sea lay spread out before us; **sus terrenos se extienden sobre muchos kilómetros** his lands spread over many miles; **no se extiende más al oeste** it does not go any further west.
(b) (*place:* fig) to range, extend; **las posibilidades se extienden de A a Z** the possibilities range from A to Z.
(c) (*in time*) to extend, last (*a* to, till; *de* from).
(d) (*fig: custom, knowledge*) to spread, extend; (*war*) to escalate, widen, broaden; **su venganza se extendió hasta matar a las mujeres** in his vengeance he even killed the women; **la epidemia se extendió rápidamente** the epidemic spread rapidly.
(e) (*of amount*) — **a** to amount to, reach, go as high as; (*in size*) to run to; **el libro se extiende a 400 páginas** the book runs to 400 pages.
(f) (*fig: in speech*) to spread oneself; — **sobre un tema** to enlarge on a subject.

extendido *adj* (a) spread out, open; extended; *arms* outstretched, spread wide.
(b) *custom etc* widespread; prevalent, (*pej*) rife, rampant; *knowledge* widespread.

extensamente *adv* (a) extensively, widely. (b) fully, in full, with full details.

extensible *adj* extending, extensible.

extensión *nf* (a) (*act*) extension; stretching; spreading; — **de plazo** (*Comm*) extension.
(b) extent, size; spaciousness; **un solar de mayor —** a site of greater size, a site of larger area.
(c) (*of land, sea*) expanse, stretch; **por toda la — del paisaje** over the whole (expanse) of the countryside.
(d) (*of time*) length, duration; span.
(e) (*Mus*) range, compass.
(f) (*fig: of knowledge etc*) extent, range; (*of meaning*) range; (*of plan, programme*) scope.
(g) (*SAm: Tel*) extension.

extensivo *adj* extensive; **hacer — a** to extend to, apply to, make applicable to; **la crítica se hizo extensiva a toda la ciudad** the criticism applied to the whole city.

extenso *adj* (a) extensive; vast; *room etc* big, broad, spacious; *empire* far-flung.
(b) *knowledge etc* widespread; *report, story* full; **por —** in full, with full particulars, at length.

extenuación *nf* emaciation, weakness.

extenuado *adj* emaciated, wasted, weak.

extenuar [1e] **1** *vt* to emaciate, weaken. **2 extenuarse** *vr* to become emaciated, waste away; to get weak.

exterior 1 *adj* (a) exterior, external; outer; *appearance* outward; *room* outside, outward-facing.
(b) *relations, trade* foreign; **asuntos —es** foreign affairs; **comercio —** foreign trade, overseas trade.
2 *nm* (a) exterior, outside; outward appearance; **al —, por el —** on the outside; outwardly; **avanzar por el —** (*Racing*) to come up on the outside; **de — poco agradable** of unprepossessing appearance; **con el — pintado de azul** with the outside painted blue.
(b) foreign parts; **noticias del —** foreign news, overseas news, news from abroad; **comercio con el —** foreign trade, overseas trade.
(c) (*Sport*) wing, wing-forward, winger; — **derecho** outside-right; — **izquierdo** outside-left.

exterioridad *nf* (a) outward appearance, externals.
(b) —**es** (*fig*) pomp, show; formalities.

exteriorizar [1f] *vt* to express outwardly; to show, reveal.

exteriormente *adv* outwardly.

exterminar [1a] *vt* to exterminate.

exterminio *nm* extermination.

externamente *adv* externally; outwardly.

externalizar [1f] *vt* = **exteriorizar.**

externo 1 *adj* external, outside; outward. **2** *nm,* **externa** *nf* day pupil.

extinción *nf* (*all senses*) extinction.

extinguido *adj* (a) **estar —** (*fire*) to be out, be extinguished. (b) *animal, volcano* extinct.

extinguir [3d] **1** *vt* (a) *fire etc* to extinguish, put out; *mutiny* to put down.
(b) (*Bio*) to exterminate, wipe out.
(c) *debt etc* to wipe out.
2 extinguirse *vr* (a) (*fire*) to go out.
(b) (*Bio*) to die out, become extinct.

extinto *adj* (a) extinct. (b) (*Chi, Mex, RPl: euph*) dead, deceased.

extintor *nm* (*also — de incendios*) fire extinguisher.

extirpación *nf* (a) extirpation, eradication. (b) (*Med*) removal.

extirpar [1a] *vt* (a) to extirpate, eradicate, stamp out.
(b) (*Med*) to remove (surgically); **le extirparon el ojo derecho** they removed his right eye, he had his right eye removed.
(c) (*fam*) *person* to fire (*fam*); to get rid of.

extra¹ 1 *adj invar* extra; — **de** in addition to, on top of.
2 *nm* (a) (*on menu, bill*) extra; (*on pay*) bonus. (b) (*Typ*) extra, special edition. **3** *nmf* (*Cine*) extra.

extra² . . . extra . . .

extracción *nf* extraction; (*in lottery*) draw.

extracorto *adj wave* ultra-short.

extractar [1a] *vt* (a) to make extracts from. (b) to abridge, summarize.

extracto *nm* (a) (*Chem etc*) extract. (b) (*Lit*) abstract, summary.

extractor *nm* extractor.

extradición *nf* extradition; **crimen sujeto a —** extraditable offence.

extradicionar [1a] *vt* to extradite.

extraer [2p] *vt* to extract (*also Math, Med, Min*), take out, pull out.

extrafino *adj* superfine.

extrajudicial *adj* extrajudicial.

extralimitación *nf* abuse (of authority).

extralimitarse [1a] *vr* to go too far, exceed (*or* abuse) one's authority.

extramuros *adv* outside the city.

extranjería *nf* alien status.

extranjerismo *nm* foreign word (*or* phrase *etc*).

extranjerizante *adj* tending to favour foreign ways (*etc*); *word* foreign-looking, foreign-sounding.

extranjero 1 *adj* foreign; alien.

2 *nm*, **extranjera** *nf* foreigner; alien.

3 *nm* foreign country; foreign lands; **cosas del —** things from abroad; foreign things; **estar en el —** to be abroad, be overseas, be in foreign parts; **ir al — to** go abroad; **pasó 6 años en el —** he spent 6 years abroad; **no me siento a gusto en el —** I don't feel at ease abroad.

extrañamente *adv* strangely, oddly.

extrañamiento *nm* **(a)** estrangement (*de* from). **(b)** = **extrañeza.**

extrañar [1a] **1** *vt* **(a)** to find strange, find odd, wonder at; **extrañaba la falta de autobuses** she found the absence of buses strange; **me extrañaba que no hubieras venido** I was surprised that you should not have come; **apenas es de — que . . .** it is hardly surprising that . . .; **eso me extraña** that surprises me, that puzzles me, I find that odd; **me extraña su conducta** I am surprised at your behaviour.

(b) (*SAm*) to miss; to feel the lack of, regret the absence of; to yearn for.

2 extrañarse *vr* **(a)** to be amazed, be surprised (*de* at); to marvel (*de* at); **— de que . . .** to be surprised that . . .; to marvel that . . .

(b) to refuse.

(c) (*of friends etc*) to become estranged, grow apart.

extrañeza *nf* **(a)** strangeness, oddness, oddity.

(b) surprise, amazement; uneasiness; **me miró con —** he looked at me in surprise.

(c) estrangement, alienation.

extraño *adj* **(a)** strange, odd, queer; singular; **la extraña guerra** (1939) the phoney war; **es muy —** it's very odd; **¡cosa extraña!** how strange!, how odd!; **parece — que . . .** it seems strange that . . .

(b) extraneous (*a* to); **cosas extrañas a las que tratamos** things unconnected with those we handle; **país —** foreign country.

extrañoso *adj* (*Ec*) surprised.

extraoficial *adj* unofficial; informal.

extraoficialmente *adv* unofficially; informally.

extraordinariamente *adv* extraordinarily.

extraordinario 1 *adj* extraordinary; unusual; outstanding; *edition, number, discount etc* special; *charge* extra, supplementary; **por sus servicios —s** for his outstanding services; **no tiene nada de —** there's nothing special about it.

2 *nm* **(a)** treat; **invitar a uno a un —** to stand someone a treat.

(b) (*on menu*) special dish, extra dish.

(c) (*Typ*) special issue.

extraplano *nm* (*Mountaineering*) overhang.

extrarradio *nm* (*of town*) outer parts, outlying area.

extrasensorial *adj* extrasensory.

extraterrenal *adj* (*SAm*), **extraterreno** *adj* (*SAm*) unearthly, supernatural.

extraterritorial *adj* extraterritorial.

extravagancia *nf* **(a)** (*quality*) extravagance; outlandishness; oddness, strangeness.

(b) (*una —*) whim; vagary, peculiarity; **—s** nonsense; **tiene sus —s** he has his oddities.

extravagante *adj* extravagant; outlandish, eccentric; odd, strange, nonsensical.

extravagantemente *adv* extravagantly; eccentrically; oddly, strangely; nonsensically.

extravasarse [1a] *vr* to leak out, flow out; (*blood*) to ooze out.

extraviado *adj* lost; missing; *animal* lost, stray.

extraviar [1c] **1** *vt* **(a)** *person* to mislead, misdirect; to lead astray.

(b) *article* to lose, mislay, misplace.

(c) *money* (*pej*) to embezzle.

2 extraviarse *vr* **(a)** (*person*) to lose one's way, get lost; (*animal*) to stray, wander; (*letter*) to go astray, get lost in the post, miscarry.

(b) (*morally*) to go astray, err, fall into evil ways.

extravío *nm* **(a)** loss, misplacement, mislaying; straying; wandering; (*fig*) deviation (*from* de). **(b)** (*fig: moral*) misconduct, erring, evil ways.

extremadamente *adv* extremely, exceedingly; extraordinarily.

extremado *adj* extreme; excessive; intense; extremely good; extremely bad; **frío —** extreme cold; **con extremada delicadeza** with extraordinary delicacy.

extremar [1a] **1** *vt* to carry to extremes; to force the sense of, stretch the application of; to overdo; **sin — el sentimentalismo** without overdoing the sentimentality; **el dictador extrema sus incendiarios discursos** the dictator is making even more inflammatory speeches, the dictator is being still more outrageous in his inflammatory speeches.

2 extremarse *vr* to do one's utmost, exert oneself to the full, make every effort (*en* + *infin* to + *infin*).

extremaunción *nf* extreme unction.

extremeño 1 *adj* Extremaduran. **2** *nm*, **extremeña** *nf* Extremaduran.

extremidad *nf* **(a)** end, tip, extremity; edge, outermost part. **(b)** **—es** (*Anat*) extremities.

extremismo *nm* extremism.

extremista 1 *adj* extremist. **2** *nmf* extremist.

extremo 1 *adj* **(a)** (*of place*) extreme, last; end (*attr*); far, furthest, outer, outermost.

(b) (*in order*) last.

(c) (*fig*) extreme; utmost; critical, desperate; **en caso —** as a last resort, in an extreme case.

2 *nm* **(a)** end; extremity; **— muerto** dead end; **pasar de un — a otro** to go from one end to the other, (*fig*) go from one extreme to the other.

(b) (*fig*) highest point, highest degree; lowest point; extreme; **al — de, hasta el — de** to the point of; **con —** in the extreme; **por —** extremely; **hacer —s** to gush, behave effusively; **quedó reducido al — de ir a pie** he was reduced to (the extreme of) going on foot.

(c) (*fig*) point, matter, question; **ese — no se tocó en la discusión** that point was not dealt with in the discussion.

(d) (*fig*) great care.

(e) (*Sport*) wing; (*person*) wing-forward, winger; **— derecho** outside-right; **— izquierdo** outside-left.

Extremo Oriente *m* Far East.

extremoso *adj* **(a)** *person* gushing, effusive; vehement, extreme in his (*etc*) attitudes (*or* reactions). **(b)** *landscape etc* of extremes, of violent contrasts.

extrínseco *adj* extrinsic.

extrovertido 1 *adj* extrovert; outgoing. **2** *nm*, **extrovertida** *nf* extrovert.

exuberancia *nf* **(a)** exuberance. **(b)** (*Bot*) luxuriance, lushness. **(c)** fullness, buxomness.

exuberante *adj* **(a)** exuberant. **(b)** (*Bot*) luxuriant, lush. **(c)** *figure etc* full, buxom, well-covered.

exudación *nf* exudation.

exudar [1a] **1** *vt* to exude, ooze (*de* from). **2** *vi* to exude, ooze out.

exultación *nf* exultation.

exultar [1a] *vi* to exult.

exvoto *nm* votive offering.

eyector *nm* (*Tech*) ejector.

eyaculación *nf* (*Med*) ejaculation.

eyacular [1a] *vti* (*Med*) to ejaculate.

F

fabada nf (*Asturias*) rich stew of beans, pork etc.
fábrica nf (**a**) (*Tech*) factory; works, plant; mill; (*Col*) still, distillery; **— de cerveza** brewery; **— de conservas** canning plant; **— experimental** pilot plant; **— de gas** gasworks; **— de moneda** mint; **— de papel** paper mill; **marca de —** trademark; **precio en —** price ex-factory.
(**b**) (*act*) manufacture, making.
(**c**) make; **de — alemana** of German make.
(**d**) (*Archit*) building, structure; fabric; masonry.
fabricación nf manufacture, making, production; make; **— de coches** car manufacture; **— de tejas** tile making; **de — casera** home-made; **de — nacional** made in Spain (*or* Britain *etc*); **de — propia** made on the premises, our own make; **— en serie** mass production; **estar en —** to be in production.
fabricante nm manufacturer; maker; factory owner, mill owner.
fabricar [1g] vt (**a**) to manufacture, make; to put together; (*Archit*) to build, construct; **— en serie** to mass-produce.
(**b**) (*fig: pej*) to fabricate, invent, devise.
fabril adj manufacturing.
fabriquero nm (**a**) = **fabricante**. (**b**) (*Eccl*) church-warden. (**c**) (*Mex*) distillery operator (in a sugar mill).
fábula nf (**a**) (*Lit etc*) fable; myth; tale.
(**b**) (*Lit: of play*) story, plot, action.
(**c**) rumour; piece of gossip; fib.
(**d**) (*person*) talk of the town; laughing stock.
(**e**) (*fam*) **un negocio de —** a splendid piece of business; **es una cosa de —** it's fabulous (*fam*).
fabulario nm collection of fables.
fabulista nm writer of fables.
fabulosamente adv fabulously.
fabuloso adj (**a**) fabulous; mythical; imaginary, fictitious. (**b**) (*fam*) fabulous (*fam*), fantastic; **es francamente —** it's just fabulous.
facción nf (**a**) (*Pol*) faction; (*pej*) breakaway group; hostile group, group of troublemakers.
(**b**) (*of face*) feature; **de —es irregulares** with irregular features.
(**c**) (*Mil*) routine duty; **estar de —** to be on duty.
faccioso 1 adj factious; hostile; rebellious, seditious. 2 nm rebel; hostile person, troublemaker.
faceta nf facet (*also fig*).
facial adj facial; **valor —** face value.
fácil 1 adj (**a**) easy; simple, straightforward; **es — ver que...** it is easy to see that...; **— de hacer** easy to do.
(**b**) *style etc* easy, fluent; ready; (*pej*) facile, too easy; glib.
(**c**) *person* docile, compliant; *woman* easy, loose.
(**d**) **es — que venga** he is likely to come; **no veo muy — que...** I don't think it is at all likely that...
2 adv (*fam*) = **fácilmente**.
facilidad nf (**a**) ease, easiness, facility; simplicity; straightforwardness; **con la mayor —** with the greatest ease.
(**b**) fluency; **— de palabra** fluency in speech, readiness with which one talks.
(**c**) docility, compliant nature.
(**d**) **—es** facilities; **—es de crédito** credit facilities; **"—es de pago"** (*Comm*) "easy terms"; **las —es del puerto** the port facilities; **me dieron todas las —es** they gave me every facility.
facilitar [1a] vt (**a**) to facilitate, make easy; to expedite; to help to cause.
(**b**) to provide, furnish, supply; *document* to issue; **¿quién facilitó el dinero?** who provided the money?; **me facilitó un coche** he supplied me with a car, he provided the car.
(**c**) (*Arg*) **— algo** to make something out to be easier than it really is.

fácilmente adv easily; readily; simply, straight-forwardly.
facilongo adj (*Per*) rather easy.
facineroso 1 adj criminal; wicked, villainous. 2 nm criminal; wicked person, criminal.
facistol 1 adj (**a**) (*Ant, Col, Mex, Ven*) insolent.
(**b**) (*Cu, PR*) full of jokes; given to practical joking.
2 nm (**a**) (*Eccl*) lectern; choir desk.
(**b**) (*Ant, Col, Mex, Ven*) insolent person; braggart.
facistolería nf (*Ant, Col, Mex, Ven*) insolence; boastfulness, conceit.
facón nm (*RPl*) long knife, gaucho knife.
facsímil 1 adj (**a**) (*Ant, Col, Mex, Ven*) facsimile. 2 nm facsimile.
factible adj feasible; workable, practical.
facticio adj artificial, factitious.
factor nm (**a**) (*Math*) factor.
(**b**) factor, element; **— determinante** determining factor; **— humano** human factor; **— de seguridad** safety factor; **el — suerte** the luck factor, the element of chance; **es un nuevo — de la situación** it is a new factor in the situation.
(**c**) (*Comm*) agent, factor; commission merchant.
(**d**) (*Rail*) clerk; freight agent.
factoría nf (**a**) (*Comm*) trading post; agency. (**b**) (*angl*) factory; (*Ec, Per*) foundry.
factótum nm (**a**) factotum; jack-of-all-trades. (**b**) (*pej*) busybody.
factual adj factual; based on fact(s), consisting of facts.
factura nf (**a**) (*Comm*) bill, invoice; **— simulada** pro forma invoice; **según —** as per invoice; **pasar —, presentar —** to send an invoice. (**b**) (*Arg*) buns, cakes.
facturación nm (**a**) (*Comm*) invoicing. (**b**) (*Rail*) registration.
facturar [1a] vt (**a**) (*Comm*) to invoice. (**b**) (*Rail*) *luggage* to register, check (*US*).
facultad nf (**a**) faculty.
(**b**) power, authority; permission; **tener la — de + infin** to have the power to + infin; **tener — para + infin** to be authorized to + infin.
(**c**) **—es** faculties, powers; **—es del alma** mental powers.
(**d**) (*Univ*) faculty, school; **F— de Filosofía y Letras** Faculty of Arts; **F— de Derecho** Faculty of Law.
(**e**) (*Univ: loosely*) university; **está en la —** he's at the university; **quedarse a comer en la —** to lunch at the university.
facultar [1a] vt to authorize, empower; **— a uno para hacer algo** to empower someone to do something.
facultativo 1 adj (**a**) optional.
(**b**) (*Univ*) faculty (*attr*).
(**c**) professional; (*Med*) medical; **dictamen —** medical report; **prescripción facultativa** medical prescription.
2 nm doctor, practitioner.
facundia nf eloquence.
facundo adj eloquent.
facha nf (**a**) (*fam*) look, appearance; face; (*person*) sight, object; **— a —** face to face; **estar hecho una —** to look a sight, look terrible (*fam*).
(**b**) (*Naut*) **ponerse en —** to lie to.
fachada nf (**a**) (*Archit*) façade, front; (*as measurement etc*) frontage; **con — al parque** looking towards the park, overlooking the park; **con 15 metros de —** with a frontage of 15 metres.
(**b**) (*Typ*) frontispiece.
(**c**) (*fig*) façade, outward show; **no tiene más que —** it's all just show with him; **tener mucha —** to be all show and no substance.
fachado adj: **bien —** good-looking; **mal —** ugly, plain.

fachenda (fam) **1** nf swank (fam), conceit. **2** nm swank (fam), show-off (fam).

fachendear [1a] vi (fam) to swank (fam), show off.

fachendista adj (fam), **fachendón** adj (fam), **fachendoso** adj (fam) swanky (fam), conceited, snooty (fam).

fachinal nm (Arg) swamp, swampy place.

fachoso adj (a) (SAm) = **fachendista**. (b) ridiculous, odd-looking. (c) (Arg, Per) elegant, natty.

faena nf (a) task, job, piece of work; duty; (fam) tough job, sweat, fag; (Mil) fatigue; — **doméstica** housework; —s (at home) chores; **esto es una** — this is a tough one, this is a real sweat; **estar de** — to be at work; **estar en plena** — to be hard at work; **tener mucha** — to be terribly busy.
(b) (Ant, Guat, Mex) extra work, overtime.
(c) (fam: also **mala** —) dirty trick; **hacer una — a uno** to play a dirty trick on someone; **¡menuda — la que me hizo!** a fine thing he did to me!
(d) (Taur) play with the cape; performance; **hizo una — maravillosa** he gave a splendid performance (with the cape).
(e) (Chi) gang of workers; working place.

faenar [1a] (RPl) **1** vi to work, labour. **2** vt cattle to slaughter and dress; wood to cut, work.

faenero nm (Chi) farmhand, farm worker.

fafarechero 1 adj (fam) swanky (fam), conceited. **2** nm (fam) swank (fam), show-off (fam).

failear [1a] vt (CAm, RPl: angl) to file.

fain adj (CAm: angl) fine.

fainada nf (Cu) silly thing, foolish act.

faino adj (Cu) rude; coarse, rough.

faisán nm pheasant.

faite (SAm: angl) **1** adj tough, strong.
2 nm (a) tough man, good fighter.
(b) (pej) quarrelsome sort, brawler.

faitear [1a] vi (SAm: angl) to fight (with fists).

faja nf (a) (of cloth) strip, band; (garment) sash, belt; girdle, corset; (Mil) sash; (Med) bandage, support.
(b) (Post) wrapper (also — **postal**).
(c) (fig) strip, belt, zone; **una estrecha — de terreno** a narrow strip of land.
(d) (Aut) lane.
(e) (Radio, TV) channel.
(f) (Archit) band, fascia.
(g) (Mex: Typ) spine.

fajada nf (a) (Ant) attack, rush. (b) (Arg) beating. (c) (Ven) disappointment.

fajar [1a] **1** vt (a) to wrap; to swathe; to bandage; (Post) to wrap up, put a wrapper on.
(b) (SAm) to attack, lay into (fam); to bash (fam), beat; to thrash; woman (fam) to try to seduce.
(c) (Arg, Mex) **¡que lo fajen!** tell him to wrap up! (sl).
2 vi: — **con uno** (fam) to go for someone, lay into someone (fam).
3 fajarse vr (a) to put on one's belt (or sash etc); (fig) to tighten one's belt.
(b) (SAm) to come to blows; to fight, bash each other (fam); **los boxeadores se fajaron duro** the boxers really laid into each other (fam).

fajilla nf (Arg: Post) wrapper.

fajín nm (Mil) sash.

fajina nf (a) (Agr) shock, pile, rick.
(b) kindling, brushwood, faggots.
(c) (Mil) bugle call, (esp) call to mess.
(d) (Arg) task, job (to be done quickly); hard work; **tenemos mucha** — we've a lot to do, we've a tough job on here.
(e) (Cu) extra work, overtime.
(f) (Arg) **ropa de** — working clothes; **uniforme de** — ordinary uniform.

fajo nm (a) (of papers) bundle, sheaf; (of notes) roll, wad. (b) —s swaddling clothes. (c) (Mex) blow. (d) (SAm) swig (of liquor) (fam).

falacia nf (a) deceit, fraud. (b) deceitfulness.

falange nf (a) (Mil) phalanx; **F**— Spanish fascist party. (b) (Anat) phalange.

falangista 1 adj Falangist. **2** nmf Falangist.

falanjear [1a] vt (sl) to pinch (fam), swipe (sl).

falaropo nm phalarope.

falaz adj person deceitful; treacherous; doctrine etc fallacious; appearance etc deceptive, misleading.

falca nf (a) (Col, Mex, Ven) river ferryboat. (b) (Bol) small still.

falda nf (a) (dress) skirt; (Sew) flap, fold; — **escocesa** kilt; **estar cosido a las** —s **de su madre** to be tied to mother's apron strings; **estar cosido a las** —s **de su mujer** to be dominated by one's wife; **haberse criado bajo las** —s **de mamá** to have led a very sheltered life.

(b) (Anat) lap; **sentarse en la — de una** to sit on someone's lap.
(c) (fam: person) bird (sl), dame (sl); **ser muy aficionado a** —s to be fond of the ladies.
(d) (Geog) slope, hillside; foot, bottom (of a slope); **a la — de la montaña** at the foot of the mountain.

faldellín nm (a) short skirt; underskirt. (b) (Ant, Ven) christening robe.

faldero adj: **perro** — lapdog; **hombre** — ladies' man; **es muy** — he's a great one for the ladies.

faldicorto adj short-skirted.

faldillas nfpl coattails.

faldón nm (a) (of dress) tail, skirt; coattails; (Sew) flap. (b) (Archit) gable.

falencia nf (a) deceit; error, mistake. (b) (SAm) bankruptcy.

falena nf moth.

falibilidad nf fallibility.

falible adj fallible.

fálico adj phallic.

falo nm phallus.

falsamente adv falsely; unsoundly, mistakenly; insincerely, dishonestly.

falsario nm, **falsaria** nf (a) falsifier; liar. (b) forger, counterfeiter.

falseador nm, **falseadora** nf forger, counterfeiter.

falsear [1a] **1** vt to falsify; to forge, counterfeit, fake; to fiddle (with), juggle with; lock to pick; (Tech) to bevel. **2** vi (a) to buckle, sag, give way; (fig) to flag, slacken. (b) (Mus) to be out of tune.

falsedad nf (a) (in general) falseness; falsity; unsoundness; hollowness, insincerity; dishonesty; treachery, deceit. (b) (una —) falsehood.

falsete nm (a) (Tech) plug, bung. (b) (Mus) falsetto.

falsía nf falseness, duplicity.

falsificación nf (a) (act) falsification, forging. (b) (object) forgery; fabrication.

falsificador nm, **falsificadora** nf forger, counterfeiter.

falsificar [1g] vt to falsify; coin to counterfeit; picture, stamp etc to forge, fake; election, results etc to rig, fiddle (with), juggle with.

falso 1 adj (a) false; coin false, counterfeit, bad, dud; picture, stamp etc forged, fake; bogus, sham; jewel imitation (attr); horse, mule vicious; statement false; opinion, theory unsound; mistaken; evidence false, untrue; perjured; person hollow, insincere; dishonest; friend false, treacherous.
(b) **en** — falsely; without proper support; **coger a uno en** — to catch someone in a lie; **jurar en** — to commit perjury; **dar un paso en** — to step on something that is not there, trip; (fig) to take a false step.
2 nm (CAm, Mex) false evidence.

falta nf (a) lack, want, need; absence; shortage; (Law) default; non-, eg — **de asistencia** non-attendance; — **de pago** non-payment; **a** — **de** (as prep) failing; **a** — **de, por** — **de** for want of, for lack of; — **de dinero** shortage of money; — **de peso** short weight; — **de respeto** lack of respect, disrespect; — **de seriedad** frivolity; irresponsibility; **hacer** — to be lacking, be wanting; to be missed; **el hombre que hace** — the right man, the man we (etc) want; **eso me hace (mucha)** — I need it (badly); **me hizo Vd mucha** — I missed you a lot; **aquí no haces** — you are not needed here; **¡— hacía!** and about time too!; **hacer** — + infin to be necessary to + infin; **hace** — **pintarlo** somebody ought to paint it, it needs painting.
(b) failure, shortcoming; fault, mistake; misdeed; (in manufacture etc) flaw, defect, fault; (Mech) trouble; — **de ortografía** spelling mistake; — **garrafal** stupid mistake; gross blunder; **sin** — without fail; **sacar** —s **a uno** to point out someone's defects.
(c) (Sport) foul, infringement; (Tennis) fault; **cometer una** — **contra uno** to commit a foul on someone, foul someone.

faltar [1a] **1** vt (Arg, Mex, Ven) to be rude to, show disrespect for.
2 vi (a) to be lacking, be wanting; **le falta dinero** he lacks money, he needs money; **no le faltan buenas cualidades** he is not lacking in good qualities; **nos falta tiempo para hacerlo** we lack the time to do it, we are short of time to do it, we haven't the time to do it; **lo que falta es libros** what is lacking is books.
(b) to be absent, be missing (de from); **faltaron 3 de la reunión** there were 3 missing (or absent) from the meeting; — **a clase** to miss class, not go to class; — **a una cita** to miss an appointment, break an appointment, not turn up for a date; — **al trabajo** to stay away from work; **¿falta algo?** is

anything missing?; **faltan 9** there are 9 missing, we are 9 short; **no falta quien opina que . . .** there are some who think that **. . .**; **en 8 años no he faltado ni una sola vez** I've not missed once in 8 years.

(c) (*of gun, mechanism, supply etc*) to fail, go wrong, break down.

(d) — **a principle** to be false to; **person** to fail; to offend; — **a la decencia** to offend against decency; — **a una promesa** to break a promise, go back on one's word; — **al respeto** to be disrespectful (*a* to); — **a la verdad** to lie, be untruthful; — **en los pagos** to default on one's payments.

(e) — **en hacer algo** to fail to do something; **no faltaré en comunicárselo** I shall not fail to tell him.

(f) (*of quantity, time etc*) **faltan pocos minutos para el comienzo** it's only a few minutes to go to the start; **faltan 3 semanas para las elecciones** there are 3 weeks to go to the election, the election is 3 weeks off; **falta poco para las 8** it's nearly 8 o'clock, it's getting on for 8 o'clock; **falta poco para terminar** it's almost over; it's almost finished; **falta todavía por hacer** it remains to be done, it is still to be done.

(g) (*idioms*) **¡no faltaba más!** it's the limit!; it's the last straw!; **¡lo que faltaba!**, **¡es lo único que faltaba!** that's the very end!

(h) (*esp SAm*) to be rude, be disrespectful.

falto *adj* (a) short, deficient, lacking; **estar — de** to be short of; *quality etc* to be wanting in, be lacking in; **estar — de personal** to be short-handed.

(b) (*morally*) poor, wretched, mean.

(c) (*Col*) fatuous, vain.

faltón *adj* (a) remiss, neglectful, unreliable (about carrying out duties); (*SAm*) slack (about work), often absent. (b) (*Andalusia, Cu*) disrespectful.

faltoso *adj* (a) (*CAm, Mex*)=**faltón** (a). (b) (*CAm, Mex*) disrespectful. (c) (*Col*) quarrelsome.

faltriquera *nf* fob, watch pocket; handbag; **rascarse la —** to dig into one's pocket (*fig*).

falúa *nf* launch; tender.

falla *nf* (a) fault, defect; failure; (*SAm*) lack, shortage; (*SAm*) failure to keep one's promises; — **en caja** cash shortage; **géneros que tienen —s** (*Comm*) defective goods, seconds.

(b) (*Geol*) fault.

(c) (*Mech*) failure, breakdown; — **de encendido** (*Aut*) ignition fault; — **de tiro** (*Mil*) misfire.

(d) (*Col: Cards*) void.

fallada *nf* (*Cards*) ruff, trumping.

fallar [1a] **1** *vt* (a) (*Cards*) to ruff, trump.

(b) (*Law*) to pronounce sentence on.

2 *vi* (a) (*of memory, crop, brakes etc*) to fail; (*of plans*) to go wrong, miscarry; (*of shot*) to miss, go astray; (*of rope, support etc*) to break, snap, give way; (*of gun*) to misfire, fail to go off; (*of motor*) to miss; — **a uno** to fail someone, let someone down; **algo le falla a X** there's something up with X; **algo falló en sus planes** something went wrong with his plans.

(b) (*Law*) to pronounce sentence, pass judgement.

(c) (*Cards*) to ruff, trump (in).

falleba *nf* bolt.

fallecer [2d] *vi* (a) to pass away, die. (b) to end, run out, expire.

fallecido 1 *adj* late. **2** *nm*, **fallecida** *nf* deceased, person who has lately died.

fallecimiento *nm* decease, demise, passing.

fallero *adj* (*Chi*) slack (about work), often absent.

fallido 1 *adj* (a) *effort etc* unsuccessful; *hope* disappointed; (*Mech, Mil etc*) dud; *debt* bad, uncollectable.

(b) (*Comm*) bankrupt.

2 *nm* bankrupt.

fallir [3a] *vi* (a) to fail. (b) to end, run out, expire. (c) (*Ven*) to go bankrupt.

fallo 1 *adj* (a) **estar —** (*Cards*) to be out of a suit; **estar — de** (*Cards*) to be out of, have a void in; (*Mex, PR*) to lack, be without.

(b) (*Chi*) fatuous, stupid.

2 *nm* (a) (*Mech*) failure, trouble, breakdown; (*Med*) failure; (*Sport*) mistake, tactical error, mix-up; **debido a un —** **de los frenos** because of a brake failure; — **de corazón** heart failure.

(b) (*Cards*) void; **tener un — a corazones** to have a void in hearts.

(c) (*Law etc*) sentence, verdict; decision, ruling; findings.

falluto *adj* (*RPl*) (a) unsuccessful, failed. (b) untrustworthy.

fama *nf* (a) fame; reputation, repute; **mala —** bad reputation; notoriety; **de mala —** of ill fame; **el libro que le dio —** the book which made him famous,

the book which made his name; **tener — de gran cazador** to have the reputation of being a great hunter, be known as a great hunter; **tiene — de poco escrupuloso** he is thought to be unscrupulous.

(b) report, rumour; **corre la — de que . . .** it is rumoured that . . .

famélico *adj* starving, famished; **los —s** the starving.

familia *nf* (a) family; household; — **política** relatives by marriage, in-laws; **de buena —** of good family; **tener mucha —** to have lots of children; **ser como de la —** to be one of the family; **eso viene de —** that runs in the family.

(b) (*Ant, Col, Mex, Per*) relative.

(c) (*Typ*) fount.

familiar 1 *adj* (a) family (*attr*); **los lazos —es** the family bond, the ties of blood; **subsidio —** family allowance; **dioses —es** household gods.

(b) familiar (*a* to).

(c) homely, domestic; informal; plain, ordinary; (*Ling*) colloquial, familiar; *style* familiar.

2 *nmf* relative, relation; member of the household; intimate friend, close acquaintance.

familiaridad *nf* familiarity (*con* with); homeliness; informality; familiarities.

familiarizar [1f] **1** *vt* to familiarize, acquaint (*con* with). **2 familiarizarse** *vr*: — **con** to familiarize oneself with, make oneself familiar with, get to know.

famoso *adj* (a) famous (*por* for). (b) (*fam*) famous, great (*fam*), splendid.

fan *nmf, pl* **fans** (*Cine, Mus etc: angl*) fan (*fam*).

fanal *nm* (a) lighthouse; (*harbour*) beacon; lantern; (*Aut*) headlight. (b) bell glass; lampshade.

fanático 1 *adj* fanatical.

2 *nm* fanatic; bigot; (*Cine, Sport etc*) fan (*fam*), supporter, admirer; **es un — del aeromodelismo** he's an aeromodelling fiend (*or* enthusiast); **los —s de la estrella** the star's fans, the star's admirers.

fanatismo *nm* fanaticism; bigotry; enthusiasm.

fandango *nm* (a) (*Mus*) fandango. (b) (*fam*) row, shindy; **se armó un —** there was a great row. (c) (*SAm*) spree (*fam*), carousal.

fandanguear [1a] *vi* (*Arg*) to carouse, live it up (*fam*).

fané *adj* (*SAm: gall*) messed-up, crumpled, rumpled.

fanega *nf* (a) *grain measure* (=Spain 1.58 bushels, Mex 2.57 bushels, Arg 3.89 bushels). (b) *land measure* (=Spain 1.59 acres, Ven 1.73 acres).

fanfarrear [1a] *vi*=**fanfarronear**.

fanfarria *nf* (a) bluster, bravado, bragging. (b) (*Mus*) fanfare.

fanfarrón 1 *adj* blustering, boastful; flashy. **2** *nm* blusterer, braggart; bully; flashy type.

fanfarronada *nf* bluster, bravado, swagger; bluff.

fanfarronear [1a] *vi* to bluster, boast, swagger; to rant; to talk big (*sl*), bluff.

fanfarronería *nf* blustering, boasting, bragging; ranting; big talk, bluffing.

fangal *nm* bog; quagmire, muddy place.

fango *nm* mud, mire; slush; (*fig*) mire, dirt.

fangoso *adj* muddy, miry; slushy.

fanguero 1 *adj* (*Arg*) *animal, player* suited to heavy going. **2** *nm* (*Cu, PR, Mex*)=**fango, fangal**.

fanta-ciencia *nf* science-fiction.

fantasear [1a] *vi* to dream, let one's imagination run free.

fantaseo *nm* (*SAm*) dreaming, imagining.

fantasía *nf* (a) (*faculty*) fantasy, imagination, fancy; **es obra de la —** it is a work of the imagination; **dejar correr la —** to let one's imagination roam.

(b) (*Art, Lit etc*) fantasy; fantastic tale; work of the imagination; (*Mus*) fantasia.

(c) (**una —**) whim, fancy.

(d) (*fam*) conceit, vanity, airs.

(e) (*Comm*) **de —** fancy; **joyas de —** imitation jewellery.

(f) (*Ven*) **tocar por —** to play by ear.

fantasioso *adj* (*fam*) vain, conceited, stuck-up (*fam*); **¡fantasiosa!** you vain thing!

fantasma 1 *nm* (a) ghost, phantom, apparition. (b) solemn and vain person. (c) (*TV*) ghost image. **2** *nf* bogey.

fantasmagoría *nf* phantasmagoria.

fantasmagórico *adj* phantasmagoric.

fantasmal *adj* ghostly; phantom (*attr*).

fantásticamente *adv* fantastically; weirdly; fancifully.

fantástico *adj* (a) fantastic; weird, unreal; fanciful, whimsical. (b) vain. (c) (*Arg*) capricious. (d) (*Chi*) bragging, swaggering.

fantoche *nm* (a) puppet, marionette. (b) (*fam*) mediocrity, man of straw, nonentity.

fantochesco *adj* puppet-like.

faquín *nm* porter, errand boy.

faquir *nm* fakir.

farabute *nm* (*Arg*) rogue; untrustworthy person; poor wretch.

farallón *nm* (*Geog*) steep rock, cliff; headland; (*Geol*) outcrop; (*Arg*, *Chi*) rocky peak.

faramalla *nf* (*fam*) (a) blarney, humbug, claptrap; trash. (b) empty show, sham. (c) (*Chi*) bragging, boasting.

faramallear [1a] *vi* (*Chi*, *Mex*) to brag, boast.

faramallero *adj* (*Chi*, *Mex*) bragging, boastful.

farándula *nf* (a) (*Theat*: *Hist*) troupe of strolling players.
(b) (*fam*) humbug, claptrap; pack of lies; confidence trick, confidence game (*US*), swindle; wicked gossip.

farandulero 1 *adj* (a) (*Theat*: *Hist*) theatre (*attr*).
(b) (*SAm*) = **farolero**.
2 *nm*, **farandulera** *nf* (a) (*Theat*: *Hist*) strolling player.
(b) confidence trickster, confidence man (*US*), swindler, rogue.

Faraón *m* Pharaoh.

faraónico *adj* Pharaonic.

faraute *nm* (a) (*arch*) herald. (b) (*fam*) busybody.

fardel *nm* (a) bag, knapsack; ragbag. (b) bundle.

fardo *nm* bundle; bale, pack; (*fig*) burden.

farfulla 1 *nf* (*fam*) (a) splutter, jabber. (b) = **faramalla** (a). (c) (*Chi*, *Ec*, *Per*, *PR*) bragging, boasting. 2 *nmf* (*fam*) jabberer, gabbler.

farfullador *adj* spluttering; jabbering; gabbling.

farfullar [1a] *vi* to splutter; to jabber, gabble.

farfullero *adj* (*Per*, *PR*, *SD*) (a) = **farfullador**. (b) = **fanfarrón**.

farináceo *adj* starchy, farinaceous.

faringe *nf* pharynx.

faringitis *nf* pharyngitis.

fariña *nf* (*Per*, *RPl*) manioc gratings.

farisaico *adj* Pharisaic(al), hypocritical; smug.

fariseo *nm* Pharisee, hypocrite; smug sort.

farmacéutico 1 *adj* pharmaceutical. 2 *nm* chemist, pharmacist.

farmacia *nf* (a) pharmacy. (b) chemist's (shop), drugstore (*US*); — **de guardia** all-night chemist's.

fármaco *nm* drug.

farmacológico *adj* pharmacological.

farmacología *nf* pharmacology.

farmacólogo *nm* pharmacologist.

farmacopea *nf* pharmacopoeia.

faro 1 *nm* (a) (*Naut*) lighthouse; beacon; — **aéreo** air beacon.
(b) (*Naut*) light, lantern; (*Aut*) headlamp, headlight; — **lateral** sidelight; — **piloto**, — **trasero** rear light, tail light; — **de marcha atrás** reversing light.
2 *as adj* (*fam*): **idea** — bright idea, brilliant idea.

farol *nm* (a) lantern, lamp; (*Rail*) headlamp; — **de calle**, — **público** street lamp; — **de viento** hurricane lamp; *see* **adelante** (d).
(b) lamppost; (*Gymnastics*) handstand.
(c) wrapping of cigarette packet.
(d) —**es** (*SAm*: *fig*) eyes.
(e) (*Arg*, *Bol*) bay window, glassed-in balcony.
(f) (*fam*) swank (*fam*); **marcarse un** — to shoot a line (*fam*), swank, brag; **tiene mucho** — he's terribly swanky (*fam*).

farola *nf* street lamp; lamppost.

farolazo *nm* (*CAm*, *Mex*) swig of liquor (*fam*).

farolear [1a] *vi* (*fam*) to swank (*fam*), strut around; to brag.

farolero 1 *adj* (*fam*) vain, stuck-up (*fam*), swanky (*fam*). 2 *nm* (a) lamppost. (b) lamp maker; lamplighter. (c) (*fam*) swank (*fam*); braggart.

farolillo *nm* (a) (*Elec*) fairy light, Chinese lantern. (b) (*Bot*) Canterbury bell.

farra[1] *nf* (*Fish*) salmon trout.

farra[2] *nf* (a) (*SAm*) spree (*fam*), party, carousal. (b) (*RPl*) mockery, teasing; **tomar a uno para la** — to pull someone's leg.

fárrago *nm* medley, hotchpotch.

farrear [1a] 1 *vi* (*SAm*) to make merry, carouse. 2 **farrearse** *vr* (a) (*RPl*) — **de uno** to tease someone.
(b) — **el dinero** to spend one's money on drink.

farrero 1 *adj* (*Chi*, *Per*) merry; fun-loving. 2 *nm*, **farrera** *nf* reveller.

farrista *adj* (*Chi*, *RPl*) dissipated, hard-drinking; too boisterous, too rowdy.

farruto *adj* (*Arg*, *Bol*, *Chi*) sickly, weak.

farsa *nf* (a) (*Theat*) farce; (*pej*) bad play, crude play. (b) (*fig*) humbug, sham, masquerade.

farsante *nm* (*fam*) humbug, fraud, fake.

farsear [1a] *vi* (*Arg*, *CAm*, *Chi*) to joke.

fas: por — **o por nefas** by hook or by crook, rightly or wrongly; at any cost.

fascículo *nm* fascicule, part.

fascinación *nf* fascination.

fascinador *adj* fascinating.

fascinar [1a] *vti* to fascinate; to captivate; to bewitch, cast the evil eye on.

fascismo *nm* fascism.

fascista 1 *adj* fascist. 2 *nmf* fascist.

fase *nf* (a) phase, stage; **estar fuera de** — to be out of phase. (b) (*Astron*, *Bio*, *Elec*) phase.

fastidiar [1b] 1 *vt* (a) to annoy, bother, vex; to bore; to upset, disgust, sicken, irk; **eso me fastidia terriblemente** it annoys me no end; it upsets me terribly; **¡no fastidies!** you can't mean it!, you're kidding!; **¡no me fastidies!** stop bothering me!
(b) to harm, damage.
2 **fastidiarse** *vr* (a) to get cross; to get bored; **¡fastídiate!** (*fam*) get lost! (*fam*); **¡que se fastidie!** (*fam*) tell him to go to blazes!
(b) to harm oneself.

fastidio *nm* (a) annoyance, bother, nuisance; **¡qué** —! what a nuisance! (b) boredom. (c) disgust, repugnance.

fastidioso *adj* (a) annoying, bothersome, vexing; tedious, tiresome, boring; irksome; sickening. (b) (*SAm*: *angl*) fastidious.

fasto *nm* (a) pomp, pageantry. (b) —**s** (*Lit*) annals.

fastuosamente *adv* magnificently, splendidly; lavishly; pompously.

fastuoso *adj* magnificent, splendid; lavish; pompous.

fatal *adj* (a) fatal; ill-fated, disastrous.
(b) irrevocable, unavoidable.
(c) (*fam*) awful (*fam*), ghastly (*fam*), rotten (*fam*); **tiene un ⸿inglés** — he speaks awful English; **la obra fue** — the play was rotten.

fatalidad *nf* (a) fate, fatality. (b) mischance, misfortune, ill-luck.

fatalismo *nm* fatalism.

fatalista 1 *adj* fatalistic. 2 *nmf* fatalist.

fatalizarse [1f] *vr* (a) (*Col*) to commit a grave crime. (b) (*Chi*) to suffer grave harm; (*Per*) to suffer a series of misfortunes (as a punishment for a wrong committed).

fatalmente *adv* (a) fatally; disastrously. (b) unavoidably, irremediably.

fatídicamente *adv* (a) prophetically. (b) fatefully, ominously.

fatídico *adj* (a) prophetic. (b) fateful, ominous.

fatiga *nf* (a) fatigue, weariness; — **cerebral** brain-fag, mental fatigue. (b) (*Tech*) fatigue; — **del metal** metal fatigue. (c) —**s** hardships, troubles, toils.

fatigadamente *adv* with difficulty, wearily.

fatigar [1h] 1 *vt* (a) to tire, weary, fatigue. (b) to annoy. 2 **fatigarse** *vr* to tire, get tired, grow weary; — **de andar** to wear oneself out walking.

fatigosamente *adv* painfully, with difficulty.

fatigoso *adj* (a) tiring, exhausting, fatiguing. (b) laboured, difficult; **respiración fatigosa** laboured breathing. (c) trying, tiresome.

fatuidad *nf* (a) fatuity, foolishness, inanity. (b) conceit.

fatuo *adj* (a) fatuous, foolish, inane. (b) conceited; *see* **fuego**.

fauces *nfpl* (*Anat*) fauces, gullet; (*SAm*) tusks, teeth; (*fig*) jaws, maw.

fauna *nf* fauna.

fauno *nm* faun.

Fausto *m* Faust.

fausto *nm* splendour, pomp, magnificence.

fautor *nm* accomplice, helper; instigator.

favor *nm* (a) favour, service, good turn, kindness; —**es** (*of woman*) favours; **entrada de** — complimentary ticket; **es de** — it's complimentary, it's free; **por** — please; **no es** —, **no hay** — (*in reply to "please"*) think nothing of it, it's no trouble; **haga el** — **de esperar** please wait, kindly wait; **haga de no fumar** (*severely*) please be so good as to refrain from smoking; **¿me hace el** — **de pasar la sal?** would you please pass the salt?, would you be so kind as to pass the salt?; — **que Vd me hace** you're very kind, it's good of you; — **de venir puntualmente** (*Mex etc*) please be punctual.
(b) favour, good graces; **estar en** — to be in favour; **gozar de** — **cerca de uno** to be in favour with someone.
(c) protection, support; **gracias al** — **del rey** thanks to the king's protection.
(d) (*symbol*) favour; token; gift.
(e) **a** — **de** in favour of; on behalf of; (*Comm*) to the order of; **a** — **de la marea** helped by the tide, taking advantage of the tide; **a** — **de la noche** under the cover of night, helped by the darkness.

favorable *adj* favourable; auspicious; advantageous.

favorablemente *adv* favourably; auspiciously; advantageously.

favorecedor *adj dress etc* becoming.

favorecer [2d] *vt* (a) to favour; to help, protect; to treat favourably; (*of fortune*) to favour, smile on. (b) (*of dress*) to become, flatter, look well on; (*of picture*) to flatter.

favorecido *adj* favoured; **trato de nación más favorecida** (*Comm*) most-favoured nation treatment.

favoritismo *nm* favouritism.

favorito 1 *adj* favourite. **2** *nm*, **favorita** *nf* favourite (*also Sport*).

faz *nf* (a) (*lit, fig*) face; front; aspect; — **a** — face to face; — **de la tierra** face of the earth. (b) (*of coin*) obverse.

fe *nf* (a) (*Rel*) faith (*en* in); **la** — **católica** the Catholic faith.
(b) faith, belief; reliance; **de buena** — in good faith; (*Law*) bona fide; **obrar de buena** — to act in good faith; **mala** — bad faith; **a** — **mía, por mi** — (*arch*) by my faith, upon my honour; **dar** — **a, prestar** — **a** to believe, credit, place reliance on; **tener** — **en** to have faith in, believe in.
(c) assurance; **a** — in truth; **en** — **de lo cual** in witness whereof; **dar** — **de** to testify to, bear witness to.
(d) fidelity, loyalty.
(e) certificate; — **de bautismo** certificate of baptism; — **de erratas** (*Typ*) list of errata.

fealdad *nf* ugliness, hideousness.

feamente *adj* hideously.

Febo *m* Phoebus.

febrero *nm* February.

febril *adj* (a) (*Med*) fevered, feverish. (b) (*fig*) feverish, hectic.

febrilmente *adv* (*fig*) feverishly, hectically.

fécula *nf* starch.

feculento *adj* starchy.

fecundación *nf* fertilization; — **artificial** artificial insemination.

fecundar [1a] *vt* to fertilize; — **por fertilización cruzada** to cross-fertilize.

fecundidad *nf* (a) fertility; fecundity. (b) (*fig*) fruitfulness, productiveness.

fecundizar [1f] *vt* to fertilize.

fecundo *adj* (a) fertile; fecund; prolific.
(b) (*fig*) fruitful; copious, abundant; productive; — **de palabras** fluent, eloquent; — **en** fruitful of, productive of; **una época muy fecunda en buenos poetas** a period very productive of good poets, a period in which good poets abounded; **un libro** — **en ideas** a book full of ideas.

fecha *nf* date; — **tope** closing date, last date; **de larga** — (*Fin*) long-dated; **a partir de esta** — from today, starting from today; **a 30 días** — (*Comm*) at 30 days' sight; **con** — **del 15 de agosto** dated the 15th of August; **con** — **adelantada** *cheque* postdated; **en** — **próxima** soon, at an early date; **hasta la** — to date, so far; **para estas** — **s** by this time; **por estas** — **s** now, about now; **manuscrito sin** — undated manuscript.

fechador *nm* (*Arg, Chi, Mex*) date stamp.

fechar [1a] *vt* to date.

fechoría *nf* misdeed, villainy.

federación *nf* federation.

federal *adj* federal.

federalismo *nm* federalism.

federalista *nmf* federalist.

federativo *adj* federative.

Federico *m* Frederick.

feérico *adj* fairy (*attr*).

féferes *nmpl* (*CAm, Col, Cu, Ec, Mex, SD*) junk, lumber; things (in general), thingummyjigs (*fam*).

fehaciente *adj* reliable, authentic.

feldespato *nm* felspar.

felicidad *nf* (a) happiness.
(b) good luck, good fortune; success.
(c) — **es** best wishes, congratulations; **os deseo toda clase de** — **es** I wish you every kind of happiness; **¡mis** — **es!** congratulations!

felicitación *nf* congratulation.

felicitar [1a] *vt* to congratulate (*a uno por algo* somebody on something); **¡le felicito!** congratulations!

feligrés *nm*, **feligresa** *nf* parishioner.

feligresía *nf* parish; parishioners (*collectively*).

felino *adj* feline, catlike.

Felipe *m* Philip.

feliz *adj* (a) happy; **¡— año nuevo!** happy new year!; **y vivieron felices** (*end of story*) and they lived happily ever after.

(b) *turn of phrase etc* felicitous, happy, exactly right.
(c) lucky, fortunate; successful; **la cosa tuvo un fin** — the affair had a successful outcome, the affair turned out well.

felizmente *adv* (a) happily. (b) felicitously. (c) luckily, fortunately; successfully.

felón 1 *adj* wicked, treacherous. **2** *nm* wicked person, villain.

felonía *nf* (*SAm: angl*) felony, crime.

felpa *nf* (a) plush. (b) (*fam*) hiding; dressing-down.

felpar [1a] *vt* to cover with plush; (*fig*) to carpet.

felpeada *nf* (*Arg, Mex*) dressing-down.

felpear [1a] *vt* (*Arg, Mex, Urug*) to dress down.

felpilla *nf* chenille.

felpudo 1 *adj* plush, plushy. **2** *nm* doormat.

femenil *adj* (a) feminine, womanly. (b) (*CAm, Mex*) women's (*attr*); **equipo** — women's team.

femenino 1 *adj* (a) feminine; (*Bot*) female; **deporte** — sport for women; **equipo** — women's team; **del género** — of the feminine gender. **2** *nm* (*Gram*) feminine.

fementido *adj* treacherous, false.

feminidad *nf* femininity.

feminismo *nm* feminism.

feminista *nmf* feminist.

fémur *nm* femur.

fenecer [2d] **1** *vt* to finish, conclude, close. **2** *vi* (a) to come to an end, cease. (b) (*euph*) to pass away, die; to perish.

fenecimiento *nm* (a) end, conclusion, close. (b) (*euph*) passing, demise.

Fenicia *f* Phoenicia.

fenicio 1 *adj* Phoenician. **2** *nm*, **fenicia** *nf* Phoenician.

fénix *nm* phoenix; (*fig*) marvel; **el F— de los ingenios** the Prince of Wits, the genius of our times (*Lope de Vega*).

fenol *nm* phenol.

fenomenal *adj* (a) phenomenal. (b) (*fam*) tremendous (*fam*), terrific (*fam*).

fenómeno 1 *nm* phenomenon; (*fig*) freak, accident.
2 *adj* (*fam*) great (*fam*), marvellous; **una chica fenómena** a smashing girl (*sl*); **¡él estuvo** —**!** he was great!; he was the tops! (*fam*).
3 *adv* (*sl*) **lo hemos pasado** — we had a terrific time (*fam*).

feo 1 *adj* (a) *appearance* ugly; hideous, unsightly; **más** — **que Picio, más** — **que un grajo** (*etc*) as ugly as sin.
(b) *smell etc* bad, nasty; *play* dirty, foul; *weather* foul; *situation* nasty; ugly; **es una costumbre fea** it's a nasty habit; **eso es muy** — that's nasty, that's not nice; **él me puso el problema** — he made me see the difficulties of the problem; **esto se está poniendo** — this is beginning to look bad, I don't like the look of this.
(c) (*Arg, CAm, Col, Mex*) bad, foul, foul-smelling, foul-tasting.
2 *nm* insult, slight; **hacer un** — **a uno** to insult someone, offend someone; **¿me va Vd a hacer ese** —**?** (*concerning invitation*) but you can't refuse!
3 *adv* (*SAm*) bad, badly; **oler** — to smell bad, have a nasty smell; **cantar** — to sing terribly *fam*.

feón *adj* (*SAm*) ugly; **medio** — rather ugly.

feote *adj* (*fam*) terribly ugly (*fam*).

feracidad *nf* fertility.

feraz *adj* fertile.

féretro *nm* coffin; bier.

feri *nm* (*SAm*) see **ferryboat**.

feria *nf* (a) fair, market; agricultural show; carnival; (*SAm*) village market, weekly market; **la F— de Sevilla** the Seville Fair, the Seville Carnival; — **de muestras** trade show, trade exhibition.
(b) holiday; rest, rest day.
(c) (*Mex: Fin*) change; (*CAm*) tip.

feriado *adj*: **día** — holiday, day off; **día medio** — half-holiday, half-day off.

ferial *nm* fair, market; fairground.

feriante *nmf* (a) stallholder, trader; showman. (b) fair-goer.

feriar [1b] **1** *vt* (a) to buy, sell (in a market, at a fair); to trade, exchange. (b) (*Col*) to sell cheap. **2** *vi* to take time off, take a break.

ferino *adj* savage, wild; **tos *f* ferina** whooping cough.

fermata *nf* (*Mus*) run.

fermentación *nf* fermentation.

fermentado *adj* fermented.

fermentar [1b] *vi* to ferment; **hacer** — to ferment, cause fermentation in.

fermento *nm* (a) ferment. (b) leaven, leavening.

Fernando *m* Ferdinand; **te lo han puesto como a** — **VII** (*fam*) they've given it to you on a plate.

ferocidad *nf* fierceness, ferocity, savageness; cruelty.
feroz *adj* (a) fierce, ferocious, savage; cruel. (b) (*SAm*) ugly.
ferozmente *adv* fiercely, ferociously, savagely; cruelly.
férreo *adj* (a) iron (*also fig*); (*Chem*) ferrous; **metal no —** non-ferrous metal. (b) (*Rail*) rail (*attr*).
ferrería *nf* ironworks, foundry.
ferretería *nf* (a) ironmongery, hardware. (b) (*Comm*) ironmonger's (shop), hardware store. (c) = **ferrería**.
ferretero *nm* ironmonger, hardware dealer.
férrico *adj* ferric, ferrous; **metal no —** non-ferrous metal.
ferrobús *nm* (*Rail*) diesel car.
ferrocarril *nm* railway, railroad (*US*); **— de cremallera** rack railway; **— elevado** elevated railway, overhead railway; **— funicular** funicular (railway); **— de vía estrecha** narrow-gauge railway; **— de vía única** single-track railway; **por —** by rail, by train; **de —** railway (*attr*), railroad (*attr*: *US*), rail (*attr*).
ferrocarrilero (*SAm*) 1 *adj* railway (*attr*), railroad (*attr*: *US*), rail (*attr*). 2 *nm* railway, railroad (*US*).
ferrohormigón *nm* ferroconcrete.
ferroprusiato *nm* (*Archit*, *Tech*) blueprint.
ferroso *adj* ferrous; **metal no —** non-ferrous metal.
ferrotipo *nm* (*Phot*) tintype.
ferroviario 1 *adj* railway (*attr*), railroad (*attr*: *US*), rail (*attr*). 2 *nm* railwayman.
ferryboat [feri'βot] *nm* (*SAm*: *angl*) ferryboat, railway ferry, train-ferry.
fértil *adj* fertile, fruitful, productive; rich (**en** in); **imaginación etc** fertile.
fertilidad *nf* fertility; fruitfulness; richness.
fertilizante *nm* fertilizer.
fertilizar [1f] *vt* to fertilize; to make fruitful; to enrich.
férula *nf* (a) ferule, birch, rod.
   (b) (*Med*) splint.
   (c) (*fig*) rule, domination; **vivir bajo la — de un tirano** to live under the harsh rule (*or* jackboot) of a tyrant.
férvido *adj* fervid, ardent.
ferviente *adj* fervent.
fervor *nm* fervour, ardour, passion.
fervorosamente *adv* fervently, ardently, passionately.
fervoroso *adj* fervent, ardent, passionate.
festejar [1a] *vt* (a) *person* to feast, wine and dine; to entertain; to fête.
   (b) *occasion*, *anniversary etc* to celebrate.
   (c) *woman* to woo, court.
   (d) (*SAm*) to thrash.
festejo *nm* (a) feast; entertainment; (*Per*) revelry. (b) celebration; **—s** public festivities, rejoicings. (c) wooing, courtship.
festín *nm* feast, banquet.
festinar [1a] *vt* (a) (*CAm*) to feast, wine and dine; to entertain. (b) (*SAm*) to mess up, ruin (by being overhasty). (c) (*SAm*) to hurry along, speed up.
festival *nm* festival.
festivamente *adj* wittily, facetiously, humorously; jovially.
festividad *nf* (a) festivity, merrymaking. (b) (*Eccl*) feast, festivity; holiday. (c) wit, humour; joviality.
festivo *adj* (a) festive, merry, gay. (b) **día —** holiday. (c) witty, facetious, humorous; jovial; (*Lit etc*) humorous, comic, burlesque.
festón *nm* (*Sew*) festoon, scallop; (*of flowers*) garland.
festonear [1a] *vt* to festoon, scallop; to garland.
fetén (*sl*) 1 *adj* smashing (*sl*), super (*fam*); **una chica —** a smashing girl.
   2 *nf*: **de —** smashing, super; **ser la — (y la chupén)** to be smashing; to be gospel truth.
fetiche *nm* fetish; (*fig*) mumbo jumbo, rigmarole.
fetichismo *nm* fetishism.
fetichista 1 *adj* fetishist. 2 *nmf* fetishist.
fetidez *nf* smelliness, rankness.
fétido *adj* foul-smelling, stinking, rank.
feto *nm* (a) foetus. (b) (*fam*) plain girl, ugly girl.
feúcho *adj* (*fam*) horribly ugly.
feudal *adj* feudal.
feudalismo *nm* feudalism.
feudo *nm* (a) (*Hist*) fief; manor. (b) (*Law*) **— franco** freehold.
feúra *nf* (*SAm*) (a) (*in general*) ugliness. (b) (**una —**) ugly person, ugly thing.
fiable *adj* reliable, trustworthy.
fiado *nm* (a) **al —** on trust, (*Comm*) on credit. (b) (*Law*) **en —** on bail.
fiador *nm* (a) (*person: Law*) surety, guarantor; (*Comm*) sponsor, backer; **salir — por uno** to go bail for someone, stand security for someone.

   (b) (*Mech*) catch, fastener, pawl, trigger; (*of gun*) safety catch; (*of lock*) tumbler; (*of window*) fastener, bolt.
   (c) (*fam*) bottom.
   (d) (*Chi*, *Ec*, *Urug*) muzzle; (*Chi*, *Ec*) chinstrap.
fiambre 1 *adj* (a) (*Cook*) cold, served cold.
   (b) (*fam*) news etc old, stale.
   2 *nm* (a) (*Cook*) cold meat, cold food; cold lunch, buffet lunch; **—s** cold meats, cold cuts (*US*).
   (b) (*fam*) corpse, stiff (*sl*); **el pobre está —** the poor chap is stone dead, the poor devil is cold meat now.
   (c) (*fam*) (piece of) stale news.
   (d) (*fam*) corny joke (*fam*).
   (e) (*Arg*) lifeless party, cold affair.
fiambrera *nf* (a) lunch basket, dinner pail (*US*). (b) (*RPl*) meat safe; icebox.
fiambrería *nf* (*SAm*) delicatessen store.
fianza *nf* (a) surety, security, bond; deposit; **— de aduana** customs bond; **— carcelera** bail. (b) (*person*) surety, guarantor.
fiar [1c] 1 *vt* (a) to entrust, confide (**a** to).
   (b) (*Fin etc*) to guarantee, vouch for; to stand security for; (*Law*) to go bail for.
   (c) (*Comm*) to sell on credit; (*SAm*) to buy on credit.
   2 *vi* to trust (**en** in); **ser de —** to be reliable, be trustworthy.
   3 **fiarse** *vr*: **— de uno** to trust someone; to rely on someone, depend on someone; to confide in someone; **me fié completamente de ti** I trusted in you completely; **no me fío de él** I don't trust him; **nos fiamos de Vd para conseguirlo** we rely on you to get it.
fiasco *nm* fiasco.
fíat *nm*, *pl* **fíats** fiat.
fibra *nf* (a) fibre; **— artificial** man-made fibre; **— de vidrio** fibre-glass.
   (b) (*in wood*) grain; (*Min*) vein.
   (c) (*fig*) vigour, toughness; sinews; **—s del corazón** heartstrings.
fibravidrio *nm* fibre-glass.
fibrina *nf* fibrin.
fibroso *adj* fibrous.
ficción *nf* (a) fiction; (*pej*) invention, fabrication. (b) (*SAm*: *Lit*: *angl*) fiction.
ficcioso (*Chi*) 1 *adj* bluffing; false, double-dealing. 2 *nm* bluffer; double-dealer.
ficticio *adj* fictitious; imaginary; (*pej*) fabricated.
ficha *nf* (a) (*Tel etc*) token; (*in games*) token, counter, marker; (*Poker*) chip; (*Chess etc*) piece, man; (*Comm*, *Fin*) token, tally; **— de ajedrez** chessman; **— del dominó** domino.
   (b) card; index card, record card, catalogue card; **— antropométrica** card recording personal particulars; **— policíaca** police record, police dossier.
   (c) (*Elec*) plug.
   (d) (*Arg*, *CR*, *PR*) 5-cent piece.
   (e) (*Mex*) flat bottle cap.
   (f) (*Col*, *Cu*, *Ec*, *PR*: *also* **mala —**) rogue, villain.
fichaje *nm* (*Sport*) signing-up.
fichar [1a] 1 *vt* (a) *card* to file, index.
   (b) to file the personal particulars of; **le tenemos fichado** we have his record, (*fig*) we've got him taped (*fam*), we know all about him.
   (c) *domino* to play.
   (d) (*Sport etc*) to sign up, sign on (**en un club** for a club, with a team).
   (e) (*Cu*) to swindle.
   2 *vi* (a) (*Sport etc*) to sign up, sign on; (*in factory etc*) to clock in.
   (b) (*Col*) to die.
fichero *nm* card index; filing cabinet; **— fotográfico de delincuentes** photographic records of criminals, rogues' gallery.
fidedigno *adj* reliable, trustworthy.
fideicomisario 1 *adj* trust (*attr*); **banco —** trust company. 2 *nm* trustee.
fideicomiso *nm* trust.
fidelería *nf* (*SAm*) noodles factory.
fidelidad *nf* (a) fidelity, loyalty (**a** to).
   (b) accuracy.
   (c) **alta —** (*Radio*) high fidelity; **de alta —** high-fidelity (*attr*), hi-fi.
fideo *nm* (a) (*fam*) lath, skinny person. (b) **—s** (*Cook*) noodles, vermicelli, spaghetti.
fiduciario 1 *adj* fiduciary. 2 *nm* fiduciary, trustee.
fiebre *nf* (a) (*Med*) fever; **— aftosa** foot-and-mouth disease; **— amarilla** yellow fever; **— entérica** enteric fever; **— glandular** glandular fever; **— del heno** hay fever; **— palúdica** malaria; **— reumática**

rheumatic fever; — **tifoidea** typhoid; **tener** — to have fever, be in a fever.

(b) (*fig*) fever; feverish excitement, fevered atmosphere; **la** — **del juego** the gambling fever.

(c) (*Arg, Chi*) shrewd person; tedious person.

fiel 1 *adj* **(a)** faithful, loyal; honest, reliable, trustworthy; **seguir siendo** — **a** to remain loyal to, remain true to.

(b) *account, translation etc* accurate, exact, faithful.

2 los —**es** *nmpl* (*Eccl*) the faithful.

3 *nm* **(a)** (*person*) inspector of weights and measures.

(b) (*Tech*) needle, pointer.

fielmente *adv* **(a)** faithfully, loyally; reliably. **(b)** accurately, exactly.

fieltro *nm* **(a)** (*material*) felt. **(b)** (*object*) felt, piece of felt; felt rug; felt hat; — **de la cerveza** beer mat.

fiera *nf* **(a)** wild beast, wild animal; (*Taur*) bull.

(b) (*fig*) fiend; virago, dragon; **es una** — **para el deporte** he's a fiend for sport, he's a sports fiend; **estar hecho una** — to be wild, be furious; **ella entró hecha una** — she came in absolutely furious.

(c) — **sarda** (*Col*) expert, top man.

fierecilla *nf* (*fig*) shrew; "**La** — **domada**" "The Taming of the Shrew".

fiereza *nf* **(a)** fierceness; ferocity; cruelty, frightfulness. **(b)** ugliness.

fiero 1 *adj* **(a)** fierce, ferocious; cruel; frightful. **(b)** ugly. **2** —**s** *nmpl* threats, boasts; **echar** —**s, hacer** —**s** to utter threats, bluster, brag.

fierro *nm* (*SAm: in general*) iron; (*Agr*) marking iron, brand; (*Arg*) knife; (*Arg: Aut*) accelerator; (*Mex*) cent; —**s** (*Mex: fig*) money.

fiesta *nf* **(a)** (*in house*) party, entertainment; social gathering; celebration; (*in town*) festival, fête; —**s** public festivities, public rejoicings; — **de armas** (*Hist*) tournament; **la** — **brava, la** — **nacional** bullfighting; **organizar una** — **en honor de uno** to give a party in someone's honour; **¡se acabó la** —**!** (*fig*) drop it!, that's enough of that!, joke over!; **aguar la** — to spoil the fun, be a spoilsport; **estar en** —**s** to be en fête; **para coronar la** —, **por fin de** — to round it all off, as a finishing touch; **¡tengamos la** — **en paz!** none of that!; cut it out!

(b) (*Eccl*) feast, feast day; holiday; —**s** holidays; — **de la banderita** flag day; — **fija,** — **inmoble** immovable feast; — **de guardar,** — **de precepto** day of obligation; **F**— **de la Hispanidad, F**— **de la Raza** Columbus Day; — **movible** movable feast, movable holiday; — **nacional** public holiday, bank holiday; **F**— **del Trabajo** Labour Day; **mañana es** — it's a holiday tomorrow; **la** — **del santo** the saint's feast, the saint's day; **celebrar la** —, **guardar la** — to observe the feast (*de* of); **hacer** — to take a day off.

(c) merrymaking, festivities, fun and games; **las** —**s continuaron hasta muy tarde** the festivities went on very late; **estar de** —**s** to be in high good humour; **no estoy para** —**s** I'm in no mood for jokes.

(d) —**s** endearments; soothing words, flattering words, caresses; **hacer** —**s a** to caress, fondle; (*of dog*) to fawn on; (*fig*) to make a great fuss of.

fiestero *adj* gay; fun-loving, pleasure-seeking; fond of parties.

fifí *nm* (*SAm*) playboy, young man about town.

fifiriche *adj* (*CAm, Mex*) weak, sickly.

figón *nm* cheap restaurant.

figulino *adj:* **arcilla figulina** potter's clay.

figura *nf* **(a)** (*in general, Art etc*) figure; shape, form; image; **de** — **entera** full-length; — **de nieve** snowman.

(b) (*person*) figure; **una** — **destacada** an outstanding figure; **las principales** —**s del partido** the chief figures in the party; **cuando uno es** — when one is a famous person; **hacer** — to cut a figure.

(c) face.

(d) (*Geom etc, Typ*) figure, drawing, diagram; — **celeste** horoscope.

(e) (*Ling*) figure; — **retórica** rhetorical figure, figure of speech.

(f) (*Theat*) character, role; **en la** — **de** in the role of.

(g) (*Theat*) marionette.

(h) (*Cards*) picture card, court card; (*Chess*) piece, man.

(i) (*Dancing, Skating*) figure.

(j) (*Mus*) note.

figuradamente *adv* figuratively.

figurado *adj* figurative.

figurante *nm*, **figuranta** *nf* **(a)** (*Theat*) extra, walker-on, super(numerary). **(b)** (*fig*) figurehead.

figurar [1a] **1** *vt* to figure, shape, form; to represent.

2 *vi* **(a)** to figure (*como* as, *entre* among), appear; **los nombres no figuran aquí** the names do not appear here.

(b) (*fig*) to show off, cut a dash; **todo se debe al afán de** — it's all due to the urge to cut a dash, it's the urge to be somebody that causes it all.

3 figurarse *vr* to suppose; to imagine, fancy; to figure (*US*); **¡figúrate!, ¡figúrese!** just think!, just imagine!; **¡figúrate lo que sería con dos!** imagine what it would be like with two of them!; **ya me lo figuraba** I thought as much; **me figuro que es caro** I fancy it's dear, I imagine it's dear; **¿qué se figuran que me preguntó ayer?** what do you think he asked me yesterday?; **no te vayas a** — **que . . .** don't go thinking that . . .

figurativo *adj* figurative; *art* representational.

figurín *nm* fashion plate; model; dummy; (*Theat*) design for a costume.

figurina *nf* figurine, statuette.

figurinista *nmf* (*Theat*) costume designer.

figurón *nm* **(a)** grotesque figure, huge figure; — **de proa** (*Naut*) figurehead. **(b)** (*fam*) pretentious nobody; pompous ass.

figuroso *adj* (*Chi, Mex*) showy, loud.

fija *nf* **(a)** (*Tech*) hinge; (*Archit*) trowel.

(b) (*Chi, Per, RPl: Racing*) favourite; **es una** — (*RPl*) it's a cert (*sl*); **ésa es la** — that's for sure; **ésta es la** — this is it, this is the real thing.

fijacarteles *nm, pl* **fijacarteles** billposter.

fijación *nf* **(a)** (*act*) fixing; securing; fastening; sticking (on); posting; establishing. **(b)** (*Med*) fixation.

fijador *nm* **(a)** (*Phot*) fixer; fixing bath. **(b)** — **para el pelo** hair lotion, hair cream.

fijamente *adv* firmly, steadily, securely; fixedly; **mirar** — **a uno** to stare at someone, look hard at someone.

fijapelo *nm* hair lotion, hair cream.

fijar [1a] **1** *vt* **(a)** to fix; to secure, fasten (on, down *etc*); *stamp etc* to affix, stick (on), paste on, glue on; *poster* to post, stick, put up; *hair* to set; (*Phot*) to fix; *residence* to take up, establish; *eyes* to fix (*en* on); *attention* to focus, fix (*en* on).

(b) (*fig*) to settle (on), decide, determine; *date, hour, price etc* to fix, set; **la fecha no se puede** — **con precisión** the date cannot exactly be determined; **hemos fijado una hora** we have fixed a time, we have agreed on a time.

2 fijarse *vr* **(a)** to become fixed, get set; to settle, lodge; to establish oneself.

(b) to notice, pay attention; **lo malo es que no se fija** the trouble is he doesn't pay attention; **no me había fijado** I hadn't noticed; **fíjese bien** pay close attention, watch this carefully; **¡fíjate!** fancy that!, just imagine!

(c) — **en algo** to notice something, observe something, pay attention to something; to stare at something; — **en un detalle** to seize upon a detail; **¡fíjense en los precios!** just look at these prices!; **se fijó en mí en seguida** he fixed on me at once; — **en** + *infin* to be intent on + *ger*.

fijasello *nm* stamp hinge.

fijativo *nm* fixative.

fijeza *nf* firmness, stability; constancy; fixity; **mirar con** — **a uno** to stare at someone, look hard at someone.

fijo *adj* **(a)** fixed; firm, steady, stable, secure; *date, star, price etc* fixed; *look* fixed, steady; **de** — certainly, for sure.

(b) *purpose etc* fixed, firm.

(c) *staff* permanent, established.

fil *nm:* — **derecho** leapfrog.

fila *nm* **(a)** row, line; file; (*Sport, Theat etc*) row, tier (of seats); **una** — **de coches** a line of cars; — **india** single file, Indian file; **una chaqueta de dos** —**s a** double-breasted jacket; **en** — in a row; in a line; **en** — **de a uno** in single file; **ponerse en** — to line up, get into line.

(b) (*Mil*) rank; **las** —**s** (*fig*) the ranks; **¡en** —**s!** fall in!; **apretar las** —**s** (*fig*) to close ranks; **estar en** —**s** to be with the colours, be on active service; **llamar a uno a** —**s** to call someone up, call someone to the colours; **romper** —**s** to fall out, dismiss; **¡rompan** —**s!** dismiss!; **romper las** —**s** to break ranks.

(c) (*fam*) dislike, antipathy.

filacteria *nf* phylactery.

Filadelfia Philadelphia.

filamento *nm* filament.

filantropía *nf* philanthropy.

filantrópico *adj* philanthropic.

filántropo *nm*, **filántropa** *nf* philanthropist.

filarmónico *adj* philharmonic.
filatelia *nf* philately, stamp collecting.
filatélico *adj* philatelic.
filatelista *nmf* philatelist, stamp collector.
filático *adj* (*Col*) *horse* vicious; *person* mischievous; crafty; rude.
filete *nm* (a) (*Archit*) fillet.
  (b) (*Mech*) worm; (*of screw*) thread; (*of bridle*) snaffle bit.
  (c) (*Cook*) (*meat*) fillet, tenderloin, steak; (*fish*) fillet; **darse el —** (*fam*) to neck (*fam*), pet.
  (d) (*Sew*) narrow hem.
  (e) (*Typ*) ornamental bar (*or* line).
filfa *nf* (*fam*) (a) fraud, hoax; piece of humbug. (b) fake. (c) (*Mech etc*) dud, useless object.
filiación *nf* (a) filiation; (*of ideas etc*) connection, relationship. (b) personal description; characteristics.
filial 1 *adj* filial; (*Comm*) subsidiary, affiliated. **2** *nf* (*Comm*) subsidiary, affiliated company.
filibusterismo *nm* (*SAm: Pol*) filibustering.
filibustero *nm* pirate, freebooter.
filigrana *nf* (a) (*Tech*) filigree; filigree work; (*Typ*) watermark. (b) (*Sport etc*) delicate move, clever piece of play.
filípica *nf* harangue, tirade, philippic.
Filipinas: las —, las Islas — the Philippines.
filipino 1 *adj* Philippine. **2** *nm*, **filipina** *nf* Philippine, Filipino.
filisteísmo *nm* Philistinism.
filisteo 1 *adj* Philistine. **2** *nm* (a) (*Bib*) Philistine. (b) (*fig*) big man, giant.
film *nm*, *pl* **films** [film] (*angl*) film; picture, movie (*US*).
filmación *nf* filming, shooting.
filmador *nm* film maker.
filmadora *nf* film studio.
filmar [1a] *vt* to film, shoot.
filme *nm* (*Acad*) = **film**.
fílmico *adj* film (*attr*), movie (*attr*: *US*); screen (*attr*); **obras teatrales y fílmicas** theatrical and screen works, works for stage and screen.
filmina *nf* (*Phot*) slide, transparency.
filmlet *nm*, *pl* **filmlets** ['filmlet] short advertising film, short commercial film.
filmografía *nf* study of the film; **la — de la estrella** the star's film history, the star's screen history; **la — del Oeste** the history of the Western, films (*collectively*) about the West.
filmología *nf* science of film making, art of film making.
filmoteca *nf* film library, film archive.
filo[1] *nm* (a) edge; cutting edge, blade; dividing line; ridge; **— del viento** (*Naut*) direction of the wind; **de dos —s** double-edged (*also fig*); **al — de las 12** at about 12 o'clock; **por —** exactly; **de —** (*Col*) resolutely; **dar (un) —** **a, sacar el —** **a** to sharpen, put an edge on; **dar —** **a** (*fig: Ec*) to tell off, (*SD*) to wound with a knife; **herir a uno por los mismos —s** to pay someone back in his own coin; **pasar al — de la espada** to put to the sword.
  (b) (*CAm, Mex*) hunger.
  (c) (*Arg: sl*) tale, hoax.
  (d) (*Arg: sl*) suitor; girlfriend; courtship.
filo[2] *nm* (*Bio*) phylum.
filo[3] **... philo ...,** *eg* **francófilo** *nm*, **francófila** *nf* francophile.
filocomunismo *nm* pro-communist feeling(s); fellow-travelling.
filocomunista 1 *adj* pro-communist; with communist leanings, fellow-travelling. **2** *nmf* pro-communist; fellow traveller.
filología *nf* philology.
filológico *adj* philological.
filólogo *nm* philologist.
filomela *nf*, **filomena** *nf* (*poet*) nightingale.
filón *nm* (*Min*) seam, vein, lode; (*fig*) rich seam, gold mine.
filongo *nm* (*Arg*) girlfriend (of inferior social status).
filoso *adj* (a) (*CAm, Mex, RPl*) sharp. (b) (*Hond*) hungry.
filosofal *adj*: **piedra —** philosopher's stone.
filosofar [1a] *vi* to philosophize.
filosofía *nf* philosophy; **— moral** moral philosophy; **— natural** natural philosophy; **— de la vida** philosophy of life.
filosófico *adj* philosophic(al).
filósofo *nm* philosopher.
filote *nm* (*Col*) ear of green maize; maize silk; **estar en —** (*child*) to begin to grow hair.
filotear [1a] *vi* (*Col: of maize*) to come into ear, begin to ripen; (*of child*) to grow hair.

filoxera *nf* phylloxera.
filtración *nf* filtration; seepage, leakage, loss.
filtrador 1 *adj* filtering. **2** *nm* filter.
filtrar [1a] **1** *vt* to filter; *coffee etc* to strain.
  2 *vi* and **filtrarse** *vr* (a) to filter; **— por** to filter through; to percolate (through); to seep through, leak through.
  (b) (*fig: of money etc*) to dwindle, disappear bit by bit.
filtro *nm* (a) (*Tech*) filter; (*Cook*) strainer; **— de aceite** oil filter; **— de aire** air filter; **— de café** coffee strainer; **cigarrillo con —** filter-tipped cigarette.
  (b) (*Hist*) love potion, philtre.
filudo *adj* (*SAm*) sharp.
filum *nm* (*Bio*) phylum.
filván *nm* featheredge; (*on paper*) deckle edge; (*on knife*) burr.
fimbria *nf* (*Sew*) border, hem.
fin *nm* (a) end; ending; conclusion; **"— de la cita"** "end of quote", "unquote"; **— de fiesta** (*Theat etc*) grand finale; **— de semana** weekend; **a —es del mes** at (*or* about) the end of the month; **hacia —es del siglo** towards the end of the century; **al —** finally, in the end; **al — y al cabo** at long last; in the end; after all, when all is said and done; **en —, por —** finally, at last; in short; **en —** (*fig*) well, well then; **¡en —!** so that's that!, what next?; **en — de cuentas** in the last analysis; **sin —** (*adv*) endlessly; (*adj: also Tech*) endless; **correa sin —** endless belt; **un sin —** **de** see **sinfín**; **dar — a un discurso** to end a speech, close a speech; **llevar algo a buen —** to carry something through to a successful conclusion; **poner — a** to stop, put a stop to.
  (b) aim, purpose, objective; scope; **los —es de este estudio** the aims of this study; the scope of this study; **a — de + infin** in order to + *infin*, so as to + *infin*; **a — de que ...** in order that ..., so that ...; **con el — de + infin** with the purpose of + *ger*; **con —es deshonestos** with an immoral purpose.
finado 1 *adj* late, deceased; **el — presidente** the late president. **2** *nm*, **finada** *nf* deceased.
final 1 *adj* final; last; ultimate; eventual. **2** *nm* end; conclusion; (*Mus*) finale; **al — de la calle** at the end of the street; **por —** finally. **3** *nf* (*Sport etc*) final.
finalidad *nf* (a) object, purpose, intention; **la — de este libro** the aim of this book; **¿qué — tendrá todo esto?** what can be the purpose of all this?; **perseguir algo como —** to set something as one's goal.
  (b) (*Philos etc*) finality.
finalista *nmf* finalist.
finalizar [1f] **1** *vt* (a) to end, finish.
  (b) (*Law*) *deed* to execute.
  2 *vi* and **finalizarse** *vr* to end, finish, conclude; **finalizada la ceremonia ...** once the ceremony was finished ...
finalmente *adv* finally, lastly.
finamente *adv* politely; elegantly; acutely, shrewdly; subtly; delicately.
finamiento *nm* decease, demise, passing.
financiación *nf* financing.
financiar [1b] *vt* to finance.
financiero 1 *adj* financial; **los medios —s** the financial means; **el mundo —** the financial world, the world of finance. **2** *nm* financier.
financista *nm* (*SAm*) financier; financial expert.
finanzas *nfpl* finances.
finar [1a] **1** *vi* to pass away, die. **2 finarse** *vr* to long, yearn.
finca *nf* (a) property; land, real estate; **— raíz** (*Col*) real estate.
  (b) country estate, country house; (*SAm*) farm; small rural holding; ranch; **— azucarera** sugar plantation; **— cafetera** coffee plantation; **cazar en — ajena** to poach (on somebody else's property); **penetrar en — ajena** to trespass (on somebody else's property); **tienen una — en Guadalajara** they have a country house (*or* property, estate) in Guadalajara; **pasan un mes en su —** they're spending a month at their country place.
fincar [1g] **1** *vt* (*PR*) to till, cultivate. **2** *vi* (*Col, Mex, Per, RPl*) **— en** to rest on, be based on.
finchado *adj* (*fam*) stuck-up (*fam*), conceited.
finés = **finlandés**.
fineza *nf* (a) (*quality*) fineness, excellence; purity; select quality.
  (b) (*of manner*) refinement; elegance.
  (c) (*act*) kindness, favour; courtesy, nice thing (to say *or* do *etc*); compliment; small gift, token.
fingidamente *adv* feignedly; in a sham way; as a piece of make-believe.
fingido *adj* feigned, false; fake, sham; mock; make-believe.

fingimiento nm pretence; simulation, feigning.

fingir [3c] **1** vt to sham, fake; to invent; to simulate; — **desinterés** to feign disinterest, pretend not to be interested; — **mucha humildad** to pretend to be very humble; **lo habrán fingido** I expect they invented it, I expect they faked it up.

2 vi to pretend, feign; — **dormir** to pretend to be asleep, to feign sleep.

3 fingirse vr: — **un sabio** to pretend to be an expert; — **dormido** to pretend to be asleep.

finiquitar [1a] vt account to settle and close, balance up.

finiquito nm (Comm, Fin) settlement.

finito adj finite.

finlandés 1 adj Finnish. **2** nm, **finlandesa** nf Finn. **3** nm (language) Finnish.

Finlandia f Finland.

fino adj **(a)** (in quality) fine, excellent; pure; fruit, wine etc choice, quality (attr); tobacco etc select; (Min) refined; **oro** — pure gold, refined gold.

(b) thin; person (in stature) slender, slight; fabric thin, delicate, sheer; slice thin.

(c) point sharp.

(d) person (in manner) polite, well-bred, refined; manners refined, cultured; compliment etc elegant, well-turned; **ponerse** — to turn on the charm.

(e) intelligence shrewd, acute, penetrating; taste fine, discriminating; hearing sharp, acute.

(f) distinction etc fine, subtle, delicate; irony subtle.

finta nf feint; **hacer** —s to feint, spar.

fintar [1a] vi, **fintear** [1a] vi (SAm) to feint, spar.

finura nf **(a)** fineness, excellence; purity; choiceness, high quality.

(b) politeness, courtesy, refinement; elegance; **¡qué** —! what refinement!, how charming!

(c) shrewdness, acuteness.

(d) subtlety, delicacy.

fiñe adj (Cu) small, weak, sickly.

fiordo nm fiord.

fique nm (Col, Mex, Ven) vegetable fibre, rope, cord.

firma nf **(a)** signature; (act) signing; **es de mi** — I signed that; **6 novelas de su** — 6 novels of his, 6 novels which he has written.

(b) (Comm, Fin) firm, company, concern.

firmamento nm firmament.

firmante 1 adj signatory (de to). **2** nmf signatory; **el abajo** — the undersigned.

firmar [1a] vti to sign; **firmado y lacrado, firmado y sellado** signed and sealed.

firme 1 adj **(a)** firm; steady, secure, stable; hard; solid, compact; colour fast; resistance firm; resolute; **estar en lo** — to be in the right; to be positive; **mantenerse** — to hold one's ground, not give way.

(b) (Comm, Fin) market steady; price firm, stable.

(c) person staunch, steadfast, resolute.

(d) (Mil) ¡—s! attention!; **estar en posición de** —s to stand at attention; **poner** —s **a un pelotón** to bring a squad to attention; **ponerse** —s to come to attention.

(e) **de** — firmly, strongly; steadily; **batir de** — to strike hard; **resistir de** — to resist strongly; **trabajar de** — to work hard, work solidly.

(f) (Comm) **oferta en** — firm offer; **pedido en** — firm order.

2 nm roadbed, road foundation layer; road surface; "— **ondulado**" "uneven surface"; "— **provisional**" "temporary surface"; — **del suelo** rubble filling, rubble base (of floor).

firmemente adv **(a)** firmly; securely, solidly. **(b)** staunchly, steadfastly.

firmeza nf **(a)** firmness; steadiness, stability; solidity, compactness. **(b)** (Comm, Fin) steadiness. **(c)** (moral) firmness; steadfastness, resolution.

firuletes nmpl (SAm) elaborate adornment, flourishes; (in dance) gyrations, contortions.

fiscal 1 adj fiscal, financial; tax (attr); **año** — fiscal year, financial year.

2 nm (Law) prosecutor, counsel for the prosecution, district attorney (US); — **general** attorney-general.

(b) (fam) busybody, meddler.

fiscalía nf office of the public prosecutor.

fiscalizar [1f] vt **(a)** to control, oversee, inspect (officially). **(b)** (fig) to criticize, find fault with. **(c)** (fam) to pry into, meddle with.

fisco nm treasury, exchequer; **declarar algo al** — to declare something for tax purposes.

fisga nf **(a)** fish spear; (Guat, Mex: Taur) banderilla. **(b)** (fig) banter, chaff; **hacer** — **a uno** to tease someone, banter someone.

fisgar [1h] **1** vt **(a)** fish to spear, harpoon. **(b)** (fig) to pry into, spy on. **2** vi **(a)** to pry, snoop, spy. **(b)** to mock, scoff, jeer.

fisgón (fam) **1** adj **(a)** snooping, prying, nosey. **(b)** bantering, teasing; mocking. **2** nm, **fisgona** nf **(a)** snooper, nosey-parker. **(b)** banterer, tease; mocker.

fisgonear [1a] vt (fam) to be always prying into, spy continually on.

fisgoneo nm (fam) constant prying; chronic nosiness.

física nf physics; — **nuclear** nuclear physics; — **del estado sólido** solid-state physics.

físicamente adv physically.

físico 1 adj **(a)** physical.

(b) (Cu, Mex, SD) finicky; prudish; affected.

2 nm **(a)** physicist; (Med: arch) physician.

(b) (Anat) physique; appearance, looks; **de** — regular ordinary-looking.

fisil adj fissile.

fisiología nf physiology.

fisiológico adj physiological.

fisiólogo nm physiologist.

fisión nf fission; — **nuclear** nuclear fission.

fisionable adj fissionable.

fisioterapia nf physiotherapy.

fisioterapista nmf physiotherapist.

fiso nm (SAm: sl) clock (sl), dial (sl).

fisonomía nf physiognomy, face; features.

fistol nm **(a)** (Mex) tiepin. **(b)** (fam) crafty fellow.

fístula nf fistule.

fisura nf fissure.

flaccidez nf flaccidity; softness, flabbiness.

fláccido adj flaccid; soft, flabby.

flaco 1 adj **(a)** thin, skinny, lean; **ponerse** — to get thin. **(b)** weak, feeble; memory bad, short; point, side weak. **2** nm weakness, weak spot, failing.

flacón adj (Arg, Mex, PR) very thin.

flacuchento adj (SAm) very thin.

flacura nf **(a)** thinness, skinniness. **(b)** weakness, feebleness.

flagelación nf flagellation, whipping.

flagelar [1a] vt **(a)** to flagellate, whip, scourge. **(b)** (fig) to flay, criticize severely.

flagelo nm **(a)** whip, scourge. **(b)** (fig) scourge, calamity.

flagrante adj flagrant; **en** — in the act, red-handed.

flamante adj **(a)** brilliant, flaming. **(b)** (fig) brand-new.

flameante adj flamboyant (also Archit).

flamear [1a] vi **(a)** to flame, blaze (up). **(b)** (Naut: of sail) to flap; (of flag) to flutter.

flamenco¹ nm (Orn) flamingo.

flamenco² 1 adj **(a)** Flemish.

(b) Andalusian gipsy (attr); **cante** — Andalusian gipsy singing.

(c) (pej) flashy, vulgar, gaudy.

(d) **ponerse** — (fam) to get cocky (fam); to get on one's high horse.

(e) (Hond, Mex, PR) =**flaco**.

2 nm, **flamenca** nf Fleming; **los** —s the Flemings, the Flemish.

3 nm **(a)** Andalusian gipsy singing and dancing, flamenco.

(b) (language) Flemish.

flamenquilla nf small marigold, tagetes.

flámula nf streamer.

flan mf cream caramel, caramel custard (dessert dish).

flanco nm **(a)** (Anat) side, flank. **(b)** (Mil) flank; **coger a uno por el** — to catch someone off guard.

Flandes m Flanders.

flanquear [1a] vt **(a)** to flank. **(b)** (Mil) to outflank.

flaquear [1a] vi **(a)** to weaken, grow weak; (of effort) to slacken, flag; (of timber etc) to give way; (of health) to decline, get worse; (morally) to lose heart, become dispirited.

flaquencia nf (SAm) =**flacura**.

flaqueza nf **(a)** thinness, leanness; weakness; feebleness, frailty; **la** — **de su memoria** his poor memory; **la** — **humana** human frailty.

(b) (una —) failing, weakness; **las** —s **de la carne** the frailties to which the flesh is heir.

flash [flas] nm, pl **flashes** or **flashs** [flas] **(a)** newsflash. **(b)** (Phot) flash, flashlight; **con** — by flashlight.

flato nm **(a)** flatulence, wind. **(b)** (CAm, Col, Mex, Ven) gloom, depression; (Col, Cu, Guat, Ven) fear, apprehension.

flatoso adj **(a)** flatulent, windy. **(b)** (Cu) gloomy, depressed; (CAm, Ven) apprehensive.

flatulencia nf flatulence.

flatulento adj flatulent.

flatuoso adj flatulent, windy.

flauta 1 *nf* flute; **estar hecho una —** to be as thin as a rake.
2 *nm* flautist, flute player.
3 *interj* (*Chi, Per, RPl*) gosh! (*sl*); **¡la gran —!** my God!; **¡por la —!** (*Chi*) oh dear!
flautín *nm* piccolo.
flautista *nmf* flautist, flute player; **el — de Hamelín** the Pied Piper of Hamelin.
flebitis *nf* phlebitis.
fleco *nm* fringe, fringe curls; tassel; **—s** gossamer.
flecha *nf* arrow; dart; (*Col*) sling; **— de mar** squid; **— de dirección** (*Aut*) trafficator; **como una —** like an arrow, like a shot; **con alas en —** swept-wing, with swept-back wings.
flechar [1a] *vt* **(a)** *bow* to draw, stretch.
(b) to wound (*or* kill) with an arrow, shoot (with an arrow).
(c) (*fam*) to make a hit with, (*more formally*) inspire sudden love in.
(d) (*Arg*) to prick (*esp* with a goad); (*of the sun*) to burn, scorch.
flechazo *nm* **(a)** arrow shot, bowshot; arrow wound; (*Col*) slingshot.
(b) (*fam*) love at first sight; **con nosotros fue el —** with us it was love at first sight.
(c) (*fam*) sudden illumination, revelation; **aquello fue el —** then it hit me, that was the moment of illumination.
flechero *nm* **(a)** archer, bowman; arrow maker. **(b)** quiver.
fleje *nm* iron hoop, metal band.
flema *nf* phlegm (*also fig*).
flemático *adj* phlegmatic, matter-of-fact, unruffled.
flemón *nm* gumboil.
flemudo *adj* slow, sluggish.
flequetería *nf* (*Col*) cheating, swindling.
flequetero *adj* (*Col*) tricky, dishonest.
flequillo *nm* fringe.
Flesinga Flushing.
fleta *nf* (*Col, Cu, PR, Ven*) **(a)** rub, rubbing. **(b)** thrashing.
fletamento *nm* charter, chartering; **contrato de —** chartering agreement.
fletar [1a] **1** *vt* **(a)** *plane, ship* to charter; to load, freight.
(b) (*SAm*) *vehicle etc* to hire.
(c) (*Arg, Chi, Per*) *insults* to let fly, utter; *blow* to deal.
(d) (*Arg*) to fire (*fam*), sack (*fam*); to chuck out, remove by force.
2 fletarse *vr* **(a)** (*Col, Cu, Mex*) to get out, beat it (*fam*); to slip away, get away unseen; (*Arg*) to gatecrash.
(b) (*CAm*) to be annoyed, get cross.
(c) (*Cu, Mex*) **salir fletado** to be off like a shot.
(d) (*Chi*) **"se fleta"** (*notice*) "to let".
flete *nm* **(a)** charter; **vuelo —** (*angl*) charter flight.
(b) freight, cargo; **salir sin —s** (*Col, Ven*) to leave in a hurry, be off like a shot.
(c) freightage; (*SAm*) transport charges, carriage; (*SAm*) hire, hire charge, hiring fee.
(d) (*Bol, Col, RPl*) fast horse; racehorse; (*Chi*) old nag.
(e) (*Per*) lover, companion.
fletera *nf* (*Cu*) prostitute.
fletero 1 *adj* **(a)** charter (*attr*); freight (*attr*); **avión —** (*angl*) charter plane.
(b) (*SAm*) hired, for hire; **camión —** lorry for hire.
2 *nm* **(a)** (*SAm*) owner of vehicles for hire; owner of a transport business; collector of transport charges.
(b) (*Ec, Guat*) porter.
flexibilidad *nf* flexibility; suppleness, pliability; compliant nature.
flexible 1 *adj* flexible; soft, supple, pliable; *hat* soft; *person* compliant. **2** *nm* **(a)** soft hat. **(b)** (*Elec*) flex, cord, wire.
flexión *nf* flexion; (*Ling*) inflexion.
flexional *adj* flexional, inflected.
flirt, *pl* **flirts** [flirt] (*fam: angl*) **1** *nmf* sweetheart; boyfriend, girlfriend; **la estrella vino con su — del momento** the star came with her current boyfriend.
2 *nm* flirtation, (light-hearted, semi-serious) affair; **A tuvo un — con B** A had a brief affair with B.
flirteador *nm*, **flirteadora** *nf* (*fam*) flirt.
flirtear [1a] *vi* (*fam*) to flirt (*con* with), have a light-hearted affair (*con* with).
flirteo *nm* (*fam*) **(a)** (*in general*) flirting; (*un —*) flirtation, (light-hearted, semi-serious) affair.
flojamente *adv* **(a)** loosely, slackly; limply. **(b)** weakly, feebly; lightly.

flojear [1a] *vi* to weaken; to slacken, ease up.
flojedad *nf* **(a)** looseness, slackness; limpness.
(b) weakness, feebleness; lightness.
(c) limpness, flaccidity.
(d) poor quality.
(e) slackness, laxity, negligence.
flojel *nm* (*on cloth*) nap; (*Orn*) down.
flojera *nf* (*fam*) =**flojedad**.
flojo *adj* **(a)** *rope etc* loose, slack; limp; *nut etc* loose.
(b) *effort* weak, feeble; *wind* light.
(c) (*in consistency*) soft, limp, flaccid.
(d) *tea, wine etc* weak; *literary work etc* poor, thin, weak, feeble.
(e) *student etc* poor, weak; slack, lax.
(f) *price* low, weak; *market* slack, dull.
(g) (*SAm*) lazy; timid, cowardly.
flor 1 *nf* **(a)** (*Bot*) flower, blossom, bloom; **— de harina** flour; **— de mano** artificial flower; **— del sol** sunflower; **en —** in flower, in bloom; **en plena —** in full bloom; **hijos como una —** lovely children; **de —** (*Cu, PR, Ven*) very good, splendid.
(b) (*on plum etc*) bloom.
(c) (*in leather*) grain.
(d) (*fig*) flower, best part, cream; **la — y nata de la sociedad** the cream of society, the pick of society; **es la — de la canela** it's the very best, it's the tops (*fam*); **en la — de la edad** in the flower of one's youth; **en la — de la vida** in the prime of life; **frenar a uno en —** to cut someone off in his prime.
(e) surface; **a — de level with, on a level with**; flush with; on the surface of; **a — del agua** at water level, close to the surface of the water; (*of flooded boat*) awash; **tiene el humorismo a — de piel** his humour is always ready to break out, his wit is never far below the surface; **los odios salen a — de piel** hatred comes out into the open, hatred comes to the surface.
(f) compliment, nice thing (to say); **decir** (*or* **echar**) **—es a una** to pay pretty compliments to a girl, flirt with a girl.
(g) **—es** (*Chi*) popcorn.
2 *adj* (*SAm*) splendid, excellent.
flora *nf* flora.
floración *nf* flowering; bloom.
floral *adj* floral.
florar [1a] *vi* to flower, bloom.
florcita *nf* (*SAm*) little flower; **andar de —** (*Arg*) to live in idleness.
floreado *adj* **(a)** *fabric* flowery, flowered. **(b)** *bread* of the finest flour, top-quality. **(c)** (*Mus*) elaborate, with flourishes.
florear [1a] **1** *vt* **(a)** to adorn with flowers, add a flowery design to.
(b) *flour* to sift.
(c) *cards* to stack.
2 *vi* **(a)** (*SAm*) to flower, bloom.
(b) (*Mus*) to play a flourish, play elaborate variations.
(c) to indulge in flowery compliments, flatter.
3 florearse *vr* (*SAm*) to show off; to perform brilliantly.
florecer [2d] *vi* **(a)** (*Bot*) to flower, bloom. **(b)** (*fig*) to flourish, thrive; to flower.
floreciente *adj* **(a)** (*Bot*) in flower, flowering, blooming. **(b)** (*fig*) flourishing, thriving.
florecimiento *nm* **(a)** (*Bot*) flowering, blooming. **(b)** flourishing, thriving; flowering.
Florencia Florence.
florentino 1 *adj* Florentine, of Florence. **2** *nm*, **florentina** *nf* Florentine.
floreo *nm* **(a)** (*Fencing, Mus*) flourish. **(b)** witty but insubstantial talk; compliment, nicely-turned phrase; **andarse con —s** to beat about the bush.
florería *nf* florist's (shop).
florero *nm* **(a)** florist; (street) flower seller. **(b)** vase; flower stand. **(c)** (*Art*) flower painting. **(d)** flatterer, specialist in elegant compliments.
florescencia *nf* florescence.
floresta *nf* **(a)** wood, grove; glade; beauty spot; charming rural scene; (*Col*) forest, jungle. **(b)** (*Lit*) anthology.
florete *nm* (*Fencing*) foil.
floretear [1a] *vt* to decorate with flowers.
floretista *nmf* (*SAm*) fencer.
floricultura *nf* flower growing.
floridano, floridense, florideño 1 *adj* Floridian (US). **2** *nm*, **floridana** *nf*, **florideña** *nf* Floridian (US).
florido *adj* **(a)** *field etc* flowery, full of flowers. **(b)** (*fig*) choice, select. **(c)** *style* flowery, florid.
florilegio *nm* anthology.
florín *nm* florin.
florión *nm*, **floriona** *nf* (*Col*) =**fanfarrón**.

floripón nm (SAm), **floripondio** nm (SAm) (a) big flower (in pattern, decoration etc). (b) (Lit) rhetorical flourish, extravagant figure. (c) effeminate person.

florista nmf florist.

floristería nf florist's (shop).

florón nm (a) (Bot) big flower. (b) (Archit) fleuron, rosette. (c) (Typ) tailpiece.

flota nf (a) (Naut) fleet; shipping; — **mercante** merchant marine; **la** — **española** the Spanish fleet. (b) (Aer) fleet (of civil airline). (c) (Bol, Col etc) long-distance bus, inter-city bus. (d) (SAm) lot, crowd, heap; **una** — **de** a lot of, a crowd of. (e) (Col, Pan, Ven) boast, bluff; (Ven) lie; **echar** —s (Col, Pan, Ven) to brag.

flotación nf floating, flotation; see **línea**.

flotador nm (in most senses) float; (in cistern) ball-cock.

flotante 1 adj dock, ice, population, rib etc floating; part loose, hanging loose. 2 nm (Col) braggart.

flotar [1a] vi (a) to float. (b) (of part etc) to hang, hang loose; — **al viento** (of hair etc) to stream in the wind.

flote nm: **estar a** — to be afloat; **poner a** — to float, set afloat; (also **sacar a** —) to refloat, raise; **ponerse a** — (fig) to get back on one's feet, get out of a jam; **sostenerse a** — to keep afloat.

flotear [1a] vi: — **en el aire** to hover.

flotilla nf flotilla, fleet of small ships; line of vessels being towed, string of barges.

flox [flos] nm phlox.

fluctuación nf (a) fluctuation; **las** —**es de la moda** the fluctuations of fashion, the ups and downs of fashion. (b) uncertainty, hesitation.

fluctuante adj fluctuating.

fluctuar [1e] vi (a) to fluctuate. (b) to waver, hesitate.

fluente adj fluid, flowing.

fluidez nf (a) fluidity. (b) (fig) fluency, smoothness.

fluido adj (fig) fluent, free-flowing, smooth.

flúido 1 adj fluid. 2 nm (a) fluid. (b) (Elec) current, power.

fluir [3g] vi to flow, run; to pass.

flujo nm (a) flow; stream; flux; (Naut) rising tide, incoming tide; — **y reflujo** ebb and flood, (fig) ebb and flow. (b) (Med) — **de sangre** flow of blood, loss of blood, haemorrhage; — **de vientre** diarrhoea.

fluminense (SAm) 1 adj of Río de Janeiro. 2 nmf native (or inhabitant) of Río de Janeiro; **los** —s the people of Río de Janeiro.

fluorescencia nf fluorescence.

fluorescente adj fluorescent.

fluorización nf fluoridation.

fluoruro nm fluoride.

flus nm (Ant, Col, Ven) suit of clothes.

fluvial adj fluvial, river (attr); fish river (attr), freshwater (attr).

flux [flus] nm, pl **flux** [flus] (a) (Cards) flush; — **real** royal flush. (b) (CAm) stroke of luck. (c) (Ant, Col, Ven) suit of clothes. (d) (Arg, Mex) **estar a** —, **quedarse a** — not to have a shirt to one's back; **hacer** — to squander everything without paying one's debts.

fobia nf phobia.

—**fobia** -phobia, eg **agorafobia** nf agoraphobia.

—**fobo** -phobe, eg **francófobo** nm, **francófoba** nf francophobe.

foca nf seal; — **de trompa** sea elephant.

focal adj focal.

foco nm (a) (Math, Med, Phys etc) focus; focal point, centre; (of heat, light) source; (of fire) seat; **estar fuera de** — to be out of focus. (b) (Elec) floodlight; (Theat etc) spotlight; street lamp; (SAm) electric-light bulb. (c) (fig) centre, focal point.

focha nf coot.

foche (Chi) 1 adj smelly. 2 nmf dissolute person.

fodolí adj meddlesome.

fodongo adj (Mex) filthy, slovenly.

foete nm = **fuete**.

fofadal nm (Arg) bog, quagmire.

fofo adj (a) soft, spongy; porous; fluffy. (b) (fam) fat, plump.

fogaje nm (a) (SAm) scorching heat; sultry weather. (b) (Arg, Cu, Mex) heat rash; (PR) blush. (c) (Ec) fire, blaze.

fogarada nf, **fogarata** nf (Arg), **fogata** nf blaze, bonfire.

fogón nm (a) (Cook) stove, kitchen range; (Rail) firebox; (Naut) galley. (b) (of gun, machine) vent. (c) (Arg, CAm, Chi) fire, bonfire; hearth.

fogonazo nm (a) flash, explosion. (b) (Mex) coffee with brandy added.

fogonero nm (a) (Naut) stoker. (b) (Rail) foreman, stoker. (c) (Col) chauffeur.

fogosidad nf spirit, mettle; fire, dash, verve; fieriness, friskiness.

fogoso adj spirited, mettlesome; fiery, ardent; horse fiery, frisky.

fogueado adj (a) (SAm) expert, experienced. (b) (Col) weary.

foguear [1a] vt (SAm) to fire on.

foguerear [1a] vt (Cu, Chi) brushwood to burn off; bonfire to set light to.

foguista nm (RPl) = **fogonero**.

foja nm coot.

folgo nm foot muff.

foliación nf foliation, page numbering.

foliar [1b] vt to foliate, number the pages of.

folio nm (a) folio; leaf, sheet; (Typ) running title; **al primer** — (fig) at first glance; **en** — in folio; **libro en** — folio book. (b) (Col) tip.

folklore nm (a) folklore. (b) (fam) row, shindy; **se armó un** — there was a row.

folklórico adj folklore (attr); folk (attr), popular, traditional; **es muy** — it's very quaint, it's full of local colour; it is rich in historical interest.

folklorista 1 adj folklore (attr). 2 nmf folklorist, specialist in folklore, student of folklore.

folklorizar [1f] 1 vt (a) to give a popular (or folksy) character to. 2 **folklorizarse** vr to acquire popular (or folksy) features.

follado nm (Col) petticoat.

follaje nm (a) (Bot) foliage, leaves; (Art) leaf motif. (b) (fig) excessive ornamentation; bombast, verbiage.

follar [1m] 1 vt to blow (on) with bellows. 2 vi (tabu) = **joder**. 3 **follarse** vr (tabu) to fart silently (tabu).

folletín nm newspaper serial.

folletista nmf pamphleteer.

folleto nm pamphlet; folder, brochure, leaflet.

follín nm (Chi) bad-tempered individual.

follisca nf (Ant, CAm, Col, Ven) confusion, shindy; brawl.

follón 1 adj (a) lazy, slack. (b) arrogant, puffed-up; blustering. (c) cowardly. (d) (Guat) dress roomy, loose; (Ven) dress short. 2 nm (a) (Bot) sucker. (b) good-for-nothing, layabout; conceited person. (c) noiseless rocket; (tabu) silent fart (tabu). (d) (fam) rumpus (fam), row, shindy; (of students) rag; **hubo** (or **se armó**) **un tremendo** — there was a hell of a row. (e) (Ec) skirt, petticoat. (f) (Cu, PR) drinking bout.

follonarse [1a] vr (Chi, Mex: tabu) to fart silently (tabu).

fomentación nf (Med) fomentation, poultice.

fomentar [1a] vt (Med) (a) to foment; to warm. (b) (fig) to promote, foster, encourage, foment; revolt to foment, stir up; production etc to boost. (c) (Cu, PR) business to found, promote.

fomento nm (a) (Med) fomentation. (b) promotion, fostering, encouragement, fomentation; **Ministerio de F**— ministry responsible for public works, agriculture etc.

fonda nf (Hist) inn, tavern; small restaurant; (Rail) buffet; (Chi) refreshment stall.

fondeadero nm anchorage; berth.

fondeado adj (a) (Naut) **estar** — to be anchored, be at anchor. (b) (SAm) **estar** — to be in the money, be well heeled (sl); **quedar** — (Arg) to be broke (fam).

fondear [1a] 1 vt (a) (Naut) depth to sound; ship to search; (fig) to examine. (b) (PR) to rape. (c) (CAm) to provide with money. 2 vi to anchor, drop anchor. 3 **fondearse** vr (a) (SAm) to get rich; to save for the future. (b) (SAm) to get drunk.

fondero nm (SAm) innkeeper; restaurant owner.

fondillos nmpl (a) seat (of trousers). (b) (SAm: Anat) seat, bottom.

fondilludo nm, **fondilluda** nf (SAm) person with a large backside, big ass (US: fam).

fondista nmf innkeeper; restaurant owner.

fondo nm (a) (of box, sea etc) bottom; (of room etc) back, far end; (as measurement) depth; **doble** —, — **falso** false bottom; — **del mar** bottom of the sea, sea bed, sea floor; **a** — (adj) thorough, (adv) thoroughly; **una investigación a** — a thorough investigation; **conocer algo a —** to know something thoroughly; **al — de** at the bottom of; at the back of; **de —** race long-distance (attr), endurance (attr); **de bajo —** shallow; flat; **en el —** (fig) at bottom; at heart; **en el — del corazón** deep down in one's heart; **sin —** bottomless; **dar —** to anchor; **echar un buque al —** to sink a ship; to scuttle a ship; **irse al —** to sink, founder, go to the bottom; **llegar al — de un misterio** to get to the bottom of a mystery.

(b) (Art) background, ground; (Sew) ground; **se ve una casa en el —** there is a house in the background.

(c) **bajos —s sociales** lowest strata of society, dregs of society.

(d) (Comm, Fin) fund; **—s funds**; money; finance; resources; **— de amortización** sinking fund; **—s bloqueados** frozen assets; **— de huelga** strike fund; **cheque sin —s** bad cheque; **estar sin —s** to have no money, be broke; **reunir —s** to get money together.

(e) (fig) fund, supply, reservoir; **tiene un — de alegría** he has a fund of cheerfulness.

(f) (fig) nature, disposition; **de — jovial** of cheery disposition; **tener buen —** to be good-natured.
fondongo nm (Cu, Mex: Anat) bottom.
fonducha nf (Per) = fonducho.
fonducho nm cheap restaurant.
fonema nm phoneme.
fonémico adj phonemic.
fonendoscopio nm stethoscope.
fonética nf phonetics.
fonético adj phonetic.
fonetista nmf phonetician.
fónico adj phonic.
fono nm (Chi: Tel) earpiece.
fonocaptor nm (of gramophone) pickup.
fonógrafo nm (SAm) gramophone, phonograph (US).
fonología nf phonology.
fonológico adj phonological.
fontanal nm, **fontanar** nm spring.
fontanería nf plumbing.
fontanero nm plumber.
footing ['futiŋ] nm, pl **footings** ['futiŋ] (SAm: pseudo-angl) walk, hike.
foque nm jib.
foquillos nmpl fairy lights.
forajido nm outlaw, bandit; desperado.
foral adj relative to the fueros, pertaining to the privileges of a town (or region).
foramen nm (Mex) hole.
foráneo adj foreign, strange.
forastero 1 adj alien, strange; exotic. **2** nm, **forastera** nf stranger; outsider; visitor; person from another part.
forcej(e)ar [1a] vi to struggle, wrestle; to make violent efforts; to flounder about.
forcej(e)o nm struggle; violent efforts; floundering.
forcejudo adv tough, strong, powerful.
fórceps nm, pl **fórceps** forceps.
forcito nm (SAm) little Ford (vehicle).
forense 1 adj forensic, legal; see **médico. 2** nm pathologist.
forestación nf afforestation.
forestal adj forest (attr); see **repoblación** etc.
forito nm (SAm) = fotingo.
forja nf (a) forge; foundry. (b) (act) forging.
forjado adj iron wrought.
forjar [1a] vt (a) to forge, shape, beat (into shape).

(b) to forge, shape, make; **— un plan** to make a plan, hammer out a plan; **tratamos de — un estado moderno** we are trying to build a modern state.

(c) (pej) to invent, think up, concoct; to forge.
forma nf (a) form, shape; **de — triangular** of triangular shape, triangular in shape; **en — de U** U-shaped, shaped like a U.

(b) (Tech) mould; block, pattern; hatter's block.

(c) (Sport etc) form; (Med) fitness; **estar en — to** be in (good) form; to be fit; **estar en plena — to** be on top form, be on the top of one's form; **ponerse en — to** get fit.

(d) way, means, method; **la única — de hacerlo es . . .** the only way to do it is . . .; **no hubo — de convencerle** there was no means of persuading him, it was impossible to persuade him; **— de pago** (Comm) manner of payment, method of payment; **de esta — in** this way; **de — que . . .** so that . . .; in such a way that . . .; **de todas —s** at any rate, in any case, anyway; **en debida — duly**, in due form; **ver la — de + infin** to see one's way to + infin or ger.

(e) **—s** social forms, conventions; **buenas —s** good manners.

(f) formula; **es pura — it's** just for form's sake, it's a mere formality.

(g) (Typ) format.

formación nf (a) formation. (b) (Geol) formation. (c) training, education; **sin la debida — erudita** without the proper scholarly training.
formado adj formed; grown; **bien — nicely-shaped**, well-formed; **hombre (ya) — grown man.**
formal adj (a) (relating to shape) formal.

(b) matter serious; official; promise, statement etc formal, express, definite; manner serious, earnest, inspiring confidence; person reliable, dependable; businesslike; steady, stable; (in age) adult, grown-up; child well-behaved; **es una persona muy — he** is a perfectly reliable sort; **¿has sido —? (to** child) did you behave yourself?; **¡estáte —!** behave yourself!; **siempre estuvo muy — conmigo** he was always very correct towards me.

(c) (Col) affable, pleasant.

(d) (SAm: angl) dress etc formal.
formaldehido nm formaldehyde.
formaleta nf (CAm, Col, Mex) bird trap.
formalidad nf (a) form, formality; established practice; **son las —es de costumbre** these are the usual formalities; **es pura — it's** a pure formality, it's just a matter of form; **hay muchas —es** there are a lot of formalities, there's a lot of red tape.

(b) seriousness; formal nature, express character; earnestness; reliability, dependable nature; steadiness, stability; (of child) good behaviour; **hablar con — to** speak in earnest; **¡niños, —!** kids, behave yourselves!; **¡señores, un poco de —!** gentlemen, let's be serious!
formalina nf formalin(e).
formalismo nm conventionalism; (pej: bureaucratic etc) red tape, useless formalities.
formalista nmf formalist.
formalizar [1f] **1** vt to formalize; to formulate, draw up; to put in order, give proper form to, regularize; **— sus relaciones** to become formally engaged.

2 formalizarse vr (a) to grow serious.

(b) to take offence.
formalote adj (fam) stiff, serious.
formar [1a] **1** vt (a) to form, shape, fashion, make; plan etc to make, lay; reserve, stock to build up.

(b) to form, make up, constitute; **está formado por** it is formed by, it is made up of.

(c) pupil etc to train, educate.

(d) (Mil) to form up, parade.

2 vi (Mil) to form up, fall in; (Sport) to line up; **¡a —!** (Mil) fall in!; **los equipos formaron así: . . .** the line-up of the teams was: . . .

3 formarse vr (a) to form; to take form, begin to form; to shape, develop.

(b) to be trained, be educated; **se formó en la escuela de Praga** he was trained in the school of Prague.

(c) (Mil) to form up, fall in, get into line; (Sport) to line up; **¡fórmense!** fall in line!; **el equipo se formó sin González** the team lined up without Gonzalez; the team left out Gonzalez at the start.

(d) **— una opinión** to form an opinion; **¿qué impresión se ha formado?** what impression have you formed?
formativo adj formative.
formato nm (Typ) format; (of paper) size; **papel (de) — holandesa** (approx) foolscap; **periódico de — reducido** tabloid newspaper; **¿de qué — lo quiere?** what size do you want?
fórmico adj: **ácido — formic** acid.
formidable adj (a) formidable, redoubtable; huge; forbidding. (b) (fig) terrific (fam), tremendous (fam); **¡—!** that's great! (fam), splendid!
formón nm chisel.
fórmula nf (Chem, Math, fig) formula; (Med etc) prescription; **una — para conseguir el éxito** a formula to ensure success; **por pura — just** for form's sake, purely as a matter of form.
formulación nf formulation.
formular [1a] vt to formulate; to draw up, make out; question to frame, pose; protest to make, lodge; claim to file, put in.
formulario nm formulary (also Pharm), collection of formulae; form, blank; **— de inscripción, — de solicitud** application form; **— de pedido** (Comm) order blank, order form; **llenar un — to** fill in a form.
formulismo nm red tape; useless formalities.
fornicación nf fornication.
fornicador, fornicario 1 adj fornicating. **2** nm fornicator.
fornicar [1g] vi to fornicate.
fornicio nm fornication.
fornido adj well-built, strapping, hefty.
fornitura nf (CAm, Mex, PR: angl) furniture.

foro *nm* (a) (*Hist*) forum. (b) (*Law*) court of justice; (*fig*) bar, legal profession. (c) (*Theat*) back of the stage, upstage area.
forrado *adj* (a) (*Sew etc*) lined; — **de nilón** lined with nylon; **un libro** — **de pergamino** a book bound in parchment; **un coche** — **de . . .** a car upholstered in . . .
   (b) (*fam*) well heeled (*sl*), moneyed.
   (c) (*Arg*) **estar** — to know one's stuff (*for exam*).
forraje *nm* (a) forage, fodder. (b) (*act*) foraging. (c) (*fam*) hotchpotch, mixture.
forrajear [1a] *vi* to forage.
forrar [1a] **1** *vt* (*Sew etc*) to line (*de* with); to pad; *book* to cover (*de* with), bind (*de* in); *car* to upholster; (*Tech*) to line, face, cover; *pipe, tank* to lag.
   2 forrarse *vr* (a) to line one's pockets; to make one's pile (*fam*).
   (b) to stuff oneself (*de* with).
   (c) (*Guat, Mex*) to get in provisions for a journey.
   (d) (*Arg: Univ*) to prepare oneself well for an exam.
forro *nm* (a) (*Sew*) lining; padding; (*Typ*) cover; (*Naut*) sheathing; (*Tech*) lining; facing, sheathing; (*Aut*) upholstery; **con** — **de piel** with a fur lining, fur-lined; — **de freno** (*Aut*) brake lining; **ni por el** — not by a long shot.
   (b) (*Arg*) rubber sheath.
   (c) (*Cu, Chi*) swindle, fraud.
   (d) (*Chi*) aptitude.
forsitia *nf* forsythia.
fortacho *nm* (*Arg*) strongly-built car, good car; old car, old crock.
fortalecer [2d] **1** *vt* (a) to strengthen; (*Mil*) to fortify.
   (b) (*morally*) to encourage; *morale* to stiffen; — **a uno en una opinión** to encourage someone in a belief.
   2 fortalecerse *vr* (a) to fortify oneself (*con* with).
   (b) (*of belief etc*) to become stronger.
fortalecimiento *nm* (a) strengthening; fortification, fortifying. (b) encouragement; stiffening.
fortaleza *nf* (a) (*Mil*) fortress, stronghold. (b) (*quality*) strength, toughness, vigour; (*moral*) fortitude, resolution. (c) (*Chi, Mex*) nasty smell.
fortificación *nf* fortification.
fortificar [1g] *vi* to fortify; (*fig*) to strengthen.
fortín *nm* (small) fort; pillbox, bunker, blockhouse.
fortísimo *adj superl of* **fuerte**; (*Mus*) fortissimo.
fortuitamente *adv* fortuitously; accidentally; by chance, by coincidence.
fortuito *adj* fortuitous; accidental; chance (*attr*).
fortuna *nf* (a) fortune; chance; (good) luck; **mala** — misfortune; **por** — luckily, fortunately; **tener la** — **de** + *infin* to have the good fortune to + *infin*; **probar** — to try one's luck, have a shot.
   (b) (*Naut*) **correr** — to weather a storm, ride out a storm.
   (c) (*Fin*) fortune; wealth.
fortunón *nm* (*fam*) vast fortune, pile (*fam*).
forzadamente *adv* forcibly, by force; **sonreír** — to force a smile; **reírse** — to laugh in a forced way.
forzado *adj* forced; compulsory; **sonrisa forzada** forced smile; *see* **trabajo**.
forzar [1f *and* 1m] *vt* (a) to force, compel, make; — **a uno a hacer algo** to force someone to do something, make someone do something.
   (b) *door etc* to force, break down, break open; *lock* to force, pick; *house* to break into, enter by force, force a way into; *blockade* to run; (*Mil*) to storm, take; to force a passage through; *woman* to ravish, rape.
   (c) *ears, eyes* to strain.
forzosamente *adv* necessarily; inescapably; compulsorily; **tiene** — **que ser así** it must necessarily be so; **tuvieron** — **que venderlo** they had no choice but to sell it.
forzoso *adj* necessary; inescapable, unavoidable; compulsory; *landing* (*Aer*), *sale etc* forced; **es** — **que . . .** it is inevitable that . . .; **le fue** — **hacerlo** he was forced to do it, he had no choice but to do it.
forzudo **1** *adj* strong, tough, brawny. **2** *nm* (*in circus*) strong man; (*pej*) thug, tough (*fam*).
fosa *nf* (a) pit; grave; — **de reparaciones** (*Aut*) inspection pit; — **séptica** septic tank; — (**sub**)**marina** deep trough in the ocean bed.
   (b) (*Anat*) fossa, fosse; cavity; —**s nasales** nasal cavities.
fosar [1a] *vt* to dig a ditch (*or* trench *etc*) round.
fosfato *nm* phosphate.
fosforecer [2d] *vi* to phosphoresce, glow.
fosforera *nf* matchbox.
fosforescencia *nf* phosphorescence.
fosforescente *adj* phosphorescent.

fosfórico *adj* phosphoric.
fósforo *nm* (a) (*Chem*) phosphorus.
   (b) (*esp SAm*) match; (*Col*) percussion cap.
   (c) (*Mex*) coffee laced with brandy.
   (d) (*Arg*) intelligence, wit, shrewdness.
   (e) (*Nic, Mex*) irritable person; hothead.
fosforoso *adj* phosphorous.
fosgeno *nm* phosgene.
fósil **1** *adj* fossil, fossilized. **2** *nm* fossil.
fosilizado *adj* fossilized.
fosilizarse [1f] *vr* to fossilize, become fossilized.
foso *nm* pit, hole; ditch, trench; (*Theat*) pit; (*Mil*) moat, fosse; entrenchment, defensive ditch; — **de agua** (*Sport*) water jump; — **de reconocimiento** (*Aut*) inspection pit; **irse al** —, **venirse al** — (*Theat*) to flop (*fam*), fail.
fostró *nm* (*Mus: angl*) foxtrot; (*PR, Ven*) riot, brawl.
fotingo *nm* (*SAm*) cheap car; old car, old crock.
foto *nf* photo; snap, snapshot; — **de conjunto** group photo; **sacar una** —, **tomar una** — to take a photo (*de* of); **ella saca buena** — she photographs well.
fotocalco *nm* photoprint.
fotocontrol *nm* photocontrol; **resultado comprobado por** — photo finish.
fotocopia *nf* photocopy, print.
fotocopiador *nm* photocopier.
fotocopiar [1b] *vt* to photocopy.
fotocromía *nf* colour photography.
fotoeléctrico *adj* photoelectric; **célula** *f* **fotoeléctrica** photoelectric cell.
fotogénico *adj* photogenic.
fotograbado *nm* photogravure, photoengraving.
fotografía *nf* (a) (*in general*) photography; — **aérea** aerial photography; — **en colores** colour photography.
   (b) (*una* —) photograph; — **en colores** colour photograph; — **al flash**, — **al magnesio** flashlight photograph; — **instantánea** snapshot; "— **de X**" (*caption*) "photographed by X"; **hacer una** — **de** to take a photograph of, photograph; *see also* **foto**.
fotografiar [1c] *vt* to photograph.
fotográficamente *adv* photographically.
fotográfico *adj* photographic.
fotógrafo *nm*, **fotógrafa** *nf* photographer; — **aficionado** amateur photographer; — **de prensa** press photographer.
fotograma *nm* (*Cine*) shot.
fotogrametría *nf*: — **aérea** aerial photography, mapmaking from the air.
fotómetro *nm* exposure meter, light meter, photometer.
fotón *nm* photon.
fotosíntesis *nf* photosynthesis.
fotostatar [1a] *vt* to photostat.
fotostato *nm* photostat.
fototeca *nf* collection of photographs.
fototopografía *nf* = **fotogrametría**.
fototropismo *nm* phototropism.
foul [faul] **1** *interj* (*Sport: angl*) foul! **2** *nm* (*SAm: angl*) foul.
fox [fos] *nm*, *pl* **fox** [fos] foxtrot.
frac *nm*, *pl* **fracs** *or* **fraques** dress coat, tails.
fracasado **1** *adj* failed; unsuccessful. **2** *nm*, **fracasada** *nf* failure, person who is a failure.
fracasar [1a] *vi* to fail, be unsuccessful; (*of plan etc*) to fail, come to grief, fall through.
fracaso *nm* failure; fiasco; collapse, breakdown; — **sentimental** disappointment in love, disastrous love affair; **el** — **de las negociaciones** the failure of the negotiations, the breakdown of the talks; **es un** — **total** it's a complete disaster.
fracción *nf* (a) (*Math*) fraction; — **decimal** fraction.
   (b) fraction, part, fragment.
   (c) (*Pol etc*) faction, splinter group.
   (d) (*act*) division, breaking-up (*en* into).
fraccionamiento *nm* (a) division; breaking-up (*en* into). (b) (*Mex*) real-estate development.
fraccionar [1a] *vt* to divide, break up, split up (*en* into).
fraccionario *adj* fractional.
fractura *nf* fracture (*also Med*), break; — **complicada** compound fracture.
fracturar [1a] **1** *vt* to fracture, break. **2 fracturarse** *vr* to fracture, break.
fragancia *nf* fragrance, sweet smell, perfume.
fragante *adj* (a) fragrant, sweet-smelling, scented.
   (b) = **flagrante**.
fragata *nf* frigate.
frágil *adj* fragile, frail; (*Comm*) breakable; (*fig*) frail, delicate.
fragilidad *nf* fragility, frailty; (*fig*) frailty, delicacy.
fragmentario *adj* fragmentary.

fragmento nm fragment; piece, bit.

fragor nm din, clamour, noise; uproar; crash, clash; (of machine, river etc) roar.

fragoroso adj deafening, thunderous.

fragosidad nf (a) roughness, unevenness; difficult nature; denseness. (b) (una —) rough spot; rough road.

fragoso adj rough, uneven; terrain difficult; wood dense.

fragua nf forge.

fraguado nm (a) forging. (b) hardening, setting.

fraguar [1i] 1 vt (a) to forge. (b) (fig) to hatch, concoct; to plot. 2 vi (of cement etc) to harden, set.

fraile nm (a) friar; monk; (fam and pej, any) priest; — descalzo barefooted friar; — mendicante mendicant friar (gen Franciscan); — de misa y olla ignorant friar, simple-minded friar; — predicador friar preacher (gen Dominican). (b) (Cu) bagasse, residue of sugar cane.

frailecillo nm (Orn) puffin.

frailería nf friars (collectively); monks (collectively); (pej) priests.

frailesco adj, **frailuno** adj (pej) monkish.

frambuesa nf raspberry.

frambueso nm raspberry cane.

francachela nf (fam) spread (fam), big feed (fam); spree (fam), binge (sl), jamboree (sl).

francachón adj (SAm) too direct, too outspoken, bad-mannered.

francamente adv (a) frankly, openly, forthrightly. (b) generously, liberally. (c) frankly; really, definitely; — no lo sé frankly I don't know, I really don't know; eso está — mal that is definitely wrong; es una obra — divertida it's a really funny play; estoy — harto contigo I'm frankly fed up with you, I really am fed up with you.

francés 1 adj French; a la francesa in the French manner (or style etc); despedirse a la francesa to take French leave. 2 nm Frenchman. 3 nm (language) French.

francesa nf Frenchwoman.

francesilla nf (a) (Bot) buttercup. (b) (Cook) roll.

Francia f France.

fráncico 1 adj Frankish. 2 nm (language) Frankish.

Francisca f Frances.

franciscano 1 adj Franciscan. 2 nm Franciscan.

Francisco m Francis.

francmasón nm (free)mason.

francmasonería nf (free)masonry.

franco[1] (Hist) 1 adj Frankish. 2 nm Frank.

franco[2] nm (Fin) franc.

franco[3] adj (a) frank, open, forthright, candid; seré — contigo I will be frank with you, I will be plain with you; son francas imposibilidades they are plain impossibilities, they are downright impossible; estar en franca rebeldía to be in open rebellion; estar en franca decadencia to be in full decline. (b) generous, liberal. (c) (Comm etc) free, gratis; exempt; road etc free, open; port etc free; — a bordo free on board; — de derechos duty-free; — de porte (Comm) carriage-free, (Post) post-free; — sobre vagón free on rail. (d) (SAm) on leave (from military service or duties).

franco ... franco ...

francocanadiense 1 adj French-Canadian. 2 nmf French-Canadian.

francófilo nm, **francófila** nf francophile.

francófobo nm, **francófoba** nf francophobe.

franco-hispano adj Franco-Spanish.

francote adj outspoken, blunt, bluff.

francotirador nm sniper, sharpshooter.

franchute nm, **franchuta** nf (fam: pej) Frenchy (fam), frog (fam).

franela nf (a) flannel. (b) (Col, Cu, PR, Ven) vest, undershirt (US).

frangollar [1a] 1 vt (a) to bungle, botch, rush. (b) (Chi, RPl) corn to grind. 2 vi (Bol) to dissemble.

frangollero adj (Arg, Bol) bungling.

frangollo nm (a) (Cook: SAm) crushed and boiled corn, wheat porridge; (Ant) sweet made from mashed bananas; (Arg, Cu, Mex, Per, PR) hastily-prepared meal. (b) (SAm: Orn) birdseed. (c) (Mex) muddle, mess; mixture.

frangollón (SAm) 1 adj bungling. 2 nm bungler.

franja nf (a) (Sew) fringe, border, trimming; braid. (b) fringe, strip, band; — fotoacústica sound track; — de tierra strip of land; la — de Gaza the Gaza strip.

franj(e)ar [1a] vt to fringe, trim (de with).

franqueadora nf (Post) franking machine.

franquear [1a] 1 vt (a) slave to free, liberate; taxpayer etc to free, exempt (de from). (b) right etc to grant, allow, concede (a to). (c) road, way to clear, open. (d) river etc to cross; obstacle to negotiate, overcome, get round. (e) (Post) to frank, stamp; to pay postage on; una carta franqueada a post-paid letter, a letter with the postage paid on it; una carta insuficientemente franqueada a letter with insufficient postage. 2 franquearse vr (a) to give way, fall in with someone's wishes. (b) — a uno, — con uno to unbosom oneself to someone, have a heart-to-heart talk with someone.

franqueo nm postage; franking; con — insuficiente with insufficient postage, with postage underpaid.

franqueza nf (a) frankness, openness, forthrightness, candidness; con — frankly; lo digo con toda — I say so quite frankly. (b) generosity, liberality.

franquía nf (Naut) searoom, room to manoeuvre.

franquicia nf exemption (de from); — aduanera exemption from customs duties; — postal privilege of franking letters.

franquista 1 adj pro-Franco; tendencia — tendency to support Franco, pro-Franco tendency; es una familia muy — it is a strongly pro-Franco family, it is a family which strongly supports Franco. 2 nmf supporter of Franco, pro-Franco person.

frasca nf (a) dry leaves, small twigs. (b) (CAm, Mex) riotous party.

frasco nm (a) flask, bottle; — de campaña (SAm) water bottle; — de perfume scent bottle; — al vacío vacuum flask. (b) liquid measure (Cu = 2.44 litres, Arg = 21.37 litres).

frase nf (a) (Gram) sentence; — compleja complex sentence. (b) (Ling) phrase, expression; — hecha saying, proverb; idiom; (pej) cliché, stock phrase.

fraseo nm (Mus) phrasing.

fraseología nf phraseology.

fratás nm plastering trowel.

fraterna nf (fam) ticking-off.

fraternal adj brotherly, fraternal.

fraternidad nf brotherhood, fraternity; (CAm, PR: Univ) fraternity.

fraternización nf fraternization.

fraternizar [1f] vi to fraternize.

fraterno adj brotherly, fraternal.

fratricida 1 adj fratricidal. 2 nmf fratricide (person).

fratricidio nm fratricide (act).

fraude nm (a) (quality) dishonesty, fraudulence. (b) (act) fraud, swindle; deception; por — by fraud, by false pretences.

fraudulencia nf fraudulence.

fraudulentamente adv fraudulently, by fraud; dishonestly.

fraudulento adj fraudulent; dishonest, deceitful.

fray nm (Eccl: before names) brother, friar.

frazada nf blanket.

frecuencia nf (a) frequency; con — frequently, often. (b) (Elec, Radio) frequency; alta — high frequency; de alta — high-frequency (attr).

frecuentador nm, **frecuentadora** nf frequenter.

frecuentar [1a] vt to frequent; to haunt.

frecuente adj frequent; common; custom etc common, usual, prevalent; (pej) rife.

frecuentemente adv frequently, often.

fregada nf (Arg, CAm, Mex) nuisance; misfortune, untoward event.

fregadera nm (SAm) nuisance, annoyance.

fregadero nm (a) (kitchen) sink. (b) scullery. (c) (CAm, Mex) constant nuisance; recurrent misfortune.

fregado 1 adj (a) (SAm) tiresome, annoying. (b) (SAm) affair nasty, messy, dishonest. (c) (SAm) silly, stupid. (d) (Col, Guat, Mex, Pan, Per) cunning, sly. (e) (Pan, Per, PR) pigheaded. (f) (PR) brazen, fresh. 2 nm (a) rubbing. scrubbing, scouring; washing-up; hacer el — to do the washing-up, wash up. (b) mess, messy affair; nasty affair, dishonest deal. (c) (SAm) row, tiff; tener un — con uno to have a row with someone. (d) (fam) dar un — a uno to give someone a dressing down. (e) (Chi, Col, Per) es un — he's a dead loss.

fregador nm (a) sink. (b) dishcloth; scourer; mop.

fregadura nf (a) = fregado 2 (a). (b) (Chi) = fregada.

fregancia nf (Col) = fregada.

fregandera nf (Mex) charwoman, cleaner.

fregantina nf (Bol, Col, Chi, Per) = fregada.

fregar [1h *and* 1k] *vt* (a) to rub, scrub; to scour; *floor* to mop, scrub; *dishes* to wash (up).
  (b) (*SAm*) to bother, annoy; to worry, harass; ¡no me fregue! stop bothering me!
  (c) (*Cu, PR*) to thrash; (*Sport*) to beat, thrash.
fregasuelos *nm, pl* **fregasuelos** mop.
fregazón *nm* (*Chi*) = **fregada**.
fregón *adj* (a) (*Bol, CAm, Col, Ec, Mex*) trying, tiresome, annoying. (b) (*SAm*) silly, stupid. (c) (*Ec, PR*) brazen, fresh.
fregona *nf* kitchen maid, dishwasher; (*pej*) skivvy; (*PR*) shameless hussy.
freidera *nf* (*Cu*) frying pan.
freiduría *nf* (*also* — de pescado) fried-fish shop.
freír [3m; *ptp* **frito**] 1 *vt* (a) (*Cook*) to fry; (*fig: of sun*) to burn, fry; al — será el reír the proof of the pudding is in the eating.
  (b) (*fig*) to annoy; to torment; to bore.
  2 **freírse** *vr* (a) (*Cook*) to fry, be frying; — de calor to fry in the heat, be roasted.
  (b) —la a uno (*fam*) to plan to deceive someone.
fréjol *nm* = **fríjol**.
frenaje *nm* (*Aut*) braking.
frenar [1a] *vt* (a) (*Aut, Mech*) to brake; to put the brake on, apply the brake to. (b) (*fig*) to check, curb, restrain.
frenesí *nm* frenzy.
frenéticamente *adv* frantically, frenziedly; furiously, wildly.
frenético *adj* frantic, frenzied; furious, wild.
freno *nm* (a) (*Aut, Mech etc*) brake; — de aire air brake; — de mano handbrake; — de pedal footbrake; poner el —, echar los —s to put the brake(s) on, apply the brake(s); soltar el — to release the brake.
  (b) (*horse's*) bit; bridle; morder (*or* tascar) el — (*fig*) to stop before going too far.
  (c) (*fig*) check, curb, restraint; —s y contrapesos, —s y equilibrios (*Pol*) checks and balances; poner — a to curb, check; poner — a las malas lenguas to stop the gossip.
  (d) (*Arg*) hunger.
frenología *nf* phrenology.
frenólogo *nm* phrenologist.
frentazo *nm* (*Arg, Mex*) rebuff, disappointment; pegarse un — to suffer a disappointment; to have things turn out badly for one.
frente 1 *nm* (a) front, front part; face; (*Archit*) front, face, façade; — de arranque, — de trabajo (*Min*) working face; al — in front (*de* of); al — de (*fig*) in charge of, at the head of; ¡de — (mar)! forward march!, by the right quick march!; ir de — to go forward; to face forwards; chocar de — to crash head-on; atacar de — to make a frontal attack; viajar de — a la marcha (*Rail*) to travel facing the engine; marchar 6 de — to march 6 abreast; en — opposite; in front; la casa de en — the house opposite; estar — por — de to be directly opposite; hacer — a to resist, stand up to, face; hacer — a unos grandes gastos to (have to) meet considerable expenses; hacer — a un temporal (*Naut*) to weather a storm.
  (b) (*Mil*) front; — de batalla battle front, firing line; — del oeste western front; cambiar de — to wheel.
  (c) (*Pol*) front; — popular popular front; hacer un — común con uno to make common cause with someone.
  (d) (*Meteorol*) front; — frío cold front.
  2 *nf* forehead, brow; face; — a — face to face; arrugar la —to knit one's brow, frown; llevarlo escrito en la — to make no effort to hide one's feelings.
  3 *prep*: — a opposite (to), facing; in front of; (*fig*) as opposed to, as contrasted with.
freo *nm* channel, strait.
fresa *nf* (a) (*Bot*) strawberry (*esp wild*); strawberry plant. (b) (*Tech*) milling cutter; (dentist's) drill, bit.
fresado *nm* (*Mech*) milling.
fresadora *nf* (*Mech*) milling machine; — de roscar thread cutter.
fresal *nm* strawberry bed.
fresar [1a] *vt* (*Mech*) to mill.
fresca *nf* (a) fresh air, cool air; cool part of the day; tomar la — to get some fresh air, go out for a breath of air.
  (b) (*fam*) decir cuatro —s a uno to give someone a piece of one's mind.
  (c) (*fam*) shameless woman, brazen woman; ¡es una —! she's a hussy!, she's quite brazen!
frescachón *adj* (a) glowing with health, ruddy; robust. (b) *child* bouncing, healthy. (c) *woman* buxom. (d) (*Naut*) *breeze* fresh, stiff.

frescales *nm, pl* **frescales** (*fam*) rogue; brazen person, cheeky sort.
fresco 1 *adj* (a) fresh; new, recent; *bread* new; *egg* new-laid; cosas todavía frescas en la memoria things still fresh in the memory.
  (b) cool; agua fresca cold water; bebida fresca cool drink, cooling drink, cold drink; hacer — (*Meteorol*) to be cool, be fresh.
  (c) *cloth, dress* light, thin.
  (d) *complexion* fresh, ruddy, healthy.
  (e) cool, calm, unabashed; tan — quite unabashed, quite unconcerned; me lo dijo tan — he said it to me as cool as you please; estar más — que una lechuga to be as cool as a cucumber.
  (f) (*fam*) cool, fresh; cheeky, saucy; bad-mannered; ¡qué —! what cheek!, what a nerve!; ponerse — con una to get fresh with a girl.
  2 *nm* (a) fresh air, cool air; al — in the open air, out of doors; tomar el — to get some fresh air, go for a stroll in the open; ¡vete a tomar el —! (*fam*) get lost! (*fam*).
  (b) (*Archit, Art*) fresco; pintar al — to paint in fresco.
  (c) (*fam*) fresh guy (*US fam*), shameless individual; bad-mannered person; ¡Vd es un —! you've got a nerve!; mind your manners!
  (d) (*SAm*) echar — a uno to tell someone a few home truths.
frescor *nm* freshness; coolness; gozar del — nocturno to enjoy the cool night air.
frescote *adj* blooming; buxom.
frescura *nf* (a) freshness; coolness; (*of complexion*) freshness.
  (b) coolness, calmness, unconcern; con la mayor — with the greatest unconcern, completely unconcerned.
  (c) (*fam*) cheek, sauce, nerve; ¡qué —! what a nerve!; tiene la mar de — he's got the cheek of the devil.
  (d) (*fam*) impudent remark, cheeky thing (to say); me dijo unas —s he said some cheeky things to me.
fresia *nf* freesia.
fresnada *nf* ash grove.
fresno *nm* ash, ash tree.
fresón *nm* strawberry (*esp cultivated*); strawberry plant.
fresquera *nf* meat safe; icebox.
fresquería *nf* (*SAm*) refreshment stall, ice-cream parlour.
freudiano *adj* Freudian.
freza *nf* (a) (*Fish*) spawn; (*act, season*) spawning. (b) (*Zool*) dung, droppings.
frezar [1f] *vi* to spawn.
friable *adj* friable.
frialdad *nf* (a) coldness, cold, chilliness. (b) (*fig*) coldness, coolness; indifference, unconcern. (c) (*Mex*) impotence; frigidity.
friamente *adv* (*fig*) coldly.
frica *nf* (*Chi*) beating.
fricasé *nm* fricassee.
fricativa *nf* fricative.
fricativo *adj* fricative.
fricción *nf* rub, rubbing; (*Med*) massage; (*Mech*) friction; (*fig: Pol etc*) friction, trouble.
friccionar [1a] *vt* to rub; (*Med*) to rub, massage.
friega *nf* (a) rub, rubbing; (*Med*) massage.
  (b) (*SAm*) nuisance, annoyance; bother; fuss.
  (c) (*Arg, Col, CR, Mex, Per, PR*) silliness, stupidity.
  (d) (*Arg, Cu, Chi, Per, PR*) thrashing.
  (e) (*Mex, Per*) ticking-off.
friegaplatos *nm, pl* **friegaplatos** dishwasher (*person*).
frígano *nm* caddis fly.
frigidaire *nm or f* (*SAm: angl*) refrigerator.
frigidez *nf* frigidity (*also Med*).
frígido *adj* frigid (*also Med*).
frigo *nm* (*fam*) fridge (*fam*), refrigerator.
frigocentral *nm* (*Arg*) refrigeration plant.
frigorificación *nf* (*Arg*) refrigeration.
frigorífico 1 *adj* refrigerating, cold-storage (*attr*); camión — refrigerator lorry, refrigerator truck (*US*); instalación frigorífica cold-storage plant.
  2 *nm* refrigerator; (*RPl*) cold-storage plant, meat-packing depot; (*Naut*) refrigerator ship.
fríjol *nm*, **frijol** *nm* (a) (*Bot*) kidney bean, French bean.
  (b) —es (*SAm*) food (*in general*); meterse los —es (*Cu*) to eat, have a meal.
  (c) (*Mex*) taunt; —es (*Mex*) boasts.
  (d) ¡—es! (*Cu, PR*) certainly not!, rubbish!
  (e) (*Mex, Per*) coward.

fringolear [1a] *vt* (*Chi*) to thrash, beat.
frío 1 *adj* (**a**) cold; chilly; **más — que el hielo** (*etc*) as cold as charity.
  (**b**) *bullet* spent.
  (**c**) (*fig*) cold, unconcerned, unmoved, indifferent; *reception etc* cold, cool, frigid; **¡me deja Vd —!** you amaze me!; **eso me deja —** that leaves me cold.
  2 *nm* (**a**) cold; coldness; **¡qué —!** isn't it cold!, how cold it is!; **hace —** it's cold; **hace mucho —** it's very cold; **coger —** to catch cold; **pasar —** to be cold, suffer cold; **tener —** to be cold, feel cold; **no me da ni — ni calor** it's all the same to me; *see* **helador** *etc*.
  (**b**) (*fig*) coldness, indifference.
  (**c**) **—s** (*CAm, Col, Ec, Mex*) intermittent fever; malaria.
friolento *adj person* chilly, sensitive to cold, shivery.
friolera *nf* trifle, mere nothing.
friolero *adj* =**friolento**.
frisa *nf* (**a**) (*fabric*) frieze.
  (**b**) (*Bol, Chi, RPl*) nap (on cloth); (*Chi*) fluff; (*PR, SD*) blanket; **sacar a uno la —** (*Chi*) to tan someone's hide (*fam*); **sacar la — a algo** (*Chi*) to extract the maximum advantage from something.
frisar [1a] **1** *vt cloth* to frizz, rub. **2** *vi:* **— en** to border on, be close to; **frisa en los 50** she's close on 50, she's getting on for 50.
Frisia *f* Friesland.
friso *nm* frieze; wainscot, dado.
fritada *nf* fry, fried dish.
fritanga *nf* (**a**) (*SAm: Cook*) fried food; frying. (**b**) (*Chi*) kitchen; stove; (*Mex*) portable stove. (**c**) (*Chi*) nuisance, bother.
fritar [1a] *vt* (*Arg, CAm, Col, Ven*) to fry.
frito 1 *adj* (**a**) (*Cook*) fried.
  (**b**) **tener — a uno** (*fam*), **traer — a uno** (*fam*) to worry someone to death; to defeat someone; to make someone cross; **ese hombre me trae —** that chap bothers me all day long, that chap makes me really cross; **las matemáticas me traen —** maths is getting me down, maths just defeats me.
  (**c**) (*Arg, Cu*) **estar —** to be finished, be done for.
  2 *nm* (**a**) fry, fried dish; **—s variados** mixed grill.
  (**b**) (*Ven*) daily bread; food (*in general*); **ganarse el —** to earn a living.
  (**c**) (*Arg, Ven*) **a esa mujer le gusta el —** she's no angel (though she may try to look like one).
fritura *nf* (**a**) fry, fried dish. (**b**) fritter.
frívolamente *adv* frivolously.
frivolidad *nf* frivolity, frivolousness.
frivolité *nm* (*Sew: gall*) tatting.
frívolo *adj* frivolous.
fronda *nf* frond; **—s** fronds; foliage, leaves.
frondís *adj* (*Col*) dirty.
frondosidad *nf* leafiness; luxuriance.
frondoso *adj* leafy; luxuriant.
frontal *adj* frontal.
frontera *nf* (**a**) frontier, border; frontier area, borderland (*also fig*). (**b**) (*Archit*) façade.
fronterizo *adj* (**a**) frontier (*attr*); border (*attr*). (**b**) opposite, facing; **las casas fronterizas** the houses opposite.
frontero *adj* opposite, facing.
frontis *nm* (*Archit*) façade.
frontispicio *nm* frontispiece; (*fam*) face, clock (*sl*).
frontón *nm* (**a**) (*Archit*) pediment. (**b**) (*Sport*) pelota court; front wall of a pelota court.
frotación *nf*, **frotadura** *nf*, **frotamiento** *nm* rub, rubbing; (*Mech*) friction.
frotar [1a] **1** *vt* to rub; *match* to strike; **quitar algo frotando** to rub something off. **2 frotarse** *vr* to rub, chafe; **— las manos** to rub one's hands.
frote *nm* rub.
fructífero *adj* (**a**) (*Bot etc*) productive, fruit-bearing. (**b**) (*fig*) fruitful.
fructificación *nf* (*fig*) fruition.
fructificar [1g] *vi* (**a**) (*Bot*) to produce, yield a crop, bear fruit. (**b**) (*fig*) to yield a profit; to come to fruition.
fructuosamente *adv* fruitfully.
fructuoso *adj* fruitful.
frugal *adj* frugal; thrifty; parsimonious.
frugalidad *nf* frugality; thrift, thriftiness; parsimony.
frugalmente *adv* frugally; thriftily; parsimoniously.
fruición *nf* enjoyment; satisfaction, delight; **— maliciosa** malicious pleasure.
frunce *nm* pleat, tuck, gather, shirr.
fruncido 1 *adj* (**a**) contracted; (*Sew*) pleated, gathered; *brow* wrinkled, furrowed; *face* frowning.
  (**b**) (*Arg, Chi*) prudish, demure; affected.
  2 *nm* =**frunce**.
fruncimiento *nm* =**frunce**.
fruncir [3b] *vt* to contract, pucker; to ruffle; (*Sew*) to

pleat, gather, shirr, put a tuck in; *brow* to wrinkle, knit; *lips* to purse; *see* **ceño** *etc*.
fruslería *nf* trifle, trinket; (*fig*) trifle, small thing, triviality.
frustración *nf* frustration.
frustrar [1a] **1** *vt* to frustrate, thwart. **2 frustrarse** *vr* to be frustrated; (*of plan etc*) to fail, miscarry.
fruta *nf* (**a**) fruit; **—s** (*Cook*) fruit; **— prohibida** forbidden fruit; **— de sartén** fritter; **— seca** dried fruit.
  (**b**) (*fig*) fruit, consequence.
frutal 1 *adj* fruit-bearing, fruit (*attr*); **árbol — =2** *nm* fruit tree.
frutar [1a] *vi* to fruit, bear fruit.
frutera *nf* fruit dish, fruit bowl.
frutería *nf* fruiterer's (shop), fruit shop.
frutero 1 *adj* fruit (*attr*); **plato —** fruit dish. **2** *nm* (**a**) fruiterer. (**b**) fruit dish, fruit bowl; basket of fruit.
fruticultura *nf* fruit growing.
frutilla *nf* (*SAm*) Indian strawberry; Chilean strawberry.
fruto *nm* (**a**) (*Bot*) fruit; **— del pan** breadfruit; **—s del país** (*RPl*) agricultural products; **dar —** to fruit, bear fruit.
  (**b**) (*fig*) fruits; result, consequence; profit, benefit; offspring, child; **— de bendición** legitimate offspring; **el — de esta unión** the offspring of this marriage; **sacar — de** to profit from, derive benefit from.
fu: ni — ni fa neither one thing nor the other.
fuácata *nf* (*Ant, Mex*): **estar en la —** to be broke (*fam*).
fucilazo *nm* (flash of) sheet lightning.
fuco *nm* wrack.
fucsia *nf* fuchsia.
fudiño *adj* (*Cu*) small, sickly.
fuego *nm* (**a**) fire; conflagration; **—s artificiales** fireworks; **— fatuo** will-o'-the-wisp; **apagar el —** to put out the fire; **atizar el —** to poke the fire; **encender un —** to light a fire; **se declaró el —** fire broke out; **echar — por los ojos** to glare, look daggers; **jugar con —** (*fig*) to play with fire; **matar a uno a — lento** to worry someone to death; **pegar** (*or* **prender**) **— a** to set fire to, set on fire; **poner un pueblo a — y sangre** to lay a village waste.
  (**b**) (*of gas stove*) burner; (*of oven, electric stove*) plate; **una cocina a gas de 4 —s** a gas cooker with 4 burners.
  (**c**) (*Cook*) flame, heat; **sobre un — bajo** on a low flame, on a low gas; **hervir a — lento** to simmer.
  (**d**) (*Naut etc*) beacon, signal fire.
  (**e**) (*for cigarette*) light; **¿tienes —?** have you a light?; **le pedí —** I asked him for a light.
  (**f**) (*Mil*) fire; firing; **¡—!** fire!; **¡alto el —!** cease fire!; **— de andanada** (*Naut*) broadside; **— cruzado** crossfire; **— graneado**, **— nutrido** heavy fire; **abrir — to** open fire; **hacer —** to fire (*sobre* at, on); **romper el — to** open fire.
  (**g**) (*Med*) rash, skin eruption; **— pérsico** shingles.
  (**h**) hearth, home; **un pueblo de 50 —s** a village of 50 houses (*or* families).
  (**i**) (*fig*) fire, ardour, passion; **apagar los —s de uno** to damp down someone's ardour; **atizar el —** to add fuel to the flames, stir things up.
fueguino (*Arg*) **1** *adj* of Tierra del Fuego. **2** *nm*, **fueguina** *nf* native (*or* inhabitant) of Tierra del Fuego; **los —s** the people of Tierra del Fuego.
fuel-oil [fuel'oil] *nm* paraffin, kerosene.
fuelle *nm* (**a**) bellows; blower; **— de pie** foot pump.
  (**b**) (*of car, carriage*) folding hood, folding top (*US*); (*Phot*) bellows; **— quitasol** (*Phot*) hood.
  (**c**) (*fam*) telltale.
fuente *nf* (**a**) fountain, spring; **— de beber** drinking fountain; **— termal** hot spring; **— de río** source of a river; **abrir la — de las lágrimas** (*hum*) to weep buckets.
  (**b**) (*Cook*) large dish, bowl; serving dish.
  (**c**) (*fig*) source; origin; **de — desconocida** from an unknown source; **de — fidedigna** from a reliable source; **— de suministro** source of supply.
fuer *nm:* **a — de** as a; in the manner of; **a — de caballero** as a gentleman; **a — de hombre honrado** as an honest man.
fuera 1 *adv* (**a**) outside; out; **¡—!** get out!, off with you!; chuck him out!; **"¡ruritanos —!"** (*placard etc*) "Ruritanians go home!"; **ir —** to go out, go away, go outside; **con la camisa —** with his shirt hanging out; **el perro tenía la lengua —** the dog had his tongue hanging out; **la parte de —** the outside part, the outer part; **desde —** from outside; **por —** (on the) outside; **los de —** those from outside; strangers, newcomers.
  (**b**) **estar —** (*of person*) to be out of town, be on

a trip; to be away; **estuvo — 8 semanas** he was away for 8 weeks.

(**c**) (*Sport*) **estar —** to be out, be in touch; **poner —** to put into touch; **jugar —** (*of team*) to play away (from home); **los de —, el equipo de —** the away team.

2 — de (*prep*) (**a**) outside (of); out of; **estaba — de su jaula** it was outside (*or* out of) its cage; **esperamos — de la puerta** we waited outside the door; **— de alcance** out of reach, beyond one's reach; **— de moda** out of fashion; **estar — de sí** to be beside oneself; *see* **combate** *etc.*

(**b**) (*fig*) in addition to, besides, beyond; **pero — de eso** but in addition to that; but aside from that; **todo — de mentir** everything short of lying.

fuera-borda *nm, pl* **fuera-borda; fuerabordo** *nm, pl* **fuerabordo** outboard engine, outboard motor; dinghy with an outboard engine.

fuereño *nm,* **fuereña** *nf* (*Mex*) outsider, stranger (*living temporarily in Mexico City*).

fuerino *nm,* **fuerina** *nf* (*Chi*) stranger, non-resident.

fuero *nm* (**a**) municipal charter; local (*or* regional *etc*) law code; (*of group*) privilege, exemption; **a —** according to law; **¿con qué —?** by what right?; **de — de jure**, in law.

(**b**) jurisdiction, authority; **el — no alcanza a tanto** his authority does not extend that far.

fuerte 1 *adj* (*in many senses*) strong; tough, sturdy; robust; vigorous; solid; *town, defences, wind, argument, objection, belief, will etc* strong; *terrain* rough, difficult; *blow* hard, heavy; *noise* loud; *expense, rain* heavy; *meal* heavy, big; *dish* main; rich; *bend* sharp; *taste, tea, wine etc* strong; *heat, pain etc* intense, great, considerable; *crisis* grave; *exercise* strenuous; *rigour etc* excessive, extreme; **hacerse — en una colina** to entrench oneself on a hill, make a fortified position on a hill; **se hicieron —s en la casa** they prepared to defend the house; they barricaded themselves in the house; they made a stand in the house; **ser — en filosofía** to be strong in (*or* on) philosophy, be well up in philosophy.

2 *adv* strongly; *hit* hard; *play, talk* loud, loudly; **pegar — al enemigo** to hit the enemy hard; **toca muy —** she plays very loudly; **¡más —!** (*to speaker*) speak up!; **poner la radio más —** to turn the radio up; **comer —** to eat a big meal, eat too much.

3 *nm* (**a**) (*Mil*) fort, strongpoint.

(**b**) (*Mus*) forte.

(**c**) (*fig*) forte, strong point; **el canto no es mi —** singing is not my strong point.

fuertemente *adv* strongly; loudly; intensely.

fuerza *nf* (**a**) (*in many senses*) strength; toughness, sturdiness; vigour; solidity; power; intensity; **—s** (*of person*) strength; (*of argument*) force, strength, effect; **a — de** by dint of, by force of; **a viva —** by sheer strength, by main force; **entrada a viva —** forced entry, **cobrar —s** to recover one's strength; to gather strength; **hacer — de vela** (*Naut*) to crowd on sail; **restar —s a** to weaken; **no me siento con —s para eso** I don't feel up to it; **tener —s para + infin** to have the strength to + infin, be strong enough to + infin.

(**b**) (*Mech, Phys*) force; power; **— de arrastre** pulling power; **— ascensional** (*Naut*) buoyancy; **— de brazos** manpower; **— centrífuga** centrifugal force; **— centrípeta** centripetal force; **— de gravedad** force of gravity; **— hidráulica** water power, hydraulic power; **— motriz** motive power; **— de sustentación** (*Aer*) lift.

(**c**) (*Elec*) power, current, energy; **han cortado la —** they've cut off the power.

(**d**) force, compulsion; pressure; **— mayor** force majeure; act of God; **por — mayor** by sheer force; **a la —, por —** by force; willy-nilly, against one's will; under pressure, compulsively; perforce, of necessity; **en — de** by virtue of; **es — + infin** it is necessary to + infin.

(**e**) force, violence; **— bruta** brute force; **hacer — a una mujer** to rape a woman; **recurrir a la —** to resort to force, use violence; **rendirse a la —** to yield to violence; **sin usar —** without using force, without using violence.

(**f**) (*Mil*) force, forces; **—s aéreas** air force; **—s aliadas** allied forces; **—s armadas** armed forces; **— de disuasión, — disuasoria, — disuasiva** deterrent; **— expedicionaria** expeditionary force; **—s de mar y de tierra** land and sea forces; **— pública** police (force); **—s terrestres** land forces.

fuetazo *nm* (*SAm*) lash.

fuete *nm* (*SAm: gall*) whip; **dar — a** (*Ant*) to whip.

fuetear [1a] *vt* (*SAm*) to whip.

fuga[1] *nf* (**a**) flight, escape; (*of lovers*) elopement; **— de**

la cárcel escape from prison, jailbreak; **apelar a la —, darse a la —, ponerse en —** to flee, take to flight; **poner al enemigo en —** to put the enemy to flight. (**b**) (*of gas etc*) leak, escape. (**c**) (*fig*) ardour, impetuosity.

fuga[2] *nf* (*Mus*) fugue.

fugarse [1h] *vr* (**a**) to flee, escape (*a* to); to run away (*con* with); (*of lovers*) to elope (*con* with); **— de la ley** to abscond from justice.

(**b**) (*of gas etc*) to leak out, escape.

fugaz *adj* (**a**) *moment etc* fleeting, short-lived, transitory, brief. (**b**) elusive. (**c**) **estrella —** shooting star.

fugazmente *adv* fleetingly, briefly.

fugitivo 1 *adj* (**a**) fugitive, fleeing. (**b**) = **fugaz. 2** *nm,* **fugitiva** *nf* fugitive.

fui, fuimos *etc see* **ser;** *see* **ir.**

fuina *nf* marten.

fulana *nf* (**a**) **Doña F—** Mrs So-and-so, Mrs Blank. (**b**) (*fam*) tart (*sl*), whore.

fulano *nm* so-and-so, what's-his-name; **— de tal, Don F—** Mr So-and-so, Mr Blank; Joe Soap; John Doe (*US*); **—, zutano y mengano** Tom, Dick and Harry; **me lo dijo —** somebody told me; old what's-his-name told me; **no te vas a casar con un —** you're not going to marry just anybody; **nombramos a — y ya está** we nominate some chap and that's that.

fulcro *nm* fulcrum.

fulero *adj* (**a**) useless, sham, bogus; poor-quality, poorly made; nasty. (**b**) *person* tricky, sly. (**c**) *person* blundering, incompetent.

fulgente *adj,* **fúlgido** *adj* dazzling, bright, brilliant, radiant.

fulgor *nm* brilliance, radiance, glow; (*fig*) splendour.

fulgurante *adj* (**a**) bright, shining. (**b**) (*fig*) shattering, stunning.

fulgurar [1a] *vi* to shine, gleam, glow; to flash.

fulguroso *adj* bright, shining, gleaming; flashing.

fúlica *nf* coot.

fulmicotón *nm* guncotton.

fulminación *nf* fulmination.

fulminador *nm* fulminator (*de* against), thunderer (*de* against).

fulminante 1 *adj* (**a**) *powder* fulminating; **cápsula —** percussion cap.

(**b**) (*Med*) fulminant; *see* **ataque** (**b**).

(**c**) (*fam*) *success etc* terrific (*fam*), tremendous (*fam*); **golpe —** terrific blow, smash hit; **tiro —** (*Sport*) sizzling shot.

2 *nm* (**a**) (*Arg*) match.

(**b**) (*SAm*) percussion cap.

fulminar [1a] **1** *vt* (**a**) to fulminate; *threats* to utter, thunder (*contra* against); **— a uno con la mirada** to look daggers at someone.

(**b**) to strike with lightning.

2 *vi* to fulminate, explode.

fulo *adj* (**a**) (*Pan*) blond(e), fair. (**b**) (*Arg*) furious, enraged; maddened.

fullerear [1a] *vi* (*Col*) to swank (*fam*).

fullería *nf* (**a**) cheating, cardsharping; guile, low cunning. (**b**) trick. (**c**) (*Col*) swankiness (*fam*), conceit.

fullero *nm* (**a**) cheat, cardsharper; crook; tricky individual. (**b**) (*Col*) swank (*fam*), show-off (*fam*).

fullingue *adj* (*Chi*) (**a**) *tobacco* inferior, poor-quality. (**b**) *child* small, sickly.

fumada *nf* whiff of smoke, puff of smoke.

fumadero *nm* smoking room; **— de opio** opium den.

fumador *nm,* **fumadora** *nf* smoker; **— de pipa** pipe smoker; **no —** non-smoker.

fumante *nm* (*Arg*) cigar, cigarette.

fumar [1a] **1** *vti* to smoke; **"prohibido —"** "no smoking"; **— como un carretero** to smoke like a chimney; **él fuma en pipa** he smokes a pipe; **está fumando su pipa** he is smoking his pipe; **¿puedo —?, ¿se permite —?** may I smoke?

2 fumarse *vr* (**a**) *money* to dissipate, squander; *class* to cut, miss.

(**b**) **—lo a uno** (*Arg, Cu, Mex*) to outdo someone; **— de uno** to trick someone, swindle someone.

fumarada *nf* (**a**) puff of smoke. (**b**) (*of tobacco*) pipeful.

fumigación *nf* fumigation.

fumigar [1h] *vt* to fumigate; **¡que te fumiguen!** (*fam*) get lost! (*fam*).

fumista *nm* (*Arg: gall*) joker, tease.

fumo *nm* (*Ven*) puff of smoke.

fumosidad *nf* smokiness.

fumoso *adj* smoky.

funámbulo *nm,* **funámbula** *nf* tightrope walker.

funcia *nf* (*CAm, Col, Chi, Ven: hum*) = **función.**

función *nf* (**a**) function; functioning, operation;

(b) (*of post*) duties; **presidente en —es** acting president; **entrar en —es** to take up one's duties; **excederse en sus —es** to exceed one's duty.

(c) (*Theat etc*) show, performance; entertainment; spectacle; **— benéfica** charity performance; **— de despedida** farewell performance; **— de la tarde** matinée; **— de títeres** puppet show; **— taquillera** box-office success, big draw; **mañana no hay —** there will be no performance tomorrow.

funcional *adj* functional.

funcionalidad *nf* functional character.

funcionamiento *nm* functioning, operation; (*Mech, Tech*) operation, working, running; performance; behaviour; **máquina en —** machine in working order; **sociedad en —** going concern; **entrar en —** to come into operation; **poner en —** to bring into operation, bring into service.

funcionar [1a] *vt* to function; (*Mech, Tech*) to go, work, run; to perform; to behave; "**funcionando**" (*in advert etc*) in working order, in running order; "**no funciona**" (*notice*) "out of order"; **hacer — una máquina** to operate a machine.

funcionario *nm* official, functionary; employee; civil servant; **— público** public official.

funda *nf* **(a)** case, cover, sheath; **— de almohada** pillowcase, pillowslip; **— de pistola** holster. **(b)** holdall. **(c)** (*Col*) shirt.

fundación *nf* foundation.

fundadamente *adv* with good reason, on good grounds.

fundado *adj* firm, well-founded, justified; **una pretensión mal fundada** an ill-founded claim.

fundador *nm*, **fundadora** *nf* founder.

fundamental *adj* fundamental, basic; essential.

fundamentalmente *adv* fundamentally, basically; essentially.

fundamentar [1a] *vt* **(a)** to lay the foundations of. **(b)** (*fig*) *argument etc* to base, found (*en* on).

fundamento *nm* **(a)** (*Archit etc*) foundation. **(b)** (*fig*) foundation, basis; groundwork; grounds, reason; **eso carece de —** that is groundless, that is completely unjustified; **creencia sin —** groundless belief, unfounded belief; **¿qué — tiene esta teoría?** what is the basis of this theory?, what is the basic justification for this theory? **(c)** (*moral*) reliability, trustworthiness. **(d)** (*Tech*) weft, woof. **(e)** (*Anat*) fundament. **(f)** **—s** (*fig*) fundamentals; basic essentials.

fundar [1a] **1** *vt* **(a)** to found; to institute, set up, establish; to raise, erect; (*with money*) to endow. **(b)** *theory etc* to base, found (*en* on). **2 fundarse** *vr* **(a)** to be founded, be established. **(b)** **— en** to be founded on, be based on; to base oneself on; **me fundo en los siguientes hechos** I base myself on the following facts.

fundente 1 *adj* melting. **2** *nm* (*Chem*) dissolvent; flux.

fundería *nf* foundry; **— de hierro** iron foundry.

fundición *nf* **(a)** fusing, fusion; (*Tech*) smelting; melting. **(b)** (*Tech*) foundry, forge, smelting plant; **— de hierro** iron foundry. **(c)** cast iron; casting; **— de acero** steel casting. **(d)** (*Typ*) font, fount.

fundido *adj* (*SAm: Comm*) ruined, bankrupt.

fundidor *nm* smelter, founder.

fundillos *nmpl* (*SAm*) seat (*of trousers*); (*fam*) seat, bottom; (*Arg*) pants.

fundir [3a] **1** *vt* **(a)** to fuse (together); to join, unite. **(b)** (*Tech*) to melt (down), smelt; *snow etc* to melt; (*Elec*) to fuse; *piece, part* to found, cast; (*Comm*) to merge; **el faro está fundido** the lamp is fused, the lamp is broken. **(c)** (*SAm*) to ruin. **2** *vi* (*Cine*) to fade (*a* to). **3 fundirse** *vr* **(a)** to fuse (together); to join, unite; (*of colours, effects etc*) to merge, blend (together). **(b)** to melt (*also fig*); (*Elec: of fuse*) to blow, burn out; **se le fundió el corazón** her heart melted. **(c)** (*SAm*) to ruin oneself; to be ruined.

fundón *nm* (*Col, Ven*) riding habit.

fúnebre *adj* **(a)** funeral (*attr*). **(b)** (*fig*) funereal; *sound etc* mournful, lugubrious.

funeral 1 *adj* funeral (*attr*). **2** *nm* funeral; **—es** funeral, obsequies.

funerala *nf*: **marchar a la —** to march with reversed arms; **ojo a la —** black eye.

funeraria *nf* undertaker's, undertaker's establishment, funeral parlor (*US*); **director de —** undertaker, funeral director, mortician (*US*).

funerario *adj*, **fúnéreo** *adj* funeral (*attr*); funereal.

funestamente *adv* banefully; fatally, disastrously.

funestidad *nf* (*Mex*) calamity.

funesto *adj* ill-fated, unfortunate; baneful; fatal, disastrous (*para* for).

fungir [3c] *vi* (*CAm, Mex*) to act (*de* as); (*Cu*) to substitute, stand in (*a* for).

fungoideo *adj* fungoid.

fungoso *adj* fungous.

funicular *nm* funicular (*railway*).

fuñido *adj* **(a)** (*Ven*) quarrelsome; unsociable. **(b)** (*Cu*) weak, sickly, feeble.

fuñingue *adj* (*Chi*) weak.

furcia *nf* (*sl*) tart (*sl*), whore.

furgón *nm* wagon, van, truck; (*Rail*) van; **— de cola** guard's van; caboose (*US*); **— de equipajes** luggage van, baggage car (*US*); **— de mudanzas** removal van.

furgonada *nf* wagonload, vanload.

furgonero *nm* carter, vanman.

furgoneta *nf* van; (*Aut*) shooting brake, station wagon (*US*).

furia *nf* fury; rage, violence; **a toda —** like fury; **a la —** (*RPl*) at top speed; **ella salió como una —, ella salió hecha una —** she went out furiously (angry).

furibundo *adj* furious; frenzied.

furiosamente *adv* furiously; violently; frantically.

furioso *adj* furious; violent; frantic, raging; **estar —** to be furious; **ponerse —** to get furious.

furor *nm* **(a)** fury, rage; frenzy; passion; **— uterino** nymphomania; **dijo con —** he said furiously. **(b)** (*fig*) rage; **hacer —** to be all the rage; **tener — por** (*SAm*) to have a passion for.

furquina *nf* (*Bol, Col*) short skirt.

furriel *nm*, **furrier** *nm* quartermaster.

furrusca *nf* (*Col*) row, brawl.

furtivamente *adv* furtively; in a clandestine way; slyly, stealthily.

furtivo *adj* furtive; clandestine; sly, stealthy; *edition* pirated; *see* **cazador**.

furuminga *nf* (*Chi*) intrigue, scheme, plot.

furúnculo *nm* (*Med*) boil.

fusa *nf* demisemiquaver.

fuselado *adj* streamlined.

fuselaje *nm* fuselage.

fusible *nm* fuse.

fusil *nm* rifle, gun; **— de juguete** popgun, toy gun.

fusilamiento *nm* shooting, execution.

fusilar [1a] *vt* to shoot, execute; (*Ven etc*) to kill (*in general*).

fusilazo *nm* rifle shot.

fusilero *nm* rifleman, fusileer.

fusión *nf* fusion; joining, uniting; (*of metal etc*) melting; (*Comm*) merger, amalgamation.

fusionamiento *nm* (*Comm*) merger, amalgamation.

fusionar [1a] **1** *vt* to fuse (together); (*Comm*) to merge, amalgamate. **2 fusionarse** *vr* to fuse; (*Comm*) to merge, amalgamate.

fusta *nf* **(a)** long whip; riding whip. **(b)** brushwood, twigs.

fustán *nm* **(a)** fustian. **(b)** (*SAm*) petticoat, underskirt; (*Ec, Per*) skirt.

fuste *nm* **(a)** wood, timber; **de —** wooden. **(b)** (*of weapon*) shaft; (*of chimney, column*) shaft; **de —** (*fig*) important, of some consequence. **(c)** saddle tree. **(d)** (*CAm, Ven: Anat*) bottom.

fustigar [1h] *vt* **(a)** to whip, lash. **(b)** (*fig*) to upbraid, lash (*with one's tongue*).

fútbol *nm* (*angl*) football; **— americano** American football; **— asociación** association football, soccer; **— rugby** rugby football.

futbolín *nm* table football, bar football.

futbolista *nm* footballer, football player.

futbolístico *adj* football (*attr*).

futearse [1a] *vr* (*Col: of fruit etc*) to go bad, rot.

futesa *nf* trifle, mere nothing; **—s** small talk, trivialities.

fútil *adj* trifling, trivial.

futilidad *nf* triviality, trifling nature, unimportance.

futre *nm* (*Bol, Chi, Ec, Per, RPl*) dandy, toff (*fam*), dude (*US*).

futrería *nf* (*Chi, Per*) **(a)** affected behaviour. **(b)** group of dandies, group of dudes (*US*). **(c)** dude's hangout (*US*).

futura *nf* **(a)** (*Law*) reversion. **(b)** (*fam*) fiancée.

futurismo *nm* futurism.

futurístico *adj* futuristic.

futuro 1 *adj* future; **en lo —** in (the) future. **2** *nm* **(a)** future; **en el —** in (the) future; **en un — próximo** in the very near future, very soon. **(b)** (*Gram*) future, future tense. **(c)** (*fam*) fiancé. **(d)** **—s** (*Comm*) futures.

G

gaba *nmf* (*Texas: pej*) white American, Yankee.
gabacho 1 *adj* (**a**) (*Geog*) Pyrenean.
　(**b**) frenchified.
　(**c**) (*Col: fam*) **le salió gabacha la cosa** it came to nothing, the affair was a failure.
　2 *nm*, **gabacha** *nf* (**a**) (*Geog*) Pyrenean villager.
　(**b**) (*pej*) Frenchy (*fam*), froggy (*fam*); frenchified Spaniard; (*Texas*) white American, Yankee; (*Mex*) (*any*) foreigner, outsider.
gabán *nm* overcoat, topcoat.
gabarda *nf* wild rose.
gabardina[1] *nf* gabardine; raincoat, mackintosh.
gabardino *nm*, **gabardina**[2] *nf* (*Texas: pej*) white American, Yankee.
gabarra *nf* barge, lighter, flatboat.
gabarrero *nm* bargee, bargeman, lighterman.
gabarro *nm* (**a**) (*in cloth*) flaw, defect. (**b**) (*Vet*) pip.
　(**c**) (*fig*) error, slip, miscalculation; snag; annoyance.
gabela *nf* (**a**) (*Hist*) tax, duty; (*fig*) burden. (**b**) (*Col, Ec, PR, SD, Ven*) advantage, profit.
gabinete *nm* (**a**) study, library; private sitting room; boudoir; (*Law, Med*) office; laboratory; museum; (*Art*) studio; (*Col*) enclosed balcony; **— de consulta** consulting room; **— de lectura** reading room; **— de teléfono** (*Mex*) telephone booth; **estratega de —** armchair strategist.
　(**b**) (*Pol*) cabinet.
　(**c**) suite of office furniture.
gablete *nm* gable.
gacel *nm*, **gacela** *nf* gazelle.
gaceta *nf* (**a**) gazette, official journal; (*SAm*) newspaper. (**b**) (*Ant*) gossip; telltale.
gacetero *nm* (**a**) newswriter, journalist. (**b**) newspaper seller.
gacetilla *nf* (**a**) gossip column; section of local news, section of miscellaneous news items; **"G—"** (*heading*) "News in Brief".
　(**b**) (*fam*) gossip, scandalmonger; **ella es una — andando** (*or* **con dos patas**) she's a dreadful gossip.
gacetillero *nm* newspaper reporter; gossip columnist; (*pej*) hack, penny-a-liner.
gacetista *nmf* gossip, scandalmonger.
gacilla *nf* (*CAm: Sew*) clasp, hook and eye.
gacha *f* (**a**) thin paste; watery mass, mush; **—s** (*as food*) pap; porridge; **—s de avena** oatmeal porridge; **se ha hecho unas —s** it's got mushy, it's got soggy, (*fig*) she's got mushy, she's turned all sentimental.
　(**b**) (*Col, Ven*) earthenware bowl.
gachí *nf*, *pl* **gachís** (*sl*) dame (*sl*), bird (*sl*).
gacho *adj* (**a**) bent down, turned downward; *horn* down-curved; *cow* with down-curved horns; *hat* with down-turned brim; *ears etc* drooping, floppy; **sombrero —** slouch hat.
　(**b**) (*Mex*) unpleasant.
　(**c**) **ir a gachas** to go on all fours.
gachó *nm*, *pl* **gachós** (**a**) (*sl*) chap (*fam*), bloke (*sl*).
　(**b**) *interj* bravo!, jolly good! (*fam*).
gachón *adj* (*fam*) nice, charming, sweet; *child* spoilt.
gachumbo *nm* (*Col, Ec*) hard woody shell (*of certain fruits: used to make cups etc*).
gachupín *nm* (*CAm, Mex: pej*) (*any*) Spaniard.
gaditano 1 *adj* of Cadiz. **2** *nm*, **gaditana** *nf* native (*or* inhabitant) of Cadiz; **los —s** the people of Cadiz.
gaélico 1 *adj* Gaelic. **2** *nm*, **gaélica** *nf* Gael. **3** *nm* (*language*) Gaelic.
gafa *nf* grapple; clamp; **—s** glasses, spectacles; goggles; **—s ahumadas** smoked glasses; **—s sin aros** rimless glasses; **— bifocales**, **—s graduadas** bifocals; **—s de motorista** motorcyclist's goggles; **—s negras** dark glasses; **—s protectoras** protective goggles; **—s de sol**, **—s para sol** sunglasses; **—s submarinas** underwater goggles.
gafancia *nf* (tendency to have) constant bad luck, capacity for messing things up.

gafar [1a] *vt* (**a**) to hook, claw, latch on to. (**b**) (*fam*) to bring bad luck to, put a hoodoo on; to spoil, mess up.
gafe 1 *adj* (*fam*): **ser —** to have constant bad luck, have a great capacity for messing things up. **2** *nm* (*fam*) bad luck; hoodoo.
gafete *nm* clasp, hook and eye.
gafo *adj* (**a**) (*SAm, Col, PR*) footsore, dog-tired; (*Mex*) numb. (**b**) (*Ven*) unreliable.
gag [gax] *nm*, *pl* **gags** [gax] (*angl: Theat etc*) gag.
gago (*Cu, Chi, Mex, Per, PR, Ven*) **1** *adj* stammering. **2** *nm*, **gaga** *nf* stammerer.
gagoso *adj* (*Col*) stammering.
gaguear [1a] *vi* (*Cu, Chi, Mex, Per, PR, Ven*) to stammer, stutter.
gagueo *nm* (*Cu, Chi, Mex, Per, PR, Ven*) stammer(ing).
gaguera *nf* (*Cu, Chi, Mex, Per, PR, Ven*) stammer, speech defect.
gaita 1 *nf* (**a**) (*Mus*) flute, flageolet; hurdy-gurdy; **— (gallega)** bagpipe; **ser como una —** to be very demanding; **estar de —** to be merry; **templar —s** to calm someone down, smooth things out.
　(**b**) (*fam*) neck; **sacar la —** to stick one's neck out.
　(**c**) (*Arg*) bother, nuisance; tough job.
　2 *nmf* (*SAm: hum*) Galician, (*any*) Spaniard.
gaitero 1 *adj* (**a**) gaudy, flashy. (**b**) inappropriately jocular, witty in the wrong way. **2** *nm* (bag)piper.
gajes *nmpl* pay, emoluments; perquisites; **—s del oficio** (*hum*) occupational hazards, occupational risks.
gajo *nm* (**a**) (torn-off) branch, bough, limb; (*of grapes*) small cluster, bunch.
　(**b**) (*of orange etc*) slice, segment, quarter.
　(**c**) (*of fork*) point, prong; (*Geog*) spur.
　(**d**) (*Col, Guat, Hond, SD*) curl, ringlet.
gala *nf* (**a**) full dress; best dress; court dress; **de —** state (*attr*), dress (*attr*), full-dress (*attr*); gala (*attr*); **estar de —** to be in full dress; to be in one's best dress, be all dressed up; (*town etc*) to be bedecked, be in festive mood.
　(**b**) **—s** finery, trappings; jewels, adornments; regalia; fine things; **—s de novia** bridal attire.
　(**c**) (*fig*) elegance, gracefulness; pomp, display; **hacer — de** to display, show off; to boast of, glory in; **tener algo a —** to be proud of something; **tener a — + infin** to be proud to **+ infin**.
　(**d**) (*fig*) cream, flower, pride, chief ornament; **es la — de la ciudad** it is the pride of the city.
　(**e**) delight; speciality, special accomplishment; **su mejor — está en recorrer las calles con guitarras** their special delight is to roam the streets with their guitars.
　(**f**) (*SAm*) gift, tip.
galáctico *adj* galactic.
galafate *nm* expert thief, sly thief.
galán 1 *nm* (**a**) handsome fellow, attractive young man; ladies' man; (*Hist*) young gentleman, courtier.
　(**b**) gallant, beau; suitor.
　(**c**) (*Theat*) male lead, chief male part; hero; **joven —** juvenile lead; **primer —** leading man.
　2 *adv* (*SAm: fam*)**=bien**.
galanas *nfpl* (*CAm*): **echar —** to boast, brag; **hacer —** to do naughty things, be wicked.
galanamente *adv* smartly, sprucely; elegantly, tastefully.
galancete *nm* handsome young man; (*hum*) dapper little man; (*Theat*) male juvenile lead.
galano *adj* (**a**) smart, spruce; elegant, tasteful; gaily dressed. (**b**) (*Cu*) *cow* mottled (with red and white patches).

galante adj (a) man gallant; charming, attentive (to women); polite, urbane. (b) woman flirtatious; (pej) wanton, free, licentious.

galantear [1a] vt to court, woo; to flirt with.

galantemente adj gallantly; charmingly, attentively; politely.

galanteo nm courting, courtship, wooing; flirting.

galantería nf (a) (in general) gallantry; attentiveness (to women); politeness, urbanity. (b) (remark etc) compliment; charming thing (to say), gallantry.

galanto nm (Bot) snowdrop.

galanura nf prettiness; charm; elegance, tastefulness.

galápago nm (a) (Zool) freshwater tortoise. (b) (Agr) mould board. (c) (Tech) ingot, pig. (d) light saddle; (SAm) sidesaddle.

Galápagos: Islas fpl **de (los)** — Galapagos Isles.

galardón nm (lit) reward, prize.

galardonar [1a] vt (lit) to reward, recompense (de with); (Lit) work to give a prize to; **obra galardonada por la Academia** work which won an Academy prize.

galaxia nf galaxy.

galbana nf sloth, laziness; shiftlessness.

galbanoso adj slothful, lazy; shiftless.

galembo nm (Col, Ven) turkey buzzard.

Galeno m Galen.

galeón nm galleon.

galeote nm galley slave.

galera nf (a) (Naut) galley; **echar a uno a —s** to condemn someone to the galleys. (b) (covered) wagon. (c) (Med) hospital ward; (Hist) women's prison; (CAm, Mex) shed; (CR) slaughterhouse. (d) (SAm) top hat; derby hat; felt hat; bowler hat. (e) (Typ) galley.

galerada nf (a) wagonload. (b) (Typ) galley proof.

galería nf (in many senses) gallery; passage, corridor; (Min) gallery; (on beach etc) beach hut, changing room, (at swimming pool) cubicle; (on outside of house) veranda(h); (Art) gallery; **— de columnas** colonnade; **— de popa** (Naut) stern gallery; **— secreta** secret passage; **— de tiro** shooting gallery; **— de viento** (Aer) wind tunnel; **— visitable** manhole.

galerita nf crested lark.

galerna nf, **galerno** nm violent north-west wind (on N coast of Spain).

galerón nm (CAm) shed; shed roof; (Mex) big room.

Gales m Wales.

galés 1 adj Welsh. 2 nm Welshman. 3 nm (language) Welsh.

galesa nf Welshwoman.

galga nf (a) (Zool) greyhound (bitch). (b) (Geol) boulder, rolling stone; (Tech) millstone (of an oil press). (c) (Agr) hub brake (on a cart).

galgo[1] nm greyhound; **— ruso** borzoi, Russian wolfhound; **¡échale un —!** good heavens!, you don't say!; search me! (fam); **¡vaya Vd a espulgar un —!** (fam) go to blazes!

galgo[2] adj (Col) sweet-toothed, fond of sweets.

galgón adj (Ec) =**galgo**[2].

galguear [1a] vi (CAm, RPl) to feel terribly hungry; to wander about looking for food.

Galia f Gaul.

galicano adj Gallic.

galiciano 1 adj Galician. 2 nm, **galiciana** nf Galician.

galicismo nm gallicism.

gálico nm syphilis.

galicoso 1 adj syphilitic. 2 nm syphilitic.

Galilea f Galilee.

galillo nm (Anat) uvula.

galimatías nm, pl **galimatías** rigmarole; gibberish, nonsense.

galo 1 adj Gallic. 2 nm, **gala** nf Gaul.

galocha nf clog, patten.

galón[1] nm (Sew) braid; (Mil) stripe, chevron; **quitar los —es a uno** to take his stripes away from someone, demote someone; **la acción le valió 2 —es** the action got him a couple of stripes.

galón[2] nm (measure) gallon.

galonear [1a] vt to trim with braid.

galopada nf gallop.

galopante adj (Med and fig) galloping.

galopar [1a] vi to gallop; **echar a —** to break into a gallop.

galope nm gallop; **a —, al —** (SAm), **de —** at a gallop, (fig) in great haste, in a rush; **a — tendido** at full gallop; **alejarse a —** to gallop off; **desfilar a —** to gallop past; **llegar a —** to gallop up; **medio —** canter.

galopín nm ragamuffin, urchin, street arab; scoundrel, rogue; smart-aleck (fam), clever dick (fam); (Naut) cabin boy.

galpón nm (SAm) (large) shed, storehouse; (Aut) garage; (Col) tileworks, pottery.

galucha nf (SAm) short gallop; (Cu) start of a gallop.

galuchar [1a] vi (SAm) to gallop.

galvánico adj galvanic.

galvanismo nm galvanism.

galvanizado adj galvanized.

galvanizar [1f] vt to galvanize (also fig), electroplate.

gallada nf (CAm, Chi, Col) bold deed, great achievement; piece of boasting.

gallardamente adv gracefully, elegantly; splendidly; bravely; gallantly, dashingly; nobly.

gallardear [1a] vi to be elegant, be graceful, act with ease and grace; to bear oneself well.

gallardete nm pennant, streamer.

gallardía nf gracefulness, elegance; fineness, splendidness; bravery; gallantry, dash; nobleness.

gallardo adj graceful, elegant; fine, splendid; brave; gallant, dashing; noble.

gallareta nf (SAm) South American coot; see **pato**.

gallear [1a] 1 vt (of cock) to tread. 2 vi (a) to excel, stand out. (b) to put on airs, strut; to bully, chuck one's weight about; to brag; to bluster, bawl.

gallego 1 adj (a) Galician. (b) (SAm: pej) Spanish (in general). 2 nm, **gallega** nf (a) Galician. (b) (SAm: pej) (any) Spaniard. (c) north-west wind. 3 nm (dialect) Galician.

gallera nf (SAm) cockpit; (Guat, Per) coop (for gamecocks).

gallería nf (a) (Cu) place where gamecocks are raised; (Cu) building for cockfights; (Guat) cockpit. (b) (Cu: fig) egotism, selfishness.

gallero 1 adj (SAm) fond of cockfighting. 2 nm (a) (SAm) man in charge of gamecocks (or cockfighting); cockfighting enthusiast. (b) (Chi: Rail) pilferer.

galleta nf (a) biscuit; wafer; (Naut) ship's biscuit, hardtack; (Chi) coarse bread; **— dulce** rusk; **— de perro** dog biscuit. (b) (fam) bash (fam), punch, slap. (c) (Bol, RPl, Ven) small bowl for drinking maté. (d) (Chi) ticking-off. (e) (Ven) joke; hoax, deception. (f) **colgar la — a uno, dar la — a uno** (RPl) to sack someone (fam); to jilt someone; to refuse to accept someone's advances; **hacerse una —** (RPl) to get muddled. (g) **— del tráfico** (Ven) traffic jam.

galletear [1a] vt (Chi, RPl) to sack (fam), fire (fam); to tick off. (b) to bash (fam), punch.

galletero nm (a) biscuit barrel, biscuit tin. (b) (Chi) quick-tempered person; argumentative sort, brawler.

gallina 1 nf (a) hen, fowl; **— de agua** coot; **— de Bantam** bantam; **— clueca** broody hen; **— de Guinea** guinea fowl; **— ponedora** laying hen, hen in lay; **acostarse con las —s** to go to bed early; **estar como — con huevos** to be very distrustful; **estar como — en corral ajeno** to have no freedom of movement; to be like a fish out of water; to be timid, be shy; **¡hasta que meen las —s!** (fam) till pigs learn to fly! (fam); **la — de arriba ensucia a la de abajo** (SAm) the underdog always suffers. (b) **jugar a la — ciega** to play blind man's buff. 2 nmf (a) (fam) coward. (b) (Ec: pej) Peruvian.

gallinacera nf (Ec, Per) bunch of Negroes.

gallinaza nf hen droppings.

gallinazo nm (SAm) turkey buzzard.

gallinería nf (a) flock of hens; poultry shop, chicken market. (b) (fig) cowardice.

gallinero nm (a) henhouse, coop; poultry basket. (b) chicken farmer; poulterer, poultry dealer. (c) (Theat) gods, top gallery. (d) babel, hubbub; noisy gathering.

gallineta nf (Orn) sandpiper; (SAm) guinea fowl.

gallinilla nf: **— de Bantam** bantam.

gallipavo nm (a) (Orn) turkey. (b) (Mus) false note, wrong note.

gallito nm (a) (Orn) small cock. (b) (fig) rowdy, tough (fam), troublemaker; **el — (del mundo)** the cock-o'-the walk, the top dog. (c) (Col) small arrow, dart.

gallo nm (a) (Orn) cock, cockerel, rooster; **— lira** black grouse; **— montés, — silvestre** capercaillie; **— de combate, — de pelea, — de riña** gamecock, fighting cock; **estar como — en gallinero** to be much esteemed, be well thought-of; **en menos que canta un —** in an instant; **otro — me cantara** that would be quite a different matter; **otro — que cantara si . . .** things would have turned out very differently if . . .; **comer —** (CR, Ec) to suffer a blow;

haber comido — (Mex) to be in a fighting mood; **hay** — **tapado** (SAm) I smell a rat; **no me va nada en el** — (Mex) it doesn't matter to me; **levantar el** — (Mex, PR, SD) to pack it in; **matar a uno el** — **en la mano** to floor someone (in an argument), shut someone up.
(b) (fam) boss; (SAm) expert, master; **yo he sido** — **para eso** I was a great one at that.
(c) **alzar el** —, **levantar el** — (fig) to put on airs, brag; to bawl, behave noisily; **tener mucho** — to be cocky (fam).
(d) (Fish) cork float.
(e) (Mus) false note, wrong note; break in the voice; **soltar un** — to sing a wrong note.
(f) (Arg, CAm, Mex, PR) phlegm, sputum.
(g) (Col) small arrow, dart.
(h) (Chi, Per) fire engine, hose truck.
(i) (Mex: Mus) street serenade.
(j) (Mex) secondhand article, discarded object; **vestirse de** — to wear old things.

gallofero 1 adj idle, loafing; vagabond. **2** nm idler, loafer; tramp; beggar.

gallón adj (Mex) cocky (fam).

gallote adj (CAm, Mex) cocky (fam).

gama¹ nf (Mus) scale; (fig) range, scale, gamut; **una extensa** — **de colores** an extensive range of colours; — **de frecuencias** frequency range; — **de ondas** wave range; — **sonora** sound range.

gama² nf (letter) gamma.

gama³ nf (Zool) doe (of fallow deer); **sentársele a uno la** — (Arg) to get discouraged.

gamba nf prawn; (sl) 100 pesetas.

gambado adj (Ant) knock-kneed.

gamberrada nf piece of hooliganism, loutish thing (to do).

gamberrear [1a] vi to go around causing trouble, act like a hooligan; to be a lout; to loaf.

gamberrismo nm hooliganism; loutishness.

gamberrístico adj loutish, ill-bred.

gamberro 1 adj ill-bred, loutish, rough. **2** nm lout, hooligan, troublemaker, roughneck (sl).

gambeta nf (of horse) prance, caper; (Bol, Per, RPl) dodge, avoiding action; (fig) dodge, pretext.

gambito nm gambit.

gambuza nf (Naut) store, storeroom.

gamella nf trough; washtub.

gamín nm (Col) street urchin.

gamo nm buck (of fallow deer).

gamonal nm (CAm, Col, Ec, Per) = **cacique**.

gamonalismo nm (CAm, Col, Ec, Per) = **caciquismo**.

gamuza nf (a) (Zool) chamois. (b) chamois leather, wash leather; duster.

gana nf desire, wish (de for); appetite (de for); inclination, longing (de for); **¡las** —**s!** you'll wish you had (agreed)!; **son** —**s de joder** (or **molestar** etc) they're just trying to be awkward; **es** — (Mex, Per, PR) it's a waste of time; — **tiene de coles quien besa al hortelano** it's just cupboard love; **con** —**s** (CAm, PR) really, truly; **de** — (Ec) unintentionally; as a joke, in fun; **de buena** — willingly, readily; **¡de buena** —**!** gladly!; **de mala** — unwillingly, reluctantly, grudgingly; **hasta las** —**s** (Mex) right up to the end; **comer con** — to eat heartily; **me da la** — **de** + infin I feel like + ger, I want to + infin, I have an inclination to + infin; **esto da** —**s de comerlo** it makes you want to eat it; **porque no me da la** (**real**) — because I don't (damned well) want to; **como se dé la** — just as you wish; **le entran** —**s de** + infin he begins to want to + infin, he feels the urge to + infin; **quedarse con las** —**s** to fail, to be disappointed; **quitársele a uno las** —**s de** to spoil one's appetite for; **tener** —**s de** + infin to feel like + ger, have a mind to + infin; **tengo pocas** —**s de** + infin I don't much feel like + ger.

ganadería nf (a) cattle raising, stockbreeding; ranching. (b) stock farm; cattle ranch. (c) cattle, livestock; strain, breed, race (of cattle).

ganadero 1 adj cattle (attr), stock (attr); cattle-raising (attr). **2** nm stockbreeder, rancher (US); cattle dealer.

ganado nm (a) stock, livestock; (esp SAm) cattle; (un —) herd, flock; — **asnal** donkeys; — **caballar** horses; — **cabrío** goats; — **lanar** ovejuno sheep; — **mayor** cattle, horses and mules; — **menor** sheep, goats and pigs; — **porcino** pigs; — **vacuno** cattle.
(b) (SAm) **un** — **de** (fig) a crowd of, a mob of.

ganador 1 adj winning, victorious; **el equipo** — the winning team; **apostar a** — **y colocado** to back (a horse) each way, back for a win and a place.
2 nm, **ganadora** nf winner; (Fin) earner; (fig) gainer, one who gains.

ganancia nf (a) gain; increase; (Comm, Fin) profit; —**s** earnings; profits, winnings; —**s y pérdidas** profit and loss; — **bruta** gross profit; —**s de capital** capital gains; — **líquida** net profit; **sacar** — **de** to draw profit from. (b) (SAm) extra, bonus.

ganancial adj profit (attr).

ganancioso 1 adj (a) gainful; profitable, lucrative.
(b) winning; **salir** — to emerge the winner, come out on top; to be the gainer.
2 nm, **gananciosa** nf gainer, one who gains; winner; **en esto el** — **es él** in this he is the gainer.

ganapán nm (a) messenger, porter. (b) casual labourer; odd-job man. (c) lout, rough individual.

ganar [1a] **1** vt (a) to gain; to get, acquire, obtain; (Comm, Fin) to earn; interest to draw; money to earn, make; prize to win; **gana un sueldo** he earns a salary; **¿cuánto ganas al mes?** how much do you earn (or make) a month?; **tierras ganadas al mar** land reclaimed from the sea, land won from the sea.
(b) (Sport etc) match, race, contest to win; point to score, win; opponent to beat; rival to outstrip, surpass, leave behind; — **unas oposiciones para un puesto** to win a post by public competition; **A le ganó a B esta vez** A beat B this time; **no hay quien le gane** there's nobody who can beat him; **A le gana a B en pericia** A has more expert knowledge than B; **A le gana a B trabajando** A is a better worker than B; **A le ganó 5 duros a B** A won 5 duros from (or off) B.
(c) (Mil) town etc to take, capture.
(d) to reach; — **la orilla** to reach the shore; — **la orilla nadando** to swim to the shore.
(e) (fig) to win over; support, supporters to win, get; **dejarse** — **por** to allow oneself to be won over by; **no se deja** — **en ningún momento por la desesperación** he never gives way to despair.
2 vi (a) (Sport etc) to win; to gain.
(b) (fig) to thrive, improve, do well.
(c) (also **ganarse**; SAm) to go off; to escape, take refuge; — **a la cama** to go off to bed; — **hasta la casa** to get to the house; **se ganó en la iglesia** he took refuge in the church; **el caballo ganó para el bosque** the horse moved off towards the wood, the horse made for the wood.

ganchera nf (Arg) matchmaker.

ganchero nm (Arg) helper, assistant; (Chi) odd-job man.

ganchete nm: **mirar al** — (Ven) to look askance (at); **ir de** — (SAm) to go arm-in-arm.

ganchillo nm (a) small hook; (Sew) crochet hook. (b) crochet, crochet work; **hacer** — to crochet.

gancho nm (a) hook; hanger; (Agr) shepherd's crook; (SAm) hairpin; — **de carnicero** butcher's hook; **echar el** — **a** (fig) to hook, land, capture.
(b) (person) main attraction, centre of attraction; (pej) pimp, procurer; (pej) tout.
(c) (fam) sex appeal, charm, attractiveness; **tiene muchísimo** — she's got lots of sex appeal.
(d) (Col, Ec) lady's saddle.
(e) (SAm) help; protection; **hacer** — (Arg, Guat) to lend a hand.

ganchoso adj, **ganchudo** adj hooked.

gandido adj (Col) hungry; greedy.

gandinga nf (Cu, PR) (Cook) liver stew. (b) sloth, apathy; **tener poca** — to have small sense of shame.

gandul 1 adj idle, lazy, slack; good-for-nothing. **2** nm, **gandula** nf idler, slacker; good-for-nothing.

gandulear [1a] vi to idle, loaf, slack.

gandulería nf idleness, loafing, slackness.

gandulitis nf (hum) congenital laziness.

gane nm (CAm: Sport) win, victory; **llevarse el** —, **lograr el** — to win.

gang [gan] nm, pl **gangs** [gan] (angl) gang.

ganga nf (a) (Comm) bargain; **¡una verdadera** —**!** a genuine bargain! (b) (fig) windfall; cinch (sl), gift (fam); **esto es una** — this is a gift. (c) (Mex) taunt, jeer.

ganglio nm ganglion; swelling.

gangosear [1a] vi (Arg, Col) = **ganguear**.

gangoseo nm (Arg, Col) = **gangueo**.

gangoso adj accent nasal, twanging.

gangrena nf gangrene.

gangrenarse [1a] vr to become gangrenous.

gangrenoso adj gangrenous.

gángster ['ganster] nm, pl **gángsters** ['ganster] (angl) gangster, gunman.

gangsterismo [ganste'rizmo] nm (angl) gangsterism.

ganguear [1a] vi to talk with a nasal accent, speak with a twang.

gangueo nm nasal accent, twang.

ganoso adj (a) anxious, keen; — **de** + infin anxious to + infin, keen to + infin. (b) (Chi) horse spirited, fiery.

gansa nf (a) (Orn) goose. (b) (fam) goose, silly girl.

gansada nf stupid thing (to do), piece of stupidity.

ganso nm (a) (Orn) goose, gander; — **salvaje** wild goose. (b) (fam) idiot, dimwit (fam), dolt; country bumpkin; ¡no seas —! don't be an idiot!

Gante Ghent.

ganzúa 1 nf picklock, skeleton key. **2** nmf burglar, thief; inquisitive person, smeller out of secrets.

gañán nm farmhand, labourer.

gañido nm yelp, howl; croak; wheeze.

gañir [3h] vi (of dog) to yelp, howl; (of bird) to croak; (of person) to wheeze, talk hoarsely, croak.

gañón nm (fam), **gañote** nm (fam) throat, gullet.

garabatear [1a] **1** vt to scribble, scrawl. **2** vi (a) to throw out a hook. (b) to scribble, scrawl. (c) to beat about the bush.

garabato nm (a) hook; grapple, grapnel; (Ant) long forked pole; (Naut) grappling iron; — **de carnicero** meat hook.
  (b) (in writing exercise) pothook.
  (c) (Ant) skinny person.
  (d) (Chi) coarse remark.
  (e) —s scribble, scrawl.
  (f) = **gancho** (c).

garabina nf (a) (Bol) trifle, bagatelle; cheap finery. (b) (Cu) chrysalis.

garabito nm (a) market stall. (b) (Bol) bum, tramp.

garaje nm garage; — **de varios pisos** multi-storey car park.

garajista nm garage owner; garage man, garage attendant.

garambaina nf (a) cheap finery, tawdry finery.
  (b) gaudiness.
  (c) —s (affected) grimaces; absurd mannerisms; ¡déjate de —s! stop that silly simpering!
  (d) —s scribble, scrawl.

garambetas nfpl (PR) = **garambaina** (a) and (c).

garandumba nf (Arg) (a) flatboat, flat river boat. (b) (hum) big woman.

garante 1 adj responsible. **2** nmf guarantor, surety.

garantía nf guarantee; pledge, security; undertaking; (Law) warranty; **bajo** — under guarantee; — **constitucionales** constitutional guarantees; — **en efectivo** cash guarantee, surety; **de máxima** — absolutely guaranteed.

garantir [3a; defective] vt (a) to guarantee. (b) (Chi, Per, PR) to guarantee, assure; **le garanto** I assure you, I warrant you.

garantizado adj guaranteed.

garantizar [1f] vt to guarantee, warrant; to vouch for.

garañón nm (a) stud jackass; (SAm) stallion. (b) (Chi) brothel keeper.

garapiña nf (a) sugar icing, sugar coating. (b) (SAm) iced pineapple drink. (c) (Mex) theft.

garapiñar [1a] vt ice cream etc to freeze; cream to clot; cake to ice, coat with sugar; fruit to candy.

garapiñera nf ice-cream freezer.

garapullo nm dart, arrow; (Taur) = **banderilla**.

garata nf (PR, SD) fight, brawl, row.

garatusas nfpl: **hacer — a uno** to coax someone, wheedle someone.

garba nf (Agr) sheaf.

garbanzo nm (a) (Bot) chickpea; **ser el — negro** to be the black sheep of the family.
  (b) **de —** ordinary, unpretentious, common; **gente de —** humble folk, ordinary people.

garbear [1a] **1** vt (fam) to pinch (fam), swipe (sl). **2** vi (a) to affect elegance, make a show, show oneself off. (b) = **3 garbearse** vr to get along, rub along (fam).

garbeo nm affected elegance, show; **darse un —**, **pegarse un —** to take an elegant stroll, walk to show oneself off.

garbera nf (Agr) stook, shock.

garbillar [1a] vt (Agr) to sift, sieve; (Min) to sift, screen, riddle.

garbillo nm sieve; screen, riddle.

garbo nm (a) grace, elegance; graceful bearing, fine carriage; jauntiness, jaunty bearing; (woman's) glamour, allure, attractiveness; **andar con —** to walk gracefully, carry oneself well; **hacer algo con —** to do something with grace and ease (or with style); ¡qué —! what a carriage!, (freq) isn't she lovely?
  (b) magnanimity, generosity.

garbosamente adv (a) gracefully, elegantly; in sprightly fashion; jauntily; alluringly, attractively; gracefully and easily, stylishly. (b) generously.

garboso adj (a) graceful, elegant; jaunty; glamorous, alluring, attractive; graceful and easy, stylish. (b) magnanimous, generous.

garceta nf egret.

gardel nm (Arg) toff (fam), masher (fam).

gardelear [1a] vi (Arg) to dress smartly.

gardenia nf gardenia.

garduña nf (Zool) marten.

garduño nm, **garduña** nf sneak thief.

garete nm: **estar al —**, **ir al —** to be adrift.

garfa nf claw.

garfada nf clawing, scratching.

garfio nm hook; gaff; (Tech) grapple, grappling iron, claw; (Mountaineering) climbing iron.

gargajear [1a] vi to spit phlegm, hawk.

gargajo nm phlegm, sputum.

garganta nf (a) (Anat) throat, gullet; neck; **le tengo atravesado en la —** he sticks in my gullet.
  (b) (Anat: of foot) instep.
  (c) (Mus) singing voice; **tener buena —** to have a good singing voice.
  (d) (of bottle) neck.
  (e) (Geog) gorge, ravine; narrow pass.
  (f) (Archit: of column etc) shaft.

gargantear [1a] vi (Mus) to warble, quaver, trill.

gargantilla nf necklace.

gárgara nf gargle, gargling; **hacer —s** to gargle; ¡**vaya Vd a hacer —s!** (fam) go to blazes!

gargarear [1a] vi (Chi, Guat, Per) to gargle.

gargarismo nm (a) gargle, gargling solution. (b) gargle, gargling.

gargarizar [1f] vi to gargle.

gárgol nm (Tech) groove.

gárgola nf gargoyle.

gargolet nm wren.

garguero nm gullet; windpipe.

garifo adj (a) spruce, elegant, natty. (b) (Arg, Bol) lively, merry. (c) (Col) stuck-up (fam). (d) (CR, Ec, Per) hungry, greedy.

garita nf cabin, hut, box; (Mil) sentry box; (of lorry etc) cab; (of building) porter's lodge; look-out post; (fam) water closet; (SAm: of traffic police) stand, box; — **de señales** (Rail) signal box.

garitea nf (Bol, Ec) river flatboat.

garitero nm keeper of a gaming house; gambler.

garito nm (a) gaming house, gambling den. (b) gambling profits.

garlador 1 adj garrulous. **2** nm, **garladora** nf chatterer, great talker.

garlito nm fish trap; (fig) snare, trap; **caer en el —** to fall into the trap; **coger a uno en el —** to catch someone in the act.

garlopa nf jack plane.

garnacha nf (Law: Hist) gown, robe. (b) (Mex: Cook) omelette. (c) (CAm) **a la —** violently; **ni de —** (Ven) not at all, by no means.

garnucho nm (Mex) tap, rap on the nose.

Garona m Garonne.

garra nf (a) (Zool) claw; talon; (fig) hand, paw; (Mex: fig) muscular strength; **echar la — a uno** to arrest someone, seize someone; **estar como una —** (Arg, Col) to be terribly thin.
  (b) —s (Zool) claws, talons; (fig) jaws; (fig) clutches; (fig) grip, clutch; **caer en las —s de uno** to fall into someone's clutches.
  (c) (Tech) claw, tooth, hook; (Mech) clutch; — **de seguridad** safety clutch.
  (d) (fig) bite, penetration; **esa canción no tiene —** that song has no bite to it.
  (e) (SAm) piece of (hard, wrinkled, old) leather; —s (Mex) bits, pieces, scraps; **no hay cuero sin —s** (Mex) nothing is ever perfect.
  (f) (Col) leather bag; sack.

garrafa nf carafe, decanter.

garrafal adj enormous, terrific; blunder etc monumental, terrible.

garrafón nm carboy, demijohn.

garrancha nf (fam) sword; (Col) hook.

garrapata nf (a) (Zool) tick. (b) (Mil: hum) disabled horse, useless horse.

garrapatear [1a] vi to scribble, scrawl.

garrapatero nm cowbird, buffalo bird; (SAm) tick-eater bird.

garrapato nm pothook; —s (fig) scribble, scrawl.

garrapaticida nm (SAm) insecticide, tick-killing agent.

garrear [1a] (Arg) **1** vt (a) to skin the feet of. (b) (fam) to steal. **2** vi to sponge, live at someone else's expense.

garreo nm (Arg: fam): **es de puro —** it's a cinch (sl).

garrete nm (Arg, Guat, Col, Ven) = **jarrete**.

garrido adj (a) neat, elegant, smart. (b) (arch) handsome; pretty.

garroba nf carob bean.

garrocha nf (Agr) goad; (Taur) spear; (Sport) vaulting pole.

garrón *nm* (*Orn*) spur; talon; (*Zool*) paw; heel; (*of meat*) shank; (*Arg*) hock; (*Bot*) snag, spur; **vivir de —** (*Arg*) = **garronear**.

garronear [1a] *vi* (*Arg*) to live in idleness; to sponge (*fam*), live at someone else's expense.

garrotazo *nm* blow with a stick (*or club etc*).

garrote *nm* (a) stick, club, truncheon, cudgel; **política del gran —** (*SAm*) policy of the big stick; **jugar —** (*Ven*) to get angry. (b) (*Med*) tourniquet; (*Law*) garrotte; **dar — a uno** to garrotte someone. (c) (*Mex*: *Aut*) brake; **darse —** to check oneself, hold oneself back.

garrotero 1 *adj* (*Cu*, *Chi*) stingy. **2** *nm* (a) (*Mex*) brakeman. (b) (*Chi*, *Ec*, *Per*) bully, tough (*fam*); brawler, troublemaker.

garrotillo *nm* (a) (*Med*) croup. (b) (*Arg*) very cold drizzle.

garrucha *nf* pulley.

garrudo *adj* (a) (*Mex*) tough, muscular. (b) (*Col*) *cow* terribly thin.

garrulería *nf* chatter.

garrulidad *nf* garrulity, talkativeness.

gárrulo *adj person* garrulous, chattering, talkative; *bird* twittering; *water* babbling, murmuring; *wind* noisy.

garúa *nf* (a) (*SAm*) drizzle. (b) (*PR*) row, uproar.

garuar [1e] *vi* (*SAm*) to drizzle; ¡qué le garúe fino! I wish you luck!, I hope it keeps fine for you!

garubar [1a] *vi* (*Hond*, *Urug*) = **garuar**.

garuga *nf* (*Chi*, *Nic*, *Mex*, *RPI*) = **garúa**.

garugar [1h] *vi* (*Arg*, *Chi*) = **garuar**.

garulla *nf* (a) loose grapes. (b) (*fam*) mob, rabble. (c) (*fam*) urchin.

garullada *nf* (*fam*) mob, rabble.

garullo *nm* (*fam*) lanky youth, gawky lad.

garza *nf* (*also* **— real**) heron; **— imperial** purple heron.

garzo *adj* blue, bluish; blue-eyed.

garzón *nm* (*Chi*, *RPI*: *gall*) waiter.

gas *nm* (a) gas; fumes; **— del alumbrado** coal gas; **— asfixiante**, **— tóxico** poison gas; **— butano** butane; **—es de escape** exhaust (fumes); **— hilarante** laughing gas; **— lacrimógeno** tear gas; **— mostaza** mustard gas; **— natural** natural gas; **— de los pantanos** marsh gas; **— pobre** producer gas; **asfixiar con —** to gas; **estar — (Guat)** to be in love. (b) (*CAm*, *Mex*, *PR*) petrol, gas (*US*); **ir a todo —** (*Aut*) to go full out.

gasa *nf* gauze; (*for mourning*) crêpe.

Gascuña *f* Gascony.

gaseosa *nf* aerated water, carbonated water, mineral water; (*freq*) pop (*fam*), fizz (*fam*), fizzy drink; **— de limón** fizzy lemonade.

gaseoso *adj* gaseous; aerated, carbonated; gassy; *drink* fizzy.

gásfiter *nm*, *pl* **gásfiters** (*Chi*: *angl*) plumber.

gasfitería *nf* (*Chi*, *Ec*, *Per*) plumber's (shop).

gasfitero *nm* (*SAm*: *angl*) plumber.

gasista *nm* gas fitter, gasman.

gasoducto *nm* gas pipeline.

gas-oil [ga'soil] *nm* (*angl*) diesel oil.

gasóleo *nm* (*Acad*) diesel oil.

gasolina *nf* (a) (*Aut*) petrol, motor spirit, gasoline (*US*), gas (*US fam*); **— de aviación** aviation spirit; **— de alto octanaje** high-octane petrol. (b) (*PR*) petrol station, gas station (*US*).

gasolinera *nf* (a) (*Naut*) motorboat. (b) (*Aut*) petrol station, gas station (*US*).

gasómetro *nm* gasometer.

gásquet *nm*, *pl* **gásquets** (*SAm*: *angl*) gasket.

gastable *adj* expendable; dispensable.

gastado *adj* (a) spent; used up. (b) worn out; *dress* shabby, threadbare. (c) *cliché etc* hackneyed, trite; *joke* old, corny (*fam*).

gastador 1 *adj* extravagant, lavish; wasteful. **2** *nm*, **gastadora** *nf* (a) spender; (*pej*) spendthrift. (b) (*Mil*: *Hist*) sapper, pioneer.

gastar [1a] **1** *vt* (a) *effort, money, time etc* to spend; to expend; to lay out; **han gastado un dineral** they've spent a fortune. (b) *resources etc* to use up, exhaust, consume. (c) (*pej*) to waste; **— una semana en hacer algo** to waste a week doing something; **— palabras** to waste words, waste one's breath. (d) (*Mech etc*) to wear away, wear down; *clothes, shoes* to wear out; to spoil. (e) *to have, wear, sport; to use*; to show habitually; *car etc* to have, own, run; **— barba** to have a beard, wear a beard, sport a beard; **antes no gastaba gafas** he used not to wear glasses. (f) *joke* to crack; *trick* to play (*a on*). (g) **—las** (*fam*) to act, behave.

2 *vi* to spend.

3 gastarse *vr* to become exhausted; to run out; to wear out; to waste, go to waste, spoil.

gasto *nm* (a) (*act*) spending, expenditure. (b) amount spent, expenditure, expense; **ello supone un gran — para él** it means a considerable expense for him. (c) consumption, use. (d) (*Mech etc*) wear. (e) waste. (f) (*of gas etc*) flow, rate of flow. (g) **—s** (*Comm*, *Fin*) expenses; charge(s), cost(s), rate(s); **—s de acarreo** transport charges, haulage; **—s de administración** administrative costs, overheads; **—s bancarios** bank charges; **—s de conservación**, **—s de mantenimiento** upkeep costs, maintenance expenses; **—s de correos** postal charges; **—s de defensa** (*Mil*) defence costs; **—s de explotación** operating costs, operating expenses; **—s fijos** fixed charges; **—s de flete** freight charges; **—s generales** overheads; **—s menores (de caja)** petty cash; **—s de viaje** travelling expenses; **cubrir —s** to cover expenses; **meterse en —s** to go to expense, incur expense; **pagar los —s** to pay the expenses, foot the bill.

gastoso *adj* extravagant, wasteful.

gástrico *adj* gastric.

gastritis *nf* gastritis.

gastronomía *nf* gastronomy.

gastronómico *adj* gastronomic.

gastrónomo *nm*, **gastrónoma** *nf* gastronome, gourmet; gastronomist.

gata *nf* (a) (*Zool*) cat, she-cat. (b) (*fam*) Madrid woman; (*Mex*) servant, maid. (c) (*Meteorol*) hill cloud. (d) (*Chi*, *Per*) crank, handle. (e) **a —s** on all fours; (*Bol*, *RPI*) barely, hardly; with great difficulty; **andar a —s** to go on all fours; to creep, crawl; (*of child*) to crawl. (f) **echar la —** (*CAm*), **soltar la —** (*Col*) to pilfer, steal.

gatada *nf* (a) movement (*or act etc*) typical of a cat. (b) litter of kittens. (c) scratch, clawing. (d) artful dodge, sly trick.

gateado 1 *adj* (a) catlike, feline. (b) streaked, striped. **2** *nm* (a) crawl, crawling; climb, climbing. (b) scratch, clawing. (c) (*Ant*) hard veined wood (used in cabinet-making).

gateamiento *nm* = **gateado 2** (a) *and* (b).

gatear [1a] **1** *vt* (a) to scratch, claw. (b) (*fam*) to pinch (*sl*), swipe (*sl*). (c) (*Mex*) *servants* to make love to; (*Bol*, *Ec*, *Guat*) to make love to. **2** *vi* (a) to climb, clamber (*por up*); to creep, crawl, go on all fours. (b) (*SAm*) to go looking for sexual adventure.

gatera *nf* (a) catlover. (b) cat hole (*also Naut*). (c) (*Bol*, *Ec*, *Per*) market woman, stallholder.

gatería *nf* (a) cats, collection of cats. (b) gang of louts. (c) pretended humility, assumed modesty.

gatillo *nm* (a) (*Mil*) trigger; (*Med*) dental forceps; (*Tech*) clamp. (b) (*Zool*) nape (of the neck). (c) young thief, young pickpocket.

gatita *nf* (female) kitten.

gatito *nm* kitten; puss, pussy.

gato[1] *nm* (a) (*Zool*) cat, tomcat; **— de algalia** civet cat; **— de Angora** Angora cat; **— montés** wild cat; **— romano** tabby cat; **— siamés** Siamese cat; **"El — con botas"** "Puss in Boots"; **dar a uno — por liebre** to take someone in, pull the wool over someone's eyes, sell someone a pig in a poke; **el — escaldado del agua fría huye** once bitten twice shy; **aquí hay — encerrado** I smell a rat, there's something fishy here; **no había más que 4 —s** there was hardly anybody there; **jugar al — y ratón con uno** to play a cat-and-mouse game with someone; **llevar el — al agua** to pull off something difficult; **pasar sobre algo como — sobre ascuas** to tread carefully round something. (b) (*Tech*: *Aut etc*) jack; clamp, vice, grab; (*Mex*) = **gatillo**; **— de tornillo** screw jack. (c) (*Fin*) money bag. (d) (*fam*) sneak thief, petty thief; slyboots (*fam*). (e) native of Madrid. (f) (*Mex*) servant. (g) (*CAm*, *Col*, *SD*) fleshy part of the arm. (h) (*Mex*) tip. (i) (*Ven*) syphilis. (j) (*Chi*) hot-water bottle. (k) (*RPI*) *a popular folk dance*.

gato² nm (Per) open-air market, market place.
gatuno adj catlike, feline.
gatuperio nm (a) hotchpotch. (b) fraud, piece of underhand dealing.
gaucha nf (Arg) mannish woman.
gauchada nf (RPl) (a) gauchos (collectively). (b) gaucho exploit, (pej) typical gaucho trick. (c) kind deed, favour; disinterested act.
gauchaje nm (RPl) gauchos (collectively); gathering of gauchos; (pej) riffraff, rabble.
gauchear [1a] vi (RPl) (a) to live like a gaucho, observe the customs of the gauchos. (b) to be mixed up in dangerous love affairs.
gauchesco adj (RPl) gaucho (attr); like a gaucho; of the gauchos; **vida gauchesca** gaucho life.
gaucho 1 nm (SAm) gaucho; cowboy, herdsman, rough rider; (Arg: hum) inhabitant of the coastal provinces.
  (b) (Chi, RPl) good rider, expert horseman.
  (c) (Ec) wide-brimmed straw hat.
  2 adj (a) gaucho (attr); gaucho-like.
  (b) (SAm: pej) coarse, rough; sly, tricky.
gaudeamus nm (hum) party, beano (fam).
gaveta nf drawer, till; locker.
gavia nf (a) (Naut) (main) topsail. (b) (Orn) seagull. (c) (Agr) ditch.
gavilán nm (a) (Orn) sparrowhawk. (b) (of quill pen) nib. (c) (of sword) quillon. (d) (SAm) ingrowing nail.
gavilla nf (a) (Agr) sheaf. (b) (fam) gang, band.
gaviota nf (a) (Orn) seagull, gull. (b) (Mex: hum) airman.
gavota nf (Hist) gavotte.
gaya nf (a) (Orn) magpie. (b) (in cloth) coloured stripe.
gayo adj (a) merry, gay; **gaya ciencia** (Lit: Hist) art of poetry, art of the troubadours. (b) bright, showy.
gayola nf cage; (fam) jail.
gaza nf loop; (Naut) bend, bight.
gazafatón nm (fam) = **gazapatón**.
gazapa nf (fam) fib, lie.
gazapatón nm (fam) blunder, slip; piece of nonsense.
gazapera nf (a) rabbit hole, warren. (b) (fam) den of thieves. (c) brawl, shindy.
gazapo nm (a) (Zool) young rabbit. (b) sly fellow; (SAm) liar. (c) blunder, bloomer (fam); lie; (Typ) meaningful misprint. (d) (PR) trick.
gazmoñada nf, **gazmoñería** nf (a) hypocrisy, cant. (b) prudery, priggishness; affected demureness; sanctimoniousness.
gazmoñero adj, **gazmoño** 1 adj (a) hypocritical, canting.
  (b) prudish, priggish; strait-laced; affectedly demure; sanctimonious.
  2 nm, **gazmoñera** nf, **gazmoña** nf (a) hypocrite.
  (b) prude, prig; affectedly demure person; sanctimonious person.
gaznápiro nm, **gaznápira** nf dolt, simpleton.
gaznatada nf (CAm, PR) punch, slap.
gaznate nm (a) gullet; windpipe, throttle; **remojar el —** (fam) to wet one's whistle (fam), have a swig (fam). (b) (Mex) fritter.
gaznetón nm adj (CAm, Col, Mex) loud-mouthed, bawling.
gazpacho nm (a) cold soup (esp Andalusian) made of oil, vinegar, garlic, onion, cucumber etc. (b) (Hond) residue, dregs, left-overs.
gazuza nf (a) (fam) ravenous hunger. (b) (CR) din, row, merry noise. (c) (Guat) common people. (d) (Hond) wily bird.
géiser nm (Geog) geyser.
geisha ['geiʃa] nf geisha (girl).
gelatina nf gelatin(e), jelly; **— explosiva** gelignite.
gelatinoso adj gelatinous.
gelignita nf gelignite.
gema nf (a) gem, jewel. (b) (Bot) bud.
gemelo 1 adj twin; **buque —** sister ship; **hermanas gemelas** twin sisters.
  2 (a) nm, **gemela** nf twin.
  (b) **—s** nmpl **de campo** field glasses, binoculars; **—s de teatro** opera glasses.
  (c) **—s** nmpl (Sew) cufflinks.
  (d) **G—s** mpl (Astron) Gemini.
  (e) nm (Naut) sister ship.
gemido nm groan, moan; wail, howl.
gemidor adj groaning, moaning; wailing, howling.
Géminis nm (Astron) Gemini.
gemiquear [1a] vi (Chi) to whine.
gemiqueo nm (Chi) whining.
gemir [3l] vi to groan, moan; to wail, howl; (of animal) to whine; (of wind etc) to moan, howl; (fig) to moan, lament; (in jail) to languish, rot; **"Sí" dijo gimiendo** "Yes" he groaned.
gen nm gene.

genciana nf gentian.
gendarme nm (SAm: gall) policeman, gendarme.
gendarmería nf (SAm: gall) police, gendarmerie.
genealogía nf genealogy; family tree; pedigree.
genealógico adj genealogical.
genealogista nmf genealogist.
generación nf (a) (act) generation.
  (b) (group) generation; **la — del '98** the '98 generation; **la — de 1927** (Lit) the 1927 generation; **las nuevas —es** the rising generation.
  (c) progeny, offspring; succession.
generador 1 adj generating. 2 nm generator.
general 1 adj general; wide, universal; common, prevailing, (pej) rife; usual; **es — por toda España** it is common throughout Spain, it exists in the whole of Spain; **de distribución —** of general distribution, generally distributed; **en —, por lo —** generally, as a general rule, in general; for the most part; **el mundo en —** the world in general, the world at large.
  2 nm general; **— de brigada** brigadier-general; **— de división** major-general.
  3 **—es** nfpl personal particulars.
generala nf (a) general's wife. (b) call to arms, general alert.
generalato nm generalship.
generalidad nf (a) generality; mass, majority; **la — de los hombres** the mass of ordinary people, the common run of men.
  (b) vague answer, generalization, general statement.
  (c) (Pol) **la G—** Catalan autonomous government of 1931-36.
generalísimo nm generalissimo, supreme commander; **el G— Franco** (usually called) General Franco.
generalización nf (a) generalization. (b) (of conflict) widening, escalation.
generalizar [1f] 1 vt (a) to generalize; to make more widely known, bring into general use.
  (b) (Mil) to widen, escalate, scale up.
  2 vi to generalize.
  3 **generalizarse** vr (a) to become general, become universal; to become widely known (or used etc).
  (b) (Mil) to widen, escalate.
generalmente adv generally.
generar [1a] vt to generate.
generativo adj generative.
genérico adj generic.
género nm (a) class, kind, type, sort; **— humano** human race, mankind; **le deseo todo — de felicidades** I wish you all the happiness in the world.
  (b) (Bio) genus.
  (c) (Art, Lit) genre; type; **— chico** (genre of) comic one-act pieces, short farces; zarzuela, Spanish operetta; **— novelístico** novel genre, fiction; **pintor de —** genre painter; **es todo un — de literatura** it is a whole type of literature.
  (d) (Gram) gender; **del — masculino** of the masculine gender.
  (e) (Comm) cloth, stuff, material; **—s** goods, merchandise; commodities; **—s de lino** linen goods; **—s de punto** knitwear, knitted goods; **le conozco el —** I know his sort; I know all about him, I recognize the type.
generosamente adv generously; nobly, magnanimously.
generosidad nf (a) generosity; nobility, magnanimity. (b) (Hist) nobility; valour.
generoso adj (a) generous (con, para to); noble, magnanimous.
  (b) (Hist) noble, highborn; gentlemanly; brave, valiant; **de sangre generosa** of noble blood; **en pecho —** in a noble heart.
  (c) wine rich, full-bodied.
genésico adj genetic.
génesis nf genesis.
Génesis nm (Bib) Genesis.
genética nf genetics.
genético adj genetic.
genetista nmf geneticist.
genial 1 adj (a) inspired, brilliant, of genius; **escritor —** writer of genius; **fue una idea —** it was a brilliant idea; **¡eso fue —!** it was marvellous!, it was wonderful!
  (b) pleasant, cheerful, genial.
  (c) in character, characteristic; individual; typical.
  2 nm (fam) temper, disposition.
genialidad nf (a) genius; stroke of genius, brilliant stroke, inspired move; **tiene una — para los negocios**

he has a genius for business; **eso fue una** — it was a stroke of genius; **es una** — **suya** it's one of his brilliant ideas.
(**b**) temperament.
(**c**) peculiarity, typical feature, characteristic; eccentricity.
genialmente adv (**a**) in an inspired way, brilliantly, with genius. (**b**) pleasantly, cheerfully.
genio nm (**a**) disposition, nature, character, temper; — **alegre** cheerful nature; **buen** — good nature; **de** — **franco** of an open nature; **mal** — bad temper; evil disposition; **de mal** — bad-tempered; ill-disposed; **estar de mal** — to be in a bad temper; — **vivo** quick temper, hot temper; **corto de** — dim-witted; spiritless, timid; **llevar el** — **a uno** to humour someone; not to dare to contradict someone.
(**b**) bad temper; **es una mujer de mucho** — she's a quick-tempered woman; **tiene** — he's temperamental; he has an uncertain temper, he's bad-tempered.
(**c**) genius; **¡eres un** —! you're a genius!
(**d**) genius, special nature, peculiarities; **esto va en contra del** — **de la lengua** this goes against the genius of the language.
(**e**) (Myth, Rel) spirit; genie; — **del mal** evil spirit; — **tutelar** guardian spirit.
genioso adj (Col, Mex, SD) bad-tempered.
genista nf broom, genista.
genital 1 adj genital. 2 —**es** nmpl genitals, genital organs.
genitivo 1 adj generative, reproductive. 2 nm (Gram) genitive.
genocidio nm genocide.
Génova f Genoa.
genovés 1 adj Genoese. 2 nm, **genovesa** nf Genoese.
gental nm (Col) lot, mass; **un** — **de gente** a mass of people.
gente nf (**a**) people, folk; race, nation; (Mil) men, troops, followers, retinue; (fam) relatives, folks, people; **el rey y su** — the king and his retinue; **mi** — my people, my folks; **son** — **inculta** they're rough people; **no me gusta esa** — I don't like those people; **hay muy poca** — there are very few people; — **baja** lower classes, low-class people; — **bien** upper-class people; nice people, respectable people; (pej) posh people (fam); smart set; — **de bien** honest folk, decent people; — **de capa parda** country folk; — **de color** (euph) coloured people; — **de la cuchilla** butchers; — **de mar** seafaring men; — **menuda** small fry; humble folk; children, little people; **¡— de paz!** (Mil) friend!; — **de pelo** well-to-do people; — **de medio pelo** people of limited means; — **natural** (CAm) Indians, natives; — **perdida** bad people; criminals; idlers, loafers; — **de pluma** clerks, penpushers; — **principal** nobility, gentry; — **de tomuza** (Ven) Negroes, mulattoes; — **de trato** tradespeople; **de** — **en** — from generation to generation.
(**b**) (SAm) upper-class people; nice people, respectable people; **ser** — to be somebody, to have social importance.
(**c**) (Mex, SD) person; **había dos** —**s** there were two people, there were two persons.
gentecilla nf unimportant people; (pej) rabble, riff-raff.
genterío nm (CR) = **gentío**.
gentil 1 adj (**a**) elegant, graceful, attractive; charming; pretty; courteous.
(**b**) (iro) pretty, fine; **¡— cumplido!** a fine compliment!
(**c**) (Rel) pagan, heathen; gentile.
2 nmf pagan, heathen; gentile.
gentileza nf (**a**) elegance, gracefulness; charm; prettiness; courtesy. (**b**) show, splendour, ostentation. (**c**) dash, gallantry.
gentilhombre nm (Hist) gentleman; — **de cámara** gentleman-in-waiting.
gentilicio adj national, tribal; family (attr); **nombre** — family name.
gentilidad nf, **gentilismo** nm heathendom; heathenism.
gentilmente adv (**a**) elegantly, gracefully, attractively; charmingly; prettily; courteously. (**b**) (iro) prettily.
gentío nm crowd, throng.
gentualla nf, **gentuza** nf rabble, mob; riffraff; **¡qué** —! what a shower! (sl).
genuflexión nf genuflexion.
genuflexo adj (Arg) servile, slavish.
genuinamente adv genuinely; really, truly.

genuino adj (**a**) genuine; real, pure, true. (**b**) (Col) smashing (sl), super (fam).
geodesia nf geodesy.
geodésico adj geodesic.
geofísica nf geophysics.
Geofredo m Geoffrey.
geografía nf geography.
geográfico adj geographical.
geógrafo nm geographer.
geología nf geology.
geológico adj geological.
geólogo nm geologist.
geometría nf geometry; — **del espacio** solid geometry.
geométrico adj geometric(al).
geopolítica nf geopolitics.
georgiano adj Georgian.
geranio nm geranium.
Gerardo m Gerald, Gerard.
gerencia nf (**a**) management. (**b**) managership, post of manager. (**c**) manager's office.
gerente nm manager, director; executive; — **de personal** personnel manager.
geriatra nm geriatric specialist.
geriatría nf geriatrics.
germanesco adj slang.
germanía nf thieves' slang, cant, underworld parlance.
germánico adj Germanic.
germano adj German; Germanic.
germanófilo nm, **germanófila** nf germanophile.
germanófobo nm, **germanófoba** nf germanophobe.
germen nm (**a**) (Bio, Med) germ; — **plasma** germ plasma. (**b**) (fig) germ, seed; source, origin; **el** — **de una idea** the germ of an idea.
germicida 1 adj germicidal. 2 nm germicide, germ killer.
germinación nf germination.
germinar [1a] vi to germinate; to sprout, shoot.
gerontología nf gerontology.
gerontólogo nm gerontologist.
Gertrudis f Gertrude.
gerundense 1 adj of Gerona. 2 nmf native (or inhabitant) of Gerona; **los** —**s** the people of Gerona.
gerundiano adj bombastic.
gerundiar [1b] vi (of Indians) to speak in gerunds, use the gerund a lot.
gerundino nm gerundive (Latin).
gerundio nm gerund; — **adjetivado** gerundive.
gervasio nm (Col) fellow, guy; shrewd fellow.
gesta nf (**a**) heroic deed, epic achievement: (**b**) (Lit: Hist) epic, epic poem; see also **cantar**.
gestación nf gestation.
Gestapo nf Gestapo.
gestear [1a] vi = **gesticular**.
gesticulación nf (**a**) gesticulation. (**b**) grimace, (wry) face.
gesticular [1a] vi (**a**) to gesticulate, gesture. (**b**) to grimace, make a face.
gestión nf (**a**) (Comm etc) management, conduct. (**b**) negotiation.
(**c**) measure, step; action; effort; —**es** measures, steps; **hacer las** —**es necesarias para** + infin to take the necessary steps to + infin; **hacer las** —**es preliminares** to do the groundwork, make the first steps; **donde él tenía que realizar unas** —**es** where he had some business to transact; **el gobierno tendrá que hacer las primeras** —**es** the government will have to make the first move.
gestionar [1a] vt (**a**) to manage, conduct. (**b**) to negotiate (for). (**c**) to try to arrange, strive to bring about, (take steps to) procure, work towards, work for.
gesto nm (**a**) face; expression on one's face; **estar de buen** — to be in a good mood; **estar de mal** — to be in a bad mood; **poner mal** —, **torcer el** — to make a (wry) face; to scowl, look cross.
(**b**) grimace, (wry) face; scowl; **hacer** —**s** to make faces (a at); **hacer un** — to make a face; **hizo un** — **de asco** he looked disgusted; **hizo un** — **de extrañeza** he looked surprised.
(**c**) gesture; sign; **hacer** —**s** to make gestures (a to); **con un** — **de cansancio** with a weary gesture.
gestor 1 adj managing. 2 nm manager; promoter; business agent, representative.
gestoría nf agency (for undertaking business with government departments).
Getsemaní Gethsemane.
Ghana f Ghana.
ghaneano 1 adj Ghanean. 2 nm, **ghaneana** nf Ghanean.
giba nf (**a**) hump; hunchback. (**b**) (fam) nuisance, bother.

gibado *adj* with a hump, hunchbacked.
gibar [1a] *vt* (*fam*) to annoy, bother.
gibón *nm* gibbon.
giboso *adj* with a hump, hunchbacked.
Gibraltar *m* Gibraltar.
gibraltareño 1 *adj* of Gibraltar. **2** *nm*, **gibraltareña** *nf* native (or inhabitant) of Gibraltar; **los —s** the people of Gibraltar.
giganta *nf* (**a**) giantess. (**b**) (*Bot*) sunflower.
gigante 1 *adj* giant, gigantic. **2** *nm* giant.
gigantesco *adj* gigantic, giant.
gigantez *nf* gigantic stature, vast size.
gigantón *nm* big giant; giant carnival figure.
gigoló *nm* gigolo.
gijonés 1 *adj* of Gijón. **2** *nm*, **gijonesa** *nf* native (or inhabitant) of Gijón; **los —es** the people of Gijón.
Gil *m* Giles.
gilda *nf* lollipop.
gilí *adj* (*fam*) stupid, silly.
gilipollada *nf* (*fam*) silly thing.
gilipollas *nmf*, *pl* **gilipollas** (*fam*) idiot; **¡—!** you idiot!
gilipollear [1a] *vi* (*fam*) to do silly things.
gilipollez *nf* (*fam*) stupidity, silliness.
gillet(t)e [xi'lete] *nf* (*angl*) (*any*) razor blade.
gimnasia *nf* gymnastics; physical training; **— respiratoria** deep breathing; **hacer —** to do gymnastics, do physical training.
gimnasio *nm* gymnasium, gym (*fam*).
gimnasta *nmf* gymnast.
gimnástica *nf* gymnastics.
gimnástico *adj* gymnastic.
gimotear [1a] *vi* to whine, whimper; to wail; (*of child*) to snivel, grizzle.
gimoteo *nm* whine, whining; whimpering; wailing; snivelling, grizzling.
Ginebra[1] (*Geog*) Geneva.
Ginebra[2] *f* (*Hist*) Guinevere.
ginebra[1] *nf* gin.
ginebra[2] *nf* (*fam*) bedlam, uproar, confusion.
ginecología *nf* gynaecology.
ginecólogo *nm* gynaecologist.
ginesta *nf* = **hiniesta**.
ginfizz [ʒin'fiz] *nm*, *pl* **ginfizz** (*angl*) gin with mineral water.
Gioconda: la — (the) Mona Lisa.
gira *nf* (*Mus*, *Theat etc*) tour; trip; **estar en —** to be on tour; *see also* **jira**.
girado *nm*, **girada** *nf* (*Comm*) drawee.
girador *nm*, **giradora** *nf* (*Comm*) drawer.
giralda *nf*, **giraldilla** *nf* weathercock.
girar [1a] **1** *vt* (**a**) to turn, turn round, rotate; to twist; to spin; **— la manivela 2 veces** turn the crank twice.
(**b**) to swing, swivel; **— la vista** to look round.
(**c**) (*Comm*) to draw (*a cargo de, contra* on), issue.
2 *vi* (**a**) to turn, turn round, go round; to rotate, revolve; to spin, gyrate; to wheel; (*Sport: of ball*) to spin; **— hacia la derecha** to turn (to the) right, swing right; **gira a 1600 rpm** it rotates at 1600 rpm; **el satélite gira alrededor del mundo** the satellite circles the earth, the satellite revolves round the earth; **la conversación giraba en torno de las elecciones** the conversation turned on (or centred on) the election.
(**b**) to swing (from side to side), swivel; to hinge; to pivot; **la puerta giró sobre sus goznes** the door swung on its hinges.
(**c**) (*Comm*, *Fin*) to operate, do business; **la compañía gira bajo la razón social de X** the company operates under the name of X.
(**d**) (*Comm*) to draw; **— en descubierto** to overdraw.
girasol *nm* sunflower.
giratorio *adj* revolving, rotatory; gyratory; *door, stage etc* revolving; *bridge swing* (*attr*), swivel (*attr*).
giro[1] *nm* (**a**) turn; revolution, rotation; gyration; **hacer un —** to turn, make a turn; **el coche dio un — brusco** the car swung away suddenly.
(**b**) (*fig: of events etc*) trend, tendency, course; **tomar otro —** to change one's mind, change one's tactics; **la cosa ha tomado un — favorable** the affair has taken a favourable turn; **la intriga tiene un — inesperado** the plot has an unexpected twist in it.
(**c**) (*Ling*) turn of phrase, expression.
(**d**) (*Comm*) draft; bill of exchange; **— en descubierto** overdraft; **— postal** money order, postal order; **— a la vista** sight draft.
giro[2] *adj* (**a**) (*SAm*) *cock* with some yellow colouring.

(**b**) (*Cu*) scatterbrained, thoughtless. (**c**) (*Guat*) drunk. (**d**) (*Mex*) cocky (*fam*), confident.
girocompás *nm* gyrocompass.
Gironda *m* Gironde.
giroscópico *adj* gyroscopic.
giroscopio *nm* **giróscopo** *nm* gyroscope.
gis *nm* (**a**) chalk; (*Col*) slate pencil. (**b**) (*Mex*) *pulque*, (*any*) colourless drink.
gitana *nf* gipsy; (*at fair etc*) fortuneteller.
gitanada *nf* (**a**) gipsy trick, mean trick. (**b**) wheedling, cajolery; humbug.
gitanear [1a] *vt* to wheedle, cajole.
gitanería *nf* (**a**) band of gipsies; gathering of gipsies. (**b**) gipsy (way of) life. (**c**) gipsy saying. (**d**) (*fig*) wheedling, cajolery.
gitanesco *adj* (**a**) gipsy (*attr*); gipsy-like. (**b**) (*pej*) wily, tricky.
gitano 1 *adj* (**a**) gipsy (*attr*); **las costumbres gitanas** gipsy customs. (**b**) (*fig*) wheedling, cajoling; smooth, flattering. (**c**) (*fig*) wily, tricky, sly. **2** *nm* gipsy.
glabro *adj* glabrous; hairless.
glaciación *nf* glaciation.
glacial *adj* (**a**) glacial; *wind etc* icy, bitter, freezing. (**b**) (*fig*) icy, cold, stony.
glaciar *nm* glacier.
glacis *nm*, *pl* **glacis** glacis.
gladiador *nm* gladiator.
gladio *nm*, **gladíolo** *nm* gladiolus.
glándula *f* gland; **— cerrada, — de secreción interna** ductless gland; **— endocrina** endocrine gland; **— pituitaria** pituitary (gland); **— prostática** prostate (gland); **— tiroides** thyroid (gland).
glandular *adj* glandular.
glaseado *adj* glazed, glossy; glacé.
glasear [1a] *vt* *paper etc* to glaze.
glauco *adj* green, light-green.
glaucoma *nm* glaucoma.
gleba *nf* clod.
glicerina *nf* glycerin(e).
global *adj* global; total, complete, overall; *inquiry, report etc* full, searching, comprehensive; *amount* total, aggregate; *sum* lump (*attr*).
globo *nm* (**a**) globe, sphere; **— de luz** spherical lamp, spherical lampshade; **— del ojo, — ocular** eyeball; **— terráqueo** globe, schoolroom globe.
(**b**) (*Aer*) **— (aerostático)** balloon; **— cautivo** captive balloon; **— dirigible** dirigible; **— de protección** barrage balloon.
(**c**) **en —** as a whole, all in all; (*Comm*) in bulk; (*fig*) in broad outline only.
globosidad *nf* globosity.
globoso *adj*, **globular** *adj* globular, spherical.
glóbulo *nm* (**a**) globule. (**b**) (*Anat*) corpuscle; **— blanco** white corpuscle; **— rojo** red corpuscle.
gloria *nf* glory; (*fig*) glory, delight, bliss; **una vieja —** a has-been, a great figure (*etc*) from the past; **el día es pura —** it's a wonderful day; **¡sí, —!** yes, my love!; **¡por la — de mi madre!** by all that's holy!; **estar en su** (**s**) to be in one's element, be in one's glory; **saber a —** to taste heavenly; **Dios le tenga en su santa —** God rest his soul.
gloriado *nm* (*CAm, Col, Ec*) hot drink of rum, lemon and cinnamon; (*Per*) tea drink with brandy or rum.
gloriarse [1b] *vr*: **— de algo** to boast of something, be proud of something; **— en algo** to glory in something, rejoice in something.
glorieta *nf* (**a**) bower, arbour; summerhouse. (**b**) (*Aut*) roundabout, traffic circle (*US*); circus; intersection of streets.
glorificación *nf* glorification.
glorificar [1g] **1** *vt* to glorify, extol, praise. **2 glorificarse** *vr*: **— de, — en** to boast of, be proud of, glory in.
gloriosamente *adv* gloriously.
glorioso *adj* (**a**) glorious; (*Eccl*) *saint* blessed, in glory; *memory* blessed; **la Gloriosa** (*Eccl*) the Virgin; (*Hist: fam*) the 1868 revolution (in Spain).
(**b**) (*pej*) proud, boastful.
glosa *f* gloss; comment, note, annotation.
glosar [1a] *vt* to gloss; to comment on, annotate; (*fig*) to put an unfavourable interpretation on, criticize.
glosario *nm* glossary.
glosopeda *nf* foot-and-mouth disease.
glotis *nf*, *pl* **glotis** glottis.
glotón 1 *adj* gluttonous, greedy. **2** *nm*, **glotona** *nf* glutton. **3** *nm* (*Zool*) glutton; **— de América** wolverine.
glotonear [1a] *vi* to be greedy, be gluttonous, gormandize.
glotonería *nf* gluttony, greediness.
glucosa *nf* glucose, grape sugar.

gluglú nm (a) (of water) gurgle, gurgling; **hacer — to** gurgle. (b) (of turkey) gobble, gobbling; **hacer — to** gobble.

gluglutear [1a] vi (of turkey) to gobble.

gluten nm gluten.

glutinoso adj glutinous.

gneis [neis] nm gneiss.

gnomo ['nomo] nm gnome.

gobelino nm hand-woven wall tapestry.

gobernable adj (a) (Pol) governable; **un pueblo difícilmente —** a people hard to govern, an unruly people. (b) (Naut) navigable, steerable.

gobernación nf (a) (act) governing, government; **Ministerio m de la G—** Ministry of the Interior, Home Office (Brit), Department of the Interior (US); **Ministro m de la G—** Minister of the Interior, Home Secretary (Brit), Secretary of the Interior (US).
   (b) governor's residence, governor's office.

gobernador 1 adj governing, ruling. 2 nm governor, ruler; **— general** governor-general.

gobernalle nm rudder, helm.

gobernanta nf (SAm: gall) governess.

gobernante 1 adj ruling, governing. 2 nmf ruler, governor; (fig) self-appointed boss (or leader etc).

gobernar [1k] 1 vt (a) (Pol) to govern, rule.
   (b) (in general) to govern; to guide, direct; to control, manage, run; to handle.
   (c) (Naut) to steer, sail.
   2 vi (a) (Pol) to govern, rule; **— mal** to misgovern.
   (b) (Naut) to handle, steer.

gobierno nm (a) (Pol) government; **el — español** the Spanish government; **— fantasma** shadow cabinet.
   (b) (in general) guidance, direction; control, management, running; handling; **— doméstico, — de la casa** housekeeping, running of the household; **para su —** for your guidance; **servir de — a** to act as a guide to, serve as a norm for.
   (c) (post) governorship.
   (d) (Naut) steering; helm; **buen — navigability**, good steering qualities; **de buen — navigable**, easily steerable.
   (e) **mirar contra el —** (PR, RPl) to squint.

gobio nm gudgeon.

goce nm enjoyment; possession.

gocho nm (a) (fam) pig. (b) (Col) ear; handle.

godo 1 adj Gothic.
   2 nm, **goda** nf (a) (Hist) Goth.
   (b) (SAm: pej) Spaniard; (Hist: early 19th century) loyalist; (modern Pol) conservative, reactionary.
   (c) (Canaries) (peninsular) Spaniard.

Godofredo m Geoffrey, Godfrey.

gofio nm (Canaries, SAm) roasted maize meal mixed with sugar.

gol nm (angl) goal (score); ¡—! goal!

gola nf (a) (Anat) throat, gullet. (b) (Mil: Hist) gorget; (Sew: Hist) ruff. (c) (Archit) cyma, ogee.

goleada nf quantity of goals, avalanche of goals.

goleador nm goal scorer; **el máximo — de la liga** the top goal scorer in the league.

golear [1a] 1 vt to score a goal against; **Eslobodia goleó a Ruritania por 13 a 0** Slobodia overwhelmed Ruritania by 13-0; **A fue goleado por B** A had a lot of goals scored against it by B.
   2 vi to score (a goal).

goleta nf schooner.

golf nm (angl) golf; golf course; **— miniatura** miniature golf (course).

golfa nf (fam) tart (sl), whore.

golfán nm waterlily.

golfante nm oaf, lout; rascal.

golfear [1a] vi to loaf, idle; to live like a street urchin.

golfería nf (a) loafers (collectively); street urchins (collectively). (b) loafing, idling; life of idleness; life in the gutter. (c) dirty trick.

golfillo nm urchin, street urchin.

golfista nmf golfer.

golfístico adj golf (attr), golfing (attr).

golfo[1] nm (Geog) (a) gulf, bay; **G— de Méjico** Gulf of Mexico; **G— Pérsico** Persian Gulf; **— de Vizcaya** Bay of Biscay.
   (b) open sea.
   (c) (fig) gulf, abyss.
   (d) (fig) chaos, confusion.

golfo[2] nm urchin, street urchin; tramp; oaf, lout; loafer.

Goliat m Goliath.

golilla nf (a) (Sew: Hist) ruff, gorget; magistrate's collar; (Bol, RPl) neckcloth, neckerchief; **andar de — (Bol, RPl)** to be in full regalia.
   (b) (SAm: Orn) collar, ruff.
   (c) (Tech) flange (of a pipe).
   (d) (Cu) debt.
   (e) (Cu) trick, ruse.
   (f) **alzar — (Guat)** to be brave; (Mex) to show fear.
   (g) **de — (Hond)** free, for nothing.

golondrina nf (a) swallow; **— de mar** tern; **una — no hace verano** one swallow does not make a summer. (b) (Chi) furniture van.

golondrino nm (a) tramp; (Mil) deserter. (b) (Med) tumour under the armpit.

golondro nm (fam) fancy, yen (fam), longing; **andar de —s** to cherish foolish hopes; **campar de — to** sponge (fam), live on other people.

golosina nf (a) titbit, delicacy, dainty; sweet.
   (b) bauble, trifle; useless object.
   (c) desire, longing; fancy.
   (d) sweet tooth, liking for sweet things; greed.

goloso adj (a) sweet-toothed, fond of dainties. (b) (pej) greedy.

golpe nm (a) blow; hit, punch, knock; smack; bump; (with oar etc) stroke; (of heart) beat, throb; (of clock etc) tick; **se dio un — en la cabeza** he got a bump on his head, he banged his head; **A le dio a B un — en el pecho** A punched B on the chest; **A dio a B un — con un palo** A gave B a blow with his stick, A hit B with his stick; **— aplastante** crushing blow, knockout blow; **— bien dado** hit, well-aimed blow; **— de gracia** coup de grâce (also fig); **— mortal** death blow; **dar —s en la puerta** to thump the door, pound (at, on) the door; **descargar —s sobre uno** to rain blows on someone; **darse —s de pecho** to beat one's breast; **no dar —** not to do a stroke, be bone-idle; **¡qué —!** (fam) what a joke!; **a — dado no hay quite** (CAm) what's done cannot be undone.
   (b) (Tech) stroke; **— de émbolo** piston stroke.
   (c) (Sport: Boxing) blow, punch; (Football etc) kick; (Baseball, Golf, Tennis etc) hit, stroke, shot; **con un total de 280 —s** (Golf) with a total of 280 strokes; **— de abajo arriba** (Boxing) uppercut; **— de acercamiento** (Golf) approach shot; **— de castigo** (Football etc) penalty kick; **— franco** (Football) free kick; **— franco indirecto** indirect free kick; **— de martillo** (Tennis) smash; **— de salida** (Golf) drive, drive-off; **— de voleo** volley.
   (d) (fig) blow, (hard) knock, misfortune; **ha sufrido un — duro** he has had a hard knock.
   (e) (fig) shock, clash.
   (f) (fig) surprise, astonishment.
   (g) (fam: of criminal) job (fam); **él preparaba su primer —** he was planning his first job; **dieron un — en un banco** they did a bank job.
   (h) (fig) **— de agua** heavy fall of rain; **— de estado** coup d'état; **— de fortuna** stroke of luck; **— maestro** master stroke, stroke of genius; **— de mano** rising; sudden attack; **— de mar** heavy sea, surge; **— de sol** sunstroke; **— de teatro** coup de théâtre; **— de tos** fit of coughing; **— de viento** gust of wind; **— de vista** look, glance.
   (i) (phrases with prep) **a — seguro** with an assurance of success, without any risk; **ir a — de calcetín** (fam) to go on Shanks' pony; **al — (Cu)** instantly; **de — (y porrazo)** suddenly, unexpectedly; **de un —** at one stroke, in one go; outright; at a stretch; **abrir una puerta de —** to fling open a door; **la puerta se abrió de —** the door flew open; **cerrar una puerta de —** to slam a door.
   (j) (fig) crowd, mass; abundance; **— de gente** crowd of people.
   (k) (Mech) spring lock; **de —** spring (attr), eg **pestillo de —** spring bolt.
   (l) (Sew) pocket flap; (Col) facing.
   (m) (Mex) sledgehammer.
   (n) (Ven) swig (of liquor) (fam).

golpeador nm (Col, Chi, Guat) door knocker.

golpeadura nf = golpeo.

golpear [1a] 1 vt to strike, knock, hit; to beat, pound (on, at); to punch; to thump, bang; to tap.
   2 vi to throb, tick; (Aut, Mech) to knock; **el — de las olas** the buffeting of the waves, the pounding of the sea.

golpecito nm (light) blow, tap, rap; **dar —s en** to tap (on), rap (on).

golpeo nm striking, knocking, hitting; beating, pounding; punching, thumping, banging; tapping; (Aut, Mech) knock, knocking.

golpetear [1a] vti to beat (repeatedly); to knock, hammer, drum, tap; to rattle.

golpeteo *nm* beating; knocking, hammering, drumming, tapping; rattling.

golpiza *nf* (*SAm*) bash (*fam*), bashing (*fam*), beating-up (*fam*); **dar una — a uno** to bash someone, beat someone up.

gollería *nf* dainty, titbit, delicacy; extra, special treat; **pedir —s** to ask too much.

golleroso *adj* affected; pernickety.

gollete *nm* throat, neck; (*of bottle*) neck.

goma *nf* (**a**) (*in general*) gum; rubber; (*Sew*) elastic; **— arábiga** gum arabic; **— espumosa** foam rubber; **— de mascar** chewing gum; **— de pegar** gum, glue.
(**b**) (*una* **—**) rubber band, elastic band; length of elastic, piece of elastic; (*Aut*) tyre; (*fam*) rubber sheath, condom; (*SAm*) rubber overshoe; **— de borrar** rubber, eraser; **— de borrar de máquina** typewriter rubber.
(**c**) **estar de —** (*CAm*) to have a hangover.

goma-espuma *nf* foam rubber.

gomal *nm* (*Col, Ec, Per*) rubber plantation.

gomero 1 *adj* gum (*attr*); rubber (*attr*). **2** *nm* (**a**) (*Bot*) gum tree; rubber tree. (**b**) (*person*) rubber planter, rubber producer; rubber-plantation worker.

gomina *nf* (*SAm*) hair lotion, hair groom (*US*).

gomita *nf* rubber band, elastic band.

gomosidad *nf* gumminess, stickiness.

gomoso 1 *adj* gummy, sticky. **2** *nm* (*fam*) toff (*fam*), masher (*fam*), dandy.

gónada *nf* gonad.

góndola *nf* (*Naut*) gondola; (*Rail*) goods wagon, freight truck (*US*), (*Chi*) bus; **— de cable** cable-car; **— del motor** (*Aer*) engine casing.

gondolero *nm* gondolier.

gong [gon] *nm*, *pl* **gongs** [gon], **gongo** *nm* gong.

gonorrea *nf* gonorrhoea.

gorda *nf* (*fam*) (**a**) fat woman.
(**b**) = **perra gorda**.
(**c**) **la G—** *the 1868 revolution (in Spain)*; **se armó la —** there was a hell of a row, there was a tremendous fuss; **aquí se va a armar la —** there's going to be trouble; **ahora nos va a tocar la —** now we're for it.
(**d**) (*Mex*) thick maize omelette.

gordal 1 *adj* fat, big, thick. **2** *nm* kind of large olive.

gordiflón *adj*, **gordinflón** *adj* (*fam*) podgy, chubby; **¡—!** fatty! (*fam*).

gordo 1 *adj* (**a**) *person* fat; stout, plump; *object* big; *cloth, thread etc* thick, coarse, rough; *event* important, big; *prize* first, big, main; **está más — que nunca** he's fatter than ever; **en mi vida las he visto más gordas** (*fig*) I've never been in a tougher spot; **el desastre más — de su historia** it was the biggest (*or* worst) disaster in their history.
(**b**) *food, matter* fatty, greasy, oily.
(**c**) *water* hard.
(**d**) (*fam*) unpleasant; **ese tipo me cae —** that chap gets on my nerves, I can't bear that fellow.
2 *adv* (*fam*): **hablar —** to talk big (*sl*).
3 *nm* (**a**) fat man; **¡—!** fatty! (*fam*).
(**b**) (*Cook*) fat, suet.
(**c**) (*fam*) first prize, big prize; **ganar el —** to win the big prize; **sacarse el —** (*fig*) to bring home the bacon (*fam*).

gordolobo *nm* mullein.

gordura *nf* (**a**) fat, fatness; corpulence, stoutness. (**b**) (*Cook*) grease, fat. (**c**) (*Arg, PR*) cream.

gorgojo *nm* (**a**) (*Ent*) grub; weevil. (**b**) (*fig*) dwarf, runt.

gorgón *nm* (*Col*) concrete.

gorgoritear [1a] *vi* to trill, warble.

gorgorito *nm* trill, warble.

górgoro *nm* (*Mex*) bubble.

gorgotear [1a] *vi* to gurgle.

gorgoteo *nm* gurgle.

gorguera *nf* ruff; (*Mil: Hist*) gorget.

gori *nm*: **armar el —** (*fam*) to make a row, kick up a fuss.

gorigori *nm* (*fam*) funeral chanting, dirge; (*fig*) wailing, gloomy chanting.

gorila 1 *nf* (*Zool*) gorilla. **2** *nm* (*fam*) tough (*fam*), thug, bruiser (*fam*).

goriloide *nm* (*fig*) brute, thug.

gorja *nf* throat, gorge; **estar de —** (*fam*) to be very cheerful.

gorjear [1a] **1** *vi* to chirp, twitter, trill. **2 gorjearse** *vr* (*of child*) to crow, gurgle, burble.

gorjeo *nm* (**a**) chirping, twittering, trilling; crowing, gurgling, burbling.

gorobeto *adj* (*Col*) twisted, bent, warped.

gorra 1 *nf* (peaked) cap; (*baby's*) bonnet; (*Mil*) bearskin, busby; (*Univ*) cap; **— de montar** riding cap; **— de paño** cloth cap; **— de punto** knitted cap;

— de visera peaked cap; **— de yate** yachting cap.
2 *nm* (*fam*) cadger, sponger (*fam*), parasite; **andar** (*or* **ir**, **vivir**) **de —** to cadge, sponge (*fam*), scrounge (*fam*), live at someone else's expense; **colarse de —** to gatecrash; **comer de —** to scrounge a meal (*fam*).

gorrear [1a] **1** *vt* (*Chi*) to cuckold. **2** *vi* (*Ec*) to sponge (*fam*), live as a parasite.

gorrero *nm* (*fam*) = **gorra 2**.

gorriada *nf* (**a**) (number of) pigs. (**b**) (*fig*) dirty trick.

gorrinera *nf* pigsty.

gorrinería *nf* (**a**) dirt. (**b**) (*fig*) dirty trick.

gorrino *nm*, **gorrina** *nf* (**a**) small pig, sucking-pig; hog, sow. (**b**) (*fig*) dirty individual.

gorrión *nm* sparrow; **de —** (*SD*) = **de gorra**.

gorrista *nmf* (*fam*) = **gorra 2**.

gorro *nm* cap; (*baby's*, *woman's*) bonnet; **— de baño** bathing cap; **— de dormir** nightcap; **— de montaña** Balaclava (helmet); **— de papel** paper hat; **poner el — a uno** to embarrass someone by petting in his (*etc*) presence.

gorrón¹ *nm* (**a**) pebble; cobblestone. (**b**) (*Mech*) pivot, journal, gudgeon.

gorrón² *nm* (*fam*) = **gorra 2**.

gorrona *nf* tart (*sl*), whore.

gorronear [1a] *vi* (*fam*) to cadge, sponge (*fam*), scrounge (*fam*), live at someone else's expense.

gorronería *nf* (*CAm*) greedy selfishness.

gota *nf* (**a**) drop; bead; blob; **—s amargas** bitters; **a — drop by drop; caer a —s** to drip; **parecerse como dos —s de agua** to be as like as two peas; **sudar la — gorda** to sweat blood; **no ver —** to see nothing.
(**b**) (*Med*) gout; **— caduca**, **— coral** epilepsy.
(**c**) **—s de leche** (*fig*: *SAm*) child welfare clinic, welfare food centre.

goteado *adj* speckled, spotted.

gotear [1a] *vi* to drip, dribble; to trickle; to leak; (*o candle*) to gutter; (*Meteorol*) to sprinkle, rain lightly.

goteo *nm* dripping, dribbling; trickle, trickling; leak.

gotera *nf* (**a**) drip; trickle; leak.
(**b**) mark left by dripping water, stain.
(**c**) (*of canopy*) valance.
(**d**) (*Med*) chronic ailment; **estar lleno de —s** to be full of aches and pains, feel a wreck.
(**e**) **—s** (*SAm*) outskirts, environs.

gotero *nm* (*SAm: Med*) dropper.

goterón *nm* big raindrop.

gótico 1 *adj* Gothic; (*fig*) noble, illustrious. **2** *nm* (*language*) Gothic.

gotita *nf* droplet; **¡una — nada más!** (*on pouring drink*) just a drop!; **hubo dos —s de lluvia** it rained a drop or two.

gotoso *adj* gouty.

gourmet [gur'me] *nm*, *pl* **gourmets** [gur'me] (*gall*) gourmet, connoisseur (*of food*).

goyesco *adj* (**a**) of Goya, pertaining to Goya. (**b**) Goyesque, in the style of Goya, after the manner of Goya.

gozar [1f] **1** *vt* (**a**) to enjoy; to have, possess.
(**b**) (*arch*) *woman* to have, enjoy, seduce.
2 *vi* to enjoy oneself, have a good time; **— de** to enjoy; to have, possess; **— de buena salud** to enjoy good health.
3 gozarse *vr* to enjoy oneself; to rejoice; **— en +** *infin* to enjoy + *ger*, take pleasure in + *ger*.

gozne *nm* hinge.

gozo *nm* (**a**) enjoyment, pleasure; delight; joy, gladness, rejoicing; **es un — para la retina** it's a joy to see, it's a sight for sore eyes; **¡mi — en el pozo!** I'm sunk!, it's all ruined!; **no caber** (en sí) **de —** to be beside oneself with joy, be overjoyed; **da — escucharle** it's a pleasure to listen to him.
(**b**) **—s** (*Lit, Mus*) couplets in honour of the Virgin.

gozosamente *adv* joyfully, delightedly.

gozoso *adj* glad, joyful, delighted (*con, de* about).

gozque *nm* small yapping dog.

grabación *nf* recording; **— en cinta**, **— magnetofónica** tape recording.

grabado 1 *adj* music *etc* recorded; on tape.
2 *nm* engraving, print; (*in book*) illustration, picture, print; **— al agua fuerte** etching; **— al agua tinta** aquatint; **— en cobre** copperplate; **— en madera** woodcut; **— rupestre** rock carving.

grabador *nm* engraver.

grabadora *nf* (**a**) (*Tech*) graver, cutting tool. (**b**) (*Elec etc*) recorder; **— de cinta** tape recorder.

grabadura *nf* (act of) engraving.

grabar [1a] *vt* (a) (*Art*) to engrave; — **al agua fuerte** to etch.

(b) (*on disc, tape*) to record.

(c) (*fig*) to engrave, impress; — **algo en el ánimo de uno** to impress something on someone's mind; **la 'escena está grabada en mi memoria** the scene is engraved on my memory.

gracejada *nf* (*CAm, Mex*) clownish act, stupid (and tasteless) joke.

gracejo *nm* (a) charm, grace; charming manner. (b) wit, humour; repartee. (c) (*Guat, Mex*) clown.

gracia *nf* (a) grace, gracefulness; attractiveness; **sin** — graceless, unattractive.

(b) favour, kindness; **de** — free, gratis; **hacer a uno** — **de algo** to excuse someone from something, free someone from something.

(c) graciousness.

(d) grace, good graces, favour; **caer de la** — **de uno** to lose someone's favour; **caer en** — **a uno** to find favour with someone, please someone, make a hit with someone.

(e) (*Law*) pardon, mercy.

(f) joke, witticism; **hacer una** — **a uno** to play a (practical) joke on someone.

(g) humour, funniness; wit; point (of a joke); **por** — in fun, as a joke; **¡qué** —**!** how funny!, (*iro*) what a nerve!, the very idea!; **coger** (*or* **pescar**) **la** — to see the point (of a joke); **dar en la** — **de** + *infin* to fall into the (amusing) habit of + *ger*; **dar en la** — **de decir algo** to mention something repeatedly, harp on something; **hacer** — **a uno** to amuse someone, strike someone as funny; **no nos hace** — we are not amused; **no me hace** — **la idea** I'm not keen on the idea; **tener** — to be funny, be amusing; **el tío tiene mucha** — **hablando** the chap talks very amusingly, the fellow is an amusing talker; **si lo haces se va la** — if you do it it breaks the spell.

(h) (*fam*) name; **¿cuál es su** —? what's your name?

(i) (*Rel*) grace; — **de Dios** (*fig*) sunshine, fresh air; **por la G**— **de Dios** (*on coin etc*) by the grace of God; **estar en** — (**de Dios**) to be in a state of grace.

(j) **en** — **a** for the sake of; on account of, because of; **en** — **a la brevedad** for brevity's sake, to be brief.

(k) —**s** thanks; **¡**—**s!** thanks!, thank you!; **¡muchas** —**s!**, **¡muchísimas** —**s!** many thanks!, thanks very much!; —**s a Dios** thank heaven; —**s a la ayuda de otros** thanks to the help of others; —**s a que** . . . thanks to the fact that . . ., because of the fact that . . .; **toma eso**, **¡y** —**s!** take that and be thankful!; **con anticipadas** —**s** thanking you in advance; **con repetidas** —**s** thanking you again; **dar las** —**s a uno por algo** to thank someone for something.

(l) **las G**—**s** (*Myth*) the Three Graces.

graciable *adj* (a) gracious; affable. (b) *concession etc* easily granted.

grácil *adj* graceful; slender; small, delicate; **un coche de líneas** —**es** a car of graceful lines, an elegantly designed car.

graciosamente *adv* (a) gracefully; pleasingly, elegantly. (b) graciously. (c) funnily, amusingly; wittily; comically.

graciosidad *nf* (a) grace, gracefulness; elegance; beauty. (b) graciousness. (c) funniness, amusing qualities; wittiness.

gracioso 1 *adj* (a) graceful; pleasing, elegant.

(b) gracious; **su graciosa Majestad** her gracious Majesty.

(c) funny, amusing; witty; comical; **una situación muy graciosa** a very amusing situation; **¡qué** —**!** how funny!, that's rich!; **es un tío de lo más** — he's a most amusing chap; **lo** — **del caso es que** . . . the funny thing about it is that . . .

(d) free.

2 *nm* (*Theat: Hist*) comic character, fool, funny man.

grada *nf* (a) step, stair; (*Eccl*) altar step; —**s** (flight of) steps.

(b) (*Sport, Theat etc*) tier, row (of seats).

(c) —**s** (*Naut*) slips, slipway; —**s de construcción** shipyard, shipbuilding yard.

(d) (*Agr*) harrow; — **de disco** disk harrow; — **de mano** hoe, cultivator.

(e) —**s** (*Chi, Per*) paved terrace (in front of a building).

gradación *nf* (a) gradation; graded series. (b) (*Rhetoric*) climax; (*Gram*) comparison.

gradar [1a] *vt* (*Agr*) to harrow; to hoe.

gradería *nf*, **graderío** *nm* (a) (flight of) steps. (b) (*Sport, Theat etc*) tiers, rows (of seats); — **cubierta** covered stand, grandstand.

grado *nm* (a) step.

(b) degree; stage, step; measure; rate; **el** — **que ahora hemos alcanzado** the stage we have now reached; **está en el segundo** — **de elaboración** it is now in the second stage of production; — **de velocidad** (rate of) speed; **es lo mismo pero en mayor** — it's the same only more so; **de** — **en** —, **por** —**s** by degrees, gradually, step by step; **en sumo** —, **en** — **superlativo** in the highest degree; in the extreme; vastly.

(c) grade, quality; (*Mil*) rank; **de** — **superior** of superior quality.

(d) (*School*) class, year, grade (*US*).

(e) (*Univ*) degree; — **universitario** university degree.

(f) (*Geog, Math, Phys*) degree; — **de latitud** degree of latitude; **en un ángulo de 45** —**s** at an angle of 45 degrees; **la temperatura es de 40** —**s** the temperature is 40 degrees.

(g) (*Gram*) degree (of comparison).

(h) (*of relationship*) degree; **dentro de los** —**s prohibidos** within the prohibited degrees.

(i) willingness; **de** —, **de buen** — willingly; **de mal** —, **mal de mi** — unwillingly; **de** — **o por fuerza** willy-nilly.

(j) —**s** (*Eccl*) minor orders.

graduable *adj* adjustable, that can be adjusted.

graduación *nf* (a) gradation, grading; graduation.

(b) rating, grading; (*of drink*) alcoholic strength, proof grading; — **octánica** octane rating.

(c) (*Mil*) rank; **de alta** — of high rank, high-ranking.

graduado *nm*, **graduada** *nf* graduate.

gradual *adj* gradual.

gradualmente *adv* gradually.

graduar [1e] **1** *vt* (a) to grade, classify (*de, por* as); to appraise; to gauge, measure; (*Tech*) to calibrate; *sight* to test; *thermometer etc* to graduate.

(b) (*Univ*) to confer a degree on.

(c) (*Mil*) to confer a rank on, commission; — **a uno de capitán** to confer the rank of captain on someone.

2 graduarse *vr* (a) to graduate, take one's degree; — **de** to take the degree of.

(b) (*Mil*) to take a commission (*de* as).

grafía *nf* (*Ling*) graphy, signs representing the sound of a word; (way of) spelling; **se inclina por la** — "jira" he prefers the spelling "jira".

gráfica *nf* graph; diagram; — **de fiebre**, — **de temperatura** (*Med*) temperature chart.

gráficamente *adv* graphically.

gráfico 1 *adj* (a) graphic; pictorial, illustrated. (b) (*fig*) graphic, vivid, lively. **2** *nm* (*Math etc*) graph; diagram; chart; (*Rail etc*) timetable; = **gráfica**.

grafito *nm* graphite, black lead.

grafología *nf* graphology.

gragea *nf* small coloured sweets; (*Med*) sugar-coated pill.

graja *nf* rook.

grajea *nf* (*Col*) fine shot, birdshot.

grajear [1a] *vi* (*Orn*) to caw; (*of baby*) to crow, gurgle.

grajiento *adj* (*SAm*) sweaty, smelly.

grajilla *nf* jackdaw.

grajo *nm* (a) rook. (b) (*SAm*) body odour, smell of sweat; underarm odour.

grama *nf* (*esp SAm*) grass.

gramática *nf* (a) grammar. (b) — **parda** native wit, horse sense; **andar a la** — to look out for oneself.

gramatical *adj* grammatical.

gramático 1 *adj* grammatical. **2** *nm* grammarian.

gramil *nm* (*Tech*) gauge.

gramilla *nf* (*RPl*) grass.

gramillar *nm* (*RPl*) meadow, grassland.

gramo *nm* gramme, gram (*US*).

gramófono *nm* gramophone, phonograph (*US*).

gramola *nf* gramophone, phonograph (*US*); (*in cafe etc*) jukebox.

grampa *nf* (*SAm*) = **grapa**.

gran *adj* (*apocopated form*) *see* **grande**.

grana[1] *nf* (*Bot*) (a) small seed; **dar en** — to go to seed, run to seed. (b) seeding; seeding time.

grana[2] *nf* (*Zool etc*) cochineal; (*dye*) kermes; (*colour*) scarlet; scarlet cloth; **de** — scarlet, bright red; **ponerse como la** — to turn scarlet.

granada *nf* (a) (*Bot*) pomegranate. (b) (*Mil*) shell; grenade; — **fallida** dud shell; — **de mano** hand grenade; — **de metralla** shrapnel shell; **a prueba de** — shellproof.

granadero *nm* grenadier.

granadilla *nf* passionflower; passionfruit.

granadino 1 adj of Granada. **2** nm, **granadina** nf native (or inhabitant) of Granada; **los —s** the people of Granada.

granado[1] nm pomegranate tree.

granado[2] adj (a) fine, choice, select; mature; distinguished, illustrious; **lo más — de** the cream of, the pick of. (b) tall, full-grown.

granar [1a] vi to seed, run to seed.

granate nm garnet.

granazón nf seeding.

Gran Bretaña f Great Britain.

grande 1 adj (a) (in size) big, large; (in stature) big, tall; number, speed etc high, great; **en cantidades más —s** in larger quantities; **hay una diferencia no muy —** there is not a very big difference; **los zapatos le están muy —s** the shoes are too big for her; **con gran placer** with great pleasure; **¿cómo es de —?** how big is it?, what size is it?

(b) (morally etc) great; **un gran hombre** a great man; **fue una gran hazaña** it was a great achievement.

(c) grand, grandiose, impressive.

(d) **en —** as a whole; on a large scale, on a grand scale, in a big way; **estar en —** to be going strong; **pasarlo en —** to have a tremendous time (fam); **hacer algo en —** to do something in style, make a splash; **vivir en —** to live in style.

(e) **grandísimo** (hum or iro) great big, huge; **un coche —** a whacking big car (fam), a car and a half; **¡grandísimo tunante!** you awful old rogue!

2 adv (RPl) much, a lot.

3 nm (a) **los —s** the great.

(b) **— (de España)** grandee.

4 nf (a) (Arg) first prize, big prize (in the lottery). (b) (Chi, Col) naughty thing, misdeed.

grandemente adv greatly, extremely; **— equivocado** greatly mistaken.

grandeza nf (a) bigness; size, magnitude.

(b) greatness.

(c) grandness, grandiose quality, impressiveness; grandeur, magnificence.

(d) status of grandee.

(e) grandees (collectively), nobility.

grandilocuencia nf grandiloquence.

grandilocuente adj (SAm) boastful, arrogant.

grandílocuo adj grandiloquent.

grandiosidad nf = **grandeza** (c).

grandioso adj grand, impressive, magnificent; (pej) grandiose.

grandor nm size.

grandote adj great big, huge; see also **—ote.**

grandullón adj overgrown, oversized.

grandura nf (Arg) = **grandeza** (b) and (c).

granear [1a] vt (a) seed to sow. (b) (Tech) to grain, stipple.

granel nm heap of corn; **a —** in abundance; by the score, by the ton; lavishly; at random; (Comm) in bulk, loose; in quantity; **vino a —** wine in bulk, wine in the barrel.

granero nm granary, barn; (fig) granary, corn-producing area.

granetario nm precision balance.

granete nm (Tech) punch.

granilla nf grain (in cloth).

granítico adj granitic, granite (attr).

granito[1] nm (Geol) granite.

granito[2] nm (Agr etc) small grain; granule; (Med) pimple.

granizada nf (a) (Meteorol) hail, hailstorm. (b) (fig) hail; shower, volley; vast number; **una — de balas** a hail of bullets. (c) (Chi, Guat) iced drink.

granizado nm iced drink; **— de café** iced coffee.

granizal nm (Col, Chi, Guat, Mex) hailstorm.

granizar [1f] vi to hail; (fig) to rain, shower.

granizo nm hail.

granja nf farm; farmhouse; dairy; country house; **— avícola** chicken farm, poultry farm; **— colectiva** collective farm.

granjear [1a] **1** vt to gain, earn; to win; (Chi) to steal. **2 granjearse** vr to win for oneself, gain for oneself.

granjería nf (a) (Comm, Fin) profit, earnings; (Agr) farm earnings. (b) (Agr) farming, husbandry.

granjero nm farmer.

grano nm (a) (Agr, Bot) grain; seed; berry; **—s** grain, corn, cereals; **— de arroz** grain of rice; **— de trigo** grain of wheat; **— de café** coffee bean; **—s panificables** bread grains; **tomarlo con un — de sal** to take it with a pinch of salt; **ir al —** to get to the point, get down to brass tacks; **¡vamos al —!** let's get on with it!

(b) particle, grain; speck; **— de arena** grain of

sand; **no es — de anís** (or **arena**) it's not just a small thing, you can't laugh this one off.

(c) (in stone, wood etc) grain; **de — fino** fine-grained; **de — gordo** coarse-grained.

(d) (Med) pimple, spot.

(e) (Pharm) grain.

granoso adj granular; granulated.

granuja 1 nf loose grapes; grape seed. **2** nm urchin, ragamuffin; rogue.

granujería nf urchins (collectively), rogues (collectively).

granujiento adj, **granujoso** adj pimply, spotty.

granulación nf granulation.

granular[1] adj granular.

granular[2] [1a] **1** vt to granulate. **2 granularse** vr (a) to granulate, become granulated. (b) (Med) to break out in pimples, become spotty.

gránulo nm granule.

granuloso adj granular.

grapa nf (for papers) staple; clip, fastener; (Mech) dog, clamp; (Archit) cramp.

grasa nf (a) (in general) grease; (Cook) fat; suet; **— de ballena** blubber; **— de pescado** fish oil; **— vegetal** vegetable fat.

(b) (Aut, Mech) oil; grease; **— para ejes** axle grease.

(c) (Anat) fat, fattiness; **tener mucha —** to be very fat.

(d) (Mex) shoe polish.

(e) (pej) grease, greasy dirt, filth.

(f) **—s** (Min) slag.

grasiento adj greasy, oily; road surface greasy, slippery; (pej) filthy.

grasilla nf (Bot) sundew.

graso 1 adj fatty; greasy; food oily. **2** nm fattiness; greasiness; oiliness.

grata nf (Comm) favour (letter).

gratamente adv pleasingly, pleasantly, agreeably; gratifyingly.

gratificación nf (a) (Fin etc) reward, recompense; tip; gratuity; bonus (on wages); bounty. (b) (angl: esp SAm) gratification, pleasure, satisfaction.

gratificador adj (SAm) gratifying, pleasurable, satisfying.

gratificar [1g] vt (a) (Fin etc) to reward, recompense; to tip, give a gratuity to; to give a bonus to, pay extra to; **"se gratificará"** (adverts) "a reward is offered".

(b) to gratify; to give pleasure to, satisfy; longing to gratify, indulge.

gratis adv gratis, free, for nothing; **"entrada —"** "admission free"; **de —** (SAm) gratis.

gratitud nf gratitude.

grato adj (a) pleasing, pleasant; agreeable; welcome, gratifying; **una decisión muy grata para todos** a very welcome decision for everybody; **recibir una impresión grata** to get a pleasing impression; **nos es — informarle que . . .** we are pleased to inform you that . . .

(b) (Bol, Chi) grateful; **le estoy — por ello** I am grateful to you for it.

gratuitamente adv (a) free, for nothing. (b) gratuitously; unfoundedly.

gratuito adj (a) free, free of charge. (b) remark etc gratuitous, uncalled-for; charge unfounded, unjustified.

gratulatorio adj congratulatory.

grava nf gravel; crushed stone; road metal.

gravamen nm burden, obligation; (Law) lien, encumbrance; (Fin) tax, impost; **libre de —** unencumbered, free from encumbrances.

gravar [1a] **1** vt to burden, encumber (de with); property (Law) to place a lien upon; (Fin) to assess for tax; **— con impuestos** to burden with taxes; **— un producto con un impuesto** to place a tax on a product.

2 gravarse vr (SAm) to get worse, become more serious.

gravativo adj burdensome.

grave adj (a) heavy, weighty.

(b) (fig) grave, serious; critical; important, momentous; loss etc grave, severe, grievous; **un deber muy —** a very grave duty; **la situación es —** the situation is grave (or critical); **me es muy — tener que + infin** it is very hard for me to + infin.

(c) (in character) serious, sedate, dignified; **y otros hombres —s** and other worthy men.

(d) (Med) illness, condition grave, serious; wound severe; **estar —** to be seriously ill, be critically ill.

(e) (Mus) note, pitch low, deep.

(f) (Ling) accent grave; word paroxytone, stressed on the penultimate syllable (eg padre, romance).

gravedad *nf* (a) (*Phys*) gravity.
  (b) (*fig*) gravity, seriousness; importance; severity, grievousness.
  (c) seriousness, dignity.
  (d) (*Med*) gravity; **estar de —** to be seriously ill, be dangerously ill; **estar herido de —** to be severely injured (*or* wounded); **tiene heridas de —** he has serious injuries; **parece que la lesión es sin —** it seems that the injury is not serious.
  (e) (*Mus*) depth.

gravemente *adv* gravely, seriously; critically; severely, grievously; **habló —** he spoke gravely; **estar — enfermo** to be critically ill.

grávido *adj* (a) pregnant; (*Zool*) with young, carrying young.
  (b) (*fig*) full (*de* of), heavy (*de* with); **me sentí — de emociones** I was heavy with emotions, I was weighed down with emotions.

gravilla *nf* gravel.

gravitación *nf* gravitation.

gravitacional *adj* gravitational.

gravitar [1a] *vi* (a) (*Phys*) to gravitate (*hacia* towards). (b) **— sobre** to rest on; to bear down on, weigh down on; (*fig*) to be a burden to; to encumber.

gravitatorio *adj* gravitational.

gravoso *adj* (a) burdensome, oppressive, onerous; **ser — a** to be a burden to, weigh on.
  (b) (*Fin*) costly, expensive; burdensome; *charge* extortionate.
  (c) tiresome, vexatious.

graznar [1a] *vi* to squawk; (*of crow*) to caw, croak; (*of goose*) to cackle; (*of duck*) to quack; (*of singer: hum*) to croak.

graznido *nm* squawk; caw, croak; cackle; quack.

grébano *nm* (*Arg: pej*) Italian.

Grecia *f* Greece.

greco *adj*, *n* (*lit*) = **griego**.

greda *nf* (*Geol*) clay; (*Tech*) fuller's earth.

gredal *nm* claypit.

gredoso *adj* clayey.

gregario *adj* (a) gregarious; **instinto —** herd instinct.
  (b) (*fig*) servile, slavish.

gregarismo *nm* gregariousness.

gregoriano *adj* Gregorian.

Gregorio *m* Gregory.

greguería *nf* (a) hubbub, uproar. (b) (*Lit*) brief, *humorous and often mildly poetic comment or aphorism about life.*

gremial 1 *adj* (a) (*Hist*) guild (*attr*). (b) (*modern Pol*) trade-union (*attr*), trades-union (*attr*); (*SAm*) trade (*attr*). **2** *nm* union member.

gremio *nm* (a) (*Hist*) guild, corporation, company.
  (b) (*modern Pol*) union; **— obrero, — de obreros** trade union, trades union.

greña *nf* (a) (*also* **—s**) shock of hair, mat (*or* mop) of hair, matted hair.
  (b) (*fig*) tangle, entanglement; **andar a la — to** bicker, squabble.
  (c) **en —** (*Mex*) *silk* raw; *silver* unpolished.

greñudo *adj hair* tangled, matted; *person* dishevelled.

gres *nm* (a) (*Geol*) potter's clay. (b) earthenware, stoneware.

gresca *nf* uproar, hubbub; row, shindy; **andar a la —** to row, brawl.

grey *nf* (*Eccl*) flock, congregation.

Grial *nm*: **Santo —** Holy Grail.

griego 1 *adj* Greek, Grecian.
  2 *nm*, **griega** *nf* (a) Greek.
  (b) (*fam*) cheat.
  3 *nm* (*language*) (a) Greek; **— antiguo** ancient Greek.
  (b) (*fig*) gibberish, double Dutch; **para mí es —** it's Greek to me; **hablar en —** to talk double Dutch.

grieta *nf* fissure, crack; chink; crevice; chasm; (*on skin*) chap, crack; (*Pol etc*) rift.

grietarse [1a] *vr* = **agrietarse**.

grifa *nf* (*Mex*) marijuana.

grifear [1a] *vi* (*Mex*) to smoke marijuana.

grifería[1] *nf* taps (*collectively*), faucets (*collectively: US*).

grifería[2] *nf* (*Ant*) Negroes (*collectively*).

grifo[1] *nm* (a) tap, faucet (*US*); cock; **cerveza (servida) al —** draught beer, beer on draught. (b) (*Per*) petrol station, gas station (*US*); dive (*fam*); drink shop.

grifo[2] **1** *adj* (a) (*Mex*) **estar —** to be drunk; to be mad; to be high on pot (*sl*), be under the influence of marijuana.
  (b) (*Col*) vain, stuck-up (*fam*).
  2 *nm* (*Mex*) (a) marijuana, pot (*sl*).
  (b) marijuana addict, pot smoker (*sl*).
  (c) drunkard.

grifo[3] (*Ant*) **1** *adj* (a) *hair* curly, kinky. (b) *person* (*euph*) coloured. **2** *nm* (a) kinky hair. (b) (*euph*) Negro, coloured person.

grifo[4] *nm* (*Myth*) griffin.

grigallo *nm* blackcock.

grilla *nf* (a) (*Ent*) female cricket; **¡ésa es — (y no canta)!** (*fam*) that's a likely story! (*iro*). (b) (*Col, Ec, Per*) annoyance, bother. (c) (*Col*) row, slanging match (*fam*).

grillera *nf* cage for crickets; cricket hole.

grillete *nm* fetter, shackle.

grillo *nm* (a) (*Ent*) cricket; **— cebollero, — real** mole cricket. (b) (*Bot*) shoot, sprout. (c) **—s** fetters, shackles, irons; (*fig*) shackles.

grima *nf* (a) horror, loathing, disgust; aversion, reluctance; uneasiness; annoyance, irritation, displeasure; **me da —** it gets on my nerves, it gives me the shivers; it sickens me.
  (b) (*Chi*) bit, small particle.
  (c) (*Col*) **en —** alone; **estar solo en —** to be all alone.

grimillón *nm* (*Chi*) lot, heap.

grímpola *nf* pennant.

gringada *nf*, **gringaje** *nm* (*RPl*) gringos (*collectively*); group of gringos.

gringo 1 *adj* (a) (*SAm*) foreign (see **2**).
  (b) (*SAm*) *language* foreign, unintelligible.
  (c) (*Per*) blond(e), fair.
  2 *nm*, **gringa** *nf* (a) (*SAm, freq pej*) foreigner (*in 19th century esp* Briton, Anglo-Saxon, *now esp* North American, Yankee; *RPl freq* Italian).
  (b) (*Chi, Per*) blond(e), fair-haired person.
  (c) (*SAm*) gibberish, unintelligible speech; **hablar en —** to talk double Dutch.

gringuería *nf* (*SAm*) group of gringos.

gripe *nf* influenza, flu.

gris 1 *adj* grey; *day, weather* grey, dull; **— perla** pearl-grey. **2** *nm* grey; **hace un —** there's a cold wind.

grisáceo *adj* greyish.

grisma *nf* (*Chi, Guat, Hond*) strand, shred, bit.

grisú *nm* firedamp.

grita *nf* uproar, hubbub; shouting; (*Theat*) catcalls, booing; **dar — a** to boo, hoot (at).

gritadera *nf* (*SAm*) loud shouting, clamour.

gritar [1a] *vti* to shout, yell; to scream, shriek, cry out; to hoot, boo; **¡no grites!** stop shouting!

gritería *nf*, **griterío** *nm* shouting, uproar, clamour.

grito *nm* (a) shout, yell; scream, shriek, cry; hoot, boo; bellow; (*Zool*) cry, sound; (*Orn*) call, cry; **a —s, a — herido, a — pelado, a voz en —** at the top of one's voice; **llorar a —s** to weep and wail; **poner el — en el cielo** to make a great fuss, scream blue murder (*fam*); **es el último —** (*gall*) it's the very latest, it's the latest craze.
  (b) (*SAm*) proclamation; **— de independencia** proclamation of independence; **el — de Dolores** *the proclamation of Mexican independence* (1810).

gritón *adj* loud-mouthed; screaming, shouting.

gro *nm* grosgrain.

groenlandés 1 *adj* Greenland (*attr*). **2** *nm*, **groenlandesa** *nf* Greenlander.

Groenlandia *f* Greenland.

groggy ['grogi] *adj*, **grogui** *adj* (*Boxing etc*) groggy.

grosella *nf* (red)currant; **— espinosa** gooseberry; **— negra** blackcurrant; **— roja** redcurrant.

grosellero *nm* currant bush.

groseramente *adv* rudely, discourteously; coarsely, crudely, vulgarly, indelicately; roughly, loutishly; grossly, stupidly.

grosería *nf* (a) (*in general*) rudeness, discourtesy; coarseness, crudeness, vulgarity; roughness; stupidity.
  (b) (*remark etc*) rude thing, coarse thing, vulgar remark (*etc*).

grosero *adj* rude, discourteous; coarse, crude, vulgar, indelicate; rough, loutish; *error etc* gross, stupid.

grosor *nm* thickness.

grosura *nf* (a) fat, suet. (b) (*Med*) meat diet.

grotescamente *adv* grotesquely; bizarrely, absurdly.

grotesco *adj* grotesque; bizarre, absurd.

grúa *nf* (*Tech*) crane; derrick; **— corredera, — corrediza, — móvil** travelling crane; **— de pescante** jib crane; **— (de) puente** overhead crane; **— de torre** tower crane.

gruesa *nf* gross, twelve dozen.

gruesamente *adv* (a) thickly; bulkily. (b) (*Comm etc*) in bulk.

grueso 1 *adj* (a) thick; bulky, stout, massive, solid; big, heavy; *person* stout, thickset; *artillery, sea* heavy; *intestine* large; *chest* large; *trunk etc* thick, massive.
  (b) *quality etc* coarse.

2 *nm* **(a)** thickness; bulkiness, bulk, size; density. **(b)** thick part; main part, major portion; (*of crowd, troops etc*) main body, mass; **el — del pelotón** (*Racing*) the ruck of the runners; **va mezclado con el — del pasaje** he is mingling with the mass of the passengers.
　(c) (*Comm*) **en —** in bulk.

grujidor *nm* glass cutter, glazier.

grulla *nf* (*Orn*) crane (*also —* **común**).

grullo 1 *adj* **(a)** (*fam*) uncouth, rough. **(b)** (*Mex*) sponging (*fam*), cadging. **(c)** (*Guat, Mex*) *horse*, mule grey.
　2 *nm* (*Mex*) grey (horse); (*RPl*) big colt, large stallion.

grumete *nm* cabin boy, ship's boy.

grumo *nm* **(a)** clot, lump; dollop; (*of blood*) clot; **— de leche** curd. **(b)** (*of grapes etc*) bunch, cluster.

grumoso *adj* clotted; lumpy.

gruñido *nm* grunt, growl; snarl; (*fig*) grouse (*fam*), grumble; **dar —s = gruñir.**

gruñidor 1 *adj* grunting, growling; snarling; (*fig*) grumbling. **2** *nm* (*fig*) grumbler.

gruñir [3h] *vi* to grunt, growl; to snarl; (*fig*) to grouse (*fam*), grumble; (*of door etc*) to creak.

gruñón 1 *adj* grumpy, grumbling. **2** *nm* grumbler.

grupa *nf* crupper; hindquarters, rump (of horse).

grupera *nf* (*of horse*) pillion (seat); **ir en la —** to sit behind the rider, be carried on the horse's crupper.

grupo *nm* **(a)** group; (*of trees etc*) cluster, clump; (*Pol*) group; **— del dólar** dollar block; **— de presión** pressure group; **— sanguíneo** blood group; **discusión en —** group discussion; **reunirse en —s** to gather in groups; **reunirse en — en torno a** to gather round, cluster round.
　(b) (*Elec, Tech etc*) unit, set, plant; assembly; **— compresor** compressor unit; **— dental** dentist's operating equipment; **— electrógeno, — generador** generating set, power plant.

gruta *nf* cavern, grotto.

gua *interj* (*SAm: distress*) oh dear!; (*surprise*) well!; (*scorn*) get away!

gua . . . : *for some words so spelled in SAm, see also* **hua . . .**

guabiroba *nf* (*RPl*) dugout canoe.

guaca *nf* **(a)** (*SAm*) (*Indian*) tomb, funeral mound; buried treasure; wealth, money; (*Bol, CR, Cu, Mex, Ven*) moneybox; **hacer —** (*Bol, Col, Cu, Mex*) to make money, make one's pile (*fam*); **hacer su —** (*Cu, Chi, PR*) to make hay while the sun shines.
　(b) (*Cu*) ticking-off.
　(c) (*Mex*) double-barrelled shotgun.
　(d) (*Ven*) large sore; **se sacó la —** he got fleeced, he was cheated.

guacal *nm* (*SAm*) wooden crate; gourd, vessel.

guacamayo 1 *adj* (*RPl*) absurdly dressed; (*PR*) flashily dressed. **2** *nm* **(a)** macaw. **(b)** (*PR*) flashily-dressed person; (*Cu: pej*) Spaniard.

guacarnaco *adj* **(a)** (*Col, Cu, Chi, Ec*) silly, stupid. **(b)** (*Chi*) long-legged.

guachafita *nf* **(a)** (*Col, SD, Ven*) hubbub, din; disorder. **(b)** (*Ven*) gambling joint (*sl*). **(c)** (*PR, Ven*) mockery, jeering.

guachaje *nm* (*Chi*) orphaned animal; group of calves separated from their mothers.

guachalomo *nm* (*Chi*) sirloin steak.

guachapear [1a] **1** *vt* **(a)** *water* to dabble in, splash about in.
　(b) to botch, mess up, bungle.
　(c) (*Chi*) to pinch (*fam*), borrow.
　(d) (*Col*) *brushwood* to clear, cut.
　2 *vi* to rattle, clatter, bang about.

guachar [1a] *vt* (*Mex: angl*) to watch.

guáchara *nf* (*Cu, PR*) lie.

guache *nm* (*Col, Ven*) common sort, uneducated person; (*pej*) layabout, loafer.

guachicar(ro) *nm* (*Mex: angl*) parking attendant.

guachimán *nm* (*CAm, Mex: angl*) watchman.

guachinanga *nf* (*Cu*) wooden bar (on door etc).

guachinango 1 *adj* (*Col, Cu, PR*) soapy, smooth; teasing. **2** *nm* **(a)** (*Cu: pej*) Mexican. **(b)** (*Ant*) smooth person, flatterer.

guacho 1 *adj* (*esp Chi, Per, RPl*) **(a)** *person* homeless, orphaned, abandoned; *animal* motherless.
　(b) *shoe etc* odd.
　2 *nm* **(a)** baby bird, chick.
　(b) (*Chi, Per, RPl*) homeless child, abandoned child; orphan, foundling; illegitimate child; (*Agr*) motherless animal.
　(c) (*Chi, Per, RPl*) odd one (of a pair); isolated object.

guadal *nm* (*Col, RPl*) sandy bog.

guadalajareño 1 *adj* of Guadalajara. **2** *nm*, **guadalajareña** *nf* native (*or* inhabitant) of Guadalajara; **los —s** the people of Guadalajara.

guadaloso *adj* (*RPl*) boggy.

guadamecí *nm* embossed leather.

guadaña *nf* scythe.

guadañadora *nf* mowing machine.

guadañar [1a] *vt* to scythe, mow.

guadañero *nm* mower.

guadaño *nm* (*Cu, Mex*) small harbour boat.

guagua[1] *nf* (*Cu, PR, Canaries*) bus.

guagua[2] **1** *adj* (*Ec*) small, little. **2** *nf* (*in parts also m*) **(a)** (*SAm*) baby. **(b)** trifle, small thing; **de —** (*Cu, Mex*) free, for nothing.

guaguarear [1a] *vi* (*Guat, Mex*) to burble, chatter.

guaguatear [1a] *vt* (*Chi, Guat, RPl*) *baby* to breastfeed; to carry in one's arms.

guaguatera *nf* (*RPl*) nurse.

guagüero 1 *adj* **(a)** (*Ant*) sponging (*fam*), parasitical. **(b)** (*Cu*) bus (*attr*).
　2 *nm*, **guagüera** *nf* **(a)** (*Cu*) bus driver.
　(b) (*Ant*) bargain hunter, person looking for something for nothing.

guaica *nf* (*Arg*) bead; (*Bol*) rosary beads; (*Col*) bead necklace.

guaico *nm* (*Arg, Col, Chi, Ec*) hollow, dip, depression; ravine; (*Col*) hole, pit; (*Col*) out-of-the-way place, lonely spot; (*Per*) mountain torrent; (*Per*) avalanche; (*Bol*) dung heap, rubbish tip.

guaina 1 *nf* (*Arg*) girl, young woman. **2** *nm* (*Bol, Chi*) youth, young man.

guaino *nm* (*Arg, Per*) young man; small man; (*Sport*) jockey.

guaipe *nm* (*SAm: angl*) wiper, cloth.

guáiper *nm* (*CAm: angl*) windscreen wiper, windshield wiper (US).

guaira *nf* **(a)** (*CAm*) Indian flute. **(b)** (*Arg, Bol, Chi, Per*) earthenware smelting furnace (*for silver ore*). **(c)** (*Cu, Ven*) triangular sail.

guairana *nf* (*Per*) lime kiln; **= guaira.**

guairo *nm* (*Cu, Ven*) small coastal vessel (*with 2 triangular sails*).

guajada *nf* (*Mex*) stupid thing.

guajalote (*Mex, PR*) **= guajolote.**

guaje 1 *adj* (*Hond, Mex*) silly, stupid; **hacer — a uno** to fool someone.
　2 *nm* **(a)** (*Hond, Mex*) gourd, calabash.
　(b) (*Hond, Mex*) idiot, fool.
　(c) (*CAm*) old thing, piece of junk.

guajear [1a] *vi* (*Mex*) to play the fool, be silly.

guajería *nf* (*Mex*) **(a)** idiocy, foolishness. **(b)** stupid thing, foolish act.

guajero *nm*, **guajera** *nf* (*Cu*) (white) peasant; (*SD*) peasant; (*Guat*) countryman; outsider.

guajolote (*Mex*) **1** *adj* silly, stupid. **2** *nm* **(a)** turkey. **(b)** (*fam*) fool, idiot.

gualdo *adj* yellow, golden.

gualdrapa *nf* **(a)** (*Hist*) trappings. **(b)** (*fam*) tatter, ragged end.

gualdrapear [1a] *vi* **(a)** (*Naut: of sail*) to flap. **(b)** (*Cu: of horse*) to walk slowly.

gualicho *nm* **(a)** (*Arg, Bol, Chi*) devil, evil spirit; evil spell; hurt, harm. **(b)** (*Arg*) powerful talisman, good-luck charm.

Gualterio *m* Walter.

guama *nf* **(a)** (*CAm, Col,Ven*) lie. **(b)** (*Col*) big foot; big hand. **(c)** (*Col, Ven*) calamity, disaster, misfortune; annoyance.

guambra *nmf* **(a)** (*Bol*) peasant, Indian. **(b)** (*Col, Ec, Per*) child, baby; (*fam*) sweetheart.

guampa *nf* (*Bol, PR*) horn; drinking vessel.

guámparo *nm* (*Chi*) horn; drinking vessel.

guanacada *nmf* (*SAm*) simpleton, dimwit (*fam*); rustic.

guanaco 1 *adj* (*SAm*) simple, silly; slow.
　2 *nm* **(a)** (*Zool*) guanaco.
　(b) (*SAm*) simpleton, dimwit (*fam*); rustic.
　(c) (*Guat*) Honduran; (*any*) Central American.

guanajada *nf* (*Ant*) silly thing, foolish act.

guanajo *nm*, **guanaja** *nf* (*Ant*) **(a)** (*Orn*) turkey. **(b)** (*fam*) fool, idiot.

guanay *nm* (*Chi*) oarsman; longshoreman; (*fig*) tough man.

guanear [1a] **1** *vt* **(a)** (*Per*) to fertilize with guano. **(b)** (*Bol*) to dirty, soil. **2** *vi* (*SAm: of animals*) to defecate.

guanera *nf* (*SAm*) guano deposit.

guanero *adj* (*SAm*) guano (*attr*), pertaining to guano.

guanín *nm* (*Ant, Col, Chi: Hist*) base gold.

guano[1] *nm* (*SAm*) **(a)** guano; artificial manure; (*Chi, Per*) dung, manure. **(b)** (*Cu, PR: hum*) money, brass (*sl*); **meter —** to work hard.

guano[2] *nm* (*Ant*) palm tree; palm leaf.
guantada *nf*, **guantazo** *nm* slap.
guante *nm* (a) glove; — **de boxeo** boxing glove; — **de cabritilla** kid glove; — **de goma** rubber glove; — **con puño** gauntlet; **se ajusta como un** — it fits like a glove; **me conviene como un** — it suits me down to the ground; **arrojar el** — to throw down the gauntlet; **recoger el** — to take up the challenge; **echar un** — to take a collection (*a beneficio de* for, on behalf of); **echar el** — **a uno** to catch hold of someone, seize someone; (*fig*) to catch someone out, come down on someone.
   (b) (*Chi*) whip, cat-o'nine-tails.
   (c) —s tip, commission.
guantear [1a] *vt* (*Chi, Mex*) to slap, hit.
guantelete *nm* gauntlet.
guantera *nf* (*Aut*) glove compartment.
guantería *nf* (a) glove shop; glove factory. (b) glove making.
guantero *nm*, **guantera** *nf* glover.
guantón *nm* (*SAm*) slap, hit, blow.
guañusco *adj* (*Arg*) (a) withered, faded. (b) burned, burned up.
guapear [1a] *vi* (*fam*) (a) to cut a dash, dress flashily. (b) to bluster, swagger.
guapetón 1 *adj* (a) good-looking, handsome; dashing. (b) (*pej*) flashy. **2** *nm* bully, roughneck (*sl*).
guapeza *nf* (a) good looks; prettiness, attractiveness. (b) smartness, elegance; (*pej*) flashiness. (c) boldness, dash; (*pej*) bravado.
guapo 1 *adj* (a) good-looking; *girl* pretty, attractive; *man* handsome; **¡oye, guapa!** hey, beautiful!
   (b) smart, elegant, well-dressed; (*pej*) flashy, overdressed; **¡hombre, qué** — **estás!** how smart you're looking!
   (c) bold, dashing.
   2 *nm* (a) lover, gallant, beau.
   (b) swell (*fam*), toff (*fam*); (*pej*) bully, tough guy (*US fam*); braggart.
guaposo *adj* (*Cu*) bold, dashing.
guapucha *nf* (*Col*) cheating (*at cards*).
guaquear [1a] *vt* (*Cam, Col, Per*) *tomb* to rob (*in search of archaeological valuables*).
guaqueo *nm* (*CAm, Col, Per*) tomb robbing.
guaquero *nm* (*CAm, Col, Per*) tomb robber.
guara *nf* (a) (*Per*) lot, heap. (b) (*Arg, Chi*) —s tricks, wiles.
guaraca *nf* (*Col, Chi, Ec, Per*) sling; whip; (*Per*) sling shot; (*Chi*) cosh, blunt instrument.
guaracha *nf* (a) (*Ant*) merry song, merry dance.
   (b) (*Ant*) din, hubbub; quarrel; spree (*fam*), carousal.
   (c) (*Cu*: *pej*) small-time band.
   (d) (*PR*) joke.
   (e) (*Bol*) litter, rough bed.
   (f) —s (*Guat*) old shoes.
guarache *nm* (*Mex*) (a) sandal, light shoe. (b) (*Aut*) tyre patch.
guarachear [1a] *vi* (*Ant*) to revel, carouse.
guaragua *nf* (a) (*Bol, Per*) adornments; tawdry finery.
   (b) (*Guat, Hond*) lie; hoax.
   (c) (*CR*) liar, taleteller.
   (d) (*Chi, Ec, Per*) rhythmical movement (*of the body in dancing*).
guaral *nm* (*Col,Ven*) rope, line.
guarango *adj* (a) (*Chi, Per, RPl*) rough, rude, ill-bred. (b) (*Bol*) ragged, dirty.
guaranguear [1a] *vi* (*Chi, RPl*) to act in an ill-bred way, be rude.
guaranguería *nf* (*Chi, RPl*) roughness, rudeness, lack of breeding.
guaranismo *nm* word (*or expression etc*) from the Guaraní language.
guarapazo *nm* (*Col*) (a) sugar-cane liquor. (b) blow, knock; hard fall.
guarapear [1a] *vi* and **guarapearse** *vr* (*Per*) to drink sugar-cane liquor; (*SD*) to drink, get drunk.
guarapo *nm* (*SAm*) sugar-cane liquor; (*PR, SD*) watered-down drink; (*Ven*) fermented pineapple juice; **menear el** — (*Cu,Ven*) to get things moving; **se le enfrió el** — he lost the urge.
guarapón *nm* (*Bol, Chi, Per*) broad-brimmed hat.
guarda 1 *nm* guard; keeper, custodian; (*Arg*) bus conductor, tram conductor; (*Arg*: *Rail*) guard, brakeman; — **de coto**, — **forestal**, — **jurado** gamekeeper, game warden; — **de dique** lock keeper; — **nocturno** night watchman.
   2 *nf* (a) guard, guarding; safekeeping; custody.
   (b) (*of law*) observance.
   (c) (*of lock*) ward; (*of sword, machine*) guard; (*Typ*) flyleaf, endpaper.
   (d) (*Per, RPl*: *Sew*) ribbing, trimming.

guarda(a)gujas *nm*, *pl* **guarda(a)gujas** (*Rail*) switchman.
guarda(a)almacén *nm* storekeeper.
guardabarrera *nm* (a) (*Rail*: *person*) crossing keeper. (b) (*Rail*) level-crossing gate(s), grade-crossing gate(s) (*US*).
guardabarros *nm*, *pl* **guardabarros** mudguard, fender (*US*).
guardabosque(s) *nm* gamekeeper, game warden; ranger, forester.
guardabrisa *nf* (*Aut*) windscreen, windshield (*US*); (*Mex*) screen.
guardacabo *nm* (*Naut*) thimble.
guardacabras *nm*, *pl* **guardacabras** goatherd.
guardacalor *nm* cosy, cover.
guardacantón *nm* kerbstone; roadside post.
guardacartas *nm*, *pl* **guardacartas** letter file.
guardacenizas *nm*, *pl* **guardacenizas** ash pan.
guardacoches *nm*, *pl* **guardacoches** parking attendant.
guardacostas *nm*, *pl* **guardacostas** coastguard vessel, revenue cutter.
guardador 1 *adj* (a) protective.
   (b) observant, watchful.
   (c) (*pej*) mean, stingy.
   2 *nm* (a) keeper; guardian; protector.
   (b) (*of laws*) observer.
   (c) (*pej*) mean person.
guardaespaldas *nm*, *pl* **guardaespaldas** bodyguard, henchman.
guardafango *nm* mudguard, fender (*US*).
guardafrenos *nm*, *pl* **guardafrenos** (*Rail*) guard, brakeman.
guardafuego *nm* fireguard; fender.
guardajoyas *nm*, *pl* **guardajoyas** jewel case.
guardalado *nm* railing, parapet.
guardalodos *nm*, *pl* **guardalodos** mudguard, fender (*US*).
guardamano *nm* guard (*of a sword*).
guardameta *nm* goalkeeper.
guardamuebles *nm*, *pl* **guardamuebles** furniture repository.
guardapapeles *nm*, *pl* **guardapapeles** filing cabinet.
guardapelo *nm* locket.
guardapolvo *nm* (a) dust cover, dust sheet. (b) (*dress*) dust coat; overalls; outdoor coat. (c) (*of watch*) inner lid.
guardapuerta *nf* outer door, storm door.
guardapuntas *nm*, *pl* **guardapuntas** top (*of pencil etc*).
guardar [1a] **1** *vt* (a) to guard; to watch over, protect, take care of, keep safe; to maintain, preserve; *flock etc* to watch over, tend; **¡Dios guarde a la Reina!** God save the Queen!; **Dios os guarde** (*Hist*) may God be with you.
   (b) to keep, hold, hold on to, retain; to put away, put by, lay by, store away; to save; — **algo para sí** to keep something for oneself; **lo guardó en el bolsillo** he put it away in his pocket; **te lo puedes** — you keep it, you can keep it; **guardo los sellos para mi hermano** I save the stamps for my brother.
   (c) *promise, secret* to keep.
   (d) *commandment etc* to keep; *law* to observe, respect.
   (e) *respect etc* to have, show (*a* for); *malice etc* to bear, have (*a* for, towards); see **cama**, **silencio** etc.
   2 *vi*: **¡guarda!** look out!, watch out!
   3 guardarse *vr* (a) to be on one's guard, look out for oneself.
   (b) — **de algo** to avoid something; to look out for something; to refrain from something; to protect oneself against something; — **de** + *infin* to be careful not to + *infin*; to refrain from + *ger*; to avoid + *ger*; to guard against + *ger*; **guárdate de no ofenderle** take care not to upset him; **¡ya te guardarás de hacerlo!** I bet you won't!; you wouldn't dare!
   (c) —**la a uno** to keep a rod in pickle for someone, have it in for someone.
guardarropa 1 *nm* (a) (*room*) cloakroom, checkroom (*US*). (b) (*cupboard*) wardrobe. **2** *nmf* cloakroom attendant.
guardarropía *nf* (*Theat*) wardrobe; properties, props (*fam*); **de** — make-believe, (*pej*) sham, fake.
guardatrén *nm* (*RPl*: *Rail*) guard, brakeman.
guardavalla *nm* (*SAm*) goalkeeper.
guardavía *nm* (*Rail*) linesman.
guardavidas *nm*, *pl* **guardavidas** (*Arg*) lifeguard (*on beach*).
guardavista *nm* visor, sunshade.

guardería *nf*: — **infantil** crèche, day nursery.
guardia 1 *nf* (a) (*in general*) custody, care; defence, protection; (*Mil etc*) guarding; **estar de** — to be on guard, be on duty; to keep watch; **estar en** — **contra** to be on one's guard against; **montar (la)** — to mount guard; **poner a uno en** — to put someone on his guard.
(b) (*body of men*) guard; (*Mil*) guard; police; (*Naut*) watch; — **de asalto** riot police; **G— Civil** Civil Guard; — **de corps** bodyguard; — **de cuartillo** (*Naut*) dog watch; — **de honor** guard of honour; —**s montadas** horse guards; — **municipal**, urbana town police, traffic police; — **real** household troops; — **suiza** Swiss guard; **relevar la** — to change guard.
(c) (*Fencing: position*) guard; **aflojar la** — to lower one's guard (*also fig*); **estar en** — to be on guard.
2 *nm* policeman; (*Mil*) guard, guardsman; —**s de asalto** riot police, (*Mil*) shock troops; — **de la circulación**, — **de la porra**, — **de tráfico**, — **urbano** traffic policeman; — **civil** civil guard; — **forestal** game warden, ranger; — **marina** midshipman.
guardián *nm*, **guardiana** *nf* guardian, custodian, keeper; warden; watchman; (*Zool*) keeper; — **de niño(s)** baby-sitter; — **de parque** park keeper; — **de prisiones** warder.
guardiero *nm* (*Cu*) watchman (*on an estate*).
guardilla *nf* attic, garret; attic room.
guardoso *adj* careful, thrifty; (*pej*) mean.
guare *nm* (*Ec*) punt pole.
guarearse [1a] *vr* (*CAm*) to drink sugar-cane liquor.
guarecer [2d] **1** *vt* to protect, give shelter to, take in; to preserve. **2 guarecerse** *vr* to shelter, take refuge (*de* from).
guargüero *nm* (*SAm*) throat, throttle.
guari *nm* (*Chi*) throat, throttle.
guaricha *nf* (a) (*Col, Ec, Pan, Ven*) little woman; nasty woman; (*Ven*) young (Indian) woman; (*Pan*) sly old woman.
(b) (*Pan*) brass lamp.
guariche *nm* (*Col*) = **guaricha**.
guaricho *nm* (*Ven*) young farm labourer.
guarida *nf* (*Zool*) den, lair, hideout; (*fig*) refuge, shelter; cover; (*of person*) haunt, hideout.
guarismo *nm* figure, numeral; **en** — **y por extenso** in figures and in words.
guarnecer [2d] *vt* (a) to equip, provide (*de* with); to adorn, embellish, garnish (*de* with); (*Sew*) to trim, edge (*de* with); *brakes* to line; *wall* to plaster, stucco; *jewel* to set, mount; *horse* to harness; (*Tech*) to cover, protect, reinforce (*de* with).
(b) (*Mil*) to man, garrison.
guarnecido *nm* plaster, plastering.
guarnición *nf* (a) (*act*) equipment, provision; fitting; adorning, embellishing.
(b) adornment; (*Sew*) trimming, edging, binding; (*of brake*) lining; (*of wall*) plastering; (*of jewel*) setting, mount; (*of sword*) guard; (*Mech*) packing.
(c) —**es** harness; gear; (*domestic*) fittings, fixtures; —**es del alumbrado** light fittings.
(d) (*Mil*) garrison.
guarnicionar [1a] *vt* to garrison, man.
guarnicionero *nm* harness maker.
guaro *nm* (a) (*CAm*) sugar-cane liquor, rum. (b) small parrot.
guarra *nf* sow; (*fig*) slut.
guarro 1 *adj* dirty, filthy. **2** *nm* pig, hog; (*fig*) dirty person, slovenly person.
guarrusca *nf* (*Col*) machete, big knife.
guarte *interj* (*arch*) look out!, take care!
guasa *nf* (a) joke; joking, teasing, kidding; **con** —, **de** — jokingly, in fun.
(b) dullness, insipidness.
(c) (*Chi*) peasant woman.
(d) **armar** — to kick up a row; to cause a sensation.
guasábara *nf* (*Col, PR, SD*) uprising, riot; tumult; clamour, uproar.
guasada *nf* (*RPl*) coarseness, crudity.
guasamaco *adj* rough, coarse.
guasanga *nf* (a) (*CAm, Col, Cu, Mex*) = **guasábara**; (*Guat*) quarrel, squabble. (b) (*Guat*) joke.
guasca[1] *nf* (*SAm*) leather strap, rawhide thong; **dar** — **a** (*SAm*) to whip, flog; (*Chi, RPl*) to insist stubbornly on; (*Per*) to wind up; **¡déle** — **no más!** (*Urug*) keep at it!; **pisarse la** — (*Col, Chi, RPl*) to fall into the trap; to be too clever by half; **volverse** — (*Col*) to be full of longing.
guasca[2] *nf* (*Col*) mountain peak.
guascazo *nm* (*SAm*) lash; blow, punch.
guasearse [1a] *vr* (*SAm*) to joke, tease, kid, rag.
guasería *nf* (*Bol, Chi, RPl*) coarseness, crudity.

guaserío *nm* (*Bol, Chi, RPl*) peasants, peasantry.
guaso 1 *adj* (*Cu, Ec, RPl*) coarse, crude, rough. **2** *nm*, **guasa** *nf* (*Bol, Chi, Per, RPl*) peasant, countryman. **3** *nm* (*Cu*) merry din; merrymaking, revels.
guasón 1 *adj* (a) witty, humorous; joking; **dijo** — he said jokingly, he said teasingly.
(b) dull, insipid; boring.
2 *nm*, **guasona** *nf* (a) wag, wit; joker, tease.
(b) tedious person, bore.
guasqueada *nf* (*Arg*) lash; whipping, flogging.
guasquear [1a] *vt* (*Col, Chi, Per, RPl*) to whip, flog.
guata[1] *nf* (a) (*Arg, Chi, Per*) paunch, belly; stomach; (*Cook*) tripe; **echar** — to get fat. (b) (*Chi*) warping, bulging.
guata[2] *nf* (a) raw cotton; padding; (*Bol*) twine, cord.
(b) (*Cu*) lie, fib.
(c) (*Ec*) inseparable friend.
(d) (*Guat*) double-barrelled shotgun.
guata[3] *nmf* (*Col*) inhabitant of the interior.
guataca 1 *nf* (a) (*Cu*) small hoe; wooden shovel; (b) (*Cu, SD*) big ear. **2** *nmf* (*Cu*) creep (*sl*), boot-licker (*fam*).
guataco *adj* (a) (*Col: pej*) Indian, native. (b) (*Cu*) rough, coarse. (c) (*Hond*) squat; thickset.
guatal *nm* (*CAm*) = **guate**.
guate *nm* (a) (*CAm*) maize plantation (for fodder).
(b) (*Col*) inhabitant of the interior; (*Ven*) highlander; (*Ven*) Colombian.
(c) (*Ec*) inseparable friend.
guatearse [1a] *vr* (*Chi*) to warp, bulge.
Guatemala *f* Guatemala.
guatemalteco 1 *adj* Guatemalan, of Guatemala. **2** *nm*, **guatemalteca** *nf* Guatemalan.
guatemaltequismo *nm* word (*or phrase etc*) peculiar to Guatemala.
guateque *nm* party, celebration, binge (*sl*).
guatón *adj* (*Arg, Chi, Per*) fat, paunchy, pot-bellied.
guatuso *adj* (*CAm*) blond(e), fair.
guau 1 *interj etc* bow-wow! **2** *nm* bark.
guayaba *nf* (a) (*SAm: Bot*) guava; guava jelly.
(b) (*fig and hum: SAm*) fib, lie; hoax; (*CAm*) worthless object; (*Ec*) ankle; (*Guat*) kiss; (*Guat, Salv: Pol*) power, presidency; —**s** (*CR*) (protruding) eyes.
guayabal *nm* grove of guava trees.
guayabear [1a] **1** *vt* (*Guat*) to kiss. **2** *vi* (a) (*CAm*) to pick guavas; to eat guavas. (b) (*PR, RPl*) to lie, tell fibs.
guayabera *nf* (*CAm, Cu, Mex*) light blouse.
guayabero *adj* (*Ant, Arg, Ec*) lying, deceitful.
guayabo *nm* (a) (*Bot*) guava tree. (b) (*Col*) grief, sorrow; nostalgia; (*fam*) hangover. (c) (*fam*) pretty girl, smasher (*sl*).
guayaca 1 *adj* (*Chi*) slow, dull; simple-minded. **2** *nf* (*SAm*) bag, purse.
guayacán *nm* lignum vitae.
Guayana *f* Guayana; (*earlier name*) Guiana; — **Británica** British Guiana; — **Francesa** French Guiana; — **Holandesa** Dutch Guiana.
guayanés 1 *adj* Guayanese. **2** *nm*, **guayanesa** *nf* Guayanese.
guayar [1a] **1** *vt* (*Ant: Cook*) to grate, break up; to scrape. **2** *vi* (*Ant*) to work hard. **3 guayarse** *vr* (*PR*) to get drunk.
guayo *nm* (*Ant: Cook*) grater; (*hum*) poor-quality band.
guayunga *nf* (*Ec*) lot, heap.
gubernamental 1 *adj* governmental; (*as faction*) loyalist. **2** *nmf* loyalist, government supporter; (*Mil*) government soldier.
gubernativo *adj* governmental.
gubia *nf* gouge.
guedeja *nf* long hair, lock; (*lion's*) mane.
güe—: *alternative spelling* (*prov, SAm*) *for some words, see* **hue—**: *eg for* **güevo** *see* **huevo**.
güegüecho 1 *adj* (a) (*CAm, Col*) silly, stupid.
(b) (*CAm, Mex: Med*) suffering from goitre.
2 *nm* (a) (*CAm, Mex: Med*) goitre.
(b) (*CAm, Mex: Orn*) wattle; turkey.
Guernesey *m* Guernsey.
güeñi *nm* (*Chi*) boy; servant; swarthy person.
güero *adj* (*CAm, Mex*) blond(e), fair.
guerra *nf* (a) war; warfare; struggle, fight, conflict; — **de agotamiento**, — **de desgaste** war of attrition; — **atómica** atomic war(fare); — **bacteriológica** germ warfare; — **civil** civil war; — **de** **fría** cold war; — **de guerrillas** guerrilla warfare; — **a muerte** war to the knife, war to the bitter end; — **mundial** world war; — **de nervios** war of nerves; — **nuclear** nuclear war(fare); — **relámpago** blitzkrieg; — **santa** holy war, crusade; — **a tiros** shooting war, hot

war; **— de trincheras** trench warfare; **G—** de los **Cien Años** Hundred Years' War; **G—** de los **Treinta Años** Thirty Years' War; **G—** de la **Independencia** (*Spain, also SAm*) War of Independence; **G—** de **Liberación** (*Spain, 1936-39*) Civil War; **G—** del **Transvaal** Boer War; **Primera G— Mundial** First World War; **Segunda G— Mundial** Second World War; **de —** military; war (*attr*); **Ministerio m de G—** Ministry of War, War Office (*Brit*), War Department (*US*); **estar en —** to be at war (*con* with); **dar —** to be annoying (*a* to), be a nuisance (*a* to), make trouble (*a* for); (*of child*) to carry on, make a great fuss; **dar — a uno** to rag someone; **declarar la —** to declare war (*a* on); **hacer la —** to wage war, make war (*a* on).

(b) billiards.

guerrear [1a] *vi* to wage war, fight; (*fig*) to put up a fight, resist.

guerrero 1 *adj* (a) fighting (*attr*); war (*attr*); **espíritu —** fighting spirit.

(b) warring.

(c) (*of character*) warlike, martial; **un pueblo —** a warlike people.

2 *nm* warrior, soldier, fighter.

guerrilla *nf* (a) guerrilla band; group of partisans.

(b) guerrilla warfare.

guerrillear [1a] *vi* to wage guerrilla warfare; to fight as a guerrilla band.

guerrillero *nm* guerrilla (fighter); partisan; irregular.

güi . . .: *for some words so spelled in SAm see also* **hui . . .**

guía 1 *nf* (a) (*act*) guidance, guiding; **— vocacional** vocational guidance; **para que le sirva de —** for your guidance.

(b) (*Typ*) guide, guidebook (*de* to); handbook; directory; **— de campo** (*Bio*) field guide; **— de carga** (*Rail*) waybill; **— oficial de ferrocarriles** official railway guide, official timetable; **— telefónica, — de teléfonos** telephone directory; **— del turista** tourist's guide; **— del viajero** traveller's guide.

(c) (*Mech*) guide; (*of cycle*) handlebars; (*horse*) leader, front horse; **—s reins; — sonora** (*Cine*) soundtrack.

2 *nmf* (*person*) guide; leader; adviser.

guiar [1c] **1** *vt* (a) (*in general*) to guide; to lead, direct; to manage; to advise.

(b) (*Aut etc*) to drive; (*Naut*) to steer; (*Aer*) to pilot.

(c) (*Bot*) to train.

2 guiarse *vr*: **— por** to be guided by, be ruled by, go by.

Guido *m* Guy.

guija *nf* pebble; (*on road*) cobble, cobblestone.

guijarral *nm* stony place; (*beach*) shingle, pebbles, pebbly part.

guijarro *nm* pebble; boulder; (*on road*) cobble, cobblestone.

guijarroso *adj* ground stony; boulder-strewn; *road* cobbled; *beach* pebbly, shingly.

guijo *nm* (a) gravel; (*for roadmaking*) granite chips; (*on beach*) shingle. (b) (*Col, Mex*) shaft of a water wheel; (*Cu, Mex*) shaft of a sugar mill.

güila *nf* (a) (*Mex*) whore. (b) (*Mex*) small paper kite. (c) (*CR*) small spinning top. (d) (*Chi*) rags, tatters.

guili *nm* (*fam*) bobby (*sl*), cop (*sl*).

güiliento *adj* (*Chi*) ragged, tattered.

güilo *adj* (*Mex*) maimed, crippled; (*fig*) weak, sickly.

guillado *adj* (*fam*) cracked, crazy; **estar —** to be cracked; to be in love.

guilladura *nf* (*fam*) craziness, light-headedness, idiotic joy.

guillame *nm* (*Tech*) rabbet plane.

guillarse [1a] *vr* (*fam*) to go crazy.

guillate *adj* (*fam*) crazy; **ella me vuelve —** she drives me crazy, I'm crazy about her.

Guillermo *m* William; **— el Conquistador** William the Conqueror.

guillotina *nf* guillotine; paper cutter; **ventana de —** sash window.

guillotinar [1a] *vt* to guillotine.

güincha *nf* (*Bol, Chi, Per*) (a) narrow strip of cloth; ribbon; hair ribbon; (*Sport*) tape. (b) measuring tape, tape measure.

güinche *nm* (*SAm: angl*) winch, hoist; crane.

güinchero *nm* (*SAm*) winch operator; crane operator.

guinda *nf* (a) mazzard cherry, morello cherry; **ponerse como una —** to turn scarlet.

(b) (*Naut*) height of masts.

(c) (*Cu*) guttering, spout.

(d) (*Chi*) **eso es una —** that's simple, it's a cinch (*sl*).

guindalejo *nm* (*Col, PR*) old clothes, junk, lumber.

guindaleza *nf* hawser.

guindar [1a] **1** *vt* (a) to hoist, hang up (high); (*Ven etc*) to hang (up); *criminal* (*fam*) to hang, string up (*fam*).

(b) (*fam*) to pinch (*fam*), swipe (*sl*).

2 guindarse *vr* (*fam*) to hang oneself.

guindaste *nm* (*CAm*) jib crane.

guindilla *nm* (*fam*) bobby (*sl*), cop (*sl*).

guindo *nm* mazzard (*or* morello) cherry tree.

guindola *nf* lifebuoy.

Guinea *f* Guinea; **— Española** Spanish Guinea.

guinea *nf* (*coin*) guinea.

guineo[1] **1** *adj* Guinea(n), of Guinea. **2** *nm*, **guinea** *nf* Guinean.

guineo[2] *nm* (*SAm: Bot*) banana.

guiña *nf* (*Col, Ven*) bad luck; (*Col*) witchcraft.

guiñada *nf* (a) wink; blink. (b) (*Aer, Naut*) yaw.

guiñapo *nm* (a) rag, tatter; **poner a uno como un —** to shower insults on someone. (b) slovenly person; ragamuffin; rogue, reprobate.

guiñar [1a] **1** *vt* to wink; to blink. **2** *vi* (a) to wink; to blink. (b) (*Aer, Naut*) to yaw.

guiño *nm* (a) wink; grimace, wry face; **hacer —s a** to wink at, (*of lovers*) to make eyes at. (b) (*Aer, Naut*) yaw.

guiñol *nm* art of the puppeteer, puppet theatre, Punch-and-Judy show.

guión *nm* (a) (*Zool, person*) leader.

(b) (*Typ*) hyphen, dash.

(c) (*Lit*) summary, outline; handout; explanatory text; (*Cine*) script, scenario; (*Cine*) subtitle.

(d) royal standard; (*Eccl*) processional cross, processional banner.

(e) (*Orn*) **— de codornices** corncrake.

guionista *nmf* (*Cine*) scriptwriter; writer of subtitles.

guipuzcoano 1 *adj* of Guipúzcoa. **2** *nm*, **guipuzcoana** *nf* native (*or* inhabitant) of Guipúzcoa; **los —s** the people of Guipúzcoa.

guiri *nm* (*Hist*) Carlist soldier.

guirigay *nm* (a) gibberish, jargon.

(b) hubbub, uproar; chaos, confusion; **¡esto es un —!** the place is like a bear garden!; **la nación se sumirá en un espantoso —** the country will fall into dreadful anarchy.

guirizapa *nf* (*Ven*) quarrel, squabble.

guirnalda *nf* garland; (*at funeral*) wreath; (*Art*) garland, floral motif.

güiro *nm* (a) (*SAm*) bottle gourd.

(b) (*Ant, Ven*) musical instrument made of a gourd.

(c) (*Col, Cu, PR*) head, bean (*fam*).

(d) (*Guat*) small baby.

(e) (*Cu, PR*) whore.

(f) (*Cu*) love affair.

güirro 1 *adj* (*SAm*) weak, sickly. **2** *nm* (*CR*) small baby.

guisa *nf*: **a — de** as, like, in the manner of; **de tal —** in such a way (*que* that).

guisado *nm* stew.

guisador *nm*, **guisadero** *nm* cook.

guisante *nm* pea; **— de olor** sweet pea.

guisar [1a] *vt* (a) to prepare; to arrange. (b) (*Cook*) to cook; to stew.

güisingue *nm* (*Col*) whip.

güisinguear [1a] *vt* (*Col*) to whip.

guiso *nm* (a) cooked dish; (*SAm*) stew. (b) seasoning.

guisote *nm* (*pej*) hash, poor-quality stew; concoction; grub (*sl*).

guita *nf* (a) twine; packthread. (b) (*sl*) dough (*sl*); **aflojar la —, soltar la —** to stump up (*fam*), fork out (*fam*).

guitarra *nf* guitar; **ser como — en un entierro** to be quite out of place, strike the wrong note; **chafar la — a uno** to queer someone's pitch.

guitarrear [1a] *vi* to play the guitar.

guitarrista *nmf* guitarist.

gula *nf* greed, gluttony.

guloso *adj* greedy, gluttonous.

gulusmear [1a] *vi* to nibble titbits; to sniff the cooking.

gurguciar [1b] *vt* (*CAm*) to sniff at, sniff out.

gurí *nm*, *pl* **gurís, guríes**, *or* **gurises** (*RPl*) Indian *or* half-breed child; boy, lad.

gurisa *nf* (*RPl*) Indian *or* half-breed child; girl, lass; young wife.

gurrí *nm* (*SAm*) wild duck.

gurrumina *nf* (a) (*Col, Ec, Guat, Mex*) bother, vexation; (*Col*) sadness.

(b) (*Guat, Mex*) trifle, mere nothing.

(c) (*Hond*) shrewd person.

gurrumino 1 *adj* **(a)** weak, sickly; small, puny.
   (b) *husband* henpecked, hag-ridden; uxorious.
   (c) (*Bol*) cowardly.
   (d) (*Hond*) clever, sharp.
   2 *nm* **(a)** henpecked husband; uxorious man.
   (b) (*Mex, Salv*) child.

gur(r)upié *nm* **(a)** (*SAm: gall*) croupier. **(b)** (*Cu, Ec*) false bidder (*at auction*). **(c)** (*Cu*) buddy (*esp US*), pal (*fam*). **(d)** (*PR, Ven*) servant, family retainer.

gus *nm* (*Col*) turkey buzzard.

gusanera *nf* **(a)** nest of maggots; breeding ground for maggots. **(b)** (*fig*) bunch, lot, crowd; **una — de chiquillos** a bunch of kids.

gusaniento *adj* maggoty, worm-eaten, grub-infested.

gusanillo *nm* small maggot, small worm; **me anda el —** I feel peckish; **matar el —** to have a snack, take the edge off one's appetite; to have a nip of liquor first thing in the morning.

gusano *nm* **(a)** maggot, grub, worm; (*of butterfly, moth*) caterpillar; **— de luz** glow-worm; **— de seda** silkworm; **— de tierra** earthworm.
   (b) (*fig*) worm, contemptible person; meek creature.
   (c) (*Arg, Ec, Per*) liquor; **matar el —** to have a drink.
   (d) (*Cu: Pol*) anti-Castro Cuban.

gusanoso *adj* = **gusaniento**.

gusgo *adj* (*Mex*) sweet-toothed.

gustación *nf* tasting, trying.

gustado *adj* (*SAm*) esteemed, well-liked, popular.

gustar [1a] **1** *vt* to taste, try, sample.
   2 *vi* **(a)** to please, be pleasing; **es una película que siempre gusta** it's a film which always pleases (*or* gives pleasure); **la comedia no gustó** the play was not a success, the play was not much liked; **mi número ya no gusta** my act isn't popular any more.
   (b) (*with personal indirect object*) **me gusta el té** I like tea; **¿te gusta Méjico?** do you like Mexico?; **no le gusta que le llamen Pepe** he doesn't like to be called Joe; **no me gusta mucho** I don't like it much, I'm not very struck (on it); **me gusta como anda** I like the way she walks.
   (c) (*formal phrases*) **¿gusta Vd?** would you like some?, may I offer you some?; **si Vd gusta** if you please, if you don't mind; **como Vd guste** as you wish.
   (d) **— de algo** to like something, enjoy something; **— de** + *infin* to like to + *infin*, be fond of + *ger*, enjoy + *ger*.

gustazo *nm* great pleasure; (*pej*) unhealthy pleasure, nasty pleasure.

gustillo *nm* suggestion, touch, tang.

gusto *nm* **(a)** taste (*sense*); **agregue azúcar a —** add sugar to taste.
   (b) (*of food*) taste, flavour; **tiene un — amargo** it has a bitter taste, it tastes bitter.
   (c) (*Art etc*) taste; style, fashion; **buen — good** taste; **mal —** bad taste; **de buen —** in good taste; **es de un mal — extraordinario** it is in extraordinarily bad taste; **para mi —** to my taste; **al — de hoy, según el — de hoy** in the taste of today; **ser persona de —** to be a person of taste; **sobre —s no hay disputa, de —s no hay nada escrito** there's no accounting for tastes; **tiene — para vestir** she dresses elegantly, she has taste in dresses.
   (d) pleasure; **con mucho —** with pleasure; gladly, willingly; **con sumo —** with the very greatest pleasure; **comer con —** to eat heartily; **estar a —** to be at ease, feel comfortable; **aquí me encuentro a —** I like it here, I feel at home here; **acomodarse a su —** to make oneself comfortable, make oneself at home; **sentirse mal a —** to feel ill at ease; **tengo los pies a — y calientes** my feet are nice and warm; **dar — a** to please, give pleasure to; **tener el — de** + *ger* to have the pleasure of + *ger*; **tener — en** + *infin* to be glad to + *infin*.
   (e) (*introductions*) **¡mucho —!, ¡tanto —!** how do you do?; pleased to meet you; **el — es mío** how do you do?; the pleasure is mine; **tengo mucho — en presentar al Sr X** allow me to introduce Mr X; **tengo mucho — en conocerle** I'm very pleased to meet you.
   (f) liking (*por* for); **al — de** to the liking of; **ser del — de uno** to be to someone's liking; **tener — por** to have a liking for, have an eye for; **tomar — a** to take a liking to.
   (g) whim, fancy; **a —** at will, according to one's fancy.
   (h) (*RPl: Comm*) style, design, colour; range, assortment.

gustoso *adj* **(a)** tasty, savoury, nice.
   (b) pleasant.
   (c) willing, glad; **lo hizo —** he did it gladly, he did it with pleasure; **le ofrezco — una habitación de matrimonio** I am glad to be able to offer you a double room.

gutapercha *nf* gutta-percha.

gutifarra *nf* (*SAm*) = **butifarra**.

gutural *adj* guttural (*also Ling*); throaty.

H

ha *see* **haber.**
ha *interj* ha!
haba *nf* (broad) bean; (*of coffee etc*) bean; **— de las Indias** sweet pea; **son —s contadas** we know all about that; it's a sure thing, it's a certainty; **en todas partes cuecen —s** it's the same the whole world over.
Habana: La — Havana.
habanera *nf* (*Mus*) habanera.
habanero 1 *adj* of Havana. **2** *nm*, **habanera** *nf* native (*or* inhabitant) of Havana; **los —s** the people of Havana.
habano 1 *adj and n* = **habanero. 2** *nm* Havana cigar.
hábeas corpus *nm* habeas corpus.
haber [2k] **1** *vt* (**a**) (*arch*) to have, possess.
　(**b**) (*lit*) to get; to catch, lay hands on; **lee cuantos libros puede —** he reads all the books he can lay hands on.
　(**c**) (*Rel: formulae*) **bien haya . . .** blessed be . . .; **X, que Dios haya** X, God rest his soul.
　(**d**) (*Law: formula*) **todos los inventos habidos y por haber** all inventions present and future, the present inventions and any others that may be made.
　(**e**) (*lit, journalese*) **en el encuentro habido ayer** in the fight which occurred yesterday; **la baja de temperatura habida ayer** the fall in temperature recorded yesterday; **la lista de los caídos habidos** the list of casualties suffered.
　2 *v aux* (**a**) (*used in forming compound tenses*) to have; **he comido** I have eaten; **lo hubiéramos hecho** we would have done it; **antes de —lo visto** before seeing him, before having seen him; **de —lo sabido** if I had known it.
　(**b**) **— de +** *infin*: **he de hacerlo** I have to do it, I am to do it, I must do it; **¿qué he de hacer?** what am I to do?; **ha de llegar hoy** he is due to arrive today; **ha de haberse perdido** it must have got lost; **han de ser las 9** it must be about 9 o'clock.
　3 *v impersonal* (**a**) (*general sense*) **hay** there is, there are; **hay calefacción** there is heating; **hay tanto que hacer** there is so much to be done; **no hay plátanos** there are no bananas, we have no bananas; **no lo hay** there isn't any; **no hubo discusión** there was no discussion; **"mejores no hay"** (*Comm: slogan*) "none better!"; **¿habrá tiempo?** will there be time?; **¿hay puros?** (*in shop*) have you any cigars?; **tomará lo que haya** he'll take whatever there is, he'll take whatever is going; **lo que hay es que . . .** what's happening is that . . ., it's like this . . .; **hay sol** the sun is shining, it is sunny; **¿qué hay?** what's up?, what's the matter?, what goes on?; **¡no hay de qué!** don't mention it!, not at all!; **¿cuánto hay de aquí a Cuzco?** how far is it from here to Cuzco?
　(**b**) **hay que +** *infin* it is necessary to + *infin*, one must + *infin*; **hay que trabajar** one has to work, everything must work; **hay que trabajar más** (*to individual*) you must work harder; **hay que hacerlo** it has to be done; **¡había que verlo!** you should have seen it!; **hay que ser fuertes** we must be strong; **no hay que tomarlo a mal** there's no cause to take it badly, you mustn't get upset about it; **y no hay más que conformarse** there's nothing one can do but fall into line.
　(**c**) (*expressions of time*) **3 años ha** 3 years ago; **poco tiempo ha** a short time ago.
　4 haberse *vr* (**a**) (*arch*) to behave, comport oneself; **se ha habido con honradez** he has behaved honourably.
　(**b**) **—las con uno** to be up against someone, have to do with someone, have to contend with someone; **tenemos que habérnoslas con un enemigo**

despiadado we are up against a ruthless enemy; **¡allá te las hayas!** that's your affair!
　5 *nm* income, salary; (*Comm*) assets; (*of balance sheet*) credit side; **—es** assets, property, goods; **asentar algo al — de uno, pasar algo al — de uno** to credit something to someone; **¿cuánto tenemos en el —?** how much have we on the credit side? (*also fig*).
habichuela *nf* kidney bean; **ganarse las —s** to earn one's living.
hábil *adj* (**a**) clever; skilful; able, capable, proficient; good, expert (*en* at); (*pej*) cunning, smart.
　(**b**) **— para** fit for.
　(**c**) **día —** working day.
　(**d**) (*Law*) competent.
habilidad *nf* (**a**) cleverness; skill; ability, proficiency; expertness, expertise; (*pej*) cunning, smartness; **hombre de gran — política** a man of great political skill; **tener — manual** to be clever with one's hands.
　(**b**) fitness (*para* for).
　(**c**) (*Law*) competence.
habilidoso *adj* (*esp pej*) clever, smart.
habilitación *nf* (**a**) qualification, entitlement.
　(**b**) equipment, fitting out.
　(**c**) financing; (*Arg, Par: Agr*) credit in kind; (*Guat, Mex*) loan.
　(**d**) (*Arg, Par*) offer of a partnership.
　(**e**) paymaster's office.
habilitado *nm* paymaster.
habilitar [1a] *vt* (**a**) to qualify, entitle (*para que haga* to do); to enable (*para que haga* to do); to empower, authorize (*para que haga* to do).
　(**b**) to equip, fit out, set up.
　(**c**) to finance; **— a uno** (*Arg, Par: Agr*) to make someone a loan in kind (with the next crop as security), give someone credit facilities; (*Guat, Mex*) to advance money to.
　(**d**) (*Arg, Par: Comm*) to take into partnership.
　(**e**) (*CR: Agr*) to cover, serve.
　(**f**) (*Cu*) to annoy, provoke.
hábilmente *adv* cleverly; skilfully; ably, proficiently, expertly; (*pej*) cunningly, smartly.
habiloso *adj* (*Chi*) = **habilidoso.**
habitabilidad *nf* habitability; (*of house*) quality, quality of the living accommodation.
habitable *adj* inhabitable, that can be lived in.
habitación *nf* (**a**) habitation; dwelling, abode; lodging(s), apartment; (*Bio*) habitat.
　(**b**) (*personal, hotel etc*) room; **—es (particulares)** rooms, suite; **— de dos camas, — doble, — de matrimonio** double room; **— individual** single room; **— lacustre** lake dwelling.
habitado *adj* inhabited; lived-in; *satellite etc* manned, carrying a crew.
habitante 1 *nmf* inhabitant; resident; (*of house*) occupant, tenant; **una ciudad de 10.000 —s** a city of 10,000 inhabitants (*or* people), a city with a population of 10,000.
　2 *nm* (*hum*) louse; **tener —s** to be lousy.
habitar [1a] **1** *vt* to inhabit, live in, dwell in; *house etc* to occupy, be the occupant of. **2** *vi* to live.
habitat *nm*, *pl* **habitats** habitat.
hábito *nm* (**a**) habit, custom; **una droga que conduce al — morboso** a habit-forming drug; **tener el — de +** *infin* to be in the habit of + *ger*.
　(**b**) (*Eccl*) habit; **— monástico** monastic habit; **ahorcar** (*or* **colgar**) **los —s** to leave the priesthood; **tomar el — (man)** to take holy orders, become a monk, (*woman*) to take the veil, become a nun.
habituado *nm*, **habituada** *nf* habitué(e).
habitual 1 *adj* habitual, customary, usual; *criminal* hardened; *liar* incorrigible; *sin* besetting; **su restaurante —** one's usual restaurant; **como**

lector — **de esa revista** as a regular reader of your journal.

2 nmf (of bar etc) habitué(e); (of shop) regular customer.

habituar [1e] **1** vt to accustom (a to). **2 habituarse** vr: — **a** to become accustomed to, get used to.

habla nf **(a)** (faculty in general) speech; **dejar a uno sin** — to leave someone speechless, dumbfound someone; **estar sin** — to be speechless; **perder el** — to become speechless.

(b) (national etc) language; (regional) dialect, speech; (of class, profession etc) talk, speech; (Lit) language, style; **de** — **francesa** French-speaking.

(c) talk; **¡García al** —! (Tel) García speaking!; **estar al** — to be in contact, be in touch; (Naut) to be within hail; (Tel) to be on the line, be speaking (con to); **negar** (or **quitar**) **el** — **a uno** to stop speaking to someone, not be on speaking terms with someone; **ponerse al** — **con uno** to get into touch with someone.

hablachento adj (Ven) talkative.

hablada nf **(a)** (Chi) speech.

(b) (Arg, Mex) boast.

(c) (Ec) scolding, telling-off.

(d) (Chi, Guat, Mex) hint, innuendo; piece of gossip; **echar** —s to drop hints, make innuendoes.

habladera nf **(a)** (SAm) talking, noise of talking.

(b) (Ant, CAm, Chi, Mex) = **habladuría**.

habladero nm (Chi, SD) piece of gossip.

hablado (a) adj and ptp spoken; **la palabra hablada** the spoken word.

(b) adj: **bien** — nicely-spoken, well-spoken; **mal** — coarse, rude; foul-mouthed.

hablador 1 adj **(a)** talkative; chatty; voluble.

(b) gossipy, given to gossip.

(c) (Mex) boastful, bullying.

(d) (Mex, SD) lying; loud-mouthed.

2 nm, **habladora** nf **(a)** talkative person, great talker, chatterbox.

(b) gossip.

habladuría nf rumour; nasty remark, sarcastic remark; idle chatter, piece of gossip; —s gossip, scandal.

hablanchín adj, **hablantín** adj talkative, garrulous, chatty.

hablante 1 adj speaking. **2** nmf speaker.

hablantina nf (Col, Ven) gibberish, meaningless torrent; empty talk.

hablantino(so) adj (Col) = **hablador (a)** and **(b)**.

hablar [1a] **1** vt language to speak, talk; nonsense etc to talk; **habla bien el portugués** he speaks good Portuguese, he speaks Portuguese well; **hablarlo todo** to talk too much, give the game away; **y no hay más que** — so there's no more to be said about it.

2 vi to speak, talk (a, con to; de about, of); **que hable él** let him speak, let him have his say; **¡hable!, ¡puede** —! (Tel) you're through!; **¿quién habla?** (Tel) who is it?, who's calling?; **¡ni** —! nonsense!; no fear!, not likely!; **de eso ni** — that's out of the question, that's not on; — **alto** to speak loudly, (fig) to speak out (frankly); — **bajo** to talk quietly, speak in a low voice; — **claro** (fig) to speak plainly, speak bluntly; **¡para luego hablen de coches!** as if other cars came into it!; — **por sólo** — to talk just for talking's sake; **habla por sí mismo** it speaks for itself; **los datos hablan por sí solos** the facts speak for themselves; **el retrato está hablando** the portrait is a speaking likeness; **dar que** — **a la gente** to make people talk, cause people to gossip; **hacer** — **a uno** (fig) to make someone talk; **el vino hace** — wine loosens people's tongues.

3 hablarse vr: **"se habla inglés"** (notice) "English spoken here"; **en el Brasil se habla portugués** Portuguese is spoken in Brazil; **se habla de que van a comprarlo** there is talk of their buying it; **no se hablan** they are not on speaking terms, they don't speak.

hablilla nf rumour, story; (piece of) gossip, tittle-tattle.

habloteo nm incomprehensible talk.

Habsburgo Hapsburg.

hacedero adj practicable, feasible.

hacedor nm, **hacedora** nf maker; **el (Supremo) H—** the Maker; **el** — **de reyes** the kingmaker.

hacendado 1 adj landed, property-owning. **2** nm landowner, property owner; gentleman farmer; (SAm) rancher.

hacendario nm (CAm, Mex) treasury.

hacendista nm economist, financial expert.

hacendoso adj industrious, hard-working; busy, bustling.

hacer [2s] **1** vt **(a)** to make, create; (Tech) to make, manufacture; to build, construct; dress etc to make; work of art to make; to fashion; (Lit, Mus) to compose; money to make, earn; smoke etc to make, give off, emit, produce; war to fight, wage; — **algo** to have something made.

(b) to make, prepare; bed to make; meal to make, prepare, get, cook; suitcase to pack; tie to tie; balance (Comm) to strike; bet to lay; objection to make, raise; question to put, ask; order to give; speech to make, deliver; visit to pay; — **la barba a uno** to shave someone (see also **barba**[1]); — **el pelo a una** to do someone's hair; — **un recado** to run a message, go on an errand.

(c) to cause, make; shadow to cast; **el árbol hace sombra** the tree gives shade, the tree casts a shadow.

(d) eg — **cine** to make films, be engaged in film work, be working for the cinema; **este año hace turismo en África** this year he's gone touring (or as a tourist) in Africa.

(e) to do; to execute, perform, put into practice; play to do, perform; wonders etc to do, work, perform; **no sé qué** — I don't know what to do; **haga lo que quiera** do as you please; **¿qué haces ahí?** what are you doing?, what are you up to?; **¿qué le vamos a** —? what shall we do with him?, what can we do about him?; — **por** — to do something for the sake of doing it, do something even though it is not necessary; **la ha hecho buena** (iro) a fine mess he's made of it; see **bien, mal** etc.

(f) (substitute verb in repetitions) to do; **él protestó y yo hice lo mismo** he protested and I did the same; **no viene como lo solía** — he doesn't come as he used to (do).

(g) — **algo pedazos** (etc): see **pedazo** etc.

(h) (Theat) — **el malo** to play the (part of the) villain, act the villain.

(i) to imagine, think, assume; **yo le hacía más viejo** I thought he was older; **te hacíamos en el Perú** we thought you were in Peru, we assumed you were in Peru.

(j) **me hizo con dinero** he provided me with money.

(k) to accustom, inure; — **el cuerpo al frío** to inure the body to cold, get the body used to cold.

(l) (with verb construction) to make, force, oblige, compel; **les hice venir** I made them come; **nos hizo que fuésemos** he made us go; **yo haré que vengan** I'll see to it that they come; **hágale entrar** show him in, have him come in; **me lo hizo saber** he told me it, he informed me of it; — **construir una casa** to have a house built, get a house built; **hago lavar la ropa a mi vecina** I have a neighbour (to) wash my clothes.

(m) (numerals) to make (up), amount to; **6 y 3 hacen 9** 6 and 3 make 9; **éste hace 100** this one makes 100.

(n) (with adj) to make, turn, render, send; **el vino lo hizo borracho** the wine made him drunk; **la tinta lo hizo azul** the ink made (or turned) it blue; **esto lo hará más difícil** this will make (or render) it more difficult.

2 vi **(a)** to act, behave; to pretend; — **como que** . . ., — **como si** . . . to act as if . . .; — **uno como que no quiere** to be reluctant, seem not to want to; — **de** to act as, (Theat) act, play the part of; — **el muerto** to pretend to be dead (see also **muerto**); — **el tonto** to act the fool, play the fool.

(b) **dar que** — to cause trouble; to make work; **daban que** — **a la policía** they gave the police trouble, they caused trouble to the police.

(c) — **para** + infin, — **por** + infin to try to + infin, make an effort to + infin.

(d) to be important, matter; **no le hace** it doesn't matter, never mind; see **caso**.

(e) to be suitable, be fitting; **hace a todo** he's good for anything; **¿hace?** will it do?, is it all right?; **la llave hace a todas las puertas** the key fits (or does for) all the doors.

3 v impersonal **(a)** (Meteorol) to be; see **calor, frío, tiempo** etc.

(b) (SAm) **hace sed** I'm thirsty; **hace sueño** I'm sleepy.

(c) (of time) ago; **hace 3 años** 3 years ago; **hace 2 años que se fue** he left 2 years ago, it's 2 years since he left; **desde hace 4 años** for (the last) 4 years; **está perdido desde hace 15 días** it's been lost for a fortnight; **hace poco** a short while back, a short time ago; **no hace mucho** not long ago; see **tiempo** etc.

4 hacerse vr **(a)** to be made, be done etc; **se**

hará de ladrillos it will be built of brick; todavía no se ha hecho it still has not been done; ¡eso no se hace! that's not done!

(b) (*mutual*) — cortesías to exchange courtesies.

(c) (*personal*) se hizo cortar el pelo she had her hair cut; me hago confeccionar un traje I'm having a suit made; — un retrato, — retratar to have one's portrait painted; — afeitar to have a shave, have oneself shaved.

(d) (*with noun complement*) to become; se hicieron amigos they became friends; — enfermera to become a nurse, take up nursing, go into nursing.

(e) (*with noun complement: idiom*) to pretend; — el sordo to pretend not to hear, turn a deaf ear; — el sueco (*fam*) to pretend not to hear (*or* understand); to act dumb, not let on (*fam*); — el tonto to act the fool, play the fool.

(f) (*with adj complement*) to become, grow; to turn (into), come to be; esto se hace pesado this is becoming tedious; si las cosas se hacen difíciles if things get difficult, if things turn awkward; — grande to grow tall, get tall; — viejo to grow old, get old; — cristiano to turn Christian, become a Christian, be converted to Christianity; se me hace imposible trabajar it's becoming impossible for me to work, I'm finding it impossible to work.

(g) — a + *infin* to get used to + *ger*, become accustomed to + *ger*.

(h) se me hace que . . . (*esp SAm*) I think that . . ., it seems to me that . . ., I get the impression that . . .

(i) — con algo to get hold of something; to take something, appropriate something; logró — con una copia he managed to get hold of a copy.

(j) — a un lado to stand aside (*also fig*), move over; — atrás to move back, fall back; *for many phrases, see the adj or noun.*

hacia *prep* (a) (*of place*) towards, in the direction of; about, near; — abajo down, downwards; — arriba up, upwards; ir — las montañas to go towards the mountains; eso está más — el este that's further over to the east, that is more in an easterly direction; vamos — allá let's go in that direction, let's go over that way.

(b) (*of time*) about; — mediodía about noon, towards noon.

(c) (*of attitude*) towards; su hostilidad — la empresa his hostility towards the undertaking.

hacienda *nf* (a) property; country estate, large farm; (*SAm*) ranch; (*SAm*) plantation; — de azúcar (PR) sugar mill.

(b) (*RPl*) cattle, livestock.

(c) — pública public finance; (Ministerio de) H— Treasury, Exchequer, Ministry of Finance.

(d) —s household chores.

hacina *nf* pile, heap; (*Agr*) stack, rick.

hacinamiento *nm* heaping (up); (*Agr*) stacking; (*fig*) crowding, overcrowding; accumulation.

hacinar [1a] *vt* to pile (up), heap (up); (*Agr*) to stack, put into a stack (*or* rick); (*fig*) to crowd, overcrowd; to accumulate, amass; to hoard.

hacha[1] *nf* (a) axe; chopper; hatchet; — de armas battle-axe.

(b) (*fig*) genius, wizard; ¡eres un —! you're a wizard!; es un — para el bridge he's a genius at bridge, he's a brilliant bridge player.

(c) (*phrases*) — y tiza (Arg) tough, virile, (*pej*) brawling; de — (*adv*: Chi) unexpectedly, without warning; ser — para la ropa (Mex) to be hard on one's clothes; estar — (Mex) to be ready.

hacha[2] *nf* torch, firebrand; large candle; como — de muerto light dim, weak.

hachador *nm* (Arg, Cu, Guat, Ven) woodman, lumberjack.

hachar [1a] *vt* (*SAm*) = hachear.

hachazo *nm* (a) axe blow, stroke with an axe; hack, cut.

(b) (*SAm*) gash, open wound.

(c) (*Col*) bolt, dash (*of startled horse*).

hache *nf* name of the letter h; llámele Vd — call it what you will; volverse —s y erres (Col), volverse —s y cúes (Chi) to come to nothing, fall through.

hachear [1a] **1** *vt* to hew, cut (down *etc*). **2** *vi* to wield an axe.

hachero[1] *nm* woodman, lumberjack; (*Mil*) sapper.

hachero[2] *nm* torch stand.

hacheta *nf* adze; small axe, hatchet.

hachich *nm* hashish.

hacho *nm* beacon.

hachón *nm* (large) torch, firebrand.

hachuela *nf* = hacheta.

hada *nf* fairy; — madrina fairy godmother; cuento de —s fairy tale.

hadado *adj* fated; bien — lucky; mal — ill-fated, ill-starred.

hado *nm* fate, destiny.

haga, hago *etc*: see hacer.

hagiografía *nf* hagiography.

haiga *nm* (*fam*) big car, posh car (*fam*).

Haití *m* Haiti.

haitiano 1 *adj* Haitian. **2** *nm*, **haitiana** *nf* Haitian.

hala *interj* (a) hi!, hoy!

(b) come on!, let's go!

(c) get on with it!, hurry up!

(d) (*Naut*) heave!; see also jalar.

halaco *nm* (*CAm*) piece of junk, useless object.

halagar [1h] *vt* (a) to show affection to, make up to.

(b) to please, gratify; to allure, attract; es una perspectiva que me halaga it's a possibility which pleases me.

(c) to flatter; to cajole.

halago *nm* (a) (*also* —s) pleasure, delight; gratification; allurement, attraction; blandishment; los —s de la vida rural the attractions of country life, the blandishments of country life.

(b) (*also* —s) flattery; cajolery.

halagüeño *adj* pleasing, gratifying, alluring, attractive; *opinion, remark* flattering (*para* to); *outlook* promising, rosy, hopeful.

halar [1a] *vt and vi* = jalar.

halcón *nm* falcon; — común peregrine; — abejero honey buzzard; los —es y las palomas (*Pol etc*) the hawks and the doves.

halconería *nf* falconry, hawking.

halconero *nm* falconer.

halda *nf* (a) skirt; de —s o de mangas at all costs, by hook or by crook. (b) sackcloth, coarse wrapping material.

haleche *nm* anchovy.

halibut [ali'βu] *nm*, *pl* **halibuts** [ali'βu] (*angl*) halibut.

hálito *nm* breath; vapour, exhalation; (*poet*) gentle breeze.

halitosis *nf* halitosis.

halo *nm* halo.

halógeno *nm* halogen.

halón *nm* (*SAm*) = jalón (c).

hall [xol] *nm*, *pl* **halls** [xol] (*angl*) hall; (*Theat*) foyer; (*of hotel*) lounge, foyer.

hallador *nm*, **halladora** *nf* finder.

hallar [1a] **1** *vt* to find; to discover; to locate; to find out; *approval, opposition etc* to meet with, run up against.

2 hallarse *vr* to be; to find oneself; se hallaba fuera he was away at the time; ¿dónde se halla la catedral? where is the cathedral?; se halla sin dinero he has no money, he finds himself out of money; — enfermo to be ill; — mejor to be better; aquí me hallo a gusto I'm all right here, I'm comfortable here; no se halla bien con el nuevo jefe he doesn't get on with the new boss; — con un obstáculo to encounter an obstacle, be up against an obstacle; se halla en todo he's mixed up in everything.

hallazgo *nm* (a) (*act*) finding, discovery.

(b) (*object*) find, thing found; un — interesantísimo a most interesting find.

(c) finder's reward; "500 pesos de —" (*notice*) "500 pesos reward".

hamaca *nf* hammock; (Arg) swing; (Arg, Par) reclining chair; — plegable deckchair.

hamacar [1g], **hamaquear** [1a] (*SAm*) **1** *vt* (a) to rock, swing.

(b) (Mex) — a uno (*fig*) to keep someone waiting for a decision.

(c) (PR, Ven) to beat, ill-treat.

2 hamacarse, hamaquearse *vr* to rock (oneself), swing.

hambre *nf* (a) hunger; famine; starvation; — canina ravenous hunger; estar con —, padecer —, pasar — to be hungry, go hungry, starve; entretener el — to stave off hunger; matar el — to satisfy one's hunger; morir de — to die of (*or* from) starvation, starve to death; hacer morir de — to starve to death; tener — to be hungry; tener mucha — to be very hungry; vengo con mucha — I'm terribly hungry, I've got a vast appetite.

(b) (*fig*) hunger, keen desire, longing (*de* for); tener — de to hunger for, be hungry for.

hambreado *adj* (*SAm*) = hambriento.

hambrear [1a] **1** *vt* to starve. **2** *vi* to starve, be hungry, be famished.

hambriento 1 adj (a) starving, hungry, famished.
(b) (fig) — de starved of, hungry for, longing for.
2 nm, **hambrienta** nf starving person; **los —s** the hungry, the starving.
hambruna nf (Arg, Col), **hambrusia** nf (Mex, PR) ravenous hunger; **tener —** to be ravenously hungry.
Hamburgo Hamburg.
hamburguesa nf hamburger.
hamo nm fish hook.
hampa nf underworld, low life, criminal classes; (Hist) rogue's life, vagrancy; **gente del —** people of the underworld, criminals, riffraff.
hampante nm criminal, underworld character.
hampesco adj underworld (attr), criminal.
hampón nm tough (fam), rowdy, thug.
hámster nm, pl **hámsters** (angl) hamster.
han see **haber**.
handicap [andi'kap] nm, pl **handicaps** [andi'kap] (angl) handicap.
handicapar [1a] vt (angl) to handicap.
hangar nm (Aer) hangar.
Hanovre m Hanover.
haragán 1 adj idle, lazy, good-for-nothing. **2** nm, **haragana** nf idler, layabout, good-for-nothing.
haraganear [1a] vi to idle, waste one's time; to lounge about, loaf around.
haraganería nf idleness, laziness.
harapiento adj ragged, tattered, in rags.
harapo nm rag, tatter; **estar hecho un —** to go about in rags; **poner a uno como un —** to shower insults on someone, make someone feel a heel.
haraposo adj = **harapiento**.
haraquiri nm hara-kiri.
harén nm harem.
harina nf (a) flour; meal; powder; **— de avena** oatmeal; **— de huesos** bone meal; **— lacteada** malted milk; **— leudante** self-raising flour; **— de maíz** cornflour, corn meal; **— de trigo** wheat flour; **eso es — de otro costal** that's another story, that's a horse of a different colour; **estoy hecho —** I'm exhausted.
(b) (Col) small piece; **una — de pan** a bit of bread.
(c) (Ant: hum) money, dough (sl).
harinear [1a] vi (SD, Ven) to drizzle.
harineo nm (SD, Ven) drizzle.
harinero 1 adj flour (attr). **2** nm (a) flour merchant. (b) flour bin.
harinoso adj floury.
harnear [1a] vt (Col, Chi, Mex) to sieve, sift.
harnero nm sieve.
harpagón adj (Col) very thin.
harpillera nf sacking, sackcloth.
hartar [1a] **1** vt (a) to satiate, surfeit, glut, more than satisfy (con, de with).
(b) (fig) to weary, tire.
(c) **— a uno de algo** (fig) to overwhelm someone with something; **— a uno de palos** to rain blows on someone.
(d) (Guat) to malign, slander; (Ven) to insult.
2 hartarse vr (a) to eat one's fill (con of), gorge (con on), be satiated; **comer hasta —** to eat to repletion; **— de uvas** to stuff oneself with grapes, eat too many grapes.
(b) (fig) to weary, get weary (de of); to get fed up (de with); **— de reír** to laugh fit to burst; **no se hartaron de reír** they couldn't stop laughing.
hartazgo nm surfeit, satiety; repletion; glut; **darse un —** to eat to repletion, eat one's fill, overeat; **darse un — de** to eat one's fill of; (fig) to overdo, have too much of.
harto 1 adj (a) full (de of), satiated; glutted (de with).
(b) (fig) **estar —** de to be fed up with, be tired of; **¡estamos —s ya!** we're fed up!, enough is enough!; **¡estoy — de decírtelo!** I'm fed up with telling you so!
2 adv (lit) enough; very, quite; **una tarea —difícil** a very difficult task, a difficult enough task.
hartón 1 adj (a) (CAm, Mex, SD) greedy, gluttonous.
(b) (Mex) stupid; annoying. **2** nm (Col, Mex, PR) large banana.
hartura nf (a) surfeit; glut; abundance, plenty; **con —** in abundance, in plenty. (b) full satisfaction (of a desire).
has see **haber**.
hasta 1 adv even; **y — la pegó** and he even hit her; **— en Valencia hiela a veces** even in Valencia it freezes sometimes.
2 prep (a) (of place) as far as; up to, down to; **lo llevó — la iglesia** he carried it as far as the

church; **los árboles crecen — los 4.000 metros** the trees grow up to 4,000 metres.
(b) (of time) till, until; as late as; up to; se **quedará — el martes** she will stay till Tuesday; **siguió en pie — el siglo pasado** it stood until (or up to, as late as) the last century; **no me levanto — las 9** I don't get up until (or before) 9 o'clock; **no iré — después de la reunión** I shan't go till after the meeting; see **luego, vista** etc.
3 conj — **que** till, until; — **que me lo des** until you give it to me.
hastial[1] nm (Archit) gable end.
hastial[2] nm lout, roughneck (sl).
hastiar [1c] **1** vt to weary, bore; to sicken, disgust.
2 hastiarse vr: **— de** to tire of, get fed up with.
hastío nm weariness; boredom; disgust, loathing.
hatajo nm lot, collection.
hatillo nm = **hato**.
hato nm (a) clothes, set of clothing; personal effects, possessions; **— y garabato** (Cu, Ec) all that one has; **liar el —** to pack up, get ready to go; **menear el —a uno** to beat someone up; **revolver el —** to stir up trouble.
(b) provisions.
(c) shepherd's hut; stopping place (of migratory flocks etc).
(d) (Agr) flock, herd; (of people) group, crowd, collection; (pej) bunch, band, gang; (of objects, remarks etc) lot, collection.
(e) (Cu, Ec, PR, Ven) cattle ranch.
Hawai: **Islas** fpl — Hawaii.
hawaiano 1 adj Hawaiian. **2** nm, **hawaiana** nf Hawaiian.
haxix [a'tʃitʃ] nm hashish.
hay, haya etc: see **haber**.
Haya: **La —** The Hague.
haya nf beech, beech tree.
hayaca nf (Ven) mince pie.
hayal nm, **hayedo** nm beechwood.
hayuco nm beechnut; beechnuts, beechmast (also **—s**).
haz[1] nm (a) bundle, bunch; (Agr: of corn) sheaf, (of straw) truss; **haces** (Hist) fasces.
(b) (of light, TV etc) beam; **— de luz** beam of light, pencil of light.
haz[2] nf (Anat: lit) face; (fig) face, surface; (of cloth) right side; **— de la tierra** face of the earth; **de dos haces** two-faced.
haz[3] see **hacer**.
hazaña nf feat, exploit, deed, achievement; **las —s del héroe** the hero's exploits, the hero's great deeds; **sería una —** it would be a great thing to do, it would be a great achievement.
hazañería nf fuss, exaggerated show; histrionics.
hazañero adj person dramatic, histrionic, given to making a great fuss; act histrionic, exaggerated.
hazañoso adj person heroic, gallant, dauntless; deed heroic, doughty.
hazmerreír nm laughing stock, joke.
he[1] see **haber**.
he[2] adv (lit): — **aquí** here is, here are; this is, these are; (more dramatically) behold; **¡heme aquí!, ¡héteme aquí!** here I am!; **¡helo aquí!** here it is!; **¡helos allí!** there they are!; **— aquí la razón de que..., — aquí por qué...** that is why...; **— aquí los resultados** these are the results, here you have the results.
hebdomadario 1 adj weekly. **2** nm (Typ) weekly.
hebilla nf buckle, clasp.
hebra nf (Sew) thread; piece of thread, length of thread; (Bot etc) fibre; strand; (of silkworm) thread; (of wood) grain; (of metal) vein, streak; (fig) thread (of the conversation); **—s** (poet) hair; **ni —** (Col) nothing; **tabaco de —** loose tobacco; **de una —** (Chi, Mex) all at once; in one go; **pegar la —** to start a conversation; to chatter, talk nineteen to the dozen; **romperse la —** (Mex: of friendship etc) to break up, come to an end.
hebraico adj Hebraic.
hebreo 1 adj Hebrew. **2** nm, **hebrea** nf Hebrew; (fam, pej) usurer, extortioner; pawnbroker. **3** nm (language) Hebrew.
Hébridas fpl Hebrides.
hebroso adj fibrous; meat stringy.
hecatombe nf hecatomb; (fig) slaughter, butchery; **¡aquello fue la —!** what a disaster that was!, you should have seen it!
hectárea nf hectare (= 2.471 acres).
héctico adj consumptive.
hectogramo nm hectogramme, hectogram (US).
hectolitro nm hectolitre, hectoliter (US).
hechicera nf sorceress, enchantress, witch.
hechicería nf (a) (in general) sorcery, witchcraft. (b) (una —) spell. (c) (fig) spell, enchantment, charm.

hechicero 1 *adj* magic(al); bewitching, enchanting. **2** *nm* wizard, sorcerer, enchanter; (*African etc*) witch doctor.

hechizar [1f] *vt* (a) to bewitch, cast a spell on. (b) (*fig*) to charm, enchant, fascinate; (*pej*) to bedevil.

hechizo 1 *adj* (a) artificial, false, fake.
(b) detachable, removable.
(c) (*Tech*) manufactured.
(d) (*CAm, Chi, Mex, Per*) home-made, locally produced, craft (*attr*); (*Mex, Per: pej*) home-made, rough and ready.
2 *nm* (a) (*in general*) magic, witchcraft; (*un —*) magic spell, charm.
(b) (*fig*) magic, spell, enchantment; glamour; fascination; **—s** (*of woman etc*) charms.

hecho 1 *ptp of* **hacer** done; **¡—!** agreed!, it's a deal!; **a lo — pecho** we must make the best of it now; **lo — está** — what's done cannot be undone; **bien —** well done; well made; *person* well-proportioned; **¡bien —!** well done!; **mal —** badly done; poorly made; *person* ill-proportioned; **él, — un . . .** he, like a . . .; **ella, hecha una furia, se lanzó . . .** she hurled herself furiously . . ., she threw herself in a fury . . .; **estar — a** to be used to, be inured to; *see* **basilisco, fiera** *etc.*
2 *adj* (a) complete, finished; mature; perfect; (*Sew*) ready-made, ready-to-wear; made-up; *phrase* stock; **— y derecho** complete, right and true, as it should be in every way; **un hombre — y derecho** a real man, every inch a man.
(b) (*Cook*) **muy —** overdone, well-cooked; **no muy —, poco —** underdone, undercooked.
3 *nm* (a) deed, act, action; **— de armas** feat of arms; **H—s de los Apóstoles** Acts of the Apostles; **—s y no palabras** deeds not words.
(b) fact; factor; matter; event; **esto es un —** this is a fact; **el — es que . . .** the fact is that . . ., the position is that . . .; **volvamos al —** let's get back to the matter in hand; **de —** in fact, as a matter of fact; (*Pol etc: adj and adv*) **de facto; de — y de derecho** de facto and de jure; **en — de verdad** as a matter of solid fact.

hechor *nm* (a) (*SAm*) stud donkey. (b) (*Chi*) = **malhechor.**

hechura *nf* (a) (*act*) making, creation; **no tiene —** it can't be done.
(b) (*object etc*) creation, product; **somos — de Dios** we are God's handiwork.
(c) form, shape; (*of person*) build; (*of suit*) cut; **a — de** like, after the manner of; **tener —s de algo** to show an aptitude for something; **no tener uno —** (*Arg, Mex*) to be a dead loss.
(d) (*Sew*) making-up, confection; **—s** cost of making up; **de — sastre** tailor-made.
(e) (*Tech*) craftsmanship, workmanship; **de exquisita —** of exquisite workmanship.
(f) (*fig*) creature, puppet; **él es una — del ministro** he is a creature of the minister.

heder [2g] *vi* (a) to stink, smell, reek (*a* of). (b) (*fig*) to annoy, be unbearable.

hediondez *nf* (a) stink, stench. (b) stinking thing.

hediondo *adj* (a) stinking, foul-smelling, smelly. (b) filthy; repulsive; obscene. (c) (*fig*) annoying, unbearable.

hedonismo *nm* hedonism.

hedonista *nmf* hedonist.

hedor *nm* stink, stench, smell (*a* of).

hegemonía *nf* hegemony.

hégira *nf* hegira.

helada *nf* frost; freeze, freeze-up; **— blanca** hoar-frost.

heladera *nf* (*RPl*) refrigerator; (*Mex*) ice-cream dish.

heladería *nf* (*esp SAm*) ice-cream stall, ice-cream parlour.

heladero *nm* (*Chi, RPl*) ice-cream man.

helado 1 *adj* (a) frozen; freezing, icy; icebound.
(b) (*fig*) chilly, cold, disdainful.
(c) **dejar — a uno** to dumbfound someone, shatter someone; **¡me deja Vd —!** you amaze me!
(d) (*Ven: Cook*) iced.
2 *nm* ice cream.

helador *adj* wind *etc* icy, freezing; **hace un frío —** it's icy cold, it's perishing cold.

heladora *nf* freezing unit, freezer (*in refrigerator*); (*esp Chi, RPl*) refrigerator, icebox.

helaje *nm* (*Col*) intense cold; chilly feeling.

helar [1k] **1** *vt* (a) (*Meteorol*) to freeze; to ice (up); *liquid* to congeal, harden; *drink etc* to ice, chill.
(b) (*fig*) to dumbfound, shatter, amaze; to discourage.
2 *vi* to freeze.

3 helarse *vr* (*Meteorol*) to freeze; to be frozen; (*Aer, Rail etc*) to ice (up), freeze up; (*liquid*) to congeal, harden, set.

helecho *nm* bracken, fern.

Helena *f* Helen.

helénico *adj* Hellenic, Greek.

heleno *nm*, **helena** *nf* Hellene, Greek.

hélice *nf* (a) spiral; (*Anat, Elec, Math*) helix. (b) (*Aer*) propeller, airscrew; (*Naut*) propeller, screw.

helicoidal *adj* spiral, helicoidal, helical.

helicóptero *nm* helicopter.

helio *nm* helium.

heliógrafo *nm* heliograph.

helioterapia *nf* heliotherapy, sun-ray treatment.

heliotropo *nm* heliotrope.

helipuerto *nm* heliport.

hematites *nf*, **hematita** *nf* bloodstone.

hembra *nf* (a) (*Bot, Zool*) female; (*human*) woman, (*pej*) female; **el armiño —** the female stoat, the she-stoat; **el pájaro —** the female bird, the hen bird; **una real —** a fine figure of a woman; **5 hijos, esto es 2 varones y 3 hembras** 5 children, that is 2 boys and 3 girls.
(b) (*Mech*) nut; **— de terraja** die.
(c) (*Sew*) eye.

hembraje *nm* (*SAm*) female flock, female herd; (*hum*) womenfolk.

hembrería *nf* (*Mex*), **hembrerío** *nm* (*Ant, Mex: pej*) group of women, crowd of women; excessive number of women.

hembrilla *nf* (*Mech*) nut; eyebolt.

hemiciclo *nm* semicircular theatre; (*Parl*) chamber; floor.

hemiplejía *nf* hemiplegia.

hemisferio *nm* hemisphere.

hemistiquio *nm* hemistich.

hemofilia *nf* haemophilia.

hemofílico 1 *adj* haemophilic. **2** *nm*, **hemofílica** *nf* haemophiliac, bleeder.

hemoglobina *nf* haemoglobin.

hemorragia *nf* (*Med*) haemorrhage; bleeding, loss of blood; (*fig*) drain, loss.

hemorroides *nfpl* haemorrhoids, piles.

henal *nm* hayloft.

henar *nm* meadow, hayfield.

henchir [3h] **1** *vt* to fill (up), stuff, cram (*de* with). **2 henchirse** *vr* (a) to swell; (*person*) to stuff oneself (with food).
(b) **— de orgullo** to swell with pride.

hendedura *nf* crack, fissure, crevice; cleft, split, slit; (*Geol*) rift, fissure.

hender [2g] *vt* to crack; to cleave, split, slit; *waves* to cleave, breast; to make one's way through; (*fig*) to split.

hendidura *nf* = **hendedura.**

hendija *nf* (*SAm*) crack, crevice.

hendir [3i] *vt* (*SAm*) = **hender.**

heneador *nm* hay-turner; haymaker.

henequén *nm* (*SAm*) agave, henequen.

henificación *nf* haymaking.

henil *nm* hayloft.

heniquén *nm* (*Cu, Mex*) = **henequén.**

heno *nm* hay.

hepático *adj* hepatic, liver (*attr*).

heráldica *nf* heraldry.

heráldico *adj* heraldic.

heraldo *nm* herald.

herbáceo *adj* herbaceous.

herbaje *nm* (a) herbage; grass, pasture. (b) (*Naut*) coarse woollen cloth.

herbaj(e)ar [1a] **1** *vt* to graze, put out to pasture. **2** *vi* to graze.

herbario 1 *adj* herbal. **2** *nm* (a) herbarium, plant collection. (b) (*person*) herbalist; botanist.

herbazal *nm* grassland, pasture.

herbicida *nm* weed-killer; **— selectivo** selective weed-killer.

herbívoro *adj* herbivorous.

herbolario 1 *adj* (*fig*) crazy, cracked. **2** *nm* herbalist.

herborizar [1f] *vi* to gather herbs, pick herbs; (*as collector*) to botanize, collect plants.

herboso *adj* grassy.

hercúleo *adj* Herculean.

Hércules *m* Hercules; **h—** (*in circus*) strong man; **es un —** (*fig*) he's awfully strong.

heredable *adj* inheritable, that can be inherited.

heredad *nf* landed property; country estate, farm.

heredar [1a] *vt* (a) *property* to inherit (*de* from); to be heir to. (b) *person* to name as one's heir. (c) (*SAm*) to leave, bequeath (*a* to).

heredera *nf* heiress.

heredero *nm* heir (*de* to); inheritor (*de* of); — **forzoso** heir apparent; — **único** universal heir; **príncipe** — crown prince; — **del trono** heir to the throne.

hereditario *adj* hereditary.

hereje 1 *adj* (a) (RPl: Rel) indifferent, agnostic; lacking in respect (*for traditions etc*).
(b) (*Ven*) excessive; **un trabajo** — a heavy task.
2 *nmf* heretic; ¡—! (*fam*) you brute!

herejía *nf* (a) (Rel) heresy. (b) (*fig*) dirty trick, low deed. (c) (Ec, Mex, RPl) silly remark, stupid thing.

herencia *nf* inheritance, estate, legacy; (*fig*) heritage; (*Bio*) heredity.

hereque *nm* (Ven: Med) skin disease; (*Bot*) *a disease of coffee.*

herético *adj* heretical.

herida *nf* (a) wound, injury. (b) (*fig*) wound, insult, outrage; **lamer las** —s to lick one's wounds.

herido 1 *adj* (a) injured; (*Mil etc*) wounded.
(b) (*fig*) wounded, offended.
2 *nm* (a) injured man; (*Mil*) wounded man; **los** —s (Mil) the wounded; **el número de los** —s **en el accidente** the number of people hurt in the accident, the number of casualties in the accident.
(b) (Chi, Mex) ditch, channel.

herir [3i] *vt* (a) to injure, hurt; (*Mil etc*) to wound; — **a uno en el brazo** to wound someone in the arm.
(b) to beat, strike, hit; (*Mus*) to pluck, strike, play; (*of sun*) to strike on; to beat down on; **un sonido hirió el oído** a sound reached (*or* struck) my ear; **es un color que hiere la vista** it's a colour which impinges (*or* strikes) on the eye.
(c) (*fig*) heart etc to touch, move, sway.
(d) (*fig*) to offend, hurt.

hermafrodita 1 *adj* hermaphrodite. 2 *nm* hermaphrodite.

hermana *nf* (a) sister; **media** — half-sister; **prima** — first cousin; — **gemela** twin sister; — **política** sister-in-law.
(b) (Eccl) sister; — **lega** lay sister.
(c) (1 of pair) twin; other half (*of pair*), corresponding part.

hermanable *adj* (a) fraternal. (b) compatible. (c) matching, that can be matched.

hermanar [1a] *vt* to match, put together; to join; to relate; to harmonize, bring into harmony; (Chi) to put into pairs.

hermanastra *nf* stepsister.

hermanastro *nm* stepbrother.

hermandad *nf* (a) (*state*) brotherhood; close relationship, intimacy.
(b) (*group etc*) brotherhood, fraternity; sisterhood; (Hist) brotherhood.

hermano 1 *adj* similar; matched, matching; **ship** sister.
2 *nm* (a) brother; **medio** — half-brother; **primo** — first cousin; — **carnal** full brother; — **gemelo** twin brother; — **de leche** foster brother; — **político** brother-in-law; **mis** —s my brothers, my brothers and sisters.
(b) (Eccl) brother; —s brothers, brethren.
(c) (1 of pair) twin; other half (*of pair*), corresponding part; — **gemelo** (Naut) sister ship.
(d) (CR) ghost.

herméticamente *adv* hermetically.

hermético *adj* hermetic; airtight, watertight; (*fig*) *theory* watertight; *mystery* impenetrable.

hermetismo *nm* (*fig*) tight secrecy, close secrecy.

hermosamente *adv* beautifully; handsomely.

hermosear [1a] *vt* to beautify, embellish, adorn.

hermoso *adj* (a) beautiful, lovely; fine, splendid; *man* handsome; **un día** — a fine day, a lovely day; ¡**qué escena más hermosa!** what a lovely scene!; **seis** —s **toros** six magnificent bulls.
(b) (SAm) large, robust; *person* large, impressive, stout.

hermosura *nf* (a) beauty, loveliness; splendour; handsomeness. (b) (*person*) beauty, belle.

hernia *nf* rupture, hernia.

Herodes *m* Herod.

héroe *nm* hero.

heroicamente *adv* heroically.

heroicidad *nf* (a) heroism. (b) (*una* —) heroic deed.

heroico *adj* heroic.

heroicocómico *adj* mock-heroic.

heroína[1] *nf* heroine.

heroína[2] *nf* (Pharm) heroin.

heroísmo *nm* heroism.

herpes *nmpl or fpl* (Med) herpes, shingles.

herrada *nf* (a) bucket. (b) (Col: Agr) branding.

herrador *nm* farrier, blacksmith.

herradura *nf* horseshoe; **curva en** — (Aut) hairpin bend; **mostrar las** —s (*fig*) to kick over the traces.

herraje *nm* (a) ironwork, iron fittings. (b) (Arg) horseshoe. (c) (Mex) silver harness fittings.

herramental *nm* toolkit, toolbag.

herramienta *nf* (a) tool; implement, appliance; set of tools; — **de filo** edge tool; — **de mano** hand tool; — **mecánica** power tool.
(b) (*fam*) horns (*of bull*); teeth.

herranza *nf* (Col) branding.

herrar [1k] *vt* (Agr) *horse* to shoe; *cattle* to brand; (Tech) to bind with iron, trim with ironwork.

herrería *nf* (a) smithy, forge, blacksmith's (shop).
(b) ironworks.
(c) blacksmith's trade, craft of the smith.
(d) (*fig*) uproar, tumult.

herrerillo *nm* (Orn) tit.

herrero *nm* blacksmith, smith; — **de grueso** foundry worker.

herrete *nm* metal tip, ferrule, tag; (SAm) branding-iron, brand.

herrumbre *nf* (a) rust; **a prueba de** — rustproof, rust-resistant. (b) (*Bot*) rust. (c) (*fig*) iron taste, taste of iron.

herrumbroso *adj* rusty.

hervederas *nfpl* (PR) heartburn, indigestion.

hervidero *nm* (a) (*act*) boiling; bubbling, seething.
(b) hot spring; bubbling spring.
(c) (*fig*) swarm, throng, crowd; **un** — **de gente** a swarm of people.

hervido 1 *ptp and adj* boiled. 2 *nm* (Arg, Chi, Ven) stew.

hervidor *nm* kettle; boiler, boiling pan.

hervir [3i] 1 *vt* (*esp* SAm) to boil; to cook.
2 *vi* (a) to boil; to bubble, seethe; (*of sea etc*) to seethe, surge; — **a fuego lento** to simmer; **dejar de** — to stop boiling, go off the boil; **empezar a** — to begin to boil, come to the boil.
(b) (*fig*) — **de**, — **en** to swarm with, seethe with, teem with; **la cama hervía de pulgas** the bed was swarming with fleas.

hervor *nm* (a) (*act*) boiling; seething; **alzar el** —, **levantar el** — to come to the boil.
(b) (*fig*) fire, fervour (*of youth*); passion; restlessness.

hervoroso *adj* (a) boiling, seething; *sun* burning.
(b) (*fig*) = **fervoroso**.

heteo 1 *adj* Hittite. 2 *nm*, **hetea** *nf* Hittite.

heterodoxo *adj* heterodox, unorthodox.

heterogéneo *adj* heterogeneous.

heterosexual 1 *adj* heterosexual. 2 *nmf* heterosexual.

heterosexualidad *nf* heterosexuality.

heticarse [1g] *vr* (PR, SD) to contract tuberculosis.

hético *adj* consumptive.

hetiquencia *nf* (PR) tuberculosis.

hexagonal *adj* hexagonal.

hexágono *nm* hexagon.

hexámetro *nm* hexameter.

hez *nf* (*esp* **heces** *pl*) sediment, dregs; (*fig*) dregs, scum; **la** — **de la sociedad** the scum of society.

hiato *nm* (Ling) hiatus.

hibernación *nf* hibernation.

hibernal *adj* wintry, winter (*attr*).

hibernar [1a] *vi* to hibernate.

hibridación *nf* hybridization.

hibridar [1a] *vti* to hybridize.

hibridismo *nm* hybridism.

híbrido 1 *adj* hybrid. 2 *nm*, **híbrida** *nf* hybrid.

hice *etc see* **hacer**.

hidalga *nf* noblewoman.

hidalgo 1 *adj* noble; illustrious; (*fig*) gentlemanly, honourable; generous.
2 *nm* (a) nobleman, hidalgo.
(b) (Mex) 10-peso gold coin.

hidalguía *nf* nobility; (*fig*) nobility, gentlemanliness, honourableness; generosity.

hidra *nf* hydra; **H—** (Myth) Hydra.

hidratar [1a] *vt* to hydrate; to moisturize.

hidrato *nm* hydrate; — **de carbono** carbohydrate.

hidráulica *nf* hydraulics.

hidráulico *adj* hydraulic, water (*attr*); **fuerza hidráulica** water power, hydraulic power.

hidro . . . hydro . . ., water- . . .

hidroala *nf* hovercraft.

hidroavión *nm* seaplane, flying boat.

hidrocarburo *nm* hydrocarbon.

hidrocefalía *nf* (Med) hydrocephalus, water on the brain.

hidrodinámica *nf* hydrodynamics.

hidroeléctrico *adj* hydroelectric.

hidrófilo *adj* absorbent; (*fam*) bibulous, boozy.

hidrofobia *nf* hydrophobia; rabies.

hidrofóbico adj, **hidrófobo** adj hydrophobic.
hidrófugo adj damp-proof, damp-resistant, water-repellent.
hidrógeno nm hydrogen.
hidrografía nf hydrography.
hidrólisis nf hydrolysis.
hidrolizar [1f] **1** vt to hydrolyze. **2 hidrolizarse** vr to hydrolyze.
hidropesía nf dropsy.
hidrópico adj dropsical.
hidroplaneador nm glider.
hidroplano nm seaplane.
hidrovelero nm glider.
hidróxido nm hydroxide.
hiedra nf ivy.
hiel nf (a) (Anat) gall, bile; **echar la** — to overwork, sweat one's guts out. (b) (fig) gall, bitterness; **no tener** — to be very sweet-tempered. (c) **—es** (fig) troubles, upsets.
hielo nm (a) ice; frost; — **a la deriva**, — **flotante**, — **movedizo** drift ice; **romper el** — (fig) to break the ice. (b) (fig) coldness, indifference.
hiena nf hyena; **hecho una** — furious; **ponerse como una** — to get furious.
hierba nf grass; small plant; (Med) herb, medicinal plant; **—s** grass, pasture; **mala** — weed, (fig) evil influence; — **cara** groundsel; — **gatera** catmint; — **lombriguera** ragwort; — **mate** maté; — **mora** nightshade; — **rastrera** cotton grass; — **de San Juan** St John's-wort; **y otras —s** (fig) and so forth, and suchlike; **oír** (or **sentir**, **ver**) **crecer la** — to be pretty smart; **pisar mala** — to have bad luck.
hierbabuena nf mint.
hierra nf (SAm) branding.
hierro nm (a) iron; — **acanalado** corrugated iron; — **batido** wrought iron; — **bruto** crude iron, pig iron; — **colado** cast iron; — **forjado** wrought iron; — **de fundición**, — **fundido** cast iron; — **en lingotes** pig iron; — **ondulado** corrugated iron; — **viejo** scrap iron, old iron; **a** — **candente batir de repente** strike while the iron is hot; **como el** — like iron, tough, strong; **de** — iron (attr); **llevar** — **a Vizcaya** to carry coals to Newcastle; **machacar en** — **frío** to beat one's head against a wall, flog a dead horse; **el que a** — **mata**, **a** — **muere** those that live by the sword die by the sword; **quitar** — **to** minimize something, cut things down to their proper size. (b) iron object; tool; (of arrow etc) head; (Agr) brand, branding-iron; (Golf) iron; **—s** irons.
higa nf rude sign, obscene gesture; (fig) scorn, derision.
hígado nm (a) (Anat) liver; **echar los —s** to wear oneself out; **tener** — **de indio** (CAm, Mex) to be a disagreeable sort. (b) **—s** (fig) guts, pluck. (c) (CAm, Mex) **ser un** — to be tedious, be a nuisance.
higadoso adj (CR, Mex) tedious, annoying.
higiene nf hygiene.
higiénico adj hygienic; sanitary.
higienizar [1f] **1** vt (SAm) to clean up. **2 higienizarse** vr (Arg) to wash, bath.
higo nm (a) (Bot) fig, green fig; — **chumbo**, — **de tuna** prickly pear; — **paso**, — **seco** dried fig; **de —s a brevas** once in a blue moon; see **importar** etc. (b) (Vet) thrush.
higuera nf fig tree; — **chumba**, — **de tuna** prickly pear (cactus), Indian fig tree; — **del infierno**, — **infernal** castor-oil plant; **caer de la** — to come down to earth with a bump; **estar en la** — to be naïve; to be at a loss, not know what to do; to be day-dreaming.
higuerilla nf (Mex) castor-oil plant.
hija nf daughter; child; (in direct address, usually not translated, eg) —, **no te lo puedo decir** I can't tell you; — **política** daughter-in-law; — **del mar** mermaid.
hijastra nf stepdaughter.
hijastro nm stepson.
hijo nm (a) son; child; **—s** (freq) children; sons and daughters; offspring, descendants; **sin —s** childless, without children; **¿cuántos —s tiene?** how many children has she?; **Pitt** — Pitt the Younger, the younger Pitt; **Juan Pérez**, — Juan Pérez Junior; — **de bendición** legitimate child; — **de la cuna** foundling; — **de leche** foster child; — **natural** illegitimate child; — **político** son-in-law; **nombrar a uno** — **predilecto de la ciudad** to give someone the freedom of the city; — **pródigo** prodigal son; **cada** — **de vecino** everyone, every mother's son; — **de**

puta bastard, son of a bitch; **ser** — **de sus obras** to be a self-made man; **ser** (**muy**) — **de papá** to be daddy's boy, be a spoiled child; **to have led a very sheltered life**; **entró en el negocio como** — **de papá** he just followed his father in the business (so it was easy for him). (b) (in direct address: to child) son, sonny (fam), my boy; (to adult) man, old chap (fam) (but often not translated); **¡— de mi alma!**, **¡— de mis entrañas!** my precious child! (c) **hacer a una un** — to get someone with child; **hacer a uno un** — **macho** (SAm) to do someone harm.
hijuela nf (a) little girl; small daughter. (b) (Tech etc) accessory. (c) (Law) estate of a deceased person; share, portion, inheritance; list of bequests. (d) (Arg, Chi, Per) rural property, piece of land (resulting from division of estate). (e) (Sew) piece of material (for widening a garment). (f) (Agr) small irrigation channel. (g) (Mex: Min) seam of ore.
hijuelo nm (a) little boy; small son; **—s** small children, (Zool) young. (b) (Bot) shoot. (c) (Col) side road, minor road.
hijuna (SAm) interj you bastard!
hila nf (a) row, line; **a la** — in a row, in single file. (b) thin gut; **—s** (Med) lint. (c) (Ven) **irse a la** — to fail, come to nothing.
hilacha nf ravelled thread; shred; fibre, filament; — **de acero** steel wool; — **de vidrio** spun glass; **—s** (Med) lint; **mostrar la** — (RPl) to show oneself in one's true colours.
hilachento adj (SAm) ragged, tattered; frayed; shabby.
hilacho nm = **hilacha**; **—s** (Mex) rags, tatters; shabby clothing.
hilachudo adj (Mex) = **hilachento**.
hilada nf row, line; (Archit) course.
hilado 1 adj and ptp spun; **seda hilada** spun silk. **2** nm (a) spinning. (b) thread, yarn.
hilador nm spinner.
hiladora nf (a) (person) spinner. (b) (Tech) spinning jenny.
hilandería nf (a) (craft) spinning. (b) spinning mill; — **de algodón** cotton mill.
hilandero nm, **hilandera** nf spinner.
hilangos nmpl (Col) rags, tatters.
hilar [1a] vt (a) to spin (also Zool). (b) (fig) to reason, infer; — (**muy**) **delgado** to draw it fine, (pej) to split hairs.
hilaracha nf = **hilacha**.
hilarante adj hilarious; merry, mirthful; **gas** — laughing gas.
hilaridad nf hilarity; merriment, mirth.
hilaza nf yarn, coarse thread; **descubrir la** — to show oneself in one's true colours.
hilera nf (a) row, line; string; (Mil etc) rank, file; (Archit) course; (Agr) row, drill. (b) (Sew) fine thread.
hilo nm (a) (Sew etc) thread, yarn; (Bot etc) fibre, filament; — **bramante** twine; — **de perlas** string of pearls; **a** — uninterruptedly, continuously; **coser al** — to sew on the straight; **escapar con el** — **en una pata** (Arg, PR, Urug) to get oneself cleverly out of a jam; **colgar** (or **pender**) **de un** — to hang by a thread; **contar algo del** — **al ovillo** to tell something without omitting a single detail; **estar al** — to be watchful, be on the look-out; **estar hecho un** — to be as thin as a rake; **tela de** — (Col, Ven) cotton cloth. (b) (of metal) thin wire; (Elec) wire; flex; — **de tierra** earth wire, ground wire (US); **el** — **rojo** (Tel) the hot line. (c) (of liquid) thin line, thin stream, trickle; (of people) thin line; — **de humo** thin line of smoke, plume of smoke; **decir algo con un** — **de la voz** to say something in a barely audible voice; **irse tras el** — **de la gente** to follow the crowd. (d) (cloth) linen; **traje de** — linen dress. (e) (fig: of conversation, speech) thread, theme; (of life) course; (of thought) train; **coger el** — **to** pick up the thread; **perder el** — to lose the thread.
hilván nm tacking, basting; (Chi) basting thread; (Ven) hem.
hilvanar [1a] vt (a) (Sew) to tack, baste. (b) (fig) job to do hurriedly; construction to throw together, knock up hurriedly; **bien hilvanada** well done, well constructed.
Himalaya m: **el —**, **los montes** — the Himalayas.
himen nm hymen, maidenhead.

himeneo nm (lit) nuptials (lit), wedding.
himnario nm hymnal, hymnbook.
himno nm hymn; — **nacional** national anthem.
hincada nf (a) (Col, Cu, Per, PR, Ven) thrust. (b) (Chi, PR) genuflection. (c) (Per, PR) sharp rheumatic pain.
hincadura nf (a) thrust, thrusting, driving. (b) — **de alfiler** pinprick.
hincapié nm: **hacer** — to make a stand, take a firm stand; **hacer** — **en** to insist on; to dwell on, emphasize, make a special point of.
hincapilotes nm, pl **hincapilotes** (Arg) piledriver.
hincar [1g] **1** vt to thrust (in), drive (in), push (in); tooth to sink (en into); foot etc to set (firmly) (en on); **hincó la mirada en ella** he fixed his gaze on her, he stared at her fixedly; **hincó el bastón en el suelo** he stuck his stick in the ground, he thrust his stick into the ground; see **diente, rodilla**.
　　2 hincarse vr: — **de rodillas** to kneel (down).
hinco nm (Chi) post, stake.
hincha **1** nf (a) ill will, animosity, bad blood; grudge; **tener** — **a uno** to have a grudge against someone; **tomar** — **a uno** to take a dislike to someone.
　　(b) (person, thing) pet aversion; **es mi** — he's my pet aversion, he's one of my special dislikes.
　　2 nmf (a) (Sport etc) fan (fam), supporter, rooter (US); **los** —**s del Madrid** the Madrid supporters.
　　(b) (Per) pal (fam), chum.
hinchada nf (Col, RPl) mass of supporters, group of fans (fam).
hinchado |adj (a) swollen. (b) (fig) person arrogant, vain; style etc pompous, high-flown, windy.
hinchador nm (Chi, RPl) bore, nuisance.
hinchar [1a] **1** vt (a) to swell; to distend, enlarge; tyre etc to blow up, inflate, pump up.
　　(b) (fig) to exaggerate.
　　(c) (RPl) to annoy.
　　2 vi (RPl): — **por** to shout for, root for.
　　3 hincharse vr (a) to swell (up); to get distended; (fam) to stuff oneself (de with).
　　(b) (fig) to get conceited, become vain.
　　(c) — **a correr** (etc) to run (etc) hard, run (etc) about a lot; — **a reír** to laugh a lot, have a good laugh.
hinchazón nf (a) (Med etc) swelling; bump, lump. (b) (fig) arrogance, vanity, conceit; (of style etc) pomposity, windiness.
hindú **1** adj Hindu. **2** nm, **hindúa** nf Hindu.
hiniesta nf (Bot) broom.
hinojo[1] nm (Bot, Cook) fennel.
hinojo[2] nm (Anat: arch) knee; **de** —**s** on bended knee; **ponerse de** —**s** to kneel (down), go down on one's knees.
hipar [1a] **1** vi (a) to hiccup, hiccough.
　　(b) (of dog) to pant; — **por algo** to long for something, yearn for something; — **por** + infin to long to + infin, yearn to + infin.
　　(c) (fig) to be worn out, be exhausted.
　　2 vi [xi'par] to whine, whimper.
hipato adj (Col) full, replete; swollen; (Col, Cu, Mex) = **jipato**.
hipear [1a] vi (Mex) = **hipar**.
hiper... hyper...
hiperacidez nf hyperacidity.
hipérbaton nm, pl **hipérbatos** hyperbaton.
hipérbola nf hyperbola.
hipérbole nf hyperbole.
hiperbólico adj hyperbolic(al), exaggerated.
hipercrítico adj hypercritical; carping, censorious.
hipersensibilidad nf hypersensitivity.
hipersensible adj hypersensitive.
hipertensión nf hypertension.
hipiar [1b] vi (Mex) = **hipar**.
hípico adj horse (attr); equine.
hipnosis nf hypnosis.
hipnótico **1** adj hypnotic. **2** nm hypnotic.
hipnotismo nm hypnotism.
hipnotista nmf hypnotist.
hipnotizador adj hypnotizing.
hipnotizar [1f] vt to hypnotize, mesmerize.
hipo nm (a) hiccup(s), hiccough(s); **quitar el** — **a uno** to cure someone's hiccups, (fig) to take someone's breath away; **tener** — to have hiccups.
　　(b) (fig) longing, yearning; **tener** — **por** to long for, crave.
　　(c) (fig) disgust; grudge, ill will; **tener** — **contra uno** to have a grudge against someone, have it in for someone.
hipocampo nm sea horse.
hipocondria nf hypochondria.
hipocondríaco **1** adj hypochondriac(al). **2** nm, **hipocondríaca** nf hypochondriac.

hipocorístico adj: **nombre** — pet name, affectionate form of a name (eg Jim for James).
Hipócrates m Hippocrates.
hipocresía nf hypocrisy.
hipócrita **1** adj hypocritical. **2** nmf hypocrite.
hipócritamente adv hypocritically.
hipodérmico adj hypodermic; **aguja hipodérmica** hypodermic needle.
hipódromo nm racetrack, racecourse; (Hist) hippodrome.
hipopótamo nm hippopotamus.
hiposulfito nm: — **sódico** (Phot) hypo, sodium thiosulphate.
hipoteca nf mortgage; **redimir una** — to pay off a mortgage.
hipotecar [1g] vt to mortgage.
hipotecario adj mortgage (attr).
hipotenusa nf hypotenuse.
hipótesis nf, pl **hipótesis** hypothesis, supposition.
hipotéticamente adv hypothetically.
hipotético adj hypothetic(al).
hiriente adj remark, tone wounding, cutting; contrast striking.
hirsuto adj (a) hairy, hirsute; bristly. (b) (fig) brusque, gruff, rough.
hirvición nf (Ec) abundance, multitude.
hirviendo (as adj) boiling.
hirviente adj boiling, seething.
hisca nf birdlime.
hisopear [1a] vt (Eccl) to sprinkle with holy water.
hisopo nm (a) (Eccl) sprinkler, aspergillum. (b) (Bot) hyssop. (c) (SAm) paintbrush; (Par) dishcloth.
hispalense **1** adj Sevillian. **2** nmf Sevillian.
Híspalis (lit) Seville.
hispánico adj Hispanic, Spanish.
hispanidad nf (a) Spanishness; Spanish quality, Spanish characteristics.
　　(b) (Pol) Spanish world, Hispanic world; **Día de la H—** Columbus Day (12 October).
hispanismo nm (a) word (or phrase etc) peculiar to Spain; word (etc) borrowed from Spanish, hispanicism.
　　(b) (Univ etc) Hispanism, Hispanic studies; **el H—** holandés Hispanic studies in Holland.
hispanista nmf (a) (Univ etc) hispanist, Spanish scholar, student of Spain. (b) lover of Spain; **yo soy muy** — I am a great lover of Spain.
hispanizar [1f] vt to hispanicize.
hispano **1** adj Spanish, Hispanic. **2** nm Spaniard.
hispano-... Hispano-..., Spanish-... eg **pacto hispano-ruritano** Hispano-Ruritanian pact.
Hispanoamérica f Spanish America, Latin America.
hispanoamericano **1** adj Spanish-American, Latin-American. **2** nm, **hispanoamericana** nf Spanish-American, Latin-American.
hispanófilo nm, **hispanófila** nf hispanophile.
hispanófobo nm, **hispanófoba** nf hispanophobe.
hispanomarroquí adj Spanish-Moroccan.
histerectomía nf hysterectomy.
histeria nf hysteria.
histéricamente adv hysterically.
histérico adj hysterical; **paroxismo** — hysterics.
histerismo nm hysteria; hysterics.
histología nf histology.
historia nf (a) story; tale; —**s** (pej) tales, gossip; (Mex, RPl) confused tale; ins-and-outs; (Mex, RPl) worthless excuses; evasions; **la** — **es larga de contar** it's a long story; **dejarse de** —**s** to come to the point, stop beating about the bush; **no me vengas con** —**s** don't come telling tales to me.
　　(b) history; **en toda la** — **humana** in the whole of human history; — **antigua** ancient history; — **del arte** history of art, art history; — **natural** natural history; **H— Sacra, H— Sagrada** Biblical history, (School) Scripture; — **universal** world history; **es una mujer que tiene** — she's a woman with a past; **ser de** — to be famous; (pej) to be notorious; **pasar a la** — to go down in (or to) history (como as); **picar en** — to be a serious matter.
historiador nm, **historiadora** nf historian; chronicler, recorder.
historial **1** adj historical. **2** nm record; dossier; (Med) case history; **el brillante** — **del club** the club's brilliant record.
historiar [1b] vt (a) to tell the story of; to write the history of; to record, chronicle, write up. (b) (Art etc) to paint, depict.
histórico adj historical; (esp fig) historic.
historiero adj (Arg) gossipy, intriguing.
historieta nf short story, tale; anecdote; — **muda** (Typ) strip cartoon.

historiografía *nf* historiography, writing of history.
histrión *nm* actor, player; (*pej*) playactor; buffoon.
histrionismo *nm* (a) (*Theat*) acting, art of acting.
(b) (*fig*) histrionics. (c) actors (*collectively*),
theatre people.
hita *nf* (a) (*Tech*) brad, headless nail. (b) = **hito**.
hitita 1 *adj* Hittite. 2 *nmf* Hittite. 3 *nm* (*language*)
Hittite.
hito *nm* (a) boundary post, boundary mark; milestone;
— **kilométrico** kilometre stone.
(b) (*fig*) landmark, milestone; **es un** — **en nuestra
historia** it is a landmark in our history; **esto
marca un** — **histórico** this marks a historical
milestone.
(c) (*Sports*) quoits.
(d) (*Mil*) target; (*fig*) aim, goal; **a** — fixedly; **dar
en el** — to hit the nail on the head; **mudar de** —
to change one's methods.
(e) **mirar a uno de** — **en** — to look someone up
and down; to stare at someone.
hocicar [1g] 1 *vt* (of *pig*) to root among; (of *person
etc*) to nuzzle.
2 *vi* (a) to root; to nuzzle; — **con**, — **en** to put
one's nose against (or into *etc*).
(b) (*Naut*: of *bow*) to dip.
(c) to fall on one's face.
(d) (*fig*) to run into trouble, come up against it.
hocico *nm* (a) (*Zool*) snout, muzzle, nose; (of *person*)
snout (*sl*); face, mug (*sl*); **caer** (or **dar**) **de** —**s** to fall
on one's face; **dar de** —**s contra algo** to bump into
something, go slap into something; **cerrar el** —
(*fam*) to shut one's trap (*sl*); **estar de** — to be in a
bad mood; **meter el** — to meddle, shove one's nose
in.
(b) (*fig*) angry face, grimace; **poner** — to show
one's anger (or resentment) in one's expression.
hocicudo *adj* (*Guat, Per, PR*) disgusted, disagreeable.
hociquear [1a] *vti* = **hocicar**.
hociquera *nf* (*Cu, Per*) muzzle.
hockey ['oki or 'xoki] *nm* (*angl*) hockey; — **sobre
patines**, — **sobre hielo** ice hockey.
hogaño *adv* (*arch or lit*) this year; these days,
nowadays.
hogar *nm* (a) fireplace, hearth; fireside; (*Tech*)
furnace; (*Rail*) firebox.
(b) (*fig*) home, house; home life, family life; —
nacional judío Jewish national home; **los que han
quedado sin** — the homeless, those left homeless;
no tienen — they have no home.
hogareño *adj* home (*attr*), family (*attr*); fireside
(*attr*); *person* home-loving, stay-at-home.
hogaza *nf* large loaf, cottage loaf.
hoguera *nf* bonfire; blaze; **la casa estaba hecha una**
— the house was ablaze, the house was an inferno.
hoja *nf* (a) (*Bot*) leaf; petal; — **de parra** (*fig*) figleaf;
de — **ancha** broad-leaved; **de** — **caduca** deciduous;
de — **perenne** evergreen.
(b) (of *paper*) leaf, sheet; (*Typ*) leaf, page;
(*official etc*) sheet, form, document; — **de guarda**
flyleaf; — **de ruta** waybill; — **de servicios** record
(of service); — **volante** leaflet, handbill, pamphlet;
doblar la — (*fig*) to change the subject; **volver la** —
to turn the page; (*fig*) to change the subject; (*fig*)
to turn over a new leaf.
(c) (of *metal*) sheet; thin plate; (of *door*) leaf;
(of *sword*) blade; (of *skate*) blade; (of *glass*) sheet,
pane; — **de afeitar** razor blade; — **de estaño**
tinfoil; — **de lata** tin, tinplate; — **plegadiza** flap
(of *table etc*); — **de tocino** side of bacon, flitch.
hojalata *nf* tin, tinplate.
hojalatería *nf* (a) tinwork; sheet-metal work. (b)
tinsmith's (shop).
hojalaterío *nm* (*CAm, Col, Mex*) tinware.
hojalatero *nm* tinsmith.
hojalda *nf* (*SAm*), **hojaldra** *nf* (*SAm*), **hojaldre**
gen m puff pastry.
hojarasca *nf* (a) dead leaves, fallen leaves. (b) (*fig*)
rubbish, trash, worthless stuff; empty verbiage.
hojear [1a] 1 *vt* to turn the pages of, leaf through;
to skim through, glance through.
2 *vi* (a) (*Mex*: *Bot*) to put out leaves.
(b) (*CAm, Mex*: *Agr*) to eat leaves.
(c) (of *surface*) to scale off, flake off.
hojerío *nm* (*CAm*) leaves, foliage.
hojoso *adj* leafy.
hojuela *nf* (a) (*Bot*) leaflet, little leaf.
(b) flake; (of *metal*) foil, thin sheet; — **de estaño**
tinfoil.
(c) (*Cook*) pancake; (*SAm*) ordinary fare, daily
food; (*Cu, Mex*) = **hojaldre**.

hola *interj* (greeting) hullo!; (*surprise*) hullo!, hey!, I
say!
holán *nm* (a) cambric, fine linen. (b) (*Mex*) flounce,
frill.
Holanda *f* Holland.
holandés 1 *adj* Dutch. 2 *nm* Dutchman; **los** —**es** the
Dutch. 3 *nm* (*language*) Dutch.
holandesa *nf* Dutchwoman.
holgadamente *adv* (a) loosely, comfortably.
(b) idly; in leisurely fashion.
(c) **vivir** — to live comfortably, live in luxury, be
well off.
holgado *adj* (a) *dress etc* loose, full, comfortable;
roomy; baggy; **demasiado** — too big.
(b) idle, unoccupied, free; leisured.
(c) (*Fin*) comfortably off, well-to-do; **vida
holgada** comfortable life, life of luxury.
holganza *nf* (a) idleness; rest; leisure, ease. (b)
amusement, enjoyment.
holgar [1h *and* 1m] 1 *vi* (a) to rest, take one's ease,
be at leisure; (of *worker etc*) to be idle, be out of work;
(of *thing*) to lie unused.
(b) to be unnecessary, be superfluous; **huelga
toda protesta** no protest is necessary, it is not
necessary to protest; **huelga decir que...** it goes
without saying that..., needless to say, ...
(c) = 2 **holgarse** *vr* to amuse oneself, enjoy
oneself, have a good time; —(**se**) **con algo** to take
pleasure in something; —(**se**) **con una noticia** to
be pleased about a piece of news; —(**se**) **de que...**
to be pleased that..., be glad that...; **huelgo de
saberlo** I'm delighted to hear it.
holgazán 1 *adj* idle, lazy, slack. 2 *nm*, **holgazana** *nf*
idler, slacker, loafer; ne'er-do-well.
holgazanear [1a] *vi* to laze around, be idle, slack,
loaf.
holgazanería *nf* idleness, laziness, slackness.
holgazanitis *nf* (*hum*) congenital laziness, workshyness.
holgorio *nm* = **jolgorio**.
holgura *nf* (a) (*Sew etc*) looseness, fullness; roominess,
bagginess; (*Mech*) play, free movement.
(b) freedom, leisure; ease, comfort.
(c) enjoyment; merriment, merrymaking.
(d) comfortable living, luxury; **vivir con** — to
live well, live comfortably, live in luxury.
holocausto *nm* (*Rel: Hist*) holocaust, burnt offering;
(*fig*) sacrifice.
hollar [1m] *vt* (a) to tread, tread on; to trample
down, trample underfoot. (b) (*fig*) to trample
underfoot; to humiliate, humble.
hollejo *nm* (*Bot*) skin, peel.
hollín *nm* soot.
holliniento *adj*, **hollinoso** *adj* sooty, covered in soot.
hombracho *nm*, **hombrachón** *nm* hulking great
brute, big tough fellow.
hombrada *nf* (a) manly deed, brave act. (b) (*pej*)
piece of bravado; show of courage.
hombradía *nf* manliness; courage, guts.
hombre 1 *nm* man; (*in general*) man, mankind; **su**
— (*fam*) her man, her husband; **pobre** — poor devil;
(*pej*) poor fish, weak man; slow-witted chap; **es un
pobre** — he's a poor fish; **está hecho un pobre** —
he's now a man to be pitied, he's a shadow of his
former self; **una charla de** — **a** — a man-to-man
talk; **el** — **propone, pero Dios dispone** man
proposes, but God disposes; **ser muy** — to be a real
man, be pretty tough; **no me fastidien, pues sé ser
muy** — don't provoke me, because I can get tough;
¡—**al agua!**, ¡— **al mar!** man overboard!; — **de
armas** man-at-arms; — **de bien** honest man, good
man; — **blanco** white man; paleface; — **bueno**
(*Law*) arbiter; **el** — **de** (or **en**) **la calle** the man in
the street; — **de las cavernas** caveman; — **de
confianza** right-hand man; — **de estado** statesman;
el — **fuerte de Ruritania** the strong man of
Ruritania; — **hecho** grown man; — **de letras** man
of letters; — **de mar** seafaring man, seaman; **el** —
masa, **el** — **medio, el** — **del montón** the average man,
the ordinary man, the man in the street; — **mun-
dano** man-about-town; — **de mundo** man of the
world; — **de negocios** businessman; **el abominable**
— **de las nieves** the abominable snowman; — **de
pro**, — **de provecho** worthy man, honest man;
— **del tiempo** weather man.
2 *interj* (a) (*in ordinary address*) old chap (*fam*), my
boy, man (*but often not translated*); **sí** — yes, yes of
course.
(b) (*surprise*) well!, good heavens!, you don't say!
(c) (*pitying*) dear me!; yes I know!
(d) (*protesting*) come now!, but my dear fellow!,
heavens man!

hombre-anuncio *nm, pl* **hombres-anuncio** sandwich-board man.

hombrear[1] **1** *vi* **(a)** (*of youth*) to play the man, act grown-up; (*of man*) to act tough, try to be somebody; (*Mex: of woman*) to be mannish, behave like a man.

    (b) — **con** = **2 hombrearse** *vr:* — **con uno** to try to keep up with someone, strive to equal someone.

hombrear[1a] *vt* **(a)** to shoulder; to push with one's shoulder, put one's shoulder to.

    (b) (*Arg, Col, Mex*) to help, lend a hand to, back.

hombrecillo *nm* **(a)** little man, little fellow. **(b)** (*Bot*) hop.

hombrera *nf* (*of dress*) shoulder strap; (*in dress*) shoulder pad; (*Mil*) epaulette.

hombre-rana *nm, pl* **hombres-rana** frogman.

hombría *nf* manliness; — **de bien** honesty, uprightness, worthiness.

hombro *nm* shoulder; — **a** —, — **con** — shoulder to shoulder; **¡armas al** —!, **¡sobre el** — **armas!** shoulder arms!; **arrimar el** —, **poner el** — (*Arg*) to put one's shoulder to the wheel, lend a hand; **cargar algo sobre los** —**s** to shoulder something; **echar algo al** — (*fig*) to shoulder something, take something upon oneself; **encogerse de** —**s** to shrug one's shoulders; **enderezar los** —**s** to square one's shoulders, straighten up; **mirar a uno por encima del** — to look down on someone; **sacar a uno en** —**s** to carry someone out on (their) shoulders; **el vencedor salió en** —**s** the victor was carried out shoulder-high.

hombruno *adj* mannish, manlike.

homenaje *nm* **(a)** (*Law, Hist etc*) homage; allegiance; **rendir** — **a** to do (*or* pay, render) homage to, swear allegiance to.

    (b) (*fig*) tribute, testimonial; **en** — **a** in honour of; in recognition of; **rendir** — **a**, **tributar** — **a** to pay a tribute to; **una cena** — **para don XY** a dinner in honour of don XY; **partido** — benefit match.

    (c) (*SAm*) celebration; gathering (*in honour of someone*).

    (d) (*Chi*) gift, favour.

homenajeado *nm*, **homenajeada** *nf:* **el** — the person being honoured, the guest of honour.

homenajear [1a] *vt* (*SAm*) to honour, pay tribute to.

homeópata *nm* homeopath.

homeopatía *nf* homeopathy.

homérico *adj* Homeric.

Homero *m* Homer.

homicida 1 *adj* murderous, homicidal. **2** *nm* murderer. **3** *nf* murderess.

homicidio *nm* murder, homicide; manslaughter.

homilía *nf* homily.

homogeneidad *nf* homogeneity.

homogéneo *adj* homogeneous.

homógrafo *nm* homograph.

homónimo 1 *adj* homonymous. **2** *nm* homonym; (*person*) namesake.

homosexual 1 *adj* homosexual. **2** *nmf* homosexual.

homosexualidad *nf* homosexuality.

honda *nf* sling; (*SAm*) catapult.

hondear[1] [1a] *vt* (*Naut*) **(a)** to sound. **(b)** to unload.

hondear[2] [1a] *vt* (*SAm*) to hit with a slingshot, kill with a sling; to hit with a catapult.

hondo 1 *adj* **(a)** deep; low.

    (b) (*Cu*) *river etc* swollen, high.

    (c) (*fig*) profound, deep, heartfelt; **con** — **pesar** with deep regret, with profound sorrow.

    2 *nm* depth(s); bottom.

hondón *nm* **(a)** (*of cup, valley etc*) bottom; (*of stirrup*) footrest. **(b)** (*of needle*) eye.

hondonada *nf* **(a)** hollow, coombe; dip, depression; gully, ravine. **(b)** lowland.

hondura *nf* **(a)** depth; profundity. **(b)** depth; deep place; **meterse en** —**s** to get out of one's depth, get into deep water (*also fig*).

Honduras *f* Honduras; — **Británica** British Honduras.

hondureñismo *nm* word (*or* phrase *etc*) peculiar to Honduras.

hondureño 1 *adj* Honduran. **2** *nm*, **hondureña** *nf* Honduran.

honestamente *adv* **(a)** decently, properly, decorously.

    (b) modestly; purely.

    (c) fairly, justly, reasonably.

    (d) honourably; (*angl: esp SAm*) honestly.

honestidad *nf* **(a)** decency, decorum. **(b)** modesty; purity, chastity. **(c)** fairness, justice. **(d)** honourableness; (*angl: esp SAm*) honesty.

honesto *adj* **(a)** decent, proper, decorous. **(b)** modest; pure, chaste. **(c)** fair, just, reasonable. **(d)** honourable; (*angl: esp SAm*) honest.

hongo *nm* **(a)** (*Bot*) fungus; (*edible*) mushroom; (*poisonous*) toadstool; **un enorme** — **de humo** an enormous mushroom of smoke; **surgen como** —**s** they grow like mushrooms.

    (b) bowler, bowler hat, derby (*US*).

Honolulú Honolulu.

honor *nm* honour; (*of woman*) honour, virtue, good name; (*fig*) glory; —**es** (*Mil etc*) honours, honorary status (*or* rank); — **profesional** professional etiquette; **en** — **a la verdad** to be fair, for the sake of truth; **en** — **de uno** in someone's honour; **13 puntos de** —**es** (*Cards*) 13 honours points; **hacer** — **a un compromiso** to honour a pledge; **hacer** — **a su firma** to honour one's signature; **hacer los** —**es de la casa** to do the honours (of the house); **hacer los debidos** —**es a una comida** to do full justice to a meal; **sepultar a uno con todos los** —**es militares** to bury someone with full military honours; **tener el** — **de** + *infin* to have the honour to + *infin*, to be proud to + *infin*; **el poeta X,** — **de esta ciudad** the poet X in whom this city glories, the poet X who is this city's claim to fame.

honorable *adj* honourable, worthy.

honorario 1 *adj* honorary, honorific. **2** *nm* honorarium; —**s** (professional) fees, charges.

honorífico *adj* honourable; honorific; **mención honorífica** honourable mention.

honra *nf* self-esteem, sense of personal honour, dignity; (*of woman*) honour, virtue, good name; chastity; good name, reputation; —**s fúnebres** last honours, funeral rites; **¡a mucha** —! I'm honoured!, delighted!; **tener algo a mucha** — to be proud of something, consider something an honour; **tener a mucha** — + *infin* to be proud to + *infin*, deem it an honour to + *infin; see* **atentado**.

honradamente *adv* honestly; honourably, uprightly.

honradez *nf* honesty; honourableness, uprightness, integrity.

honrado *adj* honest; honourable, upright; **hombre** — honest man, decent man, honourable man.

honrar [1a] **1** *vt* **(a)** to honour, revere, respect; to do honour to.

    (b) (*Comm etc*) to honour.

    2 honrarse *vr:* — **con algo** to be honoured by something; — **de** + *infin* to be honoured to + *infin*, deem it an honour to + *infin*.

honrilla *nf:* **por la negra** — out of concern for what people will say, out of a sense of shame; for the sake of appearances.

honrosamente *adv* honourably.

honroso *adj* honourable; respectable, reputable; **es una profesión honrosa** it is an honourable profession, it is a respectable profession.

hontanar *nm* spring, group of springs.

hopa[1] *nf* cassock.

hopa[2] *interj* **(a)** (*RPl*) stop it!, that hurts! **(b)** (*Col, Guat, Mex*) = **hola**.

hopear [1a] *vi* (*Ven*) to call, shout.

hopo ['xopo] *nm* (fox's) brush, tail.

hora *nf* **(a)** hour; (*more generally*) time; **media** — half an hour; **durante 2** —**s** for 2 hours; **esperamos** —**s y** —**s** we waited hours and hours; **en la** — **de su muerte** at the moment of his death, at the time of his death; **¿a qué** —? at what time?; **¿qué** — **es?** what is the time?, what time is it?; **¡la** —!, **¡es la** —! time's up!; **es** — **de** + *infin* it is time to + *infin*; **es** — **de irnos** it's time we went, it's time for us to go; **¡ya es** — **de que . . .!** it is high time that . . .!; **¡ya era** —! and about time too!; **éstas son las** —**s mías** this is my time, this is the time I like.

    (b) (*with adj or prep*) **a altas** —**s, en las altas** —**s** in the small hours, late at night; **a una** — **avanzada** at a late hour; **a buena** — opportunely; **¡a buena** —, **mangas verdes!** a fine time you choose to tell me that!, it's too late now!; **en buena** — fortunately; safely; — **de comer** mealtime; **a la** — **de comer** at lunchtime; —**s extra**, —**s extraordinarias** overtime; —**s de insolación** hours of sunshine; — **legal** official time, standard time; —**s libres** free time, spare time; **en mala** — unluckily; — **oficial** official time, standard time; —**s de oficina** business hours, office hours; **a primera** — first thing in the morning; — **punta** peak hour, rush hour; —**s punta** peak hours, rush hours; — **de recreo** playtime; —**s suplementarias** overtime; —**s de trabajo** working hours; working day; **"última** —" (*Press*) "stoppress"; **a última** — at the last moment; in the nick of time; at the eleventh hour; last thing at night; **noticias de última** — last-minute news; **dejar las cosas hasta última** — to leave things until the last moment; — **de verano** summertime; **a la** — punctually, on the dot; **a la** — **justa** on the stroke of time; **a estas —s** now, at this time; **fuera de —s** out of hours, out of working hours; **por —s** by the hour; **trabajar por —s** to be paid by the hour; to work part-time.

    (c) (*with verb*) **dar —** to fix a time, offer an appointment; **dar la —** to strike (the hour); **poner el reloj en —** to set one's watch, put one's watch right; **tener —** to have an appointment; **no ver la — de algo** to be scarcely able to wait for something, look forward impatiently to something.

    (d) **—s** (*Eccl*) book of hours; **—s canónicas** canonical hours.

horaciano *adj* Horatian.

Horacio *m* Horace.

horadar [1a] *vt* to bore (through), pierce, drill, perforate; to tunnel (into).

hora-hombre *nf, pl* **horas-hombre** man-hour.

horario 1 *adj* hourly; hour (*attr*), time (*attr*).

    2 *nm* hour hand; (*Aer, Rail etc; also SAm: School*) timetable; **llegar a —** (*SAm*) to arrive on time, be on schedule.

horca *nf* (a) gallows, gibbet; **condenar a uno a la —** to condemn someone to the gallows.

    (b) (*Agr*) pitchfork; hayfork; manure fork.

    (c) (*of garlic, onions*) string.

    (d) (*PR, Ven*) birthday present, present given on one's saint's day.

horcadura *nf* fork (of a tree).

horcajadas: a — *adv* astride.

horcajo *nm* (a) (*Agr*) yoke. (b) (*of river, tree*) fork.

horcar [1g] *vt* (*SAm*) = **ahorcar**.

horcón *nm* (a) (*Agr*) pitchfork. (b) (*Agr*) forked prop (*for branches of fruit trees*); (*SAm*) prop, support (*for beam of roof*).

horchata *nf* orgeat.

horchatería *nf* refreshment stall.

horda *nf* horde; (*fig*) gang.

hordiate *nm* barley water.

horero *nm* (*Bol, Ec, Guat, Mex*) hour hand.

horita *adv* (*SAm*) = **ahorita**.

horizontal *adj* horizontal.

horizontalmente *adv* horizontally.

horizonte *nm* horizon (*also fig*); (*also* **línea del —**) skyline.

horma *nf* (a) (*Tech*) form, mould; **— de sombrero** hat block; **— (de calzado)** last, boot tree; **encontrar(se con) la — de su zapato** to meet one's match.

    (b) dry-stone wall.

hormadoras *nfpl* (*Col*) petticoat.

hormiga *nf* (a) ant; **— blanca** white ant; **— león** ant lion.

    (b) **—s** (*Med*) itch; pins and needles.

    (c) (*Arg, Mex*) **ser una —** to be hard-working; to be thrifty.

hormigón *nm* concrete; **— armado** reinforced concrete; **— pretensado** pre-stressed concrete.

hormigonera *nf* concrete mixer.

hormiguear [1a] *vi* (a) to itch; to have pins and needles; to have a feeling as though insects were crawling over one. (b) to swarm, teem.

hormigueo *nm* (a) itch, itching; tingling, prickly feeling, feeling as though insects were crawling over one.

    (b) (*fig*) anxiety, uneasiness.

    (c) swarming.

hormiguero 1 *adj* ant-eating; **oso —** anteater. 2 *nm* (a) ant-hill. (b) (*fig*) ant-hill; swarm of people, place swarming with people.

hormiguillo *nm* = **hormigueo** (a).

hormón *nm* (*Acad*), **hormona** *nf* hormone.

hornacina *nf* (vaulted) niche.

hornada *nf* (a) batch (of loaves *etc*), baking. (b) (*fig*) batch, collection, crop.

hornalla *nf* (*RPl*) furnace; firebox (of oven).

hornazo *nm* (a) batch (of cakes *etc*), baking. (b) Easter cake.

hornear [1a] 1 *vt* (*SAm*) to cook, bake. 2 *vi* to bake, be a baker.

hornero *nm*, **hornera** *nf* baker.

hornillo *nm* (a) (*Tech*) small furnace; (*Cook*) cooker, stove; portable stove; (*of pipe*) bowl; **— eléctrico** hotplate; **— de gas** gas ring.

    (b) (*Mil: Hist*) mine.

horno *nm* (*Cook*) oven; (*Tech*) furnace; (*for pottery*) kiln; **alto —** blast furnace; **— de cal** lime kiln; **— crematorio** crematorium; **— de fundición** smelting furnace; **— de ladrillos** brick kiln; **asar al — to bake**; **el — no está para bollos** this is the wrong moment, this is a bad time to ask.

horóscopo *nm* horoscope.

horqueta *nf* (*all senses*) fork.

horquetear [1a] 1 *vt* (a) (*Arg*) *ears* to prick up; to listen suspiciously to.

    (b) (*Col, Mex, Urug*) to bestride, sit astride.

    2 *vi* (*Col, Mex, Urug*) to grow branches, put out branches.

horquilla *nf* hairpin, hairclip; (*Agr*) pitchfork; **— (de cavar)** garden fork; (*of bicycle*) fork; (*Mech*) yoke; (*Tel*) rest, cradle; (*on stilt*) footrest.

horrarse [1a] *vr* (*SAm: Agr*) to abort.

horrendo *adj* horrible; hideous; dire, frightful.

hórreo *nm* (*prov*) (raised) granary.

horrible *adj* (a) horrible, dreadful, ghastly.

    (b) (*fig*) dreadful, nasty, terrible (*fam*); **¡qué persona más —!** what a dreadful man!; **la película es —** the film is dreadful.

horriblemente *adv* (a) horribly, dreadfully. (b) (*fig*) dreadfully, terribly (*fam*).

horripilante *adj* hair-raising, horrifying; harrowing; grisly; creepy.

horripilar [1a] 1 *vt:* **— a uno** to make someone's hair stand on end, horrify someone, give someone the creeps.

    2 **horripilarse** *vr* to be horrified, be terrified; **era para —** it was enough to make your hair stand on end.

horror *nm* (a) horror, dread, terror (*a* of); abhorrence (*a* of); enormity; frightfulness; **¡qué —!** how ghastly!; **isn't it dreadful?**; (*fam*) well!, goodness!; **la fiesta ... ¡un —!** the party was ghastly! (*fam*); **tener — a algo** to have a horror of something; **tener algo en —** to loathe something, loathe something.

    (b) (*act*) atrocity, terrible thing.

    (c) (*as adv: fam*) **me gusta un —** I like it awfully (*fam*); **hoy he trabajado un —** today I worked awfully hard (*fam*); **se divirtieron —es** they had a tremendous time (*fam*).

horrorizar [1f] 1 *vt* to horrify; to terrify, frighten. 2 **horrorizarse** *vr* to be horrified, be aghast.

horrorosamente *adv* (a) horrifyingly; horribly, frightfully. (b) (*fig*) dreadfully, awfully (*fam*).

horroroso *adj* (a) horrifying, terrifying; horrible, frightful. (b) (*fig*) ghastly (*fam*), dreadful, awful (*fam*); hideous, ugly.

horrura *nf* filth, dirt; rubbish.

hortaliza *nf* (a) vegetable; **—s** vegetables, garden produce. (b) (*Mex*) vegetable garden.

hortelano *nm* gardener; market gardener, truck farmer (*US*).

hortensia *nf* hydrangea.

hortera 1 *nf* wooden bowl. 2 *nm* (*Madrid*) shop assistant, grocer's boy.

hortícola 1 *adj* horticultural; garden (*attr*). 2 *nmf* = **horticultor**.

horticultor *nm* horticulturist; gardener; nurseryman.

horticultura *nf* horticulture; gardening.

hosco *adj* (a) dark; gloomy. (b) *person* sullen; morose; grim.

hospedaje *nm* (cost of) board and lodging.

hospedar [1a] 1 *vt* to put up, lodge, give a room (*etc*) to; to receive as a guest, entertain.

    2 **hospedarse** *vr* to stay, stop, put up, lodge (*con* with, *en* at).

hospedera *nf* hostess; innkeeper's wife.

hospedería *nf* (a) hostelry, inn. (b) guest room. (c) (*Eccl*) hospice, guest quarters.

hospedero *nm* host; innkeeper, landlord.

hospiciano *nm*, **hospiciana** *nf*, **hospiciante** *nmf* inmate of a poorhouse.

hospicio *nm* poorhouse; orphanage; (*Eccl*) hospice.

hospital *nm* hospital; infirmary; **— de aislamiento, — de contagiosos** isolation hospital; **— de (primera) sangre** field dressing station.

hospitalario *adj* hospitable.

hospitalidad *nf* hospitality.

hospitalizar [1f] 1 *vt* to send (*or* take) to hospital, hospitalize. 2 **hospitalizarse** *vr* (*SAm*) to go into hospital.

hosquedad *nf* sullenness; moroseness; grimness.

hostelería *nf* hotel trade, hotel business.

hostelero *nm* innkeeper, landlord.

hostería *nf* inn, hostelry.

hostia *nf* (a) (*Eccl*) host, consecrated wafer.

    (b) (*fam*) punch, bash (*fam*).

    (c) **no entiendo ni —** I don't understand a word of it.

    (d) **¡—!** damn it!

hostigar [1h] *vt* (a) to lash, whip, scourge. (b) (*fig*) to harass, plague, pester; to bore. (c) (*SAm: of food*) to surfeit, cloy.

hostigoso *adj* (*CAm, Col, Chi, Per*) *food* sickening, cloying; *person* annoying, tedious.

hostil *adj* hostile.

hostilidad nf (a) hostility. (b) hostile act; **romper las —es** to start hostilities.

hostilizar [1f] vt (Mil) to harry, harass, worry; (fig) to antagonize.

hotel nm (a) hotel. (b) detached house, suburban house, villa.

hotelero 1 adj hotel (attr); **la industria hotelera** the hotel trade. 2 nm hotelkeeper, hotel manager.

hoy 1 adv (a) today; now, nowadays; **la juventud de —** the youth of today; **en el correo de —** in today's post; **— día, — en día** nowadays; in this day and age; **— por —** at the present time, right now; **de — en ocho días, de — en una semana** today week, a week today; **de — en quince (días)** today fortnight, a fortnight today; **de — a mañana** any time now, when one least expects it; **está para llegar de — a mañana** it might happen any day now; **de — en adelante** from now on, henceforward; **de — no pasa que le escriba** I'll write to him this very day; **desde —** from now on, starting from now; **¡y hasta —!** and I've heard no more about it!, and that was the last I heard!; **por —** for the present. (b) (SAm) now; this year.
2 nm present time; **el — cubano** Cuba at the present time, the present state of affairs in Cuba.

hoya nf (a) pit, hole; grave; **— de arena** (Golf) bunker. (b) (Geog) vale, valley; (SAm) riverbed, river basin. (c) (Agr) seedbed.

hoyada nf hollow, depression.

hoyador nm (Col, Cu, Mex) dibber, seed drill.

hoyanco nm (Mex:Aut) pothole.

hoyar [1a] vt (Cu, Guat, Mex) to make holes (for sowing seeds).

hoyito nm (SAm) dimple.

hoyo nm (a) hole, pit; hollow, cavity; grave. (b) (Golf) hole; **en el — 18** at the 18th hole. (c) (Med) pockmark. (d) (Theat) **irse al —** to flop (fam), be a disaster.

hoyuelo nm dimple.

hoz nf (a) (Agr) sickle. (b) (Geog) defile, narrow pass, gorge. (c) **de — y coz** wildly, recklessly.

hozar [1f] vt (of pig) to root in, root among.

hua . . .: for some words so spelled in SAm, see also **gua . . .**, eg for **huaico** see **guaico**.

huaca nf etc see **guaca** etc.

huacalón adj (Mex) (a) rough-voiced, gruff. (b) fat.

huaco adj (SAm) toothless.

huachafería nf (Per) middle-class snobs, would-be social climbers.

huachafo nm, **huachafa** nf (Per) middle-class snob, would-be social climber.

huacho nm (Per) section of a lottery ticket.

huahua nf (Ec, Mex, Per) = **guagua**.

huaica nf (Per) bargain sale.

huáncar nm, **huáncara** nf (Bol, Per) Indian drum.

huasicama nmf (Ec) Indian servant.

hube etc see **haber**.

hucha nf (a) chest, bin; moneybox. (b) (fig) savings; **tener una buena —** to have money laid by, have a nest egg.

hueco 1 adj (a) hollow; empty; (on paper) blank. (b) soft, spongy. (c) voice, sound resonant, resounding, booming. (d) person conceited; style pompous, affected.
2 nm hollow, cavity, hole; gap, opening; empty space; (Archit) recess, window space; (of staircase) well; (of lift) shaft; (fam) vacancy; **— de la mano** hollow of the hand; **deja un — que será difícil llenar** he leaves a gap which it will be hard to fill.

huecograbado nm (Typ) photogravure.

huelán adj (a) (Chi) immature, not fully developed; wood unseasoned; herbage withered; corn unripe. (b) decayed, in decline, that has come down in the world.

hueleflor nmf (PR) idiot.

hueleguisos nm, pl **hueleguisos** (Per) sponger (fam).

huelehuele nmf (PR) idiot.

huelga nf (a) rest, repose; leisure; idleness; recreation. (b) (Pol etc) strike; stoppage, walkout; **— de brazos caídos** sit-down strike; **— de hambre** hunger strike; **— patronal** lockout; **— por solidaridad** sympathy strike; **los obreros en —** the workers on strike, the striking workers; **estar en —** to be on strike; **declarar la —, declararse en —, ponerse en —** to come out on strike, go on strike; to walk out. (c) (Mech) play, free movement.

huelgo nm (a) breath; **tomar —** to take breath, pause. (b) room, space. (c) (Mech) play, free movement.

huelguear [1a] vi (Per) to strike, be on strike.

huelguista nmf striker.

huella nf (a) (act) tread, treading. (b) trace, mark, sign, imprint; footprint; footstep; (of animal, vehicle) track; **— dactilar, — digital** fingerprint; **sin dejar —** without leaving a trace, leaving no sign; **seguir las —s de uno** to follow in someone's footsteps. (c) (of stair, tyre) tread. (d) **— del sonido** (Cine) sound track.

huellear [1a] vt (Col) to track, follow the trail of.

huellero adj (Col): **perro —** tracking dog.

huello nm condition of the ground etc (for walking); **camino de buen —** good road for walking; **camino de mal —** bad road for walking, badly-surfaced road.

huérfano 1 adj orphan, orphaned; (fig) unprotected, defenceless, uncared-for; **una niña huérfana de madre** a motherless child, a child that has lost her mother.
2 nm, **huérfana** nf orphan.

huero adj (a) egg addled, rotten. (b) (fig) empty, sterile; rotten; dud. (c) (Guat, Mex) blond(e).

huerta nf (a) vegetable garden, kitchen garden; (large) market garden, truck farm (US). (b) (esp Murcia, Valencia) irrigated region, fertile irrigated area. (c) (Ec) cocoa plantation.

huertero nm (Arg, Chi, Mex, Per) gardener.

huerto nm kitchen garden, (small) market garden, truck garden (US); orchard; back garden.

huesa nf grave.

huesear [1a] vi (a) (CAm) to beg. (b) (Mex) to work.

hueserío nm (Per) unsaleable merchandise.

huesero nm, **huesera** nf (Cu) slum dweller.

huesillo nm (Chi, Per) sun-dried peach.

huesista nm (CAm) government employee.

hueso nm (a) (Anat) bone; **— de la alegría** funny bone; **un — duro de roer** a hard nut to crack, a tough assignment; **— de la suerte** wishbone; **sin —** boneless; **la sin —** the tongue; **soltar la sin — (fam)** to shoot one's mouth off (fam); **no dejar — sano a uno** to pull someone to pieces; **estar en los —s** to be nothing but skin and bone; **meterse a — de puerco** (Mex) to brag; **tener los —s molidos** to be fagged out (fam), ache all over. (b) (Bot) stone, pit (US); core. (c) (Col) unsaleable article, drug on the market. (d) (fig) hard work, drudgery. (e) (CAm, Mex) government job, sinecure, political plum; soft job. (f) **ser un — (fig)** to be terribly strict, be an old battle-axe (fam). (g) (Ec) mule. (h) (Mex) **— colorado** strong northerly wind.

huesoso adj bony; bone (attr).

huésped nm (a) guest; lodger, boarder, resident. (b) host. (c) (Hist) innkeeper, landlord.

huéspeda nf (a) guest; lodger, boarder, resident. (b) hostess. (c) (Hist) innkeeper's wife; **no contar con la —** to fail to take something into account.

huesudo adj bony; big-boned, raw-boned.

hueva nf (Fish) (hard) roe; **—s** eggs, spawn.

huevada nf (a) (SAm) nest of eggs, clutch of eggs; number of eggs. (b) (Chi, Per) foolish remark, piece of nonsense, crazy idea.

huevera nf eggcup.

huevo nm (a) egg; **— en cáscara** boiled egg; **— crudo** raw egg; **— duro** hard-boiled egg; **— escalfado** poached egg; **— estrellado, — frito, — al plato** fried egg; **— fresco** new-laid egg; **— pasado por agua, — tibio** (CAm, Col, Mex) soft-boiled egg; **—s pericos** (Col), **—s revueltos** scrambled eggs; **ser como el — de Colón** to be simple, be easy; **¡que le frían un —!** (fam) get knotted! (sl); **pensar en los —s del gallo** (CAm, Col) to be in a daydream. (b) (tabu) ball (tabu), testicle; **me costó un — it** took me a lot of trouble, it was hard work; **tener —s** to have guts, be tough.

huevón 1 adj ·(a) (Cu, Chi, Guat, Mex, RPl) slow; lazy; stupid, dim; cowardly. (b) (Nic) tough, brave.
2 nm (a) (Ant, CAm, Mex) slowness; idleness, laziness; (Chi, Per, PR, Ven) stupidity; (Chi) cowardice. (b) (Nic) courage, guts, toughness.

Hugo m Hugo.

hugonote 1 adj Huguenot. 2 nm, **hugonota** nf Huguenot.

hui . . .: for some words so spelled in SAm, see also **gui . . ., güi . . .**, eg for **huinche** see **güinche**.

huida nf (a) flight, escape. (b) (of horse) shy, bolt.

huidizo *adj* (a) *person etc* shy; elusive. (b) *impression etc* fleeting.

huido *adj* very shy, easily scared.

huile *nm* (Mex) roasting grill.

huilón *adj* (Ec, Per) elusive.

huilla *nf* (Ven) cork (of bottle).

huir [3g] **1** *vt* to run away from, flee (from), escape (from); to avoid, shun.
   2 *vi* and **huirse** *vr* to run away, flee, escape; (of time) to fly; (SAm) to elope.

huira *nf* (Chi, Per) rope; halter, tether; **dar — a uno** to thrash someone; **sacar las —s a uno** to beat someone up.

huiro *nm* (Chi) seaweed.

huisachear [1a] *vi* (CAm, Mex) (a) to go to law, engage in litigation. (b) to practise law without a qualification.

huisachería *nf* (CAm, Mex) (a) lawyer's tricks, legal intricacies. (b) practice of law without a qualification.

huisachero *nm* (CAm, Mex) (a) shyster lawyer, unqualified lawyer. (b) (Mex) scribbler, pen-pusher.

hulado *nm* (CAm) oilskin, rubberized cloth.

hular *nm* (Mex) rubber plantation.

hule[1] *nm* (a) rubber. (b) oilskin, oilcloth. (c) (CAm, Mex) rubber tree.

hule[2] *nm* (Taur) goring; (fam) row; **habrá — there** is going to be trouble.

hulear [1a] *vi* (CAm) to extract rubber (from trees).

hulero 1 *adj* (CAm) rubber (attr). **2** *nm* rubber worker.

huloso *adj* (CAm) rubbery, elastic.

hulla *nf* coal, soft coal.

hullera *nf* colliery, coalmine.

hullero *adj* coal (attr).

humanar [1a] **1** *vt* to humanize.
   2 humanarse *vr* (a) to become more human; **— a + infin** (SAm) to condescend to + *infin*.
   (b) (Eccl: of Christ) to become man.

humanidad *nf* (a) humanity, mankind. (b) (quality) humanity. (c) (fam) corpulence. (d) **las —es** the humanities.

humanismo *nm* humanism.

humanista *nmf* humanist.

humanístico *adj* humanistic.

humanitario 1 *adj* humanitarian; humane. **2** *nm* humanitarian.

humanización *nf* humanization.

humanizar [1f] **1** *vt* to humanize, make more human.
   2 humanizarse *vr* to become more human.

humano 1 *adj* (a) human. (b) *act, character etc* humane. (c) **ciencias humanas** humane learning, humanistic learning, humanities. **2** *nm* human.

humarasca *nf* (CAm), **humareda** *nf* cloud of smoke.

humazo *nm* dense smoke, cloud of smoke; **dar — a uno** to smoke someone out.

humeante *adj* smoking, smoky; steaming.

humear [1a] **1** *vt* (a) (Col, Mex, Ven) to fumigate.
   (b) (Chi, Mex) to beat, thrash.
   2 *vi* (a) to smoke, give out smoke; to fume, steam, give off fumes.
   (b) (fig: of memory etc) to be still alive.
   (c) (fig) to give oneself airs, be conceited.

humectador *nm* humidifier; humidor.

humectar [1a] *vt* = **humedecer**.

humedad *nf* humidity; damp, dampness; moisture; **a prueba de — damp-proof**; **sentir la —** (Per, Ven) to feel the consequences of one's act.

humedecer [2d] **1** *vt* to dampen, wet, moisten; to humidify. **2 humedecerse** *vr* to get damp, get wet.

húmedo *adj* humid; damp, wet; moist.

humera *nf* (a) (PR) cloud of smoke. (b) = **jumera**.

humero *nm* (a) chimney, smokestack; flue. (b) (Col) cloud of smoke.

húmero *nm* humerus.

humildad *nf* (a) humbleness, humility; meekness. (b) humbleness; lowliness.

humilde *adj* (a) *character etc* humble; meek; *voice* small.
   (b) *class etc* low, modest; lowly, lowborn, humble; **son gente —** they are humble people, they are poor people.

humildemente *adv* humbly; meekly.

humillación *nf* humiliation; humbling.

humillante *adj* humiliating; humbling; degrading.

humillar [1a] **1** *vt* to humiliate; to humble; *head* to bow, bend; *revolt etc* to crush.
   2 humillarse *vr* to humble oneself; **— a** to bow to, bow down before; to grovel to.

humo *nm* (a) smoke; fumes; vapour, steam; **a — de pajas** thoughtlessly, heedlessly; **quedó en — de pajas** it all came to nothing; **hacer —, echar — to smoke**; **lo que hace — es porque está ardiendo, donde se hace — es porque hay fuego** there's no smoke without fire; **hacerse —, irse todo en — to go up in smoke**; (fig) to disappear completely, vanish without trace; **írsele al — a uno** (Mex, RPl) to fall suddenly on someone, jump someone (sl); **tomar la del —** (fam) to beat it (fam).
   (b) **—s** (fig) homes, hearths.
   (c) **—s** (fig) conceit, airs; **bajar los —s a uno** to take someone down a peg; **tener muchos —s** to be terribly vain, have a swelled head; **tener —s para + infin** to have the nerve to + *infin*; **vender —s** to brag, talk big.

humor *nm* (a) mood, humour; temper, disposition; **buen —** good humour, good mood, high spirits; **estar de buen —** to be in a good mood; **mal —** bad mood, bad temper; **en un tono de mal —** in an ill-tempered tone; **seguir el — a uno** to humour someone, go along with someone's mood.
   (b) (angl) humour; humorousness.

humorada *nf* (a) joke, witticism, pleasantry. (b) caprice, whim.

humorado *adj*: **bien —** good-humoured, good-tempered; **mal —** bad-tempered, cross, peevish.

humorismo *nm* humour; humorousness.

humorista *nmf* humorist.

humorísticamente *adv* humorously, facetiously.

humorístico *adj* humorous, funny, facetious.

humoso *adj* smoky.

humus *nm* humus.

hundible *adj* sinkable.

hundido *adj* sunken; *eyes* deep-set, hollow.

hundimiento *nm* (a) sinking. (b) collapse, fall, ruin, destruction; cave-in, subsidence.

hundir [3a] **1** *vt* (a) to sink; to submerge, engulf.
   (b) *building etc* to ruin, destroy, cause the collapse of; *plan etc* to sink, ruin; (in argument) to confound.
   2 hundirse *vr* (a) (Naut) to sink; (in sand, mud etc) to sink; (of swimmer etc) to plunge, go down.
   (b) (of building etc) to collapse, tumble (down), fall (down); (of ground) to cave in, subside.
   (c) (fig) to be destroyed, be ruined; to disappear, vanish; **se hundió la economía** the economy collapsed; **se hundieron los precios** prices slumped; **se hundió en el estudio de la historia** he plunged into the study of history, he became absorbed in the study of history; **se hundió en la meditación** he became lost in meditation.

húngaro 1 *adj* Hungarian. **2** *nm*, **húngara** *nf* Hungarian. **3** *nm* (language) Hungarian.

Hungría *f* Hungary.

huno *nm* Hun.

huracán *nm* hurricane.

huracanado *adj*: **viento —** hurricane wind, violent wind.

huraco *nm* (SAm) hole.

huranía *nf* shyness; unsociableness; elusiveness.

huraño *adj* shy; unsociable; *animal* shy, elusive, wild.

hure *nm* (Col) large pot, vessel.

hureque *nm* (Col) = **huraco**.

hurgar [1h] **1** *vt* (a) to poke, jab; to stir (up); *fire* to poke, rake.
   (b) (SAm) = **hurguetear**.
   (c) (fig) to stir up, excite, provoke.
   2 hurgarse *vr* (also **— las narices**) to pick one's nose.

hurgón *nm* (a) poker, fire rake. (b) thrust, stab (with weapon).

hurgonada *nf*, **hurgonazo** *nm* poke, jab; poking, raking.

hurgonear [1a] *vt fire* to poke, rake (out); to thrust at, jab (at).

hurgonero *nm* poker, fire rake.

hurguete *nm* (Chi, RPl) busybody, nosey-parker.

hurguetear [1a] *vt* (SAm) to finger, turn over, rummage (inquisitively) among; to shove one's nose into, pry into.

hurí *nf* houri.

hurón 1 *adj* (a) shy, unsociable.
   (b) (Chi) greedy.
   2 *nm* (a) (Zool) ferret.
   (b) (fig) shy person, unsociable person.
   (c) (fig: pej) busybody, nosey-parker, snooper.

huronear [1a] *vt* (fig) to ferret out; to pry into, shove one's nose into.

huronera *nf* ferret hole; (fig) den, lair; hiding place.

hurra *interj* hurray!, hurrah!

hurtadillas: a — *adv* stealthily, by stealth, on the sly.

hurtar [la] **1** *vt* (**a**) to steal; (*Lit etc*) to plagiarize, pinch (*fam*), lift.

(**b**) (*of sea*) to eat away, erode, encroach on.

(**c**) — **el cuerpo** to dodge, move (one's body) out of the way.

2 hurtarse *vr* to withdraw; to make off; to keep out of the way.

hurto *nm* (**a**) (*act*) theft, robbery; (*in general*) thieving, robbery; — **doméstico** burglary, housebreaking; **a** — stealthily, by stealth, on the sly.

(**b**) thing stolen, (piece of) stolen property, loot.

húsar *nm* hussar.

husillo *nm* (**a**) (*Mech*) spindle, shaft; (*of a press etc*) screw, worm. (**b**) drain.

husma *nf* snooping, prying; **andar a la** — to go snooping around, go prying (*de* after, for).

husmear [la] **1** *vt* (**a**) to scent, get wind of, sniff out.

(**b**) (*fig*) to smell out; to nose into, pry into.

2 *vi* (*of meat*) to (begin to) smell high, be smelly.

husmeo *nm* (**a**) scenting. (**b**) (*fig*) smelling-out; prying, snooping.

husmo *nm* high smell, strong smell, gaminess; **estar al** — to watch one's chance.

huso *nm* (**a**) (*Tech*) spindle; bobbin; (*of lathe, windlass*) drum. (**b**) (*Chi*) kneecap.

huy *interj* (*pain*) ow!, ouch!; (*surprise*) well!; (*relief*) phew!

huyente *adj* forehead receding.

huyón (*SAm*) **1** *adj* cowardly; shy, unsociable. **2** *nm* coward; shy person, unsociable person.

I

iba *etc see* **ir.**
Iberia *f* Iberia.
ibérico *adj* Iberian.
ibero, íbero 1 *adj* Iberian. **2** *nm*, **ibera** *nf*, **íbera** *nf* Iberian.
Iberoamérica *f* Latin America.
iberoamericano 1 *adj* Latin-American. **2** *nm*, **iberoamericana** *nf* Latin-American.
íbice *nm* ibex.
ibicenco 1 *adj* of Ibiza. **2** *nm*, **ibicenca** *nf* native (*or* inhabitant) of Ibiza; **los —s** the people of Ibiza.
ibis *nf*, *pl* **ibis** ibis.
ibón *nm* Pyrenean lake, tarn.
iceberg *nm* [iθe'βer], *pl* **icebergs** [iθe'βer] iceberg.
—ico, —ica *n and adj etc suffix* (*regional variation; in some combinations* —(e)cico, —(e)cica): *see* **—ito.**
icono *nm* ikon, icon.
iconoclasta 1 *adj* iconoclastic. **2** *nmf* iconoclast.
ictericia *nf* jaundice.
id *nm* id.
ida *nf* **(a)** going, departure; **—s y venidas** comings and goings; **en dos —s y venía** in an instant; **dejar las —s por las venidas** to miss the boat; **(viaje de) —** outward journey, trip out; **— y vuelta** round trip.
　(b) (*Hunting*) track, trail.
　(c) (*fig*) rash act; rashness, hastiness.
idea *nf* **(a)** idea, notion; **— faro** (*fam*), **— genial, — luminosa** bright idea, brilliant idea; **— fija** fixed idea, obsession, idée fixe; **— monstruo** fantastic idea; **una persona de mala —** a malicious person, an evil-minded person; **¡ni —!** I haven't a clue!, search me! (*fam*); **meterse una — en la cabeza** to get an idea into one's head; **no tengo la menor —, no tengo la más remota —** I haven't the faintest (*or* foggiest) idea; **no tenía la menor — de que . . .** I had no idea that . . .
　(b) idea, opinion, estimate; **¿qué — tienes de él?** what impression do you have of him?; **darse una — de, hacerse una — de** to get an idea of, form an impression of.
　(c) idea, intention; **con la — de + infin** with the idea of + *ger*; **cambiar de —, mudar de —** to change one's mind; **hace falta que cambie de —** he'll have to alter his outlook; he'll have to buck his ideas up; **llevar — de + infin** to have the idea of + *ger*, intend to + *infin*.
　(d) ingenuity, inventiveness.
ideación *nf* conception, thinking-out.
ideal 1 *adj* ideal; **nuestra casa —** our ideal house, our dream house. **2** *nm* ideal.
idealismo *nm* idealism.
idealista 1 *adj* idealistic **2** *nmf* idealist.
idealización *nf* idealization.
idealizar [1f] *vt* to idealize.
idealmente *adv* ideally.
idear [1a] *vt* to think up; to contrive, invent, devise; to plan, design.
ideario *nm* set of ideas; ideology; ideological formation.
ideático *adj* **(a)** (*SAm*) eccentric, having odd ideas, full of whims. **(b)** (*Hond*) ingenious, full of ideas.
ídem 1 *pron* ditto, the same, idem. **2** *nm*: **ser un — de lienzo** to be another of the same sort, be tarred with the same brush.
idénticamente *adv* identically.
idéntico *adj* identical; the same, the very same.
identidad *nf* identity; sameness, similarity.
identificación *nf* identification; **— errónea** mistaken identity.
identificar [1g] **1** *vt* to identify; to recognize, spot, pick out; **víctima sin —** unidentified victim. **2 identificarse** *vr*: **— con** to identify oneself with.

ideología *nf* ideology.
ideológico *adj* ideological.
ideólogo *nm* ideologist.
ideoso *adj* (Arg, Bol, Mex) full of strange notions; odd, eccentric; nervous, suspicious.
idílico *adj* idyllic.
idilio *nm* idyll.
idioma *nm* language; (*of group*) speech, idiom.
idiomático *adj* language (*attr*), linguistic; idiomatic.
idiosincrasia *nf* idiosyncrasy.
idiosincrásico *adj* idiosyncratic.
idiota 1 *adj* idiotic, stupid. **2** *nmf* idiot; **¡—!** you idiot!
idiotez *nf* idiocy.
idiotismo *nm* **(a)** (*Gram*) idiom, idiomatic expression. **(b)** ignorance.
idiotizar [1f] *vt* (*SAm*): **— a uno** to drive someone crazy.
ido 1 *adj* (*fam*) **(a)** (*SAm*) absent-minded.
　(b) (*SAm*) potty (*fam*), barmy (*sl*); **estar — (de la cabeza)** to be crazy, be wild.
　(c) (*CAm, Mex*) tight.
　2 *nmpl*: **los —s** the dead, the departed.
idólatra 1 *adj* idolatrous. **2** *nmf* idolater, (*f*) idolatress.
idolatrar [1a] *vt* to worship, adore; (*fig*) to idolize.
idolatría *nf* idolatry.
idolátrico *adj* idolatrous.
ídolo *nm* idol.
idoneidad *nf* suitability, fitness; aptitude, ability.
idóneo *adj* suitable, fit, fitting.
idus *nmpl* ides.
iglesia *nf* church; **I— Anglicana** Church of England, Anglican Church; **— catedral** cathedral; **I— Católica** Catholic Church; **— colegial** collegiate church; **— parroquial** parish church; **casarse por la —** to get married in church, have a church wedding; **casarse por detrás de la —** to set up house together, form a permanent union (without benefit of clergy); **cumplir con la —** to fulfil one's religious obligations; **llevar a una a la —** to lead someone to the altar; **¡con la — hemos topado!** now we're really up against it!
iglesiero *adj* (*SAm*) churchy (*fam*), much given to church-going.
iglú *nm* igloo.
Ignacio *m* Ignatius.
ignaro *adj* ignorant.
ígneo *adj* igneous.
ignición *nf* ignition.
ignominia *nf* ignominy, shame, disgrace.
ignominiosamente *adv* ignominiously, shamefully.
ignominioso *adj* ignominious, shameful, disgraceful.
ignorado *adj* unknown; obscure, little-known.
ignorancia *nf* ignorance; **por —** through ignorance.
ignorante 1 *adj* ignorant; uninformed. **2** *nmf* ignoramus.
ignorar [1a] *vt* **(a)** not to know, be ignorant of, be unaware of; **lo ignoro en absoluto** I don't know at all, I've no idea; **ignoramos su paradero** we don't know his whereabouts; **no ignoro que . . .** I am fully aware that . . . , of course I know that . . .
　(b) (*SAm: angl*) to ignore.
ignoto *adj* unknown; undiscovered.
igual 1 *adj* **(a)** equal (*a* to); (the) same; alike, similar; **no vi nunca cosa —** I never saw the like; **1 kilómetro es — a 1.000 metros** a kilometre is equal to 1,000 metres, a kilometre equals 1,000 metres; **A es — a B** A is like B, A is the same as B; **es — it** makes no difference, it's all the same; **me es —** it's all the same to me.
　(b) even, level; uniform, constant, unvarying, unchanging; smooth; *temperature* even; *climate* equable; **ir —es** (*in race*) to be level, be even.

(c) — que (as prep) like, the same as; **A,** — que **B, no sabe** A, like B, doesn't know.

(d) al — que (as prep or conj) like, just like; while, whereas; **Chile, al** — que **Argentina, estima que . . .** Chile, (just) like Argentina, thinks that . . .

2 nmf equal; **al** —, **por** — equally, on an equal basis; **sin** — without equal, matchless; **ser el** — **de** to be the equal of, be a match for; **no tener** — to be unrivalled, have no equal; **alternar de** — **a** — to be on an equal footing; **tratar a uno de** — **a** — to treat someone as an equal.

3 nm (Math) equals sign, sign of equality.

iguala nf **(a)** equalization. **(b)** (Comm) agreement; agreed fee.

igualación nf equalization; evening up, levelling; (Math) equating.

igualada nf (Sport) equalizer, equalizing goal (etc).

igualado adj (Guat, Mex) free and easy, excessively familiar (to a superior); (Mex, Nic) cheeky; (Salv) sly.

igualar [1a] **1** vt **(a)** to equalize, make equal; (Math) to equate (a to); (fig) to compare, match (a with).

(b) to level, level off, level up; to even, even out; to smooth; (fig) to even out, adjust.

(c) (Comm) to agree upon.

2 vi and **igualarse** vr **(a)** to be equal; — **a**, — **con** to equal, be equal to, be the equal of.

(b) (Sport) to equalize, score the equalizer; to tie.

(c) (Comm) to come to an agreement.

(d) (Guat, Mex) to be excessively familiar (to a superior).

igualatorio nm (Med) association.

igualdad nf **(a)** equality; sameness; (Math) equality; — **de retribución** equal pay; **en** — **de condiciones** on the same conditions, on an equal basis.

(b) evenness, levelness; uniformity; smoothness; — **de ánimo** equanimity.

igualitariedad nf egalitarianism.

igualitario adj egalitarian.

igualmente adv **(a)** equally.

(b) evenly; uniformly.

(c) likewise, also.

(d) (replying to good wishes etc) the same to you.

iguana nf iguana.

ijada nf **(a)** flank, side, loin. **(b)** (Med) stitch, pain in the side; **esto tiene su** — this has its weak side.

ijadear [1a] vi (Zool) to pant.

ijar nm flank, side.

ilación nf inference; connection, relationship; sequence.

ilativo adj inferential; (Gram) illative.

ilegal adj illegal, unlawful.

ilegalidad nf illegality, unlawfulness.

ilegalmente adv illegally, unlawfully.

ilegible adj illegible, unreadable.

ilegítimamente adv illegitimately.

ilegitimidad nf illegitimacy.

ilegítimo adj **(a)** illegitimate; unlawful. **(b)** false, spurious.

ilerdense 1 adj of Lérida. **2** nmf native (or inhabitant) of Lérida; **los** —**s** the people of Lérida.

ileso adj unhurt, unharmed; untouched; **salió** — **del accidente** he came out of the accident unharmed, he got out of the accident unscathed; **los pasajeros resultaron** —**s** the passengers were unhurt.

iletrado adj uncultured, illiterate.

Ilíada nf Iliad.

iliberal adj illiberal.

ilícitamente adv illicitly, illegally, unlawfully.

ilicitano 1 adj of Elche. **2** nm, **ilicitana** nf native (or inhabitant) of Elche; **los** —**s** the people of Elche.

ilícito adj illicit, illegal, unlawful.

ilimitado adj unlimited, limitless, unbounded.

ilógicamente adv illogically.

ilógico adj illogical.

iluminación nf **(a)** illumination, lighting; floodlighting; — **indirecta** indirect lighting. **(b)** (fig) enlightenment.

iluminado 1 adj illuminated, lighted, lit; **estar** — (fam) to be lit up (sl). **2** nm, **iluminada** nf visionary; illuminist; **los I**—**s** the Illuminati.

iluminador 1 adj illuminating. **2** nm illuminator.

iluminar [1a] vt **(a)** to illuminate, light, light up; to floodlight. **(b)** (fig) to enlighten.

ilusión nf **(a)** illusion; delusion; — **de óptica** optical illusion; **todo es** — it's all an illusion.

(b) (unfounded) hope, dream; piece of wishful thinking; hopefulness; **con** — hopefully; **el hombre de sus** —**es** the man of her dreams; **su** — **era comprarlo** her dream was to buy it, she dreamed of buying it; **forjarse** —**es, hacerse** —**es** to build up

(false) hopes, deceive oneself with false hopes, indulge in wishful thinking; **no te hagas** —**es** don't get any false ideas; **se hace la** — **de que . . .** she fondly imagines that **. . . ; tendió la mano con** — she put her hand out hopefully.

(c) excitement, thrill; eagerness; hopeful anticipation; **¡qué** —**!** how thrilling!, how exciting!; **comer con** — to eat eagerly; **trabajar con** — to work with a will; **el viaje me hace mucha** — I am so looking forward to the trip, I am getting very excited about the trip; **tu carta me hizo mucha** — I was thrilled to get your letter; **me hace una gran** — **que . . .** it gives me a thrill that . . .

ilusionado 1 adj hopeful; excited, eager; **el viaje me trae muy** — I am so looking forward to the trip, I am getting very excited about the trip.

2 nm, **ilusionada** nf hopeful; **joven** — young hopeful.

ilusionar [1a] **1** vt (SAm) to deceive; to give grounds for false hopes to, encourage falsely.

2 ilusionarse vr to have unfounded hopes, indulge in wishful thinking; **no te ilusiones** don't get any false ideas.

ilusionismo nm **(a)** wishful thinking. **(b)** conjuring.

ilusionista nmf conjurer, illusionist.

iluso 1 adj easily deceived; deluded. **2** nm, **ilusa** nf dreamer, visionary; **¡**—**!** you're hopeful!

ilusorio adj illusory, deceptive, unreal; empty, ineffectual.

ilustración nf **(a)** illustration.

(b) illustration, picture, drawing.

(c) learning, erudition; enlightenment; **la I**— the Enlightenment, the Age of Enlightenment (18th century).

ilustrado adj **(a)** illustrated. **(b)** learned, erudite; enlightened.

ilustrador 1 adj illustrative; enlightening. **2** nm, **ilustradora** nf illustrator.

ilustrar [1a] **1** vt **(a)** to illustrate.

(b) to explain, elucidate, make clear.

(c) to instruct, enlighten.

(d) to make famous, make illustrious.

2 ilustrarse vr **(a)** to acquire knowledge, become enlightened.

(b) to become famous.

ilustrativo adj illustrative.

ilustre adj illustrious, famous.

ilustrísimo adj most illustrious; **Su Ilustrísima** His Grace; **Vuestra Ilustrísima** Your Grace.

illanco nm (Per) slow stream, quiet-flowing stream.

—illo, —illa n and adj etc suffix (in some combinations —(e)cillo, —(e)cilla): see —**ito**.

imagen nf **(a)** image; (mental) picture; likeness; **ser la viva** — **de** to be the living image of; **hacer a uno a su** — to make somebody in one's own image.

(b) (Eccl) image, statue; **quedar para vestir imágenes** to be an old maid.

(c) (TV) picture; — **fantasma** ghost image.

(d) (Lit) image; **imágenes** (collectively) imagery.

imaginable adj imaginable, conceivable.

imaginación nf imagination; fancy; **ni por** — on no account; **no se me pasó por la** — **que . . .** it never even occurred to me that **. . . ; ella se deja llevar por la** — she lets her imagination run away with her.

imaginar [1a] **1** vt to imagine; to visualize; to think up, invent; **cosas que nadie imagina** things that no-one imagines; **¿quién imaginó esto?** who thought this one up?

2 vi and **imaginarse** vr to imagine, fancy, suppose; to picture (to oneself); **¡imagínate!** just imagine!, just fancy!; **imagínese que . . .** suppose that **. . .**, imagine that **. . . ; me imagino que . . .** I suppose that **. . . ; sí, me imagino** yes, I can imagine.

imaginaria nf (Mil) guard, night guard.

imaginario adj imaginative.

imaginativa nf imagination, imaginativeness.

imaginativo adj imaginary, fanciful.

imaginería nf **(a)** (Eccl) images, statues. **(b)** (Llt) imagery.

imaginero nm maker (or painter) of religious images.

imán nm magnet (also fig); — **de herradura** horseshoe magnet.

iman(t)ación nf magnetization.

iman(t)ar [1a] vt to magnetize.

imbatible adj unbeatable.

imbatido adj unbeaten.

imbécil 1 adj **(a)** (Med) imbecile, feeble-minded. **(b)** silly, stupid.

2 nmf **(a)** (Med) imbecile.

(b) imbecile, idiot; **¡**—**!** you idiot!

imbecilidad nf (a) (Med) imbecility, feeble-mindedness. (b) silliness, stupidity, idiocy; **decir —es** to say silly things.

imberbe adj beardless.

imbibición nf imbibing.

imbíbito adj (Guat, Mex) included (in the total).

imbombera nf (Ven) pernicious anaemia.

imbombo adj (Ven) anaemic.

imbornal nm scupper; **irse por los —es** (SAm) to get off the beam, wander.

imborrable adj ineffaceable, indelible.

imbricación nf (esp SAm) overlapping; interweaving, interdependence.

imbricar [1g] (SAm) **1** vt to overlap; to interweave. **2 imbricarse** vr to overlap; to be interwoven.

imbuir [3g] vt to imbue, infuse (de, en with); **imbuido de la cultura de** imbued with the culture of, full of the culture of.

imbunchar [1a] vt (Chi) (a) to bewitch. (b) to swindle, cheat.

imbunche nm (Chi) (a) spell, piece of witchcraft. (b) mess; fuss, row.

imitable adj imitable.

imitación nf (a) imitation; mimicry; **a — de** in imitation of; **desconfíe de las —es** (Comm) beware of imitations.
(b) **de —** imitation (attr); **joyas de —** imitation jewellery.
(c) (Theat) imitation, impersonation.

imitador 1 adj imitative. **2** nm, **imitadora** nf imitator; follower; (Theat) imitator, impersonator.

imitar [1a] vt (a) to imitate; to mimic, ape; to follow. (b) to counterfeit.

imitativo adj imitative.

impaciencia nf impatience.

impacientar [1a] **1** vt to make impatient; to irritate, exasperate.
2 impacientarse vr to get impatient (ante, por about, at; con with), lose patience, get worked up; to fret; **— por + infin** to be impatient to + infin.

impaciente adj impatient; anxious; fretful.

impacientemente adv impatiently; anxiously; fretfully.

impacto nm impact; (Mil) hit; (SAm: Boxing) punch, blow; **— directo** (Mil) direct hit; **— político** political impact.

impagable adj unpayable.

impagado adj unpaid, still to be paid.

impago 1 adj unpaid, still to be paid. **2** nm non-payment.

impalpable adj impalpable.

impar 1 adj (Math) odd; **los números —es** the odd numbers. **2** nm odd number.

imparable adj (Sport) unstoppable.

imparcial adj impartial, unbiassed, fair.

imparcialidad nf impartiality, lack of bias, fairness.

imparcialmente adv impartially, fairly.

impartible adj indivisible.

impartir [3a] vt teaching etc to impart, give, convey; order to give.

impase nm (Bridge) finesse; **hacer el — a uno** to finesse against someone.

impasible adj impassive, unmoved.

impávidamente adv (a) intrepidly; dauntlessly. (b) (SAm) cheekily.

impavidez nf (a) intrepidity; dauntlessness. (b) (SAm) cheek, cheekiness.

impávido adj (a) intrepid; dauntless, undaunted. (b) (SAm) cheeky.

impecable adj impeccable, faultless.

impecablemente adv impeccably, faultlessly.

impedido adj crippled, disabled; **estar — para algo** to be unfit for something.

impedimenta nf (Mil) impedimenta.

impedimento nm (a) impediment (also Law), obstacle, hindrance. (b) disability.

impedir [3l] vt (a) to impede, obstruct, hinder, hamper; to deter; **— el tráfico** to block the traffic, obstruct the traffic.
(b) to stop, prevent; to thwart; **— algo a uno** to keep someone from doing something, to make something impossible for someone; **— a uno hacer algo, — que uno haga algo** to stop someone doing something, prevent someone (from) doing something; **me veo impedido para ayudar** I find it impossible for me to help; **lo que no se puede —** what cannot be prevented.

impeditivo adj preventive.

impeler [2a] vt (a) (Mech) to drive, propel.
(b) to drive, impel; to urge; **— a uno a hacer algo** to drive someone to do something; to urge someone to do something; **impelido por la necesidad** impelled by necessity.

impenetrabilidad nf impenetrability.

impenetrable adj impenetrable (also fig); impervious; (fig) obscure, incomprehensible.

impenitencia nf impenitence.

impenitente adj impenitent, unrepentant.

impensable adj unthinkable.

impensadamente adv (a) unexpectedly. (b) at random, by chance. (c) inadvertently.

impensado adj (a) unexpected, unforeseen. (b) random, chance (attr).

impepinable adj (fam) certain, inevitable.

impepinablemente adv (fam) inevitably; **— se le olvida** he's sure to forget, he always forgets.

imperante adj ruling (also Comm), prevailing.

imperar [1a] vi (a) to rule, reign; to be in command. (b) (fig) to reign, prevail; (of price etc) to be in force, be current.

imperativamente adv (a) imperatively. (b) say etc imperiously, in a commanding tone.

imperativo 1 adj (a) imperative (also Gram). (b) imperious, commanding. **2** nm imperative (mood).

imperceptible adj imperceptible, undiscernible.

imperceptiblemente adv imperceptibly.

imperdible nm safety pin.

imperdonable adj unpardonable, unforgivable, inexcusable.

imperdonablemente adv unpardonably, inexcusably.

imperecedero adj imperishable, undying.

imperfección nf imperfection; flaw, fault, blemish.

imperfectamente adv imperfectly.

imperfecto 1 adj (a) imperfect, faulty. (b) unfinished, incomplete. (c) (Gram) imperfect. **2** nm imperfect (tense).

imperial 1 adj imperial. **2** nf (of bus) top, upper deck; (of coach) top, roof.

imperialismo nm imperialism.

imperialista 1 adj imperialist(ic). **2** nmf imperialist.

imperialmente adv imperially.

impericia nf unskilfulness; lack of experience, inexperience; **a prueba de —** foolproof.

imperio nm (a) empire; **I— Español** Spanish Empire; **vale un —, vale siete —s** it's worth a fortune. (b) rule, authority; sway. (c) (fig) haughtiness, pride.

imperiosamente adv (a) imperiously. (b) urgently; imperatively, overridingly.

imperioso adj (a) imperious; lordly. (b) urgent; imperative, overriding; **necesidad imperiosa** absolute necessity, pressing need.

imperito adj inexpert, unskilled; inexperienced; clumsy.

impermanente adv impermanent.

impermeabilidad nf impermeability, imperviousness.

impermeabilizar [1f] vt to waterproof, make waterproof.

impermeable 1 adj impermeable, impervious (a to); waterproof. **2** nm raincoat, mackintosh, mac.

impersonal adj impersonal.

impersonalidad nf impersonality.

impersonalismo nm (SAm) disinterestedness.

impersonalmente adv impersonally.

impertérrito adj unafraid, unshaken, undaunted.

impertinencia nf (a) irrelevance. (b) fussiness; peevishness. (c) impertinence; intrusion.

impertinente 1 adj (a) irrelevant, not pertinent; uncalled for. (b) touchy, fussy; peevish. (c) impertinent; intrusive. **2 —s** nmpl lorgnette.

impertinentemente adv (a) irrelevantly. (b) impertinently.

imperturbable adj imperturbable; unruffled, unflappable; impassive.

imperturbablemente adv imperturbably; impassively.

imperturbado adj unperturbed.

impétigo nm impetigo.

impetrar [1a] vt to beg for, beseech.

ímpetu nm (a) impetus, impulse; momentum. (b) rush, onrush. (c) haste; violence; impetuosity.

impetuosamente adv impetuously, impulsively; violently; hastily.

impetuosidad nf impetuousness, impulsiveness; violence; haste, hastiness.

impetuoso adj person impetuous, impulsive; headstrong; torrent etc rushing, violent; act hasty, impetuous.

impiedad nf impiety, ungodliness; wickedness, cruelty; pitilessness, heartlessness.

impío adj impious, ungodly; wicked, cruel; pitiless, heartless.

implacable adj implacable, relentless, inexorable.

implacablemente adv implacably, relentlessly, inexorably.

implantación nf implantation; introduction.

implantar [1a] vt to implant; to introduce.

implementar [1a] (SAm) **1** vt to implement. **2** vi to help, give aid.

implemento nm (SAm) means; tool, implement; (Agr) implement.

implicación nf (a) contradiction (in terms). (b) involvement, implication, complicity. (c) (SAm) implication.

implicancia nf (SAm) implication.

implicar [1g] vt (a) to implicate, involve. (b) to imply; **esto no implica que ... this does not imply that ...**, this does not mean that ...

implícitamente adv implicitly.

implícito adj implicit, implied.

imploración nf supplication, entreaty.

implorar [1a] vt to implore, beg.

implume adj featherless; unfledged.

impolítico adj (a) impolitic, imprudent, tactless, undiplomatic. (b) impolite.

impoluto adj unpolluted, pure.

imponderable 1 adj imponderable; inexpressible, unutterable. **2** –s nmpl imponderables.

imponencia nf (SAm) imposing character, impressiveness; stateliness, grandness.

imponente 1 adj (a) imposing, impressive; stately, grand. (b) terrific (fam), tremendous (fam), smashing (sl).
2 nmf (Comm, Fin) investor; depositor; lender.

imponer [2r] **1** vt (a) (general sense) to impose; (Eccl, Typ) to impose; obligation, penalty, silence etc to impose (a on); burden to lay, thrust (a upon); task to set; tax to put, impose (a, sobre on).
(b) obedience etc to exact (a from), demand (a from), enforce (a upon); respect to command (a from); fear etc to inspire (a in).
(c) to impute falsely (a to).
(d) to inform, instruct (en in).
(e) (Comm, Fin) to invest, deposit.
(f) (Mex) to accustom; **estoy impuesto a madrugar** I'm used to getting up early.
2 imponerse vr (a) **– un deber** to assume a duty, take on a duty.
(b) to assert oneself, get one's way; **– a to** dominate, impose one's authority on, exact obedience from.
(c) to prevail (a over); (of custom) to grow up; **se impondrá el buen sentido** good sense will prevail.
(d) to be necessary, to impose itself; **la conclusión se impone** the conclusion is inescapable, the conclusion imposes itself.
(e) **– de** to acquaint oneself with, inform oneself about.
(f) (Mex) to get accustomed (a + infin to + infin).

imponible adj (Fin) taxable, subject to tax; dutiable, subject to duty; **no – free** of tax, tax-free, tax-exempt (US).

impopular adj unpopular.

impopularidad nf unpopularity.

importación nf (a) importation, importing; **artículo de – imported** article; **comercio de – import** trade. (b) import; imports.

importador nm, **importadora** nf importer.

importancia nf importance; significance; weight; size, magnitude; **de cierta – of** some importance; **sin – unimportant**, insignificant, minor; **carecer de – to** be unimportant; **conceder (or dar) mucha – a to** attach great importance to, make much of, put the emphasis on; **no dar – a to** consider unimportant; to make light of; **darse – to** give oneself airs; **restar – a to** diminish the importance of; to make light of; **no tiene – it's** nothing, it's not important.

importante adj (a) important; significant, weighty, momentous; **lo – es ..., lo más – es ... the** main thing is ...; **poco – unimportant**.
(b) loss, quantity, sum considerable, sizeable.

importantizarse [1f] vr (Ven) to give oneself airs.

importar¹ [1a] vt (Comm) to import (a, en into; de from).

importar² [1a] **1** vt (a) (Fin) to amount to; to cost, be worth; **la cuenta importa 5 pesos** the bill amounts to 5 pesos; **el libro importa 5 dólares** the book costs 5 dollars.
(b) to involve, imply, carry with it.
2 vi to be important, be of consequence, matter;

– a to concern; **esto importa mucho** this is very important; **no importa** it doesn't matter; **¡no importa!** never mind!; **¿qué importa?** what does it matter?, what difference does it make?; who cares?; **no le importa** he doesn't care, it doesn't bother him; **(no) me importa un bledo** (or **higo** etc) I don't care two hoots (de about); **¿te importa prestármelo?** would you mind lending it to me?; **no le importa conducir todo el día** he doesn't mind driving all day; **"no importa precio"** (adverts) "cost no object"; **lo comprará a no importa que precio** he'll buy it at any price, he'll buy it regardless of the price; **iremos no importa el tiempo que haga** we'll go whatever the weather.

importe nm amount; value, cost; **– total** final total, grand total; **hasta el – de** up to the amount of; **el – de esta factura** the amount of this bill.

importunación nf importuning, pestering.

importunar [1a] vt to importune, bother, pester.

importunidad nf (a) importunity, pestering. (b) annoyance.

importuno adj (a) importunate, troublesome, annoying. (b) inopportune, ill-timed.

imposibilidad nf (a) impossibility. (b) **mi – para + infin** my inability to + infin.

imposibilitado adj (a) (Med) disabled, crippled; (Fin) helpless, without means.
(b) **estar – para + infin, verse – para + infin** to be unable to + infin, be prevented from + ger.

imposibilitar [1a] vt (a) to disable; to make unfit, incapacitate (para for).
(b) to make impossible, preclude, prevent; **esto me imposibilita hacerlo** this makes it impossible for me to do it, this prevents me from doing it.

imposible 1 adj (a) impossible; intolerable, unbearable; **es – it's** impossible, it's out of the question; **es – de toda imposibilidad** it's utterly impossible; **es – de predecir** it's impossible to forecast.
(b) person difficult, awkward, impossible.
(c) (SAm) slovenly, dirty, repulsive.
2 nm the impossible; impossible thing; **hacer los –s to** do one's utmost (para + infin to + infin).

imposición nf (a) (general sense) imposition.
(b) (Comm, Fin) tax, impost, imposition.
(c) (Typ) imposition, make-up.
(d) (Fin) deposit; **efectuar una – to** make a deposit; to deposit money.
(e) (Eccl) **– de manos** laying-on of hands.

impositiva nf (SAm) tax office.

impositivo adj (a) (SAm) tax (attr); **sistema – taxation**, tax system. (b) (Arg) authoritative, domineering; imperative.

impositor nm (Fin) depositor.

impostor nm, **impostora** nf (a) impostor, fraud. (b) slanderer.

impostura nf (a) imposture, fraud; sham. (b) aspersion, slur, slander.

impotable adj undrinkable.

impotencia nf (a) impotence, powerlessness, helplessness. (b) (Med) impotence.

impotente (a) impotent, powerless, helpless. (b) (Med) impotent.

impracticabilidad nf impracticability.

impracticable adj (a) impracticable, unworkable. (b) road impassable, unusable.

imprecación nf imprecation, curse.

imprecar [1g] vt to curse.

imprecisión nf lack of precision, vagueness.

impreciso adj imprecise, vague.

impredecible adj (CAm, Mex, PR), **impredictible** adj unpredictable.

impregnación nf impregnation.

impregnar [1a] vt to impregnate (de with); to saturate (de with); (fig) to pervade.

impremeditado adj unpremeditated.

imprenta nf (a) printing, art of printing. (b) press, printing house, printing office. (c) print, letterpress. (d) printed matter.

imprentar [1a] vt (a) (Chi: Sew) to put a permanent crease into. (b) (SAm) to mark.

imprescindible adj essential, indispensable; **cosas –s** essential things, things one cannot do without; **es – que ... it** is essential that ..., it is imperative that ...

impresentable adj unpresentable.

impresión nf (a) impression; imprint; **– dactilar, – digital** fingerprint.
(b) (Typ) printing; print; edition, impression, issue; **quinta – fifth** impression; **una – de 5.000 ejemplares** an edition of 5,000 copies; **– en color(es)** colour printing.
(c) (Phot) print.

(d) (*fig*) impression; **cambiar —es** to exchange impressions, compare notes; **da la — de** + *infin* it gives the impression of + *ger*; **formarse una — de** to get an idea of; **hacer buena —** to make a good impression, impress; **no me hizo buena —** I was not impressed (with it); **¿qué — te produjo?** how did it impress you?, what impression did it make on you?; **tener la — de que . . .** to have the impression that . . .

impresionable *adj* impressionable.

impresionado *adj* **(a)** impressed. **(b)** (*Phot*) exposed; **excesivamente —** overexposed.

impresionante *adj* impressive; striking; moving, affecting.

impresionar [1a] **1** *vt* **(a)** *record* to cut; (*Phot*) to expose; **película sin —** unexposed film.

(b) (*fig*) to impress, strike; to move, affect; **me impresionó mucho** it greatly impressed me; **no se deja fácilmente —** he is not easily impressed.

2 *vi* to impress, make an impression; **lo hace sólo para —** he just does it to impress.

3 impresionarse *vr* to be impressed; to be moved, be affected.

impresionismo *nm* impressionism.

impresionista **1** *adj* impressionist(ic). **2** *nm* impressionist.

impreso **1** *adj* printed. **2** *nm* **(a)** printed paper, printed book (*etc*). **(b)** form; **— de solicitud** application form. **(c)** **—s** printed matter.

impresor *nm* printer.

imprevisible *adj* unforeseeable; *person* unpredictable.

imprevisión *nf* improvidence; lack of foresight; thoughtlessness.

imprevisor *adj* improvident; lacking foresight; thoughtless, happy-go-lucky.

imprevisto **1** *adj* unforeseen, unexpected. **2 —s** *nmpl* incidentals, unforeseen expenses.

imprimar [1a] *vt* (*Art*) to prime.

imprimátur *nm* imprimatur.

imprimible *adj* printable.

imprimir [3a; *ptp* **impreso**] *vt* **(a)** to imprint, impress, stamp (*a, en* on; *also fig*). **(b)** (*Typ*) to print.

improbabilidad *nf* improbability, unlikelihood.

improbable *adj* improbable, unlikely.

improbidad *nf* dishonesty.

improbo *adj* **(a)** dishonest, corrupt. **(b)** *task* arduous, thankless, tough; *effort etc* tremendous, awful, strenuous.

improcedencia *nf* **(a)** wrongness; inappropriateness, inapplicability. **(b)** (*Law*) inadmissibility.

improcedente *adj* **(a)** wrong, not right; inappropriate, inapplicable. **(b)** (*Law*) unfounded, inadmissible.

improductivo *adj* unproductive.

impronta *nf* stamp, impress, impression; (*fig*) stamp, mark.

impronunciable *adj* unpronounceable.

improperio *nm* insult, taunt.

impropiamente *adv* improperly; inappropriately, unsuitably.

impropicio *adj* inauspicious, unpropitious.

impropiedad *nf* **(a)** inappropriateness, unsuitability. **(b)** impropriety, infelicity (of language).

impropio *adj* improper (*also Math, Gram*); inappropriate, unsuitable; **— de** inappropriate for; unbecoming to; foreign to.

impróvidamente *adv* improvidently.

impróvido *adj* improvident.

improvisación *nf* improvisation; (*Mus*) extemporization, impromptu.

improvisado *adj* improvised; makeshift; (*Mus etc*) extempore, impromptu.

improvisamente *adv* unexpectedly, suddenly.

improvisar [1a] *vi* to improvise; (*Mus etc*) to extemporize.

improviso *adj* **(a)** unexpected, unforeseen. **(b)** **al —, de —** unexpectedly, suddenly; on the spur of the moment; **hablar de —** to speak extempore, speak unprepared; **tocar de —** to play impromptu.

improvisto *adj* unexpected, unforeseen; **de —** unexpectedly, suddenly.

imprudencia *nf* imprudence; rashness; indiscretion; carelessness.

imprudente *adj* unwise; imprudent; rash; indiscreet; *driver etc* rash, careless; ill-judged.

imprudentemente *adv* unwisely, imprudently; rashly; carelessly.

impublicable *adj* unprintable.

impudencia *nf* shamelessness, brazenness.

impudente *adj* shameless, brazen.

impúdicamente *adv* immodestly, shamelessly; lewdly; lecherously.

impudicia *nf* immodesty, shamelessness; lewdness; lechery.

impúdico *adj* immodest, shameless; lewd; lecherous.

impudor *nm* = **impudicia**.

impuesto **1** *ptp of* **imponer**; **estar — de, quedar — de** to be informed about; **estar — en** to be well versed in. **2** *nm* tax; duty, levy (*sobre* on); **—s** taxes, (*collectively, as system*) taxation; **sujeto a —** taxable, dutiable; **— sobre apuestas** betting tax; **— sobre los bienes heredados, — sobre herencias, —sobre las sucesiones** estate duty; **— sobre espectáculos** entertainments tax; **— de plusvalía** capital gains tax; **— sobre la propiedad** property tax; **— sobre la renta** income tax; **— del timbre** stamp duty; **— de venta** sales tax, purchase tax.

impugnar [1a] *vt* to oppose, contest, challenge; *theory etc* to impugn, refute.

impulsador *nm* (*Aer*) booster.

impulsar [1a] = **impeler**.

impulsión *nf* **(a)** impulsion; (*Mech*) propulsion, drive; **— por correa** belt drive; **— por reacción** jet propulsion. **(b)** (*fig*) impulse.

impulsividad *nf* impulsiveness.

impulsivo *adj* impulsive.

impulso *nm* **(a)** impulse; (*Mech*) drive, thrust; impetus, momentum.

(b) (*fig*) impulse; stimulus, urge; **los —s del corazón** the promptings of the heart; **a —s del miedo** driven on by fear; **no resisto al — de decir que . . .** I can't resist saying that . . .

impulsor **1** *adj* drive (*attr*), driving. **2** *nm* drive.

impune *adj* unpunished.

impunemente *adv* with impunity.

impunidad *nf* impunity.

impuntual *adj* unpunctual.

impuntualidad *nf* unpunctuality.

impureza *nf* **(a)** impurity. **(b)** (*fig*) unchastity, lewdness.

impurificar [1g] *vt* **(a)** to adulterate, make impure. **(b)** (*fig*) to corrupt, defile.

impuro *adj* **(a)** impure. **(b)** (*fig*) impure, unchaste, lewd.

imputable *adj*: **fracasos que son —s a** failures which can be attributed to, failures which are attributable to.

imputación *nf* imputation.

imputar [1a] *vt*: **— a** to impute to, attribute to.

-in, -ina *n and adj etc suffix* (*regional variation*): *see* **-ito**.

inabordable *adj* unapproachable.

inacabable *adj* endless, interminable.

inacabablemente *adv* endlessly, interminably.

inacabado *adj* unfinished.

inaccesibilidad *nf* inaccessibility.

inaccesible *adj* inaccessible.

inacción *nf* inaction; inactivity, idleness; drift.

inacentuado *adj* unaccented, unstressed.

inaceptable *adj* unacceptable.

inactividad *nf* inactivity; laziness, idleness; (*Comm, Fin*) dullness.

inactivo *adj* inactive; lazy, idle; (*Comm, Fin*) dull.

inactual *adj* (*SAm*) lacking present validity, no longer applicable; old-fashioned, out-of-date.

inadaptable *adj* unadaptable.

inadaptación *nf* maladjustment; failure of adjustment, failure to adjust (*a* to).

inadaptado **1** *adj* maladjusted, who fails to adjust (*a* to). **2** *nm*, **inadaptada** *nf* misfit; person who fails to adjust.

inadecuación *nf* inadequacy; unsuitability, inappropriateness.

inadecuado *adj* inadequate; unsuitable, inappropriate.

inadmisibilidad *nf* inadmissibility.

inadmisible *adj* inadmissible.

inadvertencia *nf* **(a)** inadvertence; **por — inadvertently**, through inadvertence. **(b)** (*una —*) oversight, slip.

inadvertidamente *adv* inadvertently.

inadvertido *adj* **(a)** *person* unobservant, inattentive; careless. **(b)** unnoticed, unobserved; **pasar —** to escape notice, slip by.

inafectado *adj* unaffected.

inagotable *adj* inexhaustible.

inaguantable *adj* intolerable, unbearable.

inaguantablemente *adv* intolerably, unbearably.

inajenable *adj* inalienable; not transferable.

inalámbrico *adj* wireless.

inalcanzable *adj* unattainable.

inalienable *adj* inalienable; not transferable.

inalterabilidad *nf* inalterability, unchangingness; immutability.

inalterable *adj* unalterable, unchanging; immutable; *colour* fast; *gloss etc* permanent.

inalterado *adj* unchanged, unaltered.

inamistoso *adj* (SAm) unfriendly.

inamovible *adj* fixed, immovable; undetachable.

inanición *nf* starvation, (Med) inanition; **morir de** — to die of starvation.

inanidad *nf* inanity.

inánime *adj* lifeless.

inapagable *adj* unquenchable; inextinguishable.

inapeable *adj* (a) incomprehensible. (b) obstinate, stubborn.

inapelable *adj* (Law) unappealable; (fig) inevitable.

inapercibido *adj* unperceived.

inapetencia *nf* lack of appetite, loss of appetite.

inaplazable *adj* which cannot be postponed.

inaplicable *adj* inapplicable, not applicable.

inaplicado *adj* slack, lazy.

inapreciable *adj* invaluable, inestimable.

inaprehensible *adj* indefinite, hard to pin down.

inapto *adj* unsuited (*para* to).

inarmónico *adj* unharmonious, unmusical.

inarrugable *adj* crease-resisting, which does not crease.

inarticulado *adj* inarticulate.

inasequible *adj* unattainable, out of reach; unobtainable.

inasistencia *nf* absence.

inastillable *adj* *glass* unsplinterable, non-splinter.

inatacable *adj* unassailable.

inatención *nf* inattention.

inatento *adj* inattentive.

inaudible *adj* inaudible.

inaudito *adj* unheard-of; unprecedented; outrageous.

inauguración *nf* inauguration; opening; unveiling; **— privada** (Art) private view.

inaugural *adj* inaugural; opening; *voyage etc* maiden.

inaugurar [1a] *vt* to inaugurate; *bridge, canal, exhibition etc* to open (formally); *statue etc* to unveil.

inca *nmf* Inca.

incachable *adj* (SAm) useless.

incaico *adj* Inca.

incalculable *adj* incalculable.

incalificable *adj* indescribable, unspeakable.

incanato *nm* (Per) Inca period; reign of an Inca.

incandescencia *nf* incandescence; white heat; glow.

incandescente *adj* incandescent; white hot; glowing.

incansable *adj* tireless, untiring, unflagging.

incansablemente *adv* tirelessly, untiringly.

incapacidad *nf* incapacity; unfitness (*para* por); inadequacy, incompetence; **su — para** + *infin* his inability to + *infin*.

incapacitado *adj* incapacitated; unfitted (*para* for).

incapacitar [1a] *vt* to incapacitate, render unfit, handicap (*para* for); to disqualify (*para* for).

incapaz *adj* (a) incapable (*de* of); unfit; inadequate, incompetent; (Law) incompetent; **— de** + *infin* unable to + *infin*. (b) (Guat, Mex) child trying, difficult.

incario *nm* (Bol, Ec, Per) = **incanato**.

incasable *adj* unmarriageable.

incásico *adj* (SAm) Inca.

incautación *nf* seizure, confiscation.

incautamente *adv* unwarily, incautiously.

incautarse [1a] *vr:* **— de** to seize, confiscate, impound; to take possession of.

incauto *adj* unwary, incautious.

incendiar [1b] **1** *vt* to set on fire, set fire to, set alight; (fig) to kindle, inflame.
　2 incendiarse *vr* to catch fire.

incendiario 1 *adj* (a) incendiary.
　(b) (fig) inflammatory.
　2 *nm*, **incendiaria** *nf* fire-raiser, pyromaniac; incendiary; **— de la guerra** warmonger.

incendio *nm* fire; conflagration; **— intencionado**, **— malicioso**, **— premeditado** arson, fire-raising; **echar** (*or* **hablar**)**—s de uno** (Arg, Chi, Per) to speak ill of someone, curse someone; to attribute evil deeds to someone.

incensar [1k] *vt* (Eccl) to cense, incense; (fig) to flatter.

incensario *nm* censer.

incentivo *nm* incentive.

incertidumbre *nf* uncertainty, doubt.

incesable, **incesante** *adj* incessant, unceasing.

incesantemente *adv* incessantly, unceasingly.

incesto *nm* incest.

incestuoso *adj* incestuous.

incidencia *nf* (a) (Math etc) incidence. (b) incident.

incidental *adj* incidental.

incidente 1 *adj* incidental. **2** *nm* incident.

incidentemente *adv* incidentally.

incidir [3a] **1** *vt* (Med) to incise.
　2 *vi:* **— en** to fall upon; to influence, affect, impinge on; **— en un error** to fall into error; **el impuesto incide más en ellos** the tax falls most heavily on them, the tax affects them worst; **la familia ha incidido fuertemente en la historia** the family has influenced history a lot, the family has made itself strongly felt in history.

incienso *nm* (Eccl) incense; (Bib) frankincense; (fig) flattery.

inciertamente *adv* uncertainly.

incierto *adj* uncertain, doubtful; inconstant.

incineración *nf* incineration; **— de cadáveres** cremation.

incinerador *nm* incinerator.

incinerar [1a] *vt* to incinerate, burn; *corpse* to cremate.

incipiente *adj* incipient.

incircunciso *adj* uncircumcised.

incisión *nf* incision.

incisivo 1 *adj* sharp, cutting; (fig) incisive. **2** *nm* incisor.

inciso *nm* (Gram) clause, sentence; comma.

incitación *nf* incitement; provocation.

incitante *adj* provoking, provocative, inviting.

incitar [1a] *vt* to incite, rouse, spur on; **— a uno a hacer algo** to urge someone to do something; **— a uno contra otro** to incite someone against another person.

incivil *adj* uncivil, rude.

incivilidad *nf* incivility, rudeness; **una —** an incivility, a piece of rudeness.

incivilizado *adj* uncivilized.

inclasificable *adj* unclassifiable, nondescript.

inclemencia *nf* harshness, severity, inclemency; **la — del tiempo** the inclemency of the weather; **dejar algo a la —** to leave something exposed to wind and weather.

inclemente *adj* harsh, severe, inclement.

inclinación *nf* (a) inclination; slope, incline; slant, pitch, tilt; (*of body*) stoop; **— lateral** (Aer) bank; **a una — de 45 grados** at an inclination of 45 degrees.
　(b) bow; (*of head*) nod.
　(c) (fig) inclination, leaning, propensity; **de malas —es** evilly inclined.

inclinado *adj* (a) inclined, sloping, leaning, slanting; *plane* inclined.
　(b) (*esp* SAm: fig) **estar — a** + *infin* to be inclined to + *infin*.

inclinar [1a] **1** *vt* (a) to incline; to slope, slant, tilt; *head* to incline, bend, nod; to bow.
　(b) (fig) **— a uno a hacer algo** to induce someone to do something; to persuade someone to do something.
　2 *vi:* **— a uno** to take after someone, resemble someone.
　3 inclinarse *vr* (a) to incline; to slope, slant, tilt, be inclined.
　(b) (*person*) to stoop, bend; to bow; **— ante** (fig) to bow to, bow down before.
　(c) **— a uno** to take after someone, resemble someone.
　(d) **— a hacer algo** to be inclined to do something, tend to do something; **me inclino a decir que . . .** I am inclined to say that . . .

ínclito *adj* illustrious, renowned.

incluir [3g] *vt* to include; to comprise, contain; to incorporate; (*in letter*) to enclose; **todo incluido** (Comm) inclusive terms; all found, all-in.

inclusa *nf* foundling hospital.

inclusero *nm*, **inclusera** *nf* foundling.

inclusión *nf* inclusion; **con — de** including.

inclusivamente *adv* inclusive, inclusively.

inclusive 1 *adv* inclusive, inclusively. **2** *prep* including.

inclusivo *adj* inclusive.

incluso 1 *adj* included; enclosed.
　2 *adv* (a) including.
　(b) even, actually; **— la pegó** he even hit her, he actually hit her.

incoar [1a] *vt* to start, initiate.

incobrable *adj* irrecoverable; *debt* bad.

incógnita *nf* (Math) unknown quantity; (fig) unknown quantity; unknown factor; hidden motive.

incógnito 1 *adj* unknown. **2** *nm* incognito; **viajar de —** to travel incognito.

incoherencia *nf* incoherence; disconnectedness.

incoherente *adj* incoherent; disconnected.

incoloro *adj* colourless.

incólume *adj* safe; unhurt, unharmed; **salir — del accidente** to emerge unharmed from the accident.

incombustible *adj* incombustible, fire-resisting; fireproof.

incomible *adj* uneatable, inedible.

incómodamente *adv* inconveniently; uncomfortably.

incomodar [1a] **1** *vt* to inconvenience, trouble, put out.

2 incomodarse *vr* **(a)** to put oneself out, take trouble; ¡no se incomode! don't bother!, don't trouble yourself!

(b) to get cross, get annoyed (*con* with); **— con** to fall out with; **estar incomodado con** to be cross with; to be at odds with.

incomodidad *nf* **(a)** inconvenience; discomfort, uncomfortableness. **(b)** annoyance, annoying thing, vexation.

incomodo *nm* (*SAm*) = **incomodidad (b)**.

incómodo 1 *adj* inconvenient; uncomfortable; tiresome, annoying; **un bulto —** an awkward package, a cumbersome package; **una casa incómoda** an inconvenient house; **sentirse —** to feel uncomfortable, feel ill-at-ease; **estar — con uno** (*Arg, Chi*) to be fed up with someone, be cross with someone.

2 *nm* = **incomodidad (b)**.

incomparable *adj* incomparable.

incomparablemente *adv* incomparably.

incomparecimiento *nm*: **pleito perdido por —** suit lost by default, undefended suit.

incompasivo *adj* unsympathetic; pitiless.

incompatibilidad *nf* incompatibility.

incompatible *adj* incompatible.

incompetencia *nf* incompetence.

incompetente *adj* incompetent.

incompletamente *adv* incompletely.

incompleto *adj* incomplete, unfinished.

incomprendido 1 *adj* *person* misunderstood; not appreciated.

2 *nm,* **incomprendida** *nf* misunderstood person; person who is not appreciated.

incomprensibilidad *nf* incomprehensibility.

incomprensible *adj* incomprehensible.

incomprensión *nf* incomprehension, lack of understanding; lack of appreciation.

incomunicación *nf* isolation; lack of communication; (*Law*) solitary confinement.

incomunicado *adj* isolated, cut off; (*Law*) in solitary confinement, incommunicado.

incomunicar [1g] **1** *vt* to cut off the communications of, leave without communications; to cut off, isolate; (*Law*) to put into solitary confinement.

2 incomunicarse *vr* to isolate oneself, withdraw from society.

inconcebible *adj* inconceivable, unthinkable.

inconcebiblemente *adv* inconceivably.

inconciliable *adj* irreconcilable.

inconcluso *adj* unfinished, incomplete.

inconcluyente *adj* inconclusive.

inconcuso *adj* indisputable, undeniable.

incondicional 1 *adj* **(a)** unconditional; *faith* implicit, complete, unquestioning; *support* wholehearted; *assertion* unqualified; *friend, supporter etc* staunch, stalwart.

(b) (*SAm*) servile, fawning.

2 *nmf* **(a)** stalwart, staunch supporter (*etc*); (*pej*) diehard, hardliner.

(b) (*SAm*) toady, yes man (*sl*).

incondicionalismo *nm* (*SAm*) toadyism, servility.

incondicionalmente *adv* unconditionally, unreservedly; implicitly, unquestioningly; wholeheartedly; staunchly.

inconexión *nf* disconnectedness; incongruity.

inconexo *adj* unconnected; disconnected, disjointed; unrelated; incongruous.

inconfesable *adj* which cannot be told (*or* confessed); shameful, disgraceful.

inconfeso *adj* unconfessed.

inconformismo *nm* nonconformism.

inconformista 1 *adj* nonconformist. **2** *nmf* nonconformist.

inconfundible *adj* unmistakable.

incongruencia *nf* incongruity.

incongruente *adj,* **incongruo** *adj* incongruous.

inconmensurable *adj* immeasurable, vast; incommensurate.

inconmovible *adj* unshakeable.

inconmutable *adj* immutable.

inconocible *adj* unknowable; **lo —** the unknowable.

inconquistable *adj* unconquerable; (*fig*) inconquerable, unyielding.

inconsciencia *nf* **(a)** (*Med*) unconsciousness. **(b)** (*fig*) unawareness. **(c)** (*fig*) thoughtlessness; recklessness.

inconsciente *adj* **(a)** (*Med*) unconscious; **lo —** the

unconscious; **le encontraron —** they found him unconscious.

(b) (*fig*) unconscious, unaware (*de* of); oblivious (*de* to); unwitting.

(c) (*fig*) thoughtless, reckless, carefree; **es más — que malo** he's thoughtless rather than wicked; **son gente —** they're thoughtless people.

inconscientemente *adv* **(a)** unconsciously; unawares, unwittingly. **(b)** thoughtlessly; recklessly; in a carefree manner.

inconsecuencia *nf* inconsistency; inconsequence.

inconsecuente *adj* inconsistent; inconsequent, inconsequential.

inconsideración *nf* inconsiderateness, thoughtlessness; rashness, haste.

inconsideradamente *adv* inconsiderately, thoughtlessly; rashly, hastily.

inconsiderado *adj* inconsiderate, thoughtless; rash, hasty.

inconsistencia *nf* lack of firmness; unevenness; weakness; looseness; flimsiness.

inconsistente *adj* lacking firmness, not solid; uneven; *argument* weak; *earth etc* loose; *cloth* flimsy, thin.

inconsolable *adj* inconsolable.

inconstancia *nf* inconstancy; unsteadiness; fickleness; inconsistency.

inconstante *adj* inconstant, changeable; unsteady; fickle; inconsistent.

inconstantemente *adv* inconstantly; unsteadily; in a fickle way; inconsistently.

inconstitucional *adj* unconstitutional.

inconstitucionalmente *adv* unconstitutionally.

incontable *adj* countless, innumerable.

incontenible *adj* uncontrollable, unstoppable.

incontestable *adj* unanswerable; undeniable, unchallengeable, indisputable.

incontestablemente *adv* unanswerably; undeniably, indisputably.

incontestado *adj* unanswered; unchallenged, unquestioned.

incontinencia *nf* incontinence (*also Med*).

incontinente 1 *adj* incontinent (*also Med*). **2** *adv* = **incontinenti**.

incontinenti *adv* at once, instantly, forthwith.

incontrastable *adj* *difficulty* insuperable; *argument* unanswerable; *person* unshakeable, unyielding.

incontrolable *adj* uncontrollable.

incontrolado *adj* uncontrolled.

incontrovertible *adj* incontrovertible.

inconveniencia *nf* **(a)** unsuitability, inappropriateness; inadvisability; inconvenience. **(b)** impoliteness. **(c)** silly remark, tactless remark.

inconveniente 1 *adj* **(a)** unsuitable, inappropriate; inadvisable; inconvenient.

(b) impolite.

2 *nm* obstacle, difficulty; disadvantage, drawback; objection; **el — es que . . .** the trouble is that . . ., the difficulty is that . . .; **no hay — en + infin,** no **hay — para + infin** there is no objection to + *ger*; **poner un —** to raise an objection; **no tengo —** I have no objection, I don't mind; **¿tienes algún — en + infin?** do you mind + *ger*?; **no veo —** I see no objection, I see no difficulty.

inconvertibilidad *nf* inconvertibility.

inconvertible *adj* inconvertible.

incordiar [1b] *vt* (*fam*) to bother, annoy; **¡déjate de —!** stop bothering me; **¡no incordies!** stop it!, behave yourself!

incordio *nm* (*fam*) nuisance.

incorporación *nf* incorporation, embodiment.

incorporado *adj* (*Tech*) built-in; **con antena incorporada** with built-in aerial.

incorporal *adj* = **incorpóreo**.

incorporar [1a] **1** *vt* **(a)** to incorporate (*a, con, en* into, in); to embody (*a, con, en* in); to mix.

(b) **— a uno** to make someone sit up (in bed), help someone to sit up.

2 incorporarse *vr* **(a)** to sit up, raise oneself; **— en la cama** to sit up in bed.

(b) **— a** *regiment, society etc* to join.

incorpóreo *adj* incorporeal, bodiless; intangible.

incorrección *nf* **(a)** incorrectness, inaccuracy.

(b) irregularity.

(c) discourtesy; piece of bad manners, gaffe; impropriety; **cometer una —** to commit a faux pas.

incorrectamente *adv* **(a)** incorrectly, inaccurately, wrongly. **(b)** discourteously; improperly.

incorrecto *adj* **(a)** incorrect, inaccurate, wrong.

(b) *features* irregular, odd.

(c) *conduct* discourteous, bad-mannered; improper; **ser — con una** to take liberties with someone.

incorregible *adj* incorrigible.
incorruptible *adj* incorruptible.
incorrupto *adj* (**a**) *body* uncorrupted. (**b**) (*fig*) pure, chaste, undefiled.
incredibilidad *nf* incredibility.
incredulidad *nf* incredulity, unbelief.
incrédulo 1 *adj* incredulous, unbelieving, sceptical. **2** *nm*, **incrédula** *nf* unbeliever, sceptic.
increíble *adj* incredible, unbelievable; **es — que . . .** it is unbelievable that . . .
increíblemente *adv* incredibly, unbelievably.
incremento *nm* increment; increase, rise, addition; **— de temperatura** rise in temperature; **tomar —** to increase.
increpación *nf* reprimand, rebuke.
increpar [1a] *vt* to reprimand, rebuke.
incriminación *nf* accusation; incrimination.
incriminar [1a] *vt* (**a**) to accuse; to incriminate. (**b**) *fault etc* to magnify. (**c**) *goods etc* to obtain illegally.
incruento *adj* bloodless.
incrúspido *adj* (*Col, Mex, Nic*) awkward, clumsy.
incrustación *nf* (**a**) incrustation; (*fig*) grafting. (**b**) (*Art*) inlay, inlaid work.
incrustar [1a] *vt* to incrust (*de* with); to inlay (*de* with); (*fig*) to graft (*en* on to), introduce (*en* into); **una espada incrustada de joyas** a sword encrusted with jewels; **la palabra se ha incrustado en nuestro idioma** the word has been grafted on to our language.
incubación *nf* incubation.
incubadora *nf* incubator.
incubar [1a] *vt* to incubate; to hatch (*also fig*).
íncubo *nm* incubus; nightmare.
incuestionable *adj* unquestionable, unchallengeable.
incuestionablemente *adv* unquestionably.
inculcar [1g] **1** *vt* to instil, inculcate (*en* in, into). **2 inculcarse** *vr* to be obstinate.
inculpable *adj* blameless, guiltless.
inculpación *nf* charge, accusation.
inculpar [1a] *vt* to charge (*de* with), accuse (*de* of); to blame (*de* for); **los crímenes que se le inculpan** the crimes with which he is charged.
incultamente *adv* in an uncultured way; uncouthly.
incultivable *adj* uncultivable, unworkable.
inculto *adj* (**a**) (*Agr*) uncultivated, unworked, untilled; **dejar un terreno —** to leave land uncultivated. (**b**) (*fig*) uncultured; uncivilized; uncouth.
incultura *nf* lack of culture; uncouthness.
incumbencia *nf* obligation, duty, concern; **no es de mi —** it is not my job, it is not my concern.
incumbir [3a] *vi:* **— a** to be incumbent upon; **no me incumbe a mí** it's not my job, it is no concern of mine; **le incumbe hacerlo** it is his business to do it; it behoves him to do it.
incumplido *adj* unfulfilled.
incumplimiento *nm* non-fulfilment; **— de contrato** breach of contract; **— de promesa matrimonial** breach of promise; **por —** by default.
incunable *nm* incunable, incunabulum; **—s** incunabula.
incurable 1 *adj* (*Med*) incurable; (*fig*) hopeless, irremediable. **2** *nmf* incurable.
incuria *nf* negligence; carelessness, shiftlessness; **por —** through negligence.
incurrir [3a] *vi:* **— en** *error* to fall into; *crime etc* to commit; *debt, hatred, wrath etc* to incur; *disaster etc* to bring on oneself, become a victim of.
incursión *nf* raid, incursion, attack.
indagación *nf* investigation, inquiry.
indagador *nm*, **indagadora** *nf* investigator (*de* into, of), inquirer (*de* into).
indagar [1h] *vt* to investigate, inquire into; to find out, ascertain.
indebidamente *adv* unduly; improperly; illegally, wrongfully.
indebido *adj* undue; improper; illegal, wrongful.
indecencia *nf* (**a**) indecency; obscenity. (**b**) filth; wretchedness. (**c**) indecent act.
indecente *adj* (**a**) indecent, improper; obscene. (**b**) filthy; miserable, wretched; low, mean; **algún empleadillo —** some wretched clerk; **un cuchitril —** a miserable pigsty of a place; **la calle está — de lodo** the street is terribly muddy; **es una persona —** he's a low sort, he's a mean character.
indecentemente *adv* (**a**) indecently; obscenely. (**b**) miserably, wretchedly.
indecible *adj* unspeakable, unutterable; indescribable; **sufrir lo —** to suffer terribly.
indeciblemente *adv* unspeakably, unutterably; indescribably.
indecisión *nf* indecision, hesitation

indeciso *adj* (**a**) undecided; hesitant, irresolute; vague. (**b**) *result etc* indecisive.
indeclinable *adj* (**a**) (*Gram*) indeclinable. (**b**) unavoidable.
indecoro *nm* unseemliness, indecorum; indelicacy.
indecorosamente *adv* indecorously, unbecomingly; indelicately.
indecoroso *adj* unseemly, indecorous, unbecoming; indelicate.
indefectible *adj* unfailing, infallible.
indefectiblemente *adv* unfailingly, infallibly.
indefendible *adj* indefensible.
indefenso *adj* defenceless.
indefinible *adj* indefinable; inexpressible.
indefinidamente *adv* indefinitely.
indefinido *adj* indefinite; undefined, vague; (*Gram*) indefinite; **por tiempo —** for an indefinite time, indefinitely.
indeleble *adj* indelible.
indemne *adj* undamaged; *person* unharmed, unhurt.
indemnidad *nf* indemnity.
indemnizable *adj* that can be indemnified, recoverable.
indemnización *nf* (**a**) (*act*) indemnification. (**b**) (*payment*) indemnity, compensation; **—es** (*eg* 1918) reparations; **— de despido** severance pay; **pagó un dólar de —** he paid a dollar in damages (*or* in compensation).
indemnizar [1f] *vt* to indemnify (*de* against, for), compensate (*de* for).
independencia *nf* independence.
independiente 1 *adj* independent; self-sufficient, self-contained; **hacerse —** to become independent. **2** *nmf* independent.
independientemente *adv* independently.
independizar [1f] **1** *vt* to emancipate, free; to make independent, grant independence to. **2 independizarse** *vr* to become free, become independent (*de* of).
indescifrable *adj* undecipherable, indecipherable; *mystery* impenetrable.
indescriptible *adj* indescribable.
indescriptiblemente *adv* indescribably.
indeseable 1 *adj* undesirable. **2** *nmf* undesirable (person); **es un —** he's an unsavoury sort, he's beyond the pale.
indeshilachable *adj* non-fraying.
indesmallable *adj* *stocking etc* ladderproof, which does not ladder, runproof.
indestructible *adj* indestructible.
indeterminado *adj* (**a**) indeterminate; inconclusive; (*Gram*) indefinite. (**b**) *person* irresolute.
India *f:* **la —** India; **las —s** the Indies; **—s Occidentales** West Indies; **—s Orientales** East Indies.
indiada *nf* (**a**) (*SAm*) group of Indians, crowd of Indians; (*Arg: pej*) collection of ignorant people, mob. (**b**) (*SAm*) typically Indian thing to do (*or* say etc).
indiana *nf* printed calico.
indiano 1 *adj* (Spanish-)American. **2** *nm* Spaniard returning rich from America, equivalent to nabob; **— de hilo negro** miser.
indicación *nf* (**a**) indication, sign; (*Med*) sign, symptom. (**b**) hint, suggestion; **por — de** at the suggestion of; **aprovechó la —** he took the hint; **seguiré sus —es** I will follow your suggestion, I will do what you say. (**c**) piece of information; (*of dial, thermometer etc*) reading. (**d**) **—es** (*Comm etc*) instructions, directions; **—es para el empleo** instructions for use.
indicado *adj* right, suitable, proper; obvious; likely; **el sitio más —** the most obvious place; **una elección indicada** an obvious choice; **es el más — para el puesto** he is the most suitable man for the job, he is the best man for the job; **tú eres el menos — para hacerlo** you're the last person to do it, you're the least suitable person to do it.
indicador *nm* indicator; gauge, meter, dial; hand, pointer; roadsign; **— de dirección** (*Aut*) indicator, trafficator; **— de velocidades** speedometer.
indicar [1g] *vt* (**a**) (*Tech etc*) to indicate, show; to register, record; (*of thermometer etc*) to read. (**b**) to indicate, point out, point to; to show; to suggest, hint, intimate; **me indicó que . . .** he told me that . . ., he suggested to me that . . .
indicativo 1 *adj* indicative (*also Gram*). **2** *nm* (**a**) (*Gram*) indicative. (**b**) (*Radio*) call sign; **— de nacionalidad** (*Aut*) national identification plate.

índice *nm* (a) (*Typ etc*) index; (library) catalogue; — **de materias** table of contents.
(b) index; ratio, rate; — **de compresión** (*Mech*) compression ratio; — **del coste de (la) vida** cost-of-living index; — **expurgatorio** (*Eccl*) Index; — **de mortalidad** death rate; — **de natalidad** birth rate; — **de vida** expectation of life, life expectancy.
(c) (*Tech*) pointer, needle, hand; (*of clock*) hand.
(d) (*Anat*) index finger, forefinger.
(e) (*Math*) index.
indiciario *adj*: **prueba indiciaria** circumstantial proof.
indicio *nm* (a) indication, sign; token; piece of evidence, clue (*de* to); trace, vestige; **es — de** it is an indication of, it is a sign of; **no hay el menor — de él** there isn't the faintest sign of him, there isn't the least trace of him; **dar —s de sorpresa** to show surprise, evince surprise.
(b) —**s** (*Law*) evidence; —**s vehementes** circumstantial evidence.
indiferencia *nf* indifference; apathy, lack of interest.
indiferente *adj* (a) indifferent (*a* to), unconcerned (*a* about); apathetic, uninterested.
(b) indifferent, immaterial; **me es —** it is immaterial to me, it makes no difference to me.
indiferentemente *adv* indifferently.
indiferentismo *nm* indifference; apathy; (*Rel*) scepticism, unbelief.
indígena 1 *adj* indigenous (*de* to), native (*de* to); (*SAm*) Indian. 2 *nmf* native; (*SAm*) Indian.
indigencia *nf* poverty, destitution, indigence.
indigenismo *nm* word (*or* phrase *etc*) borrowed from a native language.
indigente 1 *adj* destitute, poverty-stricken, indigent. 2 *nmf* poor person.
indigerible *adj* undigestible.
indigestar [1a] 1 *vt* to cause indigestion to.
2 **indigestarse** *vr* (a) (*person*) to get indigestion, have indigestion.
(b) (*food*) to cause indigestion, be indigestible; **esa carne se me indigestó** that meat gave me indigestion, I couldn't digest that meat.
(c) (*fig*) to be insufferable; **se me indigesta ese tío** I can't stand that fellow.
(d) (*SAm*) to get worried, get alarmed.
indigestible *adj* indigestible.
indigestión *nf* indigestion.
indigesto *adj* undigested; indigestible, hard to digest; (*fig*) muddled, turgid, badly thought-out.
indignación *nf* indignation, anger; **descargar la — sobre** to vent one's spleen on, take out one's anger on.
indignado *adj* indignant, angry (*con*, *contra* with; *por* at, about).
indignamente *adv* (a) unworthily. (b) contemptibly, meanly.
indignante *adj* outrageous, infuriating, unworthy, humiliating.
indignar [1a] 1 *vt* to anger, make indignant; to provoke, stir up.
2 **indignarse** *vr* to get angry, get indignant; — **con uno** to get indignant with someone; — **por algo** to get indignant about something, get angry about something.
indignidad *nf* (a) unworthiness. (b) unworthy act; indignity, insult; **sufrir la — de** + *infin* to suffer the indignity of + *ger*.
indigno *adj* (a) unworthy (*de* of). (b) contemptible, mean, low.
índigo *nm* indigo.
indino *adj* (a) (*CAm*, *Cu*) cheeky. (b) (*Ec*, *PR*) mean, stingy.
indio 1 *adj* (a) Indian.
(b) blue.
2 *nm*, **india** *nf* (a) Indian (*of India, of West Indies, of America*).
(b) **hacer el —** to play the fool; **le salió el —** (*Arg*) he behaved like the lout he is; he got angry for no reason at all; **se le subió el —** (*CAm*) he got angry.
indirecta *nf* hint; insinuation, innuendo; — **del padre Cobos** broad hint; **soltar una —** to drop a hint, make an insinuation.
indirectamente *adv* indirectly.
indirecto *adj* indirect; roundabout.
indiscernible *adj* indiscernible.
indisciplina *nf* indiscipline, lack of discipline; insubordination.
indisciplinado *adj* undisciplined; lax.
indiscreción *nf* indiscretion; tactless thing (to do), tactless remark (*etc*), gaffe; **. . ., si no es — . . .,** if I may say so; **cometió la — de** + *infin* he

committed the indiscretion of + *ger*, he was so tactless as to + *infin*.
indiscretamente *adv* indiscreetly; tactlessly.
indiscreto *adj* indiscreet; tactless.
indisculpable *adj* inexcusable, unforgivable.
indiscutible *adj* indisputable, unquestionable.
indiscutiblemente *adv* indisputably, unquestionably.
indisoluble *adj* indissoluble; inseparable.
indisolublemente *adv* indissolubly; inseparably.
indispensable *adj* indispensable, essential.
indisponer [2r] 1 *vt* (a) *plan etc* to spoil, upset.
(b) (*Med*) to upset, make ill, make unfit.
(c) — **a uno con otro** to set someone against another person, prejudice someone against another person.
2 **indisponerse** *vr* (a) (*Med*) to become ill, fall ill.
(b) — **con uno** to fall out with someone.
indisponible *adj* not available, unavailable.
indisposición *nf* (a) (*Med*) indisposition, slight illness. (b) disinclination, unwillingness.
indispuesto *adj* (a) (*Med*) indisposed, unwell, slightly ill; **sentirse —** to feel slightly ill, feel queer. (b) disinclined, unwilling.
indisputable *adj* indisputable, unquestioned; unchallenged.
indistinción *nf* (a) indistinctness; vagueness. (b) lack of discrimination. (c) lack of distinction, sameness, identity.
indistinguible *adj* indistinguishable (*de* from).
indistintamente *adv* (a) indistinctly; vaguely. (b) without distinction, indiscriminately.
indistinto *adj* (a) indistinct; vague; faint, dim. (b) indiscriminate.
individua *nf* (*fam*) whore.
individual 1 *adj* (a) individual; peculiar, special; *room* single.
(b) (*Col*, *Chi*, *Ven*) alike, similar, identical; **A es — a B** A is like B, A is identical to B.
2 *nm* (*Sport*) singles, singles match; — **femenino** women's singles; — **masculino** men's singles.
individualidad *nf* individuality.
individualismo *nm* individualism.
individualista 1 *adj* individualistic. 2 *nmf* individualist.
individualizar [1f] *vt* to individualize.
individualmente *adv* individually.
individuar [1e] *vt* to individualize.
individuo 1 *adj* individual.
2 *nm* (a) individual; (*pej*) individual, fellow; **el — en cuestión** the person in question.
(b) (*of society*) member, fellow.
indivisible *adj* indivisible.
indiviso *adj* undivided.
indo 1 *adj* Hindu. 2 *nm*, **inda** *nf* Hindu.
indo . . . Indo . . .
Indo *m* (*Geog*) Indus.
indócil *adj* unmanageable, headstrong; disobedient.
indocilidad *nf* unmanageableness, headstrong character; disobedience.
indocto *adj* ignorant, unlearned.
indoctrinar [1a] *vt* (*SAm*) to indoctrinate.
indocumentado 1 *adj* without identifying documents, who carries no identity papers. 2 *nm* person who carries no identity papers.
Indochina: la — Indochina.
indoeuropeo 1 *adj* Indo-European. 2 *nm*, **indoeuropea** *nf* Indo-European. 3 *nm* (*language*) Indo-European.
índole *nf* (a) nature; character, disposition. (b) class, kind, sort; **cosas de esta —** things of this kind.
indolencia *nf* indolence, laziness; apathy.
indolente *adj* indolent, lazy; apathetic.
indoloro *adj* painless.
indomable *adj* indomitable; *animal* untameable; (*fig*) unmanageable, uncontrollable.
indomado *adj* wild, untamed.
indomesticable *adj* untameable.
indómito *adj* = **indomable**.
Indonesia *f* Indonesia.
indonesio 1 *adj* Indonesian. 2 *nm*, **indonesia** *nf* Indonesian.
indormia *nf* (*Col*, *Ven*) trick, wangle (*fam*), wheeze (*fam*).
Indostán *nm* Hindustan.
indostanés 1 *adj* Hindustani. 2 *nm*, **indostanesa** *nf* Hindustani.
indostaní *nm* (*language*) Hindustani.
indostánico 1 *adj* Hindustani. 2 *nm* (*language*) Hindustani.
indotado *adj* without a dowry.
indubitable *adj* indubitable, undoubted.
indubitablemente *adv* indubitably, undoubtedly.

inducción *nf* (a) (*Elec, Philos*) induction; **por —** by induction, inductively. (b) inducement, persuasion.

inducido *nm* (*Elec*) armature.

inducir [3o] *vt* (a) (*Elec*) to induce; (*Philos*) to infer. (b) to induce, persuade; **— a uno a hacer algo** to induce someone to do something; **— a uno en el error** to lead someone into error.

inductivo *adj* inductive.

indudable *adj* undoubted, indubitable; unquestionable; **es — que . . .** there is no doubt that . . .

indudablemente *adv* undoubtedly, doubtless; unquestionably.

indulgencia *nf* (a) indulgence; forbearance; **proceder sin — contra** to proceed ruthlessly against. (b) (*Eccl*) indulgence; **— plenaria** plenary indulgence.

indulgente *adj* indulgent (*con* towards).

indulgentemente *adv* indulgently.

indultar [1a] **1** *vt* (a) (*Law*) to pardon, reprieve (*de* from). (b) to exempt, excuse (*de* from). **2 indultarse** *vr* (a) (*Bol*) to meddle, pry. (b) (*Cu*) to get oneself out of a jam.

indulto *nm* (a) (*Law*) pardon, reprieve. (b) exemption, excusal.

indumentaria *nf* (a) clothing, apparel, dress. (b) (history of) costume.

indumentario *adj* clothing (*attr*); **elegancia indumentaria** elegance of dress, sartorial elegance.

indumento *nm* clothing, apparel, dress.

industria *nf* (a) industry; **— algodonera** cotton industry; **— del automóvil** car industry, automobile industry (*US*); **— básica** basic industry; **— pesada** heavy industry; **— siderúrgica** iron and steel industry; **Ministro de — y Comercio** President of the Board of Trade (*Brit*), Secretary of Industry and Trade (*US*). (b) industry, industriousness. (c) ingenuity, skill, expertise; **de —** on purpose.

industrial 1 *adj* industrial. **2** *nm* industrialist, manufacturer.

industrialismo *nm* industrialism.

industrialista *nm* (*SAm*) industrialist.

industrialización *nf* industrialization.

industrializar [1f] **1** *vt* to industrialize. **2 industrializarse** *vr* to become industrialized.

industriarse [1b] *vr* to manage, find a way; **—las para + infin** to manage to + *infin*, contrive to + *infin*.

industriosamente *adv* (a) industriously. (b) skilfully, resourcefully.

industrioso *adj* (a) industrious. (b) skilful, resourceful, versatile, handy.

inédito *adj* (a) (*Lit*) unpublished; **un texto rigurosamente —** a text never published previously in any form. (b) (*fig*) new; not known hitherto, hitherto unheard of; **una experiencia inédita** a completely new experience.

ineducable *adj* ineducable.

ineducado *adj* (a) uneducated. (b) ill-bred, badmannered, uncouth.

inefable *adj* indescribable, inexpressible, ineffable.

ineficacia *nf* (a) ineffectiveness. (b) inefficiency.

ineficaz *adj* (a) ineffective, ineffectual. (b) inefficient.

ineficazmente *adv* (a) ineffectively, ineffectually. (b) inefficiently.

ineficiencia *nf* inefficiency.

ineficiente *adj* inefficient.

inelástico *adj* inelastic.

inelegancia *nf* inelegance, lack of elegance.

inelegante *adj* inelegant.

inelegantemente *adv* inelegantly.

inelegible *adj* ineligible.

ineluctable *adj*, **ineludible** *adj* unavoidable, inescapable.

inenarrable *adj* inexpressible.

inencogible *adj* unshrinkable, non-shrink, which will not shrink.

inencontrable *adj* unobtainable.

inepcia *nf* (a) ineptitude, incompetence; stupidity. (b) (*SAm*) silly thing (to say *etc*); **decir —s** to say silly things.

ineptitud *nf* ineptitude, incompetence.

inepto *adj* inept, incompetent; stupid; **— de toda ineptitud** utterly incompetent.

inequívoco *adj* unequivocal, unambiguous; unmistakable.

inercia *nf* (a) (*Phys*) inertia. (b) (*fig*) passivity; sluggishness, slowness.

inerme *adj* unarmed; defenceless, unprotected.

inerte *adj* (a) (*Phys*) inert. (b) (*fig*) passive, inactive; sluggish, slow.

Inés *f* Agnes.

inescrupuloso *adj* unscrupulous.

inescrutabilidad *nf* inscrutability.

inescrutable *adj* inscrutable.

inesperadamente *adv* unexpectedly; without warning, suddenly.

inesperado *adj* unexpected, unforeseen; sudden.

inesquivable *adj* unavoidable; which cannot be overlooked.

inestabilidad *nf* instability, unsteadiness.

inestable *adj* unstable, unsteady.

inestimable *adj* inestimable, invaluable.

inevitabilidad *nf* inevitability.

inevitable *adj* inevitable, unavoidable.

inevitablemente *adv* inevitably, unavoidably.

inexactitud *nf* inaccuracy; incorrectness, wrongness.

inexacto *adj* inaccurate; incorrect, untrue; **esto es —** this is not so, this is incorrect.

inexcusable *adj* (a) inexcusable, unforgivable. (b) essential.

inexcusablemente *adv* inexcusably, unforgivably.

inexhausto *adj* (a) unused, still to be used; unspent. (b) inexhaustible.

inexistencia *nf* non-existence.

inexistente *adj* non-existent; which no longer exists, defunct.

inexorable *adj* inexorable.

inexorablemente *adv* inexorably.

inexperiencia *nf* inexperience; unskilfulness, lack of skill.

inexperto *adj* inexperienced; unskilled, inexpert.

inexplicable *adj* inexplicable, unaccountable.

inexplicablemente *adv* inexplicably, unaccountably.

inexplicado *adj* unexplained.

inexplorado *adj* unexplored; *sea etc* uncharted.

inexplotado *adj* unexploited, unused.

inexpresable *adj* inexpressible.

inexpresivo *adj* inexpressive; dull, flat, wooden.

inexpuesto *adj* (*Phot*) unexposed.

inexpugnable *adj* (a) (*Mil*) impregnable. (b) (*fig*) firm, unyielding, unshakeable.

inextinguible *adj* inextinguishable, unquenchable.

inextirpable *adj* ineradicable.

inextricable *adj* inextricable.

infalibilidad *nf* infallibility; certainty.

infalible *adj* infallible; certain, sure; foolproof; *aim* unerring.

infaliblemente *adv* infallibly; surely; unerringly.

infamación *nf* defamation.

infamador 1 *adj* defamatory, slanderous. **2** *nm*, **infamadora** *nf* slanderer.

infamar [1a] *vt* to dishonour, discredit; to defame, slander.

infamatorio *adj* defamatory, slanderous.

infame 1 *adj* infamous, odious, vile; *task* terrible, thankless; **esto es —** this is monstrous, this is infamous. **2** *nmf* vile person, villain.

infamia *nf* infamy; disgrace.

infancia *nf* (a) infancy, childhood; (*fig*) infancy. (b) children.

infanta *nf* (a) infant. (b) (*Hist*) infanta, princess.

infante *nm* (a) infant. (b) (*Hist*) infante, prince; (*Mil: Hist*) infantryman.

infantería *nf* infantry; **— de marina** marines.

infanticida *nmf* infanticide (*person*), child-killer.

infanticidio *nm* infanticide (*act*).

infantil *adj* (a) infant; child's, children's; **de tamaño —** child's size; **para el uso —** for children (to use). (b) childlike, innocent; (*pej*) infantile, childish.

infanzón[1] *nm*, **infanzona** *nf* (*Hist*) *member of the lowest rank of the nobility*.

infanzón[2] *nm* (*Cu*) boast.

infatigable *adj* tireless, untiring.

infatigablemente *adv* tirelessly, untiringly.

infatuación *nf* vanity, conceit.

infatuar [1d] **1** *vt* to make conceited. **2 infatuarse** *vr* to get conceited (*con* about).

infausto *adj* unlucky; ill-starred, ill-fated.

infección *nf* infection.

infeccioso *adj* infectious.

infectar [1a] **1** *vt* (a) to infect. (b) to contaminate, corrupt; to pervert. **2 infectarse** *vr* to become infected (*de* with; *also fig*).

infecto *adj* infected (*de* with); foul; corrupt, tainted.

infecundidad *nf* infertility; sterility, barrenness.

infecundo *adj* infertile; sterile, barren; **la época infecunda de la mujer** the woman's infertile period.

infelicidad *nf* unhappiness; misfortune.

infeliz 1 *adj* **(a)** unhappy; unfortunate, miserable, wretched.
   (b) simple, kind-hearted, good-natured; (*pej*) gullible.
   (c) (*Arg, Guat, Mex*) trifling, insignificant.
   2 *nmf* **(a)** wretch, poor devil.
   (b) good-natured simpleton.
infelizmente *adv* unhappily.
infelizón *nm* (*fam*), **infelizote** *nm* (*fam*) = **infeliz 2 (a)**.
inferencia *nf* inference; **por —** by inference.
inferior 1 *adj* **(a)** (*physically*) lower (*a* than); **la parte —** the lower part; **el lado —** the underside, the side underneath; **el Egipto —** lower Egypt.
   (b) (*in quality, rank*) inferior (*a* to), lower (*a* than); **de calidad —** of inferior quality; **no ser — a nadie** to be inferior to none; **le es — en talento** he is inferior to him in talent.
   (c) (*Math*) lower; **cualquier número — a 9** any number under 9, any number below 9, any number less than 9; **una cantidad —** a lesser quantity.
   2 *nm* inferior, subordinate; (*pej*) underling.
inferioridad *nf* inferiority.
inferir [3i] *vt* **(a)** to infer, deduce; **— una cosa de** (or **por**) **otra** to infer one thing from another.
   (b) to lead to, cause, bring on.
   (c) *wound* to inflict (*a, en* on); *insult* to offer (*a* to).
infernáculo *nm* hopscotch.
infernal *adj* infernal; (*fig*) infernal, hellish, devilish; **un ruido —** a hell of a noise (*fam*), a hellish noise.
infértil *adj* infertile.
infestación *nf* infestation.
infestar [1a] *vt* **(a)** to infect; to infest, overrun, invade. **(b)** (*fig*) to harass, beset.
inficionar [1a] *vt* = **infectar**.
infidelidad *nf* **(a)** infidelity, unfaithfulness; **— conyugal** marital infidelity. **(b)** (*Eccl*) unbelief, lack of faith. **(c)** (*Eccl*) unbelievers, infidels.
infidencia *nf* **(a)** disloyalty, faithlessness; treason. **(b)** disloyal act; breach of trust.
infiel 1 *adj* **(a)** unfaithful, disloyal (*a, con, para* to); **fue — a su mujer** he was unfaithful to his wife.
   (b) (*Eccl*) unbelieving, infidel.
   (c) *account etc* inaccurate; **la memoria le fue —** his memory failed him.
   2 *nmf* (*Eccl*) unbeliever, infidel.
infielmente *adv* **(a)** unfaithfully, disloyally. **(b)** inaccurately.
infiernillo *nm* (*also* **— de alcohol**) spirit lamp, spirit stove; **— campestre** camp stove; **— de gasolina** petrol stove.
infierno *nm* **(a)** hell.
   (b) (*fig and in phrases*) hell, inferno; hades; **¡anda al —!** go to hell!; **está en el quinto —** it's at the back of beyond, it's right off the map; **mandar a uno al quinto —** to tell someone to go to hell.
infiltración *nf* infiltration.
infiltrar [1a] **1** *vt* to infiltrate (*en* into); (*fig*) to inculcate (*en* in). **2 infiltrarse** *vr* to infiltrate (*also fig; en* into), filter (*en* in, through); to percolate.
ínfimo *adj* lowest; (*fig*) very poor, of very poor quality; vile, mean; least; **a precios —s** at very low prices, at ridiculously low prices.
infinidad *nf* **(a)** (*Math etc*) infinity.
   (b) great quantity, enormous number; **— de an** infinity of, vast numbers of; **durante una — de días** for days on end; **— de veces** times out of number; **hay — de personas que ...** there are great numbers of people who ...
infinitamente *adj* infinitely.
infinitesimal *adj* infinitesimal.
infinitivo 1 *adj* infinitive. **2** *nm* infinitive (mood).
infinito 1 *adj* **(a)** (*Math etc*) infinite.
   (b) (*fig*) infinite; boundless, limitless, endless; **hasta lo —** ad infinitum.
   2 *adv* infinitely, immensely.
   3 *nm* (*Math*) infinity; **el —** (*Philos etc*) the infinite.
infinitud *nf* infinitude.
inflación *nf* **(a)** inflation (*also Econ*); swelling. **(b)** (*fig*) pride, conceit.
inflacionismo *nm* (*Econ*) inflation, inflationism.
inflacionista *adj* inflationary, inflationist.
inflador *nm* (*SAm*) bicycle pump.
inflamable *adj* inflammable.
inflamación *nf* **(a)** ignition, combustion; **— espontánea** spontaneous combustion. **(b)** (*Med*) inflammation.
inflamar [1a] **1** *vt* **(a)** to set on fire, ignite.
   (b) (*Med*) to inflame.
   (c) (*fig*) to inflame, excite, arouse.
   2 inflamarse *vr* **(a)** to catch fire, flame up,

ignite; **se inflama fácilmente** it is highly inflammable.
   (b) (*Med*) to become inflamed.
   (c) (*fig*) to become inflamed (*de, en* with), get excited.
inflamatorio *adj* inflammatory.
inflar [1a] **1** *vt* **(a)** to inflate, blow up, pump air into.
   (b) (*fig*) to inflate, exaggerate; to make conceited.
   2 inflarse *vr* **(a)** to swell.
   (b) (*fig*) to get conceited.
inflatorio *adj* inflationary.
inflexibilidad *nf* inflexibility; unyielding nature.
inflexible *adj* inflexible; unbending, unyielding; **— a los ruegos** unmoved by appeals, unresponsive to appeals; **regla —** strict rule, hard-and-fast rule.
inflexión *nf* inflexion.
infligir [3c] *vt* to inflict (*a* on).
influencia *nf* influence (*sobre* on); **bajo la — de** under the influence of.
influenciable *adj* impressionable, easily influenced.
influenciar [1b] *vt* to influence.
influenza *nf* (*esp SAm*) influenza.
influir [3g] **1** *vt* to influence; **A, influido por B ...** A, influenced by B ...
   2 *vi* **(a)** to have influence, carry weight, have pull (*con* with); **es hombre que influye** he's a man of influence, he's a man who carries weight.
   (b) **— en, — sobre** to influence, affect, have an influence on; to have a hand in.
influjo *nm* influence (*sobre* on).
influyente *adj* influential.
información *nf* **(a)** (*in general*) information; news; (*Mil*) intelligence; **una —** a piece of information, a piece of news; **— secreta** secret information, classified information.
   (b) report, account; reference, testimonial; (*in newspaper, as heading*) section; **— de crédito** credit report; **— deportiva** sports section, sporting page; **— extranjera** news from abroad, foreign news; **— periodística** newspaper report.
   (c) (*Law*) legal proceedings; judicial inquiry, investigation; **abrir una —** to begin proceedings.
informador *nm*, **informadora** *nf* informant.
informal *adj* **(a)** irregular, incorrect; *behaviour etc* bad, unmannerly; unconventional.
   (b) *person* unreliable, untrustworthy; shifty; unbusinesslike, disorganized; offhand, bad-mannered; frivolous.
informalidad *nf* **(a)** irregularity, incorrectness; unmannerliness; unconventionality.
   (b) unreliability, untrustworthiness, shiftiness; unbusinesslike nature; offhandedness, bad manners; frivolity, levity.
informalmente *adv* **(a)** irregularly; badly; unconventionally. **(b)** unreliably; shiftily; in an unbusinesslike way; offhandedly; frivolously.
informante *nmf* informant.
informar [1a] **1** *vt* **(a)** to inform, tell (*de* of, *sobre* about).
   (b) to form, shape.
   2 *vi* **(a)** to report (*acerca de, de* on); **el profesor informará de su descubrimiento** the professor will report on his discovery.
   (b) (*Law*) to plead.
   (c) (*Law*) to inform (*contra* against), lay information (*contra* against).
   3 informarse *vr* to find out, inform oneself; **— de** to find out about, acquaint oneself with, inquire into; **— sobre algo** to gather information about something.
informativo *adj* **(a)** informative; news (*attr*); **un folleto —** a booklet of information, an explanatory booklet. **(b)** *body etc* consultative, advisory.
informe[1] *adj* shapeless.
informe[2] *nm* **(a)** report, statement; (*Parl*) report, white paper; **el — del ministro** the minister's statement.
   (b) (*Mil*) briefing.
   (c) piece of information; **—s** information; data, particulars, references; **según mis —s** according to my information; **dar — sobre** to give information about; **pedir —s** to ask for information, make inquiries (*a* of, *sobre* about); **tomar —s** to gather information.
   (d) (*Law*) plea; **— forense, — jurídico** legal speech, speech in court.
infortunado *adj* unfortunate, unlucky.
infortunio *nm* misfortune, ill luck; mishap.
infra ... infra ...
infracción *nf* infraction, infringement (*de* of); breach

(de of); (Aut etc) offence (de against); — **de contrato** breach of contract.

infractor nm offender (de against).

infraescrito 1 adj undersigned; undermentioned. 2 nm, **infraescrita** nf: **el** — the undersigned; (SAm: hum) the present speaker, I myself.

infraestructura nf substructure; (fig) underlying structure.

in fraganti adv: **coger a uno** — to catch someone red-handed.

infrahumano adj subhuman.

inframundo nm underworld.

infrangible adj unbreakable.

infranqueable adj impassable; (fig) unsurmountable.

infrarrojo adj infrared.

infrecuencia nf infrequency.

infrecuente adj infrequent.

infringir [3c] vt to infringe, break, contravene.

infructuosamente adv fruitlessly, unsuccessfully; unprofitably.

infructuoso adj fruitless, unsuccessful; unprofitable.

ínfulas nfpl conceit; **darse** — to put on airs, get on one's high horse; **tener (muchas)** — **de** to fancy oneself as.

infumable adj (a) unsmokable. (b) (Mex) unbearable, intolerable.

infundado adj unfounded, baseless.

infundia nf (SAm) = **enjundia**.

infundio nm (fam) fairy tale, fib.

infundir [3a] vt (a) to infuse (a, en into). (b) (fig) to instil (a, en into); — **ánimo a uno** to encourage someone; — **miedo a uno** to scare someone, frighten someone, fill someone with fear; — **un espíritu nuevo a un club** to inject new life into a club, to put new life into a club.

infusión nf infusion; — **de té** infusion of tea.

ingeniar [1a] 1 vt to devise, think up, contrive. 2 **ingeniarse** vr to manage, find a way, get along; — **con algo** to manage with something, make do with something; — **para** + infin to manage to + infin, contrive to + infin (also —**las**).

ingeniería nf engineering.

ingeniero nm engineer (also Mil, Naut); — **agrónomo** agronomist, agricultural expert; — **de caminos, canales y puentes** civil engineer; — **forestal**, — **de montes** forestry expert; — **de minas** mining engineer; — **naval** shipbuilder, naval architect; — **químico** chemical engineer.

ingenio nm (a) ingenuity, inventiveness; talent; creativeness; wit, wits; **aguzar el** — to sharpen one's wits. (b) clever person, talented person; (Hist) wit. (c) (Mech) apparatus, engine, device; (Mil) device; — **nuclear** nuclear device. (d) (Tech) mill, plant; — (**de azúcar**) sugar mill, sugar refinery; (Bol, Per) foundry, smelting plant.

ingeniosamente adv (a) ingeniously, cleverly. (b) wittily.

ingeniosidad nf (a) ingenuity, ingeniousness, cleverness, resourcefulness. (b) (una —) clever idea. (c) wittiness.

ingenioso adj (a) ingenious, clever, resourceful. (b) witty.

ingénito adj innate, inborn.

ingente adj huge, enormous.

ingenuamente adv ingenuously, naïvely; with candour; simply, unaffectedly.

ingenuidad nf ingenuousness, naïveté; candour; simplicity.

ingenuo adj ingenuous, candid; simple, unaffected.

ingerido adj (Col, Mex, Ven) ill.

ingerir [3i] vt to swallow; to ingest, consume, take in; **el automovilista había ingerido 3 litros de alcohol** the motorist had taken 3 litres of alcohol.

ingestión nf swallowing; ingestion.

Inglaterra f England; (often loosely used by foreigners when strict usage requires) Great Britain, United Kingdom; **la batalla de** — the Battle of Britain (1940).

ingle nf groin.

inglés 1 adj English; (often loosely used by foreigners when strict usage requires) British. 2 nm Englishman; Briton, Britisher (US); **los** —**es** the English, the British. 3 nm (language) English.

inglesa nf Englishwoman; Briton, Britisher (US); **montar a la** — to ride sidesaddle.

inglesismo nm anglicism.

inglete nm dovetail.

ingobernable adj uncontrollable, unmanageable; (Pol) ungovernable.

ingratitud nf ingratitude.

ingrato adj (a) (person) ungrateful; ¡—! you wretch! (b) (taste) unpleasant, disagreeable; task etc thankless, unrewarding.

ingravidez nf weightlessness.

ingrávido adj weightless; very light.

ingrediente nm ingredient; —s (Arg) dish of hors d'oeuvres on the bar counter.

ingresado nm, **ingresada** nf (Univ etc) entrant, new student.

ingresar [1a] 1 vt money to deposit, pay in; — **dinero en una cuenta** to pay money into an account. 2 vi (a) to come in, enter; — **en una sociedad** to join a club, become a member of a club, be admitted to a society; — **en la Academia** to be admitted to the Academy, be received into the Academy; — **en el ejército** to join the army, join up; — **en el hospital** to be admitted to hospital; **pero ingresó cadáver** but he was dead on arrival (at hospital). (b) (of money, profits) to come in. 3 **ingresarse** vr (Mex) to join, become a member; (Mex: Mil) to join up.

ingreso nm (a) entry (en into), joining; admission (en to); **su** — **en la Academia** his admission to the Academy; **examen de** — entrance examination. (b) (Comm) entry; deposit; sum received. (c) —s (Comm, Fin) income; revenue; receipts, takings; —s **accesorios** additional earnings, earnings on the side; fringe benefits; —s **anuales** annual income; —s **brutos** gross receipts; **vivir con arreglo a los** —s to live within one's income.

íngrimo adj all alone.

inguandia nf (Col) fib, tale.

inhábil adj (a) unskilful, inexpert, clumsy; incompetent. (b) unfit (para for, para + infin to + infin). (c) **día** — non-working day.

inhabilidad nf (a) unskilfulness; clumsiness; incompetence. (b) unfitness (para for).

inhabilitación nf (a) disqualification; see nota. (b) disablement.

inhabilitar [1a] vt (a) to disqualify (para + infin from + ger). (b) to disable; to render unfit (para for).

inhabitable adj uninhabitable.

inhabitado adj uninhabited.

inhabituado adj unaccustomed (a to).

inhalación nf inhalation.

inhalador nm (Med) inhaler.

inhalante nm inhalant.

inhalar [1a] vt to inhale.

inherente adj inherent (a in).

inhibición nf inhibition.

inhibir [3a] 1 vt to inhibit; (Law) to restrain, stay. 2 **inhibirse** vr to keep out (de of), to stay away (de from); to keep out of the way, lie low.

inhibitorio adj inhibitory.

inhospitalario adj inhospitable; (fig) bleak, cheerless, uninviting.

inhospitalidad nf inhospitality.

inhóspito adj inhospitable.

inhumación nf burial, inhumation.

inhumanamente adv inhumanly.

inhumanidad nf inhumanity.

inhumano adj inhuman; (Chi) dirty, disgusting.

iniciación nf initiation; beginning.

iniciado 1 adj initiate(d). 2 nm, **iniciada** nf initiate.

iniciador nm initiator, starter; pioneer.

inicial 1 adj initial. 2 nf initial.

iniciar [1b] vt (a) to initiate (en into); — **a uno en un secreto** to initiate someone into a secret. (b) to begin, start, initiate; to originate, set on foot; to pioneer.

iniciativa nf initiative, enterprise; lead, leadership; — **privada** private enterprise; **bajo su** — on his initiative; **por** — **propia** on one's own initiative; **carecer de** — to lack initiative; **tomar la** — to take the initiative.

inicuamente adv wickedly, iniquitously.

inicuo adj wicked, iniquitous.

inigualado adj unequalled.

inimaginable adj unimaginable, inconceivable.

inimitable adj inimitable.

ininteligente adj unintelligent.

ininteligibilidad nf unintelligibility.

ininteligible adj unintelligible.

ininterrumpidamente adv uninterruptedly; continuously, without a break; steadily.

ininterrumpido adj uninterrupted; continuous, without a break; steady; prolonged, sustained.

iniquidad nf wickedness, iniquity; injustice.

injerencia *nf* interference, meddling (*en* in).
injerir [3i] **1** *vt* (**a**) to insert, introduce (*en* into); (*Agr*) to graft (*en* on, on to). (**b**) = **ingerir**. **2 injerirse** *vr* to interfere, meddle (*en* in).
injertar [1a] *vt* (*Agr*, *Med*) to graft (*en* on, on to); (*fig*) to graft; to inject (*en* into).
injerto **1** *nm* (**a**) grafting. (**b**) (*Agr*, *Med*) graft; — **de piel** skin graft. **2** *nm*, **injerta** *nf* (*Per*) mestizo with Chinese blood.
injuria *nf* (**a**) insult, offence, affront (*para* to); outrage, injustice; —**s** insults, abuse; **llenar a uno de** —**s** to heap abuse on someone. (**b**) damage, harm.
injuriar [1b] *vt* (**a**) to insult, abuse, revile; to wrong. (**b**) to injure, damage, harm.
injuriosamente *adv* (**a**) insultingly, offensively; outrageously. (**b**) harmfully.
injurioso *adj* (**a**) insulting, offensive; outrageous. (**b**) harmful, damaging.
injustamente *adv* unjustly, unfairly; wrongfully.
injusticia *nf* injustice; unfairness; **una solemne** — a terrible injustice; **con** — unjustly.
injustificable *adj* unjustifiable.
injustificadamente *adv* unjustifiably.
injustificado *adj* unjustified, unwarranted.
injusto *adj* unjust, unfair; wrong, wrongful; **ser** — **con uno** to be unjust to someone.
inllevable *adj* unbearable, intolerable.
inmaculado *adj* immaculate.
inmadurez *nf* immaturity.
inmancable *adj* (*Col*, *PR*, *SD*) unfailing, infallible.
inmanejable *adj* unmanageable.
inmanente *adj* immanent; inherent (*a* in).
inmarcesible *adj*, **inmarchitable** *adj* imperishable, undying, unfading.
inmaterial *adj* immaterial.
inmaturo *adj* immature; unripe.
inmediaciones *nfpl* neighbourhood, surroundings, environs; immediate area; **en las** — **de** in the neighbourhood of.
inmediatamente *adv* immediately, at once.
inmediatez *nf* immediacy.
inmediato *adj* (**a**) (*of time*) immediate; prompt; **de** — immediately, promptly. (**b**) (*of place*) immediate, next; adjoining; — **a** close to, next to.
inmejorable *adj* unsurpassable; —**s recomendaciones** excellent references; **precios** —**s** unbeatable prices; **de calidad** — of the very best quality.
inmemorable *adj*, **inmemorial** *adj* immemorial.
inmensamente *adv* immensely, vastly.
inmensidad *nf* immensity, hugeness, vastness.
inmenso *adj* immense, huge, vast.
inmensurable *adj* immeasurable.
inmerecidamente *adv* undeservedly.
inmerecido *adj*, **inmérito** *adj* undeserved; uncalled-for.
inmergir [3c] *vt* to immerse.
inmersión *nf* immersion; (*by diver etc*) dive, plunge.
inmigración *nf* immigration.
inmigrado *nm*, **inmigrada** *nf* immigrant.
inmigrante **1** *adj* immigrant. **2** *nmf* immigrant.
inmigrar [1a] *vi* to immigrate.
inminencia *nf* imminence.
inminente *adj* imminent, impending.
inmiscuirse [3g] *vr* to interfere, meddle (*en* in).
inmisericorde *adj* insensitive, hard-hearted.
inmisericordioso *adj* merciless.
inmobiliaria *nf* building society.
inmobiliario *adj* real-estate (*attr*).
inmoble *adj* (**a**) immovable; motionless. (**b**) (*fig*) unmoved, unshaken.
inmoderadamente *adv* immoderately, excessively.
inmoderado *adj* immoderate, excessive.
inmodestamente *adv* immodestly.
inmodestia *nf* immodesty.
inmodesto *adj* immodest.
inmolar [1a] *vt* to immolate.
inmoral *adj* immoral; unethical.
inmoralidad *nf* immorality; unethical nature.
inmortal **1** *adj* immortal. **2** *nmf* immortal.
inmortalidad *nf* immortality.
inmortalizar [1f] *vt* to immortalize.
inmotivado *adj* motiveless, unmotivated, without motive.
inmoto *adj* unmoved.
inmovible *adj* immovable.
inmóvil *adj* (**a**) immovable; immobile; motionless, still; **quedar** — to remain (*or* be, stand *etc*) motionless; (*vehicle etc*) to remain stationary. (**b**) (*fig*) steadfast, unshaken.
inmovilidad *nf* immovability; immobility; stillness.
inmovilismo *nm* (*fig*) stagnation, deadness; do-nothing policy.

inmovilizar [1f] *vt* to immobilize; to stop, paralyse, bring to a standstill; *capital* (*Fin*) to tie up, lock up.
inmueble **1** *adj*: **bienes** —**s** real estate, landed property. **2** *nm* property; —**s** real estate, landed property.
inmundicia *nf* filth, dirt; nastiness; —**s** filth, rubbish.
inmundo *adj* filthy, dirty; foul, nasty.
inmune *adj* (**a**) (*Med*) immune (*contra* against, to). (**b**) (*fig*) exempt, free (*de* from).
inmunidad *nf* (**a**) immunity; — **diplomática** diplomatic immunity; — **parlamentaria** parliamentary immunity. (**b**) exemption.
inmunizar [1f] *vt* to immunize.
inmutabilidad *nf* immutability.
inmutable *adj* immutable, changeless.
inmutarse [1a] *vr* to change countenance, turn pale, lose one's self-possession; **se inmutó** his face fell, he seemed disappointed; **siguió sin** — he carried on unperturbed, he showed no sign of what he was feeling.
innato *adj* innate, inborn; inbred.
innatural *adj* unnatural.
innavegable *adj* *river etc* unnavigable; *ship* unseaworthy.
innecesariamente *adv* unnecessarily.
innecesario *adj* unnecessary.
innegable *adj* undeniable.
innoble *adj* ignoble.
innocuo *adj* innocuous, harmless.
innominado *adj* nameless, unnamed.
innovación *nf* innovation; novelty, new thing.
innovador *nm*, **innovadora** *nf* innovator.
innovar [1a] *vt* to introduce.
innumerable *adj*, **innúmero** *adj* innumerable, countless.
inobediencia *nf* disobedience.
inobediente *adj* disobedient.
inobjetable *adj* (*SAm*) unobjectionable.
inobservado *adj* unobserved.
inobservancia *nf* non-observance (*de* of); disregard (*de* for); neglect; (*of law*) violation, breaking (*de* of).
inocencia *nf* innocence.
inocentada *nf* (**a**) naïve remark, simple-minded thing; blunder. (**b**) practical joke, April Fool joke; hoax.
inocente[1] **1** *adj* (**a**) innocent (*de* of); harmless. (**b**) simple, naïve. **2** *nmf* (**a**) innocent, innocent person. (**b**) simple soul, naïve person.
inocente[2] *nm* (**a**) (*Chi*, *Ec*) avocado pear. (**b**) (*Ec*) masquerade.
inocentemente *adv* innocently.
inocentón **1** *adj* simple, naïve, gullible. **2** *nm*, **inocentona** *nf* simple soul, naïve person.
inocuidad *nf* innocuousness, harmlessness.
inoculación *nf* inoculation.
inocular [1a] *vt* (**a**) (*Med*) to inoculate (*contra* against, *de* with). (**b**) (*fig*) to corrupt, contaminate (*de* with).
inocuo *adj* = **innocuo**.
inodoro **1** *adj* odourless, having no smell. **2** *nm* lavatory, toilet.
inofensivo *adj* inoffensive, harmless.
inoficioso *adj* (*SAm*) useless.
inolvidable *adj* unforgettable.
inolvidablemente *adv* unforgettably.
inope *adj* impecunious, indigent.
inoperable *adj* (*Arg*, *Guat*, *Mex*: *Med*) inoperable.
inoperante *adj* (**a**) inoperative; unworkable. (**b**) (*SAm*) useless, fruitless, unproductive; inactive.
inopia *nf* indigence, poverty.
inopinadamente *adv* unexpectedly.
inopinado *adj* unexpected.
inoportunamente *adv* (**a**) inopportunely, at the wrong time. (**b**) inconveniently; inappropriately.
inoportunidad *nf* (**a**) inopportuneness, untimeliness. (**b**) inconvenience; inexpediency; inappropriateness.
inoportuno *adj* (**a**) inopportune, untimely, ill-timed. (**b**) inconvenient; inexpedient; inappropriate.
inorgánico *adj* inorganic.
inoxidable *adj* rustless; *steel* stainless.
inquebrantable *adj* (**a**) unbreakable. (**b**) (*fig*) unshakeable, unyielding, unswerving.
inquietador *adj* = **inquietante**.
inquietamente *adv* (**a**) anxiously, uneasily. (**b**) restlessly.
inquietante *adj* worrying, disturbing.
inquietar [1a] **1** *vt* to worry, disturb, trouble, upset; to torment. **2 inquietarse** *vr* to worry, get worried, upset oneself; **¡no te inquietes!** don't worry!

inquieto adj (a) anxious, worried, uneasy; **estar — por** to be anxious about, be worried about. (b) restless, unsettled.

inquietud nf (a) anxiety, worry, uneasiness, disquiet. (b) restlessness.

inquilinaje nm (Chi) = **inquilinato**; (Mex) tenants, tenantry.

inquilinato nm (a) tenancy; (Law) lease, leasehold. (b) rent; (**impuesto de**) — rates. (c) (Arg) tenement house.

inquilino nm, **inquilina** nf tenant; lessee; (Chi) tenant farmer.

inquina nf dislike, aversion; ill will, spite; **tener — a uno** to have a grudge against someone, have one's knife in someone.

inquiridor 1 adj inquiring. 2 nm, **inquiridora** nf inquirer; investigator.

inquirir [3i] 1 vt to enquire into, investigate, look into. 2 vi to inquire.

inquisición nf inquiry, investigation; **la I—** the Inquisition.

inquisidor nm inquisitor.

inquisitorial adj inquisitorial.

insaciable adj insatiable.

insaciablemente adv insatiably.

insalubre adj unhealthy, insalubrious; insanitary.

insanable adj incurable.

insania nf insanity.

insano adj (a) insane, mad. (b) unhealthy.

insatisfacción nf dissatisfaction.

insatisfactorio adj unsatisfactory.

insatisfecho adj unsatisfied; dissatisfied.

inscribir [3a; ptp **inscrito**] 1 vt to inscribe (also Math); to list, enter (on a list); to enrol; to register, record. 2 **inscribirse** vr to enrol, register.

inscripción nf (a) (act) inscription; enrolment; registering, recording. (b) inscription; lettering.

insecticida nm insecticide.

insectívoro adj insectivorous.

insecto nm insect.

inseguridad nf unsafeness; insecurity; unsteadiness; uncertainty.

inseguro adj unsafe; insecure; unsteady; uncertain.

inseminación nf insemination; — **artificial** artificial insemination.

inseminar [1a] vt to inseminate, fertilize.

insensatez nf folly, foolishness, stupidity.

insensato adj senseless, foolish, stupid.

insensibilidad nf (a) insensitivity; lack of feeling, callousness. (b) (Med) insensibility, unconsciousness; numbness.

insensibilizar [1f] vt to desensitize.

insensible adj (a) insensitive (a to); unfeeling, callous. (b) imperceptible. (c) (Med) insensible, unconscious; limb numb, without feeling.

insensiblemente adv (a) insensitively; unfeelingly. (b) imperceptibly.

inseparable adj inseparable.

inseparablemente adv inseparably.

insepulto adj unburied; without burial.

inserción nf insertion.

insertar [1a] vt to insert.

inservible adj useless.

insidia nf snare, trap; ambush.

insidiosamente adv insidiously; treacherously.

insidioso adj insidious; treacherous.

insigne adj distinguished; notable, famous.

insignia nf (a) badge, device, emblem; decoration. (b) flag, banner; (Naut) pennant. (c) —s insignia.

insignificancia nf insignificance.

insignificante adj insignificant; trivial, tiny, petty.

insinceridad nf insincerity.

insincero adj insincere.

insinuación nf insinuation.

insinuador adj insinuating.

insinuante adj (a) insinuating. (b) ingratiating. (c) cunning, crafty.

insinuar [1e] 1 vt (a) to insinuate, hint at, imply; — **que . . .** to hint that . . . , imply that . . .
(b) — **una observación** to slip in a comment.
2 **insinuarse** vr (a) — **con uno** to ingratiate oneself with somebody.
(b) — **en** to worm one's way into, creep into, slip into; — **en el ánimo de uno** to work one's way gradually into someone's mind.

insipidez nf insipidness, tastelessness; (fig) dullness, flatness.

insípido adj insipid, tasteless; (fig) dull, flat, tedious.

insistencia nf insistence (en on); persistence; **con — machacona** with wearisome insistence.

insistente adj insistent; persistent.

insistentemente adv insistently; persistently.

insistir [3a] vi to insist; to persist; — **en algo** to insist on something; to stress something, emphasize something; — **en una idea** to press an idea; — **en hacer algo** to insist on doing something; — **en que se haga algo** to insist that something should be done; — **en que algo es así** to insist that something is so.

insobornable adj incorruptible.

insociabilidad nf unsociability.

insociable adj unsociable.

insolación nf (a) (Meteorol) sunshine; **horas de —** hours of sunshine; **la — media diaria es de . . .** the daily sunshine average is . . .
(b) exposure (to the sun); (Med) sunstroke; **darse** (or **coger**) **una —** to get sunstroke.

insolar [1a] 1 vt to expose to the sun, put in the sun. 2 **insolarse** vr (Med) to get sunstroke.

insoldable adj irremediable; unmendable.

insolencia nf (a) insolence, effrontery. (b) piece of rudeness, rude thing.

insolentarse [1a] vr to be insolent (con to), become insolent.

insolente adj (a) insolent, rude; unblushing. (b) haughty, contemptuous. (c) sound harsh, grating.

insolentemente adv (a) insolently, rudely; unblushingly. (b) haughtily, contemptuously.

insólito adj unusual, unwonted.

insoluble adj insoluble.

insolvencia nf insolvency, bankruptcy.

insolvente adj insolvent, bankrupt.

insomne 1 adj sleepless. 2 nmf insomniac.

insomnio nm sleeplessness, insomnia.

insondable adj bottomless; (fig) unfathomable, impenetrable, inscrutable.

insonorización nf soundproofing.

insonorizado adj soundproof; **estar —** to be soundproofed.

insonoro adj noiseless, soundless.

insoportable adj unbearable, intolerable.

insoportablemente adv unbearably, intolerably.

insoria nf (Ven) insignificance.

insoslayable adj undeniable; problem etc unavoidable, which cannot be got round.

insospechado adj unsuspected.

insostenible adj untenable.

inspección nf inspection, examination; check; survey; — **ocular** visual examination.

inspeccionar [1a] vt to inspect, examine; to check; to survey; to supervise.

inspector nm inspector; superintendent, supervisor.

inspectorado nm inspectorate.

inspiración nf (a) inspiration. (b) (Med) inhalation.

inspirador adj inspiring.

inspirar [1a] 1 vt (a) to inspire; — **algo a uno** to inspire someone with something; to inspire something in someone. (b) (Med) to inhale, breathe in.
2 **inspirarse** vr: — **en** to be inspired by, find inspiration in.

inspirativo adj inspiring; inspirational.

instable adj = **inestable**.

instalación nf (a) (act) installation, instalment. (b) installation; fittings, equipment; (Tech) plant; — **de fuerza** power plant; —**es portuarias** harbour installations; — **sanitaria** sanitation, plumbing.

instalador nm installer; fitter; — **sanitario** plumber.

instalar [1a] 1 vt to install; to set up, erect, fit up, lay on. 2 **instalarse** vr to install oneself, establish oneself, settle (down).

instancia nf (a) request; application; (Law) petition; **a — de** at the request of; **pedir algo con — to** demand something insistently, demand something urgently. (b) application form.

instantánea nf (Phot) snap, snapshot.

instantáneamente adv instantaneously, instantly.

instantáneo adj instantaneous, instant; **café —** instant coffee.

instante nm instant, moment; **al — instantly, at** once; (a) **cada — every single moment, all the time; en un — in a flash; por —s incessantly, all the time; hace un — a moment ago.

instantemente adv insistently, urgently.

instar [1a] 1 vt to urge, press; — **a uno a hacer algo,** — **a uno para que haga algo** to urge someone to do something. 2 vi to be urgent, be pressing.

instauración nf (a) restoration, renewal. (b) establishment, setting-up.

instaurar [1a] vt (a) to restore, renew. (b) to establish, set up (again).

instigación nf instigation; **a — de** at the instigation of.

instigador nm, **instigadora** nf instigator; — **de un delito** instigator of a crime, (Law) accessory before the fact.

instigar [1h] *vt* to instigate; to abet; — **a uno a hacer algo** to incite someone to do something, induce someone to do something.

instilar [1a] *vt* to instil (*a, en* into).

instintivamente *adv* instinctively.

instintivo *adj* instinctive.

instinto *nm* instinct; impulse, urge; — **sexual** sexual urge, sexual desire; **por** — by instinct, instinctively.

institución *nf* (a) (*act*) institution, establishment. (b) institution; establishment; — **benéfica** charitable foundation; — **pública** public institution, public body. (c) —**es** (*of a study etc*) principles.

institucional *adj* institutional.

instituir [3g] *vt* to institute, establish; to found, set up.

instituto *nm* (a) institute, institution; **el benemérito** — the Civil Guard; — (**de segunda enseñanza**) state grammar school, high school (US); — **laboral** technical grammar school. (b) principle, rule; (*Eccl*) rule.

institutriz *nf* governess.

instrucción *nf* (a) instruction; education, teaching; (*Mil etc*) training, drill; (*Sport*) coaching, training; — **primaria** primary education; — **pública** state education.
   (b) knowledge, learning, instruction; **tener poca** — **en** to have little knowledge of, know little about.
   (c) (*Law*) proceedings.
   (d) —**es** instructions, orders, direction; **de acuerdo con sus** —**es** in accordance with your instructions; —**es para el uso** directions for use.

instructivo *adj* instructive; illuminating, enlightening; *film etc* educational.

instructor *nm* instructor, teacher; (*Sport*) coach, trainer.

instructora *nf* instructress, teacher; (*Sport*) coach, trainer.

instruido *adj* well-educated; well-informed.

instruir [3g] **1** *vt* (a) to instruct, teach (*de, en, sobre* in, about); to educate; (*Mil etc*) to train, drill; (*Sport*) to coach, train.
   (b) (*Law*) *case* to prepare, draw up; to investigate.
   2 instruirse *vr* to learn, teach oneself (*de, en, sobre* about).

instrumentación *nf* orchestration, scoring.

instrumental 1 *adj* instrumental. **2** *nm* instruments, set of instruments.

instrumentar [1a] *vt* to score, orchestrate; **está instrumentado para** it is scored for.

instrumentista *nmf* instrumentalist; instrument maker.

instrumento *nm* (a) instrument; tool, implement; —**s científicos** scientific instruments; —**s de mando** (*Aer etc*) controls; — **de precisión** precision instrument; —**s quirúrgicos** surgical instruments; —**s topográficos** surveying instruments; **volar por** —**s** (*Aer*) to fly on instruments.
   (b) (*Mus*) instrument; — **de batería**, — **de percusión** percussion instrument; — **de cuerda** stringed instrument; — **musical**, — **músico** musical instrument; — **de viento** wind instrument.
   (c) (*fig*) instrument, tool; **fue solamente el** — **del dictador** he was merely the dictator's tool, he was just a tool in the dictator's hands.
   (d) (*Law*) deed, legal document, instrument.

insubordinación *nf* insubordination; turbulence, unruliness.

insubordinado *adj* insubordinate; turbulent, rebellious, unruly.

insubordinar [1a] **1** *vt* to stir up, rouse to rebellion. **2 insubordinarse** *vr* to become unruly; to rebel.

insuficiencia *nf* (a) insufficiency, inadequacy; lack, shortage; — **de franqueo** underpaid postage; **debido a la** — **de personal** through shortage of staff.
   (b) incompetence.

insuficiente *adj* (a) insufficient, inadequate. (b) *person* incompetent.

insuficientemente *adv* insufficiently, inadequately.

insuflar [1a] *vt* to breathe into, introduce by blowing.

insufrible *adj* unbearable, insufferable.

insufriblemente *adv* unbearably, insufferably.

insular *adj* insular.

insularidad *nf* insularity.

insulina *nf* insulin.

insulsez *nf* (a) tastelessness, insipidity. (b) (*fig*) flatness, dullness.

insulso *adj* (a) tasteless, insipid. (b) (*fig*) flat, dull.

insultante *adj* insulting; abusive.

insultar [1a] *vt* to insult.

insulto *nm* (a) insult (*para* to). (b) (*Arg, Ven*) fainting fit; (*Mex, Nic*) indigestion.

insumergible *adj* unsinkable.

insumiso *adj* unsubmissive, rebellious.

insuperable *adj* insuperable, unsurmountable; *quality* unsurpassable.

insuperado *adj* unsurpassed.

insurgente 1 *adj* insurgent. **2** *nmf* insurgent.

insurrección *nf* revolt, insurrection.

insurreccional *adj* insurrectionary.

insurreccionar [1a] **1** *vt* to rouse to revolt, incite to rebel. **2 insurreccionarse** *vr* to rebel, rise in revolt.

insurrecto 1 *adj* rebel, insurgent. **2** *nmf* rebel, insurgent.

insustancial *adj* unsubstantial.

insustituible *adj* irreplaceable.

intacto *adj* untouched; whole, intact, undamaged; pure.

intachable *adj* irreproachable; faultless, perfect, not open to criticism on any score.

intangible *adj* intangible, impalpable.

integérrimo *adj superl of* **íntegro.**

integración *nf* integration; — **racial** racial integration.

integrado *adj* (a) integrated; in one piece, all of a piece; *society* integrated; *school* comprehensive (*Brit*). (b) **un grupo** — **por** a group made up of, a group consisting of.

integral 1 *adj* integral; (*Mech etc*) built-in; (*Math*) integral; *bread* wholemeal. **2** *nf* (*Math*) integral; **integral sign.**

íntegramente *adv* (a) wholly, entirely, completely. (b) (*fig*) uprightly, with integrity.

integrante 1 *adj* integral. **2** *nmf* member; **los** —**s del conjunto** the members of the group.

integrar [1a] *vt* (a) to make up, compose, form; **y los que integran el otro grupo** and those who make up the other group. (b) (*Math and fig*) to integrate. (c) (*Fin*) to repay, reimburse; (*Arg, Col, Mex*) to hand over.

integridad *nf* (a) wholeness, completeness. (b) (*fig*) uprightness, integrity. (c) (*fig*) virginity.

íntegro *adj* (a) whole, entire, complete; integral; **la cantidad íntegra** the whole sum, the sum in full; **versión íntegra** (*Lit*) unabridged version; **en versión íntegra de Pérez** in Pérez's edition of the complete text.
   (b) (*fig*) honest, upright.

integumento *nm* integument.

intelectiva *nf* intellect, mental faculty.

intelecto *nm* intellect; understanding; brains.

intelectual 1 *adj* intellectual; brain (*attr*). **2** *nmf* intellectual.

intelectualidad *nf* (a) intellectuality. (b) intelligentsia, intellectual people.

intelectualmente *adv* intellectually.

inteligencia *nf* (a) intelligence; mind, wits, understanding; ability; **de mediocre** — of mediocre intelligence; **una persona de fina** — a person with a sharp mind.
   (b) understanding; **la buena** — **entre los pueblos** good understanding between peoples.
   (c) (*SAm: Mil etc*) intelligence.
   (d) (*pej*) secret agreement, collusion.

inteligente *adj* (a) intelligent; clever, brainy, talented. (b) skilful; skilled, trained (*en* in).

inteligentemente *adv* intelligently.

inteligibilidad *nf* intelligibility.

inteligible *adj* intelligible.

inteligiblemente *adv* intelligibly.

intemperancia *nf* intemperance, excess.

intemperante *adj* intemperate, excessive.

intemperie *nf* inclemency (of the weather); bad weather, rough weather; **estar a la** — to be out in the open, be exposed to wind and weather, be at the mercy of the elements; **aguantar la** — to put up with wind and weather; **una cara curtida a la** — a face tanned by wind and weather.

intempestivamente *adv* in an untimely way, at a bad time; unseasonably.

intempestivo *adj* untimely, ill-timed; unseasonable.

intención *nf* intention; purpose; plan; **mis** —**es** my intentions, my plans; — **delictiva** criminal intent; —**es delictivas** criminal intentions; **segunda** — duplicity, underhandedness; **con** — deliberately; **con segunda** — meaningfully; with a second meaning, implying something else; (*pej*) nastily; **con la** — **de** + *infin* with the idea of + *ger*, intending to + *infin*; **de** — on purpose; **aceptar las** —**es de uno** to accept someone's advances, respond to someone's advances; **sin hacer la menor** — **de** + *infin* without making the least move to + *infin*; **tener la** — **de** + *infin* to intend to + *infin*, mean to + *infin*.

intencionadamente *adv* (a) meaningfully; nastily. (b) deliberately.

intencionado *adj* (a) meaningful. (b) deliberate. (c) **bien** — well-meaning; **mal** — ill-disposed, hostile, unkind; malicious.

intencional *adj* intentional.

intencionalmente *adv* intentionally.

intendencia *nf* (a) management, administration. (b) manager's office. (c) (*Mil: also* **cuerpo de** —, *approx*) service corps. (d) (*Arg*) mayoralty.

intendente *nm* (a) manager. (b) — **de ejército** quartermaster general. (c) (*Arg*) mayor.

intensamente *adv* intensely; powerfully, strongly; vividly, profoundly.

intensar [1a] **1** *vt* to intensify. **2 intensarse** *vr* to intensify.

intensidad *nf* intensity; power, strength; vividness; deepness; (*Elec, Tech*) strength.

intensificación *nf* intensification.

intensificar [1g] *vt* to intensify.

intensión *nf* intensity, intenseness.

intensivamente *adv* intensively.

intensivo *adj* intensive.

intenso *adj* intense; *feeling* intense, powerful, strong; *impression* vivid, profound; *tan* deep; *colour* deep, intense; (*Elec etc*) strong.

intentar [1a] *vt* (a) to try, attempt; — **algo** to try something; — + *infin* to try to + *infin*, attempt to + *infin*, endeavour to + *infin*. (b) to mean, intend (*con* by); — + *infin* to mean to + *infin*.

intento *nm* (a) intention, intent, purpose; **al** — **de** + *infin* (*Arg, Chi*) with the aim of + *ger*; **de** — on purpose. (b) attempt; — **fracasado** failed attempt, unsuccessful attempt; **acusado de** — **de violación** charged with attempted rape.

intentona *nf* foolhardy attempt, wild attempt; (*Pol*) putsch, rising.

inter . . . **inter** . . .

interacción *nf* interaction, interplay.

interamericano *adj* inter-American.

interandino *adj* inter-Andean, concerning areas on both sides of the Andes.

intercalación *nf* intercalation, insertion.

intercalar [1a] *vt* to intercalate, insert.

intercambiable *adj* interchangeable.

intercambiar [1b] *vt* to change over, interchange; *publications, prisoners etc* to exchange; *stamps etc* to exchange, swap.

intercambio *nm* interchange; exchange; swap, swapping.

interceder [2a] *vi* to intercede; — **con A por B** to intercede with A on B's behalf, to plead with A for B.

interceptación *nf* interception; stoppage, holdup.

interceptar [1a] *vt* to intercept, cut off; to stop, hold up.

interceptor *nm* (a) interceptor. (b) (*Mech*) trap; separator.

intercesión *nf* intercession; mediation.

interclub *adj* (*SAm*) *game* inter-club, between two clubs.

intercomunicación *nf* intercommunication.

intercomunión *nf* intercommunion.

interconectar [1a] *vt* to interconnect.

interconfesional *adj* interdenominational.

intercontinental *adj* intercontinental.

interdecir [3p] *vt* to forbid, prohibit.

interdependencia *nf* interdependence.

interdependiente *adj* interdependent.

interdicción *nf* prohibition, interdiction.

interdicto *nm* prohibition, ban, interdict.

interés *nm* (a) interest; concern; **con gran** — with great interest; **de gran** — of great interest, very interesting; **su** — **en, su** — **por** his interest in; his concern for; **poner** — **en** to take an interest in; **sentir** — **por** to be interested in, feel an interest in; **no tiene** — it has no interest. (b) interest, share, part; —**es** interests, affairs; **los** —**es españoles en África** Spanish interests in Africa; —**es creados** vested interests; **en** — **de** in the interest of; **en** — **de la higiene** in the interest of hygiene, for the sake of cleanliness; **fomentar los** —**es de uno** to promote someone's interests; **tener** — **en** to hold a share in, have a part in. (c) (*pej*) self-interest; selfishness, egotism; **todo es cuestión de** — it's all a matter of self-interest. (d) (*Comm, Fin*) interest; **con** — **de 9 por cien, con un** — **del 9 por cien** at an interest of 9%; — **compuesto** compound interest; — **devengado** accrued interest, earned interest; — **simple** simple interest; **dar a** — to lend at interest; **devengar** —**es** to bear interest; **poner a** — to put out at interest, invest.

interesado 1 *adj* (a) interested; concerned; **estar** — **en** to be interested in, have an interest in; **la compañía está interesada en comprarlo** the company is interested in buying it. (b) biassed, prejudiced; **actuar de una manera interesada** to act in a biassed way. (c) selfish, self-seeking; having an ulterior motive; mercenary. **2** *nm*, **interesada** *nf* (a) person concerned, interested party; **los** —**s** those interested, those concerned. (b) (*in applications*) the undersigned, the applicant.

interesante *adj* interesting.

interesar [1a] **1** *vt* (a) to interest, be of interest to; to appeal to; **¿te interesa el fútbol?** are you interested in football?; **no me interesan los toros** I'm not interested in bullfighting, bullfighting does not appeal to me; **la propuesta no nos interesa** the proposal is of no interest to us. (b) to interest (*in* en); **logré** —**le en mi idea** I succeeded in interesting him in my idea. (c) to concern, involve; **el asunto interesa a todos** the matter concerns everybody. (d) (*Med*) to affect, involve; **la lesión interesa la región lumbar** the injury affects the lumbar region. **2** *vi* to be of interest; to be important; **la idea no interesó** the idea was of no interest, the idea did not interest anybody. **3 interesarse** *vr* to be interested, take an interest (*en, por* in); — **en una empresa** to participate in an enterprise, concern oneself with an enterprise.

interestatal *adj* inter-state.

interestelar *adj* interstellar.

interferencia *nf* (a) (*Phys, Radio*) interference, (*deliberate*) jamming. (b) (*angl*) interference (*en* in); **no** — non-interference.

interferir [3i] **1** *vt* (a) (*Phys, Radio*) to interfere with, (*deliberately*) jam. (b) (*angl*) to interfere with, upset, affect; **su acción ha interferido nuestras operaciones** his action has interfered with our operations. **2** *vi* (*angl*) to interfere (*en* in, with). **3 interferirse** *vr* (*angl*) to interfere (*en* in, with); **no está en posición de** — **en el conflicto** he is in no position to interfere in the conflict.

ínterin 1 *adv* meanwhile. **2** *conj* while; until. **3** *nm* (a) interim; **en el** — in the interim, in the meantime. (b) temporary incumbency.

interinamente *adv* (a) in the interim, meanwhile. (b) temporarily, as a temporary holder of the post (*etc*), as a stopgap.

interinar [1a] *vt post* to occupy temporarily, occupy in an acting capacity.

interinato *nm* (a) (*Arg*) temporary nature (of a post). (b) (*Arg*) period of temporary occupation of a post. (c) (*Arg, Chi, Guat, Hond*) temporary post.

interino 1 *adj* (a) provisional, temporary, interim. (b) *person* acting. **2** *nm*, **interina** *nf* temporary holder of a post, acting official (*etc*); stopgap, stand-in; (*Eccl, Med*) locum, locum tenens.

interior 1 *adj* interior, inner, inside; *thoughts etc* inward, inner; *politics, trade* domestic, internal; (*Geog*) inland, *part of country* inner; **en la parte** — inside, on the inside; **pista** — (*Sport*) inside track; *see* **ropa** *etc*. **2** *nm* (a) interior, inside; inner part. (b) (*fig*) mind, soul; **en su** — in one's heart, deep inside one; **dije para mi** — I said to myself. (c) **Ministerio del I**— Ministry of the Interior, Home Office (*Brit*), Department of the Interior (*US*). (d) (*Sport*) inside-forward; — **derecho** inside-right; — **izquierdo** inside-left. (e) —**es** (*Anat*) insides.

interioridad *nf* (a) inwardness; **en su** —, **sabe que** . . . (*CAm*) in his heart he knows that . . . , deep inside himself he knows that . . . . (b) —**es** family secrets, private affairs; inner history, secret goings-on; ins and outs; **explicó las** —**es de la lucha** he explained the inner history of the struggle; **desconocen las** —**es del mercado** they don't know all the ins and outs of the market.

interiorizar [1f] (*SAm*) **1** *vt* to look into, investigate closely. **2 interiorizarse** *vr*: — **algo** to familiarize oneself with something.

interiormente adv internally, inwardly; **lo que pasa — what** goes on inside.

interjección nf interjection.

interlineado nm space between the lines.

interlineal adj interlinear.

interlinear [1a] vt (a) to interline, write (or print etc) between the lines. (b) (Typ) to space, lead.

interlocutor nm, **interlocutora** nf speaker, interlocutor; **mi —** the person I was speaking to, the person who spoke to me.

intérlope 1 adj interloping, intrusive; (Mex) fraudulent. 2 nm (Comm) interloper, unauthorized trader.

interludio nm interlude.

intermediario 1 adj (a) intermediary.
(b) mediating.
2 nm, **intermediaria** nf (a) intermediary.
(b) mediator.
3 nm (Comm) middleman.

intermedio 1 adj (a) intermediate, halfway (entre between).
(b) intervening; **el período —** the intervening period, the period between.
2 nm (a) interval (also Theat); (Parl) recess.
(b) **por — de** (SAm) through, by means of.

intermezzo [inter'metso] nm intermezzo.

interminable adj endless, interminable.

interminablemente adv endlessly, interminably.

intermisión nf intermission.

intermitente 1 adj intermittent. 2 nm (Aut) flashing light, indicator.

internacional 1 adj international. 2 nf: **I—** International(e).

internacionalismo nm internationalism.

internacionalizar [1f] vt to internationalize.

internada nf (Sport) tackle.

internado 1 nm, **internada** nf (Mil etc) internee. 2 nm boarding school; boarding; (pupils collectively) boarders.

internamiento nm internment.

internar [1a] 1 vt (a) (Mil) to intern; **— a uno en un manicomio** to put someone into an asylum, commit someone to an asylum.
(b) to send inland.
2 **internarse** vr (a) to advance (deeply); to penetrate; **el jugador se interna** the player goes deep into the opponent's half.
(b) **— en** to go into, go deeply into, penetrate into; **se internó en el edificio** he went into the building, he disappeared into the building; **— en un país** to go into the interior of a country.
(c) **— en un estudio** to go deeply into a subject, study a subject in depth.

interno 1 adj internal, interior; inside; **la política interna** internal politics, domestic politics; **por vía interna** (Med) internally. 2 nm, **interna** nf boarder.

interpelación nf appeal, plea.

interpelar [1a] vt (a) to implore, beseech; to beg for the aid of. (b) to address, speak to; (Parl) to ask for explanations, question formally.

interplanetario adj interplanetary.

interpolación nf interpolation.

interpolar [1a] vt (a) to interpolate. (b) to interrupt briefly.

interponer [2r] 1 vt (a) to interpose, put in, insert.
(b) (Law) appeal to lodge, put in.
(c) (in speech) to interpose, interject.
2 **interponerse** vr to intervene.

interposición nf (a) insertion. (b) lodging, formulation. (c) interjection.

interpretación nf (a) interpretation; **mala —** misinterpretation, misunderstanding.
(b) interpretation, translation.
(c) (Mus) rendition, performance; interpretation.
(d) (Theat) performance; playing.

interpretar [1a] vt (a) to interpret; **— mal** to misinterpret, misunderstand, misconstrue.
(b) (Ling) to interpret, translate; **— del chino al ruso** to translate from Chinese into Russian.
(c) (Mus) to render, perform; to interpret; (Theat) play to perform; part to play.

interpretativo adj interpretative.

intérprete nmf (a) (Ling) interpreter, translator.
(b) (Mus) performer; exponent; artist(e).

interracial adj interracial.

interregno nm interregnum; (SAm) interval, intervening period.

interrelación nf interrelation.

interrelacionado adj interrelated.

interrelacionar [1a] vt to interrelate.

interreligioso adj: **contactos —s** contacts between religions.

interrogación nf (a) interrogation. (b) question. (c) question mark.

interrogador nm, **interrogadora** nf interrogator; questioner.

interrogante 1 adj questioning. 2 nmf interrogator; questioner. 3 nf question mark; (fig) question mark, query.

interrogar [1h] vt to question, interrogate; (Law) to examine.

interrogativo 1 adj interrogative. 2 nm interrogative.

interrogatorio nm (a) questioning; (Law) examination. (b) questionnaire.

interrumpir [3a] vt speaker etc to interrupt; holiday etc to interrupt, cut short; supply to cut off; traffic etc to block, hold up; (Elec) to switch off.

interrupción nf interruption; stoppage, holdup.

interruptor nm (Elec) switch; **— de dos direcciones** two-way switch.

intersecarse [1g] vr to intersect.

intersección nf intersection; (Aut) intersection, crossing, junction.

intersticio nm interstice; crack; interval, gap; (Mech) clearance.

intertanto (SAm) 1 adv meanwhile. 2 conj: **— que él llegue** until he comes, while we wait for him to come. 3 n: **en el —** in the meantime.

interurbano adj inter-city; (Tel) long-distance, trunk (attr).

intervalo nm (in time) interval; break; (Mus) interval; (in space) gap; **a —s** at intervals; intermittently; every now and then.

intervención nf (a) supervision, control.
(b) (Comm) audit, auditing.
(c) (Med) operation; **— quirúrgica** surgical operation.
(d) (Tel) tapping.
(e) intervention (en in); participation (en in); contribution (en to); **su — en la discusión** his contribution to the discussion; **la política de no —** the policy of non-intervention, the non-intervention policy.

intervenir [3s] 1 vt (a) to supervise, control.
(b) (Comm) to audit.
(c) (Med) to operate on.
(d) (Tel) to tap.
2 vi (a) to intervene (en in); to take part, participate (en in); to contribute (en to); **no intervino en el debate** he did not take part in the debate, he did not contribute to the debate; **él no intervino en la decisión** he did not have a hand in the decision; **una reyerta en la que intervino X** a brawl in which X was involved.
(b) to intercede; to mediate; **— por uno** to intercede for someone.

interventor nm inspector, supervisor; (Comm) auditor (also **— de cuentas**).

interviú nf interview; **hacer una — a uno** to interview someone.

interviuvada nf series of interviews, interview session.

interviuvador nm, **interviuvadora** nf interviewer.

interviuvar [1a] vt to interview, have an interview with.

intestado adj intestate.

intestinal adj intestinal.

intestino 1 adj internal; domestic, civil. 2 nm intestine; gut; **— ciego** caecum; **— delgado** small intestine; **— grueso** large intestine.

intimación nf intimation, announcement, notification.

íntimamente adv intimately.

intimar [1a] 1 vt to intimate, announce, notify (a to); to order, require (que that).
2 vi and **intimarse** vr to become intimate, become friendly (con with); **ahora intiman mucho** they're very friendly now.

intimidación nf intimidation.

intimidad nf (a) intimacy, familiarity; **disfrutar de la — de uno** to be on close terms with someone, enjoy someone's confidence; **entrar en — con uno** to become friendly with someone.
(b) privacy, private life; **conocido en la — como X** known in private life as X; **la ceremonia se celebró en la —** the wedding took place privately, it was a quiet wedding.

intimidar [1a] 1 vt to intimidate, overawe; to bully, scare.
2 **intimidarse** vr to be intimidated, be overawed; to get scared.

íntimo adj intimate; relationship intimate, close; thoughts inner, innermost; life etc private; **una boda**

íntima a quiet wedding, a private wedding; **es —
amigo mío** he is a close friend of mine; **en lo más
— de su corazón** in one's heart of hearts.
intitular [1a] *vt* to entitle, call.
intocable 1 *adj* untouchable. **2** *nmf* untouchable.
intolerable *adj* intolerable, unbearable.
intolerancia *nf* intolerance; narrow-mindedness,
bigotry.
intolerante *adj* intolerant (*con*, *para* of); narrow-
minded, bigoted (*en* about).
intonso *adj* book uncut.
intoxicación *nf* poisoning; **— alimenticia** food
poisoning.
intoxicar [1g] *vt* to poison.
intra . . . **intra** . . .
intradós *nm* inside surface of an arch (*or* vault); side
of a window frame.
intraducible *adj* untranslatable.
intragable *adj* unpalatable (*also fig*).
intramuros *adv* within the city, within the walls.
intranquilidad *nf* worry, uneasiness, disquiet,
anxiety.
intranquilizar [1f] **1** *vt* to worry, disquiet, make
uneasy. **2 intranquilizarse** *vr* to get worried, feel
uneasy, be anxious.
intranquilo *adj* worried, uneasy, anxious; restless.
intranscendente *adj* (*SAm*) unimportant, insignificant.
intranscribible *adj* unprintable.
intransferible *adj* untransferable, not transferable.
intransigencia *nf* intransigence; uncompromising
attitude.
intransigente *adj* intransigent; uncompromising,
unyielding; diehard.
intransitable *adj* impassable.
intransitivo *adj* intransitive.
intratable *adj* problem intractable; awkward, tough;
person unsociable; difficult, impossible; **¡son —s!**
they're impossible!
intravenoso *adj* intravenous.
intrépidamente *adv* intrepidly, dauntlessly.
intrepidez *nf* intrepidity, intrepidness.
intrépido *adj* intrepid, dauntless.
intriga *nf* intrigue; plot, scheme; (*Theat*) plot; **—
secundaria** subplot.
intrigante 1 *adj* (*a*) (*pej*) intriguing, scheming. (*b*)
(*angl*) intriguing, interesting, puzzling. **2** *nmf*
intriguer.
intrigar [1h] **1** *vt* (*a*) to intrigue, interest, puzzle.
(*b*) (*SAm*) *affair* to conduct in a surprising way.
2 *vi* to intrigue, scheme, plot.
3 intrigarse *vr* (*SAm*) to be intrigued, be puzzled.
intrincadamente *adv* (*a*) densely, impenetrably.
(*b*) (*fig*) intricately.
intrincado *adj* (*a*) dense, impenetrable; tangled.
(*b*) (*fig*) intricate; involved, complicated.
intrincar [1g] *vt* to entangle; to confuse, complicate.
intríngulis *nm* (*fam*) ulterior motive; hidden snag;
puzzle, mystery.
intrínsecamente *adv* intrinsically; inherently.
intrínseco *adj* intrinsic; inherent.
intro . . . **intro** . . .
introducción *nf* introduction; insertion; creation.
introducir [3o] **1** *vt* to introduce; *visitor etc* to bring
in, show in; *object* to insert, introduce, put in;
discord etc to create, sow, cause.
2 introducirse *vr* (*a*) to get in, slip in, gain
access (*en* to); (*fig*) to insinuate oneself, worm one's
way (*en* into).
(*b*) (*fig*) to interfere, meddle.
introductor *adj* introductory.
introito *nm* (*Theat*) prologue; (*Eccl*) introit.
intromisión *nf* (*a*) introduction, insertion. (*b*) (*pej*)
interference, meddling.
introspección *nf* introspection.
introspectivo *adj* introspective.
introversión *nf* introversion.
introvertido 1 *adj* introvert. **2** *nm*, **introvertida** *nf*
introvert.
intrusión *nf* intrusion; (*Law*) trespass.
intruso 1 *adj* intrusive. **2** *nm*, **intrusa** *nf* intruder,
interloper; outsider; (*at party etc*) gatecrasher;
(*Law*) trespasser.
intuición *nf* intuition; **por —** by intuition, intuitively.
intuir [3g] **1** *vt* to know by intuition.
2 intuirse *vr*: **eso se intuye** that can be guessed;
se intuye que . . . one can tell intuitively that . . .,
one can guess that . . .; **el hombre se intuye
observado** the man guesses he is being watched,
the man realizes he is under observation.
intuitivamente *adv* intuitively.

intuitivo *adj* intuitive.
intuito *nm* glance, look; **por — de** in view of.
inundación *nf* flood, flooding.
inundadizo *adj* (*SAm*) liable to flooding.
inundar [1a] *vt* to flood, inundate, swamp (*all also
fig*; *de*, *en* with); **— el mercado de un producto** to
flood the market with a product; **quedamos
inundados de ofertas** we are swamped with offers;
la lluvia inundó la campiña the rain flooded the
countryside, the rain left the countryside under
water.
inusitado *adj* (*a*) unusual, unwonted, rare. (*b*)
obsolete.
inútil *adj* useless; *attempt etc* vain, fruitless; *effort*
vain; **todo es —** nothing is any use; **es — que Vd
proteste** it is useless for you to protest, it's no good
your protesting.
inutilidad *nf* uselessness.
inutilización *nf* disablement; spoiling; (*of stamp*)
cancellation.
inutilizar [1f] **1** *vt* to make useless, render useless;
ship etc to disable, put out of action; to spoil, ruin;
effort etc to nullify; *stamp* to cancel.
2 inutilizarse *vr* to become useless; to be disabled;
to be spoiled.
inútilmente *adv* uselessly; vainly, fruitlessly.
invadeable *adj* unfordable; (*fig*) impassable; (*fig*)
unsurmountable.
invadir [3a] *vt* (*a*) to invade; to overrun; **la turba
invadió las calles** the mob poured out on to the
streets. (*b*) (*fig*) *rights etc* to encroach upon.
invalidar [1a] *vt* to invalidate, nullify.
invalidez *nf* (*a*) disablement; unfitness. (*b*) in-
validity, nullity.
inválido 1 *adj* (*a*) (*Med*) invalid, disabled; unfit.
(*b*) (*Law etc*) invalid, null and void; **declarar
inválida una elección** to declare an election invalid.
2 *nm*, **inválida** *nf* (*Med*) invalid.
3 *nm* (*Mil: Med*) disabled soldier, wounded
soldier; pensioner.
invaluable *adj* (*SAm*) invaluable.
invariable *adj* invariable.
invariablemente *adv* invariably.
invasión *nf* (*a*) invasion (*also Med*); attack. (*b*)
(*fig*) encroachment (*de* on); inroad (*de* into).
invasor 1 *adj* invading. **2** *nm*, **invasora** *nf* invader,
attacker.
invectiva *nf* invective; **una —** a piece of invective,
a tirade.
invectivar [1a] *vt* to inveigh against.
invencibilidad *nf* invincibility.
invencible *adj* invincible; *obstacle* unsurmountable,
insuperable.
invenciblemente *adv* invincibly; insuperably.
invención *nf* invention; discovery, finding; (*pej*)
fabrication; (*Poet etc*) fiction, tale, fable.
invendible *adj* unsaleable, unmarketable.
inventar [1a] *vt* to invent; to devise; (*pej*) to make up,
fabricate, concoct.
inventariar [1b] *vt* to inventory, make an inventory
of.
inventario *nm* inventory; stocktaking; **hacer — de**
to make an inventory of, take stock of.
inventiva *nf* inventiveness; ingenuity, resourcefulness.
inventivo *adj* inventive; ingenious, resourceful.
invento *nm* invention.
inventor *nm*, **inventora** *nf* inventor.
invernáculo *nm* greenhouse, hothouse; conservatory.
invernada *nf* (*a*) winter season.
(*b*) wintering; hibernation.
(*c*) (*Arg*, *Col*, *Per*, *Urug*) winter pasture.
(*d*) (*Ven*) heavy rainstorm.
invernadero *nm* (*a*) = **invernáculo**. (*b*) (*SAm*)
winter pasture.
invernal *adj* wintry, winter (*attr*).
invernar [1k] *vi* to winter, spend the winter; (*Zool*)
to hibernate.
invernazo *nm* (*PR*, *SD*) rainy season (*July to
September*).
inverne *nm* (*SAm*) winter pasturing; winter fattening.
invernizo *adj* wintry, winter (*attr*).
inverosímil *adj* unlikely, improbable; implausible.
inverosimilitud *nf* unlikeliness, improbability;
implausibility.
inversamente *adv* inversely; **e —** and vice versa.
inversión *nf* (*a*) inversion; reversal; (*Aut*, *Mech*)
reversing; **— de marcha** reversing, backing; **—
sexual** homosexuality.
(*b*) (*Comm*, *Fin*) investment (*en* in); **— de
capitales** capital investment.

inversionista nmf (Comm, Fin) investor.
inverso adj inverse, inverted; reverse, contrary; **a la inversa** inversely, the other way round; (fig) vice versa; on the contrary.
inversor nm, **inversora** nf (SAm: Comm, Fin) investor.
invertebrado 1 adj invertebrate. **2** nm invertebrate.
invertido 1 adj (a) inverted; reversed. (b) homosexual. **2** nm homosexual.
invertir [3i] vt (a) to invert, turn upside down; to reverse, put the other way round; to change over, change the order of; (Aut, Mech) to reverse.
(b) effort, time to spend, put in (en on); **invirtieron 5 días en el viaje** they spent 5 days on the journey.
(c) (Comm, Fin) to invest (en in).
investidura nf investiture.
investigación nf (a) investigation; inquiry (de into); — **policíaca** police investigation.
(b) (Univ etc) research, research work (de in, into).
investigador nm, **investigadora** nf (a) investigator.
(b) (Univ etc) research worker, researcher.
investigar [1h] vt (a) to investigate; to inquire into, look into.
(b) (Univ etc) to do research into, do research work on.
investir [3l] vt: — **a uno con algo**, — **a uno de algo** to invest someone with something, confer something on someone.
inveterado adj inveterate; confirmed, hardened; habit deep-seated, well-established.
invicto adj unconquered, unbeaten.
invidencia nf sightlessness.
invierno nm (a) winter, wintertime. (b) (CAm, Col, Ec, Ven) rainy season. (c) (Ven) heavy shower.
inviolabilidad nf inviolability; — **parlamentaria** parliamentary immunity.
inviolable adj inviolable.
inviolado adj inviolate.
invisibilidad nf invisibility.
invisible 1 adj invisible. **2** nm (Arg) hairpin; (Mex) hairnet.
invitación nf invitation (a to).
invitado nm, **invitada** nf guest.
invitar [1a] vt (a) to invite; — **a uno a hacer algo** to invite someone to do something; to call on someone to do something; **hoy invito a café** today I'll buy the coffee, today I'll stand coffees all round; **dio las gracias a los que le habían invitado** he thanked his hosts.
(b) to attract, entice.
invocar [1g] vt (a) to invoke, call on; — **la ley** to invoke the law.
(b) to beg for, implore; — **la ayuda de** to beg for the help of.
involucrar [1a] **1** vt: — **algo en un discurso** to bring something irrelevant into a speech.
2 involucrarse vr (esp SAm) to meddle, interfere (en in); to get involved (en in); **las personas involucradas en el caso** the people involved in the affair, the persons concerned in the matter.
involuntariamente adv involuntarily; unintentionally.
involuntario adj involuntary; offence etc unintentional.
invulnerabilidad nf invulnerability.
invulnerable adj invulnerable.
inyectable adj serum, vaccine.
inyección nf injection, shot; **hacerse** (or **ponerse**) **una** — to give oneself an injection.
inyectado adj: ojos —**s** (**en sangre**) bloodshot eyes.
inyectar [1a] vt to inject (en into); — **algo en uno** to inject someone with something.
inyector nm injector; (Tech) nozzle.
ion nm ion.
iónico adj ionic.
ionizar [1f] vt to ionize.
ionosfera nf ionosphere.
iota nf iota.
ipecacuana nf ipecacuanha.
ir [3t] **1** vi (a) (general sense) to go; to move; to travel; (on foot) to go, walk; (in car etc) to go, drive; (on cycle, horse etc) to go, ride; — **a Quito** to go to Quito; **este camino va a Huesca** this road goes to Huesca, this is the road to Huesca; — **hacia Sevilla** to go towards Seville, go in the direction of Seville; — **hasta León** to go as far as León; **fui en coche** I went by car, I drove; **fui en tren** I went by train, I went by rail; — **despacio** to go slow(ly); — **con tiento** to go carefully, go cautiously; **vaya donde vaya, encontrará** . . . wherever you go, you will find . . .; **ya ha ido** (fam) you've had it (fam);

¡voy! I'm coming! (answering a call); **¡vamos!** let's go! (see also (**k**)); **¿quién va?** (Mil etc) who goes there?; — **por leña** to fetch wood, go and fetch wood, go for wood; **voy por el médico** I'll (go and) fetch the doctor, I'll call the doctor; — **tras una** to chase someone, chase after someone.
(b) (idioms) — **de mal en peor** to go from bad to worse, get worse; **esto va de veras** this is serious; I'm in earnest; **en lo que va de año** so far this year; **a eso voy** I'm coming to that; **si vamos a eso** for that matter, as for that; — **a lo suyo** to go one's own way; (pej) to act selfishly, think only of oneself; **va para los 40** he's going on for 40, he's knocking on 40 (fam); **va para viejo** he's getting old; **con éste van 30** that makes 30.
(c) (of progress) to go; (Med) to be, go, get along; **¿cómo va eso?** how are things going?; **¿cómo le va?** how goes it?; **¿cómo va el ensayo?** how are you getting on with the essay?; **no me va bien el inglés** I can't get on with English; **el enfermo va mejor** the patient is better, the patient is getting along nicely.
(d) (of difference) **va mucho de A a B** there's a lot of difference between A and B, A is very different from B; **¡lo que va del padre al hijo!** what a difference there is between father and son!; **de 7 a 9 van 2** 7 from 9 leaves 2.
(e) (of intention) **eso no va por Vd** I wasn't referring to you, that wasn't meant for you; it's not your fault.
(f) (of concern) **va mucho en esto** a lot depends on it; **¿qué te va en ello?** what does it matter to you?; **no le va la vida en esto** it's not as though his life depends on it.
(g) (of betting) **van 5 duros a que no lo haces** I bet 5 duros that you won't do it; **¿cuánto va?** how much do you bet?
(h) (of career etc) **va para ingeniero** he's going to become an engineer, he's going into engineering.
(i) (Cards) to lead; to go.
(j) (of clothes) to suit, become; **¿me va bien esto?** does this suit me?; **no le va bien el sombrero** the hat doesn't suit her.
(k) (interj) etc **¡vaya!** well!, there!, I say!; **¡vaya coche!** what a car!, there's a car for you!, that's some car!; **¡vaya susto que me pegué!** what a fright I got!; **¡vaya, vaya!** well I'm blowed!; come now!; **¡vamos!** well!; **vamos, no es difícil** come now, it's not difficult; **una chica, vamos, una mujer** a girl, well . . . a woman; **¡qué va!** rubbish!; nonsense!; **¡vaya por Pepe!** here's to Joe!
(l) (in continuous tenses) **iba anocheciendo** it was getting dark; **iban fumando** they were smoking; **voy comprendiendo que** . . . I am beginning to see that . . ., I am in the process of learning that . . .
(m) (with ptp) **iba cansado** he was tired; **van escritas 3 cartas** that's 3 letters I've written; **va vendido todo** everything has been sold.
(n) (ir a + infin) **voy a hacerlo** I'm going to do it; **vamos a hacerlo** we are going to do it; let's do it; **fui a verle** I went to see him, I went and saw him; **¿qué le vamos a hacer?** what can we do about him?
(o) ir de + noun: see the corresponding noun entry.
2 irse vr (a) **por aquí se va a Jaca** this is the way to Jaca; **¿por dónde se va al aeropuerto?** which way to the airport?
(b) to go away, leave, depart; **se fueron** they went, they went off, they left; **es hora de irnos** it's time we went, it's time for us to go; **¡vete!** go away!, get out!; **¡vete ya!** off with you!; **¡no te vayas!** don't go!; **¡vámonos!** let's go!; (Rail etc) all aboard!; — **de algo** to discard something; **me voy de con Vd** (CAm) I'm leaving you.
(c) (of mano, pie etc) to slip, lose one's balance; (of wall etc) to give way.
(d) (of container) to leak; to overflow; (of contents) to leak out, overflow, ooze out; to evaporate; **se fue el vino** the wine leaked out; the wine overflowed; **el neumático se va** the tyre is losing air.
(e) (euph) to be dying; to die; **se nos va el amo** the master is dying; **se nos fue hace 3 años** he departed from us 3 years ago, he passed away 3 years ago.
ira nf anger, rage, wrath (lit); (of elements) fury, violence.
iracundia nf ire; irascibility.
iracundo adj irate; irascible.
Irak: el — Iraq.
iraki see **iraquí**.

Irán: el — Iran, Persia.
iranés = iraní.
iraní 1 adj Iranian, Persian. **2** nmf Iranian, Persian.
iranio = iraní.
iraquí 1 adj Iraqui. **2** nmf Iraqui.
irascibilidad nf irascibility.
irascible adj irascible.
iridescencia nf iridescence.
iridescente adj iridescent.
iris nm rainbow; (Anat) iris.
irisación nf iridescence.
irisado adj iridescent.
irisar [1a] vi to be iridescent, iridesce.
Irlanda f Ireland; **— del Norte** Northern Ireland, Ulster.
irlandés 1 adj Irish. **2** nm Irishman; **los —es** the Irish. **3** nm (language) Irish.
irlandesa nf Irishwoman.
ironía nf irony; **con —** ironically.
irónicamente adv ironically.
irónico adj ironical.
ironizar [1f] vt to ridicule.
irracional 1 adj irrational; unreasoning; **ser —** brute, brute creature. **2** nm brute, brute creature.
irracionalidad nf irrationality; unreasonableness.
irracionalmente adv irrationally; unreasonably, unreasoningly.
irradiación nf irradiation.
irradiar [1b] vt to irradiate, radiate.
irrazonable adj unreasonable.
irreal adj unreal.
irrealidad nf unreality.
irrealizable adj unrealizable; unworkable; impossible to carry out; objective etc unattainable.
irrebatible adj unanswerable, irrefutable, unassailable.
irreconciliable adj irreconcilable; inconsistent, incompatible.
irreconocible adj unrecognizable.
irrecuperable adj irrecoverable, irretrievable.
irrecusable adj unimpeachable.
irredimible adj irredeemable.
irreducible adj irreducible.
irreductible adj defender etc uncompromising, unyielding.
irreembolsable adj deposit non-returnable.
irreemplazable adj irreplaceable.
irreflexión nf thoughtlessness; rashness, impetuosity.
irreflexivamente adv thoughtlessly, unthinkingly; rashly.
irreflexivo adj thoughtless, unthinking; rash, impetuous; act rash, ill-considered.
irrefrenable adj violence etc unrestrained, unbridled, uncontrollable; person irrepressible; unmanageable.
irrefutable adj irrefutable, unanswerable.
irregular adj irregular; abnormal.
irregularidad nf irregularity; abnormality.
irregularmente adv irregularly; abnormally.
irrelevante adj (SAm) irrelevant.
irreligioso adj irreligious; ungodly.
irremediable adj irremediable; incurable.
irremediablemente adv irremediably; incurably.
irremisible adj irremissible, unpardonable; loss irretrievable.
irremisiblemente adv unpardonably; **— perdido** irretrievably lost, lost beyond hope of recovery.
irremunerado adj unremunerated.
irreparable adj irreparable.
irreparablemente adv irreparably.
irreprimible adj irrepressible.
irreprochable adj irreproachable.
irresistible adj irresistible.
irresistiblemente adv irresistibly.
irresoluble adj unsolvable; unresolved.
irresolución nf irresolution, hesitation, undecidedness.
irresoluto adj (a) irresolute, hesitant, undecided. (b) problem unresolved.
irrespetuosamente adv disrespectfully.
irrespetuoso adj disrespectful.
irresponsabilidad nf irresponsibility.
irresponsable adj irresponsible.
irresuelto adj = **irresoluto (a).**
irreverencia nf irreverence; disrespect.
irreverente adj irreverent; disrespectful.
irreversible adj irreversible.
irrevocable adj irrevocable, irreversible.
irrevocablemente adv irrevocably.
irrigación nf (a) (Med) irrigation. (b) (SAm: Agr) irrigation.
irrigador nm sprinkler.

irrigar [1h] vt (Agr, Med) to irrigate.
irrisible adj laughable, absurd; price absurdly low, bargain (attr).
irrisión nf (a) derision, ridicule. (b) laughing stock.
irrisorio adj derisory, ridiculous, absurd; price absurdly low, bargain (attr).
irritabilidad nf irritability.
irritable adj irritable.
irritación nf irritation.
irritador adj irritating.
irritante 1 adj irritating. **2** nm irritant.
irritar [1a] **1** vt (a) to irritate, anger, exasperate.
    (b) (fig) to stir up, inflame.
    (c) (Med) to irritate, inflame.
    2 irritarse vr to get angry, lose one's temper (de about, at, with).
irrompible adj unbreakable.
irrumpir [3a] vi **: — en** to burst into, rush into; to invade.
irrupción nf irruption; inrush; invasion.
Isaac m Isaac.
Isabel f Isabel, Elizabeth; (queens of England) Elizabeth.
isabelino adj: **la España isabelina** Isabelline Spain, the Spain of Isabel (II); **la Inglaterra isabelina** Elizabethan England, the England of Elizabeth.
Isabelita f Betty; Bess, Bessie; Liz.
Iseo f Iseult, Isolde.
—ísimo adj suffix (a) **un asunto importantísimo** a very important matter, a most important matter; **una cuestión discutidísima** a highly controversial question; **un desarrolladísimo sentido de orgullo** a very highly developed sense of pride; **es dificilísimo** it is extremely difficult; **resultó incomodísimo** it was extremely uncomfortable; **le golpeó violentísimamente** he hit him with considerable violence.
    (b) (more emotionally) **es amabilísimo** he's terribly kind (fam); **¡es simpatiquísimo!** he's awfully nice! (fam); **¡es guapísima!** she is awfully pretty (fam), she just is pretty.
    (c) (hum, iro) **un grandísimo libro** an enormous great book, a shockingly heavy book; **una comida costosísima** a shockingly expensive meal.
    (d) **aquel españolísimo plato** that most Spanish of all dishes, that most typically Spanish dish; **la madrileñísima plaza de Santa Ana** St Anne's square which is so typical of Madrid, St Anne's square which sums up so much of Madrid.
isla nf (a) island; isle.
    (b) (Archit) block.
    (c) (Mex, PR) isolated cluster of trees, isolated patch of scrub.
Isla f: **—s Británicas** British Isles; **— de Francia** Mauritius; for other names, see the second element.
Islam m Islam.
islámico adj Islamic.
islandés 1 adj Icelandic. **2** nm, **islandesa** nf Icelander. **3** nm (language) Icelandic.
Islandia f Iceland.
islándico adj Icelandic.
isleño 1 adj island (attr). **2** nm, **isleña** nf islander.
isleta nf islet.
islote nm small island, rocky isle.
iso . . . iso . . .
isobara nf isobar.
isoca nf (RPI) caterpillar, grub.
Isolde f Iseult, Isolde.
isósceles adj: **triángulo —** isosceles triangle.
isoterma nf isotherm.
isótopo nm isotope.
Israel m Israel.
israelí 1 adj Israeli. **2** nmf Israeli.
israelita 1 adj Israelite. **2** nmf Israelite.
istmeño 1 adj of the Isthmus, (loosely) Panamanian. **2** nm, **istmeña** nf native (or inhabitant) of the Isthmus, Panamanian.
istmo nm isthmus; neck; **— de Panamá** Isthmus of Panamá.
itacate nm (Mex) food, provisions.
Italia f Italy.
italianismo nm italianism, word (or phrase etc) borrowed from Italian.
italiano 1 adj Italian. **2** nm, **italiana** nf Italian. **3** nm (language) Italian.
ítem 1 nm item. **2** adv also, moreover.
itemizar [1f] vt (SAm) to itemize, specify; to divide into sections.
iterar [1a] vt to repeat.
itinerante adj roving, travelling; ambassador roving, at large.

itinerario *nm* itinerary, route.

—ito, —ita *n and adj etc suffix (in some combinations* **—(e)cito, —(e)cita**). **(a)** *(diminutive)* **un caballito** a little horse; **Juanito** Johnny; **su hijito** her small son, her baby boy; **es más bien bajita** she's rather on the short side; **es mayorcito ya** he's quite tall now; **¡un momentito!** just a moment!

(b) *(superlative)* **ahora mismito** this very instant; **estaba solito** he was completely alone; **están calentitos** they're extra hot, they're piping hot; **salimos tempranito** we left very early; **lo mejorcito que haya** the very best there is.

(c) *(emotive)* **¡pobrecito!** poor old chap! *(fam)*, poor little fellow!; **¡una limosnita!** surely you can spare a copper or two?

(d) *(suffix added from habit, without extra sense:* *esp SAm)* **allacito** = **allá**; **lueguito** = **luego**; *see* **adiosito**, **ahorita** *etc.*

izar [1f] *vt* (*Naut*) to hoist, haul up; *flag* to hoist, run up; **la bandera está izada** the flag is flying.

izcuinche *nm* (*Mex*) **(a)** mangy dog, mongrel. **(b)** ragged child, urchin.

izquierda *nf* **(a)** left hand; left side, left-hand side; **estar a la —** **de** to be on the left of; **torcer a la —** to turn (to the) left; **conducción por la —** (*Aut*) left-hand drive; **el árbol de la —** the tree on the left; **seguir por la —** to keep (to the) left.

(b) (*Pol*) left.

izquierdista 1 *adj* leftist, left-wing. **2** *nmf* leftist, left-winger.

izquierdo *adj* **(a)** left; left-hand. **(b)** left-handed. **(c)** (*fig*) crooked, twisted.

J

ja *interj* ha!
jaba *nf* (a) (*SAm*) stout basket, crate.
  (b) (*Ven*) hollow gourd; (*fig*) poverty.
  (c) (*Cu*) beggar's bag; **llevar** (*or* **tener**) **algo en —** (*fig*) to have something in the bag; **no poder ver a otro con — grande** to envy someone; **soltar la —** to go up in the world, acquire polish.
  (d) (*SAm*) = **haba.**
jabado *adj* (*Ant, Mex, Ven*) off-white with dark spots; (*Cu*) half-bred with pretentions to be white; (*fig*) hesitant, undecided.
jabalí *nm* wild boar.
jabalina *nf* (a) (*Zool*) wild sow, female wild boar.
  (b) (*Sport*) javelin.
jabato 1 *adj* (*Cu, Mex*) rough, uncouth; ill-tempered. **2** *nm* young wild boar.
jábega *nf* (a) seine; sweep net, dragnet. **(b)** fishing smack.
jabón *nm* (a) soap; (**un —**) piece of soap, tablet of soap; **— de afeitar** shaving soap; **— en escama** soapflakes; **— de olor, — de tocador** toilet soap; **— en polvo** soap powder, washing powder; **— de sastre** French chalk; **no es lo mismo — que hilo negro** (*Per, PR*) they're as different as chalk from cheese.
  (b) (*fam*) soft soap (*sl*), flattery; **dar — a uno** to soft-soap someone (*sl*).
  (c) (*fam*) **dar un — a uno** to tell someone off.
  (d) (*Arg*) **hacer —** to laze around.
  (e) (*Arg, Mex, PR*) fright, fear; **agarrarse un —** to have a scare.
jabonada *nf* (a) (*SAm*) = **jabonadura.** **(b)** (*Arg, Chi, Mex*) telling-off.
jabonado *nm* (a) soaping. **(b)** wash, laundry.
jabonadura *nf* (a) soaping. **(b)** **—s** lather, soapsuds.
  (c) (*fam*) telling-off; **dar una — a uno** to tell someone off.
jabonar [1a] *vt* (a) to soap; *clothes* to wash; *beard* to soap, lather. **(b)** (*fam*) to tell off, dress down.
jaboncillo *nm* (piece of) toilet soap; **— de sastre** French chalk.
jabonera *nf* soapdish.
jabonería *nf* soap factory.
jabonete *nm* piece of toilet soap.
jabonoso *adj* soapy.
jabuco *nm* (*Cu*) large basket, big crate.
jaca *nf* (a) pony, small horse; (*Cu*) gelding. **(b)** (*Arg*) (old) fighting cock.
jacal *nm* (*Guat, Mex, Ven*) shack, hut; **al — viejo no le faltan goteras** old age is bound to have its problems; **no tener — donde meterse** to be terribly poor.
jacalear [1a] *vi* (*Mex*) to wander about gossiping.
jacalón *nm* (*Mex*) shed; tumbledown building; (*Theat*) fleapit (*fam*).
jácara *nf* (a) (*Lit: Hist*) comic ballad of low life; (*Mus: Hist*) a merry dance; band of night revellers; **estar de —** to be very merry; **tener mucha —** to have a fund of stories.
  (b) (*fam*) fib, story; hoax.
  (c) (*fam*) annoyance.
jacarandá *nm or f* jacaranda.
jacarandoso *adj* merry, jolly; lively; spirited, stylish.
jacaré *nm* (*SAm*) alligator.
jacarear [1a] *vi* (a) to sing in the streets at night, go serenading.
  (b) (*fig*) to cause a commotion; to be rude, make offensive remarks.
jacarero *nm* amusing person, wag.
jácena *nf* girder.
jacinto *nm* (*Bot*) hyacinth; (*Min*) jacinth.
jaco *nm* small horse, young horse; (*pej*) nag, hack.
jacobino 1 *adj* Jacobin. **2** *nm*, **jacobina** *nf* Jacobin.
Jacobo *m* Jacob.

jactancia *nf* boasting, bragging; boastfulness.
jactanciosamente *adv* boastfully.
jactancioso *adj* boastful.
jactarse [1a] *vr* to boast, brag; **— de** to boast about, boast of; **— de +** *infin* to boast of + *ger*.
jachudo *adj* (*Ec*) strong, tough; obstinate.
jade *nm* (*Min*) jade.
jadeante *adj* panting, gasping, breathless.
jadear [1a] *vi* to pant, gasp for breath, puff and blow.
jadeo *nm* panting, gasping, puffing and blowing.
jaez *nm* (a) harness, piece of harness; **jaeces** trappings.
  (b) (*fig*) kind, sort; **y gente de ese —** (*pej*) and people of that sort.
jaguar *nm* jaguar.
jagüel *nm*, **jagüey** *nm* (*SAm*) pool; tank, cistern.
jaiba 1 *nf* (a) (*SAm*) crab.
  (b) (*Col*) mouth; **abrir la —** to show oneself greedy for money.
  2 *nmf* (*Ant, Mex*) sly person, sharp businessman.
jáibol *nm* (*SAm: angl*) highball (*US*).
jaibón *adj* (*CAm: angl*) stuck-up (*fam*), pretentious, snobbish.
jailaif (*SAm: angl*) **1** *adj* high-life (*attr*). **2** *nf* high life.
jailoso *adj* (*Col: angl*) well-bred; (*pej*) stuck-up (*fam*), pretentious, snobbish.
Jaime *m* James.
jalada *nf* (*Mex*) (a) pull, tug, heave. **(b)** harsh remark, rebuke. **(c)** (*Per: Univ*) failure.
jalar [1a] **1** *vt* (a) to pull, haul; (*Naut*) to heave; (*Per etc*) to push, push at, shove.
  (b) (*fam*) = **jamar.**
  (c) (*Col, Ven*) to make, do, perform.
  2 *vi* (a) (*SAm*) to go, go off; to clear out; **— para su casa** to go off home.
  (b) (*Per: Univ*) to fail.
  (c) (*CAm*) to make love; to be courting.
  (d) (*Mex*) **—le a una cosa** to get fond of something, be fond of something.
  3 jalarse *vr* (a) (*CAm*) to make love; to be courting.
  (b) (*SAm*) to get drunk.
  (c) = *vi* (a).
jalbegar [1h] *vt* to whitewash; *face* (*fam*) to make up, paint.
jalbegue *nm* whitewash; whitewashing; (*fam*) make-up, paint.
jalde *adj*, **jaldo** *adj* bright yellow.
jalea *nf* jelly; **— de guayaba** guava jelly; **estar hecho una —** (*person*) to be as sweet as can be, (*pej*) to be soapy.
jalear [1a] **1** *vt* (a) *dogs* to urge on; *dancers* to encourage (by shouting and clapping).
  (b) (*Chi, Mex*) to pester; (*Mex*) to tease, mock.
  2 *vi* (*Mex*) to amuse oneself noisily.
jaleo *nm* (a) spree (*fam*), binge (*sl*); **estar de —** to make merry, have a good time.
  (b) row, racket, uproar; fuss; **armar un —** to kick up a row; **se armó un tremendo —** there was a hell of a row.
  (c) (*Hunting*) hallooing.
  (d) (*Mus*) shouting and clapping (*to encourage dancers*).
jalisco[1] *adj* (*Guat, Mex*) drunk.
jalisco[2] *nm* (*Guat, Mex*) straw hat.
jalón *nm* (a) stake, pole; surveying rod.
  (b) (*fig*) stage.
  (c) (*SAm*) pull, tug; **hacer algo de un —** (*Mex*) to do something in one go.
  (d) (*Ant, CAm, Mex, Per, Ven*) distance, stretch; **hay un buen —** it's a good way.
  (e) (*CAm, Mex*) swig (*fam*), drink.
  (f) (*CAm*) lover, sweetheart; suitor.

jalona nf (CAm) flirt, flighty girl.
jalonar [1a] vt to stake out, mark out; (fig) to mark; **el camino está jalonado por plazas fuertes** the route is marked out by a series of strongholds, a line of strongholds marks the route.
jalonazo nm (CAm, Mex) pull, tug.
jalonear [1a] **1** vt (Mex) to pull, tug, drag. **2** vi (a) (CAm, Mex) to pull, tug. (b) (CAm, Mex) to haggle.
jallo adj (Mex) vain, stuck-up (fam); showy; quick to take offence.
Jamaica f Jamaica.
jamaica[1] nf (CAm, Mex) charity fair, function held to raise funds.
jamaica[2] nm (Jamaica) rum.
jamaicano, jamaiquino (SAm) **1** adj Jamaican. **2** nm, **jamaicana** nf, **jamaiquina** nf Jamaican.
jamar [1a] vi (fam) to eat to excess, stuff oneself.
jamás adv never; (not) ever; **¿se vio — tal cosa?** did you ever see such a thing?; **¡—!** never!; see **nunca** etc.
jamba nf jamb; **— de puerta** jamb, door post.
jambado adj (Mex) greedy, gluttonous; **estar —** to be feeling over-full.
jambarse [1a] vr (CAm, Mex) to overeat; to eat greedily.
jamelgo nm wretched horse, nag, jade.
jamón nm (a) ham; **— en dulce** boiled ham; **¡y un — (con chorreras)!** you're hopeful!, you want jam on it!
(b) (sl) **una mujer jamón** a knockout (of a woman) (sl); **ella es un —** she's a smasher (sl).
(c) (Ven) bargain.
jamona nf (fam) buxom (middle-aged) woman.
jampa nf (Ec) threshold.
jámparo nm (Col) canoe, small boat.
jamurar [1a] vt (Col) to rinse; to bale out.
jan nm (Cu) stout pointed stake, fencing post; **ensartarse en los —es** to get involved in an unprofitable piece of business.
jandinga nf (Cu) food.
janearse [1a] vr (Cu) (a) to leap into the saddle. (b) to stand still; to come to a complete stop.
jangada[1] nf (Naut) raft.
jangada[2] nf stupid remark; dirty trick.
Japón: el — Japan.
japonés 1 adj Japanese. **2** nm, **japonesa** nf Japanese. **3** nm (language) Japanese.
jaque nm (a) (Chess) check; **¡— (al rey)!** check!; **— continuo** continuous check; **— mate** checkmate; **¡— de aquí!** get out of here!; **dar — a** to check; **dar — mate a** to checkmate, mate; **tener en —** to check; (fig) to hold a threat over; (fig) to keep in check, hold at bay.
(b) (fam) bully, braggart.
jaquear [1a] vt (Chess) to check; (Mil and fig) to harass.
jaqueca nf (severe) headache, migraine; **dar — a** (fig) to bore.
jaquetón nm (fam) bully, braggart.
jáquima nf (a) (SAm) headstall. (b) (CAm, Mex) drunkenness, drunken state.
jaquinón nm (SAm) headstall, halter.
jara[1] nf (a) (Bot) a species of Cistus; clump, thicket. (b) dart, arrow; (Mex) arrow. (c) (Mex: sl) **la —** the cops (sl).
jara[2] nf (Bol) halt, rest.
jarabe nm syrup; sweet drink; **— de arce** maple syrup; **— de pico** (fig) mere words, lip service; **— para la tos** cough syrup, cough mixture; **dar — a uno** (fam) to butter someone up (fam); **estar hecho un —** see **jalea**.
jaral nm (a) ground covered with jaras, scrub; thicket. (b) (fig) difficult affair, thorny question.
jaramago nm hedge mustard.
jaramillo nm (fam) row; **armar un —** to kick up a row.
jarana nf (a) spree (fam), binge (sl), carousal; rumpus (fam), row; **andar de —** to roister, carouse; to lark about, have a high old time; **ir de —** to go on the spree (fam).
(b) trick, deceit; (SAm) joke, practical joke, hoax; (Col) fib; **la — sale a la cara** (CAm) a hoax can have a boomerang effect.
(c) (Mus: Bol, Per) dance; (Col, Ec, PR) hop (fam), informal dance; (Per) festival of regional dances.
(d) (Mus: Mex) small guitar.
(e) (Fin: Col) debt.
jaranear [1a] **1** vt (CAm, Col) to cheat, swindle. **2** vi (a) to go on a spree (fam); to roister, carouse; to lark about, have a high old time.

(b) (Bol, Per, PR) to make merry at an informal dance.
(c) (CAm) to get into debt.
jaranero adj (a) merry, roistering, rowdy. (b) (CAm) deceitful, tricky.
jaranista adj (SAm) = **jaranero** (a).
jarano nm (Mex) broad hat, sombrero.
jarcia nf (a) tackle, fishing tackle; (Naut: also —s) ropes, rigging; (Cu, Mex) rope (made from agave fibre).
(b) (Guat, Mex, Nic) agave.
(c) heap, mess.
jardín nm garden, flower garden; **— alpestre, — rocoso** rock garden; **— botánico** botanical garden; **— de (la) infancia** kindergarten, nursery school; **— zoológico** zoo.
jardinaje nm (SAm) gardening.
jardinera nf (a) (woman) gardener.
(b) window box.
(c) (RPl) light two-wheeled handcart, barrow.
(d) (Col) jacket.
jardinería nf gardening.
jardinero nm gardener.
jarea nf (Mex) hunger, keen appetite.
jarear[1] [1a] vi (Bol) to halt, stop for a rest.
jarearse[2] [1a] vr (Mex) (a) to be dying of hunger. (b) to flee. (c) to rock, sway.
jareta nf (a) (Naut) cable, rope. (b) (CR, Par) trouser flies. (c) (Ven) snag, setback.
jarete nm (Ven) paddle.
jarifo adj (lit) elegant, showy, spruce.
jaro nm arum lily.
jarope nm syrup; (fam) brew, concoction, nasty drink.
jarra nf jar, pitcher; (for milk) churn; (for beer) mug, tankard; **de —s, en —s** with arms akimbo.
jarrada nf (SAm) jarful, jugful.
jarrete nm (Anat) back of the knee; (horse's) hock; (Col) heel.
jarro nm jug, pitcher; **echar un — de agua fría a una idea** to pour cold water on an idea.
jarrón nm vase; (Archit) urn.
jartón adj (CAm, Mex) greedy, gluttonous.
Jartum, Jartún Khartoum.
jaspe nm jasper.
jaspeado adj mottled, speckled, marbled; streaked.
jaspear [1a] **1** vt to speckle, marble; to streak. **2 jaspearse** vr (Ven) to get cross.
jato nm (a) calf.
(b) (PR) stray dog, mongrel.
(c) (Mex) implement and load of a mule.
(d) (Mex) stopping place (of muleteers).
(e) (Per) saddle.
(f) see **hato**.
Jauja, jauja nf (a) promised land, earthly paradise; **¡esto es —!** this is the life!; **¿estamos aquí o en —?** where do you think you are?; **vivir en —** to live in luxury, have a marvellous life.
(b) (Chi) rumour, tale.
jaula nf cage; (Min) cage; (for packing, milk bottles etc) crate; (in asylum) cell; (fam) lock-up; (Aut) lock-up garage; (Mex: Rail) cattle truck; (PR) Black Maria, police wagon (US); **hacer —** (Mex) to dig one's heels in.
jauría nf pack of hounds.
Javier m Xavier.
jayán nm big strong man; (pej) hulking great brute.
jáyaro adj (Ec) rustic, uncouth.
jazmín nm jasmine; **— del Cabo, — de la India** gardenia.
jazz [jaθ or jas] nm jazz.
jazzístico [ja'θistiko] adj jazz (attr).
jebe nm (a) (SAm: Bot) rubber plant. (b) club, cudgel; **llevar —** to suffer a lot.
jebero nm (SAm) rubber-plantation worker.
jeep [jip] nm jeep.
jefa nf (woman) head, (woman) boss; manageress.
jefatura nf (a) leadership; chieftainship; **bajo la — de** under the leadership of; **dimitir la — del partido** to resign the party leadership.
(b) headquarters; central office; **— de policía** police headquarters.
jefe nm (a) chief, head, boss; leader; manager; (Mil) field officer, officer in command; **— de bomberos** fire officer; **— de camareros** head waiter; **— de cocina** chef; **— de estación** station master; **— de estado** head of state, chief of state; **— de estado mayor** chief of staff; **— de los mozos** head groom; **— de redacción** editor-in-chief; **— supremo** commander-in-chief; **— de taller** foreman; **— de tren** guard, conductor (US); **— de ventas** sales

manager; **comandante en —** commander-in-chief; **¡sí, —!** (*esp SAm*) yes, boss!; **ser el —** (*fig*) to be the boss.

 (b) (*of tribe*) chief.

Jehová *m* Jehovah.

jején *nm* **(a)** (*SAm*) gnat; **sabe donde el — puso el huevo** (*Cu, PR*) he's pretty smart.

 (b) (*Mex*) great number, lot; **un — de cosas** a lot of things, a mass of things.

jelenque *nm* (*Cu, Mex*) brawl, squabble, set-to (*fam*).

jemiquear [1a] *vi* (*Chi*) = **jeremiquear.**

jengibre *nm* ginger.

jenízaro *adj* mixed, hybrid.

Jenofonte *m* Xenophon.

jeque *nm* sheik(h).

jerarca *nm* chief, leader; important person; (*pej*) big shot (*fam*).

jerarquía *nf* hierarchy; (high) rank; **una persona de —** a high-ranking person.

jerárquico *adj* hierarchic(al).

Jeremías *m* Jeremy; (*Bib*) Jeremiah.

jeremiquear [1a] *vi* (*SAm*) to snivel, whimper; to make repeated requests.

jerez *nm* sherry.

jerezano 1 *adj* of Jerez. 2 *nm*, **jerezana** *nf* native (*or* inhabitant) of Jerez; **los —s** the people of Jerez.

jerga¹ *nf* coarse cloth, sackcloth; (*SAm*) horse blanket; (*Col*) coarse cloak.

jerga² *nf* jargon; slang, cant; gibberish; **— de germanía** thieves' cant; **— publicitaria** sales talk, salesman's patter.

jergón *nm* palliasse, straw mattress; (*fam*) ill-fitting garment; (*fam*) awkward-looking person.

Jericó Jericho.

jerigonza *nf* **(a)** = **jerga**². **(b)** silly thing, piece of folly.

jeringa *nf* **(a)** syringe; **— de engrase** grease gun. **(b)** (*SAm*) annoyance, bother; (*Arg*) pest, annoying person.

jeringador *adj* (*SAm*) annoying, bothersome, vexing.

jeringar [1h] *vt* **(a)** to syringe; to inject; to squirt. **(b)** (*SAm*) to annoy, bother, plague.

jeringazo *nm* syringing; injection; squirt.

jeringón 1 *adj* (*SAm*) = **jeringador.** 2 *nm* (*SAm*) pest, annoying person.

jeringuear [1a] *vt* (*SAm*) = **jeringar (b).**

jeringuilla *nf* mock orange.

jeroglífico 1 *adj* hieroglyphic. 2 *nm* hieroglyph(ic); (*fig*) puzzle.

Jerónimo *m* Jerome.

jerónimo¹ (*Eccl*) 1 *adj* Hieronymite. 2 *nm* Hieronymite.

jerónimo² (*hum*): **sin — de duda** without a shadow of doubt.

jersé *nm*, **jersei** *nm*, **jersey** [xer'sei] *nm*, *pl* **jerseys** [xer'seis] jersey, sweater, pullover; jumper; (*SAm*) knitted cloth.

Jerusalén Jerusalem.

jeruza *nf* (*Guat, Hond: sl*) clink (*sl*), jail.

Jesucristo *m* Jesus Christ.

jesuita 1 *adj* (*Eccl*) Jesuit; (*fig*) Jesuitic(al). 2 *nm* (*Eccl*) Jesuit; (*SAm*) hypocrite, sly person.

jesuítico *adj* Jesuitic(al).

Jesús *m* Jesus; **¡—!** good heavens!; (*on sneezing*) bless you!; **en un decir —** in an instant, before one can say Jack Robinson; **morir sin decir —** to die very suddenly.

jet [jet] *nm*, *pl* **jets** [jet] (*angl*) jet, jet plane.

jeta *nf* **(a)** thick lips; **poner —** to pout, make a wry face.

 (b) (*Zool*) snout; (*sl*) face, mug (*sl*), dial (*sl*); **estirar la —** (*Chi, RPl*) to die; (*Arg*) to make a wry face.

 (c) (*fam*) nerve, neck (*fam*); **¡qué — tienes!** you've got a nerve!

jetear [1a] *vi* (*Arg*) to eat at someone else's expense.

jetón *adj* **(a)** (*SAm*) thick-lipped. **(b)** (*Chi*) stupid.

jibarear [1a] *vi* (*SD*) to flirt.

jíbaro 1 *adj* (*Ant, Mex*) peasant, rustic; shy; (*SD*) wild, untamed.

 2 *nm*, **jíbara** *nf* (*SD*) peasant; (*PR*) (white) peasant, rustic.

 3 *nm* **(a)** (*Hond*) big strong man.

 (b) (*Cu*) wild dog.

jibia *nf* cuttlefish.

jicaque *adj* (*Guat, Hond*) uncouth.

jícara *nf* **(a)** small cup (for drinking-chocolate *etc*).

 (b) (*CAm, Mex*) gourd, drinking vessel made from a gourd; (*CAm: hum*) head; bald head; face; **sacar la — a uno** to shower someone with attentions.

jicarazo *nm* (*CAm, Mex*) cupful.

jícaro *nm* (*CAm, Mex*) **(a)** calabash tree. **(b)** bowl.

jicarón *adj* (*CR*) big-headed.

jicarudo *adj* (*Mex*) broad-faced, broad-browed.

jicote *nm* (*CAm, Mex*) wasp.

jicotera *nf* (*CAm, Mex*) wasps' nest; buzzing of wasps; **armar una —** to kick up a row.

jiche *nm* (*CAm, Mex*) tendon, sinew.

jiennense 1 *adj* of Jaén. 2 *nmf* native (*or* inhabitant) of Jaén; **los —s** the people of Jaén.

jifero 1 *adj* (*fam*) filthy. 2 *nm* **(a)** slaughterer, butcher. **(b)** butcher's knife.

jifia *nf* swordfish.

jijene *nm* sandfly.

jilguero *nm* goldfinch.

jilibioso *adj* (*Chi*) person weepy, tearful; finicky, hard to please; *horse* nervous.

jilote *nm* (*CAm, Mex*) green ear of maize.

jilotear [1a] *vi* (*CAm, Mex*) to come into ear.

jimagua (*Cu*) 1 *adj* twin; identical. 2 *nmf* twin.

jimba *nf* (*Ec*) pigtail, tress; (*Mex*) bamboo, long pole of bamboo.

jimbal *nm* (*Mex*) bamboo thicket.

jimbito *nm* (*Guat, Hond*) small wasp; wasps' nest.

jimbo *adj* (*Mex*) drunk.

jinaiste *nm* (*Mex*) group of children, mob of kids.

jindama *nf* (*sl*) fear, funk (*fam*).

jineta *nf* horsewoman, rider.

jinete *nm* horseman, rider; (*Mil*) cavalryman.

jinetear [1a] 1 *vt* (*SAm*) to break in; to ride; **— la burra** (*CAm*) to go the whole hog, stake everything.

 2 *vi* to ride around, show off one's horsemanship.

 3 **jinetearse** *vr* **(a)** (*Col, Mex*) to get into the saddle, manage to stay in the saddle; (*fig*) to stand firm.

 (b) (*Col*) to be vain.

jingo *nm* (*angl*) jingoist, jingo.

jingoísmo *nm* jingoism.

jingoísta 1 *adj* jingoistic. 2 *nmf* jingoist, jingo.

jiote *nm* (*CAm, Mex: Med*) shingles.

jipa *nf* (*Col*) straw hat.

jipatera *nf* (*Col, Mex, PR, Ven*), **jipatez** *nf* (*Mex, PR, Ven*) paleness, wanness.

jipato *adj* (*SAm*) pale, wan, anaemic; (*Cu*) tasteless; (*Guat*) drunk.

jipe *nm* (*Mex, Per*) straw hat.

jipi *nm* (*Cu, Mex*) straw hat.

jipijapa *nf* (*SAm*) fine woven straw; straw hat.

jira¹ *nf* (*of cloth*) strip.

jira² *nf* excursion, outing; picnic (*also* **— campestre**); **ir de —** to go on an outing, go for a picnic; *see also* **gira.**

jirafa *nf* giraffe; (*of microphone etc*) jib, arm, boom.

jiribilla *nf* (*Mex*) spin, turn; **tener — (— Cu)** to have its awkward points; (*PR*) to be anxious.

jirimiquear [1a] *vi* (*SAm*) = **jeremiquear.**

jirón *nm* **(a)** rag, shred, tatter; **en —es** in shreds; **hacer algo —es** to tear something to shreds.

 (b) (*fig*) bit, shred.

 (c) (*Per*) avenue, boulevard.

jit *nm*, *pl* **jits** [xit] (*CAm: angl*) hit.

jitazo *nm* (*Mex: angl*) hit, blow; (*Sport*) hit, stroke.

jitomate *nm* (*Mex*) tomato.

jiu-jitsu *nm* jiu-jitsu.

Job *m* Job.

jockey ['joki] *nm*, *pl* **jockeys** ['jokis] (*angl*) jockey; (*SAm*) jockey cap.

joco *adj* **(a)** (*CAm, Mex*) sharp, sour, bitter. **(b)** (*Col*) hollow.

jocolote *nm* (*Hond*) hut, shanty.

jocoque *nm* (*Mex*) sour milk, sour cream.

jocosamente *adv* humorously, comically.

jocoserio *adj* seriocomic.

jocosidad *nf* humour; (*una —*) joke.

jocoso *adj* humorous, comic, jocular.

joda *nf* (*SAm: tabu*) **(a)** annoyance; bother; harm. **(b)** joke; **lo dijo en —** he said it as a joke.

joder [2a] (*tabu in all senses; in SAm used only in fig senses*) 1 *vt* **(a)** to fuck (*tabu*), screw (*tabu*); **¡—!** (*annoyance*) damn it!, damnation!; (*surprise*) well I'm damned!

 (b) (*fig*) to annoy, vex, upset; to harm, spoil; **esto me jode** this really feeds me up (*fam*), I'm fed up with this; **son ganas de —** they're just trying to be awkward; **¡no me jodas!** stop bothering me!; come off it!, tell us another!

 (c) to pinch (*fam*), steal; **alguien le jodió el puesto** someone pinched the job from him.

 2 *vi* to fuck (*tabu*), screw (*tabu*).

 3 **joderse** *vr* **(a)** **¡que te jodas!** get stuffed! (*sl*); **¡hay que —!** this is the end!, to hell with it all!

 (b) to fail; to get spoiled, get messed up; **se jodió todo** everything was spoiled; **se ha jodido la función** the show was a failure.

jodido adj (tabu in all senses) (a) awkward, difficult;
es un libro — it's a very difficult book.
    (b) **estoy —** I'm worn out, I'm shagged (tabu).
    (c) bloody; **ni una jodida peseta** not one bloody peseta.
    (d) **todo está —** it's all ruined, everything's in a mess.
    (e) (SAm) person selfish; evil, wicked; awkward, prickly; soapy, oily.
jodienda nf (Arg, Chi, Mex: tabu) bother, annoyance.
jodón adj (SAm: tabu) (a) annoying; given to stupid jokes. (b) tricky, untrustworthy.
jodontón adj (tabu) randy, oversexed, wolfish (fam).
jofaina nf washbasin.
jojoto adj (Cu, PR) fruit partly spoiled; (SD) fruit undeveloped; person anaemic; (Ven) fruit, maize soft, tender.
jolgorio nm (a) fun, merriment; revelry; rowdiness.
    (b) (un —) spree (fam), binge (sl); lark; **ir de —** to go on a binge.
jolín, jolines interj (fam) cor! (fam).
jolinche adj, **jolino** adj (Mex) short-tailed, bob-tailed.
jolón nm (Mex) wasp; wasps' nest.
jolongo nm (Cu) bag, bundle.
jolote nm (CAm, Mex) turkey.
joma nf (Mex) hump.
jombado adj (Mex) hunchbacked.
Jonás m Jonah.
jónico adj (Archit) Ionic.
jonja nf (Chi) imitation, mimicry.
jonjear [1a] vt (Chi) to tease, make fun of.
jonjolear [1a] vt (Col) to spoil, lavish attentions upon.
jonrón nm (SAm: Sport: angl) home run.
jonronear [1a] vi (SAm: Sport: angl) to make a home run.
jopo[1] interj get out!, be off!
jopo[2] nm = **hopo.**
jora nf (SAm) maize specially prepared for making high-grade chicha.
Jordán m Jordan (river).
Jordania f Jordan (country).
jorga nf (Ec) band of crooks, gang.
Jorge m George.
jorguín nm sorcerer, wizard.
jorguina nf sorceress, witch.
jorguinería nf sorcery, witchcraft.
jorgón nm (Ec) lot, abundance.
jornada nf (a) day's journey; stage (of a journey); **a largas —s** (Mil) by forced marches; **al fin de la —** at the end, in the end.
    (b) working day; hours of work; shift; (fig) lifetime, span of life; **— de 8 horas** 8-hour day; **— legal** maximum legal working hours; **hay — limitada en la industria** there is short-time working in the industry; **trabajar en —s reducidas** to work short-time.
    (c) (Mil) expedition; **la — de Orán** the expedition against Oran.
    (d) (Theat: Hist) act.
    (e) (Chi) day's wage.
jornal nm (day's) wage; day's work; **— mínimo** minimum wage; **política de —es y precios** prices and incomes policy; **trabajar a —** to work for a day wage, be paid by the day.
jornalero nm (day) labourer.
joro nm (Ven) small basket.
joroba 1 nf (a) hump, hunched back. (b) (fig) nuisance, bother, annoyance. 2 nm hunchback.
jorobado 1 adj hunchbacked. 2 nm, **jorobada** nf hunchback.
jorobar [1a] 1 vt to annoy, pester, bother; **esto me joroba** I'm fed up with this, this gives me the hump; **¡no me jorobes!** stop bothering me!
    2 **jorobarse** vr to get cross, get worked up; to get fed up; **¡hay que —!** to hell with it!
jorobeta nf (Arg) nuisance.
jorobón adj (SAm) annoying.
joronche nm (Mex: euph) hunchback.
jorongo nm (Mex) poncho, peasant's blanket.
jorro nm (Cu, PR) poor-quality cigarette, slow-burning tobacco.
jorungo 1 adj (Cu) annoying, vexing. 2 nm (Ven) foreigner, gringo.
José m Joseph.
Josefina f Josephine.
Josué m Joshua.
jota[1] nf (a) name of the letter J.
    (b) (fig) jot, iota; **no entendió —** he didn't understand a word of it; **sin faltar una —** to a T, with complete accuracy, just as it should be; **no saber —** to have no idea; not to know what it's all about.

jota[2] nf Spanish dance and tune (esp Aragonese).
jote nm (Chi) buzzard; large kite; unattractive person; (pej) priest.
joto 1 adj (Mex) effeminate. 2 nm (Col) bundle; (Mex) effeminate person.
joven 1 adj young; appearance etc youthful.
    2 nm young man, youth; **los —es** young people, youth, the young; **¡eh, —!** I say, young man!
    3 nf young woman, young lady, girl.
jovencito nm, **jovencita** nf, **jovenzuelo** nm, **jovenzuela** nf youngster.
jovial adj jolly, cheerful, jovial.
jovialidad nf jolliness, cheerfulness, joviality.
jovialmente adv in a jolly way, cheerfully, jovially.
joya nf (a) jewel, gem, piece of jewellery; **— de familia** heirloom.
    (b) **—s** jewels, jewellery; (bride's) trousseau; **— de fantasía, —s de imitación** imitation jewellery.
    (c) (fig) gem, treasure, precious thing; (person) gem, treasure.
joyería nf (a) jewellery, jewels. (b) jeweller's (shop).
joyero nm (a) jeweller. (b) jewel case.
juagar [1h] vt (Col, Ec) = **enjuagar.**
Juan m John; **don —** don John, don Juan; (Mus) Don Giovanni; **San — Bautista** St John the Baptist; **un buen —** a simple soul, a good-natured fool; **— Lanas, — Vainas** (CAm, PR) even-tempered person, calm sort; (pej) simpleton, ninny; **— Palomo** lone wolf, independent sort; **— Zoquete** rustic, idiot.
juan nm (Bol, Mex) common soldier.
Juana f Joan, Jean, Jane; **— de Arco** Joan of Arc.
juana nf (a) (Col) whore. (b) (Mex) marijuana.
juancho nm (Col) boyfriend, lover.
juanear [1a] vt (Arg) to swindle.
juanete nm (a) bunion; prominent cheekbone. (b) (Naut) topgallant sail. (c) (Col, Hond) hip.
juanillo nm (Chi, Per) tip, gratuity.
juapao nm (Ven) beating, thrashing.
jubilación nf (a) retirement. (b) pension, retirement pension.
jubilado 1 adj (a) retired; **vivir —** to live in retirement.
    (b) (Col, Cu) wise, sagacious, expert.
    (c) (Col: pej) stupid; wretched.
    2 nm retired person, pensioner.
jubilar [1a] 1 vt (a) person to pension off, retire.
    (b) (fig) person to shunt aside, put out to grass; thing to discard, get rid of, cast aside.
    2 vi to rejoice.
    3 **jubilarse** vr (a) to retire, take one's pension.
    (b) (CAm, Ven) to play truant.
    (c) (Col, Cu, Mex) to acquire skill, gain experience.
    (d) (Col) to deteriorate, go downhill; to go mad.
jubileo nm jubilee; (fam) comings and goings; **por — once in a lifetime.**
júbilo nm joy, jubilation, rejoicing; **con — joyfully,** with jubilation.
jubiloso adj jubilant.
jubón nm doublet, jerkin, close-fitting jacket; (woman's) bodice.
jud nm (CAm, Mex: Aut: angl) bonnet, hood (US).
Judá m Judah.
judaico adj Jewish, Judaic.
judaísmo nm Judaism.
Judas m Judas; (fig) traitor, betrayer.
judas nm (a) (SAm) peephole.
    (b) (Mex) saint's day, name day (of person).
    (c) (Chi) snooper, inspector.
    (d) (CAm, Mex) naughty child.
Judea f Judea.
judería nf (a) Jewish quarter, ghetto. (b) Jewry.
    (c) (Guat, Mex) prank, lark.
judía nf (a) Jewess, Jewish woman.
    (b) (Bot) kidney bean; **— blanca** haricot bean; **— colorada, — escarlata, — de España, — negra** runner bean; **— de la peladilla** Lima bean.
judiada nf (a) cruel act, cruel thing. (b) (Fin) extortion.
judicatura nf (a) judicature. (b) judgeship, office of judge.
judicial adj judicial; **recurrir a la vía —** to go to law, have recourse to the law.
judío 1 adj (a) Jewish. (b) (pej) extortionate, usurious.
    2 nm Jew.
Judit f Judith.
judo nm judo.
juego[1] etc (verb) see **jugar.**
juego[2] nm (a) play, playing; sport; fun, amusement; **los niños en el —** children at play; **— duro** rough

play; — **limpio** fair play; — **sucio** foul play, dirty play; **el balón está en** — the ball is in play; **entrar en** — (person) to take a hand, (factor) come into play; **poner algo en** — to set something in motion, bring something into play; **estar fuera de** — (person) to be offside, (ball) be out, be out of play; **por** — in fun, for fun.

(b) (un —) game, sport; **es solamente un** — it's only a game; —**s atléticos** (athletic) sports; — **de azar** game of chance; — **de las bochas** bowls; — **de (las) bolas** American skittles; — **de las bolitas**, — **de las canicas** marbles; — **de bolos** ninepins, skittles, tenpin bowling; — **de cartas** card game; — **de damas** draughts, checkers (US); — **de destreza** game of skill; —**s infantiles** children's games; —**s malabares** juggling; — **de manos** conjuring trick; —**s de manos** conjuring; — **de naipes** card game; **J**—**s Olímpicos** Olympic Games; — **de palabras** pun, play on words; — **de prendas** (game of) forfeits; — **del tejo** hopscotch.

(c) (complete or finished) game; (Tennis) game; (Bridge) rubber; —, **set y partido** game, set and match.

(d) (fig) game; **le conozco el** —, **le veo el** — I know his little game, I know what he's up to.

(e) gambling, gaming; **el** — **es un vicio** gambling is a vice; **lo perdió todo en el** — he lost the lot gambling; **lo que está en** — what is at stake.

(f) (Mech) play, movement; **estar en** — to be in gear, be in mesh.

(g) (of light etc) play; **el** — **de luces sobre el agua** the play of light on the water; **el** — **de los colores** the interplay of the colours.

(h) field, pitch, court; **en el** — **de pelota** on the pelota court.

(i) set; (of dishes) set, service; (of furniture) suite; (of tools etc) set, kit, outfit; (of cards) hand; pack; — **de bolas** (Mech) ball bearing, set of ball bearings; — **de café** coffee set; — **de campanas** peal of bells; — **de comedor** dining-room suite; — **de mesa** dinner service; **una falda a** — **con un jersey** a skirt with a jersey to match; a skirt which goes with a jersey; **con falda a** — with skirt to match; **hacen** — they match, they go well together.

juepucha interj (RPl: euph) well I'm damned!

juerga nf (a) binge (sl), spree (fam), carousal; good time; **correr las grandes** —**s** to live it up (fam); **¡vaya que nos vamos a correr con ellas!** what a time we'll have with them!; **ir de** — to go on a spree, go out for a good time.

juerguista nm reveller.

jueves nm, pl **jueves** Thursday; **J**— **Santo** Maundy Thursday; **no es cosa del otro** — it's nothing to write home about.

juez nm (a) (Law) judge (also fig); — **árbitro** arbitrator, referee; — **de instrucción** examining magistrate; — **municipal** magistrate; — **de paz** justice of the peace; **parece un** — he looks terribly serious.

(b) (Sport) judge; — **de línea** linesman; — **de llegada**, — **de meta**, — **de raya** (Arg) judge; — **de salida** starter.

jugada nf (a) play; playing.

(b) piece of play; move; stroke, shot; throw; **una bonita** — a pretty piece of play, a pretty shot; **con dos** —**s más** in two more moves; **hacer una** — to make a move, make a shot (etc).

(c) (mala) — bad turn, dirty trick; **hacer una mala** — **a uno** to play someone a dirty trick.

(d) (Mex) dodge, duck, evasive movement.

jugado adj (Col, Mex) expert, experienced.

jugador nm, **jugadora** nf player; gambler; — **de bolsa** speculator, gambler on the stock exchange; — **de fútbol** footballer, football player; — **de manos** juggler, conjurer.

jugar [1h and 1o] 1 vt (a) card, trick, role etc to play; **¡me la han jugado!** (fam) they've done it on me!

(b) to gamble, stake; — **5 dólares a una carta** to stake (or put) 5 dollars on a card; **lo jugó todo** he gambled it all away.

(c) weapon to handle, wield.

2 vi (a) to play (con with, contra against); — **limpio** to play fair, play the game; — **sucio** to play unfairly, indulge in dirty play; **yo no juego** I don't play, I can't play; — **al tenis** to play tennis; — **al ajedrez** to play chess; **la niña juega a ser madre** the little girl plays at being mother; — **con** (pej) to play about with; to finger, handle, mess up; (fig) to toy with, trifle with; **solamente está jugando contigo** he's just trifling with you, he's just having a game with you; **un coche de** — a toy car, a model car; **de jugando** (Arg, Guat, PR) in fun, for fun.

(b) to play, make a move; **¿quién juega?** whose move is it?, whose turn is it?, who's to play next?

(c) to gamble; (Fin) to speculate, gamble; see **bolsa** etc.

(d) (SAm) to have room, move about; **la varilla juega dentro de la unión** the rod moves about inside the joint.

(e) to match, go together.

3 **jugarse** vr to gamble (away), risk; **se jugó 500 dólares** he staked 500 dollars; **esto es** — **la vida** this means risking one's life; — **el todo por el todo** to stake one's all, (fig) go to extremes, go the whole hog.

jugarreta nf (a) bad move, poor piece of play. (b) dirty trick; **hacer una** — **a uno** to play a dirty trick on someone.

juglar nm (Hist) minstrel, jongleur; juggler, tumbler, entertainer.

juglaresco adj (Hist): **arte** — art of the minstrel(s); **estilo** — minstrel's style, popular style.

juglaría nf (Hist) minstrelsy, art of the minstrel(s).

jugo nm (a) (Bot etc) juice; sap; (of meat) juice; gravy; — **de naranja** orange juice; — **de muñeca** (fam) elbow grease (fam).

(b) (fig) essence, substance, pith; **sacar el** — **a uno** to pick someone's brains.

jugosidad nf (a) juiciness, succulence. (b) (fig) substantial nature, pithiness.

jugoso adj (a) juicy, succulent.

(b) (fig) substantial, pithy; meaty, full of good stuff, full of solid sense; **un discurso** — a solid sort of speech, a speech full of good things.

juguete nm (a) toy; **un cañón de** — a toy gun.

(b) (fig) toy, plaything; **fue el** — **de las olas** it was the plaything of the waves.

(c) joke.

(d) (Theat) skit, sketch.

juguetear [1a] vi to play, romp, sport; — **con** to play with, sport with.

jugueteo nm playing, romping.

juguetería nf (a) toy trade, toy business. (b) toyshop.

juguetón adj playful; frisky, frolicsome.

juicio nm (a) (faculty) judgement, reason.

(b) sanity, reason; good sense, prudence, wisdom; **asentar el** — to come to one's senses, return to sanity; **lo dejo a su** — I leave it to your discretion, I leave it to you to decide; **estar en su (cabal)** — to be in one's right mind; **estar fuera de** — to be out of one's mind; **perder el** — to lose one's reason, go mad; **no tener** — to lack common sense; **¿se te ha vuelto el** —? are you mad?, have you gone out of your mind?

(c) opinion; — **de valor** value judgement; **a mi** — in my opinion, to my mind.

(d) (Law) trial; — **de Dios** trial by ordeal; **pedir a uno en** — to sue someone.

(e) (Law) verdict, judgement; **J**— **Final** Last Judgement; — **en rebeldía** judgement by default.

juicioso adj judicious, wise, prudent, sensible.

juilipio nm (Per) sparrow.

juilón adj (Mex) cowardly.

julepe nm (a) julep.

(b) (fam) telling-off, dressing-down.

(c) (SAm) scare, fright; **irse de** —, **salir de** — (Ec) to run away in terror.

(d) (Cu, Mex, Ven) fag, hard work; trouble.

(e) (Col, Per) **meter un** — to hurry on, speed up.

julepear [1a] 1 vt (a) (RPl) to scare, terrify.

(b) (Mex) to wear out, tire out.

(c) (Col) to hurry along, speed up.

2 **julepearse** vr (RPl) to get scared; (Chi) to smell danger.

julia nf (Mex: sl) Black Maria, police wagon (US).

Julián m, **Juliano** m Julian.

Julieta f Juliet.

Julio m Julius; — **César** Julius Caesar.

julio nm July.

juma nf (SAm) drunkenness, drunken state.

jumadera nf (Mex) (a) drunkenness, drunken state.

(b) = **humareda**.

jumado adj (SAm) drunk.

jumarse [1a] vr (SAm) to get drunk.

jumatán nm (Cu) habitual drunkard.

jumazo nm (PR) cigarette.

jumeado adj (Per) drunk.

jumento nm donkey; beast of burden; (fig) dolt.

jumo adj (SAm) drunk.

juncal 1 adj (a) rushy, reedy. (b) (fig) willowy, lissom. 2 nm = **juncar**.

juncar nm ground covered in rushes.

juncia nf sedge.

junco[1] nm rush, reed; (Hond) fine straw; — **de Indias** rattan.

junco² nm (Naut) junk.

juncoso adj (a) rushy, reedy, reed-like. (b) *place* covered in rushes.

jungla nf jungle.

junio nm June.

junior nm (a) (Eccl) novice monk. (b) ['junior] (Sport: angl) junior.

Juno f Juno.

junquera nf rush, bulrush.

junquillo nm (a) jonquil; reed. (b) (Cu, Mex, PR) golden necklace.

junta nf (a) meeting, assembly; session; — **de acreedores** meeting of creditors; — **general** general meeting; — **general extraordinaria** special general meeting; **celebrar** — to hold a meeting; to sit.
(b) board, council, committee; (Comm, Fin) board; **la** — **de la asociación** the committee of the association; — **directiva** board of management; **J**— **para Ampliación de Estudios** Council for Research; **J**— **Nacional del Carbón** National Coal Board (Brit).
(c) junction, (point of) union.
(d) (Tech) joint; coupling; — **cardán,** — **universal** universal joint.
(e) (Tech) washer, gasket.

juntadero nm (Arg) meeting place.

juntamente adv (a) **hacer algo** — to do something together; to do something at the same time.
(b) **A** — **con B** A together with B; **ella y yo** — she and I together, she and I jointly.

juntar [1a] **1** vt (a) to join, unite; to assemble, put together; to collect, gather (together), amass; *money* to collect, raise.
(b) *door* to half-close, leave ajar.
2 juntarse vr (a) to join, come together; (persons) to meet, assemble, gather (together); — **con uno** to join someone; to meet (up with) someone; to associate with someone; **se juntaron para oírle** they assembled to hear him, they came together to hear him; **se juntó con ellos en la estación** he met them at the station, he joined them at the station.
(b) (Zool) to mate, copulate.
(c) (Mex: euph) to live together.

juntillo etc see **pie**.

junto 1 adj (a) joined, united; together; **fuimos** —**s** we went together; **tenía los ojos muy** —**s** his eyes were very close together.
(b) (Col) —**s** both.
2 adv near, close; together; (de) **por** —, **en** — in all, all together; (Comm) wholesale; **demasiado** — too close; **muy** — very close, very near; **ocurrió todo** — it happened all at once.
3 prep: — **a** near (to), close to, next to; — **con** together with.

juntura nf join, junction; (Anat) joint; (Tech) seam; (Tech) joint, coupling.

jupa nf (CAm, Mex) gourd; (hum) head.

jupiarse [1b] vr (CAm) to get drunk.

Júpiter m Jupiter.

jura¹ nf oath, pledge.

jura² nm (Cu, Guat: sl) cop (sl).

juraco nm (CAm) hole.

jurado nm (a) jury; (in contest, quiz etc) panel (of judges). (b) juror, juryman; member of a panel.

juramentar [1a] **1** vt to swear in, administer the oath to. **2 juramentarse** vr to be sworn in, take the oath.

juramento nm (a) oath; **bajo** — on oath; **prestar** — to take the oath (sobre on); **tomar** — **a uno** to swear someone in, administer the oath to someone.
(b) oath, swearword, curse; **decir** —**s a uno** to swear at someone.

jurar [1a] **1** vti to swear; — **decir la verdad** to swear to tell the truth; **le juro a Vd que ...** I swear to you

that . . .; **¡no jures!** don't swear!; — **en falso** to commit perjury.
2 jurarse vr: —**las a uno** to have it in for someone.

jurel nm (Cu) (a) fish used for food (Caranx latus). (b) fear, dread. (c) drunkenness, drunken state.

jurero nm (Chi, Ec, Per) perjurer, false witness.

jurgo nm, **jurgonera** nf (Col) = **jorga**.

jurídico adj juridical; legal; **departamento** — (Comm) legal department.

jurisdicción nf (a) jurisdiction. (b) district, administrative area.

jurisdiccional adj: **aguas** —**es** territorial waters.

jurisprudencia nf jurisprudence, (study of the) law.

jurista nmf jurist, lawyer.

jurungo nm (Ven) = **jorungo**.

juro nm right of perpetual ownership; pension; **a** — (Col, Ven), **de** — certainly.

justa nf joust, tournament; (fig) contest.

justamente adv (a) justly, fairly.
(b) just, precisely, exactly; ¡—! precisely!, that's just it!; **de eso se trata** — that's just the point, that's exactly the point; **son** — **las que no se venden** they are precisely the ones which are not for sale.

justar [1a] vi to joust, tilt.

justicia nf (a) justice; fairness, equity, rightness; right; — **poética** poetic justice; **de** — justly, deservedly; **lo estimo de** — I think it right; **es de** — **añadir que . . .** it is only right to add that . . .; **en** — by rights; **hacer** — **a** to do justice to; **hacerse** — **por sí mismo** to take the law into one's own hands.
(b) —**s y ladrones** (fam) cops and robbers (fam).

justiciable adj (a) actionable. (b) subject to review by a court; subject to arbitration.

justiciero adj (strictly) just, righteous.

justificable adj justifiable.

justificación nf justification.

justificante nm voucher.

justificar [1g] vt to justify; to verify, substantiate; *suspect* to clear (de of), vindicate.

justillo nm jerkin.

justipreciar [1b] vt to evaluate, appraise.

justiprecio nm evaluation, appraisal.

justo 1 adj (a) just, fair, right; **una decisión justa** a just decision; **los** —**s** the righteous; **me parece muy** — it seems perfectly fair to me; **más de lo** — more than is proper, more than usual.
(b) *quantity etc* exact, correct; **el peso** — the correct weight; ¡—! that's it!, correct!, right!
(c) *dress* tight; **el traje me viene muy** — the suit is rather tight for me, the suit is a very tight fit.
2 adv (a) justly.
(b) right.
(c) tightly; **vivir muy** — to be hard up, have only just enough to live on.

jute nm (Guat, Hond) edible snail.

juvenil adj (a) youthful; **obra** — youthful work, early work; **en los años** —**es** in one's early years, in one's youth; **de aspecto** — youthful in appearance.

juventud nf (a) youth; early life. (b) (young people; **la** — **de hoy** young people today, today's youth; **J**—**es Hitlerianas** Hitler Youth (Movement).

juyungo nm, **juyunga** nf (Col, Ec) Negro.

juzgado nm court, tribunal.

juzgar [1h] vti to judge; — **mal** to misjudge; **júzguelo Vd mismo** see for yourself, form your own judgement; **lo juzgo mi deber** I consider it my duty, I deem it my duty; **juzgue Vd mi sorpresa** imagine my surprise; — **de** to judge of, pass judgement on, appraise; **a** — **por** to judge by, judging by; **a** — **según lo que hemos visto** to judge by (or from) what we have seen.

juzgón adj (Guat, Mex) hypercritical, carping, fault-finding.

K

kaki *nm* (*SAm*) = **caqui**.
karting ['kartin] *nm* (*SAm: angl*) go-kart; go-kart racing.
kayac *nm*, **kayak** *nm* kayak.
Kenia *f* Kenya.
kermese *nf* charity fair, bazaar.
kerosén *nm*, **kerosene** *nm*, **kerosín** *nm* (*CAm*), **kerosina** *nf* (*CAm*) kerosene, paraffin.
kilate *nm* see **quilate**.
kilo *nm* kilo.
kilociclo *nm* kilocycle.
kilogramo *nm* kilogramme, kilogram (*US*).
kilolitro *nm* kilolitre, kiloliter (*US*).
kilometraje *nm* distance (*or* rate *etc*) in kilometres, (*equivalent to*) mileage.

kilométrico 1 *adj* (**a**) kilometric; **billete** — runabout ticket, mileage book. (**b**) (*fam*) very long; **palabra kilométrica** very long word, multisyllabic word. **2** *nm* = **billete** —.
kilómetro *nm* kilometre, kilometer (*US*).
kilovatio *nm* kilowatt.
kilovatios-hora *nmpl* kilowatt-hours.
kimona *nf* (*Cu, Mex*), **kimono** *nm* (*RPl*) kimono.
kiwi *nm* kiwi.
knock-out [kaw] *nm*, **K.O.** [kaw] *nm*, (*angl*) knock-out; knockout blow; **dejar a uno** —, **poner a uno** — to knock someone out, give someone a knockout blow.
kodak *nf, pl* **kodaks** [ko'ðak] (*SAm: angl*) (*any kind of*) small camera.

L

la[1] *def art f* the (*see* **el**[1] *for usage examples*).

la[2] *pron* (*person*) her; (*corresponding to Vd*) you; (*thing*) it.

la[3] *dem pron:* **mi casa y — de Vd** my house and yours; **esta chica y — del sombrero verde** this girl and the one in the green hat; **— de Pedro es mejor** Peter's is better; **y — de todos los demás** and that of everybody else; **— de Rodríguez** Mrs Rodríguez.

la[4]: **— que** *rel pron: see* **el**[3] **que.**

laberintero *adj* (*Mex*) = **laberintoso.**

laberíntico *adj* labyrinthine; *house etc* rambling.

laberinto *nm* (**a**) labyrinth, maze; (*fig*) maze, tangle. (**b**) (*SAm*) uproar, confused shouting; row, fuss.

laberintoso *adj* (*Mex, Per*) rowdy, brawling; gossipy.

labia *nf* fluency, persuasive verbosity, blarney; (*pej*) glibness; **tener mucha —** to have the gift of the gab (*fam*), be terribly persuasive.

labial 1 *adj* labial. **2** *nf* labial.

labihendido *adj* harelipped.

labio *nm* lip; (*of vessel etc*) lip, edge, rim; (*fig*) tongue; **—s lips, mouth; — inferior** lower lip; **— superior** upper lip; **— leporino** harelip; **lamerse los —s** to lick one's lips; **no morderse los —s** to be outspoken, pull no punches; **no descoser los —s** to keep one's mouth shut; **sin desplegar los —s** without uttering a word.

labiolectura *nf* lip-reading.

labiosear [1a] *vt* (*CAm*) to flatter; to blarney, chat up (*sl*).

labiosidad *nf* (*CAm, Ec*) flattery.

labioso *adj* (*SAm*) talkative; flattering; persuasive, glib; sly.

labor *nf* (**a**) labour, work; (*una —*) job, task, piece of work; **— de equipo** teamwork. (**b**) (*Agr*) farm work, cultivation; ploughing. (**c**) (*Guat, Mex, Salv*) small farm, smallholding. (**d**) (*Sew*) needlework, sewing, embroidery; **una — a** piece of needlework (*etc*): **— de aguja, —es femeninas** needlework; **— de ganchillo** crochet, crocheting. (**e**) **—es** (*Min*) workings.

laborable *adj* workable; arable; *see* **día.**

laboral *adj* labour (*attr*); technical; *see* **escuela** *etc*.

laboratorio *nm* laboratory.

laborar [1a] **1** *vt* to work, till. **2** *vi* (**a**) (*CAm*) to work. (**b**) (*pej*) to scheme, plot.

laborear [1a] *vt* to work (*also Min*); (*Agr*) to work, till.

laboreo *nm* (*Agr*) working, cultivation, tilling; (*Min*) working.

laborero *nm* (**a**) (*Bol, Chi, Per*) foreman. (**b**) (*Chi*) tanner.

laboriosamente *adv* industriously; painstakingly.

laboriosidad *nf* (**a**) industry; painstaking skill. (**b**) laboriousness.

laborioso *adj* (**a**) *person* hard-working, industrious, painstaking. (**b**) *work* tough, hard, laborious.

laborismo *nm* (*SAm*) labour movement, workers' movement; (*of Brit Pol*) Labour Party, Labour Movement.

laborista 1 *adj* (**a**) (*SAm*) labour (*attr*). (**b**) (*of Brit Pol*) Labour (*attr*); **Partido L—** Labour Party; **miembro —** Labour member. **2** *nmf* (**a**) (*Guat*) small farmer, smallholder. (**b**) (*Brit Pol*) Labour Party member, supporter of the Labour Party; Labour member of parliament.

labradío *adj* arable.

labrado 1 *adj* worked; *metal* wrought; *wood etc* carved; *cloth* patterned, embroidered. **2** *nm* cultivated field; **—s** cultivated land.

labrador *nm* farmer; farm labourer; ploughman; peasant; (*Mex*) lumberjack.

labradora *nf* peasant (woman).

labrantío *adj* arable.

labranza *nf* (**a**) farming; cultivation. (**b**) farm; farmland.

labrar [1a] *vt* to work; to fashion, shape; *metal* to work; *wood etc* to carve; *tree* (*Guat, Mex*) to fell and smooth; *land* to work, farm, till; *cloth* to embroider; (*fig*) to cause, bring about.

labriego *nm*, **labriega** *nf* farmhand, labourer; peasant.

laburno *nm* laburnum.

laca *nf* (**a**) (*also* **goma —**) shellac; (*varnish*) lac, lacquer; (*colour*) lake; **— de uñas, — para uñas** nail polish, nail varnish. (**b**) (*Chi*) = **lacra.**

lacayo *nm* footman; (*fig*) lackey.

laceada *nf* (*Arg*) whipping.

lacear [1a] *vt* (**a**) to beribbon, adorn with bows; to tie with a bow; *horse's load* (*Guat, Mex*) to tie on firmly, strap securely. (**b**) (*Arg*) to whip. (**c**) (*Hunting*) to snare, trap; to beat, drive.

laceración *nf* laceration; (*fig*) damage, spoiling.

lacerar [1a] *vt* to lacerate, tear, mangle; (*fig*) to damage, spoil.

lacería *nf* poverty, want; distress, wretchedness; toil.

laciar [1b] *vt* (*SAm*) *curly hair* to straighten.

Lacio *m* Latium.

lacio *adj* (*Bot*) withered, faded; *hair* lank, straight; *movement etc* limp, languid.

lacón *nm* shoulder of pork.

lacónicamente *adv* laconically, tersely.

lacónico *adj* laconic, terse.

laconismo *nm* laconic style (*or* manner *etc*), terseness.

lacra *nf* (**a**) (*Med*) mark, trace, scar; (*SAm*) sore, ulcer. (**b**) (*fig*) blot, blemish; **la prostitución es una — social** prostitution is a blot on society, prostitution is a disgrace to society.

lacrar[1] [1a] **1** *vt* (**a**) (*Med*) to injure the health of; to infect, strike (with a disease). (**b**) (*fig*) to injure, harm, cause damage (*or* loss) to. **2 lacrarse** *vr:* **— con algo** to suffer harm (*or* damage, loss *etc*) from something; **— con el trabajo excesivo** to harm oneself through overwork.

lacrar[2] [1a] *vt* to seal (*with sealing wax*).

lacre 1 *adj* (*SAm*) bright red. **2** *nm* sealing wax.

lacrimógeno *adj* (**a**) tear-producing; *gas* **—** tear gas. (**b**) (*fig*) tearful, highly sentimental; **canción lacrimógena, comedia lacrimógena** tear-jerker.

lacrimoso *adj* tearful, lachrymose.

lacrosse [la'kros] *nf* lacrosse.

lactación *nf*, **lactancia** *nf* lactation; nursing.

lactante *adj:* **mujer —** nursing mother.

lactar [1a] **1** *vt* to nurse, suckle; to feed on milk. **2** *vi* to suckle; to feed on milk.

lácteo *adj* lacteal, milk (*attr*); (*fig*) milky, lacteous.

láctico *adj* lactic.

lactosa *nf* lactose.

lacustre *adj* lake (*attr*), lacustrine; (*SAm*) marshy.

lachear [1a] *vt* (*Chi*) to court.

lacho *nm* (*Chi, Per*) lover; beau, gallant.

ladeado *adj* (**a**) tilted, leaning, inclined. (**b**) (*Arg*) slovenly. (**c**) (*Arg*) wily. (**d**) (*Arg*) **andar —** to be in a bad temper; **andar — con uno** to feel hostile to someone.

ladear [1a] **1** *vt* (**a**) to tilt, tip; to incline (to one side); (*Aer*) to bank, turn; *head* to tilt, put on one side. (**b**) *hill etc* to skirt, go round the side of. **2** *vi* (**a**) to tilt, tip, lean. (**b**) to turn aside, turn off. **3 ladearse** *vr* (**a**) to lean, incline (*also fig: a*

towards); **(Aer)** to bank, turn; **ladea al otro partido** he leans towards the other party.
(b) — **con** to be equal to, be even with.
(c) **(Chi)** to fall in love **(con** with).
ladeo nm **(a)** tilting, inclination, leaning; **(Aer)** banking, turning. **(b)** (fig) inclination.
ladera nf slope, hillside.
ladero 1 adj side (attr), lateral. **2** nm (Arg) helper, backer.
ladilla nf crab louse.
ladillento adj (Guat, Mex) lousy.
ladinazo adj (Arg) cunning, shrewd.
ladino 1 adj **(a)** cunning, wily; smart, shrewd.
(b) **(CAm, Col, Ec, Per, RPl)** Indian Spanish-speaking.
(c) **(CAm, Mex)** half-breed, mestizo; non-Indian, white, of Spanish descent.
(d) **(Col, SD)** talkative, loquacious.
(e) **(Mex)** voice high-pitched, fluty.
2 nm **(a)** (CAm, Col, Ec, Per, RPl) Spanish-speaking Indian.
(b) **(CAm, Mex)** half-breed, mestizo; non-Indian, white man.
(c) **(Ling)** Ladin (Rhaeto-Romance dialect); Ladino, Sephardic (mixed Spanish and Hebrew).
lado nm **(a)** (in most senses) side; — **débil** weak spot; — **izquierdo** left(-hand) side; — **a** — side by side; **al** — near, at hand; **al** — **de** by the side of, beside; **estuvo a mi** — she was at my side, she was beside me; **al otro** — **de la calle** on the other side of the street, across the street; **llevar algo al otro** — **del río** to carry something across (or over) the river; **al** — **de aquello, esto no es nada** beside (or in comparison with) that, this is nothing; **la casa de al** — the house next door; **viven al** — **de nosotros** they live next door to us; **ir de un** — **a otro** to go to and fro, walk up and down; **poner algo de** — to put something sideways (or edgeways); **por el** — **del mar** towards the sea, on the sea side; **por el** — **de Madrid** in the direction of Madrid; **salieron corriendo cada uno por su** — they all ran off in different directions; **por todos** —**s** on all sides, all round; **por un** — . . ., **por otro** . . . on the one hand . . ., on the other . . .; **dar a uno de** — to disregard someone, be unconcerned about someone; **dejar a un** — to skip, omit, pass over; to leave aside; **echar a un** — to cast aside; **hacer** — to make room (a for); **hacerse a un** — to stand aside (also fig), move over; **mirar de (medio)** — to look askance at; **to steal a glance at; **poner a un** — to put aside.
(b) (Mil) flank.
(c) (Sport) end; **cambiar de** — to change ends.
(d) (genealogical) side; **por el** — **de la madre** on the mother's side.
(e) (Pol etc) side; faction; **ponerse al** — **de uno** to side with someone.
(f) favour, protection; **tener buenos** —**s** to have good connections.
ladrar [1a] vi to bark.
ladrería nf (Col, Cu, Mex), **ladrerío** nm (Mex) barking.
ladrido nm bark, barking; (fig) slander, scandal.
ladrillado nm brick floor; tile floor.
ladrillar 1 nm brickworks. **2** vt to brick, pave with bricks.
ladrillería nf (SAm) brickworks.
ladrillo nm brick; tile; (of chocolate) block; — **de fuego,** — **refractario** firebrick.
ladrón 1 adj thieving. **2** nm, **ladrona** nf thief; — **de corazones** ladykiller; **¡al** —**!** stop thief!
ladronera nf **(a)** den of thieves. **(b)** robbery, theft.
lagaña nf = **legaña.**
lagar nm wine press; oil press.
lagarta nf **(a)** lizard; **¡—, —!** look out! **(b)** (Ent) gipsy moth; — **falsa** lackey moth. **(c)** sly woman; **¡—!** you bitch!
lagartear [1a] vt **(a)** (Chi) to pinion. **(b)** (Col) to fiddle (fam), wangle (fam).
lagartera nf lizard hole.
lagartija nf (small) lizard, wall lizard.
lagartijo nm (Mex) young man-about-town, elegant idler.
lagarto nm **(a)** lizard: — **de Indias** alligator; **¡—, —!** look out!; (Ec, Mex, Per) God forbid!
(b) sly fellow, fox.
(c) (Ec) shopkeeper who charges high prices; (Mex, Nic) grasping sort, greedy person; (Col) unemployed man seeking to live at government expense; intriguer, wirepuller (fam).
lagartón adj (Guat, Mex) greedy; sharp, shrewd; sly.

lago nm lake; **los Grandes L**—**s** the Great Lakes.
lágrima nf tear; drop; —**s de cocodrilo** crocodile tears; —**s de San Pedro** (Arg, Chi) June rains; **beberse las** —**s** to hold back one's tears; **deshacerse en** —**s** to burst into tears; **llorar a** — **viva** to sob one's heart out, cry uncontrollably.
lagrimar [1a] vi to cry.
lagrimear [1a] vi (of person) to shed tears easily, be tearful; (of eyes) to water, fill with tears.
lagrimilla nf (Chi) unfermented grape juice.
lagrimoso adj person lachrymose, tearful; eyes watery.
laguna nf **(a)** (Geog) pool; (near coast) lagoon. **(b)** (Lit etc) gap, lacuna; (in process) hiatus, gap, break.
lagunajo nm pool, pond; puddle.
lagunato nm (Cu, Hond) = **lagunajo.**
lagunoso adj marshy, swampy.
laicado nm laity.
laical adj lay.
laicidad nf (SAm), **laicismo** nm laicism (doctrine of the independence of the state etc from church interference).
laicizar [1f] vt to laicize.
laico 1 adj lay. **2** nm layman.
laísmo nm use of la and las as indirect objects.
laísta 1 adj that uses la and las as indirect objects. **2** nmf user of la and las as indirect objects.
laja[1] nf **(a)** (Arg, Chi, Hond) sandstone (easily broken into slabs); slab, flagstone. **(b)** (Ec) steep ground, steep place.
laja[2] nf (Col) fine rope.
Lalo m (SAm) pet name for **Eduardo.**
lama[1] nf **(a)** mud, slime, ooze. **(b)** (Bol, Col, Mex) mould, verdigris; (Mex) moss; duckweed.
lama[2] nf (Sew) lamé.
lama[3] nm (Rel) lama.
lambarear [1a] vi (Cu) to wander aimlessly about.
lambeculo nmf (Arg, Mex) creep (sl), toady.
lambeladrillos nm, pl **lambeladrillos** (Col) hypocrite.
lambeplatos nmf, pl **lambeplatos** (SAm) **(a)** bootlicker (fam). **(b)** poor wretch.
lamber [2a] vt (SAm) **(a)** = **lamer. (b)** to fawn on, toady to, suck up to (fam).
lambeta nmf (Arg) creep (sl), toady.
lambetada nf (Arg, Mex, PR) **(a)** lick. **(b)** servile action; remark designed to flatter.
lambetazo nm (SAm) **(a)** lick. **(b)** = **lambetada.**
lambetear [1a] vt (SAm) **(a)** to lick; to lick greedily, lick noisily. **(b)** to suck up to (fam).
lambiche adj (Mex) = **lambiscón.**
lambida nf (SAm) lick.
lambido adj (SAm) prim, affected; vain; (Col, Ec, Mex, PR, SD) shameless, cynical; (Per) disrespectful towards women.
lambioche adj (Mex) servile, soapy, fawning.
lambiscón adj (Mex, Per) **(a)** greedy, gluttonous. **(b)** = **lambioche. (c)** prim, affected.
lambisconear [1a] (Col, Mex, Per) **1** vt **(a)** to lick greedily. **(b)** (fig) to suck up to (fam). **2** vi (fig) to creep (sl), crawl.
lambisconería nf (Mex, Per) **(a)** greediness, gluttony. **(b)** servility, soapiness. **(c)** primness, affectation.
lambisquear [1a] (Col, Mex, Per) = **lambisconear.**
lambón adj (SAm) = **lambioche.**
lambraña nmf (Col) wretch.
lambrijo adj (Mex) very thin.
lambrusquear [1a] vt (Chi, Mex) to lick.
lambuzo adj (Col, Ec, Mex, Ven) **(a)** greedy, gluttonous. **(b)** shameless, brazen.
lameculos nmf, pl **lameculos** (fam) bootlicker (fam), toady.
lamedero nm (Agr) salt lick.
lamedura nf lick, licking.
lamentable adj regrettable; lamentable; pitiful; **es** — **que . . .** it is regrettable that . . .
lamentablemente adv regrettably.
lamentación nf lamentation; sorrow; **ahora no sirven** —**es** it's no good crying over spilt milk.
lamentar [1a] **1** vt to be sorry about, regret; loss etc to lament, bemoan, bewail; death to mourn; — **que . . .** to be sorry that . . ., regret that . . .; **lamentamos mucho que . . .** we very much regret that . . .
2 lamentarse vr to lament, wail, moan (de, por about, over); to mourn (de, por over); to complain (de, por about).
lamento nm lament; moan, wail; —**s** lamentation.
lamentoso adj **(a)** = **lamentable. (b)** plaintive.
lameplatos nmf, pl **lameplatos (a)** person who eats scraps. **(b)** (Mex) toady; poor wretch; worthless individual.

lamer [2a] *vt* to lick; (*of water*) to lap, lap against.
lametada *nf* lick; lap.
lamido *adj* (a) very thin; pale. (b) scrubbed. (c) prim, affected.
lámina[1] *nf* (*of metal, glass etc*) sheet; (*Metal, Phot, Typ*) plate; (*in book etc*) plate, illustration, picture; engraving; **—s de acero** steel in sheets, sheet steel.
lámina[2] *nmf* (*Col*) rogue, rascal.
laminadero *nm*: **— de hierro** steel rolling mill.
laminado *adj* (a) laminate(d). (b) (*Tech*) sheet (*attr*), rolled; **cobre —** sheet copper, rolled copper.
laminador *nm* rolling mill.
laminar [1a] *vt* to laminate; (*Tech*) to roll.
lamiscar [1g] *vt* to lick greedily, lick noisily.
lampa *nf* (*SAm*) spade, hoe.
lampalague *nf* (*Arg, Chi*) boa constrictor. (b) (*Chi: fig*) glutton.
lámpara 1 *nf* lamp, light; bulb; (*Radio*) valve, tube (*US*); **—s** (*SAm*) eyes; **— de alcohol** spirit lamp; **— de arco** arc lamp; **— de bolsillo** torch, flashlight; **— de lectura** reading lamp; **— de mesa** table lamp; **— de pared** wall light; **— de pie** standard lamp; **— de señales** signalling lamp; **— de soldar** blowlamp, blow torch; **— de techo** overhead lamp; **— solar ultravioleta** sun-ray lamp; **atizar la —** (*fam*) to fill up the glasses; **quebrar la —** (*Ven*) to ruin everything.
 2 *nmf* (*Cu*) bore; (*Ven*) thief, swindler.
lamparero *nm* lampmaker; lamplighter.
lamparilla *nf* (a) small lamp; nightlight. (b) (*Bot*) aspen.
lamparín *nm* (a) (*Chi*) candle. (b) (*Per*) paraffin lamp.
lamparista *nm* = **lamparero**.
lámparo *adj* (*Col*) penniless, broke (*fam*).
lamparón *nm* (a) (*Med*) scrofula. (b) large grease spot.
lampazo[1] *nm* (*Bot*) burdock.
lampazo[2] *nm* (a) (*Naut*) swab; (*Arg*) floor mop. (b) (*Col, Ven*) whipping.
lampear [1a] *vt* (*Per*) to shovel.
lampiño *adj* hairless; *person* clean-shaven.
lampión *nm* Chinese lantern.
lampista *nm* (a) = **lamparero**. (b) tinsmith.
lampón[1] *adj* (*Col*) starving, hungry.
lampón[2] *nm* (*Ec*) spade, hoe.
lamprea *nf* (a) (*Fish*) lamprey. (b) (*Med*) sore, ulcer.
lamprear [1a] *vt* (*CAm*) to whip.
lana[1] *nf* (a) wool; fleece; woollen cloth; **— de acero** steel wool; **de —, hecho de —** wool (*attr*), woollen; **ir por — y volver trasquilado** to get nothing for one's pains, be disappointed in one's hopes.
 (b) (*Mex*) money.
 (c) (*Mex*) lie.
 (d) (*CAm*) trickster, swindler; rotter.
lana[2] *nf* (*CR, Guat*) = **lama**[1] (b).
lanar *adj* wool (*attr*), wool-bearing; **ganado —** sheep.
lance *nm* (a) (*of net etc*) throw, cast.
 (b) (*Fish*) catch, quantity of fish caught.
 (c) (*in games etc*) stroke, move, piece of play.
 (d) incident, event, occurrence, episode; chance, accident; **— de honor** affair of honour, duel; **el libro tiene pocos —s** the book is dull, not much happens in the book; **tirarse (a) un —** (*Arg, Par*) to take a chance.
 (e) critical moment, difficult moment.
 (f) row, quarrel.
 (g) (*Chi*) duck, dodge; **sacar — to** dodge, duck away.
 (h) (*Arg, Par: Archit*) section, range; **casa de 3 —s** house in 3 sections.
 (i) **de —** (*Comm*) secondhand; cheap; **libros de —** secondhand books; **comprar algo de —** to buy something secondhand, buy something cheap.
lancear [1a] *vt* to spear.
lancero 1 *nm* (*Mil*) lancer; **—s** (*Mus*) lancers. 2 *nmf* (*Arg*) excessively optimistic person, irresponsible person.
lanceta *nf* (a) (*Med etc*) lancet; **abrir con — to** lance. (b) (*SAm*) goad.
lancinante *adj* pain piercing.
lancinar [1a] *vt* to lance, pierce.
lancha[1] *nf* launch; (*small*) boat; lighter, barge; **— automóvil** motor launch, motorboat; **— cañonera** gunboat; **— de carga** lighter, barge; **— de carreras** speedboat; **— de desembarco** landing craft; **— motora** motorboat, speedboat; **— neumática** (*Aer etc*) rubber dinghy; **— de pesca** fishing boat; **— rápida** speedboat; **— salvavidas, — de socorro** lifeboat; **— torpedera** torpedo boat.
lancha[2] *nf* (*Ec*) mist, fog; (hoar)frost.
lanchaje *nm* (*Mex*) freight charge.

lanchar [1a] *vi* (*Ec*) to become overcast; to freeze.
lanchero *nm* boatman; lighterman, bargee.
lanchón *nm* lighter, barge.
landó *nm* landau.
landra *nf*: **¡mala — te coma!** curse you!
lanería *nf* (a) woollen goods. (b) wool shop.
lanero 1 *adj* wool (*attr*); woollen; **la industria lanera** the wool industry. 2 *nm* (a) woolman, wool dealer. (b) wool warehouse.
lángara *nmf* (*Mex*) untrustworthy individual.
lángaro *adj* (a) (*CAm*) vagrant, wandering, idle; (*Col, Mex*) starving, poverty-stricken; (*Mex*) wicked; sly, untrustworthy. (b) (*CR*) lanky.
langarucho *adj* (*CAm, Mex*), **langarutano** *adj* (*Ec*) lanky.
langosta *nf* (a) lobster. (b) (*Ent*) locust.
langostera *nf* lobster pot.
langostín *nm*, **langostino** *nm* prawn; crayfish.
languceta *adj* (*Chi*), **languciento** *adj* (*Chi, Mex*), **langucio** *adj* (*Chi*) starving; weakly.
lánguidamente *adv* languidly; weakly, listlessly.
languidecer [2d] *vi* to languish, pine (away).
languidez *nf* languor, lassitude; listlessness.
lánguido *adj* languid; weak, listless, drooping.
languso *adj* (*Mex*) (a) sly, shrewd. (b) lanky.
lanilla *nf* nap (*on cloth*); thin flannel cloth.
lanolina *nf* lanolin(e).
lanoso *adj* woolly, fleecy.
lanudo *adj* (a) woolly, fleecy. (b) (*Ec, Ven*) rustic, uncouth.
lanza 1 *nf* (a) (*Mil*) lance, spear; **estar — en ristre** to be ready for action, be all set to go; **medir —s** to cross swords; **ser una —** to be pretty sharp; (*Mex*) to be sly, be a rogue.
 (b) (*of wagon*) pole.
 (c) (*of hose*) nozzle.
 2 *nm* (*Col, CR, Ven*) swindling businessman, dishonest dealer, shark (*fam*).
lanzabombas *nm, pl* **lanzabombas** (*Aer*) bomb release; (*Mil*) trench mortar.
lanzacohetes *nm, pl* **lanzacohetes** rocket launcher.
lanzada *nf* spear thrust; spear wound.
lanzadera *nf* shuttle.
lanzador *nm* (a) thrower; (*Sport*) pitcher; **— de cuchillos** knife-thrower. (b) (*Comm, Fin*) promoter.
lanzaespumas *nm, pl* **lanzaespumas** foam extinguisher.
lanzallamas *nm, pl* **lanzallamas** flamethrower.
lanzamiento *nm* (a) throw, cast; throwing, casting, hurling; (*Aer*) drop (*by parachute*), jump, descent; **— de pesos** putting the weight.
 (b) (*Naut*) launch, launching.
 (c) (*Comm, Fin*) launching; promotion.
 (d) (*Law*) dispossession, eviction.
lanzaminas *nm, pl* **lanzaminas** minelayer.
lanzar [1f] 1 *vt* (a) to throw, cast, fling, hurl; (*Sport, ball* to pitch, bowl (*a* at, to); *weight* to put; (*Aer*) to drop (*by parachute*); (*Med*) to bring up, throw up, vomit; *challenge* to throw out, throw down.
 (b) *cry* to give, utter; *look* to give, cast (*a* at).
 (c) (*Naut*) to launch.
 (d) (*Bot*) *leaves etc* to put forth.
 (e) (*Comm, Fin*) to launch, promote.
 (f) (*Law*) to dispossess, evict.
 2 **lanzarse** *vr* (a) to throw oneself, hurl oneself, fling oneself (*a, en* into; *sobre* on); to rush (*sobre* at, on), fly (*sobre* at); (*Aer*) to jump (*by parachute*), bale out; **se lanzó a la pelea** he rushed into the fray; **se lanzó al río** he jumped into the river, he dived into the river.
 (b) **— a** (*fig*) to launch into; to embark upon, undertake.
Lanzarote *m* Lancelot.
lanzatorpedos *nm, pl* **lanzatorpedos** torpedo tube.
laña *nf* clamp; rivet.
lañar [1a] *vt* to clamp (together); to rivet.
Laos *m* Laos.
laosiano 1 *adj* Laotian. 2 *nm*, **laosiana** *nf* Laotian.
lapa *nf* (a) (*Zool*) limpet.
 (b) (*CAm*) odd-looking person, outlandish individual; (*Mex*) scrounger (*fam*).
 (c) (*Chi*) soldiers' camp follower.
 (d) (*Chi, Per*) half gourd (*used as bowl etc*).
 (e) (*Ec*) large flat-topped hat.
lapalada *nf* (*Mex*) drizzle.
lape *adj* (*Chi*) (a) massed, packed tight; matted. (b) *dance etc* merry, lively.
lapicera *nf* (*Chi, RPl*) = **lapicero**.
lapicero *nm* propelling pencil; pencil-holder; (*SAm*) penholder, pen; (*Per etc*) ball-point pen.

lápida *nf* stone, stone tablet, memorial tablet; — **conmemorativa** commemorative tablet; — **mortuoria** headstone, gravestone; — **mural** tablet let into a wall; — **sepulcral** tombstone.

lapidar [1a] *vt* (a) to stone, throw stones at; to stone to death. (b) (Col, Guat, Hond, Mex, Per) *gem* to cut.

lapidario 1 *adj* lapidary. **2** *nm* lapidary.

lapislázuli *nm* lapis lazuli.

lápiz *nm* (a) pencil; crayon; — **de cejas** eyebrow pencil; — **labial**, — **de labios** lipstick; — (**de**) **plomo** lead pencil; **escribir algo a** (or **con**) — to write something in pencil; **está añadido a** — it is added in pencil; it is pencilled in.
(b) (Min) blacklead, graphite.

lapo *nm* (a) (sl) bash (fam), swipe; **de un** — (Col) at one go. (b) (Col, Ec, Ven) swig (fam). (c) (Ven) simple soul.

lapón *nm*, **lapona** *nf* Lapp, Laplander.

Laponia *f* Lapland.

lapso *nm* lapse; — **de tiempo** interval of time, passage of time.

lapsus *nm*, *pl* **lapsus**; — **calami** slip of the pen; — **linguae** slip of the tongue.

laqueado *adj* lacquered; varnished.

laquear [1a] *vt* to lacquer; *nails* to varnish.

lard(e)ar [1a] *vt* to lard, baste.

lardo *nm* lard, animal fat.

lardoso *adj* lardy, fatty; greasy.

lares *nmpl* (Hist) household gods, lares; (fig) home; **volver a los** — to return home.

largamente *adv* (a) for a long time; *tell* at length, fully; **conversamos** — we talked at length, we had a long conversation.
(b) *live* comfortably, at ease.
(c) *reward, treat etc* generously.

largar [1h] **1** *vt* (a) to let go, let loose, release; to loosen, slacken; *rope* to let out, pay out; *flag, sail* to unfurl; *boat* to launch, put out.
(b) *blow* to give, fetch, deal.
(c) *curse etc* to let fly.
(d) (Arg, Mex, Par) to throw, hurl.
(e) (Col) to give, lend.
2 largarse *vr* (a) (fam) to beat it (fam), hop it (fam); to quit; **¡lárgate!** clear off!
(b) (Naut) to set sail, start out.
(c) (SAm) to start, begin; — **a** + *infin* to start to + *infin*.

largo 1 *adj* (a) (of distance, measure) long; (of time) long, lengthy; — **de pelo** long-haired; — **de uñas** light-fingered, thieving; —**s años** long years, many years; **no es bastante** — it's not long enough; **es muy** — **de contar** it's a long story.
(b) (fam) **¡**— (**de aquí**)**!** clear off!
(c) (with **de**) **estar de** — to be in a long dress; **ponerse de** — to put on grown-up clothes, dress as an adult (for the first time); **pasar de** — to pass by, go by (without stopping); **dejar pasar a uno de** — to give someone a wide berth.
(d) (with **lo**) **a lo más** — at the most; **a lo** — *put* lengthways; *tell* at great length, lengthily; *see etc* in the distance, far off; **a lo** — **de** along; alongside; (of time) all through, throughout; **a lo** — **del río** along the river; **a lo** — **del túnel** throughout the tunnel.
(e) (of quantity) full, good; **tardó media hora larga** he took a good (or full) half-hour; **los aventajó en un minuto** — he beat them by a full minute; **le costó 50 dólares** —**s** it cost him all of 50 dollars, it cost him a good 50 dollars.
(f) (*larga*) **a la larga** in the long run; eventually, in the end; **dar largas a un asunto** to delay a matter, put off making a decision about a matter; **me dio largas con una promesa** she put me off with a promise; **saberla larga** to be shrewd; to know one's way about.
(g) generous; lavish; **tirar de** — to spend lavishly.
(h) abundant, copious; *crop, harvest* heavy.
(i) *person* sharp, shrewd; quick.
(j) (Naut) *rope* loose, slack.
2 *nm* (a) length; **el** — **de las faldas** the length of skirts; **tiene 9 metros de** — it is 9 metres long; **¿cuánto tiene de** —**?** how long is it?
(b) (Mus) largo.

largona *nf* (a) (Chi, Per) delay. (b) (Chi) **darse una** — to take a rest.

largor *nm* length.

largucho *adj* (SAm) lanky.

larguero 1 *adj* (a) (Arg, Chi) long, lengthy; *person* slow, slow-working; (Sport) trained for long-distance running.
(b) (Chi) generous; lavish; abundant, copious.
2 *nm* (Archit) main beam, chief support; (of door) jamb; (Sport) goal-post, crossbar; (of bed) bolster.

largueza *nf* generosity.

larguirucho *adj* lanky, gangling.

largura *nf* length.

largurucho *adj* (SAm) lanky, gangling.

lárice *nm* larch.

laringe *nf* larynx.

laringitis *nf* laryngitis.

larva *nf* larva; grub, maggot.

las *def art fpl etc: see* **los.**

lasca *nf* chip of stone.

lascadura *nf* (Mex) sore, abrasion.

lascar [1g] **1** *vt* (a) (Naut) to slacken. (b) (Mex) to graze, bruise; *stone* to chip, chip off. **2** *vi* (Mex) to chip off, flake off.

lascivamente *adv* lewdly, lasciviously; lustfully; (fig) playfully, wantonly.

lascivia *nf* lewdness, lasciviousness; lust, lustfulness; (fig) playfulness.

lascivo *adj* lewd, lascivious; lustful; (fig) playful, wanton.

lasitud *nf* lassitude, weariness.

laso *adj* weary; weak; limp, slack, languid.

lástima *nf* (a) (feeling) pity; compassion; shame; **¡qué** —**!** what a pity!, what a shame!, that's too bad!; **¡qué** — **de hombre!** isn't he pitiful?; **es una** — it's a shame; **es** — **que . . .** it's a pity that . . ., it's too bad that . . .; **dar** — to be pitiful, rouse to pity; **eso me da mucha** — I feel very sorry about that; **es una película que da** — it's a pathetic film; (pej) it's a pathetically bad film; **todos me dan** — I feel sorry for them all.
(b) pitiful object, pitiful sight; **estar hecho una** — to be a sorry sight, be in a dreadful state.
(c) complaint.

lastimada *nf* (Guat, Mex) = **lastimadura.**

lastimador *adj* harmful, injurious.

lastimadura *nf* (SAm) wound, injury; bruise; sore.

lastimar [1a] **1** *vt* (a) to hurt, harm, injure; to wound, bruise.
(b) to offend, distress.
(c) to pity, sympathize with, feel pity for.
(d) to move to pity.
2 lastimarse *vr* (a) to hurt oneself, injure oneself; **se lastimó el brazo** he hurt his arm.
(b) — **de** to complain about.
(c) — **de** to feel sorry for, pity.

lastimero *adj* (a) harmful, injurious. (b) = **lastimoso.**

lastimón *nm* (SAm) = **lastimadura.**

lastimosamente *adv* pitifully, pathetically.

lastimoso *adj* piteous, pitiful, pathetic.

lastrar [1a] *vt* to ballast.

lastre *nm* (a) (Tech) ballast; **en** — (Naut) in ballast. (b) (fig) ballast; dead weight, useless load. (c) good sense, steadiness.

lata *nf* (a) (metal) tinplate; tin, can; (Col) food, daily ration; **sardinas en** — tinned sardines, canned sardines; **sonar a** — (Mus etc) to sound tinny.
(b) (fam) nuisance, bore, bind (sl); **es una** — **tener que . . .** it's a nuisance having to . . .; **¡vaya una** —**!**, **¡qué** —**!** what a nuisance!; **dar** — (Nic, Per) to talk nonsense; **dar la** — to be a nuisance, be annoying, be boring; **dar la** — **a uno** to annoy someone.
(c) (wood) lath.
(d) **estar sin** — (fam), **estar en la(s)** —**(s)** (CAm, Col) to be penniless, be broke (fam).
(e) (CAm) whippersnapper, young rascal.

latazo *nm* (fam) nuisance, bore, bind (sl).

latear [1a] *vi* (SAm) (a) to be a nuisance, be annoying. (b) to talk a lot, chatter away pointlessly.

latente *adj* (a) latent. (b) (SAm) alive, intense, vigorous; *memory* fresh, alive.

lateral 1 *adj* lateral, side (attr). **2** *nm* (Theat) wings, side of the stage.

lateralmente *adv* laterally; sideways.

latería *nf* (CAm) tinplate; (Arg, Cu, Par) tinsmith's workshop; tinworks.

laterío *nm* (Mex) tinned goods, canned goods.

latero *nm* (SAm) (a) tinsmith. (b) bore, tedious person.

látex *nm* latex.

latido *nm* (a) (of heart) beat, beating; throb, throbbing; palpitation. (b) (of dog) bark, yelp.

latifundia *nf* latifundia, large estates.

latifundio *nm* large estate.

latifundista *nm* (SAm) important landowner, owner of a large estate.

latigazo *nm* (a) lash; crack (of a whip). (b) (fig) harsh reproof; verbal lashing. (c) (fam) swig (fam), swallow; strong nightcap.

látigo nm **(a)** whip; (Col, Ec, Hond, Per) lash; crack (of a whip).
(b) (Chi: Sport) finishing post, finishing line; **salir al —** to complete a task.
(c) (Arg, Per, Urug) horseman, rider.
latigudo adj (SAm) leathery.
latigueda nf (Ec, Hond, Mex, Nic) whipping, thrashing.
latiguear [1a] vt (Arg, Ec, Hond, Mex) to whip, thrash.
latiguera nf (Per) whipping, thrashing.
latín nm **(a)** Latin; **bajo —** Low Latin; **— clásico** Classical Latin; **— tardío** Late Latin; **— vulgar** Vulgar Latin; **saber (mucho) —** (fam) to be pretty sharp.
(b) —es Latin tags, learned quotations and references.
latinajo nm dog Latin, bad Latin; **—s** Latin tags, learned quotations and references.
latinidad nf latinity.
latinismo nm latinism.
latinista nmf latinist.
latinización nf latinization.
latinizar [1f] vti to latinize.
latino 1 adj Latin; (SAm: angl) Latin-American. 2 nm, **latina** nf Latin; (SAm: angl) Latin-American.
Latinoamérica f Latin America.
latinoamericano 1 adj Latin-American. 2 nm, **latinoamericana** nf Latin-American.
latir [3a] 1 vt **(a)** (Mex) **me late que todo saldrá bien** I have a feeling that all will be well, something tells me that everything will be all right.
(b) (Ven) to annoy, upset.
2 vi **(a)** (heart) to beat, throb, palpitate.
(b) (dog) to bark, yelp.
latitud nf (Geog and fig) latitude; breadth; area, extent.
latitudinal adj latitudinal.
lato adj broad, wide, extensive; sense broad.
latón nm **(a)** brass. **(b)** (RPl) big tin, large tin container; (Per, PR) tin bucket.
latoso adj annoying, tiresome; boring.
latrocinio nm robbery, theft.
Latvia f Latvia.
latvio 1 adj Latvian. 2 nm, **latvia** nf Latvian. 3 nm (language) Latvian, Lettish.
lauca nf (Chi) baldness, loss of hair; alopecia.
laucadura nf (Chi) baldness.
laucar [1g] vt (Chi) to fleece, shear, remove the hair (or wool) from.
lauco adj (Chi) bald, hairless.
laucha nf (Chi, RPl) mouse; (fig) thin person, small-featured person; (Arg) dirty old man; (Col) **= baquiano; ser una —, ser una lauchita** (Chi, RPl) to be very sharp, be quick; **aguaitar la —, catear la —** (Chi, RPl) to await a favourable opportunity, bide one's time.
laúd nm (Mus) lute.
laudable adj laudable, praiseworthy.
laudablemente adv laudably, in a praiseworthy way.
láudano nm laudanum.
laudatorio adj laudatory.
laudo nm (Law) award, decision, finding.
laureado 1 adj honoured, distinguished, famous. 2 nm laureate.
laurear [1a] vt to crown with laurel; (fig) to honour, reward.
laurel nm laurel; (fig) laurels; honour, reward; **— rosa** rosebay, oleander; **descansar** (or **dormirse**) **sobre sus —es** to rest on one's laurels.
lauréola nf **(a)** laurel wreath, crown of laurel; halo. **(b)** (Bot) daphne.
lauro nm laurel; (fig) laurels; glory, fame.
Lausana Lausanne.
lava[1] nf (Geol) lava.
lava[2] nf (Min) washing; **camisa de — y pon** drip-dry shirt.
lavable adj washable.
lavabo nm **(a)** washbasin; washstand. **(b)** (euph) lavatory, washroom (euph), toilet (euph).
lavacara nf (Col, Ec) washbasin.
lavacaras nmf, pl **lavacaras** (fam) toady, creep (sl).
lavacoches nm, pl **lavacoches** car wash.
lavada nf (SAm) wash, washing.
lavadedos nm, pl **lavadedos** finger bowl.
lavadero nm **(a)** laundry, wash house; (in river) washing place. **(b)** (SAm) gold-bearing sands (in river).
lavado nm **(a)** (act) wash, washing; **— de cabeza** shampoo; **— de cerebro** brainwashing; **— químico, — en seco** dry cleaning.
(b) (clothes) wash, laundry.
(c) (Art) wash.

lavador nm **(a)** (Arg, Par) washbasin. **(b)** (Guat) = **lavabo** (b).
lavadora nf **(a)** washing machine; **— de coches** car wash; **— de platos** dish-washer. **(b)** (Col, Ec) laundress, washerwoman.
lavadura nf **(a)** washing. **(b)** dirty water.
lavagallos nm (Col, Ven) poor-quality brandy, firewater.
lavaje nm (Chi, RPl) **(a)** = **lavadura. (b)** (Med) enema.
lavamanos nm, pl **lavamanos** washbasin.
lavanda nf lavender.
lavandera nf **(a)** laundress, washerwoman. **(b)** (Orn) wagtail.
lavandería nf laundry; **— automática** launderette.
lavandero nm launderer, laundryman.
lavándula nf lavender.
lavaojos nm, pl **lavaojos** eye bath.
lavaplatos nm, pl **lavaplatos** **(a)** (machine) dish-washer. **(b)** (Arg: person) dishwasher, washer-up. **(c)** (Chi, Mex) sink.
lavar [1a] 1 vt **(a)** to wash; **— y marcar** hair to shampoo and set; **— en seco** to dry-clean; **— la cabeza** to wash one's hair.
(b) (fig) to wipe away; to wipe out.
2 **lavarse** vr to wash, have a wash; **— las manos** to wash one's hands; (fig) to wash one's hands of it.
lavativa nf **(a)** (Med) enema. **(b)** (fig) nuisance, bother, bore.
lavatorio nm **(a)** washstand. **(b)** (SAm: angl) lavatory, washroom (euph). **(c)** (Med) lotion.
lavavajillas nm, pl **lavavajillas** dishwasher.
lavazas nfpl dishwater, dirty water, slops.
lavoteo nm (fam) quick wash, cat-lick (fam).
laxante 1 adj laxative. 2 nm laxative.
laxar [1a] vt to ease, relax, slacken; bowels to loosen.
laxativo adj laxative.
laxitud nf laxity, slackness.
laxo adj lax, slack.
laya nf **(a)** spade; **— de puntas** (garden) fork. **(b)** (fig) kind, sort; **de esta —** of this kind.
lazada nf bow, knot.
lazar [1f] vt to lasso, rope; (Mex, Nic) = **enlazar.**
lazariento adj (Arg, Mex, Nic) leprous.
lazarillo nm blind man's guide.
lazarino 1 adj leprous. 2 nm leper.
Lázaro m Lazarus.
lazo nm **(a)** bow, knot; loop; lasso, lariat; **— corredizo** slipknot; **— de zapato** bootlace.
(b) (Hunting) snare, trap (also fig); **caer en el —** to fall into the trap; **tender un — a uno** to set a trap for someone.
(c) (Aut) hairpin bend.
(d) (fig) link, bond, tie; **los —s culturales entre A y B** cultural ties between A and B; **los —s familiares** the family bond, the ties of blood.
le personal pron **(a)** (acc) him; (relating to Vd) you; **no le veo** I don't see him; **¿le ayudo?** shall I help you?
(b) (dative) (to) him, (to) her, (to) it; (relating to Vd) (to) you; **le hablé** I spoke to him, I spoke to her; **quiero darle esto** I want to give you this; **le he comprado esto** I bought this for you; **uno de los mejores papeles que le hayamos visto** one of the best performances we have seen from him; **no se le conoce otra obra** no other work of his is known.
leal loyal, faithful, trustworthy.
lealmente adv loyally, faithfully.
lealtad nf loyalty, fidelity; trustworthiness.
Leandro m Leander.
lebrato nm leveret.
lebrel nm greyhound.
lebrón adj (Mex) **(a)** sharp, wide-awake. **(b)** boastful, insolent. **(c)** sly; evil-minded.
lección nf **(a)** lesson (also Eccl); (School) lesson, class, (Univ) lecture, class; (fig) warning, example; **— particular** private lesson; **— práctica** object lesson (de in); **dar —es** to teach, give lessons; **dar una — a uno** (fig) to teach someone a lesson; **¡que te sirva de —!** let that be a lesson to you!; **tomar —** to have a lesson.
(b) (Lit: of MS etc) reading.
leco adj (Mex) crazy, stupid.
lectivo adj school (attr); see **año, día** etc.
lector nm, **lectora** nf **(a)** reader. **(b)** (School, Univ) conversation assistant.
lectura nf reading; reading matter; **una persona de mucha —** a well-read person; **dar — a** to read (publicly).
lecha nf milt, (soft) roe.
lechada nf **(a)** whitewash; paste; grout; (in paper making) pulp. **(b)** (SAm) milking.

lechal 1 *adj* sucking. **2** *nm* milk (*fig*), milky juice.
lechar [1a] *vt* (**a**) (*SAm*) to milk; (*CAm, Col, Ec*) to give suck to, produce milk for. (**b**) (*CAm, Mex*) to whitewash.
lechazo *nm* young lamb.
leche *nf* (**a**) milk; **— condensada** condensed milk; **— desnatada** skim(med) milk; **— de magnesia** milk of magnesia; **— pasterizada** pasteurized milk; **— en polvo** powdered milk; **estar con** (*or* **tener**) **la — en los labios** (*fig*) to be young and inexperienced, be wet behind the ears (*fig*).
   (**b**) (*Bot*) milk, milky juice; (*Bol*) rubber; (*Ant*) rubber tree.
   (**c**) (*tabu*) semen, spunk (*tabu*); ¡—! hell!; **un tío de mala —** a nasty sort, an evil person; a disagreeable chap; **tener mala —** to be vindictive, be nasty; **hay mucha mala — entre ellos** there's a lot of bad blood between them; **aquí hay mucha mala —** there's a lot of ill-feeling here.
   (**d**) (*SAm*) good luck; **estar con —, estar de —, tener —** to be lucky.
lecheada *nf* (*Arg*) = **lechada.**
lechear [1a] *vt* (*SAm*) to milk.
lechecillas *nfpl* sweetbreads.
lechera *nf* (**a**) milkmaid, dairymaid. (**b**) milk can, milk churn. (**c**) (*SAm*) cow.
lechería *nf* (**a**) dairy, creamery; (*Col, Chi*) milking parlour. (**b**) (*Chi*) cows, herd. (**c**) (*Col, Mex, Ven*) meanness.
lecherita *nf* milk jug.
lechero 1 *adj* (**a**) milk (*attr*); dairy (*attr*); **producción lechera** milk production; *see* **vaca.**
   (**b**) (*SAm*) lucky.
   (**c**) (*Mex, Ven*) mean, stingy.
   (**d**) (*Ant*) greedy, grasping.
   2 *nm* dairyman; milkman.
lechigada *nf* litter, brood; (*fig*) gang.
lecho *nm* (**a**) bed; couch; (*Agr*) bedding; **— mortuorio** deathbed. (**b**) (*of river*) bed; bottom, floor; (*Geol*) layer; **— de roca** bedrock.
lechón *nm* (**a**) piglet, sucking-pig. (**b**) (*fig*) pig, filthy person.
lechona *nf* (**a**) sow. (**b**) (*fig*) pig, sow; slob (*sl*).
lechoncillo *nm* piglet, sucking-pig.
lechoso *adj* (**a**) milky. (**b**) (*CAm, Ven*) lucky.
lechucear [1a] *vi* (*Per*) to be on night duty.
lechucero *nm* (*Ec, Per*) (**a**) night worker; night taxi driver. (**b**) night taxi.
lechudo *adj* (*SAm*) lucky.
lechuga 1 *nf* (**a**) lettuce; **— Cos** cos lettuce. (**b**) (*Sew*) frill, flounce. (**c**) (*Cu, PR*) banknote. **2** *nm* (*fam*) rotter, cad, heel (*sl*).
lechuguilla *nf* (*Sew*) frill, flounce, ruff.
lechuguino *nm* (**a**) young lettuce. (**b**) (*fam*) toff (*fam*), dude (*US*).
lechuza *nf* (**a**) (*Orn*) owl; **— común** barn owl. (**b**) (*Chi, Mex*) albino, light blond(e). (**c**) (*Cu, Mex*) whore.
leer [2e] *vti* to read; **— en la boca** to lip-read; **— entre líneas** to read between the lines; **— la mano a uno** to read someone's palm; **"al que leyere"** "to the reader".
lega *nf* lay sister.
legación *nf* legation.
legado *nm* (**a**) legate. (**b**) (*Law*) legacy, bequest.
legajar *vt* (*Col, Chi, Ec, Mex*) to file.
legajo *nm* file, bundle (of papers).
legal *adj* (**a**) legal, lawful; **time standard.** (**b**) *person* trustworthy, truthful; (*Mex*) upright. (**c**) (*Per*) fine, marvellous.
legalidad *nf* legality, lawfulness.
legalización *nf* legalization; authentication.
legalizar [1f] *vt* to legalize, make lawful; *document* to authenticate.
legalmente *adv* legally, lawfully.
légamo *nm* slime, mud, ooze; clay.
legamoso *adj* slimy, oozy; clayey.
legaña *nf* rheum.
legañoso *adj* bleary.
legar [1h] *vt* to bequeath (*also Law, fig*), leave (*a* to).
legatario *nm*, **legataria** *nf* legatee.
legendario *adj* legendary.
legibilidad *nf* legibility.
legible *adj* legible.
legiblemente *adv* legibly.
legión *nf* legion; **L— Extranjera** Foreign Legion; **son — they are legion; el autor — (***Lit***) the author whose name is legion, the collectivity of anonymous authors (***of ballads etc***).
legionario 1 *adj* legionary. **2** *nm* legionary; legionnaire.
legislación *nf* legislation.

legislador *nm*, **legisladora** *nf* legislator.
legislar [1a] *vi* to legislate.
legislativo *adj* legislative.
legislatura *nf* (*SAm*) legislature, legislative body.
legista 1 *nm* jurist, legist. **2** *adj* (*SAm*): **médico —** forensic expert, criminal pathologist.
legítimamente *adv* legitimately, rightfully; justly; genuinely.
legitimar [1a] **1** *vt* to legitimize; to legalize. **2 legitimarse** *vr* to establish one's identity; to establish one's title (*or* claim *etc*).
legitimidad *nf* legitimacy; justice; authenticity.
legitimista 1 *adj* loyalist. **2** *nmf* loyalist.
legítimo *adj* legitimate, rightful; just; genuine, authentic, real.
lego 1 *adj* (**a**) (*Eccl*) lay; secular. (**b**) (*fig*) ignorant, uninformed. **2** *nm* layman; lay brother; **los —s** the laity.
legón *nm* hoe.
legua *nf* league; **a la — far** away, a mile away; **eso se ve a la —** you can tell it a mile away.
leguaje *nm* (**a**) (*Mex, Nic*) distance in leagues. (**b**) (*Per: Parl*) travelling expenses.
leguario *nm* (*Bol, Chi*) milestone.
leguleyo *nm* pettifogging lawyer.
legumbre *nf* vegetable.
leguminoso *adj* leguminous.
leíble *adj* legible.
Leida, Leide(n) (*n*) Leyden.
leída *nf* (*SAm*) reading; **de una — in** one reading, at one go; **dar una — a** to read.
leído *adj person* well-read.
leísmo *nm* use of **le** instead of **lo** and **la** (*direct objects*).
leísta 1 *adj* that uses **le** instead of **lo** and **la** (*direct objects*). **2** *nmf* user of **le** instead of **lo** and **la.**
lejanía *nf* distance, remoteness; remote place.
lejas *adj pl*: **de — tierras** of (*or* from) some distant land.
lejano *adj* distant, remote, far off.
Lejano Oriente *m* Far East.
lejía *nf* (**a**) bleach; lye. (**b**) (*fam*) dressing-down.
lejos 1 *adv* far, far away, far off; **a lo — in** the distance, far off; **de —, desde — from** afar, from a long way off; **más — further** (off); **está muy — it's** a long way (away); **¿está —?** is it far?; **eso queda demasiado —** that's too far (away); **ir — to** go far (*also fig*); **para no ir más — (***fig***) to take an obvious example.
   2 — de *prep* far from; **estoy muy — de pensar que . . .** I am very far from thinking that . . .
   3 *nm* distant view; appearance from a distance; glimpse; (*Art*) background; **tiene buen — it** looks all right at a distance.
lejura *nf* (*Col, Ec*) distance; **—s** (*Arg*) remote place, remote area.
lele *adj* (*CAm, Chi*), **lelo** *adj* silly, stupid.
lema *nm* motto, device; theme; (*Pol etc*) slogan, watchword.
lempira *nf* standard monetary unit of Honduras.
lempo 1 *adj* (*Col*) big, large. **2** *nm* (**a**) (*Col, Ec*) bit, piece. (**b**) (*Col*) **un — de caballo** a big horse.
lémur *nm* lemur.
lencería *nf* (**a**) linen, drapery; (*woman's*) lingerie. (**b**) draper's (shop). (**c**) linen cupboard.
lencero *nm* draper.
lendroso *adj* lousy.
lengón *adj* (*Col, Mex*) = **lenguón.**
lengua *nf* (**a**) (*Anat or Zool*) tongue; **mala —, — larga** (*SAm*), **— de trapo** (*SAm*) gossip; **de — en — from** mouth to mouth; **andar en —s** to be the talk of the town; **atar la — a uno** (*fig*) to silence someone; **beber con la — to** lap up; **buscar la a uno** to pick a quarrel with someone; **dar a la — to** chatter, talk too much; **estar con la — fuera** (*fig*) to be dead beat, be exhausted; **hacerse —s de** to praise to the skies, rave about; **írsele a uno la — to** talk too much; to let the cat out of the bag; **morderse la — to** hold one's tongue; to keep something back; **no morderse la — not** to mince one's words, not to pull one's punches; **nacer con la — fuera** to be born idle; **sacar la — a uno** (*fig*) to cock a snook at someone (*fam*); **soltar la — (***fam***) to spill the beans (*sl*); **tirar de la — a uno** to draw someone out, make someone talk; to provoke someone; **se le trabó la — he** began to stammer.
   (**b**) (*of bell*) clapper.
   (**c**) (*Geog*) **— de tierra** spit of land, tongue of land.
   (**d**) (*Ling*) language, tongue; **— franca** lingua franca; **— madre** parent language; **— materna** mother tongue; **— moderna** modern language; **— muerta** dead language; **— viva** living language; **hablar en — (***Per***) to speak Quichua.

lenguado *nm* (*Fish*) sole.

lenguaje *nm* (**a**) (*in general*) language; (faculty of) speech.

  (**b**) idiom, parlance, (mode of) speech; — **comercial** business language; — **periodístico** newspaper language, journalese; — **vulgar** common speech, ordinary speech; **en** — **llano** in plain English (*etc*).

  (**c**) (*Lit*) style, diction.

lenguaraz *adj* talkative; (*pej*) foul-mouthed.

lenguaz *adj* garrulous.

lengüeta *nf* (**a**) tab, small tongue; (*Carp, Mus, of shoe*) tongue; (*Anat*) epiglottis; (*of balance etc*) needle, pointer; (*of arrow*) barb.

  (**b**) (*SAm*) chatterbox; gossip.

  (**c**) (*SAm*) paper cutter.

  (**d**) (*SAm*) fringe of a petticoat.

lengüetada *nf* lick.

lengüetazo *nm* (*SAm*) lick; rapid movement of the tongue.

lengüetear [1a] **1** *vt* (*SAm*) to lick (with the tip of the tongue). **2** *vi* (*SAm*) to stick one's tongue out; (*Ant*) to jabber, chatter.

lengüeterías *nfpl* (*SAm*) gossip, tales.

lengüetero *adj* (*Ant*) garrulous; gossiping.

lengüicorto *adj* (*fam*) shy, timid.

lengüilargo *adj*, **lengüisucio** *adj* (*Mex, PR*) foul-mouthed.

lengüón (*SAm*) **1** *adj* garrulous; outspoken; gossiping. **2** *nm* gossip, talebearer.

lenidad *nf* lenience.

Leningrado Leningrad.

lenitivo 1 *adj* lenitive. **2** *nm* lenitive.

lenocinio *nm* pandering, procuring; (**casa de**) — brothel.

lentamente *adv* slowly.

lente *nm or f* lens; eyeglass; —s (*Hist*) spectacles; — **de aumento** magnifying glass; —s **de contacto** contact lenses.

lenteja *nf* lentil.

lentejuela *nf* spangle, sequin.

lentitud *nf* slowness; **con** — slowly.

lento *adj* slow.

leña *nf* (**a**) firewood; sticks, kindling; — **de oveja** (*RPl*) sheep droppings; **echar** — **al fuego** to add fuel to the flames; **llevar** — **al monte** to carry coals to Newcastle.

  (**b**) (*fam*) thrashing; **cargar de** —, **dar** — **a**, **hartar de** — to lay it on, thrash.

leñador *nm* woodcutter, woodman.

leñar [1a] *vt* (*Arg, Mex*), **leñatear** [1a] *vt* (*Col*) to make into firewood, cut up for firewood.

leñateo *nm* (*CAm, Col*) woodpile.

leñatero *nm* (*RPl*) woodcutter, woodman.

leñazo *nm* blow with a stick.

leñe *nm* (*euph*) = **leche**.

leñera *nf* woodshed.

leñero *nm* (**a**) dealer in wood. (**b**) woodshed.

leño *nm* (**a**) log; timber, wood, piece of wood. (**b**) (*fam*) blockhead.

leñoso *adj* woody.

León *m* Leon; — (**de Francia**) Lyons.

león *nm* lion (*also fig*); (*SAm*) puma; — **marino** sea lion; **estar hecho un** — to be furious; **ponerse como un** — to get furious.

leona *nf* (**a**) lioness. (**b**) (*Chi*) confusion, mess, mix-up.

leonado *adj* tawny.

leonera *nf* (**a**) lion's cage; lion's den; **parece una** — it's shockingly dirty.

  (**b**) (*fam*) gambling den, dive (*fam*); lumber room, attic; (*Mex*) bawdy house; (*Arg, Ec, PR*) communal prison cell; (*Per*) noisy gathering; (*Col, Chi*) underworld gathering.

leonés 1 *adj* Leonese. **2** *nm*, **leonesa** *nf* Leonese. **3** *nm* (*dialect*) Leonese.

leonino *adj* leonine.

Leonor *f* Eleanor.

leontina *nf* watch chain.

leopardo *nm* leopard; — **cazador** cheetah.

leopoldina *nf* fob, short watch chain.

Lepe: ir donde las — (*Chi*) to make a bloomer (*in calculating*) (*fam*); **saber más que** — to be pretty smart, have lots of savoir-faire.

leperada *nf* (*CAm, Mex*) coarse remark; dirty trick, rotten thing to do) (*fam*).

lépero *nm*, **lépera** *nf* (*CAm, Mex*) low-class person, plebeian; (*pej*) rotter, heel (*sl*), villain; (*Cu*) clever person, quick-witted person.

leperusco *adj* (*Mex*) low-class, plebeian; (*pej*) rotten (*fam*), villainous.

lepidópteros *nmpl* lepidoptera, butterflies and moths.

lepisma *nf* silverfish.

leporino *adj* leporine; hare-like; **labio** — harelip.

lepra *nf* leprosy.

leprosería *nf* leper colony.

leproso 1 *adj* leprous. **2** *nm*, **leprosa** *nf* leper.

lerdear [1a] *vi* (*Arg, CAm*) to be slow (about doing things), do things unwillingly.

lerdera *nf* (*CAm*) = **lerdez**.

lerdez *nf*, **lerdeza** *nf* (*CAm*) slowness; heaviness, dullness; slow-wittedness; clumsiness.

lerdo *adj* slow; heavy, dull; slow-witted; clumsy.

lerdura *nf* (*RPl*) = **lerdez**.

leridense 1 *adj* of Lérida. **2** *nmf* native (*or* inhabitant) of Lérida; **los** —s the people of Lérida.

les *personal pron* (**a**) (*acc*) them; (*relating to* **Vds**) you.

  (**b**) (*dative*) (to) them; (*relating to* **Vds**) (to) you; *for usage examples, see* **le**.

lesa majestad *nf* lese-majesty.

lesbiana *nf* lesbian.

lesbianismo *nm* lesbianism.

lésbico *adj* lesbian.

lesbio *adj* lesbian.

lesera *nf* (*Chi, Per*) stupidity.

lesión *nf* wound, lesion; injury (*also fig*).

lesionado *adj* hurt, injured; *player* injured, unfit.

lesionar [1a] **1** *vt* to hurt, injure; to wound. **2 lesionarse** *vr* to get hurt.

lesivo *adj* harmful, damaging.

lesna *nf* awl.

leso *adj* (**a**) hurt; injured, offended.

  (**b**) (*Bol, Chi, Per*) simple, stupid; **no está para** — (*Chi*) he's not easily taken in; **hacer** — **a uno** (*Chi*) to play a trick on someone.

lesura *nf* (*Chi*) stupidity.

letal *adj* deadly, lethal.

letanía *nf* (*Eccl*) litany; (*fig*) rigmarole; long list; tedious recitation.

letárgico *adj* lethargic.

letargo *nm* lethargy.

Lete(o) *m* Lethe.

letón 1 *adj* Latvian. **2** *nm*, **letona** *nf* Latvian. **3** *nm* (*language*) Latvian, Lettish.

letra *nf* (**a**) (*of alphabet*) letter; — **gótica** Gothic script, black letter; — **de imprenta** print; — **inicial** initial letter; — **mayúscula** capital letter; — **minúscula** small letter; **en** —**s de molde** in print; in block letters; — **muerta** dead letter; — **negrilla** bold type, heavy type; — **versal** capital letter; — **versalita** small capital.

  (**b**) (*fig*) letter, literal meaning; **a la** — to the letter; **atarse a la** — to stick to the literal meaning.

  (**c**) —s piece of writing; **poner unas** (*or* **dos**) —s **a uno** to drop someone a line.

  (**d**) writing, handwriting; — **cursiva** cursive writing; **tiene buena** — he writes a good hand; **tiene malísima** — his writing is shocking.

  (**e**) (*Comm*) letter, bill, draft; — **abierta** letter of credit; — **aceptada** accepted letter; — **de cambio** bill (of exchange), draft; — **a la vista** sight draft; **pagar a** — **vista** to pay on sight.

  (**f**) (*Mus*) words, lyric.

  (**g**) —s (*fig*) letters, learning; (*Univ*) Arts; **bellas** —s belles lettres, literature; —s **humanas** humanities; **primeras** —s elementary education, three Rs; —s **sagradas** Scripture.

letrado 1 *adj* learned; (*pej*) pedantic. **2** *nm* laywer.

letrero *nm* sign, notice; placard, poster; label; inscription; words, (piece of) writing.

letrina *nf* latrine, privy; (*fig*) sewer, sump, filthy place; **el río es una** — the river is an open sewer.

letrista *nmf* songwriter.

leucemia *nf* leukaemia.

leudante *adj*: **harina** — self-raising flour.

leudar [1a] **1** *vt* to leaven. **2 leudarse** *vr* (*of bread etc*) to rise.

leva *nf* (**a**) (*Naut*) weighing anchor.

  (**b**) (*Mil*) levy.

  (**c**) (*Mech*) lever; cam.

  (**d**) (*CAm, Col*) trick, swindle, ruse; **bajar la** — **a uno** (*Bol, Chi*) to do someone a mischief; **caer de** — (*CAm*) to play the fool; **echar** —s (*Col*) to boast; to bluster, utter threats; (*Mex*) to tell lies; **encender la** — **a uno** (*Cu*) to bash someone (*fam*); **ponerse la** — (*Col*) to play truant; to stay away from work; to beat it (*fam*).

levada *nf* (*of horse*) prance.

levadizo *adj* that can be raised; **puente** — drawbridge.

levadura *nf* yeast, leaven; — **de cerveza** brewer's yeast; — **en polvo** baking powder.

levantador *nm*: — **de pesos** weight lifter.

levantamiento *nm* (**a**) raising, lifting; elevation; — **de pesos** weight lifting. (**b**) (*Pol*) rising, revolt.

levantar [1a] **1** *vt* (**a**) to raise, lift (up); to elevate; *fallen object* to raise up, stand up; to straighten; *dropped object* to pick up; *weight* (*Sport*) to lift; (*Archit*) to raise, build, erect; *bump etc* (*Med*) to raise; *army* to raise, recruit; *census* to take; *dust* to raise; *game* to flush, put up; *house* to move, remove; *plan, survey* to make, draw up; *session* to adjourn; *siege* to raise; *tone, voice* to raise; **levantó la mano** he raised his hand, he put up his hand; **— los ojos** to look up, raise one's eyes; **¡no levantes la voz!** keep your voice down!; **fue imposible —lo** it was impossible to lift it.

(**b**) (*fam*) to lift (*fam*), steal.

(**c**) *table, tablecloth* to clear away; *camp* to strike; *tent* to take down.

(**d**) *ban* to raise, lift.

(**e**) *person* (*fig*) to uplift, hearten, cheer up; *spirits* to raise; (*Pol*) to rouse, stir up.

2 levantarse *vr* (**a**) to rise; to get up, stand up, rise to one's feet; to straighten up; **— (de la cama)** to get up, get out of bed.

(**b**) (*of fog*) to lift; (*of wind etc*) to rise.

(**c**) (*on horizon etc*) to stand up, stick up, stand out; **se levanta por encima de los demás edificios** it stands up higher than the other buildings.

(**d**) (*of session*) to be adjourned; to conclude, be concluded.

(**e**) **— con algo** to make off with something.

(**f**) (*Pol*) to rise, revolt, rebel.

levantaválvulas *nm, pl* **levantaválvulas** valve tappet.

Levante *nm* (**a**) Levant; **el —** the Levant, the (Near) East. (**b**) (*Spain*) east coast, south-east coast.

levante[1] *nm* (*Geog*) (**a**) east. (**b**) east wind.

levante[2] *nm* (**a**) (*PR*) uprising; riot.

(**b**) (*Ven*) driving of cattle.

(**c**) (*CAm, PR*) slander; **armar un —** to invent a slander.

(**d**) (*Col*) arrogance, haughtiness.

(**e**) (*Arg*) **dar** (*or* **pegar**) **un — a uno** to give someone a dressing-down.

levantino 1 *adj* (**a**) Levantine.

(**b**) of the eastern coast (*or* provinces *etc*) of Spain.

2 *nm*, **levantina** *nf* (**a**) Levantine.

(**b**) native (*or* inhabitant) of the eastern provinces of Spain; **los —s** the people of the east of Spain.

levantisco *adj* restless, turbulent.

levar [1a] **1** *vt*: **— anclas** to weigh anchor. **2 levarse** *vr* to weigh anchor, set sail.

leve *adj* light; slight; trivial, small, unimportant; **una herida —** a slight wound; **sin el más — optimismo** without the slightest optimism.

levedad *nf* lightness; (*fig*) levity.

levemente *adv* lightly; slightly.

leviatán *nm* leviathan.

levita[1] *nf* frock coat.

levita[2] *nm* Levite.

léxico 1 *adj* lexical. **2** *nm* lexicon, dictionary; vocabulary; word list.

lexicografía *nf* lexicography.

lexicográfico *adj* lexicographical.

lexicógrafo *nm* lexicographer.

ley *nf* (**a**) law; (*Parl*) act, bill, measure; (*Sport etc*) rule, law; **— de la calle, — de Lynch** mob law, lynch law; **la — del embudo** "might is right"; **— no escrita** unwritten law; **— marcial** martial law; **— de Moisés** the Law (*Jewish*); **— natural** law of nature; **— de préstamos y arriendos** Lend-Lease Act; **a — de** on the word of; **de acuerdo con la —, según la —** in accordance with the law; by law, in law; **es la —** it's the law; **su palabra es —** his word is law; **está fuera de la —** he's outside the law; **un fuera de —** an outlaw; **está por encima de la —** he's above the law; **recurrir a la —** to go to law.

(**b**) (*fig*) loyalty, devotion; **tener — a** to be devoted to; to have great respect for.

(**c**) (*Metal*) legal standard of fineness; **oro de — standard** gold; **bajo de —** base; **de buena —** (*fig*) genuine, reliable; **de mala —** (*fig*) base, disreputable; **en buena —** really; **entonces me toca esperar en buena —** then I really do have to wait.

leyenda *nf* (**a**) legend; **la — negra** the black legend. (**b**) (*Typ*) legend, inscription; key.

leyente *nmf* reader.

leyista *nm* (*Cu*) pettifogging lawyer.

leyoso *adj* (*Col*) cunning, sly; sophistical.

lezna *nf* awl.

lía *nf* (*SAm*) plaited esparto grass.

liana *nf* (*SAm*) liana.

liar [1c] **1** *vt* to tie, tie up; to do up; to bind; to wrap

up; *cigarette* to roll; (*fig*) to embroil, confuse; **—las** (*fam*) to beat it (*fam*); to kick the bucket (*sl*).

2 liarse *vr* (**a**) to get tied up; to entwine.

(**b**) (*fig*) to get involved (*con* with), get embroiled (*con* in); to get involved in a love affair (*con* with), form a liaison (*con* with).

(**c**) **— a + infin** (*fam*) to start to + *infin*.

libación *nf* libation; **—s** libations, potations.

libanés 1 *adj* Lebanese. **2** *nm*, **libanesa** *nf* Lebanese.

Líbano: el — the Lebanon.

libar [1a] *vt* to suck; to sip; to taste.

libelista *nm* lampoonist, writer of lampoons.

libelo *nm* (**a**) lampoon, satire (*contra* of). (**b**) (*Law*) petition.

libélula *nf* dragonfly.

liberación *nf* liberation; release.

liberado *adj* (*Comm, Fin*) paid-up, paid-in (*US*).

liberal 1 *adj* (**a**) (*Pol*) liberal. (**b**) *character* liberal, generous; lavish. **2** *nmf* liberal.

liberalidad *nf* liberality, generosity, lavishness.

liberalismo *nm* liberalism.

liberalizar [1f] *vt* to liberalize.

liberalmente *adv* liberally, generously; lavishly.

liberar [1a] *vt* (**a**) to free, liberate.

(**b**) (*SAm*) **— a uno de una obligación** to release someone from a duty; **— a uno de una contribución** to exempt someone from a tax.

Liberia *f* Liberia.

libertad *nf* liberty, freedom; licence; (undue) familiarity; **"¡—!"** (*slogan*) "freedom!"; **— de comercio** free trade; **— condicional, — vigilada** (*Law*) probation; **estar en — condicional** (*or* **vigilada**) to be on probation; **— de cultos** freedom of worship, religious freedom; **— de imprenta** freedom of the press; **— de (la) palabra** freedom of speech; **estar en —** to be free, be at liberty; **poner a uno en —** to set someone free, release someone, set someone at liberty; **tomarse una —** to take a liberty; **tomarse la — de + infin** to take the liberty of + *ger*, presume to + *infin*.

libertador 1 *adj* liberating. **2** *nm*, **libertadora** *nf* liberator.

libertar [1a] *vt* to set free, liberate, release (*de* from); to exempt, release (*de* from); to save, deliver (*de* from); **— a uno de la muerte** to save someone from death.

libertinaje *nm* licentiousness; profligacy.

libertino 1 *adj* (**a**) loose-living, rakish, profligate.

(**b**) (*Rel Hist*) freethinking. **2** *nm* (**a**) libertine, rake.

(**b**) (*Rel Hist*) freethinker.

Libia *f* Libya.

libídine *nf* libido.

libidinoso *adj* lustful, libidinous.

libido *nf* libido.

libio 1 *adj* Libyan. **2** *nm*, **libia** *nf* Libyan.

liborio *nm* (*Cu*): **el —** the Cuban people.

libra *nf* pound; **— esterlina** pound sterling.

libraco *nm* boring book, worthless book.

librado *nm*, **librada** *nf* (*Comm*) drawee.

librador *nm*, **libradora** *nf* (*Comm*) drawer.

libramiento *nm* rescue, delivery (*de* from).

librante *nmf* (*Comm*) drawer.

libranza *nf* (*Comm*) draft, bill of exchange; **— de correos** (*SAm*), **— postal** (*SAm*) money order.

librar [1a] **1** *vt* (**a**) to save, free, rescue, deliver (*de* from); (*Law*) to exempt, free, release (*de* from); **— a uno de una obligación** to free someone from an obligation; **¡Dios me libre!** Heaven forbid!; **¡líbreme Dios de . . .!** Heaven forbid that I . . .!

(**b**) *confidence, hope* to place (*en* in).

(**c**) *sentence* to pass; *edict etc* to issue.

(**d**) (*Comm*) to draw; *cheque* to make out; **— a cargo de** to draw on.

(**e**) *battle* to fight, wage; to join.

2 *vi* (**a**) to be delivered of a child.

(**b**) **— bien** to fare well, succeed; **— mal** to fare badly, fail.

3 librarse *vr* to free oneself, escape; **— de** to escape from, get out of, get away from; to get rid of; **de buena nos hemos librado** we did well to get out of that, we're well out of that.

libre *adj* (**a**) (*in most senses*) free (*de* from, of); **¿estás —?** are you free?; **esa plaza no está —** that seat is not free; **cada cual es — de hacer lo que quiera** everyone is free to do as he wishes; **por fin estamos —s de él** at last we're rid of him; **— de derechos** free of duty, duty-free; **al aire —** in the open air.

(**b**) (*pej*) free, outspoken; licentious, loose, immoral; **de vida —** loose-living, immoral.

(**c**) (*Sport*) free, free-style; **los 200 metros —s** the 200 metre free-style race.

2 *nm* (**a**) (*Sport*) free kick.

(**b**) (*Mex*) taxi.

librea 1 *nf* livery, uniform. **2** *nm* (*Chi*) footman.
librecambio *nm* free trade.
librecambista 1 *adj* free-trade (*attr*). **2** *nm* free-trader.
librepensador *nm*, **librepensadora** *nf* freethinker.
librepensamiento *nm* freethinking.
librera *nf* (*RPl*) bookcase.
librería *nf* (a) bookshop; — **anticuaria** antiquarian bookshop; — **de ocasión**, — **de viejo** secondhand bookshop.
(b) bookcase; (personal, private) library.
(c) bookselling, book trade, book business.
librero *nm* (a) bookseller; — **de viejo** secondhand bookseller. (b) (*Cu, Mex, Par*) bookcase.
libresco *adj* bookish.
libreta *nf* (a) notebook; (*Comm*) account book; — **de banco**, — **de depósitos** bank book, pass book.
(b) one-pound loaf.
librete *nm* booklet.
libretista *nmf* librettist.
libreto *nm* libretto.
libro *nm* book; — **de actas** minute book; — **de apuntes** notebook; — **de cabecera** bedside book; — **de caja** cashbook; — **de cálculos hechos** ready reckoner; — **de cocina** cookery book, cookbook (*US*); — **de consulta** reference book, work of reference; — **de cuentas** account book; — **de cuentos** storybook; — **de cheques** cheque book; — **diario** journal; — **de encargos** order book; — **escolar** school report; — **genealógico** (*Agr*) herd-book; — **de hojas cambiables** loose-leaf book; — **de honor** visitors' book; — **de imágenes** picture book; — **de lectura** reader; — **mayor** ledger; — **parroquial** parish register; — **de pedidos** order book; — **de reclamaciones** complaints book; **L— Rojo** (*Pol*) White Paper; — **en rústica** paperback (book); — **talonario** receipt book; book of tickets, book of counterfoils; — **de texto** textbook; — **de visitas** visitors' book; — **de vuelos** (*Aer*) logbook; **ahorcar los —s, arrimar los —s** (*fig*) to lay aside one's books, give up studying; **no estar en el —** (*Arg*), **no tener el —** (*Arg*) to be unaware of a matter; to be uninterested in a matter, have no intention of pursuing a matter; **hacer — nuevo** to turn over a new leaf.
librote *nm* big book, tome.
licencia *nf* (a) (*general sense*) licence, permission; **sin mi —** without my permission; **dar su —** to give one's permission, grant permission.
(b) (*document*) licence, permit; — **de armas** gun licence; — **de caza** game licence, hunting permit; — **de conducir**, — **de conductor**, — **de manejar** (*SAm*) driving licence; — **de matrimonio** marriage licence.
(c) (*Mil etc*) leave; — **por enfermedad** sick leave; — **sin sueldo** leave without pay, unpaid leave; **estar de —** to be on leave; **ir de —** to go on leave.
(d) (*Mil*) discharge (*also* — **absoluta**); — **honrosa** honourable discharge.
(e) (*moral*) licence, licentiousness; — **poética** poetic licence.
(f) (*Univ: Hist*) degree.
licenciado *nm*, **licenciada** *nf* (a) (*Univ*) licenciate, bachelor; **L— en Filosofía y Letras** Bachelor of Arts.
(b) (*SAm*) lawyer (*not translated as title before proper name*).
licenciar [1b] **1** *vt* (a) to license, grant a permit (*or* licence) to.
(b) to permit, allow.
(c) (*Mil*) to discharge.
(d) (*Univ*) to confer a degree on.
2 licenciarse *vr* to graduate, take one's degree.
licenciatura *nf* (a) degree, licentiate. (b) graduation.
(c) degree course, university degree.
licencioso *adj* licentious.
liceo *nm* lyceum; (*Chi, Mex*) secondary school; (*Arg*) secondary school for girls.
licitación *nf* bidding (*at auction*).
licitador *nm* bidder; (*SAm*) auctioneer.
licitar [1a] **1** *vt* (a) to bid for. (b) (*SAm*) to sell by auction. **2** *vi* to bid.
lícito *adj* lawful, legal, licit; fair, just; permissible; **si es —** **preguntarlo** if one may ask.
licitud *nf* legality; fairness, justness; **la controversia sobre la — del aborto** the controversy about whether abortion should be permitted.
licor *nm* (a) (*in general*) liquid. (b) (alcoholic) liquor, spirits; liqueur; —**es espiritosos** hard liquor.
licorería *nf* (*SAm*) distillery.
licorero *nm* (*SAm*) distiller.
licorista *nmf* distiller; dealer in liquor, seller of liquor.

licoroso *adj* wine etc strong, of high alchoholic content.
licuar [1d] *vt* to liquefy, turn into liquid.
licuefacción *nf* liquefaction.
líchigo *nm* (*Col*) provisions, food.
lid *nf* fight, combat; dispute, controversy; **en buena —** in (a) fair fight, (*fig*) by fair means, fairly.
líder *nm*, *pl* **líderes** *or* **lideres** (*angl*) leader; (*Sport*) leader, league leader, top club (*etc*).
liderato *nm* leadership; (*Sport*) lead, leadership, top position.
lidia *nf* (a) (*Taur*) bullfight; bullfighting; **toro de —** fighting bull. (b) (*Mex, RPl*) trouble, nuisance; **dar —** to be trying, be a nuisance.
lidiadera *nf* (*Ec, Guat*) quarrel; **andar en —s** to quarrel, bicker.
lidiador *nm* fighter; (*Taur*) bullfighter.
lidiar [1b] **1** *vt* bull to fight. **2** *vi* to fight (*also fig*; **con**, **contra** against, **por** for).
liebre *nf* hare; (*fig*) coward; — **corrida** (*Mex*) old hand, experienced person; whore; **levantar la —** to blow the gaff.
Lieja Liège.
liencillo *nm* (*SAm*) thin cotton material.
liendre *nf* nit.
lienzo *nm* (a) linen; (*Art*) canvas; handkerchief; **un —** a piece of linen (*etc*).
(b) (*Archit*) wall; face, front; (*SAm*) section (*of fence etc*); (*Mex*) corral, pen.
liga *nf* (a) (*Pol etc*) league.
(b) (*Sew*) band; suspender, garter.
(c) (*Metal*) alloy; mixture.
(d) (*Bot*) mistletoe.
(e) birdlime.
(f) (*Cu, Guat, Hond, Mex*) binding; state of being bound.
(g) (*RPl*) piece of luck.
(h) (*Col*) theft.
(i) (*Ec*) bosom friend.
ligado *nm* (*Mus*) slur, tie; (*Typ*) ligature.
ligadura *nf* bond, tie; (*Naut*) lashing; (*Med, Mus*) ligature.
ligamento *nm* ligament.
ligamiento *nm* bond, tie.
ligar [1h] **1** *vt* (a) to tie, bind; (*Metal*) to alloy; to mix; (*Med*) to put a ligature on, bind up; (*Mus*) to slur; (*fig*) to join, bind together; — **dos bebidas** to mix two drinks, blend two drinks; **estar ligado por contrato a** to be bound by contract to.
(b) (*Col*) to pinch (*fam*).
(c) (*Cu: Agr*) to contract in advance for.
2 *vi* (a) to mix (well), blend, go well together; **ligan A y B** (*Arg, Per*) A and B get on well together.
(b) (*Cu, Mex, PR*) to have a bit of luck, be lucky; **la cosa le ligó** (*CAm, Col*) the affair went well for him.
(c) (*Cu, Mex, PR*) to look, stare.
(d) (*Guat, Per, PR, SD*: *of wish*) to be fulfilled.
(e) (*prov, Mex*) — **con una** to flirt with someone; to pick a girl up.
3 ligarse *vr* (a) to unite, band together.
(b) to bind oneself, commit oneself.
ligazón *nf* (a) (*Naut*) rib, beam. (b) (*fig*) bond, tie, union.
ligeramente *adv* (a) lightly. (b) know etc slightly. (c) judge etc hastily.
ligerear [1a] *vi* (*Chi*) to walk fast, move quickly.
ligereza *nf* (a) lightness; thinness.
(b) swiftness, quickness, speed.
(c) agility, nimbleness.
(d) slightness.
(e) superficiality, shallowness; flippancy; frivolity; **obrar con —** to act rashly, act thoughtlessly.
(f) — **de espíritu** light-heartedness, gaiety.
(g) (*act*) indiscretion.
ligero 1 *adj* (a) (*of weight*) light; material light, light-weight, thin; meal, sleep light; tea weak; — **de ropa** lightly clad, scantily clad, not wearing much; **más — que un corcho** (*or* **una pluma** etc) as light as a feather.
(b) (*of speed*) swift, quick, rapid; — **de dedos** light-fingered; — **de pies** light-footed, quick; **corrió — por el puente** she ran quickly over the bridge; **más — que una bala** (*or* **el viento** etc) as quick as a flash.
(c) (*in movement*) agile, quick, nimble.
(d) (*of gravity, importance*) slight; **un — conocimiento** a slight acquaintance, a superficial acquaintance.
(e) (*of character*) superficial, shallow, flippant; frivolous, flighty; — **de cascos** scatterbrained, frivolous; **hacer algo a la ligera** to do something

quickly; to do something without fuss; (*pej*) to do something perfunctorily; **juzgar a la ligera** to judge hastily, jump to conclusions; **obrar de —** to act rashly, act thoughtlessly.
2 *adv* (*SAm*) lightly; quickly, swiftly.
lignito *nm* lignite.
ligón *nm* hoe.
liguero *nm* suspender belt, garter belt (*US*).
ligustro *nm* privet.
lija *nf* (**a**) (*Zool*) dogfish. (**b**) (*Tech: also* **papel de —**) sandpaper; **— esmeril** emery paper. (**c**) **darse —** (*Cu*) to give oneself airs.
lijar [1a] *vt* to sandpaper.
lijoso *adj* (*Cu*) vain, stuck-up (*fam*).
Lila Lille.
lila[1] *nf* (*Bot*) lilac.
lila[2] *nm* (*fam*) boob (*sl*), twit (*fam*).
lilailas *nfpl* (*fam*) tricks.
lilaya *nm* (*fam*) sissy.
lile *adj* (*Chi*) weak, weak-willed.
liliputiense 1 *adj* Lilliputian. **2** *nmf* Lilliputian.
liliquear [1a] *vi* (*Chi*) to tremble nervously, shake.
lima[1] *nf* (*Bot*) lime, sweet-lime tree.
lima[2] *nf* (*Tech*) (**a**) file; **— de uñas, — para las uñas** nail file.
  (**b**) (*act*) filing, polishing.
  (**c**) (*fig*) polish, finish; **dar la última — a una obra** to give a work its final polish.
limadura *nf* (**a**) (*act*) filing; polishing. (**b**) **—s** filings.
limar [1a] *vt* (*Tech*) to file, file down, file off; to smooth (over); (*fig*) to polish (up), put the final polish on.
limatón *nm* (*SAm*) crossbeam, roofbeam.
limaza *nf* slug.
limazo *nm* slime, sliminess.
limbo *nm* limbo; **estar en el —** to be in limbo; (*fig*) to be distracted, be bewildered.
limeño 1 *adj* of Lima. **2** *nm*, **limeña** *nf* native (*or* inhabitant) of Lima; **los —s** the people of Lima.
limero *nm* lime (tree).
limeta *nf* (**a**) (*Arg*) broad brow, domed forehead; bald head. (**b**) (*Par*) bottle.
limitación *nf* limitation; limit; **— de velocidad** speed limit; **sin —** unlimited.
limitado *adj* (**a**) limited (*also Comm*). (**b**) slow-witted, dim.
limitar [1a] **1** *vt* to limit, restrict; to cut down, reduce; **— a uno a + infin** to limit someone to + *ger*, restrict someone to + *infin*.
  2 *vi*: **— con** to border on, be adjacent to, be bounded by.
  3 limitarse *vr* to limit oneself, restrict oneself; **— a + infin** to limit oneself to + *infin*, confine oneself to + *infin*.
límite *nm* limit; end; (*Geog, Pol*) boundary, border; **— forestal** timber line, tree line; **— de velocidad** speed limit; **asciende a 100 como —** it goes up to 100 at the most; **se celebrará en octubre como —** it will be held in October at the latest; **sin —** limitless; **poner un — a** to set a limit to; (*fig*) to draw the line at; **no tener —s** to have no limits, know no bounds.
limítrofe *adj* bordering, neighbouring.
limo *nm* slime, mud.
limón *nm* lemon; **— mejicano** lime.
limonada *nf* lemonade; **— natural** lemon juice, lemon squash.
limonado *adj* lemon, lemon-coloured.
limonar *nm* lemon grove.
limonero *nm* lemon tree.
limosina *nf* limousine.
limosna *nf* alms; charity; **¡una —, señor!** can't you spare something, sir?; **vivir de —** to live by begging, live on charity.
limosnear [1a] *vi* to beg, ask for alms.
limosnera *nf* collecting tin (*for charity*).
limosnero 1 *adj* charitable. **2** *nm* (**a**) (*Hist*) almoner. (**b**) (*SAm*) beggar.
limoso *adj* slimy, muddy.
limpia 1 *nf* (**a**) cleaning; (*CAm, Mex: Agr*) weeding, cleaning, clearing; (*fig: Pol etc*) clean-up, purge. (**b**) (*Col, Mex, Par*) beating.
  2 *nm* (*fam*) bootblack.
limpiabarros *nm, pl* **limpiabarros** scraper; door-mat.
limpiabotas *nm, pl* **limpiabotas** bootblack.
limpiacristales *nm, pl* **limpiacristales** window cleaner.
limpiachimeneas *nm, pl* **limpiachimeneas** chimney-sweep.
limpiada *nf* (**a**) (*SAm*) clean, clean-up. (**b**) (*Arg, Par*) treeless area, bare ground; clearing in a wood.

limpiadientes *nm, pl* **limpiadientes** toothpick.
limpiadora *nf* cleaner.
limpiadura *nf* (**a**) cleaning, cleaning-up. (**b**) **—s** dirt, dust, scourings.
limpiamanos *nm, pl* **limpiamanos** (*CAm, Mex*) hand towel.
limpiamente *adv* cleanly; neatly; honestly; skilfully.
limpiametales *nm, pl* **limpiametales** metal polish.
limpiaparabrisas *nm, pl* **limpiaparabrisas** windscreen wiper, windshield wiper (*US*).
limpiapiés *nm, pl* **limpiapiés** scraper; (*Mex*) door-mat.
limpiaplumas *nm, pl* **limpiaplumas** penwiper.
limpiar [1b] **1** *vt* (**a**) to clean; to cleanse; to wipe, wipe off, wipe clean; to wipe away; *shoes* to shine, polish; **— en seco** to dry-clean; **— las narices a un niño** to wipe a child's nose.
  (**b**) (*fig*) to cleanse, purify, clean up; (*Mil etc*) to mop up; (*of police*) to clean up; (*Bot*) to prune, cut back.
  (**c**) (*fam: at gambling*) to clean out (*sl*).
  (**d**) (*sl*) to swipe (*sl*).
  (**e**) (*Arg, Mex*) to hit, bash (*fam*), beat.
  2 limpiarse *vr* to clean oneself; to wipe oneself; **— las narices** to wipe one's nose.
limpiavía *nm* (*SAm: Rail*) cowcatcher.
límpido *adj* limpid.
limpieza *nf* (**a**) (*act*) clean; cleaning, cleansing; shine, shining, polishing; **— en seco** dry cleaning; **— de primavera** spring cleaning; **hacer la —** to clean (up).
  (**b**) (*act: fig*) cleansing, cleaning-up; (*Mil*) mopping-up; (*by police*) clean-up.
  (**c**) (*state*) cleanness, cleanliness; **— de sangre** purity of blood, racial purity.
  (**d**) (*moral quality*) purity; integrity, honesty; (*Sport etc*) fair play.
  (**e**) skill.
limpio 1 *adj* (**a**) clean; neat, tidy; *blood* pure; *water etc* pure, clean; **— de** free from, clear of; **más — que el oro** (*etc*) as clean as can be.
  (**b**) (*morally*) pure; honest; *play* fair, clean.
  (**c**) (*Fin*) clear, net; **50 dólares de ganancia limpia** 50 dollars of clear profit.
  (**d**) alone; **se defendieron a pedrada limpia** they defended themselves with stones alone; **lo hizo a clavo —** he simply nailed it together, he did it just using nails; **luchar a puñetazo —** to fight with bare fists.
  (**e**) **estar —** (*fam*) not to know a single thing; **quedar(se) —** (*fam*) to be cleaned out (*sl*).
  2 *adv* play fair, clean.
  3 *nm* (**a**) **en —** (*as adv*) clearly; (*Fin*) clear, net; **copia en —** fair copy; **estar** (*or* **quedar**) **en —,** **estar — y soplado** (*Col*) to be broke (*fam*); **poner algo en —** to make a fair copy of something; **quedó en — que . . .** it was clear that . . .; **sacar algo en —** to make sense of something; **no pude sacar nada en —** I couldn't make anything of it.
  (**b**) (*Mex*) treeless area, bare ground; clearing in a wood.
limpión *nm* (**a**) wipe, (quick) clean; **dar un — a algo** to give something a wipe.
  (**b**) cleaning rag, cleaning cloth; (*Col, CR, Ven*) dishcloth.
  (**c**) cleaner.
  (**d**) (*Col*) ticking-off.
limusina *nf* limousine.
lina *nf* (*Chi*) (**a**) coarse wool. (**b**) pigtail, long hair.
linaje *nm* (**a**) lineage, family; **de — de reyes** descended from royalty, of royal descent; **de — honrado** of decent family, of good parentage.
  (**b**) **—s** (local) nobility, noble families.
  (**c**) class, kind; **— humano** mankind; **de otro —** of another kind.
linajudo *adj* highborn, noble, blue-blooded.
linar *nm* flax field.
linaza *nf* linseed.
lince 1 *nm* (**a**) lynx; (*Mex, Salv*) wild cat.
  (**b**) **ser un —** (*fig*) to be very observant, be sharp-eyed; to be shrewd, be crafty.
  2 *adj*: **ojos —s** sharp eyes; **es muy —** he's very observant, he's very sharp-eyed; he's pretty shrewd.
linchamiento *nm* lynching.
linchar [1a] *vt* to lynch.
linche *nm* (*Ec*) knapsack; **—s** (*Mex*) saddlebags.
lindamente *adv* (**a**) prettily; daintily; elegantly. (**b**) (*iro*) well, jolly well (*fam*). (**c**) (*esp SAm*) excellently, marvellously, jolly well (*fam*).
lindante *adj* bordering (*con* on), adjoining, adjacent (*con* to).

lindar [1a] *vi* to adjoin, be adjacent; — **con** to border on, adjoin, be adjacent to; to extend to, be bounded by; (*Archit*) to abut on.

linde *nm* or *f* boundary.

lindero 1 *adj* adjoining, bordering. **2** *nm* edge, border; boundary.

lindeza *nf* (a) prettiness; daintiness; elegance.
  (b) (*esp SAm*) niceness; excellence, high quality.
  (c) witticism.
  (d) —s pretty things; pretty ways, charming ways.
  (e) —s (*iro*) insults, improprieties.

lindo 1 *adj* (in all senses, more used in SAm than in Spain) (a) pretty; dainty; exquisite, elegant, delicate.
  (b) (*iro*) fine, pretty.
  (c) nice, lovely; fine, excellent, first-rate, marvellous; **un — coche** a nice car, a fine car; **un — partido** a first-rate game; **un — concierto** a marvellous concert; **de lo —** a lot, a great deal; wonderfully, marvellously, jolly well (*fam*); **es de —** (*SAm*) it's fine, it's marvellous.
  2 *adv* (*SAm*) nicely, well, marvellously; **baila —** she dances beautifully.
  3 *nm* (*Hist*) fop.

lindura *nf* (a) (*Chi, RPl*) prettiness, loveliness; **estar hecha una —** to look very pretty.
  (b) (*Chi, PR, Ven*) outstanding person; ace, champion; expert; **ella es una — en el vestir** she's an expert on clothes.

línea *nf* (a) (in most senses) line; (*Elec*) line, cable; (*Rail, Tel etc*) line; —s (*Mil*) lines; — **aérea** (*Aer*) airline; (*Elec*) overhead cable; — **de alto el fuego** ceasefire line; — **de banda** sideline, touchline; — **de base** (*Surveying*) base line; — **de batalla** line of battle, battle line; — **de carga** load line; — **de medio campo**, — **de centro** halfway line; — **delantera** forward line; — **derivada** (*Tel*) extension; — **divisoria** dividing line; — **férrea** railway; — **de flotación** water line; — **de fuego** firing line; — **de gol** goal line; — **lateral** sideline, touchline; — **de meta** goal line; (in race) finishing line; — **de montaje** assembly line; production line; — **primera —** front line; — **de puerta** goal line; — **de puntos** dotted line; — **recta** straight line; — **de saque** base line, service line; — **de alta tensión** high-tension cable; — **de tiro** line of fire; — **de toque** touchline; — **de la vida** life line; **explicar algo a grandes —s, explicar algo en sus —s generales** to set something out in broad outline, give the broad outline of something; **de —** (*Mil*) regular, front-line, (*Naut*) of the line; **en — in** (a) line, in a row; **en — recta** in a straight line; **en toda la —** all along the line; **leer entre —s** to read between the lines; **poner unas —s a uno** to drop a line to someone; **tirar una —** to draw a line.
  (b) (woman's) figure; (of ship etc) lines, outline; **guardar la —** to keep one's figure (trim); **la — de 1902** the 1902 line, the fashion line of 1902.
  (c) (genealogical) line (also fig); **en — directa** in an unbroken line; **es único en su —** it is unique in its line, it is the only one of its kind; **en esa — no tenemos nada** we have nothing in that line.
  (d) (moral, Pol etc) line; — **de conducta** course of action; — **dura** (*Pol*) hard line; — **de partido** party line; **ser de (una or una sola) —** (*Arg, Chi, PR*) to be honest, be absolutely straight.

lineal *adj* linear; **dibujo —** line drawing.

lineamento *nm* lineament.

linear [1a] *vt* (a) to line, draw lines on. (b) (*Art*) to sketch, outline.

linfa *nf* lymph.

linfático *adj* lymphatic.

lingote *nm* ingot.

lingüista *nmf* linguist, language specialist, linguistician.

lingüística *nf* linguistics.

lingüístico *adj* linguistic.

linimento *nm* liniment.

lino *nm* (a) (*Bot*) flax. (b) (*Arg, PR*) linseed. (c) linen; canvas; **géneros de —** linen goods.

linóleo *nm* lino, linoleum.

linón *nm* lawn (*fabric*).

linotipia *nf* linotype.

linotipo *nm* (*SAm*) linotype.

linterna *nf* lantern; lamp; (*Elec*) spotlight; —s (*SAm*) eyes; — **eléctrica**, — **de bolsillo**, — **a pila** torch, flashlight; — **mágica** magic lantern.

linyera (*RPl*) **1** *nf* knapsack; poor man's belongings, bundle of belongings. **2** *nm* tramp, bum (*US*).

lío *nm* (a) bundle; package, parcel; (*Arg*) truss.
  (b) (fam) row, fuss; mess, mix-up, confusion, muddle; jam; **ese — de los pasaportes** that fuss about the passports; **armar un —** to make a fuss,

kick up a row; to cause confusion; **se armó un tremendo —** there was an almighty row (*fam*); **hacerse un —** to get all mixed up, get into a muddle; **meterse en un —** to get into a jam.
  (c) (fam) affair, liaison; **tener un — con una** to be having an affair with someone.
  (d) (*SAm*) tale, piece of gossip; **no me venga con —s** don't come telling tales to me, I don't want to know.

Liorna Leghorn.

lioso *adj* (*Arg*) gossiping, talebearing.

lipa *nf* (*Ven*) belly.

lipe *nm* (*SAm: also piedra —*) vitriol; copper sulphate.

lipidia 1 *nf* (a) (*CAm*) poverty.
  (b) (*Cu, Mex*) impertinence.
  (c) (*Ec, Per*) indigestion; stomach upset.
  2 *nmf* (*Cu, Mex*) annoying person, pest.

lipidiar [1b] *vt* (*Cu, Mex, PR*) to annoy, bother, pester.

lipidioso *adj* (*Cu, Mex, PR*) silly; annoying.

lipón *adj* (*Ven*) fat, pot-bellied.

liquen *nm* lichen.

líquida *nf* (*Ling*) liquid.

liquidación *nf* (a) (*Chem*) liquefaction.
  (b) (*Comm, Fin*) liquidation; winding-up; (of account) settlement; **entrar en —** to go into liquidation.
  (c) (also **venta de —**) sale, clearance sale; **vender en —** to sell up.
  (d) (*Pol*) liquidation.

liquidar [1a] **1** *vt* (a) (*Chem*) to liquefy.
  (b) (*Comm, Fin*) to liquidate; *account* to settle; *business* to wind up; *debt* to settle, pay off, clear; *stocks* to sell off, sell up.
  (c) (*Pol*) to liquidate; (*SAm*) to kill, kill off.
  (d) (*SAm*) to destroy, ruin, render useless.
  2 liquidarse *vr* (*Chem*) to liquefy.

liquidez *nf* liquidity, fluidity.

líquido 1 *adj* (a) liquid; fluid.
  (b) (*Ling*) liquid.
  (c) (*Comm*) net; **ganancia líquida** net profit.
  (d) (*SAm*) exact; accurate, right, correctly measured; **4 varas líquidas** exactly 4 yards; **una líquida vez** once only, just once.
  2 *nm* (a) liquid; fluid.
  (b) (*Comm, Fin*) net amount, net profit; — **imponible** net taxable income.

lira *nf* (*Mus*) lyre; (*Italian: Fin*) lira; (*Lit*) a 5-line stanza popular in the 16th century.

lírica *nf* lyrical poetry; **la — provenzal** the Provençal lyric, Provençal lyrical poetry.

lírico 1 *adj* (a) (*Lit*) lyric(al); (*Theat*) musical.
  (b) (*SAm*) person dreamy, full of idealistic plans, given to making Utopian projects; (*Arg, Mex, Nic, Ven*) plan Utopian, fantastic.
  2 *nm* (*Arg*) dreamer, Utopian.

lirio *nm* iris; — **de los valles** lily of the valley.

lirismo *nm* (a) lyricism; lyrical feeling, sentimentality, (pej) gush, effusiveness.
  (b) (*SAm*) fantasy, dreams, Utopian ideals; dreaminess, fancifulness.

lirón *nm* dormouse; (fig) sleepyhead; **dormir como un —** to sleep like a log.

lirondo: see **mondo**.

lisamente *adv* smoothly, evenly; **lisa y llanamente** plainly, in plain language.

Lisboa Lisbon.

lisboeta 1 *adj* of Lisbon. **2** *nmf* native (or inhabitant) of Lisbon; **los —s** the people of Lisbon.

lisbonense, lisbonés = **lisboeta**.

lisiado 1 *adj* injured, hurt; lame, crippled. **2** *nm*, **lisiada** *nf* cripple; — **de guerra** wounded ex-serviceman.

lisiar [1b] *vt* to injure (permanently), hurt (seriously); to cripple, maim.

liso 1 *adj* (a) smooth, even; *hair* straight; *sea* calm; *race* flat; **los 400 metros —s** the 400-metre flat race.
  (b) (fig) plain, unadorned; — **y llano** plain, simple.
  (c) (*Mex, Per*) fresh, impudent; **irse —** (*Ven*) to depart without saying good-bye.
  2 *nm* (*Arg*) tall beer glass.

lisol *nm* lysol.

lisonja *nf* flattery.

lisonjear [1a] *vt* (a) to flatter. (b) to please, delight.

lisonjeramente *adv* (a) flatteringly; gratifyingly.
  (b) pleasingly, agreeably.

lisonjero 1 *adj* (a) flattering; gratifying. (b) pleasing, agreeable. **2** *nm*, **lisonjera** *nf* flatterer.

lista *nf* (a) list; catalogue; (*Mil*) roll; roll call; (*School*) roll, register; — **de comidas** menu; — **de**

correos poste restante; — **electoral** electoral roll, register of voters; — **de espera** waiting list; — **negra** blacklist; — **de pagos** payroll; — **de platos** menu; — **de precios** price list; — **de raya** (*Mex*) payroll; — **de tandas** duty roster, rota; — **de vinos** wine list; **pasar** — (*Mil*) to call the roll, (*School*) to call the register, call the roll.

(b) (*of cloth*) strip; (*of paper*) slip.

(c) stripe; **tela a** —**s** striped material.

listadillo *nm* (*Col, Mex, PR*) striped (white and blue) cotton cloth.

listado 1 *adj* striped. **2** *nm* (*Col, Per, PR, SD, Ven*) = **listadillo.**

listar [1a] *vt* to list, enter on a list.

listero *nm* (*SAm*) timekeeper, wages clerk.

listín *nm* telephone directory; (*SD*) newspaper.

listo *adj* (a) ready, prepared; **una pintura lista para usar** a ready-to-use paint; **un traje** — (*Mex*) a ready-made suit; **el avión estará** — **para volar en 6 meses** the plane will be ready to fly in 6 months; **¿estás** —**?** are you ready?; **todo está** — everything is ready, everything is in order.

(b) **¡**—**!** (*interj: SAm*) all right!, OK!; that's the lot!, it's all over!

(c) (*of character*) clever, smart, sharp, quick; **¡**—**!** (*iro*) wake up!, you're a bright one!; **es la mar de** — (*fam*) he's terribly clever (*fam*); **ser más** — **que el hambre** to be as smart as they come; **pasarse de** — to be too clever by half.

listón *nm* (*Sew*) ribbon; (*of wood*) strip, lath; (*Sport: high-jump etc*) bar; (*in vaulting*) pole; (*of metal, rubber etc*) strip; (*Archit*) fillet.

lisura *nf* (a) smoothness, evenness; straightness; calmness.

(b) plainness; sincerity; naïvety.

(c) (*SAm*) shamelessness, brazenness, impudence.

(d) (*SAm*) shameless remark, impudent remark, disrespectful thing (to say); (*Per*) coarse remark, rude thing (to do or say).

lisurero *adj* (*Per*) fresh, brazen, impudent.

litera *nf* litter; (*in dormitory*) bunk, bunk bed; (*Naut, Rail*) bunk, berth.

literal *adj* literal.

literalmente *adv* literally (*also fig*).

literario *adj* literary.

literata *nf* woman writer, literary lady; (*pej*) blue-stocking.

literato *nm* man of letters, writer; —**s** (*freq*) literati.

literatura *nf* literature.

litigación *nf* litigation.

litigante *nmf* litigant.

litigar [1h] **1** *vt* to dispute at law; to fight. **2** *vi* (*Law*) to go to law; to indulge in lawsuits; (*fig*) to argue, dispute.

litigio *nm* litigation; lawsuit; (*fig*) dispute; **en** — at stake, in dispute.

litigioso *adj* litigious; contentious.

litio *nm* lithium.

litisexpensas *nfpl* (*Law*) costs.

litografía *nf* (a) (*art*) lithography. (b) (*picture*) lithograph.

litografiar [1c] *vt* to lithograph.

litoral 1 *adj* coastal, littoral, seaboard (*attr*). **2** *nm* seaboard, littoral, coast.

litre *nm* (*Chi*) nausea.

litro[1] *nm* litre, liter (*US*).

litro[2] *nm* (*Chi*) coarse woollen cloth.

Lituania *f* Lithuania.

lituano 1 *adj* Lithuanian. **2** *nm*, **lituana** *nf* Lithuanian. **3** *nm* (*language*) Lithuanian.

liturgia *nf* liturgy.

litúrgico *adj* liturgical.

livianamente *adv* (a) in a fickle way; frivolously; in a trivial way. (b) lewdly.

liviandad *nf* (a) fickleness; frivolity, triviality. (b) lewdness. (c) (*SAm*) lightness.

liviano 1 *adj* (a) fickle; frivolous, trivial. (b) lewd. (c) (*SAm*) light. **2** —**s** *nmpl* lights, lungs.

lividez *nf* (a) lividness. (b) (*SAm*) paleness, pallor.

lívido *adj* (a) livid; black and blue. (b) (*SAm*) pale, pallid.

living ['liβin] *nm, pl* **livings** ['liβin] (*angl*) living room.

Livio *m* Livy.

lixiviar [1b] **1** *vt* to leach. **2 lixiviarse** *vr* to leach.

liza *nf* (*Hist*) lists; (*fig*) contest.

lo[1] "neuter" *def art* (a) — **bello** the beautiful, what is beautiful, that which is beautiful; — **difícil** what is difficult; — **difícil es que** ... the difficult thing about it is that ...; **quiero** — **justo** I want what is just; **defiendo** — **mío** I defend what is mine; **visto** — **ocurrido** in view of what has happened; — **insospechado del caso** what was unsuspected about the

matter; — **totalmente inesperado del descubrimiento** the completely unexpected nature of the discovery; — **mejor de la película** the best part of the film, the best thing about the film; **sufre** — **indecible** she suffers terribly.

(b) **construido a** — **campesino** built in peasant style; **viste a** — **americano** he dresses in the American style, he dresses like an American.

(c) **no saben** — **aburrido que es** they don't know how boring it is; **me doy cuenta de** — **amables que ellas son** I realize how kind they are.

lo[2] *pron* (*person*) him; (*thing*) it; — **tengo aquí** I have it here; — **creo** I think so; (*not translated in such cases as*) — **veo** I see, — **sé** I know; **no** — **hay** there isn't any; "**¿anarquista?**" ... "**no** — **soy**" "an anarchist?" ... "I'm not"; "**¿estás cansado?**" ... "—**estoy**" "are you tired?" ... "I am" (*or* "yes"); **guapa sí que** — **es** she's certainly very pretty, I should jolly well say she's pretty (*fam*).

lo[3] *dem pron*: — **de** that matter of, that business about; — **de ayer** what happened yesterday; — **de Suez** the Suez affair; — **de no traer dinero** that business about not having any money.

lo[4] *rel pron*: — **que** (a) what, that which; — **que digo es** ... what I say is ...; **toma** — **que quieras** take what(ever) you want; **con** — **que él gana** with what he earns; **¡**— **que sufre un hombre honrado!** what an honourable man has to suffer!; — **que pasa es que** ..., — **que hay es que** ... what's happening is that ..., it's like this ...; **empezó a tocar**, — **que le fastidió** she began to play, which made him cross.

(b) (*idioms*) — **que es eso** as for that; **¡**— **que has tardado!** how late you are!; **¡**— **que cuesta vivir!** isn't living expensive!; **¡**— **que es saber lenguas!** isn't it wonderful to speak several languages!; **¡**— **que he dicho!** I stand by what I said!; **¡**— **que ves!** can't you see?, it's there for you to see!

loa *nf* (a) praise. (b) (*Theat: Hist*) prologue, playlet. (c) (*CAm, Mex*) reproof.

loable *adv* praiseworthy, commendable, laudable.

loablemente *adv* commendably.

loar [1a] *vt* to praise.

loba *nf* (a) (*Zool*) she-wolf. (b) (*Agr*) ridge (between furrows).

lobanillo *nm* wen, cyst.

lobato *nm* wolf cub.

lobelia *nf* lobelia.

lobero *adj* wolf (*attr*); **perro** — wolfhound.

lobezno *nm* wolf cub.

lobito *nm* (*RPl*) otter (*also* — **de río**).

lobo[1] *adj* (*Mex*) shrewd, cunning; (*Chi*) shy; (*SD*) green, raw.

2 *nm* wolf; — **de mar** old salt, sea dog, (*Chi*) seal; — **marino** seal; **son** —**s de una camada** they're birds of a feather; **arrojar a uno a los** —**s** to throw someone to the wolves; **gritar ¡el** —**!** to cry wolf; **pillar un** — (*fam*) to get boozed.

3 *nm* (*SAm*) half-breed.

lóbrego *adj* dark, murky, gloomy.

lobreguez *nf* darkness, murk(iness), gloom(iness).

lóbulo *nm* lobe.

lobuno *adj* wolf (*attr*); wolfish, wolflike.

loca *nf* (a) madwoman, lunatic. (b) (*RPl*) whore. (c) **dar** (*or* **venir**) **a uno la** — (*RPl*) to get cross, get into a temper.

local 1 *adj* local; **equipo** — home team; **los** —**es** (*Sport*) our boys, the home team.

2 *nm* place; site, scene; rooms; premises; **en el** — on the spot; on the premises.

localidad *nf* (a) locality; location. (b) (*Theat*) seat, ticket; **sacar** —**es** to get tickets; "**no hay** —**es**" "house full", "sold out".

localización *nf* location; placing, siting; finding.

localizar [1f] *vt* (a) to locate; to place, site; to find, track down; **el sitio donde se va a** — **la nueva industria** the place where the new industry is to be sited.

(b) to localize.

locamente *adv* madly; wildly; — **enamorado** madly in love.

locatario *nm*, **locataria** *nf* (*SAm*) tenant, lessee.

locatis *nm, pl* **locatis** madman, crackpot, crazy sort.

locería *nf* (*Col, Mex*) china, chinaware; (*Col*) pottery.

locero *nm* (*CAm, Col, Mex*) potter.

loción *nf* lotion; wash; — **capilar**, — **para el cabello** hair restorer; — **facial**, — **para después del afeitado** after-shave lotion.

lock-out ['lokaut] *nm, pl* **lock-outs** ['lokaut] (*angl*) lock-out.

loco 1 *adj* (a) mad, crazy; (*fig*) wild, mad; — **de atar**, — **rematado** (*SAm*) raving mad; — **de verano** (*Arg*) cracked, crazy; — **lindo** (*Arg*) mad in a nice sort of way; **más — que una cabra** as mad as a hatter; **andar — con algo** to be worried to death about something; **ando — con el examen** the exam is driving me crazy; **estar — de alegría** to be mad with joy; **estar — por una chica** to be mad about a girl; **estar — por hacer algo** (*SAm*) to be mad keen to do something; **esto me tiene** (*or* **trae**) **—** it's driving me crazy; **volver — a uno** to drive someone mad; **volverse —** to go mad; **esto es para volverse —** it's maddening, it's enough to drive you mad; **estar para volverse —** to be at one's wit's end.

(b) (*Mech*) loose, free.

(c) (*fam*) huge, tremendous (*fam*); **un éxito —** a huge success; **estoy con** (*or* **tengo**) **una prisa loca** I'm in a tremendous rush; **he tenido una suerte loca** I've been fantastically lucky.

2 *nm* madman; lunatic; maniac; **correr como un —** to run like mad; **gritar como un —** to shout like a madman.

locomoción *nf* locomotion.

locomotora *nf* (*Rail*) engine, locomotive; **— de maniobras** shunting engine, switch engine (*US*).

locomóvil *nf* traction engine.

locrear [1a] *vi* (*SAm*) to eat, have a meal.

locro *nm* (*SAm*) meat and vegetable stew.

locuacidad *nf* loquacity, talkativeness.

locuaz *adj* loquacious, voluble, talkative.

locución *nf* expression, phrase.

locuelo *nm*, **locuela** *nf* madcap.

locura *nf* **(a)** madness, lunacy, insanity; **¡qué —!** it's madness!, what lunacy!; **me gusta con —** (*fam*) I'm crazy about it; **es una casa de —** (*fam*) it's a smashing house (*sl*).

(b) (*act*) mad thing, crazy thing; **—s** folly; **es capaz de hacer cualquier —** he is capable of any madness.

locutor *nm*, **locutora** *nf* (*Radio*) announcer; commentator; (*TV*) newscaster, newsreader; (*of comedy show*) compère; (*at fashion show etc*) presenter.

locutorio *nm* (*Eccl*) parlour; (*Tel*) telephone box; **— radiofónico** studio.

locha *nf* loach.

loche *nm* (*Col*) reddish colour.

locho *adj* (*Col*) red, reddish.

lodacero *nm* (*Ec*), **lodazal** *nm* muddy place, mudhole, quagmire.

lodo *nm* mud, mire; sludge; **—s** (*Med*) mudbath.

lodoso *adj* muddy.

loga *nf* **(a)** (*CAm*) eulogy; **echar una — a uno** (*iro*) to tell someone off. **(b)** (*Chi*) ballad, short poem.

logaritmo *nm* logarithm.

logia *nf* **(a)** (*masonic etc*) lodge. **(b)** (*Archit*) loggia.

lógica *nf* logic.

lógicamente *adv* logically.

lógico 1 *adj* logical; natural, right, reasonable; **es — que . . .** it is natural that . . ., it stands to reason that . . . **2** *nm* logician.

logística *nf* logistics.

logístico *adj* logistic.

logradamente *adv* successfully.

logrado *adj* successful.

lograr [1a] *vt* **(a)** to get, obtain; to achieve, attain; **por fin lo logró** eventually he achieved it, eventually he managed it; **logra cuanto quiere** he gets whatever he wants; **¡no lo lograrán!** they shan't get away with it!

(b) **— hacer algo** to manage to do something, succeed in doing something; **— que uno haga algo** to (manage to) get someone to do something, persuade someone to do something.

logrear [1a] *vi* to lend money at interest, be a moneylender.

logrero *nm* **(a)** moneylender, (*pej*) profiteer. **(b)** (*SAm*) sponger (*fam*), parasite.

logro *nm* **(a)** achievement, attainment; success; **uno de sus mayores —s** one of his greatest successes (*or* achievements).

(b) (*Comm, Fin*) profit; (*pej*) usury; **a —** at (a high rate of) interest.

logroñés 1 *adj* of Logroño. **2** *nm*, **logroñesa** *nf* native (*or* inhabitant) of Logroño; **los —es** the people of Logroño.

Loira *m* Loire.

loísmo *nm* use of *lo* instead of *le* (*indirect object*).

loísta 1 *adj* that uses *lo* instead of *le* (*indirect object*). **2** *nmf* user of *lo* instead of *le*.

Lola *f*, **Lolita** *f* pet names for **María de los Dolores**.

loma *nf* hillock, low ridge; **en la — del diablo** (*Arg*) at the back of beyond.

lomada *nf* (*SAm*) =**loma**.

lombarda *nf* (*Agr*) red cabbage.

Lombardía *f* Lombardy.

lombardo 1 *adj* Lombard. **2** *nm*, **lombarda** *nf* Lombard.

lombriciento *adj* (*SAm*) suffering from worms.

lombriz *nf* worm, earthworm; **— solitaria** tapeworm.

lomería *nf*, **lomerio** *nm* (*Guat, Mex*) group of low hills, series of ridges.

lometón *nm* (*Cu, Mex*) isolated hillock.

lomillería *nf* (*RPl*) **(a)** harness maker's; harness shop. **(b)** harness, harness accessories.

lomillero *nm* (*RPl*) harness maker; harness seller.

lomillo *nm* **(a)** (*Sew*) cross-stitch. **(b)** **—s** (*SAm*) pads (of a pack saddle).

lomo *nm* **(a)** (*Anat*) back; (*of meat*) loin; **—s** ribs; **iba a —s de una mula** he was riding a mule, he was mounted on a mule. **(b)** (*Agr*) balk, ridge; (*of hill*) shoulder; (*Rail*) gradient. **(c)** (*of book*) spine, back.

lona *nf* canvas; sailcloth; (*Mex, RPl*) sackcloth.

loncha *nf* =**lonja¹**.

lonchar [1a] (*SAm*) **1** *vt* to have for lunch. **2** *vi* to have lunch, lunch.

lonche *nm* (*SAm*: *angl*) lunch, midday snack; (*Per*) tea, afternoon snack.

lonchear [1a] *vt* (*Mex*) to have for lunch.

lonchería *nf* (*SAm*) lunch counter, snack bar, restaurant.

loncho *nm* (*Col*) bit, piece, slice.

londinense 1 *adj* London (*attr*), of London. **2** *nmf* Londoner; **los —s** the people of London, (the) Londoners.

Londres London.

londri *nm* (*SAm*: *angl*) laundry.

loneta *nf* (*SAm*) coarse cotton cloth.

longanimidad *nf* forbearance, magnanimity.

longánimo *adj* forbearing, magnanimous.

longaniza *nf* **(a)** long pork sausage. **(b)** (*Chi*) string, series.

longevidad *nf* longevity.

longevo *adj* long-lived; **las mujeres son más longevas que los hombres** women live longer than men.

longitud *nf* **(a)** length; **— de onda** wavelength. **(b)** (*Geog*) longitude.

longitudinal *adj* longitudinal.

longitudinalmente *adv* longitudinally; lengthways.

longo *nm* (*Ec*) Indian youth.

longui(s) *nm* (*fam*): **hacerse el —** to pretend not to know; to pretend not to be interested.

lonja¹ *nf* **(a)** slice; (*of bacon*) rasher. **(b)** (*RPl*) strip of leather; tip of a whiplash; **sacar —s a uno** to thrash someone severely.

lonja² *nf* (*Comm*) **(a)** market, exchange; **— de granos** corn exchange; **— de pescado** fish market; **manipular la —** to rig the market.

(b) grocer's (shop).

lonjear [1a] *vt* (*RPl*) *leather* to cut into strips; *person* to thrash severely.

lonjista *nm* grocer.

lontananza *nf* (*Art*) background; **en —** far away, in the distance.

loor *nm* praise.

loquear [1a] *vi* to play the fool; to make merry, have a high old time.

loqueo *nm* (*Urug*) uproar, hullaballoo (*fam*).

loquera *nf* **(a)** madhouse, lunatic asylum. **(b)** (*SAm*) madness.

loquería *nf* (*Chi, Per*) madhouse, lunatic asylum.

loquero *nm* **(a)** (*RPl*) nurse in an asylum. **(b)** (*RPl*) confusion, pandemonium.

loquira *nf* (*Col*) foolish thing, idiocy.

loquircho *adj* (*Arg*) crazy, cracked.

lor *nm* (*angl*) lord.

lora *nf* **(a)** (*SAm*: *Orn*) female parrot. **(b)** (*Chi, RPl*) ugly woman; chatterbox. **(c)** (*Col, Ec, PR, Ven*) severe wound, open wound.

Lorena *f* Lorraine.

Lorenzo *m* Laurence, Lawrence.

loro *nm* **(a)** parrot.

(b) (*SAm*) chatterbox; (*Chi*) spy; thieves' lookout man.

(c) (*Chi*) bedpan.

(d) (*Arg, Chi*) **sacar los —s** to pick one's nose.

(e) pointed and curved knife.

los¹ *def art mpl*, **las** *def art fpl* the (see **el** for *usage examples*).

los², **las** *pron* them; **¿los hay?** are there any?; **los hay** there are some.

los³, **las** *dem pron*: **mis libros y los de Vd** my books and yours; **nuestros cines y los de París** our cinemas and those of Paris, our cinemas and the Paris ones; **las de Juan son verdes** John's are green; **una inocentada de las de niño pequeño** a practical joke typical of a small child, a practical joke such as a small child might play; **un bombardeo de los de cataclismo** a really shattering bombardment.

los[4], **las: los que, las que** rel pron: see **el que**.

losa nf (stone) slab, flagstone; — **sepulcral** gravestone, tombstone.

losange nm diamond (shape); (Math) rhomb; (Her) lozenge; (Sport) diamond.

lote[1] nm (a) portion, share; (Comm etc) lot.
(b) land measure: (Mex) = about 100 hectares; (Arg) = about 400 hectares.
(c) (Chi) **al** — in a rough and ready way, crudely, without bothering much.

lote[2] nm (Arg: sl) idiot, clot (sl).

lotear [1a] vt (Arg, Chi) to divide into lots.

lotería nf lottery; **le cayó la** —, **le tocó la** — he won a big prize in the lottery, (fig) he struck lucky, he struck it rich.

lotero nm, **lotera** nf seller of lottery tickets.

lotificar [1g] vt (Guat, Mex), **lotizar** [1f] vt (Per) to divide into lots.

loto nm lotus.

Lovaina Louvain.

loza nf crockery; earthenware; — **fina** china, chinaware; **hacer la** — to wash up.

lozanamente adv (a) luxuriantly; rankly; profusely; vigorously; in a lively fashion, in a sprightly way. (b) haughtily, proudly.

lozanear [1a] vi (Bot) to flourish, do well, grow strongly; to grow profusely; (person) to be full of life, be vigorous, flourish.

lozanía nf (a) lushness, luxuriance; vigour; liveliness, sprightliness. (b) haughtiness, pride.

lozano adj (a) (Bot) lush, luxuriant; rank; profuse; person, animal vigorous, lusty; lively, sprightly. (b) haughty, proud.

lubricación nf lubrication.

lubricador 1 adj lubricating. **2** nm lubricator.

lubricante 1 adj lubricant, lubricating. **2** nm lubricant.

lubricar [1g] vt to lubricate, oil, grease.

lubricidad nf (a) slipperiness. (b) lewdness, lubricity.

lúbrico adj (a) slippery. (b) (fig) lewd, lubricious.

lubrificar [1f] vt etc see **lubricar** etc.

Lucano m Lucan.

Lucas m Luke, Lucas; (Eccl) Luke.

lucas adj invar (Mex) crazy, cracked.

lucense 1 adj of Lugo. **2** nmf native (or inhabitant) of Lugo; **los** —**s** the people of Lugo.

lucera nf skylight.

lucerna nf chandelier.

lucernario nm skylight.

lucero nm (a) (Astron) bright star, (esp) Venus; — **del alba** morning star; — **de la tarde**, — **vespertino** evening star. (b) (fig) brilliance, radiance.

lucidez nf (a) lucidity, clarity. (b) (Arg, Chi, Guat) brilliance.

lúcido adj lucid, clear.

lucido adj (a) splendid, brilliant; sumptuous, magnificent; elegant; successful.
(b) **estar** —, **quedar(se)** — (iro) to do splendidly (iro), make a mess of things; **¡estamos** —**s!** (iro) a fine mess we're in!

luciente adj bright, shining, brilliant.

luciérnaga nf glow-worm.

Lucifer m Lucifer.

lucimiento nm brilliance, lustre, splendour; show, ostentation; dash, verve; success; **hacer algo con** — to do something outstandingly well, do something very successfully.

lucio[1] nm (Fish) pike.

lucio[2] adj = **lúcido**.

lución nm slow-worm.

lucir [3f] **1** vt (a) to illuminate, light up.
(b) to show off, display; to sport; — **las habilidades** to show off one's talents; **lucía traje nuevo** he was sporting a new suit.
2 vi (a) to shine; to sparkle, glitter, gleam.
(b) (fig) to shine, be brilliant; to be a success; (in dress etc) to look nice, cut a dash; to show off; **no lucía en los estudios** he did not shine at his studies.
3 lucirse vr (a) to dress up, dress elegantly; = vi (b).
(b) (iro) to make a fool of oneself, make a mess of things; **¡te has lucido!** (iro) a fine thing you've done! (iro), what a mess you've made!

lucrarse [1a] vr to do well out of a deal; (pej) to enrich oneself, feather one's nest.

lucrativo adj lucrative, profitable, remunerative; **institución no lucrativa** non-profitmaking institution.

Lucrecia f Lucretia.

Lucrecio m Lucretius.

lucro nm profit; —**s y daños** (Fin) profit and loss.

luctuoso adj mournful, sad, tragic.

lucubración nf lucubration.

lúcuma nf (Chi) a pear-shaped fruit; (fam) head.

Lucha f pet name for **Luz, Lucía**.

lucha nf (a) fight, struggle (por for); conflict; contest, dispute; — **de clases** class war; — **contra la subversión** struggle against subversive elements; witch hunt.
(b) (Sport) — **de la cuerda** tug-of-war; — **grecorromana**, — **libre** wrestling.

luchador nm fighter; (Sport) wrestler.

luchar [1a] vi (a) to fight, struggle (por algo for something; por hacer to do); **luchaba con los mandos** he was struggling (or wrestling) with the controls; — **con uno**, — **contra uno** to fight (against) someone.
(b) (Sport) to wrestle (con with).

luche nm (Chi) (a) hopscotch. (b) an edible seaweed.

ludibrio nm mockery, derision.

ludir [3a] vt to rub (con, contra against).

luego adv then, next; presently, soon; later (on), afterwards; (also Mex) at once, instantly, immediately; (SAm) later; (Col, Mex, Par, Per, PR) sometimes, from time to time; (Par) already, earlier, previously; **¿y** —? what next? what happened then?; **desde** — naturally, of course; **desde** — **que no** of course not; **¡hasta** —! I see you later, so long!; **¡para** — **es tarde!** (Guat, Mex) prove it to us right now!; — **de eso** immediately after that; — **de haberlo dicho** immediately after saying it; — **que . . .** as soon as . . .

lueguito adv (a) (Arg, Chi, Guat, Mex, Par) at once, immediately. (b) (Chi, Guat, Mex) near; **aquí** — right here, near here.

lúes nf syphilis.

luengo adj (arch, lit, also SAm) long.

lugar nm (a) place, spot; position; — **seguro** safe place; **el** — **del crimen** the scene of the crime; **una emisión de algún** — **de Europa** a broadcast from somewhere in Europe; **en** — **de** instead of, in place of; **en primer** — in the first place, firstly; for one thing . . .; **yo en su** — if I were him; in his place, I . . .; **estar fuera de** — to be out of place (also fig); **dejar a uno en mal** — to let someone down, leave someone in the lurch; **devolver un libro a su** — to put a book back (in its place); **ocupar el** — **de** to take the place of; **poner las cosas en su** — (fig) to put things straight, put the record straight; **póngase en mi** — put yourself in my place; **ponerse en su** — to stand on one's dignity; **tener** — to take place, happen, occur.
(b) room, space; **¿hay** —? is there any room?; **hacer** — **para** to make room for, make way for.
(c) village, town, place.
(d) reason (para for), cause; **no hay** — **para preocupaciones** there is no cause for concern, there is no need for worry.
(e) opportunity; **si se me da el** — if I have the chance; **dar** — **a** to give rise to, occasion; **dejar** — **a** to allow, permit of.
(f) — **común** commonplace, cliché, platitude.

lugareño 1 adj village (attr). **2** nm, **lugareña** nf villager.

lugarteniente nm deputy.

lugre nm lugger.

lúgubre adj mournful, lugubrious, dismal.

luir [3g] vt (Chi) to rumple, mess up; pottery to polish.

Luis m Louis.

Luisa f Louise.

Luisiana f Louisiana.

lujo nm (a) luxury; sumptuousness, lavishness; **de** — de luxe, luxury (attr); **vivir en el** — to live in luxury.
(b) (fig) profusion, wealth, abundance; **con** — **de fuerza** with an excessive show of force.

lujosamente adv luxuriously; sumptuously, lavishly; ostentatiously; profusely.

lujoso adj luxurious; sumptuous, lavish; ostentatious; profuse.

lujuria nf lust, lechery; lewdness.

lujuriante adj (a) luxuriant, lush. (b) lustful.

lujuriar [1b] vi to lust.

lujurioso adj lustful, lecherous; lewd, sensual.

lulo 1 adj (Chi) (a) object long and cylindrical; person lank, slender.
(b) character dull, colourless.
2 nm (a) (Chi) cylindrical object; bundle; curl.
(b) — **del ojo** (Col) eyeball.

lullir [3h] vt (Col, CR, Mex) to rub (con, contra against, on).

lumbago nm lumbago.

lumbar *adj* lumbar.
lumbre *nf* (a) fire; **cerca de la —** near the fire, at the fireside; **echar —** to be furious.
(b) (*for cigarette*) light; **¿tienes —?, ¿me das —?** have you got a light?
(c) light; brightness, brilliance, splendour; **— del agua** surface of the water.
(d) (*Archit*) light, opening (in a wall); skylight.
lumbrera *nf* (a) luminary; (*Archit*) skylight.
(b) (*Mech*) vent, port; **— de escape** exhaust vent.
(c) (*fig*) luminary, leading light, authority; **estaba rodeado de —s literarias** he was surrounded by leading literary figures.
(d) (*Mex: Taur, Theat*) box.
luminar *nm* luminary; =**lumbrera** (c).
luminaria *nf* altar lamp; **—s** illuminations, lights.
lumínico *adj* light (*attr*).
luminiscenia *nf* luminescence.
luminosidad *nf* (a) brightness (*also TV*), luminosity.
(b) (*fig*) brightness, brilliance.
luminoso *adj* (a) bright, luminous, shining; **sign** illuminated. (b) (*fig*) *idea* bright, brilliant.
luna *nf* (a) moon; **— creciente** crescent moon, waxing moon; **— llena** full moon; **media —** half-moon, (*fig*) crescent; **— menguante** waning moon; **— nueva** new moon; **— de miel** honeymoon; **estar de buena —** to be in a good mood; **estar de mala —** to be in a bad mood; **estar en la —** to be wool-gathering; **eso es hablar de la —** that's nonsense; **quedarse a la — de Valencia** (*or de Paita: Chi, Ec, Per*) to be disappointed, be left in the lurch; **vivir en la —** to be completely out of touch with reality, have one's head in the clouds.
(b) plate glass; mirror; lens.
lunar 1 *adj* lunar.
2 *nm* (*Anat*) mole, spot; (*fig*) defect, flaw, blemish; (*moral*) stain, blot; black spot; **— postizo** beauty spot; **hay —es en la prosperidad general** there are black spots in the general prosperity.
lunarejo *adj* (*SAm*) spotty, spotty-faced.
lunático 1 *adj* lunatic. **2** *nm* lunatic.
lunch [lunʃ] *nm, pl* **lunchs** [lunʃ] (*angl*) lunch; midday snack; formal luncheon, luncheon party.
lunchería *nf* (*SAm: angl*) =**lonchería**.
lunes *nm, pl* **lunes** Monday; **hacer San L—** (*SAm*) to stay away from work on Monday; **no ocurre cada — y cada martes** it doesn't happen every day of the week.
luneta *nf* (a) lens, glass (of spectacles). (b) half-moon shape, crescent. (c) (*Theat: Hist, Mex*) stall.
lunfa *nm* (*Arg: sl*) thief.
lunfardismo *nm* (*RPl*) word (*or* phrase *etc*) from thieves' slang.
lunfardo *nm* (*Per, RPl*) (a) thieves' slang, language of the underworld; slang (*in general*). (b) thief.
lupa *nf* lens, magnifying glass.
lupanar *nm* brothel.
Lupe *f pet name for* **Guadalupe**.
lupia¹ *nf* (a) wen, cyst. (b) (*Col; also* **—s**) small amount of money; small change.
lupia² *nmf* (*Hond*) quack doctor.
lúpulo *nm* (*Bot*) hop, hops.
luquete *nm* (*Chi*) unploughed patch of land; bald patch (*on head*); grease spot (*on clothing*).
lurio *adj* (*Mex*) in love; crazy, cracked.
lusitano 1 *adj* Portuguese; (*ancient Hist*) Lusitanian. **2** *nm*, **lusitana** *nf* Portuguese; (*ancient Hist*) Lusitanian.
luso *adj* =**lusitano**.
lustrabotas *nm, pl* **lustrabotas** (*esp SAm*) bootblack.
lustrada *nf* (*SAm*) shoeshine.

lustrador *nm* (a) (*Tech*) polisher. (b) (*SAm*) bootblack.
lustrar [1a] *vt* to shine, polish.
lustre *nm* (a) polish, shine, gloss, lustre; **dar — a** to polish, put a shine on.
(b) polish; **— para calzado** shoe polish; **— para metales** metal polish.
(c) (*fig*) lustre, glory.
lustrín *nm* (a) (*Chi*) shoeshine parlour. (b) (*Ec*) = **lustrina** (a).
lustrina *nf* (a) (*Arg, Par*) shiny material of alpaca; (*Ec*) silk cloth. (b) (*Chi*) shoe polish.
lustro *nm* lustrum, period of five years.
lustroso *adj* glossy, bright, shining.
luteranismo *nm* Lutheranism.
luterano 1 *adj* Lutheran. **2** *nm*, **luterana** *nf* Lutheran.
Lutero *m* Luther.
luto *nm* (a) mourning; grief, sorrow; **medio —** half-mourning; **— riguroso** deep mourning; **estar de —, llevar —** to be in mourning (*por* for); **dejar el —** to come out of mourning.
(b) **—s** mourning (clothes), crêpe.
Luxemburgo *m* Luxembourg.
luz *nf* (a) (*in general*) light; daylight; **— y sombra** light and shade; **la — del día** the light of day; **a la — del día** (*fig*) in the cold light of day; **como la — del día** as clear as daylight; **— eléctrica** electric light; **— de la luna** moonlight; **— del sol, — solar** sunlight; **a la — de una vela** by the light of a candle; **a — primera** at first light; **espectáculo de — y sonido** son et lumière show; **entre dos luces** at twilight; (*fam*) mellow, tipsy; **dar a —** to give birth; **dar a — un niño** to give birth to a child; **dar a — un libro** to publish a book; **negar la — del día a uno** to concede absolutely nothing to someone; **quitar la — a uno** to stand in someone's light; **sacar a — to** bring to light; *book* to publish; **salir a —** to come to light; (*book*) to appear, come out, be published.
(b) (*Elec: fam*) electricity, electric current, juice (*sl*).
(c) (*fig*) light; **a la — de** in the light of; **a la — de un nuevo descubrimiento** in the light of a new discovery; **a todas luces** anyway; evidently; by any reckoning; **arrojar — sobre** to cast (*or* shed, throw) light on; **estudiar algo a nueva —** to study something in a new light; **tuvo una larga experiencia de estar a la — de la publicidad** he had long experience of the limelight, he was used to being in the public eye.
(d) (*Elec etc*) light, lamp; **— de costado** sidelight; **— de cruce** dipped headlight; **— destelladora** winking light; **luces de detención, luces de freno** braking lights; **luces de estacionamiento** parking lights; **— intermitente** winking light; **— lateral** sidelight; **— piloto, — de situación** sidelight, parking light; **— relámpago** (*Phot*) flashlight; **— roja** red light; **luces de tráfico** traffic lights; **luces traseras** rear lights, tail lamps; **— verde** green light; **apagar la —** to switch off (*or* put off, turn off) the light; **poner la —** to switch on (*or* put on, turn on) the light; **poner una lámpara a media —** to dim a light.
(e) (*Archit etc*) light; window, opening; (*of bridge*) space, span; (*RPl*) distance between two objects; **dar — a uno** (*RPl: Sport*) to give someone a start; **te doy 10 metros de —** I'll give you 10 metres' start.
(f) **luces** (*fig*) enlightenment; intelligence; **corto de luces, de pocas luces** dim, stupid; **el Siglo de las Luces** the Age of Enlightenment (*18th century*).
Lyón Lyons.

LL

llacsa *nf* (*Chi*) molten metal.
llaga *nf* (a) wound; ulcer, sore; ¡por las —s! damnation!
(b) (*fig*) sore, affliction, torment; las —s de la guerra the afflictions of war, the havoc of war.
llagar [1h] *vt* (a) to make sore; to wound, injure.
(b) (*fig*) to wound, injure.
llalla *nf* (*Chi*) see **yaya**.
llama[1] *nf* (*Zool*) llama.
llama[2] *nf* (a) flame; blaze; — **piloto** pilot light (*on stove*); **arder sin** — to smoulder; **entregar algo a las —s** to commit something to the flames; **estallar en —s** to burst into flames; **salir de las —s y caer en las brasas** (*fig*) to jump out of the frying pan into the fire.
(b) (*fig*) flame; passion, ardour.
llamada *nf* (a) call; (*at door*) knock, ring; (*Tel*) call; (*Mil*) call to arms; — **a larga distancia**, — **interurbana** long-distance call, trunk call; — **al orden** call to order.
(b) signal, sign, gesture.
(c) (*Typ*) reference mark.
(d) (*Mex*) cowardliness; timidity.
llamado 1 *adj* so-called. 2 *nm* (*SAm*) = **llamada**.
llamador *nm* (a) (*person*) caller. (b) door-knocker; bell; push-button.
llamamiento *nm* call; **hacer un** — **a uno para que** + *subj* to call on someone to + *infin*.
llamar [1a] 1 *vt* (a) to call, name; **le llamaron el Gordo** they called him Fatty (*fam*); **¿cómo le van a —?** what are they going to call him?
(b) to call; to summon; to invoke, call upon; (*with gesture*) to beckon; (*Tel*) to call, ring up, telephone (to); **¿quién me llama?** who's asking for me?; **que me llamen a las 7** please have them call me at 7; **le llamaron a palacio** they called (*or* summoned) him to the palace; **le llaman desde París** they're calling you from Paris; — **a uno a hacer algo** to call on someone to do something.
(c) to draw, attract; *attention* to attract.
(d) **estar llamado a** + *infin* to be destined to + *infin*; **esto está llamado a ser de gran utilidad** this is destined to be very useful; **estaba llamado a fracasar** it was doomed to failure.
2 *vi* (a) to call; **¿quién llama?** (*Tel*) who's calling?, who's that?; **"llama D de Dulcinea"** (*Aer etc*) "this is D for Dulcinea (calling)"; — **por ayuda** to call for help.
(b) to knock, ring; — **a la puerta** to knock at the door; **¿quién llama?** who's there?
3 **llamarse** *vr* to be called, be named; **me llamo Mimi** my name is Mimi, they call me Mimi; **¿cómo te llamas?** what's your name?; ¡**eso sí que se llama cantar!** that's what you really call singing!; ¡**eso sí que se llama hablar!** now you're talking!, that's more like it!; ¡**como me llamo Rodríguez, que lo haré!** as sure as my name's Rodríguez, I'll do it!
llamarada *nf* flare-up, sudden blaze; (*on face*) sudden flush; (*fig*) flare-up, outburst.
llamarón *nm* (*CAm, Col, Chi*) = **llamarada**.
llamativo *adj* gaudy, flashy, showy; *colour* loud; **de modo** — in such a way as to draw attention.
llame *nm* (*Chi*) bird trap.
llamear [1a] *vi* to blaze, flame, flare.
llamón *adj* (*Mex*) cowardly; timid.
llampo *nm* (*Arg, Bol, Chi*) ore, pulverized ore; pebble deposit.
llana *nf* (a) (*Geog*) plain; flat ground. (b) (*Archit*) mason's trowel.
llanada *nf* plain; flat ground.
llanamente *adv* (a) smoothly, evenly. (b) plainly, simply; clearly, straightforwardly; openly, frankly; see **lisamente**.
llanca *nf* (*Per*) earthworm.

llanero *nm*, **llanera** *nf* plainsman, plaindweller.
llaneza *nf* (*fig*) plainness, simplicity; clearness, straightforwardness; naturalness; modesty; openness, frankness; informality.
llano 1 *adj* (a) level, flat, smooth, even.
(b) (*fig*) plain, simple, unadorned; clear, easy, straightforward; open, frank; **en lenguaje** — in plain language; **a la llana** simply; openly, frankly; **decir algo por lo** — to put matters bluntly, say things straight out; **de** — openly.
2 *nm* plain, flat ground.
llanque *nm* (*Per*) rustic sandal.
llanta[1] *nf* tyre (*esp SAm*); rim (*of a wheel*); (*PR*) large finger-ring; — **de oruga** caterpillar track.
llanta[2] *nf* (*Bol, Per*) sunshade, awning.
llantén *nm* plantain.
llantería *nf* (*Chi*) weeping, wailing.
llanto *nm* weeping, crying; tears; (*fig*) lamentation; (*Lit*) dirge, funeral lament; **dejar el** — to stop crying.
llanura *nf* (a) flatness, smoothness, evenness. (b) (*Geog*) plain; prairie.
llapa *nf* see **yapa**.
llapango *adj* (*Ec*) barefoot.
llauto *nm* (*Bol, Per*) headband.
llave *nf* (a) (*to door*) key; (*Tech*) key; — **de cambio** shift key; — **de contacto** (*Aut*) ignition key; — **espacial** spacing bar; — **maestra** skeleton key, master key; ¡**por las —s de San Pedro!** by heaven!; **bajo —, debajo de** — under lock and key; **cerrar una puerta con** — to lock a door; **echar la** — (a) to lock up; **tener las —s de la caja** (*fig*) to hold the purse strings.
(b) (*for gas, water etc*) tap, faucet (*US*); (*Elec*) switch; — **de bola**, — **de flotador** ballcock; — **de cierre** stopcock.
(c) (*Mech*) spanner; — **ajustable** adjustable spanner; — **inglesa** wrench, monkey wrench.
(d) (*Mus*) stop, key.
(e) (*Wrestling*) lock.
(f) (*of gun*) lock.
(g) (*Arg: Archit*) beam, joist.
(h) (*Mex: Taur*) —s horns.
llavero *nm* (a) key ring. (b) (*person: also* — **de cárcel**) turnkey.
llavín *nm* latchkey.
llegada *nf* arrival, coming.
llegar [1h] 1 *vt* to bring up, bring over, draw up.
2 *vi* (a) to arrive, come; — **a** to arrive at, reach; **por fin llegamos** we're here at last; **llegue** tell me when he comes; **cuando llegue eso** when that happens; **le llegó el año pasado** (*SAm*) he died last year.
(b) (*SAm*) to arrive, get to the top, triumph.
(c) (*of extent etc*) to reach; to be enough; (*of quantity, money etc*) to amount to, equal, be equal to; **esta cuerda no llega** this rope won't reach, this rope isn't long enough; **las personas no llegan a 100** the people don't amount to 100, the people are fewer than 100; **el importe llega a 50 pesos** the total is 50 pesos; **con ese dinero no va Vd a** — you won't have enough money; **el pobrecito no llega a Navidades** the poor chap won't last out (*or* live) till Christmas; **hacer** — **el dinero** to make one's money last out, eke out one's money; **hacer** — **el sueldo** to make both ends meet (*on one's salary*); **este libro no me llega** this book is no help (*or* use) to me.
(d) (*with following verb*) — **a** + *infin* to reach the point of + *ger*; to manage to + *infin*, succeed in + *ger*; **por fin llegó a hacerlo** he managed to do it eventually; **llegué a creerlo** I even believed it; — **a saber algo** to find something out; to get wind of something; **si llego a saberlo** if I had known it; — **a ser** + *adj or n* to become + *adj or n*; —**a**

ser el jefe to become the boss; **el país llegará a ser una nulidad** the country will become a nonentity.

3 llegarse *vr* to come near, draw near, approach; **llégate más a mí** come closer to me.

llenador *adj* (Arg, Chi) food filling, satisfying.

llenar [1a] **1** *vt* **(a)** to fill (de with); *surface etc* to cover (de with); *space, time etc* to fill, occupy, take up (de with); *form* to fill in, fill up, fill out (US).

(b) *duty etc* to fulfil; *wish* to satisfy; *requirements* to meet, satisfy.

(c) (fig) **— a uno de elogios** to heap praises on someone; **— a uno de insultos** to heap insults on someone, revile someone.

2 llenarse *vr* **(a)** to fill, fill up (de with); (fam) to stuff oneself (de with); **la superficie se llenó de polvo** the surface got covered in dust.

(b) (fig) to get cross, get annoyed.

llenazón *nm* (Mex) blown-out feeling, indigestion.

lleno 1 *adj* full (de of), filled (de with); full up; **— hasta el borde** brimful (de of); **estar — a reventar** to be full to bursting; **estar — de polvo** to be covered in dust; **estar — de sí mismo** to be full of oneself, be conceited; **de —** fully, entirely.

2 *nm* **(a)** abundance, plenty; perfection.

(b) (Theat) full house, sellout.

(c) (Astron) full moon.

llevadero *adj* bearable, tolerable.

llevar [1a] **1** *vt* **(a)** to carry, take, transport, convey; **¿me llevas esta carta?** will you take this letter for me?; **yo llevaba la maleta** I was carrying the case; **es muy pesado para —lo los dos** it's too heavy for the two of us to carry; **— adelante** *plan etc* to carry forward, go on with; **— a uno por delante** (SAm: Aut) to run someone over.

(b) *clothes etc* to wear; *small objects* to have, wear, carry (on one); *arms, name, title* to bear; **llevaba traje azul** he wore a blue suit; **llevaba puesto un sombrero raro** she had an odd hat on, she was wearing an odd hat; **no llevo dinero encima** (or **conmigo**) I have no money on me, I have no money about me; **lleva un rótulo que dice . . .** it has a label which says . . .; **el libro lleva el título de . . .** the book has the title of . . ., the book is entitled . . .; **el tren no lleva coche-comedor** the train has no dining car; **el avión no llevaba paracaídas** the plane had no parachutes, the plane was not carrying parachutes.

(c) (with personal object) to take (a to); to lead (a to); **este camino nos lleva a Bogotá** this road takes us to Bogotá; **le llevamos al teatro** we took him to the theatre; **— a uno de la mano** to lead someone by the hand; **¿adónde me llevan Vds?** where are you taking me?; **me llevaron de suplente** they took me along as a substitute.

(d) course, direction to follow, keep to; **¿qué dirección llevaba?** what direction was he going in?, what route was he following?

(e) to carry off, take away, cut off; **el viento llevó una rama** the wind carried a branch away; **la bala le llevó dos dedos** the shot cut off two of his fingers.

(f) prize etc to win, get, carry off; **llevó el primer premio** he carried off the first prize.

(g) price to charge; **¿cuánto me van a —?** what are you going to charge me?

(h) (Agr) to bear, produce; (Comm, Fin) to bear, carry; **no lleva fruto este año** it has no fruit this year; **los bonos llevan un 8 por cien de interés** the bonds bear interest at 8%.

(i) life to lead; **— una vida tranquila** to live a quiet life, lead a quiet life.

(j) to bear, stand, put up with; **— las desgracias con paciencia** to bear misfortunes patiently.

(k) (of time) to spend; **llevo 3 días aquí** I have been here for 3 days, I have so far spent 3 days here; **¿cuánto tiempo llevas aquí?** how long have you been here?; **el tren lleva una hora de retraso** the train is an hour late.

(l) (as v aux) **llevo 3 meses buscándolo** I have been looking for it for 3 months; **lleva conseguidas muchas victorias** he has won many victories; **llevo estudiados 3 capítulos** I have studied 3 chapters, I have covered 3 chapters; **llevaba hecha la mitad** he had done half of it.

(m) affair, negotiation etc to conduct, direct, manage; **— una finca** to manage an estate; **— los libros** (Comm) to keep the books; **— la casa** to run the house (see also **casa**).

(n) to exceed; **ella me lleva 2 años** she's 2 years older than I am; **él me lleva la cabeza** he's taller than me by a head; **les llevamos una gran ventaja** we have a great advantage over them.

(o) (Math) to carry.

(p) **— a uno a creer que . . .** to lead someone to think that . . .; **esto me lleva a pensar que . . .** this leads me to think that . . .

(q) (idioms) **la lleva hecha** he's got it all worked out; **llevo las de perder** I'm likely to lose, I'm in a bad way; **— lo mejor** to get the best of it; **— lo peor** to get the worst of it; **no las lleva todas consigo** he's not all there; **¡la que llevaba encima aquella noche!** (fam) how drunk he was that night!

2 *vi* (of road) to go, lead; **esta carretera lleva a La Paz** this road goes to La Paz.

3 llevarse *vr* **(a)** object, person to carry off, take away, remove; **se lo llevaron al cine** they took him off to the cinema; **se llevó mi máquina** he took my camera, he went off with my camera; **los ladrones se llevaron la caja** the thieves took the safe away; **¡que se lo lleve el diablo!** to hell with it!; **el pistolero se llevó 10.000 libras** the gunman got away with £10,000.

(b) **— bien** to get on well (together); **no se lleva bien con el jefe** he doesn't get on (or along) with the boss.

(c) **— a uno por delante** (SAm) to offend someone; to ride roughshod over someone.

llimo *adj* (Chi) small-eared; earless.

llocalla *nm* (Bol) boy.

lloquena *nf* (Bol, Per) fish spear, harpoon.

llora *nf* (Ven) funeral wake.

llorado *adj*: **el — rey** the (late) lamented king; **un hombre no —** an unlamented man.

llorar [1a] **1** *vt* to weep, weep for, cry about, to bewail, lament; loss, death to mourn.

2 *vi* **(a)** (of person) to cry, weep; **¡no llores!** don't cry!; **— a cuajo, — lágrima viva, — a moco y baba, — a moco tendido** to sob one's heart out, cry uncontrollably; **— como una fuente** (or **criatura** etc) to weep buckets.

(b) (of eyes) to water; (of tap etc) to drip.

(c) (Chi) to suit, be becoming, look nice (a on).

(d) (Per, PR, RPl) to be very unbecoming.

lloretas *nmf, pl* **lloretas** (Col, CR) crybaby.

lloriquear [1a] *vi* to snivel, whimper.

lloriqueo *nm* snivelling, whimpering.

llorisquear [1a] *vi* (PR, RPl) etc **=lloriquear** etc.

llorón 1 *adj* weeping, tearful; snivelling, whining; willow weeping.

2 *nm*, **llorona** *nf* tearful person, weepy sort; crybaby.

3 llorona *nf* (Mex) ghost, soul in torment.

4 lloronas *nfpl* (Col, RPl) large spurs.

lloroso *adj* weeping, tearful; sad.

llovedera *nf* (Col, Guat, Ven), **llovedero** *nm* (Arg) (period of) continuous rain.

llovedizo *adj* **(a)** roof leaky. **(b)** **agua llovediza** rain-water.

llover [2h] **(a)** *vi* to rain; **llueve, está lloviendo** it is raining; **— a cántaros, — a cubos, — a chuzos, — a mares, — a torrentes** to rain cats and dogs, rain in torrents; **como llovido (del cielo)** unexpectedly; **ser una cosa llovida del cielo** to come just right, be a godsend; **llueva o no** rain or shine, come what may; **mucho** (or **ya) ha llovido desde entonces** much water has flowed under the bridge since then; **¡como ahora llueve pepinos** (or **uvas)!** (Col) rubbish!; see **mojado**.

(b) (fig) to rain; **le llovieron regalos encima** gifts were rained on him, he was showered with gifts.

llovida *nf* (SAm) rain, shower.

llovido *nm* stowaway.

llovizna *nf* drizzle.

lloviznar [1a] **1** *vi* to drizzle. **2 lloviznarse** *vr* to get wet.

lloviznoso *adj* drizzly.

llueca *nf* broody hen.

lluqui *adj* (Ec) left-handed.

lluvia *nf* rain; shower; (as quantity) rainfall; (of insecticide etc) spray; (of missiles, bullets) hail, shower; (of watering can) rose; (Chi, RPl) shower, shower bath; (fig) shower, mass, abundance; **día de — rainy day; — fría, — menuda** fine rain, drizzle; **—s monzónicas** monsoon rains; **— de oro** (Bot) laburnum; **— radiactiva** radioactive fallout; **— torrencial** torrential rain; **una — de regalos** a shower of gifts; **la — cae sobre los buenos como sobre los malos** it rains on the just as well as on the unjust.

lluvioso *adj* rainy, wet.

M

maca[1] *nf* flaw, defect; spot; (*on fruit*) bruise, blemish, bad patch.
maca[2] *nf* (*Ant*) parrot.
macabí *nm* (a) (*Col*) shrewd person. (b) (*SD*) bandit.
macabro *adj* macabre.
macaco 1 *adj* (a) (*SAm*) deformed, misshapen; ugly. (b) (*PR*) silly.
2 *nm* (a) (*Zool*) macaque. (b) (*Ec, Mex, Pan, Per*) half-breed peasant; (*RPl: pej*) Brazilian. (c) (*Mex*) bogie. (d) (*interj: to child*) you rascal!; (*to person*) little man!
macadán *nm* macadam.
macadamizar [1f] *vt* to macadamize.
macagua *nf* (*SAm*) macaw.
macana *nf* (a) (*SAm*) club; cudgel, truncheon. (b) (*Bol, Chi, Pan, RPl*) absurdity, piece of nonsense, silly thing; doubtful thing; fib, falsehood; tale. (c) (*Arg*) bad job, botch. (d) (*Arg*) long boring conversation; ¡qué —! what a bind! (*sl*). (e) (*Cu*) de — undoubtedly; es de — que . . . of course . . .
macanazo *nm* (a) (*Ant*) blow (with a club). (b) (*Chi, RPl*) = **macana** (b); nuisance, bore.
macaneador (*RPl*) **1** *adj* deceitful; unreliable. **2** *nm*, **macaneadora** *nf* charlatan.
macanear [1a] **1** *vt* (a) (*Ant*) to beat, hit. (b) (*Col, Ven*) = **desbrozar; = rozar.** (c) (*Col, Ven*) *matter* to handle. **2** *vi* (a) (*Bol, Col, Chi, RPl, Ven*) to talk nonsense, say silly things; to exaggerate wildly, tell tall stories, fib. (b) (*Col, Hond*) to work hard.
macanero *adj* (*Bol, Chi, RPl*) given to talking nonsense, silly; given to telling tall stories.
macanudo *adj* (a) (*esp SAm*) smashing (*sl*), super (*fam*); first-rate; great (*fam*). (b) (*Chi*) big; overlarge, disproportionate. (c) (*Col, Ec*) strong, tough; *task* tough, difficult.
macaquear [1a] **1** *vt* (*CAm*) to steal. **2** *vi* (*Chi, RPl*) to make faces.
macarrón[1] *nm* (a) (*also* — **de almendras**) macaroon. (b) —**es** macaroni.
macarrón[2] *nm* (*Naut*) bulwark, stanchion.
macarrónico *adj* macaronic.
macarse [1g] *vr* (*fruit*) to get bruised, (begin to) rot.
macear [1a] **1** *vt* to hammer, pound. **2** *vi* = **machacar** 2.
maceración *nf* maceration; (*fig*) mortification.
macerar [1a] **1** *vt* to macerate; (*pej*) to mortify. **2** **macerarse** *vr* to macerate; (*fig*) to mortify oneself.
macero *nm* macebearer.
maceta 1 *adj* (a) (*Bol, Chi, RPl*) slow, sluggish; **ponerse** — to get old. (b) (*PR*) miserly.
2 *nf* (a) flowerpot; pot of flowers; (*Chi*) bouquet, bunch of flowers. (b) mallet, small hammer; stonecutter's hammer; (*RPl*) club, cudgel. (c) (*Mex*) head; **ser duro de** — (*Arg, Bol*) to be pretty thick.
macetero *nm* flowerpot stand (*or* holder); (*Arg, Chi, Per, PR*) flowerpot.
macetón *nm* tub (*for plants*).
macia *nf* = **macis**.
macicez *nf* massiveness; solidity; stoutness.
macilento *adj* wan, haggard; gaunt; emaciated.
macillo *nm* (*Mus*) hammer.
macis *nf* mace (*spice*).
macizamente *adj* massively; solidly; stoutly.

macizar [1f] *vt* to fill up, fill in, pack solid.
macizo 1 *adj* massive; *door, gold, tyre etc* solid; solidly made, stoutly made; *person* solid, stoutly built; **de roble** — of solid oak; — **de gente** solid with people.
2 *adv* (*CAm, Mex*) quickly, fast.
3 *nm* (a) mass; lump, chunk, solid piece. (b) (*Geog*) massif. (c) (*Hort*) bed, plot. (d) (*Aut*) solid tyre. (e) (*Archit*) stretch, section (of a wall).
macolla *nf* bunch, cluster.
macro . . . macro . . .
macró *nm* (*Per, RPl: gall*) pimp.
macrocosmo *nm* macrocosm.
macuco 1 *adj* (a) (*Arg, Chi, Per, Ven*) crafty, cunning. (b) (*Ec*) old, useless. (c) (*Arg, Bol, Col, Chi, Ven*) big, great; overgrown.
2 *nm* (*Arg, Bol, Col*) overgrown boy, big lad.
macuenco *adj* (a) (*Cu, PR*) thin, weak, feeble. (b) (*SD*) useless. (c) (*Col*) big; overgrown, extra large; (*fig*) splendid, terrific (*fam*).
mácula *nf* (a) (*mostly fig*) stain, spot, blemish; (*Anat*) blind spot; — **solar** sunspot. (b) trick, fraud.
macular [1a] *vt* to stain, spot.
macundales *nmpl* (*Col, Ven*), **macundos** *nmpl* (*Ven*) things, gear (*fam*), junk.
macuteno *nm* (*Mex*) pickpocket.
macuto *nm* (a) knapsack; satchel. (b) (*Cu, SD, Ven*) begging basket.
macha *nf* (*Bol, Per, SD*) mannish woman.
machaca 1 *nf* crusher, pounder. **2** *nmf* (*person*) pest, bore.
machacadora *nf* crusher, pounder.
machacar [1g] **1** *vt* (a) to crush, pound; to grind (up); to mash. (b) (*fig*) *object* to knock to bits; *enemy* to maul, crush; (*in argument*) to crush, flatten, make mincemeat of; *price* to slash.
2 *vi* (a) to go on, keep on; to nag; — **en un asunto** to keep on about a matter, harp on a matter; ¡no machaques! don't go on so!, stop harping on it!; *see* **hierro.** (b) (*Univ etc*) to swot (*fam*).
3 machacarse *vr* (*fam*): — **el verano** to spend the summer swotting (*fam*).
machacón 1 *adj* tiresome, wearisome; insistent; monotonous; **con insistencia machacona** with wearisome insistence.
2 *nm*, **machacona** *nf* pest, bore.
machado *nm* hatchet.
machamartillo: a — *adv*: **creer a** — to believe firmly, (*pej*) to believe blindly; **cumplir a** — to carry out a task to the letter, perform a task down to the last detail; **eran cristianos a** — they were absolutely convinced Christians.
machango *adj* (a) (*Cu*) coarse, rough. (b) (*Chi*) stupid; annoying, tedious.
machaquear [1a] *vti* (*Mex*) = **machacar.**
machaqueo *nm* crushing, pounding.
machaquería *nf* tiresomeness; insistence, harping (on a subject); monotony.
macharse [1a] *vr* (*Arg, Bol, Ec*) to get drunk.
machetazo *nm* (*SAm*) (a) large *machete*. (b) blow (*or* slash) with a *machete*.
machete *nm* (*SAm*) *machete*, cane knife, big knife.
machetear [1a] **1** *vt* (a) (*SAm*) *cane etc* to cut down with a *machete*; *person* to slash (*or* wound, stab *etc*) with a *machete*. (b) (*Col*) to sell cheap.
2 *vi* (a) (*Col, Mex*) to insist, be stubborn. (b) (*Mex*) to work; (*of student*) to plod on.

machetero nm (a) (SAm: Agr) cane cutter.
(b) (Mex) slave, drudge.
(c) (Ant) revolutionary; — **de salón** armchair radical.
(d) (Mex) plodding student.
(e) (Ven) soldier.
machi nm, **machí** nm (SAm) medicine man.
machiega nf queen bee.
machihembrado nm (Carp) dovetail (joint).
machihembrar [1a] vt to dovetail.
machina nf (a) crane, derrick; pile driver. (b) (PR) merry-go-round.
machirulo nm tomboy; mannish woman.
macho 1 adj (a) (Bio) male; **la flor** — the male flower.
(b) (fig) masculine; strong, tough; **es muy** — he's very tough.
(c) (Mech) male.
(d) (fam) stupid.
(e) (Col) big, huge, splendid, terrific (fam).
2 nm (a) (Bio) male; (Zool) mule; — **cabrío** he-goat, billy-goat; — **de varas** leading mule; (fig) person in charge.
(b) (Mech) pin, peg; (Elec) pin; plug; (Sew) hook.
(c) (Tech) sledgehammer.
(d) (Archit) buttress.
(e) (fig: person) tough guy (US fam), he-man (fam); **pej** idiot.
(f) (SAm) **parar el** — **a uno** to restrain someone; to take the wind out of someone's sails.
machón nm buttress.
machona nf (Bol, Ec, PR, RPl) mannish woman; tomboy.
machota nf (a) mannish woman. (b) (Tech) hammer, mallet; rammer. (c) **a la** — (Col, Cu) carelessly; (CAm) rudely, roughly.
machote nm (a) (fam) tough guy (US fam), he-man (fam). (b) (SAm) rough draft, sketch; model; pattern. (c) (Mex) blank form.
machucar [1g] vt (a) to pound, crush; to beat; to dent; to knock about, damage.
(b) (Med) to bruise.
(c) (Col, Mex, PR) horse to tire out (before a race).
(d) (Cu) clothes to wash badly.
machucón nm (SAm) bruise.
machucho adj (a) elderly, getting on in years. (b) prudent; sedate; wise beyond one's years. (c) (Col, Mex) cunning, sly, shrewd.
madama nf (Bol, Per, RPl) madame, brothel keeper.
madeja nf (of wool) skein, hank; (of hair) mass, mop; — **de nervios** bundle of nerves; **se está enredando la** — the affair is getting complicated, the plot thickens.
Madera Madeira.
madera[1] nm Madeira (wine).
madera[2] nf (a) wood; — (**de construcción** etc) timber; (una —) piece of wood; — **contrachapada,** — **laminada** plywood; — **de deriva** driftwood; — **dura** hardwood; — **fósil** lignite; **de** — wood, wooden; **¡toca** —! touch wood!
(b) (Zool) horny part (of hoof).
(c) (fig) nature, temperament; aptitude; **tiene buena** — there's a lot (of good) in him, he's made of solid stuff; **tiene** — **de futbolista** he'll make a footballer, he's got football in him.
maderable adj: **árbol** — tree useful for its wood; **bosque** — wood containing useful timber.
maderaje nm, **maderamen** nm timber, wood; woodwork, timbering.
maderero nm timber merchant; lumberman.
madero nm (a) beam; log; (piece of) timber. (b) (fig) ship, vessel. (c) (fam) oaf, blockhead.
Madona f Madonna.
madrastra nf stepmother; (fig) unloving mother.
madre 1 adj (a) mother; **buque** — mother ship; **lengua** — parent language; **acequia** — main channel; **alcantarilla** — main sewer, principal sewer.
(b) (SAm) tremendous (fam), terrific (fam); **una regañada** — a tremendous dressing-down, the father and mother of a telling-off.
2 nf (a) mother; (in orphanage etc) matron; — **adoptiva** foster mother; — **política** mother-in-law; **M— de Dios** Mother of God; **¡M— de Dios!** good heavens!; **futura** — expectant mother; **su señora** — your mother; **sin** — motherless; **¡— mía!** well!; oh dear!; **ahí está la** — **del cordero** that's just the trouble.
(b) the word enters into a number of very strong insults which have no equivalents in English, eg **¡la —!, ¡tu —!; mentar la** — **a uno** to insult someone violently.

(c) (fig: of civilization etc) origin, cradle.
(d) (games) **la** — home.
(e) (Anat) womb.
(f) (of river) bed; **sacar de** — **a uno** to provoke someone, upset someone; **salirse de** — (river) to overflow, burst its banks; (person) to lose all self-control; (process etc) to go beyond its normal limits.
(g) (of wine etc) dregs, lees; sediment.
(h) (Agr) main channel, main irrigation ditch; (Tech) main sewer.
(i) (Col) dead skin, scab.
madrejón nm (Agr) watercourse.
madreperla nf mother-of-pearl; — **de río** freshwater mussel.
madreselva nf honeysuckle.
madrigal nm madrigal.
madriguera nf (a) (Zool) den; burrow. (b) (fig) den.
madrileño 1 adj of Madrid; **madrileñísimo** typical of Madrid, full of the character of Madrid; **la madrileñísima Cibeles** Cibeles Square which is so typical of Madrid, Cibeles Square which sums up so much of Madrid.
2 nm, **madrileña** nf native (or inhabitant) of Madrid; **los** —**s** the people of Madrid.
Madriles mpl: **Los** — (fam) Madrid.
madrina nf (a) godmother; (of enterprise etc) patron(ess), protectress; — **de boda** (approx) bridesmaid.
(b) (Archit etc) prop, shore; (Tech) brace.
(c) (Agr) leading mare.
(d) (SAm) tame animal (used in breaking in or catching others).
madroño nm strawberry tree, arbutus.
madrugada nf early morning; dawn, daybreak; **levantarse de** — to get up early; **a las 4 de la** — at 4 o'clock in the morning, at 4 a.m.
madrugador 1 adj early rising, who gets up early.
2 nm, **madrugadora** nf early riser; (fig) early bird.
madrugar [1h] **1** vt (Arg, Mex) — **a uno** to forestall someone, get in ahead of someone.
2 vi (a) to get up early; to be an early riser; **a quien madruga, Dios le ayuda** God helps those who help themselves.
(b) (fig) to get ahead; to get in first (in replying etc); (Sport) to jump the gun.
madrugón nm: **darse** (or **pegarse**) **un** — to get up terribly early.
maduración nf ripening; maturing.
madurar [1a] **1** vt (a) fruit to ripen.
(b) (fig) to mature; person to mature; to toughen (up); plan etc to think out.
2 vi (a) fruit to ripen.
(b) (fig) to mature.
3 madurarse vr to ripen.
madurez nf (a) ripeness. (b) (fig) maturity; mellowness; sageness, wisdom.
maduro 1 adj (a) fruit ripe; **poco** — unripe, underripe.
(b) (fig) mature; mellow; **de edad madura** middle-aged; **la cosa está madura para la reforma** the business is ripe for reform; **el divieso está** — the boil is about to burst.
2 nm (SAm) (ripe) banana.
maesa nf queen bee.
maestra nf (a) teacher (also fig); — **de escuela** schoolteacher. (b) (Ent) queen bee. (c) (Archit) guide line.
maestranza nf (a) arsenal, armoury; (Naut) naval dockyard. (b) staff of an arsenal (or dockyard). (c) (SAm) machine shop.
maestrazgo nm (Hist) office of grand master.
maestre nm (Hist) grand master (of a military order).
maestrear [1a] vt (a) to direct, manage. (b) (Agr) to prune.
maestría nf mastery; skill, expertise; **lo hizo con** — he did it very skilfully, he did it in a masterly fashion.
maestro 1 adj (a) masterly; skilled, expert.
(b) (Tech) main, principal; master (attr); **cloaca maestra** main sewer; **llave maestra** skeleton key, master key; **obra maestra** masterpiece; **viga maestra** main beam.
(c) (Ent) **abeja maestra** queen bee.
(d) animal trained; **halcón** — trained hawk.
2 nm (a) (in general) master; teacher; authority; — (**de escuela**) schoolteacher; (Tech) master craftsman; **el** — **de todos los medievalistas españoles** the greatest authority among the Spanish medievalists; **beber en los grandes** —**s** to absorb wisdom from the great teachers.
(b) (in apposition) master . . .; — **albañil** mason, skilled building craftsman; — **sastre** master tailor; **"Los** —**s cantores"** "The Mastersingers".

(c) (*Mus*) maestro; **el — Falla** the great musician (*or* composer) Falla.

(d) **— de armas, — de esgrima** fencing master; **— de ceremonias** master of ceremonies; **— de cocina** chef; **— de coros** choirmaster; **— de maquillaje** make-up expert; **— de obras** master builder; foreman.

(e) (*SAm*) skilled workman, craftsman; **— de caminos** skilled road-construction man.

mafioso *nm* (*Per, RPl*) mafioso, member of the Mafia.

Magallanes *m* Magellan.

magancear [1a] *vi* (*Col, Chi*) to idle, loaf.

magancia *nf* (*Chi*) villainy.

maganciero *adj* (*Chi*) villainous.

maganto *adj* (a) wan, wasted. (b) worried; lifeless, dull.

maganza *nf* (*Col, Ec*) idleness.

maga(n)zón *nm* (*SAm*) lazy person, idler, loafer.

Magdalena *f* Magdalen, Madeleine.

magenta *nf* magenta.

magia *nf* magic; **— negra** black magic; **por arte de —** (as if) by magic.

magiar 1 *adj* Magyar. 2 *nmf* Magyar.

mágico 1 *adj* magic, magical. 2 *nm* magician.

magín *nm* (*fam*) fancy, imagination; mind; **todo eso salió de su —** it all came out of his own head.

magisterio *nm* (a) teaching; teaching profession; **dedicarse al —** to go in for teaching; **ejerció el — durante 40 años** he taught for 40 years.

(b) teachers (*collectively*).

(c) (*fig*) pompousness, pedantry.

magistrado *nm* magistrate; judge.

magistral 1 *adj* (a) magisterial. (b) (*fig*) masterly. (c) pompous, pedantic. 2 *nm* wall clock.

magistratura *nf* magistracy; judgeship.

magnánimamente *adv* magnanimously.

magnanimidad *nf* magnanimity.

magnánimo *adj* magnanimous.

magnate *nm* magnate; tycoon; (*Hist*) baron; **los —s de la industria** the top people in industry, the big industrialists; **— de la prensa** press baron, press lord.

magnavoz *nm* (*Mex*) loudspeaker.

magnesia *nf* magnesia.

magnesio *nm* (*Chem*) magnesium; (*Phot*) flash, flashlight.

magnéticamente *adv* magnetically.

magnético *adj* magnetic.

magnetismo *nm* magnetism.

magnetizar [1f] *vt* to magnetize.

magneto *nf* magneto.

magnetofón *nm*, **magnetófono** *nm* tape recorder.

magnetofónico *adj* tape (*attr*), recording (*attr*); **cinta magnetofónica** recording tape.

magnicidio *nm* assassination (of an important person).

magníficamente *adv* splendidly, wonderfully, superbly, magnificently.

magnificar [1g] *vt* to praise, extol.

magnificencia *nf* (a) splendour, magnificence. (b) lavishness, generosity.

magnífico *adj* splendid, wonderful, superb, magnificent; **¡—!** splendid!, that's grand!; **es un muchacho —** he's a fine boy; **tenemos un — profesor** we have a splendid teacher.

magnitud *nf* magnitude (*also Astron*); **de primera —** (*Astron*) of the first magnitude.

magnolia *nf* magnolia.

mago *nm* magician, wizard; **los Reyes Magos** the Magi, the Three Wise Men.

magra *nf* (a) lean part (*of meat*). (b) slice; rasher. (c) **¡—!** (*fam*) rubbish!, not on your nelly! (*fam*).

magrez *nf* leanness.

magro *adj* (a) *person* thin, lean. (b) *meat* lean. (c) *land* poor, thin.

magrura *nf* leanness.

magua *nf* (*Ant, Ven*) disappointment; failure, setback.

maguarse [1i] *vr* (*Cu, PR, Ven*) (a) (*party etc*) to be a failure, be spoiled. (b) (*person*) to suffer a disappointment; to get depressed.

maguey *nm* (*Bot*) maguey.

maguillo *nm* wild apple tree.

magulladura *nf* bruise.

magullar [1a] *vt* to bruise; to hurt, damage; to batter, bash (*fam*); (*Per, PR*) to crumple, rumple.

magullón *nm* (*SAm*) bruise.

Maguncia Mainz.

maharajá *nm* maharajah.

Mahoma *m* Mahomet.

mahometanismo *nm* Mahommedanism.

mahometano 1 *adj* Mahommedan. 2 *nm*, **mahometana** *nf* Mahommedan.

maicena *nf* (*SAm*) cornflour, corn starch (*US*).

maicero *adj* maize (*attr*), corn (*attr: US*).

maitines *nmpl* matins.

maíz *nm* maize, corn (*US*), sweet corn, Indian corn; **— en la mazorca** corn on the cob.

maizal *nm* maize field, cornfield (*US*).

maja *nf* woman (*or* girl) of the people, low-class woman (*esp of Madrid*).

majada *nf* (a) sheepfold. (b) dung. (c) (*Chi, RPl*) (flock of) sheep, goats.

majaderear [1a] *vt* (*SAm*) to bother, annoy.

majadería *nf* (a) silliness; absurdity. (b) (**una —**) silly thing, absurdity; **—s** nonsense.

majadero 1 *adj* silly, stupid; rotten (*fam*), lousy (*fam*), caddish.

2 *nm* (a) idiot, fool; **— rotter**, villain, cad; **¡—!** you idiot!

(b) (*Tech*) pestle.

(c) (*Sew*) bobbin.

majador *nm* pestle.

majagranzas *adj etc* = **majadero**.

majar [1a] *vt* (a) to pound, crush, grind; to mash; (*Med*) to bruise. (b) (*fam*) to bother, pester.

majareta *adj* (*fam*) cracked, potty (*fam*).

majestad *nf* majesty; stateliness; **Su M—** His (*or* Her) Majesty; **M—, Vuestra M—** Your Majesty.

majestuosamente *adv* majestically.

majestuosidad *nf* majesty, stateliness.

majestuoso *adj* majestic, stately, imposing.

majo 1 *adj* (a) nice; pretty, attractive, handsome; lovely.

(b) smart, natty; (*pej*) flashy, gaudy.

2 *nm* (a) toff (*fam*), masher (*fam*), sport (*esp from the lower classes of Madrid, 19th century*); (*pej*) flashy sort.

(b) (*pej*) lout, bully; **echársela de —** to brag, give oneself airs.

mal 1 *adv* (a) badly; poorly; wrongly; hardly, with difficulty; **¡—!** that's bad!, oh dear!; **lo hace muy —** he does it very badly; **hace — en + infin** he is wrong to **+ infin**, he is mistaken in **+ ger**, it is unwise of him to **+ infin**; **oigo —** I don't hear well, I have difficulty in hearing; **ahora veo bastante —** my sight is rather weak now; **huele —** it smells bad; **sabe —** it tastes nasty; **estar —** to be ill; **sentirse —** to feel ill, feel bad; **está muy — escrito** it's very badly written; **lo hice lo menos — que pude** I did it as well as I could; **me entendió —** he misunderstood me; **pero digo —** but I am wrong to say . . .; **— puedo hablar yo de este asunto** I can hardly talk about this matter, I'm hardly the right person to talk about this.

(b) (*idioms*) **— que bien** willy-nilly; rightly or wrongly; **hacer algo — que bien** to do something somehow; **ir de — en peor** to go from bad to worse, get worse; **¡menos —!** that's a relief!; **menos — que . . .** it's just as well that . . ., it's a good job that . . .

2 *conj* **— que le pese** however much he resents it, even though he hates the idea.

3 *adj* (*apocopated form before m sing noun*) see **malo.**

4 *nm* (a) (*in general*) evil, wrong; **el bien y el —** good and evil, right and wrong; **caer en el —** to fall into evil ways; **combatir el —** to fight against evil; **echar algo a —** to despise something; to waste something, squander something; **el — está en que . . .** the trouble is . . .; **estar a — con uno** to be on bad terms with someone; **no hay — que por bien no venga** it's an ill wind that blows nobody any good; it may be a blessing in disguise; **parar en — to come** to a bad end.

(b) harm, hurt, damage; misfortune; **no le deseo ningún —** I don't wish him any harm (*or* ill); **hacer — a uno** to do someone harm; **ya está hecho el —** the harm is done now; **no hay ningún —** there's no harm done; **¡— haya quien . . .!** a curse on whoever . . .!; **decir — de uno** to speak ill of someone, slander someone; **llevar** (*or* **tomar**) **algo a —** to take something amiss, be offended about something.

(c) (*Med*) disease, illness; (*fig*) suffering; **—es** (*fig*) ills; **— caduco** epilepsy; **— francés** (*Hist*) syphilis; **— de mar** seasickness; **— de ojo** evil eye; **— de la tierra** homesickness; **los —es de la economía** the things that are wrong with the economy; **dar — a uno** to make someone suffer; **darse — to** torment oneself.

(d) (*Med: SAm*) epileptic fit.

mala¹ *nf* (*Ec*) bad luck.

mala² *nf* (*Post*) mailbag; mail, post.

malabar *adj*: **juegos —es** juggling.

malabarismo nm (a) juggling, conjuring. (b) —s (fig) juggling; balancing act.

malabarista nmf juggler, conjurer.

Malaca f Malaya.

malacate nm winch, capstan; (Guat, Mex) spindle.

malaconsejado adj ill-advised.

malacostumbrado adj (a) having bad habits, vicious. (b) spoiled, pampered.

malacostumbrar [1a] vt (CAm): — a uno to get someone into bad habits.

malacrianza nf (SAm) =malcriadez.

malagradecido adj ungrateful.

malagueño 1 adj of Málaga. 2 nm, **malagueña** nf native (or inhabitant) of Málaga; los —s the people of Málaga.

malamente adj badly; poorly; wrongly; **estar** — **de dinero** to be badly off for money; **tenemos gasolina** — **para** + infin we hardly have enough petrol to + infin.

malandante adj unfortunate.

malandanza nf misfortune.

malandrín nm, **malandrina** nf (arch or hum) scoundrel, rogue.

malanga 1 adj (Cu, PR) incompetent. 2 nf (Ant, CAm, Mex) tuber resembling a sweet potato.

malapata nmf (fam) pest, nuisance; tedious individual; clumsy sort.

malaria nf malaria.

Malasia f Malaysia.

malasombra nmf (fam) =**malapata**.

malavenido adj: estar —s to be in disagreement, be in conflict.

malaventura nf misfortune.

malaventurado adj unfortunate.

malaya interj (SAm) damn!

Malaya f Malaya.

malayo 1 adj Malay(an). 2 nm, **malaya** nf Malay. 3 nm (language) Malay.

Malaysia f Malaysia.

malbaratar [1a] vt (Comm) to sell off cheap, sell at a loss; (fig) to squander.

malcarado adj ugly, repulsive; fierce-looking, cross-looking.

malcasado adj unhappily married; errant, unfaithful.

malcasarse [1a] vr to make an unhappy marriage.

malcomer [2a] vi to have a poor meal, eat badly.

malcontento 1 adj discontented. 2 nm, **malcontenta** nf malcontent.

malcriadez nf (SAm) bad breeding, lack of breeding.

malcriado adj rude, bad-mannered, coarse.

malcriar [1c] vt child to spoil, pamper.

maldad nf (a) evil, wickedness. (b) (una —) wicked thing.

maldecir [approx 3p] 1 vt (a) to curse.
(b) to loathe, detest.
2 vi: — de (a) to speak ill of; to slander; to disparage, run down.
(b) to curse, complain bitterly of.

maldiciente 1 adj that speaks ill of everything, forever criticizing; foul-mouthed. 2 nmf grumbler, complainer; malcontent; slanderer.

maldición nf curse; ¡—! curse it!, damn!; **parece que ha caído una** — **sobre este programa** there seems to be a curse on this programme.

maldispuesto adj ill-disposed; (Med) ill, indisposed.

maldita nf (a) tongue; **soltar la** — to talk too much; to explode angrily, blow up (fam). (b) (Cu, PR) sore, swelling; (PR, Ven) insect bite.

maldito 1 adj (a) damned (also Eccl), accursed.
(b) damned; ¡— sea! damn it!; ese — niño that wretched child, that blessed child; ese — libro that damned book; — lo que me importa I don't care a damn; no le hace — el caso he doesn't take a blind bit of notice; no le encuentro maldita la gracia I don't find it in the least amusing; no sabe maldita la cosa de ello he knows damn-all about it.
(c) wicked.
(d) (Mex) crafty.
2 nm (a) el — the devil.
(b) (Theat) extra.

maleabilidad nf malleability.

maleable adj malleable.

maleante 1 adj wicked; villainous, rascally; unsavoury. 2 nmf malefactor, unsavoury character, suspicious person; vagrant.

malear [1a] 1 vt to damage, spoil, harm; land to sour; (fig) to corrupt, pervert. 2 **malearse** vr to spoil, be harmed; to be corrupted.

malecón nm pier, jetty, mole.

maledicencia nf slander, scandal.

maleficiar [1b] vt (a) to bewitch, cast an evil spell on. (b) to harm, damage.

maleficio nm curse, spell; witchcraft.

maléfico adj harmful, damaging, evil.

malejo adj (fam) rather bad, pretty bad.

malentendido nm misunderstanding; **tiene que haber algún** — there must be some misunderstanding.

malestar nm (a) (Med) discomfort; indisposition. (b) (fig) uneasiness, malaise; (Pol etc) unrest.

maleta[1] adj (a) (CAm, Mex, Per, PR) naughty; mischievous; wicked. (b) (Chi, RPl) stupid; useless. (c) (Chi, RPl) sly. (d) (Arg, Mex) lazy.

maleta[2] 1 nf (a) case, suitcase; travelling bag; **hacer la** —, **hacer las** —s to pack (up); **ya puede preparar la** — he's on his way out, the skids are under him (fam).
(b) (Aut) boot, trunk (US).
(c) (Arg, Chi, Guat) saddlebag.
(d) (CAm, Col, Chi, Ec) bundle of clothes.
(e) (Col, Cu, PR: Anat) hump.
2 nm (fam) bungler, clumsy novice; (Taur) clumsy bullfighter; (Sport) poor player, rabbit (fam); (Theat) ham (sl).

maletera nf (a) (Col, Mex) saddlebag. (b) (Per: Aut) boot, trunk (US).

maletero nm (a) (Aut) boot, trunk (US). (b) (person) porter.

maletín nm small case, bag; satchel; — de excursiones picnic case; — de grupa (Mil) saddlebag.

maletón adj (Col) hunchbacked.

maletudo (Col, Cu, Ec, Per) 1 adj hunchbacked. 2 nm hunchback.

malevaje nm (Bol, RPl) malefactors (collectively), underworld.

malevo nm (Bol, RPl) malefactor.

malevolencia nf malevolence, malice, spite, ill will; **por** — out of spite; **sin** — **para nadie** with malice toward none.

malévolo adj malevolent, malicious, spiteful.

maleza nf (a) (Agr) weeds. (b) scrub; undergrowth; brushwood; thicket. (c) (Arg, Chi: Med) pus.

malezal nm (a) (Arg, Chi, PR) mass of weeds. (b) (Chi: Med) pus.

malformación nf malformation.

malgastador 1 adj spendthrift, thriftless, wasteful. 2 nm spendthrift.

malgastar [1a] vt money, resources to waste, squander; effort, time to waste; health to ruin.

malgeniado adj, **malgenio(so)** adj (SAm) bad-tempered.

malhablado adj coarse, rude; foul-mouthed.

malhadado adj ill-fated, ill-starred.

malhaya interj (SAm) damn!

malhecho nm misdeed.

malhechor nm, **malhechora** nf malefactor, criminal, wrongdoer.

malhumorado adj bad-tempered, cross, peevish.

malicia nf (a) wickedness.
(b) evil intention; spite, malice, maliciousness; **lo dijo sin** — he said it without any evil intention.
(c) (of animal) viciousness, vicious nature; (of child etc) mischief, mischievous nature.
(d) (of look, joke etc) roguishness, naughtiness, provocative nature; **contó un chiste con mucha** — he told a very naughty story; **el niño tiene demasiada** — **para su edad** the kid is too knowing for his age.
(e) slyness, guile.
(f) —s suspicions; **tengo mis** —s I have my suspicions.

maliciarse [1b] vr to suspect, have one's suspicions; **ya me lo maliciaba** I thought as much, it's just what I suspected.

maliciosamente adv (a) wickedly. (b) spitefully, maliciously. (c) viciously; mischievously. (d) roguishly, naughtily, provocatively. (e) slyly.

malicioso adj (a) wicked, evil.
(b) ill-intentioned; spiteful, malicious.
(c) vicious; mischievous.
(d) roguish, naughty, provocative; **una mirada maliciosa** a roguish look, a provocative glance.
(e) sly, crafty.

malignidad nf (a) (Med) malignancy. (b) evil nature, viciousness; harmfulness; malice.

maligno 1 adj (a) (Med) malignant; pernicious. (b) person evil, vicious; influence evil, pernicious, harmful; remark, attitude malicious. 2 nm: el — the devil.

malintencionado adj ill-disposed, hostile, unkind; malicious.

malísimamente adv very badly, dreadfully, appallingly.

malísimo adj very bad, dreadful, appalling.

malmandado *adj* disobedient; obstinate, bloody-minded (*sl*).

malmirado *adj* **(a) estar —** to be disliked. **(b)** thoughtless, inconsiderate.

malmodado *adj* (*Cu, Mex*) rude, rough.

malnutrido *adj* undernourished.

malo 1 *adj* (**mal** *before m sing noun*) **(a)** (*in most senses*) bad; poor; wretched, dreadful; *smell etc* bad, nasty, unpleasant; *jewel* false; *tooth, finger etc* bad, sore; *child* bad, naughty, disobedient; **este papel es — para escribir** this paper is bad for writing; **ir por mal camino** to be on the wrong road; **¡no seas —!** don't be naughty!, behave yourself!; that's a wicked thing to say!

(b) (*Med*) **estar —** to be ill; **sentirse —** to feel ill, feel bad; **ponerse — de risa** to die of laughing.

(c) es muy — de vencer he's very hard to beat; **es un animal — de domesticar** it's a difficult animal to tame.

(d) (*idioms*) **¡—!** oh dear!, that's bad!; **lo — es que . . .** the trouble is that . .; **a la mala** if the worst comes to the worst; (*Cu, Per, PR*) by force, forcibly; (*Chi, Mex, PR*) treacherously; **andar a malas con uno** to be on bad terms with someone; **los dos se pusieron a malas** the two fell out; **ponerse a malas con uno** to fall foul of someone, get on the wrong side of someone; **estar de malas** to be out of luck; to be in a bad mood; **venir de malas** to have evil intentions; **por las malas** by force, willy-nilly.

2 *nm* **(a)** (*Rel*) **el —** the devil.

(b) (*Theat*) villain.

3 mala *nf* spell of bad luck.

maloca *nf* **(a)** (*Chi, RPl: Hist*) Indian raid. **(b)** (*Bol, Col*) village of uncivilized Indians.

malogrado *adj* **(a)** *plan etc* abortive; ill-fated; *effort etc* wasted. **(b)** *person* who died before his time, who died early; **el — ministro** the late-lamented minister.

malograr [1a] **1** *vt* to spoil, upset, ruin; *chance, time* to waste.

2 malograrse *vr* **(a)** (*plan etc*) to fail, miscarry, come to grief.

(b) (*person*) to die before one's time, die early, come to an untimely end.

malogro *nm* **(a)** failure; waste. **(b)** early death, untimely end.

maloliente *adj* stinking, smelly.

malón *nm* (*Chi, RPl*) **(a)** (*Hist*) Indian raid. **(b)** rowdy party. **(c)** dirty trick, bad turn.

malparado *adj*: **salir —** to come off badly; **salir — de** to get the worst of.

malparar [1a] *vt* to damage; to harm, impair, wreck; *person* to ill-treat.

malparir [3a] *vt* to have a miscarriage.

malparto *nm* miscarriage.

malpensado *adj* nasty, evil-minded; **¡no seas —!** don't be nasty!, don't be so horrid! (*fam*).

malquerencia *nf* dislike.

malquistar [1a] **1** *vt*: **— a dos personas** to cause a rift between two people, set one person against another; **— a A con B** to set A against B.

2 malquistarse *vr* **(a)** (*person*) **— con uno** to incur the dislike of someone, become estranged from someone.

(b) (*2 persons*) to fall out, become estranged.

malquisto *adj*: **estar —** to be disliked, be unpopular; **los dos están —s** the two are estranged.

malsano *adj* **(a)** *climate, atmosphere etc* unhealthy, bad. **(b)** (*Med*) *mind* sickly, morbid.

malsín *nm* slanderer; informer, talebearer.

malsonante *adj* *word* nasty, rude, offensive.

malsufrido *adj* impatient.

Malta *f* Malta.

malta *nf* malt.

maltés 1 *adj* Maltese. **2** *nm*, **maltesa** *nf* Maltese. **3** *nm* (*language*) Maltese.

maltón *nm*, **maltoncillo** *nm* (*SAm*) young animal; child.

maltraer [2p] *vt* **(a)** to insult, abuse. **(b)** to ill-treat.

maltraído *adj* (*Arg, Bol, Chi, Per*) shabby, untidy.

maltratamiento *nm* = **maltrato**.

maltratar [1a] *vt* **(a)** to ill-treat, maltreat; to handle roughly, knock about, damage. **(b)** (*also — de palabra*) to abuse, insult.

maltrato *nm* **(a)** ill treatment, maltreatment; rough handling, damage. **(b)** abuse, insults.

maltrecho *adj* battered, damaged; injured; **dejar — a uno** to leave someone in a bad way.

malucho *adj* (*Med: fam*) poorly, under the weather.

malura *nf* (*Chi*) pain, discomfort; indisposition; **— de estómago** stomach ache.

malva *nf* mallow; **— loca, — real, — rósea** holly-

hock; **(de) color de —** mauve; **ser como una —** to be very meek and mild.

malvado 1 *adj* evil, wicked, villainous. **2** *nm* villain.

malvarrosa *nf* hollyhock.

malvavisco *nm* (*Bot*) marshmallow.

malvender [2a] *vt* to sell off cheap, sell at a loss.

malversación *nf* embezzlement, misappropriation.

malversador *nm* embezzler.

malversar [1a] *vt* to embezzle, misappropriate.

Malvinas: Islas *fpl* — Falkland Isles.

malviviente *nmf* (*Mex*) = **maleante**.

malvón *nm* (*Mex, RPl*) geranium.

malla *nf* **(a)** mesh; network; **— de alambre** wire mesh, wire netting; **hacer —** to knit.

(b) (*Sport*) **las —s** the net.

(c) (*Hist*) chain mail.

(d) (*Theat etc*) **—s** tights.

mallo *nm* mallet.

Mallorca *f* Majorca.

mallorquín 1 *adj* Majorcan. **2** *nm*, **mallorquina** *nf* Majorcan. **3** *nm* (dialect of *Catalán*) Majorcan.

mama *nf* mammary gland; breast; udder.

mamá *nf* **(a)** (*fam*) mummy (*fam*), mum (*fam*), mamma (*mainly US*), mom (*US*).

(b) (*CAm, Mex etc*) mother; **futura —** expectant mother, mother-to-be.

mamada *nf* **(a)** suck; milk; feeding time. **(b)** (*SAm*) cinch (*sl*); soft job, plum, sinecure; bargain. **(c)** (*RPl*) drunkenness.

mamadera *nf* (*Ant, Arg, CAm*) rubber teat; (*SAm*) feeding bottle.

mamado *adj* **(a)** (*SAm*) drunk. **(b)** (*Cu, PR*) silly, stupid.

mamagrande *nf* (*Arg, Mex, Par*) grandmother.

mamaíta *nf* (*fam*) = **mamá** (**a**).

mamalón *adj* (*Ant, Ven*) idle; sponging (*fam*).

mamamama *nf* (*Per*) grandmother.

mamandurria *nf* (*SAm*) = **mamada** (**b**).

mamantear [1a] *vt* (*CAm, Cu, PR*) **(a)** to nurse, feed, suckle. **(b)** (*fig*) to spoil, pamper.

mamar [1a] **1** *vt* **(a)** *breast, milk* to suck.

(b) (*fig*) to absorb, assimilate; to acquire in infancy.

(c) (*fam*) *food* to wolf, bolt; *resources etc* to milk, suck dry; *funds* to pocket (illegally); **¡cómo la mamamos!** this is the life!, we never had it so good!

2 *vi* to suck; **dar de —** a to feed, suckle.

3 mamarse *vr* **(a)** *advantage, post etc* to wangle (*fam*), fiddle (*fam*); *to land, manage* to get.

(b) **— un susto** to give oneself a scare.

(c) **— a uno** to get the best of someone; (*Col, Chi, Mex*) to cheat someone; (*Pan*) to do someone in (*sl*).

(d) (*esp SAm*) to get tight.

(e) (*Col*) to go back on one's word.

mamario *adj* mammary.

mamarracha *nf*, **mamarracho** *nm* grotesque object, ridiculous sight; mess, botch; (*person*) sight, object, scarecrow; (*Art*) daub; **ella estaba hecha una —** she looked a complete mess.

mamá-señora *nf* (*Arg, Col, Cu, Nic, Par*) grandmother.

mameluca *nf* (*Chi*) whore.

mameluco *nm* **(a)** (*Hist*) Mameluke. **(b)** (*SAm*) Brazilian mestizo, half-breed. **(c)** (*fam*) chump (*fam*), idiot. **(d)** (*SAm: also —s*) rompers; overalls.

mamey *nm* (*SAm*) mamey, mammee.

mamífero 1 *adj* mammalian, mammal (*attr*). **2** *nm* mammal.

Mammón *m* (*Bib*) Mammon (*also fig*).

mamola *nf* chuck under the chin; **dar** (*or* **hacer**) **la — a uno** to chuck someone under the chin; (*fig*) **to make a sucker out of someone** (*sl*).

mamón 1 *adj* small, baby, suckling.

2 *nm* **(a)** small baby, baby still at the breast.

(b) (*Bot*) sucker, shoot.

(c) (*Bol, RPl*) papaya tree (*or* fruit).

(d) (*Arg, Mex, Par*) suck.

(e) (*Guat, Hond*) club, stick.

(f) (*Mex*) soft spongecake.

(g) (*Cu*) tobacco from the second crop.

mamonear [1a] *vt* **(a)** (*Guat, Hond*) to beat. **(b)** (*SD*) to postpone; *time* to waste.

mamotreto *nm* **(a)** hefty tome, whacking great book (*fam*). **(b)** (*Arg, Mex*) = **armatoste**. **(c)** (*PR, SD*) shapeless object.

mampara *nf* screen; partition.

mamparo *nm* (*Naut*) bulkhead.

mamplora *nf* (*CAm*) queer (*fam*).

mamporro *nm* (*fam*) bash (*fam*), punch, clout; (*on falling*) bump; **atizar un — a uno** to give someone a swipe; **liarse a —s con uno** to come to blows with someone.

mampostería nf masonry; rubblework.
mampuesto nm (a) rough stone. (b) wall, parapet. (c) (SAm) rest (used in aiming a gun). (d) de — spare, emergency (attr), extra.
mamut nm mammoth.
mana nf (a) (CAm, Col) spring, fountain. (b) (SAm) =maná.
maná nm manna.
manada nf (a) (Zool) herd, flock; (of wolves) pack; (of lions) pride. (b) (fam) crowd, mob; a —s, en — in a mob; in crowds.
manadero nm shepherd, herdsman, drover.
manager ['manaʒer] nm, pl **managers** ['manaʒer] (Sport, Theat) manager.
manantial 1 adj: agua — running water, flowing water. 2 nm (a) spring, fountain; agua de — spring water. (b) (fig) source, origin; cause.
manantío adj running, flowing.
manar [1a] 1 vt to run with, flow with; — sangre to run with blood.
2 vi (a) (of liquid) to run, flow (de from, en with); to pour out, stream, gush forth; to well up.
(b) (fig) to abound, be plentiful; — de to spring from, flow from; — en to flow with, abound in.
manare nm (Col, Ven) wicker basket; sieve.
manatí nm manatee.
manaza nf (a) great big hand; dirty hand. (b) ser un —s to be clumsy.
manazo nm punch, slap.
mancar [1g] vt (a) to maim, cripple. (b) (Arg) — el tiro to miss.
mancarrón nm (a) (Arg, Urug) worn-out horse, nag. (b) (Arg, Chi, Per) disabled workman. (c) (Chi, Per) small dam.
manceba nf whore; lover, mistress.
mancebía nf brothel.
mancebo nm (a) youth, young man. (b) bachelor. (c) (Comm) clerk; (Pharm) assistant, dispenser.
mancera nf plough handle.
mancilla nf stain, blemish; sin — unblemished, (Rel) immaculate, pure.
mancillar [1a] vt honour to stain, sully.
manco 1 adj (a) one-handed, one-armed; armless; crippled, maimed, disabled; — de la izquierda with a maimed left hand, lacking a left hand.
(b) (fig) defective, faulty.
(c) no ser — to be useful, be active; (fam) to be light-fingered, have thievish propensities; to be quite unscrupulous; A, jugador que tampoco es — A, who is a pretty useful player; no ser — en not to be backward in, not be lacking in skill (etc) in.
2 nm, manca nf (a) cripple, disabled person; one-armed person, one-handed person.
(b) (Chi) old horse, nag.
mancomún: de — adv, also **mancomunadamente** adv jointly, conjointly, together; by common consent; obrar de mancomún con uno to act jointly with someone.
mancomunar [1a] 1 vt persons to unite, associate, bring together; interests to combine; resources to pool; (Law) to make jointly responsible.
2 mancomunarse vr to unite, merge, combine, join together.
mancomunidad nf union, association; pool; community; (Pol) commonwealth; (Law) joint responsibility; la M— Británica the British Commonwealth.
mancornar [1m] vt (a) bull to seize by the horns; to hobble. (b) (fig) to join, couple.
mancornas nfpl (SAm), **mancuernas** nfpl (Mex), **mancuernillas** nfpl (CAm, Mex) cufflinks.
mancha nf (a) (Zool etc) spot, mark; speckle; (on pattern) spot, fleck; (of dirt) spot, stain, mark; (of ink etc) blot, smudge; (Med) spot; bruise, mark; (of vegetation etc) patch, small area; (Art) shading, shaded area; — solar sunspot; —s del sarampión measles spots.
(b) (fig) stain, stigma; blemish, blot; sin — unblemished.
(c) (Col, PR) cloud, swarm (of locusts etc).
manchado adj skin spotty; animal spotted; dappled; bird speckled; pied; paper etc smudged, smudgy, covered with smudges (etc); un abrigo — de barro a coat stained (or bespattered) with mud.
manchar [1a] 1 vt (a) to spot, mark; to soil, dirty, stain; to smudge.
(b) (fig) honour etc to stain, sully; person to soil; — a otro to smear someone else's reputation.
2 mancharse vr (a) to get dirty.
(b) (fig) to stain one's reputation; to dirty one's hands, soil oneself.

manchego 1 adj of La Mancha. 2 nm, manchega nf native (or inhabitant) of La Mancha; los —s the people of La Mancha.
manchón[1] nm large stain, big spot (etc); patch; (Bot) patch of dense vegetation.
manchón[2] nm (Arg, Chi) muff.
Manchuria f Manchuria.
manchuriano 1 adj Manchurian. 2 nm, manchuriana nf Manchurian.
manda nf (a) bequest. (b) (SAm) religious vow.
mandadero nm messenger; errand boy, office boy.
mandado nm order; commission, errand, job; muchacho de —s errand boy, office boy; hacer los —s, ir a los —s to run errands.
mandamiento nm (a) order, command.
(b) (Law) writ; warrant; — de entrada y registro search warrant; — judicial warrant; — de venir summons.
(c) (Eccl) commandment; los diez —s the Ten Commandments.
mandar [1a] 1 vt (a) to order; — que . . . to order that . . ., give orders that . . .; — a uno hacer algo to order someone to do something; — hacer un traje to order a suit, have a suit made; — reparar el coche to get (or have) the car repaired; — llamar a uno to send for someone; — salir a uno to order someone out; mándele sentarse please ask him to take a seat.
(b) (Comm) to order, ask for; ¿qué manda Vd? what can I do for you?; ¿manda Vd algo más? is there anything else?
(c) (Mil etc) to lead, command; group to be in charge of, lead, be the leader of; country to rule (over).
(d) to send; le manda muchos recuerdos he sends you warmest regards; se lo mandaremos por correo we'll send it to you by post, we'll post it to you.
(e) to bequeath.
(f) (SAm) to throw, hurl; to throw away.
(g) (SAm) blow to give, strike, fetch; person to hit, punch.
2 vi (a) to be in charge, be in command; to be in control; ¿quién manda aquí? who's in charge here?; aquí mando yo I give the orders here, I'm the boss.
(b) to give the orders; ¡mande Vd! at your service!; ¿mande? pardon?, what did you say?; — por uno to send for someone, fetch someone.
(c) (pej) to be bossy, boss people about.
3 mandarse vr (a) (Med) to get about by oneself, manage unaided.
(b) (Archit: of rooms) to communicate (con with).
(c) (Ant, Chi) to go away, slip away; to disappear secretly.
(d) (SAm) — algo to eat something up.
(e) (Arg: Mus) — una sinfonía to play (or perform) a symphony.
(f) (SAm) mándese entrar please come in; — cambiar, — mudar to go away, leave; to get out; — con uno to be rude to someone, be bossy to someone.
mandarín nm (a) mandarin; (pej) petty bureaucrat, jack-in-office. (b) (SAm) domineering person, bossy individual.
mandarina nf (a) (Bot) tangerine, mandarin (orange). (b) (language) Mandarin.
mandarino nm mandarin (orange) tree.
mandatario nm (a) (Law) agent, attorney. (b) (SAm: Pol) leader.
mandato nm (a) order; (Law) writ, warrant; — judicial (search) warrant; — de prisión warrant of arrest.
(b) (Law) power of attorney.
(c) (Pol) mandate; territorio bajo — mandated territory.
(d) (Pol) term (of office); durante su — during his term of office.
(e) (Eccl) maundy.
(f) (Post) — internacional international money order.
mandíbula nf jaw (also Tech), mandible; reírse a — batiente to laugh one's head off.
mandil nm (a) (leather) apron; (woman's) pinafore dress. (b) (Arg, Chi) horse blanket.
mandilón nm (fam) coward.
mandinga 1 adj (a) (CAm, RPl) effeminate. (b) (Arg, Ven) impish, mischievous. 2 nm (a) (SAm) devil; goblin; evil spirit. (b) (Col, Ec, Per, PR) Negro.
mandioca nf cassava, tapioca, manioc.
mando nm (a) command; rule; control; authority; leadership; alto — high command; un oficial al — de un pelotón an officer in command of a squad; un

pelotón al — de un oficial a squad under the command of (or led by) an officer; **ejercer el** —, **estar al** —, **tener el** — to be in command, be in control; **entregar el** — to hand over command (or control).

(b) (in race) lead; **tomar el** — to take the lead.

(c) —s (persons) leaders, leadership, top people.

(d) (Mech) drive; — **a la izquierda** left-hand drive.

(e) (Mech) control; — **a distancia**, — **remoto** remote control; — **por botón** push-button control; **palanca de** — control lever.

(f) (Radio, Tech etc) —s controls.

(g) (Pol etc) term of office.

mandoble nm **(a)** two-handed blow, blow struck with two hands. **(b)** large sword, broadsword. **(c)** (fam) ticking-off.

mandolina nf mandolin(e).

mandón 1 adj bossy, domineering. **2** nm (Arg) mine foreman; (Chi: Racing) starter.

mandrágora nf mandrake.

mandria 1 adj worthless. **2** nm useless individual.

mandril[1] nm (Zool) mandrill.

mandril[2] nm (Tech) mandrel.

manducar [1g] vt (fam) to scoff (fam), stuff oneself with.

manea nf hobble.

maneador nm (Mex, RPl) hobble; (Arg) whip; (Mex) halter.

manear [1a] **1** vt to hobble. **2 manearse** vr (Col, Mex) to trip over one's own feet.

manecilla nf **(a)** (Tech) pointer, hand; (of watch) hand; — **grande** minute hand; — **pequeña** hour hand. **(b)** (of book) clasp.

maneco adj (Arg, Mex, PR) maimed; with deformed hands (or feet); knock-kneed.

manejable adj manageable; tool etc handy, easy to use; aircraft etc manoeuvrable.

manejador nm, **manejadora** nf (Mex: Aut) driver, motorist.

manejar [1a] **1** vt **(a)** language, tool, horse etc to handle; machine to run, work, operate; house etc to run, manage.

(b) person to manage; **ella maneja a su marido** she manages her husband, she bosses her husband about.

(c) (SAm: Aut) to drive.

2 vi **(a)** " — **con cuidado**" "handle with care".

(b) (SAm) to drive.

3 manejarse vr **(a)** to act, behave.

(b) to manage; **se maneja bien con los chiquillos** she manages all right with the kids; **¿cómo te manejas para hacer eso?** how do you manage to do that?, how do you set about doing that?; **ya se manejarán** they'll manage, they'll find a way.

(c) (Med) to get about unaided.

manejo nm **(a)** handling; running, working, operation; management; — **a distancia** remote control; — **doméstico**, — **de la casa** housekeeping, running the house; **una casa de fácil** — an easily-run house, a house which is easy to run; **llevar todo el** — **de** to be in sole charge of.

(b) confidence, ease of manner; savoir-faire, shrewdness; **no tiene bastante** — he's not sufficiently wide-awake.

(c) address, quickness, speed of action; **hay que ver el** — **que tiene la chica** you should see how quick the girl is.

(d) (pej) intrigue; stratagem; shady deal; —s **turbios** intrigues, underhand dealing.

(e) (SAm: Aut) driving.

manera nf **(a)** way, manner, fashion; — **de obrar** way of going about things; conduct; — **de ser** way of life; manner (of person); **no me gusta su** — **de ser** I don't like his manner; **hay varias** —s **de hacerlo** there are various ways of doing it; **no hay** — there's no solution, there's nothing one can do; **no hay** — **con él** he's hopeless; **no hay** — **de** + infin there's no way of + ger; **no había** — **de persuadirle** there was no convincing him; **¡qué** — **de** + infin!, **¡vaya una** — **de** + infin!** what a way to + infin!

(b) (phrases with prep) **a la** — **de** in the manner of, after the fashion of; **siguen arando a la** — **de los abuelos** they still plough as their grandfathers did; **a mi** — **de ver** in my view, as I see it; **de esta** — (in) this way, like this; **¡llovía de una** —! it just was raining!, you should have seen how it rained!; **de la** — **que sea** in whatever way you (etc) like; however he (etc) does it; **la pegó de mala** — he hit her really hard; **le han estafado de mala** — they really have cheated him, they've properly done him down; **de la misma** — in the same way; **de otra** — otherwise, if not; **de ninguna** — by no means; **¡de ninguna** —!

certainly not!, never!; **de tal** — **que . . .** in such a way that . . .; to such a degree that . . .; **de** — **que . . .** so that . . .; **¿de** — **que esto no le gusta?** so you don't like it?; **de todas** —s at any rate; **en cierta** — up to a point, to some degree; **en gran** — in great measure; greatly, extremely; **sobre** — exceedingly; for other phrases, compare **modo** (a) and (b).

(c) (lit) kind, sort; **es otra** — **de afirmación** it is another kind of affirmation; it is another method of saying yes; **que es otra** — **de valentía** which is another kind of courage.

(d) (Art, Lit etc) manner, style; **la segunda** — **de Picasso** Picasso's second manner; **las dos** —s **de Góngora** the two styles of Góngora.

(e) —s (of person) manners; **de** —s **muy groseras** with very rude manners; **se lo dije con buenas** —s I told him politely; **tener** —s (SAm) to have good manners, show breeding.

maneto adj (Col, Guat, Hond, PR) = **maneco**.

manflor(ita) nm (SAm) pansy (fam), queer (fam).

manga nf **(a)** sleeve; — **de camisa** shirtsleeve; **estar en** —s **de camisa** to be in one's shirtsleeves; **sin** —s sleeveless; **estar de** — to be in league; **ser de** — **ancha, tener** — **ancha** to be easy-going, be over-indulgent, be too lenient; to be broad-minded; (pej) to be not overscrupulous; **andar** — **por hombro** to be terribly poor; **pegar las** —s (sl) to kick the bucket (sl).

(b) (also — **de riego**) hose, hosepipe; — **de incendios** fire hose.

(c) (Cook) filter, strainer.

(d) (Aer) windsock, windgauge.

(e) portmanteau.

(f) (Meteorol) cloudburst; — **marina** waterspout; — **de viento** whirlwind.

(g) (Naut) beam, breadth.

(h) (Bridge) game; **ir a** — to go to game.

(i) (SAm) crowd, mob, swarm.

(j) (SAm: Agr) funnel, narrow entrance (to a corral etc).

(k) (CAm) poncho, coarse blanket.

(l) (Col) pasture.

mangal nm (SAm) = **manglar**.

mangana nf lasso, lariat.

manganear [1a] vt **(a)** to lasso. **(b)** (Per) to bother, annoy. **(c)** (Guat, Urug) to pillage, plunder; to steal.

manganeso nm manganese.

manganeta nf (SAm), **manganilla** nf (Mex) disappearing trick; (fig) swindle, dodge, racket.

mangante 1 adj brazen. **2** nm beggar, scrounger (fam); brazen individual.

mangar [1h] **1** vt **(a)** to plug in, fit together.

(b) (fam) to swipe (sl), pinch (fam).

(c) (fam) to beg (for), scrounge (fam).

2 vi (Arg) to live by scrounging (fam), live on graft.

mangazón adj (SAm) lazy.

manglar nm mangrove swamp.

mangle nm mangrove.

mango[1] nm (Bot) mango.

mango[2] nm handle, haft; — **de escoba** broomstick, (Aer: fam) joystick; — **de pluma** penholder.

mangón nm (Arg, Bol, Col) pasture; cattle ranch.

mangoneador nm **(a)** meddler, interfering sort; bossy individual. **(b)** (SAm) corrupt official, grafter.

mangonear [1a] **1** vt **(a)** person to manage, boss about.

(b) (fam) to swipe (sl), pinch (fam).

(c) (SAm) to pillage, plunder.

2 vi **(a)** to meddle, interfere (en in); to dabble (en in).

(b) to boss people about; to take charge and insist on doing everything oneself; to thrust oneself brazenly forward.

(c) (SAm) to graft, be on the fiddle (fam).

mangoneón, mangonero 1 adj meddlesome, interfering; bossy; brazen. **2** nm busybody; bossy individual; brazen sort.

mangosta nf mongoose.

manguear [1a] **1** vt (Arg, Chi, Mex) cattle to drive; game to beat, put up.

2 vi **(a)** (Col, PR, Ven) to pretend to be working. **(b)** (Ant, Ven) to beckon.

manguera nf **(a)** hose, hosepipe; pipe, tube; — **de aspiración** suction pump; — **de incendios** fire hose.

(b) (Col) bicycle tyre.

(c) (Meteorol) waterspout.

(d) (Chi, RPl) corral, yard.

manguillo nm (Mex) penholder.

manguito nm **(a)** muff. **(b)** (Tech) sleeve; coupling; — **incandescente** gas mantle.

maní nm, pl **maníes** or **manises (a)** (SAm) peanut; groundnut plant. **(b)** (Cu, PR: fam) dough (sl), money. **(c)** (RPl) **¡—!** never!

manía *nf* (a) (*Med*) mania; **— de grandezas** megalomania; **— persecutoria** persecution mania.
(b) (*fig*) mania; rage, craze (*de* for); whim, fad; peculiarity, oddity; **la — del fútbol** the soccer craze; **la — de la minifalda** the fashion for miniskirts; **tiene —s** she's rather odd, she has her little ways; **tiene la — de + infin** she has the (odd) habit of + *ger*; **ha dado en la — de salir sin abrigo** she's taken to going out without a coat.
(c) (*pej*) dislike; spite, ill will; **tener — a uno** to dislike someone; **el maestro me tiene —** the teacher has got it in for me; **tiene — a los eslobodos** he can't stand the Slobodians.

maniabierto *adj* (*PR, SD*) lavish, generous.

maníaco 1 *adj* maniac(al). **2** *nm*, **maníaca** *nf* maniac; **— sexual** sex maniac.

maniacodepresivo 1 *adj* manic-depressive. **2** *nm*, **maniacodepresiva** *nf* manic-depressive.

maniatar [1a] *vt person* to tie the hands of; to handcuff; *animal* to hobble.

maniático 1 *adj* (a) maniacal.
(b) (*fig*) crazy; odd, eccentric, peculiar; cranky.
(c) stubborn.
2 *nm*, **maniática** *nf* (a) maniac.
(b) (*fig*) maniac; odd individual, eccentric, crank.

manicero *nm* (*SAm*) peanut seller.

manicomio *nm* lunatic asylum, mental hospital.

manicura *nf* manicure.

manicuro *nm*, **manicura** *nf* manicurist.

manida *nf* lair, den.

manido *adj* (a) *meat* high, gamy; smelly. (b) *subject etc* trite, stale.

manierismo *nm* (*Art, Lit*) mannerism.

manierista 1 *adj* mannerist. **2** *nmf* mannerist.

manifestación *nf* (a) (*of emotion etc*) manifestation; show; sign; **una gran — de entusiasmo** a great show of enthusiasm.
(b) (*of policy etc*) statement, declaration.
(c) (*Pol*) demonstration; mass meeting; riot.

manifestante *nmf* demonstrator; rioter.

manifestar [1k] **1** *vt* (a) *emotion etc* to show, manifest, demonstrate, reveal.
(b) *policy etc* to state, declare; to express.
2 manifestarse *vr* (a) (*emotion etc*) to show, be manifest; to become apparent; **— en** to be evident in (*or* from), be revealed by, be shown by.
(b) (*Pol*) to demonstrate; to hold a mass meeting; to riot.

manifiesto 1 *adj* clear, manifest; evident, obvious; *error* glaring, obvious; *truth* manifest; **poner algo de —** to make something clear; to disclose something, reveal something; **quiero poner de — que . . .** I wish to state that . . .; **quedar —** to be plain, be clear.
2 *nm* (a) (*Naut*) manifest.
(b) (*Pol*) manifesto.

manigua *nf* (*Ant, Mex*) swampy scrubland, jungle; (*fig*) countryside; **irse a la —** to take to the hills (in revolt).

manigual *nm* (*Ant*) = **manigua**.

manigueta *nf* (a) handle, haft; crank; (*RPl: Aut*) starting handle. (b) hobble.

manija *nf* (a) handle. (b) (*Mech*) clamp, collar; (*Rail*) coupling. (c) (*Agr*) hobble.

manilargo *adj* (a) open-handed. (b) (*SAm*) light-fingered, thievish.

manilense 1 *adj* of Manila. **2** *nmf* native (*or* inhabitant) of Manila; **los —s** the people of Manila.

manileño = **manilense**.

manilla *nf* (a) bracelet; **—s (de hierro)** handcuffs, manacles. (b) (*of watch*) hand.

manillar *nm* handlebar(s).

maniobra *nf* (a) (*act*) handling; manoeuvring; operation, control; (*Rail*) shunting; **hacer —s** to manoeuvre; (*Rail*) to shunt.
(b) (*Naut*) seamanship, (art of) navigation; handling.
(c) (*Naut*) gear, rigging.
(d) **—s** (*Mil*) manoeuvres.
(e) (*fig*) manoeuvre, move; (*pej*) trick, stratagem; **mediante una hábil —** by a clever move; **es una — para expulsar al jefe** it's a manoeuvre to get rid of the chief.

maniobrabilidad *nf* manoeuvrability; handling qualities.

maniobrable *adj* manoeuvrable; easy to handle.

maniobrar [1a] **1** *vt* to handle, operate; to manoeuvre; (*Rail*) to shunt. **2** *vi* to manoeuvre (*also fig*).

maniota *nf* hobble.

manipulación *nf* manipulation.

manipulador 1 *nm*, **manipuladora** *nf* manipulator; handler. **2** *nm* (*Elec, Tel*) key, tapper.

manipular [1a] **1** *vt* to manipulate; to handle. **2** *vi*: **— con, — en** to manipulate.

maniquí 1 *nm* (a) (tailor's) dummy, manikin; (*Fencing etc*) dummy figure. (b) (*fig*) puppet. **2** *nf* mannequin, model.

manirroto 1 *adj* lavish, extravagant, prodigal. **2** *nm* spendthrift.

manisero *nm* (*SAm*) = **manicero**.

manita *nf* little hand; **—s de cerdo** (*etc*) trotters; **—s de plata** (*or* **de oro**) delicate hands, artistic hands, talented hands; **echar una — a uno** to lend someone a hand; **hacer —s** (*of lovers*) to hold hands (*con* with).

manito[1] *nm* (*SAm*) = **hermanito (hermano)**; (*in direct address*) mate (*fam*), chum.

manito[2] *nm* (*SAm*) = **manita**.

manivacío *adj* empty-handed.

manivela *nf* crank; **— de arranque** starting handle.

manjar *nm* (tasty) dish, special dish; **— blanco** blancmange; **— delicado, — exquisito** tasty morsel; **— espiritual** food for the mind, spiritual sustenance.

mano[1] *nf* (a) (*Anat*) hand; (*Zool*) foot, forefoot, paw; (*elephant's*) trunk; (*of bird*) foot, (*of hawk*) claws, talons.
(b) (*in fig phrases, mostly*) hand; **— derecha** (*fig*) right-hand man; **—s muertas** (*Law*) mortmain; **— de santo** sure remedy; **última —** final touch, finishing touch; **¡—s a la obra!** to work!, let's get on with it!; **¡—s quietas!** hands off!, keep your hands to yourself!; **¡qué —!** (*SAm*) what luck!; what a surprise!; how ghastly! (*fam*), how horrid! (*fam*).
(c) (*phrases with prep*) **a —** by hand; **bordado a —** hand-embroidered; **hecho a —** handmade; **escribir a —** to write in longhand, write out; **girar una manivela a —** to turn a crank by hand; **mandar algo a —** to send something by hand; **estar a (la) —** to be at hand, be on hand, be handy; to be within one's grasp; **¡eso está a la —!** that's obvious!; **a — airada** violently; **robo a — armada** armed robbery; **a — salva** without risk; **estar** (*or* **quedar**) **a —** (*SAm*) to be quits, be even; **a —s llenas** lavishly, generously; **dirigir una carta a —s de uno** to send a letter care of (*c/o*) someone; **morir a —s de** to die at the hands of; **llegó a mis —s** it reached me, it came into my hands; **llegar a las —s** to come to blows; **si a — viene** when it comes to the point; yet; **¡arriba las —s!** hands up!; **bajo —** in secret, behind the scenes; in an underhand way; **coger a uno con las —s en la masa** to catch someone red-handed, catch someone in the act; **de — hand** (*attr*), *eg* **equipaje de —** hand-luggage; **los dos iban de la —** the two were walking hand-in-hand; **llevar a uno de la —** to lead someone by the hand; **de buena —** on good authority; **de primera —** (at) first-hand; **de segunda —** (at) secondhand; **de —s de** at the hands of; **recibir algo de —s de uno** to receive something from someone; **de —s a boca** unexpectedly, suddenly; **vivir de la — a la boca** to live from hand to mouth; **dar de — a** to stop working; **darse de —s con uno** to come across someone; **dejar a una —** to abandon someone; **no pude dejar el libro de la —** I couldn't put the book down; **ponerse de —s** (*horse*) to rear (up); **en —s de** in the hands of, into the hands of; **ha hecho cuanto ha estado en su —** he has done all in his power (*para* + *infin* to + *infin*); **traer un asunto entre —s** to have a matter in hand; **to have a matter on one's hands**; **¡fuera las —s!** hands off!, keep your hands to yourself!; **ganar por la — a uno** to beat someone to it; **tomarse la justicia por su —** to take justice into one's own hands; **estar — sobre —** to be idle, be out of work.
(d) (*phrases with verb*) **alzar la — a** (*or* **contra**) to raise one's hand against; **cargar la —** to overdo it; to press too hard, be too exacting; (*Comm*) to overcharge; (*Cook*) to put too much spice (*etc*) in; **darse las —s** to join hands; to shake hands; **déle la — y se tomará el pie** give him an inch and he'll take a yard; **echar una —** to lend a hand (*a* to); **echar — a** to lay hands on; **echar — de** to make use of; to resort to; **estrechar la — a uno** to shake someone's hand; **hacerse la —, hacerse las —s** to get one's hand in; **se le fue la —** his hand slipped (*also fig*); **meter — a uno** to bring someone to book; **meter — a una** to make a pass at a girl; **no hay quien le meta —** there's nobody to touch him; **pasar la — a uno** (*SAm*) to flatter someone, suck up to someone (*fam*); **sentar la — a uno** to beat someone, (*fig*) to bring someone to heel; (*Comm*) to overcharge someone; **tener buena —** to be lucky; to have the knack; **tener mala —** to be clumsy, be awkward; **tener — con** to have a way with; **tener — para** to be clever

at; **tener las —s largas** to be light-fingered; **untar la — a uno** to grease someone's palm; **¡venga esa —!** shake!, put it there!

(e) (*Sport*) handling, handball; **¡—!** handball!

(f) (*of watch*) hand.

(g) (*of paint*) coat; (*of soap*) wash, soaping; **dar una — de jabón a la ropa** to give the clothes a soaping.

(h) (*Cards etc*) hand; round; game; **echar una — de mus** to have a game (*or* hand) of *mus*; **ser —, tener la —** to lead; **soy —** it's my lead.

(i) (*Mus*) scale.

(j) **— de almirez** pestle.

(k) lot, series; (*CAm, Chi, Ec, Mex*) group of 5 (*or* 4, 6) things of the same kind; (*SAm: of bananas*) bunch, hand; **una — de bofetadas** a series of punches; **una — de papel** a quire of paper.

(l) **— de obra** labour, manpower; labour force; **— de obra especializada** skilled labour.

(m) **—s** (*fig*) hands, workmen; **contratar —s** to sign up workmen.

(n) (*SAm*) misfortune, mishap; unexpected event.

mano² *nm* (*SAm*)=**hermano**; (*in direct address*) mate (*fam*), chum.

manojo *nm* handful, bunch; (*fam*) bunch; (*Cu, PR*) bundle of raw tobacco (*about 2 lbs*); **— de hierba** tuft of grass; **— de llaves** bunch of keys; **— de pillos** bunch of rogues.

manoletina *nf* (*Taur*) a kind of pass with the cape.

Manolo *m* pet name for **Manuel**.

manolo *nm* toff (*fam*), masher (*fam*) (*esp Madrid equivalent of cockney*).

manómetro *nm* (*pressure*) gauge; **— de aceite** oil gauge; **— de combustible** fuel gauge.

manopla *nf* **(a)** flannel, face flannel. **(b)** (*Hist, Tech etc*) gauntlet. **(c)** (*Chi, PR*) knuckleduster.

manoseado *adj* (*fig*) hackneyed, well-worn.

manosear [1a] *vt* **(a)** to handle, finger, touch; to rumple, mess up; to paw; to fiddle with, mess about with; (*SAm*) to caress, fondle, feel (*sexually*).

(b) theme etc to overwork, repeat.

manoseo *nm* **(a)** handling, fingering, touching; rumpling; pawing; (*SAm*) caressing, fondling. **(b)** overworking, repetition.

manotada *nf* **(a)** slap, smack. **(b)** (*Col, Chi, Mex*) handful, fistful.

manotazo *nm* slap, smack.

manoteador *nm* (*Arg, Mex*) **(a)** bag-snatcher. **(b)** gesticulator.

manotear [1a] **1** *vt* to slap, smack, cuff. **2** *vi* to gesticulate, move (*or* use) one's hands.

manoteo *nm* gesticulation.

manque *conj* (*SAm: fam*)=**aunque**.

manquear [1a] *vi* to be maimed, be crippled; to pretend to be crippled; (*Mex, RPl*) to limp.

manquedad *nf*, **manquera** *nf* **(a)** disablement, crippled state, bodily incapacity. **(b)** (*fig*) defect.

mansalino *adj* (*Chi*) huge; extraordinary.

mansalva: a — without risk, without any danger; **le dispararon a —** they shot him with complete certainty of hitting him; **estar a — de** to be safe from.

mansamente *adv* gently, mildly, meekly.

mansarda *nf* (*Arg, Chi, Mex*) attic.

mansedumbre *nf* **(a)** gentleness, meekness. **(b)** tameness.

mansión *nf* (*esp SAm: angl*) mansion.

manso *adj* **(a)** gentle, mild, meek. **(b)** animal tame.

manta *nf* **(a)** blanket; shawl; **— eléctrica** electric blanket; **— de viaje** travelling rug; **a — (de Dios)** plentifully, abundantly; **liarse la — a la cabeza** to decide to go the whole hog; to press on regardless; **tirar de la —** to let the cat out of the bag, give the game away.

(b) (*Col, Mex, Ven*) coarse cotton cloth; (*Chi, Ec*) poncho.

(c) (*fam*) hiding.

mantear [1a] *vt* **(a)** to toss in a blanket. **(b)** (*Arg, PR*) to ill-treat, abuse. **(c)** (*Mex, PR*) to set on, beat up.

manteca *nf* **(a)** (*animal*) fat; (*SAm*) butter; **— de cacahuete** peanut butter; **— de cacao** cocoa butter; **— de cerdo** lard; **— de vaca** butter; **— vegetal** vegetable fat.

(b) (*Col*) servant, girl.

mantecado *nm* (*approx*) ice cream.

mantecón *nm* (*fam*) milksop, mollycoddle.

mantecoso *adj* fat, greasy; lardy; buttery.

mantel *nm* tablecloth; (*Eccl*) altar cloth; **levantar los —es** to clear the table; **poner los —es** to lay the table.

mantelería *nf* table linen.

mantelillo *nm* table runner.

mantención *nf* (*SAm*)=**manutención**.

mantenedor *nm* (*of contest*) chairman, president; **— de la familia** breadwinner.

mantener [2l] **1** *vt* **(a)** (*Archit, Tech etc*) to hold up, support; **— algo en equilibrio** to keep something balanced.

(b) idea, opinion to support, defend, maintain; person to sustain, support.

(c) fire etc to keep in, keep going; (*of food*) to sustain; **le mantiene la esperanza** he is sustained by hope, hope keeps him going.

(d) (*Fin*) to maintain, support.

(e) (*Mech etc*) to maintain, service.

(f) custom, discipline, relations etc to keep up, maintain.

(g) **— + adj** to keep + adj; **— la comida caliente** to keep the food hot; "**Mantenga limpia España**" "Keep Spain clean".

2 mantenerse *vr* **(a)** **se mantiene todavía en pie** it is still standing.

(b) **— firme** to hold one's ground, not give way; **— en vigor** to stand, remain in force; **— en un puesto** to stay in one's job, keep one's post; **— en contacto con** to keep up one's contacts with.

(c) to sustain oneself, subsist, keep going (*con, de* on); **se mantiene con leche** she keeps going on milk.

mantenido *nm* (*Guat, Mex*) pimp; kept man, gigolo; sponger (*fam*), parasite.

mantenimiento *nm* maintenance; upkeep; support, sustenance.

mantequera *nf* **(a)** churn. **(b)** butter dish.

mantequería *nf* dairy, creamery; grocer's (*shop*).

mantequilla *nf* butter.

mantequillera *nf* (*SAm*) butter dish.

mantilla *nf* **(a)** mantilla; **— de blonda, — de encajes** lace mantilla.

(b) **—s** baby clothes; **estar en —s** (*person*) to be terribly innocent; (*plan*) to be in the very early stages, be in its infancy; **dejar a uno en —s** to leave someone helpless.

mantillo *nm* humus, mould.

mantillón *nm* (*CAm, Mex*) coloured horse blanket.

mantis *nf, pl* **mantis** mantis; **— religiosa** praying mantis.

manto *nm* **(a)** cloak; (*Eccl, Law etc*) robe, gown.

(b) (*Zool*) mantle.

(c) (*Archit: also* **— de chimenea**) mantel.

(d) (*Min*) layer, stratum.

(e) (*fig*) cloak, mantle.

mantón *nm* shawl.

mantudo *adj* **(a)** bird with drooping wings. **(b)** (*CAm*) masked, in disguise.

manuable *adj* handy, easy to handle.

manual 1 *adj* **(a)** manual, hand (*attr*); **habilidad —** manual skill; **tener habilidad —** to be clever with one's hands; **obrero —** manual worker, worker who uses his hands; **trabajo —** manual labour.

(b) =**manuable**.

2 *nm* manual, handbook, guide.

manualmente *adv* manually, by hand.

manubrio *nm* **(a)** handle, crank; winch. **(b)** (*SAm*) handlebar(s). **(c)** (*Mus*) barrel organ.

manudo *adj* (*SAm*) with big hands.

Manuel *m* Emmanuel.

manufactura *nf* **(a)** (*act, product*) manufacture. **(b)** factory.

manufacturar [1a] *vt* to manufacture.

manufacturero 1 *adj* manufacturing. **2** *nm* (*SAm*) manufacturer.

manuscrito 1 *adj* handwritten, manuscript. **2** *nm* manuscript.

manutención *nf* **(a)** maintenance; support; keep, board. **(b)** (*Mech etc*) maintenance.

manyar [1a] *vti* (*Chi, PR, RPl*) to eat.

manzana *nf* **(a)** apple; **— de la discordia** (*fig*) apple of discord, bone of contention; **— silvestre** wild apple, crab apple.

(b) (*SAm: Anat*) **— de Adán** Adam's apple.

(c) (*Archit: esp SAm*) block.

(d) (*Arg*) land measure, =2.5 acres; (*CAm*) land measure, =1.75 acres.

manzanal *nm* **(a)** apple orchard. **(b)** apple tree.

manzanar *nm* apple orchard.

manzanilla *nf* **(a)** (*Bot*) camomile; camomile tea. **(b)** a variety of small olive. **(c)** manzanilla (*a very dry sherry-type wine*).

manzano *nm* apple tree.

maña *nf* **(a)** (*in general*) skill, dexterity; ingenuity; (*pej*) craft, guile; **con —** craftily, slyly; **darse — para + infin** to contrive to + infin.

(b) (*una —*) trick, knack; (*malas*) **—s** evil ways, bad habits, vices; (*of child etc*) naughty ways; **tiene**

— **para hacerlo** he's got the knack of doing it; **es una — para conseguir algo** it's a trick (or ruse) to get something.

(c) (Col) idleness; **hacer —** to kill time.

mañana 1 adv (a) tomorrow; **— por la —** tomorrow morning; **¡hasta —!** see you tomorrow!; **pasado —** the day after tomorrow; **— temprano** early tomorrow.

(b) later, some other time; in time to come; **vuelva Vd —** come back later.

2 nm future; **el — es incierto** the future is uncertain.

3 nf (a) morning; tomorrow; **a la —** in the morning; **a la — siguiente** (on) the following morning, the morning after; **a las 7 de la —** at 7 o'clock, at 7 a.m.; **de —, por la —** in the morning; **muy de —** very early in the morning; **— es otro día** there's a new day tomorrow.

(b) (SAm) **tomar la —** to take a shot of liquor before breakfast.

mañanero 1 adj early-rising, who gets up early. **2** nm, **mañanera** nf early riser.

mañanita nf (a) early morning; **de —** very early in the morning, at the crack of dawn. (b) bed jacket.

mañear [1a] **1** vt to manage cleverly, contrive skilfully. **2** vi to act shrewdly, go about things cunningly; (pej) to get up to one's tricks.

mañero adj (a) = **mañoso** (a). (b) (RPl) animal vicious; obstinate; shy, nervous.

mañosamente adv cleverly, ingeniously, skilfully; (pej) craftily.

mañosear [1a] vi (Arg, Col, Chi, Ven) = **mañear** 2; (Arg, Mex: of child) to be difficult (esp about food).

mañoso adj (a) clever, ingenious, skilful; (pej) sharp, crafty, wily.

(b) (Col) lazy, indolent.

(c) (Arg, CAm, Mex, Per) animal vicious; obstinate; shy, nervous; (Arg, Mex) child difficult (esp about food).

mapa nm map; **— geológico** geological map; **— meteorológico** weather map; **— mural** wall map; **en relieve** relief map.

mapache nm rac(c)oon.

mapamundi nm globe; world map.

mapeango adj, **mapiango** adj (Cu, Mex) useless, incompetent.

mapurito nm (CAm) skunk.

maque nm lacquer.

maquear [1a] vt to lacquer.

maqueta nf model, scale model, mock-up, maquette.

maquiavélico adj Machiavellian.

Maquiavelo m Machiavelli.

maquillador nm, **maquilladora** nf (Theat etc) make-up assistant.

maquillaje nm make-up; (act) making-up.

maquillar [1a] **1** vt to make up. **2 maquillarse** vr to make up.

máquina nf (a) machine; (Rail) engine, locomotive; (Phot) camera; (fam) bike (fam); (Cu) car; taxi; **— de afeitar** (safety) razor; **— de afeitar eléctrica** electric razor, shaver; **— de calcular, — computadora** computer; **— de contabilidad, — de sumar** adding machine; **— copiadora** copier, copying machine; **— de coser** sewing machine; **— de direcciones** Addressograph (Protected Trade Name); **— de discos** juke box; **— electrónica, — tragaperras** fruit machine, one-armed bandit; (Comm) slot machine; (Mus) juke box; **— de escribir** typewriter; **— fotográfica** camera; **— herramienta** machine tool; **— de lavar** washing machine; **— de matasellar** franking machine; **— para hacer punto, — de tricotar** knitting machine; **— registradora** (SAm) cash register; **— de vapor** steam engine; **hecho a —** machine-made; script typed; **acabar a —, coser** (etc) **a —** to machine; **escribir a —** to type; **entrar en —** to go to press.

(b) (Archit) imposing building; edifice; structure.

(c) (fig) machinery, workings; scheme of things.

(d) (fig) plan, project.

maquinación nf machination, scheme, plot.

maquinador nm, **maquinadora** nf schemer, plotter.

maquinal adj (fig) mechanical, automatic.

maquinalmente adv (fig) mechanically, automatically.

maquinar [1a] vti to plot, machinate.

maquinaria nf (a) machinery; plant; **— agrícola** agricultural machinery, farm implements. (b) (of watch etc) mechanism, works.

maquinilla nf small machine; winch; (for hair) clippers; **— de afeitar** (safety) razor; **— eléctrica** electric razor, shaver; **— para liar cigarrillos** cigarette(-rolling) machine.

maquinista nm (Rail) engine driver, engineer (US); (Naut etc) engineer; (Tech) operator, machinist.

maquinístico adj (fig) mechanical; materialistic.

mar¹ nm and f (a) sea; ocean; tide; **— de fondo** groundswell; **— gruesa** heavy sea; **— llena** high tide; **— adentro, — afuera** out at sea, out to sea; **caer al —** to fall into the sea, (from ship) to fall overboard; **de alta —** boat seagoing, ocean-going; fishing deepwater (attr); **en alta —** on the high seas; **por —** by sea, by boat; **arar en el —** to labour in vain; **echar a la —** to launch; **es hablar de la —** its all very vague; it's just a dream; **hacerse a la —** to put to sea; to stand out to sea.

(b) **M— Adriático** Adriatic Sea; **M— de las Antillas, M— Caribe** Caribbean Sea; **M— Báltico** Baltic Sea; **M— Caspio** Caspian Sea; **M— Mediterráneo** Mediterranean Sea; **M— Muerto** Dead Sea; **M— Negro** Black Sea; **M— del Norte** North Sea; **M— Rojo** Red Sea.

(c) **un — de confusiones** a sea of confusion, a welter of confusion; **hay un — de diferencia** there's a world of difference.

(d) **estar hecho un — de lágrimas, llorar a —es** to weep floods; **llover a —es** to rain cats and dogs, rain in torrents.

(e) (fam) **la — (as adv)** a lot; **la — de cosas** lots of things, no end of things, ever so many things; **es la — de tonto** he's no end of a fool; **es la — de guapa** she's awfully pretty (fam); **está la — de contento** he's terribly happy (fam).

mar² nf: euph for **madre** (in obscene expressions).

mar³ interj (Mil) march!; see **frente** etc.

maraca nf (a) (SAm) maraca, rattle. (b) (Chi) whore. (c) (Col, PR, Ven) useless person.

maraña nf (a) (Bot) thicket; tangle of plants. (b) (of threads etc) tangle. (c) (fig) mess, tangle; jungle; puzzle. (d) (fam) trick, ruse. (e) (Col) small tip.

marañero 1 adj scheming. **2** nm schemer.

marañón nm (Bot) cashew.

maraquear [1a] vt (SAm) to shake, rattle.

marasmo nm (a) (Med) wasting; atrophy. (b) (fig) paralysis, stagnation.

maravedí nm, pl **maravedíes** or **maravedises** old Spanish coin.

maravilla nf (a) marvel, wonder; wonderment; **las siete —s del mundo** the seven wonders of the world; **hacer —s** to work wonders; **ir a —, ir a las mil —s** to go wonderfully well, go extremely well; to go swimmingly; **lo hace a —** he does it perfectly, he does it splendidly; **por —** for a wonder; by chance; very seldom.

(b) (Bot) marigold.

maravillar [1a] **1** vt to astonish, amaze. **2 maravillarse** vr to be astonished, be amazed (con, de at); **— con, — de** to wonder at, marvel at.

maravillosamente adv wonderfully, marvellously.

maravilloso adj wonderful, marvellous.

marbete nm (a) label; tag, ticket, docket; **— engomado** sticker. (b) (Sew) edge, border.

marca 1 nf (a) mark; stamp; name tab; (of foot) footprint, footmark; (in paper) watermark; (Comm) trademark; (Comm) make, brand; **— de agua, — transparente** watermark; **— de fábrica** trademark; **— de ley** hallmark; **— registrada** registered trademark; **de — excellent, outstanding; de — mayor** absolutely outstanding; really big; **coches de 3 —s distintas** cars of 3 different makes; **productos de varias —s** various brands of products.

(b) (Naut) seamark; marker, buoy; landmark.

(c) (Sport) record; **batir la —, mejorar la —** to break the record; **establecer una —** to set up a record.

(d) (Cards) bid.

(e) (tool) stamp.

(f) (Hist) march, frontier area; **la M— Hispánica** the Spanish March (Catalonia).

2 nm (Rowing) stroke.

marcable adj (Cards) biddable.

marcación nf (Naut) bearing.

marcadamente adv markedly.

marcado 1 adj marked, strong, pronounced; distinct; **con — acento argentino** with a marked Argentinian accent. **2** nm hairnet.

marcador nm (a) marker (also Billiards); bookmark; **— de caminos** roadsign. (b) (Sport) scoreboard; (person) scorer.

marcar [1g] **1** vt (a) (general sense) to mark (de with); to brand, stamp (de with); ground etc to mark off, mark out; clothing to put one's name on, embroider a name on.

(b) (fig) to mark, indicate, point to; (of dial, thermometer etc) to show, register, record, read, say;

las agujas marcan las 2 the hands point to 2 o'clock; **el tanteador marca 3 goles** the scoreboard shows 3 goals; **mi reloj marca la hora exacta** my watch keeps exact time.

(c) *numbers etc* to keep a tally (*or* score) of, record; *score* (*Sport*) to keep.

(d) (*Mus etc*) *pace, step* to mark; *time* to beat, keep.

(e) (*Tel*) to dial.

(f) (*Cards*) to bid.

(g) (*Sport*) *goal, point* to score (*also fig*); — **un tanto en la discusión** to score a point in the argument.

(h) *task* to assign, set; *policy* to lay down.

(i) (*Comm*) to put a price on.

(j) *hair* to set.

2 *vi* (a) (*Sport*) to score.

(b) (*Tel*) to dial.

3 marcarse *vr* (a) (*Naut*) to take one's bearings.

(b) (*Sport*) to score.

(c) (*fam*) to make one's mark, stand out; — **con relieve** to stand out in relief.

Marcial *m* Martial.

marcial *adj law etc* martial; *bearing, discipline* military.

marciano 1 *adj* Martian. **2** *nm*, **marciana** *nf* Martian.

marco *nm* (a) (*Art, Archit,* of *mirror etc*) frame; — **de chimenea** mantelpiece; — **para cuadro** picture frame; — **de ventana** window frame; **poner** — **a un cuadro** to frame a picture.

(b) (*Sport*) goal-posts.

(c) (*fig*) setting; **el paisaje ofreció un bello** — **para la fiesta** the countryside made a splendid setting for the festivity.

(d) (*fig:* of *scheme etc*) framework.

(e) (*Fin*) mark.

(f) (of *weights etc*) standard.

márcola *nf* (*prov*) pruning hook.

Marcos *m* Mark.

marcha *nf* (a) (*Mil etc*) march; — **forzada** forced march; — **del hambre** hunger march; **a largas** —**s** speedily; **a** —**s forzadas** (*fig*) with all speed, as a matter of great urgency; **abrir la** — to come first, be at the head of the procession (*etc*); **cerrar la** — to come last, bring up the rear; **¡en** —**!** (*Mil*) forward march!; (*fig*) let's go!, (*to someone else*) get going!, get moving!; (*fig*) here goes!; **España es país en** — Spain is a country on the move; **estar en** — to be in motion, be going; (*Naut*) to be under way; (*fig*) to be on the move; **poner en** — to start; (*fig*) to get going, set in motion, set on foot; **ponerse en** — to start, get going.

(b) (*Sport*) walk; — **atlética,** — **de competición** walk, walking race.

(c) (of *vehicle*) speed; "— **moderada**" (*Aut*) "drive slowly"; **moderar la** — **de un coche** to slow a car down, reduce the speed of a car; **a toda** — at full speed, at top speed; (*fig*) at full blast, full-blast.

(d) (*Mech*) running, working, functioning, operation; **estar en** — to be working; to be in working order.

(e) (*Aut, Mech*) gear; speed; **primera** — first gear, bottom gear; — **directa** top gear; — **atrás** reverse gear; **dar** — **atrás, poner en** — **atrás, invertir la** — to reverse, put into reverse; **el coche tiene cinco** —**s** the car has five gears.

(f) (*Mus*) march; — **fúnebre** funeral march, dead march; — **lenta** slow march; — **nupcial** wedding march.

(g) (*fig*) progress; march; trend, course; (of *hurricane*) path, track; **la** — **de los acontecimientos** the march of events, the course of events; **coger la** — **de algo** to get into the way (*or* habit) of something, get the hang of something.

(h) (*Cu, PR:* of *horse*) walk, walking pace.

(i) (*Mex: Aut*) self-starter.

marchantaje *nm* (*SAm*) clients, clientèle.

marchante *nm*, **marchanta** *nf* (a) dealer, merchant; (*SAm*) pedlar. (b) (*SAm*) client, customer. (c) (*Ant*) trickster.

marchantía *nf* (*CAm, PR, Ven*) clients, clientèle.

marchar [1a] **1** *vi* (a) to go; to move, travel; (*Mil*) to march.

(b) = **marcharse.**

(c) (*Mech etc*) to go; to run, function, work; (of *train etc*) to run; **el motor no marcha** the engine isn't working, the engine won't work; **el motor marcha mal** the engine is running badly; — **en vacío** to tick over; **el reloj marcha atrasado** the watch is slow.

(d) (*fig*) to go, proceed; **todo marcha bien** everything is going well; **el proyecto marcha bien** the

plan is coming along nicely; **el negocio no marcha** the business is getting nowhere, the deal is making no progress.

(e) (*Cu, Chi, PR:* of *horse*) to walk.

2 marcharse *vr* to go (away), leave; — **a otro sitio** to go somewhere else, leave for another place; — **de la capital** to leave the capital; **¿os marcháis?** are you leaving?, must you go?; **con permiso me marcho** if you don't mind I must go.

marchitar [1a] **1** *vt* to wither, fade, shrivel, dry up.

2 marchitarse *vr* (a) (*Bot*) to wither, fade, shrivel up.

(b) (*fig*) to languish, fade away; to go into a decline.

marchitez *nf* withered state, faded condition.

marchito *adj* (a) withered, faded. (b) (*fig*) faded; in decline.

marea *nf* (a) tide; — **alta** high tide, high water; — **baja** low tide, low water; — **creciente** rising tide; — **menguante** ebb tide; — **muerta** neap tide; — **viva** spring tide.

(b) (*fig*) tide; **la** — **de la rebelión** the tide of revolt.

(c) light sea breeze.

(d) drizzle; (*Chi*) sea mist.

mareado *adj:* **estar** — (a) to feel sick; to feel dizzy; (*Naut*) to be (*or* feel) seasick. (b) (*fam*) to be a bit drunk.

mareaje *nm* (a) navigation, seamanship. (b) ship's course.

marear [1a] **1** *vt* (a) (*Naut*) to sail, navigate.

(b) (*Med*) — **a uno** to make someone feel sick; to make someone seasick; to make someone feel dizzy.

(c) (*fig*) to annoy, upset, disturb; to burden with (useless) things to do.

(d) (*Mex, PR*) to cheat.

2 marearse *vr* (a) (*Med*) to feel sick; to be (*or* get, feel) seasick; to feel dizzy, feel giddy; to feel faint.

(b) **no te marees con esto** don't bother your head about this.

(c) (*fam*) to get a bit drunk.

(d) (*Arg, Cu, PR: cloth*) to fade.

marejada *nf* (a) (*Naut*) swell, heavy sea, surge. (b) (*fig*) undercurrent (of unrest *etc*).

maremagno *nm*, **maremágnum** *nm* (*fig*) ocean, abundance; (*fig*) noisy confusion.

maremoto *nm* tidal wave.

mareo *nm* (a) (*Med*) sick feeling; travel sickness, seasickness; dizziness, giddiness.

(b) (*fig*) irritation; confusion; nervy state; boredom.

(c) nuisance, bore; **es un** — **tener que . . .** it is a nuisance having to . . .; **¡qué** — **de hombre!** what a bore that man is!

marfil *nm* (a) ivory. (b) (*SAm*) fine-toothed comb.

marfileño *adj* ivory, like ivory.

marga *nf* marl, loam.

margal *nm* marly patch; marlpit.

margarina *nf* margarine.

Margarita *f* Margaret.

margarita *nf* (a) (*Zool*) pearl; **echar** —**s a los cerdos** to cast pearls before swine. (b) (*Zool*) winkle. (c) (*Bot*) daisy.

margen 1 *nm* (a) border, edge, fringe; (of *paper, Typ*) margin; **al** — in the margin.

(b) (*Lit*) marginal note.

(c) (*fig*) margin; gap, space; leeway; — **de beneficio,** — **de ganancia** profit margin; — **de confianza** credibility gap; — **de error** margin of (*or* for) error; — **de seguridad** safety margin; **hay un** — **de aproximación de 8 días** we allow a week each way; **le digo el número con un** — **de unos 20** I'm telling you the number, give or take about 20.

(d) (*fig*) **dejar a uno al** — to leave someone out (in the cold); **mantenerse al** — to keep out, stand aside.

(e) (*fig*) occasion, opportunity; **dar** — **para** to give an opportunity for.

2 *nf* (of *river etc*) bank.

marginal *adj* marginal.

marginar [1a] *vt* (a) *page* to leave margins on. (b) *text* to add marginal notes to, write marginal notes against.

margoso *adj* marly, loamy.

margullo *nm* (*Cu, Ven*) shoot, runner.

Mari *f* pet name for **María.**

María *f* Mary; — **Antonieta** Marie Antoinette; — **Estuardo** Mary Stuart; — **la Sangrienta** Bloody Mary.

marial *adj*, **mariano** *adj* Marian.

marica 1 *nf* (*Orn*) magpie. **2** *nm* (*fam*) weak character; milksop, sissy, mollycoddle; (*fam*) = **maricón.**
Maricastaña: en los días de —, en tiempos de — way back, long ago; in the good old days.
maricón *nm* (*fam*) queer (*fam*), pansy (*fam*).
maridaje *nm* (a) conjugal life, marriage ties. (b) (*fig*) marriage, close association, intimate connection. (c) (*pej*) collusion.
marido *nm* husband.
marijuana *nf* (*also* **mariguana, marihuana**) marijuana, cannabis, Indian hemp.
marimacha *nf* (*Per*) = **marimacho.**
marimacho *nm* (*fam*) mannish woman.
marimba *nf* (a) (*Mus*) kind of drum; (*SAm*) marimba, kind of xylophone; (*Arg, PR*) tuneless instrument. (b) (*RPl*) beating. (c) (*Col*) large goitre.
marimoña *nf* buttercup.
marimorena *nf* fuss, row, shindy; **armar una — to** kick up a row.
marina *nf* (a) (*Geog*) coast, coastal area. (b) seamanship; navigation; **término de —** term from navigation, nautical term. (c) ships; **— (de guerra)** navy; **la — española** the Spanish navy, the Spanish fleet; **— mercante** merchant navy; **servir en la —** to serve in the navy. (d) (*Art*) sea piece, seascape.
marinar [1a] *vt* (*Cook*) to marinade, marinate.
marinería *nf* (a) seamanship. (b) ship's crew; seamen, sailors (*collectively*).
marinero 1 *adj* (a) = **marino.** (b) *people* sea (*attr*), seafaring. (c) *ship* seaworthy. (d) **a la marinera, a lo —** in a seamanlike way; sailor-fashion. **2** *nm* sailor, seaman; mariner, seafarer; **— de agua dulce** landlubber; **— de cubierta** deckhand; **— de primera** able seaman.
marinesco *adj* seamanly; **a la marinesca** in a seamanlike way; sailor-fashion.
marino 1 *adj* sea (*attr*), marine; **pez —** sea fish; **fauna marina** marine life, sea creatures. **2** *nm* sailor, seaman.
mariolatría *nf* mariolatry.
marioneta *nf* marionette, puppet; (*fig*) puppet; **régimen —** puppet régime.
mariposa *nf* (a) (*Ent*) butterfly; **— (nocturna)** moth; **— de la col** cabbage-white butterfly; **— cabeza de muerte, — de calavera** death's head moth. (b) (*Swimming*) butterfly stroke; **100 metros —** 100 metres butterfly. (c) (*Col, Hond*) toy windmill. (d) (*Col*) blind man's bluff.
mariposear [1a] *vi* (a) to flutter about, flit to and fro. (b) (*fig*) to be fickle, act capriciously; to flirt; **— alrededor de uno** to dance attendance on someone, be constantly fluttering round someone.
mariposilla *nf* small moth, (*esp*) clothes moth.
mariposón *nm* (a) flirt, wolf (*fam*). (b) (*Per*) queer (*fam*), pansy (*fam*).
Mariquita *f* pet name for **María.**
mariquita 1 *nf* (a) (*Ent*) ladybird. (b) (*Orn*) parakeet. **2** *nm* = **marica 2.**
marisabidilla *nf* (*fam*) bluestocking; know-all.
mariscal *nm* (*Hist*) blacksmith, farrier; (*Hist*) major-general; **— de campo** field marshal.
mariscos *nmpl* shellfish, seafood.
marisma *nf* marsh, swamp; mud flats.
marisquería *nf* shellfish bar, seafood restaurant.
marital *adj* marital.
maritatas *nfpl* (*Andalusia, SAm*), **maritates** *nmpl* (*CAm, Mex*) gear, tackle, tools; (*pej*) things, junk.
marítimo *adj* maritime; marine, sea (*attr*); *agent etc* shipping (*attr*); **ciudad marítima** seaside town, coastal town; **ruta marítima** ocean route, seaway, route by sea; **seguro —** marine insurance.
maritornes *nf, pl* **maritornes** sluttish servant; wench, tart (*sl*).
marjal *nm* marsh, fen, bog.
marmita *nf* (a) (*Cook*) pot; (*Mil*) mess tin. (b) (*Geol*) **— de gigante** pothole.
marmitón *nm* kitchen boy, scullion.
mármol *nm* marble.
marmolejo *nm* small marble column.
marmóreo *adj* marble; marmoreal.
marmosete *nm* (*Typ*) tailpiece, vignette.
marmota *nf* (a) (*Zool*) marmot; **— de Alemania** hamster; **— de América** woodchuck; **dormir como una —** to sleep like a log. (b) (*fig*) sleepyhead.
maroma *nf* (a) rope. (b) (*SAm*) tightrope; acrobatic performance; (*SD*) circus. (c) (*SAm*) **—s** acrobatics, acrobatic stunts; **hacer —s = maromear.**

maromear [1a] *vi* (*SAm*) (a) to walk (on) a tightrope; to do acrobatic stunts. (b) (*fig*) to change one's political allegiance, climb on the bandwaggon; to keep in with all parties, do a political balancing act.
maromero *nm* (*SAm*) (a) tightrope walker, acrobat. (b) (*fig*) clever politician, politician who manages to be on good terms with all parties.
marqués *nm* marquis.
marquesa *nf* marchioness.
marquesina *nf* glass canopy, porch; glass roof, cantilever roof; (*Rail*) roof, cab (*of locomotive*).
marquetería *nf* marquetry, inlaid work.
marrajo 1 *adj* *bull* vicious, dangerous; *person* sly. **2** *nm* (a) shark. (b) (*Mex*) skinflint.
marramizar [1f] *vi* (*of cat*) to howl, caterwaul.
marrana *nf* (a) (*Zool*) sow. (b) (*fam*) slut.
marranada *nf*, **marranería** *nf* (a) filthiness. (b) (*una —*) filthy act; dirty trick, vile deed.
marrano 1 *adj* filthy, dirty. **2** *nm* (a) (*Zool*) pig, boar. (b) (*fam*) swine; dirty pig. (c) (*Hist*) Jew, converted Jew.
marrar [1a] **1** *vt*: **— el tiro** to miss; **— el golpe** to miss (with a blow). **2** *vi* (a) to miss; (*fig*) to miss the mark. (b) (*fig*) to fail, miscarry, go astray; **no me marra una** everything's going well for me.
marras *adv* (a) **de —** old; long-standing; well-known, that you (*etc*) know all about; in question, aforementioned; **es el problema de —** it's the same old problem; **volver a lo de —** to go back over the same old stuff. (b) (*Bol, Ec*) **hace — que no le veo** it's ages since I saw him.
marrazo *nm* mattock; short *machete*; (*Mex*) bayonet.
marrón 1 *adj* chestnut, brown; maroon. **2** *nm* (a) chestnut (colour); maroon. (b) (*Cook*) marron glacé. (c) (*SAm*) (descendant of) fugitive Negro slave. (d) (*Col*) curlpaper.
marroncito *nm* (*Ven*) coffee with milk.
marroquí 1 *adj* Moroccan. **2** *nmf* Moroccan. **3** *nm* (*Tech*) morocco (leather).
marrubio *nm* (*Bot*) horehound.
marrueco = marroquí 1 *and* **2.**
Marruecos *m* Morocco; **el — Español** Spanish Morocco.
marrullería *nf* (a) (*quality*) smoothness, glibness, plausibility. (b) (*una —*) plausible excuse; **—s** smooth approach, cajolery, wheedling.
marrullero 1 *adj* smooth, glib, plausible; cajoling, wheedling. **2** *nm* smooth type, plausible individual.
Marsella Marseille.
Marsellesa *nf* Marseillaise.
marsopa *nf* porpoise.
marsupial 1 *adj* marsupial. **2** *nm* marsupial.
marta *nf* (pine) marten; (*fur*) sable; **— cebellina** sable.
martajar [1a] *vt* (*SAm*) (a) *maize* to pound, grind. (b) **— el español** to speak broken Spanish.
Marte *m* Mars.
martellina *nf* sledgehammer.
martes *nm, pl* **martes** Tuesday; **— de carnaval, — de carnestolendas** Shrove Tuesday.
martillada *nf* hammer blow, blow with a hammer.
martillar [1a] *vt* (a) to hammer; to pound. (b) (*fig*) to worry, torment.
martillazo *nm* (heavy) blow with a hammer; **a —s** by hammering; **formar algo a —s** to hammer something out (*or* into shape).
martillear [1a] **1** *vt* = **martillar. 2** *vi* (*of engine*) to knock.
martilleo *nm* hammering; pounding.
martillero *nm* (*SAm*) auctioneer.
martillo *nm* (a) hammer; (*of chairman etc*) gavel; **— de madera** mallet; **— mecánico** power hammer; **— de orejas, — sacaclavos** claw-hammer; **— picador** pneumatic drill. (b) (*Comm*) auction room. (c) (*Archit*) projecting part, house (*etc*) that sticks out from the row; (*SAm*) wing (of a building). (d) (*fig: person*) hammer, scourge.
Martín *m* Martin; **San —** St Martin, (*as festivity*) Martinmas, (*Agr*) season for slaughtering pigs; **a cada puerco le llega su San —** everything has to come to an end sometime; *see* **veranillo.**
martín *nm*: **— pescador** kingfisher.
martinete *nm* drop hammer; pile driver; (*Mus*) hammer.
martingala *nf* (*fam*) knack, trick; (*pej: SAm*) trick, cunning device, fiddle (*fam*).
Martinica *f* Martinique.
mártir *nmf* martyr.

martirio nm (a) (Eccl) martyrdom. (b) (fig) torture, torment.

martirizador adj (fig) agonizing, excruciating.

martirizar [1f] vt (Eccl) (a) to martyr. (b) (fig) to torture, torment.

martirologio nm martyrology.

Marucha f, Maruja f pet names for **María.**

marusa nf (Ven) knapsack, bag.

maruto nm (Ven) (a) (Anat) navel. (b) (Med) wart; bruise, welt.

marxismo nm Marxism.

marxista 1 adj Marxist. **2** nmf Marxist.

marzal adj March (attr), of March.

marzo nm March.

más 1 adv and adj (a) (basic comparisons: comp) more, (superl) most; **A es — difícil que B** A is more difficult than B, A is harder than B; **ella es la — guapa de todas** she is the prettiest of all; **él es el — inteligente** he is the most intelligent (one); **es el que sabe —** he's the one who knows most; **tiene — dinero que yo** he has more money than I (do); **un libro de lo — divertido** a most amusing book, a highly amusing book; **es de lo — verde** it's as dirty as can be, it's as dirty as they come; **un hombre de lo — desaprensivo** a completely unscrupulous man.

(b) (examples of use with certain verbs) **correr — to run faster; durar —** to last longer; **trabajar —** to work harder; **ha viajado —** he has travelled more (widely); **— quiero + infin** I would rather + infin, I would prefer to + infin.

(c) (idiomatic use with adjs) **¡qué perro — feo!** what an ugly dog!; **¡ya verán qué cena — rica!** you wait and see what a splendid supper it will be!; **¡es — bueno!** (fam) he's so kind!, he's ever so kind!

(d) (comparisons of quality and quantity) **— de, — de lo que, — que** more than; **— de 10** more than 10; **con — dinero de lo que creíamos** with more money than we thought; **no veo — solución que de . . .** I see no other solution than to . . . (or but to); **se trata de voluntad — que de fuerza** it's more a question of will power than of strength, it's a matter of will power rather than of strength; **se estima en — de mil** it is reckoned at more than a thousand; **no — que ayer** only yesterday; **hace no — de 3 semanas** only 3 weeks ago, no longer than 3 weeks ago; **nadie lo sabe — que yo** nobody knows it better than I do.

(e) (other uses, and idioms with prep) **— y — more and more; o menos — o menos** more or less; **el que — y el que menos** every single one; the whole lot; **los — most people; los — de most of, the majority of; es — . . .** furthermore . . .; **a —** in addition, besides; **a — de** in addition to, besides; **a lo —** at most, at the most; **a las 8 a — tardar** at 8 o'clock at the latest; **está nevando a — y mejor** it really is snowing, it's snowing harder than ever; **como el que —** as well as anyone, as well as the next man; **llevaba 3 de —** he was carrying 3 too many; **trae una manta de — bring an extra blanket; estar de —** to be unnecessary, be superfluous; **aquí yo estoy de —** I'm not needed here, I'm de trop here, I'm in the way here; **está de — decir que . . .** it is unnecessary to say that . . .; **de — en —** more and more; **hasta no — to** the utmost, to the limit; **nada —** nothing else; **¡nada —!** that's all!, that's the lot!; **¿nada —?** anything else?; **ocurrió nada — iniciado el partido** it happened when the game had scarcely begun; **aparecen nada — terminado el invierno** they come when the winter is hardly over; **ni — ni menos** neither more nor less; just; **es un genio ni — ni menos** he's nothing more nor less than a genius, he's a real genius; **no — no more; habían llegado no —** they had just arrived; **vengo no — a verlo** I've come just to see it; **ayer no —** (SAm) only yesterday; **¡espera no —!** (SAm) just you wait!; **no trabaja —** he no longer works, he doesn't work any more; **por — que se esfuerce** however much (or hard) he tries, no matter how (hard) he tries; **por — que quisiera ayudar** much as I should like to help; **¿qué —?** what else?; what next?; **sin — (ni —)** without more ado; **todo lo —** at most, at the most; see **allá, bien, cuento, nunca** etc.

2 conj and, plus; **2 — 3 son 5** 2 and 3 are 5, 2 plus 3 are 5; **con éstos — los que había antes** with these and (or together with) what there were before; **España — Portugal** Spain together with Portugal.

3 nm (a) (Math) plus, plus sign.

(b) **tiene sus — y sus menos** it has its good and bad points, there are things to be said on both sides.

mas conj (lit) but.

masa¹ nf (a) (Cook) dough. (b) (RPl) small bun, tea-

cake; (Chi, Ec) puff pastry. (c) (Archit) mortar, plaster.

masa² nf (a) (Phys etc) mass; (fig) mass; bulk; volume, quantity; **las —s** the masses; **— coral** choir; **en — en masse; in a body, all together; (Arg, Chi, Per) as a whole, altogether; reunir(se) en —** to mass; **llevar algo en la — de la sangre** to have something in one's blood, have a natural inclination towards something.

(b) (Elec) earth, ground (US); **conectar un aparato con —** to earth a piece of apparatus, ground a piece of apparatus (US).

masacrar [1a] vt to massacre.

masacre nf massacre.

masada nf farm.

masadero nm farmer.

masaje nm massage; **dar — a** to massage; **hacerse dar —s** to have oneself massaged.

masajista 1 nm masseur. **2** nf masseuse.

masato nm (SAm) drink made from fermented maize, bananas, yucca etc.

mascada nf (a) (SAm) plug of chewing tobacco. (b) (CAm, Ec) buried treasure; store of money, nest egg; (Col, Ec) money; (RPl) illicit gains; rake-off (fam), cut. (c) (CAm) rebuke. (d) (Guat, Mex) silk handkerchief.

mascadura nf chewing.

mascar [1g] **1** vt (a) food to chew.

(b) (fam) words to mumble, mutter.

(c) (fam) **— un asunto, dar mascado un asunto** to explain something in very simple terms.

2 vi to chew; (SAm, esp) to chew tobacco.

máscara 1 nf (a) mask; **— antigás** gasmask; **— para esgrima** fencing mask; **— de oxígeno** oxygen mask.

(b) **—s** masque, masquerade.

(c) (fig) mask; disguise; **quitar la — a uno** to unmask someone; **quitarse la —** to reveal oneself.

2 nmf masked person.

mascarada nf (a) masque, masquerade. (b) (fig) masquerade; farce, charade.

mascarilla nf mask (also Med); plaster cast (of the face); **— mortuoria** death mask.

mascarón nm large mask; **— de proa** figurehead.

mascota nf mascot.

masculinidad nf masculinity, manliness.

masculino 1 adj masculine, manly; (Bio) male; (Gram) masculine; **ropa masculina** men's clothing. **2** nm (Gram) masculine.

mascullar [1a] vt to mumble, mutter.

masera nf kneading trough.

masía nf (Aragon) farm.

masilla nf putty.

masillo nm (Cu) plaster.

masita nf (Bol, RPl, SD) small bun, teacake, pastry.

masitero nm (Bol, RPl, SD) pastrycook, confectioner.

masivo adj attack, dose etc massive; evacuation etc en masse, general; execution mass (attr), wholesale.

masocotudo adj (Chi, Per) heavy, ponderous; thick.

masón nm (free)mason.

masonería nf (free)masonry.

masónico adj masonic.

masoquismo nm masochism.

masoquista 1 adj masochistic. **2** nmf masochist.

mastate nm (CAm, Mex) loincloth; short skirt.

mastelero nm topmast.

masticación nf mastication.

masticar [1g] vt to masticate, chew.

mástil nm (a) pole, post, support; flagpole; (Naut) mast; (Archit) upright; **— de tienda** tent pole. (b) (Mus) neck. (c) (of feather) shaft.

mastín nm mastiff; **— danés** Great Dane.

mastique nm plaster; cement; putty.

mastitis nf mastitis.

masto nm (Agr, Hort) stock (for grafting).

mastodonte nm mastodon.

mastodóntico adj (fig) elephantine.

mastoides 1 adj mastoid. **2** nf mastoid.

mastuerzo nm (a) (Bot) cress; **— de agua** watercress. (b) (fam) dolt.

masturbación nf masturbation.

masturbarse [1a] vr to masturbate.

mata nf (a) bush, shrub; (esp SAm: any) plant; **— de coco** (Ant) coconut palm; **— de plátano** (Ant) banana tree; **— rubia** kermes oak.

(b) sprig; tuft, blade; clump, root; bunch.

(c) **—s** thicket, bushes; scrub.

(d) (Agr) field, plot, patch; **— de olivos** field of olive trees, olive grove.

(e) (SAm) clump, group (of trees), grove; (Col) orchard; (Mex, Ven) forest, jungle; **— de bananos** clump of banana trees, banana plantation.

(f) **— de pelo** head of hair; mop of hair.

mataburro nm (CAm, Col, Ec) liquor, rum.

mataburros nm, pl **mataburros** (Cu, RPl: hum) dictionary.

matacán nm (a) (Ec, Ven) fawn, young deer. (b) (Hond) calf.

matachín nm bully.

matadero nm (a) slaughterhouse, abattoir. (b) (fig) drudgery. (c) (fig: Mil) exposed position, dangerous place. (d) (Mex, RPl) brothel.

matador 1 adj (a) killing.
(b) (fam) ridiculous; absurd; **el vestido le está —** the dress looks absurd on her.
2 nm, **matadora** nf killer.
3 nm (Taur) matador, bullfighter.

matadura nf (Vet) sore.

matafuego nm fire extinguisher.

mátalas callando nm (fam) smooth type, sly sort.

matalobos nm, pl **matalobos** aconite, wolf's-bane.

matalón 1 adj horse old, broken-down. **2** nm broken-down old horse.

matamoros nm, pl **matamoros** swashbuckler, braggart.

matamoscas nm, pl **matamoscas** fly swat; flypaper.

matanza nf (a) slaughter, killing; (Agr) slaughtering, (esp) pig-killing; slaughtering season; (fig) slaughter, massacre, butchery.
(b) (Ven) slaughterhouse; (Col) butcher's (shop); (CAm) meat market.

mataperrear [1a] vi (Arg, Ec, Per) to behave like a hooligan.

mataperros nm, pl **mataperros** nm (fam) urchin, hooligan.

matar [1a] **1** vt (a) to kill; to slay, slaughter; **— a uno a disgustos** to wear someone out with burdens, heap troubles on someone; **así me maten . . .** for the life of me . . .; **que me maten si . . .** I'll eat my hat if . . .; believe me, I never . . .; **—las callando** to do oneself a lot of good on the quiet, go about things slyly.
(b) (fig) time to kill; hunger to stay; dust to lay; lime to slake; corner, edge etc to file down, smooth, round off; colour to tone down; violence etc to diminish, reduce.
2 vi (a) to kill; **no mataréis** thou shalt not kill; **estar a — con uno** to be at daggers drawn with someone.
(b) (Chess) to mate.
3 matarse vr (a) to kill oneself, commit suicide; (in accident) to be killed, get killed.
(b) (fig) to wear oneself out, kill oneself; **— a trabajar** to kill oneself with work, overwork; **— por + infin** to struggle to + infin, make a great effort to + infin.

matarife nm butcher, slaughterman; **— de caballos** knacker.

matarratas nm rat poison; (fig) hooch, bad liquor.

matasanos nm, pl **matasanos** (fam) quack (doctor).

matasellado nm cancellation, postmark.

matasellos nm, pl **matasellos** cancellation, postmark.

matasiete nm braggart, bully.

matasuegras nm, pl **matasuegras** streamer, blower (toy).

matazón nm (CAm, Col, Cu, Ven) = **matanza**.

match [matʃ] nm, pl **matchs** [matʃ] (Sport: angl) rnatch.

mate¹ adj dull, matt, unpolished.

mate² nm (Chess) mate, checkmate; **dar — a** to mate, checkmate.

mate³ nm (SAm) (a) maté, Paraguayan tea (herb and drink similar to tea).
(b) gourd, drinking vessel; maté pot; **pegar — ** (CAm) to go crazy; **tener mucho — ** (CAm) to be sly, be sharp.
(c) (Chi, RPl: fam) head, nut (sl).

matear¹ [1a] **1** vt (Agr) to plant at regular intervals, sow in groups. **2** vi (a) (Bot) to sprout. (b) (Hunting: of dog) to hunt among the bushes.

matear² [1a] vi (SAm) to drink maté.

matear³ [1a] vt (Chi) to checkmate.

matemáticamente adv mathematically.

matemáticas nfpl mathematics; **— aplicadas** applied mathematics; **— puras** pure mathematics.

matemático 1 adj mathematical. **2** nm mathematician.

Mateo m Matthew.

materia nf (a) matter (also Med, Phys); material; stuff; **— colorante** dyestuff; **— prima** raw material.
(b) (Lit etc) matter, subject matter; (School etc) subject; **índice de —s** table of contents; **en — de** in the matter of, on the subject of; as regards; **entrar en —** to begin on one's subject (after a preamble); **será — de muchas discusiones** it will be

the subject of a lot of argument, it will give rise to a lot of argument.

material 1 adj (a) material.
(b) physical; **la presencia — de uno** someone's physical (or bodily) presence; **dolor —** physical pain; **daños —es** physical damage; damage to property.
(c) real, true; literal; **el autor — del hecho** the real instigator of the deed, the person really responsible for the affair.
2 nm (a) (in general) material; **hecho de mal —** made of bad material(s); **— bélico, — de guerra** war material; **— de construcción** building material; **—es de derribo** rubble; **—es plásticos** plastics, plastic materials.
(b) (Tech) equipment, plant; materials; **— escolar** teaching materials, school equipment; **— fijo** permanent way; **— de limpieza** cleaning materials; **— móvil, — rodante** rolling stock; **el nuevo — de la fábrica** the new factory plant.
(c) (Typ) copy.
(d) (of footwear) leather.
(e) (SAm) de **—** made of adobe; made of bricks, brick-built.

materialidad nf material nature; outward appearance; literalness; substance; **percibe solamente la — del asunto** he sees only the basic aspects of the question; **no hablo de la — del insulto** I'm not talking about the substance of the insult, I'm not talking about what the insult actually consisted of.

materialismo nm materialism.

materialista 1 adj materialist(ic). **2** nmf materialist. **3** nm (Mex) lorry driver, truckdriver (US).

materializar [1f] **1** vt to materialize. **2 materializarse** vr to materialize.

materialmente adv (a) materially; physically, in the physical sense.
(b) absolutely; literally; **nos es — imposible** it is quite (or absolutely) impossible for us; **estaba — mojado** he was literally soaked.

maternal adj motherly; maternal.

maternidad nf (a) motherhood, maternity. (b) (also **casa de —**) maternity hospital.

materno adj (a) language etc mother (attr); home etc mother's. (b) **abuelo —** maternal grandfather, grandfather on the mother's side.

matero adj (Chi, RPl) (a) of maté, relating to maté. (b) fond of drinking maté.

matete nm (Arg, Urug) (a) confused mess, mixture, hash. (b) (fig) quarrel, brawl. (c) (fig) confusion.

Matilde f Mat(h)ilda.

matinal adj morning (attr).

matiz nm (a) shade, hue, tint. (b) (of meaning) shade, nuance; (of irony etc) touch.

matizado adj: **— de, — en** tinged with, touched with (also fig).

matizar [1f] vt (a) (Art) to blend.
(b) to tinge, tint (de with; also fig); **— un discurso de ironía** to introduce ironical notes into a speech, give a speech an ironical slant.
(c) tone etc to vary, introduce some variety into.

matojal nm (Cu, PR), **matojo** nm (Ant, Col, Mex) = **matorral**.

matón nm bully, lout, thug.

matonismo nm bullying, loutishness.

matorral nm thicket; brushwood, scrub.

matorro nm (Col) = **matorral**.

matra nf (RPl) horseblanket.

matraca 1 nf (a) rattle.
(b) (fam) nuisance, bore; chaff, banter; **dar — a uno** to pester someone, keep bothering someone; to banter someone.
2 nmf (fam: person) nuisance, bore.

matraquear [1a] vt (a) to rattle. (b) (fam) = **dar matraca a**.

matraz nm (Chem) flask.

matreraje nm (RPl) banditry, brigandage.

matrero 1 adj (a) cunning, sly, knowing. (b) (SAm) suspicious, distrustful. **2** nm (SAm) bandit, brigand; trickster.

matriarca nf matriarch.

matriarcado nm matriarchy.

matriarcal adj matriarchal.

matricida nmf matricide (person).

matricidio nm matricide (act).

matrícula nf (a) register, list, roll; (Naut) register.
(b) (act: Naut) registration; (Univ) registration, matriculation; **un buque de — extranjera** a foreign ship, a ship with foreign registration; **un barco con — de Bilbao** a boat registered in Bilbao; **en los exámenes le dieron una — de honor** as a result of the examinations his fees for the following year were remitted.

(c) licence; (*Aut*) registration number; licence plate.

matriculación *nf* registration; enrolment; licensing.

matricular [1a] **1** *vt* to register; to enrol; to license. **2 matricularse** *vr* to register; to enrol, sign on; — en el curso de . . . to sign on for the course in . . .

matrimonial *adj* matrimonial; **enlace** — link by marriage; **capitulaciones** —**es** marriage settlement; **vida** — married life, conjugal life.

matrimonio *nm* (a) (*in general*) marriage, matrimony; married state; (*act*) marriage; — **civil** civil marriage; — **clandestino** secret marriage; — **de conveniencia**, — **de interés** marriage of convenience; — **por la iglesia** church marriage; **contraer** — (**con**) to marry. (b) (*persons*) couple, married couple; **el** — **García** the Garcías, Mr and Mrs García; **de** — bed etc double.

matritense = **madrileño**.

matriz 1 *nf* (a) (*Anat*) womb, uterus. (b) (*Tech*) mould, die; (*Typ*) matrix. (c) (*Math*) matrix. (d) (*of cheque book etc*) stub. (e) (*Law*) original, master copy. **2** *attr*: **casa** — (*Comm etc*) head office; parent company; **convento** — (*Eccl*) parent house.

matrona *nf* (a) matron. (b) (*Med*) midwife.

matronal *adj* matronly.

matungo (*Ant, RPl*) **1** *adj* old, worn-out. **2** *nm* old horse, nag; thin person, weakling.

maturrango 1 *adj* (*Arg, Chi, Urug*) clumsy, awkward; (*Arg, Per, Urug*) rider poor, incompetent. **2** *nm* (*Per, RPl*) poor rider, incompetent horseman.

matute *nm* (a) smuggling, contraband; **de** — (*Comm*) smuggled, contraband; (*as adv*) secretly, stealthily; **introducir una idea de** — to bring in a (dangerous) notion from outside. (b) smuggled goods, contraband. (c) gambling den.

matutero *nm* smuggler.

matutino *adj* morning (*attr*).

maula 1 *adj* (*SAm*) *animal* useless, vicious, lazy; (*Arg, Mex*) *person* good-for-nothing, unreliable; (*Arg*) cowardly. **2** *nf* (a) (*Sew*) remnant. (b) piece of junk, useless object; white elephant. (c) (*person*) useless individual, dead loss. (d) dirty trick, fraud. **3** *nmf* (a) idler, slacker. (b) cheat, trickster; tricky individual; (*Fin*) bad payer.

maulería *nf* cunning, trickiness.

maulero *nm* (a) cheat, trickster; smooth and deceitful type. (b) (*Ec*) conjurer.

maullar [1a] *vi* to mew, miaow.

maullido *nm* mew, miaow.

Mauricio[1] *m* Maurice.

Mauricio[2] *m* (*Geog*) Mauritius.

mausoleo *nm* mausoleum.

maxifalda *nf* maxiskirt.

maxilar 1 *adj* maxillary. **2** *nm* jaw, jawbone.

máxima *nf* maxim.

máxime *adv* especially; principally; all the more so.

máximo 1 *adj* maximum; top; highest, greatest; **el** — **premio** the highest award, the top prize; **su** — **esfuerzo** their greatest effort; **llegar al punto** — to reach the highest point; **es lo** — **en la moda juvenil** (*sl*) it's the most in young people's fashions (*sl*). **2** *nm* maximum; **como** — at most, at the outside; **al** — to the maximum, to the utmost.

máximum *nm* maximum.

maya[1] *nf* (a) (*Bot*) daisy. (b) May Queen, Queen of the May.

maya[2] (*Hist*) **1** *adj* Mayan. **2** *nmf* Maya, Mayan.

mayal *nm* flail.

mayo *nm* (a) May. (b) maypole.

mayonesa *nf* mayonnaise.

mayor 1 *adj* (a) *part etc* main, major, larger; **y otros animales** —**es** and other larger animals. (b) *altar, mass, street etc* high; *square* main, principal; *mast* main; see **colegio, libro** etc. (c) (*Mus*) major. (d) *person* grown up, adult; of age; elderly; **ser** — **de edad** to be of age, be adult; **hacerse** — to grow up. (e) (*of rank etc*) head, chief; **montero** — head huntsman. **2** *adj comp* (a) (*in size*) bigger, larger, greater (*que* than). (b) (*in age*) older (*que* than), elder; (*in rank*) senior (*que* to). **3** *adj superl* (a) (*in size*) biggest, largest, greatest

(*also fig*); **su** — **cuidado** his biggest worry; **su** — **enemigo** his greatest enemy; **viven en la** — **miseria** they live in the greatest poverty. (b) (*in age*) oldest, eldest; (*in rank*) most senior. **4** *nmf* (a) (*of rank*) chief, boss, superior; (*in office*) chief clerk. (b) — **de edad** adult, person legally of age; —**es** grown-ups, adults; elders (and betters); **eso es sólo para** —**es** that's only for grown-ups; **¡más respeto con los** —**es!** be more respectful to your elders (and betters)! (c) —**es** ancestors, forefathers. (d) **llegar a** —**es** (*of situation*) to get out of hand, get out of control. **5** *nm*: **al por** — wholesale (*also fig*); **vender al por** — to sell wholesale; **repartir golpes al por** — to deal out punches wholesale, throw punches left and right.

mayoral *nm* (*Tech etc*) foreman, overseer, gaffer; (*Agr*) head shepherd; steward; farm manager; (*Arg*) tram conductor; (*Hist*) coachman.

mayorazgo *nm* (a) primogeniture. (b) entailed estate. (c) eldest son, first-born.

mayordomo *nm* steward, butler; (*Naut*) steward; (*of estate*) steward; (*Chi*) foreman; (*Per*) servant.

mayoreo *nm* (*Chi, Mex*) wholesale (trade).

mayoría *nf* (a) majority, greater part, larger part; **la** — **de los españoles** the majority of Spaniards, most Spaniards; **en la** — **de los casos** in most cases; **en su** — in the main; **la abrumadora** —, **la inmensa** — the overwhelming majority, the vast majority; **por una** — **arrolladora** by an overwhelming majority. (b) (*Pol etc*) majority; **una** — **de las cuatro quintas partes** a four-fifths majority; **gobierno de la** — majority rule, majority government. (c) — **de edad** majority, adult age; **cumplir** (*or* **llegar a**) **la** — **de edad** to come of age.

mayorista *nmf* wholesaler.

mayoritario *adj* majority (*attr*); **gobierno** — majority government.

mayormente *adv* chiefly, mainly; especially; all the more so.

mayúscula *nf* capital (letter).

mayúsculo *adj* (a) *letter* capital. (b) (*fig*) big, tremendous; **un susto** — a big scare; **un error** — a tremendous mistake.

maza *nf* (a) (*Hist*) mace; war club; (*Sport*) bat; (*in polo*) stick, mallet; (*Mus*) drumstick; (*of billiard cue etc*) thick end; (*Tech*) flail; — **de fraga** drop hammer; — **de gimnasia** Indian club. (b) (*fam*) pest, bore. (c) (*SAm*) hub. (d) (*Col, Cu, PR*) drum (of a sugar mill).

mazacote *nm* (a) hard mass; (*Cook*) dry doughy food; (*Archit*) concrete; **el arroz se ha hecho un** — the rice has gone lumpy, the rice has set like concrete. (b) (*Art, Lit etc*) crude piece of work; mess, hotchpotch. (c) (*fam*) bore.

mazacotudo *adj* = **amazacotado**.

mazada *nf* (a) bash (*fam*), blow (with a club); **dar** — **a** (*fig*) to hurt, injure. (b) (*fig*) blow; **fue una** — **para él** it came as a blow to him.

mazamorra *nf* (a) (*SAm*) maize mush, maize pudding, porridge. (b) (*CAm, Col, Cu, PR*) blister (on a horse's hoof); sore, soreness (on the foot).

mazapán *nm* marzipan.

mazmorra *nf* dungeon.

mazo *nm* (a) club; mallet; pestle; (*Sport*) club, bat, (*for croquet*) mallet; (*Agr*) flail; (*Aragon: of bell*) clapper. (b) bunch, handful; bundle, packet; — **de papeles** sheaf of papers, bundle of papers; — **de naipes** stack of cards; — **de billetes** wad of notes (*or* bills: US). (c) (*fam*) bore.

mazorca *nf* (a) (*Bot*) spike; (*of maize*) cob, ear; — **de maíz** corncob; **maíz en la** — corn on the cob. (b) (*Tech*) spindle. (c) (*Chi, RPl*) despotic government; political gang, terrorist band.

mazorquero *nm* (*Chi, RPl*) member of a despotic government; member of a political gang.

me *personal pron* (a) (*acc*) me. (b) (*dative*) (to) me; **¡dámelo!** give it to me!; **me lo compró** he bought it from me; he bought it for me; **me rompí el brazo** I broke my arm. (c) (*reflexive*) (to) myself; **me lavé** I washed, I washed myself; **me retiro** I withdraw.

meada *nf* (a) (*tabu*) piss (*tabu*). (b) mark (*or* stain etc) of urine.

meadero *nm* (*tabu*) bog (*sl*), jakes (*fam*).

meados *nmpl* (*tabu*) piss (*tabu*).

meaja *nf* crumb.

meandro *nm* meander.

mear [1a] (*tabu*) **1** *vt* to piss on (*tabu*).
    2 *vi* to piss (*tabu*), have a piss (*tabu*).
    3 mearse *vr* to wet oneself; **— de risa** to laugh so much that one has an accident.

Meca: La — Mecca.

meca *nf* (*Ec, Per*) prostitute.

mecachis *interj* (*euph for* ¡me cago!) *see* **cagar.**

mecánica *nf* (a) mechanics. (b) mechanism, works.

mecánicamente *adv* mechanically.

mecánico 1 *adj* (a) mechanical; power-driven, power-operated; machine (*attr*).
    (b) *trade etc* manual.
    2 *nm* mechanic; machinist; fitter, repair man; (*Aut*) driver, chauffeur; (*Aer*) rigger, fitter.

mecanismo *nm* (a) mechanism; works, machinery; gear; **— de dirección** steering gear.
    (b) action, movement.
    (c) (*fig*) mechanism; machinery, structure; process.

mecanización *nf* mechanization.

mecanizar [1f] *vt* to mechanize.

mecanografía *nf* typing, typewriting; **— al tacto** touch-typing.

mecanografiado 1 *adj* typewritten, typescript. **2** *nm* typescript.

mecanografiar [1c] *vt* to type.

mecanógrafo *nm*, **mecanógrafa** *nf* typist.

mecapalero *nm* (*CAm, Mex*) porter.

mecatazo *nm* (*CAm*) (a) lash, slash. (b) swig of liquor (*fam*).

mecate *nm* (*CAm, Col, Mex, Ven*) (a) strip of pita fibre; string, cord; twine. (b) coarse individual.

mecateada *nf* (*CAm, Mex*) lashing, beating.

mecatear¹ [1a] **1** *vt* (a) (*CAm, Mex*) to tie up; to lash, whip.
    (b) (*Ven*) to fawn on, flatter.
    2 mecatearse *vr* (*Mex*): **—las** to run away, beat it (*fam*).

mecatear² [1a] *vi* (*Col*) to eat cakes.

mecato *nm* (*Col*) cakes, pastries.

mecedor 1 *adj* rocking; swinging. **2** *nm* (a) swing. (b) (*Cu, Mex, Pan*) rocking chair. (c) (*Cu*) stirrer, spoon.

mecedora *nf* rocking chair.

Mecenas *m* Maecenas; **m—** (*fig*) patron.

mecenazgo *nm* patronage.

mecer [2b] **1** *vt* (a) to swing; *cradle etc* to rock; *child* to rock (to and fro), dandle; *branch etc* to sway, move to and fro.
    (b) *container, liquid* to stir, shake (up), agitate.
    2 mecerse *vr* to swing; to rock (to and fro); to sway, move to and fro.

meción *nm* (*CAm, PR*) jerk, jolt.

meco *adj* (*Mex*) *Indian* uncivilized; rebellious, treacherous; (*CAm, Mex*) coarse, rough, vile.

mecha *nf* (a) wick; (*Mil etc*) fuse; **— tardía** time fuse; **aguantar (la) —** (*fig*) to take one's punishment; to put up with everything.
    (b) (*Cook*) slice of bacon.
    (c) **=mechón.**
    (d) (*Arg, Chi, Per*) bit (*of brace*).
    (e) (*Col, Ec, Ven*) joke.
    (f) (*Mex*) fear.

mechar [1a] *vt* (*Cook*) to lard; to stuff.

mechera *nf* shoplifter.

mechero *nm* (a) cigarette lighter; (*of stove*) burner; jet; (*Arg, Col*) oil lamp; **— Bunsen** Bunsen burner; **— encendedor** pilot light; **— de gas** gas burner, gas jet.
    (b) (*Guat, Mex*) mop of hair.
    (c) (*Ven*) joker.

mechificar [1g] *vt* (*Ec, Per, Ven*) to trick, deceive; to mock.

mecho *nm* (*Guat, Col*) candle; candle end; candlestick.

mechón *nm* tuft, wisp; (*of threads*) bundle; (*of hair*) lock.

mechudo *adj* (*SAm*) tousled, unkempt.

medalla *nf* medal.

medallón *nm* (a) medallion. (b) locket. (c) (*Typ*) inset.

médano *nm*, **medaño** *nm* sand dune; sandbank.

media *nf* (a) stocking; (*SAm: man's*) sock; **— de malla** net stocking; **— de nylon** nylon stocking.
    (b) **de —** knitting (*attr*); *knitting* plain; **hacer —** to knit.
    (c) (*Sport*) half-back line.
    (d) (*Math*) mean.

mediación *nf* (a) mediation; intercession. (b) instrumentality.

mediado *adj* (a) half full; halfway through, half completed; **el local estaba —** the place was half full; **mediada la tarde** halfway through the afternoon; **llevo — el trabajo** I am halfway through the job, I have completed half the work.
    (b) **a —s de marzo** in the middle of March, halfway through March; **hacia —s del siglo pasado** about the middle of last century.

mediador *nm*, **mediadora** *nf* mediator.

medial *adj* medial.

medialuna *nf* croissant, breakfast roll.

medianamente *adv* moderately, fairly; moderately well; **un trabajo — bueno** a moderately good piece of work; **quedó — en los exámenes** he did moderately well in the exams.

medianera *nf* (*RPl*) party wall, dividing wall.

medianería *nf* (a) party wall. (b) (*Mex, Ven*) partnership.

medianero 1 *adj* (a) *wall* party (*attr*), dividing; *fence* boundary (*attr*).
    (b) adjacent, next.
    2 *nm* (a) owner of the adjoining house (*or property etc*).
    (b) (*Ven*) partner.

medianía *nf* (a) average; halfway point; middling position; (*Econ*) moderate means, modest circumstances; undistinguished social position.
    (b) (*person*) ordinary sort, mediocrity; **no pasa de ser una —** he's no better than average, he's rather a mediocrity.

mediano *adj* middling, medium, average; indifferent, undistinguished; (*euph*) mediocre (*euph*), rather poor; **de tamaño —** medium-sized; **es — de talento** he has average talent; **es mediana de guapa** she has average looks, she's not outstandingly pretty.

medianoche *nf* midnight.

mediante *prep* by means of, through, by.

mediar [1b] *vi* (a) to be in the middle; to get to the middle, get halfway; **entre A y B median 30 kms** there are 30 kms between A and B; **entre estas 2 casas median otras 3** there are 3 other houses between those 2; **media un abismo entre los dos gobiernos** there is a wide gap between the two governments; **entre los dos sucesos mediaron varios años** several years elapsed between the two events, there were some years between the two events; **mediaba el otoño** autumn was half over; **mediaba el mes de julio** it was halfway through July.
    (b) to come up, happen; to intervene; to exist; **pero medió la muerte de su madre** but his mother's death intervened; **media el hecho de que . . .** there is the fact that . . . to be considered; there is an obstacle in the fact that . . .; **median relaciones cordiales entre los dos** cordial relations exist between the two.
    (c) to mediate (**en** in, **entre** between), intervene; **— con uno** to intercede with someone.

médica *nf* woman doctor.

medicación *nf* medication, treatment.

médicamente *adv* medically.

medicamento *nm* medicine, drug; **— de patente** patent medicine.

medicastro *nm* (*pej*) quack (doctor).

medicina *nf* medicine; **— forense, — legal** forensic medicine; **— preventiva** preventive medicine; **estudiante de —** medical student.

medicinal *adj* medicinal.

medicinar [1a] **1** *vt* to treat, prescribe for. **2 medicinarse** *vr* to dose oneself.

medición *nf* measurement, measuring; **hacer —es** to take measurements.

médico 1 *adj* medical.
    2 *nm* doctor; medical practitioner, physician; **— de cabecera** family doctor; **— dentista** dental surgeon; **— forense** forensic surgeon, expert in forensic medicine; **— general** general practitioner; **— partero** obstetrician; **— puericultor** paediatrician; **— residente** house physician, resident, intern (*US*).

medida *nf* (a) (*Math*) measurement; (*act*) measuring, measurement; **a la —** in proportion; suitable; **el precio es a la — del tamaño** the price goes according to the size; **una caja a la —** a specially made box, a box made for the purpose; **un traje a la —, un traje hecho a la —** a made-to-measure suit; **tiene una novia a la —** he has a girl who is just right for him; **es una solución a la —** the solution is exactly the right one; **a la — de mi deseo** just as I would have wished, exactly as I wanted (it); **a — de** in proportion to, in keeping with; **a — que . . . as . . .**, according as . . ., in keeping with the rate at which . . .; **a — que vaya bajando el agua** as the water goes down; **en cierta —** up to a point, in a way; **en gran — to** a great extent; **—s vitales** vital statistics; **tomar las —s a uno** to measure someone, take someone's measurements; (fig) to size someone up; **tomar sus —s** to size a situation up.

(**b**) (system, container etc) measure; **pesos y —s** weights and measures; **— agraria** land measure; **— para áridos** dry measure; **— para líquidos** liquid measure; **esto colma la — (**fig) this is the last straw; **con esto se colmó la — de la paciencia de su padre** this finally exhausted her father's patience.

(**c**) (of shirt, shoe etc) size, fitting.

(**d**) (Lit) (correct) scansion.

(**e**) (fig) measure, step, move; **— preventiva** preventive measure; **— represiva** deterrent, check (contra to); **tomar —s** to take steps (para que to ensure that).

(**f**) (fig) moderation, prudence; restraint; **sin —** immoderately, in an unrestrained fashion.

medidor nm (SAm) meter; gauge; **— de lluvia** rain gauge.

mediería nf hosiery.

medieval adj medieval.

medievalismo nm medievalism.

medievalista nmf medievalist.

medio 1 adj (**a**) half (a).

(**b**) **media naranja** half an orange, a half orange; **media hora** half an hour; **nos queda media botella** we've half a bottle left; **media luna** half-moon, (fig) crescent; **medio luto** half-mourning; **media luz** half-light; **acudió media provincia** half the province turned up.

(**c**) point etc mid, midway, middle; **clase —** middle class(es); **dedo —** middle finger; **a media tarde** halfway through the afternoon; **café de media mañana** (mid-)morning coffee.

(**d**) (Math) mean, average; (fig) average; **el hombre —** the average man, the ordinary man, the man in the street; see **término** etc.

(**e**) (SAm) big, huge.

(**f**) **a medias** half; by halves; **está escrito a medias** it's half-written; **lo dejó hecho a medias** he left it half-done; **estoy satisfecho sólo a medias** I am only partly satisfied; **ir a medias** to go fifty-fifty (con with), divide the costs (etc) equally; **lo pagamos a medias** we share the cost.

2 adv half; **— dormido** half asleep; **estar — borracho** to be half drunk; **está — escrito, está a — escribir** it is half-written; **eso no está ni — bien** that isn't at all right.

3 nm (**a**) middle, centre; halfway point (etc); (Math) mean; **— aritmético** arithmetical mean; **justo —** happy medium, golden mean; fair compromise; **equivocarse de — a —** to be completely wrong; **en —** in the middle; in between; **en — de la plaza** in the middle of the square; **en — de tanta confusión** in the midst of such confusion; **la casa de en —** the middle house; the house in between; **quitar algo de en —** to remove something; to get rid of something, get something out of the way; **quitarse de en —** to get out of the way; to duck, dodge; to remove oneself; **pasar por — de** to go through (the middle of); **tomar algo por el —** to grasp something round the middle; **de por — in** between; **hay dificultades de por —** there are snags in the way; **meterse de por —** to intervene; **día (de) por — (**SAm) every other day.

(**b**) (Sport) half-back; **— centro** centre-half.

(**c**) (Spiritualism) medium.

(**d**) means, way, method; medium; measure, expedient; **—s de transporte** means of transport; **por — de** by means of, by, through; **por todos los —s** by all possible means, in every possible way; **no hay — de conseguirlo** there is no way of getting it; **poner todos los —s para + infin**, **no regatear — para + infin** to spare no effort to + infin.

(**e**) **—s** (Econ, Fin) means, resources.

(**f**) atmosphere; milieu, ambience; environment; circle; (Bio: also **— ambiente**) environment; **— de cultivo** culture medium; **en los —s financieros** in financial circles; **encontrarse en su —** to be in one's element.

mediocre adj middling, average; (pej) mediocre, rather poor.

mediocridad nf middling quality; (pej) mediocrity; **es una —** he's a nonentity, he's a dead loss.

mediodía nm (**a**) midday, noon; **a —** at noon. (**b**) (Geog) south.

Medio Oriente m Middle East.

mediquillo nm (pej) quack (doctor).

medir [3I] **1** vt (**a**) to measure; to survey, plot; **— a**

millas, **— por millas** to measure in miles; **— a uno (con la vista:** fig) to size someone up.

(**b**) plan, possibility etc to weigh up.

(**c**) (Lit) verse to scan (properly).

2 vi (**a**) to measure, be; **la tela mide 90 cms** the cloth measures 90 cms; **el papel mide 20 cms de ancho** the paper is 20 cms wide; **ella mide 1,50 m** she is 1.50 m tall; **mide 88 cms de pecho** she is 88 cms round the chest, her bust measurement is 88 cms.

(**b**) (Lit) to scan (properly).

3 medirse vr (**a**) **— con uno** to measure up to someone; to test oneself against someone.

(**b**) (fig) to be moderate, act with restraint.

(**c**) (SAm: Sport) to play each other, meet; to quarrel, come to blows.

meditabundo adj pensive, thoughtful.

meditación nf meditation; pondering; **—es** meditations (sobre on).

meditar [1a] **1** vt to ponder, think over, meditate (on); plan etc to think out, work out, plan. **2** vi to ponder, think, meditate; to muse.

Mediterráneo m Mediterranean.

mediterráneo adj Mediterranean.

médium nm, pl **médiums** medium.

medo nm: los **—s y los persas** the Medes and the Persians.

medra nf increase, growth; improvement; (Econ etc) prosperity.

medrar [1a] vi to increase, grow; to improve, do well, do better; (Econ etc) to prosper, thrive, do well; (animal, plant) to grow, thrive; **¡medrados estamos!** (iro) a fine thing you've done!

medro nm = **medra**.

medroso adj fearful, timid, fainthearted.

médula nf, **medula** nf (**a**) (Anat) marrow; medulla; **— espinal** spinal cord; **hasta la — (**fig) to the core; through and through; **estoy convencido hasta la —** I am profoundly convinced.

(**b**) (Bot) pith.

(**c**) (fig) essence; substance; pith.

medusa nf jellyfish.

Mefistófeles m Mephistopheles.

megaciclo nm megacycle.

megáfono nm megaphone.

megalítico adj megalithic.

megalito nm megalith.

megalomanía nf megalomania.

megalómano nm, **megalómana** nf megalomaniac.

megatón nm megaton.

megavatio nm megawatt.

megavoltio nm megavolt.

mejicanismo nm mexicanism, word (or phrase etc) peculiar to Mexico.

mejicano 1 adj Mexican. **2** nm, **mejicana** nf Mexican.

Méjico m Mexico.

mejido adj egg beaten.

mejilla nf cheek.

mejillón nm mussel.

mejor 1 adj (**a**) (comp) better (que than).

(**b**) (superl) best; bidder highest; **es el — de todos** he's the best of all; **lo — the** best thing, the best part (etc); **lo — de la novela** the best part of the novel, the best thing about the novel; **lo — de la vida** the prime of life; **hice lo — que pude** I did the best I could, I did my best; **llevar lo — to** get the best of it; **a lo —** probably, maybe; with any luck; suddenly, when least expected; **"¿crees que lo hará?" ... "a lo —"** "do you think he'll do it?" ... "he may do" (or "maybe").

2 adv (**a**) (comp) better; **A canta — que B** A sings better than B; **— quisiera + infin** I would rather + infin; **¡—!** good!, that's fine!; **— que —** better and better, all the better; **tanto —** all the better, so much the better (para for); **está mucho —** he's much better; **"nunca habéis estado —"** (slogan) "you never had it so good".

(**b**) (superl) best.

mejora nf (**a**) improvement; **—s** (to property) improvements; alterations, repairs. (**b**) (at auction) higher bid. (**c**) (Mex: Agr) weeding, cleaning.

mejorable adj improvable; **esto es fácilmente —** this can easily be improved.

mejoramiento nm improvement.

mejorana nf marjoram.

mejorar [1a] **1** vt (**a**) to improve, make better, ameliorate; to enhance; bid to raise; offer to improve, increase; record to break.

(**b**) **— a** to be better than, be superior to.

2 vi and **mejorarse** vr (**a**) to improve, get better; (Med) to get better; (Meteorol) to improve, clear up;

(*Fin etc*) to do well, prosper; **los negocios mejoran** business is improving, business is picking up; **¡que se mejore!** get well soon!

(b) (*at auction*) to raise one's bid.

mejoría *nf* improvement; recovery; **¡que siga la —!** I hope the improvement continues.

mejunje *nm* **(a)** brew, mixture, concoction. **(b)** (*fam*) fraud. **(c)** (*Arg, Mex, PR*) mess, tangle, mix-up.

melado 1 *adj* honey-coloured. **2** *nm* treacle, syrup; (*SAm*) cane syrup.

meladura *nf* (*Cu, Mex*) cane syrup.

melancolía *nf* melancholy, gloom(iness), sadness; (*Med*) melancholia.

melancólicamente *adv* gloomily, sadly, in a melancholy way; wistfully.

melancólico *adj* melancholy, gloomy, sad; dreamy, wistful.

melanismo *nm* melanism.

melarchía *nf* (*CAm*) = **melancolía**.

melaza *nf* (*also —s*) molasses; treacle.

melcocha *nf* molasses; treacle; candy, molasses toffee.

melcochado *adj* fruit etc candied; (*in colour*) golden, honey-coloured.

melcocharse [1a] *vr* to thicken (*in boiling*).

mêlée [me'le] *nf* (*Rugby*) scrum.

melena *nf* long hair; loose hair, flowing hair; (*pej*) mop of hair, bushy hair; (*as style*) ponytail; (*Zool*) mane; **andar a la —** to pull one another's hair, (*fig*) to quarrel; **estar en —** to have one's hair down; **soltar la —** (*fig*) to break out, shatter the conventions; to lose all restraint.

melenudo *adj* long-haired.

melga *nf* (*Arg, Mex*) plot of land prepared for sowing; (*Chi*) furrow.

melifluo *adj* mellifluous, sweet.

melindre *nm* **(a)** sweet cake, iced bun; honey fritter. **(b)** **—s** daintiness, dainty ways; (*pej*) affectation, affected ways; squeamishness; prudery, prudishness; **gastar —s** = **melindrear**.

melindrear [1a] *vi* to be affected, indulge in affectation; to be squeamish; to be prudish; to be excessively finicky, be terribly fussy.

melindroso *adj* affected; squeamish; prudish; finicky, fussy.

melisca *nf* (*Arg*) gleaning.

melocotón *nm* peach.

melocotonero *nm* peach tree.

melodía *nf* **(a)** (*una —*) melody; tune, air. **(b)** (*quality*) melodiousness.

melódico *adj* melodic.

melodiosamente *adv* melodiously, tunefully.

melodioso *adj* melodious, tuneful.

melodrama *nm* melodrama.

melodramáticamente *adv* melodramatically.

melodramático *adj* melodramatic.

melón[1] *nm* **(a)** (*Bot*) melon. **(b)** (*fam*) head, nut (*sl*). **(c)** (*fam*) idiot.

melón[2] *nm* (*Zool*) = **meloncillo**.

melonada *nf* (*fam*) silly thing, idiotic remark (*etc*).

meloncillo *nm* (*Zool*) ichneumon, (kind of) mongoose.

melosidad *nf* **(a)** sweetness; (*pej*) sickliness. **(b)** (*fig*) sweetness; gentleness; (*pej*) smoothness.

meloso *adj* **(a)** honeyed, sweet; (*pej*) sickly, cloying. **(b)** (*fig*) voice etc sweet, musical; gentle; (*pej*) smooth, soapy.

mella *nf* **(a)** nick, dent, notch; (*in teeth etc*) gap; **hacer —** (*fig*) to make an impression, sink in, strike home; **hacer — en** (*or* **a**) to make an impression on, tell on.
(b) (*fig*) harm, damage; **hacer — en** to do damage to, harm.

mellado *adj* edge jagged, nicked, ragged; *person* gap-toothed.

mellar [1a] *vt* **(a)** to nick, dent, notch; to take a chip out of. **(b)** (*fig*) to damage, harm.

mellizo 1 *adj* twin. **2** *nm*, **melliza** *nf* twin.

membrana *nf* **(a)** membrane; (*Orn*) membrane, web; **— mucosa** mucous membrane; **— virginal** hymen. **(b)** (*Chi*) diphtheria.

membranoso *adj* membranous.

membrete *nm* letterhead, heading.

membrillero *nm* quince tree.

membrillo *nm* quince; (**carne de**) **—** quince jelly.

membrudo *adj* burly, brawny, tough.

memela *nf* (*CAm, Mex*) thick pancake of maize flour.

memez *nf* silly thing; farce, absurdity.

memo 1 *adj* silly, stupid. **2** *nm* idiot.

memorable *adj* memorable.

memorablemente *adv* memorably.

memorando *nm* (*Acad*), **memorándum** *nm*, *pl* **memorándums** **(a)** notebook. **(b)** (*Pol etc*) memorandum.

memoria *nf* **(a)** (*in general*) memory; **de buena —**, **de feliz —** of happy memory; **digno de —** memorable; **falta de —** forgetfulness; **flaco de —** forgetful; **aprender algo de —** to learn something by heart; to memorize something, commit something to memory; **hablar de —** to speak from memory; **se le fue de la —** he forgot it, it slipped his mind; **en — de** in memory of; **la peor tormenta de que hay —** the worst storm in living memory; the worst storm on record; **hacer — de algo** to recall something, bring something to mind; **no queda — de eso** there is no memory (*or* record) of that; **tener mala —** to have a bad memory; **si tengo buena —** if my memory serves me; **traer algo a la —** to recall something.
(b) note, report, statement; record; aide-mémoire, memorandum; petition; (learned) paper; **— anual** annual report; **—s** (*of person*) memoirs, (*of society*) transactions.
(c) **—s** (*to person*) regards, remembrances.

memorial *nm* memorial, petition; (*Law*) brief.

memorialista *nm* amanuensis.

memorión *nm* (*fam*) good memory, amazing memory.

memorioso *adj* (*SAm*) having a retentive memory, that remembers everything.

memorista *adj* (*SAm*) having a retentive memory; **es —** (*pej*) he just memorizes things.

memorización *nf* (*SAm*) memorizing.

memorizar [1f] *vt* (*SAm*) to memorize.

mena *nf* ore.

menaje *nm* **(a)** family, household; **vida de —** (*SAm*) family life, domestic life.
(b) housekeeping; housework, upkeep of the house.
(c) (*Comm etc*) household equipment, furnishings; **sección de —** (*in store*) hardware and kitchen department.

mención *nf* mention; **— honorífica** honourable mention; **hacer — de** to mention.

mencionado *adj* aforementioned.

mencionar [1a] *vt* to mention, refer to; to name; **sin —** . . . let alone . . .; **dejar de —** to fail to mention, leave unmentioned.

mendacidad *nf* **(a)** mendacity, untruthfulness. **(b)** (*una —*) untruth, gross lie.

mendaz *adj* mendacious; lying, untruthful.

mendeliano *adj* Mendelian.

mendelismo *nm* Mendelism, Mendelianism.

mendicante 1 *adj* mendicant. **2** *nmf* mendicant.

mendicidad *nf* begging; mendicity.

mendigar [1h] **1** *vt* to beg (for). **2** *vi* to beg (for alms).

mendigo *nm*, **mendiga** *nf* beggar.

mendrugo *nm* **(a)** (hard) crust. **(b)** (*fam*) dolt, blockhead.

mene *nm* (*Col, Ven*) pitch, asphalt.

menear [1a] **1** *vt* **(a)** to move, shift; *head etc* to shake, toss; *tail* to wag; *hips* to sway, swing, waggle; **sin — el dedo** without lifting a finger; **peor es meneallo** it's best to leave that alone; don't go stirring all that up.
(b) **— cálamo** to wield a pen.
(c) *affair* to get on with, get moving; *business etc* to handle, conduct.
2 menearse *vr* **(a)** to move; to shake; to wag; to sway, swing, waggle.
(b) to hustle, bestir oneself, get a move on; **¡—!** get going!, jump to it!

Menelao *m* Menelaus.

meneo *nm* **(a)** movement; shake, toss; wag; sway(ing), swing(ing); waggle; jerk, jolt; **dar un — a** to jerk, jolt, move suddenly. **(b)** (*fam*) hiding.

menequear [1a] *vt*, **menequetear** [1a] *vt* (*Arg, Mex*) to shake, wag.

meneque(te)o *nm* (*Arg, Mex*) shaking, wagging.

menester *nm* **(a)** **ser —** to be necessary; **cuando sea —** when it is necessary; **es — + infin** it is necessary to + *infin*, we (*etc*) must + *infin*; **todo es —** everything is welcome.
(b) job, piece of business; errand; **—es** duties, jobs, business; occupation; function; **salir para un —** to go out on an errand; **hacer sus —es** (*euph*) to do one's business (*euph*).
(c) **—es** (*Tech*) gear, tackle, tools.

menesteroso *adj* needy.

menestra *nf* **(a)** vegetable soup, stew. **(b)** **—s** dried vegetables.

menestral *nm* workman, artisan.

mengano *nm*, **mengana** *nf* Mr (*etc*) So-and-so; *see* **fulano**.

mengua *nf* **(a)** decrease, diminishment; dwindling;

decay, decline; **ir en — de** to contribute to the lessening of, assist the decrease (or restriction etc) of; **sin —** complete, whole; untouched.
(**b**) lack, want; loss.
(**c**) poverty.
(**d**) (of person) spinelessness, weakness of character.
(**e**) discredit; **ir en — de uno** to be to someone's discredit.
menguadamente adv (**a**) (fig) wretchedly; weakly, spinelessly. (**b**) meanly. (**c**) foolishly.
menguado 1 adj (**a**) decreased, diminished.
(**b**) (fig) wretched, miserable; weak, spineless, weak in character; cowardly.
(**c**) unlucky; **en hora menguada** at an unlucky moment.
(**d**) mean.
(**e**) foolish.
2 nm (knitting) decrease.
menguante 1 adj decreasing, diminishing; dwindling; decaying; moon waning; tide ebb (attr).
2 nf (**a**) (Naut) ebb tide, low water.
(**b**) (of moon) waning.
(**c**) (fig) decay, decline; **estar en —** to be in decline.
menguar [1i] **1** vt (**a**) to lessen, diminish, reduce; (knitting) to decrease (by).
(**b**) (fig) to discredit.
2 vi (**a**) to diminish, get less, dwindle, decrease; (of number, tide etc) to go down; (of moon) to wane.
(**b**) (fig) to wane, decay, decline.
mengue nm (fam) the devil; **¡malos —s te lleven!** go to hell!
meningitis nf meningitis.
menjunje nm, **menjurje** nm see **mejunje**.
menopausia nf menopause.
menor 1 adj (Eccl) order minor; (Mus) minor.
2 adj comp (**a**) (in size) smaller (que than); less, lesser; **en — número** in smaller numbers; **celidonia — lesser** celandine.
(**b**) (in age) younger (que than); junior (que to); **el hermano —** the younger brother; **Juanito es — que Pepe** Johnnie is younger than Joe; see **edad**.
3 adj superl (**a**) (in size) smallest; least; **éste es el — de todos** this is the smallest of the lot; **no le concedo la — importancia** I don't attach the least (or slightest) importance to it.
(**b**) (in age) youngest; most junior; **ella es la — de todas** she is the youngest of all.
4 nmf young person, juvenile, (Law) minor; **un — de 14** an under-14; **los —es de edad** those who are under age, the juveniles; **apto para —es** (Cine) for all ages, "Universal" (U); **no apto para —es** (Cine) not suitable for juveniles.
5 nm (**a**) **al por —** (Comm) retail; **vender un género al por —** to sell goods retail.
(**b**) **contar algo por —** to recount something in detail.
Menorca f Minorca.
menoría nf (**a**) (Law) minority. (**b**) inferiority; subordination.
menorista (Chi, Mex) **1** adj retail (attr). **2** nmf retailer.
menorquín 1 adj Minorcan. **2** nm, **menorquina** nf Minorcan.
menos 1 adj (**a**) (Math) sign minus.
(**b**) (comp) less; fewer; **con — ruido** with less noise; **con — hombres** with fewer men; **A tiene — ventajas que B** A has fewer advantages than B; **A tiene — años que B** A is younger than B; **éste es — coche que el anterior** (fam) this is not such a good car as the old one.
(**c**) (superl) least; fewest; **es el que — culpa tiene** least blame attaches to him, he is least to blame.
2 adv (**a**) (comp) less, (superl) least; **hoy se va** people don't go so much nowadays, nowadays people go less; **es el — inteligente de los 4** he is the least intelligent of the 4; **no quiero alquilarlo ni — comprarlo** I don't want to rent it and still less to buy it; **¿qué —?** (fam) what else did you expect?; **— de, — de lo que, — que** less than; **— de lo que piensas** less than you think; **fue nada — que un rey** he was nothing less than a king, he was a king no less; **hay 7 de —** we're 7 short, there are 7 missing; **me dieron un paquete con medio kilo de —** they gave me a packet which was half a kilo short (or under weight); **me han pagado 2 libras de —** they have underpaid me by £2.
(**b**) (phrases with lo) **lo — 10** 10 at least; **lo — posible** as little as possible; **eso es lo de —** that's the least of it; **es lo — que se puede esperar** it's the

least one can expect; **al —, a lo —, por lo —** at least.
(**c**) (idioms) **a — de** without; **tener a — + infin** to consider it beneath oneself to **+ infin; ir a —, venir a —** to come down in the world; to decline, decay; to run to seed; **darse de —** to underestimate oneself, hide one's light under a bushel; **echar a uno de —** to miss someone; **hacer a uno de —** to despise someone; to belittle someone; **no se quedó en —** he was not to be outdone; see **cuando, mucho, poder.**
3 prep (**a**) except; **todos — él** everybody except him; **¡todo — eso!** anything but that!
(**b**) (Math) minus, less; **7 — 2 son 5** 2 from 7 leaves 5, 7 take away 2 leaves 5; **las 7 — 20** (time) 20 to 7.
4 conj: **a — que** . . . unless . . .
5 nm (**a**) (Math) minus sign (-).
(**b**) see **más.**
menoscabar [1a] vt (**a**) to lessen, reduce, diminish; to damage, harm, impair. (**b**) to discredit.
menoscabo nm lessening, reduction; damage, harm; loss; **con — de, en — de** to the detriment of; **sin —** unimpaired; **sufrir —** to suffer damage, suffer loss.
menospreciable adj contemptible.
menospreciador adj scornful.
menospreciar [1b] vt (**a**) to scorn, despise. (**b**) to slight. (**c**) to underrate, undervalue.
menospreciativo adj scornful, contemptuous; slighting.
menosprecio nm (**a**) scorn, contempt.
(**b**) underrating, undervaluation.
(**c**) disrespect; **con — del sexo de la víctima** without regard for the sex of the victim.
mensaje nm message; **— de buenos augurios** goodwill message; **— de la corona** (Parl) speech from the throne.
mensajero nm, **mensajera** nf messenger.
menso adj (Mex) silly, stupid.
menstruación nf menstruation.
menstrual adj menstrual.
menstruar [1e] vi to menstruate.
menstruo nm (**a**) menstruation. (**b**) menses.
mensual adj monthly; **50 dólares —es** 50 dollars a month.
mensualidad nf monthly payment (or salary, instalment etc).
mensualmente adv monthly.
mensuario nm (SAm) monthly journal.
ménsula nf bracket; (Archit) corbel.
mensura nf (SAm) measurement.
mensurable adj measurable.
mensuración nf mensuration.
menta nf mint; **— romana, — verde** spearmint.
mentado adj (**a**) aforementioned. (**b**) well-known, famous.
mental adj mental; capacity, work etc intellectual.
mentalidad nf mentality, mind.
mentalmente adv mentally.
mentar [1k] vt to mention, name.
mentas nfpl (Arg, Bol, Urug) (**a**) reputation. (**b**) rumours, gossip.
mente nf mind; intelligence, understanding; **— consciente** conscious mind; **— subconsciente** subconscious mind; **cambiar de —** to change one's mind; **no está en mi — + infin**, no tengo en **— + infin** it is not in my mind to **+ infin**, it is not my intention to **+ infin; se le fue completamente de la —** it completely slipped his mind.
mentecatería nf, **mentecatez** nf stupidity, foolishness.
mentecato 1 adj silly, stupid. **2** nm, **mentecata** nf idiot, fool.
mentidero nm place where people gossip.
mentir [3i] **1** vt (lit) to feign, pretend; to suggest (falsely) to; **la sed me mintió un arroyo cercano** my thirst led me to suppose there was a stream nearby.
2 vi to lie, tell a lie, tell lies; to be deceptive; **¡miento!** sorry, I'm wrong!, my mistake!; **¡esta carta no me dejará —!** this letter will bear me out!, this letter will confirm what I say!
mentira nf (**a**) (una —) lie, falsehood; (in general) lying, untruthfulness, deceitfulness; (Lit) fiction, invention; (in text) error, misprint; **¡—!** it's a lie!; **una mentira como una casa** a whopping great lie (sl); **— oficiosa, — piadosa** white lie; **¡parece —!** well (I never)!; you don't say so!; **aunque parezca —** however incredible it seems; **parece — que . . . it** seems impossible that . . .; **parece — que no te acuerdas** I'm surprised you don't remember it; **no**

hay — que no salga truth will out; **coger a uno en una** — to catch someone in a lie.
(b) white mark (on fingernail).
(c) (Arg, Chi, CAm) cracking of knuckles; **sacar —s** to crack one's knuckles.

mentirijillas: es de —, **va de** — it's only a joke; (to child) just pretend, it's just make-believe; **jugar de** — to play for fun (ie not for money).

mentirilla nf fib; white lie.

mentirosillo nm, **mentirosilla** nf fibber.

mentiroso 1 adj (a) lying, deceitful, untruthful; deceptive, false. (b) text full of errors, full of misprints. **2** nm, **mentirosa** nf liar; deceiver.

mentís nm, pl **mentís** denial; **dar el** — **a** to refute, deny, give the lie to.

mentol nm menthol.

mentolado adj mentholated.

mentón nm chin.

mentor nm mentor.

menú nm menu.

menudear [1a] 1 vt (a) to repeat frequently, do repeatedly; story etc to tell in great detail.
(b) (Col) to sell retail.
2 vi (a) to be frequent, happen frequently; (of missiles etc) to rain, come thick and fast; to come in abundance.
(b) to go into great detail.
(c) (Arg, Mex) to abound; to increase, grow in number.

menudencia nf (a) trifle, small thing; —s little things, odds and ends. (b) minuteness; exactness; meticulousness. (c) —s pork products; offal.

menudeo nm (Comm) retail trade; **vender al** — to sell retail.

menudillos nmpl giblets.

menudo 1 adj (a) small, tiny, minute; (fig) slight, petty, insignificant; **moneda menuda** small change, coins of low denomination.
(b) person exact, meticulous.
(c) (iro) fine, some; **¡— negocio!'** some deal!; **¡menuda plancha!** what a bloomer! (fam); **¡menuda vidorra nos vamos a dar!** we won't half live it up! (fam); **¡menuda me la han hecho!** they've done it on me!
(d) (with prep) **a** — frequently, often; **a la menuda, por la menuda** (Comm) retail; **contar algo por** — to tell something in detail.
2 nm (a) small change.
(b) —s offal; giblets.

meñique 1 adj tiny, very small; **dedo** — = **2** nm little finger.

meollo nm (a) (Anat) marrow, brains.
(b) (of bread) soft part, inside, crumb.
(c) (fig: of person) brains.
(d) (fig: of matter etc) gist, essence, core; solid substance, solid part, meat.

meón 1 adj child that constantly wets itself. **2** nm, **meona** nf baby (boy, girl).

meque nm (Cu) slap, punch.

mequetrefe nm good-for-nothing, whippersnapper.

meramente adv merely, only, solely.

merca nf (Mex) shopping, purchases.

mercachifle nm (a) small-time trader, dealer; hawker, huckster. (b) (fig) money grubber.

mercadear [1a] vi to deal, trade.

mercadeo nm marketing.

mercader nm (esp Hist) merchant.

mercadería nf commodity; —s goods, merchandise.

mercado nm market; **M— Común** Common Market; — **de dinero** money market; — **exterior** overseas market; — **interior,** — **nacional** home market; — **libre** free market (de in); — **mundial** world market; — **negro** black market; — **de valores** stock market; — **de viejo** rag fair; — **de signo favorable al comprador** buyer's market; — **de signo favorable al vendedor** seller's market; **inundar el** — **de** to flood the market with.

mercadotecnia nf marketing; **estudios de** — market research.

mercancía 1 nf commodity; —s goods, merchandise. **2** —s nm goods train, freight train (US).

mercante 1 adj merchant (attr), trading, commercial; **buque** — = **2** nm merchantman, merchant ship.

mercantil adj mercantile, trading, commercial; law commercial.

mercantilismo nm mercantilism.

mercar [1g] vt to buy.

merced nf (a) (arch) favour; benefit, reward; pleasure, will; **hacer la** — **de** + infin to do someone the favour of + ger; **tenga la** — **de** + infin please be so good as to + infin.
(b) — **a** thanks to.

(c) (arch) **vuestra** — your honour, your worship, sir.
(d) **estar a la** — **de** to be at the mercy of.

mercenario 1 adj mercenary. **2** nm (Mil) mercenary; (Agr) day labourer; (fig) hack, hireling.

mercería nf (a) haberdashery, notions (US).
(b) haberdasher's (shop), notions store (US); (Mex, Per, PR) draper's (shop), dry-goods store (US); (Chi) hardware store.

mercero nm haberdasher; (Mex, Per, PR) draper.

mercurial adj mercurial.

Mercurio m Mercury.

mercurio nm mercury.

merdoso adj (tabu) filthy; sluttish.

merecedor adj deserving, worthy (de of); — **de crédito** solvent; — **de confianza** trustworthy; **ser** — **de** to deserve, be deserving of.

merecer [2d] 1 vt (a) to deserve, be worthy of, merit; — + infin to deserve to + infin; **merece que se le dé el premio** he deserves (to receive) the prize.
(b) (Col, Ec) to catch; to snatch, pinch (fam); to find.
2 vi to be deserving, be worthy; — **mucho** to be very deserving; — **bien de la patria** to deserve well of one's country, deserve one's country's gratitude.
3 merecerse vr: — **algo** to earn something.

merecidamente adv deservedly.

merecido 1 adj well deserved, fully deserved; **bien** — **lo tiene** it serves him right. **2** nm (just) deserts; **llevar su** — to get one's deserts.

merecimiento nm (a) deserts. (b) merit, worthiness.

merendar [1k] 1 vt (a) to have for tea.
(b) — **lo que escribe otro** to look at what someone else is writing; — **las cartas de otro** to peep at someone else's cards, take a sly look at an opponent's cards.
2 vi to have tea; (in country) to picnic, take tea out.
3 merendarse vr (fam) (a) — **algo** to wangle something (fam), get something by a fiddle (fam).
(b) — **una fortuna** to squander a fortune.
(c) — **a uno** (Col) to beat someone; (Col, Chi, Mex) to kill someone.

merendero nm tearoom; picnic spot.

merengue nm (a) (Cook) meringue. (b) (Ant, Col, Chi, Per) sickly person, invalid. (c) (Arg) row, fuss.

meretriz nf prostitute.

mergo nm cormorant.

meridiana nf (a) divan, couch; chaise longue. (b) **a la** — at noon.

meridiano nm meridian.

meridional 1 adj southern. **2** nmf southerner.

merienda nf tea; afternoon snack; (on journey) packed meal; (in country) picnic, picnic tea (also — **campestre**); — **de negros** (fam) bedlam; (fam) crooked deal, dishonest share-out; **ir de** — to go for a picnic; **juntar** —s (fig) to join forces, pool one's resources.

merienda-cena nf high tea.

merino 1 adj merino. **2** nm merino (sheep); merino wool.

mérito nm merit; worth, value; excellence; **de** — worthy, of merit; —s **de guerra** equivalent to mention in dispatches; **hacer** — **de** to mention; **hacer** —s **to** strive to be deserving; **restar** — **de** to detract from; **alega los siguientes** —s he quotes the following facts in support (or in his favour).

meritocracia nf meritocracy.

meritorio 1 adj meritorious, worthy, deserving; praiseworthy. **2** nm unpaid employee, apprentice, (esp) office boy.

merla nf = **mirlo**.

Merlín m Merlin; **saber más que** — to know the lot.

merlo¹ nm (Fish) black wrasse.

merlo² nm (SAm) idiot.

merluza nf (a) (Fish) hake. (b) (sl) **coger una** — to get sozzled (sl); **estar** —, **estar con la** — to get boozed up.

merma nf decrease; shrinkage; wastage, loss.

mermar [1a] 1 vt to reduce, lessen; to deplete; pay, rations etc to cut down.
2 vi and **mermarse** vr to decrease, dwindle; to be depleted; (liquid) to go down; (fig) to waste away.

mermelada nf jam; — **de albaricoques** apricot jam; — **de manzanas** apple sauce; — **de naranjas amargas** marmalade.

mero¹ 1 adj (a) mere; pure, simple.
(b) (Mex) exact, real.
2 adv (a) (Col, Ven) only.
(b) (Guat, Mex, Salv) soon.
(c) (Guat) really, truly.
(d) (Mex) just; right, exactly; **aquí** — right here; **él va** — **adelante** he's just ahead.

mero² nm (Fish) grouper.

merodeador 1 *adj* marauding; prowling. **2** *nm* (*Mil etc*) marauder; raider; (*at night*) prowler.
merodear [1a] *vi* (**a**) (*Mil etc*) to maraud; (*at night*) to prowl (about), rove about. (**b**) (*Mex*) to make money by illicit means.
merodeo *nm* marauding; prowling, roving.
merolico *nm* (*Mex*) quack, seller of quack remedies.
merovingio 1 *adj* Merovingian. **2** *nm*, **merovingia** *nf* Merovingian.
mes *nm* (**a**) month; **50 dólares al** — 50 dollars a month; — **lunar** lunar month; **el** — **corriente** the current month, this month; **el** — **que viene, el** — **próximo** next month.
(**b**) (*Fin*) month's pay; monthly payment.
(**c**) (*Med*) menses.
mesa *nf* (**a**) table; (*also* — **de trabajo**) desk; (*Comm*) counter; — **de alas abatibles** gate-leg(ged) table, table with flaps; — **de billar** billiard table; — **de café** coffee table; café table; — **de despacho** office desk; — **de noche** bedside table; — **de operaciones**, — **operatoria** operating table; — **redonda** (*restaurant*) table d'hôte; (*Hist*) Round Table; (*Pol*) round table; — **de tijera** folding table; **alzar la** —, **levantar la** —, **quitar la** — (*SAm*) to clear away; **bendecir la** — to say grace; **poner la** — to lay the table; **sentarse a la** — to sit down to table; **servir a la** — to wait at table; **vino de** — table wine.
(**b**) board; — **y cama** bed and board; **tratar a uno a** — **y mantel** to entertain someone royally.
(**c**) (*Geog*) meseta, tableland, plateau.
(**d**) (*Archit*) landing.
(**e**) (*of tool, blade*) side, flat.
(**f**) (*persons*) presiding committee, board.
mesana *nf* mizzen.
mesarse [1a] *vr* (**a**) (*of 2 persons*) to pull each other's hair. (**b**) — **el pelo** (*or* **los cabellos**) to tear one's hair.
mescalina *nf* mescaline.
mescolanza *nf* = **mezcolanza**.
mesenterio *nm* mesentery.
mesera *nf* (*Mex*) waitress.
mesero *nm* (*Mex*) waiter.
meseta *nf* (**a**) (*Geog*) meseta, tableland, plateau. (**b**) (*Archit*) landing.
mesiánico *adj* messianic.
Mesías *m* Messiah.
mesilla *nf* (**a**) small table, side table, occasional table; — **de chimenea** mantelpiece; — **de noche** bedside table; — **plegable** folding table; — **de ruedas** trolley.
(**b**) (*Cu*) market stall.
mesmeriano *adj* mesmeric.
mesmerismo *nm* mesmerism.
mesón[1] *nm* (*Phys*) meson.
mesón[2] *nm* (**a**) (*arch*) inn; (*modern*) hotel with period décor, olde-worlde pub. (**b**) (*Chi*) counter; bar.
mesonero, mesonera *nf* (*arch*) innkeeper; landlord, landlady.
mesteño (*Mex*) **1** *adj* horse wild, untamed. **2** *nm* mustang.
mestizaje *nm* (**a**) crossbreeding; miscegenation. (**b**) half-castes (*collectively*).
mestizar [1f] *vt* to crossbreed; *race* to adulterate by crossbreeding.
mestizo 1 *adj* half-caste, half-breed, racially mixed; (*Zool*) crossbred; hybrid; mongrel.
2 *nm*, **mestiza** *nf* half-caste, half-breed; (*Zool*) crossbred animal; hybrid; mongrel.
mesura *nf* (**a**) gravity, dignity, calm. (**b**) moderation, restraint. (**c**) courtesy.
mesurado *adj* (**a**) grave, dignified, calm. (**b**) moderate, restrained. (**c**) courteous.
mesurar [1a] **1** *vt* (**a**) to restrain, temper. (**b**) (*SAm*) to measure. **2 mesurarse** *vr* to restrain oneself, act with restraint.
meta 1 *nf* (**a**) (*Sport*) goal; (*in race*) winning post, finishing line. (**b**) (*fig*) goal, aim, objective. **2** *nm* goalkeeper.
metabólico *adj* metabolic.
metabolismo *nm* metabolism.
metacarpiano *nm* metacarpal.
metafísica *nf* metaphysics.
metafísico 1 *adj* metaphysical. **2** *nm* metaphysician.
metáfora *nf* metaphor.
metafórico *adj* metaphorical(al).
metal *nm* (**a**) metal; (*Mus*) brass; (*Mex*) ore; — **en láminas**, — **laminado** sheet metal; **el vil** — filthy lucre. (**b**) (*of voice*) timbre; (*fig*) quality.
metalero *adj* (*Bol, Chi, Per*) metal (*attr*).
metálico 1 *adj* metallic; metal (*attr*). **2** *nm* (**a**) specie, bullion, coin; cash; **pagar en** — to pay (in) cash; **premio en** — cash prize. (**b**) metalworker.
metalista *nm* metalworker.

metalistería *nf* metalwork.
metalizado *adj* mercenary, dedicated to making money; who sees everything in terms of money.
metalizarse [1f] *vr* (*fig*) to become mercenary.
metalurgia *nf* metallurgy.
metalúrgico 1 *adj* metallurgic(al). **2** *nm* metallurgist.
metamórfico *adj* metamorphic.
metamorfosear [1a] **1** *vt* to metamorphose, transform, change (*en into*). **2 metamorfosearse** *vr* to be metamorphosed, be transformed, change.
metamorfosis *nf*, *pl* **metamorfosis** metamorphosis, transformation, change.
metano *nm* methane.
metatarsiano *nm* metatarsal.
metate *nm* (*CAm, Mex*) flat stone for grinding.
metátesis *nf*, *pl* **metátesis** metathesis.
metedor *nm* smuggler.
metedura *nf* (**a**) putting, placing; insertion. (**b**) — **de pata** (*fam*) blunder, bloomer (*fam*), clanger (*sl*).
meteduría *nf* smuggling.
metejón *nm* (**a**) (*Arg*) violent love; passion, fanatical enthusiasm. (**b**) (*Col*) fuss.
metelón *adj* (*Mex*) meddling.
meteórico *adj* meteoric (*also fig*).
meteorito *nm* meteor, meteorite.
meteoro *nm* (*esp fig*) meteor.
meteoroide *nm* meteoroid.
meteorología *nf* meteorology.
meteorológico *adj* meteorological, weather (*attr*).
meteorologista *nmf* meteorologist.
meter [2a] **1** *vt* (**a**) (*general sense*) to put, place; to insert, introduce (*en in, into*); to fit in; to squeeze in; (*Cook*) *ingredient* to add (*en to*), put (*en in*); *tool* to use, ply; **le están poniendo inyecciones a todo** — they're pumping injections into him as fast as they can.
(**b**) (*Sport*) *goal* to score (*a against*).
(**c**) (*Comm*) *goods* to smuggle (in; *also* — **de contrabando**).
(**d**) to make, cause; — **ruido** to cause a stir (*and see* **ruido**); — **un lío** to make a fuss, stir up trouble; — **miedo a uno** to scare someone, frighten someone, fill someone with fear; — **un susto a uno** to put the wind up someone; — **prisa a uno** to make someone get a move on.
(**e**) *money* to stake, wager (*en on*); (*Fin*) to invest (*en in*).
(**f**) **no hay quien le meta aquello** nobody seems able to make him understand that, nobody is able to get that idea into his head.
(**g**) *person* to involve (*en in*); **tú me metiste en este lío** you got me into this mess; **A le metió a B en muchos disgustos** A let B in for a lot of trouble; **¿quién le mete en esto?** who told you to interfere?
(**h**) — **a uno a trabajar** to put someone to work; — **a uno a un oficio** to put someone to a trade; — **a un chico de panadero** to apprentice a lad to a baker, put a lad to the baking trade.
(**i**) (*Sew*) *dress* to take in, take up, gather.
(**j**) (*fam*) *blow* to give, deal.
(**k**) (*fam*) — **algo a uno** to palm something off on someone; to force someone to accept something; **nos metió un largo discurso** he gave us a terribly long speech; **le metieron 5 años de cárcel** they did him for 5 years (*fam*); **nos van a** — **más trabajo** they're going to lumber us with more work; **no me meta esas peras** don't try to foist those pears off on me.
(**l**) (*Col*) —**las** to beat it (*fam*).
2 meterse *vr* (**a**) — **en** to go into, get into, enter; — **en un agujero** to get into a hole, squeeze into a hole; **se metió en la tienda** he went into the shop; — **en un negocio turbio** to take part in a shady deal, get involved in a shady deal; — **en peligro** to get into danger; — **en sí mismo** to withdraw into one's shell; **¿dónde se habrá metido el lápiz?** where can the pencil have got to?
(**b**) (*Geog*) to extend, project; **el cabo se mete en el mar** the cape extends (*or* goes out) into the sea; **el río se mete en el mar** the river flows into the sea.
(**c**) — **en** (*fig*) to interfere in, meddle in; **¡no se meta en lo que no le importa!**, **¡no se meta donde no le llaman!** mind your own business!
(**d**) — **con uno** to provoke someone, pick a quarrel with someone; to accost someone, molest someone.
(**e**) — **con una herramienta** to misuse a tool, use a tool in ways for which it was not designed.
(**f**) — **monja** to become a nun; — **a escritor to**

become a writer, (*pej*) set oneself up as a writer; — **de aprendiz en un oficio** to go into a trade as an apprentice.

(g) — **a + infin** to start (without due preparation) to + *infin*; to take it upon oneself to + *infin*.

meterete *nm*, **metereta** *nf* (*RPl*), **metete** *nm* (*CAm, Chi, Per*), **meticón** *nm* (*fam*) busybody, meddler.

meticulosamente *adv* meticulously, scrupulously, thoroughly.

meticulosidad *nf* meticulousness, scrupulousness, thoroughness.

meticuloso *adj* meticulous, scrupulous, thorough; (*esp SAm: pej*) fussy, petty, small-minded.

metiche *adj* (*Mex*) meddling, meddlesome.

metido 1 *adj* (a) — **en sí**, — **para adentro** introspective.

(b) **estar muy — en un asunto** to be deeply involved in a matter.

(c) — **en años** elderly, advanced in years; **está algo metidita en años** she must be getting on a bit now; — **en carnes** plump.

(d) **estar muy — con uno** to be well in with someone.

(e) (*SAm*) meddling, meddlesome.

(f) (*PR, SD, Urug*) half tight.

2 *nm* (*fam*) (a) ticking-off; **dar** (*or* **pegar**) **un — a uno** to give someone a dressing-down.

(b) touch (*sl*); **pegar un — a uno** to touch someone for money (*sl*).

(c) **pegar un buen — a una tarta** to make a cake look silly (*fam*), dispose of a good chunk out of a cake.

metijón *nm* (*fam*) busybody, meddler.

metilado *adj*: **alcohol —** methylated spirit.

metilo *nm* methyl.

metimiento *nm* (a) insertion. (b) (*fig*) influence, pull.

metódicamente *adv* methodically.

metódico *adj* methodical.

metodismo *nm* Methodism.

metodista 1 *adj* Methodist. **2** *nmf* Methodist.

método *nm* method.

metodología *nf* methodology.

metomentodo *nm* meddler, busybody.

metraje *nm* (*Cine*) length; **cinta de largo —** full-length film; *see* **cortometraje.**

metralla *nf* shrapnel.

metralleta *nf* submachine gun, tommy gun.

métrica *nf* metrics.

métrico *adj* metric(al).

metro[1] *nm* (a) (*Math*) metre, meter (*US*); — **cuadrado** square metre; — **cúbico** cubic metre.

(b) (*Math*) rule, ruler (*also* — **plegable**); — **de cinta** tape measure.

metro[2] *nm* (*Rail*) underground, tube, subway (*US*); — **aéreo** overhead railway, elevated railway.

metrónomo *nm* metronome.

metrópoli *nf* metropolis; (*of empire*) mother country.

metropolitano 1 *adj* metropolitan. **2** *nm* (a) (*Eccl*) metropolitan. (b) (*Rail*) = **metro**[2].

mexicano (*SAm*) = **mejicano.**

México *m* (*SAm*) Mexico.

mezcla *nf* (a) (*act*) mixing.

(b) (*substance*) mixture; (*fig*) blend, combination; medley; (*Sew*) mixture; tweed; **sin —** pure, unadulterated; *drink* neat; — **explosiva** explosive mixture; (*fam*) unholy mixture.

(c) (*Archit*) mortar.

mezclador *nm* mixing bowl.

mezcladora *nf* (*Cook*) mixer; — **de hormigón** concrete mixer.

mezclar [1a] **1** *vt* (a) to mix, mix up (together); to blend; to merge, combine; *cards* to shuffle.

(b) (*fig*) — **a A con B** to involve A with B, get A into trouble with B; — **a la Iglesia en el debate** to drag the Church into the debate.

2 mezclarse *vr* (a) to mix, mingle (*con* with); to blend (*con* with).

(b) — **con cierta gente** to mix with certain people; **hizo mal en — con esa familia** she did wrong to marry (beneath herself) into that family.

(c) — **en** to get mixed up in, get involved in; to meddle in.

mezcolanza *nf* hotchpotch, jumble.

mezquinar [1a] **1** *vt* (a) (*SAm*) to be stingy with, give sparingly.

(b) (*Arg*) — **el cuerpo** to dodge, duck; — **el saludo** to refuse to greet someone.

(c) (*Col*) — **a uno** to defend someone; — **a un niño** to let a child off a punishment.

2 *vi* (*SAm*) to be mean, be stingy.

mezquindad *nf* (a) (*quality*) meanness, stinginess;

poor spirit; pettiness; ignoble nature; paltriness, wretchedness. (b) (*act*) mean action, petty deed.

mezquino 1 *adj* (a) mean, stingy.

(b) poor-spirited; small-minded, petty; ignoble, materialistic, lacking the finer sentiments.

(c) *quality etc* miserable, paltry, tiny; *pay etc* wretched, wretchedly small.

2 *nm* (a) mean person, miser; petty individual, wretch.

(b) (*CAm, Col, Mex*) wart, callosity.

mezquita *nf* mosque.

mezzo-soprano ['metso-] *nf* mezzo-soprano.

mi *poss adj* my.

mí *pron* (*used after prep*) me; myself; **¡a —!** help!; **¡a — con ésas!** come off it!, tell me another!; **¿y a — qué?** so what?, what has that got to do with me?; **para — no hay duda** so far as I'm concerned there's no doubt, I don't believe there can be any doubt; **por —, puede ir** so far as I'm concerned she can go; **por — mismo** by myself; on my own account.

miaja *nf* (a) crumb.

(b) (*fig*) bit, tiny portion; **ni (una) — de** not the least little bit of.

(c) (*as adv*) a bit; **me quiere una —** she likes me a bit.

miasma *nm* miasma.

miau *nm* mew, miaow.

mica[1] *nf* (*Min*) mica.

mica[2] *nf* (*Col*) chamberpot.

mica[3] *nf* (*CAm*) drunkenness; **ponerse una —** to get drunk.

micada *nf* (*CAm, Mex*) affected expression, simper.

mico *nm*, **mica** *nf* (a) (*Zool*) monkey, (*esp*) long-tailed monkey.

(b) (*fam*) ugly devil; conceited person, swank (*fam*); flirt; randy man, old goat; **¡—!** (*to child*) you little monkey!

(c) **dar —, hacer —** to miss a date, fail to turn up for an appointment (*a* with); **dar el —** to cheat; to disappoint, behave differently from what had been hoped; **volverse — para hacer algo** to be at one's wit's end to know how to do something.

micología *nf* mycology.

micro . . . micro . . .; mini . . .

micro[1] *nm* (*Radio*) mike (*sl*), microphone.

micro[2] *nm* (*Chi, Per*) bus.

microbiano *adj* microbial.

microbio *nm* microbe.

microbiología *nf* microbiology.

microbiólogo *nm* microbiologist.

microbús *nm* minibus.

microcosmo(s) *nm* microcosm.

microfilm *nm*, *pl* **microfilms**, **microfilme** *nm* (*Acad*) microfilm.

micrófono *nm* microphone; (*Tel*) mouthpiece.

microfundio *nm* smallholding, small farm.

microlentillas *nfpl* contact lenses.

micrómetro *nm* micrometer.

microorganismo *nm* microorganism.

microscopia *nf* microscopy.

microscópico *adj* microscopic.

microscopio *nm* microscope.

microsurco *nm* microgroove; **disco (de) —** long-playing record (*L.P.*).

microtaxi *nm* minicab.

microteléfono *nm* (*Tel*) handset; mouthpiece.

miche *nm* (a) (*Mex*) cat. (b) (*Ven*) liquor, rum. (c) (*Ven*) native hut. (d) (*Chi*) game of marbles. (e) (*CR*) fight, brawl.

micho *nm*, **micha** *nf* (*fam*) puss, pussy cat.

Midas *m* Midas.

mieditis *nf* (*fam*) permanent fear, funkiness (*fam*).

miedo *nm* (a) fear, dread (*a, de* of); apprehension, nervousness; — **cerval**, — **espantoso** great fear; — **público** (*Theat*) stage fright; **por — a**, **por — de** for fear of; **por — de que . . .** for fear that . . .; **dar — a**, **infundir — a**, **meter — a** to scare, frighten, fill with fear; **me da —** he scares me, he makes me nervous; **le daba — hacerlo** he was nervous about doing it; **en este punto siempre me entra un — terrible** I always get terribly nervous at this point; **tener — a** to be afraid (*a* of); **tener — de + infin** to be afraid to + *infin*, be afraid (*or* nervous) of + *ger*.

(b) (*fam*) **¡qué —!** how awful! (*fam*); **de —** (*adj*) wonderful, smashing (*sl*), marvellous; (*pej*) awful, ghastly (*fam*); (*adv*) wonderfully, marvellously; (*pej*) awfully; **es un coche de —** it's a smashing car (*sl*); **eso fue de —** it was tremendous (*fam*), (*pej*) it was ghastly (*fam*); **hace un frío de —** it's terribly cold (*fam*).

miedoso *adj* fearful, fainthearted; timid, nervous, shy.
miel *nf* (a) honey.
    (b) (*esp SAm*) molasses (*also* — de caña, — negra *etc*).
    (c) (*idioms*) es — sobre hojuelas it's marvellous, it's even better than I (*etc*) expected; no hay — sin hiel nothing is ever entirely perfect; dejar a uno con la — en los labios to snatch something away from someone, spoil someone's fun; hacerse de — to be excessively kind, be almost too sweet; hazte de — y te comerán las moscas if you are too nice people will take advantage of you.
mielga *nf* alfalfa.
miembro 1 *nm* (a) (*Anat*) limb, member; — viril male member, penis.
    (b) (*Gram, Math etc*) member.
    (c) (*person*) member; fellow, associate; no — non-member; hacerse — de to become a member of.
    2 *as adj* member; los países —s the member countries.
mientes: ¡ni por —! never!, not on your life!; parar — en to reflect on, consider carefully; traer a las — to recall; se le vino a las — it occurred to him, it came to his mind.
mientras 1 *conj* (a) while; as long as; — duraba la guerra while the war lasted, as long as the war lasted; — él estaba fuera while he was abroad; — no venga until he comes.
    (b) — (que) whereas; — más tienen más quieren the more they have the more they want.
    2 *adv* meanwhile, meantime (*also* y —, — tanto); all the while.
miércoles *nm, pl* **miércoles** Wednesday; — de ceniza Ash Wednesday.
mierda *nf* (*tabu*) (a) shit (*tabu*); (*fig*) filth, dirt.
    (b) (*fig*) es una — he's a shit (*tabu*); es un don M— he's a nobody; coger (*or* pillar) una — to get sozzled (*sl*); ¡vaya Vd a la —! go to hell!
mies *nf* (a) (ripe) corn, wheat, grain. (b) harvest time.
    (c) —es cornfields.
miga *nf* (a) crumb; (*fig*) bit; —s (*Cook*) fried bread-crumbs.
    (b) (*fig*) core, substance, essence; esto tiene su — there's something in this; there's more in this than meets the eye.
    (c) hacer algo —s to break something up, smash something into little pieces; hacer —s a uno to leave someone in a sorry state; tener los pies hechos —s to be footsore; hacer buenas —s to get on well, hit it off (*con* with).
migajas *nfpl* crumbs; bits; (*fig*) leavings.
migar [1h] *vt* to crumble, break up.
migración *nf* migration.
migraña *nf* migraine.
migratorio *adj* migratory.
Miguel *m* Michael; — Ángel Michaelangelo.
miguelear [1a] *vt* (*CAm*) to court.
miguelero *nm* (*CAm*) wolf (*fam*).
mijo *nm* millet.
mil *adj and* —s *nm* thousand; tres — coches three thousand cars; — doscientos dólares one thousand two hundred dollars; lo ha hecho — veces he's done it hundreds of times; —es y —es thousands and thousands; a las — at some ungodly hour, terribly late.
miladi *nf* (*angl*) milady.
milagro *nm* miracle; (*fig*) miracle, wonder, marvel; ¡ni de —! not a bit of it!; es un — que . . . it is a miracle (*or* wonder) that . . .; (*sería*) que . . . it would be a miracle if . . .; salvarse de — to escape miraculously, have a miraculous escape; vivir de — to have a hard time of it, keep going somehow; to manage to stay alive; hacer —s (*fig*) to work wonders.
milagrosamente *adv* miraculously.
milagroso *adj* miraculous.
Milán Milan.
milano *nm* (*Orn*) kite.
mildeu (*also* **mildiu, mildiú**) *nm* mildew.
mildo *adj* (*Chi*) timid, shy.
milenario 1 *adj* millennial; (*fig*) very ancient, age-old. **2** *nm* millennium.
milenio *nm* millennium.
milenrama *nf* yarrow.
milésima *nf* thousandth.
milésimo 1 *adj* thousandth. **2** *nm* thousandth.
mili *nf* (*fam*) military service; estar en la — to be in the army; hacer la — to do one's military service.
miliar *adj*: piedra — milestone.
milicia *nf* (a) militia; military, soldiery.
    (b) art of war; science of warfare; soldiering, military profession.
    (c) (period of) military service.

    (d) M—s universitarias *equivalent to* cadet corps, O.T.C.
miliciano *nm*, **milico** *nm* (*Bol, Chi, RPl*) militiaman, conscript.
miligramo *nm* milligramme, milligram (*US*).
mililitro *nm* millilitre, milliliter (*US*).
milímetro *nm* millimetre, millimeter (*US*).
militante 1 *adj* militant. **2** *nmf* militant.
militar 1 *adj* military; spirit etc warlike; ciencia — art of war.
    2 *nm* soldier, military man; serviceman.
    3 [1a] *vi* (a) (*Mil*) to serve (in the army); to soldier.
    (b) (*fig*) — en un partido to belong to a party, be a member of a party.
    (c) (*fig*) — contra to militate against; — en defensa de, — en favor de to speak for, argue in favour of, lend weight to.
militarada *nf* military rising, putsch.
militarismo *nm* militarism.
militarista 1 *adj* militaristic. **2** *nmf* militarist.
militarizar [1f] *vt* to militarize.
militarote *nm* (*SAm: pej*) rough soldier; blustering soldier; sergeant-major type.
milonga *nf* (a) (*Arg, Bol, Chi*) kind of dance; cabaret; party. (b) (*Bol, RPl*) gossip.
milord [mi'lor] *nm* (*angl*) milord.
milpa *nf* (*CAm, Mex*) maize field, cornfield (*US*).
milpear [1a] **1** *vt* (*CAm, Mex*) to prepare for the sowing of maize. **2** *vi* (a) (*CAm, Mex*) to make a maize field. (b) (*Mex: of maize*) to sprout.
milpero *nm* (*CAm, Mex*) maize grower.
milla *nf* mile; — marina nautical mile.
millar *nm* thousand; a —es in thousands, by the thousand; los había a —es they were there in thousands.
millarada *nf* (about a) thousand.
millas-pasajero *nfpl* passenger miles.
millo *nm* (*CAm, Mex*) (variety of) millet.
millón *nm* million; un — de sellos a million stamps; 3 —es de niños 3 million children; ¡un — de gracias! a thousand thanks!
millonada *nf* (*fam*) million.
millonario *nm*, **millonaria** *nf* millionaire.
millonésimo 1 *adj* millionth. **2** *nm* millionth.
mimado *adj* spoiled.
mimar [1a] *vt* child etc to spoil, pamper, indulge; powerful person to humour, flatter.
mimbre *nm or f* (a) (*Bot*) osier, willow. (b) (*material*) wicker; de — wicker, wickerwork.
mimbrearse [1a] *vr* to sway.
mimbrera *nf* osier, willow.
mimbreral *nm* osier bed.
mimeografiar [1c] *vt* to mimeograph.
mimeógrafo *nm* mimeograph.
mimetismo *nm* mimicry.
mimetizarse [1f] *vr* (*SAm: Zool*) to change colour, camouflage oneself.
mímica *nf* (a) sign language; gesticulation. (b) mimicry; (una —) mime.
mímico *adj* mimic; imitative; lenguaje — sign language.
mimo *nm* (a) (*Theat: Hist*) mime; hacer — de to mime, mimic.
    (b) affectionate caress; nice remark (*etc*); (in general) pampering, indulgence; dar —s a un niño to spoil a child; hacer —s a uno to make a great fuss of someone, fuss over someone; hacer —s a los poderosos to humour the powerful, flatter the great.
mimosa *nf* mimosa.
mimoso *adj* (a) spoilt, pampered; soft; fussy, finicky. (b) (to opposite sex) arch, coy, provocative; kittenish.
mina *nf* (a) (*Min*) mine; — de carbón, — hullera coalmine.
    (b) underground passage; gallery; shaft.
    (c) (*Mil, Naut*) mine.
    (d) (of pencil) lead; refill.
    (e) (*fig*) mine, storehouse; gold mine; — de información mine of information.
minador *nm* (a) (*Mil*) sapper; (*Min*) mining engineer. (b) (*Naut: also buque* —) minelayer.
minar [1a] *vt* (a) (*Min*) to mine. (b) (*Mil, Naut*) to mine. (c) (*fig*) to undermine, sap, wear away.
minarete *nm* minaret.
mineral 1 *adj* mineral. **2** *nm* (*Geol*) mineral; (*Min*) ore; - de hierro iron ore.
mineralogía *nf* mineralogy.
mineralogista *nmf* mineralogist.
minería *nf* mining.
minero 1 *adj* mining. **2** *nm* miner; — de carbón coalminer.
minga[1] *nf* (*tabu*) prick (*tabu*).

minga² nf (SAm) (a) voluntary communal labour, cooperative work. (b) crew, team, gang (of cooperative workers).

mingaco nm (Chi, Per)=**minga²** (a).

mingar [1h] vt (a) (Arg, Chi, Ec) to work communally on, contribute cooperatively to.

(b) (Arg, Chi, Ec) workers to call together for a communal task.

(c) (Col) to set on, attack.

mini . . . **mini** . . ; (as hum prefix) **minibikini** microscopic bikini; **mininovillo** (Taur) baby bull, tiny bull.

miniatura 1 adj miniature; dog etc toy; **golf —** miniature golf (course); **relojes —** miniature watches. **2** nf miniature; **en —** in miniature.

minicoche nm minicar.

minifalda nf miniskirt.

minifaldero adj short-skirted, miniskirted.

minifundio nm smallholding, small farm.

minimizar [1f] vt to minimize.

mínimo 1 adj minimum; minimal; smallest, slightest, least; **cifra mínima** minimum number, smallest figure; **sin el más — esfuerzo** without the slightest effort; **no contribuye en lo más —** it doesn't help at all, it doesn't help in the least; **no me importa en lo más —** it doesn't matter to me in the least.

2 nm minimum; **como —** as a minimum, at the very least; **— de presión** (Meteorol) low-pressure area, trough.

mínimum nm minimum.

minina nf (fam) prick (tabu); (child's) John Thomas.

minino nm, **minina** nf (fam) puss, pussy cat.

minio nm red lead, minium.

ministerial adj ministerial; governmental.

ministerio nm ministry; see **asunto, gobernación** etc.

ministro nmf minister; **primer —** prime minister; **— sin cartera** minister without portfolio.

minoración nf reduction, diminution.

minorar [1a] vt to reduce, diminish.

minoría nf minority; **— de edad** minority.

minoridad nf minority (of age).

minorista nm (Ant, Chi, RPl) retailer, retail trader.

minoritario adj minority (attr); **gobierno —** minority government.

minorizar [1f] vt to minimize.

Minotauro m Minotaur.

minucia nf trifle, insignificant detail; mere nothing; morsel, tiny bit; **—s** petty details, minutiae.

minuciosamente adv thoroughly, meticulously; in a very detailed way; minutely.

minuciosidad nf thoroughness, meticulousness; detailed nature; minuteness.

minucioso adj thorough, meticulous; very detailed; minute.

minué nm minuet.

minúscula nf small letter.

minúsculo adj tiny, minute, minuscule; (Typ) small.

minuta nf (a) rough draft, first draft; carbon copy.

(b) note, memorandum.

(c) list, roll.

(d) (Cook) menu; **a la —** (Ant, RPl) rolled in breadcrumbs.

(e) (Chi) junk, trash; secondhand goods; junk shop.

minutar [1a] vt to draft.

minutario nm minute book.

minutero nm minute hand.

minutisa nf sweet william.

minuto nm minute.

miñango nm (Bol, RPl) bit, small piece; **hecho —s** smashed to pieces.

miñoco nm (Col) wry face; grimace.

miñón adj (SAm: gall) sweet, cute.

mío adj and pron mine, of mine; **es —, es el —** it is mine; **lo —** (what is) mine, what belongs to me; **no es amigo —** he's no friend of mine; **¡hijo —!** my dear boy!; **los —s** (freq) my people, my relations, my family.

miope 1 adj short-sighted, myopic. **2** nmf short-sighted person.

miopía nf short-sightedness, myopia.

mira nf (a) **estar a la —** to be on the look-out, keep watch (de for).

(b) (Mil, Tech etc) sight(s); **— de bombardeo** bombsight; **— telescópica** telescopic sight; **con la — puesta en** (fig) with one's sights set on.

(c) (Mil) watchtower, look-out post.

(d) (fig) aim, intention; **con la — de +** infin with the aim of + ger; **con —s a** with a view to; **llevar una — interesada** to have a selfish end in view; **poner la — en** to aim at, aspire to; **tener —s sobre** to have designs on.

(e) (fig) **de amplias —s** broad in outlook; tolerant,

broad-minded; **de —s estrechas** narrow-minded; insular, parochial.

mirada nf (a) look, glance, gaze; **— fija** stare; hard look; **— de soslayo** sidelong glance; **— perdida, — vaga** vague look, distant look; **apartar la —** to look away (de from); **apuñalar a uno con la —** to look daggers at someone; **echar una — a** to glance at; to keep an eye on; **lanzar una — a** to glance at, cast a glance at; **levantar la —** to raise one's eyes; **no levanta la — del libro** he never takes his eyes off the book; **resistir la — de uno** to stare back at someone, stare someone out.

(b) (of face) look, expression; **con una — triste** with a sad look.

miradero nm (a) look-out, vantage point. (b) cynosure (of every eye), person (etc) that attracts every eye.

mirado adj (a) **bien —** well thought of, well liked, highly regarded; **no está bien — que** . . . it is not thought proper that . . .; **mal —** disliked (see also **malmirado**).

(b) sensible; well-behaved; considerate, thoughtful; **ser — en los gastos** to be sensible about what one spends, be a careful spender.

(c) (pej) finicky, fussy.

(d) **bien —** (as adv) by rights, in justice, if everything is weighed up.

mirador nm (a) (Archit) bay window; (enclosed) balcony; **— de popa** (Naut) stern gallery. (b) viewpoint, vantage point.

miramiento nm (a) considerateness; courtesy; **sin —** without consideration, discourteously.

(b) caution, circumspection, care; (pej) timidity, excessive caution.

(c) **—s** courtesies, attentions; **sin —s** unceremoniously; high-handed(ly); **sin —s de** regardless of; **tratar sin —s a uno** to treat someone without consideration, ride roughshod over someone.

mirar [1a] **1** vt (a) to look at; to gaze at; to watch; **miraba la foto** she was looking at the photo; **miraba los barcos** she was watching the boats; **la miré subir la escalera** I watched her go (or going) upstairs; **le miraron la cartera** they looked at his wallet; **— fijamente a uno** to stare at someone, look hard at someone; **— algo por encima** to glance over something, glance cursorily at something.

(b) (fig) to consider, think over, think carefully about; **lo hago mirando el porvenir** I do it bearing the future in mind; **no mira las dificultades** he doesn't take account of the difficulties; **mirándolo bien** all in all; by rights; on second thoughts; **¡mira lo que haces!** just think what you're doing!; **¡mira con quien hablas!** just remember who you're talking to!

(c) (fig) **— a uno como** to look on someone as, consider someone to be.

(d) (fig) to watch, keep an eye on, be careful about; **conviene — el bolso** it's best to keep an eye on your handbag.

(e) (fig) to value, think highly of (also **— bien**); **— mal** to dislike, have a poor opinion of.

(f) (SAm) to see.

2 vi (a) to look; to glance; **no habla pero mira mucho** he never speaks but he keeps on looking; **¡mira!, ¡mire!** look!; (as protest) look here!; **¡pero mire!** now look here!; **¡mira que no tenemos dinero!** remember that we haven't any money!; **¡mira que tenemos que aguantar!** look at what we have to put up with!; **¡mira que si es mentira!** just suppose it isn't true!, what if it's not true?; **mira si ha venido el taxi** look and see if the taxi has come; **— alrededor** to look around; **— atrás** to look back (fig), think about the past; **— hacia otro lado** to look the other way; **— por la ventana** to look out of the window; **— por un agujero** to look through a hole; **— de través** to squint (see also **través** 2).

(b) (Archit) to face; to look on to, open on to; **la casa mira al sur** the house faces south.

(c) (fig) **— a** to aim at, have in mind.

(d) **por lo que mira a** as far as, as regards.

(e) (fig) **— por** to look after, take care of; **— por sí** to look out for oneself, consider one's own safety.

3 mirarse vr (a) to look at oneself; **— al espejo** to look at oneself in the mirror.

(b) (2 persons) to look at one another; **nos miramos asombrados** we looked at each other in amazement; **— a los ojos** to look into each other's eyes.

(c) **— muy bien de hacer algo** to be very careful about doing something; to think carefully before doing something; **— en ello** to watch one's step.

mirasol nm sunflower.
miríada nf myriad; —(s) **de moscas** a myriad flies.
mirilla nf peephole, spyhole; (Phot) viewer.
miriñaque nm (a) (Hist) crinoline, hoop skirt. (b) (Arg: Rail) cowcatcher. (c) (Cu) thin cotton cloth.
miriópodo nm millipede.
mirlarse [1a] vr to put on airs, act important.
mirlo nm (a) (Orn) blackbird.
(b) — **blanco** (fig) exceptional thing, highly unusual thing; one in a million; impossible dream.
(c) (fig) self-important air, pompousness.
mirobrigense 1 adj of Ciudad Rodrigo. 2 nmf native (or inhabitant) of Ciudad Rodrigo; **los —s** the people of Ciudad Rodrigo.
mirón 1 adj inquisitive, curious.
2 nm, **mirona** nf onlooker, watcher, observer; (pej) nosey-parker; (Cards) kibitzer; **los —es son de piedra** those watching the game are not allowed to speak; **estar de —** to look on (without doing anything), to stand by (doing nothing); **ir de —** to go along just to see.
mirra nf myrrh.
mirtilo nm bilberry, whortleberry.
mirto nm myrtle.
misa nf mass; — **del gallo** midnight mass (on Christmas Eve); — **mayor** high mass; — **de prima** early mass; — **rezada** low mass; **como en —** in dead silence; **celebrar —** to celebrate mass; **ir a —** to go to mass, go to church; **oír —** to go to mass, attend mass; **ser como — de pobre** to last all too short a time; **no saber de la — la media** to be woefully ill-informed; to know only a part of the story; **estos datos van a —** (fig) these facts are utterly trustworthy.
misal nm missal.
misantropía nf misanthropy.
misantrópico adj misanthropic.
misántropo nm misanthrope, misanthropist.
misario nm acolyte, altar boy.
miscelánea nf (a) miscellany. (b) (Mex) small shop, (esp) hardware store.
misceláneo adj miscellaneous.
miserable 1 adj (a) person mean, stingy; miserly; sum etc miserable, paltry, pitifully small.
(b) (morally) rotten (fam), vile, contemptible, despicable; ¡—! you rotter!, you wretch!
(c) place, room etc squalid, sordid.
2 nmf wretch; rotter, cad; ¡**eres un —!** you're a rotter!
miserando adj (esp SAm) pitiful.
miseria nf (a) poverty, destitution; want; **caer en la —** to fall into abject poverty; **vivir en la —** to live in poverty.
(b) squalor, squalid conditions.
(c) fleas, lice; **estar lleno de —** to be covered with vermin.
(d) (Fin) **una —** a tiny sum, a mere pittance; a tiny amount.
(e) meanness, stinginess.
misericordia nf (a) pity, compassion. (b) forgiveness; mercy.
misericordioso adj (a) compassionate. (b) forgiving; merciful.
misero adj (fam) churchy (fam), fond of going to church.
mísero adj (a) wretched. (b) =**miserable**.
mísil nm (angl) missile; — **antimísil** antimissile missile; — **autodirigido** guided missile.
misión nf mission; —**es** (Eccl) overseas missions, missionary work; — **de buena voluntad** goodwill mission.
misional adj missionary.
misionero nm, **misionera** nf missionary.
Misisipí m Mississippi.
misiva nf missive.
mismamente adv (fam) only, just; literally; **ayer —vino** it was only yesterday he came.
mismísimo adj superl selfsame, very same; **por mis —s ojos** with my very own eyes; **es Vd el — diablo** you're the very devil in person; **estuvo el —obispo** the bishop himself was there; **es el — que yo perdí** it's the very (same) one I lost.
mismo 1 adj (a) same (que as, that); **el — coche** the same car; **viven en la misma calle** they live in the same street; **es el — que vi ayer** it's the same (one) as I saw yesterday; **el policía y el ladrón son el —** the policeman and the thief are one and the same; **quedar en las mismas** to be no further forward, show no progress.
(b) (with lo) **lo —** the same, the same thing; **es lo —** it's the same thing, it comes to the same thing; **no es lo —** it's not the same (at all); **él diría lo —**

he would say the same; **por lo —** for the same reason; **lo — A que B** both A and B; **o lo que es lo —** or what amounts to the same thing; **lo — si viene que si no viene** whether he comes or not; see **dar**.
(c) (with personal pron) -self; **yo —** I myself; **yo — lo vi** I saw it myself; **lo hizo por sí —** he did it by himself; **perjudicarse a sí —** to harm one's own interests.
(d) (emphatic) very; selfsame; **en ese — momento** at that very moment; **en Argentina misma, en la misma Argentina** in Argentina itself; **estuvo el —ministro** the (very) minister himself was there; **ella es la misma caridad** she is charity itself; **eso —digo yo** that's just what I say.
2 adv right; **aquí —** right here, on this very spot; **ayer —** only yesterday; **delante — de la casa** right in front of the house.
3 as conj: **lo — que** just like, just as (if); **lo — que Vd es médico yo soy ingeniero** just as you are a doctor I am an engineer; **nos divertimos lo — que si hubiéramos ido al baile** we had just as good a time as if we had gone to the dance; **lo — que me levanto a las 6 me levantaría a las 5** just as I get up at 6 so I would gladly get up at 5.
misogamia nf misogamy.
misógamo nm, **misógama** nf misogamist.
misoginia nf misogyny.
misógino nm misogynist.
miss [mis] nf (angl) beauty queen; **M— España 1978** Miss Spain 1978.
misterio nm (a) mystery; **no hay —** there's no mystery about it.
(b) secrecy; **obrar con —** to go about something secretly, go to work in secrecy.
(c) (Theat: Hist) mystery play.
misteriosamente adv mysteriously; puzzlingly.
misterioso adj mysterious; mystifying, puzzling.
mística nf, **misticismo** nm mysticism.
místico 1 adj mystic(al). 2 nm, **mística** nf mystic.
mistificación nf hoax, practical joke; hocus-pocus.
mistificar [1g] vt (a) to hoax, play a practical joke on.
(b) to mix up, make a mess of.
Misurí m Missouri.
mitad nf (a) half; — **y** — half-and-half; (fig) so-so, yes and no; **es — blanco y — rojo** it's half white and half red; **mi otra —, mi cara —** my better half; **me queda la —** I have half left; **a — de precio** half-price, at half the cost; **reducir en una —** to cut by half, halve.
(b) middle; **a — de, en — de** halfway along (or through etc); **a — de la distancia entre A y Z** halfway between A and Z; **estar a — de camino** to be halfway there; **hacia la — de la película** halfway through the film; **cortar por la —** to cut down the middle; **partir a uno por la —** (fig) to upset someone's plans, queer someone's pitch; see **dividir**.
mítico adj mythical.
mitigación nf mitigation; relief; quenching; appeasement; tempering; reduction.
mitigar [1h] vt to mitigate, allay; pain to relieve; thirst to quench; anger to appease, mollify; harshness etc to temper, mitigate; worry to allay; heat to reduce; solitude to alleviate, relieve.
mitin nm (esp Pol: angl) meeting; — **popular** mass meeting.
mito nm myth.
mitología nf mythology.
mitológico adj mythological.
mitón nm mitten.
mitote nm (Mex) a kind of dance; brawl; uproar; —**s** rowdyism; merrymaking.
Mitra m Mithras.
mitra nf mitre.
mitrado nm bishop, prelate.
mitraico adj Mithraic.
mitraísmo nm Mithraism.
mítulo nm mussel.
mixomatosis nf myxomatosis.
mixtión nf mixture.
mixto 1 adj (all senses) mixed. 2 nm (a) match; (Mil) explosive compound. (b) (Rail) passenger and goods train.
mixtolobo nm Alsatian (dog).
mixtura nf mixture (also Pharm).
mixturar [1a] vt to mix.
mnemotécnica nf mnemonics.
mnemotécnico adj mnemonic.
moaré nm moiré.
mobiliario nm furniture; household goods; suite (of furniture).
moblaje nm =**mobiliario**.
moca[1] nf mocha.

moca[2] nf (Ec) quagmire, muddy place.
moca[3] nm (Mex) coffee-flavoured cake (or biscuit).
mocasín nm moccasin.
mocear [1a] vi to play around, live a bit wildly, sow one's wild oats.
mocedad nf (a) youth; **en mis —es** in my young days. (b) **—es** youthful pranks; wild living; **pasar las —es** to sow one's wild oats.
moceril adj youthful; typical of youth.
mocerío nm young people, lads and lasses (collectively).
mocero adj rakish, loose-living; fond of the girls.
mocetón nm strapping youth.
mocetona nf big girl, hefty wench.
moción nf (a) motion, movement.
(b) (Parl etc) motion; **— de censura** motion of censure, censure motion; **hacer (or presentar) una — to** propose a motion.
mocionante nmf (SAm) proposer (of a motion).
mocionar [1a] vti (SAm) to move, propose.
mocito 1 adj very young. **2** nm, **mocita** nf youngster.
moco nm (a) mucus; snot (fam); **limpiarse los —s** to blow one's nose; **llorar a — y baba, llorar a — tendido** to sob one's heart out, cry uncontrollably; **soltar el —** to burst into tears.
(b) (Orn) crest; **no es — de pavo** it's not just a small thing; you can't laugh this one off. (c) (of candle) snuff, burnt wick; candle grease; **a — de candil** by candlelight. (d) (Tech) slag.
mocoso 1 adj snivelling; (fig) ill-bred, rude. **2** nm (fam) brat.
mochales adj (fam): **estar —** to be round the bend (sl).
mochar [1a] vt (a) = **desmochar**.
(b) (Per, PR) to chop off, hack off (clumsily); (Col, PR) to amputate.
(c) (Arg) to pinch (fam). (d) (Col) to fire (fam), sack (fam).
mochila nf rucksack, knapsack; (Mil) pack.
mocho 1 adj (a) cut off, short, truncated; stubby; tool etc blunt, short; tree lopped, pollarded; cow hornless, polled; tower flat-topped; person (fam) close-cropped, shorn.
(b) (Col) big, huge.
(c) (Guat, Mex) reactionary.
2 nm (a) butt; blunt end, thick end.
(b) (fam) burden, chore, bind (sl); blame; **cargar el —** to get landed with it; to carry the can (sl); **le echaron el —** they gave him the job; they made him carry the can (sl).
(c) (Cu) **— de tabaco** cigar butt.
(d) (Col, PR, Ven) nag.
mochuelo nm (a) (Orn: also **— común**) little owl; **cada — a su sitio** everything in its place. (b) (fam) = **mocho**(b).
moda nf fashion; style; **a la —** (adj) in fashion, fashionable; (adv) fashionably; **un sombrero a la —** a fashionable hat; **a la — de** after the fashion of; **estar a la —** to be in fashion, be fashionable; **ponerse a la —** to smarten up, get some new clothes; (fam) to get with it (fam); **de —** in fashion, fashionable; **fuera de —** out of fashion; **pasado de —** old-fashioned, out-dated; **pasarse de —** to go out of fashion; **ponerse de —** to become fashionable; **estar muy de —** to be highly fashionable; **ha entrado la — de las medias amarillas** the fashion for yellow stockings has begun, yellow stockings are in.
modal 1 adj modal. **2 —es** nmpl manners.
modalidad nf form, kind, variety; fashion; modality; **una nueva — teatral** a new dramatic form; a new fashion in the theatre; **hay varias —es del juego** there are various forms of the game, there are several ways of playing the game.
modelado nm modelling.
modelador nm, **modeladora** nf modeller.
modelar [1a] **1** vt (a) to model (sobre, según on). (b) to fashion, shape, form. **2 modelarse** vr: **— sobre** to model oneself on.
modelo 1 nm model; pattern; standard; **presentar algo como un —** to hold something up as a model; **servir de —** to serve as a model; **tomar por —** to take as a model; **— de maridos** model husband.
2 nmf (Art, Phot, Fashion etc) model; **servir de — a un pintor** to sit for a painter, pose for a painter.
3 as adj model; **cárcel — model** prison; **empresa — model** company; pilot plant.
moderación nf moderation; **con —** in moderation.
moderadamente adv moderately.
moderado adj (all senses) moderate.

moderar [1a] **1** vt to moderate; violence etc to restrain, control; speed to reduce.
2 moderarse vr (fig) to restrain oneself, control oneself; to calm down.
modernamente adv nowadays, in modern times; recently.
modernidad nf modernity.
modernismo nm modernism.
modernista 1 adj modernist(ic). **2** nmf modernist.
modernización nf modernization.
modernizar [1f] **1** vt to modernize. **2 modernizarse** vr to modernize (oneself); to catch up, get up to date.
moderno adj modern; present-day; up-to-date; **a la moderna** in the modern way; modern.
modestamente adv modestly.
modestia nf modesty.
modesto adj modest.
modicidad nf reasonableness, fairness, moderateness.
módico adj reasonable, fair, moderate.
modificación nf modification.
modificar [1g] vt to modify.
modismo nm idiom.
modista nf dressmaker, modiste; **— de sombreros** milliner.
modistilla nf dressmaker, seamstress.
modisto nm fashion designer, couturier.
modo nm (a) way, manner; fashion; mode, method; **"— de empleo"** (on label) "instructions for use"; **— de gobierno** form of government; **— de pensar** way of thinking; **según mi — de pensar** according to my way of thinking; **— de ser — manera de ser; a mi — de ver** in my view; as I see it.
(b) (phrases with prep) **a mi —** in my (own) way; **lo interpretan a su —** they interpret it each in his own way; **a — de** like; **uno a — de saco** a sort of bag, some kind of bag; **al — inglés** in the English way (or style); **de este —** (in) this way, like this; **de ese —** (fig) at that rate; **del mismo — (que), de igual — (que)** in the same way (as), just (as); **de igual —, . . .** in the same way, . . .; **de diversos —s** in various ways; **declaraba su edad de diversos —s** she gave her age variously; **de un — o de otro** (in) one way or another; **by some means or other;** for numerous other phrases, see **manera** (a) and (b).
(c) **—s** (of person) manners; **buenos —s** good manners; **contestar con buenos —s** to answer courteously.
(d) (Mus) mode.
(e) (Gram) mood; **— imperativo** imperative mood; **— indicativo** indicative mood; **— subjuntivo** subjunctive mood.
(f) (fig) moderation; **beber con —** to drink in moderation.
modorra nf (a) drowsiness, heaviness. (b) (Vet) staggers.
modorro adj (a) drowsy, heavy. (b) fruit soft, sleepy. (c) (fam) dull, stupid.
modoso adj quiet, well-mannered, nicely-behaved; girl demure.
modulación nf modulation; **— de frecuencia** (Radio) frequency modulation.
modulado adj modulated.
modular [1a] vt to modulate.
moer nm mohair.
mofa nf (a) (in general) mockery, ridicule, derision; **exponer a uno a la — pública** to hold someone up to public ridicule; **hacer — de** to scoff at, jeer at.
(b) (una —) jibe, taunt, sneer.
mofador 1 adj mocking, scoffing, sneering. **2** nm mocker, scoffer.
mofar [1a] **1** vi to mock, scoff, sneer. **2 mofarse** vr: **— de** to mock, scoff at, sneer at.
mofeta nf (a) (Zool) skunk. (b) (Min) firedamp. (c) (fam) fart (tabu).
moflete nm (a) fat cheek. (b) **—s** (fig) chubbiness.
mofletudo adj fat-cheeked, chubby.
mogol 1 adj Mongol, Mongolian. **2** nm, **mogola** nf Mongol, Mongolian; **el Gran M—** the Great Mogul. **3** nm (language) Mongol.
Mogolia f: **la —** Mongolia.
mogolismo nm mongolism.
mogollón nm (fam) sponger (fam), hanger-on; spiv (sl); **colarse de — en un sitio** to get into a place without paying; **comer de —** to scrounge a meal (fam); **lograr un puesto de —** to get a job without effort, get a job the easy way.
mogote nm flat-topped hillock; heap, pile; (of sheaves etc) stack, rick.
mohín nm (wry) face, grimace; pout; **hacer un —** to make a face; **con un leve — de chanza** with a faintly humorous expression.

mohina nf (a) annoyance, displeasure; resentment.
(b) (una —) grudge. (c) the sulks, sulkiness; **ser fácil a las —s** to be easily depressed.

mohino adj gloomy, depressed; sulky, sullen, resentful; peevish.

moho nm (a) (on metal) rust.
(b) (Bot) mould, mildew; **cubierto de —** mouldy, mildewed.
(c) lazy feeling; workshyness; **no cría —** he's not exactly idle, he's always on the go; **no dejar criar — a uno** to keep someone on the go.

mohoso adj (a) rusty. (b) mouldy, mildewed; musty. (c) (fig) joke etc stale.

Moisés m Moses.

moisés nm Moses basket, cradle; carrycot.

mojada nf (a) wetting, soaking. (b) stab (wound).

mojado adj wet; damp, moist; drenched, soaked; **llover sobre —** to be quite unnecessary, be entirely superfluous; **luego llovió sobre —** then on top of all that something else happened; **llueve sobre —** it never rains but it pours.

mojadura nf wetting, soaking.

mojama nf salted tuna.

mojar [1a] **1** vt (a) to wet; to damp(en), moisten; to drench, soak; **la lluvia mojó a todos** the rain soaked everybody; **moje ligeramente el sello** moisten the stamp a little; **— la ropa en un líquido** to soak (or steep) clothes in a liquid.
(b) **— la pluma en la tinta** to dip one's pen into the ink; **— el pan en el café** to dip one's bread into one's coffee.
(c) (Ling) to palatalize.
(d) to stab.
(e) (PR, SD) to tip; (PR) to bribe.
2 vi **— en** (fig) to dabble in; to meddle in, get involved in.
3 mojarse vr to get wet; to get drenched, get soaked.

mojarra nf (SAm) short broad knife.

mojicón nm (a) (Cook) sponge cake; bun. (b) (fam) punch in the face, biff (fam), slap.

mojiganga nf (a) (Hist) masquerade, mummery; farce, piece of clowning. (b) (fam) pretentious thing.

mojigatería nf hypocrisy; sanctimoniousness, affected piety; prudery, prudishness.

mojigato 1 adj hypocritical; sanctimonious, affectedly pious; prudish, strait-laced. **2** nm, **mojigata** nf hypocrite; sanctimonious person; prude.

mojinete nm (a) (of roof) ridge; (of wall) tiling, coping. (b) (Arg, Chi) gable.

mojón nm landmark, boundary stone; (also **— kilométrico**) milestone; signpost; heap, pile.

mola nf rounded mountain.

molar nm molar.

molde nm (a) (Tech) mould; (Cook) mould, shape; (of plaster etc) cast.
(b) (Sew) pattern; knitting needle.
(c) (fig) model.
(d) **de —** very suitably; **el vestido le está de —** the dress suits her perfectly, the dress is just right for (or on) her; **venir de —** to come just right; see **letra**.

moldear [1a] vt (a) to mould, shape; (in plaster etc) to cast. (b) (fig) to mould, shape, form.

moldura nf moulding.

mole nf mass, bulk; (of building) pile; **se sentó con toda su —** he sat down with his full weight; **la enorme — del buque** the vast mass of the ship; **esa mujer es una —** that woman is a lump.

molécula nf molecule.

molecular adj molecular.

moledor 1 adj (a) grinding, crushing. (b) (fam) boring. **2** nm (a) (Tech) grinder, crusher; roller. (b) (fam) bore.

moledora nf (Tech) grinder, crusher; mill.

moler [2h] vt (a) to grind, crush; to pound; to mill; (fam) to chew (up); **— a uno a palos** to give someone a beating.
(b) (fig) to tire out, weary, exhaust.
(c) (fig) to annoy; to bore.

molestar [1a] **1** vt to annoy; to bother, inconvenience, put out; to upset; (of pain) to trouble, bother, hurt; **me molesta ese ruido** that noise upsets me, that noise gets on my nerves; **¿le molesta el ruido?** do you mind (or object to) the noise?, does the noise bother you?; **los niños me molestan para estudiar** the kids disturb my work, the kids stop me working; **me molesta tener que repetirlo** I hate having to repeat it; **¿le molesta que abra la ventana?** do you mind if I open the window?; **¿le molesta que fume?** will it bother you if I smoke?

2 vi to be a nuisance; to get in the way, be awkward; **no quiero —** I don't want to intrude, I don't want to be in the way, I don't wish to cause any trouble.

3 molestarse vr (a) to bother (con about); to go to trouble, put oneself out; **— en + infin** to bother to **+ infin**; **¡no se moleste!** don't bother!, don't trouble yourself!
(b) to get cross; to take offence, get upset.

molestia nf bother, trouble, nuisance; inconvenience; (Med) discomfort; **es una —** it's a nuisance; **no es —** it's no trouble; **ahorrarse —s** to save oneself trouble, spare oneself effort; **darse la — de + infin, tomarse la — de + infin** to take the trouble to **+ infin**, go out of one's way to **+ infin**.

molesto adj (a) troublesome, annoying; trying, tiresome; arrangement inconvenient; task irksome; smell, taste nasty; **es muy —** it's very inconvenient for me; **si no es — para mí** it's very inconvenient for me; **si no es — para Vd** if it's no trouble to you; **es una persona muy molesta** she's a very trying person.
(b) discontented; restless; ill-at-ease; uncomfortable; upset, offended; embarrassed; **estar — (Med)** to be in some discomfort; **estar — con uno** to be cross with someone; **me sentí —** I felt uncomfortable; I felt embarrassed.

molestoso adj (Cu, Chi, Ec, PR) annoying.

moletón nm flannelette.

molibdeno nm molybdenum.

molicie nf (a) softness. (b) (fig) soft living, luxurious living; effeminacy.

molido adj (a) ground, crushed; powdered. (b) **estar — (fig)** to be exhausted, be dead beat.

molienda nf (a) (act) grinding; milling. (b) quantity of corn (etc) to be ground. (c) mill. (d) (fam) weariness. (e) (fam) nuisance.

molinero nm miller.

molinete nm (toy) windmill.

molinillo nm (a) hand mill; **— de café** coffee mill, coffee grinder; **— de carne** mincer. (b) (toy) windmill.

molino nm (a) mill; grinder; **— de agua** water mill; **— de viento** windmill. (b) (fam) restless person; bore, tedious individual.

molo nm (Chi, Ven) breakwater, sea wall.

molote nm (a) (Mex) ball of wool (etc). (b) (Mex) fried maize pancake. (c) (Col, Mex) dirty trick. (d) (CAm, Cu, SD) riot, commotion.

molusco nm mollusc.

mollar adj (a) fruit soft, tender; easily shelled; (pej) mushy, rotten. (b) meat lean. (c) (fam) gullible.

molledo nm (a) (Anat) fleshy part (of a limb). (b) (of bread) crumb.

molleja nf gizzard; **—s** sweetbreads.

mollejón nm fat listless man.

mollera nf (Anat) crown of the head; (fam) brains, sense; **cerrado de —, duro de —** dense, dim; pigheaded; **secar la — a uno** to drive someone crazy; **tener buena —** to have brains, be brainy.

mollete nm (a) (Cook) muffin. (b) (Anat) fleshy part of the arm; fat cheek.

momentáneamente adv momentarily.

momentáneo adj momentary.

momento nm (a) moment; instant; time; **—s después** a few moments later; **al —** at once; **a cada —** every instant, all the time; **de —** at the moment, for the moment; **no los vi de —** I didn't see them at first; **de un — a otro** at any moment; **en el — actual** at the present time; **en el — bueno** at the right moment, at the proper time; **en este —** at this moment; right now; **hace un —** not a moment ago; **por el —** for the moment; **está cambiando por —s** it is changing all the time; **atravesamos un — difícil** we are going through a difficult time; **ha llegado el — de + infin** the time has come to **+ infin**.
(b) (Mech) momentum; moment.
(c) (fig) consequence, importance; **de poco —** unimportant.

momería nf mummery, clowning.

momia nf mummy.

momificación nf mummification.

momificar [1g] **1** vt to mummify. **2 momificarse** vr to mummify, become mummified.

momio 1 adj meat lean. **2** nm bargain; extra; cushy job (sl); profitable deal; **de — free**, gratis.

momo nm (a) funny face. (b) clowning, buffoonery.

mona nf (a) (Zool) female monkey; (species) Barbary ape; **estar hecho una —** to be embarrassed, be quite

put out; **mandar a uno a freír —s** (*fam*) to tell someone to go to blazes.
(**b**) (*fam: person*) ape, copycat (*fam*).
(**c**) (*fam*) drunk (*fam*); hangover; **coger** (*or* **pillar**) **una —** to get tight; **dormir la —** to sleep off a hangover.
(**d**) (*Col*) blonde.

monacal *adj* monastic.

monacato *nm* monasticism; monastic life, monk's way of life.

monacillo *nm* acolyte, altar boy.

monada *nf* (**a**) (*act*) monkey face; monkeyish way (*or* movement *etc*); silly habit; silly thing (to say *etc*).
(**b**) (*child's*) charming habit, sweet little way.
(**c**) (*quality*) silliness, childishness.
(**d**) (*fam*) lovely thing; beauty, cute little thing; (*person*) pretty girl; **la casa es una —** the house is lovely, the house is a gem; **¡qué —!** isn't it cute?, isn't it lovely?; **¡hola, —!** hullo, beautiful!
(**e**) (*fam*) **—s** flattery.

mónada *nf* monad.

monago *nm*, **monaguillo** *nm* acolyte, altar boy.

monarca *nm* monarch, ruler.

monarquía *nf* monarchy.

monárquico **1** *adj* monarchic(al); (*Pol*) royalist, monarchist. **2** *nm* royalist, monarchist.

monarquismo *nm* monarchism.

monasterio *nm* monastery.

monástico *adj* monastic.

monda[1] *nf* (**a**) (*act*) pruning, lopping, trimming; peeling. (**b**) pruning season. (**c**) peel, peelings, skin. (**d**) (*Col, Cu, Mex, PR*) beating.

monda[2] *nf* (*fam*): **¡es la —!** (**a**) it's great! (*fam*); (*pej*) it's the limit, it's the end; it's sheer hell (*fam*); **este nuevo baile es la —** this new dance is the greatest (*fam*), (*pej*) this new dance is awful (*fam*).
(**b**) (*of person*) he's the most (*sl*), he's a knockout (*sl*); (*pej*) he's a shocker, he's a terror.

mondadientes *nm*, *pl* **mondadientes** toothpick.

mondadura *nf* (**a**) =**monda**[1] (**a**); cleaning, cleansing. (**b**) **—s** =**monda**[1] (**c**).

mondar [1a] **1** *vt* (**a**) *tree* to prune, lop, trim.
(**b**) *fruit* to peel, skin; *potato* to peel; *nut, peas* to shell; *stick* to peel, pare, remove the bark from; **— a uno** to cut someone's hair.
(**c**) to clean, cleanse; *canal etc* to clean out.
(**d**) (*fam*) to fleece, strip bare, clean out (*sl*).
(**e**) (*fam*) **¡que te monden!** get away!, rubbish!
(**f**) (*Col, Cu, PR*) to beat, thrash; (*Cu: Sport etc*) to wipe the floor with (*fam*).
2 mondarse *vr*: **— los dientes** to pick one's teeth.

mondo *adj* (**a**) clean; pure; plain; neat; *head* completely shorn.
(**b**) (*fig*) bare, plain, without addition; **el asunto — es esto** the plain fact of the matter is; **tiene su sueldo — y nada más** he has his bare salary and nothing more; **me he quedado —** I'm cleaned out (*sl*), I haven't a cent; **— y lirondo** (*fam*) fact, truth *etc* plain, pure and simple.

mondongo *nm* guts, insides.

mondongudo *adj* (*esp RPl*) fat, potbellied.

monear [1a] *vi* (**a**) to act like a monkey; to make monkey faces. (**b**) (*Chi, Mex, Urug*) to boast, swank (*fam*).

moneda *nf* (**a**) (*in general*) currency, money, coinage; **— blanda, — débil** soft currency; **— dura, — fuerte** hard currency; **— menuda, — suelta** small change, coins of low denomination; **en — española** in Spanish money; **pagar a uno con** (*or* **en**) **la misma —** to pay someone back in his own coin.
(**b**) (*una —*) coin, piece; **— falsa** false coin, dud coin; **una — de 5 dólares** a 5-dollar piece; **es tan probable como que ahora lluevan —s de 5 duros** it's about as likely as my becoming pope.

moned(e)ar [1a] *vt* =**amonedar**.

monedero *nm* (**a**) **— falso** counterfeiter. (**b**) purse.

monería *nf* (**a**) funny face, monkey face; mimicry.
(**b**) antic, prank, playful trick. (**c**) (*pej*) trifle, triviality.

monetario *adj* monetary, financial.

Mongolia *f* =**Mogolia**.

moni *nf* (*SAm: angl*) money.

monigote *nm* (**a**) rag doll; puppet; grotesque figure; **— de nieve** snowman.
(**b**) (*fig*) colourless individual, weak character, little man; **¡—!** (*to child*) you chump! (*fam*).
(**c**) (*Art*) humorous sketch, cartoon; (*pej*) bad painting (*or statue*), daub; doodle.

monises *nmpl* (*fam: angl*) brass (*sl*), dough (*sl*).

monitor *nm* monitor.

monitorio *adj* admonitory.

monja *nf* nun; sister.

monje *nm* monk.

monjil **1** *adj* nun's, of (*or* like) a nun; (*fig*) excessively demure. **2** *nm* nun's habit.

mono[1] *nm* (**a**) (*Zool*) monkey, ape; **¡—!** (*to child*) you little monkey!
(**b**) (*fig*) ape, mimic; **— de imitación** (*child etc*) copycat (*fam*).
(**c**) (*fam*) brash youth; affected youth.
(**d**) (*Art*) =**monigote** (**c**).
(**e**) (*Cards*) joker.
(**f**) (*fam*) ugly devil, ugly monkey.
(**g**) (*fam*) sign (*between lovers etc*); **hacerse —s** to make eyes at each other, make little signs to each other.
(**h**) (*idioms*) **no lo aguantaría ni que fuera yo un —** I wouldn't put up with it at any price; **no me mirarían más ni que tuviera —s en la cara** they couldn't have stared at me more if I had come from the moon; **estar de —s** to be at daggers drawn; **meter los —s a uno** (*Col, Cu, PR*) to put the wind up someone.

mono[2] *adj* pretty, lovely, attractive; nice, charming, cute; **una chica muy mona** a very attractive girl, a very nice girl; **¡qué sombrero más —!** what a cute little hat!

mono[3] *nm* overalls; boiler suit; (*child's*) rompers.

mono[4] **1** *adj* (*Col*) yellow; blond, reddish blond; yellow with age. **2** *nm* (*Chi*) pile (*of fruit etc*); slice of melon; bunch of cherries.

mono ... mono ...

monocarril *nm* monorail.

monocromo **1** *adj* monochrome. **2** *nm* monochrome.

monóculo *nm* monocle.

monocultivo *nm* monoculture, single crop; one-crop farming; **el — es un peligro para muchos países** in many countries dependence upon a single crop is dangerous.

monogamia *nf* monogamy.

monógamo *adj* monogamous.

monografía *nf* monograph.

monográfico *adj*: **estudio —** monograph.

monograma *nm* monogram.

monohombre *adj* one-man (*attr*).

monolingüe *adj* monolingual.

monolítico *adj* monolithic.

monolito *nm* monolith.

monologar [1h] *vi* to soliloquize.

monólogo *nm* monologue.

monomanía *nf* monomania; mania, obsession; **— de grandezas** megalomania.

monomio *nm* monomial.

monomotor *adj* single-engined.

monoplano *nm* monoplane.

monoplaza *nm* single-seater.

monopolio *nm* monopoly.

monopolizar [1f] *vt* to monopolize.

monorail *nm* monorail.

monorrimo *adj* *stanza etc* having the same rhyme throughout.

monosabio *nm* (**a**) (*Zool*) trained monkey. (**b**) (*Taur*) picador's assistant; employee who leads the horse team dragging the dead bull.

monosilábico *adj* monosyllabic.

monosílabo **1** *adj* monosyllabic. **2** *nm* monosyllable.

monoteísmo *nm* monotheism.

monoteísta **1** *adj* monotheistic. **2** *nmf* monotheist.

monotipia *nf* Monotype (*Protected Trade Name*).

monotonía *nf* (*sound*) monotone; (*fig*) monotony; sameness, dreariness.

monótono *adj* on one note; (*fig*) monotonous; humdrum, dreary.

monóxido *nm* monoxide; **— de carbono** carbon monoxide.

monseñor *nm* monsignor.

monserga *nf* (**a**) gibberish, jargon. (**b**) drivel, tedious talk; **dar la —** to get on someone's nerves, be a bore.

monstruo **1** *nm* monster (*also fig*); (*Bio*) freak, sport, monster.
2 *as adj* (*invar*) (*fam*) fantastic, fabulous (*fam*); **idea —** fantastic idea; **es un plan —** it's a fabulous scheme.

monstruosidad *nf* monstrosity; (*Bio*) freak.

monstruoso *adj* monstrous, huge, monster (*attr*); (*Bio*) freakish, freak (*attr*); (*fig*) monstrous, hideous; **es — que ...** it is monstrous that ...

monta *nf* (**a**) (*act*) mounting.
(**b**) (*Math*) total, sum.
(**c**) (*fig*) value; **de poca —** of small account, unimportant.
(**d**) (*Agr*) stud; mating season (*of horses*).

montacargas *nm*, *pl* **montacargas** service lift, hoist, freight elevator (*US*).

montado *adj* (a) mounted; **artillería montada** horse artillery; **guardias montadas** horse guards. (b) (*Tech*) built-in.

montador *nm* (a) mounting block. (b) (*person*) fitter; — **de escena** (*Cine*) design craftsman.

montadura *nf* (a) mounting. (b) = **montura**.

montaje *nm* (a) (*Mech etc*) assembly; fitting-up; (*Archit*) erection.
  (b) (*Radio*) hookup.
  (c) (*Art, Cine, Phot*) montage; (*Theat*) stage designing, décor.

montante *nm* (a) (*Hist*) broadsword.
  (b) (*Tech*) upright, post; stanchion; (*Archit*) transom; (*of window*) mullion.
  (c) (*Archit*) small window over a door.
  (d) (*SAm*) total, amount.

montaña *nf* (a) mountain; mountains, mountainous area; — **rusa** switchback, scenic railway. (b) (*Per, PR*) forest.

montañero 1 *adj* mountain (*attr*). **2** *nm*, **montañera** *nf* mountaineer, climber.

montañés 1 *adj* (a) mountain (*attr*); hill (*attr*); highland (*attr*).
  (b) of (*or* from) the Santander region.
  2 *nm*, **montañesa** *nf* (a) highlander.
  (b) native of the Santander region.

montañismo *nm* mountaineering, climbing.

montañoso *adj* mountainous.

montaplatos *nm*, *pl* **montaplatos** service lift, dumbwaiter (*US*).

montar [1a] **1** *vt* (a) *horse etc* to mount, get on; to ride; **hoy ella monta mi caballo** she's riding my horse today.
  (b) — **a uno sobre un tronco** to lift someone on to a log; **montó al niño en el burro** he lifted the child on to the donkey, he put the child up on the donkey, he sat the child on the donkey.
  (c) (*Bio*) to cover, mate with.
  (d) to overlap; — **un color sobre otro** to overlap one colour with another, to cover one colour partially with another.
  (e) (*Mech*) to assemble, fit (up), put together, set up; (*Archit*) to erect, put up; *jewel* to set, mount; *gun* to cock; *clock, spring* to wind (up); *stitches* to cast on; *guard* to mount.
  (f) — **una casa** to set up house; — **una tienda** to open a shop; — **un negocio** to start a business, found a business.
  (g) (*Cook*) *egg* to beat, whip.
  2 *vi* (a) to mount (*a un caballo, en un caballo* a horse), get up (*a, en* on); to get on; to ride; — **a caballo** to ride; — **en bicicleta** to ride a bicycle, cycle; **me ayudó a** — he helped me up; he helped me to mount; **montó en la bicicleta y desapareció** he got on his bicycle and disappeared; **mi hermana monta a diario** my sister rides every day; — **para una cuadra de carreras** to ride for a racing stable.
  (b) to overlap; **el mapa monta sobre el texto** the map overlaps the text, the map covers part of the text.
  (c) — **en cólera**, — **en indignación** to get angry.
  (d) (*Fin*) — **a** to amount to, come to, add up to.
  (e) **tanto monta** it makes no odds; it's all the same, it doesn't matter either way; **tanto monta que vengas o no** it's all the same whether you come or not.
  3 montarse *vr* = **2** (a) (b) *and* (c).

montaraz 1 *adj* (a) mountain (*attr*), highland (*attr*). (b) wild, untamed; (*pej*) rough, coarse, uncivilized; unsociable. **2** *nm* gamekeeper, game warden.

montarrón *nm* (*Col*) forest.

monte *nm* (a) mountain; **M—s Apalaches** Appalachians; **M—s Cárpatos** Carpathians; **M—de la Mesa** Table Mountain; **los M—s Pirineos** the Pyrenees; **echarse al** — to take to the hills.
  (b) woodland; wilds, wild country; — **alto** forest; — **bajo** scrub; **batir el** — to beat for game, go hunting.
  (c) — **de piedad** (state-owned) pawnshop.
  (d) (*Cu, Pan, PR, Urug, Ven*) outskirts, surrounding country.
  (e) (*Mex*) grass, pasture.
  (f) (*Cards*) pile; bank; *a card game*.
  (g) (*fam*) obstacle, snag; **todo se le hace un** — he sees difficulties everywhere, he makes a mountain out of every molehill.

montear [1a] *vt* to hunt.

montecillo *nm* mound, hummock, hump.

montepío *nm* (a) charitable fund for dependents, friendly society. (b) (*SAm*) pawnshop.

montera *nf* cloth cap; bullfighter's hat.

montería *nf* (a) (art of) hunting; hunt, chase. (b) (*Art*) hunting scene. (c) hunting party. (d) (*SAm*) animals, game; hunting ground. (e) (*Bol, Ec*) canoe.

montero *nm* huntsman, hunter; beater.

montés *adj* *cat etc* wild.

montevideano 1 *adj* Montevidean. **2** *nm*, **montevideana** *nf* Montevidean.

montículo *nm* = **montecillo**.

monto *nm* total, amount.

montón *nm* (a) heap, pile; (*of snow*) drift.
  (b) (*fig*) **del** — ordinary, average, commonplace; **un hombre del** — an ordinary chap; **salirse del** — to be exceptional, stand out from the crowd.
  (c) (*fam*) stack (*fam*), heap, lot; (*of people*) crowd, mass; **un** — **de gente** a crowd, a mass of people, masses of people; **tengo un** — **de cosas que decirte** I have lots (*or* heaps, stacks) of things to tell you; **tenemos** —**es** we have heaps (*or* tons, loads: *fam*); **a** — **together**, all lumped together; **a** —**es** in great abundance, by the score (*etc*), galore.

montonera *nf* (a) (*SAm*) band of guerrilla fighters.
  (b) (*PR*) pile, heap; (*Col*) haystack, strawstack.

montonero 1 *adj* (*Mex etc*) *person* overbearing, that chucks his weight about. **2** *nm* (*SAm*) guerrilla fighter.

montuno *adj* (a) mountain (*attr*); forest (*attr*). (b) (*SAm*) wild, untamed; rustic.

montuosidad *nf* hilliness, mountainous nature.

montuoso *adj* hilly, mountainous.

montura *nf* (a) mount.
  (b) saddle; harness, trappings; **cabalgar sin** — to ride bareback.
  (c) (*of jewel etc*) mount, mounting, setting; (*of spectacles etc*) frame.

monumental *adj* monumental; (*fam*) tremendous (*fam*), terrific (*fam*).

monumento 1 *nm* (a) monument (*also fig*); memorial; —**s prehistóricos** prehistoric remains; **visitar los** —**s de una ciudad** to see the sights of a town, visit the places of interest in a city.
  (b) (*historical*) —**s** documents, source material.
  2 *as adj* (*fam*) **un éxito** — a tremendous success (*fam*), a huge success.

monzón *nm or f* monsoon.

monzónico *adj* monsoon (*attr*); **lluvias monzónicas** monsoon rains.

moña *nf* (a) hair ribbon, bow; bullfighter's ribbon; sash, prize ribbon. (b) (*fam*) doll. (c) (*fam*) **estar con la** — to be tight.

moño *nm* (a) bun, chignon; topknot; (*Chi*) man's hair; (*Chi*) horse's forelock; **agarrarse del** — to tear each other's hair; **estar hasta el** — (*fam*) to be fed up to the back teeth; **ponerse** —**s** (*fam*) to give oneself airs, put it on.
  (b) (*Orn*) crest.
  (c) = **moña** (a).
  (d) —**s** (*fig*) frippery, buttons and bows.
  (e) (*SAm*) pride, haughtiness; **bajar el** — **a uno** to take someone down a peg.

moquero *nm* handkerchief.

moqueta *nf* moquette.

moquete *nm* punch on the nose.

moquillo *nm* (*Vet*) distemper; pip.

mora[1] *nf* (a) (*Bot*) mulberry; blackberry. (b) (*Bol*) bullet.

mora[2] *nf* (*Law*) delay; **ponerse en** — to default, get into arrears.

mora[3] *nf* (*Chi*) blood sausage, black pudding.

morada *nf* (a) dwelling, abode, home; **la eterna** — the great beyond; **última** — (last) resting place; **no tener** — **fija** to be of no fixed abode.
  (b) stay, period of residence.

morado 1 *adj* purple, violet; **pasarlas moradas** to have a tough time of it. **2** *nm* bruise.

morador *nm*, **moradora** *nf* inhabitant.

moradura *nf* bruise.

moral[1] *nm* (*Bot*) mulberry tree.

moral[2] **1** *adj* moral. **2** *nf* (a) morals, morality; (*as study*) ethics. (b) (*of army etc*) morale.

moraleja *nf* moral.

moralidad *nf* (a) morals, morality, ethics. (b) (*of story etc*) moral.

moralista *nmf* moralist.

moralizador 1 *adj* moralizing. **2** *nm*, **moralizadora** *nf* moralist.

moralizar [1f] *vt* to moralize.

moralmente *adv* morally.

morapio *nm* (*fam*) red wine.

morar [1a] *vi* to live, dwell; to stay.

moratoria *nf* moratorium.

morbidez *nf* (*Art etc*) softness, delicacy.

mórbido *adj* (a) morbid; diseased. (b) (*Art etc*) soft, delicate.

morbosidad *nf* (a) morbidity, morbidness; unhealthiness. (b) (*of nation*) state of health; medical statistics.

morboso *adj* (a) morbid; unhealthy, likely to cause disease(s). (b) (*fig*) diseased, morbid.

morcilla *nf* (a) (*Cook*) blood sausage, black pudding. (b) (*Theat*) gag, unscripted lines, improvised part.

morcillo *adj horse* black with reddish hairs.

morcón *nm* (a) (*Cook*) big blood sausage. (b) (*fam*) stocky person. (c) (*fam*) sloppy individual, shabby sort.

mordacidad *nf* sharpness, pungency; bite.

mordaga *nf* (*fam*), **mordaguera** *nf* (*fam*) drunkenness; **coger** (or **pillar**) **una —** to get boozed.

mordaz *adj wit etc* biting, scathing, pungent.

mordaza *nf* (a) gag. (b) (*Tech*) clamp, jaw.

mordazmente *adv* bitingly, scathingly.

mordedura *nf* bite.

mordelón 1 *adj* (a) (*CAm, Mex*) given to taking bribes. (b) (*Col, Ven*) dog snappy. **2** *nm* (*Mex: fam*) traffic cop (*sl*).

morder [2h] **1** *vt* (a) to bite; to nip; to nibble (at). (b) (*Chem*) to corrode, eat away, eat into; *resources etc* to eat into. (c) (*Mech*) to catch; to clutch, seize. (d) (*fam*) to gossip about, run down. (e) (*Ant, Mex, Ven*) to cheat; (*CAm, Mex*) **to** exact a bribe from.
2 *vi* to bite (*also fig*); **estoy que muerdo** I'm simply furious; **está que muerde** he's hopping mad.

mordicar [1g] *vi* to smart, sting.

mordida *nf* (a) (*SAm*) bite. (b) (*CAm, Mex*) bribe; money obtained by graft, illegal payment.

mordiscar [1g] **1** *vt* to nibble at, gnaw at; to nip; (*of horse*) to champ. **2** *vi* to nibble; to champ.

mordisco *nm* (a) bite, nip; nibble; **deshacer algo a —s** to bite something to pieces. (b) bite, piece bitten off.

mordisquear [1a] = **mordiscar.**

morena[1] *nf* (*Geol*) moraine.

morena[2] *nf* (*Fish*) moray.

morena[3] *nf* dark girl, brunette.

moreno *adj* (dark) brown; *person* dark; swarthy; dark-haired; *hair* dark, black; (*euph*) coloured (*euph*), Negro; (*Cu, Ec, PR*) mulatto.

morera *nf* mulberry tree.

morería *nf* (*Hist*) Moorish lands, Moorish territory; (*in town*) Moorish quarter.

morfema *nm* morpheme.

morfina *nf* morphia, morphine.

morfinómano 1 *adj* addicted to drugs. **2** *nm*, **morfinómana** *nf* drug addict.

morfología *nf* morphology.

morfológico *adj* morphological.

morganático *adj* morganatic.

morgue *nf* (*CAm*) morgue.

moribundo 1 *adj* dying; (*esp fig*) moribund. **2** *nm*, **moribunda** *nf* dying person.

moricho *nm* (*Ven*) hammock.

morigerado *adj* well-behaved, law-abiding.

morigerar [1a] *vt* to restrain, moderate.

morillo *nm* firedog.

morir [3k; *ptp* **muerto**] **1** *vt* (*only in ptp and perfect tense*) to kill; **le han muerto** they have killed him; **fue muerto en un accidente** he was killed in an accident; **fue muerto a tiros** he was shot (dead).
2 *vi* (a) to die (*also fig*); **— de difteria** to die of diphtheria; **— joven** to die young; **— de vejez** to die of old age; **— ahogado** to drown; **— ahorcado** to be hanged, die by hanging; **— de frío** to die of cold, freeze to death; **— fusilado** to be shot; **— de hambre** to die of (or from) starvation, starve to death; **— sin decir Jesús** to die very suddenly; **¡muera!** kill him!; **¡muera el tirano!** down with the tyrant!; **¡así se muera!** (*fam*) God rot him!
(b) (*of fire*) to die down, burn low; to go out; (*of light*) to get dim, go out; **moría el día** the day was almost over, night was falling.
(c) (*Rail etc: of line*) to end (*en* at); (*of street*) to come out (*en* at).
3 morirse *vr* (a) to die; **se le murió el tío** an uncle of his died; **se nos va a — el burro** the donkey is going to die on us; **— de hambre = morir de hambre; ¡me muero de hambre!** (*fig*) I'm starving!; **no es cosa de —** it's not as bad as all that.
(b) (*fig*) to be dying; **me moría de vergüenza** I nearly died of shame; **me moría de miedo** I was half-dead with fright; **se van a — de risa** they'll die of laughing.
(c) **— por algo** to be dying for something; **— por uno** to be crazy about someone; **se muere por el**

fútbol he's mad keen on football; **— por** + *infin* to be dying to + *infin*.
(d) (*limb*) to go to sleep, go numb.

morisco 1 *adj* Moorish; (*Archit*) Mauresque, in the Moorish style.
2 *nm*, **morisca** *nf* (a) (*Hist*) Moslem convert to Christianity, subject Moslem (*of 15th and 16th centuries*).
(b) (*Mex*) quadroon.

morisqueta *nf* fraud, dirty trick.

mormón *nm*, **mormona** *nf* Mormon.

mormónico *adj* Mormon.

mormonismo *nm* Mormonism.

moro 1 *adj* (a) Moorish.
(b) *horse* dappled, piebald.
2 *nm*, **mora** *nf* (a) Moor; **— de paz** peaceful person; **¡hay —s en la costa!** watch out!; **dar a — muerto gran lanzada** to kick a man when he's down.
(b) (*SAm*) piebald horse.

morocha *nf* (*Ven*) double-barrelled gun.

morocho 1 *adj* (a) (*SAm*) dark, swarthy; brunette.
(b) (*Col, Chi, Ec, PR*) strong, tough; well-preserved.
(c) (*Ven*) twin.
2 *nm* (a) (*SAm*) hard maize, corn (*US*).
(b) (*Col, Chi, Ec, PR*) tough person.
(c) (*Ven*) twin.

morondaga *nf* hotchpotch.

morondo *adj* (a) bald; leafless, bare. (b) (*fig*) bare, plain.

moronga *nf* (*CAm, Mex*) blood sausage, black pudding.

morosidad *nf* slowness, sluggishness; dilatoriness; apathy.

moroso 1 *adj* (a) slow, sluggish; dilatory; (*Comm, Fin*) slow to pay up; **deudor —** slow payer, defaulter; **una película de acción morosa** a film with slow action, a slow-moving film.
(b) **delectación morosa** lingering enjoyment, (*pej*) morbid enjoyment, unhealthy enjoyment.
2 *nm* (*Comm, Fin*) slow payer, bad debtor; defaulter.

morra *nf* top of the head; **andar a la —** to exchange blows.

morrada *nf* butt; bang on the head; bash (*fam*), punch.

morral *nm* (a) haversack, knapsack; (*Hunting*) pouch, gamebag; (*horse's*) nosebag. (b) (*fam*) lout, rough type.

morrillo *nm* (*Zool*) fleshy part of the neck; (*fam*) neck, back of the neck.

morriña *nf* depression, depressed state, blues; **— de la tierra** homesickness.

morrión *nm* (*Mil*) helmet, bearskin.

morro *nm* (a) (*Zool*) snout, nose; (*fam*) lip, thick lip; **andar de — con uno** to be at odds with someone; **estar de —s** to be in a bad mood; **estar de —(s) con uno** to be cross with someone; **¡cierra los —s!** shut your trap! (*sl*); **poner —, torcer el —** to look cross.
(b) (*Aer, Aut etc*) nose; **caer de —** to nose-dive (into the ground).
(c) (*Geog*) headland, promontory.
(d) pebble.
(e) small rounded hill, rounded rock.

morrocotudo *adj* (*fam*) (a) smashing (*sl*), terrific (*fam*), splendid; *row, blow etc* tremendous.
(b) strong; heavy.
(c) *affair* sticky, awkward; important, weighty.
(d) (*Arg, Mex, Urug*) big.
(e) (*Col*) rich.
(f) (*Chi*) dull, monotonous.

morrocoyo *nm* (*Ant*) (a) turtle. (b) (*fam*) fat person; deformed person.

morrongo *nm*, **morronga** *nf* cat.

morronguero *adj* (*Cu*) mean; cowardly.

morroñoso *adj* (a) (*CAm*) rough. (b) (*Per*) small, feeble; mean.

morrudo *adj* (a) thick-lipped. (b) (*Arg*) tough, brawny.

morsa *nf* walrus.

mortaja *nf* (a) shroud. (b) (*Tech*) mortise. (c) (*SAm*) cigarette paper.

mortal 1 *adj* (a) mortal.
(b) *wound etc* mortal, fatal; *blow* deadly.
(c) (*fam*) *distance, wait etc* deadly, unending.
(d) (*fam*) **quedarse —** to be utterly taken aback.
2 *nmf* mortal.

mortalidad *nf* (a) mortality. (b) mortality; loss of life, toll, number of victims; death rate; **— infantil** (rate of) infantile mortality.

mortalmente *adv* (a) mortally. (b) fatally.

mortandad *nf* toll, loss of life, number of victims; (*Mil*) slaughter, carnage.

mortecino *adj* (a) weak, failing; **hacerse la mortecina** to pretend to be dead. (b) *light* dim, fading, failing; *colour* dull, faded.

mortero *nm* (*all senses*) mortar.

mortífero *adj* deadly, lethal.

mortificación *nf* mortification; humiliation.

mortificar [1g] **1** *vt* (a) (*Med*) to damage, affect seriously.
(b) *flesh* to mortify; (*of insect, shoe*) to torment, plague; **me han mortificado toda la noche los mosquitos** the mosquitos tormented me all night; **estos zapatos me mortifican** these shoes are killing me.
(c) (*fig*) to mortify, humiliate; to spite.
2 mortificarse *vr* (*Mex*) to feel ashamed; to be embarrassed, feel bashful.

mortuorio *adj* mortuary, death (*attr*); **casa mortuoria** house of mourning, home of the deceased.

morueco *nm* (*Zool*) ram.

Mosa *m* Meuse.

mosaico[1] *adj* Mosaic, of Moses.

mosaico[2] *nm* mosaic; tessellated pavement; **— de madera** marquetry.

mosca *nf* (a) (*Ent*) fly; **— de burro** horsefly; **— de la carne** meat fly; **— doméstica** housefly; **— de España** Spanish fly, cantharides; **— muerta** (*fig*) hypocrite, slyboots (*fam*); **— tsetsé** tsetse fly; **por si las —s** just in case; **estar — to** smell a rat, be distrustful; **estar —** to be utterly fed up; **estar — con uno** to be cross with someone; **mandar a uno a capar —s** to tell someone to go to blazes; **papar —s** to gape, gawp (*fam*); **pescar a —** to fish with a fly; **le picó la —** (*fig*) he suddenly got worried; **tener la — en** (*or* **detrás de**) **la oreja** to be wary, be suspicious.
(b) (*sl*) dough (*sl*); **aflojar la —, soltar la —** to fork out (*fam*), stump up.
(c) (*fam: person*) pest, bore.
(d) tuft of hair, small growth of hair; small goatee beard.
(e) **—s** sparks; **—s volantes** spots before the eyes.
(f) (*Mex*) sponger (*fam*).

moscarda *nf* blowfly, bluebottle.

moscardón *nm* (a) (*Ent*) botfly, blowfly; hornet.
(b) (*fam*) pest, bore, nuisance.

moscatel[1] **1** *adj grape* muscatel. **2** *nm* muscatel.

moscatel[2] *nm* (a) bore, pest. (b) big lad, overgrown lad.

moscón *nm* (a) (*Ent*) = **moscarda**. (b) (*Bot*) maple.
(c) (*fam*) pest, nuisance.

Moscú Moscow.

Mosela *m* Moselle.

mosqueado *adj* spotted.

mosqueador *nm* fly-whisk; (*fam*) tail (*of horse etc*).

mosquearse [1a] *vr* (*fig*) to get cross, take offence.

mosquete *nm* musket.

mosquetero *nm* (*Hist: Mil*) musketeer; (*Theat*) groundling.

mosquita *nf:* **— muerta** (*fig*) hypocrite, slyboots (*fam*); **hacerse la — muerta** to look as if butter would not melt in one's mouth.

mosquitero *nm* mosquito net.

mosquito *nm* mosquito; gnat.

mostacera *nf*, **mostacero** *nm* mustard pot.

mostacho *nm* moustache.

mostachón *nm* macaroon.

mostaza *nf* mustard.

mostela *nf* sheaf.

mosto *nm* must, unfermented grape juice.

mostrador *nm* (a) counter; (*of café, pub etc*) bar.
(b) (*of clock*) face, dial.

mostrar [1m] **1** *vt* to show; to display, exhibit; to point out; to explain; to demonstrate.
2 mostrarse *vr* (a) to show oneself; to appear.
(b) (*with adj*) to appear, show oneself to be; **se mostró muy amable** he was very kind, he proved to be very kind; **se mostró ofendido** he appeared (to be) cross; **no se muestra muy imaginativa** she does not seem to be very imaginative.

mostrenco *adj* (a) ownerless, unclaimed; *title* in abeyance; *animal* stray; *person* (*fam*) homeless, rootless.
(b) (*fam*) *person* dense, slow; fat.
(c) (*fam*) *object* crude, roughly made.

mota *nf* (a) speck, tiny piece; piece of fluff; **— de carbonilla** smut, speck of coaldust; **— de polvo** speck of dust; **ver la — en el ojo ajeno** to see the mote in someone else's eye.
(b) (*in pattern*) dot; **diseño a —s** design with (*or* of) dots.

(c) (*in cloth*) burl, kink; (*fig*) fault, blemish, defect.
(d) **no ... —** nothing, no, *eg* **no hace — de aire** there isn't a breath of air.
(e) (*Geog*) hillock.
(f) (*Agr*) ridge, boundary mark.
(g) (*Agr*) turf, clod (*used to block off irrigation channel*).
(h) (*SAm*) lock of kinky hair.
(i) (*Cu, Mex, PR*) powder puff.
(j) (*Mex*) marijuana plant.

mote[1] *nm* (a) (*Hist*) motto, device. (b) nickname, by-name.

mote[2] *nm* (*SAm*) boiled maize, boiled corn (*US*).

moteado *adj skin* speckled, mottled, dappled (*de* with); *fabric etc* dotted, with a design of dots.

motear [1a] *vt* to speck (*de* with); to speckle, dapple.

motejar [1a] *vt* to nickname; **— a uno de** to brand someone as, accuse someone of being.

motel *nm* (*angl*) motel.

motete *nm* motet.

motín *nm* revolt, rising; riot, disturbance.

motivación *nf* motivation.

motivar [1a] *vt* (a) to cause, motivate, give rise to.
(b) to explain, justify (*con, en* by, by reference to).

motivo 1 *adj* motive.
2 *nm* (a) motive, reason (*de* for), cause (*de* of); **—s de divorcio** grounds for divorce; **— oculto** ulterior motive; **con — de** because of, owing to; **on the occasion of; fue allí con — de la boda de su hija** he went there for his daughter's wedding; **con este — for** this reason, because of this; **por cuyo — for** which reason, on account of which; **sin — for** no reason at all, without good reason; **un crimen sin —** a crime without a motive, a pointless crime; **tengo mis —s** I have my reasons.
(b) (*Art, Mus*) motif; **— conductor** leitmotif; **— principal** (*of musical etc*) theme song.

moto[1] *nf* (*fam*) motorbike (*fam*); scooter.

moto[2] *adj* (a) (*CAm*) orphaned, abandoned. (b) (*Bol*) tailless.

motobomba *nf* fire engine.

motocarro *nm* three-wheeler, light delivery van.

motocicleta *nf* motorcycle; **— con sidecar** motorcycle combination.

motociclista *nmf* motorcyclist; **— de escolta** outrider.

moto-cross *nm* (*angl*) moto-cross.

motón *nm* (*Naut*) pulley.

motonave *nf* motor ship, motor vessel.

motoniveladora *nf* bulldozer.

motor 1 *adj* (a) (*Tech*) motive; **potencia motora** motive power.
(b) (*Anat*) motor.
2 *nm* motor, engine; **con 6 —es** 6-engined; **— de arranque, — de puesta en marcha** starter, starting motor; **— de aviación** aircraft engine; **— de combustión interna, — de explosión** internal combustion engine; **— a chorro** jet engine; **— delantero** front-mounted engine; **— Diesel** Diesel engine; **— de fuera de borda** outboard motor; **— de pistón** piston engine; **— radial** radial engine; **— de reacción** jet engine; **— refrigerado por aire** air-cooled engine; **— trasero** rear-mounted engine.

motora *nf*, **motorbote** *nm* motorboat, speedboat.

motorismo *nm* motorcycling.

motorista *nm* (a) motorcyclist. (b) (*SAm*) motorman.

motorización *nf* motorization.

motorizado *adj* motorized.

motorizar [1f] *vt* to motorize.

motosierra *nf* mechanical saw.

motosilla *nf* scooter, light motorcycle.

motoso *adj* (*Arg, Col, Ec, Per*) kinky.

motriz *adj* motive, driving; *see* **fuerza**.

motudo *adj* (*Chi*) *hair* kinky.

movedizo *adj* (a) easily moved, movable; loose, unsteady, shaky; *sands* shifting. (b) *person* fickle; *situation etc* shifting, unsettled, changeable; troubled.

mover [2h] **1** *vt* (a) *object etc* to move; to shift; to move about, move along; *head* to shake; to nod; *tail* to wag; (*Chess etc*) to move.
(b) (*Mech*) to drive, power, work; to pull; **el agua mueve la rueda** the water turns (*or* drives) the wheel; **la máquina mueve 14 coches** the engine pulls 14 coaches; **el vapor mueve el émbolo** the steam drives (*or* works) the piston.
(c) (*fig*) to cause, provoke, induce; *trouble etc* to stir up; **— un jaleo** to cause a row, make a fuss; **— guerra a uno** to wage war on someone; **— pleito a uno** to take proceedings against someone; **— a uno a piedad** to move someone to pity, arouse compassion in someone; **— a uno a risa** to make someone

laugh; — **a uno a hacer algo** to move (*or* prompt, lead) someone to do something.

2 *vi* (a) (*Bot*) to bud, sprout.

(b) (*fam*) to start to leave, get ready to go, make a move.

3 moverse *vr* (a) to move; to stir (*de* from); **no se ha movido de su asiento** he has not stirred from his place.

(b) (*sea*) to get rough; (*wind*) to rise.

(c) (*fig*) to move oneself, get a move on; **to be on the move; hay que** — we must get a move on; **si no te mueves lo perderás** if you don't hustle (*or* unless you do something) it will be lost; **la moda masculina se mueve** men's fashions are changing, men's fashions are on the move.

movible *adj* (a) movable; mobile. (b) (*fig*) changeable; fickle.

movida *nf* (*Chess etc*) move.

movido *adj* (a) (*Phot*) blurred (*by camera shake etc*).

(b) *person* active; restless, always on the go; *meeting etc* lively; turbulent.

(c) (*Col, CR, Chi*) egg soft-shelled.

(d) (*CAm, Col, Chi*) weak, feeble; stiff; paralytic; (*CAm, Mex*) slow, sluggish; irresolute.

móvil 1 *adj* =**movible** (a) and (b); *see* **material** *etc*.

2 *nm* motive (*de* for); incentive.

movilidad *nf* mobility.

movilización *nf* mobilization.

movilizar [1f] *vt* (a) to mobilize. (b) (*Arg*) to un-block, free.

movimiento *nm* (a) (*in general*) movement; (*Mech, Phys*) motion; (*statistical etc*) movement; (*of head*) shake; nod; — **ascensional de los precios** upward trend (*or* movement) of prices; — **ascendente de las líneas** (*Archit etc*) upward sweep of the lines; — **continuo,** — **perpetuo** perpetual motion; — **de mercancías** (*Comm*) turnover, volume of business; — **de pinza** (*Mil*) pincer movement; — **de los precios** changes in prices; — **sísmico** earth tremor; **estar en** — to be in motion, be moving; **to be on the move; mantener algo en** — to keep something moving; **mantener en** — **la circulación** to keep the traffic on the move; **poner algo en** — to set something in motion, start something, get something going.

(b) (*of street etc*) movement; activity; bustle, stir; (*Aut*) traffic; **una tienda de mucho** — a busy shop, a much-frequented shop; — **máximo** (*Aut*) peak traffic; **había mucho** — **en el tribunal** there was great activity in the court.

(c) (*Lit, Theat etc*) action; **el libro no tiene bastante** — the book does not have enough action, not enough happens in the book.

(d) (*Mus*) tempo.

(e) (*of emotions*) change, alteration; — **de ánimo** perturbation; **en un** — **de celos** in a rush of jealousy; **obró en un** — **de pasión** he acted in a surge of passion.

(f) (*Art, Lit, Pol etc*) movement; **el** — **revolucionario** the revolutionary movement; **el** — **iniciado por Picasso** the movement started by Picasso; **el M**— (*Spain, 1936 etc*) the Falangist Movement.

moviolas *nfpl* magic-lantern (show); (*Cine*) hand viewer for film editing.

moza *nf* girl; servant; (*pej*) wench; **buena** —, **real** — handsome girl, good-looking girl; — **de partido** prostitute; — **de servicio** maid of all work; — **de taberna** barmaid.

mozalbete *nm* lad.

mozárabe 1 *adj* Mozarabic. **2** *nmf* Mozarab. **3** *nm* (*dialect*) Mozarabic.

mozo 1 *adj* (a) young.

(b) single, unmarried.

2 *nm* youth, young fellow, lad; servant; (*in café*) waiter; (*Rail etc*) porter; **buen** — handsome lad; well set-up young man; — **de caballos** groom; — **de café** waiter; — **de cámara** cabin boy; — **de cuerda,** — **de estación,** — **de equipajes** porter; — **de hotel** page, buttons, bellhop (*US*); — **de laboratorio** laboratory assistant; — **de panadería** baker's boy.

mozuela *nf* girl; (*pej*) wench.

mozuelo *nm* (young) lad.

muaré *nm* moiré.

mucama *nf* (*SAm*) maid, servant.

mucamo *nm* (*RPl*) servant, houseboy.

muceta *nf* (*Univ*) hood.

mucilaginoso *adj* mucilaginous.

mucílago *nm* mucilage.

mucosa *nf* mucous membrane; mucus.

mucosidad *nf* mucus.

mucoso *adj* mucous.

muchá *nmf* (*SAm*) =**muchacho, muchacha.**

muchacha *nf* (a) girl. (b) maid, servant (*also* — **de servicio**).

muchachada *nf* childish prank.

muchacha-guía *nf*, *pl* **muchachas-guías** girl guide, girl scout (*US*).

muchachería *nf* (a) childish prank. (b) boys and girls, kids (*collectively*) (*fam*); crowd of kids (*fam*).

muchachil *adj* boyish, girlish.

muchacho *nm* (a) boy, lad. (b) (*SAm*) clamp, holdfast; (*RPl*) reel; (*Chi*) shoehorn; (*Per*) miner's lamp; (*Per*) prop.

muchedumbre *nf* crowd, mass, throng; (*pej*) mob, herd; **una** — **de** a great crowd of, a great number of.

muchísimo *adj, adv superl of* **mucho**; very much, a very great deal (*etc*).

mucho 1 *adj* (a) (*sing*) a lot of; much, great; — **tiempo** a long time (*and see* **tiempo**); — **dinero** a lot of money; **con** — **valor** with much courage, with great courage; **hace** — **calor** it's very hot.

(b) (*sing, collective*) **había** — **borracho** there were a lot of drunks (*fam*); **aquí hay** — **maricón** there are lots of queers here (*fam*).

(c) (*sing: fam*) **es** — **jugador** he's a great player; **es mucha mujer** what a woman she is!, there's a woman for you!; **ésta es mucha casa para nosotros** this house is far too big for us.

(d) (*pl*) —**s** many, lots of; many a; **hay** —**s conejos** there are lots of rabbits; —**s de los ausentes** many of those absent; **somos** —**s** there are a lot of us; **son** —**s los que no quieren** there are many who don't want to.

2 *pron:* **tengo** — **que hacer** I have a lot to do; —**s dicen que . . .** a lot of people say that . . .

3 *adv* (a) a lot, a great deal, much; — **más** much more, a lot more; — **menos** much less; — **peor** much worse; **toca** — she plays a lot, she plays a great deal; **me alegro** — I'm very glad; **correr** — to run fast; **trabajar** — to work hard; **viene** — he comes a lot, he comes often; **es** — it's a lot, it's too much; **si no es** — **pedir** if that's not asking too much; **se guardará muy** — **de hacerlo** (*fam*) he'll jolly well be careful not to do it (*fam*); *see* **antes** *etc*.

(b) (*of time*) long; **¿te vas a quedar** —**?** are you staying long?

(c) (*used alone, in answers*) very; **¿estás cansado?** . . . **¡**—**!** are you tired? . . . very (*or* I certainly am, yes indeed).

(d) (*idioms*) **¡**— **que sí!** I should jolly well think so! (*fam*), of course!; **con** — by far, far and away, easily; **con** — **el mejor** far and away the best; **ni con** — not nearly, nothing like; not by a long chalk; **ni** — **menos** far from it; **no es** — **que . . .** it is no wonder that . . .; **no es para** — it's not up to much; **tener a uno en** — to think highly of someone, have a high opinion of someone.

muda *nf* (a) change of clothing. (b) (*Orn, Zool*) moult; (*of snake*) slough. (c) moulting season. (d) **está de** — (*boy*) his voice is breaking.

mudable *adj* changeable, variable; shifting; *character etc* fickle.

mudanza *nf* (a) change; **sufrir** — to undergo a change.

(b) (*of house*) move, removal; **camión de** —**s** removal van; **estar de** — to be moving.

(c) (*Dancing*) figure.

(d) —**s** (*fig*) fickleness; moodiness, uncertainty of mood.

mudar [1a] **1** *vt* (a) to change, alter; — **en** to change into, transform into; **me van a** — **la pluma** they're going to change the pen for me; **le han mudado a otra oficina** they've moved (*or* switched) him to another office; **esto mudó la tristeza en alegría** this changed (*or* turned, transformed) the sadness into joy; **le mudan las sábanas todos los días** they change his sheets every day.

(b) (*Orn, Zool*) to shed, moult; *skin* to slough.

2 *vi* to change; — **de ropa** to change one's clothes; — **de color** to change colour; **he mudado de parecer** I've changed my mind.

3 mudarse *vr* (a) = *vi*.

(b) to move, move house (*also* — **de casa**).

(c) (*of voice*) to break.

mudéjar 1 *adj* Mudejar. **2** *nmf* (*Hist*) Mudejar (*Moslem permitted to live under Christian rule*).

mudenco *adj* (*CAm*) stuttering; silly.

mudengo *adj* (*Per*) silly.

mudez *nf* dumbness.

mudo *adj* (a) dumb, silent, mute; **quedarse** — **de** (*fig*) to be dumb with; **quedarse** — **de asombro** to be dumbfounded, be speechless; **se quedó** — **durante 3 horas** he remained silent for 3 hours, he did not speak for 3 hours.

(b) (*Ling*) *letter* mute, silent.

(c) *film* silent; **papel** — (*Theat*) walking-on part.

mueblaje *nm* =**mobiliario.**

mueble 1 *adj* movable.

2 *nm* piece of furniture; —s furniture; (*of shop etc*) fittings; **con** —s furnished; **sin** —s unfurnished; — **combinado,** — **de elementos adicionables** piece of unit furniture; —s **y enseres** furniture and fittings.

mueble-bar *nm* cocktail cabinet.

mueblería *nf* furniture factory; furniture shop.

mueca *nf* (wry) face, grimace; **hacer** —s **a** to make faces at.

muela *nf* **(a)** (*Anat*) tooth, (*strictly*) molar, back tooth; — **del juicio** wisdom tooth; **dolor de** —s toothache; **está que echa las** —s he's hopping mad.
(b) (*Tech*) millstone; grindstone.
(c) (*Geog*) mound, hillock.
(d) (*Col*) gluttony.
(e) (*Ant*) trickery.

muellaje *nm* wharfage.

muelle[1] *adj* **(a)** soft; delicate; springy, bouncy.
(b) (*fig*) life soft, easy, luxurious.
2 *nm* spring; — **real** mainspring; **colchón de** —s spring mattress, interior sprung mattress.

muelle[2] *nm* **(a)** (*Naut*) wharf, quay; pier. **(b)** (*Rail*) unloading bay.

muérdago *nm* mistletoe.

muérgano *nm* **(a)** (*Col, Ven*) useless object, piece of junk. **(b)** (*Col*) shabby person; (*Ec*) ill-bred person, lout. **(c)** (*Col*) vicious horse.

muerte *nf* **(a)** death (*also fig*); murder; — **civil** loss of civil rights; — **a mano airada,** — **violenta** violent death; — **natural** natural death; — **repentina** sudden death; **dar** — **a** to kill; **causar la** — **a, producir la** — **a** to kill (*in an accident*), cause the death of, bring about the death of; **encontrar la** — to meet one's death; **estar a la** — to be at death's door.
(b) (*fig phrases*) **guerra a** — war to the knife, war to the bitter end; **luchar a** — to fight to the death; **un susto de** — a terrible fright; **odiar a uno de** — to hate someone implacably; **aburrirse de** — to be bored to death; **un empleo de mala** — an awful job (*fam*), a lousy job (*fam*).

muerto 1 *adj* **(a)** dead; lifeless; **nacido** — stillborn; **más** — **que vivo** half-dead, more dead than alive; **más** — **que mi abuela, más** — **que una piedra** as dead as a doornail, stone-dead; **dar por** — **a uno** to give someone up for dead; **no tener donde caerse** — to be utterly destitute, not have a thing; **resultó** — **en el acto** he died instantly.
(b) (*fig*) **estar** — **de cansancio** to be dead tired, be dog-tired; **estar** — **de hambre** to be dying of hunger; **estar** — **de miedo** to be half-dead with fear, be panic-stricken.
(c) colour dull.
(d) language dead; see **marea, naturaleza** *etc*.
(e) lime slaked.
2 *nm,* **muerta** *nf* dead man, dead woman; deceased; corpse; **los** —s the dead; **callarse como un** — to keep absolutely quiet; **cargar con el** — (*fam*) to carry the can (*sl*); **doblar a** —, **tocar a** — to toll (for a death); **echar el** — **a uno** to put the blame on someone else; **no hablan los** —s dead men tell no tales; **hacer el** — (*of swimmer*) to float; **hacerse el** — to pretend to be dead.
3 *nm* (*Cards*) dummy.

muesca *nf* notch, nick; groove, slot.

muestra *nf* **(a)** indication, sign; example; demonstration; proof; token; **es** — **de cariño** it is a token of affection; **el no hacerlo es** — **de desprecio** not doing it is an indication of contempt; **quieren hacer una** — **de su poder** they want to give a demonstration of their power; **da** —s **de deterioro** it's showing signs of wear.
(b) (*Comm etc*) sample; specimen; — **gratuita** free sample.
(c) (*statistical*) sample.
(d) model, pattern, guide; (*Sew*) pattern; **es** — **de cómo debe hacerse** it is a model of how it should be done.
(e) (*of watch*) face.
(f) (*of shop etc*) sign, signboard.

muestrario *nm* collection of samples (*or specimens*); pattern book.

muestreo *nm* (*statistical*) sampling.

mugido *nm* moo, lowing; bellow; roar, howl.

mugir [3c] *vi* (*cow*) to moo, low; (*bull*) to bellow; (*with pain*) to roar, howl; (*of sea etc*) to roar.

mugre *nf* dirt, filth; grease, grime.

mugriento *adj* dirty, filthy; greasy, grimy.

mugrón *nm* (*of vine*) sucker, layer; shoot, sprout.

muguete *nm* lily of the valley.

mujer *nf* **(a)** woman; — **alegre,** — **de vida alegre,** —

de (mala) vida, — **pública** prostitute; — **de la limpieza** charwoman, cleaner; **ser muy** — **de su casa** to be a good housewife; to be very houseproud; — **fatal** femme fatale; — **policía** policewoman.
(b) wife; **mi** — my wife; **tomar** — to take a wife, marry.
(c) ¡—!: in direct address, not translated.

mujeraza *nf* shrew, bitch, horrid woman.

mujerengo *adj* (*CAm, RPl*) **(a)** effeminate. **(b)** fond of women.

mujerero *adj* (*SAm*) fond of women.

mujeriego 1 *adj* **(a)** fond of women, given to chasing the girls, wolfish (*fam*).
(b) **cabalgar a mujeriegas** to ride sidesaddle.
2 *nm* man who is fond of the women, wolf (*fam*).

mujeril *adj* womanly.

mujerzuela *nf* whore.

mújol *nm* grey mullet.

mula *nf* **(a)** mule. **(b)** (*Mex*) trash, junk, unsaleable goods. **(c)** (*Guat, Hond*) shame. **(d)** (*Col*) pipe. **(e)** (*Col*) idiot. **(f)** (*Mex*) tough guy (*US fam*).

mulada *nf* drove of mules.

muladar *nm* dungheap, dunghill, midden.

mulato 1 *adj* mulatto. **2** *nm,* **mulata** *nf* mulatto.

mulero *nm* muleteer.

muleta *nf* **(a)** crutch. **(b)** (*Taur*) matador's stick with red cloth attached. **(c)** (*fig*) prop, support.

muletilla *nf* **(a)** cross-handled cane; (*Tech*) wooden toggle; large wooden button; (*Taur*) =**muleta (b).**
(b) (*fig*) pet word, tag, cliché.

mulo *nm* mule.

mulón *adj* (*Chi, Per*) stammering; slow in learning to talk, backward.

multa *nf* fine; (*Sport etc*) penalty; **echar una** — **a, imponer una** — **a** to impose a fine (*or* penalty) on.

multar [1a] *vt* to fine; (*Sport etc*) to penalize; — **a uno en 100 dólares** to fine someone 100 dollars.

multi... multi...

multicanal *adj* (*TV*) multichannel.

multicolor *adj* multicoloured, many-coloured; motley, variegated.

multicopista *nm* duplicator.

multiforme *adj* manifold, multifarious; multiform; having different forms.

multilaminar *nm* plywood.

multilateral *adj,* **multilátero** *adj* mutilateral, many-sided.

multimillonario *nm,* **multimillonaria** *nf* multimillionaire.

múltiple *adj* **(a)** (*Math*) multiple; (*fig*) many-sided.
(b) —s (*fig*) many, numerous; manifold, multifarious; **tiene** —s **actividades** he has very numerous activities.

multiplicación *nf* multiplication.

multiplicado *nm* multiplicand.

multiplicar [1g] **1** *vt* (*Math and fig*) to multiply (**por** by); possibilities etc to increase; (*Mech*) to gear up.
2 multiplicarse *vr* **(a)** (*Math, Bio etc*) to multiply; to increase.
(b) (*fig*) to be everywhere at once; to attend to a lot of things all at once.

multiplicidad *nf* multiplicity.

múltiplo 1 *adj* multiple. **2** *nm* multiple; **mínimo común** — lowest common multiple.

multirracial *adj* multiracial.

multisecular *adj* age-old, centuries-old, very ancient.

multitud *nf* multitude; (*of people*) crowd; **la** — (*pej*) the multitude, the masses; — **de** (*fam*) lots of, heaps of; **tengo** — **de cosas que hacer** I have lots of things to do.

multitudinario *adj* multitudinarious; of the multitude, mass (*attr*).

mullido 1 *adj* **(a)** bed etc soft, sprung; fluffy; grass etc soft, springy.
(b) (*fam*) **dejar a uno** — to leave someone all in (*fam*), wear someone out.
2 *nm* stuffing, filling.

mullir [3a] *vt* **(a)** wool etc to make fluffy, fluff up; to soften; bed to shake up; earth to hoe, loosen.
(b) plants to hoe round, loosen the earth round.

mullo *nm* (red) mullet.

mundanal *adj* (*lit*) worldly, of the world.

mundanalidad *nf* (*lit*) worldliness.

mundanería *nf* worldliness.

mundano 1 *adj* **(a)** worldly, of the world.
(b) society (*attr*); fashionable; social; **son gente muy mundana** they're great society people; **una reunión mundana** a fashionable gathering, a gathering of society people.
2 *nm,* **mundana** *nf* society person, socialite.

mundial *adj* world-wide, universal; record, war, distribution etc world (*attr*); **las comunicaciones** —es world communications; **un invento de aplicación —** an invention of world-wide application; **otra guerra —** another world war.

mundialmente *adv* throughout the world; universally; **— famoso** world-famous; **hacer algo — popular** to make something universally popular.

mundillo *nm* (a) world, circle; **en el — teatral** in the theatre world, in theatrical circles. (b) (*Bot*) viburnum.

mundo *nm* (*in most senses*) world, people; society; (*Eccl*) world, secular life; **— antiguo** ancient world; **Nuevo M—** New World; **el — hispánico** the Hispanic world; **el gran —** high life, high society; **el — del espectáculo** show business; **este pícaro —** this wicked world; **en el — de las ideas** in the world of ideas, in the realm of ideas; **estaba medio —** there were hordes of people; **el otro —** the other world, the next world; **no es nada del otro —** it's nothing extraordinary; **hacer algo del otro —** to do something quite extraordinary; **todo el —** everybody; **en todo el —** everywhere; throughout the world; **es lo que más desea en el —** it's what she wants most in the world; **por esos —s (de Dios)** there; all over, in all parts; **el — es un pañuelo** it's a small world; **desde que el — es —** since time began; **echar al —** to bring into the world; **echarse al —** to take to prostitution; **aunque se hunda el —** come what may; **no por eso se hundirá el —** it won't be too much of a disaster; **así va el —** that's the way it is; **ponerse el — por montera** to care nothing for public opinion; **tener (mucho) —** to be experienced, be sophisticated, know one's way around; **tener poco —** to be inexperienced; **ver —** to see life, see the world; **ha visto mucho —** he's knocked around a lot.

mundología *nf* (*iro*) worldly-wisdom, experience of the world.

mundonuevo *nm* peep show.

munición *nf* (a) (*also* **—es**) ammunition; munitions; stores, supplies; **—es de boca** provisions.
(b) **de —** army (*attr*), service (*attr*); **botas de —** army boots.
(c) (*CAm*) uniform.

municionera *nf* (*Ven*) ball bearing.

municipal 1 *adj* municipal; town (*attr*). 2 *nm* policeman.

municipalidad *nf* municipality.

municipio *nm* (a) municipality; town, township. (b) corporation; town council.

munificiencia *nf* munificence.

munífico *adj* munificent.

muñeca *nf* (a) (*Anat*) wrist. (b) (*child's*) doll; (*tailor's*) dummy, manikin; **— de trapo** rag doll. (c) bunch of rags, cleaning (*or* polishing) rag.

muñeco *nm* (a) figure; (boy) doll, guy, scarecrow; puppet, marionette; (*tailor's*) dummy; **— de nieve** snowman.
(b) (*fig*) puppet, pawn.
(c) (*fam*) pretty little boy, little angel; (*pej*) sissy.

muñequera *nf* wristband; wrist watch.

muñir [3h] *vt* (a) to summon, convoke, call. (b) (*pej*) to rig, fix, arrange in a fraudulent fashion.

muñón *nm* (a) (*Anat*) stump. (b) (*Mech*) trunnion; pivot, journal.

mural *adj* 1 *adj* mural, wall (*attr*); **mapa —** wall map. 2 *nm* mural.

muralla *nf* (city) wall, walls; rampart; (*SAm*) (*any*) wall.

murar [1a] *vt* to wall.

murciano 1 *adj* Murcian. 2 *nm*, **murciana** *nf* Murcian.

murciélago *nm* bat.

murga *nf* (a) band of street musicians. (b) (*fam*) bore, nuisance, bind (*sl*).

murguista *nm* (a) street musician; (*fam*) bad musician, poor player. (b) (*fam*) bore.

murmullo *nm* (a) murmur(ing); whisper(ing); mutter(ing). (b) murmur, rippling; rustle, rustling; hum(ming).

murmuración *nf* gossip; slanderous talk, backbiting; constant complaining.

murmurador 1 *adj* gossip; backbiting; critical; complaining, grumbling. 2 *nm*, **murmuradora** *nf* gossip; backbiter; critic; complainer, grumbler.

murmurar [1a] *vi* (a) (*person*) to murmur, whisper; to mutter.
(b) (*of water*) to murmur, ripple; (*of leaves, wind etc*) to rustle; (*of bees, crowd etc*) to hum.
(c) (*fig*) to gossip (*de* about); to criticize (*de uno* someone), grumble (*de* about), mutter (*de* about);

siempre están murmurando del jefe they're always grumbling about the boss, they're always criticizing the boss.

muro *nm* wall; **— de contención** containing wall.

murria *nf* depression, blues; sulks; **tener —** to feel blue, be down in the dumps (*fam*); to feel sulky.

murrio *adj* depressed, dejected; sulky, sullen.

mus[1] *nm* a card game.

mus[2] *see* **chus**; **sin decir ni —** without saying a word.

musa *nf* Muse; **las M—s** the Muses.

musaraña *nf* (a) (*Zool*) shrew; (*any*) small creature, bug, creepy-crawly (*fam*).
(b) speck floating in the eye; **mirar a las —s** to stare vacantly; **pensar en las —s** to go woolgathering.

muscovita 1 *adj* Muscovite. 2 *nmf* Muscovite.

muscular *adj* muscular.

musculatura *nf* muscles, musculature; **preparar su —** to flex one's muscles (*also fig*).

músculo *nm* muscle.

musculoso *adj* muscular; tough, brawny.

muselina *nf* muslin.

museo *nm* museum; gallery; **— de arte, — de pintura** art gallery; **— de cera** waxworks.

musgaño *nm* shrew.

musgo *nm* moss.

musgoso *adj* mossy, moss-covered.

música *nf* (a) music; **— de cámara** chamber music; **— celestial** (*fam*) bunk (*sl*), drivel; **— coreada** choral music; **— de fondo** background music; **— mundana, — de las esferas, — de los planetas** music of the spheres; **— sagrada** sacred music; **poner — a** to set to music; **irse con la — a otra parte** to take one's troubles elsewhere; to go away, go somewhere else; **¡con la — a otra parte!** off with you!, get out!
(b) (*persons*) band.
(c) **—s** (*fam*) drivel; **no estoy para —s** I'm not in the mood to listen to such drivel.

musical *adj* musical.

musicalidad *nf* musicality, musical quality.

músico 1 *adj* musical. 2 *nm* musician, player; **— mayor** bandmaster.

musicología *nf* musicology.

musicólogo *nm* musicologist.

musitar [1a] *vti* to mumble, mutter.

muslo *nm* thigh.

mustango *nm* (*SAm*) mustang.

mustela *nf* weasel.

mustio *adj* (a) (*Bot*) withered, faded. (b) soft, slack. (c) depressed, gloomy. (d) (*Mex*) hypocritical.

musulmán 1 *adj* Moslem. 2 *nm*, **musulmana** *nf* Moslem.

mutabilidad *nf* mutability; changeableness.

mutación *nf* (a) (sudden) change. (b) (*Bio*) mutation. (c) (*Ling*) mutation. (d) (*Theat*) change of scene.

mutante *nm* mutant.

mutil *nm* (*Hist*) Carlist soldier.

mutilación *nf* mutilation.

mutilado *nm*, **mutilada** *nf* cripple, disabled person; **— de guerra** war cripple.

mutilar [1a] *vt* (a) to mutilate; to cripple, maim, disable. (b) (*fig*) *text etc* to mutilate, hack about, spoil; *tale* to garble; *object* to deface.

mutis *nm*, *pl* **mutis** (*Theat*) exit; **¡—!** sh!; **hacer —** (*Theat*) to exit, go off; (*fig*) to say nothing, keep quiet.

mutismo *nm* dumbness; (*fig*) silence, uncommunicativeness.

mutualidad *nf* (a) mutuality, mutual character. (b) mutual aid, reciprocal aid. (c) (*Fin*) friendly society, mutual benefit society.

mutuamente *adv* mutually, reciprocally.

mutuo *adj* mutual, reciprocal; joint.

muy *adv* very; greatly, highly; too; **— bueno** very good; **— lentamente** very slowly; **— buscado** very much sought-after, highly prized; **— de noche** very late at night; **tener — en cuenta** to bear very much in mind; **venir — tarde** to come too late; **es — de sentir** it is much to be regretted; **eso es — español** that's very Spanish, that's typically Spanish; **eso es — de él** that's just like him; **una enfermera — de minifalda** a nurse in a very short skirt, a nurse in what one could undoubtedly describe as a miniskirt; **es — hombre** he's a real man, he's pretty tough; **es — mujer** she's very feminine; as a woman she's terribly attractive; **el — bestia de Pedro** that great idiot of a Peter; **¡el — bandido!** the rotter!

N

naba *nf* (*Bot*) rape.
nabab *nm* nabob.
nabina *nf* rapeseed.
nabo *nm* (**a**) (*Bot*) turnip; (*any*) root vegetable, thick root; — **gallego** rape; — **sueco** swede.
    (**b**) (*Anat*) root of the tail.
    (**c**) (*Archit*) newel, stair post.
    (**d**) (*Naut*) mast.
    (**e**) (*Anat: tabu*) prick (*tabu*).
Nabucodonosor *m* Nebuchadnezzar.
nácar *nm* mother-of-pearl, nacre.
nacarado *adj*, **nacarino** *adj* mother-of-pearl (*attr*), pearly, nacreous.
nacatete *nm* (*Mex*), **nacatón** *nm*, **nacatona** *nf* (*CAm, Mex*) unfledged chick.
nacedera *nf* (*CAm: also* **cerca** —) hedge.
nacencia *nf* (*SAm*) =**nacimiento.**
nacer [2d] **1** *vi* (**a**) to be born; (*from egg*) to hatch; **nací en Cuba** I was born in Cuba; **cuando nazca el niño** when the baby is born; — **al amor** to awaken to love; **con esa exposición nació a la vida artística** that exhibition saw the beginning of his artistic career; **no nació para sufrir** she was not born to suffer; **nació para poeta** he was born to be a poet; **nadie nace enseñado** we all have to learn.
    (**b**) (*Bot*) to sprout, bud; to come up; (*of star etc*) to rise; (*of river*) to rise; (*of water*) to spring up, appear, begin to flow; (*of roads*) to begin, start (*de from, en* in); **le nacieron alas** it grew wings; **le nació mucho pelo** it sprouted a lot of hair.
    (**c**) (*fig: of idea etc*) to be born; to begin, originate, have its origin (*en* in); **nació una sospecha en su mente** a suspicion formed in her mind; **el error nace del hecho de que . . .** the error springs (*or* stems) from the fact that . . .; **entre ellos ha nacido una fuerte simpatía** a strong friendship has sprung up between them; **¿de dónde nace la idea?** whence comes the idea?
    2 nacerse *vr* (**a**) (*Bot*) to bud, sprout.
    (**b**) (*seam*) to split.
nacido 1 *adj* born; — **a la libertad** born to be free; — **para el amor** born to love; — **de padres ricos** born of wealthy parents; **bien** — of noble birth; well-bred; **mal** — mean, base, wicked; ill-bred; **recién** — newborn.
    2 *nm* (**a**) human being; **todos los** —**s** everybody, all mankind; **ningún** — nobody.
    (**b**) (*Med*) tumour, growth; boil.
    (**c**) (*Sew*) split.
naciente 1 *adj* nascent; new, recent; growing; *sun* rising; **el** — **interés por . . .** the new-found interest in . . ., the growing interest in . . .
    2 *nm* (**a**) east.
    (**b**) (*Arg, Par: also* —**s**) spring, source.
nacimiento *nm* (**a**) birth; (*Orn etc*) hatching; **ciego de** — blind from birth; **tonto de** — born fool; **este defecto lo tiene de** — he has had this defect since birth, he was born with this defect.
    (**b**) (*fig*) descent, family; **de** — **noble** of noble birth, of noble family.
    (**c**) (*of water*) spring; (*of river*) source.
    (**d**) (*fig*) birth; origin, beginning, start; **dar** — **a** to give rise to; **el partido tuvo su** — **en . . .** the party had its origins in . . .
    (**e**) (*Art, Eccl*) nativity (scene).
nación 1 *nf* nation; people; **N**—**s Unidas** United Nations; **de** — **ruritana** Ruritanian by birth, of Ruritanian nationality. **2** *nmf* (*Arg*) foreigner.
nacional 1 *adj* national; *industry, product etc* home.
2 *nmf* national; **los** —**es** (*Spain, 1936 etc*) the Franco forces.
nacionalidad *nf* nationality.
nacionalismo *nm* nationalism.
nacionalista 1 *adj* nationalist(ic). **2** *nmf* nationalist.

nacionalización *nf* (**a**) naturalization. (**b**) nationalization.
nacionalizar [1f] **1** *vt* (**a**) *person* to naturalize. (**b**) *industry* to nationalize. **2 nacionalizarse** *vr* to become naturalized.
naco 1 *adj* (*Mex*) stupid.
    2 *nm* (**a**) (*CAm*) coward; milksop.
    (**b**) (*Bol, RPl*) chewing tobacco.
    (**c**) (*Col*) *maize kernels cooked with salt*; mashed potatoes.
    (**d**) (*Arg*) fright, scare.
    (**e**) —**s** (*Arg*) roll of banknotes.
nada 1 *pron* nothing; **no dijo** — she said nothing, she didn't say anything; **¡—, —!** not a bit of it!; — **de eso** nothing of the kind, far from it; **¡— de eso!** not a bit of it!; **¡— de excusas!** no excuses!; — **de marcharse!** forget about leaving!; **no tiene** — **de particular** there's nothing special about it; — **entre dos platos** a lot of fuss, much ado about nothing; *see* **más**; **a cada de** — (*SAm*) every moment, at every step; **antes de** — very soon, right away; **antes de** — **tengo que . . .** before I do anything else I must . . .; **casi** — next to nothing; **como si** — as if it didn't matter, as if it were only a small thing; **¡de** —**!** not at all!, don't mention it!; **estuvo en** — **que lo perdiesen** they very nearly lost it; **quedar(se) en** — to come to nothing; **no reparar en** — to stop at nothing; **en** — **de tiempo** in no time at all; **hace** — just a moment ago; **¡ni curas ni** —**!** blow the priests!; I don't want to hear about the priests!; **no los mencionó para** — he never mentioned them at all; **no servir para** — to be no use at all, be utterly useless; **llorar por** — to cry for no reason at all; **por** — **del mundo** not for anything in the world; **por menos de** — for two pins; **no lo hago por** — **ni por nadie** I won't do it and that's flat; **¡pues** —**!** not to worry!; **no ha sido** — it's nothing; **y** — **and that was that**, so there it was.
    2 *adv* not at all, by no means; **no es** — **fácil** it's not at all easy, it's far from easy.
    3 *nf* nothingness; **la** — the void; **el avión parecía salir de la** — the aircraft seemed to come from nowhere.
nadaderas *nfpl* water wings.
nadador *nm*, **nadadora** *nf* swimmer.
nadar [1a] *vi* (**a**) to swim; (*of cork etc*) to float; (*Col*) to take a bath.
    (**b**) (*Sew*) **en estos pantalones va nadando** he rattles about inside these trousers, these trousers are much too big for him.
    (**c**) — **en** (*fig*) to wallow in, be rolling in.
nadería *nf* small thing, mere trifle.
nadie *pron* (**a**) nobody, no-one; — **lo tiene, no lo tiene** — nobody has it; **no le visto a** — I haven't seen anybody; **apenas** — hardly anybody.
    (**b**) **no es** — he's nobody (that matters); **es un don** — he's a nobody.
nadir *nm* nadir.
nadita (*SAm*) =**nada.**
nado: cruzar (*or* **pasar**) **a** — to swim, swim across.
nafta *nf* naphtha; (*Arg*) petrol, gasoline (*US*).
naftaleno *nm*, **naftalina** *nf* naphthaline.
nagual *nm* (**a**) (*CAm, Mex*) sorcerer, wizard. (**b**) (*Guat, Hond*) inseparable companion. (**c**) (*Mex*) lie.
nagualear [1a] *vi* (*Mex*) (**a**) to lie. (**b**) to go thieving at night; to spend the night in revelry.
naguas *nfpl* petticoat.
nagüeta *nf* (*CAm*) overskirt.
nailon *nm* (*angl*) nylon.
naipe *nm* playing card; — **de figura** court card, picture; —**s** cards.
naipeador *adj* (*Arg*) fond of cards.
naipear [1a] *vi* (*Arg*) to play cards.
naja: salir de — (*fam*) to get out, beat it (*fam*).

najarse [1a] *vr* (*fam*) to beat it (*fam*).
najencia *interj* (*fam*) scram! (*sl*).
nalga *nf* buttock; —s buttocks, backside, rump; **dar de** —s to fall on one's bottom.
nalgada *nf* (a) (*Cook*) ham, shoulder. (b) smack on the bottom; —s spanking.
nalguiento *adj* (*Per*), **nalgón** *adj* (*SAm*), **nalgudo** *adj* big-bottomed, broad in the beam (*fam*).
nana¹ *nf* (a) grandma (*fam*), granny (*fam*); *see* año. (b) (*Mus*) lullaby, cradlesong. (c) baby's sleeping bag. (d) (*CAm, Mex*) wet-nurse; nurserymaid.
nana² *nf* (*Chi, RPl*) minor ailment of children.
nanai *interj* (*sl*) no!
napias *nfpl* (*sl*) nose, snitch (*sl*).
Napoleón *m* Napoleon.
napoleónico *adj* Napoleonic.
Nápoles Naples.
napolitano 1 *adj* Neapolitan. 2 *nm*, **napolitana** *nf* Neapolitan.
naranja *nf* (a) orange; — **cajel** Seville orange; — **sanguina** blood orange. (b) (*fam*) ¡—s!, ¡—s chinas!, ¡—s de la China! nonsense!, rubbish! (c) **la media** — one's better half; **esperar la media** — to wait for Mr Right; **encontrar su media** — to find one's life partner. (d) (*PR*) bitter orange.
naranjada *nf* orangeade, orange squash.
naranjado *adj* orange, orange-coloured.
naranjal *nm* orange grove.
naranjo *nm* orange tree.
Narbona Narbonne.
narcisismo *nm* narcissism.
narcisista *adj* narcissistic.
narciso *nm* (a) narcissus; — **atrompetado**, — **trompón** daffodil. (b) (*fig*) dandy, fop.
narcosis *nf* narcosis.
narcótico 1 *adj* narcotic. 2 *nm* narcotic; sleeping pill; —s (*loosely*) drugs, dope.
narcotismo *nm* narcosis.
narcotizar [1f] *vt* to narcotize; (*loosely*) to drug, dope.
nardo *nm* nard; spikenard.
narguile *nm* hookah.
naricear [1a] *vt* (*Per*) to smell (out).
narigón 1 *adj* big-nosed. 2 *nm* (*Cu, Mex, SD*) ring (in *animal's* nose).
narigudo *adj* big-nosed.
narigueta *adj* (*Arg, Chi*) big-nosed.
nariz *nf* (a) nose; nostril. (b) **narices** *pl* nostrils; (*fam*) nose; **¡narices!** (*fam*) rubbish!, nonsense!; **cerrar la puerta en las narices de uno** to shut the door in someone's face; **dar de narices** to fall flat on one's face; **dar de narices contra la puerta** to bang one's face on the door; **estar hasta las narices** to be completely fed up; **hablar por las narices** to talk through one's nose, speak with a nasal twang; **hacer algo por narices** to do something under compulsion; **se le hincharon las narices** he got very cross; **meter las narices en algo** to poke one's nose into something. (c) sense of smell. (d) (*of wine*) bouquet.
narizota *nf* big nose; ¡—s! (*fam*) you villain!; you idiot!
narizudo *adj* (*CAm, Mex, PR*) big-nosed.
narración *nf* narration, account.
narrador *nm*, **narradora** *nf* narrator.
narrar [1a] *vt* to tell, narrate, recount.
narrativa *nf* (a) narrative, story. (b) narrative skill, skill in storytelling.
narrativo *adj* narrative.
narval *nm* narwhal.
nasa *nf* bread bin, flour bin; (*Fish*) basket, creel; (*Fish*) fish trap.
nasal 1 *adj* nasal. 2 *nf* nasal.
nasalidad *nf* nasality.
nasalizar [1f] *vt* to nasalize.
nasalmente *adv* nasally.
nata *nf* (a) cream; (on *custard etc*) skin; — **batida** whipped cream. (b) (*fig*) cream, choicest part, best part; *see* flor.
natación *nf* (a) swimming. (b) style (of swimming), stroke; — **a braza**, — **de pecho** breast-stroke; — **de costado**, — **en cuchillo** sidestroke; — **de espalda** backstroke; — **submarina** underwater swimming; skin diving.
natal *adj* natal; *soil etc* native; *town etc* home (*attr*).
natalicio 1 *adj* birthday (*attr*). 2 *nm* birthday.
natalidad *nf* birth rate.
natillas *nfpl* custard.
natividad *nf* nativity.
nativo 1 *adj* (a) native; *country etc* native, home

(*attr*); **lengua nativa** native language, mother tongue. (b) natural, innate. (c) (*Min*) native. 2 *nm*, **nativa** *nf* native; **los —s son gente pacífica** the natives are friendly.
nato *adj* born; **un actor** — a born actor; **un criminal** — a hardened criminal, an incorrigible criminal; **es un pintor** — he's a natural painter.
natural 1 *adj* (a) (in *most senses*) natural; **es — que ...** it is natural that ... (b) *fruit* fresh, raw. (c) (*Mus*) natural. 2 *nmf* native, inhabitant; **fue — de Sigüenza** he was a native of Sigüenza; **trató sin miramientos a los —es** he treated the inhabitants unceremoniously. 3 *nm* (a) nature, disposition, temperament; **buen** — good nature. (b) **fruta al** — fruit in its own juice; **ginebra al** — neat gin, gin with nothing added; **una descripción al** — a true-to-life description, a realistic description; **vivir al** — to live according to nature; **está muy guapa al** — she is very pretty just as she is (without make-up *etc*); **pintar del** — to paint from life, paint from nature. (c) (*Taur*) a kind of pass with the cape.
naturaleza *nf* (a) (in *most senses*) nature. (b) — **muerta** (*Art*) still life. (c) (*Pol*) nationality; **una mujer de** — **suiza** a woman of Swiss nationality. (d) (*Pol*) citizenship (*granted to a foreigner*); **carta de** — naturalization papers.
naturalidad *nf* naturalness; **con la mayor** — (**del mundo**) as if nothing had happened; as if it were the most natural thing in the world; **lo dijo con la mayor** — he said it in a perfectly ordinary tone; **allí le pegan un tiro con la mayor** — they'll shoot you there and think nothing of it.
naturalismo *nm* naturalism; realism.
naturalista 1 *adj* naturalistic; realistic. 2 *nmf* naturalist.
naturalización *nf* naturalization.
naturalizar [1f] 1 *vt* to naturalize. 2 **naturalizarse** *vr* to become naturalized.
naturalmente *adv* (a) naturally; in a natural way. (b) ¡—! naturally!, of course!; you bet!
naturismo *nm* naturism.
naturista *nmf* naturist.
naufragar [1h] *vi* (a) (*ship*) to be wrecked, sink; (*person*) to be shipwrecked. (b) (*fig*) to fail, miscarry, suffer a disaster.
naufragio *nm* (a) shipwreck. (b) (*fig*) failure, disaster, ruin.
náufrago 1 *adj* shipwrecked. 2 *nm* shipwrecked sailor, shipwrecked person; castaway.
náusea *nf*, **náuseas** *nfpl* nausea, sick feeling; (*fig*) disgust, repulsion; **dar —s a** to nauseate, sicken, disgust; **tener —s** to feel nauseated, feel sick, (*fig*) to be nauseated, be sickened.
nauseabundo *adj* nauseating, sickening.
náutica *nf* navigation, seamanship.
náutico *adj* nautical.
nautilo *nm* nautilus.
navaja *nf* (a) clasp knife, jack-knife; penknife; — (**de afeitar**) razor. (b) (*Zool: of boar*) tusk; (*mollusc*) razor shell; (*Ent*) sting. (c) (*fig*) sharp tongue, evil tongue.
navajada *nf*, **navajazo** *nm* slash, gash, razor wound.
naval *adj* naval; ship (*attr*), sea (*attr*).
Navarra *f* Navarre.
navarro 1 *adj* Navarrese. 2 *nm*, **navarra** *nf* Navarrese. 3 *nm* (*dialect*) Navarrese.
nave *nf* (a) (*Naut*) ship, vessel; **quemar las —s** to burn one's boats; **la N— de San Pedro** (*Eccl*) the Roman Catholic Church. (b) (*Aer*) — **espacial** spaceship, spacecraft. (c) (*Archit*) nave; — **lateral** aisle. (d) (*Tech*) large building, large shed; factory, mill, plant; — **de laminación** rolling mill.
navegable *adj* navigable.
navegación *nf* (a) navigation. (b) sea voyage; — **costanera** coasting, coastal traffic; — **fluvial** sailing by inland waterways, river navigation. (c) ships, shipping; **cerrado a la** — closed to shipping.
navegador *nm*, **navegante** *nm* navigator.
navegar [1h] 1 *vt* to sail; to navigate; — **los mares** to sail the seas. 2 *vi* to sail; — **a 15 nudos** to sail at 15 knots, go at 15 knots; — **a la vela** to sail, go sailing.

Navidad *nf* Christmas; (**día de**) — Christmas Day; —**es** Christmas time; **por** —**es** at Christmas time; ¡**feliz** —! happy Christmas!

naviero 1 *adj* shipping (*attr*). **2** *nm* shipowner.

navío *nm* ship; — **de alto bordo**, — **de línea** (*Hist*) ship of the line.

náyade *nf* naiad.

nazarenas *nfpl* (*Bol*, *Chi*, *RPl*) large *gaucho* spurs.

nazareno 1 *adj* Nazarene. **2** *nm*, **nazarena** *nf* Nazarene.

Nazaret Nazareth.

nazi 1 *adj* Nazi. **2** *nmf* Nazi.

nazismo *nm* Nazism.

nazista *adj* Nazi.

neblina *nf* mist; mistiness; (*fig*) fog.

nebulosa *nf* nebula.

nebulosidad *nf* (a) nebulosity; cloudiness; mistiness; gloominess. (b) (*fig*) vagueness; obscurity.

nebuloso *adj* (a) (*Astron*) nebular, nebulous; *sky* cloudy; *air* misty, foggy; dark, gloomy. (b) (*fig*) nebulous, vague; obscure.

necedad *nf* (a) foolishness, silliness. (b) (*una* —) silly thing; —**es** nonsense.

necesariamente *adv* necessarily.

necesario *adj* necessary; **es** — **que lo hagas** it is necessary that you should do it, it is necessary for you to do it; **todo es** — it all helps, every little helps.

neceser *nm* toilet case, dressing case; holdall; — **de belleza** vanity case; — **de costura** workbox; — **de fin de semana** weekend bag, weekend case.

necesidad *nf* (a) necessity; need (**de** for); — **imperiosa**, — **primordial** absolute necessity, pressing need; **de** —, **por** — of necessity; **esto es de primera** — this is absolutely essential; **no hay** — **de** + *infin* there is no need to + *infin*; **satisfacer las** —**es de uno** to satisfy someone's needs.

(b) necessity; tight spot, awkward situation; **en caso de** — in case of need; **encontrarse en una** — to be in a difficult situation.

(c) need, necessity, want; poverty; **están en la mayor** — they are in great need.

(d) —**es** hardships; **pasar** —**es** to suffer hardships.

(e) (*euph*) business (*euph*); **hacer sus** —**es** to do one's business, relieve oneself; **sentir una gran** — to be dying to relieve oneself.

necesitado *adj* (a) — **de** in need of; **estamos** —**s de mano de obra** we need workers, we are in need of labour.

(b) needy, necessitous; **los** —**s** the needy, those in need.

necesitar [1a] **1** *vt* to need, want; to necessitate, require; **necesitamos 2 más** we need 2 more; **necesita un poco de cuidado** it needs (*or* requires, takes) a little care; — + *infin* to need to + *infin*, **must** + *infin*; **no necesitas hacerlo** you don't need to do it, you don't have to do it.

2 *vi*: — **de** to need.

3 necesitarse *vr* to be needed, be wanted; "**necesítase coche**" (*advert*) "car wanted".

neciamente *adv* foolishly, stupidly.

necio *adj* (a) silly, stupid.

(b) (*Col etc*) peevish.

(c) (*Arg*, *Col*, *PR*) touchy, hypersensitive.

(d) (*Guat etc*) *illness* stubborn, long-lasting.

necrófago *nm* ghoul.

necrología *nf* obituary (notice), necrology.

necrológico *adj* necrological, obituary (*attr*).

necromancia *nf*, **necromancía** *nf* necromancy.

necrópolis *nf*, *pl* **necrópolis** necropolis.

néctar *nm* nectar (*also fig*); **el** — **de la amabilidad humana** the milk of human kindness.

nectarina *nf* nectarine.

neerlandés 1 *adj* Dutch, Netherlands (*attr*). **2** *nm*, **neerlandesa** *nf* Dutchman, Dutchwoman, Netherlander. **3** *nm* (*language*) Dutch.

nefando *adj* unspeakable, abominable.

nefario *adj* nefarious.

nefasto *adj* unlucky, ill-fated, inauspicious.

nefato *adj* (*Ven*) stupid, dim.

nefritis *nf* nephritis.

negación *nf* (a) negation; refusal, denial. (b) (*Gram*) negation; negative.

negado *adj* (a) dull, stupid. (b) — **para** inept at, unfitted for.

negar [1h *and* 1k] **1** *vt* (a) *fact*, *truth etc* to deny; *charge* to deny, reject, refute; — **que algo sea así** to deny that something is so.

(b) *permission etc* to deny, refuse (*a* to); to withhold (*a* from); — **la mano a uno** to refuse to shake hands with someone; — **el saludo a uno** to cut someone; **le negaron el paso por la frontera** they refused to let him cross the frontier; **pasé por la casa**

pero me la negaron I called at the house but they refused to let me see her.

(c) *relationship*, *responsibility etc* to disclaim, disown.

2 negarse *vr* (a) — **a** + *infin* to refuse to + *infin*.

(b) — **a una visita** to refuse to see a visitor, be not at home to a caller.

negativa *nf* (a) negative; denial, refusal; — **rotunda** flat refusal; **la** — **a comer es peligrosa** the refusal to eat is dangerous.

(b) (*Phot*) negative.

negativamente *adv* negatively; **contestar** — to answer in the negative.

negativo 1 *adj* (a) negative. (b) (*Math*) minus. (c) (*Phot*) negative. **2** *nm* (*Phot*) negative.

negligencia *nf* negligence; neglect, slackness, carelessness; nonchalance.

negligente *adj* negligent; neglectful, slack, careless; *posture etc* careless, nonchalant.

negligentemente *adv* negligently; slackly, carelessly; nonchalantly.

negociable *adj* negotiable.

negociación *nf* negotiation; deal, transaction; (*of cheque*) clearance; **entrar en** —**es con** to enter into negotiations with.

negociado *nm* (a) department, section. (b) (*Chi*) shop, store. (c) (*Arg*, *Chi*, *Ec*, *Per*) illegal transaction, shady deal.

negociador *nm*, **negociadora** *nf* negotiator.

negociante *nm* businessman; merchant, dealer.

negociar [1b] **1** *vt* to negotiate. **2** *vi* (a) (*Pol etc*) to negotiate. (b) (*Comm*) — **en** to deal in, trade in.

negocio *nm* (a) affair; **mal** — bad business; ¡**mal** —! it looks bad!; **eso es** — **tuyo** that's your affair.

(b) (*Comm*, *Fin*) business; **el** — **del libro** the book trade, the book business; **el** — **del espectáculo** show business; **montar un** — **de frutas** to start a fruit business; **traspasar un** — to transfer a business, sell a business.

(c) (*Comm*, *Fin*) deal, transaction, piece of business; (*iro*) bargain; **buen** — profitable deal, (good) bargain; — **sucio**, — **turbio** shady deal; **hacer un buen** — to pull off a profitable deal; ¡**hiciste un buen** —! (*iro*) that was a fine deal you did!; **hacer su propio** — to look after one's own interests.

(d) —**s** (*Comm*, *Fin*: *in general*) business; trade; **hombre de** —**s** businessman; **el mundo de los** —**s** the business world; "**los** —**s**, **como de costumbre**" "business as usual"; **a malos** —**s sombrero de copa** one must accept losses with dignity, one must make the best of a bad job; **estar de** —**s** to be (away) on business; **retirarse de los** —**s** to retire from business.

(e) (*Arg*, *Chi*, *Per*, *Urug*) firm, business house; place of business.

(f) (*Per*, *PR*, *Ven*) **el** — the fact, the truth; **pero el** — **es que** — ... but the fact is that ...

(g) (*Col*) tale, piece of gossip.

negocioso *adj* industrious; businesslike.

negra *nf* (a) Negress, black woman.

(b) (*Mus*) crotchet.

(c) (*Chess*) black piece.

(d) (*CAm*: *fig*) black mark.

(e) bad luck; **tener la** — to be out of luck, have a run of bad luck; **le tocó la** — he had bad luck; **ése me trae la** — he brings me bad luck; he mucks things up for me.

negrada *nf* (*SAm*) (a) group of Negroes; Negroes (*collectively*). (b) remark (*or* act *etc*) typical of a Negro.

negrear [1a] *vi* to turn black; to look black, appear black.

negrería *nf* (*SAm*), **negrerío** *nm* (*SAm*) = **negrada** (a).

negrero *nm* slave trader; (*RPl*) exploiter of labour, cruel boss.

negrilla *nf* (a) (*Typ*) = **negrita** (a). (b) (*Bot*) elm.

negrita *nf* (a) (*Typ*) bold face; **en** — in bold type, in heavy type. (b) (*CAm*: *fig*) black mark.

negrito *nm* golliwog.

negro 1 *adj* (a) black; dark; *person* Negro; dark, swarthy; — **como boca de lobo**, — **como un pozo** as black as pitch, pitch-dark; as black as your hat; **más** — **que el azabache** (*etc*) as black as ink, coal-black.

(b) (*fig*) mood, state *etc* sad; black, gloomy; *luck* awful (*fam*), atrocious; **pasarlas negras** to have a tough time of it; **la cosa se pone negra** it's not going well, it looks bad; **ve muy** — **el porvenir** he's very gloomy about the future; **lo ve todo** — he's terribly pessimistic about everything; **verse** — to be in a jam;

verse — **para** + *infin* to have one's work cut out to + *infin*; **nos veíamos —s para salir del apuro** we had a tough time getting out of it.

(c) (*fam*) cross, peeved (*fam*); **estoy — con esto** I'm getting desperate about it; **poner — a uno** (*fam*) to make someone cross, upset someone; **ponerse —** (*fam*) to get cross, cut up rough.

2 *nm* (a) (*colour*) black; **en —** (*Phot*) in black and white; **— de humo** lampblack.

(b) (*person*) Negro, black; **¡no somos —s!** we won't stand for it!, you can't do that to us!; **sacar lo que el — del sermón** to understand nothing of what has been said.

(c) (*SAm: in direct address*) dear, honey (US).

negroide *adj* negroid.

negrura *nf* blackness.

negruzco *adj* blackish.

neme *nm* (*Col*) asphalt.

nemorosa *nf* wood anemone.

nene *nm*, **nena** *nf* baby, small child; **¡sí, nena!** (*to woman*) yes dear!, yes darling!

nenúfar *nm* water lily.

neo *nm* neon.

neo . . . neo . . .

neoclasicismo *nm* neoclassicism.

neoclásico *adj* neoclassical.

neofascismo *nm* neofascism.

neofascista **1** *adj* neofascist. **2** *nmf* neofascist.

neófito *nm*, **neófita** *nf* neophyte.

neolatino *adj*: **lenguas neolatinas** Romance languages.

neolítico *adj* neolithic.

neologismo *nm* neologism.

neón *nm* neon.

neonazi **1** *adj* neonazi. **2** *nmf* neonazi.

neonazista *adj* neonazi.

neoperonista *adj* (*Arg*) neoperonist.

neoplatónico *adj* neoplatonic.

neoplatonismo *nm* neoplatonism.

neoplatonista *nmf* neoplatonist.

neoyorquino **1** *adj* New York (*attr*), of New York. **2** *nm*, **neoyorquina** *nf* New Yorker.

neozelandés **1** *adj* New Zealand (*attr*), of New Zealand. **2** *nm*, **neozelandesa** *nf* New Zealander.

Nepal *m* Nepal.

nepalés **1** *adj* Nepalese. **2** *nm*, **nepalesa** *nf* Nepalese.

nepotismo *nm* nepotism.

Neptuno *m* Neptune.

nereida *nf* nereid.

Nerón *m* Nero.

nervadura *nf* (*Archit, Bot*) ribs; (*Ent*) veins (*of wing*).

nervio *nm* (a) (*Anat*) nerve; **crispar los —s a uno, poner los —s en punta a uno** to get on someone's nerves; to jar on someone, grate on someone; **tener los —s en punta** to be all keyed up, have one's nerves on edge.

(b) (*Anat*) tendon, sinew; (*in meat*) sinew, tough part.

(c) (*Archit, Bot*) rib; (*Ent*) vein; (*of book*) rib, fillet; (*Mus*) string.

(d) (*fig*) vigour, strength; fibre; stamina, toughness; moral fibre, moral strength; **un hombre sin —** a weak man, a spineless man; **tener —** to have character.

(e) (*fig: person*) soul, leading light, guiding spirit; **él es el — de la sociedad** he is the guiding spirit of the club.

(f) (*fig: of question*) core, crux.

nerviosamente *adv* nervously.

nerviosidad *nf*, **nerviosismo** *nm* nervousness; nervous anticipation, nerves; agitation, restlessness, impatience.

nervioso *adj* (a) (*Anat*) nerve (*attr*), nervous; **centro —** nerve centre; **crisis nerviosa** nervous breakdown; **sistema —** nervous system.

(b) (*Anat*) hand *etc* sinewy, wiry.

(c) *person* (*by temperament*) nervy, highly-strung, excitable; (*temporarily*) nervous, nervy; restless, impatient; overwrought; upset, agitated; **poner — a uno** to make someone nervous, get on someone's nerves; to get someone worked up; to make someone cross; **ponerse —** to get nervous; to get worked up; to get upset, get cross; to get rattled; **¡no te pongas —!** take it easy!, keep calm!

(d) *style etc* vigorous, forceful.

nervoso *adj* (a) *person* = **nervioso** (c). (b) *meat* sinewy, tough.

nervudo *adj* (a) tough, strong. (b) *hand etc* sinewy, wiry.

nesga *nf* (*Sew*) flare, gore.

nesgado *adj* *skirt etc* flared.

nesgar [1h] *vt* (*Sew*) to flare, gore.

netamente *adv* clearly; purely; genuinely; **una construcción — española** a purely Spanish construction, a genuinely Spanish construction.

neto *adj* (a) clear; clean, pure; neat; *truth etc* pure, simple; **tiene su sueldo —** he has (just) his bare salary.

(b) (*Comm, Fin*) net; **peso —** net weight; **sueldo —** net salary, salary after deductions.

neumático **1** *adj* pneumatic; air (*attr*). **2** *nm* tyre; **— de recambio, — de repuesto** spare tyre.

neural *adj* neural.

neuralgia *nf* neuralgia.

neurastenia *nf* (a) neurasthenia; nervous exhaustion.

(b) excitability, highly-strung nature, nerviness.

neurasténico *adj* (a) neurasthenic. (b) excitable, highly-strung, nervy, neurotic.

neuritis *nf* neuritis.

neurología *nf* neurology.

neurólogo *nm* neurologist.

neurona *nf* neuron, nerve cell.

neurópata *nmf* neuropath.

neurosis *nf*, *pl* **neurosis** neurosis; **— de guerra** shell-shock.

neurótico **1** *adj* neurotic. **2** *nm*, **neurótica** *nf* neurotic.

neutral **1** *adj* neutral. **2** *nmf* neutral.

neutralidad *nf* neutrality.

neutralismo *nm* neutralism.

neutralista **1** *adj* neutralist. **2** *nmf* neutralist.

neutralización *nf* neutralization.

neutralizar [1f] *vt* to neutralize; *tendency etc* to counteract.

neutro *adj* (a) (*in most senses*) neutral.

(b) (*Bio*) neuter, sexless, without sex; **abeja neutra** worker bee.

(c) (*Gram*) neuter; **género —** neuter; **verbo —** intransitive verb.

neutrón *nm* neutron.

nevada *nf* snowstorm; snowfall; **una copiosa —** a heavy snowfall.

nevado **1** *adj* (a) snow-covered; *mountain* snow-capped; (*Arg*) permanently snow-covered.

(b) (*fig*) snowy, snow-white.

2 *nm* (*Chi, Ec*) snow-capped mountain.

nevar [1k] **1** *vt* to cover with snow; (*fig*) to whiten. **2** *vi* to snow.

nevasca *nf* snowstorm.

nevazón *nf* (*Arg, Chi, Ec*) snowstorm.

nevera *nf* refrigerator, icebox; (*fig*) icebox.

nevero *nm* snowfield, icefield, place of perpetual snow.

nevisca *nf* light snowfall, flurry of snow; sleet.

neviscar [1g] *vi* to snow lightly; to sleet.

nevoso *adj* snowy.

nexo *nm* link, connection; nexus.

ni *conj* (a) nor, neither; **no bebe — fuma** he neither smokes nor drinks; **— el uno — el otro** neither one nor the other; **— vino — llamó por teléfono** he neither came nor rang up; **no quiere — sal — mostaza** he doesn't want either salt or mustard; **sin temor — favor** without fear or favour; **sin padre — madre** without father or mother; **— yo** nor me; *see* **siquiera.**

(b) **not . . . even; no lo sabrán — por fuerza** they won't find it out even by force; **— a ti te lo dirá** he won't tell even you.

(c) **— que . . . not even if . . .; — que fueses su mujer** not even if you were his wife; **— que fuera de plomo pesaría tanto** it wouldn't weigh so much even if it were lead.

Niágara *m* Niagara.

niara *nf* (*Agr*) stack, rick.

nica *nmf* (*CAm: fam*) Nicaraguan.

Nicaragua *f* Nicaragua.

nicaragüense **1** *adj* Nicaraguan. **2** *nmf* Nicaraguan.

nicaragüismo *nm* word (*or phrase etc*) peculiar to Nicaragua.

Nicolás *m* Nicholas.

nicotina *nf* nicotine.

nicho *nm* niche; recess; hollow.

nidada *nf* (*of eggs*) sitting, clutch; (*of chicks*) brood.

nidal *nm* (a) nest; nesting box. (b) nest egg. (c) (*fam*) haunt, hangout (*fam*); hiding place. (d) (*of bird-watcher*) hide.

nido *nm* (a) nest; **— de amor** love nest; **caer del —** (*fig*) to come down to earth with a bump; **se ha caído de un —** he's dreadfully innocent, he's terribly naïve (*fam*); **manchar el propio —** to foul one's own nest.

(b) (*fig*) nest, haunt, abode, den; **— de ladrones** nest of thieves, den of thieves.

(c) (*fig*) hiding place; secret store.

(d) (*fig*) centre, hotbed; **el reparto de premios fue**

un — de polémicas the prize giving was a centre of controversy, the prize giving gave rise to heated arguments.

niebla nf (a) fog, mist; — **artificial** smoke screen; **un día de** — a foggy day; **hay** — it is foggy. (b) (fig) fog, confusion. (c) (Bot) mildew.

nieta nf granddaughter.

nieto nm (a) grandson; —**s** grandchildren. (b) (fig) descendant.

nieve nf (a) snow; **las primeras** —**s** the first snows, the first snowfall; — **abundante, copiosa** — heavy snow. (b) (SAm) sherbet, ice cream.

Nigeria f Nigeria.

nigeriano 1 adj Nigerian. 2 nm, **nigeriana** nf Nigerian.

nigromancia nf, **nigromancía** nf necromancy, black magic.

nigromante nm necromancer.

nihilismo nm nihilism.

nihilista 1 adj nihilistic. 2 nmf nihilist.

Nilo m Nile.

nilón nm (Acad) nylon.

nimbo nm (Art, Astron, Eccl) halo; (Meteorol) nimbus.

nimiamente adv (a) trivially; with a host of petty details. (b) fussily; small-mindedly; long-windedly. (c) excessively.

nimiedad nf (a) (quality) triviality; fussiness; small-mindedness; long-windedness; excess; **tratar un asunto con** — to discuss a subject in great detail, treat a theme exhaustively; (pej) to discuss a subject in excessive detail. (b) (una —) very small thing, tiny detail; **riñeron por una** — they quarrelled over some triviality.

nimio adj (a) insignificant, trivial, tiny; **un sinfín de detalles** —**s** a host of petty details. (b) person fussy (about details), too meticulous; small-minded; long-winded. (c) excessive (en in).

ninfa nf nymph.

ninfilla nf, **ninfita** nf nymphet.

ninfómana nf nymphomaniac.

ninfomanía nf nymphomania.

ninfómano adj nymphomaniac.

ningún see ninguno.

ningunear [1a] vt (Mex) to deny; to refuse; — **a uno** to look down one's nose at someone; to pretend that someone is not there, pay no attention to someone; to make someone feel small; to treat someone badly.

ninguno 1 adj (**ningún** before m sing noun) no; **ningún hombre** no man; **ninguna belleza** no beauty; **no hay ningún libro que valga más** there is no book that is worth more; **en ninguna fiesta me he divertido tanto** I haven't enjoyed myself so much at any other party; **sin ningún sentimiento** without any regret, without regret of any kind; **no es ningún tonto** he's no fool, he's no sort of fool.

2 pron nobody, no-one; none; neither; **no lo sabe** — nobody knows; — **de ellos** none of them; — **de los dos** neither of them; **¿cuál prefieres?** . . . — which do you prefer? . . . neither (of them).

niña nf (a) girl, little girl, child; — **exploradora** girl guide, girl scout (US). (b) (fam) tart (sl), whore. (c) (SAm: in direct address) miss, mistress; **la** — the mistress of the house. (d) (Anat) pupil; **ser las** —**s de los ojos de uno** to be the apple of someone's eye.

niñada nf = niñería.

niñear [1a] vi to act childishly.

niñera nf nursemaid, nanny.

niñería nf (a) (quality) childishness. (b) (act) childish thing, silly thing, triviality; **llora por cualquier** — she cries about any triviality.

niñero adj fond of children.

niñez nf childhood; infancy (also fig); **segunda** — second childhood.

niño 1 adj (a) young; immature, inexperienced; (pej) childish; **es muy** — **todavía** he's still very young (or small). (b) (Col) fruit green, unripe.

2 nm (a) boy, little boy, child; (in general) child; (unborn, newborn) baby; (in direct address) my boy, my lad; **¡**—**!** (fam) look out!, be careful!; **los** —**s the children; el N**— the Child, Jesus; **el N— Jesús** the Christ-child, (less formally) Baby Jesus; — **azul** blue baby; — **bien,** — **bonito,** — **gótico** playboy, elegant layabout; — **de coro** choirboy; — **explorador** boy scout; — **expósito** foundling; — **de pecho** small baby, babe-in-arms; — **prodigio** child prodigy; **de**

— as a child; when a child; **desde** — since childhood, since I (etc) was a child; **¡no seas** —! don't be such a baby!; **ser el** — **mimado de uno** to be someone's pet, be someone's white-haired boy (fam); **hacer un** — **a una** to get a girl in the family way; **va a tener un** — she's going to have a baby; **cuando nazca el** — when the baby (or child) is born. (b) (SAm: in direct address) master, sir; **el** — the (young) master. (c) (Chi) unsavoury individual.

nipón 1 adj Japanese. 2 nm, **nipona** nf Japanese.

níquel nm (a) nickel; (Tech) nickel-plating, chromium-plating. (b) (SAm) small coin, nickel (US); —**es** (esp Arg, Mex) money, wealth.

niquelado adj nickel-plated, chromium-plated.

niquelar [1a] vt to nickel-plate; to chromium-plate.

niquelera nf (Col) purse.

níspero nm, **níspola** nf medlar.

nítidamente adv brightly, cleanly; spotlessly; clearly, sharply.

nitidez nf (a) brightness; spotlessness; clarity, sharpness. (b) (fig) unblemished nature.

nítido adj (a) bright, clean; spotless; outline (also Phot) clear, sharp. (b) (fig) pure, unblemished.

nitral nm nitrate deposit.

nitrato nm nitrate.

nitrera nf (Chi) nitrate deposit.

nítrico adj nitric.

nitro nm nitre, saltpetre.

nitrogenado adj nitrogenous.

nitrógeno nm nitrogen.

nitroglicerina nf nitroglycerin(e).

nitroso adj nitrous.

nivel nm (a) (Geog etc) level, height; — **de(l) aceite** (Aut etc) oil level; — **del agua** water level; — **del mar** sea level; **a los 900 m sobre el** — **del mar** at 900 m above sea level, at a height of 900 m; **la nieve alcanzó un** — **de 1,5 m** the snow reached a depth of 1½ m; **a** — level; true; flush; horizontal; **al** — **de** on the same level as, on a level with, at the same height as. (b) (fig) level, standard; **el** — **cultural del país** the cultural standard of the country; — **de vida** standard of living; **alto** — **de trabajo** high level of employment; **conferencia al más alto** —, **conferencia de alto** — high-level conference, top-level conference; **estar al** — **de** to be on a level with, be equal to; **no está al** — **de los demás** he is not up to the standard of the others; **estar al** — **de las circunstancias** to rise to the occasion. (c) (Tech) — **de aire,** — **de burbuja** spirit level.

nivelación nf levelling.

nivelado adj level, flat; flush.

niveladora nf bulldozer.

nivelar [1a] vt (a) to level (out); (Rail etc) to grade. (b) (fig) to level (up), even (out, up), make even; (Fin etc) to balance (con against), adjust (con to).

níveo adj (lit) snowy, snow-white.

Niza Nice.

no adv (a) (used alone) no; not; (qualifying verb) not; **¡no! no!; ¡yo no! not I!; ¡rey no!** we don't want a king!; **¡Paco no, Pepe sí!** Paco out, Pepe in!; **no sé** I do not know, I don't know; **me rogó no hacerlo** he asked me not to do it; **¿vives aquí, no?** see **¿no es verdad?** (in verdad); **decir que no** to say no; **creo que no** I don't think so; **¡que no!** I tell you it isn't! (or doesn't etc); **¡a que no!** I bet you can't!, I bet you it isn't! (etc); **¿oh no?, ¿a que no?** oh no?; do you dare me to?, do you think I can't?; **¡a que no lo sabes!** I bet you don't know!; **está de que no** he is in a mood to refuse, I guess he'll say no; **no sea que . . . lest . . .; ¡no** si not if not, otherwise; unless you (etc) do; **todavía no** not yet; see **más, sino** etc. (b) (in double negatives) **no tengo nada** I have nothing, I don't have anything; see **nada, nunca** etc. (c) (in compounds) eg **el no conformismo** non-conformism; **pacto de no agresión** non-aggression pact; **la política de no intervención** the policy of non-intervention, the non-intervention policy; **cosa no esencial** non-essential thing, inessential; **la no necesidad del latín en partes de la misa** the fact that Latin is not to be insisted upon in parts of the mass; for other cases, see the noun or adj.

nobiliario adj (a) title etc noble. (b) book etc genealogical.

noble 1 adj noble; honest, upright. 2 nm noble, nobleman; **los** —**s** the nobles, the nobility.

noblemente adv nobly; honestly, uprightly.

nobleza nf (a) (quality) nobility; honesty, uprightness. (b) (persons) nobility, aristocracy.

nocaut nm (SAm: angl) knockout.

noción nf (a) notion, idea; **no tener la menor —de algo** to have not the faintest idea about something.
(b) **—es** elements, rudiments; smattering; **tiene algunas —es de árabe** he has a smattering of Arabic.

nocional adj notional.

nocivo adj harmful, injurious (para to).

noctambulismo nm sleepwalking.

noctámbulo nm, **noctámbula** nf sleepwalker.

noctiluca nf (Ent) glow-worm.

nocturno 1 adj night (attr); evening (attr); (Zool etc) nocturnal; **clase nocturna** evening class; **vida nocturna** night life. **2** nm (Mus) nocturne.

noche nf night; night-time; (late) evening; dark, darkness (fig); **ayer —** last night; **esta —** tonight; **¡buenas —s!** good evening!, (on parting or going to bed) good night!; **— de estreno** (Theat) first night; **—toledana** sleepless night; **— vieja** New Year's Eve; **a primera —** shortly after dark; **a la —** at nightfall; **de —** (adv) at night, by night, in the night-time; **de —** (adj) late-night (attr), evening (attr), eg **función de —** late-night show, evening performance, **traje de —** evening dress; **de la — a la mañana** overnight (also fig); **en toda la —** all night; **hasta muy entrada la —** until late at night; on into the small hours; **por la —** at night, during the night; **se ha cerrado la —** the darkness has come down, night has closed in; **hacer — en un sitio** to spend the night in a place; **se hace de —** it's getting dark, night is falling; **pasar la — en blanco, pasar la — de claro en claro** to have a sleepless night.

Nochebuena nf Christmas Eve.

nochecita nf (SAm) dusk, nightfall.

nocherniego 1 adj nocturnal, that goes out (etc) at night, given to wandering about at night. **2** nm night-bird (fig).

nochero 1 adj (SAm) =**nocherniego**. **2** nm (a) (Col, Chi) night watchman; (Guat) night worker. (b) (Guat) bedside table.

nodo nm node.

nodriza nf wet-nurse.

nodular adj nodular.

nódulo nm nodule.

Noé m Noah.

nogal nm walnut (wood); walnut tree.

nogalina nf imitation walnut (wood).

noguera nf walnut tree.

nómada 1 adj nomadic. **2** nmf nomad.

nomadismo nm nomadism.

nomás adv (SAm) just; only.

nombradía nf fame, renown.

nombrado adj (a) aforementioned. (b) (fig) famous, renowned.

nombramiento nm (a) naming; designation. (b) mention. (c) nomination; appointment; commission.

nombrar [1a] vt (a) to name; to designate.
(b) to mention.
(c) to nominate; to appoint; (Mil) to commission; **— a uno embajador** to nominate someone as ambassador, appoint someone ambassador.

nombre nm (a) name; **mal —** nickname; **A, por mal — B** A, nicknamed B; A, wrongly named B; A, improperly called B; **— y apellidos** name in full, full name; **— artístico** nom de plume, pen name; **— comercial** trade name; **— gentilicio** family name; see **hipocorístico**; **— de lugar** place name; **— de pila** first name, Christian name; **— propio** proper name; **— de religión** name in religion; **bajo el — de** under the name of; **de — by name, eg de García García** by name; **conocer a uno de — to** know someone by name; **era rey tan sólo de —, de rey no tenía más que el —** he was king in name only; **no existe sino de —** it exists in name only; **en — de** in the name of, on behalf of; **en — de la libertad** in the name of liberty; **¡abran en — de la ley!** open up, in the name of the law!; **por — de** by the name of, called; **sin —** nameless; **poner — a** to call, name; **¿qué — le van a poner?** what are they going to call him, what name are they giving him?; **le pusieron el — de su abuelo** they named him after his grandfather; **su conducta no tiene —** his conduct is utterly despicable.
(b) (Gram) noun.
(c) (fig) name, reputation; **un médico de — a** famous doctor; **tiene — en el mundo entero** it has a world-wide reputation.

nomenclatura nf nomenclature.

nomeolvides nf, pl **nomeolvides** forget-me-not.

nómina nf list, roll; (Comm, Fin) payroll; **tiene una — de 500 personas** he has 500 on his payroll.

nominación nf (esp SAm) nomination.

nominal adj (a) head, king etc nominal, titular, in name only. (b) value face (attr), nominal; salary etc nominal. (c) (Gram) noun (attr), substantival.

nominalismo nm nominalism.

nominalmente adv nominally, in name; **al menos —** at least in name.

nominativo 1 adj (a) (Gram) nominative.
(b) (Comm, Fin) bearing a person's name, made out to an individual; **el cheque será — a favor de X** the cheque should be made out to X.
2 nm (Gram) nominative.

non 1 adj number odd, uneven.
2 nm odd number; **pares y —es** odds and evens; **los —es** the odd ones; **un zapato de —** an odd shoe; **queda uno de —** there's an odd one, there's one left over; **estar de —** (person) to be odd man out, (fig) be useless; **andar de —es** to have nothing to do.

nonada nf trifle, mere nothing.

nonagenario 1 adj nonagenarian, ninety-year old.
2 nm, **nonagenaria** nf nonagenarian, person in his (or her) nineties.

nonagésimo adj ninetieth.

nonato adj unborn.

noneco adj, **nonejo** adj (CAm, Pan) dolt.

nones adv (fam) no; **decir que —** to say no.

nono adj ninth.

nopal nm prickly pear.

nopalera nf patch of prickly pears, area where prickly pears grow.

noqueada nf (esp SAm: angl) knockout; knockout blow.

noquear [1a] vt (esp SAm: angl) to knock out.

noray nm bollard.

norcoreano 1 adj North Korean. **2** nm, **norcoreana** nf North Korean.

nordeste 1 adj part north-east, north-eastern; direction north-easterly; wind north-east, north-easterly.
2 nm (a) north-east.
(b) north-east wind.

nórdico 1 adj (a) northern, northerly; **es la ciudad más nórdica de Europa** it is the most northerly city in Europe.
(b) (Hist) Nordic, Norse.
2 nm, **nórdica** nf (a) northerner.
(b) (Hist) Northman.
3 nm (language) Norse.

noreste see **nordeste**.

noria nf (a) (Agr) waterwheel, chain pump. (b) (at fair) big wheel.

norma nf (a) standard, norm, rule; pattern; method; **— de comprobación** (Phys etc) control; **—s de conducta** (of newspaper) policy; **— de vida** standard of living; **está sujeto a ciertas —s** it is subject to certain rules.
(b) (Archit, Tech) square.

normal adj normal; regular, usual, natural; gauge etc standard; **es perfectamente —** it's perfectly normal, it's completely usual.

normalidad nf normality, normalcy; (Pol) calm, normal conditions; **la situación ha vuelto a la —** the situation has returned to normal; **la vuelta a la — es completa en la provincia** calm has been completely restored in the province.

normalizar [1f] **1** vt to normalize, restore to normal; (Tech) to standardize.
2 normalizarse vr to return to normal, settle down.

normalmente adv normally; usually.

Normandía f Normandy.

normando 1 adj Norman; **— francés** Norman-French; **Islas Normandas** Channel Isles.
2 nm, **normanda** nf Norman; Northman, Norseman.
3 nm (language) **— francés** Norman-French.

normánico adj (Archit) Norman.

normar [1a] vt (SAm) to lay down rules for, establish norms for.

normativo adj: **es — en todos los coches nuevos** it is standard in all new cars, it is the norm in all new cars.

noroeste 1 adj part north-west, north-western; direction north-westerly; wind north-west, north-westerly.
2 nm (a) north-west.
(b) north-west wind.

norsa nf (SAm: angl) nurse; governess; nursemaid.

nortada nf (steady) northerly wind.

norte 1 adj part north, northern; direction northerly; wind north, northerly.
2 nm (a) north; **en la parte del —** in the northern part; **al — de Segovia** to the north of Segovia, on the

north side of Segovia; **eso cae más hacia el —** that lies further (to the) north.
   (b) north wind.
   (c) (*fig*) guide; aim, objective; lodestar.
   (d) (*Cu*) *used loosely to refer to the* United States.
   (e) (*Cu, PR*) drizzle.
Norteamérica *f* North America.
norteamericano 1 *adj* North American, (*esp*) American. **2** *nm*, **norteamericana** *nf* North American, (*esp*) American.
nortear *vi* (*CAm, Per, PR*): **nortea** the north wind is blowing.
norteño 1 *adj* northern. **2** *nm*, **norteña** *nf* northerner.
nortino =**norteño**.
Noruega *f* Norway.
noruego 1 *adj* Norwegian. **2** *nm*, **noruega** *nf* Norwegian. **3** *nm* (*language*) Norwegian.
norvietnamita 1 *adj* North Vietnamese. **2** *nmf* North Vietnamese.
nos *personal pron pl* **(a)** (*acc*) us.
   (b) (*dative*) (to) us; **— lo dará** he will give it to us; **— lo compró** he bought it from us; he bought it for us; **— cortamos el pelo** we had our hair cut.
   (c) (*reflexive*) (to) ourselves; (*reciprocal*) (to) each other; **— lavamos** we washed; **no — hablamos** we don't speak to each other; **— levantamos a las 7** we get up at 7.
nosotros, nosotras *personal pron pl* **(a)** (*subject*) we.
   (b) (*after prep*) us; ourselves; **no irán sin —** they won't go without us; **no pedimos nada para —** we ask nothing for ourselves.
nostalgia *nf* nostalgia, homesickness; longing.
nostálgico *adj* nostalgic, homesick; longing.
nostalgioso *adj* (*Chi*) =**nostálgico**.
nota *nf* **(a)** note; memorandum; (*Lit*) footnote, marginal note; (*Comm*) account; (*in newspaper*) note; (*SAm*) IOU, promissory note; **— de gastos** expense account; **— de inhabilitación** (*Aut*) endorsement (*in licence*); **— de la redacción** editor's note; **— de sociedad** gossip column, column of society news; **texto con —s de . . .** text edited with notes by . . ., text annotated by . . .; **tomar —s** to take notes.
   (b) (*school etc*) grade, mark, class; (*terminal*) report; **obtener buenas —s** to get good marks.
   (c) (*Mus and fig*) note; **— de adorno** grace note; **una — de buen gusto** a tasteful note; **como — de color** as a colourful note; as a bit of local colour; **— dominante** dominant feature; **entonar la —** to pitch a note, give the note (*for singers to start*).
   (d) (*fig*) reputation; **de — of** note, famous; **de mala —** notorious; of ill fame; **tiene — de tacaño** he has a reputation for meanness.
   (e) **digno de —** notable, worthy of note; **tomar —** to take note.
notabilidad *nf* **(a)** noteworthiness, notability. **(b)** (*person*) notable, worthy.
notable 1 *adj* noteworthy, notable; remarkable; outstanding. **2** *nmf* notable, worthy.
notablemente *adv* notably; remarkably, outstandingly.
notación *nf* notation.
notar [1a] **1** *vt* **(a)** to note, notice; to feel, perceive; to see; **no noto frío alguno** I don't feel cold at all; **no lo había notado** I hadn't noticed it; **hacer — que . . .** to note that . . ., observe that . . .; **hacerse —** to stand out, catch the eye, draw attention to oneself.
   (b) to note down.
   (c) to mark, indicate.
   (d) to criticize; to discredit; **— a uno de oscuro** to brand someone as obscure, criticize someone for being obscure.
   2 notarse *vr* to show, be apparent, be obvious; **se nota que . . .** one observes that . . ., one notes that . . .; **la combinación no se le nota** your slip doesn't show; **su origen extranjero no se nota en absoluto** his foreign origin is not in the least obvious, you can't tell at all that he is foreign.
notaría *nf* **(a)** profession of notary. **(b)** notary's office.
notarial *adj* notarial; *style etc* legal, lawyer's.
notario *nm* notary, notary public; (*in some functions, equivalent to*) solicitor.
noticia *nf* **(a)** piece of news; (*in newspaper etc*) news item; **—s** news; information; **— necrológica** notice of a death, obituary notice; **según nuestras —s** according to our information; **estar atrasado de —s** to be behind the times, lack up-to-date information; **tener —s de uno** to have news of someone, hear from someone; **hace tiempo que no tenemos —s suyas** we haven't heard from her for a long time.
   (b) knowledge; notion; **no tener la menor — de algo** to know nothing at all about a matter, be completely ignorant of something.

noticiar [1b] *vt* to notify.
noticiario *nm* (*Radio*) news bulletin; (*Cine*) newsreel.
noticiero 1 *adj* **(a)** news-bearing, news-giving. **(b)** fond of receiving news. **2** *nm* **(a)** newspaper, gazette. **(b)** (*Cu*) newsreel.
noticioso *adj* **(a)** *source etc* well-informed.
   (b) **— de que Vd quería verme . . .** hearing that (*or* on being informed that) you wished to see me . . .
notificación *nf* notification.
notificar [1g] *vt* to notify, inform.
notoriamente *adv* obviously; glaringly, blatantly, flagrantly; **una sentencia — injusta** a glaringly injust sentence.
notoriedad *nf* fame, renown; wide knowledge.
notorio *adj* **(a)** well-known, publicly known; **un hecho —** a well-known fact; **es — que . . .** it is well-known that . . .
   (b) obvious; glaring, blatant, flagrant.
novador 1 *adj* innovating, revolutionary. **2** *nm* innovator.
noval *adj* ground newly-broken.
novatada *nf* **(a)** rag, ragging, hazing (*US*) (*of new member etc*). **(b)** beginner's mistake, elementary blunder.
novato 1 *adj* raw, green, new. **2** *nm* beginner, tyro.
novecientos *adj* nine hundred.
novedad *nf* **(a)** (*quality*) newness, novelty; strangeness.
   (b) (*object etc*) novelty; surprise; **—es** (*newspaper*) latest news; **—es, últimas —es** (*Comm*) novelties, latest fashions, latest models.
   (c) new feature, new development, change; **sin — en el frente** all quiet on the front; **llegar sin —** to arrive without mishap, arrive safely; **la jornada ha sido sin —** it has been a quiet (*or* normal) day, it has been a day without incident; **el enfermo sigue sin —** the patient's condition is unchanged.
novedoso *adj* **(a)** novel; full of novelties. **(b)** (*Arg, Chi, Mex*) =**novelesco**.
novel 1 *adj* new; inexperienced; **una escritora —** a new writer. **2** *nm* beginner.
novela *nf* novel; **— de amores** love story, romance; **—s científicas** science fiction; **— por entregas** serial; **— histórica** historical novel; **— policíaca** detective story, whodunit (*sl*); **— radiofónica** radio serial; **la — española en el siglo XX** the 20th century Spanish novel.
novelar [1a] **1** *vt* to make a novel out of; to tell in novel form. **2** *vi* to write novels.
novelero 1 *adj* **(a)** *person* highly imaginative; dreamy, romantic.
   (b) *person* fond of novelty.
   (c) *person* fond of novels.
   (d) *story etc* romantic, novelettish.
   (e) *person* (*pej*) gossipy, fond of gossiping.
   2 *nm*, **novelera** *nf* novel reader.
novelesco *adj* **(a)** (*Lit*) fictional; **el género —** fiction, the novel. **(b)** romantic, fantastic, novelettish.
novelista *nmf* novelist.
novelística *nf*: **la —** fiction, the novel.
novelón *nm* big novel, three-decker novel.
novelucha *nf* (*pej*) cheap novel, yellowback, shocker.
noveno *adj* ninth.
noventa *adj* ninety; ninetieth.
noventón 1 *adj* ninety-year old, ninetyish. **2** *nm*, **noventona** *nf* person of about ninety.
novia *nf* girlfriend, sweetheart; fiancée; bride, newly-married girl; **echarse una —** to get oneself a girlfriend; **Juan y su —** John and his girlfriend, John and his fiancée; **traje de —** bridal gown, wedding dress.
noviar [1b] *vi* (*RPl*): **— con** to court, keep company with.
noviazgo *nm* engagement.
noviciado *nm* apprenticeship, training; (*Eccl*) novitiate.
novicio *nm*, **novicia** *nf* beginner, novice; apprentice; (*Eccl*) novice.
noviembre *nm* November.
noviero *adj* (*CAm, Mex*) =**enamoradizo**.
novilunio *nm* new moon.
novilla *nf* heifer.
novillada *nf* (*Taur*) bullfight with young bulls (and novice bullfighters).
novillero *nm* **(a)** (*Taur*) novice, young bullfighter. **(b)** (*fam*) truant.
novillo *nm* **(a)** young bull, bullock, steer; **—s =** **novillada**.
   (b) (*fam*) cuckold.
   (c) hacer —s to stay away, not turn up, (*School*) play truant.

novio *nm* boyfriend, sweetheart; fiancé; bridegroom, newly-married man; los —s the engaged couple; the bride and groom; the newly-weds; **ser** —**s formales** to be formally engaged; **Maruja y su** — Mary and her boyfriend, Mary and her fiancée; **viaje de** —**s** honeymoon.

novísimo *adj* newest, latest, most recent; brand-new.

nubada *nf*, **nubarrada** *nf* (a) downpour, sudden shower. (b) (*fig*) shower; abundance; mass.

nubarrón *nm* storm cloud.

nube *nf* (a) cloud; — **de lluvia** raincloud; — **de tormenta** storm cloud.
(b) (*fig: of insects, smoke etc*) cloud; crowd, mass, multitude; **una** — **de pordioseros** a crowd of beggars; **una** — **me críticas** a storm of criticism.
(c) (*Med: in eye*) cloud, film.
(d) **los precios están por las** —**s** prices are terribly high; **poner a uno en** (*or* **por, sobre**) **las** —**s** to praise someone to the skies; **ponerse por las** —**s** (*person*) to go up the wall (*fam*); (*price*) to rocket, soar; **andar por las** —**s, estar en las** —**s** to be up in the clouds, be daydreaming, be remote from it all.

núbil *adj* marriageable, nubile.

nublado 1 *adj* cloudy, overcast.
2 *nm* (a) storm cloud, black cloud; **todo** — **tiene su claridad** every cloud has a silver lining.
(b) (*fig*) threat; impending danger.
(c) (*fig*) swarm, crowd, multitude; **un** — **de a** swarm of, a host of.
(d) (*fig*) anger, black mood.

nublar [1a] **1** *vt* (a) to darken, obscure. (b) (*fig*) *sight* to cloud, disturb; *reason* to affect; *happiness etc* to cloud, destroy. **2 nublarse** *vr* to become cloudy, cloud over.

nublazón *nm* (*SAm*) = **nublado**.

nublo *adj* (*SAm*) cloudy.

nuboso *adj* (a) cloudy. (b) (*fig*) unlucky, unfortunate; gloomy.

nubosidad *nf* cloudiness.

nuboso *adj* cloudy.

nuclear *adj* nuclear.

nuclearizado *adj*: **países** —**s** countries possessing nuclear weapons.

núcleo *nm* nucleus; (*Elec*) core; (*Bot*) kernel, stone; (*fig*) core, essence; — **rural** (new) village, village settlement.

nudillo *nm* knuckle.

nudismo *nm* (*angl*) nudism.

nudista *nmf* (*angl*) nudist.

nudo *nm* (a) knot; — **corredizo** slipknot; — **llano,** — **de rizos** reef knot.
(b) (*Naut*) knot.
(c) (*Bot*) knot; node.
(d) thick part, thickening, lump; **con un** — **en la garganta** with a lump in one's throat; **se me hizo un** — **en la garganta** I got a lump in my throat.
(e) (*of communications etc*) centre; (*of road system*) cloverleaf, system of flyovers.
(f) (*fig*) bond, tie, link.
(g) (*fig: of problem*) knotty point; core, crux; (*of play etc*) crisis, point of greatest complexity.

nudoso *adj wood etc* knotty, full of knots; *trunk* gnarled; *stick* knobbly.

nuégado *nm* nougat.

nuera *nf* daughter-in-law.

nuestro 1 *poss adj* our; (*after n*) of ours, *eg* **un barco** — a boat of ours, one of our boats; **no es amigo** — he's no friend of ours; **lo** — (what is) ours, what belongs to us. **2** *poss pron* ours, of ours; **es el** —it is ours; **los** —**s** (*freq*) our people, our relations, our family; our men, our side.

nueva *nf* piece of news; —**s** news; **me cogió de** —**s** it was news to me, it took me by surprise; **hacerse de** —**s** to pretend that one had not heard a piece of news before.

Nueva Escocia *f* Nova Scotia.

Nueva Gales *f* **del Sur** New South Wales.

Nueva Guinea *f* New Guinea.

Nueva Inglaterra *f* New England.

nuevamente *adv* again; anew.

Nueva Orléans New Orleans.

Nueva York New York.

Nueva Zelanda *f* New Zealand.

nueve 1 *adj* nine; (*date*) ninth; **las** — nine o'clock.
2 *nm* nine.

nuevo *adj* (in most senses) new; fresh; novel; further, additional; *stamp* mint, unused; **es** — **en la ciudad** he's new to the town; **es** — **en el oficio** he's new to the trade; **somos** —**s aquí** we're new here; **no hay nada** — there's nothing fresh; **no hay nada** — **bajo las estrellas** there's nothing new under the sun; **es más** — **que yo** he is junior to me; **con** —**s argumentos** with new arguments, with further arguments; **la**

casa es nueva the house is new; **la casa está nueva** the house is as good as new; **¿qué hay de** —? (*fam*) what's new? (*fam*), what's the news?

nuevomejicano 1 *adj* New Mexican. **2** *nm*, **nuevomejicana** *nf* New Mexican.

Nuevo Méjico *m* New Mexico.

nuez *nf* nut, (*esp*) walnut; — **moscada** nutmeg; — **de la garganta** Adam's apple.

nulidad *nf* (a) (*Law*) nullity. (b) incompetence, incapacity. (c) (*person*) nonentity; **es una** — he's a dead loss, he's useless.

nulo 1 *adj* (a) (*Law*) void, null and void; invalid, without force.
(b) *person* useless; **es** — **para la música** he's useless at music, he's no good at music, he's a dead loss as a musician.
(c) (*Sport*) game drawn, tied.
2 —**s** *nmpl* (*Cards*) misère; **bridge con** —**s** bridge with the misère variation.

numen *nm* inspiration; talent, inventiveness; — **poético** poetic inspiration; **de propio** — out of one's head.

numeración *nf* (a) numeration. (b) numbers, numerals; — **arábiga** Arabic numerals; — **romana** Roman numerals.

numerador *nm* numerator.

numeral 1 *adj* numeral, number (*attr*). **2** *nm* numeral.

numerar [1a] **1** *vt* to number; **páginas sin** — unnumbered pages. **2 numerarse** *vr* (*Mil etc*) to number off.

numerario *nm* hard cash.

numéricamente *adv* numerically.

numérico *adj* numerical.

número *nm* (a) number (*also Gram, Tel*); numeral; — **arábigo** Arabic numeral; — **cardinal** cardinal number; — **entero** whole number; — **impar** odd number; — **de matrícula** (*Aut etc*) registration number; — **ordinal** ordinal number; — **par** even number; — **primo** prime number; — **quebrado** fraction; — **redondo** round number; **en** —**s redondos** in round numbers, in round figures; — **de referencia** reference number; — **romano** Roman numeral; — **de serie** serial number; **el jugador** — **uno de su país** the number one player of his country; **en** — **de** to the number of; **miembro de** — full member; **sin** — (*fig*) numberless, unnumbered; countless.
(b) (*of shoe etc*) size.
(c) (*of journal etc*) number, issue; — **atrasado** back number; — **extraordinario** special edition, special issue.
(d) (*in programme*) item, number; (*Theat etc*) turn, act, number; sketch.
(e) (*Arg*) **de** — best, first.
(f) **¡vaya** —! (*fam*) what a character!

numeroso *adj* numerous; **familia numerosa** large family.

numismática *nf* numismatics.

numismático 1 *adj* numismatic. **2** *nm* numismatist.

nunca *adv* never; ever; **no viene** —, — **viene** he never comes, he doesn't ever come; **¡**—**!** never!; **casi** — almost never, hardly ever; **¡hasta** —**!** I don't care if I never see you again!; **más que** — more than ever; — **jamás,** — **más** never again, nevermore; **¿has visto** — **cosa igual?** have you ever seen anything like this?

nunciatura *nf* nunciature.

nuncio *nm* (a) (*Eccl*) nuncio; — **apostólico** papal nuncio; **¡cuéntaselo al** —**!** tell that to the marines!; **¡que lo haga el** —**!** get someone else to do it!
(b) messenger; (*fig*) herald, harbinger; — **de la primavera** harbinger of spring.

nunquita *adv* (*SAm*) = **nunca**.

nupcial *adj* wedding (*attr*), nuptial.

nupcias *nfpl* wedding, nuptials; **casarse en segundas** — to marry again, get married a second time; **A, que se casó en segundas** — **con B** A, who made a second marriage to B.

nurse ['nurse] *nf* (*angl*) nurse; governess; nursemaid.

nutria *nf* otter.

nutrición *nf* nutrition.

nutrido *adj* (a) **bien** — well-nourished; **mal** — undernourished.
(b) (*fig*) large, considerable; numerous; abundant; — **de** full of, abounding in; **una nutrida concurrencia** a large attendance; —**s aplausos** deafening applause; **fuego** — (*Mil*) heavy fire.

nutrimento *nm* nutriment, nourishment.

nutrir [3a] *vt* (a) to feed, nourish. (b) (*fig*) to feed, strengthen; to support, foment, encourage.

nutritivo *adj* nourishing, nutritious; **valor** — nutritional value, food value.

nylon [ni'lon, 'nailon] *nm* (*angl*) nylon.

Ñ

ña *nf* (*SAm: fam*) = **doña, señora.**
ñácara *nf* (*CAm*) ulcer, sore.
ñame *nm* yam.
ñandú *nm* (*RPl*) rhea, American ostrich.
ñanga *nf* (a) (*CAm*) marsh, swampy estuary. (b) (*Ec*) bit, small portion.
ñangada *nf* (*CAm*) (a) nip, bite. (b) harmful and foolish act.
ñangado *adj* (*Cu*) knock-kneed; bow-legged.
ñango *adj* (a) (*Arg, Urug*) awkward, clumsy. (b) (*Chi*) short-legged, waddling. (c) (*Mex*) weak, feeble. (d) (*PR*) = ñangado.
ñangotarse [1a] *vr* (a) (*Col, PR*) to squat, crouch down. (b) (*PR*) to get scared.
ñaña *nf* (a) (*Arg, Chi*) elder sister; (*Chi, PR*) nursemaid, wet-nurse. (b) (*CAm*) excrement.
ñaño 1 *adj* (a) (*Col, Chi, Ec, Pan*) *friend* close; (*Col, Pan*) spoiled, pampered. (b) (*Chi*) silly.
  2 *nm* (*Col, Chi, Ec, Pan*) close friend, chum; (*Arg, Ec*) elder brother; (*Col, Per*) baby, child; **estar —s** to be on very close terms.
ñapa *nf* (*SAm*) extra, bonus; tip; **de —** (*Col, PR*) as an extra, in addition.
ñapango *nm* (*Col*) mulatto, mestizo, half-breed.
ñaque *nm* junk, worthless stuff; odds and ends.
ñata *nf* (a) (*SAm*) nose. (b) (*Per*) death.
ñato *adj* (a) (*SAm*) flat-nosed, snub-nosed. (b) (*Col*) nasal, twangy. (c) (*Arg*) ugly; bent, deformed; wicked. (d) (*Pan*) effeminate.
ñeque 1 *adj* (*CAm, Chi, Ec, Ven*) strong; vigorous; clever, capable; (*CAm, Cu*) brave. 2 *nm* (a) (*CAm, Col, Chi, Ec, Per, Ven*) strength; energy, vigour; courage. (b) (*CAm, Mex*) blow, punch. (c) **—s** (*Ec*) fists.

ñique *nm* (*CAm, Chi*) butt, thrust; (*CAm*) punch.
ñiquiñaque *nm* (a) trash, junk, rubbish. (b) worthless individual.
ñisca *nf* (a) (*CAm, Chi, Ec, Per*) bit, small piece. (b) (*CAm, Col*) excrement.
ñoca *nf* (*Col*) crack, fissure.
ñoco 1 *adj* (*Col, PR, SD, Ven*) lacking a finger; one-handed. 2 *nm* (*Chi*) straight punch.
ñola *nf* (a) (*Col, Guat*) excrement. (b) (*Guat, Hond*) ulcer, sore.
ñongarse [1h] *vr* (*Col*) (a) to squat, crouch down. (b) **— el pie** to twist one's foot.
ñongo *adj* (a) (*Cu, Chi*) stupid; (*Chi*) slow, lazy; good-for-nothing; excessively humble. (b) (*Col, Ven*) crippled; damaged, defective. (c) (*Ven*) tricky, deceitful; unsightly; of ill omen; touchy.
ñoñería *nf*, ñoñez *nf* (a) insipidness; spinelessness; shyness, bashfulness, fussiness. (b) (*Arg, Chi*) senility; dotage. (c) (*Cu*) inanity, stupid thing. (d) (*PR, SD*) endearment; caress.
ñoño 1 *adj* (a) characterless, insipid; unsubstantial; *person* spineless. (b) shy, bashful. (c) fussy, finicky. (d) (*SAm*) senile, decrepit. (e) (*Per, PR, SD*) vain, that likes to be flattered. 2 *nm*, ñoña *nf* spineless person, drip (*sl*).
ñorbo *nm* (*CAm, Ec, Per*) passionflower.
ñudoso *adj* = nudoso.
ñufla *nf* (*Chi*) worthless object.
ñusca *nf* (*Col, Ec*) excrement.
ñutir [3a] *vi* (*Col*) to grunt.

O

o *conj* or; — . . .— either . . . or.
oasis *nm, pl* **oasis** oasis.
obcecación *nf* blindness, blind obstinacy; mental blockage, disturbance; **en un momento de** — when the balance of his (*etc*) mind was disturbed.
obcecadamente *adv* blindly; stubbornly, obdurately; in a disturbed state.
obcecado *adj* blind, mentally blinded; stubborn, obdurate; disturbed.
obcecar [1g] *vt* to blind (mentally), disturb the mind of; **el amor le ha obcecado** love has blinded him (to all else).
obedecer [2d] *vti* (a) to obey.
   (b) — **a** (*of disease etc*) to yield to, respond to (treatment by).
   (c) — **a,** — **al hecho de que . . .** to be due to . . ., arise from . . .; **su viaje obedece a dos motivos** his journey has two reasons.
obediencia *nf* obedience.
obediente *adj* obedient.
obelisco *nm* obelisk; (*Typ*) dagger.
obenques *nmpl* (*Naut*) shrouds.
obertura *nf* overture.
obesidad *nf* obesity.
obeso *adj* obese.
óbice *nm* obstacle, impediment; **eso no es** — **para que lo haga** that is not an obstacle to my doing it.
obispado *nm* bishopric.
obispo *nm* bishop.
óbito *nm* (*lit*) decease, demise (*lit*).
obituario *nm* (*SAm*) (a) decease, demise. (b) (*angl*) obituary; obituary section (*of a newspaper*).
objeción *nf* objection; **hacer** —**es** to raise objections; **no hacen ninguna** — they make (*or* raise) no objection.
objetable *adj* objectionable, open to objection.
objetante *nmf* objector; (*in meeting*) heckler, protester.
objetar [1a] *vti* to object; *objection* to make, offer, raise; *argument* to present, put forward; **le objeté que no había dinero para ello** I pointed out to him (*or* I protested to him) that there was no money for it.
objetivamente *adv* objectively.
objetividad *nf* objectivity.
objetivo 1 *adj* objective. **2** *nm* (a) objective, aim, end. (b) (*Mil*) objective, target. (c) (*Phot*) lens; object lens.
objeto *nm* (a) object, thing; —**s de escritorio** writing materials; —**s de tocador** toilet articles.
   (b) object, aim, end, purpose; **al** — **de** + *infin* with the object of + *ger*, with the aim of + *ger*; **esta carta tiene por** — + *infin* this letter has the aim of + *ger*, this letter aims to + *infin*.
   (c) (*of speech etc*) theme, subject matter.
   (d) (*Gram*) object.
objetor *nm* objector; — **de conciencia** conscientious objector.
oblación *nf* oblation, offering.
oblar [1a] *vt* (*Arg*) *debt* to pay in cash.
oblata *nf* oblation, offering.
oblea *nf* (a) (*Eccl and fig*) wafer; very thin slice; **quedar como una** — to be as thin as a lath. (b) (*Chi: Post*) stamp.
oblicuamente *adv* obliquely.
oblicuar [1d] **1** *vt* to slant, place obliquely, cant, tilt. **2** *vi* to deviate from the perpendicular.
oblicuidad *nf* obliquity, oblique angle (*or* position *etc*).
oblicuo *adj* oblique; slanting; *glance* sidelong.
obligación *nf* (a) obligation; duty; responsibility; —**es** (*esp*) family responsibilities; **cumplir con una** — to fulfil a duty; **faltar a sus** —**es** to fail in one's duty, fail to carry out one's obligations; **tener** — **de** + *infin* to have a duty to + *infin*, be under an obligation to + *infin*; **primero es la** — **que la devoción** business before pleasure.
   (b) (*Comm, Fin*) bond; —**es** bonds, securities; — **de banco** bank bill.
obligacionista *nmf* bondholder.
obligar [1h] **1** *vt* (a) to force, compel, oblige; — **a uno a hacer algo** to force (*or* compel) someone to do something; **verse obligado a** + *infin* to be obliged to + *infin*, find oneself compelled to + *infin*; **estar** (*or* **quedar**) **obligado a uno** to be obliged to someone, be in someone's debt.
   (b) *shoes etc* to force, stretch; **el libro sólo entra allí obligándolo** the book goes in there but only with a hard push (*or* but only by forcing it).
   2 obligarse *vr* to put oneself under an obligation; — **a** + *infin* to bind oneself to + *infin*.
obligatoriedad *nf* obligatory nature.
obligatorio *adj* obligatory, compulsory; binding; **es** — + *infin* it is obligatory to + *infin*; **escolaridad obligatoria** compulsory schooling, compulsory attendance at school.
obliteración *nf* (*Med*) obliteration.
obliterar [1a] *vt* (a) (*Med*) to obliterate. (b) (*SAm: angl*) to obliterate, efface, destroy.
oblongo *adj* oblong.
oboe *nm* (a) oboe. (b) oboist, oboe player.
óbolo *nm* (*fig*) mite, small contribution.
obra *nf* (a) (*in general*) work; piece of work; — **de arte** work of art; — **benéfica,** — **de misericordia,** — **piadosa** charity; **buenas** —**s,** —**s de caridad** good works; — **maestra** masterpiece; — **pía** religious foundation; —**s públicas** public works; **Ministerio de O**—**s Públicas** Ministry of Works; **es** — **de benedictinos** (*or* **romanos**) it's a huge task, it's a long job; **¡manos a la** —**!** to work!, let's get on with it!; **por** — **de** thanks to, thanks to the efforts of; **poner algo por** — to carry something out, put something into effect; —**s son amores y no buenas razones** actions speak louder than words.
   (b) (*Lit*) work, book; — **de consulta** reference book, work of reference; — **literaria** literary work; — **de vulgarización** popular work; —**s completas** complete works, collected works; **las** —**s de Cervantes** the works of Cervantes.
   (c) (*Theat: also* — **dramática,** — **de teatro**) play.
   (d) (*Mus*) work, opus, composition.
   (e) (*Archit: also* —**s**) work; construction, building; (*Arg*) building under construction; — **de hierro** ironwork; —**s** (*freq*) repairs, alterations; "**cerrado por** —**s**" "closed for repairs (*or* alterations)"; **estamos en** —**s** there are building repairs going on; we have the workmen in; **se han comenzado las** —**s del nuevo embalse** work has been begun on the new dam.
   (f) workmanship, craftsmanship; handiwork; **la** — **es buena pero con malos materiales** the workmanship is good but the materials were bad.
   (g) (*Chi*) brickworks.
   (h) — **de** about; **en** — **de 8 semanas** in about 8 weeks, in a matter of 8 weeks.
obradera *nf* (*Col, Guat, Pan*) diarrhoea.
obrador *nm* working table, bench; workroom, workshop.
obraje *nm* (a) (*Bol, RPl*) sawmill, timberyard. (b) (*Mex*) pork butcher's (shop).
obrajero *nm* (a) foreman, overseer. (b) (*RPl*) lumberman. (c) (*Bol*) craftsman, skilled worker. (d) (*Mex*) pork butcher.
obrar [1a] **1** *vt* (a) *wood etc* to work.
   (b) (*of medicine*) to work on, have an effect on.
   (c) (*Arg*) to build.
   (d) *miracle etc* to work, bring about.
   2 *vi* (a) to act, behave; to proceed; — **de acuerdo**

con to proceed in accordance with; **— con precaución** to act cautiously, proceed warily.

(**b**) (*of medicine*) to work, have an effect.

(**c**) (*formal phrases*) **su carta obra en mi poder** I have received your letter, your letter is to hand; **el acusado obra en manos del juez** the accused man is in the judge's hands.

(**d**) (*fam*) to relieve nature.

obrerismo *nm* working-class movement.

obrero 1 *adj class* working; *action, union etc* labour (*attr*); **el movimiento —** the working-class movement; **condiciones obreras** working conditions.

2 *nm* worker (*also Pol*), workman; man, hand; labourer; **— escenógrafo** stagehand; **— portuario** dock worker.

3 obrera *nf* worker, woman worker.

obscenamente *adv* obscenely.

obscenidad *nf* obscenity.

obsceno *adj* obscene.

obscu ... see oscu ...

obsceder [2a] *vt* (*SAm*) to obsess.

obsequiar [1b] *vt* (**a**) to lavish attentions on, make a fuss of; **le obsequiaron con un reloj** they presented him with a clock, they gave him a clock; **le van a — con un banquete** they are going to hold a dinner for him, they are going to honour him with a dinner.

(**b**) (*SAm*) **le obsequiaron un reloj** they presented him with a clock.

obsequio *nm* (**a**) present, gift; (*on retirement etc*) presentation; **ejemplar de —** complimentary copy, presentation copy.

(**b**) attention, kindness, courtesy; **en — de** in honour of; **hágame el — de +** *infin* please **+** *infin*.

obsequiosamente *adv* obligingly, helpfully.

obsequioso *adj* (**a**) obliging, helpful, attentive. (**b**) (*Mex*) fond of giving presents.

observable *adj* observable.

observación *nf* (**a**) observation; (*of law*) observance.

(**b**) observation, remark, comment; objection; **hacer una —** to make a remark, comment, observe; **hacer una — a** (*freq*) to raise an objection to.

observador 1 *adj* observant. **2** *nm*, **observadora** *nf* observer; **— extranjero** foreign observer.

observancia *nf* observance.

observar [1a] *vt* (**a**) to observe, watch; to see, notice, spot; (*Astron*) to observe; **— que . . .** to observe that . . ., notice that . . .

(**b**) *law* to observe, respect; to keep; *rule* to abide by, adhere to; **— buena conducta** (*Per*) to behave oneself.

(**c**) (*SAm*) **— algo a uno** to point out something to someone, draw someone's attention to something.

observatorio *nm* observatory; **— del tiempo** weather station.

obsesión *nf* obsession.

obsesionante *adj* haunting; obsessive.

obsesionar [1a] *vt* to obsess, haunt; **estar obsesionado con** (*or* **por**) **algo** to be obsessed by something; to have something on the brain.

obsesivo *adj* obsessive.

obseso *adj* obsessed, haunted.

obsidiana *nf* obsidian.

obsoleto *adj* (*SAm: angl*) obsolete.

obstaculizar [1f] *vt* to hinder, hamper, hold up; to prevent, stand in the way of.

obstáculo *nm* obstacle; hindrance; handicap, drawback; (*Mil, Sport etc*) obstacle; **no es — para que yo +** *subj* it is no obstacle to my **+** *ger*.

obstante: no — 1 *adv* nevertheless, however; all the same. **2** *prep* in spite of.

obstar [1a] *vi*: **— a, — para** to hinder; to prevent; **eso no obsta para que lo haga** that is no obstacle to his doing it, that does not prevent him from doing it.

obstetricia *nf* obstetrics.

obstétrico 1 *adj* obstetric(al). **2** *nm* obstetrician.

obstinación *nf* obstinacy, stubbornness.

obstinadamente *adv* obstinately, stubbornly.

obstinado *adj* obstinate, stubborn.

obstinarse [1a] *vr* to be obstinate; to dig one's heels in; **— en +** *infin* to persist in **+** *ger*, continue obstinately to **+** *infin*.

obstrucción *nf* obstruction (*also Parl*).

obstruccionar [1a] *vt* (*SAm*) to obstruct.

obstruccionismo *nm* obstructionism.

obstruccionista 1 *adj* obstructionist, obstructive. **2** *nmf* obstructionist.

obstructivo *adj*, **obstructor** *adj* obstructive.

obstruir [3g] *vt* to obstruct; to block; to hinder, impede; to interfere with.

obtención *nf* obtaining, securing.

obtener [2l] *vt* to get, obtain, secure; **— un subproducto del carbón** to obtain a by-product from coal.

obtenible *adj* obtainable.

obturación *nf* plugging, stopping; sealing off; filling.

obturador *nm* plug, stopper; (*Aut*) choke; (*Phot*) shutter.

obturar [1a] *vt* to plug, stop (up); to seal off; *tooth* to fill.

obtuso *adj* (**a**) *edge etc* blunt, dull. (**b**) (*Math and fig*) obtuse.

obús *nm* (**a**) (*Mil*) howitzer; shell. (**b**) (*Aut*) tyre valve.

obvención *nf* bonus, perquisite.

obvencional *adj* bonus, extra; incidental.

obviar [1c] **1** *vt* to obviate, remove. **2** *vi* to stand in the way.

obvio *adj* obvious.

oca *nf* goose.

ocasión *nf* (**a**) occasion, time; **con — de** on the occasion of; **en algunas —es** sometimes; **en aquella —** on that occasion; **venir en una mala —** to come at a bad moment.

(**b**) chance, opportunity, occasion; **aprovechar la —** to take one's chance, seize one's opportunity; **dar a uno la — de +** *infin* to give someone a chance (*or* opportunity) to **+** *infin*.

(**c**) cause, motive; **no hay — para quejarse** there is no cause to complain.

(**d**) **de —** (*Comm*) secondhand; old, used; **librería de —** secondhand bookshop.

(**e**) (*SAm*) bargain; **precio de —** bargain price, reduced price.

ocasional *adj* (**a**) chance, accidental; incidental. (**b**) *composition etc* occasional.

ocasionalmente *adv* by chance, accidentally; incidentally.

ocasionar [1a] *vt* to cause, produce, occasion.

ocaso *nm* (**a**) (*Astron*) sunset; (*of star*) setting. (**b**) (*Geog*) west. (**c**) (*fig*) decline, end, fall.

occidental 1 *adj* western. **2** *nmf* westerner.

occidentalizar [1f] *vt* to westernize.

occidente *nm* west.

occipucio *nm* occiput.

occiso *nm*, **occisa** *nf*: **el —** the deceased, (*of crime*) the victim.

Oceanía *f* Oceania.

oceánico *adj* oceanic.

océano *nm* ocean; **O— Atlántico** Atlantic Ocean; **O— Glacial Ártico** Arctic Ocean; **O— Índico** Indian Ocean; **O— Pacífico** Pacific Ocean.

oceanografía *nf* oceanography.

ocelote *nm* ocelot.

ocio *nm* (**a**) leisure, idleness; (*pej*) idleness; **—s, ratos de —** leisure, spare time, free time; **entretener los —s de uno** to help someone to enjoy his leisure, occupy someone's spare time.

(**b**) **—s** pastime, diversion.

ociosamente *adv* idly.

ociosear [1a] *vi* (*Arg, Bol, Chi, Ec*) to be at leisure; (*pej*) to idle, loaf about.

ociosidad *nf* idleness; **la — es madre de todos los vicios** the devil finds work for idle hands.

ocioso *adj* (**a**) idle; at leisure; inactive; **estar —** to be idle.

(**b**) *act, words etc* useless, pointless, idle; **dinero —** money lying idle; **es — especular** it is idle to speculate.

oclusión *nf* (**a**) (*Ling etc*) occlusion. (**b**) (*Meteorol*) occluded front.

oclusiva *nf* (*Ling*) occlusive, plosive.

oclusivo *adj* (*Ling*) occlusive, plosive.

ocote *nm* (*CAm, Mex*) torch; *a species of pine*.

ocre *nm* ochre; **— amarillo** yellow ochre; **— rojo** red ochre.

octaedro *nm* octahedron.

octagonal *adj* octagonal.

octágono *nm* octagon.

octanaje *nm* octane number; **de alto —** high-octane (*attr*).

octano *nm* octane.

octava *nf* (*Mus, Poet*) octave.

octavilla *nf* pamphlet, leaflet.

octavín *nm* piccolo.

Octavio *m* Octavian.

octavo 1 *adj* eighth. **2** *nm* (**a**) eighth. (**b**) (*Typ*) **libro en —** octavo book. (**c**) **—s de final** (*Sport*) quarter finals.

octeto *nm* octet(te).

octogenario 1 *adj* octogenarian, eighty-year-old. **2** *nm*, **octogenaria** *f* octogenarian, person in his (*or* her) eighties.

octogésimo *adj* eightieth.

octosílabo 1 adj octosyllabic. **2** nm octosyllable.
octubre nm October.
ocular 1 adj ocular; eye (attr); **testigo** — eyewitness. **2** nm eyepiece.
oculista nmf oculist.
ocultamente adv secretly; mysteriously; stealthily.
ocultar [1a] **1** vt to hide, conceal (a, de from); to screen, mask.
2 ocultarse vr to hide (oneself); — **a la vista** to keep out of sight; — **con**, — **tras** to hide behind; **se me oculta la razón** I do not know the reason, the reason is a mystery to me.
ocultismo nm occultism.
ocultista nmf occultist.
oculto adj **(a)** hidden, concealed; **permanecer** — to stay hidden, remain in hiding.
(b) (fig) secret; mysterious; science occult; thought secret, inner; motive ulterior.
ocupación nf (all senses) occupation.
ocupado adj **(a)** place etc occupied, taken; **¿está ocupada la silla?** is that seat taken?
(b) la línea esta ocupada (Tel) the line is engaged, the line is busy (US); **señal de** — engaged tone, busy signal (US).
(c) person busy; **estoy muy** — I'm very busy (en with).
(d) estar ocupada (woman) to be pregnant.
ocupante nmf occupant.
ocupar [1a] **1** vt **(a)** seat, space etc to occupy, fill, take up; room to occupy, live in, inhabit; atmosphere to fill, pervade; country, town (Mil) to occupy; to take over, take control of.
(b) post to occupy, fill.
(c) person to occupy, engage; to keep busy; workers to employ, provide work for; **las obras ocupan más de 1000 hombres** the work keeps more than 1000 men busy, the work employs more than 1000 men.
(d) time to occupy, fill up, take up; **ocupa sus ratos libres pintando** he uses his spare time to paint, he paints in his spare time.
(e) object to seize, confiscate; **la policía le ocupó la navaja con que hirió a su mujer** the police took from him (or found on him) the razor with which he wounded his wife; **les ocuparon todo el contrabando** they seized all the contraband from them.
(f) (Mex) to use.
2 ocuparse vr: — **con**, — **de**, — **en** to concern oneself with; to pay attention to; to busy oneself with; to take care of, look after; **los críticos no se ocuparon del libro** the critics paid no attention to the book, the critics did not take note of the book; **me ocuparé de ello mañana** I will deal with it tomorrow; I will look into it tomorrow; **en esta sección el autor se ocupa de los peces** in this section the author deals with fish; **conviene** — **de lo suyo** it's best to mind one's own business.
ocurrencia nf **(a)** occurrence; incident, event.
(b) idea, bright idea; **me dio la** — **de** + infin it occurred to me to + infin, I had the idea of + ger; **¡qué** —! what a bright idea!
(c) witty remark, witticism.
ocurrente adj witty; bright, clever.
ocurrido adj **(a) lo** — what has happened. **(b)** (Ec, Per) witty.
ocurrir [3a] **1** vi to happen, occur; **¿qué ocurre?** what's going on?; **por lo que pudiera** — because of what might happen.
2 ocurrirse vr: **se le ocurre** + infin it occurs to him to + infin; **si se le ocurre huir** if he takes it into his head to escape; **se me ocurre que ...** it occurs to me that . . .; **nunca se me había ocurrido** it had never crossed my mind.
ochar [1a] **1** vt **(a)** (Arg, Chi) dog to urge on, provoke to attack. **(b)** (Chi) to spy on. **2** vi (Arg) to bark.
ochavado adj eight-sided, octagonal.
ochavero nm miser, skinflint.
ochenta adj eighty; eightieth.
ochentón 1 adj eighty-year-old, eightyish. **2** nm, **ochentona** nf person of about eighty.
ocho 1 adj eight; (date) eighth; **las** — eight o'clock. **2** nm eight.
ochocientos adj eight hundred.
oda nf ode.
odalisca nf odalisque.
odiar [1b] vt **(a)** to hate. **(b)** (Chi) to irk, annoy.
odio nm **(a)** hatred; ill will; dislike; — **de clases** class hatred; — **de sangre** feud, vendetta; **almacenar** — to store up hatred; **tener** — **a** to hate.
(b) (Chi) annoyance, bother.
odiosear [1a] vt (Chi, Per) to weary, annoy.

odiosidad nf **(a)** odiousness, hatefulness; nastiness.
(b) (Arg, Chi, Per, SD) irksomeness, annoyance.
odioso adj **(a)** odious, hateful, detestable; nasty, unpleasant; **hacerse** — **a uno** to incur someone's dislike.
(b) (Arg, Chi, Per) irksome, annoying.
Odisea f Odyssey; **o**— odyssey.
Odiseo m Odysseus.
odómetro nm odometer.
odontología nf dentistry, dental surgery, odontology.
odontólogo nm dentist, dental surgeon, odontologist.
odorífero adj sweet-smelling, odoriferous.
odorífico adj (pej) smelly.
odre nm **(a)** wineskin. **(b)** (fam) toper, old soak (fam).
oeste 1 adj part west, western; direction westerly; wind west, westerly.
2 nm **(a)** west; **en la parte del** — in the western part; **al** — **de Bilbao** to the west of Bilbao, on the west of Bilbao; **eso cae más hacia el** — that lies further (to the) west.
(b) west wind.
Ofelia f Ophelia.
ofender [2a] **1** vt **(a)** to offend, slight, insult; to wrong; **por temor a** —**le** for fear of offending him.
(b) sense to offend, be offensive to; — **a la vista** to offend one's sight.
2 ofenderse vr to take offence (de, por at).
ofendido adj offended; **darse por** — to take offence.
ofensa nf offence; slight; wrong.
ofensiva nf offensive; — **de paz** peace offensive; **tomar la** — to take the offensive.
ofensivo adj **(a)** (Mil) offensive. **(b)** offensive; rude, insulting; nasty, disgusting.
ofensor 1 adj offending. **2** nm, **ofensora** nf offender.
oferta nf **(a)** offer; proposal, proposition.
(b) (Comm) offer; tender; bid; — **y demanda** supply and demand; **la** — **es superior a la demanda** the supply exceeds the demand; **estar en** — to be on offer.
(c) gift, present.
ofertar [1a] vt **(a)** (Chi, Guat, Mex, RPl) to offer.
(b) (Comm) to tender.
ofertorio nm offertory.
off [of] nm: **voz en** — (Cine etc: angl, gall) voice off; **hay una discusión en** — there is an argument offstage, there is an argument spoken by unseen actors.
office ['ofis] nm (gall) pantry; scullery.
offset [of'set] nm (Typ: angl) offset.
offside [or'sai] interj (Sport: angl) offside!
oficial 1 adj official.
2 nm official, officer; (Mil) officer; (Tech) skilled workman; craftsman; journeyman; (in office) clerk; **primer** — (Naut) mate; — **del día** orderly officer; — **de enlace** liaison officer; — **de guardia** (Naut) officer of the watch; — **mayor** chief clerk; — **médico** medical officer; — **pagador** paymaster.
oficiala nf skilled woman worker; clerk.
oficialada nf (Mex, RPl)=**oficialidad**.
oficialidad nf (Mil) officers (collectively).
oficializar [1f] vt (CAm) to make official, give official status to.
oficialmente adv officially.
oficiante nm (Eccl) officiant.
oficiar [1b] **1** vt to inform officially. **2** vi **(a)** (Eccl) to officiate. **(b)** — **de** to officiate as, act as.
oficina nf office; (Mil) orderly room; (Pharm) laboratory; (Tech) workshop; (Chi) nitrate works; **horas de** — business hours, office hours; — **de colocación** labour exchange, employment agency; — **de información** information bureau; — **meteorológica** weather bureau; — **de objetos perdidos** lost-property office, lost-and-found department (US).
oficinesco adj office (attr); clerical, white-collar (attr); (pej) bureaucratic.
oficinista nmf office worker, clerk; white-collar worker.
oficio nm **(a)** job, profession, occupation; (Tech) craft, trade; **es del** — he's an old hand; **sabe su** — he knows his job; **aprender un** — to learn a trade; **mi** — **es enseñar** my job is to teach; my profession is teaching.
(b) job, role, post; office; (Mech etc) function; **los deberes del** — the duties of the post; **el** — **de esta pieza es de ...** the function (or job) of this part is to . . .
(c) buenos —**s** good offices; **ofrecer sus buenos** —**s** to offer one's good offices.
(d) Santo O— (Hist) Holy Office, Inquisition.
(e) official letter.
(f) (Eccl) service; mass; — **de difuntos** office for

the dead, funeral service; — **divino** divine service; canonical hours.

(**g**) (*Archit*) scullery.

(**h**) **de** —: **miembro de** — ex officio member; **4 matones de** — 4 professional thugs, 4 hired toughs (*fam*); **fue enterrado de** — he was buried at the State's expense; **le informaremos de** — we will inform you officially.

oficiosamente *adv* (**a**) semiofficially; informally. (**b**) helpfully. (**c**) (*pej*) officiously.

oficiosidad *nf* (**a**) helpfulness. (**b**) (*pej*) officiousness, meddlesomeness.

oficioso *adj* (**a**) semiofficial; unofficial, informal; **de fuente oficiosa** from a semiofficial source.

(**b**) kind, helpful, obliging.

(**c**) (*pej*) officious, meddlesome, interfering.

(**d**) see **mentira**.

ofrecer [2d] **1** *vt* (*in most senses, also Comm*) to offer; to present; *thanks* to give, offer; *respects* to pay; *welcome* to extend; — **a uno hacer algo** to offer to do something for someone; **me ha ofrecido no fumar más** she has promised me that she won't smoke any more.

2 ofrecerse *vr* (**a**) to offer oneself, volunteer; — **a** + *infin* to offer to + *infin*, volunteer to + *infin*; **me ofrezco de guía** I offer myself as a guide.

(**b**) (*of object, view etc*) to offer itself, present itself.

(**c**) to occur; **¿qué se ofrece?** what's going on?, what's happening?; **se me ofrece una duda** a doubt occurs to me.

(**d**) **¿se le ofrece algo?** do you want anything?; is there anything I can get you?; **no se me ofrece nada por ahora** I don't want anything for the moment.

ofrecimiento *nm* offer, offering; — **de paz** peace offer.

ofrenda *nf* offering, gift; (*Eccl*) offering; (*fig*) tribute.

ofrendar [1a] *vt* to give, contribute.

oftalmía *nf* ophthalmia.

oftálmico *adj* ophthalmic.

oftalmología *nf* ophthalmology.

oftalmólogo *nm* ophthalmologist.

ofuscación *nf*, **ofuscamiento** *nm* (*fig*) dazzled state; blindness; bewilderment, confusion, mystification.

ofuscar [1g] *vt* (**a**) to dazzle.

(**b**) (*fig*) to dazzle; to bewilder, confuse, mystify.

(**c**) (*fig*) to blind; **estar ofuscado por la cólera** to be blinded by anger.

ogro *nm* ogre.

oh *interj* oh!

ohmio *nm* ohm.

oíble *adj* audible.

oída *nf* hearing; **de —s** by hearsay.

oído *nm* (**a**) (sense of) hearing; **duro de** — hard of hearing.

(**b**) (*Anat*) ear; — **interno** inner ear; **¡— a la caja!, ¡— al parche!** pay attention!; **aguzar los —s** to prick up one's ears; **dar —s a** to listen to, give ear to; **apenas pude dar crédito a mis —s** I could scarcely believe my ears; **decir algo al** — **de uno** to whisper something to someone, whisper something in someone's ear; **entra por un** — **y sale por otro** it goes in one ear and out (of) the other; **hacer —s sordos a** to turn a deaf ear to; **es una canción que se pega al** — it's a catchy song; **prestar** —(**s**) **a** to give ear to; **ser todo —s** to be all ears; **le estarán zumbando los —s** his ears must be burning.

(**c**) (*Mus*) ear; **de** — by ear; **duro de** — tone-deaf; **tener (buen)** — to have a good ear.

oidor *nm* (*Hist*) judge.

oigo *etc see* **oír.**

oír [3q] *vti* (**a**) to hear; to listen (to); *confession* to hear; *mass* to go to, attend, hear; *advice* to hear, pay attention to, heed; — **decir que** ... to hear about ..., hear of ...; — **hablar de** to hear about, hear of; — **de** (*SAm: angl*) to hear from; **le oí abrir la puerta** I heard him open (*or* opening) the door; **como lo oyes, lo que oyes** it really is so, just like I'm telling you; **lo oyó como quien oye llover** she paid no attention, she turned a deaf ear to it.

(**b**) (*as interj etc*) **¡oye!, ¡oiga!** listen!, listen to this!; (*calling attention*) hi!, hey!; I say!; (*objecting*) now look here!; (*surprise*) I say!, say! (*US*); **¡oiga!** (*Tel*) hullo?

(**c**) *entreaty* to hear, heed, answer; **Dios oyó mi ruego** God answered my prayer.

(**d**) (*Law*) *case* to hear.

ojada *nf* (*Col*) skylight.

ojal *nm* buttonhole.

ojalá 1 *interj* (*used alone*) if only it were so!, if only it would! (*etc*); no such luck!, some hope!; "**mañana**

puede que haga sol" ... "**¡—!**" "it may be fine tomorrow" ... "I hope it will be!" (*or pessimistically*, "some hope!").

2 *conj* (*also* — **que**) (**a**) I wish ...!, if only ...!, (*rhetorically*) would that ...!; **¡— venga pronto!** I hope he comes soon!, I wish he'd come!; **¡— pudiera!** I wish I could!, if only I could!

(**b**) (*SAm*) even though; **no lo haré,** — **me maten** I won't do it even if they kill me.

ojazos *nmpl* big eyes, wide eyes; **echar los — a uno** to make eyes at someone.

ojeada *nf* glance; **echar una** — **a** to glance at, take a quick look at.

ojeador *nm* (*Hunting*) beater.

ojear[1] [1a] *vt* to eye; to stare at; **voy a** — **cómo va el trabajo** I'm going to see how the work is getting on.

ojear[2] [1a] *vt* (**a**) to drive away, drive off, shoo. (**b**) (*Hunting*) *game* to beat, put up, drive.

ojeo *nm* (*Hunting*) beating.

ojera *nf* (**a**) ring under the eye; **tener —s** to have rings (*or* circles) under the eyes. (**b**) eyebath.

ojeriza *nf* spite, ill will; **tener** — **a** to have a grudge against, have it in for.

ojeroso *adj* with rings under the eyes; tired, haggard; seedy.

ojete *nm* (**a**) (*Sew*) eyelet. (**b**) (*SAm: tabu*) arse (*tabu*).

ojillos *nmpl* bright eyes; lovely eyes; roguish eyes; **¡tiene unos —!** you should see what eyes she's got!

ojinegro *adj* black-eyed.

ojituerto *adj* cross-eyed.

ojiva *nf* ogive, pointed arch.

ojival *adj* ogival, pointed.

ojo *nm* (**a**) eye; **—s de almendra** almond eyes; — **de cristal** glass eye; — **a la funerala,** — **amoratado** black eye; **—s saltones** bulging eyes, goggle eyes; **—s que hablan** expressive eyes; **a los —s de** in the eyes of; **a** — (**de buen cubero**) by guesswork; roughly, at a rough guess; **a —s cerrados** blindly; on trust; **dependiente a —s cerrados en** blindly dependent on; **a** — **vistas** publicly, openly; **grow etc** before one's (very) eyes; *happen etc* right under one's nose; **con buenos —s** kindly, favourably; **delante de mis propios —s** before my very eyes; **estar hasta los —s de trabajo** to be up to one's eyes in work; — **por** — an eye for an eye; tit for tat; **abrir el** — to keep one's eyes open; **abrir los —s a uno** to open someone's eyes to something; **en un abrir y cerrar de —s** in the twinkling of an eye; **avivar el** — to be on the alert; **cerrar los —s a algo** (*fig*) to shut one's eyes to something; **clavar los —s en** to fix one's eyes on, stare at; **costar un** — **de la cara** to cost a small fortune; **dar en los —s** to be conspicuous; to be self-evident; **echar el** — **a** to have one's eye on, covet; **guiñar el** — to wink (**a** at); to turn a blind eye (**a** on); **hacer del** — to wink; **se le fueron los —s tras la chica** he couldn't keep his eyes off the girl; **pasar los —s por algo** to look something over; **no pegué los —s en toda la noche** I didn't get a wink of sleep all night; **en mi vida le puse los —s encima** I never set eyes on him in my life; **recrear los —s en** to feast one's eyes on; **ser todo —s** to be all eyes; **¡no es nada lo del —!** there's a lot more to it than that!; **tener a uno entre —s** to loathe someone; **tener los —s puestos en** (*fig*) to have set one's heart on; **torcer los —s** to squint; **—s que no ven, corazón que no siente** out of sight, out of mind; *see* **alerta, avizor, besugo, blanco** *etc*.

(**b**) (*of needle etc*) eye; (*in cheese etc*) hole; — **de la llave** keyhole.

(**c**) (*of bridge*) span; space underneath the span; **un puente de 4 —s** a bridge with 4 arches (*or* spans).

(**d**) (*SAm*) — **de agua** spring.

(**e**) — **del culo** (*tabu*) arse (*tabu*).

(**f**) (*Archit*) skylight; — **de buey** (*Naut*) porthole; (*Mex*) round church window.

(**g**) — **de gallo,** — **de pollo** (*SAm*) corn, callus; — **de pescado** (*Ant*) callus (on the hand).

(**h**) (*fig*) perspicacity; judgement; sharpness; **tener** — **para conocer algo** to have the perspicacity to recognize something.

(**i**) (*fig*) care, caution; **¡—!** careful!, look out!; (*as marginal sign*) N.B.; **hay que tener mucho — con los carteristas** one must be very careful of pickpockets, one must beware of pickpockets.

ojón *adj* (*SAm*) big-eyed, having big eyes.

ojota *nf* (**a**) (*SAm*) sandal. (**b**) (*Arg, Bol, Chi*) tanned llama leather.

ojotes *nmpl* (*CAm, Col*) bulging eyes, goggle eyes.

ojuelos *nmpl* = **ojillos.**

ola *nf* wave (*also fig*); — **de calor** heat wave; — **de frío** cold wave; — **de marea,** — **sísmica** tidal wave; **la nueva** — the latest fashion, the current trend, the most modern style; (*persons*) the new generation; (*Cine*) the new wave; **batir las —s** (*fig*) to ply the seas.

olé *interj* bravo!; well done!, jolly good! (*fam*).

oleada *nf* (**a**) (*Naut*) big wave; surge, swell.

(**b**) (*fig*) wave; surge; **una gran — de gente** a great surge of people; **la primera — del ataque** the first wave of the attack; **esta última — de huelgas** this latest wave of strikes.

(**c**) (*Mex*) run of luck.

oleaginoso *adj* oily, oleaginous.

oleaje *nm* swell, surge; surf.

oleo ... oleo ...

óleo *nm* (**a**) (*Eccl*) oil; (*Art*) oil; **santo —** holy oil.

(**b**) (*Art*) oil painting; **pintar al —** to paint in oils.

(**c**) (*SAm*) baptism.

oleoducto *nm* (oil) pipeline.

oleoso *adj* oily.

oler [2i] **1** *vt* (**a**) to smell.

(**b**) (*fig*) to pry into, poke one's nose into.

(**c**) (*fig*) to smell out, sniff out, uncover.

2 *vi* to smell (*a* of, like; *also fig*); **huele mal** it smells bad.

oletear [1a] *vt* (*Per*) to pry into.

oletón *adj* (*Per*) prying.

olfa *nmf* (*Rpl*) creep (*sl*), bootlicker (*fam*).

oifatear [1a] *vt* (**a**) to smell, sniff (*also fig*); (*of dog*) to smell out, scent out, nose out (*also fig*).

(**b**) (*fig*) to pry into, poke one's nose into.

olfativo *adj* olfactory.

olfato *nm* (**a**) (sense of) smell. (**b**) (*fig*) good nose; instinct, intuition.

olfatorio *adj* olfactory.

oligarquía *nf* oligarchy.

oligárquico *adj* oligarchic(al).

olimpíada *nf* Olympiad; **las O—s** the Olympics.

olímpico *adj* Olympian; *games* Olympic.

Olimpo *m* Olympus.

oliscar [1g] **1** *vt* (**a**) to smell, sniff (gently). (**b**) (*fig*) to investigate, look into. **2** *vi* to smell (bad).

olisco *adj* (*Arg, Chi, Mex*), **oliscón** *adj* (*Per*), **oliscoso** *adj* (*Cu, Ec*) smelly.

olisquear [1a] = **oliscar**.

oliva *nf* (**a**) olive; olive tree. (**b**) (*Orn*) = **lechuza**.

oliváceo *adj* olive, olive-green.

olivar *nm* olive grove.

Oliverio *m* Oliver.

olivo *nm* olive tree; **tomar el —** (*fam*) to beat it (*fam*).

olmeda *nf*, **olmedo** *nm* elm grove.

olmo *nm* elm, elm tree.

ológrafo **1** *adj* holograph. **2** *nm* holograph.

olor *nm* (**a**) smell; odour, scent; **buen —** nice smell, pleasant smell; **mal —** bad smell, nasty smell, stink; **tiene mal —** it smells bad; **— de santidad** odour of sanctity.

(**b**) (*fig*) smell; suspicion; **acudir al — del dinero** to come to where the money is, get wind of the money.

(**c**) (*Chi, Mex*) spice.

oloroso *adj* sweet-smelling, scented, fragrant.

olote *nm* (*CAm, Mex*) (**a**) corncob. (**b**) (*fig*) **un — a** nobody, a nonentity.

olotear [1a] *vi* (*CAm, Mex*) to gather maize, gather corn (*US*).

olotera *nf* (*CAm, Mex*) (**a**) head of corncobs. (**b**) maize thresher.

olvidadizo *adj* forgetful; absent-minded.

olvidado *adj* (**a**) forgotten.

(**b**) *person* forgetful; **— de** forgetful of, oblivious to.

(**c**) (*fig*) ungrateful.

(**d**) (*Arg, Col, Par*) = **olvidadizo**.

olvidar [1a] **1** *vt* to forget; to leave behind; to leave out, omit; **— hacer algo** to forget to do something.

2 olvidarse *vr* (**a**) **se me olvidó** I forgot; **se me olvidó el paraguas** I forgot my umbrella; **se me olvida la fecha** I forget the date, the date escapes me, I can't think of the date; **— de hacer algo** to forget to do something, neglect to do something.

(**b**) (*fig*) to forget oneself.

olvido *nm* (**a**) (*state*) oblivion; **caer en el —** to fall into oblivion; **echar al —** to forget; **enterrar** (*or* **hundir**) **en el —** to forget (deliberately), cast into oblivion.

(**b**) (*state*) forgetfulness; (*act*) omission, oversight; slip; **ha sido por —** it was an oversight.

olvidón *adj* (*Ec*) forgetful.

olla *nf* (**a**) (*vessel*) pot, pan; kettle; **— eléctrica** electric kettle; **— exprés. — de** (*or* **a**) **presión** pressure cooker.

(**b**) (*Cook*) stew; **— podrida** Spanish stew, (*fig*) hotchpotch.

(**c**) (*of river*) pool; eddy, whirlpool.

(**d**) (*Mountaineering*) chimney.

ollero *nm* maker of (*or* dealer in) pots and pans.

ombligo *nm* navel; **encogérsele el — a uno** to get the wind up, get cold feet; **meter a uno el — para dentro** to put the wind up someone.

ombliguera *nf* (*Per*) striptease artiste.

omega *nf* omega.

ominoso *adj* (**a**) awful, dreadful. (**b**) ominous.

omisión *nf* (**a**) omission; oversight; **su — de + infin** his failure to + *infin*, the fact that he omits to + *infin*. (**b**) (*quality*) neglect.

omiso *adj see* **caso**.

omitir [3a] *vt* (**a**) to leave out, miss out, omit. (**b**) **— hacer algo** to omit to do something, fail to do something.

ómnibus **1** *adj see* **tren**. **2** *nm* (*Hist*) omnibus.

omnímodo *adj* all-embracing.

omnipotencia *nf* omnipotence.

omnipotente *adv* omnipotent, all-powerful.

omnipresencia *nf* omnipresence.

omnipresente *adj* omnipresent.

omnisapiente *adj* omniscient, all-knowing.

omnisciencia *nf* omniscience.

omnisciente *adj*, **omniscio** *adj* omniscient, all-knowing.

omnívoro *adj* omnivorous.

omóplato *nm* shoulder blade.

—ón, —ona *n and adj suffix* (**a**) (*augmentative*) **librón** big book, massive tome; **fortunón** vast fortune, pile (*fam*); **barrigón** fat, potbellied; *see* **gritón, llorón** etc.

(**b**) (*pej*) **hombrón** hulking great brute; **caserón** large (ramshackle) house, barracks (of a place); *see* **solterona, valentón** etc.

(**c**) (*of age*) *see* **sesentón** etc.

(**d**) (*of blow*) *see* **empujón**.

(**e**) (*of habit*) *see* **mirón, tragón** etc.

onanismo *nm* onanism.

once **1** *adj* eleven; (*date*) eleventh; **las —** eleven o'clock; **las —** (*fam*) elevenses (*fam*), mid-morning snack, (*Col, Chi, Ven*) tea, afternoon snack.

2 *nm* eleven.

oncear [1a] *vi* (*Col, Ven*) to have an afternoon snack.

onceno *adj* eleventh.

onda *nf* (*in most senses*) wave; (*Sew*) scallop; **— corta** short wave; **de — corta** shortwave (*attr*); **— de choque, — sísmica** shock wave; **— extracorta** ultra-short wave; **— larga** long wave; **— luminosa** light wave; **— media** medium wave; **— sonora** sound wave; **tratamiento de — ultravioleta** ultraviolet treatment.

ondeante *adj* = **ondulante**.

ondear [1a] **1** *vt* *flag* to wave; *hair* to wave; (*Sew*) to pink, scallop.

2 *vi* to wave (up and down), undulate; to be wavy; to fluctuate; (*of water*) to ripple; (*of flag etc*) to fly, flutter, wave; (*of hair*) to flow, fall, (*in wind*) to stream; **la bandera ondea en lo alto del edificio** the flag flies (*or* flutters) from the top of the building; **la bandera ondea a media asta** the flag is flying at half mast.

3 ondearse *vr* to swing, sway.

ondímetro *nm* wavemeter.

ondulación *nf* undulation; wavy motion; (*in water*) wave, ripple; (*in hair*) wave; **—es** (*of surface*) undulations, ups and downs; unevenness; **— permanente** permanent wave.

ondulado **1** *adj* *hair etc* wavy; *surface* undulating, uneven; *road* uneven, rough; *country* undulating, rolling; *iron, paper etc* corrugated.

2 *nm* (in hair) wave.

ondulante *adj* (**a**) *movement* undulating; from side to side, (gently) swaying; *sound* rising and falling. (**b**) = **ondulado**.

ondular [1a] **1** *vt* *hair* to wave; **hacerse — el pelo** to have one's hair waved. **2** *vi and* **ondularse** *vr* to undulate; to sway; to wriggle.

ondulatorio *adj* undulatory, wavy.

oneroso *adj* onerous, burdensome.

ónice *nm* onyx.

onomástica *nf* personal names, proper names; study of personal names.

onomástico **1** *adj* onomastic, name (*attr*), of names; **lista onomástica** list of names; **fiesta onomástica =**

2 *nm* one's saint's day, one's name day (*celebrated in Spain etc as equivalent to one's birthday*).

onomatopeya *nf* onomatopoeia.

onomatopéyico *adj* onomatopoeic.

ontología *nf* ontology.

ontológico *adj* ontological.

onubense **1** *adj* of Huelva. **2** *nmf* native (*or* inhabitant) of Huelva; **los —s** the people of Huelva.

onza *nf* ounce.

oolítico adj oolitic.

oolito nm oolite.

opa[1] adj (Bol, Per, RPl) **(a)** deaf and dumb. **(b)** (fig) stupid.

opa[2] interj (SAm) =hola; (Arg) stop it!

opacar [1g] **1** vt (SAm) to make opaque; to darken; to mist up; to dull, tarnish.
   2 opacarse vr **(a)** (SAm) to become opaque; to darken; to mist up; to lose its shine, become tarnished.
   (b) (Col, Guat) to cloud over.

opacidad nf **(a)** opacity, opaqueness. **(b)** (fig) dullness, lifelessness. **(c)** gloominess.

opaco adj **(a)** opaque; dark; **una pantalla opaca a los rayos X** a screen which does not let X-rays through, a screen resistant to X-rays.
   (b) (fig) dull, lustreless, lifeless.
   (c) (fig) gloomy, sad.

opalescencia nf opalescence.

opalescente adj opalescent.

ópalo nm opal.

opción nf **(a)** option, choice; **no hay —** there is no choice, you (etc) do not have the option.
   (b) right; **tiene — a viajar gratis** he has the right to travel free.
   (c) (Comm) option (a on); **con — a 8 más, con — para 8 más** with an option on 8 more; **este dispositivo es de —** this gadget is optional; **suscribir una — para la compra de** to take out an option on.

opcional adj optional.

opear [1a] vi (Bol, Per, RPl) to act the fool.

ópera nf opera; **— bufa** comic opera; **— semiseria** light opera; **— seria** grand opera.

operación nf **(a)** (Med) operation; **— cesárea** Caesarean operation; **— quirúrgica** surgical operation; **— de estómago** stomach operation, operation on the stomach.
   (b) (Mil etc) operation; **— de ablandamiento** softening-up operation; **—es conjuntas** joint operations; **— de limpieza** mopping-up operation; **—es de rescate, —es de salvamento** rescue operations.
   (c) (Comm) transaction, deal; operation; **—es de bolsa** stock-exchange transaction; **— mercantil** business deal.
   (d) (Math) operation.
   (e) (SAm: Min) operation; working, exploitation; (Comm) management.

operacional adj operational.

operador nm operator; (Med) surgeon; (Cine) cameraman, film cameraman; (in cinema) projectionist, operator; **— del telégrafo** (SAm) telegraph operator.

operante adj **(a)** operating. **(b)** powerful, influential; active; **los medios más —s del país** the most influential circles in the country.

operar [1a] **1** vt **(a)** cure, change etc to produce, bring about, effect; miracle to work.
   (b) (Med) to operate on; **— a uno de apendicitis** to operate on someone for appendicitis.
   (c) (SAm) machine to use, operate; business to manage; (Min) to work, exploit.
   2 vi **(a)** to operate (also Math).
   (b) (Comm) to operate; to deal, do business; **hoy no se ha operado en la bolsa** there has been no dealing on the stock exchange today.
   3 operarse vr **(a)** to occur, come about; **se han operado grandes cambios** great changes have come about, there have been great changes.
   (b) (Med) to have an operation (de for).

operario nm, **operaria** nf operative; worker, hand; **— de máquina** machinist.

operativo adj operative.

opereta nf operetta, light opera.

opería nf (Bol, Per, RPl) stupidity.

operista nmf opera singer.

operístico adj operatic, opera (attr).

opiata nf opiate.

opimo adj plentiful, abundant, rich.

opinable adj debatable, open to a variety of opinions.

opinar [1a] vi **(a)** to think; **— que ...** to think that ..., be of the opinion that ...
   (b) **— bien de** to think well of, have a good opinion of.
   (c) to give one's opinion; **fueron opinando uno tras otro** they gave their opinions in turn; **hubo un 7 por 100 que no quisieron —, no opinaron el 7 por 100** (in poll) there were 7% "don't knows".

opinión nf opinion, view; **— pública** public opinion; **en mi —** in my opinion; **abundar en la — de uno** to share someone's opinion (or view) wholeheartedly; **cambiar** (or **mudar**) **de —** to change one's mind;

formarse una — to form an opinion; **ser de — que ...** to be of the opinion that ..., take the view that ...

opio nm opium; **dar el — a uno** (fam) to fill someone with wonder, leave someone open-mouthed; **ella le dio el —** she knocked him all of a heap (fam).

opíparo adj meal sumptuous.

oponente nmf (angl) opponent; opposite number; **tener de — a uno** to have someone as one's opposite number, (Theat) play opposite someone.

oponer [2r] **1** vt **(a)** **— A a B** to pit A against B, set up A in opposition to B; to play off A against B; **— dos opiniones** to contrast two views.
   (b) objection to raise (a to); resistance to put up, offer (a to); weapon to use (a against); **— la razón a la pasión** to use reason against passion, rely on reason and not passion; **— un dique al mar** to set up defences against the sea.
   2 oponerse vr to be opposed; (of 2 persons) to oppose each other, be in opposition; **yo no me opongo** I don't oppose it, I don't object; **— a to** oppose, be opposed to, be against; to object to; to defy, resist; **se opone a hacerlo** he resists the idea of doing it, he is unwilling to do it, he objects to doing it; **se opone rotundamente a ello** he is flatly opposed to it.

oportunamente adv opportunely, in a timely way; appropriately, suitably; conveniently; expediently.

oportunidad nf **(a)** (quality) opportuneness; timeliness; appropriateness; expediency.
   (b) (una —) opportunity, chance; **igualdad de —es** equality of opportunity; **en la primera —** at the first opportunity; **tener la — de + infin** to have the chance of + ger, have a chance to + infin.

oportunismo nm opportunism.

oportunista 1 adj opportunist. **2** nmf opportunist.

oportuno adj **(a)** opportune, timely; appropriate, suitable; convenient; expedient; **una respuesta oportuna** a suitable reply; **en el momento —** at the right moment; at a convenient time; **las medidas que se estimen oportunas** the measures which may be considered appropriate; **sería — hacerlo en seguida** it would be best to do it at once.
   (b) person witty.

oposición nf **(a)** opposition.
   (b) **—es** public competition (for a post), public entrance (or promotion) examination; **hacer —es a, presentarse a unas —es a** to be a candidate for, go in for; **hacer —es para una cátedra** (etc) to try to win a chair (etc) by public competitive examination; **ganar unas —es** to be successful in a public competition.

opositar [1a] vi to go in for a public competition (for a post), sit for a public entrance (or promotion) examination; **— a una cátedra** (etc) to try to win a chair (etc) by public competitive examination.

opositor nm, **opositora** nf competitor, candidate (a for).

opresión nf **(a)** oppression; oppressiveness. **(b)** (Med) difficulty in breathing, tightness of the chest; **sentir —** to find it difficult to breathe.

opresivo adj oppressive.

opresor nm, **opresora** nf oppressor.

oprimir [3a] vt **(a)** to squeeze, press, exert pressure on; handle etc to grasp, clutch; button etc to press; gas to compress; (of clothing) to be too tight for, constrict; to strangle.
   (b) (fig) to oppress; to burden, weigh down, bear down on; to crush.

oprobio nm shame, ignominy, opprobrium.

oprobioso adj shameful, ignominious, opprobrious.

optar [1a] vi **(a)** to choose, decide; **— entre** to choose between; **— por** to choose, decide on, opt for; **— por + infin** to choose to + infin.
   (b) **poder — a** to (have the right to) apply for, go in for; **ésos no pueden — a las becas** those do not have the right to apply for scholarships.

optativo 1 adj **(a)** optional. **(b)** (Gram) optative. **2** nm (Gram) optative.

óptica nf optics.

óptico 1 adj optic(al). **2** nm optician.

optimismo nm optimism.

optimista 1 adj optimistic, hopeful. **2** nmf optimist.

óptimo adj very good, very best; conditions etc optimum.

optometrista nm optometrist.

opuesto adj **(a)** angle, side etc opposite; **en dirección opuesta** in the opposite direction. **(b)** opinion etc contrary, opposing, opposite.

opugnar [1a] vt to attack.

opulencia nf opulence; luxury; affluence; **vivir en la —** to live in luxury, live in affluence.

opulento *adj* opulent, rich; luxurious; affluent.
opúsculo *nm* booklet; short work, tract, brief treatise.
oquedad *nf* hollow, cavity; (*fig*) void; hollowness, emptiness.
oquedal *nm* wood of grown timber, plantation.
ora *adv* (*lit*): — A, — B now A, now B; sometimes A, at other times B.
oración *nf* (a) oration, speech; — **fúnebre** funeral oration; **pronunciar una** — to make a speech.
(b) (*Eccl*) prayer; —**es por la paz** prayers for peace; **estar en** — to be at prayer.
(c) (*SAm, freq*) pagan invocation, magic charm.
(d) (*Gram*) sentence; clause; — **compuesta** complex sentence; — **subordinada** subordinate clause; **partes de la** — parts of speech.
oráculo *nm* oracle.
orador *nm*, **oradora** *nf* speaker, orator.
oral *adj* oral.
orangután *nm* orang-outang.
orante 1 *adj*: **actitud** — kneeling position, posture of prayer. 2 *nmf* worshipper.
orar [1a] *vi* (a) (*Eccl*) to pray (*a* to, *por* for). (b) to speak, make a speech.
orate *nmf* lunatic.
orático *adj* (*CAm*) crazy, lunatic.
oratoria *nf* oratory.
oratorio 1 *adj* oratorical. 2 *nm* (*Mus*) oratorio; (*Eccl*) oratory, chapel.
orbe *nm* (a) orb, sphere. (b) (*fig*) world; **en todo el** — throughout the world.
órbita *nf* orbit (*also fig*); **estar en** — to be in orbit; **entrar en** — **alrededor de la luna** to go into orbit round the moon.
orbital *adj* orbital.
orbitar [1a] *vt* to orbit.
orca *nf* grampus, killer whale.
Órcadas *fpl* Orkneys, Orkney Islands.
órdago: de — *adj* (*fam*) first-class, jolly good (*fam*), swell (*US*).
ordalías *nfpl* (*Hist*) ordeal, trial by ordeal.
orden 1 *nm* (a) order; arrangement; — **del día** agenda; **de primer** — first-rate, of the first order; **en** — in order; **en** — **a** with regard to; **en** — **de batalla** in battle order; **en** — **de marchar** in marching order; **fuera de** — out of order; out of turn; **por (su)** — in order; **por** — **de antigüedad** in order of seniority; **por** — **cronológico** in chronological order; **poner en** — to put in order, arrange (properly); to tidy up.
(b) (*Law etc*) order; — **público** public order, law and order; **las fuerzas del** — the forces of law and order; **llamar al** — to call to order; **mantener el** — to keep order.
(c) **una cifra del** — **de 600** a figure of the order of 600.
(d) (*Archit*) order; — **dórico** Doric order.
2 *nf* (a) order; (*Law*) order, warrant, writ; — **del día** (*Mil*) order of the day; **eso ahora está a la** — **del día** that is now the order of the day; **O** — **Real** Order in Council; **a la** — (*Comm*) to order; **a la** — **de Vd, a sus** —**es** at your service; **¡a las** —**es!** (*Mil*) yes sir?; **hasta nueva** — till further orders; **por** — **de** on the orders of, by order of; **¡es una** —**!** that's an order!; **dar una** — to give an order; **dar la** — **de** + *infin* to give the order to + *infin*.
(b) (*Eccl*) order; —**es menores** minor orders; — **monástica** monastic order; — **religiosa** religious order; —**es sagradas** holy orders; **O** — **de San Benito** Benedictine Order.
(c) (*Hist, Mil*) — **de caballería** order of knighthood; — **militar** military order; **O** — **del Imperio Británico** Order of the British Empire.
(d) (*SAm: Comm: angl*) order.
ordenación *nf* (a) order; arrangement; (*act*) ordering, arranging. (b) (*Eccl*) ordination.
ordenada *nf* ordinate.
ordenadamente *adv* in an orderly way; tidily; methodically.
ordenado *adj* (a) orderly; tidy; well arranged. (b) *person* methodical; tidy. (c) (*Eccl*) in holy orders.
ordenador *nm* computer.
ordenancista *nm* disciplinarian, martinet.
ordenando *nm* (*Eccl*) ordinand.
ordenanza 1 *nf* ordinance, decree; —**s municipales** by-laws; **ser de** — to be the rule.
2 *nm* (*Comm etc*) office boy, messenger; errand boy; (*Mil*) orderly, batman.
ordenar [1a] 1 *vt* (a) to arrange, put in order; to marshal; to draw up; — **sus asuntos** to put one's affairs in order; — **su vida** to arrange one's life.

(b) to order; — **a uno hacer algo** to order someone to do something.
(c) (*Eccl*) to ordain.
2 **ordenarse** *vr* (*Eccl*) to take holy orders, be ordained (*de* as).
ordeña *nf* (*Chi, Mex*) milking.
ordeñadero *nm* milking pail.
ordeñadora *nf* milking machine.
ordeñar [1a] *vt* to milk.
ordeñe *nm* (*Cu*), **ordeño** *nm* milking.
ordinal 1 *adj* ordinal. 2 *nm* ordinal.
ordinariamente *adv* ordinarily, usually.
ordinariez *nf* (a) (*quality*) commonness, coarseness, vulgarity. (b) (*una* —) coarse remark (*or* joke *etc*), piece of vulgarity.
ordinario 1 *adj* (a) ordinary; usual; current; *expenses* daily; **de** — usually, ordinarily.
(b) common, coarse, vulgar; *joke* coarse, crude; **son gente muy ordinaria** they're very common people.
2 *nm* (a) daily household expenses.
(b) carrier, delivery man.
orear [1a] 1 *vt* to air. 2 **orearse** *vr* (a) to air. (b) (*person*) to get some fresh air, take a breather.
orégano *nm* marjoram.
oreja *nf* (a) (*Anat*) ear; **con las** —**s gachas** (*fig*) ashamed; embarrassed; **aguzar las** —**s** to prick up one's ears; **asomar** (*or* **descubrir, enseñar**) **la** — to give oneself away, reveal one's true nature; **calentar las** — **a uno** to box someone's ears; **estar hasta las** —**s** to be utterly fed up; **hacer** —**s de mercader** to turn a deaf ear.
(b) (*of shoe etc*) tab; tag; (*of vessel*) lug, handle; (*Mech*) lug, flange; (*of chair*) wing; (*of book jacket*) flap.
(c) (*SAm*) curiosity; eavesdropping; caution.
(d) (*SAm*) secret police.
orejano 1 *adj* (a) (*SAm*) *animal* unbranded, ownerless.
(b) (*SAm*) shy, easily scared; unsociable.
(c) (*Ven*) cautious.
2 *nm* (*Pan, SD*) peasant, countryman.
orejear [1a] *vi* (a) (*CAm, Chi, Mex, Per, PR*) to eavesdrop.
(b) (*Ant, Bol, Chi*) to suspect, be distrustful.
(c) (*RPl*) to uncover one's cards one by one.
orejera *nf* earflap.
orejero 1 *adj* (a) (*SAm*) suspicious; cautious. (b) (*Arg*) telltale. (c) (*Col*) malicious. 2 *nm* (*Arg*) boss's right-hand man.
orejeta *nf* (*Tech*) lug.
orejón 1 *adj* (a) (*SAm*)=**orejudo**.
(b) (*CAm, Col, Mex*) rough, coarse.
2 *nm* (a) pull on the ear, tug at one's ear.
(b) strip of dried peach (*or* apricot).
(c) (*Col*) goitre.
(d) (*Col*) herdsman, plainsman.
(e) (*Mex*) complaisant husband.
(f) (*Per*) Inca nobleman.
orejonas *nfpl* (*Col, Ven*) big spurs.
orejudo *adj* big-eared, with big ears.
orensano 1 *adj* of Orense. 2 *nmf* native (*or* inhabitant) of Orense; **los** —**s** the people of Orense.
orfanato *nm*, **orfanatorio** *nm* (*SAm*) orphanage.
orfandad *nf* (a) orphanhood. (b) (*fig*) helplessness, destitution.
orfebre *nm* goldsmith, silversmith.
orfebrería *nf* gold work, silver work, craftsmanship in precious metals.
orfelinato *nm* (*gall*) orphanage.
Orfeo *m* Orpheus.
orfeón *nm* glee club, choral society.
organdí *nm* organdie.
orgánicamente *adv* organically.
orgánico *adj* organic.
organillero *nm* organ-grinder.
organillo *nm* barrel organ, hurdy-gurdy.
organismo *nm* (a) (*Bio*) organism.
(b) (*Pol etc*) organization; body, institution; —**s de gobierno** organs of government, state bodies; — **de sondaje** public-opinion poll, institute of public opinion.
organista *nmf* organist.
organito *nm* (*RPl*)=**organillo**.
organización *nf* organization; **O** — **de Estados Americanos** Organization of American States; **O** — **de las Naciones Unidas** United Nations Organization.
organizador *nm*, **organizadora** *nf* organizer.
organizar [1f] *vt* to organize.
órgano *nm* (a) (*Anat, Mech etc*) organ. (b) (*Mus*) organ. (c) (*fig*) organ, means, medium.
orgasmo *nm* orgasm.
orgía *nf* orgy.

orgiástico *adj* orgiastic.
orgullo *nm* pride; (*pej*) pride, haughtiness.
orgullosamente *adv* proudly; haughtily.
orgulloso *adj* proud; haughty; **estar — de algo** to be proud of something; **estar — de** + *infin* to be proud to + *infin.*
orientación *nf* (**a**) orientation, position(ing); direction, course; (*Archit*) aspect, prospect; **la — actual del partido** the party's present course (*or* position); **una casa con — sur** a house with a southerly aspect, a house facing south.
(**b**) (*of person*) guidance; training; **me ayudó en la — bibliográfica** he helped me with bibliographical information; **importa mucho en la — de los maestros** it is very important in the training of teachers; **lo hizo para mi —** he did it for my guidance.
oriental 1 *adj* oriental; eastern. **2** *nmf* oriental.
orientar [1a] **1** *vt* (**a**) to orientate, position; to point (*hacia* towards); to give a direction to, direct; (*Naut*) sail to trim; **la casa está orientada hacia el suroeste** the house faces (*or* looks) south-west; **hay que — las investigaciones en otro sentido** you will have to change the direction of your inquiries, you will have to pursue your researches in another direction.
(**b**) *person* to guide, direct; to train; **me ha orientado en la materia** he has guided me through the subject, he has given me guidance about the subject.
2 orientarse *vr* (**a**) (*object etc*) to point, face (*hacia* towards).
(**b**) (*person*) to get one's bearings, orient oneself, get orientated; (*fig*) to get one's bearings; to establish oneself; to decide on a course of conduct (*etc*); **es difícil — en este terreno** it's hard to get one's bearings (*or* find one's way about) in this country.
oriente *nm* (**a**) east.
(**b**) **el O—** the Orient, the East; **Cercano O—, Próximo O—** Near East; **Extremo O—, Lejano O—** Far East; **O— Medio** Middle East.
(**c**) east wind.
(**d**) masonic lodge.
orificación *nf* gold filling.
orificar [1g] *vt* tooth to fill with gold.
orificio *nm* orifice, hole; vent.
origen *nm* origin; source; **los —es de la guerra** the origins of the war, the causes of the war; **país de —** country of origin; **de — argentino** of Argentinian origin; **dar — a** to cause, give rise to.
original 1 *adj* (**a**) original.
(**b**) (*fig*) original; novel; odd, eccentric, strange.
(**c**) = **originario** (**b**).
2 *nm* (**a**) original; **el — es mejor que la copia** the original is better than the copy.
(**b**) (*Typ*) manuscript, original; copy; **tenemos exceso de —** we have too much copy.
(**c**) (*person*) character, eccentric, original type.
originalidad *nf* (**a**) originality. (**b**) eccentricity, oddness.
originar [1a] **1** *vt* to originate; to start, cause, give rise to. **2 originarse** *vr* to originate (*de* from, *en* in); to be started, be caused.
originariamente *adv* originally.
originario *adj* (**a**) original; **en su forma originaria** in its original form.
(**b**) **ser — de** to originate from, be a native of; **una familia originaria de Sicilia** a family originating from Sicily.
(**c**) **país —** country of origin, native country.
(**d**) **una decisión originaria de disgustos** a decision which gave rise to trouble, a decision which was a source of trouble.
orilla *nf* (**a**) edge, border; (*of river*) bank; (*of lake*) side, shore; (*of sea*) shore; (*of table etc*) edge; (*of cup, vessel*) rim, lip; **— del mar** seashore; **a —s de** on the banks of; **vive — de mi casa** (*fam*) he lives next door to me.
(**b**) (*Sew*) edge, border, trimming; hem.
(**c**) (*Ant*) **de —** trivial, of no account; worthless.
orillar [1a] *vt* (**a**) (*Sew*) to edge, trim (*de* with).
(**b**) *lake, wood etc* to skirt, go round; to pass along the edge of.
(**c**) *subject* to touch briefly on.
(**d**) *affairs* to put in order, tidy up; to wind up.
(**e**) *obstacle* to overcome; *difficulty* to avoid, get round.
orillero *adj* (*SAm*) = **arrabalero**.
orillo *nm* selvage.
orín *nm* rust; **tomarse de —** to get rusty.
orina *nf* urine.
orinacamas *nm, pl* **orinacamas** dandelion.
orinal *nm* chamberpot; **— de cama** bedpan.

orinar [1a] **1** *vti* to urinate. **2 orinarse** *vr* to urinate (involuntarily); to wet oneself; **— en la cama** to wet one's bed.
orines *nmpl* urine.
oriundo 1 *adj*: **— de** native to; **ser — de** to be a native of, come from, hail from. **2** *nm*, **oriunda** *nf* native, inhabitant.
orla *nf*, **orladura** *nf* border, fringe, trimming.
orlar [1a] *vt* to border, edge, trim (*de* with).
ornamentación *nf* ornamentation, adornment.
ornamental *adj* ornamental.
ornamentar [1a] *vt* to adorn (*de* with).
ornamento *nm* (**a**) ornament, adornment; **—s** (*Eccl*) ornaments, vestments. (**b**) **—s** (*fig*) good qualities, moral qualities.
ornar [1a] *vt* to adorn (*de* with).
ornato *nm* adornment, decoration.
ornitología *nf* ornithology.
ornitológico *adj* ornithological.
ornitólogo *nm* ornithologist.
ornitorrinco *nm* platypus.
oro *nm* (**a**) gold; **— en barras** gold bars, bullion; **— batido** gold leaf; **— laminado** rolled gold; **— molido** ormulu; **— en polvo** gold dust; **de — gold**, golden; **como un —** like new; spick and span; **no es — todo lo que reluce** all that glitters is not gold; **es de —** (*fig*) he's a treasure; he's a marvel; he has a heart of gold; **tiene una voz de —** she has a marvellous voice; **apalear —** to be rolling in money; **guardar algo como — en paño** to treasure something; **tratar algo como — en paño** to treat something as if it were terribly fragile; **hacerse de — to** make a fortune; **poner a uno de — y azul** to lay into someone (verbally) (*fam*), heap insults on someone; **prometer el — y el moro** to promise the moon.
(**b**) (*Cards*) **—s** hearts.
orondo *adj* (**a**) *pot etc* big, big-bellied, rounded; *person* fat, potbellied.
(**b**) *person* smug, self-satisfied; pompous.
(**c**) (*SAm*) calm, serene.
oropel *nm* tinsel; **de —** flashy, bright but tawdry; unsubstantial; **gastar mucho —** to put on a bold front; **tener mucho —** to be all show, (*esp*) make a pretence of being wealthy.
oropéndola *nf* golden oriole.
oroya *nf* (*Bol, Per*) basket of a rope bridge (*for conveying people across ravines*).
orozuz *nm* liquorice.
orquesta *nf* orchestra; **— de baile** dance band; **— de jazz** jazz band; **— sinfónica** symphony orchestra.
orquestación *nf* orchestration.
orquestal *adj* orchestral.
orquestar [1a] *vt* to orchestrate.
orquídea *nf* orchid, orchis.
ortiga *nf* nettle, stinging nettle.
ortodoncia *nf* orthodontics.
ortodoxia *nf* orthodoxy.
ortodoxo *adj* orthodox.
ortografía *nf* spelling; orthography.
ortográfico *adj* spelling (*attr*); orthographic(al); **reforma ortográfica** spelling reform.
ortopedia *nf* orthopaedics.
ortopédico *adj* orthopaedic.
ortopedista *nmf* orthopaedist.
oruga *nf* (**a**) (*Ent, Tech*) caterpillar; **tractor de —** caterpillar tractor. (**b**) (*Bot*) rocket.
orujo *nm* refuse of grapes (*or* olives) after pressing.
orza *nf* (*Naut*) luff, luffing.
orzar [1f] *vi* (*Naut*) to luff.
orzuelo *nm* (*Med*) stye.
os *personal pron pl* (**a**) (*acc*) you.
(**b**) (*dative*) (to) you; **— lo di** I gave it to you; **— lo compré** I bought it from you; I bought it for you; **— quitáis el abrigo** you take off your coats.
(**c**) (*reflexive*) (to) yourselves; (*reciprocal*) (to) each other; **vosotros — laváis** you wash yourselves; **cuando — marchéis** when you leave.
osa *nf* she-bear; **O— Mayor** Ursa Major, Great Bear; **O— Menor** Ursa Minor, Little Bear; **¡anda la —!** what a carry-on! (*fam*).
osadamente *adv* daringly, boldly.
osadía *nf* daring, boldness.
osado *adj* daring, bold.
osamenta *nf* bones; skeleton.
osar [1a] *vi* to dare; **— hacer algo** to dare to do something.
osario *nm* ossuary, charnel house.
oscense 1 *adj* of Huesca. **2** *nmf* native (*or* inhabitant) of Huesca; **los —s** the people of Huesca.
oscilación *nf* (**a**) oscillation; swing, sway, to and fro movement; rocking; winking, blinking. (**b**) fluctuation. (**c**) hesitation, wavering.

oscilador 1 *adj* oscillating. **2** *nm* oscillator.

oscilante *adj* oscillating.

oscilar [1a] *vi* **(a)** to oscillate; to swing, sway, move to and fro; to rock; (*of light*) to wink, blink.
(b) (*fig*) to fluctuate (*entre* between); to range (*entre* between); **la distancia oscila entre los 100 y 500 m** the distance ranges between 100 and 500 m; **los precios oscilan mucho** prices are fluctuating a lot.
(c) (*person*) to hesitate; to waver (*entre* between); **oscila entre la alegría y el pesimismo** he passes from cheerfulness to pessimism.

oscilatorio *adj* oscillatory.

oscular [1a] *vt* (*lit*) to osculate, kiss.

ósculo *nm* (*lit*) osculation, kiss; **— de paz** kiss of peace.

oscuramente *adv* obscurely; in an obscure way.

oscurana *nf* (*Hond*) cloud of volcanic dust; (*Mex, Per*) darkness.

oscurantismo *nm* obscurantism.

oscurantista 1 *adj* obscurantist. **2** *nmf* obscurantist.

oscurear [1a] (*Mex*) = **oscurecer**.

oscurecer [2d] **1** *vt* **(a)** to obscure, darken; to dim; to black out.
(b) (*fig*) *issue* to confuse, cloud, fog; *rival* to overshadow, put in the shade; *fame* to dim, tarnish.
(c) (*Art*) to shade.
2 *vi* to grow dark, get dark.

oscuridad *nf* **(a)** darkness, obscurity; gloom, gloominess. **(b)** (*fig*) obscurity.

oscuro *adj* **(a)** dark; dim, gloomy, obscure; *outline* confused, indistinct; **a oscuras** in the dark (*also fig*), in darkness.
(b) *colour* dark, deep; **un hermoso azul —** a beautiful dark blue.
(c) (*Meteorol*) overcast, cloudy.
(d) (*fig*) obscure; confused; *future etc* uncertain; **de origen —** of obscure origin(s).

óseo *adj* bony, osseous.

osezno *nm* bear cub.

osificación *nf* ossification.

osificar [1g] **1** *vt* to ossify. **2 osificarse** *vr* to ossify, become ossified.

osito *nm*: **— de felpa** teddy bear.

osmosis *nf*, **ósmosis** *nf* osmosis.

osmótico *adj* osmotic.

oso *nm* **(a)** bear; **— blanco** polar bear; **— gris** grizzly bear; **— hormiguero** anteater; **— pardo** brown bear; **— de peluche** teddy bear; **ser un —** to be a prickly sort; **hacer el —** to play the fool; to play the sentimental lover.
(b) (*Cu*) braggart; bully.

Ostende Ostend.

ostensible *adj* obvious, evident; **hacer algo —** to reveal something, make something clear; **procurar no hacerse —** to keep out of the way, lie low.

ostensiblemente *adv* obviously, evidently; openly; perceptibly, visibly; **se mostró — conmovido** he was visibly affected.

ostenta *nf* (*Chi, Ec*) = **ostentación**.

ostentación *nf* **(a)** ostentation, display; pomp. **(b)** (*act*) show, display; **hacer — de** to show off, display, parade.

ostentar [1a] *vt* **(a)** to show; (*pej*) to show off, display, make a parade of, flaunt.
(b) to have, carry, show; **ostenta todavía las cicatrices** he still has (*or* carries) the scars.
(c) *legal powers etc* to have, possess; *title, honour* to have, hold; **— el título mundial en el deporte** to hold the world title in the sport, be the world record holder.

ostentativo *adj* ostentatious.

ostentosamente *adv* ostentatiously.

ostentoso *adj* ostentatious.

osteoartritis *nf* osteoarthritis.

osteópata *nm* osteopath.

osteopatía *nf* osteopathy.

ostión *nm* large oyster.

ostra *nf* **(a)** (*Zool*) oyster; **— perlera** pearl oyster.
(b) (*fig*) dull person; retiring individual; **las —s del café** the café regulars, the café habitués; **es una —** he's a fixture here.

ostracismo *nm* ostracism.

ostral *nm* oyster bed.

ostrero *nm* **(a)** oyster bed. **(b)** (*Orn*) oystercatcher.

osuno *adj* bear-like.

otario *adj* (*Arg, Urug*) simple, gullible.

otate *nm* (*Mex*) bamboo; cane, stick.

-ote, -ota *n and adj suffix* **(a)** (*augmentative*) **un toro grandote** a whacking great bull (*fam*), a whopping bull (*sl*).
(b) (*pej*) **barbarote** terribly rough (*fam*), awfully

uncouth (*fam*); **presumidote** awfully vain (*fam*); **papelote** useless bit of paper, worthless document; (*Lit*) trashy piece of writing; *see* **machote, palabrota** *etc*.
(c) (*diminutive*) **islote** small island, rocky isle.

otear [1a] *vt* **(a)** to descry, make out, glimpse; to look down on, look over; to watch (from above), spy on. **(b)** (*fig*) to examine, look into.

Otelo *m* Othello.

otero *nm* low hill, hillock, knoll.

otitis *nf* earache.

otomana *nf* ottoman.

otomano 1 *adj* Ottoman. **2** *nm*, **otomana** *nf* Ottoman.

otomía *nf* (*Mex*) = **atomía**.

Otón *m* Otto.

otoñada *nf* autumn, fall (*US*).

otoñal *adj* autumnal, autumn (*attr*), fall (*attr: US*).

otoño *nm* autumn, fall (*US*).

otorgamiento *nm* **(a)** (*act*) granting, conferring; consent; (*Law*) execution. **(b)** (*Law*) legal document, deed.

otorgar [1h] *vt* **(a)** to grant, give (*a* to); to confer (*a* on); *prize etc* to award (*a* to); *privilege etc* to grant; (*Law*) *deed etc* to execute; *will* to make.
(b) to consent, agree to.

otramente *adv* in a different way.

otro 1 *adj* (*sing*) another, (*pl*) other; **otra taza de café** another cup of coffee; **con —s trajes** with other dresses; with different dresses; **con otras 8 personas** with another 8 people, with 8 other people; **¡otra!** (*Theat*) encore!; **otra cosa** something else; **tropezamos con otra nueva dificultad** we run up against yet another (*or* a further) difficulty; **va a ser — Manolete** he's going to be another (*or* a second) Manolete; **— que** other than; different from; **fue no — que el obispo** it was none other than the bishop, it was no lesser person than the bishop; **ser muy —** to be quite changed; **los tiempos son —s** times have changed.
2 *pron* (*sing*) another one, (*pl*) others; **el — the** other one; **los —s** the others; the rest; **¿—? another one?; **lo — es más triste** the rest of it is sadder; **lo — no importa** the rest isn't important; **tomar el sombrero de — to take somebody else's hat; **conformarse con las costumbres de los —s** to adapt oneself to other people's habits; **algún —** somebody else; **que lo haga —** let somebody else do it; **— dijo que ...** somebody else said ...; **como dijo el —** as someone said; **¡— que tal!** here we go again!, we've heard all that before!; *see* **alguno, parte, tanto** *etc*.

otrora *adv* (*arch, lit*) formerly, in older times; **el — señor del país** the one-time ruler of the country.

ovación *nf* ovation.

ovacionar [1a] *vt* to cheer, applaud, give an ovation to.

oval *adj*, **ovalado** *adj* oval.

óvalo *nm* oval.

ovario *nm* ovary.

oveja *nf* **(a)** sheep, ewe; **— negra** (*fig*) black sheep (of the family); **cada — con su pareja** it's best to stick to people like oneself; birds of a feather flock together; **apartar las —s de los cabritos** (*fig*) to separate the sheep from the goats; **cargar con la — muerta** to be left holding the baby.
(b) (*Arg*) whore.

ovejera *nf* (*Mex*) sheepfold.

ovejería *nf* (*Chi*) sheep farm; sheep farming.

ovejo *nm*, **ovejón** *nm* (*SAm*) ram.

ovejuno *adj* sheep (*attr*).

overear [1a] *vt* (*Bol, RPl*) to cook to a golden colour, brown.

overol *nm* (*SAm: angl*) overalls.

ovetense 1 *adj* of Oviedo. **2** *nmf* native (*or* inhabitant) of Oviedo; **los —s** the people of Oviedo.

Ovidio *m* Ovid.

oviducto *nm* oviduct.

oviforme *adj* egg-shaped, oviform.

ovillar [1a] **1** *vt* *wool etc* to wind, wind into a ball. **2 ovillarse** *vr* to curl up into a ball.

ovillo *nm* (*of wool etc*) ball; (*fig*) tangle; **hacerse un —** to curl up into a ball; (*in fear*) to crouch, cower; (*in speech etc*) to get tied up in knots.

ovino *adj* sheep (*attr*), ovine; **ganado —** sheep.

ovíparo *adj* oviparous.

ovoide **1** *adj* ovoid. **2** *nm* ovoid.

ovulación *nf* ovulation.

óvulo *nm* ovule, ovum.

oxálico *adj* oxalic.

oxear [1a] *vt* to shoo (away).

oxiacanta *nf* hawthorn.

oxiacetilénico *adj* oxyacetylene (*attr*).
oxidación *nf* rusting; (*Chem*) oxidation.
oxidado *adj* rusty; (*Chem*) oxidized.
oxidar [1a] **1** *vt* to rust; (*Chem*) to oxidize. **2 oxidarse**
  vr to rust, go rusty, get rusty; (*Chem*) to oxidize.
óxido *nm* oxide.
oxigenación *nf* oxygenation.
oxigenado 1 *adj* (**a**) (*Chem*) oxygenated.
    (**b**) *hair* peroxided, bleached; **una rubia
oxigenada** a peroxide blonde.
    2 *nm* peroxide (*for hair*).

oxigenar [1a] **1** *vt* to oxygenate. **2 oxigenarse** *vr* (**a**)
  to become oxygenated. (**b**) (*fig*) to get some fresh air.
oxígeno *nm* oxygen.
oxte *interj* shoo!; get out!, hop it! (*fam*); **sin decir
  — ni moxte** without a word.
oye, oyendo *etc see* **oír.**
oyente *nmf* (**a**) listener, hearer; "**queridos —s . . .**"
  (*Radio*) "dear listeners . . .".
    (**b**) (*Univ*) unregistered student, occasional
student.
ozono *nm* ozone.

P

pabellón *nm* (a) bell tent.
  (b) (*of bed*) canopy, hangings.
  (c) (*Archit*) pavilion; (*in garden*) summerhouse, hut; (*of hospital etc*) block, section; — **de caza** shooting box; — **de conciertos**, — **de música** bandstand; — **de hidroterapia** pumproom.
  (d) (*of trumpet etc*) mouth; — **de la oreja** outer ear.
  (e) (*Mil*) stack.
  (f) flag; — **de conveniencia** flag of convenience; — **nacional** national flag; **un buque de — panameño** a ship of Panamanian registration, a ship flying the Panamanian flag.
pabilo *nm*, **pábilo** *nm* wick; snuff.
Pablo *m* Paul.
pábulo *nm* (a) food.
  (b) (*fig*) food, fuel; encouragement; **dar — a to** feed, encourage; **dar — a las llamas** to add fuel to the flames; **dar — a los rumores** to encourage rumours.
Paca *f pet name for* **Francisca**.
paca[1] *nf* bale.
paca[2] *nf* (*SAm: Zool*) paca, spotted cavy.
pacatería *nf* (a) timidity. (b) excessive modesty, prudishness.
pacato *adj* (a) timid. (b) excessively modest, prudish, shockable.
pacense 1 *adj* of Badajoz. 2 *nmf* native (*or* inhabitant) of Badajoz; **los —s** the people of Badajoz.
paceño 1 *adj* of La Paz. 2 *nm*, **paceña** *nf* native (*or* inhabitant) of La Paz; **los —s** the people of La Paz.
pacer [2d] 1 *vt* (a) (*grass etc*) to eat, graze. (b) (*flocks*) to graze, pasture. 2 *vi* to graze.
paciencia *nf* patience; forbearance; **¡—!** be patient!; **¡— y barajar!** keep trying!, don't give up!; **se me acaba** (*or* **agota**) **la —, no tengo más —** my patience is exhausted; **armarse** (*or* **cargarse, revestirse**) **de —** to arm oneself with patience, resolve to be patient; **perder la —** to lose one's temper.
pacienzudo *adj* (*Chi, Ec*) patient.
paciente 1 *adj* patient. 2 *nmf* patient.
pacientemente *adv* patiently.
pacienzudo *adj* very patient, long-suffering.
pacificación *nf* pacification.
pacificador 1 *adj*: **operación pacificadora** peace-keeping operation. 2 *nm*, **pacificadora** *nf* peacemaker.
pacíficamente *adv* pacifically, peaceably.
pacificar [1g] 1 *vt* to pacify; to calm; to appease. 2 **pacificarse** *vr* to calm down.
Pacífico *nm* (*also* **Océano —**) Pacific (Ocean).
pacífico *adj* pacific, peaceable; peace-loving.
pacifismo *nm* pacifism.
pacifista 1 *adj* pacifist. 2 *nmf* pacifist.
Paco *m pet name for* **Francisco**; **ya vendrá el tío — con la rebaja** the day of reckoning will come.
paco[1] *nm* (*Mil*) sniper, sharpshooter.
paco[2] *nm* (*Col, Chi, Ec, Pan, Per*) policeman.
paco[3] 1 *adj* (*Chi, Per, RPl*) reddish. 2 *nm* (*Chi, Per*) alpaca.
pacota *nf* (*Mex*) = **pacotilla**.
pacotilla *nf* (a) trash, junk, inferior stuff; **de —** trashy, shoddy; **hacer su —** to be doing nicely, make a nice profit.
  (b) (*Chi, Ec, Guat*) rabble, crowd, mob.
pacotillero 1 *adj* (*Ec*) rustic, uncouth. 2 *nm* (*Chi, Ec, Ven*) pedlar, peddler (*US*), hawker.
pactar [1a] 1 *vt* to agree to, agree on; to stipulate, contract for. 2 *vi* to come to an agreement; to compromise.
pacto *nm* pact; agreement, covenant; — **de no agresión** non-agression pact.
pachá *nm* pasha.
pachaco *adj* (*CAm*) weak, feeble; useless.

pachacho *adj* (*Chi*) chubby, squat.
pachamama *nf* (*Arg, Bol, Ec, Per*) the good earth, Earth (*as a deity*).
pachamanca *nf* (*Per*) barbecue; (*fig*) disorder, confusion.
pacho *adj* (a) (*CAm, Chi*) chubby, squat; (*CAm*) *object* flat, flattened. (b) (*Cu*) slow, phlegmatic.
pachocha *nf* (*SAm*) = **pachorra**.
pachol *nm* (*Mex*) mat of hair.
pachón 1 *adj* (a) (*Chi, Hond*) shaggy, hairy; (*Guat, Mex*) woolly.
  (b) (*Per*) plump.
  (c) (*Per*) dim, dense.
  2 *nm* (a) dull person, slow sort.
  (b) (*also* **perro —**) pointer.
pachorra *nf* slowness, sluggishness; phlegm, phlegmatic nature; **Juan, con su santa —** ... John, as slow as ever ...
pachorrada *nf* (*Ant, Par*) = **patochada**.
pachorrear [1a] *vi* (*CAm*) to be slow, be sluggish.
pachorriento *adj* (*Per, RPl*), **pachorro** *adj* (*Col, Per, PR*), **pachorrudo** *adj* slow, sluggish; phlegmatic.
pachotada *nf* (*Mex, Per*) = **patochada**.
pachuco *adj* (*Mex*) flashy, flashily dressed; coarse, common.
pachucho *adj fruit* overripe; soft, sleepy; *person* droopy, off-colour, poorly.
padecer [2d] *vti* to suffer; to endure, put up with; *error etc* to labour under, be a victim of; — **de** to suffer from; **padece del corazón** he suffers with his heart, he has heart trouble; **padece en su amor propio** his self-respect suffers; **ella padece por todos** she suffers on everybody's account; **eso hace — el metal de los goznes** that puts a strain on the metal of the hinges; **se embala bien para que no padezca en el viaje** it is well packed so that it should not get damaged on the journey.
padecimiento *nm* suffering.
padrastro *nm* (a) stepfather; (*fig*) harsh father, cruel parent. (b) (*fig*) obstacle, difficulty. (c) (*Anat*) hangnail.
padrazo *nm* indulgent father.
padre 1 *nm* (a) father; (*Zool*) father, sire; **—s** father and mother, parents; ancestors; **García —** García senior, the elder García; — **de familia** father of a family, man with family responsibilities, (*in census etc*) head of a household; — **de pila** godfather; — **político** father-in-law; **su señor —** your father; **es el — de estos estudios** he is the father of this discipline.
  (b) (*Eccl*) father; **el P— Las Casas** Father Las Casas; — **espiritual** confessor; **P— Nuestro** Lord's Prayer, Our Father; **P— Santo** Holy Father, Pope.
  (c) (*fam*) **una paliza de — y muy señor mío** a terrific bashing (*fam*), a beating and a half, the father and mother of a thrashing.
  2 *adj* (*fam*) huge, tremendous (*fam*); **un éxito —** a terrific success (*fam*); **un lío —** an almighty row (*fam*); **un susto —** an awful fright (*fam*).
padrejón *nm* (*Arg*) stallion.
padrenuestro *nm* Lord's Prayer, paternoster; **en menos que se reza un —** in no time at all.
padrillo *nm* (*Per, RPl*) stallion.
padrinazgo *nm* godfathership; (*fig*) sponsorship, patronage.
padrino *nm* (*Eccl*) godfather; (*also* — **de boda**) best man; (*in duel*) second; (*fig*) sponsor, patron; **—s** godparents.
padrón *nm* (a) list of inhabitants, roll, census; (*of members etc*) register.
  (b) (*Tech*) pattern.
  (c) (*Archit*) inscribed column, commemorative column.
  (d) (*fig*) stain, blot (*also* — **de ignominia**); **el**

trabajo es un — **para su autor** the work is a disgrace to its author; **será un — para todos nosotros** it will be a stain on all of us.
   (e) (*fam*) indulgent father.
   (f) (*SAm*) stallion; (*Col*) breeding bull.
padrote *nm* (a) (*SAm*) stallion; breeding bull. (b) (*Mex*) brothel keeper; pimp.
paella *nf* (originally *Valencian*) dish of rice with meat, shellfish etc.
paf *interj* bang!; plop!, splash!
paga *nf* (a) payment; **entrega contra —** cash on delivery. (b) pay, wages; fee. (c) (*fam*) **mala —** bad payer.
pagadero *adj* payable, due; **— a la entrega** payable on delivery; **— a plazos** payable in instalments.
pagado *adj* (*fig*) pleased; **— de sí mismo** self-satisfied, smug.
pagador *nm* (a) payer; **mal —** bad payer. (b) (in *bank*) teller, cashier; (*Mil*: also **oficial —**) paymaster.
pagaduría *nf* paymaster's office.
paganismo *nm* paganism, heathenism.
pagano[1] 1 *adj* pagan, heathen. 2 *nm*, **pagana** *nf* pagan, heathen.
pagano[2] *nm*, **pagana** *nf* person who pays for others; scapegoat, dupe.
pagar [1h] 1 *vti* (a) to pay; *debt* to pay, pay off, repay; *purchase* to pay for; *insurance policy* to pay out on; **su tío le paga los estudios** his uncle is paying for his education; **no lo podemos —** we can't afford it; **paga 20 dólares de habitación** he pays 20 dollars for his room; **a —** (*Post*) postage due; **cuenta a —, cuenta por —** unpaid bill, outstanding account; **— por adelantado** to pay in advance; **— al contado** to pay (in) cash.
   (b) (*fig*) *favour* to repay; *love* to return, requite; *visit* to return; *crime, offence* to pay for, atone for; **lo pagó con la vida** he paid for it with his life; **¡me las pagarás!** I'll pay you out for this!, I'll get you for this!; **¡las vas a —!** you'll catch it! (*fam*), you've got it coming to you!
   2 *vi* (a) (*SAm*) to pay; **el negocio no paga** the business doesn't pay.
   (b) (*Arg, Chi*) to take bets, make a book.
   3 **pagarse** *vr* (a) **— con algo** to be content with something.
   (b) **— de algo** to be pleased with something; to take a liking to something; (*pej*) to boast of something; **— de sí mismo** to be conceited, be smug; **se paga mucho de su pelo** she's terribly vain about her hair.
pagaré *nm* promissory note, IOU.
página *nf* page.
paginación *nf* pagination.
paginar [1a] *vt* to paginate, number the pages of; **con 6 hojas sin —** with 6 unnumbered pages.
pago[1] 1 *nm* (a) payment; repayment; **— anticipado** advance payment; **— al contado** cash payment; **— a cuenta** payment on account; **— a la entrega, — contra recepción** cash on delivery; **— en especie** payment in kind; **— inicial** first payment, down payment, deposit; **— a plazos** payment by instalments, deferred payment; **"nada de —"** (at *customs*) "nothing to declare"; **atrasarse en los —s** to be in arrears; **efectuar un —** to make a payment; **faltar en los —s** to default on one's payments; **suspender los —s** to stop payments.
   (b) (*fig*) return, reward; **en — de** in return for; as a reward for.
   2 *adj* paid; **estar —** to be paid; (*fig*) to be even, be quits.
pago[2] *nm* district; estate, property (*esp* planted with vines or olives); (*Arg, Urug*) region, area; home area, native part.
pagoda *nf* pagoda.
pagote *nm* (*fam*) scapegoat.
pagua *nf* (*Chi*) hernia; large swelling.
paguacha *nf* (*Chi*) (a) = **pagua**. (b) gourd, vessel; (*any*) large round fruit; moneybox; (*Anat*) hump; (*fam*) head.
paguala *nf* (*PR*) swordfish.
pai *nm* (*SAm*: angl) pie.
paila *nf* large pan; (*SAm*) frying pan.
pailero *nm* (a) (*Col, Mex*) immigrant Italian. (b) (*Cu, Mex, Nic*) coppersmith; tinker.
pailón *nm* (a) (*Col, Cu*) pot, pan. (b) (*Bol, Ec, Hond*: Geog) bowl, round flat area. (c) (*Ven*) whirlpool.
paiño *nm* petrel.
país *nm* (a) country; land, region, area; landscape; **— natal** native land; **— satélite** satellite country; **los —es miembros, los —es participantes** the member countries; **vivir sobre el —** to live off the country.

   (b) **P—es Bajos** Low Countries; **P— de los Lagos** Lake District; **P— Vasco** Basque Country.
paisa *nmf* (*SAm*: fam) = **paisano**.
paisaje *nm* landscape, countryside, scenery.
paisajista *nmf* landscape painter.
paisajístico *adj* landscape (*attr*), scenic.
paisanada *nf* (*RPl*) group of peasants, peasants (collectively).
paisanaje *nm* (a) civil population. (b) (*RPl*) = **paisanada**.
paisano 1 *adj* of the same country.
   2 *nm*, **paisana** *nf* (a) (*Mil*) civilian; **vestir de —** (soldier) to be in mufti, be in civvies (*fam*), (policeman) be in plain clothes.
   (b) compatriot, fellow countryman, fellow countrywoman; **es — mío** he's a fellow countryman (of mine).
   (c) (*Arg*) countryman, peasant; (*Ec, Per*) (Indian) highlander; (*Mex*) Spaniard; (*Chi, Per*) Chinese.
paja *nf* (a) straw; (*SAm*) dried brushwood; **hombre de —** (*fam*) stooge (*sl*); **techo de —** thatched roof; **hacerse una —** (*fam*) to masturbate; **riñeron por un quítame allá esas —s** they fell out over some tiny thing, they quarrelled over some trifle; **ver la — en el ojo ajeno y no la viga en el propio** to see the mote in someone else's eye and not the beam in one's own.
   (b) (*fig*) trash, rubbish; (*Lit*) padding, waffle (*fam*); **hinchar un libro con mucha —** to pad a book out.
   (c) (*CAm, Col*) **— de agua** tap, faucet (*US*); canal.
pajar *nm* straw loft; straw rick.
pájara *nf* (a) (*Orn*) hen, hen bird; (*esp*) hen partridge.
   (b) kite; paper bird.
   (c) loose woman; thieving woman.
   (d) **— pinta** (game of) forfeits.
   (e) (*Col, CR*) **dar — a uno** to swindle someone.
pajarada *nf* (*Ec*) flock of birds.
pajarear [1a] 1 *vt* (a) (*SAm*) *birds* to scare, keep off.
   (b) (*Col*) to watch intently.
   (c) (*Col*) to murder.
   2 *vi* (a) to loaf; to loiter.
   (b) (*SAm*: of horse) to shy.
   (c) (*Chi*) to pay no attention, be absent-minded.
   (d) (*Mex*) to take notice, listen carefully.
pajarera *nf* aviary.
pajarero 1 *adj* (a) (*Orn*) bird (*attr*).
   (b) person merry, fun-loving.
   (c) dress etc gaudy, flashy, loud.
   (d) (*SAm*) horse nervous; (*Mex, Per, PR*) horse spirited.
   (e) (*Ven*) meddlesome.
   2 *nm* bird catcher; bird fancier, breeder of birds; (*Col, Guat*) bird-scarer.
pajarilla *nf* paper kite; **se le alegraron las —s** he laughed himself silly.
pajarita *nf* (a) **— de las nieves** white wagtail. (b) paper kite; paper bird. (c) bow tie.
pajarito *nm* (a) baby bird, fledgling; (*hum*) birdie; (*fig*) very small person; **quedarse como un —** to die peacefully, fade away.
   (b) (*PR*) bug, insect.
pájaro 1 *nm* (a) bird; **— de mal agüero** bird of ill omen; **P— del Alba** Early Bird (*satellite*); **— azul** bluebird; **— bobo** penguin; **— cantor, — cantarín** songbird; **— carpintero** woodpecker; **— mosca** hummingbird; **matar dos —s de un tiro** to kill two birds with one stone; **más vale — en mano que ciento volando** a bird in the hand is worth two in the bush; **tener la cabeza a —s** (or **llena de —s**) to be featherbrained.
   (b) (*fam*: person) bird (*sl*), chap (*fam*), guy (*US fam*); (*pej*) clever fellow, sharp sort; **— de cuenta** big shot (*fam*).
   2 *adj* (a) (*Arg*) scatty, featherbrained; shady, dubious; loud, flashy.
   (b) (*Cu*) effeminate; queer (*fam*).
   (c) (*Chi*) vague, distracted.
   (d) (*SD*) (*any*) animal.
pajarón (*Arg*) 1 *adj* vague, ineffectual, stupid.
   2 *nm*, **pajarona** *nf* (a) untrustworthy sort, unbusinesslike person.
   (b) flashily dressed person.
pajarota *nf* (*fam*) hoax.
pajarraco *nm* (a) big bird; mysterious bird. (b) (*fam*) slyboots (*fam*).
paje *nm* page; (*Naut*) cabin boy.
pajera *nf* straw loft.
pajilla *nf* (*Cu, Mex, Pan*) straw hat.
pajita *nf* (drinking) straw.

pajizo *adj* (a) straw, made of straw; *roof* thatched. (b) straw-coloured.

pajolero *adj* (*fam*) blessed, wretched, annoying.

pajón *adj* (*Mex*) *hair* straight, lank.

pajonal *nm* (*SAm*) weedy place, scrubland.

pajoso *adj* (a) *grain* full of chaff. (b) straw-coloured; like straw.

pajuela *nf* spill; (*Bol*) match; (*Bol, Col, Chi*) toothpick; (*Ven: Mus*) plectrum.

Pakistán *m* Pakistan.

pakistaní 1 *adj* Pakistani. **2** *nmf* Pakistani.

pala *nf* (a) shovel, spade; scoop; — **mecánica** power shovel; — **de patatas** potato fork; — **topadora** (*Arg*) bulldozer.
(b) (*Cook*) slice; — **para el pescado** fish slice.
(c) (*Sport*) bat; racquet.
(d) (*of oar, propeller*) blade.
(e) — **matamoscas** fly swat.
(f) (*of shoe*) uppers.
(g) (*fig*) cunning, wiliness.

palabra *nf* (a) word; —**s cruzadas** crossword; —**s gruesas**, —**s mayores** strong words, abuse; **dos** —**s**, **cuatro** —**s** a couple of words; ¡**ni una** — **más!** not another word!; **a media** — at the least hint; **de** — by word of mouth; **en una** — in a word; — **por** word for word; verbatim; **a** —**s necias, oídos sordos** it's best not to listen to such nonsense; **ser la última** — **en lujo** to be the last word in luxury; **cambiar unas** —**s con uno** to have a few words with someone; **coger a uno la** — to take someone at his word; **sin chistar** — without a word; **dejar a uno con la** — **en la boca** to interrupt someone; **no encuentro** —**s para expresarme** words fail me; **no entiendo** — it's Greek to me; **gastar** —**s** to waste words, waste one's breath; **negar la** — **de Dios a uno** to concede absolutely nothing to someone; **quedarse con la** — **en la boca** to stop short; **tuvo** —**s de elogio para el ministro** he praised the minister; **trabarse de** —**s** to get involved in an argument; to wrangle, squabble.
(b) speech, power of speech, faculty of speech; **de** — **fácil** fluent; **perder la** — to lose one's power of speech.
(c) (*Parl*) right to speak; **conceder la** — **a uno** to invite someone to speak; **dirigir la** — **a uno** to address someone; **hacer uso de la** —, **tomar la** — to speak; **pedir la** — to ask to be allowed to speak; **tener la** — to have the floor; **Vd tiene la** — the floor is yours; **yo no tengo la** — it's not for me to say.
(d) word, promise; — **de casamiento**, — **de matrimonio** promise to marry; — **de honor** word of honour; **bajo** — (*Mil*) on parole; **es hombre de** — he is a man of his word; **dar su** —, **empeñar su** — to give one's word, give a pledge; **faltar a su** — to go back on one's word.

palabrear [1a] *vt* (a) (*Col, Chi, Ec*) to agree verbally to; — **a una** to promise to marry someone. (b) (*Chi*) to abuse.

palabreja *nf* strange word; nasty-sounding word.

palabrería *nf*, **palabrerío** *nm* (*Guat, RPl*) wordiness; verbiage, hot air.

palabrero 1 *adj* wordy, windy. **2** *nm*, **palabrera** *nf* windbag.

palabrota *nf* rude word, swearword.

palabrudo *adj* (*Chi*) foulmouthed.

palacete *nm* small palace; outlying building of a palace; court, manor.

palacial *adj* (*SAm: angl*) palatial.

palaciego 1 *adj* palace (*attr*), court (*attr*). **2** *nm* courtier.

palacio *nm* palace; mansion, large house; — **episcopal** bishop's palace; — **de justicia** courthouse; — **municipal** city hall; — **real** royal palace; **el** — **de los Marqueses de Tal** the house of the Marquis of Tal; **ir a** — to go to court; **tener un puesto en** — to have a post at court.

palada *nf* (a) shovelful, spadeful. (b) (*of oar*) stroke.

paladar *nm* (hard) palate, roof of the mouth; (*fig*) palate, taste; **tener un** — **delicado** to have a delicate palate.

paladear [1a] *vt* to taste; to relish, savour; **beber algo paladeándolo** to sip a drink (to see what it tastes like).

paladeo *nm* tasting; relishing, savouring; sipping.

paladín *nm* (*Hist*) paladin; (*fig*) champion.

paladinamente *adv* openly, publicly.

paladino *adj* open, public.

palafrén *nm* palfrey.

palafrenero *nm* groom.

palana *nf* (*Per*) = **pala**.

palanca *nf* (a) lever; crowbar; (*Mech*) lever; — **de cambio** gear-lever, gearshift (*US*); — **de freno** brake lever; — **de mando** control lever.
(b) (*fig*) lever; pull, influence; **mover** —**s** to pull strings.
(c) (*Col, Mex, Ven*) punting pole.

palangana 1 *nf* (a) washbasin.
(b) (*CAm, Col*) platter, wooden bowl.
2 *nmf* (also —**s**; *Chi*) intruder; (*SAm*) shallow person; charlatan; braggart.

palanganear [1a] *vi* (*SAm*) to brag; to show off.

palanganero *nm* washstand.

palanquear [1a] **1** *vt* (*Ec, Guat*) to lever (along), move with a lever; (*Col, Mex, Ven*) *boat* to punt, pole along.
2 *vi* (*Cu, Per, RPl: fig*) to pull strings.

palanquera *nf* stockade.

palanquero *nm* (*Bol, Chi: Rail*) brakeman; (*Col*) lumberman; (*Chi*) burglar, housebreaker.

palanqueta *nf* small lever; (*burglar's*) jemmy; (*Chi, Mex*) metal bar, weight (*in weight lifting*).

palatal 1 *adj* palatal. **2** *nf* palatal.

palatalizar [1f] **1** *vt* to palatalize. **2 palatalizarse** *vr* to palatalize.

palatinado *nm* palatinate.

palatino *adj* (a) (*Pol*) palace (*attr*), court (*attr*), palatine. (b) (*Anat*) palatal.

palatosquisis *nf* cleft palate.

palco *nm* (*Theat etc*) box; — **de la presidencia** (*Taur*) president's box; — **de proscenio** stage box.

palde *nm* (*Chi*) pointed digging tool; dagger.

palear [1a] *vt* (a) (*SAm*) *boat* to punt, pole. (b) (*SAm*) *earth* to shovel; *trench* to dig. (c) (*Arg*) to thresh.

palenque *nm* (a) fence, stockade, palisade.
(b) arena, ring, enclosure; (*for cockfighting*) pit.
(c) (*Bol, RPl*) tethering post, rail.
(d) (*Chi*) noisy place.

palenquear [1a] *vt* (*RPl*) to hitch, tether.

paleo ... pal(a)eo ...

paleografía *nf* paleography.

paleógrafo *nm* paleographer.

paleolítico *adj* paleolithic.

paleontología *nf* paleontology.

Palestina *f* Palestine.

palestino 1 *adj* Palestinian. **2** *nm*, **palestina** *nf* Palestinian.

palestra *nf* arena; (*fig*) lists; **salir a la** — (*fig*) to take the field, take the floor.

paleta *nf* (a) small shovel, small spade; scoop; fire shovel; (*Archit*) trowel.
(b) (*Art*) palette.
(c) (*Tech: of turbine etc*) blade; vane; (*of wheel*) paddle; bucket.
(d) (*Anat*) shoulder blade.
(e) (*SAm*) wooden paddle for beating clothes.
(f) (*SAm*) lollipop.

paletear [1a] **1** *vt* (*Arg*) *horse* to pat; (*fig*) to flatter. **2** *vi* (*Chi*) to lose one's job.

paletero *nm* (*Ec*) tuberculosis.

paletilla *nf* shoulder blade.

paleto *nm* (a) (*Zool*) fallow deer. (b) (*fam*) yokel, country bumpkin.

palia *nf* altar cloth, pallium.

paliar [1b] *vt* (a) to palliate, mitigate, alleviate; *pain* to relieve; *effect* to lessen, cushion; *importance* to diminish.
(b) *defect* to conceal, gloss over.
(c) *offence etc* to mitigate, excuse.

paliativo 1 *adj* palliative; mitigating; concealing. **2** *nm* palliative.

palidecer [2d] *vi* to pale, turn pale.

palidez *nf* paleness, pallor; wanness; sickliness.

pálido *adj* pale, pallid (*also fig*); wan; sickly.

palidoso *adj* (*Per*) = **pálido**.

palillo *nm* (a) small stick; toothpick; (*Mus*) drumstick; (*CAm, Mex*) penholder; —**s** (*Mus*) castanets; —**s chinos** chopsticks; **unas piernas como** —**s de dientes** legs like matchsticks.
(b) (*hum*) very thin person; **estar hecho un** — to be as thin as a rake.

palimpsesto *nm* palimpsest.

palindromo *nm* palindrome.

palinodia *nf* recantation; **cantar la** — to recant.

palio *nm* cloak; canopy; (*Eccl*) pallium.

palique *nm* (*fam*) chat; small talk, chitchat; **estar de** — to be chatting, have a chat.

palitroque *nm* (*Chi*) skittles, bowling (*US*); skittle alley, bowling alley (*US*).

paliza *nf* (a) beating, thrashing; beating-up; **dar una**

— **a uno** to give someone a beating, beat someone up.
(**b**) (*fig: Sport etc*) beating, drubbing; ¡qué — aquélla! what a beating that was!; **el viaje fue una** — the journey was ghastly (*fam*); **le espera una** — **en la oficina** he'll get a dressing-down at the office, he's got it coming to him at the office; **los críticos le dieron una** — **a la novela** the critics panned the novel (*sl*), the novel took a beating from the critics.
palizada *nf* (**a**) fence, stockade, palisade. (**b**) fenced enclosure.
palma *nf* (**a**) (*Anat*) palm; **batir** —**s**, **dar** —**s** to clap hands, applaud; (*Mus*) to clap hands; **como la** — **de la mano** as flat as the palm of one's hand; very easy, straightforward.
(**b**) —**s** (*fig*) clapping, applause.
(**c**) (*Bot*) palm, palm tree; palm leaf; **ganar la** —, **llevarse la** — to carry off the palm, triumph, win.
palmada *nf* (**a**) slap, pat (*on the shoulder etc*); **darse una** — **en la frente** to clap one's hand to one's brow.
(**b**) —**s** clapping, applause; **dar** —**s** to clap, applaud.
palmadita *nf* pat, light tap.
palmar[1] *nm* (*Bot*) palm grove, cluster of palms.
palmar[2] [1a] *vi* (*fam*) to die, peg out (*sl*).
palmar[3] *adj*, **palmario** *adj* clear, obvious, self-evident.
palmarote *nm* (*Ven*) rustic, peasant.
palmatoria *nf* (**a**) candlestick. (**b**) (*for punishment*) cane.
palmeado *adj* foot webbed.
palmear [1a] *vi* to clap.
palmera *nf*, **palmero** *nm* (*Arg, Ec, Mex*) palm, palm tree.
palmeta *nf* cane; caning, swish with a cane; — **matamoscas** fly swat.
palmetazo *nm* caning, swish with a cane; (*fig*) blow, slap in the face.
palmillas *nfpl*: **llevar a uno en** — to treat someone with great consideration.
palmípedo *adj* web-footed.
palmista *nmf* (*Cu, Mex, PR: angl*) palmist.
palmito *nm* (*SAm*) top of the palm tree (*an edible delicacy*).
palmo *nm* span; (*fig*) few inches, small amount; — **a** — inch by inch; **avanzar** — **a** — to go forward inch by inch; **conocer el terreno** — **a** — (*or* **a** —**s**), **tener medido el terreno a** —**s** to know every inch of the ground; **crecer a** —**s** to shoot up; **dejar a uno con un** — **de narices** to disappoint someone greatly, leave someone very crestfallen; **no hay un** — **de A a B** there's hardly any distance (*or* difference) between A and B.
palmotear [1a] *vi* to clap, applaud.
palmoteo *nm* clapping, applause.
palo *nm* (**a**) stick; post, pole; club; (*of tool etc*) handle, haft, shaft; (*Sport*) club; bat; — **ensebado** greasy pole; — **de escoba** broomstick; — **de golf** golf club; — **de tienda** tent pole; **de tal** — **tal astilla** like father like son; **estar hecho un** — to be as thin as a rake; **meter** —**s en las ruedas** (*fig*) to put a spanner in the works.
(**b**) (*Naut*) mast; spar; — **mayor** mainmast; — **de mesana** mizzenmast; — **de trinquete** foremast.
(**c**) (*Bot*) stalk (*of grape etc*).
(**d**) wood; **cuchara de** — wooden spoon.
(**e**) (*esp SAm*) tree; — **dulce** liquorice root; — **de hule** (*Guat etc*) rubber tree; — **de mango** mango tree; — **santo** lignum vitae.
(**f**) (*Typ: of letter*) upright, straight part.
(**g**) blow, hit (*with a stick*); **andar a** —**s** to be always squabbling; **dar un** — **a uno** (*fig*) to criticize someone severely, take someone to task; **los críticos le dieron un** — **a la obra** the critics lashed (*or* panned: *sl*) the play; **dar de** —**s a uno**, **doblar** (*or* **moler**) **a uno a** —**s** to give someone a beating; **dar** —**s de ciego** to lash out wildly.
(**h**) (*Cards*) suit; **seguir el** —, **servir del** — to follow suit.
(**i**) (*SAm*) swig (*fam*), draught of liquor; **a medio** — half-drunk; **darse al** — to take to drink; **pegarse unos** —**s** to have a few drinks.
(**j**) **a** — **seco** bare; by itself, pure, with nothing else; **vermut a** — **seco** straight vermouth; **beber a** — **seco** to drink without having anything to eat; **tiene el sueldo a** — **seco** he has just his salary, he has his bare salary and nothing else.
(**k**) (*SAm*) **un** — **de casa** a splendid house, a marvellous house; **es un** — **de hombre** he's a great guy (*US fam*); **cayó un** — **de agua** there was a tremendous lot of rain (*fam*).
(**l**) (*Chi*) — **grueso** (*fig*) big shot (*fam*).

paloma *nf* (**a**) (*Orn*) dove, pigeon; — **mensajera** carrier pigeon, homing pigeon; — **torcaz** woodpigeon, ringdove.
(**b**) (*fig*) meek and mild person.
(**c**) (*Sport*) handstand.
(**d**) (*Cu, Hond*) kite.
(**e**) (*Naut*) —**s** white caps (*of waves*), white horses.
palomar *nm* dovecot(e), pigeon loft.
palomear [1a] *vt* (**a**) (*Cu*) to swindle. (**b**) (*Ec, Per*) enemies to hunt down one by one; to shoot to kill, shoot dead.
palomilla *nf* (**a**) (*Ent*) moth; moth which is a pest on stored grain; (*stage*) nymph, chrysalis.
(**b**) (*Tech*) wing nut.
(**c**) (*Tech*) wall bracket, angle iron.
(**d**) (*of horse*) back, backbone.
(**e**) (*Chi, Per*) urchin, ragamuffin; (*Chi, Hond, Mex*) mob of kids (*fam*); crowd of layabouts, band of hooligans.
palomino 1 *adj* (*Arg, Mex, Per*) horse white. **2** *nm* (**a**) young pigeon. (**b**) (*Arg, Mex, Per*) white horse, palomino horse.
palomitas *nfpl* popcorn.
palomo 1 *adj* (*Arg, Col, Mex*) = **palomino. 2** *nm* (cock) pigeon; — **de arcilla** clay pigeon.
palotada *nf*: **no dar** — not to do a stroke of work; to do nothing; to get nothing right.
palote *nm* (**a**) (*Mus*) drumstick. (**b**) (*in writing*) downstroke; pothook. (**c**) (*Arg, Cu*) rolling pin; (*Chi*) tall thin person.
palotear [1a] *vi* to bicker, wrangle.
paloteo *nm* bickering, wrangling.
palpable *adj* palpable; (*fig*) tangible, palpable; concrete.
palpar [1a] **1** *vt* (**a**) to touch, feel; (*amorously*) to feel, caress, fondle; *wall etc* to feel one's way along, grope one's way past.
(**b**) — **a uno** (*of police etc*) to frisk someone, search someone for weapons.
(**c**) (*fig*) to feel; to appreciate, understand; **ahora palpa las consecuencias** now he's really feeling the consequences; **ya palparás lo que es esto** one day you'll really understand all this.
2 palparse *vr* (*fig*) to be felt; **se palpaba el descontento** you could feel the restlessness; **es una enemistad que se palpa** it's a hostility which one can feel.
palpitación *nf* palpitation, throb(bing), beat(ing); quiver(ing); stutter(ing).
palpitante *adj* (**a**) palpitating, throbbing. (**b**) (*fig*) interest, question burning.
palpitar [1a] *vi* (**a**) to palpitate; to throb, beat; to quiver; to flutter.
(**b**) (*fig*) to throb; **en la poesía palpita la emoción** the poem throbs with emotion.
(**c**) (*RPl*) **me palpita** I have a hunch; **ya me palpitaba ese fracaso** I had a hunch about that disaster, I had a presentiment of that disaster.
palpite *nm*, **pálpito** *nm* (*Chi, Per, RPl*) hunch, presentiment; **tener un** — to have a hunch.
palta *nf* (*SAm*) avocado pear.
paltó *nm* (*Col, CR, Ven: gall*) jacket.
palúdico *adj* marshy; (*Med*) malarial.
paludismo *nm* malaria.
palurdo 1 *adj* rustic; coarse, uncouth. **2** *nm* rustic, yokel, hick (*US*); (*pej*) lout.
palustre[1] *nm* (*Tech*) trowel.
palustre[2] *adj* marsh (*attr*); marshy.
palla *nf* (*Chi, Per*) mistress, kept woman.
pallador *nm* (*SAm*) *etc see* **payador** *etc*.
pallar *nm* (*Arg, Chi, Per*) Lima bean.
pallasa *nf* (*Chi, Per: gall*) mattress.
pamela *nf* (*woman's*) broad straw hat.
pamema *nf* (**a**) silly thing, stupid remark (*etc*); —**s** nonsense, humbug; ¡déjate de —**s**! stop your nonsense!
(**b**) triviality, trifle.
(**c**) —**s** flattery; coaxing, wheedling.
(**d**) —**s** fuss; ¡déjate de —**s**! stop your fussing!, that's enough of that!
pampa[1] *nf* (**a**) (*SAm*) pampa(s), prairie; **la P**— the Pampas.
(**b**) (*Chi*) region of nitrate deposits; open area on the outskirts of a town.
(**c**) **a la** — (*SAm*) in the open, out of doors; **en** — (*Chi, Guat*) in the open; naked; disappointed, frustrated.
pampa[2] **1** *adj* (**a**) (*Arg, Bol, Urug*) deal shady, dishonest.
(**b**) (*Bol*) weak, feeble.
2 *nmf* (*Arg*) pampean Indian.
3 *nm* language of the pampean Indians.

pámpana *nf* (a) vine leaf. (b) (*fam*) **zurrar la** — **a uno** to give someone a hiding.

pámpano *nm* vine shoot, vine tendril.

pampeano *adj* (SAm) of (*or* from) the pampas.

pampear[1] *vi* (Arg) to travel over a plain.

pampear[2] [1a] *vt* (Col) (a) to tap, pat (on the shoulder). (b) *pastry* to roll out.

pampero (SAm) **1** *adj* of (*or* from) the pampas. **2** *nm* (a) inhabitant of the pampas, plainsman. (b) strong wind (*blowing over the pampas from the Andes*).

pampino 1 *adj* (SAm) of (*or* from) the pampas. **2** *nm*, **pampina** *nf* (Chi) inhabitant of the Chilean pampas.

pamplina *nf* (a) (Bot) chickweed. (b) (*fam*) silly remark; —s nonsense; fuss; ¡—s! rubbish!; **esas son** —**s** that's a load of rubbish; **no me venga Vd con** —**s** don't come to me with such nonsense.

pamplinero *adj* (a) silly, nonsensical. (b) fussy, emotional, given to making a great fuss. (c) vain.

pamplonada *nf* (SAm) triviality; silly thing, piece of nonsense.

pamplonés *adj and nm*, **pamplonesa** *nf* = **pamplonica**.

pamplonica 1 *adj* of Pamplona. **2** *nmf* native (*or* inhabitant) of Pamplona; **los** —**s** the people of Pamplona.

pamporcino *nm* cyclamen.

pan[1] *nm* (a) (*in general*) bread; (*un* —) loaf; (*fig*) bread, daily bread; — **candeal**, — **de flor** white bread; — **de centeno** rye bread; — **integral** wholemeal bread; **el** — **nuestro de cada día** our daily bread; **estar a** — **y agua** to be on (*or* condemned to a diet of) bread and water; **ganarse el** — to earn one's living.
(b) (Bot) wheat; —**es** (*fig*) crops, harvest; **año de mucho** — good year for wheat, year of a heavy wheat crop; **tierras de** — **llevar** arable land, corn-growing land.
(c) — **de azúcar** sugar loaf; — **de higos** block of dried figs; — **de jabón** bar of soap, cake of soap.
(d) (Tech) gold leaf, silver leaf.
(e) — **de cuco** (Bot) stonecrop.
(f) (*idioms*) **eso es** —**comido** it's a cinch (*sl*); **contigo** — **y cebolla** (with you I'd gladly have) love in a cottage; **con su** — **se lo coma** that's his look-out, let him get on with it; **echar** —**es** (Arg, Bol) to boast, brag; **llamar al** — — **y al vino vino** to call a spade a spade; **venderse como** — **bendito** to sell like hot cakes.

pan[2] ... **pan** ..., *eg* **panasiático** pan-Asiatic.

pana[1] *nf* velveteen, corduroy.

pana[2] *nf* (SAm: Aut: *gall*) breakdown.

pana[3] *nf* (Chi) liver; (*fig*) guts, courage.

panacea *nf* panacea, cure-all.

panadería *nf* bakery, bakehouse; baker's (shop).

panadero *nm* baker.

panadizo *nm* (Med) whitlow.

panal *nm* honeycomb.

Panamá *m* Panama.

panamá *nm* (SAm) panama hat.

panameñismo *nm* word (*or* phrase *etc*) peculiar to Panama.

panameño 1 *adj* Panamanian. **2** *nm*, **panameña** *nf* Panamanian.

panamericanismo *nm* Pan-Americanism.

panamericano *adj* Pan-American.

panamitos *nmpl*, **panamos** *nmpl* (Per) beans; (*fig*) food, daily bread.

panca *nf* (Bol, Per) green leaf of maize.

pancarta *nf* placard, banner.

pancista *adj* unprincipled; always ready to compromise, concerned only to keep on good terms with those in power.

páncreas *nm* pancreas.

pancreático *adj* pancreatic.

pancromático *adj* panchromatic.

pancha *nf* (*fam*) = **panza**.

pancho[1] *adj* (a) (Chi) brown, tan. (b) (Col, Ven) broad and flat; squat.

pancho[2] *adj* calm, unruffled; **estar tan** — to remain perfectly calm.

panda[1] *nf* (Zool) panda.

panda[2] *nf* (Cu) = **pandeo**.

panda[3] *nf* (*fam*) = **pandilla**.

pandear [1a] *vi and* **pandearse** *vr* to bend, warp; to sag; to bulge.

pandeo *nm* bend; sag(ging); bulge, bulging.

pandereta *nf* tambourine; **zumbar la** — **a uno** (*fam*) to tan someone's hide (*fam*).

panderetear [1a] *vi* to play the tambourine.

pandero *nm* (a) (Mus) tambourine. (b) kite. (c) (*fam*) idiot.

pandilla *nf* set, group; (*pej*) clique, coterie; (*criminal etc*) gang; (Comm) ring.

pandillero *nm* member of a clique (*etc*); (SAm) gangster.

pando *adj* (a) *beam etc* sagging, warped. (b) *dish* shallow; flat. (c) *river, person* slow.

Pandora *f*: **la caja de** — Pandora's box.

pandorga *nf* (a) fat woman. (b) kite. (c) (Col) bother, nuisance. (d) (Mex) practical joke, hoax; student rag.

pandorgo *adj* (a) (Mex) dim, stupid. (b) (PR) fat and slow-moving.

panecillo *nm* roll.

panegírico *nm* panegyric.

panel *nm* panel; plywood; —**es** (Archit) panelling.

panela *nf* (a) (SAm) brown sugar, coarse sugar; sugar loaf. (b) (Mex) straw hat. (c) (Col, Mex, Ven) bore, tedious person; flatterer, smooth type.

pánfilo *adj* (a) simple, gullible; stupid. (b) (Col) pale, discoloured.

panfletario *adj* (SAm) *style* violent, highly-coloured.

panfletista *nm* (SAm: *angl*) pamphleteer; satirist, lampoonist.

panfleto *nm* (*angl*) pamphlet; (SAm) satire, lampoon, scandal sheet.

panga *nf* (Mex, Nic, Pan) barge, lighter.

paniaguado *nm* (Hist) henchman; protégé.

paniaguarse [1i] *vr* (Mex) to become friends, pal up (*fam*).

pánico 1 *adj* panic. **2** *nm* (a) panic, fear; **yo le tengo un** — **tremendo** (*fam*) I'm scared stiff of him. (b) **de** — = **de miedo**.

panizo *nm* (a) millet; maize. (b) (Chi) mineral deposit; (*fig*) treasure, gem, valuable object; (Comm) profitable deal, gold mine.

panocha *nf*, **panoja** *nf* (a) corncob, ear of maize; ear of wheat (*etc*). (b) (Mex) brown sugar; brown sugar candy. (c) (Col, CR, Chi) large pancake of maize and cheese.

panolis *nmf*, *pl* **panolis** (*fam*) chump (*fam*), idiot.

panoplia *nf* panoply.

panorama *nm* panorama (*also fig*); vista, view, scene; (Art, Phot) view.

panoramicar [1g] *vti* (Cine) to pan.

panorámico *adj* panoramic; **punto** — viewpoint, vantage point.

panqué *nm* (Cu, Guat: *angl*), **panqueque** *nm* (SAm: *angl*) pancake.

pantaleta *nf* (SAm) bloomers, drawers.

pantalón *nm*, **pantalones** *nmpl* (a) (*man's*) trousers, pants (US); (*woman's: outer*) slacks, trousers, (*inner*) knickers; —**es cortos** shorts; —**es de esquí** ski pants; —**es (de) pirata**, —**es tejanos**, —**es vaqueros** jeans. (b) (Ec, Per) man, male. (c) (Ant) guts, courage.

pantalla *nf* (a) screen; shade, lampshade. (b) (Cine *etc*) screen; — **de radar** radar screen; — **de televisión** television screen; **los personajes de la** — screen personalities; **llevar una historia a la** — to film a story. (c) (SAm) fan. (d) (*fig*) blind, pretext; decoy; **servir de** — **a** to be a blind for. (e) (SAm) henchman, bodyguard. (f) (Guat) large mirror.

pantanal *nm* marshland.

pantano *nm* (a) (*natural*) marsh, swamp, bog; (*artificial*) reservoir, artificial lake; **los nuevos** —**s del Tajo** the new artificial lakes along the Tagus. (b) (*fig*) jam, fix (*fam*), difficulty; **salir de un** — to get out of a jam.

pantanoso *adj* marshy, swampy, boggy.

panteísmo *nm* pantheism.

panteísta 1 *adj* pantheistic. **2** *nmf* pantheist.

panteón *nm* (a) pantheon; — **familiar** family vault; **el** — **de los reyes** the burial place of the royal family, the pantheon of the kings. (b) (Andalusia, SAm) cemetery. (c) (Chi) ore, mineral.

panteonero *nm* (SAm) gravedigger.

pantera *nf* (a) panther; (Ven) jaguar, ocelot. (b) (Cu, PR) trickster; (Mex) bully; bold person.

pantógrafo *nm* pantograph.

pantomima *nf* pantomime, dumb show.

pantoque *nm* (Naut) bilge; **agua de** — bilge water.

pantorrilla *nf* (a) calf (of the leg). (b) (Ec, Per) brazenness, nerve.

pantorrilludo adj (a) fat in the leg, thick-calved. (b) (Ec, Per) brazen, cheeky.

pantufla nf, **pantuflo** nm slipper.

panul nm (Chi) celery.

panza nf belly, paunch; — **de burro** (Mountaineering) overhang; — **mojada** (Mex) wetback (US).

panzada nf (fam) (a) bellyful; **darse una** —, **darse las grandes** —s to have a blow-out (sl).
(b) blow in the belly.
(c) (fig) **una** — **de** a lot of, a bellyful of.

panzazo nm (a) (Arg, Par, Per) blow in the belly. (b) (Mex) = **panzada**.

panzón adj, **panzudo** adj paunchy, fat, potbellied.

pañal nm (a) nappy, diaper (US); shirttail.
(b) —es baby clothes, swaddling clothes; (fig) early stages, infancy; **de humildes** —es of humble origins; **criarse en buenos** —es to be born with a silver spoon in one's mouth; **estar todavía en** —es to be very innocent still.

pañería nf drapery; draper's (shop), dry-goods store (US), clothier's (shop).

pañero nm draper, dry-goods dealer (US), clothier.

pañete nm (a) light cloth. (b) —s shorts, trunks. (c) (Col) coat of fine plaster. (d) (Chi) horse blanket.

pañi nm (Chi) sun trap, sunny place.

pañito nm table runner; traycloth.

paño nm (a) (in general) cloth; stuff, material; **el buen** — **en el arca se vende** good wine needs no bush; **le conozco el** — I know his sort, I know all about him, I recognize the type.
(b) (un —) (piece of) cloth; duster, rag, cleaning cloth; (Eccl) altar cloth; —s **calientes** (fig) half-measures, ineffective remedies; **no andarse con** —s **calientes** to pull no punches, not go in for half-measures; — **de cocina** dishcloth; — **higiénico** sanitary towel, sanitary napkin (US); — **de lágrimas** (fig) standby, consolation; — **de manos** towel; — **mortuorio** pall; — **de los platos**, — **de secar** tea towel; **jugar a dos** —s to play a double game.
(c) (Sew) piece of cloth, width; panel.
(d) —s clothes; (Art) drapes; —s **menores** underclothes, undies (fam).
(e) **al** — (Theat) offstage.
(f) (Archit) stretch, length (of wall).
(g) (on glass etc) mist, cloud, cloudiness.
(h) (Cu) fishing net.
(i) (Cu, Mex) plot of land made ready for cultivation.

pañol nm (Naut) store, storeroom; — **del agua** water store; — **del carbón** coal bunker.

pañoleta nf fichu.

pañolón nm shawl.

pañuelo nm handkerchief; scarf, headscarf, shawl.

papa[1] nm (Eccl) pope.

papa[2] nf (a) (esp SAm) potato. (b) see **entender** etc. (c) (Arg) bash (fam), blow. (d) (Cu) soft job, plum. (e) (Mex) lie, fib; hoax.

papa[3] adj (Arg, Chi) jolly good (fam), first-rate.

papá nm (a) (fam) dad, daddy, papa, pop (US). (b) (CAm, Mex etc) father; —s mother and father, parents; **felicitamos a los** —s **de la damita** we congratulate the young lady's parents.

papacote nm (CAm) kite.

papachar [1a] vt (Mex) to pat, caress.

papada nf double chin; dewlap.

papadilla nf dewlap.

papado nm papacy.

papagayo nm (a) (Orn) parrot.
(b) (fig) parrot; chatterbox; person who repeats parrot fashion.
(c) (Cu, Mex) large kite.
(d) (Per) chamberpot.

papal[1] adj (Eccl) papal.

papal[2] nm (SAm) potato field.

papalina nf (a) cap with earflaps; bonnet; mobcap. (b) (fam) binge (sl); **coger una** — to get tight.

papalón nm (Mex) cad, rotter.

papalote nm (Ant, Guat, Mex) kite.

papalotear [1a] vi (Guat, Mex) to roam, wander.

papamoscas nm, pl **papamoscas** (a) (Orn) flycatcher. (b) = **papanatas**.

papanatas nm, pl **papanatas** simpleton, sucker (sl).

papanatería nf, **papanatismo** nm gullibility, simple-mindedness.

papandujo adj soft, overripe.

papapa nf (CAm) stupidity.

papar [1a] vt to swallow, gulp (down).
2 **paparse** vr: — **algo** (fam) to eat up, scoff (fam); **se lo papó todo** he scoffed the lot; **¡pápate ésa!** put that in your pipe and smoke it! (fam).

paparrucha nf (a) piece of nonsense, silly thing. (b) botch, worthless object. (c) hoax.

paparruta nmf (Chi) humbug.

papas nfpl pap, mushy food; (fam) grub (sl).

papaya nf (a) (Bot: SAm) papaya. (b) (Cu, PR, Ven: tabu) cunt (tabu).

papayo nm (SAm) papaya tree.

papel nm (a) (in general) paper; — **atrapamoscas** flypaper; — **de calcar** tracing paper; — **biblia**, — **de China** India paper; — **carbón** carbon paper, carbon; — **de cartas** notepaper, stationery; — **cuadriculado** squared paper; — **de embalar**, — **de envolver** brown paper, wrapping paper; — **de empapelar** wallpaper; — **encerado** wax(ed) paper; — **de estaño** tinfoil; — **engomado** gummed paper; — **de estraza** brown paper, wrapping paper; **es como el** — **de estraza** it's worthless, it's not worth the paper it's written on; — **de excusado** toilet paper; — **de filtro** filter paper; — **de fumar** cigarette paper; **entre A y B no cabía un** — **de fumar** you couldn't have got a razor's edge between them; — **de lija** sandpaper; — **para máquinas de escribir** typing paper; — **mojado** (fig) scrap of paper, worthless bit of paper; — **de oficio** (SAm) official foolscap paper; — **ondulado** corrugated paper; — **de paja de arroz** rice paper; — **de paredes**, — **pintado** wallpaper; — **de plata** silver paper; — **prensa** newsprint; — **sanitario** (CAm) toilet paper; — **secante** blotting paper; blotter; — **sellado** stamped paper; — **de tina** handmade paper; — **de tornasol** litmus paper; — **transparente** tracing paper; — **vitela** vellum paper; **sobre el** — (fig) on paper, in theory.
(b) (un —) piece of paper, sheet (of paper); —es papers; —es **usados**, —es **viejos** waste paper.
(c) (official) —es papers, documents; identification papers; **los** —es, **por favor** your papers, please; **tiene los** —es **en regla** his papers are in order.
(d) (Fin) — **moneda** paper money, banknotes; **mil dólares en** — a thousand dollars in notes.
(e) (Fin) stocks and shares; — **del Estado** government bonds.
(f) (Col) one-peso note.
(g) (Cine, Theat etc) part, role; **desempeñar un** — (fig), **hacer un** — to play a part; **el** — **del gobierno en este asunto** the government's role in this matter; **hizo el** — **de Cleopatra** she played the part of Cleopatra; **el equipo hizo un buen** — **en el torneo** the team did well in the tournament, the team put up a good show in the tournament; **tuvo que desempeñar un** —secundario he had to play second fiddle, he had to take a minor role.

papelada nf (CAm) farce, pretence, charade.

papelear [1a] vi (a) to rummage through papers. (b) to make a splash, draw attention to oneself.

papeleo nm (fig) red tape.

papelera nf (a) litter bin; wastepaper basket. (b) desk.

papelería nf (a) stationery. (b) stationer's (shop). (c) mass of papers, heap of papers; sheaf of papers.

papelerío nm (SAm) = **papelería** (c).

papelero 1 adj (SAm) paper (attr). **2** nm (a) stationer; paper manufacturer. (b) (Mex) paper-boy. (c) (RPl) ridiculous person.

papeleta nf slip of paper, bit of paper; card, index card, file card; (Pol) voting paper, ballot paper; (School) report; (Guat) visiting card, calling card (US); — **de empeño** pawn ticket; **¡vaya** —! this is a tough one.

papelillo nm cigarette.

papelista nmf (Arg, Cu, PR) = **picapleitos**.

papelito nm slip of paper, bit of paper.

papelón nm (a) (piece of) wastepaper; pasteboard. (b) impostor; bluffer, show-off (fam). (c) ridiculous act, ridiculous state; **hacer un** — to do something ridiculous, make oneself a laughing stock. (d) (Col, Ven) sugar loaf.

papelonero adj (RPl) ridiculous.

papelucho nm, **papelucho** nm useless bit of paper; worthless document; (Lit) trashy piece of writing.

papera nf goitre; (also —s) mumps.

papero 1 adj (a) (SAm) potato (attr). (b) (Mex) lying, deceitful. **2** nm potato grower; potato dealer.

papilla nf (a) pap, mush. (b) (fig) guile, deceit. (c) **estar hecho** — to be smashed to pieces (or to pulp); to be dog-tired.

papiro nm papyrus.

pápiro nm (fam) thousand-peseta note; —s (fig) dough (sl), brass (sl); **tener afán de** —s to be greedy for money.

papirotazo nm, **papirote** nm flick.

papismo nm papistry, popery.

papista 1 *adj* papist, popish. **2** *nmf* papist.
papo *nm* (**a**) (*Orn*) crop; (*Zool*) dewlap; (*of person*) jowl, double chin. (**b**) (*Med*) goitre.
papudo *adj* with a heavy jowl, double-chinned.
papujado *adj* swollen, puffed up.
papujo *adj* (**a**) (*Mex*) swollen, puffed up; (*Col*) fat-cheeked. (**b**) (*Mex*) wan, sickly, anaemic.
paquebote *nm* packet boat, packet.
paquete 1 *nm* (**a**) packet, parcel (*also Post*), package; **—s postales** (*as service*) parcel post; **— de cigarrillos** packet (pack *US*) of cigarettes; **— de flores** bunch of flowers.
(**b**) (*Naut*) packet boat, packet.
(**c**) (*fam*) toff (*fam*), dandy; **estar hecho un —** to be all dressed up, be dressed in style.
(**d**) (*Mil: fam*) **meter un — a uno** to put someone on a charge.
(**e**) (*SAm*) nuisance, bore; **¡menudo —!, ¡vaya —!** what a bore!
(**f**) (*Guat, Mex*) **darse —** to give oneself airs.
2 *adj* (*SAm*) chic, elegant, spruce.
paquetear [1a] *vi* (*SAm*) to be very smart.
paquetería *nf* (*RPl*) (**a**) adornments, accessories.
(**b**) excess of adornment, overdressed state.
paquetudo *adj* (*SAm*) = **paquete 2.**
paquidermo *nm* pachyderm.
paquistaní (*Acad*) = **pakistaní.**
Paquita *f* pet name for **Francisca.**
Paquito *m* pet name for **Francisco.**
par 1 *adj* like, equal; *number* even.
2 *nm* (**a**) pair; couple; **un — de guantes** a pair of gloves; **por un — de dólares** for a couple of dollars; **solamente un — de veces** only a couple of times; **a —es** in pairs, in twos.
(**b**) equal; **al —** equally; together, jointly; **es útil a — que** (*or* **y al —**) **divertido** it is both useful and amusing, it is useful and amusing at the same time; **está al — de los mejores** it is on a level with the best, it's up to the standard of the best; **caminar al — de** to walk abreast of; **sin —** matchless, peerless; unparalleled; **no tener —** to have no parallel, be unique.
(**c**) (*Math*) even number; **—es o nones** odds or evens.
(**d**) (*Golf*) par; **lo hizo con 4 por debajo del —** he did it in 4 under par.
(**e**) (*Mech*) **— de fuerzas** couple; **— de torsión** torque.
(**f**) **estar abierto de — en —** to be wide open.
(**g**) (*person*) peer; **los doce —es** the twelve peers.
3 *nf* (*esp Comm, Fin*) par; **a la —** at par; (*fig*) **= al par; estar a la —** to be at par; **estar por encima de la —** to be above (*or* over) par; **estar por debajo de la —** to be under (*or* below) par.
para *prep* (**a**) (*destination, aim, use etc*) for; intended for; **un regalo — ti** a present for you; **lo traje — ti** I brought it for you; **un hotel — turistas** a hotel (intended) for tourists, a tourist hotel; **una taza — café** a coffee cup, a cup for coffee; **no es — comer** it's not for eating, it's not to be eaten; **nació — poeta** he was born to be a poet; **ir — casa** to go home, head for home; **salir — Panamá** to leave for Panama; **decir — sí** to say to oneself; **léelo — ti** read it to yourself; **esto, podíamos habernos quedado en casa** if this is all it is we might as well have stayed at home.
(**b**) **¿— qué?** why?, for what purpose?, what's the use?; **¿— qué lo quieres?** why do you want it?
(**c**) **— + infin** (*purpose*) to **+** infin, in order to **+** infin; **lo hizo — salvarse** he did it (in order) to save himself; **— comprarlo necesitas 5 dólares más** to buy it you need another 5 dollars.
(**d**) (*bastante, demasiado, muy*) **— + infin:** **tengo bastante — vivir** I have enough to live on; **es demasiado cara — nuestros recursos** it's too dear for our means; **tiene demasiada inteligencia — pensar así** he's too intelligent to think that.
(**e**) **— que** in order that, so that; **lo traje — que lo veas** I brought it so that you could see it, I brought it for you to see; **— que eso fuera posible habría que trabajar mucho** you would have to work hard for that to be possible (*or* to bring that about).
(**f**) **— + infin** (*result*) only to **+** infin; **se casaron — separarse en seguida** they married only to separate at once.
(**g**) (*expressions of time*) **mañana —** for tomorrow; **by tomorrow; lo dejamos — mañana** we left it till tomorrow; **lo tendré listo — fin de mes** I'll have it ready by (*or* for) the end of the month; **— las 2 estaba lloviendo** by 2 o'clock it was raining; **ahora — la feria de agosto hará un año** it'll be a

year ago this (*or* come the) August holiday; *see* **ir** etc.
(**h**) (*relationships: also* **— con**) to, towards; **tan amable — todos** so kind to everybody; **no hay hombre grande — su ayuda de cámara** no man is a hero to (*or* in the eyes of) his valet.
(**i**) (*contrasts*) **— profesor habla muy mal** he talks very badly for a professor; **— niño lo hace muy bien** he does it very well for a child; **es mucho — lo que suele dar** this is a lot in comparison with what he usually gives; **¿quién es Vd — gritar así?** who are you to shout like that?
(**j**) *see* **estar 1** (**r**) *and* (**s**); *see* **ir 1** (**b**) *etc.*
parabién *nm* congratulations; **dar el — a uno** to congratulate someone (*por* on).
parábola *nf* (**a**) (*Math*) parabola. (**b**) (*Lit*) parable.
parabólico *adj* parabolic.
parabrisas *nm, pl* **parabrisas** windscreen, windshield (*US*).
paracaídas *nm, pl* **paracaídas** parachute; **lanzar algo en —** to send something down by parachute; **lanzarse en —** to parachute (down), (*in emergency*) bale out.
paracaidista *nm* parachutist; (*Mil*) paratrooper; **los —s** (*Mil*) the paratroops.
parachoques *nm, pl* **parachoques** (*Aut*) bumper, fender (*US*); (*Rail*) buffer(s); (*Mech etc*) shock absorber.
parada *nf* (**a**) stop; stopping; stopping place; (*of industry etc*) shutdown, stoppage; standstill; (*of payments*) suspension; **— de autobús** bus stop; **— discrecional** request stop; **— en seco** sudden stop; **— de taxis** taxi stand, cab rank.
(**b**) (*of horses*) relay, team.
(**c**) bet, stake.
(**d**) dam.
(**e**) (*Fencing*) parry.
(**f**) (*of horses*) stud, breeding establishment.
(**g**) (*Mil etc*) parade; (*CAm, Mex, Per, PR*) civic procession; **formar en —** to parade.
(**h**) (*CAm, Mex*) clip of cartridges.
(**i**) (*SAm*) vanity, pride, presumption; boastfulness; **meter —** to boast, be proud.
(**j**) (*Col*) crafty trick.
(**k**) (*Per*) farmer's market (*US*), open market.
paradear [1a] *vi* (*RPl*) to brag; to swank, show off; **— con algo** to brag about something, show something off.
paradero *nm* (**a**) whereabouts; **no sabemos su —** we do not know where it is; **averiguar el — de** to ascertain the whereabouts of, locate.
(**b**) stopping place; lodging; (*SAm: Rail*) wayside halt; (*Col*) bus stop.
(**c**) end; **seguramente tendrá mal —** he'll surely come to a bad end.
paradigma *nm* paradigm.
paradisíaco *adj* heavenly.
parado 1 *adj* (**a**) **estar —** (*person*) to be motionless, be standing still; (*factory*) to be closed, be at a standstill; (*car*) to be stopped, be standing; **salida parada** (*Sport*) standing start.
(**b**) **estar —** (*worker*) to be unemployed, be idle; **los —s** the unemployed.
(**c**) **estar —** (*SAm*) to be standing (up); **estuve — durante 2 horas** I was standing for 2 hours, I stood for 2 hours.
(**d**) **dejar a uno —** (*fig*) to amaze someone; to bewilder someone, leave someone confused; to leave someone in doubt; **¡me deja Vd —!** you amaze me!; **me quedé —** I was completely confused.
(**e**) **salir bien —** to come off well, come out of it well; **salió mejor — de lo que cabía esperar** he came out of it better than could be expected; **estar bien —** (*SAm*) to be well placed; to have influence; (*Ec, Per, PR*) to be lucky; **estar mal —** (*Ec, Per, PR*) to be unlucky; **caer — (como los gatos)** to land on one's feet, be lucky.
(**f**) **ser —** (*person*) to be slow, be dull, be inactive; to lack character, be weak.
(**g**) (*SAm*) hair stiff, straight; *post etc* upright.
(**h**) (*Chi, PR*) proud, haughty; vain.
2 *nm* (*Mex*) air, look, resemblance.
paradoja *nf* paradox.
paradójicamente *adv* paradoxically.
paradójico *adj* paradoxical.
parador *nm* (**a**) (*Hist*) inn; (*modern*) tourist hotel.
(**b**) (heavy) gambler.
paraestatal *adj* body semi-official, public.
parafina *nf* paraffin wax.
parafrasear [1a] *vt* to paraphrase.
paráfrasis *nf, pl* **paráfrasis** paraphrase.

paragolpes nm, pl **paragolpes** (RPl) = **parachoques**.

paraguas nm, pl **paraguas** (a) umbrella. (b) (Col, Cu, Mex) fungus.

Paraguay: el — Paraguay.

paraguayismo nm word (or phrase etc) peculiar to Paraguay.

paraguayo 1 adj Paraguayan. **2** nm, **paraguaya** nf Paraguayan. **3** nm (a) (Bol) whip. (b) (Cu) long straight knife.

paragüero nm umbrella stand.

paraíso nm (a) paradise, heaven. (b) (Theat) upper gallery, gods.

paraje nm place, spot.

paral nm (Mex) shore, prop; post.

paralela nf parallel (line); —s parallel bars.

paralelamente adv parallel; (fig) in a parallel way, comparably.

paralelismo nm parallelism.

paralelo 1 adj parallel (also fig: a to). **2** nm (all senses) parallel; **en** — (Elec) in parallel.

paralelogramo nm parallelogram.

parálisis nf paralysis; — **cerebral** cerebral palsy; — **infantil** infantile paralysis; — **progresiva** creeping paralysis.

paralítico 1 adj paralytic. **2** nm, **paralítica** nf paralytic.

paralización nf paralysation.

paralizar [1f] **1** vt to paralyse (also fig); **estar paralizado de un brazo** to be paralysed in one arm; **estar paralizado de miedo** to be paralysed with fright.
2 paralizarse vr to become paralysed; (fig) to be paralysed, come to a standstill; to stagnate.

paramar nm (Col, Ec, Ven) season of wind and snow.

param(e)ar [1a] vi (Col, Ec, Ven) to drizzle.

paramento nm (a) ornament, ornamental cover; hangings; (of horse) trappings; —s **sacerdotales** liturgical vestments. (b) (of stone, wall) face.

paramera nf (a) high moorland. (b) (Ven) mountain sickness.

paramero 1 adj (Col, Ven) upland, highland. **2** nm, **paramera** nf highlander.

paramilitar adj paramilitary.

páramo nm (a) bleak plateau, high moor. (b) waste land. (c) (Bol, Col, Ec) drizzle; storm of wind and snow. (d) (Ven) mountain heights.

paramoso adj (Col) drizzly.

paramuno adj (Col) upland, highland.

paranera nf (SAm) grassland.

parangón nm comparison; **sin** — incomparable, matchless.

parangonable adj comparable (con to).

parangonar [1a] vt to compare (con to).

paraninfo nm (Univ) central hall.

paranoia nf paranoia.

paranoico nm paranoic.

paranza nf (Hunting) hide.

parapetarse [1a] vr (a) to protect oneself, shelter (tras behind). (b) (fig) — **tras una razón** to take refuge in a reason (for not doing something).

parapeto nm parapet, breastwork; defence, barricade.

paraplejía nf paraplegia.

parapléjico 1 adj paraplegic. **2** nm, **parapléjica** nf paraplegic.

parar [1a] **1** vt (a) to stop; breathing, car, engine etc to stop; progress to stop, check, halt.
(b) blow, threat to ward off; (Fencing) to parry; pass (Sport) to intercept, cut off; shot to stop, save.
(c) attention to fix (en on).
(d) (fig) to lead; **ahí le paró esa manera de vida** that's where that way of life led him.
(e) (Cards etc) to bet, lay, stake.
(f) to prepare, arrange; (esp SAm) to stand upright.
2 vi (a) to stop; to come to rest; to come to an end; ¡**pare**! stop!; **el coche ha parado** the car has stopped; **el autobús para enfrente** the bus stops opposite; **sin** — without stopping; without a break; — **en seco** to stop dead, stop suddenly; **no parará hasta conseguirlo** he won't give up until he gets it; ¡**y no para**! (of speaker) he just goes on and on!, there's no stopping him!; **vino a** — **a mis pies** it came to rest at my feet.
(b) — **de** + infin to stop + ger; **ha parado de llover** it has stopped raining; **no para de quejarse** he never stops complaining, he complains all the time; . . . **y pare Vd de contar** . . . and that's the lot, . . . and that was it.
(c) — **en** (of plan etc) to end up as, result in,

come down to; (of person) to end up at; **no sabemos en qué va a** — **todo esto** we don't know where all this is going to end; **el edificio paró en hotel** the building ended up as a hotel; **fueron a** — **en la comisaría** they finished (or ended) up at the police station; **irá a** — (en) **mal** he'll come to a bad end.
(d) to stay, put up, lodge (en at); **siempre paro en este hotel** I always stay at this hotel.
(e) (Hunting: of dog) to point.
3 pararse vr (a) (person etc) to stop; (car etc) to stop, pull up, draw up; (process) to come to a halt; (work etc) to stop, come to a standstill, cease; — **a** + infin to stop to + infin, pause to + infin.
(b) — **en algo** to pay attention to something, notice something.
(c) (SAm) to stand up, get up; to straighten up; sit (etc) erect; (from bed) to get up; (hair) to stand on end.
(d) (Arg, Cu, Ec, Guat) to prosper, become wealthy.

pararrayos nm, pl **pararrayos** lightning conductor.

parasitario adj, **parasítico** adj parasitic(al).

parasitismo nm parasitism.

parásito 1 adj parasitic (de on). **2** nm (a) parasite (also fig). (b) (Radio) —s atmospherics, statics.

parasitología nf parasitology.

parasol nm parasol, sunshade.

paratifoidea nf paratyphoid.

paratopes nm, pl **paratopes** (Rail) buffer(s).

Parcas: las — the Parcae.

parcela nf plot, piece of ground; smallholding.

parcelar [1a] vt to divide into plots; estate to break up, parcel out.

parcial adj (a) partial; part-. (b) partial, prejudiced, biassed; partisan.

parcialidad nf (a) partiality, prejudice, bias; partisanship. (b) party, faction, group, (esp) rebel group.

parcidad nf = **parquedad**.

parcamente adv frugally, sparingly; parsimoniously; moderately.

parco adj frugal, sparing; parsimonious; moderate, temperate; **muy** — **en comer** very frugal in one's eating habits; — **en elogios** sparing in one's praises.

parcómetro nm parking meter.

parchar [1a] vt (SAm) to patch, put a patch on, mend.

parche nm (a) (Med) sticking plaster; (Aut etc) patch; (fig) patch, mend, botch.
(b) (Mus) drumhead; drum.
(c) **pegar un** — (fam) to get money by a trick.

parcho nm (Ant, Ven) = **parche**.

pardal nm (a) (Orn) sparrow; linnet. (b) (Bot) aconite. (c) (fam) sly fellow, rogue; ¡—! (to child) you rascal!

pardear [1a] vi to look brown(ish).

pardiez interj good heavens!

pardillo nm (a) brown cloth; **gente del** — country folk. (b) (person) yokel, rustic. (c) (Orn) linnet (also — **común**).

pardo 1 adj brown; dun; drab, dark grey; cloud, beer black, dark; sky overcast. **2** nm (Ant, Arg) mulatto, half-breed; (Mex) low-class person.

pardusco adj = **pardo**.

parear [1a] **1** vt (a) to match, put together; to form pairs of. (b) (Bio) to mate, pair. **2 parearse** vr to pair off.

parecer 1 nm (a) opinion, view; **a mi** — in my opinion; **al** — apparently, seemingly; **por el bien** (or **buen**) — for form's sake, as a matter of courtesy; in order not to seem rude; **soy de** — **que** . . . I am of the opinion that . . . , I take the view that . . . ; **mudar de** — to change one's mind.
(b) looks; **de buen** — good-looking, nice-looking, handsome; **de mal** — plain, ugly.
2 [2d] vi (a) to seem; to look; **parece muy difícil** it seems very difficult, it looks very difficult; **parecía volar** it seemed to fly; **así parece** so it seems; **a lo que parece, según parece** evidently, apparently; **aunque no lo parezca** surprising though it may seem, incredible though it is; **parece como si quisieras** . . . it looks as if you wanted to . . . ; **parece que va a llover** it looks as though it's going to rain, it seems that it's going to rain.
(b) (hum comparisons) **parece un alfeñique** he's terribly thin (fam); **parece una ballena** (fam) she's as fat as a cow (fam); **parece un juez** he looks terribly serious (fam).
(c) (with personal pron) **me parece que** . . . I think (that) . . . , it seems to me that . . . ; **como te parece, si a Vd le parece** as you wish; if you think so, if you want to; ¿**qué te parece**? what do you

think (of it)?; **vamos a la piscina, ¿te parece?** do you fancy the swimming pool?, what about going to the swimming pool?; **me parece bien que vayas** I think you should go, it seems to be proper you should go; **si a Vd le parece mal** if you don't like it; **le parece mal que no vayas** she takes a poor view of your not going, she doesn't like the idea of your not going; **¡me parece muy mal!** I think it's shocking!

(d) to look like, seem like, resemble; **una casa que parece un palacio** a house that looks like a palace; **¡pareces una reina!** you look like a queen!

(e) to appear, show; (*person*) to turn up, show up, appear; (*lost object*) to turn up, reappear; **pareció el sol entre las nubes** the sun showed (or shone) through the clouds; **cuando la luna parezca** when the moon comes up; **ya parecieron los guantes** the gloves turned up; **¡ya pareció aquello!** so that was it!

3 parecerse *vr* (a) (*2 objects etc*) to look alike, resemble each other; **se parecen mucho** they look very much alike, they resemble each other closely; **ni cosa que se parezca** nor anything of the sort; far from it.

(b) — **a** to look like, resemble; **se parece al abuelo** he takes after his grandfather, he has his grandfather's looks; **el retrato no se le parece** the picture isn't a bit like him.

parecido 1 *adj* (a) similar (*de, en* in, in respect of); — **a** like, similar to; **son muy** —**s** they are very similar, they are very much alike.

(b) **bien** — good-looking, nice-looking, handsome; **no es mal parecida** she's not bad-looking.

2 *nm* similarity, likeness, resemblance (*a* to, *entre* between); **tienen mucho** — they are very alike.

parecimiento *nm* (a) (*Arg, Mex, Par*) = **parecido 2.** (b) (*Chi*) appearance.

pared *nf* wall; — **medianera** party wall; — **por medio** next door; **ni que hablara uno a la** — I might as well talk to a brick wall; **ponerse como la** — to go as white as a sheet; **subirse por las** —**es** (*fam*) to go up the wall (*fam*); **me hace subirme por las** —**es** it drives me up the wall (*fam*).

paredaño *adj* adjoining, next-door (*con* to).

paredón *nm* (a) thick wall; standing wall (*of ruined house etc*).

(b) wall of rock, rock face.

(c) **llevar a uno al** — to put someone up against a wall, shoot someone; **¡al** —**!** shoot him!

pareja *nf* (a) pair, couple; pair of Civil Guards; (*Cards*) pair.

(b) other one (of a pair); — **de baile** dancing partner; **no encuentro la** — **de este guante** I can't find the glove that goes with this one, I can't find the other half of my pair of gloves; **correr** —**s** to be on a par, go together, keep pace (*con* with).

(c) (*SAm*) pair of horses; team of draught animals; yoke of oxen.

parejería *nf* (*Ant, Ven*) vanity, conceit.

parejero 1 *adj* (a) (*Cu, PR, SD*) bold, brazen; presumptuous.

(b) (*Ven*) vain, conceited; given to social climbing.

2 *nm* (a) (*SAm*) racehorse.

(b) (*Ven*) friend, companion.

parejo 1 *adj* (a) equal; **6 todos** —**s** 6 all the same; **por** — on a par; **ir** —**s** to be neck and neck; **ir** — **con** to be on a par with, be paralleled by.

(b) *joint etc* smooth, even, flush; (*SAm*) flat, level.

2 *adv* (a) (*SAm*) at the same time, together.

(b) (*Ven*) often.

3 *nm* (*Ant, CAm*) dancing partner, escort.

parentela *nf* relations.

parentesco *nm* relationship, kinship.

paréntesis *nm, pl* **paréntesis** (a) (*Ling*) parenthesis; digression; aside.

(b) (*Typ*) parenthesis, bracket; — **rectos** square brackets; **entre** — (*adj*) parenthetical, incidental; (*adv*) parenthetically, incidentally; **y, entre** — . . . and, by the way . . . , and, I may add in passing . . .

(c) (*fig*) interruption, interval, break.

paria *nmf* pariah.

parián *nm* (*SAm*) market.

parida *nf* woman who has recently given birth.

paridad *nf* (a) parity, equality; similarity. (b) comparison.

parienta *nf* (a) relative, relation. (b) (*fam*) **la** — the wife (*fam*), the missus (*fam*).

pariente *nm* (a) relative, relation; — **político** relative by marriage; **los** —**s políticos** the in-laws.

(b) (*fam*) **el** — the old man, my (*etc*) hubby (*fam*).

parietal *adj* parietal.

parihuela *nf* stretcher.

parir [3a] **1** *vt* to give birth to, bear.

2 *vi* (*woman*) to give birth, have a baby; to be delivered; (*cow*) to calve (*and similar words for many other species*); **ha parido 4 veces** she has had 4 children, she has given birth 4 times.

París Paris.

parisién *adj*, **parisiense** *adj*, **parisino** *adj* Parisian.

parisiense *nmf* Parisian.

parla *nf* chatter, gossip.

parlador *adj* talkative; **ojos** —**es** eyes that speak, expressive eyes.

parlamentar [1a] *vi* to converse, talk; (*of enemies*) to parley.

parlamentario 1 *adj* parliamentary. **2** *nm*, **parlamentaria** *nf* parliamentarian; member of parliament.

parlamento *nm* (a) (*Pol*) parliament. (b) (*between enemies*) parley. (c) (*Law, Theat*) speech.

parlanchín 1 *adj* loose-tongued, indiscreet. **2** *nm*, **parlanchina** *nf* (a) chatterbox, great talker. (b) indiscreet person.

parlante *adj* machine *etc* talking.

parlar [1a] *vi* to chatter (away), talk (a lot), gossip; (*of parrot*) to talk.

parlero *adj* (a) talkative, garrulous; gossipy. (b) bird talking; singing, song (*attr*); stream musical; eyes expressive.

parleta *nf* chat, small talk.

parlotear [1a] *vi* to chatter, prattle.

parloteo *nm* chatter, prattle.

Parnaso *m* Parnassus.

parné *nm* (*sl*) dough (*sl*), brass (*sl*).

paro[1] *nm* (*Orn*) tit.

paro[2] *nm* (a) stoppage (of work); standstill; **hay** — **en la industria** work in the industry is at a standstill.

(b) (*also* — **forzoso,** — **obrero**) unemployment; — **estacional** seasonal unemployment; **subsidio de** — unemployment benefit, unemployment compensation (*US*).

(c) (*Col, SD, Ven*) throw (at dice).

(d) (*Col*) **en** — all at once, in one go.

parodia *nf* parody, travesty, takeoff; (*fig*) travesty.

parodiar [1b] *vt* to parody, travesty, take off.

parodista *nmf* parodist, writer of parodies.

parola *nf* (a) fluency; verbosity; gift of the gab (*fam*).

(b) chitchat; wearisome talk; —**s** (*Arg*) empty talk, hot air.

parón *nm* sudden halt, complete stop.

paroxismo *nm* paroxysm; — **histérico** hysterics; — **de risa** convulsions of laughter; **en un** — **de celos** in a fit of jealousy, in a paroxysm of jealousy.

parpadear [1a] *vi* (*eye*) to blink, wink; (*light*) to blink, flicker; (*star*) to twinkle.

parpadeo *nm* blinking, winking; flickering; twinkling.

párpado *nm* eyelid; **restregarse los** —**s** to rub one's eyes.

parque *nm* (a) park; — **de automóviles,** — **de estacionamiento** carpark, parking lot (*US*); — **de atracciones** fun fair, fairground; — **nacional** national park; — **zoológico** zoo.

(b) (*Mil etc*) depot; — **de artillería** artillery depot, artillery stores; — **de bomberos** fire station; **el** — **nacional de automóviles** the total number of cars in the country; **el** — **provincial de tractores** the number of tractors in use in the province.

(c) — **de jugar** playpen.

(d) (*SAm: Mil*) equipment; ammunition.

parqué *nm* (*Acad*) parquet.

parqueadero *nm* (*Col*) carpark, parking lot (*US*); parking place.

parquear [1a] *vti* (*SAm: angl*) to park.

parquedad *nf* frugality, sparingness; parsimony; moderation.

parqueo *nm* (*SAm: angl*) parking; carpark, parking lot (*US*); parking place.

parquet [par'ke] *nm* (*gall*) parquet.

parquímetro *nm* parking meter.

parra *nf* grapevine; climbing vine, trained vine; **subirse a la** — (*fam*) to blow one's top (*fam*).

párrafo *nm* paragraph; **echar un** — (*fam*) to have a chat (*con* with).

parral *nm* vine arbour.

parranda *nf* (a) spree (*fam*), party; **andar** (*or* **ir** *etc*) **de** — to go on a binge (*sl*), have a party. (b) (*Col, Chi, Mex*) lot, group, heap; **una** — **de** a lot of.

parricida *nmf* parricide (*person*).

parricidio *nm* parricide (*act*).

parrilla *nf* (a) grating, gridiron, grille; (*Cook*) grill; **carne a la** — grilled meat. (b) grillroom, steak restaurant.

parrillada *nf* grill; barbecue.
párroco *nm* parish priest.
parroquia *nf* (a) (*Eccl*) parish; parish church.
(b) (*Comm*) clientèle, customers; **hoy hay poca** — there are few customers today; **una tienda con mucha** — a shop with a large clientèle, a well-patronized shop.
parroquial *adj* parochial, parish (*attr*).
parroquiano *nm*, **parroquiana** *nf* (a) (*Eccl*) parishioner.
(b) (*Comm*) client, customer, patron; **ser** — **de** to be a regular client of, shop regularly at, patronize.
parsi *nmf* Parsee.
parsimonia *nf* (a) carefulness (about money *etc*); sparingness.
(b) deliberateness, calmness; phlegmatic nature; **con** — deliberately, calmly, unhurriedly.
parsimonioso *adj* (a) sensible, careful (about money *etc*); economical; sparing. (b) slow, deliberate, calm, unhurried; phlegmatic.
parte[1] *nm* (*Tel*) message; report; (*Mil*) dispatch, communiqué; — **meteorológico** weather report, weather forecast; **dar** — **a uno** to report to someone, inform someone.
parte[2] *nf* (a) (*in general*) part; portion, section; **cuarta** — quarter, fourth part; **tercera** — third; **reducir algo en una tercera** — to reduce something by a third; **la mayor** — de most of; the greater part of, the great majority of; **la mayor** — **de los argentinos** most Argentinians, most of the Argentinians; — **del mundo** part of the world; **en las cinco —s del mundo** in the four corners of the earth; — **de la oración** part of speech; **ser** — **esencial** (*or* **integral, integrante**) **de** to be an essential part of; **de algún tiempo a esta** — for some time past; **como** — **del pago** in part payment; in part exchange; **de una** — **a otra** back and forth, to and fro; **de** — **a** — through and through, right through; **de** — **de** from, on behalf of; in the name of; **de** — **de todos nosotros** on behalf of us all; **salúdale de mi** — give him regards from me, give him my regards; **en** — in part, partly; **en gran** — to a large extent, in large measure; **por** — **de** on the part of; **con concesiones por ambas —s** with concessions on both sides; **por —s** bit by bit; stage by stage, systematically; **por otra** — (or) again, on the other hand; **por una** — **. . . por otra** (—) on the one hand, **. . .** on the other; **yo por mi** — I for my part; **por la mayor** — mostly, for the most part; **echar algo a mala** — to look on something with disapproval, be offended about something; **echar una palabra a mala** — to use a word incorrectly; (**entrar a**) **formar** — **de** to form a part of, be a part of; (*person*) to be a member of; **no formaba** — **del equipo** he was not in the team; **tomar algo en buena** — to take something in good part.
(b) share; **la** — **del león** the lion's share; **a —s iguales** in equal shares; **ir a la** — to go shares; **llevar la mejor** — to have the advantage, be on the way to winning; **llevarse la mejor** — to come off best, get the best of it; **tener** — **en** to share in; **tomar** — to take part (**en**).
(c) (*of place, Geog etc*) part; **en alguna** — somewhere; **en alguna** — **de Europa** somewhere in Europe; **en cualquier** — anywhere; **por ahí no se va a ninguna** — that leads nowhere, (*fig*) this is getting us nowhere; **en ninguna** — **del país** in no part of the country, nowhere in the country; **de ninguna** — **esperes ayuda** don't expect help from any quarter; **ir a otra** — to go somewhere else; **mirar a otra** — to look the other way, look in another direction; **ha de estar en otra** — it must be somewhere else; **¿en qué** — **del país?** in which part of the country? **¿en qué** — **lo dejaste?** whereabouts did you leave it?; **en todas —s** everywhere; **en todas —s de España** in all parts of Spain, everywhere in Spain, all over Spain; **por todas —s se va a Roma** all roads lead to Rome.
(d) (*of object*) side; **por cualquier** — **que lo mires** from whichever side you look at it.
(e) (*Mus, Theat*) part.
(f) (*of relationship*) side; **por** — **de madre** on the mother's side.
(g) (*person*) contender; (*Law*) party, side; — **actora** prosecution; plaintiff; **las —s contratantes** the contracting parties; — **contraria** opposing party, other side; **tercera** — third party; **ponerse de** — **de** to take the side of, side with.
(h) —**s** (*of person*) parts, qualities, talents; **buenas** —**s** parts; —**s pudendas** pudenda, private parts; **la** — **donde la espalda pierde su**

honesto nombre (*hum, euph*) one's anatomy; **le dio en salva sea la** — (*euph*) it hit her on a part of her anatomy.
(j) (*Mex: Mech*) = **pieza**.
parteaguas *nm*, *pl* **parteaguas** divide, ridge; — **continental** continental divide.
partear [1a] *vt* woman to deliver.
partenogénesis *nf* parthenogenesis.
partenueces *nm*, *pl* **partenueces** nutcracker.
partera *nf* midwife.
partición *nf* division, sharing-out; (*Pol etc*) partition.
participación *nf* (a) (*act*) participation, taking part.
(b) share; (*Fin*) share, stock (*US*), investment; — **en los beneficios** profit-sharing; **su** — **en estos asuntos** his share (*or* part) in these matters.
(c) (*Sport*) entry; **hubo una nutrida** — there was a big entry, there were numerous entrants.
(d) (*part of a*) lottery ticket.
(e) notice, notification; — **de boda** notice of a forthcoming wedding; **dar** — **a uno de algo** to inform someone of something.
participante *nmf* participant; (*Sport*) entrant, entry.
participar [1a] **1** *vt* to notify, inform; — **algo a uno** to notify someone of something; **le participo que . . .** I have to tell you that . . . ; I warn you that . . .
2 *vi* (a) to take part, participate (**en in**); — **en una carrera** to enter for a race, run in a race, take part in a race.
(b) — **de** (*or* **en**) **una herencia** to share in an estate; — **en una empresa** (*Fin*) to invest in an enterprise.
(c) — **de una cualidad** to share a quality, partake of a quality, have a quality in common.
partícipe *nmf* participant; **hacer** — **a uno de algo** to share something with someone, inform someone of something.
participial *adj* participial.
participio *nm* participle; — **de pasado** past participle; — **de presente** present participle.
partícula *nf* particle.
particular **1** *adj* (a) particular, special; peculiar (**a** to); **nada de** — nothing special; **lo que tiene de** — **es que . . .** what's remarkable about it is that . . . ; **en** — in particular; **en este caso** — in this particular case; **tiene un sabor** — it has a special flavour, it has a flavour of its own.
(b) private, personal; **tiene coche** — he has a car of his own, he has a car to himself; **secretario** — private secretary; **en** — in private.
2 *nm* (a) particular, point, matter; **no dijo mucho sobre el** — he didn't say much about the matter.
(b) individual, private individual; **no comerciamos con —es** we don't do business with individuals.
particularidad *nf* (a) particularity, peculiarity; **tiene la** — **de que . . .** one of its special features is . . . , it has the characteristic that . . .
(b) friendship, intimacy.
particularizar [1f] **1** *vt* (a) to distinguish, characterize, mark out.
(b) to particularize, specify.
(c) to show special friendship to.
(d) to give details about.
2 particularizarse *vr* (a) to distinguish itself, stand out, mark itself out; (*person*) to make one's mark, do something outstanding.
(b) — **con uno** to single someone out (for special treatment *etc*).
partida *nf* (a) departure.
(b) register; certificate; entry (in a register *etc*); — **de bautismos** register of baptisms; — **de bautismo** certificate of baptism; — **de defunción** death certificate; — **de matrimonio** marriage certificate, marriage lines; — **de nacimiento** birth certificate.
(c) (*Comm, Fin: of account*) entry, item; (in budget *etc*) item, section, heading; — **doble** double entry; — **simple** single entry.
(d) (*Comm: of goods*) consignment.
(e) (*Cards*) game, hand; (*Chess etc*) game; — **de dobles** doubles match; — **de individuales**, — **de simples** singles match; **echar una** — to have a game.
(f) stake, wager, bet.
(g) (*persons*) party; (*Mil etc*) band, group; faction; — **de caza** hunting party; — **de campo** picnic (party); — **de excursión** group of trippers.
(h) (**mala**) —, — **serrana** dirty trick.

partidario 1 *adj* partisan. **2** *nm,* **partidaria** *nf* (a) supporter, follower (*de* of); partisan. (b) (*Cu, Ec*) sharecropper.

partidismo *nm* partisanship, bias; partisan spirit; (*Pol, pej: also* —s) party feeling, party politics.

partidista 1 *adj* partisan. **2** *nmf* partisan.

partido *nm* (a) (*Pol etc*) party; — **político** political party; — **de la reforma** reforming party; — **republicano** republican party; **sistema de —** **único** one-party system, single-party system.

(b) (*Sport etc*) game, match; fixture; — **amistoso** friendly game; — **de fútbol** football match; — **internacional** international match.

(c) (*Sport etc: persons*) team, side.

(d) (*also* — **judicial**) district, administrative area.

(e) **darse a —, venir(se) a —** to give way; **tomar —** to decide, make up one's mind; to take sides.

(f) advantage, profit; **sacar — de** to profit from, benefit from; **to put to use.**

(g) support; **tiene — en todas las clases** he has support among all classes.

(h) **de —** *bachelor* eligible; **Lola es un —** (*sl*) Lola's a girl with money; Lola's hot stuff (*sl*).

(i) (*Chi: Cards*) hand.

(j) (*Mex*) smallholding; portion of a crop given to the landlord.

(k) (*Bol, Cu*) **a —, al —** equal shares.

partija *nf* (a) partition, division. (b) (*pej*) = **parte².**

partir [3a] **1** *vt* (a) to split (up, into two *etc*), divide (up); *nut etc* to crack; to break open, split open; — **la cabeza a uno** to split (*or* crack) someone's head open.

(b) *slice etc* to cut off.

(c) to share (out), distribute, divide (up); — **algo con otros** to share something with others.

(d) *cards* to cut.

2 *vi* (a) to start, set off, set out, depart (*de* from, *para* for, *con rumbo a* for, in the direction of).

(b) to start (*de* from); **a — del lunes** from Monday, starting on (*or* from) Monday; **es el tercero a — de la esquina** it's the third one counting from the corner; **a — de estos datos** starting from these data; **hemos partido de un supuesto falso** we have started from a false assumption.

3 partirse *vr* to crack, split, break (in two *etc*).

partisano 1 *adj* partisan. **2** *nm* (*Mil*) partisan.

partitivo *adj* partitive.

partitura *nf* (*Mus*) score.

parto *nm* (a) birth, childbirth; delivery; labour; **asistir un —** to deliver a baby; **estar de —** to be in labour; **tener un — difícil** to have a difficult labour.

(b) (*fig*) product, creation; — **del ingenio** brainchild; **el ensayo ha sido un — difícil** I sweated blood over the essay.

parturición *nf* parturition.

parturienta *nf* woman in labour; woman who has just given birth.

party *nm or f* (*angl*) party.

parva *nf* (heap of) unthreshed corn; (*fig*) heap, pile.

parvada *nf* (*SAm*) flock.

parvedad *nf* littleness, smallness; fewness; **una —** a very small amount, a tiny bit.

parvulario *nm* nursery school, kindergarten.

párvulo *nm,* **párvula** *nf* child, infant; (*School*) infant.

pasa *nf* raisin; — **de Corinto** currant; — **de Esmirna** sultana.

pasable *adj* (a) passable, tolerable. (b) (*SAm*) *stream etc* fordable, that can be forded. (c) (*Arg*) saleable.

pasablemente *adv* passably, tolerably (well).

pasada *nf* (a) (*act*) passing, passage; (*with cloth etc*) rub, clean, polish; — **de pintura** coat of paint; **dar dos —s de jabón a la ropa** to soap the clothes twice.

(b) **de —** in passing, incidentally.

(c) (*Sew*) row of stitches; tacking stitch; —s patch, mend, botch.

(d) **mala —** dirty trick.

(e) (*fam*) **una — de** a lot of, a whole heap of.

(f) (*CAm, Arg*) telling-off.

(g) (*Col*) shame, embarrassment.

pasadera *nf* stepping stone.

pasadero *adj* passable, tolerable.

pasadizo *nm* passage, corridor; passageway, alley, (*with shops*) arcade; gangway; catwalk.

pasado 1 *adj* (a) past; **lo —** the past; **lo —, —** let bygones be bygones; **el mes (próximo) —** last month; — **mañana** the day after tomorrow; —s **dos días** after two days.

(b) *food* stale, bad; *fruit* overripe; *cooked dish* overdone; *news, story* stale; *idea* antiquated, out of date; *clothing etc* old, worn, threadbare; *beauty* faded; **la carne está pasada** the meat is off (*or* bad); **ella está un poco pasada** she's a little past her best.

2 *nm* (a) past.

(b) (*Gram*) past (tense).

(c) —s ancestors.

pasador *nm* (a) (*of window etc*) bolt, fastener; (*for hair, tie etc*) pin; (*Tech*) bolt; split pin.

(b) (*Cook*) colander; (*Tech*) filter.

(c) —**es** cufflinks; (*Per*) shoelaces.

(d) (*person*) smuggler.

pasaje *nm* (a) (*act*) passage, passing; (*Naut*) voyage, crossing.

(b) fare; **cobrar el —** to collect fares.

(c) passengers (collectively).

(d) passageway, alleyway; (*with shops*) arcade; (*Arg, Cu, Mex*) cul-de-sac.

(e) (*Lit, Mus*) passage.

(f) (*Col, Ven*) story, anecdote.

(g) (*Col*) tenement building.

pasajeramente *adv* fleetingly.

pasajero 1 *adj* (a) passing, fleeting, transient.

(b) **pájaro —** bird of passage, migratory bird.

(c) *street etc* busy.

2 *nm,* **pasajera** *nf* passenger; traveller.

3 *nm* (*Mex*) ferryman.

pasamano(s) *nm* (a) rail, handrail; bannister(s).

(b) (*Arg, Chi*) strap (*for standing passenger*). (c) (*Chi*) tip.

pasamontaña(s) *nm* Balaclava (helmet).

pasante *nm* assistant; assistant teacher.

pasapasa *nm* sleight of hand.

pasaporte *nm* passport; **dar el — a uno** (*sl*) to bump someone off (*sl*).

pasapurés *nm, pl* **pasapurés** grinder, mincer.

pasar [1a] **1** *vt* (a) (*general sense*) to pass; *object* to hand, give, pass (*a* to); *message, news* to give, pass on; *bill* to send; *property* to transfer; *person* to take, lead, conduct (*a* to, into); **¿me pasas la sal, por favor?** would you please pass the salt?; **nos pasaron a otra habitación** they led us into another room; **nos pasaron a ver al director** they took us to see the director; *see* **lista, revista** *etc*.

(b) *illness* to give, infect with; **me has pasado tu tos** you've given me that cough.

(c) *visit etc* to make, carry out; **el médico pasará visita** the doctor will call.

(d) *river, street etc* to cross, go over.

(e) *armour etc* to pierce, penetrate, go through; *barrier* to pass through (*or* across, over), go through; *boundary etc* to cross, go beyond; **el túnel pasa la montaña** the tunnel goes right through the mountain; **esto pasa los límites de lo razonable** this goes beyond anything that is reasonable.

(f) *pin etc* to insert, put in; to put through; — **el café por el colador** to put the coffee through a filter, strain the coffee.

(g) *drink, pill etc* to swallow; (*SAm*) to bear, stand, put up with; **no puedo — este vino** I can't get this wine down; **no puedo — a ese hombre** (*SAm*) I can't bear that chap.

(h) *exam etc* to pass.

(i) *fault etc* to overlook, tolerate; *person* to forgive, indulge, be soft on; **no te voy a — más** I'm not going to indulge you any more.

(j) *false coin* to pass (off); *goods* to smuggle (in, out); **a ése se le puede — cualquier cosa** you can get anything past him.

(k) to surpass, excel; *competitor* to do better than, beat, outdistance; (*Aut*) to pass, overtake; **él me pasa ya 3 cms** he's already 3 cms taller than I am.

(l) *event, date etc* to pass, go past; *illness* to get over; **hemos pasado el aniversario** we are past the anniversary, the anniversary is behind us.

(m) to omit, leave out, pass over; to skip; to overlook; *see* **alto 3 (f).**

(n) *time* to spend, pass; — **las vacaciones** to spend one's holidays; **fuimos a — el día en la playa** we went to the seaside for a day; —**lo bien** to have a good time; **¡que lo pases bien!** have a good time!, enjoy yourself!; **lo pasaremos tan ricamente** we'll have such a good time; —**lo mal** to have a bad time (of it); —**las moradas** (*etc*) to have a tough time of it.

(o) *hardships* to suffer, endure, go through.

(p) — **la mano por algo** to pass (*or* run) one's hand over something; to stroke something; — **el rosario** to tell one's beads; — **el cepillo por el pelo** to run a brush through (*or* over) one's hair.

2 *vi* (a) (*general sense*) to pass, go; **pasó de mis manos a las suyas** it passed from my hands into his; **la cuerda pasa de un lado a otro de la calle** the rope goes from one side of the street to the other; **el hilo pasa por el agujero** the thread goes through the hole; **el río pasa por la ciudad** the river flows (*or* goes, runs) through the city; **el autobús pasa por nuestra casa** the bus goes past our house.

(b) (*general sense: of person*) to pass, go; to move; to come in, go in; **¡pase Vd!** come in!; after you!; **— a un cuarto contiguo** to go into an adjoining room, move into an adjoining room; **no se puede —** you can't go in; you can't go through; **pasamos directamente a ver al jefe** we went straight in to see the chief; **nos hicieron —** they showed us in (*a to*), they ushered us in; **— a decir algo** to go on to say something; **y luego pasaron a otra cosa** and then they went on to something else; **los moros pasaron a España** the Moors crossed into (*or* over to) Spain; **— adelante** to go on, continue, proceed; **— de Inglaterra al Canadá** to move (*or* go, migrate) from England to Canada; **— de teniente a general** to go from lieutenant to general; **— por una crisis** to go through a crisis; **pasaré por tu casa** I'll call on you (at home), I'll drop in.

(c) (*of proposal*) to pass, get through, be approved; (*of excuse*) to be accepted; **puede —** it's passable, it's O.K. (*fam*); **esta moneda no pasa** this coin is a dud, this coin is no good.

(d) **— de** to go beyond; to exceed; **— de los límites** to exceed the limits; **pasa ya de los 70** he's over 70; **esto pasa de ser una broma** this goes beyond a joke; **no pasa de ser una mediocridad** he's no more than a mediocrity; **no pasan de 60 los que lo tienen** those who have it do not number more than 60; **de ésta no pasa** this is the very last time; **de hoy no pasa que le escriba** I'll write to him this very day; **yo de ahí no paso** that's as far as I can go; I draw the line at that; there I stick.

(e) (*Cards*) to pass; **paso** I pass, no bid.

(f) **Juan pasa por francés** John could be taken for a Frenchman; **pasa por buen pintor** he is considered to be a good painter; **pasa por sabio** he has a reputation for learning; **se hace — por médico** he passes himself off as a doctor, he poses as a doctor.

(g) **ir pasando** (*fig*) to get by, manage (somehow); **— con poco** to get along with very little; **tendrá que — sin coche** he'll have to get along without a car; **pasa por todo con tal que no le hagan trabajar** he'll put up with anything as long as they don't make him work.

(h) (*of time*) to pass, go by, elapse; **han pasado 4 años** 4 years have gone by; **¡cómo pasa el tiempo!** how time passes!

(i) (*of event, state etc*) to be over; to pass away; (*of effect*) to pass off, wear off; **ha pasado la crisis** the crisis is over; **ya pasó aquello** that's all over (and done with) now.

(j) to happen; **aquí pasa algo misterioso** something odd is going on here; **¿qué pasa?** what's happening?, what's going on?, what's up?; **¿qué le pasa a ése?** what's the matter with him?; **algo le pasa al motor** something's the matter with the engine; **lo que pasa es que . . . ,** **pasa una cosa y es que . . .** what's happening is that . . . , it's like this . . . ; **como si no hubiese pasado nada** as if nothing (unusual) had happened; **pase lo que pase** whatever happens, come what may; **no me ha pasado otra (igual) en la vida** nothing like it has ever happened to me before.

3 pasarse *vr* (a) (*state, effects etc*) to pass, pass off; **ya se te pasará** you'll get over it.

(b) **se me pasó el turno** I missed my turn; **no se te pase la oportunidad** don't miss the chance this time.

(c) (*movement etc*) = **1** (a); **— al enemigo** to go over to the enemy.

(d) (*flower, beauty etc*) to fade; (*fruit*) to go soft, get overripe; (*food*) to go bad, go off, get stale; (*tea*) to stew; (*cloth*) to wear, show signs of wear, get threadbare; (*woman*) to lose her charms; **no se pasará si se tapa la botella** it will keep if you put the cap on the bottle.

(e) to go too far, go over the line (*etc*); (*fig*) to overdo it; to say too much, go too far; **se pasa en mostrar agradecimiento** he overdoes the gratitude.

(f) (*time*) = **1** (n); **se ha pasado todo el día leyendo** he has spent the whole day reading.

(g) **— con, — sin**; see **2** (g).

(h) **no se le pasa nada** nothing escapes him, nothing gets past him, he misses nothing; **se me pasó + infin** I forgot to + *infin*.

(i) **— de + adj** to be too + *adj*, be excessively + *adj*; **se pasa de generoso** he's too generous; see **listo**.

4 *nm*: **un modesto —** modest means, modest income; **tener un buen —** to be well off.

pasarela *nf* footbridge; catwalk; (*Naut*) gangway, gangplank.

pasarrato *nm* (*Mex, PR*) = **pasatiempo**.

pasatiempo *nm* pastime, (leisure) pursuit; hobby; amusement.

pascana *nf* (a) (*Arg, Bol, Per*) wayside inn. (b) (*Arg, Bol, Per*) stage, part (of a journey); (*Col, Ec*) part of a journey done without stopping.

Pascua *nf*, **pascua** *nf* (a) **— florida, — de Resurrección** Easter; **— de Navidad** Christmas; **— de Pentecostés** Whitsun, Whitsuntide; **—s** Christmas holiday, Christmas time (*strictly, Christmas Day to Twelfth Night*); **¡felices —s!** merry Christmas!

(b) **— de los hebreos, — de los judíos** Passover.

(c) (*idioms*) **. . . y santas —s . . .** and that's that, . . . and that's the lot; . . . and there's nothing one can do about it; **de —s a Ramos** once in a blue moon; **estar como unas —s** to be as happy as a sandboy; **hacer la — a uno** (*fam*) to do the dirty on someone.

pascual *adj* paschal.

pase *nm* (*all senses*) pass.

paseandero *adj* (*Arg, Chi, Par*) fond of strolling.

paseante *nmf* (a) walker, stroller; passer-by; (*pej*) loafer, idler. (b) (*of woman*) suitor.

pasear [1a] **1** *vt* (a) *child, dog etc* to take for a walk, walk; *child* (*fig*) to keep amused, entertain.

(b) *banner etc* to parade, show off, exhibit; to walk about (the streets) with.

(c) **— la calle a una muchacha** to prowl up and down the street where a girl lives.

(d) (*CAm*) *money* to squander.

2 *vi and* **pasearse** *vr* (a) to walk, go for a walk, stroll; to walk about, walk up and down; **— en bicicleta** to go for a ride, go cycling; **— en coche** to go for a drive, go driving, go for a run; **— a caballo** to ride, go riding; **— en bote** (*etc*) to go sailing, go on a trip.

(b) **pasearse** (*fig*) to idle, loaf about.

(c) **pasearse por un tema** to deal superficially with a subject.

(d) **pasear** (*Mex*) to take a day off.

paseíllo *nm* (*Taur*) inaugural procession (*or* ceremonial entry) of bullfighters.

paseo *nm* (a) (*act*) stroll, walk; outing; **— en bicicleta, — a caballo** ride; **— en coche** drive, run, ride, outing; **— de vigilancia** round, tour of inspection; **dar un —** to go for a walk, take a walk (*or* stroll); to go for a ride (*etc*); **dar el — a uno** (*sl*) to bump someone off (*sl*); **estar de —** to be out for a walk; **enviar** (*or* **mandar**) **a uno a —** to tell someone to go to blazes; to chuck someone out, send someone packing; **¡vete a —!** get lost! (*fam*); **llevar** (*or* **sacar**) **a un niño de —** to take a child out for a walk.

(b) parade, avenue; **— marítimo** promenade, esplanade.

(c) (*distance*) short walk; **entre las dos casas no hay más que un —** it's only a short walk between the two houses.

(d) (*SAm*) **— cívico** civic procession.

pasero *nm* (*Col*) ferryman.

pasillo *nm* (a) passage, corridor; (*Parl: fig*) lobby; (*Naut*) gangway. (b) (*Theat*) short piece, sketch.

pasión *nf* (a) (*in most senses*) passion; **tener — por** to be passionately fond of, have a passion for. (b) (*pej*) bias, prejudice, partiality.

pasional *adj* (a) *person etc* passionate; **crimen —** crime of passion. (b) temperamental.

pasionaria *nf* passionflower.

pasito *adv* gently, softly.

pasivamente *adv* passively.

pasividad *nf* passiveness, passivity.

pasivo 1 *adj* (a) passive; inactive. (b) (*Gram*) passive. **2** *nm* (a) (*Comm, Fin*) liabilities, debts; (*of account*) debit side. (b) (*Gram*) passive (voice).

pasmado *adj* (a) **dejar — a uno** to amaze someone; **estar** (*or* **quedar**) **— de** to be amazed at, be astonished at.

(b) (*fam*) **estar** (*or* **quedar**) **—** to stand gaping, be bewildered, look silly; **se quedó ahí —** he just stood there gaping; **¡oye, —!** hey, you idiot!

(c) (*SAm*) *wound* infected, unhealthy; *person* unhealthy-looking, ill-looking, seedy.

(d) (*CAm, Mex*) dull, stupid; clumsy.

(e) (*CAm, PR*) sluggish, phlegmatic.

pasmar [1a] **1** vt **(a)** to amaze, astonish, astound; to stun, dumbfound.

(b) to chill (to the bone); *plants* to nip, cut.

2 pasmarse vr **(a)** to be amazed (*etc*; *de* at); to be dumbfounded; to marvel, wonder (*de* at).

(b) to be chilled to the bone; to catch a chill.

(c) (*SAm*) to become infected; to fall ill, look seedy; to catch a fever.

(d) (*Mex*, *PR*: *fruit*) to dry up, wither.

pasmarota nf, **pasmarotada** nf display of shocked surprise, exaggerated reaction.

pasmazón nm (*CAm*, *Mex*, *PR*) = **pasmo**.

pasmo nm **(a)** amazement, astonishment; awe; (*fig*) wonder, marvel, prodigy; **es el — de cuantos lo ven** it is a marvel (*or* a source of wonder) to all who see it.

(b) (*Med*) lockjaw, tetanus.

(c) (*Med*) chill.

(d) (*SAm*) fever; inflammation.

pasmosamente adv amazingly; awesomely; wonderfully.

pasmoso adj amazing, astonishing; awesome, breathtaking; wonderful.

paso[1] adj *fruit* dried.

paso[2] **1** nm **(a)** (*act*) passing, passage; crossing; (*Aut*) overtaking, passing; (*Orn*, *Zool*) migration, passage; (*fig*) transition; progress; **el — del tiempo** the passage of time; **lo recogeré al —** I'll pick it up when I'm passing; **salir al — a** (*or* **de**) to waylay; to confront; (*fig*) to nip in the bud; to strangle at birth; **de —** in passing; by the way, incidentally; **estar de —** to be passing through; **entrar de —** to drop in, call in (for a moment).

(b) way through, passage; (*Archit*) passage; **¡—!** make way!, gangway!; **— elevado, — a distinto nivel** (*Aut*) flyover; **— franco, — libre** free passage, free access; clear way through; **— inferior** underpass; **— a nivel** level crossing, grade crossing (*US*); **— de** (*or* **para**) **peatones** pedestrian crossing; **— subterráneo** subway, underpass (*US*); **"prohibido el —"** "no thoroughfare" (*Aut*), "no entry"; **abrir — para** to make way for; **abrirse —** to make one's way (*entre*, *por* through), force a way through; **abrirse — luchando** to fight one's way through; **abrirse — a tiros** to shoot one's way through; **ceder el —** to make way; (*Aut*) to give way, yield (*US*); **"ceda el —"** (*Aut*) "give way"; **ceder el — a** (*fig*), **dar — a** to give way to, give place to; **cerrar el —** to block the way.

(c) (*Geog*) pass; (*Naut*) strait.

(d) (*of foot*) steps, pace; (*mark*) footprint; (*sound*) footstep, footfall; (*distance*) pace; **— atrás** step backwards, (*fig*) backward step; **— a —** step by step; **a cada —** at every step, at every turn; **a grandes —s, a —s agigantados** (*fig*) by leaps and bounds; **a dos —s de aquí** two steps from here, very near here; **estar a un — mínimo de** to border on, verge closely on; **por sus —s contados** step by step, systematically; **coger el —** to fall into step (*con* with; *also fig*); **dar un — to take a step; dar un — en falso** to step on something that is not there, trip; (*fig*) to take a false step; **no da un — sin hacer alguna barbaridad** he can't take a step without doing something awful; **llevar el —** to keep in step, keep time; **marcar el —** (*SAm*) to keep time, (*fig*) to mark time; **seguir los —s a uno** to tail someone, shadow someone; **seguir los —s de uno** to follow in someone's footsteps; **volver sobre los —s** to retrace one's steps.

(e) walk, gait; speed, pace, rate; (*of horse*) gait; **— de andadura** amble; **buen —** quick step, good pace; **a buen —** quickly; (*fig*) at a good rate; **a — lento** at a slow pace, slowly; **a — ligero** (*Mil*), **a — redoblado** (*SAm*) at the double; **a — de tortuga** at a snail's pace; **a ese —** (*fig*) at that rate; **al — slowly**; **al — que vamos** at the rate we're going; **al — que . . .** (*as conj*) at the same time as . . . ; while . . . , whereas . . . ; **acelerar** (*or* **apretar, avivar** *etc*) **el —** to go faster, quicken one's pace; **aflojar el —** to slow down, slacken one's pace; **establecer el —** to make the pace, set the pace; **romper el —** to break step.

(f) (*of dance*) step; **— a dos** pas de deux; **— de vals** waltz step.

(g) (*fig*) step, move; measure; **es un — hacia nuestro objetivo** it's a step towards our objective; **andar en malos —s** to be mixed up in shady affairs; **dar un mal —** to take a false step, make a false move; to get in the family way; **dar los primeros —s** to make the first moves; *see also fig senses in* **(d)**.

(h) episode, incident, event.

(i) (*Theat*: *Hist*) sketch, interlude; (*Eccl*) float (*or series of sculptures etc*) *representing part of the Easter story, carried in procession*.

(j) (*Elec*, *Tech*) pitch.

(k) **— de armas** (*Mil*: *Hist*) passage of arms.

(l) difficulty, awkward situation, crisis; **salir del —** to get out of a jam, get out of trouble.

(m) (*SAm*) ford.

2 adv softly, gently; **¡—!** not so fast!, easy there!

pasoso adj **(a)** (*Col*, *Chi*, *Guat*, *Per*, *Ven*) porous, permeable; absorbent. **(b)** (*Chi*) perspiring, sweaty.

(c) (*Ec*) contagious.

paspa nf (*Bol*, *Ec*, *Per*), **paspadura** nf (*RPl*) chapped skin, cracked skin.

pasparse [1a] vr (*SAm*: *skin*) to chap, crack.

paspartú nm passe-partout.

pasquín nm skit, satire, lampoon.

pasta nf **(a)** (*in general*) paste; **— de carne** meat paste; **— de dientes, — dentífrica** toothpaste; **— de madera** wood pulp.

(b) (*of tooth*) filling; (*of pencil*) lead.

(c) cardboard; papier mâché; (*Typ*) boards; **— española** marbled leather binding; **media —** half-binding; **libro en —** book in boards.

(d) (*Cook*) dough; pastry (mixture); **—s** pastries, cakes; noodles, spaghetti.

(e) (*sl*) money, dough (*sl*).

(f) de buena — equable; kindly, good-natured.

pastaje nm (*Arg*, *Col*, *Guat*, *Urug*) pasture.

pastal nm (*SAm*) pasture, grazing land.

pastar [1a] vti to graze.

pastear [1a] vt to graze.

pastejón nm solid mass, lump.

pastel nm **(a)** (*Cook*: *of fruit etc*) cake; (*of meat etc*) pie; **—es** pastry, confectionery.

(b) (*Art*) pastel; pastel drawing (*also* **pintura al —**).

(c) (*Cards*) sharp practice; (*fig*) plot; undercover agreement, cynical compromise, deal; **se le descubrió el —** his little game was found out.

(d) (*fam*) botch, mess.

pastelear [1a] vi **(a)** to indulge in sharp practice; to make an undercover agreement. **(b)** to stall, spin it out to gain time.

pastelería nf **(a)** (*art of*) confectionery, pastry-making. **(b)** pastry, pastries (*collectively*). **(c)** confectioner's, pastry shop, cake shop.

pastelero 1 adj (*Arg*) meddlesome, intriguing. **2** nm, **pastelera** nf pastrycook; confectioner.

pastelillo nm small cake; **— de mantequilla** pat of butter; **— de hígado de ganso** pâté de foie gras.

pastelón nm (*Chi*) large paving stone.

pasteurización nf pasteurization.

pasteurizado adj pasteurized.

pasteurizar [1f] vt to pasteurize.

pastilla nf tablet, pastille; (*of soap etc*) cake, bar; (*of chocolate*) bar, piece; **— para la tos** cough drop, throat lozenge.

pastinaca nf parsnip.

pastizal nm pasture.

pasto nm **(a)** grass, herbage, fodder; grazing; **un sitio abundante en —s** a place with rich grazing.

(b) (*any*) food, feed (*for cattle*).

(c) pasture, field; (*SAm*) grass, lawn; **echar el ganado al —** to put animals out to pasture.

(d) (*fig*) food, nourishment; fuel; **fue — del fuego** it was fuel to the flames, the flames devoured it; **es — de la murmuración** it is a subject for gossip, gossip thrives on it; **— espiritual** spiritual nourishment.

(e) a — abundantly; **había fruta a —** there was fruit in unlimited quantities; **beber a todo —** to drink for all one is worth, drink to excess; **cita refranes a todo —** he quotes vast quantities of proverbs, he greatly overdoes the proverbs.

(f) **vino de —** ordinary wine.

pastor nm **(a)** (*Agr*) shepherd; herdsman, goatherd, cowman (*etc*). **(b)** (*Eccl*) (*protestant*) minister, clergyman, pastor. **(c) el Buen P—** the Good Shepherd.

pastora nf shepherdess.

pastoral 1 adj pastoral. **2** nf pastoral, idyll.

pastorear [1a] vt **(a)** *flock* to pasture, shepherd; to look after; (*Eccl*) to guide, lead.

(b) (*CAm*, *Arg*, *Urug*) to lie in wait for.

(c) (*CAm*) to spoil, pamper.

(d) (*Arg*, *Urug*) to court.

pastorela nf (*Lit*) pastourelle.

pastoril adj (*Lit*) pastoral.

pastoso adj **(a)** *material* doughy; soft; pasty. **(b)** *voice* rich, mellow, pleasant. **(c)** (*Arg*, *Chi*) grassy.

(d) (*Col*) lazy.

pastura nf (a) pasture. (b) food, fodder, ration of feed.

pasudo adj (Mex) hair kinky.

pata nf (a) (Zool) foot, leg; paw; (Orn) foot; (of person, hum) foot; (of furniture etc) leg; — de cabra (Tech) crowbar; — de gallina (Ant, Col, Ven) crow's-feet (wrinkles); — de gallo crow's-feet; (fam) silly remark, piece of nonsense; bloomer (fam); — hendida cloven hoof; la — coja, la — sola (Col) hopscotch; eso lo sé hacer a la — coja I can do that blindfold; —s arriba on one's back, upside down; (fig) upside down, topsy-turvy; a — on foot; a cuatro —s on all fours; a la — la llana plainly, simply, directly; bluntly; andar a —s (child) to crawl, go on all fours; andar a — renca (SAm) to limp; enseñar la —, sacar la — to give oneself away; estirar la — (sl) to peg out (sl); meter la — to put one's foot in it, make a blunder; to blot one's copybook; to butt in; ser —(s) to be even, tie; es un diccionario con dos —s he's a walking dictionary; es la virtud con dos —s she is virtue personified; tener buena — to be lucky; tener mala — to be unlucky; to be clumsy; ser de mala — to be unlucky, bring bad luck.
(b) (Zool) (female) duck.
(c) P—s the devil; —s cortas shorty, little man.

patacón nm (a) (Col) slice of fried banana. (b) (Chi) bruise, welt.

patache nm (a) (Arg) flat-bottomed boat. (b) (Ec, Per) soup; food (in general).

patacho nm (a) (Arg, Par) flat-bottomed boat. (b) (CAm, Mex) train of mules.

patada nf kick; stamp; a —s in abundance, in great quantity; (treat etc) roughly, inconsiderately; dar —s to kick; to stamp; dar —s para conseguir algo to take steps to obtain something; dar la — a uno (fam) to give someone the boot (fam); dar a uno una — en el culo (fam) to kick someone up the backside (fam); me da cien —s it gets on my nerves; he gives me a pain in the neck, I can't stand him; echar a uno a —s to kick someone out.

patagón 1 adj Patagonian. 2 nm, **patagona** nf Patagonian.

patagónico adj Patagonian.

patalear [1a] vi (a) to stamp (angrily).
(b) por mí, que patalee so far as I'm concerned he can make all the fuss he likes.
(c) (child etc) to kick out, kick about.

pataleo nm stamping; kicking.

patán nm rustic, yokel; (pej) lout.

pataplún (SAm) = cataplum.

patarata nf (a) gush, affectation, emotional fuss; excessive show of feeling. (b) silly thing; triviality; —s nonsense, tomfoolery.

pataratero adj (a) gushing, affected. (b) silly.

pataruco adj (Ven) coarse, rough. (b) cowardly.

patata nf (a) potato; — de siembra seed potato; — temprana early potato; —s enteras potatoes in their jackets; —s a la española, —s fritas chips, French fries (US); —s inglesas crisps, potato chips (US); —s mojadas, puré de —s mashed potatoes.
(b) no se me da una —, (no) me importa una — I don't care two hoots (de about); no entendió una — he didn't understand a word of it.

patatal nm, **patatar** nm potato field, potato patch.

patato adj (Cu), **patatuco** adj (Cu) chubby, plump.

patatús nm dizzy spell, queer turn.

pateada nf (Arg) long tiring walk; = pateadura.

pateadura nf, **pateamiento** nm (a) stamping, kicking. (b) (in argument) flat denial; violent interjection; (Theat) noisy protest.

patear [1a] 1 vt (a) to stamp on, trample (on); to kick, boot.
(b) (fig) to trample on, treat roughly, treat inconsiderately.
(c) (Ven) to abuse.
2 vi (a) to stamp (with rage), stamp one's foot; (Theat etc) to stamp.
(b) (SAm: of animal, gun) to kick.
(c) (Chi, RPl: of food etc) to cause an upset, be harmful.
(d) (Chi, RPl) to go long distances on foot.
(e) (fam) to be always on the go, bustle about.

patena nf paten.

patentado adj patent; proprietary.

patentar [1a] vt to patent.

patente 1 adj (a) patent, obvious, evident; hacer — to show clearly, establish.
(b) (Comm etc) patent.
2 nf (a) grant; warrant; (Comm) patent; — de invención patent; — de navegación ship's certificate of registration; — de privilegio letters patent; — de sanidad bill of health; de — patent; (Chi) first-rate.
(b) (Arg, Par: Aut) licence plate.
2 nm (Cu) patent medicine.

patentizar [1f] vt to show, reveal, make evident.

pateo nm stamping; (Theat) stamping, noisy protest, the bird (sl).

páter nm (fam): el — the pater (fam).

paternal adj fatherly, paternal.

paternalmente adv paternally, in a fatherly fashion.

paternidad nf (a) (in general) fatherhood, parenthood. (b) (of child) paternity; — literaria authorship.

paterno adj paternal; abuelo — paternal grandfather, grandfather on the father's side.

patero adj (a) (Chi) fawning. (b) (Per) tricky, untrustworthy.

patéticamente adv pathetically, movingly, poignantly.

patético adj (a) pathetic, moving, poignant. (b) (Chi) clear, evident.

patetismo nm pathos, poignancy.

patiabierto adj bow-legged.

patibulario adj (a) horrifying, harrowing. (b) person of criminal appearance.

patíbulo nm scaffold; gallows, gibbet.

patidifuso adj (fam) aghast, shattered; open-mouthed; nonplussed; dejar a uno — to shatter someone; to nonplus someone.

patiestevado adj bandy-legged.

patihendido adj cloven-hoofed.

patilla 1 nf (a) (Arg) bench.
(b) (Col, Ven) watermelon.
(c) (Chi: Bot) layer.
(d) —s whiskers, sideburns.
2 —s nm: P—s Old Nick; ser un —s to be a weak character, be a poor fish.

patín nm skate; (of sledge) runner; (Aer) skid; — de cola (Aer) tailskid; — de cuchilla, — de hielo iceskate; — de ruedas roller skate.

pátina nf patina.

patinadero nm skating rink.

patinador nm, **patinadora** nf skater.

patinadura nf (Ven) skid, skidding.

patinaje nm skating; — artístico, — de figuras figure skating.

patinar [1a] vi (a) (person) to skate. (b) (Aut etc) to skid, slip. (c) (fam) to boob (sl), make a blunder. (d) (Arg) to fail.

patinazo nm (a) skid. (b) (fam) boob (sl), blunder; dar un —, pegar un — to make a boob, blunder.

patinete nm (child's) scooter.

patio nm court, courtyard, patio; (Theat) pit; (Mex) shunting yard; — de recreo playground.

patiquín nm (Ven) fop, dandy.

patita nf: see calle (a).

patitieso adj (a) paralysed with cold (or fright etc).
(b) (fig) = patidifuso. (c) (fig) vain, conceited.

patito nm duckling.

patituerto adj with crooked legs.

patizambo adj knock-kneed.

pato nm (a) duck; — (macho) drake; — real, — silvestre mallard, wild duck; pagar el — (fam) to foot the bill; to take the blame, carry the can (sl); ser el — de la boda (or fiesta) (SAm) to be the one who pays; to be an object of ridicule, be a laughing stock; salga — o gallareta (SAm) whatever the results.
(b) (fam) bore, dull person; estar hecho un — to be terribly dull.
(c) (fam) boredom; boring time; boring party (etc).
(d) (Col) stowaway; sponger (fam); gatecrasher.
(e) (Ec) victim (of a swindle).
(f) (Arg) ser un —, estar — to be broke (fam).
(g) (SAm) bedpan.

patochada nf blunder, bloomer (fam).

patojo 1 adj (SAm) having deformed legs (or feet); waddling; lame. 2 nm, **patoja** nf (CAm, Col) child; sweetheart; (pej) street urchin, ragamuffin.

patología nf pathology.

patológico adj pathological.

patólogo nm pathologist.

patomachera nf (Ven) loud argument.

patoso 1 adj boring, tedious; would-be clever. 2 nm bore; smart-aleck (fam).

patota nf (RPl) street gang, mob of young thugs.

patotero nm (RPl) rowdy, young thug.

patraña nf story, fib; hoax; long involved story.

patraquear [1a] vt (Chi) object to steal; person to hold up, attack.

patraquero nm (Chi) thief; holdup man.

patria nf native land, mother country; fatherland; — **adoptiva** country of adoption; — **chica** home town, home area; **madre** — mother country; **luchar por la** — to fight for one's country; see **merecer**.
patriada nf (RPl) rising, revolt.
patriarca nm patriarch.
patriarcado nm patriarchy.
patriarcal adj patriarchal.
Patricia f Patricia.
Patricio m Patrick.
patricio 1 adj patrician. **2** nm, **patricia** nf patrician.
patrimonial adj hereditary.
patrimonio nm **(a)** inheritance.
  (b) (fig) heritage; birthright; **el — artístico de la nación** our national art heritage, the national art treasures; **nuestro — forestal** our national stock of trees, the forestry resources we have inherited.
patrio adj **(a)** native, home (attr); **el suelo** — one's native land, one's native soil. **(b)** (Law) power etc paternal.
patriota 1 nmf patriot. **2** nm (CAm) banana.
patriotería nf ostentatious patriotism, flag-wagging; chauvinism; jingoism.
patriotero 1 adj ostentatiously patriotic; chauvinistic; jingoistic. **2** nm, **patriotera** nf flag-wagger; chauvinist; jingoist.
patrióticamente adv patriotically.
patriótico adj patriotic.
patriotismo nm patriotism.
patrocinador nm, **patrocinadora** nf sponsor, patron(ess).
patrocinar [1a] vt to sponsor, act as patron to; to back, support; **un movimiento patrocinado por . . .** a movement under the auspices of . . . (or under the patronage of).
patrocinio nm sponsorship, patronage; backing, support.
patrón nm **(a)** patron; (Eccl: also **santo** —) patron saint; (of slave) master; (fig) master, boss, chief; (Naut) skipper; (of boarding house etc) landlord.
  (b) (Sew, Tech) pattern; (for measurement etc) standard; — **oro** gold standard; — **picado** stencil.
  (c) (Agr) prop, shore.
  (d) (Agr) stock (for grafting).
patrona nf patron(ess); (Eccl) patron saint; employer, owner; (of boarding house etc) landlady.
patronal adj **(a)** **organización** — employers' organization, owners' organization; **la clase** — management, the managerial class; **cerrado por acto** — closed by the employers, closed by the owners (or management).
  (b) (Eccl) of a patron saint.
patronato nm **(a)** (act) patronage; sponsorship; **bajo el — de** under the auspices of, under the patronage of.
  (b) (Comm, Fin) employers' association, owners' organization; (Pol) the owners (as a class), management; **el — francés** (loosely) French industrialists, French capitalism.
  (c) board of trustees, board of management; **el — de turismo** the tourist board, the tourist organization.
patronímico 1 adj patronymic. **2** nm patronymic.
patronizar [1a] vt (SAm: angl) to patronize.
patrono nm patron; sponsor; protector, supporter; (Eccl) patron saint; (Comm, Fin) owner, employer.
patrulla nf patrol.
patrullar [1a] **1** vt to patrol, police. **2** vi to patrol.
patrullero nm patrol boat.
patucho adj (Ec) short, squat.
patudo nm (Per): **el** — the devil.
patueco adj (CAm) = **patojo**.
patulea nf (fam) mob, rabble.
patuleco adj (SAm), **patulejo** adj (Chi), **patuleque** adj (Cu) = **patojo**, **patituerto**.
patullar [1a] vi **(a)** to trample about, stamp around. **(b)** to bustle about, keep very busy, be always on the go. **(c)** to chat.
paturro adj (Col, Chi) chubby, plump; squat.
paulatinamente adv gradually, slowly.
paulatino adj gradual, slow.
paulina nf (fam) **(a)** telling-off. **(b)** poison-pen letter.
Paulo m Paul.
pauperismo nm pauperism.
paupérrimo adj very poor, terribly poor.
pausa nf **(a)** pause; break, respite; interruption; (Mus) rest. **(b)** **con** — slowly, deliberately.
pausadamente adv slowly, deliberately.
pausado adj slow, deliberate.
pausar [1a] **1** vt to slow down; to interrupt. **2** vi to go slow.

pauta nf **(a)** line, guide line.
  (b) ruler.
  (c) (fig) guide, guide lines, model; standard, norm; outline, plan, key; **dar** (or **marcar**) **la** — to set a standard, lay down a norm; **servir de — a** to act as a model for.
pautado adj: **papel** — ruled paper.
pautar [1a] vt **(a)** paper to rule. **(b)** (fig: esp CAm) to establish a norm for, lay down a pattern for, give directions for.
pava nf **(a)** (Orn) turkey (hen); — **real** peahen; **pelar la** — (fam: of lovers) to talk, whisper sweet nothings, canoodle (sl).
  (b) (Arg, Bol, Per, Urug) kettle; teapot; pot for making maté.
  (c) (Col, Ec, PR, Ven) broad-brimmed straw hat.
  (d) (Col, CR) fringe.
  (e) (Chi, Mex) chamber pot.
  (f) (Bol, Chi, Per) coarse banter; tasteless joke; **hacer la** — **a** to play a joke on.
  (g) (Ec, Pan) fag end.
  (h) (fam) **es una** — she's a dull person.
pavada nf (RPl) **(a)** silly thing; silliness, stupidity.
  (b) triviality; very small amount.
pavear [1a] **1** vt **(a)** (Col) to kill treacherously.
  (b) (Chi, Per) to play a joke on.
  2 vi **(a)** (Chi, RPl) to act the fool, do silly things.
  (b) (Arg, Chi) = **pelar la pava**.
  (c) (Ec, Pan) to play truant; (PR) to malinger, slack.
pavería nf (Chi, RPl) silliness, stupidity.
pavero nm, **pavera** nf (Chi, Per) practical joker.
pavimentar [1a] vt to pave; to floor.
pavimento nm pavement, paving; (inside house) flooring.
pavisoso adj (fam), **pavitonto** adj (fam) nice but a bit dull.
pavo nm **(a)** (Orn) turkey (cock); — **real** peacock.
  (b) **comer** — (fam) to be a wallflower (at a dance); (SAm) to be disappointed; to get embarrassed.
  (c) (fam) silly thing, idiot; **¡no seas** —! don't be silly!
  (d) (sl) 5 pesetas, one duro.
  (e) **ponerse hecho un** —, **subirse a uno el** — to blush like a lobster; **tener mucho** — to blush a lot.
  (f) (Col) large kite.
  (g) (Col) big shot (fam); evil-looking person.
  (h) (SAm) **ir de** — (on bus etc) to travel free, travel without paying one's fare.
  (i) (Ant) telling-off.
pavón nm **(a)** (Orn) peacock. **(b)** (Tech) bluing, bronzing.
pavonearse [1a] vr to swagger, strut (about); to swank, show off.
pavoneo nm swagger(ing), strutting; swanking (fam), showing-off.
pavor nm dread, terror.
pavorosamente adv frighteningly, terrifyingly.
pavoroso adj dreadful, frightening, terrifying.
pavoso adj (Ven) unlucky; that brings bad luck.
payacate nm (Mex) handkerchief.
payada nf (Chi, RPl) extemporary song (of gaucho minstrel); — **de contrapunto** contest between two payadores.
payador nm (Chi, RPl) gaucho minstrel, popular musician (poet and guitarist).
payar [1a] vi (Chi, RPl) to improvise songs to a guitar accompaniment.
payasada nf clownish trick, stunt; (pej) ridiculous thing (to do); —**s** clowning, tomfoolery; (Theat etc) slapstick, knockabout humour.
payasear [1a] vi (SAm) to clown, do clownish things.
payaso nm clown (also fig).
payés nm (Catalonia, Balearics) peasant farmer.
payo 1 adj **(a)** (Arg) albino. **(b)** (Mex) rustic, simple. **(c)** (Mex) dress etc loud, flashy, tasteless. **2** nm (in gipsy speech) non-gipsy.
payuelas nfpl chickenpox.
paz nf **(a)** peace; peacefulness, tranquility; **¡a la — de Dios!** God be with you!; **en — y en guerra** in peace and war, in peacetime and wartime; **no dar — a** to give no rest (or respite to); **no dar — a la lengua** to keep on and on; **dejar a uno en** — to leave someone alone, leave someone in peace; **¡déjame en** —! leave me alone!; **descansar en** — to rest in peace; **su madre, que en** — **descanse**, lo decía her mother (God rest her soul) used to say so; **estar en** — to be at peace; (fig) to be even, be quits, be all square (con with); **¡haya** —! stop it!, that's enough!; **mantener la** — to keep the peace; **¡aquí** — **y después gloria!** and that's that!, and Bob's your uncle! (fam).

(b) peace, peace treaty; **la — de los Pirineos** the Peace of the Pyrenees (1659); **hacer las paces** to make peace, (*fig*) to make it up.
pazguato *adj* (a) simple, stupid. (b) prudish.
pe: de — a pa from A to Z, from beginning to end.
peaje *nm* toll.
peal *nm* (*SAm*) lasso.
pealar [1a] *vt* (*SAm*) to lasso.
peana *nf* stand, pedestal, base.
peatón *nm* pedestrian, person on foot; walker.
pebete 1 *nm* (a) joss stick. (b) (*Mil*) fuse. (c) (*fam*) small object. **2** *nm*, **pebeta** *nf* (*RPl*) kid (*fam*), child; short person.
peca *nf* freckle.
pecado *nm* sin; **— capital, — grave, — mortal** mortal sin; **— de comisión** sin of commission; **— nefando** sodomy; **— original** original sin; **— venial** venial sin; **por mis —s** for my sins; **sería un — no aprovecharlo** it would be a crime (*or* sin, pity) not to make use of it.
pecador 1 *adj* sinful, sinning. **2** *nm*, **pecadora** *nf* sinner.
pecaminoso *adj* sinful.
pecar [1g] *vi* (a) (*Eccl*) to sin; (*fig*) to err, go astray; **si he pecado en esto, ha sido por . . .** if I have been at fault in this, it has been because . . .; **si me lo pones delante, acabaré pecando** if you put temptation in front of me, I shall fall.
(b) (*fig*) **— de + adj** to be too + *adj*; **peca de generoso** he is too generous, he is excessively generous; **nunca se peca por demasiado cuidado** one can't be too careful; **peca por exceso de confianza** he is too confident, he errs on the side of overconfidence.
pececillos *nmpl* (*Fish*) fry.
pecera *nf* fishbowl, fishtank.
pecios *nmpl* flotsam, wreckage.
pécora *nf* (*esp mala —*) bitch; loose woman, whore.
pecoso *adj* freckled.
pecotra *nf* (*Chi*: *Anat*) bump, swelling; (*on wood*) knot.
pectina *nf* pectin.
pectoral 1 *adj* pectoral. **2** *nm* (*Eccl*) pectoral cross.
pecuaca *nf* (*Col, Ec, Ven*) = **pecueca**.
pecuario *adj* cattle (*attr*).
pecueca *nf* (*Col, Ec, Ven*) hoof; (*hum*) smell of feet.
peculado *nm* peculation.
peculiar *adj* special, peculiar; typical, characteristic.
peculiaridad *nf* peculiarity; special feature, characteristic.
peculio *nm* one's own money; modest savings.
pecunia *nf* (*fam*) brass (*sl*), cash.
pecuniario *adj* pecuniary, money (*attr*).
pecha *nf* (*Arg, Chi*), **pechada** *nf* (*SAm*) push, shove.
pechar¹ [1a] *vti* to pay (as a tax).
pechar² [1a] *vt* (a) (*SAm*) to push, shove. (b) (*SAm*) **— a uno** to touch someone for a loan (*sl*). (c) (*Chi*) to collar (*fam*), grab.
pechazo *nm* (*SAm*) push, shove; (*fig*) bold act, unprincipled deed; (*fam*) touch (for a loan: *sl*).
pechblenda *nf* pitchblende.
peche (*CAm*) **1** *adj* skinny, weak. **2** *nm* child.
pechera *nf* (a) shirt front; (*of dress*) front, bosom; (*Mil etc*) chest protector; **— postiza** dicky. (b) (*Anat*: *hum*) (big) bosom. (c) (*Chi*: *Tech*) apron.
pechero¹ *nm* (*Hist*) commoner, plebeian.
pechero² *nm* (*Sew*) front (*of dress*); bib.
pechicato *adj* (*Cu*) = **pichicato**.
pecho¹ *nm* (a) (*Anat*) chest; **de — plano** flat-chested; **a — descubierto** unarmed, defenceless; (*fig*) openly, frankly; **dar el —** to face things squarely; **estar de —s sobre una barandilla** to be leaning on a railing; **gritar a todo —** (*Col, PR*) to shout at the top of one's voice; **quedarse con algo entre — y espalda** to keep something back; to have something on one's mind; **sacar el —** to thrust one's chest out, draw oneself up.
(b) (*woman's*) breast; **los —s** the breasts, the bosom, the bust; **dar el — a** to feed, suckle, nurse.
(c) (*fig*) heart, breast; **abrir** (*or* **descubrir**) **su — a uno** to unbosom oneself to someone; **no le cabía en el —** he just had to talk about it; he was bursting with happiness; **tomar algo a —** to take something to heart.
(d) (*fig*) courage, spirit; **¡— al agua!** courage!
(e) (*Geog*) slope, gradient.
pecho² *nm* (*Hist*) tax, tribute.
pechoño *adj* (*Bol, Chi*) sanctimonious.
pechuga *nf* (*of chicken etc*) breast; (*hum*: *woman's*) bosom; cleavage.
(b) (*Geog*) slope, hill.

(c) (*SAm*) sangfroid; (*pej*) nerve, insolence.
(d) (*Ec, Pan, Per*) abuse of trust.
(e) (*Guat, Hond, Nic, Pan*) trouble, annoyance.
pechugón 1 *adj* (a) (*Arg, Mex, PR*) big-bosomed.
(b) (*SAm*) shameless, brazen, insolent; sponging (*fam*), parasitical; on the make (*fam*).
(c) (*Chi*) bold, single-minded.
2 *nm* (*SAm*) shameless individual, impudent person; sponger (*fam*), parasite; go-getter.
pechuguera *nf* (*Bol, Col, Mex*) hoarseness; chest trouble, bronchitis.
pedagogía *nf* pedagogy.
pedagógico *adj* pedagogic(al).
pedagogo *nm* teacher; educator; (*pej*) pedagogue.
pedal *nm* pedal; **— de acelerador** accelerator (pedal); **— de embrague** clutch (pedal); **— de freno** footbrake, brake (pedal); **— dulce, — piano, — suave** (*Mus*) soft pedal; **— fuerte** (*Mus*) loud pedal.
pedalear [1a] *vi* to pedal; **— en agua** to tread water.
pedante 1 *adj* pedantic. **2** *nm* pedant.
pedantería *nf* pedantry.
pedantescamente *adv* pedantically.
pedantesco *adj* pedantic.
pedazo *nm* (a) piece, bit; scrap; morsel; **un — de papel** a piece of paper; **un — de pan** a bit of bread, a scrap of bread; **es un — de pan** (*fig*) he's a terribly nice person; **trabaja por un — de pan** he works for a mere pittance; **hacer algo a —s** to do something in pieces, do something piecemeal; **hacer —s** to break to pieces, tear (*or* pull) to pieces; to shatter, smash; **se hizo —s** it fell to pieces, it came apart; it broke up; it shattered, it smashed (itself); **estoy hecho —s** I'm worn out.
(b) (*fig*) **— del alma, — de las entrañas, — del corazón** one's darling, the apple of one's eye; (*in direct address*) my darling; **— de animal** blockhead; **¡— de animal!, ¡— de bruto!** you idiot!; you beast!
pederasta *nm* pederast.
pederastia *nf* pederasty.
pedernal *nm* flint; **como un —** (*fig*) of flint, flinty.
pederse [2a] *vr* (*tabu*) to fart (*tabu*).
pedestal *nm* pedestal, stand, base.
pedestre *adj* (a) *traveller etc* on foot; walking. (b) (*fig*) pedestrian.
pedestrismo *nm* walking (*as a sport*).
pediatra *nmf* paediatrician.
pediatría *nf* paediatrics.
pedicura *nf* chiropody.
pedicuro *nm* chiropodist.
pedidera *nf* (*CAm, Col, Ec, Ven*) = **petición**.
pedido *nm* (*Comm*) order; **— de ensayo** trial order; **— de repetición** repeat order; **a — on** request; **a — de** at the request of.
pedigüeño *adj* insistent, importunate; demanding.
pedilón 1 *adj* (*SAm*) = **pedigüeño**. **2** *nm* (*SAm*) pest, nuisance.
pedimento *nm* petition; (*Law*) claim, bill.
pedir [3l] **1** *vt* (a) to ask for, request; *meal* to order; (*Comm*) to order (*a from*); **— algo a uno** to ask someone for something; **— la paz** to sue for peace; **— que . . .** to ask that . . .; **me pidió que cerrara la puerta** he asked me to shut the door; **pidió que se volviera a estudiar la cuestión** he asked that the matter should be studied afresh; **el pescado es tal que no hay más que —** the fish is as good as it could possibly be.
(b) (*Comm*) *price* to ask; **¿cuánto piden por él?** how much are they asking for it?
(c) **— a una joven** to ask for a girl's hand in marriage; **fue anoche a —la a su padre** he went last night to ask for permission to marry the girl.
(d) (*Law*) to file a claim against.
(e) (*fig*) to need, demand, require; to cry out for; **la casa está pidiendo una mano de pintura** the house is crying out for a dab of paint; **ese color pide una cortina azul** that colour needs a blue curtain to go with it; **el triunfo pide que bebamos algo** the victory demands to be celebrated with a drink.
2 *vi* (a) to ask.
(b) (*also* **— por Dios**) to beg.
(c) *see* **boca** (a).
pedo *nm* (*tabu*), **pedorrera** *nf* (*tabu*) fart (*tabu*).
pedorrero *adj* (*tabu*) given to farting (*tabu*), windy.
pedrada *nf* (a) throw of a stone; hit (*or* blow) from a stone; **matar a uno a —s** to stone someone to death; **pegar una — a uno** to throw a stone at someone.
(b) (*fig*) wounding remark, snide remark, dig.
(c) **la cosa le sentó como una —** he took it very ill, the affair went down very badly with him; **me sienta como una — tener que irme** I don't in the

least want to go; **venir como — en ojo de boticario** to come just right, be just what the doctor ordered.

pedrea nf (a) stone-throwing, fight with stones. (b) (Meteorol) hailstorm. (c) small prizes in the lottery.

pedregal nm stony place, rocky ground.

pedregón nm (SAm) big stone, rock, boulder.

pedregoso adj stony, rocky.

pedregullo nm (RPl, Ven) crushed stone, grit; small loose stones.

pedrejón nm big stone, rock, boulder.

pedrera nf stone quarry.

pedrería nf precious stones, jewels.

pedrero nm (a) quarryman, stone cutter. (b) (CAm, Col, Chi) = **pedregal**.

pedrisco nm (a) shower of stones; (Meteorol) hailstorm. (b) heap of stones.

Pedro m Peter; **entrar como — por su casa** to come in as if one owned the place.

pedrusco nm (a) rough stone; piece of stone, lump of stone. (b) (Meteorol) hailstorm; hailstones. (c) (SAm) = **pedregal**.

pedúnculo nm stem, stalk.

peerse [2a] vr = **pederse**.

pega nf (a) (act) sticking.
(b) beating; beating-up.
(c) practical joke; hoax, trick.
(d) snag, difficulty; **todo son —s** there's nothing but problems; **poner —s** to raise objections; to make trouble.
(e) searching question; catch question, trick question.
(f) **de —** false, dud; fake, sham, bogus; **un billete de —** a dud banknote.
(g) (Cu, Chi) job.
(h) (Cu) birdlime.
(i) (Chi: of disease) infectious period.
(j) (Chi) **estar en la —** to be at one's best.

pegada nf (Arg) (a) fib, lie. (b) piece of luck.

pegadillo nm (Ec) lace.

pegadizo 1 adj (a) sticky.
(b) (Med) infectious, catching.
(c) (Mus) tune catchy.
(d) sham, imitation.
(e) person parasitic, sponging (fam).
2 nm sponger (fam), hanger-on.

pegado 1 adj (fig) **dejar a uno —** to leave someone nonplussed; **estar —** to have no idea, not have a clue; **quedarse —** to be bewildered, be nonplussed.
2 nm patch, sticking plaster.

pegadura nf (Col, Ec) practical joke.

pegajoso adj (a) sticky, adhesive; viscous.
(b) (Med) infectious, catching; (fig) contagious; tempting.
(c) person over-sweet; sloppy, cloying; too free with one's hands.

pegamento nm gum, sticky stuff; **— de caucho** (Aut etc) rubber solution.

pegar [1h] 1 vt (a) to stick (on, together, up); to glue, gum, paste; poster to post, stick up; (Sew) to sew (on), fasten (on); parts to join, fix together; **— un sello** to stick a stamp on; **— una estantería a una pared** to put a set of shelves against a wall; **— una silla a una pared** to move a chair up against a wall.
(b) (Med) disease to give, infect with; idea etc to give, communicate (a to).
(c) blow to give, hit, deal; ball to hit; person to hit, strike; to smack, slap; **dicen que pega a su mujer** they say he knocks his wife about; **es un crimen — a los niños** it's a crime to hit (or smack) children; **"pegad fuerte a Eslobodia"** (slogan) "hit Slobodia hard"; **hazlo o te pego** do it or I'll bash you (fam).
(d) (fam) **— un grito** to let out a yell; **— un puntapié a uno** to give someone a kick; **— un salto** to jump (with fright etc); see **susto, fuego** etc.
(e) (SAm) **—la** to be lucky; to manage it, get what one wants; to make a hit (con with).
(f) (Mex) to tie, fasten (down); horse etc to hitch up.
(g) (Ven) work to start.
2 vi (a) to stick, adhere; see **cola**.
(b) **— en** to touch; **el piano pega en la pared** the piano is touching the wall.
(c) (Bot) to take root; (of remedy) to take; (of fire) to catch.
(d) **— con uno** to run into someone.
(e) (of colours etc) to match, go together; **— con** to match, go with; **ese sombrero no pega con el abrigo** that hat doesn't go with the coat.
(f) to hit; to beat; **— en** to hit, strike (against); **la flecha pegó en el blanco** the arrow hit the target;

pegaba con un palo en la puerta he was hitting (or pounding on) the door with a stick; **las ramas pegan en los cristales** the branches beat against the windows.
(g) (of sun) to strike hot; **a estas horas el sol pega fuerte** the sun strikes very hot at this time; **el sol pega en esta ventana** the sun comes (or shines) in through this window.
3 **pegarse** vr (a) to stick.
(b) (2 persons) to hit each other, fight.
(c) **— a uno** to stick to someone, attach oneself to someone; **— a una reunión** to intrude on a meeting, go to a meeting uninvited.
(d) (Med) to be catching.
(e) (Cook) to catch, burn.
(f) (fam) **ella se la pega a su marido** she's deceiving her husband, she's unfaithful to her husband.
(g) **— un tiro** to shoot oneself; **se pega una vida de millonario** (fam) he lives the life of Riley, he has a whale of a time (see also **vida**).

Pegaso m Pegasus.

pegativo adj (Chi, Hond) sticky.

pegoste nm (CAm, Col, Mex, Ven) sticking plaster.

pegote nm (a) sticking plaster; (fig) patch, ugly mend, botch.
(b) (Cook: fam) sticky mess, sticky lump.
(c) (fam) botch, clumsy job.
(d) (fam) sponger (fam), hanger-on.

pegotear [1a] vi (fam) to sponge (fam), cadge.

peina nf ornamental comb.

peinada nf combing; **darse una —** to comb one's hair, have a brush up.

peinado 1 adj (a) **bien —** well combed; neat, well-groomed.
(b) (fig) foppish, over elegant, overdressed; affected, overdone.
2 nm hairdo; coiffure, hair style.

peinador nm (a) hairdresser. (b) peignoir, dressing gown. (c) (SAm) dressing table.

peinadora nf hairdresser.

peinadura nf (a) combing. (b) **—s** combings.

peinar [1a] 1 vt (a) hair to comb; to do, arrange, style; horse, skin to dress.
(b) (SAm) rock to cut.
(c) (Arg) to flatter.
2 **peinarse** vr to comb one's hair, do one's hair; **— a la griega** to do one's hair in the Greek style.

peine nm comb; **¡ya pareció el —!** so that was it!

peinecillo nm fine comb.

peineta nf ornamental comb.

peinilla nf (Col, Ven) machete.

peje 1 adj (Mex) stupid. 2 nm (a) fish. (b) (fam) sly fellow, twister (fam).

pejiguera nf (fam) bother, nuisance.

Pekín Peking.

pela nf (a) peeling. (b) (sl) one peseta. (c) (SAm) beating. (d) (Mex) slog, hard work.

pelada nf (a) (SAm) haircut.
(b) (Chi, RPl) bald head; head of close-cropped hair.
(c) (Col, Ec, Guat, Pan, Ven) blunder.
(d) (Cu, Chi, Ec) **la —** death.
(e) (Mex) **la —** the plain truth.

peladar nm (Arg, Mex) bare land, wasteland.

peladera nf (CAm, Mex) (a) gossip, backbiting. (b) = **peladar**.

peladero nm (CAm, Col, Chi, Mex) = **pelador**.

peladez nf (a) (Col) poverty. (b) (Mex) rudeness.

pelado 1 adj (a) head etc shorn; hairless; trunk etc bare, smooth; bone clean; apple peeled; field etc treeless, bare; countryside bleak.
(b) (fig) bare; **cobra el sueldo —** he gets just the bare salary; **el cinco mil —** exactly five thousand; five thousand as a round number.
(c) (SAm) poor; broke (fam), penniless.
(d) (Mex) coarse, rude.
(e) (CAm, PR) impudent; barefaced.
2 nm (a) bare patch.
(b) poor man, member of the lowest class; (fig) poor devil, wretch.
(c) (Mex) fellow, chap (fam).
(d) (Bol, Col, Pan) child, baby.

peladura nf (a) (act) peeling. (b) bare patch. (c) **—s** peel, peelings.

pelafustán nm, **pelafustana** nf layabout, good-for-nothing.

pelagallos nm, pl **pelagallos** = **pelagatos**.

pelagatos nm, pl **pelagatos** poor man, member of the lowest class; poor devil, wretch.

pelágico adj pelagic.

pelaje *nm* (a) (*Zool*) fur, coat. (b) = **pelambre** (a). (c) (*fig*) appearance; quality; **y otros de ese —** and others like him, and others of that ilk.

pelambre *nm* (a) thick hair, long hair, mop of hair; unkempt hair. (b) fur, fleece (*cut from animal*). (c) bare patch. (d) (*Chi*) gossip, slander.

pelambrera *nf* = **pelambre** (a).

pelanas *nm, pl* **pelanas** = **pelado** 2 (b).

pelar [1a] **1** *vt* (a) to cut the hair of, shear; *dead animal* to flay, skin; *fowl* to pluck; *fruit* to peel, skin, take the skin off; *potatoes etc* to peel; *peas etc* to shell.
(b) (*fam*) to blacken, slander, speak ill of; to criticize.
(c) (*fam: Cards etc*) to fleece, clean out (*sl*).
(d) (*SAm*) to beat.
2 *vi*: **hace un frío que pela** it's bitterly cold.
3 pelarse *vr* (a) to peel off.
(b) (*person*) to lose one's hair; **voy a pelarme** I'm going to get my hair cut.
(c) **—las por algo** (*fam*) to crave (for) something; **—las por + infin** (*fam*) to crave to + *infin*, long to + *infin*.
(d) (*fam*) **corre que se las pela** he runs like nobody's business (*fam*).

pelazón *nf* (*CAm, Mex*) (a) gossip, backbiting. (b) chronic poverty.

peldaño *nm* step, stair; (*of ladder*) rung.

pelea *nf* (a) fight, tussle, scuffle; quarrel, row; **armar una —** to kick up a row, start a fight. (b) **— de gallos** cockfight; **gallo de —** gamecock, fighting cock.

peleador *adj* brawling; combative, quarrelsome.

pelear [1a] **1** *vi* to fight; to scuffle, brawl; (*fig*) to fight, struggle (*por* for); to vie.
2 pelearse *vr* (a) to fight; to scuffle, brawl; to come to blows; **— con uno** to fight someone (*por* for).
(b) (*fig*) to fall out, quarrel (*con* with; *por* about, over); **estamos peleados** (*SAm*) we're at daggers drawn.

pelechar [1a] *vi* (a) to moult, shed its hair; to get new hair.
(b) (*fig*) to regain one's strength, be on the mend; (*RPl, Ven*) to improve one's position, prosper.

pelecho *nm* (*Mex, RPl*) (a) moulted fur; sloughed skin. (b) old clothing.

pelele *nm* (a) guy, dummy, figure of straw; (*fig*) tool, cat's-paw, puppet. (b) (*child's*) rompers.

peleón *adj* pugnacious, aggressive; quarrelsome; argumentative.

peleona *nf* row, set-to (*fam*); brawl.

peleonero *adj* (*SAm*) = **peleón**.

pelero *nm* (a) (*CAm, Chi*) horse blanket. (b) (*Ven*) = **pelambre**.

pelete *nm* = **pelado** 2 (b); **en —** stark naked.

peletería *nf* furrier's, fur shop; (*Cu*) shoe shop.

peletero *nm* furrier.

peliagudo *adj* *subject* tricky, ticklish.

pelicano *adj* grey-haired.

pelícano *nm* pelican.

pelicorto *adj* short-haired.

película *nf* (a) film; thin covering.
(b) (*Cine*) film, movie (*US*), motion picture (*US*); **— en colores** colour film; **— de dibujos (animados)** cartoon film; **— estereofónica** stereophonic film; **— muda** silent film; **— sonora** talkie.
(c) (*Phot*) film; roll of film, reel of film.
(d) (*Ant*) silly remark; row, rumpus (*fam*).

peliculero 1 *adj* film (*attr*), cine (*attr*), movie (*US attr*). **2** *nm* film maker; scenario writer; film actor.

peligrar [1a] *vi* to be in danger; **— de + infin** to be in danger of + *ger*.

peligro *nm* danger, peril; risk; menace, threat; **"— de muerte"** (*notice*) "danger"; **con — de la vida** at the risk of one's life; **estar en —** to be in danger; to be at stake; **estar fuera de —** to be out of danger; **correr —** to be in danger; to run a risk; **correr — de + infin** to run the risk of + *ger*; **poner algo en —** to endanger something; **estar enfermo de —** to be seriously ill, be dangerously ill.

peligrosamente *adv* dangerously; riskily.

peligrosidad *nf* danger; riskiness.

peligroso *adj* dangerous; risky; *wound etc* ugly, nasty.

pelillo *nm* slight annoyance; triviality; **echar —s a la mar** to make it up, bury the hatchet; **no se para en —s** he doesn't stick at trifles, he won't let a little thing like that deter him.

pelinegro *adj* black-haired.

pelirrojo *adj* red-haired, red-headed; **la pequeña pelirroja** the little redhead.

pelirubio *adj* fair-haired.

pelma 1 *nmf* (*fam*) bore; **¡no seas —!** don't be such a bore!, don't go on about it! **2** *nm* lump, solid mass.

pelmazo *nm* = **pelma** 1 *and* 2.

pelo *nm* (a) hair; (*of beard, moustache*) whisker; (*of animal*) hair, fur, coat; (*of corn*) beard; (*of bird, fruit*) down; (*of carpet, cloth*) nap, pile; (*Tech*) fibre, filament, strand; (*in jewel*) flaw; (*of watch*) hairspring; **un — rubio** a blonde hair; **tiene — rubio** she has blonde hair; **— de camello** camel-hair, camel's hair (*US*); **dos caballos del mismo —** two horses of the same colour; **cortarse el —** to have one's hair cut; **hacer el — a una** to do someone's hair.
(b) (*idioms etc*) **a —** bareheaded, hatless; **a medios —s** (*fam*) half-seas over; **al —** just right; **venir al —** to come just right, be exactly what one needs; **con (sus) —s y señales** with full details, with chapter and verse; **de medio —** person of no social standing, socially unimportant; *thing* mediocre; **hombre de — en pecho** brave man; real man, he-man (*fam*), tough guy; (*pej*) hard-hearted man; **en —** bareback; (*fam*) naked; **por los —s** by the skin of one's teeth; **escaparse por un —** to have a narrow escape, have a close shave; **pasó el examen por los —s** he scraped through the exam; **agarrarse** (*or* **asirse**) **a un —** to clutch at any opportunity; **cortar un — en el aire** (*fig*) to be pretty smart; **dar a uno para el —** to knock someone silly; (*in argument*) to flatten someone; to dress someone down; **estuvo en un — que lo perdiéramos** we very nearly lost it; **no se mueve un — de aire** (*or* **viento**) there isn't a breath of air stirring; **se me pusieron los —s de punta** my hair stood on end; **soltarse el —** to burst out, drop all restraint; **tener el — de la dehesa** to betray one's rustic (*or* humble) origins; **no tiene — de tonto** he's no fool; **no tener —s en la lengua** to be outspoken, not mince words; to talk nineteen to the dozen; **no tocar un — de la ropa a uno** not to lay a finger on someone; **tomar el — a uno** to pull someone's leg, to rag someone.
(c) (*Tech*) hairline, fine crack.
(d) (*Tech*) fine saw.

pelón 1 *adj* (a) hairless; bald; close-cropped.
(b) (*fam*) poor; broke (*fam*), penniless.
(c) (*Ec*) hairy, long-haired.
2 *nm* (a) (*fam*) = **pelado** 2 (b).
(b) (*SAm*) child, baby.
(c) (*Arg*) smooth-skinned peach.
(d) (*Guat, Mex*) **el —** death.
(e) (*Ven*) blunder.

pelona *nf* (a) baldness. (b) (*fam*) **la —** death.

peloso *adj* hairy.

pelota 1 *nf* (a) ball; (*sl*) nut (*sl*), head; **— base** baseball; **— vasca** pelota; **devolver la — a uno** (*fig*) to turn the tables on someone; **la — sigue en el tejado** (*fig*) the situation is still unresolved.
(b) **en —** stark naked; **dejar a uno en —** to strip someone of all that he has; **estar en —s** (*fam*) to be broke (*fam*).
(c) (*SAm*) ferryboat.
(d) (*Cu, Mex, Nic, Ven*) passion; **tener — por** to have a passion for; to be madly in love with.
(e) (*Cu, Mex, Nic, Ven*) girlfriend, mistress.
2 *nm* (*fam*) = **pelotillero**.

pelotari *nm* pelota player.

pelotear [1a] **1** *vt account* to audit.
2 *vi* (a) to knock (*or* kick) a ball about; (*Tennis*) to knock up (*before a game*).
(b) to bicker, argue.
(c) (*SAm*) to cross by ferry.

peloteo *nm* (*Tennis*) knock-up (*before a game*); rally, long exchange of shots.

pelotera *nf* row, scrap (*fam*), set-to (*fam*).

pelotero *nm* (*SAm*) ball player, sportsman, (*esp*) footballer, baseball player.

pelotilla *nf*: **hacer la — a** (*fam*) to suck up to (*fam*), ingratiate oneself with.

pelotillero (*fam*) **1** *adj* creeping (*sl*), soapy. **2** *nm* toady, creep (*sl*); yes man (*sl*), stooge (*sl*).

pelotón *nm* (a) big ball.
(b) (*of threads etc*) mass, tangle, mat.
(c) (*of people*) knot, crowd.
(d) (*Mil*) squad, party, detachment; **— de ejecución** firing squad.

pelotudo *adj* (*RPl*) good-for-nothing, useless; slack, negligent.

peltre *nm* pewter.

peluca *nf* (a) wig. (b) (*fam*) dressing-down.

peluco *nm* (*sl*) watch.

pelucón 1 *adj* (*Per*) long-haired. **2** *nm* (*Chi*) conservative; (*Ec*) bigwig, big shot (*fam*).

peluche *nm* felt; *see* **oso**.

peludo 1 *adj* hairy, shaggy; *animal* long-haired, shaggy; furry; *beard etc* bushy.
  2 *nm* **(a)** round felt mat.
  (b) (*Arg, Urug*) (species of) armadillo.
  (c) (*Arg, Urug*) **agarrarse un —** to get drunk.
peluquearse [1a] *vr* (*SAm*) to have a haircut.
peluquería *nf* hairdresser's, barber's (shop), barbershop (*US*).
peluquero *nm* **(a)** hairdresser, barber. **(b)** wigmaker.
pelusa *nf* **(a)** (*Bot*) down; (*on face*) down, fuzz; (*of cloth*) fluff; (*under furniture etc*) fluff, dust. **(b)** (*fam*) envy, jealousy.
pelusiento *adj* (*Per, PR*) hairy, shaggy.
pélvico *adj* pelvic.
pelvis *nf* pelvis.
pella *nf* **(a)** ball, pellet, round mass; roll; dollop; (*Cook*) lump of raw lard. **(b)** (*Bot*) head. **(c)** (*fam*) sum of money.
pelleja *nf* **(a)** skin, hide. **(b)** (*fam*) whore. **(c)** (*fam*) thin person.
pellejería *nf* **(a)** skins, hides. **(b)** tannery. **(c)** (*Arg, Chi*) difficulty, jam; setback; **—s** hard work to no avail.
pellejo *nm* **(a)** (*of animal*) skin, hide, pelt; (*of person: esp SAm*) skin; (*Bot*) skin, peel, rind.
  (b) wineskin; (*fam*) drunk (*fam*), toper.
  (c) (*fam*) whore.
  (d) (*fig*) skin, hide; **perder el —** to lose one's life; **no quisiera estar en su —** I wouldn't like to be in his shoes; **quitar el — a uno** to flay someone, criticize someone harshly; **salvar el —** to save one's skin; **no tener más que el —** to be all skin and bones.
pellingajo *nm* (*Col, Chi*) **(a)** floor cloth.
  (b) (*fig*) shabby individual; worthless object.
pellizcar [1g] *vt* to pinch, nip; *food etc* to take a small bit of.
pellizco *nm* **(a)** pinch, nip. **(b)** small bit; **un — de sal** a pinch of salt. **(c)** (*in hat*) pinch, dent.
pellón *nm* (*SAm*) sheepskin (*used as a saddle cushion*).
pena *nf* **(a)** grief, sadness, sorrow; distress; anxiety; regret; ¡**allá —s!** I don't care!, that's not my worry!; **es una —** it's a shame, it's a pity (*que* that); **me dan — verlos así** it grieves me to see them like that; **da — que no vengan más** it's a pity they don't come more often; ¡**qué —!** what a shame!; **merecer la —, valer la —** to be worthwhile; **no merece la —** it's not worth the trouble; **merece la — (de) ir a verlo** it's worth taking the trouble to go and see it, it's worth seeing; **morir de —** to die of a broken heart.
  (b) (*fam*) pain; **tener una —** to have a pain.
  (c) trouble; **—s** hardships; toil; **alma en —** soul in torment; **a duras —s** with great difficulty; (*fig*) hardly, scarcely; **ahorrarse la —** to save oneself trouble; **pasar las —s del purgatorio** (*fig*) to go through purgatory; **con muchas —s llegamos a la cumbre** after much toil we reached the top.
  (d) (*Law*) punishment, penalty; (*Comm*) penalty; **— capital** capital punishment; **— de muerte** death penalty; **— pecuniaria** fine; **bajo — de, so — de** on pain of, on penalty of.
  (e) (*SAm*) bashfulness; shyness, timidity.
  (f) (*Per*) ghost.
penable *adj* punishable.
penacho *nm* **(a)** (*Orn*) tuft, crest; (*on helmet*) plume.
  (b) (*of smoke etc*) plume; wreath; pall. **(c)** (*fig*) pride, arrogance.
penado 1 *adj* = **penoso. 2** *nm* convict.
penal 1 *adj* penal; criminal. **2** *nm* **(a)** prison. **(b)** (*SAm: Sport*) foul (in the penalty area); penalty (kick).
penalidad *nf* **(a)** trouble, hardship. **(b)** (*Law*) penalty, punishment.
penalista *nm* penologist, expert in criminal law.
penalización *nf* penalty; penalization.
penalizar [1f] *vt* (*SAm: angl*) to penalize.
penálty *nm*, *pl* **penálty(e)s, penalties** (*etc*) (*angl*) penalty (kick).
penar [1a] **1** *vt* to penalize; to punish.
  2 *vi* **(a)** to suffer; (*of soul*) to be in torment; **— de amores** to be unhappy in love, go through the pains of love; **ella pena por todos** she takes everybody's sufferings upon herself.
  (b) **— por** to pine for, long for.
  3 penarse *vr* to grieve, mourn.
penca *nf* **(a)** fleshy leaf; main rib of a leaf; (*SAm*) palm leaf; (*Cu*) fan; (*Mex: of knife*) blade.
  (b) **hacerse de —s** to have to be coaxed into doing something.
  (c) (*Col*) **— de hombre** a fine man; **— de casa** a great big house.
  (d) (*SAm*) **agarrar una —** to get drunk.

penco 1 *adj* (*CAm*) rustic; stupid. **2** *nm* **(a)** (*Mex, Nic*) horse. **(b)** (*Col*) **un — de hombre** a fine man.
pendango *adj* (*Cu*) effeminate; (*PR*) cowardly.
pendejada *nf* (*SAm*) **(a)** foolish act; cowardly act.
  (b) foolishness, stupidity; cowardliness.
pendejear [1a] *vi* (*Col, Mex*) to act the fool; to act irresponsibly.
pendejeta *nmf* (*Col*) idiot.
pendejo 1 *adj* **(a)** (*CAm, Mex, Ven*) silly, stupid; irresponsible; contemptible; cowardly.
  (b) (*Col, Per*) alert; cunning.
  2 *nm* (*RPl*) lad, youth; (*pej*) pretentious adolescent.
pendencia *nf* quarrel; fight, brawl; **armar —** to fight, brawl; to stir up trouble.
pendenciero 1 *adj* quarrelsome, argumentative; brawling, given to fighting. **2** *nm* rowdy, lout, tough (*fam*).
pender [2a] *vi* **(a)** to hang (*de, en* from; *sobre* over); to hang down, dangle; to droop.
  (b) (*Law*) to be pending.
  (c) (*fig: of threat etc*) **— sobre** to hang over.
pendiente 1 *adj* **(a)** hanging; **estar —** to be hanging; to hang, dangle.
  (b) (*fig*) *matter* pending, unsettled; *account* outstanding, unpaid.
  (c) (*fig*) **estar — de un cabello** to hang by a thread; **estar — de los labios de uno** to hang on someone's lips (*or* words); **estamos —s de lo que él decida** we are dependent on what he may decide, everything hangs for us on his decision.
  2 *nm* earring; pendant.
  3 *nf* (*Geog*) slope, incline; (*Aut etc*) hill, slope; (*Archit*) pitch.
pendil *nm* (woman's) cloak; **tomar el —** (*fam*) to pack up, clear out.
péndola *nf* **(a)** pen, quill. **(b)** (*of bridge etc*) suspension cable.
pendolear [1a] *vi* **(a)** (*SAm*) to write a lot; (*Arg*) to write neatly. **(b)** (*Mex*) to be good in difficult situations, know how to manage people sensibly.
pendolista *nm* penman, calligrapher.
pendón *nm* **(a)** banner, standard; pennant. **(b)** (*fam*) tall shabby person. **(c)** (*fam*) lazy woman; worthless woman, slut; whore.
pendona *nf* (*fam*) whore.
pendonear [1a] *vi* (*fam*) to loaf around the streets.
pene *nm* penis.
peneque *adj* (*sl*): **estar —** to be pickled (*sl*).
penetrable *adj* penetrable.
penetración *nf* **(a)** (*act*) penetration. **(b)** (*quality*) penetration, sharpness, acuteness; insight.
penetrador *adj* = **penetrante (c)**.
penetrante *adj* **(a)** *wound* deep.
  (b) *weapon* sharp; *cold, wind* biting; *sound* penetrating, piercing; *look* searching; sharp, penetrating; *sight* acute; *irony etc* biting.
  (c) *person, mind* sharp, acute, keen.
penetrar [1a] **1** *vt* **(a)** to penetrate, pierce; to permeate.
  (b) *mystery etc* to fathom, grasp, see the explanation of; *secret* to lay bare, understand; *intention* to see through, grasp; *meaning* to grasp.
  2 *vi* **(a)** to penetrate; to go in; (*of liquid etc*) to sink in, soak in; **— en, — entre, — por** to penetrate; **el cuchillo penetró en la carne** the knife went into (*or* entered, penetrated) the flesh; **penetramos poco en el mar** we did not go far out to sea; **el frío penetra en los huesos** the cold gets right into one's bones.
  (b) (*of person*) to enter, go in; **— en un cuarto** to go into a room.
  (c) (*of emotion etc*) to pierce; **la ingratitud penetró hondamente en su corazón** the ingratitude pierced him to the heart (*or* wounded him deeply).
  3 penetrarse *vr*: **— de (a)** to become imbued with.
  (b) to understand fully, become fully aware of (the significance of).
penga *nf* (*Bol*) bunch of bananas.
penicilina *nf* penicillin.
península *nf* peninsula; **P— Ibérica** Iberian Peninsula.
peninsular *adj* peninsular.
penique *nm* penny.
penitencia *nf* **(a)** (*condition*) penitence.
  (b) (*act, punishment*) penance; **en —** as a penance; **imponer una — a uno** to give someone a penance; **hacer — (Eccl)** to do penance (*por* for); to do something unpleasant; (*fam*) to take potluck.
penitenciado *nm* (*SAm*) convict.
penitencial *adj* penitential.

penitenciar [1b] *vt* to impose a penance on.
penitenciaría *nf* prison, penitentiary (*esp US*).
penitenciario 1 *adj* penitentiary, prison (*attr*). **2** *nm* (*Eccl*) confessor.
penitente 1 *adj* (**a**) (*Eccl*) penitent. (**b**) (*Ec*) silly. **2** *nmf* (*Eccl*) penitent. **3** *nm* (*Arg, Chi*) rock pinnacle, isolated cone of rock; snowman.
penol *nm* yardarm.
penosamente *adv* (**a**) painfully, distressingly. (**b**) laboriously, with difficulty.
penoso *adj* (**a**) painful, distressing. (**b**) arduous, laborious, difficult. (**c**) (*Col, Mex, Ven*) bashful; timid, shy.
pensado *adj* (**a**) **un proyecto poco —** a badly thought-out scheme; **lo tengo bien —** I have thought it over (*or* out) carefully; **tengo — hacerlo mañana** I had formed the intention of doing it tomorrow.
   (**b**) **bien —** well-intentioned; **mal —** *see* **malpensado.**
   (**c**) **en el momento menos —** when least expected; much sooner than one thinks.
pensador *nm* thinker.
pensamiento *nm* (**a**) (*faculty*) thought; **como el —** (*fig*) in a flash.
   (**b**) mind; **acudir** (*or* **venir**) **al —** to come to someone's mind; **no le pasó por el —** it never occurred to him.
   (**c**) (**un —**) thought; **mal —** nasty thought, wicked thought; **el — de Quevedo** Quevedo's thought; **nuestro — sobre este tema** our thinking on this subject; **adivinar los —s de uno** to read someone's thoughts.
   (**d**) idea, intention; **mi — es +** *infin* my idea is to + *infin.*
   (**e**) (*Bot*) pansy.
pensante *adj* thinking.
pensar [1k] **1** *vt* (**a**) *thought etc* to think; **— que . . .** to think that . . .; **cuando menos lo pensamos** when we least expect it; **¿qué piensas de ella?** what do you think of her?, what is your opinion of her?; **dar que — a uno** to give someone food for thought; to give someone pause; **dar que — a la gente** to arouse suspicions, set people thinking; **¡ni —lo!** not a bit of it!
   (**b**) *problem etc* to think over, think out; **lo pensaré** I'll think about it; **esto es para —lo** this needs thinking about; **pensándolo bien** on reflection, after mature consideration.
   (**c**) **— que . . .** to decide that . . ., come to the conclusion that . . .
   (**d**) **— +** *infin* to intend to + *infin*, plan to + *infin*, propose to + *infin.*
   (**e**) *scheme etc* to think up, invent; **¿quién pensó este plan?** who thought this one up?
   2 *vi* (**a**) to think; **— en** to think of, think about; **¿en qué piensas?** what are you thinking about?; **— entre sí, — para sí** to think to oneself; **— sobre** to think about, think over; **sin —** without thinking; rashly; involuntarily; unexpectedly.
   (**b**) **— en** to aim at, aspire to; **piensa en una cátedra** he's aiming at a chair.
pensativamente *adv* thoughtfully, pensively.
pensativo *adj* thoughtful, pensive.
penseque *nm* (*fam*) excuse.
Pensilvania *f* Pennsylvania.
pensión *nf* (**a**) (*Fin*) pension; allowance; **— de retiro** retirement pension; **— vitalicia** annuity.
   (**b**) (*Univ etc*) scholarship, fellowship; travel grant.
   (**c**) boarding house, guest-house, lodging house; (*for students etc*) lodgings.
   (**d**) board and lodging; **— completa** full board, room and all meals.
   (**e**) (*fig*) nuisance; burden.
   (**f**) (*Col, Chi, Mex*) worry, anxiety; regret.
pensionado 1 *nm* boarding school. **2** *nm*, **pensionada** *nf* pensioner.
pensionar [1a] *vt* (**a**) to pension, give a pension to; *student* to give a grant to. (**b**) (*Chi, Ec, Per*) to cause trouble to, make work for; to worry.
pensionista *nmf* (**a**) pensioner, old-age pensioner. (**b**) lodger, paying guest. (**c**) boarder; boarding-school pupil.
pentagonal *adj* pentagonal.
pentágono *nm* pentagon; **el P—** (*Washington*) the Pentagon.
pentagrama *nm* (*Mus*) stave, staff.
pentámetro *nm* pentameter.
Pentateuco *nm* Pentateuch.
pentatlon *nm* pentathlon.
pentatónico *adj* pentatonic; **escala pentatónica** pentatonic scale.

Pentecostés *nm* (*sometimes f*) (**a**) Whitsun, Whitsuntide; **domingo de —** Whit Sunday. (**b**) (*Jewish*) Pentecost.
penúltima *nf* (*Gram*) penult.
penúltimo *adj* penultimate, last but one, next to last.
penumbra *nf* penumbra; half-light, semi-darkness; shadows; **sentado en la —** seated in the shadows.
penuria *nf* shortage, dearth.
peña *nf* (**a**) cliff, crag; **— viva** bare rock, living rock.
   (**b**) group, circle; (*pej*) coterie, clique; **— deportiva** (*Sport*) supporters' club; **forma parte de la —** he's a member of the circle; **hay — en el café los domingos** the group meets in the café on Sundays.
   (**c**) (*Ec, Guat, PR*) deaf person.
   (**d**) (*Chi*) pawnshop; moneylender's.
peñascal *nm* rocky place; rocky hill.
peñasco *nm* (**a**) large rock, boulder. (**b**) rock, crag; pinnacle of rock.
peñascoso *adj* rocky, craggy.
peñón *nm* mass of rock; wall of rock, crag; **el P—** the Rock (of Gibraltar).
peños *nmpl* (*sl*) ivories (*sl*), teeth.
peñusco *nm* (*Arg, PR*) crowd, squash.
peón *nm* (**a**) (*Tech*) unskilled workman; (*Agr, esp SAm*) labourer, farmhand; (*Mex*) apprentice; **— de albañil** building labourer, bricklayer's mate; **— caminero** navvy, roadman, roadmender.
   (**b**) (*Mil: Hist*) infantryman, foot-soldier.
   (**c**) (*Chess*) pawn.
   (**d**) spinning top.
   (**e**) (*Mech*) spindle, shaft, axle.
peonada *nf* (**a**) (*Agr*) day's stint. (**b**) gang of workmen, gang of labourers.
peonaje *nm* labourers (*collectively*), group of labourers.
peonar [1a] *vi* (*Arg*) to work as a labourer.
peonía *nf* peony.
peonza *nf* (**a**) spinning top, whipping top. (**b**) (*fam*) busy little person. (**c**) (*fam*) **ir a —** to go on foot, walk it.
peor *adj and adv* (*comp*) worse; (*superl*) worst; **— que —** worse and worse; **A es — que B** A is worse than B; **Z es el — de todos** Z is the worst of all; **lo — es que . . .** the worst of it is that . . .; **llevar lo —** to get the worst of it; **o si no, será — para Vd** or if you don't, it will be the worse for you; *see* **mal, tanto etc.**
peoría *nf* worsening, deterioration.
Pepa *f pet name for* **Josefa**; **¡viva la —!** as if he (*etc*) cared!, and to blazes with everybody else!; jolly good! (*fam*).
pepa *nf* (**a**) (*SAm*) seed, pip, stone. (**b**) (*SAm*) marble. (**c**) (*Col*) lie; fraud, hoax. (**d**) (*Ec*) rogue.
pepazo *nm* (**a**) (*SAm*) shot, hit, throw; accurate shot. (**b**) (*Col*) **= pepa** (**c**).
Pepe *m pet name for* **José.**
pepe *nm* (**a**) (*Bol, Ven*) fop, toff (*fam*). (**b**) (*Guat, Hond*) feeding bottle.
pepenado *nm*, **pepenada** *nf* (*CAm, Mex*) orphan; foundling.
pepenar [1a] *vt* (**a**) (*CAm, Col, Mex*) to pick up; to search out; to choose; to get, obtain.
   (**b**) (*Mex*) to grab hold of; to go through the pockets of; to steal; *orphan* to take in, bring up.
pepinillo *nm* gherkin.
pepino *nm* cucumber; **no se me da un —, (no) me importa un —** I don't care two hoots (*de* about).
Pepita *f pet name for* **Josefa.**
pepita *nf* (**a**) (*Vet*) pip; **no tener — en la lengua** to be outspoken, not mince words; to talk nineteen to the dozen.
   (**b**) (*Bot*) pip.
   (**c**) (*Min*) nugget.
Pepito *m pet name for* **José.**
pepito *nm* (*Col, Pan, Ven*) fop, toff (*fam*).
pepitoria *nf* (*fig*) hotchpotch, mixture.
pepsina *nf* pepsin.
péptico *adj* peptic.
peptona *nf* peptone.
peque *nmf* (*fam*) kid (*fam*), child.
pequeñez *nf* (**a**) smallness, littleness, small size; shortness; (*of child*) infancy.
   (**b**) (*pej*) pettiness, small-mindedness.
   (**c**) trifle, triviality; **preocuparse por pequeñeces** to worry about trifles.
pequeño *adj* small, little; *number, figure* small, low; (*in stature*) short; **los —s** the children, the kids (*fam*), the little ones; **un castillo en —** a miniature castle; **un negocio en —** a small-scale business.
pequero *nm* (*RPl*) cardsharper.
pequinés *nm* (*dog*) Pekinese.
pera¹ *nf* (**a**) (*Bot*) pear; (*sl*) nut (*sl*), head; **partir —s con uno** to fall out with someone; **eso es pedir —s**

al olmo that's asking the impossible; **poner a uno las —s a cuarto** to tell someone a few home truths. **(b)** goatee; (Chi) chin. **(c)** (of spray, horn etc) bulb. **(d)** (Elec) bulb; switch. **(e)** (sl) **hacerse una —** to masturbate.

pera² adj invar (sl) elegant; classy (fam), posh (fam); **niño —** spoiled upper-class child; **es un pollo —** he's a real toff (fam); **fuimos a un restaurante muy —** we went to a really swish restaurant (sl).

peral nm pear tree.

perca f (Fish) perch.

percal nm, **percala** nf (Mex, Per) percale.

percán nm (Chi) mould.

percance nm **(a)** misfortune, mishap; (in plan etc) setback, hitch; **sufrir un —, tener un —** to have a mishap. **(b)** (Fin) perquisite.

percanque nm (Chi) mould.

percatarse [1a] vr: **— de** to notice, take note of; to heed; to guard against.

percebe nm **(a)** (Zool) barnacle. **(b)** (fam) idiot.

percepción nf **(a)** perception; **— extrasensoria** extrasensory perception. **(b)** notion, idea. **(c)** (Comm, Fin) collection; receipt.

perceptible adj **(a)** perceptible, noticeable, detectable. **(b)** (Comm, Fin) payable, receivable.

perceptiblemente adv perceptibly, noticeably.

perceptivo adj perceptive.

perceptor nm, **perceptora** nf recipient; (of taxes etc) receiver.

percibir [3a] vt **(a)** to perceive, notice, detect; to see, observe; danger etc to sense, scent; **— que ...** to perceive that ..., observe that ... **(b)** (Comm, Fin) salary to earn, receive, get.

percollar [1a] vt (Arg) to acquire illegally; (Bol, Per) to monopolize.

percuchante nm (Ec, Per) fool.

percudir [3a] vt to tarnish, dull; clothing etc to dirty, mess up; complexion to spoil.

percusión nf percussion; **instrumento de —** percussion instrument.

percusor nm, **percutor** nm (Tech) striker, hammer.

percutir [3a] vt to strike, tap.

percha nf **(a)** pole, support; rack; coat stand, hallstand; coat hanger; (Orn) perch; **— de herramientas** toolrack. **(b)** (Col, Ec) elegance, luxury; showiness; **tener —** (Arg) to be smart. **(c)** (Col) new clothes, smart clothing; (Cu) jacket; (SD) suit, dress. **(d)** (Chi) pile. **(e)** (Mex) bunch, crowd (of people).

perchero nm clothes rack, hallstand.

perchudo adj (Col), smart, elegant.

perdedor 1 adj **(a)** team, trick etc losing. **(b)** forgetful, given to losing things. **2** nm, **perdedora** nf loser; **buen —** good loser, good sport.

perder [2g] **1** vt **(a)** (general sense) to lose; **¿dónde lo perdió?** where did you lose it?; **he perdido 5 kilos** I've lost 5 kilos; **he perdido la costumbre** I have got out of the habit (and see **costumbre**). **(b)** effort, time, words etc to waste; chance to miss, lose, waste; train etc to miss; (Law) to lose, forfeit, give up; **no pierde nada** he doesn't miss a thing; **sin — un momento** without wasting a moment. **(c)** to ruin, spoil; **ese vicio le perderá** that vice will be his ruin, that vice will destroy him; **ese error le perdió** that mistake was his undoing. **(d)** (Univ) course to fail. **2** vi **(a)** to lose; **el equipo perdió por 2-5** the team lost 2-5; **salir perdiendo** to lose, be the loser; to lose on a deal; **tener buen —** to be a good loser. **(b)** to decline, deteriorate, go down(hill); to lose influence; **ha perdido mucho en mi estimación** he has gone down a lot in my estimation; **era guapísima, pero ha perdido bastante** she used to be very pretty, but she's deteriorated a bit. **(c)** (of cloth) to fade, discolour. **(d)** **echar a —** food etc to spoil, ruin; chance to waste; **echarse a —** to be spoiled, be ruined; to go downhill. **3 perderse** vr **(a)** to get lost (also fig), lose oneself; to stray; to lose one's way; **se perdieron en el bosque** they got lost in the wood; **se perdió en un mar de contradicciones** he got lost in a mass of contradictions. **(b)** to disappear, be lost (to view); **el tren se perdió en la niebla** the train disappeared into the fog, the train was lost to sight in the fog; **el arroyo**

se pierde en la roca the stream disappears into the rock. **(c)** to be wasted; to go (or run) to waste. **(d)** to be ruined, get spoiled; **con la lluvia se ha perdido la mitad de la cosecha** with so much rain half the crop has been ruined (or lost). **(e)** (Naut) to sink, be wrecked. **(f)** (person) to be ruined; **se perdió por el juego** he was ruined through gambling. **(g)** **— por** to be mad about, long for; **— por + infin** to be mad keen to + infin, long to + infin. **(h)** (SAm) to become a prostitute.

perdición nf perdition (also Rel), undoing, ruin; **fue su —** it was his undoing; **será mi —** it will be the ruin of me.

pérdida nf loss; (of time etc) waste; (Law) forfeiture, loss; **—s** (Fin, Mil etc) losses; (of liquid etc) wastage; **¡no tiene —!** you can't miss!, you can't go wrong!; **vender algo con —** to sell something at a loss.

perdidamente adv: **— enamorado** passionately in love, hopelessly in love.

perdidizo adj: **hacer algo —** to hide something away, deliberately lose something; **hacerse el —** to lose deliberately (in a game); to make oneself scarce, hide oneself away.

perdido 1 adj **(a)** lost; bullet stray; moments idle; spare; **dar algo por —** to give something up for lost; **darse por —** to give oneself up for lost. **(b)** vicious; incorrigible; drinker etc inveterate, hardened. **(c)** **estar — por** to be mad about, be crazy about. **(d)** (SAm) idle; down and out. **2** nm rake, libertine, profligate.

perdidoso adj **(a)** team etc losing. **(b)** easily lost, easily mislaid.

perdigar [1h] vt to half-cook, brown.

perdigón nm **(a)** young partridge. **(b)** pellet; **— zorrero** buckshot; **—es** shot, pellets.

perdiz nf partridge; **— blanca, — nival** ptarmigan.

perdón nm pardon (also Law), forgiveness; mercy; (of sin etc) remission; **¡—!** sorry!, I beg your pardon!; **¡le pido —!** I am so sorry!, do forgive me!; **pedir — a uno** to ask someone's forgiveness, apologize to someone; **con —** if I may, if you don't mind, by your leave; excuse me; **con — de los presentes** present company excepted; **hablando con —** if I may say so, if you'll pardon the expression; **no cabe —** it's inexcusable.

perdonable adj pardonable, excusable.

perdonador adj forgiving.

perdonar [1a] vti **(a)** offence etc, person to pardon (also Law), forgive, excuse; **¡perdone (Vd)!** sorry!, I beg your pardon!; **perdone, pero me parece que ...** excuse me, but I think ...; **perdónanos nuestras deudas** forgive us our trespasses; **Dios le haya perdonado** may God have mercy on him. **(b)** **— la vida a uno** to spare someone's life. **(c)** (from duty etc) to exempt, excuse; **les he perdonado las clases** I have excused them from classes. **(d)** **no — esfuerzo** to spare no effort; **no — ocasión** to miss no chance (de + infin to + infin); **no — medio para + infin** to use all possible means to + infin; **sin — detalle** without omitting a single detail.

perdonavidas nm, pl **perdonavidas** bully, tough (fam), thug.

perdulario 1 adj **(a)** forgetful, given to losing things. **(b)** careless, sloppy, inefficient. **(c)** (pej) vicious, dissolute. **2** nm rake.

perdurable adj lasting, abiding; everlasting.

perdurar [1a] vi to last, endure, survive; to stand, still exist.

perecedero adj perishable; life etc transitory, which must come to an end; person mortal.

perecer [2d] **1** vi **(a)** to perish, die; (hum) to expire; (of object) to shatter; **— ahogado** to drown; to suffocate. **2 perecerse** vr **(a)** **— de risa** to die (of) laughing; **— de envidia** to be dying of jealousy. **(b)** **— por algo** to be dying for, crave; **— por una mujer** to be crazy about a woman; **se perece por los calamares** he's passionately fond of squid; **— por + infin** to long to + infin, be dying to + infin.

peregrinación nf **(a)** long tour, travels; (hum) peregrination. **(b)** (Eccl) pilgrimage; **ir en —** to go on a pilgrimage, make a pilgrimage (a to).

peregrinar [1a] vi **(a)** to go to and fro; to travel extensively (abroad). **(b)** (Eccl) to go on a pilgrimage (a to).

peregrino 1 *adj* **(a)** *person* wandering; travelling; *bird* migratory.

(b) *custom, plant etc* alien, newly introduced; adventitious.

(c) (*fig*) odd, strange, surprising.

(d) (*fig*) *beauty etc* fine, extraordinary, rare; exotic.

2 *nm*, **peregrina** *nf* pilgrim.

perejil *nm* **(a)** (*Bot*) parsley.

(b) (*fam*) —**es** buttons and bows, trimmings, fripperies.

(c) —**es** (*fam*) extra titles, handles (to one's name) (*fam*).

perendengue *nm* trinket, cheap ornament; silly adornment.

perenne *adj* everlasting, constant, perennial; (*Bot*) perennial; **de hoja** — evergreen.

perennemente *adv* everlastingly, constantly, perennially.

perentoriamente *adv* urgently, peremptorily.

perentorio *adj* **(a)** urgent, peremptory. **(b)** *term* set, fixed.

pereza *nf* **(a)** sloth, laziness; slowness; idleness. **(b)** (*Ven*) deck chair. **(c)** (*Col*) nuisance.

perezosa *nf* (*Arg, Per*) deck chair.

perezosamente *adv* lazily; slowly; sluggishly.

perezoso 1 *adj* slothful, lazy; slow, sluggish, idle. **2** *nm* **(a)** (*Zool*) sloth. **(b)** (*Cu, Mex*) safety pin. **(c)** headrest.

perfección *nf* **(a)** perfection; **a la** — to perfection. **(b)** (*act*) completion.

perfeccionamiento *nm* perfection; improvement.

perfeccionar [1a] *vt* **(a)** to perfect; to improve. **(b)** *process etc* to complete, finish.

perfeccionista *nmf* perfectionist.

perfectamente *adv* perfectly; ¡—! precisely!, just so!; of course!

perfectibilidad *nf* perfectibility.

perfectible *adj* perfectible.

perfecto 1 *adj* **(a)** perfect. **(b)** complete, finished; perfected. **2** *nm* (*Gram*) perfect (tense).

pérfidamente *adv* perfidiously, treacherously.

perfidia *nf* perfidy, treachery.

pérfido *adj* perfidious, treacherous.

perfil *nm* **(a)** profile; silhouette, outline; (*Archit, Geol etc*) section, cross section, sectional view; (*Phot*) side view; — **aerodinámico** streamlining; **en** — in profile, from the side.

(b) —**es** (*fig*) features, characteristics.

(c) —**es** (*fig*) social courtesies; finishing touches.

perfilado *adj* well-shaped, well-finished; *face* long; *nose* well-formed, shapely; (*Aer*) streamlined.

perfilar [1a] **1** *vt* **(a)** to outline; (*fig*) to shape, give character to; **son los lectores los que perfilan los periódicos** it is the readers who shape their newspapers.

(b) (*Aer etc*) to streamline.

(c) (*fig*) to put the finishing touches to; to round off, perfect.

2 perfilarse *vr* **(a)** (*person*) to show one's profile, give a side view; (*Taur*) to draw oneself up (and prepare for the kill); (*building etc*) to show in outline, appear in silhouette.

(b) (*fig*) to take shape; to become more definite; **el proyecto se va perfilando** the plan is taking shape.

(c) (*SAm*) to slim, get slim.

(d) (*Arg: Sport*) to dribble and shoot.

perforación *nf* **(a)** perforation; piercing; drilling, boring; punching. **(b)** (*for oil*) drilling; drill, bore.

perforadora *nf* punch; drill; — **neumática** pneumatic drill.

perforar [1a] **1** *vt* to perforate; to pierce; to puncture; *hole* to make, drill, bore; *well* to sink; *card etc* to punch, punch a hole in.

2 *vi* (*for oil etc*) to drill, bore.

performance [per'formans] *nm or f* (*Aut, Mech, Sport etc: angl*) performance.

perfumado *adj* scented; sweet-smelling.

perfumar [1a] *vt* to scent, perfume.

perfume *nm* scent, perfume.

perfumería *nf* perfume shop; perfumery.

pergamino *nm* parchment; **una familia de muchos** —**s** a very blue-blooded family, a very ancient family.

pergenio *nm* **(a)** (*SAm*) small unpleasant person; ragamuffin. **(b)** (*Arg*) bright boy, clever youngster.

pergeñar [1a] *vt* **(a)** to sketch; to do roughly, do in rough; *text etc* to do a draft of, prepare. **(b)** (*fam*) to fix up, arrange.

pergeño *nm* **(a)** aspect, appearance. **(b)** sketch; rough draft. **(c)** (*fam*) arrangement.

pérgola *nf* pergola.

perica *nf* **(a)** (*Col, Pan*) razor, knife; *machete*; short sword. **(b)** (*Col, Ec, Pan*) **agarrar una** — to get drunk.

pericia *nf* skill, skilfulness; expertness, expertise.

pericial *adj*: **testigo** — expert witness.

Perico *m* Pete; — **el de los palotes** anybody, somebody; so-and-so; any Tom, Dick or Harry; **ser p— entre ellas** to be a ladies' man.

perico *nm* **(a)** (*Orn*) parakeet.

(b) wig, toupé.

(c) (*fam*) chamberpot.

(d) (*Col*) coffee with milk.

(e) —**s** (*Col, Ven*) scrambled eggs with fried onions.

pericote *nm* **(a)** (*Arg, Bol, Ec, Per*) mouse. **(b)** (*Arg, Per*) child.

periferia *nf* periphery; (*of town*) outskirts.

periférico *adj* peripheral.

perifollo *nm* **(a)** chervil. **(b)** —**s** (*fig*) buttons and bows, trimmings, fripperies.

perífrasis *nf*, *pl* **perifrasis** periphrasis.

perifrástico *adj* periphrastic.

perilla *nf* pear-shaped ornament, drop; switch; doorknob; goatee; — **de la oreja** lobe of the ear; — **del timbre** bell-push; **venir de** —**s** to come just right, be very welcome, be perfect.

perillán *nm* (*fam*) rogue, rascal; ¡—! (*to child*) you rascal!

perímetro *nm* perimeter.

perinola *nf* teetotum.

periódicamente *adv* periodically.

periodicidad *nf* periodicity; regular recurrence, regular nature.

periódico 1 *adj* periodic(al); (*Math*) recurrent. **2** *nm* newspaper; periodical; — **del domingo** Sunday newspaper; — **de la tarde** evening newspaper.

periodicucho *nm* (*fam: pej*) rag (*fam*).

periodismo *nm* journalism.

periodista *nmf* journalist; (*m*) pressman, newsman, newspaperman.

periodístico *adj* **(a)** journalistic; newspaper (*attr*); **estilo** — journalistic style, journalese. **(b)** *report etc* newsworthy.

período *nm* **(a)** period (*also Med*). **(b)** (*Gram*) sentence, period.

peripatética *nf* (*hum*) whore.

peripatético *adj* peripatetic.

peripecia *nf* vicissitude; sudden change, unforeseen change; —**s** vicissitudes, ups and downs; adventures, incidents.

periplo *nm* journey, tour; wanderings; (*hum*) peregrination.

peripuesto *adj* (*fam*) dressed up, smart; overdressed, dressy; **tan** — all dressed up (to the nines).

periquete *nm* (*fam*): **en un** — in a tick.

periquito *nm* parakeet.

periscopio *nm* periscope.

peristilo *nm* peristyle.

peritaje *nm* **(a)** expert work; report of an expert; specialist's report. **(b)** expert's fee. **(c)** professional training.

perito 1 *adj* skilled, skilful; expert; experienced, seasoned; — **en** skilled in, expert at.

2 *nm* expert; skilled man, qualified man; technician; — **electricista** qualified electrician; — **forense** legal expert; — **en metales** metal expert, specialist in metals.

peritoneo *nm* peritoneum.

peritonitis *nf* peritonitis.

perjudicar [1g] *vt* **(a)** to damage, harm, impair; *chances etc* to damage, prejudice; **me perjudica que digan eso** for them to say that lowers me in the eyes of others.

(b) to be unbecoming to; **ese sombrero le perjudica** that hat does not become her, she doesn't look well in that hat.

perjudicial *adj* harmful, injurious, damaging (*a, para* to); detrimental, prejudicial (*a, para* to).

perjuicio *nm* damage, harm; (*Fin*) financial loss; **en** — **de** to the detriment of; **redundar en** — **de** to be detrimental to, harm; **sin** — **de** without prejudice to; **sufrir grandes** —**s** to suffer great damage.

perjurar [1a] **1** *vi* **(a)** to perjure oneself, commit perjury. **(b)** to swear a lot. **2 perjurarse** *vr* to perjure oneself.

perjurio *nm* perjury.

perjuro 1 *adj* perjured. **2** *nm* perjurer.

perla *nf* **(a)** pearl; — **cultivada** cultivated pearl, cultured pearl; —**s de imitación** imitation pearls.

(b) (*fig*) pearl (*de of, among*), gem; **me está de** —**s, me viene de** —**s** it comes just right; it suits me perfectly; **me parece de** —**s** it all seems splendid to me.

perlático adj paralytic, palsied.

perlesía nf paralysis, palsy.

perlífero adj pearl-bearing; **ostra perlífera** pearl oyster.

perlino adj pearly.

permanecer [2d] vi (a) to stay, remain; **¿cuánto tiempo vas a —?** how long are you staying?
   (b) **— + adj** to go on being + adj, remain + adj; **— indeciso** to remain undecided; **— dormido** to go on sleeping.

permanencia nf (a) permanence. (b) stay.

permanente 1 adj permanent; constant; colour fast; committee, army etc standing.
   2 nf permanent wave, perm (fam); **hacerse una —** to have one's hair permed.

permanentemente adv permanently; constantly.

permanganato nm permanganate.

permeabilidad nf permeability, pervious nature.

permeable adj permeable, pervious (a to).

permisible adj allowable, permissible.

permisionario nm (SAm) official agent, official agency, concessionaire.

permisivo adj permissive.

permiso nm (a) (in general) permission; **con —** if I may; excuse me; **con — de Vds me voy** excuse me but I must go, if you don't mind I must go; **dar su —** to give one's permission; **tener — para + infin** to have permission to + infin.
   (b) (document) permit, licence; **— de conducción, — de conducir, — de conductor** driving licence; **— de entrada** entry permit; **— de exportación** export permit; **— de importación** import permit; **— de salida** exit permit.
   (c) (Mil etc) leave; **— de convalecencia** sick leave; **estar de —** to be on leave.

permitir [3a] **1** vt to permit, allow; to allow of; **— a uno hacer algo** to allow someone to do something; **¿me permite?** may I?, do you mind?; **permítame que le diga que ...** permit me to tell you that ...; **si lo permite el tiempo** weather permitting; **la fábrica permitirá una producción anual de ...** the factory will provide an annual production of ..., the factory will make possible an annual production of ...
   2 permitirse vr (a) to be permitted, be allowed; **eso no se permite** that is not allowed; **si se me permite la expresión** if you'll pardon the expression; so to speak; **no se permite fumar** no smoking, you can't smoke here; **¿se permite fumar?** may I smoke?
   (b) **— algo** to permit oneself something; to (be able to) afford something.

permuta nf barter, exchange; interchange.

permutación nf (a) (Math etc) permutation. (b) = permuta.

permutar [1a] **1** vt (a) (Math etc) to permute.
   (b) to exchange (con with, por for); to interchange (con with); **— algo con uno** to exchange something with someone; **— destinos con uno** to exchange jobs with someone.
   2 vi: **— con uno** to exchange (jobs) with someone, swap with someone.

pernear [1a] vi (a) to shake one's legs; to kick one's legs. (b) to stamp one's foot (with rage). (c) (fam) to hustle, get cracking (fam).

pernera nf trouser leg.

perneta nf: **en —s** bare-legged, with bare legs.

perniabierto adj bow-legged.

pernicioso adj pernicious (also Med); person wicked, evil; insect etc injurious (para to).

pernicorto adj short-legged.

pernil nm (a) (Zool) upper leg, haunch; (Cook) leg.
   (b) trouser leg.

pernio nm hinge.

perno nm bolt.

pernoctar [1a] vi to spend the night, stay for the night.

pero¹ 1 conj (a) but; yet.
   (b) (fam) **una chica guapa, — muy guapa** what you really call a pretty girl, a pretty girl and no mistake; **hizo muy mal, — muy mal** he was wrong, a thousand times wrong; I should jolly well say he was wrong (fam); **— vamos a ver** well let's see; **¡— que muy bien!** jolly good! (fam); **¡— si no tiene coche!** I tell you he hasn't got a car!
   2 nm (a) flaw, defect; snag; **el plan no tiene —** there's nothing wrong with the plan, the plan hasn't any snags; **he encontrado un —** I've found a snag.
   (b) objection; **poner —s a** to raise objections to, find fault with; **el programa tiene dos —s** the programme is open to two objections; **¡no hay — que valga!** there are no buts about it!

pero² nm (Arg, Bol) pear tree.

perogrullada nf platitude, truism.

Pero Grullo: verdad de — platitude, truism.

perol nm pan; (Cu) saucepan; (Chi, Mex) metal pot, pot with legs and handles; (Ven) kitchen utensil; (Ven: fig) piece of junk, worthless object.

perolero nm (Ven) tinsmith; plumber.

peroné nm fibula.

peronista (Arg etc) **1** adj Peronist. **2** nmf Peronist, supporter of Perón.

peroración nf (a) peroration, speech. (b) conclusion of a speech.

perorar [1a] vi to make a speech; (hum) to orate (hum), spout.

perorata nf long-winded speech; violent speech, harangue.

peróxido nm peroxide; **— de hidrógeno** hydrogen peroxide.

perpendicular 1 adj (a) perpendicular (a to).
   (b) at right angles (a to); **el camino es — al río** the road is at right angles to the river.
   2 nf perpendicular; vertical; **salir de la —** to be out of the perpendicular (or vertical).

perpendicularmente adv perpendicularly; vertically.

perpetración nf perpetration.

perpetrador nm, **perpetradora** nf perpetrator.

perpetrar [1a] vt to perpetrate.

perpetuación nf perpetuation.

perpetuamente adv perpetually; everlastingly, ceaselessly.

perpetuar [1e] vt to perpetuate.

perpetuidad nf perpetuity; **a —** in perpetuity, for ever; **condena a —** life sentence, sentence of life imprisonment; **le condenaron a prisión a —** he was sentenced to life imprisonment.

perpetuo adj perpetual; everlasting; ceaseless; exile, sentence etc life (attr); (Bot) everlasting.

Perpiñán Perpignan.

perplejamente adv perplexedly; in a puzzled way; in perplexity.

perplejidad nf (a) perplexity; bewilderment; puzzlement; hesitation. (b) perplexing situation; dilemma.

perplejo adj perplexed; bewildered; puzzled; **me miró —** he looked at me in perplexity, he looked at me in a puzzled way; **dejar a uno —** to perplex someone, puzzle someone; **se quedó — un momento** he looked perplexed for a moment, he hesitated a moment.

perra nf (a) (Zool) bitch; female dog, lady dog (euph).
   (b) (Fin: fam) **— chica** 5-céntimo coin; **— gorda** 10-céntimo coin; **—s** small change; **costó unas —s** it cost a few coppers.
   (c) (fam) tantrum (fam), pet; **el niño cogió una —** the child had a tantrum, the child began to cry violently.
   (d) (fam) mania, crazy idea; **está con la — de un abrigo de pieles** she's got the crazy idea that she must have a fur coat; **le cogió la — de ir a Eslobodia** he got an obsession about going to Slobodia.
   (e) (Chi) old hat; leather water bottle.

perrada nf (a) pack of dogs. (b) (fam) dirty trick.

perraje nm (Col, Ven) pack of dogs.

perramus nm (Bol, RPl) raincoat.

perrera nf (a) kennel; kennels.
   (b) cart in which stray dogs are picked up.
   (c) badly-paid job; drudgery.
   (d) (fam) = perra (c).
   (e) (Cu, Ven) row, shindy.

perrería nf (a) pack of dogs; (fig) gang of villains.
   (b) harsh word, angry word; **decir —s de uno** to say harsh things about someone.
   (c) (fam) dirty trick.

perrillo nm (a) puppy; small (breed of) dog; miniature dog; (sentimentally) doggie. (b) (Mil) trigger.

perrito, perrita nf puppy.

perro 1 nm (a) (Zool) dog; **"— peligroso"** "beware of the dog"; **— afgano** Afghan hound; **— de aguas** spaniel; **— callejero** mongrel; **— cobrador** retriever; **— danés** Great Dane; **— dogo** (angl) bulldog; **— esquimal** husky; **— faldero** lapdog; **— guardián** watchdog; **— del hortelano** dog in the manger; **— de lanas** poodle; **— lebrel** whippet; **— lobo** alsatian; **— marino** dogfish; **— de muestra** pointer, setter; **— pastor** sheepdog; **— pequinés** Pekinese; **— policía** police dog; **— de presa** bulldog; **— raposero** foxhound; **— rastreador, — rastrero** tracker dog; **— (de) San Bernardo** St Bernard; **— tejonero** dachshund; **— de Terranova** Newfoundland dog.
   (b) (idioms) **ser — viejo** to be an old hand; to be an old fox; **tiempo de —s** dirty weather, awful weather (fam); **¡a otro — con ese hueso!** tell that to the marines!; **darse a —s** to get wild; **echar a uno los**

—s encima to persecute someone, keep after someone; **echar una hora a** —s to waste a whole hour, get absolutely nothing done in an hour; **hacer** — **muerto** (*Bol, Per*) to avoid paying; **heder a** — **muerto** to stink to high heaven; **se llevan como** —s **y gatos** they're always squabbling; **meter los** —s **en danza** to set the cat among the pigeons; — **que ladra no muerde,** — **ladrador, poco mordedor** his bark is worse than his bite.

   (c) (*pej*) dog, swine, hound.

   (d) (*Col*) drowsiness.

   2 *adj* (*fam*) awful (*fam*), wretched; **esta perra vida** this wretched life; **he pasado una temporada perra** I've had a ghastly time (*fam*).

perrucho *nm* (*pej*) hound, cur.

perruna *nf* dog biscuit.

perruno *adj* canine, dog (*attr*); *devotion etc* doglike.

persa 1 *adj* Persian. **2** *nmf* Persian. **3** *nm* (*language*) Persian.

persecución *nf* (a) pursuit, hunt, chase; **estar en plena** — to be in full cry. (b) (*Eccl, Pol etc*) persecution.

persecutorio *adj*: **manía persecutoria** persecution mania; **trato** — cruel treatment.

perseguidor *nm*, **perseguidora** *nf* (a) pursuer. (b) (*Eccl, Pol etc*) persecutor.

perseguimiento *nm* pursuit, hunt, chase; **en** — **de** in pursuit of.

perseguir [3d *and* 3I] *vt* (a) *fugitive, prey* to pursue, hunt, chase; to hunt out, hunt down.

   (b) (*fig*) *post, girl etc* to chase after, go after; *aim* to pursue; **la persiguió durante 2 años** he was after her for 2 years, he pursued her for 2 years.

   (c) (*Eccl, Pol etc*) to persecute; (*fig*) to persecute, harass; to pester, annoy; **me persiguieron hasta que dije que sí** they pestered me until I said yes; **le persiguen los remordimientos** he is gnawed by remorse, his conscience pricks him constantly; **le persigue la mala suerte** he is dogged by ill luck.

perseverancia *nf* perseverance, persistence.

perseverante *adj* persevering, persistent.

perseverantemente *adv* perseveringly.

perseverar [1a] *vi* to persevere, keep on, persist; — **en** to persevere in, persist with.

Persia *f* Persia.

persiana *nf* (Venetian) blind; slatted shutter (*also* — **enrollable**).

persignarse [1a] *vr* to cross oneself.

persistencia *nf* persistence.

persistente *adj* persistent.

persistentemente *adv* persistently.

persistir [3a] *vi* to persist (**en** in; **en** + *infin* in + *ger*).

persoga *nf* (*CAm, Mex*) halter (of plaited vegetable fibre.)

persona *nf* person; **20** —s 20 people; **aquellas** —s **que lo deseen** those who wish; **es para animales y no para** —s it's for animals not people; **es buena** — he's a good sort, he's a decent chap (*fam*); **tercera** — third party; (*Gram*) third person; **un pronombre de primera** — a first person pronoun; — **no grata persona** non grata; — **de historia** person with a past, dubious individual; — **jurídica** legal entity; —s **reales** royalty, king and queen; **en** — in person; **in the flesh; en la** — **de** in the person of; **3 caramelos por** — 3 sweets per person, 3 sweets each; **pagaron 2 dólares por** — they paid 2 dollars a head (*or* each).

personaje *nm* (a) personage, important person; celebrity; **ser un** — to be somebody, to be important. (b) (*Lit, Theat etc*) character.

personal 1 *adj* (a) personal.

   (b) *room, seat etc* single, for one person.

   2 *nm* (a) personnel, staff; (*as total*) establishment; (*esp Mil*) force; (*Naut*) crew, complement; — **de tierra** (*Aer*) ground crew, ground staff; **estar falto de** — to be short-handed.

   (b) (*fam*) people; **había exceso de** — **en el cine** there were too many people in the cinema.

personalidad *nf* (a) personality; — **desdoblada** split personality. (b) (*Law*) legal entity.

personalísimo *adj* intensely personal, highly individualistic.

personalismo *nm* (a) personal reference, personal nature (*of attack etc*); **tenemos que proceder sin** —s we must proceed without indulging in personalities (*or* personal attacks).

   (b) selfishness, egoism.

   (c) personal preference, partiality; **obrar sin** —s to act with partiality towards none, act fairly with regard to the persons involved.

personalizar [1f] **1** *vt* to personalize; *virtue etc* to embody, personify. **2** *vi* to make a personal reference. **3 personalizarse** *vr* to become personal.

personalmente *adv* personally.

personarse [1a] *vr* to appear in person; — **en** to present oneself at; to report to; — **en forma** (*Law*) to be officially represented; **el juez se personó en el lugar del accidente** the judge made an official visit to the scene of the accident.

personería *nf* (*RPl*) personality; aptitude, talent.

personificación *nf* personification; embodiment.

personificar [1g] *vt* (a) to personify; to embody, be the embodiment of.

   (b) **en esta mujer el autor personifica la maldad** the author makes this woman a symbol of wickedness.

   (c) (*in speech etc*) to single out for special mention.

perspectiva *nf* (a) (*Art and fig*) perspective; **en** — in perspective; **le falta** — he lacks a sense of perspective.

   (b) view, scene, panorama.

   (c) outlook, prospect; future development; **"buenas** —s **de mejora"** (*job advert*) "good prospects"; **las** —s **de la cosecha son favorables** the harvest outlook is good; **es una** — **nada halagüeña** it's a most unwelcome prospect; **se alegró con la** — **de pasar un día en el campo** he cheered up with the prospect of spending a day in the country; **encontrarse ante la** — **de** + *infin* to be faced with the prospect of + *ger*; **tener algo en** — to have something in view, have a prospect of something; **hay ocupaciones en** — there's a busy time ahead.

perspicacia *nf* (a) keen-sightedness. (b) (*fig*) perspicacity, shrewdness, discernment.

perspicaz *adj* (a) *sight* keen; *person* keen-sighted. (b) (*fig*) perspicacious, shrewd, discerning.

perspicuidad *nf* perspicuity, clarity.

perspicuo *adj* clear, intelligible.

persuadir [3a] **1** *vt* to persuade; to convince, prevail upon; — **a uno a hacer algo** to persuade someone to do something; **dejarse** — to allow oneself to be persuaded.

   2 persuadirse *vr* to be persuaded, become convinced.

persuasión *nf* (a) (*act*) persuasion. (b) (*state*) conviction; **tener la** — **de que . . .** to have the conviction that . . ., be convinced that . . .

persuasiva *nf* persuasiveness.

persuasivo *adj* persuasive; convincing.

pertenecer [2d] *vi* (a) to belong (**a** to). (b) (*fig*) — **a** to concern; to apply to, pertain to; **le pertenece a él hacerlo** it's his job to do it.

perteneciente *adj* (a) **los países** —s the member countries, the countries which belong. (b) — **a** pertaining to, relevant to.

pertenencia *nf* (a) ownership; **las cosas de su** — the things which belong to him, his possessions, his property.

   (b) —s possessions, property; estate.

   (c) (*of estate etc*) —s appurtenances, accessories.

pértica *nf* *land measure* = 2.571m, *approx* = rod.

pértiga *nf* pole; — **de trole** trolley pole.

pertinacia *nf* (a) persistence; prolonged nature. (b) pertinacity, obstinacy.

pertinaz *adj* (a) *cough etc* persistent; *drought* persistent, long-lasting, prolonged. (b) *person* pertinacious, obstinate.

pertinencia *nf* relevance, pertinence; appropriateness.

pertinente *adj* (a) relevant, pertinent; appropriate; **no es** — **hacerlo ahora** this is not the appropriate time to do it.

   (b) — **a** concerning, relevant to; **en lo** — **a libros** as regards books, as far as books are concerned.

pertinentemente *adv* relevantly, pertinently; appropriately.

pertrechar [1a] **1** *vt* to supply (**con, de** with); to equip (**con, de** with); (*Mil*) to supply with ammunition and stores.

   2 pertrecharse *vr*: — **de algo** to provide oneself with something.

pertrechos *nmpl* implements, equipment; gear; (*Mil*) supplies and stores, provisions; (*Mil*) ammunition.

perturbación *nf* (a) (*Meteorol, Pol etc*) disturbance; — **del orden público** breach of the peace.

   (b) (*Med*) upset, disturbance; (*mental*) perturbation, (*serious*) mental disorder, alienation.

perturbado 1 *adj* mentally unbalanced. **2** *nm*, **perturbada** *nf* mentally unbalanced person.

perturbador 1 *adj* (a) perturbing, disturbing.

   (b) unruly, disorderly; subversive.

   2 *nm* disturber (of the peace); (*Pol*) disorderly element, unruly person; subversive.

perturbar [1a] vt (a) order etc to disturb; calm to disturb, ruffle, upset.
(b) (Med) to upset, disturb; (mentally) to perturb; to cause mental disorder in.
Perú: el — Peru.
peruanismo nm word (or phrase etc) peculiar to Peru.
peruano 1 adj Peruvian. **2** nm, **peruana** nf Peruvian.
peruétano 1 adj (Col, Cu, Mex) boring, tedious; stupid. **2** nm (Col, Cu, Mex) bore; dolt; (Chi) meddlesome youngster; (Mex) rascal.
perulero nm (SAm: hum) Peruvian.
perversamente adv perversely; wickedly.
perversidad nf (a) perversity; depravity; wickedness.
(b) (una —) evil deed, wrongdoing.
perversión nf (a) perversion; — **sexual** sexual perversion. (b) wickedness.
perverso adj perverse; depraved; wicked.
pervertido 1 adj perverted. **2** nm, **pervertida** nf pervert.
pervertimiento nm perversion, corruption.
pervertir [3i] **1** vt to pervert, corrupt; text etc to distort, corrupt; taste to corrupt. **2 pervertirse** vr to become perverted.
pervinca nf periwinkle.
pesa nf (a) weight; (Sport) weight, shot; dumbbell. (b) (CAm, Col, Ven) butcher's shop.
pesadamente adv (a) heavily; **caer** — to fall heavily. (b) slowly, ponderously; sluggishly; stiffly. (c) boringly, tediously.
pesadez nf (a) heaviness; weight.
(b) slowness, ponderousness; sluggishness.
(c) drowsiness; dull feeling, heavy feeling.
(d) tediousness, boring nature; annoyance; **es una** — **tener que** . . . it's a bore having to . . .
pesadilla nf (a) nightmare, bad dream.
(b) (fig) worry, obsession, nightmare; bogey; (person) pet aversion; bogeyman; **ese equipo es nuestra** — that is our bogey team; **ha sido la** — **de todos** it has been a nightmare for everybody.
pesado 1 adj (a) heavy (also fig), weighty.
(b) person etc slow, slow-moving, ponderous; sluggish; work etc slow; mechanism stiff.
(c) (Meteorol) heavy, sultry.
(d) sleep deep, heavy.
(e) **tengo la cabeza pesada** my head feels heavy, I can hardly keep my head up, my head feels like lead; **tener el estómago** — to feel blown out.
(f) task etc tough, hard; tedious; boring; reading etc boring, stodgy; person tedious, boring, annoying; **esto se hace** — this is becoming tedious; **la lectura del libro resultó pesada** the book was heavy going, I got bored with the book; **es una persona de lo más** — he's a terribly dull sort, he's a person of the most boring kind; **es** — **tener que** . . . it's such a bore having to . . .; it's tough having to . . .; **¡no seas** —! come off it!; don't be so difficult!
(g) (Col) very good, excellent.
2 nm, **pesada** nf boring person, bore; **es un** — he's such a bore.
pesador nm (CAm, Col, Ven) butcher.
pesadumbre nf grief, sorrow, affliction.
pésame nm expression of condolence, message of sympathy; **dar el** — to express one's condolences, send one's sympathy (por for, on).
pesantez nf weight, heaviness; (Phys) gravity.
pesar [1a] **1** vt (a) to weigh.
(b) to weigh down, be heavy for; **me pesa el abrigo** the coat weighs me down.
(c) (fig) to weigh heavily on; **le pesa tanta responsabilidad** so much responsibility bears heavily on him (or is a burden to him).
(d) (fig) to weigh; to appraise, value; to reckon up; — **las posibilidades** to weigh up one's chances; — **las palabras** to weigh one's words.
(e) (fig) to grieve, afflict, distress; **me pesa mucho** it grieves me, I am very sorry about it (or to hear it etc); **no me pesa haberlo hecho** I'm not sorry I did it; **le pesa que no le hayan nombrado** it grieves him that they should not have nominated him; **¡ya le pesará!** you'll be sorry!; **pese a las dificultades** in spite of the difficulties; **pese a quien pese** regardless of the consequences; in spite of everything; see **mal**.
2 vi (a) to weigh; (Phys) to have weight; **pesa 5 kilos** it weighs 5 kilos.
(b) to weigh a lot, be heavy; (of time) to drag, hang heavy; **ese paquete no pesa** that parcel isn't heavy, that parcel hardly weighs anything; **¿pesa mucho?** is it heavy?
(c) (fig) to weigh heavily; **sobre ella pesan muchas obligaciones** many obligations bear

heavily on her; **la hipoteca que pesa sobre la finca** the mortgage with which the estate is burdened.
(d) (fig: of opinion etc) to carry weight, count for a lot; **esa consideración no ha pesado conmigo** that consideration has not weighed with me (or influenced me).
(e) (CAm, Col, Ven) to sell meat.
3 nm (a) regret; grief, sorrow; **a mi** — to my regret; **con gran** — **mío** much to my sorrow; **causar** — **a uno** to grieve someone, cause grief to someone; **tener** — **por no haber** . . . to regret not having . . .
(b) **a** — **de** in spite of, despite; **a** — **de eso** in spite of that, notwithstanding that; **a** — **de que no tiene dinero** in spite of the fact that he has no money.
pesario nm pessary.
pesaroso adj sorrowful, regretful, sad.
pesca nf (a) fishing; — **de altura** deep-sea fishing; — **en bajura** shallow water fishing, coastal fishing; — **de la ballena** whaling; — **de perlas** pearl fishing; — **submarina** underwater fishing; skin diving; **allí la** — **es muy buena** the fishing is very good there; **ir de** — to go fishing; **andar a la** — **de** (fig) to fish for, angle for.
(b) catch, quantity (of fish) caught; **la** — **ha sido mala** it's been a poor catch.
pescada nf hake.
pescadera nf fishmonger; (esp pej) fishwife.
pescadería nf fish market; fish shop.
pescadero nm fishmonger.
pescadilla nf whiting; small hake.
pescado nm (a) fish. (b) (Ec, RPl: hum) secret police.
pescador nm fisherman; — **de caña** angler, fisherman; — **a mosca** fly fisherman.
pescaduría nf fishery; — **de perlas** pearl fishery.
pescante nm (a) coachman's seat, driver's seat. (b) (Theat) wire. (c) (Tech) jib; (Naut) davit.
pescar [1g] **1** vt (a) to catch; to land.
(b) to fish for, try to catch; **¿qué pescáis aquí?** what are you fishing for here?, what fish are you after here?
(c) (fam) to catch, get hold of, land; job etc to land, manage to get; meaning to grasp; facts etc to dredge up; **viene a** — **un marido** she's come to get a husband; **logró** — **unos cuantos datos** he managed to bring up a few facts, he was able to find a few facts.
(d) (fam) person to catch (out), catch in a lie; to catch unawares; **¡ya te pesqué!** now I've found you out!
2 vi (a) to fish; to go fishing; — **a mosca** to fish with a fly; — **al arrastre**, — **a la rastra** to trawl.
(b) (fam) **la chica viene a ver si pesca** the girl is coming to see if she can get hitched (sl).
(c) (Col, RPl) to nod, doze.
3 pescarse vr: **no sabe lo que se pesca** (fam) he hasn't a clue, he has no idea.
pescocear [1a] vt (SAm) to punch.
pescozudo adj thick-necked, fat in the neck.
pescuezo nm (a) neck; scruff of the neck; **retorcer el** — **a una gallina** to wring a chicken's neck; **¡calla, o te retuerzo el** —! shut up, or I'll wring your neck!
(b) (fig) vanity; haughtiness.
pescuezón adj (SAm) (a) = **pescozudo**. (b) long-necked.
pese: — **a** (as prep) see **pesar 1** (e).
pesebre nm (a) manger; stall. (b) (SAm) Nativity scene, crib.
pesebrera nf (Chi, Mex) = **pesebre** (b).
pesero nm (a) (CAm, Col, Ven) butcher; slaughterman. (b) (Mex) small bus.
peseta nf peseta; **cambiar la** — (fam) to be sick.
pesetada nf (SAm) joke, trick.
pesetera nf (fam) prostitute.
pesetero adj (a) money-grubbing, mercenary. (b) (Mex) dealer small-time. (c) (Cu) mean. (d) (Ant, Guat, Per, Ven) sponging (fam), parasitic.
pésimamente adv abominably, wretchedly.
pesimismo nm pessimism.
pesimista 1 adj pessimistic. **2** nmf pessimist.
pésimo adj abominable, wretched, vile.
peso nm (a) (in general) weight; weightiness, heaviness; (Phys) gravity; **—s y medidas** weights and measures; — **atómico** atomic weight; — **bruto** gross weight; **—específico** specific gravity; — **muerto** dead weight; — **neto** net weight; — **en vivo** live weight; **comprar algo a** — **de oro** to buy something at a very high price; **vender a** — to sell by weight; **de poco** — light, lightweight; **de mucho** — (very) heavy; **eso cae de su** — that goes without saying, that's obvious; **coger algo en** — to catch something in the

air; **echar a uno en — por una ventana** to throw someone bodily through a window; **sostener algo en —** to support the full weight of something; **lleva toda la dirección en —** he carries all the burden of the management; **llevar el — de un ataque** to bear the brunt of an attack.

(b) (object) weight, weighty object; burden, load; (Sport) weight; shot; **lanzar el —** to put the shot; **levantamiento de —s** weight lifting.

(c) (Boxing) weight; **— completo** (CAm, Mex), **— fuerte** heavyweight; **— gallo** bantam-weight; **— ligero** lightweight; **— medio** middle-weight; **medio fuerte** light heavyweight, cruiser weight; **— mosca** flyweight; **— pesada** heavyweight; **— pluma** featherweight.

(d) heavy feeling, dull feeling (in head etc).

(e) (fig) weight; **el — de los años** the weight of the years, the burden of age; **argumento de —** weighty argument.

(f) scales, balance, weighing machine; **— de baño** bathroom scales; **— de muelle** spring balance.

(g) (Fin) standard monetary unit of certain SAm countries.

pesor nm (Ant, CAm) weight, heaviness.
pespunt(e)ar [1a] vti to backstitch.
pespunte nm backstitch(ing).
pesquera nf (a) fishing ground, fishery. (b) (on river) weir.
pesquería nf fishing ground, fishery.
pesquero 1 adj fishing (attr). **2** nm fishing boat.
pesquisa nf (a) investigation, inquiry; search. (b) (Ec, RPl: euph) secret police.
pesquisador nm (Ec, RPl: euph) member of the secret police, detective.
pesquisar [1a] vt to investigate, inquire into.
pesquisidor nm investigator, inquirer.
pestaña nf (a) (Anat) eyelash; (Anat, Bot etc) fringe (of hairs); **no pegué —** (fam) I didn't get a wink of sleep. (b) (Tech) flange; (of tyre) rim.
pestañar [1a] vi (SAm), **pestañear** [1a] vi to blink, wink; **sin —** without batting an eyelid.
pestañeo nm blink(ing), wink(ing).
peste nf (a) (Med) plague, epidemic; (Per, PR) bubonic plague; (Chi) smallpox; (Col, Per) cold; (RPl) (any) infectious disease; **— aviar** fowl pest; **— bubónica** bubonic plague; **— negra** Black Death.

(b) (fig) plague; evil menace; nuisance; **una — de ratones** a plague of mice; **los chiquillos son una —** the kids are a pest, the kids are a nuisance (fam).

(c) stink, stench, foul smell; **¡qué — hay aquí!** what a stink!

(d) **echar —s de** to swear about, fume at, utter bitter words about.

pesticida nm pesticide.
pestífero adj pestiferous; smell foul; influence etc noxious, harmful.
pestilencia nf (a) pestilence, plague. (b) stink, stench.
pestilencial adj pestilential.
pestilente adj (a) pestilent. (b) smelly, foul.
pestillo nm bolt, latch; catch, fastener.
petaca 1 nf (a) cigarette case, cigar case; tobacco pouch.

(b) wicker basket; hamper; (SAm) leather-covered chest; (Mex) suitcase, grip; piece of luggage.

(c) (CAm: Anat) hump; **—s** (Ant, Mex) buttocks; big breasts.

2 nmf (SAm) (a) short squat person.

(b) lazy person.

3 adj invar (a) (SAm) idle, lazy; (Chi) slow, ponderous, sluggish.

(b) (PR) coarse.

petacón adj (a) (Mex, Per, RPl) plump; squat, short. (b) (Col) lazy. (c) (Col) potbellied, fat; (Mex) broad in the beam (fam). (d) (CAm) bent.
petacudo adj (a) (Bol) stout, fat; (Guat) hunchbacked; (Mex) broad in the beam (fam). (b) (SAm) slow, ponderous, sluggish.
pétalo nm petal.
petardear [1a] **1** vt to cheat, swindle. **2** vi (Aut) to backfire.
petardista nm cheat, swindler; (in strike) blackleg; (Mex) crooked politician.
petardo nm (a) firework, firecracker; (Mil) petard. (b) (fam) fraud, swindle; **pegar un —** to practise a fraud, pull a fast one (a on).
petate nm (a) grass mat; (SAm) mat of palm leaves, sleeping mat.

(b) roll of bedding; baggage; **liar el —** (fam) to pack up; to pack up and go, clear out; to peg out (sl).

(c) (fam) cheat, trickster.

(d) (fam) poor fish, worthless individual.

petatearse [1a] vr (Mex) to peg out (sl), die.
peteneras nfpl: **salir por —** to butt in with some silly remark, say (or do) something quite inappropriate.
peteretes nmpl sweets.
petición nf request, plea; petition; (Law) plea; claim; **a —** by request; **a — de** at the request of; **programa a — de radioyentes** listeners' request programme; **— de aumento de salarios** demand for higher wages, wage demand, wage claim; **— de divorcio** petition for divorce; **cometer — de principio** to beg the question.
peticionar [1a] vt (SAm) to petition.
peticionario nm, **peticionaria** nf petitioner.
petimetre nm fop, dandy.
petirrojo nm robin.
petizo (Bol, Chi, RPl) **1** adj small, short; stocky; chubby. **2** nm small horse; small person.
petizón adj (Bol, Chi, RPl) = **petizo 1**.
peto nm bodice; bib; (Mil) breastplate; (Taur) protective covering of picador's horse.
petral nm breast-strap (of harness).
Petrarca m Petrarch.
petrarquismo nm Petrarchism.
petrarquista adj Petrarchan.
petrel nm petrel.
pétreo adj stony; rocky.
petrificación nf petrifaction.
petrificado adj petrified.
petrificar [1g] **1** vt to petrify (also fig), turn to stone. **2 petrificarse** vr to petrify, become petrified (also fig), turn to stone.
petróleo nm (Min) oil, petroleum; **— de alumbrado** paraffin (oil); **— combustible** fuel oil; **— crudo** crude oil.
petrolero 1 adj oil (attr), petroleum (attr). **2** nm (a) (Comm) oil man. (b) (fam) extremist, revolutionary. (c) (Naut) tanker.
petrolífero adj petroliferous, oil-bearing.
petrología nf petrology.
petulancia nf vanity, self-satisfaction, opinionated nature.
petulante adj vain, self-satisfied, opinionated.
petunia nf petunia.
peuquino adj (Chi) greyish.
peyorativo adj pejorative.
pez¹ nm (a) fish; **— de color(es)** goldfish; **— espada** swordfish; **— mujer** manatee; **— sierra** sawfish; **— volador, — volante** flying fish; **estar como el — en el agua** to feel completely at home.

(b) (fam) **— gordo** big shot (fam), big pot (fam).

(c) (fam) **buen —** rogue, rascal.

(d) **estar — de** (or **en**) **algo** to be completely ignorant of something, know nothing at all about something.

pez² nf pitch, tar.
pezón nm (a) (Anat) teat, nipple. (b) (Bot) stalk. (c) (Mech) **— de engrase** nipple, lubrication point.
pezonera nf (Arg) feeding bottle.
pezuña nf (a) hoof. (b) (Mex, Per) dirt hardened on the feet.
piache nm (Ven) medicine man; quack doctor.
piada nf (a) (Orn) cheep, cheeping. (b) (fig) catch phrase.
piadosamente adv (a) piously, devoutly. (b) kindly, mercifully.
piadoso adj (a) (Rel) pious, devout. (b) kind, merciful (para con to); see **mentira**.
piafar [1a] vi (horse) to paw the ground, stamp.
pial nm (etc) see **peal** (etc).
Piamonte m Piedmont.
piamontés 1 adj Piedmontese. **2** nm, **piamontesa** nf Piedmontese.
pianista nmf pianist.
piano nm piano; **— de cola** grand piano; **— de media cola** baby grand; **— mecánico** pianola; **— recto, — vertical** upright piano; **tocar el —** to play the piano, (fam) do the washing up; **tocar —** (SAm) to rob, steal.
piar [1c] vi (a) (Orn) to cheep. (b) (fam) **— por** to cry for, be dying for.
piara nf herd; drove.
piastra nf piastre.
pibe nm, **piba** nf (Bol, Chi, RPl) kid (fam), child.
pica¹ nf (Orn) magpie.
pica² nf (Mil) pike; (Taur) goad; **poner una — en Flandes** to bring off something difficult, achieve a signal success.
pica³ nf (Col, Ec, Per) tapping (of rubber trees).
pica⁴ nf (Col) pique, resentment; (Chi) annoyance, impatience.
pica⁵ nf (Col, Ec, Guat, Ven) forest trail, narrow path.

picacera nf (Chi, Per) pique, resentment.
picacho nm peak, summit.
picada[1] nf (a) prick; sting; bite; peck. (b) (Chi) bad temper, anger.
picada[2] nf (SAm) forest trail, narrow path; (Bol) ford.
picadero nm (a) riding school. (b) (Col) slaughterhouse.
picadillo nm mince, minced meat.
picado 1 adj (a) material pricked, perforated; with a row of holes; surface pitted; — **de viruelas** pockmarked.
　(b) meat etc minced; tobacco cut; sea choppy.
　(c) **estar** — to be offended, be cross.
　(d) **estar** — **por algo** (SAm) to go for something in a big way.
　2 nm (a) (Aer, Orn) dive.
　(b) (Mus) pizzicato.
picador nm (a) horse-trainer, horse-breaker. (b) (Taur) picador, bullfighter's assistant (mounted, with a pike). (c) (Min) faceworker.
picadora nf: — **de carne** mincer, mincing machine.
picadura nf (a) prick; puncture; sting; bite. (b) cut tobacco.
picaflor nm (SAm) (a) hummingbird. (b) (fam) wolf (fam), flirt; lover, boyfriend.
picafuego nm poker.
picajón adj (fam), **picajoso** adj (fam) touchy.
picamaderos nm, pl **picamaderos** woodpecker.
picana nf (SAm) spur, goad.
picanear [1a] vt (SAm) to spur on, goad on.
picante 1 adj (a) food, flavour hot; peppery; highly seasoned.
　(b) (fig) remark sharp, stinging, cutting; joke etc racy, spicy; situation, contrast piquant.
　2 nm (a) hot taste.
　(b) (fig) sharpness, pungency; raciness, spiciness; piquancy.
　(c) (Bol, Chi, Per) highly seasoned sauce (or dish).
picantería nf (Bol, Chi, Per) restaurant specializing in seasoned dishes.
picapedrero nm stonecutter, quarryman.
picapica: polvos nmpl **de** — itching powder.
picapleitos nm, pl **picapleitos** (pej) lawyer; litigious person.
picaporte nm door-handle; latch; doorknocker; latchkey.
picar [1g] **1** vt (a) to prick, puncture; paper etc to prick (a line of) holes in, pierce with holes, perforate; surface to pit, pock; (Art) to stipple; (Sew) to pink; ticket to punch, clip.
　(b) (of insect) to sting; to bite; (of snake) to bite; (of thorn) to prick.
　(c) (of bird) to peck; to peck at; (of person) food to nibble (at), pick at; (of fish) to bite.
　(d) horse to put spurs to, spur on; bull to stick, prick (with the goad); (fig) to incite, goad, stimulate; (fig) to wound; to pique; to annoy, bother; **le pican los celos** jealousy is pricking him, he is feeling pangs of jealousy.
　(e) (Mus) to play pizzicato.
　(f) stone to chip, chip pieces off; millstone to sharpen; stone to grind (up); (Cook) to mince, chop (up); tobacco to cut.
　(g) tongue to burn, sting.
　(h) (Mil) to harass.
　2 vi (a) (of thorn) to prick; (of insect) to sting, bite; **no es de los que pican** it's not the kind that stings.
　(b) (of bird) — **en** to peck at; (of person etc) to nibble at, pick at; (fig) to dabble in, study superficially; **ha picado en todos los géneros literarios** he's dabbled in (or had a go at) all the literary genres.
　(c) (of fish) to bite, take the bait; (fig) to rise to the bait; **por fin picó** he swallowed the bait eventually; **ha picado mucha gente** lots of people have fallen for it, it has caught on with lots of people.
　(d) — **en** (fig) to border on, be akin to; **eso pica en frescura** that borders (or verges) on cheek.
　(e) (Med) to itch, sting; **me pican los ojos** my eyes hurt; **me pica la lengua** my tongue is smarting (or stinging); **me pica el brazo** my arm itches.
　(f) (of sun) to burn, scorch; **hoy sí pica el sol** the sun is really burning today.
　(g) (Aer, Orn) to dive.
　(h) — **muy alto** to aim too high, be overambitious.
　(i) (Aut) — **por autoencendido** to pink.
　3 picarse vr (a) (clothing) to get moth-eaten; (substance) to get holes in it; (tooth) to decay.

　(b) (wine etc) to turn sour, go off; (fruit etc) to spoil, go rotten.
　(c) (sea) to get choppy.
　(d) (person) to take offence, get piqued; to get cross; to bridle (por at).
　(e) — **con algo** to get a longing for, get an obsession about; to take a strong liking to.
　(f) — **de puntual** to take a pride in being punctual, make a strong point of punctuality; — **de caballero** to boast of being a gentleman.
　(g) (Ant) — **de pecho** to become consumptive.
picarazado adj (Cu, PR) pockmarked.
picardear [1a] **1** vt: — **a uno** to get someone into bad habits, lead someone into evil ways.
　2 vi to play about; to play up, be mischievous.
　3 picardearse vr to get into evil ways, go to the bad.
Picardía f Picardy.
picardía nf (a) (quality) crookedness; villainy, knavery; slyness, craftiness; naughtiness.
　(b) (una —) dirty trick; naughty thing (to do), mischievous act.
　(c) rude thing (to say), naughty word; insult; **le gusta decir** —**s a las chicas** he likes saying naughty things to the girls.
picaresco adj (a) roguish, rascally. (b) (Lit) novel picaresque, of roguery.
pícaro 1 adj (a) crooked; villainous, knavish; sly, crafty; child naughty, mischievous.
　(b) child etc precocious, knowing, (esp) sexually aware before the proper age.
　(c) (hum) naughty, wicked; **¡este** — **siglo!** what naughty times we live in!; **tiene inclinación a los** —**s celos** she gives way to that wicked jealousy.
　2 nm (a) crook; villain, knave, scoundrel, rogue, rascal; sly sort; (child) rascal, scamp; **¡**—**!** you rascal!
　(b) (Lit) rogue, pícaro.
picarón nm (a) rogue. (b) (Chi, Mex, Per) fritter.
picaruelo adj look etc roguish, naughty, sly; **me miró picaruela** she gave me a roguish look.
picatoste nm fried bread.
picaza nf magpie.
picazo nm peck; jab, poke.
picazón nf (a) itch; sting, stinging feeling; smart, smarting. (b) (fig) annoyance, pique; uneasy feeling, pang of conscience.
piccolo nm piccolo.
pícea nf spruce.
pick-up [pi'kap or pi'ku] nm (angl) pickup.
pico nm (a) (Orn) beak, bill; (Ent etc) beak; (hum) mouth, lips; **callar** (or **cerrar**) **el** — (fam) to shut one's trap (sl), keep one's trap shut (sl); **hincar el** — (fam) to peg out (sl); to give up, give in.
　(b) corner, peak, sharp point; (of page) corner; **sombrero de tres** — cocked hat, three-cornered hat; **andar** (or **irse**) **de** —**s pardos** to go on the spree (fam); to go whoring.
　(c) (of jug etc) lip, spout.
　(d) (Tech) pick, pickaxe.
　(e) (Geog) peak, summit; pinnacle of rock.
　(f) **y** — **and a bit**; **son las 3 y** — it's just after 3; **tiene 50 libros y** — he has 50-odd books; **quédese con el** — keep the change, keep the odd amount; **me costó un** — it cost me quite a bit.
　(g) (Orn: species) woodpecker.
　(h) (fam) talkativeness; **ser un** — **de oro, tener buen** (or **mucho**) — to have the gift of the gab (fam), be a great talker; **irse del** — to talk too much; **perderse por el** — to harm oneself by saying too much.
　(i) (Cards) —**s** spades.
　(j) (Col, Guat, Mex) kiss.
　(k) (Chi: tabu) prick (tabu).
picolargo adj (Arg) pert, saucy; backbiting; intriguing, scheming.
picón 1 adj (a) (Col, PR) pert, saucy. (b) (Per, PR) touchy. (c) (PR) mocking. **2** nm (Col) gossip, talebearer.
picor nm = **picazón** (a).
picoreto adj (CAm, Col, PR, Ven) talkative, indiscreet.
picoso adj pockmarked.
picota nf (a) pillory; **poner a uno en la** — (fig) to ridicule someone, show someone up (for what he is). (b) (Archit) point, top; (Geog) peak.
picotada nf, **picotazo** nm peck; sting, bite.
picotear [1a] **1** vt to peck. **2** vi (a) to nibble, pick. (b) (fam) to chatter, gas (fam), gab (fam). **3 picotearse** vr to squabble.
picotero (fam) **1** adj chattering, gossipy, talkative. **2** nm, **picotera** nf gossip, chatterer, gasbag (fam).

picotón nm (Arg, Chi, Ec) peck.
picto 1 adj Pictish. **2** nm, **picta** nf Pict. **3** nm (language) Pictish.
pictóricamente adv pictorially.
pictórico adj **(a)** pictorial.
   (b) scene etc worth painting.
   (c) gift, skill etc artistic; **tiene dotes pictóricas** she has artistic gifts, she has talent for painting.
picúa nf (Cu, PR) **(a)** small kite. **(b)** sharp business-man. **(c)** prostitute.
picuda nf **(a)** (Orn) woodcock. **(b)** (Cu, PR: Fish) barracuda.
picudo adj **(a)** pointed, with a point; jar with a spout; person long-nosed, sharp-nosed.
   (b) (fam) = **picotero 1**.
   (c) (Cu) = **cursi**.
   (d) (Mex) crafty, clever.
picure nm **(a)** (Col) fugitive; slacker. **(b)** (Ven) highly seasoned sauce.
picurearse [1a] vr (Col, Ven) to flee.
picha[1] nf (Mex) blanket; (hum) mistress.
picha[2] nf (tabu) prick (tabu).
pichado adj (RPl) easily embarrassed.
pichana nf (Arg, Chi, Per) bass broom.
pichanga nf (Col) bass broom.
pichango nm (Chi) dog.
piche nm **(a)** (CAm) miser, skinflint.
   (b) (Arg, Bol, Chi) (kind of) armadillo.
   (c) (Arg, Cu) fear, cowardice.
   (d) (Col) shove.
   (e) (Col) whey.
   (f) (Col) red.
pichel nm tankard, mug.
pichicata nf (Per) cocaine powder.
pichicatero nm, **pichicatera** nf (Per) dope addict.
pichicato adj (SAm) mean, miserly.
pichicote adj (Bol, Ec) mean, miserly.
pichilingo nm (Mex) lad, kid.
pichincha nf (Bol, RPl) bargain; low price, reduced price; advantageous deal, lucky break.
pichingo nm (CAm) jar, vessel; piece of junk.
pichirre adj (Per, Ven) mean, stingy.
picholear [1a] vi **(a)** (Chi, Hond) to make merry.
   (b) (Guat) to win by cheating. **(c)** (Hond, Mex) to lay small bets.
pichón 1 nm **(a)** young pigeon; (SAm) chick, young bird; **— de barro** clay pigeon.
   (b) (SAm) novice, greenhorn; tyro; young player, inexperienced player.
   (c) (Arg) **un — de hombre** a well-bred man.
   2 nm, **pichona** nf darling, dearest.
pichonear [1a] **1** vt **(a)** (Arg, Mex) to swindle.
   (b) (Col, Pan) to catch out; to kill, murder.
   (c) (Chi) = **pinchar**.
   (d) (Ec, Pan etc) to borrow, use temporarily; to occupy temporarily.
   2 vi (Arg, Col, Mex) to beat an inexperienced player.
pichuleador nm (RPl) money grubber.
pichulear [1a] vi **(a)** (CAm, RPl) to be in a small-time business; to be mercenary, be greedy for money. **(b)** (CR, Mex) to lay small bets; to spend very little.
pichuleo nm **(a)** (RPl) meanness. **(b)** (Mex, Nic) small business, retail business; small-time gambling.
pídola nf leapfrog.
pie nm **(a)** (Anat etc) foot; **— de atleta** athlete's foot; **— de cabra** crowbar; **— marino** sea legs; **—s planos** flat feet; **ligero de —s** light-footed, quick; **a — on** foot; **ir a —** to go on foot, walk; **a cuatro —s** on all fours; **a — enjuto** dry-shod, (fig) without danger, without any risk; **a — firme** steadfastly; **a — juntillo, a —s juntillos** with both feet together, (fig) believe firmly, absolutely; **al —** close, handy; **con el —** bien sentado calmly, thoughtfully with due care; **con —s de plomo** warily, gingerly; **andar con —s de plomo** to go very carefully; **con un — en el hoyo** with one foot in the grave; **entrar con buen —** (or **con — derecho**) to get off to a good start; **hacer algo con los —s** to bungle something, make a mess of something; **estar de —** to be standing (up); **ponerse de** (or **en**) **—** to stand up, get up, rise; **caer de —** (fig) to fall on one's feet; **nacer de —** to be born with a silver spoon in one's mouth, be born lucky; **cojear del mismo —** to have the same faults as someone else; **saber de qué — cojea uno** to know someone's weak spots (or weaknesses); **de —s a cabeza** from head to foot, from top to toe; **soldado de a —** (Hist) foot-soldier; **en —** standing; upright; **mantenerse en —** to remain upright; **la duda sigue en —** the doubt remains; **saltar en —** to leap to one's feet; **irse** (or **salir**) **por —s** to make off;

argumento sin —s ni cabeza pointless argument, absurd argument; **asentar el —** to make a cautious start; **buscar tres —s al gato** to split hairs, quibble; to look for trouble; **no dar — con bola** to do everything wrong, be no good at anything; **se le fueron los —s** he slipped, he stumbled; **parar los —s a uno** to curb someone, clip someone's wings; to stop someone going too far; to take someone down a peg; **poner el —** to tread, put one's foot; **poner los —s en** (fig) to set foot in; **sacar los —s del plato** to abandon all restraint; to kick over the traces; **tomar —** (Aer) to land, come down; **volverse —s atrás** to retrace one's steps.
   (b) (Math) foot; **— cuadrado** square foot; **— cúbico** cubic foot; **tiene 6 —s de largo** it is 6 feet long.
   (c) trunk, stem; (of rose etc) root, stock, stand; (of glass) stem; (of statue) foot, base; (of bed, hill, page, slope, stairs etc) foot, bottom; (of document, letter) ending; (of picture, photo) caption; **— de imprenta** imprint; **al — del monte** at the foot (or bottom) of the mountain; **a los —s de la cama** at the foot of the bed; **al — de la fábrica** cost price, ex works; **al — de la letra** quote etc literally, verbatim; copy exactly, word for word; **morir al — del cañón** to die in harness.
   (d) (Theat) cue.
   (e) (of wine etc) sediment.
   (f) (fig) motive, basis; pretext; **dar — a** to give cause for; **dar — para que uno haga algo** to give someone a motive for doing something; **tomar — para hacer algo** to use something as a basis for action.
   (g) (fig) foothold; **perder el —** to lose one's foothold, slip.
   (h) (fig) standing, footing; **en — de guerra** on a war footing; **estar sobre un (mismo) — de igualdad** to be on an equal footing, be on equal terms (con with).
   (i) (Lit) foot; measure, verse form.
piedad nf **(a)** (Rel) piety, devotion, devoutness; respect; **— filial** filial respect.
   (b) pity; mercy; **¡por —!** for pity's sake!; **mover a uno a —** to move someone to pity, arouse compassion in someone; **tener — de** to take pity on; **¡ten un poco de —!** show some sympathy!; **no tuvieron — de ellos** they showed him no mercy.
piedra nf **(a)** stone; rock; (of lighter etc) flint; (Med) stone; (Meteorol) hailstone; hail; **un puente de —** a stone bridge; **tener el corazón de —** to be hard-hearted; **primera —** foundation stone; **— de afilar** hone; **— de amolar** grindstone; **— angular** corner-stone (also fig); **— arenisca** sandstone; **— de cal, — caliza** limestone; **— de escándalo** source of scandal; bone of contention; **— filosofal** philosopher's stone; **— fundamental** (fig) basis, cornerstone; **— imán** lodestone; **— miliar** milestone; **— de molino** mill-stone; **— pómez** pumice (stone); **— preciosa** precious stone; **— de toque** touchstone; **a tiro de —** within a stone's throw; **no dejar — sobre —** to raze to the ground; **no dejar — por mover** to leave no stone unturned; **¿quién se atreve a lanzar la primera —?** which of you shall cast the first stone?; **pasar a uno por la —** to put someone through the mill; **quedarse de —** to be thunderstruck.
   (b) (Cu, PR) bore.
piel 1 nf **(a)** (Anat) skin.
   (b) (Zool) skin, hide, pelt; fur; leather; **— de ante** buckskin, buff, suède; **— de becerro, — de ternera** calf, calfskin; **— de cabra** goatskin; **— de cerdo** pigskin; **— de Suecia** suède; **abrigo de —es** fur coat; **artículos de —** leather goods; **una maleta de —** a leather suitcase.
   (c) (Bot) skin, peel, rind.
   2 nmf: **— roja** redskin; **los —es rojas** the redskins.
piélago nm (lit) **(a)** ocean, deep. **(b)** (fig) **un — de dificultades** a sea of difficulties.
pienso[1] nm (Agr) feed, fodder; **—s** feeding stuffs.
pienso[2]: **¡ni por —!** never!, the very idea!
pierna nf **(a)** leg; **— artificial** artificial leg; **en —s** bare-legged; **estirar las —s** (fig) to stretch one's legs; see **dormir**.
   (b) (of letter) stroke; (with pen) downstroke.
   (c) (Arg) player; partner.
piernicorto adj short-legged.
pierrot [pie'ro] nm pierrot.
pieza 1 nf **(a)** piece; (of cloth) piece, roll; **— de museo** museum exhibit, (fig) object fit only for a museum; **— de ropa** piece of clothing, article of clothing; **de una —** in one piece; solid; (SAm) person straight, honest; **formar — única con** to be all of a piece

with, (*Mech*) be integral with; **traje de dos —s** two-piece costume; **dejar a uno de una —** to strike someone all of a heap; **quedarse de una —** to be dumbfounded; **vender algo por —s** to sell something by the piece.

(**b**) (*Mech*) part; **— de recambio, — de repuesto** (*SAm*) spare, spare part, extra (*US*).

(**c**) (*Fin*) coin, piece; **— de oro** gold coin, gold piece.

(**d**) (*Chess etc*) piece, man.

(**e**) (*Hunting*) example; **cobró dos bellas —s** he obtained (*or* shot *etc*) two fine specimens (*or* examples.)

(**f**) (*Archit*) room; **— amueblada** furnished room; **— de recibo** reception room.

(**g**) (*Mus*) piece, composition; (*Theat*) piece, work, play; **— corta** sketch; **— oratoria** speech.

(**h**) **— de artillería** piece, gun.

(**i**) **— de convicción** (*Law*) exhibit, document, piece of evidence; (*fig*) convincing argument; **— de examen** thing worth examining; point to bear in mind.

(**j**) **buena —** (*iro*) rogue, villain.

2 *nm*: **un dos —s** a two-piece (costume *etc*).
pífano *nm* fife.
pifia *nf* (**a**) (*Billiards*) bad shot.

(**b**) (*fig*) blunder, bloomer (*fam*).

(**c**) (*Arg, Chi, Per*) joke; mockery; **hacer — de** to joke about, mock.

(**d**) (*Ec, Per*) hiss.
pifiador *adj* (*Chi, Per*) joking, mocking.
pifiar [1b] **1** *vt* (*Arg, Chi, Per*) to joke about, mock; to hoax; to play a practical joke on.

2 *vi* (**a**) (*RPl*) to fail, come a cropper (*fam*); to mess up one's game.

(**b**) (*Col, CR, Ec*) to be disappointed, suffer a setback.

(**c**) to blunder, make a bloomer (*fam*).
pigmentación *nf* pigmentation.
pigmentado 1 *adj* pigmented; *person* (*euph*) coloured.
2 *nm*, **pigmentada** *nf* (*euph*) coloured person.
pigmento *nm* pigment.
pigmeo 1 *adj* pigmy. **2** *nm*, **pigmea** *nf* pigmy.
pignorar [1a] *vt* to pawn.
pigricia *nf* (**a**) laziness; sluggishness. (**b**) (*Chi, Ec, Per*) trifle, bagatelle; small bit, pinch.
pija *nf* (*SAm: tabu*) prick (*tabu*).
pijama *nm* pyjamas.
pije *nm* (*Chi*) toff (*fam*), fop.
pijotada *nf* (*Mex*) (**a**) nuisance, annoying thing. (**b**) insignificant sum.
pijotear [1a] *vi* (*Col, Mex, RPl*) to haggle over trifles; to behave meanly.
pijotería *nf* (**a**) (*fam*) nuisance, small annoyance; trifling request.

(**b**) (*SAm*) insignificant sum, tiny amount; trifle, small thing.

(**c**) (*SAm*) meanness.
pijotero 1 *adj* (**a**) (*fam*) tedious, annoying; wretched.

(**b**) (*SAm*) mean, given to haggling over small amounts.

(**c**) (*Arg*) untrustworthy.

2 *nm* (*fam*) wretch, rogue; **¡no seas —!** don't be a beast!
pila[1] *nf* (**a**) heap, pile; stack.

(**b**) (*fam*) heap; **tengo una — de cosas que hacer** I have heaps (*or* stacks) of things to do (*fam*).

(**c**) (*SAm*) **una — de** a heap of, a lot of; **una — de años** very many years; **una — de ladrones** a whole lot of thieves.
pila[2] *nf* (**a**) sink; trough; drinking trough; (*of fountain*) basin; (*SAm*) fountain; **— de cocina** kitchen sink.

(**b**) (*Eccl: also* **— bautismal**) font; **— de agua bendita** holy-water stoup; **sacar de — a uno** to act as godparent to someone.

(**c**) (*Elec*) battery; cell; **— atómica** atomic pile; **— seca** dry cell.

(**d**) (*Cu*) tap, faucet (*US*).
pilado *adj* (*Col*) sure (to succeed); easy, simple.
pilar[1] *nm* (**a**) post, pillar; milestone.

(**b**) (*Post*) pillar box.

(**c**) (*Archit*) pillar; column, pier.

(**d**) (*fig*) prop, (chief) support, mainstay; **un — de la monarquía** a mainstay of the monarchy.
pilar[2] *nm* (*of fountain*) basin, bowl.
pilastra *nf* pilaster; (*Chi: of door etc*) frame.
Pilatos *m* Pilate.
pilatuna *nf* (*SAm*) dirty trick; vile deed.
pilatuno *adj* (*Col*) manifestly unjust.
pilcate *nm* (*Mex*) grubby child; child.
pilcha *nf* (**a**) (*Chi, RPl*) garment, article of clothing;

—s old clothes; fine clothes. (**b**) (*Arg*) mistress, one's beloved.
pilche *nm* (*Bol, Col, Ec*) gourd, calabash.
píldora *nf* pill; **— anticonceptiva** contraceptive pill; **— antifatiga** anti-fatigue pill, pep pill (*fam*); **dorar la —** to gild the pill.
pileta *nf* (**a**) basin, bowl; sink; **— de cocina** kitchen sink. (**b**) (*Arg*) **— de natación** swimming pool.
pilgua *nf* (*Chi*) wicker basket.
pilígüe 1 *adj* (*CAm*) *fruit* shrivelled, empty. **2** *nmf* (*CAm, Mex*) poor fish, weak person.
pililo *nm* (*Chi*) tramp; ragged person.
pilintruca *nf* (*Chi*) slut.
pilmama *nf* (*Mex*) wet-nurse; nursemaid.
pilón[1] *nm* (**a**) pillar, post; (*Elec etc*) pylon; **— de azúcar** sugar loaf. (**b**) (*of steelyard*) weight. (**c**) (*Cu: Agr*) dump, store.
pilón[2] *nm* (**a**) drinking trough; (*of fountain*) basin; (*Mex*) drinking fountain. (**b**) mortar. (**c**) (*Chi*) pannier. (**d**) (*Mex, Ven*) tip, gratuity.
pilongo *adj* thin, lean.
pilotar [1a] *vt plane* to pilot; *car* to drive; *ship* to steer, navigate; (*fig*) to guide, direct.
pilote *nm* (*Archit*) pile.
pilotear [1a] *vt* (**a**) **=pilotar**. (**b**) (*SAm*) *person* to guide, direct; *business* to run, manage. (**c**) (*Chi*) *person* to exploit.
piloto 1 *nm* (**a**) (*Aer*) pilot; **— automático** automatic pilot; **— de caza** fighter pilot; **— de prueba** test pilot.

(**b**) (*Naut*) first mate; navigator, navigation officer; **— de puerto** harbour pilot.

(**c**) (*Aut*) driver.

(**d**) (*fig*) guide; (*in exploration*) pathfinder.

(**e**) (*Elec*) rear light, tail light.

2 *attr*: **planta —** pilot plant; *see* **luz.**
pilpinto *nm* (*Arg, Bol*) butterfly.
pilsen *nf* (*Chi*) (any) beer.
piltrafa *nf* (**a**) useless bit of meat, skinny meat; **—s** offal, scraps.

(**b**) (*fig*) useless lump, worthless object; (*person*) poor specimen, poor fish, weakling.

(**c**) (*Chi, Per*) bargain; piece of luck; profit.

(**d**) (*SAm*) **—s** rags, old clothes.
piltrafiento *adj* (**a**) (*Chi, Mex*) ragged. (**b**) (*Chi*) withered.
piltrafoso *adj* (*Per*) ragged.
piltrafudo *adj* (*Per*) weak, languid.
piltre *adj* (**a**) (*Col, Cu, Ven*) foppish. (**b**) (*Chi*) overripe; shrivelled, dried up; *person* wizened.
pilucho *adj* (*Chi*) naked (from the waist down).
pillada *nf* (**a**) dirty trick. (**b**) (*RPl*) surprise revelation; surprise encounter.
pillaje *nm* pillage, plunder.
pillar [1a] *vt* (**a**) to pillage, plunder, sack.

(**b**) (*fam*) to grasp, seize, lay hold of; (*of dog*) to catch, worry; **la puerta le pilló el dedo** the door trapped his finger, he got his finger caught in the door; **el perro le pilló el pantalón** the dog seized his trouser leg (in its teeth).

(**c**) (*fam*) *culprit etc* to catch; (*fig*) to catch, catch out, catch in the act; **por fin le pilló la policía** the police nabbed him eventually; **¡te he pillado!** got you!

(**d**) (*fam*) *bargain, job etc* to get, land, lay hold of.

(**e**) (*fam*) *meaning* to grasp, catch on to.

(**f**) (*of horse, coach etc: fam*) to knock down.

(**g**) (*fam*) **— una enfermedad** to catch a disease; **— una borrachera** to get drunk.
pillastre *nm* (*fam*) scoundrel.
pillería *nf* (**a**) dirty trick. (**b**) gang of scoundrels.
pillete *nm*, **pillín** *nm* rascal, scamp.
pillo 1 *adj* villainous, knavish; blackguardly; sly, crafty; *child* naughty. **2** *nm* rascal, rogue; scoundrel; rotter; (*child*) rascal, scamp.
pilluelo *nm* **=pillo**; urchin.
pimentero *nm* (**a**) pepperpot. (**b**) (*Bot*) pepper plant.
pimentón *nm* cayenne pepper, red pepper; paprika.
pimienta *nf* pepper; **— inglesa** allspice.
pimiento *nm* (**a**) pepper, pimiento; **no se me de un —, (no) me importa un —** I don't care two hoots (*de about*). (**b**) (*Bot*) pepper plant.
pimpante *adj* (*fam*) (**a**) charming, attractive; chic. (**b**) (*pej: esp* **tan —**) smug, self-satisfied.
Pimpinela *m*: **el — escarlata** the Scarlet Pimpernel.
pimpinela *nf* pimpernel.
pimpollo *nm* (**a**) (*Bot*) sucker, shoot; sapling; rosebud. (**b**) (*fam*) bonny 'child; attractive woman;| **estar hecho un —** to look very smart; to look very young (still).
pinabete *nm* fir, fir tree.
pinacoteca *nf* art gallery.

pináculo *nm* pinnacle.

pinar *nm* pinewood, pine grove.

pinaza *nf* pinnace.

pincel *nm* (a) paintbrush, artist's brush; **estar hecho un —** to be very smartly dressed. (b) (*fig*) painter.

pincelada *nf* brush-stroke; **última —** (*fig*) finishing touch.

pinciano 1 *adj* of Valladolid. 2 *nm*, **pinciana** *nf* native (*or* inhabitant) of Valladolid; **los —s** the people of Valladolid.

pinchar [1a] 1 *vt* (a) to prick, pierce, puncture; *tyre* to puncture; **no — ni cortar** (*fam*) to cut no ice; **tener un neumático pinchado** to have a puncture, have a flat tyre; **— a uno** (*Med: fam*) to give someone a jab (*or* injection).
(b) (*fig*) to prod; **hay que —le** he needs prodding; **le pinchan para que se case** they keep prodding him to get married.
(c) (*fig*) to wound, mortify; to provoke, stir up.
2 **pincharse** *vr* (a) to prick oneself.
(b) (*tyre*) to get punctured, go flat, burst.

pinchazo *nm* (a) prick; puncture (*also Aut*), flat (*US Aut*). (b) (*fig*) prod.

pinche *nm* (a) kitchen boy, scullion. (b) (*Arg*) minor office clerk. (c) (*Mex, PR*) rascal. (d) (*Col*) bad horse, nag. (e) (*Arg*) hatpin.

pinchitos *nmpl* hors d'oeuvres, snacks (*served on bar counter*).

pincho *nm* (a) point; pointed stick, spike; (*RPl*) spike, prickle. (b) **—s** (*Cook*) = **pinchitos**.

pindárico *adj* Pindaric.

Píndaro *m* Pindar.

pindonga *nf* (*fam*) gadabout.

pinga *nf* (*Col, Cu, Mex, PR: tabu*) prick (*tabu*).

pingajo *nm* rag, shred; tag.

pinganilla *nm* (a) (*SAm*) poor man with pretensions to elegance; (*Arg*) toff (*fam*), masher (*fam*).
(b) **en —s** (*Col, Mex*) on tiptoe; (*Mex*) squatting; in an unsteady position.

pinganillo *adj* (a) (*Bol, Ec*) smart, elegant. (b) (*Col*) chubby.

pinganitos: estar en — to be well up, be well-placed socially; **poner a uno en —s** to give someone a leg up (socially).

pingo *nm* (a) rag, shred; tag; old garment, shabby dress; **—s** (*fam*) clothes; odds and ends; **no tengo ni un — que ponerme** (*fam*) I haven't a single thing I can wear; **andar** (*or* **ir**) **de —** to gad about; **poner a uno como un —** to abuse someone.
(b) (*fam*) slut; prostitute.
(c) (*RPl*) horse; good horse; (*Chi, Per*) worthless horse, nag.
(d) (*Mex*) naughty child; **el —** the devil.
(e) (*RPl*) lively child.

pingonear [1a] *vi* (*fam*) to gad about.

pingorotear [1a] *vi* (*SAm*), **pingotear** [1a] *vi* (*SAm*) to skip about, jump.

ping-pong ['pinpon] *nm* (*angl*) ping-pong.

pingucho (*Chi*) 1 *adj* poor, wretched. 2 *nm* urchin, ragamuffin.

pingüe *adj* (a) greasy, fat. (b) (*fig*) abundant, copious; *profits* rich, fat; *crop* heavy, bumper, rich; *business* lucrative.

pingüino *nm* penguin.

pininos *nmpl* (*SAm*), **pinitos** *nmpl*: **hacer —** (*child*) to toddle, walk alone, take one's first steps; (*convalescent*) to start to get about again; (*novice*) to take one's first steps, try for the first time.

pino[1] *nm* (*Bot*) pine, pine tree; **— albar** Scots pine; **— bravo, — marítimo, — rodeno** cluster pine; **— de tea** pitch pine; **vivir en el quinto —** to live at the back of beyond; **eso está en el quinto —** that's terribly far away.

pino[2] *nm* (a) **en —** upright, vertical; standing. (b) **—s = pinitos**.

pinocha *nf* pine needle.

pinsapo *nm* Spanish fir.

pinta[1] *nf* (a) spot, dot; (*Zool etc*) spot, mark, marking; **una tela a —s azules** a cloth with blue spots.
(b) (*Cards*) spot (*indicating value*); **¿a qué —?** what's trumps?, what suit are we in?
(c) (*of water etc*) drop, drop of rain; (*fam*) drink, drop to drink; **una — de grasa** a grease spot.
(d) (*fig*) appearance, look(s); **tener buena —** to look good, look well; **tener — de listo** to look clever, have a bright look about one; **tiene — de criminal** he has a criminal look.
(e) (*fam*) worthless creature.
(f) (*Arg, Per, PR: Zool etc*) colouring, coloration; (*Arg, Col, Ec, Mex, PR*) family characteristic, distinguishing mark.
(g) (*Bol, Chi, Per*) draughts.

(h) (*Chi*) high-grade ore.
(i) **hacer la —** (*Mex*), **irse de —** (*CAm*) to play truant.
(j) (*SD*) **ser de la —** to be a Negro, be of the Negro race.

pinta[2] *nf* (*British measure*) pint.

pintado *adj* (a) spotted; mottled, dappled; (*fig*) many-coloured, colourful.
(b) (*fam*) **podría pasarle al más —** it could happen to anybody; **lo hace como el más —** he does it with (*or* as well as) the best.
(c) (*fam*) **me sienta que ni —, viene que ni —** it comes just right; it suits me a treat.
(d) (*SAm*) like, identical; **el niño salió — al padre** the boy looked exactly like his father.

pintar [1a] 1 *vt* (a) to paint; *letter, sign etc* to draw, make; **— algo de azul** to paint something blue.
(b) (*fig*) to paint, depict, describe; **lo pinta todo con colores muy negros** he paints it all very black.
(c) (*fam*) **—la** to put it on, show off.
(d) (*fam*) **no pinta nada** he cuts no ice, he doesn't count; he has no say.
(e) (*SAm*) to flatter.
2 *vi* (a) to paint; "**ojo, que pinta**" (*notice*) "wet paint"; **— como querer** to daydream, indulge in wishful thinking.
(b) (*Bot*) to ripen, turn red.
(c) (*fam*) to show; to turn out (as), give signs of (being).
3 **pintarse** *vr* (a) to use make-up; to put on make-up, (*pej*) paint oneself.
(b) **—las solo para algo** to manage to do something by oneself.

pintarraj(e)ar [1a] *vti* (*fam*) to daub.

pintarrajo *nm* (*fam*) daub.

pintear [1a] *vi* to drizzle, spot with rain.

pintiparado *adj* (a) identical (*a to*). (b) **me viene (que ni) —** it comes just right, it's just what the doctor ordered.

pintiparar [1a] *vt* to compare.

pinto *adj* (a) (*SAm*) spotted; mottled, dappled; marked (*esp* with black and white); motley, colourful; *complexion* blotchy.
(b) (*Cu*) clever; (*pej*) sharp, shrewd.

Pinto: estar entre — y Valdemoro (*fam*) to be unable to decide between two alternatives.

pintor *nm*, **pintora** *nf* painter; **— de brocha gorda** house painter, (*fig*) bad painter, dauber; **— decorador** house painter, decorator.

pintoresco *adj* picturesque.

pintura *nf* (a) (*in general*) painting; (*fig*) painting, depiction, description.
(b) (*una —*) painting; **— a la acuarela, — a la aguada** watercolour; **— al óleo** oil painting; **— al pastel** pastel drawing; **— rupestre** cave painting.
(c) (*material*) paint; **— a la cola, — al temple** distemper, (*Art*) tempera.

pinturero (*fam*) 1 *adj* conceited, swanky (*fam*). 2 *nm*, **pinturera** *nf* show-off (*fam*), swank (*fam*).

pinza *nf* (*also* **—s**) clothes peg, clothespin (*US*); tweezers, forceps; tongs; (*Tech*) pincers; (*Zool*) claw; **—s de azúcar** sugar tongs; **no se lo sacan ni con —s** wild horses won't drag it out of him.

pinzón *nm* finch; **— vulgar** chaffinch; **— real** bullfinch.

piña *nf* (a) pine cone.
(b) (*also* **— de América, — de las Indias**) pineapple.
(c) (*fig*) group; cluster, knot; (*pej*) clique, closed circle.
(d) (*Ant, Mex*) hub.
(e) (*Mex, RPl*) punch, bash (*fam*); **darse —s** to fight, exchange blows.
(f) (*Mex: of revolver*) chamber.

piñal *nm* (*SAm*) pineapple plantation.

piñata *nf* (*Chi*) brawl, scrap (*fam*).

piñatería *nf* (*Chi*) armed holdup.

piño *nm* (*Chi*) lot, crowd.

piñón[1] *nm* (*Bot*) pine kernel; **estar a partir un —** to be bosom pals (*fam*).

piñón[2] *nm* (*Orn, Tech*) pinion.

piñonate *nm* candied pine kernel.

piñonear [1a] *vi* to click.

piñoneo *nm* click.

Pío *m* Pius.

pío[1] *adj* *horse* piebald, dappled.

pío[2] *adj* (a) (*Rel*) pious, devout; (*pej*) sanctimonious; excessively pious. (b) merciful.

pío[3] *nm* (a) (*Orn*) cheep, chirp; **no decir ni —** not to breathe a word; **¡de esto no digas ni —!** you keep your mouth shut about this!
(b) (*fam*) **tener el — de algo** to long for something.

piocha nf (a) jewel (worn on the head). (b) (SAm:
gall) pickaxe. (c) (Mex) goatee.
piojería nf (a) lousy place, verminous place. (b)
poverty. (c) (fam) tiny amount, very small portion.
piojo nm (a) louse; — **resucitado** (fam) jumped-up
fellow, vulgar parvenu; **estar como —s en costura** to
be packed in like sardines. (b) (Col) gambling den.
piojoso adj (a) lousy, verminous; (fig) dirty, ragged.
(b) (fig) mean.
piojuelo nm louse.
piola nf (a) (SAm) rope, tether. (b) (Per, Ven) cord,
string, twine.
piolet [pio'le] nm, pl **piolets** [pio'les] (gall) ice axe.
piolín nm (SAm) cord, twine.
pionco adj (a) (Chi) naked from the waist down. (b)
(Mex) squatting. (c) (Mex) horse short-tailed.
pionero (angl) 1 adj pioneering. 2 nm pioneer.
piorrea nf pyorrhoea.
pipa nf (a) pipe; **fumar una —, fumar en —** to smoke
a pipe.
(b) (of wine) cask, barrel; (as measure) pipe.
(c) (Bot) pip, seed, edible sunflower seed.
(d) (Mus) reed.
(e) (SAm) belly.
(f) (CR, Ec, Pan) green coconut.
pipeta nf pipette.
pipí nm (fam) weewee (fam); **hacer —** to go weewee
(fam).
pipiar [1c] vi to cheap, chirp.
pipiciego adj (Col) short-sighted.
pipil nm (CAm: hum) Mexican.
pipiolero nm (Mex) crowd of kids (fam).
pipiolo nm (a) youngster; (SAm) little boy; (fig)
novice, greenhorn, tyro. (b) (Ec) short person. (c)
(Arg, Ven) fool. (d) —s (CAm) money.
pipiripao nm (a) (fam) slap-up do (fam), spread
(fam). (b) (SAm) **de —** worthless.
pipo 1 adj (Ant, Ec) potbellied; **estar —** (PR) to be
blown out.
2 nm (a) (Ant, Ec) child.
(b) (Ant, Ec) crooked employee.
(c) (Col) punch, bash (fam).
(d) (Col) contraband liquor.
pipón adj (Ant, Ec, RPl) potbellied; full, blown out
(after a meal).
pipote nm keg, cask.
pique[1] nm (a) pique, resentment; ill will; grudge;
rivalry, competition; self-respect; **estar de —** to
have a grudge, be at loggerheads; **tener un — con
uno** to have a grudge against someone.
(b) **estar a — de + infin** to be on the point of +
ger; to be in danger of + ger; **estuvo a — de hacerlo**
he very nearly did it.
(c) **echar a — ship** to sink; (fig) to wreck, ruin;
irse a — to sink, founder; (hope, family etc) to be
ruined.
(d) (SAm) bounce, rebound.
(e) (Chi, Hond) mine shaft; (Mex) drill, well.
(f) (Arg, Guat) trail, narrow path.
pique[2] nm (Cards: gall) spades.
piquera nf (a) hole, vent. (b) (CAm, Mex) night-club
hostess.
piquero nm (a) (Hist) pikeman. (b) (Chi, Ec) miner.
piqueta nf pick, pickaxe.
piquetazo nm (SAm) = **picotazo**; (Col) = **tijeretazo**.
piquete nm (a) prick, jab, slight wound.
(b) small hole (in clothing).
(c) (Mil) squad, party; (of strikers) picket.
(d) (Arg) yard, small corral.
(e) (Col) picnic.
(f) (Cu) small band; poor-quality band.
piquiña nf (a) (Ant, Col, Ven) = **picazón**. (b) (PR)
envy; grudge.
pira nf pyre.
piragua nf canoe; (Sport) shell.
piragüismo nm canoeing.
piragüista nmf canoeist; oarsman.
piramidal adj (a) pyramidal. (b) (Col) terrific (fam),
tremendous (fam).
pirámide nf pyramid.
piraña nf (SAm) piranha.
pirarse [1a] vr (fam; also **—las**) (a) to beat it (fam).
(b) (Univ) to cut class.
pirata nm (a) pirate. (b) (fig) hard-hearted person.
(c) (fam) plagiarist, borrower of other people's
ideas (etc).
piratear [1a] vi to buccaneer, practise piracy; (fig) to
steal.
piratería nf piracy; (fig) theft, stealing; —s depredations.
pirático adj piratical.
piraya nf (SAm) piranha.

pirca nf (SAm) dry-stone wall.
pirenaico adj Pyrenean.
pirético adj pyretic.
piretro nm pyrethrum.
pirgua nf (Arg, Bol, Chi) shed, outhouse, small barn.
pirineo adj Pyrenean.
Pirineo m, **Pirineos** mpl Pyrenees; **el — catalán** the
Catalan (part of the) Pyrenees.
pirinola nf (Mex) kid (fam), child.
piripez nf (fam): **coger una —** to get sozzled (sl).
piripi adj (fam): **estar —** to be sozzled (sl).
piritas nfpl pyrites.
pirlán nm (Col) doorstep.
piro . . . pyro . . .
pirófago nm fire-eater.
piropear [1a] vt to pay an amorous compliment to,
make a flirtatious remark to.
piropo nm (a) amorous compliment, flirtatious
remark; nice (and witty) thing to say; **echar —s a =
piropear**.
(b) garnet; ruby.
(c) (Col) ticking-off.
pirotecnia nf pyrotechnics; firework display (also
fig).
pirotécnico adj pyrotechnic, firework (attr).
pirrarse [1a] vr (fam): **— por** to rave about, be crazy
about.
pírrico adj: **victoria f pírrica** Pyrrhic victory.
pirueta nf (a) pirouette; caper. (b) (fig) remark which
helps someone out of an awkward situation. (c) —s
(fig) balancing act (between two policies etc).
piruetear [1a] vi to pirouette; to caper.
pirulí nm toffee apple; (Ant, CAm, Mex, RPl)
lollipop.
pirulo nm, **pirula** nf (Chi, RPl) slim child.
pisa nf (a) treading (of grapes etc). (b) (fam) beating.
pisada nf footstep, footfall, tread; footprint.
pisadera nf (Per) carpet.
pisadero nm (Mex) brothel.
pisapapeles nm, pl **pisapapeles** paperweight.
pisar [1a] 1 vt (a) to tread (on), walk on; (accidentally)
to step on; (destructively) to flatten, crush, trample
(on, underfoot); grapes etc to tread; earth to tread
down; — **el acelerador** to step on the accelerator,
press the accelerator; **no volvimos a — ese sitio**
we never went to that place again.
(b) (Mus) key to play, strike, press; string to
pluck.
(c) to lie on, cover (part of).
(d) (fig) to trample on, walk all over; to disregard; to abuse; **no se deja — por nadie** he doesn't
let anybody trample over him.
(e) (fam) honey, pinch, steal; **A le pisó la
novia a B** A pinched B's girl; — **una baza a uno**
to trump someone's trick; **otro le pisó el puesto**
someone got in first and collared the job (fam); **el
periódico le pisó la noticia** the newspaper got in
first with the news.
2 vi (a) to tread, step, walk; **hay que — con
cuidado** you have to tread carefully.
(b) (fig) — **fuerte** to act determinedly; to make a
strong showing, make a real impression; **entrar
pisando fuerte** to get off to a good start.
3 **pisarse** vr (Arg) to be mistaken.
pisaverde nm fop, toff (fam).
pisca nf (Mex) maize harvest, corn harvest (US).
piscador nm (Mex) harvester.
piscar [1g] vi (Mex) to harvest maize (or corn: US).
piscina nf (a) swimming pool. (b) fishpond, fishtank.
pisco[1] nm (Col) (a) turkey. (b) (fig) fellow, guy
(US fam).
pisco[2] nm (SAm) brandy, liquor.
piscoiro nm, **piscoira** nf (Chi) kid (fam), child.
piscolabis nm, pl **piscolabis** (fam) snack.
pisicorre nm (Ant) small bus.
piso nm (a) floor; flooring.
(b) (Archit) storey, floor; (of bus) deck; (of rocket)
stage; — **alto** top floor; — **bajo** ground floor,
first floor (US); **primer —** first floor, second floor
(US); **un edificio de 8 —s** an 8-storey building;
viven en el quinto — they live on the fifth floor;
autobús de dos —s double-decker bus; **ir en el — de
arriba** to travel on the top deck, travel upstairs.
(c) flat, apartment (US); **poner un — a una** to
make a girl one's mistress.
(d) (Aut: of tyre) tread.
(e) (of shoe) sole; **poner — a un zapato** to sole a
shoe.
(f) (Min) set of workings; (Geol) layer, stratum.
(g) (Chi) stool; bench.
(h) (Chi, Mex) table runner; (Chi, Per) long narrow
rug.

pisón nm (a) ram, rammer. (b) (SAm) = **pisotón**. (c) (RPl) mortar.

pisotear [1a] vt (a) to tread down, trample (on, underfoot); to stamp on. (b) (fig) to trample on; law etc to abuse, disregard.

pisotón nm (a) stamp on the foot. (b) (fam) newspaper scoop, reporting scoop.

pispar [1a] vi (Chi, RPl) to keep watch, spy.

pisporra nf (CAm) wart.

pista nf (a) (Zool and fig) track, trail; (fig) clue; — falsa false trail, false clue; (in argument etc) red herring; **estar sobre la** — to be on the scent; **estar sobre la** — **de uno** to be on someone's trail, be after someone; **seguir la** — **de uno** to be on someone's track, trail someone; **la policía tiene una** — **ya** the police already have a lead (or clue).

(b) (Sport etc) track, course; court; (Aut) motorway; — **de aterrizaje** runway; landing strip; — **de baile** dance floor; — **de bolos** bowling alley; — **de carreras** racetrack; — **de ceniza** dirt track; — **de esquí** ski run; — **de hielo** ice rink; — **de patinaje** skating rink; — **de tenis** tennis court; **atletismo en** — track events.

pistacho nm pistachio.

pistero adj (CAm) mercenary, fond of money.

pistilo nm pistil.

pisto nm (a) (Med) chicken broth. (b) (Cook) fried vegetable hash. (c) (fig) mixture, hotchpotch. (d) a —s little by little; sparingly. (e) **darse** — (fam) to show off, swank (fam). (f) (CAm, Per) money. (g) (Col) barrel (of gun). (h) (Mex) shot of liquor.

pistola nf pistol; (Tech) spray, sprayer; — **ametralladora** submachine gun, tommy gun; — **engrasadora**, — **de engrase** grease gun; — **de juguete** toy pistol; — **rociadora de pintura** paint spray.

pistolera nf holster.

pistolero nm gunman, gangster.

pistoleta nf (Arg, Col, Chi) pistol.

pistoletazo nm pistol shot.

pistolete nm pocket pistol.

pistón nm (a) (Mech) piston. (b) (Mus) key; (SAm) bugle, cornet. (c) (fam) **de** — = **pistonudo**.

pistonudo adj (fam) smashing (sl), terrific (fam).

pistudo adj (CAm) rich.

pita nf (SAm) agave; pita fibre, pita thread.

pitada nf (a) whistle; hiss. (b) (SAm) puff (at cigarette etc). (c) (fam) silly remark.

pitador nm, **pitadora** nf (SAm) smoker.

Pitágoras m Pythagoras.

pitandero nm (Chi) smoker.

pitanza nf (a) dole, daily ration; (fam) grub (sl). (b) (fam) price. (c) (Chi) bargain; profit.

pitar [1a] 1 vt (a) whistle to blow. (b) referee etc to whistle at, boo; actor, play to hiss, give the bird to (sl). (c) (SAm) to smoke.
2 vi (a) to whistle, blow a whistle; to hiss, boo; (Aut) to sound one's horn. (b) (SAm) to smoke. (c) (fam) **esto no pita** this is no good, this doesn't work; — **bien** to give a good account of oneself; **salir pitando** to beat it (fam).

pitay nm (Arg, Bol) rash.

pitazo nm (Mex, Per) whistle, hoot.

pitear [1a] vi (SAm) = **pitar** 2 (a).

pitido nm whistle.

pitillera nf cigarette case.

pitillo nm (a) cigarette; **echarse un** — to have a smoke. (b) (Ec, Ven) drinking straw.

pitiyanqui nmf, **pitiyanki** nmf (PR) slavish imitator of Yankee mannerisms.

pito nm (a) whistle; (Aut) horn, hooter; (Rail etc) whistle, hooter; **tener voz de** — to have a squeaky voice.
(b) (Orn) — **real** green woodpecker. (c) (SAm: Zool) tick. (d) cigarette; (SAm) pipe. (e) (SAm: tabu) prick (tabu). (f) (idioms) —s **flautos** (fam) tomfoolery, absurdities; **cuando** —s, **flautas** it's always the same, one way or another it always happens; **no se me da un** —, (no) **me importa un** — I don't care two hoots (de about); **en este asunto no toca** — he's got nothing to do with this matter; **me tomaron por el** — **del sereno** they thought I was something the cat had brought in; **no vale un** — it's not worth tuppence.

pitón[1] nm (Zool) python.

pitón[2] nm bump, lump, protuberance; (Zool) budding horn; (Bot) sprig, young shoot; (of jar etc) spout; (SAm: of hose) nozzle; — **de roca** sharp point of rock.

pitongo[1] adj (Chi) drunk.

pitongo[2] adj (sl): **niño** — spoiled upper-class child.

pitonisa nf fortuneteller; witch, sorceress.

pitorrearse [1a] vr: — **de** (fam) to scoff at, make fun of.

pitorro nm spout.

pitra nf (Chi) rash.

pitre adj (Col, Cu, PR, Ven) foppish.

pituitario adj pituitary; **glándula pituitaria** pituitary (gland).

pituco nm (RPl) fop, toff (fam).

piuco adj (Chi) timid, scared.

piular [1a] vi to cheep, chirp.

pivote nm pivot.

píxide nf pyx.

piyama nm (SAm) pyjamas.

pizarra nf (a) slate; shale. (b) (School etc) blackboard.

pizarral nm slate quarry; shale bed.

pizarrín nm slate pencil.

pizarrón nm (SAm: School) blackboard; (Sport) scoreboard.

pizarroso adj slaty.

pizca nf (a) pinch, spot; crumb; **una** — **de sal** a pinch of salt. (b) (fig) spot, speck, trace, jot; **ni** — not a bit, not a scrap; **no tiene ni** — **de verdad** there's not a jot of truth in it.

pizcar [1g] vt to pinch, nip.

pizco nm pinch, nip.

pizpireta nf (fam) bright girl, lively (little) girl; smart little piece (sl).

placa nf (a) plate; thin piece of material, (thin) sheet; tab; plaque, tablet; dental plate, denture; — **conmemorativa** commemorative plaque; — **giratoria** turntable; — **de matrícula** number plate, registration plate; — **del nombre** nameplate. (b) (Phot: also — **fotográfica**) plate; — **esmerilada** focusing screen. (c) (Mus) gramophone record, phonograph record (US). (d) badge, insignia. (e) (SAm) blotch, skin blemish.

placaminero nm persimmon.

pláceme nm congratulations, message of congratulations; **dar el** — **a uno** to congratulate someone.

placenta nf placenta.

placentero adj pleasant, agreeable.

placentino 1 adj of Plasencia. 2 nm, **placentina** nf native (or inhabitant) of Plasencia; **los** —s the people of Plasencia.

placer[1] 1 nm (a) pleasure; enjoyment, delight; **a** — at one's pleasure; as much as one wants; **es un** — + infin it is a pleasure to + infin; **con mucho** —, **con sumo** — with great pleasure; **tengo** — **en** + infin it is my pleasure to + infin, I have pleasure in + ger. (b) pleasure; **los** —es **del ocio** the pleasures of idleness; **darse a los** —es to give oneself over to pleasures.
2 [2x] vt to please; **me place poder** + infin I am glad to be able to + infin.

placer[2] nm (a) (Geol, Min) placer. (b) (Naut) sandbank. (c) (Col) ground prepared for sowing; plot, patch; (Cu) field.

placero nm, **placera** nf (a) stallholder, market trader. (b) (fig) loafer, gossip.

placeta nf (Chi) piece of level ground.

plácidamente adv placidly.

placidez nf placidity.

plácido adj placid.

plaga nf (a) (Agr: Zool) pest, (Bot) blight; — **del jardín** garden pest; — **de la vid** pest of vines, pest on the vine; —s **forestales** pests on timber, forest pests. (b) (Med, of locusts etc) plague; (fig) scourge; calamity, disaster; blight; **aquí la sequía es una** — drought is a menace here; **una** — **de gitanos** a plague of gipsies. (c) (fig) glut, abundance; **ha habido una** — **de lechugas** there has been a glut of lettuces. (d) (fig) hardship.

plagar [1h] 1 vt (a) to infest, plague; to fill; **han plagado la ciudad de carteles** they have covered (or plastered) the town with posters; **un texto plagado de errores** a text full of errors, a text riddled with errors. (b) — **de minas** to sow with mines.
2 **plagarse** vr to become infested with.

plagiar [1b] vt (a) to plagiarize. (b) (SAm) to kidnap.

plagiario nm, **plagiaria** nf (a) plagiarist. (b) (SAm) kidnapper.

plagio nm (a) plagiarism. (b) (SAm) kidnapping.
plan nm (a) plan; scheme; idea, intention; — **de desarrollo** development plan; — **del ensanche de la capital** plan for the expansion of the capital; — **quinquenal** five-year plan; **mi — era comprar otro nuevo** my idea was to buy a new one; **realizar su** — to put one's plans into effect.
  (b) (fam) (idea for an) activity, amusement; **ha sido un — muy pesado** it turned out to be a very tedious kind of amusement; **tengo un — estupendo para mañana** I've got a splendid idea about what to do tomorrow.
  (c) (fam: between sexes) date; (pej) affair; **¿tienes — para esta noche?** are you booked for tonight?, have you a date for tonight?; **tiene un — con la mujer del alcalde** he's having an affair with the mayor's wife.
  (d) programme; — **de estudios** curriculum, syllabus.
  (e) (Med) régime; course of treatment; **estar a —** to be on a course of treatment.
  (f) (Surveying) level; height.
  (g) (fam) **a todo —** with great ceremony; in a very posh way (fam).
  (h) (fam) **no me hace —** + infin it doesn't suit me to + infin.
  (i) (fam) set-up, system, arrangement; basis; footing; attitude; **en — económico** in an economical way, on the cheap; **en ese —** in that way; at that rate; **como sigas en ese —** if you go on like that; **si te pones en ese —** if that's your attitude; **no puedo con este — de esperar** I can't stand this business of waiting; **está en un — imposible** it's on an impossible basis, it's an impossible set-up; **en — de** as; on a basis of; **vamos en — de turismo** we're going as tourists; **estaban en — de viaje** they were making preparations for the trip; **unos jóvenes en — de divertirse** some youngsters out for a good time; **está en — de rehusar** he's in a mood to refuse, he's likely to refuse at the moment.
  (j) (Mex, RPl) flat bottom (of boat etc).
  (k) (Chi, Guat, Mex, Ven) level ground; plain; (Arg, Chi) flat area at the foot of a hill.
  (l) (Cu, Ec, Guat, Ven) flat (of a sword etc).
plana nf (a) sheet (of paper), page; (School) writing exercise, copy writing; (Typ) page; — **de anuncios** advertisement page; **en primera —** on the front page; **noticias de primera —** front-page news; **corregir** (or **enmendar**) **la — a uno** to put someone right, (pej) find fault with someone; to improve upon someone's efforts.
  (b) (Mil) — **mayor** staff; (fig) persons in charge.
  (c) (Tech) trowel; cooper's plane.
planazo nm (a) (SAm) blow with the flat of a sword (etc). (b) (Cu) shot of liquor.
plancha nf (a) plate, sheet; slab; (Typ) plate; (Naut) gangway; (Med) dental plate; **hacer la —** (bather) to float.
  (b) iron; (act) ironing; pressing; ironed clothes; clothes to be ironed, ironing; — **eléctrica** electric iron.
  (c) (fam) bloomer (fam); **hacer una —, tirarse una —** to make a bloomer, drop a clanger (sl).
planchada nf (SAm) (a) landing stage. (b) (fam) = **plancha** (c).
planchado 1 adj (a) clothes ironed; pressed.
  (b) (Arg, Guat, Salv) very smart, dolled up.
  (c) (Cu, Chi, Per) broke (fam).
  (d) (Mex) clever; brave.
  2 nm ironing; pressing; **dar un — a** to iron; to press; **prenda que no necesita —** non-iron garment.
planchar [1a] 1 vt (a) clothes to iron; suit, trousers to press; **prenda de no —** non-iron garment.
  (b) (SAm) to flatter, suck up to (fam).
  2 vi (a) to iron, do the ironing.
  (b) (SAm) to sit out (a dance), be a wallflower.
  (c) (Chi, RPl) to make a bloomer (fam), drop a clanger (sl); to make oneself look ridiculous.
planchear [1a] vt to plane.
plancheta nf (a) (Surveying) plane table. (b) (fam) **echárselas de —** to show off, swank (fam).
planchón nm (SAm) snowcap; ice field.
planeador nm glider.
planeadora nf leveller, bulldozer.
planear [1a] 1 vt to plan. 2 vi (Aer) to glide.
planeta nm planet.
planetario 1 adj planetary. 2 nm planetarium.
planicie nf plain; flat area, level ground; flat surface.
planificación nf planning; — **de familia, — familiar** family planning.
planificador 1 adj planning (attr). 2 nm planner.
planificar [1g] vt to plan.

planilla nf (a) (SAm) list; table, tabulation; payroll.
  (b) (SAm: Rail etc) ticket.
  (c) (Ec, Per, RPl) form, application form, blank; (Fin) account; expense account.
  (d) (CAm, Ec, Mex) voting paper; (Pol) ticket.
planimetría nf surveying, planimetry.
plankton nm plankton.
plano 1 adj (a) flat, level, even; plane (also Math, Mech); smooth; **caer de —** to fall flat.
  (b) **de —** (fig): **le daba el sol de —** the sun shone directly on it; the sun was directly over it; **confesar de —** to make a full confession; **rechazar algo de —** to turn something down flat, reject something outright; see **cortar**.
  2 nm (a) (Math, Mech) plane; — **focal** focal plane; — **inclinado** inclined plane.
  (b) (fig) plane; position, level; **de distinto — social** of a different social level; **están en un — distinto** they're on a different plane.
  (c) (Cine, Phot) shot; **primer —** foreground; close-up; **un primer — de la famosa actriz** a close-up of the famous actress.
  (d) (Aer) plane; — **de cola** tailplane.
  (e) (Archit, Mech etc) plan; (Geog) map; (of city) map, street plan; — **acotado** contour map; **levantar el — de** country to survey, map, make a map of; building etc to draw up the designs for.
  (f) (of sword) flat.
planta nf (a) (Anat) sole of the foot, foot; **asentar sus —s en** to establish oneself in.
  (b) (Archit) ground plan; **construir un edificio de (nueva) —** to build a completely new building, rebuild from the foundations up.
  (c) (Archit) floor, storey; — **baja** ground floor, first floor (US); **una ventana de la — baja** a downstairs window, a ground-floor window.
  (d) (Dancing, Fencing) position (of the feet).
  (e) **de buena —** well-built; shapely; **tener buena —** to have a fine physique; to be good-looking.
  (f) (Tech) plant; — **de ensamblaje** assembly plant; — **piloto** pilot plant.
  (g) plan, programme, scheme.
  (h) (Bot) plant.
  (i) (fam) **echar —s** to swagger; to brag.
plantación nf (a) (act) planting. (b) plantation; — **de tabaco** tobacco plantation.
plantado adj (a) (fam) **dejar a uno —** to leave someone suddenly, leave someone in mid-sentence; to leave someone in the lurch, leave someone high and dry; **dejar — al novio** to jilt one's boyfriend, walk out on one's boyfriend; (on a date) to stand one's boyfriend up (fam).
  (b) **bien —** well-built; shapely; good-looking.
plantador nm (a) (Agr) dibber. (b) (person) planter.
plantaje nm (Col, Ec, PR) looks.
plantar [1a] 1 vt (a) (Bot) to plant.
  (b) post etc to put in; monument etc to erect, set up; tent to pitch; belief, reform etc to implant; institution to set up.
  (c) blow to plant (en on).
  (d) remark to make.
  (e) — **a uno en la calle** to pitch someone into the street, chuck someone out; — **a un obrero en la calle** to sack a workman (fam).
  (f) (fam) — **a uno** to curb someone, check someone; **le planté para que no dijera más** I stopped him before he could say any more.
  (g) (fam) **dejar plantado** (see **plantado** (a)).
  2 **plantarse** vr (a) to stand firm, stay resolutely where one is; to plant oneself; (fig) to stand firm, dig one's heels in, refuse to compromise.
  (b) (horse) to balk, refuse.
  (c) — **en** to reach, get to; **en 3 horas se plantó en Sevilla** he got to Seville in 3 hours.
  (d) (Cards) to stick.
  (e) (CAm, Col, Mex) to doll oneself up.
plante nm stand, agreed basis for resistance, common programme of demands.
plantear [1a] vt (a) belief, reform etc to implant; change to get under way; institution to set up, establish.
  (b) to plan.
  (c) problem to create, pose; difficulty, question to raise; discussion, lawsuit etc to start; **nos ha planteado muchos problemas** it has created a lot of problems for us; **se lo plantearé** I'll put it to him; I'll have it out with him.
plantel nm (a) (Hort) nursery.
  (b) training establishment, nursery.
  (c) (RPl) stud animals; best animals on a farm; (fig) group, set, establishment.
  (d) (Mex) school.

plantificarse [1g] *vr* (a) (*Cu, Mex, RPl*) to plant oneself. (b) (*CAm, Mex*) to doll up.

plantilla *nf* (a) (*of shoe*) inner sole, insole; (*of stocking etc*) sole.

(b) (*Tech*) pattern, template; stencil.

(c) (*persons*) establishment, personnel; list, roster; — **de personal** staff; **ser de** — to be established, be on the establishment.

plantío *nm* (a) (*act*) planting. (b) plot, bed, patch.

plantista *nm* braggart.

plantón *nm* (a) (*Bot*) seedling; cutting.

(b) (*Mil etc*) guard, sentry.

(c) (*fam*) long wait, tedious wait; **dar (un) — a uno** to stand someone up (on a date; *fam*); **estar de** — to be stuck, have to wait around; **tener a uno de** — to keep someone waiting around.

plañidera *nf* (paid) mourner.

plañidero *adj* mournful, plaintive.

plañir [3h] *vt* to mourn, grieve over.

plasma *nm* plasma.

plasmar [1a] **1** *vt* to mould, shape, form; to create; to represent, give visible (*or* concrete) form to. **2** *vi*: — **en** to take the form of, emerge as.

plasta *nf* (a) soft mass, lump; flattened mass.

(b) (*fam*) botch, mess; **es una — de edificio** it's a mess of a building; **el plan es una** — the plan is one big mess, the plan is a complete botch.

plástica *nf* (art of) sculpture, modelling.

plasticidad *nf* (a) plasticity. (b) (*fig*) expressiveness, descriptiveness; richness, evocative character.

plasticina *nf* plasticine.

plástico 1 *adj* (a) (*in most senses*) plastic; **artes plásticas** plastic arts.

(b) (*fig*) *image etc* expressive, descriptive; *description* rich, poetic, evocative. **2** *nm* plastic.

plastificado *adj* treated with plastic.

plastrón *nm* (*SAm*) floppy tie, cravate.

plata *nf* (a) silver; silverware; (*Fin*) silver, silver coin(s); **como una** — shining bright, like a new pin.

(b) (*esp SAm*) money; wealth; **apalear** — to be rolling in money.

(c) **hablar en** — to speak bluntly, speak frankly.

platada *nf* (*SAm*) dish, plateful.

plataforma *nf* (a) platform; stage; (*Rail*) turntable; — **de lanzamiento** launching pad; — **de perforación** submarine drilling rig.

(b) (*SAm: Pol: angl*) platform.

platal *nm* (*SAm*) fortune; wealth.

platanal *nm*, **platanar** *nm*, **platanera** *nf* (*Col, Mex, PR*) banana plantation.

platanero 1 *adj* banana (*attr*). **2** *nm* (*CAm, Mex*) banana grower; dealer in bananas.

plátano *nm* (a) plane; plane tree. (b) banana; banana tree.

platea *nf* (*Theat*) pit, orchestra (US).

plateado 1 *adj* (a) silver; silvery; (*Tech*) silver-plated. (b) (*Mex*) wealthy. **2** *nm* silver-plating.

platear [1a] *vt* (a) to silver; to silver-plate. (b) (*Mex, Nic*) to sell, turn into money.

platense *adj* (*SAm*) = **rioplatense**.

platería *nf* (a) silversmith's craft. (b) silversmith's; jeweller's.

platero *nm* silversmith; jeweller.

plática *nf* talk, chat; (*Eccl*) sermon; **estar de** — to be chatting, have a talk.

platicar [1g] *vi* (a) to talk, chat. (b) (*Mex*) to say, tell.

platija *nf* plaice.

platillo *nm* (a) saucer; small plate; collecting bowl; — **de balance** scale, pan (*of scales*); — **volador,** — **volante** flying saucer; **pasar el** — to pass the hat round, make a collection.

(b) **—s** (*Mus*) cymbals.

(c) (*CAm, Mex*) dish; course; **el tercer — de la comida** the third course of the meal.

platina *nf* microscope slide.

platino 1 *nm* platinum; **—s** (*Aut*) contact points. **2** *as adj*: **rubia** — platinum blonde.

plato *nm* (a) plate, dish; (*Tech*) plate; (*of balance*) scale, pan; — **frutero** fruit dish; — **hondo,** — **sopero** soup dish; **del — a la boca se pierde la sopa** there's many a slip 'twixt cup and lip; **fregar** (*or* **lavar**) **los** — **s** to wash the dishes, wash up; **pagar los** — **s rotos** to pay for the damage, (*fig*) to carry the can (*sl*); *see* **nada**.

(b) plateful, dish; **un — de arroz** a dish of rice; **vender algo por un — de lentejas** to sell something for a mess of pottage.

(c) dish; course; — **dulce** sweet course; — **fuerte** main course; heavy dish, meal in itself; **sopa y 4 —s** soup and 4 courses; **es un — típico español** it's a

typical Spanish dish; **es mi — favorito** it's my favourite dish (*or* meal); **ser — de segunda mesa** (*fam*) to be second-best; to feel neglected, be left out in the cold.

plató *nm* (*Cine*) set.

Platón *m* Plato.

platón *nm* (*SAm*) (a) large dish; serving dish. (b) washbasin.

platónicamente *adv* Platonically.

platónico *adj* Platonic.

platonismo *nm* Platonism.

platonista *nmf* Platonist.

platudo *adj* (*SAm*) rich, well heeled (*sl*).

plausible *adj* (a) commendable, laudable, praiseworthy. (b) *reason etc* acceptable, admissible.

plausiblemente *adv* commendably, laudably.

playa *nf* (a) shore, beach; **una — de arenas doradas** a beach of golden sands; **pasar el día en la** — to spend the day on the beach; **pescar desde la** — to fish from the beach.

(b) (*fig*) seaside; seaside resort; **ir a veranear a una** — to spend the summer at the seaside, go to the seaside for one's summer holidays.

(c) (*Arg, Bol, Ven*) flat open space; (*Rail*) yard; — **de estacionamiento** carpark, parking place, parking lot (US); — **de juegos** playground.

playeras *nfpl* sandals, sandshoes; tennis shoes.

playero *adj* beach (*attr*).

playo *adj* (*Mex, RPl*) shallow.

plaza *nf* (a) square; public square, open space; market (place); — **de armas** parade ground; — **mayor** main square; — **de toros** bullring; **hacer la** — to do the daily shopping.

(b) (*Comm*) town, city, centre; **en esa** — there, in your town.

(c) room, space; place; (*on vehicle etc*) seat, place; **¡—! make way!; abrir** — to make way; **el avión tiene 90 —s** the plane has 90 seats, the plane carries 90 passengers; **de dos —s** (*Aut etc*) two-seater; **reservar una** — to reserve a seat.

(d) post, job; vacancy; **cubrir una** — to fill a job, appoint to a post; **sentar** — (*Mil*) to enlist, sign on (**de** as).

(e) (*Mil*) fortress, fortified town (*also* — **fuerte**).

plazo *nm* (a) time, period, term; time limit; date, expiry date; (*Comm, Fin*) date; **en un — de 6 meses** in the space of 6 months, in a period of 6 months; **within a term of 6 months**, before 6 months are up; **nos dan un — de 8 días** they allow us a week, they give us a week's grace; **¿cuándo vence el —?** when is the payment due?, what is the time limit?; **se ha cumplido el** — the time is up; **a** — (*Comm*) on credit; **a corto** — *loan* short-dated, (*fig*) short-term; **a largo** — *loan* long-dated, (*fig*) long-term; **es una tarea a largo** — it's a long-term job.

(b) instalment, payment; **pagar el — de marzo** to pay the March instalment; **comprar a —s** to buy on hire purchase, pay for in instalments.

plazoleta *nf*, **plazuela** *nf* small square.

pleamar *nf* high tide.

plebe *nf*: **la** — the common people, the masses, the mass of the population; (*pej*) the plebs; the mob, the rabble.

plebeyez *nf* plebeian nature; (*fig*) coarseness, commonness.

plebeyo 1 *adj* plebeian; (*pej*) coarse, common. **2** *nm*, **plebeya** *nf* plebeian, commoner; (*pej*) plebeian.

plebiscito *nm* plebiscite.

plectro *nm* plectrum.

plegable 1 *adj* pliable, that bends; *chair etc* folding, that folds up, collapsible. **2** *nm* playpen.

plegadera *nf* paper knife.

plegadizo *adj* = **plegable 1**.

plegado *nm*, **plegadura** *nf* (a) (*act*) folding; bending; creasing. (b) fold; crease.

plegar [1h *and* 1k] **1** *vt* to fold; to bend; to crease; (*Sew*) to pleat. **2 plegarse** *vr* (a) to bend; to crease. (b) (*fig*) to yield, submit (*a* to).

plegaria *nf* prayer.

pleitear [1a] *vi* (a) to plead, conduct a lawsuit; to go to law (*con, contra* with; *sobre* over), indulge in litigation. (b) (*esp SAm*) to argue.

pleitesía *nf*: **rendir — a** to show respect for, treat respectfully, show courtesy to; (*SAm*) to pay tribute to.

pleitista 1 *adj* litigious; (*fig*) quarrelsome, argumentative. **2** *nmf* litigious person; quarrelsome individual.

pleitisto *adj* (*SAm*) quarrelsome, argumentative.

pleito *nm* (a) (*Law*) lawsuit, case; **—s** litigation; — **de acreedores** bankruptcy proceedings; — **civil** civil action; **andar a —s** to be engaged in lawsuits;

entablar — to bring an action, bring a lawsuit; **ganar el** — to win one's case; **poner** — to sue, bring an action; **poner** — **a uno** to bring an action against someone, take someone to court.
   (**b**) (*fig*) dispute, feud; controversy; (*SAm*) quarrel, argument; **estar a** — **con uno** to be at odds with someone.
   (**c**) — **homenaje** homage.
plenamente *adj* fully; completely.
plenario *adj* plenary, full.
plenilunio *nm* full moon.
plenipotenciario *nm* plenipotentiary.
plenitud *nf* plenitude, fullness; abundance; **en la** — **de** in the fullness of; at the height of.
pleno 1 *adj* full; complete; *powers* full; *session* plenary, full; **en** — **día** in broad daylight; **en** — **verano** at the height of summer; **tiene frío en** — **mes de julio** he's cold even though it's July; **en plena rebeldía** in open revolt; **en plena vista** in full view; **le dio en plena cara** it hit him full in the face.
   2 *nm* (**a**) plenum.
   (**b**) **en** — as a whole, collectively; unanimously.
pleonasmo *nm* pleonasm.
pleonástico *adj* pleonastic.
plepa *nf* sickly person.
plétora *nf* plethora, abundance; flood; excess, surplus.
pletórico *adj* abundant; — **de** abounding in, full of, brimming with.
pleuresía *nf* pleurisy.
plexiglás *nm* perspex (*Protected Trade Name*).
plexo *nm*: — **solar** solar plexus.
plica *nf* sealed envelope, sealed document; (*in competition*) sealed entry.
pliego *nm* (**a**) sheet; folder; (*Typ*) gathering.
   (**b**) sealed letter, sealed document; — **cerrado** (*Naut*) sealed orders; — **de condiciones** details, specifications (*of a tender etc*); — **de cargos** list of accusations; *see* **descargo**.
pliegue *nm* (**a**) fold, crease; (*Sew*) pleat, crease; tuck. (**b**) (*Geol etc*) fold.
Plinio *m* Pliny; — **el Joven** Pliny the Younger; — **el Viejo** Pliny the Elder.
plinto *nm* plinth.
plisado *nm* pleating.
plisar [1a] *vt* to pleat.
plomada *nf* (*Archit etc*) plumb; (*Naut*) lead; (*on fishing net*) weights, sinkers.
plomar [1a] *vt* to seal with lead.
plomazo *nm* (*CAm, Mex*) shot; bullet wound.
plombagina *nf* plumbago.
plomería *nf* (**a**) (*Archit*) leading, lead roofing. (**b**) (*SAm*) plumbing; plumber's workshop, plumber's shop.
plomero *nm* (*SAm*) plumber.
plomizo *adj* (**a**) leaden, lead-coloured. (**b**) (*fig*) leaden.
plomo 1 *nm* (**a**) lead; — **derretido** molten lead; **soldado de** — tin soldier.
   (**b**)=**plomada**; (*Fishing*) weight, sinker; **a** — plumb, true, vertical(ly); (*fig*) just right, exactly right; **caer a** — to fall heavily, fall flat.
   (**c**) (*Elec*) fuse; **se ha fundido el** — it's fused.
   (**d**) (*esp SAm*) bullet, shot.
   (**e**) (*fam*) bore, dull affair, dull person.
   (**f**) (*Mex*) gunfight.
   2 *adj* (*SAm*) leaden, lead-coloured.
plomoso *adj* (*CAm*) boring.
plugo, pluguiere *etc see* **placer**[1].
pluma *nf* (**a**) (*Orn*) feather; quill; (*adornment*) plume, feather; **colchón de** — **s** feather bed; **hacer algo a** — **y a pelo** to waste nothing, do something using every scrap.
   (**b**) pen (*also fig*); — **esferográfica** (*SAm*) ball-point pen; — **estilográfica** fountain pen; **y otras obras de su** — and other works from his pen; **dejar correr la** — to write spontaneously; **escribir a vuela** — to write quickly, write without much thought.
   (**c**) (*fig*) penmanship, writing.
   (**d**) (*CAm*) fib, tale; hoax.
   (**e**) (*Arg, Mex*) prostitute.
   (**f**) (*Col, PR, Urug*) tap, faucet (*US*).
   (**g**) (*Chi*) crane, derrick.
plumada *nf* stroke of the pen; flourish.
plumado *adj* feathered, with feathers; *chick* fledged.
plumafuente *nf* (*SAm*) fountain pen.
plumaje *nm* (**a**) (*Orn*) plumage, feathers. (**b**) (*adornment*) plume, crest; bunch of feathers.
plumario *nm*, **plumaria** *nf* (*CAm, Mex*) hack journalist.

plumazo *nm* (**a**) stroke of the pen (*also fig*); **de un** — with one stroke of the pen.
   (**b**) piece of rapid writing (*or sketching*).
   (**c**) feather mattress; feather pillow.
plúmbeo *adj* leaden.
plúmbico *adj* plumbic.
plumear [1a] **1** *vt* (*CAm, Mex*) to write. **2** *vi* (*Mex*) to be (*or* become) a prostitute.
plumero *nm* (**a**) feather duster.
   (**b**) (*adornment*) plume; bunch of feathers; **se le ve el** — (*fam*) you can see what he's really thinking.
   (**c**) penholder.
   (**d**) (*Col, Ec*) plumber.
   (**e**) (*Chi*) powder puff.
plumífero *nm* (*hum*) poor writer, hack; hack journalist.
plumilla *nf*, **plumín** *nm* nib, pen nib.
plumista *nm* clerk, scrivener.
plumón *nm* (**a**) (*Orn*) down. (**b**) feather bed.
plumoso *adj* feathery, downy.
plural 1 *adj* (**a**) plural. (**b**) (*fig: esp SAm*) many, manifold, numerous. **2** *nm* plural; **en** — in the plural.
pluralidad *nf* (**a**) plurality.
   (**b**) — **de votos** majority of votes.
   (**c**) **una** — **de** a number of; numerous, diverse; **el asunto tiene** — **de aspectos** there are a number of sides to this question; **existe una** — **de textos para esta asignatura** there is a duplication of textbooks for this course.
plurilingüe *adj* multilingual.
plurivalencia *nf* many-sided value; diversity of uses (*etc*); wide applicability.
plurivalente *adj* having numerous values; having diverse uses (*etc*); widely applicable.
plus *nm* extra pay, bonus; — **de carestía de vida** cost-of-living bonus; **con 5 dólares de** — with a bonus of 5 dollars.
pluscafé *nm* (*SAm*) liqueur.
pluscuamperfecto *nm* pluperfect.
plusmarca *nf* record; **batir la** — to break the record.
plusmarquista *nmf* record holder; record breaker; top scorer.
plusvalía *nf* appreciation, added value.
Plutarco *m* Plutarch.
plutocracia *nf* plutocracy.
plutócrata *nmf* plutocrat.
plutocrático *adj* plutocratic.
Plutón *m* Pluto.
plutonio *nm* plutonium.
pluvial *adj* rain (*attr*).
pluviómetro *nm* rain gauge, pluviometer.
pluvioso *adj* rainy.
población *nf* (**a**) population; — **activa** working population. (**b**) town, city; village; (*Arg*) small hamlet; (*on ranch*) main building and outbuildings.
poblacho *nm* down-at-heel town, miserable village.
poblachón *nm* dump (*fam*), one-horse town.
poblada *nf* (**a**) (*Bol, Col, Chi, Ec, Per, Ven*) riot; revolt, armed rising. (**b**) (*Chi, Ec, Per, Ven*) crowd.
poblado 1 *adj* (**a**) inhabited.
   (**b**) **poco** — underpopulated, with a sparse population; **densamente** — thickly populated; **la ciudad más poblada del país** the most populous city in the country.
   (**c**) — **de** peopled with, populated with; (*fig*) full of, filled with; covered with.
   (**d**) *beard* big, thick; *eyebrows* bushy.
   2 *nm* village; town; inhabited place; (*Aut etc*) built-up area; — **de absorción** new town, satellite town.
poblador *nm*, **pobladora** *nf* settler, colonist; founder.
poblano 1 *adj* (*SAm*) village (*attr*), town (*attr*); (*Mex*) of Puebla. **2** *nm*, **poblana** *nf* (*SAm*) villager; (*Mex*) native of Puebla.
poblar [1m] **1** *vt* (**a**) *place* to settle, people, colonize; *hive, river etc* to stock (*de* with); *ground* to plant (*de* with).
   (**b**) to people, inhabit; **los peces que pueblan las profundidades** the fish that inhabit the depths; **las estrellas que pueblan el espacio** the stars that dwell in (*or* fill) space.
   2 **poblarse** *vr* (**a**) to fill (*de* with); to fill up, become stocked (*de* with); to become covered (*de* with).
   (**b**) (*Bot*) to come into leaf.
pobo *nm* white poplar.
pobre 1 *adj* (*all senses*) poor (*de, en* in); **¡— de mí!** poor old me!; **¡— de él!** poor fellow!; **¡— de ti si te pillo!** it'll be tough on you if I catch you!
   2 *nmf* (**a**) poor person; beggar, pauper; **un** — a poor man; **los** —**s** the poor, poor people.

(b) (*fig*) poor wretch, poor devil; **la — estaba mojada** the poor girl was wet through; **el — está fatal de los ojos** (*fam*) he's terribly short-sighted, poor chap (*fam*).

pobremente *adv* poorly.

pobrería *nf*, **pobrerío** *nm* (*SAm*) poor people (*collectively*).

pobrete 1 *adj* poor, wretched. **2** *nm*, **pobreta** *nf* poor thing, poor wretch.

pobretería *nf* **(a)** poor people (*collectively*); gathering of poor people. **(b)** poverty. **(c)** miserliness, meanness.

pobretón 1 *adj* terribly poor. **2** *nm* poor man.

pobreza *nf* poverty; work, penury; **— de espíritu** poorness of spirit, small-mindedness; **— no es vileza** poverty is not a crime.

poca *nm* (*SAm*), **pócar** *nm* (*Mex*) poker.

pocero *nm* well-digger.

pocerón *nm* (*CAm, Mex*) pool.

pocilga *nf* piggery, pigsty; (*fig*) pigsty.

pocillo *nm* (*SAm*) cup; (*Mex*) tankard.

pócima *nf*, **poción** *nf* (*Pharm*) potion, draught; (*Vet*) drench; (*fig*) brew, concoction, nasty drink.

poco 1 *adj* **(a)** (*sing*) little; small; slight, scanty; **con — respeto** with little respect, with scant respect; **de — interés** of small interest; **de poca extensión** of small extent, not extensive; **hay — queso** there isn't much cheese; **nos queda — tiempo** we haven't much time; **el provecho es —** the gain is small; **con lo — que me quedaba** with what little I had left; **ya sabes lo — que me interesa** you know how little it interests me.

(b) (*pl*) **—s** few; **unos —s** a few, some; **—s de entre ellos** few of them; **—s niños saben que . . .** few (*or* not many) children know that . . .; **—s son los que . . .** there are few who . . .; **me quedan pocas probabilidades** I don't have much chance; **un canalla como hay —s** a real rotter, an absolute rotter.

2 *adv* **(a)** little, not much; only slightly; **cuesta —** it doesn't cost much; **ahora trabaja —** he only works a little now; **los estiman —** they hardly value it at all; **— a —** little by little; **¡— a —!** gently!, easy there!; **— más o menos** more or less; **ser para —** to be weak, be characterless, be very negative; **tener a uno en —** to think little of someone, have no use for someone; **tiene la vida en —** he holds his life cheap.

(b) (*with adj: often translated by prefixes dis-, un-*) **— dispuesto a ayudar** disinclined to help; **— amable** unkind; **— inteligente** unintelligent.

(c) **por —** almost, nearly; **por — me ahogo** I very nearly drowned; **en — estuvo que el coche le atropellara** the car almost knocked him down.

(d) (*time expressions*) **a —** shortly (after), presently; **a — de haberlo firmado** shortly after he had signed it; **dentro de —** shortly; soon after; **hace — a** short while back, a short time ago.

(e) (*SAm*) **¿a —?** not really!, you don't say!

3 *nm*: **un —** a little, a bit; **estoy un — triste** I am a little sad; **le conocía un —** I knew him slightly; **un — de dinero** a little money, some money.

pocha *nf* (*Chi*) lie; trick.

pochismo *nm* (*Mex etc*) gross anglicism introduced into Spanish.

pocho 1 *adj* **(a)** faded, discoloured; *person* pale; *fruit* soft, overripe; withered.
(b) (*fig*) depressed, gloomy.
(c) (*Chi*) chubby; squat.

2 *nm*, **pocha** *nf* (*Mex etc*) United States national of Mexican origin; Mexican influenced in language etc by North America.

pochola *nf* (*fam*) nice girl, attractive girl; (*in direct address*) dear, darling.

pocholez *nf* (*fam*) gem, treasure; **el vestido es una —** it's a dear little dress.

poda *nf* **(a)** (*act*) pruning. **(b)** pruning season.

podadera *nf* pruning knife, billhook; pruning shears, secateurs.

podar [1a] *vt* **(a)** to prune; to lop, trim (off). **(b)** (*fig*) to prune, cut out.

podenco *nm* hound.

poder 1 [2t] *vi* **(a)** (+ *infin*) can, to be able to; **puede venir** he can come, he is able to come; **no puede venir** he cannot come; **puede ser** maybe, it may be so; **puede ser que . . .** it may be that . . .; **puede que esté en la biblioteca** he may be in the library, perhaps he's in the library; **este vino no se puede beber** this wine is not fit to drink.

(b) (+ *infin*) may; **puede no venir** he may not come, it is possible that he won't come; **por lo que pudiera pasar** because of what might happen;

¡podías habérmelo dicho! you might have told me!; **bien puedes pasar la noche aquí** you might as well spend the night here.

(c) (*absolutely*) can; **lo haré si puedo** I'll do it if I can; **no puedo** I can't; **¡puede!** who knows!, maybe!; **¿se puede?** may I?, may I come in?; do you mind?; **los que pueden** those who can, those who are able (to); **el dinero puede mucho** money can do anything, money talks; **él puede mucho en el partido** he has great influence in the party; **causas respecto a las cuales nada puede el fabricante** causes over which the manufacturer has no control; **¿tú puedes con eso?** can you manage that?; **no puedo con él** I can't stand him; **no puedo con la maleta** I can't manage the case; **no puedo más** I've had enough; I can't go on any longer; I'm exhausted; **a más no —** to the utmost; as hard as possible, for all one is worth; **es terco a más no —** he's utterly obstinate, he's as obstinate as they come; **comió a más no —** he ate to excess; **me gusta al cine a más no —** I'm passionately fond of the cinema; **no — menos de +** *infin* not to be able to help + *ger*; to have no alternative but to + *infin*.

(d) **puede que vaya** I may go, I might go; **puede que tenga uno ya** he may have one already; **puede que sí** it may be, maybe.

(e) (*fam*) **A le puede a B** A can beat B; A is tougher than B; A is more than a match for B.

(f) (*CAm, Mex*) to affect, upset; **me pudo esa broma** that joke upset me.

2 *nm* **(a)** power; authority; possession; **— adquisitivo, — de compra** purchasing power; **— de repercusión** resilience, recuperative power; **a — de** by dint of; **bajo el — de** in the hands of; under the power of; **estar en — de** to be in the hands of, be in the possession of; **pasar a — de** to pass to, pass into the possession of; **el dinero es —** money is power; **tiene — para arruinarnos** he has the power to ruin us; **esa droga no tiene — contra la enfermedad** that drug has no power (*or* is not effective) against the disease.

(b) (*Mech*) power; strength; capacity; **el — del motor** the power of the engine; **tiene — para levantar X kilos** it has the power to lift X kilos.

(c) (*Pol etc*) power; authority; **— absoluto** absolute power; **— ejecutivo** executive power; **— legislativo** legislative power; **división de poderes** separation of powers; **estar en el —, ocupar el —** to be in power.

(d) (*Law*) power of attorney, proxy; **plenos poderes** full power, full authority (to act); **por poder(es)** by proxy.

poderhabiente *nmf* (*Law*) proxy.

poderío *nm* **(a)** power; might; authority, jurisdiction. **(b)** (*Fin*) wealth.

poderosamente *adv* powerfully.

poderoso *adj* (*all senses*) powerful.

podiatría *nf* podiatry.

podio *nm* podium; (*Mex*) rostrum; **estar en el — de la actualidad** to be in the limelight, be the centre of current interest.

podómetro *nm* pedometer.

podón *nm* billhook.

podre *nf* pus.

podredumbre *nf* **(a)** (*matter*) pus; rotten part, rot.
(b) (*quality*) rottenness, putrefaction; (*fig*) rottenness, decay, corruption.
(c) (*fig*) gnawing doubt, secret uneasiness.

podrido *adj* **(a)** rotten, bad; putrid.
(b) (*fig*) rotten, corrupt; **"algo está — en Dinamarca"** "something is rotten in the state of Denmark"; **está — por dentro** he's rotten inside; **están —s de dinero** they're rotten with money (*fam*).

podrir [3a] **= pudrir.**

poema *nm* **(a)** poem, (*esp*) long poem. **(b)** (*fig*) **fue todo un —** it was just like a fairy tale; it was all terribly romantic (*fam*); (*hum*) it was a proper farce.

poemario *nm* book of poems.

poemático *adj* poetic.

poesía *nf* **(a)** (*in general*) poetry; **la — del Siglo de Oro** Golden Age poetry. **(b)** (*una —*) poem, (*esp*) short poem, lyric.

poeta *nm* **(a)** poet. **(b)** (*SAm*) writer, author, literary man.

poetastro *nm* poetaster.

poética *nf* poetics, art of poetry, theory of poetry.

poéticamente *adv* poetically.

poético *adj* poetic(al).

poetisa *nf* poetess.

poetizar [1f] **1** *vt* to poeticize; to idealize; to turn into poetry, make poetry out of. **2** *vi* to write poetry.

pogrom(o) *nm* pogrom.
póker *nm* (*Cards: angl*) poker.
polaco 1 *adj* Polish. **2** *nm*, **polaca** *nf* Pole. **3** *nm* (*language*) Polish.
polaina *nf* (a) gaiter, legging. (b) (*Arg, Bol, Hond*) annoyance; setback.
polar *adj* polar.
polaridad *nf* polarity.
polarización *nf* polarization.
polarizar [1f] **1** *vt* to polarize. **2 polarizarse** *vr* to polarize (*en torno a* around).
polca *nf* (a) (*Mus*) polka. (b) (*Ec, Per*) blouse; (*Chi, Per*) long jacket.
polea *nf* pulley; (*Naut*) tackle, tackle block.
polémica *nf* (a) (*in general*) polemics. (b) (*una —*) polemic, controversy.
polémico *adj* polemic(al).
polemista *nmf* polemicist; debater, controversialist.
polemizar [1f] *vi* to indulge in a polemic, argue (*en torno a* about); **no quiero —** I have no wish to get involved in an argument; **con uno en la prensa** to have a debate with someone in the press.
polen *nm* pollen.
poli 1 *nm* (*fam*) bobby (*sl*), copper (*sl*), cop (*sl*). **2** *nf* (*fam*): **la —** the cops (*sl*).
poli . . . poly . . ., many . . .
poliandria *nf* polyandry.
poliándrico *adj* polyandrous.
policía 1 *nm* policeman; **— femenino** policewoman.
  2 *nf* (a) police; police force; **— fluvial** river police; **— militar** military police; **— montada** mounted police; **— secreta** secret police; **— de tráfico** traffic police.
  (b) administration, (good) government; public order.
  (c) courtesy, politeness.
  (d) cleanliness.
policíaco *adj* police (*attr*); *see* **novela**.
policial 1 *adj* police (*attr*). **2** *nm* (*CAm*) policeman.
policromo *adj*, **polícromo** *adj* polychromatic; many-coloured, colourful.
Polichinela *m* Punch.
polietileno *nm* polythene, polyethylene (*US*).
polifacético *adj* person, talent etc many-sided, versatile.
Polifemo *m* Polyphemus.
polifonía *nf* polyphony.
polifónico *adj* polyphonic.
poligamia *nf* polygamy.
polígamo 1 *adj* polygamous. **2** *nm* polygamist.
poligloto *nm*, **poliglota** *nf* (*also* **políglото** *nm*, **políglota** *nmf*) polyglot.
poligonal *adj* polygonal.
polígono *nm* (a) (*Math*) polygon.
  (b) site (for development), building lot; area; housing estate; **— industrial** industrial estate; **— de descongestión** industrial overspill area.
polígrafo *nm* writer on a wide variety of subjects.
polilla *nf* moth, (*esp*) clothes moth; grub, destructive larva; bookworm.
polimerización *nf* polymerization.
polímero *nm* polymer.
polimorfismo *nm* polymorphism.
polimorfo *adj* polymorphic.
Polinesia *f* Polynesia.
polinesio 1 *adj* Polynesian. **2** *nm*, **polinesia** *nf* Polynesian.
polinización *nf* pollination; **— cruzada** cross-pollination.
polio *nf* polio.
poliomielitis *nf* poliomyelitis.
pólipo *nm* polyp, polypus.
polisílabo 1 *adj* polysyllabic. **2** *nm* polysyllable.
polisón *nm* bustle.
polista *nm* polo player.
politeísmo *nm* polytheism.
politeísta *adj* polytheistic.
politene *nm*, **politeno** *nm* polythene, polyethylene (*US*).
política *nf* (a) (*Pol*) politics; **la — ruritana en la posguerra** postwar Ruritanian politics; **mezclarse en la —** to go in for politics, get mixed up in politics.
  (b) policy; **— agraria** farming policy, agricultural policy; **— económica** economic policy; **— exterior** foreign policy; **— de ingresos y precios, — de jornales y precios** prices and incomes policy; **— de mano dura** strong-arm policy, tough policy.
  (c) tact, skill; politeness; good manners.
políticamente *adv* politically.
politicastro *nm* (*pej*) politician.

político 1 *adj* (a) (*Pol*) political.
  (b) politic; tactful, skilful; polite, well-mannered, courteous.
  (c) stiff, reserved, stand-offish.
  (d) (*of family relationships*) in-law, eg **padre —** father-in-law; **es tío — mío** he's an uncle of mine by marriage; *see* **familia** etc.
  2 *nm* politician.
politicón *adj* (*fam*) (a) strongly political, keenly interested in politics. (b) very ceremonious, obsequious.
politiquear [1a] *vi* to play at politics, dabble in politics; to talk politics.
politiqueo *nm*, **politiquería** *nf* party politics, the political game; political gossip.
politiquero *nm* (*pej*) politician, party politician; political intriguer.
póliza *nf* (a) certificate, voucher; (*Fin*) draft; (*Fin*) insurance certificate; insurance policy; **— dotal** endowment policy; **— de seguro(s)** insurance policy; **pagar una —** to pay out on an insurance.
  (b) tax stamp, fiscal stamp.
polizón *nm* (a) tramp, vagrant, bum (*US*). (b) (*Aer, Naut, etc*) stowaway; **viajar de —** to stow away (*en* on).
polizonte *nm* (*sl*) bobby (*sl*), copper (*sl*), cop (*sl*).
polo[1] *nm* (a) (*Geog*) pole; **P— Norte** North Pole; **P— Sur** South Pole; **— magnético** magnetic pole, magnetic north; **de — a —** from pole to pole.
  (b) (*Elec*) pole; terminal; pin, point; **— negativo** negative pole; **— positivo** positive pole; **una clavija de 4 —s** a 4-pin plug.
  (c) (*fig*) pole; focus, centre; **— de atracción** focus of interest, centre of attraction; **los dos generales son —s opuestos** the two generals are at opposite extremes; **esto es el — opuesto de lo que dijo antes** this is the exact opposite of what he said before.
  (d) (*fig: Comm etc*) **— de desarrollo, — de promoción** growth point; development area.
  (e) **— helado** iced lolly.
polo[2] *nm* (*Sport*) polo; **— acuático** water polo.
polo[3] *nm* polo-necked sweater.
polola *nf* (*Chi, Ec*) flirtatious girl; steady girlfriend.
pololear [1a] (*Bol, Chi, Ec, Per*) **1** *vt* to court; to flirt with. **2** *vi* to flirt (*con* with); to be going steady (*fam*).
pololo *nm* (*Chi*) (a) (*species of*) buzzing insect. (b) bore, tedious person; flirt; steady boyfriend; (persistent) suitor. (c) pimp.
polonesa *nf* polonaise.
Polonia *f* Poland.
poltrón *adj* idle, lazy.
poltrona *nf* reclining chair, easy chair.
poltronear [1a] *vi* (*Arg, Chi, Mex*) to idle, loaf.
polución *nf* pollution; **— de la atmósfera** air pollution.
polvareda *nf* (a) dust cloud, cloud of dust. (b) (*fig*) storm, fuss, rumpus (*fam*); **levantar una —** to create a storm, cause a rumpus.
polvera *nf* (a) powder compact, vanity case. (b) (*Mex*) = polvareda.
polvero *nm* (a) (*Col, CR, Mex, Ven*) = polvareda. (b) (*CAm*) handkerchief.
polvillo *nm* (a) (*Arg, Col*) blight. (b) (*Chi, Per*) tobacco refuse. (c) (*CAm*) leather for shoemaking. (d) (*Ec, Per*) rice bran.
polvo *nm* (a) dust; **lleno de —** dusty; dust-covered; **limpiar un mueble de —, quitar el — de** (*or* **a**) **un mueble** to dust a piece of furniture; **hacer algo —** to smash something, ruin something; **hacer — a uno** to shatter someone; to wear someone out; to depress someone; (*in argument*) to flatten someone, crush someone; **estoy hecho —** I'm worn out; **hacer morder el — a uno** to make someone bite the dust; **matar el — to** lay the dust; **sacudir el — a uno** to thrash someone; to beat someone up.
  (b) (*Chem, Cook, Med etc*) powder (*freq* **—s**); **—s** (*esp*) **de arroz** rice powder; **—s de blanqueo** bleaching powder; **—s de hornear, —s de levadura** baking powder; **dentífrico, —s para dientes** tooth powder; **—s de talco** talcum powder; **en —** powdered, in powdered form; **ponerse —s** to powder one's face.
  (c) pinch; **un — de rapé** a pinch of snuff.
  (d) (*sl: tabu*) screw (*tabu*); **echar un —** to have a screw (*tabu*).
pólvora *nf* (a) gunpowder; **— de algodón** guncotton; **no ha descubierto** (*or* **inventado**) **la —** he'll never set the Thames (*or* world) on fire; **gastar la — en salvas** to waste time and energy, fuss around uselessly; **propagarse como la —** to spread like wildfire.
  (b) fireworks.
  (c) (*fig*) bad temper, crossness.
  (d) (*fig*) life, liveliness.

polvorear [1a] *vt* to powder, dust, sprinkle (*de* with).
polvoriento *adj* (a) *surface etc* dusty. (b) *substance* powdery.
polvorilla *nmf* (*fam*) (a) live wire, lively spark (*fam*). (b) touchy person, bad-tempered person.
polvorín *nm* (a) fine powder; **—es atómicos** atomic dust, atomic fallout.
  (b) (*Mil*) powder magazine; (*fig*) powder keg.
  (c) (*Arg*) =**jején**.
  (d) (*Chi, Mex*) =**polvorilla** (b).
  (e) (*Col, PR*) cloud of dust.
polvorosa: poner pies en — (*fam*) to beat it (*fam*).
polvoroso *adj* (*SAm*) dusty.
polvoso *adj* = **polvoriento**.
polla *nf* (a) (*Orn*) pullet; chick; **— de agua** moorhen.
  (b) (*Cards*) pool, kitty; (*Arg, Chi, Guat, Per*) stakes, pool.
  (c) (*fam*) girl, chick (*fam*), bird (*sl*).
  (d) (*Anat: tabu*) prick (*tabu*).
pollada *nf* (*Orn*) brood.
pollastre *nm* (*fam*) = **pollo** (b).
pollastro, pollastrón *nm* (*fam*) sly fellow.
pollera *nf* (a) hencoop; chicken run; basket for chickens. (b) (*Bol, Chi, RPl*) skirt, overskirt; (*Chi: Eccl*) soutane.
pollería *nf* poulterer's (shop).
pollero *nm* (a) chicken farmer; poulterer. (b) (*SAm*) gambler.
pollerudo *adj* (*RPl*) (a) cowardly; backbiting, gossipy. (b) *priest* (*pej*) holy, sanctimonious.
pollino *nm*, **pollina** *nf* (a) donkey. (b) (*fam*) ass, idiot.
pollita *nf* young pullet.
pollito *nm* (a) (*Orn*) chick. (b) (*fam*) = **pollo** (b).
pollo *nm* (a) (*Orn*) chicken; chick, young bird; (*Cook*) chicken; **— asado** roast chicken.
  (b) (*fam*) young man; elegant youth, playboy; **¿quién es ese —?** who is that chap? (*fam*); **es un — nada más** he's only a youngster.
  (c) (*fam*) spittle, sputum.
polluelo *nm* chick.
poma *nf* (a) (*fig*) apple. (b) (*Chi*) small flask; scent bottle; (*Ec*) carafe. (c) (*Mex*) pumice (stone).
pomada *nf* pomade.
pomar *nm* apple orchard.
pomelo *nm* grapefruit.
pómez: piedra *f* **—** pumice (stone).
pomo *nm* (a) (*Bot*) pome, fruit with pips. (b) scent bottle. (c) (*of sword*) pommel; (*of door*) round knob, handle. (d) (*Col*) powder puff.
pompa *nf* (a) bubble; **— de jabón** soap bubble. (b) (*Naut*) pump. (c) pomp, splendour; show, display; procession; pageant, pageantry; **—s fúnebres** funeral.
Pompeya Pompeii.
Pompeyo *m* Pompey.
pompo *adj* (*Col*) blunt.
pomposamente *adv* splendidly, magnificently; majestically; (*pej*) pompously.
pomposidad *nf* splendour, magnificence; majesty; (*pej*) pomposity.
pomposo *adj* splendid, magnificent; majestic; (*pej*) pompous.
pómulo *nm* cheekbone; (*fig*) cheek.
Poncio Pilatos *m* Pontius Pilate.
ponchada[1] *nf* bowlful of punch.
ponchada[2] *nf* (*Chi, RPl*) large quantity, large amount; **costó una —** it cost a lot.
ponchar [1a] *vt* (*Ant, Mex: angl*) (a) *ticket* to punch. (b) *tyre* to puncture.
ponche *nm* punch.
ponchera *nf* (a) punch bowl. (b) (*Col, Mex, Ven*) washbasin; (*Col*) bath.
poncho[1] *adj* (a) lazy, indolent; quiet, peaceable. (b) (*Col*) chubby.
poncho[2] *nm* (*SAm*) poncho, blanket, cape.
ponderación *nf* (a) weighing, consideration; deliberation. (b) high praise. (c) weighting. (d) calmness, steadiness, balance.
ponderado *adj* calm, steady, balanced.
ponderar [1a] *vt* (a) to weigh up, consider.
  (b) to praise highly, speak in praise of; **— algo a uno** to speak warmly of something to someone, tell someone how good something is; **le ponderan de inteligente** they speak highly of his intelligence.
  (c) (*Statistics*) to weight.
ponedero *nm* nest, nesting box.
ponedora *adj*: **gallina —** laying hen, hen in lay; **ser buena —** to be a good layer.
ponencia *nf* (learned) paper, communication; report.
poner [2r] **1** *vt* (a) (*general sense*) to put; to place, set; *clothes, hat* to put on; *care* to take, exercise (*en* in);

objection to raise; *table* to lay, set; *window* (*Comm*) to dress, arrange; *emphasis* to place (*en* on); **— algo a secar al sol** to put something (out) to dry in the sun; **— la experiencia al servicio de** to put one's experience at the disposal of; **— algo como ejemplo** to give (*or* quote) something as an example, use something as an illustration; **— a uno por testigo** to cite someone as a witness; **— algo en duda** to cast doubt on something, call something in question; **— algo aparte** to put something aside, put something on one side.
  (b) *egg* to lay.
  (c) *watch etc* to adjust, set (right); **pone el reloj por esa campana** he sets his watch by that bell.
  (d) *radio etc* to switch on, turn on, put on; **ponlo más fuerte** turn it up.
  (e) *letter, telegram* to send (*a* to).
  (f) *problem* to set; *fine, tax* to impose (*a* on); *task* to give, assign (*a* to); **nos pone mucho trabajo** he gives us a lot of work.
  (g) *shop* to open, set up, establish; *house* to fit up, equip; **han puesto la casa con todo lujo** they have fitted the house up most luxuriously.
  (h) *money* to contribute, subscribe, give; (*in gambling*) to stake; (*Fin*) to put, invest; (*fig*) to contribute; *time* to put, give; **yo pongo el dinero pero ella escoge** I put up the money but she chooses; **he puesto 5 minutos en firmarlo** it took me 5 minutes to sign it; **esto no pone nada para la solución del problema** this does not contribute at all towards solving the problem.
  (i) *name* to give; **al niño le pusieron Luis** they called the child Louis; **¿qué nombre le van a —?** what are they going to call him?, what name are they giving him?
  (j) **— a uno de cochino** to call someone a swine.
  (k) to add; **pongo 3 más para llegar a 100** I'll add 3 more to make it 100.
  (l) (*Theat*) *play* to put on, do, perform; *film* to show, put on; to screen; **¿qué ponen en el cine?** what's on at the cinema?
  (m) *emotion, fear etc* to cause; **me pone miedo** it frightens me, it scares me.
  (n) *words, language etc* to translate, put (*en* into); **puso el discurso en alemán** he translated the speech into German.
  (o) to suppose; **pongamos 120** let's say 120, let's put it at 120; **pongamos que...** let us suppose that ...; **poniendo que...** supposing that ..., assuming that ...
  (p) (*Tel*) **— a X con Y** to connect X to Y, give X a line to Y; **póngame con el conserje** get me the porter, put me through to the porter; **le pongo en seguida** I'm trying to connect you.
  (q) **poner a P bien con Q** to reconcile P and Q, make things up between P and Q; **poner a Z mal con A** to cause a rift between Z and A, make Z fall out with A.
  (r) (+ *adj*) to make, turn; **si añades eso lo pones azul** if you add that you turn it blue; **la medicina le puso bueno** the medicine made him better; **la has puesto colorada** now you've made her blush; **para no —le de mal humor** so as not to make him cross.
  (s) **— a uno a** + *infin* to set someone to + *infin*; to start someone + *ger*.
  (t) **puso a su hija de sirvienta** she got her daughter a job as a servant; **puso a sus hijos a trabajar** she sent her children out to work; *see* **aprendiz**; *for many other uses and idioms, see noun entries.*
2 *vi* (a) (*Orn*) to lay, lay eggs.
  (b) **no pongo a la lotería** I don't go in for the lottery, I don't invest in the lottery.
  (c) **eso pone mucho** that's asking a lot.
3 ponerse *vr* (a) to put oneself, place oneself; **se ponía debajo de la ventana** he used to stand under the window; *see* **cómodo** *etc*.
  (b) **— un traje** to put a suit on; *see* **largo** *etc*.
  (c) **— de barro** to get covered in mud.
  (d) **— de conserje** to take a job as a porter.
  (e) **— a** (*place*), **— en** to reach, get to, arrive at; **en 2 horas se puso a su lado** in 2 hours he reached her side, in 2 hours he was at her side.
  (f) (*sun etc*) to set.
  (g) **— delante** to get in the way; to intercede, intervene; (*difficulty*) to arise, come up; **destruye al que se le pone delante** he destroys anyone who gets in his way.
  (h) **— a bien con uno** to get on good terms with someone, (*pej*) get in with someone; **— a mal con uno** to get on the wrong side of someone.
  (i) **— con uno** to quarrel with someone; to

oppose someone; to compete with someone, play (against) someone.

(j) (+ *adj*) to turn, get, become; **se puso serio** he became serious; **en el agua se pone verde** it turns green in the water; **¡no te pongas así!** don't be like that!; *see* **furioso** *etc.*

(k) — **a** + *infin* to begin to + *infin*, set about + *ger*; to proceed to + *infin*; **se pusieron a gritar** they started to shout.

poney ['poni] *nm, pl* **poneys** ['ponis] (*angl*) pony.

ponga, pongo[1] *etc see* **poner**.

pongaje *nm* (*Bol, Chi, Ec, Per*) *domestic service which Indian tenants are obliged to give free*.

pongo[2] *nm* orang-outang.

pongo[3] *nm* (*Bol, Chi, Ec, Per*) Indian servant, Indian tenant.

poniente *nm* (a) west. (b) west wind.

pontaje *nm* (*SAm*), **pontazgo** *nm* toll.

pontevedrés 1 *adj* of Pontevedra. **2** *nm,* **pontevedresa** *nf* native (*or* inhabitant) of Pontevedra; **los —es** the people of Pontevedra.

pontificado *nm* papacy, pontificate.

pontifical *adj* papal, pontifical.

pontificar [1g] *vi* to pontificate (*also fig*).

pontífice *nm* pope, pontiff; **el Sumo P—** His Holiness the Pope.

pontificio *adj* papal, pontifical.

pontón *nm* (a) pontoon; (*Aer: of seaplane*) float. (b) pontoon bridge (*also* — **flotante**); bridge of planks. (c) (*Naut*) hulk.

pony ['poni] *nm, pl* **ponys** ['ponis] (*angl*) pony.

ponzoña *nf* poison, venom; (*fig*) poison.

ponzoñoso *adj* poisonous, venomous; (*fig*) *attack etc* venomous; *propaganda* poisonous; *custom, idea etc* harmful.

popa *nf* stern; **a —** astern, abaft; **de — a proa** fore and aft, from stem to stern.

popar [1a] *vt* (a) *child etc* to spoil; (*fig*) to make a fuss of, flatter. (b) to scorn, jeer at.

popelín *nm*, **popelina** *nf* (*Acad*), **poplín** *nm* (*SAm*) poplin.

poporo *nm* (a) (*Col, Ven*) bump, swelling. (b) (*Ven*) stick.

popote *nm* (*Mex*) long thin stem; tough grass used for making brooms; drinking straw.

populachería *nf* cheap popularity, playing to the gallery.

populachero *adj* common, vulgar; cheap; *speech, policy* rabble-rousing; *politician* demagogic, who appeals to the lower orders, who plays to the gallery.

populacho *nm* populace, plebs, mob.

popular *adj* (*in most senses*) popular; *word etc* colloquial; *culture etc* of the people; folk (*attr*).

popularidad *nf* popularity.

popularismo *nm* colloquial word (*or* phrase *etc*).

popularización *nf* popularization.

popularizar [1f] **1** *vt* to popularize. **2 popularizarse** *vr* to become popular.

populoso *adj* populous.

poquedad *nf* (a) scantiness, paucity; smallness; fewness. (b) (*una —*) small thing, trifle; small quantity. (c) (*fig*) timidity.

póquer *nm* poker.

poquísimo *adj* (a) (*sing*) very little; hardly any, almost no. (b) (*pl*) **—s** very few, terribly few (*fam*).

poquito *nm* (a) **un —** a little bit (*de of*); (*as adv*) a little, a bit. (b) **a —s** bit by bit; in dribs and drabs; **¡— a poco!** gently!, easy there!

por *prep* (a) (+ *infin*) in order to; **— no llegar tarde** in order not to be late, so as not to arrive late; **lo hizo — complacerle** he did it to please her; **hablar — hablar** to talk just for talking's sake; **moverse — no estar quieto** to move about simply so as to have a change from sitting still; *see also* (c).

(b) (*objective*) for; **luchar — la patria** to fight for one's country; **trabajar — dinero** to work for money; **su amor — la pintura** his love for painting; **hazlo — mí** do it for me, do it for my sake.

(c) (*cause*) out of, because of, from; **fue — necesidad** it was from (*or* out of, because of) necessity; **— temor** from fear; **— temor a** for fear of; **lo hago — gusto** I do it because I like to; **no se realizó — escasez de fondos** it was not put into effect because of lack of money; **— venir tarde perdió la mitad** through coming late he missed half of it; **se hundió — mal construido** it collapsed because it was badly built; **le expulsaron — revoltoso** they expelled him as a troublemaker; **lo dejó — imposible** he gave it up as (being) impossible.

(d) (*evidence*) **— lo que dicen** from what they say, judging by what they say; **— las señas no piensa**

hacerlo judging by the signs he's not intending to do it.

(e) (*person affected*) **— mí, que se vaya** so far as I'm concerned (*or* for myself, for my part) he can go.

(f) (*agent*) by; **— su propia mano** by his own hand; **— correo** by post, through the post; **— mar** by sea, by boat; **— sí mismo** by oneself; **hablar — señas** to talk by signs, communicate by means of signs; **lo obtuve — un amigo** I got it through a friend, I got it with the help of a friend.

(g) (*Math*) **7 — 2 son 14** 7 times 2 are 14.

(h) (*manner*) in; by; according to; **— centenares** by the hundred, by hundreds; **— orden** in order; **están dispuestos — tamaños** they are arranged according to size (*or* by sizes, in sizes); **punto — punto** point by point; **día — día** day by day.

(i) (*of place*) by, by way of; through; along; **ir a Bilbao — Santander** to go to Bilbao via Santander; **— el lado izquierdo** on (*or* along) the left side; **cruzar la frontera — Canfranc** to cross the frontier at Canfranc; **— la calle** along the street; **— la caña** through the pipe, along the pipe; **— todo el país** over the whole country, throughout the country; **llevar periódicos — las casas** to deliver papers round the houses; **pasar — Madrid** to pass through Madrid; to go via Madrid; **pasearse — el parque** to walk round the park, stroll through the park.

(j) (*of time*) **— la mañana** in the morning; during the morning; **no sale — la noche** he doesn't go out at night.

(k) (*of present and future time*) for; **se quedarán — 15 días** they will stay for a fortnight; **será — poco tiempo** it won't be for long.

(l) for, in exchange for; **te doy éste — aquél** I'll swap you this one for that one; **le dieron uno nuevo — el viejo** they gave him a new one (in exchange) for the old one; **se vendió — 15 dólares** it was sold for 15 dollars; **me dieron 13 francos — una libra** they gave me 13 francs for a pound; **ha puesto B — V** he has put B as being equivalent to V.

(m) **vino — su jefe** he came instead of (*or* in place of) his boss; **interceder — uno** to intercede for someone, intercede on someone's behalf; **hablo — todos** I speak on behalf of (*or* in the name of) everybody.

(n) **contar a uno — amigo** to count someone as a friend; **no se admite — válido** it is not accepted as valid; *see* **tener, tomar** *etc.*

(o) (*rate*) **tres dólares — hora** three dollars an hour; **revoluciones — minuto** revolutions per minute; *see* **persona** *etc.*

(p) (*approximation*) **eso está allá — el norte** that's somewhere up in the north; **— la feria** about carnival time, round about the carnival; *see* **fecha, Navidad** *etc.*

(q) **— difícil que sea** however hard it is, however hard it may be; **por mucho que lo quisieran** however much they would like to; *see* **más**.

(r) (*fam*) **ir a — uno** to go for someone, go and fetch someone; *see* **ir —, venir —** *etc.*

(s) **— qué** why; **¿ — qué?** why?

porcachón *adj* (*fam*) filthy, dirty.

porcada *nf* (*fam*) = **porquería**.

porcallón *adj* (*fam*) filthy, dirty.

porcelana *nf* porcelain; china, chinaware; **tienda de — china** shop.

porcentaje *nm* percentage; proportion, ratio; rate; **un elevado — de** a high percentage of, a high proportion of; **el — de defunciones** the death rate.

porcentual *adj* percentage (*attr*).

Porcia *f* Portia.

porcino 1 *adj* porcine; pig (*attr*); **ganado —** pigs. **2** *nm* (a) young pig. (b) (*Med*) bump, swelling.

porción *nf* (a) portion; part, share; (*in recipes etc*) quantity, amount, part; (*of chocolate bar*) piece, segment.

(b) **una — de** (*fig*) a number of; **tengo una — de cosas que hacer** I have a number of things to do; **tuvimos una — de problemas** we had quite a few problems.

porcuno *adj* pig (*attr*).

porche *nm* (a) arcade (*of shops, round village square etc*). (b) (*of house*) porch.

pordiosear [1a] *vi* to beg (*also fig*).

pordiosero *nm*, **pordiosera** *nf* beggar.

porende *adv* (*arch or lit*) hence, therefore.

porfía *nf* (a) persistence; obstinacy, stubbornness. (b) dispute; continuous struggle, continuous competition. (c) **a — in** competition.

porfiadamente *adv* persistently; obstinately, stubbornly.

porfiado 1 *adj* persistent; obstinate, stubborn. **2** *nm* (*SAm*) doll; manikin, dummy.

porfiar [1c] *vi* to persist, insist; to argue stubbornly, doggedly maintain one's point of view; — **con uno** to argue with someone; — **en algo** to persist in something; **porfía en que es así** he insists that it is so, he will have it that it is so; — **por** + *infin* to struggle obstinately to + *infin*.

pórfido *nm* porphyry.

pormenor *nm* detail, particular.

pormenorizar [1f] **1** *vt* to detail, set out in detail; to particularize; to describe in detail. **2** *vi* to go into detail, particularize.

pornografía *nf* pornography.

pornográfico *adj* pornographic.

poro[1] *nm* (*Anat*) pore.

poro[2] *nm* (*Mex*) leek.

porongo *nm* (*SAm*) gourd, calabash.

pororó *nm* (*RPl*) popcorn.

porosidad *nf* porousness, porosity.

poroso *adj* porous.

porotal *nm* (*SAm*) (a) beanfield, bean patch. (b) (*fig*) **un** — **de** a lot of, a whole heap of.

poroto *nm* (a) (*Arg, Chi, Per*) bean; (*fig*) food (*in general*). (b) (*Arg: Sport etc*) point. (c) (*Chi, RPl*) weak person, inferior individual. (d) (*Chi*) child.

porque *conj* (a) (+ *indic*) because; since, for. (b) (+ *subj*) so that, in order that.

porqué *nm* (a) reason (*de* for), cause (*de* of); the whys and wherefores; **el** — **de la revolución** the factors that underlie the revolution; "El — de los dichos" "Origins of our Sayings". (b) (*fam: Fin*) wherewithal; **no tenemos el** — we haven't the wherewithal.

porquería *nf* (a) (*substance*) filth, muck, dirt; **me lo devolvieron cubierto de** — they gave it back to me filthy all over; **estar hecho una** — to be covered in muck, be dirty all over. (b) (*quality*) nastiness; indecency. (c) (*objects*) small thing, trifle; —**s** old things, junk, lumber; **le regalaron alguna** — they gave her some worthless present; **lo vendieron por una** — they sold it for next to nothing. (d) (*act*) dirty trick, mean action; indecent act; **me han hecho una** — they've played a dirty trick on me. (e) (*Cook*) nasty food, awful meal (*fam*); attractive but unwholesome dish. (f) (*fig*) rubbish; **la novela es una** — the novel is just rubbish; **escribió 3 o 4** —**s** he wrote 3 or 4 rubbishy books.

porqueriza *nf* pigsty.

porquerizo *nm*, **porquero** *nm* pigman, swineherd (*arch*).

porra *nf* (a) stick, club, cudgel; truncheon; (*Mus*) drumstick; (*Tech*) large hammer; (*Anat: tabu*) prick (*tabu*). (b) (*fam*) bore. (c) (*fam*) swank (*fam*), conceit; **gasta mucha** — he's got loads of swank. (d) (*fam*) ¡ —**s!** bother!, dash it!; (*to another person*) rubbish! (e) (*fam*) **mandar a uno a la** — to chuck someone out, send someone packing; ¡**vete a la** —! go to blazes! (f) (*Bol, RPl*) curl, forelock. (g) (*CAm, Mex*) political gang; terrorist band; (*Theat*) claque.

porracear [1a] *vt* (*Mex, Ven*) to hit, beat.

porrada *nf* (a) thwack, thump, blow. (b) (*fam*) pile, heap; lot; **una** — **de** a whole heap of, a lot of.

porrazo *nm* (a) thwack, thump, blow (*in falling*) bump. (b) (*SAm*) **de** — in one go, at one blow.

porrear [1a] *vi* to go on and on, harp on a theme.

porrería *nf* (*fam*) (a) annoying request, footling demand. (b) stupidity.

porreta *nf* (a) (*Bot*) green leaf. (b) (*fam*) **en** — stark naked.

porretada *nf* = **porrada** (b).

porrillo: a — *adv* in abundance, by the ton.

porro (*fam*) **1** *adj* stupid, oafish. **2** *nm* idiot, oaf.

porrón[1] *adj* slow, stupid; dull; sluggish.

porrón[2] *nm* glass wine jar with a long spout.

porrudo *adj* (a) big, bulging. (b) (*Arg, Urug*) long-haired; tousle-headed. (c) (*Arg, Urug*) big-headed.

porsiacaso *nm* (*Arg, Ven*) knapsack.

porta *nf* (*Naut*) port.

porta(a)viones *nm*, *pl* **porta(a)viones** aircraft carrier.

portacargas *nm*, *pl* **portacargas** crate; (*of bicycle*) carrier.

portación *nf* (*SAm*): — **de armas** carrying (of) a weapon.

portacubiertos *nm*, *pl* **portacubiertos** knife box, cutlery box.

portada *nf* (a) (*Archit*) main front; façade; porch, doorway. (b) (*Typ*) frontispiece, title page; (*of magazine*) cover.

portado *adj*: **bien** — well-dressed; well-behaved; respectable.

portador *nm*, **portadora** *nf* carrier, bearer; (*Comm, Fin*) bearer; payee; — **de gérmenes** germ carrier; **el** — **de esta carta** the bearer of this letter.

portaequipajes *nm*, *pl* **portaequipajes** (*Aut etc*) boot, trunk (*US*); luggage rack, grid; (*on bicycle*) carrier.

portaestandarte *nm* standard bearer.

portafolio *nm* (*Ven*) briefcase.

portafusil *nm* rifle sling.

portahachón *nm* torchbearer.

portal *nm* (a) vestibule, hall. (b) porch, doorway; street door, main door; (*of city*) gate; —**es** arcade. (c) (*Sport*) goal. (d) (*Eccl*) — **de Belén** Nativity scene, crèche.

portalada *nf* large doorway; imposing entrance; gate.

portalámpara(s) *nm*, *pl* **portalámparas** lamp-holder, socket.

portaligas *nm*, *pl* **portaligas** suspender belt, garter belt (*US*).

portalón *nm* (a) (*Archit*) = **portalada**. (b) (*Naut*) gangway.

portamaletas *nm*, *pl* **portamaletas** (*Aut*) luggage rack, grid.

portamantas *nm*, **portamantas** valise.

portamanteo *nm* travelling bag.

portaminas *nm*, *pl* **portaminas** propelling pencil.

portamonedas *nm*, *pl* **portamonedas** pocketbook, purse.

portañuela *nf* fly (*of trousers*).

portaobjeto(s) *nm*, *pl* **portaobjetos** slide; stage (*of microscope*).

portapapeles *nm*, *pl* **portapapeles** briefcase.

portaplacas *nm*, *pl* **portaplacas** (*Phot*) plateholder.

portaplumas *nm*, *pl* **portaplumas** penholder.

portar [1a] **1** *vt* (*lit*) to carry, bear. **2 portarse** *vr* (a) to behave, conduct oneself; — **mal** to misbehave, behave badly; **se ha portado como un cochino** he has behaved like a swine; **se portó muy bien conmigo** he was very decent to me, he treated me very well. (b) (*fam*) to show up well, come through creditably. (c) (*SAm*) to behave well; to behave nobly (*or* bravely).

portarretratos *nm*, *pl* **portarretratos** picture frame, photograph frame.

portátil *adj* portable.

portatostadas *nm*, *pl* **portatostadas** toast rack.

portaviandas *nm*, *pl* **portaviandas** lunch tin, dinner pail (*US*).

portavoz *nm* (a) megaphone, loudhailer. (b) (*person*) spokesman; (*pej*) mouthpiece.

portazgo *nm* toll.

portazo *nm* bang (*of a door*), slam; **dar un** — to slam the door.

porte *nm* (a) (*Comm*) carriage, transport; (costs of) carriage, transport charges; (*Post*) postage; — **pagado** (*Comm*) carriage paid, (*Post*) post-paid; **franco de** — (*Comm*) carriage free, (*Post*) post-free. (b) (*esp Naut*) capacity. (c) conduct, behaviour. (d) bearing, demeanour; air, appearance; **de** — **distinguido** with a distinguished air.

porteador *nm* carrier; (*Mountaineering etc*) porter; (*Hunting etc*) porter.

portear[1] [1a] *vt* (*Comm*) to carry, convey, transport.

portear[2] [1a] *vi* (a) (*of door*) to slam, bang. (b) (*Arg*) to get out in a hurry.

portento *nm* marvel, wonder, prodigy; **es un** — **de belleza** she is extraordinarily beautiful.

portentosamente *adv* marvellously, extraordinarily; extraordinarily well.

portentoso *adj* marvellous, extraordinary.

porteño 1 *adj* of Buenos Aires. **2** *nm*, **porteña** *nf* native (*or* inhabitant) of Buenos Aires; **los** —**s** the people of Buenos Aires.

porteo *nm* carriage, transport, conveyance.

portera *nf* portress.

portería *nf* (a) porter's lodge, porter's office. (b) (*Sport*) goal.

portero *nm* (a) porter, janitor; doorman; caretaker. (b) (*Sport*) goalkeeper.

portezuela *nf* (a) little door; (*of vehicle*) door. (b) (*Sew*) pocket flap.

portezuelo *nm* (Arg, Chi: *Geog*) pass.

pórtico *nm* (a) portico, porch; (*fig*) gateway (*de* to). (b) arcade.

portilla *nf* porthole.

portillo *nm* (a) gap, opening; breach; wicket, wicket gate; side entrance, private door. (b) (*Geog*) narrow pass. (c) (*of vessel etc*) dent; chip. (d) (*fig*) weak spot, vulnerable point; opening (*affording solution to a problem*).

pórtland *nm or f* (*esp SAm*) cement.

portón *nm* large door, main door; (*SAm*) gate; (*Chi*) back door.

portorriqueño 1 *adj* Puerto Rican. 2 *nm*, **portorriqueña** *nf* Puerto Rican.

portuario *adj* port (*attr*), harbour (*attr*); dock (*attr*); **trabajador** — docker.

Portugal *m* Portugal.

portugués 1 *adj* Portuguese. 2 *nm*, **portuguesa** *nf* Portuguese. 3 *nm* (*language*) Portuguese.

portuguesimo *nm* portuguesism, word (*or* phrase *etc*) borrowed from Portuguese.

porvenir *nm* future; **en el** —, **en lo** — in the future; **un hombre sin** — a man with no future, a man with no prospects; **le espera un brillante** — a brilliant future awaits him.

pos: en — **de** *prep* after, in pursuit of; **ir en** — **de** to chase (after), pursue; **ella va en** — **de un marido** she's after a husband.

posada *nf* (a) shelter, lodging; **dar** — **a** to give shelter to, take in. (b) inn; lodging house. (c) house, dwelling, abode.

posaderas *nfpl* backside, buttocks.

posadero *nm* innkeeper.

posar [1a] 1 *vt* load to lay down, put down; *hand etc* to place, put gently; — **los ojos en** to look vaguely at, glance briefly at.
2 *vi* (*Art, Cine, Phot*) to sit, pose.
3 **posarse** *vr* (a) (*bird, insect*) to alight, settle, rest; (*bird*) to perch, sit; (*aircraft*) to land, come down; **el avión se encontraba posado** the aircraft was on the ground. (b) (*liquid*) to settle, form sediment; (*dust*) to settle.

posas *nfpl* backside, buttocks.

posdata *nf* postscript.

pose [pouz *or* 'pose] *nf* (*angl, gall*) (a) (*Art, Cine, Phot*) pose; (*Phot*) time exposure. (b) (*fig*) attitude. (c) (*fig*) composure; poise. (d) (*fig*) pose; affectedness; affected posture.

poseedor *nm*, **poseedora** *nf* owner, possessor; (*of post, record*) holder.

poseer [2e] *vt* to have, possess, own; *advantage* to have, enjoy; *language, subject* to know perfectly, have a complete mastery of; *post, record* to hold.

poseído 1 *adj* (a) possessed (*por* by); (*fig*) maddened, crazed. (b) **estar muy** — **de** to be very vain about, have an excessively high opinion of.
2 *nm*, **poseída** *nf*: **gritar como un** — to shout like one possessed.

posesión *nf* (a) (*in general*) possession; (*of office*) tenure, occupation; (*of language, subject*) complete knowledge, perfect mastery; **dar** — **a** to hand over to, make formal transfer to; **él está en** — **de las cartas** he is in possession of the letters; **las cartas están en** — **de su padre** the letters are in the possession of his father; **está en** — **del récord** he holds the record; **tomar** — to take over, enter upon office (*etc*); **tomar** — **de** to take possession of, take over; **tomar** — **de un oficio** to take up a post. (b) (*una* —) possession (*also Pol*); property; piece of property, estate. (c) (*Chi*) country house and lands; (*Ven*) ranch, estate.

posesionar [1a] 1 *vt*: — **a uno de algo** to hand something over to someone. 2 **posesionarse** *vr*: — **de** to take possession of, take over.

posesivo 1 *adj* possessive. 2 *nm* possessive.

poseso = **poseído**.

posfechar [1a] *vt* to postdate.

posibilidad *nf* possibility; chance; **no existe** — **alguna de que venga** there is no possibility of his coming; **tiene pocas** —**es** he hasn't much chance.

posibilitar [1a] *vt* to make possible, facilitate, permit; to make feasible.

posible 1 *adj* possible; feasible; **una** — **tragedia** a possible tragedy; **todas las concesiones** —**s** all possible concessions; **a serme** — if I possibly can; **de**

ser — if possible; **en lo** — as far as possible; **lo antes** — as soon as possible; as quickly as possible; **lo más frecuentemente** — as often as possible; **hacer lo** — to do all that one can (*para* or *por* + *infin* to + *infin*); **es** — **que** + *subj* it is possible that . . .; perhaps . . .; **¿es** —? surely not?; can it really be true?; **¿será** — **que haya venido?** can he really have come (after all)?; **¿será** — **que no haya venido?** surely he has come, hasn't he?; **si es** — if possible; **si me es** — if I possibly can; *see* **dentro, pronto** *etc*.
2 —**s** *nmpl* means; funds, assets; **vivir dentro de sus** —**s** to live within one's means.

posiblemente *adv* possibly.

posición *nf* (a) (*in most senses*) position; status, standing, social position. (b) (*Sport*) position; (*in table etc*) place, position; **terminar en primera** — to finish first; **ganó A con B en segunda** — A won with B in second place. (c) (*SAm: angl*) position, post, job.

positiva *nf* (*Phot*) positive, print.

positivamente *adv* positively.

positivismo *nm* positivism.

positivista 1 *adj* positivist. 2 *nmf* positivist.

positivo 1 *adj* (*in most senses*) positive; (*Math*) positive, plus; *idea* useful, practical, constructive.
2 *nm* (a) (*Ling*) positive. (b) (*Phot*) positive, print.

pósito *nm* (a) (public) granary. (b) cooperative, association.

positrón *nm* positron.

posma *nmf* (*fam*) bore, dull person.

poso *nm* sediment, deposit; dregs.

posponer [2r] *vt* (a) — **A a B** to put A behind (*or* below) B; — **el amor propio al interés general** to subordinate one's self-respect to the general interest; — **a uno** to assign an unduly low position (*etc*) to someone. (b) (*esp SAm: angl*) to postpone.

posposición *nf* (a) postposition; relegation; subordination. (b) postponement.

posta 1 *nf* (a) (*of horses*) relay, team; stage; staging post; **a** — on purpose, deliberately; **por la** — posthaste, as quickly as possible. (b) (*Cards*) stake. (c) slice (*of meat etc*). (d) (*Hunting*) slug, pellet.
2 *nm* courier.

postal 1 *adj* postal. 2 *nf* postcard; — **ilustrada** picture postcard.

poste *nm* post, pole; pillar; stake; (*Sport*) post, upright; —**s** (*Sport*) goalposts, goal; — **de cerca** fencing post; — **indicador** signpost; — **de llegada** winning post; — **de portería** goalpost; — **de salida** starting post; — **telegráfico** telegraph pole; **dar** — **a uno** (*fam*) to keep someone hanging about; **oler el** — to scent danger, see trouble ahead; to smell a rat.

postema *nf* (a) (*Med*) abscess, tumour; (*Mex*) pus; (*Mex*) boil. (b) (*fam*) bore, dull person.

postemilla *nf* (*SAm*) gumboil.

postergación *nf* (a) passing over, ignoring. (b) delaying; deferment, postponement.

postergar [1h] *vt* (a) *person* to pass over, disregard; to ignore the seniority (*or* better claim) of. (b) (*esp SAm*) to delay; to defer, postpone.

posteridad *nf* posterity.

posterior *adj* (a) (*place*) back, rear; posterior; *engine* rear-mounted. (b) (*in order*) later, following. (c) (*time*) later, subsequent; **ser** — **a** to be later than.

posterioridad *nf* later nature; **con** — later, subsequently; **con** — **a** subsequent to, later than.

posteriormente *adv* later, subsequently, afterwards.

postglacial *adj* postglacial.

postgraduado 1 *adj* postgraduate. 2 *nm*, **postgraduada** *nf* postgraduate.

pos(t)guerra *nf* postwar period; **los años de la** — the postwar years; **en la** — in the postwar period, after the war.

postigo *nm* (a) wicket, wicket gate; postern; small door, side door. (b) shutter.

postillón *nm* postillion.

postimpresionismo *nm* post-impressionism.

postimpresionista 1 *adj* post-impressionist. 2 *nmf* post-impressionist.

postín *nm* (*fam*) (a) elegance, luxury, poshness (*fam*), tone (*fam*); **de** — posh (*fam*), swanky (*fam*), smart. (b) side (*fam*), swank (*fam*); **darse** — to show off, swank (*fam*); **se da mucho** — **de que su padre es ministro** he swanks about his father being a minister.

postinear [1a] *vi* (*fam*) to show off, swank (*fam*).

postinero adj (fam) (a) person, vain, conceited (de about); swanky (fam). (b) dress etc posh (fam), swish (sl).

postizas nfpl castanets.

postizo 1 adj false, artificial; teeth false; collar detachable; front etc dummy; smile etc false, phoney (fam), sham. 2 nm switch, false hair, hairpiece.

postludio nm postlude.

postmeridiano adj postmeridian.

postnatal adj postnatal.

postor nm bidder; **mejor** — highest bidder.

postración nf prostration; — **nerviosa** nervous exhaustion.

postrado adj prostrate (also fig); — **por el dolor** prostrate with grief.

postrar [1a] 1 vt (a) to cast down, overthrow; to humble. (b) (Med) to weaken, exhaust, prostrate. 2 **postrarse** vr to prostrate oneself.

postre 1 nm (also —s) sweet, sweet course; dessert; **¿qué hay de —?** what is there for dessert?; **para —** (fam) to crown it all, on top of all that; **llegar a los —s** (fig) to come too late, come after everything is over.
2 nf: **a la —** at last, in the end; when all is said and done.

postremo adj, **postrero** adj (**postrer** before m sing noun) last; rear, hindermost.

postrimerías nfpl (a) dying moments; final stages, closing stages; **en las — del siglo** in the last few years of the century, right at the end of the century. (b) (Eccl) four last things.

postulación nf (a) postulation. (b) collection.

postulado nm postulate, proposition; assumption, hypothesis.

postulante nmf petitioner; (Eccl) postulant, candidate.

postular [1a] vt (a) to postulate.
(b) to seek, demand; to petition for; to claim; **en el artículo postula la reforma de . . .** in the article he sets out demands for the reform of . . .
(c) to collect (for charity).
(d) (CAm, Mex) candidate to nominate.

póstumo adj posthumous.

postura nf (a) (of body) posture, position; stance; pose. (b) (fig) attitude, position; stand; **adoptar una — poco razonable** to take an unreasonable attitude; **la — del gobierno en este asunto** the government's position in this matter.
(c) (in auction) bid; (Gambling) bet, stake; **hacer una —** to lay a bet; to make a bid.
(d) (Orn) egg-laying; eggs (laid).

post-venta adj after-sales (attr); **servicio** (or **asistencia**) **de —** after-sales service.

potable adj drinkable; **agua —** drinking water.

potaje nm (a) (Cook) stew; —s mixed vegetables; (dish of) dried vegetables. (b) (fig) mixture; jumble.

potasa nf potash.

potasio nm potassium.

pote nm (a) pot; jar; jug; (Pharm) jar; (Mex) tin, can; (Mex) tankard; (Hort) flowerpot, pot; (Ec, PR) flask; **a —** in plenty; see **beber**.
(b) (Prov) stew.
(c) (fam) pout.
(d) (fam) **darse —** to show off, swank (fam).

potencia nf (a) (in general) power; potency; — **electoral** voting power, power in terms of votes; — **hidráulica** hydraulic power; — **muscular** muscular power, muscular strength.
(b) (Mech) power; capacity; — (**en caballos**) horsepower; — **al freno** brake horsepower; — **real** effective power.
(c) (Pol) power; **las —s** the Powers; **las grandes —s** the great powers; — **colonial** colonial power; — **mundial** world power; **éramos una — naval** we used to be a naval power.
(d) (Math) power.
(e) (Rel) —s **del alma** faculty.
(f) **en —** potential, in the making; **es una guerra civil en —** it is a civil war in the making.

potencial 1 adj potential. 2 nm (a) potential. (b) (Gram) conditional.

potencialidad nf potentiality.

potencialmente adv potentially.

potentado nm potentate; (fig) tycoon; baron; magnate; big shot (fam).

potente adj (a) powerful. (b) (fam) big, mighty, strong; **un grito —** a great yell.

potestad nf power, authority, jurisdiction; — **marital** husband's authority; **patria —** paternal authority.

potestativo adj optional, not mandatory; permissive.

potingue nm (fam) concoction, brew.

poto nm (a) (Arg, Bol, Chi, Per) backside, bottom; lower end. (b) (Chi, Ec, Per) calabash; earthenware vessel.

potoco adj (Bol, Chi) squat.

potón (Chi) 1 adj coarse. 2 nm rustic, peasant.

potosí nm fortune; **cuesta un —** it costs the earth; **vale un —** it's worth a fortune; **ella vale un —** she's a treasure; **en ese negocio tienen un —** they've got a gold mine in that business.

potra nf (a) (Zool) filly. (b) (Med) rupture, hernia. (c) (fam) **tener —** to be lucky.

potranca nf filly, young mare.

potranco nm (Col, CR, Mex, PR) colt, young horse.

potrear [1a] 1 vt (a) (Guat, Per) to beat. (b) (Mex, PR) to break, tame. 2 vi (Arg, Hond, Urug) to gambol, caper about, chase around.

potrero nm (a) pasture; paddock. (b) (SAm) cattle ranch. (c) (Arg) playground.

potrillo nm (a) (Chi, RPl) colt. (b) (Chi) tall glass. (c) (Col, Ec) small canoe.

potro nm (a) (Zool) colt; — **de madera** vaulting horse. (b) rack (for torture); stocks; shoeing frame. (c) (SAm) hernia, tumour.

poyo nm stone bench.

poza nf puddle, pool; (Mex) pool, backwater (of river).

pozanco nm puddle, pool.

pozo nm (a) well; — **artesiano** artesian well; — **negro** cesspool; — **de petróleo** oil well; — **séptico** septic tank; **caer en el —** (fig) to fall into oblivion.
(b) (Geog) deep pool, deep part (of river).
(c) (Min) shaft; pit; — **de aire** air shaft; — **de registro,** — **de visita** manhole; inspection hatch; — **de ventilación** ventilation shaft.
(d) (fig) **ser un — de ciencia** to be immensely learned; **es un — de maldad** he is utterly wicked.

práctica nf (in most senses) practice; method; skill; **en la —** in practice; —s **restrictivas** (**de la competencia**) restrictive practices; —s **profesionales** professional training, practical training for a profession; **la — hace maestro** practice makes perfect; **aprender con la —** to learn by practice; **hacer —s de piano** to practise (on) the piano; **hacer — de clínica** to do one's hospital training, walk the wards (fam); **poner algo en —** to put something into practice.

practicable adj (a) practicable; workable, feasible. (b) road etc passable, usable. (c) door that opens, that is meant to open.

prácticamente adv practically.

practicante 1 adj (Eccl) practising. 2 nmf practitioner; (Med) medical assistant, doctor's assistant; male nurse.

practicar [1g] 1 vt (a) skill, virtue etc to practise, exercise.
(b) activity etc to practise; sport to go in for, play; profession to practise; — **el francés con su profesor** to practise one's French with one's teacher.
(c) to perform, carry out; arrest to make.
(d) hole to cut, make; to bore, drill.
2 **practicarse** vr: — **en la enseñanza** to do teaching practice, do one's school practice.

práctico 1 adj (a) practical; tool etc handy; house etc convenient; clothing sensible, practical; **no resultó ser muy —** it turned out to be not very practical; **resulta — vivir tan cerca de la fábrica** it's convenient (or handy) to live so close to the factory.
(b) study, training etc practical.
(c) person skilled, expert (en at); **ser muy — en** to be very skilled at, be very adept at.
2 nm (Med) practitioner; (Naut) pilot.

pradera nf meadow, meadowland; (Canada etc) prairie; **unas extensas —s** extensive grasslands.

pradería nf meadowlands, grasslands.

prado nm meadow, field; pasture; green grassy area; — **de juego** playground, play area.

Praga Prague.

pragmático adj pragmatic.

pragmatismo nm pragmatism.

pragmatista nmf pragmatist.

preámbulo nm (a) preamble, introduction.
(b) (pej) evasive talk, annoying digression; **gastar —s** to talk evasively, beat about the bush; **decir algo sin —s** to say something without beating about the bush.

prebélico adj prewar.

prebenda nf (a) (Eccl) prebend. (b) (fam) sinecure, soft job.

prebendado nm prebendary.

preboste nm provost.

precalentar [1k] vt to preheat.

precariamente adv precariously.

precario adj precarious; **estar de** — to be in a precarious position.
precaución nf (a) (act) precaution; preventive measure; **tomar** —**es** to take precautions.
(b) (quality) foresight; caution, wariness; **ir con** — to go cautiously, proceed warily; **lo hicimos por** — we did it to be on the safe side.
precautorio adj (SAm) precautionary.
precaver [2a] 1 vt to guard against, try to prevent; to forestall; to stave off.
2 **precaverse** vr to be on one's guard, take precautions, be forewarned; — **contra** to guard against; — **de** to be on one's guard against, beware of.
precavidamente adv cautiously, warily.
precavido adj cautious, wary.
precendencia nf precedence; priority; greater importance, superiority.
precedente 1 adj preceding, foregoing; former; **cada uno mejor que el** — each one better than the one before.
2 nm precedent; **de acuerdo con el** — according to precedent; **contra todos los** —**s** against all the precedents; **sin** —(**s**) unprecedented; unparalleled; **establecer un** —, **sentar un** — to establish (or set up) a precedent.
preceder [2a] 1 vt: — **a** (a) to precede, go before; **le precedía un coche** he was preceded by a car; **el título precede al nombre** the title goes before the name.
(b) (fig) to have priority over; to take precedence over.
2 vi to precede; **todo lo que precede** all the preceding (part), all that which comes before.
preceptista nmf theorist.
precepto nm precept; order, rule; **de** — (Eccl) obligatory.
preceptor nm teacher; (private) tutor.
preceptorado nm tutorship.
preceptoral adj tutorial.
preces nfpl prayers, supplications.
preciado adj (a) esteemed, valuable. (b) presumptuous.
preciarse [1b] vr to boast; — **de algo** to pride oneself on something, boast of being something; — **de inteligente** to think oneself clever, pride oneself on one's intelligence; — **de** + infin to boast of + ger.
precintado adj sealed, presealed; (Comm) prepackaged.
precinto nm seal.
precio nm (a) price; cost; value, worth; (of journey) fare; (in hotel etc) rate, charge; — **de compra** purchase price; — **al contado** cash price; — **de coste** cost price; **a** — **de coste, a** — **costo** at cost price; — **en fábrica** price ex-factory; — **irrisorio, — de oportunidad, — de situación** (SAm) bargain price; — **de lista** list price; — **de mercado** market price; — **neto** net price; — **obsequio** giveaway price; — **de pensión** school fees; — **tope** top price, ceiling price; **último** — closing price; — **de venta** sale price; — **del viaje** fare (for the journey); **al** — **de** (fig) at the cost of; **lo hará a cualquier** — he'll do it whatever the cost; **evítelo a cualquier** — avoid it at all costs; **"no importa** —**"** "cost no object"; **poner** (or **señalar**) — **a la cabeza de uno** to put a price on someone's head; **no tener** — (fig) to be priceless.
(b) (fig) value, worth; **hombre de gran** — a man of great worth.
preciosamente adv (fam) beautifully; charmingly.
preciosidad nf (a) preciousness; value, worth.
(b) (pej) preciosity.
(c) (fam) beautiful thing; precious object; **es una** — it's lovely, it's really beautiful; **¡oye,** —**!** hey, beautiful!
preciosismo nm (Lit etc) preciosity.
preciosista (Lit etc) 1 adj precious, affected. 2 nmf precious writer, affected writer (etc).
precioso adj (a) precious; valuable.
(b) (fam) pretty, lovely, beautiful; charming; **una edición preciosa** a beautiful edition; **tienen un niño** — they have a lovely child; **¿verdad que es** —? isn't it lovely?
preciosura nf (SAm) =**preciosidad** (c).
precipicio nm (a) cliff, precipice.
(b) (fig) chasm, abyss; **tiene el** — **abierto a sus pies** the chasm yawns before him, he stands on the brink of disaster.
(c) (fig) ruin.
precipitación nf (a) haste; rashness; **con** — hastily; rashly, precipitately. (b) (Meteorol) precipitation, rainfall. (c) (Chem) precipitation.
precipitadamente adv headlong; hastily, suddenly; rashly, precipitately.

precipitado 1 adj flight etc headlong; departure etc hasty, sudden; act hasty, rash, precipitate. 2 nm (Chem) precipitate.
precipitar [1a] 1 vt (a) to hurl down, cast down, throw (desde from).
(b) to hasten; to speed up, accelerate; to precipitate; **aquello precipitó su salida** that affair hastened his departure; **la dimisión precipitó la crisis** the resignation precipitated (or brought on, sparked off) the crisis.
(c) (Chem) to precipitate.
2 **precipitarse** vr (a) to throw oneself, hurl oneself (desde from); to launch oneself.
(b) to rush, dash; to dart; — **a hacer algo** to rush to do something, hasten to do something; — **sobre** (bird etc) to swoop on, pounce on; — **sobre uno** to rush at someone, hurl oneself on someone; — **hacia un sitio** to rush towards a place.
(c) to act rashly; **se ha precipitado rehusándolo** he acted rashly in rejecting it, it was rash of him to refuse it.
precipitoso adj (a) place precipitous, steep, sheer.
(b) act etc =**precipitado** 1.
precisado adj (Arg, CAm, Mex): **verse** — **a** + infin to be obliged to + infin.
precisamente adv (a) precisely, in a precise way.
(b) precisely, exactly, just; **¡**—**!** exactly!, precisely!; just so!; — **por eso** for that very reason, precisely because of that; — **fue él quien lo dijo** it so happens it was he who said it, as a matter of fact he said it; — **estábamos hablando de eso** we were just talking about that; **llegó** — **cuando nos íbamos** he arrived just as we were leaving; **yo no soy un experto** — I'm not exactly an expert; **no es eso** — it's not quite that, it's not really that.
precisar [1a] 1 vt (a) to need, require; **no precisa lavado** it needs no washing; **"vendedores precisa agencia internacional"** (advert) "salesmen wanted by international agency"; **precisa que vengas** you must come; **no precisamos que el candidato tenga experiencia** we do not insist (or demand) that the candidate should be experienced.
(b) to determine exactly, fix; to pinpoint, put one's finger on; details etc to specify, state precisely; **hay alguna rareza que no puedo** — there is some oddity which I cannot pin down (or put my finger on).
2 vi to be necessary; to be urgent; — **de algo** to need something; **precisamos de más tiempo** we need more time.
precisión nf (a) precision; preciseness, accuracy, exactness; **instrumento de** — precision instrument.
(b) need, necessity; **tener** — **de algo** to need something, have need of something.
(c) (Mex) urgency.
preciso adj (a) precise; exact, accurate; **una descripción precisa** a precise description.
(b) **en aquel** — **momento** at that precise moment, at that very moment, just at that moment.
(c) necessary, essential; **las cualidades precisas** the essential qualities, the requisite qualities; **tener el tiempo** — **para** + infin to have (just) enough time to + infin; **cuando sea** — when it becomes necessary; **es** — **que lo hagas** it is essential that you should do it, you must do it; **es** — **tener coche** it is essential to have a car.
precitado adj above-mentioned.
preclaro adj (lit) illustrious.
precocidad nf precociousness, precocity; (Bot etc) earliness.
precognición nf precognition.
precolombino adj pre-Columbian; **la América precolombina** America before Columbus.
preconcebido adj preconceived; **idea preconcebida** preconception.
preconcepción nf preconception.
preconizable adj foreseeable, that can be envisaged.
preconización nf (a) recommendation; favouring.
(b) visualizing, envisaging.
preconizar [1f] 1 vt (a) to advise, recommend; policy to favour.
(b) to foresee, visualize, envisage (que that).
2 **preconizarse** vr: **se preconiza que . . .** it is envisaged that . . . , it is thought that . . .
precordillera nf (Arg) Andean foothills.
precoz adj precocious; forward; baldness etc premature; (Bot etc) early.
precursor nm, **precursora** nf predecessor, forerunner.
predador nm, **predator** nm predator.
predecesor nm, **predecesora** nf predecessor.
predecir [3p] vt to predict, foretell, forecast.

predestinación *nf* predestination.
predestinado *adj* predestined; **ser — a** + *infin* to be predestined to + *infin*.
predestinar [1a] *vt* to predestine.
predeterminación *nf* predetermination.
predeterminar [1a] *vt* to predetermine.
prédica *nf* sermon; harangue; **—s** preaching (*also fig*).
predicación *nf* (a) preaching. (b) (*una —*) = **prédica**.
predicado *nm* predicate.
predicador *nm* preacher.
predicamento *nm* (a) standing, prestige; **no goza ahora de tanto —** it has less prestige now, it is not so well thought of now. (b) (*SAm: angl*) predicament.
predicar [1g] *vti* to preach.
predicativo *adj* predicative.
predicción *nf* prediction; forecast; **— del tiempo** weather forecast(ing).
predicho *adj* aforementioned.
predilección *nf* predilection; **tener — por** to have a predilection for; **—es y aversiones** likes and dislikes.
predilecto *adj* favourite.
predio *nm* property, estate; **— rústico** country estate; **— urbano** town property.
predisponer [2r] *vt* to predispose; (*pej*) to prejudice, bias (*contra* against).
predisposición *nf* predisposition, inclination; (*pej*) prejudice, bias (*contra* against); (*Med*) tendency, predisposition (*a* to).
predispuesto *adj* predisposed; **ser — a los catarros** to have a tendency to get colds; **ser — al abatimiento** to be inclined to depression; **estar — contra uno** to be prejudiced against someone.
predominante *adj* predominant; major; prevailing; (*Comm*) *interest* controlling.
predominantemente *adv* predominantly.
predominar [1a] **1** *vt* to dominate, predominate over. **2** *vi* (a) to predominate; to prevail. (b) **esta casa predomina a áquella** this house is higher than that one.
predominio *nm* predominance; prevalence; sway, ascendancy, influence; superiority.
preeminencia *nf* pre-eminence, superiority.
preeminente *adj* pre-eminent; superior.
preeminentemente *adv* pre-eminently.
preempción *nf* pre-emption.
preenfriar [1c] *vt* to precool.
pre(e)scoger [2c] *vt players* to seed.
preestreno *nm* preview, press view, private showing.
preexistencia *nf* pre-existence.
preexistente *adj* pre-existent, pre-existing.
preexistir [3a] *vti* to pre-exist, exist before.
prefabricado *adj* prefabricated.
prefabricar [1g] *vt* to prefabricate.
prefacio *nm* preface, foreword.
prefecto *nm* prefect.
prefectura *nf* prefecture.
preferencia *nf* preference; **de —** for preference, preferably; **localidad de —** reserved seat; **tratamiento de —** preferential treatment; **mostrar — por** to show preference to, be biassed in favour of.
preferente *adj* (a) preferred; preferable. (b) (*Fin*) *share* preference (*attr*); *duty, treatment etc* preferential; *right* prior.
preferentemente *adv* preferably.
preferible *adj* preferable (*a* to).
preferiblemente *adv* preferably.
preferir [3i] *vt* to prefer; **— té a café** to prefer tea to coffee; **¿cuál prefieres?** which do you prefer?; **prefiero ir a pie** I prefer to walk, I'd rather go on foot.
prefiguración *nf* foreshadowing, prefiguration.
prefigurar [1a] *vt* to foreshadow, prefigure.
prefijar [1a] *vt* (a) to fix beforehand, arrange in advance, prearrange. (b) (*Gram*) to prefix (*a* to).
prefijo *nm* prefix.
pregón *nm* proclamation, announcement; (*Comm*) street cry, vendor's cry; **— literario de un acto** speech (*etc*) about a forthcoming public ceremony.
pregonar [1a] *vt* to proclaim, announce; *secret* to disclose, reveal; *wares* to cry, hawk, advertise verbally; *merits etc* to praise publicly, proclaim (for all to hear).
pregonero *nm* town crier.
preguerra *nf* prewar period; **el nivel de la —** the prewar level; **en la —** in the prewar period, before the war.
pregunta *nf* question; **— capciosa** catch question, loaded question; **— retórica** rhetorical question; **andar** (*or* **estar**) **a la cuarta —** (*fam*) to be broke (*fam*); **contestar a una —** to answer a question; **hacer una —** to ask (*or* put) a question; **estrechar a uno a —s** to press someone closely with questions.

preguntar [1a] **1** *vt* to ask; to question, interrogate; **— algo a uno** to ask someone something; **— si** to ask if, ask whether; **le fue preguntada su edad** he was asked his age; *see* **caber**.
2 *vi* to ask, inquire; **— por uno** to ask for someone, inquire for someone; **— por la salud de uno** to ask after someone's health, ask about someone's health.
3 preguntarse *vr* to wonder; **me pregunto si vale la pena** I wonder if it's worth while.
preguntón *adj* inquisitive.
prehistoria *nf* prehistory.
prehistórico *adj* prehistoric.
preignición *nf* preignition.
prejuiciado *adj* (*SAm: angl*) prejudiced (*contra* against).
prejuicio *nm* (a) prejudgement. (b) (*pej*) prejudice, bias (*contra* against); preconception.
prejuzgar [1h] *vt* to prejudge.
prelación *nf* priority.
prelado *nm* prelate.
preliminar 1 *adj* preliminary. **2** *nm* preliminary.
preludio *nm* (a) (*Mus and fig*) prelude (*de* to). (b) (*Mus*) tuning up, practice notes, scales.
preludir [1b] **1** *vt* to announce, herald; to introduce; to start off. **2** *vi* (*Mus*) to tune up, play a few scales.
premarital *adj* premarital.
prematuramente *adv* prematurely.
prematuro *adj* premature.
premeditación *nf* premeditation; **con —** with premeditation, deliberately.
premeditadamente *adv* with premeditation, deliberately.
premeditado *adj* premeditated, deliberate; *wilful; insult etc* studied.
premeditar [1a] *vt* to premeditate; to plan, think out (in advance).
premiado 1 *adj novel etc* prize (*attr*), prize-winning. **2** *nm*, **premiada** *nf* prizewinner.
premiar [1b] *vt* to reward (*con* with); to give a prize to, make an award to; **salir premiado** to win a prize.
premio *nm* (a) reward, recompense; **como — a sus servicios** as a reward for his services.
(b) (*in competition*) prize; award; **— de consolación** consolation prize; **— extraordinario** award (*of a degree etc*) with special distinction; **— gordo** first prize, big prize.
(c) (*Comm, Fin*) premium; **a —** at a premium.
premioso *adj* (a) *dress etc* tight.
(b) *order etc* strict.
(c) *person* tongue-tied, slow of speech; slow in writing; slow in movement, heavy, awkward.
(d) (*fig*) troublesome.
premisa *nf* premise.
premonición *nf* premonition.
premonitorio *adj* indicative, warning.
premunirse [3a] *vr* (*SAm*) = **precaverse**.
premura *nf* (a) pressure; **con — de tiempo** under (time) pressure, with very little time; **debido a — de espacio** because of pressure on space.
(b) haste, urgency.
prenatal *adj* antenatal, prenatal.
prenda *nf* (a) pledge; (*fig*) pledge, token; **dejar algo en —** to pawn something; to leave something as security; **en — de** as a pledge of, as a token of; **no doler —s** to make a promise without conditions; to spare no effort (*or* expense *etc*); **a mí no me duelen —s** I don't mind saying nice things about others, it doesn't worry me that I'm not as good as others; **no soltar —** to give nothing away, avoid committing oneself; to give someone no chance (*or* opening).
(b) (*also — de vestir*) garment, article of clothing; **— interior** undergarment, piece of underclothing; **—s de cama** bedclothes; **—s de mesa** table linen.
(c) **—s** (*fig*) talents, gifts; (*also* **buenas —s**) good qualities.
(d) **—s** (*game*) forfeits.
(e) (*esp SAm*) jewel.
(f) (*in direct address*) darling!, my treasure!
(g) (*RPl*) **la —** one's sweetheart, one's lover.
prendar [1a] **1** *vt* to captivate, enchant; to win over; **volvió prendado con** (*or* **de**) **la ciudad** he came back enchanted with the town.
2 prendarse *vr*: **— de** to be captivated by, be enchanted with; to take a fancy to; **— de uno** to fall in love with someone.
prendedera *nf* (*Col*) waitress.
prendedero *nm*, **prendedor** *nm* clasp, brooch.
prender [2a] **1** *vt* (a) *person* to catch, capture; to arrest.
(b) (*Sew etc*) to fasten; to pin, attach (*en* to); to

tie, do up; — **el pelo con horquillas** to fix one's hair with grips, put grips in one's hair.

(c) (*esp SAm*) *fire, oven etc* to light; *match* to strike; *light* to switch on; *cigarette, candle* to light; *room* to light up.

2 *vi* (a) to catch, stick; to grip; **el ancla prendió en el fondo** the anchor buried itself in the seabed, the anchor gripped firmly.

(b) (*of fire*) to catch; (*of injection*) to take; (*of plant*) to take, take root; **el mal prendió más en la juventud** the evil spread most among young people, the evil infected youth most strongly.

3 prenderse *vr* (a) to catch fire (*en* on).

(b) (*woman*) to dress up.

prendería *nf* secondhand (clothes) shop; pawnbroker's (shop).

prendero *nm* secondhand (clothes) dealer, junk dealer; pawnbroker.

prendido 1 *adj*: **quedar** — to be caught (fast), be stuck; (*fig*) to be captivated. **2** *nm* clip, brooch.

prendimiento *nm* (a) capture, seizure; arrest. (b) (*Chi*) constipation.

prensa *nf* (a) (*Mech*) press; (*Mech*) gland, stuffing box; (*Typ*) press, printing press; (*of racquet*) press, frame; — **de copiar** printing frame; — **hidráulica** hydraulic press; — **de ropa** linen press, clothes press; — **rotativa** rotary press.

(b) (*fig*) **la P—** the press; **aprobar un libro para la** — to pass a book for (the) press; **dar algo a la** — to publish something; **entrar en** — to go to press; **estar en** — to be in press; **tener mala** — to have (*or* get) a bad press; **"libros en —"** (*advert*) "books in press", "forthcoming publications".

prensado *nm* sheen, shine, gloss.

prensador *nm* press, pressing machine; — **de paja** (*Agr*) straw baler.

prensaestopas *nm, pl* **prensaestopas** (*Mech*) packing gland.

prensalimones *nm, pl* **prensalimones** lemon squeezer.

prensar [1a] *vt* to press.

prensil *adj* prehensile.

preñada *adj* pregnant; (*Zool*) pregnant, with young.

preñado 1 *adj* (*fig*) (a) *wall* bulging, sagging.

(b) — **de** pregnant with, full of; **una situación preñada de peligros** a situation full of danger, a situation fraught with dangers; **ojos —s de lágrimas** eyes filled with tears, eyes brimming with tears.

2 *nm* pregnancy.

preñar [1a] *vt* (*fam*) to get pregnant; (*Zool*) to impregnate, fertilize.

preñez *nf* pregnancy.

preocupación *nf* (a) worry, anxiety, concern, preoccupation.

(b) prejudice.

(c) preconception; unfounded fear, silly fear; notion, silly idea; **tiene la** — **de que su mujer le es infiel** he has the silly idea that his wife is unfaithful to him.

(d) (*SAm*) special consideration, priority, preference.

preocupado *adj* worried, anxious, concerned, preoccupied.

preocupar [1a] **1** *vt* (a) to worry, preoccupy; to bother, exercise; **esto me preocupa muchísimo** this worries me greatly; **me preocupa cómo decírselo** it bothers me to know how to tell him; **no le preocupa el qué dirán** public opinion doesn't bother him.

(b) to prejudice, influence.

2 preocuparse *vr* (a) to worry, care (*de, por* about); to concern oneself (*de* about); **¡no se preocupe!** don't worry!, don't bother!; **no te preocupes por eso** don't worry about that; **no se preocupa en lo más mínimo** he doesn't care in the least.

(b) **yo me preocuparé de que esté listo** I'll see to it that everything is ready; **tú preocúpate de que todo esté listo** you ensure that (*or* see to it that) everything is ready.

(c) (*SAm*) — **de algo** to give special attention to something, give something priority.

preparación *nf* (a) (*act*) preparation; **estar en** — to be in preparation.

(b) (*state*) preparedness, readiness; — **militar** military preparedness.

(c) training (*also Sport*); **le falta** — **matemática** he lacks mathematical training, he is not trained in maths.

(d) (*Bio, Pharm*) preparation.

preparado 1 *adj* prepared (*para* for); (*Cook*) ready to serve, ready cooked; **¡—s, listos, ya!** ready, steady, go!

2 *nm* (*Pharm*) preparation.

preparador *nm* (*Sport*) trainer, coach; (*of horse*) trainer.

preparar [1a] **1** *vt* (a) to prepare, get ready; (*Tech*) to prepare, process, treat.

(b) to teach, train; (*Sport*) to train, coach; **X le prepara a Y de física** X is coaching Y in physics.

2 prepararse *vr* (a) to prepare, prepare oneself, get ready; — **a** + *infin*, — **para** + *infin* to prepare to + *infin*, get ready to + *infin*.

(b) (*storm, trouble etc*) to be brewing.

preparativo 1 *adj* preparatory, preliminary.

2 —s *nmpl* preparations; preliminaries; **hacer sus —s** to make one's preparations (*para* + *infin* to + *infin*).

preparatorio *adj* preparatory.

preponderancia *nf* preponderance; superiority.

preponderante *adj* preponderant; superior.

preponderar [1a] *vi* to preponderate; to dominate, prevail.

preposición *nf* preposition.

preposicional *adj* prepositional.

prepucio *nm* foreskin, prepuce.

prerrogativa *nf* prerogative, right, privilege.

presa *nf* (a) (*act*) capture, seizure; **hacer** — to seize.

(b) clutch, hold; — **de pie** foothold; **hacer** — **en** to clutch (on to), seize; to get a hold on; **el fuego hizo** — **en la cortina** the fire set light to (*or* caught, began to burn) the curtain.

(c) (*object*) capture, catch, prize; (*Mil*) spoils, booty; loot; (*Naut*) prize; (*Orn*) prey; (*Zool*) prey, catch; **ave de** — bird of prey; **ser** — **de** (*fig*) to be a prey to, be a victim of.

(d) (*Orn*) claw; (*Zool*) tusk, fang.

(e) (*in river etc*) dam; weir, barrage.

(f) (*Agr*) ditch, channel.

(g) (*esp SAm*) piece of food, piece of meat (*esp* chicken).

presagiar [1b] *vt* to betoken, forebode, presage.

presagio *nm* omen, portent.

presbicia *nf* long-sightedness.

presbiopía *nf* presbyopia.

présbita *adj*, **présbite** *adj* long-sighted.

presbiteriano 1 *adj* Presbyterian. **2** *nm*, **presbiteriana** *nf* Presbyterian.

presbiterio *nm* presbytery, chancel.

presbítero *nm* priest.

presciencia *nf* prescience, foreknowledge.

presciente *adj* prescient.

prescindencia *nf* (*SAm*) doing without, going without; non-participation (in a dispute).

prescindente *adj* (*SAm*) non-participating.

prescindible *adj* dispensable; expendable; **y cosas fácilmente —s** and things we can easily do without.

prescindir [3a] *vi*: — **de** to do without, go without; to dispense with, get rid of; to disregard; to omit, overlook; **han prescindido del coche** they've given up their car, they've got rid of their car; **no podemos** — **de él** we can't manage without him; **prescindamos de todo aquello** let's forget about all that, let's leave all that aside.

prescribir [3a; *ptp* **prescrito**] *vt* to prescribe.

prescripción *nf* prescription; — **facultativa** medical prescription.

prescrito *adj* prescribed.

presea *nf* jewel; treasure, precious thing.

preselección *nf* (*Sport*) seeding.

preseleccionar [1a] *vt* (*Sport*) to seed.

presencia *nf* (*all senses*) presence; — **de ánimo** presence of mind; **en** — **de** in the presence of; **tener (buena)** — to have a good presence, be impressive, have an impressive bearing.

presencial *adj*: **testigo** — eyewitness.

presenciar [1b] *vt* to be present at; to attend; to see, witness, watch.

presentable *adj* presentable.

presentación *nf* (a) presentation; introduction; — **en (la) sociedad** coming-out, début. (b) (*SAm*) petition.

presentador *nm* (*TV etc*) compère.

presentar [1a] **1** *vt* (a) (*general sense*) to present; to offer; to show, display; *arms, excuse, petition, proof etc* to present; *resignation* to tender; *motion* to propose, put forward; **presenta señales de deterioro** it shows signs of wear; **el coche presenta ciertas modificaciones** the car has certain modifications.

(b) *play* to perform, put on; *film* to show; *star* to present, feature.

(c) *person* to introduce; **le presento a Vd a mi hermana** may I introduce my sister to you?; **ser presentada en (la) sociedad** to come out, make one's début.

2 presentarse *vr* (a) to present oneself; to appear

(unexpectedly), turn up; — **a la policía** to report to the police, (*criminal*) give oneself up to the police; **hay que — el lunes a las 9** you should report at 9 on Monday; **se presentó en un estado lamentable** he turned up in a dreadful state.

(b) to introduce oneself (*a* to); — **en (la) sociedad** to come out, make one's début.

(c) (*as candidate*) to run, stand; — **a** *post* to put in for, apply for; — **para** *exam* to sit (for), enter for.

(d) to present itself; to show, appear; **el día se presenta muy hermoso** it looks like being a lovely day, there are prospects of a fine day; **se presentó un caso singular** a strange case came up.

presente 1 *adj* **(a)** *person* present; ¡—! present!, here!; **los —s** those present; **los señores aquí —s** the gentlemen here present; **estar — en** to be present at; **mejorando lo —, salvando a los —s** present company excepted.

(b) la — carta, la — this letter.

(c) *time, tense* present; **hacer —** to state, declare; **tener —** to remember, bear in mind; **ten —s a nosotros** don't forget us; **ten muy — que . . .** be sure to remember that . . .; understand clearly that . . .

2 *nm* **(a)** present; **al —** at present; **hasta el —** up to the present.

(b) (*Gram*) present (tense).

presentimiento *nm* premonition, presentiment; foreboding.

presentir [3i] *vt* to have a premonition of; — **que . . .** to have a premonition that . . .

preservación *nf* protection, preservation.

preservar [1a] *vt* **(a)** to protect, preserve (*contra* against, *de* from). **(b)** (*SAm: angl*) to keep, preserve.

presidencia *nf* presidency; chairmanship; **ocupar la —** to preside, be in (*or* take) the chair.

presidencial *adj* presidential.

presidente *nm* (*Pol, of association, Taur etc*) president; (*of committee, meeting*) chairman; (*Parl*) speaker; (*Law*) presiding magistrate (*etc*).

presidiario *nm* convict.

presidio *nm* **(a)** prison, penitentiary; **echar a uno a —** to put someone in prison.

(b) hard labour, penal servitude.

(c) (*Pol*) praesidium.

(d) (*Mil*) garrison; fortress.

presidir [3a] **1** *vt* **(a)** to preside at, preside over; to take the chair at.

(b) (*fig*) to dominate, rule, be the dominant element in.

2 *vi* to preside; to take the chair.

presilla *nf* **(a)** fastener, clip. **(b)** loop. **(c)** (*SAm*) shoulder badge, flash; (*Mex*) epaulette.

presión *nf* **(a)** pressure; (*with hand etc*) press, squeeze; (*Meteorol, Phys, Tech*) pressure; (*of explosion*) blast; — **arterial, — sanguínea** blood pressure; — **atmosférica** atmospheric pressure, air pressure; **a — under** pressure; **de —** (*Tech*) pressure (*attr*); **hacer —** to press (*sobre* on).

(b) (*fig*) pressure; **ejercer** (*or* **hacer**) — **para que se haga algo** to press for something to be done; **hay —es dentro del partido** there are pressures within the party.

presionar [1a] **1** *vt* **(a)** *button etc* to press.

(b) (*fig*) to press, put pressure on; **el ministro, presionado por los fabricantes, accedió** the minister, under pressure from the manufacturers, agreed.

2 *vi* to press; — **para,** — **por** to press for; — **para que sea permitido algo** to press for something to be granted.

preso 1 *ptp of* **prender; llevar — a uno** to take someone away under arrest; **estar — de un terror pánico** to be panic-stricken.

2 *nm,* **presa** *nf* convict, prisoner.

prestación *nf* **(a)** lending, loan; — **de ayuda** giving of help; — **personal** obligatory service (*of individual on communal work*).

(b) — **de juramento** oath-taking, swearing.

prestado *adj:* **dar algo —** to lend something; **eso está —** that is on loan; **pedir — algo, tomar — algo** to borrow something; **vivir de —** to live at someone else's expense, live on what one can borrow.

prestador *nm,* **prestadora** *nf* lender.

prestamista *nm* moneylender; pawnbroker.

préstamo *nm* **(a)** (*act*) loan, lending, borrowing. **(b)** loan. **(c)** (*Ling*) loanword.

prestancia *nf* distinction, excellence; elegance, dignity.

prestar [1a] **1** *vt* **(a)** *money etc* to lend, loan.

(b) (*fig*) to lend, give; *help, support* to give; *attention* to pay (*a* to); *service* to do, render; *enchantment etc* to lend.

(c) *oath* to take, swear.

(d) (*SAm*) to borrow (*a* from).

(e) (*Arg, Ven*) to do good to, be good for; to suit; **no le prestó el viaje** the trip was not good for him.

2 *vi* **(a)** to give, stretch.

(b) — **para** to be big enough for.

3 prestarse *vr* **(a) no se presta a esas maniobras** he does not lend himself to manoeuvres of that kind; **la situación se presta a muchas interpretaciones** the situation lends itself to many interpretations.

(b) — **a** + *infin* to offer to + *infin*, volunteer to + *infin*.

prestatario *nm,* **prestataria** *nf* borrower.

presteza *nf* speed, promptness; alacrity; **con — promptly**, with alacrity.

prestidigitación *nf* conjuring, juggling; sleight of hand.

prestidigitador *nm* conjurer, juggler.

prestigiado *adj* (*SAm*) worthy, estimable, prestigious.

prestigiar [1b] *vt* to give prestige to; to make famous; to honour (*con* with).

prestigio *nm* **(a)** prestige; face; good name. **(b)** (*magic*) spell. **(c)** trick.

prestigioso *adj* worthy, estimable, prestigious; reputable; famous.

prestímano *nm* conjurer, juggler.

presto 1 *adj* **(a)** quick, prompt. **(b)** ready (*para* for). **(c)** (*Mus*) presto. **2** *adv* quickly; at once, right away.

presumible *adj* presumable; probable; **es —** it is to be presumed.

presumido *adj* conceited.

presumir [3a] **1** *vt* **(a)** to presume, conjecture, surmise; — **que . . .** to presume that . . ., guess that . . .

(b) (*Arg, Bol*) to court; to flirt with.

2 *vi* **(a) según cabe —** as may be presumed, presumably.

(b) to be conceited; to give oneself airs, swank (*fam*), show off; **para — ante las amistades** in order to show off before one's friends; **no presumas tanto** don't be so conceited; — **de listo** to think oneself very smart, boast of being clever; — **de experto** to pride oneself on being an expert; — **demasiado de las fuerzas** to overestimate one's strength.

presunción *nf* **(a)** supposition, presumption; (*pej*) suspicion. **(b)** (*quality*) conceit, presumption; pretentiousness.

presunto *adj* supposed, presumed; so-called; *heir* presumptive; **el — asesino** the alleged murderer; **estos —s expertos** these so-called experts.

presuntuosamente *adv* conceitedly, presumptuously; pretentiously.

presuntuoso *adj* conceited, presumptuous; pretentious.

presuponer [2r] *vt* to presuppose.

presuposición *nf* presupposition.

presupuestal *adj* (*Mex etc*) budgetary, budget (*attr*).

presupuestar [1a] *vt* to budget for; to reckon up, estimate for.

presupuestario *adj* budgetary, budget (*attr*).

presupuestívoro *nm* (*SAm: hum, pej*) public employee.

presupuesto *nm* (*Fin*) budget; (*for job, plan etc*) estimate.

presurosamente *adv* quickly, promptly; hastily.

presuroso *adj* quick, prompt, speedy; hasty; *step etc* light, quick.

pretal *nm* (*esp SAm*) strap, girth.

pretencioso *adj* **(a)** pretentious, presumptuous; showy. **(b)** (*SAm*) vain, boastful.

pretender [2a] *vt* **(a)** — + *infin* to try to + *infin*, seek to + *infin*, endeavour to + *infin*; **pretendió convencerme** he sought to convince me; **han pretendido robarme** they have attempted to rob me; **¿qué pretende Vd decir con eso?** what do you mean by that?; **no pretendo ser feliz** it's not happiness I'm after.

(b) to claim; — **ser rico** to claim to be rich, profess to be rich; — **haber hecho algo** to claim to have done something; **el libro pretende ser importante** the book tries to look (*or* make out that it is) important; **esto pretende poder curarlo todo** this purports to cure everything; **pretende que el coche le atropelló** he alleges that the car knocked him down.

(c) to seek, try for; *post* to apply for; *honour* to aspire to; *objective* to aim at, try to achieve; **¿qué pretende Vd?** what are you after?; what do you hope to achieve?

(d) — **que** + *subj* to expect that . . ., suggest that . . ., intend that . . .; **él pretende que yo le**

escriba he suggests that I should write to him, he wants me to write to him; ¿**cómo pretende Vd que lo compre yo?** how do you expect me to buy it?

(e) *woman* to woo, court; to seek the hand of.

pretendido adj supposed, pretended; alleged.

pretendiente 1 nm suitor. **2** nm, **pretendienta** nf claimant; (*for post*) candidate, applicant (a for); (*royal*) pretender (a to).

pretensado adj prestressed.

pretensión nf (a) claim.

(b) aim, object; aspiration.

(c) (*pej*) pretension; exaggerated claim, false claim; **tener —es de** to have pretensions to, lay claim to; **tener pocas —es** to be undemanding, be content with very little; **tiene la — de que le acompañe yo** he expects me to go with him, he says unreasonably that I ought to go with him.

(d) (*SAm*) vanity; presumption.

pretensioso adj (*SAm*) = **pretencioso (b)**.

pretérito 1 adj (a) (*Gram*) past. (b) past, former; **las glorias pretéritas del país** the country's former glories. **2** nm preterite, past historic.

preternatural adj preternatural.

pretextar [1a] vt to plead, use as an excuse; **— que . . .** to plead that . . ., allege that . . .

pretexto nm pretext; excuse, plea; **a — de** on the pretext of; **so — de** under pretext of.

pretil nm (a) parapet; handrail, guardrail, railing. (b) (*Ec*) forecourt; (*Mex, Ven*) bench; (*Mex*) kerb.

pretina nf girdle, belt, waistband; (*Arg, Col, Urug*) leather strap; (*Cu*) trouser fly.

preuniversitario 1 adj pre-university; **curso — course taken between the end of one's school career and beginning of university studies.**

2 nm, **preuniversitaria** nf student on a pre-university course.

prevalecer [2d] vi (a) to prevail (*sobre* against, over); to triumph, win through; to come to dominate. (b) (*Bot*) to take root and grow.

prevaleciente adj prevailing, prevalent; dominant.

prevalerse [2q] vr: **— de** to avail oneself of; (*pej*) to take advantage of.

prevención nf (a) preparation; (*state*) preparedness, readiness; **las —es para la ceremonia** the preparations for the ceremony.

(b) prevention.

(c) (*quality*) foresight, forethought; **obrar con —** to act with foresight.

(d) precaution; precautionary measure, safety measure; **de —** spare, reserve, emergency (*attr*); **hemos tomado ciertas —es** we have taken certain precautions.

(e) prejudice; **tener — contra uno** to have a prejudice against someone, be prejudiced against someone.

(f) police station; (*Mil*) guardroom, guardhouse.

prevenido adj (a) **ser —** to be cautious; to be far-sighted.

(b) **estar —** to be prepared, be ready; to be forewarned, be on one's guard (*contra* against); **hombre — vale por dos** forewarned is forearmed.

prevenir [3s] **1** vt (a) to prepare, get ready, make ready (*para* for).

(b) **— a uno de algo** to provide someone with something.

(c) to prevent; to alert; to forestall; **hay accidentes que no se pueden —** some accidents cannot be prevented.

(d) **— a uno** to warn someone, forewarn someone, put someone on his guard (*contra* against, *de* about); **pudieron —le a tiempo** they were able to warn him in time.

(e) to foresee, anticipate; to provide for.

(f) to prejudice, bias (*a favor de* in favour of, *en contra de* against).

2 prevenirse vr (a) to get ready, prepare; **— para un viaje** to get ready for a trip; **— de ropa adecuada** to provide oneself with suitable clothing.

(b) **— contra** to take precautions against, prepare for.

(c) **— en contra de uno** to take up a hostile attitude to someone.

preventivo adj preventive, precautionary; (*Med*) preventive.

prever [2v] vt (a) to foresee.

(b) to anticipate, envisage, visualize; **— que . . .** to anticipate that . . ., envisage that . . ., expect that . . .; **ya lo preveía** I expected as much.

previamente adv previously.

previo 1 adj previous, prior, earlier; *exam* preliminary.

2 as *prep* after, following; **— acuerdo de los otros**

subject to the agreement of the others; **— pago de los derechos** on payment of the fees.

3 nm (*Cine*) playback.

previsible adj foreseeable.

previsión nf (a) (*quality*) foresight, far-sightedness; caution.

(b) (*act*) precaution, precautionary measure; **en — de** as a precaution against.

(c) **— social** social security.

(d) forecast; **— del tiempo** weather forecast(ing); **las —es del plan quinquenal** the forecasts of the five-year plan.

previsivo adj (*Mex*) = **previsor**.

previsor adj far-sighted; thoughtful.

prez nf honour, glory.

prieto adj (a) blackish, dark; (*SAm*) dark, swarthy; *woman* brunette.

(b) *person* mean.

(c) tight, compressed, tightly packed; **un siglo — de historia** a century packed full of history, a century rich in history.

prietuzco adj (*Ant, CAm, Mex*) blackish.

prima nf (a) (*female*) cousin.

(b) (*on wages etc*) bonus, extra payment; (*insurance*) premium; (*on exports etc*) subsidy; **— de incentivo** incentive bonus; **— por rendimiento** output bonus; **— por trabajos peligrosos** danger money.

(c) (*Eccl*) prime.

(d) (*RPl*) **bajar la —** to moderate one's language; **subir la —** to use strong language.

primacía nf (a) primacy, first place; priority; supremacy; **— de paso** (*Aut*) priority, right of way; **tener la — entre** to be supreme among.

(b) (*Eccl*) primacy.

primada nf (*fam*) (a) piece of stupidity; silly mistake. (b) trick, hoax.

primado nm (*Eccl*) primate.

primadon(n)a nf prima donna.

primal 1 adj yearling. **2** nm, **primala** nf yearling.

primar [1a] vi to occupy first place, be supreme; **— sobre** to have priority over, take precedence over; to outweigh.

primariamente adv primarily.

primario adj primary.

primate nm (a) (*Zool*) primate. (b) important person, outstanding figure.

primavera 1 nf (a) spring; springtime (*also fig*). (b) (*Orn*) blue tit. (c) (*Bot*) primrose. **2** nm (*fam*): **ser un —** to be a simple soul.

primaveral adj spring (*attr*); springlike.

primer adj see **primero**.

primera nf (a) (*Aut etc*) first gear, bottom gear.

(b) (*Rail*) first class; **viajar en —** to travel first.

(c) (*fam*) **de —** first-class, first-rate; **comer de —** to eat really well, have a first-class meal; **estar de —** to feel fine.

(d) (*Comm*) **— de cambio** first of exchange; see **cambio (c)**.

primeramente adv first, firstly; chiefly.

primerear [1a] vi (*RPl*) to land the first blow, get in first.

primerizo 1 adj green, inexperienced. **2** nm, **primeriza** nf novice, beginner.

primero 1 adj (**primer** before m sing noun) (a) first; former; *page* first, front; **en los —s años del siglo** in the early years of the century; **en los —s años treinta** in the early thirties; **a —s de siglo** at the start of the century, early in the century; **llegar el —** to arrive first; **ser el — en + infin** to be the first to **+ infin**.

(b) (*fig*) first; prime; basic, fundamental; urgent; *material* raw; **lo —es que . . .** the fundamental thing is that . . .; **es nuestro primer deber** it is our first duty; **es el primer país en estos estudios** it is the foremost country in these studies.

2 adv (a) first.

(b) rather, sooner; **— se quedará en casa que pedir permiso para salir** she'd rather stay at home than have to ask for permission to go out; **¡— morir!** we'd rather die!

primicias nfpl (a) first fruits. (b) (*fig*) first fruits, first effort, first attempt.

primitivamente adv (a) at first; originally. (b) primitively, in a primitive way.

primitivo adj (a) early; first, original; **el texto — the original text; quedan 200 de los —s 850** there remain 200 from the original 850; **es una obra primitiva** it is an early work; **devolver algo a su estado — to restore something to its original state.

(b) *colour* primary.

(c) (*Fin*) *share* ordinary.

(d) (*Hist etc*) primitive; uncivilized; **en condiciones primitivas** in primitive conditions.

primo 1 *adj* (a) (*Math*) prime.
    (b) *material* raw.
    2 *nm* (a) cousin; — **carnal,** — **hermano** first cousin; **ser** —**s carnales** (*fig*) to be extraordinarily alike, be very closely related.
    (b) (*fam*) fool; dupe, sucker (*sl*); **hacer el** — to be easily taken in, be taken for a sucker (*sl*); to carry the can (*sl*).
primogénito *adj* first-born.
primogenitura *nf* primogeniture; birthright.
primor *nm* (a) exquisiteness, beauty; elegance; delicacy.
    (b) care, skill; **hecho con** — done most skilfully, delicately made.
    (c) fine thing, lovely thing; **hace** —**es con la aguja** she makes lovely things with her needlework; **cose que es un** — she sews beautifully, she sews in a way that is a delight to see; **hijos que son un** — delightful children, charming children.
primordial *adj* basic, fundamental, essential; **es de interés** — it is of fundamental concern; **es** — **saberlo** it is essential to know it.
primordialmente *adv* basically, fundamentally.
primorosamente *adv* exquisitely, delicately, elegantly; neatly, skilfully.
primoroso *adj* exquisite, fine, delicate, elegant; neat, skilful.
princesa *nf* princess.
principado *nm* principality.
principal 1 *adj* (a) principal, chief, main; foremost; *floor* first, second (*US*); **lo** — **es . . .** the main thing is to . . .
    (b) *person* illustrious.
    2 *nm* (a) (*person*) head, chief, principal.
    (b) (*Fin*) principal, capital.
    (c) (*Theat*) dress circle.
principalmente *adv* principally, chiefly, mainly.
príncipe *nm* (a) prince; — **consorte** prince consort; — **encantador** Prince Charming; — **heredero** crown prince. (b) *see* **edición.**
principesco *adj* princely.
principiante 1 *adj* who is beginning; novice; inexperienced, green. **2** *nm,* **principianta** *nf* beginner; learner; novice.
principiar [1b] *vti* to begin; — **a** + *infin* to begin to + *infin,* begin + *ger*; — **con** to begin with.
principio *nm* (a) beginning, start; origin; early stage; **al** — at first, in the beginning; **a** —**s de** at the beginning of; **a** —**s del verano** at the beginning of the summer, early in the summer; **desde el** — from the first; **desde el** — **hasta el fin** from start to finish, from beginning to end; **en un** — at first; **dar** — **a** to start off; **tener** (*or* **tomar**) — **en** to start from, be based on.
    (b) —**s** (*of subject*) rudiments, first notions; "**P**—**s de física**" "Introduction to Physics", "Outline of Physics".
    (c) (*moral*) principle; **persona de** —**s** man of principles; **en** — in principle; **por** — on principle; **es inmoral por** — it is immoral in principle; **sin** —**s** unprincipled.
    (d) (*Philos*) principle; (*Chem*) element, constituent.
    (e) (*Cook*) entrée.
principote *nm* (*fam*) swank (*fam*), show-off (*fam*); parvenu, social climber.
pringar [1h] **1** *vt* (a) (*Cook*) to dip in fat (*etc*); *roast* to baste; — **el pan en la sopa** to dip one's bread in the soup.
    (b) to dirty, soil (with grease); to splash grease (*or* fat) on; (*esp SAm*) to splash.
    (c) (*fam*) — **a uno** to wound someone, make someone bleed.
    (d) (*fam*) to blacken, run down.
    (e) (*fam*) — **a uno en un asunto** to involve someone in a matter.
    (f) (*Chi*) disease to give.
    (g) (*Chi*) *woman* to put in the family way.
    (h) (*sl*) —**las** to peg out (*sl*).
    2 *vi* (a) (*fam*) to take a beating, lose badly; to come a cropper (*fam*); **hemos pringado** we're done for.
    (b) (*Mil etc*) to sweat one's guts out (*fam*).
    (c) (*fam*) — **en** to dabble in; to take a hand in, get mixed up in.
    (d) (*CAm, Mex, Ven*) to drizzle.
    3 pringarse *vr* (a) to get splashed, get soiled (*con,* **de** with).
    (b) (*fam*) = **2** (c).
    (c) (*fam*) to make money on the side; to get a rake-off (*fam*); to make a packet (*fam*).
pringo *nm* (*SAm*) drop (of liquid); **con un** — **de leche** with a drop of milk.

pringón 1 *adj* dirty, greasy. **2** *nm* (a) grease stain, grease spot. (b) (*fam*) rake-off (*fam*); packet (*fam*).
pringoso *adj* greasy.
pringue *nm* (*sometimes f*) (a) grease, fat, dripping.
    (b) grease stain, grease spot; (*any*) dirty object, sticky thing.
    (c) (*fam*) nuisance; cause of trouble; **es un** — **tener que . . .** it's a bind having to . . . (*sl*).
    (d) (*CAm, Mex*) drop (of liquid); (*Mex, Nic*) splash (of mud *etc*); (*Ec*) burn.
prior *nm* prior.
priora *nf,* **prioresa** *nf* prioress.
priorato *nm* priory.
prioridad *nf* priority; seniority, greater age; **tener** — to have priority (*sobre* over).
prioritario *adj* prior, priority (*attr*); **un proyecto de carácter** — a plan with top priority, a plan in the priority class.
prisa *nf* hurry, haste; speed; (sense of) urgency; **temporada de más** —(**s**) rush period, busy period; **a** —, **de** — quickly, hurriedly; **a toda** — as quickly as possible; **estar de** — to be in a hurry; **voy con mucha** — I'm in a great hurry; **correr** — to be urgent; **¿te corre** —? are you in a hurry?; **¿corren** — **estas cartas?** are these letters urgent?, is there any hurry for these letters?; **dar** — **a uno, meter** — **a uno** to make someone get a move on; **darse** — to hurry (up); **¡date** —! hurry (up)!, come along!; **tener** — to be in a hurry.
prisco *nm* (*esp SAm*) apricot.
prisión *nf* (a) prison. (b) imprisonment; **cinco años de** — five years' imprisonment, prison sentence of five years. (c) —**es** shackles, fetters.
prisionero *nm* prisoner (of war); **hacer** — **a uno** to take someone prisoner.
prisma *nm* prism.
prismático 1 *adj* prismatic. **2** —**s** *nmpl* binoculars, field glasses.
prístino *adj* pristine, original.
privación *nf* (a) (*act*) deprivation, deprival; **sufrir** — **de libertad** to suffer loss of liberty. (b) (*state*) deprivation; want, privation; —**es** hardships, privations.
privadamente *adv* privately.
privado 1 *adj* (a) private; personal; " — **y confidencial**" "private and confidential".
    (b) (*SAm*) mad, senseless; (*Ven*) weak, faint.
    2 *nm* (a) (*Pol*) favourite, protégé; (*Hist*) royal favourite, chief minister.
    (b) **en** — privately, in private.
privanza *nf* favour; **durante la** — **de Lerma** when Lerma was royal favourite, when Lerma was chief minister.
privar [1a] **1** *vt* (a) — **a uno de algo** to deprive someone of something, take something away from someone; — **a uno del conocimiento** to render someone unconscious; **le privaron del carnet de conducir** they suspended his driving licence, they took away his driving licence; **nos vemos privados de . . .** we find ourselves without . . ., we find ourselves bereft of . . .
    (b) — **a uno de** + *infin* to forbid someone to + *infin,* prevent someone from + *ger*; **lo cual me privó de verlos** which prevented me from seeing them; **no me prives de verte** don't forbid me to come to see you, don't tell me not to come again.
    (c) to delight, overwhelm.
    2 *vi* (a) (*Pol*) to be in favour (at court).
    (b) to obtain, be present; to prevail; (*fam*) to be in fashion, be the thing; **la cualidad que más priva entre ellos** the quality which is most strongly present in them; **en ese período privaba la minifalda** at that time miniskirts were in (*fam*).
    3 privarse *vr:* — **de** to deprive oneself of; to give up, go without, forgo; **no se privan de nada** they lack nothing, they have everything they want.
privativo *adj* exclusive; — **de** exclusive to; **esa función es privativa del presidente** that function is the president's alone; **la planta es privativa del Brasil** the plant is peculiar to Brazil, the plant is restricted to Brazil.
privilegiado 1 *adj* privileged; *memory etc* exceptionally good. **2** *nm,* **privilegiada** *nf* privileged person; **los** —**s** the privileged.
privilegiar [1b] *vt* to grant a privilege to; to favour.
privilegio *nm* privilege; concession; immunity, exemption; (*Law*) sole right; (*Lit*) copyright; — **fiscal** tax concession; — **de invención** patent.
pro 1 *nm and f* profit, advantage; **hombre de** — worthy man, honest man; **los** —**s y los contras** the pros and the cons, for and against; **buena** — **le haga** and much good may it do him; **en** — **de** for, on behalf of; for the benefit of.

2 *prep* for, on behalf of; **campaña — paz** peace campaign; **asociación — ciegos** association for (aid to) the blind.

pro . . . pro- . . ., *eg* **prosoviético** pro-Soviet.

proa *nf* (*Naut*) bow, bows; prow; (*Aer*) nose; **de —** bow (*attr*), fore; **en la —** in the bows; **poner la — a** (*Naut*) to head for, set a course for; (*fig*) to aim at; **poner — a la tempestad** to ride out the storm (*also fig*); **poner la — a uno** to take a stand against someone.

probabilidad *nf* (a) probability, likelihood; **según toda — in** all probability.

(b) chance, prospect; **—es** chances; **—es de vida** expectation of life; **hay pocas —es de que venga** there is little prospect of his coming; **apenas tiene —es** he hasn't much chance.

probable *adj* probable, likely; **es — que** + *subj* it is probable (*or* likely) that . . .; **es — que no venga** he probably won't come.

probablemente *adv* probably.

probado *adj* *remedy etc* proven.

probador *nm* (a) (*person*) taster (*of wine etc*). (b) fitting room. (c) (*SAm*) tailor's dummy.

probanza *nf* proof, evidence.

probar [1m] **1** *vt* (a) *fact, case etc* to prove; to show, demonstrate; to establish; **— que . . .** to prove that . . .

(b) *apparatus, weapon etc* to test, try (out); *garment* to try on.

(c) *food etc* to try, taste, sample; **prueba un poco de esto** try a bit of this; **no han probado nunca un jerez fino** they have never tasted fine sherry; **no lo pruebo nunca** I never touch it.

2 *vi* (a) to try; **¿probamos?** shall we try?, shall we have a go?; **— a** + *infin* to try to + *infin*.

(b) **— de = 1** (c).

(c) to suit; **no me prueba (bien) el café** coffee doesn't agree with me; **le probó mal ese oficio** that trade did not suit him.

3 probarse *vr*: **— un traje** to try a suit on.

probatorio *adj* (a) evidential; **documentos —s del crimen** documents in proof of the crime, documents which prove the crime. (b) convincing.

probeta *nf* test tube; graduated cylinder.

probidad *nf* integrity, honesty, rectitude.

problema *nm* problem; puzzle.

problemático *adj* problematic.

probo *adj* honest, upright.

probóscide *nf* proboscis.

procacidad *nf* (a) insolence, impudence; brazenness. (b) indecency.

procaz *adj* (a) insolent, impudent; brazen. (b) indecent.

procedencia *nf* (a) source, origin; point of departure; (*Naut*) port of origin. (b) properness; (*Law*) propriety.

procedente *adj* (a) **— de** coming from, proceeding from, originating in. (b) reasonable; proper, fitting; (*Law*) proper; duly established.

proceder [2a] **1** *vi* (a) to proceed; **— a una elección** to proceed to an election; **— contra uno** (*Law*) to take proceedings against someone.

(b) **— de** to come from, originate in; to flow from, spring from; **todo esto procede de su negativa** all this springs from his refusal; **estas patatas proceden de Israel** these potatoes come from Israel; **de donde procede que . . .** (from) whence it happens that . . .

(c) to act; to proceed, behave; **ha procedido precipitadamente** he has acted hastily; **conviene — con cuidado** it is best to go carefully.

(d) to be right (and proper), be fitting; **si el caso procede** if the case warrants it; **no procede obrar así** it is not right to act like that; **luego, si procede, . . .** then, if appropriate, . . .

2 *nm* course of action; behaviour, conduct.

procedimiento *nm* procedure; process; means, method; (*Law*) proceedings; **un — para abaratar el producto** a method of making the product cheaper; **por un — deductivo** by a deductive process.

proceloso *adj* (*lit*) stormy, tempestuous.

prócer *nm* worthy, notable; important person; (*Pol*) great man, leader.

procesado *nm*, **procesada** *nf* accused (person).

procesal *adj* (a) (*Parl etc*) procedural. (b) (*Law*) *costs etc* legal.

procesar [1a] *vt* to try, put on trial; to prosecute; to sue, bring an action against.

procesión *nf* procession; **la — va por dentro** still waters run deep; there is more in this than meets the eye; **la — le va por dentro** he's a quiet one; he keeps his troubles to himself.

procesional *adj* processional.

proceso *nm* (a) process (*also Anat, Chem etc*); **— mental** mental process; **— de datos** data processing; **— de una enfermedad** course (*or* progress) of a disease.

(b) lapse of time; **en el — de un mes** in the course of a month.

(c) (*Law*) trial; prosecution; action, lawsuit, proceedings; **— verbal** record; **abrir** (*or* **entablar, formar**) **—** to bring a suit (*a* against).

proclama *nf* (a) proclamation. (b) poster; **— electoral** election poster. (c) **—s** (*Eccl*) banns.

proclamación *nf* proclamation.

proclamar [1a] **1** *vt* to proclaim. **2 proclamarse** *vr*: **— rey** to proclaim oneself king.

procreación *nf* procreation, breeding.

procrear [1a] *vti* to procreate, breed.

procura *nf* (*SAm*) obtaining, getting; **andar en — de algo** to be trying to get something.

procuración *nf* (*Law*) power of attorney; proxy.

procurador *nm* (a) (*Law*) attorney, (*approx*) solicitor. (b) (*Law*) proxy. (c) (*Pol*) **— en Cortes, — a Cortes** (*Hist*) deputy, member of (the Spanish) parliament.

procurar [1a] **1** *vt* (a) **—** + *infin* to try to + *infin*, endeavour to + *infin*; **procura conservar la calma** do try to keep calm; **procura que no te vean** take care not to let them see you, don't let them see you.

(b) to get, obtain; to secure; to yield, produce; **— un puesto a uno** to get someone a job, find a job for someone; **esto nos procurará grandes beneficios** this will bring us great benefits, this will secure great benefits for us.

(c) **—** + *infin* to manage to + *infin*, succeed in + *ger*; **por fin procuró dominarse** eventually he managed to control himself.

2 procurarse *vr*: **— algo** to secure something for oneself.

Procustes *m*, **Procusto** *m* Procrustes; **lecho de —** Procrustes' bed.

prodigalidad *nf* (a) bounty; richness. (b) lavishness, generosity. (c) (*pej*) prodigality; extravagance, wastefulness.

pródigamente *adv* (a) bountifully; richly. (b) lavishly. (c) (*pej*) prodigally; wastefully.

prodigar [1h] **1** *vt* to lavish, give lavishly; (*pej*) to squander; **prodiga las alabanzas** he is lavish in his praise (*a* of); **nos prodigó sus atenciones** he was very generous in his kindnesses to us.

2 prodigarse *vr* to be generous with what one has, lay oneself out to please.

prodigio *nm* prodigy; wonder, marvel; **niño —** child prodigy; **es un — de talento** he is wonderfully talented.

prodigiosamente *adv* prodigiously, marvellously.

prodigioso *adj* prodigious, marvellous.

pródigo 1 *adj* (a) bountiful; rich; productive; **— en** rich in, generous with; **la pródiga naturaleza** bountiful nature.

(b) lavish, generous (*de* with); **ser — de sus talentos** to be generous in offering one's talents.

(c) (*pej*) prodigal; extravagant, wasteful; **hijo — prodigal** son.

2 *nm*, **pródiga** *nf* spendthrift, prodigal.

producción *nf* (a) production; output; yield; **— en serie** mass production. (b) (*object*) product; (*Cine*) production.

producido *nm* (*Arg, Mex*) profit, yield.

producir [3o] **1** *vt* (*in most senses*) to produce; to make; to give, yield; to cause, generate; *change etc* to bring about; *impression* to give, cause; *interest* (*Fin*) to bear; **le produjo gran tristeza** it caused her much sadness; **¿qué impresión le produce?** how does it impress you?, what impression do you get from it?; **Ruritania no produce cohetes** Ruritania does not make rockets; **estos factores produjeron la revolución** these factors caused the revolution; **— en serie** to mass-produce.

2 producirse *vr* (a) to be produced, be made (*etc*).

(b) (*change etc*) to come about; (*difficulty, crisis*) to arise; (*accident*) to happen, take place; (*riot etc*) to break out; **así se produjo la nueva creencia de que . . .** in this way there arose the new belief that . . .; **en ese momento se produjo una explosión** at that moment there was an explosion; **a no ser que se produzca un cambio** unless a change takes place, unless there is a change.

productividad *nf* productivity.

productivo *adj* productive; *business* profitable; **— de interés** *bond etc* that bears interest.

producto *nm* product (*also Math*); production; (*Comm, Fin*) yield, profit; proceeds, revenue; **—s** products, (*Agr*) produce; **—s agrícolas** agricultural

produce, farm produce; **— alimenticio** foodstuff; **— bruto** gross (national) product; **— de desecho** waste product; **—s estancados** goods sold by state monopoly; **—s de marca** branded goods; **— secundario** by-product; **— terminado** finished product.
productor 1 *adj* productive, producing; **clase productora** producing class, class of producers; **nación productora** producer nation.
2 *nm*, **productora** *nf* producer (*also Cine*).
produje, produzco *etc see* **producir**.
proemio *nm* preface, introduction.
proeza *nf* (a) exploit, feat, heroic deed. (b) (*Col, Mex*) boast.
profanación *nf* desecration.
profanar [1a] *vt* to desecrate, profane; to defile; **— la memoria de uno** to blacken the memory of someone, slander someone who is dead.
profano 1 *adj* (a) profane, secular.
   (b) irreverent.
   (c) lay; ignorant.
   (d) indecent, immodest.
   2 *nm* layman; **soy — en música** I'm ignorant of music, I'm a layman in matters of music.
profecía *nf* prophecy.
proferir [3i] *vt word, sound* to utter; *hint* to drop, throw out; *sigh* to fetch; *insult* to hurl, let fly (*contra* at); *curse* to utter.
profesar [1a] **1** *vt* (a) *admiration, belief etc* to profess; to declare.
   (b) *subject* to teach; to hold a chair in.
   (c) *profession* to practise.
   2 *vi* (*Eccl*) to take vows.
profesión *nf* (a) (*of faith etc*) profession, declaration; avowal; (*Eccl*) taking of vows.
   (b) profession; calling, vocation; **abogado de —**, **de — abogado** a lawyer by profession; **— liberal** liberal profession.
profesional 1 *adj* professional; **no — non**-professional. **2** *nmf* professional.
profesionalismo *nm* professionalism.
profesionalmente *adv* professionally.
profeso *adj* (*Eccl*) professed.
profesor *nm*, **profesora** *nf* (a) (*in general*) teacher; instructor; **— de esgrima** fencing master; **— de gimnasia** gym instructor; **— de natación** swimming instructor; **— de piano** piano teacher; **— robot** teaching machine.
   (b) (*School: in general*) teacher; **— (de instituto)** schoolmaster, schoolmistress; **— de biología** biology teacher (*or* master, mistress).
   (c) (*Univ*) professor; lecturer; **— adjunto** (*kind of*) assistant lecturer, associate professor (*US*); **— agregado** assistant professor (*US*); **— numerario**, **— titular** full professor; **es — de griego** he is professor of Greek, he is a lecturer in Greek; **nuestros —es de universidad** our university teachers; **se reunieron los —es** the staff met, the faculty met (*US*).
profesorado *nm* (a) teaching profession; teaching, lecturing. (b) teaching staff, faculty (*US*). (c) professorship.
profesoral *adj* professorial.
profeta *nm* prophet.
proféticamente *adv* prophetically.
profético *adj* prophetic.
profetisa *nf* prophetess.
profetizar [1f] *vti* to prophesy.
profiláctico 1 *adj* prophylactic. **2** *nm* prophylactic.
profilaxis *nf* prophylaxis.
prófugo *nm* fugitive; (*Mil*) deserter; **— de la justicia** fugitive from justice.
profundamente *adv* deeply, profoundly; *sleep* deeply, soundly.
profundidad *nf* (a) depth; (*Math*) depth, height; **la poca — del río** the shallowness of the river; **tener una — de 30 cm** to be 30 cm deep (*or* in depth).
   (b) **las —es del océano** the depths of the ocean.
   (c) (*fig*) depth, profundity.
profundizar [1f] **1** *vt* (a) to deepen, make deeper.
   (b) (*fig*) *subject* to study in depth, make a profound study of, go deeply into; *mystery* to fathom, get to the bottom of.
   2 *vi* (a) **— en** to penetrate into, enter.
   (b) **— en** (*fig*) **=1** (b).
profundo *adj* (a) deep; **poco —** shallow; **tener 20 cm de —** to be 20 cm deep (*or* in depth); **¿cuánto tiene de —?** how deep is it?
   (b) (*fig*) *bow* low; *breath, sigh, voice* deep; *note* low, deep; *sleep* deep, sound; *darkness* deep; *effect, impression etc* deep; *mystery* profound; *thinker* profound; **conocedor — del arte** a very knowledgeable expert in the art; **en lo — del alma** in the depths of one's soul.

profusamente *adv* profusely; lavishly, extravagantly.
profusión *nf* profusion; wealth, extravagance.
profuso *adj* profuse; lavish, extravagant.
progenie *nf* (a) progeny, offspring; (*pej*) brood. (b) family, lineage.
progenitor *nm* ancestor; **—es** (*hum*) parents.
progenitura *nf* offspring.
programa *nm* programme; plan; **— continuo** (*Cine*) continuous showing; **— de estudios** curriculum, syllabus.
programación *nf* programming; programme planning.
programado *adj* programmed; *visit etc* planned.
programador *nm*, **programadora** *nf* programmer.
programar [1a] *vt* (a) (*for computer etc*) to program. (b) (*Arg, Ec, Mex*) to plan; to draw up a programme for.
progresar [1a] *vi* to progress, make progress.
progresión *nf* progression; **— aritmética** arithmetic progression; **— geométrica** geometric progression.
progresista (*Pol*) **1** *adj* progressive. **2** *nmf* progressive.
progresivamente *adv* progressively; gradually, little by little.
progresivo *adj* progressive; gradual; continuous; (*Gram*) continuous.
progreso *nm* progress; advance; **—s** progress; **hacer —s** to progress, make progress, advance.
prohibición *nf* prohibition (*de* of); ban (*de* on); embargo (*de* on); **levantar la — de** to remove the ban on, lift the embargo on.
prohibicionismo *nm* prohibitionism.
prohibicionista 1 *adj* prohibitionist. **2** *nmf* prohibitionist.
prohibir [3a] **1** *vt* to prohibit, forbid, stop, ban; **— una droga** to prohibit a drug, ban a drug; **— algo a uno** to forbid someone something; **— a uno + *infin*** to forbid someone to + *infin*; to stop someone + *ger*, ban someone from + *ger*; **"prohibido fumar"** "no smoking"; **está prohibido fumar aquí** smoking is not allowed here, you can't smoke in here; **queda terminantemente prohibido + *infin*** it is strictly forbidden to + *infin*.
   2 prohibirse *vr*: **"se prohíbe fumar"** "no smoking".
prohibitivo *adj* prohibitive.
prohibitorio *adj* prohibitory.
prohijar [1a] *vt* to adopt (*also fig*).
prohombre *nm* outstanding man, great man; leader.
prójima *nf* woman of dubious character, loose woman.
projimidad *nf* (*Arg, Per, PR*) fellow feeling, compassion (for one's fellows).
prójimo *nm* fellow man, fellow creature, neighbour; **nuestros —s los animales** our fellow animals.
prolapso *nm* prolapse.
prole *nf* offspring; (*pej*) brood, spawn; **padre de numerosa —** father of a large family.
proletariado *nm* proletariat.
proletariar [1b] *vt* to proletarianize.
proletario 1 *adj* proletarian. **2** *nm*, **proletaria** *nf* proletarian.
proletarismo *nm* proletarianism.
proliferación *nf* proliferation; **— de armas nucleares** proliferation of atomic weapons, spread of nuclear arms.
proliferar [1a] *vi* to proliferate.
prolífico *adj* prolific (*en* of).
prolijamente *adv* long-windedly; tediously; with an excess of detail.
prolijidad *nf* prolixity, long-windedness; tediousness; excess of detail.
prolijo *adj* prolix, long-winded; tedious; excessively detailed; excessively meticulous. (b) (*RPl*) untiring.
prologar [1h] *vt* to preface, write an introduction to; **un libro prologado por Ortega** a book with a preface by Ortega.
prólogo *nm* (a) prologue (*de* to); preface, introduction; **un texto con — y notas de X** a text edited by X. (b) (*fig*) prelude (*de* to).
prolongación *nf* (a) (*act*) prolongation, extension.
   (b) extension; **por la — de la Castellana** along the new part of the Castellana, along the extension of the Castellana.
prolongado *adj* *envelope, room etc* long; *meeting, stay* lengthy.
prolongar [1h] **1** *vt* to prolong, extend; *line* (*Math*) to produce; *tube etc* to make longer, extend; *meeting* to prolong.
   2 prolongarse *vr* to extend; to go on; **la carretera**

se prolonga más allá del bosque the road goes on (or extends, stretches) beyond the wood; el paisaje se prolonga hasta lo infinito the countryside stretches away to infinity; la sesión se prolongó bastante the meeting went on long enough, it was a pretty long meeting.

promediar [1b] **1** vt (a) object etc to divide into two halves, divide equally.
(b) (Math etc) to work out the average of, average (out).
2 vi (a) to mediate (entre between).
(b) **promediaba el mes** it was halfway through the month; **antes de — el mes** before the month is halfway through.

promedio nm (a) average; **el — de asistencia diaria** the average daily attendance; **el — es de 35 por 100** the average is 35%.
(b) (of distance etc) middle, mid-point.

promesa nf **1** promise; pledge; **— de matrimonio** promise of marriage; **absolver a uno de su —** to release someone from his promise; **faltar a una —** to break a promise, go back on one's word.
2 attr: **jugador —** promising player, bright hope among players.

promesante nmf (Arg), **promesero** nm, **promesera** nf (Arg, Col, Per) pilgrim.

prometedor adj promising.

Prometeo m Prometheus.

prometer [2a] **1** vt to promise; to pledge; **— hacer algo** to promise to do something, (Eccl) to take a vow to do something; **esto promete ser interesante** this promises to be interesting; **esto no nos promete nada bueno** this does not look at all hopeful for us, this promises to be pretty bad for us.
2 vi to have promise, show promise; **es un jugador que promete** he's a promising player, he's a player with promise.
3 prometerse vr (a) to expect, promise oneself; **— algo bueno** to promise oneself a treat; **nos habíamos prometido algo mejor** we had expected something better; **se prometía que todo iba a ser fácil** he anticipated that everything was going to be easy.
(b) (2 persons) to get engaged; **se prometió con él en abril** she got engaged to him in April.

prometida nf fiancée.

prometido 1 adj (a) promised. (b) engaged; **estar — con** to be engaged to. **2** nm (a) fiancé. (b) promise.

prominencia nf (a) protuberance; swelling, bump; (in ground) rise. (b) (fig: esp SAm) prominence.

prominente adj (a) prominent, protuberant; that sticks out. (b) (fig) prominent.

promiscuidad nf (a) mixture, jumble, confusion; confused nature. (b) ambiguity.

promiscuo adj (a) mixed (up), in disorder; crowd, gathering motley. (b) sense ambiguous.

promisión nf: **tierra de —** land of promise, promised land.

promoción nf (a) promotion, advancement, furtherance; (in table, Sport etc) promotion; **— de ventas** sales promotion.
(b) (professional) promotion; class, year; **la — de 1975** the 1975 class; **fue de mi —** he belonged to the same class as I did, he graduated (or got his commission etc) at the same time as I did.

promocionar [1a] vt (Comm) to promote.

promontorio nm promontory, headland.

promotor nm promoter; pioneer; instigator, prime mover; **— de ventas** sales promoter; **el — de los disturbios** the instigator of the rioting.

promovedor nm promotor; instigator.

promover [2h] vt (a) process etc to promote, advance, further; interests to promote; plan etc to pioneer; action to begin, set on foot, get moving; lawsuit to bring.
(b) scandal etc to cause; riot, trouble to instigate, stir up.
(c) person, team to promote (a to).

promulgación nf promulgation; (fig) announcement, publication.

promulgar [1h] vt to promulgate; (fig) to proclaim, announce publicly.

pronombre nm pronoun; **— personal** personal pronoun; **— posesivo** possessive pronoun; **— reflexivo** reflexive pronoun.

pronominal adj pronominal.

pronosticación nf prediction, prognostication, forecasting.

pronosticador nm forecaster; (Racing) tipster.

pronosticar [1g] vt to predict, foretell, forecast, prognosticate.

pronóstico nm (a) prediction, forecast; omen; **— del tiempo** weather forecast; **—s para el año nuevo** predictions for the new year, prognostications for the new year.
(b) (Med) prognosis; **de — leve** slight, not serious; **de — reservado** of uncertain gravity, of unknown extent, possibly serious.

prontitud nf (a) speed, quickness, promptness. (b) (of mind) quickness, sharpness.

pronto 1 adj (a) ready; **la comida está pronta** lunch is ready; **estar — para + infin** to be ready to + infin.
(b) reply etc prompt, quick, (esp Comm) early; cure speedy; service quick, rapid, prompt.
(c) person quick, sharp; **de inteligencia pronta** of keen (or sharp) intelligence; **es — en las decisiones** he is quick about taking decisions; **estuvo muy — para resolver** he was quick to make up his mind, he decided on the spot.
2 adv (a) quickly, promptly, speedily; at once, right away; soon; **lo más — posible** as soon as possible, as quickly as possible; **tan — como** as soon as; **tan — como lo traigan** as soon as they bring it to me; **¡—!** hurry!, get on with it!; **al —** at first; **de —** suddenly; unexpectedly, without warning; **¡hasta —!** see you soon!; **por de —, por lo —** meanwhile, for the present; at least, anyway.
(b) early; **levantarse —** to get up early; **todavía es — para hacerlo** it's too early yet to do it, it's too soon to be doing it yet; **todavía es — para decidir si . . .** it's early days to decide whether to . . .; **iremos a comer un poco —** we'll go and lunch a bit early.
3 nm urge, strong impulse; sudden feeling; **tener —s de enojo** to be quick-tempered.

prontuario nm handbook, manual, compendium.

prónuba nf bridesmaid.

pronuncia nf (Mex) = **pronunciamiento**.

pronunciación nf pronunciation; **— figurada** phonetic transcription.

pronunciado adj pronounced, strong; bend etc sharp; feature etc marked, noticeable.

pronunciamiento nm revolt, insurrection, military rising.

pronunciar [1b] **1** vt (a) (Ling) to pronounce; to make, utter.
(b) (fig) speech to make, deliver; toast to propose; **— palabras de elogio para . . .** to say a few words of tribute to . . .
(c) (Law) sentence to pass, pronounce.
2 pronunciarse vr (a) to be pronounced; **ese sonido se pronuncia más abierto** that sound is pronounced more openly.
(b) to declare oneself, state one's opinion; to make a pronouncement; **— a favor de** to pronounce in favour of, declare oneself in favour of; **— sobre** to pronounce on, make a pronouncement about.
(c) (Pol) to revolt, rise, rebel.
(d) (fig) to become (more) pronounced.

pronuncio nm (Col) = **pronunciamiento**.

propagación nf propagation; (fig) propagation, spread(ing), dissemination.

propaganda nf (a) propaganda. (b) (Comm) advertising; **hacer — de un producto** to advertise a product.

propagandista nmf propagandist.

propagandístico adj propaganda (attr); (Comm) advertising (attr).

propagar [1h] **1** vt (Bio) to propagate; (fig) to propagate, spread, disseminate. **2** propagarse vr (Bio) to propagate; (fig) to spread, be disseminated.

propalar [1a] vt to divulge, disclose; to publish an account of.

propasarse [1a] vr to go too far, overstep the bounds; (sexually) to take liberties, overstep the bounds of propriety.

propela nf (Cu, Mex: angl) propeller; outboard motor.

propender [2a] vi: **— a** to tend towards, incline to; **— a + infin** to tend to + infin, have a tendency to + infin.

propensión nf inclination, propensity, tendency (a to).

propenso adj: **— a** inclined to; prone to, subject to; **ser — a + infin** to be inclined to + infin, have a tendency to + infin.

propi nf (fam) = **propina**.

propiamente adv properly; really, exactly; see dicho.

propiciación nf propitiation.

propiciar [1b] vt (a) to propitiate, to win over.
(b) to favour; to cause, give rise to; **tal secreto**

propicia muchas conjeturas such secrecy causes a lot of speculation.

propiciatorio *adj* propitiatory.

propicio *adj* propitious, auspicious; *moment etc* favourable; *person* kind, well-disposed, helpful.

propiedad *nf* (a) possession, ownership; **ser de la — de** to be the property of, belong to; **una finca de la — del marqués** an estate belonging to the marquis; **ceder algo a uno en —** to transfer something completely to someone, transfer to someone the full rights over something.

(b) (*object etc*) property; **— particular** private property; **una — a** property, a piece of property; **es — del municipio** it is the property of the town.

(c) (*Chem etc*) property; (*fig*) property, attribute.

(d) (*quality*) propriety, properness; suitability, appositeness; **discutir la — de una palabra** to discuss the appropriateness of a word.

(e) (*quality*) accuracy, faithfulness; naturalness; **lo reproduce con toda —** he reproduces it faithfully.

(f) (*Comm etc*) right(s); **— industrial** patent rights; **— intelectual, — literaria** copyright; **"es —"** "copyright".

propietaria *nf* owner, proprietress.

propietario 1 *adj* proprietary. **2** *nm* owner, proprietor; (*Agr etc*) landowner.

propina *nf* tip, gratuity; **dar algo de —** to give something extra, give something as a bonus; **con dos más de —** (*fig*) with two more into the bargain.

propinar [1a] **1** *vt* (a) to tip, give a tip to.

(b) **— a uno** to treat someone to a drink, buy someone a drink.

(c) (*fam*) *blow* to deal, hit; *beating* to give; **le propinó una serie de consejos** he gave him a lot of advice, he made him listen to several bits of advice.

2 propinarse *vr:* **— algo** to treat oneself to something.

propincuidad *nf* propinquity, nearness, proximity.

propincuo *adj* near.

propio 1 *adj* (a) own, of one's own; **con su propia mano** with his own hand; **lo vi con mis —s ojos** I saw it with my own eyes; **los rizos son —s** her curls are natural, her curls are her own; **lo hizo en beneficio —** he did it for his own good; he did it in his own interest; **tienen casa propia** they have a house of their own; **ahora tiene una bicicleta suya propia** now she has a bicycle of her very own.

(b) peculiar (*de* to); special; characteristic, typical (*de* of); of one's own; **una bebida propia del país** a typical drink of the country; **hace un sol — de país mediterráneo** this sunshine is more typical of a Mediterranean country; **fruta propia del tiempo** fruit in season; **eso es muy — de él** that's very characteristic of him; **tiene un olor muy —** it has a very special smell, it has a smell of its own.

(c) proper; correct, suitable, fitting (*para* for); **con los honores que le son —s** with the honours which are proper (*or* due) to him; **ese bikini no es — para esta playa** that bikini is not suitable for this beach.

(d) selfsame, very; **sus propias palabras** his very words; **me lo dijo el — ministro** the minister himself told me so; **yo haría lo — que tú** I'd do the same as you, I'd do exactly what you're doing.

(e) *sense* proper, true; basic.

(f) **de —** especially, deliberately, expressly.

2 *nm* (*fam*) messenger.

proponente *nmf* proposer.

proponer [2r] **1** *vt scheme etc* to propose, put forward; *theory* to propound; *problem* to pose; to outline, put up (for discussion); *motion* to propose; *candidate* to propose, nominate, put forward; **— a uno para una beca** to propose someone for a scholarship; **le propuse que fuéramos juntos** I proposed to him that we should go together.

2 proponerse *vr* (a) **— hacer algo** to propose to do something, plan to do something, intend to do something.

(b) (*pej*) **te has propuesto hacerme perder el tren** you set out deliberately to make me miss the train.

proporción *nf* (a) proportion; (*Math etc*) ratio; relationship; rate; **—es** proportions, (*fig*) dimensions; size, scope; **la — entre azules y verdes** the proportion of blues to greens; **en — con** in proportion to; **en una — de 5 a 1** in a ratio of 5 to 1; at a rate of 5 to 1; **guarda bien las —es** it remains in proportion; **esto no guarda — con lo otro** this is out of proportion to the rest; **una máquina de gigantescas —es** a machine of huge proportions (*or* size); **se descono-**

cen las **—es del desastre** the size (*or* extent, scope) of the disaster is unknown.

(b) chance, opportunity, right moment.

(c) (*SAm*) **de —es** huge, vast; considerable; (*Mex*) wealthy.

proporcionadamente *adv* proportionately, in proportion.

proporcionado *adj* (a) proportionate (*a* to).

(b) medium, middling, just right; **de tamaño —** of the right size.

(c) **bien —** well proportioned; shapely, of pleasing shape.

proporcional *adj* proportional.

proporcionalmente *adv* proportionally.

proporcionar [1a] *vt* (a) to give, supply, provide, furnish; (*fig*) to lend; **— dinero a uno** to give someone money, supply someone with money; **esto le proporciona una renta anual de ...** this brings him in a yearly income of ...; **esto proporciona gran encanto a la narración** this lends (*or* gives) great charm to the story.

(b) to adjust, adapt (*a* to).

proposición *nf* proposition; proposal.

propósito *nm* purpose; aim, intention, objective; **buenos —s** good intentions; good resolutions; **¿cuál es su —?** what is his aim?; **nuestro — es de + infin** our aim is to + *infin*; **hacer(se) el — de + infin** to form an intention to + *infin*, set oneself the aim of + *ger*; **a —** (*as adj*) appropriate, suitable, fitting (*para* for); *remark etc* relevant, apt; **a —** (*as adv*) by the way, incidentally; **a — de** about, with regard to; **y a — de los toros ...** and talking of bulls ..., and while we're on the subject of bulls ...; **eso no viene a —** that's not relevant, that's nothing to do with it; **de —** on purpose, purposely, deliberately; **fuera de —** irrelevant(ly), off the point, out of place; **sin — fijo** aimless(ly), pointless(ly).

propuesta *nf* proposal.

propulsado *adj:* **— a cohete** rocket-driven; **— a chorro** jet-propelled.

propulsar [1a] *vt* (a) (*Mech*) to drive, propel. (b) (*fig*) to promote, encourage.

propulsión *nf* (a) propulsion; **— a cohete** rocket propulsion; **— a chorro, — por reacción** jet propulsion; **con — a chorro** jet-propelled.

propulsor *nm* propellent, fuel.

prorrata *nf* share, quota; prorate (*US*); **a — pro rata**, proportionately.

prorratear [1a] *vt* to share out, apportion, distribute proportionately; to prorate (*US*); **prorratearemos el dinero** we will share out the money pro rata.

prorrateo *nm* sharing (in proportion), apportionment; **a —** pro rata, proportionately.

prórroga *nf* prorogation; (*Comm*) extension; (*Mil*) deferment; (*Law*) stay (of execution), respite; (*Sport*) extra time.

prorrogable *adj* which can be extended.

prorrogación *nf* prorogation.

prorrogar [1h] *vt sitting etc* to prorogue, adjourn; *period* to extend; (*Mil*) to defer; (*Law*) to grant a stay of execution to; *decision etc* to defer, postpone; **prorrogamos una semana las vacaciones** we extended our holiday by a week.

prorrumpir [3a] *vi* to burst forth, break out; **— en gritos** to start shouting; **— en lágrimas** to burst into tears.

prosa *nf* (a) (*Lit*) prose.

(b) (*fig*) prosaic nature, tedium; **la — de la vida** the tedium of life, the ordinariness of life.

(c) (*fam*) chatter, idle talk.

(d) (*Chi*) vanity, haughtiness.

(e) (*Ec, Guat, Per*) pomposity, affectation.

prosador *nm*, **prosadora** *nf* (a) (*Lit*) prose writer. (b) (*fam*) chatterbox, great talker, gossip.

prosaicamente *adv* (a) prosaically. (b) (*fig*) prosaically; tediously, monotonously.

prosaico *adj* (a) (*Lit*) prosaic, prose (*attr*). (b) (*fig*) prosaic, prosy; tedious, monotonous; ordinary.

prosaísmo *nm* (*fig*) prosaic nature; tediousness, monotony; ordinariness.

prosapia *nf* lineage, ancestry.

proscenio *nm* proscenium.

proscribir [3a; *ptp* **proscrito**] *vt* to prohibit, ban; *party etc* to proscribe; *criminal* to outlaw; to banish; *subject etc* to ban; **— un tema de su conversación** to banish a topic from one's conversation.

proscripción *nf* prohibition (*de* of), ban (*de* on); proscription; outlawing; banishment.

proscrito 1 *ptp of* **proscribir**. **2** *adj* banned; outlawed; proscribed; **un libro —** a banned book. **3** *nm* exile; outlaw.

prosecución *nf* continuation; pressing; pursuit.

proseguir [3d *and* 31] **1** *vt* to continue, carry on, go on with, proceed with; *demand* to go on with, push, press; *investigation, study* to pursue.
   2 *vi* (a) — **en** (*or* **con**) **una actitud** to continue in one's attitude, maintain one's attitude.
   (b) (*of state etc*) to continue, go on; **prosiguió con el cuento** he went on with the story; **¡prosigue!** continue!; **prosigue el mal tiempo** the bad weather continues.

proselitismo *nm* proselytism.
proselitista *adj* proselytizing.
prosélito *nm*, **prosélita** *nf* proselyte.
prosificación *nf* prose version; rewriting as prose, turning into prose.
prosificar [1g] *vt* to rewrite as prose, write a prose version of.
prosista *nmf* prose writer.
prosodia *nf* (set of) rules for pronunciation and accentuation.
prosopopeya *nf* (a) (*Lit*) personification. (b) (*fig*) pomposity, affectation.
prospección *nf* exploration; (*Mil*) prospecting (**de** for); — **del petróleo** prospecting for oil, drilling for oil.
prospectivo *adj* (*SAm: angl*) prospective.
prospecto *nm* prospectus; (*Comm etc*) leaflet, sheet of instructions.
prospector *nm* prospector.
prósperamente *adv* prosperously; successfully.
prosperar [1a] *vi* to prosper, thrive, flourish; (*of idea etc*) to prosper.
prosperidad *nf* prosperity; success; **en época de** — in a period of prosperity, in good times; **desear a uno muchas** —**s** to wish someone success.
próspero *adj* (a) prosperous, thriving, flourishing; successful. (b) **con próspera fortuna** with good luck, favoured by fortune.
próstata *nf* prostate.
prosternarse [1a] *vr* to prostrate oneself; to bow low, bow humbly.
prostético *adj* (*Gram, Med*) prosthetic.
prostíbulo *nm* brothel.
prostitución *nf* prostitution (*also fig*).
prostituir [3g] **1** *vt* to prostitute (*also fig*). **2 prostituirse** *vr* to prostitute oneself, take up prostitution, become a prostitute.
prostituta *nf* prostitute; — **callejera** streetwalker.
prosudo *adj* (*Chi, Ec, Per*) affectedly solemn, pompous.
protagonista *nmf* protagonist; (*Lit etc, freq*) main character; hero, heroine.
protagonizar [1f] *vt* to take the chief role in, play the main part in.
protección *nf* protection.
proteccionismo *nm* protectionism.
proteccionista **1** *adj* *policy* protectionist; *duty etc* protective. **2** *nmf* protectionist.
protector **1** *adj* (a) protective, protecting. (b) *tone etc* patronizing. **2** *nm*, **protectora** *nf* protector; (*Lit etc*) patron; (*of tradition etc*) guardian.
protectorado *nm* protectorate.
protectoramente *adv* (a) protectively. (b) patronizingly.
proteger [2c] *vt* to protect (**contra** against, **de** from); to shield; to defend; to act as patron to.
protegida *nf* protégée.
protegido *nm* protégé.
proteico *adj* protean.
proteína *nf* protein.
protervidad *nf* wickedness, perversity.
protervo *adj* wicked, perverse.
protesta *nf* (a) protest; **bajo** — under protest. (b) (*of innocence etc*) protestation; **hacer** —**s de lealtad** to protest one's loyalty.
protestación *nf* protestation; — **de lealtad** protestation of loyalty, declaration of loyalty; — **de fe** profession of faith.
protestante **1** *adj* Protestant. **2** *nmf* Protestant.
protestantismo *nm* Protestantism.
protestar [1a] **1** *vt* (a) *innocence etc* to protest, declare, avow; *faith* to profess.
   (b) (*Fin*) **cheque protestado por falta de fondos** cheque referred to drawer (R/D).
   2 *vi* (a) to protest (**contra, de** about, against; **de que** that); to object, remonstrate; — **contra una demora** to protest about a delay; **¡protesto contra esa observación!** I resent that!, I object to that remark!
   (b) — **de** *innocence etc* to protest.
proto . . . proto . . .
protocolario *adj* (a) established by protocol, required by protocol. (b) (*fig*) formal.

protocolo *nm* (a) (*Pol*) protocol. (b) (*fig*) protocol, social etiquette, convention. (c) (*fig*) **sin** —**s** informal(ly); without formalities, without a lot of fuss.
protón *nm* proton.
protoplasma *nm* protoplasm.
prototipo *nm* prototype.
protuberancia *nf* protuberance.
protuberante *adj* protuberant.
provecto *adj*: **de edad provecta** elderly.
provecho *nm* advantage, benefit, profit; (*Fin*) profit; **de** — *deal* profitable; *activity* useful; *person* worthy, honest; **¡buen** —**!** *phrase used to those at table, hoping they will enjoy their meal*; **¡buen** — **le haga!** and much good may it do him!; **en** — **de** to the benefit of; **en** — **propio** to one's own advantage, for one's own profit; **ese alimento no le hace** — **a uno** that food(stuff) doesn't do one any good; **sacar** — **de algo** to benefit from something, profit by (*or* from) something.
provechosamente *adv* advantageously, beneficially, profitably.
provechoso *adj* advantageous, beneficial, profitable; useful; (*Fin*) profitable.
proveedor *nm*, **proveedora** *nf* supplier, purveyor; dealer; — **casero** roundsman, deliveryman (US); **"**—**es de la Real Casa"** "by appointment to His (*or* Her) Majesty"; **consulte a su** — **habitual** consult your usual dealer.
proveer [2a; *ptp* **provisto** *and* **proveído**] **1** *vt* (a) to provide, supply, furnish (**de** with).
   (b) to provide, get ready; — **todo lo necesario** to provide all that is necessary (**para** for).
   (c) *vacancy* to fill.
   (d) *business* to transact, dispatch.
   (e) (*Law*) to decree.
   2 *vi*: — **a** to provide for; — **a las necesidades de uno** to provide for someone's wants; — **a un vicio de uno** to pander to someone's vice.
   3 proveerse *vr*: — **de** to provide oneself with.
provenir [3s] *vi*: — **de** to come from, arise from, stem from; **esto proviene de no haberlo curado antes** this comes from (*or* is due to) not having treated it earlier.
Provenza *f* Provence.
provenzal **1** *adj* Provençal. **2** *nm* Provençal. **3** *nm* (*language*) Provençal.
proverbial *adj* proverbial.
proverbialmente *adv* proverbially.
proverbio *nm* proverb.
próvidamente *adv* providently.
providencia *nf* (a) (*quality*) foresight; forethought, providence; (**Divina**) **P**— (Divine) Providence.
   (b) —**s** measures, steps; **dictar** (*or* **tomar**) —**s para** + *infin* to take steps to + *infin*.
   (c) (*Law*) ruling, decision.
providencial *adj* providential.
providencialmente *adj* providentially.
providente *adj*, **próvido** *adj* provident.
provincia *nf* province; **las P**—**s Vascongadas** the Basque Provinces, the Basque Country; **un pueblo de** —(**s**) a provincial town, a country town; **la vida en** — provincial life.
provincial **1** *adj* provincial. **2** *nm*, **provinciala** *nf* (*Eccl*) provincial.
provincialismo *nm* (*Ling*) provincialism, dialect(al) word (*or* phrase *etc*).
provincianismo *nm* provincialism; — **de cortas luces**, — **de vía estrecha** narrow provincialism, deadening provincialism.
provinciano **1** *adj* (a) provincial (*also pej*); country (*attr*).
   (b) Basque, of the Basque Provinces.
   2 *nm*, **provinciana** *nf* (a) provincial (*also pej*); country dweller.
   (b) Basque.
provisión *nf* (a) (*act*) provision.
   (b) provision, supply; —**es** provisions, supplies, stores.
   (c) (*Fin*) — **de fondos** financial cover; **cheque sin** — bad cheque.
   (d) (*precautionary*) measure, step.
provisional *adj* provisional.
provisionalidad *nf* provisional nature, temporary character.
provisionalmente *adv* provisionally.
provisorio *adj* (*SAm*) provisional.
provista *nf* (*RPl*) provisions, supplies.
provisto **1** *ptp of* **proveer**. **2** *adv*: — **de** provided with, supplied with; having, possessing.
provocación *nf* provocation.
provocador *adj* provocative, provoking.

provocar [1g] **1** *vt* **(a)** *person* to provoke; to rouse, stir up (to anger *etc*); to tempt, invite; **— a uno a cólera** (*or* **indignación**) to rouse someone to fury; **— a uno a lástima** to move someone to pity; **— a uno a risa** to make someone laugh; **el mar provoca a bañarse** the sea tempts one to bathe, the sea invites one to go for a swim.

(b) *change etc* to bring about, lead to; *process to* promote; *explosion, protest, war etc* to cause, spark off.

(c) (*of woman*) to rouse, stir, stimulate (sexually). **2** *vi* (*fam*) to be sick.

provocativo *adj* **(a)** provocative, provoking.

(b) *woman* provocative, sexually stimulating; (*pej*) openly sexy; *dress* daring, immodest; *laugh, gesture etc* inviting.

proxeneta *nmf* go-between; pimp, procurer.

próximamente *adv* shortly, soon.

proximidad *nf* nearness, closeness, proximity.

próximo *adj* **(a)** near, close; neighbouring; *relative* close; **en fecha próxima** soon, at an early date; **— a** to be close to, be near; **estar — a** + *infin* to be on the point of + *ger*, be about to + *infin*.

(b) next; **el mes —** next month; **el mes — pasado** last month; **el — 5 de junio** on 5th June next; **se bajarán en la próxima parada** they will get off at the next stop.

proyección *nf* **(a)** (*act etc, part*) projection.

(b) (*Cine*) showing; **el tiempo de — es de 35 minutos** the showing lasts 35 minutes, the film runs for 35 minutes.

(c) (*Cine, Phot*) slide, projection; transparency.

(d) (*fig*) hold, sway, influence; **la — de los periódicos sobre la sociedad** the hold of newspapers over society, the influence which newspapers have on society.

proyectable *adj*: **asiento —** (*Aer*) ejector seat.

proyectar [1a] *vt* **(a)** *object* to hurl, throw; *light to* cast, shed, project; *jet, liquid etc* to send out, give out; to direct (*hacia* at); *shadow* to cast.

(b) (*Cine, Phot*) to project; to screen, show.

(c) (*Math etc*) to project.

(d) (*Archit etc*) to plan; (*Mech*) to design; **está proyectado para** + *infin* it is designed to + *infin*.

(e) **—** + *infin* to plan to + *infin*.

proyectil *nm* projectile, missile; (*Mil: of gun*) shell, (*with rocket*) missile; **— de aire a aire** air-to-air missile; **— balístico intercontinental** intercontinental ballistic missile; **— (tele)dirigido** guided missile; **— de iluminación** flare, rocket.

proyectista *nm* planner; (*Aer, Aut, Tech etc*) designer; draughtsman.

proyecto *nm* **(a)** (*Tech*) plan, design; project.

(b) (*fig*) plan; scheme, project; **cambiar de —** to change one's plans; **tener —s para** to have plans for; **tener algo en —** to be planning something; **tener sus —s sobre algo** to have designs on something.

(c) (*Fin*) detailed estimate.

(d) (*Parl*) **— de ley** bill.

proyector *nm* **(a)** (*Cine*) projector. **(b)** (*Mil etc*) searchlight; (*Theat*) spotlight.

prudencia *nf* wisdom, prudence; care; soundness, sound judgement.

prudencial *adj* **(a)** prudential; sensible.

(b) *amount, distance etc* roughly correct, more or less correctly guessed.

prudenciarse [1b] *vr* (*CAm, Col, Mex*) to be sensible; to remain calm, control oneself.

prudente *adj* sensible, wise, prudent; *driver etc* careful; *choice etc* sensible, judicious, sound.

prudentemente *adv* sensibly, wisely, prudently; carefully; judiciously, soundly.

prueba *nf* **(a)** proof (*also Math*); (*Law*) proof, evidence; **—s** (*Law*) documents; **— documental** documentary evidence; **— indiciaria** circumstantial proof; **a la — me remito** the proof of the pudding is in the eating, the event will show; **en — de** in proof of; **en — de lo cual** in proof whereof; **en — de que no es así te lo ofrezco gratis** to prove that it isn't so I offer it to you free; **¿tiene Vd — de ello?** can you prove it?; do you have proof?

(b) (*fig*) proof, sign, token; **es buena —** it's a good sign; **sin dar la menor — de ello** without giving the faintest sign of it.

(c) (*Tech etc*) test, trial; (*Chem etc*) experiment; **—s** (*Aer, Aut, Naut*) trials; **— por carretera** road trials; **— de fuego** (*fig*) acid test; **— de inteligencia** intelligence test; **— nuclear** nuclear test; **por un procedimiento de — y desacierto** by a process of trial and error; **a —** (*Tech*) on trial; (*Comm*) on approval, on trial; **ingresar con un nombramiento a —** to take up a post for a probationary period; to

come in with a probationary appointment; **a — de** proof against; **a — de agua** waterproof; **a — de bala** bulletproof; **a — de bombas** bombproof, shell-proof; **a — de choques** shockproof; **a — de grasa** greaseproof; **a — de herrumbre** rustproof, rust-resistant; **a — de impericia** foolproof; **a — de ladrones** burglarproof; **a — de lluvia** rainproof; **a — de ruidos** soundproof; **a — de viento** windproof; **poner a —, someter a —** to test, put to the test, try out; **poner a — los nervios de uno** to test someone's nerves; **poner a — la paciencia de uno** to try someone's patience; **hacer — de** to tesr, put to the test.

(d) (*of food etc: act*) testing, sampling; (*quantity*) taste, sample.

(e) (*Sew*) fitting, trying on; **sala de —s** fitting room.

(f) (*Typ*) **—s** proofs; **primeras —s** first proofs, galleys; **—s de planas** page proofs.

(g) (*Phot*) proof, print; **— negativa** negative; **— positiva** positive, print.

(h) (*Sport*) event; **—s** trials; **— clasificatoria, — eliminatoria** heat; **— de vallas** hurdles, hurdles race.

(i) (*SAm*) circus act; acrobatic act, piece of juggling (*or* contortionism *etc*), display of acrobatic (*etc*) skill; (*Ec, Per*) circus show, performance.

pruebista *nmf* **(a)** (*SAm*) acrobat, tightrope walker; conjurer, juggler; contortionist. **(b)** (*Arg*) proof-reader.

prurito *nm* **(a)** (*Med*) itch.

(b) (*fig*) itch; urge (to perfectionism); **tener el — de** + *infin* to have the urge to + *infin*; **por un — de exactitud** out of an excessive desire for accuracy, because of his urge to get everything just right.

Prusia *f* Prussia.

prusiano 1 *adj* Prussian. **2** *nm*, **prusiana** *nf* Prussian.

pse . . ., psi . . .: *the Academy recommends the spellings* **se . . ., si . . .**; *all forms are pronounced* [se—, si—].

psefología *nf* psephology.

psefólogo *nm* psephologist.

psic . . ., psiqu . . . psych . . .

psicoanálisis *nm* psychoanalysis.

psicoanalista *nmf* psychoanalyst.

psicoanalizar [1f] *vt* to psychoanalyse.

psicología *nf* psychology.

psicológicamente *adv* psychologically.

psicológico *adj* psychological.

psicólogo *nm* psychologist.

psiconeurosis *nf, pl* **psiconeurosis** psychoneurosis.

psicopatología *nf* psychopathology.

psicópata *nmf* psychopath.

psicopático *adj* psychopathic.

psicosis *nf, pl* **psicosis** psychosis.

psicosomático *adj* psychosomatic.

psicoterapia *nf* psychotherapy.

psicótico 1 *adj* psychotic. **2** *nm*, **psicótica** *nf* psychotic.

Psique *f* Psyche.

psique *nf* **(a)** psyche. **(b)** cheval glass.

psiquedélico *adj* psychedelic.

psiquiatra *nmf* psychiatrist.

psiquiatría *nf* psychiatry.

psiquiátrico *adj* psychiatric.

psíquico *adj* psychic(al).

psitacosis *nf* psittacosis.

pterodáctilo [te—] *nm* pterodactyl.

ptomaína [to—] *nf* ptomaine.

ptomaínico [to—] *adj*: **envenenamiento m —** ptomaine poisoning.

púa *nf* sharp point; (*Bot, Zool*) prickle, spike, spine; (*of hedgehog*) quill; (*of comb*) tooth; (*of fork*) prong, tine; (*of hook, wire*) barb; (*SAm: of fighting cock*) spur; (*Mus*) plectrum; (*Mus*) gramophone needle, phonograph needle (*US*); (*Bot*) graft, cutting.

puazo *nm* (*SAm*) slash (*with cock's spur*).

púber 1 *adj* adolescent. **2** *nmf* adolescent child, child approaching puberty.

pubertad *nf* puberty.

pubescencia *nf* pubescence.

pubescente *adj* pubescent.

púbico *adj* pubic.

pubis *nm* pubis.

publicación *nf* publication.

públicamente *adv* publicly.

publicar [1g] *vt* (*in most senses*) to publish; to publicize; *secret etc* to make public, disclose, divulge.

publicidad *nf* **(a)** publicity; **dar — a** to publicize, give publicity to.

(b) (*Comm*) advertising; **— de lanzamiento** advance publicity, advertising campaign to launch a product; **hacer — por** to advertise; **se ha prohibido la — de cigarrillos** cigarette advertising has been banned.

publicista *nmf* publicist.
publicitario *adj* advertising (*attr*); publicity (*attr*).
público 1 *adj* public; **hacer —** to publish, make public; to disclose.
  2 *nm* public; (*Mus, Theat etc*) audience; (*Sport*) spectators, crowd; (*of restaurant etc*) clients, clientèle, patrons; (*of newspaper*) readers, readership; **hay poco —** there aren't many people; **el — que se paseaba por la calle** the people who were strolling in the street; **hubo un — de 800** there was a crowd (*or* gathering, audience *etc*) of 800; **el gran —** the general public; **en —** in public.
puco *nm* (*SAm*) earthenware bowl.
pucha[1] *nf* (**a**) (*Cu, PR*) bouquet. (**b**) (*Mex*) ring-shaped loaf.
pucha[2] *nf* (*SAm: euph*)=**puta**; **¡(la) —!** well I'm damned!
puchera *nf* stew.
pucherazo *nm* (*fam*) electoral fiddle (*fam*); **dar —** to rig an election, fiddle the votes (*fam*).
puchero *nm* (**a**) (*Cook*) cooking pot. (**b**) (*Cook*) stew; (*fig*) daily bread, ordinary sustenance; **apenas gana para el —** he hardly earns enough to live on. (**c**) (*fam*) pout; **hacer —s** to pout, make a face, screw up one's face.
puches *nmpl* porridge, gruel.
puchito *nm*, **puchita** *nf* (*Chi, Ec*) youngest child.
pucho *nm* (**a**) fag end, cigar stub.
  (**b**) (*SAm*) scrap, left-over(s); dregs; (*Sew*) remnant; (*Fin*) coppers, small change; (*fig*) trifle, mere nothing; **a —s** in dribs and drabs.
  (**c**) (*Chi, Ec*) youngest child.
pude *etc see* **poder**.
pudendo 1 *adj*: **partes pudendas** pudenda, private parts. **2** *nm* penis.
pudibundez *nf* false modesty, affected modesty; excess of modesty.
pudibundo *adj* affectedly modest; over-shy (*about sexual matters*), excessively modest; prudish.
pudicicia *nf* modesty; chastity.
púdico *adj* modest; chaste.
pudiendo *see* **poder**.
pudiente *adj* wealthy, well-to-do; powerful, influential; **las gentes menos —s** the less well-off.
pudín *nm* (*angl*) pudding.
pudinga *nf* pudding stone.
pudor *nm* (**a**) modesty; shyness; (sense of) shame, (sense of) decency; **con —** modestly; discreetly. (**b**) chastity, virtue; **atentado al —** indecent assault.
pudorosamente *adv* (**a**) modestly; shyly. (**b**) chastely, virtuously.
pudoroso *adj* (**a**) modest; shy. (**b**) chaste, virtuous.
pudrición *nf* (**a**) rotting. (**b**) rot, rottenness; **— seca** dry rot.
pudridero *nm* rubbish heap, midden.
pudrimiento *nm* (**a**) rotting. (**b**) rot, rottenness.
pudrir [3a] **1** *vt* (**a**) to rot.
  (**b**) (*fam*) to upset, vex, annoy.
  2 *vi* (*fig*) to rot, be dead and buried.
  3 pudrirse *vr* (**a**) to rot, decay; to rot away.
  (**b**) (*fig*) to rot, languish; **mientras se pudría en la cárcel** while he was languishing in jail; **te vas a — de aburrimiento** you'll die of boredom; **¡que se pudra!** let him rot!
pueblada *nf* (*SAm*) riot; revolt, uprising; (*Arg*) mob, gathering of workers.
pueblerino 1 *adj* countrified, small-town (*attr*); *person* rustic, provincial. **2** *nm*, **pueblerina** *nf* rustic, country person, provincial.
pueblero (*SAm*) **1** *adj* town (*attr*), city (*attr*). **2** *nm* townsman, city dweller; (*pej*) city slicker (*US*); (*pej*) toff (*fam*), fop.
pueblo *nm* (**a**) (*Pol etc*) people, nation; **— elegido** chosen people; **el — español** the Spanish people; **la voluntad del —** the nation's will; **hacer un llamamiento al —** to call on the people, call on the nation.
  (**b**) (*pej*) common people, lower orders; **— de mala muerte** dregs of the populace.
  (**c**) village; small town, country town.
puedo *etc see* **poder**.
puente *nm* (**a**) bridge (*also fig*); **— aéreo** airlift; **— de barcas, — de pontones** pontoon bridge; **— colgante** suspension bridge; **— giratorio** swing bridge; **— levadizo** drawbridge; **— para peatones** footbridge; **tender un —** (*fig*) to offer a compromise, go part-way to meet someone's wishes.
  (**b**) (*fig: of glasses, Mus etc*) bridge.
  (**c**) (*Naut*) bridge (*also* **— de mando**); deck; **— del timón** wheelhouse.
  (**d**) (*fig*) gap; hiatus; **habrá que salvar el — de una cosecha a otra** something will have to be done to fill the gap between one harvest and the next.

  (**e**) (*fam*) **hacer (el) —** to take a long weekend, take extra days off work between two public holidays.
  (**f**) (*Col*) collarbone.
puerca *nf* (**a**) sow. (**b**) (*fam*) slut. (**c**) woodlouse.
puercada *nf* (*CAm, Per, PR*) dirty trick, mean act; obscene remark.
puercamente *adv* (**a**) dirtily. (**b**) nastily, disgustingly; coarsely. (**c**) vilely, meanly.
puerco 1 *nm* (**a**) pig, hog (*US*); wild boar; **— espín** porcupine; **— jabalí, — montés, — salvaje** wild boar, wild pig; **— de mar** porpoise; **— marino** dolphin; *see* **Martín**.
  (**b**) (*fam*) pig; swine, rotter.
  2 *adj* (**a**) dirty, filthy.
  (**b**) nasty, disgusting; coarse.
  (**c**) vile, rotten (*fam*), mean.
puericia *nf* boyhood.
puericultor *nm* (*also* **médico —**) paediatrician.
puericultura *nf* paediatrics.
pueril *adj* (**a**) childish, child (*attr*); **edad —** childhood.
  (**b**) (*pej*) puerile, childish.
puerilidad *nf* puerility, childishness.
puerperal *adj* puerperal.
puerqueza *nf* (*Arg, Par*) (**a**) dirty thing, filthy object. (**b**) dirty trick. (**c**) (*Zool*) bug, creepy-crawly (*fam*).
puerro *nm* leek.
puerta *nf* door; gate; doorway; (*esp fig*) gateway (*de* to); **— accesoria** side door; **— de artistas** stage door; **— de corredera** sliding door; **— de cristales** glass door; **— excusada** private door, side door; **— chica** side door, private door; **entrar por la — chica** (*fam*) to get in by the back door (*fig*); **— giratoria** swing door, revolving door; **— principal** front door; main entrance; **— de servicio** tradesmen's entrance; **— trasera** back door; **— ventana** French window; **— vidriera** glass door; **a — cerrada** behind closed doors; **a las —s de la muerte** at death's door; **tenemos la guerra a las —s** war is upon us, the threat of war is imminent; **coche de 2 —s** 2-door car; **coche de 4 —s** 4-door car; **política de — adentro** home policy; **lo que pasa de —s afuera** what happens abroad, foreign affairs; **de — en —** from door to door; **abrir la — a** (*fig*) to open the door to; **coger la —** (*fam*) to leave in a huff; **coger a uno detrás de la —** to catch someone at a disadvantage; **enseñar la — a uno** to show someone the door; **franquear las —s a uno** to welcome someone in; **querer poner —s al campo** to try to stem the tide; **salir por la — de los carros** to fail, be a disaster; **tomar la —** (*fam*) to leave, get out.
puertaventana *nf* shutter.
puertear [1a] *vi* (*SAm*) to stand about in the doorway.
puerto *nm* (**a**) port, harbour; seaport; **— comercial** trading port; **— de escala** port of call; **— de entrada** port of entry; **— franco** free port; **— de origen** home port; **— naval** naval port, naval harbour; **pesquero** fishing port; **entrar a —, tomar —** to enter port, come into port.
  (**b**) (*fig*) haven, refuge; **llegar a —** to solve a problem, get over a difficulty, come through safely.
  (**c**) (*Geog*) pass.
Puerto *m* **Rico** Puerto Rico.
puertorriqueñismo *nm* word (*or* phrase *etc*) peculiar to Puerto Rico.
puertorriqueño 1 *adj* Puerto Rican. **2** *nm*, **puertorriqueña** *nf* Puerto Rican.
pues 1 *adv* (**a**) then; well, well then; so; **— no voy** well I'm not going, in that case I'm not going; **¿no vas con ella, —?** aren't you going with her after all?; so you're not going with her?; **llegó, —, con 2 horas de retraso** so he arrived 2 hours late; **— sí** well yes, why yes; certainly; **— no** well no; not at all; **¡— qué!** come now!; what else did you expect!; **¿—?** so?, well?; what next?
  (**b**) (*hesitant*) **—...no sé** well ... I don't know.
  (**c**) (*affirmation*) **¡—!** yes!, certainly!; *see* **ahora, bien** *etc*.
  2 *conj* since, for; **cómpralo, — lo necesitas** buy it, since you need it; **nos marchamos, — no había más remedio** we went, since there was no alternative.
puesta *nf* (**a**) **— en marcha** starting; **— en escena** staging.
  (**b**) (*Astron*) setting; **— del sol** sunset.
  (**c**) (*Orn*) egg-laying; **una — anual de 300 huevos** an annual lay (*or* output) of 300 eggs.
  (**d**) (*Cards etc*) stake, bet.
  (**e**) (*RPl*) **¡—!** it's a tie!, it's a draw!; (*Racing*) it's a dead heat!
puestero *nm* (**a**) (*SAm*) stallholder, market vendor.
  (**b**) (*Chi, RPl*) farm overseer; small farmer, tenant farmer.

puesto 1 *ptp of* **poner.**
    2 *adj* (a) **con el sombrero** — with one's hat on, wearing a hat; **una mesa puesta para 9** a table laid for 9.
    (b) **bien** — well dressed, smartly turned out.
    3 *nm* (a) place; position; **el** — **de la especie en la clasificación** the place of the species in the classification; **ocupa el tercer** — **en la liga** it is in third place in the league; **ceder el** — **a uno** to give up one's place to someone; **quedar** (*or* **mantener**) **su** — to know one's place; to keep the proper distance.
    (b) post, position, job; **tiene un** — **de conserje** he has a post as a porter; **se creará 200** — **s de trabajo** 200 new jobs will be created.
    (c) (*Mil etc*) post; — **de escucha** listening post; — **de policía** police post, police station; — **de socorro** first-aid post.
    (d) (*Hunting*) stand, place.
    (e) (*Comm*) stall; stand, booth; kiosk; pitch; — **de mercado** market stall.
    (f) (*RPl*) small farm.
    3 — **que** *conj* since, as.
puf *interj* ugh!
púgil *nm* boxer.
pugilato *nm* boxing.
pugilista *nm* (*SAm*) boxer.
pugío *nm* (*Arg, Per*) spring.
pugna *nf* battle, struggle, conflict; **entrar en** — **con** to clash with, come into conflict with; **estar en** — **con** to clash with, conflict with.
pugnacidad *nf* pugnacity, aggressiveness.
pugnar [1a] *vi* (a) to fight; — **en defensa de** to fight in defence of; — **por** to fight for.
    (b) to struggle, fight, strive (*por* + *infin* to + *infin*); — **por no reírse** to struggle not to laugh.
    (c) — **con** (*of opinion etc*) to clash with, conflict with.
pugnaz *adj* pugnacious, aggressive.
puja *nf* (a) attempt, effort. (b) (*at auction*) bid. (c) **sacar de la** — **a uno** to get ahead of someone; to get someone out of a jam. (d) (*Col*) ticking-off.
pujante *adj* strong, vigorous; powerful; pushful, forceful.
pujanza *nf* strength, vigour; power; pushfulness, forcefulness, drive.
pujar [1a] **1** *vt price* to raise, push up.
    2 *vi* (a) (*at auction*) to bid, bid up; (*Cards*) to bid.
    (b) to struggle, strain; — **para hacer algo** to struggle to do something; — **para adentro** (*SAm*) to grin and bear it.
    (c) to falter, dither, hesitate.
    (d) to struggle for words, be at a loss for words.
    (e) to be on the verge of tears.
puje *nm* (*Per*) ticking-off.
pujo *nm* (a) (*Med*) difficulty in relieving oneself.
    (b) (*fig*) longing, strong urge; **sentir** — **de llorar** to be on the verge of tears; **sentir** — **de reírse** to have an uncontrollable urge to laugh.
    (c) (*fig*) attempt, try, shot; —**s pretensions; tiene** —**s de caballero** he has pretensions to being a gentleman.
pulcramente *adv* neatly, tidily, smartly; exquisitely; delicately.
pulcritud *nf* neatness, tidiness, smartness; exquisiteness, delicacy.
pulcro *adj* neat, tidy, smart; smartly dressed, smartly turned out; *style etc* exquisite; dainty, delicate.
pulga *nf* (a) flea.
    (b) (*idioms*) **un tío de malas** —**s** a bad-tempered chap, a peppery individual; **tener malas** — to be bad-tempered, be violent, be unpredictable; **no aguantar** —**s** (*fam*) to stand no nonsense; **buscar las** —**s a uno** to tease someone, needle someone (*fam*); **hacer de una** — **un elefante** to make a mountain out of a molehill.
pulgada *nf* inch.
pulgar *nm* thumb.
pulgarada *nf* (a) flick, flip. (b) (*of snuff etc*) pinch.
Pulgarcito *m* Tom Thumb.
pulgón *nm* plant louse; bug.
pulgoso *adj*, **pulguiento** *adj* (*SAm*) full of fleas, verminous.
pulidamente *adv* (a) neatly, tidily; carefully; in a polished way; (*pej*) affectedly. (b) courteously.
pulido *adj* neat, tidy; clean; careful; polished; refined; (*pej*) over-nice, affected, finicky.
pulidor *nm*, **pulidora** *nf* polisher.
pulimentar [1a] *vt* to polish; to put a gloss on, put a shine on; to smooth.
pulimiento *nm* (a) polish, shine; gloss. (b) (*substance*) polish.

pulir [3a] **1** *vt* (a) to polish; to put a gloss on, put a shine on.
    (b) to smooth; to finish (off).
    (c) (*fig*) to polish up, touch up, rub up; *person* to polish up.
    (d) (*fam*) to pinch (*fam*); to sell, flog (*fam*).
    2 pulirse *vr* (*fig*) to acquire polish; to spruce oneself up.
pulmón *nm* lung; — **de acero** iron lung; **a pleno** — breathe deeply; shout at the top of one's voice.
pulmonar *adj* pulmonary, lung (*attr*).
pulmonía *nf* pneumonia; — **doble** double pneumonia.
pulóver *nm* (*angl*) pullover.
pulpa *nf* pulp; soft mass; (*of fruit, plant*) flesh, soft part; (*Anat*) soft flesh; (*RPl*) boneless meat, fillet; — **de madera** wood pulp.
pulpejo *nm* fleshy part, soft part.
pulpería *nf* (*SAm*) general store, food store; bar, tavern.
pulpero *nm* (*SAm*) storekeeper, grocer; tavern-keeper.
púlpito *nm* pulpit.
pulpo *nm* octopus.
pulposo *adj* pulpy; soft, fleshy.
pulque *nm* (*Ec, Mex*) *fermented drink made from maguey juice.*
pulquear [1a] (*Mex*) **1** *vi* to drink *pulque*. **2 pulquearse** *vr* to get drunk on *pulque*.
pulquería *nf* (*Mex*) bar, tavern.
pulquérrimo *adj superl of* **pulcro.**
pulsación *nf* (a) beat, pulsation; (*Anat*) throb(bing), beat(ing). (b) (*on typewriter etc*) tap; (*of pianist, typist*) touch.
pulsador *nm* button, push-button; (*Elec*) switch.
pulsar [1a] **1** *vt* (a) *key etc* to strike, touch, tap; *button, switch* to press; (*Mus*) to play.
    (b) (*Med*) — **a uno** to take someone's pulse, feel someone's pulse.
    (c) (*fig*) *opinion etc* to sound out, take, explore.
    2 *vi* to pulsate; to throb, beat.
pulsear [1a] *vi* (*RPl*) to aim at a target.
pulsera *nf* wristlet, bracelet; — **para reloj** watch strap; **reloj de** — wristwatch.
pulso *nm* (a) (*Anat*) pulse; **tomar el** — **a uno** to take someone's pulse, feel someone's pulse; **tomar el** — **a la opinión** to sound out opinion.
    (b) (*Anat*) wrist; (*fig*) strength of wrist; **a** — by sheer strength; with arm upraised, with arm up in the air; (*fig*) by sheer hard work; (*fig*) unaided, all alone; the hard way; **a** — **sudando** by the sweat of one's brow; **dibujo** (**hecho**) **a** — freehand drawing; **tomar un mueble a** — to lift a piece of furniture clean off the ground.
    (c) (*fig*) steadiness, steady hand, firmness of touch; **tener** — (*RPl*) to have a good aim.
    (d) (*fig*) tact, good sense; **con mucho** — very sensibly; with great tact.
    (e) (*Col*) = **pulsera.**
pulular [1a] **1** *vt* (*SAm*) to infest, swarm in, overrun. **2** *vi* to swarm, abound.
pulverización *nf* (a) pulverization. (b) spray; spraying.
pulverizador *nm* spray, sprayer, spray gun.
pulverizar [1f] *vt* (a) *substance* to pulverize; to powder, convert into powder. (b) *liquid* to spray. (c) (*fig*) *enemy, city* to pound, pulverize, smash.
pulverulento *adj* (a) powdered, powdery. (b) *surface* dusty.
pulla *nf* (a) cutting remark, wounding remark; taunt; dig. (b) obscene remark, rude word.
pum *interj* bang!; thud!; pop!
puma *nf* puma.
puna *nf* (*SAm*) (a) high Andean plateau, bleak upland. (b) (*Med*) mountain sickness.
punción *nf* (*Med*) puncture.
punch *nm* (*SAm: angl*) (a) punch. (b) (*fig*) vigour, strength, energy; agility.
punchar [1a] *vt* (*SAm: angl*) to punch.
punching ['punʃin] *nm* (*angl*) punchball.
pundonor *nm* self-respect, amour propre; honour; face.
pundonoroso *adj* honourable; punctilious, scrupulous.
punga 1 *nf* (*Arg*) thieving. **2** *nmf* (*Chi*) pickpocket, thief.
punguista *nm* (*Arg, Urug*) pickpocket, thief.
pungir [3c] *vt* (a) to prick, puncture; to sting. (b) to cause suffering to.
punible *adj* punishable.
punición *nf* punishment.
púnico 1 *adj* Punic. **2** *nm* (*language*) Punic.
punitivo *adj* punitive.

punta 1 *nf* **(a)** end; tip, point, sharp end; (*of timber etc*) thin end; (*Geog*) point; headland; (*Sew etc*) corner; — **de lanza** spearhead (*also fig*); **con la — de la lengua** with the tip of one's tongue; **tener algo en la — de la lengua** to have something on the tip of one's tongue; — **del pie** toe; **de —** on end; endways; **de — a —** from one end to the other; **ir de — en blanco** to be all dressed up to the nines; **hacer —** to be first, go first; **sacar — a** to sharpen, point, put a point on; **sacar — a una observación** to read too much into a remark, force the sense of a remark; **sacar — a una máquina** to get the most out of a machine; to use a machine in ways which were never intended; **se le pusieron los pelos de —** her hair stood on end; **estoy hasta la — de los pelos con él** I'm utterly fed up with him.

(b) (*fig*) touch, trace; tinge; **tiene — de loco** he has a streak of madness; he's a bit mad; **tiene sus —s de filósofo** there's a little of the philosopher about him.

(c) (*fig: idioms*) **andar** (*or* **estar**) **de —** to be at odds (*con* with); **estar de —** to be edgy; to be in a bad mood; **ponerse de — con uno** to fall out with someone; to adopt a hostile attitude to someone; **tener de — a uno** to be at daggers drawn with someone.

(d) (*Tech*) small nail.

(e) (*of cigar*) stub, butt.

(f) (*Zool: of bull*) horn; (*of antler*) point, tine.

(g) (*Agr*) group of cows.

(h) (*Cu, PR*) leaf of best tobacco.

(i) (*Mex*) sharp weapon.

(j) (*Ven*) taunt, snide remark.

(k) (*SAm*) group, gathering; lot; **una — de a** lot of, a bunch of.

(l) (*CAm*) **en —** wholesale.

2 *attr*: **horas —** peak hours, rush hours; **velocidad —** maximum speed, top speed.

puntada *nf* **(a)** (*Sew*) stitch; **— cruzada** cross-stitch; **— invisible** invisible mending; **dar unas —s en** to put a few stitches in, stitch up; **no ha dado —** (*fig*) he hasn't done a stroke; he's done nothing at all about it.

(b) (*fam*) hint; **pegar** (*or* **soltar**) **una —** to drop a hint.

(c) (*SAm: Med*) stitch; sharp pain.

(d) (*Mex*) witty remark.

puntal *nm* **(a)** (*Archit*) prop, shore, support; (*Agr*) prop; (*Tech*) strut, crosspiece; stanchion. **(b)** (*fig*) prop, support; chief supporter. **(c)** (*SAm*) snack.

puntapié *nm* kick; **echar a uno a —s** to kick someone out; **pegar un — a uno** to give someone a kick.

puntazo *nm* (*Taur*) jab (*with a horn*); (*SAm*) jab, poke; stab; stab wound, knife wound.

punteado 1 *adj* dotted, covered with dots; stippled; flecked (*de* with); *design* of dots.

2 *nm* **(a)** series of dots; stippling; flecking.

(b) (*Mus*) twang; twanging; plucking.

puntear [1a] **1** *vt* **(a)** to dot, cover (*or* mark) with dots; to stipple; to fleck.

(b) *items* to tick, put a mark against; (*SAm*) *list* to check off.

(c) (*Sew*) to stitch (up).

(d) (*Mus*) to pluck; to twang.

(e) (*Chi, RPl*) *ground* to fork over.

(f) (*Chi, RPl*) *march etc* to head, lead.

2 *vi* (*Naut*) to tack.

punteo *nm* plucking, twanging.

puntera *nf* **(a)** toecap. **(b)** pencil top. **(c)** (*fam*) kick.

puntería *nf* **(a)** aim, aiming; **enmendar** (*or* **rectificar**) **la —** to correct one's aim; **hacer la — de un cañón** to aim a gun, sight a gun.

(b) (*fig*) marksmanship; **tener buena —** to be a good shot; **tener mala —** to be a bad shot.

puntero *nm* **(a)** pointer.

(b) stonecutter's chisel.

(c) outstanding individual; leader, top man.

(d) (*SAm*) leading team, team which is ahead; leading animal (*of a flock or team*); leader (*of a procession*).

(e) (*SAm: of watch*) hand.

puntiagudo *adj* sharp, sharp-pointed.

puntilla *nf* **(a)** (*Tech*) tack, brad.

(b) (*of pen*) point, nib.

(c) (*Sew*) lace edging.

(d) (*Taur*) short dagger for giving the coup de grâce; **dar la —** to give the coup de grâce, finish off the bull.

(e) de —s on tiptoe; **andar de —s** to walk on tiptoe.

puntillismo *nm* pointillisme.

puntillo *nm* punctilio; exaggerated sense of honour, excessive amour propre.

puntilloso *adj* punctilious; touchy, sensitive.

punto *nm* **(a)** (*in design etc*) dot, spot; fleck; (*on plumage etc*) spot, speckle; (*on card, domino*) spot, pip; **diseño a —s** design of dots, pattern of dots.

(b) (*Typ*) point; (*also* **— final**) full stop; **dos —s** colon; **— y coma** semicolon; **— de admiración**, **— de exclamación** exclamation mark; **— de interrogación** question mark, query; **—s suspensivos** dots, suspension points (. . .); **— acápite** full stop, new paragraph; **" — y aparte"** (*in dictating*) "new paragraph"; **sin faltar — ni coma** accurately, faithfully; minutely; **poner los —s sobre las íes** to dot the i's and cross the t's.

(c) (*in scoring*) point; (*in exam*) mark; **con 8 —s a favor y 3 en contra** with 8 points for and 3 against; **vencer por —s** to win on points.

(d) (*in argument, discussion*) point; item, matter, question; **contestar — por —** to answer point by point; **— capital** crucial point, basic point; crux; **—s de consulta** terms of reference; **—s a tratar** matters to be discussed, agenda.

(e) — **de taxis** taxi stand, cabrank.

(f) (*Mus*) pitch.

(g) (*Sew*) stitch; (*of fabric*) mesh; (*in stocking*) ladder, run; (*Med*) stitch; **— de media** plain knitting; **hacer —** to knit; **¡— en boca!** mum's the word!, keep it under your hat!; **chaqueta de —** knitted jacket.

(h) (*Med*) **— de costado** stitch, pain in the side.

(i) (*in strap, belt etc*) hole; **darse dos —s en el cinturón** to let out one's belt, (*fig*) overeat; **calzar muchos —s** to know a lot; **calzar pocos —s** to know very little, be pretty dim.

(j) (*of place etc*) spot, place, point; (*Geog*) point; (*Math*) point; (*of process*) point, stage; (*in time*) point, moment; **— de apoyo** fulcrum; **— de arranque** starting point; **— cardinal** cardinal point; **— céntrico** central point; **— ciego** (*Anat*) blind spot; **— clave de las defensas** key point in the defences; **— de congelación** freezing point; **— de contacto** point of contact; **— crítico** critical point, critical moment; **— culminante** culminating moment; topmost point, limit; **— débil**, **— flaco** weak spot, weak point; **— de ebullición** boiling point; **— de fuga** vanishing point; **— de fusión** melting point; **— de inflamación** flash point; **— muerto** (*Mech*) dead centre; (*Aut etc*) neutral (gear); (*fig*) deadlock, stalemate; **las negociaciones están en un — muerto** the negotiations are deadlocked, there is stalemate in the talks; **hemos llegado a un — muerto** we have reached deadlock; **— neutro** (*Mech*) dead centre; (*Aut etc*) neutral (gear); **— panorámico** viewpoint, vantage point; **— de partida** starting point; **— de referencia** point of reference; **— de veraneo** summer resort, holiday resort; **— de vista** point of view, viewpoint; criterion; **él lo mira desde otro — de vista** he looks at it from another point of view.

(k) (*idioms etc with prep*) **a —** ready; **con sus máquinas a — para disparar** with their cameras ready to shoot; **llegar a —** to come just at the right moment; **al llegar a este —** at this moment, at this stage; **saber algo a — fijo** to know something for sure; **al —** at once, instantly; **está a —** it's ready; **estar a — de** + *infin* to be on the point of + *ger*, be about to + *infin*; **poner un motor a —** to tune an engine; **de todo —** completely, absolutely; **bajar de —** to decline, fall off, fall away; **subir de —** to grow, increase; to get worse; **a las 7 en —** at 7 sharp, at 7 on the dot, punctually at 7; **en — a** with regard to; **estar en su —** (*Cook*) to be done to a turn; **una medida muy puesta en su —** a very timely (*or* proper) measure; **para dejar las cosas en su —** to be absolutely precise; **pongamos las cosas en su —** let's be absolutely clear about this; **poner algo en su —** to bring something to perfection; **hasta el — de** + *infin* to the extent of + *ger*; **hasta cierto —** up to a point, to some extent; **hasta tal — que . . .** to such an extent that . . .

(l) (*fam*) **¡vaya un —!**, **¡está hecho un — filipino!** he's a right rogue! (*fam*).

puntuable *adj*: **una prueba — para el campeonato** a race which counts towards (*or* scores in) the championship.

puntuación *nf* **(a)** (*Gram, Typ*) punctuation.

(b) (*act: School etc*) marking; (*Sport*) scoring; **sistema de —** system of scoring.

(c) (*School etc*) mark(s); class, grade; (*Sport*) score.

puntual *adj* **(a)** *person* reliable, conscientious; prompt, (*in timing*) punctual.

(b) *arrival etc* punctual.

(c) *report etc* reliable; precise; *calculation* exact, accurate.

puntualidad nf (a) reliability, conscientiousness; promptness; punctuality. (b) precision; exactness, accuracy.

puntualizar [1f] vt (a) to fix, specify, state in detail; to settle, determine. (b) to fix in one's mind (or memory).

puntualmente adv (a) reliably, conscientiously; promptly; punctually. (b) precisely, exactly, accurately.

puntuar [1c] 1 vt (a) (Gram, Typ) to punctuate. (b) exam to mark. 2 vi (Sport etc) to score, count; **eso no puntúa** that doesn't count.

puntudo adj (SAm) sharp.

puntura nf puncture, prick.

punzada nf (a) puncture, prick; jab. (b) (Med) stitch; twinge (of pain), shooting pain; spasm. (c) (fig) pang, twinge (of regret etc). (d) (Cu) silliness.

punzante adj (a) pain shooting, sharp. (b) tool etc sharp. (c) (fig) remark etc biting, caustic.

punzar [1f] 1 vt (a) to puncture, prick, pierce; (Tech) to punch; to perforate. (b) (fig) to hurt, grieve; **le punzan remordimientos** he feels pangs of regret, his conscience pricks him. 2 vi (of pain) to shoot, stab; to sting.

punzó adj (SAm) bright red.

punzón nm (Tech) punch; graver, burin; bodkin.

puñada nf punch, clout; **dar de —s en** to punch, pound, beat on.

puñado nm handful (also fig); **a —s** by handfuls; **in plenty, galore**.

puñal nm dagger; **poner el — al pecho a uno** (fig) to put someone on the spot.

puñalada nf (a) stab, thrust; **— de misericordia** coup de grâce; see **coser**. (b) (fig) stab, grievous blow; **— encubierta** stab in the back, treacherous thrust.

puñeta nf (a) ¡—!, ¡qué —(s)! hell!, damnation! (b) **hacer —s** (tabu) to masturbate; **mandar a uno a hacer —s** to tell somebody to go to hell.

puñetazo nm punch; **a —s** with (blows of) one's fists; **dar a uno de —s** to punch someone.

puñetero adj (fam) bloody.

puño nm (a) (Anat) fist; **— de hierro** knuckleduster; **a — cerrado** with one's clenched fist; **apretar los —s** (fig) to struggle hard; **comerse los —s** to be starving; **como un —** house etc tiny, very small; truth etc obvious; tangible, visible; (see also **verdad**); **mentiras como —s** whopping great lies (sl); **de propio —** in one's own handwriting **de — y letra del poeta** in the poet's own handwriting; **meter a uno en un —** to intimidate someone, cow someone; to bring someone under control; **su mujer le tiene en un —** his wife's got him completely under her thumb. (b) (quantity) handful, fistful. (c) (Sew) cuff. (d) (of sword) hilt; (of tool) handle, haft, grip; (of vessel) handle. (e) (fig) **—s** strength; brute force; **es hombre de —s** he's strong, he's tough; **ganar algo con los —s** to get something by sheer hard work; **hacer algo a —** to do something by hand. (f) (fig) **un — de casa** a tiny house, a very small house.

pupa nf (a) (Med) pimple, blister; lip sore, ulcer. (b) (Ent) pupa.

pupila nf (a) (Anat) pupil. (b) (Law) ward. (c) (Chi, RPl) prostitute.

pupilo nm (a) (of institution) inmate; boarder. (b) (Law) ward.

pupitre nm desk.

pupo nm (Arg, Chi, Ec, Per) navel.

pupón adj (Arg, Mex) (a) replete, full (of food). (b) pot-bellied, fat.

puque nm (Mex) rotten, bad; weak, sickly; sterile.

puquío nm (SAm) spring, fountain.

puramente adv purely, simply.

pura-sangre nmf, pl **pura-sangres** thoroughbred.

puré nm purée, (thick) soup; **— de patatas** mashed potatoes; **— de guisantes** (fig) pea souper, thick fog.

purear [1a] vi (Ec) to drink one's liquor neat.

pureza nf purity (also fig).

purga nf (a) (Med) purge, cathartic, purgative. (b) (Pol) purge. (c) (Mech) venting, draining, airing; **válvula de —** vent.

purgación nf (a) purging, purgative. (b) menstruation. (c) **tener —es** (fam) to have the clap (fam).

purgante nm purgative.

purgar [1h] 1 vt (a) to purge, cleanse (de of); (Mech) to vent, drain, air; (Pol) to purge, liquidate. (b) to purify, refine. (c) (Med) to purge, administer a purgative to. (d) (fig) sin to purge, expiate; passions to purge. 2 **purgarse** vr (a) (Med) to take a purge. (b) (fig) **— de** to purge oneself of.

purgativo adj purgative.

purgatorio nm purgatory (also fig); ¡**fue un —!** it was purgatory!

puridad nf (lit) secrecy; **en —** plainly, directly; in secret.

purificación nf purification.

purificar [1g] vt to purify; to cleanse; (Tech) to purify, refine.

Purísima adj superl: **la —** the Virgin.

purismo nm purism.

purista nmf purist.

puritanismo nm puritanism.

puritano 1 adj attitude etc puritanical; church, tradition etc puritan. 2 nm, **puritana** nf puritan.

puro 1 adj (a) substance, colour, language etc pure; unadulterated; gold solid; sky clear. (b) (fig) pure, simple; sheer; truth plain, simple; **de — aburrimiento** out of sheer boredom; **por pura casualidad** by sheer chance. (c) (morally) pure, virtuous, chaste. (d) (SAm) only, just; **me queda una pura porción** I have just one ration left, I have only one ration left. (e) (Mex, Ven) identical; **el hijo es — el padre** the son is exactly like his father. 2 as adv: **de — bobo** out of sheer stupidity; **de — cansado** out of sheer tiredness; **no se le ve el color de — sucio** it's so dirty you can't tell what colour it is. 3 nm (a) cigar. (b) **a — de** by dint of, thanks only to.

púrpura nf purple.

purpurado nm (Eccl) cardinal.

purpurar [1a] vt to dye purple.

purpúreo adj, **purpurino** adj purple.

purpurina nf (Ec, Per) metallic paint (gold, silver etc).

purrela nf (a) bad wine, cheap wine. (b) (fig) **una — a** mere trifle, chicken feed.

purrete nm (RPl) kid (fam), child.

purulento adj purulent.

pus nm pus, matter.

puse etc see **poner**.

pusilánime adj fainthearted, pusillanimous.

pusilanimidad nf faintheartedness, pusillanimity.

pústula nf pustule, sore, pimple.

puta nf (a) whore, prostitute; **— callejera** streetwalker; **casa de —s** brothel; **ir de —s** to go whoring. (b) (SAm: Cards) jack.

putañear [1a] vi to go whoring, consort with prostitutes.

putañero adj that consorts with prostitutes; (fig) randy, oversexed, wolfish (fam).

putativo adj putative, supposed.

puteada nf (Mex, RPl) shower of gross insults.

putear [1a] vi =**putañear**.

putería nf (a) prostitution, whoring. (b) gathering of prostitutes; brothel. (c) (fam) womanly wile(s).

putrefacción nf (a) (act) rotting, putrefaction; decay. (b) rot, rottenness; **— fungoide** dry rot; **sujeto a —** food etc perishable.

putrefacto adj rotten, putrid; decayed.

putrescente adj rotting, putrefying, putrescent.

pútrido adj putrid, rotten.

puya nf goad, pointed stick; point; (Taur) point of the picador's lance.

puyar [1a] 1 vt (a) (SAm) to jab, wound, prick. (b) (Ant, CAm) to upset, needle (fam). 2 vi (Ven: of plant) to shoot, sprout.

puyo nm (Arg) coarse woollen poncho.

puyón nm (a) (Arg, Bol) cock's spur; (Mex) sharp point; (Mex: Bot) prickle, spine, thorn; (CAm, Col, Mex) shoot, bud. (b) (Col, Guat, PR) jab, prick.

Q

que[1] **1** *rel pron* **(a)** (*of person: subject*) who, that; (*acc*) whom, that; (*but relative often omitted, eg*) **la joven —invité** the girl I invited.

(b) (*of thing*) that, which; (*but relative often omitted, eg*) **el coche — compré** the car I bought; **la cama en — pasé la noche** the bed in which I spent the night, the bed I spent the night in; **el día — ella nació** the day (that) she was born, the day when she was born; **la reunión a — yo asistí** the meeting I attended, the meeting at which I was present; **los disgustos — tiene que aguantar** the unpleasantness he has to put up with.

2 *rel pron* (*with article*) see **el**[3], **lo**.

que[2] *conj* **(a)** (*following verb*) that; (*but often omitted, eg*) **creo — va a venir** I think (that) he will come; **no sabía — tuviera coche** I didn't know he had a car; **decir — sí** to say yes; **la idea de — haya oro en Ruritania** the idea that there is gold in Ruritania; **estoy seguro de — lloverá** I am sure (that) it will rain; **¿— no estabas allí?** (are you telling me) you weren't there?; *see* **claro, decir** *etc*.

(b) (*introducing subj verb*) that; **esperar — uno haga algo** to hope that somebody will do something; **querer — uno haga algo** to want someone to do something; **alegrarse de — uno haya llegado** to be glad (that) someone has arrived; **no digo — sea traidor** I'm not saying (that) he's a traitor; **¡— lo haga él!** let him do it!, get him to do it!; **¡— entre!** let him come in!, send him in!; **¡— venga pronto!** let's hope he comes soon!

(c) (*elliptical*) **¡a — no!** *etc: see* **no (a)**.

(d) el que + *subj* the fact that . . .; **el — tenga dos hermanas guapas no me interesa** the fact that he has two pretty sisters doesn't concern me; **el — quiera estar con su madre es natural** it is natural (that) he should want to be with his mother.

(e) (*result*) that; **soplaba tan fuerte — no podíamos salir** it was blowing so hard (that) we couldn't go out; **huele — es un asco** it smells so much that it's disgusting; *see* **bendición, primor** *etc*.

(f) (*idiom*) **siguió toca — toca** he just kept on playing, he played and played; **estuvieron habla — habla toda la noche** they talked and talked all night.

(g) for, since, because; **vine un poco pronto —está lloviendo** I came a bit early because it's raining; **¡vamos, — cierro!** off with you, (because) I'm closing!; **¡cuidado, — nos vamos!** hold tight, we're off!; **¡suélteme, — voy a gritar!** let go or I'll scream!

(h) (*comparisons*) than; *see* **más** *etc*.

(i) (*idiom*) **yo — tú** if I were you, if I were in your place.

qué **1** *interrog pron*: **¿—?** what?; **¿— dijiste?** what did you say?; **no sé — quiere decir** I don't know what it means; **¿a —?** why?; **¿y a mí —?** so what?, what has that got to do with me?; **¿y —?** so what?, well?; **¿con — lo vas a pagar?** what are you going to pay with?; how are you going to pay it?; **¿de — le conoces?** how do you recognize him?; **¿en — lo notas?** in what way do you see that?; **sin — ni para —** without rhyme or reason; *see* **más, para** *etc*.

2 *adj* **(a)** (*interrog*) **¿— libro?** what book?; which book?; **¿— edad tiene?** what age is he?, how old is he?; **¿— traje te vas a poner?** which dress are you wearing?; **¿a — velocidad?** at what speed?, how fast?; **¿de — tamaño es?** what size is it?, how big is it?; **dime — libro buscas** tell me which book you are looking for.

(b) (*excl*) **¡— día más espléndido!** what a glorious day!; **¡— bonito!** isn't it pretty!, how pretty it is!; very nice too! (*also iro*); **¡— asco!** how revolting!; **¡— susto!** what a scare!; **¡— de cosas te diría!** what a lot I'd have to say to you!; **¡— de gente había!** what a lot of people there were!

quebrada *nf* **(a)** gorge, ravine; gap, pass. **(b)** (*SAm*) brook, stream.

quebradero *nm*: **— de cabeza** headache, worry.

quebradizo *adj* **(a)** fragile, brittle, delicate; *pastry* short; *biscuit etc* crumbly.

(b) (*Med*) sickly, frail.

(c) emotionally fragile, sensitive, readily upset.

(d) (*morally*) frail, easily tempted.

quebrado **1** *adj* **(a)** *ground* broken, rough, uneven, *line* irregular, zigzag.

(b) *face* pale; *complexion* pallid.

(c) (*Med*) ruptured.

(d) (*Fin*) bankrupt.

2 *nm* **(a)** (*Math*) fraction.

(b) (*Fin*) bankrupt.

quebradura *nf* **(a)** fissure, slit, crack. **(b)** (*Geog*) =**quebrada (a)**. **(c)** (*Med*) rupture.

quebraja *nf* fissure, slit, crack.

quebrantadura *nf*, **quebrantamiento** *nm* **(a)** (*act*) breaking; cracking; weakening; forcing; violation.

(b) (*state*) exhaustion, exhausted state; broken health.

quebrantar [1a] **1** *vt* **(a)** to break; to crack; to shatter.

(b) *foundations, fury, morale etc* to weaken; *resistance* to break, weaken; *health, position* to undermine, shatter, destroy; *person* to shatter, break.

(c) *lock* to force; *safe, seal* to break open; *prison* to break out of; *sanctuary* to break into, violate; *forbidden ground etc* to trespass on.

(d) *law, promise* to break.

(e) *colour* to tone down.

(f) (*SAm*) *horse* to break in.

2 quebrantarse *vr* (*person*) to be shattered, be broken (in health *etc*).

quebranto *nm* **(a)** damage, harm; severe loss. **(b)** exhaustion, weakness; broken health; depression, shattered state. **(c)** sorrow, affliction.

quebrar [1k] **1** *vt* **(a)** to break, smash.

(b) *body* to bend (at the waist); to twist.

(c) *career, training, process etc* to interrupt; to alter the course of, interfere seriously with.

(d) *colour* to tone down.

(e) =**quebrantar** (*various senses*).

2 *vi* **(a)** (*Fin*) to fail, go bankrupt.

(b) to weaken.

(c) — con uno to break with someone.

3 quebrarse *vr* **(a)** to break, smash, get broken.

(b) (*Med*) to be ruptured; to have a rupture.

quebraza *nf* crack; (*Med*) crack (on the skin), chap.

quebrazón *nf* (*SAm*) smash-up, general shattering, multiple breakage.

quebroso *adj* (*Per*) brittle, fragile.

queco *nm* (*Arg*) brothel.

queche *nm* smack, ketch.

queda *nf* curfew.

quedada *nf* (*Mex, Nic, SD*) spinster, old maid.

quedado *adj* (*Chi, Mex*) feeble, slow, lazy.

quedar [1a] **1** *vi* **(a)** to stay, remain; **quedamos una semana** we stayed a week; **— atrás** to remain behind; to fall behind.

(b) (*in state*) to remain, be; **— asombrado** to be amazed; **— inmóvil** to remain (*or* be, stand *etc*) motionless; (*vehicle etc*) to remain stationary; **— de pie** to remain standing; **— ciego** to go blind; **— cojo** to go lame; **después de eso ha quedado en ridículo** as a result of that he was ridiculed; **A pretendía que B quedara en ridículo** A was trying to make B look ridiculous; **ha quedado sin hacer** it remained undone, nothing was done about it; **el proyecto quedó sin realizar** the plan was never carried out; **ir quedando lejos** to fall behind; **con las reformas el edificio queda feo** as a result of the alterations the building is ugly; **la cosa queda así** there the matter rests, that's how the affair stands; **¿cuánto te quedo a deber?** how much do I owe you?; **quedó heredero del título** he became heir to the title, that made him heir to the title.

(c) (— **bien** etc) — **bien** to come off well; to do oneself justice; — **bien con uno** to be on good terms with someone, stand well with someone; **por — bien** in order to do the right thing; — **mal** to do badly, come off badly; — **mal con uno** to be at odds with someone; **por no — mal** in order to do the right thing, so as not to cause any offence; **ha quedado como un canalla** he showed himself to be a rotter, he was shown up as the rotter he is.

(d) (place) to be; **eso queda muy lejos** that's a long way (away); **queda un poco más al oeste** it is (or lies) a little further west; **esa cuestión queda fuera de nuestros límites** that matter lies (or falls, is) outside the bounds of our inquiry.

(e) to remain, be left; **quedan 6** there are 6 left; **me quedan 6** I have 6 left; **nos queda poco dinero** we haven't much money left; **no quedan más que escombros** there is nothing left but rubble; **ya no queda motivo para ello** there is no longer any reason for it; **no me queda otro remedio** I have no alternative (left).

(f) to be . . . still; **quedan pocos días para la fiesta** only a few days remain till the party, there are only a few days to go to the party; **nos quedan 12 kms para llegar al pueblo** there are still 12 kms to go to the village.

(g) — **en** to turn out to be, result in, end up as; **todo ese trabajo quedó en nada** all that work came to nothing; **las discusiones quedaron en un informe más** the discussions merely resulted in one more report.

(h) — **en** + infin to agree to + infin, arrange to + infin; — **en que** . . . to agree that . . .; **¿en qué quedamos?** what do we decide to do then?

(i) — **por** + infin to be still to be + ptp, remain to be + ptp; **las cartas quedan aún por escribir** the letters are still to be written; **eso queda todavía por estudiar** that remains to be studied.

(j) — + ger to be + ger, go on + ger; **él quedaba trabajando en casa** he went on working at home.

2 quedarse vr (a) in basic sense, = 1 (a) and (b), eg — **atrás** to remain behind; to fall behind; (additional senses) to stay on, stay behind, linger (on); — **en una pensión** to stay at a boarding house, put up at a boarding house; — **con unos amigos** to stay with some friends; **se me queda pequeña esta camisa** this shirt has got too small for me, I've outgrown this shirt; — **sin** to find oneself out of, run out of; **nos hemos quedado sin café** we've run out of coffee.

(b) (sea, wind) to fall calm.

(c) — **con** to keep, hold on to, retain; to acquire, get hold of; (fig) to take, prefer; **se quedó con mi pluma** he kept my pen, he walked off with my pen; **quédese con la vuelta** keep the change; **entre A y B, me quedo con B** if I have to choose between A and B, I'll take B; **así que me quedé con la más fea de las tres** so I got left with the plainest of the three.

(d) — **con uno** (fam) to swindle someone, cheat someone.

(e) (idioms) **no se queda con la cólera dentro** he can't control his anger, he can't keep his anger bottled up; — **en nada** to come to nothing; **no se quedó en menos** he was not to be outdone.

(f) (Chi: limb) to become paralysed; (person) to die.

(g) — + ger to be + ger, go on + ger; **se nos quedó mirando asombrado** he stood (etc) looking at us in amazement.

quedito adv very softly, very gently.

quedo 1 adj (a) still. (b) voice quiet, soft, gentle; step etc soft. **2** adv softly, gently; **¡—!** gently now!

quehacer nm job, task; —**es (domésticos)** household jobs, chores; **agobiado de —** overburdened with work; **tener mucho —** to have a lot to do.

queja nf (a) complaint; protest; grumble, grouse (fam); grudge, resentment; (Law) protest; **una — infundada** an unjustified complaint; **formar — de uno** to make a complaint about someone; **tener — de uno** to have a complaint to make about someone; **tengo — de ti** I've a bone to pick with you.

(b) moan, groan; — **de dolor** groan of pain.

quejadera nf (Col, Mex), **quejambre** nf (Col, Mex) moan.

quejarse [1a] vr (a) to complain (de about, of), grumble (de about, at); to protest (de about, at);

— **de que** . . . to complain (about the fact) that . . .; — **a un oficial** to complain to an official.

(b) to moan, groan; to whine.

quejica nmf (fam), **quejicoso** nm, **quejicosa** nf (fam) = **quejón**.

quejido nm moan, groan; whine; **dar —s** to moan, groan; to whine.

quejón (fam) **1** adj grumbling, complaining. **2** nm, **quejona** nf grumbler, constant complainer.

quejoso adj person complaining; tone querulous, whining; plaintive.

quejumbre nf moan, groan.

quejumbroso adj = **quejoso**.

quelite nm (CAm, Mex) greens, vegetables; shoot, tip, green part.

quelonia nf (Ven) turtle.

quelpo nm kelp.

quema nf (a) fire; burning, combustion. (b) (Arg) rubbish dump. (c) (Mex) burning-off (of scrub). (d) (Mex: fig) danger.

quemado adj (a) burned, burnt; **aquí huele a —** I smell something burning in here; **esto sabe a —** this has a burnt taste. (b) (Arg, Mex) very dark.

quemador nm burner; — **de gas** gas burner.

quemadura nf (a) burn; scald; sunburn; (of fuse) blowing, blow-out. (b) (Bot: by frost) cutting, withering. (c) (Bot: disease) smut.

quemar [1a] **1** vt (a) to burn (also Cook; of acid, sun); to burn up; to set on fire, kindle; to scorch; (with liquid) to scald; fuse to blow, burn out.

(b) plants (of frost) to cut, wither, burn.

(c) (fig) fortune etc to burn up, squander; sum to spend quickly, get through in no time; prices to slash, cut.

(d) (fig) to annoy, upset; **estar muy quemado** to have suffered an unpleasant experience.

(e) (CAm, Mex) to denounce, inform on.

(f) (Cu, Mex, PR) to swindle.

(g) (Ven) to shoot.

2 vi (a) to be burning hot; **esto está que quema, está quemando** it's burning hot; **es una especia que quema en la lengua** it's a spice that tastes really hot, it's a spice that burns the tongue.

(b) (of skin) to get tanned.

3 quemarse vr (a) to burn up, burn away; to burn down; to scorch, get scorched; to get sunburnt; — **con la sopa** to burn one's mouth on the soup; **¡que me quemo!** (fig) I'm scorching!, I'm terribly hot!

(b) (in search) to get warm; **¡que te quemas!** you are getting warm!

(c) (fig) to fret.

(d) (Arg, Cu) to get depressed.

quemarropa: a — adv point-blank (also fig).

quemazón nf (a) burn; burning, combustion; (Ant, CAm, Mex) fire.

(b) intense heat.

(c) burning sensation; (fig) itch; smarting, sting.

(d) (fig) cutting remark, wounding thing (to say).

(e) (fig) pique, resentment, annoyance.

(f) (Comm: fam) bargain sale, cut-price sale.

(g) (Bol, Chi) mirage (on the pampas).

quena nf (Arg, Bol, Per) rustic flute.

quepo etc see **caber**.

queque nm (SAm) pancake; (CAm, Mex) bun, cake.

querella nf (a) complaint. (b) (Law) charge, accusation. (c) dispute, controversy.

querellante 1 adj actionable; giving grounds for complaint. **2** nmf (Law) plaintiff.

querellar [1a] **1** vt to scold, reprimand.

2 querellarse vr (a) to complain.

(b) (Law) to file a complaint, bring an action (ante before; contra, de against).

querencia nf (a) (Zool) lair, haunt; (fig) favourite spot, home ground, haunt; **buscar la —** to home, head for home.

(b) (Zool) homing instinct; (fig) longing for home, homesickness.

querendón (SAm) **1** adj affectionate, loving, of an affectionate nature; susceptible to women. **2** nm favourite, pet; spoiled child.

querer [2u] **1** vti (a) to want, wish (for); **¿cuál quieres?** which one do you want?; **no quiero más** I don't want any more; **¿qué más quieres?** what more do you want?; **¿cuánto quieren por el coche?** how much do they want for the car?, what are they asking for the car?; **como Vd quiera** as you wish, as you please; **ven cuando quieras** come when you like; **quiera o no, quiera que no** willy-nilly, whether he (etc) likes it or not; **lo hizo queriendo** (fam) he did it deliberately; **lo hizo sin —** he didn't mean to do it, he did it inadvertently, he did it by mistake; — **es poder** where there's a will there's a way.

(b) (*with verb construction*) — **hacer algo** to want to do something, wish to do something; — **que uno haga algo** to want someone to do something; **no quiso pagar** he didn't want to pay; he refused to pay; **ha querido quedarse en casa** he preferred to stay at home, he decided to stay at home; **¿quiere abrir la ventana?** would you mind opening the window?, please open the window?; **más quiero** + *infin* I would rather + *infin*, I would prefer to + *infin*; **mejor quisiera** + *infin* I would rather + *infin*; **la ley quiere que seamos buenos** the law wants us to be good; **este crítico quiere que Góngora haya sido loco** this critic tries to make out that Góngora was mad, this critic would have us believe that Góngora was mad; **la tradición quiere que** . . . tradition has it that . . .; **éste quiere que le rompan la cabeza** (*fam*) this fellow is asking for a crack on the head.

(c) (*absolute*) **¡no quiero!** I won't!, I refuse!; **sí quiero** (*marriage*) I will; **lo hago porque quiero** I do it because I want to; **pero no quiso** but he refused; but he was unwilling; **¿quiere?** do you want some?, would you like some?

(d) to need, demand; **tal traje quiere un sombrero ancho** that dress needs a big hat to go with it; **¡esto quiere unas copas!** we must have a drink on that!, that deserves a drink to celebrate it!

(e) (*impersonal use*) **quería amanecer** dawn was about to break; **parece que quiere llover** it looks like rain, it seems that it's trying to rain.

(f) *person* to love; to like; — **bien a uno** to be fond of someone; **¡te quiero, bobo!** I love you, you idiot!; **en la oficina le quieren mucho** he is well liked at the office; **¿no me quieres siquiera un poquito?** don't you like me just a little bit?; **hace tiempo que te quiero** I've been in love with you for a long time; **hacerse** — **por uno** to endear oneself to someone; **¡por lo que más quieras!** by all that's sacred!; **me quiere** . . . **no me quiere** (*picking off petals etc*) she loves me . . . she loves me not.

(g) **como quiera** *etc: see* **comoquiera, cuandoquiera, dondequiera.**

2 *nm* love, affection; **tener** — **a** to be fond of.

querida *nf* **(a)** darling, beloved; **¡sí, —!** yes, darling! **(b)** (*pej*) mistress.

querido 1 *adj* dear, darling, beloved; (*in letters*) dear; **nuestra querida patria** our beloved country.

2 *nm* darling, beloved; **¡sí, —!** yes, darling!; **el** — **de las musas** the darling of the muses.

querindongo *nm*, **querindonga** *nf* (*SAm*) lover.

querosén *nm*, **queroseno** *nm* (*Acad*), **querosín** *nm* (*SAm*) kerosene, paraffin.

querúbico *adj* cherubic.

querubín *nm* cherub.

quesera *nf* **(a)** dairymaid; cheesemaker. **(b)** cheese-dish.

quesería *nf* dairy; cheese factory.

quesero *nm* dairyman; cheesemaker.

queso *nm* cheese; — **de bola** Dutch cheese; — **crema** cream cheese; — **helado** ice-cream brick; — **rallado** grated cheese; **darla a uno con** — (*fam*) to swindle someone, pull a fast one on someone.

quetzal *nm* standard monetary unit of Guatemala.

quiá *interj* never!, not on your life!; surely not!

quicio *nm* hinge; **estar fuera de** — (*fig*) to be out of joint; **sacar a uno de** — (*fig*) to irritate someone, get on someone's nerves; to get someone worked up; **estas cosas me sacan de** — these things make me see red.

Quico: ponerse como el — (*fam*) to stuff oneself; to get as fat as a pig.

quichuista *nm* **(a)** (*SAm*) Quichua specialist. **(b)** (*Arg, Bol, Per*) Quichua speaker.

quid *nm* gist, core, root, crux; **dar en el** — to hit the nail on the head.

quídam *nm* **(a)** somebody, somebody or other. **(b)** (*pej*) nobody, nonentity.

quiebra *nf* **(a)** crack, fissure; slit.

(b) (*Fin*) bankruptcy; failure; (*Econ*) slump, crash, collapse; (*fig*) failure; risk of failure; **es una cosa que no tiene** — it just can't go wrong, it's a venture that carries no risk.

quiebro *nm* **(a)** (*Taur etc*) dodge, swerve; avoiding action; **dar el** — **a uno** (*fig*) to dodge someone. **(b)** (*Mus*) grace note(s), trill.

quien *rel pron* **(a)** (*subject*) who; (*acc*) whom; **la señorita con** — **hablaba** the young lady to whom I was talking, the young lady I was talking to; **las personas con —es estabas** the people you were with; **esta señora es a** — **tienes que dar el recado** this is the lady to whom you are to give the message.

(b) (*indefinite*) — **dice eso es tonto** whoever says

that is a fool; — **lo sepa, que lo diga** *or* **que lo diga** — **lo sepa** let whoever knows it speak up about it; — **habla más trabaja menos** he who talks most works least; **contestó como** — **no quería** he answered as if he was reluctant to.

(c) — **más,** — **menos tiene sus problemas** everybody has problems.

quién *interrog pron* (*subject*) who, (*acc*) whom; **¿— es?** who is it?; who's there?; (*Tel*) who's calling?; **"¿Q— es Q—?"** "Who's Who?"; **¿a — lo diste?** to whom did you give it?, who did you give it to?; **¿a quién le toca jugar?** whose turn is it to play?, whose go is it?; **¿con — estabas anoche?** who were you with last night?; **¿de — es la bufanda esa?** whose scarf is that?, who does that scarf belong to?; **¿— de ustedes lo reconoce?** which of you recognizes it?; **no sé — lo dijo primero** I don't know who said it first.

quienquiera *indef pron*, *pl* **quienesquiera** whoever; **le cazaremos** — **que sea** we'll catch him whoever he is.

quietismo *nm* quietism.

quietista *nmf* quietist.

quieto *adj* **(a)** still; motionless; **¡—!** (*to dog*) down boy!; **¡estáte —!** keep still!, stop fidgeting!; behave yourself!; **dejar** — **a uno** to leave someone alone; **estar** — **como un poste** (*or* **una estatua**) to stand stock-still.

(b) *character* calm, staid, placid.

quietud *nf* stillness; quietude; calm.

quijada *nf* jaw, jawbone.

quijotada *nf* quixotic act.

quijote *nm* quixotic person; hopelessly unrealistic person, do-gooder (*fam*); well-meaning busybody; **Don Q—** Don Quixote.

quijotería *nf* **(a)** =**quijotismo.** **(b)** =**quijotada.**

quijotescamente *adv* quixotically.

quijotesco *adj* quixotic.

quijotismo *nm* quixotism.

quilatar [1a] *vt* =**aquilatar.**

quilate *nm* carat.

quilco *nm* (*Chi*) large basket.

quiligua *nf* (*Mex*) large basket.

quilo¹ *nm* (*Anat*) chyle; **sudar el** — (*fam*) to have a tough time; to slave, work like a nigger.

quilo² *nm* kilo, kilogramme.

quilo . . . *alternative spelling of* **kilo** . . .

quilombear [1a] *vi* (*RPl*) to patronize brothels.

quilombera *nf* (*RPl*) prostitute.

quilombo *nm* **(a)** (*Bol, Chi, Per, RPl*) brothel. **(b)** (*Bol, Chi, Per, RPl*) row, set-to (*fam*). **(c)** (*Col, Ec, Ven*) out-of-the-way spot; rustic hut, shack.

quiltrear [1a] *vt* (*Chi*) to annoy.

quiltro *nm* (*Chi*) **(a)** small dog, yapping dog. **(b)** nobody, nonentity.

quilla *nf* (*all senses*) keel; **colocar la** — **de un buque** to lay down a ship; **dar de** — to keel over.

quillango *nm* (*Bol, Chi, RPl*) fur blanket.

quimba *nf* **(a)** (*Col, Ec, Ven*) sandal. **(b)** (*Ec*) grimace. **(c)** (*Col*) —**s** difficulties; debts.

quimbo *nm* (*Ant*) knife, *machete*.

quimera *nf* **(a)** (*Myth*) chimera.

(b) hallucination; fancy, fantastic idea; impossible notion, pipe dream.

(c) unfounded suspicion; **tener la** — **de que** . . . to suspect quite wrongly that . . .

(d) quarrel.

quimérico *adj* fantastic, fanciful; *hope, plan etc* impossible.

quimerista 1 *adj* quarrelsome; rowdy. **2** *nmf* quarrelsome person; rowdy, brawler.

quimerizar [1f] *vi* to indulge in fantasy, indulge in pipe dreams.

química *nf* chemistry.

químico 1 *adj* chemical. **2** *nm* chemist.

quimono *nm* kimono.

quina *nf* quinine, Peruvian bark.

quincalla *nf* hardware, ironmongery.

quincallería *nf* ironmonger's (shop), hardware store (US).

quincallero *nm* ironmonger, hardware dealer (US).

quince 1 *adj* fifteen; (*date*) fifteenth; — **días** (*freq*) fortnight; **dar** — **y raya a uno** to be able to beat someone hollow (**en** at), be more than a match for someone (**en** at).

2 *nm* fifteen.

quinceañero 1 *adj* fifteen-year old, (*loosely*) teenage. **2** *nm*, **quinceañera** *nf* fifteen-year old, (*loosely*) teenager.

quincena *nf* **(a)** fortnight. **(b)** fortnight's imprisonment. **(c)** fortnightly pay.

quincenal *adj* fortnightly.

quinceno *adj* fifteenth.
Quincuagésima *f* Quincuagesima.
quincuagésimo *adj* fiftieth.
quincha *nf* (*SAm*) wall (*or* roof *etc*) made of rushes and mud.
quinchar [1a] *vt* (*SAm*) to build walls (*etc*) of *quincha*.
quincho *nm* (*Arg, Urug*) mud hut; (*Bol, Chi*) mud fence.
quindécimo *adj* fifteenth.
quinfa *nf* (*Col*) sandal.
quingentésimo *adj* five-hundredth.
quingo *nm* (*Col, Per*) twist, turn; zigzag.
quinguear [1a] *vi* (*Ec, Col*) to twist, turn; to zigzag.
quiniela *nf* pools coupon; —s football pool(s).
quinielista *nmf* punter, participant in a football pool.
quinientos *adj* five hundred.
quinina *nf* quinine.
quinqué *nm* (**a**) oil lamp. (**b**) (*fam*) know-how, shrewdness; **tener mucho** — to know what's going on, know what the score is.
quinquenal *adj* quinquennial; **plan** — five-year plan.
quinquenio *nm* quinquennium, five-year period.
quinqui *nm* (*fam*) bandit, gangster.
quinta *nf* (**a**) villa, country house; (*SAm*) estate on the outskirts of a town.
  (**b**) (*Mil*) draft, call-up; **la** — **de 1978** the 1978 call-up, the class called up in 1978; **ser de la** — **de uno** to be the same age as someone; **entrar en** —**s** to reach the call-up age; to be called up.
  (**c**) (*Mus*) fifth.
quintacolumnista *nmf* fifth columnist.
quintada *nf* (*fam*) rag, trick.
quintaescencia *nf* quintessence.
quintal *nm* (*Castile*) measure of weight, = 46 kg; — **métrico** = 100 kg.
quintar [1a] *vt* (*Mil*) to call up, conscript, draft (*US*).
quintería *nf* farmhouse.
quintero *nm* farmer; farmhand, labourer.
quinteto *nm* quintet(te).
quintilla *nf* (*Lit: Hist*) a five-line stanza.
quintillizos *nmpl*, **quintillizas** *nfpl* quintuplets.
quinto 1 *adj* fifth. **2** *nm* (**a**) (*Math*) fifth. (**b**) (*Mil*) conscript, recruit, national serviceman. (**c**) (*fam*) bingo.
quintuplicar [1g] **1** *vt* to quintuple. **2 quintuplicarse** *vr* to quintuple.
quíntuplo 1 *adj* quintuple, fivefold. **2** *nm* quintuple; **X es el** — **de Y** X is five times the size of Y.
quinzavo *adj* fifteenth.
quiñazo *nm* (*SAm*) smash, collision.
quiosco *nm* (*in street*) kiosk, stand, stall; (*in garden*) summerhouse, pavilion; (*in park: also* — **de música**) bandstand; — **de necesidad** public lavatory; — **de periódicos** news stand.
quipe *nm* (*Bol, Ec*) knapsack, bag; (*Per*) bundle, roll.
quiquiriquí *nm* cock-a-doodle-doo.
quirico *nm* (*Ven*) servant; messenger; petty thief.
quirófano *nm* operating theatre.
quiromancia *nf* palmistry.
quiromántico *nm*, **quiromántica** *nf* palmist.
quiropedia *nf* chiropody.
quiropodista *nmf* chiropodist.
quirúrgico *adj* surgical.
quise *etc see* **querer**.
quisicosa *nf* (*fam*) puzzle, conundrum.
quisling ['kizliŋ] *nm*, *pl* **quislings** ['kizliŋ] quisling.
quisquilla *nf* (**a**) trifle, triviality.
  (**b**) slight snag, minor difficulty.
  (**c**) —**s** quibbles, quibbling, hair-splitting; **¡déjate de** —**s!** stop fussing!; don't quibble! **pararse en** —**s** to bicker; to quibble.
  (**d**) (*Zool*) shrimp.
quisquilloso *adj* (**a**) touchy, oversensitive; irritable; pernickety (*fam*), choosy (*fam*). (**b**) quibbling, hair-splitting.
quiste *nm* cyst.
quisto *adj*: **bien** —, **mal** — *see* **bienquisto, malquisto**.
quita *nf* (**a**) release (from a debt); (*SAm*) rebate.
  (**b**) **de** — **y pon** *see* **quitapón**.

quitaesmalte *nm* nail-polish remover.
quitagusto *nm* (*Ec, Per*) intruder, gatecrasher.
quitalodos *nm*, *pl* **quitalodos** boot-scraper.
quitamanchas *nm*, *pl* **quitamanchas** (**a**) cleaning material, stain remover. (**b**) (*person*) dry cleaner; dry-cleaner's (shop).
quitamiedos *nm*, *pl* **quitamiedos** handrail.
quitamotas *nm*, *pl* **quitamotas** (*fam*) bootlicker (*fam*).
quitanieves *nm*, *pl* **quitanieves** snowplough.
quitapelillos *nm*, *pl* **quitapelillos** (*fam*) bootlicker (*fam*).
quitapenas *nm*, *pl* **quitapenas** (*fam*) pistol, rod (*US sl*).
quitapesares *nm*, *pl* **quitapesares** comfort; distraction.
quitapiedras *nm*, *pl* **quitapiedras** (*Rail*) cowcatcher.
quitapón: **pieza** *f* **de** — detachable part, removable part.
quitar [1a] **1** *vt* (**a**) to take away, remove; *clothing etc* to take off; *stain* to remove, get rid of, get out; *pain etc* to relieve, stop, kill; *happiness* to destroy; *life* to take; *part* (*Mech etc*) to remove, take out, take off; *table* to clear; *abuse, difficulty, obstacle* to remove, do away with, put an end to; *time* to take (up); *trouble, worry* to save, prevent; (*Math*) to take away, subtract; *value etc* to reduce; (*pej*) to remove, steal; — **extensión a un campo** to reduce the size of a field; — **importancia a un acontecimiento** to diminish the importance of an event; **no quita nada de su valor** it does not detract at all from its value; **me quita mucho tiempo** it takes up a lot of my time; **le van a** — **ese privilegio** they are going to take that privilege away from him; **le quitaron la cartera en el tren** he had his wallet stolen on the train; **me quitó las ganas de comer** it took away my appetite; **el café me quita el sueño** coffee stops me sleeping; **quitando 3 o 4, van a ir todos** except for 3 or 4 everybody is going; *see* **medio** *etc*.
  (**b**) *blow* to avert, ward off; (*Fencing*) to parry.
  (**c**) — **a uno de hacer algo** to stop someone doing something, prevent someone (from) doing something; **eso no quita para que me ayudes** that doesn't stop you helping me, that is no bar to your helping me.
  2 *vi* (**a**) **¡quita!**, **¡quita de ahí!** get away!
  (**b**) **ni quito ni pongo** I'm not saying one thing or the other; I'm strictly neutral.
  3 quitarse *vr* (**a**) to remove oneself; to withdraw (**de** from); — **de la vista de uno** to remove oneself from someone's sight; **esa mancha de vino no se quita** that wine stain won't come off (*or* come out); **¡quítate de ahí!** come (*or* get) out of there!, off with you!; *see* **medio** *etc*.
  (**b**) — **algo de encima** to get rid of something; to cast something off, shake something off; — **la ropa** to take off one's clothing; — **una jaqueca andando** to walk off a headache.
  (**c**) — **de un vicio** to give up a vice, wean oneself away from a vice; — **del tabaco** to give up smoking; **se me ha quitado el gusto de fumar** I've lost my taste for smoking; **quitémonos de tonterías** let's stop being silly.
quitasol *nm* sunshade, parasol.
quite *nm* (**a**) removal.
  (**b**) (*Fencing*) parry.
  (**c**) dodge, sidestep, swerve; (*Taur*) *manoeuvre whereby bullfighters draw the bull away from an injured colleague*; **estar al** — to be ready to go to someone's aid; **esto no tiene** — there's no help for it.
  (**d**) (*SAm: Sport*) tackle.
quiteño 1 *adj* of Quito. **2** *nm*, **quiteña** *nf* native (*or* inhabitant) of Quito; **los** —**s** the people of Quito.
quitrín *nm* (*Ant, Chi, Guat*) open two-wheeled carriage.
quizá(s) [ki'θa] *adv* perhaps, maybe.
quórum ['korum] *nm*, *pl* **quórums** ['korum] quorum; **constituir** — to constitute (*or* make up) a quorum.

R

rabada *nf* hindquarter, rump.
rabadán *nm* head shepherd.
rabadilla *nf* (*Anat*) coccyx.
rábano *nm* radish; — **picante** horseradish; **¡un —!**
(*fam*) get away!; **no se me da un —,** (**no**) **me importa
un —** I don't care two hoots (*de* about); **tomar el —
por las hojas** to get hold of the wrong end of the
stick, bark up the wrong tree.
rabear [1a] *vi* (*dog*) to wag its tail.
rebelasiano *adj* Rabelaisian.
rabí *nm* (*before name*) rabbi.
rabia *nf* (**a**) (*Med*) rabies.
(**b**) (*fig*) fury, rage, anger; bad feeling; **¡qué —!**
isn't it infuriating!; **me da —** it maddens me, it
infuriates me; **tener — a uno** to have a grudge
against someone, have it in for someone; **el maestro
le tiene —** the teacher has it in for him, the teacher
doesn't like him; **tomar — a** to take a dislike to.
(**c**) **con —** (*SAm*) extremely, terribly (*fam*); **es fea
con —** she's terribly ugly.
rabiadero *nm* (*Col*) annoyance.
rabiar [1b] *vi* (**a**) (*Med*) to have rabies.
(**b**) (*fig*) to suffer terribly, be in great pain; **estaba
rabiando de dolor de muelas** she had raging
toothache.
(**c**) (*fig*) **esto quema** (*or* **pica**) **que rabia** this is hot
enough to burn your mouth; **este cóctel está que
rabia** this cocktail has got a real kick to it.
(**d**) (*fig*) to rage, rave, be furious; — **contra** to
storm at, rave about; **hacer — a uno** to rouse someone to a fury; **las cosas así le hacen —** things like
that make him see red; **está que rabia** he's hopping
mad, he's furious; **¡para que rabies!** so there!; just to
turn you green with envy!
(**e**) (*fig*) — **por algo** to long for, be dying for; —
por — + *infin* to be dying to + *infin*.
(**f**) **me gusta a —** I'm terribly fond of it (*fam*).
rabiasca *nf* (*Cu, PR*) fit of temper.
rabieta *nf* (*fam*) fit of temper; paddy (*fam*), pet,
tantrum (*fam*); **tomarse una —** to get cross, fly into
a rage.
rabietas *nmf, pl* **rabietas** (*fam*) touchy sort, bad-
tempered person.
rabillo *nm* (**a**) (*Anat*) small tail.
(**b**) (*Bot*) leaf stalk.
(**c**) tip; corner; thin part; thin strip of material;
mirar con el — del ojo to look out of the corner of
one's eye.
rabimocho *adj* (*Col, Mex, Per, PR*) cut-tailed.
rabina *nf* rapeseed.
rabínico *adj* rabbinical.
rabino *nm* rabbi; **gran —** chief rabbi.
rabión *nm* (*also* **—es**) rapids.
rabiosamente *adv* (*fig*) furiously; terribly, violently;
rabidly.
rabioso *adj* (**a**) (*Med*) rabid, suffering from rabies;
perro — (*fig*) mad dog.
(**b**) (*fig*) furious; *pain* terrible, raging, violent;
supporter etc rabid; *taste* hot; **poner — a uno** to
enrage someone.
rabo *nm* (**a**) (*Anat*) tail; **con el — entre las piernas**
crestfallen, dejected; **queda el — por desollar** we've
still got the most difficult part to do.
(**b**) (*fig*) tail, train, hanging part; =**rabillo** (**b**) *and*
(**c**).
rabón *adj* (**a**) short-tailed; bobtailed; tailless.
(**b**) (*SAm*) short, small.
(**c**) (*Chi*) stark naked; half-naked.
(**d**) (*Arg, Ven*) *knife* damaged.
(**e**) (*Mex*) wretched.
rabona *nf* (**a**) **hacer —** to play truant. (**b**) (*SAm*)
camp follower.
rabonear [1a] *vi* (*SAm*) to play truant.
rabosear [1a] *vt* to mess up, rumple, crumple.

rabotada *nf* rude remark; coarse expression.
rabudo *adj* long-tailed.
racanear [1a] *vi* (*fam*) to slack; to swing the lead
(*fam*).
racaneo *nm* (*fam*) slackness, idleness.
rácano *nm* (*fam*) (**a**) slacker, idler; **hacer el —** to
slack; to swing the lead (*fam*). (**b**) (*Aut*) grid, old car.
racial *adj* racial, race (*attr*); **odio —** race hatred.
racimo *nm* bunch, cluster; (*Bot*) raceme.
raciocinación *nf* ratiocination.
raciocinar [1a] *vi* to reason.
raciocinio *nm* (**a**) (*faculty*) reason. (**b**) (*act*) reasoning.
ración *nf* (**a**) ratio; portion, helping; **—es** (*Mil*)
rations; — **de hambre** starvation ration; — **de
reserva** emergency ration; iron ration.
(**b**) (*Eccl*) prebend.
racional *adj* (**a**) (*Math, Philos etc*) rational. (**b**)
rational, reasonable, sensible.
racionalidad *nf* rationality.
racionalismo *nm* rationalism.
racionalista **1** *adj* rationalist. **2** *nmf* rationalist.
racionalización *nf* rationalization.
racionalizar [1f] *vt* to rationalize.
racionalmente *adv* rationally, reasonably, sensibly.
racionamiento *nm* rationing.
racionar [1a] *vt* (**a**) to ratio; **estar racionado** to be
rationed, be on the ration. (**b**) to ration out, share
out.
racionero *nm* (*Eccl*) prebendary.
racionista *nmf* (**a**) person living on an allowance. (**b**)
(*Theat*) player of bit parts; ham (*sl*), third-rate actor
(*or* actress).
racismo *nm* racialism, racism.
racista **1** *adj* racial, racialist. **2** *nmf* racialist.
racha *nf* (**a**) (*Meteorol*) gust of wind; squall.
(**b**) (*fig*) string, series; **buena —** piece of luck,
stroke of luck, lucky break; **mala —** piece of bad
luck; unlucky spell, spell when everything goes
wrong; **a —s** by fits and starts.
racheado *adj* *wind* gusty, squally.
rada *nf* (*Naut*) roads, roadstead; natural bay.
radar *nm* radar.
radiación *nf* (**a**) radiation. (**b**) broadcasting.
radiactividad *nf* radioactivity.
radiactivo *adj* radioactive.
radiado *adj* (**a**) (*Bot etc*) radiate. (**b**) radio (*attr*),
broadcast; **en una interviú radiada** in a radio
interview.
radiador *nm* radiator.
radial *adj* (**a**) (*Mech etc*) radial. (**b**) (*SAm*) radio
(*attr*), broadcasting (*attr*).
radiante *adj* (*Phys and fig*) radiant; **estaba —** she was
radiant (*de* with).
radiar[1] [1b] *vt* (**a**) (*Phys etc*) to radiate; to irradiate.
(**b**) to broadcast. (**c**) (*Med*) to treat with X-rays.
radiar[2] [1b] *vt* (*SAm*) to delete, cross off (a list); to
expel; to remove.
radical **1** *adj* radical. **2** *nm* (**a**) (*Gram, Math*) root;
square-root sign. (**b**) (*Pol*) radical.
radicalismo *nm* radicalism.
radicalmente *adv* radically.
radicar [1g] **1** *vi* (**a**) (*Bot and fig*) to take root.
(**b**) to be, be situated, lie.
(**c**) (*of difficulty etc*) — **en** to lie in.
2 radicarse *vr* to establish oneself, put down one's
roots (*en* in).
radícula *nf* (*Bot*) radicle.
radio[1] *nm* (**a**) (*Math*) radius; — **de acción** sphere of
jurisdiction, extent of one's authority; (*Aer*) range;
un avión de largo — de acción a long-range aircraft; **en un — de 10 km alrededor de la ciudad**
within a radius of 10 km round the city.
(**b**) (*of wheel*) spoke.
(**c**) (*Anat*) radius.

(d) (*Chem*) radium.
(e) (*fam*) wireless message.
(f) (*SAm*) =**radio**[2].
radio[2] *nf* **(a)** (*in general*) radio, wireless; broadcasting; **R— Eslobodia** Radio Slobodia; **por —** by radio, on the radio, over the radio; **hablar por —** to talk on the radio.
(b) radio (set), wireless (set).
radio ... radio ...
radioactivo *adj* =**radiactivo**.
radioastronomía *nf* radio astronomy.
radiobiología *nf* radiobiology.
radiocaptar [1a] *vt* station to monitor.
radiodifusión *nf* broadcasting.
radiodifusora *nf* (*SAm*) radio station, transmitter.
radiodifusorio *adj* broadcasting (*attr*).
radioemisora *nf* radio station, transmitter.
radioescucha *nmf* listener.
radioexperimentador *nm* radio fan, ham (*sl*).
radiofaro *nm* radio beacon, wireless beam.
radiofonía *nf* radio, wireless.
radiofónico *adj* radio (*attr*).
radiofonógrafo *nm* (*SAm*) radiogram.
radiogoniómetro *nm* direction finder.
radiografía *nf* **(a)** (*in general*) radiography, X-ray photography. **(b)** (*una —*) radiograph, X-ray photograph (*or picture*).
radiografiar [1c] *vt* **(a)** (*Med*) to X-ray. **(b)** to radio, send by radio.
radiográfico *adj* X-ray (*attr*).
radiograma *nm* wireless message.
radiogramola *nf* radiogram; **— tragamonedas, — tragaperras** jukebox.
radioisótopo *nm* radioisotope.
radiología *nf* radiology.
radiólogo *nm* radiologist.
radiooperador *nm* (*SAm*) radio operator, wireless operator.
radiorreceptor *nm* radio (set), wireless (set), receiver; **— de contrastación** monitor set.
radioscopia *nf* radioscopy.
radiotelefonía *nf* radiotelephony.
radioteléfono *nm* radiotelephone.
radiotelegrafía *nf* radiotelegraphy, wireless (telegraphy).
radiotelegrafista *nm* radio operator, wireless operator.
radiotelescopio *nm* radiotelescope.
radioterapia *nf* radiotherapy.
radioyente *nmf* listener.
raedera *nf* scraper.
raedura *nf* **(a)** scrape, scraping; (*Med*) abrasion, graze. **(b)** —**s** scrapings, filings.
raer [2z] **1** *vt* **(a)** to scrape; to scrape off; to erase; (*Med*) to abrade, graze; to chafe; *cloth etc* to fray.
(b) contents *of vessel* to level off, level with the brim.
2 raerse *vr* to chafe; (*cloth*) to fray.
Rafael *m* Raphael.
ráfaga *nf* **(a)** (*Meteorol*) gust, squall; sudden blast.
(b) (*of shots*) burst.
(c) (*of light, intuition*) flash.
(d) (*Arg, Per*) run of luck; **estar de** (*or* **en**) **—** to have a spell of bad luck.
rafañoso *adj* (*Arg*) dirty; coarse, common.
rafia *nf* raffia.
raglán *nm* raglan.
raicear [1a] *vi* (*CAm, Ven*) to take root.
raicero *nm* (*SAm*) mass of roots, root system.
raid [raid] *nm, pl* **raids** [raid] (*angl, gall*) **(a)** (*Mil*) raid, attack; expedition.
(b) police raid; criminal raid.
(c) attempt, endeavour; enterprise; heroic undertaking.
(d) endurance test; (*Aer*) long-distance flight; (*Aut*) rally drive; transcontinental expedition by car.
(e) (*Mex: Aut*) lift.
raído *adj* **(a)** *cloth* frayed, threadbare; *garment, person* shabby. **(b)** (*fig*) shameless.
raigambre *nf* (*often m*) **(a)** (*Bot*) mass of roots; root system.
(b) (*fig*) tradition; antecedents, history; **una familia de fuerte — local** a family with deep roots in the area; **tienen — liberal** they have a liberal tradition.
raigón *nm* (*Bot*) thick root, stump; (*Anat*) root, stump.
rail, raíl *nm* (*angl*) rail.
Raimundo *m* Raymond.
raíz *nf* **(a)** (*Bot etc*) root; **arrancar algo de —** to root something out completely, destroy something root

and branch; **cortar un peligro de —** to nip a danger in the bud; **echar raíces** to take root (*algo fig*).
(b) (*Math*) root; **— cuadrada** square root; **— cúbica** cube root.
(c) root.
(d) (*fig*) root, origin; **a — de** immediately after, immediately following; as a result of.
raja *nf* **(a)** slit, split; crack; gash, chink.
(b) sliver, splinter, thin piece; (*of lemon etc*) slice.
(c) (*fam*) **sacar —** to get a rake-off (*fam*), get a share.
(d) (*PR*) **tener —** to have Negro blood.
rajá *nm* rajah.
rajada *nf* **(a)** (*Arg*) flight, hasty exit. **(b)** (*Mex*) cowardly act; backing down, going back on one's word.
rajador *adj* (*Arg*) fast.
rajadura *nf* =**raja (a)** *and* **(b)**.
rajamacana *nm* (*Ven*) **(a)** hard work, drudgery; tough job. **(b)** tough character; stubborn person. **(c)** expert. **(d) a —** =**a rajatabla**.
rajante *adj* (*Arg*) peremptory, sharp.
rajar [1a] **1** *vt* **(a)** to split, crack; to cleave; to slit; *fruit etc* to slice; *log etc* to chop (up), split.
(b) (*SAm*) to slander, run down.
(c) (*SAm: Univ*) to plough (*sl*).
(d) (*Col, Per, PR*) to crush, defeat; to ruin; to annoy.
(e) (*Arg*) *worker* to fire (*fam*).
2 *vi* **(a)** (*fam*) to chatter, talk a lot; to brag.
(b) (*SAm*) to rush off, rush out.
3 rajarse *vr* **(a)** to split, crack.
(b) (*esp SAm*) to back out (*de of*), quit; to get cold feet; to go back on one's word; **¡me rajé!** that's enough for me!, I'm quitting!
(c) (*Ant, Bol, Arg*) to run away; to rush off; **salir rajando** to go off at top speed.
(d) (*Arg, Col*) to be mistaken.
(e) (*PR*) to get drunk.
(f) (*CAm, Chi, Per, PR*) **— con** to give generously, dish out lavishly; to make a splurge with (*fam*).
rajatabla: a — ** *adv* strictly, rigorously; exactly; without fear or favour; at all costs; regardless (of the consequences); **cumplir las órdenes a — to carry out one's orders to the letter; **pagar** (*etc*) **a —** (*SAm*) to pay (*etc*) on the dot, pay (*etc*) promptly.
rajatablas *nm, pl* **rajatablas** (*Col, Ven*) ticking-off.
raje *nm* (*Arg*) firing (*fam*), sacking (*fam*); **dar el — a uno** to fire someone (*fam*); **tomar(se) el —** to flee; to rush off.
rajo *nm* (*SAm*) tear, rip.
rajón 1 *adj* **(a)** (*Andalusia, Ant, CAm, Chi, Per*) generous, lavish, free-spending.
(b) (*Andalusia, CAm, Mex*) easily scared, cowardly; readily disheartened; (*Mex*) unreliable.
2 *nm* **(a)** (*Ant, Col, Guat, Urug*) tear, rip.
(b) (*Andalusia, CAm, Mex*) quitter.
(c) (*CAm, Mex*) bully; braggart.
rajonada *nf* (*CAm*) **(a)** boast, brag; bragging. **(b)** ostentation.
rajuñar [1a] *vt* (*Arg*) =**rasguñar**.
rala *nf* (*Col*) birdlime.
rale *nm* (*Chi*) wooden bowl, wooden trough.
ralea *nf* (*pej*) kind, sort, breed; **de esa —** of that ilk; **de baja —** evil, wicked; wretched.
ralear [1a] *vi* to become thin, become sparse; to thin out; to become less dense.
ralenti *nm* (*gall*) **(a)** (*Cine*) slow motion; **al —** in slow motion. **(b)** (*Aut*) neutral; **estar al —** to be ticking over.
ralo *adj* *hair etc* thin, sparse; *cloth* loosely woven; *woodland* open; (*Phys*) rare; (*Arg*) unsubstantial, lacking body.
rallado *adj* *cheese etc* grated.
rallador *nm* grater.
rallar [1a] *vt* **(a)** (*Cook*) to grate. **(b)** (*fam*) to grate on; to annoy, needle (*fam*). **(c)** (*Cu*) to goad.
rallo *nm* (*Cook*) grater; (*Tech*) file, rasp.
rallye ['rali] *nm* (*angl, gall: Aut*) rally.
rallye-paper *nm* (*angl, gall*) paper chase.
rama *nf* (*all senses*) branch; **en —** cotton, silk raw; *book* unbound; **— de olivo** olive branch; **andarse por las —s** to beat about the bush; to get bogged down in details; **poner algo en la última —** to leave something till last; to consider something unimportant.
ramada *nf* **(a)** branches, foliage. **(b)** (*SAm*) shed, hut; shelter (*or covering etc*) made of branches.
ramadán *nm* Ramadan.
ramaje *nm* branches, foliage.
ramal *nm* **(a)** strand (of a rope); halter. **(b)** (*fig*) offshoot; (*Aut*) branch, branch road; (*Rail*) branch line.

ramalazo nm (a) lash; weal, bruise, mark left by a lash.
(b) (fig) stab of pain, sharp pain; fit of depression, sudden grief; blow; fit of madness.
(c) (fig) gust of wind; lash of rain.
(d) (fig: Pol etc) backlash, reaction; outbreak of violence.
ramazón nf (Arg, CAm, Mex) antler, horns.
rambla nf (a) watercourse; stream, torrent. (b) avenue.
ramera nf whore.
ramificación nf ramification.
ramificarse [1g] vr to ramify, divide, branch (out).
ramillete nm (a) bouquet, bunch of flowers, posy; (worn on dress) corsage; (Bot) cluster. (b) (fig) collection; choice bunch, select group.
ramita nf twig, spring; (of flowers) spray.
ramo nm (a) (of tree) branch (also fig).
(b) (fig) branch; (Comm) section, department; (of goods) line.
(c) (Med; also —s) touch; **tiene —s de loco** he has a streak of madness.
ramojo nm brushwood.
Ramón m Raymond.
ramonear [1a] vt (a) trees to lop, lop the twigs of. (b) (of sheep) to browse on, nibble.
rampa nf ramp, incline; **— de lanzamiento** launching ramp.
ramplón adj common, coarse, uncouth.
ramplonería nf commonness, coarseness, uncouthness.
rana nf frog; **— toro** bullfrog; **no es —** (fig) he's no fool, he knows his stuff; **pero salió —** (fam) but he turned out badly, but he was a big disappointment; **cuando las —s críen pelo** when pigs learn to fly; **¡hasta que las —s críen pelo!** if I never see you again it'll be too soon!
rancidez nf, **ranciedad** nf (a) age, mellowness; (pej) rankness, rancidness; mustiness. (b) (fig) great age, antiquity; (pej) antiquatedness.
rancio 1 adj (a) wine old, mellow; food (pej) rank, rancid, stale; musty.
(b) (fig) lineage ancient; tradition etc very ancient, time-honoured; (pej) antiquated, old-fashioned.
2 nm =**rancidez.**
rancotán adv (Col, Pan, PR, Ven) in cash.
ranchada nf (a) (CAm) canoe. (b) (Arg, Par) shed, improvised hut.
ranchar [1a] vi (a) (Arg, Mex) to wander from farm to farm. (b) (Col, Mex, Ven) to spend the night, make a camp; to settle.
ranchear [1a] 1 vt (Cu, Mex, PR) to loot, pillage; to rob. 2 vi (SAm) (a) to build a camp, make a settlement. (b) (Arg, Per) to have a meal.
ranchería nf (a) (RPl) =**rancherío.** (b) (Per) labourers' quarters (on an estate). (c) (Ven) poor country inn.
rancherío nm (SAm) settlement.
ranchero nm 1 adj (Mex) uncouth. 2 (a) (SAm) rancher, farmer. (b) mess cook.
rancho nm (a) hut, thatched hut; (Col, Per) shed; (Per) country house, villa.
(b) (Naut) crew's quarters.
(c) (SAm) ranch, large farm; (Mex) small farm.
(d) (of gipsies etc) camp, settlement; (Mex) village.
(e) (Mil etc) mess, communal meal; (pej) bad food, grub; **asentar el —** to prepare a meal; (fig) to get things organized, settle in; **hacer —** to make room; **hacer el —** to have a meal; **hacer — aparte** to set up on one's own, go one's own way.
(f) (RPl) straw hat.
randa nm (fam) pickpocket, petty thief; suspicious character, prowler.
randevú nm (RPl: gall) rendez-vous.
randevuses nmpl (RPl: gall) courtesies.
ranfaña nm (Chi, Per) shabby person.
ranfañoso nm (Arg) shabby person; mean individual; (Comm) crook.
ranfla nf (Col, Mex) ramp, incline.
ranga nf (Col, Ec) nag, old horse.
rango[1] nm (a) rank; standing, status, class; **de — of** high standing, of some status. (b) (SAm) luxury; pomp, splendour.
rango[2] nm (Col) =**ranga.**
rangosidad nf (Chi) generosity.
rangoso adj (CAm, Cu, Chi) generous.
Rangún Rangoon.
rantifuso adj (Arg) dirty, grubby; common; suspicious.
ranúnculo nm ranunculus, (esp) buttercup.
ranura nf groove; slot.

rapacidad nf rapacity, greed.
rapadura nf (a) shave, shaving; close haircut. (b) (SAm) brown sugar; home-made sweet.
rapapolvo nm ticking-off; **echar un — a uno** to give someone a ticking-off, tick someone off.
rapar [1a] vt (a) to shave; to crop, cut very close. (b) (fam) to pinch (fam).
rapaz[1] 1 adj rapacious, greedy; thieving; (Zool) predatory; (Orn) raptorial, of prey. 2 nf (Zool) predatory animal; (Orn) bird of prey.
rapaz[2] nm lad, youngster; kid; **sí, —** yes, my lad.
rapaza nf lass, girl, youngster.
rape nm (a) quick shave, rough haircut; **al — cut** close. (b) (fam) ticking-off.
rapé nm snuff.
rápida nf (Mex) chute.
rápidamente adv rapidly, fast, quickly, swiftly.
rapidez nf rapidity, speed; speediness, swiftness.
rápido 1 adj (a) rapid, fast, quick, swift; train fast, express.
(b) (Col, Chi, Ven) field open; country flat, monotonous.
(c) (Ven) weather clear.
2 adv (fam) quickly; **¡y —, eh?** and make it snappy!
3 nm (a) (Rail) express.
(b) (Col, Chi, Ven) open field, bare field.
(c) **—s** rapids.
rapiña nf robbery (with violence); see **ave.**
rapiñar [1a] vt to steal.
raposa nf fox (also fig), vixen.
raposera nf foxhole.
raposero adj: **perro —** foxhound.
raposo nm (a) fox, dog fox. (b) (Ec, PR) urchin.
rapsodia nf rhapsody.
rapsódico adj rhapsodic.
raptar [1a] vt to kidnap, abduct; to carry off.
rapto nm (a) kidnapping, abduction; carrying-off.
(b) (fig) sudden impulse; **en un — de celos** in a sudden fit of jealousy. (c) (fig) ecstasy, rapture.
raptor nm kidnapper.
raque[1] nm beachcombing.
raque[2] nm (Cu) bargain.
raquear[1] [1a] vi to go beachcombing.
raquear[2] [1a] vt (Cu) to rob, hold up.
Raquel f Rachel.
raquero nm beachcomber.
raqueta nf racquet; **— de nieve** snowshoe.
raquetazo nm (SAm) shot, hit, stroke.
raquítico adj (a) (Med) rachitic; tree etc weak, stunted. (b) (fig) small, inadequate, miserly.
raquitis nf, **raquitismo** nm rickets.
raramente adv rarely, seldom.
rarefacción nf rarefaction.
rareza nf (a) (quality) rarity, rareness, scarcity.
(b) (object) rarity.
(c) (fig) oddity, peculiarity; eccentricity; **tiene alguna —** there's something odd about him; **tiene sus —s** he has his peculiarities, he has his little ways.
raridad nf rarity.
rarificar [1g] vt to rarefy.
rarifico adj (Chi) =**raro (b).**
raro adj (a) rare, scarce, uncommon; **son —s los que saben hacerlo** very few people know how to do it; **con alguna rara excepción** with rare exceptions.
(b) odd, peculiar, strange; eccentric; notable, remarkable; **de rara perfección** of rare perfection, of remarkable perfection; **es — que . . .** it is odd that . . ., it is strange that . . .; **¡qué —!** how (very) odd!; **¡(qué) cosa más rara!** how strange!, most odd!; **es un hombre muy —** he's a very odd man.
(c) (Phys) rare, rarefied.
ras[1] nm leveleness, evenness; **— con —** level, on a level; flush; **a — de** level with; flush with; **volar a — de tierra** to fly (almost) at ground level.
ras[2] interj snap!
rasar [1a] 1 vt (a) contents to level (with the rim).
(b) to skim, graze; **la bala pasó rasando su sombrero** the bullet grazed his hat.
(c) =**arrasar.**
2 **rasarse** vr (sky) to clear.
rascacielos nm, pl **rascacielos** skyscraper.
rascadera nf scraper.
rascado adj (a) (SAm) drunk. (b) (CAm) feather-brained.
rascador nm (a) scraper; file, rasp. (b) hairpin.
rascaespalda nf backscratcher.
rascamoño nm (a) hairpin. (b) (Bot) zinnia.
rascar [1g] 1 vt (a) to scrape, rasp; to scrape off; to scratch.
(b) (Mus: hum) to scrape, scratch away.
2 vi (Chi) to itch.

3 rascarse *vr* (**a**) to scratch, scratch oneself.
(**b**) (*SAm*) to get drunk.
(**c**) — **juntos** (*Arg, Guat*) to band together (for a criminal purpose); — **la barriga**, — **la panza** (*Mex, RPl*) to take it easy; **no** — **con uno** (*Col*) not to hit it off with someone.

rascatripas *nm, pl* **rascatripas** (*fam*) fiddler, third-rate violinist.

rascón[1] *adj* (**a**) sharp, sour. (**b**) (*Mex*) quarrelsome.

rascón[2] *nm* (*Orn*) water rail.

rascuache *adj* (*Guat, Mex*) poor, penniless; (*Mex*) wretched; ridiculous, in bad taste; worthless; coarse, vulgar.

rasete *nm* satinet(te).

rasgado *adj* (**a**) *window* wide; *eyes* wide, large; almond-shaped; *mouth* wide, big. (**b**) (*SAm*) outspoken. (**c**) (*Col*) generous.

rasgadura *nf* tear, rip, slash.

rasgar [1h] *vt* (**a**) to tear, rip, slash; *paper* to tear up, tear to pieces. (**b**) =**rasguear**.

rasgo *nm* (**a**) (*with pen*) stroke, flourish; adornment; dash; —**s** characteristics (*of one's handwriting*); **a grandes** —**s** (*fig*) with broad strokes, in outline.
(**b**) —**s** (*Anat*) features; **de** —**s enérgicos** of energetic appearance, with an energetic look.
(**c**) (*fig*) characteristic, feature, trait; —**s característicos** typical features; —**s distintivos** distinctive features.
(**d**) generous deed; noble gesture; — **de ingenio** flash of wit; stroke of genius.
(**e**) (*Chi*) irrigation channel.
(**f**) (*Chi*) plot of land); piece, portion.

rasgón *nm* tear, rent.

rasguear [1a] *vt* (**a**) (*Mus*) to strum. (**b**) to write with a flourish; (*fig*) to write.

rasguñadura *nf* (*SAm*) scratch.

rasguñar [1a] *vt* (**a**) to scratch. (**b**) (*Art*) to sketch, draw in outline.

rasguño *nm* (**a**) scratch; **salir sin un** — to come out of it without a scratch. (**b**) sketch, outline drawing.

rasmillar [1a] *vt* (*Chi*) to scratch.

rasmillón *nm* (*Chi*) scratch.

raso 1 *adj* (**a**) flat, level; clear, bare, open; smooth; *seat* backless.
(**b**) *sky* clear; **está** — the sky is clear, the weather is clear.
(**c**) level (with the brim); **una cucharada rasa** a level teaspoonful.
(**d**) *ball, flight etc* very low, almost at ground level.
(**e**) **soldado** — private.
2 *adv*: **tirar** — (*Sport*) to shoot low.
3 *nm* (**a**) (*Sew*) satin.
(**b**) flat country; open country; **al** — in the open.

raspa *nf* (**a**) (*Bot: of corn*) beard; (*of grape*) stalk.
(**b**) (*Fish*) fishbone, (*esp*) backbone.
(**c**) (*fam*) sharp-tongued woman.
(**d**) (*SAm*) scolding; dressing-down.
(**e**) (*Ant, Mex*) brown sugar.
(**f**) (*RPl*) scolding.

raspada *nf* (*Mex, PR*) scolding; dressing-down.

raspado *adj* (*CR, Ven*) shameless.

raspador *nm* scraper, rasp.

raspadura *nf* (**a**) scrape, scraping, rasping. (**b**) —**s** scrapings; filings. (**c**) scratch, mark; erasure. (**d**) (*SAm*) brown sugar.

raspante *adj wine* sharp, rough.

raspar [1a] **1** *vt* (**a**) to scrape; to rasp, file; to smooth (down); *paint etc* to scrape off, remove by scraping; *surface* to scratch; *skin* to chafe; to graze; *word* to erase, scratch out.
(**b**) (*fig*) to skim, graze; to scrape past.
(**c**) **este vino raspa la boca** this wine is rough on the mouth, this wine takes the skin off your mouth.
(**d**) (*fam*) to pinch (*fam*).
(**e**) (*Ven*) to kill.
(**f**) (*Mex, PR*) to scold; to dress down.
(**g**) (*Mex*) to say unkind things to, make wounding remarks to.
2 *vi* (**a**) (*of hands*) to be rough.
(**b**) (*of wine*) to be sharp, have a rough taste.
(**c**) (*Ven*) to leave, go off; to die.

raspear [1a] **1** *vt* (*Chi, Ec*) to tick off. **2** *vi* (*of pen*) to scratch.

raspón *nm* (**a**) scratch, graze; (*SAm*) abrasion; bruise.
(**b**) (*Col, Chi, Hond, Mex*) scolding; ticking-off.
(**c**) (*Mex*) cutting remark.
(**d**) (*Col*) straw hat.

rasponear [1a] *vt* (*Col*) to scold; to tick off.

rasposo *adj* (**a**) sharp-tasting, rough. (**b**) (*Mex*) joking, teasing. (**c**) (*Arg*) stingy.

rasqueta *nf* (*SAm*) scraper, rasp; currycomb.

rasquetear [1a] *vt* (*SAm*) *horse* to brush down; (*Arg*) to scrape.

rasquiña *nf* (*SAm*) itch.

rastacuerismo *nm* (*SAm*) social climbing; rich living; ostentation, display; public lavishness.

rastacuero *nm* (*SAm*) upstart, parvenu, wealthy social climber.

rastra *nf* (**a**) (*Agr*) rake; harrow.
(**b**) =**rastro**; =**ristra**.
(**c**) sledge (*for moving heavy objects*); weighty object, thing being pulled along.
(**d**) (*Fish*) trawl; dredge; **pescar a la** — to trawl.
(**e**) (*Arg, Urug*) thick leather belt, gaucho's belt.
(**f**) (*Mex*) prostitute.
(**g**) (*fig*) unpleasant consequence, disagreeable result; punishment; deserts.
(**h**) **a** —**s** by dragging, by pulling; (*fig*) unwillingly; **avanzar a** —**s** to crawl (along), drag oneself along; **llevar un piano a** —**s** to pull a piano along; **andar a** —**s** (*fig*) to have a difficult time of it, suffer hardships.

rastreador *nm* (**a**) tracker. (**b**) (*Naut: also* **barco** —) trawler; — **de minas** minesweeper.

rastrear [1a] **1** *vt* (**a**) to track, trail, follow the trail of; *satellite* to track; to track down, trace, run to ground.
(**b**) to dredge (up), drag (up); to trawl; *mines* to sweep.
2 *vi* (**a**) (*Agr*) to rake, harrow.
(**b**) (*Fish*) to trawl.
(**c**) (*Aer*) to skim the ground; to fly low, hedgehop.

rastreo *nm* (**a**) dredging, dragging; trawling. (**b**) (*of satellite*) tracking.

rastrerismo *nm* (*SAm*) toadyism, bootlicking (*fam*).

rastrero *adj* (**a**) (*Zool*) creeping, crawling; (*Bot*) creeping.
(**b**) *dress etc* trailing, hanging close to the ground; (*Aer*) *flight* very low.
(**c**) (*fig*) *conduct* mean, despicable; *method* low; *apology* abject, humble; *person* cringing; soapy, bootlicking (*fam*), fawning.

rastrillada *nf* (*RPl*) track, trail.

rastrillar [1a] **1** *vt* (**a**) (*Agr*) to rake; to rake up, rake together; to rake smooth.
(**b**) *flax etc* to dress.
(**c**) (*SAm*) *weapon* to fire; *match* to strike.
(**d**) (*CR, Mex*) *feet* to drag.
2 *vi* (**a**) (*Col, Cu, RPl*) to miss (with a shot).
(**b**) (*Chi*) to shoplift, steal from shops.

rastrillazo *nm* (*CAm*) light sleep; light meal, snack.

rastrillero *nm*, **rastrillera** *nf* (*Chi*) shoplifter.

rastrillo *nm* (**a**) (*Agr etc*) rake.
(**b**) (*Tech*) hackle, flax comb.
(**c**) (*of key*) ward.
(**d**) (*Mil*) portcullis; (*Archit etc*) spiked gate.
(**e**) (*Rail*) — **delantero** cowcatcher.
(**f**) (*Col*) barter; deal.

rastro *nm* (**a**) (*Agr etc*) rake; harrow.
(**b**) track, trail; mark on the ground; scent; (*of rocket etc*) track, course; (*of storm*) path; **perder el** — to lose the scent; **seguir el** — **de uno** to follow someone's trail.
(**c**) (*fig*) trace, sign; **desaparecer sin dejar** — to vanish without trace; **no quedaba ni** — **de ello** not a trace of it was to be seen.
(**d**) slaughterhouse; **el R**— secondhand market in Madrid.

rastrojear [1a] *vi* (*Col, Chi, Guat, Mex*) to glean; (*of animals*) to feed in the stubble.

rastrojera *nf* stubble field.

rastrojero *nm* (**a**) (*Chi, Mex*) stubble field. (**b**) (*Arg*) jeep. (**c**) (*Mex*) maize plant, corn plant (*US*) (*used as fodder*).

rastrojo *nm* (**a**) stubble. (**b**) —**s** (*SAm*) waste, remains, left-overs.

rasura *nf* (**a**) flatness, levelness; smoothness. (**b**) shave, shaving; scrape, scraping. (**c**) —**s** scrapings; filings.

rasurado *nm* shave.

rasurador *nm*, **rasuradora** *nf* (electric) shaver, electric razor.

rasurar [1a] **1** *vt* (**a**) to shave. (**b**) (*Tech*) to scrape. **2 rasurarse** *vr* to shave.

rata 1 *nf* rat. **2** *nm* (*fam*) sneak thief.

rataplán *nm* drumbeat, rub-a-dub.

ratear[1] [1a] **1** *vt* to steal, pilfer; to filch. **2** *vi* to crawl, creep (along).

ratear[2] [1a] *vt* (**a**) to share out. (**b**) to reduce proportionately.

ratera *nf* (*Mex*) rattrap.

ratería nf (a) petty larceny, small-time thieving, pilfering. (b) (una —) theft. (c) (quality) crookedness, dishonesty.

raterismo nm (SAm) art of thieving; tendency to thievishness.

ratero 1 adj thievish, light-fingered. **2** nm pickpocket, sneak thief, small-time thief.

raticida nm (SAm) rat poison.

ratificación nf ratification.

ratificar [1g] vt to ratify.

Ratisbona Regensburg, Ratisbon.

rato nm (short) time, while; spell, period; **un —** (as adv) a while, a time; **un buen —, largo —** a long time, a good while; **—s libres, —s de ocio** leisure, spare time, free time; **a —s** at times, from time to time; **a —s perdidos** at (or in) odd moments; **al poco —** shortly after; **¡hasta cada —!** (SAm), **¡hasta otro —!** so long!; **matar el —, pasar el —** to kill time, pass the time, while away the time; **pasar un buen —** to have a good time; **pasar un mal —** to have a bad time of it, have a rough time; **dar malos —s a uno** to give someone a hard time of it; to cause someone a lot of worry; **hay para —** there's still a long way to go; **tenemos para —** we've still a lot to do, we're still far from finished.

ratón nm (a) mouse; **— de archivo, — de biblioteca** bookworm; **— almizclero** muskrat; **mandar a uno a capar —es** (fam) to tell someone to go to blazes. (b) (Ven) squib, cracker. (c) (Ven) hangover. (d) (fam) ball of fluff.

ratonar [1a] vt to gnaw, nibble.

ratonera nf (a) mousetrap. (b) mousehole. (c) (Arg, Chi, Per) hovel, slum; (PR, Ven) poky little shop.

ratonero nm buzzard.

raudal nm (a) torrent, flood. (b) (fig) plenty, abundance; great quantity; **a —es** in abundance, in great numbers; **entrar a —es** to pour in, come flooding in.

raudo adj swift; rushing, impetuous.

raya[1] nf (a) line; streak; (on stone etc) scratch, mark; (on hand) line; (on cloth, pattern) stripe, pinstripe; **— de puntos** dotted line; **— en negro** black line; **a —s** striped.
(b) (in hair) parting; (in trousers) crease; **hacerse la —** to part one's hair.
(c) line, boundary, limit; (Sport) line, mark; **hacer —** to mark off (also fig); **pasar de la —** to overstep the mark, go too far; **poner a —** to check, hold back; **tener a —** to keep off, keep at bay, keep in check, control.
(d) (Typ) line, dash; (Tel) dash.
(e) (Mex) pay, wages.

raya[2] nf (Fish) ray, skate.

rayado 1 adj paper ruled; cheque crossed; cloth, pattern striped. **2** nm ruling, ruled lines; crossing; stripes, striped pattern; (Tech) rifling.

rayador nm (a) (Mex) paymaster, accountant. (b) (Chi) umpire. (c) (RPl) =**rallador**.

rayano adj (a) adjacent, contiguous; borderline. (b) **— en** bordering on.

rayar [1a] **1** vt (a) paper to line, rule lines on; cheque to cross; stone etc to scratch, score, mark; text to underline, underscore; mistake to cross out; (as pattern) to stripe, streak; (Tech) to rifle.
(b) (Mex) to pay (his wages to).
(c) (RPl) =**rallar**.
(d) (SAm) horse to spur on.
2 vi (a) **— con** to border on, be next to, be adjacent to.
(b) **— en** (fig) to border on, verge on; **esto raya en lo increíble** this verges on the incredible, this is well-nigh incredible.
(c) to scratch, make scratches; **este producto no raya al fregar** this product scrubs without scratching.
(d) **al — el alba** at break of day, at first light.
(e) (Mex) to draw one's wages; to earn.
3 rayarse vr (a) to get scratched.
(b) (Col, Mex) to get all one wants; to get rich.

rayero nm (RPl) umpire, judge.

rayo[1] nm (a) ray, beam; shaft (of light); **— de luna** moonbeam; **— de sol, — solar** sunbeam, ray of sunlight; **—s catódicos** cathode rays; **—s cósmicos** cosmic rays; **—s gamma** gamma rays; **—s infrarrojos** infrared rays; **—s luminosos** light rays; **—s ultravioleta** ultraviolet rays; **—s X** X-rays.
(b) (Tech) spoke.
(c) (Meteorol) lightning, flash of lightning; thunderbolt; **cayó un — en la torre** the tower was struck by lightning; **como un —** like lightning, like a shot; **la noticia cayó como un —** the news was a bombshell; **entrar como un —** to dash in; **salir como un —** to dash out; **pasar como un —** to rush past, flash past; **echar —s y centellas** to rage, fume; **¡que le parta un —!, ¡mal — le parta!** God's curse on him!
(d) (fig) blow, misfortune.
(e) (fig: person) fast worker, speedy and efficient person; **es un —** he's like lightning.

rayo[2] etc see **raer**.

rayón nm rayon.

raza[1] nf race; breed, strain; stock; (Bio) race; **— blanca** white race; **— humana** human race; **— negra** black race; **de —, de pura —** horse thoroughbred; dog etc pedigree.

raza[2] nf (a) crack, slit, fissure; (in cloth) run. (b) ray of light.

razano adj (Col, Ec) thoroughbred.

razón nf (a) (faculty) reason; **hacer que uno entre en —, meter (or poner) a uno en —** to make someone see sense; **meterse en —** to see sense, listen to reason; **perder la —** to lose one's reason, go out of one's mind; **muy puesto en —** very reasonable; **¡eso es ponerse en —!** that's better!, now you're talking!
(b) right, rightness; justice; **con — o sin ella** rightly or wrongly; **le asiste la —** he has right on his side; **cargarse de —** to justify oneself completely; **dar la — a uno** to agree that someone is right; **tener —** to be right; **no tener —** to be wrong; **tener plenamente — en** + infin to be fully justified in + ger; **tratar de quitar a uno la —** to try to put someone in the wrong.
(c) reason, motive, cause; **"—: Princesa 4"** "inquiries to 4 Princesa Street"; "for further details, apply to 4 Princesa Street"; **¿cuál es la —?** what is the reason?; **la — por qué** the reason why; **la — por la que lo hizo** the reason why he did it, the reason for his doing it; **— de estado** reasons of state; **— de más** all the more reason (para + infin to + infin); **— de ser** raison d'être; **con —** with good reason; **¡con —!** naturally!; **en —** de with regard to; **no atiende a —es** he'll not listen to reason, he's not open to argument; **dar — de** to give an account of, report on; to give information about; **nadie me daba — de ella** nobody could tell me anything about her; **dar — de sí** to give an account of oneself; **tener — para** + infin to have cause to + infin.
(d) (Comm) **—** social trade name, firm's name.
(e) (fam) message; **mandar a uno — de que haga algo** to send someone a message telling him to do something.
(f) (Math) ratio, proportion; rate; **a — de 5 a 7** in the ratio of 5 to 7; **a — de 8 por persona** at the rate of 8 per head; **abandonan el país a — de 800 cada año** they are leaving the country at the rate of 800 a year; **en — directa con** in direct ratio to.

razonable adj reasonable.

razonablemente adv reasonably.

razonado adj reasoned; account etc itemized, detailed.

razonamiento nm reasoning.

razonar [1a] **1** vt (a) to reason, argue. (b) problem etc to reason out. (c) account to itemize. **2** vi (a) to reason, argue. (b) to talk (together).

re . . . (a) (prefix) re . . .
(b) (intensifying prefix) very, awfully (fam), terribly (fam), eg **rebueno** very good, jolly good (fam); **reguapa** awfully pretty; **resalada** terribly attractive; **¡rebomba!** how utterly amazing!; **¡rediez!** well I'm damned!

reabastecer [2d] **1** vt (also **— de combustible, — de gasolina**) to refuel. **2 reabastecerse** vr to refuel.

reabastecimiento nm refuelling.

reabrir [3a; ptp **reabierto**] **1** vt to reopen. **2 reabrirse** vr to reopen.

reacción nf (a) reaction (a, ante to; also Med); response (a to); **— en cadena** chain reaction; **la —** **blanca** the white backlash.
(b) (Pol) reaction.
(c) (Tech) **avión a (or de) —** jet plane; **propulsión por —** jet propulsion.

reaccionar [1a] vi to react (a, ante to; contra against; sobre on); to respond (a to); **¿cómo reaccionó?** how did she react?

reaccionario 1 adj reactionary. **2** nm, **reaccionaria** nf reactionary.

reacio adj stubborn; **ser — a, estar — a** to be opposed to, resist (the idea of); to be unwilling to accept (the need for); **estar — a** + infin to be unwilling to + infin.

reacondicionar [1a] vt to recondition.

reactivo nm reagent.

reactor nm (a) (Phys) reactor; **— nuclear** nuclear reactor; **— generador, — reproductor** breeder reactor. (b) (Aer) jet engine; jet plane.

readaptación *nf*: — **profesional** industrial re-training.

readmisión *nf* readmission.

readmitir [3a] *vt* to readmit.

readquirir [3a] *vt power etc* to recover.

reafirmación *nf* reaffirmation; reassertion.

reafirmar [1a] *vt* to reaffirm; to reassert.

reagrupación *nf* regrouping.

reagrupar [1a] **1** *vt* to regroup. **2 reagruparse** *vr* to regroup.

reagudizarse [1f] *vr* (*Med*) to become acute again, get worse again.

reajustar [1a] **1** *vt* to readjust. **2 reajustarse** *vr* to readjust.

reajuste *nm* readjustment; (*fig*) readjustment, reappraisal; — **agonizante,** — **doloroso** agonizing reappraisal.

real[1] *adj* real.

real[2] **1** *adj* (a) royal.
  (b) (*fig*) royal; grand, splendid; *see* **moza** *etc*. **2** *nm* (a) (*Hist*) army camp; fairground.
  (b) (*Fin*) coin of 25 céntimos, one quarter of a *peseta*; **costó 6 reales** it cost 1½ pesetas; **está sin un** —, **no tiene un** — (*fam*) he hasn't a bean (*fam*).

realada *nf* (*Mex*) roundup, rodeo.

realar [1a] *vt* (*Mex*) *cattle* to round up.

realce *nm* (a) (*Tech*) raised work, embossing.
  (b) (*Art*) highlight.
  (c) (*fig*) lustre, splendour; importance, significance; enhancement; **dar** — a to add lustre to, enhance the splendour of; **un asunto sin** — a matter of no importance.

realengo *adj* (a) (*SAm*) *animal* stray, lost, ownerless.
  (b) (*Mex, Ven*) idle; out of work; carefree.

realeza *nf* royalty.

realidad *nf* reality; truth; **la** — **de la política** the realities of politics; **atengámonos a la** — let's stick to realities; **en** — in fact, really, actually; **la** — **es que** . . . the fact of the matter is that . . .

realismo *nm* realism.

realista 1 *adj* realistic. **2** *nmf* realist.

realizable *adj* (a) *assets etc* realizable. (b) *aim* attainable; *plan* practical, feasible.

realización *nf* (a) (*Fin*) realization; sale, selling-up; — **de plusvalías** profit-taking. (b) realization; fulfilment, carrying out; achievement.

realizador *nm* (*TV etc*) producer.

realizar [1f] **1** *vt* (a) (*Fin*) *assets* to realize; *stock* to sell off, sell up; *profit* to take.
  (b) *aim etc* to attain, achieve, realize; *promise* to fulfil, carry out; *plan* to carry out, put into effect.
  (c) *journey etc* to make; *visit* to carry out; *expedition, flight etc* to undertake, make; *purchase* to make.
  (d) — **que** (*SAm: angl*) to realize that . . .
  2 realizarse *vr* (*dream etc*) to come true; to materialize; (*plan*) to be carried out.

realmente[1] *adv* really; in fact, actually.

realmente[2] *adv* (*fig*) royally.

realquilar [1a] *vt* to sublet, sublease; to relet.

realzar [1f] *vt* (a) (*Tech*) to emboss, raise. (b) (*Art*) to highlight. (c) (*fig*) to enhance, heighten, add to.

reanimar [1a] **1** *vt* (a) to revive. (b) (*fig*) to revive, encourage, stimulate; to give new life to. **2 reanimarse** *vr* to revive; to acquire new life.

reanudación *nf* renewal; resumption.

reanudar [1a] *vt* to renew; *story, journey etc* to resume.

reaparecer [2d] *vi* to reappear; to return; to recur.

reaparición *nf* reappearance; return; recurrence.

reapertura *nf* reopening.

reaprovisionamiento *nm* replenishment, restocking.

reaprovisionar [1a] *vt* to replenish, restock.

rearmar [1a] **1** *vt* to rearm. **2 rearmarse** *vr* to rearm.

rearme *nm* rearmament.

reasegurar [1a] *vt* to reinsure; to underwrite.

reaseguro *nm* to reinsure.

reasumir [3a] *vt* to resume, reassume.

reata *nf* (a) rope (*joining string of pack animals*); (*SAm*) rope, lasso; strap; (*Ec*) strip of cotton cloth.
  (b) string (of horses *etc*), pack train; **de** — in single file, one after the other; (*fig*) submissively.
  (c) (*Ant, Col, Mex*) flowerbed, border.

rebaja *nf* lowering, lessening, reduction; (*Comm*) discount, rebate; (*in sale*) reduction; "**grandes** —**s**" "big reductions".

rebajamiento *nm* (a) =**rebaja.** (b) — **de sí mismo** self-abasement.

rebajar [1a] **1** *vt* (a) *ground etc* to lower, lower the level of.
  (b) *price* to reduce, lower, cut (down); *value* to detract from, reduce; — **el precio a uno en un 5 por**

100 to give someone a discount of 5%, knock 5% off the price for someone.
  (c) *intensity etc* to lessen, diminish; *colour* to tone down; *sound* to turn down, reduce; *heat* to lessen.
  (d) *person etc* to humble; to bring down a peg or two, deflate; *advantages etc* to decry, disparage; **llamarlo así es** —**lo de categoría** calling it by that name reduces its (real) importance, calling it that makes it less important than it is.
  2 rebajarse *vr*: — **ante uno** to bow before someone; — **a** + *infin* to humble oneself sufficiently to + *infin*; to stoop to + *ger*, descend to + *ger*, condescend to + *infin*.

rebajo *nm* recess; (*Tech*) rabbet.

rebalsa *nf* pool, puddle.

rebalsar [1a] **1** *vt* (a) *water* to dam, dam up. (b) (*SAm*) *banks etc* to burst, overflow. **2 rebalsarse** *vr* to form a pool (or lake); to become dammed up.

rebanada *nf* (a) slice. (b) (*Mex*) latch.

rebanar [1a] *vt food* to slice, cut in slices; *tree etc* to slice through, slice down; *limb etc* to slice off.

rebañar [1a] *vt* (a) to scrape up, scrape together; to sweep up, sweep into a pile; **logró** — **ciertos fondos** he managed to scrape some money together; — **el plato del arroz** to scrape a dish clean of rice.
  (b) (*fig*) — **una tienda de joyas** to clear a shop of jewellery, clean out all the jewellery from a shop.

rebaño *nm* flock, herd; (*fig*) flock.

rebasar [1a] *vt* (*also vi*: — **de**) (in *quality, number*) to exceed, surpass; (*in race, progress*) to overtake, leave behind; (*Aut*) to overtake, pass; *point* to pass, go beyond; (*Naut*) to sail past; *time limit* to exceed; (*of water*) to overflow, rise higher than; **han rebasado ya los límites razonables** they have already gone beyond all reasonable limits; **la cifra no rebasa de mil** the number does not exceed a thousand.

rebatible *adj* (a) *argument* easily refuted. (b) *seat* tip-up.

rebatinga *nf* (*Mex*) =**rebatiña.**

rebatiña *nf* (*CAm, Mex*) scramble, rush; **les echó caramelos a la** — he threw sweets so that they could scramble for them; **andar a la** — **de algo** to scramble for something, fight over something; (*fig*) to argue fiercely over something.

rebatir [3a] *vt* (a) *attack* to repel; *thrust* to parry, ward off.
  (b) *arguments etc* to reject, rebut, refute; *temptation* to resist; *suggestion* to reject.
  (c) *sum* to reduce; *discount* to deduct, knock off.

rebato *nm* (*Mil*) alarm, warning of attack, call to arms; surprise attack; **llamar** (*or* **tocar**) **a** — to sound the alarm (*also fig*).

rebautizar [1f] *vt* to rechristen.

Rebeca *f* Rebecca.

rebeca *nf* cardigan.

rebeco *nm* chamois, ibex.

rebelarse [1a] *vr* to revolt, rebel, rise; — **contra** (*fig*) to rebel against.

rebelde 1 *adj* (a) rebellious; mutinous; **el gobierno** — the rebel government; **ser** — **a** (*fig*) to be in revolt against, rebel against; to resist.
  (b) *child etc* unruly; unmanageable, uncontrollable; stubborn; *problem etc* difficult; *cough etc* persistent, hard to cure; *substance* difficult to work, awkward to treat.
  2 *nmf* (a) (*Mil, Pol*) rebel.
  (b) (*Law*) defaulter; person in contempt of court.

rebeldía *nf* (a) rebelliousness; defiance, disobedience; **estar en plena** — to be in open revolt.
  (b) (*Law*) default; contempt of court; **caer en** — to be in default; to be in contempt of court; **fue juzgado en** — he was sentenced by default.

rebelión *nf* revolt, rebellion, rising.

rebelón *adj horse* restive.

rebencudo *adj* (*Cu*) stubborn.

rebenque *nm* (*SAm*) whip.

rebenquear [1a] *vt* (*SAm*) to whip.

reblandecer [2d] *vt* to soften.

reblandecimiento *nm* softening; — **cerebral** softening of the brain.

rebolludo *adj* thickset, chunky (*fam*).

reborde *nm* ledge; (*Tech*) flange, rim; border.

rebosadero *nm* overflow.

rebosante *adj*: — **de** brimming with, overflowing with (*also fig*).

rebosar [1a] *vi* (a) (*of container, liquid*) to overflow, run over; **el café rebosa de la taza** the coffee cup is running over, the coffee is running over the cup.
  (b) to abound, be plentiful; **allí rebosa el mineral** the mineral abounds there, a lot of the mineral is

found there; **le rebosa la alegría** merriment bubbles out of him.
(c) **— de, — en** to overflow with, be brimming with; **— de salud** to be busting with health, be brimming with health; **ellos rebosan en dinero** they have pots of money.

reboso nm (Arg, PR) driftwood.

rebotar [1a] **1** vt (a) ball to bounce; attack to repel; rays etc to send back, turn back, cause to bounce off.
(b) nail to clinch.
(c) person to annoy; to put out, upset.
(d) (Col, Mex) water to muddy, stir up.
2 vi (of ball etc) to bounce; to rebound (de off); (of bullet) to ricochet (de off), glance (de off).

rebote nm bounce, rebound; **de —** on the rebound; (fig) indirectly, as an indirect consequence.

rebozado adj (Cook) fried in batter (or breadcrumbs etc).

rebozar [1f] **1** vt (a) to muffle up, wrap up. (b) (Cook) to roll in batter (or breadcrumbs etc), fry in batter.
2 rebozarse vr to muffle (oneself) up.

rebozo nm (a) muffler, wrap; (SAm) shawl. (b) (fig) disguise; dissimulation; **de —** secretly; **sin —** (adv) openly, frankly, (adj) plain, straight; aboveboard.

rebufar [1a] vi to recoil.

rebufo nm recoil.

rebujo nm mass, knot, tangle, ball; badly-wrapped parcel.

rebultado adj bulky.

rebullicio nm hubbub, uproar; agitation.

rebullir [3a] **1** vt (Mex) to stir up. **2** vi and **rebullirse** vr to stir, begin to move; to show signs of life.

rebumbio nm (Mex) shouting, row, hubbub.

rebusca nf (a) search.
(b) (Agr) gleaning.
(c) leavings, left-overs, remains.
(d) (Arg, Ec) small business; undercover business, illicit trading; (Col) profit made on the side.

rebuscado adj recherché; out-of-the-way; studied, elaborate; (SAm) affected.

rebuscar [1g] **1** vt (a) object etc to search carefully for, search out; (Agr) to glean.
(b) place to search carefully; pile etc to search through, rummage in.
2 vi to search carefully; (Agr) to glean.
3 rebuscarse vr (Col, RPl) to look for work.

rebuznar [1a] vi to bray.

rebuzno nm bray; braying.

recabar [1a] vt (a) to obtain by entreaty, manage to get (de from).
(b) to claim as of right, assert one's claim to.
(c) (SAm) to ask for, apply for; to ask insistently for.

recadero nm messenger; errand boy, deliveryman; carrier.

recado nm (a) message; errand; gift, small present; **coger** (or **tomar**) **un —** (Tel etc) to take a message; **dejar —** to leave a message; **enviar a uno a un —** to send someone on an errand; **mandar —** to send word.
(b) provisions, daily shopping.
(c) equipment, materials; **— de escribir** writing case, set of writing materials.
(d) **—s** regards, remembrances.
(e) (SAm) saddle and trappings, horseman's equipment.

recaer [2o] vi (a) (Med) to suffer a relapse.
(b) (of criminal etc) to fall back, relapse (en into); to backslide.
(c) **— en** (of choice etc) to fall on, fall to; (of bequest) to pass to; (of duty) to devolve upon; (of prize) to go to; **las sospechas recayeron sobre el conserje** the suspicions fell on the porter; **este peso recaerá más sobre los pobres** this burden will bear most heavily on the poor; **la acusación recayó sobre él mismo** the charge recoiled upon him.
(d) (Archit) **— a** to look out on, look over.

recaída nf relapse (en into); backsliding.

recalar [1a] **1** vt to saturate, soak. **2** vi (a) to sight land, reach port. (b) (SAm) to end up (en at). (c) (SAm) **— a uno** to go to someone for help.

recalcar [1g] **1** vt (a) contents to press down, press in, squeeze in; container to cram, stuff (de with).
(b) (fig) to stress, emphasize; to make great play with; **— algo a uno** to insist on something to someone; **— a uno que . . .** to tell someone emphatically that . . .
2 vi (Naut) to list, heel.
3 recalcarse vr (SAm): **— un hueso** to dislocate a bone.

recalcitrante adj recalcitrant.

recalcitrar [1a] vi (a) to take a step back (the better to resist). (b) to resist, be stubborn, refuse to take heed.

recalentado adj warmed-up (also fig).

recalentar [1k] **1** vt (a) to overheat. (b) food etc to warm up, reheat. **2 recalentarse** vr to become overheated, get too hot.

recalmón nm lull.

recamado nm embroidery.

recamar [1a] vt to embroider.

recámara nf (a) side room; dressing room; (CAm, Col, Mex) bedroom.
(b) (of gun) breech, chamber.
(c) (fig) caution, wariness; reserve; **tener mucha —** to be on the careful side, be wary by nature.

recamarera nf (Mex) chambermaid.

recamarero nm (Mex) houseboy, hotel servant.

recambiar [1b] vt part to change over.

recambio nm spare; refill; **—s** spares, spare parts, extras (US); **neumático de —** spare tyre.

recapacitar [1a] **1** vt to think over, reflect on. **2** vi to think things over, reflect.

recapitulación nf recapitulation, summing-up, summary.

recapitular [1a] vti to recapitulate, sum up, summarize.

recargado adj (a) overloaded. (b) adornment, style etc overelaborate.

recargar [1h] vt (a) to overload; to overload on one side, unbalance.
(b) (Fin) to put an additional charge on, increase (the price of, the tax on etc).
(c) (Law) sentence to increase.
(d) (Tech) to reload, recharge; battery to recharge.
(e) (fig) to overload (de with); **— a uno de deberes** to overload someone with duties; **— el café de azúcar** to put too much sugar in the coffee, make the coffee too sweet; **— un diseño de adornos** to overload a pattern with decoration.

recargo nm (a) new burden; extra load, additional load.
(b) (Fin) extra charge, surcharge; increase.
(c) (Law) new charge, further charge; increase of sentence.
(d) (Med) rise in temperature.

recatado adj (a) woman modest, shy, demure. (b) cautious, circumspect.

recatar [1a] **1** vt to hide.
2 recatarse vr (a) to hide oneself away (de from).
(b) to act discreetly; **sin —** openly.
(c) to be cautious; to hesitate; **— de algo** to fight shy of something.

recato nm (a) modesty, shyness, demureness. (b) caution, circumspection; reserve, restraint; **sin —** openly, unreservedly.

recatón nm (Col) miner's pick.

recauchutado nm (a) retread. (b) (process) retreading, remoulding.

recauchutar [1a] vt tyre to retread, remould.

recaudación nf (a) (act) collection; recovery. (b) (sum) takings, sum taken, income; (Sport) gate, gate money. (c) tax office.

recaudador nm: **— de contribuciones** tax collector.

recaudar [1a] vt taxes to collect; sum to collect, take (in), receive; debt to recover.

recaudo nm (a) (Fin) collection.
(b) (Law) surety, security.
(c) care, protection; precaution; **estar a buen —** to be in safekeeping; **poner algo a buen —** to put something in a safe place.
(d) (Chi, Guat, Mex) spices, condiments.
(e) (Chi, Guat, Mex) daily supply of vegetables.

recechar [1a] vt game to stalk.

recelar [1a] **1** vt: **— que . . .** to suspect that . . ., fear that . . .
2 vi and **recelarse** vr: **— de** to suspect, fear, distrust; **recelarse + infin** to be afraid of + ger.

receloso adj suspicious, distrustful; apprehensive.

recensión nf recension.

recepción nf (a) (act) reception, receiving; (Radio) reception; (to academy etc) admission.
(b) (ceremony) reception.
(c) drawing room; (at hotel) reception, reception desk.

recepcionar [1a] vt (SAm) to receive.

recepcionista nf (hotel) receptionist.

receptáculo nm receptacle; holder.

receptividad nf receptivity.

receptivo adj receptive.

receptor nm (all senses) receiver; **— de control** (TV) monitor; **— de televisión** television receiver, television set; **descolgar el —** (Tel) to pick up the receiver.

recesión nf (Comm, Fin) recession; slump.

recesivo adj (Bio) recessive.

receso *nm* (*SAm: Parl*) recess.
receta *nf* (*Cook*) recipe (*de* for); (*Med*) prescription.
recetar [1a] *vt* (a) (*Med*) to prescribe. (b) (*Guat, Mex*) *blow* to deal, hit.
recial *nm* rapids.
reciamente *adv* strongly; severely; intensely; loudly.
recibí *nm* "received with thanks", receipt; **poner el —** **en** to sign one's receipt on.
recibida *nf* (*Arg*) reception, welcome.
recibidero *adj* receivable.
recibidor *nm*, **recibidora** *nf* receiver, recipient.
recibimiento *nm* (a) (*act*) reception, welcome; **dispensar a uno un — apoteósico** to give someone an enthusiastic welcome.
(b) anteroom, vestibule, lobby; hall; reception room.
recibir [3a] **1** *vt* (a) (*general sense*) to receive.
(b) *person* to welcome, receive, greet; to go and meet; *proposal etc* to receive; to welcome, greet; **— a uno con los brazos abiertos** to welcome someone with open arms; **el torero recibe al toro** the bullfighter awaits the bull's charge; **le recibió el ministro** the minister received him, the minister granted him an interview; **la oferta fue mal recibida** the offer was badly received.
(c) *degree etc* to receive, take.
2 *vi* to receive; to entertain; **reciben mucho en casa** they entertain at home a good deal; **la baronesa recibe los lunes** the baroness receives visitors on Mondays, the baroness's "at home" day is Monday.
3 recibirse *vr*: **— de** to qualify as; *see* **abogado**; **— de doctor** to take one's doctorate, receive one's doctor's degree.
recibo *nm* (a) **= recibimiento** (a) *and* (b); **acusar —** to acknowledge receipt (*de* of); **estar de —** (*dress etc*) to be ready for collection; (*person*) to be at home (to callers).
(b) (*Comm*) receipt.
recidiva *nf* (*Med*) relapse.
reciedumbre *nf* strength, toughness; solidity; severity, harshness; loudness.
recién *adv* (a) newly, recently (+ *ptp*).
(b) (*SAm*) just, recently; **— llegó** he has just arrived, he arrived recently; **— se acordó** he only just then remembered it; **— ahora** right now, this very moment; **— aquí** right here, just here.
recién casado *adj* newly-wed; **los —s** the newly-weds.
recién hecho *adj* newly-made.
recién llegado 1 *adj* newly arrived. **2** *nm*, **recién llegada** *nf* newcomer, new person; (*at party etc*) latecomer.
recién nacido 1 *adj* newborn. **2** *nm*, **recién nacida** *nf* newborn child.
recién puesto *adj* egg new-laid.
reciente *adj* recent; *bread etc* new, fresh, newly-made.
recientemente *adv* recently.
recinto *nm* enclosure; precincts; area, spot, place; **— amurallado** walled enclosure; **— fortificado** fortified place; strongpoint; **dentro del — universitario** within the university precincts.
recio 1 *adj* (a) *rope etc* thick, strong; *person* strong, tough, robust; *ground* solid; *test etc* tough, demanding, severe.
(b) *voice* loud.
(c) *weather* harsh, severe.
(d) swift, fast, quick.
(e) **en lo más — del combate** in the thick of the fight; **en lo más — del invierno** in the depths of winter.
2 *adv* hard; *blow* hard, strongly; *pass etc* swiftly; *shout, sing* loud, loudly.
recipiente *nm* (a) (*person*) recipient. (b) recipient, receptacle, container.
recíproca *nf* (*Math*) reciprocal.
reciprocación *nf* reciprocation.
recíprocamente *adv* reciprocally, mutually.
reciprocar [1g] *vt* to reciprocate.
reciprocidad *nf* reciprocity; mutual character; **usar de —** to reciprocate.
recíproco *adj* (a) reciprocal, mutual. (b) inverse. (c) **a la recíproca** vice versa; **estar a la recíproca** to be ready to respond.
recitación *nf* recitation.
recitado *nm* recitation; (*Mus*) recitative.
recital *nm* (*Mus*) recital; (*Lit*) reading; **— de poesías** poetry reading.
recitar [1a] *vt* to recite.
recitativo *nm* recitative.
reclamable *adj* reclaimable.
reclamación *nf* (a) reclamation. (b) claim, demand; **— salarial** wage claim. (c) objection; complaint, protest; **formular una —** to make (*or* lodge) a complaint.

reclamar [1a] **1** *vt* (a) to claim, demand (*de* from); **— algo para sí** to claim something for oneself; **su porción de la herencia** to claim one's share of the estate; **esto reclama toda nuestra atención** this demands our full attention.
(b) **— a uno ante los tribunales** to take someone to court, file a suit against someone.
2 *vi*: **— contra** to protest against, complain about; **— contra una sentencia** (*Law*) to appeal against a sentence.
reclame *nm and f* (*SAm*) advertisement; **mercadería de —** loss leader.
reclamo *nm* (a) (*Orn*) call, bird call; (*Hunting*) decoy, lure.
(b) (*to person*) call; **acudir al —** to answer the call.
(c) (*Typ*) catchword.
(d) (*fig*) inducement, lure, attraction; (*Comm*) advertisement; advertising slogan; publisher's blurb.
(e) (*Law*) claim.
reclinar [1a] **1** *vt* to lean, recline (*contra* against, *sobre* on). **2 reclinarse** *vr* to lean; to recline, lean back.
recluir [3g] **1** *vt* to shut away; to confine; (*Law*) to imprison. **2 recluirse** *vr* to shut oneself away.
reclusión *nf* (a) seclusion; (*Law*) imprisonment, confinement; **— perpetua** life imprisonment. (b) place of imprisonment, prison.
recluso 1 *adj* imprisoned; **población reclusa** prison population. **2** *nm*, **reclusa** *nf* (a) recluse. (b) (*Law*) inmate (of a prison), prisoner.
recluta 1 *nf* recruitment. **2** *nm* recruit.
reclutamiento *nm* recruitment.
reclutar [1a] *vt* (a) (*Mil*) to recruit. (b) (*Arg*) *cattle* to round up; (*RPl*) *workmen* to sign up, engage; *members etc* to recruit.
recobrar [1a] **1** *vt* to recover, get back, retrieve; *fugitive, city etc* to recapture; *friendship etc* to win back; *time* to make up (for).
2 recobrarse *vr* (a) (*Med*) to recover, convalesce; to come to, regain consciousness.
(b) (*fig*) to collect oneself.
recobro *nm* recovery, retrieval; recapture.
recocer [2b and 2h] **1** *vt* (a) (*Cook*) to cook again, warm up; to overcook.
(b) (*Metal*) to anneal.
(c) (*Urug*) to cook.
2 recocerse *vr* (*fam*) to be eaten up inside, suffer a lot.
recocina *nf* scullery.
recodar [1a] *vi* to twist, turn; to form a bend.
recodo *nm* turn, bend; elbow; loop.
recogedor *nm* (a) (*person*) picker, harvester; gleaner. (b) (*tool*) rake, scraper; (*container*) pan.
recoger [2c] **1** *vt* (a) *fallen object* to pick up; *scattered objects* to gather (up), gather together; *ball* (*Sport*) to gather, stop, field; *detail, information etc* to pick up, come across; to collect; **este romance fue recogido en Esmirna** this ballad was picked up in Smyrna.
(b) *money etc* to collect, get together; *stamps etc* to collect.
(c) *newspaper etc* to take up, ban; **las autoridades recogieron todos los ejemplares** the authorities took up all the copies; **van a — las monedas antiguas** they are going to call in the old coins.
(d) (*Agr*) *crop* to harvest, get in; *fruit* to pick; (*fig*) to harvest, reap; to get as one's reward; **no recogió más que censuras** all he got was criticisms; **de todo esto van a — muy poco** they won't get much back out of all this.
(e) *water etc* to absorb, take up; *dust* to gather; (*in receptacle*) to collect.
(f) *rope, sails* to take in; *wings* to fold; *horns etc* to draw in; *skirt* to roll up, lift, gather up; *sleeves* to roll up; (*Sew*) to take in, reduce, shorten.
(g) *washing* to take in, get in; *apparatus, materials, crockery etc* to put away.
(h) *person* to pick up; to get, fetch, come for; **te vendremos a — a las 8** we'll come for you at 8 o'clock; **me recogieron en la estación** they picked me up at the station.
(i) *needy person* to take in, shelter.
2 recogerse *vr* (a) to withdraw, retire; to go home; to go to bed; to take shelter; to go off alone (to meditate etc).
(b) (*Fin*) to retrench.
recogida *nf* (a) withdrawal, retirement.
(b) (*Agr*) harvest; (*of post, rubbish etc*) collection; **hay 6 —s diarias** there are 6 collections daily.
(c) (*Arg, Mex: Agr*) roundup; (*Arg: by police*) sweep, raid.

recogido 1 adj (a) life quiet; place, setting secluded; character modest, retiring, (pej) shy, inhibited; **ella vive muy recogida** she lives very quietly.
(b) small; bunched up, tight.
2 nm tuck, gathering.

recogimiento nm (a) (act) harvesting, picking; collection; gathering.
(b) (act) withdrawal, retirement; (Fin) retrenchment.
(c) (state) absorption, concentration; seclusion; quietness.
(d) (Eccl) retreat, withdrawal.

recolección nf (a) (act) harvesting, picking; collection; gathering.
(b) (time) harvest time, picking season.
(c) (Lit) compilation; summary.
(d) (Eccl) retreat.

recolecta nf (Mex) collection.

recolectar [1a] vt = **recoger** (d).

recomendable adj recommendable; laudable; advisable; **poco —** inadvisable.

recomendación nf (a) recommendation; suggestion.
(b) praise.
(c) (written) reference, testimonial; **carta de —** letter of introduction (para to); **tiene muchas —es** he is strongly recommended to us, (fig) there's a lot to be said for him.
(d) (Eccl) **— del alma** prayers for the dying.

recomendar [1k] vt (a) to recommend; to suggest, advise; **— a uno que haga algo** to recommend someone to do something, advise someone to do something; **se lo recomiendo** I recommend it to you.
(b) to entrust, confide (a to).
(c) to praise, command.

recomendatorio adj recommendatory.

recomenzar [1f and 1k] vti to begin again, recommence.

recomerse [2a] vr to bear a secret grudge, harbour resentment.

recompensa nf recompense, reward; compensation (de una pérdida for a loss); **en — de** in return for, as a reward for.

recompensar [1a] vt to reward, recompense (por for); to compensate (algo for something).

recomponer [2r] **1** vt (a) (Tech) to mend, repair; (Typ) to reset. (b) (fam) person to dress up, doll up.
2 recomponerse vr (fam) to dress up, doll up.

reconcentrar [1a] **1** vt (a) attention etc to concentrate (en on), devote (en to).
(b) persons etc to bring together.
(c) solution to make more concentrated; to reduce the volume of, compress, increase the density of.
(d) emotion to hide.
2 reconcentrarse vr (a) to concentrate hard, become totally absorbed.
(b) emotion to harbour, conceal in one's heart.

reconciliable adj reconcilable.

reconciliación nf reconciliation.

reconciliar [1b] **1** vt to reconcile. **2 reconciliarse** vr to become (or be) reconciled.

reconcomerse [2a] vr to bear a secret grudge, harbour resentment.

reconcomio nm (a) grudge, resentment. (b) urge, longing, itch. (c) suspicion.

recóndito adj recondite; **en lo más — de** in the depths of; **en lo más — del corazón** in one's heart of hearts.

reconfortante 1 adj comforting; cheering. **2** nm (SAm) tonic; strengthening food (or drink), pick-me-up.

reconfortar [1a] **1** vt to comfort; to cheer, encourage; (Med) to strengthen. **2 reconfortarse** vr: **— con** to fortify oneself with.

reconocer [2d] vt (a) to recognize (por by); to identify, know, tell, distinguish (por by); **se le reconoce por el pelo** you can recognize him by his hair.
(b) to recognize (por as); child, government, signature etc to recognize; **no le reconocieron por jefe** they did not recognize (or accept) him as their leader; **le reconocen por inteligente** they agree that he is intelligent; **reconoció al niño por suyo** he recognized that the child was his, he recognized the child as his.
(c) merit, obligation, quality, right etc to recognize, admit, acknowledge; **— los hechos** to face the facts; **— que . . .** to admit that . . .; to realize that . . .; **reconozco que no existen pruebas de ello** I realize that there is no proof of it; **hay que — que no es normal** one must admit that it isn't normal; **por fin reconocieron abiertamente que era falso** eventually they openly admitted that it was untrue.
(d) gift, service etc to be grateful for.

(e) person to search; luggage etc to search, inspect, examine; terrain to survey; (Mil) to reconnoitre, spy out; (Med) to examine.

reconocible adj recognizable.

reconocido adj (a) leader etc recognized, accepted. (b) **estar —** to be grateful.

reconocimiento nm (a) recognition; identification.
(b) recognition, admission, acknowledgement.
(c) gratitude; **en — de** in gratitude for.
(d) search(ing); inspection, examination; survey; (Mil) reconnaissance; (Med) examination, checkup; **vuelo de —** reconnaissance flight.

reconquista nf reconquest; recapture; **la R—** the Reconquest (of Spain).

reconquistar [1a] vt (a) (Mil) territory to reconquer; position, town to recapture (a from). (b) (fig) esteem etc to recover, win back.

reconsideración nf reconsideration.

reconsiderar [1a] vt to reconsider.

reconstitución nf reconstitution, reforming; reconstruction.

reconstituir [3g] vt to reconstitute, reform; crime, scene to reconstruct.

reconstituyente nm tonic, restorative, pick-me-up.

reconstrucción nf reconstruction; reshuffle.

reconstruir [3g] vt (in most senses) to reconstruct; cabinet to reshuffle.

recontar [1m] vt (a) quantity to recount, count again; to count up carefully. (b) story to retell, tell again.

recontra (a) (SAm: intensifying prefix) extremely, terribly; eg **recontracaro** terribly dear, **recontrabueno** jolly good. (b) **¡—!** interj (euph) well I'm . . .!

reconvención nf (a) reprimand; expostulation, remonstrance. (b) (Law) countercharge.

reconvenir [3s] vt (a) to reprimand; to expostulate with, remonstrate with. (b) (Law) to countercharge.

reconversión nf reconversion; **— profesional** industrial retraining.

reconvertir [3i] vt to reconvert (en to); **— profesionalmente** to retrain for industry, give industrial retraining to.

recopilación nf summary; compilation; (Law) code; **la R—** Spanish law code of 1567; **la Nueva R—** Spanish law code of 1775.

recopilador nm compiler.

recopilar [1a] vt (a) to compile, gather, collect (together); to summarize. (b) laws to codify.

record, récord [re'kor, 'rekor] (angl) **1** adj invar record; **cifras —** record quantities; **en un tiempo — in a record time.
2 nm, pl **records, récords** [re'kor, 'rekor] record; **batir el —** to break the record.

recordable adj memorable.

recordación nf recollection; remembrance; **de feliz — of happy memory; **de infeliz (or triste) — of unhappy memory; **digno de —** memorable.

recordar[1] [1m] **1** vt (a) to remember; to recollect, recall; **no lo recuerdo** I don't remember it; **recuerda haberlo dicho** he remembers having said it.
(b) to recall; to call up, evoke (memories of), bring to mind; **esto recuerda aquella escena de la película** this recalls that scene in the film; **la frase recuerda a Garcilaso** the phrase is reminiscent of Garcilaso, the phrase has echoes of Garcilaso.
(c) to remind; — **algo a uno** to remind someone of something; — **a uno que haga algo** to remind someone to do something; **recuérdale que me debe 5 dólares** remind him that he owes me 5 dollars.
(d) (Arg, Mex) to rouse, awaken.
2 vi to remember; **no recuerdo** I don't remember; **que yo recuerde** as far as I can remember; **creo —, si mal no recuerdo** if my memory serves me right; see **desde.**
3 recordarse vr (a) **— que . . .** to remind oneself that . . .
(b) (Arg, Mex) to wake up.

recordar[2] [1m] vt (CAm, Mex, PR: angl) voice etc to record.

recordativo adj reminiscent; **carta recordativa** follow-up letter, reminder.

recordatorio nm (a) reminder; memento. (b) notice of death.

recordman nm, pl **recordmans** (angl, gall) record holder; champion; outstanding player (etc).

recorrer [2a] vt (a) area, place to go over, go across, go through, traverse; country to cross, tour, travel; (of searchers) to cover, range, scour; distance to travel, cover, do; (Mech) to travel (along); — **una provincia a pie** to go over a province on foot, have a walking tour through a province; — **un escrito** to run one's eye over a document, look through a document; **en 14 días los Jones han recorrido media Europa** the Jones have done half Europe in a fortnight.

(b) to look over, go over, survey; to check; to search. **(c)** (*Mech etc*) to repair, mend; to overhaul. **(d)** *chairs etc* to move along, put closer together; (*Typ*) *letters* to take over.

recorrido *nm* **(a)** run, journey; route, course, path; distance covered, distance travelled; (*of roundsman, golf, show jumping etc*) round; (*of piston etc*) stroke; **el — del primer día fue de 450 km** the first day's run was 450 kms; **un — en 5 bajo par** a round in 5 under par; **un — sin penalizaciones** a clear round; **— de aterrizaje** (*Aer*) landing run. **(b)** (*Mech etc*) repair; overhaul. **(c)** (*fam*) detailed reprimand.

recortable *nm* cutout.

recortadito *adj* (*fam*) fussy, very particular, strict.

recortado 1 *adj* **(a)** *edge* jagged; uneven, irregular. **(b)** (*Cu, Mex*) squat. **(c)** (*Nic, Ven*) needy. **2** *nm* (*Arg, Per, Ven*) sawn-off rifle, pistol.

recortar [1a] *vt* **(a)** *excess* to cut away, cut off, cut back, trim; *hair* to trim; *cutting, figure, picture etc* to cut out. **(b)** (*Art*) to draw in outline. **(c)** (*fig*) to cut out, remove, suppress; *rations etc* to cut down. **2 recortarse** *vr* to stand out, be outlined, be silhouetted (*en, sobre* against).

recorte *nm* **(a)** (*act*) cutting, trimming; (*of hair*) trim. **(b)** (*child's*) cutout. **(c)** **—s** trimmings, clippings; **—s de periódico** newspaper cuttings, press clippings; **álbum de —s** scrapbook; **el libro está hecho de —s** (*pej*) the book is a scissors-and-paste job. **(d)** (*CAm, Mex*) nasty remark, piece of gossip.

recoser [2a] *vt* to patch up, darn.

recosido *nm* patch, darn.

recostado *adj* reclining, recumbent; **estar — to be** lying down.

recostar [1m] **1** *vt* to lean (*en* on). **2 recostarse** *vr* **(a)** to recline, lie back; to lie down. **(b)** (*fig*) to have a short rest.

recotín *adj* (*Chi, Mex*) nervous, restless.

recova *nf* **(a)** poultry business, dealing in poultry; poultry market. **(b)** (*Bol, Chi, Ec, Per, Urug*) food market; (*Arg*) butcher's (shop). **(c)** (*RPl*) arcade, covered corridor (*along the front of a house*); porch.

recoveco *nm* **(a)** (*in street etc*) turn, bend. **(b)** (*in house*) nook, odd corner; cubbyhole. **(c)** **—s** (*fig*) ins and outs; **el asunto tiene muchos —s** it's a very complicated matter, the affair has lots of pitfalls. **(d)** **—s** (*fig: of person*) subterfuges, devious ways; **sin —s** plainly, frankly.

recreación *nf* **(a)** recreation. **(b)** = **recreo**.

recrear [1a] **1** *vt* **(a)** to recreate. **(b)** to amuse, divert, entertain. **2 recrearse** *vr* to enjoy oneself; to amuse oneself, entertain oneself (*con* with); **— viendo algo** (*pej*) to enjoy watching something, take a fiendish delight in seeing something.

recreativo *adj* recreative; recreational.

recrecer [2d] **1** *vt* to increase. **2** *vi* **(a)** to increase, grow. **(b)** to happen again. **3 recrecerse** *vr* to cheer up, recover one's spirits.

recreo *nm* **(a)** recreation, relaxation; amusement. **(b)** (*School*) break, playtime, recreation.

recriminación *nf* recrimination; **— mutua** mutual recrimination.

recriminar [1a] **1** *vt* to reproach. **2** *vi* to recriminate. **3 recriminarse** *vr* to reproach each other, indulge in mutual recrimination.

recrudecer [2d] **1** *vt* to cause to break out again; to worsen, exacerbate. **2** *vi and* **recrudecerse** *vr* to recrudesce, break out again; to worsen.

recrudecimiento *nm*, **recrudescencia** *nf* recrudescence, new outbreak, upsurge.

recrudescente *adj* recrudescent.

recta *nf* straight line; **la —** (*Sport*) the straight; **— de llegada** home straight.

rectal *adj* rectal.

rectangular *adj* = **rectángulo 1.**

rectángulo 1 *adj* rectangular, oblong; *triangle etc* right-angled. **2** *nm* rectangle, oblong.

rectificable *adj* rectifiable; **fácilmente —** easily rectified, easy to put right.

rectificación *nf* rectification; correction; **publicar una —** to publish a correction.

rectificador *nm*, **rectificadora** *nf* (*Mech*) rectifier.

rectificar [1g] **1** *vt* **(a)** *road etc* to straighten (out). **(b)** (*Mech etc*) to rectify; to balance; *cylinder* to rectify, rebore. **(c)** *calculation etc* to rectify, correct; *conduct* to change, reform. **2** *vi* to correct oneself; **"No, eran 4", rectificó** "No", he said, correcting himself, "there were 4".

rectilíneo *adj* rectilinear.

rectitud *nf* **(a)** straightness. **(b)** (*fig*) rectitude, honesty, uprightness.

recto 1 *adj* **(a)** *line etc* straight; *angle* right; *part etc* upright; *course* straight, direct, unswerving; **la flecha fue recta al blanco** the arrow went straight to the target. **(b)** (*fig*) *person* honest, upright; *judge etc* fair, just, impartial; *judgement* sound; *intention* lawful, proper. **(c)** (*fig*) *sense* literal, proper, basic; **en el sentido — de la palabra** in the proper sense of the word. **(d)** (*Gram*) *case* nominative. **2** *nm* (*Anat*) rectum.

rector 1 *adj person* leading; governing, managing; *idea, principle* guiding, governing; **los deberes —es del régimen** the régime's duty to govern; **una figura rectora** an outstanding figure, a leading figure. **2** *nm* **(a)** head, chief, leader; principal. **(b)** (*Univ*) rector, president (*US*), (*approx*) vice-chancellor.

rectorado *nm* (*Univ*) **(a)** rectorship, presidency (*US*), (*approx*) vice-chancellorship. **(b)** rector's office.

rectorar [1a] *vt* (*CAm*) to rule, govern, direct.

rectoría *nf* **(a)** = **rectorado (a)** *and* **(b)**. **(b)** (*Eccl*) rectory.

recua *nf* mule train, train of pack animals.

recubrir [3a; *ptp* **recubierto**] *vt* to cover (*con, de* with); to coat (*con, de* with).

recuento *nm* count, recount; inventory, survey; **hacer el — de** to make a survey of, draw up an inventory of; to count up, reckon up.

recuerdo 1 *adj* (*Ven*) awake. **2** *nm* **(a)** memory; recollection; reminiscence; **"R—s de la vida de hace 80 años"** "Reminiscences of life 80 years ago"; **contar los —s** to reminisce; **guardar un feliz — de uno** to have happy memories of someone. **(b)** souvenir, memento, keepsake; **"R— de Mallorca"** "A present from Majorca"; **toma esto como —** take this as a keepsake. **(c)** **—s** regards, best wishes; **¡dale —s míos!** give him my regards!, remember me to him!; **os manda muchos —s para todos** he sends you all his warmest regards.

recuero *nm* muleteer.

recuesto *nm* slope.

reculada *nf* **(a)** backward movement; (*of gun*) recoil. **(b)** (*fig*) retreat; backing down, weakening.

recular [1a] *vi* **(a)** (*of animal, vehicle*) to go back, back; (*of gun*) to recoil; (*of army etc*) to fall back, retreat. **(b)** (*fig*) to back down, weaken (in one's resolve).

reculativa *nf* (*Mex*) = **reculada (b).**

reculón *nm* **(a)** (*SAm*) = **reculada.** **(b)** **andar a —es** to go backwards.

recuperable *adj* recoverable, retrievable.

recuperación *nf* recovery, recuperation, retrieval.

recuperar [1a] **1** *vt* **(a)** to recover, recuperate, retrieve; *loss* to recoup; *lost time* to make up. **(b)** (*Tech*) *waste etc* to reclaim, process for re-use. **2 recuperarse** *vr* (*Med etc*) to recover, recuperate.

recuperativo *adj* recuperative.

recurrente *adj* recurrent.

recurrir [3a] *vi* **(a)** **— a** *means etc* to resort to, have recourse to; to fall back on; *person* to turn to, appeal to. **(b)** (*Law*) to appeal (*a* to; *contra, de* against).

recurso *nm* **(a)** recourse, resort; means; expedient; **como último —** as a last resort. **(b)** **—s** (*Fin etc*) resources; means; **—s económicos** economic resources; **—s naturales** natural resources; **la familia está sin —s** the family has nothing to fall back on. **(c)** (*Law*) appeal.

recusante 1 *adj* recusant. **2** *nmf* recusant.

recusar [1a] *vt* **(a)** to reject, refuse. **(b)** (*Law*) to challenge (the authority of).

rechazamiento *nm* **(a)** repelling, beating off; driving back; reflection. **(b)** rejection; refusal; resistance.

rechazar [1f] *vt* **(a)** *person* to push back, push away; *attack* to repel, beat off; *enemy* to throw back, drive back; *light etc* to reflect, turn back; *water etc* to throw off. **(b)** *accusation, idea, motion* to reject; *offer* to reject, refuse, turn down; *temptation* to resist.

rechazo nm (of ball) bounce, rebound; (of gun) recoil; (fig) repulse, rebuff; **de —** on the rebound; (of bullet) as it glanced off, as it richocheted; (fig) in consequence, as a result.

rechifla nf (a) whistle, whistling. (b) hissing, hooting, booing; (Theat) catcall. (c) (fig) mockery, derision.

rechiflar [1a] 1 vt to whistle at, hiss, hoot, boo. 2 vi to whistle, hiss. 3 **rechiflarse** vr (a) to take things as a joke. (b) (Arg) to get cross.

rechín nm (Col) piece of burnt food; **oler a —** to smell burnt.

rechinamiento nm creaking, grating; squeaking; clanking, clattering; humming, whirring; grinding, gnashing (of teeth).

rechinar [1a] 1 vi (a) to creak, grate; to squeak; (of wood, door etc) to creak; (of machine) to clank, clatter; (of unoiled parts) to grate; (of engine) to hum, whirr; (of teeth) to grate, grind, gnash; **hacer — los dientes** to grind one's teeth, gnash one's teeth.

(b) (fig) to do (or accept etc) something with an ill grace.

(c) (Arg, Col, Mex, Per) to rage; (Ven) to grumble; (Ven) to answer rudely.

2 **rechinarse** vr (a) (CAm, Mex) to burn, overcook.

(b) (Arg) to get furious.

rechinido nm, **rechino** nm = **rechinamiento**.

rechoncho adj thickset, stocky, squat; plump.

rechupete: de — (fam) 1 adj splendid, jolly good (fam); meal delicious, scrumptious (fam).

2 adv splendidly, jolly well (fam); **me ha salido de —** it turned out marvellously for me; **pasarlo de —** to have a fine time.

red nf (a) (Fish etc) net; hairnet; mesh, meshes; (Rail) rack; fence; grille; **— de alambre** wire mesh, wire netting; **— barredera** trawl.

(b) (fig) network, system; (Elec, of water etc) mains, supply system; (of shops etc) chain; **— de emisoras** radio network; **— de espionaje** spy network; spy ring; **— ferroviaria** railway network, railway system; **— rastreadora**, **— de rastreo** tracking network; **con agua de la —** with mains water, with water from the mains; **estar conectado con la —** to be connected to the mains.

(c) (fig) snare, trap; **aprisionar a uno en sus —es** to have someone firmly caught in one's toils, have someone well and truly snared; **caer en la —** to fall into the trap; **tender una — para uno** to set a trap for someone.

redacción nf (a) (act) writing, redaction; editing. (b) wording. (c) newspaper office. (d) (persons) editorial staff.

redactar [1a] vt (a) to write; to draft, draw up; to word, express; **una carta mal redactada** a badly-worded letter. (b) newspaper etc to edit.

redactor nm (a) writer, drafter. (b) editor; sub-editor.

redada nf (a) (act) cast, casting, throw. (b) (by police) sweep, raid. (c) catch, haul (also fig).

redaje nm (Ec) net; mass, tangle.

redaño nm (a) (Anat) mesentery; caul. (b) **—s** (fam) guts, pluck.

redargüir [3g] 1 vt (Law) to impugn, hold to be invalid. 2 vi to turn an argument against its proposer; **— que . . .** to argue on the other hand that . . .

redecilla nf hairnet.

rededor: al — see **alrededor**.

redención nf redemption.

redentor 1 adj redeeming. 2 nm redeemer; **R—** Redeemer, Saviour; **meterse a —** to intervene (with the best intentions).

redescubrir [3a; ptp **redescubierto**] vt to rediscover.

redespachar [1a] vt (Arg) to send on, forward (directly).

redicho adj (fam) affected, overrefined, stilted.

redil nm sheepfold.

redimible adj redeemable.

redimir [3a] vt to redeem (also Fin, fig); captive to ransom; slave to purchase the freedom of.

rédito nm interest, yield, return.

redituar [1e] vt to yield, produce, bear.

redoblado adj (a) (Mech) part reinforced, extra strong; person stocky, thickset. (b) zeal etc redoubled. (c) pace double-quick.

redoblante nm drum.

redoblar [1a] 1 vt (a) paper etc to bend back, bend over, bend down; nail to clinch.

(b) watchfulness, zeal etc to redouble.

(c) (Bridge) to redouble.

2 vi (Mus) to play a roll on the drum; (of thunder) to roll, rumble.

redoble nm (Mus) drumroll, drumbeat; (of thunder) roll, rumble.

redoma nf (a) flask, phial. (b) (Chi) fishbowl. (c) (Ven) large lamp.

redomado adj (a) sly, artful. (b) rogue etc complete, utter, out-and-out.

redomón adj (SAm) horse half-tamed, half-trained; (Chi, Mex) person untrained; (Mex) rustic.

redonda nf (a) (Mus) semibreve.

(b) (Typ) roman, rounded characters, ordinary letters.

(c) **en muchas millas a la —** for many miles round about; **se olía a un kilómetro a la —** you could smell it a mile off.

redondear [1a] 1 vt (a) to round, round off. (b) (fig) to round off. 2 **redondearse** vr (a) to acquire money, become wealthy. (b) to get clear of debts.

redondel nm (a) bullring, arena. (b) (fam) ring, circle. (c) (Aut) roundabout, traffic circle (US).

redondez nf roundness; **en toda la — de la tierra** in the whole wide world.

redondilla nf (Lit: Hist) quatrain.

redondo adj (a) round; rounded; **3 m en —** 3 metres round; **¿cuánto tiene de —?** how far is it round?; **caer —** to fall in a heap; **girar en —** to turn right round; **rehusar en —** to give a flat refusal, refuse flatly.

(b) number, quantity round; **en números —s** in round numbers, in round figures.

(c) trip round.

(d) refusal etc straight, flat, square; oath etc frank.

(e) deal etc complete, finished; successful; **todo le ha salido —** it all went well for him.

(f) (Mex) person dim, dense; weak, unresisting.

redopelo nm (a) (fam) row, shindy. (b) **a — = a contrapelo; traer al — a uno** to treat someone very badly, ride roughshod over someone.

redro adv (fam) behind; backwards.

redrojo nm (a) (Bot) late fruit, withered fruit.

(b) puny child, runt; (Mex) worthless individual, poor fish; poor wretch.

(c) (Arg) surplus, remainder.

(d) (Mex) rag.

reducción nf (a) reduction; diminution, lessening, cut. (b) (Med) setting. (c) (SAm: Hist) settlement of converted Indians.

reducible adj reducible.

reducido adj (a) reduced; limited; number etc small; income, resources limited, small; space confined, limited; price low. (b) **quedar — a** to be reduced to.

reducir [3o] 1 vt (a) number, quantity etc to reduce; to diminish, lessen, cut (down); speech etc to cut down, abridge; size to reduce, cut down; activity, intervention etc to limit (a to).

(b) (Math etc) to reduce (a to), convert (a into); **— las millas a kilómetros** to convert miles into kilometres; **— los dólares en pesetas** to change dollars into pesetas; to express dollars as pesetas; **— una casa a escombros** to reduce a house to rubble; **todo lo reduce a cosas materiales** he reduces everything to material terms.

(c) country etc to subdue; rebels to overcome, bring under control; fortress to reduce; **— a uno al silencio** to silence someone, reduce someone to silence; **— a uno a la obediencia** to bring someone to heel.

(d) (Med) bone to set.

2 **reducirse** vr (a) to diminish, lessen, fall, be reduced (a to).

(b) (Fin) to economize.

(c) **— a** to come down to, amount to no more than; **el escándalo se redujo a un simple chisme** the scandal amounted to nothing more than a piece of gossip; **— a + infin** to come down to + ger, find oneself reduced to + ger.

reductible adj (Arg, Mex) reducible.

reducto nm (Mil and fig) redoubt; **el último — de the** last redoubt of.

reduje etc see **reducir**.

redundancia nf redundancy, superfluity.

redundante adj redundant, superfluous.

redundar [1a] vi: **— en** to redound to; **— en beneficio de** to be to the advantage of.

reduplicación nf reduplication; redoubling.

reduplicar [1g] vt to reduplicate; effort etc to redouble.

reedición nf reissue, reprint(ing).

reedificación nf rebuilding.

reedificar [1g] vt to rebuild.

reeditar [1a] vt to reissue, republish, reprint.

reeducación nf re-education; **— profesional** industrial retraining.

reeducar [1g] *vt* to re-educate; — **profesionalmente** to give industrial retraining to.
reelección *nf* re-election.
reelegible *adj* re-elegible.
reelegir [3c *and* 3l] *vt* to re-elect.
reembalar [1a] *vt* to repack.
reembolsable *adj* repayable; returnable; **no** — (*Fin*) stock irredeemable; *deposit* non-returnable.
reembolsar [1a] **1** *vt person* to reimburse; to repay; *money* to repay, pay back; *deposit* to refund, return.
  2 reembolsarse *vr* to reimburse oneself; — **una cantidad** to recover a sum.
reembolso *nm* reimbursement; repayment; refund; **enviar algo contra** — to send something cash on delivery (*abbr:* C.O.D.).
reemplazable *adj* replaceable.
reemplazante *nmf* (*Mex*) replacement, substitute.
reemplazar [1f] *vt* (*all senses*) to replace (**con** with, **por** by).
reemplazo *nm* (a) replacement. (b) (*Mil*) reserve; annual draft of recruits; **de** — reserve (*attr*), from the reserve.
reencarnación *nf* reincarnation.
reencarnar [1a] **1** *vt* to reincarnate. **2** *vi* to be reincarnated.
reencender [1k] *vt* to light again, rekindle.
reencuadernar [1a] *vt* to rebind.
reengancharse [1a] *vr* to re-enlist.
reentrada *nf* re-entry.
reenvasar [1a] *vt* to repack, rewrap.
reenviar [1c] *vt* to forward, send on; to send back.
reestatificación *nf* renationalization.
reestatificar [1g] *vt* to renationalize.
reestrenar [1a] *vt* (*Theat*) to revive, put on again; (*Cine*) to reissue.
reestreno *nm* (*Theat*) revival; (*Cine*) reissue.
reexaminación *nf* re-examination.
reexaminar [1a] *vt* to re-examine.
reexpedir [3l] *vt* to forward; to redirect.
reexportar [1a] *vt* to re-export.
refacción *nf* (a) light refreshment, refection.
  (b) (*SAm: Archit, Mech*) repair(s).
  (c) (*Cu, Mex, Per, PR*) upkeep costs.
  (d) (*Mex, PR*) short-term loan, financial aid.
  (e) (*Mex: Mech*) spare part.
refaccionar [1a] *vt* (a) (*SAm*) to repair. (b) (*Cu, Mex, Per, PR*) to give financial aid to, subsidize.
refajo *nm* flannel underskirt; short extra skirt; slip.
refalar [1a] **1** *vt* (a) (*Chi, RPl*) — **algo a uno** to take something from (*or* off) someone.
  (b) (*Arg, Bol*) to steal.
  2 refalarse *vr* (*RPl*) (a) — **los zapatos** to take one's shoes off.
  (b) to leave, make off; to beat it (*fam*); to slip.
refaloso *adj* (*Arg*) (a) slippery. (b) shy, timid.
refectorio *nm* refectory.
referencia *nf* (a) (*in most senses*) reference; **con** — **a** with reference to; **hacer** — **a** to refer to, allude to.
  (b) account, report; **una** — **completa del suceso** a complete account of what took place.
referente *adj:* — **a** relating to, about, concerning.
referéndum *nm*, *pl* **referéndums** referendum.
referí *nm* (*SAm: angl*) referee, umpire.
referible *adj:* — **a** referable to.
referir [3i] **1** *vt* (a) to recount, report; to tell; — **que . . .** to say that . . ., tell how . . ., relate how . . .
  (b) — **al lector a un apéndice** to refer the reader to an appendix.
  (c) to refer, apply, relate; **todo lo refiere a su teoría favorita** he refers (*or* relates) everything to his favourite theory; **han referido el cuadro al siglo XVII** they have referred the picture to the 17th century, they have placed the picture in the 17th century.
  (d) — **a** (*Fin*) to convert into, express in terms of.
  (e) (*CAm*) to abuse, insult.
  (f) (*Mex*) — **algo a uno** to reproach someone with something.
  2 referirse *vr:* — **a** to refer to; **me refiero a lo de anoche** I refer to what happened last night; **por lo que se refiere a eso** as for that, as regards that.
refilón: de — *adv* obliquely, slantingly, aslant; **el sol da de** — the sun strikes obliquely, the sun comes slanting in; **mirar a uno de** — to take a sideways glance at; to take a quick look at.
refinación *nf* refining.
refinado *adj* refined.
refinador *nm* refiner.
refinadura *nf* refining.
refinamiento *nm* refinement; **con todos los** —**s modernos** with all the modern refinements.

refinar [1a] *vt* (a) (*Tech*) to refine. (b) (*fig*) *system etc* to refine, perfect; *style etc* to polish.
refinería *nf* refinery.
refino 1 *adj* extra fine, pure, refined. **2** *nm* refining.
refirmar [1a] *vt* (*SAm*) to reaffirm.
refistolería *nf* (a) (*CAm, Ven*) scheming nature; scheming, troublemaking.
  (b) (*Ant, Ec, Mex*) conceit; affectation; pedantry.
  (c) (*Cu, SD*) oiliness, soapiness.
refistolero *adj* (a) (*CAm, Ven*) intriguing, scheming; mischievous. (b) (*Ant, Ec, Mex*) vain, stuck-up (*fam*), affected; pedantic. (c) (*Cu, SD*) oily, soapy.
reflector *nm* (a) reflector; — **posterior** (*Aut*) rear reflector. (b) (*Elec*) spotlight; (*Aer, Mil*) searchlight.
reflejar [1a] **1** *vt* (a) to reflect. (b) (*fig*) to reflect, mirror, show, reveal. **2 reflejarse** *vr* to be reflected (*also fig*).
reflejo 1 *adj* (a) *light* reflected.
  (b) *action* reflex.
  (c) (*Gram*) *verb* reflexive.
  2 *nm* (a) reflection; **mirar su** — **en el agua** to look at one's reflection in the water.
  (b) (*fig*) reflection.
  (c) (*Anat etc*) reflex; reflex action.
  (d) —**s** gleam, glint; **tiene** —**s metálicos** it has a metallic glint.
  (e) (*for hair*) rinse; **darse un** — **azul** to give one's hair a blue rinse.
reflexión *nf* (a) (*Phys*) reflection. (b) (*fig*) reflection; thought; meditation; **mis** —**es sobre el problema** my reflections on the problem.
reflexionar [1a] **1** *vt* to reflect on, think about, think over.
  2 *vi* to reflect (**en**, **sobre** on); (*before acting*) to think, pause, reflect; **¡reflexione!** you think it over!, think for a moment!
reflexivamente *adv* (a) (*Gram*) reflexively. (b) thoughtfully, reflectively.
reflexivo *adj* (a) (*Gram*) *verb* reflexive. (b) *person etc* thoughtful, reflective. (c) *act* considered.
refluir [3g] *vi* to flow back.
reflujo *nm* ebb, ebb tide.
refocilación *nf* huge enjoyment, great pleasure; unhealthy pleasure, cruel pleasure; coarse merriment.
refocilar [1a] **1** *vt* to give great pleasure to; to amuse hugely, amuse in a coarse way; to cheer up.
  2 *vi* (*RPl: of lightning*) to flash.
  3 refocilarse *vr* (a) to enjoy oneself hugely; to enjoy oneself in a coarse way; — **con algo** to enjoy something hugely, have a fine time with something; — **viendo lo que sufre otro** to take a cruel pleasure in watching someone else's sufferings.
  (b) to cheer up no end.
refocilo *nm* (a) = **refocilación**. (b) (*RPl*) lightning, flash of lightning.
reforma *nf* (a) reform; reformation; improvement; **R—** (*Eccl*) Reformation; — **agraria** land reform.
  (b) (*Archit etc*) —**s** alterations, repairs, improvements; "**cerrado por** —**s**" "closed for repairs".
reformación *nf* reform, reformation.
reformado *adj* reformed.
reformador *nm*, **reformadora** *nf* reformer.
reformar [1a] **1** *vt* (a) to reform; to change, alter, improve; to reorganize; *abuse etc* to correct, put right; *text* to revise.
  (b) to re-form.
  (c) (*Archit etc*) to alter, repair; to improve; (*Mech*) to mend, repair; (*Sew*) to alter.
  2 reformarse *vr* to reform, mend one's ways.
reformatorio *nm* reformatory; — **de menores** remand home.
reformista *nmf* reformist, reformer.
reforzador *nm* (*Elec*) booster; (*Phot*) intensifier.
reforzamiento *nm* reinforcement, strengthening.
reforzar [1f *and* 1m] *vt* (a) (*Archit etc*) to reinforce, strengthen; (*Mil*) to reinforce; (*Elec etc*) to boost, raise, step up; *dose* to increase.
  (b) (*fig*) *resistance etc* to strengthen, buttress, bolster up; *person* to encourage.
refracción *nf* refraction.
refractar [1a] *vt* to refract.
refractario *adj* (a) (*Tech*) fireproof, heat-resistant; (*Cook*) ovenproof.
  (b) (*fig*) refractory, recalcitrant; stubborn; **ser** — **a una reforma** to resist a reform, be opposed to a reform; **ser** — **a las lenguas** to have a total blank where languages are concerned.
refractivo *adj* refractive.
refractor *nm* refractor.
refrán *nm* proverb, saying; **como dice el** — as the saying goes.

refranero nm collection of proverbs.

refraniento adj (Chi) much given to quoting proverbs.

refregar [1h and 1k] vt (a) to rub (hard), brush (repeatedly); to scrub.
(b) (fig) — algo a uno to rub something in so that someone remembers it, drive something home; to harp on something to someone; to reproach someone with something.

refregón nm (a) rub(bing); brush(ing); scrub(bing).
(b) mark left by rubbing (etc).

refrenar [1a] vt (a) horse to rein back, rein in; to hold back. (b) (fig) to curb, restrain, hold in check.

refrendar [1a] vt (a) to endorse, countersign; to authenticate; to give one's approval to; passport to stamp. (b) (fam) to do again, repeat; food to order more of, have a second helping of. (c) (Mex) to redeem (from pawn).

refrescante adj refreshing, cooling.

refrescar [1g] 1 vt (a) to refresh, to cool (down).
(b) memory to refresh; knowledge, subject to brush up, polish up.
(c) action to repeat; enmity etc to renew.
2 vi (a) (Meteorol) to get cooler, cool down.
(b) (person) to refresh oneself; to take the air, go out for a walk.
(c) (person) to take some refreshment, have a drink.
(d) (Mex: Med) to get better.
3 **refrescarse** vr =vi (esp b).

refresco nm cool drink, soft drink; —s refreshments; "R—s" "Refreshments".

refresquería nf (SAm) refreshment stall.

refriega nf scuffle, set-to (fam); affray, brawl.

refrigeración nf refrigeration; (Mech) cooling; air conditioning; — por agua water-cooling; — por aire air-cooling.

refrigerado adj cooled; cinema, room etc air-conditioned; — por agua water-cooled; — por aire air-cooled.

refrigerador nm refrigerator; cooling unit, cooling system.

refrigeradora nf (SAm) refrigerator.

refrigerante 1 adj cooling, refrigerating. 2 nm (Chem) refrigerant.

refrigerar [1a] vt to cool, refresh; (Tech) to refrigerate; (Mech) to cool; room to air-condition.

refrigerio nm (a) snack; cooling drink. (b) (fig) relief.

refucilar [1a] vi (Arg, Ec) =**refocilar** 2.

refucilo nm (Arg) =**refocilo** (b).

refuerzo nm (a) (act) strengthening; reinforcement (also Mil). (b) (Tech) brace, support. (c) —s (Mil) reinforcements. (d) (fig) aid.

refugiado 1 adj refugee. 2 nm, **refugiada** nf refugee.

refugiarse [1b] vr to take refuge; to shelter (en in); to go into hiding; — en un país vecino to flee to a neighbouring country, seek asylum in a neighbouring country.

refugio nm (a) (in general) refuge, shelter; asylum; (Eccl) sanctuary; (fig) refuge, haven; acogerse a un — to take refuge, shelter (en in); to seek sanctuary.
(b) refuge, shelter; (Aut) street island; — alpino, — de montaña mountain hut; — antiaéreo air-raid shelter; — subterráneo (Mil) underground shelter, dugout.

refulgencia nf brilliance, refulgence.

refulgente adj brilliant, refulgent.

refulgir [3c] vi to shine (brightly).

refundición nf (a) (act) revision, recasting. (b) new version, adaptation, rehash; revision.

refundidor nm, **refundidora** nf reviser, adapter.

refundir [3a] 1 vt (a) (Tech) to recast.
(b) (Lit etc) to adapt, rehash; to revise, rewrite; to remodel.
(c) (CAm, Col, Mex) to lose, mislay.
(d) (Arg) to ruin, crush; candidate to plough (sl).
(e) (Guat, Mex) to keep carefully.
2 **refundirse** vr (CAm, Col, Mex) to get lost, be mislaid.

refunfuñar [1a] vi to growl, grunt; to grumble.

refunfuño nm growl, grunt; grumble.

refunfuñón (fam) 1 adj growling, grunting; grumbling, grouchy (fam). 2 nm grumbler, groucher (fam).

refutable adj refutable; **fácilmente** — easily refuted.

refutación nf refutation.

refutar [1a] vt to refute.

regadera nf (a) sprinkler; (Hort) watering can. (b) (Mex) shower bath. (c) (fam) estar como una —, ser una — to have a memory like a sieve; to be crazy.

regadío 1 adj irrigable. 2 nm irrigated land, irrigable

land (also tierra de —); cultivo de — crop that grows on irrigated land, crop that needs irrigation.

regadizo adj irrigable.

regador nm (Chi) watering can.

regadura nf sprinkling, watering; (Agr) irrigation.

regala nf gunwale.

regaladamente adv live in luxury.

regalado adj (a) life etc of luxury; comfortable, pleasant; (pej) soft.
(b) dainty, delicate.
(c) (Comm, Fin) free, given away; me lo dio medio — he gave it to me for a song; no lo quiero ni — I won't have it at any price, I don't want it even as a present.

regalar [1a] 1 vt (a) to give, present; to give away; — algo a uno to give someone something, make someone a present of something; en su jubilación le regalaron este reloj they gave him this clock on his retirement, they presented him with this clock on his retirement; están regalando plumas they're giving pens away, they're issuing pens free.
(b) person to treat royally, make a great fuss of; (pej) to indulge, pamper; — a uno con un banquete to entertain someone to a dinner, (less formally) treat someone to a dinner; le regalaron con toda clase de atenciones they regaled him with all manner of hospitality, they lavished attentions on him.
2 **regalarse** vr (a) to indulge oneself, pamper oneself; to do oneself well.
(b) — con to regale oneself with.

regalía nf (a) —s (Hist) royal prerogatives.
(b) (fig) privilege, prerogative; (Fin) perquisite, bonus.
(c) (Ant, CAm, Col) gift, present.
(d) (Arg, Cu, Mex) royalty; advance payment.
(e) (Ven) excellence, goodness; beauty.

regaliz nm, **regaliza** nf liquorice, licorice.

regalo nm (a) gift, present; — de boda wedding present; entrada de — complimentary ticket.
(b) (fig) pleasure; (food) treat, delicacy, dainty; es un — del oído it's a treat to listen to.
(c) (fig) luxury, comfort.

regalón adj (a) child spoiled, pampered; person comfort-loving, (pej) soft, lapped in luxury.
(b) life of luxury, comfortable; (pej) soft.
(c) (Arg) éste es el — de su padre this is the son that his father spoils most, this is daddy's pet.

regalonear [1a] 1 vt (Arg, Chi) to spoil, pamper.
2 vi (Chi) to allow oneself to be pampered.

regañada nf (CAm, Mex, Per) =**regaño**.

regañadientes: a — adv unwillingly, reluctantly.

regañado adj: estar — con uno to be at odds with someone.

regañar [1a] 1 vt to scold; to tell off, reprimand; to nag (at).
2 vi (a) (of dog) to snarl, growl.
(b) (of person) to grumble, grouse (fam); to nag.
(c) (of two persons) to fall out, quarrel.

regaño nm (a) snarl, growl; scowl; grumble, grouse (fam). (b) scolding; telling-off; merecerse un — to get a telling-off.

regañón adj grumbling, grouchy (fam); irritable; woman nagging, shrewish.

regar [1h and 1k] 1 vt (a) plant to water; land to water, irrigate; street to water, hose (down), wash; wound etc to wash, bathe (con, de with); (with insecticide etc) to spray (con, de with); — la garganta to spray one's throat; — un papel de lágrimas to let tears fall on a sheet of paper, cover a sheet of paper with teardrops.
(b) (Geog: of river) to water; (of sea) to wash, lap against; una costa regada por un mar tranquilo a coast washed by a calm sea.
(c) (fig) to sprinkle, strew (in all directions), scatter; iba regando monedas he was dropping money all over the place.
(d) (Col, CR) to spill; to knock over.
(e) (PR) to hit.
2 vi (a) (PR) to joke; to fib.
(b) (Ven) to act rashly.
3 **regarse** vr (a) (CAm, Mex, Ven) to scatter (in all directions).
(b) (SD) to get cross.

regata[1] nf (Agr) irrigation channel.

regata[2] nf (Naut) race, boat race; regatta.

regate nm (a) swerve, dodge; (Sport) dribble. (b) (fig) dodge, ruse.

regatear[1] [1a] vi (Naut) to race.

regatear[2] [1a] 1 vt (a) (Comm) deal, object to haggle over, bargain over; price to try to beat down.
(b) supply etc to be mean with, economize on; to give (or issue etc) sparingly; su padre no le regata

dinero her father does not keep her short of money; **aquí regatean el vino** they are mean with their wine here; **no hemos regateado esfuerzo para** + *infin* we have spared no effort to + *infin*.
　(c) (*fig*) to deny, refuse to allow; **no le regateo buenas cualidades** I don't deny his good qualities.
　2 *vi* (a) (*Comm*) to haggle, bargain; (*fig*) to bicker.
　(b) to swerve, dodge; to duck; (*Sport*) to dribble.
regateo *nm* (a) haggling, bargaining. (b) (*Sport*) dribbling.
regatón[1] *nm* (*of stick*) tip, ferrule.
regatón[2] 1 *adj* (*Comm*) haggling; (*fig*) bickering, niggling, argumentative. 2 *nm* (a) (*Ven*) dregs. (b) (*Mex*) retailer, small-time dealer.
regazo *nm* lap (*also fig*).
regencia *nf* regency.
regeneración *nf* (a) regeneration. (b) (*Tech*) reclaiming.
regenerado *adj* regenerate.
regenerador *adj* regenerative.
regenerar [1a] *vt* (a) to regenerate. (b) (*Tech*) to reclaim, process for re-use.
regentar [1a] *vt* (a) *chair etc* to occupy, hold; *post* to hold temporarily; (*fig*) *destinies etc* to guide, preside over. (b) (*fam*) to domineer, boss.
regente 1 *adj* (a) *prince etc* regent.
　(b) *director etc* managing.
　2 *nm* (*also f, and* **regenta** *nf*) (a) (*Pol*) regent.
　(b) (*of estate, factory*) manager; (*Pharm*) chief pharmacist; (*Typ*) foreman.
regiamente *adv* regally.
regicida *nmf* regicide (*person*).
regicidio *nm* regicide (*act*).
regidor *nm* (*Hist*) alderman.
regiego = **rejego**.
régimen *nm* (a) (*Pol*) régime; rule; **antiguo —** ancien régime; **— marioneta** puppet régime; **bajo el — del dictador** under the dictator's régime (*or* rule).
　(b) (*Med*) diet (*also* **— alimenticio**); **— lácteo** milk diet; **estar a — to be on a diet; poner a uno a —** to put someone on a diet.
　(c) rules, set of rules, régime, system; way of life; **he cambiado de —** I have changed my whole way of life, I have made myself a new set of rules.
　(d) (*Gram*) government.
regimentación *nf* regimentation.
regimiento *nm* (a) administration, government, organization. (b) (*Mil*) regiment. (c) (*SAm*) regiment, mass, crowd.
Reginaldo *m* Reginald.
regio *adj* (a) royal, regal; kingly. (b) (*fig*) royal; splendid, majestic.
región *nf* (a) region; district, area, part; (*Pol*) region. (b) (*Anat*) region, tract.
regional *adj* regional.
regionalismo *nm* regionalism.
regionalista 1 *adj* regionalist. 2 *nmf* regionalist.
regir [3c *and* 3l] 1 *vt* (a) *country etc* to rule, govern; *college etc* to run, be in charge of, be at the head of; *business* to manage, run, control.
　(b) (*Law, Gram etc*) to govern; **según que rige esos casos** according to the statute which governs these cases; **ese verbo rige el dativo** that verb takes the dative; **los factores que rigen los cambios del mercado** the factors which govern (*or* determine, control) changes in the market.
　2 *vi* (a) (*Law*) to be in operation, be in force, apply; (*of price*) to be in force; (*of condition etc*) to prevail, obtain; **esa ley ya no rige** that law no longer applies; **el mes que rige** the present month, the current month; **cuando estas condiciones ya no rijan** when these conditions no longer obtain.
　(b) (*Mech*) to work, go; **el timbre no rige** the bell doesn't work.
　(c) (*fam*) **no — to have a screw loose** (*fam*), be not all there (*fam*).
　3 **regirse** *vr*: **— por** to be ruled by, be guided by, go by.
registrado *adj* registered.
registrador *nm* recorder, registrar.
registrar [1a] 1 *vt* (a) *fact etc* to register, record; to enter; to file.
　(b) (*Mus etc*) to record; **— la voz en una cinta** to record one's voice on tape.
　(c) *luggage, person, place* to search; *archive, document* to survey, inspect; to look through; **lo hemos registrado todo de arriba abajo** we have searched the whole place from top to bottom.
　2 **registrarse** *vr* (a) (*person*) to register.
　(b) (*fact etc*) to be recorded; (*event, accident*) to happen; **se han registrado algunos casos de tifus**

a few cases of typhus have been reported; **no se ha registrado nunca nada parecido** nothing of the kind has ever been recorded before; **el cambio que se ha registrado en su actitud** the change which has occurred in his attitude.
registro *nm* (a) (*act*) registration, recording.
　(b) register; visitor's book; **— de casamientos** register of marriages; **— de defunciones** register of deaths; **— electoral** voting register, electoral roll; **— de hotel** hotel register; **— de nacimientos** register of births; **— parroquial** parish register; **firmar el —** to sign the register.
　(c) list, roll, record; note; **— de erratas** list of errata.
　(d) entry (in a register).
　(e) registry, record office; **— civil** register office; **— de patentes y marcas** patents office; **— de la propiedad** land registry (office).
　(f) search; survey, inspection; **— domiciliario** search of a house; **— policíaco** police search; **practicar un —** to make a search (**en** of).
　(g) (*Mus etc*) recording; **es un buen — de la sinfonía** it is a good recording of the symphony.
　(h) (*Mus*) register; (*of organ*) stop; (*of piano*) pedal; **salir por** (*or* **adoptar**) **un — muy raro** (*fig*) to adopt a very odd tone, adopt a most inappropriate tone; **tocar todos los —s** (*fig*) to pull out all the stops.
　(i) (*Tech*) manhole, manhole cover; (*of fire*) damper; inspection plate, inspection hatch.
　(j) bookmark.
　(k) (*of watch*) regulator.
　(l) (*Typ*) register; **estar en —** to be in register.
　(m) (*Bol, RPl*) wholesale textiles store.
regla *nf* (a) ruler, rule; **— de cálculo** slide rule; **— de un pie** foot rule; **— en T**, **— en T** T-square.
　(b) rule; regulation; (*Sport etc*) rule; (*scientific*) law, principle; norm; **—s del juego** rules of the game, laws of the game; **—s de la circulación** traffic regulations; **—s para utilizar una máquina** instructions for the use of a machine, points to be observed in using a machine; **no hay — sin excepción** every rule has its exception; **en —** in order; **todo está en —** everything is in order; all is as it should be; **poner algo en —** to put something straight; **no tenía los papeles en —** his papers were not in order; **por — general** generally, usually, as a rule; on the average; **hacerse una — de** + *infin* to make it a rule to + *infin*; **ser de —** to be the rule, be usual, be the norm; **salir de —** to overstep the mark; to be abnormal, have abnormal features.
　(c) (*Math*) rule; law; **— de 3** rule of 3.
　(d) (*Eccl*) rule, order; **viven según la — benedictina** they live according to the Benedictine rule.
　(e) (*Med*) **—s** period.
　(f) (*fig*) moderation, restraint; **comer con —** to eat in moderation.
reglaje *nm* (a) (*Mech*) checking, overhaul; adjustment. (b) (*Mil*) correction (of aim).
reglamentación *nf* (a) (*act*) regulation. (b) rules, regulations (*collectively*).
reglamentar [1a] *vt* to regulate; to make rules for, establish regulations for.
reglamentariamente *adv* in due form, according to the rules; properly.
reglamentario *adj* regulation (*attr*); set; statutory; proper, due; **en el traje —** in the regulation dress; **en la forma reglamentaria** in due form, in the properly established way; **es — + *infin*** the law requires that . . ., the regulation makes it obligatory to + *infin*.
reglamento *nm* rules, regulations (*collectively*); (*of meeting, society*) standing order(s); (*municipal etc*) by-law; (*of profession*) code of conduct; **— de aduana** customs regulations; **— del tráfico** rule of the road, highway code.
reglar [1a] 1 *vt* (a) *line etc* to rule.
　(b) (*Mech*) to check, overhaul; to adjust; (*Mil*) *aim* to correct.
　(c) (*fig*) to regulate, make regulations for.
　2 **reglarse** *vr*: **— a** to abide by, conform to; **— por** to be guided by.
regleta *nf* (*Typ*) space.
regletear [1a] *vt* (*Typ*) to space out.
regocijadamente *adv* merrily; joyously, joyfully; exultantly.
regocijado *adj* (a) *character* jolly, cheerful, merry. (b) *state* merry; joyous, joyful; exultant.
regocijar [1a] 1 *vt* to gladden, delight, cheer (up); **un chiste que regocijó a todos** a joke which made everyone laugh; **crear un personaje para — a los niños** to create a character to amuse children; **la**

noticia regocijó a la familia the news delighted the family, the news filled the family with joy.
2 regocijarse *vr* (a) to rejoice, be glad, express one's happiness (*de*, *por* about, at).
(b) to laugh; — **con un chiste** to laugh at a joke.
(c) to make merry, have a merry time, celebrate.
(d) (*pej*) to exult; — **por un desastre ajeno** to exult in someone else's misfortune, take a cruel pleasure in a disaster which has befallen someone else.
regocijo *nm* (a) joy, happiness; rejoicing; elation; gaiety, merriment.
(b) (*pej*) exultation; unhealthy pleasure, cruel delight (*por* in).
(c) —**s** festivities, rejoicings, celebrations; —**s navideños** Christmas festivities; —**s públicos** public rejoicings.
regodearse [1a] *vr* (a) to crack jokes (*fam*); to indulge in coarse humour.
(b) to be glad, be delighted; — **haciendo algo** to enjoy oneself hugely doing something; (*pej*) — **con**, — **en** to take a cruel delight in; — **porque otro está sufriendo** to be perversely glad that somebody else is suffering.
(c) (*Col, Chi, Ven*) to be fussy, be hard to please.
regodeo *nm* (a) joking; coarse humour. (b) delight; huge enjoyment; (*pej*) cruel delight, perverse pleasure.
regodeón *adj* (*Col, Chi*) fussy, hard to please.
regodiente *adj* (*Col, Ven*) fussy, hard to please.
regoldar [1m] *vi* to belch.
regordete *adj* person chubby, plump; *hands etc* fat.
regosto *nm* longing, craving (*de* for).
regresar [1a] **1** *vt* (*SAm*) to give back, return. **2** *vi* to come back, go back, return. **3 regresarse** *vr* (*SAm*) = **2**.
regresión *nf* regression; (*fig*) retreat; backward step; fall, decrease.
regresivo *adj* movement backward; (*fig*) regressive, retrogressive, backward; downward.
regreso *nm* return; **viaje de** — return trip, homeward journey; **emprender el** — **a** to return to, come back to; **estar de** — to be back, be home.
regüeldo *nm* belch, belching.
reguera *nf* (a) (*Agr*) irrigation channel. (b) (*Naut*) cable, mooring rope, anchor chain.
reguero *nm* (a) (*Agr*) irrigation ditch; (*SAm*) furrow.
(b) track; streak, line, mark; (*of blood etc*) trickle; (*of gunpowder etc*) train; (*of smoke, vapour*) trail; **propagarse como un** — **de pólvora** to spread like wildfire.
reguío *nm* (*Col, Ec, SD*) = **riego**.
regulable *adj* adjustable.
regulación *nf* regulation; adjustment; control; — **de la natalidad** birth control; — **del tráfico** traffic control; — **del volumen sonoro** (*Radio*) volume control.
regulador *nm* (*Mech*) regulator, throttle, governor; (*Radio etc*) control, knob, button; — **del volumen sonoro** volume control.
regular 1 *adj* (a) (*in most senses, also Eccl, Math, Mil*) regular; normal, usual, customary; ordinary; *life etc* regular, orderly, well-organized; **a intervalos** —**es** at regular intervals; **tiene un latido** — it has a regular beat.
(b) (*fig*) regular; middling, medium, average; fair; (*pej*) fair, so-so, not too bad; (*fam: euph*) tremendous (*fam*), whopping (*sl*); **es una novela** — it's an average sort of novel, it's a fair novel; **de tamaño** — medium-sized, fair-sized; "**¿cómo es la chica?**" . . . "**—**" "what's the girl like?" . . . "an ordinary sort of girl" (*or* "not too bad", "nothing outstanding").
(c) **por lo** — as a rule, generally.
2 *adv* (*fam*) **estar** — to be all right, be so-so; "**¿qué tal estás?**" . . . "**—**" "how are you?" "so-so" (*or* "all right", "can't complain").
3 [1a] *vt* (a) to regulate, control; (*of law etc*) to govern; *traffic* to control, direct; *price etc* to control.
(b) (*Mech etc*) to adjust, regulate; *watch* to put right; *alarm clock* to set.
(c) (*Mex*) to calculate.
regularcillo *adj* (*fam*) = **regular 1**(b).
regularidad *nf* regularity; **con** — regularly.
regularizar [1f] *vt* to regularize; to standardize, bring into line.
regularmente *adv* regularly.
regurgitación *nf* regurgitation.
regurgitar [1a] *vt* to regurgitate.
regustado *adj* (*Cu, PR*) satisfied.
regustar [1a] *vt* (*Cu, Mex*) to taste, relish, savour.
regusto *nm* (a) aftertaste (*also fig*). (b) additional pleasure; unhealthy pleasure.

rehabilitación *nf* (a) rehabilitation; reinstatement. (b) restoration; overhaul.
rehabilitar [1a] *vt* (a) *person* to rehabilitate; (*in office*) to reinstate. (b) (*Archit etc*) to restore, renovate; (*Mech*) to overhaul.
rehacer [2s] **1** *vt* (a) to redo, do again; to repeat.
(b) to remake; to mend, repair; to refurbish, renew, do up.
2 rehacerse *vr* (a) (*Med*) to recover; to regain one's strength; (*fig*) to recover one's calm (*or* self esteem *etc*).
(b) (*Mil*) to re-form; to rally.
rehecho *adj* thickset, chunky (*fam*).
rehén *nm* hostage.
rehenchir [3l] *vt* to fill, stuff, pack (*de* with).
rehilar [1a] *vi* (a) to quiver, shake. (b) (*of arrow etc*) to whizz.
rehilete *nm* (a) dart (*also Taur*). (b) shuttlecock; badminton. (c) (*fig*) dig, cutting remark, taunt.
rehuir [3g] *vt* to shun, avoid; to shrink from; — + *infin* to avoid + *ger*, shrink from + *ger*.
rehusar [1a] **1** *vt* to refuse, decline; — **hacer algo** to refuse to do something. **2** *vi* to refuse (*also of horse*).
reidero *adj* (*fam*) amusing, funny.
reidor *adj* merry, laughing.
reilón *adj* (*Ec, Ven*) given to laughing a lot, giggly; merry.
reimponer [2r] *vt* to reimpose.
reimpresión *nf* reprint(ing).
reimprimir [3a] *vt* to reprint.
reina *nf* queen (*also Chess, Ent etc*); — **de belleza** beauty queen; — **de la fiesta** carnival queen; — **madre** queen mother; — **viuda** dowager queen.
reinado *nm* reign; **bajo el** — **de** in the reign of.
Reinaldos *m* Reginald.
reinante *adj* (a) reigning. (b) (*fig*) prevailing.
reinar [1a] *vi* (a) (*Pol*) to reign, rule.
(b) (*fig*) to reign; to prevail, be general; **reinan las bajas temperaturas** there are low temperatures everywhere; **reina una confusión total** total confusion reigns; **entre la población reinaba el descontento** unrest was rife in the population; there was widespread discontent in the population.
reincidencia *nf* relapse (*en* into).
reincidente *nmf* recidivist; hardened offender; backslider.
reincidir [3a] *vi* to relapse (*en* into); to repeat an offence; to backslide.
reincorporarse [1a] *vr*: — **a** to rejoin.
reingresar [1a] *vi*: — **en** to re-enter.
reingreso *nm* re-entry (*en* into).
reino *nm* (*all senses*) kingdom.
reinoso *nm* (a) (*Col*) inlander, inhabitant of the interior (*esp of the cold eastern upland*). (b) (*Ven*) Colombian.
reinstalar [1a] *vt* to reinstall; *person* to reinstate.
reintegrable *adj* deposit returnable, repayable.
reintegración *nf* (a) reinstatement (*a* in). (b) (*Fin*) refund, repayment, reimbursement. (c) return (*a* to).
reintegrar [1a] **1** *vt* (a) to make whole again, reintegrate.
(b) *person* to reinstate (*a* in).
(c) (*Fin*) — **a uno una cantidad** to refund (*or* repay, pay back) a sum to someone, reimburse someone for a sum; **ha sido reintegrado de todos sus gastos** he has been reimbursed in full for all his expenses.
(d) *sum* to pay back.
(e) *document* to attach a fiscal stamp to.
2 reintegrarse *vr* (a) — **a** to return to.
(b) — **de una cantidad** to recover a sum, recoup a sum, secure repayment of a sum; — **de los gastos** to reimburse oneself for one's expenses.
reintegro *nm* (a) refund, repayment, reimbursement; (*from bank account*) withdrawal. (b) (*in lottery*) return of one's stake. (c) (*cost of a*) fiscal stamp.
reinversión *nf* reinvestment.
reinvertir [3i] *vt* to reinvest.
reír [3m] **1** *vt* to laugh at; **todos le ríen los chistes** everybody laughs at his jokes.
2 *vi* (a) to laugh; **sólo para hacer** — just to make people laugh, just for a laugh; **el último que ríe, ríe más fuerte** he who laughs last laughs longest.
(b) (*fig: of eyes etc*) to laugh, sparkle, be merry; (*of morning, nature, countryside*) to smile, be bright.
3 reírse *vr* to laugh (*con*, *de* about, at, over); — **con uno** to laugh at someone's jokes; — **de uno** to laugh at someone, make fun of someone; **¿se ríe Vd de mí?** are you laughing at me?; **¡déjeme que me ría!** that's a good one!; **fue para** — it was utterly absurd; *see* **echar** *etc*.
(b) (*fam*) to tear, come apart; **la chaqueta se me**

ríe por los codos my jacket is out at the elbows, my jacket is coming apart at the elbows.

reiteración *nf* reiteration, reaffirmation; repetition.

reiteradamente *adv* repeatedly.

reiterado *adj* repeated.

reiterar [1a] *vt* to reiterate, reaffirm; to repeat.

reiterativo *adj* reiterative; (*pej*) repetitive, repetitious.

reivindicable *adj* recoverable (at law).

reivindicación *nf* (a) claim (*de* to). (b) vindication; restoration. (c) (*Law*) recovery.

reivindicar [1g] **1** *vt* (a) to claim (the right to), claim as of right; to assert one's claim to.
(b) *reputation etc* to vindicate; to restore; to win back.
(c) (*Law*) *right* to recover.
2 reivindicarse *vr* (*SAm*) to vindicate oneself; to restore one's reputation.

reja *nf* (a) grating, grid, gridiron; (*of window*) bars, grille; **estar entre —s** to be behind bars.
(b) (*Agr*) **— del arado** ploughshare.
(c) (*SAm*) prison.
(d) (*Mex*) darning.
(e) (*Chi*) cattle truck.

rejado *nm* grille, grating.

rejeada *nf* (*CAm, Col*) thrashing.

rejear [1a] *vt* (*CAm*) to jail, put in jail.

rejego **1** *adj* (a) (*CAm, Mex*) wild, untamed; troublesome, unruly. (b) (*Mex*) slow, sluggish. **2** *nm* (*CAm*) stud bull.

rejiego *adj* (*Cu, Mex*) =**rejego.**

rejilla *nf* (a) grating, grille; lattice; screen; (*Radio*) grille; (*Rail*) luggage rack; (*of furniture*) wickerwork; **silla de —** wicker chair.
(b) small stove, footwarmer.
(c) (*Chi*) meat safe.

rejo *nm* (a) spike, sharp point.
(b) (*Ent*) sting.
(c) (*Bot*) radicle.
(d) (*fig*) strength, vigour, toughness.
(e) (*SAm*) whip; (*Col, Ven*) strip of raw leather.
(f) (*Ven*) stick, club.
(g) (*Ec*) milking; herd of cows.

rejón *nm* pointed iron bar; (*Taur*) lance.

rejoneador *nm* (*Taur*) *mounted bullfighter who uses the lance.*

rejonear [1a] (*Taur*) **1** *vt* to wound the bull with the lance. **2** *vi* to fight the bull on horseback with the lance.

rejudo *adj* (*Col, Ven*) sticky, viscous.

rejugado *adj* (*CAm, Col, Cu*) shy.

rejunta *nf* (*Arg, Mex*) roundup, rodeo.

rejuntar [1a] *vt* (*Mex, RPl*) to collect, gather in; *cattle* to round up; *sum* to add up.

rejuvenecer [2d] **1** *vt* to rejuvenate. **2 rejuvenecerse** *vr* to be rejuvenated, become young again.

relación *nf* (a) relation, relationship (*con* to, with); **—es** relations, relationship; **la — entre X y Z** the relationship between X and Z; **sus —es con el jefe** his relations with the boss; **buenas —es** good relations; **—es amistosas** friendly relations; **—es carnales** sexual relations; **—es comerciales** business connections, trade relations; **—es humanas** human relations, (*as department, profession*) personnel management; **—es públicas** public relations; **estar en buenas —es con** to be on good terms with; **mantener —es con** to keep in touch with; **romper las —es con** to break off relations with; **con — a**, **en — a** in relation to; **un aumento de 3 por cien con — al año anterior** an increase of 3% over the previous year.
(b) (*Math*) ratio; proportion; **en una — de 7 a 2** in a ratio of 7 to 2; **— real de intercambio** terms of trade; **guardar cierta — con** to bear a certain relation to; **no guardar — alguna con** to be out of all proportion to, bear no relation whatsoever to.
(c) **—es (amorosas)** courting, courtship; **—es formales** engagement; **—es ilícitas** illicit sexual relations; **llevan varios meses de —es** they've been going out (*or* courting) for some months; **A está en (*or* tiene) —es con B** A and B are going out together, A and B are courting.
(d) **—es (*persons*)** acquaintances; (*esp*) influential friends, contacts, connections; **para eso conviene tener —es** for that it helps to have contacts; **tener buenas —es** to be well connected, have powerful friends.
(e) account, report; story; (*of difficulties etc*) tale, recital; **hizo una larga — de su viaje** he gave a lengthy account of his trip.
(f) list; record, (official) return.

(g) (*Theat*) long speech.
(h) (*Mex*) buried treasure.

relacionado *adj* (a) related; **un tema — con Lorca** a subject that has to do with Lorca, a subject that concerns Lorca; **A está íntimamente — con B** A is closely connected with B; A is much bound up with B.
(b) **una persona relacionada** (*SAm*), **una persona bien relacionada** a well-connected person.

relacionar [1a] **1** *vt* to relate (*con* to), connect (*con* with).
2 relacionarse *vr* (a) **es hombre que se relaciona** he's a man with (powerful) connections.
(b) (*two things etc*) to be connected, be related.
(c) **— con uno** to get to know someone; to get into touch with someone.
(d) **en lo que se relaciona con** as for, with regard to.

relai(s) [re'le] *nm* (*Elec*) relay.

relajación *nf* (a) relaxation; slackening, loosening; weakening. (b) (*fig*) relaxation, amusement. (c) (*fig*: *moral*) laxity, looseness. (d) (*Med*) hernia, rupture.

relajado *adj* (a) *life etc* dissolute, loose. (b) (*Med*) ruptured.

relajadura *nf* (*Mex*) hernia, rupture.

relajante 1 *adj* (a) (*Med*) laxative. (b) (*Arg, Chi*) *food* cloying, excessively sweet; repellent. **2** *nm* laxative.

relajar [1a] **1** *vt* (a) to relax; to slacken, loosen; to weaken.
(b) (*fig*: *morally*) to weaken, corrupt, make lax.
(c) (*SAm*: *of food*) to cloy, sicken, disgust.
(d) (*Ant*) to mock; to abuse, be disrespectful to.
2 relajarse *vr* (a) to relax; to slacken, loosen; to weaken.
(b) (*fig*) to relax; **tiene mucha facilidad para —** he has a great capacity for relaxing.
(c) (*fig*: *morally*) to become dissolute, go to the bad; (*morality etc*) to become lax.
(d) (*Med*) **— un tobillo** to lose the use of an ankle, lose the feeling in an ankle; **— un órgano** to rupture an organ.

relajo *nm* (*SAm*) (a) laxity, dissipation, depravity; lewdness.
(b) immoral act; indecent act.
(c) boisterous gathering; lewd party; commotion, disorder.
(d) rude joke; practical joke; derision; **cuento de —** blue joke; **echar algo a —** to make fun of something.

relajón *adj* (*Ant*) (a) mocking; coarsely humorous.
(b) depraved, lewd.

relamer [2a] **1** *vt* to lick repeatedly.
2 relamerse *vr* (a) (*animal*) to lick its chops; (*person*) to lick one's lips (*also* — **los labios**).
(b) (*fig*) **— con algo** to relish something in advance, relish the prospect of something; to smack one's lips over (the idea of) something; (*pej*) to gloat over the prospect of something.
(c) (*fig*) to brag.
(d) (*fig*) to paint one's face.

relamido *adj* (a) prim and proper; affected; overdressed. (b) (*CAm, Cu, Mex*) shameless, brazen.

relámpago 1 *nm* lightning, flash of lightning; (*fig*) flash; **— difuso** sheet lightning; **como un —** as quick as lightning, in a flash.
2 *as adj* lightning; **guerra —** blitzkrieg; **visita —** rushed visit, rapid visit; **viaje —** lightning trip.

relampaguear [1a] *vi* (*Cu, Mex*) to twinkle; to flicker; to gleam.

relampagueo *nm* (*Cu, Mex*) twinkle; flicker, gleam.

relampagueante *adj* flashing.

relampaguear [1a] *vi* to lighten; to flash; **relampagueó toda la noche** the lightning was flashing all night, there was lightning all night.

relampagueo *nm* flashing.

relampuso *nm* (*Cu*) shameless, brazen.

relance *nm* (*Chi*) =**piropo.**

relanzar [1f] *vt* to repel, repulse.

relatar [1a] *vt* to relate, tell; to report.

relativamente *adv* relatively.

relativismo *nm* relativism.

relativista 1 *adj* relativistic. **2** *nmf* relativist.

relativo 1 *adj* relative (*also Gram*); **— a** a relative to; regarding, relating to. **2** *nm* (*Gram*) relative.

relato *nm* story, tale; account, report.

relator *nm* teller, narrator; (*Law*) court reporter.

relauchar [1a] *vi* (*Chi*) to knock off work for a rest.

relé *nm* (*Elec: Acad*) relay.

releer [2e] *vt* to reread.

relegación *nf* (a) relegation. (b) (*Hist*) exile, banishment.

relegar [1h] vt (a) to relegate; — **algo al olvido** to banish something from one's mind; to consign something to oblivion. (b) (Hist) to exile, banish.

releso adj (Chi) stupid.

relevación nf (a) relief (also Mil); replacement. (b) (Law) exoneration; release (de from).

relevante adj outstanding.

relevar [1a] vt (a) (Tech) to emboss; to carve (or paint etc) in relief.
(b) (Mil) guard to relieve.
(c) — **a uno de una obligación** to relieve someone of a duty, free someone from an obligation; — **a uno de la culpa** to exonerate someone, free someone from blame; **relevar a uno de** + infin to free someone from the obligation to + infin.
(d) — **a uno de un cargo** to relieve someone of his post, replace someone in his post; **ser relevado de su mando** to be relieved of one's command.

relevo nm (a) (Mil: act) relief, change; (persons) relief; — **de los tiros** change of horses. (b) (Sport) —s relay (race); **100 metros** —s 100 metres relay.

relicario nm (a) (Eccl) shrine; reliquary. (b) locket.

relieve nm (a) (Art, Tech) relief; raised work, embossing; raised part; **alto** — high relief; **bajo** — bas-relief; **en** — raised pattern, embossed pattern, pattern in relief; **película en** — stereoscopic film, three-dimensional (abbr: 3-D) film; **estampar en** — to emboss.
(b) importance, prominence; social standing; **un personaje de** — an important man, a man of some importance; **dar** — **a** to enhance; to give prominence to, bring out; **poner algo de** — to emphasize (the importance of), point out the interest of, stress the qualities of.
(c) —s left-overs.

religión nf (a) religion.
(b) (fig) religion, cult; **tiene la** — **de la promesa** he believes utterly in keeping his word.
(c) religiousness; religious sense, piety.
(d) (Eccl) the religious life, religion; **entrar en** — to take vows, enter a religious order.

religiosa nf nun.

religiosamente adv religiously.

religiosidad nf religiosity, religiousness; (fig) religiousness.

religioso 1 adj religious (also fig). 2 nm religious, member of a religious order, monk.

relimpio adj absolutely clean; spick and span.

relinchada nf (Mex) = **relincho**.

relinchar [1a] vi to neigh, whinny, snort.

relincho nm neigh(ing), whinny(ing), snort(ing).

reliquia nf (a) (Eccl) relic; (Mex) votive offering.
(b) relic; —s relics, remains; traces, vestiges; — **de familia** heirloom, family treasure.
(c) (Med) —s after-effects, lingering effects, resultant weakness.

reloj [re'lo] nm clock; watch; (Tech) clock, meter; — **de arena** sandglass, hourglass; — **automático** timer, timing mechanism; — **de bolsillo** pocket watch; — **de caja** grandfather clock; — **de carillón** chiming clock; — **despertador** alarm clock; — **eléctrico** electric clock; — **de estacionamiento** parking meter; — **de la muerte** (Ent) deathwatch beetle; — **de pie** grandfather clock; — **de pulsera** wristwatch; — **registrador** time clock; — **de sol** sundial; **como un** — like clockwork; **estar como un** — (fam) to feel on top of the world, be on top form; to be as fit as a fiddle; **contra** (**el**) — against the clock.

relojear [1a] vt (Arg) (a) race to time. (b) (fig) to watch, spy on; to check.

relojería nf (a) watchmaking, clockmaking. (b) watchmaker's (shop). (c) (also **aparato de** —) clockwork; **bomba de** — time bomb.

relojero nm watchmaker, clockmaker.

reluciente adj (a) shining, brilliant; glittering, gleaming, sparkling; bright. (b) person sleek; well-fed; healthy-looking.

relucir [3f] vi (a) to shine; to glitter, gleam, sparkle; to be bright. (b) **sacar algo a** — to bring something out, show something off.

relujar [1a] vt (Guat, Mex) shoes to shine.

relumbrante adj brilliant, dazzling; glaring.

relumbrar [1a] vi to shine brilliantly, be bright; to dazzle; to glare.

relumbrón nm (a) flash; sudden glare. (b) (fig) flashiness, ostentation; **joyas de** — flashy jewellery; **vestirse de** — to dress flashily, dress ostentatiously.

rellano nm (Archit) landing.

rellena nf (Col, Mex) black pudding.

rellenado nm refill; replenishment; (Aer etc) refuelling.

rellenar [1a] 1 vt (a) to refill, replenish; (Aer etc) to refuel.
(b) to fill up; to pack, stuff, cram (de with); (Cook) to stuff; (Sew etc) to pad; spaces etc to fill in; form to fill in, fill up.
2 **rellenarse** vr to stuff oneself (de with).

relleno 1 adj packed, stuffed, crammed (de with); very full, full right up (de of); (Cook) stuffed.
2 nm filling; (Archit) plaster filling; (Cook) stuffing; (Sew) padding; wadding; (Mech) packing.

remachado adj (Col) quiet, reserved.

remachador nm rivetter.

remachar [1a] 1 vt (a) (Tech) nail etc to clinch; metals to rivet.
(b) (fig) point to hammer home, drive home; to stress; **para** —**lo todavía** to clinch matters; to make it entirely certain.
2 **remacharse** vr (Col) to remain stubbornly silent.

remache nm (a) (Tech) rivet. (b) (act) clinching; rivetting. (c) (Col) stubbornness.

remada nf stroke.

remador nm rower, oarsman.

remadura adj (SAm) overripe.

remandingo nm (Cu) row, uproar.

remanente 1 adj remaining; (Phys) remanent; (Comm etc) surplus. 2 nm remainder; (Comm, Fin) balance; (of production) surplus.

remansarse [1a] vr to form a pool; to become stagnant.

remanso nm (a) pool; backwater. (b) (fig) quiet place, peaceful area; **un** — **de paz** an oasis of peace, a haven of peace.

remar [1a] vi (a) to row. (b) (fig) to toil, struggle; to suffer hardships.

remarcable adj (SAm: angl) remarkable.

remarcar [1g] vt (SAm: angl) (a) to notice, observe, remark on. (b) to distinguish.

rematadamente adv terribly, hopelessly; — **mal** terribly bad; **es** — **tonto** he's utterly stupid.

rematado adj (a) hopeless, complete, out-and-out; **es un loco** — he's a raving lunatic; **es un tonto** — he's an utter fool. (b) child very naughty.

rematador nm (Bol, RPl) auctioneer.

rematante nm highest bidder.

rematar [1a] 1 vt (a) person to finish off; to kill off; animal to shoot dead, kill instantly.
(b) (fig) work etc to finish off, bring to a conclusion; process to finish, round off; abuse to put an end to; drink etc to finish up, drink (etc) the last of.
(c) (Archit etc) to top, be at the very top of, crown.
(d) (Comm) to sell off cheap (to clear).
(e) (Comm) — **algo a uno** to knock something down to someone (en for).
(f) (SAm) to buy at an auction; to sell at auction; (CAm, Mex) to sell.
(g) (Chi) horse to rein in suddenly.
2 vi (a) to end, finish off; **remató con un par de chistes** he finished with a couple of jokes.
(b) — **en** to end in, come to; **es del tipo que remata en punta** it's the sort which comes to a point; **fue una broma que remató en tragedia** it was a joke which ended in tragedy.
(c) (Sport) to shoot, score; — **de cabeza** to head a goal.

remate nm (a) (act) finishing (off); killing.off.
(b) (of object) end; tip, point; (Archit) top, crest; (of sideboard etc) ornamental top.
(c) (fig) conclusion; finishing touch; **de** — = **rematado** (a); **para** — to crown it all, on top of all that; **por** — finally, as a finishing touch; **poner** — **a** to cap; to put the finishing touch to, round off.
(d) (Comm) highest bid.
(e) (Comm) sale (by auction); (Bridge) bidding, auction; (SAm) auction.

rematista nm (Per, PR) auctioneer.

remecer [2d] 1 vt to rock, swing (to and fro); (Mex) to shake; to wave. 2 **remecerse** vr to rock, swing (to and fro).

remedar [1a] vt to imitate, copy; (pej) to ape; (jokingly) to ape, mimic.

remediable adj remediable, that can be remedied; **fácilmente** — easy to remedy, easily remedied.

remediar [1b] vt (a) damage, loss to make good, repair; to make up for; abuse to correct, put right, put a stop to; **llorando no remedias nada** you won't do any good by crying.
(b) needs etc to meet, help with; needy person to help (out); endangered person to help, save.
(c) to avoid, prevent; **sin poder** —**lo** without being able to prevent it; **a ver si lo remediamos** let's

see if we can do anything about it; **no poder — el
echarse a reír** not to be able to help laughing.
remedio nm (a) remedy (also Med; contra against);
help; — **casero** ordinary remedy, simple domestic
remedy; — **heroico** extreme remedy, extreme
measure; **como último** — as a last resort; **sin —**
inevitable; irremediable; **es un tonto sin —** he's a
hopeless idiot, he's so stupid he's past redemption;
no se podía encontrar ni para un — it couldn't be
had for love nor money; **¡ni por un —!** not on your
life!; **no hay más —** there's no help for it, there's
nothing one can do, there's no other way; **no hay
más — que +** infin the only thing is to + infin; **no
hay — para él** it's all up with him; **esto no tiene —**
it is unavoidable; there's nothing one can do about
it; it's beyond repair; **no tiene —** he's hopeless,
he's past redemption; **¿qué — tengo?** what else
can I do?; **no tener más — que +** infin to have
no alternative but to + infin; **poner — a un abuso**
to correct an abuse, put a stop to an abuse.
  (b) relief, help; **buscar — en su aflicción** to look
for some relief in one's distress.
  (c) (Law) remedy, recourse.
remedo nm imitation, copy; (pej) poor imitation,
travesty, parody.
rememorar [1a] vt (lit) to remember, recall.
remendar [1k] vt (a) to mend, repair; to patch, darn.
  (b) (fig) to correct.
remendón nm cobbler.
remero nm oarsman.
remesa nf remittance; shipment, consignment.
remesar [1a] vt money to remit, send; goods to send,
ship, consign.
remeter [2a] vr to put back; bedclothes, shirt etc to
tuck in.
remezón nm (SAm) earth tremor, slight earthquake.
remiendo nm (a) (act) mending; patching.
  (b) mend; patch, darn; **a —s** piecemeal; **echar un
— a** to patch, put a patch on.
  (c) (fig) correction.
  (d) (Zool) spot, patch.
remilgado adj prudish, prim; affected; finicky, fussy,
particular, overnice; squeamish, oversensitive.
remilgarse [1h] vr to react prudishly; to show one's
affectation; to be fussy; to be squeamish.
remilgo nm (a) prudery, primness; affectation; fussiness; squeamishness, excess of sensitivity.
  (b) prim look; simper; smirk; **hacer —s a** to react
in a prudish (etc) way to; **él no hace —s a ninguna
clase de trabajo** he won't turn up his nose at any
kind of work.
  (c) **don R—s** (hum) Lord Muck.
remilgoso adj (SAm) = **remilgado**.
reminiscencia nf reminiscence.
remirado adj (a) cautious, circumspect, careful;
(pej) overcautious. (b) (pej) prudish; affected, overnice; fussy, pernickety (fam).
remirar [1a] 1 vt to look at again; to look hard at. 2
remirarse vr to be extra careful (en about), take
great pains (en over).
remise nm or f (Arg: gall) hired car, taxi.
remisión nf (a) sending; (SAm) shipment, consignment.
  (b) reference (a to).
  (c) postponement; adjournment.
  (d) remission (also Med); slackening.
  (e) (Eccl) forgiveness, remission.
remiso adj (a) slack, slow (to obey), remiss. (b)
movement slow, sluggish.
remisor nm (SAm: Comm) sender.
remitente nmf sender.
remitido nm (a) (in newspaper) paid insertion; note
(or article) reprinted from another newspaper. (b)
(Mex) shipment, consignment.
remitir [3a] 1 vt (a) (Post) to send; money to remit;
(Comm) to send, ship, consign.
  (b) reader, user to refer (a to).
  (c) event etc to postpone; session to adjourn.
  (d) **— una decisión a uno** to leave a decision to
someone, refer a matter to someone for a decision.
  (e) sins to forgive, pardon.
  2 vi (a) to slacken, diminish, let up.
  (b) **"remite: X . . ."** (on envelope) "sender:
X . . ."
remo nm (a) oar; **a — y vela** (fig) speedily; **andar al
—** (fig) to be hard at it; **cruzar un río a —** to row
across a river; **pasaron los cañones a —** they rowed
the guns across.
  (b) (as sport) rowing; **practicar el —** to row, go in for
rowing.
  (c) (Anat) arm, leg; (Orn) wing.
  (d) (fig) toils, hardships.

remoción nf (a) removal. (b) (Mex) sacking (fam),
dismissal.
remodelar [1a] vt to remodel.
remojar [1a] vt (a) to steep, soak (en in); to dip (en
in, into); (accidentally) to soak, drench (con with);
biscuit etc to dip, dunk (en in).
  (b) (fam) event to celebrate with a drink.
remojo nm (a) steeping, soaking; drenching; dip,
dipping; **dejar la ropa en —** to leave clothes to soak;
poner los garbanzos a — to put chickpeas in to soak.
  (b) (SAm) gift made to mark an occasion; tip.
remojón nm (a) soaking, drenching. (b) (Cook)
piece of bread soaked in milk (etc).
remolacha nf beet, beetroot; — **azucarera** sugar beet.
remolcador nm (Naut) tug; (Aut) tow car, breakdown lorry.
remolcar [1g] vt to tow, tow along; to take in tow.
remoledor adj (Chi, Per) roistering, merry.
remoler [2h] 1 vt (a) to grind up small. (b) (Guat,
Per) to annoy. 2 vi (Chi, Per) to live it up (fam).
remolienda nf (Chi, Per) carousal, revelry.
remolinar(se) [1a], **remolinear(se)** [1a] = **arremolinarse**.
remolino nm (a) (of water) swirl, eddy; whirlpool;
(of air) whirl; disturbance; whirlwind; (of dust,
smoke) whirl, cloud.
  (b) (of hair) tuft.
  (c) (of people) crowd, throng, crush, moving mass.
  (d) (fig) commotion.
remolón 1 adj (a) stubborn; awkward, cantankerous.
  (b) slack, lazy. 2 nm, **remolona** nf stubborn individual; slacker, shirker; **hacerce el — = remolonear**.
remolonear [1a] vi (a) to be stubborn, refuse to
budge; to hold out on someone. (b) to slack, shirk.
remolque nm (a) (act) towing; **a —** on tow, being
towed; **ir a —** to be on tow; **llevar un coche a —**
to tow a car; **lo hizo a —** (fig) he did it reluctantly;
they had to push him to do it, he did it because
somebody made him; **dar — a** to tow, take in tow.
  (b) (Naut) towrope; cable, hawser; (Aut etc) towrope.
  (c) (vehicle etc: Aut) tow; car being towed;
trailer, caravan; (Naut) ship on tow.
remonda nf (sl): **¡es la —!** this is the end!; it's sheer hell!
remonta nf (a) mending, repair. (b) (Mil) remount,
supply of cavalry horses; cavalry horses; cavalry
depot.
remontar [1a] 1 vt (a) stocking to mend (a ladder in);
shoes to mend, repair, resole.
  (b) **— el vuelo** to soar (up).
  (c) river etc to go up.
  (d) obstacle to negotiate, get over, surmount.
  (e) (Mil) cavalry to remount.
  (f) watch to wind.
  (g) Hunting game to frighten away.
  2 **remontarse** vr (a) (Aer, Orn etc) to rise, soar;
(building) to soar, tower; (fig) to soar; **— en alas de
la imaginación** to take flight on the wings of fantasy.
  (b) (Fin) **— a** to amount to.
  (c) (in time) **— a** to go back to; **sus recuerdos se
remontan al siglo pasado** her memories go back to
the last century; **este texto se remonta al siglo XI**
this text dates from (or back to) the 11th century;
tenemos que remontarnos a los mismos orígenes
we must get back to the very origins.
remoquete nm (a) punch. (b) (fig) cutting remark,
dig. (c) nickname; **poner — a uno** to give someone a
nickname. (d) (fam) flirting, spooning (fam); suitor.
rémora nf (fig) drawback; hindrance.
remorder [2h] 1 vt person to grieve, distress; to cause
remorse to; conscience to prick; mind to afflict, prey
upon.
  2 **remorderse** vr to suffer (or show) remorse; to
suffer inwardly, harbour a grudge (or jealousy etc).
remordimiento nm remorse, regret (also **—s**);
tener —s to feel remorse, suffer pangs of conscience.
remotamente adv (a) resemble, remember vaguely,
slightly; **no se le parece ni —** he doesn't look even
remotely like him. (b) think etc vaguely, tentatively.
remotidad nf (CAm) (a) remoteness. (b) remote spot,
distant place.
remoto adj (all senses) remote; **¡ni por lo más —!** not
on your life!
remover [2h] vt (a) earth etc to turn over, dig up;
objects to move round, change over, shift about;
cocktail etc to shake; porridge etc to stir (round);
feelings to disturb, upset; **— un asunto** to turn a
matter over, go into a matter again; **— el pasado**
to stir up the past; to rake up the past; **— un
proyecto** to revive a scheme.
  (b) obstacle etc to remove; (Med) to excise, cut out;
person to discharge, remove (from office).

removimiento *nm* removal.

remozamiento *nm* rejuvenation.

remozar [1f] **1** *vt person etc* to rejuvenate; *appearance etc* to brighten up, polish up.

2 remozarse *vr* to|be rejuvenated; to look much younger; **la encuentro muy remozada** I find her looking much younger.

rempujar [1a] *vt* (*fam*) to shove, jostle.

rempujón *nm* (*fam*) shove, push.

remuda *nf* change, alteration; replacement; **— de caballos** change of horses; **— (de ropa)** change of clothes, spare clothes.

remudar [1a] *vt* to remove; to change, alter; to replace.

remuneración *nf* remuneration.

remunerado *adj*: **trabajo mal —** badly-paid job.

remunerador *adj* remunerative; rewarding, worthwhile; **poco —** unremunerative.

remunerar [1a] *vt* to remunerate; to pay; to reward.

renacentista *adj* Renaissance (*attr*).

renacer [2d] *vi* (a) to be reborn; (*Bot*) to appear again, come up again.
(b) (*fig*) to revive; to acquire new vigour (*or* life); **hacer —** to revive; **hoy me siento —** today I feel renewed, I feel I am coming to life again today; **sentían — la esperanza** they felt new hope.

renaciente *adj* renascent.

renacimiento *nm* rebirth, revival; **R—** Renaissance.

renacuajo *nm* (a) (*Zool*) tadpole. (b) (*fam*) shrimp; (*pej*) runt, little squirt (*fam*); **¡ven, —!** (*to child*) come along, pet!

renal *adj* renal, kidney (*attr*).

Renania *f* Rhineland.

renano *adj* Rhenish, Rhine (*attr*).

rencilla *nf* (a) quarrel; feud; **—s** dissension; arguments, bickering. (b) bad blood; ill will; grudge; **me tiene —** he's got it in for me, he bears me a grudge.

rencilloso *adj* quarrelsome.

renco *adj* lame.

rencor *nm* rancour, bitterness; ill feeling, resentment; spitefulness; **guardar —** to bear malice, have a grudge (*a* against); **no le guardo —** I bear him no malice.

rencorosamente *adv* (a) spitefully, maliciously. (b) resentfully; bitterly.

rencoroso *adj* (a) (*ser*) spiteful, nasty, malicious. (b) (*estar*) resentful; bitter, embittered.

rendición *nf* (a) (*Mil etc*) surrender; **— incondicional** unconditional surrender. (b) (*Fin*) yield, profit(s), return. (c) (*Arg*) trading balance.

rendidamente *adv* submissively; obsequiously; humbly, devotedly.

rendido *adj* (a) submissive; obsequious; *admirer* humble, devoted. (b) **estar — (de cansancio)** to be exhausted, be all in.

rendidor *adj* (*SAm*) highly productive; (*Fin*) highly profitable.

rendija *nf* (a) crack, cleft, crevice; chink; aperture. (b) (*fig*) rift, split. (c) (*Law*) loophole.

rendimiento *nm* (a) usable part, proportion of usable material.
(b) (*Mech*) efficiency, performance; capacity; output; **el — del motor** the performance of the engine; **aumentar el — de una máquina** to increase the output of a machine.
(c) (*Fin*) yield, profit(s), return; **ley del — decreciente** law of diminishing returns.
(d) (*quality*) submissiveness; obsequiousness; devotion; **su — total a la voluntad de ella** his complete submissiveness to her will.
(e) exhaustion.

rendir [3l] **1** *vt* (a) to produce, yield, bear; *product, total etc* to produce; *profit etc* to yield; *interest* to bear.
(b) *enemy* to defeat, conquer, overcome; *country* to conquer, subdue; *fortress* to take, capture, reduce.
(c) *person* to exhaust, tire out; **le rindió el sueño** sleep overcame him.
(d) *will* to subject to one's own will, dominate, assume control of; **logró — el albedrío de la joven** he came to dominate the young woman's will completely; **había que — su entereza** he had to overcome his honest doubts, he had to fight down his moral objections.
(e) to give back, return; to hand over; (*Mil*) to surrender; (*Mil*) *guard* to hand over; (*fam*) to vomit, bring up.
(f) (*Comm*) *account* to send.
(g) (*Mil*) *flag* to dip; *arms* to lower, reverse.
(h) *tribute* to pay; *homage* to do, pay; *thanks* to give; **— culto a** to worship; (*fig*) to pay homage to, pay tribute to.

(i) (*RPl*) **— examen** to sit an exam, take an exam.

2 *vi* (a) to yield, produce; **el negocio no rinde** the business doesn't pay; **este año ha rendido poco** it has done poorly this year; **la finca rinde para mantener a 8 familias** the estate produces enough to keep 8 families.
(b) (*SAm*) to last longer than usual.
(c) (*SAm*) to swell up (in the cooking *etc*).

3 rendirse *vr* (a) to yield (*a* to); (*Mil*) to surrender; to give oneself up; **— a la evidencia** to bow before the evidence; **— a la fuerza** to yield to violence; **— a la razón** to yield to reason.
(b) to wear oneself out, exhaust oneself.

renegado 1 *adj* (a) renegade.
(b) (*fam*) gruff; cantankerous, bad-tempered.
2 *nm*, **renegada** *nf* (a) renegade; turncoat.
(b) (*fam*) bad lot, nasty piece of work (*fam*).

renegar [1h *and* 1k] **1** *vt* (a) to deny vigorously, deny repeatedly.
(b) to abhor, detest.
2 *vi* (a) to turn renegade, turn one's coat, be a traitor; (*Eccl*) to apostatize.
(b) **— de** to forsake, disown; to renounce, give up; **— de su familia** to disown one's family; **— de la amistad de uno** to break completely with someone; **reniego de ti** I want nothing more to do with you.
(c) **— de** to abhor, detest.
(d) to curse, swear; (*Rel*) to blaspheme.
(e) to grumble; to protest, complain.
(f) (*Mex, Per, RPl*) to get angry, be upset.

renegón *adj* (*fam*) grumbling, cantankerous, grouchy (*fam*).

renegrido *adj* (*SAm*) very black, very dark; blackened.

renglón *nm* (a) line (of writing); **a — seguido** in the very next line, (*fig*) straight after, without a break; **escribir un —, poner unos —s a** to drop a line to; **leer entre —es** to read between the lines; **estos pobres —es** these humble jottings.
(b) (*Comm etc*) item (of expenditure).
(c) (*SAm: Comm*) line of goods.

renguear [1a] *vi* (a) (*SAm*) to limp, hobble. (b) (*Arg*) to be courting.

renguera *nf* (*SAm*) limp, limping; lameness.

reniego *nm* (a) curse, oath; (*Rel*) blasphemy, blasphemous remark. (b) grumble; complaint.

reno *nm* reindeer.

renombrado *adj* renowned, famous.

renombre *nm* (a) renown, fame; **de —** renowned, famous. (b) surname.

renovable *adj* renewable.

renovación *nf* (a) renewal; renovation; **— espiritual** spiritual renewal; **— de la suscripción** renewal of one's subscription.
(b) (*Archit etc*) renovation; restoration; redecoration.
(c) (*Pol etc*) reorganization, remodelling, transformation.

renovado *adj* renewed, redoubled; **con renovada energía** with renewed energy.

renoval *nm* (*Arg, Chi, Mex*) area of young trees.

renovar [1m] *vt* (a) (*general sense*) to renew; *warning etc* to renew, repeat; *subscription* to renew.
(b) (*Archit etc*) to renovate; to restore; *room* to redecorate.
(c) (*Pol etc*) to reorganize, remodel, transform.

renquear [1a] *vi* (a) to limp, hobble. (b) (*fam*) to get along, manage with difficulty.

renta *nf* (a) income; (*from stock etc*) interest, return, yield; **política de —s** incomes policy; **—, gravable,** **— imponible** taxable income; **— nacional** national income; **— bruta nacional** gross national income; **—s públicas** revenue; **— del trabajo** earned income; **— vitalicia** annuity; **tiene —s particulares** she has a private income; **vivir de sus —s** to live on one's income.
(b) public debt, national debt.
(c) (*for a property etc*) rent.

rentabilidad *nf* profitability.

rentable *adj* profitable; **no —** unprofitable; uneconomical; **el avión no es —** the aircraft is not an economic proposition; **la línea ya no es —** the line is no longer economic (to run).

rentado *adj* (*Arg, Chi*) work paid.

rentar [1a] *vt* (a) to produce, yield. (b) (*Mex*) to let, rent out; **"rento casa"** "house to let".

rentero *nm* tenant farmer.

rentista *nmf* (a) stockholder, person who lives on income from shares, (*as member of class*) rentier; person of independent means. (b) financial expert.

rentístico *adj* financial.
renuencia *nf* (a) unwillingness, reluctance. (b) awkwardness.
renuente *adj* (a) *person* unwilling, reluctant. (b) *material* awkward, difficult.
renuevo *nm* (a) (*act*) renewal. (b) (*Bot*) shoot, sprout.
renuncia *nf* renunciation; resignation; relinquishment; abdication.
renunciar [1b] **1** *vt* (*also vi*: — **a**) *right etc* to renounce (*en* in favour of), surrender, relinquish; *plan, habit etc* to give up; *claim* to drop, waive; *post, responsibility* to resign; *throne* to abdicate (*en* in favour of); **— a hacer algo** to give up doing something, stop doing something.
2 *vi* (*Cards*) to revoke.
renuncio *nm* (a) (*Cards*) revoke. (b) **coger a uno en un —** to catch someone in a fib, catch someone out.
reñidamente *adv* fight *etc* bitterly, hard, stubbornly.
reñidero *nm*: **— de gallos** cockpit.
reñido *adj* (a) *battle, contest* bitter; **un partido — a** hard-fought game; a bitter struggle; **en lo más — de la batalla** in the thick of the fight.
(b) **estar — con uno** to be at odds with someone, be on bad terms with someone; **está — con su familia** he has fallen out with his family.
(c) **estar — con** (*of principle etc*) to be at variance with, be divorced from, be in opposition to.
reñidor *adj* quarrelsome.
reñir [3h *and* 3l] **1** *vt* (a) to scold; to tell off, reprimand (*por* for).
(b) *battle* to fight, wage.
2 *vi* to quarrel, fall out (*con* with); to fight, scrap, come to blows; **ha reñido con su novio** she's fallen out with her boyfriend; she's broken it off with her fiancé; **se pasan la vida riñendo** they spend their whole time quarrelling; **riñeron por cuestión de dinero** they quarrelled about (*or* over) money.
reo *nmf* (a) culprit, offender; criminal; (*Law*) accused, defendant; **— de estado** person accused of a crime against the state; **— de muerte** person under sentence of death.
(b) (*Arg*) shabby individual, tramp.
reojo: mirar a uno de — to look at someone out of the corner of one's eye; (*fig*) to look askance at someone, look dubiously at someone.
reorganización *nf* reorganization.
reorganizar [1f] **1** *vt* to reorganize. **2 reorganizarse** *vr* to reorganize.
reorientar [1a] *vt* to reorientate; to give a new direction to; to readjust.
reóstato *nm* rheostat.
repanchigarse [1h] *vr*, **repantigarse** [1h] *vr* to lounge, sprawl, loll (*back*); **estar repanchigado en un sillón** to loll back in a chair.
reparable *adj* repairable.
reparación *nf* (a) (*act*) repairing, mending.
(b) (*Tech*) repair; **"—es en el acto"**, **"—es instantáneas"** "repairs while you wait"; **efectuar —es en** to carry out repairs to.
(c) (*fig*) amends, reparation, redress.
reparador 1 *adj* (a) *person* critical, faultfinding.
(b) *food* fortifying, strengthening, restorative.
2 *nm* (*Tech*) repairer.
3 *nm*, **reparadora** *nf* carping critic, faultfinder.
reparar [1a] **1** *vt* (a) (*Tech*) to repair, mend.
(b) *energies etc* to repair, restore; *fortunes* to retrieve.
(c) *offence etc* to make amends for; *damage, loss* to make good; *bad effect* to undo.
(d) *blow* to parry.
(e) to observe, notice.
(f) (*RPl*) to mimic, imitate.
2 *vi* (a) **— en** to observe, notice, note, see; **no reparó en la diferencia** he didn't notice the difference; **sin — en que ya no funcionaba** without noticing that it was no longer working.
(b) **—** to pay attention to, take heed of; to consider; **no — en las dificultades** to take no heed of the difficulties, refuse to consider the difficulties; **repara en lo que vas a hacer** reflect on what you are going to do; **sin — en los gastos** heedless of expense, regardless of the cost; **no — en nada** to stop at nothing.
(c) (*Guat, Mex*: *of horse*) to rear, buck.
3 repararse *vr* to check oneself, restrain oneself.
reparista *adj* (*CAm, Col, PR*), **reparisto** *adj* (*CAm, Ven*) =**reparón 1.**
reparo *nm* (a) (*Tech*) repair; (*Archit etc*) restoration.
(b) (*Fencing*) parry; (*fig*) defence, protection.
(c) (*Med*) remedy; restorative.
(d) objection; criticism; doubt; **poner —s** to raise

objections (*a* to); to criticize, express one's doubts; (*pej*) to find fault (*a* with).
(e) hesitation; scruple, doubt; **no tuvo — en + infin** he did not hesitate to + *infin*; he did not scruple to + *infin*.
(f) (*CAm, Mex*) buck, rearing; **tirar un —** to rear, buck.
reparón 1 *adj* carping, critical, faultfinding. **2** *nm*, **reparona** *nf* critic, faultfinder.
repartición *nf* (a) distribution; sharing out, division. (b) (*Chi, RPl*) government department, administrative section.
repartida *nf* (*Arg, Guat*) =**repartición (a).**
repartido *nm* (*Post*) delivery; (*of milkman etc*) round.
repartidor *nm* distributor; (*Comm*) roundsman, deliveryman; **— de leche** milkman; **— de periódicos** paperboy.
repartija *nf* (*RPl*: *pej*) share-out, carve-up (*fam*).
repartimiento *nm* distribution; division; (*of tax*) assessment.
repartir [3a] **1** *vt* to distribute; to divide (up), share (out); to parcel out; *task* to allot, assign; *land* to parcel up, divide, split up; *country* to partition; *pamphlets etc* to give out, hand out; *food* to serve out; *drinks, glasses* to hand round; *dividend* to declare, pay out; *bread, milk, papers, post etc* to deliver; *cards* to deal; *parts* (*Theat*) to cast; *punishments* to issue, impose, mete out; **las cartas están repartidas en 4 palos** the cards are distributed among 4 suits; **las guarniciones están repartidas por toda la costa** the garrisons are distributed all round the coast, there are garrisons dotted about all along the coast.
2 repartirse *vr* to be distributed, be shared out (*etc*): **"se reparte a domicilio"** "home delivery service".
reparto *nm* (a) (*act*) =**repartición (a).**
(b) distribution (*also Bridge*); **un — poco uniforme** a very uneven distribution.
(c) (*Comm, Post*) delivery.
(d) (*Theat*) cast(ing); cast list; **dar — francés a uno** to put someone at the top of the bill.
(e) (*Cu, Mex*) building site, building lot (*US*); (*Mex*) suburb, real-estate development.
repasador *nm* (*Arg*) dishcloth.
repasar [1a] *vt* (a) *place* to pass (by) again; *street* to go along again; **pasar y — una calle** to go up and down a street repeatedly.
(b) **— la plancha por una prenda** to put the iron again over a garment.
(c) (*Sew*) to sew, sew up, darn; to mend.
(d) (*Mech*) to check, overhaul.
(e) *accounts etc* to check; *text* to revise, re-examine; *notes* to go over again; to read through rapidly, flick through; *lesson* to revise; *publication etc* to put the finishing touches to, polish up.
(f) (*Arg*) *plates etc* to dust, rub the cloth over; *furniture* to polish; *clothes* to brush down.
repasata *nf* (*fam*) ticking-off.
repaso *nm* review, revision; check; (*Sew*) mending; (*Mech*) checkup, overhaul; rapid reading, quick rereading; **— general** general overhaul; **curso de —** revision course, refresher course; **ropa de —** mending, darning; **dar un — a una lección** to revise a lesson; **los técnicos daban el último — al cohete** the technicians were giving the rocket a final check.
repatriación *nf* repatriation.
repatriado 1 *adj* repatriated. **2** *nm*, **repatriada** *nf* repatriate, repatriated person.
repatriar [1b] **1** *vt* to repatriate; *criminal etc* to deport; to send home, send back to one's country of origin; **van a — el famoso mármol** they are going to send the famous marble back to its original country.
2 repatriarse *vr* to return home, go back to one's own country.
repecho *nm* (a) sharp gradient, steep slope; **a —** uphill. (b) (*Mex*) parapet; shelter, refuge, hut.
repela *nf* (*CAm, Col, Ec*) gleaning (*of coffee crop*).
repelar [1a] **1** *vt* (a) to leave completely bare, shear; *grass* to nibble, crop; *nails* to clip.
(b) **— a uno** to pull someone's hair.
(c) (*Mex*) to raise objections to.
(d) (*Mex*) to reprimand.
2 repelarse *vr* (*Chi*) to feel uneasy; to feel unwell; to feel regret.
repelencia *nf* (*Per, PR, Ven*) revulsion, disgust.
repelente *adj* (a) repellent, repulsive, disgusting. (b) (*SAm*) tedious, annoying.
repeler [2a] **1** *vt* (a) *enemy etc* to repel, repulse, drive back; *person* to push away.
(b) **este material repele el agua** this material resists water, this material makes water roll off it;

la pared repele la pelota the wall sends the ball back, the ball bounces off the wall.
    (c) *idea, offer* to reject.
    (d) *(fig)* to repel, disgust, fill with repulsion.
  2 **repelerse** *vr:* **los dos se repelen** the two are (mutually) incompatible.

repelo *nm* (a) hair out of place, hair *(etc)* that sticks up; *(in wood)* snag, knot; *(Anat)* hangnail.
    (b) *(fam)* tiff, slight argument.
    (c) *(fig)* aversion.
    (d) *(Ec, Mex)* old dress; worn-out object; piece of junk; *(Mex)* rag, tatter.

repelón 1 *adj (Mex)* grumbling, complaining, grouchy *(fam)*.
    2 *nm* (a) tug (at one's hair).
    (b) *(Sew)* ruck, snag.
    (c) small bit, tag, pinch.
    (d) *(of horse)* dash, short run.
    (e) *(Mex)* sharp reprimand.

repelús *nm (fam)* inexplicable fear; **me da** — it gives me the willies *(sl)*, it gives me the shivers.

repeluzno *nm (fam)* nervous shiver, slight start of fear.

repellar [1a] *vt* to plaster, stucco; *(SAm)* to whitewash.

repello *nm* (a) *(SAm)* whitewash(ing). (b) *(Cu etc)* lewd movement, lewd gesture *(in a dance)*.

repensar [1k] *vt* to rethink, reconsider, think out again.

repente *nm* (a) sudden movement, start, jerk; *(fig)* sudden impulse; — **de ira** fit of anger.
    (b) **de** — suddenly; unexpectedly; all at once.
    (c) *(Mex)* fit, fainting fit.

repentinamente *adv* suddenly; unexpectedly; **torcer** — to turn sharply, make a sharp turn.

repentino *adj* (a) sudden; unexpected; *change* sudden, swift; *turn* sharp. (b) **tener repentina compasión** to be quick to pity.

repentizar [1f] *vi (Mus)* to sight-read, improvise.

repentón *nm (fam)* violent start.

repercusión *nf* (a) repercussion; reverberation; re-echo.
    (b) *(fig)* repercussion; **las —es de esta decisión** the repercussions of this decision; **de amplia —, de ancha —** far-reaching, of profound effects; **tener —(es) en** to have repercussions on.

repercutir [3a] 1 *vt (Col)* to contradict.
  2 *vi* (a) *(object)* to rebound, bounce off; *(sound)* to re-echo; to reverberate, go on sounding *(or* beating *etc)*.
    (b) *(fig)* — **en** to have repercussions on, have effects on.
    (c) *(Mex)* to smell bad.
  3 **repercutirse** *vr* to reverberate.

reperiquete *nm (Mex)* (a) cheap adornment. (b) brag, boast.

repertorio *nm* (a) list, index, compendium. (b) *(Theat)* repertoire, repertory.

repeso *nm (Col)* bonus, extra.

repetición *nf* (a) repetition; recurrence. (b) *(Theat etc)* encore; **pedir la — de una canción** to encore a song. (c) **fusil de** — repeater rifle.

repetidamente *adv* repeatedly.

repetido *adj* (a) repeated; numerous; **el tan — aviso** the oft-repeated warning; **repetidas veces** repeatedly, over and over again. (b) aforementioned.

repetidor *nm (Radio, TV)* booster, booster station.

repetir [3l] 1 *vt* (a) to repeat; to say again, do again; *(Theat)* to give as an encore, sing *(etc)* again; *lesson* to recite, rehearse, go over; *sound* to echo; *recording* to repeat, play back; **le repito que es imposible** I repeat that it is impossible, I tell you again it is impossible; **los niños repiten lo que hacen las personas mayores** children imitate adults, children ape their seniors.
  2 *vi* (a) to repeat; **el pepino repite mucho** cucumber keeps coming back, cucumber gives one bad hiccups.
    (b) — **de un plato** to have a second helping of a dish.
  3 **repetirse** *vr* (a) to repeat oneself; *(artist etc)* to copy oneself, use an earlier theme *(etc)* again.
    (b) *(event)* to recur.

repicar [1g] 1 *vt* (a) *meat etc* to chop up small.
    (b) to prick (again).
    (c) *bells* to ring, peal (merrily).
    (d) *(fam)* — **gordo un acontecimiento** to celebrate an event in style.
  2 **repicarse** *vr* to boast *(de* about, of).

repintar [1a] 1 *vt* to repaint; to paint hastily, paint roughly. 2 **repintarse** *vr* to pile the make-up on.

repipi *adj (fam)* posh *(fam)*; la-di-dah *(fam)*, affected;

arty *(fam)*; precocious, knowing for one's years; stuck-up *(fam)*; **es una niña** — she's a little madam, she's an insufferably affected child.

repique *nm* (a) *(Mus)* peal(ing), ringing; chime. (b) *(fam)* tiff, squabble.

repiquete *nm* (a) *(Mus)* merry peal(ing). (b) *(Mil)* clash. (c) *(Chi: Orn)* trill, song. (d) *(Col)* pique, resentment.

repiquetear [1a] 1 *vt* (a) *bells* to peal joyfully, ring merrily.
    (b) *drum, table etc* to tap, beat rapidly, drum lightly on.
  2 *vi* (a) *(Mus)* to peal out, ring.
    (b) *(of machine)* to clatter.
  3 **repiquetearse** *vr (fam)* to squabble.

repiqueteo *nm* (a) *(Mus)* joyful peal(ing), merry ringing. (b) tapping, drumming; clatter.

repisa *nf* ledge, shelf; (wall) bracket; — **de chimenea** mantelpiece; — **de ventana** windowsill.

replana *nf (Per)* underworld slang.

replantar [1a] *vt* to replant.

replantear [1a] *vt question* to raise again, reopen.

replantigarse [1h] *vr (SAm)* =**repanchigarse**.

repleción *nf* repletion.

replegable *adj* folding, that folds (up); *(Aer)* undercarriage retractable.

replegar [1h *and* 1k] 1 *vt* to fold over; to fold again, refold; *undercarriage* to retract, draw up.
  2 **replegarse** *vr (Mil)* to withdraw, fall back (in good order; *sobre* on).

repletar [1a] 1 *vt* to fill completely, stuff full, pack tight. 2 **repletarse** *vr* to eat to repletion.

repleto *adj* (a) replete, full up; — **de** filled with, absolutely full of, crammed with; **la plaza estaba repleta de gente** the square was solid with people; **una colección repleta de rarezas** a collection containing innumerable rarities.
    (b) **estar** — to be full up *(with food)*, be replete.
    (c) *appearance* sleek, well-fed.

réplica *nf* (a) answer; retort, rejoinder; rebuttal; *(Law)* answer to a charge; —**s** backchat. (b) *(Art)* replica, copy.

replicar [1g] *vi* to answer, retort, rejoin; *(pej)* to argue, answer back; **¡no repliques!** don't answer back!, I don't want any backchat!

replicón *adj (fam)* argumentative; cheeky, saucy.

repliegue *nm* (a) fold, crease. (b) *(Mil)* withdrawal, retirement.

repoblación *nf* repopulation, repeopling; restocking; — **forestal** (re)afforestation.

repoblar [1m] *vt area, country* to repopulate; repeople; *river etc* to restock; *(Bot)* to (re)afforest, plant trees on.

repollo *nm* cabbage.

repolludo *adj* tubby, chunky *(fam)*.

reponer [2r] 1 *vt* (a) to replace, put back; *person* to reinstate; *fuel, stock etc* to replenish; *(Fin)* to plough back, reinvest; *damaged article etc* to replace, pay for (the replacement of).
    (b) *(Theat)* to revive, put on again.
    (c) to reply *(que* that).
  2 **reponerse** *vr (Med etc)* to recover; — **de** to recover from, get over.

reportaje *nm* report, article, news item; — **gráfico** illustrated report, story in pictures.

reportar [1a] 1 *vt* (a) to bring, fetch, carry.
    (b) *benefit etc* to obtain.
    (c) to give, bring; **esto le habrá reportado algún beneficio** this will have brought him some benefit; **la cosa no le reportó sino disgustos** the affair brought him nothing but trouble.
    (d) *(fig)* to check, restrain.
    (e) *(SAm: angl)* to report; to denounce, accuse; to notify.
  2 **reportarse** *vr* to control oneself; to calm down; **¡repórtate!** control yourself!

reporte *nm (CAm, Cu, Mex: angl)* report.

reportear [1a] *vt (SAm)* to interview (for the purpose of writing an article); to photograph (for the press).

repórter *nm*, **reportero** *nm (angl)* reporter.

reposacabezas *nm*, *pl* **reposacabezas** headrest.

reposadamente *adv* quietly; gently, restfully; unhurriedly, calmly.

reposado *adj* quiet; gentle, restful; unhurried, calm.

reposaplatos *nm*, *pl* **reposaplatos** tablemat.

reposar [1a] 1 *vt:* — **la comida** to let one's meal go down, settle one's stomach.
  2 *vi* to rest, repose; to sleep; *(of dead)* to lie, rest.
  3 **reposarse** *vr (liquid)* to settle.

reposición *nf* (a) replacement. (b) *(Fin)* ploughing back, reinvestment. (c) *(Theat)* revival. (d) *(Med and fig)* recovery.

repositorio nm repository.

reposo nm rest, repose; **— absoluto** (Med) complete rest.

repostada nf (CAm) rude reply, sharp answer.

repostar [1a] **1** vt stock etc to replenish, renew; **— combustible, — gasolina** (Aer) to refuel, (Aut) to fill up (with petrol).
2 vi to refuel.
3 repostarse vr to replenish stocks, take on supplies; **— de combustible** to refuel.

repostería nf (a) confectioner's (shop), cake shop. (b) confectionery; (art of) pastrymaking. (c) larder, pantry.

repostero nm, **repostera** nf confectioner, pastrycook.

repostón adj (CAm, Mex) rude, surly.

repregunta nf (Law) cross-examination, cross-questioning.

repreguntar [1a] vt (Law) to cross-examine, cross-question.

reprender [2a] vt to reprimand, tell off, take to task; child to scold; **— algo a uno** to reprimand someone for something; to criticize someone about something, reproach someone for something.

reprensible adj reprehensible.

reprensión nf reprimand, rebuke; scolding; criticism, reproach.

represa nf (a) recapture. (b) repression; check, stoppage. (c) (on river) dam; weir; pool, lake; **— de molino** millpond.

represalia nf reprisal; **como — por** as a reprisal for; **tomar —s** to take reprisals, retaliate (contra against).

represar [1a] vt (a) (Naut) to recapture. (b) to repress; to check, put a stop to; to restrain. (c) water to dam (up); (fig) to stem.

representable adj (Theat): **la obra no es —** the play cannot actually be staged, it is not a play for the stage.

representación nf (a) (in most senses) representation; **— proporcional** proportional representation; **en — de** representing, as a representative of; **por —** by proxy; **hacer —es a** to make representations to. (b) (Theat) performance; production; (of actor) playing, acting; **una serie de 350 —es** a run of 350 performances. (c) (fig) importance, standing; **hombre de —** man of some standing.

representante nmf (a) (Comm, Pol etc) representative. (b) (Theat) performer, actor, actress.

representar [1a] **1** vt (a) (general sense) to represent; to act for; to stand for, symbolize; to express. (b) (Theat) play to perform, put on, do; to produce; part to act, play, take. (c) age etc to look; **representa unos 55 años** he looks about 55, from his appearance he's about 55; **ella no representa los años que tiene** she doesn't look her age; **el conserje no representaba ser muy listo** the porter didn't seem to be any too intelligent; **ese traje no representa lo que has gastado en él** that suit does not look as though it's worth what you paid for it. (d) details, facts etc to state, explain; to enumerate; to express; **— una dificultad a uno** to represent a difficulty to someone, explain a snag to someone. (e) to mean; **tal acto representaría la guerra** such an act would mean war.
2 representarse vr: **— una escena** to imagine a scene, picture a scene to oneself; **— una solución** to envisage a solution; **se me representa la cara que pondrá** I can just imagine what a face he'll pull.

representativo adj representative.

represión nf repression; suppression.

represivo adj repressive.

reprimenda nf reprimand, rebuke.

reprimido adj repressed.

reprimir [3a] **1** vt to repress, suppress; to curb, check; giggle, yawn etc to suppress, hold in, smother; revolt etc to suppress.
2 reprimirse vr: **— de + ger** to stop oneself from + ger.

reprisar [1a] vt (Arg, Chi, Mex, Nic: gall) play to revive, put on again.

reprise nf (SAm: Theat: gall) revival.

reprobable adj blameworthy, to be condemned, reprehensible.

reprobación nf reproval, reprobation; blame; condemnation; **escrito en — de ...** written in condemnation of ...

reprobador adj look etc reproving, disapproving.

reprobar [1m] vt (a) to reprove, condemn; to blame; to damn. (b) candidate to fail.

reprobatorio adj = **reprobador**.

réprobo adj (Eccl) damned.

reprochar [1a] **1** vt to reproach; to condemn, censure; **— algo a uno** to reproach someone for something; **le reprochan (por) su descuido** they reproach him for his negligence.
2 reprocharse vr to reproach oneself; **no tienes nada que reprocharte** you have nothing to reproach yourself for (or about).

reproche nm reproach (a for); reflection (a on); **es un — a su honradez** it is a reflection on his honesty; **nos miró con —** he looked at us reproachfully.

reproducción nf reproduction.

reproducir [3c] **1** vt to reproduce; (Bio) to reproduce, breed.
2 reproducirse vr (a) to reproduce; to breed. (b) (conditions etc) to be reproduced; (event) to happen again, recur; **se le ha reproducido la enfermedad** the complaint has made a reappearance; **si se reproducen los desórdenes** if the disorders happen again.

reproductor adj reproductive.

reps nm (fabric) rep.

reptar [1a] vi to creep, crawl; to snake along.

reptil 1 adj reptilian. **2** nm reptile.

república nf republic; **R— Dominicana** Dominican Republic; **R— Árabe Unida** United Arab Republic; **Segunda R— Española** Second Spanish Republic.

republicanismo nm republicanism.

republicano 1 adj republican. **2** nm, **republicana** nf republican.

repudiación nf repudiation.

repudiar [1b] vt wife, violence etc to repudiate; to disown, disavow; inheritance to renounce.

repudio nm repudiation.

repudrir [3a] **1** vt (a) to rot. (b) (fig) to gnaw at, eat up, devour.
2 repudrirse vr to suffer inwardly, suffer gnawing doubts (etc); to eat one's heart out, pine away.

repuesto nm (a) stock, store; supply. (b) replacement; refill. (c) (Aut, Mech) spare, spare part, extra (US); **rueda de —** spare wheel; **y llevamos otro de —** and we have another as a spare (or in reserve). (d) (Cook) sideboard, buffet.

repugnancia nf (a) disgust, loathing, repugnance; aversion (hacia, por to). (b) (moral) repugnance. (c) reluctance; **lo hizo con —** he did it reluctantly. (d) (Philos) opposition.

repugnante adj disgusting, loathsome, revolting.

repugnar [1a] **1** vt (a) to disgust, revolt, nauseate; to fill with loathing; **ese olor me repugna** that smell revolts me, I loathe that smell; **me repugna tener que mirarlo** I hate having to watch it, I loathe having to watch it. (b) to hate, loathe; **siempre repugnaba el engaño** he always hated deceit.
2 vi (a) to be disgusting, be revolting. (b) **= 3 repugnarse** vr to conflict, be in opposition; to contradict each other; **las dos teorías se repugnan** the two theories are not compatible; the two theories contradict each other.

repujar [1a] vt to emboss, work in relief.

repulgado adj affected.

repulgar [1h] vt (a) (Sew) to hem, edge. (b) (Cook) to edge, put an edging on.

repulgo nm (a) (Sew) hem; hemstitch. (b) (Cook) fancy edging, decorated border; **— de empanada** (fig) mere trifle.

repulido adj (a) polished, repolished. (b) (fig) dressed up, dolled up; spick and span, very smart.

repulir [3a] **1** vt (a) to polish up; to repolish. (b) (fig) to try to make absolutely perfect, seek the greatest perfection in. (c) (fig) to dress up; to spruce up.
2 repulirse vr (fig) to dress up, doll up; to smarten up.

repulsa nf (a) (Mil) check. (b) (fig) rejection, refusal; rebuff; **sufrir una —** to meet with a rebuff. (c) (fig) strong condemnation; severe reprimand.

repulsar [1a] vt (a) (Mil) to repulse; to check. (b) (fig) request to reject, refuse; offer, person to rebuff. (c) (fig) to condemn in strong terms.

repulsión nf (a) = **repulsa**. (b) (feeling) repulsion, disgust, aversion. (c) (Phys) repulsion.

repulsivo adj disgusting, revolting, loathsome.

repunta nf (a) (Geog) point, headland. (b) sign, indication, hint. (c) pique. (d) slight upset, tiff. (e) (SAm: Agr) roundup. (f) (Col, Per) sudden rise (of a river).

repuntar [1a] **1** *vt* (*Chi, Mex, RPl*) *cattle* to round up.
2 *vi* (a) (*of tide*) to turn.
  (b) (*SAm*) to begin to show, give the first signs;
(*of person*) to turn up unexpectedly.
  (c) (*SAm: of river*) to rise suddenly.
  (d) (*RPl*) to recover lost ground.
3 repuntarse *vr* (a) (*wine*) to begin to sour, turn.
  (b) (*person*) to get cross.
  (c) (*two persons*) to fall out, have a tiff.
repunte *nm* (a) (*Naut*) turn of the tide. (b) (*SAm:
Agr*) roundup. (c) (*RPl: Fin*) rise in share prices.
reputación *nf* reputation; standing.
reputado *adj* (*also bien* —) highly reputed, reputable.
reputar [1a] *vt* to repute; to esteem; to deem, consider; — **a uno de** (*or* **por**) **inteligente** to consider
someone intelligent; **le reputan no apto para el
cargo** they think him unsuitable for the post; **una
colección reputada en mucho** a highly esteemed
collection.
requebrar [1k] *vt* to say nice things to, flatter, compliment; — **a una de amores** to court someone.
requemado *adj* scorched; parched; *skin* tanned,
bronzed; *food* overdone.
requemar [1a] **1** *vt* (a) (*of fire etc*) to scorch; *plant* to
parch, scorch, dry up; *skin* to tan; *food* to overdo,
burn; *tongue* to burn, sting.
  (b) (*fig*) *blood* to inflame, set afire.
2 requemarse *vr* (a) to scorch; to parch, get
parched, dry up; to tan; to burn.
  (b) (*fig*) to harbour resentment, smoulder with
indignation (*etc*).
requenete *adj* (*Ven*), **requeneto** *adj* (*Col, Ven*) =
rechoncho.
requerimiento *nm* (a) request; demand; summons
(*also Law*). (b) notification.
requerir [3i] *vt* (a) to need, require; **esto requiere
cierto cuidado** this requires some care.
  (b) to request, ask, invite; — **a uno para que haga
algo** to ask someone to do something.
  (c) to send for, call for; *person* to send for, summon; **el ministro requirió sus gafas** the minister
sent for his spectacles; **el ministro le requirió para
que lo explicara** the minister summoned him to
explain it.
  (d) *woman* (*also* — **de amores a**) *see* **requebrar**.
requesón *nm* cottage cheese; curd(s).
requeté *nm soldier of the Carlist forces* (*esp 19th
century*).
requete . . . *intensifying prefix* (*fam*), *eg* **requeteguapa**
quite extraordinarily pretty; **me parece requetebién**
it seems absolutely splendid to me; **una joven
requetemonísima** a fabulously attractive girl; **una
requetesuperminifalda** an ultrashort miniskirt.
requiebro *nm* amorous compliment, flirtatious
remark.
réquiem *nm, pl* **réquiems** requiem.
requilorios *nmpl* (a) tedious formalities, annoying
bits of red tape; petty conditions.
  (b) silly adornments, unnecessary frills.
  (c) time-wasting preliminaries; roundabout way of
saying something.
  (d) bits and pieces.
requintar [1a] **1** *vt* (a) (*SAm*) *rope* to tighten,
tauten.
  (b) (*Col, Mex*) — **a uno** to impose one's will on
someone, exact obedience from someone.
  (c) (*Per*) to insult, abuse.
2 *vi* (*PR*) to resemble each other.
requisa *nf* (a) survey, inspection. (b) (*Mil*) requisition. (c) (*Arg*) seizure, confiscation.
requisar [1a] *vt* (a) (*Mil*) to requisition. (b) (*Arg*) to
seize, confiscate. (c) (*Arg*) to search.
requisición *nf* (a) (*Mil*) requisition. (b) (*Arg, Chi,
Mex*) seizure, confiscation. (c) (*Arg, Chi, Mex*)
search.
requisito *nm* requirement, requisite; qualification; —
previo prerequisite; **llenar los** —**s** to fulfil the requirements; **tener los** —**s para un cargo** to have the
essential qualifications for a post.
requisitoria *nf* (*SAm: Law*) examination, interrogation.
res *nf* (a) beast, animal; — **lanar** sheep; — **vacuna**
cow, bull, ox; **100** —**es** 100 animals, 100 head of
cattle. (b) (*SAm: Cook*) steak. (c) (*RPl*) body.
resabiado *adj* knowing, crafty; that has learned his
lesson; *horse* vicious.
resabiarse [1b] *vr* to acquire a bad habit, get into
evil ways.
resabido *adj* (a) thoroughly well known; **lo tengo
sabido y** — of course I know all that perfectly well.
  (b) (*fam*) pretentious, pedantic, would-be knowledgeable.

resabio *nm* (a) nasty taste (in the mouth), unpleasant
aftertaste; **tener** —**s de** (*fig*) to smack of. (b) bad
habit, unpleasant way; (*of horse*) vicious nature.
resabioso *adj* (*Cu, Mex, Per*) = **resabiado**.
resaca *nf* (a) (*Naut*) undertow, undercurrent; backward movement (of the waves).
  (b) (*fam*) hangover.
  (c) (*fig*) reaction, backlash; **la** — **blanca** the white
backlash.
  (d) (*CAm, Col, Mex*) high-quality liquor; bad
liquor.
  (e) (*Arg, Chi, Urug*) line of driftwood and rubbish
(*left by the tide*).
  (f) (*Arg, Chi, Urug*) worthless individual; very
poor person.
  (g) (*Cu, PR*) beating.
  (h) (*Mex*) the best thing (*etc*) of its kind; (*iro*)
hardened criminal.
resacado 1 *adj* (*Mex*) mean; weak; stupid. **2** *nm* (*Col,
Ec*) (contraband) liquor.
resacar [1g] *vt* (*Col, Ec, Mex*) to distil (a second time).
resalado *adj* lively, vivacious, attractive; *see* **re . . .**
resaltante *adj* (*SAm*) outstanding.
resaltar [1a] *vi* (a) to jut out, stick out, stick up,
project.
  (b) (*fig*) to stand out; to be outstanding; **hacer** —
algo to throw something into relief, set something
off (*contra* against a background of); (*fig*) to emphasize something.
resalte *nm*, **resalto** *nm* projection.
resanar [1a] *vt* to restore, repair, make good.
resaque *nm* (*Ven*) = **resaca** (d).
resaquero *adj* (*CAm*) = **remolón**.
resarcimiento *nm* repayment; indemnification, compensation.
resarcir [3b] **1** *vt* to repay; to indemnify, compensate;
— **a uno de una cantidad** to repay someone a sum;
— **a uno de una pérdida** to compensate someone for
a loss.
2 resarcirse *vr*: — **de** to make up for, compensate
oneself for; to retrieve.
resbalada *nf* (*SAm*) slip.
resbaladero *nm* slippery place; slide.
resbaladizo *adj* slippery.
resbalar [1a] **1** *vi* (a) to slip, slip up (*en, sobre* on);
to slide, slither (*por* along, down); (*Aut etc*) to skid;
el embrague resbala the clutch is slipping; **le
resbalaban las lágrimas por las mejillas** tears were
trickling down her cheeks.
  (b) (*fig*) to slip up, make a slip.
2 resbalarse *vr* = **1**.
resbalón *nm* (a) slip; slide, slither; skid. (b) (*fig*)
slip, error; **dar un** — to slip up.
resbaloso *adj* (*SAm*) slippery.
rescatar [1a] *vt* (a) *captive* to ransom; *town etc* to
recapture, recover; *pledge* to redeem.
  (b) *person in danger etc* to save, rescue.
  (c) *object, money etc* to get back, recover, regain
possession of.
  (d) *lost time* to make up; *misdeeds* to atone for,
redeem, expiate.
  (e) *land* to reclaim.
  (f) (*Mex*) to resell.
2 *vi* (*Col*) to peddle goods from village to village.
rescate *nm* (a) ransom; recapture, recovery; redemption.
  (b) rescue; **operaciones de** — rescue operations;
acudir al — **de** to go to the rescue of.
  (c) recovery.
  (d) atonement, expiation.
  (e) reclamation; — **de terrenos** land reclamation.
rescindir [3a] *vt* to rescind, cancel; to withdraw.
rescisión *nf* cancellation; withdrawal.
rescoldo *nm* (a) embers, hot ashes. (b) (*fig*) lingering
doubt, scruple; **avivar el** — (*fig*) to stir up the dying
embers.
rescontrar [1m] *vt* (*Comm, Fin*) to offset, balance.
resecar[1] [1g] **1** *vt* to dry off, dry thoroughly; to parch,
scorch, burn. **2 resecarse** *vr* to dry up, get too dry.
resecar[2] [1g] *vt* (*Med*) to cut out, remove; to amputate.
resección *nf* resection.
reseco *adj* (a) very dry, too dry; parched. (b) (*fig*)
skinny, lean.
reseda *nf*, **resedá** *nf* (*SAm*) mignonette.
resellarse [1a] *vr* (*fam*) to switch parties, change one's
views.
resembrar [1k] *vt* to resow, reseed.
resentido *adj* resentful; bitter; sullen; **es un** — he's
bitter, he's got a chip on his shoulder, he feels hard
done by.
resentimiento *nm* resentment; bitterness.

resentirse [3i] *vr* (a) — **con algo,** — **por algo** to resent something, be offended about something, feel bitter about something.

(b) to remain weak, be weakened, suffer; **con los años se resintió su salud** his health suffered (*or* was affected) over the years; **los cimientos se resintieron con el terremoto** the foundations were weakened by the earthquake.

(c) — **de** *defect* to suffer from, labour under; *consequences etc* to feel the effects of; **me resiento todavía del golpe** I can still feel the effects of the injury.

reseña *nf* (a) outline, account, summary; (*Lit*) review; (*Sport etc*) report (*de* on), account (*de* of). (b) brief description (*for identification purposes*). (c) (*Mil*) review.

reseñar [1a] *vt* (a) to describe (*for identification purposes*); to write up, write a brief account of; (*Lit*) to review; *match* to report on. (b) (*fam*) *offender* to book (*fam*); **la policía le reseñó por alguna infracción** the police booked him for some offence.

resero *nm* (*Arg, Bol, Guat*) cowboy, herdsman; cattle dealer.

reserva *nf* (a) (*act*) reservation; **la** — **de asientos no se paga** there is no charge for seat reservation (*or for* reserving seats).

(b) reserve (*also Comm*); stock, holding; — **en metálico** cash reserves; — **de oro** gold reserve; **las** —**s mundiales de petróleo** world reserves of oil; **de** — spare, reserve (*attr*); emergency (*attr*); **tener algo de** — to have something in reserve, keep something for an emergency.

(c) (*Geog etc*) reserve, reservation; — **de indios** Indian reservation; — **natural** nature reserve.

(d) (*Mil*) reserve.

(e) (*quality*) reserve; discretion, reticence; (*pej*) coldness, distance.

(f) privacy; **con** — in confidence; **escribir con la mayor** — to write in the strictest confidence; **"absoluta** —**"** (*adverts*) "strictest confidence".

(g) reserve, reservation; — **mental** mental reservation; **con ciertas** —**s** with certain reservations; **hay que tomar esa noticia con** — that news should be taken with reservations; **sin** —**(s)** unreservedly.

(h) **a** — **de except for; a** — **de que ... unless ...,** unless it should turn out that ...

reservación *nf* reservation.

reservadamente *adv* confidentially, privately.

reservado 1 *adj* (a) *seat etc* reserved. (b) *person, manner* reserved; discreet, reticent; (*pej*) cold, distant. (c) *matter etc* confidential, private.

2 *nm* (*in restaurant etc*) private room; (*Rail*) reserved compartment.

reservar [1a] **1** *vt* (a) to reserve; to keep, keep in reserve, set aside; *seats etc* to reserve, book; **lo reserva para el final** he's keeping it till last; **ha reservado lo mejor para sí** he has kept the best part for himself.

(b) to conceal; to keep to oneself, refuse to tell; *opinion etc* to reserve; **prefiero** — **los detalles** I prefer to keep the details to myself.

2 reservarse *vr* (a) to save oneself (*para* for); to keep up one's strength; to bide one's time; **no bebo porque me reservo para más tarde** I'm not drinking because I have to be fit for later on.

reservista *nm* reservist.

reservón *adj* (*fam*) excessively reserved.

resfriado 1 *adj* (*Arg*) indiscreet. **2** *nm* cold; chill; **coger un** — to catch a cold.

resfriar [1c] **1** *vt* (a) to cool, chill. (b) (*fig*) *ardour* to cool. (c) (*Med*) — **a uno** to give someone a cold.

2 *vi* (*Meteorol*) to turn cold.

3 resfriarse *vr* (a) (*Med*) to catch (a) cold. (b) (*fig*: *relations*) to cool off.

resguardar [1a] **1** *vt* to protect, shield (*de* from); to safeguard.

2 resguardarse *vr* (a) to defend oneself, protect oneself; to safeguard oneself. (b) to go warily, proceed with caution.

resguardo *nm* (a) defence, protection; safeguard; **servir de** — **a uno** to be a protection to someone; — **de consigna** cloakroom check.

(b) (*Comm etc*) voucher, certificate; guarantee; slip, check, cover note, receipt. (c) (*Naut*) sea room; safe distance.

residencia *nf* residence; (*Univ*) hall of residence, hostel; — **para ancianos,** — **para jubilados** rest home, old people's home.

residencial *adj* residential.

residenciar [1b] **1** *vt* (*Law*) to conduct a judicial inquiry into, investigate. **2 residenciarse** *vr* to take up residence, establish oneself, settle.

residente 1 *adj* resident; **no** — non-resident. **2** *nmf* resident; **no** — non-resident.

residir [3a] *vi* (a) to reside, live, dwell. (b) (*fig*) — **en** to reside in, lie in; to consist in; **la autoridad reside en el gobernador** authority rests with the governor; **la dificultad reside en que ...** the difficulty lies in the fact that ...

residual *adj* residual, residuary; **aguas** —**es** sewage.

residuo *nm* residue; (*Math*) remainder; (*Chem etc*) residuum; —**s** remains; refuse, waste; rubbish; left-overs; —**s atmosféricos,** —**s radiactivos** fallout.

resignación *nf* resignation.

resignadamente *adv* resignedly, with resignation.

resignado *adj* resigned.

resignar [1a] **1** *vt* to resign, give up, renounce; *command* to hand over (*en* to); *post* to resign.

2 resignarse *vr* to resign oneself (*a, con* to); — **a** + *infin* to resign oneself to + *ger*.

resina *nf* resin.

resinoso *adj* resinous.

resistencia *nf* (a) (*in most senses*) resistance; stand; **la R**— (*Pol*) the Resistance; — **a la enfermedad** resistance to disease; — **pasiva** passive resistance; **oponer** — **a** to resist, oppose, stand out against.

(b) (*of body etc*) endurance, stamina; strength; staying power; toughness; (*of material*) strength, toughness; **carrera de** — endurance race, long-distance race; **la** — **que necesitan tener los montañistas** the toughness (*or* stamina) which mountaineers need.

(c) opposition; **luchar con la** — **de sus colegas** to fight against the opposition of one's colleagues, try to overcome the hostility of one's colleagues.

resistente *adj* resistant (*a* to); *material* strong, tough; hard-wearing; (*Bot*) hardy; — **al calor** resistant to heat, heat-resistant; **hacerse** — (*Med*) to build up a resistance (*a* to).

resistible *adj* resistible.

resistir [3a] **1** *vt* (a) *weight* to bear, support; *pressure etc* to bear, withstand.

(b) *enemy* to resist; *attack* to resist, withstand; to stand up to; *proposal* to resist, oppose, make a stand against; *temptation* to resist.

(c) *disappointment, tiredness etc* to put up with, endure, withstand; **no puedo** — **este frío** I can't bear (*or* stand) this cold; **no lo resisto un momento más** I'm not putting up with this a moment longer.

(d) — **la mirada de uno** to stare back at someone; to stare someone out.

2 *vi* (a) to resist; to struggle; to put up a fight, fight back; to hold out.

(b) to last, still go on, endure; **el coche resiste todavía** the car is still going; **el equipo no puede** — **mucho tiempo más** the team can't last out much longer; **no podíamos** — **de cansados** we were so tired we couldn't go on any longer.

3 resistirse *vr* (a) = 2 (a).

(b) — **a** + *infin* to refuse to + *infin*, find it hard to + *infin*, resist + *ger*; **no me resisto a citar algunos versos** I can't resist quoting a few lines; **me resisto a creerlo** I refuse to believe it; **se me resiste pasar sin saludarle** I cannot possibly pass by without calling on him.

(c) **se le resiste la química** she can't get on with chemistry, chemistry comes very hard to her.

resma *nf* ream.

resobado *adj* (*fig*) hackneyed, trite, well-worn.

resobar [1a] *vt* (a) to finger, paw; to muck about. (b) (*fig*) *subject* to work to death.

resobrino *nm*, **resobrina** *nf* second cousin.

resol *nm* glare of the sun; reflected sunlight.

resolana *nf* (*SAm*) sunlight; warmth of the sun; = **resol**; = **resolano.**

resolano *nm* suntrap, sunny place.

resoltarse [1m] *vr* (*Col*) to overstep the mark.

resolución *nf* (a) decision; — **fatal** decision to take one's own life; **tomar una** — to take a decision.

(b) (*of problem*) solving; solution; **un problema de** — **nada fácil** a problem which it is not easy to (re)solve.

(c) (*Parl etc*) resolution; motion; — **judicial** legal ruling.

(d) (*quality*) resolution, resolve, determination; decisiveness; **obrar con** — to act with determination, act boldly.

(e) **en** — in a word, in short, to sum up.

resoluto *adj* = **resuelto.**

resolver [2h; *ptp* **resuelto**] **1** *vt* (a) *problem* to solve, resolve; *doubt* to settle; *matter* to decide, settle; *course of action* to decide on.
(b) (*Chem*) to dissolve.
(c) *body of material etc* to analyse, divide up, resolve (en into).
2 *vi* (a) to resolve, decide; **— a favor de uno** to resolve in someone's favour.
(b) **— hacer algo** to resolve to do something.
3 resolverse *vr* (a) (*problem etc*) to resolve itself, work out.
(b) **— en** to resolve itself into; to be transformed into; **todo se resolvió en una riña más** in the end it came down to one more quarrel.
(c) to decide, make up one's mind; **— a +** *infin* to resolve to + *infin*; **— por algo** to decide on something; **hay que — por el uno o el otro** you'll have to make up your mind one way or the other.
resollar [1m] *vi* (a) to breathe heavily, breathe noisily; to puff and blow; to wheeze.
(b) (*fig*) **escuchar sin —** to listen without saying a word in reply, listen scarcely daring to breathe; **hace tiempo que no resuella** he has given no sign of life for some time, it's a long time since we heard from him.
resonador *nm* resonator.
resonancia *nf* (a) resonance; echo. (b) (*fig*) wide importance, widespread effect; **tener —** to have repercussions, cause a stir, have a considerable effect.
resonante *adj* (a) resonant; ringing, echoing, re-sounding. (b) (*fig*) *success etc* tremendous, resounding.
resonar [1m] *vi* to resound, ring, echo (*de* with).
resoplar [1a] *vi* = **resollar**; (*with anger etc*) to snort.
resoplido *nm* (a) heavy breathing, noisy breathing; puff, puffing; wheeze; snort; **dar —s** to breathe heavily, puff; (*of engine*) to chug, puff; to labour.
(b) (*fig*) sharp answer.
resopón *nm* nightcap.
resorber [2a] *vt* to reabsorb.
resorción *nf* resorption, reabsorption.
resorte *nm* (a) spring.
(b) (*quality*) elasticity; springiness, resilience.
(c) (*fig*) means, expedient; contact; influence; **tocar —s** to pull strings; **tocar todos los —s** to mobilize all one's influential friends, bring influence to bear from all sides.
(d) (*SAm*) elastic band.
(e) (*SAm*) responsibility; concern; (*Law*) author-ity; jurisdiction; **no es de mi —** it's not my concern.
respaldar [1a] **1** *vt* (a) *document* to endorse.
(b) (*fig*) to back, support.
(c) (*SAm*) to ensure; to guarantee, safeguard.
2 respaldarse *vr* (a) to lean back, sprawl, loll (*contra* against, *en* on).
(b) (*fig*) **— con, — en** to take one's stand on, base oneself on.
respaldo *nm* (a) (*of chair etc*) back.
(b) (*Hort*) wall.
(c) (*of documents*) back; endorsement; **firmar al —, firmar en el —** to sign on the back.
(d) (*fig*) support, backing; (*esp SAm*) help; guarantee.
respectar [1a] *vt* to concern, relate to; **por lo que respecta a** as for, with regard to.
respectivamente *adv* respectively.
respectivo 1 *adj* respective. **2 en lo — a** *as prep* as regards, with regard to.
respecto *nm*: **al —** in the matter, with regard to the subject under discussion; **a ese —** on that score; **bajo ese —** in that respect; **(con) — a, — de** with regard to, in relation to.
respetabilidad *nf* respectability.
respetable *adj* (*all senses*) respectable.
respetablemente *adv* respectably.
respetar [1a] *vt* to respect; **hacerse —** to win respect; to establish oneself, win a proper position; to impose one's will.
respeto *nm* (a) respect, regard, consideration; **— a la opinión ajena** respect for somebody else's opinion; **— de sí mismo** self-respect; **— a la conveniencia, —s humanos** respect for the conventions, considera-tion for the susceptibilities of others; **por — a** out of consideration for; **campar por sus —s** to act independently, strike out on one's own; (*pej*) to show no consideration for others, be entirely self-centred; **faltar al —, perder el —** to be disrespect-ful (*a* to).
(b) **—s** respects; **presentar sus —s a** to pay one's respects to.
(c) **de —** spare, reserve (*attr*); special; **cuarto de —** spare room; **estar de —** to be all dressed up.

respetuosamente *adv* respectfully.
respetuosidad *nf* respectfulness.
respetuoso *adj* respectful.
réspice *nm* (a) sharp answer, curt reply. (b) severe reprimand.
respingado *adj* nose snub, turned-up.
respingar [1h] **1** *vi* (a) (*of horse*) to shy, balk; to start.
(b) (*fig*) to kick, show oneself unwilling, dig one's heels in.
(c) = **2 respingarse** *vr* (*dress*) to ride up, curl up.
respingo *nm* (a) shy; start, sudden movement (*of alarm etc*); wince (*of pain*); jump (*of surprise*); **dar un —** to start, jump.
(b) (*fig*) gesture of disgust; flounce.
(c) (*Sew*) part that is too short, part that rides up; **la chaqueta me hace un — aquí** the jacket rides up here.
(d) (*fig*) = **réspice** (a) *and* (b).
respingón *adj* nose snub, turned-up.
respiración *nf* (a) breathing, respiration; breath; **contener la —** to hold one's breath; **quedarse sin —** to be knocked all of a heap (*fam*); **llegar sin —** to arrive exhausted.
(b) (*of room etc*) ventilation.
respiradero *nm* (a) (*Tech*) vent, valve. (b) (*fig*) respite, breathing space.
respirador *nm* breathing tube, snorkel.
respirar [1a] **1** *vt* to breathe; *gas etc* to breathe in, inhale.
2 *vi* (a) to breathe; to draw breath; **— con dificultad** to breathe with difficulty, gasp for breath; **sin —** without a break, without respite; **paramos durante 5 minutos para —** we stopped for 5 minutes to get our breath back.
(b) (*fig*) (*after shock, effort etc*) to breathe again; **¡respiro!** that's a relief!; **no dejar — a uno** to keep on at someone, badger someone, make someone's life a misery; **no poder —** to be all in; to be up to one's eyes (with work *etc*).
(c) **no —** to say absolutely nothing; **estuvo escuchándole sin —** he listened to him in complete silence; **los niños le miraban sin —** the children watched him with bated breath.
(d) (*of room*) to be ventilated.
(e) (*fig*) **respira confianza** he oozes confidence, he breathes out confidence through every pore.
respiratorio *adj* respiratory; breathing (*attr*).
respiro *nm* (a) breathing. (b) (*fig*) respite, breathing space; rest; (*Comm etc*) extension of time, period of grace; (*Law*) suspension; reprieve.
respis *nm* see **réspice**.
resplandecer [2d] *vi* (a) to shine; to gleam, glitter, glow; to blaze. (b) (*fig*) to shine; **— de felicidad** to shine with happiness, be radiant with happiness.
resplandeciente *adj* (a) shining; gleaming, glittering, glowing; blazing. (b) (*fig*) radiant (*de* with).
resplandor *nm* (a) brilliance, brightness, radiance; gleam, glitter, glow; blaze. (b) (*Arg, Mex*) = **resolana**.
responder [2a] **1** *vt* to answer; to reply to; **pero él responde con injurias** but he answers with insults.
2 *vi* (a) to answer, reply; (*of echo*) to answer; **— a una pregunta** to answer a question.
(b) (*fig*) to reply, respond; **— con grosería a una cortesía** to return rudeness for courtesy, answer a courteous request rudely.
(c) (*fig: after order etc*) to answer back.
(d) **— a** *need* to answer, obey; *controls etc* to obey; *situation, treatment etc* to respond to; **la cápsula no responde a los mandos** the capsule is not obeying the controls; **pero no respondió a tal tratamiento** but he did not respond to such treatment.
(e) (*of material*) to be workable, be easily worked.
(f) (*of results etc*) to correspond (*a* to); **— a una descripción** to fit a description, agree with a descrip-tion; **la obra no responde al título** the book is not what the title implies.
(g) **— de** to be responsible for; to answer for; **yo no respondo de lo que hagan mis colegas** I am not responsible for what my colleagues may do; **yo no respondo de él** I cannot answer for him; **en estas circunstancias, ¿quién responde?** who is responsible in these circumstances?
(h) **— por uno** to vouch for someone, guarantee someone.
(i) **— al nombre de** to be called, go by the name of.
respondón *adj* cheeky, saucy.
responsabilidad *nf* responsibility; liability; **— solidaria** joint responsibility; **de — limitada** limited liability (*attr*); **bajo mi —** on my responsibility.

responsabilizar [1f] **1** vt (SAm): — **a uno** to make someone responsible; to put someone in charge.
2 responsabilizarse vr to make oneself responsible; to acknowledge one's responsibility; to take charge.

responsable adj (a) responsible (de for); **la persona** — the person in charge; **la policía busca a los —s** the police are hunting for those responsible; **hacer a uno —** to hold someone responsible (de for); **hacerse — de algo** to assume responsibility for something; to acknowledge one's responsibility for something; **no me hago — de lo que pueda pasar** I take no responsibility for what may happen.
(b) accountable, answerable; **ser — ante uno de algo** to be answerable to someone for something.

responsorio nm (Eccl) response.

respuesta nf answer, reply; response.

resquebra(ja)dura nf crack, split, cleft.

resquebrajar [1a] **1** vt to crack, split. **2 resquebrajarse** vr to crack, split.

resquebrar [1k] vi to begin to crack.

resquemar [1a] vt (a) to burn slightly; (Cook) to burn; tongue to burn, sting; plant to parch, dry up.
(b) (fig) to cause bitterness to, upset.

resquemor nm (a) burn, sting, stinging feeling; (Cook) burnt taste. (b) (fig) resentment, bitterness; concealed anger; secret suspicion.

resquicio nm (a) chink, crack.
(b) (fig) chance, possibility; opening, opportunity.
(c) (Col, Per, PR, Ven) sign, vestige, trace.
(d) (Cu, PR, Ven) bit, small piece.

resta nf (Math) (a) subtraction. (b) remainder.

restablecer [2d] **1** vt to re-establish; to restore. **2 restablecerse** vr (Med) to recover.

restablecimiento nm re-establishment; restoration; (Med) recovery.

restallar [1a] vi to crack; to click one's tongue; to crackle.

restallido nm crack; click; crackle.

restante adj remaining; **lo —** the rest, the remainder; **los —s** the remaining ones, the rest, those that are left (over).

restañar [1a] vt to stanch, stop (the flow of).

restañasangre nm bloodstone.

restar [1a] **1** vt (a) to take away, reduce; to deduct; (Math) to take away, subtract (de from); **— autoridad a uno** to take away authority from someone, reduce someone's authority.
(b) (Sport) ball to return.
2 vi to remain, be left; **restan 3 días para terminarse el plazo** there are 3 days left before the period expires.

restauración nf restoration.

restaurador 1 nm, **restauradora** nf restorer. **2** nm: **— del cabello** hair restorer.

restaurán nm, **restaurante** [resto'ran] nm restaurant.

restaurar [1a] vt (all senses) to restore.

restinga nf sandbar, shoal, mudbank.

restitución nf return; restoration.

restituir [3g] **1** vt (a) to return, give back, restore (a to). (b) (Archit etc) to restore. **2 restituirse** vr: **— a** to return to, go back to, rejoin.

resto nm (a) rest, remainder; (Math) remainder; **—s** remains; (Cook) left-overs, scraps; (Naut etc) wreckage; debris, rubble; **—s de edición** remainders; **—s humanos** human remains; **—s mortales** mortal remains.
(b) (Sport) return (of a ball); (person) receiver.
(c) stake; **a — abierto** with no limit on stakes; (fig) without limit; **echar el — (fam)** to stake all one's money; (fig) to go all out, go the whole hog; **echar el — por + infin** to do one's utmost to + infin.

restorán nm restaurant.

restregar [1h and 1k] vt (a) to scrub; to rub (hard).
(b) (of furniture etc) to rub on, rub against.

restricción nf restriction; limitation; restraint; **— mental** mental reservations; **—es eléctricas** electricity cuts; **sin — de** without restrictions as to, with no limitation upon; **hablar sin —es** to talk freely.

restrictivo adj restrictive.

restrillar [1a] **1** vt (Per, PR) whip to crack. **2** vi (Per, PR: of wood) to crack, creak.

restringido adj restricted, limited.

restringir [3c] vt to restrict, limit (a to).

resucitación nf resuscitation.

resucitar [1a] **1** vt (a) to resuscitate, revive.
(b) (fig) to revive; to resurrect, give a new existence to.
2 vi (a) to revive, return to life.
(b) (fig) to be resuscitated, be resurrected; to revive.

resudar [1a] vti to sweat a little; (of bottle etc) to leak slightly.

resueltamente adv resolutely, with determination; boldly; steadfastly.

resuelto 1 ptp of **resolver**.
2 adj resolute, resolved, determined; bold; steadfast; **estar — a algo** to be set on something; **estar — a + infin** to be determined to + infin.

resuello nm (a) breath; breathing; **corto de —** short of breath, short-winded.
(b) puff; heavy breathing; wheeze.
(c) **meter a uno el — en el cuerpo** to put the wind up someone, give someone a nasty fright; to puncture someone's vanity.
(d) (SAm) breathing space; rest; **tomar un —** to take a breather.

resulta nf result; **de —s de** as a result of.

resultado nm result; outcome, sequel; effect; **dar —** to produce results.

resultante adj resultant, consequential.

resultar [1a] vi (a) to be; to prove (to be), turn out (to be); **si resulta (ser) verdadero** if it proves (to be) true; **el conductor resultó muerto** the driver was killed; **resultó (ser) el padre de mi cocinera** he turned out to be my cook's father, it emerged that he was my cook's father; **la casa nos resulta muy pequeña** we find the house very small; **resulta difícil decidir si ...** it is difficult to decide whether ...; **resulta que ...** it follows that ...; it seems that ..., it emerges that ...; **ahora resulta que no vamos** now it turns out that we're not going; **resulta de todo esto que no lo podemos pagar** it follows from all this that we can't afford it.
(b) **— de** to result from; to stem from; to be evident from; **— en** to result in, produce; **de ese negocio resultaron 4 más** from that deal there resulted 4 others, that deal produced 4 more; **me resultan 8 menos que a ti** that leaves me with 8 less than you.
(c) (in absolute use) to ensure; **con lo que después resultó** with what ensued, with what happened in consequence; **no resultó** it didn't work; **no me resultó muy bien aquello** that didn't work out very well for me; **este tema no me resulta** I can't get along with this subject.
(d) (Fin) to cost, work out at, amount to; **la serie completa nos resultó en 50 dólares** the complete set cost us 50 dollars; **resultan con unos y otros a 80 pesetas** all together they amount to 80 pesetas.
(e) (fam) **— + infin** to be best to + infin, be wise to + infin; **no resulta dejar el coche fuera** it's best not to leave the car outside.
(f) (fam) to look well, have a pleasing effect; **esa corbata no resulta con ese traje** that tie doesn't go with the suit.

resumen nm summary, résumé; abstract; **en —** to sum up; in short.

resumidero nm (SAm) =**sumidero**.

resumir [3a] **1** vt to sum up; summarize; to abridge, shorten, cut down.
2 resumirse vr (a) **la situación se resume en pocas palabras** the situation can be summed up in a few words.
(b) **— en** to be reduced to, come down to; **todo se resumió en algunos porrazos** the affair amounted to no more than a few bashes (fam).

resurgimiento nm resurgence; revival.

resurgir [3c] vi (a) to reappear, revive; to be resurrected. (b) to acquire a new spirit, pick up again; (Med) to recover.

resurrección nf resurrection.

retablo nm reredos, altarpiece.

retacarse [1g] vr (Chi) to refuse to budge; to go back on a promise (etc).

retacear [1a] vt (RPl) grant etc to give grudgingly, give in small amounts.

retacón adj (Per, RPl) short, squat.

retachar [1a] vti (SAm) to bounce.

retador 1 adj challenging; defiant. **2** nm (SAm: Sport) challenger.

retaguardia nf rearguard; **a — in** the rear; **3 millas a —** 3 miles to the rear, 3 miles further back.

retahíla nf string, series; (of abuse etc) volley, stream.

retajado adj (Arg) castrated, gelded.

retajar [1a] vt (a) to cut out, cut round. (b) (SAm) to castrate, geld.

retal nm remnant, piece left over.

retaliación nf (SAm: angl) retaliation.

retama nf (Bot), **retamo** nm (SAm: Bot) broom.

retar [1a] vt (a) to challenge; to defy. (b) to reprimand, tell off; to scold. (c) (Chi, RPl) to insult, abuse.

retardación nf retardation, slowing down; delaying; (Mech) deceleration.

retardar [1a] vt to slow down, slow up, retard; progress etc to hold up, retard; train etc to delay, make late; clock to put back.

retardatriz adj (f) action etc delaying.

retardo nm delay; time lag.

retazar [1f] vt to cut up, snip into pieces; to divide up; firewood to chop.

retazo nm remnant; snippet; bit, piece, fragment; —s (Lit etc) snippets, bits and pieces; disjointed fragments.

rete ... intensifying prefix (fam) very ... eg, **retebién** very well, jolly well (fam); **una persona retefina a** terribly refined person (fam).

retemblar [1k] vi to shudder, shake (de at, with).

retemplar [1a] vt (Arg, Chi, Guat, Per) to cheer up, revive, raise the spirits of.

retén nm (a) (Tech) stop, catch; lock. (b) reserve, store. (c) police post; post of armed men kept in reserve for an emergency.

retención nf (a) retention (also Med). (b) (Fin) deduction, part (of pay etc) withheld.

retener [2l] vt to retain; to keep (back), hold back; (Fin) to deduct; to withhold (part of); attention to hold; memory to retain; borrowed article to keep, hold on to; treasures, rationed goods to hoard; — a uno preso to keep someone in detention.

retenida nf guy-rope.

retentivo adj retentive.

reteñir [3h and 3l] vt to redye.

reticencia nf (a) insinuation, (malevolent) suggestion; implication; irony, sarcasm. (b) half-truth, misleading statement. (c) (angl) reticence, reserve.

reticente adj (a) insinuating; ironical, sarcastic; full of (unpleasant) implications. (b) deceptive, misleading. (c) (angl) reticent, reserved.

retícula nf (Opt) reticle; (Phot) screen.

reticular adj reticulated.

retículo nm reticle; net, network; (in measuring etc) grid.

retina nf retina.

retintín nm (a) tinkle, tinkling; jingle, jangle; (in the ears) ringing. (b) (fig) sarcastic tone; **decir algo con** — to say something sarcastically.

retinto adj (SAm) complexion very dark.

retiñir [3a] vi to tinkle; to jingle, jangle; to go on ringing (in one's ears).

retirada nf (a) (Mil) retreat, withdrawal; **batirse en** —, **emprender la** — to retreat.
(b) (of money, ambassador etc) withdrawal.
(c) retreat, safe place, place of refuge.

retiradamente adj live quietly, in seclusion.

retirado adj (a) life quiet; place remote, secluded, quiet. (b) officer etc retired.

retirar [1a] 1 vt (a) chair etc to move away, move back; to put away, take away, remove; horn, tentacle etc to draw in; cover, hand etc to draw back; lid to take off; part (Mech) to take out, remove; (Mil) forces to withdraw.
(b) (Fin) to withdraw (de from), take out; ambassador to recall, withdraw; horse, runner to scratch.
(c) coins, stamps etc to withdraw (from circulation); permission to withdraw, cancel; driving licence to suspend, confiscate, take away.
(d) person to retire, pension off.
(e) accusation, words to withdraw.
2 **retirarse** vr (a) to move back, move away (de from); (Mil) to retreat, withdraw; — **ante un peligro** to shrink back from a danger.
(b) (Sport) to retire; to scratch.
(c) to go into seclusion, go off into retreat, withdraw from active life; (with pension) to retire (de from); **se retiró a vivir a Mallorca** he went off to live in Majorca, he retired to Majorca; **cuando me retire de los negocios** when I retire from business.
(d) to retire (to one's room or to bed), go off to bed.

retiro nm (a) (act) retirement; withdrawal; (Sport) retirement; scratching; (of money etc) withdrawal.
(b) (state) retirement; **un oficial en** — an officer in retirement, a retired officer.
(c) (Fin) retirement pay, pension.
(d) quiet place, secluded spot; seclusion; retreat; **vivir en el** — to live in seclusion; live quietly.
(e) (Eccl) retreat.

reto nm (a) challenge; threat, defiant statement (etc). (b) (Chi, RPl) reprimand; scolding. (c) (Chi) insult.

retobado adj (a) (SAm) animal wild, untamed;

person wild, unruly, rebellious; obstinate; sullen; unpredictable, capricious.
(b) (CAm, Ec, Mex) grumbling; saucy, cheeky.
(c) (Col, Chi, Per, RPl) sly, crafty.

retobar [1a] 1 vt (a) (SAm) to line (or cover) with leather; (Chi, Per) crate etc to line (or cover) with leather (or sacking or oilcloth).
(b) (Col) hides to tan.
2 vi and **retobarse** vr (SAm) to be stubborn, dig one's heels in; to rebel; to grumble, protest.

retobo nm (a) (SAm) lining, covering; (Chi) sacking, oilcloth, wrapping material.
(b) (SAm) stubbornness; rebelliousness; grumble, protest; whim.
(c) (Col, Hond: Agr) old stock, useless animals; (fig) useless person, worthless object; junk, rubbish.

retobón adj (Arg) =**retobado**.

retocar [1g] vt (a) to retouch, touch up. (b) recording to play back.

retoñar [1a] vi (a) (Bot) to sprout, shoot. (b) (fig) to reappear, recur.

retoño nm (Bot) sprout, shoot, new growth.

retoque nm (a) retouching, touching-up; finishing touch. (b) (Med) symptom, sign, indication.

retorcer [2b and 2h] 1 vt (a) arm etc to twist; hands, neck, washing to wring; strands to twine (together).
(b) (fig) argument to turn, twist; sense to twist, force.
2 **retorcerse** vr (a) (string etc) to get into knots, twist up, curl up.
(b) — **el bigote** to twirl one's moustache.
(c) (person) to writhe; to squirm; — **de dolor** to writhe in pain, squirm with pain; — **de risa** to double up with laughter.

retorcido adj (a) style involved. (b) person, manner crafty, devious.

retorcijón nm (SAm) =**retortijón**.

retorcimiento nm (a) twisting; wringing; entwining; writhing. (b) (fig) involved nature. (c) (fig) craftiness, deviousness.

retórica nf (a) rhetoric; (pej) affectedness, windiness, grandiloquence. (b) —s (fam) hot air, mere words; quibbles.

retóricamente adv rhetorically.

retórico 1 adj (a) rhetorical; (pej) affected, windy; grandiloquent. 2 nm rhetorician.

retornar [1a] 1 vt (a) to return, give back. (b) to replace, return to its place. (c) to move back. 2 vi to return, come back, go back.

retorno nm (a) return. (b) reward; repayment; exchange, barter; (of present, service etc) return. (c) (Elec) — **terrestre** earth wire, ground wire (US).

retorsión nf =**retorcimiento** (a).

retorta nf (Chem) retort.

retortero: andar al — to bustle about, have heaps of things to do; **andar** — **por algo** to crave for something; **andar** — **por uno** to be madly in love with someone; **llevar** (or **traer**) **a uno al** — to have someone under one's thumb; to keep someone constantly on the go; (fig) to push someone around.

retortijón nm rapid twist; — **de tripas** gripe, stomach cramp.

retostar [1m] vt to burn, overcook.

retozar [1f] vt to romp, frolic, frisk about; to gambol.

retozo nm (a) romp, frolic; gambol; —s romping, frolics; gambolling. (b) — **de la risa** giggle, titter, suppressed laugh.

retozón adj (a) playful, frolicsome, frisky. (b) laughter bubbling.

retracción nf retraction, retractation.

retractable adj retractable.

retractación nf retraction, recantation.

retractar [1a] 1 vt to retract, withdraw. 2 **retractarse** vr to retract, recant; **me retracto** I take that back.

retráctil adj (Aer etc) retractable.

retraer [2p] 1 vt (a) horns etc to draw in, retract.
(b) to bring back, bring again.
(c) (fig) to dissuade.
2 **retraerse** vr to withdraw, retire, retreat (de from); — **a** to take refuge in; — **de** (fig) to withdraw from; to give up, avoid, shun.

retraído adj retiring, shy, reserved; aloof, unsociable.

retraimiento nm (a) (act) withdrawal, retirement; (state) seclusion. (b) (quality) retiring nature, shyness, reserve; aloofness. (c) (place) refuge, retreat.

retranca nf (SAm) brake.

retrancar [1g] 1 vt (SAm) to brake. 2 **retrancarse** vr (a) (SAm) to brake, apply the brakes. (b) (Mex) to be held up, reach deadlock.

retransmisión nf repeat broadcast, rebroadcast.

retransmitir [3a] vt message to relay, pass on; (Radio, TV) to repeat, rebroadcast, retransmit; to broadcast live (direct from a theatre etc), do an outside broadcast of.

retrasado adj (a) estar — (of person, industry etc) to be behind, be behindhand, lag behind; **está — en química** he is behind in chemistry, he has a lot to make up in chemistry; **vamos —s en la producción** we lag behind in production, our production is lagging; **estar — en los pagos** to be behind in one's payments, be in arrears.

(b) estar — (of watch) to be slow; **tengo el reloj 8 minutos** — my watch is 8 minutes slow.

(c) country backward, underdeveloped; way of life antiquated, old-fashioned.

(d) food etc unused, left over; **tengo trabajo** — I have work piling up, I am behindhand in my work.

(e) (Med) child subnormal, mentally retarded.

retrasar [1a] **1** vt (a) departure, event etc to delay, put off, postpone; development, progress to retard, slow down; to hold up.

(b) watch to put back.

2 vi and **retrasarse** vr (watch) to be slow; (person, train etc) to be late, be behind time; (in production, studies etc) to lag behind; (production etc) to decline, fall away.

retraso nm (a) delay; time lag; slowness, lateness; **llegar con** — to be late, arrive late; **llegar con 25 minutos de** — to be 25 minutes late; **llevo un** — **de 6 semanas** I'm 6 weeks behind (with my work etc).

(b) (of country) backwardness, backward state.

(c) (Med) — **mental** subnormality, mental deficiency.

(d) —s (Comm, Fin) arrears; deficit, debts.

retratar [1a] **1** vt (a) to portray; (Art) to paint a picture of, paint the portrait of; (Phot) to photograph, take a picture of; **hacerse** — to have one's portrait painted.

(b) (fig) to portray, depict, describe.

2 retratarse vr (a) to have one's picture painted; (Phot) to have one's photograph taken.

(b) (sl) to pay (up), fork out (fam).

retratería nf (SAm) photographer's (studio).

retratista nmf (Art) portrait painter; (Phot) photographer.

retrato nm (a) (Art) portrait; (Phot) photograph, portrait.

(b) (fig) portrayal, depiction, description.

(c) (fig) likeness; **ser el vivo** — **de** to be the very image of.

retrato-robot nm identikit picture.

retrechería nf (a) (fam: act) dodge, wheeze (fam), crafty trick; (hum) rascally trick.

(b) (fam) —s winning ways, charming ways.

(c) (fam: quality) charm, attractiveness.

(d) (SAm) meanness; deceitfulness; suspicious nature.

retrechero adj (a) (fam) full of dodges; wily, crafty; (hum) rascally.

(b) (fam) child, woman winning, charming, attractive.

(c) (SAm) mean; unreliable, deceitful; suspicious.

retreparse [1a] vr to lean back; to sprawl, loll, lounge.

retreta nf (a) (Mil) retreat; tattoo, display. (b) (SAm) open-air band concert. (c) (SAm) series, string.

retrete nm lavatory.

retribución nf (a) pay, payment; reward; compensation. (b) (Tech) compensation.

retribuido adj work paid; post salaried, that carries a salary; **un puesto mal** — an ill-paid post.

retribuir [3g] vt (a) to pay; to reward, compensate.

(b) (SAm) favour etc to repay, return.

retro . . . retro . . .

retroactivo adj retroactive, retrospective; **dar efecto** — **a un pago** to backdate a payment.

retrocarga: de — breechloading; **arma de** — breechloader.

retroceder [2a] vi (a) (of person) to move back; to draw back, stand back; to go backwards; (on journey) to turn back; (Mil) to fall back, retreat; (of gun) to recoil; (of water level etc) to fall, go down; **retrocedió unos pasos** he went back a few steps; **la policía hizo** — **a la multitud** the police forced the crowd back, the police pushed the crowd back.

(b) (fig) to back down; to give up; to flinch (ante un peligro from a danger); **no** — to stand firm.

retroceso nm (a) backward movement; drawing back; (Mil) withdrawal, retreat; (of gun) recoil.

(b) (fig) backing down.

(c) (Comm, Fin) recession (of trade), slump, depression.

(d) (Med) renewed attack, new outbreak.

retrocohete nm retrorocket.

retrogradación nf retrogression.

retrógrado adj retrograde, retrogressive; (Pol etc) reactionary.

retrogresión nf retrogression.

retronar [1m] vi =**retumbar.**

retropropulsión nf retropropulsion; (Aer) jet propulsion.

retrospección nf retrospection.

retrospectivamente adv retrospectively; in retrospect.

retrospectivo adj retrospective; **escena retrospectiva** flashback; **mirada retrospectiva** backward glance, look back (a at).

retrotraer [2p] vt to carry back (in time), take back; **retrotrajo su relato a los tiempos del abuelo** he carried his tale back into his grandfather's day; **ahora podemos** — **su origen al siglo XI** now we can take its origin further back to the 11th century; **piensa** — **el problema a su origen** he hopes to trace the problem back to its origin.

retrovisor 1 adj: **espejo** — = **2** nm driving mirror, rear-view mirror.

retrucar [1g] vt (a) argument to turn against its user.

(b) (Prov, SAm) to retort; **le retruqué diciendo que . . .** I retorted to him that . . .

retruécano nm pun, play on words.

retruque nm (a) (Per, RPl) sharp retort, brusque reply. (b) (Chi, Mex) **de** — on the rebound; as a consequence.

retumbante adj (a) booming, rumbling; resounding.

(b) (fig) bombastic.

retumbar [1a] vi (of guns, thunder etc) to boom, roll, thunder, rumble; (of voice, steps) to echo, resound; to reverberate; **la cascada retumbaba a lo lejos** the waterfall boomed (or roared) in the distance; **la caverna retumbaba con nuestros pasos** the cave echoed with our steps; **sus palabras retumban en mi cabeza** his words are still reverberating in my mind.

retumbo nm boom, roll, thunder, rumble; echo; reverberation.

reuma nm, **reúma** nm rheumatism.

reumático adj rheumatic.

reumatismo nm rheumatism.

reumatoideo adj rheumatoid.

reunificación nf reunification.

reunificar [1g] vt to reunify.

reunión nf (a) meeting, gathering; social gathering, party; (Pol) meeting; rally; (Sport) meeting; — **en la cumbre** summit meeting; — **plenaria** plenary session.

(b) reunion.

reunir [3a] **1** vt (a) parts etc to reunite, join (together); — **dos cuartos** to knock two rooms together, make one room out of two.

(b) scattered objects etc to gather (together), get together, put together; data etc to assemble, collect, gather; resources to pool; collection to make; money to collect; funds to raise; **los 4 reunidos no valen lo que él** the 4 of them together are not as good as he is; **la producción de los demás países reunidos no alcanzará al nuestro** the production of the other countries put together will not come up to ours.

(c) persons to assemble, bring together, invite together; **reunió a sus amigos para discutirlo** he assembled his friends to talk it over.

(d) qualities to combine; **la casa reúne la comodidad con la economía** the house combines comfort with economy.

2 reunirse vr (a) to unite, join together; to re-unite.

(b) (persons) to meet, gather, assemble; to get together; — **para** + infin to get together to + infin; — **con uno para una excursión** to join someone for an outing.

(c) (circumstances) to conspire (para + infin to + infin).

reválida nf (School etc) final examination.

revalidar [1a] vt (a) to confirm, ratify. (b) (School etc) to sit a final examination for, take a final examination in.

revalor(iz)ación nf revaluation; reassessment.

revalorar [1a] vt, **revalorizar** [1f] vt to revalue; to reassess.

revaluación nf (SAm) revaluation.

revancha nf (a) revenge; **tomar su** — to get one's revenge, get one's own back. (b) (Sport) return match; (Boxing) return fight.

revejido adj (Col) weak, feeble.

revelación nf revelation; disclosure; **fue una** — **para mí** it was a revelation to me.

revelado nm (Phot) developing.

revelador 1 adj revealing; telltale. **2** nm (Phot) developer.

revelar [1a] *vt* (a) to reveal; to disclose; to betray, show; to give away. (b) (*Phot*) to develop.

revendedor *nm* retailer; (*pej*) speculator; vendor, hawker, seller; (*Sport, Theat etc*) ticket tout.

revender [2a] *vt* to resell; to retail; (*pej*) to speculate in; to hawk; *tickets* to tout.

revendón *nm* (*Ec, Per*) middleman.

revenirse [3s] *vr* (a) to shrink.
(b) (*food*) to go bad, go off; (*wine etc*) to sour, turn.
(c) (*plaster etc*) to dry out; to give off moisture.
(d) (*Cook*) to get tough; get leathery.
(e) (*fig*) to give way (at last).

reventa *nf* resale; speculation; hawking; touting.

reventadero *nm* (a) rough ground; steep terrain. (b) (*fig*) tough job, heavy work, grind. (c) (*Col, Mex*) bubbling spring. (d) (*Chi*) =**rompiente**.

reventar [1k] **1** *vt* (a) *balloon etc* to burst, explode, pop; *pipe, tyre etc* to burst; *barrier etc* to break, smash; **tengo una cubierta reventada** I have a puncture, I have a burst tyre, I have a flat (*US*).
(b) *horse* to flog, ride hard, ride to death; *person* to work to death, overwork, exhaust.
(c) (*fam*) *plan etc* to sink, ruin; *play* to hiss off the stage.
(d) (*fam*) *person* to do down, do serious harm to.
(e) (*fam*) to annoy, rile (*fam*); **me revienta tener que ponérmelo** it riles me to have to wear it; **me revienta de aburrimiento** it bores me to tears.
2 *vi* (a) (*of balloon etc*) to burst, pop, go off pop; to explode; (*of shell, pipe, tyre etc*) to burst; (*of contents*) to burst forth, burst out.
(b) (*of wave*) to break.
(c) (*sl*) to peg out (*sl*).
(d) — **de** (*fig*) to be bursting with; — **de indignación** to be bursting with indignation; **casi reventaba de ira** he almost exploded with anger; — **de risa** to burst out laughing, split one's sides; — **de ganas de decirlo todo** to be bursting to tell all about it; — **por algo** to crave something; — **por** + *infin* to be bursting to + *infin*, be dying to + *infin*.
3 reventarse *vr* (a) =**2** (a).
(b) (*horse*) to die of overwork, die of exhaustion; (*in race*) to blow up.
(c) (*sl*) to peg out (*sl*); **se revienta trabajando** he's killing himself with work, he's working his guts out.

reventazón *nf* (a) (*Arg*) low ridge. (b) (*Mex*) flatulence. (c) (*Mex*) bubbling spring.

reventón *nm* (a) burst, bursting; explosion; (*Aut*) puncture, blow-out, flat (*US*); **dar un** — to burst, explode.
(b) (*fam*) death (from overeating); **dar un** — to peg out (*sl*).
(c) steep slope; tough climb.
(d) (*fam*) killing effort; toil, slog; **le dio un** — **al caballo** he flogged his horse, he half-killed his horse; **darse un** —, **pegarse un** — to slog, flog oneself (*fam*), sweat one's guts out (*para* + *infin* to + *infin*).
(e) jam, difficulty.
(f) (*Arg, Chi*) outcrop of ore.
(g) (*Chi*) violent outburst; (*Med*) relapse.
(h) (*CR*) shove.

rever [2v] *vt* (a) to see again, look again at. (b) (*Law*) *sentence* to review; *case* to retry.

reverberación *nf* reverberation.

reverberador *nm* reverberator.

reverberar [1a] *vi* (a) (*of light*) to play, be reflected; (*of surface*) to shimmer, shine; (*of snow etc*) to glare; **la luz reverberaba en el agua** the light played (*or* danced) on the water; **la luz del farol reverberaba en la calle** the lamplight lay in a pool on the street, the lamplight was reflected on the street.
(b) (*of sound*) to reverberate.

reverbero *nm* (a) play, reflection; shimmer, shine; glare; **el** — **de la nieve** the glare of the snow, the dazzle of the snow.
(b) reverberation.
(c) reflector; adornment of glass (*or* steel).
(d) (*CAm, Col, Mex*) small spirit stove.
(e) (*Mex*) brazier.

reverdecer [2d] *vi* (a) (*Bot*) to grow green again. (b) (*fig*) to come to life again, revive, acquire new vigour.

reverencia *nf* (a) reverence. (b) bow, curtsy; **hacer una** — to bow, curtsy. (c) (*as title*) **R**— (*also* **Su R**—, **Vuestra** —) Your Reverence.

reverencial *adj* reverential.

reverenciar [1b] *vt* to revere, venerate.

reverendísimo *adj* right reverend.

reverendo *adj* (a) respected, revered.
(b) (*Eccl*) reverend; **el** — **padre X** Reverend Father X.
(c) (*fam*) solemn.
(d) (*SAm*) big, tremendous (*fam*), awful (*fam*); **un** — **imbécil** an awful idiot.

reverente *adj* reverent.

reverentemente *adv* reverently.

reversa *nf* (*Col, Cu, Mex, PR*: *Aut*) reverse.

reversible *adj* reversible.

reversión *nf* reversion.

reversionario *adj* reversionary.

reverso *nm* back, other side; wrong side; (*of coin*) reverse; **el** — **de la medalla** (*fig*) the other side of the coin; the exact opposite.

revertir [3i] *vi* (a) (*of possession*) to revert (*a* to).
(b) — **a su estado primitivo** to revert to its original state.
(c) — **en** to end up as, come to be.
(d) — **en beneficio de** to be to the advantage of; — **en perjuicio de** to be to the detriment of.

revés *nm* (a) back; other side, wrong side; underside.
(b) backhand (blow *or* shot *etc*); slap, swipe; (*Sport*) backhand.
(c) (*fig*) reverse (*also fig*), setback; **sufrir un** — to suffer a setback; **los** —**es de la fortuna** the blows of fate.
(d) **al** — the wrong (*or* other) way round; upside down; *dress etc* inside out; **y al** — and vice versa; **entender algo al** — to get hold of the wrong end of the stick; to have quite a different idea; **todo nos salió al** — it all turned out wrong for us; **al** — **de lo que se cree** contrary to what is believed; **al** — **de lo corriente** against the usual practice, contrary to what normally happens; **llevar algo del** — to wear something the wrong way round (*or* inside out); **volver algo del** — to turn something round (the other way); to turn something inside out.

revesado *adj* (a) *matter* complicated, involved. (b) *child etc* unruly, uncontrollable.

revesero *adj* (*Col*) treacherous.

revestimiento *nm* (*Tech*) coating, facing, covering; lining; (*Mil*) revetment.

revestir [3l] **1** *vt* (a) *dress* to put on, don; to wear.
(b) (*Tech*) to coat, face, cover (*de* with); to line (*de* with); to sheathe (*de* in); (*fig*) *floor etc* to carpet (*de* with).
(c) (*fig*) to cloak, disguise (*de* in); *person* to invest (*con, de* with); *tale etc* to adorn (*de* with); **revistió su acto de generosidad** he gave his action an appearance of generosity.
(d) *importance, quality* to have, possess; **el acto revestía gran solemnidad** the ceremony had great dignity, the ceremony was a very solemn one.
2 revestirse *vr* (a) (*Eccl*) to put on one's vestments.
(b) (*fig*) to deck oneself in, put on; **los árboles se revisten de hojas** the trees put on their leaves again.
(c) (*fig*) — **con**, — **de** *authority etc* to be invested with, have; *quality etc* to arm oneself with; **se revistió de valor y fue a hablarle** he screwed up his courage and went to speak to her; *see also* **paciencia**.
(d) (*fig*) to get carried away; to be vain, be haughty.

reviejo *adj* very old.

revirado *adj* (*RPl*) (a) bad-tempered; unruly, uncontrollable. (b) crazy.

revirar [1a] **1** *vt* to turn (round), twist (round); to turn over. **2 revirarse** *vr* (a) (*Cu, Chi, RPl*) to disobey, rebel. (b) (*Arg*) to go crazy.

revirón 1 *adj* (*Cu*) disobedient, rebellious, unruly. **2** *nm* (*Ant, CAm, Mex*) disobedience, revolt.

revisación *nf* (*RPl*), **revisada** *nf* (*SAm*) =**revisión**.

revisar [1a] *vt* (a) *notes, text etc* to revise, look over, go through; *edition* to revise; *account* to check; to audit; (*Law*) to review; *case, theory etc* to re-examine, review.
(b) (*Mil*) *troops* to review.
(c) (*Mech*) to check, overhaul.

revisión *nf* (a) revision; check, checking; re-examination, review; — **aduanera** customs inspection; — **de cuentas** audit. (b) (*Mech*) check, overhaul.

revisionismo *nm* revisionism.

revisionista 1 *adj* revisionist. **2** *nmf* revisionist.

revisor *nm* reviser; inspector; (*Rail*) ticket collector, inspector, conductor (*US*); — **de cuentas** auditor.

revista *nf* (a) review, revision; inspection; (*Law*) retrial; **pasar** — **a** to review, revise, re-examine.
(b) (*Mil*) review, inspection; (*Naut*) review; **pasar** — **a** to review, inspect.

(c) review, journal, magazine; — **comercial** trade paper; — **cómica** comic; — **gráfica** illustrated paper; — **juvenil** teenage magazine; — **literaria** literary review; — **de modas** fashion paper; — **para mujeres** women's magazine; — **semanal** weekly review.

(d) (*Lit*) section, page; — **de libros** book review section, literary page; — **de toros** bullfighting page, section of bullfight reports.

(e) (*Theat*) revue; variety show, vaudeville show (*US*).

revistar [1a] *vt* (*Mil*) to review, inspect; (*Naut*) to review.

revistero *nm* (a) reviewer, critic; contributor; — **deportivo** sporting journalist; — **literario** literary critic, book reviewer. (b) magazine rack.

revitalizar [1f] *vt* (*SAm: angl*) to revitalize.

revivificar [1g] *vt* to revitalize.

revivir [3a] **1** *vt event etc* to revive memories of; to relive, live again; *suspicions* to revive. **2** *vi* to revive, be revived; to come to life again; **hacer** — = **1**.

revocación *nf* revocation, repeal; reversal.

revocar [1g] *vt* (a) *decision* to revoke, repeal; to cancel; to reverse.

(b) *smoke etc* to send in a different direction, blow back, blow the wrong way.

(c) *person* to dissuade (*de* from).

(d) (*Archit*) to plaster, stucco; to whitewash.

revocatoria *nf* (*SAm*) revocation, repeal; reversal.

revoco *nm* (a) = **revocación**. (b) = **revoque**.

revolar [1m] *vi* to take to flight again; to flutter about, fly around.

revolcadero *nm* (*Zool*) mudhole, mudbath.

revolcar [1g *and* 1m] **1** *vt* (a) *person* to knock down, knock over, send flying; (*Taur*) to knock down and trample on.

(b) (*fam*) *opponent* to floor, crush; to wipe the floor with (*fam*).

(c) *proud person* to deflate, puncture.

(d) (*Univ: sl*) to plough (*sl*).

2 revolcarse *vr* (a) to roll about, flounder about; to turn over and over; (*animal*) to wallow; — **en la tumba** to turn over in one's grave; — **en los vicios** to wallow in vice.

(b) (*fig*) to dig one's heels in.

revolcón *nm* (*fam*) fall, tumble; (*Fin*) slump; **dar un** — **a uno** (*fig*) to floor someone, crush someone; to wipe the floor with someone (*fam*); to deflate someone.

revolear [1a] **1** *vt* (*Mex, RPl*) *lasso* to whirl, twirl. **2** *vi* to fly round.

revolotear [1a] *vi* to flutter, fly about; to flit; to wheel, circle; to hover.

revoloteo *nm* fluttering; flitting; wheeling, circling; hovering.

revoltijo *nm*, **revoltillo** *nm* (a) jumble, confusion; mess, litter; (*fig*) mess; — **de huevos** scrambled eggs.

(b) (*Arg, Guat, Mex*) badly-tied bundle.

revoltoso 1 *adj* rebellious, unruly, turbulent; *child* naughty, uncontrollable. **2** *nm* rebel; (*Pol*) trouble-maker, agitator; rioter.

revoltura *nf* (a) (*Ant, Col, Chi, Mex*) confusion, jumble. (b) (*Mex*) mixture; (*Cook*) mixed egg and vegetable dish; (*Archit*) plaster; concrete.

revolución *nf* (*all senses*) revolution; —**es por minuto** revolutions per minute.

revolucionar [1a] *vt* (a) *fashion etc* to revolutionize, cause a revolution in.

(b) *person* to arouse intense excitement in, rouse to a pitch of excitement.

(c) (*Pol*) to stir up, sow discontent among; to rouse to revolt.

revolucionario 1 *adj* revolutionary. **2** *nm*, **revolucionaria** *nf* revolutionary.

revoluta *nf* (*CAm*) revolution.

revolvedora *nf* (*Arg, Mex*) concrete mixer.

revolver [2h; *ptp* **revuelto**] **1** *vt* (a) *objects* to move about; *object* to turn round, turn over, turn upside-down; (*Cook*) to turn over; *earth* to turn over, turn up, dig over; *container* to shake; *liquid etc* to stir; *papers etc* to look through; to rummage through, rummage among.

(b) *order, ordered things* to disturb, disarrange, mix up, mess up; **han revuelto toda la casa** they've messed up the whole house, they've turned the whole house upside-down.

(c) *affair* to go into, inquire into, investigate; — **algo en la cabeza** to turn something over in one's mind.

(d) (*Pol etc*) to stir up, rouse, cause unrest among; *person* to provoke, rouse to anger; — **a Eslobodia con Ruritania** to stir up trouble between Slobodia and Ruritania; — **al secretario con el jefe** to get the secretary into trouble with his boss.

(e) *eyes, head, horse* to turn.

(f) *parcel* to wrap up.

(g) (*Col*) to weed.

2 *vi* — **en una maleta** to rummage (about) in a case, hunt through the contents of a case; — **en los bolsillos** to feel in one's pockets, fumble in one's pockets.

3 revolverse *vr* (a) to turn (right) round; to turn over; (*in bed*) to toss and turn; (*with pain*) to writhe, squirm; (*Astron*) to revolve; — **al enemigo** to turn to face the enemy; **hay tantos muebles que resulta imposible** — there is so much furniture you can't turn round; **se revolvía en su silla** he was fidgeting about on his chair; he was squirming uncomfortably on his chair.

(b) (*fig*) — **contra uno** to turn on someone, turn against someone, attack someone.

(c) (*sediment*) to be stirred up, be disturbed; (*liquid*) to become cloudy.

(d) (*Meteorol*) to break, turn stormy.

(e) (*Col*) to have a piece of luck, begin to do well; (*pej*) to look after number one.

revólver *nm* revolver.

revoque *nm* (a) (*act*) plastering; whitewashing. (b) (*material*) plaster, stucco; whitewash.

revuelco *nm* fall, tumble.

revuelo *nm* (a) second flight; wheeling flight.

(b) mass flight.

(c) flutter(ing).

(d) (*fig*) stir, commotion, disturbance; row, rumpus; **de** — incidentally, in passing; **armar** (*or* **levantar** *etc*) **un gran** — to cause a great stir.

revuelta *nf* (a) turn; **dar vueltas y** —**s a algo** to go on turning something over and over.

(b) (*in road etc*) bend, turn.

(c) (*fig*) commotion, disturbance; fuss; quarrel, row; (*Pol*) disturbance, riot; revolt.

(d) (*Col, Ven*) weeding.

revuelto 1 *ptp of* **revolver**.

2 *adj* (a) *objects* mixed up, in disorder, confused; *eggs* scrambled; *water* cloudy, muddy; *sea* rough; *weather* unsettled, changeable; stormy; **todo estaba** — everything was in disorder, everything was upside-down; **los tiempos están** —**s** the times are out of joint, these are disturbed times; **viven** —**s los animales y las personas** people and animals live on top of each other.

(b) *character* unruly; restless, discontented; *child etc* mischievous, naughty; *populace* rebellious, mutinous; **la gente está revuelta por tales abusos** people feel mutinous about such scandals, people are properly on the boil about such abuses.

(c) *matter* complicated, involved.

3 *nm* (a) (*Arg*) mixed egg and vegetable dish.

(b) (*Col*) must, grape juice.

revulsar [1a] *vt* (*Mex*) to vomit, bring up.

revulsivo *nm* (a) enema, revulsive. (b) (*fig*) nasty but salutary shock.

rey *nm* king (*also Cards, Chess and fig*); **los** —**es** (*freq*) the king and queen; royalty; **los Reyes Católicos** the Catholic Monarchs (*Ferdinand and Isabella of Castile and Aragon*); **los Reyes Magos** see **Mago**; — **de armas** king of arms; — **de la evasión** escapologist; **ni** — **ni roque** no-one at all, not a single living soul; **lo mismo me da** — **que roque** it's all the same to me.

reyerta *nf* quarrel; fight, brawl, affray.

reyezuelo *nm*: — **sencillo** goldcrest.

rezaga *nf* (*SAm*) = **zaga**.

rezagado 1 *adj* **quedar** — to be left behind; to be late, be behindhand; (*in payment, progress etc*) to fall behind, be backward.

(b) (*Mex, Per*) **carta rezagada** unclaimed letter. **2** *nm* latecomer, loiterer, dawdler; (*Mil*) straggler.

rezagar [1h] **1** *vt* (a) to leave behind; to outpace, outdistance.

(b) *event etc* to postpone.

2 rezagarse *vr* to stay behind, fall behind, get left behind; to lag (behind); to loiter, dawdle; to struggle; **nos rezagamos en la producción** we are falling behind in production.

rezago *nm* (a) left-over goods (*etc*); unused material which is left over; (*Arg*) unsold goods, articles being remaindered.

(b) group of straggling cattle.

(c) (*Mex, Per*) unclaimed letters.

rezar [1f] **1** *vt* (a) *prayer* to say.
(b) to call for, plead for; **el periódico reza agua** the paper says we need rain.
2 *vi* (a) (*Rel*) to pray (*a* to); to say one's prayers; to be at prayer.
(b) (*of text*) to read, say, run, go; **el anuncio reza así** the notice reads as follows.
(c) (*fam*) to grumble.
(d) (*fam*) — **con** to concern, have to do with; **eso no reza conmigo** that has nothing to do with me; that doesn't apply to me.
rezo *nm* (a) prayer(s); devotions; daily service; **estar en el** — to be at prayer. (b) (*act, in general*) praying.
rezongador *adj* =**rezongón**.
rezongar [1h] **1** *vt* (*Arg, CAm*) to reprimand; to scold. **2** *vi* to grumble; to mutter; to growl.
rezongo *nm* (a) grumble, moan. (b) (*CAm*) reprimand; scolding.
rezongón *adj* grumbling, grouchy (*fam*), cantankerous.
rezumar [1a] **1** *vt* to ooze, exude; to leak.
2 *vi* (a) (*of contents*) to ooze (out), seep, leak out; (*of container*) to ooze, leak.
(b) (*fig*) to ooze; **le rezuma el orgullo** he oozes pride; **le rezuma el entusiasmo** he is bursting with enthusiasm, he overflows with enthusiasm.
3 rezumarse *vr* (a) =**2** (a).
(b) (*fig*) to leak out, become known.
ría[1] *etc* see **reír**.
ría[2] *nf* estuary.
riachuelo *nm* brook, stream.
riada *nf* flood (*also fig*).
ribazo *nm* steep slope, steep bank.
ribera *nf* (a) (*of river, lake*) bank; (*of sea*) beach, shore; (*as area*) riverside.
(b) (*Agr*) irrigated plain.
(c) (*Mex, RPl*) group of riverside houses; shantytown, slum quarter.
riberano *adj* (*SAm*) =**ribereño**.
ribereño **1** *adj* riverside (*attr*); (*Law*) riparian. **2** *nm*, **ribereña** *nf* person who lives near a river.
ribete *nm* (a) (*Sew*) edging, border, trimming.
(b) (*fig*) addition, adornment; —**s** (*of story*) embellishments, trimmings, personal touches.
(c) (*fig*) —**s** touch, quality; **tiene sus** —**s de pintor** he has some pretensions to being a painter, he is not without some of the painter's talents.
ribetear [1a] *vt* to edge, border, trim (*de* with).
ribo *nm* (*Col*) bank; shore.
ricacho *nm*, **ricachón** *nm* (*fam*) fabulously rich man (*fam*); nouveau riche; (*Pol: as abuse*) well-heeled bourgeois (*sl*), dirty capitalist (*fam*).
ricamente *adv* (a) richly.
(b) (*fig*) **muy** —, **tan** — very well, jolly well (*fam*); **comeremos tan** — we'll have a really good meal; **he dormido tan** — I've slept splendidly; **viven muy** — **sin él** they manage perfectly well without him.
Ricardo *m* Richard.
ricino *nm* castor-oil plant; **aceite de** — castor oil.
rico **1** *adj* (a) (*Fin*) rich, wealthy.
(b) (*fig*) soil, vein *etc* rich; — **de**, — **en** rich in.
(c) *gem etc* valuable, precious; *furnishings etc* luxurious, sumptuous, valuable; *cloth* fine-quality, rich.
(d) *food* delicious, tasty; *fruit* luscious; **estos pasteles son riquísimos** these cakes are exceptionally tasty, these cakes are really lovely.
(e) *child* bonny; cute, lovely; (*in direct address*) ¡—! darling!; ¡oye, rica! hey, beautiful! (*fam*); hullo, gorgeous! (*fam*); ¡qué — está el pequeño! isn't he a lovely baby!; ¡qué —! (*iro*) isn't that just splendid?
2 *nm*, **rica** *nf* rich person; wealthy man, wealthy woman; **nuevo** — nouveau riche.
rictus *nm* (*involuntary*) curl of the lip; sneer; grin; — **de dolor** wince of pain; — **de amargura** bitter smile.
ricura *nf* (*fam*) (a) (*of food*) tastiness, delicious quality.
(b) smashing girl (*sl*); ¡oye, —! hey, beautiful! (*fam*); hullo, gorgeous (*fam*)!
(c) ¡qué — de pastel! aren't these cakes lovely?, what smashing cakes! (*sl*); ¡qué — de criatura! what a lovely baby!
ridículamente *adv* ridiculously, absurdly.
ridiculez *nf* absurdity.
ridiculizar [1f] *vt* to ridicule, to deride; to mock, guy, parody; — **a sus adversarios** (*Sport etc*) to make one's opponents look silly.
ridículo **1** *adj* ridiculous, absurd, ludicrous.
2 *nm* (a) **hacer el** — to make oneself ridiculous.
(b) **ridiculle; exponerse al** — to lay oneself open to ridicule; **poner a uno en** — to ridicule someone, make a fool of someone; **ponerse en** — to make oneself ridiculous, make a fool of oneself.

riego *nm* watering; irrigation; (*fig*) sprinkling; — **por aspersión** watering by spray, watering by sprinklers; **la política del** — **en esta provincia** irrigation policy in this province; **con el** — **se triplica la producción** productivity is increased threefold by irrigation.
riel *nm* (a) (*Rail*) rail; —**es** rails, track, permanent way. (b) (*Tech*) ingot.
rielar [1a] *vi* (*poet*) to shimmer; to glitter, gleam.
rielero *nm* (*Mex*) railwayman.
rienda *nf* rein; (*fig*) restraint, moderating influence; **a** — **suelta** at top speed; (*fig*) without the least restraint; violently; **aflojar las** —**s** to let up; **dar** — **suelta a** to give free rein to; **dar** — **suelta al llanto** to weep uncontrollably; **dar** — **suelta a los deseos** to indulge one's desires freely; **dar** — **suelta a uno** to give someone a free hand; **empuñar las** —**s** to take charge; **llevar las** —**s** to be in charge, be in control; **soltar las** —**s** to relinquish control; to take off the brakes; to kick over the traces.
riente *adj* (a) laughing, merry. (b) (*fig*) *countryside etc* bright, pleasant.
riesgo *nm* risk, danger; **con** — **de** at the risk of; **seguro a** (*or* **contra**) **todo** — comprehensive insurance; **correr** — **de** + *infin* to run the risk of + *ger*, be in danger of + *ger*.
riesgoso *adj* (*SAm*) risky, dangerous.
rifa *nf* (a) raffle. (b) quarrel, dispute, fight.
rifar [1a] **1** *vt* to raffle; — **algo para fines benéficos** to raffle something for charity.
2 *vi* to quarrel, fight.
3 rifarse *vr* (*fam*): — **algo** to quarrel over something, fight for something; — **el amor de una** to vie for someone's love.
rifeño **1** *adj* Riffian, of the Riff. **2** *nm*, **rifeña** *nf* Riffian.
rifle *nm* rifle; sporting rifle; hunting gun.
riflero **1** *adj* (*Arg, Chi, Mex*) *marksman* expert, crack. **2** *nm* (a) (*Mil*) rifleman. (b) (*Arg, Chi, Mex*) marksman, crack shot.
rígidamente *adv* (a) rigidly, stiffly. (b) (*fig*) rigidly. (c) (*fig*) strictly, sternly, harshly. (d) *stare etc* woodenly.
rigidez *nf* (a) rigidity, stiffness; — **cadavérica** rigor mortis. (b) (*fig*) rigidity; inflexibility. (c) (*fig*) strictness, sternness, harshness. (d) woodenness.
rígido *adj* (a) rigid, stiff; **quedarse** — to go rigid; to get stiff (with cold).
(b) (*fig: in attitude*) rigid, inflexible, unadaptable.
(c) (*fig: morally*) strict, stern (*con, para* towards), harsh, unbending.
(d) *face* wooden, expressionless.
rigor *nm* (a) severity, harshness; strictness; toughness; stringency.
(b) (*Meteorol*) harshness, severity; **el** — **del verano** the worst of the summer, the hottest part of the summer; **los** —**es del clima** the rigours of the climate.
(c) rigour; exacting nature; accuracy, meticulousness; **con todo** — **científico** with complete scientific rigour; **una edición hecha con el mayor** — **crítico** an edition produced with absolute meticulousness.
(d) **ser de** — to be de rigueur, be absolutely essential; **después de los saludos de** — after the inevitable greetings; **me dio los consejos de** — he gave the expected advice, he gave me the advice which he felt he had to; **en** — strictly speaking.
(e) (*Col*) **un** — **de cosas** a whole lot of things.
(f) (*RPl*) **dar un** — **a uno** to give someone a thrashing.
rigorismo *nm* strictness, severity; austerity.
rigorista *nmf* strict disciplinarian; strict observer (*de* of), stickler (*de* for).
rigurosamente *adv* (a) severely, harshly; strictly; stringently.
(b) rigorously; accurately, meticulously.
(c) **un estudio** — **científico** an absolutely scientific study; **eso no es** — **exacto** that is not strictly accurate, that is not wholly true.
rigurosidad *nf* rigour, harshness, severity.
riguroso *adj* (a) *attitude, discipline etc* severe, harsh; *application etc* strict; *measure* severe, tough, stringent; **su tratamiento** — **de los empleados** his harsh treatment of the employees.
(b) (*Meteorol*) harsh, severe, hard; extreme.
(c) *method, study etc* rigorous; exacting; accurate; meticulous.
(d) (*lit*) cruel; **los hados** —**s** the cruel fates.
rija *nf* quarrel, dispute, fight.
rijio *nm* (a) (*Guat*) =**rijo**. (b) (*Mex, Nic*) spirit, spirited temperament (*of a horse*).
rijioso *adj* (*CAm, Mex*) =**rijoso**.
rijo *nm* lustfulness.

rijosidad *nf* (a) sensitivity, susceptible nature; quarrelsomeness. (b) lustfulness, sensuality; randiness.

rijoso *adj* (a) sensitive, susceptible; quarrelsome. (b) lustful, sensual; randy.

rikisha *nf* rickshaw.

rila *nf* (a) (*Col, Mex*) gristle. (b) (*Col*) bird droppings.

rima *nf* (a) rhyme; — **imperfecta** assonance, half-rhyme; **octava** — ottava rima; **tercia** — terza rima. (b) —s poems, verse, poetry.

rimador *nm*, **rimadora** *nf* rhymester.

rimar [1a] *vti* to rhyme (**con** with).

rimbombancia *nf* (a) resonance, echo. (b) (*fig*) pomposity, bombast. (c) (*fig*) showiness, flashiness.

rimbombante *adj* (a) resounding, echoing. (b) (*fig*) pompous, bombastic. (b) (*fig*) showy, flashy.

rimbombar [1a] *vi* to resound, echo, boom.

rimel *nm* (*esp SAm*) mascara; eyeshadow.

rimero *nm* stack, pile, heap.

Rin *m* Rhine.

rincón *nm* (a) (inside) corner. (b) (*fig*) corner, nook; retreat; niche. (c) (*Agr: esp SAm*) patch of ground.

rinconada *nf* corner.

rinconera *nf* (a) corner piece (of furniture); corner cupboard, dresser. (b) (*Archit*) wall between corner and window.

rinche[1] *adj* (*Col*) full to the brim.

rinche[2] *nm* (*fam*) secret place, hiding place.

rinde *nm* (*Arg: also* —s) yield, revenue.

ringla *nf*, **ringle** *nm*, **ringlera** *nf* row, line; (*Agr*) swath.

ringorrango *nm* (a) (*in writing*) flourish. (b) —s frills, buttons and bows, useless adornments.

ringuelete *nm* (a) (*Arg, Col, Chi*) restless person; busybody, gadabout. (b) (*Col*) dart; toy windmill.

ringueletear [1a] *vi* (*Col, Chi*) = **callejear**.

rinoceronte *nm* rhinoceros.

riña *nf* quarrel, argument; fight, brawl, scuffle; — **de gallos** cockfight.

riñón *nm* (a) (*Anat*) kidney; (*loosely*) lower part of the back; **tener el** — **bien cubierto** (*fam*) to be well heeled (*sl*); **me costó un** — (*fam*) it cost the earth. (b) (*fig*) heart, core; innermost part; **aquí en el** — **de Castilla** here in the very heart of Castile.

río[1] *nm* river; (*fig*) stream, torrent; — **abajo** downstream; — **arriba** upstream; **un** — **de gente** a stream of people, a flood of people; **es un** — **de oro** it's a gold mine; **a** — **revuelto, ganancia de pescadores** there are bound to be pickings for some, it's an ill wind that blows nobody any good; **cuando el** — **suena, agua lleva** there's no smoke without fire.

río[2], **rió** *etc see* **reír**.

riojano 1 *adj* Riojan, of La Rioja. 2 *nm*, **riojana** *nf* Riojan. 3 *nm* (*wine*) Riojan.

riolada *nf* (*fam*) flood, stream.

rioplatense 1 *adj* of the River Plate region. 2 *nmf* native (or inhabitant) of the River Plate region; **los** —s the people of the River Plate region.

riostra *nf* brace, strut.

ripiado *adj* (a) (*Col*) ragged. (b) (*Cu*) very poor.

ripiar [1b] *vt* (a) (*Archit*) to fill with rubble. (b) (*Ant, Col*) to cut up, cut into shreds; to crumble. (c) (*Col, Cu*) to squander. (d) (*Col*) *person* to leave badly off; *two persons* to mix up. (e) (*Mex*) to glean. (f) (*Ant*) to hit.

ripiería *nf* mob, populace.

ripio *nm* (a) refuse, waste; (*Archit*) rubble; debris. (b) (*Lit*) padding, word (or phrase) put in to fill up the line; (*fig*) padding, verbiage, empty words; **no perder** — not to miss a trick, to miss nothing of what is going on.

ripioso *adj* (*Col, SD*) ragged.

riquerío *nm* (*Chi*) rich people (*collectively*).

riqueza *nf* (a) wealth, riches; — **imponible** part of one's property qualifying for the wealth tax; **vivir en la** — to live in luxury. (b) (*fig: quality*) richness.

riquiña *nf* (*Ven*) wicker basket.

risa *nf* (*una* —) laugh; (*in general, also* —s) laughter; **hubo** —s there was laughter; **no es cosa de** — it's no laughing matter; **¡qué** —! how very funny!, what a joke!; **el libro es una verdadera** — the book is a laugh from start to finish; — **retozona** suppressed giggle, titter; **caerse** (*or* **descoserse, desternillarse, mondarse, morirse**) **de** — to split one's sides with laughing, die of laughing; **causar** — **a uno, mover** (*or* **provocar**) **a uno a** — to make someone laugh; **soltar la** — to burst out laughing; **tomar algo a** — to take something as a joke, laugh something off.

risco *nm* (a) cliff, crag; steep rock. (b) —s rough parts, difficult pieces (*of a terrain*).

riscoso *adj* steep, craggy.

risible *adj* ludicrous, laughable.

risotada *nf* guffaw, loud laugh.

rispiar [1b] *vi* (*CAm*) to rush off.

rispidez *nf* (*Ec, Mex*) roughness, coarseness.

risquería *nf* (*Chi*) craggy place.

ristra *nf* string (*also fig*).

ristre *nm*: **en** — at the ready, all set; *see* **lanza**.

risueño *adj* (a) *face* smiling; **muy** — smiling all over, with a big smile, wreathed in smiles. (b) *disposition etc* cheerful, sunny, gay; *countryside etc* smiling, pleasant. (c) *outlook* bright.

rítmico *adj* rhythmic(al).

ritmo *nm* (a) (*Mus*) rhythm. (b) (*fig*) rhythm; rate, pace; speed; — **de crecimiento**, — **de expansión** rate of growth; **el trabajo se mantiene a un** — **intenso** the work is going on at a good rate (or pace); **trabajar a** — **lento** (*of workers*) to go slow; **de acuerdo con el** — **de las estaciones** in keeping with the rhythm of the seasons.

rito *nm* rite, ceremony.

ritual 1 *adj* ritual. 2 *nm* ritual; **de** — ritual, customary.

ritualismo *nm* ritualism.

ritualista 1 *adj* ritualistic. 2 *nmf* ritualist.

rival 1 *adj* rival, competing. 2 *nmf* rival, competitor; contender.

rivalidad *nf* rivalry, competition; enmity.

rivalizar [1f] *vi* to vie, compete, contend; — **con** to rival, compete with; **los dos rivalizan en habilidad** they rival each other in skill.

rizado *adj* *hair* curly; *surface* ridged, crinkly; undulating.

rizador *nm* curling iron, hair-curler.

rizar [1f] 1 *vt* *hair* to curl; to ruffle; *surface* to ridge, crinkle; *water* to ripple, ruffle; *see* **rizo** (b). 2 **rizarse** *vr* (*water*) to ripple.

rizo[1] 1 *adj* curly. 2 *nm* (a) curl, ringlet; (*of surface*) ridge; (*on water*) ripple. (b) (*Aer*) loop; **hacer el** —, **rizar el** — to loop the loop.

rizo[2] *nm* (*Naut*) reef; **tomar** —s to reef in (the sails).

rizoma *nm* rhizome.

roano 1 *adj* roan. 2 *nm* roan (horse).

robar [1a] *vt* (a) *possessor* to rob; *object* to steal (*a* from); *house etc* to break into, burgle; *safe* to break open, break into, rifle (the contents of); — **algo a uno** to steal something from someone, rob someone of something; **en ese negocio me han robado** I was cheated in that deal. (b) *person* to steal away, kidnap, abduct. (c) (*fig*) *attention etc* to steal, capture; *interest* to command; *patience* to exhaust; *peace of mind* to destroy; *life* to take; — **el corazón a uno** to steal someone's heart; **tuve que** — 3 **horas al sueño** I had to use up 3 hours when I should have been sleeping. (d) (*of river*) to carry away. (e) (*Cards*) to draw, take (from the pile).

Roberto *nm* Robert.

roblar [1a] *vt* to rivet, clinch.

roble *nm* oak, oak tree; **de** — oak (*attr*), oaken; **de** — **macizo** of solid oak.

robledal *nm*, **robledo** *nm* oakwood.

roblón *nm* rivet.

roblonar [1a] *vt* to rivet.

robo *nm* (a) (*un* —) theft; (*in general*) robbery, theft, thieving; — **con escalamiento** housebreaking, burglary; — **relámpago** smash-and-grab raid; — **en la vía pública** highway robbery; **¡esto es un** —! this is sheer robbery! (b) stolen article, stolen goods.

robot [ro'βo] *nm*, *pl* **robots** [ro'βo] (a) robot. (b) (*fig*) puppet, tool.

robustecer [2d] 1 *vt* to strengthen. 2 **robustecerse** *vr* to grow stronger.

robustez *nf* strength, toughness, robustness.

robusto *adj* strong, tough, robust.

roca *nf* rock; **en** — **viva** in(to) the living rock.

rocalla *nf* small stones, pebbles; stone chippings.

rocalloso *adj* pebbly, stony.

roce *nm* (a) (*act*) rub, rubbing; (*Tech*) friction. (b) rub, mark of rubbing; (*on skin*) graze, chafing mark. (c) (*fam*) close contact; familiarity; **tener** — **con** to be in close contact with, have a lot to do with.

rociada *nf* (a) shower, spray, sprinkling; (*in drink etc*) dash, splash; (*Agr*) spray. (b) (*fig: of stones*) shower; (*of bullets*) hail; (*of shot*) scatter; (*of abuse etc*) hail, stream, torrent.

rociadera *nf* watering can.

rociador nm spray, sprinkler.

rociar [1c] **1** vt to sprinkle, spray (de with); (with mud etc) to spatter, bespatter (de with); (with bullets) to spray (de with).
　　2 vi: **empieza a —** the dew is beginning to fall; **rocía esta mañana** there is a dew this morning.

rocín nm (a) hack, nag, poor horse; (Arg) riding horse; (Bol) draught ox. (b) (fam) lout, ignorant fellow.

rocinante nm broken-down old horse.

rocío nm (a) (Meteorol) dew; light drizzle. (b) (fig) sprinkling; dew; drops of condensation (etc).

rococó 1 adj rococo. **2** nm rococo.

rocosidades nfpl rocky places.

rocoso adj rocky.

rocote nm, **rocoto** nm (SAm) large pepper, large chili.

Rochela: La — La Rochelle.

rochela nf (Col, Mex, PR, Ven) noisy gathering, rowdy party.

rochelear [1a] vi (Col, PR, Ven) to play about, live it up (fam).

rochelero adj (PR, Ven) unruly, rowdy; mischievous; quarrelsome.

roda nf (Naut) stem.

rodaballo nm turbot; **— menor** brill.

rodada nf (a) rut, wheel track. (b) (Mex, RPl) fall (from a horse).

rodadero nm (Ec) cliff, precipice.

rodado 1 adj (a) traffic wheeled, on wheels.
　　(b) stone etc rounded; **esto vino —** this just happened (without my having to do anything); by luck the chance came up.
　　(c) horse dappled.
　　(d) style well-rounded, fluent.
　　2 nm (Arg, Chi) wheeled vehicle.

rodadura nf (a) roll, rolling. (b) rut. (c) (of tyre) tread.

rodaja nf (a) small wheel; small disc; (of furniture) castor. (b) (of bread, fruit etc) slice; **limón en —s** sliced lemon.

rodaje nm (a) (Tech) wheels, set of wheels. (b) (Cine) shooting, filming. (c) (Aut) running-in; "**en —**" "running in". (d) (Per) vehicle tax.

rodamiento nm (a) **— a bolas, — de bolas** ball bearing. (b) (Aut: on tyre) tread.

Ródano m Rhône.

rodante adj rolling; **material —** rolling stock.

rodapié nm skirting board, baseboard (US).

rodar [1m] **1** vt (a) vehicle to wheel (along); object to roll, drag (along).
　　(b) staircase to roll down, go tumbling down.
　　(c) area to travel, go over; **ha rodado medio mundo** he's been over half the world.
　　(d) car, make of car to race, drive; **new car** to run in.
　　(e) (Cine) to shoot, film.
　　(f) (Ven) to seize; to imprison.
　　(g) (SAm) **— (a patadas)** to knock down, knock over.
　　2 vi (a) to roll (por along, down, over etc); (on wheels) to go, run, travel; **— de suelo** (Aer) to taxi; **se oía el — de los carros** one could hear the rumbling of the tanks; **echarlo todo a — (**fig) to mess it all up, spoil everything; to throw one's hand in.
　　(b) (on axle etc) to go round, turn, rotate.
　　(c) **andar** (or **ir**) **rodando** (of person) to move about (from place to place), to roll around, drift; **no hace más que ir rodando** he just drifts about; **me han hecho ir rodando de acá para allá** they kept shunting me about from place to place.
　　(d) (fig) to be still going, exist still; **no sabía que ese modelo rodaba todavía por esos mundos** I didn't know that model was still about.
　　(e) **— por uno** to be at someone's beck and call, dance attendance on someone.
　　(f) (Cine) to shoot, film; **llevamos 2 meses de — en Méjico** we've spent 2 months filming in Mexico.
　　(g) (Arg, Mex: of horse) to stumble, fall forwards.

Rodas f Rhodes.

rodear [1a] **1** vt (a) to surround (de by, with); to ring, encircle, enclose, shut in; (of arms, dress etc) to encircle, enclose; **los soldados rodearon el edificio** the soldiers surrounded the building; **le rodeó el cuello con los brazos** she threw her arms round his neck.
　　(b) (SAm) cattle to round up.
　　2 vi (a) to go round, go by an indirect route; to make a detour.
　　(b) (fig) to beat about the bush.
　　3 rodearse vr (a) **— de** to surround oneself with.
　　(b) to turn round; to turn over (and over), toss and turn.

rodela nf (a) (Hist) buckler, round shield. (b) (Chi) padded ring (for carrying loads on one's head).

rodeo nm (a) long way round, roundabout way; detour.
　　(b) (in pursuit) dodge; (fig) dodge, stratagem, subterfuge.
　　(c) (in speech) circumlocution; evasion; **andarse con —s, ir por —s** to beat about the bush; **no andarse con —s, dejarse de —s** to talk straight, stop beating about the bush; **hablar sin —s** to speak out plainly.
　　(d) (SAm) roundup, rodeo.

rodera nf rut, wheel track.

Rodesia f Rhodesia.

rodesiano 1 adj Rhodesian. **2** nm, **rodesiana** nf Rhodesian.

rodete nm (a) (of hair) coil, bun; (of fat) roll; (to support weight) pad. (b) (of lock) ward. (c) (Tech) articulator.

rodilla nf (a) (Anat) knee; **de —s** kneeling; **caer de —s** to fall on one's knees; **doblar** (or **hincar**) **la —** to kneel down; (fig) to bow, humble oneself, bend the knee (ante to); **estar de —s** to kneel, be kneeling (down); **hincarse de —s, ponerse de —s** to kneel (down); **poner de —s a un país** to bring a country to its knees.
　　(b) (to support weight) pad.
　　(c) floorcloth, mop.

rodillazo nm push with the knee; **dar un —** a to knee.

rodillera nf (a) knee guard; kneepad, patch on the knee. (b) baggy part (in knee of trousers). (c) (to support weight) pad.

rodillo nm roller; (Cook) rolling pin; (Typ) ink roller; (of typewriter) cylinder, roller; (for washing) mangle; (Agr) roller; **— pintor** paint roller; **— de vapor** steamroller.

rodillón nm (Col) old man, feeble individual.

rodillona nf (Ven) old maid.

rododendro nm rhododendron.

Rodrigo m 'Roderick; **— el último godo** Roderick, the last of the Goths.

rodrigón nm (Agr) stake, prop, support.

roedor 1 adj (a) (Zool) gnawing. (b) (fig) regret etc gnawing, ever-present, nagging. **2** nm rodent.

roer [2z] vt (a) food to gnaw; to nibble at; bone to gnaw, pick.
　　(b) metal to corrode, eat away, eat into.
　　(c) (fig) capital etc to eat into bit by bit.
　　(d) (fig) (of remorse etc) to gnaw, nag, torment.

rogación nf (a) petition. (b) (Eccl) **—es** rogations.

rogar [1h and 1m] **1** vt (a) person to beg; to plead with; thing to ask for, beg for, plead for; **— a uno + infin** to ask someone to + infin, beg someone to + infin; **— que + subj** to ask that . . .; **ruegue a este señor que nos deje en paz** please ask this gentleman to leave us alone.
　　(b) (Rel) to pray.
　　2 vi (a) to beg, plead; **hacerse —** to have to be coaxed, be unwilling to agree; **no se hace de —** he doesn't have to be asked twice.
　　(b) (Rel) to pray.
　　3 rogarse vr: "**se ruega la mayor puntualidad**" "please be punctual"; "**se ruega no fumar**" "please do not smoke".

rogativas nfpl (Eccl) rogations.

rogatoria nf (SAm) request; pleading.

rojear [1a] vi (a) to redden, turn red; to show red. (b) to tend towards red.

rojete nm rouge.

rojez nf redness.

rojiblanco adj red-and-white.

rojillo adj (Pol) pink; suspicious, subversive.

rojizo adj reddish; ruddy.

rojo 1 adj (a) red; ruddy; **— cereza** cherry red; **poner — a uno** to make someone blush; **ponerse —** to turn red, blush.
　　(b) hair red; sandy.
　　(c) (Pol) red; (in Nationalist parlance in Spain, 1936 and subsequently) Republican.
　　2 nm (a) red, red colour; **calentar al —** to make red-hot; **la atmósfera está al — vivo** the atmosphere is electric; **la emoción está al — vivo** excitement is at fever pitch.
　　(b) **— de labios** rouge, lipstick.
　　(c) (Pol) red; Republican (see **1** c).

rojura nf redness.

rol nm (a) list, roll; catalogue; (Naut) muster. (b) SAm: Theat and fig) role, part.

rola 1 nf (Ven) police station. **2** nmf (Chi) lout; dimwit (fam).

Rolando m Roland.

rolar [1a] **1** *vt* (a) (Arg, Bol, Chi, Per) to touch on (in conversation).
(b) (Arg, Chi, Per) to associate with, be in contact with.
(c) (Mex) to pass from hand to hand.
2 *vi* (a) (Naut: of wind) to veer round.
(b) (Arg) to be a social climber.
(c) (Bol, Chi) to talk, converse (con with).
Roldán *m* Roland.
rollista *nmf* (fam) bore.
rollizo *adj* (a) *object* round, cylindrical. (b) *person* plump; stocky; *child* chubby; *woman* plump, buxom.
rollo 1 *adj* (fam) boring, tedious.
2 *nm* (a) (of cloth, film, paper etc) roll; (of rope) coil; (Hist) scroll; **en —** rolled, rolled up; *log* whole, uncut.
(b) (Cook) rolling pin.
(c) round log, uncut log.
(d) (Cook) roll.
(e) (Anat: fam) roll of fat.
(f) (fam) bore; boring speech; tedious explanation, lengthy justification; sermon; **la conferencia fue un —** the lecture was an awful bore (fam); **¡menudo — nos colocó!** some sermon he gave us!; **iba a soltarnos un —** he was about to start off on a lengthy explanation.
(g) (Bol, RPl) **largar el —** to be sick.
Roma Rome; **— no se construyó en un día** Rome was not built in a day; **por todas partes se va a —** all roads lead to Rome; **revolver — con Santiago** to leave no stone unturned.
romadizo *nm* head cold; catarrh; (PR) rheumatism.
romana *nf* steelyard; **cargar la —** (RPl) to heap the blame on somebody.
romance 1 *adj language* Romance.
2 *nm* (a) (Ling) Romance language; Spanish, Spanish language; **hablar en —** (fig) to speak plainly.
(b) (Lit) ballad.
(c) (angl) romance, love affair.
romancear [1a] **1** *vt* to translate into Spanish. **2** *vi* (Chi) (a) to waste time chatting. (b) to flirt.
romancero *nm* collection of ballads; **el R—** the Spanish ballads (collectively).
románico *adj* (a) (Ling) Romance. (b) (Archit) Romanesque, Romanic; (in England) Norman.
romanizar [1f] **1** *vt* to romanize. **2 romanizarse** *vr* to become romanized.
romano 1 *adj* Roman. **2** *nm,* **romana** *nf* Roman.
románticamente *adv* romantically.
romanticismo *nm* romanticism.
romántico 1 *adj* romantic. **2** *nm* romantic.
romaza *nf* dock, sorrel.
rombal *adj* rhombic.
rombo *nm* rhomb, rhombus.
romboidal *adj* rhomboid.
romboide *nm* rhomboid.
romereante *nmf* (Ec, PR) pilgrim.
romería *nf* (a) (Eccl) pilgrimage; gathering at a local shrine; **ir en —** to go on a pilgrimage. (b) (fig) trip, excursion; fair, open-air dance; festivities.
romero[1] *nm,* **romera** *nf* pilgrim.
romero[2] *nm* (Bot) rosemary.
romo[1] *adj* (a) blunt; *person* snub-nosed. (b) (fig) dull, lifeless.
romo[2] *nm* (Ant, Ven) rum.
rompecabezas *nm, pl* **rompecabezas** (a) puzzle; riddle; jigsaw (puzzle). (b) (fig) puzzle; problem, teaser, headache.
rompedero 1 *adj* breakable, delicate, fragile. **2** *nm* (Arg) **— de cabeza** puzzle, problem.
rompedora-cargadora *nf* (Min) power loader.
rompehielos *nm, pl* **rompehielos** icebreaker.
rompehuelgas *nm, pl* **rompehuelgas** strikebreaker, blackleg.
rompeolas *nm, pl* **rompeolas** breakwater.
rompenueces *nm, pl* **rompenueces** nutcrackers.
romper [2a; *ptp* **roto**] **1** *vt* (a) *plate, toy etc* to break, smash, shatter; *barrier, fence etc* to break down, break through; to breach; *rope etc* to snap, break; *paper, cloth* to tear (up), rip (up); *mist, clouds* to break through.
(b) *clothing, shoes* to wear out, wear a hole in.
(c) *waves* (of breakwater) to break the force of; (of ship) to cleave.
(d) *land* to break (up), plough.
(e) (Mil) *line etc* to break (through); see **fila.**
(f) *continuity, fast, silence, succession etc* to break.
(g) *contract, pact* to break; *friendship, relations* to break off.
(h) **— el fuego** to open fire; **— las hostilidades** to start hostilities.

2 *vi* (a) (of waves) to break.
(b) (of bud) to open, burst.
(c) (of war) to break out.
(d) **— la naturaleza** to reach puberty; to begin to menstruate.
(e) (of tooth) to break through; (of sun) to break through, appear, begin to shine; (of dawn, day) to break; **— entre** to burst one's way through; **— por** to break through.
(f) **— a + infin** to start (suddenly) to + infin; **— a proferir insultos** to begin to pour forth abuse; **— a llorar** to burst into tears; **luego rompió a hacer calor** then it suddenly began to get hot.
(g) **— en llanto** to burst into tears.
(h) **— con uno** to fall out with someone, break with someone; **ha roto con su novio** she has broken it off with her fiancé.
(i) **de rompe y rasga** brash, tearaway, impetuous; full of self-confidence; utterly inconsiderate; **rompe por todo** he presses on regardless (fam).
3 romperse *vr* to break, smash; to snap; to tear, rip; to wear out.
rompiente *nm* (a) reef, shoal. (b) **—s** breakers, surf.
rompimiento *nm* (a) (act) breaking, smashing, shattering; breaching; snapping; tearing.
(b) opening, breach; crack.
(c) (act: fig) break (con with); **— de relaciones** breaking-off of relations.
(d) **— de hostilidades** outbreak of hostilities.
romplón: de — *adv* (CAm, Mex) suddenly, unexpectedly.
rompopo *nm* (CAm, Mex) eggnog.
Rómulo *m* Romulus.
ron *nm* rum; **— de laurel, — de malagueta** bay-rum.
ronca *nf* (a) (Zool) roar (of rutting stag); rutting season. (b) (fig) threat; **echar —s** to bully, threaten.
roncadoras *nfpl* (SAm) large spurs.
roncar [1g] *vi* (a) to snore. (b) (of stag, sea, wind) to roar. (c) to threaten, bully; (Arg) to be bossy, domineer; to be jealous of one's authority.
roncear [1a] **1** *vt* (a) to cajole, pester, keep on at. (b) (SAm) =**ronzar**[1]. (c) (SAm) to keep watch on, spy on. **2** *vi* to work (etc) unwillingly; to slack, kill time.
roncería *nf* (a) unwillingness. (b) cajolery.
roncero *adj* (a) (Naut) slow, slow-moving, sluggish.
(b) *person* unwilling; slack, slow; **estar —** to find reasons for shirking work (etc).
(c) *person* grumpy, grouchy (fam).
(d) *person* smooth, smarmy (fam).
(e) (CAm, Col) sly.
ronco *adj person* hoarse; *voice* throaty, husky; *sound* harsh, raucous.
roncón *adj* (Col, Ven) boastful.
roncha *nf* bruise, weal, welt; (of sting) swelling.
ronda *nf* (a) (esp Hist) night patrol, night watch; (of policeman) beat; (persons) watch, patrol, guard; **ir de —** to go the rounds, do one's round.
(b) (Mus) group of serenaders.
(c) (of drinks etc, negotiations) round; **pagar una —** to pay for a round.
(d) (Cards) hand, round, game; (in competition) round.
(e) (Mil) sentry walk (on wall).
(f) outer road, ring road.
(g) (Arg, Chi) ring-a-ring-a-roses.
(h) (Arg) **en —** in a ring, in a circle.
rondalla *nf* (a) band of street musicians. (b) fiction, invention.
rondana *nf* (SAm) pulley; winch.
rondar [1a] **1** *vt* (a) (Mil etc) to patrol; to inspect, go the rounds of; (fig) to haunt, frequent, hang about; **— la calle a una joven** to patrol up and down (or hang about) the street where a girl lives.
(b) *person* to hang round; to harass, pester; *girl* to court.
(c) *light* (of moth) to flutter round, fly about.
(d) (fig) **me está rondando un catarro** I've got a cold hanging about.
2 *vi* (of police) to patrol, go on patrol, go the rounds; (fig) to prowl round, go up and down, hang about; to roam the streets after dark; (Mus) to go serenading.
rondín[1] *nm* (Bol, Chi) policeman; night watchman.
rondín[2] *nm* (Bol, Ec, Per) harmonica.
rondó *nm* (Lit) rondeau; (Mus) rondo.
rondón: de — *adv* unexpectedly; unannounced, without warning; **entrar de —** to rush in.
ronquear [1a] *vi* to be hoarse, talk hoarsely.
ronquedad *nf,* **ronquera** *nf* hoarseness; huskiness.
ronquido *nm* snore; snoring; (fig) roar(ing); snort.
ronronear [1a] *vi* to purr.
ronroneo *nm* purr.

ronzal nm halter.

ronzar[1] [1f] vt (Naut) to move with levers, lever along.

ronzar[2] [1f] **1** vt to munch, crunch, eat noisily. **2** vi to crunch.

roña 1 nf (a) (Vet: on sheep) scab, (on dog) mange; (Bot) rust.

 (b) crust of dirt, filth, grime; (on metal) rust.

 (c) (Bot) pine bark.

 (d) (fig) moral danger, contagion.

 (e) (fig) meanness, stinginess.

 (f) stratagem.

 (g) (Cu, PR) envy; rancour; (Mex) grudge, ill will.

 (h) (Col) feigned illness.

 (i) **jugar a la —** to play for fun, play without money stakes.

2 nmf (fam) mean person.

3 adj (Arg, CR) mean, stingy.

roñería nf meanness, stinginess.

roñoso adj (a) (Vet) scabby, mangy.

 (b) dirty, filthy, grimy; rusty; (fig) wretched, broken down, useless.

 (c) (fig) mean, stingy.

 (d) (Col, Ec) rough, unpolished, coarse.

 (e) (Ec) tricky.

 (f) (Mex, PR) bitter, hostile.

ropa nf clothes, clothing; dress; **— blanca** linen; **— blanca de mujer** lingerie; **— de cama** bed linen, bedclothes; **— hecha** ready-made clothes; **— interior** underwear, underclothes; **— lavada, — por lavar** washing; **— de mesa** table linen; **— planchada** ironing; **— sucia** dirty clothes, washing; **— usada** used clothing, secondhand clothes; **a quema —** pointblank; **hay — tendida** be careful what you say, walls have ears; **guardar la —** to speak cautiously; **nadar y guardar la —** to be able to do two things well at the same time; **tentarse la —** to think long and hard (before doing anything); **no tocar la — a uno** not to touch a hair of someone's head, keep one's hands off someone; see **ligero** etc.

ropaje nm (a) gown, robes, ceremonial garb; **—s** (Eccl) vestments.

 (b) (fig) drapes, drapery.

 (c) (pej) odd garb; heavy clothing, excessive amount of clothes.

 (d) (Lit) trappings, rhetorical adornments.

ropavejero nm old-clothes dealer.

ropería nf (a) clothier's, clothes shop. (b) clothing trade.

ropero 1 adj for clothes, clothes (attr); **armario —** wardrobe, clothes cupboard.

2 nm (a) clothier, dealer in ready-made clothing.

 (b) wardrobe, clothes cupboard.

ropón nm (a) long robe; loose coat, housecoat. (b) (Col, Chi, Ven) woman's riding habit.

roque nm (Chess) rook, castle.

roquedal nm rocky place.

roqueño adj (a) rocky. (b) hard as rock, rock-like, flinty.

rorro nm (a) (fam) baby, kid (fam). (b) (Mex) fair blue-eyed person.

Rosa f Rose.

rosa 1 nf (a) (Bot) rose; **— almizcleña** musk rose; **no hay — sin espinas** there's no rose without a thorn; **un cutis como una —** a skin as soft as silk; **estar como una —** to be fresh and clean; to feel as fresh as a daisy; **estar como las propias —s** to feel entirely at ease.

 (b) **de —, color de —** pink, rose, rose-coloured; **vestidos color de —** pink dresses; see also **color**.

 (c) (Anat) red spot, red mark, birth mark.

 (d) (Archit) rose window.

 (e) **— náutica, — de los vientos** compass (card), compass rose.

 (f) **—s** popcorn.

2 adj pink, rose, rose-coloured.

rosáceo adj = **rosado 1**.

rosado 1 adj pink, rosy, roseate. **2** nm rosé.

rosal nm (a) rosebush, rosetree; **— silvestre** wild rose, dog rose; **— de China, — japonés** japonica. (b) (Chi, PR, RPl) rosebed, rosegarden.

rosaleda nf rosebed, rosegarden.

rosario nm (a) rosary; chaplet, beads; **rezar el —** to say one's rosary, tell one's beads.

 (b) (Agr) chain of buckets (of a waterwheel).

 (c) (fam) backbone.

 (d) (fig) string, series; **un — de maldiciones** a string of curses.

 (e) (Archit) beading.

rosbif nm roast beef.

rosca nf (a) coil, spiral, ring; (Cook) ring, ring-shaped

roll; **estaba hecho una —** he was all curled up in a ball.

 (b) (of screw) thread; (of spiral) turn; **hacer la — a uno** (fam) to suck up to someone (fam); **pasarse de —** (screw) to have a crossed thread; (fig) to go too far, overdo it.

 (c) (Anat etc) swelling; (Anat) roll of fat.

 (d) (Chi) pad (for carrying loads on the head).

 (e) (Chi) circle (of card players).

 (f) (Arg, Chi) noisy argument, general set-to (fam); uproar, commotion.

 (g) (Univ sl) **tirarse una —** to plough (sl).

rosedal nm (Arg) = **rosaleda**.

Rosellón m Roussillon.

róseo adj rosy, roseate.

roseta nf (a) (Bot) small rose.

 (b) (Sport etc) rosette.

 (c) (of watering can) rose, nozzle.

 (d) (Anat) red spot (on the cheek).

 (e) (Arg, Mex) prickly fruit, prickly seed, burr.

 (f) (Per, RPl) rowel (of a spur).

 (g) **—s** (Cook) popcorn.

rosetón nm (a) (Archit) rose; rose window. (b) (Sport etc) rosette. (c) (Aut) cloverleaf (junction).

rosicler nm dawn pink, rosy tint of dawn.

rosita nf (a) (Bot) small rose. (b) (Chi) earring. (c) **de —** (Bol, Mex) free, gratis; **andar de —** (Arg, Mex) to be out of work. (d) **—s** (Cook) popcorn.

rosquero adj (Chi) quarrelsome.

rosquete nm (a) (CAm, Per) bun. (b) (Per) queer (fam), homosexual.

rosquilla nf (a) (of smoke) ring. (b) (Ent) grub, small caterpillar.

rosticería nf (Mex) = **rotisería**.

rostro nm (a) (Anat) countenance, **face** (for idioms and phrases, compare **cara**). (b) (Naut) beak. (c) (Zool, Hist etc) rostrum.

rotación nf rotation; turn, revolution; (Tech: of production etc) turnover; **— de cultivos** rotation of crops; **— de la tierra** rotation of the earth.

rotariano adj and nm (SAm) = **rotario**.

rotario 1 adj Rotarian. **2** nm Rotarian.

rotativo 1 adj rotary, revolving; **press rotary**. **2** nm newspaper.

rotería nf (Chi) (a) common people, plebs. (b) dirty trick; coarse remark, coarse action.

rotisería nf (Arg, Mex: gall) grillroom, steak restaurant.

roto 1 ptp of **romper**.

2 adj (a) broken, smashed; dress etc torn; ragged; life shattered, destroyed; wasted.

 (b) (fig) debauched, dissipated.

3 nm (a) (in dress) hole, torn piece, worn part; **nunca falta un — para un descosido** you can always find someone else just as contemptible as he (etc) is.

 (b) (Chi) very poor person, down-and-out; (iro) fop, toff (fam).

 (c) (Arg, Per) nickname given to a Chilean.

 (d) (Ec) half-breed.

rotograbado nm rotogravure.

rotonda nf (Archit) rotunda; circular gallery; (Rail) engine shed, roundhouse.

rotor nm rotor.

rotoso adj (a) (SAm) ragged, shabby. (b) (Chi) low-class, common.

rótula nf (a) (Anat) kneecap. (b) (Mech) ball-and-socket joint.

rotulación nf (a) labelling; lettering. (b) (as profession) sign painting.

rotular [1a] vt object to label, put a label (or ticket etc) on; map etc to letter, inscribe; letter, document to head, entitle.

rotulata nf (a) labels, inscriptions etc (collectively). (b) (fam) = **rótulo**.

rotulista nm sign painter.

rótulo nm (on goods) label, ticket, tag; (on specimen etc) label; (on document) heading, title; (on map etc) lettering; inscription; (Comm) sign; placard, poster.

rotundamente adv deny flatly, roundly; agree etc emphatically.

rotundidad nf (a) rotundity. (b) forthrightness. (c) well-rounded character, expressiveness.

rotundo adj (a) round. (b) denial etc flat, round, forthright; **me dio un "sí" —** he gave me an emphatic "yes". (c) style well-rounded, expressive.

rotura nf (a) (act) breaking etc (see **rompimiento** (a)). (b) opening, breach; crack; (in cloth) tear, rip, hole. (c) (act: fig) break (con with); **— de relaciones** breaking-off of relations.

roturación nf breaking-up, ploughing.

roturar [1a] vt to break up, plough.

roya nf (Bot) rust, blight.

roza nf (a) (Archit) groove, hollow (in a wall). (b) (Prov, Chi, Mex) weeds, brushwood. (c) (Col) planting in newly-broken ground.

rozado adj worn, grazed.

rozador nm (Ven) machete.

rozadura nf mark of rubbing, chafing mark; (Med) abrasion, graze, sore place.

rozagante adj (a) dress etc showy, gorgeous; striking. (b) (fig) proud.

rozamiento nm (a) rubbing, chafing; (Mech) friction; wear. (b) (fam) **tener un — con uno** to have a slight disagreement with someone.

rozar [1f] **1** vt (a) to rub (on), rub against; to scrape (on); to chafe; (Mech) to grate on, cause friction with; (Med) to chafe, graze; (of vehicle etc) to graze, shave, touch lightly; surface etc (of bird) to skim; **— a uno al pasar** to brush past someone.
(b) dress to rumple, crumple; to dirty.
(c) (fig) to touch on, border on; **es cuestión que roza la política** it's a question which partly concerns politics.
(d) (Archit) to make a groove (or hollow) in.
(e) (Agr) grass to graze, crop, nibble.
(f) (Agr) land to clear.
2 vi (a) **— en** = **1** (a).
(b) **= con** (fig) = **1** (c).
3 rozarse vr (a) **— el cuello** to rub (or wear, chafe) one's collar; **— los puños** to graze one's knuckles.
(b) to get worn, get rubbed (etc).
(c) (fam) to trip over one's own feet.
(d) (fam) **— con** to hobnob with, rub shoulders with, mix with.
(e) **— en un sonido** to stutter over a sound, have trouble pronouncing a sound.

roznar[1] [1a] vti = **ronzar**.

roznar[2] [1a] vi to bray.

roznido nm bray(ing).

Ruán Rouen.

ruana nf (Col, Ven) peasant poncho.

ruanetas nmf, pl **ruanetas** (Col) peasant.

ruano adj and nm = **roano**.

rubéola nf German measles.

rubí nm ruby; (of watch) jewel.

rubia nf (a) blonde; **— de bote, — de frasco** peroxide blonde; **— platino** platinum blonde. (b) (Aut) shooting brake, station wagon. (c) (sl) one-peseta coin.

rubiales nmf, pl **rubiales** (fam) blond(e), fair-headed person.

Rubicón m Rubicon; **pasar el —** to cross the Rubicon.

rubicundo adj (a) ruddy, rubicund. (b) reddish.

rubio adj (a) hair, person fair, fair-haired, blond(e); animal, fur etc light-coloured, golden. (b) **tabaco —** Virginian tobacco.

rublo nm rouble.

rubor nm (a) bright red. (b) (on face) blush, flush; **causar — a una** to make someone blush (also fig). (c) (fig) bashfulness.

ruborizado adj blushing; flushed.

ruborizar [1f] **1** vt to cause to blush, make blush (also fig). **2 ruborizarse** vr to blush, flush, redden (de at).

ruboroso adj (a) **ser —** to have a tendency to blush, blush easily. (b) **estar —** to blush, be blushing, have a flush; (fig) to feel bashful.

rúbrica nf (a) red mark. (b) flourish (added to a signature). (c) title, heading, rubric; **bajo la — de** under the heading of. (d) **de —** = **de rigor**.

rubricar [1g] vt to sign with a flourish; (loosely) to sign and seal.

rubro nm (a) (SAm) heading, title; (Typ) headline; section heading.
(b) (Chi, RPl) book-keeping entry.
(c) (Chi, RPl) section, department (of a business).
(d) (Arg) **— social** trading name, firm's name.

ruca nf (a) (Arg, Chi) hut, cabin. (b) (Mex) old maid.

rucio 1 adj horse grey, silver-grey; person grey-haired; (Chi) fair, blond(e). **2** nm grey (horse).

ruco adj (CAm) worn-out, useless.

rucho adj (Col) (a) rough. (b) fruit overripe.

ruda nf rue.

rudamente adv simply, plainly; (pej) roughly, coarsely.

rudeza nf (a) simplicity; plainness; (pej) roughness, coarseness, commonness. (b) stupidity (also **— de entendimiento**).

rudimental adj, **rudimentario** adj rudimentary.

rudimento nm (Anat etc) rudiment. (b) **—s** rudiments.

rudo adj (a) wood etc rough; unpolished, unworked. (b) (Mech) part stiff.

(c) person simple, uncultured; plain; (pej) rough, coarse, common.
(d) blow hard.
(e) (in intelligence) simple, stupid.

rueca nf distaff.

rueda nf (a) (Mech etc) wheel; (of furniture) roller, castor; **— de agua, — hidráulica** waterwheel; **— de alfarero** potter's wheel; **—s de aterrizaje** (Aer) landing wheels; **— de atrás** rear wheel, back wheel; **— de cadena** sprocket wheel; **— dentada** cog, cog wheel; gear wheel; **— de la fortuna** wheel of fortune; **— libre** freewheel; **— de molino** millwheel; **— de paletas** paddle wheel; **— de recambio** spare wheel; **— de trinquete** ratchet wheel; **ir sobre —s** (fam) to go smoothly; to go with a swing.
(b) (of objects, persons) circle, ring; **en —** in a ring; **— de prensa** press conference.
(c) (Cook) slice, round.
(d) (of tournament) round.
(e) (Hist) rack.
(f) (Fish) sunfish.
(g) (Orn: of peacock) spread tail; **hacer la —** to spread its tail; **hacer la — a una** to court someone; **hacer la — a uno** (fig) to play up to someone, ingratiate oneself with someone.

ruedecilla nf small wheel; roller, castor.

ruedero nm wheelwright.

ruedo nm (a) turn, rotation. (b) edge, circumference; border; (of skirt) hem, bottom. (c) (Taur) bullring, arena. (d) (round) mat.

ruego nm request, entreaty; **a — de** at the request of; **accediendo a los —s de . . .** in response to the requests of . . .; **"—s y preguntas"** (on agenda) "any other business".

rufián nm (a) pimp, pander. (b) lout, hooligan; scoundrel.

rufiancete nm villain, rogue.

rufianesca nf criminal underworld.

rufianesco adj (a) pimping, pandering. (b) loutish; villainous.

rufo adj (a) sandy-haired, red-haired; curly-haired. (b) (fam) smug, self satisfied; cocky (fam), boastful.

rugbista nm rugby player.

rugby ['rugbi] nm rugby.

rugido nm roar; bellow; howl; **— de dolor** howl of pain; **— de tripas** intestinal rumblings, collywobbles (fam).

rugir [3c] vi (of lion etc) to roar; (of bull) to bellow; (of sea) to roar; (of storm, wind) to roar, howl, rage; (of person) to roar; (of stomach) to rumble; **— de dolor** to roar with pain, howl with pain.

rugoso adj wrinkled, creased; ridged; rough.

ruibarbo nm rhubarb.

ruido nm (a) noise, sound; din, row; noisiness; **— de fondo** background noise; **sin —** quietly, soundlessly, without making a noise; **no hagas —** don't make a sound; **no hagas tanto —** don't make such a noise; **mucho — y pocas nueces** much ado about nothing; **es más el — que las nueces** there's a lot of talk but nothing much gets done.
(b) (fig) commotion, stir; fuss; row, rumpus (fam); outcry; **hacer —, meter —** to cause a stir, be a sensation; to have repercussions; to cause an outcry; **quitarse de —s** to keep out of trouble.

ruidosamente adv (a) noisily, loudly. (b) (fig) sensationally.

ruidoso adj (a) noisy, loud. (b) (fig) sensational; much talked-of.

ruin 1 adj (a) person mean, despicable, low, contemptible; treatment etc mean, shabby; heartless, callous.
(b) mean, stingy.
(c) (in size) small, weak.
(d) animal vicious.
2 nm mean person (etc); **en nombrando al — de Roma, luego asoma** talk of the devil!; well, look who's here!

ruina nf (a) (Archit etc) ruin; **—s** ruins, remains; **estar hecho una —** to be a wreck; to be a shadow of one's former self.
(b) (Archit: act) collapse; **amenazar —** to threaten to collapse, be about to fall down.
(c) (fig) ruin, destruction; (of empire) fall, decline; (of person) ruin, downfall; (of hopes) destruction; **será mi —** it will be the ruin of me; **la empresa le llevó a la —** the venture ruined him (financially).

ruindad nf (a) (quality) meanness, lowness; shabbiness; callousness. (b) (act) mean act, low trick, piece of villainy.

ruinoso adj (a) (Archit) ruinous; tumbledown. (b) (Fin etc) ruinous, disastrous.

ruiseñor nm nightingale.

rula nf (a) roulette. (b) (Col, Pan) hunting knife.

rulemán nm (Arg) ball bearing, roller bearing.
rulenco, rulengo adj (Chi) weak, underdeveloped.
ruleta nf roulette.
ruletero nm (Mex) taxi driver.
rulo[1] nm (a) ball, round mass. (b) roller; (Cook) rolling pin. (c) hair-curler. (d) (Arg) (natural) curl.
rulo[2] nm (Chi) well-watered ground.
rulota nf (gall) caravan, trailer (US).
ruma nf (SAm) heap, pile.
Rumania f Rumania.
rumano 1 adj Rumanian. **2** nm, **rumana** nf Rumanian. **3** nm (language) Rumanian.
rumba[1] nf (a) (Mus) rumba. (b) (Ant) party, celebration, spree (fam).
rumba[2] nf (Chi) = **ruma**.
rumbar [1a] **1** vt (Col, Hond) to throw. **2** vi (a) (Col) to buzz. (b) (Col, Chi) to follow a direction; to get one's bearings. **3 rumbarse** vr (Col) to go off.
rumbeador nm (Bol, RPl) pathfinder, tracker, man with expert knowledge of the countryside.
rumbear [1a] vi (a) (SAm: Mus) to dance the rumba.
(b) (SAm) to follow a direction; to find one's way, get one's bearings.
(c) (Ant, Guat, Mex, Per) to have a party, carouse, go on the spree (fam).
(d) (Mex) to open up a forest path.
rumbero 1 adj (a) (Col) knowledgeable about the countryside, expert in pathfinding.
(b) (Ant) merry, fond of carousing.
2 nm (Col) pathfinder, guide; (Per) river guide.
rumbo[1] nm (a) route, direction; (Naut) course; bearing; **con — a** in the direction of; **ir con — a** to be heading for, be going in the direction of, be bound for; (Naut) to be bound for; **corregir el —** to correct one's course; **hacer — a** (or **hacia**) to head for; **poner — a** (Naut) to set a course for; **ir al —** find one's way by guesswork.
(b) (fig) course of events; line of conduct; **— nuevo** new departure; **los nuevos —s de la estrategia occidental** the new lines of western strategy; **tomar — nuevo** to set off on a different tack, change one's approach; **los acontecimientos vienen tomando un — sensacional** events are taking a sensational turn.
(c) (fig) generosity, lavishness; lavish display; showiness, pomp; **de mucho —** = **rumboso**; **viajar con —** to travel in style, travel in state.
(d) (CAm) party, binge (sl).
(e) (Arg) cut on the head.
rumbo[2] nm (Col) hummingbird.
rumbón adj (fam) = **rumboso**.
rumboso adj (a) person generous, lavish; free-spending. (b) present lavish; wedding etc big, splendid, slap-up (fam).
rumia nf, **rumiación** nf rumination.
rumiante 1 adj ruminant. **2** nm ruminant.

ruminar [1b] **1** vt (a) to chew.
(b) (fig) matter to chew over; to brood over, ponder (over).
2 vi (a) to chew the cud.
(b) (fig) to ruminate, brood, ponder; (pej) to take too long to make up one's mind.
rumor nm (a) murmur, mutter; confused noise, low sound; (of voices) buzz; (of water) murmur. (b) (fig) rumour.
rumorearse [1a] vr: **se rumorea que . . .** it is rumoured that . . .
rumoreo nm murmur(ing).
rumoroso adj full of sounds; stream etc murmuring, musical.
runa nf rune.
runcho adj (a) (Col) stupid. (b) (Pan) mean.
rundir [3a] (Mex) **1** vt to keep; to hide, put away. **2** vi to become drowsy. **3 rundirse** vr to fall fast asleep.
rundún nm (Arg) hummingbird.
runfla nm (SAm) mass, lot, heap; crowd; gang.
rúnico adj runic.
runrún nm (a) sound of voices, buzz of conversation, murmur. (b) (fig) rumour, buzz (fam). (c) (of machine etc) whirr.
runrunearse [1a] vr: **se runrunea que . . .** it is rumoured that . . .
runruneo nm = **runrún** (a).
ruñir [3h] vti (Col, Mex, PR, Ven) = **roer**.
rupestre adj rock (attr); **pintura —** cave painting; **planta —** rock plant.
rupia nf rupee.
ruptura nf (fig) rupture; split; (of contract) breaking; (of relations) breaking-off.
rural adj rural, country (attr).
Rusia f Russia; **— Soviética** Soviet Russia.
ruso 1 adj Russian. **2** nm, **rusa** nf Russian. **3** nm (language) Russian.
rústica nf: **libro en —** paperback (book).
rusticidad nf (a) rusticity, rural character. (b) coarseness, uncouthness; crudity; unmannerliness.
rústico 1 adj (a) rustic, rural, country (attr). (b) (pej) coarse, uncouth; crude; unmannerly. **2** nm rustic, peasant, yokel.
ruta nf route; (fig) course, course of action; **— aérea** air route, airway.
rutilante adj (lit) shining, sparkling, glowing.
rutilar [1a] vi (lit) to shine, sparkle, glow.
rutina nf routine; **— diaria** daily routine, daily round; **por —** as a matter of course, as a matter of routine; (fig) from force of habit.
rutinariamente adv in a routine way; unimaginatively.
rutinario adj (a) routine; ordinary, everyday. (b) person ordinary; unimaginative.
rutinero 1 adj who sticks to routine; ordinary; unimaginative. **2** nm person who sticks to routine; ordinary sort, unimaginative person.

S

sábado *nm* Saturday; (*Jewish*) Sabbath; **S— de Gloria, S— Santo** Easter Saturday; **hacer —** to have a good cleanup, do the weekly clean.

sábalo *nm* (*Fish*) shad.

sabana *nf* (*SAm*) savannah.

sábana *nf* (**a**) sheet; (*Eccl*) altar cloth; **— de agua** (*fig*) sheet of rain; **estirarse más de lo que dan de sí las —s** to bite off more than one can chew, overreach oneself; **se le pegan las —s** he gets up late.

(**b**) (*sl*) 1000-*peseta note*.

sabandija *nf* (**a**) bug, insect, creepy-crawly (*fam*), creature; **—s** bugs, vermin. (**b**) (*fig*) wretch, louse.

sabanear [1a] **1** *vt* (**a**) (*CAm*) to catch.

(**b**) (*CAm*) to flatter.

(**c**) (*Guat, Ven*) to pursue.

2 *vi* (*SAm*) to travel over a plain; to round up cattle on the savannah, scour the plain for cattle.

sabanero 1 *adj* (*SAm*) plain (*attr*), savannah (*attr*); of (*or* from) the plains. **2** *nm* (**a**) (*SAm*) plainsman.

(**b**) (*CAm*) bully, thug.

sabanilla *nf* small sheet, piece of cloth; (*Eccl*) altar cloth; (*Chi*) bedspread.

sabañón *nm* chilblain.

sabara *nf* (*Ven*) light mist, haze.

sabatario 1 *adj* sabbatarian. **2** *nm*, **sabataria** *nf* sabbatarian.

sabateño *nm* (*Ven*) boundary stone.

sabático (*Rel*) sabbatical.

sabedor *adj*: **ser — de** to know about; to be aware of.

sabelotodo *nm* (*fam*) know-all.

saber [2n] **1** *vti* (**a**) (*general sense*) to know; **— de** to know about, be aware of; to know of; **desde hace 6 meses no sabemos nada de él** we haven't heard from him for 6 months, it's 6 months since we had news of him; **lo sé** I know; **sin —lo yo** without my knowledge; **hacer — algo a uno** to inform someone of something, let someone know about something.

(**b**) (*in past tenses, freq*) to find out, learn; to hear, get to know; **cuando lo supe** when I heard about it; **lograron — el secreto** they managed to learn the secret.

(**c**) (*phrases and idioms*) **a —** namely; **a — dónde lo tiene guardado** I wonder if he really has got it hidden away; **a — si realmente lo compró** I wonder whether he really did buy it; **es a —** namely, that is to say; **¡haberlo sabido!** if only I'd known!; **¡yo qué sé!, ¡qué sé yo!** how should I know!, search me! (*fam*); **demasiado sé que . . .** I know only too well that . . .; **que yo sepa** as far as I know; **que sepamos** as far as we know; **ya lo sabía yo** I thought as much; **un no sé qué** a certain something; **un no sé qué de afectado** a certain (element of) affectation; **nos sirvió no sé qué vino** he gave us some wine or other; **¿tú qué sabes?** what do you know about it?; **vete a —** your guess is as good as mine; **¡vete a — de dónde ha venido!** goodness only knows where he came from!; **cualquiera sabe si . . .** it's anybody's guess whether . . .; **¿sabe?** (*fam*) you know?, you know what I mean?; **costó muy caro, ¿sabe Vd?** it was very dear, you know; **¿quién sabe?** who knows?, who can tell?, who's to say?; **sepa Vd, para que lo sepa** let me tell you, just for your information; see **cuánto, más, convenir, Briján** *etc.*

(**d**) **—** + *infin* to know how to + *infin*, can + *infin*; **sé conducir** I can drive, I know how to drive; **¿sabes nadar?** can you swim?; **tiene que — contenerse** he must know how to control himself, he must be able to control himself.

(**e**) **—** + *infin* (*verbs of motion*): **— ir a un sitio** to know one's way to a place; **no sabe todavía andar por la ciudad** he still doesn't know his way about the town.

(**f**) (*SAm*) **—** + *infin* to be in the habit of + *ger*; **no sabe venir por aquí** he doesn't usually come

this way, he's not in the habit of coming along here.

2 *vi*: **— a** to taste of, taste like; (*fig*) to smack of; **esto sabe a queso** this tastes of cheese; **esto sabe mal, sabe a demonio(s)** this tastes awful (*fam*); **le sabe mal que otro la saque a bailar** it upsets him that anybody else should ask her to dance, he doesn't like other people dancing with her.

3 saberse *vr* (**a**) **se sabe que . . .** it is known that . . ., we know that . . .; **no se sabe** nobody knows; **¿se puede — si . . .?** may one inquire whether . . .?; **¿quién es Vd, si puedo —?** who are you, may I ask?; **tiene que perder sépase cuánto tiempo para recuperarlo** he has to waste goodness knows how much time getting it back.

(**b**) **se supo que . . .** it was learnt that . . ., it was discovered that . . .; **por fin se supo el secreto** finally the secret was revealed.

4 *nm* knowledge, learning; **según mi leal — y entender** to the best of my knowledge, as far as I can honestly tell.

sabiamente *adv* (**a**) learnedly; expertly. (**b**) wisely, sensibly.

sabichoso *adj* (*Ant*) = **sabihondo**.

sabidillo *nm*, **sabidilla** *nf* (*fam*) know-all.

sabido 1 *ptp* of **saber; es — que . . .** it is well known that . . .; **como es —** as we know, as is well known.

2 *adj* (**a**) = **consabido**.

(**b**) (*iro*) highly knowledgeable, learned.

(**c**) **de —** for sure, certainly.

(**d**) (*Col*) lively.

sabiduría *nf* wisdom; learning, knowledge; **— popular** popular knowledge; folklore.

sabiendas: a — *adv* knowingly; consciously, deliberately; **a — de que . . .** knowing full well that . . ., in the full knowledge that . . .

sabihondo 1 *adj* know-all. **2** *nm*, **sabihonda** *nf* know-all, self-proclaimed expert; smart-aleck.

sabio 1 *adj* (**a**) *person* (*in a subject*) learned; expert; (*iro*) know-all.

(**b**) *person* (*in acting*) wise, sensible, judicious.

(**c**) *act, decision etc* wise, sensible.

(**d**) *animal* trained.

2 *nm*, **sabia** *nf* learned man, learned woman; wise person; scholar, expert, savant; (*Hist*) sage; **¡hay que escuchar al —!** (*iro*) just listen to the professor!

sablazo *nm* (**a**) sword wound; slash with a sword.

(**b**) (*fam*) sponging (*fam*); **dar un —, pegar un —** to make a touch (*sl*; **de** for); **dar un — a uno** to touch someone for a loan (*sl*); **vivir de —s** to live by sponging (*fam*).

sable[1] *nm* sabre, cutlass.

sable[2] *nm* (*Her*) sable.

sablear [1a] *vi* (*fam*) to live by sponging (*fam*); to ask for a loan.

sablista *nmf* (*fam*) sponger (*fam*), cadger.

sabor *nm* taste, flavour; savour, savouriness; (*fig*) flavour; **con — a queso** with a cheese flavour(ing), cheese-flavoured; **con ligero — arcaico** with a slightly archaic flavour (to it); **sin —** tasteless; **le deja a uno mal — de boca** (*fig*) it leaves a nasty taste in the mouth.

saborcillo *nm* slight taste.

saborear [1a] **1** *vt* (**a**) to savour, relish (the savour of); to taste; to enjoy.

(**b**) to flavour, add a flavour to.

(**c**) (*fig*) to relish, enjoy; **— el triunfo** to enjoy one's triumph, relish one's victory (to the full).

2 saborearse *vr* (**a**) to smack one's lips (in anticipation).

(**b**) **— algo** (*fig*) to relish the thought of something.

saborete *nm* slight taste.

sabotaje *nm* sabotage.

saboteador *nm* saboteur.
sabotear [1a] *vt* to sabotage (*also fig*).
Saboya *f* Savoy.
sabré *etc see* **saber**.
sabrosera *nf* (*CAm*) tasty thing, delicacy.
sabroso *adj* (a) *food* tasty, delicious; nice, rich.
   (b) (*Cook*) too salty.
   (c) (*fig*) *lecture etc* solid, meaty.
   (d) (*fig*) *story etc* salty, racy, daring.
   (e) (*Col, Ven*) lovely, nice, pleasant.
   (f) (*Mex, Per, PR, SD*) talkative.
sabrosón *adj* (a) (*SAm*)=**sabroso** (a). (b) (*Cu, Per, PR, Ven*) talkative.
sabrosura *nf* (*SAm*) (a) tastiness. (b) pleasantness, delightfulness, sweetness; delight, enjoyment.
sabueso *nm* (a) (*Zool*) bloodhound. (b) (*fig*) sleuth.
saburra *nf* coat, fur (*on tongue etc*).
saca¹ *nf* (a) big sack; — **de correo(s)** mailbag. (b) (*SAm*) herd of cattle.
saca² *nf* taking out; withdrawal; (*Comm*) export; **estar de** — (*Comm*) to be on sale; (*fig*) to be at the right age to marry.
sacabocados *nm*, *pl* **sacabocados** (*Tech*) punch.
sacabotas *nm*, *pl* **sacabotas** bootjack.
sacabuche *nm* sackbut.
sacaclavos *nm*, *pl* **sacaclavos** nail-puller, pincers.
sacacorchos *nm*, *pl* **sacacorchos** corkscrew.
sacacuartos *nm*, *pl* **sacacuartos**=**sacadineros**.
sacada *nf* (*Arg, Col, Per*)=**sacadura**.
sacadera *nf* (*Fish*) landing net.
sacadineros *nm*, *pl* **sacadineros** (a) cheap trinket.
   (b) money-wasting spectacle, worthless sideshow (*etc*), small-time racket. (c) (*person*) cheat.
sacador *nm* (*Tennis*) server.
sacadura *nf* (*Col, Chi, Per*) extraction, removal.
sacafaltas *nmf*, *pl* **sacafaltas** faultfinder.
sacamanchas *nm*, *pl* **sacamanchas** cleaning material.
sacamuelas *nm*, *pl* **sacamuelas** (*hum*) dentist.
sacapuntas *nm*, *pl* **sacapuntas** pencil sharpener.
sacar [1g] *vt* (a) (*general sense*) to take out, get out; to pull out, draw out, extract; (*Chem*) to extract; *coal etc* to mine, bring up; (*from pocket etc*) to get out; *weapon* to draw; *money* (*from bank*) to draw out, withdraw; (*from list etc*) to remove, exclude; to except.
   (b) (*general and fig sense*) to get (out); — **una información a uno** to get information out of someone; **los datos están sacados de 2 libros** the data is taken from 2 books; — **un secreto a uno** to get (*or* worm) a secret out of someone; **¿de dónde has sacado esa idea?** where did you get that idea?; **no conseguirán** —**le nada** they'll get nothing out of him; **lo que se saca de todo esto es que ...** what I gather from all this is that ...
   (c) *stain etc* to remove, get out, get off.
   (d) (*Tennis*) to serve; (*Football*) to throw in.
   (e) *part of body* to stick out, put out, thrust out; — **la barbilla** to stick one's chin out; — **la lengua** to put one's tongue out; — **la mano** (*Aut etc*) to put one's hand out.
   (f) *garment* (*Sew*) to let out.
   (g) *clothing etc* (*esp SAm*) to take off; — **la funda a un fusil** to take the cover off a rifle.
   (h) *tickets etc* to get; *reservations* to make, book.
   (i) *answer, solution* to reach, obtain, get; *conclusion* to draw.
   (j) *piece of work* to produce, make; *product* to make; *novel etc* to bring out, publish; *new model* to bring out; *fashion* to create; *song etc* to compose, make up; **aquí sacan 200 coches diarios** they make 200 cars a day here; **he sacado 20 páginas de notas** I've made 20 pages of notes; **a este propósito han sacado unos versos** they've made up some verses about this.
   (k) (*Phot*) to take; *copy* to make, have made; **saca buen retrato** he takes well; **nos quiso** — **una foto** he wanted to take a photo of us; **no tenía la intención de** — **ese coche** I didn't mean to include that car in the photograph.
   (l) *prize, benefit, legacy, post etc* to get; to receive; *profit* to make; (*fig*) to derive (**de** from); **sacó el premio gordo** he got (*or* won) the big prize; **así no vas a** — **nada** you won't get anything that way; **sacó un buen número para la lotería** he drew a good number for the lottery; **la sociedad saca una ganancia de ...** the company makes a profit of ...
   (m) (*Parl etc*) to elect; **han sacado 35 diputados** they have got 35 members elected; **por fin sacaron presidente a X** they finally elected X (as) president.
   (n) *quality etc* to show; **en esto sacó por fin su habilidad** in this he finally showed (*or* demonstrated,

proved) his skill; — **faltas a uno** to point out someone's defects.
   (o) *polish etc* to put on, bring up, bring out; — **los colores a la cara de uno** to bring the colour to someone's cheeks, put some colour into someone's cheeks.
   (p) (*in newspaper etc*) to mention, put; **no me vayas a** — **en tu discurso** don't mention me in your speech; **le han sacado en el periódico** they've put him in the paper.
   (q) (*fam*) **le saca 10 cm a su hermano** he is 10 cm taller than his brother, he has an advantage in height of 10 cm over his brother; **al terminar la carrera le sacaba 10 metros al adversario** at the end of the race he was 10 metres ahead of his rival.
   (r) — **adelante** *child* to bring up; *graduate, trainee etc* to produce, turn out; *business* to carry on, go on with; — **a una adelante** (*fam*) to get a girl in the family way.
   (s) — **a uno de sí** to infuriate someone.
   (t) (*CAm, Ec*) to flatter, fawn on.
   (u) (*Ec, Mex*) — **algo a uno** to reproach someone for something.
sacarina *nf* saccharin(e).
sacarino *adj* saccharine.
sacatín *nm* (*Col*) still.
sacerdocio *nm* priesthood.
sacerdotal *adj* priestly.
sacerdote *nm* priest; — **obrero** worker priest; **sumo** — high priest.
sacerdotisa *nf* priestess.
saciado *adj*: — **de** (*fig*) steeped in, saturated in, full of.
saciar [1b] **1** *vt* (a) to satisfy, satiate.
   (b) (*fig*) *desires etc* to appease; *curiosity, longing etc* to satisfy; *ambition* to fulfil, more than satisfy.
   2 saciarse *vr* to satiate oneself; to be satiated (**con, de** with).
saciedad *nf* satiation, satiety; **demostrar algo hasta la** — to prove something up to the hilt; **repetir algo hasta la** — to repeat something over and over again.
saco¹ *nm* (a) bag; sack; (*Mil*) kitbag; (*as measure*) bagful; sackful; — **de arena** (*Mil*) sandbag, (*Sport*) punchball; — **de dormir**, — **manta** sleeping bag; — **de mano**, — **de noche**, — **de viaje** travelling bag; — **terrero** sandbag; **a** —**s** (*fig*) by the ton; **no echar algo en** — **roto** to be careful not to forget something; **no es** (*or* **no parece**) — **de paja** he can't be written off as unimportant.
   (b) (*Anat*) sac.
   (c) (*fam*) **ser un** — **de gracia** to be very witty; **es un** — **de picardías** he's full of tricks; **ser un** — **de huesos** (*SAm*) to be a bag of bones.
   (d) long coat, loose-fitting jacket; (*Arg*) woman's outdoor coat.
   (e) (*sl*) 1000 *pesetas*.
saco² *nm* (*Mil*) sack; **entrar a** — **en** to sack, loot, plunder.
sacón 1 *adj* (*CAm*) (a) talebearing, sneaking. (b) flattering, soapy.
   2 *nm*, **sacona** *nf* (*CAm*) flatterer, soapy individual.
   3 *nm* (*Arg*) woman's outdoor coat.
saconear [1a] *vt* (*CAm*) to flatter, soap up (*fam*).
saconería *nf* (*CAm*) flattery, soft soap (*sl*).
sacramental *adj* (a) (*Eccl*) sacramental. (b) (*fig*) ritual, ritualistic; time-honoured; **pronunció las palabras** —**es** he spoke the time-honoured words.
sacramentar [1a] *vt* to administer the last sacraments to.
sacramento *nm* sacrament; **el Santísimo S**— the Blessed Sacrament; **recibir los** —**s** to receive the last sacraments.
sacrificar [1g] **1** *vt* (a) to sacrifice (*also fig; a* to).
   (b) *animal* (*for meat*) to slaughter; *pet* to put to sleep, destroy painlessly.
   2 sacrificarse *vr* to sacrifice oneself; to make a sacrifice.
sacrificio *nm* (a) sacrifice (*also fig*); **el** — **de la misa** the sacrifice of the mass. (b) slaughter(ing); painless destruction.
sacrilegio *nm* sacrilege.
sacrílego *adj* sacrilegious.
sacristán *nm* verger, sacrist(an); sexton.
sacristía *nf* vestry, sacristy.
sacro¹ *adj* sacred, holy.
sacro² *nm* (*Anat*) sacrum.
sacrosanto *adj* most holy; (*fig*) sacrosanct.
sacudida *nf* (a) shake, shaking; jerk; jolt, jar, bump; (*of earthquake*) shock; (*of explosion*) blast; (*with head*) jerk, toss; — **eléctrica** electric shock; **dar una** — **a una alfombra** to beat a carpet; **el coche avanzaba dando** —**s** the car moved forward

in a series of jolts, the car went jerkily forwards; **la — de la bomba llegó hasta aquí** the blast of the bomb was felt as far away as this.

(b) (*fig*) violent change; sudden jolt; (*Pol etc*) upheaval; **hay que darle una —** he needs a jolt.

sacudido *adj* (a) ill-disposed, unpleasant; intractable. (b) determined.

sacudidura *nf*, **sacudimiento** *nm* = sacudida.

sacudir [3a] **1** *vt* (a) *building, ground, limb, person, tree etc* to shake; *person (as punishment)* to beat, thrash; *wing etc* to flap, move up and down; *carpet* to beat; *mattress* to shake (the dust out of); *rope etc* to jerk, tug; *passenger, vehicle etc* to shake, jolt, jar, bump; to rock (to and fro); *head* to jerk, toss.

(b) *flies etc* to chase away, brush off; *burden* to shake off.

(c) (*of emotion etc*) to shake; **una tremenda emoción sacudió a la multitud** a great wave of excitement ran through the crowd; **— a uno de su depresión** to shake someone out of his depression; **— los nervios a uno** to shatter someone's nerves.

(d) (*fam*) **— a uno** to belt someone (*fam*); to beat someone up; to shoot someone.

2 sacudirse *vr*: **— (de) un peso** to shake off a burden, get rid of a burden; **por fin se le han sacudido** they've finally got rid of him; **el caballo se sacudía las moscas con la cola** the horse brushed off the flies with his tail.

sacudón *nm* (*SAm*) violent shake, severe jolt; (*fig*) big shake-up, almighty upheaval (*fam*).

sacha *adj invar* (*SAm*) (a) false, sham; **— médico** quack. (b) bungling, unskilled; **— carpintero** clumsy carpenter.

sádico *adj* sadistic.

sadismo *nm* sadism.

sadista *nmf* sadist.

saeta *nf* (a) (*Mil*) arrow, dart.

(b) (*Mech*) hand; magnetic needle.

(c) (*Mus*) sacred song in flamenco style sung during Holy Week processions.

(d) (*Rel*) short prayer.

saetera *nf* (*Mil*) loophole.

saetín *nm* (a) millrace. (b) (*Tech*) tack, brad.

safado *adj* (*SAm*) impudent, shameless.

safagina *nf* (*Col*) uproar, commotion.

safari *nm* safari; **estar de —** to be on safari.

saga *nf* saga.

sagacidad *nf* shrewdness, cleverness, sagacity; astuteness.

sagaz *adj* (a) shrewd, clever, sagacious; astute. (b) *dog* keen-scented.

sagazmente *adv* shrewdly, cleverly, sagaciously; astutely.

sagrado 1 *adj* sacred, holy (*also fig*); *orders, scripture etc* holy. **2** *nm* sanctuary, asylum; **acogerse a —** to seek sanctuary.

sagú *nm* sago.

Sahara *m*, **Sáhara** *m* Sahara.

sahumar [1a] *vt* to perfume (with incense); to smoke, fumigate.

saibó *nm* (*SAm: angl*), **saibor** *nm* (*Col, Ven: angl*) sideboard.

saín *nm* (a) animal fat, grease; fish oil (*used for lighting*). (b) (*on clothing*) dirt, grease.

sainete *nm* (a) (*Cook*) seasoning, sauce; (*fig*) titbit, delicacy, pleasant adornment, nice extra.

(b) (*fig*) spice, relish, tastiness.

(c) (*Theat*) one-act farce (*or* comedy); comic sketch, skit.

sajar [1a] *vt* (*Med*) to cut open, lance.

sajín *nm* (*CAm*), **sajino** *nm* (*CAm*) underarm odour.

sajón 1 *adj* Saxon. **2** *nm*, **sajona** *nf* Saxon.

Sajonia *f* Saxony.

sajornar [1a] *vt* (*Cu*) to bother, upset.

sal¹ *nf* (a) salt; **— amoníaca** sal ammoniac; **—es (aromáticas)** smelling salts; **—es de baño** bath salts; **— de cocina**, **— gorda** kitchen salt, cooking salt; **— de fruta(s)** fruit salts; **— gema** rock salt; **— de la Higuera** Epsom salts; **— de mesa** table salt; **— volátil** sal volatile.

(b) (*fig*) salt; wit, wittiness; charm, liveliness; **— de la tierra** salt of the earth; **esto es la — de la vida** this is the spice of life; **tiene mucha —** he's a great wit, he's very amusing, he's good company; **ella tiene mucha —** she's delightful, she's absolutely charming.

(c) (*fig: CAm, SD*) misfortune, bad luck.

sal² *see* **salir**.

sala *nf* (a) (*in house: also* **— de estar**) drawing room; (large) room; hall; (*Theat*) house, auditorium; (*Law*) court; (*Med*) hospital ward, section; **— de alum-**

bramiento delivery ward; **— capitular** chapter house, meeting room; **— de lo civil** civil court; **— de conferencias** lecture room, lecture hall; **— de lo criminal** criminal court; **— de espectáculos** concert room, hall; **— de espera** waiting room; **— de fiestas** dance hall; **— de juntas** (*Comm*) boardroom; **— de justicia** law court; **— de lectura** reading room; **— de máquinas** (*Naut*) engine room; **— de muestras** showroom; **— de operaciones** operating theatre; **— de pruebas** fitting room; **— de recibo** parlour; **— de subastas** saleroom, auction room; **— del trono** throne room; **deporte en —** indoor sport, indoor game.

(b) suite of drawing-room (*etc*) furniture.

salacidad *nf* salaciousness, prurience.

saladar *nm* salt marsh, saltings.

salado *adj* (a) (*Cook*) salt, salty; *water* salt; **muy —** strongly salted, over-salted.

(b) (*fig*) witty, amusing; lively; charming, attractive, cute; *language* rich, racy; **es un tipo muy —** he's a very amusing chap, he's a very lively sort; **¡qué —!** how amusing!, (*iro*) very droll!, wasn't that clever of you?

(c) (*SAm*) unlucky, unfortunate; wretched.

(d) (*Chi, RPl*) *article* expensive; *price* very high.

salamanca *nf* (*Chi, RPl*) (a) cave, grotto; dark place. (b) witchcraft, sorcery.

salamandra *nf* salamander.

salamanquesa *nf* lizard.

salame *nm* (*Arg*) idiot.

salami *nm* salami.

salar 1 *nm* (*Arg, Bol, Chi*) salt mine; salt pan. **2** [1a] *vt* (a) (*Cook*) to put salt in, add salt to.

(b) (*Cook*) to salt, cure.

(c) (*Col, Ec*) *cattle* to feed salt to.

(d) (*Ant, CAm, Ec, Mex, Per*) to ruin, spoil; to bring bad luck to.

(e) (*Cu, Hond*) to dishonour.

salarial *adj* wage (*attr*); **reclamación —** wage claim.

salario *nm* wages, pay; (*SAm: angl*) salary.

salaz *adj* salacious, prurient.

salazón *nf* (*Ant, Guat, Par*) bad luck.

salceda *nf*, **salcedo** *nm* willow plantation.

salcochar [1a] *vt* to boil in salt water.

salchicha *nf* pork sausage.

salchichería *nf* pork butcher's (shop).

salchichón *nm* (salami-type) sausage.

saldar [1a] *vt* (a) *bill* to pay; *debt* to pay off. (b) (*fig*) *differences* to settle, resolve; *see* **cuenta**. (c) *stocks* to sell off, sell up; *books* to remainder.

saldo *nm* (a) (*act*) settlement; payment.

(b) balance (*also fig*); **— acreedor**, **— a favor** credit balance; **— deudor**, **— en contra** debit balance, adverse balance; **el — es a su favor** (*fig*) the balance is in his favour, on balance he comes off best.

(c) (*Comm*) clearance sale.

(d) remnant(s), remainder, left-over(s).

saledizo 1 *adj* projecting. **2** *nm* projection; overhang; **en —** projecting, overhanging.

salera *nf* (*Chi*) = **salina**.

salero *nm* (a) (*Cook*) saltcellar. (b) salt store. (c) (*Agr*) salt lick. (d) (*fig*) wit, wittiness; charm; sex appeal, allure, glamour. (e) (*Chi*) = **salina**.

saleroso *adj* (*fam*) = **salado** (b).

salida *nf* (a) (*act*) leaving, going out, exit; emergence; (*Aer, Rail etc*) departure; (*Astron*) rising; (*of gas etc*) leak, escape; (*Sport*) start; (*Theat*) appearance, entry, coming-on; (*Theat*) curtain call; **"S—s"** (*Rail*) "Departures"; **— lanzada** running start, flying start; **— parada** standing start; **— del sol** sunrise; **la — fue triste** leaving was sad, our departure was sad; **a la — del trabajo** on leaving work; **a la — del teatro** as we (*etc*) came out of the theatre; **para García, dos orejas y — en hombros** (*Taur*) García won two ears and was carried out shoulder-high.

(b) (*Mil*) sally, sortie; (*Aer*) sortie.

(c) (*Cards*) lead; **si la — es a trébol** if the lead is in clubs.

(d) (*Tech*) output, production; (*Fin*) outlay.

(e) (*place etc*) exit, way out; (*Mech*) outlet, vent, valve; (*Geog*) outlet; **"S—"** "Exit", "Way Out"; **— de artistas** (*Theat*) stage door; **— de emergencia**, **— de urgencia** emergency exit; **dar — a su indignación** to vent one's anger; **tener — a** (*Archit*) to lead to, open on to; (*Geog*) have an outlet to.

(f) (*fig*) way out; pretext, loophole; dodge; **es una — cómoda** it's a simple solution; **no hay —** there's no way out of it; **no tenemos otra — que firmarlo** there's nothing we can do but sign it, there is no solution open to us except to sign it;

dio con una — ingeniosa he hit upon a clever way out.

(g) (*fig*) issue, result, outcome.

(h) (*fig*) argument, counterargument.

(i) (*Comm*) sale, sales outlet, opening; **dar — a** to sell, place, find an outlet for; **tener —** to sell well; **el bikini no tiene — en Groenlandia** bikinis don't sell in Greenland; **tener una — difícil** to be a hard sell; **tener una — fácil** to have a ready market, be a soft sell.

(j) (*on surface*) projection, protuberance.

(k) — de baño bathrobe; **— de teatro** evening wrap.

(l) (*Comm: in account*) item.

(m) (*fig*) crack (*fam*), joke, witty remark; **tener —s** to be amusing, be full of wisecracks; to have amusing ideas.

(n) (*fig*) **— de pie de banco, — de tono** inept remark, ill-judged remark, unfortunate intervention.

salido *adj* **(a)** projecting, sticking out; bulging. **(b)** **estar salida** (*Zool*) to be on heat.

salidor *adj* (*Chi, RPl, Ven*) restless, roving; fond of going out a lot.

saliente 1 *adj* **(a)** (*Archit etc*) projecting, protuberant; raised, overhanging; *feature* prominent.

(b) (*fig*) salient; outstanding.

(c) sun rising.

(d) *member etc* outgoing, retiring.

2 *nm* projection; (*of road etc*) shoulder; (*Mil*) salient.

salina *nf* salt mine; salt pan; **—s** saltworks.

salinera *nf* (*Per, PR*) =**salina.**

salinidad *nf* salinity; saltness, saltiness.

salino *adj* saline; salty.

salir [3t] **1** *vi* **(a)** (*general sense: of person*) to come out, go out (*de* of); to leave; to appear, emerge (*de* from); to get out (*de* of), escape (*de* from); **salimos a la calle** we went out into the street; **— a ver algo** to go out to see something; **— de** to leave; **al — del cine** on leaving the cinema, when we (*etc*) came out of the cinema; **lo buscaremos al — de aquí** we'll look for it on the way out of here; **¿de dónde ha salido Vd?** where did you spring from?; **— del coma** to emerge from a coma; **— del enojo** to get over one's anger; **— de un apuro** to get out of a jam; **— de un puesto** to leave one's post, give up one's post; **este año sale de presidente** this year he ceases to be chairman, he gives up the chairmanship this year; **por fin salió de pobre** he finally left poverty behind him; **— para** to leave for.

(b) (*general sense: other subjects*) to come out; to emerge, appear; (*Astron*) to rise, come up; (*Bot*) to appear, come up, show; (*of journal etc*) to come out, appear, be published; (*of fashion etc*) to come in; (*of stain, dirt*) to come off, come out; **el agua sale aquí** the water comes out here; **le salió un diente** he cut a tooth; **esta calle sale a la plaza** this street comes out in the square, this street leads to the square; **el vino sale de la uva** wine comes from grapes; **el anillo no le sale del dedo** the ring won't come off her finger, she can't get the ring off her finger; **le salió la satisfacción a la cara** satisfaction showed in his face; **la noticia salió en el periódico de ayer** the news came out in yesterday's paper; **por fin salió la causa de todo ello** eventually the reason for the whole thing came to light; **¡ya salió aquello!** so that was it!, so now we know!; **cuando salga la ocasión** when the opportunity comes up (*or* arises, presents itself); **si sale un puesto a propósito** if the right job comes up; **no le sale novio** she doesn't seem to get a boyfriend; **— adelante** to do well, make progress, get on.

(c) (*of result etc*) to turn out; to prove, be, turn out to be; **salga lo que salga** (*or* **saliere**) come what may; regardless of the consequences; whatever turns up; **si sale verdad** if it proves (to be) true; **nos salió la criada muy trabajadora** the girl turned out to be very hard-working; **el conserje salió un sinvergüenza** the porter turned out to be a rogue; **si sale cara** (*tossing coin*) if it comes down heads; **este crucigrama no me sale** this crossword won't work out, I can't do this crossword; **le salen los problemas sin dificultad** he works problems out with no trouble at all; **— a** (*of price*) to come to, amount to, work out at; **el traje le salió muy caro** the suit worked out very expensive for him; **esto nos va a — carísimo** this is going to cost us a fortune; **me sale a menor precio que a ti** it's working out cheaper for me than it is for you; **— ganando** to gain, be the gainer; to come out on top; to emerge as the winner; to gain on a deal; **— perdiendo** to lose, be the loser; to lose on a deal; **— bien** (*person*)

to succeed, make good; to do well; (*in exam*) to pass; (*event*) to go off well; **— mal** (*person*) to fail, do badly, come unstuck; (*in exam*) to fail; (*event*) to be a failure; **les salió mal el proyecto** the scheme miscarried, the plan went badly for them.

(d) (*Theat: also* **— a escena**) to enter, come on; **sale vestido de policía** he comes on dressed as a policeman; **"sale el rey"** (*stage direction*) "enter the king".

(e) (*of bus, train etc*) to leave, depart; (*Naut*) to sail; **sale a las 8** it departs at 8; **— para** to leave for.

(f) — con (*of boyfriend etc*) to go out with, date (*US*); **salen juntos desde hace 2 años** they've been going around together for two years.

(g) (*of chick, egg*) to hatch.

(h) (*Archit etc*) to project, jut out; to stick out; to overhang; **sale un poco más cada día** it comes out a little further each day; **el balcón sale unos 2 metros** the balcony projects about 2 metres.

(i) (*of lottery number etc*) to come up, win (a prize); (*Pol: also* **— elegido**) to be elected, win; **salió alcalde por 3 votos** he was elected mayor by 3 votes.

(j) (*Cards*) to lead; (*Chess*) to have first move; (*Sport*) to start; **— con un as** to lead an ace.

(k) — con una observación to come out with a remark, come up with some (inept) remark.

(l) — por uno to come out in defence of someone.

(m) — con un propósito to carry out a plan; **— con una pretensión** to succeed in a claim; **ella sale con todo el trabajo** she manages to keep up with all the work; she is fully up to all the work.

(n) — a to take after; **salió a su padre** he took after his father, he was exactly like his father.

(o) (*Fin*) **— a los gastos de uno** to meet (or pay, defray) someone's expenses; **— por uno** to back someone financially; to stand security for someone.

2 salirse *vr* **(a)** (*in most senses*) =**1**; **— del tema** to wander from the point; to make a digression, go outside one's subject; **se salió del partido** he left the party.

(b) (*animal, bird etc*) to escape (*de* from), get out (*de* of); (*air, liquid etc*) to leak out; to overflow; to boil over; (*container*) to leak; to overflow; to boil over; **el barril se sale** the barrel is leaking.

(c) (*Mech*) to become disconnected; **— de la vía** (*Rail*) to leave the rails, jump the track.

(d) — de costumbre to break with custom, depart from tradition; **— de lo normal** to go beyond what is normal; **— de los límites** to go beyond the limits.

(e) — de un compromiso to get out of an obligation.

salitre *nm* saltpetre, nitre.

salitrera *nf* nitre works; nitrate fields.

saliva *nf* saliva, spit; **gastar —** (*fig*) to waste one's breath (*en* on); **tragar —** to swallow one's feelings; to swallow hard.

salivación *nf* salivation.

salivadera *nf* (*Andalusia, Chi, RPl*) spittoon, cuspidor (*US*).

salival *adj* salivary.

salivar [1a] *vi* to salivate.

salivazo *nm* spittle, gobbet, spit; **arrojar un —** to spit.

salivera *nf* (*RPl*) spittoon, cuspidor (*US*).

salmantino 1 *adj* of Salamanca. **2** *nm*, **salmantina** *nf* native (*or* inhabitant) of Salamanca; **los —s** the people of Salamanca.

salmear [1a] *vi* to sing psalms.

salmo *nm* psalm.

salmodia *nf* **(a)** (*Eccl*) psalmody. **(b)** (*fam*) monotonous singing; drone, singsong.

salmodiar [1b] *vi* **(a)** to sing psalms. **(b)** (*fig*) to drone, sing monotonously; to chant.

salmón *nm* salmon.

salmonete *nm* red mullet.

salmuera *nf* pickle, brine.

salobre *adj* salt, salty; *water* salt, brackish.

saloma *nf* sea shanty, sea song; working song.

Salomón *m* Solomon.

salón *nm* **(a)** drawing room, lounge; (*Art and Hist*) salon; hall, assembly room; (*Naut*) saloon; (*of college etc*) common room; **— del automóvil** motor show; **— de baile** ballroom, dance hall; **— de belleza** beauty parlour; **— de demostraciones** showroom; **— de fiestas** dance hall; **— de fumar** smoking room; **— de pintura** art exhibition, art gallery; **— de sesiones** assembly hall; (*Pol*) chamber; **— de té** tearoom; **juego de —** parlour game.

(b) suite of drawing-room furniture.

(c) (*Mex, Pan: angl*) saloon (*US*).

saloncillo nm (Theat etc) private room; rest room.

salpicado adj (a) — de splashed with, spattered with; sprinkled with; **un diseño — de puntos rojos** a pattern with red dotted about in it; **una llanura salpicada de granjas** a plain with farms dotted about on it, a plain dotted with farms.
(b) **un discurso — de citas latinas** a speech sprinkled with Latin quotations, a speech full of Latin quotations.
(c) (Arg, Mex) animal spotted, dappled, mottled.

salpicadura nf (a) (act) splashing, spattering; sprinkling; flecking. (b) splash, spatter; sprinkle; dot, fleck. (c) (fig) spatter, peppering; sprinkling.

salpicar [1g] vt (a) (with mud, paint etc) to splash, spatter (de with); (with water etc) to sprinkle (de with); flowers etc to scatter, strew (about); cloth, design to dot, fleck (de with); — **un coche de barro** to splash a car with mud, splash mud over a car; — **agua sobre el suelo** to sprinkle water on the floor; **la multitud de islas que salpican el océano** the host of islands dotted about the ocean.
(b) (fig) conversation, speech etc to sprinkle, interlard (de with); to pepper (de with).

salpicón nm (a) = salpicadura. (b) (Cook) salmagundi. (c) (Ec) drink of cold fruit juice.

salpimentar [1a] vt (a) (Cook) to season, add salt and pepper to. (b) (fig) to season, improve, sweeten (de with).

salpiquear [1a] vt (Col, PR) = salpicar.

salpresar [1a] vt to salt (down).

salpreso adj (Cook) salted, salt.

salpullido nm (a) (Med) rash, skin disease. (b) flea-bite, swelling (from a bite).

salsa nf (a) sauce; (with roast) gravy; (with sweet) sauce; (with salad) dressing; — **de ají** chili sauce; — **mayonesa** mayonnaise; — **de tomate** tomato sauce, ketchup; — **tártara** tartar sauce.
(b) (fig) seasoning, spice; appetizer; **es la — de la vida** it's the spice of life.

salsera nf sauce boat; gravy boat.

salsifí nm salsify.

saltabanco nm (a) (Hist) quack, mountebank. (b) rogue. (c) = saltimbanqui.

saltado adj (a) estar — to be chipped, be damaged; **la corona tiene varias piedras saltadas** the crown has several stones missing. (b) eyes bulging.

saltador nm (a) (Sport) jumper. (b) skipping rope.

saltadura nf chip.

saltamontes nm, pl **saltamontes** grasshopper.

saltante adj (Chi, Per) outstanding.

saltaperico nm (a) (Cu) squib, firecracker. (b) (Ven) row, uproar.

saltar [1a] 1 vt (a) to jump (over), leap (over), vault.
(b) to remove; **le saltó 3 dientes** he knocked out 3 of his teeth; **me has saltado un botón** you've torn off one of my buttons.
(c) (fig) meal, name, passage etc to skip, miss out, leave out; **saltó un párrafo entero** he skipped a whole paragraph; **me he saltado dos renglones** I've left out a couple of lines.
2 vi (a) (of persons etc) to jump, leap, spring (a on to, into; por, por encima de over); to vault; to bound; (of child) to hop, skip; to gambol; — **a la silla** to leap into the saddle; — **al agua** to jump (or dive, plunge) into the water; — **de la cama** to leap out of bed; — **de alegría** to jump with joy, jump for joy; — **en una silla** to jump up on (to) a chair; — **en tierra** to leap ashore; **en paracaídas** to jump, come down by parachute; — **por una ventana** to jump out of a window, leap from a window; — **sobre uno** to pounce on someone; **hacer — un caballo** to jump a horse, make a horse jump.
(b) (fig: in speech etc) to skip about, skip from one subject to another.
(c) (of ball) to bounce, fly up; (of spring) to unroll suddenly; (of liquid) to spurt up, shoot up; (of tears) to well up; (of figure) to leap (up); — **a la mente** to leap to one's mind; **estar a lo que salta** to watch out for an opportunity, look for an opening; to live for the day; **la mayoría ha saltado a 900 votos** the majority has shot up (or leaped up) to 900 votes.
(d) (of part) to come off, fly off; (of cork) to blow out, pop out; (of chip etc) to fly off; (of button) to come off; (of wood etc) to crack, snap, break; (of spring) to break; (of vessel) to crack; (of explosive) to explode, burst; **hacer — un edificio** to blow a building up; **hacer — una trampa** to spring a trap.
(e) (fig: with anger) to explode, blow up (fam).

(f) (fig) — **con una observación** to come out with a remark, make a ridiculous remark.
(g) (fig) — **de un puesto** to leave a post, give up a job; **hacer — a uno de un puesto** to boot someone out of a job.
(h) (Bio) — **atrás** to revert (to type).
3 **saltarse** vr (a) — **un párrafo** to skip a paragraph; see 1 (c).
(b) — **todas las reglas** to break all the rules.
(c) (of part) to come off, fly off; see 2 (d).

saltarín 1 adj restless; full of movement, always on the go; (pej) unstable. 2 nm, **saltarina** nf dancer.

salteado adj (Cook) sauté.

salteador nm (also — **de caminos**) holdup man; (Hist) highwayman, footpad.

salteamiento nm robbery, holdup.

saltear [1a] 1 vt (a) to hold up; to rob, assault, attack; to take by surprise.
(b) (fig: of doubt etc) to assail, overcome suddenly.
(c) (Cook) to sauté.
2 vi to work (etc) fitfully, do something by fits and starts; **lo leyó salteando** he read bits of it here and there.

salterio nm (a) (Eccl) psalter; (Bib) Book of Psalms. (b) (Mus) psaltery.

saltimbanqui nm juggler; acrobat; tightrope walker, mountebank; (fig) playboy.

salto nm (a) jump, leap; bound, spring; vault; hop, skip; (into water) jump, dive, plunge; (on to prey) pounce; — **a ciegas** leap in the dark; **el gran —** (hacia) **adelante** the great leap forward; **a —s** by jumping, in a series of jumps; (fig) by fits and starts; **avanzar a —s** to jump along, go hopping along; **de un —** at one bound, with one jump; **subió de un —** he jumped up; **bajó de un —** he jumped down; **en un —** (fig) in a jiffy; **en dos —s estoy de vuelta** I'll be back in a moment; **dar un —, pegar un —** to jump (with fright etc); **me daba —s el corazón** my heart was pounding; **vivir a — de mata** to live from hand to mouth, keep one's head just above water; to keep one jump ahead of justice; **escapar a — de mata** to flee headlong; **hacer algo a — de mata** to do something thoughtlessly, do something unmethodically.
(b) (Sport etc) jump; (into water) dive; — **de altura** high jump; high dive; — **de cabeza** header; — **de carpa** jack-knife dive; — **a la** (or **con**) **garrocha**, **con** (or **de**) **pértiga** pole vault; — **de longitud** long jump; — **mortal** somersault; — **ornamental** fancy dive; **triple —** hop, step and jump; — **de trampolín** springboard dive.
(c) (Bio) — **atrás** throwback, reversion to type.
(d) (Geol) fault; chasm, rift.
(e) (fig) gap; jump; passage skipped, part missed; **aquí hay un — de 50 versos** there is a gap here of 50 lines; **de él al otro hermano hay un — de 9 años** there is a gap of 9 years between him and the other brother, there are 9 years between him and the other brother.
(f) (Sport) jump; fence; hurdle, obstacle; — **de agua** water jump.
(g) — **de agua** (Geog) waterfall, cascade; (Tech) chute.
(h) — **de cama** négligé, peignoir.
(i) (Cu) **a —** in cash.

saltón 1 adj (a) eyes bulging, popping; teeth prominent, protruding.
(b) (Col, Chi, Ven) undercooked, half raw.
2 nm grasshopper; (Mex) immature locust.

saltona nf (RPl) immature locust.

salubre adj healthy, salubrious.

salubridad nf (a) healthiness, salubrity, salubriousness. (b) health statistics.

salud nf (a) (Med) health; state of health; **estar bien de —** to be in good health; **estar mal de —** to be in bad health; **¿cómo vamos de —?** how are we today?; **mejorar de —** to improve in health, get better; **devolver la — a uno** to give someone back his health, restore someone to health.
(b) (fig) health; welfare, wellbeing; **la — moral de la nación** the country's moral welfare.
(c) ¡—!, ¡a su —!, ¡— y pesetas! good health!, here's to you!, here's luck!; **beber a la — de** to drink to the health of.
(d) (Rel) salvation; state of grace.

saludable adj (a) (Med) healthy. (b) (fig) salutary, good, beneficial; **un aviso —** a salutary warning.

saludar [1a] vt (a) to greet; to bow to, take off one's hat to; **ir a — a uno** to go and say hullo to someone, drop in to see someone; **salude de mi parte a X** give my regards to X; **no — a uno** to cut someone, refuse to acknowledge someone.

(b) (*formula in letter*) **le saluda atentamente** yours faithfully.

(c) (*Mil*) to salute.

(d) (*fig*) to salute, hail, welcome.

saludo *nm* **(a)** greeting; bow.

(b) (*formula in letter*) **—s** best wishes, greetings, regards; **un — afectuoso, un — cordial** yours sincerely; **os envía muchos —s** he sends you warmest regards.

(c) (*Mil*) salute.

Salustio *m* Sallust.

salutación *nf* greeting, salutation.

salva *nf* **(a)** (*Mil etc*) salute, salvo; (*fig: of applause*) storm, volley. **(b)** greeting. **(c)** oath, solemn promise.

salvabarros *nm*, *pl* **salvabarros** mudguard.

salvación *nf* **(a)** rescue, delivery (*de* from), salvation.

(b) (*Rel*) salvation; **— eterna** eternal salvation.

salvada *nf* (*SAm*) =**salvación (a)**.

salvado *nm* bran.

salvador *nm* rescuer, saviour; **el S—** the Saviour.

salvadoreñismo *nm* word (*or* phrase *etc*) peculiar to Salvador.

salvadoreño 1 *adj* Salvadoran. **2** *nm*, **salvadoreña** *nf* Salvadoran.

salvaguardar [1a] *vt* to safeguard.

salvaguardia *nf* safe-conduct; (*fig*) safeguard.

salvajada *nf* savage deed, piece of savagery; barbarity, atrocity; brutal act.

salvaje 1 *adj* **(a)** (*Bot, Zool etc*) wild; *land* wild, uncultivated. **(b)** *people, tribe etc* savage. **2** *nmf* savage (*also fig*).

salvajería *nf* =**salvajada**.

salvajez *nf* =**salvajismo**.

salvajino *adj* **(a)** wild, savage. **(b) carne salvajina** meat from a wild animal.

salvajismo *nm* savagery.

salvamanteles *nm*, *pl* **salvamanteles** tablemat.

salvamento *nm* **(a)** rescue; delivery; salvage; (*fig*) salvation; **de —** life-saving (*attr*); rescue (*attr*); **bote de —** lifeboat; **operaciones de —** rescue operations.

(b) place of safety, refuge; haven.

salvaplatos *nm*, *pl* **salvaplatos** tablemat.

salvar [1a] **1** *vt* **(a)** *person etc* to save, rescue (*de* from); *ship* to salvage; *appearances* to save, keep up; **me salvó la vida** he saved my life; **apenas salvaron nada del incendio** they hardly rescued anything from the fire; **— a uno de tener que + infin** to save someone from having to + *infin*.

(b) (*Rel*) to save.

(c) *barrier, line, mountains, river etc* to cross; *rapids* to shoot; *ditch, stream* to jump across, jump over, clear; *difficulty* to overcome, resolve; *obstacle* to get round, negotiate.

(d) *distance* to cover, do, travel; **el tren salva la distancia en 2 horas** the train covers the distance in 2 hours.

(e) to except, exclude.

(f) (*of building, tree etc*) to rise above.

(g) (*of water level etc*) to reach, rise as high as; **el agua salvaba el peldaño más alto** the water came up to the topmost step.

2 salvarse *vr* **(a)** to save oneself, escape (*de* from); **¡sálvese el que pueda!** every man for himself!

(b) (*Rel*) to save one's soul, be saved.

salvavidas *nm*, *pl* **salvavidas (a)** lifebelt. **(b)** (*as adj*) life-saving (*attr*); **bote —** lifeboat; **cinturón —** lifebelt.

salvedad *nf* reservation, qualification, proviso; **con la — de que . . .** with the proviso that . . .; **hacer una — to** make a qualification.

salvia *nf* (*Bot*) sage.

salvilla *nf* salver, tray; (*Chi*) cruet.

salvo 1 *adj* safe; *see* **sano**.

2 *adv and prep* **(a)** except (for), save; barring; **— aquellos que ya contamos** except for those we have already counted; **de todos los países — de Ruritania** from all countries except Ruritania.

(b) a — safely; out of danger; **a — de** safe from; **en —** out of danger, in a safe place; **dejar algo a —** to make an exception of something, leave something out of it; **para dejar a — su reputación** in order to keep his reputation safe; **poner algo a —** to put something in a safe place, put something out of harm's way; **ponerse a —** to escape, reach safety; **nada ha quedado a — de sus ataques** nothing has been safe from his attacks.

3 — que, — si *conj* unless . . .; except that . . .; **iré — que me avises al contrario** I'll go unless you tell me not to.

salvoconducto *nm* safe-conduct.

salvohonor *nm* (*hum*) backside.

samaritano 1 *adj* Samaritan. **2** *nm*, **samaritana** *nf* Samaritan; **buen —** good Samaritan.

samaruco *nm* (*Chi*) hunter's pouch, gamebag.

samba *nf* (*SAm*) samba.

sambenito *nm* (*fig*) dishonour, disgrace, infamy; **echar el — a otro** to pin the blame on someone else; **quedó con el — toda la vida** he was disgraced for life.

sambumbia *nf* **(a)** (*Col, Mex, PR*) badly-made drink, watery drink; badly-made object.

(b) (*Cu*) drink of sugar-cane syrup, water and peppers; (*Mex*) pineapple drink; (*Mex*) barley-water drink.

(c) (*Col*) old thing, battered object; **volver algo —** to smash something to pieces.

sambutir [3a] *vt* (*Mex*) =**embutir**.

samotana *nf* (*CAm*) row, uproar.

samovar *nm* samovar.

sampablera *nf* (*Ven*) noisy argument; fuss, row.

sampán *nm* sampan.

Samuel *m* Samuel.

samurar [1a] *vi* (*Ven*) to walk with bowed head.

San *nm* (*apocopated form of* **santo**) saint; **San Juan** Saint John, (*mostly written*) St John; **cerca de San Martín** near St Martin's (church); **se casarán por San Juan** they'll get married sometime in midsummer (*strictly*, round about St John's Day); *see also* **santo**.

sanable *adj* curable, susceptible to treatment.

sanaco *adj* (*Ant*) silly.

sanalotodo *nm* cure-all, universal remedy.

sanamente *adv* healthily; wholesomely.

sananería *nf* (*Ant*) silly thing, stupid remark.

sanar [1a] **1** *vt* to heal; to cure (*de* of). **2** *vi* (*of person*) to recover, get well; (*of wound*) to heal.

sanativo *adj* healing, curative.

sanatorio *nm* sanatorium; (*private*) nursing home.

sanción *nf* sanction; **imponer —es** to impose sanctions; **levantar —es a uno** to lift sanctions against someone.

sancionable *adj* punishable.

sancionado *nm* guilty person; **los —s** (*Pol*) those who have been punished for a political offence, those guilty of political crimes.

sancionar [1a] *vt* (*all senses*) to sanction.

sancochado *nm* (*Per*) =**sancocho**.

sancochar [1a] *vt* to parboil.

sancocho *nm* **(a)** undercooked food, parboiled meat. **(b)** (*SAm*) stew (of meat, yucca *etc*). **(c)** (*CAm, Mex, PR, Ven*) fuss; confusion; row. **(d)** (*Cu*) pigswill.

San Cristóbal *m* **(a)** (*Eccl*) St Christopher. **(b)** (*Geog*) St Kitts.

sancho *nm* **(a)** (*Prov*) pig. **(b)** (*Mex*) ram, lamb; billy-goat; (*any*) domestic animal.

sandalia *nf* sandal.

sándalo *nm* sandal, sandalwood.

sandez *nf* **(a)** (*quality*) foolishness. **(b)** (*act*) stupid thing, piece of stupidity; **decir sandeces** to talk nonsense; **fue una — obrar así** it was silly to do that.

sandía *nf* watermelon.

sandío *adj* foolish, silly, stupid.

sandunga *nf* **(a)** (*fam*) charm; wit. **(b)** (*Chi, Mex, Per, PR*) carousal, celebration.

sandunguero *adj* (*fam*) charming; witty, amusing.

sandwich [saŋ'gwitʃ, sam'bitʃ] *nm*, *pl* **sandwichs** *or* **sandwiches** (*angl*) sandwich.

saneamiento *nm* **(a)** draining; drainage (system), sanitation; sewerage.

(b) (*fig*) remedy; ending; cleaning-up.

(c) guarantee; insurance.

(d) compensation, indemnification.

sanear [1a] *vt* **(a)** *land* to drain; *house* to remove the dampness from; (*Tech*) to instal drainage (*or* sewerage) in, lay sewers in.

(b) (*fig*) *damage* to remedy, repair; *abuse* to end; *centre of vice* to clean up.

(c) *goods* to guarantee; to insure.

(d) (*Law*) *purchaser* to compensate, indemnify.

sanfasón: a la — adv (*SAm: gall*) unceremoniously, informally; (*pej*) carelessly.

sanforizar [1f] *vt* to sanforize (*Protected Trade Name*).

sangradera *nf* **(a)** (*Med*) lancet. **(b)** (*Agr*) irrigation channel; sluice, outflow.

sangradura *nf* **(a)** (*Anat*) inner angle of the elbow. **(b)** (*Med*) cut made into a vein; bleeding, blood-letting. **(c)** (*Agr*) outlet, drainage channel.

sangrante *adj* **(a)** *person, wound* bleeding. **(b)** (*fig*) *injustice etc* crying, flagrant.

sangrar [1a] **1** *vt* **(a)** (*Med*) to bleed.

(b) (*Agr etc*) to drain, drain the water from;

water to drain off, let out, allow to drain away; *tree* to tap; *furnace* to tap.
(c) (*Typ*) to indent.
(d) (*fam*) to filch, filch from.
2 *vi* (a) to bleed (*also fig*).
(b) (*fig*) **estar sangrando** to be still fresh, be very new still; to be obvious; **aún sangra la humillación** the humiliation still rankles.

sangre *nf* blood (*also fig*); — **azul** blue blood; — **fría** sangfroid, coolness; (*pej*) callousness; **a** — **fría** in cold blood, callously; **mala** — bad blood; **pura** — (*nmf*) thoroughbred; — **vital** lifeblood; **a** — by animal power, by horsepower; **a** — **caliente** in the heat of the moment; **a** — **y fuego** by fire and sword; **es de** — **de reyes** he has royal blood, he is of the blood royal; **fue de** — **de conquistadores** he came of a line of conquerors; **le bulle la** — **(en las venas)** he is full of youthful vigour, he is bursting with energy; **esto chorrea** — this cries out to heaven; **chupar la** — **a uno** (*fig*) to exploit someone, suck out someone's lifeblood; to bleed someone white; **dar su** — to give one's blood; **echar** — to bleed (*de* from); **echar** — **por los ojos** to be furious; **encender** (*or* **quemar, revolver**) **la** — **a uno** to infuriate someone, make someone's blood boil; **freír la** — **a uno** (*fam*) to rile someone (*fam*), needle someone (*fam*); **se me heló la** — my blood froze, my blood ran cold; **llegar a la** — to come to blows; **sin que la** — **llegue al río** without disastrous results, without going to extremes; **no creo que llegue la** — **al río** I don't think it will be too disastrous; **sudar** — to undergo hardships; to slog, toil; **tener la** — **gorda** (*or* **de horchata**), **no tener** — **en las venas** to be excessively phlegmatic, be unemotional, be stone cold; to be dull, be boring.

sangregorda *nmf* (*fam*) bore.

sangría *nf* (a) (*Med*) bleeding, bloodletting; — **suelta** excessive flow of blood; (*fig*) outflow, drain, continuous loss.
(b) (*Anat*) inner angle of the elbow.
(c) (*Agr*) irrigation channel; outlet, outflow; ditch; drainage.
(d) (*Tech*) tapping (*of a furnace*); stream of molten metal.
(e) (*Cook*) sweetened and chilled drink of red wine with fruit, (*approx*) fruit cup.
(f) (*Typ*) indentation.

sangrientamente *adv* bloodily.

sangriento *adj* (a) *wound* bleeding.
(b) *dress, weapon etc* bloody, bloodstained, gory.
(c) *battle, clash* bloody.
(d) (*lit*) blood-red.
(e) (*fig*) *injustice etc* crying, flagrant; *insult* deadly; *joke* cruel.

sangrigordo *adj* (*Ant*) tedious; annoying.

sangriligero *adj* (*SAm*), **sangriliviano** *adj* (*SAm*) pleasant, nice, congenial.

sangripesado *adj* (*SAm*), **sangrón** *adj* (*Cu, Mex*), **sangruno** *adj* (*PR*) rude; unpleasant, nasty, uncongenial.

sanguarañas *nfpl* (*Arg, Ec, Per*) circumlocutions.

sanguijuela *nf* leech (*also fig*).

sanguinario *adj* bloodthirsty, cruel, callous.

sanguíneo *adj* (a) (*Anat*) blood (*attr*); **vaso** — blood vessel. (b) (*fig*) blood-red.

sanguinolento *adj* (a) bleeding; bloody, bloodstained; streaked (*or* tinged) with blood; *eyes* bloodshot.
(b) (*Cook*) underdone, rare.
(c) (*fig*) blood-red.

sanidad *nf* (a) health, healthiness; (*fig*) salubrity.
(b) public health; sanitation; **Ministerio de S**— Ministry of Health; — **pública** public health (department); **inspector de** —, **oficial de** — sanitary inspector.

sanitario *adj* sanitary; health (*attr*); sanitation (*attr*).

sano *adj* (a) (*Med etc*) healthy; fit; *organ, wood etc* sound; *fruit* good; **cortar por lo** — to take extreme measures, go right to the root of the trouble; to cut one's losses.
(b) *climate etc* healthy; *food* good, wholesome.
(c) *object* whole, intact, undamaged; — **y salvo** safe and sound; **esa silla no es muy sana** that chair is not too strong; **no ha quedado plato** — **en toda la casa** there wasn't a plate left whole (*or* unbroken) in the house.
(d) (*fig*) (morally) healthy, wholesome; *doctrine, teaching* sound; *desire* earnest, sincere; *objective etc* worthy.

sánscrito 1 *adj* Sanskrit. 2 *nm* Sanskrit.

sanseacabó (*fam*): **y** — and that's the end of it, and there's no more to be said.

Sansón *m* Samson; **es un** — he's tremendously strong.

santa *nf* saint; *see* **santo**.

santabárbara *nf* (*Naut*) magazine.

santamente *adv*: **vivir** — to live a saintly (*or* holy) life.

santanderino 1 *adj* of Santander. 2 *nm*, **santanderina** *nf* native (*or* inhabitant) of Santander; **los** —**s** the people of Santander.

santateresa *nf* (*Ent*) praying mantis.

santería *nf* (a) (*SAm*) shop selling religious images, prints etc. (b) (*fam*) = **santidad**.

santero 1 *nm* (*SAm*) maker (*or* seller) of religious images, prints etc. 2 *nm*, **santera** *nf* person excessively devoted to the saints.

Santiago *m* St James; — **de Compostela** St James of Compostella.

santiamén *nm*: **en un** — in an instant.

santidad *nf* holiness, sanctity; saintliness; **su S**— His Holiness.

santificación *nf* sanctification.

santificar [1g] *vt* (a) to sanctify, make holy, hallow; to consecrate; *festivity* to keep; **santificado sea Tu Nombre** hallowed be thy name. (b) (*fam*) to forgive.

santiguar [1i] 1 *vt* (a) to make the sign of the cross over; to bless.
(b) (*SAm*) to heal (by blessing).
(c) (*fam*) to slap, hit.
2 **santiguarse** *vr* (a) to cross oneself, make the sign of the cross.
(b) (*fam*) to make a great fuss, react in an exaggerated way, overdo the emotion.

santísimo *adj superl* (most) holy.

santo 1 *adj* (a) holy; sacred; *ground* holy, consecrated; *person* saintly; *martyr* blessed.
(b) (*fig*) *remedy etc* wonderful, miraculous.
(c) (*fam*) utter, complete; blessed; — **y bueno** well and good; **todo el** — **día** the whole livelong day; **the whole blessed day**; **y él con su santa calma** and he utterly unmoved, and he so completely calm; *see* **voluntad** *etc*.
2 *nm* (a) (*Eccl*) saint; — **patrón**, — **titular** patron saint; **S**— **Domingo** (*Eccl*) St Dominic; (*Geog*) Santo Domingo, Dominican Republic; **S**— **Tomás** St Thomas; *see also* **san**.
(b) (*idioms*) **¿a qué** —? what on earth for?; **¿a** — **de qué . . .?** why on earth . . .?; **¡por todos los** —**s!** for pity's sake!; **no es** — **de mi devoción** I'm not very keen on him; **alzarse con el** — **y la limosna** to clear off with the whole lot; **comerse los** —**s** to be terribly devout; **desnudar a un** — **para vestir otro** to rob Peter to pay Paul; **se le fue el** — **al cielo** he forgot what he was about to say; **llegar y besar el** — to pull it off at the first attempt; **nacer con el** — **de espaldas** to be born unlucky; **poner a uno como un** — to give someone a telling-off; **quedar para vestir** —**s** to be on the shelf; **tener el** — **de cara** to have tremendous luck.
(c) (*fig*) saint; **es un** — he's a saint; **estaba hecho un** — he was terribly sweet (*fam*).
(d) (*fig*) saint's day; — **y seña** (*Mil*) password; (*fig*) watchword, slogan; **mañana es mi** — tomorrow is my saint's day, tomorrow is my name day (*celebrated in Spain etc as equivalent to a birthday*).
(e) (*Chi: Sew*) patch, darn.

santuario *nm* (a) sanctuary, shrine. (b) (*Col, Ven*) native idol; buried treasure.

santulario *adj* (*RPl*) = **santurrón**.

santurrón 1 *adj* sanctimonious; hypocritical. 2 *nm*, **santurrona** *nf* sanctimonious person; hypocrite.

saña *nf* anger, rage, fury; cruelty; (*fig*) fury, viciousness.

sañoso *adj* = **sañudo**.

sañudamente *adv* angrily, furiously; cruelly; viciously.

sañudo *adj* furious, enraged; cruel; *blow etc* vicious, cruel.

sapaneco *adj* (*CAm*) plump, chubby.

sáparo *nm* (*Col*) wicker basket.

sapo[1] *nm* (a) (*Zool*) toad; (*fig*) small animal, bug, creature; **echar** —**s y culebras** to produce a stream of abuse, swear black and blue.
(b) (*prov, SAm*) game of throwing coins into the mouth of an iron toad.

sapo[2] *adj* (*Chi, Par, Per*) sly, cunning; hypocritical; (*Pan*) telltale.

saporro *adj* (*CAm, Col*) chubby.

sapotear [1a] *vt* (*Col*) to finger, handle.

saque *nm* (a) (*act: Tennis*) service, serve; (*Football*) throw-in, (*Rugby; also* — **de banda**) line-out; — **de castigo** penalty kick; — **de esquina** corner kick; —

inicial kick-off; — **libre** free kick; — **de portería,** — **de puerta** goal-kick.

(**b**) (*Tennis: person*) server.

(**c**) **tener buen —** to eat heartily, be a good trencherman.

(**d**) (*Chi*) distilling; distillery.

saqueador *nm* looter.

saquear [1a] *vt* (*Mil*) to sack; to loot, plunder, pillage; (*fig*) to rifle, ransack; to turn upside down.

saqueo *nm* sacking; looting, plundering; (*fig*) rifling, ransacking.

saquito *nm* small bag; sachet; — **de papel** paper bag.

saracutear [1a] *vi* (*RPl*) to move about restlessly, be always on the go.

sarampión *nm* measles.

sarao *nm* soirée, evening party.

sarape *nm* (*Guat, Mex*) blanket.

saraviado *adj* (*Col*) spotted, mottled; *person* freckled.

sarazo (*SAm*) = **zarazo.**

sarazón *adj* (*Mex*) = **zarazo.**

sarcasmo *nm* sarcasm.

sarcásticamente *adv* sarcastically.

sarcástico *adj* sarcastic.

sarcófago *nm* sarcophagus.

sardina *nf* sardine; — **arenque** pilchard; — **noruega** brisling; **como —s en banasta** packed like sardines.

sardinero *adj* sardine (*attr*).

sardo 1 *adj* Sardinian. **2** *nm,* **sarda** *nf* Sardinian.

sardónico *adj* (*esp SAm*) sardonic; ironical, sarcastic.

sargentear [1a] **1** *vt* (*Mil*) to command; (*fam*) to boss about. **2** *vi* (*fam*) to be bossy, boss people about.

sargento *nm* sergeant; **ser — de caballería** (*of woman*) to be very tough and mannish.

sargentona *nf* (*fam*) tough mannish woman.

sargo *nm* bream.

sari *nm* sari.

sarita *nf* (*Per*) straw hat.

sarmentoso *adj* (**a**) *plant* twining, climbing. (**b**) *finger etc* long and thin; gnarled.

sarmiento *nm* vine shoot.

sarna *nf* itch, scabies; (*Vet*) mange.

sarniento *adj* (*CAm, Mex*), **sarnoso** *adj* (**a**) itchy, infected with the itch; (*Vet*) mangy. (**b**) (*fig*) weak, feeble. (**c**) (*Arg, Bol*) contemptible, lousy (*fam*).

sarpullido *nm* = **salpullido.**

sarraceno 1 *adj* Saracen. **2** *nm,* **sarracena** *nf* Saracen.

sarracina *nf* (**a**) quarrel; brawl, free fight.

(**b**) mass slaughter; (*fig*) wholesale destruction.

(**c**) (*Univ: fam*) **han hecho una —** they've ploughed almost everybody (*sl*).

Sarre *m* Saar.

sarro *nm* (**a**) incrustation, deposit; (*on teeth*) tartar; (*on kettle, tongue*) fur. (**b**) (*Bot*) rust.

sarroso *adj* incrusted; covered with tartar; furred, furry.

sarta *nf,* **sartal** *nm,* **sartalada** *nf* (*Chi*) string; line, row, series; (*fig*) string; **una — de mentiras** a string of lies.

sartén *nf* frying pan; **coger la — por donde quema** to act rashly; **saltar de la — y dar en la brasa** to jump out of the frying pan into the fire; **tener la — por el mango** to be the master, rule the roost.

sarteneja *nf* (*Ec, Mex*) dried-out pool; (*Mex*) deep bog.

sasafrás *nm* sassafras.

sastre *nm* tailor; — **de teatro** costumier; **hecho por —** tailor-made.

sastrería *nf* (**a**) tailoring, tailor's trade. (**b**) tailor's (shop).

Satanás *m* Satan.

satánico *adj* satanic; devilish, fiendish.

satélite 1 *nm* (**a**) (*Astron*) satellite; — **artificial** artificial satellite.

(**b**) (*person*) satellite; minion; henchman; boon companion, crony.

2 *as adj* satellite; **ciudad —** satellite town; **país —** satellite country.

satén *nm* sateen.

satín *nm* (*SAm*) sateen, satin.

satinado 1 *adj* glossy, shiny. **2** *nm* gloss, shine.

satinar [1a] *vt* to gloss, make glossy.

sátira *nf* satire.

satíricamente *adv* satirically.

satírico *adj* satiric(al).

satirizar [1f] *vt* to satirize.

sátiro *nm* satyr.

satisfacción *nf* (**a**) (*in most senses*) satisfaction; **a — de** to the satisfaction of; **a su entera —** to his complete satisfaction; **con — de todos** to the general satisfaction.

(**b**) (*for an offence*) satisfaction, redress; apology;

pedir una — a uno to demand an apology from someone, demand satisfaction from someone.

(**c**) — **de sí mismo** self-satisfaction, smugness.

satisfacer [2s] **1** *vt* (**a**) (*in most senses*) to satisfy; (*of achievement etc*) to gratify, please; *need, request* to meet, satisfy; *debt, wages etc* to pay; *draft* (*Comm*) to honour; *expenses* to meet.

(**b**) *guilt* to expiate; *loss* to make good.

(**c**) — **a uno de** (*or* **por**) **una ofensa** to give someone satisfaction for an offence.

2 satisfacerse *vr* (**a**) to satisfy oneself, be satisfied; — **con muy poco** to be content with very little.

(**b**) to obtain redress, obtain satisfaction; to take revenge.

satisfactoriamente *adv* satisfactorily.

satisfactorio *adj* satisfactory.

satisfecho *adj* (**a**) satisfied; content(ed); **darse por — con algo** to declare oneself satisfied (*or* content) with something; **dejar —s a todos** to satisfy everybody.

(**b**) (*also* — **consigo mismo,** — **de sí mismo**) self-satisfied, smug; conceited; **nos miró —** he looked at us smugly.

saturación *nf* saturation; permeation.

saturar [1a] *vt* to saturate; to permeate.

saturnales *nfpl* Saturnalia.

saturnino *adj* saturnine.

Saturno *m* Saturn.

sauce *nm* willow; — **de Babilonia,** — **llorón** weeping willow.

saucedal *nm* willow plantation.

saúco *nm* (*Bot*) elder.

Saúl *m* Saul.

sauna *nf* sauna.

saurio *nm* saurian.

savia *nf* sap.

saxífraga *nf* saxifrage.

saxofón *nm,* **saxófono** *nm* saxophone.

saya *nf* (**a**) skirt; petticoat; dress. (**b**) (*Col*) woman.

sayal *nm* coarse woollen cloth.

sayo *nm* smock, tunic; loose garment, long loose gown.

sayón *nm* (**a**) (*Law*) executioner. (**b**) (*fig*) cruel henchman; (*fam*) fierce-looking chap (*fam*), ugly customer (*fam*).

sayuela *nf* (*Cu*) serge skirt.

sazo *nm* (*sl*) hankie (*fam*).

sazón 1 *nf* (**a**) (*Agr*) good heart; proper condition (*of land*) for planting.

(**b**) (*of fruit*) ripeness, maturity; **en —** ripe, ready (to eat); (*fig*) opportunely; **fuera de —** at the wrong moment, inopportunely.

(**c**) (*lit*) time, moment, season; **a la —** then, at that time.

(**d**) (*Cook*) flavour.

2 *adj* (*CAm, Mex, Per*) ripe.

sazonado *adj* (**a**) *fruit etc* ripe; mellow; *dish* tasty. (**b**) — **de** (*Cook*) seasoned with, flavoured with. (**c**) (*fig*) witty.

sazonar [1a] **1** *vt* (**a**) *fruit* to ripen, bring to maturity. (**b**) (*Cook*) to season, flavour (**de** with). (**c**) PR) to sweeten. **2** *vi* to ripen.

se[1] *reflexive pron* (**a**) (*sing: m*) himself, (*f*) herself, (*of thing*) itself, (*relating to* **Vd**) yourself; (*pl*) themselves, (*relating to* **Vds**) yourselves; **se está lavando, está lavándose** he's washing, he's washing himself; **se retira** he withdraws; **se tiró al suelo** she threw herself to the ground; **¡siéntese!** sit down!

(**b**) (*reciprocal*) each other, one another; **se ayudan** they help each other; **se miraron el uno al otro** they looked at one another; **no se hablan** they are not on speaking terms, they don't speak; **procuran no verse** they try not to run into each other.

(**c**) (*in general*) oneself; **conviene lavarse de vez en cuando** it is advisable to wash oneself occasionally.

(**d**) (*dative use*) **se ha comprado un sombrero** he has bought himself a hat, he has bought a hat for himself; **se rompió la pierna** he broke his leg; **han jurado no cortarse la barba** they have sworn not to cut their beards.

(**e**) (*impersonal use: often translated by English passive, by* one, *by* some *or* people) **se compró hace 3 años** it was bought 3 years ago; **se comprende que . . .** it can be understood that . . ., it is understandable that . . .; **no se sabe por qué** it is not known why; **en esa parte se habla galés** in that area Welsh is spoken, in that area people speak Welsh; **en ese hotel se come realmente bien** the food is really good in that hotel, you eat (*or* one eats) really well in that hotel; **se hace cuando se puede** one does it when one can; **se avisa a los interesados que . . .** those concerned are informed that . . .; **"véndese: solar . . ."** (*advert*) "for sale: plot . . ."; **"véndese coche"** (*advert*) "car for sale".

se[2] *personal pron* (*corresponding to* **le, les**): **se lo arrancó** he snatched it from her; **voy a dárselo** I'll give it to him; **se lo buscaré** I'll look for it for you; **no se lo agradecerán** they won't thank you for it.

sé *see* **saber, ser.**

sebear [1a] *vi* (*Ven*) to make love.

sebo *nm* (a) grease, fat; (*for candles*) tallow; (*Cook*) suet.
(b) (*fam: on person*) fat; (*on object*) grease, filth, grime.
(c) **helarse a uno el —** (*Arg, Bol*) to fail; to peg out (*sl*); **hacer un —** (*RPl*) to idle, loaf; **dar — a** (*Col, Ven*) to pester; **hacer** (*or* **volver**) **— a** (*Cu*) to finish off, ruin.

sebón *adj* (*Arg, Guat*) idle, lazy.

seboso *adj* (a) greasy, fatty; tallowy; suety. (b) (*fam*) greasy, filthy, grimy.

seca *nf* (a) (*Agr*) drought; (*Meteorol*) dry season. (b) (*Naut*) sandbank.

secadero *nm* (a) place where fruit (*etc*) is laid to dry. (b) (*Col*) dry land.

secador *nm* (a) place where clothes are hung to dry. (b) **— de cabello, — para el pelo** hair-drier; **— centrífugo** spin-drier.

secadora *nf* wringer; **— centrífuga** spin-drier.

secamente *adv* brusquely, sharply, curtly; drily.

secano *nm* (a) (*Agr: also* **tierra de —**) dry land, dry region; unirrigated land; **cultivo de —** crop of dry regions, crop not requiring irrigation; crop suitable for a region of low rainfall. (b) (*Naut*) sandbank; small sandy island. (c) (*fig*) very dry thing.

secante[1] **1** *adj* (a) *wind etc* drying; **papel — =2**. (b) (*RPl*) annoying. **2** *nm* blotting paper, blotter.

secante[2] *nf* (*Math*) secant.

secar [1g] **1** *vt* (a) to dry, dry up, dry off; *dish, surface* to wipe dry; *tears* to dry; *brow* to wipe, mop; *spilt liquid* to mop up; *ink* to blot; *plant* to dry up, wither.
(b) (*fig*) to annoy, vex; to bore.
2 secarse *vr* (a) (*washing etc*) to dry, dry off; (*river*) to dry up, run dry; (*plant*) to dry up, wither, wilt; (*person*) to dry oneself, get dry (*con una toalla* on a towel, with a towel).
(b) (*wound*) to close up, heal up.
(c) (*fam: person*) to get thin.
(d) (*fam: also* **— de sed**) to have a raging thirst.

secarropa *nm* clothes horse.

sección *nf* (a) (*Archit, Math etc*) section; (*also* **— transversal**) cross-section; **— cónica** conic section; **— longitudinal** longitudinal section; **— vertical** vertical section.
(b) (*fig*) section; division, department, branch.
(c) (*Mil*) section, platoon.

seccional *adj* sectional.

seccionar [1a] *vt* to divide up, divide into sections.

secesión *nf* secession.

secesionista 1 *adj* secessionist. **2** *nmf* secessionist.

seco *adj* (a) (*general sense*) dry; *fruit etc* dried; *plant* dried up, withered, dead; *battery, climate, lake, season etc* dry; **— al tacto** touch-dry; **estar en —** (*Naut and fig*) to be high and dry.
(b) *person* thin, skinny.
(c) *character* cold; disagreeable; blunt; *manner, reply etc* brusque, sharp, curt; *style* plain, bare, flat, inexpressive; *explanation* plain, unvarnished; *subject, study* dry.
(d) *blow, sound, thud etc* dull; *cough* dry.
(e) bare; *brandy* pure, unadulterated; **vivir a pan —** to live on bread alone, eat only bread; **tiene el sueldo —** he has just his salary.
(f) **dejar a uno —** to kill someone stone-dead; (*fig*) to dumbfound someone; **quedarse —** to be dumbfounded.
(g) **a secas: habrá pan a secas** there will be just bread; **decir algo a secas** to say something curtly, say something abruptly; **se llama Rodríguez a secas** he is called plain Rodríguez, he is just called Rodríguez.
(h) **callarse en —** to stop talking suddenly; to stop talking at once; **frenar en —** to brake sharply, pull up sharply; **parar en —** to stop dead, stop suddenly.

secoya *nf* redwood, sequoia.

secreción *nf* secretion.

secretamente *adv* secretly.

secretar [1a] *vt* to secrete.

secretaría *nf* (a) secretariat. (b) secretary's office. (c) secretaryship.

secretariado *nm* (a) secretariat. (b) secretaryship. (c) (*SAm*) secretarial course. (d) (*SAm*) career as a secretary, profession of secretary.

secretario *nm*, **secretaria** *nf* secretary; **— general** general secretary, (*Pol*) secretary general; **— municipal** town clerk; **— particular** private secretary.

secretear [1a] *vi* (a) to talk confidentially, exchange secrets. (b) to whisper unnecessarily; to whisper ostentatiously.

secreter *nm* (*gall*) writing desk.

secreto 1 *adj* (a) secret; hidden; *information* secret, confidential, (*Mil*) classified; **todo es de lo más —** it's all highly secret.
(b) *person* secretive.
2 *nm* (a) (*un* **—**) secret; **— de confesión** confessional secret; **— de estado** state secret; **— de fabricación** industrial secret; **— a voces** open secret; **estar en el —** to be in on the secret; **guardar un —** to keep a secret; **hacer — de algo** to be secretive about something.
(b) (*quality*) secrecy; **— de correspondencia** sanctity of the mails; **en —** in secret, secretly, in secrecy; **lo han hecho con mucho —** they have done it in great secrecy.
(c) (*of desk*) secret drawer.
(d) (*of lock*) combination.

secta *nf* sect; denomination.

sectario 1 *adj* sectarian; denominational; **no — non-sectarian**, non-denominational.
2 *nm*, **sectaria** *nf* follower, devotee; member; (*Eccl*) sectarian, member of a sect (*or* denomination).

sectarismo *nm* sectarianism.

sector *nm* sector; (*of opinion etc*) section; **— privado** (*Comm*) private sector; **— público** (*Comm*) public sector.

secuaz *nm* follower, supporter; (*pej*) underling, hireling.

secuela *nf* consequence.

secuencia *nf* (*Cine, Gram etc*) sequence.

secuestración *nf* sequestration; **= secuestro.**

secuestrador *nm*, **secuestradora** *nf* kidnapper.

secuestrar [1a] *vt* (a) *child* to kidnap; *person* to kidnap, abduct. (b) (*Law*) *goods* to seize, confiscate.

secuestro *nm* (a) kidnapping, abduction. (b) (*Law*) seizure, confiscation.

secular *adj* (a) (*Eccl*) secular; lay. (b) century-old; (*fig*) centuries-old, age-old, ancient; **según una tradición —** according to an age-old tradition.

secularización *nf* secularization.

secularizar [1f] *vt* to secularize.

secundar [1a] *vt* to second, help, support.

secundario *adj* secondary; minor, of lesser importance; *question* (*Parl*) supplementary.

secundinas *nfpl* afterbirth.

secuoia *nf* (*SAm*) **= secoya.**

sed *nf* thirst; thirstiness; (*Agr*) thirst, drought, dryness; (*fig*) thirst, lust, longing (*de* for); **— inextinguible, — insaciable** unquenchable thirst; **apagar la —** to quench one's thirst; **tener —** to be thirsty; **tener mucha —** to be very thirsty; **tener — de** (*fig*) to thirst for, long for.

seda *nf* (a) silk; **— artificial** artificial silk; **— de coser** sewing silk; **— floja** floss silk; **— hilada** spun silk; **— en rama** raw silk; **como una — (*adj*)** as smooth as silk, beautifully smooth; *person* very meek, very sweet-tempered; (*adv*) smoothly; **de — silk** (*attr*); silken, silky.
(b) (*Zool*) bristle.

sedal *nm* fishing line.

sedalina *nf* artificial silk.

sedán *nm* (*Aut*) sedan (*US*).

sedante 1 *adj* sedative; (*fig*) soothing, calming. **2** *nm* sedative.

sedativo *adj* sedative.

sede *nf* (a) (*of government*) seat; (*of company, society*) headquarters, central office; **— social** head office, central office. (b) (*Eccl*) see; **Santa S—** Holy See.

sedentario *adj* sedentary.

sedeño *adj* (a) silken, silky. (b) (*Zool*) bristly.

sedería *nf* (a) silk raising, silk manufacture, sericulture; silk trade. (b) silks, silk goods. (c) silk shop.

sedero 1 *adj* silk (*attr*); **industria sedera** silk industry. **2** *nm* silk dealer; draper, haberdasher.

sedicente *adj* self-styled; so-called, would-be.

sedición *nf* sedition.

sedicioso 1 *adj* seditious; mutinous, rebellious. **2** *nm*, **sediciosa** *nf* subversive element, disloyal individual; rebel; troublemaker.

sediento *adj* (a) thirsty (*also Agr*). (b) (*fig*) thirsty, eager (*de* for).

sedimentación *nf* sedimentation.

sedimentar [1a] **1** *vt* (a) to deposit. (b) (*fig*) to calm, quieten. **2 sedimentarse** *vr* (a) to settle. (b) (*fig*) to calm down, quieten down.

sedimentario *adj* sedimentary.

sedimento *nm* sediment, deposit.

sedosidad *nf* silkiness.

sedoso *adj* silky, silken.

seducción *nf* (a) (*act*) seduction. (b) (*quality*) seductiveness; charm, allure; lure, fascination.

seducir [3o] **1** *vt* (a) *woman* to seduce.

(b) (*fig*) to lead on, seduce from one's duty; to bribe.

(c) (*fig*) to charm, attract, captivate, fascinate; **seduce a todos con su simpatía** she captivates everyone with her charm; **la teoría ha seducido a muchos** the theory has attracted many people.

2 *vi* to be charming, be fascinating; **es una película que seduce** it's a captivating film.

seductivo *adj* = **seductor 1**.

seductor 1 *adj* (a) seductive. (b) (*fig*) charming, captivating, fascinating; tempting. **2** *nm* seducer.

sefardí 1 *adj* Sephardic. **2** *nmf* Sephardi, Sephardic Jew(ess); **sefardíes** Sephardim (*descendants of the Jews expelled from Spain in 1492*).

segable *adj* corn ready to cut.

segadera *nf* sickle.

segador *nm* harvester, reaper.

segadora *nf* (a) (*person*) harvester, reaper. (b) (*Mech*) mower, reaper, mowing machine; — **de césped** lawnmower.

segadora-atadora *nf* binder.

segadora-trilladora *nf* combine harvester.

segar [1h *and* 1k] *vt* (a) (*Agr*) *corn etc* to reap, cut, harvest; *grass, hay* to mow, cut; *other object* to cut off.

(b) (*fig*) to mow down.

(c) (*fig*) *hopes etc* to ruin, destroy; — **la juventud de uno** to cut someone off in his prime.

seglar 1 *adj* secular, lay. **2** *nm* layman.

segmento *nm* segment; — **de émbolo** piston ring.

segoviano 1 *adj* of Segovia. **2** *nm*, **segoviana** *nf* native (*or* inhabitant) of Segovia; **los** —**s** the people of Segovia.

segregación *nf* (a) segregation; — **racial** racial segregation, apartheid. (b) (*Anat*) secretion.

segregacionista *nmf* segregationist, supporter of racial segregation.

segregar [1h] *vt* (a) to segregate, separate. (b) (*Anat*) to secrete.

seguida *nf* (a) normal way (of doing something); proper rhythm, habitual speed; **coger la** — to get into the swing of it, get into the proper way (of doing something).

(b) **a** — = **seguidamente**; **de** — uninterruptedly, straight off; at once; **en** — at once, right way; **en** — **termino** I've very nearly finished, I shan't be long now; **en** — **tomó el avión para Madrid** he immediately caught the plane to Madrid.

seguidamente *adv* (a) uninterruptedly, straight off, without a break; continuously. (b) immediately after, next; **dijo** — **que** ... he went on at once to say that ...

seguido 1 *adj* (a) *row etc* continuous, unbroken.

(b) *road, route etc* straight.

(c) —**s** consecutive, successive; **5 días** —**s** 5 days running; **5 blancos** —**s** 5 bull's-eyes in a row, 5 consecutive bull's-eyes.

(d) long-lasting; **una enfermedad muy seguida** a very lengthy illness, a long drawn-out illness.

2 *adv* (a) straight; **vaya Vd todo** — just keep straight on; **por aquí** — straight on past here.

(b) after; **ese coche iba primero y** — **el mío** that car was in front and mine was immediately behind it.

seguidor *nm*, **seguidora** *nf* follower; (*Sport*) fan (*fam*), follower, supporter.

seguimiento *nm* chase, pursuit; continuation; **estación de** — tracking station; **ir en** — **de** to go in pursuit of, chase (after).

seguir [3d *and* 3l] **1** *vt* (a) (*general sense*) to follow; to follow on, come next to, come after.

(b) *quarry* to chase, pursue; to hound; *track* to follow; *satellite* to track; *steps* to dog; *clue* to follow up; *woman* to court.

(c) *authority, leader, instruction, inclination, text etc* to follow; *advice* to follow, adopt, take.

(d) *career, course* to follow, pursue.

(e) — **su camino** to continue on one's way.

2 *vi* (a) (*general sense*) to follow; to follow on, come next, come after; **y los que siguen** and the next ones, and those that come next; **como sigue** as follows.

(b) to continue, to carry on, go on; ¡**siga**! go on!; (*Col*) come in!; **siga a la derecha** keep to the right; — **con una idea** to go on with an idea; **sigue en su sitio** it is still in its place; **sigue en Caracas** he is still in Caracas; **seguía en su error** he continued in his error; — **adelante** to go on, carry on; to go straight on; (*Aut*) to drive on, go straight ahead; **siga Vd adelante hasta Toboso** go straight ahead as far as Toboso; — **por un camino** to carry on along a path; **hacer** — **una carta** to forward a letter; ¿**cómo sigue?** how is he?; **sigue bien, que siga Vd bien** I hope you keep well, look after yourself.

(c) (*with adj or n etc*) to be still, go on being; **sigue enfermo** he's still ill; **si el tiempo sigue bueno** if the weather continues fine; **sigue tan misterioso como antes** it's still as mysterious as ever; **sigue soltera** she's still single; **sigue sin poderlo comprar** he is still unable to buy it; **sigo sin comprender** I still don't understand.

(d) — + *ger* to go on + *ger*, keep (on) + *ger*; **sigue lloviendo** it's still raining; **sigue siendo lo mismo** it's still the same, it remains unchanged; **siguió mirándola** he went on looking at her; **siguió sentado** he stayed sitting down, he remained seated.

3 seguirse *vr* (a) to follow; **una cosa se sigue a otra** one thing follows another.

(b) to follow, ensue, happen in consequence; **de esto se sigue que** ..., **síguese que** ... it follows that ...

según 1 *adv* (*fam*) according to circumstances; — **y como**, — **y conforme** it all depends; "¿**lo vas a comprar?**" ... "—" "are you going to buy it?" ... "it all depends".

2 *prep* (a) according to; in accordance with, in line with; — **el jefe** according to the boss; — **este mapa** according to this map; **obrar** — **las instrucciones** to act in accordance with one's instructions; — **lo que dice** from what he says, according to what he says; **iremos o no,** — **el tiempo** we'll go or not, depending on the weather; **eso es** — **el dinero de que se disponga** that depends on what money is available.

(b) **está** — **lo dejaste** it is just as you left it.

3 *conj* as; — **me consta** as far as I know; — **esté el tiempo** depending on the weather; — **que vengan 3 or 4** depending on whether 3 or 4 come.

segunda *nf* (a) (*Mus*) second. (b) second meaning, veiled meaning; **decir algo con** —(**s**) to say something with an implied second meaning.

segundante *nm* (*Boxing*) second.

segundar [1a] **1** *vt* (a) to do again. (b) (*RPl*) *blow* to return. (c) (*Mex*) to earth up. **2** *vi* to come second, be in second place.

segundero *nm* second hand (*of a watch*).

segundo 1 *adj* second.

2 *nm* (a) second; second one; second in authority; (*Naut*) mate; **ser el** — **de a bordo** (*fig*) to be second in command; **sin** — unrivalled.

(b) (*of time*) second.

(c) (*Mex*) —**s** upstairs seats (*in a theatre etc*).

segundón *nm* second son, younger son.

segur *nf* sickle; axe.

seguramente *adv* (a) *know etc* for sure, with certainty.

(b) surely; — **tendrán otro** surely they'll have another, they must have another; "¿**lo va a comprar?**" ... "—" "is he going to buy it?" ... "I should think so".

(c) (*SAm*) probably, possibly.

seguridad *nf* (a) safety; security; safeness; (*Mil, Pol*) security; — **en la carretera** road safety; — **colectiva** collective security; — **contra incendios** fire precautions; — **social** social security; **de** — safety (*attr*), *eg* **cinturón de** — safety belt; **con la mayor** — with (*or* in) complete safety; **para mayor** — to be on the safe side, for safety's sake; **estar en** — to be in a safe place.

(b) certainty; **en la** — **de su victoria** in the certainty of winning, being sure of winning; **con toda** — with complete certainty; **no lo sabemos con** — we don't know for sure; **tener la** — **de que** ... to have the certainty that ..., be sure that ...; **tengan Vds la** — **de que** ... rest assured that ...

(c) (*also* — **en sí mismo**) confidence, self-confidence.

(d) trustworthiness; reliability.

(e) firmness; stability, steadiness.

(f) (*Law*) security, surety.

seguro 1 *adj* (a) safe; secure; **un puerto** — a safe harbour; **está más** — **en el banco** it's safer in the bank; **lo más — es** + *infin* the safest thing is to + *infin*, the best thing is to + *infin*; **conviene atenerse a lo —** it's best to be on the safe side.

(b) *method, result etc* sure, certain; bound to come, certain to happen; **ir a una muerte segura** to go to certain death; **es — que . . .** it is certain that . . .; **en estas investigaciones no hay nada —** nothing is certain in these researches.

(c) *(of person)* sure, certain; **¿estás —?** are you sure?; **estar — de** to be sure of; **estar — de que . . .** to be sure that . . .

(d) **estar — de sí mismo** to be confident, be self-confident, be sure of oneself.

(e) *friend etc* firm, sure, trustworthy; *source* reliable, dependable, trustworthy.

(f) *object* firm; firmly fastened, securely tied *(etc)*; stable, steady; *date etc* firm, definite.

(g) *(SAm)* honest, straight.

2 *adv* (a) for sure; **todavía no lo ha dicho —** he still hasn't said for sure.

(b) **¡—!** sure!, I'm sure it is! *(etc)*.

3 *nm* (a) safety device; *(of lock)* tumbler; *(Mil)* safety catch; *(Tech)* catch, pawl, lock, stop.

(b) *(fig)* safety, certainty, assurance; **a buen —, de —** surely; truly; **en —** in a safe place; **sobre —** safely, without risk; **ir sobre —** to be on safe ground.

(c) *(Comm, Fin)* insurance; **S— de Enfermedad** equivalent to National Health Insurance; **— de incendios** fire insurance; **— social** social insurance, social security; **— contra terceros** third-party insurance; **— a** *(or* **contra) todo riesgo** comprehensive insurance; **— de vida, — sobre la vida** life insurance.

seibó *nm (Col, PR, SD, Ven: angl)* sideboard.
seis 1 *adj* six; *(date)* sixth; **las —** six o'clock. 2 *nm* six.
seiscientos *adj* six hundred.
seísmo *nm* tremor, shock, earthquake.
selección *nf* selection; **—es** *(Lit, Mus)* selections; **— biológica, — natural** natural selection.
seleccionador *nm (Sport)* selector.
seleccionar [1a] *vt* to pick, choose, select.
selectividad *nf* selectivity.
selectivo *adj* selective.
selecto *adj* (a) *(in quality)* select, choice, fine; *club etc* select, exclusive. (b) *(Lit) works* selected.
seltz [selθ,sel]: **agua (de) —** seltzer (water).
selva *nf* forest, woods; jungle.
selvático *adj* (a) woodland *(attr)*, sylvan; *(fig)* rustic. (b) *(Bot etc)* wild.
selvoso *adj* wooded, well-wooded.
sellado 1 *adj* sealed; stamped, franked. 2 *nm* (a) sealing; stamping. (b) *(Arg)* postage, value in stamps.
selladura *nf* (a) seal. (b) *(act)* sealing; stamping.
sello *nm* (a) seal; *(official etc)* stamp; signet; **— de caucho, — de goma** rubber stamp.

(b) impression, mark; stamp; *(Comm)* brand, seal; **— fiscal** revenue stamp; **lleva el — de esta oficina** it carries the stamp of this office.

(c) *(Post)* stamp; **— aéreo** airmail stamp; **— conmemorativo** commemorative stamp; **— de correo** postage stamp; **— de urgencia** express-delivery stamp.

(d) *(Med)* capsule, pill.

(e) *(fig)* hallmark, stamp *(also* **— distintivo); lleva el — de su genialidad** it carries the hallmark of his genius.

semáforo *nm (Naut etc)* semaphore; *(Rail)* signal; *(Aut)* traffic lights.
semana *nf* week; **— inglesa** working week of 5½ days; **— laboral** working week; **S— Santa** Holy Week; **entre —** during the week; **vuelo de entre —** mid-week flight.
semanal *adj* weekly.
semanalmente *adv* weekly, each week.
semanario 1 *adj* weekly. 2 *nm* weekly.
semanero *nm,* **semanera** *nf (SAm)* weekly-paid worker; worker specially engaged for a week's work.
semántica *nf* semantics.
semántico *adj* semantic.
semblante *nm (lit)* face, visage; *(fig)* face, appearance; outlook; aspect; **alterar** *(or* **demudar) el — a uno** to make someone look alarmed, upset someone; **componer el —** to regain one's composure; **mudar de —** to change colour.
semblantear [1a] *vt* (a) *(Chi, Guat, Mex, RPl) person* to look straight in the face, scrutinize the face of. (b) *(Mex)* to study, examine, look at.
semblanza *nf* biographical sketch.
sembradera *nf* seed drill.
sembrado *nm* sown field.

sembrador 1 *nm,* **sembradora** *nf* sower. 2 **sembradora** *nf (Mech)* seed drill.
sembradura *nf* sowing.
sembrar [1k] *vt* (a) *(Agr) field, seed* to sow; **— de** to sow with.

(b) *(Naut)* **— minas en un estrecho, — un estrecho de minas** to mine a strait, lay mines in a strait.

(c) *(fig) objects* to sprinkle, scatter about, spread around; *surface* to sprinkle, strew *(de* with); *discord* to sow; *news* to spread; **el que siembra recoge** one reaps what one has sown.

(d) *(Mex) rider* to throw; to knock down.

sembrío *nm (SAm)* sown field.
semejante 1 *adj* (a) similar; **—s** alike, similar, the same; **— a** like; **es — a ella en el carácter** she is like her in character; **son muy —s** they are very much alike.

(b) *(Math)* similar.

(c) such; **nunca hizo cosa —** he never did such a thing, he never did anything of the kind; **¿se ha visto frescura —?** did you ever see such cheek?

(d) *(Arg, Mex)* huge.

2 *nm* (a) fellow man, fellow creature; **nuestros —s** our fellow men.

(b) **no tiene —** it has no equal, there is nothing to equal it.

semejanza *nf* similarity, resemblance; **a — de** like, as; **— de familia** family likeness; **tener — con** to look like, resemble, bear a resemblance to.
semejar [1a] 1 *vi* to seem like, resemble, seem to be. 2 **semejarse** *vr* to look alike, be similar, resemble each other; **— a** to look alike, resemble.
semen *nm* semen.
semental 1 *adj* stud, breeding *(attr)*. 2 *nm* sire, stud animal.
sementera *nf* (a) sowing. (b) seedtime, sowing season. (c) sown land, sown field. (d) *(fig)* hotbed *(de* of), breeding ground *(de* for).
semestral *adj* half-yearly, biannual.
semestralmente *adv* half-yearly, biannually.
semestre *nm* (a) period of six months; *(US: Univ etc)* semester. (b) *(Fin)* half-yearly payment.
semi . . . semi . . ., half- . . .
semibola *nf (Bridge)* small slam.
semibreve *nf* semibreve.
semicircular *adj* semicircular.
semicírculo *nm* semicircle.
semiconsciente *adj* semiconscious, half-conscious.
semiconsonante *nf* semiconsonant.
semicorchea *nf* semiquaver.
semicualificado *adj* semiskilled.
semicultismo *nm* half-learned word.
semiculto *adj* half-learned.
semicupio *nm (Cu, Guat)* hip-bath.
semidesierto *adj* half-empty.
semidesnudo *adj* half-naked.
semidiós *nm* demigod.
semidormido *adj* half-asleep.
semiexperto *adj* semiskilled.
semifallo *nm (Bridge)* singleton *(a* in).
semifinal *nf* semifinal.
semifinalista *nmf* semifinalist.
semilla *nf* (a) *(Bot)* seed; **— de césped** grass seed. (b) *(Arg, Par)* brad, tack. (c) *(Chi)* baby, child; kids *(collectively; fam)*.
semillero *nm* (a) seedbed; nursery.

(b) *(fig)* hotbed *(de* of), breeding ground *(ae* for); **un — de delincuencia** a hotbed of crime; **la decisión fue un — de disgustos** the decision caused a host of troubles, the decision became a battleground of controversy.

semimedio *nm (Boxing)* welterweight.
seminal *adj* seminal.
seminario *nm* (a) *(Agr)* seedbed; nursery. (b) *(Eccl)* seminary. (c) *(Univ etc)* seminar.
seminarista *nm* seminarist.
semioficial *adj* semi-official.
semiprecioso *adj* semiprecious.
semiseparado *adj* semidetached.
semisótano *nm* semibasement.
semita 1 *adj* Semitic. 2 *nmf* Semite.
semítico *adj* Semitic.
semitono *nm* semitone.
semiverdad *nf* half-truth.
semivocal *nf* semivowel.
sémola *nf* semolina.
sempiterna *nf* evergreen.
sempiterno *adj* everlasting.
sen *nm,* **sena** *nf (Bot, Med)* senna.
Sena *m* Seine.
senado *nm* senate; *(fig)* assembly, gathering.

senador *nm* senator.
senatorial *adj* senatorial.
sencillamente *adv* simply; **es — imposible** it's simply impossible.
sencillez *nf* (a) simplicity, plainness. (b) simplicity, straightforwardness. (c) naturalness, unaffectedness, lack of sophistication; (*pej*) simplicity.
sencillo 1 *adj* (a) (*general sense*) simple, plain, unadorned; *custom, dress, style etc* simple.
  (b) *matter, problem* simple, easy, straightforward; **es muy —** it's very simple.
  (c) *person* natural, unaffected, unsophisticated; (*pej*) simple.
  (d) *flower, thread, ticket etc* single.
  2 *nm* (*SAm*) small change, loose change.
senda *nf* path, track; (*fig*) path; (*Aut*) lane.
sendero *nm* path, track.
sendos *adj pl:* **les dio — golpes** he hit both of them, he gave each of them a blow; **llevaban — sombreros** they both wore hats, each of them wore a hat; **con sendas peculiaridades** with individual peculiarities.
Séneca *m* Seneca.
senectud *nf* old age.
Senegal: El — Senegal.
senegalés 1 *adj* Senegalese. 2 *nm,* **senegalesa** *nf* Senegalese.
senil *adj* senile.
senilidad *nf* senilidad.
seno[1] *nm* (a) (*Anat*) bosom, bust; **—s** breasts; **— frontal** sinus; **— materno** womb; (*fig*) bosom; **en el — de Abrahán** on Abraham's bosom; **morir en el — de la familia** to die in the bosom of one's family; **lo escondió en su —** she hid it in her bosom, she put it down the front of her dress.
  (b) hollow, cavity; (*Naut*) trough (*between waves*).
  (c) (*Geog*) small bay, inlet; gulf.
  (d) (*fig*) refuge, haven.
  (e) (*of club etc*) headquarters.
seno[2] *nm* (*Math*) sine.
sensación *nf* (a) sensation, feeling; sense; feel; **una — de placer** a feeling of pleasure; **tengo una — de inutilidad** I have a feeling of being useless.
  (b) (*fig*) sensation; **causar —, hacer —** to cause a sensation.
sensacional *adj* sensational.
sensacionalismo *nm* sensationalism.
sensacionalista *adj* sensationalist.
sensatamente *adv* sensibly.
sensatez *nf* good sense, sensibleness.
sensato *adj* sensible.
sensibilidad *nf* sensitivity (*a* to), sensitiveness; sensibility; **— artística** artistic feeling, sensitivity to art.
sensibilizado *adj* sensitized; (*Phot*) sensitive.
sensibilizar [1f] *vt* to sensitize.
sensible *adj* (a) *creature* feeling, sentient; sensitive (*a* to); (*Med*) *spot* sensitive, tender, sore; (*Phot*) sensitive; **un aparato muy —** a very sensitive (*or* delicate) piece of apparatus; **una placa — a la luz** a plate sensitive to light; **es muy — a los cambios de temperatura** it is very sensitive to changes in temperature.
  (b) *person* sensitive (*a* to); responsive (*a* to); impressionable, emotional.
  (c) *change etc* perceptible, appreciable, noticeable; *difference etc* tangible, palpable; *blow* heavy; *loss* heavy, considerable; **una — mejoría** a noticeable improvement, a marked improvement.
  (d) **— de** capable of; **— de mejora** capable of improvement, having a capacity for improvement.
  (e) **soy — del honor que se me hace** I am conscious of the honour being done me.
  (f) regrettable, lamentable; **es muy —** it is highly regrettable; **es — que . . .** it is regrettable that . . .
sensiblemente *adv* perceptibly, appreciably, noticeably; markedly.
sensiblería *nf* sentimentality; mushiness, sloppiness; squeamishness.
sensiblero *adj* sentimental; mushy, sloppy; squeamish.
sensitiva *nf* (a) (*Bot*) mimosa. (b) (*fam*) highly sensitive person, delicate flower.
sensitivo *adj* (a) *organ etc* sense (*attr*). (b) *being etc* sentient; sensitive.
sensorio *adj* sensory.
sensual *adj* (a) sensual; sensuous. (b) (*esp SAm*) attractive, alluring, sexy.
sensualidad *nf* sensuality; sensuousness.
sensualismo *nm* sensualism.
sensualista *nmf* sensualist.

sentada *nf* (a) sitting; **de una —, en una —** at one sitting. (b) (*Pol etc*) sit-down (*protest*); sit-in.
sentadera *nf* (*SAm*) seat (*of a chair etc*).
sentadero *nm* seat.
sentado *adj* (a) **estar —** to sit, be sitting (down), be seated; **permanecer —** to remain seated.
  (b) (*fig*) settled, established; firm; **dar algo por —** to take something for granted, assume something; **dejar algo —** to establish something firmly; **dejar — que . . .** to lay down that . . ., have it clearly understood that . . .
  (c) (*fig*) *character* solid, sensible, steady; sedate.
sentador *adj* (*Chi, RPl*) *dress* becoming, smart.
sentadura *nf* mark (*on skin, fruit etc*).
sentar [1k] 1 *vt* (a) *person* to sit, seat.
  (b) *object* to place (firmly), settle (in its place); **— el último ladrillo** to tap the last brick into place; **— las costuras** to press the seams.
  (c) (*Comm*) **— una suma en la cuenta de uno** to put a sum down to someone's account.
  (d) *basis, foundations* (*fig*) to lay, establish, create; *principle* to set up, establish; *precedent* to lay down, set up.
  (e) (*Col, PR*) *person* to crush, squash.
  (f) (*Col*) *horse* to rein in sharply.
  2 *vti* (a) (*of dress etc*) to suit; to fit; to look well on, be becoming to; **ese peinado le sienta horriblemente** that hair style doesn't suit her one little bit, she looks awful with that hairdo (*fam*).
  (b) (*of food*) **— bien a** to agree with; **— mal a** to disagree with; **no me sientan las gambas** prawns disagree with me.
  (c) (*fig*) **— bien** to go down well; **— mal** to go down badly, produce a bad impression; **le ha sentado mal que lo hayas hecho tú** he took it badly that you should do it, he didn't like your doing it.
  3 **sentarse** *vr* (a) (*person*) to sit, sit down; to seat oneself; to settle oneself; **¡siéntese!** (do) sit down, take a seat; **sentémonos aquí** let's sit (down) here; **se sentó a comer** he sat down to eat.
  (b) (*sediment etc*) to settle.
  (c) (*weather etc*) to settle (down); to become steady, stabilize.
  (d) (*Archit*) to settle.
  (e) (*shoes etc*) to leave a mark, rub.
sentencia *nf* (a) (*Law*) sentence; (*fig*) decision, ruling; opinion; **— de muerte** death sentence; **dictar —, pronunciar —** to pronounce sentence.
  (b) (*Lit*) maxim, saying; dictum.
sentenciar [1b] 1 *vt* (a) (*Law*) to sentence (*a* to).
  (b) (*SAm*) **— a uno** to swear vengeance against someone. 2 *vi* to pronounce, give one's opinion.
sentenciosamente *adv* (a) pithily. (b) sententiously; dogmatically.
sentenciosidad *nf* (a) pithiness; oracular nature.
  (b) sententiousness; dogmatism.
sentencioso *adj* (a) *saying* pithy; oracular. (b) *person* sententious; dogmatic.
sentidamente *adv* (a) regretfully. (b) sincerely, with great feeling.
sentido 1 *adj* (a) regrettable; deeply felt; **una pérdida muy sentida** a deeply felt loss, a most regrettable loss.
  (b) *sympathy etc* sincere, deeply felt, keen; **le doy mi más — pésame** I send my deepest sympathy.
  (c) *character* sensitive, tender, easily wounded.
  (d) (*Arg, Mex*) having sharp hearing.
  2 *nm* (a) (*bodily*) sense; **los cinco —s** the five senses; **— del olfato** sense of smell; **— del color** sense of colour; **— del humor** sense of humour; **— de la medida, — de las proporciones** sense of proportion; **— de orientación** sense of direction; **no tiene — del ritmo** he has no sense of rhythm; **sin —** senseless, unconscious; **aguzar el —** to prick up one's ears; **costar un —** (*fam*) to cost the earth; **embargar los —s a uno** to enrapture someone; **perder el —** to lose consciousness; **poner los cinco —s en algo** to give one's whole attention to something; **recobrar el —** to regain consciousness.
  (b) (*fig*) sense; discernment, judgement; **buen —** good sense; **— común** common sense; **tener — para distinguir algo** to have enough sense to distinguish something.
  (c) (*Ling*) sense, meaning; **doble —** double meaning; **— figurado** figurative sense; **en el buen — de la palabra** in the best sense of the word; **en el — amplio** in the broad sense; **en el — estricto** in the strict sense; **en cierto —** in a sense; **en tal —** to this effect; **sin —** meaningless; **cobrar —** to begin to make sense; **no le encuentro ningún —** I can't

make any sense of it; **tener —** to make sense; **no tiene — que lo haga él** it doesn't make any sense for him to do it.

(**d**) (*in reading, for music etc*) feeling; **leer con —** to read with feeling; **tener — a la música** to have a feeling for music.

(**e**) (*Geog*) direction; way; **"— único"** "one way (street)"; **en — contrario, en — opuesto** in the opposite direction, the other way; **algo en este —** (*fig*) something along these lines; **iban en — inverso al nuestro** they were travelling in the opposite direction to us.

(**f**) (*Mex*) ear.

sentimental *adj* (**a**) sentimental; *look* soulful. (**b**) *affair, life etc* love (*attr*); **aventura —** love affair, affair of the heart.

sentimentalismo *nm* sentimentality.

sentimentero *adj* (*Mex, PR*) = **sensiblero.**

sentimiento *nm* (**a**) feeling, emotion, sentiment; **un — de insatisfacción** a feeling of dissatisfaction; **buenos —s** fellow-feeling, sympathy; **herir los —s de uno** to hurt (*or* wound) someone's feelings.

(**b**) sense; **— del deber** sense of duty; **— de la responsabilidad** sense of responsibility.

(**c**) regret, grief, sorrow; **con profundo —** with profound regret; *see* **acompañar.**

sentina *nf* (**a**) (*Naut*) bilge; (*in town*) sewer, drain. (**b**) (*fig*) sink, sewer.

sentir [3i] **1** *vt* (**a**) (*general sense*) to feel; to perceive, sense; to hear (*esp SAm*); to smell; *emotion* to feel; *dignity, responsibility etc* to feel, be aware of, realize; *music, painting etc* to feel, have a feeling for; **— un dolor** to feel a pain; **— el ruido de un coche** to hear the noise of a car; **sin — el frío** without feeling the cold; **— ganas de +** *infin* to feel an urge to + *infin*; **lo siento ajeno a mí** I feel it is foreign to me, I feel detached from it; **siente la profesión como un sacerdocio** he feels the profession like a sacred calling; **dejarse —, hacerse —** to let itself be felt.

(**b**) *illness etc* to feel the effects of, suffer from the aftermath of.

(**c**) to regret, be sorry for; **lo siento** I'm sorry; **¡lo siento muchísimo!, ¡cuánto lo siento!** I'm very sorry!, I'm so sorry!; **sintió profundamente esa pérdida** he felt (*or* regretted, mourned *etc*) that loss deeply; **— que . . .** to regret that . . ., be sorry that . . .; **sentiré que me obligue Vd a venderlo** I shall be sorry if you force me to sell it; **siento no haberlo hecho antes** I am sorry not to have done it before; **siento molestarle** I'm sorry to bother you.

2 *vi* (**a**) to feel; **estaba que ni oía ni sentía** he was in such a state that he could neither hear nor feel anything; **sin —** without noticing, quite inadvertently; imperceptibly, so quickly (*or* smoothly *etc*) that one does not notice.

(**b**) to feel sorry; **dar que —** to give cause for regret.

3 sentirse *vr* (**a**) to feel; **— pesimista** to feel pessimistic; **— herido** (*fig*) to feel hurt; **— mal(o)** to feel ill, feel bad; **— como en su casa** to feel at home; **— en ridículo** to feel ridiculous; **— actor** to feel oneself to be an actor.

(**b**) (*Med*) **— del costado** to have a pain in one's side; **— del paludismo** to suffer from malaria.

(**c**) to be offended, feel resentful (*de* about, at); **— de una observación** to take offence at a remark.

(**d**) (*SAm*) to get cross, get angry; **— con uno** to fall out with someone.

(**e**) (*container, vessel*) to crack.

4 *nm* opinion, judgement; **a mi —, en mi —** in my opinion; **compartir el — de** to share the view of, echo the opinion of.

sentón *nm* (**a**) (*CAm, Mex*) bump on one's bottom, heavy fall. (**b**) (*CAm, Ec*) **dar un —** to rein in suddenly.

seña *nf* (**a**) mark, distinguishing mark; **—s** description; **—s personales** personal description; **las —s son mortales** (*fam*) we know all about that already; **dar las —s de uno** to give a personal description of someone.

(**b**) sign; (*fig*) sign, token; secret sign; (*Mil*) password; **por las —s** so it seems; **por más —s** just to prove it, to clinch matters; into the bargain, moreover; **dar —s de** to show signs of; **hablar por —s** to talk by signs, communicate by means of signs; **hacer una — a uno** to make a sign to someone; **hacer una — a uno para que +** *subj* to signal to someone to + *infin*.

(**c**) (*Post*) **—s** address.

señal *nf* (**a**) sign; symptom; token, indication; **en —**

de as a token of, as a sign of, in sign of; **es buena —** it's a good sign; **dar —es de** to show signs of; **hacer la — de la cruz** to make the sign of the Cross.

(**b**) (*Comm, Fin*) token payment; deposit; pledge; **dejar una suma en —** to leave a sum as a deposit.

(**c**) (*with hand*) sign, signal; **dar la — de** (*or* **para**) to give the signal for; **hacer una — a uno** to make a sign to someone; **hacer una — grosera** to make a rude sign; **al hacerse una — predeterminada** at a prearranged signal.

(**d**) mark; trace, vestige; sign; (*Med*) scar, mark; (*on animal*) mark, marking; brand; (*Geog*) landmark; (*Lit*) bookmark; **sin la menor — de** without the least trace of, without the slightest sign of; **no quedaba ni — there** wasn't the slightest trace of it; **lo hicieron sin dejar —** they did it without leaving a trace.

(**e**) (*Aut, Rail etc*) signal; **— de alto** stop sign; **— de auxilio** distress signal; **— de carretera** road sign; **—es luminosas, —es de tráfico** traffic lights, traffic signals; **— óptica** (*Aut*) trafficator; **— de peligro** danger signal.

(**f**) (*Radio*) signal; **— horario** time signal.

(**g**) (*Tel*) signal, tone; buzz; **— de llamada** calling signal; **— para marcar** dialling tone; **— de ocupado** (*or* **comunicando**) engaged tone, busy signal (*US*).

(**h**) (*SAm*) earmark.

señala *nf* (*Chi*) earmark.

señaladamente *adv* (**a**) especially. (**b**) clearly, plainly.

señalado *adj* (**a**) **estar — como** to be marked down as, be known to be.

(**b**) **dejar — a uno** to scar someone permanently.

(**c**) distinct, clear, plain.

(**d**) *day, favour etc* special; *person* distinguished, notable, (*pej*) notorious.

señalar [1a] **1** *vt* (**a**) to mark; to denote, betoken; **señalan la llegada de la primavera** they announce the arrival of spring; **eso señaló el principio del descenso** that marked the start of the decline.

(**b**) *paper etc* to mark; to stamp; *person* to mark (for life), scar (permanently); (*Med*) to leave a scar on; (*SAm*) *livestock* to brand.

(**c**) *road etc* to put up signs on; *route* to signpost.

(**d**) (*with finger*) to point to, point out, indicate; (*fig*) to show, indicate; (*of clock hand etc*) to show, point to, say; **iba señalando los edificios notables** he went round pointing out the interesting buildings; **tuve que —le varios errores** I had to point out several mistakes to him.

(**e**) (*in conversation*) to allude to; (*pej*) to criticize.

(**f**) *date, price etc* to fix, settle; *task* to set; *person* to appoint; **¿qué precio ha señalado al cuadro?** what price has he put on the picture?; **se negó a —me hora** he refused to offer me an appointment.

2 señalarse *vr* to make one's mark (*como* as); to distinguish oneself (*por* by, by reason of), achieve distinction.

señalero *nm* (*Chi*) signalman.

señalización *nf* signposting; system of signs (*or* signals), signal code.

señalizar [1f] *vt* *road etc* to put up signs on; *route* to signpost.

señor 1 *nm* (**a**) man; gentleman; **le espera un —** there's a gentleman waiting to see you; **es todo un —** he's a real gentleman; **hacer el —** to lord it; **quiere parecer un —** he tries to look like a gentleman.

(**b**) (*of property*) owner, master; (*of servants*) master; (*fig*) master; **el — de la casa** the master of the household; **¿está el —?** is the master in?; **no es — de sus pasiones** he cannot control his passions.

(**c**) (*before proper name*) Mister (*always written* Mr); **es para el Sr Meléndez** it's for Mr Meléndez; **los —es Poblet** the Poblets, Mr and Mrs Poblet; **Señor Don Jacinto Benavente** (*on envelope*) Mr J. Benavente, J. Benavente Esq.

(**d**) (*before professional title: not translated*) **el — alcalde** the mayor; **el — cura** the priest; **el — presidente** the president (*but see* (**e**)).

(**e**) (*in direct address*) sir (*but often not translated*); (*to noble*) my lord; **—es** (*in speech*) gentlemen; **¡mire Vd, —!** look here!; **¡oiga Vd, —!** I say!; **— alcalde** Mr Mayor; **— director . . .** (*to editor*) Dear Sir . . .; **— juez** my lord; **— presidente** Mr Chairman, Mr President; **¡no —!** (*fig*) not a bit of it!, never!, absolutely not!; **¡sí —!** (*fig*) yes indeed!,

I should jolly well think it is! (*fam*), it certainly does! (*etc*); **pues sí** — well that's how it is.

(f) (*Comm etc*) **muy — mío** Dear Sir; **muy —es nuestros** Gentlemen.

(g) (*Hist*) noble, lord; **— feudal** feudal lord; lord of the manor; **— de horca y cuchillo** (*fig*) despot.

(h) (*Rel*) **El S—** The Lord; **Nuestro S—** Our Lord; **S— de los Ejércitos** Lord of Hosts; **recibir al S—** to take communion.

2 *adj* (*fam*) (a) lordly; **un coche muy —** a really lordly car.

(b) real, really big; **una casa para un —** a house for a gentleman who really is a gentleman; **eso es un — melón** now that really is a melon, that's some melon; **fue una señora herida** it was a real big wound.

señora *nf* (a) lady; **— de compañía** chaperon; companion; **le espera una —** there's a lady waiting to see you.

(b) (*of property*) owner, mistress; **¿está la —?** is the mistress in?

(c) wife; **mi —** my wife; **el jefe y su —** the boss and his wife; **la — de Smith** Mrs Smith.

(d) (*in direct address*) madam (*but often not translated*); (*to noble*) my lady; **¡—s y señores!** ladies and gentlemen!; **sí, —** yes, madam; **¡oiga Vd, —!** I say!

(e) (*Comm etc*) **muy — mía** Dear Madam.

(f) (*Rel*) **Nuestra S—** (*to Catholics*) Our Lady, (*to Protestants*) the Virgin (Mary).

señorear [1a] **1** *vt* (a) (*as ruler*) to rule, control; to domineer, lord it over.

(b) (*of building*) to dominate, soar above, tower over.

(c) *passions* to master, control.

2 señorearse *vr* (a) to control oneself.

(b) to adopt a lordly manner.

(c) **— de** to seize, seize control of.

señoría *nf* (a) rule, sway. (b) (*titles*) **su S—** (*also* **vuestra S—**) your lordship, his lordship, your ladyship, her ladyship; my lord, my lady.

señorial *adj*, **señoril** *adj* lordly; aristocratic; noble, majestic, stately.

señorío *nm* (a) (*Hist*) manor, feudal estate; domain.

(b) (*fig*) rule, sway, dominion (*sobre* over).

(c) (*quality*) lordliness; majesty, stateliness.

(d) (*fam*) distinguished people; (*pej*) toffs (*fam*), nobs (*sl*).

señorita *nf* (a) young lady.

(b) (*before proper name*) Miss.

(c) (*in direct address, not translated*) **¿qué busca Vd, —?** what are you looking for?

(d) (*SAm*) schoolteacher.

señorito *nm* (a) young gentleman; (*in servants' parlance*) master, young master. (b) (*pej*) playboy, toff (*fam*), young swell (*fam*).

señorón *nm* (*fam*) big shot (*fam*).

señuelo *nm* (a) decoy. (b) (*fig*) bait, lure. (c) (*Arg, Bol*) leading ox.

separable *adj* separable; (*Mech etc*) detachable, removable.

separación *nf* (a) (*act etc*) separation; division; (*Mech*) removal; (*from post*) removal, dismissal (*de* from); **— del matrimonio** legal separation; **— racial** racial segregation.

(b) gap, distance.

separadamente *adv* separately.

separado *adj* separated; separate; (*Mech*) detached; **vive — de su mujer** he is separated from his wife, he doesn't live with his wife; (*Post*) **por —** separately; individually, one by one; (*Post*) **under separate cover**; **firmar una paz por —** to sign a separate peace.

separador *nm* separator.

separar [1a] **1** *vt* (a) *object* to separate (*de* from); *chair etc* to move away (*de* from), take away, remove; **— un trozo de pan** to put aside a piece of bread.

(b) *fighters etc* to separate, pull apart, keep apart; *syllables, words* to divide; *connection* to sever, cut; *letters etc* to sort (out); **saber — las buenas de las malas** to know how to separate (*or* tell, distinguish) the good ones from the bad; **los negocios le separan de su familia** business keeps him away from his family.

(c) (*Mech*) *part* to detach, remove (*de* from).

(d) *person* (*from post*) to remove, dismiss (*de* from).

2 separarse *vr* (a) (*part*) to come away, detach itself (*de* from); (*parts*) to come apart; (*Pol*) to secede.

(b) (*person*) to leave, go away, withdraw; **— de un grupo** to leave a group; to part company with a group; **se ha separado de todos sus amigos** he has cut himself off from all his friends; **me separé de ella a las 11** I left her at 11; **se ha separado de su mujer** he has left his wife.

(c) (*Law*) to withdraw (*de* from).

separata *nf* offprint.

separatismo *nm* separatism, separatist tendency.

separatista 1 *adj* separatist. **2** *nmf* separatist.

separo *nm* (*Mex*) cell.

sepia *nf* (a) (*Fish*) cuttlefish. (b) (*Art etc*) sepia.

sepsis *nf* sepsis.

septentrión *nm* north.

septentrional *adj* north, northern.

septicemia *nf* septicaemia.

séptico *adj* septic.

se(p)tiembre *nm* September.

séptimo 1 *adj* seventh. **2** *nm* seventh.

septuagenario 1 *adj* septuagenarian, seventy-year-old. **2** *nm*, **septuagenaria** *nf* septuagenarian, person in his (*or* her) seventies.

septuagésimo *adj* seventieth.

séptuplo *adj* sevenfold.

sepulcral *adj* sepulchral; (*fig*) sepulchral, gloomy, dismal.

sepulcro *nm* tomb, grave; (*esp Bib*) sepulchre; **— blanco, — blanqueado** whited sepulchre.

sepultación *nf* (*Chi*) burial.

sepultar [1a] *vt* (a) to bury; (*fig: in mine etc*) to bury, entomb; **quedaban sepultados en la caverna** they were trapped in the cave, they were cut off in the cave.

(b) (*fig*) to hide away, bury, conceal.

sepultura *nf* (a) (*act*) burial; **dar — a** to bury; **dar cristiana — a uno** to give someone a Christian burial; **recibir —** to be buried.

(b) grave, tomb.

sepulturero *nm* gravedigger, sexton.

sequedad *nf* (a) dryness. (b) (*fig*) bluntness; brusqueness, curtness; plainness, bareness (*see* seco).

sequía *nf* (a) drought; dry season. (b) (*Prov, Col*) thirst.

sequiar [1c] *vi* (*Arg: of smoker*) to inhale.

séquito *nm* (a) retinue, suite, entourage.

(b) (*Pol etc*) group of supporters, adherents, devotees.

(c) (*of events*) train; aftermath; **con todo un — de calamidades** with a whole train of disasters.

ser [2w] **1** *vi* (a) (*general sense: absolute, of character, identity etc*) to be; **— o no —** to be or not to be; **es difícil** it's difficult; **él es pesimista** he's a pessimist, he's a pessimist sort; **soy ingeniero** I'm an engineer; **soy yo** it's me, it is I (*lit*); **¡soy Pedro!** (*Tel*) this is Peter, Peter here, Peter speaking; **¿quién es?** who is it?; who's there?; (*Tel*) who's calling?; **es él quien debiera hacerlo** it is he who should do it, he's the one who ought to do it; **¿qué ha sido?** what happened?, what goes on?

(b) (*origin*) **— de** to be from, come from; **ella es de Calatayud** she's from Calatayud; **estas naranjas son de España** these oranges come from Spain; **¿de dónde es Vd?** where are you from?

(c) (*material*) **— de** to be (made) of; **es de piedra** — it is of stone, it is made of stone, it's a stone one.

(d) (*possession*) **— de** to belong to; **éste es suyo** this is his; **el parque es del municipio** the park belongs to the town; **esta tapa es de otra caja** this top belongs to another box; **¿de quién es este lápiz?** whose is this pencil?, who does this pencil belong to?

(e) (*destination*) **¿qué será de mí?** what will become of me?; **¿qué ha sido de él?** what has become of him?, what happened to him?

(f) (*appropriateness*) **esas finuras no son para mí** those niceties are not for me; **ese coche no es para correr mucho** that car isn't made to go very fast; **esa manera de hablar no es de una dama** that talk does not come well from a lady, one does not expect to hear a lady say such things.

(g) (*time of day*) **es la una** it is one o'clock; **son las 7** it is 7 o'clock; **serán las 8** it would be about 8 o'clock; **serían las 9 cuando llegó** it would have been about 9 when he arrived; *see* hora *etc*.

(h) (*special use of imperfect: in games*) **yo era la reina** pretend I was the queen, let's pretend I'm the queen.

(i) (*special use of preterite: of offices*) **presidente que fue de Ruritania** ex-president of Ruritania, former(ly) president of Ruritania.

(j) (*as equivalent to estar*) **soy en todo con Vd**

I entirely agree with you, I'm with you all the way; **en un momento soy con Vd** I'll be with you in a moment.

(**k**) (— de + infin) **es de creer que** . . . it may be assumed that . . .; **es de desear que** . . . it is to be wished that . . .; **es de esperar que** . . . it is to be hoped that . . .; **era de ver** it was worth seeing, you ought to have seen it.

(**l**) (idioms with indicative) **siendo así que** . . . since . . .; **¡o somos o no somos!** (fam) let's get on with it!, make your minds up!; **érase que se era** once upon a time; **a no — por** but for; were it not for, had it not been for; **a no — que** . . . unless . . .; **¡ahí fue ella!** what a row there was!, you should have heard the fuss!; **¿cómo es que** . . .? how is it that . . .?, how does it happen that . . .? **¡cómo ha de ser!** what else do you expect!; **hizo como quien es** he acted as one might expect, he did what one could expect of him; **con — ella su madre** even though she is his mother, despite the fact that she's his mother; **de no — esto así** if it were not so, were it not so.

(**m**) (idioms with subjunctive) **¡sea!** agreed!, all right!; **o sea** . . . that is to say . . ., or rather . . .; **sea . . . sea** . . . either . . . or, whether . . . or whether; **sea lo que sea** (or **fuere**) be that as it may; **no sea que** . . . lest . . ., for fear that . . .; **hable con algún abogado que no sea Pérez** speak to some lawyer other than Pérez, consult any lawyer you like except Pérez.

2 v aux used to form passive: **fue construido** it was built; **ha sido asaltada una joyería** there has been a raid on a jeweller's; **será fusilado** he will be shot; **está siendo estudiado** it is being examined.

3 nm being; life; essence; — **humano** human being; — **imaginario** imaginary being; **S—Supremo** Supreme Being; — **vivo** living creature, living organism; **la que le dio su** — she who gave him life, she who brought him into the world; **en lo más íntimo de su** — in his inmost being, deep within himself.

sera nf pannier, basket.

seráficamente adv angelically, like an angel.

seráfico adj (**a**) angelic, seraphic. (**b**) (fam) poor, humble.

serafín nm (**a**) seraph; (fig) angel; cherub. (**b**) (Ven) fastener.

serbal nm, **serbo** nm service tree.

serenamente adv (**a**) calmly, serenely. (**b**) peacefully, quietly.

serenar [1a] **1** vt (**a**) to calm; to quieten, pacify. (**b**) (liquid) to clarify.
2 vi (Col) to drizzle.
3 serenarse vr (**a**) (person etc) to calm down, grow calm; to compose oneself. (**b**) (sea) to grow calm; (weather) to clear up. (**c**) (liquid) to clear, settle.

serenata nf serenade.

serenera nf (CAm, Col, Ven) cape, wrap.

serenero nm headscarf.

serenidad nf (**a**) calmness, serenity. (**b**) peacefulness, quietness.

sereno 1 adj (**a**) person calm, serene, unruffled. (**b**) weather settled, fine; sky cloudless, clear. (**c**) atmosphere calm, peaceful, quiet. (**d**) (fam) **estar** — to be sober.
2 nm (**a**) night dew, night dampness; **dormir al** — to sleep out in the open; **le perjudica el** — the night air is harmful to her. (**b**) night watchman.

serial nm serial; — **radiofónico** radio serial.

seriamente adv seriously.

sericultura nf silk raising, sericulture.

serie nf series (also Bio, Elec, Math); set, sequence, succession; (Lit, Radio etc) series, serial; **una inacabable de** an endless series of; **arrollado en** — (Elec) series-wound; **fabricación en** — mass production; **fabricar en** — to mass-produce; **casas construidas en** — mass-produced houses, prefabricated houses; **matanzas en** — mass murders; **fuera de** — out of order, not in the proper sequence; (fig) special; **artículos fuera de** — (Comm) goods left over, remainders, remnants.

seriedad nf (**a**) seriousness; gravity, solemnity; staidness; **hablar con** — to speak seriously, speak in earnest. (**b**) dignity; properness; seriousness, (sense of) responsibility; **falta de** — frivolity; irresponsibility. (**c**) (in business etc) reliability, dependability, trustworthiness; straightness, honesty; fair-mindedness. (**d**) (of crisis etc) gravity, seriousness.

serio adj (**a**) person, attitude, expression etc serious; grave, solemn; staid; **ponerse** — to look serious, adopt a solemn expression (etc); **se quedó mirándome muy** — he looked at me very seriously, he stared gravely at me; **pareces muy** — you're looking very serious.
(**b**) person, attitude etc dignified; proper; serious, responsible; **el negro es el único color** — **para esto** black is the only proper colour for this; **un traje** — a formal suit; **poco** — undignified; frivolous, not to be taken seriously; **es una persona poco seria** he's an irresponsible sort, he's rather a silly individual.
(**c**) (in business etc) person reliable, dependable, trustworthy; responsible; fair-minded; deal, dealing straight, honest; **poco** — unreliable; irresponsible; **es una casa seria** it's a reliable firm.
(**d**) book, study etc serious.
(**e**) crisis, illness, loss etc grave, serious; **esto se pone** — this is getting serious.
(**f**) **en** — seriously; **hablo perfectamente en** — I'm perfectly serious, I'm in dead earnest; **tomar un asunto en** — to take a matter seriously.

sermón nm sermon (also fam); **el S— de la Montaña** the Sermon on the Mount.

sermonear [1a] (fam) **1** vt to lecture, read a lecture to. **2** vi to sermonize.

sermoneo nm (fam) lecture, sermon.

sernambí nm (Bol, Col, Ven) inferior rubber.

serón nm pannier, large basket.

seroso adj serous.

serpa nf (Bot) runner.

serpenteante adj (fig) winding, twisting; meandering.

serpear [1a] vi, **serpentear** [1a] vi (**a**) (Zool) to wriggle; to creep. (**b**) (fig: of road) to wind, snake, twist and turn; (of river) to wind, meander.

serpenteo nm (**a**) wriggling; creeping. (**b**) (fig) winding, twisting; meandering.

serpentín nm coil.

serpentina nf (**a**) (Min) serpentine. (**b**) (of paper) streamer.

serpentino adj snaky, sinuous; winding, meandering; serpentine.

serpiente nf snake; serpent; — **boa** boa constrictor; — **de cascabel** rattlesnake; — **de mar** sea serpent; — **pitón** python; — **de vidrio** slow worm.

serpol nm thyme.

serpollo nm sucker, shoot.

serrado adj serrated; toothed; jagged, uneven, rough.

serraduras nfpl sawdust.

serrallo nm seraglio, harem.

serranía nf mountainous area, hilly country; range of mountains.

serraniego adj = serrano.

serrano 1 adj (**a**) (Geog) highland (attr), hill (attr), mountain (attr). (**b**) (fig) coarse, rustic. (**c**) **partida serrana** dirty trick. **2** nm highlander.

serrar [1k] vt to saw (off, up).

serrería nf sawmill.

serrín nm sawdust.

serrote nm (Mex) = serrucho.

serruchar [1a] vt (SAm) to saw (off, up).

serrucho nm (**a**) saw, handsaw. (**b**) (Cu) whore. (**c**) (Col, Cu) **al** — by halves; fifty-fifty. (**d**) (Ant, Col) **hacer un** — to split the cost.

Servia f Serbia.

servible adj serviceable, usable.

servicial 1 adj helpful, obliging. **2** nm (Bol, Col) servant.

servicio nm (**a**) (general sense) service; **a su** — at your service; **al** — **de** in the service of; **estar al** — **de** to be in the service of; **estar al** — **del gobierno** to be on government service; **estar de** — to be serviceable, be in service; **entrar en** — to come into service; **tiene 8 camiones en** — he has 8 lorries in service; **hacer un** — **para uno** to do someone a service; **hacer un flaco** — **a uno** to do someone an ill turn, play a dirty trick on someone.
(**b**) (Mil etc) service; — **activo** active service; — **militar** military service; — **apto para el** — fit for military service; **en condiciones de** — operational; **estar de** — to be on duty; **beber estando de** — to drink while on duty; **prestar** — to serve, see service (de as).
(**c**) (individual —s) — **aduanero**, — **de aduana** customs service; — **de asistencia**, — **de atención**, — **post-venta** after-sales service; — **de contra-espionaje** secret service; — **doméstico** domestic service; domestic help; (persons) servants; — **a**

domicilio delivery service; "— a domicilio" "we deliver"; — de incendios fire service; — de información (Mil) intelligence service; — médico medical service; —s postales postal services; —s públicos public services; — secreto secret service; —s sociales social services; welfare work; — de transportes transport service.

(d) (Cook etc) service, set; — de café coffee set; — de mesa set of dishes; — de tocador toilet set.

(e) (euph: esp SAm) lavatory; chamberpot.

(f) —s (of house) services; (euph) sanitation; "todos —s" "all main services".

(g) (Eccl) service; — divino divine service.

(h) (in hotel etc) service, service charge.

(i) (Tennis) serve, service.

servidor nm, **servidora** nf (a) servant; un — (referring to speaker or writer) my humble self; your humble servant; aquí tiene un — para lo que se le ofrezca I am always at your service, please count on me for whatever it may be; ¡— de Vd! at your service!

(b) (in class etc) ¡—! present!

(c) (formulae in letters) su seguro —, atento y s.s. (= seguro servidor) yours faithfully.

servidumbre nf (a) servitude; — de la gleba serfdom.

(b) (fig) compulsion.

(c) (Law) obligation; — de paso right of way.

(d) (persons) servants, staff.

servil adj (a) slave (attr), serf's; work etc menial. (b) attitude etc servile; obsequious, grovelling; imitation etc slavish.

servilismo nm servility; obsequiousness; slavishness.

servilla nf slipper, pump.

servilleta nf serviette, napkin.

servilletero nm serviette ring.

servio 1 adj Serbian. 2 nm, **servia** nf Serb. 3 nm (language) Serbo-Croat.

servir [31] 1 vt (a) (general sense) to serve; to do a favour to, oblige; — a Dios to serve God; — a la patria to serve one's country; dígame en qué puedo —le tell me in what way I can be of service, tell me how I can help you; para —le at your service; ser servido de + infin to be pleased to + infin.

(b) diners to wait on, serve.

(c) (Comm) customer to serve; order to attend to, fill; ¿ya le sirven, señora? are you being attended to, madam?

(d) (Cook) food to serve (out or up); — patatas a uno to serve someone with potatoes, help someone to potatoes; la cena está servida dinner is served; — vino a uno to pour out wine for someone.

(e) post to hold, fill; duties to carry out.

(f) gun to man; machine to tend, mind, man.

(g) (Tennis etc) to serve.

2 vi (a) (general sense) to serve; (of servant) to be in service; sirvió 10 años he served 10 years, he did 10 years; está sirviendo (Mil) he's doing his military service; para — a Vd at your service.

(b) (at table) to serve, wait (a at, on).

(c) to serve (de as, for); to be of use, be useful; eso no sirve that's no good, that won't do; — en lugar de to do duty for; — de guía to act as guide, serve as a guide; no sirve de nada que vaya él it's no use his going; — para to be good for, be used for; no sirve para nada it's no use at all, it's utterly useless; él no sirve para nada he's a dead loss; yo no serviría para futbolista I shouldn't be any good as a footballer.

(d) (Cards) — del palo to follow suit.

3 servirse vr (a) (at table) to serve oneself, help oneself; se sirvió patatas he helped himself to potatoes; se sirvió café he poured himself some coffee; ¡sírvete más! have some more!; ¿no se sirve más guisantes? wouldn't you like more peas?

(b) — de algo to make use of something, use something; to put something to use.

(c) — + infin to be kind enough to + infin; to deign to + infin, condescend to + infin; sírvase sentarse please sit down; si la señora se sirve pasar por aquí if madam would care to come this way.

servocroata 1 adj Serbo-Croatian. 2 nmf Serbo-Croatian. 3 nm (language) Serbo-Croat.

sésamo nm sesame; ¡— ábrete! open sesame!

sesear [1a] vt to pronounce c (before e, i) and z [θ] as [s] (a feature of Andalusian and much SAm pronunciation).

sesenta adj sixty; sixtieth.

sesentón 1 adj sixty-year old, sixtyish. 2 nm, sesentona nf person of about sixty.

seseo nm pronunciation of c (before e, i) and z [θ] as [s].

sesera nf (Anat) brainpan; (fam) brains, intelligence.

sesgado adj slanted, slanting, oblique; leaning; awry, askew.

sesgar [1h] vt (a) to slant, slope, place obliquely; to put askew, twist to one side.

(b) (Sew) to cut on the slant, cut on the bias; (Tech) to bevel.

(c) (Aut) to cut across, cut in on.

sesgo nm (a) slant, slope; warp, twist, twisted position; (Sew) bias; (Tech) bevel; estar al — to be aslant, be awry; cortar algo al — to cut something on the bias.

(b) (fig) direction; twist, turn; ha tomado otro — it has taken a new turn.

(c) (fam) dodge.

sésil adj sessile.

sesión nf (a) (Parl etc) session, sitting, meeting; — secreta secret session; abrir la — to open the meeting; levantar la — to close the meeting, adjourn.

(b) (Theat) show, performance; — de espiritismo séance; — de prestidigitación conjuring show, exhibition of conjuring; — de lectura de poesías poetry reading.

(c) (Cine) showing; — continua continuous showing; iremos a la segunda — we'll go to the second house; hay 3 —es diarias there are 3 showings a day.

sesionar [1a] vi to sit; to be in session; to hold a meeting.

seso nm (a) (Anat) brain; —s (Cook) brains.

(b) (fig) brains, sense, intelligence; calentarse los —s, devanarse los —s to rack one's brains; perder el — to go off one's head (por over); eso le tiene sorbido el — he's crazy about it.

sesquipedal adj sesquipedalian.

sestear [1a] vi to take a siesta, have a nap.

sesteo nm (SAm) siesta, nap.

sesudamente adv sensibly, wisely.

sesudo adj (a) sensible, wise. (b) brainy. (c) (Chi) stubborn.

set nm, pl set or sets (Tennis) set.

seta nf (a) mushroom. (b) (tabu) vagina.

setecientos adj seven hundred.

setenta adj seventy; seventieth.

setentón 1 adj seventy-year old, seventyish. 2 nm, setentona nf person of about seventy.

setiembre nm September.

seto nm (a) fence; — vivo hedge. (b) (PR, SD) wall, partition.

seudo ... pseudo ...

seudónimo 1 adj pseudonymous. 2 nm pseudonym; pen name, nom de plume.

severamente adv (a) severely, harshly; strictly. (b) severely; grimly, sternly.

severidad nf (a) severity, harshness; strictness; stringency. (b) severity; grimness, sternness.

severo adj (a) character etc severe, harsh; discipline strict; critic, punishment harsh; parent etc strict, harsh; conditions harsh, stringent; ser — con uno to be hard on someone, treat someone harshly.

(b) winter etc severe, harsh, hard; cold bitter.

(c) expression severe; grim, stern; dress, style etc severe.

seviche nm = cebiche.

Sevilla Seville.

sevillano 1 adj Sevillian. 2 nm, sevillana nf Sevillian.

sexagenario 1 adj sexagenarian, sixty-year old. 2 nm, sexagenaria nf sexagenarian, person in his (or her) sixties.

sexagésimo adj sixtieth.

sexar [1a] vt chicks to sex.

sexo nm sex; el bello — the fair sex; el — débil the gentle sex; el — femenino the female sex; el — masculino the male sex; de ambos —s of both sexes; sin — sexless.

sexología nf sexology.

sexólogo nm sexologist.

sextante nm sextant.

sexteto nm sextet(te).

sexto 1 adj sixth. 2 nm sixth.

séxtuplo adj sixfold.

sexual adj sexual; sex (attr); vida — sex life.

sexualidad nf (a) sexuality. (b) sex; determinar la — de to determine the sex of.

sexualmente adv sexually.

sexy nm (false angl) sex appeal.

shock [ʃok] nm, pl shock or shocks [ʃok] (angl) shock.

si *conj* (a) if; — **lo quieres te lo doy** if you want it I'll give it to you; — **me lo pedía se lo daba** if he asked me for it I gave it to him; — **me lo hubiese pedido se lo hubiera dado** if he had asked me for it I would have given it to him; — **lo sé te lo digo** (*fam*) if I had known about it I would have told you.

(b) if, whether; **me pregunto** — **vale la pena** I wonder whether (*or* if) it's worth the trouble; **no sé** — **hacerlo o no** I don't know whether to do it or not; **hablaban de** — **hacerlo o no** they were talking about whether to do it or not; **que** — **lavar los platos, que** — **limpiar el suelo, que** . . . what with washing up and sweeping the floor and . . .

(c) (*idioms etc*) — **no** if not; otherwise, or else; **¿— vendrá?** I wonder if he'll come?; **¿— será verdad?** what if it's true?; **¿— nos lo roban?** what if someone steals it?, suppose it gets stolen?; **lleva un revólver por** — **resulta útil** he carries a gun in case it should come in handy; **¡— fuera verdad!** if only it were true!; **¡— viniese pronto!** I wish he'd come!; **¡— no sabía que estabas allí!** but I didn't know you were there!; **¡— es el cartero!** why, it's the postman!

sí[1] **1** *adv* (a) yes; indeed, certainly; **él no quiere pero yo** — he doesn't want to but I do; **ellos no van pero nosotros** — they aren't going but we are; **—, pero menos** (*iro*) that's a bit much, that's pushing things a bit; **creo que** — I think so; **¡que —, hombre!** I tell you it is! (*etc*); **está de que** — (*fam*) he seems likely to agree; **¡(pues) — que estoy yo para bromas!** (*iro*) I should say I'm in the mood for jokes!; **por** — **o por no** in any case, just in case; **porque** — because that's the way it is; because I say so; **lo hizo porque** — he did it because he just felt like doing it; he did it because he thought it had to be done; (*pej*) he did it out of sheer cussedness; **una semana** — **y otra no** in alternate weeks, every other week.

(b) (*emphatic*) **ella** — **vendrá** she will certainly come, she is sure to come; **ellos** — **tienen uno** they certainly have one; **¡— que lo es!** I'll say it is!, you're dead right there!; **¡eso** — **que no!** never!, not on your life!

2 *nm* consent, agreement; **dar el** — to agree, consent; (*of woman*) to accept a proposal; **todavía no tengo el** — I have not yet received his consent, he still hasn't said yes.

sí[2] *reflexive pron* (*used after preps*) (a) (*sing: m*) himself, (*f*) herself, (*of thing*) itself, (*relating to* Vd) yourself, (*used generally*) oneself; (*pl*) themselves, (*relating to* Vds) yourselves; — **mismo** himself *etc*; **lo quieren todo para** — they want the whole lot for themselves; **no lo podrá hacer por** — **solo** he won't be able to do it by himself; **conviene guardarlo para** — it's best to keep it to oneself; **se ríe de** — **misma** she laughs at herself.

(b) (*reciprocal*) each other; **cambiaron una mirada entre** — they exchanged a look, they gave each other a look.

(c) (*idioms*) **de** — in itself; spontaneously; **el problema es bastante difícil de** — the problem is difficult enough in itself; **de por** — in itself; per se; separately, individually; **estar en** — to be in one's right mind; **pensar entre** —, **pensar para** — to think to oneself; **estar fuera de** — to be beside oneself; **estar sobre** — to be on one's guard; to be puffed up with conceit; *see* **decir, volver** *etc*.

Siam *m* Siam.

siamés 1 *adj* Siamese. **2** *nm*, **siamesa** *nf* Siamese.

sibarita 1 *adj* sybaritic, luxury-loving; epicurean. **2** *nmf* sybarite, lover of luxury; epicure, bon vivant.

sibarítico *adj* sybaritic, luxury-loving; epicurean.

sibaritismo *nm* sybaritism, love of luxury; epicureanism.

Siberia *f* Siberia.

siberiano 1 *adj* Siberian. **2** *nm*, **siberiana** *nf* Siberian.

sibil *nm* cave; vault, underground store; cornstorage pit.

Sibila *f* Sibyl.

sibila *nf* sibyl.

sibilante 1 *adj* sibilant. **2** *nf* sibilant.

sibilino *adj* sibylline.

sic . . . = **psic** . . ., *eg for* **sicología** *see* **psicología**.

sicalipsis *nf* eroticism, suggestiveness; pornography.

sicalíptico *adj* erotic, suggestive; pornographic.

Sicilia *f* Sicily.

siciliano 1 *adj* Sicilian. **2** *nm*, **siciliana** *nf* Sicilian. **3** *nm* (*dialect*) Sicilian.

sicofante *nm* sycophant.

sicomoro *nm*, **sicómoro** *nm* sycamore.

sicote *nm* (Ant, CR), **sicotera** *nf* (Ant) smell of dirty feet.

sidecar ['saikar] *nm* (*angl*) sidecar.

sideral *adj*, **sidéreo** *adj* astral, sidereal; space (*attr*).

siderurgia *nf* iron and steel industry.

siderúrgico *adj* iron and steel (*attr*); **la siderúrgica** iron and steel works.

sidra *nf* cider.

siega *nf* (a) reaping, harvesting; mowing. (b) harvest (time).

siembra *nf* (a) sowing; **patata de** — seed potato. (b) sowing time.

siembre *nm* (Ven) sowing.

siempre 1 *adv* (a) always; all the time; ever; **como** — **as usual**, as always; **la hora de** — the usual time; **somos amigos de** — we're old friends; **es lo de** — it's the same thing as it always is, it's the same old story; **lo vienen haciendo así desde** — they've always done it this way; **para** —, **por** — for ever; for good (and all); **por** — **jamás** for ever and ever.

(b) (SAm) certainly, for sure; (Mex) — **no** certainly not; — **sí** indeed yes, of course.

2 *conj*: — **que** . . . (a) (+ *indic*) whenever; each time that . . ., as often as . . .

(b) (+ *subj*) provided that . . .

sien *nf* (Anat) temple.

siena *nf* sienna.

sierpe *nf* snake, serpent.

sierra *nf* (a) (Tech) saw; — **de arco para metales** hacksaw; — **de calados** fretsaw; — **circular** circular saw; — **de espigar** tenon saw; — **mecánica** power saw; — **de vaivén** jigsaw.

(b) (Geog) mountain range, sierra; **van a la** — **a pasar el fin de semana** they're off to the mountains for the weekend.

Sierra *f* **Leona** Sierra Leone.

siervo *nm*, **sierva** *nf* slave; — **de la gleba** serf.

siesta *nf* (a) hottest part of the day, afternoon heat.

(b) siesta, nap; **dormir la** —, **echarse una** —, **tomar una** — to have one's afternoon nap, have a doze.

siete[1] **1** *adj* seven; (*date*) seventh; **las** — seven o'clock; **hablar más que** — to talk nineteen to the dozen. **2** *nm* seven.

siete[2] *nm* (SAm: *euph*) arse (*tabu*).

sietecueros *nm*, *pl* **sietecueros** (SAm) gumboil, whitlow.

sífilis *nf* syphilis.

sifilítico 1 *adj* syphilitic. **2** *nm*, **sifilítica** *nf* syphilitic.

sifón *nm* (a) (Tech) trap, U-bend; siphon. (b) siphon (of soda water); **whisky con** — whisky and soda.

siga *nf* (Chi) pursuit, chase; **ir a la** — **de** to chase after.

sigilo *nm* secrecy; discretion; (*pej*) stealth; slyness; — **sacramental** secrecy of the confessional; **con mucho** — with great secrecy.

sigilosamente *adv* secretly; discreetly; (*pej*) stealthily, slyly.

sigiloso *adj* secret; discreet; (*pej*) stealthy, sly.

sigla *nf* symbol; abbreviation; acronym, *set of initials pronounced as a word* (*eg* NATO, CAMPSA).

siglo *nm* (a) century; **S—** **de las Luces** Age of Enlightenment (*18th century*); — **de oro**, — **dorado** (*Myth*) golden age; **S—** **de Oro** Golden Age (*Spain: about 1492-1650*); **los —s medios** the Middle Ages.

(b) (*fig*) age, time, times.

(c) (*fig*) age(s); **hace un** — **que no le veo** I haven't seen him for ages.

(d) (Rel) **por los —s de los —s** world without end.

(e) (Eccl) **el** — the world; worldly affairs; **retirarse del** — to withdraw from the world, become a monk.

signar [1a] **1** *vt* (a) to seal; to put one's mark on.

(b) to sign.

(c) (Rel) to make the sign of the cross over.

2 signarse *vr* to cross oneself.

signatario 1 *adj* signatory. **2** *nm* signatory.

signatura *nf* (a) (Mus, Typ) signature. (b) (*of library*) catalogue number, press mark.

significación *nf* significance.

significado 1 *adj* well-known; outstanding.

2 *nm* significance; (*of word etc*) meaning; **su** — **principal es** . . . its chief meaning is . . .; **una palabra de** — **dudoso** a word of uncertain meaning.

significante *adj* (*esp* SAm) significant.

significar [1g] **1** *vt* (a) to mean; to signify (*also fig*); **¿qué significa "nabo?"** what does "nabo" mean?; **5 dólares significan muy poco para él** 5 dollars doesn't mean much to him; **significará la ruina de la sociedad** it will mean the ruin of the company; **él no significa gran cosa en estos asuntos** he doesn't count for much in these matters.

(b) to make known, express (*a* to); **le significó**

la condolencia de la familia **real** he expressed (or conveyed) the royal family's sympathy.

2 significarse vr (**a**) to become known, make a name, become famous (or notorious); — **como** to become known as, be recognized as.

(**b**) **no** — to refuse to take sides.

significativamente adv significantly; meaningly.

significativo adj significant; glance etc meaning, expressive; **es** — **que** ... it is significant that ...

signo nm (**a**) (in most senses) sign; (Math) sign, symbol; (of illiterate) mark; — **de admiración** exclamation mark; — **de la cruz** sign of the Cross; — **igual** equals sign; — **de interrogación** question mark; — (**de**) **más**, — **de sumar** plus sign; — (**de**) **menos** minus sign; — **positivo** positive sign; — **de puntuación** punctuation marks; — **del zodíaco** sign of the zodiac.

(**b**) (fig) quantity; tendency; **una situación de** — **alentador** an encouraging situation; see **mercado**.

sigo etc see **seguir**.

siguetear [1a] vti (Per) = **seguir**.

siguiente adj following; next; **dijo lo** — he said the following; **¡que pase el** —! next please!; **el día** — the following day, next day.

sílaba nf syllable.

silabario nm spelling book.

silabear [1a] vt to syllabicate, divide into syllables; to pronounce syllable by syllable.

silabeo nm syllabication, division into syllables.

silábico adj syllabic.

silba nf hissing, catcalls; **armar una** —, **dar una** — (**a**) to hiss.

silbar [1a] **1** vt (**a**) tune to whistle; whistle etc to blow.

(**b**) speaker, play etc to hiss.

2 vi (**a**) (Mus) to whistle; (Anat) to wheeze; (of wind) to whistle; (of bullet) to whistle, whine; (of arrow etc) to whizz, swish, hum.

(**b**) (Theat etc) to hiss, catcall, boo.

silbatina nf (Chi, Per, RPl) hissing.

silbato nm whistle.

silbido nm, **silbo** nm whistle, whistling; hiss; wheeze; whine, whizz, swish, hum; — **de oídos** ringing in the ears.

silenciador nm silencer.

silenciar [1b] vt (**a**) event etc to hush up; fact etc to keep silent about, pass over in silence. (**b**) person etc to silence. (**c**) (Tech) to silence.

silencio 1 nm (**a**) silence; quiet, hush; ¡—! silence!, quiet!; — **administrativo** policy of doing nothing about a matter; **en** — in silence; **en el** — **más absoluto** in dead silence; **entregar algo al** — to cast something into oblivion; **guardar** — to keep silent, say nothing (sobre about); **había un** — **sepulcral** it was as quiet as the grave; **imponer** — **a uno** to make someone be quiet; to force someone to remain silent; **mantener el** — **radiofónico** to keep radio silence; **pasar algo en** — to pass over something in silence; **reducir al** — person to silence, reduce to silence; guns to silence.

(**b**) (Mus) rest.

2 adj (CAm, Ec, Mex) silent, quiet; still.

silenciosamente adv silently, quietly; soundlessly; noiselessly.

silencioso 1 adj silent, quiet; soundless; machine silent, noiseless. **2** nm silencer, muffler.

silense adj of Silos, of Santo Domingo de Silos (Riojan monastery).

sílex nm silex, flint.

sílfide nf sylph (also fig).

silfo nm sylph.

silicato nm silicate.

sílice nf silica.

silíceo adj siliceous.

silicio nm silicon.

silicosis nf silicosis.

silo nm (Agr) silo; underground store; storage pit.

silogismo nm syllogism.

silogístico adj syllogistic.

silueta nf silhouette; (of building) outline; (of city) skyline; (of person) figure; (Art) silhouette, outline drawing.

silvático adj = **selvático**.

silvestre adj (Bot) wild; (fig) rustic, rural.

silvicultor nm forestry expert.

silvicultura nf forestry.

silla nf (**a**) seat; chair; — **alta** high chair; — **de balanza**, — **de hamaca** (SAm) rocking chair; — **eléctrica** electric chair; — **de manos** sedan chair; — **plegadiza**, — **de tijera** folding chair, folding stool, camp stool; — **de ruedas** wheelchair; **calentar la** — to stay too long, overstay one's welcome.

(**b**) (also — **de montar**) saddle.

sillar nm block of stone, ashlar.

sillería nf (**a**) chairs, set of chairs; seating; (Eccl) choir stalls. (**b**) chairmaker's workshop. (**c**) (Archit) masonry.

sillero nm (**a**) chairmaker. (**b**) (Arg) horse, mule.

silleta nf (**a**) small chair; (SAm) seat, chair; (SAm) low stool. (**b**) (Med) bedpan.

sillico nm chamberpot; commode.

sillín nm saddle.

sillita nf small chair; — **de ruedas** pushchair.

sillón 1 adj (Chi, RPl, SD) saddle-backed.

2 nm (**a**) armchair; easy chair; (SAm) rocking chair; — **de lona** deckchair; — **de orejas** wing chair; — **de ruedas** wheelchair.

(**b**) woman's saddle, sidesaddle.

sima nf abyss, chasm; pit; deep fissure, pothole.

Simbad m Sinbad; — **el marinero** Sinbad the sailor.

simbar [1a] vt (Arg) to plait.

simbiosis nf symbiosis.

simbólicamente adv symbolically.

simbólico adj symbolic(al); token.

simbolismo nm symbolism.

simbolista 1 adj symbolist. **2** nmf symbolist.

simbolizar [1f] vt to symbolize; to represent, stand for, be a token of; to typify.

símbolo nm symbol; — **de los apóstoles**, — **de la fe** Creed; — **de prestigio** status symbol.

simetría nf symmetry; (fig) harmony.

simétricamente adv symmetrically; (fig) harmoniously.

simétrico adj symmetrical; (fig) harmonious.

símico adj = **simiesco**.

simiente nf seed.

simiesco adj simian, apish.

símil 1 adj similar. **2** nm comparison; (Lit) simile.

similar adj similar.

similitud nf similarity, resemblance, similitude.

similor nm pinchbeck; **de** — (fig) showy but valueless; fake, sham.

simiñaca nf (Cu) tangle, complicated affair.

Simón m Simon.

simonía nf simony.

simpatía nf (**a**) liking; affection; — **hacia**, — **por** liking for; —**s y antipatías** likes and dislikes; **coger** — **a uno** to take to someone, take a liking to someone; **ganarse la** — **de todos** to win everybody's affection, come to be well liked by everybody; **tener** — **a** to like; **no le tenemos** — **en absoluto** we don't like him at all; **no tiene** —**s en el colegio** nobody at school likes him, he has no friends at school.

(**b**) (of atmosphere etc) friendliness, warmth, congeniality; (of person, place etc) charm, attractiveness, likeableness; **la famosa** — **andaluza** that well-known Andalusian charm.

(**c**) fellow feeling; mutual support, solidarity, sympathy; **mostrar su** — **por** to show one's support for, show one's solidarity with.

(**d**) (angl) sympathy, compassion.

simpático adj person nice, likeable, genial, pleasant; kind; charming, attractive; atmosphere etc congenial, agreeable; **¡qué policía más** —! what a nice policeman!; **no le hemos caído muy** —**s** she didn't much take to us; **siempre procura hacerse** — he's always trying to ingratiate himself; **me es** — **ese muchacho** I like that lad.

simpatizante nmf sympathizer (de with).

simpatizar [1f] vi (**a**) (of 2 persons) to get on (well together); **pronto simpatizaron** they hit it off at once, they soon became friends.

(**b**) — **con** to get on well with, take to, hit it off with; to be congenial to.

simplada nf (CAm, Col) simplicity, stupidity; stupid thing (to do etc).

simple 1 adj (**a**) simple; uncomplicated, unadorned, bare; (Chem, Gram etc) simple; (Bot) single; method etc simple, easy, straightforward.

(**b**) (preceding n) mere; pure; sheer; alone; **por** — **descuido** through sheer (or pure) carelessness; **es cosa de una** — **plumada** it's a matter of a mere stroke of the pen; **me basta con tu** — **palabra** your word alone is good enough for me.

(**c**) (preceding n) ordinary; **un** — **soldado** an ordinary soldier.

(**d**) person simple, simple-minded, innocent; gullible; (pej) foolish, silly.

2 nm (**a**) (person) simpleton.

(**b**) (Col) liquor.

(**c**) —**s** (Bot) simples.

(**d**) —**s** (Tennis) singles.

simplemente adv (**a**) simply. (**b**) simply, merely; purely.

simpleza *nf* (a) *(quality)* simpleness, simple-mindedness; gullibility; *(pej)* foolishness.
(b) *(una —)* silly thing (to do *etc*); **—s** nonsense.
(c) *(fig)* trifle, small thing; **se contenta con cualquier —** she's happy with any little thing.
simplicidad *nf (all senses)* simplicity, simpleness.
simplificable *adj* simplifiable.
simplificación *nf* simplification.
simplificar [1g] *vt* to simplify.
simplón 1 *adj* simple, gullible. **2** *nm,* **simplona** *nf* simple soul, gullible person.
simplote = **simplón.**
simposio *nm* symposium.
simulación *nf* simulation; make-believe; *(pej)* pretence.
simulacro *nm* (a) simulacrum; image, idol. (b) semblance; sham, pretence; **un — de ataque a** mock attack; **un — de combate** a sham fight.
simulado *adj* simulated; feigned; mock, sham.
simular [1a] *vt* to simulate; to feign, sham.
simultáneamente *adv* simultaneously.
simultanear [1a] *vt:* **— dos cosas** to do two things simultaneously; **— A con B** to contrive to do A at the same time as B, fit in A and B at the same time, synchronize A and B; **jugar con 16 tableros simultaneados** *(Chess)* to play 16 boards simultaneously.
simultaneidad *nf* simultaneity.
simultáneo *adj* simultaneous.
simún *nm* sandstorm.
sin 1 *prep* (a) without; with no . . .; apart from, not counting, not including; **— nosotros** without us; **costó 5 dólares — los gastos de envío** it cost 5 dollars not counting postage and packing; **salió — sombrero** he went out without a hat *(or* hatless); **me he quedado — cerillas** I've run out of matches; **— protección contra el sol** with no protection against the sun.
(b) **— + infin** without + *ger, eg* **— verlo** without seeing it; **— verlo yo** without my seeing it; *(often translated by* un *prefix* + *ptp, eg)* **— lavar** unwashed, **— pagar** unpaid.
2 — que *conj* without + *ger*; **— que lo sepa él** without his knowing; **entraron — que nadie les observara** they came in without anyone seeing them.
sinagoga *nf* synagogue.
sinalefa *nf* elision.
sinalefar [1a] *vt* to elide.
sinapismo *nm* (a) *(Med)* mustard plaster; **hay que ponerle un — ** *(fam)* he needs shaking up, you'll have to give him a jolt.
(b) *(fam)* bore; nuisance, pest.
sinceramente *adv* sincerely.
sincerarse [1a] *vr* to vindicate oneself; **— a, — con** to open one's heart to; to square oneself with, give a full explanation to; **— ante el juez** to justify one's conduct to the judge; **— de su conducta** to explain one's conduct, justify one's conduct.
sinceridad *nf* sincerity; **con toda —** in all sincerity.
sincero *adj* sincere.
síncopa *nf* (a) *(Ling)* syncope. (b) *(Mus)* syncope, syncopation.
sincopar [1a] *vt* to syncopate.
síncope *nm* (a) *(Ling)* syncope. (b) *(Med)* syncope; fainting fit, queer turn.
sincronía *nf* synchronous character; simultaneity.
sincrónico *adj* synchronous; *(Tech)* synchronized; *events etc* simultaneous, coincidental; *(Ling)* synchronic.
sincronismo *nm* synchronism; simultaneity; *(of dates etc)* coincidence.
sincronización *nf* synchronization.
sincronizar [1f] *vt* to synchronize *(con* with).
síncrono *adj* synchronous.
sindical *adj* union *(attr),* trade-union *(attr); (Pol)* syndical.
sindicalismo *nm* trade(s) unionism; *(Pol)* syndicalism.
sindicalista 1 *adj* union *(attr),* trade-union *(attr); (Pol)* syndicalist. **2** *nmf* trade(s) unionist; *(Pol)* syndicalist.
sindicar [1g] **1** *vt workers* to unionize, form into a trade(s) union.
2 sindicarse *vr (worker)* to join a union; *(workers)* to form themselves into a union.
sindicato *nm* (a) syndicate. (b) trade(s) union, labor union (US).
síndico *nm* trustee; *(Law)* official receiver.
síndrome *nm* syndrome.
sinécdoque *nf* synecdoche.
sinecura *nf* sinecure.
sinfín *nm* = **sinnúmero.**

sinfonía *nf* (a) symphony. (b) *(Ven)* harmonica.
sinfónico *adj* symphonic; **orquesta sinfónica** symphony orchestra.
Singapur Singapore.
singar [1h] *vt (Cu)* to bother, annoy.
singladura *nf (Naut)* day's run; nautical day *(from noon to noon).*
singuisarra *nf (Col, Ven)* row, shindy.
singular 1 *adj* (a) *(Gram)* singular.
(b) **combate —** single combat.
(c) *(fig)* outstanding, exceptional; *(pej)* singular, peculiar, odd.
2 *nm (Gram)* singular; **en —** in the singular; *(fig)* **en —** in particular; **se refiere a él en —** it refers to him in particular; **que hable él en —** let him speak solely for himself.
singularidad *nf* singularity, peculiarity, oddity.
singularizar [1f] **1** *vt* to single out; to refer specifically to.
2 singularizarse *vr* to distinguish oneself, stand out, excel; to be conspicuous; **— con uno** to single someone out for special treatment.
singularmente *adv* (a) singularly, peculiarly, oddly.
(b) especially.
sinhueso *nf (fam)* tongue; **soltar la —** to shoot one's mouth off *(fam).*
siniestrado *nm,* **siniestrada** *nf* victim (of an accident *etc),* person who has suffered a loss *(or* damage).
siniestro 1 *adj* (a) *(lit)* left.
(b) *(fig)* sinister; ominous; evil, malign.
(c) *(fig)* fateful, disastrous.
2 *nm* natural disaster, catastrophe, calamity; accident; **— marítimo** shipwreck, disaster at sea.
siniquitate *nm (PR, Ven)* fool.
sinnúmero *nm:* **un — de** a great many, no end of, a huge number of.
sino[1] *nm* fate, destiny.
sino[2] *conj* (a) but; **no son 8 — 9** there are not 8 but 9; **no cabe otra solución — que vaya él** there is no other solution but that he should go; **no lo hace sólo para sí — para todos** he's not doing it only for himself but for everybody.
(b) except, save; only; **todos aplaudieron — él** everybody except him applauded; **no te pido — una cosa** I ask only *(or* but) one thing of you; **no deseo — verte** my sole wish is to see you; **no lo habría dicho — en broma** he could only have said it jokingly, he wouldn't have said it except as a joke.
sino . . . Chinese . . ., Sino . . .
sínodo *nm* synod.
sinonimia *nf* synonymy.
sinónimo 1 *adj* synonymous *(con* with). **2** *nm* synonym.
sinopsis *nf, pl* **sinopsis** synopsis.
sinóptico *adj* synoptic(al).
sinrazón *nf* wrong, injustice, outrage.
sinsabor *nm* (a) trouble, unpleasantness. (b) *(of mind)* sorrow; uneasiness, worry.
sinsílico *adj (Mex)* stupid.
sinsombrerismo *nm* hatlessness, custom of going hatless.
sinsonte *nm* mockingbird.
sinsustancia *nmf (fam)* idiot.
sintáctico *adj* syntactic(al).
sintaxis *nf* syntax.
síntesis *nf, pl* **síntesis** synthesis.
sintéticamente *adv* synthetically.
sintético *adj* synthetic(al).
sintetizar [1f] *vt* to synthesize.
síntoma *nm* symptom; sign, indication.
sintomático *adj* symptomatic.
sintonía *nf* (a) *(Elec)* syntomy; *(Radio)* tuning. (b) *(Mus, Radio)* signature tune.
sintonización *nf (Radio)* tuning.
sintonizar [1f] *vt* (a) *(Elec)* to syntonize; *(Radio) station* to tune (in) to, pick up.
sinuosidad *nf* (a) sinuosity; waviness. (b) bend, curve, wave; **las —es del camino** the windings of the road, the bends in the road.
sinuoso *adj* (a) *road etc* winding, sinuous; *line* wavy; *course* devious. (b) *person, means etc* devious.
sinusitis *nf* sinusitis.
sinvergonzón *nm (fam)* rotter, bounder *(fam).*
sinvergüencería *nf* (a) *(quality)* villainy; rottenness, caddishness; shamelessness. (b) *(act)* = **sinvergüenzada.**
sinvergüenza *nmf* (a) scoundrel, villain, rascal; rotter, cad; **¡—!** *(hum)* you villain! (b) shameless person.
sinvergüenzada *nf (SAm)* villainous trick, rotten thing (to do) *(fam).*

sinvergüenzura nf (SAm) shamelessness.
Sión m Zion.
sionismo nm Zionism.
sionista 1 adj Zionist. **2** nmf Zionist.
sipo adj (Ec) pockmarked.
sipotazo nm (CAm) slap, punch.
siqu ... = psiqu ..., eg for siquiatría see psiquiatría.
siquiera 1 adv **(a)** at least; **una vez — once** at least, just once; **dame un abrazo —** at least give me a hug; **deja — trabajar a los demás** at least let the others work.
  (b) ni —, ni ... — not even, not so much as; **ni él — vino** not even he came; **ella ni me miró —** she didn't even look at me.
  2 conj **(a)** even if, even though; **ven — sea por pocos días** do come even if only for a few days.
  (b) — venga, — no venga whether he comes or not.
Siracusa Syracuse.
sirena nf **(a)** siren; mermaid; **— de la playa** bathing beauty. **(b)** (Tech) siren, hooter; **— de buque** ship's siren; **— de niebla** foghorn.
sirga nf towrope.
sirgar [1h] vt to tow.
Siria f Syria.
sirimba nf (Cu) faint, fainting fit.
sirimbo adj (Cu) silly.
sirimbombo adj (Cu) weak; cowardly, timid.
Sirio m Sirius.
sirio 1 adj Syrian. **2** nm, **siria** nf Syrian.
siró nm (PR), **sirope** nm (SAm: angl) syrup.
sirsaca nf seersucker.
sirte nf shoal, sandbank.
sirvienta nf servant, maid.
sirviente nm servant; waiter.
sisa nf **(a)** petty theft; dishonest profit (made by a servant); **—s** pilfering, petty thieving. **(b)** (Sew) dart; armhole.
sisal nm sisal; sisal plant.
sisar [1a] vt **(a)** to thieve, pilfer, filch; person to cheat; account to cheat on. **(b)** (Sew) to put darts in, take in.
sisear [1a] vti to hiss.
siseo nm hiss(ing).
Sísifo m Sisyphus.
sísmico adj seismic.
sismo nm = **seísmo.**
sismografía nf seismography.
sismógrafo nm seismograph.
sismología nf seismology.
sisón[1] **1** adj thieving, light-fingered. **2** nm, **sisona** nf petty thief.
sisón[2] nm (Orn) little bustard.
sistema nm system; method; **— de calefacción** heating (system); **— impositivo, — tributario** taxation, tax system; **— nervioso** nervous system; **— pedagógico** educational system; teaching method; **— rastreador** (in space research) tracking system; **trabajar con —** to work systematically, work methodically; **yo por — lo hago así** I make it a rule to do it this way.
sistemáticamente adv systematically.
sistemático adj systematic.
sistematización nf systematization.
sistematizar [1f] vt to systematize.
sitiador nm besieger.
sitial nm seat of honour; ceremonial chair.
sitiar [1b] vt to besiege, lay siege to; (fig) to surround, hem in.
sitio nm **(a)** place; spot; part; site, location; **— real** royal residence; **en cualquier —** anywhere; **en todos los —s** everywhere, all over; **en el mejor — de la ciudad** in the best part of the city; **cambiar de —** to shift, move; **cambiar de — con uno** to change places with someone; **dejar a uno en el —** to kill someone (on the spot); **poner a uno en su —, volver a uno a su —** (fig) to put someone firmly in his place; **quedarse en el —** to die instantly, die on the spot.
  (b) room, space; **¿hay —?** is there any room?; **hay — de sobra** there's plenty of room; **hacer —** to make room (a uno for someone).
  (c) (Mil) siege; **en estado de —** in a state of siege; under martial law; **levantar el —** to raise the siege; **poner a —** to besiege.
  (d) (Arg, Chi, Guat) building site, vacant lot.
  (e) (Cu, Mex) small farm.
  (f) (SAm) taxi rank.
sito adj situated, located (en at, in).
situación nf situation, position; (social) position, standing; **— económica** financial position; **crearse una —** to attain a position of financial security,

make good; **estar en — de + infin** to be in a position to + infin.
situado adj **(a)** situated, placed. **(b)** (Fin) **estar —** to be financially secure, be well placed.
situar [1e] vt **(a)** to place, put, set; building etc to locate, situate, site; (Mil) to post, station; **sitúan esta etapa en el siglo XIII** they place this stage in the 13th century; **esto le sitúa entre los mejores** this places him among the best.
  (b) (Fin) money to place, invest; to bank; grant etc to set aside; to assign, earmark; **— una pensión para uno** to settle an income on someone; **ha venido situando fondos en el extranjero** he has been placing money in accounts abroad.
siútico adj (Chi) = **cursi.**
siutiquería nf (Chi) = **cursilería.**
slam [ez'lam] nm (Bridge: angl) slam; **gran —** grand slam; **pequeño —** little slam.
slip [ez'lip] nm, pl **slips** [ez'lip] (angl) briefs, pants; (SAm) bathing trunks.
slogan [ez'loɣan] nm, pl **slogans** [ez'loɣan] (angl) slogan.
smoking [ez'mokin] nm, pl **smokings** [ez'mokin] (false angl) dinner jacket, tuxedo (US).
snack [ez'nak] nm, pl **snacks** [ez'nak] (angl) snack; snack bar.
snob [ez'noβ] etc see **esnob** etc.
so[1] prep under; see **capa** etc.
so[2] interj **(a)** whoa! **(b)** (SAm) quiet!, shut up! **(c)** (PR) shoo!
so[3] as interj (contraction of señor): **¡— indecente!** you swine!; **¡— burro!** you idiot!, you great oaf!
soba nf **(a)** kneading. **(b)** (fam) slap, punch; hiding; **dar — a uno** to wallop someone. **(c)** (fam) telling-off.
sobacal adj underarm (attr).
sobaco nm (Anat) armpit; (Sew) armhole.
sobado adj **(a)** worn, shabby; rumpled, crumpled, messed up; book well-thumbed, dog-eared.
  (b) (fig) subject well-worn.
  (c) (Cook) pastry short.
  (d) (Chi) big, huge.
sobador nm **(a)** (Col, Mex) bonesetter; quack. **(b)** (Ec, Mex, Per, PR) flatterer.
sobajar [1a] vt **(a)** to crush, rumple, mess up. **(b)** (Ec, Mex, Ven) to humiliate.
sobajear [1a] vt (SAm) to handle; to squeeze, press; to mess up.
sobandero nm (Col, Ven) bonesetter; quack.
sobaquera nf **(a)** (Sew) armhole. **(b)** shoulder holster. **(c)** (CAm, Mex, PR) underarm odour.
sobaquina nf underarm odour.
sobar [1a] **1** vt **(a)** material to handle, finger, dirty (with one's fingers); dress etc to crush, rumple, crumple, mess up; dough to knead; putty etc to squeeze (in the hands), soften; muscle to massage, rub.
  (b) person to fondle, feel (amorously); (pej) to finger, paw, lay hands on.
  (c) (SAm) bones to set.
  (d) (Col) to skin, flay.
  (e) (fam) to wallop.
  (f) to pester; to annoy.
  (g) (Ec, Mex, Per, PR) to flatter.
  (h) (Guat etc) to tell off.
  2 sobarse vr (lovers) to pet, fondle, cuddle.
sobasquera nf (CAm, Mex, PR) = **sobaquina.**
soberanamente adv (fig) supremely.
soberanía nf sovereignty.
soberano 1 adj **(a)** (Pol etc) sovereign.
  (b) (fig) supreme.
  (c) (fam) real, really big; **una soberana paliza** a real walloping.
  2 nm, **soberana** nf sovereign; **los —s** the king and queen, the royal couple.
soberbia nf **(a)** pride; haughtiness, arrogance. **(b)** (fig) magnificence, grandeur, pomp. **(c)** anger; irritable nature.
soberbio adj **(a)** proud; haughty, arrogant. **(b)** (fig) magnificent, grand, superb; **¡—!** splendid! **(c)** angry; irritable. **(d)** (fam) = **soberano** (c).
sobijo nm **(a)** (CAm, Col, Pan) = **soba. (b)** (Col) skinning, flaying.
sobijón nm (CAm) = **sobijo.**
sobón adj **(a)** too free with one's hands, given to pawing; (fig) fresh, too familiar by half; lovers mushy, spoony (fam).
  (b) lazy, workshy.
  (c) (Per) soapy.
sobornable adj bribable, venal.
sobornar [1a] vt to bribe, suborn; to buy off; (hum) to get round.

soborno nm (a) (un —) bribe; (el —) bribery, graft.
 (b) (Arg, Bol, Chi) extra load; extra, bonus.
sobra nf (a) excess, surplus; —s leavings, left-overs, scraps; (Sew) remnants.
 (b) de — spare, surplus, extra; **aquí tengo de —** I've more than enough here, I've got plenty (and to spare) here; **tuvo motivos de —** he had plenty of justification, he was more than justified; **lo sé de —** I know it only too well; **aquí estoy de —** I'm not needed here; I'm in the way here.
sobradamente adv too; amply; over...; know only too well; **con eso queda — satisfecho** he is only too happy with that, with that he is more than fully satisfied.
sobradero nm overflow pipe.
sobradillo nm penthouse.
sobrado 1 adj (a) more than enough; superfluous; excessive; superabundant; **hay tiempo —** there's plenty of time; **tuvo razón sobrada** he was amply justified; **sobradas veces** repeatedly.
 (b) **estar — de algo** to have more than enough of something, be well provided with something.
 (c) wealthy; **no anda muy —** he's not very well off.
 (d) bold, forward.
 (e) (Chi) colossal.
 2 adv too, exceedingly.
 3 nm (a) attic, garret.
 (b) (Arg) kitchen shelf.
 (c) (Andalusia, Chi) —s left-overs.
sobrancero adj unemployed.
sobrante 1 adj spare, remaining, extra, surplus; **worker** redundant.
 2 nm (a) surplus, remainder; (Comm, Fin) surplus; balance in hand.
 (b) —s odds and ends.
 3 nmf redundant worker, person made redundant.
sobrar [1a] **1** vt to exceed, surpass.
 2 vi to remain, be left (over), be to spare; to be more than enough; to be superfluous; **por este lado sobra** there's too much on this side; **no es que sobre talento** it's not that there's a surplus of talent; **todo lo que has dicho sobra** all that you've said is quite unnecessary; **nos sobra tiempo** we have plenty (or lots, heaps) of time; **al terminar me sobraba medio metro** I had half a metre left over when I finished; **veo que aquí sobro** I see that I'm not needed here; I see that I'm in the way.
sobre[1] nm envelope; **— de primer día (de circulación)** first-day cover; **— de paga** pay packet; **— de sellos** packet of stamps; **— de té** tea bag.
sobre[2] prep (a) (of place) on, upon; on top of; over, above; **está — la mesa** it's on the table; **volamos — Cádiz** we're flying over Cadiz; **prestar juramento — la Biblia** to swear on the Bible.
 (b) (of quantity etc) over, over and above; more than; (of addition) in addition to, on top of, besides; **un aumento — el año anterior** an increase over last year; **10 dólares — lo estipulado** 10 dollars over and above what was agreed; **— todas mis obligaciones hay una nueva** on top of all my duties here comes another; **crimen — crimen** crime upon crime; **— ser traidor es asesino** in addition to being a traitor he is a murderer.
 (c) **estar — uno** (fig) to keep on at someone; to keep constant watch over someone.
 (d) (of loan etc) on; **un préstamo — una propiedad** a loan on a property; **un tributo — las medias** a tax on stockings.
 (e) (of numbers) about; **— las 6** at about 6 o'clock; **ocupa — 20 páginas** it fills about 20 pages, it fills about 20 pages, it occupies roughly 20 pages.
 (f) (of proportions) in, out of; **3 — 100** 3 in a 100, 3 out of every 100.
 (g) (of subject) about, on; **un libro — Tirso** a book about Tirso.
sobre... super..., over...
sobreabundancia nf superabundance, overabundance.
sobreabundante adj superabundant, overabundant.
sobreabundar [1a] vi to superabound (en in, with), be very abundant.
sobrealimentado adj (Mech) supercharged.
sobrealimentador nm supercharger.
sobrealimentar [1a] vt (a) person etc to overfeed. (b) (Mech) to supercharge.
sobreañadir [3a] vt to give in addition, add (as a bonus); to superinduce.
sobrecalentar [1k] vt to overheat.
sobrecama nm bedspread.
sobrecarga nf (a) extra load; excess weight; (fig) new burden.

 (b) (Comm) surcharge; (Post) surcharge, overprint(ing); **— de importación** import surcharge.
 (c) rope.
sobrecargar [1h] vt (a) lorry etc to overload; (Elec) to overcharge; person to weigh down, overburden; **— el mercado** (Arg) to glut the market.
 (b) (Comm) to surcharge; (Post) to surcharge, overprint (de with).
sobrecargo nm (Naut) supercargo, purser.
sobreceño nm (a) frown. (b) (Archit) lintel.
sobreceño nm frown.
sobrecoger [2c] **1** vt to startle, take by surprise; to scare, frighten.
 2 sobrecogerse vr (a) to be startled, start (a at, de with); to get scared, be frightened.
 (b) to be overawed (de by); **— de emoción** to be overcome with emotion.
sobrecubierta nf outer cover; (of book) jacket.
sobredicho adj aforementioned.
sobredorar [1a] vt to gild; (fig) to gloss over.
sobre(e)ntender [2g] **1** vt to understand; to guess, deduce, infer.
 2 sobre(e)ntenderse vr: **aquí se sobre(e)ntienden dos palabras** here two words are understood; **se sobre(e)ntiende que...** it is implied that..., one infers that...
sobre(e)stimación nf overestimate.
sobre(e)stimar [1a] vt to overestimate.
sobre(e)xcitación nf overexcitement.
sobre(e)xcitado adj overexcited.
sobre(e)xcitar [1a] **1** vt to overexcite. **2 sobre(e)xcitarse** vr to get overexcited.
sobre(e)xponer [2r] vt to overexpose.
sobre(e)xposición nf (Phot) overexposure.
sobrefunda nf (CAm) pillowslip.
sobregirar [1a] vti to overdraw.
sobregiro nm overdraft.
sobrehumano adj superhuman.
sobreimpresión nf (Post) overprint(ing).
sobreimprimir [3a] vt (Post) to overprint.
sobrellevar [1a] vt burden to carry, help to carry, help with; another's burden to ease; illness, disaster, troubles etc to bear, endure; another's faults to be tolerant towards.
sobremanera adv exceedingly.
sobremarca nf (Bridge) overbid; raise (in a suit).
sobremarcha nf (Aut) overdrive.
sobremesa nf (a) table cover.
 (b) dessert.
 (c) sitting on after a meal; **charla de —** after-dinner speech; **conversación de —** table talk; **un cigarro de —** an after-dinner cigar, a postprandial cigar; **hablaremos de eso de —** we'll talk about that after dinner.
sobrenadar [1a] vi to float.
sobrenatural adj supernatural; weird, unearthly; **lo —** the supernatural; **ciencias —es** occult sciences; **vida —** life after death.
sobrenombre nm by-name, extra name; nickname.
sobrentender etc see **sobre(e)ntender** etc.
sobrepaga nf extra pay, bonus; rise, raise (US).
sobreparto nm confinement; **dolores de —** after-pains; **morir de —** to die in childbirth.
sobrepasar [1a] vt to exceed, surpass, outdo; limit to exceed; hope etc to surpass; competitor, record to beat; runway (Aer) to overshoot.
sobrepelo nm (RPl) saddlecloth.
sobrepelliz nf surplice.
sobrepeso nm extra load; excess weight.
sobrepoblación nf overcrowding.
sobreponer [2r] **1** vt (a) to put on top (en of), superimpose (en on), add (en to).
 (b) **— A a B** to give A preference over B, give more weight to A than to B.
 2 sobreponerse vr (a) to master oneself, pull oneself together; to win through, pull through, overcome adversity (etc).
 (b) **— a una enfermedad** to pull through an illness; **— a un rival** to triumph over a rival; **— a un enemigo** to overcome an enemy; **— a un susto** to get over a fright, recover from a fright.
sobreprecio nm surcharge; increase in price.
sobreproducción nf overproduction.
sobrepuesto adj added, superimposed.
sobrepujar [1a] vt to outdo, excel, surpass; **sobrepuja a todos en talento** he excels all the rest in talent.
sobrero adj extra, spare.
sobresaliente 1 adj (a) projecting; overhanging.
 (b) (fig) outstanding, excellent; (Univ etc) mark first class.
 2 nmf substitute; (Theat) understudy.
 3 nm (Univ etc) first class (mark), distinction.

sobresalir [3r] *vi* (a) to project, jut out; to overhang; to stick out, protrude; to stick up, stand up.
　(b) (*fig*) to stand out, be outstanding, excel.
sobresaltar [1a] **1** *vt* to startle, scare, frighten. **2 sobresaltarse** *vr* to start, be startled (*con, de* at).
sobresalto *nm* start; scare; sudden shock; **de —** suddenly.
sobresanar [1a] *vi* (*Med*) to heal superficially; (*fig*) to conceal itself, hide its true nature.
sobrescrito *nm* address; superscription.
sobreseer [2e] **1** *vt*: **— una causa** (*Law*) to stop a case, rule that a case should not continue. **2** *vi*: **— de** to desist from, give up.
sobresello *nm* double seal.
sobrestante *nm* foreman, overseer; site manager.
sobresueldo *nm* = **sobrepaga**.
sobretasa *nf* surcharge.
sobretiro *nm* (*Mex*) offprint.
sobretodo *nm* overcoat.
sobrevalorar [1a] *vt* to overvalue.
sobrevenir [3s] *vi* to happen (unexpectedly), come up, supervene; to follow, ensue.
sobreviviente = **superviviente**.
sobrevivir [3a] *vi* to survive; **— a** *disaster etc* to survive; *person* to survive, outlive; to outlast.
sobrevolar [1m] *vt* to fly over, overfly.
sobriedad *nf* soberness; moderation, restraint; quietness; plainness.
sobrina *nf* niece.
sobrino *nm* nephew.
sobrio *adj* sober; moderate, temperate, restrained; *colour* quiet; *style etc* plain, sober; **ser — en la bebida** to be temperate in one's drinking habits; **ser — de palabras** to speak with restraint.
sobros *nmpl* (*CAm*) leavings, scraps.
soca[1] *nf* (a) (*Bol*) young shoots of rice; (*Ec*) top leaf of tobacco plant, high-quality tobacco. (b) (*CAm*) drunkenness.
soca[2] *nm* (*fam*): **hacerse el —** to act dumb (*fam*).
socaire *nm* (*Naut*) lee; **al —** to leeward; **al — de** (*fig*) enjoying the protection of; **using . . . as an excuse; estar** (*or* **ponerse**) **al —** (*fig*) to shirk.
socaliña 1 *nf* craft, cunning; clever persistence. **2** *nmf* (*fam*) twister (*fam*), swindler.
socaliñar [1a] *vt* to get by a swindle.
socaliñero *adj* crafty, cunning; cleverly persistent.
socapa *nf* (*fam*) dodge, subterfuge; **a —** surreptitiously.
socapar [1a] *vt* (*Bol, Ec, Mex*): **— a uno** to cover up for someone.
socar [1g] **1** *vt* (*CAm*) (a) to press down, squeeze, compress.
　(b) (*fig*) to annoy, upset.
　2 socarse *vr* (*CAm*) (a) to get drunk.
　(b) **— con uno** to fall out with someone, get into a fight with someone.
socarrar [1a] *vt* to scorch, singe.
socarrón *adj* (a) sarcastic, ironical; *humour* sly. (b) crafty, cunning.
socarronería *nf* (a) sarcasm, irony; sly humour. (b) craftiness, cunning.
socava *nf*, **socavación** *nf* undermining.
socavar [1a] *vt* (a) to undermine; to dig under, dig away; (*of water*) to hollow out. (b) (*fig*) to sap, undermine.
socavón *nm* (a) (*Min*) gallery, tunnel; hollow; cavern; (*in street*) hole. (b) (*Archit etc*) subsidence, sudden collapse.
sociabilidad *nf* sociability, friendliness; gregariousness; conviviality.
sociable *adj person* sociable, friendly; *animal* social, gregarious; *gathering etc* convivial.
sociablemente *adv* sociably; gregariously; convivially.
social *adj* (a) social. (b) (*Comm, Fin*) company (*attr*), company's.
socialdemócrata *nmf* social democrat.
socialdemocrático *adj* social-democratic.
socialismo *nm* socialism.
socialista 1 *adj* socialist(ic). **2** *nmf* socialist.
socialización *nf* socialization; nationalization.
socializar [1f] *vt* to socialize; to nationalize.
socialmente *adv* socially.
sociedad *nf* (a) (*in general*) society; **los males de la — actual** the ills of contemporary society; **la — benéfica** the welfare state; **la — opulenta** the affluent society; **hacer —** to join forces.
　(b) society, association; body; **— científica, — docta** learned society; **— inmobiliaria** building society; **S— de Jesús** Society of Jesus; **S— de las Naciones** League of Nations; **— secreta** secret society; **— de socorro mutuo** friendly society, provident society.

　(c) (*Comm, Fin*) company; partnership; **— anónima** limited liability company, corporation; **Góngora y Quevedo S— Anónima** (*abbr* SA) Góngora and Quevedo Limited (Incorporated US); **— de cartera, — de control** holding company; **— mercantil** company, trading company.
　(d) society; **alta —, buena —** (high) society; **notas de —** gossip column, column of society news; **entrar en —, presentarse en (la) —** to come out, make one's début.
socio *nm*, **socia** *nf* (a) associate; (*of club*) member; (*of learned society etc*) fellow; **se ruega a los señores —s . . .** members are asked to . . .; **— honorario, — de honor** honorary member; **— de número** full member.
　(b) (*Comm, Fin*) partner; **— comanditario, — pasivo** sleeping partner, silent partner (US).
socioeconómico *adj* socioeconomic.
sociología *nf* sociology.
sociológico *adj* sociological.
sociólogo *nm* sociologist.
soco 1 *adj* (a) (*CAm*) drunk.
　(b) *see* **zoco 1**.
　2 *nm* (a) (*Col: Anat, Bot*) stump.
　(b) (*Col*) short blunt machete.
　(c) *see* **zoco 2**.
socola *nf* (*CAm, Col*) clearing of land.
socolar [1a] *vt* (a) (*CAm, Col, Ec, Pan*) *land* to clear, clear of scrub.
　(b) (*Col*) to bungle, do clumsily.
socollón *nm* (*CAm, Cu*) violent shake.
socollonear [1a] *vt* (*CAm*) to shake violently.
soconusco *nm* (a) snack, bite to eat, refreshment. (b) (*Cu*) chocolate; (*Guat, Mex*) high-quality chocolate. (c) (*Cu: fig*) shady deal.
socorrer [2a] *vt person* to help; *needs* to relieve, meet, help with; *city* to relieve; *expedition etc* to bring aid to.
socorrido *adj* (a) *place* well-stocked. (b) *object etc* handy; useful. (c) *person* helpful, obliging, co-operative. (d) (*fig*) hackneyed, trite, well-worn.
socorrismo *nm* life-saving.
socorro *nm* (a) help, aid, assistance; relief (*also Mil*); **¡—!** help!; **—s mutuos** mutual aid; **trabajos de —** relief work, rescue work.
　(b) (*Chi*) advance payment.
socoyote *nm* (*Mex*) youngest son.
socucha *nf*, **socucho** *nm* (*Mex, RPl*) small room, den; small house; ruinous house, slum.
soche *nm* (*Col*) tanned sheepskin (*or* goatskin).
Sócrates *m* Socrates.
socrático *adj* Socratic.
soda *nf* (a) soda. (b) soda water.
sodio *nm* sodium.
sodomía *nf* sodomy.
sodomita *nm* sodomite.
soez *adj* dirty, rude, obscene.
sofá *nm* sofa, settee.
sofá-cama *nm* studio couch, sofa bed.
sofero *adj* (*Per*) huge, tremendous.
Sofía *f* Sophia.
sofión *nm* sharp rebuke; sharp retort.
sofisma *nm* sophism.
sofista *nm* sophist; (*fig*) quibbler.
sofistería *nf* sophistry.
sofisticación *nf* sophistication; (*pej*) affectation.
sofisticado *adj* sophisticated; (*pej*) affected.
sofístico *adj* sophistic(al); false, fallacious.
soflama *nf* (a) dull glow, flicker. (b) (*of face*) blush. (c) (*fig*) fiery speech, harangue. (d) (*fig*) deceit. (e) (*Mex*) unimportant piece of news.
soflamar [1a] *vt* (a) to scorch; (*Cook*) to singe. (b) *person* to shame, make blush. (c) (*fam*) to deceive, swindle, blarney.
sofocación *nf* (a) suffocation. (b) (*fig*) = **sofoco** (b).
sofocado *adj*: **estar —** (*fig*) to be out of breath; to feel stifled; to be hot and bothered.
sofocante *adj* stifling, suffocating.
sofocar [1g] **1** *vt* (a) *person* to suffocate, stifle; to get out of breath.
　(b) *fire* to smother, put out; *revolt etc* to crush, put down; *epidemic* to stop.
　(c) (*fig*) **— a uno** to make someone blush; to put someone to shame; to embarrass someone; to anger someone, get someone worked up, provoke someone, upset someone.
　2 sofocarse *vr* (a) to suffocate, stifle; to get out of breath, (begin to) pant; to choke.
　(b) (*fig*) to blush; to feel embarrassed; to get angry, get worked up, get upset, upset oneself; **no vale la pena de que te sofoques** it's not worth upsetting yourself about it.

Sófocles m Sophocles.
sofoco nm (a) suffocation; stifling sensation. (b) (fig) embarrassment; anger, rage, feeling of indignation. (c) **pasar un —** to have an embarrassing time.
sofocón nm (fam) nasty blow; **se le dio un —** he really blew up (fam), he got really worked up.
sofoquina nf (fam) (a) stifling heat; **hace una —** it's stifling hot. (b) = **sofocón**.
sofreír [3m; ptp **sofrito**] vt to fry lightly.
sofrenada nf (a) sudden check, sudden jerk on the reins. (b) (fam) ticking-off.
sofrenar [1a] vt (a) horse to rein back sharply. (b) (fig) to restrain, control. (c) (fam) to tick off.
soga nf rope, cord; halter; hangman's rope; **dar — a uno** to make fun of someone; **echar la — tras el caldero** to chuck it all up, throw in one's hand; **estar con la — al cuello** to be in imminent danger, be in a real fix; **hablar de la — en casa del ahorcado** to say something singularly inappropriate; **hacer — to lag behind.**
soguear [1a] vt (a) to measure with a rope; (Arg, CAm, Ec) to tie with a rope; (Cu) to lasso. (b) (Cu) to tame. (c) (Col) to make fun of.
soguero adj (Cu) tame.
sois see **ser**.
soja nf soya; **semilla de —** soya bean.
sojuzgar [1h] vt to conquer; to subdue; to rule despotically.
sol nm (a) sun; sunshine, sunlight; **— naciente** rising sun; **— poniente** setting sun; **como un —** as bright as a new pin; **día de —** sunny day; **de — a —** from sunrise to sunset; **dejar algo al —** to leave something in the sun; **tostarse al —** to sit in the sun, acquire a sun tan; **arrimarse al — que más calienta** to know which side one's bread is buttered; **no dejar a uno a — ni a sombra** to chase someone all over, pester someone continually; **hay —, hace —** it is sunny, the sun is shining; **salga el — por donde quiera** come what may; press on regardless (fam); **tomar el —** to sun oneself, sunbathe, bask. (b) standard monetary unit of Peru.
solada nf sediment.
solado nm tiling, tiled floor.
solamente adv only; solely; just.
solana nf sunny spot, suntrap; sun lounge, solarium.
solanera nf scorching sunshine; (Med) sunburn; sunstroke.
solano nm east wind.
solapa nf (a) (of jacket) lapel; (of envelope, book, pocket) flap. (b) (fig) pretext.
solapadamente adv slyly, in an underhand way, by underhand means.
solapado adj sly, underhand, sneaky.
solapar [1a] 1 vt (a) to overlap. (b) (fig) to cover up, cloak, keep dark. 2 vi to overlap. 3 **solaparse** vr: **se ha solapado** it has got covered up, it has got hidden underneath.
solapo nm (a) (Sew) lapel; overlap. (b) **a —** (fam) = **solapadamente**.
solar[1] nm (a) (Archit) lot, piece of ground, site; **— para edificaciones** building site. (b) ancestral home, family seat; (fig) family, lineage, line. (c) (CAm, Ven) backyard. (d) (Cu, Per) tenement house.
solar[2] [1m] vt floor to floor, tile; shoes to sole.
solar[3] adj solar, sun (attr).
solariego adj (a) casa solariega family seat, ancestral home. (b) (Hist) family ancient and noble; rights etc manorial; **tierras solariegas** demesne.
solaz nm recreation, relaxation; solace, spiritual relief.
solazar [1f] 1 vt to amuse, provide relaxation for; to console; to comfort, cheer. 2 **solazarse** vr to enjoy oneself, amuse oneself, relax.
solazo nm (fam) = **solanera**.
soldada nf pay.
soldadesca nf (a) military profession. (b) (pej) soldiery, brutal and licentious soldiery.
soldadesco adj soldierly.
soldadito nm: **— de plomo** tin soldier.
soldado[1] nm (a) soldier; **— de infantería** infantryman; **— de marina** marine; **— de plomo** tin soldier; **— de primera** lance-corporal; **— raso** private; **la tumba del S— Desconocido** the tomb of the Unknown Warrior.
soldado[2] adj seam etc welded; **totalmente —** welded throughout.
soldador nm (a) (Tech) soldering iron. (b) (person) welder.

soldadura nf (a) (material) solder. (b) (act) soldering, welding; **— autógena** welding. (c) soldered joint, welded seam.
soldar [1m] 1 vt (a) (Tech) to solder, weld. (b) to join, unite; to cement; diverse parts to weld together; quarrel to patch up. 2 **soldarse** vr (bones) to knit (together).
soleado adj sunny.
solear [1a] vt to put in the sun; to bleach.
solecismo nm solecism.
soledad nf (a) solitude; loneliness. (b) grieving, mourning. (c) lonely place; **—es** wilderness.
solemne adj (a) solemn; dignified, impressive. (b) (fam) lie downright; nonsense utter; mistake complete, terrible.
solemnemente adv solemnly; impressively.
solemnidad nf (a) solemnity; impressiveness; formality, gravity, dignity. (b) (act) solemnity, solemn ceremony; **—es** solemnities. (c) **—es** (bureaucratic) formalities. (d) (fam) **pobre de —** miserably poor; **rico de —** stinking rich (fam).
solemnización nf solemnization, celebration.
solemnizar [1f] vt to solemnize, celebrate.
solenoide nm solenoid.
soler [2h; defective] vi (a) **— + infin** to be in the habit of + ger, be accustomed to + infin, be wont to + infin; **suele pasar por aquí** he usually comes this way; **solíamos ir todos los años** we used to go every year; **como se suele** as is normal, as is customary; **¿beber? pues no suele** drink? well he doesn't usually. (b) (Chi) to occur rarely, happen only occasionally.
solera nf (a) prop, support; plinth. (b) (of ditch etc) bottom. (c) lower millstone. (d) (Mex) floor tile, paving stone. (e) (Chi) kerb. (f) inherited character, collective character; traditional nature; **éste es país de — celta** this is a country of basically Celtic character; **es de — de médicos** he comes from a line of doctors; **vino de —** vintage wine; **es un barrio con —** it is a typically Spanish (etc) quarter, it is a quarter with a strong flavour to it.
soleta nf (a) (Sew) patch, darn. (b) (fam) shameless woman. (c) (fam) **dar — a uno** to chuck someone out; **tomar —** to beat it (fam). (d) (Mex) wafer, ladyfinger.
solevantamiento nm (a) pushing up, raising. (b) (Pol) rising; upheaval.
solevantar [1a] vt (a) to push up, raise, heave up. (b) (Pol etc) to rouse, stir up.
solfa nf (a) (Mus) solfa; musical notation; (fig) music. (b) (fam) tanning (fam). (c) (fam) **poner a uno en —** to make someone look ridiculous, hold someone up to mockery.
solfear [1a] vt (a) (Mus) to solfa. (b) (fam) to tan (fam). (c) (fam) to tick off.
solfeo nm (a) (Mus) solfa. (b) (fam) tanning (fam); ticking-off.
solicitación nf request; solicitation; canvassing.
solicitante nmf applicant; petitioner.
solicitar [1a] vt (a) permission etc to ask for, request, seek; approval to seek; post to apply for; support to solicit, canvass for; votes to canvass; **— algo a uno** to ask someone for something, request something of someone. (b) attention, interest, (also Phys) to attract. (c) person to pursue, chase after, try to attract; woman to court; **le solicitan en todas partes** he is in great demand all over, he is much sought after.
solícito adj diligent, careful; solicitous, concerned (por about, for); affectionate.
solicitud nf (a) (quality) diligence, care; solicitude, concern; affection. (b) (act) request (de for); petition; application (de un puesto for a post); **a —** on request; **presentar una —** to put in an application, make an application; **denegar (or desestimar etc) una —** to refuse a request, reject an application.
sólidamente adv solidly.
solidariamente adv jointly, mutually.
solidaridad nf solidarity; **por — con** (Pol etc) out of sympathy with, out of solidarity with.
solidario adj (a) obligation etc mutually binding, jointly shared, shared in common; participación etc joint, common; person jointly liable.

(b) hacerse — de to sympathize with, declare one's solidarity with; **hacerse — de una opinión** to echo an opinion.

solidarizarse [1f] *vr*: **— con** to declare one's solidarity with, affirm one's support for, line up with.

solidez *nf* solidity; hardness.

solidificación *nf* solidification; hardening.

solidificar [1g] **1** *vt* to solidify, harden. **2 solidificarse** *vr* to solidify, harden.

sólido[1] **1** *adj* **(a)** solid (*also Math, Phys*); hard.
(b) (*Tech etc*) solidly made; well built; *shoes etc* stout, strong; *colour* fast.
(c) (*fig*) solid, sound; firm, stable, secure; *basis, principle, morality etc* sound.
2 *nm* solid.

sólido[2] *adj* (*Andalusia, Per*) lonely.

soliloquiar [1b] *vi* to soliloquize, talk to oneself; to meditate aloud.

soliloquio *nm* soliloquy, monologue.

solimán *nm* corrosive sublimate; (*fig*) poison.

solio *nm* throne.

solipsismo *nm* solipsism.

solista *nmf* soloist.

solitaria *nf* tapeworm.

solitario 1 *adj* **(a)** *person, life* lonely, solitary; **vivir — to live alone.**
(b) *place* lonely, desolate; bleak; **a tal hora la calle está solitaria** at such a time the street is deserted (*or* empty).
2 *nm,* **solitaria** *nf* recluse; hermit; solitary person.
3 *nm* (*game, diamond*) solitaire.

sólito *adj* usual, customary.

soliviantar [1a] *vt* **(a)** to stir up, rouse (to revolt).
(b) to anger; to irritate, exasperate.
(c) to worry, cause anxiety to; **le tienen soliviantado los celos** he is eaten up with jealousy.
(d) to fill with longing; to buoy up with false hopes; to make vain, fill with conceit; **anda soliviantado con el proyecto** he has tremendous hopes for the scheme.

soliviar [1b] **1** *vt* **(a)** to lift, push up. **(b)** (*Arg*) to steal. **2 soliviarse** *vr* to half rise, partly get up; to get up on one elbow.

solo 1 *adj* **(a)** single, sole; only one; unique; **hay una sola dificultad** there is just one difficulty; **con esta sola condición** with this single condition; **su sola preocupación es ganar dinero** his one concern is to make money; **no hubo ni una sola objeción** there was not a single objection; **es — en su género** it is unique of its kind.
(b) alone; lonely; by oneself; **venir — to come** alone; **pasa los días — en su cuarto** he spends the days alone in his room; **iré — I'll go alone; estos días me siento muy — I feel very lonely nowadays; dejar — a uno** to leave someone all alone; **tendremos que comer pan — we shall have to eat plain bread, we shall have to eat bread and nothing with it; se quedó — a los 7 años** he was left an orphan (*or* alone in the world) at 7; **se queda — en esta especialidad** there's nobody to touch him in this particular field.
(c) a solas alone, by oneself; **lo hizo a solas** he did it (all) by himself; **volar a solas** to fly solo; **vuelo a solas** solo flight.
(d) (*Mus*) solo; **cantar — to sing solo.**
2 *nm* **(a)** (*Mus*) solo; **un — para tenor** a tenor solo.
(b) (*Cards*) solitaire, patience.
(c) (*Arg*) tedious conversation.

sólo *adv* only, solely, merely, just; **— quería verlo** I only (*or* just) wanted to see it; **es — un teniente** he's only a lieutenant; **no — A sino también B** not only A but also B; **— que . . .** except that . . .; but for the fact that . . .; **ven aunque — sea para media hora** come even if it's just for half an hour; **con — que sepas tocar algunas notas** even if you only know how to play a few notes; **con — que estudies dos horas diarias** by studying for as little as two hours a day; **tan — only, just.**

solomillo *nm* sirloin.

solomo *nm* sirloin; loin of pork.

solón *nm* (*Ven*) scorching heat.

solsticio *nm* solstice; **— de estío** summer solstice; **— de invierno** winter solstice.

soltar [1m] **1** *vt* **(a)** (*from hand etc*) to let go of; to drop; to release; *knot* to undo, untie; *mooring* to cast off; *buckle etc* to undo, unfasten, loosen; *clutch* (*Aut*) to release, disengage; *brake* to release, take off; *rope etc* to loosen, slacken; to pay out; *tangled rope etc* to free; *water* to let out, run off; *captive* to release, let go, set free; *animals* to let out,

turn out, turn loose; to set free; *prey* to let go of; *money* (*fam*) to cough up (*fam*); *post, privilege etc* (*fam*) to give up; **¡suéltame, querido!** let go of me, dear!; **¡suélteme, señor!** unhand me, sir! (*lit*); **no quiere — el puesto por nada del mundo** he won't give up the job for anything.
(b) *exclamation, laugh, sneeze etc* to let out; *sigh* to fetch, heave; *oath etc* to utter, come out with, let fly; *hint* to drop; *truth* to let out, let slip; **soltó un par de palabrotas** he came out with a couple of rude words, he let fly a couple of obscenities; **les volvió a — el mismo sermón** he read them the same lecture all over again.
(c) *blow* to deal, strike, let fly.
(d) *skin* (*of snake*) to cast, slough.
(e) *difficulty* to solve; *doubt* to resolve; *objection etc* to satisfy, deal with.
(f) (*Col*) to cede, give, hand over.
2 soltarse *vr* **(a)** (*knot, laces etc*) to come undone, come untied; (*seam etc*) to come unstitched; (*animal etc*) to get loose, break loose, free itself; to escape; (*Mech: part*) to work loose; to come off, fly off, fall off; **— de las manos de uno** to escape from someone's clutches; **se le soltó un grito** a cry escaped him, he let out a yell; **no se vaya a — el perro** don't let the dog get out (*or* get loose *etc*); **— del estómago** to have diarrhoea.
(b) (*fig*) to achieve one's independence, win freedom.
(c) (*fig*) to lose control (of oneself); **— a su gusto** to let fly, let oneself go.
(d) (*fig: in a skill etc*) to become expert, acquire real proficiency; (*in a language*) to become fluent.
(e) — a + infin to begin to + *infin*.
(f) — con una idea absurda to come up with a silly idea; **— con una contribución de 50 dólares** to come up with a 50-dollar contribution; **por fin se soltó con algunos peniques** he eventually parted with a few coppers.

soltera *nf* single woman, unmarried woman, spinster; **apellido de — maiden name.**

solterear [1a] *vi* (*Arg*) to stay single.

soltería *nf* single state, unmarried state; bachelorhood, spinsterhood.

soltero 1 *adj* single, unmarried. **2** *nm* bachelor, unmarried man.

solterón *nm* confirmed bachelor, old bachelor.

solterona *nf* spinster, maiden lady; (*pej*) old maid; **tía — maiden aunt.**

soltura *nf* **(a)** (*of rope etc*) looseness, slackness; (*Mech*) looseness; (*of limbs*) agility, nimbleness, ease of movement, freedom of action.
(b) (*Med, also* **— de vientre**) looseness of the bowels, diarrhoea.
(c) (*in speaking etc*) fluency, ease; **habla árabe con — he speaks Arabic fluently.**
(d) (*pej*) shamelessness; licentiousness; dissipation.

solubilidad *nf* solubility.

soluble *adj* **(a)** (*Chem*) soluble; **— en agua** soluble in water. **(b)** *problem* solvable, that can be solved.

solución *nf* **(a)** (*Chem*) solution.
(b) (*of problem etc*) solution; answer (*de* to); **esto no tiene — there's no answer to this, there's no solution to this one.**
(c) (*Theat*) climax, dénouement.
(d) **— de continuidad** break in continuity, interruption.

solucionar [1a] *vt* to solve; to resolve, settle.

solucionista *nmf* solver.

solvencia *nf* **(a)** (*Fin*) solvency.
(b) (*Fin: act*) settlement, payment.
(c) (*fig*) **— moral** character; **de toda — moral** of excellent character, completely trustworthy.

solventar [1a] *vt* **(a)** *account, debt* to settle, pay. **(b)** *difficulty* to resolve; *matter* to settle.

solvente 1 *adj* solvent, free of debt. **2** *nm* (*Chem*) solvent.

sollamar [1a] *vt* to scorch, singe.

sollastre *nm* rogue, villain.

sollo *nm* sturgeon.

sollozar [1f] *vi* to sob.

sollozo *nm* sob; **decir algo entre —s** to sob something.

somalí 1 *adj* Somali. **2** *nm* Somali.

Somalia *nf* Somaliland.

somanta *nf* beating.

somatada *nf* (*CAm, Pan*) blow, bang; punch.

somatar [1a] **1** *vt* **(a)** (*CAm*) to beat, thrash; to punch.
(b) (*Hond*) to sell off cheap.
2 somatarse *vr* (*CAm, Pan*) to fall heavily, knock oneself about badly.

somatón *nm* (*CAm*) = **somatada.**

sombra nf (a) (cast by object) shadow; (as protection etc) shade; (Art) shaded part, shaded area, dark part; —s shadows, darkness; **luz y** — light and shade; **lugar de** — shady spot; **a la** — **de** in the shade of; (fig) under the protection of; thanks to the support of; (pej) under the cloak of; **estar a la** — to be in the shade; (sl) to be in clink (sl); **dar** —, **hacer** — (of tree etc) to give shade; to cast a shadow; **dar** — **a** to shade; **hacer** — **a uno** (fig) to put someone in the shade; **no quiere que otros le hagan** — he doesn't want to be overshadowed by anybody else, he refuses to tolerate any rivals; **se ha cons-tituido en** — **de sí mismo** he is a shadow of his former self.

(b) (fig) —s darkness, obscurity; ignorance; sombreness, pessimism.

(c) (Rel) shade, ghost.

(d) (on mirror etc) dark patch, stain; (fig) stain, blot; **es una** — **en su carácter** it is a stain on his character.

(e) (fig) shadow; sign, trace, bit; **sin** — **de avaricia** without a trace of greed; **sin** — **de duda** without a shadow of doubt; **no tiene ni** — **de talento** he hasn't the least bit of talent; **tiene una** — **de parecido con su tío** he has a faint resemblance to his uncle; **ni por** — by no means; not in the least bit.

(f) luck; **tener buena** — to be lucky; **ser de mala** — to be unlucky.

(g) charm; wit; talent, aptitude; **tiene mucha** — **para contar chistes** he's got a great talent for telling jokes; **tener buena** — to be likeable, have lots of charm; **tener mala** — to be a nasty piece of work; to have an unfortunate effect (on people etc); **el cuento tiene (buena)** — it's a good story.

(h) (CAm, Chi) parasol, sunshade; (CAm) awning; porch.

(i) (CAm, Chi) guide lines (in writing).

sombraje nm, **sombrajo** nm shelter from the sun; **hacer** —s to get in the light.

sombreado 1 adj shady. 2 nm (Art etc) shading; hatching.

sombreador nm: — **de ojos** eyeshadow.

sombrear [1a] vt to shade; (Art etc) to shade; to hatch.

sombrerera nf (a) milliner. (b) hatbox. (c) (Ec, Per, PR) hatstand.

sombrerería nf (a) hats, millinery. (b) hat shop; hat factory.

sombrerero nm (a) hatter, hatmaker. (b) (Arg, Col) hatstand.

sombrerete nm (a) little hat. (b) (of mushroom) cap. (c) (Tech) bonnet; (of hub etc) cap; (of chimney) cowl.

sombrero nm (a) hat; headgear; — **apuntado**, — **de candil**, — **de tres picos** cocked hat, three-cornered hat; — **de bola** (Mex), — **hongo** bowler (hat); — **de copa**, — **de pelo** (SAm) top hat; — **flexible** soft hat, trilby; — **gacho** slouch hat; — **de jipijapa** Panama hat; — **de paja** straw hat; **quitarse el** — (y hacer reverencia) a (fig) to take off one's hat to. (b) (Bot) cap.

sombríamente adv sombrely; dismally; gloomily.

sombrilla nf parasol, sunshade.

sombrío 1 adj (a) place shaded, (too much) in the shade, dark.

(b) (fig) place sombre, sad, dismal; person gloomy; outlook etc sombre.

2 nm (Mex) shady place.

someramente adv superficially.

somero adj superficial; shallow.

someter [2a] 1 vt (a) country to conquer; person to subject to one's will, force to yield.

(b) — **una decisión a lo que se resuelva en una reunión** to make one's decision depend on what is resolved in a meeting; — **su opinión a la de otros** to subordinate one's opinion to that of others.

(c) report etc to present, submit (a to); to send in; — **algo a la aprobación de uno** to submit something for someone's approval; — **un trabajo a la censura** to send a work to the censor.

(d) — **un asunto a una autoridad** to refer a matter to an authority for decision.

(e) — **a** test etc to put to, subject to; — **una sustancia a la acción de un ácido** to subject a substance to the action of an acid; see **prueba** etc.

2 **someterse** vr (a) to give in, yield, submit; — **a la mayoría** to give way to the majority.

(b) — **a una operación** to undergo an operation; — **a un tratamiento con drogas** to have treatment with drugs.

sometico adj (Col), **sometido** adj (CR, Ec) = **entrometido.**

sometimiento nm (a) (state) submission, subjection. (b) (act) presentation, submission; reference.

somier nm, pl **somiers** (gall) spring mattress.

somnambulismo nm sleepwalking, somnambulism.

somnámbulo nm, **somnámbula** nf sleepwalker, somnambulist.

somnífero 1 adj sleep-inducing. 2 nm sleeping pill.

somnílocuo 1 adj given to talking in one's sleep. 2 nm, **somnílocua** nf person who talks in his (or her) sleep.

somnolencia nf sleepiness, drowsiness, somnolence.

somnolento adj = **soñoliento.**

somorgujar [1a] 1 vt to duck; to plunge, dip, submerge. 2 **somorgujarse** vr to dive, plunge (en into).

somormujo nm grebe; — **menor** dabchick.

somos see **ser.**

son[1] nm (a) sound; pleasant sound, sweet sound; **a** — **de** to the sound of; **a los** —**es de la marcha nupcial** to the sounds (or strains) of the wedding march.

(b) (fig) rumour; **corre el** — **de que** ... there is a rumour that ...

(c) (fig) manner, style; **¿a qué** — ...?, **¿a** — **de qué** ...? why ...?; **en** — **de** as, like, in the manner of; by the way of; **en** — **de broma** as a joke; **en** — **de guerra** in a warlike fashion; **lo dijo en** — **de riña** he said it as though he was trying to pick a quarrel; **no vienen en** — **de protesta** they're not coming in a protesting mood; **por este** — in this way; **sin** — for no reason at all; see **bailar.**

son[2] see **ser.**

sonado adj (a) talked-of; famous; sensational; scandalous; **un crimen muy** — a particularly ghastly crime, a most notorious crime; **un suceso muy** — a much talked-of event, an event which made a great stir.

(b) **hacer una (que sea) sonada** to do something really frightful; to cause a major scandal.

sonaja nf little bell.

sonajera nf (Arg, Chi), **sonajero** nm rattle.

sonante adj audible; resounding; tinkling, jingling; see **contante.**

sonar [1m] 1 vt (a) bell, coin to ring; trumpet etc to play, blow; hooter to blow.

(b) — (las narices) a un niño to blow a child's nose.

2 vi (a) to sound, make a noise; to sound out, make itself heard, be heard; (Mus) to play; (of bell) to ring; (of clock) to chime, strike; **han sonado las 10** it has struck 10; **le estaban sonando las tripas** his stomach was rumbling; — **a cascado** to sound cracked; — **a hueco** to sound hollow.

(b) (Ling) to be sounded, be pronounced; **la h de "hombre" no suena** the h in "hombre" is not pronounced (or is silent); **en esa región "fue" suena casi como "juez"** in that area "fue" sounds (or is pronounced) almost like "juez".

(c) (fig) to sound; **esas palabras suenan extrañas** those words sound strange; **no me suena bien** it sounds all wrong to me; **no le ha sonado muy bien aquello** that did not make a good impression on him, he wasn't very well impressed with that; **me suena a camelo** it sounds like a hoax to me; **se llama Anastasio, así como suena** he's called Anastasius, just like I'm telling you.

(d) (fig) to be talked-of; **es un nombre que suena** it's a name that's in the news, it's a name that people are talking about; **no quiere que suene su nombre** he doesn't want his name mentioned; **el asunto no ha sonado para nada en la reunión** the matter did not come up at all at the meeting.

(e) (fig) to sound familiar, seem familiar; **no me suena el nombre** the name doesn't ring a bell with me; **me suena ese coche** that car looks familiar.

(f) (Arg) to have a setback, suffer a disappoint-ment.

(g) (Arg, Chi) **hacer** — **a uno** to punish someone severely.

3 **sonarse** vr (a) (also — las narices) to blow one's nose.

(b) **se suena que** ... it is rumoured that ...

sonata nf sonata.

sonda nf (a) (act) sounding. (b) (Naut) lead; (Tech) bore, drill; (Med) probe; — **acústica** echo-sounder.

sondaje nm (Naut) sounding; (Tech) boring, drilling; **conversaciones de** — exploratory talks; **organismo de** — public-opinion poll, institute of public opinion.

sond(e)ar [1a] vt (Naut) to sound, take soundings of; (Med) to probe, sound; (Tech) to bore, bore into, drill; (fig) ground etc to explore; mystery to plumb, delve into, inquire into; person, intentions etc to sound out.

sondeo *nm* sounding; (*Tech*) boring, drilling; (*fig*) poll, inquiry, investigation; (*Pol etc*) feeler, overture, approach.

sonería *nf* (*of clock*) chimes.

soneto *nm* sonnet.

songa *nf* (a) (*Cu*, *PR*) sarcasm, irony. (b) (*Mex*) coarseness, vulgarity. (c) (*CAm*, *Chi*, *Ec*) **a la songasonga** slyly.

songo 1 *adj* (a) (*Col*, *Mex*) stupid. (b) (*Col*, *Mex*) sly, crafty. 2 *nm* (*Col*) buzz, hum.

sónico *adj* sonic, sound (*attr*).

sonido *nm* sound.

sonoridad *nf* sonority, sonorousness.

sonorizar [1f] (*Ling*) 1 *vt* to voice. 2 **sonorizarse** *vr* to voice, become voiced.

sonoro *adj* (a) sonorous; loud, resonant, resounding; *verse etc* sonorous; *cave etc* echoing.
(b) (*Ling*) voiced.
(c) **banda sonora** sound track; **efectos —s** sound effects.

sonreír [3m] 1 *vi* (a) to smile; **— a uno** to smile at someone, beam at someone; **— de un chiste** to smile at a joke; **— forzadamente** to force a smile.
(b) (*fig*) **le sonríe la fortuna** fortune smiles upon him; **el porvenir le sonríe** he has a bright future. 2 **sonreírse** *vr* to smile.

sonriente *adj* smiling.

sonrisa *nf* smile; **— amarga** bitter smile, wry smile; **— forzada** forced smile.

sonrojar [1a] 1 *vt*: **— a uno** to make someone blush. 2 **sonrojarse** *vr* to blush, flush (*de* at).

sonrojo *nm* (a) blush. (b) offensive word, naughty remark (that brings a blush).

sonrosado *adj* rosy, pink.

sonrosarse [1a] *vr* to turn pink.

sonsacar [1g] *vt* to get by cunning; to remove surreptitiously; *servant etc* to entice away; **— a uno** to pump someone for information; **— un secreto a uno** to worm a secret out of someone.

sonsear [1a] *vi* (*Chi*, *RPl*) see **zoncear**.

sonsera *nf*, **sonsería** *nf* (*SAm*) see **zoncera** etc.

sonso *adj* (*SAm*) see **zonzo**.

sonsonete *nm* (a) tap, tapping; rattle; jangling; monotonous din.
(b) monotonous delivery, singsong (voice), chant.
(c) jingle, rhyming phrase.
(d) mocking undertone.

sonsoniche *nm* (*Cu*) = **sonsonete**.

sonza *nf* (a) (*Cu*) slyness, deceit. (b) (*Mex*) sarcasm, mockery.

soñación: **¡ni por —!** not on your life!

soñado *adj* (a) dreamed-of, that one has dreamed of; **el hombre —** one's ideal man, one's dream man; Mr Right.
(b) (*fam*) **hemos encontrado un sitio que ni —** we've found an absolutely perfect spot; **me va que ni —** it suits me a treat (*fam*).

soñador 1 *adj* dreamy. 2 *nm*, **soñadora** *nf* dreamer.

soñar [1m] *vti* to dream (*also fig*); **— con algo** to dream of something; **soñé contigo anoche** I dreamed about you last night; **soñaba con una lavadora** she dreamed of one day having a washing machine; **— con + infin, — en + infin** to dream of + ger; **— que ... — en + infin** to dream that ...; **— despierto** to day-dream; **— en voz alta** to talk in one's sleep; **¡ni —lo!** (*fam*) not on your life!

soñarra *nf*, **soñarrera** *nf*, **soñera** *nf* (a) drowsiness, deep desire to sleep. (b) deep sleep.

soñolencia *nf* = **somnolencia**.

soñolientamente *adv* sleepily, drowsily.

soñoliento *adj* sleepy, drowsy, somnolent.

sopa *nf* (a) soup; **— de cebolla** onion soup; **— del hortelano** vegetable soup; **— de pastas** noodle soup; **comer** (*or* **andar a, vivir a**) **la — boba** to scrounge one's meals (*fam*), live on other people; **poner a uno como — de Pascua** to give someone a ticking-off.
(b) (*in milk etc*) sop; **—s de leche** bread and milk; **dar —s con honda a uno** to be streets ahead of someone; **estar hecho una —** to be sopping wet.
(c) (*Mex*: *also* **— seca**) dish.
(d) (*fam*) hangover; **quitar la — a uno** to sober someone up; **quitarse la —** to sober up.

sopapear [1a] *vt* to punch, bash (*fam*); to shake violently.

sopapié *nm* (*Col*) kick.

sopapina *nf* series of punches, bashing (*fam*).

sopapo *nm* punch (on the jaw), bash (*fam*).

sopar [1a] (*Arg*) 1 *vt* bread etc to dip, dunk. 2 *vi* to meddle.

sopera *nf* soup tureen.

sopero 1 *adj*: **plato — = 2** *nm* soup plate.

sopesar [1a] *vt* to try the weight of, try to lift.

sopetón *nm* (a) punch.
(b) **de —** suddenly, unexpectedly; **entrar de —** to pop in, drop in; **entrar de — en un cuarto** to burst into a room, appear unexpectedly in a room.

sopimpa *nf* (*Cu*) series of punches; beating, bashing (*fam*).

soplado *adj* (a) clean; extra smart, overdressed; affected; stuck-up (*fam*). (b) (*fam*) **estar —** to be tight.

soplador *nm* (a) glass blower. (b) fan, ventilator. (c) (*fig*) troublemaker. (d) (*Ec*, *Guat*: *Theat*) prompter.

soplamocos *nm*, *pl* **soplamocos** (a) punch, slap. (b) (*Mex*) rude remark.

soplar [1a] 1 *vt* (a) *dust etc* to blow away, blow off; *surface* to blow on; *candle* to blow out; *balloon* to blow up, inflate; *glass* to blow; *fire*, *ashes* to blow on.
(b) (*fig*: *of muse etc*) to inspire.
(c) **— a uno** to whisper to someone; to prompt someone, help someone along; (*CAm*: *Theat*) to prompt; **— a X algo referente a Y** to tell X something to Y's discredit.
(d) (*fam*) to split on (*fam*).
(e) (*fam*) to pinch (*fam*).
(f) (*fam*) to charge, rush (*sl*), sting (*fam*); **¿cuánto te soplaron?** what did they rush you?; **me han soplado 8 dólares** they stung me for 8 dollars.
(g) (*fam*) *blow* to deal, fetch.
2 *vi* (a) (*of person*, *wind*) to blow; to puff; **¡sopla!** well I'm blowed!
(b) (*fam*) to split (*fam*), squeal (*sl*).
(c) (*fam*) to drink, booze.
3 **soplarse** *vr* (a) (*fam*) **— un pastel** to wolf a cake.
(b) (*fam*) to get conceited.
(c) (*fam*) **— de uno** to split on someone (*fam*), sneak on someone.

soplete *nm* (a) blowlamp, torch; **— oxiacetilénico** oxyacetylene burner; **— soldador** welding torch.
(b) (*Chi*, *RPl*) = **soplón**; (*Theat*) prompter.

soplido *nm* strong puff, blast.

soplo *nm* (a) (*from mouth*) blow, puff; (*of wind*) puff, gust; (*Tech*) blast; **la semana pasó como** (*or* **en**) **un —** the week sped by, the week seemed no more than an instant.
(b) (*fam*) tip, tip-off, secret warning; denunciation, informing; **dar el —** to tell tales; to split (*fam*), squeal (*sl*); to inform; **ir con el — al director** to take one's tales to the headmaster, go and split to the head.
(c) (*fam*) telltale, talebearer, sneak (*fam*); (*of police etc*) informer.

soplón *nm*, **soplona** *nf* (a) (*fam*) = **soplo** (c). (b) (*Mex*) policeman; (*Per*) member of the secret police. (c) (*CAm*: *Theat*) prompter.

soponcio *nm* queer turn, dizzy spell.

sopor *nm* (*Med*) drowsiness; (*fig*) torpor, lethargy.

soporífero 1 *adj* sleep-inducing; (*fig*) soporific. 2 *nm* nightcap; (*Med*) sleeping pill, sleeping draught.

soportable *adj* bearable.

soportal *nm* (a) porch; portico. (b) **—es** arcade; colonnade.

soportar [1a] *vt* (a) (*Archit etc*) to bear, carry, support, hold up; *pressure etc* to resist, withstand.
(b) (*fig*) to stand, bear, endure, put up with.

soporte *nm* (a) support; base, stand, mounting; holder, bracket. (b) (*Her*) supporter. (c) (*fig*) pillar, support.

soprano *nf* soprano.

sor *nf* (*before names*) Sister; **S— María** Sister Mary.

sorber [2a] *vt* (a) (*with lips*) to sip; to suck up; **— por una paja** to drink through a straw; **— por las narices** to sniff (in, up); (*Med*) to inhale.
(b) (*of sponge*) to soak up, absorb, suck up; (*of blotter*) to dry up; (*with cloth*) to mop up.
(c) (*fig*: *of sea*) to suck down, swallow up.
(d) (*fig*) *words* to drink in.

sorbete *nm* (a) sherbet; iced fruit drink, water ice.
(b) (*PR*, *Urug*) drinking straw. (c) (*Mex*) top hat.

sorbetera *nf* (a) ice-cream freezer. (b) (*fam*) top hat.

sorbetón *nm* gulp, mouthful.

sorbito *nm* sip.

sorbo *nm* sip; gulp, swallow; sniff; **un — de té** a sip of tea; **beber a —s** to sip.

sordamente *adv* dully, in a muffled way.

sordera *nf* deafness.

sordidez *nf* (a) dirt, dirtiness, squalor. (b) (*fig*) meanness.

sórdido *adj* (a) dirty, squalid. (b) *word etc* nasty, dirty. (c) (*fig*) mean.

sordina nf (a) (Mus) mute, muffle, damper. (b) a la — on the quiet, surreptitiously, by stealth.

sordo 1 adj (a) person deaf; — como una tapia as deaf as a post, stone-deaf; quedarse — to go deaf; a la sorda, a sordas on the quiet, surreptitiously, by stealth; mostrarse — a, permanecer — a (fig) to remain deaf to.

(b) machine etc quiet, noiseless; noise dull, muffled; pain dull; (Ling) voiceless; anger, emotion suppressed, inward.

2 nm, sorda nf deaf person; hacerse el — to pretend not to hear, turn a deaf ear.

sordomudez nf condition of being deaf and dumb.

sordomudo 1 adj deaf and dumb. **2** nm, sordomuda nf deaf-mute.

sorgo nm sorghum.

soriano 1 adj of Soria. **2** nm, soriana nf native (or inhabitant) of Soria; los —s the people of Soria.

Sorlinga, Sorlingen: Islas fpl — Scilly Isles.

sorna nf (a) slyness; sarcasm, sarcastic tone; con — slyly, mockingly, sarcastically. (b) slowness; (humorous) deliberation.

sorocharse [1a] vr (a) (Bol, Chi, Ec, Per) = asorocharse. (b) (Chi) to blush.

soroche nm (a) (SAm) mountain sickness, sickness caused by great altitudes. (b) (Chi) blush(ing). (c) (Bol, Chi) galena, silver-bearing ore.

sorprendente adj surprising; amazing; startling; no es — que ... it is hardly surprising that ..., it is small wonder that ...

sorprender [2a] **1** vt (a) to surprise; to amaze; to startle.

(b) (Mil etc) to surprise; to catch unawares, take by surprise; conversation to overhear; secret to find out, discover; hiding place to come across; — a uno en el hecho to catch someone in the act.

2 sorprenderse vr to be surprised (de at), be amazed (de at); no me sorprendería de que fuera así I shouldn't be surprised if it were like that; se sorprendió mucho he was very surprised.

sorpresa 1 nf (a) (emotion) surprise; amazement; causar — a, producir — a to surprise; con gran — mía, para mí — much to my surprise, to my great surprise.

(b) (act) surprise; ¡qué —!, ¡vaya —! what a surprise!; coger a uno de — to take someone by surprise, come as a surprise to someone.

(c) (fig) surprise package.

(d) (Mil) surprise attack; coger por — to surprise.

2 as adj surprise (attr); resultado — surprise result.

sorpresivo adj (SAm) surprising; sudden, unexpected.

sorrajar [1a] vt (Mex) to hit; to wound.

sorrasear [1a] vt (Mex) to roast partially, grill.

sorrongar [1h] vi (Col) to grumble.

sorrostrigar [1h] vt (Col) to pester, annoy.

sortario adj (Ven) lucky.

sortear [1a] **1** vt (a) to draw lots for, decide by lot; to draw out of a hat; object etc to raffle (for charity); (Sport) ends to toss up for.

(b) obstacle to dodge, avoid; to get round; to manage to miss, swerve past; el torero sorteó al toro the bullfighter eluded the bull; el esquiador sorteó muy bien las banderas the skier swerved round the flags skilfully.

(c) (fig) difficulty to avoid; to get round, overcome; question to handle, deal with (skilfully).

2 vi to draw lots; to toss, toss up.

sorteo nm (a) draw, drawing lots; raffle; (Sport) toss; ganar el — to win the toss. (b) dodging, avoidance; swerving.

sortija nf (a) ring; — de sello signet ring. (b) curl, ringlet.

sortilegio nm (a) sorcery; fortunetelling; magical prediction. (b) (un —) spell, charm. (c) (fig) charm, magical attraction; unnatural influence.

sosa nf soda; — cáustica caustic soda.

sosco nm (Col) bit, piece.

sosegadamente adv quietly, calmly, peacefully; gently.

sosegado adj (a) quiet, calm, peaceful; gentle. (b) person calm, sedate, steady.

sosegar [1h and 1k] **1** vt to calm, quieten; to lull; mind etc to reassure; doubts, fears to allay.

2 vi to rest.

3 sosegarse vr to calm down, become calm; to quieten down.

sosería nf (a) insipidness. (b) (fig) dullness; flatness; colourlessness. (c) es una — it's boring, it's terribly dull.

sosiego nm (a) calm(ness), quiet(ness); peacefulness.

(b) calmness, sedateness, steadiness, composure; hacer algo con — to do something calmly.

soslayar [1a] vt (a) to put across, put sideways, place obliquely. (b) (fig) difficulty to get round; question to dodge, sidestep; meeting to avoid.

soslayo: al —, de — adv obliquely, sideways, aslant; mirada de — sidelong glance; mirar de — to look out of the corner of one's eye (at); (fig) to look askance (at), look down one's nose (at).

soso adj (a) (Cook) tasteless, insipid; unsalted; unsweetened. (b) (fig) dull, uninteresting, flat, colourless.

sospecha nf (all senses) suspicion.

sospechar [1a] **1** vt to suspect. **2** vi: — de to suspect, be suspicious of, have one's suspicions about.

sospechosamente adv suspiciously.

sospechoso 1 adj suspicious; suspect; todos son —s everybody is under suspicion; es — de desafecto al régimen he is suspected of being hostile to the régime, it is suspected that he is hostile to the régime; tiene amistades sospechosas some of his acquaintances are suspect.

2 nm, sospechosa nf suspect.

sosquín nm (Cu) (a) wide corner, obtuse angle. (b) treacherous blow.

sosquinar [1a] vt (Cu) to hit (or wound etc) treacherously.

sostén nm (a) (Archit etc) support, prop; stand; pillar, post.

(b) (woman's) brassière, bra (fam).

(c) sustenance, food, nourishment.

(d) (fig) support, pillar, mainstay; el principal — del gobierno the mainstay of the government; el único — de su familia the sole support of his family.

sostener [2l] **1** vt (a) (Archit etc) to hold up, support; to prop up; load to carry; weight to bear; (of person) to hold up, hold on to; ¡sostén! hold this!; los dos sosteníamos la cuerda we were both holding the rope; la cinta le sostiene el pelo the ribbon keeps her hair in place.

(b) (fig) person to support, back; to help; to defend; su partido le sostiene en el poder his party keeps him in power; esta manifestación de apoyo sirve para —me this demonstration of support strengthens my resolve; le sostienen los nervios his nerves keep him going.

(c) (with food) to sustain, keep going.

(d) (Mus) note to hold.

(e) (fig) charge etc to maintain; opinion to stand by, stick to, uphold; promise to stand by; proposition, theory to maintain; pressure to keep up, sustain; resistance to strengthen, boost, bolster up; — que ... to maintain that ..., hold that ...

(f) (fig) position, speed, struggle etc to keep up, maintain.

(g) (Fin) to maintain, pay for; costs to meet, defray.

(h) — la mirada de uno to stare someone out, look someone in the eye without flinching.

2 sostenerse vr (a) to hold oneself up, support oneself; to stand up; apenas podía — de puro cansado he was so utterly tired he could hardly stand.

(b) (fig) to support oneself; to keep (oneself) going; to last out; en el poder to stay in power; — vendiendo corbatas to support oneself by selling ties.

(c) (fig) to continue, remain; el mercado se sostiene firme the market remains firm, the market continues steady; se sostiene el régimen lluvioso rainy conditions prevail.

sostenidamente adv steadily, continuously.

sostenido 1 adj (a) steady, continuous, sustained; prolonged. (b) (Mus) sharp. **2** nm (Mus) sharp.

sostenimiento nm (a) support; holding up; maintenance; upholding; strengthening; bolstering. (b) (Fin) maintenance; (of body) sustenance.

sota[1] nf (a) (Cards) jack, knave. (b) (fam) hussy, brazen woman; whore.

sota[2] nm (Chi) overseer, foreman.

sotabanco nm (a) attic, garret. (b) (Arg) poky little room, dirty room.

sotabarba nf double chin, jowl.

sotacura nm (Arg, Col, Chi) curate.

sotana nf (a) (Eccl) cassock, soutane. (b) (fam) hiding.

sotanear [1a] vt (fam) to tick off.

sótano nm basement; cellar; (of bank etc) vault.

sotavento: Islas fpl de — Leeward Isles.

sotavento nm lee, leeward; a — to leeward; de — leeward (attr).

sotechado nm shed.

soterrar [1k] vt to bury; (fig) to bury, hide away.
soto nm (a) thicket; grove, copse. (b) (Ec) rough patch, bump (on the skin); knot, tangle.
sotobosque nm undergrowth.
sotreta nf (Bol, RPl) (a) vicious horse; useless horse, old horse. (b) (person) useless individual; idler; unreliable person.
soturno adj taciturn, silent; unsociable.
soviet [so'βie] nm, pl **soviets** [so'βie] soviet.
soviético 1 adj Soviet (attr). 2 nm: **los —s** the Soviets, the Russians.
soy see **ser**.
spleen [es'plin] nm (angl) see **esplín**.
sport [es'por] nm (angl) sport; **chaqueta (de) —** sports coat; **un hombre vestido de —** a man wearing sports clothes.
sprint [es'prin] nm (angl) etc see **esprint** etc.
stand [es'tan] nm, pl **stands** [es'tan] (angl) stand.
stándard [es'tandar] adj and nm etc (angl) see **estándar** etc.
stárter [es'tarter] nm (a) (Aut: angl) self-starter, starting motor. (b) (SAm, Sport: angl) starter; starting gate.
statu quo nm status quo.
status nm, pl **status** status.
stock [es'tok] nm, pl **stocks** [es'tok] (Comm: angl) stock, supply.
stop [es'top] nm (angl) (a) (Tel) stop. (b) (Aut) stop sign, halt sign.
store [es'tor] nm (gall) sunblind, awning.
su poss adj (a) (one possessor) his, hers, its; one's; (relating to Vd) your. (b) (plural possessors) their; (relating to Vds) your.
suampo nm (CAm: angl) swamp.
suato adj (Mex) silly.
suave adj (a) surface smooth, even; skin smooth; mixture, paste etc smooth.
　(b) colour, curve, slope, movement, touch, rebuke, wind etc gentle; air soft, mild, sweet; climate mild; work easy; working of machine smooth, easy; music, voice soft, sweet, mellow; noise soft, gentle, quiet; smell sweet; flavour smooth, mild.
　(c) person, character gentle; meek, docile; **estuvo muy — conmigo** he was very sweet to me, he was very helpful to me, he behaved very nicely to me.
　(d) (Chi, Mex) big, huge; outstanding.
　(e) (Mex) charming, attractive; splendid; **¡—!** yes of course!
suavemente adv smoothly; gently; softly, sweetly.
suavidad nf smoothness, evenness; gentleness; softness, mildness; sweetness.
suavizador nm razor strop.
suavizar [1f] vt (a) to smooth (out, down); to soften; paste etc to make smoother; razor to strop; slope etc to ease, make more gentle; colour to tone down; tone to soften.
　(b) person to mollify, soften, make gentler; character to mellow; harshness to soften, temper.
sub... sub..., under..., eg **subempleo** underemployment, **subprivilegiado** underprivileged, **subvalorar** to undervalue.
suba nf (CAm) rise (in prices).
subalimentación nf underfeeding, undernourishment.
subalimentado adj underfed, undernourished.
subalpino adj subalpine.
subalterno 1 adj importance etc secondary; personnel etc minor, auxiliary. 2 nm subordinate.
subametralladora nf submachine gun.
subarrendador nm, **subarrendadora** nf subtenant.
subarrendar [1k] vt to sublet, sublease.
subarrendatario nm, **subarrendataria** nf subtenant.
subarriendo nm subtenancy, sublease.
subártico adj subarctic.
subasta nf (a) auction, sale by auction; (for work etc) tender(ing); **poner en** (or **sacar a**) **pública —** to put up for auction, sell at auction.
　(b) (Cards) auction.
subastador nm auctioneer.
subastar [1a] vt to auction, auction off, sell at auction.
subcampeón nm runner-up.
subcomisión nf subcommittee.
subconsciencia nf subconcious.
subconsciente 1 adj subconscious. 2 nm: **el —** the subconscious; **en el —** in the subconscious.
subcontinente nm subcontinent.
subcontratista nmf subcontractor.
subcontrato nm subcontract.
subcutáneo adj subcutaneous.
subdesarrollado adj underdeveloped.

subdesarrollo nm underdevelopment.
subdirector nm, **subdirectora** nf subdirector; **— de biblioteca** sub-librarian.
súbdito 1 adj subject. 2 nm, **súbdita** nf (Pol) subject.
subdividir [3a] 1 vt to subdivide. 2 **subdividirse** vr to subdivide.
subdivisión nf subdivision.
subespecie nf subspecies.
subestación nf substation.
subestimación nf underestimation; undervaluation; understatement.
subestimar [1a] vt capacity, enemy etc to underestimate, underrate; object, property to undervalue; case to understate.
subexpuesto adj (Phot) underexposed.
subida nf (a) climb, climbing; ascent; **una — en globo** a balloon ascent; **en la — había muchas flores** there were a lot of flowers on the way up; **es una — difícil** it's a tough climb.
　(b) (in price, quantity etc) rise, increase (de in); (in rank) promotion (a to); **esto va de —** this is increasing, this is on the increase; **el calor va de —** it's getting hotter.
　(c) slope, hill; (as street name) rise, hill.
subido adj (a) price etc high. (b) colour bright, strong, intense; smell strong; see **color**. (c) person vain, proud.
subienda nf (Col: Fish) shoal.
subilón adj (Per) liquor strong, heady.
subilla nf awl.
subinquilino nm, **subinquilina** nf subtenant.
subir [3a] 1 vt (a) object to raise, lift up; to put up; to take up, get up; head etc to raise; **que me suban los equipajes** please see that my luggage is brought up (or taken up); **lo subieron a la reja** they put it up on the rack.
　(b) slope, street etc to go up; stairs to climb, mount, ascend.
　(c) person to promote (a to).
　(d) (Archit) to build, raise, put up; **— una pared** to build a wall.
　(e) price, salary etc to raise, put up, increase; article to put up the price of.
　(f) (Mus) to raise the pitch of.
　2 vi (a) to go up, come up; to move up; to climb; (on horse etc) to get on, mount; (into vehicle) to get in, get on; **le subieron los colores a la cara** she blushed; **el vino me sube a la cabeza** wine goes to my head; **— a caballo** to mount, get on one's horse; **— al tren** to get into the train, get on to the train; **seguíamos subiendo** we went on climbing; **bajar es peor que —** coming down is worse than going up.
　(b) (of mercury, river, tide etc) to rise.
　(c) (Fin) — a to amount to.
　(d) (of person: fig) to be promoted (a to), rise, move up.
　(e) (of price, value etc) to rise, increase, go up; (of epidemic etc) to spread; (of fever etc) to get worse; **sigue subiendo la bolsa** the market is still rising; **— de tono** to get louder, increase in volume.
　3 **subirse** vr (a) to get up, climb (a on to); to go up, rise; **— al tren** to get on the train; **el niño se le subió a las rodillas** the child climbed on to her knees; **se me sube el vino a la cabeza** wine goes to my head; see **tono** etc.
　(b) (fig) to get conceited; to become bolder; to forget one's manners.
　(c) (Bot) to grow very tall, shoot up.
súbitamente adv suddenly; unexpectedly.
súbito 1 adj (a) sudden; unexpected. (b) (fam) hasty, rash. (c) (fam) irritable. 2 adv (also **de —**) suddenly; unexpectedly.
subjetivamente adv subjectively.
subjetividad nf subjectivity.
subjetivismo nm subjectivism.
subjetivo adj subjective.
subjuntivo 1 adj subjunctive. 2 nm subjunctive (mood).
sublevación nf revolt, rising.
sublevar [1a] 1 vt (a) to rouse to revolt, stir up a revolt among.
　(b) (fig) to upset, put out, irritate; to rouse to fury.
　2 **sublevarse** vr to revolt, rise, rebel.
sublimación nf sublimation.
sublimado nm (Chem) sublimate.
sublimar [1a] vt (a) person to exalt, praise. (b) desires etc to sublimate. (c) (Chem) to sublimate.
sublime adj (a) sublime; noble, lofty, grand; **lo —** the sublime. (b) (lit) high, tall, lofty.
sublimemente adv sublimely.
sublimidad nf sublimity.

subliminal *adj* subliminal.
submarinista *nmf* underwater fisherman, underwater diver (*or* explorer *etc*).
submarino 1 *adj* underwater, submarine. **2** *nm* submarine.
suboficial *nm* non-commissioned officer; sergeant-major.
subordinación *nf* subordination.
subordinado 1 *adj* subordinate; **X queda — a Y** X is subordinate to Y. **2** *nm*, **subordinada** *nf* subordinate.
subrayable *adj* worth emphasizing; **el punto más —** the point which is particularly to be noted, the most important point.
subrayado 1 *adj* underlined; italicized, in italics. **2** *nm* underlining; italics; **el — es mío** my italics, the italics are mine.
subrayar [1a] *vt* (a) to underline; to italicize, put in italics. (b) (*fig*) to underline, emphasize.
subrepticiamente *adv* surreptitiously.
subrepticio *adj* surreptitious.
subsanable *adj* excusable; repairable; **un error fácilmente —** an error which is easily rectified; **un obstáculo difícilmente —** an obstacle which is hard to overcome.
subsanar [1a] *vt* *fault* to overlook, excuse; *damage, defect* to repair, make good; *error* to rectify, put right; *shortcoming* to make up for; *difficulty, obstacle* to get round, overcome.
subscr . . . see suscr . . .
subsecretaría *nf* undersecretaryship.
subsecretario *nm*, **subsecretaria** *nf* undersecretary.
subsector *nm* subsection.
subsecuente *adj* subsequent.
subsidiario *adj* subsidiary.
subsidio *nm* (a) subsidy, grant; aid, financial help; benefit; **— de enfermedad** sick benefit, sick pay; **— de exportación** export subsidy; **— familiar** family allowance; **— de huelga** strike pay; **— de natalidad** maternity benefit; **— de paro** unemployment benefit, unemployment compensation (US); **— de vejez** old-age pension.
(b) (*Col, Ec*) anxiety, worry.
subsiguiente *adj* subsequent.
subsistencia *nf* subsistence; sustenance.
subsistente *adj* lasting, enduring; surviving; **una costumbre aún —** a still surviving custom.
subsistir [3a] *vi* (a) to subsist, live (*con, de* on); to survive, last out, endure; **todavía subsiste el edificio** the building still stands; **es una creencia que subsiste** it is a belief which still exists; **sin ayuda económica no podrá — el colegio** the college will not be able to survive without financial aid.
(b) (*Per*) to live together.
subsónico *adj* subsonic.
subst . . . see sust . . .
subsuelo *nm* subsoil.
subteniente *nm* sub-lieutenant, second lieutenant.
subterfugio *nm* subterfuge.
subterráneo 1 *adj* underground, subterranean.
2 *nm* (a) underground passage; underground store (*or* cellar *etc*).
(b) (*SAm*) underground railway, subway (US).
subtitular [1a] *vt* to subtitle.
subtítulo *nm* subtitle, subheading.
subtropical *adj* subtropical.
suburbano 1 *adj* suburban. **2** *nm* suburban train.
suburbio *nm* (a) suburb, outlying area. (b) slum quarter; shantytown, collection of shacks.
subvención *nf* subsidy, subvention, grant; **— estatal** state subsidy; **—es agrícolas** agricultural subsidies.
subvencionar [1a] *vt* to subsidize, aid.
subvenir [3s] *vi:* **— a** *costs* to meet, defray; *needs etc* to provide for; **con eso subviene a sus vicios** with that he pays for his vices; **así subviene a la escasez de su sueldo** in that way he makes up for his low salary.
subversión *nf* (a) (*in general*) subversion.
(b) (*una —*) revolution; **la — del orden establecido** the overthrow of the established order.
subversivo *adj* subversive.
subvertir [3i] *vi* to subvert; to overthrow, undermine; to disturb.
subyacente *adj* underlying.
subyugación *nf* subjugation.
subyugador *adj* (*fig*) captivating, enchanting.
subyugar [1h] *vt* (a) *country etc* to subjugate, subdue; *enemy* to overpower; *will etc* to dominate, gain control over.
(b) (*fig*) to captivate, charm.
succión *nf* suction.
succionar [1a] *vt* to suck; to apply suction to;

(*Tech*) to absorb, soak up, suck up; **— su pipa** to suck (at) one's pipe, puff (at) one's pipe.
sucedáneo *nm* substitute (food).
suceder [2a] **1** *vti* (a) to happen; **pues sucede que no vamos** well it happens we're not going; **no le había sucedido eso nunca** that had never happened to him before; **suceda lo que suceda** come what may, whatever happens; **¿qué sucede?** what's going on?, whatever's all this?; **lo que sucede es que . . .** the fact is that . . ., the trouble is that . . .; **lo más que puede — es que . . .** the worst that can happen is that . . .; **llevar algo por lo que pueda —** to take something just in case.
(b) to succeed, follow; to inherit; **— a uno en un puesto** to succeed someone in a post; **— al trono** to succeed to the throne; **— a una fortuna** to inherit a fortune; **al otoño sucede el invierno** winter follows autumn; **a este cuarto sucede otro mayor** a larger room leads off this one, a large room lies beyond this one.
2 sucederse *vr* to follow one another.
sucesión *nf* (a) succession (*a* to); sequence, series; **una — de acontecimientos** a succession of events, a series of happenings; **en rápida —** in quick succession; **la princesa ocupa el quinto puesto en la línea de — al trono** the princess is fifth in the line of succession to the throne.
(b) inheritance; estate.
(c) issue, offspring; **morir sin —** to die without issue.
sucesivamente *adv* successively, in succession; **y así — and so on.**
sucesivo *adj* successive, following; consecutive; **3 días —s** 3 days running; 3 successive days; **en lo —** henceforth, in future; (*in past*) thereafter, thenceforth.
suceso *nm* (a) event, happening; incident; **capítulo de —s** (*newspaper*) section of accident and crime reports.
(b) issue, outcome; **buen —** happy outcome.
sucesor *nm*, **sucesora** *nf* successor; heir.
suciamente *adv* (a) dirtily, filthily. (b) (*fig*) vilely, meanly; obscenely, unfairly.
suciedad *nf* (a) dirt, filth, grime; dirtiness; filthiness.
(b) (*fig*) vileness, meanness; obscenity; unfairness.
(c) (*una —*) dirty act; filthy remark; obscenity.
sucintamente *adv* succinctly, concisely, briefly.
sucinto *adj* (a) succinct, concise, brief. (b) *garment* short, brief, scanty.
sucio 1 *adj* (a) (*general sense*) dirty; filthy, grimy, grubby, soiled; *colour* dirty; blurred, smudged; *sketch etc* rough, messy; *tongue* coated, furred.
(b) (*fig*) *conduct* vile, mean, despicable; *act, word etc* dirty, filthy, obscene; *play* foul, dirty; *tactics* unfair.
(c) *conscience* bad.
2 *adv:* **jugar —** to play unfairly, indulge in dirty play.
3 *nm* (*Col*) smut, bit of dirt.
suco[1] *adj* (*Bol, Ven*) muddy, swampy.
suco[2] *adj* (*Ec*) bright reddish; blond, fair; (*Per*) orange.
sucre *nm* *standard monetary unit of Ecuador.*
sucrosa *nf* sucrose.
suculencia *nf* tastiness, richness; succulence, lusciousness, juiciness.
suculento *adj* tasty, rich; succulent, luscious, juicy.
sucumbir [3a] *vi* to succumb (*a* to).
sucursal *nf* branch, branch office; subsidiary.
sucusumuco: a lo — *adv* (*Col, Cu, PR*) in a mock-foolish way, as if one were stupid.
suche 1 *adj* (*Ven*) sharp, bitter.
2 *nm* (a) (*Arg*) pimple.
(b) (*Chi*) subordinate.
(c) (*Chi*) pimp.
súchil *nm* (*Mex*) bouquet of sweet-smelling flowers.
sucho *adj* (*Arg, Ec*) maimed, paralytic.
sud *nm* south.
sudafricano 1 *adj* South African. **2** *nm*, **sudafricana** *nf* South African.
Sudamérica *f* South America.
sudamericano 1 *adj* South American. **2** *nm*, **sudamericana** *nf* South American.
Sudán *m* Sudan.
sudanés 1 *adj* Sudanese. **2** *nm*, **sudanesa** *nf* Sudanese.
sudar [1a] **1** *vt* (a) to sweat; *see* **sangre** *etc*.
(b) (*Bot etc*) to ooze, give out, give off; (*of container*) to ooze, give out; (*of wall etc*) to sweat, give off moisture.
(c) *garment etc* to make sweaty, make damp with sweat.
(d) (*fam*) **— un aumento de sueldo** to sweat for

a rise in pay, work hard for some extra money; **ha sudado el premio** he really sweated to get the prize.

(e) (*sl*) *money* to cough up (*sl*), part with.

2 *vi* to sweat; **hacer — a uno** (*fig*) to make someone sweat.

sudario *nm* shroud.

sudeste 1 *adj part* south-east, south-eastern; *direction* south-easterly; *wind* south-east, south-easterly.

2 *nm* (a) south-east.

(b) south-east wind.

sudoeste *adj and nm see* **suroeste**.

sudón *adj* (*SAm*) sweaty.

sudor *nm* sweat; (*fig: also* **—es**) sweat, toil, labour; **con el — de su frente** by the sweat of one's brow.

sudoriento *adj*, **sudoroso** *adj*, **sudoso** *adj* sweaty, sweating; covered with sweat; **trabajo sudoroso** thirsty work, work that makes one sweat a lot.

Suecia *f* Sweden.

suecia *nf* suède.

sueco 1 *adj* Swedish.

2 *nm*, **sueca** *nf* Swede; **hacerse el —** (*fam*) to pretend not to hear (*or* understand); to act dumb (*fam*), not let on.

3 *nm* (*language*) Swedish.

suegra *nf* mother-in-law.

suegro *nm* father-in-law.

suela *nf* (a) (*of shoe*) sole; piece of strong leather; (*Tech*) tap washer; **media —** half sole; (*fig*) patch, botch; (*fig*) temporary remedy; temporary relief; **A no le llega a la — del zapato a B** A can't hold a candle to B.

(b) **—s** (*Eccl*) sandals; **de siete —s** utter, downright.

(c) (*Fish*) sole.

suelazo *nm* (*SAm*) heavy fall, nasty bump.

sueldo *nm* salary, pay; **estar a —** to be on a salary, earn a salary; **estar a — de una potencia extranjera** to be in the pay of a foreign power.

suelear [1a] *vt* (*Arg*) to throw, hurl.

suelo *nm* (a) ground; surface; **— natal, — patrio** native land, native soil; **arrastrar** (*or* **poner, tirar**) **por los —s** to blacken, run down, speak ill of; **caer al —** to fall to the ground; **caerse al —** (*fig*) to fail, collapse; **echar al —** *building* to demolish; *hopes* to dash; *plan* to ruin; **echarse al —** to hurl oneself to the ground; to fall on one's knees; **los precios están por el —** prices are at rock-bottom; **esos géneros están por los —s** those goods are dirt cheap; **medir el —** to measure one's length (on the ground), fall full-length; **venirse al —** (*fig*) to fail, collapse, be ruined.

(b) (*of house etc*) floor; flooring.

(c) (*Arg*) ground, soil, land; **— vegetal** topsoil.

(d) (*of vessel etc*) bottom.

sueltista *nmf* (*SAm*) freelance journalist.

suelto 1 *adj* (a) free; untied, undone; detached, unattached, separate; loose; unhampered; *dress etc* loose, loose-fitting; **— de lengua** talkative; cheeky, given to answering back; not to be trusted with secrets; foulmouthed; **— de vientre** loose; **el libro tiene dos hojas sueltas** the book has two pages loose; **llevas —s los cordones** your shoelaces are undone; **el perro anda —** the dog is loose; **lo ató con el cabo —** he tied it up with the free (*or* loose) end; **lo dejamos —** we leave it untied, we leave it free.

(b) *fragment, passage etc* detached, isolated; individual; *number, volume* single; **es un trozo — de la novela** it's a separate piece from the novel, it's an isolated passage from the novel; **son 3 poesías sueltas** these are 3 separate poems; **los tomos no se venden —s** the volumes are not sold singly (*or* separately); **hay un calcetín —** there is one odd sock; **una mesa con números —s de revistas** a table with odd copies of magazines.

(c) (*in movement*) free; light; quick, agile, unhampered; *style* fluent, free, flowing.

(d) (*morally*) free and easy; daring; licentious, lax.

(e) (*Lit*) *verse* blank.

2 *nm* (a) (*Fin*) change, loose change, small change.

(b) (*Typ*) paragraph; (*in paper*) item, note, short article.

sueñera *nf* (*SAm*) drowsiness, sleepiness.

sueño *nm* (a) sleep; **— eterno** (*euph*) eternal rest; **— invernal** (*Zool*) winter sleep; **— pesado, — profundo** deep sleep, heavy sleep; **coger el —, conciliar el —** to get to sleep; **descabezar un —, echarse un —** to have a nap; **pasar una noche sin —** to have a sleepless night; **perder el — por algo**

to lose sleep over something; **tener el — ligero** to be a light sleeper; **tener el — pesado** (*or* **profundo**) to be a heavy sleeper.

(b) sleepiness, drowsiness; **caerse de —** to be so sleepy one can hardly stand; **espantar el —** to struggle to keep awake; **tener —** to be sleepy.

(c) dream (*also fig*); **¡ni en —s!, ¡ni por —!** not on your life!; **es su — dorado** it's the dream of his life, it's his great dream; **ver algo en** (*or* **entre**) **—s** to see something in a dream; **vive en un mundo de —s** she lives in a dream world; **tiene una casa que es un —** she has a real dream of a house.

suero *nm* (a) (*Med*) serum. (b) whey; **— de manteca** buttermilk.

suerte *nf* (a) fate, destiny; chance, fortune; **por —** by chance, as it happened; **confiar algo a la —** to leave something to chance; **dejar a uno a su —** to abandon someone to his fate; **la — que les espera** the fate which awaits them; **quiso la — que ...** as fate would have it . . ., as luck would have it . . .; **seguir la — a uno** to keep track of someone; **tentar a la —** to tempt fate; **unirse a la — de uno** to throw in one's lot with someone, make common cause with someone.

(b) lot; **caber en — a uno, caer en — a uno** to fall to someone, fall to someone's lot; **no me cupo la —** I had no such luck; **echaron —s entre los 4** the 4 of them drew lots, the 4 of them tossed up; **lo echaron a —s** they drew lots for it, they tossed up for it; **la — está echada** the die is cast.

(c) luck; **buena — luck, good luck; ¡buena —!** good luck!; **mala — bad luck, hard luck; hombre de — lucky man; un número de mala — an unlucky number; por — luckily, fortunately; dar —, traer — to bring luck; trae mala — escupir allí** it's unlucky to spit there; **estar de — to be in luck; probar — to try one's luck; tener — to be lucky; to have a piece of luck; ¡que tengas —!** good luck!, I wish you luck!, and the best of luck!; **tuvo una — loca** he was fantastically lucky; **tuvo la — de que hacía buen tiempo** he was lucky that it was fine.

(d) lot; state, condition; **mejorar de — to improve one's lot.**

(e) lottery ticket.

(f) sort, kind; **es una — de** it is a kind of; **no podemos seguir de esta —** we cannot go on in this way; **de otra —** otherwise, if not; **de — que ...** in such a way that . . ., so that . .; **¿de — que no hay más dragones?** so there are no more dragons?

(g) (*Taur*) stage, part (*of the bullfight*); **— de varas** opening section (*of play with the capes*).

(h) (*Arg*) lot, piece of ground.

suertero 1 *adj* (*SAm*) lucky. **2** *nm* (*CAm, Per*) seller of lottery tickets.

suertoso *adj* (*Ec*) lucky.

suertudo *adj* (*SAm*) lucky.

sueste *nm* (a) (*Naut etc*) sou'wester. (b) (*SAm*) south-east wind.

suéter *nm* (*angl*) sweater.

Suetonio *m* Suetonius.

Suez Suez; **Canal de —** Suez Canal.

suficiencia *nf* (a) sufficiency; adequacy; **una — de ...** enough . . .; **con —** sufficiently, adequately.

(b) competence; suitability, fitness; adequacy; capacity; **demostrar su —** to prove one's competence, show one's capabilities.

(c) (*pej*) self-importance; superiority; condescension; smugness, self-satisfaction, complacency; *see* **aire.**

suficiente *adj* (a) enough, sufficient (*para* for); adequate.

(b) *person* competent; suitable, fit; adequate; capable.

(c) (*pej*) self-important; superior; condescending; smug, self-satisfied, complacent.

suficientemente *adv* sufficiently, adequately.

sufijo *nm* suffix.

suflé *nm* soufflé.

sufragáneo *adj* suffragan.

sufragar [1h] **1** *vt* (a) to aid, help, support.

(b) *costs* to meet, defray, cover; *project etc* to pay for, defray the costs of.

2 *vi* (*SAm*) to vote (*por* for).

sufragio *nm* (a) vote; **los —s emitidos a favor de X** the votes cast for X.

(b) suffrage; franchise; **— universal** universal suffrage.

(c) help, aid.

(d) (*Eccl*) intercession for souls in purgatory.

sufragista *nf* suffragette.

sufrible *adj* bearable.

sufrido 1 *adj* **(a)** *person* tough; long-suffering, patient.
(b) *cloth etc* hard-wearing, long-lasting, tough; *colour* that does not show the dirt, that wears well.
(c) *husband* complaisant.
2 *nm* complaisant husband.
sufridor 1 *adj* suffering. **2** *nm* **(a)** sufferer. **(b)** *(Col, Ven)* saddlecloth.
sufrimiento *nm* **(a)** *(state)* suffering; misery, wretchedness.
(b) *(quality)* toughness; patience; tolerance; **tener — en las dificultades** to be patient in hard times, bear troubles patiently.
sufrir [3a] **1** *vt* **(a)** *(general sense)* to suffer; *accident, attack* to have, suffer; *consequences, disaster, disappointment etc* to suffer; *change* to undergo, experience; *loss* to suffer, sustain; *operation* to have, undergo.
(b) to bear, stand, put up with; **no sufre la menor descortesía** he won't tolerate the slightest rudeness; **A no le sufre a B** A can't stand B.
(c) *object* to hold up, support.
(d) *exam, test* to take, undergo.
2 *vi* to suffer; **— de** to suffer from, suffer with; **sufre de reumatismo** she suffers from (*or* with) rheumatism; **sufre mucho de los pies** she suffers a lot with her feet; **aprender a — silenciosamente** to learn to suffer in silence.
sugerencia *nf* suggestion.
sugerente *adj* full of suggestions, rich in ideas, thought-provoking.
sugerible *adj* = **sugestionable**.
sugerir [3i] *vt* to suggest; to hint, hint at; *thought etc* to prompt; **— que ...** to suggest that ...
sugestión *nf* **(a)** suggestion; hint; prompting, stimulus; **las —es del corazón** the promptings of the heart; **un sitio de muchas —es** a place rich in associations.
(b) autosuggestion, self-hypnotism.
(c) fascination (for others), hypnotic power, power to influence others; **emanaba de él una fuerte —** a strong hypnotic power flowed from him.
sugestionable *adj* impressionable, suggestible; open to influence, readily influenced.
sugestionar [1a] **1** *vt* to influence, dominate the will of, hypnotize; to exercise a powerful fascination over; **— a uno para que haga algo** to influence someone to do something.
2 **sugestionarse** *vr* to indulge in autosuggestion; **es probable que se haya dejado — por ...** he may have allowed himself to be influenced by . . .; **te lo has sugestionado** you've talked yourself into it.
sugestivo *adj* **(a)** stimulating, thought-provoking.
(b) attractive; fascinating.
suicida 1 *adj* suicidal.
2 *nmf* suicidal case, person with a tendency to suicide; person who has committed suicide; **es un — conduciendo** he drives in a suicidal way.
suicidarse [1a] *vr* to commit suicide, kill oneself.
suicidio *nm* suicide.
Suiza *f* Switzerland.
suiza[1] *nf* **(a)** *(CAm, Cu)* skipping, skipping game. **(b)** *(CAm, Ec, Ven)* beating.
suizo[1] **1** *adj* Swiss. **2** *nm*, **suiza**[2] *nf* Swiss.
suizo[2] *nm* sugared bun.
sujeción *nf* **(a)** *(state)* subjection. **(b)** *(act)* fastening; seizure; *(fig)* subjection (*a* to); **con — a** subject to.
sujetador *nm* fastener; *(for hair)* clip, pin, grip; *(for papers)* clip; *(of pen)* clip; *(garment)* brassière, bra *(fam)*; **— de libros** book end.
sujetapapeles *nm*, *pl* **sujetapapeles** paper clip.
sujetar [1a] **1** *vt* **(a)** *nation, people* to subdue, conquer; to hold down, keep down, keep under; to exercise control over; **— A a B** to put A under B's authority, subordinate A to B.
(b) *object* to seize, clutch, lay hold of; to hold tight; *person* to hold down, keep hold of; *(Tech)* to fasten; to nail down, stick down, screw down *(etc)*; *hair etc* to keep in place, hold in place; *papers etc* to fasten together.
2 **sujetarse** *vr*: **— a** to subject oneself to; *rule* to abide by; *circumstance, pay etc* to act in accordance with, recognize the limitations of; *authority* to submit to; **— a + infin** to agree to + *infin*, give way before the necessity of + *ger*.
sujeto 1 *adj* **(a)** fastened, secure; firm; tight; **la cuerda está bien sujeta** the rope is securely fastened.
(b) **— a** subject to; liable to; **— a la aprobación de** subject to the approval of; **— a derechos** subject to duty, dutiable; **ser — a cambios inesperados** to be liable to sudden changes.
2 *nm* **(a)** *(Gram)* subject.

(b) individual; *(Med etc)* subject, case; *(fam)* fellow, character *(fam)*, chap *(fam)*; **un — sospechoso** a suspicious character; **buen —** good chap.
sulfa *nf*: **fármacos —** sulpha drugs.
sulfato *nm* sulphate; **— de cobre** copper sulphate.
sulfonamida *nf* sulphonamide.
sulfurar [1a] **1** *vt* **(a)** *(Chem)* to sulphurate.
(b) *(fam)* to annoy, rile *(fam)*.
2 **sulfurarse** *vr* *(fam)* to get riled *(fam)*, see red, blow up *(fam)*.
sulfúreo *adj* sulphurous.
sulfúrico *adj* sulphuric.
sulfuro *nm* sulphide.
sulfuroso *adj* sulphurous.
sultán *nm* sultan.
sultana *nf* sultana.
sultanato *nm* sultanate.
suma *nf* **(a)** *(Math: act)* adding (up), addition; *(quantity)* total, sum; *(of money)* sum: **"— y sigue"** *(in account)* "carried forward"; *(fam)* and it's still going on; **— global** lump sum; **en —** in short.
(b) *(fig)* summary; essence; **una — de perfecciones** perfection itself; **es la — y compendio de todas las virtudes** she is the personification of all the virtues.
sumadora *nf* adding machine.
sumamente *adv* extremely, exceedingly, highly.
sumar [1a] **1** *vt* **(a)** *(Math)* to add (up), total; *(fig)* *argument etc* to summarize, sum up.
(b) to collect, gather.
(c) la cuenta suma 6 dólares the bill adds up to (*or* comes to, amounts to, works out at) 6 dollars.
2 *vi* to add up.
3 **sumarse** *vr*: **— a un partido** to join a party; **— a una protesta** to associate oneself with a protest, join in a protest.
sumariamente *adv* summarily.
sumario 1 *adj* brief, concise; *(Law)* summary.
2 *nm* **(a)** summary. **(b)** *(Law)* indictment.
sumergible *adj* submersible; that can go under water.
sumergido *adj* submerged, sunken.
sumergimiento *nm* submersion, submergence.
sumergir [3c] **1** *vt* **(a)** to submerge; to sink; to immerse, dip, plunge (*en* in).
(b) *(fig)* to plunge (*en* into).
2 **sumergirse** *vr* **(a)** to submerge, sink beneath the surface; to dive.
(b) *(fig)* **— en** to immerse oneself in, become absorbed in.
sumersión *nf* **(a)** submersion, submergence; immersion. **(b)** *(fig)* absorption (*en* in).
sumidero *nm* **(a)** drain, sewer; sink; *(Tech)* sump; *(Per, PR)* cesspool.
(b) *(PR)* quagmire.
(c) *(PR)* drain; **es el gran — de las reservas** it is the chief drain on our reserves.
suministrador *nm*, **suministradora** *nf* supplier.
suministrar [1a] *vt* *goods, information etc* to supply, furnish, provide; *person* to supply; **me ha suministrado muchos datos** he has given me a lot of data, he has supplied me with a lot of information.
suministro *nm* supply; *(act)* supplying, furnishing, provision; **—s** *(Mil)* supplies; **—s de combustible** fuel supply.
sumir [3a] **1** *vt* **(a)** to sink, plunge, submerge; *(of sea)* to swallow up, suck down.
(b) *(fig)* to plunge (*en* into); **el desastre le sumió en la tristeza** the disaster plunged him into sadness.
(c) *(SAm)* **— el resuello a uno** to kill someone.
(d) *(Mex)* to dent.
2 **sumirse** *vr* **(a)** *(object)* to sink; *(water etc)* to run away, disappear.
(b) *(mouth, chest etc)* to sink, be sunken, become hollow.
(c) **— en el estudio** to become absorbed in one's work; **— en la tristeza** to plunge into grief, give oneself over entirely to one's grief.
(d) *(SAm)* to cower, cringe; to lose heart; to fall silent from fear.
(e) *(SAm)* **— el sombrero** to pull one's hat right down.
sumisamente *adv* submissively, obediently; unresistingly; uncomplainingly.
sumisión *nf* **(a)** *(act)* submission. **(b)** *(quality)* submissiveness, docility.
sumiso *adj* submissive, docile, obedient; unresisting; uncomplaining.
sumo *adj* **(a)** great, extreme, supreme; **con suma dificultad** with the greatest difficulty; **con suma indiferencia** with supreme indifference.
(b) *(in rank)* high, highest; **— sacerdote** high

priest; see **pontífice; la suma autoridad** the highest authority, the supreme authority.

(c) **a lo** — at most.

sunco adj (Col) = **manco.**

sungo adj (Col) Negro; with a shiny skin, tanned.

suntuario adj sumptuary.

suntuosamente adj sumptuously, magnificently; lavishly, richly.

suntuosidad nf sumptuousness, magnificence; lavishness.

suntuoso adj sumptuous, magnificent; lavish, rich.

supeditar [1a] **1** vt (a) to subordinate (a to); **tendrá que ser supeditado a lo que decidan ellos** it will have to depend on what they decide.

(b) to subdue; to oppress, crush.

2 supeditarse vr: **— a** to make oneself subordinate to, come to depend on; to give way to, allow oneself to be overridden by; **no voy a supeditarme a su capricho** I am not going to depend on her whims.

super . . . super . . ., over . . .; eg (a) **superambicioso** overambitious; **superdesarrollo** overdevelopment; **superpetrolero** supertanker.

(b) as prefix to adj, often equivalent to superlative: **superfamoso** extremely famous; **superreservado** excessively shy; **un texto supercomentado** a text which has so often been commented on.

superable adj difficulty surmountable, that can be overcome; task etc that can be performed; **un obstáculo difícilmente** — an obstacle not easily surmounted.

superabundancia nf superabundance.

superabundante adj superabundant.

superación nf (a) overcoming, surmounting; transcending; excelling. (b) improvement, doing better; see **afán.**

superar [1a] **1** vt (a) rival to surpass, excel (in en), beat, do better than; opponent to overcome; expectations to exceed; limit, point to go beyond, transcend; record to break; **las escenas superan a toda imaginación** the scenes are more extraordinary than anyone could imagine, the scenes defeat one's imagination; **— a uno en brillantez** to outshine someone; **superó 2 veces la marca de los 200 metros** he twice broke the 200-metre record.

(b) difficulty to overcome, surmount; task to perform, carry out.

(c) period to get past, leave behind, emerge from; **ya hemos superado lo peor** we're over the worst now.

2 superarse vr to do extremely well, excel oneself.

superávit nm, pl **superávits** surplus.

supercarburante nm high-grade fuel.

supercarretera nf superhighway.

superconsumo nm overconsumption.

supercotizado adj much sought-after, in very great demand.

superchería nf fraud, trick, swindle.

superchero adj fraudulent; sham, bogus.

superdirecta nf (Aut) overdrive.

superempleo nm overemployment.

superentender [2g] vt to supervise, superintend.

supererogación nf supererogation.

superestructura nf superstructure.

superferolítico adj (fam) (a) affected; excessively refined. (b) overnice, finicky, choosy (fam).

superficial adj (a) measurement etc surface (attr), of the surface; wound etc superficial, skin (attr). (b) (fig) interest, glance etc superficial; brief, perfunctory; character superficial, shallow; facile.

superficialidad nf superficiality; shallowness.

superficialmente adv superficially.

superficie nf (a) surface; face; outside; (of sea etc) surface; — **inferior** lower surface, underside; — **de rodadura** (Aut) tread; **el ave rozó la** — the bird skimmed the surface; **el submarino salió a la** — the submarine surfaced, the submarine came to the surface; **ruta de** — surface route, land (or sea) route.

(b) (in measurements etc) area; **se regará una** — **de 200 hectáreas** an area of 200 hectares will be irrigated; **todo quedó destruido en una extensa** — everything was destroyed over a wide area.

(c) (fig) surface, outward appearance.

superfino adj superfine.

superfluamente adv superfluously.

superfluidad nf superfluity.

superfluo adj superfluous.

superfosfato nm superphosphate.

superhombre nm superman.

superintendencia nf supervision, superintendence.

superintendente nm supervisor, superintendent; overseer; — **de división** sectional head; (Comm) floorwalker.

superior 1 adj (a) (in position etc) upper; uppermost, top; higher; class upper; study advanced, higher; **labio** — upper lip; **vive en el piso** — he lives on the upper (or top) floor; **viven en el piso** — **al mío** they live on the floor above mine; **un estudio de nivel** — **a los existentes** a study on a higher plane than the present ones.

(b) (in quality etc) superior, better; **ser** — **a** to be superior to, be better than; **de calidad** — of superior quality.

(c) (in number) higher, greater, larger; **cualquier número** — **a 12** any number above (or higher than) 12.

2 nm superior; **mis** —**es** my superiors, those above me (in rank); (fig) my betters.

superiora nf mother superior.

superioridad nf superiority.

superlativo 1 adj superlative. **2** nm superlative.

superlujo nm: **hotel de** — super-luxury hotel; **tiene categoría de** — it is in the extra luxurious class.

supermercado nm supermarket.

superministro nm minister with an overall responsibility, senior minister, overlord.

supernumerario 1 adj supernumerary. **2** nm supernumerary.

superpetrolero nm supertanker.

superpoblación nf overpopulation, excess of population; overcrowding, congestion.

superpoblado adj country, region overpopulated; quarter etc overcrowded, congested.

superponer [2r] vt to superimpose, superpose, put on top.

superposición nf superposition.

superpotencia nf superpower, great power.

superproducción nf overproduction.

superrealismo nm (Art, Lit) surrealism.

supersecreto adj top secret.

supersimplificación nf oversimplification.

supersónico adj supersonic.

superstición nf superstition.

supersticiosamente adv superstitiously.

supersticioso adj superstitious.

supertalla nf (Sew) outsize.

supervalorar [1a] vt to overvalue, overstate.

supervigilancia nf (SAm) supervision.

supervisar [1a] vt to supervise.

supervisión nf supervision.

supervisor nm supervisor.

supervivencia nf survival; — **de los más aptos,** — **de los mejor dotados** survival of the fittest.

superviviente 1 adj surviving. **2** nmf survivor.

supino 1 adj supine. **2** nm supine.

súpito adj (a) = **súbito.** (b) (Col) dumbfounded.

suplantación nf (a) supplanting; impersonation. (b) (Col) fraudulent alteration, forgery.

suplantar [1a] vt (a) to supplant; to take the place of (fraudulently), impersonate. (b) (Col) to alter fraudulently, forge.

suplefaltas nmf, pl **suplefaltas** (a) scapegoat. (b) substitute, stopgap, fill-in.

suplemental adj supplementary.

suplementario adj supplementary; extra, additional; **empleo** —, **negocio** — sideline; **tren** — extra train, relief train.

suplementero nm (Chi) newsboy.

suplemento nm supplement; (Rail etc) excess fare.

suplencia nf (SAm) substitution, replacement; period during which one deputizes (etc).

suplente 1 adj substitute, deputy; reserve; **maestro** — supply teacher.

2 nmf substitute, deputy; replacement; (Sport) reserve; (Theat) understudy.

supletorio adj supplementary; extra, reserve, additional; stopgap (attr); **con la ventaja supletoria de que . . .** with the additional advantage that . . .; **llevar una lámpara supletoria** to take a spare bulb.

súplica nf request; entreaty, supplication; (Law) petition; —**s** entreaties, pleading; **acceder a las** —**s de uno** to grant someone's request; **se publica a** —**(s) de . . .** it is published at the request of . . .

suplicante 1 adj tone etc imploring, pleading. **2** nmf applicant; (Law) petitioner, suplicant.

suplicar [1g] **1** vt (a) thing to beg (for), plead for, implore.

(b) person to beg, plead with, implore; — **a uno**

no hacer algo to implore someone not to do something.

(c) (*Law*) to appeal to, petition (*de* against).

2 suplicarse *vr*: "se suplica cerrar la puerta" (*sign*) "please shut the door".

suplicio *nm* torture; (*Hist*) punishment, execution; (*fig*) torment, torture; (*mental*) anguish; ordeal; — **de Tántalo** torments of Tantalus; **es un — tener que escucharle** it's torture having to listen to him.

suplir [3a] **1** *vt* (a) *need, omission* to supply; *lack* to make good, make up for; *missing word etc* to supply; to understand.

(b) — **A con B** to replace A by B, substitute B for A; **suplen el aceite con grasa animal** they replace olive oil by animal fat.

2 *vi*: — **a, — por** to replace, take the place of, substitute for, do duty for; **suple en el equipo al portero lesionado** he's replacing the injured goalkeeper in the team.

suponer [2r] **1** *vt* (a) to suppose, assume; **supongamos que** . . . let us suppose (*or* assume) that . . .; **supongo que sí** I suppose so; **era de — que** . . . it was to be expected that . . .; **con las dificultades que son de —** with all the difficulties that one might expect.

(b) to think, imagine; to guess; **ya puedes — lo que ella sufría** you can just imagine how she was suffering; **Vd puede — lo que pasó** you can guess what happened; **no puedes — lo bruto que es** you can't begin to imagine what a lout he is; **es un —** I was only thinking aloud, of course that's just guesswork.

(c) to attribute; to credit (with); **le supongo unos 60 años** I give him an age of about 60; **se le supone una gran antigüedad** it is thought to be very ancient, it is credited with great antiquity, great antiquity is attributed to it; **hubo poco público y se ve que el equipo no tenía tanta "fuerza" como se le suponía** there were few spectators and it is clear that the team did not have the "pull" it was credited with.

(d) to mean, imply, involve, entail; **el traslado le supone grandes gastos** the move involves a lot of expense for him; **tal distancia no supone nada yendo en coche** that distance doesn't amount to anything in a car; **esa cantidad supone mucho para ellos** that amount means a lot to them.

2 *vi* to have authority, count (for a lot); **casi no supone en la organización** he hardly counts for anything in the organization.

suposición *nf* (a) supposition, assumption, surmise. (b) authority; distinction. (c) slander; imposture.

supositorio *nm* suppository.

supra . . . supra . . .

supradicho *adj* aforementioned.

supranacional *adj* supranational.

supremacía *nf* supremacy.

supremo *adj* supreme.

supresión *nf* suppression; abolition; removal, elimination; cancellation, lifting; deletion, omission; banning.

supresivo *adj* suppressive.

supresor *nm* (*Elec*) suppressor.

suprimido *adj book etc* suppressed, banned.

suprimir [3a] *vt revolt, criticism etc* to suppress; *custom, right, institution etc* to abolish; *difficulty, obstacle, waste* to remove, eliminate; *restrictions* to cancel, lift; *detail, passage etc* to delete, cut out, omit; *book etc* to suppress, ban.

supuestamente *adv* (*SAm*) supposedly.

supuesto 1 *ptp* of **suponer**.

2 *adj* (a) supposed, ostensible; self-styled; **el — jefe del movimiento** the self-styled leader of the movement; **bajo un nombre —** under an assumed name, under a false name.

(b) **dar por — algo** to take something for granted; **demos por — que** . . . let us take it for granted that . . .

3 — que *conj* since; granted that; inasmuch as.

4 *nm* (a) assumption, hypothesis; **— previo** prior assumption; **en el — de que** . . . on the assumption that . . .

(b) **¡por —!** of course!, naturally!

supuración *nf* suppuration.

supurar [1a] *vi* to suppurate, discharge, fester.

sur 1 *adj part* south, southern; *direction* southerly; *wind* south, southerly.

2 *nm* (a) south; **en la parte del —** in the southern part; **al — de León** to the south of Leon, on the

south side of Leon; **eso cae más hacia el —** that lies further (to the) south.

(b) south wind.

sura *nm* sura.

surazo *nm* (*Arg, Bol*) strong southerly wind.

surafricano = **sudafricano**.

surcar [1g] *vt* (a) *earth* to plough (through), furrow; *surface* to cut, score, groove; to make lines across; **una superficie surcada de** . . . a surface lined with . . ., a surface criss-crossed with . . .

(b) (*fig*) *water* to cut through, cleave; **los barcos que surcan los mares** (*lit*) the ships which ply the seas; **las aves que surcan los aires** (*lit*) the birds which ride the winds.

surco *nm* (*Agr etc*) furrow; (*of wheel*) rut, track; (*on metal etc*) groove, score, line; (*on record*) groove; (*Anat*) wrinkle; (*on water*) track, wake; **echarse al —** to sit down on the job; to knock off, think one has done enough.

surcoreano 1 *adj* South Korean. **2** *nm*, **surcoreana** *nf* South Korean.

sureño *nm*, **sureña** *nf* (*Chi, SD*) southerner.

surero *nm* (*Bol*) cold southerly wind.

surestada *nf* (*RPl*) persistent wet south-easterly wind.

sureste *adj and nm see* **sudeste**.

surgir [3c] *vi* (a) to arise, emerge, spring up, appear; (*of liquid*) to spout (out), spurt (up), gush (forth); (*in fog etc*) to loom up; (*of person*) to appear unexpectedly; (*of difficulty*) to arise, come up, crop up; **la torre surge en medio del bosque** the tower rises (*or* soars up) in the middle of the woods; **han surgido varios problemas** several problems have arisen.

(b) (*Naut*) to anchor.

suriano *adj* (*Mex*) southern.

suroeste 1 *adj part* south-west, south-western; *direction* south-westerly; *wind* south-west, south-westerly.

2 *nm* (a) south-west.

(b) south-west wind.

surrealismo *nm* surrealism.

surrealista 1 *adj* surrealist(ic). **2** *nmf* surrealist.

surtido 1 *adj* (a) mixed, assorted, varied.

(b) **estar bien — de** to be well supplied with, have good stocks of; **estar mal — de** to be badly off for.

2 *nm* selection, assortment, range; supply, stock; **gran —** large assortment, wide range; **artículo de —** article from stock.

surtidor *nm* (a) jet, spout; fountain. (b) **— de gasolina** petrol pump.

surtir [3a] **1** *vt* (a) to supply, furnish, provide; **— a uno de combustible** to supply someone with fuel; **— el mercado** to supply the market; **— un pedido** to fill an order.

(b) *effect* to have, produce; *see* **efecto** (a).

2 *vi* to spout, spurt (up), rise.

3 surtirse *vr*: **— de** to provide oneself with.

suruco *nm* (*Chi*) excrement.

surumbático *adj* (*SAm*) = **zurumbático**.

surumbiar [1b] *vt* (*Arg*) to beat, whip.

surumbo *adj* (*CAm*) = **zurumbo**.

surumpe *nm* (*Bol, Per*) inflammation of the eyes (*caused by snow glare*).

surupa *nf* (*Ven*) cockroach.

survietnamita 1 *adj* South Vietnamese. **2** *nmf* South Vietnamese.

susceptibilidad *nf* (a) susceptibility (*a* to); sensitivity; touchiness; impressionable nature.

(b) **—es** susceptibilities; **ofender las —es de uno** to offend someone's sensibilities.

susceptible *adj* (a) **— de** capable of; **— de mejora(r)** capable of improvement, open to improvement; **— de sufrir daño** liable to suffer damage.

(b) *person* susceptible; sensitive; touchy; impressionable.

suscitar [1a] *vt revolt etc* to stir up; *trouble, scandal, stir etc* to make, cause, provoke; *discussion* to start; *doubt, problem* to raise; *interest, hostility, suspicion* to arouse.

suscribir [3a; *ptp* **suscrito**] **1** *vt* (a) *contract, petition etc* to sign; *promise* to make, agree to, ratify.

(b) *opinion* to subscribe to, endorse.

(c) *shares etc* to take out an option on.

(d) **— a uno a una revista** to enter someone as a subscriber to a journal, put someone on the subscription list of a journal; **A le suscribió a B por 100 dólares** A put B down for a 100-dollar contribution.

2 suscribirse *vr* to subscribe (*a* to, for); **¿te vas a suscribir?** are you going to subscribe?

suscripción nf subscription; **abrir una —** to take out a subscription; **cerrar su —** to cancel one's subscription.

suscriptor nm, **suscriptora** nf subscriber.

susodicho adj above-mentioned.

suspender [2a] vt **(a)** object to hang, hang up, suspend (de from, on).

(b) (fig) payment, work etc to stop, suspend; meeting, session to adjourn; process etc to interrupt; **— hasta más tarde** to put off till later, postpone for a time.

(c) (Univ etc) candidate, subject to fail.

(d) (fig) to astound, astonish; to fill with wonder, cause to marvel.

suspense nm (Lit, Theat etc: angl) suspense.

suspensión nf **(a)** (act) hanging (up), suspension.

(b) (Aut, Mech) suspension.

(c) (fig) stoppage, suspension; adjournment; interruption; postponement; (Law) stay; **— de fuego, — de hostilidades** ceasefire, cessation of hostilities; **— de pagos** suspension of payments.

(d) astonishment; wonderment; (Lit, Theat etc) suspense.

suspensivo adj: **puntos —s** dots, suspension points (. . .).

suspenso 1 adj **(a)** hanging, suspended; hung (de from).

(b) (Univ etc) candidate failed.

(c) (fig) **estar —, quedarse —** to be astonished, be amazed; to be filled with wonder; to be bewildered, be baffled.

2 nm **(a)** (Univ etc) fail, failure.

(b) estar en —, quedar en — to be in suspense, be pending; (Law) to be suspended, be in abeyance; (case) to stand over, be postponed.

suspensores nmpl (SAm) braces, suspenders (US).

suspensorio 1 adj suspensory. **2** nm jockstrap; (Med) suspensory (bandage).

suspicacia nf suspicion, mistrust.

suspicaz adj suspicious, distrustful.

suspirado adj longed-for, yearned-for.

suspirar [1a] vi to sigh (also fig; por for).

suspiro nm sigh; (fig) sigh, breath, rustle, whisper; **deshacerse en —s** to sigh deeply, fetch a great sigh; **exhalar el último —** to breathe one's last.

sustancia nf substance; essence; matter; **— gris** (Anat) grey matter; **en —** in substance, in essence; **sin —** lacking in substance; shallow, superficial.

sustancial adj **(a)** substantial; essential, vital, fundamental. **(b) = sustancioso.**

sustancialmente adv substantially; essentially, vitally, fundamentally.

sustancioso adj speech etc solid; meaty; food solid, substantial, nourishing.

sustantivar [1a] vt to use as a noun.

sustantivo 1 adj substantive; (Gram) substantival, noun (attr). **2** nm noun, substantive.

sustentación nf sustenance; support; (Aer) lift.

sustentar [1a] **1** vt **(a)** object to hold up, support, bear (the weight of).

(b) (of food) to sustain, nourish, feed, keep going.

(c) (fig: of hope etc) to sustain, keep going, buoy up.

(d) idea, theory to maintain, uphold, defend.

2 sustentarse vr: **— con** to sustain oneself with, subsist on; **— de esperanzas** to sustain oneself with hopes, buoy oneself up with hopes; **— del aire** to live on air.

sustento nm support; sustenance, food; maintenance; (fig) livelihood; **ganarse el —** to earn one's living, earn a livelihood; **es el — principal de la institución** it is the lifeblood of the institution.

sustitución nf substitution (por for), replacement (por by).

sustituible adj replaceable; expendable.

sustituir [3g] **1** vt to substitute, replace; **— A por B** to substitute B for A, replace A by B, replace A with B, put A in place of B; **tendremos que — el neumático pinchado** we shall have to change (or replace) the flat tyre; **le quieren —** they want to remove him, they want him replaced.

2 vi to substitute; to deputize; **— a** to replace; to substitute for, deputize for; **los sellos azules sustituyen a los verdes** the blue stamps are replacing the green ones.

sustitutivo 1 adj substitute. **2** nm substitute (de for); **es un — del café** it is a coffee substitute.

sustituto nm, **sustituta** nf substitute, replacement; deputy.

susto nm **(a)** fright; scare; **¡qué —!** what a scare!; **dar un — a uno** to give someone a fright (or scare); **darse un —, pegarse un —** (fam) to have a fright, give oneself a fright; **meter un — a uno** to put the wind up someone.

(b) (Per) nervous breakdown; tuberculosis.

sustracción nf **(a)** removal; (Math) subtraction, taking away; deduction; extraction. **(b)** theft.

sustraer [2p] **1** vt to remove, take away; (Math) to subtract, take away; to deduct; water etc to extract.

2 sustraerse vr: **— a** to avoid; to withdraw from, contract out of; **— a + infin** to avoid + ger, get out of + ger; **no pude sustraerme a la tentación** I could not resist the temptation; **me era imposible sustraerme a un terrible dolor de cabeza** I couldn't shake off (or get rid of) an awful headache.

sustrato nm substratum.

susurrante adj whispering, murmuring; rustling.

susurrar [1a] **1** vi **(a)** (of person) to whisper; **— al oído de uno** to whisper to someone, whisper in someone's ear.

(b) (fig: of wind) to whisper; (of insects) to hum; (of stream) to murmur; (of leaves) to rustle.

2 susurrarse vr: **se susurra que . . .** it is being whispered that . . ., it is rumoured that . . .

susurro nm **(a)** whisper. **(b)** (fig) whisper; hum, humming; murmur; rustle.

sutil adj **(a)** strand etc fine, delicate, tenuous; slice thin; material thin, light; very soft; air thin; scent delicate; subtle; breeze etc gentle.

(b) difference fine, subtle, nice.

(c) mind, person sharp, keen, observant; subtle; observation subtle.

sutileza nf **(a)** fineness, delicacy; thinness; subtlety, subtleness; sharpness, keenness. **(b)** (una —) subtlety; (pej) artifice, artful deceit.

sutilizar [1f] **1** vt **(a)** object etc to thin down, fine down; (fig) to polish, perfect; (fig) to refine (upon).

(b) concept etc (pej) to quibble about, split hairs about.

2 vi (pej) to quibble, split hairs.

sutura nf suture.

suturar [1a] vt to suture; to stitch.

suyo poss adj and pron **1** (following verb ser or with article) **(a)** (one possessor) his, hers, its, one's; (relating to Vd) yours; **es —, es el —** it is his (etc); **¿es — esto?** is this yours?; **lo —** (what is) his, what belongs to him; **los —s** (freq) his people, his relations, his family.

(b) (plural possessors) theirs; (relating to Vds) yours.

2 (after n) **(a)** (one possessor) of his, of hers; of its own, of one's own; (relating to Vd) of yours; **no es amigo —** he is no friend of hers.

(b) (plural possessors) of theirs; (relating to Vds) of yours.

3 adj and pron (idioms): **de —** in itself, per se; intrinsically; on its own; **eso es muy —** that's just like him, that's typical of him; **aguantar lo —** to shoulder one's burden; to put up with a lot; **eso cae de —** that's obvious, that goes without saying; **estar en lo mejor —** (fam) to be on top form, be in one's best form; **hizo suyas mis palabras** he echoed my words, he supported what I had said; **hacer de las suyas** to get up to one's old tricks; **ir a la suya, ir a lo —** to go one's own way; (pej) to act selfishly, think only of oneself; **salirse con la suya** to get one's way; (in argument) to carry one's point; **valorar lo —** to be worth one's keep; **cada cual a lo —** it's best to mind one's own business.

svástica nf swastika.

T

taba nf (Anat) ankle bone; (game) knucklebones, jackstones (US); **menear las —s** (fam) to bustle about; to get cracking (fam), get moving; **tomar la —** (fam) to start speaking; to show who is boss.

tabacal nm (SAm) tobacco field; tobacco plantation.

Tabacalera nf Spanish state tobacco monopoly.

tabacalero 1 adj tobacco (attr). **2** nm tobacconist; tobacco grower, tobacco merchant.

tabaco 1 nm (**a**) tobacco; cigarettes, cigar (esp SAm); (Bot) tobacco plant; **— de hebra** loose tobacco; **— de pipa** pipe tobacco; **— en polvo** snuff; **— en rama** leaf tobacco; **— rubio** Virginian tobacco; **— turco** Turkish tobacco; **¿tienes —?** have you any cigarettes?; **se me acabó el —** I ran out of cigarettes, I had nothing left to smoke; **se le acabó el —** (Arg, Chi: fig) he ran out of money; **estar de mal —** (CAm) to be in a bad mood; **estaba hecho —** (fam) he was all in; it was all torn to pieces.
(**b**) (Cu) punch, blow.
2 adj (SAm) dusty brown.

tabacón nm (Mex) marijuana.

tabacoso adj tobacco-stained.

tabalada nf punch; knock, bump, blow (from a fall).

tabalear [1a] **1** vt to rock; to shake. **2** vi to drum (with one's fingers), tap.

tabaleo nm rocking; shaking; drumming, tapping.

tabanco nm (CAm) attic.

tábano nm horsefly.

tabaqueada nf (Mex) beating-up; fist fight.

tabaquear [1a] vi (Col) to smoke.

tabaquera nf tobacco jar; snuffbox; (of pipe) bowl; (SAm) tobacco pouch, cigar case, cigarette case.

tabaquería nf tobacconist's (shop), cigar store (US).

tabaquero 1 adj (SAm) tobacco (attr). **2** nm tobacconist; (SAm) tobacco grower, tobacco merchant.

tabaquito nm (SAm) small cigar.

tabarra nf (fam) nuisance, bore; **dar la —** to be a nuisance, be a bore; **dar la — a uno** to get on someone's nerves, annoy someone.

tabear [1a] vi (RPl) to chat, gossip; to gossip about someone not present.

taberna nf bar, pub; (Hist) tavern; (Arg) gambling joint; (Cu) = **pulpería**.

tabernáculo nm tabernacle.

tabernario adj rude, dirty.

tabernero nm publican, landlord; barman, bartender.

tabicar [1g] **1** vt to wall up; to partition off. **2** **tabicarse** vr to get stopped up.

tabique nm thin wall, partition (wall).

tabla nf (**a**) (of wood) plank, board; shelf; (of stone etc) slab; (Art) panel; (Cu) shop counter; **— de lavar** washboard; **— de picar** chopping board; **— de planchar** ironing board; **— de salvación** (fig) last resort, sole hope; thing that saves one's life; **— del suelo** floorboard; **escaparse** (or **salvarse**) **en una —** to have a narrow escape, have a close shave; **hacer — rasa** to make a clean sweep; to clear away all obstacles; **hacer — rasa de** (pej) to disregard utterly, ride roughshod over.
(**b**) **—s** (Taur) boards, fence.
(**c**) **—s** (Theat) boards, stage; **pisar las —s to** walk the stage; **salir a las —s** to go on the stage, become an actor; **tener muchas —s** to be an old hand, be an expert.
(**d**) **—s** (Chess) draw; tie; (fig) stalemate, deadlock; **—s por ahogado** stalemate; **hacer —s, quedar (en) —s** to draw, reach a drawn position; (fig) to reach stalemate, be deadlocked; **el partido quedó —s** the game was a draw, the game was drawn.
(**e**) (Anat) flat area, wide part.
(**f**) (Agr) plot, patch, bed.
(**g**) (Sew) broad pleat.
(**h**) (Comm) meat stall.

(**i**) (fig) table, list, chart; (Math) table; (Typ) table, index; **— de materias** table of contents; **— de multiplicar** multiplication table.
(**j**) (Arg, Col) tablet, pastille.

tablada nf (Bol, RPl) stockyard, cattlepen; (Par) slaughterhouse.

tablado nm plank floor, boards; stand, stage, platform; (Hist) scaffold; (Theat) stage.

tablaje nm, **tablazón** nf planks, planking, boards.

tablear [1a] vt (**a**) wood to cut into boards (or planks).
(**b**) land to divide up into plots.
(**c**) ground to level off; dough (Chi) to roll out.
(**d**) (Sew) to pleat.

tablero nm (**a**) (of wood) board(s), plank(s); panel; (of marble etc) slab; (School etc) blackboard; (Comm) counter; (for games) board; (RPl) notice board, bulletin board (US); (Elec) switchboard; **— de ajedrez** chessboard; **— de dibujo** drawing board; **— de instrumentos** instrument panel, (Aut) dashboard; **— posterior** tail board.
(**b**) (Agr) bed(s), plot(s).
(**c**) gambling den.

tableta nf (**a**) small board. (**b**) writing pad, tablet.
(**c**) (Med) tablet; (of chocolate) bar, stick.

tabletear [1a] vi to rattle, clatter; (of machine gun) to rattle.

tableteo nm rattle, clatter.

tablilla nf (**a**) small board; (Med) splint. (**b**) (Mex) bar (of chocolate).

tablón nm (**a**) plank, beam; **— de anuncios** notice board, bulletin board (US).
(**b**) (fam) **coger un —, pillar un —** to get tight.
(**c**) (SAm: Agr) plot, bed.

tablonazo nm (Cu) trick, swindle.

tabú nm taboo.

tabuco nm slum, shack; tiny room, poky little room.

tabular 1 [1a] vt to tabulate. **2** adj tabular.

taburete nm stool.

tacana nf (**a**) (Arg, Bol) cultivated hillside terrace.
(**b**) (Arg, Mex) pestle.

tacanear [1a] vt (Arg) to tread down; to pound, crush.

tacañería nf (**a**) meanness, stinginess. (**b**) craftiness.

tacaño adj (**a**) mean, stingy. (**b**) crafty.

tacar [1g] vt (Col) (**a**) to shoot at. (**b**) to fill, pack tightly (de with).

tacita nf small cup; **la T— de Plata** (affectionate name for) Cadiz; **como una — de plata** as bright as a new pin.

tácitamente adv tacitly.

Tácito m Tacitus.

tácito adj tacit; comment etc unspoken; law unwritten; (Ling) unexpressed, understood.

taciturnidad nf taciturnity, silent nature; moodiness, sullenness; glumness.

taciturno adj taciturn, silent; moody, sullen, sulky; glum.

tacizo nm (**a**) (Col, Ven) narrow-bladed axe. (**b**) (Col) small prison cell.

taco[1] nm (**a**) wad, wadding; wooden peg; stopper, plug, bung.
(**b**) (in boot) stud; (SAm) heel.
(**c**) pad; calendar; book of travel tickets (or coupons etc); stub; **— de papel** writing pad, pad of notepaper.
(**d**) (Billiards) cue.
(**e**) (Mil: Hist) ramrod.
(**f**) popgun.
(**g**) snack, bite; swig of wine (fam).
(**h**) (fam) rude word, swearword; **dice muchos —** he swears a lot; **soltar un —** to swear.
(**i**) (fam) tangle, mess; **armarse un —, hacerse un —** to get into a mess, get all tied up; **dejar a uno hecho un —** to flatten someone (in an argument).
(**j**) (Chi, Mex) obstruction, blockage.

(k) (*Mex*) rolled pancake.

(l) (*Arg, Chi*) short stocky person.

(m) (*CAm, PR*) worry, anxiety; fear.

taco² **1** *adj* (*Cu, PR*) **(a)** foppish. **(b)** bold, enterprising. **2** *nm* **(a)** (*Ant, CAm, Mex*) fop, dandy, toff (*fam*); **darse** — to put on airs. **(b)** (*Col*) big shot (*fam*).

tacómetro *nm* tachometer.

tacón *nm* heel; — **(de) aguja** stiletto heel; **—es altos** high heels; **de** — **alto** high-heeled.

taconazo *nm* heel tap; kick with one's heel, blow with the heel; **—s** (*Mil etc*) heel-clicking; **entró y dio un** — he came in and clicked his heels.

taconear [1a] **1** *vt* (*Chi*) to pack tight, fill right up. **2** *vi* **(a)** to tap (*or* stamp) with one's heels; (*Mil etc*) to click one's heels; to walk noisily on one's heels.

(b) (*fam*) to bustle about.

taconeo *nm* tapping (*or* stamping) with one's heels; heel-clicking; noisy walking on one's heels.

tacote *nm* (*Mex*) marijuana.

táctica *nf* tactics; (*una* —) tactic, move, method; gambit; — **de cerrojo** stonewalling, negative play.

tácticamente *adv* tactically.

táctico **1** *adj* tactical. **2** *nm* tactician.

táctil *adj* tactile.

tacto *nm* **(a)** (*bodily*) touch, sense of touch; (*of typist etc*) touch. **(b)** (*act*) touch, touching; feel; **ser áspero al** — to feel rough, be rough to the touch. **(c)** (*quality*) feel; **tiene un** — **viscoso** it has a sticky feel (to it). **(d)** (*fig*) tact.

tacuaco *adj* (*Chi*) chubby.

tacuache *nm* (*Cu*) fib, lie.

tacuche *nm* (*Mex*) bundle of rags; (*Univ: fam*) dress; (*fig*) worthless object, useless person, dead loss.

tacha¹ *nf* **(a)** (*Tech*) large tack, brad, stud. **(b)** (*SAm*) = **tacho**.

tacha² *nf* flaw, blemish, defect; **sin** — perfect, flawless; **poner** — **a** to find fault with.

tachadura *nf* erasure, correction.

tachar [1a] *vt* **(a)** to cross out, erase; to correct. **(b)** to criticize, attack, find fault with; *witness* (*Law*) to challenge; — **a uno de incapaz** to accuse someone of being incompetent.

tachero *nm* (*Arg, Chi*) tinsmith.

tachines *nmpl* (*sl*) feet.

tacho *nm* (*SAm*) boiler, large boiling pan; sugar pan, sugar evaporator; bin, container; (*RPl*) washbasin; — **para la basura** dustbin, garbage can (*US*); — **para lavar la ropa** clothes boiler; **irse al** — to be ruined, fail.

tachón¹ *nm* **(a)** (*Tech*) large stud, ornamental stud, boss. **(b)** (*Sew*) trimming.

tachón² *nm* erasure, stroke, crossing-out.

tachonado *adj*: — **de estrellas** star-studded, star-spangled.

tachonar [1a] *vt* to stud, adorn with studs; to trim; (*fig*) to stud (*de* with).

tachoso *adj* defective, faulty.

tachuela *nf* **(a)** tack, tintack; (*Cu*) long pin. **(b)** (*Col, Cu, Ven*) metal pan, boiler, bowl; (*Mex, Ven*) metal cup, dipper. **(c)** (*Arg, Chi, Guat, Mex*) short stocky person, runt.

tafetán *nm* **(a)** taffeta; — **adhesivo,** — **inglés** sticking plaster. **(b)** **—es** (*fig*) flags; (*fam*) frills, buttons and bows.

tafia *nf* (*SAm*) rum.

tafilete *nm* morocco leather.

tagarnia *nf* (*CAm, Col*) surfeit, blow-out (*sl*); drunkenness.

tagarnina *nf* **(a)** (*Mex*) leather tobacco pouch. **(b)** (*Col, Guat, Mex*) drunkenness.

tagarote *nm* **(a)** (*Zool*) sparrowhawk. **(b)** (*fam*) tall shabby person. **(c)** (*fam*) lawyer's clerk, penpusher. **(d)** (*CR, Per*) big shot (*fam*).

tagua *nf* (*Ec*) ivory palm.

tahalí *nm* swordbelt.

Tahití *m* Tahiti.

tahona *nf* bakery, bakehouse; flourmill.

tahonero *nm* baker; miller.

tahur *nm* gambler; (*pej*) cardsharper, cheat.

taifa *nf* (*fam*) gang, crew; gang of thieves.

Tailandia *f* Thailand.

tailandés **1** *adj* Thai. **2** *nm*, **tailandesa** *nf* Thai. **3** *nm* (*language*) Thai.

taima *nf* **(a)** slyness, craftiness, slickness. **(b)** (*Chi*) obstinacy, sullenness.

taimado *adj* **(a)** sly, crafty, slick. **(b)** sullen. **(c)** (*Arg, Ec*) lazy.

taimarse [1a] *vr* **(a)** to get sly, adopt crafty tactics. **(b)** to be stubborn, be sullen, sulk.

taita *nm* **(a)** (*fam*) dad, daddy; uncle. **(b)** (*Arg, Chi, Par etc*) in direct address, term of respect used before a name. **(c)** (*Arg*) tough (*fam*), bully; quarrelsome person. **(d)** pimp.

taja *nf* **(a)** cut. **(b)** division (of taxes).

tajada *nf* **(a)** (*Cook*) slice; slab, chunk. **(b)** (*fam*) rake-off (*fam*); **sacar** — to get one's share, get something out of it; to get a rake-off, take one's cut; (*fig*) to look after number one. **(c)** (*Med*) hoarseness. **(d)** (*fam*) **coger una** —, **pillar una** — to get tight. **(e)** cut, slash; **¡te haré —s!** I'll cut you up!

tajadera *nf* **(a)** chopper; cold chisel. **(b)** chopping block.

tajadero *nm* chopping block.

tajado *adj* rock sheer.

tajalán *adj* (*Cu*) lazy.

tajaleo *nm* (*Cu*) **(a)** food, grub (*sl*). **(b)** row, brawl.

tajamar *nm* **(a)** (*Naut*) stem; (*of bridge*) cutwater. **(b)** (*CAm, Chi*) mole; (*Per, RPl*) dam, dike.

tajante *adj* **(a)** sharp, cutting. **(b)** (*fig*) incisive, sharp, emphatic; *distinction etc* sharp; **contestó con un "no"** — he answered with an emphatic "no"; **una crítica** — **del gobierno** some sharp criticism of the government; **es una persona** — he's an incisive person.

tajantemente *adv* (*fig*) incisively, sharply, emphatically.

tajar [1a] *vt* to cut, slice, chop.

tajarrazo *nm* (*CAm, Mex*) slash, wound; (*fig*) damage, harm.

tajeadura *nf* (*Chi, RPl*) long scar.

tajear [1a] *vt* (*SAm: fam*) to cut up, chop; to slash.

Tajo *m* Tagus.

tajo *nm* **(a)** cut, slash; **darse un** — **en el brazo** to cut one's arm; **tirar —s a uno** to slash at someone. **(b)** (*Geog*) cut, cleft; steep cliff, sheer drop. **(c)** working area; (*fam*) work, job; **largarse al** — to get off to work, go back on the job; **¡vamos al** —**!** let's get on with it! **(d)** cutting edge. **(e)** (*Cook*) chopping block; (*Hist*) block (*for executions*). **(f)** (*Sew: Hist*) slash. **(g)** small three-legged stool.

tajón *nm* (*Mex*) slaughterhouse.

tal **1** *adj* such; — **cosa** such a thing; **—es cosas** such things; **no hay** — **cosa** there's no such thing; **con** — **atrevimiento** with such boldness; **con un resultado** — with such a result; **el** — **país no existió nunca** such a country never existed; **necesitas tanto dinero para** — **cosa** you need so much money for such-and-such a thing; **un** — **García** a man called García, one García; **el** — **cura** this priest, the aforementioned priest, this priest we were talking about; (*pej*) this priest person.

2 *pron* such a one, someone; such a thing, something; **el** — this man (*etc*) I mentioned, this man we're talking about; such a person; **una** — (*euph*) a prostitute; **no haré** — I won't do anything of the sort; **¡no hay —!** nothing of the sort!; **en la calle de —.** in such-and-such a street; **— como** such as; **— como es, todavía vale algo** such as it is, it is still worth something; **y como** —, **tiene que pagar los derechos** and as such, he has to pay the fees; **se para aquí** — **cual autocar** an odd coach stops here, a coach stops occasionally; **vive en** — **o cual hotel** he lives in such-and-such a hotel; **son** — **para cual** they're two of a kind; **sí** — yes indeed, yes of course; — **hay que lo piensa** there are some who think so; **hablábamos de que si** — **que si cual** we were talking about this that and the other; **había ruritanos y eslobodos y** — there were Ruritanians and Slobodians and such (*or* such like, others of that kind); **fuimos al cine y** — we went to the pictures and that kind of thing.

3 *adv* so; in such a way; — **como** just as; **estaba** — **como lo dejé** it was just as I had left it; — **cual** (*adv*) just as it is; **es** — **cual siempre deseaba** it is just what he had always wanted; **ella sigue** — **cual** she's so-so, she's middling fair; — **la madre, cual la hija** like mother, like daughter; **tomaremos algo ligero** — **que una tortilla** (*fam*) we'll have something light such as an omelette; **¿qué** —**?** how goes it?, how's things?; **¿qué** — **el partido?** what was the game like?, how did the game go?;

¿**qué — tu tío?** how's your uncle?; **¿qué — del profesor?** what's the news of the professor?; **¿qué — te gusta?** what do you think of it?, how do you like it?; *see also* **cual** *for other comparative phrases*.

4 *conj* **con — (de) que . . .** provided (that) . . ., on condition that . . **.; con — de no volver nunca** on condition that he (*etc*) never comes back; **no importa el frío con — de ir bien abrigado** the cold doesn't matter if you're well wrapped up.

tala *nf* (a) tree felling, wood cutting; (*fig*) havoc, destruction. (b) (*Ven*) axe. (c) (*PR*) vegetable garden. (d) (*Chi*) grazing.

talabarte *nm* swordbelt.

talabartería *nf* saddlery, harness-maker's shop.

talabartero *nm* saddler, harness maker.

talacha *nf*, **talache** *nm* (*Mex*) mattock.

taladradora *nf* drill; **— de fuerza** power drill; **— neumática** pneumatic drill.

taladrar [1a] *vt* (a) to bore, drill, punch, pierce; *ticket* to punch; *lobe of ear* to pierce.
(b) (*fig: of pain, sound*) to pierce; **un ruido que taladra los oídos** an ear-splitting noise; **es un ruido que taladra** it's a shattering noise.

taladro *nm* (a) drill; auger, gimlet; borer; **— neumático** pneumatic drill. (b) drill hole.

talaje *nm* (a) (*Arg, Chi*) pasture. (b) (*Chi, Mex*) grazing, pasturage.

tálamo *nm* marriage bed.

talamoco *adj* (*Ec*) albino.

talante *nm* (a) mood, disposition, frame of mind; will, willingness; **estar de buen —** to be in a good mood, be in the right frame of mind; **hacer algo de buen —** to do something willingly; **recibir a uno de buen —** to give someone a warm welcome; **estar de mal —** to be in a bad mood; **responder de mal —** to answer with an ill grace, answer bad-temperedly.
(b) mien, look, appearance.

talar [1a] *vt* (a) *tree* to fell, cut down. (b) (*fig*) to lay waste, devastate. (c) (*Prov, SAm*) to prune.

talco *nm* talcum powder; (*Min*) talc.

talcualillo *adj* (*fam*) so-so, middling, fair (*also Med*).

talega *nf* (a) sack, bag. (b) baby's nappy, diaper (*US*). (c) **—s** (*fig*) money.

talegada *nf*, **talegazo** *nm* heavy fall, severe bump.

talego *nm* (a) big sack, long sack, poke. (b) (*fam: person*) fat person, lump. (c) (*fam*) **tener —** to have money stashed away (*fam*), have brass (*sl*).

taleguilla *nf* bullfighter's breeches.

talento *nm* (a) talent; ability, gift; **—s** talents; accomplishments. (b) (*Bib*) talent.

talentoso *adj* talented, gifted.

talero *nm* (*Chi, RPl*) whip.

talidomida *nm* thalidomide.

talismán *nm* talisman.

talmente *adv* so, in such a way; to such an extent; exactly, literally; **la casa es — una pocilga** the house is such a pigsty, the house is literally a pigsty.

Talmud *m* Talmud.

talmúdico *adj* Talmudic.

talón *nm* (a) (*Anat*) heel; (*of shoe etc*) heel; **— de Aquiles** Achilles' heel; **pisar los —es a uno** to be on someone's heels, follow close behind someone; (*fig*) to run someone very close.
(b) (*Aut*) flange, rim (*of tyre*).
(c) (*Comm etc*) stub, counterfoil; (*Rail*) luggage receipt.

talonar [1a] *vt* to heel.

talonario 1 *adj*: **libro —** = **2** *nm* receipt book; book of tickets, book of counterfoils; **— de cheques** cheque book.

talonear [1a] **1** *vt* (*SAm*) to dig one's heels into, spur along. **2** *vi* to walk briskly, hurry along.

talonera *nf* (*Col*) heel.

talquina *nf* (*Chi*) deceit, treachery.

talud *nm* slope, bank; (*Geol*) talus.

talla[1] *nf* (a) (*Art*) carving; sculpture; engraving (*also* **obra de —**).
(b) (*of person*) height, stature; (*fig*) stature; (*of garment*) size, fitting; **camisas de todas las —** shirts in all sizes; **tener poca —** to be short, be on the short side; **ha crecido de —** (*fig*) he has grown in stature.
(c) measuring rod.
(d) (*Med*) gallstones operation.
(e) (*Cards*) hand.
(f) (*Law*) reward (*for capture of a criminal*); **poner a uno a —** to offer a reward for the capture of someone.

talla[2] *nf* (a) (*CAm*) fib, lie. (b) (*Chi, RPl*) gossip, chitchat. (c) (*Col*) beating.

tallado 1 *adj* (a) carved; sculpted; engraved.
(b) **bien —** shapely, well-formed; **mal —** misshapen.
2 *nm* carving; sculpting; engraving; **— en madera** wood carving.

tallador *nm* (a) carver; sculptor; engraver. (b) (*SAm: Cards*) dealer, banker.

tallar[1] [1a] **1** *vt* (a) to carve, shape, work; to sculpt; to engrave; *gem* to cut.
(b) *person* to measure (the height of).
(c) (*Cards*) to deal.
2 *vi* (*Cards*) to deal, be banker.

tallar[2] [1a] **1** *vt* (a) (*Col*) to bother, annoy.
(b) (*Col*) to beat.
2 *vi* (*Chi, RPl*) to chat, gossip; to gossip maliciously; (*Chi*) to exchange sweet nothings.

tallarín *nm* (*Cook*) noodle.

talle *nm* (a) (*Anat, Sew*) waist; **— de avispa** wasp waist.
(b) (*Sew etc*) waist and chest measurements; size, fitting.
(c) (*Anat: woman's*) figure; (*man's*) build, physique; **de — esbelto** with a slim figure; **tiene buen —** she has a good figure.
(d) (*fig*) look, appearance; outline.
(e) (*Chi, Guat*) bodice.

taller *nm* (*Tech*) workshop; mill, factory; (*Art*) studio; (*Sew*) workroom; (*industrial and trade-union parlance*) shop; **— agremiado** union shop, closed shop; **—es gráficos** printing works; **— de máquinas** machine shop; **— de montaje** assembly shop; **— de reparaciones** repair shop; (*Aut*) service station.

tallero *nm* (*SAm*) vegetable merchant, greengrocer.

tallista *nm* = **tallador** (a), (*esp*) wood carver.

tallo *nm* (a) stem, stalk; (*of grass*) blade, sprig; shoot.
(b) (*Col*) cabbage.
(c) (*SAm*) **—s** vegetables, greens.
(d) (*Cook*) candied peel; crystallized fruit.

talludo *adj* (a) (*Bot*) tall; *person* big, tall, lanky; (*fig*) grown-up; **ya eres una talluda** you're a big girl now, you're too big for that age; **es una talluda ya** (*pej*) she's not exactly a youngster, she's no chicken.
(b) (*CAm, Mex*) tough, leathery; hard to peel.
(c) (*CAm, Mex*) *person* old but still active; *object* old but still useful.

tamal *nm* (a) (*SAm: Cook*) tamale.
(b) (*Chi*) bundle of clothing; (*Mex*) shapeless mass, rough bundle.
(c) (*SAm: fig*) fraud, trick, hoax; intrigue; **hacer un —** to prepare a trick, set a trap.

tamalero (*SAm*) **1** *adj* (a) fond of tamales. (b) intriguing, fond of intrigue. **2** *nm* tamale maker, tamale seller.

tamango *nm* (*Chi, RPl*) (a) clog, sandal, rough shoe; old shoe. (b) baby boy.

tamañito *adj*: **dejar a uno —** to make someone feel very small; to crush someone, flatten someone (in an argument); **me quedé —** I felt about so high; I felt utterly bewildered.

tamaño 1 *adj* so big, such a big; so small, such a small; **parece absurdo que cometiera — error** it seems absurd that he should make so grave an error (*or* such a great error); **una piedra tamaña como una naranja** a stone as big as an orange.
2 *nm* size; **de — bolsillo** pocket-size; **de — extra, de — extraordinario** outsize, extra large; **de — natural** full-size, life-size; **ser del mismo —, tener el mismo —** to be the same size; **¿de qué — es?** what size is it?, how big is it?

tamarindo *nm* (a) tamarind. (b) (*Mex: fam*) policeman, cop (*sl*).

tamarisco *nm*, **tamariz** *nm* tamarisk.

tambache *nm* (*Mex*) bundle of clothes.

tambaleante *adj* staggering, tottering; *gait* unsteady; *vehicle* swaying.

tambalearse [1a] *vr* (*person*) to stagger, totter, reel; to zigzag; to wobble (from side to side); (*vehicle*) to lurch, sway; **ir tambaleándose** to stagger along; to lurch along, sway about (as one walks *etc*).

tambar [1a] *vt* (*Ec*) to swallow.

tambarria *nf* (*CAm, Col, Ec*) party, carousal.

tambero *nm* (*Chi, RPl*) innkeeper; dairy farmer.

también *adv* also, as well, too; besides; **¿Vd —?** you too?; **y bebe —** and he drinks as well, he also drinks; **no sólo A sino — B** not only A but also B; **"¿y es guapa?" . . . "—"** "and is she pretty?" . . . "she's that as well".

tambo *nm* (*Bol, Col, Ec, Per*) country inn, roadside inn; (*RPl*) milking yard; (*Chi*) brothel.

tambor nm (a) (Mus, Tech) drum; (Archit, Sew) tambour; (Anat) eardrum; — **de tostar café** coffee roaster; — **del freno** brake drum; **venir a —batiente** to come out with flying colours, emerge in triumph.
(b) (Mus) drummer; — **mayor** drum major.
(c) (Cu, Mex) burlap, sackcloth.
tambora nf (a) (Mus) bass drum. (b) (Cu) lie, fib.
tamboril nm small drum.
tamborilada nf, **tamborilazo** nm bump on one's bottom, severe jolt; slap on the shoulder.
tamborilear [1a] 1 vt (fam) to praise up, boost. 2 vi (Mus) to drum, play the drum; to drum with one's fingers; (of rain) to patter, drum.
tamborileo nm drumming; patter(ing).
tamborilero nm drummer.
tambre nm (Col) dam.
tamegua nf (CAm, Mex) weeding, cleaning.
tameguar [1d] vt (CAm, Mex) to weed, clean.
Tamerlán m Tamberlane.
Támesis m Thames.
tamiz nm sieve.
tamizar [1f] vt to sieve, sift.
tamo nm fluff, down, dust; (Agr) dust; chaff.
tampa nf (Arg) matted hair.
tampoco adv neither, not ... either; nor; **ni A ni B —** neither A nor B, not A nor B either; **yo — lo compré, yo no lo compré —** I didn't buy one either; **ni yo —** nor I; **"¿lo sabes tú?" ... "—"** do you know?" ... "No, I don't either"; **"pero ¿vendrás a la fiesta?" ... "—" "**but you'll be coming to the party?" ... "No, I shan't come to that either".
tampón nm plug (also Med); (Med) tampon; — **de entintar** inking pad.
tamuga nf (CAm, Pan) bundle, pack; knapsack.
tan adv so; — **rápido** so fast; — **rápidamente** so fast; **no es buena idea comprar un coche — grande** it's not a good idea to buy such a big car; **¡qué idea — rara!** what an odd notion!; **A es — feo como B** A is as ugly as B; **es — caro que nadie puede comprarlo** it's so expensive that nobody can afford it; **no te esperaba — pronto** I wasn't expecting you so soon; **de — rico resulta incomible** it's so rich that one can't eat it; — **es así que ...** so much so that ...
tanaca nf (Bol) slut.
tanaceto nm tansy.
tanate nm (CAm, Mex) (a) basket, pannier. (b) —**s** (fig) odds and ends, bits and pieces, gear (fam).
tanda nf (a) series, set; batch; (of eggs etc) layer; (of injections) course, series; (of bricks) course; (of blows) series.
(b) (at work) shift, turn, spell; job; task, piece of work; (in irrigation) turn (to use water); (persons) shift, relay; gang; — **de noche** nightshift, spell of night work; **ahora estás de —** now it's your turn.
(c) (Billiards etc) game; (Baseball) innings.
(d) (SAm: Theat) show, performance; (Chi) light comedy, farce, musical; **primera —** first show, early performance.
tándem nm tandem; **en —** (Elec) tandem.
tanganear [1a] vt (Col, Ec, Ven) to beat.
tanganillas: en — — adv unsteadily; (fig) uncertainly, dubiously; unsafely.
tanganillo nm prop, wedge, temporary support.
tangencial adj tangential; (fig) oblique.
tangencialmente adv tangentially; (fig) obliquely.
tangente nf tangent; **salirse por la —** (fig) to go off at a tangent; to dodge the issue, give an evasive answer.
Tánger Tangier(s).
tangerino 1 adj of Tangier(s). 2 nm, **tangerina** nf native (or inhabitant) of Tangier(s); **los —s** the people of Tangier(s).
tangibilidad nf tangibility.
tangible adj tangible; (fig) tangible, concrete.
tango nm tango.
tanguear [1a] vi (a) (SAm) to tango; to dance. (b) (Ec) to reel drunkenly.
tánico adj tannic; **ácido —** tannic acid.
tanino nm tannin.
tano nm (Arg, Urug: pej) Neapolitan, Italian.
tanque nm (in most senses) tank; water store, reservoir; (Mil) tank; (Aut) tanker, tanker lorry.
tanquero nm (Ven etc) tanker.
tanquista nm (Mil) member of a tank-crew.
tanta nf (Bol, Per) maize bread.
tantán nm gong; tomtom.
tantarán nm, **tantarantán** nm (a) drumbeat, rub-a-dub. (b) (fam) hefty punch; violent shaking.
tanteada nf (a) (SAm) = **tanteo**. (b) (Mex) dirty trick; hoax, swindle.

tanteador nm (a) scoreboard. (b) scorer.
tantear [1a] 1 vt (a) number, value etc to reckon (up), work out roughly, try to calculate, guess; cloth, quantity etc to size up, take the measure of; weight to feel, get the feel of, try the weight of; (fig) to weigh up, consider carefully.
(b) to test, try out; to probe; intentions, person to sound out; — **si la superficie está bien segura** to test the surface to see if it is safe, see if the surface is safe.
(c) (Art) to sketch in, draw the outline of.
(d) (Sport) to keep the score of.
(e) (Hond, Mex) to lie in wait for.
(f) (Mex) to swindle; to make a fool of, take for a ride (fam).
2 vi (a) (Sport) to score, keep (the) score.
(b) (SAm) to grope, feel one's way; **¡tantee Vd!** fancy that!
tanteo nm (a) reckoning, rough calculation, guesswork; weighing up, careful consideration; **a —, por —** by guesswork.
(b) test(ing), trial; trial and error; **al —** by trial and error; **conversaciones de —** exploratory conversations.
(c) (Sport) scoring.
tantico: un — — adv (fam) a bit, quite a bit; **es un — difícil** it's a wee bit awkward (fam).
tantísimo adj superl so much; —**s** so many; **había tantísima gente** there was such a crowd, there were so many people; **te lo he dicho tantísimas veces** I've told you lots of times.
tanto 1 adj so much, as much; so many, as many; **tiene — dinero como yo** he has as much money as I have; **tiene — dinero que no sabe qué hacer con él** he has so much money he doesn't know what to do with it; **hay —s sellos verdes como azules** there are as many green stamps as (there are) blue ones; **hubo tanta manzana** there were so many apples; **es uno de —s** it's one of many, it's one of a number; **hay otros —s candidatos** there are as many other candidates; **quedan por ver otros —s candidatos** there are as many candidates again still to be seen; **se dividen el trabajo en otras tantas porciones** they divide up the work into a like number of parts; **20 y —s** 20-odd; **hay ciento y —s concursantes** there are 100-odd competitors; **a —s de marzo** on such-and-such a day in March; **a —s de —** on such-and-such a day in this or that month; **volver a casa a las tantas** to come home terribly late; **estar fuera hasta las tantas** to stay out until all hours.
2 adv so much, as much; **permanecer —** to stay so long; **trabajar —** to work so hard; **venir —** to come so often; **él gasta — como yo** he spends as much as I do; **gastó — que se quedó sin dinero** he spent so much that he ran out of money; — **A como B** both A and B; — **como eso ...** I don't think it's as bad as all that, I think you're exaggerating; **es — más difícil** it is all the more difficult; **es — más loable cuanto que ...** it is all the more praiseworthy because ...; — **mejor** all the better, so much the better (para for); — **peor** so much the worse; **¡y —!** and how!, I'll say it is! (etc); — **es así que ...** so much so that ...; — **si viene como si no viene** whether he comes or whether he doesn't; **en —, entre —** meanwhile, meantime; **no es para —** it's not as bad as all that; there's no need to make such a fuss; **por —, por —** so, therefore; **¡ni — así!** not a scrap!; **no le tengo ni — así de lástima** I haven't a scrap of pity for him.
3 conj **con — que ...** provided (that) ...; **en que ... while ...;** until ...; **hasta — que ...** until (such time as) ...
4 nm (a) (Comm, Fin etc) certain amount, so much; — **alzado** agreed price; overall estimate; **por un — alzado** for a lump sum; — **por palabra** rate per word, so much a word; — **por ciento** percentage; rate; **un — por cada semana de trabajo** so much for each week's work; **al —** at the same price.
(b) (Sport) point; goal; (Gambling) counter, chip; — **en contra** point against; — **a favor** point for; **apuntar los —s** to keep score; **apuntarse un —** to score a point; (fig) to stay one up.
(c) **estar al —** to be fully informed; to know the score (fig); **estar al — de los acontecimientos** to be fully abreast of events, be in touch with events; **poner a uno al —** to give someone the news (de about), put someone in the picture (de about).
(d) **al — de —** because of; **al — de que ...** because of the fact that ...; with the excuse that ..., on the pretext that ...

(e) algún —, un — (as adv) rather, somewhat; estoy un — cansado I'm rather tired; es un — difícil it's a bit awkward.

Tanzanía f Tanzania.

tañer [2f] **1** vt (Mus) to play; bell to ring; **2** vi to drum with one's fingers.

tañido nm (Mus) sound; strains, notes; (of bell) ringing, pealing.

tapa nf **(a)** lid; cover, top, cap; (of book) cover; (of cylinder) head; — de registro manhole cover, inspection cover; — de los sesos brainbox, skull; levantarse la — de los sesos to blow one's brains out.
(b) (of shoe) heelplate.
(c) (of canal) sluice gate.
(d) (Cook) dish of hors d'oeuvres; snack, delicacy (taken at the bar counter with drinks).

tapa(a)gujeros nm, pl **tapa(a)gujeros** (fam) **(a)** jerry-builder. **(b)** (fig) stopgap, temporary measure.

tapabalazo nm (Col, Hond, Mex) trouser fly.

tapabarro nm (Chi, Per) mudguard.

tapaboca nf, **tapabocas** nm, pl **tapabocas** **(a)** slap. **(b)** muffler.

tapacubos nm, pl **tapacubos** hub cap.

tapadera nf lid, cover; cap.

tapadero nm stopper.

tapadillo: de — adv secretly, stealthily.

tapado 1 adj **(a)** (Chi, RPl) animal all one colour. **(b)** (Col, Per) lazy, slack; ignorant.
2 nm **(a)** (Arg, Bol, Per) buried treasure. **(b)** (Chi, RPl, Salv) woman's coat; child's coat; (SAm) headscarf, shawl.
(c) (Col, Guat, Hond) dish of plantain and meat.

tapalcate nm (CAm, Mex) piece of junk, useless object; useless person.

tapalodo nm (Per, PR) mudguard.

tapanca nf **(a)** (Col, Chi, Ec, Per) horse trappings. **(b)** (Chi) backside.

tapaojo nm (SAm) blindfold, bandage (over the eyes); patch.

tapar [1a] **1** vt **(a)** (general sense) to cover, cover up (de with); container, pot to put the lid on; bottle to put the cap on, put the stopper in, stopper, cork; face to cover up, hide; to muffle up; (in bed) to wrap up; pipe etc to stop (up), block (up), obstruct; hole to plug; (Archit) to fill up, wall up, wall in; (SAm) tooth to fill; object to hide; view to obstruct, block; el árbol tapa el sol a la ventana the tree keeps the sunlight off the window, the tree prevents the sun from reaching the window; el muro nos tapaba el viento the wall protected us from the wind.
(b) (fig) defeat etc to cover up, conceal; fugitive to hide, conceal; criminal to cover up for.
(c) (Col) to crush, flatten; to rumple.
(d) (Col: fig) to abuse, insult.
2 taparse vr to wrap (oneself) up, (esp) to wrap up warmly (in bed).

tapara nf (Arg, Ven) calabash, gourd.

táparo nm (Col) **(a)** tinderbox. **(b)** one-eyed person; (fig) dolt.

tapayagua nf (CAm, Mex), **tapayagüe** nm (Mex) stormcloud; drizzle.

tapeque nm (Bol) equipment for a journey.

tapera nf (SAm) ruined farm, tumbledown house; abandoned village.

taperujarse [1a] vr (fam) to cover up one's face.

tapesco nm (CAm, Mex) hurdle (used as a bed), rough bed.

tapete nm table runner, table cover; — verde card table; estar sobre el — (fig) to be under discussion.

tapetusa nf (Col) contraband goods, contraband liquor.

tapia nf garden wall; mud wall, adobe wall.

tapial nm = **tapia**.

tapialera nf (Ec) = **tapia**.

tapiar [1b] vt to wall in; (fig) to block, stop up.

tapicería nf **(a)** (art) tapestry making; upholstery. **(b)** tapestry; (collectively) tapestries, hangings; (of furniture, car etc) upholstery.

tapioca nf tapioca.

tapir nm tapir.

tapisca nf (CAm, Mex) maize harvest, corn harvest (US).

tapiscar [1g] vt (CAm, Mex) maize to harvest.

tapiz nm tapestry; carpet.

tapizado nm tapestries; carpeting; upholstery.

tapizar [1f] vt **(a)** wall to hang with tapestries; furniture to upholster, cover; car to upholster; floor to carpet, cover.
(b) (fig) to carpet (con, de with).

tapón 1 adj (Pan, Par, Urug) tailless.
2 nm **(a)** (of bottle) stopper, cap, top; cork; (Tech)

plug, bung, wad; (Med) tampon; al primer —, zurrapa (fam) well, the first shot was a failure.
(b) (fam) chubby person.
(c) (Aut: fam) slowcoach, slow driver.
(d) (PR: Aut) traffic jam.

taponar [1a] vt bottle to stopper, cork, put the cap on; pipe to plug, stop up, block; (Med) to tampon; — los oídos to stop up one's ears.

taponazo nm pop (of a cork).

tapujarse [1a] vr (fam) to muffle oneself up.

tapujo nm **(a)** muffler.
(b) (fam) deceit, humbug; subterfuge, dodge; sin —s honestly, openly, aboveboard; without beating about the bush; andar con —s to behave deceitfully, be involved in some shady business; llevan no sé qué — entre manos they're up to some dodge or other.

taquear [1a] **1** vt **(a)** (SAm) to shoot at. **(b)** (SAm) to fill right up, pack tight (de with).
2 vi **(a)** (Arg, Mex, Per) to play billiards. **(b)** (Cu) to dress in style. **(c)** (Mex) to have a snack.
3 taquearse vr (Col) to get rich.

taquería nf (Cu) brazenness.

taquigrafía nf shorthand, stenography.

taquigráficamente adv: coger un discurso — to take a speech down in shorthand.

taquigráfico adj shorthand (attr).

taquígrafo nm, **taquígrafa** nf shorthand writer, stenographer.

taquilla nf **(a)** (Rail) booking office, ticket office; ticket window; (Theat) box office.
(b) (Theat: Fin) takings; (Sport etc) gate money, proceeds.
(c) file; filing cabinet; (for tools etc) locker.
(d) (CAm) bar, liquor store.
(e) (CR, Chi, Ec, Per) tack, brad.

taquillero 1 adj: ser — to be good (for the) box office, be a draw, be popular; función taquillera box-office success, big draw; el actor más — del año the actor who has been the biggest box-office draw of the year.
2 nm, **taquillera** nf clerk, ticket clerk.

taquimeca nf (fam), **taquimecanógrafa** nf shorthand typist.

taquímetro nm speedometer; (Surveying) tachymeter.

tara¹ nf **(a)** (Comm) tare. **(b)** (fig) defect, blemish. **(c)** (Arg) —s physical defects.

tara² nf tally stick.

tarabilla 1 nf **(a)** (Orn) stonechat. **(b)** (fam) chatter.
2 nmf chatterbox; featherbrained person; useless individual, dead loss.

tarabita nf **(a)** tongue (of belt, buckle). **(b)** (Col, Ec, Per) cable of a rope bridge (with hanging basket for carrying passengers across ravines).

taracea nf inlay, marquetry.

taracear [1a] vt to inlay.

tarado adj **(a)** (Comm etc) damaged, defective, imperfect; animal etc maimed, weak. **(b)** (RPl) person physically impaired, crippled; odd, eccentric.

tarambana(s) nmf (fam) **(a)** harum-scarum, fly-by-night; crackpot; unreliable person. **(b)** chatterbox.

taranta nf **(a)** (Arg, Ec) tarantula. **(b)** (CR, Ec) mental disturbance, madness; (Hond) bewilderment. **(c)** (Mex) drunkenness.

tarantear [1a] vi (Arg) to do something unexpected; to chop and change a lot; to behave strangely, be eccentric.

tarantela nf tarantella.

tarantín nm **(a)** (CAm, Cu) kitchen utensil. **(b)** (Cu) scaffold. **(c)** (Ven) mean little shop. **(d)** (CAm, Mex) —es things, gear (fam), odds and ends.

taranto adj (Col) dazed, bewildered.

tarántula nf tarantula.

tarar [1a] vt (Comm) to tare.

tararear [1a] vti to hum.

tarasca nf **(a)** carnival dragon, monster.
(b) (fig) glutton; person who is a drain on one's resources.
(c) (fam) old hag, old bag (sl).
(d) (CR, Chi, Per) big mouth; deformed mouth.

tarascada nf **(a)** bite; snap. **(b)** (fam) tart reply, snappy answer.

tarascar [1g] vt to bite, snap at.

tarasco nm (Ec) bite; snap.

tarascón nm (SAm) bite; snap.

tarasquear [1a] vt (Arg, Mex, Nic) to bite, snap at; to bite off.

tardanza nf **(a)** slowness. **(b)** delay.

tardar [1a] vi **(a)** to take a long time, be long; to be late; to delay, linger (on); a más —, a todo — at the latest; aquí tardan mucho they are very slow here, they take a long time here; **he tardado un poco debido a la lluvia** I'm a bit late because of the rain, I took longer (to get here) because of the rain; **tardamos 3 horas de A a B** we took 3 hours (to get) from A to B; **escribiré sin —** I'll write without delay.

   (b) — a + *infin* to delay + *ger*, be slow to + *infin*; **no tardes a hacerlo** don't put off doing it.

   (c) — en + *infin* to be slow to + *infin*, take a long time to + *infin*, be long in + *ger*, to be late in + *ger*; **tardó mucho en repararlo** he took a long time to repair it; **tardó 3 horas en encontrarlo** it took him 3 hours to find it, he spent 3 hours looking for it; **no tarde Vd en informarme** tell me at once, inform me without delay; **¿cuánto tardaremos en terminarlo?** how long shall we take to finish it?; **el público no tardó en reaccionar** the spectators were not slow to react.

tarde 1 *adv* late; too late; **un poco más —** a little later; **de — en —** from time to time; **— o temprano** sooner or later; **se hace —** it's getting late; **es — para eso** it's too late for that.

   2 *nf* afternoon; evening; early evening; **¡buenas —s!** good afternoon!; good evening!; **a la —** in the evening; by evening; **por la —** in the afternoon, in the evening; **función de la —** matinée; **de la — a la mañana** overnight, during the night; (*fig*) in no time at all.

tardecer [2d] *vi* = **atardecer**.

tardecica *nf*, **tardecita** *nf* nightfall, dusk.

tardecito *adv* (*Arg, Guat, PR*) rather late.

tardíamente *adv* late, belatedly; too late.

tardío *adj* late; overdue, belated, slow to arrive (*etc*); *fruit, vegetable* late.

tardo *adj* **(a)** slow, sluggish; dilatory. **(b)** slow (of understanding), dull, dense; **— de oído** hard of hearing.

tardón *adj* (*fam*) **(a)** slow; dilatory. **(b)** dim.

tarea *nf* job, task; chore; set piece of work, stint, amount of work set; **— de ocasión** chore; **— suelta** odd job; **todavía me queda mucha —** I've still got a lot left to do; **es una — poco grata** it's not a very satisfying job; **¡— le mando!** (*fam*) you've got a job on there!; you'll have your work cut out!

tareco *nm* (*Cu, Ec, Ven*) old thing, piece of junk; **—s** (*fig*) things, gear (*fam*), odds and ends.

tarifa *nf* tariff; rate; price list, list of charges; (*on vehicle*) fare; **— de agua** water rate, water charges; **— de suscripción** subscription rate; **— turística** tourist class, tourist rates.

tarifar [1a] **1** *vt* to price. **2** *vi* to fall out, quarrel.

tarima *nf* platform; low dais; stand; low bench, stool; bunk.

tarimaco *nm* (*Cu*) = **tareco**.

tarja¹ *nf* tally, tally stick.

tarja² *nf* (*fam*) swipe, bash (*fam*).

tarjar [1a] *vt* **(a)** to keep a tally of, notch up. **(b)** (*Chi, Per*) to cross out.

tarjeta *nf* card; **— de crédito** credit card; **— de identidad** identity card; **— de Navidad, — navideña** Christmas card; **— postal** postcard; **— de visita** visiting card, calling card (*US*); **dejar —** to leave one's card; **pasar —** to send in one's card.

tarpón *nm* tarpon.

tarquín *nm* mud, slime, ooze.

tarraconense 1 *adj* of Tarragona. **2** *nmf* native (*or* inhabitant) of Tarragona; **los —s** the people of Tarragona.

tarrajazo *nm* **(a)** (*Ec, PR*) unpleasant happening. **(b)** (*Guat*) blow; wound.

tarramenta *nf* (*Cu, Mex*) horns.

tarrayazo *nm* **(a)** (*Ant, Col, Mex, Ven*) cast (of a net). **(b)** (*PR, Ven*) violent blow.

tarrear [1a] *vt* (*Cu*) to cuckold.

tarro *nm* **(a)** pot, jar.
   (b) (*Chi, Per, RPl*) tin, can; drum.
   (c) (*Cu, Mex, PR, Urug*) horn.
   (d) (*Bol, Col, Ec, Per*) top hat.
   (e) (*Arg*) stroke of luck, fluke.
   (f) (*Cu*) cuckolding.
   (g) (*Cu*) difficult matter, complicated affair.

tarsana *nf* (*SAm*) soapbark.

tarso *nm* tarsus.

tarta *nf* cake; tart; sponge; **— de cumpleaños** birthday cake; **— de Reyes** Christmas cake.

tártago *nm* **(a)** (*Bot*) spurge.
   (b) (*fam*) mishap, misfortune.
   (c) (*fam*) practical joke.
   (d) darse un — (*fam*) to slave, slog; to bustle about.

tartajear [1a] *vi* to stammer.

tartajeo *nm* stammer(ing).

tartajoso *adj* stammering, tongue-tied.

tartalear [1a] *vi* **(a)** to walk in a daze; to stagger, reel. **(b)** to stammer, be stuck for words.

tartamudear [1a] *vi* to stutter, stammer.

tartamudeo *nm* stutter(ing), stammer(ing).

tartamudez *nf* stutter, stammer, speech defect.

tartamudo 1 *adj* stuttering, stammering. **2** *nm*, **tartamuda** *nf* stutterer, stammerer.

tartán *nm* tartan.

tartancho *adj* (*Arg, Bol*) = **tartamudo**.

Tartaria *f* Tartary.

tartárico *adj* tartaric; **ácido —** tartaric acid.

tártaro¹ *nm* (*Chem etc*) tartar.

tártaro² **1** *adj* Tartar. **2** *nm*, **tártara** *nf* Tartar.

tarugo 1 *adj* **(a)** (*Guat, Mex, RPl*) stupid.
   (b) (*SD*) fawning.
   2 *nm* **(a)** lump, chunk (of wood *etc*); wooden peg; plug, stopper; chunk of stale bread; wooden paving block.
   (b) (*Cu*) fright, scare.
   (c) (*Guat, Mex, RPl*) chump (*fam*), blockhead.

tarumba *adj* (*fam*): **volver — a uno** to get someone all mixed up; to daze someone, fog someone; **volverse —** to get all mixed up, get completely bewildered; **esa chica me tiene —** I'm crazy about that girl.

tasa *nf* **(a)** (*act*) valuation; estimate, appraisal.
   (b) measure, standard, norm.
   (c) fixed price, official price, standard rate; **— de interés** rate of interest; **sin —** (*fig*) boundless, limitless; unstinted.

tasable *adj* ratable.

tasación *nf* valuation, assessment; (*fig*) appraisal; **— de un artículo** fixing of a price for an article.

tasadamente *adv* sparingly.

tasador *nm* valuer.

tasajear [1a] *vt* (*SAm*) = **atasajar**.

tasajo *nm* **(a)** dried beef, jerked beef; (*any*) piece of meat. **(b)** (*Col*) tall thin person.

tasajudo *adj* (*SAm*) tall and thin.

tasar [1a] *vt* **(a)** *article* to fix a price for, price (*en at*); to regulate; *work etc* to rate (*en at*).
   (b) (*fig*) to value, appraise, assess (*en at*).
   (c) to limit, put a limit on, restrict; to be sparing with, (*pej*) be mean with, stint; **les tasa a los niños hasta la leche** she even stints her children for milk.

tasca *nf* (*fam*) pub (*fam*), bar; dive (*fam*), joint (*sl*); **ir de —s** to go on a pub crawl (*fam*).

tascar [1g] *vt* **(a)** *flax etc* to swingle, beat. **(b)** *grass* to munch, champ; *bit* to champ; (*Ec*) to chew, crunch.

Tasmania *f* Tasmania.

tata 1 *nm* **(a)** (*Murcia, SAm: fam*) dad, daddy. **(b)** (*SAm*) = **taita**. **2** *nf* **(a)** (*fam*) nanny, nursemaid; maid. **(b)** (*SAm*) younger sister.

tatarabuelo *nm* great-great-grandfather; **los —s** one's great-great-grandparents.

tataranieto *nm* great-great-grandson.

tatas: andar a — to toddle; to crawl, get down on all fours.

tate *interj* (*surprise*) good heavens!, well well!; (*admiration*) bravo!; (*anger*) come now!; watch your step!; (*understanding*) so that's it!; oh I see!; (*warning*) look out!

tato *nm* (*prov, SAm: fam*) younger brother.

tatuaje *nm* **(a)** tattoo. **(b)** (*act*) tattooing.

tatuar [1d] *vt* to tattoo.

taumaturgo *nm* miracle-worker; (*fig*) wonder-worker.

taurino *adj* bullfighting (*attr*); **el negocio —** the bullfighting business; **leía una revista taurina** he was reading a bullfighting magazine.

taurómaco 1 *adj* bullfighting (*attr*). **2** *nm* bullfighting expert.

tauromaquia *nf* (art of) bullfighting, tauromachy.

tauromáquico *adj* bullfighting (*attr*).

tautología *nf* tautology.

tautológico *adj* tautological.

taxativamente *adv* in a restricted sense, specifically.

taxativo *adj* limited, restricted; *sense* particular, concrete; specific.

taxi *nm* taxi, cab, taxicab.

taxidermia *nf* taxidermy.

taxidermista *nmf* taxidermist.

taxímetro *nm* taximeter, clock (*fam*).

taxista *nm* taxidriver, taximan, cabby (*fam*).

taxonomía *nf* taxonomy.

taxonomista *nmf* taxonomist.

taza *nf* **(a)** cup; cupful; **— de café** cup of coffee; **— para café** coffee cup, cup for coffee.
   (b) (*of fountain*) basin, bowl; (*of lavatory*) bowl.
   (c) (*Chi*) washbasin.
   (d) (*Arg*) **— de noche** chamberpot.

tazado adj dress frayed, worn; person shabby.
tazar [1f] **1** vt (a) to cut; to cut up, divide. (b) to fray. **2 tazarse** vr to fray.
tazón nm large cup; bowl, basin; (Prov) washbasin.
te personal pron (a) (acc) you; (arch, to God) thee.
(b) (dative) (to) you; (arch, to God) to thee; **te he traído esto** I've brought you this, I've brought this for you; **¿te duele mucho el brazo?** does your arm hurt much?
(c) (reflexive) (to) yourself; (arch, to God) (to) thyself; **te vas a caer** you'll fall; **te equivocas** you're wrong; **¡cálmate!** calm yourself!
té nm (a) tea; tea party; **dar un —** to give a tea party. (b) (fam) **dar el — a uno** to bore someone to tears.
tea nf (a) torch; firelighter. (b) (fam) **coger una —, pillar una —** to get tight.
teatral adj (a) theatre (attr); dramatic; **obra —** dramatic work; **temporada —** theatre season.
(b) (fig) theatrical, dramatic; (pej) histrionic, stagey.
teatralidad nf drama; sense of the theatre, stage sense; (pej) showmanship; histrionics, staginess.
teatralmente adv (a) dramatically. (b) (fig) theatrically, dramatically; (pej) histrionically.
teatro nm (a) (in general) theatre; **el —** (as profession) the theatre, the stage, acting; **— de aficionados** amateur theatre, amateur theatricals; **— de la ópera** opera house; **— de variedades** variety theatre, music hall, vaudeville theater (US); **escribir para el —** to write for the stage; **en el — es una persona muy distinta** she's a very different person on the stage; **hacer que se venga abajo el —** to bring the house down.
(b) (Lit) drama, plays; **el — de Cervantes** Cervantes' plays, Cervantes' dramatic works; **selecciones del — del siglo XVIII** selections from 18th century drama.
(c) (of event) scene; (Mil) theatre; **— de guerra** theatre of war, front.
(d) (fig) **hacer —** to exaggerate, act affectedly; **ella tiene mucho —** she's terribly dramatic, she's given to histrionics.
Tebas Thebes.
tebeo nm children's comic.
teca nf teak.
tecla nf (Mus, of typewriter etc) key; **— de cambio** shift key; **dar en la —** (fam) to get it right; to get the hang of something; **dar en la — de + infin** (fam) to fall into the habit of + ger; **hay que tocar muchas —s a la vez** (fam) there are too many things to think about all together; **no le queda ninguna — por tocar** there's nothing else left for him to try.
teclado nm (Mus, of typewriter) keyboard, keys; (of organ) manual.
tecle adj (Chi) weak, sickly.
teclear [1a] **1** vt (a) (SAm) instrument to play clumsily, mess about on; typewriter to use clumsily.
(b) (fam) problem to approach from various angles.
2 vi (a) (Mus) to strum, thrum, play a few chords.
(b) (fam) to drum, tap (with one's fingers).
(c) (Arg, Chi) to be weak, be ill.
(d) (Chi) to be very poor.
(e) (Col, Chi, RPl: of business) to be going very badly.
tecleo nm (a) (Mus) fingering, playing; touch; strumming, thrumming. (b) (fam) drumming, tapping.
técnica nf technique; method; craft, skill **— electrónica** electronics.
técnicamente adv technically.
tecnicidad nf technicality.
tecnicismo nm (a) technical nature. (b) (Ling) technical term, technicality.
técnico 1 adj technical. **2** nm technician; expert, specialist; **es un — en la materia** he's an expert on the subject.
tecnicolor nm Technicolor (Protected Trade Name); **en —** in Technicolor.
tecnología nf technology.
tecnológico adj technological.
tecnólogo nm technologist.
teco adj (CAm, Mex) drunk.
tecolote 1 adj (a) (CR) reddish-brown. (b) (CAm, Mex) drunk. **2** nm (a) (CAm, Mex) eagle owl. (b) (Mex) policeman, cop (sl).
tecomate nm (CAm, Mex) gourd, calabash; earthenware cup, pan.
tecorral nm (Mex) dry-stone wall.

tecuán 1 adj (CAm, Mex) greedy, voracious. **2** nm monster.
techado nm roof, covering; **bajo —** under cover, indoors.
techar [1a] vt to roof (in, over).
techo nm (a) roof; ceiling; **bajo —** under cover, indoors; **tenis bajo —** indoor tennis. (b) (Aer) ceiling.
techumbre nf roof.
tedio nm (a) boredom, tedium. (b) lack of interest; depression; sense of emptiness; **a mí no me produce sino —** it just depresses me.
tedioso adj boring, tedious; wearisome; depressing.
tefe nm (a) (Col, Ec) strip of leather, strip of cloth. (b) (Ec) scar on the face; bruise.
tegumento nm tegument.
teísmo nm theism.
teísta 1 adj theistic. **2** nmf theist.
teja¹ nf tile; **pagar a toca —** to pay cash; to pay on the nail; **de —s abajo** in this world, in the natural way of things; **de —s arriba** in the next world; up aloft; with God's help.
teja² nf lime (tree).
tejadillo nm top, cover.
tejado nm roof, tiled roof; (fig) housetop; **tiene el — de vidrio** he himself is open to the same charge, he lives in a glass house and should not throw stones.
tejamaní nm, **tejamanil** nm (SAm) roofing board, shingle.
tejano 1 adj Texan. **2** nm, **tejana** nf Texan. **3 —s** nmpl jeans.
tejar [1a] vt to tile, roof with tiles.
Tejas m Texas.
tejaván nm (SAm) shed; corridor, gallery; eaves; rustic dwelling.
tejavana nf shed; shed roof, plain tile roof.
tejedor nm, **tejedora** nf (a) weaver. (b) (Chi, Per) intriguer, meddler.
tejedura nf (a) weaving. (b) weave, texture.
tejeduría nf (a) (art of) weaving. (b) textile mill.
tejemaneje nm (fam) (a) bustle; fuss, to-do (fam); **se trae un tremendo — con sus papeles** he's making a tremendous to-do with his papers, he's getting all worked up with his papers.
(b) intrigue, shady business.
tejer [2a] **1** vt (a) to weave; to make; cobweb to make, spin; cocoon to spin; (esp SAm) to knit; to sew; to crochet.
(b) (fig) to weave; to bring about little by little; lie, scandal etc to fabricate.
2 vi: **— y destejer** to chop and change, blow hot and cold.
tejido nm (a) weave, woven material; web; fabric; **—s** textiles; **— de punto** knitting; knitted fabric. (b) weave, texture. (c) (Anat) tissue.
tejo¹ nm (a) ring, quoit. (b) hopscotch.
tejo² nm (Bot) yew (tree).
tejoleta nf bit of tile, sherd; brickbat.
tejón nm badger.
tela nf (a) cloth, fabric, material; **—s del corazón** (fig) heartstrings; **— cruzada** twill; **— metálica** wire netting; **— de saco** sackcloth; **en —** (Typ) clothbound.
(b) (SAm: Art) canvas, painting.
(c) (Ent etc) web; **— de araña** spider's web, cobweb.
(d) (on liquid) skin, film.
(e) (Bot) skin.
(f) (sl) dough (sl).
(g) (fig) subject, matter; **hay — que cortar, hay — para rato** there's plenty of material, there's lots to talk about; it's a long job; it's a tricky business.
(h) **poner algo en — de juicio** to question, call in question, cast doubt on.
(i) (Col) thin maize pancake.
telabrejos nmpl (SAm) things, gear (fam), odds and ends.
telar nm (a) loom; **—es** (fig) textile mill. (b) (Theat) gridiron.
telaraña nf spider's web, cobweb.
tele nf (fam) telly (fam).
tele . . . tele . . .
telebrejos nmpl (Mex) = **telabrejos**.
telecomando nm remote control.
telecomunicación nf telecommunication.
telecontrol nm remote control.
telediario nm television news bulletin.
teledifusión nf telecast.
teledirigido adj remote-controlled, radio-controlled.
teleférico nm ski lift; cable railway, cableway.
telefilm nm, **telefilme** nm (Acad) telefilm.

telefonazo nm telephone call; **te daré un —** I'll give you a ring, I'll call you up.
telefonear [1a] vti to telephone.
telefonema nm telephone message.
telefonía nf telephony.
telefónico adj telephonic; telephone (attr).
telefonista nmf (telephone) operator, telephonist.
teléfono nm telephone, phone; **el — rojo** (Pol) the hot line; **está hablando por —** he's on the phone; **llamar a uno al** (or **por) —** to telephone someone, phone someone, ring someone up, call someone (up); **le llaman al —** you're wanted on the phone.
telefoto(grafía) nf telephoto.
telefotográfico adj telephoto (attr).
telegrafía nf telegraphy.
telegrafiar [1c] vti to telegraph.
telegráfico adj telegraphic; telegraph (attr).
telegrafista nmf telegraphist.
telégrafo nm (a) telegraph. (b) **—s** (fam) telegram boy.
telegrama nm telegram; **poner un — a uno** to send someone a telegram.
teleimpresor nm teleprinter.
telémetro nm rangefinder.
telengues nmpl (CAm) things, gear (fam), odds and ends.
telenque adj (Chi) weak, feeble.
teleobjetivo nm telephoto lens.
teleología nf teleology.
telépata nmf telepathist.
telepático adj telepathic.
telescopar [1a] **1** vt to telescope. **2 telescoparse** vr to telescope.
telescópico adj telescopic.
telescopio nm telescope.
telesilla nm skilift, chairlift.
telespectador nm, **telespectadora** nf viewer, televiewer.
telesquí nm ski lift.
teletipista nmf teletypist, teleprinter operator.
teletipo nm teletype, teleprinter; **el — rojo** (Pol) the hot line.
teletubo nm cathode-ray tube, television tube.
televidente nmf viewer, televiewer.
televisar [1a] vt to televise.
televisión nf television; **— en colores** colour television; **— pagada** pay-television; **mirar la —** to watch television; **hacer —** to be doing television, be working in television, be engaged in television work.
televisivo adj television (attr); **serie televisiva** television serial (or series).
televisor nm television set.
telón nm (a) (Theat) curtain; **— de boca** front curtain; **— de fondo, — de foro** backcloth, backdrop; **— metálico** fire curtain; **— de seguridad** safety curtain. (b) (Pol) **— de acero** iron curtain.
telúrico adj of the earth, telluric; (fig) earthy.
tema[1] nm (a) theme; subject, topic; (Mus) theme, motif; (Art) subject; **— de actualidad** current issue; **—s de actualidad** current affairs; **el — de su discurso** the theme (or subject) of his speech; **es un tema muy manoseado** it's a subject which has often been discussed; **las autoridades tienen — de meditación** the authorities have food for thought, the authorities have something to think about. (b) (Gram) stem.
tema[2] nf (a) fixed idea, mania, obsession; **tener —** to be stubborn. (b) ill will, unreasoning hostility; **tener — a uno** to have a grudge against someone.
temar [1a] vi (Arg, Par) (a) to have a mania, be obsessed. (b) to bear ill will; **— con uno** to have a grudge against someone.
temario nm set of themes, collection of subjects; (of meeting) agenda, subjects for discussion.
temascal nm (CAm, Mex) bathroom; (fig) hot place, oven.
temático adj (a) thematic. (b) (Gram) stem (attr). (c) (Col) injudicious, tasteless.
tembladera nf (a) (fam) violent shaking. (b) (SAm) = **tembladeral**.
tembladeral nm (Arg, Mex, Urug) quaking bog, quagmire.
temblar [1k] vi (a) (of person: with fear) to tremble, shake; (with cold) to shiver; (of building etc) to shake, quiver, shudder; **— de frío** to shiver with cold; **— de miedo** to tremble with fright; **— ante una escena** to shudder at a sight; **— como un azogado** to shake like a leaf, tremble all over; **dejar una botella temblando** (fam) to use most of a bottle, make a bottle look pretty silly (fam). (b) (fig) to tremble; **tiemblo de pensar en lo que pueda ocurrir** I tremble (or shudder) to think what may happen; **— por su vida** to fear for one's life.

tembleque nm (a) (fam) violent shaking; **le entró un —** he began to shake violently. (b) (SAm) sickly person, weakling.
temblequear [1a] vi (fam) to shake violently, be all of a quiver.
temblequera nf (Per, PR) fear; cowardice.
temblón 1 adj trembling, shaking; tremulous; **álamo — 2** nm aspen.
temblor nm trembling, shaking; shiver, shivering, shudder, shuddering; (SAm) **= — de tierra** earthquake; **le entró un — violento** he began to shake violently.
tembloroso adj trembling, tremulous; quivering; shivering; **con voz temblorosa** in a shaky voice, in a tremulous tone.
tembo adj (Col) featherbrained, stupid.
temer [2a] **1** vt (a) to fear, be afraid of; to dread; to go in awe of; **— + infin** to fear to + infin; **— a Dios** to fear God.
(b) (fig) **temo que lo ha perdido** I'm afraid he has lost it, I fear he has lost it; **teme que no vaya a volver** she's afraid (lest) he won't come back.
2 vi to be afraid; **no temas** don't be afraid, (fig) don't worry; **— por la seguridad de uno** to fear for someone's safety.
3 temerse vr = **1 (b)**.
temerariamente adv rashly, recklessly; boldly; hastily.
temerario adj act, person rash, reckless; bold; judgement etc hasty, rash.
temeridad nf (a) rashness, recklessness; boldness; hastiness. (b) rash act, folly.
temerón 1 adj bullying, ranting, loud-mouthed. **2** nm bully, ranter.
temerosamente adv timidly, fearfully.
temeroso adj (a) timid; fearful, frightened. (b) **— de Dios** full of the fear of God. (c) dread, frightful.
temible adj fearsome, dread, frightful; opponent etc redoubtable.
temor nm fear, dread; suspicion, mistrust; **— a** fear of; **— de Dios** fear of God; **por —** from fear; **por — a** for fear of; **sin —** a fearless of; regardless of; **sin — ni favor** without fear or favour.
témpano nm (a) (also **— de hielo**) ice floe; **quedarse como un —** (fam) to be chilled to the marrow. (b) (Mus) small drum, kettledrum. (c) (Mus) drumhead. (d) (Archit) tympan. (e) (Cook) **— de tocino** flitch of bacon.
temperadero nm (SAm) summer resort.
temperado adj (Col) = **templado**.
temperamental adj (a) temperamental. (b) (angl) temperamental.
temperamento nm (a) temperament, nature, disposition.
(b) constitution.
(c) (angl) temperament; **tener —** to have a temperament, be temperamental.
(d) (Pol etc) compromise.
(e) (SAm) climate, weather; summer.
temperancia nf temperance, moderation.
temperante (SAm) **1** adj teetotal. **2** nmf teetotaller, abstainer.
temperar [1a] **1** vt to temper, moderate; to calm; to relieve. **2** vi (SAm) to spend the summer, summer; to go to a warmer climate; to have a change of air.
temperatura nf temperature.
temperie nf state of the weather.
tempestad nf storm (also fig); **— en un vaso de agua** storm in a teacup; **levantar una — de protestas** to cause a storm of protests.
tempestuoso adj stormy (also fig).
templado adj (a) moderate, restrained; (in eating) frugal; (in drinking) of sober habits, abstemious. (b) water lukewarm; climate mild, temperate; zone (Geog) temperate. (c) (Mus) in tune, well-tuned. (d) (fam) bold, forthright; courageous. (e) (fam) child bright, lively; (CAm, Mex) clever; competent. (f) (Col) severe. (g) (SAm) half drunk. (h) (Bol, Col, Chi) **estar —** to be in love.
templanza nf (a) moderation, restraint; frugality; abstemiousness. (b) (Meteorol) mildness.
templar [1a] **1** vt (a) (general sense) to temper; to moderate, soften; anger to restrain, control; climate to make mild; heat to reduce; solution to dilute.
(b) room, water to warm up (slightly).
(c) (Mus) to tune (up).
(d) (Mech) to adjust; screw etc to tighten up; spring etc to set properly.

(e) *steel* to temper.
(f) (*Art*) *colours* to blend.
(g) (*Col, Ec*) to knock down; (*CR*) to hit; to beat; (*Ec, Per*) to kill.
2 *vi* (a) (*of cold etc*) to moderate.
(b) (*Cu*) to flee.
3 templarse *vr* (a) (*person*) to be moderate, be restrained, act with restraint; **— en la comida** to eat frugally.
(b) (*water*) to warm up, get warm.
(c) (*Ec, Guat, Hond*) to die.
(d) (*Arg, Cu*) to flee; **—las** (*Cu, Mex*) to flee.
(e) (*Col, Per, PR*) to get drunk.
(f) (*Chi*) to fall in love.
(g) (*Chi*) to go too far, overstep the mark.
(h) (*Col*) **—las** to stand firm.
templario *nm* Templar.
temple *nm* (a) (*Tech*) temper; tempering.
(b) (*Mus*) tuning.
(c) (*Meteorol*) state of the weather, temperature.
(d) (*of person*) mood; **estar de mal —** to be in a bad mood.
(e) (*of person*) spirit, temper, mettle; (*SAm*) courage, boldness, resoluteness.
(f) distemper; (*Art*) tempera; **pintar al —** to distemper; (*Art*) to paint in tempera.
templete *nm* bandstand; pavilion.
templo *nm* (*pagan, masonic, fig*) temple; (*Eccl*) church, chapel; **— metodista** Methodist chapel; **— protestante** Protestant church; **como un —** (*esp SAm*) huge, tremendous; first-rate, excellent.
temporada *nf* time, period, spell; (*Meteorol*) spell; (*of year, social, sporting etc*) season; **— de fútbol** football season; **— de ópera** opera season; **— de exámenes** examination period; **— de lluvias** rainy spell; rainy season; **en plena —** at the height of the season; **estar fuera de —** to be out of season.
temporal 1 *adj* (a) temporary.
(b) (*Eccl etc*) temporal; **poder —** temporal power.
2 *nm* (a) storm; rainy weather, spell of rough weather; **capear el —** to weather the storm, ride out the storm (*also fig*).
(b) (*Cu*) shady character.
temporalmente *adv* temporarily.
temporáneo *adj* temporary.
témporas *nfpl* ember days.
temporero *adj worker* temporary, casual.
temporizar [1f] *vi* to temporize.
tempozonte *adj* (*Mex*) hunchbacked.
tempranal *adj land, plant etc* early.
tempranear [1a] *vi* (a) (*SAm*) to get up early. (b) (*Arg*) to sow early.
tempranero *adj* (a) (*Bot*) early. (b) *person* early, early-rising.
temprano 1 *adj* (a) *fruit etc* early.
(b) *years* youthful; *period, work etc* early.
2 *adv* early; too early, too soon; **lo más — posible** as soon as possible.
tenacidad *nf* (a) toughness. (b) tenacity. (c) ingrained nature; persistence; stubbornness.
tenacillas *nfpl* sugar tongs; curling tongs; (*Med etc*) tweezers, forceps; (*for candle*) snuffers.
tenamaste 1 *adj* (*CAm, Mex*) stubborn. **2** *nm* (a) (*CAm, Mex*) cooking stone. (b) (*Guat*) **= cachivache.**
tenaz *adj* (a) *material* tough, durable, resistant.
(b) *person* tenacious.
(c) *stain etc* hard to remove, that sticks fast; ingrained; *pain* persistent; *belief, resistance etc* stubborn.
tenaza *nf* (a) (*Bridge*) squeeze (*a in*). (b) **—s** (*Tech*) pliers, pincers; tongs; forceps; **unas —s** a pair of pliers (*etc*).
tenazmente *adv* tenaciously; stubbornly.
tenazón: a —, de — *adv* suddenly; *shoot* without taking aim.
tenca[1] *nf* (*Fish*) tench.
tenca[2] *nf* (*Chi*) lie, swindle.
tencal *nm* wicker box, wicker poultry cage.
tendajo *nm* **= tendejón.**
tendal *nm* (a) awning.
(b) sheet spread to catch olives (*when shaken from the tree*).
(c) (*SAm*) heap, lot, abundance; lot of scattered objects (*or bodies etc*); confusion, disorder; **un — de** a lot of, a whole heap of.
(d) (*RPl*) shearing shed; (*Col, PR*) brickworks, tileworks; (*Cu, Nic*) sunny place for drying coffee; (*Chi*) small travelling shop.
(e) (*Bol*) flat field.
tendalada *nf* (*SAm*) **= tendal** (c).
tendalera *nf* mess, litter (of scattered objects).

tendear [1a] *vi* (*Mex*) to go window shopping.
tendedera *nf* (a) (*Cu, Guat, Mex*) clothesline. (b) (*Col*) **= tendal** (c).
tendedero *nm* drying place; clothesline, frame for drying clothes.
tendejón *nm* small shop; stall, booth.
tendencia *nf* tendency; trend; inclination; **— imperante** dominant trend, prevailing tendency; **— del mercado** (*Fin*) run of the market, price movement; **la — hacia el sinsombrerismo** the tendency (*or* trend) towards hatlessness; **una palabra con —** a word tending to become archaic; **tener — a** + *infin* to have a tendency to + *infin*, tend to + *infin*, be inclined to + *infin*; **tener —s de zurdo** to have a tendency towards left-handedness.
tendenciosidad *nf* tendentiousness.
tendencioso *adj* tendentious.
ténder *nm* (*Rail*) tender.
tender [2g] **1** *vt* (a) to stretch; to spread, spread out, extend, lay out; *paint etc* to put on, apply; *tablecloth* to lay, spread; **tendieron el cadáver sobre el suelo** they stretched the corpse out on the floor.
(b) *washing* to hang out; *rope etc* to stretch (*a to, de from*), hang (*de from*); *hand* to stretch out, reach out; *bridge, railway* to build; *cable, track* to lay.
(c) *bow* to draw; *trap* to set (*a for*).
(d) (*SAm*) **— la cama** to make the bed; **— la mesa** to lay the table.
2 *vi*: **— a** to tend to, tend towards, have a tendency towards; **— a** + *infin* to tend to + *infin*; **las plantas tienden a la luz** plants grow (*or* turn) towards the light; **el color tiende a verde** the colour tends towards green; **ella tiende al pesimismo** she has a tendency to be pessimistic.
3 tenderse *vr* (a) to lie down, stretch (oneself) out.
(b) (*fig*) to let oneself go; to give up, let things go, stop bothering.
(c) (*horse*) to run at full gallop.
(d) (*Cards*) to lay down.
tenderete *nm* (a) **= tendedero.** (b) stall, barrow, market booth. (c) display of goods for sale (*etc*); (*fig*) litter (of objects); mess.
tendero *nm*, **tendera** *nf* shopkeeper, (*esp*) grocer.
tendida *nf* (*Arg*) shy, start (*of horse*).
tendido 1 *adj* (a) lying down; flat.
(b) *gallop* fast, flat out.
2 *nm* (a) (*Archit*) coat of plaster.
(b) (*also* **—s**) washing, clothes (hung out to dry).
(c) (*Taur*) front rows of seats.
(d) (*of cable, track*) laying.
(e) (*Cook*) batch of loaves.
(f) (*Col, Ec, Mex*) bedclothes.
(g) (*Cu, Pan*) long tether, rope.
(h) (*Mex*) stall, booth.
tendinoso *adj* sinewy.
tendón *nm* tendon, sinew.
tendré *etc see* **tener.**
tenducho *nm* poky little shop.
tenebrosidad *nf* (a) darkness; gloom(iness). (b) (*fig*) gloominess, dimness, blackness. (c) (*fig*) sinister nature, shadiness. (d) (*fig*) obscurity.
tenebroso *adj* (a) dark; gloomy, dismal. (b) (*fig*) *outlook etc* gloomy, dim, black. (c) (*pej*) *plot etc* sinister, dark, shady. (d) (*fig*) *style etc* obscure.
tenedor *nm* (a) (*Cook*) fork.
(b) (*Comm, Fin etc*) holder, bearer; **— de acciones** shareholder; **— de libros** book-keeper; **— de obligaciones** bondholder; **— de póliza** policyholder.
teneduría *nf*: **— de libros** book-keeping.
tenencia *nf* (a) tenancy, occupancy; (*of office*) tenure; (*of property*) possession; **— ilícita de armas** illegal possession of weapons.
(b) mayorship, period of office as mayor.
(c) (*Mil*) lieutenancy.
tener [2l] **1** *vt* (a) (*general sense*) to have; to have got; to possess; **— ojos azules** to have blue eyes; **hemos tenido muchas dificultades** we have had a lot of difficulties; **hoy no tenemos clase** we have no class today, we are not having a class today; **¿tienes una pluma?** have you got a pen?; **¿tiene Vd permiso para esto?** do you have permission for this?, have you (got) permission for this?; **va a — un niño** she's going to have a baby; **tiene un tío en Venezuela** he has an uncle in Venezuela; **tiene muchas preocupaciones encima** he has a lot of worries, he is burdened with anxieties; **el cargo tiene una buena retribución** the post carries a good salary; **de bueno no tiene nada** there's nothing good about it; *see* **particular, suerte** *etc.*
(b) (*idiomatic uses with certain nouns*) **— 7 años**

to be 7, be 7 years old; **— hambre** to be hungry; **— mucha sed** to be very thirsty; **— calor** to be hot; **— mucho frío** to be very cold; *for a full exposition see the noun in question, also* **celos, cuidado, ganas, miedo** *etc.*

(c) *(measurements)* **— 5 cm de ancho** to be 5 cm wide; *see* **ancho, largo** *etc.*

(d) *object* to hold; to hold on to, hold up, grasp; to carry, bear; **ten esto** take this, hold on to this; **¡ten!, ¡tenga!** here you are!; catch!; **lo tenía en la mano** he was holding it in his hand; he was carrying it in his hand; **los dos que tenían la bandera** the two who were carrying the flag.

(e) *(of container)* to hold, contain; **una caja para — el dinero** a box to hold the money, a box to keep (*or* put) the money in.

(f) *promise* to keep.

(g) *(of feelings etc)* to have, profess (*a* for); **— gran admiración a uno** to have (a) great admiration for someone; **le tengo mucho cariño** I'm very fond of him; *see* **cariño** *etc.*

(h) to think, consider, deem; **— a bien** + *infin* to see fit to + *infin*, deign to + *infin*; to think it proper to + *infin*; **— a menos** + *infin* to consider it beneath oneself to + *infin*; **— a uno en más** to think all the more of someone; **te tendrán en más estima** they will hold you in higher esteem; **— para sí que ...** to think that ...; **— a uno por** + *adj* to think someone + *adj*, consider someone to be + *adj*, deem someone to be + *adj*; **no quiero que me tengan por informal** I don't want them to think me unreliable; **le tengo por poco honrado** I consider him to be rather dishonest; **lo tienen por cosa cierta** they believe it to be true; **ten por seguro que ...** rest assured that ...; *see* **más, mucho** *etc*; *see* **gala, honra** *etc.*

(i) (+ *adj*) **procura — contentos a todos** he tries to keep everybody happy; **me tiene perplejo la falta de noticias** the lack of news perplexes me, I am bewildered by the absence of news; *see* **cuidado, frito** *etc.*

(j) (+ *infin*) **no tengo nada que deciros** I have nothing to tell you; **tengo trabajo que hacer** I have work to do.

(k) **— que** + *infin* to have to + *infin*, must + *infin*; **tengo que comprarlo** I have to buy it; **tenemos que marcharnos** we have to leave, we must go; **así tiene que ser** it has to be this way; **¡tú tenías que ser!** it would be you!, it had to be you!

(l) (+ *ptp*) **tenemos alquilado un piso** we have rented a flat; **tenía el sombrero puesto** he had his hat on; **te lo tengo dicho muchas veces** I've told you hundreds of times; **nos tenían preparada una sorpresa** they had prepared a surprise for us; **teníamos andados unos 10 kilómetros** we had walked (*or* covered) some 10 kilometres.

(m) *(idioms)* **¿qué tienes?** what's the matter with you?; **¿ésas tenemos?** what's all this?; what on earth ...? **no —las todas consigo** to be worried, feel uneasy; **no las tengo todas conmigo de que lo haga** I'm none too sure that he'll do it; **ten con ten** (*as n*) good sense, tact; ability to find a middle way.

(n) *(SAm)* **tienen 3 meses de no cobrar** they haven't been paid for 3 months; **este cadáver tiene un mes de muerto** this corpse has been dead for a month.

2 tenerse *vr* (a) to stand, stand up; **la muñeca se tiene de pie** the doll stands up; **— firme** to stand upright; *(fig)* to stand firm; **no poder —** to be all in, be tired out; to be incapable (with drink).

(b) **— sobre algo** to lean on something, support oneself on something.

(c) *(fig)* to control oneself; to stop in time.

(d) **— por** to consider oneself to be, think oneself; **se tiene por muy listo** he thinks himself very clever; **— en mucho** to have a high opinion of oneself; *(fig)* to be dignified; to be incapable of a mean action.

teneraje *nm* (SAm) calves.

tenería *nf* tannery.

tenga, tengo *etc see* **tener.**

tenguerengue *nm* (Cu) shack.

tenia *nf* tapeworm.

tenida *nf* (a) *(SAm)* meeting, session; meeting of a masonic lodge. (b) *(Arg, Chi)* suit, dress; uniform; **— de gala** evening dress; **— de luto** mourning.

teniente *nm* lieutenant; **— coronel** lieutenant-colonel.

tenis *nm* tennis; **— de mesa** table tennis.

tenista *nmf* tennis player.

tenístico *adj* tennis (*attr*).

tenor[1] *nm* (Mus) tenor.

tenor[2] *nm* tenor; meaning, sense, purport; **el — de esta declaración** the sense of this statement, the tenor of this declaration; **a este —** like this, in this fashion; **a — de** on the lines of, like; *(Comm)* in accordance with.

tenorio *nm* ladykiller, wolf *(fam)*, Don Juan.

tensamente *adv* tensely.

tensar [1a] *vt* to tauten; *bow* to draw.

tensión *nf* (a) *(in physical sense)* tension, tautness; *(Mech)* stress, strain; rigidity; **— superficial** surface tension.

(b) *(Phys: of gas etc)* pressure.

(c) *(Elec)* voltage; tension; **alta —** high tension; **cable de alta —** high-tension cable.

(d) *(Anat)* **— arterial** blood pressure; **tener —** to have blood pressure; **tener la — alta** to have high blood pressure.

(e) *(Med)* tension; strain, stress; **— excesiva** (over)strain; **— nerviosa** nervous strain.

(f) *(fig)* tension, tenseness; **— racial** racial tension; **la — de la situación política** the tenseness of the political situation.

tenso *adj* (a) tense, taut.

(b) *(fig)* tense; strained; **es una situación muy tensa** it is a very tense situation; **las relaciones entre los dos están muy tensas** relations between the two are very strained.

tensor 1 *adj* tensile. **2** *nm* (Tech) guy, strut; (Anat) tensor; *(of collar)* stiffener.

tentación *nf* (a) temptation; **resistir (a) la —** to resist temptation; **no puedo resistir (a) la — de** + *infin* I can't resist the temptation of + *ger*; **vencer la —** to overcome temptation.

(b) *(fam)* tempting thing; **las gambas son mi —** I can't resist prawns; **¡eres mi —!** you'll be the ruin of me!

tentáculo *nm* tentacle; feeler.

tentador 1 *adj* tempting. **2** *nm* tempter.

tentadora *nf* temptress.

tentar [1k] *vt* (a) to touch, feel; *(Med)* to probe; **ir tentando el camino** to feel one's way, grope one's way along.

(b) to try, test, try out; to undertake, venture on; **— a hacer algo** to try to do something, attempt to do something.

(c) to tempt *(also Rel)*; to attract, lure, entice; **me tentó con una copita de anís** she tempted me with a glass of anise; **no me tienta nada la idea** the idea doesn't attract me at all; **— a uno a hacer algo** to tempt someone to do something; **ella podría estar tentada también a probarlo** she might be tempted to try it too.

tentativa *nf* attempt; effort; *(Law)* criminal attempt; **— de asesinato** attempted murder.

tentativo *adj* tentative.

tentempié *nm* (fam) snack, bite.

tenue *adj* (a) *stick etc* thin, slim, slender; *wire* fine.

(b) *(fig)* tenuous; insubstantial, slight; *air, scent* thin; *mist* light; *line* faint; *sound* faint, weak; *connection etc* slight, tenuous; *style* simple.

tenuidad *nf* (a) thinness, slimness, slenderness; fineness.

(b) tenuousness; slightness; thinness; lightness; faintness; simplicity.

(c) *(una —)* triviality.

teñir [3h *and* 3l] *vt* (a) to dye; to tinge, colour; to stain; **— una prenda de azul** to dye a garment blue; **el jersé ha teñido los pañuelos** the jersey has come out on the handkerchiefs.

(b) *(Art)* colour to darken.

(c) *(fig)* to tinge *(de* with); **una poesía teñida de añoranza** a poem tinged with longing.

teocali *nm* (Mex) Aztec temple.

teocracia *nf* theocracy.

teocrático *adj* theocratic.

teodolito *nm* theodolite.

teología *nf* theology.

teológico *adj* theological.

teólogo *nm* theologian, theologist.

teorema *nm* theorem.

teorético *adj* (SAm: *angl*) theoretic(al).

teoría *nf* theory; **— atómica** atomic theory; **— cuántica, — de los cuanta** quantum theory; **en —** in theory, theoretically.

teóricamente *adv* theoretically, in theory.

teórico 1 *adj* theoretic(al). **2** *nm* theoretician.

teorizante *nm* theoretician, theorist; *(pej)* theorizer.

teorizar [1f] *vi* to theorize.

teosofía *nf* theosophy.

teosófico *adj* theosophical.

teósofo *nm* theosophist.

tepalcate nm (Guat, Mex) (a) earthenware jar; old pot, broken vessel; fragment of pottery, sherd. (b) = **tapalcate**.

tepalcatero nm (Mex) potter.

tepe nm sod, turf, clod.

tepetate nm (a) (Hond, Mex) mining waste, refuse. (b) (Mex, Nic) building stone; stone block, building block.

tepocate nm (Guat, Mex) (a) stone, pebble. (b) small boy.

tequila nf (Mex) liquor, brandy, tequila.

tequío nm (CAm, Mex) trouble; burden; harm, damage.

tequioso adj (CAm, Mex) burdensome; harmful; annoying, bothersome.

terapeuta nmf therapist.

terapéutica nf therapeutics; therapy.

terapéutico adj therapeutic(al).

terapia nf therapy; — **laboral** occupational therapy.

tercamente adv obstinately, stubbornly.

tercena nf (a) (Mex) government warehouse. (b) (Ec) butcher's (shop).

tercenista nm (a) (Mex) government warehouseman. (b) (Ec) butcher.

tercer see **tercero**.

tercera nf (a) (Mus) third. (b) (pej) go-between, procuress.

tercería nf mediation, arbitration; good offices; (pej) pimping, procuring.

tercero 1 adj (**tercer** before m sing noun) third; **a la tercera va la vencida** third time lucky.
2 nm (a) mediator, arbitrator; (Law) third person, third party. (b) (pej) pimp, pander, procurer.

tercerola nf (Ven) shotgun.

terceto nm (a) (Mus) trio. (b) (Lit) tercet, triplet.

terciado adj (a) **azúcar terciada** brown sugar. (b) **llevar algo** — to wear something diagonally (or across one's chest etc); **con el sombrero** — with his hat on the slant, with his hat at a rakish angle. (c) **está terciado ya** a third of it has gone (or been used etc) already.

terciana nf (tertian) fever.

terciar [1b] **1** vt (a) (Math) to divide into three. (b) (Agr) to plough a third time. (c) to slant, slope; sash etc to wear (diagonally) across one's chest; hat etc to tilt, wear on the slant, put on at a rakish angle. (d) (Arg, Col, Mex) to hoist on to (or carry on) one's shoulder. (e) (SAm) wine etc to water down; (Mex) to mix, blend.
2 vi (a) to fill in, stand in, make up the number. (b) — **en** to take part in, join in; — **con uno** to intervene on behalf of someone; — **entre dos rivales** to mediate between two rivals.
3 terciarse vr (a) **si se tercia una buena oportunidad** if a good chance presents itself (or comes up); **si se tercia, él también sabe hacerlo** on occasion he knows how to do it too, in the right circumstances he can manage it too. (b) **si se tercia alguna vez que yo pase por allí** if I should happen sometime to go that way.

terciario adj tertiary.

tercio nm (a) third; **dos —s** two thirds. (b) (Mil: Hist) regiment, corps; — **extranjero** foreign legion; — **de la guardia civil** division of the civil guard. (c) (Taur) stage, part (of the bullfight). (d) **hacer buen** — **a uno** to do a service for someone; to serve someone well, be useful to someone; **hacer mal** — **a uno** to do someone a bad turn; **estar mejorado en** — **y quinto** to come out of it very well. (e) (SAm) pack, package, bale. (f) (Ven) fellow, chap (fam).

terciopelo nm velvet.

terco adj (a) obstinate, stubborn. (b) material hard, tough, hard to work. (c) (Ec) harsh, unfeeling; indifferent.

tere adj (Col) (a) weepy, tearful. (b) weak, sickly.

terebrante adj pain sharp, piercing.

tereco nm (Ec) = **tereque**.

Terencio m Terence.

tereque nm (Ant, Col, Ven) (a) = **cachivache**. (b) **—s** things, gear (fam), odds and ends.

Teresa f Theresa.

tergiversación nf (a) distortion, misrepresentation. (b) prevarication.

tergiversar [1a] **1** vt to distort, twist (the sense of), misrepresent. **2** vi to prevaricate; to chop and change, blow hot and cold.

terliz nm ticking.

termal adj thermal.

termas nfpl hot springs, hot baths.

termes nm, pl **termes** (Acad) termite.

térmico adj thermic, heat (attr).

terminación nf (a) (act) ending, termination. (b) (part) ending, conclusion. (c) (Gram) ending, termination.

terminacho nm ugly word; incorrect word, malapropism, linguistic monstrosity; nasty word, rude word.

terminado nm (Tech) finish, finishing.

terminajo nm = **terminacho**.

terminal 1 adj terminal. **2** nm (Elec) terminal. **3** nf (Naut, Rail etc) terminal; (SAm: Rail etc) terminus.

terminante adj final, decisive, definitive; decision final; reply categorical, conclusive; refusal flat, forthright; prohibition strict.

terminantemente adv finally, decisively, definitively; categorically, conclusively; flatly; strictly; **queda** — **prohibido** + infin it is strictly forbidden to + infin.

terminar [1a] **1** vt to end; to conclude; to finish, complete.
2 vi (a) (of object etc) to end, finish; **termina en punta** it ends in a point, it comes to a point; **esto va a** — **en tragedia** this will end in tragedy. (b) to end (up), finish; to stop; **al** — **el acto se fueron todos** at the end of the ceremony everyone went off; **¡hemos terminado!** that's an end of the matter!; — **de hacer algo** to finish doing something; to stop doing something; **cuando termine de hablar** when he finishes speaking; **terminaba de salir del baño** she had just got out of the bath; **terminó de llenar el vaso con helado** he topped (or filled) the glass up with ice cream; — **por hacer algo** to end (up) by doing something; **terminó marchándose enfadado** he ended up by going off in a huff, he finally went off very cross; **terminó diciendo que . . .** he ended by saying that . . . , he said in conclusion that . . .
3 terminarse vr to end, come to an end, draw to a close, stop.

terminista nm (Chi) pedant, affected speaker.

término nm (a) end, finish, conclusion; **dar** — **a** to finish off, conclude; **llevar a feliz** — to carry through to a happy conclusion; **poner** — **a** to put an end to, put a stop to. (b) (of land etc) boundary, limit; boundary stone. (c) (Rail etc) terminus. (d) (Pol) area, district; (Law) jurisdiction; — **municipal** township. (e) (Art, Theat) **primer** — foreground; **segundo** — middle distance; **último** — background. (f) (Math, Philos) term; — **medio** middle term; average; (fig) compromise, middle way; **de** — **medio** average; **por** — **medio** on the average; **tendrán que buscar un** — **medio** they will have to look for a compromise (or middle way); **en último** — in the last analysis; as a last resort, if there is no other way out. (g) (of contract etc) term, time, period; **en el** — **de 10 días** within a period of 10 days. (h) (in argument etc) point; **invertir los —s** to stand an argument on its head; (fig) to switch things round completely, turn a situation upside down. (i) (Ling) term; **según los —s del contrato** according to the terms of the contract; **en —s sencillos** in simple terms; **en otros —s** in other words; **en —s de la productividad** in terms of productivity; **se expresó en —s conciliatorios** he expressed himself in conciliatory terms. (j) **estar en buenos —s con uno** to be on good terms with someone.

terminología nf terminology.

terminológico adj terminological.

termita nf, **termite** nm termite.

termo¹ nm thermos (bottle, flask).

termo² . . . thermo . . .

termodinámica nf thermodynamics.

termodinámico adj thermodynamic.

termoeléctrico adj thermoelectric.

termoiónico adj thermionic.

termómetro nm thermometer.

termonuclear adj thermonuclear.

termopar nm thermocouple.

termopila nf thermopile.

Termópilas: Las — Thermopylae.

termos nm, pl **termos** = **termo¹**.

termostático adj thermostatic.

termostato nm thermostat.

ternario adj ternary.
terne 1 adj (a) tough, strong, husky; (pej) bullying. (b) stubborn; — **que** — out of sheer stubbornness. **2** nm bully, tough (fam).
ternejo adj (Ec, Per) active, vigorous.
ternera nf (a) (Agr) calf, heifer calf. (b) (Cook) veal.
ternero nm calf, bull calf.
ternerón adj (a) (fam) soft-hearted. (b) (Chi, Mex) lad overgrown, big.
terneza nf (a) tenderness. (b) —s nice things, endearments, tender words.
ternilla nf gristle, cartilage; (Cu, Mex, Nic) cartilage of the nose.
ternilloso adj gristly, cartilaginous.
terno nm (a) set of three, group of three; trio; three-piece suit; (Cu, PR) set of three jewels. (b) (fam) curse, swearword; **echar** (or **soltar**) —s to curse, swear.
ternura nf (a) tenderness; fondness, affection. (b) endearment, tender word.
Terpsícore f Terpsichore.
terquedad nf (a) obstinacy, stubbornness. (b) hardness, toughness. (c) (Ec) harshness, lack of feeling; indifference.
terracota nf terracotta.
terrado nm terrace; flat roof.
terraja nf diestock.
terral nm cloud of dust.
Terranova f Newfoundland.
terranova nm Newfoundland dog.
terraplén nm (a) (Rail etc) embankment; (Agr) terrace; (Mil) rampart, bank, earthwork; mound. (b) slope, gradient.
terraplenar [1a] vt to level (off); (Agr) to terrace; hole to fill in; to bank up, raise.
terrateniente nmf landowner.
terraza nf (a) (Archit) flat roof; balcony; terrace. (b) (Agr) terrace. (c) (Hort) flowerbed, border, plot. (d) (Cook) two-handled glazed jar.
terregal nm (SAm) clod, hard lump of earth; (Mex) loose earth, dusty soil.
terremoto nm earthquake.
terrenal adj earthly, worldly.
terreno 1 adj terrestrial; earthly, worldly.
2 nm (a) (in general, Geol etc) terrain; soil, earth, ground, land; (Agr) soil, land; **los accidentes del** — the characteristics of the terrain, the features of the landscape; — **abonado para el vicio** hotbed of vice, breeding ground of vice; **en todos los** —s in any place you care to name; **un coche para todo** — a car for every type of surface, a car for all conditions; **sobre el** — on the spot; **hay que fiarse del hombre sobre el** — you have to trust the man on the spot; **resolveremos el problema sobre el** — we will solve the problem as we go along; **ceder** —, **perder** — to give ground, lose ground (a, ante to); **ganar** — to gain ground; **llegar al** — to arrive on the scene, get to the spot; **medir el** — **a uno** to undermine someone's position; **mirar** (or **socavar**) **el** — **a uno** (fig) to see how the land lies; **preparar el** — (fig) to pave the way (a for).
(b) (un —) piece of land, piece of ground; (for building) plot, lot, site; (Agr) plot, field, patch; (Sport) field, pitch, ground; — **beneficial** (Eccl) glebe, glebe land; — **de camping** camping site; — **de fútbol** football ground, football pitch; — **de pasto** pasture; **un** — **plantado de patatas** a field planted with potatoes; **vender unos** —s to sell some land; **repartir** — **a los campesinos** to distribute land to the peasants.
(c) (fig) field, sphere; **en el** — **de la química** in the field of chemistry; **eso no es mi** — that's not (in) my field.
térreo adj earthen; earthy.
terrero 1 adj (a) earthy; of earth. (b) flight low, skimming. (c) (fig) humble. **2** nm pile, heap; (Min) dump.
terrestre adj terrestrial; earthly; ground (attr), land (attr); route land (attr), overland (attr); forces (Mil) ground (attr).
terrible adj terrible, dreadful, awful (also fam).
terriblemente adv terribly, dreadfully, awfully (also fam).
terrier nm terrier.
terrífico adj terrifying.
territorial adj territorial.
territorialidad nf territoriality.
territorio nm territory; — **bajo mandato** mandated territory.
terrón nm (a) (Geol) clod, lump, sod. (b) (of flour, sugar etc) lump; **azúcar en** — lump sugar. (c) (Agr) field, patch; —**es** (fig) land.

terronera nf (Col) terror, fright.
terror nm terror; — **pánico** panic.
terrorífico adj terrifying, frightening.
terrorismo nm terrorism.
terrorista 1 adj terrorist. **2** nm terrorist.
terroso adj earthy.
terruño nm (a) lump, clod. (b) plot, piece of ground; (fig) native soil, home (ground); **apego al** — attachment to one's native soil.
terso adj (a) smooth; glossy, polished, shining; **piel tersa** smooth skin, soft skin. (b) style smooth, polished, flowing.
tersura nf (a) smoothness; glossiness, polish, shine. (b) smoothness, flow.
tertulia nf (a) social gathering, regular informal gathering; (in café etc) group, circle, set; — **literaria** literary circle, literary gathering; **estar de** —, **hacer** — to get together, meet informally and talk; **hoy no hay** — there's no meeting today, the group is not meeting today. (b) clubroom, games room. (c) (Arg, Cu) upper gallery.
Tertuliano m Tertullian.
tertuliano nm, **tertuliana** nf member of a social gathering (etc).
tertuliar [1b] vi (SAm) to attend a social gathering; to get together, meet informally and talk.
terylene nm Terylene (Protected Trade Name).
Tesalia nf Thessaly.
tesar [1k] vt to tauten, tighten up.
tescal nm (Mex) stony ground, rocky area.
Teseo m Theseus.
tesina nf minor thesis, dissertation (for first degree).
tesis nf, pl **tesis** thesis.
teso adj taut, tight; tense.
tesón nm insistence; tenacity, persistence; firmness; **resistir con** — to resist firmly, resist staunchly.
tesonero adj (SAm) tenacious, persistent; firm.
tesorería nf treasurership, office of treasurer.
tesorero nm, **tesorera** nf treasurer.
tesoro nm (a) treasure; hoard; — **escondido** buried treasure; secret hoard; **valer un** — to be worth a fortune; (person) to be a real treasure. (b) (Fin, Pol etc) treasury; **T—** **público** Exchequer, Treasury. (c) (Lit) thesaurus. (d) (fig) treasure; **¡sí, —!** yes, my treasure!; **el libro es un** — **de datos** the book is a mine of information; **es un** — **de recuerdos** it is a treasure-house of memories; **tenemos una cocinera que es todo un** — we have a real gem of a cook, we have a cook who is a real treasure.
Tespis m Thespis.
test [tes] nm, pl **tests** [tes] (angl) test; aptitude test, psychological test.
testa nf (a) head; — **coronada** crowned head. (b) (fam) brains; gumption (fam).
testador nm testator.
testadora nf testatrix.
testaduro adj (Ant) = testarudo.
testaferro nm (a) figurehead; front man. (b) (Comm) dummy.
testamentaria nf executrix.
testamentaría nf (a) execution of a will. (b) estate.
testamentario 1 adj testamentary. **2** nm executor.
testamento nm (a) will, testament; **hacer** —, **otorgar** — to make one's will. (b) **Antiguo T** — Old Testament; **Nuevo T** — New Testament. (c) (fam) screed.
testar[1] [1a] vi to make a will.
testar[2] [1a] vt (Ec) to underline.
testarada nf, **testarazo** nm (fam) bump on the head; **darse una testarada** to bump one's head, give oneself a bang on the head.
testarudez nf stubbornness, pigheadedness.
testarudo adj stubborn, pigheaded.
testear [1a] (SAm: angl) **1** vt to test. **2** vi to do a test, undergo a test.
testera nf front, face; (Zool) forehead.
testero nm (a) = testera. (b) bedhead. (c) (Archit) wall.
testes nmpl testes.
testículo nm testicle.
testificación nf (a) testification. (b) = testimonio.
testificar [1g] **1** vt (a) to attest; to testify to, give evidence of. (b) (fig) to attest, testify to. **2** vi to testify, give evidence; — **de = 1** (a).
testigo nmf (a) (Law etc) witness;' — **de cargo** witness for the prosecution; — **de descargo** witness for the defence; — **del novio** (approx) best man; — **ocular**, — **presencial**, — **de vista** eyewitness; —

pericial expert witness; **poner a uno por —** to cite someone as a witness.

(b) (in experiment) control.

(c) (in relay race) baton.

testimoniar [1b] vt to testify to, bear witness to; (fig) to show, demonstrate.

testimonio nm testimony, evidence; affidavit; **falso —** perjured evidence; **dar —** to testify (de to), give evidence (de of); **en — de mi afecto** as a token (or mark) of my affection.

teta nf teat; nipple; (fam) breast; **dar (la) — a** to suckle, breast-feed; **quitar la — a** to wean; **niño de — baby** still at the breast.

tétanos nm tetanus.

tetelque adj (CAm, Mex) sharp, bitter.

tetera[1] nf teapot; tea urn.

tetera[2] nf (Cu, Mex, PR) rubber teat; (PR) feeding bottle; (Mex) vessel with a spout.

tetero nm (Col, PR, Ven) feeding bottle.

tetilla (a) nf (Anat) (man's) nipple. **(b)** rubber teat.

Tetis f Thetis.

tetón[1] nm bubble, swelling (on a tyre etc).

tetón[2] adj (Chi) stupid.

tetraedro nm tetrahedron.

tetrágono nm tetragon.

tetrámetro nm tetrameter.

tetramotor adj four-engined.

tétrico adj gloomy, dismal; mood gloomy, pessimistic; sullen; light dim, wan.

tetuda adj (fam) big-breasted, bosomy (fam).

tetunte nm (CAm) large shapeless mass; rough bundle.

teutón nm, **teutona** nf Teuton.

teutónico adj Teutonic.

teveo nm = **tebeo**.

textil 1 adj textile. **2 —es** nmpl textiles.

texto nm text; **grabado fuera de —** full-page illustration.

textual adj **(a)** textual. **(b)** (fig) exact; literal; **son sus palabras —** those are his exact words.

textualmente adv **(a)** textually. **(b)** (fig) exactly; literally.

textura nf texture (also fig).

tez nf complexion, skin; colouring.

ti pron (used after prep) you; yourself; (arch, to God) thee, thyself; **es para —** it's for you; **¿lo has comprado para —?** did you buy it for yourself?; **esto no se refiere a —** this doesn't refer to you.

tía (a) nf aunt; **— abuela** great-aunt; **¡no hay tu —!** nothing doing!; **¡cuéntaselo a tu —!** tell that to the marines!

(b) before name as title of respect, not translated: **unos dulces para la — Dulcinea** some sweets for Dulcinea.

(c) (sl) bird (sl), dame (sl), girl; (pej) coarse woman, old bag (sl); whore.

tiamina nf thiamine.

tiangue nm (CAm) small market; booth, stall; (Ec) cattle market.

tibante adj (Col) haughty.

tibe nm (Col, Cu) whetstone.

Tíber m Tiber.

Tiberio m Tiberius.

tiberio 1 adj (Guat, Mex) drunk. **2** nm **(a)** (fam) uproar, row; set-to (fam). **(b)** (Guat, Mex) drinking spree (fam).

Tibet: **El — Tibet.**

tibetano 1 adj Tibetan. **2** nm, **tibetana** nf Tibetan. **3** nm (language) Tibetan.

tibia nf tibia.

tibiarse [1b] vr (CAm, Col, Per, Ven) to get cross.

tibieza nf **(a)** lukewarmness, tepidness. **(b)** (fig) lukewarmness; coolness, lack of enthusiasm.

tibio adj **(a)** water etc lukewarm, tepid.

(b) (fig) person, belief etc lukewarm; cool, unenthusiastic; **estar — con uno** to be cool to someone, behave distantly towards someone.

(c) **poner — a uno** to hurl abuse at someone, give someone a verbal battering; to say dreadful things about someone.

(d) (CAm, Col, Per, Ven) cross, angry.

tiburón nm **(a)** shark. **(b)** (fig) go-getter, unscrupulous person; (Arg) wolf (fam), Don Juan.

tic nm, pl **tics** [tik] **(a)** tap; click; (of clock) tick, tick tock. **(b)** (Med) tic (also **— nervioso**).

Ticiano m Titian.

tico (CAm) **1** adj Costa Rican. **2** nm, **tica** nf Costa Rican.

tictac nm (of clock) tick, tick tock; (of heart) beat; (of typewriter) tapping, tip-tap; **hacer —** to tick; to beat, go pit-a-pat; to tip-tap.

tiempecito nm (SAm) (spell of) very bad weather.

tiempla nf (Chi) drunkenness.

tiemple nm (Chi) **(a)** love-making, courting. **(b)** lover.

tiempo nm **(a)** (in general) time; **— libre** spare time, free time, leisure; **a —** in time, in good time, early; **at the right time; a un —, al mismo —** at the same time; **a su debido —** in due course; **al poco —** very soon, soon after; **a — que ...** at the time that ..., while ...; **al mismo — que ...** at the same time as ...; **cada cierto —** every so often; **con —** in time, in good time, early; **con el —** eventually, in time; **¿cuánto — se va a quedar?** how long is he staying?; **de — en —** from time to time; **de algún — a esta parte** for some time past; **una costumbre de mucho —** a long-standing custom; **fuera de —** at the wrong time; **necesito más —** I need longer, I need more time; **no puede quedarse más —** he can't stay any longer; **mucho —** a long time, a long while; **todo el — all** the time; **el — es de oro** time is money; time is precious; **el — lo es todo** time is everything, time is of the essence; **es — perdido hablar con él** it's a waste of time talking to him; **andando el —** in due course, in time; in the fullness of time; **el — apremia** time presses; **dar — al —** to consider all the possibilities; to let matters take their course; **darse buen —** to have a good time; **el — dirá** time will tell; **apenas dispongo de mi —** I can scarcely call my time my own; **engañar el —, matar el —** to kill time; **hacer —** to while away the time; to mark time; **hace mucho —** a long time ago; **hace bastante — que lo compré** I bought it a good while ago; **desde hace mucho —** for a long time; **hace mucho — que no voy** I haven't been for a long time; **perder el —** to waste time; to fool around; **sin perder —** without delay; **tener — para** to have time for.

(b) (limited, specific) time, period, age; **—s modernos** modern times; **en — de los griegos** in the time of the Greeks; **en estos —s nuestros** in this day and age; **en los —s que corremos** in these dreadful times; **en mis —s** in my day; **en los buenos —s** in the good old days; **en mis buenos —s** when I was in my prime; **en otro —** formerly; once upon a time; **en — de Maricastaña, en — del rey que rabió** way back, long ago; in the good old days; **estar en el — de las vacas flacas** to have fallen on hard times; **los —s están revueltos** the times are out of joint, these are disturbed times; **hay que ir con los —s** one must keep abreast of the times.

(c) (of person) age; **A y B son del mismo —** A and B are the same age; **¿cuánto — tiene el pequeño?** how old is the child?

(d) (Sport) half; **primer —** first half.

(e) (Mus) tempo, time.

(f) (Mus: of symphony etc) movement.

(g) (Gram) tense; **— compuesto** compound tense; **en — presente** in the present tense.

(h) (Meteorol) weather; **si dura el mal —** if the bad weather continues; **hace buen —** it's fine, the weather is good, the weather is fine; **¿qué — hará mañana?** what will the weather be like tomorrow?; **a mal —, buena cara** one must make the best of a bad job.

(i) (Naut) stormy weather, rough weather.

(j) (Mech) cycle; **motor de 2 —s** two-stroke engine.

tienda nf **(a)** (Comm) shop, store; (esp) grocer's; (Cu, Chi, RPl, Ven) draper's, clothier's; **— de coloniales, — de comestibles, — de ultramarinos** grocer's (shop), grocery (US); **ir de —s** to go shopping; **poner — to** set up shop.

(b) (Naut etc) awning; **— de campaña** tent; **— de oxígeno** oxygen tent.

tienta nf **(a)** (Med) probe.

(b) cleverness; wisdom, good sense.

(c) **a —s** gropingly, blindly; **andar a —s** to grope one's way along, feel one's way; (fig) to feel one's way; **decir algo a —s** to throw out a remark at random, say something to see what effect it has.

tiento nm **(a)** feel, feeling, touch; (fam) touch (sl), tickle; (fam) pass; **a — by** touch; gropingly; (fig) uncertainly; **echar un — a una chica** to make a pass at a girl, try it on with a girl; **a 40 dólares nadie le echó un —** at 40 dollars nobody was biting, at 40 dollars he didn't get a tickle; **perder el —** to lose one's touch.

(b) (fig) tact; care; wariness, circumspection; **ir con —** to go carefully, go cautiously.

(c) (Art etc) steadiness of hand, steady hand.

(d) (Zool) feeler, tentacle; (Circus) balancing pole; blind man's stick.

(e) (Mus) preliminary flourish, scale, notes played in tuning up.

(f) (fam) blow, punch; **dar —s a uno** to hit someone.

(g) (*fam*) swig (*fam*); **dar un —** to take a swig (*a from*).

(h) (*SAm*) thong of raw leather, rawhide strap.

(i) (*Arg, PR*) snack.

tiernamente *adv* tenderly.

tierno *adj* (*in most senses*) tender; soft; *bread etc* new, fresh.

tierra *nf* (a) (*Astron*) earth, world.

(b) (*as surface, not sea*) land; **— firme** mainland; dry land; **— de nadie** no-man's land; **— quemada** scorched earth; **— adentro** inland; (*SAm*) interior, remote area; **por —** by land, overland; **besar la —** to fall flat; **caer a —** to fall down; **caer por —** to fall to the ground (*also fig*); **dar con algo en —** to drop something; to knock something over; (*fig*) to overthrow something; **echar a —** to demolish, pull down; to raze to the ground; **echar (*or* tirar) algo por —** to ruin something, upset something; **perder —** to lose one's footing; to get out of one's depth; **poner un avión en —** to land a plane; **poner — por medio** to get out quick, get as far away as possible; **saltar en (*or* a) — (*from boat*)** to leap ashore; **tocar — (*Aer*)** to touch down; **tomar — (*Aer*)** to land, come down; (*Naut*) to reach harbour.

(c) (*Geol etc*) land, soil, earth, ground; **— de batán** fuller's earth; **— de brezo** peat; **— vegetal** topsoil; **echar — a un asunto** to hush an affair up; to forget about a matter; **echar — a uno (*Mex, RPl*)** to speak damagingly of someone.

(d) (*Agr*) land; **—s** lands, estate(s); **— baldía** wasteland; **— de labor** agricultural land; **— de pan llevar** arable land, corn-growing land; **en cualquier — de garbanzos** all over; **heredó unas —s en la provincia** he inherited some land in the province.

(e) (*Pol etc*) country; **su —** one's own country, one's native land; one's own region, one's home area; **— natal** native land; **— prometida, — de promisión** land of promise, promised land; **ver —s** to see the world; **vamos a nuestra — a pasar las Navidades** we go home for Christmas; **no es de estas —s** he's not from these parts; **¿tienen tractores en tu —?** do they have tractors where you come from?, do they have tractors in your part of the world?

(f) (*Elec*) earth, ground (*US*); **conectar un aparato a —** to earth a piece of apparatus, ground a piece of apparatus (*US*).

(g) (*SAm*) dust.

tierrafría *nmf* (*Col*) highlander.

tierral *nm* (*SAm*) cloud of dust.

Tierra *f* **Santa** Holy Land.

tierrero *nm* (*SAm*) cloud of dust.

tieso 1 *adj* (a) stiff, rigid; erect; taut; **con las orejas tiesas** with its ears erect; **quedarse — (*fig*)** to be frozen stiff.

(b) (*fig*) fit; sprightly; chirpy; **le encontré muy — a pesar de su enfermedad** I found him very fit in spite of his illness.

(c) (*fig*) stiff (in manner); rigid (in attitude); **— como un ajo** as stiff as a poker; **me recibió muy —** he received me very stiffly.

(d) (*fam*) proud; conceited, stuck-up (*fam*); smug; **— de cogote** haughty; **iba tan — con la novia al brazo** he was walking so proudly with his girl on his arm; *see* **ajo**.

(e) stubborn; firm, confident; **— que —** as stubborn as they come; **ponerse — con uno** to stand one's ground, insist on one's rights; (*pej*) to be stubborn; **tenerlas tiesas con uno** to put up a firm resistance to someone, stand up for oneself.

2 *adv* strongly, energetically, hard.

tiesto *nm* (a) (*Hort*) flowerpot. (b) sherd, piece of pottery. (c) (*Chi, Urug*) pot, vessel; (*Chi*) chamberpot.

tiesura *nf* (a) stiffness, rigidity; erectness; tautness. (b) (*fig*) stiffness; rigidity. (c) (*fam*) conceit. (d) stubbornness; firmness, confidence.

tifiar [1b] *vt* (*Cu*) to steal.

tifitifi *nm* (*Cu, PR*) theft.

tifo *nm* (*Med*) typhus; **— de América** yellow fever; **— asiático** cholera; **— de Oriente** bubonic plague.

tifoidea *nf* (*also* **fiebre —**) typhoid.

tifón *nm* (a) typhoon. (b) waterspout. (c) (*Mex*) outcrop of ore.

tifus *nm* (a) (*Med*) typhus; **— exantemático** spotted fever; **— icteroides** yellow fever.

(b) (*Theat: fam*) persons having complimentary tickets (*or* free seats); claque; **entrar de —** to get in free.

tigra *nf* (*SAm*) female tiger; female jaguar; (*Arg, Col*) **ponerse como una — parida** to fly into a violent rage.

tigre *nm* (a) tiger; (*SAm*) jaguar. (b) (*Col*) black coffee with a dash of milk; (*Col, Ec*) cocktail.

tigrero 1 *adj* (*Arg*) brave. **2** *nm* (*SAm*) jaguar hunter.

tigresa *nf* tigress.

tigridia *nf* tiger lily.

tigrillo *nm* (*SAm*) member of the cat tribe, *eg* ocelot, lynx.

Tigris *m* Tigris.

tigrón *nm* (*Ven*) bully, braggart.

tigüila *nf* (*Mex*) trick, swindle.

tijera *nf* (a) (*SAm*) scissors.

(b) (*SAm: Zool*) claw, pincer.

(c) (*person*) gossip; **ser una buena —, tener buena —** to be a great gossip; to have a sharp tongue; to indulge constantly in backbiting, be a scandalmonger.

(d) **de —** folding; **escalera de —** steps, step-ladder; **silla de —** folding chair, folding stool, camp stool.

(e) **es un trabajo de —** it's a piece of paste-and-scissors work, he's put it together by copying from other people.

tijeras *nfpl* scissors; (*Hort etc*) shears, clippers; **— para las uñas** nail scissors; **unas —** a pair of scissors (*etc*), some scissors (*etc*).

tijereta *nf* (a) (*Ent*) earwig. (b) (*Bot*) vine tendril.

tijeretada *nf*, **tijeretazo** *nm* snip, snick, small cut.

tijeretear [1a] **1** *vt* to snip, snick, cut. **2** *vi* (a) to meddle. (b) (*Arg, Mex, Nic*) to gossip, backbite.

tijereteo *nm* (a) snipping, snicking, cutting. (b) meddling. (c) (*Arg, Mex, Nic*) gossiping, backbiting.

tila *nf* (a) (*Bot*) lime tree. (b) (*Cook*) *tila*, infusion of lime flowers.

tildar [1a] *vt* (a) (*Typ*) to put a tilde over. (b) (*fig*) **— a uno de + *adj*** to brand someone as (being) + *adj*, stigmatize someone as (being) + *adj*.

tilde *gen nf* (a) (*Typ*) tilde (~). (b) (*fig*) blemish, defect, flaw. (c) (*fig*) triviality; jot, bit; **en una — (*fam*)** in a jiffy (*fam*).

tilichera *nf* (*CAm, Mex*) hawker's box, glass-covered box.

tilichero *nm* (*CAm, Mex*) hawker, pedlar, peddler (*US*).

tiliches *nmpl* (*CAm, Mex*) fancy articles, trinkets, hawker's wares.

tilín *nm* (a) tinkle, ting-a-ling.

(b) (*fig*) **hacer —** to be well liked; **tener —** to be nice, be attractive, have a way with people.

(c) (*fig*) **a mí no me hace —** it doesn't ring a bell with me.

(d) (*Col, Chi, Ven*) **en un —** in an instant.

tilinches *nmpl* (*Mex*) rags.

tilingada *nf* (*RPl*) silly thing (to do *etc*).

tilingo (*Mex, Per, RPl*) **1** *adj* silly, stupid. **2** *nm* fool.

tilinguear [1a] *vi* (*RPl*) to act the fool, do (*etc*) silly things.

tilinguería *nf* (*Mex, RPl*) (a) silliness, stupidity. (b) **—s** nonsense.

tilintar [1a] *vt* (*CAm*) to stretch, tauten.

tilinte *adj* (a) (*CAm*) tight, taut. (b) (*Guat*) elegant. (c) (*Hond*) replete.

tilma *nf* (*SAm*) blanket, poncho.

tilo *nm* (a) (*Bot*) lime tree. (b) (*Chi, RPl*) = **tila** (b).

tiloso *adj* (*CAm*) dirty, filthy.

timador *nm* swindler, trickster.

timar [1a] **1** *vt* (a) *property* to steal; to swindle someone out of.

(b) *person* to swindle, play a confidence trick on.

2 timarse *vr* (*fam*) to make eyes at each other; **— con uno** to make eyes at someone, ogle someone.

timba *nf* (a) game of chance. (b) gambling den. (c) (*CAm, Mex, SD, Ven*) belly. (d) (*Cu, Mex, PR*) **tener —** to be a tough proposition; to be very odd.

timbal *nm* (a) (*Mus*) small drum, kettledrum. (b) (*Cook*) meat pie.

timbembe *adj* (*Chi*) weak, trembling.

timbiriche *nm* (*Cu, Mex, Ven*) small shop.

timbrar [1a] *vt* (a) to stamp; to seal. (b) (*Post*) to postmark.

timbrazo *nm* ring; **dar un —** to ring the bell.

timbre *nm* (a) (*Comm, Fin*) fiscal stamp, revenue stamp; seal; (*Fin*) stamp duty.

(b) (*SAm*) postage stamp.

(c) (*SAm*) personal description; description of goods (*etc*).

(d) (*fig*) **— de gloria** mark of honour; action (*etc*) which is to one's credit.

(e) (*Elec etc*) bell; **— de alarma** alarm bell; **tocar el —** to ring the bell.

(f) (*Mus etc*) timbre; **— nasal** (*Ling*) nasal timbre, twang.

timbusca *nf* (*Col, Ec*) thick soup; (*any*) low-class dish with a strong flavour; (*Per*) stew.

tímidamente adv timidly, shyly, nervously; bashfully.

timidez nf timidity, shyness, nervousness; bashfulness.

tímido adj timid, shy, nervous; bashful.

timo nm swindle, confidence trick, confidence game (US); gag, hoax; **dar un — a uno** to swindle someone; to hoax someone.

timón nm (a) (Aer, Naut) rudder; helm; **— de dirección** (Aer) rudder; **— de profundidad** (Aer) elevator; **poner el — a babor** to turn to port, port the helm.
(b) (of carriage) pole; (of plough) beam.
(c) (also fig) helm; **coger el —, empuñar el —** to take the helm, take charge.

timonear [1a] **1** vt (Col, Guat, Mex, SD) to direct, manage; to guide. **2** vi to steer.

timonel nm (Naut) steersman, helmsman; (of racing boat) cox.

timonera nf wheelhouse.

timonero nm = **timonel**.

timorato adj God-fearing; (pej) excessively pious; sanctimonious.

Timoteo m Timothy.

tímpano nm (a) (Anat) tympanum, eardrum. (b) (Archit) tympanum. (c) (Mus) small drum, kettledrum; **—s** (in orchestra) tympani.

tina nf vat, tub; bathtub; **— de lavar** washtub.

tinaco nm (Ec, Mex) tall earthenware vessel; (Mex) water tank.

tinaja nf large earthen jar.

tinca nf (a) (Arg, Chi) flip, flick. (b) (Per) bowls. (c) (Chi) presentiment, hunch.

tincanque nm (Chi) = **tinca** (a).

tincar [1g] vt (a) (Arg, Chi) to flip, flick. (b) (Chi) to have a presentiment of. (c) (Chi to like, fancy; **no me tinca** I don't like the idea, I don't fancy it.

tincazo nm (Arg, Chi) = **tinca** (a).

tinctura nf tincture.

tinerfeño **1** adj of Tenerife. **2** nm, **tinerfeña** nf native (or inhabitant) of Tenerife; **los —s** the people of Tenerife.

tinga nf (Mex) row, confusion, uproar.

tingar [1h] vt (Ec) to flip, flick.

tinglado nm (a) platform; shed, covering.
(b) (fig) trick; plot, intrigue; **armar un —** to lay a plot; **conocer el —** to see through it, see someone's little game.

tingo nm, **tingue** nm (Ec) = **tinca** (a).

tinieblas nfpl (a) darkness, dark; shadows; gloom.
(b) (fig) confusion, fog; black ignorance; **estamos en — sobre sus proyectos** we are in the dark about his plans, we are entirely ignorant of what he plans to do.

tino nm (a) skill, knack; feel; (sureness of) touch; (good) guesswork, (good) reckoning; (Mil) (accurate) aim, (good) marksmanship; **a —** gropingly; **a buen —** by guesswork; **coger el —** to get the feel of it, get the hang of it.
(b) (fig) tact; good judgement; insight, acumen; **sin —** foolishly; aimlessly; **obrar con mucho —** to act wisely, act with great good sense; **perder el —** to act foolishly, go off the rails; **sacar de — a uno** to bewilder someone; to exasperate someone, infuriate someone.
(c) (fig) moderation; **sin —** immoderately; **comer sin —** to eat to excess; **gastar sin —** to spend recklessly.

tinoso adj (Col, Ven) skilful, clever; sensible; moderate; tactful.

tinque nm (Arg, Chi) = **tinca** (a).

tinta nf (a) (Typ etc) ink; **— china** Indian ink; **— de imprenta** printer's ink, printing ink; **— indeleble, — de marcar** marking ink; **— simpática** invisible ink; **con — in** ink; **sudar —** (fam) to slog, slave; **saber algo de buena —** to know something on good authority.
(b) (Tech) dye.
(c) (Fish) dye, ink.
(d) (Art) colour; **—s** (fig) tints, shades, hues; **media —** half-tone, tint; **medias —s** (fig) half measures; half-baked ideas; inadequate answers; **presentar una situación bajo —s muy negras** to paint a situation very black; **recargar las —s** to exaggerate.

tinte nm (a) (act) dyeing.
(b) (Chem) dye, dyestuff; stain.
(c) (Comm) dyer's (shop); dry-cleaning establishment, dry cleaner's.
(d) (fig) tinge, colouring; **sin el menor — político** without the slightest political colouring, devoid of all political character.

(e) (fig) veneer, gloss, light covering; **tiene cierto — de hombre de mundo** he has a slight touch of the man of the world about him.

tinterillo nm (a) penpusher, small-time clerk. (b) (SAm) shyster lawyer.

tintero nm (a) inkpot, inkwell, inkstand; **lo dejó en el —, se le quedó en el —** he clean forgot about it. (b) (SAm) writing materials, desk set.

tintillo nm (Arg) red wine.

tintín nm (of bell) tinkle, tinkling; ting-a-ling; (of chain etc) jingle, chink; (of cups etc) clink, chink.

tintinear [1a] vi to tinkle; to go ting-a-ling; to jingle; to clink, chink.

tintineo nm = **tintín**.

tinto 1 adj (a) dyed; stained; tinged; **— en sangre** stained with blood, bloodstained. (b) wine red. **2** nm (a) red wine. (b) (Col) black coffee.

tintorera nf shark; (Guat, Mex, Per) female shark.

tintorería nf (a) (art) dyeing. (b) (Comm) dyeworks; dyer's (shop); dry-cleaning establishment, dry cleaner's.

tintorero nm dyer; dry cleaner.

tintura nf (a) (act) dyeing.
(b) (Chem) dye, dyestuff; (Tech) stain; (Pharm) tincture; **— de tornasol** litmus; **— de yodo** iodine.
(c) (fig) smattering; thin veneer.

tinturar [1a] vt (a) to dye; to tinge. (b) (fig) **— a uno** to give someone a rudimentary knowledge, teach someone superficially.

tiña nf (a) (Med) ringworm. (b) (fig) poverty. (c) (fig) meanness.

tiñoso adj (a) (Med) scabby, mangy. (b) (fig) poor, wretched. (c) (fig) mean.

tío nm (a) uncle; **— abuelo** great-uncle; **— carnal** real uncle; **mi — Eduardo** my uncle Edward; **T— Sam** Uncle Sam; **mis —s** (freq) my uncle and aunt.
(b) before name as title of respect, not translated: **ha muerto el — Francisco** Francis has died.
(c) (fam) old fellow; (fam) fellow, chap (fam), guy (US fam); **¿quién es ese —?** who's that chap?; **ese — del sombrero alto** that chap with the tall hat; **¡qué —!** what a fellow!; (pej) isn't he a so-and-so?; **es un — grande, es un — con toda la barba** he's a great guy.

tiovivo nm roundabout, merry-go-round.

tipa¹ nf (Arg, Bol, Per) wicker basket.

tipa² nf (SAm) bitch, awful woman.

tipear [1a] vti (SAm) to type.

tiperrita nf (Cu) typist.

tipiadora nf (fam) (a) typewriter. (b) typist.

típicamente adv typically; characteristically.

típico adj (a) typical; characteristic.
(b) custom **— típical**; quaint, picturesque; full of local colour; rich in folklore, full of folkloric interest; traditional; of interest to tourists; **es la taberna más típica de la ciudad** it's the most picturesque pub in town; **unas jóvenes con su — peinado** some girls with their hair done in the traditional (and local) fashion; **no hay que perderse tan típica fiesta** you shouldn't miss a festivity so rich in local colour and tradition.

tipificar [1g] vt to typify.

tipismo nm quaintness, picturesqueness; local colour; folkloric interest; traditionalism; **estoy harto de tanto — bobo** I'm fed up with all this nonsensical local colour and traditionalism.

tiple 1 nm (a) (Mus) treble, boy soprano. (b) soprano (voice). **2** nf soprano.

tipo nm (a) type; norm, standard; pattern, model.
(b) type, sort, kind; **un nuevo — de bicicleta** a new kind of bicycle; **de otro — pero del mismo precio** of a different type but at the same price.
(c) (Lit etc) type, character.
(d) (fam) fellow, chap (fam), guy (US fam); **dos —s sospechosos** two suspicious characters; **un — que yo conozco** a fellow I know; **¿quién es ese —?** who's that chap?
(e) (Comm, Fin) rate; **— bancario, — de descuento** bank rate; **— de cambio** exchange rate, rate of exchange; **— de interés** interest rate; **— (de) oro** gold standard.
(f) (Anat: man's) build, physique; (woman's) figure; **él tiene buen —** he's well built; **ella tiene buen —** she has a good figure; **tener mal —** to be misshapen.
(g) (Typ: also **—s**) type; **— gótico** Gothic type, black letter; **— menudo** small print.
(h) (fam) **aguantar el —** to put up with a lot; **jugarse el —** to risk one's neck.

tipografía nf (a) typography; printing. (b) printing works; printing press.

tipográfico adj typographical; printing (attr).

tipógrafo *nm* typographer; printer.
tiposo *adj* (*Per*) ridiculous, eccentric.
típula *nf* cranefly, daddy-long-legs.
tiquear [1a] *vt* (*Chi*) ticket to punch.
tíquet ['tike] *nm*, *pl* **tíquets** ['tike] (*SAm*: *angl*) ticket.
tiquete *nm* (*CAm*, *Col*, *Cu*, *Mex*: *angl*) ticket; (*Col*) label.
tiquismiquis 1 *nm*, *pl* **tiquismiquis** fussy person.
    2 *nmpl* (**a**) silly scruples.
    (**b**) affected courtesies, bowing and scraping.
    (**c**) bickering, squabbles.
    (**d**) minor irritations, pinpricks.
tira[1] **1** *nf* strip; long strip, narrow strip; band; slip of paper; **— de películas** film strip; **— cómica** comic strip.
    2 *nm*: **— y afloja** (**a**) prudence, caution; tact.
    (**b**) tug-of-war (*fig*); give and take, mutual concessions.
tira[2] *nm* (*Arg*, *Col*, *Chi*) detective.
tirabuzón *nm* (**a**) corkscrew; **sacar algo a uno con —** (*fig*) to worm something out of someone. (**b**) curl, ringlet.
tirada *nf* (**a**) (*act*) cast, throw.
    (**b**) distance; stretch; (*Sew*) length; (*fig*) series, number; time; (*Lit*) stanza; sequence; epic laisse; **de una —** at one go, in a stretch; **lo recitó todo de una —** he recited the whole lot straight off, he reeled the lot off; **estuvo con nosotros una — de días** he spent a number of days with us; **de B a C hay una — de 18 kms** from B to C there is a distance of 18 kms.
    (**c**) (*Typ*) printing, edition; **— aparte** offprint, reprint.
    (**d**) (*SAm*) boring speech, tedious discourse.
    (**e**) (*Arg*) hint.
    (**f**) (*PR*) dirty trick.
tiradera *nf* (**a**) (*CAm*, *Cu*, *Chi*) sash, belt, strap; (*Cu*) harness strap, trace. (**b**) (*Col*, *Pan*) taunt.
tirado *adj* (**a**) (*Naut*) rakish; *writing* cursive.
    (**b**) **estar —** (*Comm*) to be dirt-cheap; to be a glut on the market; (*task etc*) to be very simple; **esa asignatura está tirada** (*fam*) that subject is dead easy, that subject is a cinch (*sl*).
tirador *nm* (**a**) (*person*) marksman, shot; shooter; (*Mex*, *Nic*) hunter; **— apostado**, **— certero** sniper.
    (**b**) handle, knob, button; doorknob; (*Elec*) flex, cord; **— de campanilla** bellrope, bellpull.
    (**c**) catapult.
    (**d**) (*Art*, *Tech*) drawing pen.
    (**e**) (*Bol*, *RPl*) wide gaucho belt.
    (**f**) (*Bol*, *RPl*) **—es** braces, suspenders (*US*).
tiraje *nm* (*Arg*, *Chi*, *Mex*, *Nic*) chimney flue.
tiralevitas *nm*, *pl* **tiralevitas** (*fam*) bootlicker (*fam*); creep (*sl*).
tiralíneas *nm*, *pl* **tiralíneas** drawing pen, ruling pen.
tiranía *nf* tyranny.
tiránicamente *adv* tyrannically.
tiranicida *nm* tyrannicide (*person*).
tiranicidio *nm* tyrannicide (*act*).
tiránico *adj* tyrannical; despotic; *love* possessive, domineering; *attraction* irresistible, all-powerful.
tiranizar [1f] *vt* to tyrannize, rule despotically; to domineer.
tirano 1 *adj* tyrannical, despotic; domineering. **2** *nm*, **tirana** *nf* tyrant, despot.
tirantas *nfpl* (*Col*, *Mex*) braces, suspenders (*US*).
tirante 1 *adj* (**a**) *rope etc* tight, taut; tensed; drawn tight.
    (**b**) *relations*, *situation etc* tense, strained; **estamos algo —s** things are rather strained between us.
    (**c**) (*Fin*) tight.
    2 *nm* (**a**) (*Archit*) tie, brace, crosspiece; (*Mech*) brace, stay, strut.
    (**b**) (*of harness*) trace; (*of dress*) shoulder strap; **—s** braces, suspenders (*US*).
tirantear [1a] *vt* (*Chi*, *Guat*) to stretch.
tirantez *nf* (**a**) tightness, tautness; tension.
    (**b**) (*fig*) tension, strain; **la — de las relaciones con Eslobodia** the strained relations with Slobodia, the tense state of relations with Slobodia; **ha disminuido la —** the tension has lessened.
    (**c**) (*Fin*) tightness; stringency.
tirar [1a] **1** *vt* (**a**) to throw; to hurl, fling, cast, sling; (*accidentally*) to drop; to knock over, knock down; *building* to pull down; *shot* to fire, shoot; *rocket* to fire, launch; *bomb* to drop; **el aparato tira el proyectil a 2000 metros** the machine throws the projectile 2000 metres; **estaban tirando la fruta con palos largos** they were knocking the fruit down with long poles; **el viento ha tirado la valla** the

wind has knocked the fence down; **me tiró un beso** she blew me a kiss.
    (**b**) *rubbish etc* to throw away; to chuck out; *fortune* to waste, squander; **estos calcetines están para —los** these socks are ready to be thrown away; **hay que — los podridos** the rotten ones ought to be thrown out; **has tirado el dinero comprando eso** you've thrown your money away buying that.
    (**c**) *wire* to draw out.
    (**d**) *line* to draw, trace, rule.
    (**e**) (*Typ*) to print, run off.
    (**f**) *blow etc* to give, deal, fetch; **— una coz a uno** to give someone a kick; **— un mordisco a uno** to give someone a bite; **— tajos a uno** to slash at someone.
    (**g**) (*Col*) to use; to work with; **— azada** to hoe, work with the hoe; **— brazo** to swim; **— canoa** to sail a canoe.
    (**h**) (*Col*, *Cu*, *Chi*) to cart, haul, transport.
    (**i**) **—la de** to fancy oneself as, pose as.
    2 *vi* (**a**) (*Mil etc*) to shoot (*a* at), fire (*a* at, on); **— a matar** to shoot to kill; **— con bala** to use live ammunition; **¡no tires!** don't shoot!
    (**b**) **— de** to pull, tug; to draw (along), haul; *rope etc* to pull (on), tug (at); *handkerchief*, *wallet etc* to pull out, take out (suddenly), yank out; *sword* to draw; **— de la manga de uno** to tug at someone's sleeve; **tire de ese cabo** pull that end; **tiraron de cuchillos** they drew their knives; **"—", "tirad"** (*on doors etc*) "pull".
    (**c**) (*of magnet etc*) to draw, attract; (*fig*) to draw, pull, have a pull; to appeal; **no le tira el estudio** study does not attract him; **la patria tira siempre** one's native land always exerts a powerful pull.
    (**d**) (*of chimney etc*) to draw.
    (**e**) (*fam*) **ir tirando** to get along, manage; **vamos tirando** we manage, we keep going; **esos zapatos tirarán todavía otro invierno** those shoes will last out another winter.
    (**f**) (*fam*) to go; **tire Vd adelante** go straight on; **¡tira (adelante)!** get on with it!; **— a la derecha** to turn right; to keep right; **— por una calle** to turn down a street, go off along a street.
    (**g**) **— a** to tend to, tend towards; **— a rojo** to have some red in it, have a touch of red about it; **— a viejo** to be getting old, be elderly; **— a su padre** to take after one's father, resemble one's father; **él tira más bien a cuidadoso** he's on the careful side; **tira a hacerse servir** he tends to make others wait on him; **— para médico** to have inclinations towards a medical career, feel like becoming a doctor, be attracted towards a career in medicine.
    (**h**) **— a** to aim at being, work to become; (*pej*) to intrigue to become; **— a + infin** to aim to + *infin*; (*pej*) to intrigue in order to + *infin*, go surreptitiously to work to + *infin*.
    (**i**) (*Sport*) to shoot; to go, play, have one's turn; **tira tú ahora** it's your go now; **tiró fuera de la portería** he shot wide of the goal; **¡tira!** shoot!
    (**j**) **a todo —** at the most; **nos queda gasolina para 20 kms a todo —** we have only enough petrol for 20 kms at the outside (*or* at the most); **llegará el martes a todo —** he'll arrive on Tuesday at the latest.
    3 tirarse *vr* (**a**) to throw oneself, hurl oneself; **— al agua** to dive (*or* plunge) into the water; **— al suelo** to throw oneself to the ground; **— por una ventana** to throw oneself out of a window; to jump from a window; **— por un risco** to throw oneself over a cliff; **— en paracaídas** to parachute (down), (*in emergency*) bale out; **— en la cama** to lie down on one's bed; **— a uno** to rush at someone, spring on someone.
    (**b**) (*fig*) to cheapen oneself, demean oneself; to waste oneself in an unworthy job.
    (**c**) **— a una** (*tabu*) to screw someone (*tabu*).
tirilla *nf* (**a**) band, strip; (*Sew*) neckband. (**b**) (*Chi*) shabby dress, ragged garment.
tirillas *nmf* (*fam*) (**a**) unimportant person, nobody; **¡vete, —!** get along, little man! (**b**) undersized individual, runt.
tirillento *adj* (*SAm*) ragged, shabby.
tiritaña *nf* (*fam*) mere trifle.
tiritar [1a] *vi* (**a**) to shiver (*de* with).
    (**b**) (*fam*) **dejaron el pastel tiritando** they almost finished the cake off, they made the cake look pretty silly (*fam*); **este plato ha quedado tiritando** there isn't much left of this dish.
tiritón *nm* shiver.
tiritona *nf* shivering (fit).
Tiro Tyre.
tiro *nm* (**a**) throw.
    (**b**) (*Mil etc*) shot; sound of a shot, report; impact of a shot, hit; bullet mark; (*in general*) shooting,

firing; — **con arco** archery; — **de pichón** clay-pigeon shooting; — **al blanco** target practice, shooting practice; — **de escopeta**, — **de fusil** gunshot; **cañón de** — **rápido** quick-firing gun; **descargar un** — to fire a shot; **errar el** — to miss, miss with one's shot; **se oyó un** — a shot was heard; **se pegó un** — he shot himself; **le pegó un** — **a su novio** she shot her boyfriend; **le salió el** — **por la culata** the scheme (etc) backfired; **hacer** — **a** (fig) to have designs on, aim at; **no lo haría ni a** —**s** I wouldn't do it for love nor money; **matar a uno a** —**s** to shoot someone (dead); **tendrán que decidirlo a** —**s** they'll have to shoot it out.

(c) (Sport) shot; drive; — **a gol** shot at goal; — **de revés** backhand drive; **parar un** — to stop a shot.

(d) (Mil etc) range; **a** — **de fusil** within gunshot; **a** — **de piedra** within a stone's throw; **estar a** — to be within range; (fig) to be accessible; **si se pone a** — **se lo diré** if he comes my way I'll tell him.

(e) rifle range; shooting gallery.

(f) team of horses (etc); **caballo de** — cart-horse, draught horse.

(g) (Sew) length (of cloth etc); **andar de** —**s largos** to be all dressed up, be very smartly turned out.

(h) rope; cord, chain; bellpull; (of harness) trace, strap; —**s** (Mil) swordbelt; —**s** (Arg) braces, suspenders (US).

(i) (Archit) flight of stairs.

(j) (of chimney etc) draught; (Min) shaft; — **de mina** mineshaft.

(k) (fig) blow; setback.

(l) (fig) veiled attack; damaging allusion.

(m) (fig) trick, hoax; practical joke.

(n) (fig) petty theft; petty deceit.

(o) (Chi, Mex, Per) marble.

(p) (Arg, Chi: Racing) distance, course.

(q) (Mex) issue, edition.

(r) (Chi) hint.

(s) (Ven) craftiness, cunning.

(t) (SAm: idioms) **al** — at once, right away; **a** — **de** + infin about to + infin, on the point of + ger; **de a** — completely; **del** — consequently.

tiroideo adj thyroid.

tiroides nf (also **glándula** —) thyroid (gland).

Tirol: El — the Tyrol.

tirolés 1 adj Tyrolese. **2** nm, **tirolesa** nf Tyrolese.

tirón[1] nm (a) pull, tug, sudden jerk; hitch; **dar un** — **a** to pull at, tug at; to jerk suddenly; **me lo arrancó de un** — she suddenly jerked it away from me; **el coche se movía a** —**es** the car moved along in a series of jerks, the car went jerkily forward.

(b) **de un** — all at once; in one go, straight off, without a break; **leyó la novela de un** — he read the novel straight through; **se lo bebió de un** — he drank it down in one go; **trabajan 10 horas de un** — they work 10 hours at a stretch.

(c) (RPl) **ganar el** — to get ahead, jump the gun successfully.

tirón[2] nm tyro, novice.

tirona nf (fam) whore.

tironear [1a] vt (SAm) =**tirar 2 (b)**.

tirotear [1a] **1** vt to shoot at, fire on; to blaze away at; to snipe at. **2 tirotearse** vr to exchange shots; to blaze away at each other.

tiroteo nm firing, shooting, exchange of shots; skirmish.

tirria nf dislike; ill will; **tener** — **a** to dislike, have a grudge against.

tisana nf tisane, infusion.

tísico 1 adj consumptive, tubercular. **2** nm, **tísica** nf consumptive.

tisiqu(i)ento adj (RPl) consumptive; pale and thin.

tisis nf consumption, tuberculosis.

tisú nm tissue.

tita nf (fam) auntie, aunty (fam).

titán nm Titan.

titánico adj titanic.

titanio nm titanium.

titeador adj (Bol, RPl) mocking, given to scoffing.

titear [1a] vt (Bol, RPl) to mock, scoff at; to make fun of.

titeo nm (Bol, RPl) mockery, scoffing; **tomar a uno para el** — to scoff at someone; to make fun of someone.

títere nm (a) puppet, marionette; —**s** puppets; puppet show; puppetry; **no dejar** — **con cabeza** to turn everything upside down; to leave nothing intact, break up everything in sight.

(b) (fig) puppet; cat's-paw; weak person, colourless individual; untrustworthy person; odd-looking person.

tití nm (SAm) small monkey.

titilar [1a] vi (of eyelid etc) to flutter, tremble; (of light, star) to twinkle.

titiritaña nf (Mex) (a) puppet show. (b) (fig) triviality.

titiritero nm puppeteer; acrobat, juggler, circus artist.

tito nm (fam) uncle.

titubeante adj (a) tottery, unstable, shaky. (b) stammering; halting. (c) hesitant.

titubear [1a] vi (a) to totter; to stagger; to be unstable, be shaky, be unsteady; to reel.

(b) (Ling) to stammer; to falter.

(c) to hesitate, vacillate; **no** — **en** + infin not to hesitate to + infin.

titubeo nm (a) tottering; staggering; instability, shakiness, unsteadiness.

(b) (Ling) stammering; faltering.

(c) hesitation, vacillation; **proceder sin** —**s** to act resolutely, act without hesitation.

titulado adj (a) entitled; **escribió una obra titulada "Sotileza"** he wrote a book entitled "Sotileza".

(b) person titled.

(c) person (Univ etc) qualified; (Tech etc) trained, skilled.

titular 1 adj titular, official.

2 nm (Typ) headline.

3 nmf (of office) holder, occupant; (Eccl) incumbent; (of passport, record etc) holder.

4 vt [1a] to title, entitle, call.

5 titularse vr to be entitled, be called; to call oneself, style oneself.

titulillo nm (Typ) running title, page heading; **andar en** —**s** (fam) to watch out for every little thing.

título nm (a) (general sense) title; (Law etc) section heading; article; (of budget) item; (Typ) title; (of newspaper) headline; **a** — **de** by way of; in the capacity of; **a** — **de curiosidad** as a matter of interest; **el dinero fue a** — **de préstamo** the money was given as a loan, the money was by way of being a loan; **nos lo dijo a** — **de noticia alentadora** he told us it as being a cheering piece of news.

(b) (of person) title; — **de nobleza**, — **nobiliario** title of nobility.

(c) (fig) titled person; **casarse con un** — to marry a titled person, marry into the nobility.

(d) professional qualification; diploma, certificate; (Univ) degree; (fig) qualification; —**s** qualifications, credentials; — **universitario** university degree; **maestro sin** — unqualified teacher; **obtener un** — to obtain a qualification; to take a degree; **tener los** —**s para un puesto** to have the qualifications for a job.

(e) (of character etc) quality; **no es precisamente un** — **de gloria para él** it is not exactly a quality on which he can pride himself; **tiene varios** —**s honrosos** he has several noble qualities, he has a number of worthy attributes.

(f) (Law) title; — **de propiedad** title deed.

(g) (Fin) bond; — **al portador** bearer bond.

(h) (fig) right; **con justo** — rightly; **tener** — **de** + infin to be entitled to + infin, have the right to + infin; **le sobran** —**s para hacerlo** he has every right to do it.

tiza nf (a) chalk; whitening; **una** — a piece of chalk.

(b) (Col) exaggeration.

tizar [1f] vt (Chi) to plan; to design, model; (Per) suit to mark out for cutting.

tizate nm (CAm, Mex) chalk.

tizna nf black, grime; (Art) crayon.

tiznado nm (pej) nigger, blackie.

tiznajo nm (fam) black mark, dirty smear.

tiznar [1a] **1** vt to blacken, black; to smudge, soil, stain, spot; to smear (de with).

(b) (fig) to stain, tarnish; to defame, blacken.

2 tiznarse vr (a) — **la cara con un corcho quemado** to blacken one's face with burnt cork.

(b) to get smudged, get soiled (etc).

(c) (Chi, Guat, Mex) to get drunk.

tizne nm (a) soot; black smear, blackening; grime; smut. (b) (fig) stain.

tiznón nm smut, speck of soot; smudge.

tizo nm burning piece of wood, brand.

tizón nm (a) burning piece of wood, brand; half-burned piece of wood. (b) (Bot) smut. (c) (fig) stain.

tizonazos nmpl (fig) pains of hell.

tizonear [1a] vt to fire to poke, stir.

tizos nmpl (sl) fingers.

tlacanear [1a] vt (Mex) to touch, feel, handle.

tlacote nm (Mex) growth, tumour.

tlacual nm (Mex) (a) food; meal. (b) cooking pot.

tlachique *nm* (*Mex*) unfermented *pulque.*
tlapalería *nf* (*Mex*) paint shop.
tlapiloya *nf* (*Mex*) jail.
tlapisquera *nf* (*Mex*) shed, barn, granary.
tlecuil *nm* (*Mex*) hearth, fire; stove.
toa *nf* (*SAm*) hawser, rope, towrope.
toalla *nf* towel; **—** **de baño** bath towel; **—** **de rodillo** roller towel.
toallero *nm* towel rail.
tobar [1a] *vt* (*Col*) to tow.
tobera *nf* nozzle.
tobillera *nf* (**a**) ankle sock. (**b**) (*fam*) teenager, bobbysoxer (*US fam*).
tobillo *nm* ankle.
tobo *nm* (*Ven*) bucket.
tobogán *nm* (**a**) toboggan. (**b**) (*at fair*) switchback. (**c**) (*into pool*) chute, slide.
toca¹ *nf* headdress; bonnet; toque; **—s de viuda** widow's weeds.
toca² *nmf* (*SAm*) =**tocayo.**
tocadiscos *nm*, *pl* tocadiscos record player, phonograph (*US*); **—** **automático** auto-change record player; **—** **tragamonedas,** **—** **tragaperras** jukebox.
tocado¹ *adj* (**a**) *fruit* bad, rotten; *meat etc* tainted, bad; **estar** **—** **de la cabeza** to be weak in the head.
(**b**) **una creencia tocada de heterodoxia** a belief tinged with heterodoxy.
(**c**) **estar** **—** **de piedad** to be full of pious feelings.
tocado² **1** *adj*: **—** **con un sombrero de paja** wearing a straw hat, with a straw hat on his head.
2 *nm* (**a**) headdress, headgear, hat.
(**b**) coiffure, hair-do.
(**c**) toilet.
tocador¹ *nm* (**a**) dressing table; **jabón de —** toilet soap; **juego de —** toilet set.
(**b**) toilet case.
(**c**) boudoir, dressing room; **—** **de señoras** ladies' room.
tocador² *nm*, **tocadora** *nf* (*Mus*) player.
tocante 1 **—** **a** *prep* with regard to, about; **en lo —** **a** so far as concerns, as for. **2** *adj* (*RPl*) moving, touching.
tocar¹ [1g] **1** *vt* (**a**) to touch; to feel; to handle; **—** **las cosas de cerca** to experience things for oneself, learn about things at first hand; **sin —** **un pelo de su ropa** without laying a finger on her; **¡no me toques!** don't touch me!; **que nadie toque mis papeles** don't let anyone touch my papers, don't interfere with my papers.
(**b**) (*of objects*) to touch, be touching; **la mesa toca la pared** the table touches the wall, the table is up against the wall.
(**c**) (*Mus*) to play; *bell* to ring; to toll, peal; *drum* to play, beat; *trumpet* to play, blow, sound; *siren etc* to sound; *record* to play; *hour of day* to chime, strike; **—** **la generala** (*Mil*) to sound the call to arms; **—** **la retirada** to sound the retreat; **¡a pagar tocan!** it's time to pay up!
(**d**) (*Art*) to touch up.
(**e**) (*fig*) to touch; **—** **el corazón de uno** to touch someone's heart.
(**f**) *obstacle etc* to hit, strike, collide with, run into; (*Naut*) to go aground on, run on to; (*Hunting*) to hit, wing; *target etc* to hit.
(**g**) *subject* to touch on, refer to, allude to; **no tocó para nada esa cuestión** he didn't refer to that matter at all.
(**h**) *consequences* to suffer, undergo, come in for; **él tocará las consecuencias de todo esto** he will suffer the consequences of all this.
(**i**) (*fam*) to be related to; **X no le toca para nada a Y** X is not related at all to Y, X is no relation to Y.
2 *vi* (**a**) **—** **a una puerta** to knock on (*or* at) a door.
(**b**) **tocan a misa** they are ringing the bell for mass; **ese timbre toca a fuego** that bell sounds the fire alarm; *see* **muerto** *etc.*
(**c**) **—le a uno** to fall to someone, fall to someone's lot; to fall to someone's share; **les tocó un dólar a cada uno** each one got a dollar as his share; **¿les tocará algo de herencia?** will they get anything under the will?; **le ha tocado otro premio** he has won another prize; **te toca jugar** it's your turn (to play), it's your go; **¿a quién le toca?** whose turn is it?; **¿a quién le toca pagar esta vez?** whose turn is it to pay this time?; **le toca a Vd reprenderle** it is up to you to reprimand him.
(**d**) (*impersonal*) **no toca hacerlo hasta el mes que viene** it's not due to be done until next month; **ahora toca torcer a la derecha** now you have to turn right, now there's a right turn coming up.
(**e**) to concern, affect; **esto no te toca a ti** this doesn't concern you; **ello me toca de cerca** it con-

cerns me intimately; **por lo que a mí me toca** so far as I am concerned.
(**f**) (*Naut*) **—** **en** to call at, touch at; **el barco no toca en Barcelona** the ship does not call at Barcelona.
(**g**) (*fig*) **—** **en** to border on, verge on; **esto toca en locura** this verges on madness.
3 tocarse *vr* (**a**) to touch each other, be in contact.
(**b**) (*fam*) **—las** to beat it (*fam*).
tocar² [1g] **1** *vt* *hair* to do, arrange, set. **2 tocarse** *vr* to cover one's head, put on one's hat.
tocateja: a — *adv* on the nail.
tocayo *nm*, **tocaya** *nf* (**a**) namesake. (**b**) (*Per*) friend.
tocino *nm* bacon (*also* **—** **de panceta**); salt pork.
toco¹ *nm* (*CAm*) =**tocayo.**
toco² *nm* (*Ven*) =**tocón.**
tocolotear [1a] *vi* (*Cu*) to shuffle (the cards).
tocón 1 *adj* (*Col*) tailless; (*PR, Ven*) hornless. **2** *nm* (*Anat, Bot*) stump.
tocuyo *nm* (*Bol, Per, RPl*) coarse cotton cloth.
tochimbo *nm* (*Per*) smelting furnace.
todavía *adv* (**a**) still, yet; **—** **no** not yet; **—** **en 1970** as late as 1970, right up to 1970; **—** **no lo ha encontrado** he still has not found it, he has not found it yet; **está nevando —** it is still snowing; **es —** **más inteligente que su hermano** he is still (*or* yet) more intelligent than his brother.
(**b**) (*SAm*) not yet.
todo 1 *adj* (**a**) all; whole, entire; every; **—** **el bosque** all the wood, the whole wood, the entire wood; **el universo —** the whole universe; **lo sabe —** **Madrid** all Madrid knows it, the whole of Madrid knows it; **lo golpeó con toda su fuerza** he hit him with his full strength, he hit him with all his might; **a toda velocidad** at full speed, at top speed; **con toda prisa** in all haste, with all speed; **en toda España** all over Spain, throughout Spain; **en toda España no hay más que 5** there are only 5 in the whole of Spain; **— lo demás** all the rest, all else; **—s vosotros** all of you; **—s los libros** all the books; **todas las semanas** every week; **viene todos los martes** he comes every Tuesday; **— el que quiera . . .** everyone who wants to . . .; whoever wants to . . .; **—s los que quieran . . .** all those who want to . . .; **lo que Vd ve aquí** all that you see here; **— lo que Vd necesite** whatever you need; **con toda su inteligencia** with all his intelligence; in spite of all his intelligence; **de todas todas** (*fam*) the whole lot, all of them without exception; **¡te digo que sí de todas todas!** I tell you it's jolly well is! (*fam*); **es verdad de todas todas** it's absolutely true; *see* **cuanto** *etc.*
(**b**) (*neg sense*) **en —** **el día** not once all day; **en toda la noche he dormido** I haven't slept all night; **en toda España lo encuentra Vd** you won't find it anywhere in Spain.
(**c**) (*idiomatic use*) **es —** **un hombre** he's every inch a man; **es —** **un palacio** it's a real palace; **es —** **un héroe** he's a real hero; **la hija es toda su madre** the daughter is exactly like her mother; **tiene toda la nariz de su abuela** her nose is exactly like her grandmother's; **el niño estaba —** **ojos** the child was all eyes; **ese hombre es —** **ambición** that man is all ambition (and nothing else).
2 *adv* (**a**) all, entirely, completely; **estaba —** **rendido** he was completely worn out; **para las 8 estará —** **hecho** it will be completely finished by 8 o'clock; **lleva un vestido —** **roto** she's wearing a dress that's all torn.
(**b**) **puede ser —** **lo sencillo que Vd quiera** it can be as simple as you wish; *see* **más** *etc.*
3 con — **y** *conj* (*SAm*) in spite of; **el equipo, con —** **y estar integrado por buenos jugadores . . .** the team, in spite of being (*or* for all that it is) made up of good players . . .
4 *nm and pron* (**a**) all, everything; **—s** everybody; every one of them; **el —** the whole; **en un —** together, as a whole; **—s y cada uno** all and sundry; **lo comió —** he ate it all; **lo han vendido —** they've sold it all, they've sold the lot; **lo sabemos —** we know everything; **— o nada** all or nothing; **— es** (*or* son) **reveses** it's all setbacks, there's nothing but troubles; **y luego — son sonrisas** and then it's all smiles; **— cabe en él** he is capable of anything; **ser el —** to be the most important thing; (*of person: fam*) to be the mainstay; to run the show, dominate everything; **y — and so on,** and what not; **tienen un coche nuevo y —** they have a new car and everything; **los zapatos, viejos y —,** **durarán otro año** these shoes, old though they are, will last another year; **andando rápidamente y —,** **no llegaron a tiempo** even though they walked quickly they still didn't get there in time; *see* **jugarse** *etc.*

(b) (*phrases with prep*) **ante** — first of all, in the first place; primarily; **a pesar de** — even so, in spite of everything; all the same; **con** — still, however; in spite of everything; **de** — **como en botica** everything under the sun; **de** — **hay en este mundo de Dios, de** — **hay en la viña del Señor** it takes all sorts to make a world; **del** — wholly, completely; **no es del** — **verdad** it is not entirely true, it is not quite true; **no es del** — **malo** it is not wholly bad; **después de** — after all; **para** — all-purpose; **por** — all in all; **sobre** — especially; above all, most of all.

todopoderoso *adj* almighty, all-powerful; **el T—** the Almighty.

tofo *nm* (*Arg, Chi*) white clay; fireclay.

toga *nf* (*Hist*) toga; (*Law etc*) gown, robe; (*Univ*) gown; **tomar la** — (*approx*) to take silk.

Togolandia *f* Togoland.

tojo[1] *nm* gorse, furze.

tojo[2] *adj* (*Bol*) twin.

tol *nm* (*CAm*) gourd; large vessel; bowl.

tolda *nf* (**a**) (*Col, Ec, PR*) coarse material, canvas. (**b**) (*Col*) tent, improvised hut; shelter; (*of boat*) awning. (**c**) (*PR*) large sack. (**d**) (*Ven*) overcast sky.

toldería *nf* (*Bol, Chi, RPl*) Indian village, camp of Indian huts.

toldillo *nm* (*Ant, Col, Ven*) mosquito net.

toldo *nm* (**a**) sunshade, awning; marquee; cover, cloth, tarpaulin. (**b**) (*Bol, Chi, RPl*) Indian hut. (**c**) (*Col, Per, PR*) mosquito net. (**d**) (*Mex: Aut*) hood, top (*US*). (**e**) (*fig*) pride, haughtiness.

tole[1] *nm* (*fam*) (**a**) hubbub, commotion, uproar; outcry; **levantar el** — to kick up a fuss. (**b**) (*also* **tole tole**) gossip, rumour; slander campaign. (**c**) **coger el** —, **tomar el** — to get out, pack up and go.

tole[2] *nm* (*Col*) track, trail.

toledano 1 *adj* Toledan. **2** *nm*, **toledana** *nf* Toledan.

tolempo *nm* (*Col*) = **lempo**.

tolerable *adj* tolerable.

tolerancia *nf* (**a**) tolerance; toleration. (**b**) (*Mech*) tolerance.

tolerante *adj* tolerant.

tolerantismo *nm* religious toleration.

tolerar [1a] *vt* to tolerate; to bear, endure, put up with; to allow; **no se puede** — **esto** this cannot be tolerated; **no tolera que digan eso** he won't allow them to say that, he won't put up with their saying that; **su madre le tolera demasiado** his mother spoils him, his mother lets him get away with too much; **su estómago no tolera los huevos** eggs don't agree with him; **el cosmonauta toleró muy bien esta situación difícil** the cosmonaut stood up very well to this awkward situation; **el puente no tolera el peso de los tanques** the bridge will not support the weight of the tanks.

tolete *nm* (**a**) (*Naut*) tholepin. (**b**) (*SAm*) short club, stick, cudgel. (**c**) (*Col, Cu*) piece, bit. (**d**) (*Col*) raft.

toletero *nm* (*Ven*) rowdy, tough (*fam*).

toletole *nm* (**a**) (*Arg*) row. (**b**) (*Col*) obstinacy, persistence. (**c**) (*Ven*) gay life, roving life; *see also* **tole**[1] (**b**).

Tolomeo *m* Ptolemy.

Tolón Toulon.

toloncho *nm* (*Col*) piece of wood.

tolondro 1 *adj* scatterbrained. **2** *nm* (*Med*) bump, lump, swelling.

tolondrón *adj and nm* = **tolondro**.

Tolosa (**de Francia**) Toulouse.

tolva *nf* (**a**) hopper; chute. (**b**) (*Chi, Mex: Rail*) hopper wagon, hopper car (*US*). (**c**) (*Mex*) shed for storing ore.

tolvanera *nf* dustcloud.

tolla *nf* (**a**) marsh, quagmire. (**b**) (*Cu, Mex*) drinking trough.

tollina *nf* (*fam*) hiding; bashing (*fam*).

toma *nf* (**a**) (*general sense*) taking; — **de declaración** taking of evidence; — **de hábito** (*Eccl*) taking of vows; — **de posesión** taking over; (*by president*) taking up of office, inauguration; — **de tierra** (*Aer*) landing, touchdown. (**b**) (*Mil*) capture, taking; seizure. (**c**) amount, portion; (*Med*) dose; — **de rapé** pinch of snuff. (**d**) (*Mech etc*) inlet, intake; outlet; (*of water etc*) tap, outlet; (*Elec*) plug, socket; lead; terminal; — **de antena** (*Radio*) aerial socket; — **de corriente** power

point, plug; — **directa** (*Aut*) top gear; — **de fuerza** power takeoff; — **de tierra** earth wire, ground wire (*US*). (**e**) (*Cine, TV*) take, shot; — **directa** live shot; live broadcast. (**f**) (*SAm*) channel; irrigation ditch; (*Guat*) brook.

tomacorriente *nm* (*Elec*) plug.

tomada *nf* (*SAm: Elec*) plug.

tomadero *nm* (**a**) handle. (**b**) inlet, intake; tap.

tomado *adj* (**a**) (*also* — **de orín**) rusty. (**b**) *voice* hoarse. (**c**) **estar** — (*SAm*) to be drunk.

tomador 1 *adj* (*SAm*) drunken, boozy. **2** *nm* (**a**) (*Comm*) drawee. (**b**) (*fam*) thief. (**c**) (*SAm*) drunkard, boozer.

tomadura *nf* = **toma** (**a**) *and* (**b**); — **de pelo** hoax, deception; mockery; abuse.

tomaína *nf* ptomaine.

tomar 1 *vt* [1a] (*general sense*) to take; to accept; to get, acquire; *air, bath, bend, decision, measure, opportunity, route, step, sun, temperature etc* to take; *arms, pen etc* to take up; *attitude* to adopt, take up; to strike; *appearance, aspect, shape etc* to take on; *ball* to catch, stop; *cold* to take, get, catch; *habit* to get into, fall into, acquire; *business* to take over; *lesson* to have; *name* to take, adopt; *servant* to take on. engage; *strength* to get, gain, acquire; *ticket* to take, get, buy; **¡toma!** here you are!, here!, catch!; **¡tómate ésa!** take that!; — **y dejar pasajeros** to take up and set down passengers; — **a uno por policía** to take someone for a policeman, think that someone is a policeman; — **a uno por loco** to think someone mad; **¿por quién me toma Vd?** what do you take me for?, who do you think I am?; — **algo sobre sí** to take something upon oneself; *see* **mal, serio** *etc.*
(**b**) (*Mil*) to take, capture; to seize.
(**c**) (*Cook*) to eat, drink, have; — **el pecho** to suck, feed at the breast; **tomamos unas cervezas** we had a few beers; **¿qué quieres** —? what will you have?, what would you like?
(**d**) *bus, train etc* to take.
(**e**) (*Cine, Phot, TV*) to take; (*Cine*) to shoot; — **una foto de** to take a photo of.
(**f**) *notes* to take; *speech etc* to take down; — **por escrito** to write down; — **en taquigrafía** to take down in shorthand; — **en cinta** to record on tape.
(**g**) *affection, loathing etc* to acquire, take (*a* to); *see* **cariño** *etc.*
(**h**) (*of feeling*) to overcome; **le tomaron ganas de reír** she was overcome by an urge to laugh.
(**i**) — **la con uno** to pick a quarrel with someone; **tenerla tomada con uno** to have a down on someone (*fam*), adopt a consistently hostile attitude to someone.
(**j**) (*Col*) to upset, annoy.
2 *vi* (**a**) (*Bot*) to take, take root; (*of graft*) to take.
(**b**) — **a la derecha** to go off to the right, turn right; — **por una calle** to go off along a street, turn down a street.
(**c**) (*SAm*) to drink; **estaba tomando en varios bares** he was drinking in a number of bars.
(**d**) (*fam*) **tomó y lo rompió** he went and broke it; **tomó y se fue** off he went, he upped and went (*fam*).
(**e**) **toma y daca** (*as n*) give and take; (*pej*) mutual concessions (for selfish reasons), log rolling; **más vale un** — **que dos te daré** a bird in the hand is worth two in the bush.
(**f**) **¡toma!** well!; there!, fancy that!; I told you so!; (*to dog*) here boy!
3 tomarse *vr* (**a**) to take; — **la venganza por su mano** to take vengeance with one's own hands; **no te lo tomes así** don't take it that way; **se lo sabe tomar bien** he knows how to take it, he can take it in his stride; **se tomó unas vacaciones larguísimas** he took tremendously long holidays; **se tomó un tremendo disgusto** he received a very severe blow; **se tomó 13 cervezas seguidas** he drank down 13 beers one after the other.
(**b**) — **por** to think oneself, consider oneself to be; **¿por quién se toma aquel ministro?** who does that minister think he is?
(**c**) (**de orín**) to get rusty.

Tomás *m* Thomas; — **Moro** Thomas More.

tomatal *nm* (**a**) tomato bed, tomato field. (**b**) (*SAm*) tomato plant.

tomate *nm* tomato; **ponerse como un** — to turn as red as a beetroot.

tomatera *nf* (**a**) tomato plant. (**b**) (*Chi*) drunken spree (*fam*); rowdy party.

tomatero *nm* tomato grower; tomato dealer.

tomavistas *nm, pl* **tomavistas** film camera, cine-camera.

tómbola *nf* tombola.

tomillo *nm* thyme; — **salsero** savory.

tominero *adj* (*Mex*) mean.

tomismo *nm* Thomism.

tomista 1 *adj* Thomist. 2 *nmf* Thomist.

tomo[1] *nm* volume; **en 3** —**s** in 3 volumes.

tomo[2] *nm* bulk, size; (*fig*) importance; **de** — **y lomo** utter, out-and-out; **un canalla de** — **y lomo** a real rotter.

tomón *adj* (*Col*) teasing, jokey.

tompiate *nm* (*Mex*) basket made of palm leaves; bag, pouch, knapsack.

ton: **sin** — **ni son** for no particular reason; without rhyme or reason.

tonada *nf* (a) tune, song, air. (b) (*SAm*) accent, local peculiarity, typical intonation. (c) (*Cu*) fib, hoax.

tonadilla *nf* little tune; merry tune, light-hearted song.

tonal *adj* tonal.

tonalidad *nf* (a) (*Mus*) key; tonality; (*Radio*) tone; — **mayor** major key; — **menor** minor key; **control de** — tone control.
(b) (*Art*) shade; colour scheme; **una bella** — **de verde** a beautiful shade of green; **cambiar la** — **de un cuarto** to change the colour scheme of a room.

tonel *nm* barrel, cask, keg.

tonelada *nf* ton; — **métrica** metric ton; — **de registro** register ton; **un buque de 30.000** —**s de registro bruto** a ship of 30,000 gross register tons.

tonelaje *nm* tonnage.

tonelería *nf* cooperage, barrel making.

tonelero *nm* cooper.

tonelete *nm* (a) cask, keg. (b) short skirt; (*man's*) kilt.

tonga *nf* (a) layer, stratum; (*of bricks*) course. (b) (*Cu, Mex*) pile. (c) (*Aragón, Arg, Col*) job, task; spell of work. (d) (*Col*) nap.

tongada *nf* layer; coat, covering.

tongo[1] *nm* (*Sport*) fixing, throwing of a game (*or* fight *etc*); **¡hay** —**!** it's been fixed!, it's been rigged!; **hubo** — **en las elecciones** the elections were rigged.

tongo[2] *nm* (*Chi*) (a) bowler hat. (b) rum punch.

tongonearse [1a] *vr* (*SAm*) = **contonearse**.

tongoneo *nm* (*SAm*) = **contoneo**.

tongorí *nm* (*Arg, Bol*) liver (of cow *etc*); offal; lights.

tongoy *nm* (*SAm*) bowler hat.

tónica *nf* (*Mus*) tonic; keynote (*also fig*); **es una de las** —**s del estilo moderno** it is one of the keynotes of the modern style.

tonicidad *nf* tonicity.

tónico 1 *adj* (a) (*Mus*) tonic; (*Ling*) syllable tonic, stressed, accented. (b) (*Med*) tonic, invigorating, stimulating (*also fig*). 2 *nm* tonic (*also fig*).

tonificador *adj*, **tonificante** *adj* invigorating, stimulating.

tonificar [1g] *vt* to tone up; to invigorate, fortify.

tonillo *nm* (a) singsong, monotone, monotonous voice. (b) sarcastic tone, mocking undertone.

tono *nm* (a) (*Mus*) tone; pitch; key; — **mayor** major key; — **menor** minor key; **estar a** — to be in key; **estar a** — **con** (*fig*) to be in tune with.
(b) (*of voice etc, also fig*) tone; — **de marcar** (*Tel*) dialling tone; — **de voz** tone of voice; **a este** — **in the same fashion, in the same vein; en** — **bajo** in low tones; **en** — **de enojo** in an angry tone; **bajar el** — to lower one's voice; (*fig*) to change one's tune, quieten down; **cambiar el** (*or* **de**) — to change one's tune; **la expresión tiene un** — **despectivo** the expression has a pejorative tone; **la discusión tomó un** — **áspero** the discussion took on a harsh tone.
(c) (*social etc*) tone; **buen** — tone, good tone; **una familia de** — a good family, a family of some social standing; **de buen** — elegant, fashionable; (*hum*) genteel, refined; **de mal** — common, coarse; **eso no es de** — that's not done, that's not nice; **fuera de** — inappropriate; **dar el** — to set the tone; **darse** — to put on airs; **subirse de** — to get more haughty (*or* angry), take a more arrogant (*or* indignant) line; **no venir a** — to be inappropriate, be out of place.
(d) (*Mus*) tuning fork.
(e) (*Mus: of wind instrument*) slide.
(f) (*Anat, Med*) tone.
(g) (*of colour*) shade, hue; — **pastel** pastel shade.

tonsura *nf* tonsure.

tonsurado *adj* tonsured.

tonsurar [1a] *vt* to clip, shear; (*Eccl*) to tonsure.

tontada *nf* = **tontería**.

tontaina *nmf* (*fam*) idiot, dimwit (*fam*).

tontamente *adv* foolishly, stupidly.

tontear [1a] *vi* (*fam*) (a) to fool about, act the fool; to talk nonsense. (b) (*of lovers*) to exchange witty talk, flirt humorously.

tontería *nf* (a) (*quality*) silliness, foolishness, stupidity.
(b) (*una* —) silly thing; foolish act, stupid remark; —**s** nonsense, rubbish; **¡déjate de** —**s!** stop that nonsense!, quit fooling!; **dejémonos de** —**s** let's be serious; **hacer una** — to do a silly thing, do something silly; **no es ninguna** — it's not such a bad idea; it's not just a small thing, it's more serious than you think.
(c) (*fig*) triviality; **lo vendió por una** — he sold it for a song; **estima cualquier** — **de ese autor** he values any little thing by that writer.
(d) (*fig*) silly scruple; —**s** display of delicacy (*or* squeamishness *etc*).

tonto 1 *adj* (a) silly, foolish, stupid; (*Med*) imbecile; **¡qué** — **soy!** how silly of me!; **¡no seas** —**!** don't be silly!; **es lo bastante** — **como para** + *infin* he's fool enough to + *infin*; **dejar a uno** — to dumbfound someone.
(b) *lover* silly, soft, mushy.
(c) **a tontas y a locas** anyhow, unsystematically, haphazardly; **lo hace a tontas y a locas** he does it just anyhow; **repartir golpes a tontas y a locas** to hit out wildly, hit out blindly.
2 *nm*, **tonta** *nf* (a) fool, idiot; (*Med*) imbecile; **¡**—**!** you idiot!; **soy un** — I'm an idiot, I must be crazy; — **del bote**, — **de capirote** prize idiot, utter fool; **hacer(se) el** — to act the fool, play the fool.
(b) (*Circus, Theat*) clown, funny man.
(c) (*Col, CR, Chi*) jemmy.

tontón[1] *nm*, **tontona** *nf* (*fam*) = **tonto** 2.

tontón[2] *nm* (*fam*) smock, maternity dress.

tontura *nf* = **tontería** (a).

tontureco *adj* (*CAm*) = **tonto** 1.

tonudo *adj* (*Arg*) classy (*fam*).

tony ['toni] *nm* (*SAm: angl*) clown.

topacio *nm* topaz.

topar [1a] 1 *vt* (a) (*Zool*) to butt, horn.
(b) *person* to run into, come across, bump into; *object* to find, come across; **le topé por casualidad en el museo** I happened to bump into him in the museum.
(c) (*Chi, Mex, Per*) to wager, stake.
2 *vi* (a) — **contra**, — **en** to run into, hit, bump into, knock against.
(b) — **con** = 1 (b); — **con un obstáculo** to run up against an obstacle, encounter an obstacle.
(c) **la dificultad topa en eso** that's where the trouble lies, there's the rub.
(d) (*Mex*) to quarrel.
3 **toparse** *vr* = 2 (b).

tope[1] 1 *adj* top, maximum; **edad** — **para un puesto** maximum (*or* minimum) age for a job; **fecha** — closing date, last date; **precio** — top price, ceiling price; **sueldo** — top salary, maximum salary.
2 *nm* (a) end; top, maximum, limit; ceiling; (*Naut*) top, masthead; **al** — end to end; **hasta el** — to the brim, to the limit; **estar hasta los** —**s** (*Naut*) to be overloaded, be loaded to the gunwales; (*fig*) to be full to bursting; **estoy hasta los** —**s** I'm utterly fed up.
(b) (*Naut: person*) lookout.
(c) (*Arg, Col*) peak, summit.

tope[2] *nm* (a) bump, knock, bang; (*with head*) butt; collision.
(b) (*fig*) quarrel; scuffle.
(c) (*Mech etc*) catch, stop, check; (*Rail*) buffer; (*Aut*) bumper; (*of gun*) catch.
(d) (*fig*) snag, difficulty; **ahí está el** — that's just the trouble.

topera *nf* molehill.

toperol *nm* (*Chi, Mex*) brass tack.

topetada *nf* butt, bump, bang, collision.

topetar [1a] *vt* (a) to butt, bump. (b) (*fig*) to bump into.

topetazo *nm* = **topetada**.

topetear [1a] *vt* (*Col*) = **topetar**.

topetón *nm* = **topetada**.

tópico 1 *adj* (*Med*) local; for external application.
2 *nm* (a) commonplace, platitude; cliché; catchphrase.
(b) (*SAm: angl*) topic, subject.

topillo *nm* (*Mex*) trick, swindle.

topo[1] *nm* (a) (*Zool*) mole. (b) (*fig*) clumsy person, blunderer.

topo[2] *nm* (*SAm*) large pin.

topocho *adj* (*Ven*) (a) plump, chubby. (b) full up.

topografía *nf* topography.

topográfico *adj* topographic(al).

topógrafo *nm* topographer; surveyor.

topolino 1 *nf* teenager, bobbysoxer (*US fam*). **2** —s *nmpl* wedge-heeled shoes.

topón *nm* (*SAm*) =**topetada.**

toponimia *nf* (**a**) toponymy, place-names; **la —visigótica de España** the Visigothic place-names of Spain. (**b**) study of place-names.

topónimo *nm* place-name.

toposo *adj* (*Ven*) (**a**) meddlesome. (**b**) pedantic.

toque *nm* (**a**) (*act*) touch; **dar los primeros —s a** to make a start on; **dar el último — a** to put the finishing touch to; **faltan algunos —s para completarlo** it needs a few touches to finish it off. (**b**) (*Art*) touch; dab (of colour); **— de luz** light. (**c**) (*Chem*) test; assay; **dar un — a** to test; *person* to sound out. (**d**) (*Mus*) (*of bell*) peal, chime; stroke; ring; (*of drum*) beat; (*of siren*) hoot, blast; (*Mil*) bugle call; **— de atención** (*fig*) warning note; **— de diana** reveille; **— de difuntos** passing bell, knell; **— de queda** curfew; **— de retreta** tattoo; **al — de las doce** on the stroke of twelve. (**e**) (*fig*) crux; essence, heart of the matter; **ahí está el —** that's the crux of the matter. (**f**) (*Bol*) turn.

toquetear [1a] *vt* (**a**) to touch repeatedly, handle, keep fingering. (**b**) (*Mus*) to mess about on, play idly. (**c**) (*SAm*) to fondle, feel, caress.

toqueteo *nm* (*SAm*) fondling, feeling, caressing.

toquido *nm* (*Guat, Mex*) =**toque.**

toquilla *nf* headscarf; knitted shawl, woollen bonnet; (*Par, Per etc*) straw hat.

torácico *adj* thoracic.

torada *nf* herd of bulls.

tórax *nm* thorax.

torbellino *nm* (**a**) whirlwind; dust cloud. (**b**) (*fig*) whirl. (**c**) (*fig*) restless and unsound individual, energetic but disorganized person.

torcaz *adj*: see **paloma.**

torcecuello *nm* (*Orn*) wryneck.

torcedor *nm* (**a**) (*Tech*) spindle. (**b**) (*fig*) torture, torment.

torcedura *nf* (**a**) twist(ing); (*Med*) sprain, strain, wrench. (**b**) weak wine.

torcer [2b and 2h] **1** *vt* (**a**) (*general sense*) to twist; to bend; *wood etc* to warp; *limb* to twist, wrench, put out; *muscle* to strain; *ankle* to sprain, twist; *eyes* to turn; *ball* to spin, cut; **— el gesto, — el hocico** (*sl*) to make a (wry) face; to scowl, look cross. (**b**) *clothes, hands, neck* to wring; *strands, rope* to plait. (**c**) (*fig*) *decision, course of events* to influence, affect; *will* to bend; *thoughts* to turn (**de** from); *person* to dissuade, turn (**de** from). (**d**) (*fig*) *justice* to pervert; *person* to corrupt, bribe. (**e**) (*fig*) *sense* to twist, pervert, distort.

2 *vi* (**a**) (*of road, vehicle, traveller*) to turn; **el coche torció a la izquierda** the car turned left; **al llegar allí tuerza Vd a la derecha** when you reach there turn right. (**b**) (*of ball*) to spin; to swerve.

3 torcerse *vr* (**a**) to twist; to bend; to warp. (**b**) **— un pie** to twist one's foot, sprain one's foot. (**c**) (*fig*) to go astray, be perverted; (*Med etc*) to suffer in one's development; (*events*) to take a strange turn; (*hope, plan etc*) to go all wrong, go awry. (**d**) (*milk, wine*) to turn sour.

torcida *nf* wick.

torcidamente *adv* (**a**) in a twisted way, crookedly. (**b**) (*fig*) deviously, in a crooked way.

torcido 1 *adj* (**a**) twisted; bent; *road etc* crooked, twisty, full of turns; **el cuadro está —** the picture is askew, the picture is not straight; **llevaba el sombrero algo —** he had his hat on not quite straight. (**b**) (*fig*) devious, crooked. (**c**) (*CAm, Col, SD, Ven*) unlucky. **2** *nm* curl; (*of silk etc*) twist.

torcijón *nm* (**a**) sudden twist. (**b**) =**retortijón.**

torcimiento *nm* =**torcedura.**

tordillo *adj* dappled, dapple-grey.

tordo 1 *adj* dappled, dapple-grey. **2** *nm* (*Orn*) thrush.

torear [1a] **1** *vt* (**a**) *bull* to fight, play. (**b**) (*fig*) to dodge, avoid. (**c**) (*fig*) to keep at bay; to tease, draw on; to put off, keep guessing. (**d**) (*fig*) to plague, confuse. (**e**) (*Arg, CAm*) *animal* to provoke, enrage; (*Arg, Mex*) *person* to infuriate. (**f**) (*Bol, RPl: of dog*) to bark furiously at.

2 *vi* (**a**) (*Taur*) to fight, fight bulls; to be a bull-fighter; **toreó bien Suárez** Suárez fought well; **no volverá a —** he will never fight again; **el muchacho quiere —** the boy wants to be a bullfighter. (**b**) (*Bol, RPl*) to bark furiously.

toreo *nm* (**a**) (art of) bullfighting. (**b**) (*Mex*) illicit still.

torera *nf* (**a**) short tight jacket. (**b**) **saltarse algo a la —** to pay no attention to something.

torería *nf* (**a**) (class of) bullfighters; bullfighting world. (**b**) (*Cu, Guat*) mischief, prank.

torero *nm* bullfighter.

torete *nm* (**a**) small bull, young bull. (**b**) (*fig*) strong boy, robust child; (*pej*) rough child; bad-tempered boy.

toril *nm* bullpen.

torio *nm* thorium.

tormenta *nf* (**a**) storm. (**b**) (*fig*) storm; turmoil, upheaval; **— en un vaso de agua** storm in a teacup; **sufrió una — de celos** she suffered a great pang of jealousy; **desencadenó una — de pasiones** it unleashed a storm of passions. (**c**) (*fig*) misfortune; reverse, setback.

tormento *nm* torture; (*fig*) torture, torment; anguish, agony; **dar — a** to torture; (*fig*) to torment, plague; **darse —** to torment oneself; **estos zapatos son un —** these shoes are agony; **sus dos hijos son un — perpetuo** her two sons are a perpetual torment to her.

tormentoso *adj* stormy (*also fig*).

tormo *nm* lump, mass.

torna *nf* (**a**) return. (**b**) **volver las —s a uno** to make everything come out all wrong for someone; **se han vuelto las —s** now it's all changed, now the boot's on the other foot.

tornada *nf* return.

tornadera *nf* pitchfork, winnowing fork.

tornadizo 1 *adj* changeable; fickle. **2** *nm,* **tornadiza** *nf* (*Hist*) renegade.

tornado *nm* tornado.

tornar [1a] **1** *vt* (**a**) to give back, return. (**b**) to change, alter, transform (**en** into).

2 *vi* (**a**) to go back, come back, return. (**b**) **— a hacer algo** to do something again; **tornó a llover** it began to rain again; **tornó a estudiar el problema** he returned to the study of the problem. (**c**) **— en sí** to regain consciousness, come to.

3 tornarse *vr* (**a**) to return. (**b**) to turn, become.

tornasol *nm* (**a**) (*Bot*) sunflower. (**b**) (*Chem*) litmus; **papel de —** litmus paper. (**c**) (*fig*) sheen, iridescence.

tornasolado *adj* iridescent, sheeny; full of different lights; *fabric* shot.

tornasolar [1a] **1** *vt* to make iridescent, put a sheen on. **2 tornasolarse** *vr* to be (*or* become) iridescent, show different lights.

tornavía *nf* (*Rail*) turntable.

tornavoz *nf* baffle; sounding board; (*of pulpit*) canopy; **hacer —** to cup one's hands to one's mouth.

torneado *adj* (**a**) (*Tech*) turned (on a lathe). (**b**) *arm etc* shapely, delicately curved; pleasingly rounded.

tornear [1a] *vt* to turn (on a lathe).

torneo *nm* tournament, competition; (*Hist*) tourney, joust; **— de tenis** tennis tournament; **— por equipos** team tournament.

tornero *nm* machinist, turner, lathe operator.

tornillo *nm* (**a**) screw; bolt; **— de banco** vice, vise (*US*), clamp; **— sin fin** worm gear; **apretar los —s a uno** to apply pressure on someone, put the screws on someone; **le falta un —** (*fam*) he has a screw loose (*fam*). (**b**) (*Mil*) **hacer —** to desert.

torniquete *nm* (**a**) turnstile. (**b**) (*Med*) tourniquet.

torniscón *nm* (**a**) pinch, squeeze. (**b**) slap on the face; smack on the head, cuff.

torno *nm* (**a**) (*Tech*) winch, windlass; drum; winding machine. (**b**) (*Tech*) lathe; **— de banco** vice, vise (*US*), clamp; **— de tornero** turning lathe; **labrar a —** to turn on the lathe. (**c**) (*Tech*) **— de alfarero** potter's wheel; **— de asador** spit; **— de hilar** spinning wheel. (**d**) revolving door. (**e**) (*of cart etc*) brake. (**f**) (*of river*) bend; race, rapids. (**g**) **en —** a round, about; **se reunieron en — suyo** they gathered round him; **todo estaba inundado en muchos kilómetros en —** for many miles all round everything was flooded; **en — a este tema** on this theme, about this subject; **polemizar en — a un texto** to argue about a text.

toro nm (a) (Zool) bull; — **bravo**, — **de lidia** fighting bull; **coger el** — **por los cuernos, irse a la cabeza del** — to take the bull by the horns; **echar** (or **soltar**) **el** — **a uno** to give someone a severe dressing-down. (b) (fig) strong man, he-man (fam); solidly-built man; tough guy (fam); **ser** — **corrido** to be an old hand at it, be an old fox. (c) **los** —**s** bullfight; (art of) bullfighting; **los** —**s cuestan más cada año** the bullfighting business grows more expensive each year; **este año no habrá** —**s** there will be no bullfight this year; **ir a los** —**s, ir de** —**s** to go to the bullfight; **no me gustan los** —**s** I don't like bullfighting; **ciertos son los** —**s** it turns out that it's true; **ver los** —**s desde la barrera** to be able to take an independent view, remain uncommitted; to sit on the fence. (d) **hacer** —**s** (fam) to play truant, cut class.

torombolo adj (Cu) plump, potbellied.

toronja nf grapefruit.

toronjil nm balm.

toronjo nm grapefruit tree.

torpe adj (a) person clumsy, awkward; slow, ungainly; movement slow, sluggish, heavy. (b) handle, key etc stiff. (c) person (mentally) dense, dim, slow-witted. (d) (fig) morally vile; dishonest, dishonourable. (e) (fig) crude, obscene.

torpear [1a] vi (Chi) to be dishonest, behave dishonourably.

torpedear [1a] vt to torpedo (also fig).

torpedero nm torpedo boat.

torpedo nm torpedo.

torpemente adv (a) clumsily, awkwardly; slowly, sluggishly, heavily. (b) stiffly. (c) slow-wittedly. (d) (fig) vilely, dishonestly. (e) (fig) crudely, obscenely.

torpeza nf (a) clumsiness, awkwardness; slowness, ungainliness; sluggishness, heaviness. (b) stiffness. (c) denseness, dimness, slowness of wit. (d) (fig) moral vileness; dishonesty. (e) (fig) crudeness, obscenity. (f) (una —) mistake, error of taste, lack of tact; **fue una** — **más** it was yet another instance of tastelessness.

torpón adj (Chi) = **torpe**.

torrados nmpl toasted chickpeas.

torrar [1a] vt to toast, roast.

torre nf (a) (Archit etc) tower; (Radio, TV etc) mast, tower, (of oil well) derrick; **T— de Babel** Tower of Babel; — **de conducción eléctrica** electricity pylon; — **de control** (Aer) control tower; — **del homenaje** keep; — **de marfil** ivory tower; — **de refrigeración** cooling tower; — **de vigía** (Naut) crow's-nest. (b) (Chess) rook, castle. (c) (Aer, Mil, Naut) turret; (Mil) watchtower; — **de mando** conning tower. (d) (Ant, Mex) factory chimney.

torrefacción nf toasting, roasting.

torrefacto adj toasted, roasted.

torreja nf (SAm) (fried) slices of fruit and vegetables; (Chi) slice of fruit.

torrencial adj torrential.

torrente nm (a) rushing stream, mountain stream, torrent; **llover a** —**s** to rain cats and dogs, rain in torrents. (b) (Anat: also — **de sangre**) bloodstream. (c) (fig) stream, torrent, rush, flood; onrush; — **de palabras** torrent of words, rush of words; — **de voz** loud strong voice.

torrentera nf gully, watercourse.

torrentoso adj (SAm) torrential, rushing.

torreón nm tower; (Archit) turret.

torrero nm lighthouse keeper.

torreta nf (a) (Aer, Mil, Naut) turret; (of submarine) conning tower. (b) (Elec) pylon, mast.

torrezno nm rasher, slice of bacon.

tórrido adj torrid.

torrificar [1g] vt (Mex) to toast, roast.

torrija nf slice of fried bread.

torsión nf twist(ing); warp(ing); (Mech) torsion, torque.

torsional adj torsional.

torso nm (Anat) torso; (Art) head and shoulder; (Sculpture) bust.

torta nf (a) cake; tart, flan; (fig) cake, flat mass, round lump; **la** — **costó un pan** it worked out dearer than expected, (fig) it was more trouble than it was worth; **eso es** —**s y pan pintado** it's child's play, it's

a cinch (sl); **no entendió ni** — he didn't understand a word of it. (b) (CAm, Mex; also — **de huevos**) omelet(te). (c) (Typ) fount. (d) (fam) slap, punch, sock (fam).

tortazo nm (fam) slap, punch, sock (fam).

tortear [1a] **1** vt (Chi) dough to flatten, roll; (CAm, Mex) pancake to shape (with the palms of one's hands). **2** vi (Mex) to clap, applaud.

tortero adj (Bol, Par) round and flat, disc-shaped.

tortícolis nm, **torticolis** nm crick in the neck, stiff neck.

tortilla nf (a) omelet(te); — **a la española**, — **de patatas** Spanish potato omelette; **cambiar** (or **volver**) **la** — **a uno** to turn the tables on someone; **se le volvió la** — it came out all wrong for him, his luck let him down; **se ha vuelto la** — now the boot is on the other foot; **hacer algo una** — to smash something up; **hacer a uno una** — to beat someone up; **van a hacer el negocio una** — they're sure to mess the deal up. (b) (CAm, Mex) flat maize pancake, tortilla. (c) (tabu) lesbian intercourse.

tortillera nf (a) (CAm, Mex) nf woman who sells maize pancakes. (b) (tabu) lesbian.

tortita nf pancake.

tórtola nf turtledove.

tortoleo nm (Mex) billing and cooing (fig).

tórtolo nm (male) turtledove; (fam) lovebird, loverboy (fam); —**s** (fam) pair of lovers, lovebirds.

tortuga nf tortoise; — **marina** turtle.

tortuoso adj (a) winding, tortuous, full of bends. (b) (fig) devious.

tortura nf torture (also fig).

torturar [1a] vt to torture.

toruno nm (a) (CAm) stud bull; (RPl) old bull; (Chi, Ven) ox. (b) (Arg, Chi, Par) elderly but still robust man.

torvisca nf, **torvisco** nm spurge flax.

torvo adj grim, stern, fierce.

torzal nm cord, twist (of silk); (Chi, RPl) plaited rope.

tos nf cough; coughing; — **ferina** whooping cough.

toscamente adv coarsely, roughly, crudely.

Toscana: La — Tuscany.

toscano 1 adj Tuscan. **2** nm, **toscana** nf Tuscan. **3** nm (dialect) Tuscan; (Hist) Italian.

tosco adj coarse, rough, crude (also fig).

tosedera nf (CAm, Col, Ec) persistent cough.

toser [2a] **1** vt (fig) (a) **no le tose nadie, no hay quien le tosa** nobody can compete with him, he's in a class by himself. (b) **a mí no me tose nadie** I'll not stand for that, I'm not taking that from anybody. **2** vi to cough.

tosido nm (Chi, Guat, Mex) cough.

tósigo nm poison.

tosquedad nf coarseness, roughness, crudeness (also fig).

tostada nf (a) toast, piece of toast. (b) (fam) **dar una** — **a uno, pegar una** — **a uno** to have someone on, cheat someone. (c) (Arg) long boring conversation; interminable visit.

tostado 1 adj (a) (Cook) toasted. (b) colour dark brown, ochre, burnt; person, skin (also — **por el sol**) brown, tanned, sunburnt. **2** nm tan.

tostador nm toaster; roaster; — **eléctrico**, — **de pan** electric toaster.

tostadora nf toaster.

tostar [1m] **1** vt (a) bread etc to toast; coffee to roast; (Cook) to brown. (b) person, skin to tan. (c) (Chi, PR) to tan, beat. (d) to continue vigorously what one has begun. (e) (Mex) to offend; to harm, hurt; to kill. **2 tostarse** vr (also — **al sol**) to tan, brown, get brown.

tostón nm (a) (Cook) small cube of toast, crouton; toast dipped in oil; toasted chickpea. (b) (Cook) roast sucking-pig. (c) (Cook) piece of bread (etc) toasted too much. (d) (fam) bore, boring thing; long boring speech, tedious tale; **dar el** — to be a bore, get on everybody's nerves. (e) (fam) bad play (or film etc), dreadful piece of work. (f) (Ant, Ven) slice of fried green banana. (g) (Mex) 50-cent piece.

tostonear [1a] vti (Mex) to sell at bargain prices.

total 1 adj total; whole, complete; utter, sheer; anaesthetic general; **una revisión** — **de su teoría** a

complete revision of his theory; **ha sido una calamidad** — it was an utter disaster.
2 adv in short, all in all; and so; when all is said and done; — **que . . .** to cut a long story short . . ., the upshot of it all was that . . .; —, **usted manda** well, you're the boss, after all; — **que no fuimos so** we didn't go after all.
3 nm **(a)** (Math) total, sum; whole; **el — de la población** the whole (of the) population; **en** — in all.
(b) en — (fig) = 2.
totalidad nf whole; totality; **en su** — as a whole, in its entirety; **la — de los obreros** all the workers; **la — de la población** the whole (of the) population; **pero el hombre en su — se nos escapa** but the whole man eludes us.
totalista adj complete, thoroughgoing.
totalitario adj totalitarian.
totalitarismo nm totalitarianism.
totalizador nm totalizator.
totalizar [1f] **1** vt to totalize, add up. **2** vi to add up to; to come to, amount to.
totalmente adv totally, wholly, completely.
totazo nm **(a)** (Col) bursting, explosion. **(b)** (Col, Cu) bang on the head; (Ven) blow.
totear [1a] **1** vi (Col, Ven) to burst, explode. **2 totearse** vr (Col, Ven) to burst; to crack, split.
tótem nm, pl **tótems** totem.
totémico adj totemic.
totemismo nm worship of totems.
totora nf (SAm) reed.
totoreco adj (CAm) stupid.
totovía nf woodlark.
totuma nf **(a)** (Col, SD, Ven) gourd, calabash. **(b)** (Chi) bump, bruise; abscess; bump on the back. **(c)** (Per, Ven) head.
totumo nm **(a)** (Col, Ec, Per, Ven) calabash tree. **(b)** (Chi) bump on the head; bump on the back.
tóxico 1 adj toxic, poisonous. **2** nm poison.
toxicología nf toxicology.
toxicológico adj toxicological.
toxicólogo nm toxicologist.
toxicomanía nf drug addiction.
toxicómano 1 adj addicted to drugs. **2** nm, **toxicómana** nf drug addict.
toxina nf toxin.
tozudez nf obstinacy.
tozudo adj obstinate.
traba nf **(a)** (general sense) bond, tie; (of table etc) crosspiece; (Mech) lock; (on horse) hobble; (on prisoner) fetter, shackle.
(b) (fig) bond, link, tie; (pej) hindrance, obstacle; —**s** trammels, shackles; **desembarazado de —s** free, unrestrained; **poner —s a** to shackle; to restrain, check; **ponerse —s** to place restrictions on oneself, limit one's own freedom to act.
(c) (Cu, Mex) cockfight; cockpit.
trabacuenta nm mistake; **andar con —s** to be engaged in endless controversies.
trabado adj **(a)** joined; linked; speech etc coherent, well constructed. **(b)** (fig) strong, tough. **(c)** (Col) cross-eyed. **(d)** (Mex) stammering.
trabajado adj **(a)** person worn out, weary from overwork. **(b)** carefully worked, elaborately fashioned; (pej) forced, strained, artificial.
trabajador 1 adj hard-working, industrious. **2** nm worker, workman; labourer; (Pol) worker; — **eventual** casual worker; — **portuario** docker.
trabajar [1a] **1** vt **(a)** land to work, till; material, wood etc to work; dough to knead; ingredients to mix, stir, work in.
(b) subject, study to work at, work on; aspect, detail to give special attention to, to bring out; deal, project etc to work at, carry forward, pursue, follow up; (Comm) goods to run a line in, deal particularly with, handle; **estoy trabajando el latín** I am working away at Latin; **es mi colega quien trabaja esos géneros** it is my colleague who handles that line; **el pintor ha trabajado muy bien los árboles** the painter has taken special care over the trees.
(c) horse to train.
(d) person to work, drive, push.
(e) person (fig) to work on, get to work on, persuade; **trabaja a su tía para sacarle los ahorros** he's working on his aunt in order to get hold of her savings.
(f) mind etc to trouble, bother.
2 vi **(a)** to work (de as; en in, at); — **mucho** to work hard; — **más** to work harder; — **como un buey** (etc) to work like a Trojan; — **por horas** to be paid by the hour; to work part-time; — **a ritmo lento** (of workers) to go slow; — **por** + infin to

strive to + infin; **hacer** — money etc to put to good use, make work; water power, resources etc to harness.
(b) (fig) — **con uno para que** + subj to work on someone to + infin, persuade someone to + infin.
(c) (fig: of process, time etc) to work, operate; **el tiempo trabaja a nuestro favor** time is working for us.
(d) (fig: of soil, tree etc) to bear, produce, yield.
trabajo nm **(a)** (in general) work; (Mech) work; (un —) job, task; (Art, Lit etc) work, piece of work; — **de campo**, — **en el propio campo** fieldwork; — **a destajo** piecework; — **en equipo** teamwork; — **excesivo**, — **intenso** overwork; —**s forzados** hard labour; — **intelectual** brainwork; — **manual** manual labour; —**s manuales** (School etc) handicraft; — **nocturno** night work; — **por turno** shift work; **ropa de** — working clothes; **los sin** — the unemployed; **estar sin** — to be out of a job, be unemployed; **hacer — lento** to go slow; **ir al** — to go to work.
(b) (Pol) labour; the workers, the working class.
(c) (fig) effort, labour; trouble; —**s** troubles, difficulties, hardships; **ahorrarse el** — to save oneself the trouble; **tomarse el — de** + infin to take the trouble to + infin; **lo hizo con mucho** — he did it after a lot of trouble, it took him a lot of effort to do it; **le cuesta** — + infin he finds it hard to + infin, it is difficult for him to + infin; **dar** — to cause trouble; — **te doy**, — **te mando** it's no easy task, it's a tough job; **tener — de sobra para poder** + infin to have one's work cut out to + infin.
trabajosamente adv laboriously; painfully.
trabajoso adj **(a)** hard, laborious; painful.
(b) (Med) pale, sickly.
(c) (Arg, Mex) exacting, demanding; wily.
(d) (Col) unhelpful; bad-tempered.
(e) (Chi) annoying.
trabalenguas nm, pl **trabalenguas** tongue twister.
trabar [1a] **1** vt **(a)** to join, unite, link.
(b) to seize; to lay hold of, catch, grasp; to tie down; to shackle, fetter; (Mech) to lock, fasten; to jam; horse to hobble.
(c) (Cook etc) to thicken.
(d) saw to set.
(e) (fig) conversation, discussion etc to start (up); battle to join, engage in; friendship to strike up.
(f) (fig) to impede, hinder, obstruct.
(g) (Cu, Guat) to deceive.
2 vi (of plant) to take, strike; (of anchor etc) to grip, hold.
3 trabarse vr **(a)** (in rope etc) to get entangled, get tangled up; (of mechanism) to lock, jam; to seize up; **se le traba la lengua** he gets tongue-tied, he stammers.
(b) (SAm) to get tongue-tied, stammer.
(c) (also — **de palabras**) to get involved in an argument; to wrangle, squabble.
(d) (Cu) to ramble, lose the thread.
trabazón nf **(a)** (Tech) joining, assembly; (fig) link, bond, (close) connection. **(b)** (of liquid) consistency; (fig) coherence.
trabilla nf small strap; clasp, belt loop; dropped stitch.
trabucar [1g] **1** vt to confuse, to jumble up, mix up, mess up; sounds, words to switch over, misplace, interchange. **2 trabucarse** vr to get all mixed up.
trabuco nm (Hist) catapult; (also — **naranjero**) blunderbuss; (prov) popgun.
traca nf string of fireworks.
trácala nf **(a)** (Ec) crowd, mob. **(b)** (Mex, PR) trick, ruse. **(c)** (Mex) trickster.
tracalada nf **(a)** (SAm) crowd; lot, mass; **una — de** a lot of. **(b)** (Mex) trick, ruse.
tracalero (Mex, PR, Ven) **1** adj tricky; sly, deceitful. **2** nm cheat, trickster.
tracamundana nf (fam) **(a)** row, rumpus (fam). **(b)** swap, exchange.
tracción nf traction; haulage; (Mech) drive, traction; — **delantera** front-wheel drive; — **trasera** rear-wheel drive; — **a las cuatro ruedas** four-wheel drive.
tracería nf tracery.
tracoma nm trachoma.
tractivo adj tractive.
tractor nm tractor; — **agrícola** agricultural tractor, farm tractor; — **de oruga** caterpillar tractor.
tractorista nmf tractor driver.
tradición nf tradition.
tradicional adj traditional.
tradicionalismo nm traditionalism.
tradicionalista 1 adj traditionalist. **2** nmf traditionalist.
tradicionalmente adv traditionally.

traducción nf translation (a into, de from); (fig) rendering, interpretation.

traducible adj translatable.

traducir [3f] 1 vt to translate (a into, de from); (fig) to render, interpret; to express. 2 **traducirse** vr: — **en** (fig) to mean in practice; to entail, result in.

traductor nm, **traductora** nf translator.

traer [2p] 1 vt (a) to bring, get, fetch; to carry; to take; ¡trae!, ¡traiga! hand it over!, give it here!; **el muchacho que trae los periódicos** the lad who brings the papers; **¿has traído el dinero?** have you brought the money?

(b) (clothing etc) to wear; (object) to wear, carry, have about one.

(c) (of magnet etc) to draw, attract, pull.

(d) (fig) to bring (about), cause; to involve; consequences to bring, have; — **consigo** to involve, entail; **nos trajo grandes perjuicios** it did us great harm, it caused a lot of trouble for us.

(e) (of newspaper etc) to carry, have, print; **este periódico no trae nada sobre el particular** this newspaper doesn't carry anything about the affair.

(f) authority, reason etc to adduce, bring forward; see **colación, cuento.**

(g) — + adj etc to have + adj, keep + adj; — **de cabeza a uno** to upset someone, bother someone; **el juego le trae perdido** gambling is his ruin; **la ausencia de noticias me trae muy inquieto** the lack of news is making me very anxious; see **frito, loco** etc.

(h) (idioms) — **a mal** — **a uno** to abuse someone, maltreat someone; to upset someone; to exasperate someone; to keep someone chasing about all over the place; — **y llevar a uno** to gossip about someone; = — **a mal** —.

2 **traerse** vr (a) — algo to have something (improper) on hand; to be planning something (disreputable); **los dos se traen algún manejo sucio** the two of them are up to something shady.

(b) — **bien** to dress well; to behave properly; — **mal** to dress shabbily; to behave badly.

(c) —**las** to be annoying; to be difficult, be awkward; to be excessive; **es un problema que se las trae** it's a difficult problem; **ese punto realmente se las trae** that point really is a sticky one; **hace un calor que se las trae** this heat is too much of a good thing; **tiene un padre que se las trae** she has an excessively severe father.

trafagar [1h] vi to bustle about; to be on the move, keep on the go.

tráfago nm (a) (Comm) traffic, trade. (b) drudgery, toil; routine job. (c) bustle, hustle, intense activity.

trafaguear [1a] vi (Mex) to bustle about, keep on the go.

traficante nm trader, dealer (en in).

traficar [1g] vi (a) to trade, deal (con with, en in); to buy and sell; (pej) to traffic (en in).

(b) (pej) — **con** to deal illegally in, do illegal business in.

(c) to be on the move, keep on the go; to travel a lot.

tráfico nm (a) (Comm) trade, business; (esp pej) traffic (en in); — **en narcóticos** drug traffic.

(b) (Aut, Rail etc) traffic; — **de carga** (SAm), — **de mercancías** goods traffic; — **por ferrocarril** rail traffic.

(c) (SAm) transit, passage.

tragabalas nm, pl **tragabalas** (Mex) bully, braggart.

tragaderas nfpl (a) throat, gullet.

(b) (fig) gullibility; tolerance, broad-mindedness; **tener buenas** — to be gullible, be prepared to swallow anything; to be very easy-going, be prepared to put up with a lot, be excessively tolerant.

tragadero nm throat, gullet.

tragador nm glutton; — **de leguas** (fam) great walker.

trágala nm (fam) (a) glutton, greedy sort. (b) **cantar el** — **a uno** to mock someone's authority by doing precisely what he has forbidden.

tragaldabas nmf, pl **tragaldabas** (fam) glutton, greedy sort.

tragaleguas nmf, pl **tragaleguas** (fam) quick walker, great walker.

tragaluz nm skylight.

tragallón adj (Chi) greedy.

tragamonedas nm, pl **tragamonedas** = **traga-perras.**

tragantada nf swig, mouthful.

tragantón adj (fam) greedy, gluttonous.

tragantona nf (fam) (a) blow-out (sl), slap-up meal (fam). (b) (act of) swallowing hard.

tragaperras nm, pl **tragaperras** slot machine; see **máquina, tocadiscos** etc.

tragar [1h] 1 vt (a) (general sense) to swallow; to swallow down, drink up; (pej) to bolt, devour, swallow whole (or quickly etc); to gulp down, get down.

(b) (of land etc) to absorb, soak up, drink in; see also **3.**

(c) abuse, reprimand to have to listen to; trick etc to swallow, fall for, be taken in by; **hacer** — **algo a uno** to force someone to listen to something; to force someone to swallow something, make someone believe something.

(d) **no le puedo** — I can't stand him, I can't stomach him.

2 vi (sl) to screw (tabu); to sleep around.

3 **tragarse** vr (a) to swallow; to eat, get down; **se lo tragó entero** he swallowed it whole; **el perro se ha tragado un hueso** the dog has swallowed a bone; **eso me lo trago en dos minutos** I could eat that up in a couple of minutes.

(b) (of land etc) to absorb, soak up; (of chasm, sea) to swallow up, engulf; to suck down; material, savings etc to swallow up, use up, absorb.

(c) (fig) unpleasant fact, tale etc to swallow; **se tragará todo lo que se le diga** he'll swallow whatever he's told; **ya se lo tenía tragado** he had already learned to live with the idea, he had already prepared himself for that happening.

(d) = **1 (d).**

tragasables nm, pl **tragasables** sword-swallower.

tragasantos nmf, pl **tragasantos** excessively pious person.

tragavenado nm (Col, Ven) boa constrictor.

tragedia nf tragedy.

trágicamente adv tragically.

trágico 1 adj tragic(al); **lo** — **es que . . .** the tragedy of it is that . . ., the tragic thing about it is that . . . 2 nm tragedian.

tragicomedia nf tragicomedy.

tragicómico adj tragicomic.

trago nm (a) drink, draught; swallow, mouthful, swig (fam); sip; **beber algo de un** — to drink something at a gulp; **brindar el** — **a uno** (SAm) to stand someone a drink; **echarse un** — to have a drink, have a swig; **no vendría mal un** — **de vino** a drop of wine would not come amiss.

(b) drink, drinking; (SAm) hard liquor; **ser demasiado aficionado al** — to be too fond of the drink.

(c) (fig) **mal** —, — **amargo** hard time, rough time; nasty blow; misfortune, calamity; **fue un** — **amargo** it was a cruel blow; **nos quedaba todavía el** — **más amargo** the worst of it was still to come.

(d) **hacer algo a** —s to do something bit by bit.

tragón adj greedy, gluttonous.

traguear [1a] 1 vti (CR) to drink; (Ven) to get drunk. 2 **traguearse** vr (CAm, Col, Mex) to get drunk.

traición nf treachery; (Law etc) treason; (una —) betrayal, act of treason, treacherous act; **alta** — high treason; **matar a uno a** — to kill someone treacherously; **hacer** — **a uno** to betray someone.

traicionar [1a] vt to betray (also fig).

traicionero adj treacherous.

traída nf carrying, bringing; — **de aguas** water supply.

traído 1 adj (a) worn, old, threadbare. (b) (fig) — **y llevado** well-worn, trite, hackneyed. 2 —s nmpl (Col) presents.

traidor 1 adj person treacherous; act treasonable. 2 nm traitor; betrayer; (Theat) villain, bad character.

traidora nf traitress; betrayer.

traidoramente adv treacherously, traitorously.

traiga etc see **traer.**

tráiler nm, pl **tráilers** (Cine: angl) trailer.

trailla nf (a) (Tech) scraper, leveller; (Agr) harrow. (b) (of dog) lead, leash; lash. (c) team of dogs.

traillar [1a] vt to scrape; to level; (Agr) to harrow.

trainera nf small fishing boat.

Trajano m Trajan.

traje[1] etc see **traer.**

traje[2] nm (in general) dress, costume; (man's) suit; (esp Chi, Pan, Per) woman's dress; (fig) garb, guise; — **de baño** bathing costume, swimming costume, swimsuit; — **de calle** lounge suit; **un policía en** — **de calle** a policeman in plain clothes; — **de campaña** battledress; — **de ceremonia,** — **de etiqueta** full dress; dress suit, evening dress (man's); — **de cuartel** (Mil) undress; — **espacial** spacesuit; — **hecho** ready-made suit; — (**hecho**) **a la medida** made-to-measure suit; — **de luces** bullfighter's costume; — **de malla** tights; — **de**

montar riding habit; — **de noche** evening dress (*woman's*); — **de novia** wedding dress, bridal gown; — **de paisano** civilian clothes; — **pantalón** trouser suit; — **de playa** sunsuit; — **regional** regional costume, regional dress; **cortar un — a uno** (*fig*) to gossip about someone.

trajeado *adj*: **ir bien** — to be well dressed, be well turned out; **estar — de** to be dressed in; (*hum*) to be got up in, be rigged out in; **estar bien — para la temporada** to be well equipped with clothes for the season.

trajear [1a] **1** *vt* to clothe, dress (*de* in); (*hum*) to get up, rig out (*de* in). **2 trajearse** *vr* to dress up; to provide oneself with clothes.

trajín *nm* (a) haulage, carriage, transport.
(b) (*fam*) coming and going, movement; hustle, bustle, commotion; fuss.
(c) —**es** (*fam*) affairs, (suspicious) doings, goings-on.

trajinante *nm* (a) carrier, carter; haulage contractor.
(b) (*fam*) person who indulges in a lot of useless activity.

trajinar [1a] **1** *vt* (a) to carry, cart; to transport.
(b) (*Arg, Chi*) to swindle, deceive.
(c) (*Chi*) to search.
2 *vi* to bustle about; to travel around a lot; to be on the go, keep on the move.

trajinería *nf* carriage; haulage.
trajinista *nmf* (*Arg, Chi, PR*) busybody, snooper.
tralla *nf* whipcord, whiplash; lash.
trallazo *nm* (a) crack of a whip; lash. **(b)** (*fig*) telling-off.

trama *nf* (a) (*Tech*) weft, woof. **(b)** (*fig*) connection, link; correlation. **(c)** (*fig*) plot, scheme, intrigue; (*Lit*) plot.

tramar [1a] **1** *vt* (a) (*Tech*) to weave.
(b) (*fig*) to plan, plot; to scheme for, intrigue for; *plot* to lay, hatch; **están tramando algo** they're up to something; **¿qué estarán tramando?** I wonder what they're up to?
2 tramarse *vr* (*fig*): **algo se está tramando** there's something afoot, there's something going on.

trambucar [1g] *vi* (a) (*Col, Ven*) to be shipwrecked.
(b) (*Ven*) to go out of one's mind.
trambuque *nm* (*Col*) shipwreck.
trámil *adj* (*Chi*) awkward, clumsy.
tramitación *nf* transaction; negotiation; steps, procedure; handling.
tramitar [1a] *vt* to transact; to negotiate; to proceed with, carry forward; to handle.
trámite *nm* step, stage; transaction; —**s** procedure; (*Law*) proceedings; —**s de costumbre** usual channels; —**s oficiales** official channels; **los** —**s para la obtención de un visado** the procedure for obtaining a visa; **para acortar los** —**s de costumbre lo hacemos así** in order to get it quickly through the usual procedure we do it this way.

tramo *nm* (a) section, stretch; (*of road etc*) section, length; (*of bridge*) span; (*of stairs*) flight. **(b)** (*Agr*) plot.

tramontana *nf* (a) north wind; north. **(b)** (*fig*) conceit, pride; luxury. **(c)** (*fam*) **perder la** — to lose one's head.

tramontar [1a] **1** *vi* (*of sun*) to go behind the mountains. **2 tramontarse** *vr* to escape over the mountains.

tramoya *nf* (a) (*Theat*) piece of stage machinery. **(b)** trick, scheme, swindle; concealed part, secret part (of a deal). **(c)** (*fam*) **armar una** — to kick up a fuss.

tramoyar [1a] *vt* (*Per, Ven*) to swindle.
tramoyero *adj* (*Guat, PR*) tricky, sharp.
tramoyista *nm* (a) (*Theat*) scene shifter, stagehand. **(b)** (*fig*) swindler, trickster; humbug; impostor; schemer.

trampa *nf* (a) trapdoor; hatch.
(b) (*Hunting etc*) trap; snare; (*Golf*) bunker; (*fig*) snare; catch, pitfall; — **explosiva** (*Mil*) booby trap; — **para ratas** rat-trap; **caer en la** — to fall for it, fall into the trap; **hay** — there's a catch in it; there's something fishy here; **esto es sin** — **ni cartón** this is the real thing; **este juego no tiene** — **ni cartón** there are no catches in this game.
(c) conjuring trick; **hacer** —**s** to juggle, conjure.
(d) (*fig*) trick, swindle, fraud; wangle (*fam*); hoax; (*Fin etc*) racket; **hacer** —**s** to cheat; to be on the fiddle; **hicieron una** — **con los votos** they fiddled the voting, they juggled with the votes; **hecha la ley, hecha la** — as soon as a new law is brought in someone finds a way to beat it.
(e) (*Comm*) bad debt.
(f) (*of trousers*) fly.

trampantojo *nm* (*fam*) sleight of hand, trick; (*fig*) fiddle (*fam*), cheat; underhand method.

trampear [1a] **1** *vt* to cheat, swindle. **2** *vi* (a) to cheat; to get money by false pretences. **(b)** **ir trampeando** to manage, get by; (*of dress, shoes etc*) to last out.

trampería *nf* = **tramposería**.
trampero 1 *adj* (*Guat, Mex, Par*) = **tramposo**.
2 *nm* (a) trapper. **(b)** (*Arg, Chi*) trap for birds.
trampilla *nf* (a) peephole. **(b)** trap, hatchway; (*of trousers*) fly.
trampista *nm* = **tramposo 2**.
trampolín *nm* springboard, diving board; trampoline.
tramposería *nf* crookedness; guile, deceit.
tramposo 1 *adj* crooked, tricky, swindling. **2** *nm* crook, twister (*fam*), swindler; cardsharper; (*Fin*) bad payer.

tranca *nf* (a) stick, cudgel, club. **(b)** beam, pole; (*of door, window*) bar. **(c)** = **tranquera (b)**. **(d)** (*fam*) drunken spree (*fam*), binge (*sl*); **tener una** — (*SAm*) to be drunk. **(e)** (*Arg, Par*) safety catch. **(f)** (*PR, SD*) dollar, peso. **(g) a** —**s y barrancas** with great difficulty, against many obstacles; through fire and water.

trancada *nf* stride; **en dos** —**s** in a couple of strides; (*fig*) in a couple of ticks.
trancar [1g] **1** *vt* *door, window* to bar. **2** *vi* to stride along. **3 trancarse** *vr* (a) (*Cu, Ven*) to get drunk. **(b)** (*Chi, Mex, RPl*) to be constipated.
trancazo *nm* (a) blow, bang (with a stick). **(b)** (*Med: fam*) flu (*fam*).

trance *nm* (a) (difficult) moment, (awkward) juncture, (tough) situation; critical juncture, moment of peril; — **mortal, último** —, **postrer** — last moments, dying moments; **a todo** — at all costs; **estar en** — **de muerte** to be at the point of death, be at death's door; **estar en** — **de** + *infin* to be on the point of + *ger*, be in process of + *ger*; **puesto en tal** — placed in such a situation.
(b) hypnotic state; drugged condition; (spiritualistic) trance.

tranco *nm* (a) stride, big step; **a** —**s** (*fam*) pell-mell, hastily, in a rush; **andar a** —**s** to walk with long strides, take big steps; **en dos** —**s** in a couple of strides; (*fig*) in a couple of ticks.
(b) (*Archit*) threshold.

tranquera *nf* (a) palisade, fence. **(b)** (*SAm*) large gate in a fence (*for cattle*).
tranquero *nm* (*Col, Chi, Ven*) = **tranquera (b)**.
tranquilamente *adv* calmly; peacefully; quietly.
tranquilidad *nf* stillness, calmness, tranquillity; peacefulness; quietness; freedom from anxiety; unruffled state; **dijo con toda** — he said calmly; **perder la** — to lose patience; to get worked up.
tranquilino *nm* (*SAm*) drunkard.
tranquilizador *adj* *music etc* soothing; lulling; *fact etc* reassuring.
tranquilizante 1 *adj* = **tranquilizador**. **2** *nm* (*Med*) tranquillizer.
tranquilizar [1f] **1** *vt* to calm, quieten, still; *mind* to reassure, relieve, set at ease; *person* to calm down; to reassure.
2 tranquilizarse *vr* to calm down; to stop worrying; **¡tranquilícese!** calm yourself!; don't worry!, never fear!

tranquilo *adj* (a) still, calm, tranquil; peaceful; quiet; *sea etc* calm; *mind* calm, free of worry, untroubled; *character, state* calm, unruffled; **dejar a uno** — to leave someone alone; **ir con la conciencia tranquila** to go with a clear conscience; **¡estad tranquilos!** don't worry!; **keep calm!**; **tú estáte** — **hasta que yo vuelva** you stay put till I come back, you just sit tight till I get back.
(b) (*pej*) thoughtless, unreliable, inconsiderate; **es un tío de lo más** — he's an utterly inconsiderate chap.

tranquilla *nf* (a) latch; pin. **(b)** (*in conversation*) trap, catch.
tranquillo *nm* (*fam*) knack; **coger el** — **a un problema** to get the hang of a problem, find the knack of solving a problem.
tranquiza *nf* (*Mex*) beating.
trans . . . trans . . . ; *for alternative spellings, see also* **tras . . .**
transacción *nf* (a) (*Comm etc*) transaction; deal, bargain; — **comercial** business deal. **(b)** compromise, compromise settlement; **llegar a una** — to reach a compromise.
transalpino 1 *adj* transalpine; from the other side of the Alps, (*esp*) Italian. **2** *nm*, **transalpina** *nf* person from the other side of the Alps, (*esp*) Italian.
transandino *adj* trans-Andean.

transar [1a] *vi* (*S Am*) =**transigir**.

transatlántico 1 *adj cable etc* transatlantic; *crossing* Atlantic; **los países —s** the countries on the other side of the Atlantic. **2** *nm* (*Naut*) liner.

transbordador *nm* (a) ferry; **— para coches** car ferry. (b) **puente —** transporter bridge.

transbordar [1a] **1** *vt* to transfer, move across, switch; (*Naut*) to tranship; (*across river*) to ferry across. **2** *vi and* **transbordarse** *vr* (*Rail etc*) to change.

transbordo *nm* (a) transfer; move, switch; (*Naut*) transhipment; ferrying. (b) (*Rail etc*) change; **hacer —, realizar —** to change (*en at*).

transcribir [3a; *ptp* **transcrito**] *vt* to transcribe; (*from different alphabet*) to transliterate.

transcripción *nf* transcription; transliteration.

transcurrir [3a] *vi* (a) to pass, go by, elapse; **han transcurrido 7 años** 7 years have passed.
  (b) (*of event etc*) to be, turn out; **la tarde transcurrió aburrida** the evening was boring; **las fiestas transcurren con gran alegría** the festivities are being held in a very happy atmosphere, the celebrations are turning out to be very merry.

transcurso *nm:* **— del tiempo** course of time, passing of time, lapse of time; **en el — de 8 días** in the course of a week, in the space of a week; **en el — de los años** in the course of the years.

transepto *nm* transept.

transeúnte 1 *adj* transient, transitory; *member etc* temporary. **2** *nmf* passer-by; temporary member (*or inhabitant etc*), non-resident.

transferencia *nf* transference; (*Law, Sport*) transfer; **— bancaria** banker's order; **— de crédito** credit transfer.

transferible *adj* transferable.

transferir [3i] *vt* (a) to transfer. (b) to postpone.

transfiguración *nf* transfiguration.

transfigurar [1a] *vt* to transfigure (*en into*).

transformable *adj* transformable; (*Aut*) convertible.

transformación *nf* transformation (*en into*); change, conversion (*en into*); changeover; (*Rugby*) conversion.

transformador *nm* (*Elec*) transformer.

transformar [1a] *vt* to transform (*en into*); to change, convert (*en into*).

transformismo *nm* (*Bio*) evolution, transmutation.

transformista *nmf* (*Theat*) quick-change artist(e).

tránsfuga *nm* (*Mil*) deserter; (*Pol*) turncoat.

transfundir [3a] *vt* (a) to transfuse. (b) *news etc* to tell, spread, disseminate.

transfusión *nf* transfusion; **— de sangre** blood transfusion; **hacer una — de sangre a uno** to give someone a blood transfusion.

transgredir [3a] *vti* to transgress.

transgresión *nf* transgression.

transgresor *nm*, **transgresora** *nf* transgressor.

transiberiano *adj* trans-Siberian.

transición *nf* transition (*a to, de from*); **período de —** transitional period.

transicional *adj* transitional.

transido *adj:* **— de angustia** beset with anxiety; **— de dolor** racked with pain; **— de frío** frozen to the marrow; **— de hambre** overcome with hunger.

transigencia *nf* (a) compromise; yielding. (b) accommodating attitude, spirit of compromise.

transigente *adj* accommodating, compromising; tolerant.

transigir [3c] *vi* to compromise (*con with; en cuanto a* on, about); to give way, yield, make concessions; **— en** + *infin* to agree to + *infin*; **yo no transijo con tales abusos** I cannot tolerate such abuses, I cannot compromise with such abuses; **hemos transigido con la demanda popular** we have bowed to the people's demand.

transistor *nm* transistor.

transistorizado *adj* transistorized.

transitable *adj* passable.

transitar [1a] *vi* to go, go from place to place, travel; **— por** to go along, pass along.

transitivamente *adv* transitively.

transitivo *adj* transitive.

tránsito *nm* (a) (*act*) transit, passage, movement; **"se prohíbe el —"** "no thoroughfare"; **estar de —** to be in transit, be passing through; **el — de este camino presenta dificultades** this road has its problems, the going on this road is not easy.
  (b) (*Aut etc*) movement, traffic; **— rodado** wheeled traffic, vehicular traffic; **calle de mucho — ** busy street; **horas de máximo —** rush hours, peak traffic hours.
  (c) (*to job*) move, transfer.
  (d) (*Rel*) passing, death.

(e) (*on route*) stop; stopping place; **hacer —** to make a stop.
  (f) passageway.

transitoriedad *nf* transience.

transitorio *adj* transitory; fleeting; temporary; *period etc* transitional.

translucidez *nf* translucence.

translúcido *adj* translucent.

transmarino *adj* overseas.

transmigración *nf* migration, transmigration.

transmigrar [1a] *vi* to migrate, transmigrate.

transmisible *adj* transmissible.

transmisión *nf* (a) (*act*) transmission; (*Law etc*) transfer; **— de dominio** (*Law*) transfer of ownership.
  (b) (*Mech*) transmission.
  (c) (*Elec*) transmission; (*Radio, TV*) transmission, broadcast(ing); **— en circuito** hookup; **— exterior** outside broadcast.
  (d) **—es** (*Mil*) signals (corps).

transmisor 1 *adj* transmitting; **aparato —** transmitter; **estación transmisora** transmitter. **2** *nm* transmitter.

transmisora *nf* transmitter; radio relay station.

transmitir [3a] *vti* to transmit (*a to*); (*Radio, TV*) to transmit, broadcast; *possessions* to pass on, hand down; (*Law*) to transfer (*a to*); (*Med*) *disease* to give, infect with; *germs* to carry.

transmutable *adj* transmutable.

transmutación *nf* transmutation.

transmutar [1a] *vt* to transmute (*en into*).

transparencia *nf* transparency; clarity, clearness.

transparentar [1a] **1** *vt* to reveal, allow to be seen; *emotion etc* to show, reveal, betray.
  2 *vi* to be transparent; to allow the contents (*etc*) to show through.
  3 transparentarse *vr* (a) (*glass etc*) to be transparent, be clear; (*object etc*) to show through, be able to be seen.
  (b) (*fig*) to show clearly, become perceptible; **se transparentaba su verdadera intención** his real intention became plain, his true intention was betrayed.
  (c) (*fam: clothing*) to become threadbare, show what is underneath.
  (d) (*fam: person*) to be dreadfully thin.

transparente 1 *adj* transparent; *air* clear; *garment* diaphanous, filmy; (*fig*) transparent, clear, plain. **2** *nm* curtain, blind, shade.

transpiración *nf* perspiration; (*Bot*) transpiration.

transpirar [1a] *vi* (a) to perspire; (*Bot*) to transpire; (*of liquid*) to seep through, ooze out. (b) (*fig*) to transpire, become known.

transpirenaico *adj* *route etc* trans-Pyrenean; *traffic* passing through (*or over*) the Pyrenees; **los países —s** the countries on the other side of the Pyrenees.

transponer [2r] **1** *vt* (a) to transpose; to switch over, move about, change the places of.
  (b) to transplant.
  (c) **— la esquina** to disappear round the corner.
  2 *vi* to disappear from view; to go beyond, get past; (*of sun*) to go down, go behind the mountain (*etc*).
  3 transponerse *vr* (a) to change places.
  (b) to hide, hide behind something; (*sun*) to go down, go behind the mountain (*etc*).
  (c) (*person*) to get sleepy.

transportable *adj* transportable; **fácilmente —** easily carried, easily transported.

transportación *nf* transportation.

transportador *nm* (a) (*Mech*) conveyor, transporter; **— de banda, — de correa** belt conveyor. (b) (*Math*) protractor.

transportar [1a] **1** *vt* (a) to transport; to haul, carry, take; (*Naut*) to ship; (*of cable etc*) to carry, transmit; **el avión podrá — 100 pasajeros** the plane will be able to carry 100 passengers.
  (b) *design etc* to transfer (*a to*).
  (c) (*Mus*) to transpose.
  2 transportarse *vr* (*fig*) to get carried away, be enraptured.

transporte *nm* (a) (*act*) transport; haulage, carriage; **—s** transport, transportation; (*as business*) haulage business, transport company; removals company; **Ministerio de T—s** Ministry of Transport.
  (b) (*of design etc*) transfer.
  (c) (*Naut*) transport, troopship.
  (d) (*fig*) transport, rapture, ecstasy.

transposición *nf* transposition (*also Mus*).

transustanciación *nf* transubstantiation.

transustanciar [1b] *vt* to transubstantiate.

transvasar [1a] *vt* to decant.

transversal 1 *adj* transverse, cross; oblique; **calle — cross** street; **otra calle — de la calle mayor** another street which crosses the high street. **2** *nf* cross street.

transversalmente *adv* transversely, across; obliquely.

transverso *adj* =**transversal 1**.

transvestido 1 *adj* transvestite. **2** *nm*, **transvestida** *nf* transvestite.

transvestismo *nm* transvestism.

tranvía *nm* tram, tramcar, streetcar (*US*); (*system*) tramway.

trapacear [1a] *vi* to cheat, be on the fiddle (*fam*); to run a racket; to make mischief.

trapacería *nf* racket, fiddle (*fam*), swindle; piece of gossip, malicious tale.

trapacero 1 *adj* dishonest, swindling. **2** *nm* cheat, swindler; racketeer; gossip, mischief-maker.

trapacista *nm* =**trapacero 2**.

trapajoso *adj* (**a**) *dress* shabby, ragged. (**b**) *pronunciation* defective; incorrect; *person* who talks incorrectly; who has a speech defect.

trápala 1 *nf* (**a**) clatter, noise of hooves, clip-clop, hoofbeat. (**b**) (*fam*) row, uproar, shindy. (**c**) (*fam*) swindle. **2** *nm* (*fam*) talkativeness, garrulity. **3** *nmf* (*fam*) (**a**) chatterbox. (**b**) cheat, trickster, swindler.

trapalear [1a] *vi* (**a**) (*of horse*) to clatter, beat its hooves, clip-clop; (*of person*) to clatter, go clattering along. (**b**) (*fam*) to chatter, jabber. (**c**) to fib, lie; to be on the fiddle (*fam*).

trapalero *adj* (*Cu*) =**trapalón**.

trapalón *adj* (*fam*) lying; dishonest, swindling.

trapalonear [1a] *vi* (*Arg, Chi*) = **trapalear** (**c**).

trapatiesta *nf* (*fam*) commotion, 'shindy; roughhouse (*fam*).

trapaza *nf* =**trapacería**.

trapeador *nm* (*Chi, Guat, Mex*) floor mop.

trapear [1a] *vt* (**a**) (*SAm*) *floor* to mop. (**b**) (*CAm*) to beat, tan (*fam*); (*fig*) to insult; (*fig*) to dress down.

trapecio *nm* trapeze; (*Math*) trapezium.

trapecista *nmf* trapeze artist(e).

trapería *nf* (**a**) rags; old clothes. (**b**) old-clothes shop; junk shop.

trapero *nm* ragman.

trapezoide *nm* trapezoid.

trapicar [1g] *vi* (*Chi*) to taste very hot; to sting, smart.

trapichar [1a] *vt* (*Col, Mex*) to smuggle (in); (*Cu, PR*) to deal in.

trapiche *nm* olive-oil press; sugar mill; (*Arg, Chi, Per*) orecrusher.

trapichear [1a] *vi* (**a**) to be on the fiddle (*fam*); to be mixed up in something shady; to plot, scheme. (**b**) (*Arg, Mex*) to manage to live on small-time buying and selling.

trapicheos *nmpl* (**a**) fiddles (*fam*), shady dealing; plots, schemes, tricks. (**b**) (*Arg*) small-time business. (**c**) (*Mex*) clandestine affair.

trapichero *nm* (**a**) (*SAm*) sugar-mill worker. (**b**) (*Col, PR*) busybody. (**c**) (*Arg*) shady businessman, dishonest dealer.

trapiento *adj* ragged, tattered.

trapillo: **estar de —, ir de —** to be dressed in ordinary clothes, be informally dressed; to be all dressed up to the nines.

trapío *nm* (**a**) elegant carriage, attractive way of moving; **tener buen —** to have a fine presence, carry oneself elegantly, move beautifully; (*fig*) to have real class. (**b**) (*of bull*) fine appearance.

trapisonda *nf* (**a**) row, commotion; shindy; brawl, scuffle. (**b**) swindle; monkey business, shady affair, fiddle (*fam*); intrigue; fib.

trapisondear [1a] *vi* to scheme, plot, intrigue; to fiddle (*fam*), wangle (*fam*).

trapisondista *nm* schemer, intriguer; fiddler (*fam*), wangler (*fam*).

trapito *nm* rag; **—s** (*fam*) clothes; **—s de cristianar** (*fam*) Sunday best, glad rags (*fam*).

trapo *nm* (**a**) rag; **dejar a uno hecho un —, poner a uno como un —** to give someone a dressing-down; to haul someone over the coals; (*in argument*) to flatten someone, give someone a battering; to shower abuse on someone.
(**b**) (*also — del polvo*) duster; rag, cleaning cloth.
(**c**) (*Taur: fam*) cape.
(**d**) **—s** (*woman's*) clothes, dresses; **gasta una barbaridad en —s** she spends an awful lot on clothes; **lavar los —s sucios ante el mundo entero** to wash one's dirty linen in public; **sacar los —s a relucir** to let fly, tell someone a lot of home truths.
(**e**) (*Naut*) canvas, sails; **a todo —** with all sails

set, under full sail; (*fig*) quickly; **llorar** (*etc*) **a todo — to** cry (*etc*) uncontrollably.
(**f**) **soltar el — (a llorar)** to burst into tears; **soltar el — (a reír)** to burst out laughing, collapse in helpless laughter.

traposiento *adj* (*Per*) ragged.

traposo *adj* (**a**) (*Chi, Per, PR*) ragged. (**b**) (*Chi*) = **trapajoso** (**b**). (**c**) (*Chi*) *food* tough, stringy.

traque *nm* (**a**) crack, bang. (**b**) (*tabu*) noisy fart (*tabu*).

tráquea *nf* trachea, windpipe.

traquear [1a] **1** *vti* =**traquetear**.
2 *vt* (**a**) (*Arg, CR, Mex*) to make deep tracks on. (**b**) (*PR*) *person* to take about from place to place; (*Arg*) *cattle* to switch from place to place.
(**c**) (*PR, SD*) to test, try out; to train.
3 *vi* (**a**) (*Arg*) to pass frequently, frequent a place. (**b**) (*PR*) to drink.
4 traquearse *vr* (*Ven*) to go out of one's mind.

traqueo *nm* =**traqueteo**.

traquetear [1a] **1** *vt* (**a**) *container* to shake; *chairs etc* to rattle, bang about, make a lot of noise with.
(**b**) (*fam*) to mess up, muck about with.
2 *vi* (**a**) (*of rocket etc*) to crackle, bang; (*of vehicle etc*) to rattle, jolt; (*of machine gun*) to rattle, clatter.
(**b**) (*Arg, Mex*) to bustle about, go to and fro a lot; (*Arg*) to tire oneself out at work.

traqueteo *nm* (**a**) crack, crackle, bang; rattle, rattling, jolting; clatter. (**b**) (*Col, Mex, PR*) row, din; noisy movement.

traquidazo *nm* (*Mex*) =**traquido**.

traquido *nm* (*of whip*) crack; (*of shot*) crack, bang, report.

traquinar [1a] *vi* (*PR*) =**trajinar**.

tras[1] **1** *prep* (**a**) (*place*) behind; after; **día — día** day after day; **uno — otro** one after the other; **andar — algo, estar — algo** to be looking for something, be on the track of something; **andamos — un coche que han anunciado** we're after a car which has been advertised; **correr — uno, ir — uno** to chase (after) someone.
(**b**) (*time*) after.
(**c**) **— de** + *infin* besides + *ger*, in addition to + *ger*.
2 *nm* (*fam*) bottom, backside.

tras[2] *interj* **¡—, —!** bang, bang! (*sound of knocking on door*).

tras . . . trans . . .; for alternative spellings, see also **trans . . .**

trasalcoba *nf* dressing room.

trasaltar *nm* space behind the altar.

trasbocar [1g] *vti* (*Arg, Col, Chi*) to vomit.

trasbucar [1g] *vt* (*Chi, PR*) to upset, overturn.

trasbuscar [1a] *vt* (*Chi*) to search carefully.

trascendencia *nf* (**a**) importance, significance, momentousness; far-reaching nature; implications, consequences; **encuentro sin —** casual meeting; **discusión sin —** discussion of no particular significance.
(**b**) (*Philos*) transcendence.

trascendental *adj* (**a**) important, significant, momentous; vital; far-reaching. (**b**) (*Philos*) transcendental.

trascendente *adj* =**trascendental**.

trascender [2g] *vi* (**a**) to smell (*a* of); to reek (*a* of); **el olor de la cocina trascendía hasta nosotros** the smell of the kitchen floated across to us, the kitchen smell reached as far as us; **la carne trasciende a pasada** the meat smells bad.
(**b**) **— a** (*fig*) to reek of, smack of, be suggestive of; to evoke, suggest; **en esta novela todo trasciende a romanticismo** everything in this novel smacks of romanticism; **de su gesto trasciende cierta serenidad** his expression suggests a certain calmness, a certain serenity shines through his expression.
(**c**) (*of news*) to come out, leak out; **— a** to become known to, spread to; **por fin ha trascendido la triste noticia** the sad news has come out at last; **no queremos que ello trascienda a los demás** we do not want this to be known to the others.
(**d**) (*of event, feeling etc*) to spread, have a wide effect; **— a** to reach, get across to, have an effect on; **su influencia trasciende a los países más remotos** his influence extends to the most remote countries; **— de** to go beyond, go outside of, go beyond the limits of.

trascocina *nf* scullery.

trascolar [1m] *vt* to strain.

trasconejarse [1a] *vr* (*fam*) to get lost, be misplaced.

trascordarse [1m] *vr*: **— algo** to forget something, lose all memory of something; **estar trascordado** to be completely forgotten.

trascoro nm retrochoir.

trascorral nm (a) backyard. (b) (fam) bottom.

trascuarto nm back room.

trasegar [1h and 1k] **1** vt (a) to move about, switch round; posts to reshuffle; wine etc to decant; to pour into another container (or bottle).
(b) to mix up; to upset, turn upside down.
2 vi (fam) to drink, booze.

trasera nf back, rear.

trasero 1 adj back, rear; hind; **motor —** rear-mounted engine; **rueda trasera** back wheel, rear wheel. **2** nm (a) (Anat) bottom, buttocks; (Zool) hindquarters, rump. (b) **—s** ancestors.

trasfondo nm background; (of criticism etc) undertone, undercurrent.

trasgo nm (a) goblin, imp. (b) (child) imp.

trashojar [1a] vt book to leaf through, glance through.

trashumación nf seasonal migration, move to new pastures.

trashumante adj flock migrating, on the move to new pastures; person, tribe nomadic.

trashumar [1a] vi to make the seasonal migration, move to new pastures.

trasiego nm (a) move, switch; reshuffle; decanting. (b) mixing; upset.

trasigar [1h] vt (Ec, Per) to upset, turn upside down.

trasijado adj skinny.

traslación nf (a) (Astron) movement, passage; removal. (b) copy; copying. (c) (Lit) metaphor; figurative use.

trasladar [1a] **1** vt (a) to move; to remove; person to move, change, transfer (a to).
(b) event etc to postpone (a until), move (a to); meeting to adjourn (a to).
(c) document to copy, transcribe.
(d) feelings, thoughts etc to translate; to express, interpret; to convey in a different form; **— su pensamiento al papel** to put one's thoughts on paper; **— una novela a la pantalla** to transfer a novel to the screen, interpret a novel as a film.
(e) language to translate (a into).
2 trasladarse vr to go, move (a to); to betake oneself (a to); **— a otro puesto** to move to a new job, change to a new post; **los que se trasladan a la oficina en coche** those who go to their offices by car; **después nos trasladamos al bar** later we moved to the bar.

traslado nm (a) move; removal; change, transfer.
(b) copy; (Law) notification; **dar — a uno de una orden** to give someone a copy of an order.

traslapar [1a] **1** vt to overlap. **2 traslaparse** vr to overlap.

traslapo nm overlap, overlay.

traslaticiamente adv figuratively.

traslaticio adj figurative.

traslucir [3f] **1** vt to show, reveal, betray; **dejar — algo** to hint at something, suggest something.
2 traslucirse vr (a) to be translucent, be transparent.
(b) to show through, be perceptible.
(c) (fig) to reveal itself, to be revealed; to be plain to see; **en su cara se traslucía cierto pesimismo** a certain pessimism was revealed in his expression, a certain pessimism was written on his face.
(d) (fig: news) to leak out, come to light.
(e) (fig: person) to reveal one's inmost thoughts, betray one's hidden feelings.

traslumbrar [1a] **1** vt to dazzle.
2 traslumbrarse vr (a) to be dazzled.
(b) to appear and disappear suddenly, come and go unexpectedly.

trasluz nm (a) diffused light; reflected light, glint, gleam.
(b) **mirar algo al —** to look at something against the light; **estudió el cuadro al —** he held the picture up to the light.
(c) (PR, SD) resemblance.

trasmano (a) **a —** adv out of reach; (fig) out of the way, remote.
(b) (SAm) **por —** adv secretly, stealthily; in an underhand way.

trasminante adj (Chi) cold bitter, piercing.

trasminarse [1a] vr to filter through, pass through.

trasnochada nf (a) vigil, watch; sleepless night.
(b) (Mil) night attack.
(c) last night, previous night, night before.

trasnochado adj (a) food etc stale, old; (fig) stale, obsolete, ancient; plan etc that has been too long in the preparation, that has been overtaken by events.
(b) person wan, haggard, run-down, hollow-eyed.

trasnochador 1 adj given to staying up late; **son muy —es** they turn in very late, they keep very late hours. **2** nm night-bird (fig).

trasnochar [1a] **1** vt problem to sleep on.
2 vi (a) to stay up late, go to bed late; (fig) to have a sleepless night; (fig) to have a night out, have a night on the tiles.
(b) **— en un sitio** to spend the night in a place.
3 trasnocharse vr (SAm) = 2.

trasnocheo nm staying up late; (fig) night-time revelry, living it up in the small hours (fam).

trasoír [3q] vti to mishear.

trasojado adj haggard, hollow-eyed.

traspaís nm interior, hinterland.

traspalar [1a] vt to shovel about, move with a shovel.

traspapelar [1a] **1** vt to lose, mislay, misplace.
2 traspapelarse vr to get mislaid.

traspasar [1a] **1** vt (a) (of bullet, sword etc) to pierce, penetrate, go through; to transfix; (of liquid) to go through, come through, soak through; **la bala le traspasó el pulmón** the bullet pierced his lung; **— a uno con una espada** to run someone through with a sword.
(b) (fig) to pierce; to pain, grieve mortally; **un ruido que traspasa el oído** a noise which pierces your ear, a noise which drills into your ear; **ese grito me traspasó** that yell transfixed me; **la escena me traspasó el corazón** the scene pierced me to the core.
(c) river, street etc to cross over.
(d) bounds, limit to go beyond, overstep; to transcend; **esto traspasa los límites de lo tolerable** this goes beyond the limits of what is tolerable.
(e) law to break, infringe, transgress.
(f) player, property etc to transfer; to sell, make over; (Law) to convey; **"traspaso negocio"** (advert) "business for sale".
2 traspasarse vr to go too far, overstep the mark.

traspaso nm (a) transfer, sale; (Law) conveyance.
(b) property transferred, goods (etc) sold; (Law) property being conveyed.
(c) (Fin) sale price.
(d) (fig) anguish, pain; grief.
(e) (of law) infringement, transgression.

traspatio nm (SAm) backyard.

traspié nm (a) slip, stumble; **dar un —** to slip, trip, stumble. (b) trip. (c) (fig) slip, blunder.

traspintarse [1a] vr (a) (on paper) to come through, show through. (b) (fam) to backfire, turn out all wrong.

trasplantar [1a] **1** vt (Bot, Med) to transplant.
2 trasplantarse vr to emigrate, uproot oneself.

trasplante nm (a) (Bot) transplanting. (b) (Med) transplant, transplantation.

traspontín nm (fam) bottom, backside.

trasportín nm (a) extra seat, pillion seat. (b) (fam) = **traspontín**.

traspuesta nf (a) transposition; switching, changing over; removal.
(b) (Geog) rise.
(c) flight, escape; hiding.
(d) backyard.

traspunte nm (Theat) callboy; prompter.

traspuntín nm (a) = **trasportín**. (b) = **traspontín**.

trasque conj (SAm) in addition to the fact that . . ., besides being . . .

trasquiladura nf shearing, clipping.

trasquilar [1a] vt (a) sheep to shear, clip; hair, person to crop. (b) (fam) to cut down, curtail, chop off.

trastada nf (fam) (a) stupid act, senseless act; mischief, prank; practical joke; piece of bad behaviour.
(b) dirty trick; **hacer una — a uno** to play a dirty trick on someone.

trastajo nm piece of junk.

trastazo nm bump, bang, thump.

traste[1] nm (a) (Mus) fret.
(b) **dar al — con algo** to ruin something, spoil something, mess something up; **dar al — con una fortuna** to squander a fortune; **dar al — con los planes** to ruin one's plans; **esto ha dado al — con mi paciencia** this has exhausted my patience; **ir al —** to fail, fall through, be ruined.

traste[2] nm (a) (SAm) = **trasto**. (b) (Chi, RPI) bottom, backside.

trastear [1a] **1** vt (a) (Mus) to play (well).
(b) objects to move around; to mess up, disarrange.
(c) (Taur) to play with the cape.
(d) (fig) person to direct cleverly the way one wants, lead by the nose.

(e) (*fig*) *person* to keep waiting, keep at bay, keep dangling.

(f) (*Mex*) to feel, fondle.

2 *vi* (a) to move things around; **— con, — en** to rummage among; to mess up, disarrange.

(b) (*CAm, Col*) to move house.

(c) to make bright conversation.

trastera *nf* (a) lumber room. (b) (*Mex*) cupboard.

(c) (*PR*) heap of junk.

trastería *nf* (a) lumber, junk. (b) junkshop. (c) = **trastada**.

trastero *nm* lumber room.

trastienda *nf* (a) back room (of a shop); **obtener algo por la —** to get something under the counter; (*fig*) to get something by underhand means.

(b) (*fam*) **tiene mucha —** he's a sharp one; he's a deep one, he hides a lot inside himself.

(c) (*Chi, Mex*) bottom, backside.

trasto *nm* (a) piece of furniture; household utensil; (*pej*) piece of lumber, piece of junk; old crock, old pot; **—s viejos** lumber, junk, rubbish; **tirarse los —s a la cabeza** to have a blazing row; to be at daggers drawn.

(b) (*Theat*) **—s** scenery; stage furniture, properties.

(c) (*fam*) **—s** gear, tackle; **—s de matar** weapons; **—s de pescar** fishing tackle; **coger los —s, liar los —s** to pack up and go.

(d) (*fam*) useless individual, good-for-nothing; dead loss; nuisance; unreliable person; odd type (*fam*).

trastornado *adj person* mad, crazy; *mind* unhinged.

trastornar [1a] **1** *vt* (a) to overturn, upset; to turn upside down; *objects* to mix up, jumble up, turn upside down; *order* to confuse, disturb.

(b) (*fig*) *ideas etc* to upset, confuse; *plans* to upset; *life* to disturb, disorganize; *senses* to daze, confuse; *nerves* to shatter; *public order etc* to disturb; *person* to upset, trouble, disturb; to make dizzy.

(c) (*fig*) *mind, person* to unhinge; to drive crazy, disturb mentally; **esa chica le ha trastornado** that girl has bowled him over, that girl is driving him crazy.

(d) (*fam*) to delight; **la trastornan las joyas** she's crazy about jewels, she just lives for jewels.

2 trastornarse *vr* (a) (*plan etc*) to fall through, be ruined.

(b) (*person*) to go crazy, go out of one's mind.

trastorno *nm* (a) (*act*) overturning, upsetting; mixing up, jumbling up.

(b) (*fig*) confusion, disturbance; (*Pol*) disturbance, upheaval; **los —s políticos de Eslobodia** the Slobodian political disturbances.

(c) (*Med*) upset, disorder; **— estomacal** stomach upset.

(d) **— mental** mental disorder, breakdown.

trastrocar [1g *and* 1m] *vt* (a) to switch over, change round; *order* to reverse, invert. (b) to change, transform.

trastrueco *nm*, **trastrueque** *nm* (a) switch, changeover; reversal. (b) change, transformation.

trastumbar [1a] *vt* (*Mex*) = **transponer**.

trasudar [1a] *vi* to sweat a little.

trasudor *nm* slight sweat.

trasuntar [1a] *vt* (a) to copy, transcribe. (b) to summarize.

trasunto *nm* (a) copy, transcription.

(b) (*fig*) image, likeness; second edition; **fiel —** exact likeness; faithful representation; **esto es un — en menor escala de lo que ocurrió ayer** this is a repetition on a smaller scale of what happened yesterday.

trasvasar [1a] *vt* to pour into another container, decant.

trasvase *nm* pouring, decanting.

trasvasijar [1a] *vt* (*Chi*) = **trasvasar**.

trasvolar [1m] *vt* to fly over, cross in an aeroplane.

trata *nf* (*also* **— de esclavos, — de negros**) slave trade; **— de blancas** white slave trade.

tratable *adj* (a) friendly, sociable, easy to get on with. (b) (*Chi*) passable.

tratadista *nmf* writer (of a treatise); essayist.

tratado *nm* (a) (*Comm etc*) agreement; (*Pol*) treaty, pact; **— de paz** peace treaty.

(b) (*Lit*) treatise, tract; essay; **un — de física** a treatise on physics.

tratamiento *nm* (a) (*Chem, Med, Tech etc*) treatment; (*Tech*) processing; (*of person, problem*) treatment, handling; management; **— médico** medical treatment; **— con rayos X** X-ray treatment.

(b) title, style (of address); **— de tú** familiar address (in 2nd person singular of verb); **apear el —**

a uno to drop someone's title, address someone without formality; **dar — a uno** to give someone his full title.

tratante *nm* dealer, trader (*en* in).

tratar [1a] **1** *vt* (a) (*general sense*) to treat, handle; **la tratan muy bien en esa pensión** they treat her well in that boarding house; **hay que — los libros con cuidado** books should be handled carefully; **trata a todos con poca ceremonia** he treats everyone very unceremoniously.

(b) (*Chem, Med, Tech*) to treat (*con, por* with); to process; **— a uno con un nuevo fármaco** to treat someone with a new drug.

(c) **— a uno** to have dealings with someone, have to do with someone, know someone; **le trato desde hace 6 meses** I have known him for 6 months.

(d) **— a uno de tú** to address someone as "tú" (*familiar 2nd person singular pronoun*); **¿cómo le hemos de —?** how should we address him?, what ought we to call him?; **— a uno de vago** to call someone idle.

2 *vi* (a) **— de** (*of book*) to deal with, be about, discuss; (*of meeting, persons*) to talk about, discuss; **este libro trata de las leyendas épicas** this book is about the epic legends; **ahora van a — del programa** they're going to talk about the programme now.

(b) (*Comm*) **— con** to deal in, trade in, handle.

(c) **— con** *subject etc* to have to do with, deal with; *person* to know, have dealings with, have contacts with; *enemy* to negotiate with, treat with; **el geólogo trata con rocas** the geologist deals with rocks; **no tratamos con traidores** we do not treat with traitors, there can be no negotiations with traitors; **no había tratado con personas de esa clase** I had not had dealings with people of that class.

(d) **— de + *infin*** to try to + *infin*, endeavour to + *infin*.

3 tratarse *vr* (a) (*1 person*) **— bien** to do oneself well, live well; **ahora se trata con mucho cuidado** he looks after himself very carefully now.

(b) (*2 persons*) to treat each other, behave towards each other.

(c) (*2 persons*) **se tratan de usted** they address each other as "usted" (*polite form of verb*); **¿aquí nos tratamos de tú o de usted?** are we on "tú" or "usted" terms here?; **¿cómo nos hemos de —?** how should we address each other?

(d) **— con uno** to have to do with someone, have dealings with someone.

(e) **se trata de la nueva piscina** it's about the new pool, it's a question of the new pool; **se trata de aplazarlo un mes** it's a question of putting it off for a month; **¿de qué se trata?** what's it about?; what's up?, what's the trouble?; **ahora, tratándose de Vd . . .** now, in your case . . .; **si no se trata más que de eso** if there's no more to it than that, if that's all it is.

trato *nm* (a) (*between persons*) intercourse, dealings; relationship; **— carnal, — sexual** sexual intercourse; **— doble** double-dealing, dishonesty; **entrar en —s con uno** to enter into relations (*or* negotiations) with someone; **no querer —s con uno** to want no dealings with someone; **romper el — con uno** to break off relations with someone.

(b) (*of person; also* **—s**) treatment; **malos —s** ill treatment, rough treatment, ill usage.

(c) manner; behaviour; **de fácil —** easy to get on with; **de — agradable** pleasant, affable; **— de gentes = don de gentes; tener buen —** to be easy to get on with, have a pleasant manner, be affable.

(d) (*Comm, Law*) agreement, contract; deal, bargain; (*fig*) deal; **—s** dealings; **— colectivo** collective bargaining; **— comercial** business deal; **— equitativo** fair deal, square deal; **— preferente** preferential treatment; **¡— hecho!** it's a deal!; **cerrar un —** to do a deal, strike a bargain; **hacer buenos —s a uno** to offer someone advantageous terms.

(e) (*Ling*) title, style of address; **dar a uno el — debido** to give someone his proper title.

(f) (*Mex*) market stall.

(g) (*Mex*) small business.

trauma *nm* trauma.

traumático *adj* traumatic.

traumatismo *nm* traumatism.

travelín *nm* (*Cine*) travelling.

través 1 *nm* (a) (*Archit*) crossbeam.

(b) (*Mil*) traverse; protective wall.

(c) bend, turn; slant; bias; warp.

(d) (*fig*) reverse, misfortune; upset.

2 al — *adv* across, crossways; **de —** across, crossways; obliquely; sideways; **con el sombrero puesto de —** with his hat on askew; **hubo que introducirlo de —** it had to be squeezed in sideways; **ir de —** (*Naut*) to drift off course, be blown (*etc*) to the side; **mirar de —** to squint; **mirar a uno de —** to look at someone out of the corner of one's eye, (*fig*) look askance at.

3 a — de, al — de *prep* across; over; through; **un árbol caído a — de los carriles** a tree fallen across the lines; **lo sé a — de un amigo** I know about it through a friend.

travesaño *nm* **(a)** (*Archit*) crosspiece, crossbeam; (*Sport*) crossbar.
(b) (*of bed*) bolster.
(c) (*Cu, Mex: Rail*) sleeper.

travesear [1a] *vi* **(a)** to play around; to play up, be mischievous, be naughty; (*pej*) to live a dissipated life.
(b) (*fig*) to talk wittily, sparkle. **(c)** (*Mex*) to show off one's horsemanship.

traveseo *nm* (*Mex*) display of horsemanship.

travesero 1 *adj* cross (*attr*); slanting, oblique. **2** *nm* bolster.

travesía *nf* **(a)** cross-street, short street which joins two others; road that passes through a village.
(b) (*Naut*) crossing, voyage; (*Aer*) crossing; distance travelled, distance to be crossed.
(c) (*Naut*) crosswind; (*Chi*) west wind.
(d) (*in gambling*) amount won, amount lost.
(e) (*Arg, Bol*) arid plain, desert region.

travestido *adj* disguised, in disguise.

travesura *nf* **(a)** prank, lark, piece of mischief; escapade; **son —s de niños** they're just childish pranks; **las —s de su juventud** the wild doings of his youth, the waywardness of his young days.
(b) sly trick.
(c) wit, sparkle.

traviesa *nf* **(a)** (*Archit*) tie, crossbeam, rafter.
(b) (*Rail*) sleeper.
(c) (*Min*) cross gallery.
(d) = **travesía (b)**.

travieso *adj* **(a)** *child* naughty, mischievous; *adult* restless; lively, unpredictable; (*pej*) dissolute.
(b) bright, clever, shrewd; witty.
(c) **a campo traviesa** (*adj, adv*) across country, cross-country.

trayecto *nm* **(a)** road, route, way; stretch, section; **destrozó un — de varios kilómetros** it destroyed a stretch several kilometres long; **final del —** end of the line, terminus; **recorrer un —** to cover a distance.
(b) (*by person*) journey; (*of vehicle*) run, journey; (*of bullet etc*) flight, trajectory; **comeremos durante el —** we'll eat on the journey, we'll lunch on the way.

trayectoria *nf* **(a)** trajectory, path.
(b) (*fig*) course of development, evolution, path; **la — poética de Garcilaso** Garcilaso's poetic development; **la — actual del partido** the party's present line (or course, path).

traza *nf* **(a)** (*Archit, Tech*) plan, design; layout.
(b) (*of person etc*) looks, general appearance, air; **por las —s, según las —s** from all the signs, to judge by appearances; **llevar buena —** to look well, seem impressive; (*of plan etc*) to seem promising; **llevar** (*or* **tener**) **—s de + infin** to look like + ger; **esto tiene —s de nunca acabar** this looks as though it will never end.
(c) means; (*pej*) trick, device, expedient; **darse —** to find a way, get along, manage; **darse — para hacer algo, discurrir —s para hacer algo** to contrive (schemes) to do something, look for a way of achieving something.
(d) skill, ability; **tener** (**buena**) **— para hacer algo** to be skilful at doing something; **para pianista tiene poca —** she's not much of a pianist.
(e) (*Chi*) trace, vestige; trail.

trazado 1 *adj*: **bien —** shapely, well-formed; good-looking; **mal —** ill-favoured, unattractive.
2 *nm* **(a)** (*Archit, Tech*) plan, design; layout; outline, sketch; (*of road etc*) line, route.
(b) (*fig*) lines, outline, shape, appearance.
(c) (*Bol*) machete.

trazador 1 *adj* **(a)** (*Mil, Phys*) tracer (*attr*); **bala trazadora** tracer bullet; **elemento —** tracer element.
2 *nm* **(a)** (*person*) planner, designer.
(b) (*Phys*) tracer.

trazadora *nf* tracer, tracer bullet.

trazar [1f] *vt* **(a)** (*Archit, Tech*) to plan, design; to lay out; *line etc* to draw, trace; (*Art*) to sketch, outline; *boundaries* to mark out; *course, path* to trace, plot, follow.

(b) (*fig*) line of development *etc* to lay down, mark out.
(c) (*fig: in speech etc*) to trace, describe, explain, outline.
(d) *means etc* to contrive, devise.

trazo *nm* **(a)** line, stroke; — **de lápiz** pencil stroke, pencil mark.
(b) sketch, outline; —**s** (*of face*) lines, features, cast; **de —s enérgicos** vigorous-looking; **de —s indecisos** with an indecisive look about him (*etc*).
(c) (*Art*) fold (*in drapery*).

trébede(s) *nf*, *pl* **trébedes** trivet.

trebejos *nmpl* **(a)** equipment, gear, things; — **de cocina** kitchen utensils, kitchen things.
(b) chessmen.
(c) (*fig*) old-fashioned things.

trébol *nm* **(a)** (*Bot*) clover, trefoil. **(b)** (*Archit*) trefoil. **(c)** (*Cards*) —**es** clubs.

trece *adj* thirteen; (*date*) thirteenth; **estar** (*or* **mantenerse, seguir** *etc*) **en sus —** to stand firm, stick to one's guns.

trecho *nm* **(a)** stretch; length, distance; (*of time*) while; **andar un buen —** to walk a good way, go on a good distance; **a —s** in parts, here and there; intermittently; by fits and starts; **de — en —** at intervals, every so often; **muy de — en —** very occasionally, only once in a while.
(b) (*Agr*) plot, patch.
(c) (*fam*) bit, piece, part; **he terminado ese — de punto** I've finished that bit of knitting; **queda un buen — que hacer** there's still quite a bit to do.

trefilar [1a] *vt wire* to draw (out).

trefinar [1a] *vt* to trephine.

tregua *nf* **(a)** (*Mil*) truce. **(b)** (*fig*) lull, respite, let-up; **sin —** without respite; **dar —s** (*of pain etc*) to come and go, let up from time to time; (*of matter*) not to be urgent; **no dar —** to give no respite.

treinta *adj* thirty; (*date*) thirtieth.

treintena *nf* thirty, about thirty.

trematodo *nm* (*Zool*) fluke.

tremebundo *adj* terrible, frightening; *words etc* fierce, threatening, savage.

tremedal *nm* quaking bog.

tremendamente *adv* (*fam*) tremendously (*fam*); awfully (*fam*), terrifically (*fam*).

tremendismo *nm* crudeness, coarse realism; use of realism to shock.

tremendista 1 *adj* crude, coarsely realistic. **2** *nmf* coarsely realistic writer, writer who shocks by his realism.

tremendo *adj* **(a)** terrible, dreadful, frightful.
(b) imposing, awesome.
(c) (*fam*) tremendous (*fam*); awful (*fam*), terrific (*fam*); **una roca tremenda de alta** a terrifically high rock; **le dio una tremenda paliza** he gave him a tremendous beating.
(d) (*fam*) *person* inventive, witty, entertaining; **es —, ¿eh?** isn't he a scream?, isn't he great? (*fam*).
(e) **echar la tremenda** to speak angrily; **dar** (*or* **tomar**) **algo por la tremenda** to make a great fuss about something.

trementina *nf* turpentine.

tremolar [1a] **1** *vt* **(a)** *flag* to wave. **(b)** (*fig*) to show off, flaunt. **2** *vi* to wave, flutter.

tremolina *nf* (*fam*) row, fuss, commotion; shindy; **armar una —** to start a row, make a fuss.

tremotiles *nmpl* (*Col, PR*) tools, tackle.

trémulamente *adv* tremulously; quaveringly; timidly.

trémulo *adj* quivering, tremulous; *voice* quavering; timid, small; *light etc* flickering.

tren *nm* **(a)** (*Rail*) train; — **ascendente** up train; — **botijo**, — **de excursión**, — **de recreo** excursion train; — **de cercanías** suburban train; — **correo** slow train; (*Post*) mail train; — **descendente** down train; — **directo** through train; — **expreso** fast train; — **(de) mercancías** goods train, freight train (*US*); — **mixto** passenger and goods train; — **ómnibus** stopping train, local train, accommodation train (*US*); — **de pasajeros** passenger train; — **postal** mail train; — **rápido** express (train); — **suplementario** extra train, relief train; **cambiar de —** to change trains; **coger un —, tomar un —** to catch a train; **ir en —** to go by train.
(b) baggage; outfit, equipment; — **de viaje** equipment for a journey.
(c) (*Mech*) set; set of gears (*or* wheels *etc*); — **de aterrizaje** (*Aer*) undercarriage, landing gear; — **de laminación** rolling mill.
(d) (*Mil*) convoy.
(e) — **de vida** (flamboyant *etc*) way of life, (luxurious *etc*) style of living; **vivir a todo —** to

live in style, live expensively; **no pudo sostener ese — de vida** he could not keep up that style of living.

(f) speed; **a fuerte —** at a rapid pace, fast; **ir a buen —** to go at a good speed.

(g) (*RPl*) **en — de** in process of, in the course of; **estamos en — de realizarlo** we are carrying it out; **estar en — de recuperación** to be on one's way to recovery.

(h) (*Cu*) workshop; firm, company; **— de mudanzas** removal company; **— de lavado** laundry.

(i) (*Guat, Mex*) = **trajín.**

(j) (*Mex, Urug*) tram, streetcar (*US*).

(k) (*Cu*) stupid act, foolish remark.

trena *nf* (*sl*) clink (*sl*).

trencilla *nf*, **trencillo** *nm* braid.

trenista *nm* **(a)** (*Cu*) owner of a workshop; company manager. **(b)** (*Mex*) railwayman.

Trento *m* Trent; **Concilio de —** Council of Trent.

trenza *nf* **(a)** (*of hair*) plait; pigtail, ponytail; tress; (*Sew*) braid; (*of straw etc*) plait; (*of thread*) twist; **— postiza** switch, hairpiece; **encontrar a una en —** to find someone with her hair down.

(b) (*SAm: of onions etc*) string.

(c) (*Ven*) **—s** shoelaces.

(d) (*Arg*) hand-to-hand fight.

trenzado 1 *adj* plaited; braided; twisted together, intertwined. **2** *nm* plaits.

trenzar [1f] **1** *vt hair* to plait, braid; *straw etc* to plait; *threads etc* to twist (together), intertwine, weave.

2 *vi* (*dancers*) to weave in and out; (*horse*) to caper.

3 trenzarse *vr* **(a)** (*SAm*) **— en una discusión** to get involved in an argument.

(b) (*Chi, Per, RPl*) to come to blows; to fight hand to hand.

trepa¹ 1 *nf* **(a)** climb, climbing.

(b) somersault.

(c) (*Hunting*) hide.

(d) trick, ruse, deception.

(e) (*fam*) tanning (*fam*).

2 *nmf* (*fam*) creep (*sl*); social climber.

trepa² *nf* **(a)** (*Tech*) drilling, boring. **(b)** (*Sew*) trimming. **(c)** (*in wood*) grain.

trepadera *nf* (*Cu, Mex*) climbing irons.

trepado *nm* **(a)** (*Tech*) drilling, boring. **(b)** (*of stamp etc*) perforation.

trepador 1 *adj plant* climbing, rambling.

2 *nm* **(a)** (*Bot*) climber, rambler.

(b) (*Orn*) nuthatch.

(c) **—es** climbing irons.

trepadora *nf* (*Bot*) climber, rambler.

trepanar [1a] *vt* to trepan.

trepar¹ [1a] *vti* to climb (*a* up), clamber up; to scale; (*Bot*) to climb (*por* up); **— a un avión** to climb into an aircraft; **— a un árbol** to climb (up) a tree.

trepar² [1a] *vt* **(a)** (*Tech*) to drill, bore. **(b)** (*Sew*) to trim.

trepe *nm* (*fam*) telling-off; **echar un — a uno** to tell someone off.

trepetera *nf* (*Ven*) jargon, jibberish.

trepidación *nf* shaking, vibration.

trepidar [1a] *vi* **(a)** to shake, vibrate. **(b)** (*Chi, Per, RPl*) to hesitate, waver; **— en + infin** to hesitate to + *infin*.

treque *adj* (*Ven*) witty, funny.

tres 1 *adj* three; (*date*) third; **las —** three o'clock; **como — y 2 son 5** as sure as sure can be, without a shadow of doubt; **de — al cuarto** cheap, poor-quality; **ni a la de —** on no account, not by a long shot; not by any manner of means.

2 *nm* three.

trescientos *adj* three hundred.

tresillo *nm* **(a)** three-piece suite. **(b)** (*Mus*) triplet.

tresnal *nm* shock, stack.

treso *adj* (*Mex*) dirty.

treta *nf* **(a)** (*Fencing*) feint. **(b)** (*fig*) trick; ruse, stratagem; (*Comm etc*) stunt, gimmick; **— publicitaria** advertising gimmick.

tri . . . tri . . .; three- . . .

tríada *nf* triad.

triangulación *nf* triangulation.

triangular 1 *adj* triangular; three-cornered. **2** [1a] *vt* to triangulate.

triángulo *nm* triangle (*also Mus*).

tribal *adj* tribal.

tribu *nf* tribe.

tribual *adj* tribal.

tribulación *nf* tribulation.

tribuna *nf* **(a)** (*orator's*) platform, rostrum, dais; (*at meeting*) platform.

(b) (*Sport etc*) stand, grandstand; **— de la prensa** press box.

(c) (*Eccl*) gallery; **— del órgano** organ loft.

(d) (*Law*) **— del acusado** dock; **— del jurado** jury box.

(e) (*fig*) political oratory, public speechmaking.

tribunal *nm* **(a)** (*Law*) court; (*persons*) court, bench; **— juvenil, — (tutelar) de menores** juvenile court; **T— Supremo** High Court, Supreme Court (*US*); **en pleno —** in open court; **llevar a uno ante los —es** to take someone to court.

(b) (*Pol, of inquiry etc*) tribunal.

(c) (*Univ*) board of examiners; appointments committee.

(d) (*fig*) tribunal; forum; **— de la conciencia** one's own conscience; **el — de la opinión pública** the forum of public opinion.

tribuno *nm* tribune.

tributación *nf* **(a)** payment. **(b)** taxation.

tributar [1a] *vt* **(a)** (*Fin*) to pay. **(b)** (*fig*) *homage, respect etc* to pay; *thanks* to give; *affection etc* to have, show (*a* for).

tributario 1 *adj* **(a)** (*Geog, Pol*) tributary.

(b) (*Fin*) tax (*attr*), taxation (*attr*); **privilegio —** tax concession; **sistema —** taxation, tax system.

2 *nm* tributary.

tributo *nm* **(a)** (*Hist*) tribute (*also fig*). **(b)** (*Fin*) tax.

tricentenario *nm* tercentenary.

triciclo *nm* tricycle.

tricófero *nm* (*Arg, Chi, Mex*) hair-restorer.

tricola *nf* (*RPl*) knitted waistcoat.

tricolor 1 *adj* tricolour, three-coloured; **bandera —** = **2** *nm* tricolour.

tricornio *nm* three-cornered hat.

tricotosa *nf* (*gall*) knitting machine.

trichina *nf* (*SAm*) trichina.

tridente *nm* trident.

tridentino *adj* of Trent; **Concilio T—** Council of Trent.

tridimensional *adj* three-dimensional.

trienal *adj* triennial.

trienalmente *adv* triennially.

trienio *nm* period of three years.

trifásico *adj* (*Elec*) three-phase, triphase.

triforio *nm* triforium.

trifulca *nf* (*fam*) row, shindy.

trifurcarse [1g] *vr* to divide into three.

trigal *nm* wheat field.

trigésimo *adj* thirtieth.

trigo *nm* **(a)** (*Bot*) wheat; **— candeal** bread wheat; **— sarraceno** buckwheat; **de — entero** wholemeal; **no es — limpio** (*fig*) he's dishonest.

(b) **—s** wheat, wheat field(s); **meterse en —s ajenos** to meddle in someone else's affairs; to trespass on someone else's subject (*etc*).

(c) (*sl*) dough (*sl*), brass (*sl*).

trigonometría *nf* trigonometry.

trigonométrico *adj* trigonometric(al).

trigueño *adj hair* corn-coloured, dark blonde; *skin* olive, darkish; *person* olive-skinned, (*SAm*) dark, swarthy, (*euph*) Negro.

triguero 1 *adj* wheat (*attr*). **2** *nm* **(a)** corn merchant. **(b)** corn sieve.

trilátero *adj* trilateral, three-sided.

trilingüe *adj* trilingual.

trilogía *nf* trilogy.

trilla *nf* **(a)** (*Agr*) threshing. **(b)** (*Chi, PR*) thrashing, beating. **(c)** (*Mex*) track.

trillado 1 *adj* **(a)** (*Agr*) threshed.

(b) (*fig*) *path* beaten, well-trodden.

(c) (*fig*) *subject* trite, hackneyed, well-worn; well-known; straightforward.

2 *nm* (*Cu, PR*) path, track.

trillador *nm* thresher.

trilladora *nf* threshing machine.

trilladura *nf* threshing.

trillar [1a] *vt* **(a)** (*Agr*) to thresh. **(b)** (*fig*) to frequent; to use a lot, wear out by frequent use.

trillizos *nmpl*, **trillizas** *nfpl* triplets.

trillo *nm* **(a)** threshing machine. **(b)** (*Ant, CAm*) path, track.

trillón *nm* trillion (*Brit*), quintillion (*US*).

trimestral *adj* quarterly, three-monthly; (*Univ*) termly.

trimestralmente *adv* quarterly, every three months.

trimestre *nm* **(a)** quarter, period of three months; (*Univ*) term. **(b)** (*Fin*) quarterly payment; quarter's rent (*etc*).

trinado nm (Orn) song, warble; (Mus) trill.
trinar [1a] vi (a) (Mus) to trill; (Orn) to sing, warble. (b) (fam) to fume, be angry; (Arg) to shout; **está que trina** he's hopping mad.
trinca nf (a) group of three, set of three, threesome. (b) (Arg, Ec) band, gang; faction; meeting of plotters. (c) (Cu, PR, Mex) drunkenness. (d) (Chi) marbles.
trincar[1] [1g] **1** vt (a) to tie up, tie firmly; (Naut) to lash.
  (b) to pinion, hold by the arms; (fam) to arrest, catch.
  (c) (Arg, CAm, Mex) to squeeze, press.
  2 trincarse vr (CAm, Mex): **— a** + infin to start to + infin, set about + ger.
trincar[2] [1g] vt to break up; to chop up; to tear up.
trincar[3] [1g] **1** vti to drink. **2 trincarse** vr (Cu, Mex) to get drunk.
trinco nm (Mex, PR) drunkard.
trinchador nm carving knife.
trinchante nm (a) carving knife; carving fork. (b) side table; (RPl) sideboard.
trinchar [1a] vt (a) to carve, slice, cut up. (b) (sl) to do in (sl).
trinche nm (a) (SAm) fork. (b) (Chi, Ec, Mex) side table. (c) (Mex) pitchfork.
trinchera nf (a) trench, entrenchment; (Mil) trench; (Rail) cutting; **guerra de —s** trench warfare. (b) trench coat. (c) (SAm) fence, stockade. (d) (Mex) curved knife.
trinchete nm shoemaker's knife; (Col) table knife.
trincho nm (Col) parapet; trench, ditch.
trineo nm sledge, sleigh; **— de balancín** bobsleigh; **— de perros** dog sleigh.
Trinidad nf (a) (Rel) Trinity; **t—** (fig) trio, set of three. (b) (Geog) Trinidad.
trinitaria nf pansy; (wild) heart's-ease.
trinitrotolueno nm trinitrotoluene.
trino nm (Orn) warble; trill; (Mus) trill.
trinomio **1** adj trinomial. **2** nm trinomial.
trinque nm (Per) liquor.
trinquetada nf (Cu) period of danger; (Mex, Per) period of hardship (or bad luck).
trinquete[1] nm (Mech) pawl, trip, catch; ratchet.
trinquete[2] nm (a) (Naut) foremast; foresail. (b) pelota court.
trinquete[3] nm (Mex) (a) bribe; shady deal, corrupt affair. (b) **es un — de hombre** he really is a tough guy (US fam), he's mighty strong (fam).
trinquis nm, pl **trinquis** (fam) drink, swig (fam).
trío nm trio.
tripa nf (a) (Anat) intestine, gut; **—s** (Anat) guts, insides, innards (fam); (Cook) tripe; **me duelen las —s** I have a stomach ache; **echar las —s** to retch, vomit violently; **le gruñían las —s** his tummy was rumbling (fam); **hacer de —s corazón** to pluck up courage, screw up one's courage; **llenar la — (fam)** to eat well at someone else's expense; **quitar las —s a un pez** to gut a fish; **revolver las —s a uno** (fig) to turn someone's stomach; **¡te sacaré las —s!** I'll tear your guts out!; **tener malas —s** to be cruel. (b) (fig, fam) belly, tummy (fam); (of pregnancy) bulge; **echar —** to start to get a paunch; **tener mucha —** to be fat, be paunchy. (c) (of fruit) core, seeds. (d) (Mech: fam) **—s** innards (fam), works; parts; **sacar las —s de un reloj** to take out the works of a watch. (e) (of vessel) belly, bulge. (f) (Comm, Law etc) file, dossier. (g) (Ven) inner tube, tyre.
tripartito adj tripartite.
triperío nm (Col, Mex) guts, entrails.
tripicallos nmpl (Cook) tripe.
triple **1** adj triple; threefold; of three layers (or thicknesses etc). **2** nm triple; **es el — de lo que era** it is three times what (or as big as) it was; **su casa es el — de grande que la nuestra** their house is three times bigger than ours. **3** adv (fam): **esta cuerda es — gruesa que ésa** this string is three times thicker than that bit.
triplicado adj triplicate; **por —** in triplicate.
triplicar [1g] **1** vt to treble, triple. **2 triplicarse** vr to treble, triple.
trípode nm tripod.
tripón **1** adj fat, potbellied. **2** nm, **tripona** nf (Mex) little boy, little girl.

tríptico nm (a) (Art) triptych. (b) form in three parts, three-part document.
triptongo nm triphthong.
tripudo adj fat, potbellied.
tripulación nf crew.
tripulado adj: **vuelo —** manned flight; **— por** manned by.
tripulante nm crew member, crewman; **—s** crew, men.
tripular [1a] vt (a) ship etc to man. (b) (Aut etc) to drive. (c) (Chi) to mix (up).
tripulina nf (Chi) row, brawl.
trique nm (a) crack, sharp noise, swish. (b) **a cada —** at every moment; repeatedly. (c) (Col, Mex) trick, dodge. (d) (Mex) **—s** things, gear (fam), odds and ends.
triquina nf trichina.
triquinosis nf trichinosis.
triquiñuela nf trick, dodge; **—s** dodges, funny business; **es un tío —s** (fam) he's an artful old cuss (fam); **saber las —s del oficio** to know the tricks of the trade, know all the dodges.
triquis nmpl (Mex) see **trique (d)**.
trirreme nm trireme.
tris nm (a) crack; tearing noise; pop; swish; tinkle. (b) **está en un —** it's touch and go; **estaba en un — que lo perdiera** he very nearly lost it, he was within an inch of losing it; **los dos coches evitaron el choque por un —** the two cars avoided a collision by a hair's breadth.
trisar [1a] vt (Chi) to crack; to chip.
trisca nf (a) crunch, crushing noise. (b) uproar, rumpus (fam), row. (c) (Cu) mockery; private joke.
triscar [1g] **1** vt (a) to mix, mingle; to mix up. (b) saw to set. (c) (Col, Cu) to mock, joke about; to tease. **2** vi (a) to stamp one's feet about. (b) (of lambs etc) to gambol, frisk about; (of persons) to romp, play about.
trisecar [1g] vt to trisect.
trisemanal adj triweekly.
trisemanalmente adv triweekly, thrice weekly.
trisilábico adj trisyllabic, three-syllabled.
trisílabo **1** adj trisyllabic, three-syllabled. **2** nm trisyllable.
trismo nm lockjaw.
Tristán m Tristram.
triste **1** adj (a) (of person) state sad; miserable; gloomy; sorrowful; character gloomy, melancholy; appearance, face sad-looking; **poner — a uno** to make someone sad, make someone unhappy, make someone miserable; **ponerse —** to become sad; to look sad. (b) news, story etc sad; song sad, mournful; countryside dismal, desolate, dreary; room etc gloomy, dismal. (c) (fig) sorry, sad; **hizo un — papel** he cut a sorry figure; **la — verdad es que . . .** the sorry truth is that . . .; **es — verle así** it is sad to see him like that, it grieves one to see him like that; **es — no poder ir, es — que no podamos ir** it's a pity we can't go. (d) (fam) flower etc old, withered. (e) (fam) miserable, wretched; single; **no queda sino un — penique** there's just one miserable penny left, there's just one poor little penny left; **su padre es un — vigilante** his father is just a poor old watchman; **le mató algún — campesino** some wretched peasant killed him. (f) (SAm) poor, valueless, wretched. (g) (Bol, Mex) shy, timid. **2** nm (Bol, Ec, Per, RPl) sad love song.
tristemente adv sadly; miserably; gloomily; sorrowfully; mournfully; **el — famoso lugar** the place which is well known for such unhappy reasons, the place which enjoys a sorry fame.
tristeza nf (a) sadness; misery; gloom; sorrow; gloominess, melancholy. (b) dismalness, desolation, dreariness. (c) **—s** (fam) sad news, unhappy events.
tristón adj rather sad; given to melancholy; pessimistic, gloomy.
tristura nf (SAm) sadness.
Tritón m Triton.
tritón nm (Zool) newt.
trituración nf trituration; grinding, crushing.
trituradora nf grinder, crushing machine.
triturar [1a] vt to triturate; to grind, crush, pulverize.
triunfador **1** adj triumphant; winning. **2** nm victor, winner.
triunfal adj (a) arch etc triumphal. (b) cry, smile etc triumphant.
triunfalmente adv triumphantly.

triunfante adj (a) triumphant; winning; **salir** — to come out the winner, emerge victorious. (b) jubilant, exultant.

triunfar [1a] vi (a) to triumph (de, sobre over); to win; to emerge victorious; — **de los enemigos** to triumph over one's enemies; — **en la vida** to succeed in life, make a success of one's life; — **en un concurso** to win a competition.
(b) (pej) to exult (de, sobre over).
(c) (Cards) to trump (in), play a trump.
(d) (Cards) to be trumps; **triunfan corazones** hearts are trumps.

triunfo nm (a) triumph; win, victory; success; **ha sido un verdadero** — it has been a real triumph; **fue el sexto** — **consecutivo del equipo** it was the team's sixth consecutive win.
(b) (Mus etc) hit, success; **lista de** —**s**, **lista del** — hit parade, top ten (or twenty etc).
(c) (Cards) trump; **6 sin** —**s** 6 no-trumps; **palo del** — trump suit, trumps; **tener todos los** —**s en la mano** (fig) to hold all the cards.

triunvirato nm triumvirate.

trivial adj trivial, trite, commonplace.

trivialidad nf (a) (quality) triviality, triteness.
(b) (una —) trivial matter; trite remark (etc); —**es** trivia, trivialities; **decir** —**es** to talk trivially, talk in platitudes.

trivializar [1f] vt to minimize (the importance of), play down.

trivialmente adv trivially, tritely.

triza nf bit, fragment; shred; **hacer algo** —**s** to smash something to bits; to tear something to shreds; **hacer** —**s a uno** to wear someone out; to flatten someone, crush someone; **los críticos dejaron la obra hecha** —**s** the critics pulled the play to pieces, the critics tore the play to shreds.

trizar [1f] vt to smash to bits; to tear to shreds.

trocaico adj trochaic.

trocar [1g and 1m] **1** vt (a) (Comm) to exchange, barter (por for).
(b) money to change (en into).
(c) to change (con, por for); to interchange, switch round, move about; words to exchange (con with); — **la alegría en tristeza** to change gaiety into sadness.
(d) to mix up, confuse.
(e) food to vomit.
(f) (Chi) to sell; (Per) to buy.
2 trocarse vr to change (en into); to get switched round; to get mixed up.

trocha nf (a) by-path, narrow path; short cut. (b) (SAm: Rail) gauge; — **normal** standard gauge. (c) (Col, Ven) trot. (d) (Col, Ven) portion, helping (of meat).

trochar [1a] vi (Col, Ven) to trot.

troche: a — **y moche, a trochemoche** adv run etc helter-skelter, pell-mell; scatter etc all over the place; distribute, use etc haphazardly, unsystematically, regardless of distinctions.

trofeo nm (a) trophy. (b) (fig) victory, success, triumph.

troglodita nm (a) (Hist) caveman, cave dweller, troglodyte. (b) (fig) brute, coarse person; unsociable individual, recluse. (c) (fam) glutton.

troica nf troika.

troja nf (SAm) = **troj(e)**.

troj(e) nf granary, barn.

trola[1] nf (fam) fib, lie.

trola[2] nf (Col) slice of ham; piece of raw hide; piece of loose bark.

trole nm (a) (Elec) trolley, trolley pole. (b) (Arg) trolley bus.

trolebús nm trolley bus.

trolero nm (fam) fibber, liar.

tromba nf whirlwind; — **marina** waterspout; — **terrestre** whirlwind, tornado; — **de agua** violent downpour; — **de polvo** column of dust; **pasar como una** — to go by like a whirlwind.

trombón nm (a) trombone. (b) trombonist.

trombosis nf thrombosis.

trompa 1 nf (a) (Mus) horn; — **de caza** hunting horn; **sonar la** — **marcial** to sound a warlike note, blow a martial trumpet.
(b) humming-top; whipping top.
(c) (Ent) proboscis; (Zool) trunk; (Anat: hum) snout (fam), hooter (fam); (SAm) thick lips, blubber lips.
(d) (Anat) tube, duct.
(e) (Meteorol) = **tromba**.
(f) (fam) drunkenness; **cogerse una** — to get tight.
(g) (Mex: Rail) cow catcher.
2 nm horn player.

trompada nf, **trompazo** nm (a) bump, bang; head-on collision. (b) punch, swipe.

trompeadura nf (SAm) (a) bumping, banging. (b) series of punches; beating-up.

trompear [1a] (SAm) **1** vt to bump, bang into; to collide head-on with. **2** vi (a) to spin a top. (b) = **3 trompearse** vr to exchange blows, fight.

trompeta 1 nf (a) (Mus) trumpet; bugle; (fig) clarion. (b) (Mex) drunkenness. **2** nm (a) Mus) trumpeter; bugler. (b) (fam) worthless individual, silly little man.

trompetazo nm (Mus) trumpet blast; (fig) blast, blare.

trompetear [1a] vi to play the trumpet.

trompetero nm (orchestral) trumpet player; (Mil etc) trumpeter; bugler.

trompetilla nf (a) (also — **acústica**) ear trumpet. (b) (Cu, PR) hiss, unpleasant whistle.

trompetista nm (Mex etc) trumpet player.

trompeto adj (Mex) drunk.

trompezar [1f] vi (SAm) = **tropezar**.

trompezón nm (SAm) = **tropezón**.

trompicar [1g] **1** vt (a) to trip up.
(b) — **a uno** to fiddle someone's promotion (fam), promote someone improperly.
2 vi (a) to trip up a lot, stumble repeatedly.
(b) to turn a somersault.

trompicón nm stumble, trip; **a** —**es** in fits and starts; with difficulty.

trompis nm, pl **trompis** (fam) punch, bash (fam).

trompiza nf (Ec, Mex) punch-up (fam).

trompo nm (a) spinning top; — **de música** humming-top; **ponerse como un** — (fam) to eat to bursting point. (b) (SAm) clumsy person; rotten dancer (fam).

trompón nm (a) bump, bang; hefty punch, vicious swipe. (b) = **trompo** (b). (c) (Bot: also **narciso** —) daffodil.

trompudo adj (SAm) thick-lipped, blubber-lipped.

tronada nf, **tronadera** nf (Mex) thunderstorm.

tronado adj (a) old, broken-down, useless. (b) (fam) **estar** — to be broke (fam); to be ruined.

tronamenta nf (Col, Mex) thunderstorm.

tronar [1m] **1** vt (CAm, Mex) to shoot, execute.
2 vi (a) to thunder; (of guns etc) to thunder, rumble, boom; **por lo que pueda** — just in case, to be on the safe side.
(b) (fam) to go broke (fam); to fail, be ruined.
(c) (fam) — **con uno** to fall out with someone.
(d) (fig) to rave, rage; — **contra** to fulminate against, thunder against; to storm at.

tronazón nf (CAm, Mex) thunderstorm.

troncal adj: **línea** — main line, trunk line.

troncar [1g] vt = **truncar**.

tronco nm (a) (Bot: of tree) trunk; (of plant) stem, stalk; log; (SAm) tree stump; **estar hecho un** — to be sound asleep; to be completely deprived of movement.
(b) (Anat) trunk.
(c) (Rail) main line, trunk line.
(d) (of family) stock.

troncha nf (a) (SAm) slice; chunk, piece. (b) (SAm) sinecure, soft job. (c) (Mex) soldier's rations; meagre meal.

tronchado nm (Mex: Fin) gold mine, prosperous business.

tronchar [1a] **1** vt (a) tree to bring down; to chop down, lop off; to cut up, cut off; to split, rend, smash.
(b) (fig) life to cut off, cut short; hopes etc to shatter.
(c) (fam) person to tire out.
2 troncharse vr (a) (tree) to fall down, split.
(b) (fam) to tire oneself out.
(c) — **de risa** to split one's sides with laughing.

troncho 1 adj (Arg) maimed, crippled. **2** nm (a) (Bot) stem, stalk (of cabbage etc). (b) (Arg) piece, chunk. (c) (Col) knot, tangle.

tronera 1 nf (a) (Mil) loophole, embrasure; (Archit) small window.
(b) (Billiards) pocket.
(c) (Mex) chimney, flue.
2 nmf (fam) crazy person, harum-scarum.
3 nm (fam) rake, libertine.

tronido nm thunderclap; loud report, bang, detonation; boom; —**s** thunder, booming.

tronío nm lavish expenditure, extravagance.

trono nm throne; (fig: freq) crown; **heredar el** — to inherit the crown; **subir al** — to ascend the throne, come to the throne; **nuestra lealtad al** — our loyalty to the crown.

tronzar [1f] vt (a) to cut up; to split, rend, smash.
(b) (Sew) to pleat. (c) (fam) person to tire out.

tropa nf (a) troop, body, crowd; (pej) troop, mob.
(b) (Mil) army, military; —s troops; —s de asalto storm troops; ser de — (fam) to be in the army, be a soldier.
(c) (Mil) men, rank and file, ordinary soldiers.
(d) (SAm: Agr) flock, herd.
(e) (RPl) convoy of carts; stream of vehicles; line of cars.
(f) (CAm, Cu, Mex) ill-bred person; rake, libertine.

tropel nm (a) mob, crowd, throng. (b) jumble, mess, litter. (c) rush, haste; acudir (etc) en — to come in a mad rush, all rush together, come thronging in confusion.

tropelía nf (a) = tropel (c). (b) outrage, abuse of authority, violent act; cometer una — to commit an outrage.

tropero nm (a) (RPl) cowboy; carter. (b) (Mex) ill-bred person.

tropezar [1f and 1k] 1 vt = vi (b).
2 vi (a) to trip, stumble (con, contra, en on, over); — con to run into, run up against.
(b) (fig) — con uno to run into someone, bump into someone; — con algo to run across something.
(c) (fig) — con una dificultad to run into a difficulty, run up against a difficulty.
(d) (fig) — con uno to have an argument with someone; to fall out with someone.
(e) (fig) to slip up, blunder; (morally) to slip, fall.
3 tropezarse vr to run into each other.

tropezón nm (a) trip, stumble; dar un — to trip, stumble; proceder a —es to proceed by fits and starts; hablar a —es to talk jerkily, talk falteringly.
(b) (fig) slip, blunder; (moral) slip, lapse.
(c) (Cook: fam) small piece of meat (added to soup etc).

tropical adj (a) tropical. (b) (Arg) rhetorical, melodramatic, highly-coloured.

tropicalismo nm (Arg) rhetoric, melodramatic style, excessive colourfulness.

trópico nm (a) tropic; —s tropics; — de Cáncer Tropic of Cancer; — de Capricornio Tropic of Capricorn.
(b) (Col, Cu, PR) —s hardships, difficulties; pasar los —s to suffer hardships.

tropiezo nm (a) slip, blunder; moral lapse. (b) misfortune, mishap, setback; disappointment in love. (c) obstacle, snag; stumbling block. (d) quarrel; tiff, argument.

tropilla nf (RPl) drove, flock, herd.

tropo nm trope, figure of speech.

troquel nm (Tech) die.

troqueo nm trochee.

trotamundos nm, pl trotamundos globetrotter.

trotar [1a] vi (a) to trot. (b) (fam) to travel about, chase around here and there; to hustle.

trote nm (a) trot; — cochinero, — de perro jog-trot; ir al — to trot, go at a trot; irse al — to go off in a great rush.
(b) (fam) travelling, chasing around; bustle; yo ya no estoy para esos —s I can't go chasing around like that any more; tomar el — to dash off.
(c) de mucho — garment tough, hard-wearing; chaqueta para todo — a jacket for everyday use, a jacket for ordinary wear.
(d) (fam) —s shady affair, dark doings; meterse en malos —s to get mixed up in something improper.
(e) (fam) —s hardships; andar en malos —s to have a rough time of it, suffer hardships.

trovador nm troubadour.

Troya Troy; aquí fue — and now this is all you see, now there's nothing but ruins; ¡aquí fue —! (fam) you should have heard the fuss!; ¡arda —! press on regardless! (fam), never mind the consequences!

troyano 1 adj Trojan. 2 nm, troyana nf Trojan.

troza nf log.

trozo nm (a) bit, piece; chunk; fragment; a —s in bits, piecemeal. (b) (Lit, Mus) passage; section; —s escogidos selections, selected passages.

trucaje nm (Cine) trick photography.

truco nm (a) trick, device, dodge; knack; (Cine) trick effect, piece of trick photography; arte de los —s conjuring; — de naipes card trick; — publicitario advertising stunt, publicity gimmick; el tío tiene muchos —s the fellow is up to all the dodges; coger el — to get the knack, get the hang of it, catch on; coger el — a uno to see how someone works a trick; (fig) to catch on to someone's little game.
(b) —s billiards, pool.
(c) (Bol, Chi) punch, bash (fam).

truculento adj cruel; horrifying, terrifying; full of extravagant effects.

trucha¹ nf (a) (Fish) trout; — arco iris rainbow trout; — marina sea trout. (b) (Tech) crane, derrick.

trucha² nf (CAm) stall, portable stand.

trucha³ nmf (fam) tricky individual, wily bird (sl); cheat.

truche nm (Col) toff (fam), dude (US).

truchero nm (CAm) hawker, vendor.

trucho adj (Col) sharp, rascally.

trueco nm = trueque.

trueno nm (a) (in general) thunder; (un —) clap of thunder, thunderclap; (of gun etc) bang, boom, report.
(b) (fam) wild youth, madcap; rake.
(c) (fam) — gordo finale (of firework display); (fig) big row, major scandal.
(d) (Ven) carousal, binge (sl), noisy party.
(e) (Ven) —s stout shoes.

trueque nm (a) exchange; switch; (Comm) barter; a — de in exchange for; in place of; aun a — de perderlo even at the cost of losing it. (b) (Col) —s change.

trufa nf (a) (Bot) truffle. (b) (fam) fib, story.

trufado adj stuffed with truffles.

trufar [1a] 1 vt (a) (Cook) to stuff with truffles. (b) (fam) to take in, swindle. 2 vi (fam) to fib, tell stories.

truhán nm (a) (Hist) jester, buffoon, funny man. (b) rogue, crook, swindler; mountebank.

truhanería nf (a) (Hist) buffoonery. (b) roguery, crookedness, swindling.

truhanesco adj (a) buffoonish. (b) crooked, dishonest.

truismo nm truism.

trujal nm winepress; olive-oil press.

trulla nf (a) bustle, commotion, noise. (b) crowd, throng. (c) (Col) joke, tease.

trullada nf (Cu, PR) crowd, throng.

truncado adj truncated, shortened; incomplete.

truncamiento nm (a) truncation, shortening; curtailing; cutting; mutilation. (b) truncated state.

truncar [1g] vt (a) to truncate, shorten; text etc to cut off; to cut short, curtail; speech to cut, slash; quotation to mutilate; sense to affect, upset, destroy.
(b) (fig) career, life to cut short; hopes, plans to ruin; development to stunt, check, seriously affect.

trunco adj truncated, shortened; incomplete.

truquero (SAm) 1 adj tricky. 2 nm, truquera nf trickster.

trusa nf (Ant) bathing trunks.

trust [trus] nm, pl trusts [trus] (Fin: angl) trust, cartel.

tu poss adj your; (arch, to God) thy.

tú pers pron you; (arch, to God) thou.

tualé (SAm: gall) 1 nm toilet, lavatory. 2 nf (feminine) toilet.

tubercular adj tubercular.

tubérculo nm (a) (Bot) tuber; potato. (b) (Anat, Med etc) tubercle.

tuberculosis nf tuberculosis.

tuberculoso adj tuberculous, tubercular.

tubería nf pipes, piping; tubes, tubing; pipeline.

tubo nm tube (also Anat, TV etc); pipe; (SAm: Tel) handset, earpiece; — acústico speaking tube; — capilar capillary; — de chimenea chimney pot; — de desagüe drainpipe, waste pipe; — digestivo alimentary canal; — de ensayo test tube; — de escape exhaust (pipe); — de humo chimney, flue; — de imagen television picture tube; — intestinal intestine; — de lámpara lamp glass; — lanzatorpedos torpedo tube; — de órgano organ pipe; — de radio wireless valve, tube (US); — de rayos catódicos cathode-ray tube; — de respiración breathing-tube.

tubular 1 adj tubular. 2 nm (garment) roll-on.

tucán, **tucano** nm (Arg, Ven) toucan.

tuco¹ 1 adj (SAm) maimed, limbless; lacking a finger (or hand). 2 nm (SAm) (a) (Anat) stump. (b) cripple.

tuco² nm (Arg, Bol) glow worm.

tuco³ nm, **tuca** nf (CAm) namesake.

tucucho nm (Bol) bladder; balloon.

tucura nf (Arg, Urug) locust larva; (Bol) dragonfly; praying mantis; (fig) immoral priest.

tucuso nm (Ven) hummingbird.

tudesco 1 adj German. 2 nm, tudesca nf German.

tuerca nf nut; — mariposa wingnut.

tuerce nm (CAm) misfortune, setback.

tuerto 1 adj (a) twisted, bent, crooked.
(b) one-eyed, blind in one eye.
(c) a tuertas upside-down; back to front; a

tuertas o a derechas rightly or wrongly; by hook or by crook; thoughtlessly, hastily.
2 nm, **tuerta** nf one-eyed person, person blind in one eye.
3 nm wrong, injustice.
tuesta nf (PR, SD) binge (sl); beating.
tuétano nm (a) (Anat) marrow; (Bot) pith; **hasta los —s** through and through, utterly, to the core; **enamorado hasta los —s** head over heels in love.
(b) (fig) core, essence.
tufarada nf bad smell; gust of foul smell, cloud of evil-smelling gas (etc).
tufillas nmf, pl **tufillas** (fam) bad-tempered person.
tufo[1] nm (a) vapour, gas, exhalation.
(b) (pej) bad smell, stink; body odour; bad breath; (of room etc) fug; **se le subió el — a las narices** (fig) he got very cross.
(c) **—s** (fam) swank (fam), conceit; **tener —s** to be swanky (fam), be conceited.
tufo[2] nm curl, ringlet.
tugurio nm (Agr) shepherd's hut; hovel, slum, shack; poky little room; den, joint (sl).
tuja nf (Bol) hide-and-seek.
tul nm tulle, net.
tulenco adj (CAm) splay-footed.
tulipa nf lampshade.
tulipán nm tulip.
tulipanero nm, **tulipero** nm tulip tree.
tulis nm, pl **tulis** (Mex) thief, brigand.
tullida nf (Cu) dirty trick.
tullido 1 adj crippled; paralysed, paralytic. **2** nm, **tullida** nf cripple.
tullir [3h] vt (a) to cripple, maim; to paralyse. (b) (fig) to wear out, exhaust. (c) (fig) to abuse, maltreat.
tumba[1] nf tomb, grave; **ser (como) una —** to keep one's mouth shut; **llevar a uno a la —** (euph) to carry someone off, take someone.
tumba[2] nf (a) shake, jolt; lurch.
(b) somersault.
(c) (SAm) felling of timber, clearing of ground; ground cleared for sowing; forest clearing.
(d) (Arg, Chi) boiled meat of poor quality.
tumba[3] nf (Cu, RPl) African drum.
tumbacuartillos nm, pl **tumbacuartillos** (fam) old soak (fam).
tumbacuatro nm (Cu) braggart.
tumbadero nm (a) (Ant, Mex) ground cleared for sowing. (b) (Cu, Mex) brothel.
tumbar [1a] **1** vt (a) to knock down, knock over, knock to the ground; (of wine: fam) to lay out.
(b) (tabu) to lay, screw (tabu).
(c) (Univ: sl) to plough (sl).
(d) (fam: of smell etc) to lay out, knock back (fam); (of impression etc) to amaze, stun; **su presunción tumbó a todos** his conceit amazed everybody, his conceit knocked everybody sideways (fam).
(e) (SAm) trees to fell; land to clear.
2 vi (a) to fall down.
(b) (Naut) to capsize.
(c) (fam) **un olor que tumba** a smell which knocks you back (fam); **tiene una desfachatez que tumba de espaldas** his brazenness is enough to stun you.
3 tumbarse vr (a) to lie down; to stretch out; to sprawl, loll; **estar tumbado, quedar tumbado** to lie, be lying down.
(b) (corn etc) to go flat.
(c) (fig) to give up, decide to take it easy; to let oneself go (after achieving a success etc).
tumbo nm (a) fall, tumble; (of vehicle) shake, jolt; lurch; **dar un —** to tumble; to jolt; to lurch; **dando —s** (fig) with all sorts of difficulties, despite the upsets, after a lot of setbacks.
(b) critical moment.
tumbón adj (fam) slack, lazy, bone-idle.
tumbona nf easy chair; deckchair.
tumefacción nf swelling, tumefaction.
tumescente adj tumescent.
tumido adj swollen, tumid.
tumor nm tumour, growth; **— maligno** malignant growth, cancer.
túmulo nm tumulus, barrow, burial mound; (Geog) mound.
tumulto nm turmoil, commotion, uproar, tumult; (Pol etc) riot, disturbance; **— popular** popular rising.
tumultuario adj = **tumultuoso**.
tumultuosamente adv tumultuously; (pej) riotously; rebelliously.
tumultuoso adj tumultuous; (pej) riotous, disorderly; rebellious.
tuna[1] nf (Bot) prickly pear.

tuna[2] nf (a) (Mus) student music group (guitarists and singers).
(b) (fam) loose woman, amateur prostitute.
(c) rogue's life, vagabond life; (fig) merry life; **correr la —** to have a good time, live it up (fam).
(d) (Guat, Mex) drunkenness.
tunantada nf dirty trick, villainous act.
tunante nm rogue, villain, crook; ¡—! you villain!, (to child) you young scamp!
tunantear [1a] vi to live a rogue's life, be a crook.
tunantería nf (a) (quality) villainy, crookedness. (b) (una —) villainy, dirty trick.
tunar [1a] vi to loaf, idle, bum around (US).
tunco (CAm, Mex) **1** adj maimed, crippled. **2** nm (a) cripple. (b) (Zool) pig.
tunda[1] nf shearing.
tunda[2] nf (a) beating, thrashing. (b) **darse una —** to wear oneself out.
tundir[1] [3a] vt cloth to shear; grass etc to mow, cut.
tundir[2] [3a] vt (a) to beat, thrash. (b) (fig) to exhaust, tire out.
tundra nf tundra.
tunear [1a] vi (a) to live a rogue's life. (b) to loaf, idle; to have a good time.
tunecino 1 adj Tunisian. **2** nm, **tunecina** nf Tunisian.
túnel nm tunnel; **— aerodinámico, — de pruebas aerodinámicas** wind-tunnel.
tunes nmpl (CAm, Col) first steps (of a child); **hacer —** to start to walk, take one's first steps.
Túnez m (city) Tunis; (country) Tunisia.
tungo 1 adj (Col) short, shortened; blunt. **2** nm (a) (Col) bit, chunk. (b) (Chi) neck; jowl.
tungsteno nm tungsten.
túnica nf (a) tunic; robe, gown, long dress. (b) (Anat, Bot) tunic.
túnico nm (SAm) shift, long undergarment.
tuno nm (a) (hum) rogue, villain; scamp; **el muy —** the old rogue. (b) (Mus) member of a student tuna (see **tuna**[2]).
tunoso adj (Col) prickly.
tuntún: al (buen) — adv thoughtlessly, without due calculation; trusting to luck; **juzgar al buen —** to judge hastily, jump to conclusions.
tuntuneco adj (CAm, PR) stupid and ugly.
tuñeco adj (Ven) maimed, crippled.
tupé nm (a) toupée. (b) (fam) nerve, cheek.
tupi nm (SAm) Brazilian Indian.
tupia nf (Col) dam.
tupiar [1b] vt (Col) to dam up.
tupición nf (a) (SAm) blockage, stoppage, obstruction; (Med) catarrh.
(b) (SAm) dense crowd, throng.
(c) (Bol, Mex) dense part of a forest.
(d) (Chi) **una — de cosas** a lot of things.
(e) (SAm: fig) bewilderment, confusion; embarrassment.
tupido 1 adj (a) thick, dense; impenetrable; cloth close-woven.
(b) (SAm) blocked, stopped up, obstructed.
(c) (fig) dense, dim.
(d) (Mex) common, frequent.
2 adv (Mex) perseveringly, steadily; keenly.
tupir [3a] **1** vt (a) to pack tight, press down, compact.
(b) (SAm) to block, stop up, obstruct.
2 tupirse vr (a) (fam) to stuff oneself.
(b) (SAm) to feel silly, get embarrassed.
turba[1] nf (Geog) peat, turf.
turba[2] nf crowd, throng; swarm; (pej) mob; rabble.
turbación nf (a) disturbance. (b) perturbation, worry, alarm; embarrassment; bewilderment, confusion; trepidation.
turbado adj disturbed, worried, upset; embarrassed; bewildered.
turbador adj disturbing, alarming; embarrassing.
turbal nm peat bog.
turbamulta nf mob, rabble.
turbante nm (a) turban. (b) (Mex) gourd, calabash.
turbar [1a] **1** vt (a) order, peace, reason etc to disturb.
(b) person to disturb, worry, alarm; to disconcert; to upset; to embarrass; to bewilder.
(c) water etc to stir up.
2 turbarse vr to be disturbed, get worried, become alarmed; to be embarrassed; to be bewildered, get confused, get all mixed up.
turbera nf peat bog.
turbiedad nf (a) cloudiness, thickness.
(b) dimness, mistiness; disturbance; lack of clarity, confusion.
(c) turbulence.
(d) (pej) shadiness; dubious character.
turbina nf turbine; **— de gas** gas turbine; **— a (or de) vapor** steam engine.

turbio 1 adj **(a)** water etc cloudy, thick, turbid, muddy.
(b) vision dim, misty, blurred; disturbed; language, matter unclear, confused.
    (c) (fig) period etc restless, unsettled, turbulent.
    (d) (pej) deal shady; means dubious.
2 adv: **ver** — to have disturbed vision, not see clearly.
3 —s nmpl sediment; sludge.
turbión nm **(a)** (Meteorol) heavy shower, downpour; squall. **(b)** (fig) shower, torrent; swarm; (of bullets) hail.
turbohélice 1 adj turboprop. **2** nm turboprop (aeroplane).
turbonada nf (Arg) sudden storm, squall.
turbopropulsor, turborreactor 1 adj turbojet. **2** nm turbojet (aeroplane).
turbulencia nf **(a)** turbulence; troubled nature, unsettled character; storminess.
    (b) restlessness; unruliness, rebelliousness; disorderly state, mutinous state.
turbulento adj **(a)** elements, river etc turbulent; period troubled, unsettled, turbulent; meeting stormy.
    (b) character restless; unruly, rebellious; child noisy, troublesome, unruly; army etc disorderly, mutinous.
turca nf (fam) booze-up (fam), binge (sl); **coger** (or **pillar** etc) **una** — to get sozzled (fam).
turco 1 adj Turkish. **2** nm, **turca** nf **(a)** Turk. **(b)** (SAm) Arab, Syrian, Middle Easterner; pedlar, peddler (US), hawker. **3** nm (language) Turkish.
túrdiga nf thong, strip of leather.
Turena f Touraine.
turf nm (angl) **(a)** the turf, horse-racing. **(b)** (SAm) racetrack.
turfista (SAm: angl) **1** adj horsy, fond of horseracing. **2** nm racing man.
turgencia nf turgidity.
turgente adj, **túrgido** adj turgid, swollen.
turismo nm **(a)** tourism; touring, sightseeing; tourist trade; **hacer** — to go touring (abroad), go travelling as tourists; **ahora se hace más** — **que nunca** numbers of tourists are greater now than ever; **se desarrolla mucho el** — **en Eslobodia** facilities for tourists are being much developed in Slobodia; **el** — **constituye su mayor industria** the tourist trade is their biggest industry.
    (b) (Aut) saloon car, sedan (US); tourer.
turista nmf tourist; sightseer, visitor, holidaymaker, vacacionist (US).
turístico adj tourist (attr).
turma nf **(a)** (Anat) testicle. **(b)** (Bot) truffle; (Col) potato.
turnar [1a] vi and **turnarse** vr to take (it in) turns; **ellos se turnan para usarlo** they take it in turns to use it.
turné nm (gall) tour, trip.
turno nm **(a)** rota, order (of priority).
    (b) turn; (at work) spell, period of duty; shift; (at games) turn, go; (in meeting etc) opportunity to speak; — **de día** day shift; — **de noche** night shift; **por** — in rotation, in turn; **por** —s by turns; **trabajar por** —s to work shifts; **es su** —, **es el primero en** —, **le toca el** — it's his turn (next); **esperar su** — to wait one's turn, take one's turn; **cuando le llegue el** — when her turn comes; **estar de** — to be on duty.
turolense 1 adj of Teruel. **2** nmf native (or inhabitant) of Teruel; **los** —s people of Teruel.

turón nm polecat.
turquesa nf turquoise.
turquesco adj Turkish.
turquí adj: **color** — indigo, deep blue.
Turquía nf Turkey.
turra nf (Arg) loose woman, prostitute.
turrón nm **(a)** (Cook) a kind of nougat, made of almond, honey etc. **(b)** (sl) cushy government job (sl); sinecure, political plum.
turulato adj (fam) dazed, stunned, flabbergasted; **quedó** — **con la noticia** he was stunned by the news.
tus[1] interj good dog!, here boy!
tus[2]: **sin decir** — **ni mus** without saying a word; **no decir** — **ni mus** to remain silent, say nothing.
tusa nf **(a)** (Ant, CAm, Col) cob of maize, corncob; maize husk; (Cu) cigar rolled in a maize leaf; (Chi) cornsilk.
    (b) (Chi, RPl) horse's mane.
    (c) (Chi, RPl) clipping, shearing.
    (d) (Col) pockmark.
    (e) (Ec) fright; anxiety.
    (f) (CAm, Cu, PR) whore.
    (g) (CAm, PR) **no vale ni una** — it's worthless.
    (h) (Mex) nm field mouse.
tusar [1a] vt (SAm) to cut, clip, shear; to cut roughly, cut badly.
tuse nm (Chi, RPl) = **tusa**.
tuso adj **(a)** (Col, PR) cropped, shorn. **(b)** (PR) docked, tailless. **(c)** (Col, Ven) pockmarked.
tútano nm (SAm) = **tuétano**.
tute nm a card game similar to bezique; **darse un** — to work extra hard, make a special effort.
tutear [1a] **1** vt: — **a uno** to address someone as "tú" (familiar 2nd person singular).
    2 tutearse vr: **se tutean desde siempre** they have always addressed each other as "tú", they have always been on familiar terms.
tutela nf (Law) guardianship; (fig) protection, tutelage; (fig) guidance; **bajo** — in ward; **estar bajo la** — **de** (fig) to be under the protection of; to be under the auspices of.
tutelaje nm (SAm) = **tutela**.
tutelar 1 adj tutelary; **ángel** — guardian angel. **2** [1a] vt to protect, guard; to advise, guide.
tuteo nm addressing a person as "tú", familiar usage; **se ha extendido mucho el** — the use of "tú" has greatly increased.
tutilimundi nm (SAm) everybody.
tutiplé(n): a — adv give etc freely; haphazardly, without discernment; **eat** etc hugely, to excess.
tutor nm **(a)** (Law) guardian; (Univ) tutor; — **de curso** (School) form master. **(b)** (Agr) prop, stake.
tutora nf (Law) guardian; — **de curso** (School) form mistress.
tutoría nf guardianship.
tutú nm tutu.
tutuma nf (Chi, Per) head; bump, welt; hump (on one's back).
tutumito nm (CAm, Col) idiot.
tutururuto 1 adj **(a)** (CAm, Mex, Ven) drunk. **(b)** (CAm, Col, Ec, Ven) stupid; dumbfounded, stunned. **2** nm (Chi) pimp.
tuve etc see **tener**.
tuyo adj and pron yours, of yours; (arch, to God) thy, of thine; **es** —, **es el** — it is yours; **lo** — (what is) yours, what belongs to you; **cualquier amigo** — any friend of yours; **los** —s (freq) your people, your relations, your family.
tweed [twi] nm (angl) tweed.

U

u *conj* (*used instead of* **o** *before* **o—**, **ho—**) or; **siete u ocho** seven or eight.

ualabi *nm* wallaby.

ubérrimo *adj* exceptionally fertile, marvellously productive, very rich; (*SAm*) abundant.

ubicación *nf* placing; siting; (*esp SAm*) place, position, location, situation.

ubicado *adj*: **una tienda ubicada en la calle X** a shop situated in X street.

ubicar [1g] **1** *vt* (*SAm*) (**a**) to place, put, locate, situate; to site.
(**b**) (*fig*) *person* to instal in a place (*or* post *etc*).
(**c**) (*fig*) to classify, place, judge.
2 *vi* to be, be situated, be located; to lie, stand.
3 **ubicarse** *vr* (**a**) (*SAm*) = **2**.
(**b**) (*Arg*) to get a job, find a position; to get into a good position to see.

ubicuidad *nf* ubiquity.

ubicuo *adj* ubiquitous.

ubre *nf* udder; teat.

ubrera *nf* (*Med*) thrush.

—uco *n suffix* (**a**) (*diminutive, mock-scornful*), eg **mujeruca** odd little woman; **ventanuco** useless little window.
(**b**) (*prov: diminutive*) eg **niñuco** very small boy.

Ucrania *f* Ukraine.

ucraniano, ucranio 1 *adj* Ukrainian. **2** *nm*, **ucrania** *nf*, **ucraniana** *nf* Ukrainian.

—ucho *n and adj suffix* (**a**) (*strongly pej*) **medicucho** rotten doctor (*fam*), bungling doctor; **delgaducho** terribly thin (*fam*); *see* **casucha, periodicucho** *etc*.
(**b**) (*softening*) eg **delicaducho** rather delicate; **malucho** (*Med: fam*) poorly, under the weather.

uchuvito *adj* (*Col*) drunk.

—udo *adj suffix* (*denoting a lot or excess of*), eg **bigotudo** with a big moustache, **nalgudo** big-bottomed, broad in the beam (*fam*); *see* **peludo, tripudo** *etc*.

—uelo *n and adj suffix* (*diminutive*), eg **muchachuelo** little boy; **pequeñuelo** very small, tiny; *see* **arroyuelo, ojuelos** *etc*.

uf *interj* (*tiredness, lack of air etc*) phew!; (*repugnance*) ugh!

ufanamente *adv* proudly; cheerfully; exultantly; (*pej*) conceitedly; boastfully; smugly.

ufanarse [1a] *vr* to boast; to be vain, be conceited; **— con, — de** to boast of, pride oneself on, be vain about; to glory in.

ufanía *nf* (**a**) pride; (*pej*) vanity, conceit; boastfulness.
(**b**) (*Bot*) = **lozanía**.

ufano *adj* (**a**) proud; gay, cheerful; exultant; (*pej*) vain, conceited; boastful; overweening; smug; **iba muy — en el nuevo coche** he was going along so proudly in his new car; **está muy — porque le han dado el premio** he is very proud that they have awarded him the prize.
(**b**) (*Bot*) = **lozano**.

ujier *nm* usher; doorkeeper, attendant.

—ujo *n and adj suffix* (**a**) (*diminutive*) **pequeñujo** tiny, miserably small. (**b**) (*pej*) **papelujo** wretched bit of paper.

úlcera *nf* ulcer, sore; **— de decúbito** bedsore.

ulceración *nf* ulceration.

ulcerar [1a] **1** *vt* to make sore, make a sore on, ulcerate. **2** **ulcerarse** *vr* to ulcerate; to fester.

ulceroso *adj* ulcerous; full of sores, covered with sores.

ulecear [1a] *vt* (*Chi*) dough to roll out.

ulero *nm* (*Chi*) rolling pin.

Ulises *m* Ulysses.

ulpo *nm* (*Chi, Per*) maize gruel.

ulterior *adj* (**a**) *place* farther, further. (**b**) *occasion etc* later, subsequent.

ulteriormente *adv* later, subsequently.

ultimación *nf* completion, conclusion.

últimamente *adv* (**a**) lastly, finally. (**b**) as a last resort. (**c**) recently, lately. (**d**) (*SAm*) **¡—!** well I'm damned!, that's the absolute end!

ultimar [1a] *vt* (**a**) to finish, complete, conclude; *details, preparations* to finalize; *agreement* to conclude.
(**b**) (*SAm*) to finish off, give the coup de grâce to.

ultimátum *nm*, *pl* **ultimátums** ultimatum.

último *adj* (**a**) (*in order, time*) last; latest, most recent; (*of two*) latter; **éste —, éstos —s** the latter; **el — día del mes** the last day of the month; **a —s del mes** in the latter part of the month, towards the end of the month; **las últimas noticias** the latest news; **en estos —s años** in recent years, in the last few years; **llegó el —** he arrived last, he came last, he was last; (*in race*) he came (in) last; **ser el — en** + *infin* to be the last to + *infin*; **estar a lo — de** to be nearly at the end of, have nearly finished; **estar en las últimas** (*fam*) to be about to peg out (*sl*); to be down and out, be on one's last legs, to be down to one's last little bit (of a stock *etc*); **por —** lastly, finally; **por última vez** for the last time.
(**b**) (*in place*) furthest, most remote; back; top, topmost; lowest, bottom; **en el — rincón del país** in the furthest corner of the country; **un asiento de última fila** a seat in the back row; **el equipo en última posición** the team in the lowest position, the bottom team; **viven en el — piso** they live on the top floor.
(**c**) (*fig*) final, extreme, last; utmost; **la última solución** the final solution; **el — remedio** the ultimate remedy; **en — caso** as a last resort, in the last resort.
(**d**) (*Comm*) *price* lowest, bottom; **dígame lo —, dígame el — precio** tell me what your lowest price is.
(**e**) (*fig*) *quality* finest, best, superior.
(**f**) (*fam*) **vestido a la última** dressed in the latest style; **tienen un coche que es lo —** they have the very latest thing in cars; **¡es lo —!** it's the greatest! (*fam*), it's tremendous! (*fam*); (*pej*) this is the end!; **viven en un pueblucho que es lo —** they live in a dump which is unbelievably awful (*fam*); **pedirme eso encima ya es lo —** for him to ask that of me as well really is the limit.

ultra . . . ultra . . ., extra . . .

ultracorto *adj* ultra-short.

ultraísmo *nm* revolutionary poetic movement of the 1920's (*imagist, surrealist etc*).

ultrajador *adj*, **ultrajante** *adj* outrageous; offensive; insulting.

ultrajar [1a] *vt* (**a**) to outrage; to offend; to insult, revile, abuse. (**b**) (*lit*) to spoil, to crumple, disarrange.

ultraje *nm* outrage; insult.

ultrajoso *adj* outrageous; offensive; insulting.

ultramar *nm* countries beyond the seas, foreign parts; **de —, en —** overseas; **los países de —** the overseas countries; **productos venidos de —** products from overseas, goods from abroad; **pasó 8 años en —** he spent 8 years overseas.

ultramarino 1 *adj* overseas; foreign. **2** **—s** *nmpl* (**a**) groceries, foodstuffs; **tienda de —s =** (**b**) (*fam*) **un —s** a grocer's (shop), a grocery (*US*).

ultramoderno *adj* ultramodern.

ultramontanismo *nm* ultramontanism.

ultramontano 1 *adj* ultramontane. **2** *nm* ultramontane.

ultranza: a — ** *adv* (a**) **luchar a —** to fight to the death; **lo quiere hacer a —** he wants to do it at all costs (*or* come what may, regardless of the difficulties); **paz a —** peace at any price.
(**b**) **revolucionario a —** out-and-out revolutionary, utterly uncompromising revolutionary.

ultrapotente *adj* extra powerful.
ultrarrápido *adj* extra fast.
ultrarrojo *adj* = **infrarrojo**.
ultrasónico *adj* ultrasonic.
ultratumba *nf* what lies beyond the grave; **la vida de** — life beyond the grave, life in the next world; **una voz de** — a voice from beyond the grave.
ultravioleta *adj* ultraviolet; **rayos** — ultraviolet rays.
ulular [1a] *vi* (*of animal, wind*) to howl, shriek; (*of owl*) to hoot, screech.
ululato *nm* howl, shriek; hoot, screech.
ulluco *nm* (*Ec, Per*) a potato-like tuber.
umbilical *adj* umbilical.
umbral *nm* (a) threshold; **pasar** (*or* **traspasar**) **el — de uno** to set foot in someone's house.
(b) (*fig*) threshold; first step, beginning; **estar en los —es de** to be on the threshold of, be on the verge of, be on the point of; **eso está en los —es de lo imposible** that borders (*or* verges) on the impossible.
umbralada *nf* (*Col, Chi*), **umbralado** *nm* (*Col, Chi*), **umbraladura** *nf* (*Ec*) threshold.
umbrío *adj*, **umbroso** *adj* shady.
un, una 1 *indefinite article* a, (before a vowel and silent h) an.
2 *adj* one; **la una** one o'clock; **¡a la una, a las dos, a las tres!** (*at auction*) going, going, gone!; (*in racing*) ready, steady, go!
3 *nm* one.
unánime *adj* unanimous.
unánimemente *adv* unanimously.
unanimidad *nf* unanimity; **por** — unanimously.
uncial 1 *adj* uncial. **2** *nf* uncial.
unción *nf* (a) (*Med*) anointing. (b) (*Eccl and fig*) unction.
uncir [3b] *vt* to yoke.
undécimo *adj* eleventh.
undoso *etc see* **ondoso**.
ungido *adj* anointed; **el U— del Señor** the Lord's Anointed.
ungir [3c] *vt* (a) (*Med*) to anoint, put ointment on, rub with ointment. (b) (*Eccl*) to anoint.
ungüento *nm* ointment, unguent; (*fig*) salve, balm.
ungulado 1 *adj* ungulate, hoofed. **2** *nm* ungulate, hoofed animal.
uni . . . uni . . ., one- . . .
únicamente *adv* only; solely.
unicameral *adj* (*Pol*) single-chamber.
unicelular *adj* unicellular, single-cell.
unicidad *nf* uniqueness.
único *adj* (a) only; sole, single, solitary; unique; **hijo** — only child; **sistema de partido** — one-party system, single-party system; **la única dificultad es que . . .** the only difficulty is that . . .; **es el ejemplar que existe** it is the only copy in existence; **este ejemplar es** — this specimen is unique.
(b) (*fig*) unique; unusual, extraordinary.
unicolor *adj* one-colour, all one colour.
unicornio *nm* unicorn.
unidad *nf* (a) (*quality*) unity; oneness; togetherness; — **de acción** (*Lit*) unity of action; — **de lugar** (*Lit*) unity of place.
(b) (*Math, Mil, Tech etc*) unit; — **de cola** (*Aer*) tail unit; — **móvil** (*TV*) mobile unit; — **vecinal de absorción de Toboso** overspill town for Toboso.
unido *adj* (a) joined (*por* by), linked (*por* by).
(b) (*fig*) united; **una familia muy unida** a very united family; **mantenerse —s** to remain united, maintain their (*etc*) unity, keep together.
unificación *nf* unification.
unificar [1g] *vt* to unite, unify.
uniformado 1 *adj* uniformed. **2** *nm* man in uniform, (*esp*) policeman.
uniformar [1a] *vt* (a) to make uniform; to level up, make the same. (b) *person* to put into uniform, provide a uniform for.
uniforme 1 *adj* uniform; *surface etc* level, even, smooth; *speed, rate etc* uniform, steady; regular. **2** *nm* uniform.
uniformemente *adv* uniformly.
uniformidad *nf* uniformity; levelness, evenness, smoothness; steadiness; regularity.
unigénito *adj* (*Rel*) only-begotten; **el U—** the Only Begotten Son.
unilateral *adj* unilateral, one-sided.
unilateralmente *adv* unilaterally.
unión *nf* (a) (*act*) union, uniting, joining.
(b) (*quality*) unity; closeness, togetherness.
(c) (*Comm, Pol etc*) union; (*Law*) union, marriage;

en — **con** with, together with, accompanied by; **aduanera** customs union; **U— Panamericana** Pan-American Union; **U— Soviética** Soviet Union; **U— Sudafricana** Union of South Africa; **vivir en** — **libre con** to live with.
(d) (*Mech*) joint, union; (*also* **punto de —**) junction (*entre* between).
unipersonal *adj* for one (person); single, individual.
unir [3a] **1** *vt* (a) *objects, parts* to join, unite; to tie (*or* fasten, bolt *etc*) together; *persons* to unite; *families* to unite (by marriage); *companies, interests etc* to merge, join; to pool; *qualities* to combine (a with); **les une una fuerte simpatía** they are bound by a strong affection, there are bonds of affection between them.
(b) *liquids etc* to mix; *dough, sauce etc* to mix thoroughly, make smooth; to beat (up).
2 *vi* (*of ingredients*) to mix well, make a smooth mixture.
3 unirse *vr* (a) (2 *persons etc*) to join together, unite; (*companies*) to merge, combine; — **en matrimonio** to marry, be united in marriage.
(b) — **a** to join; — **con** to unite with, merge with; **se unen las ramas por encima** the branches meet overhead.
(c) (*of ingredients*) to mix well, cohere.
unísono *adj* unisonous, on the same tone; *voices etc* in harmony; **al** — on the same tone; (*fig*) in unison, with one voice, in harmony, harmoniously; **al** — **con** (*fig*) in tune with, in harmony with.
unitario 1 *adj* unitary; (*Eccl*) Unitarian. **2** *nm*, **unitaria** *nf* Unitarian.
unitarismo *nm* Unitarianism.
univalente *adj* univalent.
univalvo *adj* univalve.
universal *adj* universal; world (*attr*), world-wide; **historia** — world history; **de fama** — known all over the world, internationally famous; **una especie de distribución** — a species with a world-wide distribution.
universalidad *nf* universality.
universalizar [1f] *vt* to universalize, make universal; to extend widely, bring into general use.
universalmente *adv* universally; all over the world.
universidad *nf* university; — **laboral** technical college.
universitario 1 *adj* university (*attr*); academic. **2** *nm* university teacher; university student, university man.
universo *nm* universe; world.
uno 1 *adj* (a) one; one and the same, identical; **es todo** —, **es** — **y lo mismo** it's all one, it's all the same; **Dios es** — God is one; **la verdad es una** truth is one and indivisible.
(b) — some, a few (*also* —**s cuantos**); about, *eg* —**s 80 dólares** about 80 dollars.
2 *pron* (a) one; somebody; — **mismo** oneself; **ha venido** — **que dice que te conoce** somebody who says he knows you came; —**s que estaban allí protestaron** some (people) who were there protested; **los** —**s dicen que sí y los otros que no** some say yes and some say no; **es mejor hacerlo** — **mismo** it's better to do it oneself.
(b) **cada** — each one, every one; **cada** — **a lo suyo** everyone should mind his own business; **había 3 manzanas para cada** — there were 3 apples each.
(c) (*indef subject*) one, you; — **nunca sabe qué hacer** one never knows what to do; — **necesita descansar** a man has to rest, you have to rest.
(d) **uno(s) a otro(s)** each other, one another; **se detestan** —**s a otros** they hate each other; **se miraban fijamente el** — **al otro** they stared at each other.
(e) (*idioms*) — **a** —, — **por** —, **de** — **en** — one by one; **a una** all together; **juntarlo todo en** — to put it all together; **estar en** — to be at one; **no gustará a más de** — there are quite a few who will not like this; **una de dos** either one thing or the other; — **con otro salen a 3 dólares** on an average they work out at 3 dollars each; — **y otro están locos** they're both mad; **para mí es** — **de tantos** so far as I'm concerned he's just one of many; in my view he's a very ordinary sort; **lo** — **por lo otro** it comes to the same thing, what you lose on the swings you gain on the roundabouts.
untadura *nf* (a) (*act*) smearing, dabbing, rubbing; greasing; spreading. (b) (*Med*) ointment; (*Mech etc*) grease, oil. (c) mark, smear, dab.
untar [1a] **1** *vt* (a) to smear, dab, rub (*con, de* with); (*Med*) to anoint, rub (*con, de* with); (*Mech etc*) to

grease, oil; — **su pan en la salsa** to dip one's bread in the gravy, soak one's bread in the gravy; — **los dedos de tinta** to smear one's fingers with ink; — **el pan con manteca** to spread butter on one's bread, put butter on one's bread.

(b) (*fam*) to bribe, grease the palm of.

2 untarse *vr* (a) — **con,** — **de** to smear oneself with.

(b) (*fam*) to indulge in immorality, get involved in wrongdoing; (*Fin*) to take a rake-off (*fam*), get a cut in the profits; to find that somebody else's money (*etc*) has stuck to one.

unto *nm* (a) soft substance; (*Med*) ointment, unguent; (*Zool*) grease, animal fat. (b) (*Chi*) shoe polish.

untuosidad *nf* greasiness, oiliness; stickiness.

untuoso *adj* greasy, oily, sticky.

untura *nf* = **untadura**.

uña *nf* (a) (*Anat*) nail, fingernail; toenail; (*Zool etc*) claw; **ser** — **y carne** to be inseparable, be as thick as thieves; **largo de** —**s** light-fingered, thieving; **estar de** —**s con uno** to be at daggers drawn with someone; **caer en las** —**s de uno** to fall into someone's clutches; **comerse las** —**s** to bite one's nails; (*fig*) to get very impatient, get furious; (*SAm*) to be terribly poor; **se dejó las uñas en ese trabajo** he wore his fingers to the bone at that job; **enseñar** (*or* **mostrar, sacar**) **las** —**s** to show one's claws (*also fig*).

(b) (*of horse etc*) hoof; — **de caballo** (*Bot*) coltsfoot; **escapar a** — **de caballo** to ride off at full speed; — **de vaca** (*Cook*) cow heel.

(c) (*of scorpion*) sting.

(d) (*Tech*) claw; nailpuller.

(e) (*of anchor*) fluke.

uñada *nf* nail mark; scratch.

uñalarga *nmf* (*SAm*) thief.

uñarada *nf* = **uñada**.

uñatear [1a] *vt* (*Arg, Bol*) to steal.

uñero *nm* (a) whitlow. (b) ingrowing nail.

uñetas *nmf, pl* **uñetas** (*CAm, Col*) thief.

uñetear [1a] *vt* (*Chi*) to steal.

uñilargo *nm* (*Col, Per*), **uñón** *nm* (*Col, Per*) thief.

upa¹ *nm* (*Ec, Per*) idiot.

upa² *interj* up, up!

upar [1a] *vt* (*fam*) to lift up, lift in one's arms; (*SAm*) = **aupar**.

Urales *mpl* (*also* **Montes** —) Urals.

uranio *nm* uranium.

Urano *m* Uranus.

urbanidad *nf* courtesy, politeness, urbanity.

urbanismo *nm* (a) town planning; urban development. (b) (*Ven*) real-estate development.

urbanista *nm* town planner.

urbanístico *adj* town-planning (*attr*); urban, city (*attr*).

urbanización *nf* urbanization; urban development.

urbanizado *adj* built-up.

urbanizar [1f] *vt* (a) *land* to develop, build on, urbanize; to lay out and prepare for city development. (b) *person* to civilize.

urbano *adj* (a) urban, town (*attr*), city (*attr*). (b) courteous, polite, urbane.

urbe *nf* large city, metropolis; capital city; **La U**— (*in Spain*) Madrid, the Capital.

urbícola *nmf* city dweller.

urco *nm* (*Bol, Chi*) ram; male alpaca.

urdimbre *nf* (a) warp. (b) (*fig*) scheme, intrigue.

urdir [3a] *vt* (a) to warp. (b) (*fig*) to plot, scheme for, contrive.

urdu *nm* Urdu.

urea *nf* urea.

urente *adj* (*Med etc*) burning, stinging.

uréter *nm* ureter.

uretra *nf* urethra.

urgencia *nf* (a) urgency; pressure; haste, rush; **con toda** — with the utmost urgency, posthaste; **de** — urgent, pressing; (*Post*) express; **pedir algo con** — to press for something.

(b) emergency; **medida de** — emergency measure; **salida de** — emergency exit.

(c) pressing need; **en caso de** — in case of necessity, if the need arises; **acudió a mí en una** — **de dinero** he came to me with a pressing need for money.

urgente *adj* urgent; pressing; *demand etc* pressing, imperative, insistent; **carta** —special-delivery letter; **pedido** — rush order.

urgentemente *adv* urgently; imperatively, insistently.

urgir [3c] *vi* to be urgent, be pressing; **urge el dinero** the money is urgently needed; **me urge la respuesta** the reply is required with the utmost urgency; **el tiempo urge** time presses, time is short; **me urge terminarlo** I must finish it as soon as I can, I

must finish it with the utmost speed; **me urge partir** I have to leave at once; "**Úrgeme vender: dos gatos . . .**" (*advert*) "Must be sold: two cats."

úrico *adj* uric.

urinario 1 *adj* urinary. **2** *nm* urinal, public lavatory, comfort station (*US*).

urna *nf* urn; glass case; (*Pol etc: also* — **electoral**) ballot box; **acudir a las** —**s** (*fig*) to vote, go and vote, go to the polls.

uro *nm* aurochs.

urogallo *nm* capercaillie.

urogenital *adj* urogenital.

urología *nf* urology.

urólogo *nm* urologist.

urpo *nm* (*Arg, Chi*) = **ulpo**.

urraca *nf* magpie.

urticaria *nf* urticaria, nettlerash.

Uruguay: **El** — Uruguay.

uruguayismo *nm* word (*or* phrase *etc*) peculiar to Uruguay.

uruguayo 1 *adj* Uruguayan. **2** *nm,* **uruguaya** *nf* Uruguayan.

usado *adj* *stamp etc* used; *clothing* worn; secondhand; **muy** — worn out, old, shabby.

usagre *nm* (*Med*) impetigo; (*Vet*) mange.

usanza *nf* usage, custom; **a** — **india, a** — **de los indios** according to the custom of the Indians, in the Indian fashion.

usar [1a] **1** *vt* (a) to use, make use of; *clothing* to wear; **sin** — unused.

(b) — + *infin* to be accustomed to + *infin,* to be in the habit of + *ger*.

2 *vi:* — **de** to use, make use of.

3 usarse *vr* to be used, be in use; (*clothing*) to be worn; to be in fashion; to be the custom; **la chistera ya no se usa** top hats are not worn nowadays, top hats are no longer in fashion.

usina *nf* (*SAm: gall*) factory, plant; (*RPl*) power plant; gasworks; tram depot.

uslero *nm* (*Chi*) rolling pin.

uso *nm* (a) use; **objeto de** — **personal** article for personal use; **de** — **externo** (*Med*) for external application; **estar fuera de** — to be out of use, be obsolete; **estar en** — to be in use; **estar en buen** — to be in good condition; **estar en el** — **de la palabra** to be speaking, have the floor; **hacer** — **de** to make use of; **hacer** — **de la palabra** to speak; **retirar algo del** — to withdraw something from service.

(b) (*Mech etc*) wear, wear and tear; — **y desgaste** wear and tear; **deteriorado por el** — worn.

(c) custom, usage; fashion, style; **es un** — **muy antiguo** it is a very ancient custom; **al** — as is customary, in keeping with custom; **con bigotes al** — with the usual sort of moustache, with the sort of moustache which was then fashionable; **un hombre al** — an ordinary man; **al** — **de** in the style of, in the fashion of; **un libro hecho al** — **de los principiantes** a book written for beginners.

usted, *pl* **ustedes** *personal pronoun* (*normally abbr* **Vd, Vds**) you (*polite or formal address*); **el coche de** — your car; **mi coche y el de** — my car and yours; **para** — for you; **sin** — without you; **¡a** —**!** (*reciprocating thanks*) thank you!

usual *adj* usual, customary; ordinary; regular.

usualmente *adv* usually; ordinarily, regularly.

usuario *nm,* **usuaria** *nf* user; — **de la vía pública** road user.

usufructo *nm* usufruct, use; — **vitalicio** life interest (*de* in).

usufructuario *nm,* **usufructuaria** *nf* usufructuary.

usura *nf* usury; (*fig*) profiteering, racketeering.

usurario *adj* usurious.

usurear [1a] *vi* to lend money at an exorbitant rate of interest; (*fig*) to profiteer, run a racket.

usurero *nm* usurer; (*fig*) profiteer, racketeer.

usurpación *nf* usurpation; seizure, illegal taking; (*fig*) encroachment (*de* upon), inroads (*de* into).

usurpador *nm* usurper.

usurpar [1a] *vt* *crown, rights etc* to usurp; *land etc* to seize, take illegally; (*fig*) to encroach upon, make inroads into.

usuta *nf* (*Arg, Bol, Per*) = **ojota**.

utensilio *nm* tool, implement; (*Cook*) utensil; —**s de cirujano** surgeon's instruments; —**s para escribir** writing materials; —**s para pescar** fishing tackle; —**s de pintor** painter's materials; **con los** —**s de su oficio** with the tools of his craft, with the equipment of his trade.

uterino *adj* uterine; **hermanos** —**s** children born of the same mother.

útero *nm* womb, uterus.

útil 1 *adj* (a) useful; usable, serviceable; handy; **las**

plantas —es para el hombre the plants which are useful to man; **el coche es viejo pero todavía está —** the car is old but but it is still serviceable; **es muy — tenerlo aquí cerca** it's very handy having it here close by; **¿en qué puedo serle —?** can I do anything for you?, can I be of any help?

(**b**) **día —** working day, weekday.

(**c**) (*Mil*) **— para el servicio** *person* fit for military service, *vehicle etc* operational.

2 **—es** *nmpl* tools, implements; tackle, equipment; **—es de chimenea** fire irons; **—es de labranza** agricultural implements.

utilería *nf* (*Arg, Mex: Theat*) properties, props (*fam*).

utilidad *nf* (**a**) usefulness, utility; benefit. (**b**) (*Comm, Fin etc*) profit, benefit; **—es** profits, earnings; **—es líquidas** net profits.

utilitario *adj* (**a**) utilitarian. (**b**) *car, clothing etc* utility (*attr*).

utilitarismo *nm* utilitarianism.

utilitarista *nmf* utilitarian.

utilizable *adj* usable; serviceable; fit for use, ready to use; (*Tech*) *waste* reclaimable.

utilización *nf* use, utilization; (*Tech*) reclamation.

utilizar [1f] *vt* to use, make use of, utilize; *power, resources etc* to harness; (*Tech*) *waste* to reclaim.

útilmente *adv* usefully.

utillaje *nm* (set of) tools; tackle, equipment.

utopía *nf*, **utopia** *nf* Utopia.

utópico *adj* Utopian.

utopista 1 *adj* Utopian. **2** *nmf* Utopian.

utrículo *nm* utricle.

uva *nf* (**a**) grape; **— blanca** green grape; **— de Corinto** currant; **— crespa**, **— espina** gooseberry; **— moscatel** muscatel grape; **— pasa** raisin; **—s verdes** (*fig*) sour grapes; **de —s a peras** very occasionally, once in a blue moon; **estar hecho una —** to be drunk as a lord. (**b**) (*Chi*) kiss.

uve *nf* name *of the letter* V; **de forma de —** V-shaped; **escote en —** V-neck.

úvula *nf* uvula.

uvular *adj* uvular.

uxoricidio *nm* wife-murder.

—uzo *n and adj suffix* (*pej*), *eg* **carnuza** bad meat, awful meat (*fam*); *see* **gentuza** etc.

V

va *etc see* **ir**.

vaca *nf* (a) cow; — **de leche,** — **lechera** dairy cow, milking cow; (*SAm: fig*) good business, profitable deal; — **marina** manatee, sea cow; — **de San Antón** ladybird, ladybug (*US*); —**s gordas** (*fig*) period of prosperity, boom; **pasar las** —**s gordas** (*fig*) to have a grand time of it.
(b) (*Cook*) beef; cowhide.
(c) (*SAm*) enterprise with profits on a pro rata basis.
(d) (*Per*) **hacerse la** — to play hooky.

vacación *nf* vacation; —**es** holiday(s), vacation; —**es escolares** school holidays; —**es pagadas,** —**es retribuidas** holidays with pay; **estar de** —**es** to be (away) on holiday; **hacer** —**es** to take a day off; **marcharse de** —**es** to go off on holiday.

vacacionista *nmf* holidaymaker, vacationist (*US*).

vacada *nf* herd of cows.

vacaje *nm* (*Chi, RPl*) cows, cattle; herd of cows; (*Mex*) herd of beef cows.

vacante 1 *adj* vacant, empty, unoccupied; *post* vacant. **2** *nf* vacancy, place, (unfilled) post; **proveer una** — to fill a post.

vacar [1g] *vi* (a) to fall vacant, become vacant; to remain unfilled.
(b) (*of person*) to cease work; to be idle.
(c) — **a,** — **en** to attend to, engage in, devote oneself to.
(d) — **de** to lack, be without.

vacarí *adj* cowhide (*attr*).

vaccinio *nm* bilberry; blueberry (*US*).

vaciadero *nm* (a) sink, drain; sump. (b) rubbish tip, dumping ground.

vaciado 1 *adj statue etc* cast in a mould; *tool* hollowground. **2** *nm* (a) cast, mould(ing); — **yeso** plaster cast. (b) hollowing out; exca.... (c) (*Aer*) — **rápido** jettisoning.

vaciar [1c] **1** *vt* (a) *container* to em (out); *glass etc* to drain; *contents* to empty out; *liquid* to pour, pour away; to run off; to drink up; (*Aer etc*) to jettison; **vació los bolsillos en la mesa** he emptied out his pockets on the table; **vació la leche en un vaso** he poured (*or* emptied) the milk into a glass; **lo vació todo sobre su cabeza** he poured the lot over his head.
(b) *wood, stone etc* to hollow out; *statue etc* to cast.
(c) *knife etc* to grind, sharpen.
(d) *subject, theory* to expound at length.
(e) *writing, text* to copy out.
2 *vi* (*of river*) to flow, empty, run (**en** into).
3 vaciarse *vr* (a) to empty.
(b) (*also* — **por la lengua;** *sl*) to blab, spill the beans (*sl*).

vaciedad *nf* (a) emptiness. (b) (*fig*) silliness; piece of nonsense; —**es** nonsense, rubbish.

vacilación *nf* hesitancy, hesitation, vacillation; **sin** —**es** unhesitatingly.

vacilada *nf* (*Mex*) (a) spree (*fam*), binge (*sl*). (b) joke.

vacilante *adj* (a) unsteady; wobbly, tottery; *speech* faltering, halting; *memory* uncertain. (b) *light* flickering. (c) (*fig*) hesitant, uncertain, vacillating; indecisive, dithery.

vacilar [1a] *vi* (a) (*of furniture etc*) to be unsteady; to wobble, rock, move, shake; (*of person*) to totter; to reel, stagger; to stumble; (*fig: of morality etc*) to be indecisive, be collapsing; (*in speech*) to falter; (*of memory*) to fail.
(b) (*of light*) to flicker.
(c) (*fig*) to hesitate, waver, vacillate; to hang back; **sin** — unhesitatingly; — **en** + *infin* to hesitate to + *infin;* — **entre dos posibilidades** to hesitate between two possibilities; **es un hombre que vacila mucho** he is a very indecisive man, he is

a man who dithers a lot; **no vaciles en decírmelo** don't hesitate to tell me about it.
(d) (*fig*) — **entre** to vary between; **un sabor que vacila entre agradable y desagradable** a taste which varies between nice and nasty, a taste which ranges from nice to nasty.
(e) (*CAm, Mex, PR*) to get tight; to go on a spree (*fam*); to revel, carouse.

vacilón *nm* (*Mex*) reveller, merrymaker.

vacío 1 *adj* (a) empty; *post etc* vacant, unoccupied; unfilled; *flat* unfurnished; *paper* blank; — **de todo contenido serio** empty of any serious contents, devoid of any serious purpose; **el teatro estaba medio** — the theatre was half empty.
(b) (*fig*) insubstantial; superficial; *talk etc* light, idle, frivolous; *effort* vain, useless.
(c) (*fig*) vain; proud.
(d) (*fig*) idle, unemployed.
(e) (*Col, CR, SD*) **pan** — bread alone, just bread, bread by itself.
2 *nm* (*in general*) emptiness; void; (*Phys*) vacuum; (*un* —) empty space, gap; vacant place; hollow; (*Anat*) side, flank, ribs; **han dejado un** — **para el nombre** they have left a space for the name; **se nota ahora un gran** — **en la familia** one is conscious now of a big gap in the family; **el libro llenará un bien sentido** — the book will fill a long-felt want; **el camión volvió de** — the lorry came back empty; **lo pedí pero tuve que marcharme de** — I asked for it but had to go away empty-handed; **caer en el** — to fall flat; to fail, be ineffective, produce no result; **dar un golpe en** — to miss, fail to connect; **esta viga parece que está en el** — this beam seems to be unsupported, this beam seems to rest on nothing at all; **marchar en** — (*Mech*) to tick over; **hacer el** — **a uno** to send someone to Coventry, pretend that someone does not exist.

vacuidad *nf* (a) emptiness. (b) (*fig*) vacuity; superficiality, frivolity; empty-headedness.

vacuna *nf* (a) vaccine. (b) (*SAm*) vaccination.

vacunación *nf* (a) vaccination. (b) (*fig*) preparation; inuring; forearming.

vacunar [1a] *vt* (a) to vaccinate. (b) (*fig*) to prepare; to inure; to forearm.

vacuno *adj* bovine; cow (*attr*); **ganado** — cattle.

vacuo *adj* (a) empty; vacant. (b) (*fig*) vacuous; superficial, frivolous, empty-headed.

vade *nm* (*School etc*) satchel, case.

vadeable *adj* (a) fordable, which can be forded. (b) (*fig*) not impossible, not insuperable.

vadear [1a] **1** *vt* (a) *river* to ford; *water* to wade through, wade across.
(b) (*fig*) *difficulty* to surmount, get round, overcome.
(c) (*fig*) *person* to sound out.
2 *vi* to wade; **cruzar un río vadeando** to wade across a river; **llegar a tierra vadeando** to wade ashore.

vademécum *nm, pl* **vademécums** (a) vademecum. (b) (*School etc*) satchel, case.

vadera *nf* wide ford.

vado *nm* (a) ford. (b) (*fig*) way out, solution, expedient; **no hallar** — to see no way out, find no solution; **tentar el** — to look into possible solutions. (c) (*fig*) respite.

vagabundear [1a] *vi* to wander, roam, rove; to loaf, idle, bum (*US*).

vagabundeo *nm* wandering, roving; tramp's life; loafing, idling, bumming (*US*).

vagabundo 1 *adj* wandering, roving; (*pej*) vagrant; vagabond. **2** *nm,* **vagabunda** *nf* wanderer, rover; (*pej*) vagrant; vagabond, tramp, bum (*US*).

vagación *nf* (*Mech*) free play.

vagamente *adv* vaguely.
vagamundería *nf* (*SAm*) idleness, laziness.
vagamundero *adj* (*SAm*) idle, lazy.
vagancia *nf* vagrancy; idleness, laziness.
vagante *adj* (a) wandering, vagrant. (b) (*Mech*) *etc* free, loose.
vagar 1 [1h] *vi* (a) to wander (about), roam, rove; to prowl about; to saunter up and down, wander about the streets; to loiter; to idle, loaf, laze about.
　(b) (*Mech*) to be free, be loose, move about.
　2 *nm* leisure, free time; idleness; lack of anxiety, freedom from worry; **andar de** — to be at leisure; to feel at ease.
vagido *nm* (baby's) wail, cry.
vagina *nf* vagina.
vaginal *adj* vaginal.
vago 1 *adj* (a) vague; ill-defined, indistinct; indeterminate; (*Art*) blurred.
　(b) roving, wandering.
　(c) *person* lazy, slack; unreliable; idle, unemployed; *object* idle, unused; *space etc* empty.
　(d) **en** — *stand etc* unsteadily; unsupported; *strive* in vain; aimlessly, pointlessly; **dar golpes en** — to flail about, beat the air.
　2 *nm* (a) tramp, vagrant; down-and-out.
　(b) lazy sort, slacker; unreliable person; useless individual, dead loss.
vagón *nm* (*Rail:* for *passengers*) coach, carriage, car; (*for goods*) truck, wagon; car, van; — **cisterna**, — **tanque** tanker, tank wagon; — **directo** through carriage; — **de ganado**, — **de hacienda** (*Arg*), — **de reja** (*Chi*) cattle truck; — **de mercancías** goods van, freight car (*US*); — **de primera** first-class carriage; — **de segunda** second-class carriage; — **restaurante** dining car; — **tolva** hopper.
vagonada *nf* truckload, wagonload.
vagoneta *nf* light truck.
vaguada *nf* watercourse, stream bed.
vaguear [1a] *vi* = **vagar** 1.
vaguedad *nf* (a) vagueness; indistinctness; indeterminacy. (b) (*una* —) vague remark; woolly idea; **hablar sin —es** to talk in a down-to-earth way, speak with precision.
vaguería *nf* laziness, slackness; unreliability.
vaharada *nf* puff, gust of breath; whiff, reek; smell.
vahear [1a] *vi* to steam; to fume, give off fumes, smoke; to whiff, reek, smell.
vahído *nm* dizzy spell, queer turn, vertigo.
vaho *nm* (a) vapour, steam, fumes; breath; whiff, reek, smell. (b) —**s** (*Med*) inhalation.
vaina 1 *nf* (a) (*Mil etc*) sheath, scabbard; (*of tool*) sheath, case.
　(b) (*Bot*) pod; husk, shell.
　(c) (*SAm*) nuisance, troublesome thing.
　(d) (*Col*) flute, piece of luck.
　(e) (*Chi*) swindle.
　(f) (*Cu:* tabu) screw (*tabu*).
　2 *adj* (*SAm*) annoying.
vainetilla *nf* (*Per*) annoyance, vexation.
vainica *nf* (*Sew*) hemstitch.
vainilla *nf* vanilla.
vainillina *nf* vanillin.
vainita *nf* (*SD*, *Ven*) string bean.
vaivén *nm* (a) to-and-fro movement, oscillation; rocking, backward and forward movement; swing(ing), sway(ing); lurch(ing).
　(b) (*of vehicles etc*) coming and going, constant movement.
　(c) (*fig*) change of fortune; —**es** ups and downs, vicissitudes.
　(d) (*fig*: *Pol etc*) swing, seesaw, violent change of opinion.
vaivenear [1a] *vt* to oscillate; to rock, move backwards and forwards; to swing, sway.
vajear [1a] *vt* (*CAm, Cu, Mex*) (*of snake*) to fascinate, hypnotize; (*fig*) to use black magic on; (*fig*) to win over by flattery.
vajilla *nf* (in *general*) crockery, china; dishes; (*una* —) service, set of dishes; — **de oro** gold plate; — **de porcelana** chinaware; **lavar la** — to wash up.
valdré *etc* see **valer**.
vale[1] *nm* promissory note, IOU; receipt; voucher, warrant; — **de correo**, — **postal** money order; **dar el** — (*fig*) to pass as suitable; to give the go-ahead.
vale[2] *nm* (*SAm:* abbr of **valedor**) pal (*fam*), chum, buddy (*US*); — **corrido** (*Ven*) old crony; **ser** — **con** (*Col*) to be pals with.
valedero *adj* valid; — **para 6 meses** valid for 6 months; — **hasta el día 16** valid until the 16th.
valedor *nm* (a) protector. (b) (*SAm*) = **vale**[2].

valedura *nf* (a) (*Mex*) help; protection; favour. (b) (*Col, Cu*) gift made by a gambler out of his winnings.
Valencia Valencia.
valencia *nf* (*Chem*) valency.
valencianismo *nm* word (*or* phrase etc) peculiar to Valencia.
valenciano 1 *adj* Valencian. 2 *nm*, **valenciana** *nf* Valencian. 3 *nm* (dialect of *Catalan*) Valencian.
valentía *nf* (a) bravery, courage; boldness; resoluteness.
　(b) (*pej*) boastfulness.
　(c) (*una* —) brave deed, heroic exploit; bold act.
　(d) (*una* —: *pej*) brag, boast.
valentón 1 *adj* boastful; blustering, bullying; arrogant. 2 *nm* braggart; bluster, bully.
valentonada *nf* boast, brag; piece of bluster; arrogant act.
valer [2q] 1 *vt* (a) to aid, protect; to serve; to help, avail; **¡válgame (Dios)!** see **Dios**; **no le vale ser hijo del ministro** it's of no help to him being the minister's son, it doesn't help his case that he's the minister's son; **su situación privilegiada no le valió** his privileged position did not save him; **no le valdrán excusas** excuses won't help him, excuses will avail him nothing.
　(b) (*Math etc*) to equal, be equal to; to amount to, come to; **la suma vale 99** the total comes to 99; **el ángulo B vale 38°** angle B is 38°; **en ese caso X vale 9** in that case X equals 9.
　(c) to cause; to earn; to win; to lose, cost; **el asunto le valió muchos disgustos** the affair caused him lots of trouble; **esa tontería le valió un rapapolvo** that piece of stupidity got (*or* earned) him a dressing-down; **son las cualidades que le valieron el premio** these are the qualities which won him the prize; **su ausencia le valió la pérdida del contrato** his absence lost (*or* cost) him the contract.
　2 *vti* (a) (*Comm, Fin*) to be worth; to cost, be priced at, be valued at; (in *absolute sense*) to be valuable; (*fig*) to be equivalent to, represent; **este libro vale 5 dólares** this book costs (*or* is worth) 5 dollars; **ésas valen 20 pesetas el kilo** those are 20 pesetas a kilo; **esta tela vale a 60 pesetas** this cloth costs 60 pesetas; **¿cuánto vale?** how much is it?; **¿vale mucho?** is it valuable?; **4 fichas azules valen por una negra** 4 blue counters are worth one black one; **cada cupón vale por un paquete** each coupon represents (*or* counts for) a packet.
　(b) (*fig*) to be worth; **no vale nada** it's worthless, it's rubbish; **no vale un higo** (*etc*) it's not worth a brass farthing; **vale lo que pesa** it's worth its weight in gold; **esa mirada suya me valió un sinfín de cartas** that look of hers told me more (*or* was worth more to me) than a hundred letters; **más vale así** it's better this way; **A vale más que B** A is better than B; **más vale tarde que nunca** better late than never; **más vale no hacerlo** it's better not to do it; **más vale que vayas tú** it would be better for you to go; **más vale que me vaya** I had better go; see **pena**.
　(c) (*fig*: of *person*) to be worthy; to have one's merits (*or* qualities); **es un hombre que vale** he's a worthy man, he's a man of some quality, he has his points; **no vale para nada** he's useless, he's a dead loss.
　3 *vi* (a) to be of use, be useful; **es viejo pero todavía vale** it's old but it still serves; **este sombrero me vale aún** this hat is still useful to me; **hay que tirar todo lo que no vale** we must throw out everything that is no use; **este trozo no me vale para hacer la cortina** this piece is not big enough to make the curtain.
　(b) to be valid; to be applicable, apply; (in *games*) to count, score; to be permitted; **¿vale?** is that all right?, will that do?; how about that?; **¡vale!** that's right!, O.K.! (*fam*); that'll do!, that's enough!; **es una teoría que no vale ya** it is a theory which no longer holds; **esa sección no vale ahora** that section is not now applicable; **¡eso no vale!** that doesn't count!; that's not allowed!, you can't do that!; **ese tanto no vale** that point doesn't score; **no vale golpearlo segunda vez** you aren't allowed to have a second shot at it; **¡no hay "querido" que valga!** it's no good saying "darling" to me!
　(c) **hacer** — **su derecho** to assert one's right; **hacer** — **sus argumentos** to make one's arguments felt, establish the validity of one's arguments.
　(d) **está un poco chiflado, valga la expresión** he's a bit cracked, so to speak; he's a bit cracked, for want of a better way of putting it.

4 valerse vr (a) — **de** to make use of, avail oneself of; to take advantage of; *right* to exercise. **(b)** — **por sí mismo** to help oneself, shift for oneself, manage by oneself; **poder** — to be able to manage; **no poder** — to be helpless. **5** nm worth, value.

valeriana nf valerian.

valerosamente adv bravely, valiantly.

valeroso adj brave, valiant.

valet [ba'le] nm, pl **valets** [ba'le] (Cards: gall) jack, knave.

valetudinario 1 adj valetudinarian. **2** nm, **valetudinaria** nf valetudinarian.

valga etc see **valer**.

Valhala m Valhalla.

valía nf (a) worth, value; **de gran** — of great worth, very valuable; *person* worthy, estimable. **(b)** (fig) influence.

validación nf validation; ratification.

validar [1a] vt to validate, give effect to; to ratify.

validez nf validity; **dar** — **a** to validate, give effect to; to ratify.

válido adj **(a)** valid (hasta until, para for). **(b)** (Med) strong, robust; fit.

valido nm (Hist) (royal) favourite.

valiente 1 adj **(a)** brave, valiant; bold. **(b)** (pej) boastful, blustering. **(c)** (fig) fine, excellent; noble; strong; (iro) fine, wonderful; ¡— **amigo!** a fine friend you are!; ¡— **gobierno!** some government!, do you call this a government? **2** nm **(a)** brave man, gallant man; hero. **(b)** (pej) braggart.

valientemente adv **(a)** bravely, valiantly; boldly. **(b)** (pej) boastfully. **(c)** (fig) excellently; nobly; (iro) wonderfully.

valija nf **(a)** case. **(b)** valise; satchel; (Post) mailbag; (fig) mail, post; — **diplomática** diplomatic bag.

valijería nf (Chi, RPl) travel-goods shop.

valimiento nm **(a)** value; benefit. **(b)** (Pol etc) favour, protection; position of royal favourite, status of the royal favourite; — **con uno**, — **cerca de uno** influence with someone.

valioso adj **(a)** valuable; useful, beneficial; estimable. **(b)** wealthy; powerful.

valisoletano = **vallisoletano**.

valona nf **(a)** (Col, Ec, Ven) artistically trimmed mane; **hacer la** — (Cu) to shave. **(b)** (Mex) = **valedura (a)**.

valonar [1a] vt (Col, Ec, Ven) to trim, cut; to shear.

valonearse [1a] vr (CAm) to lean from the saddle.

valor nm **(a)** (general sense) value, worth; price; (of coin, stamp) value, denomination; (Math, Mus etc) value; (of words etc) value, importance; meaning; **objetos de** — valuables; **sin** — worthless, valueless; — **adquisitivo** purchasing power; — **alimenticio** food value, nutritional value; — **facial**, — **nominal** face value, nominal value; (of shares) par value; — **sentimental** sentimental value; **conceder** — **a**, **dar** — **a** to attach importance to; to value, esteem; **quitar** — **a** to minimize the importance of; **esas cosas ya no tienen** — **para mí** such things no longer have any importance for me, I no longer value such things. **(b)** (fig) great name, great figure; **Cervantes**, **máximo** — **nacional** Cervantes, one of our country's greatest figures; Cervantes, part of our great national heritage. **(c)** —**es** (Comm, Fin) securities, bonds; stock; (Arg, Col) assets; —**es en cartera**, —**es habidos** investments, holdings, share portfolio; —**es fiduciarios** fiduciary issue, banknotes. **(d)** bravery, courage, valour; — **cívico** (sense of) civic duty; **armarse de** — to gather up one's courage. **(e)** (fam) nerve, cheek; ¡**qué** —! of all the cheek!; **tuvo el** — **de pedírmelo** he had the nerve to ask me for it.

valoración nf **(a)** valuation; (fig) assessment, appraisal. **(b)** (Chem) titration.

valorar [1a] vt **(a)** to value (en at); to price; (esp fig) to assess, appraise; to rate; — **mucho** to value highly, esteem; — **poco** to attach little value to. **(b)** (Chem) to titrate.

valorizar [1f] vt **(a)** = **valorar**. **(b)** (Col, RPl) to put up the price of.

Valquiria nf Valkyrie.

vals nm, pl **vals** waltz.

valsar [1a] vi to waltz.

valse nm (SAm) waltz.

valsear [1a] vi (SAm) to waltz.

valsón nm (fam) burst of activity; **dar** —**es** to rush around, display great energy.

valuable adj (SAm) **(a)** (angl) valuable. **(b)** calculable.

valuación nf = **valoración (a)**.

valuador nm (SAm) valuer.

valuar [1e] vt = **valorar (a)**.

valumen nm **(a)** (Chi: Bot) luxuriance, rankness. **(b)** (Mex) bundle; mass, bulk.

valumoso adj **(a)** (CAm, Chi) luxuriant, rank. **(b)** (CAm, Ec, Mex) bulky. **(c)** (Ven) vain, conceited.

valva nf (Bot, Zool) valve.

válvula nf (Mech etc) valve; — **de admisión** inlet valve; — **de escape** exhaust valve; — **de purga** vent; — **de seguridad** safety valve.

valla nf **(a)** fence; (Mil) barricade; palisade, stockade; (Sport) hurdle; — **paranieves** snow fence. **(b)** (fig) barrier; limit; obstacle, hindrance; **romper las** —**s**, **saltar(se) la** — to disregard the social conventions, do away with social niceties; to burst through the barriers of convention. **(c)** (Cu, Col, Mex, PR) cockpit. **(d)** (Col) ditch.

valladar nm **(a)** = **valla (a)**. **(b)** (fig) defence, barrier.

vallado nm **(a)** = **valla (a)**. **(b)** defensive wall, rampart. **(c)** (Mex) deep ditch.

vallar [1a] vt to fence in, put up a fence round, enclose.

valle nm valley; vale, dale; — **de lágrimas** vale of tears.

vallero (Mex) **1** adj valley (attr). **2** nm, **vallera** nf valley dweller.

vallino adj (Per) valley (attr).

vallisoletano 1 adj of Valladolid. **2** nm, **vallisoletana** nf native (or inhabitant) of Valladolid; **los** —**s** the people of Valladolid.

vallisto adj (Arg, Mex) valley (attr).

vallunco adj (CAm) rustic, peasant (attr).

vamos etc see **ir**.

vampi nf (fam) = **vampiresa**.

vampiresa nf vamp.

vampiro nm **(a)** (Zool) vampire. **(b)** (fig) vampire; exploiter, bloodsucker.

vanagloria nf vainglory.

vanagloriarse [1b] vr to boast; to be vain, be arrogant; — **de** to boast of; — **de** + infin to boast of + ger, boast of being able to + infin.

vanaglorioso adj vainglorious; vain, boastful, arrogant.

vanamente adv uselessly, vainly.

vanarse [1a] vr (Col, Chi, Ven) to shrivel up; (fig) to fall through, come to nothing, produce no results.

vandálico adj Vandal(ic); (fig) loutish, destructive.

vandalismo nm vandalism.

vándalo 1 adj Vandal(ic). **2** nm, **vándala** nf (Hist) Vandal; (fig) vandal.

vanguardia nf vanguard, van (also fig); **estar en la** — **del progreso** to be in the van of progress; **ir a** —, **ir en** — to be in the vanguard; to be foremost, be ahead, be in front; **un pintor de** — an ultramodern painter, a painter with a revolutionary style; a far-out painter.

vanguardismo nm (Art, Lit etc) ultramodern manner, revolutionary style; new tendency, far-out tendencies.

vanidad nf **(a)** unreality; groundlessness; uselessness; futility; shallowness; inanity, pointlessness. **(b)** vanity; **por pura** — out of sheer vanity; **halagar la** — **de uno** to play up to someone's vanity. **(c)** —**es** vanities.

vanidoso adj vain, conceited; smug.

vano 1 adj **(a)** unreal, imaginary, vain; fear etc idle; suspicion groundless; superstition foolish, unreasonable. **(b)** attempt vain, useless; pastime idle; **en** — in vain. **(c)** person shallow, superficial; frivolous; pleasure etc empty, inane, pointless; adornment silly. **(d)** shell empty, hollow. **2** nm (Archit) space, gap.

vapor nm **(a)** vapour; (Tech) steam; fumes; (Meteorol) mist, haze; — **de agua** water vapour; **al** — by steam, (fig) very fast; **cocer un plato al** — to steam a dish; **de** — steam (attr); **acumular** — to get steam up; **echar** — to give off steam, steam. **(b)** (Naut) steamer, steamship; — **correo** mailboat; — **de ruedas** paddle steamer; — **volandero** tramp steamer. **(c)** (Med) giddiness, faintness; dizzy spell; —**es** vapours, hysteria.

vapora nf **(a)** steam launch. **(b)** (PR) steam engine.

vapor(e)ar [1a] **1** vt to evaporate. **2** vi to give off vapour. **3 vapor(e)arse** vr to evaporate.
vaporización nf vaporization.
vaporizador nm vaporizer; spray.
vaporizar [1f] **1** vt to vaporize, convert into vapour; scent etc to spray. **2 vaporizarse** vr to vaporize, turn into vapour.
vaporizo nm (Mex, PR) (a) strong heat, steamy heat. (b) (Med) inhalation.
vaporoso adj (a) vaporous; steamy, misty; steaming. (b) cloth light, airy, diaphanous.
vapulear [1a] vt (a) carpet etc to beat; person to beat; to thrash, flog; to beat up. (b) (fig) to give a tongue-lashing to.
vapuleo nm (a) beating; thrashing, flogging; beating-up. (b) (fig) tongue-lashing.
vaquerear [1a] vi (Per) to play truant.
vaquería nf (a) dairy. (b) (SAm) cattle management, cattle tending; craft of the cowboy. (c) (Cu, Per, PR) milking pail; milking parlour. (d) (Cu, PR) herd of dairy cows. (e) (Ven) hunting with a lasso. (f) (Mex) country dance in cowboy dress.
vaqueriza nf cowshed; cattle yard.
vaquerizo 1 adj cattle (attr). **2** nm cowman; herdsman.
vaquero 1 adj cattle (attr). **2** nm (a) cowman; herdsman, cattle tender; (in US, SAm) cowboy. (b) (SAm) milkman. (c) (Per) truant. (d) (Ven) rawhide whip.
vaqueta 1 nf (a) cowhide, leather. (b) (PR) razor strop. **2** nm (Cu) shifty sort.
vaquetón adj (a) (Cu) unreliable, shifty. (b) (Mex) dim-witted; phlegmatic, slow. (c) (Mex) barefaced, brazen.
vaquetudo adj (Cu, Mex) = **vaquetón, baquetudo.**
vaquilla nf (a) heifer. (b) —s amateur bullfight with young bulls.
vaquillona nf (SAm) heifer.
vara nf (a) stick, pole; rod, bar; (Mech) rod; (of carriage) shaft; (Bot) branch, twig (stripped of its leaves), wand, switch; (Bot) central stem, main stalk; — **mágica,** — **de las virtudes** magic wand; — **de medir** yardstick, measuring rod; — **de oro,** — **de San José** goldenrod; — **de pescar** fishing rod. (b) (Pol etc) wand (of office); sign of authority; — **alta** authority, power; influence; dominance; **doblar la** — **de la justicia** to pervert justice; **empuñar la** — to take over, take up office (as mayor etc). (c) (Math: prov, SAm) approx yard (=.836 m, =2.8 feet). (d) (Taur) lance, pike; wound with the lance; **poner** —**s al toro** to wound the bull with the lance.
varada nf (a) launching. (b) stranding, running aground.
varadero nm shipyard.
varado 1 adj (a) (Naut) stranded; **estar** — to be aground; to be beached. (b) **estar** — (Chi) to be without regular work; (Arg, CAm, Mex) to be helpless for lack of money. **2** nm (Chi) drifter, man without a regular job.
varadura nf stranding, running aground.
varal nm (a) long pole, stout stick; framework of poles; strut, support. (b) (fam) thin person, lamp-post.
varapalo nm (a) long pole. (b) blow with a stick; beating. (c) (fig) dressing-down. (d) (fig) setback, disappointment, blow.
varar [1a] **1** vt (a) to launch. (b) to beach, run up on the beach. **2** vi and **vararse** vr (a) (Naut) to be stranded, run aground. (b) (fig) to get stuck, get bogged down; to come to a standstill.
varayoc nm (Per) Indian Chief.
varazo nm blow with a stick.
varazón nf (a) (Col, Cu, Mex) sticks, bunch of sticks. (b) (Chi) shoal.
vardasca nf green twig; switch, swishy stick.
varear [1a] vt (a) person to beat, hit; fruit to knock down (with poles); carpet etc to beat; bull to prick with the lance, goad, stir up. (b) (Comm) cloth to sell by the yard. (c) (RPl) to exercise, train.
varec nm seaweed, wrack.
varejón nm (SAm) = **vardasca;** stick, straight branch (stripped of leaves).
vareta nf (a) twig, small stick; lime twig for catching birds. (b) (Sew) stripe. (c) insinuation; taunt; **echar** —**s** to make insinuations.

(d) (Med: fam) **estar de** —, **irse de** — to have diarrhoea.
varetazo nm (Taur) sideways thrust with the horn.
variabilidad nf variability.
variable 1 adj variable, changeable; (Math) variable. **2** nf (Math) variable.
variación nf variation (also Mus); **sin** — without varying, unchanged.
variado adj varied; mixed; assorted; surface, colours variegated.
variante 1 adj variant. **2** nm (Col) path; short cut. **3** nf variant.
variar [1c] **1** vt to vary, change, alter; to modify; menu etc to vary, introduce some variety into; positions to change round, switch about. **2** vi to vary; to change; — **de opinión** to change one's mind; **varía de 3 a 8** it ranges from 3 to 8, it goes from 3 to 8; **este producto varía mucho de precio** this article varies a lot in price; **esto varía de lo que dijo antes** this differs from what he said earlier.
varicela nf chickenpox.
várices nfpl varicose veins.
varicoso adj (a) varicose. (b) suffering from varicose veins.
variedad nf (a) variety; variation; (Bio) variety. (b) (Theat) —**es** variety show; **teatro de** —**es** variety theatre, music hall, vaudeville theater (US).
varietés nmpl (Theat: gall) = **variedades.**
varilla nf (a) (thin) stick; (Bot) twig, wand, switch; (Mech) rod, bar; link; (of wheel) spoke; (of corset) rib, stay; (of fan, umbrella) rib; (Anat) jawbone; — **mágica,** — **de virtudes** magic wand; — **de zahorí** divining rod. (b) (Mex) small wares, trinkets. (c) (Ven) = **vaina** (c).
varillaje nm (Mech) rods, links, linkage; (of fan, umbrella) ribs, ribbing.
varillar [1a] vt (Ven) racehorse to try out, train.
varillero nm (Mex) hawker, pedlar, peddler (US).
vario adj (a) varied; (in colour) variegated, motley. (b) varying, variable, changeable; fickle. (c) —s several, some; a number of; **hay varias posibilidades** there are several (or various) possibilities; **en** —**s libros que he visto** in a number of books which I have seen; **los inconvenientes son** —**s** there are several drawbacks.
varioloso adj pockmarked.
variopinto adj many-coloured, colourful; of diverse colours.
varita nf wand; — **mágica,** — **de las virtudes** magic wand.
varón 1 adj male; **hijo** — male child, boy, son. **2** nm (a) man, male; adult male; (fig) worthy man, great man; — **de Dios** saintly man; **santo** — nice old chap (fam); extraordinarily kind man; **tuvo 4 hijos, todos** —**es** she had 4 children, all boys. (b) (Col) husband. (c) (Chi, Mex) beam, timber.
varona nf, **varonesa** nf mannish woman.
varonil adj (a) manly, virile, vigorous. (b) (Bio) male. (c) **una mujer de aspecto** — a woman of mannish appearance.
Varsovia Warsaw.
vasallaje nm (Hist) vassalage; (fig) subjection, serfdom.
vasallo nm vassal.
vasar nm kitchen shelf, rack.
vasco 1 adj Basque. **2** nm, **vasca** nf Basque. **3** nm (language) Basque.
vascófilo nm expert in Basque studies.
Vascongadas: las — the Basque Provinces.
vascongado = **vasco.**
vascuence nm (Ling) Basque.
vascular adj vascular.
vase (= **se va**) see **ir.**
vaselina nf Vaseline (Protected Trade Name), petroleum jelly.
vasera nf kitchen shelf, rack.
vasija nf vessel; container, recipient.
vaso nm (a) (Cook) glass, tumbler; vessel; container; (lit) vase, urn; (Col) small cup; — **de agua** glass of water; — **para vino** wineglass; — **de engrase** (Mech) grease cup; — **de noche** chamberpot; — **litúrgico,** — **sagrado** holy vessel, chalice; **ahogarse en un** — **de agua** to get worked up about nothing at all. (b) (quantity) glassful, glass. (c) (Anat) vessel; tube, duct; — **capilar** capillary; — **sanguíneo** blood vessel. (d) (Zool) hoof. (e) (Naut) hull; boat, ship, vessel.

vástago nm (a) (Bot) shoot, sprout, bud.
   (b) (Mech) rod; stem; — **de émbolo** piston rod.
   (c) (fig) scion, offspring.
   (d) (Col, CR, Ven) trunk of the banana tree.
vastedad nf vastness, immensity.
vasto adj vast, huge, immense.
vate nm (a) (Hist) seer, prophet. (b) (Lit) poet, bard.
vatiaje nm wattage.
Vaticano m Vatican.
vaticano adj Vatican; papal.
vaticinador nm seer, prophet.
vaticinar [1a] vt to prophesy, predict.
vaticinio nm prophecy, prediction.
vatio nm watt.
vaya etc see **ir.**
vecinal adj (a) road etc local; tax local, municipal; **padrón** — list of residents. (b) (SAm) neighbouring, adjacent.
vecindad nf (a) neighbourhood, vicinity.
   (b) (persons) neighbours, neighbourhood; local community; residents (of a block of flats).
   (c) (Law etc) residence, abode; **declarar su** — to state where one lives, give one's place of abode.
vecindario nm neighbourhood; local community, residents; (as total etc) population, inhabitants.
vecino 1 adj (a) neighbouring, adjacent, adjoining; near, nearby, close; house etc next; **el garaje** — **del mío** the garage next to mine; **no aquí sino en el pueblo** — not here but in the next village; **las dos fincas son vecinas** the two estates adjoin.
   (b) (fig) alike, similar; — **a** like, similar to.
2 nm, **vecina** nf (a) neighbour.
   (b) resident, inhabitant, citizen; **un pueblo de 800** — **s** a village of 800 inhabitants; **una vecina de la calle X** a resident in X street.
vector nm vector.
Veda m Veda.
veda nf (a) (act) prohibition; imposition of a close season. (b) close season.
vedado nm preserve; — **de caza** game preserve; **cazar** (or **pescar**) **en** — to poach, hunt (or fish) illegally.
vedar [1a] vt to prohibit, forbid, ban; to stop, prevent; idea, plan etc to veto; — **a uno hacer algo** to forbid someone to do something; to stop someone doing something, prevent someone from doing something.
vedette [be'ðet] nf (gall) star; starlet; (fig) star turn, main attraction.
védico adj Vedic.
vedija nf (a) tuft of wool. (b) mat of hair, matted hair.
vega nf (a) fertile plain, rich lowland area; water meadow(s); (Ec) stretch of alluvial soil. (b) (Ant) tobacco plantation.
vegetación nf (a) vegetation. (b) growth, growing. (c) (Med) —**es adenoideas** adenoids.
vegetal 1 adj vegetable, plant (attr); **patología** — plant pathology. **2** nm plant, vegetable; —**es** (CAm, Mex: angl) vegetables.
vegetar [1a] vi (a) (Bot) to grow. (b) (fig) to vegetate, live like a vegetable, stagnate.
vegetarianismo nm vegetarianism.
vegetariano 1 adj vegetarian. **2** nm, **vegetariana** nf vegetarian.
vegetativo adj vegetative.
vegoso adj (Chi) land moist, damp.
veguero 1 adj lowland (attr), of the plain. **2** nm (a) lowland farmer. (b) (Ant) tobacco planter. (c) coarse cigar; (Arg) good-quality Cuban tobacco, good cigar.
vehemencia nf vehemence; passion, impetuosity; fervour; eagerness, violence.
vehemente adj (a) vehement; passionate, impetuous; supporter etc fervent, passionate; desire strong, eager, violent; speaker passionate, forceful.
   (b) sign, suspicion etc strong.
vehículo nm (a) (Aut etc) vehicle; — **carretero** road vehicle; — **astral,** — **cósmico** spacecraft.
   (b) (fig) vehicle (de for); (Med) carrier, transmitter (de of).
veinte adj twenty; (date) twentieth.
veintena nf twenty, about twenty, a score.
veintiuna nf (Cards) pontoon.
vejación nf vexation, annoyance; **sufrir** —**es** to suffer vexations.
vejamen nm (a) =**vejación.** (b) satire, satirical composition; shaft, taunt.
vejaminoso adj (Per, PR) vexatious, annoying.
vejancón, vejarrón (fam) **1** adj ancient, doddery. **2** nm old chap (fam), old dodderer.

vejar [1a] vt to vex, annoy; to make feel small, humiliate; to harass.
vejarano adj (SAm) ancient, doddery, decrepit.
vejatorio adj vexatious, annoying; humiliating, degrading; **es** — **para él tener que pedirlo** it is humiliating for him to have to beg for it.
vejestorio nm, **vejete** nm old chap (fam), old boy (fam).
vejez nf (a) old age; **los males de la** — the ills of old age; **lo escribió en su** — he wrote it in old age.
   (b) (fig) peevishness; grouchiness (fam), grumpiness.
   (c) (fig) old story; piece of stale news.
vejiga nf (a) (Anat) bladder; — **de la bilis** gallbladder; — **natatoria** air bladder. (b) (Med, on paint etc) blister.
vela¹ nf (a) wakefulness, state of being awake; sleeplessness; **estar en** — to be unable to get to sleep, be still awake; **pasar la noche en** — to have a sleepless night, not sleep all night.
   (b) vigil; evening work, night work; (Mil) (period of) sentry duty.
   (c) candle; — **de sebo** tallow candle; **no se le dará** — **en este entierro** he will not be given any say in this matter.
   (d) (Taur: fam) horn.
   (e) (fam) —**s** mucus, snot (fam).
   (f) (CAm, SD) funeral wake.
   (g) (Arg) nuisance, bother; ¡**qué** —! what a nuisance!; **aguantar la** — to put up with it for someone else's sake.
   (h) (Cu, Mex) telling-off; **aguantar la** — to face the music.
vela² nf (Naut) sail; — **mayor** mainsail; **a toda** —, **a** —**s desplegadas** under full sail, (fig) vigorously, energetically, straining every nerve; **barco de** — sailing ship; **estar a dos** —**s** (fam) to be broke (fam); **estar entre dos** —**s** (fam) to be half-seas over; **darse a la** —, **hacerse a la** —, **largar las** —**s** to set sail, get under way; **arriar** —**s, recoger** —**s** (fig) to back down; to give up, chuck it up.
velada nf (evening) party, social gathering, soirée; — **musical** musical evening; **pasar una buena** — to have a pleasant evening.
velado adj veiled (also fig); (Phot) fogged, blurred; sound muffled.
velador nm (a) watchman, caretaker; (Hist) sentinel.
   (b) candlestick.
   (c) pedestal table; (SAm) night table.
   (d) (RPl) night light.
   (e) (Mex) lampshade.
veladora nf (a) (Mex) table lamp, bedside lamp. (b) (Mex: Eccl) paraffin lamp.
velamen nm sails, canvas.
velar¹ [1a] **1** vt (a) to watch, keep watch over; sick person to sit up with, stay by the bedside of.
   (b) (SAm) to look covetously at.
2 vi (a) to stay awake; to go without sleep; to stay up, sit up at night; to work late, do night duty; to keep watch, (Eccl) keep vigil.
   (b) to be solicitous; — **por** to watch over, look after; to guard, protect; — **por que se haga algo** to see to it (or ensure) that something is done; **no hay quien vele por sus intereses** there is nobody to watch over his interests.
   (c) (Naut: of reef) to appear.
velar² [1a] **1** vt (a) to veil. (b) (fig) to shroud, hide, veil. (c) (Phot) to fog, blur. **2 velarse** vr (a) to hide itself. (b) (Phot) to fog, blur.
velar³ adj (Ling) velar.
velarte nm (Hist) broadcloth.
velatorio nm funeral wake.
Velázquez m Velasquez.
veleidad nf (quality) fickleness, capriciousness, flightiness. (b) (una —) whim, caprice; unpredictable mood; strange fancy.
veleidoso adj fickle, capricious, flighty.
velero 1 adj ship fast. **2** nm (a) (Naut) sailing ship. (b) (Aer) glider. (c) (Naut) sailmaker.
veleta 1 nf (a) weather vane, weather cock. (b) (Fish) float. **2** nmf person who chops and changes, fickle person.
veletería nf (Chi) chopping and changing, fickleness.
velís nm, **veliz** nm (Mex) valise; bag, grip; **velices, velises** cases, luggage.
velo nm (a) veil; **tomar el** — to take the veil, become a nun.
   (b) (fig) veil, light covering; shroud; film; (Phot) fog, veiling.
   (c) (fig) pretext, cloak.
   (d) (fig) mental fog, confusion, lack of clarity.
   (e) (Anat) — **del paladar** soft palate, velum.

velocidad *nf* (a) speed; rate, pace, velocity; speediness, swiftness; **de alta —** high-speed; **— de crucero, — económica** cruising speed; **— limitada** speed limit; **— máxima, — punta** maximum speed, top speed; **— máxima permitida** speed limit; **a gran —** at high speed; **a máxima —, a toda —** at full speed, at top speed; **¿a qué —?** at what speed?, how fast?; **¿a qué — ibas?** what speed were you doing?; **cobrar —** to pick up speed, gather speed; **disminuir —, moderar la —** to slow down; **exceder la — permitida** to speed, exceed the speed limit.
(b) (*Mech*) gear, speed; **primera —** low gear, bottom gear, first gear; **segunda —** second gear; **—es de avance** forward gears; **4 —es hacia adelante** 4 forward gears.

velocímetro *nm* speedometer.
velocípedo *nm* velocipede.
velódromo *nm* cycle track.
velomotor *nm* autocycle.
velón *nm* (a) oil lamp. (b) (*Chi, Mex, Per*) thick tallow candle. (c) (*CAm*) sponger (*fam*), parasite. (d) (*Col, Ec, SD*) person who casts covetous glances.
velorio[1] *nm* (a) party, celebration; (*Ant, Arg, Ec*) dull party, flat affair.
(b) (*esp SAm*) funeral wake, vigil for the dead; **— del angelito** wake for a dead child.
velorio[2] *nm* (*Eccl*) taking the veil.
veloz *adj* fast, quick, swift; **— como un relámpago** as quick as lightning.
velozmente *adv* fast, quickly, swiftly.
vello *nm* (*Anat*) down, fuzz, hair; (*Bot*) down; (*on fruit*) bloom; (*on antlers*) velvet.
vellocino *nm* fleece; **V— de Oro** Golden Fleece.
vellón[1] *nm* (a) fleece; sheepskin. (b) tuft of wool.
vellón[2] *nm* (a) (*Tech*) copper and silver alloy. (b) (*PR, Pan*) five-cent coin.
vellonera *nf* (*PR, SD*) musical box; jukebox.
vellosidad *nf* downiness, fuzziness, hairiness; fluffiness.
velloso *adj* downy, fuzzy, hairy; fluffy.
velludo **1** *adj* hairy, shaggy. **2** *nm* plush, velvet.
vena *nf* (a) (*Anat*) vein; **— yugular** jugular vein.
(b) (*Min*) vein, seam, lode.
(c) (*in stone, wood*) grain.
(d) (*Bot*) vein, rib.
(e) (*Geog*) underground stream.
(f) (*fig*) vein; mood, disposition; **— de loco** streak of madness; oddity, mania; **coger a uno de** (*or* **en**) **—** to catch someone in the right mood; **le daba la — por ello** he took a fancy to it, the mood took him that way; **estar de** (*or* **en**) **—** to be in the vein, be in the mood (*para* for); to be in good form.
(g) (*fig*) talent, promise; **tiene — de pintor** he has the makings of a painter, he shows a talent for painting.
venablo *nm* javelin, dart; **echar —s** (*fig*) to burst out angrily.
venado *nm* (a) deer, stag.
(b) (*Cook*) venison.
(c) (*Cu*) deerskin.
(d) (*Cu*) whore.
(e) (*Ec*) contraband.
(f) (*Guat, Mex*) **correr el —, pintar el —** to play truant.
venal[1] *adj* (*Anat*) venous.
venal[2] *adj* (a) (*Comm*) commercial, that can be bought (*or* sold). (b) (*pej*) venal, corrupt.
venalidad *nf* venality, corruptness.
venático *adj* rather crazy, a bit mad.
venatorio *adj* hunting (*attr*).
vencedor **1** *adj* *player, team* winning, victorious; *general etc* victorious, successful; *nation* conquering, victorious.
2 *nm*, **vencedora** *nf* winner, victor; conqueror.
vencejo[1] *nm* (*Orn*) swift.
vencejo[2] *nm* (*Agr*) straw plait, string (*used in binding sheaves*).
vencer [2b] **1** *vt* (a) *enemy* to defeat, beat; to conquer, vanquish, overcome; (*Sport*) to beat; *rival* to outdo, surpass; *passion etc* to master, control, fight down; *temptation* to overcome; (*of sleep etc*) to overcome; **vence a todos en elegancia** he outdoes them all in elegance, he beats them all for elegance; **por fin le venció el sueño** finally sleep overcame him; **dejarse —** to yield, give in; **no te dejes —** don't give in, don't let yourself be beaten (by it).
(b) *difficulty, obstacle* to overcome, surmount, get round.
(c) *branch, support etc* to break down, snap, prove too heavy for; **el peso de los libros ha vencido el estante** the weight of the book has broken the shelf.

(d) *mountain, slope* to get to the top of, reach the summit of.
2 *vi* (a) to win; to win through, succeed, triumph; **¡venceremos!** we shall win!; we shall overcome!
(b) (*Comm etc: of term*) to expire, end; (*of payment etc*) to fall due; (*of bond*) to mature, become due for redemption; (*of policy etc*) to become invalid, cease to apply.
3 vencerse *vr* (a) to control oneself.
(b) (*support etc*) to break, snap, collapse (under the weight); (*Chi, RPl*) to break down, get worn out.
vencido **1** *adj* (a) beaten, defeated; *team etc* losing; **¡ay de los —s!** woe to the conquered!; **darse por —** to give up, acknowledge defeat; **ir de — —** to be all in, be on one's last legs; **la enfermedad va de vencida** the illness is past its worst; **la tormenta va de vencida** the worst of the storm is over.
(b) (*Comm etc*) mature; due, payable; **con los intereses —s** with the interest which is due; **pagar por meses —s** to pay by the month in arrears.
2 *adv*: **pagar —** to pay in arrears, pay for the month (*etc*) which is past.
vencimiento *nm* (a) (*under weight*) breaking, snapping; collapse. (b) (*Comm etc*) expiration; maturity; **al —, a su —** when it matures, when it falls due.
venda *nf* bandage.
vendaje[1] *nm* (*Med*) dressing, bandaging; **— provisional** first-aid bandage.
vendaje[2] *nm* (a) commission. (b) (*SAm*) bonus, small extra.
vendar [1a] *vt* (a) *wound* to bandage, dress; *eyes etc* to cover, put a bandage over, tie a cloth (*etc*) round. (b) (*fig*) to blind; to hoodwink.
vendaval *nm* gale, strong wind, hurricane; (*fig*) storm.
vendedor *nm* seller, vendor; retailer; (*in shop*) salesman; **— ambulante** hawker, pedlar, peddler (*US*).
vendedora *nf* seller; (*in shop*) salesgirl, saleswoman.
vendeja *nf* (a) public sale. (b) collection of goods offered for sale.
vender [2a] **1** *vt* (a) to sell; to market; (*pej*) to sell (improperly); **— por las casas** to peddle round the houses; **— al contado** to sell for cash; **— al por mayor** to sell wholesale; **— al por menor** to sell retail; **estar sin —** to remain unsold; **¡a mí que las vendo!** you can't catch an old bird with chaff!, I'm not falling for that one!
(b) (*fig*) to sell, betray.
2 venderse *vr* (a) to sell; to be sold; **— a, — por —** to sell at, sell for; to fetch, bring in; **este artículo se vende muy bien** this article is selling very well; **"se vende"** (*advert*) "for sale"; **"véndese coche"** (*advert*) "car for sale"; **no se vende** not for sale.
(b) (*fig*) **— caro** to play hard to get, be terribly choosy about one's friends (*fam*).
(c) (*fig*) to betray oneself, give oneself away.
vendí *nm* certificate of sale.
vendible *adj* saleable; marketable.
vendimia *nf* (a) grape harvest, wine harvest; (*with reference to quality, year*) year; **la — de 1973** the 1973 vintage. (b) (*fig*) big profit, killing.
vendimiador *nm*, **vendimiadora** *nf* vintager.
vendimiar [1b] *vt* (a) *grapes* to harvest, pick, gather. (b) (*fig*) to take a profit from, squeeze a profit out of, make a killing with. (c) (*sl*) to bump off (*sl*).
vendré *etc* see **venir**.
venduta *nf* (a) (*Col, Cu, Guat, Mex, Ven*) auction, public sale.
(b) (*Cu, SD*) greengrocer's (shop), fruiterer's (shop); small grocery store.
(c) (*PR*) betrayal.
vendutero *nm* (a) (*Col, Cu, Guat, Mex, Ven*) auctioneer. (b) (*Cu, SD*) greengrocer, fruiterer.
Venecia Venice.
veneciano **1** *adj* Venetian. **2** *nm*, **veneciana** *nf* Venetian.
veneno *nm* poison, venom.
venenoso *adj* poisonous, venomous.
venera *nf* scallop; scallop shell.
venerable *adj* venerable.
veneración *nf* veneration; worship.
venerando *adj* venerable.
venerar [1a] *vt* to venerate, revere; to worship.
venéreo *adj* venereal; **enfermedad venérea** venereal disease.
venero *nm* (a) (*Min*) lode, seam. (b) spring. (c) (*fig*) source, origin; **— de datos** mine of information.
venezolanismo *nm* word (*or* phrase *etc*) peculiar to Venezuela.

venezolano 1 *adj* Venezuelan. **2** *nm*, **venezolana** *nf* Venezuelan.

Venezuela *f* Venezuela.

vengador 1 *adj* avenging. **2** *nm*, **vengadora** *nf* avenger.

venganza *nf* vengeance, revenge; retaliation; **tomar — en uno** to take vengeance on someone.

vengar [1h] **1** *vt* to avenge. **2 vengarse** *vr* to take revenge (*de una ofensa* for an offence; *de uno, en uno* on someone), avenge oneself; to retaliate (*en* against, on).

vengativo *adj person, spirit* vindictive; *step* retaliatory.

vengo *etc see* **venir**.

venia *nf* (a) pardon, forgiveness.
(b) permission, consent; **con su —** by your leave, with your permission; **casarse sin la — de sus padres** to marry without the consent of one's parents.
(c) (*SAm: Mil*) salute.

venial *adj* venial.

venialidad *nf* veniality.

venida *nf* (a) coming; arrival; return. (b) (*fig*) impetuosity, rashness.

venidero *adj* coming, future; **los —s** future generations, posterity, our (*etc*) descendants; **en lo —** in (the) future.

venir [3s] **1** *vi* (a) (*general sense*) to come (*a* to, *de* from); to arrive; **¡ven!, ¡venga!** come along!; **¡ven acá!** come (over) here!; **vino a vernos** she came to see us; **— por** to come for; **no me vengas con historias** don't come telling tales to me; **hacer — a uno** to summon someone; to call someone, have someone fetched; **le hicieron — desde Londres** they fetched him (all the way) from London.
(b) (*of event*) to come, happen; **le vino una desgracia** she had a mishap, something untoward happened to her; **venga lo que viniere** come what may; **con todo lo que vino después** with everything that happened afterwards, with all that ensued; **(estar a) ver —** to wait and see what happens; to sit on the fence; **se puede ver — la noche** one can face the evening ahead; **vinieron sobre él muchos desastres** a host of disasters fell upon him.
(c) (*of time*) . . . **que viene** next . . . , *eg* **el mes que viene** next month.
(d) (*fig*) to come; **— de** to come from, proceed from, stem from; to originate in; **la finca le viene de su hermano** the estate comes to him from his brother; **de ahí vienen muchos males** many evils spring from that; **de ahí viene que . . .** hence it is that . . . , and so it is that . . . ; thus it follows that . . .
(e) (*fig: of feeling etc*) to come; **le vino la idea de + infin** there came to him the idea of + *ger*; **sentía —me sueño** I felt sleep coming over me; **me vinieron ganas de llorar** I felt like crying, I had an urge to cry.
(f) **— a + infin** to come to + *infin*, serve to + *infin*; **el desastre vino a turbar nuestra tranquilidad** the disaster served to destroy our peace; **viene a llenar un gran vacío** it serves to fill a large gap; **viene a cumplir lo que habíamos empezado** it helps to finish off what we had begun; **venimos a conocerle en Bolivia** we got to know him in Bolivia; **vino a dar en la cárcel** he ended up in jail; *see* **caso, menos** *etc*.
(g) **— a ser: viene a ser lo mismo** it comes to (about) the same thing; **viene a ser 84 en total** it amounts to 84 in all, it comes to 84 all together; **viene a ser más difícil que nunca** it's turning out to be more difficult than ever.
(h) **— bien** to come just right; to be suitable, be convenient; to fit; (*Bot*) to do well, grow nicely; **eso vendrá bien para el invierno** that will come in handy for the winter; **no me viene muy bien aquello** that doesn't suit me all that well; **— bien a** (*of dress*) to suit, look well on, fit, be right for; **el tapón viene justo a la botella** the stopper fits the bottle exactly; **el abrigo te viene algo pequeño** the coat is rather small on you; **te viene estrecho por las espaldas** it's too tight round your shoulders; **— mal** to come awkwardly, be inconvenient (*a* for); **— mal a** (*of dress*) to look wrong on, not fit.
(i) (*idioms*) **¿a qué viene afligirte?** why get so worked up?, what's the point of distressing yourself?; **¡venga!** (*fam*) let's have it!, hand it over!; **¡venga la pluma esa!** let's have (a look at) that pen!; **¡venga una canción!** let's have a song!
(j) (*in continuous tenses*) **venían andando desde mediodía** they had been walking since midday; **viene gastando mucho** she has been spend-

ing a lot; **eso vengo diciendo** that's what I've been saying all along.
(k) (+ *ptp*) **vengo cansado** I'm tired; **venía hecho polvo** he was worn out.
2 venirse *vr* (a) (*of wine*) to ferment; (*of dough*) to work.
(b) **— abajo, — al suelo, — a (la) tierra** to fall down, collapse, tumble down; (*fig*) to fail, collapse, be ruined.
(c) **se nos vino encima la guerra** the war came upon us; **parece que todo se nos viene encima a la vez** everything seems to be happening to us all at once; **cualquier cosita se le viene encima** any little thing gets him down.
(d) *see* **mano** *etc*.

venoso *adj* (a) *blood* venous. (b) *leaf etc* veined, ribbed.

venta *nf* (a) (*Comm*) sale; selling; marketing; **— por balance, — postbalance** stocktaking sale; **— al contado** cash sale; **— de liquidación** sale, clearance sale; **— a plazos** hire purchase; **— al (por) mayor** wholesale; **— al (por) menor, — al detalle** retail; **— pública** public sale, auction; **precio de —** sale price; **poner algo a la —** to put something on sale, put something up for sale; to market a product; **estar de** (*or* **en**) **—** to be (up) for sale, be on the market.
(b) country inn.
(c) (*Mex, SD*) small shop, stall; (*Chi*) stall, booth (*at fair etc*).

ventada *nf* gust of wind.

ventaja *nf* (a) advantage; (*in a race*) start, advantage; (*Tennis*) vantage; (*in betting*) odds; **es un plan que tiene muchas —s** it is a plan that has many advantages; **me dio una — de 4 metros, me dio 4 metros de —** he gave me 4 metres start; **me dio una — de 20 puntos** he gave me an advantage of 20 points, he handicapped himself by 20 points; **llevar (la) — a** to have the advantage over; to be ahead of; to be one up on; **la — que A le lleva a B es grande** A has a big advantage over B; **sacar — de** to derive profit from, (*pej*) use to one's own advantage.
(b) (*Fin: esp SAm*) profit, gain; **dejar buena —** to bring in a good profit.
(c) **—s** (*in a job*) extras, perks (*fam*).

ventajear [1a] *vt* (*Col, Guat, RPI*) (a) = **aventajar**.
(b) (*pej*) **— a uno** to beat someone to it, get an improper advantage over someone.

ventajero *adj* (*SAm*) = **ventajista**.

ventajista *adj* unscrupulous; self-seeking, grasping; sly, treacherous.

ventajosamente *adv* advantageously; (*Fin*) profitably; **estar — colocado** to be well placed.

ventajoso *adj* (a) advantageous; (*Fin*) profitable.
(b) (*SAm*) = **ventajista**.

ventana *nf* (a) window; **— de guillotina** sash window; **— de la nariz** nostril; **— salediza** bay window; **tirar algo por la —** to throw something out of the window; (*fig*) to throw something away, fail to make any use of something.
(b) (*Col, Ven*) forest clearing, glade.

ventanaje *nm* windows.

ventanal *nm* large window.

ventanear [1a] *vi* to be always at the window, be forever peeping out.

ventanilla *nf* (a) small window; window (*of booking office etc*); (*Aut*) window. (b) (*Anat: also* **— de la nariz**) nostril.

ventanillo *nm* small window; peephole.

ventarrón *nm* (*fam*) gale, violent wind, blast.

ventear [1a] **1** *vt* (a) (*of dog etc*) *air* to sniff.
(b) *clothes etc* to air, put out to dry, expose to the wind.
(c) (*CAm, Mex*) *animal* to brand.
(d) (*Arg, Par*) *competitor* to get far ahead of, leave far behind.
(e) (*Col, PR*) to fan, winnow.
2 *vi* to snoop, pry, come poking about; to inquire, investigate.
3 ventearse *vr* (a) to split, crack; to blister; to get too dry, spoil.
(b) (*Anat*) to break wind.
(c) (*Arg, Chi, Per, PR*) to be outdoors a great deal; to spend a long time away from home.
(d) (*Col, Ec, Per, PR*) to get conceited.

ventero *nm*, **ventera** *nf* innkeeper.

ventilación *nf* (a) ventilation; **sin —** unventilated.
(b) draught, air. (c) ventilator, opening for ventilation. (d) (*fig*) airing, discussion.

ventilado *adj* draughty, breezy.

ventilador *nm* ventilator; fan.

ventilar [1a] **1** vt **(a)** room etc to ventilate. **(b)** clothing etc to air, put out to air, dry in the air. **(c)** (fig) matter to air, discuss, talk over. **(d)** (fig) private matter to make public, reveal. **2 ventilarse** vr **(a)** to ventilate, air. **(b)** (person) to get some air, take a breather.

ventisca nf blizzard, snowstorm.

ventiscar [1g] vi, **ventisquear** [1a] vi to blow a blizzard, snow with a strong wind; (of snow) to drift.

ventisquero nm **(a)** blizzard, snowstorm. **(b)** glacier; snowdrift; gully (etc) where the snow lies.

ventolera nf **(a)** gust of wind, blast. **(b)** (toy) windmill. **(c)** (fig) vanity, conceit; smugness; arrogance; boastfulness. **(d)** (fig) whim, wild idea; **le dio la — de** + infin he had a sudden notion to + infin. **(e)** (Mex) wind, flatulence.

ventolina nf **(a)** (Naut) light wind. **(b)** (Arg, Chi, Mex) sudden gust of wind. **(c)** (Chi) wind, flatulence.

ventorrillo nm **(a)** small inn, roadhouse. **(b)** (SAm) small shop.

ventosa nf **(a)** vent, airhole. **(b)** (Zool) sucker; (Tech) peg (etc) that adheres by suction. **(c)** (Med) cupping glass.

ventosear [1a] vi to break wind.

ventosidad nf wind; flatulence, windiness.

ventoso adj **(a)** windy. **(b)** (Anat) windy, flatulent.

ventral adj ventral.

ventregada nf brood, litter.

ventrículo nm ventricle.

ventrílocuo nm, **ventrílocua** nf ventriloquist.

ventriloquia nf ventriloquism.

ventrudo adj fat, potbellied.

ventura nf **(a)** happiness. **(b)** luck, (good) fortune; chance; **mala —** ill luck; **por su mala —** as ill luck would have it; **a la — — at random; ir a la —** to go haphazardly, go without a fixed plan; **vivir a la —** to live in a disorganized way; **todo lo hace a la —** he does it all in a hit-or-miss fashion; **por —** fortunately; perhaps, by chance, eg **¿piensas ir, por —?** are you by any chance thinking of going?; **echar la buena — a uno** to tell someone's fortune; **probar la —** to try one's luck; **te dé Dios —** I wish you luck; **viene la — a quien la procura** fortune favours the brave.

venturero adj (Mex) crop out of season; (fig) temporary; casual; irregular.

venturoso adj happy; lucky, fortunate.

Venus 1 nf Venus. **2** nm (Astron) Venus.

venus nf (fig) venery, love-making, sexual delights.

venusiano 1 adj Venusian. **2** nm, **venusiana** nf Venusian.

ver [2v] **1** vti **(a)** (general sense) to see; (esp SAm) to look at, watch; **la vi bajar la escalera** I saw her come downstairs; **lo he visto hacer muchas veces** I have often seen it done; **no lo veo** I can't see it; **desde aquí lo verás** you can see it from here; **¡lo que ves!** can't you see?, it's there for you to see!; **no veo nada en contra de eso** I see nothing against it; **— es creer** seeing is believing; **— y callar** it's best to keep one's mouth shut about this; **ir a — a uno** to go to see someone, go and see someone; **voy a —** I'll go and see; **¡a —!** let's see!, let's have a look!, show me!; (fig) I say!, hey!; **¿a —?** what's all this?; **a — qué nos dices** let's see what you've got to say; **¡a — qué pasa!** (fam) just you dare!; **a — si . . .** I wonder if . . .; **a — si acabas pronto** I hope you can finish this off quickly; **es de —** it's worth seeing, you really should see it; **eso está por —** that remains to be seen. **(b)** (fig) to see, understand; **¿ves?** do you see?, (do you) get it?; **lo veo** I see; **¡verás!** you'll see!; **veremos** we'll see (about that); **¿no ves que . . .?** don't you see that . . .?; **como vimos ayer en la conferencia** as we saw in the lecture yesterday; **como veremos más adelante** as we shall see later; **según voy viendo** as I am now beginning to see; **no veo claro por qué lo quiere** I don't really see why he wants it; **a mi modo de ver** in my view; as I see it. **(c)** (fig) to look into, examine, inquire into; **lo veremos** we'll look into it. **(d)** (Law) case, appeal to try, hear. **(e)** **— de** + infin to see about + ger. **(f)** (idioms) **¡para que veas!** so there!; **si te vi no me acuerdo** they (etc) just don't want to know; **me lo estoy viendo de almirante** I can just imagine him as an admiral; **lo estaba viendo** it's just what I expected, one could see this coming; **dejarse —**

(effect etc) **to show**, become apparent; to begin to tell; (person) to show up, show one's face; **no dejarse —** to keep away; to lie low, stay hidden; **la preocupación se dejaba — en su cara** the worry showed in his face; **echar de — algo** to notice something; **¡hay que —!** it just goes to show!; **hacer — que . . .** to point out that . . ., prove that . . .; **no le puedo —** I hate the sight of him, I can't stand him; **tener que — con** to concern, have to do with; **A no tiene nada que — con B** A has nothing to do with B; **vamos a —** let's see . . ., let me see . . .; **¿por qué no lo compraste, vamos a —?** why didn't you buy it, I'd like to know?; see also **visto**. **(g)** (SAm idioms) **¡nos estamos viendo!** (Mex) au revoir!; **eso está en veremos** (SAm) that's still a long way off, that's very much in the future; **lo dijo por —** (Ant), **lo dijo por de —** (Chi) he said it just as a joke.

2 verse vr **(a)** (two persons) to see each other; to meet; **— con uno** to see someone, have a talk (or interview) with someone; **ahora apenas nos vemos** we hardly see each other nowadays. **(b)** (one person: etc) to see oneself; to be seen; **véase la página 9** see page 9; **se le veía mucho en el parque** he used to be seen a lot in the park; **desde aquí no se ve** you can't see it from here; **ya se ve** naturally, plainly; **ya se ve que . . .** it is obvious that . . .; **¿cuándo se vio nada igual?** when did you hear of anything like this?; **no se ha visto un lío parecido** you never saw such a mess, it was the biggest mess ever; **¡hábráse visto!** did you ever! (fam); of all the cheek!; **¡que se vean los forzudos!** let's see how tough you are!; come on, you tough guys! (US fam). **(c)** to find oneself, be; **— en un apuro** to be in a jam; **se veía en la cumbre de la fama** he was at the height of his fame.

3 nm **(a)** looks, appearance; **de buen —** good-looking, of agreeable appearance; **tener buen —** to be good-looking; **no tiene mal —** she's not bad-looking. **(b)** **a mi —** in my view, as I see it. **(c)** **a más —, hasta más —** au revoir.

vera nf edge, verge, border; (of river) bank; **a la — de** near, beside, next to; **se sentó a mi —** he sat down beside me.

veracidad nf truthfulness, veracity.

veragua nf (CAm) mildew (on cloth).

veranda nf veranda(h).

veraneante nmf holidaymaker, (summer) vacationist (US).

veranear [1a] vi to spend the summer (holiday); **veranean en Jaca** they go to Jaca for the summer, they holiday in Jaca; **es un buen sitio para —** it's a nice place for a summer holiday.

veraneo nm summer holiday; **lugar de —, punto de —** summer resort, holiday resort; **estar de —** to be away on one's summer holiday; **ir de — a la montaña** to go off to spend one's summer holidays in the mountains.

veraniego adj **(a)** summer (attr). **(b)** (fig) slight, trivial.

veranillo nm **(a)** **— de San Martín** Indian summer. **(b)** (CAm) dry spell in the rainy season; **— de San Juan** (RPl) warm spell in June.

verano nm **(a)** summer. **(b)** (Ec, Mex) dry season.

veranoso adj (SAm) dry.

veras nfpl **(a)** truth, reality; serious things; hard facts; **burlas y —** light-hearted and serious things. **(b)** **de —** really, truly; sincerely; in earnest; **¿de —?** really?, indeed?, is that so?; **lo siento de —** I am truly sorry; **ahora me duele de —** now it really does hurt me; **esto va de —** this is serious; I'm in earnest; **ahora va de — que lo hago** now I really am going to do it; **esta vez va de —** this time it's the real thing.

veraz adj truthful, veracious.

verbal adj verbal; oral.

verbalmente adv verbally; orally.

verbena nf **(a)** (Bot) verbena. **(b)** fair; open-air celebration on the eve of a saint's day; open-air dance.

verbenero adj of (or relating to) a verbena (see verbena (b)); **alegría verbenera** fun of the fair; **música verbenera** fairground music.

verbigracia adv for example, eg.

verbo nm **(a)** (Gram) verb; **— activo** transitive verb; **— auxiliar** auxiliary verb; **— defectivo** defective verb; **— deponente** deponent verb; **— finito** finite verb; **— intransitivo, — neutro** intransitive verb; **— reflexivo** reflexive verb; **— transitivo** transitive verb.

(b) curse, oath; **echar** —**s** to swear, curse.
(c) (*Lit*) language, diction, style; **de** — **elegante** elegant in style.
(d) **el V**— (*Rel*) the Word.
verborragia *nf*, **verborrea** *nf* verbosity, verbal diarrhoea (*fam*); verbiage.
verbosidad *nf* verbosity, wordiness; verbiage.
verboso *adj* verbose, wordy.
verdad *nf* (a) truth; truthfulness; reliability, trustworthiness; **la** — **de su relato** the truthfulness of his tale, the reliability of his account; **la** — **lisa y llana** the plain truth; **la pura** — **es que** ... the plain truth is that ... ; **a la** — really, in truth; **de** — (*adj*) real, proper, *eg* **un héroe de** — a real hero; (*adv*) really, properly, *eg* **entonces la pegó de** — then he really did hit her; **¿de** —**?** really?; **en** — really, truly; **pues, la** — **no sé** well, the truth is I don't know; well, truth to tell, I don't know; **decir la** — to tell the truth; **decir la** — **al lucero del alba** to be very outspoken; to be utterly truthful; **faltar a la** — to lie, be untruthful; **hablar con** — to speak truthfully; **hay una parte de** — **en esto** there is some truth in this.
(b) **es** — it is true, it is so; (*as confession*) yes; I'm afraid so; **eso no es** — that is not true; **es** — **que** ... it is true that ... ; **bien es** — **que** ... it is of course true that ... , it is certainly true that ... ; **si bien es** — **que** ... even though ... , despite the fact that ... ; **¿**—**?, ¿no es** —**?** isn't it?, aren't you?, don't you? (*etc*), isn't that so?
(c) — **de clavo pasado,** — **de Pero Grullo** platitude, truism; —**es del barquero** plain truths; **es una** — **como un puño** it's as plain as a pikestaff; **decir cuatro** —**es a uno** to tell someone a few home truths, give someone a piece of one's mind.
verdaderamente *adv* really, indeed; truly; —**, no sé** I really don't know; **un hombre** — **bueno** a truly good man; **es** — **triste** it's really sad.
verdadero *adj* (a) *account, description etc* true, truthful; reliable, trustworthy.
(b) *person* truthful.
(c) (*fig*) true, real, veritable; **es un** — **héroe** he's a real hero; **fue un** — **desastre** it was a real disaster, it was a veritable disaster; **es un** — **amigo** he's a true friend.
verde 1 *adj* (a) green.
(b) *fruit etc* green, unripe; *plant* green; *vegetables* green, fresh; *wood* unseasoned; (*fig*) *plan etc* premature; **¡están** —**s!** sour grapes!; **segar la hierba en** — to cut the grass while it is still green.
(c) (*fig*) *person* unduly amorous, sexy (despite one's advanced years); **viejo** — randy old man, dirty old man; **viuda** — merry widow (*euph*).
(d) (*fig*) *joke, song etc* blue, smutty, scabrous, dirty.
(e) (*idioms*) **estar** — **de envidia** to be green with envy; **¡si piensan eso, están** —**s!** if that's what they think, they've got another think coming!; **pasar las** —**s y las maduras** to have a rough time of it; **poner** — **a uno** (*fam*) to give someone a dressing-down; to abuse someone violently; to run someone down.
2 *nm* (a) green, green colour.
(b) (*Bot*) green, green grass; foliage; (*Agr*) green fodder; **sentarse en el** — to sit on the grass.
(c) **darse un** — to eat a lot, eat one's fill (**de** of); **darse un** — **de conciertos** to have a surfeit of concerts, have one's fill of concerts.
(d) (*RPl*) grass, pasture; maté; salad.
(e) (*Col, Ec*) green banana.
(f) (*PR, Mex*) country, countryside.
(g) (*Cu*) policeman.
verdear [1a] *vi* (a) to look green; to incline to green, be greenish.
(b) to turn green, grow green.
(c) (*RPl*) to drink maté.
(d) (*RPl: Agr*) to graze.
verdecer [2d] *vi* to turn green, grow green; (*of person*) to go green.
verdegay 1 *adj* light green. **2** *nm* light green.
verdemar 1 *adj* sea-green. **2** *nm* sea green.
verde-oliva *adj invar* olive-green.
verderón *nm* (*Orn*) greenfinch.
verdete *nm* verdigris.
verdiblanco *adj* green and white.
verdín *nm* (a) bright green, fresh green. (b) (*Bot*) scum; moss; verdigris. (c) (*on clothing etc*) green stain.
verdinegro *adj* dark green.
verdino *adj* bright green.
verdirrojo *adj* green and red.

verdón 1 *adj* (*Arg*) (a) bright green. (b) *fruit* slow to ripen. **2** *nm* (a) (*Orn*) = **verderón**. (b) (*Arg*) bruise, welt.
verdor *nm* (a) greenness; (*Bot*) verdure, lushness. (b) (*fig*: *also* —**es**) youthful vigour, lustiness.
verdoso *adj* greenish.
verdugo *nm* (a) (*Hist*) executioner; hangman.
(b) (*fig*) cruel master, slave driver; tyrant; tormentor.
(c) (*fig*) torment.
(d) lash.
(e) weal, welt.
(f) (*Bot*) twig, shoot, sprout.
(g) slender rapier.
verdugón *nm* (a) weal, welt. (b) (*Bot*) twig, shoot, sprout. (c) (*Bol*) rent, rip.
verdulera *nf* (a) greengrocer. (b) (*pej*) coarse woman, fishwife.
verdulería *nf* greengrocer's (shop).
verdulero *nm* greengrocer.
verdura *nf* (a) greenness; (*Bot*) greenery, verdure. (b) —**s** (*Cook*) greens, green vegetables, (*esp*) cabbage. (c) (*fig*) smuttiness, scabrous nature.
verdusco *adj* dark green, dirty green.
verecundia *nf* bashfulness, sensitivity.
verecundo *adj* bashful, sensitive.
vereda *nf* (a) path, lane; **ir por la** — (*fig*) to do the right thing; to keep to the straight and narrow.
(b) (*SAm*) pavement, sidewalk (*US*).
(c) (*Col*) village, settlement; section of a village.
(d) (*Mex*) parting (*in the hair*).
veredicto *nm* verdict; — **de culpabilidad** verdict of guilty.
veredón *nm* (*Arg*) broad pavement, broad sidewalk (*US*).
verga *nf* (a) rod, stick; (*Naut*) yard, spar. (b) (*Anat: Zool*) penis.
vergajo *nm* (a) pizzle; lash, whip. (b) (*Col*) rotter, cad.
vergonzante *adj* (a) shamefaced, full of shame; **pobre** — poor but too ashamed to beg. (b) shameful, shaming.
vergonzosamente *adv* (a) bashfully, shyly; modestly. (b) shamefully, disgracefully.
vergonzoso *adj* (a) *person* bashful, shy, timid; modest. (b) *act, matter etc* shameful, disgraceful, shocking; **es** — **que** ... it is disgraceful that ...
(c) (*Anat*) **partes vergonzosas** private parts.
vergüenza *nf* (a) shame; sense of shame, feelings of shame; **perder la** — to lose all sense of shame, cast aside all restraints; **sacar a uno a la** — to hold someone up to shame; **tener** — to be ashamed; **tener** — **de** + *infin* to be ashamed to + *infin*; **si tuviera** — **no lo haría** if he had any shame he wouldn't do it.
(b) bashfulness, shyness, timidity; embarrassment; (*sexual*) shame, modesty; **me da** — **decírselo** I feel too shy to say it to him, it embarrasses me to say it to him, it upsets me to say it to him.
(c) disgrace; **¡qué** —**!** what a disgrace!, what a scandal!; **shame** (on you)!; **el hijo es la** — **de su familia** the son is a disgrace to his family; **es una** — **que esté tan sucio** it's a disgrace that it should be so dirty.
(d) —**s** (*Anat*) private parts.
vericueto *nm* rough part, rough track, piece of difficult terrain.
verídico *adj* true, truthful.
verificable *adj* verifiable.
verificación *nf* (a) check, checkup, inspection; testing; verification; proving. (b) carrying out; performance; holding. (c) realization.
verificar [1a] **1** *vt* (a) *machine, meter etc* to check, inspect; to test; *results* to check (up on); *facts* to verify, establish, substantiate; *will* to prove.
(b) *test etc* to carry out; *marriage, ceremony* to perform; *election* to hold.
2 verificarse *vr* (a) (*event etc*) to occur, happen; (*meeting etc*) to be held, take place.
(b) (*prediction etc*) to come true, prove true, be realized.
verija *nf* (a) (*Anat*) groin, genital region. (b) (*SAm*) flank (*of a horse*).
verijón *adj* (*Mex*) slow, sluggish.
veringo *adj* (*Col*) nude, naked.
veringuearse [1a] *vr* (*Col*) to undress.
verismo *nm* realism, truthfulness; factual nature.
verista *adj* realistic, true to life; factual.
verja *nf* grating, grille; railing(s); iron gate.
vermicida *nm* vermicide.
vermífugo *nm* vermifuge.
verminoso *adj* infected, wormy.

vermut [ber'mu] *nm*, *pl* **vermuts** [ber'mu] (*gall*)
(a) vermouth. (b) (*Chi, RPl: Theat*) early performance.

vernáculo *adj* vernacular; **lengua vernácula** vernacular.

vernal *adj* spring (*attr*), vernal.

Verónica *f* Veronica.

verónica *nf* (a) (*Bot*) veronica, speedwell. (b) (*Taur*) a kind of pass with the cape.

verosímil *adj* likely, probable; *story* credible.

verosimilitud *nf* likeliness, probability; credibility; (*Lit*) verisimilitude.

verosímilmente *adv* in a likely way; credibly.

verraco *nm* boar, male pig; (*Col*) ram; (*Cu*) wild boar.

verraquear [1a] *vi* (a) to grunt. (b) (*of child*) to wail, howl with rage.

verraquera *nf* (a) crying spell, fit of rage, tantrum (*fam*). (b) (*Cu*) drunken spell.

verruga *nf* (a) (*Anat, Bot*) wart. (b) (*fam*) bore, pest, nuisance. (c) (*fam*) defect; stain (on one's character).

verrugoso *adj* warty, covered in warts.

versación *nf* (*Arg, Chi, Mex*) expertise, expertness.

versada *nf* (*SAm*) long tedious poem.

versado *adj*: — **en** versed in, conversant with; expert in, skilled in.

versal (*Typ*) **1** *adj* capital. **2** *nf* capital (letter).

versalitas *nfpl* (*Typ*) small capitals.

Versalles Versailles.

versar [1a] *vi* (a) to go round, turn.
(b) — **sobre** to deal with, discuss, be about; to turn on.
(c) (*Cu, PR*) to versify, improvise verses.
(d) (*Cu*) to chat, talk.
(e) to tease, crack jokes.

versátil *adj* (a) (*Anat etc*) mobile, loose, easily turned. (b) (*fig*) versatile. (c) (*fig: pej*) fickle, changeable.

versatilidad *nf* (a) mobility, looseness, ease of movement. (b) (*fig*) versatility. (c) (*fig: pej*) fickleness, changeableness.

versículo *nm* (*Bible*) verse.

versificación *nf* versification.

versificador *nm*, **versificadora** *nf* versifier.

versificar [1g] **1** *vt* to versify, put into verse. **2** *vi* to write verses, versify.

versión *nf* version; translation.

verso *nm* (a) (*in general*) verse; — **libre** free verse; — **suelto** blank verse; **teatro en** — verse drama.
(b) (*un* —) line; **en el segundo** — **del poema** in the second line of the poem.
(c) (*Mex, Ven*) **echar** — to gab (*fam*), talk just for talking's sake; to talk nonsense.

vértebra *nf* vertebra.

vertebrado 1 *adj* vertebrate. **2** *nm* vertebrate.

vertebral *adj* vertebral.

vertedero *nm* (a) rubbish dump, tip. (b) =**vertedor** (a). (c) (*Arg*) slope, hillside, cliff.

vertedor *nm* (a) runway, overflow; drain, outlet; spillway. (b) (*Naut*) scoop, bailer. (c) (*in shop etc*) scoop, small shovel.

verter [2g] **1** *vt* (a) *contents, liquid etc* to pour (out); to empty (out); (*by accident*) to pour, spill; *light, blood* to shed; *rubbish* to dump, tip, shoot; — **los granos del saco en el camión** to pour grain from a sack into a lorry; — **el café sobre el mantel** to spill (*or* upset) one's coffee on the tablecloth.
(b) *container* to empty (out); to tip up; (*accidentally*) to upset.
(c) (*Ling*) to translate (*a* into).
2 *vi* (*of river*) to flow, run (*a* into); (*of slope etc*) to fall (*a* towards).

vertical 1 *adj* vertical; upright. **2** *nf* vertical.

verticalidad *nf* vertical position; vertical direction.

verticalmente *adv* vertically.

vértice *nm* (a) vertex, apex; top; — **geodésico** bench mark, survey point. (b) (*Anat*) crown of the head.

verticilo *nm* whorl.

vertiente *nf* (a) slope. (b) (*Col, Chi, Mex, RPl*) spring, fountain.

vertiginosamente *adv* (a) giddily, dizzily. (b) (*fig*) excessively; very rapidly; **los precios suben** — prices are rising rapidly, prices are spiralling up.

vertiginoso *adj* (a) giddy, dizzy, vertiginous. (b) (*fig*) *speed* dizzy, excessive; *rise etc* very rapid.

vértigo *nm* (*Med*) giddiness, dizziness, vertigo; dizzy spell; **puede provocar** —**s** it may cause giddiness; **bajar así me produce** — going down like that makes me dizzy.
(b) (*fig*) sudden frenzy; fit of madness, aberration.
(c) (*fig*) intense activity; whirl, maelstrom; frenzy; **el** — **de los negocios** the frenzied rush of

business; **el** — **de los placeres** the whirl of pleasures.
(d) **de** — (*fam*): **con una velocidad de** — at a giddy speed; **fue un jaleo de** — it was an almighty row (*fam*); **tiene un talento de** — he has a fantastic talent; **es de** — **cómo crece la ciudad** the city grows at a frenzied speed, the town spreads at a tremendous rate (*fam*).

vesania *nf* rage, fury.

vesánico *adj* raging, furious.

vesícula *nf* vesicle; blister; — **biliar** gall-bladder.

vespasiana *nf* (*Arg, Chi: gall*) public lavatory, urinal.

vespertino *adj* evening (*attr*).

vestal 1 *adj* vestal. **2** *nf* vestal.

vestíbulo *nm* vestibule, lobby, hall; (*Theat*) foyer.

vestido *nm* (a) (*in general*) dress, costume, clothing; **historia del** — history of costume.
(b) (*un* —: *woman's*) dress, frock; costume, suit; (*Chi, Pan, Per: man's*) suit; — **de debajo** undergarment; — **de encima** outer garment.

vestidor *nm* dressing room.

vestidura *nf* (a) (*lit*) clothing, apparel.
(b) (*Eccl*) —**s** vestments; —**s sacerdotales** priestly vestments; **rasgarse las** —**s** (*fig*) to make a great show of being shocked.

vestigial *adj* vestigial.

vestigio *nm* vestige, trace; sign; —**s** remains, relics; **no quedaba el menor** — **de ello** there was not the slightest trace of it.

vestimenta *nf* (a) clothing; (*pej*) gear (*fam*), stuff (*fam*), things. (b) (*Eccl*) —**s** vestments.

vestir [31] **1** *vt* (a) *body, person* to dress (*de* in), clothe (*de* in, with); *statue, surface etc* to clothe, cover, drape (*de* in, with); *wall* to hang (*de* with); to dress up, adorn, deck, embellish (*de* with); **estar vestido de** to be dressed in, be clad in; (*as disguise*) to be dressed as.
(b) *garment* to don, put on; to wear; **vestía traje azul con sombrero** he was wearing a blue suit and a hat; **lo viste siempre** she always wears it.
(c) (*of parent etc*) to clothe, pay for the clothing of.
(d) (*of tailor*) to dress, make clothes for; **le viste un buen sastre** he has his clothes made at a good tailor's.
(e) *idea etc* to express (*de* in); *defect etc* to conceal, cover up, disguise; — **el rostro de gravedad** to put on a serious expression.
2 *vi* (a) to dress; — **bien** to dress well; — **con elegancia** to dress smartly; — **de negro** to dress in black, wear black; — **de uniforme** to wear a uniform; **el mismo que viste y calza** the selfsame, the very same.
(b) (*of dress*) to look well, be right (for an occasion); **traje de (mucho)** — formal suit, (*pej*) suit that is too dressy; **el vestido negro viste más que el azul** the black dress is more formal (*or* suitable) than the blue one.
3 vestirse *vr* (a) to dress oneself, get dressed, put on one's clothes; (*fig*) to cover itself, become covered (*de* in); — **de azul** to wear blue, dress in blue; **el árbol se está vistiendo de verde** the tree is coming out in leaf, the tree is turning green; **su querida se viste en París** his mistress buys her clothes in Paris; **apenas gana para** — she hardly earns enough to keep her in clothes.
(b) (*fig: Med*) to get up again (after an illness).
(c) (*fig*) — **de cierta actitud** to adopt a certain attitude; — **de severidad** to adopt a severe tone (*etc*).

vestón *nm* (*Chi: gall*) jacket.

vestuario *nm* (a) clothes, wardrobe; (*Theat*) wardrobe, costumes; (*Mil*) uniform.
(b) (*Theat*) dressing room, (*loosely*) backstage area; (*in public building etc*) cloakroom; (*Sport*) changing room; pavilion.

Vesubio *m* Vesuvius.

veta *nf* (*Min*) seam, vein, lode; (*in wood*) grain; (*in stone, meat etc*) streak, stripe.

vetar [1a] *vt* to veto.

vetazo *nm* (*Ec*) lash.

veteada *nf* (*Ec*) flogging, beating.

veteado 1 *adj* veined; grained; streaked, striped (*de* with). **2** *nm* veining; graining; streaks, markings.

vetear [1a] *vt* (a) to grain; to streak. (b) (*Ec*) to flog, beat.

veteranía *nf* status (*or* dignity *etc*) of being a veteran; long service; seniority.

veterano 1 *adj* veteran. **2** *nm* veteran; (*fig*) old hand, old stager.

veterinaria *nf* veterinary science.

veterinario *nm* veterinary surgeon, vet (*fam*), veterinarian (*US*).

veto *nm* veto; **poner (su)** — **a** to veto; **tener** — to have a veto.

vetulio *nm* (*Ec*) old man.

vetustez *nf* (*lit*) great age, antiquity; (*iro*) venerable nature; hoariness.

vetusto *adj* (*lit*) very old, ancient, venerable; (*iro*) venerable, ancient; hoary.

vez *nf* (a) time, occasion; instance; **aquella** — **en Tánger** that time in Tangiers; **a veces** at times; **a la** — at a time, at the same time; **a la** — **que** . . . at the same time as . . . ; **alguna** —, **algunas veces** sometimes; **¿lo viste alguna** —? did you ever see it?; **alguna que otra** — occasionally, now and again; **cada** — every time; **cada** — **que** . . . (*as conj*) each time that . . . , whenever . . . ; **cada** — **más** increasingly, more and more; **iba cada** — **más lento** it went slower and slower; **le encuentro cada** — **más inaguantable** he gets more and more unbearable; **contadas veces** seldom, rarely; **¿cuántas veces?** how often?, how many times?; **de** — **en cuando** now and again, from time to time, occasionally; **en veces** by fits and starts; with interruptions; **las más veces** most of the times, mostly, in most cases; **muchas veces** often; **otra** — again; **pocas veces** seldom, rarely; **por esta** — this time, this once; **rara** — seldom, rarely; **repetidas veces** repeatedly, over and over again; **tal** — perhaps; **toda** — **que** . . . (*as conj*) since . . . ; in view of the fact that . . . ; **varias veces** several times; repeatedly.

(b) (*with numeral*) **una** — once; **una** — **que** (*as conj*) once . . . ; **una** — **dice que sí y otra que no** first he says yes and then he says no; **érase una** — once upon a time (there was); **había una** — **una princesa** there was once a princess; **de una** — in one go, all at once; outright; without a break, straight off; **¡acabemos de una** —**!** let's get it over!, let's have done with it!; **de una** — **para siempre** once and for all, for good; **dos veces** twice; **dos veces tanto** twice as much; **con una velocidad dos veces superior a la del sonido** at a speed twice that of sound; **tres veces** three times; **cien veces** (*fig*) hundreds of times, lots of times; **la primera** — **que le vi** the first time I saw him; **por primera** — for the first time; **por última** — for the last time; **por enésima** — for the umpteenth time (*fam*); **no se permite golpearlo segunda** — you can't hit it again, you aren't allowed a second shot at it.

(c) (*Math*) **7 veces 9** 7 times 9.

(d) turn; **a su** — in his turn; **en** — **de** instead of, in place of; **ceder la** — to give up one's turn, (*in queue etc*) give up one's place; **cuando le llegue la** — when his turn comes; **hacer las veces de** to take the place of, act for, stand in for; to serve as, do duty as.

veza *nf* vetch.

vía 1 *nf* (a) road; route; track; (*fig*) way; (*Rel etc*) way; — **aérea** airway; (*Post*) airmail; **por** — **aérea** by air, (*Post*) (by) airmail; — **de agua** leak; **abrirse una** — **de agua** to spring a leak; — **de circunvalación** bypass, ring road; — **de comunicación** communication route; — **férrea** railway; — **fluvial** waterway; V— **Láctea** Milky Way; **¡**— **libre!** make way!, clear the way!; — **marítima** sea route, seaway; **por** — **marítima** by sea; — **pública** public thoroughfare; — **romana** Roman road; — **terrestre** overland route, (*Post*) surface route; **por** — **terrestre** overland, by land, (*Post*) by surface mail; **por** — **de** via, by way of; through; (*fig*) by way of, as, as a kind of; **dejar la** — **libre al desafuero** to leave the way open for abuse.

(b) (*Rail*) track; line; (*in width*) gauge; — **ancha** broad gauge; — **doble** double track; **de** — **estrecha** narrow-gauge (*attr*); — **muerta** siding; — **normal** standard gauge; **de** — **única** single-track (*attr*); **el tren está en la** — **8** the train is at platform 8; **la estación tiene 18** —**s** the station has 18 platforms.

(c) (*Anat*) passage, tube; tract; —**s digestivas** digestive tract; **por** — **bucal** through the mouth, by mouth; **por** — **interna** (*Med*) internally.

(d) (*fig*) system; way, means; channel; — **judicial** process of law, legal means; **recurrir a la** — **judicial** to go to law, have recourse to the law; **por** — **oficial** through official channels; by official means; — **sumarísima** (*Law*) summary proceedings.

(e) (*fig*) **en** —**s de** in process of; **un país en** —**s de desarrollo** a developing country; **el asunto está en** —**s de una solución** the matter is on its way to a

solution, the question is in process of being solved.

2 *prep* (*Rail etc*) via, by way of; through.

viabilidad *nf* viability; feasibility.

viable *adj* viable; *plan etc* feasible.

viada *nf* (*Per*) speed.

viaducto *nm* viaduct.

viajante 1 *adj* travelling. 2 *nm* (also — **de comercio**) commercial traveller, salesman; — **en jabones** traveller in soap.

viajar [1a] *vi* to travel (also *Comm*); to journey; **ha viajado mucho** he has travelled a lot; — **en coche** to go in a car, ride (in a car); — **por Ruritania** to travel through (*or* across) Ruritania; to tour Ruritania.

viajazo *nm* (a) (*Mex*) push, shove. (b) (*Ven*) lash. (c) (*CR*) telling-off.

viaje [1] *nm* (a) journey; trip; tour; (*Naut*) voyage; **el** —, **los** —**s** (*in general*) travel; — **en coche** ride, trip by car; — **en barco** boat trip, sail; — **de buena voluntad** goodwill trip, goodwill mission; — **de ensayo** trial run; — **de ida** outward journey, trip out; — **de ida y vuelta,** — **redondo** (*SAm*) round trip, journey there and back; — **de novios** honeymoon; — **de recreo** pleasure trip; **¡buen** —**!, ¡feliz** —**!** bon voyage!, have a good trip!; **estar de** — to be travelling, be on a trip.

(b) (*Comm etc*) load; cartload, cartful (*etc*); **un** — **de leña** a load of wood.

(c) (*PR, Ven*) time; **lo repitió varios** —**s** he repeated it several times; **de un** — (*SAm*) all in one go, at one blow; all at once.

(d) (*CAm*) **echar un** — **a uno** to give someone a telling-off.

viaje [2] *nm* (*fam*) slash (with a razor); **tirar un** — **a uno** to take a slash at someone.

viajero 1 *adj* travelling; (*Zool*) migratory. 2 *nm*, **viajera** *nf* traveller; (*in vehicle, Rail etc*) passenger; **¡señores** —**s, al tren!** will passengers kindly board the train?

vial *adj* (*esp SAm*) road (*attr*); traffic (*attr*); **reglamento** — traffic control; rule of the road, highway code; **fluidez** — free movement of traffic.

vianda *nf* (a) (also —**s**) food. (b) (*Ant*) vegetables. (c) (*Chi, RPl*) lunch tin, dinner pail (*US*).

viandante *nmf* traveller, wayfarer; (*in town*) passerby; pedestrian.

viaraza *nf* (*Col, Guat, RPl*) fit of anger; spell of bad temper; **estar con la** — to be in a bad mood.

viático *nm* (a) (*Hist*) food for a journey. (b) (*Fin*) travel allowance. (c) (*Eccl*) viaticum.

víbora *nf* (a) viper (*also fig*). (b) (*Mex*) money belt.

viborear [1a] *vi* (a) (*RPl*) to twist, snake along. (b) (*Cu*) to cheat by marking the cards.

vibración *nf* (a) vibration; shaking; throbbing, pulsating. (b) (*Ling*) roll, trill.

vibrador *nm* vibrator.

vibrante 1 *adj* (a) vibrant, vibrating.

(b) (*Ling*) rolled, trilled.

(c) (*fig*) *voice, slogan etc* ringing; — **de ringing with**, vibrant with.

2 *nf* (*Ling*) vibrant.

vibrar [1a] 1 *vt* (a) to vibrate; to shake, rattle. (b) (*Ling*) to roll, trill. 2 *vi* to vibrate; to shake, rattle; to throb, beat, pulsate.

vibratorio *adj* vibratory.

viburno *nm* viburnum.

vicario *nm* (*Eccl*) curate; deputy; — **general** vicar-general; V— **de Cristo** Vicar of Christ (*the Pope*).

vice . . . **vice** . . .

vicealmirante *nm* vice-admiral.

vicecónsul *nm* vice-consul.

vicegerente *nm* assistant manager.

Vicente *m* Vincent.

vicepresidencia *nf* vice-presidency; vice-chairmanship.

vicepresidente *nm* (*Pol*) vice-president; (*of committee etc*) vice-chairman.

vicetiple *nf* chorus girl.

viceversa *adv* vice versa.

viciado *adj* (a) *air* foul, thick, stale. (b) *text* corrupt.

viciar [1b] 1 *vt* (a) *customs etc* to corrupt, pervert, subvert.

(b) (*Law*) to nullify, invalidate.

(c) *text* to corrupt, vitiate, falsify; to interpret erroneously.

(d) *substance* to adulterate; *air* to make foul; *food etc* to spoil, taint, contaminate.

(e) *object* to bend, twist, put out of shape; to warp.

2 **viciarse** *vr* (a) to take to vice, get depraved, become corrupted; *see also* **enviciarse**.

(b) (*object*) to warp, lose its shape.

vicio nm (a) vice; viciousness, depravity.

(b) bad habit, vice; — **inveterado**, — **de origen** ingrained bad habit; **tiene el — de no contestar las cartas** he has the bad habit of not answering letters; **no le podemos quitar el —** we can't get him out of the habit; **de —**, **por —** out of sheer habit; for no reason at all; **hablar de —** to chatter away; **quejarse de —** to complain for no reason at all.

(c) defect, blemish; (Law etc) error; (Ling) mistake, incorrect form; solecism; **adolece de ciertos —s** it has a number of defects, there are certain things wrong with it.

(d) (of surface etc) warp; twist, bend.

(e) (towards child) excessive indulgence.

(f) (Bot) rankness, luxuriance, lushness.

(g) (SAm) **estar de —** to be idle.

viciosamente adv (a) viciously; dissolutely. (b) (Bot) rankly, luxuriantly.

viciosidad nf viciousness.

vicioso 1 adj (a) vicious; depraved, dissolute; child spoiled.

(b) (Mech etc) faulty, defective.

(c) (Bot) rank, luxuriant, lush.

2 nm, **viciosa** nf (a) vicious person, depraved person.

(b) addict, fiend.

vicisitud nf accident, upset, mishap; sudden change; **—es** vicissitudes.

víctima nf (a) victim; (fig, also of bird etc) prey; **fue — de una estafa** she was the victim of a swindle; **es — de alguna neurosis** he is a prey to some neurosis; **no hay que lamentar —s del accidente** there were no casualties in the accident.

(b) (Hist) sacrifice.

victimar [1a] vt (SAm) to wound; to kill.

victimario nm (a) person responsible for someone's suffering (or accident etc).

(b) (SAm) person responsible for wounding (or killing).

Victoria f Victoria.

victoria nf victory; triumph; **— moral** moral victory; **— pírrica** Pyrrhic victory.

victoriano 1 adj Victorian. **2** nm, **victoriana** nf Victorian.

victoriosamente adv victoriously.

victorioso adj victorious.

victrola nf (SAm) gramophone, phonograph (US).

vicuña nf vicuna.

vichadero nm (RPl) see **bichadero**.

vich(e)ar [1a] vt (RPl) see **bichear**.

vid nf vine.

vida nf (a) (in most senses) life; way of life; lifetime; livelihood; **tuvo una — ejemplar** he lived an exemplary life; **la — de estos edificios es breve** the life of these buildings is short; **así es la —** such is life, that's life; **¿qué es de tu —?** what's the news?; **este sol es la —** this sunshine is a real tonic; **¡esto es —!** this is living!; **está escribiendo la — de Quevedo** he is writing the life (or a biography) of Quevedo.

(b) (phrases with prep) **¡hermana de mi —!** my dear sister!; **de por —** for life, for the rest of one's life; **un amigo de toda la —** a lifelong friend; **en —** during his (etc) lifetime, while still alive; **en la —**, **en mi —** (negative sense) never, never in my life; **entre — y muerte** at death's door; **¡por — de . . . !** upon my soul!; **¡por — del chápiro verde!** by the toe of the Prophet!

(c) (phrases with adj etc) **— airada** criminal life; underworld; **de — airada** criminal; loose-living, immoral; **— arrastrada** wretched life; **— eterna** everlasting life; **— íntima** private life; **de — libre** loose-living, immoral; **mala —** dissolute life; prostitution; **mujer de — alegre, mujer de mala —** prostitute; **— y milagros de uno** (fam) full details about someone; **la otra —** the next life; the life to come; **— perra**, **— de perros** dog's life, wretched life; **— privada** private life; **— sentimental** love life.

(d) (phrases with verb) **estar con —** to be still alive; **amargar la — a uno** to make someone's life a misery; **complicarse la —** to make life difficult for oneself; **cortar la — de uno** to cut someone off (in his prime); **darse buena —**, **darse — de canónigo** to live well, live in style, do oneself proud (fam); **dar la —** to sacrifice one's life; **dar mala — a uno** to ill-treat someone, give someone a wretched time of it; **enterrarse en —** to go into seclusion; **escapar con —** to escape alive; **ganarse la —** to make a living; **hacer — marital** to live together (as man and wife); **hacer por la —** (fam)

to eat; **no le va la — en esto** it's not as though his life depends on it; **meterse en —s ajenas** to pry, snoop; to meddle; **pasar a mejor —** (euph) to pass away; **pasar la — a tragos** (fam) to have a miserable life; **pegarse la gran —, pegarse la — padre** (fam) to live it up (fam), live the life of Riley; **perder la —** to lose one's life; **quitar la — a uno** to take someone's life; **quitarse la —** to kill oneself, do away with oneself; **vender cara la —** to sell one's life dearly.

(e) (of look, eyes etc) liveliness, brightness.

(f) (in direct address) **¡—!, ¡— mía!** my love!

(g) (euph) prostitution; **una mujer de la —** a prostitute, a woman on the game; **echarse a la —** to take up prostitution.

vidente nmf seer, prophet; clairvoyant(e).

vídeo nm video; **de —** video (attr).

vidorra nf (fam) gay life, easy life.

vidorria nf (a) (Arg) gay life, easy life. (b) (Col, Ven) miserable life.

vidriado 1 adj glazed. **2** nm (a) glaze, glazing. (b) glazed earthenware.

vidriar [1b] **1** vt to glaze. **2 vidriarse** vr to become glazed.

vidriera nf (a) (Eccl; also — **de colores**) stained-glass window; (also **puerta —**) glass door; glass partition.

(b) (SAm) shop window; showcase.

(c) (Cu) tobacco stall, tobacco kiosk.

vidriería nf (a) glassworks. (b) glassware.

vidriero nm glazier.

vidrio nm (a) glass; **— cilindrado** plate glass; **— de color(es)**, **— pintado** stained glass; **— deslustrado** frosted glass, ground glass; **— inastillable** laminated glass, splinter-proof glass; **— tallado** cut glass; **bajo —** under glass; **pagar los —s rotos** (fam) to carry the can (sl).

(b) (Arg) bottle of liquor.

vidrioso adj (a) glassy; glass-like; brittle, fragile, delicate.

(b) eye glassy; fishy; expression, look glazed; surface slippery as glass, glassy.

(c) person touchy, sensitive.

(d) matter delicate.

vidurria nf (Arg, Col, Ven) =**vidorria**.

vieira nf (Galicia) scallop.

vieja nf (a) old woman.

(b) (RPl: fam) **la —** my old woman (fam).

(c) (Chi) cracker, squib.

(d) (Mex) cigar stub.

viejada nf (Arg) group of old people.

viejales nm, pl **viejales** (fam) old chap (fam).

viejera nf (a) (PR, Ven) old age. (b) (PR) old useless thing.

viejo 1 adj (a) (all senses) old; **se cae de —** he's so old he can hardly walk; **hacerse —** to grow old, get old; **no parece más — de un día** he doesn't look a day older.

(b) **zapatero de —** cobbler.

(c) **Plinio el V—** Pliny the Elder.

2 nm (a) old man; see **verde**.

(b) (SAm) **mi —** (fam) my old man (fam); **los —s** the old folks.

viejón adj (Col, Mex, RPl) elderly.

Viena Vienna.

vienés 1 adj Viennese. **2** nm, **vienesa** nf Viennese.

viento nm (a) wind, breeze; **corre —, hay —, hace —** it is windy, there is a wind; **hace mucho —** it is very windy; **cuando sopla el — when the wind blows; —s alisios** trade winds; **— ascendente** (Aer) up-current; **— de cola**, **— de espalda**, **— trasero** tailwind; **— colado** draught; **— de costado** crosswind, sidewind; **— contrario**, **— de proa** headwind; **— de la hélice** slipstream; **— huracanado** hurricane wind, violent wind; **— en popa** following wind; **ir — en popa** to go splendidly; to do extremely well; (of business) to prosper, boom; **— terral** (Naut) land breeze; **estar lleno de —** to be empty, have nothing inside; **beber los —s por uno** to be crazy about someone; **echar a uno con — fresco** to chuck someone out; **¡vete con — fresco!** go to blazes!, and good riddance!; **publicar algo a los cuatro —s** to tell all and sundry about something, shout something from the rooftops; **soplan —s de fronda** there's trouble brewing; **como el —** like the wind; **contra — y marea** regardless of all the difficulties, at all costs, come what may.

(b) (Anat) wind, flatulence.

(c) (Mus) wind; wind instruments, wind section.

(d) (Hunting) scent.

(e) (of dog) keen scent, sense of smell.

(f) (*fig*) conceit, vanity; **estar lleno de —** to be puffed up (with conceit).
(g) (*of tent, post*) guy, guy-rope.
(h) (*Col*) strings of a kite.
(i) (*Pan, PR*) rheumatism.
vientre *nm* **(a)** (*Anat*) belly; womb; **bajo —** lower abdomen; **llevar un hijo en su —** to carry a child in one's womb.
(b) bowels; **— flojo** looseness of the bowels; **descargar el —, exonerar el —, hacer de —** to have a movement of the bowels.
(c) (*of slaughtered animal*) guts, entrails, offal.
(d) (*Zool*) foetus, unborn young.
(e) (*of vessel*) belly, wide part.
viernes *nm*, *pl* **viernes** Friday; **V— Santo** Good Friday.
Vietnam *m* Vietnam; **— del Norte** North Vietnam; **— del Sur** South Vietnam.
vietnamita 1 *adj* Vietnamese. **2** *nmf* Vietnamese. **3** *nm* (*language*) Vietnamese.
viga *nf* balk, timber; (*Archit*) beam, rafter; girder; **— maestra** main beam; **— transversal** crossbeam; **estar contando las —s** (*fig*) to gaze vacantly at the ceiling.
vigencia *nf* **(a)** operation; validity, applicability; **estar en —** to be in force; to be valid, apply; **entrar en —** to take effect, come into operation; **tener —** to be valid, apply; to prevail.
(b) social convention, norm of society.
vigente *adj* valid, applicable, in force; prevailing.
vigésimo 1 *adj* twentieth. **2** *nm* twentieth.
vigía 1 *nm* look-out, watchman; **los —s** (*Naut*) the watch. **2** *nf* **(a)** (*Mil etc*) watchtower. **(b)** (*Geog*) reef, rock.
vigilancia *nf* vigilance, watchfulness; **burlar la — de uno** to escape someone's vigilance.
vigilante 1 *adj* vigilant, watchful; alert.
2 *nm* **(a)** watchman, caretaker; (*of prison*) warder; (*in shop*) shopwalker, store detective; **— de noche, — nocturno** night watchman.
(b) (*Arg*) policeman.
vigilantemente *adv* vigilantly, watchfully.
vigilar [1a] **1** *vt* to watch, watch over; to look after, keep on eye on; *installations, prisoners etc* to guard; *machine* to tend; *frontier etc* to guard, police, patrol; *work etc* to supervise, superintend; **— a los niños para que no se hagan daño** to see that the children come to no harm; **— la leche para que no se salga** to keep an eye on the milk so that it does not boil over.
2 *vi* to be vigilant, be watchful, stay alert; to keep watch; **— por, — sobre** to watch over.
vigilia *nf* **(a)** wakefulness, being awake; watchfulness; **pasar la noche de —** to spend a night without sleep, stay awake all night.
(b) night work, late work; time spent working late; night-time study, lucubrations.
(c) (*Eccl*) fast; **día de —** day of abstinence; **comer de —** to fast, abstain from meat.
(d) (*Eccl*) vigil.
(e) (*Eccl*) eve (of a religious festivity).
vigor *nm* **(a)** vigour; vitality; toughness, stamina, hardiness; drive; **con —** vigorously.
(b) =**vigencia**; **en —** in force; valid, applicable, operative; **entrar en —** to take effect, come into force; **poner en —** to put into effect, put into operation, enforce; *see* **mantenerse**.
vigorizador *adj*, **vigorizante** *adj* invigorating; bracing; revitalizing; *medicine* tonic.
vigorizar [1f] *vt* to invigorate; to strengthen, encourage, stimulate; to revitalize.
vigorosamente *adv* vigorously; strongly, forcefully; strenuously.
vigoroso *adj* vigorous; strong, tough, forceful; *effort* strenuous; *protest etc* vigorous, forceful; *child* sturdy, strong.
viguería *nf* beams, rafters; girders; metal framework.
vigués 1 *adj* of Vigo. **2** *nm*, **viguesa** *nf* native (*or* inhabitant) of Vigo; **los —es** the people of Vigo.
vigueta *nf* joint, small beam.
vihuela *nf* (*Hist*) an early form of the guitar.
vihuelista *nmf* (*Hist*) vihuela player.
vijúa *nf* (*Col*) rock salt.
vikingo *nm* Viking.
vil *adj* *person* low, villainous, blackguardly; *act* vile, foul, rotten; *treatment* unjust, shabby, mean.
vileza *nf* **(a)** (*quality*) low character, villainy, vileness, foulness; injustice, shabbiness, meanness.
(b) (*una —*) vile act, base deed, villainy.
vilipendiar [1a] *vt* **(a)** to vilify, revile, abuse. **(b)** to despise, scorn.
vilipendio *nm* **(a)** vilification, abuse. **(b)** contempt, scorn; humiliation.

vilipendioso *adj* contemptible; humiliating.
vilmente *adv* villainously; vilely, foully; unjustly, shabbily, meanly.
vilo: en — *adv* **(a) en —** (up) in the air; suspended, unsupported; **sostener algo en —** to hold something up.
(b) (*fig*) **estar en —, quedar en —** to be left in the air, be left in suspense.
vilote *nm* (*Arg*) coward.
villa *nf* **(a)** (*Hist etc*) villa. **(b)** small town; (*Pol*) borough, municipality; **la V—** (*esp*) Madrid.
Villadiego: tomar las de — (*fam*) to beat it quick (*fam*).
villalata *nf* shack, tin hut.
villanaje *nm* **(a)** humble status, peasant condition. **(b)** peasantry, villagers.
villancico *nm* (*Christmas*) carol.
villanesco *adj* peasant (*attr*); village (*attr*), rustic.
villanía *nf* **(a)** (*Hist*) humble birth, lowly status.
(b) (*quality*) villainy, baseness.
(c) (*una —*) =**vileza (b)**.
(d) obscene expression, filthy remark.
villano 1 *adj* **(a)** (*Hist*) peasant (*attr*); rustic.
(b) (*fig*) coarse.
(c) (*fig*) villainous, base.
2 *nm*, **villana** *nf* **(a)** (*Hist*) villein, serf; (*esp fig*) peasant, rustic.
(b) (*fig*) low individual, rotter, cad.
(c) (*SAm: angl*) villain.
villoría *nf* country house.
villorrio *nm* one-horse town, dump (*fam*).
vinagre *nm* vinegar.
vinagrera *nf* **(a)** vinegar bottle; **—s** cruet stand. **(b)** (*SAm*) heartburn, acidity of the stomach.
vinagroso *adj* **(a)** vinegary, tart. **(b)** (*fig*) bad-tempered, sour.
vinatería *nf* **(a)** wine shop. **(b)** wine trade.
vinatero *nm* wine merchant, vintner.
vinaza *nf* nasty wine, wine from the dregs.
vinazo *nm* strong wine.
vinculación *nf* **(a)** linking, binding; (*fig*) bond, connexion. **(b)** (*Law*) entail.
vincular [1a] **1** *vt* **(a)** to link, bind, tie (*a* to); *hopes etc* to base, found (*en* on); **— su suerte a la de otro** to make one's fate depend on someone else's; **están estrechamente vinculados entre sí** they are closely bound together.
(b) (*Law*) to entail.
2 vincularse *vr* to link oneself (*a* to).
vínculo *nm* **(a)** link, bond, tie; **— de parentesco** family ties, ties of blood; **hay un fuerte — histórico** there is a strong historical link.
(b) (*Law*) entail.
vincha *nf* (*Per, RPl*) =**bincha.**
vindicación *nf* vindication.
vindicar [1g] **1** *vt* **(a)** to avenge.
(b) to vindicate.
(c) (*Law*) =**reivindicar.**
2 vindicarse *vr* **(a)** to avenge oneself.
(b) to vindicate oneself.
vine *etc see* **venir.**
vinería *nf* (*Bol, Chi, Per, RPl*) wineshop.
vínico *adj* (*Chem*) wine (*attr*).
vinícola *adj* wine (*attr*); wine-growing (*attr*); wine-making (*attr*).
vinicultor *nm* wine grower.
vinicultura *nf* wine growing, wine production.
vinificación *nf* fermentation.
vinilo *nm* vinyl.
vinillo *nm* thin wine, weak wine.
vino *nm* wine; **— añejo** mellow wine, mature wine; **— blanco** white wine; **— espumoso** sparkling wine; **— generoso** strong wine, full-bodied wine; **— de Jerez** sherry; **— de Málaga** Malaga (wine); **— de mesa** table wine; **— de Oporto** port (wine); **— de pasto** ordinary wine; **— peleón** coarse wine, pub wine; **— de postre** dessert wine; **— seco** dry wine; **— de solera** vintage wine; **— tinto** red wine; **aguar** (*or* **bautizar, cristianar**) **el —** to water the wine; **dormir el —** to sleep off a hangover; **echar agua al —** (*fig*) to water down a statement; **tener buen —** to know how to carry one's liquor; **tener mal —** to get wild after a few drinks.
vinolento *adj* boozy, fond of the bottle.
vinoso *adj* like wine, vinous; wine-coloured.
vinotería *nf* (*CAm, Mex*) wineshop.
viña *nf* **(a)** vineyard. **(b)** (*Mex*) rubbish dump.
viñador *nm* vine grower; wine grower.
viñal *nm* (*Arg*) vineyard.
viñatero *nm* (*Chi, Per, RPl*) vine grower; wine grower.
viñedo *nm* vineyard.

viñeta *nf* vignette; emblem, badge, device.
viola *nf* (a) (*Bot*) viola. (b) (*Mus*) viola; (*Hist*) viol.
violáceo *adj* violet.
violación *nf* (a) violation. (b) rape. (c) offence, infringement.
violado 1 *adj* violet. **2** *nm* violet (colour).
violador 1 *nm* rapist. **2** *nm,* **violadora** *nf* violator; offender (*de* against).
violar [1a] *vt* (a) *sanctuary, territory etc* to violate.
   (b) *woman* to rape.
   (c) *law etc* to break, offend against, infringe; *agreement, principle etc* to violate, break.
violencia *nf* (a) violence; force; (*Law*) violence, assault; (*Pol*) rule by force; **no —** non-violence; **usar — para abrir una caja** to use force to open a box; **no se consigue nada con él usando la —** you will not achieve anything with him by using force; **amenazar —** to threaten violence, (*of crowd etc*) to turn ugly; **apelar a la —** to resort to violence, use force; **hacer —** =violentar.
   (b) (*una —*) unjust act, damaging act; outrage.
   (c) embarrassment; embarrassing situation; **si eso te cuesta —** if that embarrasses you; **estar con —** to be (*or* feel) embarrassed.
violentamente *adv* (a) violently; furiously, wildly.
   (b) awkwardly, unnaturally.
   (c) embarrassingly, awkwardly.
   (d) distortedly.
   (e) (*SAm*) quickly.
violentar [1a] **1** *vt* (a) *door etc* to force; *branch etc* to bend, twist (out of shape); *house* to break into, enter forcibly.
   (b) *person* to force, use force on, persuade forcibly; to subject to violence; (*Law*) to assault.
   (c) (*fig*) *principle* to violate, outrage.
   (d) (*fig*) *sense* to distort, twist, force.
   2 violentarse *vr* to force oneself.
violento *adj* (a) violent; furious, wild; *means, person, speech, temperament etc* violent; *sport* tough, physically demanding, (*pej*) rough; **mostrarse —** to turn violent, offer violence.
   (b) *position of body etc* awkward, unnatural; cramped; *act* unnatural, forced; **me es muy — consentir en ello** it goes against the grain with me to agree with it.
   (c) *situation etc* embarrassing, awkward; **para mí todo esto es un poco —** this is all a bit awkward for me.
   (d) *person's state* embarrassed, awkward; **estar** (*or* **sentirse**) **—** to be (*or* feel) embarrassed; **me encuentro — estando con ellos** I feel awkward when I'm with them; **la discusión entre los dos me hacía estar —** the argument between them made me feel embarrassed.
   (e) (*fig*) *interpretation* forced, distorted.
violeta 1 *nf* violet; **— de genciana** gentian violet. **2** *adj invar* violet.
violín *nm* (a) violin.
   (b) violinist; **primer —** first violin.
   (c) **— de Ingrés** (*gall*) spare-time occupation (*or* art, hobby *etc*) at which one shines.
   (d) (*Ven*) bad breath.
   (e) (*Mex*) **de —** gratis, free.
   (f) (*Arg, Ven*) **embolsar el —** to be embarrassed.
violinista *nmf* violinist.
violón *nm* double bass; **tocar el —** (*fam*) to come out with something silly, reveal one's ignorance and stupidity.
violoncelista *nmf* cellist.
violoncelo *nm* cello.
viperino *adj* viperish.
vira[1] *nf* (*Mil etc*) dart.
vira[2] *nf* (of shoe) welt.
viracho *adj* (*Chi*) cross-eyed.
virada *nf* (*Naut*) tack, tacking.
virago *nf* mannish woman.
viraje *nm* (a) (*Naut*) tack; turn, going about; (*of vehicle*) turn; swerve; (*in road etc*) bend, curve; **— en horquilla** hairpin bend.
   (b) (*fig*) change of direction; (*in policy*) abrupt switch, volte-face; (*in voting*) swing.
   (c) (*Phot*) toning.
virar [1a] **1** *vt* (a) (*Naut*) to put about, turn.
   (b) (*Phot*) to tone.
   (c) (*Arg, Cu*) to turn round; to turn over, turn upside down.
   (d) (*Cu*) to whip.
   2 *vi* (a) to change direction; (*Naut*) to tack; to turn, go about, put about; (*of driver, vehicle*) to turn; to swerve; **— a estribor** to turn to starboard; **— hacia el sur** to turn towards the south; **— en redondo** to turn completely round; **tuve que —**

a la izquierda para no atropellarle I had to swerve left to avoid hitting him.
   (b) (*fig*) to change one's views, switch round; to veer (*a, hacia* towards); (*Pol: of voting*) to swing; **— en redondo** to switch round completely, veer round, make a complete volte-face; **el país ha virado a la derecha** the country has swung (to the) right.
   (c) (*Arg, Cu etc*) to turn.
virgen 1 *adj* virgin.
   2 *nf* virgin; **la V—** the Virgin; **la Santísima V—** the Blessed Virgin; **¡Santísima V—!** by all that's holy!; **es un viva la V—** (*fam*) he doesn't give a damn, he doesn't care one little bit.
Vírgenes: Islas *fpl* **—** Virgin Isles.
virgiliano *adj* Virgilian.
Virgilio *m* Virgil.
virginal *adj* (a) maidenly, virginal. (b) (*Eccl*) of (*or* relating to) the Virgin.
virginidad *nf* virginity.
virgo *nm* virginity.
Virgo *f* Virgo.
virguería *nf* silly adornment, frill.
viril *adj* virile; manly; see **edad** *etc.*
virilidad *nf* (a) virility; manliness. (b) manhood.
viringo *adj* (*Col, Ec*) (a) bare, naked. (b) skinned. skinless.
viroca *nf* (*Chi*) serious mistake.
virola *nf* (a) metal tip, ferrule; (*on lance, tool etc*) collar. (b) (*Mex, RPl*) silver ring; metal disc (*fixed to harness etc as an adornment*).
virolento *adj* pockmarked.
virología *nf* virology.
virólogo *nm* virologist.
virote *nm* (a) arrow.
   (b) (*Mex*) bread roll.
   (c) (*fam*) young man about town, idle youth; solemn person, stiff person.
   (d) (*Col, Mex, Ven*) simpleton.
virreinato *nm* viceroyalty.
virrey *nm* viceroy.
virriondo *adj* (*Mex*) =**cachondo**.
virtual *adj* (a) virtual. (b) *strength, wealth etc* potential; future, possible. (c) (*Phys*) apparent.
virtualidad *nf* potentiality; **tiene ciertas —es** it has certain potentialities.
virtualmente *adv* virtually.
virtud *nf* (a) virtue; **— cardinal** cardinal virtue.
   (b) virtue, power; efficacy; **en — de** by virtue of, by reason of; **tener la — de** + *infin* to have the virtue of + *ger*, have the power to + *infin*; **una planta que tiene — contra varias enfermedades** a plant which is effective against certain diseases.
   (c) (*Cu*) penis.
virtuosamente *adv* virtuously.
virtuosismo *nm* virtuosity.
virtuoso 1 *adj* virtuous. **2** *nm* virtuoso.
viruela *nf* (a) smallpox. (b) **—s** pockmarks; **picado de —s** pockmarked.
virulé: a la — (*gall*) *adj* (a) old; damaged; bent, twisted; shabby. (b) *person* cracked, potty (*fam*).
virulencia *nf* virulence.
virulento *adj* virulent.
virus *nm, pl* **virus** virus; **enfermedad por —** virus disease.
viruta *nf* shaving.
vis *nf*: **— cómica** comic sense, sense of comedy; **tener — cómica** to be witty, sparkle.
visa *nf* (*SAm: angl*) visa.
visado *nm* visa; permit; **— de permanencia** residence permit; **— de tránsito** transit visa.
visaje *nm* (wry) face, grimace; **hacer —s** to pull faces, grimace, smirk.
visar [1a] *vt* (a) *passport* to visa. (b) *document* to pass, approve, endorse.
vísceras *nfpl* viscera, entrails; (*fig*) guts, bowels.
visco *nm* birdlime.
viscosa *nf* viscose.
viscosidad *nf* (a) (*quality*) viscosity, stickiness; thickness. (b) (*Bot, Zool*) slime; sticky secretion.
viscoso *adj* viscous, sticky; *liquid* thick, stiff; *secretion* slimy.
visera *nf* (a) (*Mil*) visor; (*of cap*) peak; eyeshade.
   (b) (*Cu, PR*) (horse's) blinkers.
visibilidad *nf* visibility; **la — es de 200 m** there is a visibility of 200 m; **la — queda reducida a cero** visibility is down to nil; **una curva de escasa —** (*Aut*) a corner that leaves a driver with a poor view.
visible *adj* (a) visible.
   (b) (*fig*) clear, plain; evident, obvious.
   (c) *person* free (to receive a visit); **¿está — el profesor?** is the professor free?, could the professor see me?

visiblemente *adv* (a) visibly.
   (b) (*fig*) clearly; evidently; **parecía crecer** — it seemed to grow as one watched it, it seemed to get bigger before one's eyes.

visigodo 1 *adj* Visigothic. **2** *nm*, **visigoda** *nf* Visigoth.

visigótico *adj* Visigothic.

visillo *nm* (a) small curtain, lace curtain. (b) antimacassar.

visión *nf* (a) (*Anat*) vision, (eye)sight; **perder la** — **de un ojo** to lose the sight in one eye.
   (b) vision (*also Rel*); fantasy; illusion; **se le apareció en** — it came to him in a vision; **ver** —**es** to be seeing things, suffer delusions.
   (c) view; — **de conjunto** complete picture, overall view; **su** — **del problema** his view of the problem.
   (d) (*pej*) scarecrow, fright; **ella iba hecha una** — she looked a real fright; **han comprado una** — **de cuadro** they've bought a frightful picture, they've bought an absolutely ghastly picture (*fam*).

visionario 1 *adj* (a) visionary.
   (b) (*pej*) deluded, subject to hallucinations.
   2 *nm*, **visionaria** *nf* (a) visionary.
   (b) (*pej*) deluded person, crazy individual.

visir *nm* vizier; **gran** — grand vizier.

visita *nf* (a) visit; call; **derecho de** — right of search; — **de cortesía**, — **de cumplido** formal visit, courtesy call; — **de despedida** farewell visit; — **de médico** (*fam*) very short call; — **de pésame** call to express one's condolences; **estar de** — **en** to be on a visit to; **hacer una** —, **rendir una** — to visit, pay a visit; **devolver una** —, **pagar una** — to return a visit.
   (b) (*person*) visitor, caller; **hoy tenemos** — we have visitors today.
   (c) (*Per, PR*) enema.

visitación *nf* (*Eccl*) visitation.

visitador *nm*, **visitadora** *nf* (a) frequent visitor, person much given to calling.
   (b) inspector.
   (c) visitadora *nf* (*SAm*) syringe; enema.

visitante 1 *adj* visiting. **2** *nmf* visitor.

visitar [1a] **1** *vt* to visit; to call on, go and see; *museum, city etc* to visit; (*officially*) to visit; inspect.
   2 visitarse *vr* (a) (*two persons*) to visit each other.
   (b) (*Med*) to ask the doctor to call.

visiteo *nm* frequent visiting, constant calling.

visitero 1 *adj* fond of visiting, much given to calling.
   2 *nm*, **visitera** *nf* frequent visitor, constant caller.

visitón *nm* (*fam*) long and boring visit; visitation.

vislumbrar [1a] *vt* (a) to glimpse, catch a glimpse of, see briefly.
   (b) (*fig*) to glimpse, see some slight possibility of; *solution etc* to begin to see; *future* to get a slight idea of, make a conjecture about; *unknown fact etc* to surmise.

vislumbre *nf* (a) glimpse, brief view.
   (b) gleam, glimmer.
   (c) (*fig*) glimmer; slight possibility; vague idea; conjecture; **tener** —**s de** to get an inkling of, get a vague idea of.

viso *nm* (a) (*of metal*) gleam, glint.
   (b) (*of cloth*) —**s** sheen, gloss; shot-silk appearance; **negro con** —**s azules** black with a bluish sheen, black with bluish lights in it; **a dos** —**s, de dos** —**s** (*fig*) with a double purpose, two-edged; **hacer** —**s** to shimmer.
   (c) (*fig*) appearance; **hay un** — **de verdad en esto** this has the appearance of truth, there is an element of truth in this; **tiene** —**s de ser puro cuento** it looks like being just a tale; **tenía** — **de nunca acabar** it seemed that it was never going to finish.
   (d) (*Sew*) coloured undergarment (*worn under a filmy outer garment*).
   (e) (*Geog*) viewpoint, vantage point.
   (f) ser persona de — to be a somebody, have some standing.

visón *nm* mink.

visor *nm* (a) (*Aer*) bombsight. (b) (*Phot: also* — **de imagen**) viewfinder.

víspera *nf* eve, day before, evening before; — **de Navidad** Christmas Eve; **la** — **de, en** —**s de** on the eve of (*also fig*); **estar en** —**s de** + *infin* to be on the point of + *ger*, be on the verge of + *ger*.

vista 1 *nf* (a) (*Anat*) sight, eyesight, vision; (*act*) look, gaze, glance; — **de águila**, — **de lince** very keen sight, eagle eye; — **corta** short sight; — **doble** double vision; second sight; **¡** — **a la derecha!** (*Mil*) eyes right!
   (b) (*general sense: phrases with prep*) **a primera** — at first sight; on the face of it; **traducción hecha a primera** — unseen translation; **a simple** — with

the naked eye; at a glance; **lo teníamos a la** — we could see it, we had it before our eyes; **la parte que quedaba a la** — the part that was visible (*or uncovered*); **no tenemos ningún cambio a la** — we do not have any change in view; **está a la** — **que** . . . it is obvious that . . .; **estar a la** — **de** to be within sight of; **a la** — **de muchas personas** in the presence of many people; **a la** — **de todo el mundo** openly, publicly, for all to see; **a la** — **de tal espectáculo** at the sight of such a scene, on beholding such a scene; **a la** — **de sus informes** in the light of his reports; **estaré a la** — **de lo que pase** I will keep an eye on developments; **yo me quedo a la** — **del fuego** I'll keep an eye on the fire; **con la** — **puesta en** with one's eyes (*fig: thoughts*) fixed on; **conocer a uno de** — to know somebody by sight; **en plena** — in full view; **en** — **de** (*fig*) in view of; **en** — **de que** . . . in view of the fact that . . .; **¡hasta la** —! au revoir!; so long!; **hasta donde alcanza la** — as far as the eye can see; **no muy agradable para la** — not a pretty sight, not nice to look at.
   (c) (*general sense: phrases with verb*) **aguzar la** — to look sharp, look more carefully; **alzar la** — to look up; (*fig*) to raise one's eyes to; **alzar la** — **a uno** (*fig*) to turn to someone for help; **apartar la** — to look away, glance away; (*fig*) to turn a blind eye (*de to*); **bajar la** — to look down; to cast one's eyes down; **clavar la** — **en** to stare at, fix one's eyes on; to clap eyes on; **comer** (*or* **devorar**) **con la** — to look angrily at; to look curiously at; to look lovingly (*pej: lustfully*) at; **dirigir la** — **a** to look at, look towards; to turn one's gaze on; **echar una** — **a** to take a look at; **fijar la** — **en** to stare at, fix one's eyes on; **hacer la** — **gorda** to pretend not to notice, turn a blind eye; **hacer la** — **gorda a** to wink at, close one's eyes to; **luz que hiere la** — light that dazzles, light that hurts one's eyes; **medir a uno con la** — to size someone up; **se me nubló la** — my eyes became dazed; **pasar la** — **por** to look over, glance quickly at; **perder algo de** — to lose sight of something (*also fig*); **se pierde de** — (*fig*) he's very sharp, he's terribly clever; **no perder a uno de** — to keep someone in sight; **poner algo a la** — to put something on view; **recorrer algo con la** — to run one's eye over something; **salta a la** — it hits you in the eye; **torcer la** — to squint; **volver la** — to look back (*also fig*); to look away; **nunca volvió la** — **atrás** he never looked back, he never had regrets about the past.
   (d) (*Comm*) **a la** — at sight, on sight; **a 30 días** — thirty days after sight.
   (e) (*of object*) appearance, looks; **un coche con una** — **estupenda** a splendid-looking car; **de** — **poco agradable** of unattractive appearance, unprepossessing; **a la** —, **no son pobres** from what one can see, they're not poor.
   (f) foresight, perception; **ha tenido mucha** — he was very far-sighted.
   (g) (*fig*) intention; **con** —**s a una solución del problema** with a view to solving the problem.
   (h) (*of scene etc*) view, scene, vista, panorama; —**s** (*from house etc*) outlook; (*fig*) outlook, prospect; **la** — **desde el castillo** the view from the castle; — **anterior,** — **frontal** front view; **con** —**s a la montaña** with views across to the mountains; **con** —**s al mar** overlooking the sea; **con** —**s al oeste** facing west, with westerly aspect.
   (i) (*Art, Phot etc*) view; — **fija** still; — **de pájaro** bird's-eye view; **una tarjeta con una** — **de Venecia** a card with a view of Venice.
   (j) (*Law*) hearing; trial; — **de una causa** hearing of a case.
   (k) (*Hist*) —**s** meeting, conference.
   2 *nm* customs inspector.

vistazo *nm* look, glance; **de un** — at a glance; **dar un** — (*fam*) to pop in, drop in; **dar un** — **a, echar un** — **a** to glance at, take a look at, have a quick look at.

vistillas *nfpl* viewpoint, height, high place.

visto 1 *ptp of* **ver**.
   2 *ptp and adj* (a) — **todo esto** in view of all this; **por lo** — evidently, apparently; by the look of it; **ni** — **ni oído** like lightning; **cosa no vista, cosa nunca vista** an unheard-of thing.
   (b) — **bueno** approved, passed, O.K. (*fam*).
   (c) está muy — it is very commonly worn (*or* used), one sees it about a lot; (*pej*) it's old, it's right out of fashion.
   (d) está — **que** . . . it is clear that . . .; **estaba** — it had to be, it was expected all along.
   (e) lo que está bien — what is socially acceptable, what is done; **eso está muy mal** — that's not done, that is thought highly improper; **está muy**

mal — **que una joven vaya sola** it is thought most improper for a girl to go alone. **3** — **que . . .** *conj* seeing that . . .; since . . ., inasmuch as . . .
4 — **bueno** *nm* approval, O.K. (*fam*), authorization.
vistosamente *adv* showily, colourfully; attractively; (*pej*) gaudily.
vistosidad *nf* showiness, colourfulness; attractiveness; (*pej*) gaudiness.
vistoso *adj* showy, colourful; gay, attractive; (*pej*) gaudy.
visual 1 *adj* visual. **2** *nf* (a) line of sight. (b) (*fam*) look, glance; **echar una** — to take a look (*a* at).
visualizar [1f] *vt* (*SAm: angl*) (a) to see, make out, descry. (b) (*fig*) to visualize.
visualmente *adv* visually.
vital *adj* (a) life (*attr*), living (*attr*); **espacio** — living space, (*Pol*) lebensraum.
(b) (*fig*) vital, essential, fundamental; **de importancia** — of vital importance.
(c) (*fig*) person vital, full of vitality.
vitalicio 1 *adj* life (*attr*); for life; **cargo** — post held for life; **interés** — life interest. **2** *nm* life annuity.
vitalidad *nf* vitality.
vitalizar [1f] *vt* (*esp SAm: angl*) to vitalize; to revitalize.
vitamina *nf* vitamin.
vitaminado *adj* vitaminized.
vitaminar [1a] *vt* to vitaminize, add vitamins to.
vitamínico *adj* vitamin (*attr*).
vitela *nf* vellum.
vitícola *adj* vine (*attr*), vine-growing (*attr*).
viticultor *nm* vine grower; proprietor of a vineyard.
viticultura *nf* vine growing, viticulture.
vitoco *adj* (*Ven*) vain, swanky (*fam*).
vitola *nf* (a) cigar band. (b) looks, appearance, general air.
vitoquear [1a] *vi* (*Ven*) to be conceited, swank (*fam*).
vítor 1 *interj* hurrah! **2** *nm* cheer; **entre los** —**es de la multitud** among the cheers of the crowd.
vitorear [1a] *vt* to cheer, acclaim.
vítreo *adj* glassy, vitreous, glass-like.
vitrificación *nf* vitrification.
vitrificar [1g] **1** *vt* to vitrify. **2 vitrificarse** *vr* to vitrify.
vitrina *nf* (a) glass case, showcase; display cabinet. (b) (*SAm*) shop window.
vitriolo *nm* vitriol.
vitrola *nf* (*SAm*) gramophone, phonograph (*US*).
vitualla *nf*, **vituallas** *nfpl* provisions, victuals.
vituperable *adj* to be condemned, worthy of censure.
vituperación *nf* condemnation, censure.
vituperar [1a] *vt* to condemn, censure, inveigh against.
vituperio *nm* (a) condemnation; reproach, censure; insult; —**s** abuse, insults; vituperation. (b) stigma, dishonour.
vituperioso *adj* abusive; vituperative.
viuda *nf* (a) widow; — **verde** merry widow (*euph*). (b) (*Arg, Ec, Per*) ghost. (c) (*Col*) fish stew. (d) (*Cu*) large kite.
viudedad *nf* (a) (*esp SAm*) widowhood. (b) (*Fin*) widow's pension.
viudez *nf* widowhood.
viudo 1 *adj* widowed; **estar viuda** (*fam*) to be temporarily widowed, have one's husband away. **2** *nm* widower.
viva *nm* cheer; **dar un** — to give a cheer; **prorrumpir en** —**s** to start to cheer, burst out cheering.
vivac *nm*, *pl* **vivacs** bivouac.
vivacidad *nf* (a) vigour. (b) liveliness, vivacity; keenness, sharpness; brightness.
vivales *nm*, *pl* **vivales** (*fam*) person who is quick to look after his own interests, clever person on the make (*fam*).
vivamente *adv* in lively fashion; *describe, remember etc* vividly; *protest* sharply, strongly; *feel* acutely, intensely; **lo siento** — I am deeply sorry, I sincerely regret it; **se lo deseo** — I sincerely hope he gets it.
vivaque *nm* bivouac.
vivaquear [1a] *vi* to bivouac.
vivar[1] *nm* (a) (*Zool*) warren. (b) (*Fish*) fishpond; fish nursery.
vivar[2] [1a] *vt* (*SAm*) to cheer.
vivaracho *adj* person jaunty, lively, sprightly; *girl* vivacious; superficially attractive; bouncy; *eyes* bright, lively, twinkling.
vivaz *adj* (a) long-lived; enduring, lasting; (*Bot*) perennial. (b) vigorous. (c) lively; keen, sharp, quick-witted.
víveres *nmpl* provisions, stores, supplies.
vivero *nm* (a) (*Hort etc*) nursery; seedbed; tree nursery.

(b) (*Fish*) fishpond; fish nursery; (*Zool*) vivarium; — **de ostras** oyster bed.
(c) (*fig*) hotbed; **es un** — **de discordias** it's a hotbed of discord.
viveza *nf* liveliness, vividness; brightness; sharpness; strength, depth, intensity; acuteness; **la** — **de su inteligencia** the sharpness of his mind; **la** — **de sus sentimientos** the strength of his feelings; the sincerity of his regret; **contestar con** — to answer sharply, answer with spirit.
vividero *adj* habitable, inhabitable, that can be lived in.
vivido *adj* personally experienced; **un episodio** — **por el autor** an episode which the author himself lived (through).
vívido *adj* vivid, graphic.
vividor 1 *adj* (*pej*) sharp, clever; unscrupulous. **2** *nm* wide boy (*fam*).
vivienda *nf* (a) (*in general*) housing, accommodation; **escasez de** —**s** housing shortage; **el problema de la** — the housing problem.
(b) (*una* —) dwelling, accommodation unit; flat, apartment (*US*), tenement; — **campestre** small house in the country, cottage; **bloque de** —**s** block of flats, block of tenements; —**s para obreros** workers' flats.
viviente *adj* living; **los** —**s** the living.
vivificador *adj*, **vivificante** *adj* life-giving; (*fig*) revitalizing.
vivificar [1g] *vt* (a) to give life to, vivify. (b) (*fig*) to revitalize, bring to life, bring new life to; to enliven.
vivillo *adj and nm* (*RPl*) = **vividor**.
vivíparo *adj* viviparous.
vivir [3a] **1** *vt* to live through; to experience, go through; **los que hemos vivido la guerra** those of us who lived through the war; **ha vivido momentos de verdadera angustia** she went through moments of real agony.
2 *vi* (a) to live (*en* at, in); — **bien** to live well, be prosperous; to live an honest life; (*of 2 people*) to live happily together, live in harmony; — **para ver** to live and learn; **¡viva!** hurray!; **¡viva el rey!** long live the king!; hurray for the king!; **¿quién vive?** (*Mil*) who goes there?; **dar el quién vive a uno** to challenge someone; **saber** — to know how to get the best out of life; **no dejar** — **a uno** to bother someone, harass someone; **no le dejan** — **los celos** she is eaten up with jealousy; **no vivo de intranquilidad** I'm worried to death; **ya no vivo de vergüenza** the shame of it is killing me.
(b) (*Fin*) to live (*de* by, off, on); — **muy justo** to be hard up, have only just enough to live on; — **dentro de los medios** to live within one's means; — **por encima de sus posibilidades** to live beyond one's means; — **de la pluma** to live by one's pen; — **de las rentas** to live on one's income (from property *etc*); **no tienen con qué** — they haven't enough to live on; **ganar lo justo para** — to earn a bare living.
(c) (*fig*) to last (out); **el abrigo no vivirá mucho** the coat won't last much longer.
(d) (*fig: of memory*) to live, remain.
3 *nm* life, way of life; living; **de mal** — dissolute, loose-living; criminal, delinquent.
vivisección *nf* vivisection.
vivo 1 *adj* (a) (*general sense*) living; live, alive; *flesh* living, raw; *language* living; **los** —**s y los muertos** the living and the dead; **los venden en** — they sell them alive; **transmitir algo en** — to broadcast something live; **le ha llegado al** — it touched him on the raw, it really came home to him; **me dio** (*or* **hirió**) **en lo más** — it got me on the raw, it cut me to the quick.
(b) (*fig*) *description* lively, vivid, graphic; *memory, scene* vivid; *flash etc* bright, sudden; *eyes, look, rhythm* lively; *movement, pace* quick, lively; *colour* bright; rich, vivid; *edge* sharp; *protest etc* sharp, strong; *feeling* strong, deep, intense; *pain* sharp, acute; *temper* sharp, quick; *intelligence* sharp, keen, acute; *wit* ready; *imagination* lively; **¡**—**!** hurry up!; **describir algo al** — (*or* **a lo** —) to describe something to the life, describe something very realistically; **lo explica al** — (*or* **a lo** —) he explains it very expressively.
(c) (*fig*) *person* sharp, clever; lively; (*pej*) sharp; (*esp SAm*) sly, crafty; unscrupulous.
(d) (*Chi*) naughty.
2 *nm* (*Sew*) trimming, edging, border.
vizcaíno 1 *adj* Biscayan. **2** *nm*, **vizcaína** *nf* Biscayan.
Vizcaya *f* Biscay (*Spanish province*).
vizcondado *nm* viscounty.
vizconde *nm* viscount.
vizcondesa *nf* viscountess.

vocablo *nm* word; term; **jugar del —** to make a pun, play on words.

vocabulario *nm* vocabulary.

vocación *nf* vocation, calling; **errar la —** to miss one's vocation; **tener — por** to have a vocation for.

vocacional *adj* vocational.

vocal 1 *adj* vocal. **2** *nm* member (of a committee *etc*); director, member of the board of directors. **3** *nf* (*Ling*) vowel.

vocálico *adj* vocalic, vowel (*attr*).

vocalismo *nm* vowel system.

vocalista *nmf* vocalist, singer.

vocalizar [1f] **1** *vt* to vocalize. **2** *vi* (*Mus*) to hum; to sing scales, practise. **3 vocalizarse** *vr* to vocalize.

vocalmente *adv* vocally.

vocativo *nm* vocative.

voceador 1 *adj* loud, loud-mouthed, vociferous. **2** *nm* (**a**) town crier. (**b**) (*Col, Ec, Mex*) newsboy, paperboy.

vocear [1a] **1** *vt* (**a**) *wares* to cry.
(**b**) *person* to call loudly to, shout to, shout the name of.
(**c**) *person* to cheer, acclaim.
(**d**) *secret etc* to shout to all and sundry, proclaim from the rooftops; (*fig*) to proclaim; **su cara voceaba su culpabilidad** his face proclaimed his guilt.
(**e**) (*fam*) to boast publicly about, lay public claim to.
2 *vi* to shout, yell, bawl.

vocejón *nm* loud voice, big voice.

voceo *nm* shouting, yelling, bawling.

vocería *nf*, **vocerío** *nm* shouting, yelling; clamour, uproar, hullabaloo (*fam*).

vocero *nm* spokesman.

vociferación *nf* vociferation.

vociferador *adj* loud, loud-mouthed.

vociferar [1a] **1** *vt* (**a**) to shout, scream, vociferate.
(**b**) to proclaim boastfully. **2** *vi* to shout, yell, clamour.

vocinglería *nf* (**a**) clamour, uproar. (**b**) (*quality*) loudness, noisiness; garrulity.

vocinglero *adj* (**a**) vociferous, loud, loud-mouthed.
(**b**) loquacious, garrulous. (**c**) (*fig*) blatant.

vodevil *nm* (*gall*) vaudeville (*US*), music hall, variety show (*or* theatre).

vodka *nf* vodka.

vodú *nm* (*SAm*) voodoo.

voduísmo *nm* (*SAm*) voodooism.

volada *nf* (**a**) short flight, single flight. (**b**) (*SAm: various senses*) = **bolada**.

voladizo *adj* (*Archit*) projecting.

volado 1 *adj* (**a**) (*Typ*) superior, raised.
(**b**) **estar —** to be worried, feel anxious (*con about*); to be ill-at-ease.
(**c**) (*Arg, Mex*) projecting; protuberant, big.
(**d**) (*Arg, Mex*) **— de genio** quick-tempered.
(**e**) (*Cu, Guat, Mex*) **estar —** to be in love; to be full of hope.
2 *nm* (**a**) (*CAm*) = **bolado** (c).
(**b**) (*RPl, Ven*) flounce, ruffle.
(**c**) (*Mex*) game of heads or tails.
(**d**) (*Mex*) adventure; incident, happening.
3 *adv* (*Col, Guat, Mex*) hastily.

volador 1 *adj* (**a**) flying.
(**b**) (*fig*) swift; fleeting.
2 *nm* (**a**) (*Fish*) flying fish; (*Zool*) (*species of*) squid.
(**b**) rocket.
(**c**) (*CAm, Col*) toy windmill; (*Ven*) kite.

voladura *nf* blowing up, demolition; blast.

volandas: en — *adv* (**a**) in the air, through the air.
(**b**) (*fig*) swiftly, as if on wings; **¡voy en —!** (*hum*) I fly!

volandera *nf* (**a**) millstone, grindstone. (**b**) (*on wheel*) washer. (**c**) (*fam*) fib.

volandero *adj* (**a**) *part* loose, movable, not fixed; *leaf, rope etc* loose; *pain* that moves about.
(**b**) random, casual; unexpected.
(**c**) (*Orn*) fledged, ready to fly; (*fig*) *person* restless.

volanta *nf* (**a**) (*Col, PR*) flywheel; large wheel. (**b**) (*Cu, Mex, PR*) cart with big wheels; (*Mex*) small car.

volante 1 *adj* (**a**) flying; **ciervo —** stag beetle; **escuadrón —** flying squad; **hoja —** leaflet, handbill, pamphlet.
(**b**) (*fig*) unsettled.
2 *nm* (**a**) (*Tech*) flywheel; (*of watch*) balance.
(**b**) (*Aut*) steering wheel; **ir al —** to be at the wheel, be driving.
(**c**) note.
(**d**) (*Sport*) shuttlecock; (**juego del**) **—** badminton.

(**e**) (*Sport: person*) winger.
(**f**) (*Sew*) flounce, ruffle.
(**g**) (*SAm*) driver; racing driver.

volantín 1 *adj* loose, unattached. **2** *nm* (**a**) fishing line.
(**b**) (*SAm*) kite. (**c**) (*Bol*) rocket. (**d**) (*SAm*) somersault.

volantista *nm* driver; racing driver.

volantón 1 *adj* fledged, ready to fly. **2** *nm* fledgling.

volantusa *nf* (*SAm*) prostitute.

volantuzo *nm* (*Per*) toff (*fam*), dandy.

volapié *nm* (*Taur*) wounding thrust; **a —** (of bird) half walking and half flying; **de —** (*fam*) in a split second.

volar [1m] **1** *vt* (**a**) *building, bridge etc* to blow up, demolish (with explosive); *mine* to explode; *rock* to blast.
(**b**) (*Hunting*) to put up, put to flight, rouse.
(**c**) (*fam*) to irritate, upset, exasperate.
(**d**) (*SAm*) to put to flight.
(**e**) (*CAm*) **— lengua** to talk, speak; **— diente** to eat; **— pata** to walk; **— máquina** to type.
(**f**) (*Mex*) to pinch (*fam*).
(**g**) (*Mex*) to swindle.
(**h**) (*Mex*) to flirt with.
2 *vi* (**a**) (*general sense*) to fly; to fly away, fly off; to get blown away; **una alfombra que vuela** a carpet that flies, a flying carpet; **— a solas** to fly solo; **echar a — una noticia** to spread a piece of news; **echarse a —** (*fig*) to leave the parental nest.
(**b**) (*fig: of time*) to fly, pass swiftly; (*of news*) to spread rapidly.
(**c**) (*fig*) to fly; to rush, hurry; (*of car etc*) to scorch, hurtle (along, past *etc*), go like the wind; **¡volando!** get a move on!; **voy volando** I'll go as quickly as I can; **prepárame volando la cena** get my supper double-quick, please; **— a + infin**, rush to + *infin*.
(**d**) (*fam*) to fly, disappear, vanish, walk (*fam*); **han volado mis pitillos** my fags have walked.
(**e**) (*SAm: Cards*) to bluff.
3 volarse *vr* (**a**) to fly away.
(**b**) (*SAm*) to get angry, lose one's temper.
(**c**) (*Mex*) **— algo** to spirit something away.

volate *nm* (**a**) (*Col*) confusion, mess. (**b**) (*Col*) lot of odd things. (**c**) (*Ven*) great show of despair (*or* impatience *etc*).

volatería *nf* (**a**) (*Hunting*) hawking, falconry, fowling.
(**b**) (*Orn*) birds; fowls; flock of birds.
(**c**) (*fig*) random thoughts, formless collection of ideas.
(**d**) (*Ec*) fireworks.

volatero *nm* (*Ec*) rocket.

volátil *adj* (**a**) volatile. (**b**) (*fig*) changeable, inconstant.

volatilidad *nf* (**a**) volatility, volatile nature. (**b**) (*fig*) changeableness, inconstancy.

volatilizar [1f] **1** *vt* (**a**) to volatilize, vaporize.
(**b**) (*fig*) to spirit away, cause to vanish.
2 volatilizarse *vr* (**a**) to volatilize, vaporize.
(**b**) (*fig*) to vanish into thin air.

volatín *nm* (**a**) acrobatics, tightrope walking. (**b**) = **volatinero**.

volatinero *nm*, **volatinera** *nf* acrobat, tightrope walker.

volcán *nm* (**a**) volcano.
(**b**) (*Arg, Bol, Col*) summer torrent, avalanche.
(**c**) (*CAm, PR*) pile, heap; **un — de cosas** a lot of things, a whole heap of things.
(**d**) (*PR*) deafening noise; confusion, hubbub.
(**e**) (*Col*) breakdown; collapse, fall.

volcanada *nf* (*Chi*) puff of air; whiff (of smell).

volcanarse [1a] *vr* (*Col*) to break down; to collapse, fall down.

volcánico *adj* volcanic.

volcar [1g *and* 1m] **1** *vt* (**a**) *container* to upset, overturn, tip over, knock over; (*deliberately*) to empty out; *contents* to upset; to empty out; *lorry etc* to tip; *contents* to dump, shoot; *car etc* to overturn; *boat* to overturn, capsize, upset.
(**b**) (*fig*) **— a uno** to make someone dizzy, make someone's head swim.
(**c**) (*fig*) **— a uno** to force someone to change his mind.
(**d**) (*fig*) to irritate, exasperate; to upset; to tease.
2 *vi* (*of car etc*) to overturn.
3 volcarse *vr* (**a**) (*container*) to be upset, get overturned; to tip over; (*car etc*) to overturn; (*boat*) to capsize.
(**b**) (*fig*) to go out of one's way, be excessively kind; **— para** (*or* **por**) **conseguir algo** to do one's

utmost to get something; — **por complacer a uno** to lean over backwards to satisfy someone.

volea *nf* volley; **media —** half-volley.

volear [1a] *vti* to volley.

voleibol *nm* (*SAm*) volleyball.

voleo *nm* (**a**) volley; **de un —, del primer —** quickly; brusquely, suddenly; at one blow; **sembrar a** (*or* **al**) — to broadcast the seed, sow the seed by the handful; **repartir algo a** (*or* **al**) — to distribute something haphazardly.
(**b**) (*fam*) punch.

volframio *nm* wolfram.

volibol *nm* volleyball.

volición *nf* volition.

volido *nm* (*SAm*) flight; **de un —** quickly, at once.

volquete *nm* tipcart; dumping lorry, dumper, dump truck (*US*).

voltaico *adj* voltaic.

voltaje *nm* voltage.

voltario *adj* (*Chi*) (**a**) fickle, changeable. (**b**) wilful, headstrong. (**c**) spruce, dapper.

volteada *nf* (**a**) (*RPl*) roundup. (**b**) (*CAm, Chi, Mex*) defection.

volteado *nm* (*Col*) deserter; switch of political allegiance.

volteador *nm*, **volteadora** *nf* acrobat.

voltear [1a] **1** *vt* (**a**) to turn over, roll over; to turn upside down; to turn round; *container* to upset, overturn; (*SAm*) *back etc* to turn; (*Chi, Mex, RPl*) to knock down; to knock over, spill.
(**b**) *bells* to peal.
(**c**) to throw into the air; (*of bull*) to toss.
(**d**) (*esp SAm*) *lasso etc* to whirl, twirl.
(**e**) (*Col, Chi, PR*) — **a uno** to force someone to change his mind.
(**f**) (*Arg, PR*) to search all over.
2 *vi* to roll over, go rolling over and over; to somersault.
3 voltearse *vr* (*SAm*) to change one's allegiance, go over to the other side; to change one's ideas.

voltereta *nf* somersault; roll, tumble; **— sobre las manos** handspring.

voltímetro *nm* voltmeter.

voltio *nm* volt.

volubilidad *nf* fickleness, changeableness; unpredictability; instability.

voluble *adj* (**a**) (*Bot*) twining, clinging; climbing. (**b**) *person* fickle, changeable; erratic, unpredictable; unstable.

volumen *nm* (**a**) volume; bulk, bulkiness; mass; **— sonoro** volume (of sound); **— de negocios, — de ventas** amount of business done, volume of business, turnover; **— de capital invertido** amount of capital invested; **una operación de mucho —** a sizeable operation; **poner la radio a todo —** to turn the radio up full (*or* as loud as possible).
(**b**) (*Typ*) volume.

volumétrico *adj* volumetric.

voluminoso *adj* voluminous; sizeable, bulky, massive.

voluntad *nf* (**a**) will; willpower; volition; wish, desire; intention; **buena —** goodwill; good intention, honest intention; **mala —** ill will, malice; evil intent; **última —** last wish, (*Law*) last will and testament; **— débil** weak will, lack of willpower; **— divina** divine will; **— férrea, — de hierro** will of iron; **a —** at will; at one's discretion; *quantity* as much as one likes; **se abre a —** it opens whenever you want it to; **a — de uno** as one wishes; **por causas ajenas a mi —** for reasons beyond my control; **por — propia** of one's own volition, of one's own free will; **su — es + infin** his wish is to + *infin*; **no lo dije con — de + infin** I did not say so with any wish to + *infin*, I did not say it with any intention of + *ger*; **hacer su santa —** to do exactly as one pleases, have one's own way at all costs; **hace falta — para escucharlo hasta el final** you need a strong will to sit right through it; **ganar(se) la — de uno** to win someone over; to dominate someone's will; **no tener — propia** to have no will of one's own; **no tiene — para dejar de beber** he hasn't the willpower to give up drinking; **reiterar su — de + infin** to reaffirm one's intention to + *infin*; **le viene — de + infin** he feels a need to + *infin*, he feels like + *ger*.
(**b**) (*fam*) fondness, affection; **tener — a** to be fond of, feel affection for.

voluntariamente *adv* voluntarily.

voluntariedad *nf* wilfulness, unreasonableness.

voluntario 1 *adj* (**a**) voluntary. (**b**) (*Mil*) voluntary; *force etc* volunteer. **2** *nm* volunteer.

voluntariosamente *adv* (**a**) wilfully, unreasonably.
(**b**) dedicatedly, in a well-intentioned way.

voluntarioso *adj* (**a**) (*pej*) headstrong, wilful, unreasonable. (**b**) dedicated, full of honest endeavour, well-intentioned.

voluptuosamente *adv* voluptuously; (*pej*) sensually.

voluptuosidad *nf* voluptuousness; (*pej*) sensuality.

voluptuoso 1 *adj* voluptuous; (*pej*) sensual. **2** *nm*, **voluptuosa** *nf* voluptuary; sensualist.

voluta *nf* (**a**) (*Archit*) scroll, volute. (**b**) (*of smoke*) spiral, column; (*from cigarette etc*) curl, ring.

volvedor 1 *adj* (*Col, Guat, RPl*) *horse etc* that knows its way home; that tends to make for its home area.
2 *nm* (**a**) wrench; screwdriver.
(**b**) (*Col*) bonus, extra.

volver [2h; *ptp* **vuelto**] **1** *vt* (**a**) *object* to turn, turn round, turn over, turn upside down; to turn back to front; *back, head* to turn; (*Cook*) to turn (over); (*Sew*) to turn inside out; *soil* to turn over; *eyes* to turn (*a* on, towards), cast (*a* on); *weapon* to aim (*a* at), turn (*a* on); **— un calcetín** to turn a sock inside out; **tener a uno vuelto como un calcetín** (*or* **media**) to have got someone where one wants him; **— el pensamiento a Dios** to turn one's thoughts to God; **me volvió la espalda** he turned his back on me (*see also* **espalda**); **— la proa al viento** to turn the bow into the wind; **— la vista atrás** to look back.
(**b**) *page* to turn (over); *door, window* to push open, swing open; to close, pull to, swing to.
(**c**) *sleeves etc* to roll up.
(**d**) *object thrown etc* to turn back, send back; *food* to bring up; *image* to reflect.
(**e**) (*fam*) to return, give back, send back; *change* to give; *visit* to repay, return; **— algo a su lugar** to return something to its place, put something back (in its place); **— bien por mal** to return good for evil.
(**f**) to change, turn, transform; (**+ *adj***) to turn, make, render; **— la casa a su estado original** to restore a house to its original state; **vuelve fieras a los hombres** it turns men into wild beasts; **esto le vuelve furioso** this makes him mad; **todo lo volvió muy triste** it made it all very sad; **el ácido lo vuelve azul** the acid turns it blue; *see* **loco**.
(**g**) (*Ling*) to translate (*a* into).
2 *vi* (**a**) (*of road, traveller etc*) to turn (*a* to).
(**b**) to return (*a* to, *de* from), come back, go back, get back; **— atrás** to go back, turn back; **— victorioso** to come back victorious, return in triumph; **volvió muy cansado** he got back tired out; **— a una costumbre** to revert to a habit; **volviendo ahora a mi tema . . .** returning (*or* reverting) now to my theme . . .
(**c**) **— a hacer algo** to do something again; **han vuelto a pintar la casa** they have painted the house again; **he vuelto a salir con ella** I've started going out with her again.
(**d**) **— en sí** to come to, come round, regain consciousness; **— sobre sí** to give up an idea, change one's mind; **— por** to come out in defence (*or* support) of, stand up for.
3 volverse *vr* (**a**) to turn round, turn over, turn upside down, turn inside out; **se le volvió el paraguas** his umbrella turned inside out; **se volvió riendo a mí** she turned laughingly to me; **se volvió para mirarlo** he turned (round) to look at it; **— atrás** (*fig*) to look back; (*fig*) to back down, go back on one's word; **— contra uno** to turn on someone.
(**b**) = **2** (**b**); **vuélvete a buscarlo** go back and look for it.
(**c**) (**+ *adj***) to turn, become, go, get; **se ha vuelto imposible** he has become quite impossible; **en el ácido se vuelve más oscuro** it turns darker in the acid; **todo se le vuelve dificultades** troubles come thick and fast for him; *see* **loco** *etc*.
(**d**) (*wine etc*) to go off, turn sour.

vomitado *adj person* sickly, seedy.

vomitar [1a] **1** *vt* (**a**) to vomit, bring up, throw up; **— sangre** to spit blood.
(**b**) (*fig*) *flames, smoke etc* to belch, belch forth; *lava* to spew, throw up, hurl out; *insults* to hurl (*contra* at).
(**c**) (*fig*) *secret* to tell reluctantly, finally come out with; *profits etc* to disgorge, shed.
2 *vi* (**a**) to vomit, be sick.
(**b**) (*fig*) **eso me da ganas de —** that makes me sick, that turns my stomach.

vomitera *nf* (*Cu, PR*), **vomitina** *nf* vomiting, retching.

vomitivo 1 *adj* emetic. **2** *nm* (**a**) (*Med*) emetic. (**b**) (*Chi*) nuisance, bore.

vómito *nm* (**a**) (*act*) vomiting, being sick; **— de sangre** spitting of blood. (**b**) vomit.

vomitona *nf* (*fam*) bad sick turn.

voquible *nm* (*hum*) word.

voracear [1a] *vt* (*Arg*) to challenge in a loud voice.

voracidad *nf* voracity, voraciousness.

vorágine *nf* whirlpool, vortex, maelstrom; (*fig*) maelstrom; whirl.

voraz *adj* (a) voracious, ravenous; greedy. (b) (*fig*) *fire* all-devouring, fierce. (c) (*Mex*) bold.

vorazmente *adv* voraciously, ravenously; greedily.

vórtice *nm* (a) whirlpool, vortex; whirlwind. (b) (*Meteorol*) cyclone, hurricane.

vos *personal pronoun pl* (*arch*) you, ye; (*in certain SAm countries*) you (*in singular sense*).

vosear [1a] *vt* (*SAm*) to address as "vos" (ie, treat familiarly).

voseo *nm* (*SAm*) addressing a person as "vos", familiar usage.

Vosgos *nmpl* Vosges.

vosotros, vosotras *personal pronoun pl* (a) (*subject*) you.

(b) (*after prep*) you; yourselves; **entre** — among yourselves; **irán sin** — they'll go without you; **¿no pedís nada para** —? are you not asking anything for yourselves?

votación *nf* voting; vote; — **por manos levantadas** show of hands; **por** — **popular** by popular vote; **por** — **secreta** by secret vote, by secret ballot; **la** — **ha sido nutrida** voting has been heavy; **someter algo a** — to put something to the vote, take a vote on something.

votante 1 *adj* voting. 2 *nmf* voter.

votar [1a] 1 *vt* (a) (*Pol*) *candidate, party* to vote for; *bill, motion* to pass, approve (by vote).

(b) (*Eccl*) to vow, promise (a to).

2 *vi* (a) (*Pol etc*) to vote (*por* for).

(b) (*Eccl*) to vow, take a vow.

votivo *adj* votive.

voto *nm* (a) (*Pol etc*) vote; — **de calidad,** — **decisivo** casting vote; — **de censura** vote of censure; — **de confianza** vote of confidence; — **de desconfianza** vote of no confidence; — **de gracias** vote of thanks; — **secreto** secret vote, secret ballot; **dar su** — to cast one's vote (*a* for), give one's vote (*a* to); **emitir su** — to cast one's vote, (*fig*) give one's opinion; **ganar por 7** —**s** to win by 7 votes; **hubo 13** —**s a favor y 11 en contra** there were 13 votes for and 11 against; **tener** — to have a vote.

(b) (*Eccl*) vow; — **de castidad** vow of chastity; — **de pobreza** vow of poverty; —**s monásticos** monastic vows; **hacer** — **de** + *infin* to take a vow to + *infin*.

(c) (*Eccl*) ex voto.

(d) oath, curse; swearword.

(e) — wishes; good wishes; **mis mejores** —**s por su éxito** my best wishes for its success; **hacer** —**s por el restablecimiento de uno** to wish someone a quick recovery, hope that someone will get well; **hago** —**s para que se remedie pronto** I pray that it may be speedily put right, I earnestly hope that something will soon be done about it.

voy *etc see* **ir**.

voz *nf* (a) voice; — **argentina** silvery voice; — **empañada,** — **opaca** thin voice, voice weak with emotion; **la** — **de la conciencia** the voice of conscience, the promptings of conscience; **la** — **del pueblo** the voice of the people; **a una** — with one voice, unanimously; **a media** — in a low voice; **a en cuello, a** — **en grito** at the top of one's voice; **de viva** — viva voce; by word of mouth, verbally; **en alta** — loud(ly), in a loud voice; *see* **bajo**; **estar en** — to be in good voice; (*fam*) to be fit, be ready for anything; **aclarar la** — to clear one's throat; **alzar la** —, **levantar la** — to raise one's voice; **ahuecar la** — to adopt a serious tone, try to make oneself sound impressive; **se me anudó la** — (**en la garganta**) I got a lump in my throat; **desanudar la** — to manage to speak again, find one's voice; **tener la** — **tomada** to be hoarse.

(b) (*Mus etc*) sound, note; (*of thunder etc*) noise; **la** — **del órgano** the sound of the organ, the strains of the organ.

(c) (*Mus*) voice, part; **canción a cuatro voces** song for four voices, four-part song; **cantar a dos voces** to sing a duet; — **cantante** leading part; **llevar la** — **cantante** (*fig*) to be the boss, have the chief say.

(d) shout; yell; **voces** shouts, shouting, yelling; — **de mando** (*Mil*) command; **dar** (*or* **pegar**) **voces** to shout, call out, yell; **dale una** — give him a shout; **dar la** — **de alarma** to sound the alarm; **dar cuatro voces** to make a great fuss; **discutir a voces** to argue noisily; **llamar a uno a voces** to shout to someone; **está pidiendo a voces que se remedie** it's crying out (to heaven) to be put right.

(e) (*Cards*) call.

(f) (*fig*) rumour; — **común** hearsay, gossip, rumour; **corre la** — **de que** ... there is a rumour going round that ...

(g) (*fig: in meeting etc*) voice, say; vote, support; **asistir con** — **y voto** to be present as a full member; **tener** — **y voto** to have a say; to have the right to speak; **no tener** — **en capítulo** to have no say in a matter; to have no influence, not count.

(h) (*Ling*) word; **una** — **de origen árabe** a word of Arabic origin.

(i) (*Gram*) voice; — **activa** active voice; — **pasiva** passive voice.

vozarrón *nm* loud voice, big voice.

vudú *nm* voodoo.

vuduísmo *nm* voodooism.

vuelco *nm* (a) upset, overturning, spill; **dar un** — to overturn.

(b) **mi corazón dio un** — my heart missed a beat; I had a presentiment.

(c) (*fig*) collapse; catastrophe, ruin; **este negocio va a dar un** — this business is heading for a catastrophe.

vuelillo *nm* lace, frill.

vuelo *nm* (a) flight; — **a ciegas** blind flying, flying on instruments; — **de ensayo** test flight; — **espacial** space flight; — **sin etapas** non-stop flight; — **sin motor,** — **a vela** gliding; — **de órbita** orbital flight; — **en picado** dive; — **a solas** solo flight; **alzar el** — to take flight, take off; (*fig*) to dash off; (*fig*) to leave the parental nest, spread one's wings; **se oía el** — **de una mosca** you could hear a pin drop; **remontar el** — to soar (up); **tocar las campanas a** — to peal the bells; **tomar** — to grow, develop; to assume great importance; **de un** —, **en un** — (*fig*) rapidly.

(b) **al** —: **cazar** (*or* **coger**) **algo al** — to catch something in flight; (*fig*) to overhear something in passing; **tirar al** — to shoot at a bird on the wing; **cogerlas** (*or* **pescarlas, pillarlas** *etc*) **al** — (*fig*) to catch on immediately, get it at once; to be pretty smart.

(c) (*Orn: also* —**s**) flight feathers; wing, wings; **de altos** —**s** (*fig*) grandiose, ambitious, far-reaching; **cortar los** —**s a uno** to clip someone's wings.

(d) (*Sew: on cuff*) lace, frill.

(e) (*Sew: of skirt etc*) loose part; **el** — **de la falda** the spread of the skirt, the swirl of the skirt; **falda de mucho** — full skirt, wide skirt.

(f) (*Archit*) projection, projecting part.

(g) (*Bot*) timber, trees, woodland.

vuelta *nf* (a) turn; (*Astron, Mech etc*) revolution; **una** — **de la tierra** one revolution of the earth; — **al mundo** trip round the world; — **atrás** backward step (*also fig*); **¡media** —! (*Mil*) about turn!; — **en redondo** complete turn; **a** — **de** by dint of; **andar a** —**s con** to be engaged in, be immersed in; **dar la** — **a una página** to turn a page; **dar la** — **al mundo** to go round the world; **el coche dio la** — the car turned over; **dar una** — **de campana** to overturn, turn completely over, somersault; **dar media** — (*Mil*) to face about; to turn half round; (*fam*) to beat it (*fam*); **al llegar allí hay que dar media** — when you get there make a half turn; **dar** — **a una llave** to turn a key; **dar** — **a un coche** to reverse a car, turn a car round; **el libro dio la** — **por muchas oficinas** the book went round a lot of offices, the book went the rounds in many offices; **dar** —**s** to turn, revolve, go round; (*of head*) to spin, swim, be in a whirl; **dar** —**s alrededor de un eje** to spin round an axle; **dar** —**s alrededor de un planeta** to revolve round a planet, go round a planet; **dar** —**s a una manivela** to turn (*or* wind, crank) a handle; **dar** —**s a un botón** to turn a knob; **dar** —**s a un asunto** to think a matter over, turn a matter over in one's mind; **le estás dando demasiadas** —**s** you're worrying too much about it; **dar** —**s a un palo entre los dedos** to twirl a stick in one's fingers; **no hay que darle** —**s** that's the way it is, there's no mistake about it; **poner a uno de** — **y media** to heap abuse on someone; to give someone a good telling-off.

(b) (*fig*) turn, change; volte-face, reversal; — **de la marea** turn of the tide; **las** —**s de la vida** the ups and downs of life; **dar la** —, **dar una** — to change right round, alter radically.

(c) (*of river, road*) bend, curve, turn; — **cerrada** sharp turn, tight bend; **en una** — **del río** at a bend in the river; **dar** —**s** to twist and turn.

(d) (*of rope*) loop; coil; — **de cabo** (*Naut*) hitch.

(e) (*of election, talks, tournament etc*) round; (*in racing*) lap, circuit; — **ciclista** long-distance cycle race; **V**— **de Francia** Tour de France (*cycle race*); — **de honor** lap of honour; — **al ruedo** (*Taur*) *circuit of the ring made by a triumphant bullfighter*;

dio 3 —s al ruedo he went round the ring 3 times; **segunda** — (*Univ*) repeat examinations, resits.

(**f**) (*of sausage etc*) round, slice.

(**g**) (*Sew*) row of stitches.

(**h**) (*Sew*) strip; facing; cuff; (*of trousers*) turn-up, cuff (*US*).

(**i**) (*of paper, cloth etc*) back, reverse, other side; **a la** — on the next page, overleaf; **a la** — **de la esquina** round the corner; **a la** — **de varios años** after some years; **lo escribió a la** — **del sobre** he wrote it on the back of the envelope; **buscar las** —**s a uno** to try to catch someone out; **no tiene** — **de hoja** there's no alternative; there are no two ways about it; there's no gainsaying it, it's unanswerable.

(**j**) (*act*) return; (*Rail etc*) return journey, homeward journey; **a** — **de correo** by return (of post); **a la** — on one's return; **lo haré a la** — I'll do it when I get back; **de** —, **iremos a verlos** we'll go and see them on the way back; **estar de** — to be back, be home (again); (*fam*) to have no illusions, know from experience; (*fam*) to be pretty clever; **¡hasta la** —! au revoir!, good-bye for now!

(**k**) (*act*) =**devolución**.

(**l**) (*Fin: also* —**s**) change; **quédese con la** — keep the change.

(**m**) stroll, walk; **dar una** — to take a stroll, go for a walk.

(**n**) (*fam*) beating, tanning (*fam*).

vueltero *adj* (*Arg*) *person* difficult.

vuelto 1 *ptp of* **volver. 2** *nm* (*SAm*) =**vuelta (1).**

vuestro 1 *poss adj* your; (*after n*) of yours, *eg* **una idea vuestra** an idea of yours, one of your ideas; **lo** — (what is) yours, what belongs to you.

2 *poss pron* yours, of yours; **es el** — it is yours; **los** —**s** (*freq*) your people, your relations, your family; your men, your side.

vulcanita *nf* vulcanite.

vulcanización *nf* vulcanization.

vulcanizar [1f] *vt* to vulcanize.

Vulcano *m* Vulcan.

vulgar *adj* (**a**) *tongue* vulgar; *term* common, ordinary; (*pej*) vulgar; **latín** — Vulgar Latin.

(**b**) *person* ordinary, common; *features, manners etc* coarse; **el hombre** — the ordinary man, the common man.

(**c**) *event, life etc* ordinary, everyday; humdrum; *remark etc* banal, trivial, commonplace; inane.

vulgaridad *nf* (**a**) (*quality*) ordinariness, commonness; coarseness; banality; triviality; inanity.

(**b**) (*act*) vulgarity, coarse thing; coarse expression.

(**c**) —**es** banalities, trivialities, platitudes; inanities.

vulgarismo *nm* popular form (of a word); (*pej*) slang word, vulgarism, popular expression.

vulgarización *nf* (**a**) popularization; **obra de** — popular work. (**b**) (*Ling*) translation into the vernacular.

vulgarizar [1f] *vt* (**a**) to popularize; to spread a knowledge of. (**b**) (*Ling*) to translate into the vernacular.

vulgarmente *adv* commonly, ordinarily; vulgarly; **A, llamado** — **B** A, popularly (*or* commonly) known as B.

Vulgata *nf* Vulgate.

vulgo 1 *nm* common people; (*pej*) lower orders, common herd; mob.

2 *adv*: **el mingitorio,** — "**meadero**" the urinal, commonly (*or* popularly) known as the "bog".

vulnerabilidad *nf* vulnerability.

vulnerable *adj* vulnerable (*de* to).

vulnerar [1a] *vt* (**a**) to damage, harm; *custom, right etc* to interfere with, affect seriously. (**b**) *law* to break.

vulpeja *nf* fox; vixen.

vulpino *adj* vulpine; (*fig*) foxy.

vulva *nf* vulva.

W

[in initial position pronounced like Spanish b, v, but sometimes like English w]

wáter ['bater] *nm* (*angl*) lavatory, water closet.
wélter ['belter] *nm* (*angl*) welterweight.
whisk(e)y ['wiski, 'gwiski] *nm* (*angl*) whisk(e)y.

wolfram ['bolfram] *nm*, **wolframio** [b—] *nm* (*angl*) wolfram.

X

[in initial position pronounced like Spanish s]

xeno *nm* xenon.
xenofobia *nf* xenophobia.
xenófobo *nm* xenophobe.
xenón *nm* xenon.

xilófono *nm* xylophone.
xilografía *nf* (**a**) xylography. (**b**) (*una* —) xylograph, wood engraving.
xilográfico *adj* xylographic.

Y

y . . .: *for some words so spelled in* S Am, *see also* **ll** . . .
y *conj* and.
ya 1 *adv* (**a**) (*basic sense: past*) already; **lo hemos visto** — we've seen it already; **han dado las 8** — it's past 8 already; — **en el siglo X** as long ago as the 10th century, as early as the 10th century; — **no viene** he no longer comes, he doesn't come any more.
(**b**) (*present, future*) now; at once, right away; soon, presently; in due course; — **es hora de irnos** it's time for us to go now; — **viene el autobús** the bus is coming now, here's the bus; — **se lo traerán** they'll bring it for you right away; — **no lo volverás a ver** you won't see it any more; — **arreglarán todo eso** they'll soon put all that right.
(**c**) (*as interj*) ¡—! of course!, that's it!, now I remember!; at last!, so you've managed it at last!; ¡—, —! yes, yes!; all right!; O.K.! (*fam*).
(**d**) (*emphatic: often not translated*) ¡— **voy!** coming!; — **lo sé** I know; — **se acabó** it's all over; ¿— **estás aquí otra vez?** are you here again?; — **te llegará el turno a ti,** — your turn will come (don't you worry).
2 *conj* (**a**) — **por una cosa,** — **por otra** now for one thing, now for another; — **dice que sí,** — **dice que no** first he says yes, then he says no; — **te vas,** — **te quedas, me es igual** whether you go or stay is all the same to me.
(**b**) **no** — not only; **no** — **aquí, sino en todas partes** not only here, but everywhere.
(**c**) — **que** as, since; now that, seeing that.
yac *nm*, *pl* **yacs** [jak] yak.
yacaré *nm* (S Am) alligator.
yacente *adj* *statue* reclining, recumbent.
yacer [2y] *vi* (*mostly arch*) to lie; **aquí yace X** here lies X; — **con** to sleep with.
yacija *nf* (**a**) bed; rough bed; **ser de mala** — to sleep badly, have a restless night; (*fig*) to be a vagrant, be a ne'er-do-well. (**b**) grave, tomb.
yacimiento *nm* bed, deposit; — **petrolífero** oilfield.
yagua *nf* (Ant, Col, Mex, Per, Ven) royal palm; fibrous tissue from the wood of the royal palm.
yagual *nm* (C Am, Mex) padded ring (*for carrying loads on the head*).
yaguareté *nm* (Bol, RPl) jaguar.
yaguré *nm* (S Am) skunk.
yaíta *adv* (S Am)=ya.
yak *nm*, *pl* **yaks** [jak] yak.
Yakarta Jakarta.
yámbico *adj* iambic.
yana *adj* (Ec) black.
yanacón *nm*, **yanacona** *nf* (Arg, Bol, Chi, Per) Indian tenant farmer, Indian sharecropper; unpaid Indian servant.
yancófilo *adj* (S Am) pro-American, pro-United States.

yanqui (*fam*) **1** *adj* Yankee. **2** *nmf* Yank (*fam*), Yankee (*fam*).

Yanquilandia *f* (*SAm*: *hum*) United States.

yapa *nf* (**a**) (*SAm*) extra, extra bit, bonus; **dar algo de —** to add a bit, give something as a bonus; (*fig*) to add something for good measure.
(**b**) (*Mex*) tip.
(**c**) (*Chi, RPl*) attachment, end piece.

yapada *nf* (*SAm*) extra, extra bit, bonus.

yapar [1a] (*SAm*) **1** *vt* (**a**) to give as a bonus, add as an extra. (**b**) *rope etc* to stretch; to add a bit to, lengthen. **2** *vi* to add an extra, give an extra bit.

yarará *nm or f* (*Bol, RPl*) rattlesnake.

yarda *nf* (*angl*) yard.

yate *nm* yacht.

yaya *nm* (**a**) (*CAm, Col*) wound; (*Col, Cu, Chi, Per*) slight wound; scar; small pain. (**b**) (*Cu*) stick, walking stick.

yaz *nm* (*Acad*) jazz.

ye . . .: *for some words, see* **hie** . . ., *eg for* **yerra** *see* **hierra.**

yedra *nf* ivy.

yegua 1 *nf* (**a**) mare.
(**b**) (*Chi, Per, RPl*) woman; coarse woman, slattern.
(**c**) (*Bol, CAm*) cigar stub.
2 *adj* (**a**) (*CAm, PR*) stupid; rough, coarse.
(**b**) (*Chi*) big, huge.

yeguada *nf* (**a**) stud; (*RPl*) group of breeding mares. (**b**) (*CAm, PR*) piece of stupidity, foolish act (*etc*).

yeguarizo *nm* (*RPl*) (**a**) stud, group of breeding mares. (**b**) horses (*in general*).

yegüerío *nm* (*CAm, PR*) = **yeguarizo** (**a**).

yelmo *nm* helmet.

yema *nf* (**a**) (*of egg*) yoke; (*SAm*) egg: **— mejida** egg flip.
(**b**) (*Bot*) leaf bud, eye; young shoot.
(**c**) (*Anat*) **— del dedo** fingertip.
(**d**) (*fig*) best part.
(**e**) (*fig*) snag; **dar en la —** to put one's finger on the spot, hit the nail on the head.
(**f**) (*fig*) **en la — del invierno** in the dead of winter.

yendo *see* **ir.**

yerba *nf* (**a**) = **hierba.**
(**b**) (*SAm*) green.
(**c**) (*Bol, Chi, RPl*: *also* **— mate, — de mate**) maté.
(**d**) (*Mex*) marijuana.
(**e**) (*RPl*) **—s** herb, medicinal plant.

yerbal *nm* (*RPl*), **yerbatal** *nm* (*Ec*) maté plantation.

yerbatero *nm* (**a**) (*SAm*) herbalist; quack doctor.
(**b**) (*RPl*) dealer in maté.

yerbear [1a] *vi* (*RPl*) to drink maté.

yerbera *nf* (*RPl*) maté container.

yermar [1a] *vt* to lay waste.

yermo 1 *adj* uninhabited; waste, uncultivated. **2** *nm* waste land; waste, wilderness.

yerna *nf* (*Col, PR, SD*) daughter-in-law.

yerno *nm* son-in-law.

yeros *nmpl* lentils.

yerro *nm* error, mistake.

yersey *nm* (*Acad*), **yersi** *nm* (*Acad*) jersey.

yerto *adj* stiff, rigid; **— de frío** stiff with cold.

yesca *nf* (**a**) tinder; (*Arg*) flint; **—s** tinderbox; **arder como si fuera —** to burn like tinder.
(**b**) (*fig*) fuel; inflammable situation, group (*etc*) which is easily inflamed.
(**c**) (*fig*) food (*etc*) which makes one thirsty (*for wine*).
(**d**) (*Ec*) debt.

yesería *nf* plastering, plasterwork.

yesero *nm* plasterer.

yeso *nm* (**a**) (*Geol*) gypsum.
(**b**) (*Archit etc*) plaster; **— mate** plaster of Paris; **dar de — a una pared** to plaster a wall.
(**c**) (*Art etc*) plaster cast.
(**d**) (*School*) chalk.

yesquero *nm* (*Ec, Ven*) cigarette lighter.

yeta *nf* (*Mex, RPl*) bad luck, misfortune.

yetar [1a] *vt* (*RPl*) to bring bad luck to.

yeti *nm* yeti.

ye-yé (*fam*) **1** *adj* ultramodern; mod (*fam*); cool (*fam*), groovy (*sl*); trendy (*sl*); **cantante —** pop singer; **música —** pop music, beat music; **es una chica —** she's an ultramodern girl, she's really with it (*fam*).
2 *nmf* ultramodern person, member of the modern generation, mod (*fam*); person who is with it (*fam*); **ser un —** to be ultramodern, be with it, be a mod.

yeyeísmo *nm* (*fam*) ultramodern fashions (*or tendencies etc*); trendiness (*sl*); devotion to (*or cult of*) pop music *etc*.

yeyería *nf* (*fam*) (**a**) modern generation, mods (*fam*), people who are with it (*fam*). (**b**) = **yeyeísmo.**

yip *nm* (*SAm*) jeep.

yo *pers pron* (**a**) I; **soy —** it's me, it is I (*lit*). (**b**) **el —** the self, the ego.

yod *nf* yod.

yodo *nm* iodine.

yodoformo *nm* iodoform.

yoga[1] *nf* yoga.

yoga[2] *nf* (*Mex*) dagger.

yogui *nm* yogi.

yogur *nm* yogourt.

yol *nm* yawl.

yola *nf* gig, yawl; sailing boat, shell.

yóquey *nm* (*Acad*) jockey.

yuca *nf* (**a**) yucca; (*SAm*) manioc root, cassava. (**b**) (*Ant*) poverty. (**c**) (*Col*) food (*in general*). (**d**) (*Col*) leg. (**e**) (*CAm, Bol*) lie.

yugo *nm* yoke (*also fig*); **— del matrimonio** marriage tie; **sacudir el —** (*fig*) to throw off the yoke.

Yugo(e)slavia *f* Yugoslavia, Jugoslavia.

yugo(e)slavo 1 *adj* Yugoslavian, Jugoslavian. **2** *nm*, **yugo(e)slava** *nf* Yugoslav, Jugoslav.

yuguero *nm* ploughman.

yugular *adj* jugular.

yungas *nfpl* (*Bol, Chi, Ec, Per*) hot valleys.

yungla *nf* jungle.

yunque *nm* (**a**) anvil. (**b**) (*fig*) stoical person; tireless worker; **hacer de —, servir de —** to have to put up with hardships (*or abuse etc*).

yunta *nf* (**a**) yoke, team (of oxen). (**b**) (*esp SAm*) **—s** couple, pair; cufflinks.

yuntero *nm* ploughman.

yuta *nf* (**a**) (*Chi*) slug. (**b**) (*Arg, Bol*) **hacer la —** to play truant.

yute *nm* jute.

yuxtaponer [2r] *vt* to juxtapose.

yuxtaposición *nf* juxtaposition.

yuyal *nm* (*Chi, RPl*) weedy ground.

yuyerío *nm* (*Bol, Chi, RPl*) weeds; wild plants.

yuyero *nm* (*Arg*) herbalist.

yuyo *nm* (**a**) (*Bol, Chi, RPl*) weed; wild plant, useless plant; (*RPl*) medicinal plant, herb; (*Ec*) herb flavouring; (*Per*) cooking herb; **estar como un —** (*Arg, Chi*) to be weak, be lifeless.
(**b**) (*Col*) herbal poultice.
(**c**) (*CAm*) **—s** blisters on the feet.

Z

zabordar [1a] *vi* to run aground.
zabullir [3h] *vi etc* = **zambullir** *etc*.
zacapel(l)a *nf* rumpus (*fam*), row.
zacatal *nm* (*CAm*, *Mex*) pasture.
zacate *nm* (*CAm*, *Mex*) grass; hay, fodder.
zacatear [1a] (*CAm*, *Mex*) **1** *vt* to beat. **2** *vi* to graze.
zacatera *nf* (*CAm*, *Mex*) pasture; haystack.
zafacoca *nf* (**a**) (*SAm*) row, quarrel; brawl. (**b**) (*Mex*) beating. (**c**) (*Cu*) riot.
zafado *adj* (**a**) (*prov*, *SAm*) brazen, shameless; insolent. (**b**) (*RPl*) alert, sharp, wide awake. (**c**) (*Col*, *Mex*) crazy.
zafadura *nf* (*SAm*) dislocation, sprain.
zafaduría *nf* (**a**) effrontery, brazenness; insolence. (**b**) (*una* —) shameless remark (*or act etc*).
zafante *prep* (*Ant*) except (for).
zafar [1a] **1** *vt* (**a**) to loosen, untie.
    (**b**) *ship* to lighten; *surface etc* to clear, free.
    (**c**) (*Col*, *Cu*, *Mex*, *Nic*) to exclude.
    2 zafarse *vr* (**a**) to escape, run away; to slip away; to break loose; to hide oneself away.
    (**b**) (*Mech*) to slip off, come off.
    (**c**) — **de** *person* to get away from; to dodge, shake off; *duty, work* to get out of, dodge; *agreement* to get out of, wriggle out of; *difficulty* to get round.
    (**d**) (*fam*) — **con algo** to pinch something (*fam*).
    (**e**) (*SAm*) — **un brazo** to dislocate one's arm, wrench one's arm.
    (**f**) (*Arg*, *CAm*) to dodge (a blow).
    (**g**) (*Col*) to go a bit crazy.
zafarrancho *nm* (**a**) (*Naut*) clearing for action; — **de combate** call to action stations.
    (**b**) (*fig*) havoc, destruction; mess; **hacer un** — to cause havoc; to break everything up; to make a dreadful mess.
    (**c**) (*fam*) quarrel, row.
zafio *adj* coarse, uncouth.
zafiro *nm* sapphire.
zafo **1** *adj* (**a**) (*Naut*) clear; unobstructed. (**b**) unharmed; undamaged, intact; **salir** — **de** to come unscathed out of. (**c**) (*SAm*) free. **2** *prep* (*Arg*, *CAm*) except (for).
zafón *nm* (*Col*) slip, error.
zafra[1] *nf* oil jar, oil container.
zafra[2] *nf* (*esp SAm*) sugar harvest; sugar making.
zaga *nf* rear; **a la** —, **en** — behind, in the rear; **dejar en** — to leave behind, outstrip; **A no le va a la** (*or* **en**) — **a B** A is every bit as good as B, A is in no way inferior to B; **no le va a la** — **a nadie** he is second to none.
zagal *nm* boy, lad, youth; (*Agr*) shepherd boy.
zagala *nf* girl, lass; (*Agr*) shepherdess.
zagalejo *nm* lad; shepherd boy.
zagalón *nm* big boy, strapping lad.
zagalona *nf* big girl, hefty wench.
zagual *nm* paddle.
zaguán *nm* vestibule, hallway, entry.
zaguero *adj* (**a**) rear, back; *cart* too heavily laden at the back; **equipo** — bottom team, team that is trailing. (**b**) (*fig*) slow, laggard.
zahareño *adj* wild; shy, unsociable.
zaherimiento *nm* criticism; mortification; reprimand; reproach.
zaherir [3i] *vt* to criticize sharply (*or* sarcastically), attack, lash; to wound, mortify; to upbraid; — **a uno con algo** to reproach someone for something, cast something in someone's teeth.
zahones *nmpl* riding breeches.
zahorí *nm* seer, clairvoyant; water diviner; (*fig*) highly perceptive person.
zahurda *nf* (**a**) (*Agr*) pigsty. (**b**) (*fam*) hovel, shack.
zahurra *nf* (*Col*) din, hullabaloo (*fam*).
zaino[1] *adj* horse chestnut; *cow* black.

zaino[2] *adj* treacherous; *animal* unreliable, vicious; **mirar a lo** (*or* **de**) — to look sideways, look shiftily.
zainoso *adj* (*Chi*) treacherous.
zalagarda *nf* (**a**) (*Mil*) ambush, trap; ruse; (*Hunting*) trap. (**b**) row, din; noisy quarrel; shindy, hullabaloo (*fam*).
zalamerear [1a] *vi* (*Arg*, *Mex*) to flatter, cajole, wheedle.
zalamería *nf* (**a**) (*also* —**s**) flattery; cajolery, wheedling. (**b**) (*quality*) suaveness; oiliness, soapiness.
zalamero **1** *adj* flattering; cajoling, wheedling; suave; oily, soapy. **2** *nm* flatterer; wheedler; suave person; oily sort, soapy individual.
zalea *nf* sheepskin.
zalema *nf* salaam, deep bow; —**s** (*fig*) bowing and scraping, flattering courtesies.
zalenquear [1a] *vi* (*Col*) to limp.
zamarra *nf* sheepskin; sheepskin jacket, fur jacket.
zamarrazo *nm* (*fig*) blow; setback; nasty jolt.
zamarrear [1a] *vt* (**a**) (*of dog*) to shake, worry.
    (**b**) (*fam*) to shake up, knock around; to shove around.
    (**c**) (*fam*: *in argument etc*) to stamp on, humiliate, squash.
zamarro *nm* (**a**) sheepskin; sheepskin jacket. (**b**) (*Col*, *Ec*, *Ven*) —**s** riding breeches. (**c**) (*fam*) boor, yokel; sly person.
zamba *nf* (*esp SAm*) samba.
zambada *nf* (*Per*) group of half-breeds.
zambardo *nm* (**a**) (*Chi*) clumsy person. (**b**) (*Arg*, *Chi*) clumsiness; damage, breakage. (**c**) (*Arg*) fluke.
zambeque **1** *adj* (*Cu*) silly. **2** *nm* (**a**) (*Cu*) idiot. (**b**) (*Cu*, *Ven*) uproar, hullabaloo (*fam*).
zambequería *nf* (*Cu*) silliness.
zamberío *nm* (*Col*, *Ec*, *Per*) half-breeds (*collectively*).
Zambeze *m* Zambesi.
Zambia *f* Zambia.
zambo **1** *adj* knock-kneed. **2** *nm*, **zamba** *nf* (**a**) (*SAm*) half-breed (*of Negro and Indian parentage*). (**b**) (*Bol*, *Col*, *Chi*) mulatto.
zambomba *nf* (**a**) *a kind of rustic drum*. (**b**) (*fam*) ¡—! phew!
zambombazo *nm* (**a**) bang, explosion. (**b**) blow, punch.
zambombo *nm* boor, yokel.
zambra *nf* (**a**) gipsy dance. (**b**) (*fam*) uproar, shindy; commotion.
zambrate *nm* (*CAm*), **zambrera** *nf* (*Ven*) row, commotion.
zambucar [1g] *vt* (**a**) to hide, tuck away, cover up.
    (**b**) to mix up, jumble up.
zambuir [3g] *vi* (*Col*, *Ec*, *PR*) = **zambullir**.
zambullida *nf* dive, plunge; dip; ducking.
zambullir [3h] **1** *vt* (**a**) to dip, plunge (*en* into); to duck (*en* under).
    2 zambullirse *vr* (**a**) to dive, plunge (*en* into); to duck (*en* under).
    (**b**) to hide, cover oneself up.
zambullón *nm* (*Col*, *Ec*, *RPl*) = **zambullida**.
zambutir [3a] *vt* (*CAm*, *Mex*) to stuff, pack hastily (*en* into).
zamorano **1** *adj* of Zamora. **2** *nm*, **zamorana** *nf* native (*or* inhabitant) of Zamora; **los** —**s** the people of Zamora.
zampa *nf* (*Archit*) pile.
zampabollos *nmf*, *pl* **zampabollos** (*fam*) (**a**) greedy pig, glutton. (**b**) coarse individual.
zampar [1a] **1** *vt* (**a**) *object* to put away hurriedly (*en* in), whip smartly (*en* into); to dip, plunge (*en* into).
    (**b**) to hurl, dash (*en* against, to); **lo zampó en el suelo** he dashed it to the floor.
    (**c**) *food* to gobble, wolf.
    (**d**) (*SAm*) *blow* to fetch, deal.
    2 *vi* to gobble, eat voraciously.
    3 zamparse *vr* (**a**) to bump, crash, hurtle; **se**

zampó en medio del corro he thrust himself roughly into the circle.

    (**b**) (*fig*) to gatecrash, go along uninvited.

    (**c**) — **en** to dart into, whip into, shoot into; **pero se zampó en el cine** but he shot into the cinema.

    (**d**) — **algo** to wolf something, tuck something away (*fam*); **se zampó 4 porciones enteras** he wolfed 4 whole helpings.

zampatortas *nmf*, *pl* **zampatortas** (*fam*) = **zampabollos**.

zampón *adj* (*fam*) greedy.

zampoña *nf* shepherd's pipes, rustic flute.

zampullín *nm* grebe.

zampuzar [1f] *vt* = **zambullir**; = **zampar**.

zanahoria 1 *nf* carrot. 2 *nm* (*RPl*) (**a**) errand boy. (**b**) idiot, nitwit (*sl*); clumsy person; poor wretch.

zanca *nf* (*Orn*, *also fam*) shank.

zancada *nf* stride; **alejarse a grandes —s** to go off with big strides, stride away; **en dos —s** (*fig*) in a couple of ticks; very easily.

zancadilla *nf* (**a**) trip; (*fig*) stratagem, trick (*to get someone out of a job*); **echar la — a uno** to trip someone up; (*fig*) to put the skids under someone (*fam*), scheme to get someone out. (**b**) booby trap.

zancajear [1a] *vi* to rush around.

zancajo *nm* (**a**) (*Anat*, *Sew*) heel; **A no le llega a los —s a B** A can't hold a candle to B, A is much inferior to B. (**b**) (*fam*) dwarf, runt.

zancajón *adj* (*Mex*) (**a**) tall, lanky. (**b**) clumsy, misshapen.

zancarrón *nm* (**a**) leg bone; big bone. (**b**) (*fam*) old bag of bones. (**c**) (*fam*) poor teacher.

zanco *nm* stilt; **estar en —s** (*fig*) to be well up, be in a good position.

zancón *adj* (**a**) long-legged. (**b**) (*CAm*) lanky; clumsy-looking. (**c**) (*SAm*) dress too short.

zancudero *nm* (*Ant*, *CR*, *Mex*, *Ven*) swarm of mosquitoes.

zancudo 1 *adj* long-legged; **ave zancuda** wader, wading bird. 2 *nm* (*SAm*) mosquito.

zangamanga *nf* (*fam*) trick; funny business.

zanganada *nf* stupid remark, silly thing (to say).

zanganear [1a] *vi* (**a**) to idle, loaf; to fool around, waste one's time. (**b**) to make stupid remarks.

zángano *nm* (**a**) (*Ent*) drone. (**b**) (*fig*) drone; idler, slacker. (**c**) idiot, fool. (**d**) bore. (**e**) (*CAm*, *Mex*) rogue.

zangarri(an)a *nf* (**a**) (*Med*) headache, migraine; minor upset. (**b**) (*fig*) blues, depression.

zangolotear [1a] 1 *vt* to keep playing with, fiddle with; to shake, jiggle.

    2 *vi* and **zangolotearse** *vr* (**a**) (*of window etc*) to rattle, shake.

    (**b**) (*of person*) to fidget; to jiggle; to fiddle about, fuss around.

zangoloteo *nm* fiddling; shaking, jiggling; fidgeting; rattling.

zangolotino *adj*: **niño —** older boy with childish habits (*or* clothes *etc*); weedy youth, overgrown baby.

zangón *nm* big lazy lad.

zanguanga *nf* fictitious illness; **hacer la —** to swing the lead (*fam*), malinger.

zanguango 1 *adj* idle, slack. 2 *nm* slacker, shirker; malingerer.

zanja *nf* (**a**) ditch; drainage channel; trench; pit; grave; **abrir las —s** (*Archit*) to lay the foundations (*de* for).

    (**b**) (*SAm*) gully, watercourse.

    (**c**) (*Ec*) fence, low wall.

zanjar [1a] *vt* (**a**) to ditch, trench; to dig trenches in. (**b**) (*fig*) difficulty to get around, surmount; *disagreement* to resolve, clear up.

zanjón *nm* (**a**) deep ditch. (**b**) (*Cu*, *Chi*, *RPl*) cliff; gully, ravine.

zanquear [1a] 1 *vt* (*CAm*, *Mex*, *SD*) to hunt for. 2 *vi* (**a**) to walk awkwardly. (**b**) to stride along. (**c**) (*fig*) to rush about, bustle about.

zanquilargo *adj* long-legged, leggy.

zanquivano *adj* spindly-legged.

Zanzíbar *m* Zanzibar.

zapa[1] *nf* sharkskin.

zapa[2] *nf* (**a**) spade. (**b**) (*Mil*) sap, trench.

zapador *nm* sapper.

zapallada *nf* (**a**) (*Chi*, *RPl*) fluke; lucky break; lucky guess (*etc*). (**b**) (*Col*) silly remark.

zapallo *nm* (**a**) (*SAm*) gourd, pumpkin. (**b**) (*Chi*, *RPl*) = **zapallada** (**a**). (**c**) (*Ec*) fat person. (**d**) (*CAm*, *Col*) dull individual.

zapallón *adj* (*Chi*, *Ec*, *Per*) chubby, fat.

zapapico *nm* pick, pickaxe; mattock.

zapar [1a] *vti* to sap, mine.

zaparrazo *nm* claw, scratch.

zapata *nf* (**a**) half-boot. (**b**) (*Mech*, *Naut*) shoe; — **de freno** brake shoe.

zapatazo *nm* (**a**) blow with a shoe; (*fam*) thud; bump; bang; **tratar a uno a —s** (*fam*) to treat someone very rudely. (**b**) (*Naut*) violent flapping of a sail.

zapateado *nm* tap-dance.

zapatear [1a] 1 *vt* (**a**) to tap with one's foot.

    (**b**) to kick, prod with one's foot.

    (**c**) (*fam*) to ill-treat, treat roughly.

    2 *vi* (**a**) to tap with one's feet; to tap-dance; (*of rabbit*) to thump.

    (**b**) (*Naut*: *of sail*) to flap violently.

zapatería *nf* (**a**) shoemaking. (**b**) shoeshop; shoe factory, footwear factory.

zapatero 1 *adj* *potatoes etc* hard, undercooked; poor-quality.

    2 *nm* shoemaker; — **remendón**, — **de viejo** cobbler; —, **a tus zapatos** the cobbler should stick to his last.

zapatilla *nf* (**a**) slipper; pump. (**b**) (*Mech*) washer, gasket.

zapato *nm* shoe; —**s de color** brown shoes; —**s de goma** (*SAm*), —**s de hule** (*Mex*) rubber shoes, gym shoes; —**s de tenis** tennis shoes; **estaban como tres en un —** they were packed in like sardines; **meter a uno en un —** to bring someone to heel; **saber dónde aprieta el —** to be alive to all the difficulties, have the right feeling about a situation; to know which side one's bread is buttered; to know where someone's weakness lies.

zapatón *nm* (*SAm*) overshoe, galosh.

zape *interj* (**a**) shoo!, scat! (**b**) good gracious!

zapear [1a] *vt* (**a**) *cat* to shoo, scare away; *person* to shoo away, get rid of. (**b**) (*Pan*, *Per*) to spy on, watch.

zaporro *nm* (*Col*, *Ven*) dwarf, runt.

zaque *nm* (**a**) wineskin. (**b**) (*fam*) boozer, old soak (*fam*).

zaquizamí *nm* (**a**) attic, garret. (**b**) (*fig*) poky little room, hole; hovel.

zar *nm* tzar, czar.

zarabanda *nf* (**a**) (*Hist*) sarabande. (**b**) (*fig*) confused movement, rush, whirl. (**c**) (*Mex*) beating.

zaragata *nf* (**a**) (*fam*) bustle, turmoil; hullabaloo (*fam*); row, set-to (*fam*). (**b**) (*Cu*, *PR*) —**s** cajolery, wheedling.

zaragate *nm* (**a**) (*SAm*) rogue, rascal; busybody. (**b**) (*Cu*) flatterer, creep (*sl*).

zaragatero (*fam*) 1 *adj* rowdy, noisy; quarrelsome. 2 *nm* rowdy, hooligan.

Zaragoza Saragossa.

zaragozano 1 *adj* of Saragossa. 2 *nm*, **zaragozana** *nf* native (*or* inhabitant) of Saragossa; **los —s** the people of Saragossa.

zaramullo 1 *adj* (**a**) (*Col*, *Cu*, *Hond*) affected; conceited; finicky.

    (**b**) (*Ec*, *SD*) amusing, witty.

    2 *nm* (**a**) (*Bol*) silly thing.

    (**b**) (*Per*, *Ven*) busybody; fool.

zaranda *nf* (**a**) sieve. (**b**) (*Mex*) cruet. (**c**) (*Ven*) spinning top; (*Mus*) horn.

zarandajas *nfpl* (*fam*) trifles, odds and ends, little things.

zarandear [1a] 1 *vt* (**a**) to sieve, sift.

    (**b**) (*fam*) to shake vigorously to and fro, shake up, toss about.

    (**c**) (*fam*) *person* to keep on the go, keep bustling about.

    (**d**) (*SAm*) to swing, push to and fro; (*fig*) to abuse publicly.

    2 **zarandearse** *vr* (**a**) (*prov*, *SAm*) to strut about.

    (**b**) to keep on the go, bustle about.

zarandillo *nm* active person, bustler; (*pej*) restless individual; (*child*) fidget; **llevar a uno como un —** to keep someone on the go.

zarapito *nm* (*also* — **real**) curlew.

zaraza *nf* printed cotton cloth, chintz.

zarazas *nfpl* rat poison.

zarazo *adj* (*SAm*) (**a**) *fruit* half-ripe. (**b**) rather drunk, tight.

zarcillo *nm* (**a**) earring. (**b**) (*Bot*) tendril. (**c**) (*Arg*, *Mex*, *Ven*: *Agr*) earmark.

zarco *adj* light blue.

zarigüeya *nf* opossum.

zarina *nf* tsarina.

zaroche *nm* (*SAm*) = **soroche**.

zarpa *nf* (**a**) claw, paw; **echar la — a** to claw at, paw; (*fam*) to grab, lay hold of. (**b**) splash of mud, smear of mud.

zarpada nf clawing; blow with the paw; **dar una — a** to claw, scratch; to hit with its paw.

zarpar [1a] vi to weigh anchor, set sail, get under way.

zarpazo nm **(a)** =zarpada. **(b)** (fig) thud; bang, bump. **(c)** (fam) **dar un —** to beat it quick (fam).

zarpear [1a] vt (CAm, Mex) to splash with mud, bespatter.

zarrapastrón adj (fam), **zarrapastroso** adj shabby, dirty, rough-looking.

zarria nf **(a)** splash of mud, spattering of mud, smear of mud. **(b)** rag, tatter.

zarza nf bramble, blackberry (bush).

zarzal nm bramble patch, clump of brambles.

zarzamora nf blackberry.

zarzaparrilla nf sarsaparilla.

zarzo nm **(a)** (Agr etc) hurdle; (in building) wattle. **(b)** (Col) attic.

zarzuela nf operetta, light opera, (Spanish-style) musical comedy.

zarzuelista nmf composer of light opera, musical-comedy writer.

zas interj bang!, slap!; crash!; **le pegó un porrazo ..., ¡—! ... que ...** he gave him a swipe ... bang! ... which ...; **apenas habíamos puesto la radio y ... ¡—! ... se cortó la corriente** we had only just switched on the radio when ... click! ... and off went the current.

zascandil nm **(a)** featherbrained person; unreliable person; frivolous individual. **(b)** busybody.

zascandilear [1a] vi **(a)** to buzz about uselessly, fuss a lot; to behave frivolously, do featherbrained things. **(b)** to pry, meddle.

Zenón m Zeno.

zepelín nm zeppelin.

Zetlandia: Islas fpl **de —** Shetland Isles.

zigzag **1** adj zigzag. **2** nm zigzag (line etc); **relámpago en —** forked lightning, chain lightning (US).

zigzagueante adj (SAm) zigzag.

zigzaguear [1a] vi to zigzag.

zinc nm zinc.

zipizape nm (fam) set-to (fam), rumpus (fam); brawl, disturbance; **armar un —** to start a rumpus; **los dos están de —** the two of them are always squabbling.

zócalo nm **(a)** (Archit) socle; plinth, base. **(b)** skirting board, baseboard (US); panelling. **(c)** (Mex) parade ground; public square; walk, boulevard; park.

zocato **1** adj **(a)** fruit, vegetable hard, rubbery; damaged. **(b)** person left-handed. **2** nm **(a)** (Col) stale bread. **(b)** (Mex) sickly child.

zoclo nm =zueco.

zoco **1** adj **(a)** left-handed. **(b)** (Col) one-armed; (Col, Chi, PR) maimed, limbless. **2** nm **(a)** left-handed person. **(b)** (Ven) fool. **(c)** (Chi, Par) hefty punch.

zocotroco nm (Arg, Bol, Col) chunk, big lump; **— de hombre** hefty man.

zodíaco nm zodiac.

zollenco adj (Mex) big and tough.

zollipar [1a] vi to sob.

zona nf zone; belt, area; **— de desastre** disaster area; **— edificada** built-up area; **— de ensanche** zone of future urban development; **— fronteriza** border area, border land; **— de pruebas** testing ground; **— de tiendas** shopping centre; **— tórrida** torrid zone.

zonal adj zonal.

zoncear [1a] vi (Chi, Guat, RPl) to behave stupidly.

zoncera nf **(a)** (SAm) =zoncería. **(b)** (Chi, RPl) mere trifle; small amount; **costar una —** to cost next to nothing; **comer una —** to have a bite to eat.

zoncería nf silliness, stupidity; dullness; boredom, boring nature.

zonchiche nm (CAm, Mex) buzzard.

zonda nf (Arg, Bol) hot northerly wind.

zonzo **1** adj (esp SAm) silly, stupid; boring, inane; (Mex) dazed, weary. **2** nm (SAm) idiot; bore, tedious person.

zonzoneco adj (CAm), **zonzoreco** adj (CAm), **zonzoreno** adj (CAm) stupid.

zoo nm zoo.

zoo ... zoo ...

zoología nf zoology.

zoológico **1** adj zoological. **2** nm zoo.

zoólogo nm zoologist.

zoomórfico adj zoomorphic.

zopenco (fam) **1** adj dull, stupid. **2** nm clot (sl), nitwit (sl).

zopilote nm (SAm) buzzard; (fam) thief.

zopilotear [1a] vt (Mex) to eat greedily, wolf; (fig) to steal.

zopo adj crippled, maimed.

zoquetada nf (SAm) stupidity.

zoquetazo nm (Mex, RPl) swipe, punch.

zoquete nm **(a)** block, piece, chunk (of wood). **(b)** crust of old bread. **(c)** (fam) squat person. **(d)** (fam) duffer, blockhead; lout, oaf. **(e)** (SAm) body dirt, human dirt. **(f)** (Cu, Mex) punch.

zoquetillo nm shuttlecock.

zorenco adj (CAm) stupid.

Zoroastro m Zoroaster.

zorra nf **(a)** fox; vixen. **(b)** (fam) whore, tart (sl).

zorral adj **(a)** (CAm, Col) annoying. **(b)** (Ec) obstinate.

zorrera nf **(a)** foxhole; (fig) smoky room, room with a fug. **(b)** dismay; worry, anxiety. **(c)** (fig) drowsiness, lethargy.

zorrería nf **(a)** (quality) foxiness, craftiness. **(b)** (una —) sly trick.

zorrero adj foxy, crafty.

zorrillo nm (Arg), **zorrino** nm (Arg) skunk.

zorro **1** adj foxy, crafty. **2** nm **(a)** (Zool) fox, dog fox. **(b)** fox fur, foxskin. **(c)** (fig) old fox, crafty person, rascal; (at work) slacker, shirker; **hacerse el —** to act dumb; **estar hecho un —** to be very drowsy; **estar hecho unos —s** (fam) to be all in, be done up (fam).

zorruno adj foxy, fox-like.

zorzal nm **(a)** (Orn) thrush. **(b)** (fig) shrewd person; sly fellow. **(c)** (Arg, Chi) simpleton; dupe, innocent person.

zorzalear [1a] vi (Chi) to sponge (fam).

zorzalero adj (Chi) sponging (fam), parasitical.

zorzalino adj (Chi) life rich, luxurious, easy.

zosco nm (Ven) idiot.

zote (fam) **1** adj dense, dim, stupid. **2** nm dimwit (fam).

zozobra nf **(a)** (Naut) capsizing, overturning; sinking. **(b)** (fig) worry, anxiety; jumpiness, nervous state.

zozobrar [1a] vi **(a)** (Naut) to be in danger (of foundering); to capsize, overturn; to founder, sink. **(b)** (fig: of plan, intention) to fail, come to naught, collapse; (of business) to be ruined. **(c)** (fig: of person) to be anxious, worry, fret.

zueco nm clog, wooden shoe.

—zuelo, —zuela n suffix **(a)** (diminutive) eg **pernezuela** little leg. **(b)** (pej) eg **autorzuelo** scribbler, hack, penpusher; **mujerzuela** whore.

zulú **1** adj Zulu. **2** nmf Zulu.

Zululandia nf Zululand.

zulla nf (tabu) shit (tabu).

zullarse [1a] vr to dirty oneself; to fart (tabu).

zullón nm (tabu) fart (tabu).

zumaque nm sumac(h).

zumba nf **(a)** banter, chaff, teasing; humour; satirical intention; **dar — a, hacer — a** to rag, tease. **(b)** (SAm) beating. **(c)** (Mex) drunkenness.

zumbador nm **(a)** (Elec) buzzer. **(b)** (Ant, Mex) hummingbird.

zumbar [1a] **1** vt **(a)** person to rag, tease. **(b)** (Univ: sl) to plough (sl). **(c)** blow to fetch, hit. **(d)** (SAm) to throw, chuck, toss; to chuck out. **2** vi **(a)** (of insect) to buzz, hum, drone; (of machine) to hum, whirr; (of buzzer) to buzz; (of ears) to hum, sing, buzz; **me zumban los oídos** I have a buzzing in my ears (see also **oído**). **(b)** (fam) to be very close; **no está en peligro ahora, pero le zumba** he's not actually in danger now, but it's not far away. **3 zumbarse** vr **(a)** **— de** to rag, tease; to poke fun at. **(b)** (Ant, Col) to clear off. **(c)** (Cu) to overstep the mark.

zumbido nm **(a)** buzz(ing), hum(ming), drone; whirr(ing); **— de oídos** buzzing in the ears, ringing in the ears. **(b)** (fam) punch, biff (fam).

zumbo[1] nm (CAm, Col) gourd, calabash.

zumbo[2] nm =zumbido **(a)**.

zumbón **1** adj waggish, funny; tone etc teasing, bantering; sarcastic. **2** nm wag, joker, funny man; tease.

zumiento adj juicy.

zumo nm **(a)** juice; (as drink) juice, squash; **— de naranja** orange squash. **(b)** (fig) (solid) profit, (real) gain.

zumoso adj juicy.

zuncho nm band, hoop, ring.

zupia nf **(a)** dregs; muddy wine; nasty drink, evil-tasting liquid. **(b)** (fig) dregs; human trash, worthless people. **(c)** (Bol, Ven) coarse liquor.

zurcido nm **(a)** darning, mending. **(b)** darn, mend, patch.

zurcidura *nf* = **zurcido.**
zurcir [3b] *vt* **(a)** to darn, mend, sew up.
　(b) (*fig*) to join, combine, put together; *lie* to concoct, think up; *tale* to spin.
　(c) (*fam*) ¡que las zurzan! to blazes with them!
zurdazo *nm* (*SAm*) left-handed punch.
zurdear [1a] *vt* (*SAm*) to do with the left hand.
zurdo 1 *adj hand* left; *person* left-handed; **a zurdas** with the left hand, (*fig*) the wrong way, clumsily; **no es —** (*fig*) he's no fool.
　2 *nm*, **zurda** *nf* left-handed person.
zurra *nf* **(a)** (*Tech*) dressing, tanning. **(b)** (*fam*) tanning (*fam*), hiding. **(c)** (*fam*) hard grind (*fam*), drudgery. **(d)** (*fam*) roughhouse (*fam*).
zurrador *nm* tanner.
zurrapa *nf* **(a)** soft lump, dollop, spot; thread, stream (of dirt *etc*); —s dregs. **(b)** (*fig*) trash, muck, rubbish.
zurraposo *adj* full of dregs, thick, muddy.
zurrar [1a] *vt* **(a)** (*Tech*) to dress, tan.
　(b) (*fam*) to tan, wallop, lay into (*fam*).
　(c) (*fam*: *in argument*) to sit heavily on, flatten.
　(d) (*fam*) to lash into, criticize ferociously.

zurria *nf* **(a)** (*CAm, Col*) tanning (*fam*), hiding. **(b)** (*Col*) lot, crowd, mass.
zurriaga *nf* whip, lash.
zurriagar [1h] *vt* to whip, lash.
zurriagazo *nm* **(a)** lash, stroke, cut. **(b)** (*fig*) severe blow, bad knock; stroke of bad luck. **(c)** (*fig*) piece of unjust (*or* harsh) treatment.
zurriago *nm* whip, lash.
zurribanda *nf* (*fam*) = **zurra** (b) and (d).
zurriburri *nm* (*fam*) **(a)** turmoil, bustle, confusion; mess, mix-up; hubbub. **(b)** worthless individual.
zurrón *nm* pouch, bag.
zurullo *nm*, **zurullón** *nm* **(a)** lump, hard bit (*in liquid etc*). **(b)** (*tabu*) turd (*tabu*). **(c)** lout, hooligan.
zurumato *adj* (*Mex*) stunned, dazed; stupid.
zurumbanco *adj* (*CR, Mex*) **(a)** = **zurumato.** **(b)** half-drunk.
zurumbático *adj*: **estar —** to be stunned, be dazed.
zurumbo *adj* (*CAm*) **(a)** = **zurumato.** **(b)** fuddled, stupid with drink.
zutano *nm*, **zutana** *nf* (*Mr etc*) So-and-so; **si se casa fulano con zutana** if Mr X marries Miss Y; *see* **fulano.**

A

a [ei, ə], **an** [æn, ən, n] *(before words starting with a vowel sound)*, *indef art* (a) un, una.
 (b) *(omitted)* **half an hour** media hora; **a fine excuse!** ¡bonita disculpa!; **have you a passport?** ¿tiene Vd pasaporte?; *(omitted in negative uses)* **I haven't got a car** no tengo coche; **you don't stand a chance** no tienes posibilidad alguna; **without a doubt** sin duda; **without saying a word** sin decir palabra; *(omitted in apposition)* **the Duero, a Spanish river** el Duero, río de España.
 (c) *(a certain)* **a Mr Smith called to see you** vino a verle un tal Sr Smith.
 (d) *(distributive)* **2 apples a head** 2 manzanas por persona.
 (e) *(rate)* **30 miles an hour** 30 millas por hora; **£10 a week** 10 libras por semana; **3 times a month** 3 veces al mes; **he reads 3 books a week** lee 3 libros cada semana; **3 pence a dozen** 3 peniques la docena.
A 1 ['ei'wʌn] *adj* de primera clase, de primera categoría; excelente; **to be — at Lloyds** ser de máxima garantía; **to feel —** estar como un reloj.
Aachen ['ɑːxən] Aquisgrán.
aback [ə'bæk] *adv:* **to take —** desconcertar, coger de improviso; **to be taken —** quedar desconcertado; **I was quite taken — by the news** la noticia me causó gran sorpresa, la noticia me cogió de improviso.
abacus ['æbəkəs] *n*, *pl* **abaci** ['æbəsai] ábaco *m*.
abaft [ə'bɑːft] **1** *adv* a popa, en popa. **2** *prep* detrás de.
abandon [ə'bændən] **1** *vt* (a) *(leave)* abandonar, desamparar; **fog made the motorists — their cars** la niebla hizo que los conductores abandonasen sus coches; **to — someone to his fate** abandonar a uno a su suerte.
 (b) *(give up)* renunciar a; **the attempt had to be —ed** tuvieron que renunciar a la empresa; **the game was —ed after 20 minutes' play** después de 20 minutos de juego se dio por nulo el partido.
 2 *vr*: **to — oneself to** abandonarse a, entregarse a.
 3 *n* abandono *m*; libertad *f*, desenfado *m*, desenfreno *m*; **to dance with wild —** abandonarse al éxtasis del baile, bailar desenfrenadamente.
abandoned [ə'bændənd] *adj* **house etc** abandonado, desierto; *child* desamparado; *(vicious)* vicioso, entregado a los vicios; **— woman** mujer perdida; **in an — fashion** con abandono, desenfrenadamente.
abandonment [ə'bændənmənt] *n (state)* desamparo *m*, abandono *m*; *(act)* acto *m* de desamparar, el abandonar *(etc)*; *(moral)* **= abandon 3.**
abase [ə'beis] **1** *vt* humillar, rebajar, degradar; envilecer. **2** *vr:* **to — oneself** humillarse; envilecerse.
abasement [ə'beismənt] *n* humillación *f*, rebajamiento *m*, degradación *f*; envilecimiento *m*.
abash [ə'bæʃ] *vt* avergonzar; **—ed** avergonzado, confuso, corrido; **to be —ed** quedar confuso; **to be —ed at** avergonzarse de; **not a bit —ed** sin inmutarse, como si tal cosa; **he was not a bit —ed at this** no dio la menor señal de vergüenza, siguió como si tal cosa.
abate [ə'beit] **1** *vt* disminuir, reducir; *(Law)* suprimir; *price* rebajar; *violence* mitigar, suavizar; *energy* debilitar; *enthusiasm* moderar; *pride* abatir.
 2 *vi* disminuir, reducirse, ceder, menguar; *(violence, enthusiasm)* moderarse; *(wind)* calmarse, amainar; *(pain)* ceder; *(courage)* desfallecer; *(flood, price)* bajar.
abatement [ə'beitmənt] *n* disminución *f*; moderación *f*; amaine *m*; *(of pain)* alivio *m*; *(Law)* supresión *f*.
abattoir ['æbətwɑː*] *n* matadero *m*.
abbess ['æbis] *n* abadesa *f*.
abbey ['æbi] *n* abadía *f*; monasterio *m*, convento *m*.
abbot ['æbət] *n* abad *m*.
abbreviate [ə'briːvieit] *vt* abreviar.

abbreviation [ə,briːvi'eiʃən] *n (short form)* abreviatura *f*; *(act)* abreviación *f*.
ABC ['eibiː'siː] *n* abecé *m*; abecedario *m*; *(fig)* abecé *m*; **— of politics** nociones *fpl* de política, introducción *f* a la política.
abdicate ['æbdikeit] **1** *vt* **throne** abdicar; *responsibility, rights* renunciar a; *principles* abdicar de. **2** *vi* abdicar *(in favour of* en, en favor de).
abdication [,æbdi'keiʃən] *n* abdicación *f*; renuncia *f*.
abdomen ['æbdəmen, *Med* æb'dəumen] *n* abdomen *m*.
abdominal [æb'dɒminl] *adj* abdominal.
abduct [æb'dʌkt] *vt* raptar, secuestrar.
abduction [æb'dʌkʃən] *n* rapto *m*, secuestro *m*.
abductor [æb'dʌktə*] *n* raptor *m*, secuestrador *m*; *(Anat)* abductor *m*.
abed [ə'bed] *adv* en cama, acostado; **we are always — by 12** nos acostamos siempre antes de las 12.
aberrant [ə'berənt] *adj (Bio)* aberrante, anormal; *(Anat)* anómalo.
aberration [,æbe'reiʃən] *n (all senses)* aberración *f*; **in a moment of mental —** en un momento de aberración.
abet [ə'bet] *vt criminal* incitar; ayudar; *crime* instigar; **to — someone in a crime** ser cómplice de uno en un crimen; **X, aided and —ted by Y** X, persuadido y ayudado por Y; **accused of aiding and —ting** acusado de ser cómplice en un crimen.
abetter, abettor [ə'betə*] *n* instigador *m*, ora *f*, promovedor *m*, ora *f*; cómplice *mf*, fautor *m*.
abeyance [ə'beiəns] *n*: **to be in —** estar en suspenso; **to fall into —** caer en desuso.
abhor [əb'hɔː*] *vt* aborrecer, abominar (de), detestar.
abhorrence [əb'hɒrəns] *n* aborrecimiento *m*, detestación *f*; **violence fills me with —** aborrezco la violencia; **to hold in —** detestar.
abhorrent [əb'hɒrənt] *adj* aborrecible, detestable, repugnante; **war is — to me** aborrezco la guerra.
abide [ə'baid] *(irr: pret and ptp* **abode** *or* **abided)** **1** *vt* aguantar, soportar; **I can't —** him no le puedo ver; **I can't — a coward** aborrezco los cobardes; **I can't — tea** me da asco el té.
 2 *(arch: dwell)* morar; *(stay)* permanecer, continuar; **to — by** atenerse a, obrar de acuerdo con, guiarse por; *rules of competition* ajustarse a, aceptar; *promise* cumplir.
abiding [ə'baidiŋ] *adj* permanente, perdurable.
ability [ə'biliti] *n* habilidad *f*, capacidad *f*; talento *m*, aptitud *f*; **— to pay** *(Comm)* solvencia *f*, recursos *mpl*, medios *mpl*; **he has great —** tiene un gran talento *(for para)*; **his — in French su** aptitud para el francés; **to the best of my —** lo mejor que yo pueda *(or* sepa*)*; **my — to come** depende en el que yo asista depende de; **abilities** talento *m*, dotes *fpl*.
abject ['æbdʒekt] *adj* abyecto, vil; abatido; *apology* rastrero; **to live in — poverty** vivir en la mayor miseria.
abjure [əb'dʒuə*] *vt* renunciar (a), abjurar.
ablative ['æblətiv] *n* ablativo *m*; **— absolute** ablativo *m* absoluto.
ablaze [ə'bleiz] *adv* en llamas, ardiendo; **the house was — in 5 minutes** en 5 minutos la casa estuvo envuelta en llamas; **the house was — with light** brillaban todas las luces de la casa; **the garden was — with colour** resplandecía el jardín con sus flores multicolores; **— with excitement** emocionadísimo, fervoroso.
able ['eibl] **1** *adj (talented)* hábil, capaz, talentoso; *seaman* de primera; **he's a very — man** es un hombre de mucho talento; **it's an — piece of work** es un trabajo sólido, es un trabajo que vale; **— to pay** *(Comm)* solvente.
 2 **to be — to** + *infin* poder + *infin*; *(of acquired skills)* saber + *infin*, eg **you can go when you are —**

to swim te permitiré ir cuando sepas nadar; **I was eventually — to escape** por fin pude escaparme, por fin logré escaparme; **come as soon as you are —** venga en cuanto puedas.

able-bodied ['eibl'bɔdid] *adj* sano, robusto; **— seaman** marinero m de primera.

ablution [ə'bluːʃən] n ablución f; **—s** (*fam*) lavabo m.

ably ['eibli] *adv* hábilmente, con mucha habilidad.

abnegation [,æbni'geiʃən] n abnegación f.

abnormal [æb'nɔːməl] *adj* anormal; irregular; deforme, mal formado.

abnormality [,æbnɔː'mæliti] n anormalidad f; irregularidad f; deformidad f.

abnormally [æb'nɔːməli] *adv* anormalmente, de modo anormal.

aboard [ə'bɔːd] **1** *adv* a bordo; **to go —** embarcarse, ir a bordo; **to take —** tomar a bordo, embarcar, cargar; **he was not — when we sailed** no estaba a bordo cuando salimos; **all —!** (*Rail etc*) ¡señores viajeros, al tren! (*etc*).
2 *prep*: **— the ship** a bordo del barco; **— the train** en el tren.
3 *as adj*: **life — is pleasant** es agradable la vida de a bordo.

abode [ə'bəud] **1** *pret and ptp of* **abide**.
2 n domicilio m, morada f; **place of —** domicilio m; **of no fixed —** sin domicilio fijo; **to take up one's —** avecindarse, establecerse.

abolish [ə'bɔliʃ] *vt* suprimir, abolir; anular, revocar.

abolishment [ə'bɔliʃmənt] n, **abolition** [,æbəu'liʃən] n supresión f, abolición f; anulación f.

abolitionist [,æbəu'liʃənist] n abolicionista mf.

A-bomb ['eibɔm] n bomba f A.

abominable [ə'bɔminəbl] *adj* abominable; *taste etc* detestable, pésimo.

abominably [ə'bɔminəbli] *adv* abominablemente; **to behave —** comportarse de una manera detestable; **to be — rude to** estar terriblemente grosero con; **he writes —** escribe pésimamente.

abominate [ə'bɔmineit] *vt* abominar (de), detestar.

abomination [ə,bɔmi'neiʃən] n abominación f.

aboriginal [,æbə'ridʒinəl] **1** *adj* aborigen, indígena.
2 n aborigen mf, indígena mf.

aborigines [,æbə'ridʒiniːz] npl aborígenes mpl.

abort [ə'bɔːt] **1** *vt* abortar. **2** *vi* abortar, malparir.

abortion [ə'bɔːʃən] n (*Med*) aborto m (provocado); (*Vet*) abortón m; (*creature*) engendro m; (*fig*) malogro m, fracaso m; **illegal —** aborto m ilegal; **to have an —** hacerse abortar; **to procure an —** hacer abortar a una mujer.

abortionist [ə'bɔːʃənist] n abortista mf.

abortive [ə'bɔːtiv] *adj* abortivo; *attempt, plan* ineficaz, fracasado; **to prove —** fracasar, no dar resultado.

abound [ə'baund] *vi* abundar (**in, with** en).

about [ə'baut] **1** *adv* (a) (*approximately*) casi, alrededor de, más o menos; **— 20** unos 20, 20 más o menos; **— 7 years ago** hace unos 7 años; **— 2 o'clock** a eso de las 2; **— a month** un mes poco más o menos, cosa de un mes; **he must be — 40** tendrá alrededor de 40 años; **— half** alrededor de la mitad; **it's just — finished** está terminado casi; **he's — the same** sigue más o menos lo mismo; **that's — it, that's — right** eso es.
(b) (*place*) **all —** por todas partes; **to run —** correr, correr por todas partes; **to walk —** pasearse de aquí para allá; *see* **play, turn** *etc*.
(c) (*with verb to be*) **to be — again** (*after illness*) estar levantado; **we were — early** nos levantamos temprano; **is Mr Brown —?** ¿está por aquí el Sr Brown?; **he must be — somewhere** debe de andar por aquí; **there's a thief —** anda por aquí un ladrón; **there's a lot of measles —** hay mucho sarampión; **to be — to + infin** estar a punto de + infin, estar para + infin.
2 *prep* (a) (*place*) alrededor de; **the fields — the house** los campos alrededor de la casa; **all — the house** por todas partes alrededor de la casa, (*inside*) por todas partes de la casa; **— the fire** junto a la lumbre; **to walk — the house** andar por la casa; **to wander — the town** pasearse sin propósito fijo por la ciudad; **you're — the house all day** pasas todo el día en casa; **to do jobs — the house** hacer los quehaceres domésticos; **he looked — him** miró alrededor de sí, miró a su alrededor; **he took her — the waist** la cogió por la cintura; **I have no money — me** no llevo dinero encima.
(b) (*place: fig*) **he had a mysterious air — him** había algo misterioso en él; **there's something — him (that I like)** tiene un no sé qué que me gusta; **there's something — a soldier** los soldados tienen un no sé qué de atractivo; **while you're — it**

mientras lo estés haciendo; **you've been a long time — it** has tardado mucho en hacerlo.
(c) (*relating to*) de, acerca de, sobre, con respecto a; **a book — travel** un libro sobre los viajes; **I can tell you nothing — him** no le puedo decir nada acerca de él; **they fell out — money** riñeron por cuestión de dinero; **how — me?** ¿y yo?; **how — that book?** ¿y el libro ese?; **how — that?** ¿qué te parece?; **what — that book?** ¿y el libro ese?; **what — it?** (*what do you say*) ¿quieres?; (*what of it*) ¿y qué?; **what — a song?** ¿queréis que os cante algo?, ¿por qué no nos cantas algo?; **what's that book —?** ¿de qué trata ese libro?; **what's it all —?** ¿de qué se trata?, ¿qué pasa?; **what are you —?** ¿qué haces ahí?, ¿qué pretendes con eso?; **what did he talk —?** ¿de qué te habló?

about-face [ə'baut'feis] **1** n media vuelta f; cambio m de postura. **2** *vi* dar media vuelta, cambiar de postura.

above [ə'bʌv] **1** *adv* encima, por encima, arriba; (*in text*) arriba; **as —** según lo dicho antes; **as set out —** según lo arriba expuesto; **as I said —** según dije ya; **from —** desde encima, desde arriba; de lo alto; del cielo; **orders from —** órdenes de fuente superior; **the flat —** el piso de arriba; **the air —** el aire por encima; **those —** los de categoría superior; los que están en el cielo.
2 *prep* (a) (*place*) encima de; **— my head** encima de mi cabeza; **— ground** sobre la tierra; **the Tagus — Toledo** el Tajo más arriba de Toledo; (*more northerly than*) al norte de; **2000 metres — sea level** 2000 metros sobre el nivel del mar.
(b) (*place: fig*) **he is — me in rank** tiene categoría superior a la mía; **I couldn't hear — the din** no podía oír con tanto ruido; **we are — that sort of thing** nosotros quedamos por encima de aquello; **it is — criticism** queda por encima de toda crítica; **it's — me** no lo entiendo; **he is not — a bit of blackmail** es capaz de hacer un poco de chantaje.
(c) (*number*) más de; superior a; **— 100** más de 100; **there were not — 40 people** no había más de 40 personas; **any number — 12** cualquier número superior a 12; **she can't count — 10** no sabe contar más allá de 10.
3 *adj* susodicho, citado, arriba escrito.

aboveboard [ə'bʌv'bɔːd] **1** *adv* sin rebozo, abiertamente. **2** *adj* legítimo.

above-mentioned [ə'bʌv'menʃənd] *adj* sobredicho, susodicho.

abracadabra [,æbrəkə'dæbrə] n abracadabra f.

abrade [ə'breid] *vt* raer, raspar.

Abraham ['eibrəhæm] m Abrahán, Abraham.

abrasion [ə'breiʒən] n raedura f, raspadura f; (*Med*) abrasión f.

abrasive [ə'breiziv] **1** *adj* abrasivo. **2** n abrasivo m.

abreast [ə'brest] *adv* de frente, de fondo; **to march 4 —** marchar 4 de frente; **he was walking — of the last two** caminaba a par de los dos últimos; **to come — of** llegar a la altura de; **to be — of** (*fig*) estar al corriente de; **to keep — of** mantenerse al corriente de; **to keep — of the times** mantenerse al día.

abridge [ə'bridʒ] *vt* book compendiar, resumir; (*cut short*) abreviar, acortar; (*deprive*) privar (**of** de).

abridgement [ə'bridʒmənt] n compendio m, resumen m; abreviación f; privación f.

abroad [ə'brɔːd] *adv* (a) (*in foreign parts*): **to be —** estar en el extranjero; **to go —** ir al extranjero; **he had to go —** (*fleeing*) tuvo que salir del país; **troops brought in from —** tropas traídas de fuera.
(b) (*outside*) fuera; fuera de casa; **there were not many — at that hour** había poca gente por las calles a tal hora; **there is a rumour —** that corre un rumor de que; **it has got — that** se tiene noticia de que, (*falsely*) se ha divulgado la especie de que; **how did the news get —?** ¿cómo se divulgó la noticia?

abrogate ['æbrəugeit] *vt* abrogar.

abrogation [,æbrəu'geiʃən] n abrogación f.

abrupt [ə'brʌpt] *adj* (*sudden*) repentino, brusco; precipitado; *terrain* escarpado; *style* cortado, lacónico; *manner of person* áspero, brusco; **he was very — with me** me trató sin miramientos.

abruptly [ə'brʌptli] *adv* repentinamente, bruscamente; precipitadamente; **a cliff rose — before them** delante de ellos se alzaba un risco cortado a pico; **to leave —** salir repentinamente; **everything changed —** de pronto cambió todo.

abruptness [ə'brʌptnis] n brusquedad f; precipitación f; lo escarpado; lo cortado.

abscess ['æbsis] n absceso m.

abscond [əb'skɔnd] *vi* fugarse, huir de la justicia; **to — with the funds** huir (*or* largarse, alzarse) con el dinero.

absence ['æbsəns] n (of person) ausencia f; (of thing) falta f; **in the — of** person en ausencia de, thing a falta de; **sentenced in one's —** condenado en ausencia; **to be conspicuous by one's —** brillar por su ausencia; **— of mind** distracción f, despiste m.

absent ['æbsənt] adj ausente (from de), (fig) distraído; **where liberty is —** donde falta la libertad; **why were you — from class?** ¿por qué faltó Vd a la clase?

absent [æb'sent] vr: **to — oneself** ausentarse (from de).

absentee [.æbsən'ti:] n ausente mf; **— landlord** absentista f.

absenteeism [.æbsən'ti:izəm] n absentismo m.

absently ['æbsəntli] adv distraídamente.

absent-minded ['æbsənt'maindid] adj distraído, despistado.

absent-mindedly ['æbsənt'maindidli] adv distraídamente, por distracción.

absent-mindedness ['æbsənt'maindidnis] n distracción f, despiste m.

absinth(e) ['æbsinθ] n (Bot) ajenjo m; (drink) absenta f.

absolute ['æbsəlu:t] adj (Math, Gram, power, monarch, alcohol etc) absoluto; certainty, confidence etc completo; support incondicional; prohibition terminante, total; denial rotundo, categórico; liar redomado; **the —** (Philos) lo absoluto; **the man's an — idiot** es un puro imbécil; **it's — rubbish!** ¡es puro disparate!; **it's an — scandal** is simplemente escandaloso.

absolutely ['æbsəlu:tli] adv rule etc absolutamente; (wholly) completamente, totalmente; **—!** ¡perfectamente!, ¡eso es!; **that is — untrue** eso es completamente falso; **it is — forbidden to** + infin queda terminantemente prohibido + infin; **I deny it —** lo niego rotundamente.

absolution [.æbsə'lu:ʃən] n absolución f.

absolutism ['æbsəlutizəm] n absolutismo m.

absolve [əb'zɔlv] vt absolver (from de).

absorb [əb'zɔ:b] vt absorber; shock etc amortiguar; (Comm) absorber; **the business —s a lot of my time** el negocio me lleva mucho tiempo, el negocio me trae ocupadísimo; **she —s chemistry readily** le entra con facilidad la química; **the country —ed 1000 refugees** el país dio entrada a 1000 refugiados; **to be —ed in** (fig) estar absorto en; **to get —ed in** (fig) engolfarse en, empaparse de, dedicarse de lleno al estudio de.

absorbency [əb'zɔ:bənsi] n absorbencia f.

absorbent [əb'zɔ:bənt] adj absorbente; cotton etc hidrófilo.

absorbing [əb'zɔ:biŋ] adj study etc absorbente, interesantísimo; **I find history very —** la historia tiene para mí un fuerte atractivo, me apasiona la historia.

absorption [əb'zɔ:pʃən] n absorción f (also fig).

abstain [əb'stein] vi abstenerse (from de); (not drink) abstenerse de las bebidas alcohólicas; **to — from comment** no ofrecer comentario alguno.

abstainer [əb'steinə*] n (also total —; approx) abstemio m, abstinente m, persona f que no bebe alcohol.

abstemious [əb'sti:miəs] adj sobrio, abstemio, templado.

abstemiousness [əb'sti:miəsnis] n sobriedad f, moderación f.

abstention [əb'stenʃən] n abstención f; (Parl) abstención f de votar; **there were 20 —s** hubo 20 que no votaron.

abstinence ['æbstinəns] n abstinencia f (from de); **day of —** día m de ayuno.

abstinent ['æbstinənt] adj abstinente.

abstract ['æbstrækt] 1 adj abstracto (also Art, Gram); **in the —** en abstracto. 2 n resumen m, sumario m.

abstract [æb'strækt] 1 vt (remove) extractar, quitar, separar; (steal) robar; (Chem) extraer; book resumir, compendiar.

2 vr: **to — oneself** abstraerse, ensimismarse.

abstracted [æb'stræktid] adj distraído, ensimismado.

abstraction [æb'strækʃən] n abstracción f; distraimiento m, ensimismamiento m.

abstruse [æb'stru:s] adj profundo, recóndito, abstruso.

absurd [əb'sə:d] adj absurdo, ridículo, disparatado; **it is — that** es absurdo que; **how —!** ¡qué ridículo!; **don't be —!** ¡no digas tonterías!; **you look — in that hat** con ese sombrero pareces ridículo; **theatre of the —** teatro m de lo absurdo.

absurdity [əb'sə:diti] n absurdo m, disparate m; locura f; (of situation etc) lo absurdo.

absurdly [əb'sə:dli] adv absurdamente, ridículamente.

abundance [ə'bʌndəns] n abundancia f; (of heart) plenitud f; **in —** en abundancia, abundantemente, a granel; **we had an — of rain** llovió copiosamente; **we have a great — of books** tenemos gran copia de libros.

abundant [ə'bʌndənt] adj abundante (in en); copioso.

abundantly [ə'bʌndəntli] adv abundantemente; copiosamente; **to make it — clear that** hacer constar con toda claridad que.

abuse [ə'bju:s] n (a) (insults) improperios mpl, injurias fpl; **to heap — on somone** llenar a uno de injurias.

(b) (misuse) abuso m; **— of confidence, — of trust** abuso m de confianza; **— of one's authority** abuso m de su autoridad.

abuse [ə'bju:z] vt (a) (revile) maltratar (de palabra), injuriar, llenar de injurias; **he roundly —d the government** dijo mil improperios contra el gobierno.

(b) (misuse) abusar de.

abusive [ə'bju:siv] adj practice etc abusivo; (insulting) ofensivo, injurioso, insultante; **to be — to** decir cosas injuriosas a; **to become —** empezar a soltar injurias (to contra).

abut [ə'bʌt] vi confinar, estar contiguo; **to — against, to — on** confinar con, lindar con; (penthouse etc) apoyarse en; (end in) terminar en.

abutment [ə'bʌtmənt] n (Archit) estribo m, contrafuerte m, botarel m; (Carpentry) empotramiento m.

abutting [ə'bʌtiŋ] adj colindante, contiguo.

abysmal [ə'bizməl] adj abismal; (fig) profundo; **the most — ignorance** la ignorancia más profunda; **to live in — poverty** vivir en la mayor miseria; **an — result** un malísimo resultado; **an — performance** una pésima actuación; **the play was —** la obra fue una catástrofe.

abysmally [ə'bizməli] adv (fig) malísimamente, terriblemente; **— bad** terriblemente malo.

abyss [ə'bis] n abismo m, sima f.

Abyssinia [.æbi'siniə] Abisinia f.

Abyssinian [.æbi'siniən] 1 adj abisinio. 2 n abisinio m, a f.

acacia [ə'keiʃə] n acacia f.

academic [.ækə'demik] 1 adj académico; (Univ) universitario; argument bizantino, poco provechoso, estéril; question puramente teórico, sin trascendencia práctica; **— dress** vestidura f universitaria; **— freedom** libertad f de cátedra; **— interests** intereses mpl eruditos; **— year** (Univ) año m universitario, (School) año m escolar.

2 n universitario m, catedrático m (de universidad).

academicals [.ækə'demikəlz] npl vestidura f universitaria.

academician [ə.kædə'miʃən] n académico m.

academy [ə'kædəmi] n academia f; (Scot) instituto m, colegio m; **military —** escuela f militar; **— for young ladies** colegio m para señoritas; **secretarial —** escuela f para secretarias; **Royal A— (of Arts)** Real Academia f (de Bellas Artes); **the Spanish A—** la Real Academia Española.

acanthus [ə'kænθəs] n acanto m.

accede [æk'si:d] vi: **to — to** request consentir en, acceder a; office, post tomar posesión de, entrar en; party adherirse a; throne subir a; treaty firmar.

accelerate [æk'seləreit] 1 vt acelerar; apresurar. 2 vi acelerarse; darse prisa.

acceleration [æk.selə'reiʃən] n aceleración f.

accelerator [æk'seləreitə*] n acelerador m.

accent ['æksənt] n acento m; **acute —** acento m agudo; **grave —** acento m grave; **in a broken —** con marcado acento extranjero; **with a strong provincial —** con fuerte acento de provincia; **in —s of some surprise** en cierto tono de asombro; **the minister put the — on exports** el ministro subrayó la importancia de la exportación; **this year the — is on bright colours** este año están de moda los colores brillantes.

accent [æk'sent] vt acentuar.

accentuate [æk'sentjueit] vt acentuar; (fig) recalcar, subrayar, dar énfasis a.

accentuation [æk.sentju'eiʃən] n acentuación f.

accept [ək'sept] vt aceptar (also Comm); aprobar; admitir; recibir, acoger, dar acogida a; **the Academy —s the word** la Academia aprueba la palabra; **the Academy —ed the word in 1936** la Academia admitió la palabra en 1936; **to — orders** (Comm) admitir pedidos; **I do not — that way of doing it** no apruebo ese modo de hacerlo; **it is —ed that** se reconoce que; **we — that it is so** reconocemos que es así; **he was —ed as one of us** pasaba por ser uno de nosotros.

acceptable [ək'septəbl] *adj* acceptable; admisible; grato; **tea is always** — el té siempre agrada; **that would be most** — eso me gustaría muchísimo; **that would not be** — **to the government** eso no le sería grato al gobierno; **that policy is not** — esa política no es admisible; **it is not easy to find an** — **gift** no es fácil encontrar un regalo adecuado.

acceptance [ək'septəns] *n* aceptación *f* (*also* Comm); aprobación *f*; (buena) acogida *f*; **to win** — lograr la aprobación; **to meet with general** — ser bien recibido.

acceptation [,æksep'teiʃən] *n* acepción *f*.

accepted [ək'septid] *adj* acepto; **it's the** — **thing** es cosa corriente; **he's an** — **expert** es un experto reconocido como tal.

acceptor [ək'septə*] *n* aceptador *m*, ora *f*; (Comm) aceptante *mf*.

access ['ækses] *n* **(a)** acceso *m*, entrada *f*; **easy of** — asequible, de fácil acceso; *person* abordable, tratable; **to give** — **to a room** comunicar con una habitación; **this gives** — **to the garden** por aquí se sale al jardín; **to have** — **to the minister** poder libremente hablar con el ministro, tener libre acceso al ministro; **he had** — **to the family papers** pudo leer los papeles de la familia, se le facilitaron los papeles de la familia.
(b) (Med) acceso *m*, ataque *m*; **in an** — **of rage** en un arranque de cólera.

accessibility [æk,sesi'biliti] *n* accesibilidad *f*.

accessible [æk'sesəbl] *adj* accesible, asequible (*to* a); *person* tratable; **the duke is not** — **to visitors** el duque no recibe visitas.

accession [æk'seʃən] *n* acceso *m*, entrada *f*; (*increase*) aumento *m*; (*to treaty*) accesión *f*; (*new library book*) libro *m* recién adquirido; (*Law*) entrada *f* en posesión (*to an estate* de una propiedad); (*of king*) subida *f*, ascenso *m* (*to the throne* al trono); — **to power** ascenso *m* al poder; **a sudden** — **of strength** un aumento inesperado de fuerzas.

accessory [æk'sesəri] **1** *adj* accesorio.
2 *n* **(a)** accesorio *m*; **accessories** accesorios *mpl*; (Aut *etc*) complementos *mpl*; **toilet accessories** artículos *mpl* de tocador.
(b) (Law) cómplice *mf*; — **after the fact** cómplice *m* encubridor, ora *f*; — **before the fact** cómplice *m* instigador, ora *f*.

accidence ['æksidəns] *n* (Gram) accidentes *mpl*.

accident ['æksidənt] *n* accidente *m*; — **insurance** seguro *m* contra accidentes; **road** — accidente *m* de carretera; **traffic** — accidente *m* de circulación; **by** — (*by chance*) por casualidad, (*unintentionally*) accidentalmente, sin querer, por descuido; **by some** — **I found myself there** me encontré no sé cómo allí; —**s will happen** hay accidentes que no se pueden prever; **to have an** —, **to meet with an** — sufrir un accidente; **I'm sorry, it was an** — lo siento, lo hice sin querer.

accidental [,æksi'dentl] *adj* accidental, fortuito; — **death** muerte *f* por accidente.

accidentally [,æksi'dentəli] *adv* (*by chance*) por casualidad; (*unintentionally*) sin querer, por inadvertencia, por descuido; **we met quite** — nos encontramos por pura casualidad.

accident-prone ['æksidənt,prəun] *adj* con tendencia a sufrir (*or* causar) accidentes.

acclaim [ə'kleim] **1** *vt* aclamar; vitorear, ovacionar; **he was** —**ed king** le aclamaron rey; **he was** —**ed (as) the winner** le aclamaron por vencedor; **the play was** —**ed** la obra fue muy aplaudida, la obra recibió muchos aplausos. **2** *n* aclamación *f*, aplausos *mpl*.

acclamation [,æklə'meiʃən] *n* aclamación *f*, aplausos *mpl*; **amid the** —**s of the crowd** entre los vítores de la multitud; **by** — por aclamación.

acclimate [ə'klaimət] *vt* (US) aclimatar.

acclimatization [ə,klaimətai'zeiʃən] *n* aclimatación *f*.

acclimatize [ə'klaimətaiz] **1** *vt* aclimatar. **2** *vi*, *vr*: **to** — **oneself** aclimatarse (*to* a); **to become** —**d** aclimatarse.

acclivity [ə'kliviti] *n* subida *f*, cuesta *f*.

accolade ['ækəuleid] *n* (Hist) acolada *f*, espaldarazo *m*; (*fig*) premio *m*; (Mus) acolada *f*.

accommodate [ə'kɔmədeit] **1** *vt* **(a)** (*lodge, have room for*) *person* alojar, hospedar; *thing* tener espacio para, tener cabida para, contener; **can you** — **4 people in July?** ¿tiene Vd habitaciones para 4 personas en julio?; **can you** — **2 more in your car?** ¿caben 2 más en su coche?
(b) (*reconcile*) *differences* acomodar, concertar; *quarrel* componer; *quarrellers* reconciliar.
(c) (*adapt*) acomodar, adaptar (*to* a).

(d) (*supply*) proveer (*with* de); **to** — **someone with a loan** ayudar a uno prestándole dinero.
(e) (*oblige*) complacer; **we will do our best to** — **you** haremos todo lo que podamos por complacerle.
2 *vi* (*eye*) adaptarse (*to* a).

accommodating [ə'kɔmədeitiŋ] *adj* servicial, complaciente, atento; (*pej*) acomodadizo, que a todo se aviene fácilmente.

accommodation [ə,kɔmə'deiʃən] *n* **(a)** (*lodging*) alojamiento *m*; (*rooms*) habitaciones *fpl*; — **to let** se alquila habitación; **have you any** — **available?** ¿tiene Vd habitación disponible?; — **bureau** oficina *f* de hospedaje; — **train** (US) tren *m* de pasajeros.
(b) (*space*) espacio *m*, sitio *m*; cabida *f*; **seating** — plazas *fpl*, asientos *mpl*; **there is** — **for 20 passengers** hay sitio para 20 pasajeros; **the plane has limited** — el avión tiene un número fijo de plazas.
(c) (*agreement*) acuerdo *m*, convenio *m*.
(d) (*adaptation*) acomodación *f*, adaptación *f*.
(e) (*loan*) crédito *m*, préstamo *m*; — **bill,** — **note** (Comm) pagaré *m* de favor.

accompaniment [ə'kʌmpənimənt] *n* acompañamiento *m* (*also* Mus).

accompanist [ə'kʌmpənist] *n* acompañante *m*, a *f*.

accompany [ə'kʌmpəni] **1** *vt* acompañar (*by, with* de; *also* Mus, *on* con); **he accompanied this with a grimace** al decir esto hizo un visaje.
2 *vr*: **to** — **oneself on the piano** acompañarse del piano.

accomplice [ə'kʌmplis] *n* cómplice *mf*.

accomplish [ə'kʌmpliʃ] *vt* (*finish*) acabar, concluir; (*carry out*) llevar a cabo, hacer; (*bring about*) efectuar, lograr; *one's design* realizar; *prophecy* cumplir.

accomplished [ə'kʌmpliʃt] *adj* *person* experto, consumado, hábil; *fact* consumado.

accomplishment [ə'kʌmpliʃmənt] *n* (*finishing*) conclusión *f*; (*bringing about*) efectuación *f*, logro *m*, realización *f*; **a great** — una hazaña; **it's quite an** — **to** + *infin* exige mucho talento + *infin*; **difficult of** — de difícil consecución; —**s** talentos *mpl*, prendas *fpl*, dotes *fpl*.

accord [ə'kɔ:d] **1** *n* (*treaty*) acuerdo *m*, convenio *m*; (*harmony*) armonía *f*; **of one's own** — espontáneamente, de su propio acuerdo, por impulso propio; **with one** — de común acuerdo; **to be in** — estar de acuerdo (*with* con).
2 *vt* conceder, otorgar; *welcome* dar.
3 *vi* concordar (*with* con); **how does this** — **with your plan?** ¿cómo se aviene esto con su proyecto?

accordance [ə'kɔ:dəns] *n*: **in** — **with** conforme a, con arreglo a, de acuerdo con.

according [ə'kɔ:diŋ]: — **as** según que, a medida que; — **to** según; (*in accordance with*) con arreglo a, conforme a.

accordingly [ə'kɔ:diŋli] *adv* en conformidad, de acuerdo con esto; (**and**) — así pues, por consiguiente.

accordion [ə'kɔ:diən] *n* acordeón *m*.

accordionist [ə'kɔ:diənist] *n* acordeonista *mf*.

accost [ə'kɔst] *vt* abordar, dirigirse a, entablar conversación con; (*prostitute*) abordar con fines deshonestos; **he** —**ed me in the street** se dirigió a mí en la calle; **he** —**ed me for a light** se acercó a mí para pedir fuego.

account [ə'kaunt] **1** *n* **(a)** (Fin *etc*) cuenta *f*; (*invoice*) factura *f*; (*statement of* —) estado *m* de cuenta; —**s department** sección *f* de teneduría de libros; **blocked** — cuenta *f* bloqueada; **current** — cuenta *f* corriente; **deposit** — cuenta *f* a plazo fijo; **joint** — cuenta *f* indistinta; **profit and loss** — cuenta *f* de ganancias y pérdidas; — **payable** cuenta *f* a pagar; — **rendered** cuenta *f* pasada; **on** — a cuenta; **payment on** — pago *m* a cuenta; **could I have £50 on** —? ¿puede Vd darme 50 libras anticipadas?; **on his** — por él, por causa de él; **on his own** — por cuenta propia; **on** — **of** por, a causa de, por motivo de; **on that** — por eso; **on no** —, **not on any** — de ninguna manera, bajo ningún concepto; **to bring someone to** —, **to call someone to** — pedir cuentas a uno; **to charge something to someone's** — cargar algo en cuenta a uno; **to close an** — liquidar una cuenta; **to go to one's** — morir; **to keep the** —**s** llevar las cuentas; **to open an** — abrir una cuenta; **to render an** —, **to send an** — pasar factura; **to settle an** — liquidar una cuenta; **to settle** —**s with** (*fig*) ajustar cuentas con; **to turn to** — aprovechar, sacar provecho de.
(b) (*estimation*) importancia *f*; **of no** —, **of little** —, **of small** — de poca importancia; **of some** — de cierta importancia, de alguna consideración.

(c) (*report*) relato *m*, relación *f* (*of* de), informe *m* (*of* sobre); **by all —s** a decir de todos, por lo que dicen todos; **to give an —** dar cuenta de, informar sobre; **to give an — of oneself** justificar su conducta; **to give a good — of oneself** dar buena cuenta de sí; **to leave something out of —** no tomar algo en consideración; **to take something into —, to take — of something** tener algo en cuenta, tener algo presente.

2 *vt* considerar; **I — him a fool** considero que es tonto; **I — myself lucky** creo que tengo suerte; **he is —ed an expert** se le considera como un experto; **I should — it a favour if** agradecería que.

3 *vi*: **to — for** (*answer for*) responder de; (*explain*) dar cuenta de, dar razón de, justificar; (*kill*) acabar con; **that —s for it** ésa es la razón, ha sido por eso; **I can't — for it** no me lo explico; **how do you — for it?** ¿cómo lo explica Vd?; **everything is now —ed for** todo está completo ya; **there is no —ing for tastes** sobre gustos no hay disputa.

accountable [ə'kauntəbl] *adj* responsable (*for* de, *to* ante); **he is — only to himself** no reconoce más responsabilidad que ante sí mismo; **not — for one's actions** no responsable de sus propios actos.

accountancy [ə'kauntənsi] *n* contabilidad *f*.

accountant [ə'kauntənt] *n* contable *m*, contador *m*; **—'s office** contaduría *f*; **chartered —** contable *m* diplomado.

account book [ə'kauntbuk] *n* libro *m* de cuentas.

account day [ə'kauntdei] *n* día *m* de ajuste de cuentas.

accounting [ə'kauntiŋ] *n* contabilidad *f*.

accounting machine [ə'kauntiŋmə‚ʃiːn] *n* máquina *f* de contabilidad, calculadora *f*.

accoutred [ə'kuːtəd] *ptp and adj* equipado.

accoutrements [ə'kuːtrəmənts] *npl* equipo *m*, avíos *mpl*, arreos *mpl*.

accredit [ə'kredit] *vt* acreditar (*someone to someone* a uno cerca de uno); **to — something to someone, to — someone with something** atribuir algo a uno.

accredited [ə'kreditid] *adj* autorizado.

accretion [ə'kriːʃən] *n* aumento *m*, acrecentamiento *m*; (*Min*) acreción *f*; (*Law*) acrecencia *f*.

accrue [ə'kruː] *vi* (*grow*) aumentarse, acumularse; **to — from** proceder de; **to — to** corresponder a; **some benefit will — to you from this** de esto resultará algo a beneficio de Vd; **—d income** renta *f* acumulada; **—d interest** interés *m* acumulado.

accumulate [ə'kjuːmjuleit] **1** *vt* acumular, amontonar; acopiar. **2** *vi* acumularse, amontonarse.

accumulation [ə‚kjuːmju'leiʃən] *n* (*amassing*) acumulación *f*, amontonamiento *m*; (*mass*) montón *m*, acopio *m*.

accumulative [ə'kjuːmjulətiv] *adj* acumulativo; acumulador.

accumulator [ə'kjuːmjuleitə*] *n* acumulador *m*.

accuracy ['ækjurəsi] *n* exactitud *f*, precisión *f*.

accurate ['ækjurit] *adj* *number, observation etc* exacto, preciso, correcto; *copy* fiel; *answer* correcto, acertado; *shot* certero; *instrument* de precisión; **to be strictly —** para decirlo con toda exactitud.

accurately ['ækjuritli] *adv* exactamente, correctamente; fielmente; acertadamente; certeramente.

accursed, accurst [ə'kəːst] *adj* (*lit*) maldito; (*ill-fated*) infausto, desventurado; **— be he who . . .!** ¡maldito sea quien . . .!, ¡mal haya quien . . .!

accusation [‚ækju'zeiʃən] *n* acusación *f*, cargo *m*; denuncia *f*, delación *f*.

accusative [ə'kjuːzətiv] *n* acusativo *m*.

accuse [ə'kjuːz] *vt* acusar (*of* de); denunciar, delatar; echar la culpa a.

accused [ə'kjuːzd] *n* acusado *m*, a *f*.

accuser [ə'kjuːzə*] *n* acusador *m*, ora *f*.

accusing [ə'kjuːziŋ] *adj* acusatorio, lleno de reproches.

accusingly [ə'kjuːziŋli] *adv*: **he looked at me —** me lanzó una mirada acusatoria.

accustom [ə'kʌstəm] **1** *vt* acostumbrar, habituar (*to* a); **to be —ed to + infin** acostumbrar + infin, soler + infin; **I'm not really —ed to + ger** en realidad no tengo la costumbre de + infin, no estoy realmente acostumbrado a + infin; **to get —ed to something** acostumbrarse a algo, habituarse a algo; **to get —ed to + ger** acostumbrarse a + infin.

2 *vr*: **to — oneself to** acostumbrarse a; **to — oneself to + ger** acostumbrarse a + infin.

accustomed [ə'kʌstəmd] *adj* acostumbrado, usual.

ace [eis] *n* (*all senses*) as *m*; **to be within an — of** estar a dos dedos de, estar a pique de.

acerbity [ə'səːbiti] *n* aspereza *f*.

acetate ['æsiteit] *n* acetato *m*.

acetic [ə'siːtik] *adj* acético; **— acid** ácido *m* acético.

acetone ['æsitəun] *n* acetona *f*.

acetylene [ə'setiliːn] **1** *adj* acetilénico; **— lamp, — torch** soplete *m* oxiacetilénico; **— welding** soldadura *f* oxiacetilénica. **2** *n* acetileno *m*.

ache [eik] **1** *n* dolor *m*; **I have an — in my side** me duele el costado; **full of —s and pains** lleno de goteras; **with an — in one's heart** con dolor del corazón.

2 *vi* doler; **my head —s** me duele la cabeza; **it makes my head —** me da un dolor de cabeza; **I — all over** tengo dolores por todas partes; **it was enough to make your heart —** era para romper el alma; **my heart —s for you** lo siento en el alma; **I am aching for you** suspiro por ti; **I —d to help him** quería con todo mi ser acudir en su auxilio.

achieve [ə'tʃiːv] *vt* lograr, conseguir, alcanzar, realizar; llevar a cabo; acabar; **he will never — anything** él no hará nunca nada.

achievement [ə'tʃiːvmənt] *n* (*act*) realización *f*, consecución *f*; (*thing achieved*) éxito *m*, hazaña *f*; **that's quite an —** eso representa un éxito nada despreciable; **it's an — to do that** hacer aquello ya es algo.

Achilles [ə'kiliːz] *m* Aquiles; **—' heel** talón *m* de Aquiles; **—' tendon** tendón *m* de Aquiles.

aching ['eikiŋ] **1** *adj* dolorido; *heart etc* afligido. **2** *n* dolor *m*.

acid ['æsid] **1** *adj* (*Chem*) ácido; (*sour*) agrio; *comment etc* mordaz, punzante. **2** *n* ácido *m*.

acidify [ə'sidifai] **1** *vt* acidificar. **2** *vi* acidificarse.

acidity [ə'siditi] *n* acidez *f*; (*of stomach*) acedía *f*.

acid-proof ['æsidpruːf] *adj*, **acid-resisting** ['æsidri'zistiŋ] *adj* a prueba de ácidos.

acidulous [ə'sidjuləs] *adj* acídulo.

ack-ack ['æk'æk] *n* (*fam*) fuego *m* antiaéreo; (*guns*) artillería *f* antiaérea; **— gun** cañón *m* antiaéreo.

acknowledge [ək'nɔlidʒ] **1** *vt* reconocer; *truth etc* confesar; *claim* admitir; *crime* confesarse culpable de; *favour* agradecer; *letter* acusar recibo de; *present* dar las gracias por; *greeting* contestar a; **to — defeat** darse por vencido; **to — receipt** acusar recibo (*of* de); **I — that** reconozco que; **to — someone as leader** reconocer a uno por jefe; **to — someone to be superior** reconocer que uno es mejor.

2 *vr*: **to — oneself beaten** darse por vencido; **I — myself the loser** reconozco que he perdido.

acknowledged [ək'nɔlidʒd] *adj*: **an — expert** un experto reconocido como tal.

acknowledgement [ək'nɔlidʒmənt] *n* reconocimiento *m*; confesión *f*; agradecimiento *m*; contestación *f* (*of a greeting* a un saludo); (*Comm*) acuse *m* de recibo; (*reward*) recompensa *f*; **to make —** expresar su agradecimiento; **I wish to make public — of the help** quiero agradecer públicamente la ayuda; **to quote without —** citar sin mencionar la fuente.

acme ['ækmi] *n* colmo *m*, cima *f*; **— of perfection** suma perfección *f*; **he is the — of good taste** es el buen gusto en persona.

acne ['ækni] *n* acné *m*.

acolyte ['ækəulait] *n* acólito *m*.

aconite ['ækənait] *n* acónito *m*.

acorn ['eikɔːn] *n* bellota *f*.

acoustic [ə'kuːstik] *adj* acústico.

acoustics [ə'kuːstiks] *npl* acústica *f*.

acquaint [ə'kweint] **1** *vt* **(a)** **to — someone with** avisar a uno de, informar a uno sobre; poner a uno al corriente de.

(b) **to be —ed** conocerse; **to become —ed** (llegar a) conocerse.

(c) **to be —ed with** *person* conocer, *fact* saber, *situation* estar enterado de, estar al corriente de; **to become —ed with** *person* (llegar a) conocer, *fact* saber, *situation* ponerse al tanto de.

2 *vr*: **to — oneself with** informarse sobre; **I intend to make myself —ed with the facts** me propongo averiguar los hechos.

acquaintance [ə'kweintəns] *n* **(a)** conocimiento *m* (*with* de); familiaridad *f* (*with* con); **I have not the honour of his —** no tengo el honor de conocerle; **to have a nodding — with** conocer ligeramente; **it improves on —** parece mejor después de conocido; **to make someone's —** conocer a uno; **I am very glad to make your —** tengo mucho gusto en conocerle; **to scrape — with** hacerse conocer por.

(b) (*person*) conocido *m*; **we're just —s** nos conocemos ligeramente nada más; **an — of mine** una persona que yo conozco; **to have a wide circle of —s** conocer a muchísimas personas.

acquaintanceship [ə'kweintənsʃip] *n* **(a)** conocimiento *m* (*with* de), familiaridad *f* (*with* con). **(b)** (*between two persons*) relaciones *fpl*.

acquiesce [‚ækwi'es] *vi* consentir (*in* en), asentir (*in* a), conformarse (*in* con); (*unwillingly*) someterse.

acquiescence [ˌækwi'esns] n consentimiento m (in en), conformidad f (in con).

acquiescent [ˌækwi'esnt] adj condescendiente, conforme; **he was perfectly** — consintió de buena gana.

acquire [ə'kwaiə*] vt adquirir; obtener; conseguir; proporcionarse; language etc aprender; territory tomar (from a), tomar posesión de; **he —d a fine tan** se dio un espléndido bronceado; **where did you — that?** ¿dónde conseguiste eso?; **she —d many followers** se le pegaron muchos pretendientes; **to — a name for honesty** crearse una reputación de honrado; **to — a taste for** tomar gusto a, cobrar afición a; **—d character** (Bio) carácter m adquirido; **—d taste** gusto m adquirido.

acquirement [ə'kwaiəmənt] n adquisición f; **—s** conocimientos mpl.

acquisition [ˌækwi'ziʃən] n adquisición f.

acquisitive [ə'kwizitiv] adj codicioso; **— instincts** instintos mpl acaparadores.

acquisitiveness [ə'kwizitivnis] n codicia f.

acquit [ə'kwit] **1** vt absolver, exculpar (of de); debt pagar.

2 vr: **to — oneself** portarse; **how did he — himself?** ¿cómo se portó?, ¿cómo desempeñó el cometido?; **to — oneself well** tener éxito, hacerlo bien, salir airoso; **to — oneself of** duty desempeñar.

acquittal [ə'kwitl] n absolución f, exculpación f; (of debt) descargo m.

acre ['eikə*] n (= 40,47 áreas) acre m; **God's —** camposanto m; **the family's broad —s** los extensos terrenos de la familia.

acreage ['eikəridʒ] n superficie f (or extensión f) medida en acres; **the 1970 wheat —** el área sembrada de trigo en 1970; **what — have you here?** ¿cuánto miden estos terrenos?; **they farm a large —** cultivan unos terrenos muy extensos.

acrid ['ækrid] adj acre, punzante; (fig) áspero, desapacible.

acrimonious [ˌækri'məuniəs] adj áspero; remark mordaz; argument amargo, reñido.

acrimony ['ækriməni] n aspereza f, acrimonia f.

acrobat ['ækrəbæt] n acróbata mf.

acrobatic [ˌækrəu'bætik] adj acrobático.

acrobatics [ˌækrəu'bætiks] npl acrobacia f; (Aer) vuelo m acrobático.

acronym ['ækrənim] n sigla f (eg ONU = Organización de las Naciones Unidas).

Acropolis [ə'krɔpəlis] Acrópolis f.

across [ə'krɔs] **1** adv (**a**) a través, al través, de través; **don't go round, go —** no des la vuelta, ve al través; **shall I go — first?** ¿paso yo el primero?

(**b**) (from one side to the other) de una parte a otra, de un lado a otro; **we shall have to cut it —** tendremos que cortarlo por medio; **he helped an old lady —** ayudó a una vieja a cruzar la calle.

(**c**) **the plank is 4 inches —** la tabla tiene 4 pulgadas de ancho; **it's not very far —** es corta la travesía.

(**d**) (crossways) en cruz, transversalmente.

2 prep (**a**) a través de, al través de; **to go — a bridge** pasar a través de un puente.

(**b**) al otro lado de, del otro lado de; **from — the sea** desde más allá del mar; **— the street from our house** en el otro lado de la calle enfrente de nuestra casa; **he'll be — the water by now** ya estará al otro lado del mar.

(**c**) **it is 12 miles — the strait** el estrecho tiene 12 millas de ancho.

acrostic [ə'krɔstik] n acróstico m.

act [ækt] **1** vt play representar; part hacer; **to — the part of** hacer el papel de; **I have —ed Othello** he hecho el papel de Otelo; **to — the fool** hacer el tonto.

2 vi (**a**) (Theat) actuar, trabajar, representar; **I —ed in my youth** en mi juventud fui actor; **to — in a film** tener un papel en una película; **have you ever —ed?** ¿ha hecho Vd algún papel?; **who's —ing in it?** ¿quiénes hacen los papeles?; (fig: pretend) fingir; **he's only —ing** lo está fingiendo nada más; **to — ill** fingirse enfermo; **to — up** travesear.

(**b**) (function: machine) funcionar, marchar; (person) actuar; **the brakes did not —** no funcionaron los frenos; **—ing in my capacity as chairman** de acuerdo con las funciones atribuidas a mi cargo de presidente; **he declined to —** se negó a servir; **to — as** actuar de, hacer de, servir de; **it —s as a safety valve** funciona como una válvula de seguridad; **he was —ing as ambassador** estaba de embajador; **to — for someone** representar a uno.

(**c**) (behave) actuar, obrar, comportarse; **he is —ing strangely** se está comportando de una manera rara; **he always —s sensibly** obra siempre con juicio; **to — with caution** obrar con precaución;

she —ed as if she was crying hizo como si llorase; **to — up to a principle** obrar con arreglo a un principio.

(**d**) (take action) obrar, tomar medidas; **he —ed to stop it** tomó medidas para impedirlo; **now is the time to — es** hora ya de ponerse en acción; **he —ed for the best** hizo lo que mejor le parecía; **to — on a suggestion** seguir una indicación; **to — on the evidence** obrar de acuerdo con los hechos.

(**e**) (affect): **to — upon** afectar, obrar sobre; **the drug —s upon the brain** la droga afecta el cerebro; **acids — upon metals** los ácidos atacan los metales.

3 n (**a**) acto m, acción f; **A—s of the Apostles** Hechos mpl de los Apóstoles; **— of faith** acto m de fe; **— of God** fuerza f mayor; **an — of folly** una locura; **an — of treason** una traición; **we need —s not words** queremos ver hechos no palabras; **I was in the — of writing to him** precisamente le estaba escribiendo a él; **to catch someone in the —** coger a uno en flagrante, coger a uno con las manos en la masa.

(**b**) (Parl) decreto m, ley f.

(**c**) (Theat: division) acto m.

(**d**) (Theat: turn) número m; **to get into the —** introducirse en el asunto.

actable ['æktəbl] adj representable.

acting ['æktiŋ] **1** adj interino, suplente.

2 n (**a**) (Theat: of play) representación f; (by actor) desempeño m, actuación f; **what was his —like?** ¿qué tal hizo el papel?

(**b**) (as profession) profesión f de actor; **— is not in my line** yo no soy actor; **to go in for —** hacerse actor.

actinic [æk'tinik] adj actínico.

action ['ækʃən] n (**a**) acción f, acto m, hecho m; **man of —** hombre m de acción; **to bring into —**, **to put into —** poner en movimiento; **to go into —** entrar en acción; **to put out of —** inutilizar, destrozar, parar; **to suit the — to the word** unir la acción a la palabra; **to take —** tomar medidas.

(**b**) (Mil) acción f, batalla f; **killed in —** muerto en batalla; **to go into —** entrar en batalla.

(**c**) (Mech etc) mecanismo m, accionado m; funcionamiento m, movimiento m; (of horse) marcha f.

(**d**) (Law) demanda f, proceso m; **civil —** demanda f civil; **to bring an —** entablar demanda (against contra).

actionable ['ækʃnəbl] adj justiciable, procesable; querellante.

activate ['æktiveit] vt activar.

active ['æktiv] adj activo (also Gram, Comm); personality etc enérgico, vigoroso; **to take an — interest in** interesarse vivamente por; **to play an — part in** colaborar activamente a.

actively ['æktivli] adv activamente; enérgicamente, vigorosamente.

activist ['æktivist] n activista mf.

activity [æk'tiviti] n actividad f; (of personality) energía f, vigor m; (of busy scene) movimiento m, bullicio m; **in full —** en pleno vigor; **activities** actividades fpl; **his activities were wide** tuvo una ancha esfera de actividad; **social activities** vida f social.

actor ['æktə*] n actor m.

actress ['æktris] n actriz f.

actual ['æktjuəl] adj verdadero, real, efectivo; (of the present time) actual; **in — fact** en realidad; **let's take an — case** tomemos un caso concreto; **what were his — words?** ¿qué es lo que dijo, concretamente?; **is this the — book?** ¿es éste el mismo libro?; **what was the — price?** ¿cuál fue el precio real?; **there is no — contract** no hay contrato propiamente dicho.

actuality [ˌæktju'æliti] n realidad f; realismo m.

actualize ['æktjuəlaiz] vt realizar.

actually ['æktjuəli] adv (**a**) (really) realmente, en realidad, en efecto, efectivamente; **— I am her husband** en realidad soy su marido; **I wasn't — there** en realidad ya no estuve allí; **did you — see him?** ¿le vieron Vds realmente?; **what did he — say?** ¿qué es lo que dijo, concretamente?

(**b**) (even) **he — hit her** incluso llegó a pegarla; **we — caught a fish** con gran sorpresa nuestra cogimos un pez.

(**c**) **that's not true, —** eso no es verdad, que digamos; **as for — working, he didn't —** pues trabajar, como trabajar, no lo hizo.

actuary ['æktjuəri] n actuario m de seguros.

actuate ['æktjueit] vt mover, animar; (Mech) impulsar, accionar; **he was —d by envy** la envidia le movió a ello.

acuity [əˈkjuːiti] n acuidad f, agudeza f.

acumen [ˈækjumen] n perspicacia f.

acupuncture [ˈækjupʌŋktʃə*] n acupuntura f.

acute [əˈkjuːt] adj (in most senses) agudo; **the situation is** — la situación es sumamente peligrosa; — **anxiety exists** existe una honda preocupación; **that was very** — **of you** te has mostrado muy perspicaz.

acutely [əˈkjuːtli] adv agudamente; **I am** — **aware that** me doy perfectamente cuenta de que; **I feel my position** — no se me oculta que es muy difícil mi situación.

acuteness [əˈkjuːtnis] n agudeza f.

ad [æd] n (fam) = **advertisement**.

adage [ˈædidʒ] n adagio m, refrán m.

Adam [ˈædəm] m Adán; —'**s apple** nuez f de la garganta; **the old** — la inclinación al pecado; **I don't know him from** — no le conozco en absoluto.

adamant [ˈædəmənt] adj (fig) firme, inexorable; **he was** — se mostró inexorable; **he was** — **in his refusal** reiteró inexorablemente su denegación.

adapt [əˈdæpt] **1** vt (a) adaptar (to a); acomodar, ajustar (to a); **it is perfectly** —**ed to its environment** se ajusta perfectamente a su ambiente.
(b) text arreglar, refundir; **a novel** —**ed by X** una novela en versión de X; **a novel** —**ed as a play** una novela en versión dramática; —**ed from the Spanish** inspirado en una obra española.
2 vr: **to** — **oneself to** adaptarse a, ajustarse a.

adaptability [ə,dæptəˈbiliti] n adaptabilidad f; capacidad f para acomodarse.

adaptable [əˈdæptəbl] adj adaptable; person capaz para acomodarse; **he's very** — se acomoda en seguida a las circunstancias.

adaptation [,ædæpˈteiʃən] n adaptación f; (of text) arreglo m, versión f, refundición f.

adapter [əˈdæptə*] n (Elec, Radio) adaptador m.

add [æd] **1** vt añadir, agregar (to a); (to drink etc) añadir, echar, sumar (to a); (Math) sumar; **he** —**ed that** añadió que, agregó que; **we gave £100 and he** —**ed the rest** nosotros dimos 100 libras y él contribuyó con lo demás; **to** — **in** añadir, incluir; **to** — **together, to** — **up** sumar.
2 vi: **to** — **to** aumentar, acrecentar; realzar; **to** — **to our troubles** para colmo de desgracias; **to** — **up to** sumar, ascender a; (fig) venir a ser, equivaler a; querer decir; **it all** —**s up** es lógico, hace sentido; **it doesn't** — **up** no tiene sentido, no tiene ni pies ni cabeza; **it's beginning to** — **up** la cosa nos deja ya entrever una solución; **it doesn't** — **up to much** es poca cosa, no tiene gran importancia.

addendum [əˈdendəm] n, pl **addenda** [əˈdendə] adenda f, adición f, artículo m suplementario.

adder [ˈædə*] n víbora f.

addict [ˈædikt] n partidario m, a f (of de), entusiasta mf; drug — toxicómano m, a f; **I'm a guitar** — me apasiona la guitarra; **I'm a detective-story** — yo soy un apasionado de la novela policíaca.

addicted [əˈdiktid] adj: **to be** — **to something** ser adicto a algo, ser aficionado a algo, (viciously) estar enviciado con algo; **to be** — **to drugs** ser toxicómano; **to be** — **to** + ger ser aficionado a + infin, acostumbrar + infin, (viciously) tener la manía de + infin; **to become** — **to something** enviciarse con algo, entregarse a algo.

addiction [əˈdikʃən] n afición f (to a); (vicious) hábito m morboso; (to drugs) toxicomanía f.

adding machine [ˈædiŋmə,ʃiːn] n sumadora f, calculadora f.

Addis Ababa [ˈædisˈæbəbə] Addis Abeba.

addition [əˈdiʃən] n (act) el añadir; (Math) adición f, suma f; (thing added) adición f, añadidura f; — **sign** signo m de sumar; **if my** — **is correct** si he hecho bien el cálculo; **we made** —**s to our stocks** aumentamos nuestras existencias; **this is a welcome** — **to books on X** éste aumenta valiosamente nuestros libros sobre X; **in** — además; **in** — **to** además de.

additional [əˈdiʃənl] adj adicional; supletorio; **we need** — **men** necesitamos más hombres; **an** — **reason for** razón de más para; **this gave him** — **confidence** esto aumentó su confianza.

additionally [əˈdiʃənli] adv adicionalmente; **and** — y además; **this makes it** — **difficult for me** esto aumenta mis dificultades.

additive [ˈæditiv] n aditivo m.

addled [ˈædld] adj huero, podrido.

address [əˈdres] **1** n (a) (of house etc) señas fpl, dirección f.
(b) (on envelope) sobrescrito m.
(c) (Comm) consignación f.
(d) (style) tratamiento m, título m; **what form of** — **should I use?** ¿qué tratamiento debo darle?

(e) (speech) discurso m; (lecture) conferencia f; **election** —, **electoral** — carta f de propaganda electoral; **public** — **system** sistema m amplificador de discursos públicos.
(f) (Parl etc) petición f, memorial m.
(g) (skill) destreza f, habilidad f.
(h) (behaviour) modales mpl; conducta f, comportamiento m.
(i) **to pay one's** —**es to** hacer la corte a, pretender.
2 vt (a) person dirigirse a, dirigir la palabra a; meeting pronunciar un discurso ante; **he** —**ed us on politics** nos habló de política.
(b) **to** —**someone as** dar a uno el tratamiento de; **to** — **someone by his proper title** dar el debido tratamiento a uno; **to** — **someone as "tú"** tutear a uno, tratar a uno de tú.
(c) letter, protest dirigir (to a); **I** —**ed it to your home** lo mandé a su casa; **this letter is wrongly** —**ed** en esta carta se han puesto incorrectamente las señas.
(d) (Comm) consignar.
3 vr: **to** — **oneself to** person dirigirse a; problem aplicarse a.

addressee [,ædreˈsiː] n destinatario m, a f; (Comm) consignatario m.

Addressograph [əˈdresəugrɑːf] n (Protected Trade Name) máquina f de direcciones.

adduce [əˈdjuːs] vt alegar, aducir, presentar.

Aden [ˈeidn] Adén m.

adenoidal [ˈædinɔidl] adj adenoideo; **the child is** — (fam) el niño padece inflamación adenoidea.

adenoids [ˈædinɔidz] npl vegetaciones fpl adenoideas; (fam) inflamación f adenoidea.

adept [ˈædept] **1** adj experto, hábil, ducho (at, in en).
2 n experto m, perito m; **to be an** — **at** ser maestro en; **he's an** — **at thieving** es un ladrón consumado.

adequacy [ˈædikwəsi] n suficiencia f.

adequate [ˈædikwit] adj suficiente; **to feel** — **to a task** sentirse con fuerzas para una tarea.

adequately [ˈædikwitli] adv suficientemente.

adhere [ədˈhiə*] vi pegarse (to a); (fig) **to** — **to** party, policy adherirse a; promise cumplir; rule observar.

adherence [ədˈhiərəns] n adherencia f, adhesión f (to a); observancia f (to a rule de una regla).

adherent [ədˈhiərənt] **1** adj adhesivo. **2** n partidario m, a f.

adhesion [ədˈhiːʒən] n see **adherence**.

adhesive [ədˈhiːziv] adj adhesivo, pegajoso.

adieu [əˈdjuː] **1** interj ¡adiós! **2** n adiós m; **to bid** — **to** person despedirse de; thing renunciar a, separarse de; **to make one's** — despedirse.

ad infinitum [,ædinfiˈnaitəm] adv a lo infinito; **it carries on** — es inacabable, es cosa de nunca acabar; **it varies** — tiene un sinfín de variaciones.

ad interim [ˈædˈinterim] **1** adv en el ínterin, interinamente. **2** adj interino.

adipose [ˈædipəus] adj adiposo.

adiposity [,ædiˈpɔsiti] n adiposidad f.

adjacent [əˈdʒeisənt] adj contiguo, inmediato (to a); angle adyacente.

adjectival [,ædʒekˈtaivəl] adj adjetivo, adjetival.

adjective [ˈædʒektiv] n adjetivo m.

adjoin [əˈdʒɔin] **1** vt estar contiguo a, lindar con. **2** vi estar contiguo, colindar.

adjoining [əˈdʒɔiniŋ] adj contiguo, vecino, colindante; **the** — **house** la casa de al lado; **in an** — **room** en un cuarto inmediato.

adjourn [əˈdʒəːn] **1** vt (postpone) aplazar; session suspender, levantar; **the meeting was** —**ed** se suspendió la sesión.
2 vi (meeting) suspenderse; **the house then** —**ed** luego se suspendió la sesión; **to stand** —**ed** estar en suspenso; **to** — **to** trasladarse a.

adjournment [əˈdʒəːnmənt] n suspensión f, clausura f.

adjudge [əˈdʒʌdʒ] vt matter juzgar, decidir; **to** — **that** estimar que, considerar que; **he was** —**d the winner** se le decretó el premio; **to** — **someone guilty** declarar culpable a uno.

adjudicate [əˈdʒuːdikeit] **1** vt claim decidir, juzgar. **2** vi ser juez, sentenciar.

adjudication [ə,dʒuːdiˈkeiʃən] n juicio m, sentencia f, decisión f.

adjudicator [əˈdʒuːdikeitə*] n juez m, árbitro m.

adjunct [ˈædʒʌŋkt] n adjunto m, accesorio m.

adjure [əˈdʒuə*] vt ordenar solemnemente (to do hacer); suplicar, implorar.

adjust [əˈdʒʌst] **1** vt (change) modificar, cambiar; (arrange) arreglar; machine ajustar, regular; differences concertar, componer; insurance claim liquidar.
2 vr: **to** — **oneself to** adaptarse a.

adjustable [ə'dʒʌstəbl] *adj* ajustable, graduable, regulable.

adjustment [ə'dʒʌstmənt] *n* modificación *f*, cambio *m*; arreglo *m*; (*Mech*) ajuste *m*, regulación *f*; composición *f*; **to make a small — to one's plans** modificar ligeramente sus proyectos.

adjutant ['ædʒətənt] *n* ayudante *m*.

ad lib [æd'lib] (*fam*) **1** *adv* a voluntad, a discreción. **2 ad-lib** *vi* improvisar.

adman ['ædmæn] *n*, *pl* **admen** ['ædmen] hombre *m* que trabaja en una agencia de publicidad, profesional *m* de la publicidad comercial.

admass ['ædmæs] *n parte de la población que está considerada como fácilmente influida por los actuales medios de la publicidad o propaganda comercial, conjunto de consumidores que tiene poco sentido crítico.*

administer [əd'ministə*] *vt* administrar; *shock etc* proporcionar; **to — an oath to** tomar juramento a.

administration [əd,minis'treiʃən] *n* (*act*) administración *f*; (*system*) gobierno *m*, dirección *f*; (*ministry*) gobierno *m*.

administrative [əd'ministrətiv] *adj* administrativo.

administrator [əd'ministreitə*] *n* administrador *m*.

admirable ['ædmərəbl] *adj* admirable, digno de admiración, excelente; **—!** ¡muy bien!

admiral ['ædmərəl] *n* almirante *m*.

Admiralty ['ædmərəlti] *n* Ministerio *m* de Marina, Almirantazgo *m*; **First Lord of the —** Ministro *m* de Marina.

admiration [,ædmə'reiʃən] *n* admiración *f*.

admire [əd'maiə*] *vt* admirar; (*express admiration for*) manifestar su admiración por, elogiar; **she was admiring herself in the mirror** se estaba mirando satisfecha al espejo.

admirer [əd'maiərə*] *n* admirador *m*, ora *f*; (*suitor*) enamorado *m*, pretendiente *m*.

admiring [əd'maiəriŋ] *adj look* de admiración.

admiringly [əd'maiəriŋli] *adv*: **he looked at her —** le lanzó una mirada llena de admiración; **to speak — of** hablar en términos elogiosos de.

admissibility [əd,misə'biliti] *n* admisibilidad *f*.

admissible [əd'misəbl] *adj* admisible.

admission [əd'miʃən] *n* (*a*) (*entry*) entrada *f* (*to* a); (*to academy etc*) ingreso *m* (*to* en); **"— free"** "entrada gratis"; **"no —"** "se prohibe la entrada"; **we gained — by a window** logramos entrar por una ventana. (*b*) (*acknowledgement*) confesión *f* (*of* de); **it would be an — of defeat** sería reconocer nuestra derrota.

admit [əd'mit] **1** *vt* (*a*) (*allow to enter*) dejar entrar, dar entrada a; (*fig*) admitir; **children not —ted** se prohibe entrar a los menores de edad; **ticket which —s two** entrada *f* para dos personas; **to be —ed to academy etc** ingresar en. (*b*) (*accept*) aceptar. (*c*) (*acknowledge*) reconocer, confesar; **it must be —ted that** hay que reconocer que; **it is hard, I —** es difícil, lo reconozco; **he —ted himself beaten** reconoció que había sido vencido. **2** *vi*: **to — of** admitir, dar lugar a, permitir; **it —s of no delay** no admite dilación; **to — to crime** confesarse culpable de.

admittance [əd'mitəns] *n* entrada *f*; **he was refused —** se le negó la entrada; **"no —"** "se prohibe la entrada".

admittedly [əd'mitidli] *adv* se reconoce que, es verdad que, de acuerdo que.

admixture [əd'mikstʃə*] *n* mezcla *f*, adición *f*; (*fig*) dosis *f*.

admonish [əd'mɔniʃ] *vt* (*reprimand*) reprender, amonestar; (*warn*) amonestar, prevenir; (*advise*) aconsejar (*to do* hacer).

admonition [,ædmə'niʃən] *n* (*reproof*) represión *f*; (*warning*) amonestación *f*, advertencia *f*; (*advice*) consejo *m*.

ad nauseam [,æd'nɔːsiæm] *adv*: **he repeated it —** lo repitió incansablemente; **you've told me that —** ya me lo has dicho mil veces.

ado [ə'duː] *n*: **much — about nothing** mucho ruido y pocas nueces, nada entre dos platos; **without more —** sin más.

adobe [ə'dəubi] *n* adobe *m*.

adolescence [,ædəu'lesns] *n* adolescencia *f*.

adolescent [,ædəu'lesnt] **1** *adj* adolescente. **2** *n* adolescente *mf*; joven *mf*.

Adolf ['ædɔlf], **Adolphus** [ə'dɔlfəs] *m* Adolfo.

Adonis [ə'dəunis] *m* Adonis.

adopt [ə'dɔpt] *vt* adoptar; *report, motion* aprobar; *suggestion* seguir, aceptar.

adopted [ə'dɔptid] *adj child* adoptivo.

adoption [ə'dɔpʃən] *n* adopción *f*; **country of — patria *f*** adoptiva.

adoptive [ə'dɔptiv] *adj* adoptivo.

adorable [ə'dɔːrəbl] *adj* adorable; (*fam*) encantador, mono; **the child is —** el niño es un encanto.

adoration [,ædɔː'reiʃən] *n* adoración *f*.

adore [ə'dɔːrə*] *vt* adorar.

adoring [ə'dɔːriŋ] *adj look* lleno de adoración.

adoringly [ə'dɔːriŋli] *adv*: **she looked at him —** le miró con adoración.

adorn [ə'dɔːn] *vt* adornar, embellecer.

adornment [ə'dɔːnmənt] *n* adorno *m*.

adrenal [ə'driːnl] *adj* suprarrenal; **— gland** glándula *f* suprarrenal.

adrenalin [ə'drenəlin] *n* adrenalina *f*.

Adriatic (Sea) [,eidri'ætik (siː)] (*Mar m*) Adriático *m*.

adrift [ə'drift] *adv* al garete, a la deriva; **to be all —** (*fig*) ir a la deriva; **to break —** perder las anclas; **to come —** (*fig*) soltarse, desprenderse; **to cut a boat —** cortar las amarras de una barca; **to turn someone —** abandonar a uno a su suerte.

adroit [ə'drɔit] *adj* diestro, hábil.

adroitly [ə'drɔitli] *adv* hábilmente.

adroitness [ə'drɔitnis] *n* destreza *f*, habilidad *f*.

adulate ['ædjuleit] *vt* adular.

adulation [,ædju'leiʃən] *n* adulación *f*.

adult ['ædʌlt] **1** *adj* adulto; mayor. **2** *n* adulto *m*, a *f*; persona *f* mayor; **"—s only"** (*Cine*) "mayores".

adulterate [ə'dʌltəreit] *vt* adulterar.

adulteration [ə,dʌltə'reiʃən] *n* adulteración *f*.

adulterer [ə'dʌltərə*] *n* adúltero *m*.

adulteress [ə'dʌltəris] *n* adúltera *f*.

adulterous [ə'dʌltərəs] *adj* adúltero.

adultery [ə'dʌltəri] *n* adulterio *m*.

adumbrate ['ædʌmbreit] *vt* bosquejar; (*foreshadow*) presagiar, anunciar.

advance [əd'vaːns] **1** *n* (*a*) (*Mil*) avance *m*; (*progress*) avance *m*, progreso *m*, adelanto *m*. (*b*) (*loan*) anticipo *m*; préstamo *m*; (*in share price*) alza *f*, aumento *m*. (*c*) **—s** insinuaciones *fpl*; (*amorous*) requerimiento *m* amoroso; **to accept someone's —s** aceptar las intenciones de uno; **to make —s** to requerir de amores; **to make the first —s** dar los primeros pasos. (*d*) (*phrases with* in) **in —** por adelantado, de antemano; **to arrive in —** of someone llegar antes que uno; **to be in —** of adelantarse a; **to book in —** reservar con anticipación; **to let someone know a week in —** avisar a uno con ocho días de anticipación; **to pay in —** pagar por adelantado; **to thank in —** anticipar las gracias a; **thanking you in —** dándole anticipadas gracias. **2** *adj* anticipado, adelantado; **— booking office** despacho *m* de venta por adelantado; **— copy** anticipo *m* editorial; **— guard** avanzada *f*; **— party** (*Mil*) brigada *f* móvil; **— payment** anticipo *m*. **3** *vt* (*a*) (*move forward*) avanzar, adelantar; *person* (*in rank*) ascender (*to* a). (*b*) (*encourage*) promover, fomentar. (*c*) (*put forward*) *idea* proponer para la discusión; *suggestion* hacer; *claim* presentar. (*d*) *money* anticipar; *loan* prestar. **4** *vi* (*a*) (*move forward*) avanzar, adelantarse; **to — on someone** acercarse (de modo amenazador) a uno; **to — on a town** avanzar hacia una ciudad. (*b*) (*fig*) avanzar, adelantarse; **the work is advancing quickly** el trabajo se está adelantando rápidamente. (*c*) (*in rank*) ascender. (*d*) (*price*) subir.

advanced [əd'vaːnst] *adj* gen, *ideas etc* avanzado; *student* adelantado; *study* superior, alto; **— in years** entrado en años; **the corn is well —d** el trigo está muy avanzado; **the season is well —d** la estación está avanzada.

advancement [əd'vaːnsmənt] *n* adelantamiento *m*, progreso *m*; (*in rank*) ascenso *m*.

advantage [əd'vaːntidʒ] *n* ventaja *f* (*also Tennis*); **to be to someone's —** ser ventajoso para uno; **to have the — of someone** llevar ventaja a uno; **I'm sorry, you have the — of me** lo siento, pero no recuerdo su nombre; **to have the — in numbers** llevar ventaja en cuanto al número; **to show to —** lucir; **to take — of** aprovechar(se de); sacar partido de; *kindness etc* abusar de; (*euph*) seducir.

advantageous [,ædvən'teidʒəs] *adj* ventajoso, provechoso.

advent ['ædvənt] *n* advenimiento *m*, venida *f*; **A—** (*Eccl*) Adviento *m*.

adventitious [,ædven'tiʃəs] *adj* adventicio.

adventure [əd'ventʃə*] *n* aventura *f*.

adventurer [əd'ventʃərə*] n aventurero m.
adventuress [əd'ventʃəris] n aventurera f.
adventurous [əd'ventʃərəs] adj aventurero, emprendedor.
adverb ['ædvə:b] n adverbio m.
adverbial [əd'və:biəl] adj adverbial.
adversary ['ædvəsəri] n adversario m, a f, contrario m, a f.
adverse ['ædvə:s] adj adverso, contrario (to a); desfavorable (to para); balance negativo.
adversity [əd'və:siti] n infortunio m; **companion in** — compañero m de desgracias.
advert [əd'və:t] vi: **to** — **to** referirse a.
advert ['ædvə:t] n = **advertisement**.
advertise ['ædvətaiz] **1** vt (Comm etc) anunciar; publicar; weakness etc revelar públicamente.
  2 vi hacer publicidad, hacer propaganda; poner un anuncio (in a paper en un periódico; for solicitando); **to** — **for** buscar por medio de anuncios; **it pays to** — compensa hacer publicidad.
advertisement [əd'və:tismənt, US ædvər'taizmənt] n anuncio m.
advertiser ['ædvətaizə*] n anunciante mf.
advertising ['ædvətaiziŋ] **1** n publicidad f, propaganda f; (advertisements collectively) anuncios mpl; **my brother's in** — mi hermano trabaja en una agencia de publicidad.
  2 attr: — **agency** agencia f de publicidad; — **campaign** campaña f publicitaria; — **rates** tarifa f para anuncios.
advice [əd'vais] n consejo m; (report) informe m, noticia f; **a piece of** — un consejo; **my** — **to you is** + infin te aconsejo + infin; **to ask for** —, **to seek** — pedir consejos; **to take someone's** — seguir los consejos de uno; **to take legal** — consultar a un abogado; **to take medical** — consultar a un médico.
advisability [əd,vaizə'biliti] n conveniencia f, prudencia f.
advisable [əd'vaizəbl] adj aconsejable, conveniente, prudente; **it would be** — **to** + infin sería aconsejable + infin; **if you think it** — si le parece bien.
advise [əd'vaiz] **1** vt (a) (counsel) aconsejar (to do hacer); (as paid adviser) asesorar; **what do you** — **me to do?** ¿qué me aconsejas (que haga)?; **the doctor** —s **complete rest** el médico recomienda un descanso total.
  (b) (inform) avisar, informar; **to keep someone** —d **of something** tener a uno al corriente de algo.
  2 vi: **he** —s **against the plan** aconseja que no aceptemos el proyecto; **to** — **on** ser asesor en.
advised [əd'vaizd] adj: **well**— prudente; **you would be well** — **to** + infin sería aconsejable + infin.
advisedly [əd'vaizidli] adv deliberadamente; **I say so** — lo digo después de pensarlo bien.
adviser [əd'vaizə*] n consejero m; (eg business —) asesor m; **legal** — abogado m; **spiritual** — confesor m.
advisory [əd'vaizəri] adj consultivo; **in an** — **capacity** como asesor; — **board** junta f consultiva.
advocacy ['ædvəkəsi] n defensa f.
advocate ['ædvəkit] n (Law) abogado m; (of cause) defensor m, partidario m.
advocate ['ædvəkeit] vt abogar por, ser partidario de, recomendar; **what do you** — ? ¿qué nos aconseja Vd?
adze [ædz] n azuela f.
Aegean Sea [i:'dʒi:ən si:] Mar m Egeo.
aegis ['i:dʒis] n égida f; **under the** — **of** (protection) bajo la tutela de, (patronage) patrocinado por.
Aeneas [i:'ni:æs] m Eneas.
Aeneid ['i:niid] Eneida f.
aeon ['i:ən] n eón m; (loosely) eternidad f.
aerate ['εəreit] vt airear.
aerated ['εəreitid] adj: — **water** gaseosa f.
aerial ['εəriəl] **1** adj aéreo; — **cableway** funicular m aéreo; — **photograph** aerofoto f.
  2 n antena f; **directional** — antena f dirigida; **indoor** — antena f de interior; — (**mast**) torre f de antena.
aero . . . ['εərəu] aero . . .
aerobatics [,εərəu'bætiks] npl acrobacia f aérea.
aerodrome ['εərədrəum] n aeródromo m.
aerodynamic ['εərəudai'næmik] adj aerodinámico.
aerodynamics ['εərəudai'næmiks] npl aerodinámica f.
aero-engine ['εərəu,endʒin] n motor m de aviación.
aerogram ['εərəugræm] n aerograma m, radiograma m.
aerolite ['εərəlait] n aerolito m.
aeromodelling ['εərəu'mɔdliŋ] n aeromodelismo m.
aeronaut ['εərənɔ:t] n aeronauta mf.
aeronautic(al) [,εərə'nɔ:tik(əl)] adj aeronáutico.
aeronautics [,εərə'nɔ:tiks] npl aeronáutica f.

aeroplane ['εərəplein] n avión m; **model** — aeromodelo m.
aerosol ['εərəsɔl] n aerosol m.
Aeschylus ['i:skiləs] m Esquilo.
Aesop ['i:sɔp] m Esopo.
aesthete ['i:sθi:t] n esteta mf.
aesthetic(al) [i:s'θetik(əl)] adj estético.
aesthetically [i:s'θetikəli] adv estéticamente.
aestheticism [i:s'θetisizəm] n esteticismo m.
aesthetics [i:s'θetiks] npl estética f.
afar [ə'fa:*] adv: — **off** lejos, en lontananza; **from** — desde lejos.
affability [,æfə'biliti] n afabilidad f.
affable ['æfəbl] adj afable.
affably ['æfəbli] adv afablemente.
affair [ə'fεə*] n asunto m; episodio m; (event) acontecimiento m; (love —) aventura f amorosa; —s pl (business) negocios mpl; **man of** —s hombre m de negocios; **the Cuba** — el asunto de Cuba; **current** —s actualidades fpl; **foreign** —s asuntos mpl exteriores; — **of honour** lance m de honor; —s **of state** asuntos mpl de estado; — **of the heart** aventura f sentimental; **how are** —s **with you?** ¿qué tal van tus cosas?; **it was an odd** — fue una cosa rara; **it will be a big** — será un acontecimiento importante; **that's my** — eso me toca únicamente a mí, ésa es cosa mía; **that's his** — allá él, con su pan se lo coma; **to have an** — **with** andar en relaciones con, tener un plan con; **to put one's** —s **in order** arreglar sus asuntos personales.
affect [ə'fekt] vt (a) (concern) afectar, tener que ver con, influir en; (Med) interesar, afectar; (harm) perjudicar; **it did not** — **my decision** no influyó en mi decisión; **it** —s **me considerably** para mí tiene gran importancia.
  (b) (move) conmover, enternecer; **he seemed much** —**ed** estuvo muy emocionado, se conmovió mucho.
  (c) **he** —s **the rebel** se las echa de rebelde; **to** — **indifference** afectar indiferencia; **she** —**ed to cry** fingió llorar.
affectation [,æfek'teiʃən] n afectación f.
affected [ə'fektid] adj afectado.
affectedly [ə'fektidli] adv de manera afectada, con afectación.
affecting [ə'fektiŋ] adj conmovedor, enternecedor.
affection [ə'fekʃən] n afecto m, cariño m; **to have an** — **for** tener cariño a.
affectionate [ə'fekʃənit] adj cariñoso, afectuoso.
affectionately [ə'fekʃənitli] adv cariñosamente, afectuosamente; **yours** — un abrazo cariñoso.
affective [ə'fektiv] adj afectivo.
affidavit [,æfi'deivit] n declaración f jurada, afidávit m.
affiliate [ə'filieit] vi: **to** — **to**, **to** — **with** afiliarse a.
affiliated [ə'filieitid] adj company filial, subsidiario; member, society afiliado.
affiliation [ə,fili'eiʃən] n afiliación f; **political** —s relaciones fpl políticas; **its** —s **are rather with this school** está relacionado más bien con esta escuela.
affinity [ə'finiti] n afinidad f; **A has certain affinities with B** entre A y B existe cierta afinidad; **I feel no** — **whatsoever with him** no nos une ningún lazo de simpatía.
affirm [ə'fə:m] vt afirmar.
affirmation [,æfə'meiʃən] n afirmación f.
affirmative [ə'fə:mətiv] adj afirmativo; **to answer in the** — dar una respuesta afirmativa, contestar afirmativamente.
affix ['æfiks] n (Gram) afijo m.
affix [ə'fiks] vt signature etc poner, añadir; stamp poner, pegar; seal imprimir.
afflict [ə'flikt] vt afligir; **the** —**ed** los afligidos; **to be** —**ed with** sufrir de.
affliction [ə'flikʃən] n aflicción f, congoja f; infortunio m, desgracia f; (bodily) mal m; **the** —s **of old age** los males de la vejez.
affluence ['æfluəns] n riqueza f, opulencia f.
affluent ['æfluənt] **1** adj acaudalado, opulento; **the** — **society** la sociedad opulenta. **2** n afluente m.
afflux ['æflʌks] n afluencia f; (Med) aflujo m.
afford [ə'fɔ:d] vt (a) (provide) dar, proporcionar; **this** —s **me a chance to speak** esto me da la oportunidad de hablar; **that** —**ed me some relief** eso me proporcionó cierto alivio; **it** —s **shade** da sombra.
  (b) (pay for) **we can** — **it** tenemos con que comprarlo, podemos permitírnoslo; **can we** — **it?** ¿tenemos bastante dinero?
  (c) (spare, risk) **I can't** — **the time to go** no tengo bastante tiempo para ir; **we can** — **to wait** bien podemos esperar; **an opportunity you cannot** — **to miss** una ocasión que no es para desperdiciar;

I can't — to be idle no puedo permitirme el lujo de no hacer nada; **can we — the risk?** ¿podemos arriesgarnos?

afforest [æ'fɒrist] *vt* repoblar (de árboles).

afforestation [æ,fɒris'teiʃən] *n* repoblación *f* forestal.

affray [ə'frei] *n* refriega *f*, reyerta *f*.

affright [ə'frait] *vt* asustar, espantar.

affront [ə'frʌnt] **1** *n* afrenta *f*, ofensa *f*; **to offer an —** to afrentar. **2** *vt* afrentar; **he was much —ed** se ofendió mucho.

Afghan ['æfgæn] **1** *adj* afgano. **2** *n* afgano *m*, a *f*; (*dog*) perro *m* afgano.

Afghanistan [æf'gænistæn] Afganistán *m*.

afield [ə'fiːld] *adv*: **far —** muy lejos; **you'll have to go further — for that** para eso hará falta buscar más lejos.

afire [ə'faiə*] *adv*: **to be —** arder, estar en llamas; **to be — with a desire to** + *infin* anhelar ardientemente + *infin*.

aflame [ə'fleim] *adv* en llamas.

afloat [ə'fləut] *adv* a flote; **in the sea** en el mar; **by a miracle we were still —** por maravilla quedamos a flote; **to keep —** mantener(se) a flote; **to set —** poner a flote; **the largest navy —** la mayor marina del mundo; **to spend one's life —** pasar toda la vida a bordo.

afoot [ə'fut] *adv*: **there is something —** algo se está tramando; **what is —?** ¿qué estarán tramando?; **there is a plan — to** + *infin* existe un proyecto para + *infin*; **to set —** poner en movimiento.

aforementioned [ə,fɔː'menʃənd] *adj*, **aforesaid** [ə'fɔːsed] *adj* susodicho, mencionado.

aforethought [ə'fɔːθɔːt] *adj*: **with malice —** con premeditación.

afraid [ə'freid] *adj* (**a**) **to be —** tener miedo; **all were very —** todos se espantaron mucho; **don't be —** no tengas miedo, no temas; **to make someone —** infundir miedo a uno; **to be — for** temer por; **to be — of** *person* tener miedo a, *thing* tener miedo de; **to be — to** + *infin* tener miedo de + *infin*, temer + *infin*; **I'm — he won't come** me temo que no venga.
(**b**) **I'm — he's out** lo siento, pero no está; **I'm — I have to go now** siento tener que irme ahora; **I'm — so!** lo siento, pero es así.

afresh [ə'freʃ] *adv* de nuevo, otra vez; **to do something —** volver a hacer algo.

Africa ['æfrikə] África *f*.

African ['æfrikən] **1** *adj* africano. **2** *n* africano *m*, a *f*.

Afrikaans [,æfri'kɑːns] *n* africaans *m*.

Afrikander [,æfri'kændə*] *n* africander *m*.

Afro-Asian [,æfrəu'eiʃən] *adj* afroasiático.

aft [ɑːft] *adv* (*be*) en popa; (*go*) a popa.

after ['ɑːftə*] **1** *adv* (**a**) (*time, order*) después; **long —** mucho tiempo después; **soon —** poco después.
(**b**) (*place*) detrás.
2 *prep* (**a**) (*time, order*) después de; **soon — eating it** poco después de comerlo; **do you put Lope — Calderón?** ¿crees que Lope le es inferior a Calderón?
(**b**) (*place, order*) detrás de; tras; **day — day** día tras día; **one — the other** uno tras otro; **he ran — me with my umbrella** corrió tras de mí con mi paraguas; **— you!** ¡pase Vd!; **— you with the salt** ¿me das la sal, por favor?
(**c**) **this is — Goya** esto se pintó según el estilo de Goya; **— the English fashion** a la manera inglesa.
(**d**) (*on account of*) **he is named — Churchill** se le llamó así por Churchill.
(**e**) (*idioms with* to be): **the police are — him** la policía le está buscando; **I have been — that for years** eso lo busco desde hace años; **what are you —?** ¿qué pretendes con eso?; **she's — a husband** ella va en pos de un marido.
3 *conj* después (de) que.
4 *adj part* posterior, trasero; (*Naut*) de popa; **in — years** en los años siguientes, años después.

afterbirth ['ɑːftəbə:θ] *n* secundinas *fpl*.

aftercare ['ɑːftəkeə*] *n* asistencia *f* postoperatoria.

afterdeck ['ɑːftədek] *n* cubierta *f* de popa.

after-dinner ['ɑːftə'dinə*] *adj* de sobremesa.

after-effect ['ɑːftərifekt] *n* consecuencia *f*.

afterglow ['ɑːftəgləu] *n* (*in sky*) resplandor *m* crepuscular; (*bodily*) sensación *f* de bienestar.

afterlife ['ɑːftəlaif] *n* vida *f* futura; (*on earth*) resto *m* de la vida.

aftermath ['ɑːftəmæθ] *n* consecuencias *fpl*, resultados *mpl*, efectos *mpl*.

afternoon ['ɑːftə'nuːn] *n* tarde *f*; **good —!** ¡buenas tardes!

after-sales service ['ɑːftəseilz'sə:vis] *n* servicio *m* de asistencia post-venta.

after-shave lotion ['ɑːftəʃeiv'ləuʃən] *n* loción *f* para después del afeitado.

aftertaste ['ɑːftəteist] *n* dejo *m*, resabio *m*.

afterthought ['ɑːftəθɔːt] *n* ocurrencia *f* tardía, idea *f* adicional.

after-treatment ['ɑːftətriːtmənt] *n* tratamiento *m* postoperatorio.

afterwards ['ɑːftəwədz] *adv* después, más tarde; **shortly —, soon —** poco después; **long —** mucho tiempo después.

again [ə'gen] *adv* otra vez, nuevamente, de nuevo; *often translated by* volver a + *infin*, eg **he climbed up —** volvió a subir; **—, it may not be true** por otra parte, puede no ser verdad; **these are different —** también estos son distintos; **never —** nunca más; **as much —** otro tanto; **as many —** otros tantos.

against [ə'genst] *prep* (**a**) (*next to*) contra; (*close to*) al lado de, junto a, cerca de; **— over the church** enfrente de la iglesia.
(**b**) **— that, as — that** en contraste con eso.
(**c**) (*for*) **— his arrival** para su llegada.
(**d**) (*fig*) contra; en contra de; **he was — it** estaba en contra, se opuso a ello; **I see nothing —** it no veo nada en contra de eso; **I spoke — the plan** hablé en contra del proyecto; **I know nothing — him** yo no sé nada que le sea desfavorable; **what have you got — me?** ¿por qué me tiene Vd inquina?; **it's — the rules** no lo permiten las reglas; **is there a law — it?** ¿es que hay ley que lo prohíba?; **luck was — him** la suerte le era contraria; **to be up — it** estar en un aprieto.

agape [ə'geip] *adj and adv* boquiabierto.

agate ['ægət] *n* ágata *f*.

agave [ə'geivi] *n* agave *f*, pita *f*.

age [eidʒ] **1** *n* (**a**) (*in general*) edad *f*; (*old —*) vejez *f*, senectud *f*; **mental —** edad *f* mental; **middle —** mediana edad *f*; **he is 20 years of —** tiene 20 años; **when I was your —** cuando yo tenía los años de Vd; **what — are you?** ¿qué edad tiene Vd?; **she doesn't look her —** no representa la edad que tiene; **— is beginning to tell on him** los años empiezan a pesar sobre él; **at the — of** a la edad de; **at my —** a la edad que yo tengo; **of — mayor de edad; to be of an — to** ser de edad para; **to come of —** llegar a la mayoría de edad; **over —** demasiado viejo; **under —** menor de edad.
(**b**) (*period*) época *f*, era *f*, siglo *m*; **the — we live in** el siglo en que vivimos; **atomic —** era *f* atómica; **in the — of Queen Elizabeth** en la época (*or* en tiempos) de la reina Isabel; **golden —** (*Myth*) edad *f* dorada, edad *f* de oro; **Golden A— (*of Spain*)** Siglo *m* de Oro; **Bronze A—** Edad *f* de Bronce; **Iron A—** Edad *f* de Hierro; **Stone A—** Edad *f* de Piedra; **Dark A—s** Edades *fpl* Bárbaras; **Middle A—s** Edad *f* Media; **A— of Enlightenment** Siglo *m* de las Luces.
(**c**) (*long time*) siglo *m*, eternidad *f*, muchísimo tiempo *m*; **we waited an —, we waited (for) —s** esperamos una eternidad; **it's —s since I saw him** hace muchísimo tiempo que no le veo.
2 *vt* envejecer.
3 *vi* envejecer(se).

aged *adj* (**a**) ['eidʒid] viejo, anciano. (**b**) [eidʒd]: **— 15** de 15 años, que tiene 15 años.

age group ['eidʒgruːp] *n* grupo *m* de personas de la misma edad; **the 40 to 50 —** el grupo que comprende los de 40 a 50 años; **children of the same —** niños *mpl* de la misma edad; **to arrange people by —s** clasificar las personas según su edad.

ageless ['eidʒlis] *adj* eternamente joven; perenne, inmemorial.

age limit ['eidʒlimit] *n* edad *f* mínima *or* edad *f* máxima; (*retirement*) edad *f* de jubilación.

agency ['eidʒənsi] *n* (**a**) (*office*) agencia *f*; **advertising —** agencia *f* de publicidad; **news —** agencia *f* de información; **tourist —, travel —** agencia *f* de viajes.
(**b**) (*instrumentality*): **through the — of** por medio de, por la mediación de.

agenda [ə'dʒendə] *n* orden *m* del día, asuntos *mpl* a tratar.

agent ['eidʒənt] *n* (**a**) (*representative*) representante *m*, delegado *m*; (*Law*) apoderado *m*; (*Comm, Police etc*) agente *m*; (*US*) jefe *m* de estación; **foreign —** agente *m* extranjero; **special —** agente *m* especial; **he is not a free —** no puede actuar libremente; **land — (*on estate*)** administrador *m*; **literary —** agente *m* literario; **publicity —** agente *m* de publicidad; **shipping —** agente *m* marítimo; **sole —** agente *m* único; **to be sole — for** tener la representación exclusiva de.

(b) (*Chem*) **bleaching** — decolorante *m*; **chemical** — agente *m* químico.

agent provocateur ['æʒɑ̃:prɔvɔkə'tə:*] *n* agente *m* provocador.

age-old ['eidʒəuld] *adj* secular, antiquísimo.

agglomeration [ə,glɔmə'reiʃən] *n* aglomeración *f*.

agglutinate [ə'gluːtineit] **1** *vt* aglutinar. **2** *vi* aglutinarse.

agglutination [ə,gluːti'neiʃən] *n* aglutinación *f*.

agglutinative [ə'gluːtinətiv] *adj* aglutinante.

aggrandizement [ə'grændizmənt] *n* engrandecimiento *m*, agrandamiento *m*.

aggravate ['ægrəveit] *vt* agravar; (*fam*) irritar, sacar de quicio.

aggravating ['ægrəveitiŋ] *adj* (*fam*) irritante, molesto; **it's very** — es para volverse loco; **he's an** — **child** es un niño molesto.

aggravation [,ægrə'veiʃən] *n* agravación *f*; circunstancia *f* agravante; (*angering*) irritación *f*.

aggregate ['ægrigit] **1** *adj* total, global. **2** *n* agregado *m*, conjunto *m*; **in the** — en conjunto, en total.

aggregate ['ægrigeit] **1** *vt* agregar, juntar, reunir. **2** *vi* ascender a.

aggression [ə'greʃən] *n* agresión *f*.

aggressive [ə'gresiv] *adj* (*pej*) agresivo; (*zealous etc*) dinámico, enérgico.

aggressively [ə'gresivli] *adv* de manera agresiva; con dinamismo, enérgicamente, con empuje.

aggressiveness [ə'gresivnis] *n* agresividad *f*, acometividad *f*; dinamismo *m*, energía *f*, empuje *m*.

aggressor [ə'gresə*] *n* agresor *m*, ora *f*.

aggrieved [ə'griːvd] *adj*: **he was much** — se ofendió mucho; **in an** — **tone** en un tono de queja.

aghast [ə'gɑːst] *adj* horrorizado; **to be** — pasmarse (*at* de).

agile ['ædʒail] *adj* ágil.

agility [ə'dʒiliti] *n* agilidad *f*.

aging ['eidʒiŋ] **1** *adj* ya bastante viejo. **2** *n* envejecimiento *m*.

agitate ['ædʒiteit] **1** *vt* (*shake*) agitar; (*perturb*) inquietar, perturbar; **to be very** —**d** estar muy inquieto (*about* por), estar en ascuas.
2 *vi*: **to** — **for** hacer propaganda por, hacer una campaña en pro de.

agitation [,ædʒi'teiʃən] *n* (*Pol etc*) agitación *f*; propaganda *f*, campaña *f*; (*mental*) inquietud *f*, perturbación *f*; nerviosismo *m*.

agitator ['ædʒiteitə*] *n* agitador *m*, ora *f*, alborotador *m*, ora *f*, elemento *m* revoltoso; (*Chem*) agitador *m*.

aglow [ə'gləu] *adj*: **to be** — **with** brillar con; **tò be** — **with happiness** irradiar felicidad.

Agnes ['ægnis] Inés.

agnostic [æg'nɔstik] **1** *adj* agnóstico. **2** *n* agnóstico *m*, a *f*.

agnosticism [æg'nɔstisizəm] *n* agnosticismo *m*.

ago [ə'gəu] *adv*: **a week** — hace una semana; **just a moment** — hace un momento nada más; **a little while** — hace poco; **long** — hace mucho tiempo, tiempo ha; **how long** — **was it?** ¿hace cuánto tiempo?; **as long** — **as 1965** ya en 1965.

agog [ə'gɔg] *adj*: **to be** — estar ansioso, sentir gran curiosidad; **the country was** — el país estaba emocionadísimo, el país estaba pendiente de lo que pudiera pasar; **he was** — **to hear the news** tenía enorme curiosidad por saber las noticias; **to set** — emocionar, infundir curiosidad a.

agonized ['ægənaizd] *adj cry etc* angustiado, de angustia.

agonizing ['ægənaiziŋ] *adj pain* atroz, agudo; *indecision, suspense* angustioso; *moment* de angustia; *reappraisal* agonizante, doloroso.

agony ['ægəni] *n* (*pain*) dolor *m* agudo, dolor *m* punzante; (*mental anguish*) angustia *f*, aflicción *f*; — **of death, mortal** — agonía *f*; **I was in** — sufría unos dolores horrorosos; **to suffer agonies of doubt** — la obra era una birria; — **column** sección *f* de anuncios relativos a asuntos personales.

agrarian [ə'grɛəriən] *adj* agrario.

agree [ə'griː] *vi* **(a)** (*be in harmony: things*) concordar (*with* con); *also Gram*), corresponder (*with* a).
(b) (*be in agreement: persons*) estar de acuerdo (*with* con, *that* en que); **to** — **with** plan, policy aprobar; **I** — estoy conforme; **I quite** — estoy completamente de acuerdo; **I** — **that it was foolish** reconozco que era tonto; **he's an idiot, don't you** —? es un imbécil, ¿no es así?
(c) (*come to an agreement*) ponerse de acuerdo (*with* con); **eventually he** —**d** con lo consintió; **"it's impossible"**, **he** —**d** "es imposible", asintió; **you'll never get him to** — no lograrás nunca su

consentimiento; **to** — **on** convenir en; **it was** —**d that** se resolvió que, (*Parl*) se acordó que; **it is** —**d that** (*in legal contract*) se acuerda que; **to** — **to** plan convenir en, aprobar; **he'll** — **to anything se aviene** a todo; **to** — **to** + *infin* consentir en + *infin*, quedar en + *infin*; **it was** —**d to** + *infin* (*Parl etc*) se acordó + *infin*.
(d) (*get on well*) **we simply don't** —, **that's all** es que no existe simpatía entre nosotros, no congeniamos.
(e) (*of food*) **garlic does not** — **with me** el ajo no me sienta bien.

agreeable [ə'griːəbl] *adj* (*pleasing*) agradable, *person* simpático; (*in agreement*) **if you are** — si estás de acuerdo; **is that** — **to everybody?** ¿estamos de acuerdo todos?; **he was** — **to that** estaba conforme con eso, lo aprobó; **he is** — **to help** está dispuesto a ayudar.

agreeably [ə'griːəbli] *adv* agradablemente.

agreed [ə'griːd] *adj* plan etc convenido; —! ¡conformes!

agreement [ə'griːmənt] *n* **(a)** (*treaty etc*) acuerdo *m*, pacto *m*, convenio *m*; (*Comm*) contrato *m*; **gentlemen's** — acuerdo *m* verbal; — **to differ** desacuerdo *m* amistoso; **by mutual** — por acuerdo mutuo; **to come to** (*or* **reach**) **an** — ponerse de acuerdo, llegar a un acuerdo; **to enter into an** — firmar un contrato (*to* + *infin* para + *infin*).
(b) (*harmony*) concordancia *f* (*also Gram*); (*between persons*) conformidad *f*, armonía *f*; **in** — **with** de acuerdo con; **to be in** — **with** estar de acuerdo con.

agricultural [,ægri'kʌltʃərəl] *adj* agrícola; — **college** escuela-granja *f* agrícola; — **expert** agrónomo *m*.

agriculture ['ægrikʌltʃə*] *n* agricultura *f*.

agricultur(al)ist [,ægri'kʌltʃər(əl)ist] *n* agricultor *m*, ora *f*.

agronomist [ə'grɔnəmist] *n* agrónomo *m*.

agronomy [ə'grɔnəmi] *n* agronomía *f*.

aground [ə'graund] *adv*: **to be** — estar encallado; **to run** — encallar, embarrancar; **to run a ship** — hacer que encalle un barco.

ah [ɑː] *excl* ¡ah!

aha [ɑː'hɑː] *excl* ¡ajá!

ahead [ə'hed] **1** *adv*: **to be** — estar delante; **can you see who is** —? ¿ves quién va al frente?; **there's trouble** — habrá un lío, han de sobrevenir disgustos; **there's a busy time** — hay ocupaciones en perspectiva; **straight** — todo seguido; **full speed** —! ¡avante a toda máquina!; **to go** — ir adelante; continuar, avanzar; **to go** — **with one's plans** seguir adelante con sus proyectos; **go** —! ¡adelante!; **to look** — tener en cuenta el futuro; **to send someone** — enviar a uno por delante.
2 — **of** *prep* delante de; **to be** — **of** (*in progress*) llevar la ventaja a; **to be** — **of one's time** anticiparse a su época; **to get** — **of someone** adelantarse a uno; **you'll get there** — **of us** llegarás antes de nosotros.

ahoy [ə'hɔi] *excl*: **ship** —! ¡ah del barco!

aid [eid] **1** *n* ayuda *f*, auxilio *m*, socorro *m*; **audiovisual** —**s** ayudas *fpl* audiovisuales; **economic** — ayuda *f* económica; **mutual** — socorros *mpl* mutuos; **navigational** —**s**, —**s to navigation** ayudas *fpl* a la navegación; **by** (*or* **with**) **the** — **of** con la ayuda de; **in** — **of** a beneficio de, pro; **what's all this in** — **of**? ¿qué motivo tiene esto?, ¿para qué sirve esto?, ¿qué pasa aquí?; **to come to the** — **of** acudir en ayuda de, (*in argument*) acudir en defensa de.
2 *vt* ayudar, auxiliar, socorrer; —**ed by darkness** al amparo de la noche; *see* **abet**.

aide [eid] *n*, **aide-de-camp** ['eiddə'kɑ̃:ŋ] *n* edecán *m*.

aide-mémoire ['eidmei'mwɑ:] *n* memorándum *m*.

ail [eil] **1** *vt* afligir; **what** —**s you?** ¿qué tienes?, ¿qué te pasa? **2** *vi* sufrir, estar enfermo.

aileron ['eilərɔn] *n* alerón *m*.

ailing ['eiliŋ] *adj* enfermo, achacoso.

ailment ['eilmənt] *n* enfermedad *f*, achaque *m*.

aim [eim] **1** *n* (*of weapon*) puntería *f*; (*fig*) propósito *m*, intención *f*, meta *f*, blanco *m*; **his one** — **is to** + *infin* su único propósito es de + *infin*; **to have no** — **in life** no saber qué hacer con su vida; **with the** — **of** + *ger* con miras a + *infin*, con la intención de + *infin*; **to take** — apuntar (*at* a).
2 *vt* gun apuntar (*at* a); missile, remark dirigir (*at* a); blow asestar (*at* a).
3 *vi* apuntar (*at* a); **to** — **at** objective aspirar a, pretender, ambicionar; **what are you** —**ing at?** ¿qué intentas?; **to** — **high** (*fig*) picar muy alto; **to** — **to** + *infin* aspirar a + *infin*, pretender + *infin*, tener la intención de + *infin*.

aimless ['eimlis] *adj* sin propósito fijo, sin objeto.

aimlessly ['eimlisli] *adv* a la ventura.

ain't [eint] (*fam*) = **is not, are not; has not, have not.**

air [ɛə*] **1** n (a) aire m; **foul** — aire m viciado; **fresh** — aire m fresco; **he's a breath of fresh** — es una persona con ideas nuevas; **to get some fresh** — (salir a) tomar el fresco; **hot** — palabrería f; **by** — en avión, (*Post*) por avión, por vía aérea; **to be in the** — (*fig*) estar en el aire, estar en proyecto; **it's still very much in the** — está todavía en el aire, queda todavía sin resolver; **there's something in the** — se está tramando algo; **spring is in the** — se presiente ya la llegada de la primavera; **to go up in the** — (*fig*) ponerse negro, subirse por las paredes; **in mid** — entre cielo y tierra; **in the open** — al aire libre; **war in the** — la guerra f aérea; **to vanish into thin** — desaparecer por completo; **to be on the** — (*Radio*) estar en el aire, hablar por radio; **we are on the** — from 6 to 7 emitimos de 6 a 7; **one can't live on** — no se vive de aire solo; **to walk on** — estar bañado en agua de rosas; **to clear the** —, **to let in fresh** — airear la atmósfera, (*fig*) aclarar las cosas; **to fly through the** — volar por los aires; **to give someone the** — (*sl*) despedir a uno, dar calabazas a uno; **to take the** — tomar el fresco.

(b) (*Mus*) aire m, tonada f.

(c) (*appearance*) aire m, aspecto m; (*mien*) porte m, ademán m; **—s and graces** afectación f, melindres mpl; **with an** — con toda confianza, con aplomo, con garbo; **he has a distinguished** —, **he has an** — **about him** se ve que es un hombre distinguido; **to give oneself** —**s, to put on** —**s** presumir, darse tono.

2 attr aéreo; aeronáutico.

3 vt airear, ventilar; *idea, grievance* airear; **to** — **one's knowledge** lucir sus conocimientos, hacer alarde de sus conocimientos.

air base ['ɛəbeis] n base f aérea.

airborne ['ɛəbɔ:n] adj (*Mil*) aerotransportado; *germ* transmitido por el aire; *seed* llevado por el aire; **suddenly we were** — de pronto nos vimos en el aire.

air brake ['ɛəbreik] n freno m neumático.

air bubble ['ɛə,bʌbl] n burbuja f de aire.

air chamber ['ɛə,tʃeimbə*] n cámara f de aire.

air-conditioned ['ɛəkən,diʃənd] adj con aire acondicionado, refrigerado.

air conditioner ['ɛəkən,diʃənə*] n acondicionador m de aire.

air conditioning ['ɛəkən,diʃəniŋ] n acondicionamiento m de aire.

air-cooled ['ɛəku:ld] adj refrigerado por aire.

aircraft ['ɛəkrɑ:ft] n avión m.

aircraft carrier ['ɛəkrɑ:ft,kæriə*] n porta(a)viones m.

aircrew ['ɛəkru:] n tripulación f de avión.

air cushion ['ɛəkuʃən] n cojín m de aire, almohada f neumática; (*Aer*) colchón m de aire.

airdrome ['ɛə,drəum] n (*US*) see **aerodrome.**

air duct ['ɛədʌkt] n tubo m de aire.

airfield ['ɛəfi:ld] n campo m de aviación.

air force ['ɛəfɔ:s] n aviación f, fuerzas fpl aéreas.

airgun ['ɛəgʌn] n escopeta f de aire comprimido.

airhole ['ɛəhəul] n respiradero m.

air hostess ['ɛə,həustis] n azafata f.

airily ['ɛərili] adv *say etc* muy a la ligera, sin dar importancia a la cosa; confiado, satisfecho.

air intake ['ɛər,inteik] n toma f de aire.

airless ['ɛəlis] adj *room* mal ventilado; *day* sin viento.

air letter ['ɛəletə*] n carta f por correo aéreo.

airlift ['ɛəlift] n puente m aéreo.

airline ['ɛəlain] n línea f aérea.

airliner ['ɛəlainə*] n avión m de pasajeros.

airlock ['ɛəlɔk] n esclusa f de aire.

airmail ['ɛəmeil] n correo m aéreo; **by** — por avión.

airman ['ɛəmən] n, pl **—men** [mən] aviador m, piloto m.

air marshal ['ɛə'mɑ:ʃəl] n (*Brit*) mariscal m de aire.

airplane ['ɛəplein] n (*US*) avión m.

air pocket ['ɛə,pɔkit] n bache m aéreo.

airport ['ɛəpɔ:t] n aeropuerto m.

air pressure ['ɛə,preʃə*] n presión f atmosférica.

air pump ['ɛəpʌmp] n bomba f de aire.

air raid ['ɛəreid] n ataque m aéreo; **air-raid shelter** refugio m antiaéreo; — **warden** vigilante m contra ataques aéreos; — **warning** alarma f antiaérea.

airscrew ['ɛəskru:] n hélice f de avión.

air-sea base ['ɛə'si:beis] n base f aeronaval.

airship ['ɛəʃip] n aeronave f.

airsick ['ɛəsik] adj: **to be** —, **to get** — marearse (en un avión).

airspeed indicator ['ɛəspi:d'indikeitə*] n velocímetro m aéreo, tacómetro m.

airstrip ['ɛəstrip] n pista f de aterrizaje.

airtight ['ɛətait] adj hermético.

airway ['ɛəwei] n línea f aérea.

airwoman ['ɛə,wumən] n, pl **—women** [,wimin] aviadora f.

airworthy ['ɛəwə:ði] adj en condiciones de vuelo.

airy ['ɛəri] adj *place* de mucho viento; *room* bien ventilado; espacioso; *cloth etc* ligero, diáfano; (*unsubstantial*) etéreo; *step* ligero; *remark etc* dicho a la ligera.

aisle [ail] n nave f lateral; (*Theat*) pasillo m; **it had them rolling in the** —**s** los hizo desternillarse de risa.

aitch [eitʃ] n *nombre de la* h *inglesa;* **to drop one's** —**es** no pronunciar las haches.

Aix-la-Chapelle ['eikslæʃə'pel] Aquisgrán.

ajar [ə'dʒɑ:*] adv entreabierto, entornado; **to leave the door** — no cerrar completamente la puerta.

Ajax ['eidʒæks] m Áyax.

akimbo [ə'kimbəu] adv: **with arms** — en jarras.

akin [ə'kin] adj relacionado (*to* con), análogo (*to* a), semejante (*to* a).

alabaster ['æləbɑ:stə*] **1** n alabastro m. **2** adj alabastrino.

à la carte [ælæ'kɑ:t] adv a la carta.

alacrity [ə'lækriti] n: **with** — con presteza, con la mayor prontitud.

Aladdin [ə'lædin] m Aladino.

alarm [ə'lɑ:m] **1** n alarma f; (*fear etc*) inquietud f, temor m; — **and despondency** confusionismo m y desconcierto m; —**s and excursions** sobresaltos mpl; **false** — falsa alarma f; **there was some** — **at** this esto produjo cierta inquietud, esto sobresaltó a la gente; **to give** (*or* **sound, raise**) **the** — dar la alarma; **to take** — alarmarse, sobresaltarse.

2 vt alarmar; inquietar, asustar; **to be** —**ed at** alarmarse de; **don't be** —**ed** no te vayas a asustar.

alarm bell [ə'lɑ:mbel] n timbre m de alarma.

alarm clock [ə'lɑ:mklɔk] n despertador m.

alarming [ə'lɑ:miŋ] adj alarmante.

alarmingly [ə'lɑ:miŋli] adv de modo alarmante, alarmantemente.

alarmist [ə'lɑ:mist] n alarmista mf.

alarm signal [ə'lɑ:m,signəl] n señal f de alarma.

alas [ə'læs] excl ¡ay!, ¡ay de mí!; — **for the country!** ¡ay del país!

Albania [æl'beiniə] Albania f.

Albanian [æl'beiniən] **1** adj albanés. **2** n albanés m, esa f. **3** n (*language*) albanés m.

albatross ['ælbətrɔs] n albatros m.

albeit [ɔ:l'bi:it] conj (*lit*) aunque, no obstante.

Albert ['ælbət] m Alberto.

albinism ['ælbinizəm] n albinismo m.

albino [æl'bi:nəu] **1** adj albino. **2** n albino m, a f.

Albion ['ælbiən] Albión f.

album ['ælbəm] n álbum m.

albumen ['ælbjumin] n (*Bot*) albumen m; (*Chem*) albúmina f.

albumin ['ælbjumin] n (*Chem*) albúmina f.

albuminous [æl'bju:minəs] adj albuminoso.

alchemist ['ælkimist] n alquimista m.

alchemy ['ælkimi] n alquimia f.

alcohol ['ælkəhɔl] n alcohol m.

alcoholic [,ælkə'hɔlik] **1** adj alcohólico. **2** n alcohólico m, a f, alcoholizado m, a f.

alcoholism ['ælkəhɔlizəm] n alcoholismo m; **to die of** — morir alcoholizado.

alcove ['ælkəuv] n hueco m.

alder ['ɔ:ldə*] n aliso m.

alderman ['ɔ:ldəmən] n, pl **—men** [mən] concejal m (de cierta antigüedad).

ale [eil] n cerveza f.

Alec ['ælik] *nombre cariñoso de* **Alexander;** (*fam*) **smart** — sabelotodo m.

alert [ə'lə:t] **1** adj alerta (*invariable:* eg **estaban alerta**); vigilante; *character* listo; (*wide-awake*) despierto, despabilado; *expression* vivo.

2 n alerta m, alarma f; **to be on the** — estar alerta, estar sobre aviso.

3 vt alertar, poner sobre aviso, avisar.

Alexander [,ælig'zɑ:ndə*] m Alejandro; — **the Great** Alejandro Magno.

Alexandria [,ælig'zɑ:ndriə] Alejandría.

alexandrine [,ælig'zændrain] n alejandrino m.

alfalfa [æl'fælfə] n alfalfa f.

Alfred ['ælfrid] m Alfredo.

alfresco [æl'freskəu] **1** adv al aire libre. **2** adj de aire libre, al aire libre.

alga ['ælgə] n, pl **algae** ['ældʒi:] alga f.

algebra ['ældʒibrə] n álgebra f.

algebraic [,ældʒi'breiik] adj algebraico, algébrico.

Algeria [æl'dʒiəriə] Argelia f.

Algerian [æl'dʒiəriən] **1** adj argelino. **2** n argelino m, a f.

Algiers [æl'dʒiəz] Argel m.
alias ['eiliæs] 1 adv alias, por otro nombre. 2 n alias m.
alibi ['ælibai] n coartada f; (excuse) excusa f, pretexto m.
Alice ['ælis] f Alicia; — **in Wonderland** Alicia en el país de las maravillas; — **through the Looking-glass** Alicia en el país del espejo.
alien ['eiliən] 1 adj ajeno, extraño (to a); (of foreign country) extranjero. 2 n extranjero m, a f.
alienate ['eiliəneit] vt property enajenar, traspasar; friend indisponerse con, alejar, ofender; other people ganarse la antipatía de; sympathies perder, enajenar.
alienation [,eiliə'neiʃən] n (of property) enajenación f, traspaso m; (of friend) alejamiento m; (Med) enajenación f mental.
alienist ['eiliənist] n alienista mf.
alight[1] [ə'lait] adj: **to be** — (fire) estar ardiendo, estar quemando; (light) estar encendido; **to set** — pegar fuego a, incendiar.
alight[2] [ə'lait] vi bajar, apearse (from de); (from air) posarse (on sobre); (Aer) aterrizar.
align [ə'lain] 1 vt alinear. 2 vr: **to** — **oneself with** ponerse al lado de.
alignment [ə'lainmənt] n alineación f; **in** — alineados, en línea recta; **out of** — fuera de alineación.
alike [ə'laik] 1 adj semejantes, parecidos, iguales; **you're all** —! ¡todos sois iguales!; **to look** — parecerse; **they all look** — **to me** yo no veo diferencia entre ellos, para mí todos son iguales.
2 adv del mismo modo, igualmente; **winter and summer** — tanto en invierno como en verano, lo mismo en invierno que en verano.
alimentary [,æli'mentəri] adj alimenticio; **canal** digestivo.
alimony ['æliməni] n alimentos mpl.
alive [ə'laiv] adj **(a)** **to be** — estar vivo, vivir; **to be still** — vivir todavía, estar todavía con vida; — **and kicking** vivito y coleando; **dead or** — vivo o muerto; **man** —! ¡hombre!; **he's the best footballer** — es el mejor futbolista de los que ahora viven; **it's good to be** —! ¡qué bueno es vivir!; **to be buried** — ser enterrado vivo; **to keep someone** — conservar con vida a uno; **to keep a tradition** — conservar una tradición; **to keep a memory** — guardar fresco un recuerdo.
(b) — **with** lleno de, hormigueante en, rebosante de.
(c) (fig) activo, enérgico; **look** —! ¡menéarse!
(d) (fig) — **to** sensible a, consciente de; **I am** — **to the danger** estoy consciente del peligro, me doy cuenta del peligro; **I am** — **to the fact that** no ignoro que; **I am fully** — **to the honour you do me** soy consciente del honor que se me hace.
alkali ['ælkəlai] n álcali m.
alkaline ['ælkəlain] adj alcalino.
alkaloid ['ælkəlɔid] n alcaloide m.
all [ɔːl] 1 adj todo, todos; — **day** todo el día; — **men** todos los hombres; — **Spain** toda España; (with it: subject) **it's** — **done** todo está hecho, (object) **he ate it all** se lo comió todo; **and** — **that** y cosas así, y otras cosas por el estilo; **it's not as bad as** — **that** no es para tanto; **for** — **that** con todo, con todo y con todo.
2 n **(a)** (sing) todo m, (pl) todos mpl, todas fpl; **my** — todo lo que tengo; — **(that) I can tell you is** lo único que puedo decirle es; — **is lost, it's** — **up** se acabó; **it's** — **up with him** no hay remedio para él; **that's** — nada más, eso es todo; **is that** —? ¿eso es todo?, ¿nada más?; **it cost him** — **of £50** le costó 50 libras largas; — **of us** todos nosotros, nosotros todos; **what with the rain and** — con la lluvia y todo.
(b) above — sobre todo; **after** — con todo, después de todo; **did you speak at** —? ¿dijiste algo?; **if I go at** — si es que voy; **if it's at** — **possible** si existe la menor posibilidad de ello; **not at** — de ninguna manera, nada de eso, (answer to thanks) de nada, no hay de qué; **not at** — **nice** nada agradable; **I'm not at** — **tired** no estoy cansado en lo más mínimo; **you mean he didn't sing at** —? ¿quieres decir que no cantó siquiera?; **I don't know him at** — no le conozco en absoluto; **for** — **I know** que yo sepa, quizá; **for** — **his boasting** a pesar de toda su jactancia; **50 men in** — 50 hombres en total; — **in** — con todo, en resumen; **most of** — más que nada, sobre todo.
3 adv completamente, enteramente, del todo; **dressed** — **in black** vestido enteramente de negro; **it's** — **dirty** está todo sucio; — **but casi**; **he** — **but died** casi murió, por poco se nos murió; **it's** — **but impossible** es punto menos que imposible; — **but 7**

todos menos 7; **to draw 2**— empatar a 2; see **in**, **over**, **right** etc.
Allah ['ælə] Alá.
allay [ə'lei] vt pain aliviar; fears aquietar.
all clear (signal) ['ɔːl'kliə(,signəl)] n cese m de alarma.
allegation [,æle'geiʃən] n aseveración f, alegación f.
allege [ə'ledʒ] vt declarar, afirmar, pretender (that que); (with n) alegar, pretextar; **he is** —**d to be wealthy** se pretende que es rico; **he is** —**d to be the leader** se dice que él es el jefe.
alleged [ə'ledʒd] adj supuesto, pretendido.
allegedly [ə'ledʒidli] adv según se afirma.
allegiance [ə'liːdʒəns] n lealtad f; **to owe** — **to** deber lealtad a; **to swear** — **to** rendir homenaje a.
allegoric(al) [,æli'gɔrik(əl)] adj alegórico.
allegorically [,æli'gɔrikəli] adv alegóricamente.
allegorize ['æligəraiz] vt alegorizar.
allegory ['æligəri] n alegoría f.
alleluia [,æli'luːjə] n aleluya f.
all-embracing ['ɔːlim'breisiŋ] adj que lo abarca todo, de vasto alcance, universal.
allergic [ə'ləːdʒik] adj alérgico (to a).
allergy ['ælədʒi] n alergia f.
alleviate [ə'liːvieit] vt aliviar, mitigar.
alleviation [ə,liːvi'eiʃən] n alivio m, mitigación f.
alley ['æli] n callejuela f, callejón m; (in park) paseo m; **blind** — callejón m sin salida (also fig).
alleyway ['æliwei] n see **alley.**
All Fools' Day ['ɔːl'fuːlzdei] n día m de inocentes (en Inglaterra el 1 abril, en España el 28 diciembre).
All Hallows' (Day) ['ɔːl'hæləuz(dei)] n Día m de Todos los Santos (1 noviembre).
alliance [ə'laiəns] n alianza f.
allied ['ælaid] adj conexo, parecido; — **to** (fig) relacionado con.
alligator ['æligeitə*] n caimán m.
all-important ['ɔːlim'pɔːtənt] adj sumamente importante, importantísimo.
all-in ['ɔːlin] adj sum global; charge todo incluido; wrestling libre.
alliteration [ə,litə'reiʃən] n aliteración f.
alliterative [ə'litərətiv] adj aliterado.
all-metal ['ɔːl'metl] adj enteramente metálico.
all-night ['ɔːl'nait] adj café abierto toda la noche; vigil, party, journey que dura toda la noche.
allocate ['æləukeit] vt asignar, señalar (to a); repartir, distribuir.
allocation [,æləu'keiʃən] n (act) asignación f; reparto m; (share, amount) ración f, cupo m, cuota f.
allot [ə'lɔt] vt asignar, adjudicar (to a).
allotment [ə'lɔtmənt] n (act) asignación f; (share) ración f, porción f; (land) parcela f.
all-out ['ɔːl'aut] 1 adj supporter acérrimo, incondicional; effort máximo; **to make an** — **attack on poverty** desplegar todas sus fuerzas para acabar con la pobreza.
2 adv all out con todas sus fuerzas; a fondo; (of speed) a máxima velocidad; **to go** — (Sport) emplearse a fondo; **to go** — **for something** volcarse por conseguir algo.
allover ['ɔːl'əuvə*] (US) 1 adj que tiene un diseño repetido sobre toda la superficie.
2 n tela f con diseño repetido sobre toda la superficie; diseño m repetido sobre toda la superficie.
allow [ə'lau] 1 vt **(a)** (with n) permitir; (grant) dar, conceder; request, claim admitir, aceptar; discount dar; allowance pagar, dar; **it** —**s very little time** deja muy poco tiempo; **how much should I** — **for expenses?** ¿cuánto debo poner para los gastos?; — **me!** permita que le ayude (etc).
(b) to — **to** + infin permitir + infin, dejar + infin, permitir que + subj; **it is not** —**ed to speak** no se permite hablar; **smoking not** —**ed** prohibido fumar.
(c) to — **that** reconocer que, confesar que; **he is** —**ed to be strong** se reconoce que es fuerte.
2 vi: **to** — **for** tener en cuenta, tomar en consideración; **after** —**ing for** después de considerar; **to** — **of** permitir; **it** —**s of no excuse** no admite disculpa.
allowable [ə'lauəbl] adj permisible; admisible; lícito; expense deducible.
allowance [ə'lauəns] n concesión f; (amount) ración f; (payment) subsidio m, subvención f, pago m, pensión f; (discount) descuento m, rebaja f; (Mech) tolerancia f; **family** — subsidio m familiar; **subsistence** — dietas fpl; **one must make** —**s** hay que ser comprensivo, hay que ser indulgente; **to make** —**(s) for someone** ser indulgente con uno, disculpar a uno; **to make** —**(s) for something** tener algo en cuenta.

alloy ['ælɔi] n aleación f, liga f; (fig) mezcla f.
alloy [ə'lɔi] vt alear, ligar.
all-powerful ['ɔːl'pauəful] adj omnipotente.
all-purpose ['ɔːl'pəːpəs] adj universal, para todo uso.
all-round ['ɔːl'raund] adj success etc completo; view amplio, global; person que hace de todo, hábil para todo.
all-rounder ['ɔːl'raundə*] n persona f (esp jugador m) que hace de todo.
All Saints' Day ['ɔːl'seintsdei] n Día m de Todos los Santos (1 noviembre).
All Souls' Day ['ɔːl'səulzdei] n Día m de Difuntòs (2 noviembre).
allspice ['ɔːlspais] n pimienta f inglesa.
all-star ['ɔːl'stɑː] adj compuesto de primeras figuras.
all-time ['ɔːl'taim] adj: an — record un récord mundial de todos los tiempos; exports have reached an — high las exportaciones han alcanzado cifras nunca conocidas antes; to reach an — low llegar al punto más bajo.
allude [ə'luːd] vi: to — to referirse a, aludir a.
allure [ə'ljuə*] 1 n atractivo m, encanto m, fascinación f; aliciente m. 2 vt atraer, captarse la voluntad de, tentar.
alluring [ə'ljuəriŋ] adj atractivo, seductor, tentador.
allusion [ə'luːʒən] n alusión f, referencia f (to a); he said in — to dijo refiriéndose a.
allusive [ə'luːsiv] adj alusivo, referente (to a); style lleno de alusiones.
alluvial [ə'luːviəl] adj aluvial.
alluvium [ə'luːviəm] n aluvión m, depósito m aluvial.
all-weather ['ɔːl'weðə*] adj para todo tiempo.
ally ['ælai] n aliado m; the Allies los Aliados.
ally [ə'lai] vr: to — oneself to (or with) aliarse con; (by marriage) emparentar con.
ally ['æli] n bolita f, canica f.
alma mater ['ælmə'meitə*] n alma mater f, universidad f donde uno se ha graduado.
almanac ['ɔːlmənæk] n almanaque m.
almighty [ɔːl'maiti] 1 adj omnipotente, todopoderoso; (fam) imponente, enorme de grande; the A— el Todopoderoso.
2 adv (fam) terriblemente, la mar de.
almond ['ɑːmənd] n (fruit) almendra f; (tree) almendro m; burnt —s almendras fpl dulces tostadas; sugar —s almendras fpl garapiñadas.
almond-eyed ['ɑːmənd'aid] adj de ojos almendrados.
almond oil ['ɑːmənd͜ɔil] n aceite m de almendra.
almond tree ['ɑːməndtriː] n almendro m.
almoner ['ɑːmənə*] n (Hist) limosnero m; (Med) oficial mf de asistencia social (de un hospital).
almost ['ɔːlməust] adv casi; he — died en poco estuvo que muriese, por poco se nos murió.
alms [ɑːmz] n sing and pl limosna f.
alms box ['ɑːmzbɔks] n cepillo m para los pobres.
alms house ['ɑːmzhaus] n, pl — houses [ˌhauziz] hospicio m, asilo m de pobres.
aloe ['æləu] n áloe m; —s (juice) acíbar m.
aloft [ə'lɔft] adv arriba, en alto; (Naut) en la arboladura.
alone [ə'ləun] 1 adj (a) solo; to be — estar solo, estar a solas; to be all — estar completamente solo; am I — in thinking so? ¿soy yo el único en pensar así?
(b) to leave someone — dejar a uno solo; to leave (or let) someone — (fig) no molestar a uno, dejar de molestar a uno; leave me —! ¡déjame en paz!; to leave (or let) something — no tocar algo; leave it —! ¡déjalo!; I advise you to let that severely — le aconsejo no meterse de ninguna manera en eso.
(c) let — (as prep etc) sin mencionar, sin tomar en cuenta; he can't read, let — write nada de escribir, no sabe leer siquiera.
2 adv solamente, sólo, únicamente; it is mine — es todo mío; you — can do it sólo Vd puede hacerlo.
along [ə'lɔŋ] 1 adv: all — desde el principio, todo el tiempo; — with junto con; I'll be — in a moment ahora voy.
2 prep (a) a lo largo de; — the river a lo largo del río; all — the street todo lo largo de la calle.
(b) por; to go — the tunnel ir por el túnel; it's — here es por aquí.
(c) sign — this line firme Vd en este renglón.
alongside [ə'lɔŋ'said] 1 adv (Naut) al costado, costado con costado; to bring — acostar; to come — atracarse al costado.
2 prep junto a, al lado de; (Naut) al costado de; to come — a ship atracarse al costado de un navío.
aloof [ə'luːf] 1 adj character reservado, frío; he was very — with me conmigo se mostró muy reservado.
2 adv: to keep (or stand) — mantenerse a distancia, mantenerse apartado (from de).

aloofness [ə'luːfnis] n reserva f, frialdad f.
alopecia [ˌæləu'piːʃə] n alopecia f.
aloud [ə'laud] adv en voz alta, alto.
alpaca [æl'pækə] n alpaca f.
alpenstock ['ælpinstɔk] n alpenstock m, bastón m montañero.
alpha ['ælfə] n alfa f.
alphabet ['ælfəbet] n alfabeto m.
alphabetic(al) [ˌælfə'betik(əl)] adj alfabético.
alphabetically [ˌælfə'betikəli] adv alfabéticamente, en orden alfabético.
Alphonso [æl'fɔnsəu] m Alfonso.
alpine ['ælpain] adj alpino, alpestre.
alpinist ['ælpinist] n alpinista mf.
Alps [ælps] pl Alpes mpl.
already [ɔːl'redi] adv ya.
Alsace ['ælsæs] Alsacia f.
Alsace-Lorraine ['ælsæslə'rein] Alsacia-Lorena f.
Alsatian [æl'seiʃən] 1 adj alsaciano. 2 n alsaciano m, a f; (dog) perro m lobo.
also ['ɔːlsəu] adv también, además.
altar ['ɔːltə*] n altar m; high — altar m mayor; on the —s of (fig) en aras de.
altar boy ['ɔːltəbɔi] n acólito m, monaguillo m.
altar cloth ['ɔːltəklɔθ] n sabanilla f, paño m de altar.
altarpiece ['ɔːltəpiːs] n retablo m.
alter ['ɔːltə*] 1 vt cambiar, modificar, (esp for the worse) alterar; (Archit) reformar; opinion, course etc cambiar de; that —s things la cosa cambia; circumstances — cases el caso depende de las circunstancias.
2 vi cambiar(se), mudarse; I find him much —ed le veo muy cambiado.
alteration [ˌɔːltə'reiʃən] n cambio m, modificación f, (esp for the worse) alteración f (in, to de); —s (Archit) reformas fpl.
altercation [ˌɔːltə'keiʃən] n altercado m.
alter ego ['æltər'iːgəu] n álter ego m.
alternate [ɔl'təːnit] adj alterno, alternativo; on — days un día sí y otro no, cada dos días.
alternate ['ɔːltəneit] vi alternar.
alternately [ɔl'təːnitli] adv alternativamente; por turno.
alternating ['ɔːltəneitiŋ] adj alterno.
alternation [ˌɔːltə'neiʃən] n alternación f; in — alternativamente.
alternative [ɔl'təːnətiv] 1 adj alternativo.
2 n alternativa f; I have no — no tengo más remedio, no puedo hacer otra cosa; you have no — but to go Vd no tiene más remedio que ir.
alternatively [ɔl'təːnətivli] adv por otra parte.
alternator ['ɔːltəneitə*] n alternador m.
although [ɔːl'ðəu] conj aunque; si bien.
altimeter ['æltimitə*] n altímetro m.
altitude ['æltitjuːd] n altitud f, altura f.
alto ['æltəu] 1 adj alto; — saxophone saxofón m alto. 2 n contralto f.
altogether [ˌɔːltə'geðə*] adv (a) en conjunto, en total; how many are there —? ¿cuántos hay en total?; in the — (fam) en cueros.
(b) enteramente; del todo; we haven't — finished no hemos terminado del todo; I'm not — sure no estoy del todo seguro; this is — too hard esto es demasiado difícil con mucho; you're — wrong Vd está completamente equivocado.
altruism ['æltruizəm] n altruismo m.
altruist ['æltruist] n altruista mf.
altruistic [ˌæltru'istik] adj altruista.
alum ['æləm] n alumbre m.
aluminium [ˌælju'miniəm] n, **aluminum** [ə'luːminəm] n (US) aluminio m.
alumnus [ə'lamnəs] nm, pl **alumni** [ə'lamnai]; **alumna** [ə'lamnə] nf, pl **alumnae** [ə'lamni] (US) graduado m, a f.
alveolar [æl'viələ*] adj alveolar.
always ['ɔːlweiz] adv siempre; as — como siempre.
am [æm] see be.
amalgam [ə'mælgəm] n amalgama f.
amalgamate [ə'mælgəmeit] 1 vt amalgamar; companies etc unir. 2 vi amalgamarse; unirse.
amalgamation [əˌmælgə'meiʃən] n amalgamación f; unión f.
amanuensis [əˌmænju'ensis] n, pl **amanuenses** [əˌmænju'ensiːz] amanuense m.
Amaryllis [ˌæmə'rilis] f Amarilis.
amass [ə'mæs] vt amontonar, acumular.
amateur ['æmətə*] 1 n amateur mf, aficionado m, a f; (pej) principiante mf, chapucero m.
2 adj see amateurish; — tennis tenis m para aficionados (or amateur); I have an — interest in pottery me interesa como aficionado la cerámica.

amateurish ['æmətəriʃ] *adj* superficial, inexperto, torpe, chapucero.

amateurism ['æmətərizəm] *n* amateurismo *m*, estado *m* de aficionado; **there must be room for — in sport** en los deportes debe haber sitio para los aficionados.

amatory ['æmətəri] *adj* amatorio, erótico.

amaze [ə'meiz] *vt* asombrar, pasmar; **to be —d** quedar estupefacto; **to be —d at** asombrarse de; **you — me!** ¡me admiras!

amazement [ə'meizmənt] *n* asombro *m*, sorpresa *f*, estupefacción *f*; **they looked on in —** miraron asombrados; **the news caused general —** se asombraron todos al saber la noticia.

amazing [ə'meiziŋ] *adj* asombroso, pasmoso; **he's an — man** es un hombre extraordinario.

amazingly [ə'meiziŋli] *adv* milagrosamente, por maravilla; **— enough** aunque parece mentira; **—, nobody was killed** por milagro, no hubo víctimas; **he did — well** tuvo un éxito formidable; **he is — fit for his age** su estado físico es extraordinario para un hombre de su edad.

Amazon[1] ['æməzən] *n* (*Myth*) amazona *f*; (*fig*) marimacho *m*.

Amazon[2] ['æməzən] (*Geog*) Amazonas *m*.

ambassador [æm'bæsədə*] *n* embajador *m*.

ambassadorial [æm,bæsə'dɔ:riəl] *adj* embajatorio.

ambassadorship [æm'bæsədəʃip] *n* embajada *f*.

amber ['æmbə*] **1** *n* ámbar *m*. **2** *adj* ambarino, color de ámbar; *traffic light* amarillo.

ambergris ['æmbəgri:s] *n* ámbar *m* gris.

ambidextrous [,æmbi'dekstrəs] *adj* ambidextro.

ambient ['æmbiənt] *adj* ambiente.

ambiguity [,æmbi'gjuiti] *n* (*quality*) ambigüedad *f*; (*of meaning*) doble sentido *m*.

ambiguous [æm'bigjuəs] *adj* ambiguo; (*in bad sense*) doble, equívoco.

ambit ['æmbit] *n* ámbito *m*.

ambition [æm'biʃən] *n* ambición *f*; **to have an — for** ambicionar; **to have an — to be** ambicionar ser.

ambitious [æm'biʃəs] *adj* ambicioso; *idea, plan* grandioso; **to be — of** ambicionar.

ambitiously [æm'biʃəsli] *adv* ambiciosamente; grandiosamente.

ambivalence [æm'bivələns] ambivalencia *f*; (*pej*) lo equívoco, lo doble.

ambivalent [æm'bivələnt] *adj* ambivalente; (*pej*) equívoco, doble.

amble ['æmbl] **1** *n* (*horse*) paso *m* de andadura; **to walk at an —** (*person*) andar muy despacio.

2 *vi* (*horse*) amblar; (*person*) andar muy despacio; **he —d up to me** se acercó despacio a mí.

Ambrose ['æmbrəuz] *m* Ambrosio.

ambrosia [æm'brəuziə] *n* ambrosía *f*.

ambulance ['æmbjuləns] *n* ambulancia *f*; **— man** ambulanciero *m*.

ambush ['æmbuʃ] **1** *n* emboscada *f*; **to fall into an —** caer en una emboscada; **to lay an —** tender una emboscada (*for* a); **to lie in —** estar emboscado (*for* para coger).

2 *vt* tender una emboscada a, coger por sorpresa; **to be —ed** caer en una emboscada.

ameba [ə'mi:bə] *n* = amoeba.

ameliorate [ə'mi:liəreit] **1** *vt* mejorar. **2** *vi* mejorar(se).

amelioration [ə,mi:liə'reiʃən] *n* mejora *f*, mejoramiento *m*.

amen ['ɑ:'men] *interj* amén.

amenable [ə'mi:nəbl] *adj* sumiso, dócil, tratable; (*Law*) responsable; **— to argument** que se deja convencer; **— to reason** que se deja convencer por la lógica; **— to treatment** (*Med*) susceptible de ser curado, curable.

amend [ə'mend] *vt* enmendar; rectificar, corregir.

amendment [ə'mendmənt] *n* enmienda *f*; rectificación *f*, corrección *f*.

amends [ə'mendz] *n sing*: **to make —** dar cumplida satisfacción, enmendarlo; **to make — for** dar satisfacción por, enmendar, expiar.

amenity [ə'mi:niti] *n* (*pleasantness*) amenidad *f*; (*pleasant thing*) atractivo *m*, cosa *f* agradable; **amenities** atractivos *mpl*, conveniencias *fpl*, comodidades *fpl*; **the amenities of life** las cosas agradables de la vida; **a house with all amenities** una casa con todo confort.

America [ə'merikə] América *f*; (*USA*) Estados *mpl* Unidos.

American [ə'merikən] **1** *adj* americano; (*of USA*) norteamericano, estadounidense.

2 *n* americano *m*, a *f*; (*of USA*) norteamericano *m*, a *f*, estadounidense *mf*.

americanism [ə'merikənizəm] *n* americanismo *m*.

americanize [ə'merikənaiz] *vt* americanizar; **to become —d** americanizarse.

amethyst ['æmiθist] *n* amatista *f*.

amiability [,eimiə'biliti] *n* afabilidad *f*, amabilidad *f*.

amiable ['eimiəbl] *adj* afable, amable, simpático; bonachón.

amiably ['eimiəbli] *adv* afablemente, amablemente.

amicable ['æmikəbl] *adj* amistoso, amigable.

amicably ['æmikəbli] *adv* amistosamente, amigablemente.

amid [ə'mid] *prep* en medio de, entre.

amidships [ə'midʃips] *adv* en medio del navío.

amidst [ə'midst] *prep* = amid.

amiss [ə'mis] *adv*: **there's something —** pasa algo malo, no va todo bien; (*with machine etc*) esto no marcha bien; **what's —?** ¿qué pasa?; **what's — with him?** ¿qué le pasa?; **it would not be — for him to** + *infin* no le estaría mal + *infin*; **a cup of tea would not come —** me gustaría mucho una taza de té; **a little politeness would not come —** no le vendría mal un poco de cortesía; **to take something —** llevar algo a mal; **don't take it —, will you?** ¿no te vas a ofender, eh?

amity ['æmiti] *n* concordia *f*, amistad *f*.

ammeter ['æmitə*] *n* amperímetro *m*.

ammo ['æməu] *n* (*Mil sl*) = ammunition.

ammonia [ə'məuniə] *n* amoníaco *m*; **liquid —** amoníaco *m* líquido.

ammunition [,æmju'niʃən] *n* municiones *fpl*; (*fig*) argumentos *mpl*, artillería *f*.

ammunition dump [,æmju'niʃən'dʌmp] *n* depósito *m* de municiones.

amnesia [æm'ni:ziə] *n* amnesia *f*.

amnesty ['æmnisti] **1** *n* amnistía *f*, indulto *m* general; **to grant an —** amnistiar. **2** *vt* amnistiar, indultar.

amoeba [ə'mi:bə] *n* amiba *f*.

amok [ə'mɔk] *adv see* amuck.

among(st) [ə'mʌŋ(st)] *prep* entre, en medio de; **from —** de entre; **he is — those who** es de los que; **it is not — the names I have** no figura entre los nombres que tengo.

amoral [æ'mɔrəl] *adj* amoral.

amorous ['æmərəs] *adj* amoroso; enamorado, enamoradizo; **an — old man** un viejo mujeriego.

amorously ['æmərəsli] *adv* amorosamente.

amorphous [ə'mɔ:fəs] *adj* amorfo, sin forma fija.

amortize [ə'mɔ:taiz] *vt* amortizar.

amount [ə'maunt] **1** *n* cantidad *f*; (*of bill etc*) suma *f*, importe *m*; **in small —s** en pequeñas cantidades; **to the — of** hasta un total de; por la suma de, por el valor de; **we used to drink any — of** that bebíamos grandes cantidades de eso; **we have had any — of trouble** hemos tenido la mar de dificultades.

2 *vi*: **to — to** ascender a, sumar, subir a; (*fig*) equivaler a, significar; **it —s to the same thing es** igual, viene a ser lo mismo; **this —s to a refusal** esto equivale a una negativa; **he'll never — to much** siempre será una nulidad, es un pobre hombre.

amour [ə'muə*] *n* amorío *m*, intriga *f* amorosa.

amour-propre ['æmuə'prɔpr] *n* amor *m* propio.

amp [æmp] *n*, **ampère** ['æmpeə*] *n* amperio *m*.

ampersand ['æmpəsænd] *n* el signo & (*que significa* and, et).

amphibia [æm'fibiə] *npl* anfibios *mpl*.

amphibian [æm'fibiən] **1** *adj* anfibio. **2** *n* anfibio *m*.

amphibious [æm'fibiəs] *adj* anfibio.

amphitheatre ['æmfi,θiətə*] *n* anfiteatro *m*.

Amphitryon [æm'fitriən] *m* Anfitrión.

amphora ['æmfərə] *n* ánfora *f*.

ample ['æmpl] *adj* (*spacious*) amplio, ancho, extenso; (*abundant*) liberal, abundante; (*enough*) bastante, suficiente.

amplification [,æmplifi'keiʃən] *n* amplificación *f*; explicación *f*.

amplifier ['æmplifaiə*] *n* amplificador *m*.

amplify ['æmplifai] *vt* amplificar (*also Radio*), aumentar; *statement etc* explicar, añadir comentarios a.

amplitude ['æmplitju:d] *n* amplitud *f*.

amply ['æmpli] *adv* bastante, suficientemente; abundantemente; **you were — justified** Vd tuvo plenamente razón; **we are — supplied with food** tenemos abundancia de comida.

ampoule ['æmpu:l] *n* ampolla *f*.

amputate ['æmpjuteit] *vt* amputar.

amputation [,æmpju'teiʃən] *n* amputación *f*.

amuck [ə'mʌk] *adv*: **to run —** enloquecer, desbocarse; (*fig*) conducirse como un loco, hacer locuras, mostrarse violento, atacar a ciegas.

amulet ['æmjulit] *n* amuleto *m*.

amuse [ə'mju:z] **1** vt divertir, entretener, distraer; **to be —d at** (or **by**) divertirse con, reírse con; **we are not —d** no nos cae en gracia.

2 vr: **to — oneself** distraerse (doing haciendo); **run along and — yourselves** idos a jugar; **you'll have to — yourselves for a time** tendréis que buscaros algo en que ocuparos durante un rato.

amusement [ə'mju:zmənt] n (a) (amusing thing) diversión f, entretenimiento m; **— park** parque m de atracciones; **place of —** sitio m de recreo.

(b) (pastime) pasatiempo m, recreo m; **they do it for —** only lo hacen sólo para divertirse, es un pasatiempo nada más.

(c) (laughter) risa f; **there was general — at this** al oír esto se rieron todos; **much to my —** con gran regocijo mío.

amusing [ə'mju:ziŋ] adj divertido, gracioso.

amusingly [ə'mju:ziŋli] adv de modo divertido, graciosamente.

an [æn, ən, n] indef art see **a**.

anachronism [ə'nækrənizm] n anacronismo m.

anachronistic [ə,nækrə'nistik] adj anacrónico.

anaconda [,ænə'kɔndə] n anaconda f.

Anacreon [ə'nækriən] m Anacreonte.

anaemia [ə'ni:miə] n anemia f.

anaemic [ə'ni:mik] adj anémico; (fig) soso, insípido, débil.

anaesthesia [,ænis'θi:ziə] n anestesia f.

anaesthetic [,ænis'θetik] **1** adj anestésico. **2** n anestésico m.

anaesthetist [æ'ni:sθitist] n anestesista mf.

anaesthetize [æ'ni:sθitaiz] vt anestesiar.

anagram ['ænəgræm] n anagrama m.

anal ['einəl] adj anal.

analgesia [ænæl'dʒi:ziə] n analgesia f.

analgesic [,ænæl'dʒi:sik] **1** adj analgésico. **2** n analgésico m.

analogical [,ænə'lɔdʒikəl] adj analógico.

analogous [ə'næləgəs] adj análogo (to a); afín, semejante.

analogue ['ænəlɔg] n análogo m.

analogy [ə'nælədʒi] n analogía f; afinidad f, semejanza f; **on the — of** por analogía con; **to draw an — between** hacer ver la semejanza que existe entre.

analyse, (US) **analyze** ['ænəlaiz] vt analizar.

analysis [ə'næləsis] n, pl **analyses** [ə'nælisi:z] análisis m; **in the last —** en último término, en fin de cuentas.

analyst ['ænəlist] n analizador m; **public —** jefe m del laboratorio municipal.

analytic(al) [,ænə'litik(əl)] adj analítico.

anapaest ['ænəpi:st] n anapesto m.

anarchic(al) [æ'nɑ:kik(əl)] adj anárquico.

anarchism ['ænəkizm] n anarquismo m.

anarchist ['ænəkist] n anarquista mf.

anarchy ['ænəki] n anarquía f, desorden m.

anathema [ə'næθimə] n anatema m.

anathematize [ə'næθimətaiz] vt anatematizar.

anatomical [,ænə'tɔmikəl] adj anatómico.

anatomize [ə'nætəmaiz] vt anatomizar; (fig) analizar minuciosamente.

anatomy [ə'nætəmi] n anatomía f; (fig) cuerpo m, carnes fpl.

ancestor ['ænsistə*] n antepasado m; **—s** pl abuelos mpl.

ancestral [æn'sestrəl] adj ancestral, hereditario; **— home** casa f solariega, solar m.

ancestry ['ænsistri] n ascendencia f, abolengo m, linaje m.

anchor ['æŋkə*] **1** n ancla f, áncora f; **to be** (or **lie, ride**) **at —** estar al ancla, estar anclado; **to cast** (or **drop**) **—** echar anclas; **to weigh —** levar anclas.

2 vt poner sobre el ancla; (fig) sujetar, asegurar. **3** vi anclar, fondear.

anchorage ['æŋkəridʒ] n ancladero m, fondeadero m.

anchorite ['æŋkərait] n anacoreta mf.

anchovy ['æntʃəvi] n anchoa f.

ancient ['einʃənt] adj antiguo; **the —s** los antiguos; **he's getting pretty —** (fam) va para viejo.

ancillary [æn'siləri] adj subordinado (to a), auxiliar, secundario.

and [ænd, ənd, nd, ən] conj (a) y, (before i-, hi-) e; **—?** ¿y después?, ¿y qué más?; **better — better** cada vez mejor; **more — more** cada vez más.

(b) (negative sense) ni: **you can't buy — sell here** aquí no se permite comprar ni vender.

(c) **he talked — talked, but ...** habló incansablemente, pero ..., por mucho que hablase, no ...

(d) (before infins) **try — do it** trata de hacerlo, hazlo si puedes; **come — see me** ven a verme.

Andalusia [,ændə'lu:ziə] Andalucía f.

Andalusian [,ændə'lu:ziən] **1** adj andaluz. **2** n andaluz m, uza f.

Andean ['ændiən] adj andino.

Andes ['ændi:z] pl Andes mpl.

andiron ['ændaiən] n morillo m.

Andrew ['ændru:] m Andrés.

anecdote ['ænikdəut] n anécdota f.

anemia [ə'ni:miə] n etc = **anaemia** etc.

anemone [ə'neməni] n (Bot) anemone f; (Zool) anémona f (de mar).

aneroid ['ænərɔid] adj aneroide; **— barometer** barómetro m aneroide.

anesthesia [,ænis'θi:ziə] n etc = **anaesthesia** etc.

anew [ə'nju:] adv de nuevo, otra vez.

angel ['eindʒəl] n ángel m; **yes, (my) —!** ¡sí, querida!; **guardian —** ángel m custodio, ángel m de la guarda; **talk of —s!** hablando del ruin de Roma, por la puerta asoma.

angelic(al) [æn'dʒelik(əl)] adj angélico.

angelica [æn'dʒelikə] n angélica f.

angelus ['ændʒiləs] n ángelus m.

anger ['æŋgə*] **1** n cólera f, ira f; **to rouse someone to —** provocar a uno a cólera, encolerizar a uno; **to speak in —** hablar indignado, hablar coléricamente. **2** vt enojar, provocar, encolerizar.

angina pectoris [æn'dʒainə'pektəris] n angina f del pecho.

angle[1] ['æŋgl] n (a) ángulo m; **acute —** ángulo m agudo; **alternate —** ángulo m alterno; **obtuse —** ángulo m obtuso; **right —** ángulo m recto; **— iron** hierro m angular; **— of climb** (Aer) ángulo m de subida; **it is leaning at an — of 80°** esta ladeado en un ángulo de 80°; **to be at an —** to formar ángulo con; **to look at a building from a different —** contemplar un edificio desde otro sitio, tener de un edificio una nueva perspectiva.

(b) (fig) punto m de vista; opinión f; **look at it from my —** considere la cosa desde mi punto de vista; **he has a different —** tiene otro modo de enfocar la cuestión; **that's a new — to the problem** ése es otro aspecto nuevo del problema.

angle[2] ['æŋgl] vi pescar con caña (for a fish un pez); **to — for** (fig) ir a la caza de, intrigar por conseguir.

angler ['æŋglə*] n pescador m (de caña).

Angles ['æŋglz] npl anglos mpl.

Anglican ['æŋglikən] **1** adj anglicano. **2** n anglicano m, a f.

Anglicanism ['æŋglikənizəm] n anglicanismo m.

anglicism ['æŋglisizəm] n anglicismo m, inglesismo m.

anglicist ['æŋglisist] n anglicista mf.

anglicize ['æŋglisaiz] vt inglesar.

angling ['æŋgliŋ] n pesca f con caña.

Anglo ... ['æŋgləu] anglo . . .

Anglo-Catholic ['æŋgləu'kæθlik] **1** adj anglo-católico. **2** n anglocatólico m, a f.

Anglo-Catholicism ['æŋgləukə'θɔlisizəm] n anglo-catolicismo m.

Anglo-Indian ['æŋgləu'indiən] **1** adj angloindio. **2** n angloindio m, a f.

anglophile ['æŋgləufail] n anglófilo m, a f.

anglophobe ['æŋgləufəub] n anglófobo m, a f.

Anglo-Saxon ['æŋgləu'sæksən] **1** adj anglosajón. **2** n anglosajón m, ona f. **3** n (language) anglosajón m.

angora [æŋ'gɔ:rə] n angora mf.

Angoulême [ɑ̃:ŋgu'lɛm] Angulema.

angrily ['æŋgrili] adv coléricamente, airadamente.

angry ['æŋgri] **1** adj colérico, enojado, enfadado, airado; (Med) inflamado; **sky** tormentoso, que amenaza tormenta; **in an — voice** en tono colérico; **— young man** joven m airado; **to be — enfadado** (about por; at, with con); **you won't be — if I tell you?** no te vayas a ofender si te lo digo; **to get —** enfadarse, ponerse furioso, indignarse; **to make someone —** irritar a uno, provocar a uno; **this sort of thing makes me —** estas cosas me sacan de quicio.

2 n: **the angries** los airados mpl.

anguish ['æŋgwiʃ] n (bodily) dolor m agudo, tormentos mpl; (mental) angustia f.

anguished ['æŋgwiʃt] adj acongojado, afligido, angustiado.

angular ['æŋgjulə*] adj angular; **face** etc anguloso.

aniline ['ænili:n] n anilina f; **— dyes** colores mpl de anilina.

animal ['æniməl] **1** adj animal. **2** n animal m; (horse etc) bestia f; (insect etc) bicho m.

animate ['ænimit] adj vivo, que tiene vida.

animate ['ænimeit] vt animar, infundir vida a; vivificar, estimular; alentar.

animated ['ænimeitid] adj vivo, vivaz, vigoroso; **discussion** vivo; **— cartoon** película f de dibujos.

animatedly ['ænimeitidli] adv **talk** etc animadamente.

animation [ˌæni'meiʃən] n vivacidad f, viveza f, animación f; **suspended** — muerte f aparente.

animosity [ˌæni'mɔsiti] n animosidad f, rencor m, hostilidad f.

animus ['æniməs] n odio m, rencor m.

anise ['ænis] n anís m.

aniseed ['ænisi:d] n anís m; (strictly) grano m de anís.

anisette [ˌæni'zet] n anisete m, anís m.

Anjou [ɑ̃:ŋ'ʒu:] Anjeo m.

ankle ['æŋkl] n tobillo m.

anklebone ['æŋklbəun] n hueso m del tobillo.

ankle-deep ['æŋkl'di:p] adv: **to be — in something** estar metido hasta los tobillos en algo; **the water is only** — el agua llega a los tobillos nada más.

anklet ['æŋklit] n brazalete m para el tobillo, ajorca f para el pie.

ankle sock ['æŋklsɔk] n escarpín m.

Ann [æn] f Ana; **— Boleyn** Ana Bolena.

annalist ['ænəlist] n analista mf, cronista mf.

annals ['ænəlz] npl anales mpl, crónica f; **never in the — of human endeavour** nunca en la historia de los esfuerzos humanos.

Anne [æn] f Ana; **Queen —'s dead!** eso lo tenemos archisabido.

anneal [ə'ni:l] vt recocer; templar.

annex [ə'neks] vt territory anexar; document adjuntar, añadir (to a).

annexation [ˌænek'seiʃən] n anexión f.

annexe ['æneks] n pabellón m separado, dependencia f, edificio m anexo.

annihilate [ə'naiəleit] vt aniquilar.

annihilation [əˌnaiə'leiʃən] n aniquilación f, aniquilamiento m.

anniversary [ˌæni'və:səri] n aniversario m; **— dinner** banquete m para festejar el aniversario de . . .

Anno Domini ['ænəu'dɔminai] (gen abbr A.D.) (a) 250 — el año 250 después de Jesucristo; **the second century** — el siglo segundo de Cristo. (b) (fam) vejez f, edad f.

annotate ['ænəuteit] vt anotar, comentar.

annotation [ˌænəu'teiʃən] n anotación f, apunte m; **a book with —s by X** un libro con notas de X.

announce [ə'nauns] vt anunciar; proclamar; declarar; hacer saber, comunicar; **then he —d "I won't"** luego declaró "No quiero"; **it is —d from London that** se comunica desde Londres que; **we regret to — the death of** lamentamos tener que participar la muerte de.

announcement [ə'naunsmənt] n anuncio m; proclama f; declaración f; aviso m; **— of birth** natalicio m; **— of death** necrológica f.

announcer [ə'naunsə*] n (Radio) locutor m, ora f.

annoy [ə'nɔi] vt molestar, fastidiar, irritar; **to be —ed** estar enfadado (about por; at, with con); **to get —ed** enfadarse, molestarse, incomodarse.

annoyance [ə'nɔiəns] n (state) enojo m, irritación f; (thing) molestia f.

annoying [ə'nɔiiŋ] adj molesto, fastidioso, engorroso; person pesado, importuno; **it's — to have to + infin** me molesta tener que + infin.

annoyingly [ə'nɔiiŋli] adv de modo fastidioso; pesadamente, importunamente; **and then, — enough . . .** y luego, para fastidiarnos . . .; **the radio was** — loud la radio nos molestó con su ruido.

annual ['ænjuəl] **1** adj anual. **2** n (book) anuario m; (Bot) planta f anual, anual m.

annually ['ænjuəli] adv anualmente, cada año; **£500** — 500 libras al año.

annuity [ə'nju:iti] n (also life —) renta f vitalicia, pensión f vitalicia; **deferred** — cuota f de pensión; **to settle an — on** señalar una renta a.

annul [ə'nʌl] vt anular, invalidar; cancelar; law revocar.

annulment [ə'nʌlmənt] n anulación f; cancelación f; revocación f.

Annunciation [əˌnʌnsi'eiʃən] n Anunciación f.

anode ['ænəud] n ánodo m.

anodyne ['ænəudain] **1** adj anodino. **2** n anodino m.

anoint [ə'nɔint] vt untar; (Eccl) ungir.

anomalous [ə'nɔmələs] adj anómalo.

anomaly [ə'nɔməli] n anomalía f.

anon¹ [ə'nɔn] adv (arch) luego, dentro de poco; **ever and** — a menudo, de vez en cuando.

anon² [ə'nɔn] abbr = **anonymous.**

anonymity [ˌænə'nimiti] n (in general) anonimato m; (special case) anónimo m; **to preserve one's** — conservar el anónimo.

anonymous [ə'nɔniməs] adj anónimo; **he wishes to remain** — no quiere que se publique su nombre.

anonymously [ə'nɔniməsli] adv anónimamente; **the book came out** — salió el libro sin nombre de autor; **he gave £100** — dio 100 libras sin revelar su nombre.

anorak ['ænəræk] n anorak m.

another [ə'nʌðə*] **1** adj otro (no art needed, eg — **man** otro hombre); — **glass?** ¿otra copita?; **in — 10 years** en otros 10 años; **we need** — **2 men** necesitamos 2 hombres más; **there are** — **2 months to go** faltan todavía 2 meses; **that is** — **matter altogether** eso es un asunto totalmente distinto; **without** — **word** sin decir palabra.

2 pron otro m, otra f; **just such** — otro tal; — **would have done it this way** cualquier otro lo hubiera hecho de este modo.

3 reflexive pron: **they love one** — (2 persons) se quieren (uno a otro), (more than 2 persons) se quieren unos a otros; **they don't speak to one** — no se hablan.

answer ['ɑ:nsə*] **1** n (a) (to question etc) contestación f, respuesta f (to a); (Law) contestación f a la demanda, réplica f; **in** — **to** contestando a; **he smiled in** — contestó con una sonrisa; **his only** — **was to smile** por toda respuesta, se sonrió; **to know all the** —**s** saberlo todo, ser una hacha; **he's not exactly the** — **to a maiden's prayer** no es precisamente el hombre soñado.

(b) (to problem) solución f (to de); **what do you make the** —**?** ¿qué solución tienes?; **my** — **is to do nothing** yo lo resolvería no haciendo nada; **there is no easy** — esto no se resuelve fácilmente.

(c) (defence, reason) **there must be an** — debe de haber una razón, debe de haber una explicación; **he's got an** — **to everything** lo justifica todo; **he has a complete** — **to the charges** puede probar su inocencia; **there is no** — **to the H-bomb** contra la bomba H no hay defensa posible.

2 vt (a) contestar a, responder a; letter contestar (a); **that should** — **your question** eso debe resolver (or satisfacer) sus dudas; **God will** — **our prayers** Dios escuchará nuestras oraciones; **our prayers have been** —**ed** nuestras súplicas han sido oídas; **to** — **the bell, to** — **the door** acudir a la puerta; **to** — **the telephone** contestar el teléfono; **to** — **one's name** contestar a su nombre; **to** — **a call for help** acudir a una llamada de socorro; **to** — **the helm** obedecer al timón.

(b) description corresponder a, cuadrar con; expectations corresponder a; purpose convenir para.

3 vi (a) contestar, responder; **to** — **back** replicar, ser respondón; **don't** — **back!** ¡no repliques!; **to** — **for thing** responder de, ser responsable de, person responder por; **I'll not** — **for the consequences** yo no me considero responsable de las consecuencias; **he's got a lot to** — **for** tiene la culpa de muchas cosas; **to** — **to the name of** (dog) atender por.

(b) (suffice) servir, convenir.

(c) **to** — **to** description corresponder a, cuadrar con.

answerable ['ɑ:nsərəbl] adj (a) **to be** — **to someone for something** ser responsable ante uno de algo; **he's not** — **to anyone** no tiene que dar cuentas a nadie.

(b) **the question is not** — el problema no tiene solución.

ant [ænt] n hormiga f.

antacid ['ænt'æsid] **1** adj antiácido. **2** n antiácido m.

antagonism [æn'tægənizəm] n antagonismo m; oposición f, hostilidad f (to a); rivalidad f (between entre).

antagonist [æn'tægənist] n antagonista mf, adversario m, a f.

antagonistic [ænˌtægə'nistik] adj antagónico; contrario, opuesto (to a).

antagonize [æn'tægənaiz] vt enemistarse con, provocar la enemistad de; **he managed to** — **everybody** logró ponerse a malas con todo el mundo.

Antarctic [ænt'ɑ:ktik] **1** adj antártico. **2** n: **the** — el Antártico.

Antarctica [ænt'ɑ:ktikə] Antártida f.

Antarctic Circle [ænt'ɑ:ktik'sə:kl] n Círculo m Polar Antártico.

ante ['ænti] (US) **1** n apuesta f, tanto m. **2** vt apostar. **3** vi poner su apuesta; (fig, also to — **up**) contribuir, pagar su cuota.

anteater ['ænt,i:tə*] n oso m hormiguero.

antecedent [ˌænti'si:dənt] **1** adj antecedente. **2** n antecedente m; —**s** antecedentes mpl.

antechamber ['ænti,tʃeimbə*] n antecámara f.

antedate ['ænti'deit] vt (a) **this building** —**s the Norman conquest** este edificio se construyó antes de la conquista normanda; **this text** —**s that by 50 years** este texto es anterior a ése en 50 años.

(b) cheque etc antedatar.

antediluvian ['æntidi'lu:viən] adj antediluviano.

antelope ['æntiləup] n antílope m.

antenatal ['ænti'neitl] *adj* antenatal.

antenna [æn'tenə] *n, pl* **antennae** [æn'teniː] antena *f*.

antepenultimate ['æntipi'nʌltimit] *adj* antepenúltimo.

anterior [æn'tiəriə*] *adj* anterior (*to* a).

anteroom ['æntirum] *n* antecámara *f*.

anthem ['ænθəm] *n* (*Eccl*) antífona *f*, motete *m*; **national —** himno *m* nacional.

anther ['ænθə*] *n* antera *f*.

ant-hill ['ænthil] *n* hormiguero *m*.

anthology [æn'θɔlədʒi] *n* antología *f*.

Anthony ['æntəni] *m* Antonio.

anthracite ['ænθrəsait] *n* antracita *f*.

anthrax ['ænθræks] *n* ántrax *m*.

anthropoid ['ænθrəupɔid] **1** *adj* antropoide. **2** *n* antropoideo *m*.

anthropological [,ænθrəpə'lɔdʒikəl] *adj* antropológico.

anthropologist [,ænθrə'pɔlədʒist] *n* antropólogo *m*.

anthropology [,ænθrə'pɔlədʒi] *n* antropología *f*.

anthropomorphism [,ænθrəupə'mɔːfizəm] *n* antropomorfismo *m*.

anthropophagi [,ænθrəu'pɔfəgai] *npl* antropófagos *mpl*.

anti . . . ['ænti] *in compounds*: anti . . .; **he's rather —** (*fam*) está más bien opuesto a ello.

anti-aircraft ['ænti'ɛəkrɑːft] *adj* antiaéreo; **— gun** cañón *m* antiaéreo.

antibiotic ['æntibai'ɔtik] **1** *adj* antibiótico. **2** *n* antibiótico *m*.

antibody ['ænti,bɔdi] *n* anticuerpo *m*.

Antichrist ['æntikraist] *n* Anticristo *m*.

anticipate [æn'tisipeit] *vt* (a) (*forestall*) *person* anticiparse a, adelantarse a; *event* anticiparse a, prevenir; *pleasure* disfrutar de antemano.

(b) (*foresee*) prever; **you have —d my wishes** Vd se ha anticipado (*or* adelantado) a mis deseos; **you have —d my orders** Vd se ha anticipado a mis órdenes, (*wrongly*) Vd ha obrado sin esperar mis órdenes.

(c) (*expect*) esperar; contar con; **this is more than I —d** esto es más de lo que esperaba; **the police —d trouble** la policía contaba con algunos disturbios; **to — that** prever que, calcular que; **do you — that this will be easy?** ¿crees que esto va a resultar fácil?

(d) (*look forward to*) prometerse.

anticipation [æn,tisi'peiʃən] *n* (a) (*forestalling*) anticipación *f*, prevención *f*.

(b) (*foresight*) previsión *f*, prevención *f*; **in — de** antemano.

(c) (*foretaste*) anticipación *f*.

(d) (*expectation*) esperanza *f*, esperanzas *fpl*; **in — of a fine week** esperando una semana de buen tiempo; **it did not come up to our —s** no correspondió con nuestras esperanzas.

(e) (*advance excitement*) expectación *f*, ilusión *f*; **we waited with growing —** esperábamos con creciente ilusión; **we waited in great —** esperábamos muy ilusionados.

anticlerical ['ænti'klerikl] *adj* anticlerical.

anticlericalism ['ænti'kleriklizəm] *n* anticlericalismo *m*.

anticlimax ['ænti'klaimæks] *n* acontecimiento *m* (*etc*) que marca un descenso de la emoción, decepción *f*; **the book ends in —** la emoción desfallece hacia el fin de la novela, la novela termina de modo decepcionante; **the game came as an —** el partido no correspondió con las esperanzas.

anticlockwise ['ænti'klɔkwaiz] *adv* en dirección contraria a la de las agujas del reloj.

anticoagulant ['æntikəu'ægjulənt] **1** *adj* anticoagulante. **2** *n* anticoagulante *m*.

anticorrosive ['æntikə'rəuziv] *adj* anticorrosivo.

antics ['æntiks] *npl* bufonadas *fpl*, payasadas *fpl*; (*of child, animal etc*) gracias *fpl*, travesuras *fpl*; **he's up to his — again** ha vuelto a hacer de las suyas.

anticyclone ['ænti'saikləun] *n* anticiclón *m*.

anti-dazzle ['ænti'dæzl] *adj* antideslumbrante.

antidote ['æntidəut] *n* antídoto *m* (*for, against, to* contra).

antifreeze ['ænti'friːz] **1** *adj* anticongelante. **2** *n* solución *f* anticongelante.

anti-friction ['ænti'frikʃən] *adj* antifriccional.

anti-glare ['ænti'glɛə*] *adj* antideslumbrante.

Antigone [æn'tigəni] *f* Antígona.

antihistamine [,ænti'histəmin] **1** *adj* antihistamínico.

2 *n* antihistamínico *m*.

anti-knock ['ænti'nɔk] *adj* antidetonante.

Antilles [æn'tiliːz] *pl* Antillas *fpl*.

antilogarithm [,ænti'lɔgəriθəm] *n* antilogaritmo *m*.

antimacassar ['æntimə'kæsə*] *n* antimacasar *m*.

antimissile ['ænti'misail] *adj, attr* antimísil, antiproyectil.

antimony ['æntiməni] *n* antimonio *m*.

Antioch ['æntiɔk] Antioquía *f*.

antipathetic [,æntipə'θetik] *adj* antipático (*to* a).

antipathy [æn'tipəθi] *n* antipatía *f* (*between* entre; *to* por, hacia); (*thing disliked*) aversión *f*, cosa *f* aborrecida.

antiphony [æn'tifəni] *n* antífona *f*.

antipodes [æn'tipədiːz] *npl* antípodas *fpl*.

antiquarian [,ænti'kwɛəriən] **1** *adj* anticuario. **2** *n* anticuario *m*.

antiquary ['æntikwəri] *n* anticuario *m*.

antiquated ['æntikweitid] *adj* anticuado.

antique [æn'tiːk] **1** *adj* antiguo, viejo; anticuado; *furniture etc* clásico, de época.

2 *n* antigüedad *f*, antigualla *f*; **— dealer** anticuario *m*, comerciante *m* en antigüedades; **— shop** tienda *f* de antigüedades.

antiquity [æn'tikwiti] *n* antigüedad *f*; **high —** remota antigüedad *f*; **in —** en la antigüedad.

anti-roll device ['ænti'rəuldi'vais] *n* dispositivo *m* para contrarrestar el balanceo.

antirrhinum [,ænti'rainəm] *n* antirrino *m*.

anti-rust ['ænti'rʌst] *adj* antioxidante.

anti-semite ['ænti'siːmait] *n* antisemita *mf*.

anti-semitic ['æntisi'mitik] *adj* antisemítico.

anti-semitism ['ænti'semitizəm] *n* antisemitismo *m*.

antiseptic [,ænti'septik] **1** *adj* antiséptico. **2** *n* antiséptico *m*.

anti-skid ['ænti'skid] *adj* antideslizante, antiderrapante.

antisocial ['ænti'səuʃəl] *adj* antisocial.

anti-tank ['ænti'tæŋk] *adj* antitanque.

antithesis [æn'tiθisis] *n, pl* **antitheses** [æn'tiθisiːz] antítesis *f*.

antithetic(al) [,ænti'θetik(əl)] *adj* antitético.

anti-trust law ['ænti'trʌstlɔː] *n* ley *f* antimonopolios.

antivivisectionist ['ænti,vivi'sekʃənist] *n* antivivi-seccionista *mf*.

antler ['æntlə*] *n* cuerna *f*; **—s** cuernas *fpl*, cornamenta *f*.

Antony ['æntəni] *m* Antonio.

antonym ['æntənim] *n* antónimo *m*.

Antwerp ['æntwəːp] Amberes *f*.

anus ['einəs] *n* ano *m*.

anvil ['ænvil] *n* yunque *m*.

anxiety [æŋ'zaiəti] *n* (a) (*worry*) inquietud *f*, preocupación *f*; **some — is felt about it** existe cierta inquietud sobre esto; **it is a great — to me** me preocupa muchísimo.

(b) (*eagerness*) ansia *f*, anhelo *m* (*for* de; *to do* de hacer, por hacer); **in his — to be gone** he forgot his case tanto ansiaba partir que olvidó su maleta.

(c) (*Med*) ansiedad *f*; **— neurosis** neurosis *f* de ansiedad.

anxious ['æŋkʃəs] *adj* (a) (*worried*) inquieto, preocupado, angustiado; **to be — about, to be — for** inquietarse por; **I'm very — about you** me tienes muy preocupado; **in an — voice** en un tono angustiado; **with an — glance** con una mirada llena de inquietud.

(b) (*causing worry*) **it is an — time** es un período de gran ansiedad; **you gave me some — moments** en ciertas ocasiones me causaste gran inquietud; **it was an — moment** fue un momento de ansiedad.

(c) (*eager*) deseoso (*for* de; *to do* de hacer); **he is — for success** ansía el triunfo, ambiciona el triunfo; **to be — to do** desear hacer, tener ganas de hacer, tener empeño en hacer; **I am very — that he should go** quiero a toda costa que vaya; **I'm not very — to go** tengo pocas ganas de ir.

anxiously ['æŋkʃəsli] *adv* con inquietud, de manera angustiada; **we waited —** esperábamos con ansiedad.

anxiousness ['æŋkʃəsnis] *n* inquietud *f*.

any ['eni] **1** *adj* (a) algún, alguna; **— day now** algún día de éstos; **if there are — tickets left** si le queda alguna entrada.

(b) (*partitive: gen not translated*) **have you — money?** ¿tienes dinero?; **have you — bananas?** ¿hay plátanos?; **is there — man who . . .?** ¿hay hombre que . . .?

(c) (*any . . . you like*) cualquier; **— farmer will tell you** te lo dirá cualquier agricultor; **wear — hat (you like)** ponte el sombrero que quieras, ponte un sombrero no importa cuál.

(d) (*negative sense*) ningún, ninguna; **I don't see — cows** no veo ninguna vaca, no veo vaca alguna.

2 *pron* **(a)** alguno, alguna; **if there are — who ...** si hay algunos que . . .; **few, if — pocos,** si es que los hay.

(b) (*any . . . you like*) cualquiera; **take — you like** tome cualquiera.

(c) (*negative sense*) ninguno, ninguna; **I haven't — of them** no tengo ninguno de ellos.

3 *adv* (*gen not translated*) **— more** más; **don't wait — longer** no esperes más tiempo; **are there — others?** ¿hay otros?; **is he — better?** ¿está algo mejor?

(b) (*fam, esp US*) **it doesn't help us —** eso no nos ayuda en lo más mínimo.

anybody ['enibɔdi] *pron* **(a)** alguien, alguno; **did you see — ?** ¿vio a alguien?; **— but you** todos menos Vd; **— would have said he was mad** se hubiera dicho que estaba loco.

(b) (**— . . . you like**) cualquiera; **— will tell you the same** cualquiera te dirá lo mismo; **— else would have laughed** cualquier otro se hubiera reído; **it's not available to just —** no se hace asequible a todos sin distinción; **I'm not going to marry just —** yo no me caso con un cualquiera.

(c) (*negative sense*) nadie, ninguno; **I can't see —** no veo a nadie.

(d) (*person of importance*) **is he —?** ¿es una persona de importancia?

anyhow ['enihau] *adv* **(a)** (*at any rate*) de todas formas, de todos modos, con todo.

(b) (*in spite of everything*) **I shall go —** voy a pesar de todo, sin embargo voy.

(c) (*haphazard*) **he leaves things just —** deja sus cosas en la mayor confusión; **she makes the beds just —** hace las camas de cualquier modo.

anyone ['eniwʌn] *pron* **= anybody.**

anything ['eniθiŋ] *pron* **(a)** algo, alguna cosa; **is there — inside?** ¿hay algo dentro?; **are you doing — tonight?** ¿tienes compromiso para esta noche?; **— else?** (*in shop etc*) ¿algo más?, ¿alguna cosita más?; **is there — in this idea?** ¿tiene algún valor esta idea?

(b) (**— you like**) cualquier cosa; **he will give you — you ask for** te dará todo lo que pidas; **sing — you like** canta lo que quieras; **— but that** todo menos eso; **— else is ruled out** todo lo demás está excluido; **I'll read — else** leeré otra cosa cualquiera; **I'm not buying just —** yo no compro una cosa cualquiera.

(c) (*negative sense*) nada; **I can't see —** no veo nada; **can't — be done?** ¿no se puede hacer nada?; **we can't do — else** no podemos hacer otra cosa; **not for — in the world** por nada del mundo.

(d) (*fam*) **like —** hasta más no poder.

anytime ['enitaim] *adv see* **time.**

anyway ['eniwei] *adv* **= anyhow.**

anywhere ['eniwɛə*] *adv* **(a)** en todas partes, en (*or* a) cualquier parte, dondequiera; **— in the world** en todas partes del mundo; **go — you like** vaya adonde quiera; **— you go you'll see the same** dondequiera que vaya Vd verá lo mismo; **— else** en cualquier otra parte; **I'm not going to live just —** yo no voy a vivir en un sitio cualquiera; **do you see him —?** ¿le ves en alguna parte?

(b) (*negative sense*) en (*or* a) ninguna parte; **I'm not going —** yo no voy a ninguna parte; **he was first and the rest didn't come —** él se clasificó primero y los demás quedaron muy por debajo.

aorta [ei'ɔːtə] *n* aorta *f*.

apace [ə'peis] *adv* aprisa, rápidamente.

apache [ə'pætʃi] *n* apache *m*.

apart [ə'pɑːt] *adv* **(a)** aparte, separadamente; **this is something quite —** esto es una cosa totalmente distinta; **to come —** romperse, deshacerse; **but joking —** pero en serio; **to keep —** separar; mantener aislado; **they live — now** ahora están separados; **to set —** guardar, reservar (*for* para), poner aparte; **the house stands somewhat —** la casa está algo aislada; **to take —** desmontar; **to tear —** despedazar, romper; **to tell —** distinguir entre.

(b) **— from** aparte de; **but quite — from that** pero además de eso; **he lives — from his wife** vive separado de su mujer.

apartheid [ə'pɑːteit] *n* separación *f* racial.

apartment [ə'pɑːtmənt] *n* (*flat*) piso *m*, apartamento *m*; (*room*) aposento *m*; **— house** (*US*) casa *f* de pisos.

apathetic [ˌæpə'θetik] *adj* apático, indiferente; **to be — towards** ser indiferente a, no mostrar interés alguno en.

apathy ['æpəθi] *n* apatía *f*, indiferencia *f* (*towards* a), falta *f* de interés (*towards* en).

ape [eip] **1** *n* mono *m* (*esp* los antropomorfos), antropoideo *m*; (*fig*) mono de imitación *m*, imitador *m*, ora *f*. **2** *vt* imitar, remedar.

aperient [ə'piəriənt] **1** *adj* laxante. **2** laxante *m*.

apéritif [ə'peritiv] *n* aperitivo *m*.

aperture ['æpətʃjuə*] *n* abertura *f*, rendija *f*, resquicio *m*.

apex ['eipeks] *n*, *pl* **apices** ['eipisiːz] ápice *m*; (*fig*) cumbre *f*.

aphasia [æ'feiziə] *n* afasia *f*.

aphis ['eifis] *n*, *pl* **aphides** ['eifidiːz] áfido *m*.

aphorism ['æfərizm] *n* aforismo *m*.

aphrodisiac [ˌæfrəu'diziæk] **1** *adj* afrodisíaco. **2** *n* afrodisíaco *m*.

Aphrodite [ˌæfrəu'daiti] *f* Afrodita.

apiarist ['eipiərist] *n* apicultor *m*.

apiary ['eipiəri] *n* colmenar *m*.

apiculture ['eipikʌltʃə*] *n* apicultura *f*.

apiece [ə'piːs] *adv* cada uno, *eg* **they had a gun —** tenía cada uno un revólver; **he gave them an apple —** dio una manzana a cada uno; por persona, por cabeza, *eg* **the rule is a shilling —** la regla es un chelín por persona.

aplomb [ə'plɔm] *n* aplomo *m*, confianza *f*, sangre *f* fría, serenidad *f*; **with the greatest —** con la mayor serenidad.

Apocalypse [ə'pɔkəlips] *n* Apocalipsis *m*.

apocalyptic [əˌpɔkə'liptik] *adj* apocalíptico.

apocopate [ə'pɔkəpeit] *vt* apocopar.

Apocrypha [ə'pɔkrifə] *npl* libros *mpl* apócrifos de la Biblia.

apocryphal [ə'pɔkrifəl] *adj* apócrifo.

apogee ['æpəudʒiː] *n* apogeo *m*.

Apollo [ə'pɔləu] *n* Apolo.

apologetic [əˌpɔlə'dʒetik] *adj* lleno de disculpas; **with an — air** como si viniera a pedir perdón; **he was very — about it** dijo que lo sentía profundamente.

apologetically [əˌpɔlə'dʒetikəli] *adv* con aire del que pide perdón, con muchas excusas, excusándose.

apologize [ə'pɔlədʒaiz] *vi* disculparse (*for* de; *to* con), pedir perdón (*to* a); (*for absence etc*) presentar sus excusas.

apology [ə'pɔlədʒi] *n* **(a)** disculpa *f*, excusa *f*; **I demand an —** reclamo la satisfacción, insisto en que Vd pida perdón; **to make** (*or* **offer**) **an —** disculparse, presentar sus excusas.

(b) (*Lit etc*) apología *f*, defensa *f*.

(c) **an — for a house** una birria de casa; **this — for a letter** ésta que apenas se puede llamar carta.

apoplectic [ˌæpə'plektik] *adj* apopléctico; **to get —** (*fig*) enfurecerse.

apoplexy ['æpəpleksi] *n* apoplejía *f*.

apostasy [ə'pɔstəsi] *n* apostasía *f*.

apostate [ə'pɔstit] *n* apóstata *mf*.

apostatize [ə'pɔstətaiz] *vi* apostatar (*from* de).

apostle [ə'pɔsl] *n* apóstol *m*.

apostolic [ˌæpəs'tɔlik] *adj* apostólico.

apostrophe [ə'pɔstrəfi] *n* (*written sign*) apóstrofo *m*; (*address*) apóstrofe *gen m*.

apostrophize [ə'pɔstrəfaiz] *vt* apostrofar.

apothecary [ə'pɔθikəri] *n* (*Hist*) boticario *m*.

apotheosis [əˌpɔθi'əusis] *n* apoteosis *f*.

appal [ə'pɔːl] *vt* horrorizar, aterrar; **everyone was —led** se horrorizaron todos, todos quedaron aterrados; **I was —led by the news** me horrorizó la noticia.

Appalachians [ˌæpə'leiʃənz] *pl* Montes *mpl* Apalaches.

appalling [ə'pɔːliŋ] *adj* espantoso, horroroso; *taste etc* detestable, pésimo.

appallingly [ə'pɔːliŋli] *adv* espantosamente, horrorosamente; detestablemente; **it was quite — bad** fue del todo horrible; **he's — self-centred** es terriblemente egocéntrico.

apparatus [ˌæpə'reitəs] *n* aparato *m*.

apparel [ə'pærəl] (*arch or hum*) **1** *n* ropa *f*, vestidos *mpl*; (*hum*) atavío *m*. **2** *vt* vestir; (*hum*) trajear, ataviar (*in* de).

apparent [ə'pærənt] *adj* (*seeming*) aparente; (*clear*) claro, evidente, manifiesto; *heir* forzoso; **more — than real** más aparente que real; **it is — that** está claro que; **to become —** manifestarse, hacerse patente; **it is becoming — that** ya se está viendo que.

apparently [ə'pærəntli] *adv* por lo visto, según parece, al parecer.

apparition [ˌæpə'riʃən] *n* (*act*) aparición *f*; (*ghost*) fantasma *m*, aparecido *m*.

appeal [ə'piːl] **1** *n* **(a)** (*call*) llamamiento *m*; **a national — for funds** un llamamiento a todo el país para que contribuya dinero; **he made an — for calm**

hizo un llamamiento a todos para que mantuvieran la calma; **a charity** — una cuestación para obras benéficas.

(**b**) (*petition*) súplica *f*, ruego *m*, petición *f*; **an — for help** una petición de socorro.

(**c**) (*Law*) apelación *f*, recurso *m* de casación; **without** — inapelable; **there is no — from his decision** su fallo es inapelable; **to give notice of —** entablar apelación; **to lodge an** — apelar (*against* de).

(**d**) (*attraction*) atractivo *m*, encanto *m*, interés *m*; **the — of children** el encanto de los niños; **a book of general** — un libro de interés para todos.

2 *vi* (**a**) (*call, beg*) **to — for** suplicar, reclamar; **I — for its return** ruego que se me devuelva; **he —ed for silence** rogó que se callasen todos; **to — to someone for something** suplicar algo a uno; **I — to you!** ¡se lo ruego!; **it's no good —ing to me** de nada sirve acudir a mí; **to — to the country** celebrar elecciones generales; **to — to arms** recurrir a las armas; **to — to someone's finer feelings** apelar a los sentimientos nobles de uno.

(**b**) (*Law*) apelar (*against* de; *to* a).

(**c**) (*attract*) atraer, tener atractivo para, interesar; **jazz does not — to me** el jazz no tiene atractivo para mí; **it —s to the imagination** estimula la imaginación.

appealing [ə'pi:liŋ] *adj* (*begging*) suplicante; (*attractive*) atrayente, atractivo, encantador.

appealingly [ə'pi:liŋli] *adv* de modo suplicante.

appear [ə'piə*] *vi* (**a**) (*present oneself*) aparecer; mostrarse, presentarse; **he —ed from nowhere** apareció como cosa llovida del cielo; **he —ed from behind a tree** salió de detrás de un árbol; **he —ed without a tie** se presentó sin corbata; **as will — in due course** según se verá luego; **to — to someone** (*as vision*) aparecerse a uno.

(**b**) (*book etc*) salir a luz, publicarse; **the magazine —s weekly** la revista sale cada semana.

(**c**) (*Law*) comparecer (*before* ante); **to — for someone** representar a uno.

(**d**) (*seem*) parecer; **he —s tired** parece cansado; **how does it — to you?** ¿qué le parece esto?; **it —s that** resulta que, parece que; **so it —s, so it would —** según parece; **in daylight it —s red** a la luz del sol se muestra rojo.

appearance [ə'piərəns] *n* (**a**) (*act of appearing*) aparición *f*; **to make an —** aparecer, presentarse, dejarse ver; **to make one's first —** aparecer por primera vez; **to make a personal —** aparecer en persona; **to put in an —** hacer acto de presencia.

(**b**) (*Law*) comparecencia *f*; **to make an — in court** comparecer ante el tribunal.

(**c**) (*aspect*) apariencia *f*, aspecto *m*; **to have a good —** tener buen aspecto.

(**d**) **—s** (*seeming*) apariencias *fpl*; **—s are deceptive** las apariencias engañan; **to all —s** al parecer, según todos los indicios.

(**e**) (*face*) apariencias *fpl*; **for the sake of —s** para salvar las apariencias; **to keep up** (*or* **save**) **—s** salvar las apariencias.

appease [ə'pi:z] *vt* apaciguar; *hunger* satisfacer, saciar; *passion* mitigar; *person* satisfacer, dar contento a; *angry person* desenojar.

appeasement [ə'pi:zmənt] *n* apaciguamiento *m*, pacificación *f*.

appellant [ə'pelənt] *n* apelante *mf*.

appellation [ˌæpe'leiʃən] *n* nombre *m*, título *m*.

append [ə'pend] *vt* (*add*) añadir; (*enclose*) adjuntar, enviar adjunto; *signature* poner.

appendage [ə'pendidʒ] *n* añadidura *f*, apéndice *m*; (*fig*) pegote *m*.

appendectomy [ˌæpen'dektəmi] *n* apendectomía *f*.

appendicitis [ə,pendi'saitis] *n* apendicitis *f*.

appendix [ə'pendiks] *n*, *pl* **appendices** [ə'pendisi:z] apéndice *m*.

Appenines [ˈæpənainz] *pl* Apeninos *mpl*.

appertain [ˌæpə'tein] *vi*: **to — to** relacionarse con, tener que ver con.

appetite [ˈæpitait] *n* (**a**) apetito *m*; **to eat with an —** comer con buen apetito; **to whet one's —** abrir el apetito.

(**b**) (*fig*) deseo *m*, anhelo *m* (*for* de); **they had no — for further fighting** ya no les apetecía seguir luchando; **to spoil one's — for** quitar a uno las ganas de.

appetizer [ˈæpitaizə*] *n* apetite *m*, aperitivo *m*.

appetizing [ˈæpitaiziŋ] *adj* apetitoso.

applaud [ə'plɔ:d] **1** *vt* aplaudir; (*fig*) aplaudir, celebrar, alabar. **2** *vi* aplaudir, palmotear.

applause [ə'plɔ:z] *n* aplausos *mpl*; (*fig*) aplausos *mpl*, aprobación *f*; **there was loud —** sonaron fuertes aplausos; **to win the — of** ganarse la aprobación de.

apple [ˈæpl] *n* (*fruit*) manzana *f*; (*tree*) manzano *m*; **stewed —s** compota *f* de manzanas; **— of discord** manzana *f* de la discordia; **the — of one's eye** la niña de los ojos.

applecart [ˈæplkɑ:t] *n*: **to upset the —** echarlo todo a rodar; **to upset someone's —** dar al traste con los planes de uno.

apple core [ˈæplkɔ:*] *n* corazón *m* de manzana.

applejack [ˈæpldʒæk] *n* (*US*) aguardiente *m* de manzana.

apple orchard [ˈæpl,ɔ:tʃəd] *n* manzanar *m*, pomar *m*.

apple pie [ˈæpl'pai] *n* tarta *f* de manzanas; **in apple-pie order** en perfecto orden; **apple-pie bed** cama *f* en petaca.

apple-sauce [ˈæpl'sɔ:s] *n* compota *f* de manzanas; (*US sl*) coba *f*.

appliance [ə'plaiəns] *n* aparato *m*, instrumento *m*, dispositivo *m*.

applicability [ˌæplikə'biliti] *n* aplicabilidad *f*.

applicable [ə'plikəbl] *adj* aplicable (*to* a); **a rule — to all** una regla que se extiende a todos; **this is not — to you** esto no se refiere a Vd; **delete what is not —** táchese lo que no interese.

applicant [ˈæplikənt] *n* aspirante *mf*, candidato *m* (*for a post* a un puesto); suplicante *mf*, solicitante *mf*.

application [ˌæpli'keiʃən] *n* (**a**) (*in most senses*) aplicación *f*; **for external — only** (*Med*) para uso externo.

(**b**) (*request*) solicitud *f*, petición *f* (*for* de, por); **—s in triplicate** las solicitudes por triplicado; **are you going to put in an —?** ¿te vas a presentar?; **to make an — for** solicitar; **to make an — to** dirigirse a; **details may be had on — to X** para los detalles dirigirse a X.

applied [ə'plaid] *adj* *science etc* aplicado.

appliqué [æ'pli:kei] *n* (*also* **— lace**, **— work**) encaje *m* de aplicación.

apply [ə'plai] **1** *vt* aplicar (*to* a); *rule* emplear, recurrir a; *law* poner en vigor; **how can we best — this money?** ¿cómo podemos utilizar mejor este dinero?; **to — one's mind to a problem** dedicarse a resolver un problema.

2 *vi* (**a**) (*refer to*) ser aplicable, interesar; **cross out what does not —** táchese lo que no interese; **to — to** tener que ver con, ser aplicable a, referirse a; **the law applies to everybody** la ley a todos comprende.

(**b**) (*request*) presentarse, ser candidato; **are you —ing?** ¿te vas a presentar?; **to — for** solicitar, pedir, *post* solicitar, presentarse a; **patent applied for** se ha solicitado patente; **to — to** dirigirse a, acudir a; **to — to someone for something** dirigirse a uno pidiendo algo.

3 *vr*: **to — oneself to** aplicarse a, dedicarse a.

appoint [ə'pɔint] *vt* *time, date etc* fijar, señalar (*for* para); **at the —ed time** a la hora señalada.

(**b**) (*nominate*) nombrar (*to* a); **they —ed him chairman** le nombraron presidente; **they —ed him to do it** le nombraron para que lo hiciese.

(**c**) **well —ed** bien amueblado, bien equipado.

appointment [ə'pɔintmənt] *n* (**a**) (*act*) nombramiento *m* (*to* a); **by — to . . .** (*with royal arms*) proveedores de . . .

(**b**) (*engagement*) cita *f*, compromiso *m*; **I have an — at 10** tengo una cita a las 10; **have you an — tonight?** ¿tienes compromiso para esta noche?; **have you an —?** (*to caller*) ¿tiene Vd hora?; **to keep an —** acudir a una cita; **to make an —** (*2 persons*) darse una cita; **to make an — with** citarse con; **to make an — for 3 o'clock** citarse para las 3.

(**c**) (*post*) puesto *m*, empleo *m*; **—s bureau** bolsa *f* de trabajo.

(**d**) **—s** mobiliario *m*, moblaje *m*, equipo *m*.

apportion [ə'pɔ:ʃən] *vt* prorratear; repartir, distribuir; **the blame is to be —ed equally** todos tienen la culpa por partes iguales.

apposite [ˈæpəzit] *adj* apropiado (*to* a); a propósito, oportuno.

apposition [ˌæpə'ziʃən] *n* aposición *f*; **in —** en aposición.

appraisal [ə'preizəl] *n* tasación *f*, valoración *f*; (*fig*) estimación *f*, apreciación *f*.

appraise [ə'preiz] *vt* tasar, valorar; (*fig*) apreciar.

appreciable [ə'pri:ʃəbl] *adj* sensible, perceptible; **an — sum** una cantidad importante; **an — loss** una pérdida sensible.

appreciably [ə'pri:ʃəbli] *adv* sensiblemente, perceptiblemente.

appreciate [ə'pri:ʃieit] **1** *vt* (**a**) (*estimate worth of*) apreciar, valorar.

(**b**) (*estimate correctly*) apreciar, saber valorar en su justo precio.

(c) (esteem) apreciar, tener en mucho, tener un alto concepto de; **he does not — music** no sabe apreciar la música, no entiende de música; **I am not —d here** aquí no me estiman; **we much — your work** tenemos un alto concepto de su trabajo.

(d) (understand) comprender; **I — your wishes in the matter** comprendo sus deseos en este asunto; **yes, I — that** sí, lo comprendo; **to — that** comprender que; **we fully — that** comprendemos perfectamente que.

(e) (be grateful for) agradecer; **I — the gesture** agradezco el detalle.

(f) (be sensitive to) percibir; **the smallest change can be —d on this machine** en esta máquina se percibe el más pequeño cambio.

2 vi aumentar(se) en valor, subir.

appreciation [ə‚priːʃi'eiʃən] n **(a)** (estimation) aprecio m, apreciación f, estimación f; (obituary) necrológica f; (praise) elogio m; **literary —** crítica f literaria.

(b) (esteem) aprecio m; **you have no — of art** Vd no sabe apreciar el arte, Vd no entiende de arte.

(c) (gratitude) reconocimiento m, agradecimiento m; **as a token of my —** en señal de reconocimiento.

(d) (rise in value) aumento m en valor, subida f.

appreciative [ə'priːʃiətiv] adj agradecido; audience atento; **an — look** una mirada llena de agradecimiento; **he was very — of what I had done** agradeció mucho lo que yo había hecho; **he spoke in — terms of my work** habló de mi trabajo en términos elogiosos.

apprehend [‚æpri'hend] vt **(a)** (arrest) prender. **(b)** (perceive) percibir; comprender. **(c)** (fear) recelar, sospechar; **to — that** sospechar que.

apprehension [‚æpri'henʃən] n **(a)** (arrest) prendimiento m.

(b) (perception) percepción f; comprensión f.

(c) (fear) recelo m, aprensión f; **my chief — is that** sobre todo me temo que + subj.

apprehensive [‚æpri'hensiv] adj aprensivo; **to be — for** temer por, inquietarse por; **to be — that** recelar que, temer que + subj; **to grow —** inquietarse.

apprehensively [‚æpri'hensivli] adv con aprensión.

apprentice [ə'prentis] **1** n aprendiz m, iza f; (fig) novicio m, a f. **2** vt poner de aprendiz (to con); **to be —d to** estar de aprendiz con.

apprenticeship [ə'prentiʃip] n aprendizaje m; **to serve one's —** hacer su aprendizaje.

apprise [ə'praiz] vt informar, avisar (of de); **I will — him of it** se lo diré; **to be —d of** estar enterado de; **I was never —d of your decision** no se me comunicó nunca su decisión.

appro ['æprəu] (fam) = **approval**; **on — a** prueba.

approach [ə'prəutʃ] **1** vt **(a)** acercarse a; aproximarse a.

(b) (fig) **we must — the subject with care** tenemos que considerar el asunto con mucho cuidado; **it all depends on how we — it** depende de cómo enfocamos la cuestión; **I — it with an open mind** empiezo a estudiarlo sin prejuicios.

(c) person abordar, dirigirse a; **a man —ed me in the street** un hombre me abordó en la calle; **you should — the boss about that** Vd debiera dirigirse al jefe sobre aquello; **have you —ed him yet?** ¿has hablado ya con él?

(d) (approximate to) aproximarse a, parecerse a, ser semejante a; **here the colour —es blue** aquí el color tira a azul.

2 vi acercarse.

3 n **(a)** (act) acercamiento m; **— light** (Aer) luz f de acercamiento; **we watched his —** le vimos acercarse; **at the — of the enemy** al acercarse el enemigo; **at the — of night** al entrar la noche.

(b) (fig) aproximación f (to a).

(c) (to problem) aproximación f (to a), modo m de enfocar una cuestión, método m de abordar un problema; **an — to Spanish history** una aproximación a la historia de España; **I don't like your — to this matter** no me gusta su modo de enfocar esta cuestión; **we must think of a new —** tenemos que inventar otro método.

(d) (access) acceso m (to a), vía f de entrada; **— road** camino m de acceso; **—es** accesos mpl, (Mil) aproches mpl; **the northern —es of Madrid** las rutas de acceso a Madrid por la parte norte; **easy of —** asequible, de fácil acceso.

(e) (advance) propuesta f, proposición f; oferta f; **to make —es to** dirigirse a, tratar de hablar con.

approachable [ə'prəutʃəbl] adj person abordable, afable; place accesible.

approaching [ə'prəutʃiŋ] adj event próximo, venidero; car etc que se acerca; traffic que viene en dirección opuesta.

approbation [‚æprə'beiʃən] n aprobación f; consentimiento m.

appropriate [ə'prəupriit] adj apropiado, conveniente, a propósito; moment etc oportuno; authority etc competente; **— for, — to** apropiado para; **whichever seems more —** el que le parezca más apropiado; **would it be — for me to wear it?** ¿convendría que yo me lo pusiera?; **and where —** ... y en su caso ...

appropriate [ə'prəuprieit] vt thing apropiarse; funds etc asignar, destinar (for a).

appropriately [ə'prəupriitli] adv apropiadamente, convenientemente; **he was very — named Moor** tuvo el nombre tan apropiado de Moro; **in an — designed house** en una casa convenientemente distribuida.

appropriateness [ə'prəupriitnis] n propiedad f, conveniencia f.

appropriation [ə‚prəupri'eiʃən] n apropiación f; asignación f.

approval [ə'pruːvəl] n aprobación f; consentimiento m; (formal OK) visto bueno m; **on — a** prueba; **has this your —?** ¿Vd ha aprobado esto?; **to meet with someone's —** obtener la aprobación de uno; **he nodded his —** asintió con la cabeza.

approve [ə'pruːv] **1** vt aprobar; **read and —d** visto bueno.

2 vi: **to — of** aprobar, dar por bueno; **they don't — of my fiancé** no les cae en gracia mi novio; **I cannot — of your going** no puedo consentir en que vayas.

approved [ə'pruːvd] adj aprobado, acreditado; **in the — fashion** del modo acostumbrado; **— school** correccional m.

approving [ə'pruːviŋ] adj de aprobación.

approvingly [ə'pruːviŋli] adv con aprobación.

approximate [ə'prɒksimit] adj aproximado.

approximate [ə'prɒksimeit] vi aproximarse (to a).

approximately [ə'prɒksimətli] adv aproximadamente, poco más o menos.

approximation [ə‚prɒksi'meiʃən] n aproximación f.

appurtenance [ə'pəːtinəns] n (appendage) dependencia f; (accessory) accesorio m.

apricot ['eiprikɒt] n (fruit) albaricoque m; (tree) albaricoquero m.

April ['eiprəl] n abril m.

April Fools' Day ['eiprəl'fuːlz'dei] n see **All Fools' Day.**

apron ['eiprən] n delantal m; (workman's, mason's etc) mandil m; (Theat) visera f; (Aer) pista f.

apron strings ['eiprən'striŋz] npl: **tied to the — of** cosido a las faldas de.

apropos [‚æprə'pəu] **1** adv a propósito. **2** prep: **— of** a propósito de. **3** adj oportuno.

apse [æps] n ábside m.

apt [æpt] adj **(a)** (suitable) apropiado, conveniente; remark acertado, oportuno; description exacto, atinado.

(b) (tending) **to be — to** + infin tener tendencia a + infin, ser propenso a + infin; **to be rather — to** + infin tener cierta tendencia a + infin; **I am — to be out on Mondays** por regla general no estoy los lunes; **we are — to forget that** ... es fácil que olvidemos que ...; **it is — to cause trouble** suele motivar disgustos.

(c) (sharp) listo (at en); **to be an — pupil** ser un alumno aprovechado.

aptitude ['æptitjuːd] n aptitud f (for, in para), capacidad f, habilidad f; **— test** prueba f de aptitud.

aptly ['æptli] adv oportunamente, acertadamente.

aptness ['æptnis] n lo apropiado, lo acertado.

Apuleius [‚æpjə'liəs] m Apuleyo.

aqualung ['ækwəlʌŋ] n aparato m de aire comprimido (que suministra aire al buzo).

aquamarine [‚ækwəmə'riːn] **1** adj (de color) verde mar. **2** n aguamarina f.

aquatint ['ækwətint] n acuatinta f.

aquarium [ə'kwɛəriəm] n acuario m.

aquatic [ə'kwætik] **1** adj acuático. **2** n (Bot) planta f acuática; **—s** deportes mpl acuáticos.

aqueduct ['ækwidʌkt] n acueducto m.

aqueous ['eikwiəs] adj ácueo, acuoso.

aquiline ['ækwilain] adj aguileño.

Aquinas [ə'kwainəs] m Aquino.

Arab ['ærəb] **1** adj árabe. **2** n árabe mf; **street —** golfillo m.

arabesque [‚ærə'besk] n arabesco m.

Arabia [ə'reibiə] Arabia f.

Arabian [ə'reibiən] **1** *adj* árabe, arábigo; — Desert Desierto *m* Arábigo; — Sea Mar *m* de Omán; the — Nights Las Mil y Una Noches. **2** *n* árabe *mf*.
Arabic ['ærəbik] **1** *adj* árabe, arábigo; — numeral número *m* arábigo. **2** *n* árabe *m*.
arable ['ærəbl] **1** *adj* cultivable; — land = **2** *n* tierra *f* de labrantío, labranza *f*.
arachnid [ə'ræknid] *n* arácnido *m*.
Aragon ['ærəgən] Aragón *m*.
Aragonese [ˌærəgə'niːz] **1** *adj* aragonés. **2** *n* aragonés *m*, esa *f*. **3** *n* (*dialect*) aragonés *m*.
arbiter ['ɑːbitə*] *n* árbitro *m*.
arbitrarily ['ɑːbitrərili] *adv* arbitrariamente.
arbitrary ['ɑːbitrəri] *adj* arbitrario.
arbitrate ['ɑːbitreit] *vi* arbitrar (*in* en, *between* entre).
arbitration [ˌɑːbi'treiʃən] *n* arbitraje *m*; **industrial** — arbitraje *m* industrial; **the question was referred to** — se confió el asunto a un juez árbitro.
arbitrator ['ɑːbitreitə*] *n* juez árbitro *m*.
arboreal [ɑː'bɔːriəl] *adj* arbóreo.
arbour ['ɑːbə*] *n* cenador *m*, pérgola *f*.
arc [ɑːk] *n* arco *m*.
arcade [ɑː'keid] *n* (*Archit*) arcada *f*; (*round public square*) soportales *mpl*; (*with shops*) galería *f*, pasaje *m*, pasadizo *m*.
Arcadian [ɑː'keidiən] **1** *adj* árcade; (*fig*) arcádico. **2** *n* árcade *mf*.
Arcady ['ɑːkədi] Arcadia *f*.
arch[1] [ɑːtʃ] **1** *n* (a) (*Archit*) arco *m*; (*vault*) bóveda *f*; — **of heaven** bóveda *f* celeste; **horseshoe** — arco *m* de herradura; **pointed** — arco *m* ojival; **round** — arco *m* redondo; **triumphal** — arco *m* triunfal.
  (b) (*Anat*) empeine *m*; (*dental*) arcada *f*, arco *m*; **fallen** —**es** pies *mpl* planos.
  2 *vt* (a) *back, body etc* arquear; *eyebrows* enarcar.
  (b) (*Archit*) **to** — **over** abovedar.
  3 *vi* arquearse, formar un arco.
arch[2] [ɑːtʃ] *adj* (*cunning*) astuto; (*roguish*) zumbón, picaruelo; *look, remark etc* malicioso, lleno de malicia; *woman* coqueta.
arch[3] [ɑːtʃ] (*gen in compounds, see below*) principal; consumado; **the** — **criminal** el mayor de los criminales; *in compounds:* archi...
archaeological [ˌɑːkiə'lɔdʒikəl] *adj* arqueológico.
archaeologist [ˌɑːki'ɔlədʒist] *n* arqueólogo *m*.
archaeology [ˌɑːki'ɔlədʒi] *n* arqueología *f*.
archaic [ɑː'keiik] *adj* arcaico.
archaism ['ɑːkeiizəm] *n* arcaísmo *m*.
archangel ['ɑːkˌeindʒəl] *n* arcángel *m*.
archbishop ['ɑːtʃ'biʃəp] *n* arzobispo *m*.
archbishopric [ɑːtʃ'biʃəprik] *n* arzobispado *m*.
archdeacon ['ɑːtʃ'diːkən] *n* arcediano *m*.
archdiocese ['ɑːtʃ'daiəsis] *n* archidiócesis *f*.
archduchess ['ɑːtʃ'dʌtʃis] *n* archiduquesa *f*.
archduchy ['ɑːtʃ'dʌtʃi] *n* archiducado *m*.
archduke ['ɑːtʃ'djuːk] *n* archiduque *m*.
arched [ɑːtʃt] *adj* en forma de arco(s); abovedado.
arch-enemy ['ɑːtʃ'enimi] *n* archienemigo *m*; (*devil*) el enemigo malo, Satanás.
archer ['ɑːtʃə*] *n* arquero *m*.
archery ['ɑːtʃəri] *n* tiro *m* con arco.
archetype ['ɑːkitaip] *n* arquetipo *m*.
Archimedes [ˌɑːki'miːdiːz] *m* Arquímedes *f*.
archipelago [ˌɑːki'peligəu] *n* archipiélago *m*.
architect ['ɑːkitekt] *n* (a) arquitecto *m*; **naval** — constructor *m* naval. (b) (*fig*) artífice *m*; **the** — **of victory** el artífice de la victoria.
architectural [ˌɑːki'tektʃərəl] *adj* arquitectónico.
architecture ['ɑːkitektʃə*] *n* arquitectura *f*.
archive ['ɑːkaiv] *n* archivo *m*.
archivist ['ɑːkivist] *n* archivero *m*.
archness ['ɑːtʃnis] *n* astucia *f*; socarronería *f*; malicia *f*, coquetería *f*.
archway ['ɑːtʃwei] *n* arco *m*, arcada *f*.
arc lamp ['ɑːklæmp] *n* lámpara *f* de arco; (*in welding*) arco *m* voltaico.
arctic ['ɑːktik] **1** *adj* ártico; (*fig*) glacial. **2** *n*: **the A**— el Ártico.
Arctic Circle ['ɑːktik'səːkl] *n* Círculo *m* Polar Ártico.
Arctic Ocean ['ɑːktik'əuʃən] Océano *m* Glacial Ártico.
Ardennes [ɑː'denz] *pl* Ardenas *fpl*.
ardent ['ɑːdənt] *adj* ardiente, vehemente, apasionado; *supporter* fervoroso, entusiasmado; *desire* vivo; *lover* apasionado.
ardently ['ɑːdəntli] *adv* ardientemente, con vehemencia, apasionadamente; fervorosamente, con entusiasmo.
ardour ['ɑːdə*] *n* ardor *m*; fervor *m*, entusiasmo *m*; vehemencia *f*; pasión *f*; **to dampen someone's** — enfriar la pasión de uno.

arduous ['ɑːdjuəs] *adj* arduo, fuerte, riguroso; *climb, journey* penoso; *task* difícil.
arduousness ['ɑːdjuəsnis] *n* lo riguroso; lo penoso; dificultad *f*.
are [ɑː*] *see* **be**.
area ['ɛəriə] *n* (a) (*Math, surface extent*) área *f*, superficie *f*; extensión *f*.
  (b) (*Geog, space*) región *f*, zona *f*; (*Sport, eg goal* —) área *f*; **the London** — la región londinense; **postal** — distrito *m* postal; **depressed** — zona *f* deprimida, región *f* de elevado paro obrero; **prohibited** — zona *f* prohibida.
  (c) (*Archit*) corral *m*, patio *m*.
arena [ə'riːnə] *n* arena *f*, redondel *m*; (*Taur*) plaza *f*, ruedo *m*; (*Circus*) pista *f*.
aren't [ɑːnt] = **are not**.
Argentina [ˌɑːdʒən'tiːnə] la Argentina.
Argentine ['ɑːdʒəntain] **1** *adj* argentino. **2** *n*: **the** — la Argentina.
Argentinian [ˌɑːdʒən'tiniən] **1** *adj* argentino. **2** *n* argentino *m*, a *f*.
argon ['ɑːgɔn] *n* argo *m*, argón *m*.
Argonaut ['ɑːgənɔːt] *n* Argonauta *m*.
arguable ['ɑːgjuəbl] *adj* discutible; **it is** — **whether** . . . es dudoso si . . .
argue ['ɑːgjuː] **1** *vt* (a) *case* sostener; *matter* razonar acerca de; *point* discutir; **a well**—**d case** un argumento razonado; **how will you** — **the case?** ¿cómo va Vd a presentar el pleito?; **to** — **one's way out of a jam** salir de un apuro a fuerza de argumentos.
  (b) (*point to*) argüir, indicar; **it** —**s his untrustworthiness** le arguye de poco confiable; **it** —**s him to be untrustworthy** ello hace creer que es poco confiable; **to** — **that** sostener que; **I have heard it** —**d that** he oído sostener que.
  (c) **to** — **someone into** + *ger* persuadir a uno a + *infin*; **to** — **someone out of** + *ger* disuadir a uno de + *infin*; **to** — **someone out of something** persuadir a uno a abandonar algo.
  2 *vi* (a) (*two persons*) discutir, disputar (*about* acerca de, *with* con); **we** —**d all night** pasamos toda la noche discutiendo; **don't** —**!** ¡no discutas!, ¡no repliques!
  (b) (*reason*) razonar, argüir, discurrir; **I** — **this way** yo pienso de este modo, yo razono así; **he** —**s well** razona bien, presenta de modo convincente sus argumentos; **this** —**s in his favour** esto habla en su favor; **to** — **against** *person* hablar en contra de, *thing* alegar razones contra, combatir por argumentos; **to** — **for** abogar por.
argument ['ɑːgjumənt] *n* (a) (*reason*) argumento *m*. (*against* en contra de, *for* en pro de); **his** — **is that** él sostiene que; **I don't follow your** — no comprendo su razonamiento; **to be open to** — estar dispuesto a dejarse convencer.
  (b) (*debate*) discusión *f*, disputa *f*, debate *m*; **there was a heated** — hubo una discusión acalorada; **for the sake of** — pongamos por caso, como hipótesis; **to have the better of the** — salir airoso de un debate; **let's not have any** —**s** no discutamos; **you've heard only one side of the** — le han contado solamente una parte de la discusión.
  (c) (*Law*) alegato *m*.
argumentation [ˌɑːgjumən'teiʃən] *n* argumentación *f*, argumentos *mpl*.
argumentative [ˌɑːgjuˈmentətiv] *adj* discutidor, argumentador.
Argus ['ɑːgəs] *m* Argos.
aria ['ɑːriə] *n* aria *f*.
Arian ['ɛəriən] **1** *adj* arriano. **2** *n* arriano *m*, a *f*.
Arianism ['ɛəriənizəm] *n* arrianismo *m*.
arid ['ærid] *adj* árido (*also fig*).
aridity [ə'riditi] *n* aridez *f*.
aright [ə'rait] *adv* correctamente, acertadamente; **if I heard you** — si le oí bien; **if I understand you** — si le entiendo correctamente; **to set** — rectificar.
arise [ə'raiz] (*irr: pret* arose, *ptp* arisen) *vi* (a) (*lit*) levantarse, alzarse; —**!** (*slogan*) ¡arriba!
  (b) (*fig*) surgir; presentarse, producirse; **difficulties have** —**n** han surgido dificultades; **should the occasion** — si se presenta la ocasión; **should need** — si nos vemos en el caso; **a storm arose** hubo un temporal; **a great clamour arose** se produjo un tremendo clamor; **the question does not** — no hay tal, no existe ese problema; **the question** —**s whether** . . . se plantea el problema de si . . .
  (c) **to** — **from** provenir de, resultar de; **arising from this, can you say** . . .? partiendo de esta base, ¿puede Vd decir . . .?
arisen [ə'rizn] *ptp of* **arise**.
aristocracy [ˌæris'tɔkrəsi] *n* aristocracia *f*.
aristocrat ['æristəkræt] *n* aristócrata *mf*.

aristocratic [ˌærɪstə'krætik] *adj* aristocrático.
Aristophanes [ˌærɪs'tɔfəniːz] *m* Aristófanes.
Aristotelian [ˌærɪstə'tiːliən] *adj* aristotélico.
Aristotle ['ærɪstɔtl] *m* Aristóteles.
arithmetic [ə'rɪθmətik] *n* aritmética *f*; **mental —** cálculo *m* mental.
arithmetical [ˌærɪθ'metikəl] *adj* aritmético.
arithmetician [ə,rɪθmə'tiʃən] *n* aritmético *m*.
ark [ɑːk] *n* arca *f*; **A— of the Covenant** Arca *f* de la Alianza; **Noah's A—** Arca *f* de Noé.
Arles [ɑːl] Arlés.
arm[1] [ɑːm] *n* (*Anat and fig*) brazo *m*; **— in —** cogidos del brazo, de bracete; **baby in —s** niño *m* de pecho; **with open —s** con los brazos abiertos; **within —'s reach** al alcance del brazo; **to chance one's —** arriesgarse, aventurarse; **to give someone one's —** ofrecer el brazo a uno; **to keep someone at —'s length** mantener a uno a distancia; **to put one's — round someone** rodear a uno del brazo; **to take someone in one's —s** abrazar a uno.
arm[2] [ɑːm] (*Mil*) **1** *n* arma *f*; **—s** (*Her*) escudo *m*, blasón *m*; **— race** carrera *f* de armamentos; **under —s** sobre las armas; **to be up in —s** poner el grito en el cielo; **to lay down one's —s** rendir las armas; **to rise up in —s** alzarse en armas; **to take up —s** tomar las armas; **present —s!** ¡presenten armas!; **shoulder —s!**, **slope —s!** ¡armas al hombro!
 2 *vt* armar.
 3 *vr*: **to — oneself** armarse; **to — oneself with arguments** pertrecharse de argumentos.
Armada [ɑː'mɑːdə] *n*: **the —** la (Armada) Invencible.
armadillo [ˌɑːmə'dɪləu] *n* armadillo *m*.
Armageddon [ˌɑːmə'gedn] Armagedón *m*, lucha *f* suprema.
armament ['ɑːməmənt] *n* armamento *m*.
armature ['ɑːmətjuə*] *n* (*Elec, Zool, Bot*) armadura *f*; (*of dynamo*) inducido *m*.
armband ['ɑːmbænd] *n* brazal *m*, brazalete *m*.
armchair ['ɑːmtʃɛə*] **1** *n* sillón *m*, butaca *f*. **2** *attr*: **— politician** político *m* de café.
armed [ɑːmd] **1** *pret and ptp of* **arm**[2]. **2** *adj* armado, provisto de armas; **— to the teeth** armado hasta los dientes; **— robbery** robo *m* a mano armada.
-armed [ɑːmd] *adj* de brazos . . . , *eg* **strong-armed** de brazos fuertes; **one-armed** manco.
Armenia [ɑː'miːnɪə] Armenia *f*.
Armenian [ɑː'miːnɪən] **1** *adj* armenio. **2** *n* armenio *m*, a *f*.
armful ['ɑːmful] *n* brazado *m*, brazada *f*.
armhole ['ɑːmhəul] *n* sobaquera *f*.
armistice ['ɑːmɪstɪs] *n* armisticio *m*.
armlet ['ɑːmlɪt] *n* brazal *m*.
armorial [ɑː'mɔːrɪəl] *adj* heráldico; **— bearings** escudo *m* de armas.
armour, (*US*) **armor** ['ɑːmə*] **1** *n* (*Mil, Zool, fig*) armadura *f*; (*steel plates*) blindaje *m*; (*tanks*) tanques *mpl*, fuerzas *fpl* blindadas. **2** *vt* blindar, acorazar.
armour-clad, (*US*) **armor—** ['ɑːmə'klæd] *adj*, **armoured,** (*US*) **armored** ['ɑːməd] *adj* blindado, acorazado.
armourer, (*US*) **armorer** ['ɑːmərə*] *n* armero *m*.
armour-plated, (*US*) **armor—** ['ɑːmə'pleitid] *adj* blindado, acorazado.
armoury, (*US*) **armory** ['ɑːməri] *n* armería *f*; arsenal *m*.
armpit ['ɑːmpit] *n* sobaco *m*, axila *f*.
armrest ['ɑːmrest] *n* apoyo *m* para el brazo, apoyabrazos *m*.
army ['ɑːmi] *n* ejército *m*; (*fig*) ejército *m*, multitud *f*; **standing —** ejército *m* permanente; **— corps** cuerpo *m* de ejército; **— life** vida *f* militar; **— list** lista *f* de oficiales del ejército; **— doctor** médico *m* militar; **to join the —** hacerse soldado, engancharse, alistarse.
aroma [ə'rəumə] *n* aroma *m* (*of* a), fragancia *f*.
aromatic [ˌærəu'mætik] *adj* aromático, fragante.
arose [ə'rəuz] *pret of* **arise**.
around [ə'raund] **1** *adv* alrededor; a la redonda, *eg* **for 5 miles —** en 5 millas a la redonda; **all —** por todas partes, por todos lados; **is he —?** ¿está por aquí? **he must be somewhere —** debe de andar por aquí.
 2 *prep* alrededor de, en torno de; **— 50** unos 50, 50 más o menos; **all — me** por todas partes alrededor de mí; **it's just — the corner** está precisamente a la vuelta de la esquina; **to go — the world** dar la vuelta al mundo; *see also* **about, round.**
arouse [ə'rauz] *vt* despertar; (*fig*) mover, incitar, estimular; **it —d great interest** despertó mucho interés; **it should — you to greater efforts** esto deberá incitarle a esforzarse más todavía.
arrack ['ærək] *n* aguardiente *m* de palma.
arraign [ə'rein] *vt* procesar, acusar (*before* ante).

arrange [ə'reindʒ] **1** *vt* (a) (*put into order*) arreglar, ordenar, organizar; **to — one's affairs** poner en orden sus asuntos; **how did we — matters last time?** ¿cómo lo organizamos la última vez?
 (b) (*draw up*) disponer; **how is the room —d?** ¿qué disposición tienen los muebles?
 (c) (*Mus*) adaptar, refundir.
 (d) (*fix upon*) fijar, señalar; **to — a time for** fijar una hora para.
 (e) (*agree*) **it was —d that** se decidió que; **what did you — with him?** ¿qué decidieron Vds?; **a marriage has been —d between . . .** se ha concertado la boda de . . .
 2 *vi*: **to — for** prevenir, disponer; **I have —d for you to go** he hecho los arreglos para que vaya Vd; **can you — for my luggage to be sent up?** por favor, que me suban el equipaje; **I —d to meet him at the café** me cité con él en el café; **I have —d to see him tonight** nos hemos dado una cita para esta noche; **to — with someone to +** *infin* ponerse de acuerdo con uno para que **+** *subj*; **to — with someone that** convenir con uno en que **+** *subj*.
arrangement [ə'reindʒmənt] *n* (a) (*order*) arreglo *m*, orden *m*, disposición *f*.
 (b) (*act of ordering*) arreglo *m*, ordenación *f*.
 (c) (*Mus*) adaptación *f*.
 (d) (*agreement*) acuerdo *m*, convenio *m*; **to come to an —** llegar a un acomodo; **we have an — with them** existe un acuerdo con ellos; **larger orders by —** los pedidos de mayor cantidad, por acuerdo mutuo; **by — with Covent Garden** con permiso de Covent Garden; **salary by —** sueldo a convenir.
 (e) (*plan, line of action*) plan *m*, medida *f*; **—s** (*preparations*) preparativos *mpl*; (*order of events*) programa *m*; **what are the —s for your holiday?** ¿qué plan tiene Vd para sus vacaciones?; **we must make —s to help them** tenemos que tomar medidas para ayudarles; **to make one's own —s** obrar por cuenta propia; **all the —s are made** todo está arreglado; **if this — doesn't suit you** si esto no le conviene; **all the —s were made by X** todos los preparativos los hizo X.
arrant ['ærənt] *adj* *knave etc* consumado, de siete suelas; **— nonsense** puro disparate *m*.
array [ə'rei] **1** *n* (a) (*Mil*) orden *m* de batalla; **in battle —** en orden de batalla; **in close —** en filas apretadas.
 (b) (*fig*) serie *f* impresionante, colección *f* imponente; **a fine — of flowers** un bello conjunto de flores; **a great — of hats** una magnífica colección de sombreros.
 (c) (*dress*) adorno *m*, atavío *m*.
 2 *vt* (*dress*) ataviar, engalanar (*in* de).
arrears [ə'rɪəz] *npl* atrasos *mpl*; **— of rent** atrasos *mpl* de alquiler; **in —** atrasado en pagos; **to get into —** atrasarse en los pagos.
arrest [ə'rest] **1** *n* detención *f*; (*of goods*) secuestro *m*; **to be under —** estar detenido; **you're under —** queda Vd detenido.
 2 *vt* *criminal* detener, arrestar, prender; *progress, decay etc* detener, parar; *attention* llamar; *judgement* prorrogar.
arresting [ə'restiŋ] *adj* llamativo, impresionante.
arrival [ə'raivəl] *n* llegada *f*; (*fig*) advenimiento *m*; **new —** recién llegado *m*, a *f*, persona *f* que acaba de llegar; (*fam*) recién nacido *m*, a *f*; **— platform** andén *m* de vacío; **on —** al llegar.
arrive [ə'raiv] *vi* llegar (*at, in* a); (*fam*) llegar a ser un auténtico personaje, triunfar, hacerse famoso.
arriviste [ˌæri'viːst] *n* arribista *mf*.
arrogance ['ærəgəns] *n* arrogancia *f*.
arrogant ['ærəgənt] *adj* arrogante.
arrogate ['ærəugeit] *vt*: **to — something to oneself** arrogarse algo; *quality* atribuirse, apropiarse.
arrow ['ærəu] *n* flecha *f*.
arrowhead ['ærəuhed] *n* punta *f* de flecha.
arrowroot ['ærəuruːt] *n* arruruz *m*.
arse [ɑːs] *n* (*tabu*) culo *m*.
arsenal ['ɑːsinl] *n* arsenal *m*.
arsenic ['ɑːsnik] *n* arsénico *m*.
arson ['ɑːsn] *n* delito *m* de incendiar.
art[1] [ɑːt] *n* (a) arte *gen m in sing, f in pl*; (*skill*) habilidad *f*, destreza *f*; (*technique*) técnica *f*; **—s and crafts** artes *fpl* y oficios; **— exhibition** exposición *f* de arte; **— gallery** museo *m* de bellas artes; **— school** escuela *f* de arte; **work of —** obra *f* de arte; **black —s** magia *f* negra; **commercial —** arte *m* comercial; **fine —s** bellas artes *fpl*; **graphic —s** artes *fpl* gráficas; **liberal —s** artes *fpl* liberales; **the noble —** el boxeo.
 (b) **—s** (*Univ*) Artes *fpl* (*arch*), Filosofía y Letras *f*; **Faculty of A—s** Facultad *f* de Filosofía y Letras;

Bachelor of A—s (*abbr* **B.A.**) Licenciado *m*, a *f*, en Filosofía y Letras; **Master of A—s** (*abbr* **M.A.**) Maestro *m*, a *f* en Artes.

art² [ɑːt] *see* **be.**

artefact ['ɑːtifækt] *n* artefacto *m*.

arterial [ɑːˈtiəriəl] *adj* arterial; *road* principal.

arteriosclerosis [ɑːˈtiəriəusˈkliəˈrəusis] *n* arteriosclerosis *f*.

artery ['ɑːtəri] *n* arteria *f*; (*fig*) arteria *f*, vía *f* principal; (*road*) camino *m* troncal.

artesian well [ɑːˈtiːziənˈwel] *n* pozo *m* artesiano.

artful [ɑːtful] *adj* mañoso, artero, astuto; (*skilful*) ingenioso.

artfully ['ɑːtfəli] *adv* astutamente, con mucha maña; ingeniosamente.

artfulness ['ɑːtfulnis] *n* maña *f*, astucia *f*; ingenio *m*.

arthritic [ɑːˈθritik] *adj* artrítico.

arthritis [ɑːˈθraitis] *n* artritis *f*.

arthropoda [ɑːˈθrɔpədə] *npl* artrópodos *mpl*.

Arthur ['ɑːθə*] *m* Arturo; **King —** el rey Artús, el Rey Arturo.

Arthurian [ɑːˈθjuəriən] *adj* arturiano, artúrico.

artichoke ['ɑːtitʃəuk] *n* alcachofa *f*; **Jerusalem —** aguaturma *f*.

article ['ɑːtikl] **1** *n* artículo *m*; objeto *m*, cosa *f*; **—s of apprenticeship** contrato *m* de aprendizaje; **—s of association** estatutos *mpl* de asociación (de una sociedad anónima); **— of clothing** prenda *f* de vestir; **— of faith** artículo *m* de fe; **—s of value** objetos *mpl* de valor; **—s of war** código *m* militar; **definite —** artículo *m* definido; **indefinite —** artículo *m* indefinido; **leading —** artículo *m* de fondo; **toilet —s** artículos *mpl* de tocador.
2 *vt text* articular; *items* poner en lista, poner en forma detallada; *apprentice* pactar, comprometer por contrato; **to be —d to** estar de aprendiz con, servir bajo contrato a.

articulate [ɑːˈtikjulit] *adj* (*jointed*) articulado; *speech* claro, distinto; **at 2 a child is hardly —** a los 2 años el niño es apenas capaz de hablar claramente; **he's not very —** no se expresa bien, no habla con confianza.

articulate [ɑːˈtikjuleit] *vt* articular.

articulation [ɑːˌtikjuˈleiʃən] *n* articulación *f*.

artifice ['ɑːtifis] *n* artificio *m*; ardid *m*, estratagema *f*.

artificial [ˌɑːtiˈfiʃəl] *adj* artificial; *hair, teeth etc* postizo; *person* afectado; *manure* químico.

artificiality [ˌɑːtifiʃiˈæliti] *n* lo artificial; afectación *f*.

artificially [ˌɑːtiˈfiʃəli] *adv* artificialmente; afectadamente, con afectación.

artillery [ɑːˈtiləri] *n* artillería *f*; **heavy —** artillería *f* pesada.

artilleryman [ɑːˈtilərimən], *pl* **—men** [mən] *n* artillero *m*.

artisan ['ɑːtizæn] *n* artesano *m*.

artist ['ɑːtist] *n* artista *mf*.

artist(e) [ɑːˈtiːst] *n* (*Theat*) artista *mf* de teatro; (*Mus*) intérprete *mf*; **variety —** artista *mf* de variedades.

artistic [ɑːˈtistik] *adj* artístico.

artistically [ɑːˈtistikəli] *adv* artísticamente; **to be — gifted** tener talento artístico.

artistry ['ɑːtistri] *n* arte *m*, habilidad *f* artística.

artless ['ɑːtlis] *adj* natural, sencillo; ingenuo; (*clumsy*) desmañado.

arty ['ɑːti] *adj* (*fam*) ostentosamente artístico; *person* de gusto muy afectado, que se las echa de muy artista, repipi.

arty-crafty ['ɑːtiˈkrɑːfti] *adj* (*fam*), **artsy-craftsy** ['ɑːtsiˈkrɑːftsi] *adj* (*US fam*) ostentosamente artístico, afectadamente artístico.

Aryan ['ɛəriən] **1** *adj* ario. **2** *n* ario *m*, a *f*.

as [æz, əz] *adv, conj and prep* (a) (*comparisons*) como: **he does — I do** hace como yo; **— . . . — tan . . . como; — tall —** tan alto como; (*quickly —* tan rápidamente como; **is it — big — all that?** ¿tan grande es en efecto?; **the same —** it (*or* la, lo) mismo que; **such countries — France** los países tales como Francia; **large books (such) —** dictionaries los libros grandes tales como los diccionarios; **he is not so silly — to do that** no es bastante tonto para hacer eso, no es tan tonto como para hacer eso.
(b) (*comparisons: intensifying similes*) (**—**) **pale — death** pálido como la muerte; **— dead — a doornail** más muerto que mi abuela.
(c) (*comparisons*: as if etc) **— if, — though** como si + *subj*: **— if (he were) drunk** como si estuviera borracho; **— if — to** + *infin* como para + *infin*.
(d) (*concessive*) **interesting — the book is** por interesante que sea el libro; **stupid — he is** aunque es estúpido; **be that — it may** sea como fuere eso.

(e) (*in the quality or capacity of*) como: **— a husband and father** como marido y padre; **Vivien Leigh — Cleopatra** Vivien Leigh en el papel de Cleopatra; **I don't think much of him — an actor** no le estimo como (*or* en cuanto, en tanto que) actor; **he was often ill — a child** estuvo a menudo enfermo de niño; **we're going — tourists** vamos en plan de turismo; (*after certain verbs*) de: **to act —** actuar de, estar de; **to be dressed —** estar vestido de.

(f) (*concerning*) **— for that, — to that, — regards** that en cuanto a eso, por lo que se refiere a eso.

(g) (*manner*) **— often happens** como (*or* según) ocurre a menudo; **do — you wish** haga lo que quiera, haga como quiera; **to leave things — they are** dejar las cosas tal como están; **just — you are an engineer,** (so) **I am a doctor** lo mismo que Vd es ingeniero, yo soy médico; **her door is the first — you go up the stairs** su puerta es la primera según se sube la escalera; **you've got plenty —** it is Vd tiene bastante ya; **— it is we can do nothing** así las cosas, no podemos hacer nada.

(h) (*time*) **he came in — I was leaving** entró como yo salía; **— I was sitting there he came up** mientras yo estaba sentado allí se acercó; **— he learned more** a medida que iba aprendiendo más; **— I was passing the house** al pasar yo delante de la casa; **— from tomorrow** a partir de mañana.

(i) (*result*) **he did it in such a way — to please everyone** lo hizo de tal modo que logró contentar a todos.

(j) (*because*) **— I don't talk Arabic** como yo no hablo árabe; **I can't come — I have an appointment** no puedo venir, pues (*or* ya que, porque) tengo un compromiso.

asbestos [æzˈbestəs] *n* asbesto *m*, amianto *m*.

ascend [əˈsend] **1** *vt stairs, river* subir; *mountain, throne* subir a. **2** *vi* subir; (*soar*) elevarse, encaramarse.

ascendancy [əˈsendənsi] *n* ascendiente *m*, dominio *m* (*over* sobre).

ascendant [əˈsendənt] *n*: **to be in the —** predominar, tener una influencia cada vez mayor.

ascension [əˈsenʃən] *n* ascensión *f*; **A— Day** Día *m* de la Ascensión.

ascent [əˈsent] *n* (*act*) subida *f*, ascensión *f*; (*promotion*) ascenso *m*; (*slope*) cuesta *f*, pendiente *f*.

ascertain [ˌæsəˈtein] *vt* averiguar, determinar, descubrir.

ascertainable [ˌæsəˈteinəbl] *adj* averiguable.

ascertainment [ˌæsəˈteinmənt] *n* averiguación *f*.

ascetic [əˈsetik] **1** *adj* ascético. **2** *n* asceta *mf*.

asceticism [əˈsetisizəm] *n* ascetismo *m*.

ascribable [əsˈkraibəbl] *adj* atribuible.

ascribe [əsˈkraib] *vt* atribuir (*to* a).

ascription [əsˈkripʃən] *n* atribución *f*.

aseptic [eiˈseptik] *adj* aséptico.

asexual [eiˈseksjuəl] *adj* asexual.

ash¹ [æʃ] *n* (*Bot*) fresno *m*.

ash² [æʃ] *n* ceniza *f*; **—es** cenizas *fpl* (*also of dead*); **A— Wednesday** Miércoles *m* de Ceniza.

ashamed [əˈʃeimd] *adj*: **to be** (*or* feel) **—** avergonzarse, estar avergonzado (*at, of* de; *for* por; *of being*) de ser): **I am —** of you me das vergüenza; **I was — to ask for money** me daba vergüenza pedir dinero; **your generosity makes me feel —** su generosidad me produce vergüenza; **to be — of oneself** tener vergüenza de sí; **you ought to be — of yourself!** ¿no te da vergüenza esto?

ash-bin ['æʃbin] *n* cubo *m* de la basura.

ashcan ['æʃkæn] *n* (*US*) cubo *m* de la basura.

ash-coloured ['æʃkʌləd] *adj*, **ashen** ['æʃn] *adj* ceniciento; *face* pálido.

ashlar ['æʃlə*] *n* sillar *m*.

ashore [əˈʃɔː*] *adv*: **to be —** estar en tierra; **to come —, to go —** desembarcar; **to put someone —** desembarcar a uno.

ash pan ['æʃpæn] *n* guardacenizas *m*.

ashtray ['æʃtrei] *n* cenicero *m*.

ashy ['æʃi] *adj* cenizoso.

Asia ['eiʃə] Asia *f*; **— Minor** Asia *f* Menor.

Asiatic [ˌeisiˈætik] **1** *adj* asiático. **2** *n* asiático *m*, a *f*.

aside [əˈsaid] **1** *adv* aparte, a un lado. **2** *prep*: **— from** aparte de. **3** *n* (*Theat*) aparte *m*; **to say in an —** decir aparte.

asinine ['æsinain] *adj* asnal; (*fig*) estúpido.

ask [ɑːsk] **1** *vt* (a) (*inquire, inquire of*) preguntar; **to — someone something** preguntar algo a uno; **to — someone a question** hacer una pregunta a uno; **they —ed me about my passport** me hicieron preguntas acerca de mi pasaporte; **they —ed me about the new missile** me interrogaron sobre el nuevo proyectil; **don't — me!** ¡yo qué sé!

(b) (*request, demand*) pedir; **to — someone a favour** pedir un favor a uno; **how much are they —ing for it?** ¿cuánto piden por él?; **I don't — much from you** no soy muy exigente con Vds; **that's —ing the impossible** eso es pedir lo imposible; **to write —ing for help** escribir en demanda de ayuda; **that's —ing a lot** eso pone mucho; **to — something from** (*or of*) **someone** pedir algo a uno; **to — someone for something** pedir algo a uno; **to — that** pedir que + *subj*, rogar que + *subj*; **to — someone to do something** pedir que uno haga algo.

(c) (*invite*) invitar; **have they —ed you?** ¿te han invitado a ti?; **to — someone back** invitar a uno a que pague la visita; **to — someone in** rogar a uno que pase; **to — someone out** invitar a uno a que salga, rogar a uno que le dé una cita; **to — someone to dinner** invitar a uno a cenar.

2 *vi* preguntar; (*request, demand*) pedir; **I was only —ing** era una simple pregunta; **for the —ing** sin más que pedirlo, con solo pedir; **this is the third time of —ing** ésta es la tercera vez que te lo pido; **to — about, to — after, to — for** (*inquire*) preguntar por; **to — for** (*request*) pedir, reclamar; **to — for something back** pedir que se devuelva algo; **he —ed for it** (*fam*) se la buscó, bien merecido lo tiene; **it's just —ing for trouble** eso es buscar tres pies al gato.

askance [ə'skɑːns] *adv*: **to look — at** mirar con recelo, mirar con desdén.

askew [ə'skjuː] *adv* sesgado, ladeado, oblicuamente; **the picture is —** el cuadro está torcido.

aslant [ə'slɑːnt] **1** *adv* a través, oblicuamente. **2** *prep* a través de.

asleep [ə'sliːp] *adj*: **to be —** estar dormido; **to be fast** (*or* **sound**) **—** estar profundamente dormido; **to drop —, to fall —** dormirse, quedar dormido.

asp [æsp] *n* áspid *m*.

asparagus [əs'pærəgəs] *n* (*plant*) espárrago *m*; (*as food*) espárragos *mpl*.

aspect ['æspekt] *n* aspecto *m*; apariencia *f*; **to study all —s of a question** estudiar una cuestión bajo todos los aspectos; **a house with a southern —** una casa orientada hacia el sur.

aspen ['æspən] *n* álamo *m* temblón.

asperity [æs'periti] *n* aspereza *f*.

aspersion [əs'pɜːʃən] *n* calumnia *f*; **to cast —s on** difamar, calumniar.

asphalt ['æsfælt] **1** *n* asfalto *m*; (*place*) pista *f* asfaltada, recinto *m* asfaltado. **2** *vt* asfaltar.

asphyxia [æs'fiksiə] *n* asfixia *f*.

asphyxiate [æs'fiksieit] **1** *vt* asfixiar. **2** *vi* morir asfixiado.

asphyxiation [æs,fiksi'eiʃən] *n* asfixia *f*.

aspic ['æspik] *n* manjar a base de gelatina, que contiene huevos, carne etc.

aspidistra [,æspi'distrə] *n* aspidistra *f*.

aspirant ['æspirənt] *n* aspirante *mf*, candidato *m* (*after, for, to* a).

aspirate ['æspərit] **1** *adj* aspirado. **2** *n* aspirada *f*.

aspirate ['æspəreit] *vt* aspirar.

aspiration [,æspə'reiʃən] *n* (*Med, Gram*) aspiración *f*; (*fig*) anhelo *m*, deseo *m*, ambición *f*.

aspire [əs'paiə*] *vi*: **to —** aspirar a, ambicionar; **we can't — to that** nuestras pretensiones son más modestas; **he —s to a new car** anhela tener un nuevo coche; **to — to** + *infin* aspirar a + *infin*, anhelar + *infin*, tener vivo deseo de + *infin*, ambicionar + *infin*.

aspirin ['æspirin] *n* aspirina *f*.

aspiring [əs'paiəriŋ] *adj* ambicioso, deseoso de tener éxito.

ass[1] [æs] *n* asno *m*, burro *m*; (*fig*) burro *m*, imbécil *m*; **the man's an — es un imbécil**; **what an — I am!** ¡soy un imbécil!; **to make an — of oneself** ponerse en ridículo.

ass[2] [æs] *n* (*US tabu*) culo *m*.

assail [ə'seil] *vt* acometer, atacar; *task* acometer, emprender; **doubts began to — him** empezaron a asaltarle algunas dudas; **he was —ed by critics on all sides** por todos lados le atacaron los críticos; **a sound —ed my ear** un ruido penetró en mis oídos.

assailant [ə'seilənt] *n* asaltador *m*, ora *f*; agresor *m*, ora *f*; **there were 4 —s** los que le atacaron eran 4; **he disarmed his —** le quitó las armas al agresor.

assassin [ə'sæsin] *n* asesino *m*.

assassinate [ə'sæsineit] *vt* asesinar.

assassination [ə,sæsi'neiʃən] *n* asesinato *m*.

assault [ə'sɔːlt] **1** *n* asalto *m* (*on* sobre), ataque *m* (*on* a, contra); (*Law*) violencia *f*; **— and battery** violencias *fpl* físicas; **indecent —, sexual —** atentado *m* contra el pudor.

2 *vt* asaltar, atacar; (*Law*) agredir; *woman* violar, tratar de violar.

assay [ə'sei] **1** *n* ensaye *m*. **2** *vt metals* ensayar; (*fig*) intentar, probar; **to —** + *infin* intentar + *infin*.

assemblage [ə'semblidʒ] *n* reunión *f*; colección *f*; (*Mech*) montaje *m*.

assemble [ə'sembl] **1** *vt* reunir, juntar; (*Mech*) montar. **2** *vi* reunirse, juntarse.

assembly [ə'sembli] *n* reunión *f*; (*Pol etc*) asamblea *f*; (*people present*) concurrencia *f*, asistentes *mpl*; (*Mech*) montaje *m*; **unlawful —** reunión *f* ilegal.

assembly line [ə'semblilain] *n* línea *f* de montaje.

assembly room [ə'semblirum] *n* sala *f* de fiestas.

assembly shop [ə'sembliʃɔp] *n* taller *m* de montaje.

assent [ə'sent] **1** *n* asentimiento *m*, consentimiento *m*, aprobación *f*; **royal —** aprobación *f* real. **2** *vi* consentir (*to* en), asentir (*to* a).

assert [ə'sɜːt] **1** *vt* afirmar, declarar; *rights* hacer valer.

2 *vr*: **to — oneself** imponerse, hacer valer sus derechos.

assertion [ə'sɜːʃən] *n* afirmación *f*, declaración *f*.

assertive [ə'sɜːtiv] *adj* enérgico.

assess [ə'ses] *vt* valorar, apreciar, tasar, calcular (*at* en); enjuiciar, juzgar; *property* gravar (con impuestos); *tax, damages* fijar (*at* en); **how did you — this candidate?** ¿qué juicio formó Vd sobre este candidato?; **how do you — the situation now?** ¿cómo ve Vd la situación actual?

assessment [ə'sesmənt] *n* (*act*) valoración *f*, tasación *f*; (*tax*) gravamen *m*, imposición *f*; (*fig*) aprecio *m*, juicio *m*.

assessor [ə'sesə*] *n* asesor *m*; (*of taxes etc*) tasador *m*.

asset ['æset] *n* (**a**) posesión *f*; (*book-keeping item*) partida *f* del activo; (*useful quality*) ventaja *f*.

(b) **—s** (*Comm*) activo *m*, haber *m*, capital *m*, fondos *mpl*; (*fig*) valores *mpl* positivos, ventajas *fpl*; **—s in hand** bienes *mpl* disponibles; **liquid —s** activo *m* líquido; **personal —s** bienes *mpl* muebles.

asseverate [ə'sevəreit] *vt* aseverar.

asseveration [ə,sevə'reiʃən] *n* aseveración *f*.

assiduous [ə'sidjuəs] *adj* asiduo.

assiduously [ə'sidjuəsli] *adv* asiduamente.

assign [ə'sain] *vt asignar*; *reason etc* señalar, indicar; *share, task* señalar; *property* traspasar, ceder; *literary work etc* atribuir; **they —ed him to the Paris embassy** le nombraron para la embajada de París; **which is the room —ed to me?** ¿qué habitación es la que me destinan a mí?; **the event is to be —ed to the year 1600** hemos de referir este suceso al año 1600.

2 *n* (*Law*) cesionario *m*.

assignation [,æsig'neiʃən] *n* asignación *f*; traspaso *m*; nombramiento *m*; (*meeting*) cita *f* (*esp* amorosa).

assignment [ə'sainmənt] *n* (*act*) asignación *f* etc; (*task*) cometido *m*, tarea *f*; misión *f*.

assimilate [ə'simileit] **1** *vt* asimilar. **2** *vi* asimilarse.

assimilation [ə,simi'leiʃən] *n* asimilación *f*.

assist [ə'sist] **1** *vt* ayudar; *development, progress etc* favorecer, estimular, fomentar; **we —ed him to his car** le ayudamos para que llegara a su coche.

2 *vi* (*help*) ayudar; **to — at** asistir a; **to — in** tomar parte en, participar en; **to — in** + *ger* ayudar a + *infin*, contribuir a + *infin*.

assistance [ə'sistəns] *n* (**a**) ayuda *f*, auxilio *m*; **to be of —** to ayudar a, prestar ayuda a; **can I be of —?** ¿puedo ayudarle?; **to come to someone's —** acudir en auxilio de uno, socorrer a uno.

(b) (*also* **national —**) subsidio *m* al necesitado.

assistant [ə'sistənt] **1** *adj* auxiliar; **— manager** subdirector *m*; **— secretary** subsecretario *m*; **— professor** (US) profesor *m* auxiliar.

2 *n* ayudante *mf*; **laboratory —** ayudante *mf* de laboratorio; **shop —** vendedor *m*, ora *f*, dependiente *m*, a *f*.

assizes [ə'saiziz] *npl* sesión *f* de un tribunal.

associate [ə'səuʃiit] **1** *adj* asociado; *member* correspondiente; *professor* adjunto.

2 *n* asociado *m*, colega *m*; compañero *m*; (*in crime*) cómplice *m*; (*member*) miembro *m* correspondiente; (*Comm*) socio *m*, consocio *m*.

associate [ə'səuʃieit] **1** *vt* asociar; relacionar; juntar, unir; **I don't wish to be —d with** it no quiero tener nada que ver con ello; **was he —d with that scandal?** ¿estuvo mezclado con ese escándalo?

2 *vi* asociarse (*with* a, con); juntarse, unirse; **to — in** mancomunarse en, participar juntamente en; **to — with** *person* ir con, tratar con, frecuentar la compañía de.

3 *vr*: **to — oneself with someone in a venture** participar con uno en una empresa; **I should like to — myself with that** quiero hacerme eco de esa opinión.

associated [ə'səuʃieitid] *adj* asociado; conexo; *company* afiliado.

association [ə,səusi'eiʃən] *n* (**a**) asociación *f*; (*Comm*) sociedad *f*; (*producers'* —) cooperativa *f*; (*connection*) conexión *f*, relación *f*; **by — of ideas** por asociación de ideas.

(**b**) **—s** (*memories*) recuerdos *mpl*, sugestiones *fpl*; **the town has historic —s** la ciudad tiene importancia en la historia; **the word has nasty —s** la palabra hace pensar en cosas feas.

assonance ['æsənəns] *n* (*in general*) asonancia *f*; (*word*) asonante *f*; **words in —** palabras *fpl* asonantadas.

assort [ə'sɔːt] *vi* concordar (*with* con), convenir (*with* a); **it —s ill with his character** no cuadra con su carácter; **this does not — with what you said** esto no corresponde con lo que dijo Vd.

assorted [ə'sɔːtid] *adj* surtido, variado; (*hum*) **he dined with — ministers** cenó con este y con el otro ministro.

assortment [ə'sɔːtmənt] *n* (*Comm*) surtido *m*; variedad *f*, colección *f* variada; **there was a strange — of guests** los invitados pertenecían a tipos muy diversos; **quite an —!** ¡aquí hay de todo!

assuage [ə'sweidʒ] *vt feelings* calmar; *pain* aliviar; *passion* mitigar, suavizar; *desire* satisfacer; *appetite* saciar; *person* apaciguar, contentar; **he was not easily —d** no era fácil darle satisfacción, no era fácil desalterarle.

assume [ə'sjuːm] *vt* (**a**) *aspect, name, possession, importance, large proportions* tomar; *air* darse; *attitude* adoptar; *authority* (*unjustly*) apropiarse, arrogarse; *control, responsibility* asumir; *power* ocupar; *burden* asumir, tomar sobre sí.

(**b**) (*suppose*) suponer, dar por sentado; **to — that** suponer que, imaginar que; **let us — that** pongamos por caso que; **you resigned, I —** imagino que Vd dimitió; **assuming (that)** dado que.

assumed [ə'sjuːmd] *adj* falso, fingido.

assumption [ə'sʌmpʃən] *n* (**a**) (*act*) asunción *f*; el tomar, adopción *f*; **A—** (*Rel*) Asunción *f*.

(**b**) (*supposition*) suposición *f*, presunción *f*; **that is a dangerous —** es peligroso dar aquello por sentado; **on the — that** suponiendo que; **to start from a false —** partir de una base falsa.

(**c**) (*arrogance*) presunción *f*.

assurance [ə'ʃuərəns] *n* (**a**) (*guarantee*) garantía *f*, promesa *f*; **you have my —** that les aseguro que; **I can give you no — about that** no les puedo hacer ninguna promesa sobre ello.

(**b**) (*confidence*) confianza *f*; aplomo *m*, serenidad *f*.

(**c**) (*certainty*) certeza *f*, seguridad *f*; **to make — doubly sure** para mayor seguridad.

(**d**) (*insurance*) seguro *m*.

assure [ə'ʃuə*] *vt* (**a**) (*make certain*) asegurar, garantizar.

(**b**) (*insure*) asegurar; **his life is —d for £5000** su vida está asegurada en 5000 libras.

(**c**) *person* asegurar; **I —ed him of my support** le aseguré de mi apoyo; **you may rest —d that** Vd puede estar completamente seguro de que; **let me — you** that permita que le asegure que; **it is so, I — you** es así, se lo aseguro.

assured [ə'ʃuəd] **1** *adj* confiado, sereno; **you have an — future** Vd tiene un porvenir de éxito seguro. **2** *n* (*Comm*) asegurado *m*, a *f*.

assuredly [ə'ʃuəridli] *adv* seguramente, sin duda.

Assyria [ə'siriə] Asiria *f*.

Assyrian [ə'siriən] **1** *adj* asirio. **2** *n* asirio *m*, a *f*.

aster ['æstə*] *n* aster *f*.

asterisk ['æstərisk] **1** *n* asterisco *m*. **2** *vt* señalar con un asterisco, poner asterisco a.

astern [ə'stəːn] **1** *adv* a popa, por la popa; **to fall —** quedarse atrás; **to go —** ciar, ir hacia atrás; **to make a boat fast —** amarrar un barco por la popa. **2** *prep*: **— of** detrás de.

asteroid ['æstərɔid] *n* asteroide *m*.

asthma ['æsmə] *n* asma *f*.

asthmatic [æs'mætik] **1** *adj* asmático. **2** *n* asmático *m*, a *f*.

astigmatic [,æstig'mætik] *adj* astigmático.

astigmatism [æs'tigmətizəm] *n* astigmatismo *m*.

astir [ə'stəː*] *adv* activo, en movimiento; (*up and about*) levantado; **we were — early** nos levantamos temprano; **at that hour nobody was —** a tal hora todos estaban todavía en cama.

astonish [ə'stɔniʃ] *vt* asombrar, pasmar; **you — me!** ¡esto es asombroso!; **to be —ed** asombrarse (*at* de), maravillarse (*at* de, con), quedarse asombrado (*at* de).

astonishing [ə'stɔniʃiŋ] *adj* asombroso, pasmoso; **I find it — that** se me hace muy cuesta arriba creer que, para mí es increíble que.

astonishingly [ə'stɔniʃiŋli] *adv*: **it was — easy** era increíblemente fácil; **it was an — lovely scene** la escena era de una belleza totalmente inesperada; **— enough** por milagro, por maravilla.

astonishment [ə'stɔniʃmənt] *n* asombro *m*, sorpresa *f*, estupefacción *f*; **there was general —** todos quedaron estupefactos; **to my —** con gran sorpresa mía.

astound [ə'staund] *vt*, **astounding** [ə'staundiŋ] *adj etc see* **astonish, astonishing** *etc*.

astrakhan [,æstrə'kæn] *n* astracán *m*.

astral ['æstrəl] *adj* astral.

astray [ə'strei] *adv*: **to go —** extraviarse; (*fig: make a mistake*) equivocarse, (*morally*) ir por mal camino; **to lead —** llevar por mal camino; **I was led — by his voice** su voz hizo que me equivocara.

astride [ə'straid] **1** *adv* a horcajadas. **2** *prep* a caballo sobre, a horcajadas sobre.

astringent [əs'trindʒənt] *adj* (*Med*) astringente; (*fig*) adusto, austero.

astrologer [əs'trɔlədʒə*] *n* astrólogo *m*.

astrological [,æstrə'lɔdʒikəl] *adj* astrológico.

astrology [əs'trɔlədʒi] *n* astrología *f*.

astronaut ['æstrənɔːt] *n* astronauta *mf*.

astronautics [,æstrəu'nɔːtiks] *n* astronáutica *f*.

astronomer [əs'trɔnəmə*] *n* astrónomo *m*.

astronomical [,æstrə'nɔmikəl] *adj* astronómico; (*fig*) tremendo, inmenso, increíble.

astronomy [əs'trɔnəmi] *n* astronomía *f*.

astrophysics ['æstrəu'fiziks] *n* astrofísica *f*.

astute [əs'tjuːt] *adj* astuto.

astutely [əs'tjuːtli] *adv* astutamente.

astuteness [əs'tjuːtnis] *n* astucia *f*.

asunder [ə'sʌndə*] *adv*: **to tear —** hacer pedazos, romper en dos; **to put —** separar.

asylum [ə'sailəm] *n* asilo *m*; (*lunatic —, mental —*) manicomio *m*; **to afford — to** (*place*) servir de asilo a, (*person*) dar asilo a; **to ask for political —** pedir asilo político.

asymmetric(al) [,eisi'metrik(əl)] *adj* asimétrico.

at [æt] *prep* (**a**) (*position*) en; **— the edge** en el borde; **— the top** en la cumbre; **— Toledo** en Toledo; **— school** en la escuela; **— sea** en el mar; **— peace** en paz; **— John's** en casa de Juan; **— the hairdresser's** en la peluquería; **— table** a la mesa; **to stand — the door** estar a la puerta; **to be — the window** mirar por la ventana; **he came in — the window** entró por la ventana.

(**b**) (*time*) **— 4 o'clock** a las cuatro; **— midday** a mediodía; **— night** de noche, por la noche; **— this season** en esta época del año; **— Christmas** por Navidades; **— a time like this** en un momento como el actual; **two — a time** de dos en dos.

(**c**) (*price*) **— a shilling a pound** a chelín la libra; **— 4% interest** al 4 por 100 de interés; **— a high price** a un precio elevado.

(**d**) **— my request** a petición mía; **to awaken — the least sound** despertarse al menor ruido; **— his suggestion** siguiendo su sugerencia, de acuerdo con su sugerencia; **— one stroke** de un golpe; **he's good — games** tiene talento para los juegos; **I'm no good — that** yo soy inútil para eso.

(**e**) (*with verb to be*) **to be — work** estar en el trabajo; **to be hard — it** estar trabajando con ahinco; **I've been — it for 3 hours** estoy ocupado en esto desde hace 3 horas; **what are you —?** ¿qué haces ahí?; **while we are —** it mientras lo estemos haciendo; **you've been — me all day** has estado persiguiéndome todo el día; **she's — it again** ella está siempre con la misma canción.

atavism ['ætəvizəm] *n* atavismo *m*.

atavistic [,ætə'vistik] *adj* atávico.

ate [eit] *pret of* **eat**.

atheism ['eiθiizəm] *n* ateísmo *m*.

atheist ['eiθiist] *n* ateo *m*, a *f*.

atheistic [,eiθi'istik] *adj* ateo, ateísta.

Athenian [ə'θiːniən] **1** *adj* ateniense. **2** *n* ateniense *mf*.

Athens ['æθinz] Atenas *f*.

athirst [ə'θəːst] *adj* (*fig*): **to be — for** tener sed de.

athlete ['æθliːt] *n* atleta *mf*.

athlete's foot ['æθliːts'fut] *n* (*Med*) pie *m* de atleta.

athletic [æθ'letik] *adj* atlético.

athletics [æθ'letiks] *n sing* atletismo *m*.

at-home [ət'həum] *n* recepción *f* (en casa particular).

athwart [ə'θwɔːt] **1** *adv* de través, al través. **2** *prep* a través de.

Atlantic (Ocean) [ət'læntik('əuʃən)] (Océano) Atlántico *m*.

Atlantis [ət'læntis] Atlántida *f*.

atlas ['ætləs] *n* atlas *m*; **A—** Atlante *m*.

atmosphere ['ætməsfiə*] n atmósfera f; (fig) ambiente m.

atmospheric [,ætməs'ferik] adj atmosférico.

atmospherics [,ætməs'feriks] npl (Radio) mala atmósfera f, parásitos mpl.

atoll ['ætɔl] n atolón m.

atom ['ætəm] n átomo m; **if you had an — of sense** si Vd tuviera la más mínima parte de inteligencia; **to smash to —s** hacer añicos.

atomic [ə'tɔmik] adj atómico.

atomic-powered [ə'tɔmik'pauəd] adj impulsado por energía atómica.

atomize ['ætəmaiz] vt reducir a átomos; **liquid atomizer.**

atomizer ['ætəmaizə*] n atomizador m.

atom smasher ['ætəm,smæʃə*] n rompeátomos m.

atonal [æ'təunl] adj atonal.

atone [ə'təun] vi: **to — for** expiar.

atonement [ə'təunmənt] n expiación f; **Day of A—** Día m de la Expiación.

atonic [æ'tɔnik] adj átono.

atop [ə'tɔp] **1** adv encima. **2** prep encima de; sobre, en la cumbre de.

atrocious [ə'trəuʃəs] adj atroz; (fig) horrible, infame.

atrocity [ə'trɔsiti] n atrocidad f.

atrophy ['ætrəfi] **1** n atrofia f. **2** vt atrofiar. **3** vi atrofiarse.

attach [ə'tætʃ] **1** vt (a) (fasten) sujetar; (stick) pegar; (tie) atar, liar; (with pin etc) prender; (join) unir; seal poner; trailer etc acoplar, enganchar.
  (b) (in letter) adjuntar; **the document is —ed** enviamos adjunto el documento; **the —ed letter** la carta adjunta.
  (c) (fig) importance, value dar, conceder (to a); **the salary —ed to the post is £2000** el sueldo que corresponde al puesto es de 2000 libras; **to be —ed to an embassy** estar agregado a una embajada; **there are no strings —ed to this** esto es sin compromiso alguno, esto es libre de condiciones.
  (d) (Law) property incautar, embargar.
  (e) **to be —ed to** person etc tener cariño a.
  2 vi: **to — to** corresponder a, pertenecer a; **no blame —es to you** Vd no tiene culpa alguna.
  3 vr: **to — oneself to** group agregarse a, entrar a formar parte de; (in bad sense) pegarse a.

attaché [ə'tæʃei] n agregado m; **commercial —** agregado m comercial; **cultural —** agregado m cultural; **military —** agregado m militar; **naval —** agregado m naval.

attaché case [ə'tæʃeikeis] n maletín m.

attachment [ə'tætʃmənt] n (a) (act) atadura f, unión f etc.
  (b) (device) accesorio m, dispositivo m; (coupling) acoplamiento m.
  (c) (affection) cariño m, apego m (to a); (loyalty) adhesión f.
  (d) (Law) incautación f, embargo m.

attack [ə'tæk] **1** n (a) (Mil etc) ataque m (on a, contra, sobre), asalto m; (criminal — on person) agresión f; **air —** ataque m aéreo; **flank —** ataque m de flanco; **frontal —** ataque m de frente; **surprise —** ataque m por sorpresa; **— on someone's life** atentado m contra la vida de uno; **— on the security of the state** atentado m contra la seguridad del estado; **to be under —** ser atacado; **— is the best form of defence** la mejor defensa está siempre en el ataque; **to launch an —** lanzar un ataque; **to leave oneself open to —** dejarse expuesto al ataque; **to return to the —** volver al ataque.
  (b) (Med) ataque m, acceso m; **an — of pneumonia** una pulmonía; **an — of nerves** una crisis nerviosa.
  2 vt (Mil etc) atacar (also Med, Chem); acometer; (criminally) agredir, asaltar; (bull etc) embestir; (gratuitously) emprenderla con; problem acometer, tratar de resolver; opinion, theory impugnar; **we must — poverty** debemos acabar con la pobreza; **he was —ed by doubts** le asaltaron dudas.

attackable [ə'tækəbl] adj atacable.

attacker [ə'tækə*] n agresor m, ora f, asaltante mf.

attain [ə'tein] **1** vt alcanzar, lograr, conseguir. **2** vi: **to — to** llegar a.

attainable [ə'teinəbl] adj alcanzable, realizable.

attainment [ə'teinmənt] n (act) logro m, consecución f, obtención f; **—s** dotes fpl, talento m (in para), conocimientos mpl (in de); **difficult of —** de difícil consecución.

attempt [ə'tempt] **1** n (a) tentativa f, intento m, conato m; **to make an — to +** infin intentar + infin; **he made a tentativa de +** infin, intentar + infin; **he made two —s at it** trató dos veces de lograrlo; **to make an — on the record** tratar de batir la marca; **it was**

a good — fue un esfuerzo loable; **this is my first —** es la primera vez que lo intento; **we had to give up the —** tuvimos que renunciar a la empresa.
  (b) atentado m (on someone's life contra la vida de uno).
  2 vt (a) probar, ensayar, intentar; tratar de efectuar (or conseguir etc); (undertake) emprender.
  (b) **to — to +** infin intentar + infin, tratar de + infin; **to accuse someone of —ed murder** acusar a uno de tentativa de asesinato.

attend [ə'tend] **1** vt (wait on) servir; (escort) acompañar; (Med) atender, asistir; (be present at) asistir a; **a well-—ed meeting** una reunión muy concurrida; **the policy was —ed by many difficulties** la política tropezó con muchas dificultades.
  2 vi (be present) asistir; (pay attention) prestar atención; **to — to** words, work prestar atención a; task ocuparse de; (Comm) ejecutar; **can you — to this customer?** ¿está Vd libre para atender a este cliente?; **I'll — to you in a moment** un momentito y estoy con Vd.

attendance [ə'tendəns] n (a) (act) asistencia f (at a), presencia f (at en); **is my — necessary?** ¿es preciso que asista yo?
  (b) (those present) concurrencia f, asistentes mpl; **what was the — at the meeting?** ¿cuántos asistieron a la reunión?; **we need an — of 1000** hace falta atraer a un público de 1000.
  (c) (Med) asistencia f.
  (d) **to be in —** asistir; estar de servicio; **to dance — on** estar pendiente de los menores detalles de.

attendant [ə'tendənt] **1** adj: **the — crowd** la multitud que asistió a ello; **the — difficulties** las dificultades con que ello tropezó; **the — circumstances** las circunstancias concomitantes.
  2 n acompañante m; (servant) sirviente m, a f; mozo m; (Theat) acomodador m, ora f; (in carpark, museum) celador m.

attention [ə'tenʃən] n (a) atención f; **it requires daily —** hay que atenderlo a diario; **it shall have my earliest —** lo atenderé lo más pronto posible; **to attract (or catch) someone's —** llamar la atención de uno; **to call (or draw) someone's —** llamar la atención de uno sobre; **to come to someone's —** hacérsele presente a uno; **to give (or pay) —** prestar atención (to a); **he paid no —** no hizo caso (to that de eso); **to pay special — to** fijarse de modo especial en; **to turn one's — to** pasar a considerar, pasar a estudiar.
  (b) (Mil) **—!** ¡firme(s)!; **to come to —** ponerse firme(s), cuadrarse; **to stand at —** estar firme(s).
  (c) **—s** atenciones fpl, cortesías fpl.

attentive [ə'tentiv] adj (heedful) atento; (polite) cortés, obsequioso (to con).

attentively [ə'tentivli] adv atentamente; cortésmente.

attentiveness [ə'tentivnis] n atención f; cortesía f.

attenuate [ə'tenjueit] vt atenuar.

attenuating [ə'tenjueitiŋ] adj atenuante.

attest [ə'test] **1** vt atestiguar (that que); dar fe de; signature confirmar, autenticar. **2** vi: **to — to** dar fe de.

attic ['ætik] n desván m, ático m.

Attila ['ætilə] m Atila.

attire [ə'taiə*] **1** n traje m, vestido m; (hum) atavío m. **2** vt vestir (in de); (hum) ataviar (in de).

attitude ['ætitjuːd] n actitud f; (posture in painting etc) ademán m; postura f; **— of mind** actitud f, disposición f de ánimo; **to strike (or adopt, take up) an —** tomar una postura, adoptar una actitud; **if that's your —** si te pones en ese plan; **what is your — to this?** ¿cuál es su posición con respecto a esto?

attitudinize [,æti'tjuːdinaiz] vi tomar posturas afectadas.

attorney [ə'tɔːni] n (lawyer) abogado m; (representative) apoderado m, a f; **district —** (US) fiscal m; **A— General** fiscal m de la corona, (US) procurador m general; **power of —** poder m, procuración f.

attract [ə'trækt] vt atraer; attention llamar.

attraction [ə'trækʃən] n atracción f; (attractive feature) atractivo m; (inducement) aliciente m; **the film has the special — of featuring X** la película tiene el aliciente especial de presentar a X; **the main — at the party was Y** el interés de la fiesta se cifraba en Y; **one of the —s of the quiet life** uno de los encantos de la vida retirada; **spring —s in Madrid** las diversiones de la primavera madrileña.

attractive [ə'træktiv] adj atractivo; (interesting) atrayente; idea, plan sugestivo; child, girl mono, guapo, atractivo; offer interesante; prospect halagüeño.

attractively [ə'træktivli] adv atractivamente; de modo atrayente; de modo sugestivo; de modo

halagüeño; **an — designed garden** un jardín de trazado atractivo.
attributable [ə'tribjutəbl] *adj*: **— to** atribuible a.
attribute ['ætribjuːt] *n* atributo *m*.
attribute [ə'tribjuːt] *vt* atribuir; achacar; **to what would you — this?** ¿cómo explica Vd esto?
attribution [,ætri'bjuːʃən] *n* atribución *f*.
attributive [ə'tribjutiv] *adj* atributivo.
attrition [ə'triʃən] *n*: **war of —** guerra *f* de agotamiento.
attune [ə'tjuːn] *vt* (*fig*): **to — to** armonizar con; **to be —d to** estar en armonía con.
atypical [,ei'tipikəl] *adj* atípico.
aubergine ['oubəʒiːn] *n* berenjena *f*.
auburn ['oːbən] *adj* castaño rojizo.
auction ['oːkʃən] **1** *n* subasta *f*, almoneda *f*, licitación *f* (*SAm*); (*at bridge*) subasta *f*; **— sale, sale by —** subasta *f*; **Dutch —** *subasta en la que el precio se reduce poco a poco hasta encontrar comprador*; **to put up for —, to sell at —** subastar, poner en pública subasta.
  2 *vt* subastar (*also* **— off**), licitar (*SAm*).
auctioneer [,oːkʃə'niə*] *n* subastador *m*, licitador *m* (*SAm*).
auction room ['oːkʃənrum] *n* sala *f* de subastas.
audacious [oː'deiʃəs] *adj* audaz, atrevido; (*in bad sense*) descarado.
audacity [oː'dæsiti] *n* audacia *f*, atrevimiento *m*; (*in bad sense*) descaro *m*; **and you have the — to say that!** ¡y Vd me lo dice tan fresco!, ¡y usted se atreve a decirlo!
audibility [,oːdi'biliti] *n* audibilidad *f*.
audible ['oːdibl] *adj* audible, que se puede oír; **the speech was barely —** apenas se podía oír nada del discurso.
audibly ['oːdibli] *adv* de modo que se puede oír; **he said quite —** lo dijo de modo que se podía oír claramente.
audience ['oːdiəns] *n* (a) (*gathering*) auditorio *m*, público *m*; **there was a big —** asistió un público numeroso; **those in the —** los que formaban parte del auditorio.
  (b) (*interview*) audiencia *f* (*of*, *with* con); **to grant someone an —, to receive someone in —** recibir a uno en audiencia; **to have an — of** (*or* **with**) ser recibido en audiencia por.
audio-visual [,oːdiəu'vizjuəl] *adj* audiovisual.
audit ['oːdit] **1** *n* revisión *f* de cuentas, intervención *f*. **2** *vt* revisar, intervenir.
audition [oː'diʃən] **1** *n* audición *f*. **2** *vt* dar audición a; **he was —ed for the part** le hicieron una audición para el papel.
auditor ['oːditə*] *n* censor *m* de cuentas, interventor *m*.
auditorium [,oːdi'toːriəm] *m* auditorio *m*, sala *f*.
auditory ['oːditəri] *adj* auditivo.
Augean Stables [oː'dʒiːən'steiblz] *pl* establos *mpl* de Augias.
aught [oːt] *n* algo, alguna cosa *f*; (*with negation*) nada; **if there is — I can do** si puedo ayudarles en alguna manera; **for — I care** igual me da; **for — I know** que yo sepa.
augment [oːg'ment] **1** *vt* aumentar. **2** *vi* aumentar(se).
augmentation [,oːgmen'teiʃən] *n* aumento *m*.
augmentative [oːg'mentətiv] *adj* aumentativo.
augur ['oːgə*] **1** *vt* thing augurar, pronosticar; **it —s no good** esto no nos promete nada bueno.
  2 *vi*: **it —s ill** es de mal agüero; **to — well** ser de buen agüero (*for* para).
augury ['oːgjuri] *n* augurio *m*; **to take the auguries** consultar los augurios.
August ['oːgəst] *n* agosto *m*.
august [oː'gʌst] *adj* augusto.
Augustan [oː'gʌstən] *adj* augustal; **the — age** (*Latin*) el siglo de Augusto, (*English*) la época neoclásica (del siglo XVIII).
Augustine [oː'gʌstin] *m* Agustín.
Augustus [oː'gʌstəs] *m* Augusto.
auk [oːk] *n* alca *f*; **little —** mérgulo *m* marino.
aunt [ɑːnt] *n* tía *f*; **my — and uncle** mis tíos.
auntie, aunty ['ɑːnti] *n* (*fam*) tía *f*.
au pair ['əu'pɛə] *adv* au pair.
aura ['oːrə] *n* emanación *f*; (*atmosphere*) ambiente *m*.
aural ['oːrəl] *adj* aural.
au revoir [,əurə'vwɑː*] *adv* hasta la vista.
auricle ['oːrikl] *n* (*Anat*) aurícula *f*.
aurochs ['oːrɔks] *n* uro *m*.
aurora borealis [oː'roːrəbɔːri'eilis] *n* aurora *f* boreal(is).
auspices ['oːspisiz] *npl*: **under the — of** bajo los auspicios de.

auspicious [oːs'piʃəs] *adj* propicio, favorable, de buen augurio; **to make an — start** comenzar felizmente.
auspiciously [oːs'piʃəsli] *adv* propiciamente, favorablemente; **to start —** comenzar felizmente.
Aussie ['ozi] (*fam*) **= Australian**.
austere [os'tiə*] *adj* austero; *style* adusto.
austerely [os'tiəli] *adv* austeramente; adustamente.
austerity [os'teriti] *n* austeridad *f*; adustez *f*.
Australia [os'treiliə] Australia *f*.
Australian [os'treiliən] **1** *adj* australiano. **2** *n* australiano *m*, a *f*.
Austria ['ostriə] Austria *f*.
Austrian ['ostriən] **1** *adj* austríaco. **2** *n* austríaco *m*, a *f*.
authentic [oː'θentik] *adj* auténtico.
authenticate [oː'θentikeit] *vt* autenticar; autentificar.
authenticity [,oːθen'tisiti] *n* autenticidad *f*.
author ['oːθə*] *n* autor *m*, ora *f*.
authoress ['oːθəris] *n* autora *f*.
authoritarian [oː,θori'tɛəriən] **1** *adj* autoritario. **2** *n* autoritario *m*, a *f*.
authoritarianism [oː,θori'tɛəriənizəm] *n* autoritarismo *m*.
authoritative [oː'θoritətiv] *adj* *version* autorizado; *manner etc* autoritario.
authority [oː'θoriti] *n* autoridad *f*; **the authorities** las autoridades; **he is the greatest living —** es la máxima autoridad actual; **he is an — on the subject** es muy perito en la materia; **to apply to the proper —** dirigirse a la autoridad competente; **I have no — to + infin** yo no estoy autorizado para + *infin*; **to give someone an — to + infin** autorizar a uno para que + *subj*; **to do something without —** hacer algo sin tener autorización para ello; **those in —** los que tienen la autoridad; **in — over** al mando de; **who is in — here?** ¿quién manda aquí?; **on the — of Plato** con la autoridad de Platón; **I have it on good — that** sé de buena tinta que.
authorization [,oːθərai'zeiʃən] *n* autorización *f*.
authorize ['oːθəraiz] *vt* autorizar; **to — someone to + infin** autorizar a uno para + *infin*; **the A—d Version** la Versión Autorizada (de la Biblia).
authorized ['oːθəraizd] *adj* autorizado.
authorship ['oːθəʃip] *n* (a) profesión *f* de autor. (b) (*of book*) autoría *f*, paternidad *f* literaria.
autism ['oːtizəm] *n* autismo *m*.
autistic [oː'tistik] *adj* autístico.
auto¹ . . . ['oːtəu] in *compounds*: auto . . .
auto² ['oːtəu] *n* (*US*) coche *m*, automóvil *m*.
autobiographic(al) ['oːtəu,baiəu'græfik(əl)] *adj* autobiográfico.
autobiography [,oːtəubai'ogrəfi] *n* autobiografía *f*.
autocade ['oːtəukeid] *n* (*US*) caravana *f* de automóviles.
autocracy [oː'tokrəsi] *n* autocracia *f*.
autocrat ['oːtəukræt] *n* autócrata *mf*.
autocratic [,oːtəu'krætik] *adj* autocrático.
autocycle ['oːtəusaikl] *n* velomotor *m*, ciclomotor *m*.
auto-da-fé ['oːtəudɑː'fei] *n* auto *m* de fe.
autogiro ['oːtəu'dʒaiərou] *n* autogiro *m*.
autograph ['oːtəgrɑːf] **1** *adj* autógrafo *m*; **— album** álbum *m* de autógrafos.
  2 *n* (*MS*) autógrafo *m*; (*signature*) firma *f*.
  3 *vt* (*sign*) firmar; *book*, *photo* dedicar, poner su nombre en.
automate ['oːtəmeit] *vt* automatizar.
automatic [,oːtə'mætik] **1** *adj* automático. **2** *n* pistola *f* automática.
automatically [,oːtə'mætikəli] *adv* automáticamente.
automation [,oːtə'meiʃən] *n* automatización *f*.
automaton [oː'tomətən] *n*, *pl* **automata** [oː'tomətə] autómata *m*.
automobile ['oːtəməbiːl] *n* (*US*) coche *m*, automóvil *m*.
automotive [,oːtə'məutiv] *adj* automotor.
autonomous [oː'tonəməs] *adj* autónomo.
autonomy [oː'tonəmi] *n* autonomía *f*.
autopsy ['oːtopsi] *n* autopsia *f*.
autosuggestion ['oːtəusə'dʒestʃən] *n* (auto)sugestión *f*.
autumn ['oːtəm] *n* otoño *m*.
autumnal [oː'tʌmnəl] *adj* otoñal.
Auvergne [əu'vɛən] Auvernia *f*.
auxiliary [oːg'ziliəri] **1** *adj* auxiliar. **2 auxiliaries** *npl* tropas *fpl* auxiliares.
avail [ə'veil] **1** *n*: **it is of no —** es inútil; **of what — is it to + infin?** ¿de qué sirve + *infin*?; **to be of little —** ser de poco provecho; **to no —** en vano, sin resultado.
  2 *vt* aprovechar, valer.
  3 *vi*: **it —s nothing to + infin** de nada sirve + *infin*.
  4 *vt*: **to — oneself of** aprovechar(se de), valerse de.

availability [ə,veilə'biliti] n disponibilidad f.

available [ə'veiləbl] adj disponible; asequible, aprovechable; **to make something — to someone** poner algo a la disposición de uno; **is the manager —?** ¿está libre el gerente?, ¿puedo pasar a ver al gerente?; **are you — next Thursday?** ¿tienes compromiso para el jueves que viene?; **I am not — to visitors** no estoy para las visitas; **that ticket is no longer —** ese billete ya no vale.

avalanche ['ævəlɑ:nʃ] n alud m, avalancha f; (fig) torrente m, avalancha f.

avant-garde ['ævɑ̃ː'ŋ'gɑ:d] adj ultramoderno, de vanguardia, nueva ola.

avarice ['ævəris] n avaricia f.

avaricious [,ævə'riʃəs] adj avaro, avariento.

avenge [ə'vendʒ] **1** vt vengar. **2** vr: **to — oneself** vengarse (on en).

avenger [ə'vendʒə*] n vengador m, ora f.

avenging [ə'vendʒiŋ] adj vengador.

avenue ['ævənjuː] n avenida f; (fig) vía f, camino m; **to explore every —** tentar todas las vías.

aver [ə'vɜː*] vt afirmar, declarar.

average ['ævəridʒ] **1** adj medio, de término medio; regular, corriente; (pej) mediano, ordinario; **the — man** el hombre medio; **of — height** de regular estatura; **of — ability** de capacidad regular; **the — height of players** el promedio de talla por jugador.

  2 n (a) promedio m, término m medio; **on (an or the) —** por término medio; por regla general.

  (b) (Comm) avería f.

  3 vt (also **to — out**) calcular el término medio de; prorratear.

  4 vi (also **to — out at**) ser por término medio, resultar por término medio; ser por regla general; **we — 8 hours a day** trabajamos (etc) por regla general 8 horas diarias; **he —d 50 all the way** sacó un promedio de 50 millas por hora por todo el recorrido.

averse [ə'vɜːs] adj: **I am — to** siento repugnancia por, tengo antipatía a; **I am not — to an occasional drink** no me repugna tomar algo de vez en cuando; **I am — to getting up early** tengo pocas ganas de levantarme temprano.

aversion [ə'vɜːʃən] n (a) aversión f (for, from, to hacia), repugnancia f (for, from, to por); **to feel an — for** sentir repugnancia por; **I have an — to him** me resulta antipático; **I took an — to it** empezó a repugnarme.

  (b) (hated thing) cosa f aborrecida; **pet —** bestia f negra, pesadilla f; (person) hincha mf.

avert [ə'vɜːt] vt eyes, thoughts apartar (from de); suspicion desviar (from de); possibility quitar; blow impedir, desviar; accident, illness, rebellion prevenir.

aviary ['eiviəri] n pajarera f, avería f.

aviation [,eivi'eiʃən] n aviación f; **— spirit** gasolina f de aviación.

aviator ['eivieitə*] n aviador m, ora f.

avid ['ævid] adj ávido, ansioso (for, of de).

avidity [ə'viditi] n avidez f, ansia f.

avidly ['ævidli] adv ávidamente, ansiosamente; **to read —** leer con avidez.

Avignon ['ævinjɔ̃] Aviñón.

avocado [ævə'kɑ:dəu] n aguacate m.

avocation [,ævəu'keiʃən] n diversión f, distracción f, ocupación f accesoria; (loosely) vocación f.

avoid [ə'vɔid] vt evitar; guardarse de; duty etc eludir; danger salvarse de; **to — + ger** evitar + infin; **he managed to — the tree** evitó chocar con el árbol; **are you trying to — me?** ¿se está esforzando Vd por no hablar conmigo?; **I try to — him** procuro no tener nada que ver con él; **he —s all his friends** huye de todos sus amigos; **it's to be —ed like the plague** esto hay que evitarlo como la peste; **this way we — London** por esta ruta evitamos entrar en Londres.

avoidable [ə'vɔidəbl] adj evitable, eludible.

avoidance [ə'vɔidəns] n el evitar (etc), evitación f.

avoirdupois [,ævədə'pɔiz] n sistema de pesos británico y estadounidense (1 libra = 16 onzas = 453,50 gramos); (fam) peso m, gordura f.

avow [ə'vau] **1** vt reconocer, confesar. **2** vr: **he —ed himself beaten** reconoció que había perdido.

avowal [ə'vauəl] n confesión f; declaración f.

avowed [ə'vaud] adj declarado.

avowedly [ə'vauidli] adv declaradamente, abiertamente.

avuncular [ə'vʌŋkjulə*] adj como de tío.

await [ə'weit] vt esperar, aguardar; **the fate that —s him** la suerte que le espera; **we — your reply with interest** nos interesa mucho saber su contestación;

a long **—ed event** un acontecimiento que se viene esperando desde hace mucho tiempo.

awake [ə'weik] **1** adj despierto; **to lie —** quedar despierto, estar sin poder dormir; **to stay — all night** pasar toda la noche en vela; **the noise kept me —** el ruido me impidió dormir; **coffee keeps me —** el café me desvela; **to be — to** ser consciente de.

  2 (irr: pret **awoke**, ptp **awaked**) vt despertar.

  3 vi despertar(se).

awaken [ə'weikən] **1** vt despertar (also fig); **to — someone to something** hacer que uno se dé cuenta de algo.

  2 vi despertar(se) (also fig); **to — to** to darse cuenta de.

awakening [ə'weikniŋ] n despertamiento m, el despertar; **a rude —** una sorpresa desagradable.

award [ə'wɔːd] **1** n (act of —ing) adjudicación f; concesión f; (prize) premio m; (Law) sentencia f, fallo m; (Mil etc) condecoración f.

  2 vt conceder, otorgar; prize, damages etc adjudicar, decretar; medal dar; **the prize is not being —ed this year** este año el premio se declaró desierto.

aware [ə'weə*] adj (a) (alert) enterado; despierto.

  (b) **to be — of** saber, estar enterado de, ser consciente de; **not that I am — of** que yo sepa; **our employees are — of this advert** los empleados de la empresa ya conocen este anuncio; **so far as I am —** según mi leal saber y entender; **to be — that** saber que; **I am fully — that** yo sé perfectamente que; **to become — of** darse cuenta de, enterarse de.

awareness [ə'weənis] n conciencia f, conocimiento m.

awash [ə'wɔʃ] adv: **the deck is —** la cubierta está a flor de agua; **the house was —** la casa estaba inundada.

away [ə'wei] **1** adv: (a) **3 miles —** a 3 millas (de aquí); **— in the distance** allá a lo lejos; **— from the noise** lejos del ruido; **— with you!** ¡vete!, ¡fuera de aquí!; **— with him!** ¡que le lleven de aquí!; **— with taxes!** ¡abajo los impuestos!

  (b) (with verb to be) **to be — (from home)** estar fuera, estar ausente; **he's — for a week** pasa una semana fuera; **it's 10 miles —** dista de aquí 10 millas, está a 10 millas de aquí; **we are 20 miles — from London** estamos a 20 millas de Londres.

  (c) (other verbs) **I must —** tengo que marcharme; **to play —** jugar fuera.

  2 adj: **the — team** el equipo de fuera.

awe [ɔː] **1** n temor m reverencial, pavor m y respeto; **to go in — of, to hold in —, to stand in — of** tener temor reverencial a. **2** vt imponer respeto a.

awe-inspiring ['ɔːin,spaiəriŋ] adj, **awesome** ['ɔːsəm] adj imponente, pasmoso.

awe-struck ['ɔːstrʌk] adj pasmado.

awful ['ɔːfəl] adj (a) tremendo, imponente, terrible, pasmoso.

  (b) (fam) horrible, malísimo, fatal; **it was simply —** fue francamente horrible; **how —!** ¡qué horror!; **what — weather!** ¡qué tiempo más feo!; **his English is —** tiene un inglés fatal; **he's an — fool** es un puro tonto; **there were an — lot of people** había la mar de gente.

awfully ['ɔːfli] adv (fam) terriblemente; **it's — hard** es terriblemente difícil; **it's — funny** es divertidísimo; **I'm — sorry** lo siento muchísimo; **thanks —!** ¡muchísimas gracias!; **he's — nice** es simpatiquísimo.

awfulness ['ɔːfulnis] n horror m.

awhile [ə'wail] adv un rato, algún tiempo; **not yet —** todavía no.

awkward ['ɔːkwəd] adj problem, question difícil; situation violento, difícil; time inoportuno; task delicado, desagradable; shape incómodo; corner peligroso; phrasing poco elegante; (clumsy) desmañado, desgarbado, torpe; **it's — for me** es difícil para mí; **it's all a bit —** todo esto es un poco violento; **he's being — about it** está poniendo peros; **to feel —** sentirse molesto; **to be at the — age** estar en la edad del pavo; **the — squad** la sección de los bisoños.

awkwardness ['ɔːkwədnis] n dificultad f; violencia f; incomodidad f; molestia f; desmaña f, torpeza f.

awl [ɔːl] n lezna f, subilla f.

awning ['ɔːniŋ] n toldo m; (of cart) entalamadura f; (Naut) toldilla f; (over window) marquesina f.

awoke [ə'wəuk] pret and ptp of **awake**.

awry [ə'rai] adv: **to be —** estar de través, estar al sesgo, estar puesto mal; **to go —** salir mal, fracasar.

ax (US), **axe** [æks] **1** n hacha f; **when the — fell** (fig) cuando se descargó el golpe; **to have an — to grind** actuar de una manera interesada.

  2 vt (fig) reducir, cercenar; person despedir.

axial ['æksiəl] *adj* axial.

axiom ['æksiəm] *n* axioma *m*.

axiomatic [,æksiəu'mætik] *adj* axiomático.

axis ['æksis] *n*, *pl* **axes** ['æksiːz] eje *m*; (*Anat*) axis *m*; **the A—** (*Pol*) el Eje; **the A— powers** las potencias del Eje.

axle ['æksl] *n* eje *m*, árbol *m*; **rear —** eje *m* trasero.

axle-box ['ækslbɔks] *n* caja *f* de eje.

ay(e) [ai] **1** *adv* sí; **— — sir!** sí, mi capitán (*etc*).

2 *n* sí *m*; **the —s have it** se ha aprobado la moción; **there were 50 —s and 3 noes** votaron 50 a favor y 3 en contra.

aye [ei] *adv*: **for ever and —** para siempre jamás.

azalea [ə'zeiliə] *n* azalea *f*.

Azores [ə'zɔːz] *pl* Azores *fpl*.

Aztec ['æztek] **1** *adj* azteca. **2** *n* azteca *mf*.

azure ['eiʒə*] **1** *adj* azul celeste. **2** *n* azul *m* celeste; (*Her*) azur *m*.

B

baa [bɑ:] **1** n balido m. **2** interj ¡bee! **3** vi balar.

baa-lamb ['bɑ:læm] n (fam) corderito m, borreguito m.

babble ['bæbl] **1** n barboteo m; (of stream) murmullo m; **a — of voices arose** se oyó un ruido confuso de voces.

2 vt decir balbuceando.

3 vi barbullar, barbotear; (talk to excess) parlotear; (tell secrets) hablar indiscretamente; (stream) murmurar.

babe [beib] n (lit or hum) criatura f; (US sl) chica f, (in direct address) ricura f, nena f.

Babel ['beibəl] Babel m or f; **Tower of —** Torre f de Babel.

baboon [bə'buːn] n mandril m.

baby ['beibi] **1** n niño m, a f; (more sentimental) bebé mf, crío m, a f, rorro m, a f, nene m, a f; (US sl) chica f, (in direct address) ricura f, nena f; **she's having a — in May** va a tener un niño en mayo; **she's having the — in hospital** va a dar a luz en el hospital; **— of the family** benjamín m; **don't be such a —!** ¡no seas niño!

2 attr and adj: **— boy** nene m; **— girl** nena f; **— clothes**, **— linen** ropa f de niño; **— face** cara f de niño; **— car** coche m pequeño.

baby carriage ['beibi,kæridʒ] n (US) cochecito m de niño.

baby grand ['beibi'grænd] n piano m de media cola.

babyhood ['beibihud] n infancia f.

babyish ['beibiiʃ] adj infantil.

Babylon ['bæbilən], **Babylonia** [,bæbi'ləuniə] Babilonia f.

Babylonian [,bæbi'ləuniən] **1** adj babilonio, babilónico. **2** n babilonio m, a f.

baby-sit ['beibisit] vi hacer de niñero, vigilar (a los niños dormidos, en ausencia de sus padres).

baby-sitter ['beibi,sitə*] n guardián m, ana f de niños.

baby talk ['beibitɔ:k] n habla f infantil.

baccarat ['bækɑrɑ:] n bacará m, bacarrá m (Acad).

bacchanalia [,bækə'neiliə] npl bacanales fpl; (fig) bacanal f.

bacchanalian [,bækə'neiliən] adj bacanal, báquico.

Bacchic ['bækik] adj báquico.

Bacchus ['bækəs] m Baco.

baccy ['bæki] n (fam) tabaco m.

bachelor ['bætʃələ*] n **(a)** soltero m; **confirmed —, old —** solterón m; **— flat** piso m para soltero; **— girl** soltera f (que se dedica a una carrera); **— party** guateque m para hombres solos.

(b) (Univ) licenciado m, a f (of en).

bachelorhood ['bætʃələhud] n soltería f, estado m de soltero.

bacillary [bə'siləri] adj bacilar.

bacillus [bə'siləs] n, pl **bacilli** [bə'silai] bacilo m.

back ['bæk] **1** adj trasero, de atrás, posterior; **view** desde atrás; **issue**, **number** atrasado; **pay** retrasado.

2 adv **(a)** atrás, hacia atrás; **— and forth** de acá para allá, de una parte a otra; **a house standing — from the road** una casa situada no demasiado cerca de la carretera; **to make one's way —** regresar; **to fly to Madrid and —** ir en avión a Madrid y volver del mismo modo.

(b) (time) **— in the 12th century** allá en el siglo XII; **as far — as 1900** ya en 1900; **some months —** hace unos meses.

(c) (with verb to be) **to be — estar** de vuelta; **when will he be —?** ¿cuándo volverá?

3 prep: **— of** (US) = **behind.**

4 n (Anat) espalda f; (of animal, knife) lomo m; (of chair) respaldo m; (of coin) reverso m; (of cheque, document, hand) dorso m; (end of book) final m; (spine of book) lomo m; (of stage, cave etc) fondo m; (Sport) defensa m; **— to —** espalda con espalda; **— to front** al revés; **at the — of** tras, detrás de; **al fondo de**; **what's at the — of it?** ¿qué motivo oculto tendrá esto?; **who's at the — of it?** ¿quién lo está dirigiendo (entre bastidores)?; **behind one's —** a espaldas de uno, por detrás de uno (also fig); **she wears her hair down her —** el pelo le cae por la espalda; **with one's —** to de espaldas a; **to be on one's —** (Med) estar postrado (en la cama); **to carry something on one's —** llevar algo a cuestas; **he lay on his —** estaba tumbado boca arriba; **to sign on the —** firmar al dorso; **his — is broad** bien es capaz de soportarlo; **to break one's —** deslomarse; **the ship broke its —** el buque se rompió por medio; **to break the — of the work** haber terminado lo más difícil del trabajo; **to get** (or **put**) **someone's — up** enojar a uno, incordiar a uno; **to have one's — to the wall** estar entre la espada y la pared; **to put one's — into it** esforzarse al máximo, hacer todo lo que puede uno; **put your —s into it!** ¡dale!; **to scratch someone's —** (fig) hacer un favor a uno; **to see the — of someone** librarse de uno; **we were glad to see the — of him** nos alegramos de que se fuera; **to turn one's —** volver las espaldas (on a).

5 vt (support) apoyar, respaldar; defender; favorecer; (bet on) apostar a; (vehicle) dar marcha atrás a; (horse) recular; **to — up** apoyar, secundar, defender.

6 vi moverse hacia atrás, retroceder; (vehicle) dar marcha atrás; **the car —ed into the garage** el coche entró en el garaje marcha atrás; **the house —s on to the park** la parte trasera de la casa da al parque; **to — down** volverse atrás, echarse atrás, desdecirse, rajarse (fam); **to — out** retirarse (of de); **to — up** retroceder.

backache ['bækeik] n dolor m de riñones.

backbencher ['bæk'bentʃə*] n diputado m que no es ministro.

backbite ['bækbait] vi murmurar.

backbiting ['bækbaitiŋ] n murmuración f.

backbone ['bækbəun] n espinazo m; (fig) (guts) firmeza f, agallas fpl, (chief support) espina f dorsal, piedra f angular; **to the —** hasta los tuétanos.

back-breaking ['bækbreikiŋ] adj deslomador, matador.

backchat ['bæktʃæt] n réplicas fpl.

back-cloth ['bækkləθ] n telón m de foro.

backdate ['bæk'deit] vt poner fecha atrasada a; dar efecto retroactivo a; **a salary award —d to January** un aumento de sueldo con efecto retroactivo desde enero.

backdrop ['bækdrɔp] n telón m de foro.

backer ['bækə*] n (Pol) partidario m, a f; (Comm) promotor m, impulsor m, caballo m blanco; (better) apostador m.

backfire ['bæk'faiə*] **1** n (Aut) petardeo m. **2** vi (Aut) petardear; (fig) salir el tiro por la culata; **the idea —d** la idea perjudicó a sus propios inventores.

background ['bækgraund] **1** n **(a)** fondo m; (Art) fondo m, último término m; **in the —** al fondo, en el fondo, en último término; **against a dim —** sobre un fondo oscuro; **to stay in the —** preferir no destacar, no buscar la luz de la publicidad.

(b) (of person etc) antecedentes mpl, historial m, educación f; **the — to the crisis** los antecedentes de la crisis.

2 attr: **— music** música f de fondo; **— studies** estudios mpl del ambiente histórico (etc) (en que vivió un autor etc).

backhand(ed) ['bæk'hænd(id)] adj dado con la vuelta de la mano; (fig) irónico, equívoco; **— shot**, **— stroke** revés m.

backhander ['bæk'hændə*] n revés m.

backing ['bækiŋ] n apoyo m; garantía f; (Comm) respaldo m; (funds) fondos mpl.

backlash ['bæklæʃ] n reacción f, contragolpe m; **the white —** (US Pol) la resaca blanca.

backlog ['bæklɔg] *n* atrasos *mpl*; reserva *f* de pedidos pendientes.

back number ['bæk'nʌmbə*] *n* número *m* atrasado; *(fig)* cero *m* a la izquierda.

back pay ['bækpei] *n* paga *f* con efecto retroactivo.

back-pedal ['bæk'pedl] *vi* contrapedalear.

back room ['bæk'rum] *n* cuarto *m* interior, cuarto *m* en la parte trasera (de una casa); **back-room boy** investigador *m*, inventor *m* (que hace el trabajo preliminar sin reclamar ningún reconocimiento público).

back seat ['bæk'siːt] *n* asiento *m* de atrás; **to take a** — ceder su puesto, dejar de tener influencia.

backseat ['bæksiːt] *attr*: — **driver** *(Aut)* pasajero *m* que molesta al conductor dándole consejos *etc*.

backside ['bæk'said] *n* trasero *m*, culo *m*.

backslapping ['bæk,slæpiŋ] *n* espaldarazos *mpl*; mutual — bombo *m* mutuo.

backslide ['bæk'slaid] *(irr: see* slide*) vi* reincidir, volver a las andadas.

backslider ['bæk'slaidə*] *n* reincidente *mf*.

backsliding ['bæk'slaidiŋ] *n* reincidencia *f*.

backstage ['bæk'steidʒ] **1** *n* espacio *m* entre bastidores. **2** *adv*: **to be** — estar entre bastidores.

backstairs ['bæk'stɛəz] **1** *npl* escalera *f* de servicio; **by the** — *(fig)* por enchufe. **2** *attr* clandestino.

backstitch ['bækstitʃ] **1** *n* pespunte *m*. **2** *vt* pespuntar.

backstroke ['bækstrəuk] *n* braza *f* de espaldas.

backtrack ['bæktræk] *vi* volver pies atrás.

backward ['bækwəd] *adj motion etc* hacia atrás; *pupil, country* atrasado; *(shy)* tímido; **he's not** — **in coming forward** no peca de tímido.

backward(s) ['bækwəd(z)] *adv* atrás, hacia atrás; *(back to front)* al revés; **to walk** — andar de espaldas; **to read something** — leer algo para atrás; **to go** — **and forward** ir de acá para allá.

backwardness ['bækwədnis] *n* atraso *m*, estado *m* atrasado; timidez *f*.

backwash ['bækwɔʃ] *n* agua *f* de rechazo; *(fig)* reacción *f*, consecuencias *fpl*.

backwater ['bækwɔːtə*] *n* brazo *m* de río estancado, remanso *m*; *(fig)* lugar *m* atrasado, lugar *m* de agradable tranquilidad.

backwoods ['bækwudz] *npl* región *f* apartada *(freq* = Las Batuecas in Spain*).*

backwoodsman ['bækwudzmən] *n, pl* — **men** [mən] patán *m*, rústico *m*; *(Pol)* miembro de la Cámara de los Lores que rara vez asiste al Parlamento.

backyard ['bæk'jɑːd] *n* patio *m* trasero, traspatio *m*.

bacon ['beikən] *n* tocino *m* (entreverado, de panceta); **to bring home the** — *(fam)* sacarse el gordo; **to save one's** — *(fam)* salvar el pellejo.

bacterial [bæk'tiəriəl] *adj* bacteriano, bactérico.

bacteriological [bæk,tiəriə'lɔdʒikəl] *adj* bacteriológico.

bacteriologist [bæk,tiəri'ɔlədʒist] *n* bacteriólogo *m*.

bacteriology [bæk,tiəri'ɔlədʒi] *n* bacteriología *f*.

bacterium [bæk'tiəriəm] *n, pl* **bacteria** [bæk'tiəriə] bacteria *f*.

bad [bæd] **1** *adj* malo; *(ill)* malo, enfermo; *(rotten)* podrido, dañado, pasado; *(harmful)* nocivo, dañoso; *accident, mistake* grave; *air* viciado; *cheque* no cubierto, descubierto; *coin* falso; *debt* incobrable; *joke* de mal gusto, nada divertido; *law, treatment* injusto; *shot* descuidado, errado; *tooth* cariado; *voting paper* inválido; **he's a** — **man** es un hombre malo; **he's a** — **one** es un mal sujeto; **he's a very** — **poet** es un poeta malísimo; **my** — **leg** mi pierna lisiada; **to have a** — **cold** estar fuertemente acatarrado; **to talk** — **Spanish** hablar mal el español; **to be** — **at French** ser malo en francés; **I'm** — **about getting up** levantarme exige un gran esfuerzo, me repugna la idea de levantarme; **not** — bastante bueno, nada malo, *(less enthusiastic)* regular; **that's too** — es una pena; **it's really too** — **of you** te has comportado de una manera vergonzosa; **it would be** — **for you to** + *infin* sería poco aconsejable que Vd + *subj*; **it's** — **for you** te hace daño; **what's** — **about it**? ¿qué hay de malo en ello?; **he looks** — tiene mal aspecto; **this is beginning to look** — esto se está poniendo feo; **he's not as** — **as he looks** es mejor persona de lo que parece; **to go from** — **to worse** ir de mal en peor; **to be taken** — *(fam)* caer enfermo; **to go** — *(food)* echarse a perder, pasarse, alterarse.

2 *n* lo malo; **I'm £5 to the** — he perdido 5 libras; **to be in** — **with someone** estar a malas con uno; **to go to the** — echarse a perder, arruinarse; **to take the** — **with the good** aceptar lo malo con lo bueno.

baddie ['bædi] *n (US sl)* mal sujeto *m*, tipo *m* nada confiable; criminal *m*; *(Theat etc)* malo *m*.

baddish ['bædiʃ] *adj* bastante malo, más bien malo.

bade [bæd] *pret of* bid.

badge [bædʒ] *n* divisa *f*, insignia *f*; *(worn on coat)* distintivo *m*; *(metal disc)* chapa *f*, placa *f*; *(fig)* señal *f*, indicio *m*.

badger ['bædʒə*] **1** *n* tejón *m*. **2** *vt* acosar, atormentar *(for* para obtener*)*; **stop** —**ing me**! ¡no me fastidies!

badinage ['bædinɑːʒ] *n* chanzas *fpl*, bromas *fpl*.

badlands ['bædlændz] *npl (US)* tierras *fpl* malas *(región* yerma, *esp en los estados de Nebraska* y *Dakota del Sur).*

badly ['bædli] *adv* mal; **to be** — **mistaken** equivocarse gravemente; **we were** — **beaten** sufrimos una grave derrota; **we came off** — **in the deal** el negocio resultó ser desfavorable para nosotros; **I want it** — lo deseo muchísimo; **we** — **need another assistant** nos hace gran falta otro ayudante; **to be** — **off** andar mal de dinero; **how did he take it**? ... — ¿qué impresión le produjo la noticia? ... malísima.

bad-mannered ['bæd'mænəd] *adj* sin educación, grosero.

badminton ['bædmintən] *n* volante *m*.

badness ['bædnis] *n* lo malo, mala calidad *f*; *(wickedness)* maldad *f*.

bad-tempered ['bæd'tempəd] *adj (permanently)* de mal genio; *(temporarily)* de mal humor; *argument* fuerte; *tone etc* áspero, malhumorado.

baffle ['bæfl] **1** *n (also* — **plate**) deflector *m*; *(Radio)* pantalla *f* acústica.

2 *vt progress* impedir, estorbar; *mind etc* desconcertar; *searchers* confundir; **at times you** —**me** a veces no te comprendo; **the problem** —**s me** al problema no le veo solución alguna; **the police are** —**d** la policía no tiene pista alguna; **the crime** —**d the police for months** durante meses el crimen dejó perpleja a la policía; **it** —**s description** es imposible describirlo.

baffling ['bæfliŋ] *adj crime* de solución nada fácil, misterioso; *action* incomprensible; *problem* dificilísimo.

bag [bæg] **1** *n* **(a)** saco *m*; talega *f*; *(large sack)* costal *m*; *(handbag)* bolso *m*; *(suitcase)* maleta *f*; *(carried over shoulder)* zurrón *m*, mochila *f*; *(in dress)* bolsa *f*; *(in trousers)* rodillera *f*; *(sl)* puta *f*, mujeraza *f*; **diplomatic** — valija *f* diplomática; **the whole** — **of tricks** todo el negocio; **it's in the** — *(fam)* es cosa segura, está en la talega; **to pack** — **and baggage** liar el petate.

(b) *(Hunting)* cacería *f*, caza *f*, número *m* de piezas cazadas.

(c) —**s** *(fam)*: *(baggage)* equipaje *m*; *(trousers)* pantalones *mpl*; —**s under the eyes** bolsas *fpl* de los ojos; **there's** —**s of hay** un montón de, hay la mar de; **we've** —**s of time** tenemos tiempo de sobra.

2 *vt* ensacar; *(Hunting)* cazar, coger, capturar; *(shoot down)* derribar; *(sl)* birlar.

3 *vi* hacer bolsa.

bagatelle [,bægə'tel] *n* bagatela *f*.

bagful ['bægful] *n* saco *m* (lleno).

baggage ['bægidʒ] *n* equipaje *m*; *(Mil)* bagaje *m*; *(fam)* mujercilla *f*.

baggage car ['bægidʒkɑː*] *n (US)* furgón *m* de equipajes.

baggy ['bægi] *adj* muy holgado; que hace bolsa; *trousers* con rodilleras.

bagpiper ['bægpaipə*] *n* gaitero *m*.

bagpipes ['bægpaips] *npl* gaita *f*.

bag-snatcher ['bæg'snætʃə*] *n* ladrón *m* de bolsos.

Bahamas [bə'hɑːməz] *pl* Islas *fpl* Bahama, las Bahamas.

bail¹ [beil] *(Law)* **1** *n* caución *f*, fianza *f*; **on** — bajo fianza; **to be** (*or* **go, stand**) — **for** salir fiador por; **to jump one's** — *(fam)* fugarse estando bajo fianza; **to be released on** — ser puesto en libertad bajo fianza. **2** *vt* afianzar; **to** — **someone out** obtener la libertad de uno bajo fianza, *(fig)* echar un cable a uno.

bail² [beil] *vt (Naut)* achicar.

bailiff ['beilif] *n (Law)* alguacil *m*, corchete *m*; *(steward)* administrador *m*.

bairn [bɛən] *n (Scot)* niño *m*, a *f*.

bait [beit] **1** *n* cebo *m*, *(live)* carnada *f*; *(fig)* aliciente *m*, añagaza *f*; **he wouldn't rise to the** — no quería picar; **to swallow the** — tragar el anzuelo.

2 *vt hook, trap* cebar, poner cebo en; *(fig)* acosar, atormentar.

baize [beiz] *n* bayeta *f*; **green** — tapete *m* verde.

bake [beik] *vt* cocer al horno; *bricks etc* cocer; *(harden)* endurecer; **it's baking hot** hace un calor terrible.

bakehouse ['beikhaus] *n, pl* —**houses** [hauziz] tahona *f*, panadería *f*.

Bakelite ['beikəlait] *n (Protected Trade Name)* baquelita *f*.

baker ['beikə*] *n* panadero *m*; —**'s (shop)** panadería *f*.

bakery ['beikəri] n tahona f, panadería f.
baking ['beikiŋ] n cocción f; (batch) hornada f.
baking powder ['beikiŋ,paudə*] n polvos mpl de levadura.
baksheesh ['bækʃi:ʃ] n propina f.
Balaclava [,bælə'klɑ:və] n (also — helmet) pasamontañas m.
balance ['bæləns] 1 n (a) (state) equilibrio m; — of power equilibrio m político; when the — of his mind was disturbed en un momento de obcecación; to lose one's — perder el equilibrio; to throw someone off — hacer que uno pierda el equilibrio, (fig) desconcertar a uno.
(b) (scales) balanza f.
(c) (Comm) balance m; (remainder) resto m; (still to be paid over) remanente m; (eg credit —) saldo m; adverse — saldo m negativo; credit — saldo m positivo; — in hand alcance m, sobrante m; — of payments balance m de pagos; — of trade balance m de comercio; on — pensándolo bien; to be (or hang) in the — estar pendiente de un hilo; to hold the — tener una influencia decisiva.
2 vt (a) equilibrar; (make up for) contrapesar (with con); this has to be —d against that hay que pesar esto contra aquello; the match is nicely —d el partido lo podrá ganar tanto un equipo como el otro; —d diet régimen m bien equilibrado; —d personality personalidad f estable; —d view opinión f juiciosa.
(b) account saldar; budget nivelar; to — the books hacer balance, cerrar los libros.
3 vi (a) equilibrarse.
(b) (Comm) now the account —s ahora está bien, el balance de esta cuenta; to — up finiquitar.
4 vr: to — oneself equilibrarse (on en).
balance sheet ['bælənsʃi:t] n balance m, avanzo m.
balcony ['bælkəni] n balcón m; (covered) mirador m; (of block of flats) galería f, terraza f; (Theat) paraíso m.
bald [bɔ:ld] adj calvo; style escueto, desnudo; as — as a coot completamente calvo; to go — quedarse calvo.
balderdash ['bɔ:ldədæʃ] n tonterías fpl.
bald-headed ['bɔ:ld'hedid] adj calvo; to go — into (fam) meterse de ligero en.
baldly ['bɔ:ldli] adv escuetamente, desnudamente.
baldness ['bɔ:ldnis] n (a) calvicie f; premature — calvicie f precoz. (b) (fig) lo escueto, desnudez f.
bale[1] [beil] 1 n bala f, (Agr) paca f, fardo m. 2 vt (also to — up) embalar, (Agr) empacar.
bale[2] [beil] vi: to — out (Aer) lanzarse en paracaídas.
Bâle [bɑ:l] Basilea.
Balearic [,bæli'ærik] 1 adj balear. 2: the —s, — Islands pl Baleares fpl, Islas fpl Baleares.
baleful ['beilful] adj influence funesto, siniestro; look triste.
baler ['beilə*] n (Agr) empacadora f, enfardadora f.
balk [bɔ:k] 1 n (Agr) lomo m; (of timber) viga f.
2 vt (thwart) burlar, impedir; (miss) perder, no aprovechar.
3 vi (stop) detenerse bruscamente; (horse) plantarse, repropiarse (at al ver); he —ed at this se resistió a considerarlo, lo rechazó.
Balkan ['bɔ:lkən] 1 adj balcánico. 2: the —s pl los Balcanes.
ball[1] [bɔ:l] n (in general) bola f; globo m, esfera f; (eg tennis ball) pelota f; (eg football) balón m; (Mil) bala f; (of wool) ovillo m; crystal — bola f de cristal; to be on the — ser un hacha; estar al tanto; you have to be on the — for this para esto hay que fijarse mucho; to keep one's eye on the — (fig) no perder de vista lo principal del asunto; to play — jugar a la pelota, (fig) cooperar (with con), ser acomodadizo; to roll up into a — hacerse una pelota, arrollarse; to start the — rolling empezar, hablar (etc) primero.
ball[2] [bɔ:l] n (dance) baile m (gen de etiqueta).
ballad ['bæləd] n balada f, (Spanish) romance m.
ballade [bæ'lɑ:d] n (Mus) balada f.
ballast ['bæləst] 1 n (Naut and fig) lastre m; (Rail) balasto m; in — en lastre. 2 vt (Naut) lastrar; (Rail) balastar.
ball bearing ['bɔ:l'beəriŋ] n cojinete m a (or de) bolas, rodamiento m a bolas.
ballboy ['bɔ:lbɔi] n recogedor m de pelotas.
ballcock ['bɔ:lkɔk] n (Tech) llave f de bola, llave f de flotador.
ballerina [,bælə'ri:nə] f bailarina f (de ballet).
ballet ['bælei] n ballet m, baile m.
ballet dancer ['bælei,dɑ:nsə*] n bailarín m, ina f (de ballet).
ballistic [bə'listik] adj balístico.
ballistics [bə'listiks] n sing balística f.

balloon [bə'lu:n] 1 n globo m. 2 vi subir en un globo; (sail etc) hincharse como un globo (also to — out).
balloon barrage [bə'lu:n,bærɑ:ʒ] n (Mil) barrera f de globos.
balloonist [bə'lu:nist] n ascensionista mf.
ballot ['bælət] 1 n (voting) votación f; (paper) balota f, papeleta f (para votar); to take a — on something someter algo a votación; there will be a — for the remaining places se sortearán las plazas restantes.
2 vt members etc invitar a votar.
3 vi votar; to — for elegir (or determinar etc) por votación; to — for tickets rifar, sortear.
ballot box ['bælətbɔks] n urna f electoral.
ballot paper ['bælətpeipə*] n papeleta f (para votar).
ball-point pen ['bɔ:lpɔint'pen] n bolígrafo m.
ballroom ['bɔ:lrum] n salón m de baile; — dance baile m de salón.
ballyhoo [,bæli'hu:] n (fam) propaganda f sensacional.
balm [bɑ:m] n bálsamo m (also fig).
balmy ['bɑ:mi] adj balsámico; breeze etc suave, fragante.
baloney [bə'ləuni] n (sl) tonterías fpl.
balsa ['bɔ:lsə] n balsa f.
balsam ['bɔ:lsəm] n bálsamo m.
Baltic Sea ['bɔ:ltik'si:] n Mar m Báltico.
balustrade [,bæləs'treid] n balaustrada f, barandilla f.
bamboo [bæm'bu:] n bambú m.
bamboozle [bæm'bu:z] vt (fam) embaucar, capear.
ban [bæn] 1 n prohibición f (on de); to be under a — estar prohibido; to put a — on prohibir (el uso de), proscribir; to raise the — on levantar el entredicho a.
2 vt prohibir, proscribir; person excluir (from de); he was —ned from driving for life le prohibieron conducir de por vida; the bullfighter was —ned for 3 months el torero fue inhabilitado para ejercer la profesión durante 3 meses.
banal [bə'nɑ:l] adj banal, vulgar.
banality [bə'næliti] n banalidad f, vulgaridad f.
banana [bə'nɑ:nə] n plátano m, banana f (esp SAm).
banana tree [bə'nɑ:nə,tri:] n plátano m, banano m.
band [bænd] 1 n (a) (strip of material) banda f, tira f, faja f; (ribbon) cinta f; (edging) cenefa f, franja f; (armband) brazalete m; (hatband) cintillo m; (of harness) correa f; (stripe) lista f, raya f; (of territory) faja f; zona f; metal — fleje m, precinto m; rubber — goma f, gomita f.
(b) (Radio) banda f.
(c) (Mus) orquesta f; (Mil Mus) banda f, música f; (brass —) charanga f, banda f; jazz — orquesta f de jazz; to beat the — (fam) hasta más no poder.
(d) (group) grupo m; cuadrilla f; (pej) gavilla f; (gang) pandilla f.
2 vt (stripe) rayar.
3 vi: to — together juntarse, asociarse; (pej) apandillarse.
bandage ['bændidʒ] 1 n venda f, vendaje m. 2 vt vendar.
bandbox ['bændbɔks] n sombrerera f.
bandit ['bændit] n bandido m; one-armed — máquina f tragaperras.
banditry ['bænditri] n bandolerismo m, bandidaje m.
bandmaster ['bændmɑ:stə*] n director m de banda.
bandsman ['bændzmən] n, pl —men [mən] músico m de banda.
bandstand ['bændstænd] n quiosco m de música.
bandwagon ['bænd,wægən] n: to climb on the — adherirse al partido ganador; seguir la moda.
bandy[1] ['bændi] vt words, stories cambiar; don't — words with me! ¡no replique Vd!; to — someone's name about mencionar el nombre de uno en rumores.
bandy[2] ['bændi] adj, **bandy-legged** ['bændi'legd] adj estevado.
bane [bein] n: it's the — of my life será mi ruina.
baneful ['beinful] adj nocivo; funesto, fatal.
bang [bæŋ] 1 interj ¡pum!; (of a blow) ¡zas!; to go (off) — hacer explosión, estallar.
2 adv precisamente, exactamente; it hit him — on the ear le dio en la oreja precisamente; it was — on the target dio en el mismo centro del blanco.
3 n (a) (explosion) estallido m, detonación f; (of door) portazo m; (any loud noise) golpe m, estrépito m; supersonic — estampido m supersónico; it started off with a — empezó con muchísimo ímpetu; it all went with a — todo fue a las mil maravillas.
(b) (blow) golpe m.
(c) (US) flequillo m.
4 vt (explode) volar, hacer estallar; door cerrar de golpe; table etc dar golpes en; (strike) golpear; he —ed it down on the table lo arrojó violentamente sobre la mesa; I —ed his head on the table di con su

cabeza en la mesa; **I'll — your heads together!** ¡voy a dar un coscorrón a los dos!

5 *vi* hacer explosión, estallar; hacer estrépito; **the balloons were —ing** estallaban los globos; **the guns were —ing away** disparaban estrepitosamente los cañones; **she was —ing away on the piano** aporreaba el piano; **downstairs a door —ed** abajo se cerró de golpe una puerta.

6 *vr*: **he —ed himself against the wall** dio consigo contra la pared.

banger ['bæŋə*] *n* (*sl*) = **sausage**.

bangle ['bæŋgl] *n* ajorca *f*.

banish ['bænɪʃ] *vt* desterrar (*also fig*); **to — a topic from one's conversation** proscribir un tema de su conversación.

banishment ['bænɪʃmənt] *n* destierro *m*.

banisters ['bænɪstəz] *npl* barandilla *f*, pasamanos *m*.

banjo ['bændʒəʊ] *n* banjo *m*.

bank [bæŋk] 1 *n* (a) (*of river etc*) ribera *f*, orilla *f*; (*small hill*) loma *f*; (*of earth*) terraplén *m*; (*sandbank*) banco *m*; (*of snow, clouds*) montón *m*; (*rise in road*) cuesta *f*; (*escarpment*) escarpa *f*; (*of oars*) hilera *f*.

(b) (*Comm*) banco *m*; (*in games*) banca *f*; **to break the —** hacer que se quiebre la banca.

2 *vt* (*also freq* **to — up**) (*pile*) amontonar; *fire* cubrir; (*Aer*) ladear; (*Comm*) depositar, ingresar.

3 *vi* (*Aer*) ladearse; **to — on** contar con; **to — up** (*clouds etc*) amontonarse; **we — with Smith** tenemos la cuenta en el Banco Smith, (*of company*) llevamos relaciones bancarias con Smith.

bank account ['bæŋkə,kaunt] *n* cuenta *f* de banco.

bank-book ['bæŋkbuk] *n* libreta *f* (de depósitos); (*in savings bank*) cartilla *f*.

bank clerk ['bæŋkklɑːk] *n* empleado *m* de banco.

banker ['bæŋkə*] *n* banquero *m*; **to be —** (*at games*) tener la banca.

bank holiday ['bæŋk'hɔlədɪ] *n* día *m* festivo (*en que están cerrados los bancos y el comercio en general*).

banking ['bæŋkɪŋ] 1 *adj* bancario. 2 *n* (*of earth etc*) terraplén *m*, rampas *fpl*; (*Comm*) banca *f*.

banking house ['bæŋkɪŋhaus] *n*, *pl* **— houses** [,hauzɪz] casa *f* de banca.

banknote ['bæŋknəut] *n* billete *m* de banco.

bank rate ['bæŋkreit] *n* tipo *m* de interés bancario.

bankrupt ['bæŋkrʌpt] 1 *adj* quebrado, insolvente; **to be —** estar en quiebra; **to be — of ideas** estar totalmente falto de ideas; **to go —** quebrar, (*esp fraudulently*) hacer bancarrota.

2 *n* quebrado *m*; **—'s estate** activo *m* de la quiebra.

3 *vt* hacer quebrar, arruinar.

4 *vr*: **to — oneself buying pictures** arruinarse comprando cuadros.

bankruptcy ['bæŋkrəptsɪ] *n* quiebra *f*, insolvencia *f*, (*esp fraudulent*) bancarrota *f*; (*fig*) falta *f* (*of* de); **— proceedings** juicio *m* de insolvencia; **moral —** insolvencia *f* moral.

banner ['bænə*] *n* bandera *f*, estandarte *m*; (*carried in demonstration*) pancarta *f*; **— headlines** titulares *mpl* sensacionales.

banns [bænz] *npl* amonestaciones *fpl*; **to call** (*or* **put up**) **the —** correr las amonestaciones.

banquet ['bæŋkwit] 1 *n* banquete *m*. 2 *vt* festejar, banquetear. 3 *vi* banquetear.

banqueting hall ['bæŋkwitɪŋ,hɔːl] *n* comedor *m* de gala.

banshee ['bæn'ʃiː] *n* (*Scot, Ir*) *hada que anuncia una muerte en la familia*.

bantam ['bæntəm] *n* gallinilla *f* de Bantam.

bantam-weight ['bæntəmweit] *n* peso *m* gallo.

banter ['bæntə*] 1 *n* burlas *fpl*, zumba *f*. 2 *vt* chancearse con, tomar el pelo a.

baptise [bæp'taiz] *vt* bautizar (*also fig*); **he was —d John** le bautizaron con el nombre de Juan.

baptism ['bæptɪzəm] *n* (*in general*) bautismo *m*; (*act*) bautizo *m*.

baptismal [bæp'tɪzməl] *adj* bautismal.

Baptist ['bæptist] *n* baptista *mf*; **the — Church** la Iglesia Baptista; **St John the —** San Juan Bautista.

bar [bɑː*] 1 *n* (*in general, of metal, in harbour, Her*) barra *f*; (*on door*) tranca *f*; (*lever*) palanca *f*; (*of soap*) pastilla *f*; (*of chocolate*) tableta *f*; (*tavern*) bar *m*; (*counter*) mostrador *m*; (*of public opinion*) tribunal *m*; (*Mus*) compás *m*; (*hindrance*) obstáculo *m*, impedimento *m* (*to para*); (*Law*) **the B—** (*persons*) el cuerpo de abogados, (*profession*) la abogacía; **parallel —s** paralelas *fpl*; **prisoner at the —** acusado *m*, a *f*; **to be called to the B—** recibirse de abogado; **to be behind —s** estar en la cárcel; **to put someone behind —s** encarcelar a uno.

2 *vt door* atrancar; *road* obstruir; *progress* impedir; (*ban*) prohibir; (*exclude*) excluir (*from* de); **to —**

someone from doing something prohibir a uno hacer algo; **to be —red from a club** ser excluido de un club.

3 *prep*: **all — 2** todos con excepción de 2; **— none** sin excluir a ninguno, sin excepción.

barb [bɑːb] *n* lengüeta *f*; (*Zool*) púa *f*.

Barbados [bɑː'beidɔs] Barbados *m*.

barbarian [bɑː'beəriən] 1 *adj* bárbaro. 2 *n* bárbaro *m*, a *f*.

barbaric [bɑː'bærik] *adj* bárbaro, barbárico; de ruda magnificencia.

barbarism ['bɑːbərizəm] *n* barbarie *f*; (*Gram*) barbarismo *m*.

barbarity [bɑː'bæriti] *n* barbaridad *f*.

barbarous ['bɑːbərəs] *adj* bárbaro.

barbarously ['bɑːbərəsli] *adv* bárbaramente.

Barbary ['bɑːbəri] Berbería *f*.

barbecue ['bɑːbikjuː] *n* barbacoa *f*.

barbed [bɑːbd] *adj* *arrow etc* armado de lengüetas; *criticism* incisivo, mordaz.

barbed wire ['bɑːbd'waiə*] *n* alambre *m* de espino, (*Mil*) alambre *m* de púas; **barbed-wire entanglement** alambrada *f*.

barbel ['bɑːbəl] *n* (*Anat*) barbilla *f*, cococha *f*; (*Fish*) barbo *m*.

barber ['bɑːbə*] *n* peluquero *m*, barbero *m*; **—'s (shop)** peluquería *f*.

barbican ['bɑːbikən] *n* barbacana *f*.

barbiturate [bɑː'bitjurit] *n* barbiturato *m*.

barcarol(l)e [,bɑːkə'rəul] *n* barcarola *f*.

bard [bɑːd] *n* bardo *m*; **the B— of Avon** el Cisne del Avon.

bare [beə*] 1 *adj* desnudo; *head* descubierto; *landscape* pelado; *ground* raso; *room* (*casi*) desprovisto de muebles; *style* escueto, desnudo; **with one's — hands** con las manos desnudas; **— of** desprovisto de; **the trees are —** los árboles están sin hojas; **the pantry is —** la despensa está vacía; **to earn a — living** ganar lo justo para vivir; **by a — majority** por una mayoría escasa; **the — thought frightens me** me horroriza sólo pensar en ello; **to lay —** poner al descubierto, poner al desnudo.

2 *vt* desnudar; descubrir; **to — one's head** descubrirse.

bareback ['beəbæk] *adv* en pelo, sin montura.

barefaced ['beəfeist] *adj* descarado, fresco; **a — lie** una mentira descarada.

barefoot(ed) ['beə'fut(id)] *adj* descalzo, con los pies desnudos.

bareheaded ['beə'hedid] *adj* con la cabeza descubierta, sin sombrero.

barelegged ['beə'legid] *adj* en pernetas.

barely ['beəli] *adv* apenas.

bareness ['beənis] *n* desnudez *f*.

bargain ['bɑːgin] 1 *n* (*agreement*) pacto *m*; (*business deal*) negocio *m*, contrato *m*; (*cheap thing*) ganga *f*; (*advantageous deal*) negocio *m* ventajoso; **— counter** baratillo *m*; **— price** precio *m* de ganga; **— sale** saldo *m*; **into the —** por añadidura, además; **it's a real —** es una verdadera ganga; **to drive a good —** hacer un buen trato; **you drive a hard —** Vd es un hombre terrible para sacar la última peseta; **to get the better of the —** salir ganando del negocio; **to make** (*or* **strike**) **a —** cerrar un trato; **I'll make a — with you** hagamos un pacto.

2 *vt*: **to — away** regatear.

3 *vi* negociar (*about* sobre, *for* para obtener, *with* con); (*haggle*) regatear; **I wasn't —ing for that** yo no contaba con eso; **he got more than he —ed for** le resultó peor de lo que esperaba.

bargaining ['bɑːginɪŋ] *n* negociación *f*; (*haggling*) regateo *m*; **collective —** trato *m* colectivo.

barge [bɑːdʒ] 1 *n* barcaza *f*; (*towed*) lancha *f* a remolque, gabarra *f*; (*ceremonial*) falúa *f*.

2 *vt* (*fam*) empujar; (*Sport*) atajar.

3 *vi* (*fam*): **to — about** moverse pesadamente, dar tumbos; **to — in** entrar sin pedir permiso, irrumpir; (*fig*) entrometerse; **to — into** chocar contra, dar contra.

bargee [bɑː'dʒiː] *n* gabarrero *m*.

barge pole ['bɑːdʒpəul] *n*: **I wouldn't touch it with a —** no lo quiero ver ni de lejos.

baritone ['bæritəun] *n* barítono *m*.

barium ['beəriəm] *n* bario *m*.

bark[1] [bɑːk] (*Bot*) 1 *n* corteza *f*; **Peruvian —** quina *f*.

2 *vt* *tree* descortezar; *skin* raer, raspar.

bark[2] [bɑːk] 1 *n* ladrido *m*; (*fam*) tos *f*; **his — is worse than his bite** perro que ladra no muerde.

2 *vt*: **to — (out)** *order* escupir, dar en un tono muy brusco.

3 *vi* ladrar (*at* a).

barker ['bɑːkə*] *n* pregonero *m*.

barley ['bɑːli] n cebada f.
barley field ['bɑːliˈfiːld] n cebadal m.
barley sugar ['bɑːliˌʃugə*] n azúcar m cande.
barley water ['bɑːliˌwɔːtə*] n hordiate m.
barmaid ['bɑːmeid] n camarera f.
barman ['bɑːmən] n, pl —**men** [mən] barman m.
barmy ['bɑːmi] adj (sl) lelo, gili.
barn [bɑːn] n granero m, troje f; (US) establo m, cuadra f.
barnacle ['bɑːnəkl] n percebe m.
barndoor ['bɑːnˈdɔː*] n puerta f de granero; — **fowls** aves fpl de corral.
barnstorm ['bɑːnstɔːm] vi (US) hacer una campaña electoral por el campo.
barnyard ['bɑːnjɑːd] n corral m; — **fowls** aves fpl de corral.
barometer [bəˈrɔmitə*] n barómetro m.
barometric [ˌbærəuˈmetrik] adj barométrico.
baron ['bærən] n barón m; (fig) magnate m, potentado m.
baroness ['bærənis] n baronesa f.
baronet ['bærənit] n baronet m.
baronial [bəˈrəuniəl] adj baronial.
baroque [bəˈrɔk] **1** adj barroco; (fig) complicado; grotesco. **2** n barroco m.
barque [bɑːk] n (Hist, poet) barca f.
barrack ['bærək] vt befar, mofarse de; lanzar improperios a; aplaudir irónicamente.
barracking ['bærəkiŋ] n befas fpl; improperios mpl; aplausos mpl irónicos.
barrack-room ['bærəkˌrum] adj cuartelero; — **ballad** canción f cuartelera.
barracks ['bærəks] npl (a) cuartel m; **to be confined to** — estar bajo arresto en el cuartel.
(b) (house) caserón m; **a great** — **of a place** una casa enorme de grande.
barrack square ['bærəkˈskweə*] n plaza f de armas.
barrage ['bærɑːʒ] n presa f; (Mil) cortina f de fuego; (of balloons etc) barrera f; **creeping** — cortina f de fuego móvil; **a** — **of noise** un estrépito; **a** — **of questions** una descarga cerrada de preguntas; **there was a** — **of protests** estallaron ruidosamente las protestas.
barrage balloon ['bærɑːʒbəˌluːn] n globo m de barrera.
barrel ['bærəl] n tonel m, barril m; (of gun, pen) cañón m; (Tech) cilindro m, tambor m; **to scrape the bottom of the** — rebañar las últimas migas.
barrel organ ['bærəlˌɔːgən] n organillo m.
barren ['bærən] adj estéril, árido; woman estéril; — **of** falto de, desprovisto de.
barrenness ['bærənnis] n esterilidad f, aridez f.
barricade [ˌbæriˈkeid] **1** n barricada f. **2** vt barrear, cerrar con barricadas. **3** vr: **to** — **oneself in a house** hacerse fuerte en una casa.
barrier ['bæriə*] n barrera f (also fig: to para).
barring ['bɑːriŋ] prep excepto, salvo; **we shall be there,** — **accidents** iremos, si Dios quiere.
barrister ['bæristə*] n abogado m (que tiene derecho a alegar en los tribunales superiores).
barrow[1] ['bærəu] n (Hist) túmulo m.
barrow[2] ['bærəu] n carretilla f, carretón m de mano.
barrow-boy ['bærəubɔi] n carretonero m (que vende frutas etc en la calle).
bartender ['bɑːtendə*] n barman m.
barter ['bɑːtə*] **1** n permuta f, trueque m. **2** vt permutar, trocar (for por, con); **to** — **away** malvender.
Bartholomew [bɑːˈθɔləmjuː] m Bartolomé.
basalt ['bæsɔːlt] n basalto m.
base[1] [beis] **1** n base f; (Archit) basa f; **naval** — **base** f naval.
2 vt basar, fundar (on en); **to be** —**d on** (fig) estar basado en, fundarse en; (Mil) **we were** —**d on Malta** tuvimos nuestra base en Malta.
3 vr: **I** — **myself on the following facts** yo me fundo en los hechos siguientes.
base[2] [beis] adj bajo, infame, vil; metal bajo de ley.
baseball ['beisbɔːl] n béisbol m.
Basel ['bɑːzəl] Basilea.
baseless ['beislis] adj infundado.
base line ['beislain] n (Surveying) línea f de base; (Tennis) línea f de saque.
basement ['beismənt] n sótano m.
baseness ['beisnis] n bajeza f, vileza f.
bash [bæʃ] (fam) **1** n golpe m; **to have a** — **at** probar, intentar, echar un tiento a. **2** vt golpear; person aporrear, vapulear.
bashful ['bæʃful] adj tímido, vergonzoso.
bashfully ['bæʃfuli] adv tímidamente.
bashfulness ['bæʃfulnis] n timidez f, vergüenza f.
bashing ['bæʃiŋ] n (fam) tunda f, vapuleo m.

basic ['beisik] adj básico (also Chem), fundamental.
basically ['beisikli] adv fundamentalmente, en el fondo, esencialmente.
basil ['bæzl] n albahaca f.
basilica [bəˈzilikə] n basílica f.
basilisk ['bæzilisk] n basilisco m.
basin ['beisn] n (in kitchen) escudilla f, tazón m, cuenco m; (washbasin) jofaina f, palangana f; (large fixed washbasin) lavabo m; (of fountain) taza f; (Geog) cuenca f; (of port) dársena f.
basis ['beisis] n, pl **bases** ['beisiːz] base f; **on the** — **of a base de**; partiendo de una base de.
bask [bɑːsk] vi tostarse; **to** — **in the sun** tomar el sol.
basket ['bɑːskit] n cesta f; (big) cesto m; (two-handled) canasta f; (hamper) excusabaraja f.
basketball ['bɑːskitbɔːl] n baloncesto m.
basketwork ['bɑːskitwəːk] n cestería f.
basking shark ['bɑːskiŋˈʃɑːk] n cetorrino m.
Basle [bɑːl] Basilea.
Basque [bæsk] **1** adj vasco. **2** n vasco m, a f. **3** n (language) vasco m, vascuence m, éuscaro m.
Basque Country ['bæskˈkʌntri] País m Vasco.
Basque Provinces ['bæskˈprɔvinsiz] pl las Vascongadas.
bas-relief ['bæsriˌliːf] n bajorrelieve m.
bass[1] [beis] (Mus) **1** adj bajo. **2** n (voice, note) bajo m; (instrument) contrabajo m.
bass[2] [bæs] n (Fish) róbalo m.
basset ['bæsit] n perro m basset.
bassoon [bəˈsuːn] n bajón m.
basso profundo [ˌbæsəuprəˈfundəu] n bajo m profundo.
bastard ['bɑːstəd] **1** adj bastardo. **2** n bastardo m, a f.
bastardy ['bɑːstədi] n bastardía f.
baste [beist] vt (Cook) pringar.
bastion ['bæstiən] n baluarte m (also fig).
Basutoland [bəˈsuːtəulænd] Basutolandia f.
bat[1] [bæt] n (Zool) murciélago m; **to be** —**s, to have** —**s in the belfry** estar chiflado.
bat[2] [bæt] n (eg cricket —) maza f, palo m; (Baseball) bate m; (fam) golpe m; **off one's own** — sin ayuda de nadie; **right off the** — de repente, sin deliberación.
2 vt (fam) golpear.
3 vi (Baseball) batear.
bat[3] [bæt] vt: **without** —**ting an eyelid** sin pestañear.
batch [bætʃ] n colección f, serie f, grupo m, cantidad f, lote m, montoncito m; (of papers) lío m; (Cook) hornada f.
bated ['beitid] adj: **with** — **breath** sin respiración.
bath [bɑːθ] **1** n, pl **baths** [bɑːðz] baño m, bañera f; (swimming pool) piscina f; **Turkish** — baño m turco; **to have** (or take) **a** — tomar un baño.
2 vt bañar, dar un baño a.
3 vi tomar un baño.
bathchair ['bɑːθˈtʃeə*] n silla f de ruedas.
bathe [beið] **1** n baño m (en el mar etc); **to go for a** —, **to have a** —, **to go bathing** ir a bañarse.
2 vt bañar; —**d in tears** bañado en lágrimas.
3 vi bañarse.
bather ['beiðə*] n bañista mf.
bathing ['beiðiŋ] n baño m (de mar etc), el bañarse; **no** — prohibido bañarse.
bathing beauty ['beiðiŋˌbjuːti] n sirena f de la playa.
bathing cap ['beiðiŋˌkæp] n gorro m de baño.
bathing costume ['beiðiŋˌkɔstjuːm] n traje m de baño.
bathing hut ['beiðiŋˌhʌt] n caseta f.
bathing suit ['beiðiŋˌsuːt] n traje m de baño.
bathing trunks ['beiðiŋˌtrʌŋks] n taparrabo m, calzón m.
bathing wrap ['beiðiŋˌræp] n albornoz m.
bathmat ['bɑːθmæt] n estera f de baño.
bathos ['beiθɔs] n paso m de lo sublime a lo trivial.
bathrobe ['bɑːθrəub] n albornoz m.
bathroom ['bɑːθrum] n cuarto m de baño; — **fittings** aparatos mpl sanitarios; — **scales** peso m de baño.
bath salts ['bɑːθsɔːlts] npl sales fpl de baño.
bath towel ['bɑːθtauəl] n toalla f de baño.
bathtub ['bɑːθtʌb] n bañadera f.
bathwater ['bɑːθwɔːtə*] n agua f de baño.
bathysphere ['bæθisfiə*] n batisfera f.
batiste [bæˈtiːst] n batista f.
batman ['bætmən] n, pl —**men** [mən] ordenanza m.
baton ['bætən] n (Mil) bastón m; (Mus) batuta f; (in race) testigo m.
batrachian [bəˈtreikiən] n batracio m.
battalion [bəˈtæliən] n batallón m.
batten[1] ['bætn] **1** n alfarjía f, lata f, listón m. **2** vt: — **down the hatches** asegurar las escotillas con listones.

batten² ['bætn] *vi*: **to — on** vivir (*etc*) a costa de, cebarse en.

batter ['bætə*] **1** *n* batido *m* (para rebozar).

2 *vt person* apalear; (*of boxer*) magullar; (*of the elements*) embravecerse contra; (Mil) cañonear, bombardear; (*verbally etc*) criticar ásperamente, poner como un trapo; **to — down, to — in** derribar a palos.

3 *vi*: **to — at, to — away at** dar grandes golpes en.

battered ['bætəd] *adj* (*bruised*) magullado; (*damaged*) estropeado; maltrecho, malparado; *hat etc* ajado.

battering ['bætəriŋ] *n* (*blows*) paliza *f*; (Mil) bombardeo *m*; **the — of the waves** el golpear de las olas; **he got a — from the critics** los críticos le pusieron como un trapo.

battering ram ['bætəriŋræm] *n* ariete *m*.

battery ['bætəri] *n* (Mil, *for hens, of lights*) batería *f*; (Elec) pila *f*, batería *f*, acumulador *m*; (Law) violencia *f*; (*of questions*) serie *f*; **dry —** pila *f* seca.

battery charger ['bætəri,tʃa:dʒə*] *n* cargador *m* de baterías.

battle ['bætl] **1** *n* (a) batalla *f*; **pitched —** batalla *f* campal; **in — order** en orden de batalla; **to do — librar** batalla (*with* con); **to do — for** luchar por; **the — was fought in 1346** se libró la batalla en 1346; **to join —** trabar batalla.

(b) (*fig*) lucha *f* (*for control of* por el control de, *to control* por controlar); **— royal** pelotera *f*; **— of wits** duelo *m* de inteligencias; **confidence is half the —** tener confianza es vencer una buena parte de las dificultades; **to fight a losing —** ir perdiendo poco a poco, ir de vencida.

2 *vi* luchar (*against* contra, *for* por, *to do* por hacer); **the two armies —d all day** los dos ejércitos se batieron todo el día; **to — against the wind** luchar contra el viento.

battle-axe ['bætlæks] *n* hacha *f* de combate; **old —** (*fam*) arpía *f*.

battle cruiser ['bætl,kru:zə*] *n* crucero *m* de batalla.

battle cry ['bætlkrai] *n* grito *m* de combate.

battle dress ['bætldres] *n* traje *m* de campaña.

battlefield ['bætlfi:ld] *n*, **battleground** ['bætlgraund] *n* campo *m* de batalla.

battlements ['bætlmənts] *npl* almenas *fpl*.

battleship ['bætlʃip] *n* acorazado *m*.

batty ['bæti] *adj* (*fam*) lelo.

bauble ['bɔ:bl] *n* chuchería *f*.

baulk [bɔ:lk] *see* **balk**.

bauxite ['bɔ:ksait] *n* bauxita *f*.

Bavaria [bə'veəriə] *n* Baviera *f*.

Bavarian [bə'veəriən] **1** *adj* bávaro. **2** *n* bávaro *m*, a *f*.

bawd [bɔ:d] *n* alcahueta *f*.

bawdy ['bɔ:di] *adj* obsceno, indecente; *joke, song* verde.

bawdyhouse ['bɔ:dihaus] *n, pl* **—houses** [hauziz] lupanar *m*.

bawl [bɔ:l] **1** *vt*: **to — out** *song etc* cantar (*etc*) en voz muy fuerte; **to — someone out** echarle un rapapolvo a uno.

2 *vi* gritar, vocear, desgañitarse; hablar (*or* cantar *etc*) muy fuerte; **to — at** reñir en voz alta.

bay¹ [bei] *n* (Bot) laurel *m*.

bay² [bei] *n* (Geog) bahía *f*; (*small*) abra *f*; (*very large*) golfo *m*; **B— of Biscay** Golfo *m* de Vizcaya.

bay³ [bei] *n* (Archit) intercolumnio *m*; crujía *f*; (Rail) nave *f*; (*of window*) parte *f* salediza.

bay⁴ [bei] **1** *n* (*bark*) ladrido *m*, aullido *m*; **at — acorralado; to bring to —** acorralar; **to keep at —** mantener a raya. **2** *vi* ladrar, aullar.

bay⁵ [bei] **1** *adj horse* bayo. **2** *n* caballo *m* bayo.

bay leaf ['beili:f] *n* hoja *f* de laurel.

bayonet ['beiənit] **1** *n* bayoneta *f*; **with fixed —s** con las bayonetas caladas. **2** *vt* herir (*or* matar) con la bayoneta.

bayonet charge ['beiənit,tʃa:dʒ] *n* carga *f* a la bayoneta.

Bayonne [bai'jɔn] Bayona.

bay rum ['bei'rʌm] *n* ron *m* de laurel, ron *m* de malagueta.

bay window ['bei'windəu] *n* ventana *f* salediza.

bazaar [bə'za:*] *n* bazar *m*.

bazooka [bə'zu:kə] *n* bazuca *f*.

be [bi:] (*irr*: *pres* **am, is, are;** *pret* **was, were;** *ptp* **been**) **1** (*absolute*) **to — or not to —** ser *or* no ser; **as things are** tal como están las cosas; **you're busy enough as it is** estás bastante ocupado ya; **some are and some aren't** algunos lo son y otros no; **let it —!** ¡déjalo!; **let me —!** ¡déjame en paz!

2 (*with noun, pronoun, numeral or verb complement* [*but see also* **7, 8, 9, 10** *below*]) ser; **I am a man** soy hombre; **he's a pianist** es pianista; **he was a com-**

munist era comunista; **he will be pope** será papa; **I was a bullfighter for 2 days** durante 2 días fui torero; **it's a fact** es un hecho; **it is I, it's me** soy yo; **it's 8 o'clock** son las 8; **it's the 3rd of May** es el 3 de mayo; **seeing is believing** ver es creer.

3 (*with adj complement*) (a) (*when a permanent or essential quality is expressed*) ser; **I'm English** soy inglés; **she's tall** es alta; **it was very bad** fue malísimo; **I used to be poor but now I'm rich** antes era pobre pero ahora soy rico; **when I was young** cuando era joven; **when I'm old** cuando sea viejo.

(b) (*when a temporary or reversible state is indicated, also fig*) estar; **it's dirty** está sucio; **he's ill** está enfermo; **they're tired** están cansados; **the glass is empty** el vaso está vacío; **the pond is always full** el estanque siempre está lleno; **the symphony is full of tunes** la sinfonía está llena de melodías.

(c) (*of persons,* ser *+ adj indicates a permanent quality of character,* estar *+ adj indicates a more temporary mood or state*): **he's a cheerful sort** es alegre, **he's very cheerful** (*about something*) está alegre; **he's always very smart** siempre es muy elegante, **you're very smart** (*today, for once*) ¡qué guapo estás!; **they're very happy together** son muy felices, **are you happy in your work?** ¿estás contento con tu trabajo?

(d) (**to be** *+ adj, impersonal*) ser: **it is possible that . . .** es posible que . . .; **is it certain that . . .?** ¿es cierto que . . .?

4 (*expressions of authorship, origin, possession, construction*) ser: **it's a Picasso** es de Picasso; **I'm from the south** soy del Sur; **it's mine** es mío; **it's of gold, it's a gold one** es de oro.

5 (*place, geographical location, temporary circumstances*) estar: **he's here** está aquí; **it's on the table** está en la mesa; **Burgos is in Spain** Burgos está en España; **the issue was in doubt** el resultado estaba en duda; **I'm in a jam** estoy en un aprieto; **to — on a journey** estar de viaje; **to — in a hurry** estar de prisa; **to — in mourning** estar de luto.

6 (*health*) **how are you?** ¿cómo estás?; **how are you now?** ¿qué tal te encuentras ahora?; **I'm very well, thanks** estoy muy bien, gracias.

7 (*age*) **I'm 8** tengo 8 años; **how old are you?** ¿cuántos años tienes?

8 (*weather, temperatures, certain adjs*) **it is hot** (*weather*) hace calor; **I'm hot** tengo calor; **the water is hot** el agua está caliente; **it's sunny** hay sol; **it's foggy** hay niebla; **it's windy** hace viento; **to — hungry** tener hambre; **to — afraid** tener miedo.

9 (*certain expressions of time*) **we've been here a year** hace un año que estamos aquí, llevamos un año aquí; **it's a long time since I saw him** hace mucho tiempo que no le veo.

10 **there is, there are** hay; **there was, there were** había, hubo; **there may not — any** puede no haber ninguno.

11 (*idioms*) **so — it** así sea; **— that as it may** sea como fuere; **what is it to you?** ¿a ti qué te importa?; **mother to —** futura madre *f*; **my wife to —** mi futura esposa; **what's it to —?** (*in bar etc*) ¿qué vas a tomar?

12 *v aux* (a) (*conditional sentences*) **if I were to say so** si dijera eso; **if I were you** yo en tu lugar, yo que tú.

(b) (*obligation*) **I am to do it** he de hacerlo; **he was to have come** había de venir; **what am I to say?** ¿qué he de decir?

(c) (*continuous tenses*) **to be** *+ ger* estar *+ ger, eg* **I was singing** estaba cantando, **were you waiting for me?** ¿me estabas esperando?; (*but a simple tense is used in such cases as*) **he is coming tomorrow** viene (*or* vendrá) mañana, **what are you doing?** ¿qué haces?; **I shall — seeing him** voy a verle, **will you — wanting more?** ¿vas a necesitar más?

(d) (**to be** *+ ptp, passive*) ser *+ ptp*: **the window was opened by the servant** la ventana fue abierta por el criado; **it is being studied** está siendo estudiado; (*but the passive is often replaced by a reflexive or active construction*) **the window was opened by the servant** la ventana la abrió el criado; **it is being studied** se está estudiando; **it is said that** se dice que, dicen que; **he was nowhere to — seen** no se le veía en ninguna parte; **what's to — done?** ¿qué hay que hacer?; **it is to be regretted that** es de lamentar que; **it is to — hoped that** es de esperar que; **it's a film not to — missed** es una película que no hay que perder.

(e) (**to be** *+ ptp, state*) estar *+ ptp*: **the window was open** la ventana estaba abierta; **it's made of wood** está hecho de madera; **the book is bereft of ideas** el libro está desprovisto de ideas.

beach [biːtʃ] **1** n playa f. **2** vt varar.

beachcomber ['biːtʃ,kəumə*] n raquero m.

beachhead ['biːtʃhed] n cabeza f de playa.

beachwear ['biːtʃweə*] n trajes mpl de playa.

beacon ['biːkən] n almenara f; (in port) faro m, fanal m; (on aerodrome) baliza f, aerofaro m; (Radio) radiofaro m; (hill) hacho m.

bead [biːd] n cuenta f; (of glass) abalorio m; (of dew, sweat) gota f; (of gun) mira f globular; —s sarta f de cuentas, (Eccl) rosario m; **to draw a** — **on** apuntar a; **to tell one's** —s rezar el rosario.

beading ['biːdiŋ] n (Archit) astrágalo m, contero m.

beadle ['biːdl] n bedel m; (Eccl) pertiguero m.

beady ['biːdi] adj eyes parecidos a dos gotas brillantes.

beagle ['biːgl] n sabueso m.

beak [biːk] n pico m; (nose) nariz f (corva); (Naut) rostro m; (sl) magistrado m; — **of land** promontorio m.

beaked [biːkt] adj picudo.

beaker ['biːkə*] n taza f alta; (Chem) vaso m de precipitación.

be-all ['biːɔːl] n (also — **and end-all**) único objeto m, única cosa f que importa; **he is the** — **of her life** él es lo único que le importa en la vida; **money is not the** — el dinero no es lo único que vale, hay cosas que valen tanto como el dinero.

beam [biːm] **1** n (a) (Archit) viga f; travesaño m; (of plough) timón m; (of balance) astil m; (Mech) balancín m.

(b) (Naut) (timber) bao m; (width) manga f; **broad in the** — (fam) ancho de caderas, nalgudo; **on her** — **ends** a punto de volcar; **on one's** — **ends** (fam) sin un cuarto; **on the port** — a babor.

(c) (of light) rayo m; (from beacon, lamp) haz m de luz; (from radio beacon) haz m de radiofaro; (smile) sonrisa f, mirada f agradecida; **with a** — **of pleasure** con una sonrisa de placer; **to be on the** — (fam) seguir el buen camino; **to be off the** — (fam) estar despistado, estar equivocado.

2 vt light, signal emitir; **she** —**ed her thanks** me lanzó una mirada agradecida.

3 vi (shine) brillar; (smile) sonreírse alegremente (at a).

beam-ends ['biːm'endz] npl (Naut) cabezas fpl de los baos (de un buque); **she was on her** — (Naut) el buque escoraba peligrosamente; **they are on their** — (fig) están en un grave aprieto, no tienen donde caerse muertos.

beaming ['biːmiŋ] adj sonriente, radiante.

bean [biːn] n (a) (plant) runner — judía f, habichuela f; **scarlet runner** — judía f escarlata; **dwarf** —, **French** —, **kidney** — judía f enana f, fríjol m; **broad** — haba f gruesa.

(b) (served as food) —s judías fpl; (broad, haricot) habas fpl; (of coffee) granos mpl.

(c) **I haven't a** — (fam) no tengo un céntimo; **to be full of** —s (fam) rebosar de vitalidad; **to spill the** —s (sl) tirar de la manta.

beanfeast ['biːnfiːst] n, **beano** ['biːnəu] n (fam) fiesta f, juerga f; (meal) comilona f.

bear¹ [beə*] n oso m; (Comm) bajista m; — **market** mercado m bajista; **Great B**— (Astron) Osa f Mayor; **Little B**— Osa f Menor.

bear² [beə*] n (irr: pret **bore**, ptp **borne**) **1** vt (a) (carry) llevar; arms, date, inscription etc llevar; character, name, relation, responsibility tener; weight sostener; fruit dar, producir; interest devengar; child parir, tener; cost pagar, correr con; love etc sentir, tener (for para); grudge, ill will guardar, tener (against a); **it is borne in upon me that** ya voy comprendiendo que.

(b) (stand up to) inspection etc sufrir, resistir a; **it doesn't** — **close examination** no resiste a la inspección de cerca; **it doesn't** — **thinking about** da horror sólo pensar en ello; **the film will** — **a second viewing** la película vale la pena de verse por segunda vez.

(c) (endure) soportar, aguantar, resistir; **I can't** — **delays** yo no aguanto los retrasos; **I can't** — **him** no le puedo ver; **I can't** — **spiders** odio las arañas; **I can't** — **to look!** ¡no puedo mirar!; **can you** — **me to look at it?** ¿quieres dejarme verlo?; **I could** — **it no longer** ya no resistía más.

(d) **to** — **away, to** — **off** llevarse; **to** — **out** llevar; (confirm) confirmar, corroborar.

2 vi (a) **a tree that** —**s well** un árbol que rinde bien; **the ship** —**s north** el barco lleva dirección norte; **to** — **left** torcer a la izquierda.

(b) **to** — **down on** (ship etc) correr sobre, (person) avanzar hacia, acercarse majestuosamente (or de manera amenazadora etc) a; **to** — **on** person interesar, subject tener que ver con, referirse a;

it —s **hard on the old** esto pesa bastante sobre los viejos; **to** — **up** animarse; — **up!** ¡ánimo!; **to** — **with** tener paciencia con, ser indulgente con.

(c) **to bring a gun to** — **on** apuntar a; **to bring pressure to** — **on** ejercer presión sobre.

3 vr: **to** — **oneself** comportarse, portarse.

bearable ['beərəbl] adj soportable, llevadero.

beard [biəd] **1** n barba f; (Bot) arista f; **to have (or wear) a** — llevar barba. **2** vt desafiar.

bearded ['biədid] adj barbado, (pej) barbudo.

beardless ['biədlis] adj lampiño; youth imberbe.

bearer ['beərə*] n (servant) mozo m; (Comm) portador m, ora f; (of office) poseedor m, ora f.

bear garden ['beə,gaːdn] n guirigay m.

bearing ['beəriŋ] n (a) (of person) porte m, comportamiento m; **soldierly** — porte m militar.

(b) (relationship) relación f (on con); **this has no** — **on the matter** esto no tiene que ver con el asunto.

(c) (Mech) cojinete m.

(d) (Naut) marcación f; **to get one's** —s orientarse; **to lose one's** —s desorientarse; **to take a** — marcarse; **to take one's** —s orientarse.

(e) (Her) blasón m.

(f) **beyond all** — que ya no se puede sufrir más.

bearskin ['beəskin] n piel f de oso; (Mil) morrión m.

beast [biːst] n bestia f; (fig: person) bruto m, salvaje m; (thing) cosa f muy difícil; — **of burden** bestia f de carga; **wild** — fiera f; **the king of** —s el rey de los animales; **you** —! ¡animal!; **that** — **of a policeman** aquel bruto de policía; **what a** — **he is!** ¡qué bruto!; **it's a** — esto es horrible; **it's a** — **of a day** es un día horrible.

beastliness ['biːstlinis] n bestialidad f.

beastly ['biːstli] **1** adj bestial; (fam) detestable, horrible; condenado, maldito; **that was a** — **thing to do** aquello sí que fue cruel; **you were** — **to me** fuiste cruel conmigo; **where's that** — **book?** ¿dónde está el maldito libro ese?

2 adv (fam): **it's** — **awkward** es terriblemente difícil.

beat [biːt] **1** n (blow) golpe m; (of drum) redoble m; (of heart) latido m; (Mus) compás m, ritmo m; (of policeman) ronda f; **it's off my** — está fuera de mi competencia; **I like music with a** — me gusta la música de ritmo fuerte.

2 (irr: pret **beat**, ptp **beaten**) vt (a) (strike) golpear; table, door dar golpes en; metal etc batir, martillar; person pegar, (as punishment) dar una paliza a; carpet sacudir; (Cook) batir; drum tocar; time (Mus) marcar, llevar; path abrir; **he** — **him on the head** le dio un golpe en la cabeza; **he** — **him about the head** le dio una serie de golpes por la cabeza; **to** — **someone to death** apalear a uno hasta dejarlo muerto; **the bird** — **its wings** el pájaro batió las alas; **to** — **it** (fam) poner pies en polvorosa; — **it!** ¡lárgate!

(b) (Hunting) ojear.

(c) (defeat) vencer, derrotar; record batir, superar, mejorar; **to** — **someone to it** ganar por la mano a uno, llegar antes que uno.

(d) (be better than) sobrepasar; **that** —s **everything!** ¡eso es el colmo!

(e) (mystify) confundir; **the police confess themselves** —en la policía confiesa no tener pista alguna; **the problem has me** —en el problema me deja totalmente perplejo.

(f) **to** — **back** rechazar; **to** — **down** abatir, derribar a golpes; corn acamar; resistance, opponent vencer; price conseguir rebajar (regateando), seller persuadir a que venda a precio más bajo; **to** — **off** rechazar; **to** — **out** metal martillar, formar a martillazos; tune tocar (con fuerte ritmo); **to** — **up** (Cook) batir, person aporrear, vapulear.

3 vi (heart) latir, pulsar; **the rain was** —**ing down** caía la lluvia con violencia; **the drums were** —**ing** redoblaban los tambores; **to** — **on a door** dar golpes en una puerta; **the waves** — **on the shore** las olas azotaban la playa; **to** — **about** (Naut) barloventear.

4 ptp (fam) = beaten.

beaten ['biːtn] **1** ptp of beat. **2** adj (a) metal etc batido, martillado; track trillado. (b) team etc derrotado, vencido.

beater ['biːtə*] n (Hunting) ojeador m, batidor m.

beatific [,biːə'tifik] adj beatífico; **with a** — **smile** con una sonrisa de puro contento.

beatification [biː,ætifi'keiʃən] n beatificación f.

beatify [biː'ætifai] vt beatificar.

beating ['biːtiŋ] n (a) (blows) golpes mpl, golpeo m; (of waves) el batir, el azotar; (of heart) latido m, pulsación f; (*punishment*) paliza f; **to get a —** recibir una paliza.

(b) (*Hunting*) ojeo m, batida f.

(c) (*defeat*) derrota f; **to take a —** salir derrotado, ser cascado (*from por, at the hands of* a manos de).

beatitude [bi'ætitju:d] n beatitud f; **the B—s** las Bienaventuranzas.

beatnik ['bi:tnik] n beatnik m.

Beatrice ['biatris] f Beatriz.

beau [bəu] **1** adj: **— ideal** lo bello ideal. **2** n (*fop*) petimetre m, dandy m; (*ladies' man*) galán m; (*suitor*) pretendiente m; (*sweetheart*) novio m.

beauteous ['bju:tiəs] adj (*poet*) bello.

beautician [bju:'tiʃən] n especialista mf en belleza, maquillador m, ora f.

beautiful ['bju:tiful] adj hermoso, bello; precioso.

beautifully ['bju:tifli] adv maravillosamente.

beautify ['bju:tifai] vt embellecer.

beauty ['bju:ti] n (a) (*in general*) belleza f, hermosura f; (*concrete*) belleza f, eg **the beauties of Majorca** las bellezas de Mallorca.

(b) (*fig*) **the — of it is that** lo bueno es que.

(c) **B— and the Beast** la Bella y la Bestia.

(d) (*person*) belleza f, beldad f; (*thing, specimen*) ejemplar m hermoso; **it's a —** es maravilloso; **that was a —!** (*stroke etc*) ¡qué golpe más fino!; **isn't he a little —?** (*child*) ¡mira qué rico está el niño!

beauty contest ['bju:ti,kɔntest] n concurso m de belleza.

beauty cream ['bju:tikri:m] n crema f de belleza.

beauty parlour ['bju:ti,pɑ:lə*] n salón m de belleza.

beauty queen ['bju:tikwi:n] n reina f de la belleza.

beauty sleep ['bju:tisli:p] n primer sueño m; **to lose one's —** (*hum*) perder el tiempo en que uno debiera estar dormido.

beauty spot ['bju:tispɔt] n (*on face*) lunar m postizo; (*in country*) sitio m pintoresco, lugar m de excepcional belleza natural.

beaver ['bi:və*] n castor m.

becalm [bi'kɑ:m] vt: **to be —ed** estar encalmado.

became [bi'keim] pret of **become**.

because [bi'kɔz] **1** conj porque; **— he has two cars he thinks he's somebody** como tiene dos coches se cree un personaje.

2 prep: **— of** a causa de, debido a, por motivo de.

beck¹ [bek] n: **to be at the — and call of** estar a disposición de, estar sometido a la voluntad de.

beck² [bek] n (*prov*) arroyo m, riachuelo m.

beckon ['bekən] **1** vt llamar con señas; (*fig*) llamar, atraer. **2** vi: **to —** to hacer señas a.

become [bi'kʌm] (*irr: see* come) **1** vt (*of clothes etc*) sentar a, favorecer; (*action etc*) convenir a; **that thought does not — you** ese pensamiento es indigno de ti.

2 vi (a) (*absolute*) **what has become of him?** ¿qué es de él?; **what will — of me?** ¿qué será de mí?; **what can have become of that book?** ¿adónde diablos se habrá metido aquel libro?

(b) (*followed by* n: *entering profession etc*) hacerse, (*by promotion etc*) llegar a ser, (*of material things*) transformarse en, convertirse en; **to — a soldier** hacerse soldado; **to — professor** llegar a ser catedrático; **he became king in 1911** subió al trono en 1911; **to — a father** ser padre; **the gas —s liquid** el gas se convierte en líquido; **the building has become a cinema** el edificio se ha transformado en cine.

(c) (*followed by* adj) ponerse, volverse, (*by effort*) hacerse; **this is becoming difficult** esto se está poniendo difícil; **to — rich** hacerse rico; **to — mad** volverse loco; (*freq to become* + adj *is translated by a reflexive verb*) **to — red** ponerse rojo, enrojecerse; **to — ill** ponerse enfermo, enfermar; **to — angry** enfadarse; **he became quite blind** quedó totalmente ciego; **to — accustomed to** acostumbrarse a; **it became known that** se supo que, llegó a saberse que; **we became very worried** empezamos a inquietarnos muchísimo.

(d) (*of age*) **when he —s 21** cuando llegue a tener 21 años, cuando cumpla los 21 años.

becoming [bi'kʌmiŋ] adj *clothes* favorecedor, que sienta bien, que le va bien a uno; *action* decoroso, conveniente.

bed [bed] **1** n cama f, (*of animal*) lecho m; (*of river*) cauce m, lecho m; (*of flowers*) arriate m, cuadro m, macizo m; (*Geol*) capa f, estrato m, yacimiento m; (*Archit etc*) base f; **— and board** comida f y casa; **single —** cama f individual; **double —** cama f de matrimonio; **— of roses** caminito m de rosas; **to be brought to — of** dar a luz, parir; **to get out of — on the wrong side** levantarse por los pies de la cama; **to get into —** meterse en la cama; **to go to —**

acostarse (*with* con); **to give someone a — for the night** hospedar a uno una noche; **to make the —** hacer la cama; **you've made your — and you must lie on it** quien mala cama hace en ella se yace; **to put a child to —** acostar a un niño; **to put a paper to —** terminar la redacción de un número; **to stay in —** (*ill*) guardar cama, (*lazy*) seguir en la cama; **to take to one's —** encamarse.

2 vt (*Archit etc*) fijar, engastar (*also to —* **down**); **to — down** (*for the night*) hacer un lecho para; **to — out** plantar en un macizo.

bedaub [bi'dɔ:b] vt embadurnar.

bedbug ['bedbʌg] n chinche gen f.

bedclothes ['bedkləuðz] npl ropa f de cama.

bedcover ['bedkʌvə*] n colcha f, cubierta f de cama; **—s** ropa f de cama.

bedding ['bediŋ] n ropa f de cama; (*for animal*) lecho m.

Bede [bi:d] m Beda; **the Venerable —** el venerable Beda.

bedeck [bi'dek] vt adornar, engalanar.

bedevil [bi'devəl] vt endiablar; **the problem is —led by several factors** hay diversos factores que complican el problema; **the team has been —led by injuries** el equipo ha sufrido mucho de lesiones.

bedfellow ['bedfeləu] n compañero m, a f de cama.

bedhead ['bedhed] n testero m, cabecera f.

bed jacket ['beddʒækit] n mañanita f.

bedlam ['bedləm] n: **it was sheer —** la confusión era total; **— broke out** estallaron ruidosamente los gritos.

bed linen ['bedlinin] n ropa f de cama, sábanas fpl.

Bedouin ['beduin] **1** adj beduino. **2** n beduino m, a f.

bedpan ['bedpæn] n bacinilla f de cama.

bedraggled [bi'drægld] adj ensuciado, mojado.

bedridden ['bedridn] adj postrado en cama.

bedrock ['bedrɔk] n lecho m de roca, roca f sólida; **to get down to —** ir a lo fundamental.

bedroom ['bedrum] n dormitorio m, alcoba f.

bedside [bi'bedsaid] **1** n: **to wait at the —** of esperar a la cabecera de.

2 attr: **— lamp** lámpara f para leer en la cama; **— table** mesita f de noche; **to have a good — manner** tener mucho tacto con los enfermos.

bed-sitter ['bed'sitə*] n, **bed-sitting room** ['bed-'sitiŋrum] n salón m con cama.

bedsocks ['bedsɔks] npl calcetines mpl de cama.

bedsore ['bedsɔ:*] n úlcera f de decúbito.

bedspread ['bedspred] n sobrecama m, colcha f, cobertor m.

bedstead ['bedsted] n cuja f, armazón m de cama.

bedstraw ['bedstrɔ:] n cuajaleche m, amor m de hortelano.

bedtime ['bedtaim] n hora f de acostarse.

bedwetting ['bedwetiŋ] n enuresis f.

bee [bi:] n abeja f; **to have a — in one's bonnet** tener una idea fija.

beech [bi:tʃ] n haya f.

beechmast ['bi:tʃmɑ:st] n hayucos mpl.

beechnut ['bi:tʃnʌt] n hayuco m.

beech tree ['bi:tʃtri:] n haya f.

beechwood ['bi:tʃwud] n hayedo m.

beef [bi:f] **1** n carne f de vaca; (*fam*) fuerza f muscular, corpulencia f; **corned —** carne f de vaca acecinada; **roast —** rosbif m; **salt —** carne f de vaca salada.

2 vi (*sl*) quejarse.

beef cattle ['bi:f'kætl] n ganado m vacuno de engorde.

beefeater ['bi:f,i:tə*] n alabardero m de la Torre de Londres.

beefsteak ['bi:f'steik] n biftec m, bistec m.

beef tea ['bi:f'ti:] n caldo m concentrado de carne.

beefy ['bi:fi] adj (*fam*) fornido, corpulento.

beehive ['bi:haiv] n colmena f.

beekeeper ['bi:ki:pə*] n apicultor m, colmenero m.

beeline ['bi:lain] n: **to make a — for** ir en línea recta hacia, ir derecho a.

Beelzebub [bi:'elzibʌb] m Belcebú.

been [bi:n] ptp of **be**.

beer [biə*] n cerveza f; **bottled —** cerveza f de botella; **dark —** cerveza f negra; **draught —** cerveza f al grifo (*or* de barril); **light —** cerveza f clara; **small —** (*fig*) cosa f sin importancia, bagatela f; **life isn't all — and skittles** la vida no es toda diversiones.

beery ['biəri] adj *smell* a cerveza; *person* muy aficionado a la cerveza; *party* donde se bebe mucha cerveza; **it was a — affair** allí se bebió una barbaridad.

beeswax ['bi:zwæks] n cera f (de abejas).

beet [bi:t] n remolacha f.

beetle ['biːtl] **1** n escarabajo m. **2** vi: to — off (sl) marcharse.

beetroot ['biːtruːt] n (raíz f de) remolacha f.

beet sugar ['biːt͜ʃugə*] n azúcar m de remolacha.

befall [bi'fɔːl] (irr: see **fall**) **1** vt acontecer a. **2** vi acontecer.

befallen [bi'fɔːlən] ptp of **befall**.

befell [bi'fel] pret of **befall**.

befit [bi'fit] vt convenir a, venir bien a, corresponder a.

befitting [bi'fitiŋ] adj conveniente, decoroso.

befog [bi'fɔg] vt (fig) entenebrecer; person ofuscar, confundir.

before [bi'fɔː*] **1** adv (a) (place) delante, adelante; — and behind por delante y por detrás.
  (b) (time) antes; anteriormente; **a moment** — un momento antes; **the day** — el día anterior; **on this occasion and the one** — en esta ocasión y la anterior.
  2 prep (a) (place) delante de; (in the presence of, faced with) ante, en presencia de; **we still have 2 hours** — us tenemos todavía 2 horas por delante.
  (b) (time) antes de; see **long, now** etc.
  (c) (rather than) **I should choose this one** — **that** yo escogería éste antes que aquél.
  (d) (with verb) — **going out** antes de salir.
  3 conj antes (de) que.

beforehand [bi'fɔːhænd] adv de antemano, con anticipación; **to prepare something well** — preparar algo con mucha antelación.

befoul [bi'faul] vt ensuciar.

befriend [bi'frend] vt ofrecer amistad a; amparar, favorecer.

befuddled [bi'fʌdld] adj aturdido; (drunk) borracho.

beg [beg] **1** vt (a) pedir, suplicar, rogar (from, of a); **to** — **someone for something** pedir algo a uno; **he** —**ged my help** suplicó mi ayuda; **he** —**ged me to help him** me suplicó que le ayudara; **he** —**ged the book from me** rogó que le diese el libro; **I** — **you!** ¡se lo suplico!
  (b) (as beggar) mendigar; pedir; **he** —**ged a shilling** pidió un chelín.
  2 vi (a) pedir, rogar; **to** — **for** pedir, solicitar; **I** — **to inform you that** tengo el gusto de informarle que.
  (b) (as beggar) mendigar, pedir por Dios, pedir limosna; **it's going** —**ging** no se ha presentado nadie que lo quiera aceptar (or comprar etc).

began [bi'gæn] pret of **begin**.

beget [bi'get] (irr: pret **begot**, (arch) **begat**, ptp **begotten**) vt engendrar (also fig).

beggar ['begə*] **1** n mendigo m, a f; (fam) tío m, sujeto m; **lucky** —**!** ¡qué chorra tiene el tío!; **poor** —**!** ¡pobre diablo!; —**s can't be choosers** los pobres no escogen.
  2 vt empobrecer, arruinar, reducir a la miseria; (fig) excederse a; **it** —**s description** es imposible describirlo.

beggarly ['begəli] adj indigente; (fig) miserable, mezquino.

beggary ['begəri] n mendicidad f; miseria f; **to reduce to** — reducir a la miseria.

begin [bi'gin] (irr: pret **began**, ptp **begun**) **1** vt comenzar, empezar; iniciar; (undertake) emprender; **the work will be begun tomorrow** mañana se iniciará el trabajo, mañana se dará principio al trabajo; **I was foolish ever to** — **it** hice mal en emprenderlo.
  2 vi comenzar, empezar; **to** — **to** + infin comenzar (or empezar) a + infin; **to** — **talking** empezar a hablar; **it doesn't** — **to be possible** dista mucho de ser posible; **to** — **by saying** comenzar diciendo; **to** — **on** emprender; **to** — **with something** comenzar por (or con) algo; **to** — **with** (as phrase) en primer lugar, para empezar; —**ning from Monday** a partir del lunes.

beginner [bi'ginə*] n principiante mf.

beginning [bi'giniŋ] n (a) principio m, comienzo m; **at the** — **of** al principio de; **at the** — **of the century** a principios del siglo; **from the** — desde el principio; **from** — **to end** desde el principio hasta el final, de cabo a rabo; **in the** — al principio; **the** — **of the end** el comienzo del fin; **to make a** — empezar.
  (b) origen m; **from small** —**s** de orígenes modestos, de antecedentes humildes; **he had the** —**s of a beard** tenía lo que iba a ser barba.

begone [bi'gɔn] interj ¡fuera de aquí!

begonia [bi'gəuniə] n begonia f.

begot [bi'gɔt] pret of **beget**.

begotten [bi'gɔtn] ptp of **beget**; **the only B**— **Son** el Unigénito.

begrime [bi'graim] vt tiznar, ensuciar.

begrudge [bi'grʌdʒ] vt (give) dar de mala gana; (envy) tener envidia a; **I don't** — **him his success** no le tengo envidia a causa de su éxito.

beguile [bi'gail] vt (delude) engañar; (charm away) seducir; time etc entretener; **to** — **someone into doing something** persuadir a uno por engaños a hacer algo.

beguiling [bi'gailiŋ] adj seductor, persuasivo.

begun [bi'gʌn] pret of **begin**.

behalf [bi'hɑːf]: **on** —**of** prep: **on** — **of everybody** en nombre de todos; **a collection on** — **of orphans** una colecta en beneficio de los huérfanos, una colecta por huérfanos; **I interceded on his** — intercedí por él; **don't worry on my** — no os inquietéis por mí.

behave [bi'heiv] **1** vi (person) portarse (to, towards con), comportarse, conducirse; (Mech etc) comportarse, funcionar.
  2 vr: **to** — **oneself** portarse (bien); — **yourself!** ¡estate formal!; **if you** — **yourself (properly)** si te conduces debidamente.

behaviour, (US) **behavior** [bi'heivjə*] n conducta f, comportamiento m; (Mech etc) comportamiento m, funcionamiento m; **good** — buena conducta f; **to be on one's best** — estar todo lo formal que sepa uno.

behavioural, (US) **behavioral** [bi'heivjərəl] adj comportamentista, behaviorístico.

behaviourism, (US) **behaviorism** [bi'heivjərizəm] n behaviorismo m.

behead [bi'hed] vt decapitar, descabezar.

beheld [bi'held] pret and ptp of **behold**.

behest [bi'hest] n: **at the** — **of** por orden de.

behind [bi'haind] **1** adv (a) detrás, por detrás; atrás; **to come from** — venir desde atrás; **to follow close** — seguir muy de cerca; **to attack someone from** — atacar a uno por la espalda.
  (b) (with verb to be) **to be a bit** — estar un poco atrasadillo; **to be** — **with one's work** estar atrasado en su trabajo, tener atrasos de trabajo.
  2 prep detrás de; **what's** — **all this?** ¿qué motivo oculto tendrá todo esto?; **he has all of us** — **him** (fig) tiene el apoyo de todos nosotros; **we are much** — **them in technology** los somos muy inferiores en tecnología; **it's all** — **us now** todo eso ha quedado ya a la espalda.
  3 n (fam) trasero m, culo m.

behindhand [bi'haindhænd] adv atrasado, con retraso; **to be** — **with the rent** tener atrasos de alquiler.

behold [bi'həuld] (irr: see **hold**) vt contemplar; —**!** ¡fíjese bien!; — **the results!** ¡he aquí los resultados!; **see lo.**

beholden [bi'həuldən] adj: **to be** — **to** estar bajo una obligación a; **I don't want to be** — **to anybody** yo no quiero tener obligaciones con nadie.

beholder [bi'həuldə*] n espectador m, ora f, observador m, ora f.

behove [bi'həuv] vt: **it** —**s him to** + infin le incumbe + infin.

beige [beiʒ] **1** adj (color de) beige. **2** n beige m.

being ['biːiŋ] n ser m; **human** — ser m humano; **Supreme B**— Ser m Supremo; **in** — existente; **to come into** — nacer, empezar a existir.

bejewelled [bi'dʒuːəld] adj enjoyado.

belabour [bi'leibə*] vt apalear; (fig) criticar, dar un palo a.

belated [bi'leitid] adj atrasado, tardío.

belay [bi'lei] vt (Naut) amarrar (dando vueltas en una cabilla).

belch [beltʃ] **1** n eructo m. **2** vt (fig) vomitar, arrojar. **3** vi eructar.

beleaguered [bi'liːgəd] adj sitiado, asediado.

belfry ['belfri] n campanario m.

Belgian ['beldʒən] **1** adj belga. **2** n belga mf.

Belgium ['beldʒəm] Bélgica f.

Belgrade [bel'greid] Belgrado.

belie [bi'lai] vt desmentir, contradecir; hopes etc defraudar.

belief [bi'liːf] n (a) creencia f (that de que); opinión f; **a man of strong** —**s** un hombre de opiniones firmes; **to the best of my** — según mi leal saber y entender; **it is my firm** — **that** creo firmemente que; **it passes** —, **it is beyond** — es increíble (that que).
  (b) (Rel etc) fe f; **his** — **in God** su fe en Dios; **to have lost one's** — haber perdido su fe.

believable [bi'liːvəbl] adj creíble.

believe [bi'liːv] **1** vt creer; ears, story dar crédito a; **don't you** — **it!** ¡no lo creas!; **he is** —**d to be abroad** se cree que está en el extranjero.
  2 vi creer; **to** — **in God** creer en Dios; **we don't** — **in drugs** no aprobamos (el uso de) las drogas; **I** — **so** creo que sí; **I** — **not** creo que no.

believer [bɪ'liːvə*] n (Rel) creyente mf, fiel mf; (Pol etc) partidario m, a f; **I am a — in letting things take their course** yo soy partidario de dejar que las cosas se desarrollen por sí mismas.

belittle [bɪ'lɪtl] vt despreciar, minimizar, conceder poca importancia a.

bell [bel] n (church —) campana f; (hand —) campanilla f; (animal's) cencerro m; (on toy, dress etc) cascabel m; (electric) timbre m; (of trumpet) pabellón m; (Bot) campanilla f; **that rings a —** eso me suena; **it doesn't ring a —** with me no me suena.

bell-bottomed ['bel'bɔtəmd] adj acampanado, abocinado.

bellboy ['belbɔɪ] n botones m.

belle [bel] n belleza f, beldad f; **the — of the ball** la reina del baile.

belles-lettres ['bel'letr] npl bellas letras fpl.

bell glass ['belglɑːs] n campana f de cristal.

bellhop ['belhɔp] n (US) botones m.

bellicose ['belɪkəus] adj belicoso.

bellicosity [,belɪ'kɔsɪtɪ] n belicosidad f.

belligerency [bɪ'lɪdʒərənsɪ] n beligerancia f.

belligerent [bɪ'lɪdʒərənt] **1** adj beligerante; person, tone agresivo. **2** n beligerante m.

bellow ['beləu] **1** n bramido m; (of person) rugido m. **2** vt gritar, vociferar. **3** vi bramar; (person) rugir.

bellows ['beləuz] npl fuelle m; **a pair of —** un fuelle.

bell ringer ['bel,rɪŋə*] n campanero m.

bell rope ['belrəup] n cuerda f de campana.

bell-shaped ['belʃeɪpt] adj acampanado.

bell tent ['beltent] n pabellón m.

belly ['belɪ] **1** n vientre m; (with offensive connotations) barriga f, panza f; (of vessel) barriga f. **2** vi (sail) hacer bolso, llenarse de viento (also **to — out**).

bellyache ['belieɪk] **1** n dolor m de barriga. **2** vi (sl) quejarse (about de).

bellyful ['belɪful] n panzada f; **I've had a —** estoy harto ya (of de).

belly-landing ['belɪ,lændɪŋ] n (Aer) aterrizaje m de barriga.

belong [bɪ'lɔŋ] vi **(a)** (be the possession of) pertenecer (to a); **who does this — to?** ¿a quién pertenece esto?, ¿de quién es esto?; **the countryside —s to everyone** el campo es de todos.

(b) (be incumbent on): **that duty —s to me** ese deber me corresponde.

(c) (of membership etc) **to — to a club** ser socio de un club; **to — to a party** ser miembro de un partido; **why don't you —?** ¿por qué no te haces socio?

(d) (have rightful place) **this —s with that** éste va con aquél; **that card —s under K** esa ficha debiera estar en la K; **where does this —?** ¿esto dónde lo pongo?; **it —s on the shelf** tiene un puesto en el estante.

(e) (be resident, be at ease) **I — here** yo soy de aquí; **I feel I — here** aquí me siento cómodo; **that feeling of not —ing** esa sensación de estar fuera de su ambiente natural.

belongings [bɪ'lɔŋɪŋz] npl pertenencias fpl, bártulos mpl, cosas fpl.

beloved [bɪ'lʌvɪd] **1** adj querido (by, of de). **2** n querido m, amada f.

below [bɪ'ləu] **1** adv abajo, (por) debajo; **that flat —** ese piso de abajo; **the passage quoted —** el pasaje abajo citado; **here —** aquí abajo; **it was 5 —** la temperatura era de 5 grados bajo cero.

2 prep bajo, debajo de; (fig) inferior a, eg **temperatures — normal** temperaturas inferiores a las normales.

Belshazzar [bel'ʃæzə*] m Baltasar; **—'s Feast** la Cena de Baltasar.

belt [belt] **1** n cinturón m; (Med) faja f; (Mech) correa f, cinta f; (Geog and fig) zona f, faja f; **endless —** correa f sin fin; **industrial —** zona f industrial; **green —** zona f verde; **a blow below the —** un golpe bajo; **to tighten one's —** (fig) apretarse el cinturón, ceñirse.

2 vt (fam) golpear (con una correa).

3 vi (fam): **to — along** ir como una bala; **to — past** pasar como un rayo; **to — out** salir disparado.

bemoan [bɪ'məun] vt lamentar.

bemuse [bɪ'mjuːz] vt aturdir, confundir.

Ben [ben] m nombre abreviado de **Benjamin**.

ben [ben] n (Scot) montaña f; cuarto m interior.

bench [bentʃ] n banco m; (court) tribunal m; (persons) judicatura f; **to be on the —** (Law) ser juez, ser magistrado; **he's on the —** today hoy forma parte del tribunal.

bench mark ['bentʃmɑːk] n cota f, punto m topográfico.

bend [bend] **1** n curva f; recodo m, vuelta f; ángulo m; (Her) banda f; (Naut) gaza f; **hairpin —** viraje m en horquilla; **sharp —** curva f cerrada; **to be round the —** (sl) estar chiflado; **to go round the —** (sl) volverse loco.

2 (irr: pret and ptp **bent**) vt encorvar; (buckle) doblar, torcer; (cause to sag) combar; body, head inclinar; knee doblar; sail envergar; efforts, steps etc dirigir (to a); **to — someone to one's will** someter a uno a su voluntad; **to — back** doblar hacia atrás; **to — down** doblar hacia abajo, head inclinar.

3 vi encorvarse; (buckle) doblarse, torcerse; (sag) combarse; (road) torcer(se) (to the left a la izquierda); (person) encorvarse, inclinarse (also **to — down, to — over**).

bender ['bendə*] n (sl): **to go on a —** ir de juerga.

beneath [bɪ'niːθ] adv and prep = **below**; (fig) **it is — him** es indigno de él; **it is — him to do such a thing** él es incapaz de hacer tal bajeza; **she married — her** se casó con hombre de clase inferior.

Benedict ['benɪdɪkt] m Benito; (pope) Benedicto.

Benedictine [,benɪ'dɪktɪn] **1** adj benedictino. **2** n benedictino m.

benediction [,benɪ'dɪkʃən] n bendición f.

benefaction [,benɪ'fækʃən] n (gift) beneficio m.

benefactor ['benɪfæktə*] n bienhechor m.

benefactress ['benɪfæktrɪs] n bienhechora f.

benefice ['benɪfɪs] n beneficio m.

beneficence [bɪ'nefɪsəns] n beneficencia f.

beneficent [bɪ'nefɪsənt] adj benéfico.

beneficial [,benɪ'fɪʃəl] adj provechoso, beneficioso.

beneficiary [,benɪ'fɪʃərɪ] n beneficiario m, a f; (Eccl) beneficiado m.

benefit ['benɪfɪt] **1** n beneficio m; provecho m, utilidad f; (payment) subsidio m; (Theat, Sport) beneficio m; **maternity —** subsidio m de natalidad; **unemployment —** subsidio m de paro; **— match** partido homenaje m; **— performance** función f benéfica; **— society** sociedad f de socorro mutuo; **for the — of a** beneficio de; **to be to the — of** ser provechoso a; **to give someone the — of the doubt** dar a uno el beneficio de la duda; **to have the — of** tener la ventaja de; **to reap the —** of sacar el fruto de.

2 vt beneficiar, aprovechar.

3 vi aprovecharse; **to — by, to — from** sacar provecho de.

benevolence [bɪ'nevələns] n benevolencia f.

benevolent [bɪ'nevələnt] adj benévolo; **society** de socorro mutuo.

Bengal [beŋ'gɔːl] Bengala f.

benighted [bɪ'naɪtɪd] adj (fig) ignorante.

benign [bɪ'naɪn] adj benigno (also Med).

benignant [bɪ'nɪgnənt] adj benigno; (healthy) saludable.

Benjamin ['bendʒəmɪn] m Benjamín.

bent [bent] **1** adj, pret and ptp of **bend**; encorvado; doblado, torcido; (fam) sospechoso, de tendencias criminales; **on pleasure —** intentando divertirse; **to be — on** + ger estar resuelto a + infin, estar empeñado en + infin; **to be — on a quarrel** estar resuelto a provocar una riña.

2 n inclinación f (to, towards, for a); **to follow one's —** seguir su inclinación; **to have a — towards** estar inclinado a.

benumb [bɪ'nʌm] vt entumecer; (fig) entorpecer; mind etc paralizar.

Benzedrine ['benzɪdriːn] n (Protected Trade Name) bencedrina f.

benzene ['benziːn] n benceno m.

benzine ['benziːn] n bencina f.

bequeath [bɪ'kwiːð] vt legar.

bequest [bɪ'kwest] n legado m.

berate [bɪ'reɪt] vt censurar; reñir, regañar.

Berber ['bəːbə*] **1** adj bereber. **2** n bereber mf.

bereaved [bɪ'riːvd] adj afligido; **the —** los afligidos.

bereavement [bɪ'riːvmənt] n aflicción f (por la muerte de un pariente).

bereft [bɪ'reft] ptp: **to be — of** (act) ser privado de, (state) estar desprovisto de.

beret ['bereɪ] n boina f.

Berlin [bəː'lɪn] Berlín f; (attr) berlinés.

Berliner [bəː'lɪnə*] n berlinés m, esa f.

Bermuda [bəː'mjuːdə] Islas fpl Bermuda, las Bermudas.

Bernard ['bəːnəd] m Bernardo.

Berne [bəːn] Berna f.

berry ['berɪ] n baya f.

berserk [bəˈsəːk] adj: **to go —** perder los estribos.

Bert [bəːt] m nombre abreviado de **Albert, Herbert** etc.

berth [bəːθ] **1** n (place at wharf) amarradero m; (cabin) camarote m; (bunk) litera f; (fam) puesto m, lugar m; **to give someone a wide —** evitar el encuentro de uno, huir el trato de uno. **2** vti atracar.

beryl ['berɪl] n berilo m.

beseech [bi'si:tʃ] (irr: pret and ptp **besought**) vt suplicar (for something algo, to do hacer).

beseeching [bi'si:tʃiŋ] adj suplicante.

beseechingly [bi'si:tʃiŋli] adv en tono (etc) de súplica.

beset [bi'set] (irr: see **set**) vt person acosar, perseguir; road obstruir, dificultar; **a policy — with dangers** una política llena de peligros; **a way — with difficulties** un camino erizado de dificultades.

besetting [bi'setiŋ] adj obsesionante; sin dominante.

beside [bi'said] prep (a) cerca de, junto a, al lado de; **to be — oneself** (with anger) estar fuera de sí, (with anxiety) volverse loco de inquietud.

(b) (fig) **whom can we set — him?** ¿con quién podemos compararle?; **what is that — victory?** y eso ¿qué importa en comparación con la victoria?

besides [bi'saidz] **1** adv además. **2** prep además de; (with negation) excepto, fuera de.

besiege [bi'si:dʒ] vt asediar, sitiar; **we are —d with calls** nos están llamando incesantemente; **we were —d with inquiries** hubo un torrente de preguntas.

besieger [bi'si:dʒə*] n sitiador m.

besmear [bi'smi:ə*] vt embarrar, embadurnar.

besmirch [bi'smə:tʃ] vt (fig) manchar, mancillar.

besotted [bi'sɔtid] adj entontecido; **— with alcohol** embrutecido por el alcohol; **he is — with her** anda loco por ella.

besought [bi'sɔ:t] pret and ptp of **beseech**.

bespatter [bi'spætə*] vt salpicar (with de).

bespeak [bi'spi:k] (irr: see **speak**) vt (engage) apalabrar; goods etc encargar, reservar; (be evidence of) indicar.

bespectacled [bi'spektikld] adj con gafas, que lleva gafas.

bespoke [bi'spəuk] **1** pret and ptp of **bespeak**. **2** adj **— clothing** ropa f hecha a la medida; **— tailor** sastre m que confecciona a medida.

bespoken [bi'spəukən] ptp of **bespeak**.

besprinkle [bi'spriŋkl] vt salpicar, rociar (with de); espolvorear (with de).

Bess [bes], **Bessie** or **Bessy** ['besi] f Isabelita.

best [best] **1** adj superl (el, la) mejor; **to know what is — for someone** saber lo que más conviene a uno.

2 adv superl (lo) mejor; **as — I could** lo mejor que pude; **I had — go** más vale que yo vaya; **I had — see him at once** sería aconsejable verle en seguida; **you know —** Vd sabe mejor que yo; **Mummy knows —** estas cosas las decide mamá, mamá sabe lo que más conviene; **when it comes to hotels I know —** yo soy el más experto en asunto de hoteles; **to come off —** salir ganando.

3 n (a) lo mejor; **Sunday —** trapos mpl de cristianar; **to dress up in one's Sunday —** endomingarse; **the — of it is that** lo mejor del caso es que; **is that the — you can do?** y eso ¿es todo lo que Vd puede hacer?; **we have had the — of the day** el buen tiempo se acabó por hoy.

(b) (phrases with prep) **at —**, **at the —** a lo más, en el mejor de los casos; **the garden is at its — in June** en junio el jardín está en todo su esplendor; **he wasn't at his —** no estuvo en forma; **it's all for the —** todo conduce al bien a la larga; **I acted for the —** obré con la mejor intención; **we drank of the —** bebimos el mejor vino (etc); **I can sing with the — (of them)** yo canto como el que más.

(c) (phrases with verb) **to do one's —** hacer como mejor puede uno; **to get the — of it** salir ganando, imponerse; **in order to get the — out of the car** para obtener el máximo rendimiento del coche; **to look one's —** mostrarse en todo su esplendor; **she's not looking her —** está algo desmejorada; **to make the — of it** (or **of a bad job**) salir de un mal negocio lo mejor posible.

4 vt vencer.

bestial ['bestiəl] adj bestial.

bestiality [,besti'æliti] n bestialidad f.

bestir [bi'stə:*] vr: **to — oneself** menearse.

bestow [bi'stəu] vt (grant) otorgar (on a); (give) dar (on a); affections ofrecer (on a); compliment hacer (on a).

bestowal [bi'stəuəl] n otorgamiento m; donación f; ofrecimiento m.

bestraddle [bi'strædl] vt montar a horcajadas, estar a horcajadas sobre; (fig) estar a caballo sobre.

bestrew [bi'stru:] (irr: see **strew**) vt things desparramar, esparcir; surface sembrar, cubrir (with de).

bestridden [bi'stridn] ptp of **bestride**.

bestride [bi'straid] (irr: see **stride**) vt horse montar a horcajadas; stream etc cruzar de un tranco; (fig) dominar.

bestrode [bi'strəud] pret of **bestride**.

bestseller ['best'selə*] n éxito m de librería.

bet [bet] **1** n apuesta f; (sum) postura f; **to lay** (or **make, put**) **a —** on apostar a.

2 (irr: pret and ptp **bet** or **betted**) vt apostar (on a); **I — you a shilling that** te apuesto un chelín a que; **I'll — you anything you like!** ¡apuesto lo que quieras!; **you — (your life)!** ¡ya lo creo!

3 vi apostar, jugar; **I — you can't!** ¡a que no puedes!; **I — it isn't!** ¡a que no!; **I don't —** yo no juego.

betake [bi'teik] (irr: see **take**) vr: **to — oneself to** dirigirse a, trasladarse a, acudir a.

betaken [bi'teikən] ptp of **betake**.

betel ['bi:təl] n betel m.

bête noire ['beit'nwɑ:*] n bestia f negra, pesadilla f; (person) hincha mf.

bethink [bi'θiŋk] (irr: see **think**) vr: **to — oneself of** acordarse de.

Bethlehem ['beθlihem] Belén m.

bethought [bi'θɔ:t] pret and ptp of **bethink**.

betide [bi'taid] vti acontecer; see **woe**.

betimes [bi'taimz] adv temprano; con tiempo.

betoken [bi'təukən] vt presagiar, anunciar.

betook [bi'tuk] pret of **betake**.

betray [bi'trei] vt (a) person, country traicionar; **to — someone to the enemy** vender a uno al enemigo; **his accent —s him** su acento le traiciona; **his accent —s him as a foreigner** su acento le acusa de extranjero.

(b) (reveal) plot etc revelar, delatar; ignorance etc hacer patente.

(c) (show signs of) dejar ver, dar muestras de, descubrir; **his face —ed a certain surprise** su cara acusó cierto asombro.

betrayal [bi'treiəl] n (a) traición f; **— of trust** abuso m de confianza. (b) revelación f. (c) descubrimiento m.

betroth [bi'trəuð] vt prometer en matrimonio (to a); **to be —d** (act) desposarse, (state) estar desposado.

betrothal [bi'trəuðəl] n desposorios mpl, esponsales mpl.

better¹ ['betə*] **1** adj comp mejor; **— and —** cada vez mejor; **that's —** eso va mejor; **this vale así**; **that's —!** ¡bien!; **he's much —** (Med) está mucho mejor; **it couldn't be —** no podría ser mejor; **it is — to + infin** más vale + infin; **it would be — to + infin** más valdría + infin, sería aconsejable + infin; **she's no — than she ought to be** es una mujer que tiene historia; **to get —** mejorar(se), (Med) reponerse; **to go one —** hacer mejor todavía (than que).

2 adv comp mejor; **all the —, so much the —** tanto mejor (for para); **to be all the — for** haber mejorado mucho a consecuencia de; **it would be all the — for a drop of paint** no le vendría mal una mano de pintura; **they are — off than we are** son más acomodados que nosotros; **I had — go** más vale que yo vaya; **but he knew —** pero él tuvo otra idea; **he thinks he knows —** él cree que se lo sabe todo; **he knows — than the experts** él sabe más que los expertos; **to think — of it** mudar de parecer.

3 n (a) **my —s** mis superiores.

(b) **it's a change for the —** es un cambio beneficioso; **for — or worse** en la fortuna como en la adversidad; **to get the — of** vencer, quedar por encima de.

4 vt mejorar; record, score superar.

5 vr: **to — oneself** mejorar su posición.

better² ['betə*] n apostador m, ora f.

betterment ['betəmənt] n mejoramiento m.

betting ['betiŋ] **1** adj aficionado al juego; **I'm not a — man** yo no juego. Soy n juego m, el apuesta.

betting shop ['betiŋʃɔp] n oficina f de un corredor de apuestas (esp sobre las carreras de caballos).

betting slip ['betiŋslip] n boleto m de apuestas.

Betty ['beti] f Isabelita.

between [bi'twi:n] **1** adv en medio (also **in —**).

2 prep entre; **— ourselves** entre nosotros; **we bought it — 4 of us** lo compramos entre los 4; **they shared it — them** se lo repartieron; **— now and May** de ahora a mayo; **the shops are shut — 2 and 4** las tiendas están cerradas de 2 a 4.

betwixt [bi'twikst] **1** adv en medio; **— and between** entre lo uno y lo otro. **2** prep entre; en medio de.

bevel ['bevəl] **1** adj biselado. **2** n (tool) cartabón m, escuadra f falsa; (surface) bisel m. **3** vt biselar.

beverage ['bevəridʒ] n bebida f.

bevy ['bevi] n (birds) bandada f; (women etc) grupo m.

bewail [bi'weil] vt lamentar.

beware [bi'weə*] vi (a) **to — of** precaverse de, tener cuidado con, guardarse de.

(b) **—!** ¡cuidado!, ¡atención!, ¡ojo!; **— of the dog!** ¡ojo con el perro!, (as notice) "perro peligroso"; **— of pickpockets!** ¡ojo con los carteristas!; **— of imitations** desconfíe de las imitaciones.

bewilder [bi'wildə*] *vt* aturdir, dejar perplejo, desconcertar.
bewildering [bi'wildəriŋ] *adj* desconcertante.
bewilderingly [bi'wildəriŋli] *adv* de modo desconcertante; **a — complicated matter** un asunto tan complicado que desconcierta a uno.
bewilderment [bi'wildəmənt] *n* aturdimiento *m*, perplejidad *f*.
bewitch [bi'witʃ] *vt* hechizar (*also fig*).
bewitching [bi'witʃiŋ] *adj* hechicero, encantador.
beyond [bi'jɔnd] **1** *adv* más allá, más lejos.
2 *prep* (a) más allá de; **— the seas** allende los mares.
(b) (*over and above*) además, fuera de.
(c) (*fig*) **the task is — him** la tarea es superior a sus fuerzas; **it's — me** está fuera de mi alcance, no lo entiendo; **it's — me to see how** no alcanzo a ver cómo; **this is getting — me** se me está haciendo imposible esto; **it's — a doubt** está fuera de toda duda; **it's — praise** queda por encima de todo elogio; **to go — one's authority** exceder a su autoridad.
3 *n*: **the great —** el más allá; **at the back of —** en el quinto infierno.
bi . . . [bai] bi . . .
biannual [bai'ænjuəl] *adj* semestral.
bias ['baiəs] **1** *n* (a) sesgo *m*, diagonal *f*; **to cut something on the —** cortar algo al sesgo.
(b) (*inclination*) propensión *f*, predisposición *f* (*to, towards* a); **to have a — towards** tener propensión a, estar inclinado a.
(c) (*prejudice*) pasión *f*, prejuicio *m*.
2 *vt* (*fig*) influir en, torcer; **to — someone against something** predisponer a uno en contra de algo; **to be —sed** tener prejuicio (*against* contra), ser partidista (*in favour of* de).
bib [bib] *n* babero *m*, babador *m*; **in one's best — and tucker** llevando el mejor traje que tiene uno.
Bible ['baibl] *n* Biblia *f*; **the Holy —** la Santa Biblia.
Biblical ['biblikəl] *adj* bíblico.
bibliographer [,bibli'ɔgrəfə*] *n* bibliógrafo *m*.
bibliographic(al) [,bibliəu'græfik(əl)] *adj* bibliográfico.
bibliography [,bibli'ɔgrəfi] *n* bibliografía *f*.
bibliomania [,bibliəu'meiniə] *n* bibliomanía *f*.
bibliophile ['bibliəufail] *n* bibliófilo *m*.
bibulous ['bibjuləs] *adj* bebedor, borrachín.
bicameral [bai'kæmərəl] *adj* bicameral.
bicarbonate of soda [bai'ka:bənitəv'səudə] *n* bicarbonato *m* sódico.
bicentenary [,baisen'ti:nəri] *n* bicentenario *m*.
biceps ['baiseps] *n* biceps *m*.
bicker ['bikə*] *vi* reñir, altercar; (*stream*) murmurar.
bickering ['bikəriŋ] *n* riñas *fpl*, altercados *mpl*.
bicuspid [bai'kʌspid] *adj* bicúspide.
bicycle ['baisikl] **1** *n* bicicleta *f*. **2** *vi* ir en bicicleta; **to — to Dover** ir en bicicleta a Dover.
bid [bid] **1** *n* (a) (*at auction*) oferta *f*, postura *f*; **highest — mejor** postura *f*.
(b) (*Cards*) marca *f*; **no — paso.**
(c) (*fig*) tentativa *f*, conato *m*; **to make a — for control of** tratar de asegurar el control de; **to make a — to +** *infin* hacer una tentativa de + *infin*.
2 (*irr*: *pret* **bade, bid,** *ptp* **bidden, bid**) *vt* (a) (*order*) ordenar, mandar; **to — someone to do something** mandar a uno hacer algo.
(b) (*at auction*) licitar, ofrecer; **to — £10 for** ofrecer 10 libras por; **to — someone up to £12** hacer que uno siga haciendo posturas hasta 12 libras.
(c) (*Cards*) marcar, pujar, declarar.
(d) **to — someone good-day** dar a uno los buenos días; **to — defiance to** desafiar a; *see* **adieu.**
3 *vi* (a) **to — for** pujar por, hacer una oferta por; **to — up** pujar.
(b) **to — fair to +** *infin* prometer + *infin*, dar esperanzas de + *infin*.
biddable ['bidəbl] *adj* marcable.
bidden ['bidn] *ptp of* **bid.**
bidder ['bidə*] *n* (a) postor *m*; **highest — mejor** postor *m*. (b) (*Cards*) declarante *mf*.
bidding ['bidiŋ] *n* (a) (*order*) orden *f*, mandato *m*; **to do someone's —** cumplir el mandato de uno.
(b) (*at auction*) licitación *f*, ofertas *fpl*; **the — opened at £5** la primera oferta fue de 5 libras; **there was keen — for the picture** hubo una rápida serie de ofertas por el cuadro.
(c) (*Cards*) remate *m*, declaración *f*; **to open the —** abrir la declaración.
bide [baid] *vt*: **to — one's time** esperar la hora propicia.
bidet ['bi:dei] *n* bidet *m*, bidé *m* (*Acad*).
biennial [bai'eniəl] **1** *adj* bienal; (*Bot*) bianual. **2** *n* planta *f* bienal, bianual *m*.

bier [biə*] *n* féretro *m*.
biff [bif] (*fam*) **1** *n* bofetada *f*. **2** *vt* dar una bofetada a.
bifocal ['bai'fəukəl] **1** *adj* bifocal. **2** *n* lente *m* bifocal; **—s gafas** *fpl* bifocales.
bifurcate ['baifəkeit] *vi* bifurcarse.
big [big] **1** *adj* grande; abultado, voluminoso; importante; (*fam*) generoso; **my — brother** mi hermano mayor; **the B— Four** las cuatro Grandes (Potencias); **it's a — shame** es una terrible lástima; **to be — with child** estar encinta; **that's very — of you** (*fam*) es Vd muy amable.
2 *adv* (*sl*): **to talk —** darse mucha importancia, darse bombo; **to think —** hacer proyectos de gran envergadura.
bigamist ['bigəmist] *n* bígamo *m*, a *f*.
bigamous ['bigəməs] *adj* bígamo.
bigamy ['bigəmi] *n* bigamia *f*.
bighead ['bighed] *n* (*sl*) orgulloso *m*, a *f*, listillo *m*, a *f*.
bigheaded ['big'hedid] *adj* (*sl*) engreído.
big-hearted ['big'ha:tid] *adj* generoso.
bight [bait] *n* (a) (*Geog*) ensenada *f*, cala *f*; (*bend*) recodo *m*. (b) (*of rope*) gaza *f*.
bigmouth ['bigmauθ] *n* (*sl*) hablador *m*, ora *f*, charlador *m*, ora *f*; chismoso *m*, a *f*; soplón *m*.
big-mouthed ['big'mauθt] *adj* (a) de boca grande, de boca ancha, bocudo. (b) (*sl*) hablador, charlador; chismoso; soplón.
bigot ['bigət] *n* fanático *m*, a *f*, intolerante *mf*.
bigoted ['bigətid] *adj* fanático, intolerante.
bigotry ['bigətri] *n* fanatismo *m*, intolerancia *f*.
big-time ['big'taim] *adj* (*fam*) de postín, de rumbo.
bigwig ['bigwig] *n* pez *m* gordo, señorón *m*, espadón *m*.
bike [baik] (*fam*) **1** *n* bici *f*. **2** *vi* ir en bicicleta.
bikini [bi'ki:ni] *n* bikini *m*.
bilateral [bai'lætərəl] *adj* bilateral.
bilberry ['bilbəri] *n* arándano *m*.
bile [bail] *n* bilis *f*; (*fig*) mal genio *m*, displicencia *f*.
bilge [bildʒ] *n* (*Naut*) pantoque *m*; (*water*) agua *f* de pantoque; (*sl*) tonterías *fpl*.
bilge water ['bildʒwɔ:tə*] *n* agua *f* de pantoque.
bilingual [bai'liŋgwəl] *adj* bilingüe.
bilingualism [bai'liŋgwəlizəm] *n* bilingüismo *m*.
bilious ['biliəs] *adj* bilioso (*also fig*); **— attack** trastorno *m* biliar.
biliousness ['biliəsnis] *n* tendencia *f* a sufrir trastornos biliares.
bilk [bilk] *vt* estafar, defraudar.
bill[1] [bil] **1** *n* (*bird's*) pico *m*; (*of anchor*) uña *f*; (*Agr*) podadera *f*, podón *m*; (*Geog*) promontorio *m*. **2** *vi*: **— and coo** besuquearse, acariciarse.
bill[2] [bil] **1** *n* (a) (*account*) cuenta *f*; (*invoice*) factura *f*; **wages —** (*in industry*) coste *m* de salarios; **to foot the —** pagar la cuenta; correr con los gastos; (*fig*) pagar el pato.
(b) (*Parl*) proyecto *m* de ley; **— of rights** declaración *f* de derechos, ley *f* fundamental; **to fill the —** llenar los requisitos.
(c) (*banknote*) billete *m*; **— (of exchange)** letra *f* de cambio.
(d) (*notice*) cartel *m*; **stick no —s** prohibido fijar carteles.
(e) **— of fare** lista *f* (de platos), menú *m*; **— of health** (*Naut*) patente *f* de sanidad; **— of lading** conocimiento *m* de embarque; **— of sale** escritura *f* de venta.
2 *vt* (*Theat*) anunciar; **he is —ed to appear next week** figura en el programa de la semana que viene.
Bill [bil] *m nombre abreviado de* **William.**
billboard ['bilbɔ:d] *n* (*US*) cartelera *f*.
billet ['bilit] **1** *n* alojamiento *m*. **2** *vt* alojar (*on* en casa de).
billet-doux ['bilei'du:] *n* carta *f* amorosa.
billfold ['bilfəuld] *n* (*US*) billetero *m*, cartera *f*.
billhook ['bilhuk] *n* podadera *f*, podón *m*.
billiard ball ['biliəd,bɔ:l] *n* bola *f* de billar.
billiard cue ['biliəd,kju:] *n* taco *m*.
billiards ['biliədz] *n sing* billar *m*.
billiard table ['biliəd,teibl] *n* mesa *f* de billar.
billion ['biliən] *n* billón *m*, (*US*) mil millones *mpl*.
billow ['biləu] **1** *n* oleada *f*; **—s las olas,** el mar. **2** *vi* ondular, ondear; **to — out** hincharse (de viento *etc*).
billowy ['biləui] *adj* ondoso; hinchado.
billposter ['bil,pəustə*] *n*, **billsticker** ['bil,stikə*] *n* cartelero *m*.
Billy ['bili] *m nombre abreviado de* **William.**
billy goat ['biligəut] *n* macho *m* cabrío.
billy-ho ['bilihəu] *adv* (*fam*): **like —** hasta más no poder.
bimonthly ['bai'mʌnθli] **1** *adj* (*every 2 months*) bimestral; (*twice monthly*) bimensual, quincenal.

2 *adv* bimestralmente; bimensualmente, quincenalmente.

3 *n* revista *f* bimestral; revista *f* bimensual, revista *f* quincenal.

bin [bin] *n* hucha *f*, arcón *m*; (*for bread*) nasa *f*; (*for rubbish*) cubo *m*; (*for litter*) papelera *f*.

binary ['bainəri] *adj* binario.

bind [baind] (*irr: pret and ptp* **bound**) **1** *vt* **(a)** (*tie*) atar, liar (*to a*); *hands* atar; *wound* vendar (*also to — up*); *corn* agavillar; *book* encuadernar; (*Med*) estreñir; (*encircle*) rodear (*with de*), ceñir (*with con, de*); (*fig*) liar (*to a*), unir (*to con*).
(b) (*force*) obligar; **to — someone to do something** obligar a uno a hacer algo; **to — someone to a promise** obligar a uno a cumplir su promesa; **to — someone apprentice** to poner a uno de aprendiz con; **to — someone over** obligar a uno a comparecer ante el magistrado; **to — someone over to + infin** imponer a uno el deber legal de + *infin*; *see also* **bound**[1].
2 *vi* (*cement etc*) endurecerse; cuajarse; adherirse; (*parts of machine*) trabarse.
3 *n* (*sl*): **it's a —** es una lata; **what a —!** ¡qué lata!

binder ['baində*] *n* (*Agr*) agavilladora *f*; (*file*) cartera *f*, (*of book*) encuadernador *m*.

binding ['baindiŋ] **1** *adj* obligatorio (*on a, para*); *promise* que hay que cumplir; (*Med*) que estriñe. **2** *n* (*of book*) encuadernación *f*; (*Sew*) ribete *m*.

bindweed ['baindwi:d] *n* convólvulo *m*, enredadera *f*.

binge [bindʒ] *n* (*sl*) borrachera *f*; **to go on a —** ir de juerga.

bingo ['biŋgəu] *n* lotería *f* casera, quinto *m*.

binoculars [bi'nɔkjuləz] *npl* gemelos *mpl*, prismáticos *mpl*, (*Mil*) anteojo *m* de campaña.

binomial [bai'nəumiəl] **1** *adj* de dos términos. **2** *n* binomio *m*.

biochemical ['baiəu'kemikəl] *adj* bioquímico.

biochemist ['baiəu'kemist] *n* bioquímico *m*.

biochemistry ['baiəu'kemistri] *n* bioquímica *f*.

biographer [bai'ɔgrəfə*] *n* biógrafo *m*.

biographic(al) [,baiəu'græfik(əl)] *adj* biográfico.

biography [bai'ɔgrəfi] *n* biografía *f*.

biological [,baiə'lɔdʒikəl] *adj* biológico.

biologist [bai'ɔlədʒist] *n* biólogo *m*.

biology [bai'ɔlədʒi] *n* biología *f*.

biophysics [,baiəu'fiziks] *n sing* biofísica *f*.

biopsy ['baiɔpsi] *n* biopsia *f*.

bipartisan [,bai'pɑ:tizæn] *adj* *policy etc* que tienen en común los dos partidos.

bipartite [bai'pɑ:tait] *adj* bipartido.

biped ['baiped] *n* bípedo *m*.

biplane ['baiplein] *n* biplano *m*.

birch [bə:tʃ] **1** *n* abedul *m*; (*for punishment*) vara *f*, férula *f*.
2 *vt* castigar con la vara.

birch tree ['bə:tʃtri:] *n* abedul *m*.

birchwood ['bə:tʃwud] *n* bosque *m* de abedules.

bird [bə:d] *n* **(a)** ave *f*, (*gen small*) pájaro *m*; (*sl*) (*man*) tío *m*, tipo *m*, (*girl*) chica *f*, (*girlfriend*) novia *f*; **— of ill omen** ave *f* de mal agüero; **— of passage** ave *f* de paso (*also fig*); **— of prey** ave *f* de rapiña; **early —** madrugador *m*, ora *f*.
(b) (*Theat sl*) **to get the —** ganarse un abucheo, ser pateado; **to give someone the —** abuchear a uno, patear a uno.
(c) (*proverbs*) **the early — catches the worm** al que madruga Dios le ayuda; **a — in the hand is worth two in the bush** más vale pájaro en mano que ciento volando; **—s of a feather flock together** Dios los cría y ellos se juntan; **they're —s of a feather** son lobos de una camada; **to kill two —s with one stone** matar dos pájaros de un tiro.

bird brain ['bə:dbrein] *n* (*sl*) casquivano *m*, a *f*.

birdcage ['bə:dkeidʒ] *n* jaula *f* de pájaro; (*large, outdoor*) pajarera *f*.

bird call ['bə:dkɔ:l] *n* reclamo *m*.

bird fancier ['bə:d,fænsiə*] *n* pajarero *m*.

birdlime ['bə:dlaim] *n* liga *f*.

birdseed ['bə:dsi:d] *n* alpiste *m*.

bird's-eye view ['bə:dzai'vju:] *n* vista *f* de pájaro.

bird's nest ['bə:dznest] **1** *n* nido *m* de pájaro. **2** *vi* (*esp* **to go —ing**) buscar nidos.

bird watcher ['bə:dwɔtʃə*] *n* ornitólogo *m*.

birth [bə:θ] *n* nacimiento *m*; (*Med*) parto *m*; (*fig*) nacimiento *m*, origen *m*, comienzo *m*; **the — of an idea** el origen de una idea; **by —** de nacimiento; **of humble —** de nacimiento humilde; **to give — to** dar a luz, parir, (*fig*) dar lugar a, ser el origen de; **to be in at the — of** (*fig*) asistir al nacimiento de.

birth certificate ['bə:θsə'tifikit] *n* partida *f* de nacimiento.

birth control ['bə:θkən'trəul] *n* control *m* de natalidad; **method of —** método *m* anticonceptivo, método *m* anticoncepcional.

birthday ['bə:θdei] *n* cumpleaños *m*; (*of event etc*) aniversario *m*; (*the Spaniard more commonly celebrates each year his*) día *m* del santo de uno, fiesta *f* onomástica; **on my 21st —** cuando cumplí los 21 años; **in one's —** suit en cueros.

birthday present ['bə:θdei'preznt] *n* regalo *m* de cumpleaños.

birthmark ['bə:θmɑ:k] *n* rosa *f*, marca *f* de nacimiento.

birthplace ['bə:θpleis] *n* lugar *m* de nacimiento.

birth rate ['bə:θreit] *n* natalidad *f*.

birthright ['bə:θrait] *n* derechos *mpl* de nacimiento; primogenitura *f*; (*fig*) patrimonio *m*, herencia *f*; **it is the — of every Englishman** pertenece por derecho natural a todo inglés.

birthstone ['bə:θstəun] *n* piedra preciosa que simboliza las influencias astrológicas de la fecha en que uno nació.

Biscay ['biskei] Vizcaya *f*.

biscuit ['biskit] *n* galleta *f*; **that takes the —!** (*fam*) ¡eso es el colmo!

biscuit barrel ['biskit,bærəl] *n* galletero *m*.

bisect [bai'sekt] *vt* bisecar.

bisexual [bai'seksjuəl] *adj* bisexual.

bishop ['biʃəp] *n* obispo *m*; (*Chess*) alfil *m*.

bishopric ['biʃəprik] *n* obispado *m*.

bismuth ['bizməθ] *n* bismuto *m*.

bison ['baisən] *n* bisonte *m*.

bit[1] [bit] *n* (*horse's*) freno *m*, bocado *m*; (*tool*) barrena *f*; **to get the — between one's teeth** desbocarse, rebelarse.

bit[2] [bit] *n* **(a)** trozo *m*, pedacito *m*, porción *f*.
(b) (*noun phrases*) **a — of advice** un consejo; **a — of news** una noticia; **I had a — to eat** tomé un bocado; **I'll have a — of cake** tomo un poco de tarta; **they have a — of money** tienen dinerillos; **to blow something to —s** hacer algo añicos; **to come to —s** hacerse pedazos, romperse, desmontarse; **to do one's — contribuir**, hacer la debida contribución, servir como se debe (*a la patria etc*).
(c) (*adjectival uses*) **he's a — of a liar** es algo mentiroso; **I'm a — of a musician** yo sé algo de música; **I'm a — of a socialist** yo soy socialista hasta cierto punto; **it was a — of a shock** fue un golpe bastante duro; **I've a — of a cold** estoy ligeramente acatarrado; **not a — of it!** ¡ni hablar!, ¡nada, nada!; **it's not a — of use** no sirve para nada en absoluto; **every — as good as** de ningún modo inferior a; **every — a man** todo un hombre.
(d) (*adverbial uses*) **— by —** poco a poco; **it's a — awkward** es un poco difícil; **a — later** poco después, un poco más tarde; **wait a —!** ¡espere un momento!, ¡un momento, por favor!; **so I waited a — así que esperé un ratito; **it's a good — further than we thought** queda bastante más lejos de lo que creíamos; **a good — bigger** bastante más grande; **are you tired?... not a —!** ¿estás cansado?... ¡en absoluto!

bit[3] [bit] *pret of* **bite**.

bitch [bitʃ] **1** *n* **(a)** perra *f*; (*woman*) lagarta *f*, mujer *f* de mal genio; **you —!** ¡lagarta!; ¡perra salida! **(b)** (*sl*) queja *f*. **2** *vi* (*sl*) quejarse.

bitchy ['bitʃi] *adj* (*fam*) maldiciente, malicioso; de mal genio; rencoroso; *remark etc* malintencionado, horrible.

bite [bait] **1** *n* **(a)** mordedura *f*; (*toothmark*) dentellada *f*; (*of bird, insect*) picadura *f*.
(b) (*food*) bocado *m*; (*snack*) bocadillo *m*; **1 not had a —** no he comido un solo bocado; **will you have a — to eat?** ¿le traigo algo de comer?; **I'll get a — on the train** tomaré un bocadillo en el tren.
(c) (*Fishing*) **are you getting any —s?** ¿están picando?
(d) (*fig*) mordacidad *f*, penetración *f*; **a novel with —** una novela penetrante; **a speech with —** un discurso tajante; **without any —** sin garra.
2 (*irr: pret* **bit**, *ptp* **bitten**) *vt* morder; (*bird, fish, insect*) picar; (*acid*) corroer; (*Mech*) asir, trabar; **what's biting you?** (*fam*) ¿qué mosca te ha picado?; **to — off** arrancar con los dientes; **to — off more than one can chew** abarcar más de lo que se puede apretar; **once bitten twice shy** el gato escaldado del agua fría huye; **to be bitten, to get bitten** (*fig*) ser engañado; **to be bitten with** (*fam*) estar contagiado con.
3 *vi* morder; picar; (*fish*) picar; (*fig*) tragar el anzuelo; **to — at** tratar de morder; **to — into** *earth etc* devorar, tragar.

biter ['baitə*] n: the — bit el cazado cazador.
biting ['baitiŋ] adj cold, wind penetrante, cortante; criticism etc mordaz.
bitten ['bitn] ptp of **bite.**
bitter ['bitə*] **1** adj amargo; cold penetrante, cortante; battle encarnizado; enemy, hatred implacable; disappointment agudo; protest amargo; person resentido; **to feel — about something** resentirse por algo, tener rencor por motivo de algo.
2 n cerveza f clara.
bitterly ['bitəli] adv amargamente; **it's — cold** hace un frío cortante; **he protested —** se quejó amargamente; **I was — disappointed** sufrí una terrible decepción; **she spoke — of her experiences** habló con mucho rencor de sus experiencias.
bittern ['bitə:n] n avetoro m común.
bitterness ['bitənis] n amargura f; encarnizamiento m; implacabilidad f; agudeza f; **there is great — between them** entre ellos existe un odio implacable; **I accepted it without —** lo acepté sin rencor; **I have no — towards you** no le guardo rencor.
bitters ['bitəz] npl bitter m.
bittersweet ['bitəswi:t] adj agridulce.
bitumen ['bitjumin] n betún m.
bituminous [bi'tjuminəs] adj bituminoso.
bivalve ['baivælv] **1** adj bivalvo. **2** n molusco m bivalvo.
bivouac ['bivuæk] **1** n vivaque m, vivac m. **2** vi vivaquear.
bi-weekly ['bai'wi:kli] **1** adj (every 2 weeks) quincenal; (twice weekly) bisemanal.
2 adv quincenalmente; bisemanalmente.
3 n revista f quincenal; revista f bisemanal.
bizarre [bi'za:*] adj event extraño, raro; appearance etc estrafalario.
blab [blæb] **1** vt divulgar, soltar. **2** vi chismear; (to police etc) soplar.
black [blæk] **1** adj **(a)** negro; (in darkness) oscuro, tenebroso; (with smoke) negro, ennegrecido; (with dirt) sucio; event, day negro, funesto, aciago; look ceñudo, de desaprobación; **things look pretty —** la situación es desconsoladora; **a — forecast** una predicción pesimista; **a — day on the roads** una jornada trágica en las carreteras; **as — as pitch** (or **night or your hat**) negro como boca de lobo; **— man** negro m; **— woman** negra f.
(b) (trade-union parlance) **— goods** géneros mpl boicoteados; **to declare something —** boicotear algo.
(c) his face was — and blue echar la cara amoratada; **to swear — and blue** echar sapos y culebras; **— and white** photo foto f en blanco y negro; **I should like it in — and white** quisiera tenerlo por escrito; **there it is in — and white!** ¡ahí lo tiene en letra de molde!
2 n (colour) negro m, color m negro; (person) negro m, a f; (mourning) luto m; **to be in —, to wear — estar de luto; to put up a — (sl) meter la pata.
3 vt ennegrecer; shoes limpiar, lustrar; **to — someone's eye** dar a uno una bofetada en el ojo; **to — out a house** hacer que no sean visibles por fuera las luces de una casa; **the storm —ed out the town** la tormenta causó un apagón en la ciudad.
4 vi: **to — out** (Med) padecer una amnesia temporal, desmayarse.
blackball ['blækbɔ:l] vt dar bola negra a.
blackberry ['blækbəri] n (fruit) zarzamora f; (plant) zarza f.
blackbird ['blækbə:d] n mirlo m.
blackboard ['blækbɔ:d] n pizarra f, encerado m.
black box ['blæk'bɔks] n (Aer) registrador m de vuelo.
black-coated ['blæk'kəutid] adj: **— worker** oficinista mf.
blackcock ['blækkɔk] n grigallo m.
blackcurrant ['blæk'kʌrənt] n grosella f negra.
blacken ['blækən] vt ennegrecer; (by fire) calcinar; face tiznar de negro; (fig) denigrar, desacreditar.
blackguard ['blæga:d] **1** n pillo m, canalla m. **2** vt vilipendiar.
blackguardly ['blæga:dli] adj vil, canallesco.
blackhead ['blækhed] n comedón m, espinilla f.
black-hearted ['blæk'ha:tid] adj malvado, perverso.
blacking ['blækiŋ] n betún m.
blackish ['blækiʃ] adj negruzco.
blackjack ['blækdʒæk] n cachiporra f (con puño flexible).
black lead ['blæk'led] n grafito m.
blackleg ['blækleg] **1** n esquirol m. **2** vi ser esquirol, trabajar durante una huelga.
blacklist ['blæklist] **1** n lista f negra. **2** vt poner en la lista negra.
blackmail ['blækmeil] **1** n chantaje m. **2** vt chantajear, sacar dinero por chantaje a.

blackmailer ['blækmeilə*] n chantajista mf.
Black Maria ['blækmə'raiə] n coche m celular.
blackness ['blæknis] n negrura f; (darkness) oscuridad f.
blackout ['blækaut] n apagón m; (Med) amnesia f temporal, desmayo m.
Black Sea ['blæk'si:] Mar m Negro.
blackshirt ['blækʃə:t] n fascista mf.
blacksmith ['blæksmiθ] n herrero m; **—'s (forge)** herrería f.
blackthorn ['blækθɔ:n] n endrino m.
bladder ['blædə*] n vejiga f.
blade [bleid] n (of weapon etc) hoja f; (cutting edge) filo m; (sword) espada f; (of propeller) paleta f, aleta f; (of oar, hoe) pala f; (Elec) cuchilla f; **a — of grass** una brizna de hierba.
blame [bleim] **1** n culpa f; **to bear the —** tener la culpa; **to lay** (or **put**) **the — for something on someone** echar a uno la culpa de algo.
2 vt culpar, echar la culpa a; **to — someone for something** echar a uno la culpa de algo; **to be to — for** tener la culpa de; **I am not to —** yo no tengo la culpa; **who's to —?** ¿quién tiene la culpa?; **you have only yourself to —** tú eres el único culpable; **and I don't — him** y lo comprendo perfectamente.
blameless ['bleimlis] adj person inocente (of de); action intachable.
blameworthy ['bleimwə:ði] adj censurable.
blanch [bla:ntʃ] vi palidecer.
blancmange [blə'mɔnʒ] n (approx) crema f (de vainilla etc).
bland [blænd] adj suave.
blandish ['blændiʃ] vt engatusar, halagar.
blandishments ['blændiʃmənts] npl halagos mpl, lisonjas fpl.
blandly ['blændli] adv suavemente.
blank [blæŋk] **1** adj paper, space, cheque etc en blanco; verse suelto, blanco; cartridge sin bala, shell de fogueo; **a — look** una mirada sin expresión, una mirada de incomprensión; **a — stare** una mirada vaga; **when I asked him he looked —** cuando se lo pregunté puso la mirada en el vacío; **a look of — amazement** una mirada de profundo asombro; **in a state of — despair** en un estado de desesperación total; **my mind went —** no pude recordar nada.
2 n (space) blanco m, espacio m en blanco; (form) formulario m, hoja f; (coin) cospel m; (Mil) cartucho m sin bala, granada f de fogueo; **to fire —** usar municiones de fogueo; **my mind was a complete —** no pude recordar nada; **to draw a —** no encontrar nada, no tener éxito alguno.
blanket ['blæŋkit] **1** n manta f; (fig) manto m, capa f; **a — of snow** una manta de nieve; **electric —** manta f eléctrica; **wet —** aguafiestas mf.
2 adj comprensivo, general.
3 vt (fig) cubrir (in, with de), envolver (by, in, with en).
blankly ['blæŋkli] adv: **he looked at me —** me miró sin comprender.
blare [blɛə*] **1** n estrépito m, sonido m fuerte; (of trumpet) trompetazo m. **2** vt: **to — out** vociferar. **3** vi resonar, sonar muy fuerte.
blarney ['bla:ni] **1** n coba f; labia f. **2** vt dar coba a.
blasé ['bla:zei] adj hastiado; **he's very — about it** habla de ello en términos de hastío, habla con indiferencia de ello.
blaspheme [blæs'fi:m] vi blasfemar.
blasphemer [blæs'fi:mə*] n blasfemador m, ora f.
blasphemous ['blæsfiməs] adj blasfemo.
blasphemy ['blæsfimi] n blasfemia f.
blast [bla:st] **1** n **(a)** (of wind) ráfaga f; (of air) soplo m; (of sand, water) chorro m.
(b) (sound) trompetazo m; (of whistle etc) toque m.
(c) (explosive) carga f explosiva; (force of explosion) sacudida f, choque m, presión f.
(d) (of criticism etc) tempestad f, oleada f.
2 vt (with explosive) volar; (by lightning) derribar, destruir; (Mil) bombardear; (Bot) marchitar, (with blight) añublar; (fig) arruinar; criticar duramente; **to — open** abrir con carga explosiva; **— (it)!** ¡maldición!
blasted ['bla:stid] adj condenado.
blast furnace ['bla:st'fə:nis] n alto horno m.
blast-off ['bla:stɔf] n lanzamiento m, disparo m inicial.
blatant ['bleitənt] adj (shameless) descarado; agresivo; (noisy) estrepitoso, vocinglero; colour etc chillón.
blatantly ['bleitəntli] adv descaradamente.
blather ['blæðə*] **1** n disparates mpl. **2** vi charlatanear.
blaze¹ [bleiz] **1** n (with flames) llamarada f, (steady

glow) resplandor *m*; (*fire*) incendio *m*; (*bonfire*) hoguera *f*; **the garden is a — of colour** el jardín está radiante de color; **in a — in llamas; in a — of anger** en un arranque de cólera; **in a — of publicity** bajo los focos de la publicidad; **like —s** (*fam*) hasta más no poder, con todas sus fuerzas; **what the —s . . .?** ¿qué diablos . . .?; **go to —s!** ¡vete al diablo!

2 *vi* arder en llamas; (*fig*) brillar, resplandecer; **all the lights were blazing** brillaban todas las luces; **to — with anger** estar encendido de ira; **to — away** seguir tirando rápidamente; **the sun was blazing down** brillaba implacable el sol, picaba muy fuerte el sol; **to — up** (volver a) encenderse vivamente, (*fig*) estallar.

blaze² [bleiz] **1** *n* (*on animal*) mancha *f*, estrella *f*; (*on tree*) señal *f* (hecha para servir de guía). **2** *vt*: **to — a trail** abrir un camino (*also fig*).

blazer ['bleizə*] *n* chaqueta *f* ligera (de deporte *etc*).

blazing ['bleiziŋ] *adj* *sun* abrasador; *light* brillante; *anger* irreprimible; *row* violento.

blazon ['bleizn] **1** *n* blasón *m*. **2** *vt* (*fig*) proclamar.

bleach [bli:tʃ] **1** *n* lejía *f*. **2** *vt* blanquear. **3** *vi* blanquearse.

bleachers ['bli:tʃəz] *npl* (*US*) gradas *fpl* al sol.

bleaching powder ['bli:tʃiŋ,paudə*] *n* polvos *mpl* de blanqueo.

bleak [bli:k] *adj* *landscape* desierto, (*treeless*) pelado; *weather* crudo; *smile* poco afable; *welcome* inhospitalario; *prospect* nada prometedor.

bleary ['bliəri] *adj* *eye* legañoso.

bleary-eyed ['bliəriaid] *adj* de ojos legañosos.

bleat [bli:t] **1** *n* balido *m*. **2** *vi* balar; (*fig*) quejarse (*about* de).

bled [bled] *pret and ptp* of **bleed**.

bleed [bli:d] (*irr: pret and ptp* **bled**) **1** *vt* (*Med*) sangrar; (*fig*) desangrar; **to — someone white** desangrar a uno, arrancar hasta el último céntimo a uno; **to — a country white** explotar despiadadamente un país.

2 *vi* sangrar; (*tree*) exudar; **to be —ing at the nose** echar sangre por las narices; **to — to death** morir de desangramiento; **to — for** sangrar de dolor por; **those who have bled for England** los que han vertido su sangre por Inglaterra.

bleeder ['bli:də*] *n* (*Med*) hemofílico *m*.

bleeding ['bli:diŋ] *adj* (*sl*) puñetero.

bleep [bli:p] **1** *n* sonido *m* agudo; (*Radio*) señal *f* (aguda, continua). **2** *vi* (*Radio*) emitir una señal (aguda, continua).

blemish ['blemiʃ] *n* tacha *f*, mancha *f*.

blench [blentʃ] *vi* cejar, recular; palidecer.

blend [blend] **1** *n* mezcla *f*, combinación *f*.

2 *vt* mezclar, combinar, armonizar; *colours* casar. 3 *vi* combinarse, armonizarse; **to — in with** armonizarse con, formar un conjunto armonioso con; **to — into** transformarse poco a poco en.

blender ['blendə*] *n* catador *m*; **tea —** catador *m* de té.

bless [bles] *vt* bendecir; **God — you!** ¡Dios te bendiga!; **well I'm —ed!, God — my soul!** ¡caramba!; **I'm —ed if I know** que me maten si lo sé; **they were —ed with children** Dios les dio la bendición de los hijos; **she is —ed with every virtue** le adornan mil virtudes; **I — the day I bought it** bendigo el día que lo compré.

blessed ['blesid] *adj* (a) bendito, bienaventurado; **the B— Virgin** la Santísima Virgen; **— be Thy Name** bendito sea tu Nombre; **a day of — calm** un día de bendita tranquilidad.

(b) (*fig*) santo; **the whole — day** todo el santo día; **where's that — book?** ¿dónde diablos estará el libro ese?; **we didn't find a — thing** no encontramos nada en absoluto.

blessing ['blesiŋ] *n* (a) bendición *f*.

(b) (*advantage*) beneficio *m*, ventaja *f*; **the —s of electricity** los beneficios de la electricidad; **the —s of science** los adelantos que nos proporciona la ciencia; **to count one's —s** pensar en los muchos beneficios que tiene uno; **it's a — in disguise** no hay mal que por bien no venga; **it's a mixed —** está muy bien pero trae algunas desventajas, no es ganancia limpia en todos los aspectos.

blest [blest] *adj and ptp* (*poet*) of **bless**.

blether ['bleðə*] *see* **blather**.

blew [blu:] *pret* of **blow**.

blight [blait] **1** *n* (*Bot*) añublo *m*, tizón *m*, roya *f*; (*fig*) plaga *f*, infortunio *m*; desperfecto *m*, mancha *f*; **to cast a — on** (*or over*) arruinar.

2 *vt* (*Bot*) añublar, atizonar; arruinar (*also fig*).

blighter ['blaitə*] *n* (*sl*) tío *m*, sujeto *m*; **you —!** (*hum*) ¡cacho cabrón!; **what a lucky —!** ¡es un chorrón!

Blighty ['blaiti] (*Mil sl*) Inglaterra *f*.

blimey ['blaimi] *interj* (*sl*) ¡caray!

blimp [blimp] *n* globo *m*; (*person*) reaccionario *m*, militarista *m*, patriotero *m*.

blind [blaind] **1** *adj* ciego (*also fig*, *Archit*; *to a*, para; *with* de); *alley* sin salida; *corner* sin visibilidad; **— in one eye** tuerto; **as — as a bat** más ciego que un topo; **a — man** un ciego; **the — los** ciegos; **it's a case of the — leading the —** tan ciego el uno como el otro; **to be — to no ver**, (*deliberately*) hacer la vista gorda a; **he is — to all dangers** no comprende en absoluto los peligros; **he is — to her true character** se le oculta su verdadero carácter; **to fly —** volar a ciegas; **to go —** quedar ciego.

2 *n* (a) (*also* **Venetian —**) persiana *f*; (*outside window*) toldo *m*.

(b) pretexto *m*, subterfugio *m*; **it's all a —** no es más que un pretexto.

3 *vt* cegar; (*dazzle*) deslumbrar; **to be —ed in an accident** quedar ciego después de un accidente; **to be —ed by anger** estar cegado por la ira, estar ciego de ira.

blindfold ['blaindfəuld] **1** *adj* con los ojos vendados (*also fig*); *game of chess* a la ciega. **2** *n* venda *f*. **3** *vt* vendar los ojos a.

blinding ['blaindiŋ] *adj* *light* intenso, que ciega, cegador.

blindly ['blaindli] *adv* a ciegas (*also fig*).

blind man's buff ['blaindmænz'bʌf] *n* gallina *f* ciega.

blindness ['blaindnis] *n* ceguera *f*, ceguedad *f*.

blindworm ['blaindwə:m] *n* lución *m*.

blink [bliŋk] **1** *n* parpadeo *m*; (*gleam*) destello *m*.

2 *vt* guiñar, cerrar momentáneamente; **to — one's eyes** parpadear; **there is no —ing the fact that** es imposible soslayar el hecho de que.

3 *vi* parpadear, pestañear; (*light*) oscilar.

blinkers ['bliŋkəz] *npl* anteojeras *fpl*.

blinking ['bliŋkiŋ] *adj* (*fam*) maldito.

bliss [blis] (*Rel*) bienaventuranza *f*; (*happy state*) felicidad *f*; (*fig*) éxtasis *m*, arrobamiento *m*; **the concert was —!** ¡el concierto fue una gloria! **what —!** ¡qué bien!; **isn't he —?** ¡qué hombre más estupendo!

blissful ['blisful] *adj* bienaventurado; (*happy*) feliz; (*fig*) deleitoso; (*fam*) maravilloso, estupendo.

blissfully ['blisfuli] *adv* felizmente; deleitosamente; maravillosamente, estupendamente.

blister ['blistə*] **1** *n* ampolla *f*. **2** *vt* ampollar, causar ampollas en. **3** *vi* ampollarse.

blistering ['blistəriŋ] *adj* *heat* abrasador; *criticism* feroz, devastador.

blithe [blaið] *adj* alegre.

blithely ['blaiðli] *adv* alegremente.

blithering ['bliðəriŋ] *adj*: **— idiot** imbécil *mf*.

blitz [blits] **1** *n* guerra *f* relámpago; (*Aer*) bombardeo *m* aéreo; (*fig*) campaña *f* (*on* contra); **the B—** el bombardeo alemán de Inglaterra en 1940–42. **2** *vt* bombardear.

blizzard ['blizəd] *n* ventisca *f*.

bloated ['bləutid] *adj* hinchado (*also fig*; *with* de), abotagado.

bloater ['bləutə*] *n* arenque *m* ahumado.

blob [blɔb] *n* (*drop*) gota *f*; (*lump*) burujo *m*; (*blot*) borrón *m*; (*stain*) mancha *f*.

bloc [blɔk] *n* bloque *m*; **en — en** bloque.

block [blɔk] **1** *n* (*of stone, stamps, cylinder, Pol etc*) bloque *m*; (*for paving*) adoquín *m*; (*of wood*) zoquete *m*; (*butcher's, executioner's*) tajo *m*; (*children's toys*) tarugos *mpl*; (*of houses*) manzana *f*, cuadra *f* (*S Am*); (*fig*) obstáculo *m*, estorbo *m*; **— and tackle** aparejo *m* de poleas; **— of flats** bloque *m* de pisos; **to knock someone's — off** (*sl*) romper la crisma a uno.

2 *adj*: **— letter** mayúscula *f*; **please write in — letters** escribir por favor en caracteres de imprenta.

3 *vt* obstruir, cerrar; *traffic, progress* estorbar, impedir; (*Parl*) *bill* bloquear; (*Comm*) *account* bloquear; *road* **—ed** cerrado (*por obras*); **the line is —ed in 4 places** la vía está cortada en 4 lugares; **to — in, to — out** esbozar; **to — up** tapar, cegar. 4 *vi* obstruirse, cerrarse.

blockade [blɔ'keid] **1** *n* bloqueo *m*; **to run the —** forzar (*or burlar*) el bloqueo. **2** *vt* bloquear.

blockage ['blɔkidʒ] *n* obstrucción *f*; obstáculo *m*, estorbo *m*.

blockbuster ['blɔk,bʌstə*] *n* (*Mil: fam*) bomba *f* revientamanzanas.

blockhead ['blɔkhed] *n* zopenco *m*, a *f*; **you —!** ¡imbécil!

blockhouse ['blɔkhaus] *n* blocao *m*.

bloke [bləuk] *n* (*sl*) tío *m*, sujeto *m*.

blond(e) [blɔnd] **1** *adj* rubio. **2** *n* rubia *f*; **platinum —** rubia *f* platino.

blood [blʌd] n sangre f; (family) sangre f, linaje m; parentesco m; (person) galán m; **bad — mala** f leche, mala f uva; **blue — sangre** f azul; **— royal** estirpe f regia; **in cold — a sangre** fría; **that man of —** aquel monstruo; **— is thicker than water** son muy fuertes los lazos de parentesco; **it's in the —** lo lleva en la sangre; **they're out for —** están dispuestos a verter sangre; **he's after my —** me tiene un odio mortal, (hum) quiere darme una paliza; **when my — is up** cuando me encolerizo; **to draw —** hacer que sangre uno, herir, (fig) herir en lo vivo; **he has X's — on his hands** tiene las manos manchadas con la sangre de X; **it makes my — boil** me saca de quicio; **we need new — in the company** hace falta gente nueva en la compañía; **my — ran cold** se me heló la sangre; **to shed** (or **spill**) **the — of** derramar la sangre de; **without shedding — sin** efusión de sangre; **it's like trying to get — out of a stone** es como sacar agua de las piedras.

blood-and-thunder ['blʌdən'θʌndə*] **1** adj aparatosamente violento, intencionadamente cruel; melodramático.
2 n violencia f aparatosa, crueldad f intencionada; melodrama m.

blood bank ['blʌdbæŋk] n banco m de sangre.
blood bath ['blʌdbɑ:θ] n carnicería f, baño m de sangre.
blood count ['blʌdkaunt] n recuento m sanguíneo.
bloodcurdling ['blʌd,kə:dliŋ] adj espeluznante, horripilante.
blood donor ['blʌd,dəunə*] n donador m de sangre.
blood feud ['blʌdfju:d] n odio m de sangre.
blood group ['blʌdgru:p] n grupo m sanguíneo.
blood heat ['blʌdhi:t] n temperatura f de la sangre.
bloodhound ['blʌdhaund] n sabueso m.
bloodless ['blʌdlis] adj exangüe; (lacking spirit) soso; revolt sin incruento, sin efusión de sangre.
blood money ['blʌd,mʌni] n dinero m manchado de sangre.
blood orange ['blʌd,ɔrindʒ] n naranja f sanguina.
blood poisoning ['blʌd,pɔizniŋ] n envenenamiento m de la sangre.
blood pressure ['blʌd,preʃə*] n presión f sanguínea, tensión f arterial; (ie high —) hipertensión f.
blood-red ['blʌd'red] adj sanguíneo, sanguinolento.
blood relation ['blʌdri'leiʃən] n pariente m consanguíneo, parienta f consanguínea.
bloodshed ['blʌdʃed] n efusión f de sangre; mortandad f.
bloodshot ['blʌdʃɔt] adj inyectado en sangre.
blood sports ['blʌdspɔ:ts] npl caza f.
bloodstained ['blʌdsteind] adj manchado de sangre.
bloodstock ['blʌdstɔk] n caballos mpl de raza.
bloodstone ['blʌdstəun] n restañasangre m; hematites f.
bloodstream ['blʌdstri:m] n corriente f sanguínea.
bloodsucker ['blʌdsʌkə*] n (fig) sanguijuela f.
blood test ['blʌdtest] n análisis m de sangre.
bloodthirsty ['blʌdθə:sti] adj sanguinario.
blood transfusion ['blʌdtrænz'fju:ʒən] n transfusión f de sangre.
blood vessel ['blʌd,vesl] n vaso m sanguíneo.
bloody ['blʌdi] **1** adj battle sangriento, cruento; steak sanguinolento; hands, dress ensangrentado, manchado de sangre; (fig) puñetero.
2 adv (fig, fam) muy, terriblemente, condenadamente.
bloody-minded ['blʌdi'maindid] adj (sl) malintencionado; de mal genio, de malas pulgas; **to be — about a matter** mostrarse poco dispuesto a ayudar en un asunto, crear dificultades para la solución de un problema; **don't be so —!** ¡no seas malintencionado!, ¡qué mala idea!
bloody-mindedness ['blʌdi'maindidnis] n (sl) mala intención f; mal genio m; mala disposición f (para ayudar etc).
bloom [blu:m] **1** n flor f; floración f; (fig) perfección f; lozanía f; (on fruit) vello m; **in — en** flor; **in full — en** plena floración; **in the full — of youth** en la flor de su edad; **to come into — florecer**.
2 vi florecer; (fig) prosperar, lozanear, hacer eclosión.
bloomer ['blu:mə*] n (fam) plancha f.
bloomers ['blu:məz] npl pantalones mpl (de señora).
blooming ['blu:miŋ] adj floreciente; (euph, fam) condenado.
blossom ['blɔsəm] **1** n flor f; **in — en** flor.
2 vi florecer; **to — into** transformarse en, convertirse (algo inesperado) en; **to — out** desarrollarse, mostrar las muchas posibilidades que tiene uno, hacer eclosión.

blot [blɔt] **1** n borrón m (also fig); **a — on the family escutcheon** una mancha en el honor de la familia; **a — on the landscape** una cosa que afea el paisaje.
2 vt (with ink) manchar, emborronar; (with blotter) secar; reputation desacreditar; **to — out** oscurecer, hacer desaparecer; (fig) aniquilar, arrasar; **to — up** ink secar; mist beber, absorber.
3 vi (pen) echar borrones.
blotch [blɔtʃ] n mancha f; (on skin) erupción f.
blotchy ['blɔtʃi] adj manchado, lleno de manchas; skin lleno de erupciones.
blotter ['blɔtə*] n secante m tipo rodillo, secafirmas m; (sheet) hoja f de papel secante.
blotting paper ['blɔtiŋ,peipə*] n papel m secante.
blotto ['blɔtəu] adj (sl): **to be — estar** mamao.
blouse [blauz] n blusa f.
blow¹ [bləu] n **(a)** golpe m; bofetada f; (a — with may often be translated by the suffix -azo, eg) **a — with a hammer** un martillazo, **a — with the fist** un puñetazo; **at one — de** un solo golpe; **to deal** (or **strike**) **someone a — dar** (or asestar) un golpe a uno; **to strike a — for freedom** dar un golpe por la libertad; **without striking a — sin** efusión de sangre, sin violencia; **to come to —s** venir a las manos.
(b) (fig) golpe m; **that's a —!** ¡qué lástima!; **it is a cruel — for everybody** es un golpe cruel para todos; **the news came as a great — la** noticia me causó un gran disgusto; **the affair was a — to his pride** la cosa le hirió en el amor propio; **it was a final — to our hopes** esto terminó de arruinar nuestras esperanzas; **on Monday the — fell** el lunes se descargó el golpe.
blow² [bləu] **1** n soplo m, soplido m; **to go for a —** (fam) dar una vuelta.
2 (irr: pret **blew**, ptp **blown**) vt **(a)** (of wind) llevar; **the wind blew the ship towards the coast** el viento llevó el barco hacia la costa; **the wind has blown dust all over it** el viento lo ha cubierto todo de polvo.
(b) glass soplar; organ dar viento a; trumpet etc tocar, sonar; nose sonarse; bubble hacer; kiss tirar, echar; fuse quemar; money (fam) gastar, despilfarrar.
(c) — me!, well I'm —ed! ¡caramba!; **I'll be —ed if** que me cuelguen si; **— the expense!** ¡no hagamos caso del precio!
(d) to — about leaves etc llevar de acá para allá; **to — away** llevarse; arrancar; **to — down** derribar; **to — off** quitar, arrebatar; **to — the dust off a table** quitar el polvo de una mesa soplando; **to — open** door abrir de golpe, safe abrir con explosivos; **to — out** candle apagar, cheeks henchir; **to — over** derribar, volcar; **to — up** tyre etc inflar; photo ampliar; (with explosive) volar; (with publicity) dar bombo a; **to — someone up into a great novelist** hacer creer que alguien es gran novelista.
3 vi (wind, whale) soplar; (puff and —) jadear, resoplar; (siren etc) sonar; (fuse) quemarse; (sl) irse; **it's —ing a gale** hace muchísimo viento; **to — in** (sl) entrar de sopetón, llegar inesperadamente; **to — on one's fingers** soplarse los dedos; **to — on one's soup** enfriar la sopa soplando; **to — open** abrirse de golpe; **to — out** apagarse; **to — over** pasar, quedar olvidado, no tener consecuencias de importancia; **to — up** (explosive) estallar, hacer explosión; (container) reventar; (fam) reventar (de ira); **now something else has blown up** ahora ha surgido otra cosa; **it's —ing up for rain** con este viento tendremos lluvia.
blower ['bləuə*] n (sl) teléfono m.
blowfly ['bləuflai] n moscarda f, mosca f azul.
blowlamp ['bləulæmp] n soplete m, lámpara f de soldar.
blown [bləun] **1** ptp of **blow**². **2** adj **(a)** flower marchito. **(b)** bridge etc volado, destruido.
blow-out ['bləuaut] n (Aut) pinchazo m; (Elec) quemadura f; (sl) banquetazo m, atracón m.
blowpipe ['bləupaip] n cerbatana f.
blow-up ['bləuʌp] n (a) (Phot) ampliación f. (b) (fam) explosión f de ira; riña f, pelea f (between entre).
blowy ['bləui] adj ventoso; de mucho viento; **on a — day in March** un día de marzo de mucho viento; **it's — here** aquí hay mucho viento.
blowzy ['blauzi] adj desaliñado; de aspecto muy ordinario; (red in face) coloradote.
blubber¹ ['blʌbə*] n grasa f de ballena.
blubber² ['blʌbə*] **1** vt decir lloriqueando. **2** vi lloriquear, llorar a lágrima viva.
bludgeon ['blʌdʒən] **1** n cachiporra f. **2** vt aporrear; **to — someone into doing something** obligar a uno a porrazos a hacer algo.
blue [blu:] **1** adj azul; body, bruise amoratado; (Pol) conservador; blood azul, noble; joke, song verde; (sad)

deprimido, triste, melancólico; **to feel** — estar melancólico; **to look** — tener aspecto triste.
2 n **(a)** azul m; (Chem) añil m; **the** — (sky) el cielo, (sea) el mar; **electric** — azul m eléctrico; **navy** — azul m de mar; **Prussian** — azul m de Prusia; **to come out of the** — venir como cosa llovida del cielo, bajar del cielo, (bad news) caer como una bomba. **(b)** (Pol) conservador m, ora f; **a true** — un conservador de los más leales.
(c) —s melancolía f, murrias fpl, morriña f.
3 vt azular; washing añilar, dar azulete a; (fam) despilfarrar.
bluebell ['blu:bel] n campánula f azul.
blueberry ['blu:beri] n (US) vaccinio m.
bluebird ['blu:bə:d] n pájaro m azul, azulejo m de América.
blue-blooded ['blu:'blʌdid] adj de sangre noble, linajudo.
bluebottle ['blu:,bɒtl] n moscarda f, mosca f azul.
blue-eyed ['blu:,aid] adj de ojos azules.
bluejacket ['blu:,dʒækit] n marinero m (de buque de guerra).
blueness ['blu:nis] n azul m, lo azul.
blue-pencil ['blu:'pensl] vt tachar, suprimir (en la censura).
blueprint ['blu:print] n cianotipo m, ferroprusiato m; (fig) anteproyecto m (for de).
bluestocking ['blu:,stɒkiŋ] n literata f, marisabidilla f.
blue tit ['blu:tit] n primavera f.
bluff [blʌf] **1** adj escarpado; person brusco, francote.
2 n **(a)** (Geog) risco m, peñasco m.
(b) bluff m, farol m; **to call someone's** — coger a uno en un abrenuncio.
3 vt hacer un bluff a, engañar, intimidar con amenazas que no se pueden cumplir.
4 vi hacer un bluff, farolear, tirarse un farol.
bluish ['blu:iʃ] adj azulado, azulino.
blunder ['blʌndə*] **1** n patochada f, patinazo m; error m garrafal.
2 vt: **to** — **out** descolgarse con.
3 vi hacer una patochada, tirarse una plancha; **to** — **about** andar a ciegas, andar a tontas y a locas; **to** — **into** chocar con; **to** — **upon** tropezar con.
blunderbuss ['blʌndəbʌs] n trabuco m.
blunt [blʌnt] **1** adj edge embotado, desafilado; point despuntado; manner directo, franco, abrupto; statement terminante, franco; person francote; **with a** — **instrument** con un instrumento contundente.
2 vt embotar (also fig), desafilar, despuntar.
bluntly ['blʌntli] adv francamente, de modo terminante.
bluntness ['blʌntnis] n embotadura f; (fig) franqueza f, brusquedad f.
blur [blə:*] **1** n contorno m borroso, impresión f imprecisa; **my mind was a** — me veía imposibilitado de recordar con precisión nada, todo se había vuelto borroso en mi mente.
2 vt hacer borroso, oscurecer, empañar, desdibujar; **a** —**red photo** una foto desenfocada; **a** —**red image** una imagen borrosa; **my eyes were** —**red with tears** las lágrimas enturbiaban mi vista.
3 vi desdibujarse, hacerse borroso.
blurb [blə:b] n anuncio m efusivo (de un libro).
blurt [blə:t] vt: **to** — **out** descolgarse con, decir a bulto; secret revelar.
blush [blʌʃ] **1** n rubor m, sonrojo m; (glow) color m de rosa; **the first** — **of dawn** la primera luz del alba; **in the first** — **of youth** en la inocencia de la edad juvenil; **at first** — a primera vista; **it should not bring a** — **to the face of a bishop** no haría sonrojar a una hermana de la caridad; **to spare someone's** —**es** dejar de contar algo para no ofender a uno.
2 vi ruborizarse, sonrojarse, ponerse colorado (at por, with de); **to** — **like a lobster** (or tomato) ponerse colorado como un pavo; **I** — **for you** me das vergüenza; **I** — **to** + infin me avergüenzo de + infin; **to make someone** — sofocar a uno, hacer que uno se ruborice.
blushing ['blʌʃiŋ] adj ruboroso; bride candoroso.
bluster ['blʌstə*] **1** n jactancia f; fanfarronadas fpl, bravatas fpl.
2 vt: **to** — **it out** defenderse echando bravatas.
3 vi fanfarronear, echar bravatas.
blustery ['blʌstəri] adj wind tempestuoso.
boa ['bəuə] n boa f.
boar [bɔ:*] n verraco m, cerdo m padre; **wild** — jabalí m.
board [bɔ:d] **1** n **(a)** (of wood) tabla f, tablero m, tablón m; (notice-) tablón m; (table) mesa f; (in bookbinding) cartón m; (for chess etc) tablero m; **the** —**s** (Theat) las tablas; **in** —**s** (book) en cartoné; **to**

sweep the — ganar todas las bazas, (in election) copar todos los escaños.
(b) pensión f; **full** — pensión f completa; — **and lodging** comida f y casa.
(c) (Naut) **on** — a bordo; en el tren, en el autobús etc; **on** — (the) **ship** a bordo del barco; **to go on** — ir a bordo; **to go by the** — ser abandonado, ser olvidado.
(d) (persons) junta f, consejo m de administración; — **of directors** junta f directiva; **B**— **of Trade** Ministerio m de Comercio; **medical** — tribunal m médico; **planning** — comisión f planificadora; — **meeting** reunión f de la junta directiva.
2 vt (with boards) entablar, enmaderar (also to — **up**); ship ir a bordo de, embarcarse en; enemy ship abordar; bus, train subir a; person hospedar, dar pensión (completa) a.
3 vi: **to** — **with** hospedarse en casa de.
boarder ['bɔ:də*] n huésped m, eda f; (School) interno m, a f.
boarding ['bɔ:diŋ] n entablado m.
boarding house ['bɔ:diŋhaus] n, pl — **houses** [,hauziz] pensión f, casa f de huéspedes.
boarding school ['bɔ:diŋsku:l] n internado m.
board room ['bɔ:drum] n sala f de juntas.
boardwalk ['bɔ:dwɔ:k] n (US) paseo m entablado (a la orilla del mar).
boast [bəust] **1** n baladronada f; **it is his** — **that** se jacta de que.
2 vt enorgullecerse de poseer, ostentar.
3 vi jactarse; **to** — **about, to** — **of** jactarse de, hacer alarde de; **that's nothing to** — **about** eso no es motivo para vanagloriarse.
boasted ['bəustid] adj alardeado, cacareado.
boaster ['bəustə*] n jactancioso m, a f, fanfarrón m.
boastful ['bəustful] adj jactancioso, fanfarrón.
boastfully ['bəustfuli] adv jactanciosamente.
boastfulness ['bəustfulnis] n jactancia f.
boasting ['bəustiŋ] n jactancia f, baladronadas fpl.
boat [bəut] n (in general) barco m; (large ship) buque m, navío m; (small) barca f, embarcación f; (racing eight, ship's —) bote m; **we're all in the same** — todos estamos embarcados en la misma nave; **to burn one's** —**s** quemar las naves; **to go by** — ir en barco; **to launch** (or lower) **the** —**s** botar los botes al agua; **to miss the** — (fig) perder la ocasión, llegar tarde; **to push the** — **out** (sl) ir de parranda; **to rock the** — (fig) perturbar el equilibrio.
boatbuilder ['bəut,bildə*] n constructor m de barcos.
boat deck ['bəut,dek] n cubierta f de botes.
boater ['bəutə*] n sombrero m de paja.
boat hook ['bəuthuk] n bichero m.
boathouse ['bəuthaus] n cobertizo m para botes.
boating ['bəutiŋ] n canotaje m.
boatload ['bəutləud] n barcada f.
boatman ['bəutmən] n, pl —**men** [mən] barquero m.
boat race ['bəutreis] n regata f.
boatswain ['bəusn] n contramaestre m.
boat train ['bəuttrein] n tren m que enlaza con un barco.
Bob [bɒb] m nombre abreviado de **Robert**.
bob[1] [bɒb] **1** n (of hair) pelo m a lo garçon. **2** vt hair cortar a lo garçon.
bob[2] [bɒb] n (sl) chelín m.
bob[3] [bɒb] **1** n (jerk) sacudida f, meneo m, movimiento m brusco; (curtsy) reverencia f.
2 vi menearse, agitarse; **to** — **about** (in wind etc) bailar, (on water) fluctuar; **to** — **down** sentarse; agacharse; esconderse; **to** — **to someone** hacer una reverencia a uno; **to** — **up** levantarse, aparecer; (fig) surgir, presentarse inesperadamente; **to** — **up and down** subir y bajar, (person) levantarse y sentarse repetidas veces.
bobbin ['bɒbin] n carrete m, bobina f (also Elec); (Sew) canilla f.
Bobby ['bɒbi] m nombre abreviado de **Robert**.
bobby ['bɒbi] n (sl) guili m, poli m.
bobbysocks ['bɒbisɒks] npl (US) escarpines mpl.
bobbysoxer ['bɒbisɒksə*] n (US fam) tobillera f.
bobsled ['bɒbsled] n, **bobsleigh** ['bɒbslei] n bob m, trineo m de balancín.
bobtail ['bɒbteil] n cola f corta; animal m de cola corta, animal m rabón.
Boccaccio [bɒ'kætʃiəu] m Bocacio f.
Boche [bɒʃ] **1** adj alemán, tudesco. **2** n boche m, alemán m; **the** — los alemanes.
bod [bɒd] n (sl) tío m, individuo m.
bode [bəud] **1** vt presagiar; **it** —**s no good** esto no nos promete nada bueno. **2** vi: **this** —**s ill for** esto es mala señal para.
bodice ['bɒdis] n corpiño m, almilla f.

-bodied ['bɔdid] *adj* de cuerpo . . ., *eg* **small-bodied** de cuerpo pequeño; **full-bodied** *cry* fuerte, *wine* generoso.

bodily ['bɔdili] **1** *adj* corpóreo, corporal; — **needs** necesidades *fpl* corporales. **2** *adv* (*in person*) en persona; (*as a whole*) en conjunto; **to lift someone** — levantar a uno en peso.

bodkin ['bɔdkin] *n* (*Sew*) aguja *f* de jareta; (*Typ*) punzón *m*; (*for hair*) espadilla *f*.

body ['bɔdi] *n* (**a**) cuerpo *m*; (*corpse*) cadáver *m*; (*fam*) persona *f*; (*frame*) armazón *f*, bastidor *m*; (*Aut*) caja *f*, carrocería *f*; — **and soul** (*as adv*) de todo corazón, con el alma; **the** — **politic** el estado; **heavenly** — astro *m*, cuerpo *m* celeste; **over my dead** —! ¡bajo ningún concepto!; **to keep** — **and soul together** vivir justo, seguir viviendo.

(**b**) (*corporation etc*) corporación *f*; **learned** — academia *f*; **legislative** — cuerpo *m* legislativo; **public** — corporación *f* estatal.

(**c**) (*group*) grupo *m*, conjunto *m*; **a considerable** — **of evidence** una colección importante de datos; **there is a** — **of opinion that** hay quien opina que; **a large** — **of people** un nutrido grupo de personas; **main** — grueso *m*; **the main** — **of his speech** la parte principal de su discurso; **in a** — todos juntos, en bloque.

bodyguard ['bɔdigɑːd] *n* (*man*) guardaespaldas *m*; (*men*) guardia *f* personal.

bodywork ['bɔdiwəːk] *n* (*Aut*) carrocería *f*.

Boer ['bəuə*] **1** *adj* bóer. **2** *n* bóer *mf*.

Boer War ['bəuə,wɔː*] *n* Guerra *f* Bóer, Guerra *f* del Transvaal.

boffin ['bɔfin] *n* científico *m*, inventor *m*.

bog [bɔg] **1** *n* pantano *m*, ciénaga *f*; (*sl*) wáter *m*. **2** *vt*: **to get** —**ged down** quedar atascado en el lodo, hundirse en el lodo, (*fig*) empantanarse, atrancarse (*in* en).

bogey ['bəugi] *n* (*goblin*) duende *m*, trasgo *m*; (*bugbear*) pesadilla *f*; (*policeman: sl*) guindilla *m*; **that is our** — **team** ese equipo es nuestra pesadilla.

boggle ['bɔgl] *vi* sobresaltarse, pasmarse; **don't just stand and** — no sirve para nada estar ahí boquiabierto; **the imagination** —**s** la imaginación es incapaz de representárselo; **to** — **at** vacilar ante, titubear ante.

boggy ['bɔgi] *adj* pantanoso.

bogie ['bəugi] *n* (*Rail*) bogie *m*, boga *f*.

bogus ['bəugəs] *adj* falso, fraudulento; *person* fingido; (*of person's character*) artificial, afectado.

bogy ['bəugi] *n see* **bogey, bogie.**

Bohemia [bəu'hiːmiə] Bohemia *f*.

Bohemian [bəu'hiːmiən] **1** *adj* bohemio; (*fig*) bohemio. **2** *n* bohemio *m*, a *f*; (*fig*) bohemio *m*, a *f*.

boil¹ [bɔil] *n* (*Med*) divieso *m*.

boil² [bɔil] **1** *n*: **to be on the** — estar hirviendo; (*fig*) (*situation*) estar a punto de estallar, (*person*) estar furioso; **to bring to the** — calentar hasta que hierva; **to come to the** — comenzar a hervir, (*fig*) entrar en ebullición; **to go off the** — dejar de hervir.

2 *vt* hervir, hacer hervir, calentar hasta que hierva; (*Cook*) *liquid* hervir; *vegetables* herventar, cocer; *meat* salcochar; *egg* pasar por agua; **to** — **down** reducir por cocción; (*fig*) reducir a forma más sencilla.

3 *vi* hervir; **to** — **over** irse, rebosar; **it makes me** — me hace rabiar; **to** — **with rage** estar furioso; **to** — **with indignation** estar indignado; **it all** —**s down to this** la cosa se reduce a lo siguiente.

boiler ['bɔilə*] *n* caldera *f*.

boiler house ['bɔiləhaus] *n* edificio *m* de la caldera.

boiler room ['bɔilərum] *n* sala *f* de calderas.

boiler suit ['bɔiləsuːt] *n* mono *m*.

boiling ['bɔiliŋ] *adj* hirviendo (*invariable*), en ebullición; **it's** — **hot** (*weather*) hace un calor terrible; **on a** — **hot day** un día de mucho calor.

boiling point ['bɔiliŋpɔint] *n* punto *m* de ebullición.

boisterous ['bɔistərəs] *adj wind* borrascoso; *behaviour* ruidoso, turbulento; *child* bullicioso; (*in high spirits*) muy alegre, de excelente humor; *meeting* nada tranquilo, alborotado; *welcome* tumultuoso.

bold [bəuld] *adj* (*courageous*) valiente, audaz; (*excessively* —) atrevido, osado, temerario; (*shameless*) descarado; *move, stroke* enérgico; *relief*, *contrast* fuerte; *headland* escarpado; *line* claro, vigoroso; — **face**, — **type** negrita *f*; **he came up as** — **as brass** se acercó tan fresco; **if I may make so** — si Vd me lo permite; **if I may make so** — **as to** + *infin* si se me permite + *infin*.

boldly ['bəuldli] *adv* audazmente; atrevidamente, con temeridad; descaradamente; enérgicamente, vigorosamente.

boldness ['bəuldnis] *n* audacia *f*, osadía *f*; temeridad *f*; descaro *m*; energía *f*; fuerza *f*, lo marcado.

bole [bəul] *n* tronco *m*.

bolero [bə'lɛərəu] *n* bolero *m*.

Bolivia [bə'liviə] Bolivia *f*.

Bolivian [bə'liviən] **1** *adj* boliviano. **2** *n* boliviano *m*, a *f*.

boll [bəul] *n* cápsula *f*.

bollard ['bɔləd] *n* bolardo *m*, noray *m*.

Bologna [bə'ləunjə] Bolonia.

boloney [bə'ləuni] *n* (*sl*) *see* **baloney.**

Bolshevik ['bɔlʃəvik] **1** *adj* bolchevique. **2** *n* bolchevique *mf*.

Bolshevism ['bɔlʃəvizəm] *n* bolchevismo *m*.

Bolshevist ['bɔlʃəvist] **1** *adj* bolchevista. **2** *n* bolchevista *mf*.

Bolshie ['bɔlʃi] *adj* (*fam*) turbulento, rebelde.

bolster ['bəulstə*] **1** *n* travesero *m*, cabezal *m*; (*Tech*) plancha *f* de garnitura, cojín *m*. **2** *vt* (*also* **to** — **up**) reforzar; (*fig*) alentar, dar aliento a.

bolt [bəult] **1** *n* (**a**) (*of door, rifle*) cerrojo *m*; (*arrow*) cuadrillo *m*; (*of cloth*) rollo *m*; (*Tech*) perno *m*, tornillo *m*; (*of thunder*) rayo *m*; — **from the blue** suceso *m* inesperado, sorpresa *f* desagradable; **he has shot his** — ha hecho todo cuanto en él cabe.

(**b**) fuga *f* precipitada, salida *f* repentina; **to make a** — **for it** evadirse corriendo, fugarse repentinamente; **he made a** — **for the door** se precipitó hacia la puerta.

2 *as adv*: — **upright** rígido, erguido.

3 *vt door* echar el cerrojo a; (*Tech*) sujetar con tornillos, empernar; *food* engullir, comer rapidísimamente; **to** — **two things together** unir dos cosas con pernos; **to** — **someone out** dejar fuera a uno echando el cerrojo a la puerta.

4 *vi* (*escape*) fugarse; (*horse*) desbocarse, dispararse; (*rush*) precipitarse; (*US Pol*) separarse del partido; **to** — **out** salir de golpe; **to** — **past** pasar como un rayo.

bolt-hole ['bəulthəul] *n* refugio *m*.

bomb [bɔm] **1** *n* bomba *f*; **atomic** — bomba *f* atómica; **hydrogen** — bomba *f* de hidrógeno; **incendiary** — bomba *f* incendiaria.

2 *vt* bombardear; **to be** —**ed out** ser desalojado por el bombardeo.

bombard [bɔm'bɑːd] *vt* bombardear; (*fig*) asediar, llenar (*with* de); **I was** —**ed with questions** me hicieron muchísimas preguntas.

bombardment [bɔm'bɑːdmənt] *n* bombardeo *m*.

bombast ['bɔmbæst] *n* ampulosidad *f*, rimbombancia *f*; (*words*) palabras *fpl* altisonantes; (*boasts*) bravatas *fpl*.

bombastic [bɔm'bæstik] *adj* altisonante, ampuloso, rimbombante; *person* jactancioso, farolero.

bomb crater ['bɔm,kreitə*] *n* cráter *m* de bomba.

bomber ['bɔmə*] *n* bombardero *m*.

bombing ['bɔmiŋ] *n* bombardeo *m*.

bombproof ['bɔmpruːf] *adj* a prueba de bombas.

bombshell ['bɔmʃel] *n*: **it fell like a** — cayó como una bomba.

bomb shelter ['bɔm,ʃeltə*] *n* refugio *m* antiaéreo.

bombsight ['bɔmsait] *n* mira *f* de bombardeo.

bomb site ['bɔmsait] *n* lugar *m* donde ha estallado una bomba; solar *m* arrasado por una bomba.

bona fide ['bəunə'faidi] *adj* genuino, auténtico.

bona fides ['bəunə'faidiz] *n* buena fe *f*; autenticidad *f*.

bonanza [bə'nænzə] *n* (*US*) bonanza *f* (*also fig*).

bonbon ['bɔnbɔn] *n* (*arch*) bombón *m*.

bond [bɔnd] *n* lazo *m*, vínculo *m*; (*Comm*) obligación *f*, bono *m*; (*bail, customs* —) fianza *f*; —**s** (*fetters etc*) cuerdas *fpl*, cadenas *fpl*; **in** — en depósito bajo fianza.

bondage ['bɔndidʒ] *n* esclavitud *f*, cautiverio *m*.

bonded warehouse ['bɔndid'wɛəhaus] *n*, *pl* — **houses** [,hauziz] almacén *m* de depósito.

bondholder ['bɔnd,həuldə*] *n* obligacionista *mf*.

bond paper ['bɔnd,peipə*] *n* papel *m* blanco de calidad extra (para cartas).

bondsman ['bɔndzmən] *n*, *pl* —**men** [mən] (*Hist*) fiador *m*.

bone [bəun] **1** *n* hueso *m*; (*of fish*) espina *f*; —**s** (*of dead*) huesos *mpl*, (*more respectfully*) restos *mpl* mortales; — **of contention** manzana *f* de la discordia; **to feel something in one's** —**s** estar seguro de algo pero sin saber cómo, tener un presentimiento de algo; **to have a** — **to pick with someone** tener que arreglar cuentas con uno; **to make no** —**s about** + *ger* no vacilar en + *infin*; **to make no** —**s about something** no andarse con rodeos en (el asunto de) algo; **he won't make old** —**s** no llega a pájaros nuevos.

2 *vt meat* deshuesar, *fish* quitar las espinas a; (*sl*) birlar.

3 vi (US): **to — up** quemarse las cejas (on estudiando), empollar (on sobre).
bone china ['bəun'tʃainə] n porcelana f fina.
bone-dry ['bəun'drai] adj enteramente seco.
boneheaded ['bəun'hedid] adj estúpido.
bone-idle ['bəun'aidl] adj muy gandul.
bone meal ['bəunmi:l] n harina f de huesos.
boner ['bəunə*] n (US) plancha f, patochada f.
bonesetter ['bəun,setə*] n ensalmador m.
bone-shaker ['bəun,ʃeikə*] n (Aut etc) armatoste m, rácano m.
bonfire ['bɔnfaiə*] n hoguera f, fogata f.
bongo drum ['bɔŋgəudrʌm] n bongó m.
bonhomie ['bɔnɔmi:] n afabilidad f.
bon mot ['bɔn'məu] n aforismo m, chiste m, agudeza f.
bonnet ['bɔnit] n (woman's) gorra f, cofia f; (large, showy) papalina f, toca f; (baby's) capillo m; (Scot's) gorra f escocesa; (Aut) capó m.
bonny ['bɔni] adj (esp Scot) bonito, robusto, rollizo.
bonus ['bəunəs] **1** n plus m; (on wages) sobrepaga f, prima f, suplemento m; (insurance etc) prima f; **cost-of-living —** plus m de carestía de vida; **incentive —** prima f de incentivo; **output —** prima f por rendimiento.
2 adj adicional, extra.
bony ['bəuni] adj huesudo; (like bone) óseo, huesoso; (thin) descarnado, flaco.
boo¹ [bu:] (equivalents in Spain etc) **1** n silbido m, rechifla f, pateo m.
2 vt abuchear, silbar, rechiflar, patear; **to — an actor** patear a un actor; **he was —ed off the stage** tuvo que abandonar la escena a fuerza de pateo.
boo² [bu:] n: **not to say —** (to a goose) no decir chus ni mus.
boob [bu:b] (sl) **1** n (person) bobo m, a f; (mistake) patochada f. **2** vi tirar una plancha.
booby prize ['bu:bipraiz] n pequeño premio m de consolación.
booby trap ['bu:bitræp] n trampa f explosiva.
boogie-woogie ['bu:gi,wu:gi] n bugui-bugui m.
booing ['bu:iŋ] n abucheo m, silbos mpl, rechifla f.
book [buk] **1** n libro m; (notebook) libreta f, librito m; (exercise book) cuaderno m; (of cheques, tickets) libro m talonario; **reference —** libro m de consulta; **the —s** (Comm) las cuentas, el balance; **the good —** la Biblia; **to be in someone's good —s** estar bien con uno; **to be in someone's bad —s** estar mal con uno; **to bring someone to —** pedir cuentas a uno, llamar a uno a capítulo; **to close the —s** (Comm) cerrar el borrador; **to go by the —** proceder según las reglas; **to make a — on** aceptar apuestas sobre; **to read someone like a —** conocer a uno a fondo; **to suit someone's —** convenir a uno; **to throw the — at someone** echar un rapapolvo a uno.
2 vt (note down) apuntar; (Comm) asentar (to en la cuenta de), order anotar; room, place reservar; ticket sacar; performer escriturar; suspect (fam) reseñar; **the hotel is —ed up** todas las habitaciones del hotel están reservadas; **we are —ed up all summer** no tenemos nada libre en todo el verano, lo tenemos todo vendido para el verano; **are you —ed up for tonight?** ¿tienes compromiso para esta noche?
3 vi: **— well in advance** es aconsejable reservar con mucha anticipación; **to — through to** sacar un billete hasta.
bookable ['bukəbl] adj que se puede reservar de antemano.
bookbinding ['buk,baindiŋ] n encuadernación f.
bookcase ['bukkeis] n librería f, estante m para libros.
book ends ['bukendz] npl sujetalibros mpl, soportalibros mpl.
bookie ['buki] n (fam) = **bookmaker.**
booking clerk ['bukiŋ,kla:k] n taquillero m.
booking office ['bukiŋ,ɔfis] n (Rail) despacho m de billetes; (Theat) taquilla f.
bookish ['bukiʃ] adj learning libresco; person estudioso, (pej) pedantesco.
book-keeper ['buk,ki:pə*] n tenedor m de libros.
book-keeping ['buk,ki:piŋ] n teneduría f de libros; **— by double entry** contabilidad f por partida doble; **— by single entry** contabilidad f por partida simple.
book learning ['buk,lə:niŋ] n (pej) erudición f adquirida en los libros, ciencia f libresca.
booklet ['buklit] n folleto m; (learned) opúsculo m; (of tickets) bono m.
bookmaker ['bukmeikə*] n corredor m de apuestas, apostador m profesional.
bookmark ['bukma:k] n señal f, registro m (de libro).
bookplate ['bukpleit] n ex libris m.

book post ['bukpəust] n correo m de libros; tarifa f especial para libros.
bookrest ['bukrest] n atril m.
bookseller ['buk,selə*] n librero m; **—'s** librería f.
bookshelf ['bukʃelf] n estante m para libros.
bookshop ['bukʃɔp] n librería f.
bookstall ['bukstɔ:l] n quiosco m de libros.
bookworm ['bukwə:m] n polilla f; (fig) ratón m de biblioteca.
boom¹ [bu:m] n (Naut) (of jib) botalón m, (of mainsail) botavara f; (of crane) aguilón m; (across harbour) barrera f.
boom² [bu:m] **1** n estampido m, trueno m; **sonic —** estampido m sónico.
2 vi hacer estampido, tronar; (voice, radio, organ) resonar, retumbar; (gun) retumbar.
boom³ [bu:m] **1** n alza f rápida (in prices de los precios); prosperidad f repentina (in an industry de una industria); **the — started in 1968** la época de prosperidad comenzó en 1968; **there is a big — in tin** existe una gran demanda de estaño.
2 adj: **— town** ciudad f que disfruta de una prosperidad repentina; **in — conditions** en condiciones de prosperidad repentina.
3 vi (prices) estar en alza; (commodity) tener mucha demanda; (industry, town) disfrutar de gran prosperidad, estar en bonanza.
boomerang ['bu:məræŋ] **1** n bumerang m. **2** adj contraproducente, contrario a lo que se esperaba.
3 vi tener un resultado contraproducente (on para).
boon¹ [bu:n] n (arch) favor m; **it would be a — if he went** nos alegraríamos si se fuera; **the new machine is a great —** la nueva máquina representa un gran adelanto; **the servant is a — to me** la criada me ayuda muchísimo; **it should be a — to humanity** ha de ser un beneficio para el género humano.
boon² [bu:n] adj: **— companion** compañero m inseparable.
boor [buə*] n patán m.
boorish ['buəriʃ] adj palurdo, grosero.
boorishness ['buəriʃnis] n grosería f.
boost [bu:st] **1** n empuje m, empujón m, estímulo m, ayuda f; **to give a — to** = **2** vt empujar (hacia arriba); price, sales, total aumentar; product hacer publicidad por; person dar bombo a; morale reforzar; process estimular, fomentar, dar ímpetu a; (Elec) elevar.
booster ['bu:stə*] n (Elec) elevador m de tensión; (Mech) aumentador m de presión; (Radio) repetidor m.
booster rocket ['bu:stə,rɔkit] n cohete m secundario.
booster station ['bu:stə,steiʃən] n (Radio) repetidor m.
boot¹ [bu:t] **1** n bota f; (Aut) maleta f, portaequipajes m; **now the — is on the other foot** los papeles están trastrocados; **to die with one's —s on** morir al pie del cañón; **to get the —** (fam) ser despedido; **he's getting too big for his —s** tiene muchos humos; **to give someone the —** (fam) poner a uno en la calle; **to lick someone's —s** hacer la pelotilla a uno.
2 vt dar un puntapié a; **to — out** poner en la calle.
boot² [bu:t] adv: **to —** además, por añadidura.
bootblack ['bu:tblæk] n limpiabotas m.
bootee [bu:'ti:] n borceguí m, bota f de lana.
booth [bu:ð] n (in market) puesto m; (at fair) barraca f; (Tel, voting-) cabina f.
bootlace ['bu:tleis] n cordón m.
bootlegger ['bu:t,legə*] n (US) contrabandista m en licores.
bootlicker ['bu:tlikə*] n (fam) lameculos m.
boot-polish ['bu:t,pɔliʃ] n betún m.
boots [bu:ts] n sing limpiabotas m (de un hotel).
booty ['bu:ti] n botín m, presa f.
booze [bu:z] **1** n (a) (in general) bebida f, alcohol m; (in particular) vino m, cerveza f etc; **to go on the —** darse a la bebida.
(b) (outing) borrachera f; **to go on a —** ir de juerga.
2 vt beber.
3 vi beber; emborracharse.
boozer ['bu:zə*] n (person) bebedor m; (pub) bar m, taberna f.
boozy ['bu:zi] adj person borracho, aficionado a la bebida; party donde se bebe bastante; song etc tabernario.
borage ['bɔridʒ] n borraja f.
borax ['bɔ:ræks] n bórax m.
Bordeaux [bɔ:'dəu] Burdeos; **b—** (wine) burdeos m.
border ['bɔ:də*] **1** n borde m, margen m; (of cloth) orla f, orilla f, cenefa f; (Pol) frontera f; (Hort) arriate m; **the B—** la frontera entre Inglaterra y Escocia.
2 attr area, town, ballad fronterizo; guard de la frontera.

3 *vt* (*Sew*) ribetear, orlar; **it is —ed on the north by . . .** confina en el norte con . . .
4 *vi:* **to — on** lindar con, confinar con; (*fig*) rayar en, aproximarse a.
bordering ['bɔ:dəriŋ] *adj* contiguo.
borderland ['bɔ:dəlænd] *n* zona *f* fronteriza.
borderline ['bɔ:dəlain] **1** *n* línea *f* divisoria; (*Pol and fig*) frontera *f*. **2** *adj* case etc dudoso, incierto.
bore[1] [bɔ:*] **1** *n* (a) (*tool*) taladro *m*, barrena *f*; (*Geol*) sonda *f*.
(b) (*hole*) agujero *m*, barreno *m*; (*of gun*) calibre *m*, alma *f*; (*of cylinder*) alesaje *m*; (*for oil*) perforación *f*.
2 *vt* taladrar, perforar, agujerear, barrenar; **to — a hole in** practicar un agujero en; **to — one's way through** abrirse un camino por; **wood —d by insects** madera *f* carcomida.
3 *vi:* **to — for oil** hacer perforaciones en busca de petróleo.
bore[2] [bɔ:*] **1** *n* (a) (*person*) pelmazo *m*, pesado *m*, a *f*; **what a — he is!** ¡qué hombre más pesado!
(b) (*thing*) lata *f*; **it's such a —** es una lata.
2 *vt* aburrir; fastidiar, molestar, dar la lata a; **to be —d, to get —d** aburrirse; **to be —d to death** (*or* **to tears, stiff**) aburrirse como una almeja.
bore[3] [bɔ:*] *pret of* **bear**[2].
boredom ['bɔ:dəm] *n* aburrimiento *m*, fastidio *m*.
borehole ['bɔ:həul] *n* perforación *f*.
boric ['bɔ:rik] *adj:* **— acid** ácido *m* bórico.
boring ['bɔ:riŋ] *adj* aburrido, pesado, latoso.
born [bɔ:n] **1** *ptp of* **bear**[2]; **to be —** nacer; **I was — in 1927** nací en 1927; **evil is — of idleness** la pereza es madre de todos los vicios; **to be — again** renacer, volver a nacer.
2 *adj* actor, artist etc nato; liar innato; **a Londoner — and bred** londinense de casta y cuna; **in all my — days** en mi vida.
borne [bɔ:n] *ptp of* **bear**[2].
borough ['bʌrə] *n* municipio *m*.
borrow ['bɔrəu] *vt* pedir prestado, tomar prestado (*from, of* a); idea etc adoptar, apropiarse; word tomar (*from* de); **may I — your car?** ¿me prestas tu coche? **you can — it till I need it** te lo presto hasta que yo lo necesite.
borrower ['bɔrəuə*] *n* el (la) que toma prestado; (*in library*) usuario *m*, a *f*; (*Comm*) prestatario *m*, a *f*.
borrowing ['bɔrəuiŋ] *n* (*word*) préstamo *m* (*from* de).
Borstal ['bɔ:stl] *n* reformatorio *m* de menores.
Bosch [bɔʃ] *m* El Bosco.
bosh [bɔʃ] *n* tonterías *fpl*.
bosom ['buzəm] **1** *n* seno *m*, pecho *m*; (*of garment*) pechera *f*; **in the — of the family** en el seno de la familia. **2** *attr* friend íntimo, inseparable.
Bosphorus ['bɔsfərəs] Bósforo *m*.
boss[1] [bɔs] *n* protuberancia *f*; (*stud*) clavo *m*, tachón *m*; (*of shield*) ombligo *m*; (*Archit*) llave *f* de bóveda.
boss[2] [bɔs] **1** *n* jefe *m*; (*owner, employer*) patrón *m*, amo *m*; (*foreman*) capataz *m*; (*manager*) gerente *m*; (*Pol*) cacique *m*; **I'm the — here** aquí mando yo.
2 *vt* regentar, dar órdenes a, dominar.
bossy ['bɔsi] *adj* mandón, tiránico.
botanic(al) [bə'tænik(əl)] *adj* botánico.
botanist ['bɔtənist] *n* botánico *mf*, botanista *mf*.
botanize ['bɔtənaiz] *vi* herborizar.
botany ['bɔtəni] *n* botánica *f*.
botch [bɔtʃ] **1** *n:* **to make a — of =** **2** *vt* chapucear, chafullar; **to — it** arruinarlo, estropearlo; **to — up** remendar (chapuceramente).
both [bəuθ] **1** *adj and pron* ambos, los dos; **I bought — books** compré ambos libros; **we — went** fuimos los dos; **— of them** los dos; **— of us** nosotros dos.
2 *adv and conj:* **— A and B** tanto A como B; **he — plays and sings** canta y toca además; **I find it — impressive and vulgar** encuentro que es impresionante y vulgar a la vez.
bother ['bɔðə*] **1** *n* (a) molestia *f*, lata *f*; **it's such a — to clean** me molesta tener que limpiarlo, es muy incómodo limpiarlo; **what a —!** ¡qué lata!
(b) **he had a spot of — with the police** se armó un lío con la policía; **do you have much — with your car?** ¿tienes muchas dificultades con el coche?
2 *vt* molestar, fastidiar, incomodar; **— it!** ¡porras!; **does the noise — you?** ¿le molesta el ruido?; **does it — you if I smoke?** ¿le molesta que fume? **stop —ing me!** ¡no fastidies!; **please don't — me about it now** le ruego no molestarme con eso ahora; **I can't be —ed** no quiero darme el trabajo (*to +* infin *de +* infin); **to get —ed** desconcertarse, ponerse nervioso, perder la calma.
3 *vi:* **to — about, to — with** molestarse con, preocuparse por; **to — to +** infin tomarse la molestia de *+* infin.

botheration [,bɔðə'reiʃən] *interj* ¡porras!
bothersome ['bɔðəsəm] *adj* molesto.
bottle ['bɔtl] **1** *n* botella *f*; (*of ink, scent*) frasco *m*; (*baby's*) biberón *m*; **to hit the —** (*fam*) emborracharse; **to take to the —** darse a la bebida.
2 *vt* embotellar; enfrascar; **—d beer** de botella; **to — up** embotellar; emotion reprimir, contener.
bottle-fed ['bɔtlfed] *adj* alimentado con biberón.
bottle-green ['bɔtl'gri:n] **1** *adj* verde botella. **2** *n* verde *m* botella.
bottleneck ['bɔtlnek] *n* (*fig*) embotellamiento *m*, obstáculo *m*; (*on road*) estrangulamiento *m*.
bottle-opener ['bɔtl,əupnə*] *n* abrebotellas *m*, destapador *m* de botellas.
bottle party ['bɔtl,pɑ:ti] *n* guateque *m* al que cada invitado lleva su botella.
bottom ['bɔtəm] **1** *n* (*of cup, river, sea, box, garden*) fondo *m*; (*of stairs, hill, page*) pie *m*; (*of chair*) asiento *m*; (*of ship*) quilla *f*, casco *m*; (*Anat*) trasero *m*, culo *m*; false — doble fondo *m*; **— s up!** ¡salud y pesetas!; **at —** en el fondo; **at the — of the garden** en el fondo del jardín; **he's at the — of the class** es el último de la clase; **to be at the — of something** (*fig: thing*) ser el motivo de algo, (*person*) ser el causante oculto de algo; **from the — of one's heart** de todo corazón; **the — has fallen out of the market** se han derrumbado los precios; **to get to the — of a matter** llegar al fondo de un asunto, desentrañar un asunto; **to go to the —** (*Naut*) irse a pique; **to knock the — out of** desfondar; **to send a ship to the —** hundir un buque; **to touch —** tocar fondo, (*fig*) llegar al punto más bajo.
2 *adj* part más bajo, inferior; (*last*) último; **the — team** el colista.
bottomless ['bɔtəmlis] *adj* sin fondo, insondable.
boudoir ['bu:dwɑ:*] *n* tocador *m*.
bough [bau] *n* rama *f*.
bought [bɔ:t] *pret and ptp of* **buy**.
bouillon ['bu:jɔ:ŋ] *n* caldo *m*.
boulder ['bəuldə*] *n* canto *m* rodado.
boulevard ['bu:ləvɑ:*] *n* bulevar *m*.
bounce [bauns] **1** *n* (a) (re)bote *m*; **to catch a ball on the —** coger una pelota de rebote.
(b) (*fig*) fanfarronería *f*, presunción *f*.
2 *vt* hacer (re)botar; (*fam*) poner en la calle.
3 *vi* (re)botar; (*cheque*) ser incobrable; **to — in** irrumpir alegremente.
bouncer ['baunsə*] *n* (*sl*) el forzudo que echa a los alborotadores de un café etc.
bouncing ['baunsiŋ] *adj* robusto, fuerte.
bouncy ['baunsi] *adj* (a) ball de mucho rebote, que rebota fuertemente. (b) person enérgico; bullicioso, muy activo.
bound[1] [baund] **1** *pret and ptp of* **bind**.
2 *with verb:* **well I'll be —!** ¡caramba!; **to be — for** (*Naut*) navegar con rumbo a, tener . . . como puerto de destino, (*fig*) dirigirse a; **where are you — for?** ¿adónde se dirige Vd?; **to be — over** ser puesto en libertad condicional; **to be — to +** infin (*sure*) estar seguro de *+* infin, (*must*) tener que *+* infin; **we are — to win** estamos seguros de ganar; **he's — to come** es seguro que vendrá, no puede dejar de venir; **it's — to happen** tiene forzosamente que ocurrir; **you're not — to go** no es que tengas que ir; **I am — to say that** tengo el deber de decir que; **to be — by contract to someone** estar ligado por contrato a uno; **I feel — to him by gratitude** el agradecimiento me liga a él; **to be — up with** question etc estar estrechamente relacionado con; **they are — up in each other** están absortos el uno en el otro.
bound[2] [baund] **1** *n* límite *m*; **out of —s** fuera de los límites; **out of —s to civilians** prohibido el paso a los civiles; **to put a place out of —s** prohibir la entrada a un lugar; **it is within the —s of possibility** cabe dentro de lo posible; **to keep something within —s** tener algo a raya; **to set —s to one's ambitions** poner límites a sus ambiciones; **his ambition knows no —s** su ambición no tiene límite.
2 *vt* limitar, deslindar; **a field —ed by woods** un campo rodeado de bosque; **on one side it is —ed by the park** por un lado confina con el parque.
bound[3] [baund] **1** *n* (*jump*) salto *m*; **at a —, in one —** de un salto.
2 *vt* saltar por encima de.
3 *vi* saltar; (*ball*) (re)botar; **to — forward** avanzar a saltos; **his heart —ed with joy** su corazón daba brincos de alegría; **the number is —ing up** el número aumenta rápidamente.
boundary ['baundəri] *n* límite *m*, lindero *m*; (*Pol etc*) frontera *f*.
boundary-stone ['baundəri,stəun] *n* mojón *m*.

bounder ['baundə*] n (fam) calavera m.

boundless ['baundlis] adj ilimitado.

bounteous ['bauntiəs] adj, **bountiful** ['bauntiful] adj abundante; person liberal, generoso.

bounty ['baunti] n munificencia f, liberalidad f; (Mil) premio m de enganche; (Comm) prima f, subvención f.

bouquet ['bukei] n (of flowers) ramo m, ramillete m; (of wine) aroma m, nariz f.

Bourbon ['buəbən] **1** n Borbón m; **b—** (US) aguardiente m de maíz. **2** adj borbónico.

bourgeois ['buəʒwɑ:] **1** adj burgués. **2** n burgués m, esa f.

bourgeoisie [,buəʒwɑ:'zi:] n burguesía f.

bout [baut] n (spell) turno m, rato m; (Med) ataque m; (Fencing) asalto m; (fight in general) lucha f, combate m; (boxing fixture) encuentro m, match m; (of drinking) juerga f de borrachera.

bovine ['bəuvain] adj bovino; (fig) lerdo, estúpido.

bow [bəu] n (Mil, Mus) arco m; (cross-) ballesta f; (tie, knot) lazo m; **to have two strings to one's —** tener dos posibilidades.

bow¹ [bau] **1** n inclinación f, reverencia f; **to make a —** inclinarse (to delante de), hacer una reverencia (to a); **to make one's —** presentarse, debutar; **to take a —** salir a recibir aplausos.

  2 vt head etc inclinar, (in shame) bajar; (fig: also **to — down**) agobiar; **to — someone out** hacer muchas cortesías a uno que se despide; **to — one's thanks** inclinarse en señal de agradecimiento.

  3 vi inclinarse (to delante de), hacer una reverencia (to a); **to — and scrape** hacer zalamerías; **to — beneath** estar agobiado por; **to — out** retirarse; **to — to** inclinarse a, ceder ante, transigir con, someterse a; **to — to the inevitable** conformarse con lo inevitable.

bow² [bau] n (Naut) proa f; **—s** proa f; **on the port —** a babor; **shot across the —s** cañonazo m de advertencia.

bowdlerize ['baudləraiz] vt expurgar.

bowel [bauəl] n intestino m; **—s** intestinos mpl, vientre m, (fig) entrañas fpl.

bower ['bauə*] n emparrado m, enramada f; cenador m.

bowl¹ [bəul] n (Cook) escudilla f, tazón m; (for washing) jofaina f, palangana f; (of spoon) cuenco m; (of fountain) tazón m; (of pipe) hornillo m; (Geog) cuenca f.

bowl² [bəul] **1** n bola f, bocha f; **—s** juego m de las bochas, (US) boliche m.

  2 vt rodar; (Sport) arrojar; **to — over** tumbar, echar a rodar, (fig) desconcertar.

  3 vi arrojar la pelota; jugar a las bochas; **to — along** correr rápidamente, rodar.

bow-legged ['bəu,legid] adj estevado; (stance) con las piernas en arco.

bowler ['bəulə*] n (Sport) lanzador m, el que arroja la pelota; (also **— hat**) hongo m.

bowline ['bəulin] n bolina f.

bowling ['bəulin] n (US game) bolos mpl, boliche m (S Am).

bowling alley ['bəulin,æli] n bolera f.

bowling green ['bəulin,gri:n] n pista f para bochas.

bowman ['bəumən] n, pl **-men** [mən] arquero m, (cross-) ballestero m.

bowsprit ['bausprit] n bauprés m.

bowstring ['bəustrin] n cuerda f de arco.

bow tie ['bəu'tai] n corbata f de lazo.

bow window ['bəu'windəu] n ventana f salediza.

bow-wow ['bau'wau] interj ¡guau!

box¹ [bɔks] **1** n caja f, (large) cajón m; (for money etc) cofre m, arca f; (for jewels etc) estuche m; (Theat) palco m; **— of matches** caja f de cerillas; **post-office —** apartado m de correos.

  2 vt encajonar, poner en una caja; (capture) encerrar en una caja; compass cuartear; **to — someone in** encerrar a uno; **to feel —ed in** (or **up**) sentirse encerrado.

box² [bɔks] n (Bot) boj m.

box³ [bɔks] **1** n: **— on the ear** cachete m. **2** vt boxear contra; **to — someone's ear** dar un cachete a uno. **3** vi boxear.

box camera ['bɔks'kæmərə] n cámara f de cajón.

boxer ['bɔksə*] n boxeador m; (dog) boxer m.

boxing ['bɔksiŋ] n boxeo m.

Boxing Day ['bɔksiŋdei] n día en que se dan regalos a los empleados, proveedores caseros etc (26 diciembre).

boxing gloves ['bɔksiŋglʌvz] npl guantes mpl de boxeo.

boxing match ['bɔksiŋ,mætʃ] n partido m de boxeo.

boxing ring ['bɔksiŋ,riŋ] n cuadrilátero m (de boxeo).

box-number ['bɔks,nʌmbə*] n apartado m.

box office ['bɔksɔfis] **1** n taquilla f; **to be good — ser** taquillero, estar seguro de obtener un éxito. **2** attr taquillero.

box room ['bɔksrum] n trastero m.

boxwood ['bɔkswud] n boj m.

boy [bɔi] n (small) niño m; (older, also apprentice etc, and affectionately of adult) muchacho m, chico m; (son) hijo m; (servant) criado m; (boyfriend) novio m; oh **—!** ¡vaya, vaya! old **— (**of school) antiguo alumno m, (fam) vejete m; old **—!** ¡chico!; that's the **—!**, that's my **—!** ¡bravo el chico!; but my dear **—!** ¡pero hijo!; **I have known him from a —** le conozco desde chico; **—s will be —s** eso es muy de chicos; **my husband's out with the —s** mi marido ha salido con su peña; **he's one of the —s now** ahora es un personaje; **it's all jobs for the —s** los puestos se consiguen por enchufe; **to send a — to do a man's job** subestimar los recursos que se precisan para hacer algo.

boycott ['bɔikɔt] **1** n boicoteo m. **2** vt boicotear.

boyfriend ['bɔifrend] n amigo m, novio m.

boyhood ['bɔihud] n juventud f, muchachez f.

boyish ['bɔiiʃ] adj juvenil, muchachil, de muchacho.

bra [brɑ:] n (fam) sostén m.

brace [breis] **1** n (strengthening piece) abrazadera f, refuerzo m; (Archit) riostra f, tirante m; (Typ) corchete m; (Naut) braza f; (tool) berbiquí m; (pair) par m; **—s** tirantes mpl; **— and bit** berbiquí m y barrena; **in a — of shakes** en un decir Jesús.

  2 vt asegurar, reforzar.

  3 vr: **to — oneself** prepararse para resistir (una sacudida etc); (fig) fortalecer su ánimo; **we —d ourselves for bad news** nos preparamos para aguantar una noticia mala.

bracelet ['breislit] n pulsera f, brazalete m.

bracing ['breisiŋ] adj tónico, vigorizante.

bracken ['brækən] n helecho m.

bracket ['brækit] **1** n (holding) abrazadera f; (supporting) soporte m, puntal m; (angle) escuadra f; (Archit) ménsula f, repisa f; (for gas) mechero m; (sl) nariz f; (fig) clase f, categoría f; **round —s** paréntesis mpl; **square —s** corchetes mpl; **in —s** entre corchetes.

  2 vt asegurar con ménsulas (etc); (Typ) poner entre corchetes; **to — together** agrupar, poner juntos; **to — something with something else** agrupar algo con otra cosa.

brackish ['brækiʃ] adj salobre.

brad [bræd] n puntilla f, clavito m.

brae [brei] n (Scot) ladera f de monte, pendiente f.

brag [bræg] **1** n fanfarronada f, bravata f. **2** vi jactarse (about, of de; that de que), fanfarronear.

braggart ['brægət] n fanfarrón m, jactancioso m.

Brahman ['brɑ:mən], **Brahmin** ['brɑ:min] n bracmán m, ana f.

braid [breid] **1** n trenza f; (Mil) galón m; **gold —** galón m de oro. **2** vt trenzar; dress galonear.

Braille [breil] n Braille m (alfabeto de los ciegos).

brain [brein] **1** n (a) cerebro m; **—s** (Anat) sesos mpl; **electronic —** cerebro m electrónico; **to blow one's —s out** levantarse la tapa de los sesos; **to blow someone's —s out** levantar la tapa de los sesos a uno.

  (b) (fig) **—s** inteligencia f, cabeza f; capacidad f; **to cudgel (or rack) one's —s** devanarse los sesos; **to get something on the —** dejarse obsesionar por algo; **to have something on the —** estar obsesionado por algo, no poder quitar algo de la cabeza; **to have —s** ser muy inteligente; **to pick someone's —s** exprimir a uno, sacar a uno el jugo; **to turn someone's —** volver loco a uno.

  2 vt (fam) romper la crisma a.

brain-child ['breintʃaild] n parto m del ingenio.

brain-fag ['breinfæg] n fatiga f cerebral.

brainless ['breinlis] adj estúpido, insensato.

brainstorm ['breinstɔ:m] n frenesí m.

brains trust ['breinz,trʌst] n consultorio m intelectual; grupo m de consejeros expertos.

brainwash ['breinwɔʃ] vt lavar el cerebro a.

brainwashing ['brein,wɔʃiŋ] n lavado m de cerebro.

brainwave ['breinweiv] n idea f luminosa.

brainwork ['breinwɔ:k] n trabajo m intelectual.

brainy ['breini] adj muy inteligente.

braise [breiz] vt cocer a fuego lento en una vasija bien tapada.

brake¹ [breik] **1** n freno m (also fig); **emergency —** freno m de auxilio; **to put the —s on** echar los frenos, frenar; **to put a — on** (fig) frenar, detener el progreso de.

  2 vti frenar.

brake² [breik] n (vehicle) break m; (kind of car) rubia f, combi m.

brake³ [breik] n (Bot) helecho m; (thicket) soto m.

brake drum ['breikdrʌm] n tambor m de freno.
brake fluid ['breik,fluid] n líquido m para frenos.
brake horsepower ['breik'hɔːspauə*] n potencia f al freno.
brake lever ['breik,liːvə*] n palanca f de freno.
brake lining ['breik,lainiŋ] n forro m del freno, guarnición f del freno.
brake pedal ['breik,pedl] n pedal m de freno.
brake shoe ['breikʃuː] n zapata f del freno.
braking ['breikiŋ] 1 n frenar m, frenaje m.
2 attr de frenar, de frenaje.
braking distance ['breikiŋ,distəns] n distancia f de parada.
braking lights ['breikiŋ,laits] npl luces fpl de detención.
braking-power ['breikiŋ,pauə*] n potencia f al freno.
bramble ['bræmbl] n zarza f.
bran [bræn] n salvado m.
branch [braːntʃ] 1 n marca f (also Comm); (iron) división f, sección f; (Comm) sucursal f; (road, Rail) ramal m; (of river) brazo m.
2 vt (also — out) ramificarse, echar ramas; to — off salir, separarse (from de); we —ed off at Medina salimos de la carretera principal en Medina; to — out (fig) extenderse, ensanchar el campo de sus operaciones (etc).
branch line ['braːntʃlain] n ramal m, línea f secundaria.
branch-office ['braːntʃ,ɔfis] n sucursal f.
brand [brænd] 1 n marca f (also Comm); (iron) hierro m de marcar; (fire-) tizón m, tea f.
2 vt marcar (con hierro candente); to — someone as motejar a uno de; to — something as calificar algo de; to be —ed a liar quedar con la nota infamante de mentiroso; —ed goods artículos mpl de marca.
branding-iron ['brændiŋ,aiən] n hierro m de marcar.
brandish ['brændiʃ] vt blandir.
brand-new ['brænd'njuː] adj flamante, muy nuevo, novísimo.
brandy ['brændi] n coñac m, brandy m.
brash [bræʃ] adj (rough) inculto, tosco; (cheeky) descarado, respondón; (rash) impetuoso; (unwise) indiscreto; (know-all) presuntuoso.
brass [braːs] n latón m; (plate) placa f conmemorativa; (Eccl) plancha f sepulcral (de latón); (sl) pasta f; descaro m; the — (Mus) el cobre; the top — (Mil sl) los jefazos, los espadones.
brass band ['braːs'bænd] n banda f, charanga f.
brass hat ['braːs'hæt] n (Mil sl) espadón m.
brassière ['bræsieə*] n sostén m.
brassy ['braːsi] adj de latón; sound desapacible, metálico; person etc descarado.
brat [bræt] n mocoso m, braguillas m.
bravado [brə'vaːdəu] n envalentonamiento m; out of sheer — queriendo mostrarse valiente.
brave [breiv] 1 adj valiente, valeroso; esforzado; sight, show magnífico, vistoso, garboso; as — as a lion valiente como un león.
2 n valiente m; (Indian) guerrero m indio.
3 vt desafiar, arrostrar; to — the storm aguantar la tempestad; to — someone's anger no temer presentarse ante una persona encolerizada; to — it out defenderse sin confesarse culpable.
bravely ['breivli] adv valientemente, con valor; (fig) vistosamente, airosamente.
bravery ['breivəri] n valor m, valentía f.
bravo ['braː'vəu] interj ¡bravo!
bravura [brə'vuərə] n (a) arrojo m, brío m. (b) (Mus) bravura f.
brawl [brɔːl] 1 n pendencia f, reyerta f; alboroto m.
2 vi armar pendencia, alborotar.
brawn [brɔːn] n carne f en gelatina; (fig) fuerza f muscular.
brawny ['brɔːni] adj fornido, musculoso.
bray [brei] 1 n rebuzno m; (laugh) carcajada f. 2 vi rebuznar; (trumpet) sonar con estrépito.
braze [breiz] vt soldar.
brazen ['breizn] 1 adj (fig) descarado, cínico.
2 vt: to — it out defenderse con argumentos descarados.
brazenly ['breiznli] adv descaradamente, con cinismo.
brazier ['breiziə*] n brasero m.
Brazil [brə'zil] el Brasil.
Brazilian [brə'ziliən] 1 adj brasileño.
2 n brasileño m, a f.
Brazil nut [brə'zil'nʌt] n castaña f del Brasil.
breach [briːtʃ] 1 n (gap) abertura f, brecha f; (Mil) brecha f; (fig) violación f, infracción f; (between friends) rompimiento m de relaciones, (Pol) ruptura f; — of contract infracción f de contrato; — of faith (or trust) abuso m de confianza, infidencia f; — of the

law violación f de la ley; — of the peace perturbación f del orden público; — of privilege (Parl) abuso m del privilegio parlamentario; — of promise incumplimiento m de la palabra de casamiento; to heal the — hacer las paces.
2 vt romper; (Mil) abrir brecha en.
bread [bred] n pan m (also fig); daily — (Eccl and fig) pan m de cada día; white — pan m candeal; brown — pan m moreno; to be on — and water estar a pan y agua; to break — with sentarse a la mesa con; to cast one's — on the waters hacer bien sin mirar a quién; to earn one's daily — (or one's — and butter) ganarse el pan; to know which side one's — is buttered saber dónde aprieta el zapato; to live on the — line vivir muy justo; man cannot live by — alone no sólo de pan vive el hombre; to take the — out of someone's mouth quitar el pan de la boca de uno.
bread-and-butter ['bredən'bʌtə*] 1 n pan m con mantequilla; (fam) pan m de cada día.
2 adj corriente (y moliente), normal, regular; prosaico; de uso general; — letter carta f de agradecimiento que el invitado envía al anfitrión.
breadbin ['bredbin] n caja f del pan.
breadboard ['bredbɔːd] n tablero m para cortar el pan.
bread-crumb ['bredkrʌm] n migaja f; —s (Cook) pan m rallado.
breadfruit ['bredfruːt] n fruto m del pan; — tree árbol m del pan.
breadknife ['brednaif], pl —knives [naivz] cuchillo m para cortar el pan.
bread line ['bredlain] n cola f del pan; to be on the — recibir asistencia pública, (fig) vivir en la mayor miseria.
breadth [bretθ] n anchura f; (Naut) manga f; (fig) amplitud f, extensión f; to be 2 metres in — tener 2 metros de ancho.
breadwinner ['bred,winə*] n mantenedor m de la familia.
break [breik] 1 n (a) (breakage) ruptura f, rompimiento m; (between friends) ruptura f; (in voice) gallo m; (in weather) cambio m; (at billiards) partida f; at — of day al amanecer; to make a — with cortar con; romper relaciones con.
(b) (gap) abertura f; (crack) grieta f; (on paper etc) espacio m, blanco m; (of time) intervalo m; (in process) interrupción f; (in clouds) claro m; (holiday) vacación f, asueto m; (rest) descanso m; (at school) período m de recreo; — in continuity solución f de continuidad; without a — sin interrupción, sin descansar; to take a — descansar.
(c) (vehicle) break m.
(d) (chance) oportunidad f; lucky — chiripa f, racha f de suerte; to give someone a — abrir a uno la puerta.
(e) (break-out) evasión f, fuga f; to make a — for it tratar de evadirse.
2 (irr: pret broke, ptp broken) vt (a) romper; (Elec) interrumpir, cortar; ground roturar; impact, fall amortiguar; horse domar, amansar; bank quebrar, hacer saltar; news comunicar; record batir, superar, mejorar; code descifrar; ring, conspiracy deshacer; silence, spell romper; custom romper con; journey interrumpir; appointment no acudir a; promise, word faltar a; law violar, infringir, quebrantar; rival arruinar; someone's spirit abatir, vencer.
(b) to — down (shatter) derribar, echar abajo; resistance acabar con, vencer; alibi probar la falsedad de; figures etc analizar, descomponer, desglosar; clasificar; to — in forzar, romper; recruit desbastar; to — someone of a habit inducir a uno a que renuncie a una costumbre; to — off piece separar, partir; relations, engagement romper; to — open forzar, abrir por fuerza; to — up romper; desmenuzar; ship desguazar; camp levantar; estate parcelar; organization, meeting, federation disolver; industry desconcentrar.
3 vi (a) romperse, quebrarse, hacerse pedazos; (machine) estropearse; (boil) reventar; (voice) mudar; (singing voice) cascarse; (bank) quebrar; (heart, wave) romperse; (day) apuntar; (health) cascarse, empeorar; (news) saberse, revelarse; (ball) torcerse; (boxers) separarse.
(b) to — away desprenderse, separarse; (runner) despegarse, salir del pelotón; (at games) escapar; to — away from guards evadirse de; to — down (Med) perder la salud, sufrir un colapso; (Aut etc) averiarse; (machine) estropearse; (plan) fracasar; (person) romper a llorar; to — even salir sin ganar ni perder; to — in (burglar) forzar una entrada; (in

conversation) cortar, interrumpir; **to — into a house** forzar (*or* penetrar en) una casa; **to — into a run** echar a correr; **to — off** pararse repentinamente, dejar de hablar (*etc*), suspender el trabajo (*etc*); **to — out** (*fire, war*) estallar; (*riot, argument*) producirse; (*noise*) hacerse oír; (*Med*) declararse; (*exclaim*) exclamar, gritar; (*from prison*) evadirse; **to — out in spots** salir a uno granos en la piel; **to — out into abuse** empezar a soltar injurias; **to — through** (*water etc*) abrirse un camino; (*inventor etc*) hacer un descubrimiento sensacional; **to — through to miners** llegar a, abrir un camino hasta; **to — up** hacerse pedazos; (*ice*) deshacerse, romperse; desmenuzarse; (*meeting*) levantarse, (*in disorder*) disolverse; (*crowd*) dispersarse; (*federation*) desmembrarse, disgregarse; (*school*) terminar, cerrarse; **to — with** romper con.

breakable ['breikəbl] *adj* frágil, quebradizo.
breakage ['breikidʒ] *n* rotura *f*.
breakaway ['breikəwei] **1** *adj group etc* disidente, separatista. **2** *n* (*Sport*) escapada *f*.
breakdown ['breikdaun] *n* interrupción *f*; (*failure*) fracaso *m*, mal éxito *m*; (*Med*) colapso *m*, crisis *f* nerviosa; (*Aut etc*) avería *f*, pana *f*; (*of numbers etc*) análisis *m*, descomposición *f*.
breaker ['breikə*] *n* ola *f* grande, rompiente *m*.
breakfast ['brekfəst] **1** *n* desayuno *m*. **2** *vi* desayunar(se) (*off eggs, on eggs* huevos).
breaking-point ['breikiŋpɔint] *n* punto *m* de máxima tensión tolerable; **to reach —** llegar a la crisis, llegar al límite.
breakneck ['breiknek] *adj:* **at — speed** a mata caballo.
breakout ['breikaut] *n* evasión *f*, fuga *f*.
breakthrough ['breikθru:] *n* (*Mil*) ruptura *f*; (*fig*) avance *m*, adelanto *m*, invento *m* decisivo; **to achieve a —** hacer grandes progresos, hacer un descubrimiento importante.
break-up ['breikʌp] *n* disolución *f*, desintegración *f*, desmembración *f*.
breakwater ['breik,wɔːtə*] *n* rompeolas *m*.
bream [bri:m] *n* brema *f*.
breast [brest] **1** *n* (*Anat*) pecho *m*; (*woman's*) pecho *m*, seno *m*; (*of bird*) pechuga *f*; (*fig*) corazón *m*; **to beat one's —** darse golpes de pecho; **to make a clean — of** confesar con franqueza; **to make a clean — of it** confesarlo todo. **2** *vt* hacer cara a, arrostrar.
breastbone ['brestbəun] *n* esternón *m*.
breast-feed ['brest:fid] (*irr: see* **feed**) *vt* criar a los pechos.
breast-high ['brest'hai] *adv* a la altura del pecho.
breastplate ['brestpleit] *n* peto *m*.
breast-pocket ['brest,pɔkit] *n* bolsillo *m* de pecho.
breast-stroke ['breststrəuk] *n* braza *f* de pecho.
breastwork ['brestwɔːk] *n* parapeto *m*.
breath [breθ] *n* aliento *m*, respiración *f*; (*visible in air*) hálito *m*; **bad —** halitosis *f*; **the first — of spring** el primer viento suave que anuncia la primavera; **the least — of scandal** la más ligera sospecha de escándalo; **there's not a — of air stirring** no hay ni un soplo de aire; **all in the same —** todo al mismo tiempo; **in the very next — a** renglón seguido; **out of —** sofocado, jadeante, sin aliento; **to get out of —** quedar sin aliento; **short of —** corto de resuello; **under one's —** en voz baja; **to draw a deep —** respirar a fondo; **to draw one's last —** tomar el último aliento; **the best that ever drew —** el mejor que se conoció jamás; **to gasp for —** luchar por respirar; **to get one's — back** tomar aliento; **to go out for a — of air** salir a tomar el fresco; **to hold one's —** contener la respiración; **to save one's —** ahorrar las palabras; **to take a deep —** respirar a fondo; **it took my — away** me dejó pasmado; **to waste one's —** perder el tiempo (*on* hablando con).
breathe [bri:ð] **1** *vt* respirar; *sigh* dar; *prayer* decir en voz baja; **to — air into a balloon** inflar un globo soplando; **it —s the spirit of** late por todas partes el espíritu de; **to — out** exhalar.
2 *vi* respirar; (*noisily*) resollar; **to — again** respirar; **to — in** aspirar; **to — out** espirar.
breather ['bri:ðə*] *n* respiro *m*.
breathing ['bri:ðiŋ] *n* respiración *f*; **heavy —** resuello *m*.
breathing space ['bri:ðiŋspeis] *n* respiro *m*.
breathing-tube ['bri:ðiŋtju:b] *n* tubo *m* de respiración.
breathless ['breθlis] *adj* falto de aliento, jadeante.
breathlessly ['breθlisli] *adv:* **to say —** decir jadeante.
breath-taking ['breθ,teikiŋ] *adj sight* imponente, pasmoso; *speed* vertiginoso.
bred [bred] *pret and ptp of* **breed**.

breech [bri:tʃ] *n* recámara *f*.
breeches ['bri:tʃiz] *npl* calzones *mpl*; **riding —** pantalones *mpl* de montar; **to wear the —** llevar los pantalones.
breeches buoy ['bri:tʃiz'bɔi] *n* boya *f* pantalón.
breechloader ['bri:tʃ,ləudə*] *n* arma *f* de retrocarga.
breed [bri:d] **1** *n* raza *f*, casta *f*.
2 (*irr: pret and ptp* **bred**) *vt* criar, engendrar; (*fig*) engendrar, producir; **town bred** criado en la ciudad.
3 *vi* reproducirse, procrear.
breeder ['bri:də*] *n* (*person*) criador *m*, ora *f*; (*animal*) criadero *m*, paridera *f*.
breeder reactor ['bri:dəri,æktə*] *n* reactor *m* reproductor.
breeding ['bri:diŋ] *n* (*of stock*) cría *f*; (*of person*) crianza *f*, educación *f*; **bad —, ill —** mala crianza *f*, falta *f* de educación; **good —** educación *f*, cultura *f*; **he has (good) —** es una persona educada; **it shows bad —** indica una falta de educación.
breeding-season ['bri:diŋ,si:zn] *n* época *f* de reproducción.
breeze [bri:z] **1** *n* brisa *f*. **2** *vi:* **to — in** entrar como Pedro por su casa.
breezily ['bri:zili] *adv* jovialmente, despreocupadamente.
breezy ['bri:zi] *adj day, place* de mucho viento; *person's manner* animado, jovial, despreocupado; **it is —** hace viento.
brethren ['breðrin] *npl* (*irr pl of* **brother**) hermanos *mpl*.
Breton ['bretən] **1** *adj* bretón. **2** *n* bretón *m*, ona *f*. **3** *n* (*language*) bretón *m*.
breviary ['bri:viəri] *n* breviario *m*.
brevity ['breviti] *n* brevedad *f*.
brew [bru:] **1** *n* (*hum*) poción *f*, brebaje *m*.
2 *vt beer* hacer, elaborar; *tea* hacer; (*fig*) urdir, tramar.
3 *vi* (*fig*) prepararse; (*storm*) amenazar; **there's something —ing** algo se está tramando.
brewer ['bru:ə*] *n* cervecero *m*.
brewery ['bruəri] *n* fábrica *f* de cerveza.
briar ['braiə*] *n* (*rose*) escaramujo *m*, rosa *f* silvestre; (*hawthorn*) espino *m*; (*bramble*) zarza *f*.
bribe [braib] **1** *n* soborno *m*, cohecho *m*; **to take a —** dejarse sobornar (*from* por). **2** *vt* sobornar, cohechar.
bribery ['braibəri] *n* soborno *m*, cohecho *m*.
bric-à-brac ['brikəbræk] *n* curiosidades *fpl*.
brick [brik] **1** *n* ladrillo *m*; (*of ice cream*) bloque *m*; **a — wall** una pared de ladrillos; **Bath —** piedra *f* para limpiar cuchillos; **gold — (US sl)** estafa *f*; **he's a —** es un buen chico; **be a — and lend it to me** préstamelo como buen amigo; **he came down on us like a ton of —s** nos echó una bronca fenomenal; **to drop a —** tirarse una plancha.
2 *vt* (*also* **to — up**) cerrar con ladrillos.
brickbat ['brikbæt] *n* trozo *m* de ladrillo; (*fig*) palabra *f* hiriente, crítica *f*.
bricklayer ['brikleiə*] *n* albañil *m*.
brick red ['brikred] **1** *adj* rojo ladrillo. **2** *n* rojo *m* ladrillo.
brickwork ['brikwɔːk] *n* enladrillado *m*, ladrillos *mpl*.
brickworks ['brikwɔːks] *n* ladrillar *m*.
bridal ['braidl] *adj* nupcial.
bride [braid] *n* novia *f*; **the — and groom** los novios.
bridegroom ['braidgrum] *n* novio *m*.
bridesmaid ['braidzmeid] *n* dama *f* de honor.
bridge[1] [bridʒ] **1** *n* puente *m* (*also Mus*); (*Naut*) puente *m* de mando; (*of nose*) caballete *m*; **suspension —** puente *m* colgante; **much water has flowed under the — since then** mucho ha llovido desde entonces.
2 *vt* tender un puente sobre; *gap* llenar, salvar.
bridge[2] [bridʒ] *n* (*Cards*) bridge *m*; **auction —** bridge-remate *m*; **contract —** bridge-contrato *m*.
bridgehead ['bridʒhed] *n* cabeza *f* de puente.
Bridget ['bridʒit] *f* Brígida.
bridle ['braidl] **1** *n* brida *f*, freno *m*. **2** *vi:* **to — at** picarse por, ofenderse por.
bridle path ['braidlpɑːθ] *n* camino *m* de herradura.
brief [bri:f] **1** *adj* breve, corto; (*fleeting*) fugaz, pasajero; *style* lacónico; **please be as — as possible** explíquese con la mayor brevedad.
2 *n* (a) (*Eccl*) breve *m*.
(b) (*Law*) escrito *m*; **in —, to be —** en resumen; **to go beyond one's —** exceder las instrucciones; **to hold a — for** representar a; **to hold a watching — for someone** representar a un cliente a quien no interesa directamente un juicio; **to hold no — for** tener en poco, no apoyar; **to stick to one's —** atenerse a las órdenes dadas.
(c) **—s** (*man's*) calzoncillos *mpl*, (*woman's*) bragas *fpl*.
3 *vt* (*Mil etc*) dar órdenes a.

briefcase ['bri:fkeis] n cartera f.
briefing ['bri:fiŋ] n reunión f en que se dan las órdenes (a la tripulación de un avión militar); órdenes fpl; (to press) informe m.
briefly ['bri:fli] adv brevemente; en resumen, en pocas palabras.
briefness ['bri:fnis] n brevedad f.
brier ['braiə*] n see **briar**.
brigade [bri'geid] n brigada f; one of the old — un veterano.
brigadier [,brigə'diə*] n general m de brigada.
brigand ['brigənd] n bandido m, bandolero m.
brigandage ['brigəndidʒ] n bandidaje m, bandolerismo m.
bright [brait] adj (a) claro, brillante, luminoso; day luminoso, de sol; eyes claro; sun brillante; surface lustroso; colour subido; smile radiante.
  (b) (clever) listo, inteligente; idea luminoso; conversation, remark ingenioso; that was — of you en eso anduviste muy listo; you're a — one! ¡qué despiste tienes!; the child's as — as a button el niño es más listo que el hambre.
  (c) (cheerful) alegre, animado, optimista.
  (d) prospect etc prometedor, esperanzador.
brighten ['braitn] 1 vt (also to — up) abrillantar, lustrar; house hacer más alegre, poner colores en; (cheer) alegrar.
  2 vi (also to — up) (person) animarse, alegrarse; (weather) despejarse.
brightly ['braitli] adv brillantemente; ingeniosamente; answer con prontitud.
brightness ['braitnis] n claridad f; brillantez f, luminosidad f; lustre m; lo subido; inteligencia f; viveza f de ingenio.
brill [bril] n rodaballo m menor.
brilliance ['briljəns], **brilliancy** ['briljənsi] n brillo m, brillantez f.
brilliant ['briljənt] 1 adj brillante; idea genial, luminoso; student etc brillante, sobresaliente; success arrollador. 2 n brillante m.
brilliantine [,briljən'ti:n] n brillantina f.
brilliantly ['briljəntli] adv brillantemente (also fig).
brim [brim] 1 n borde m; (of hat) ala f. 2 vi: to — over desbordarse, rebosar; to — with rebosar de.
brimful ['brim'ful] adj lleno hasta el borde; — of, — with rebosante de.
brimstone ['brimstəun] n azufre m.
brindled ['brindld] adj manchado, mosqueado.
brine [brain] n salmuera f.
bring [briŋ] (irr: pret and ptp **brought**) 1 vt traer; conducir; charge hacer, formular; suit entablar; you — nothing but trouble Vd no hace más que causarme molestias; to — someone to do something inducir a uno a hacer algo; to — about ocasionar, producir; change efectuar; to — along traer consigo; to — away llevarse; to — back volver a traer, thing borrowed devolver; to — down (carry down) bajar; (Mil, Hunting) abatir, derribar; price rebajar; to — forth parir, dar a luz; (fig) producir; to — forward proposal presentar; date adelantar; (Comm) pasar a otra cuenta; to — someone home traer a uno a casa; to — something home to someone hacer que uno se dé cuenta cabal de algo; to — in bill presentar; harvest recoger, recolectar; fashion introducir; meal servir; income producir; verdict dar; person hacer entrar; — him in! ¡que entre!; this should — them in esto ha de hacerles venir en masa; to — off lograr, conseguir; success obtener; to — on causar, acarrear; acelerar el desarrollo de; to — something on oneself atraer algo sobre sí; to — out sacar; argument sacar a relucir; book sacar a luz; aspect subrayar, recalcar; person hacer más afable, ayudar a adquirir confianza; to — round (win over) ganarse la voluntad de; convencer, convertir; (Med) hacer volver en sí; to — together reunir; enemies reconciliar; to — under someter; to — up (carry up) subir; subject sacar a colación; person criar, educar; (fam) arrojar, vomitar.
  2 vr: to — oneself to + infin resignarse a + infin, convencerse de la conveniencia de + infin, cobrar suficiente ánimo para + infin.
brink [briŋk] n borde m; on the — of (fig) n en la antesala de, + ger a punto de.
brinkmanship ['briŋkmənʃip] n arte m de conducirse en el borde de la crisis; política f del borde del abismo.
briny ['braini] 1 adj salado, salobre. 2 n (fam): the — el mar.
briquette [bri'ket] n briqueta f.
brisk [brisk] adj enérgico, vigoroso; pace rápido; trade etc activo.
brisket ['briskit] n carne f de pecho (para asar).

briskly ['briskli] adv enérgicamente; rápidamente; activamente.
briskness ['brisknis] n energía f; rapidez f; actividad f.
brisling ['brizliŋ] n sardina f noruega.
bristle ['brisl] 1 n cerda f. 2 vi (hair etc) erizarse; (animal) erizar las cerdas; to — with (fig) estar erizado de.
bristly ['brisli] adj cerdoso; to have a — chin tener la barba crecida.
Britain ['britən] Gran Bretaña f, (loosely) Inglaterra f.
Britannia [bri'tæniə] figura que representa simbólicamente a Gran Bretaña.
briticism ['britisizəm] n (US) modismo (or vocablo etc) del inglés m de Inglaterra.
British ['britiʃ] adj inglés, (more formally) británico; the — los ingleses.
Britisher ['britiʃə*] n (US) natural mf de Gran Bretaña.
British Guiana ['britiʃgi'a:nə] Guayana f Inglesa.
British Honduras ['britiʃhɔn'djuərəs] Honduras f Británica.
British Isles ['britiʃ'ailz] pl Islas fpl Británicas.
Briton ['britən] n inglés m, esa f, (more formally) britano m, a f.
Brittany ['britəni] Bretaña f.
brittle ['britl] adj frágil, quebradizo.
broach [brəutʃ] vt cask espitar; bottle etc abrir; subject comenzar a hablar de, mencionar por primera vez, abordar.
broad [brɔ:d] 1 adj (a) ancho; extenso, amplio; 3 metres — ancho de 3 metros.
  (b) (fig) ancho; view comprensivo; mind tolerante, liberal; hint claro, inconfundible; accent marcado, cerrado, fuerte; story verde; sense of word ancho, lato; grin, smile jovial; it's as — as it is long lo mismo da.
  2 n (US sl) fulana f.
broad-brimmed ['brɔ:d'brimd] adj hat de ala ancha.
broadcast ['brɔ:dka:st] 1 adj (Agr) sembrado a voleo; (Radio) radiodifundido, de (la) radio.
  2 adv por todas partes.
  3 n emisión f, programa m; repeat — retransmisión f.
  4 vt (Agr) sembrar a voleo; (fig) diseminar, divulgar; (Radio) emitir, radiar.
  5 vi hablar (or tocar etc) por la radio.
broadcaster ['brɔ:dka:stə*] n conferenciante mf (or cronista mf) de radio; (announcer) locutor m, ora f.
broadcasting ['brɔ:dka:stiŋ] 1 n radiodifusión f. 2 attr de radiodifusión.
broadcasting station ['brɔ:dka:stiŋ,steiʃən] n emisora f.
broadcloth ['brɔ:dklɔθ] n (Hist) velarte m.
broaden ['brɔ:dn] 1 vt ensanchar. 2 vi ensancharse.
broadly ['brɔ:dli] adv extensamente; claramente; con fuerte acento; de modo jovial; it is — true that es en general verdad que; — speaking hablando en términos generales.
broad-minded ['brɔ:d'maindid] adj tolerante, liberal; (pej) de manga ancha.
broad-mindedness ['brɔ:d'maindidnis] n tolerancia f.
broadness ['brɔ:dnis] n anchura f, extensión f; claridad f; lo fuerte etc.
broadsheet ['brɔ:dʃi:t] n hoja f suelta impresa.
broad-shouldered ['brɔ:d'ʃəuldəd] adj ancho de espaldas.
broadside ['brɔ:dsaid] n (side) costado m; (shots) andanada f; — on de costado; to fire a — hacer fuego con todos los cañones.
broadways ['brɔ:dweiz] adv a lo ancho, por lo ancho; con la parte ancha por delante; — on to the waves con la parte ancha de cara a las olas.
brocade [brəu'keid] n brocado m.
broccoli ['brɔkəli] n brécol m.
brochure ['brəuʃjuə*] n folleto m.
brock [brɔk] n tejón m.
brogue[1] [brəug] n (shoe) abarca f.
brogue[2] [brəug] n acento m irlandés.
broil [brɔil] vt asar a la parrilla.
broiler ['brɔilə*] n pollo m para asar.
broiling ['brɔiliŋ] adj: it's — hot hace un calor terrible.
broke [brəuk] pret of **break**; to be — (fam) no tener un céntimo.
broken ['brəukən] 1 ptp of **break**.
  2 adj ground accidentado, quebrado; tone de desesperación; — in health deshecho, muy decaído; in — Spanish en castellano imperfecto.
broken-down ['brəukən'daun] adj agotado; machine descompuesto, desvencijado.

broken-hearted ['brəukən'hɑːtid] *adj* traspasado de dolor; **to be —** tener el corazón partido.

brokenly ['brəukənli] *adv say etc* en tono angustiado.

broker ['brəukə*] *n* corredor *m*, bolsista *m*; agente *m* de negocios.

brokerage ['brəukəridʒ] *n*, **broking** ['brəukiŋ] *n* corretaje *m*.

bromide ['brəumaid] *n* bromuro *m*; (*fig*) trivialidad *f*.

bronchial ['brɔŋkiəl] *adj* bronquial.

bronchitis [brɔŋ'kaitis] *n* bronquitis *f*.

bronco ['brɔŋkəu] *n* (*US*) potro *m* cerril.

bronze [brɔnz] **1** *n* bronce *m*. **2** *adj* de bronce. **3** *vt* broncear. **4** *vi* broncearse.

bronzed [brɔnzd] *adj* bronceado.

brooch [brəutʃ] *n* alfiler *m* de pecho, prendedor *m*.

brood [bruːd] **1** *n* camada *f*, cría *f*; (*of chicks*) nidada *f*; (*fig*) familia *f*, progenie *f*, (*pej*) prole *f*. **2** *adj*: **— mare** yegua *f* de cría. **3** *vi* empollar; (*fig*) meditar tristemente; **to — on, to — over** meditar tristemente; **you musn't — over** it no debes dejarte obsesionar con eso; **disaster —ed over the town** se cernía el desastre sobre la ciudad.

broody ['bruːdi] *adj* clueca; (*fig*) triste, melancólico.

brook[1] [bruk] *n* arroyo *m*.

brook[2] [bruk] *vt* aguantar, permitir.

brooklet ['bruklit] *n* arroyuelo *m*.

broom [brum] *n* escoba *f*; (*Bot*) hiniesta *f*, retama *f*, piorno *m*; **new —** (*person*) persona *f* que entra en una compañía (*etc*) y propugna grandes reformas.

broomstick ['brumstik] *n* palo *m* de escoba.

broth [brɔθ] *n* caldo *m*.

brothel ['brɔθl] *n* prostíbulo *m*, casa *f* de putas.

brother ['brʌðə*] *n* hermano *m* (*also Eccl*); **X and his — teachers** X y sus colegas profesionales; **they're —s under the skin** les une una fuerte simpatía.

brotherhood ['brʌðəhud] *n* fraternidad *f*; (*group*) hermandad *f*; (*Hist*) cofradía *f*.

brother-in-law ['brʌðərinlɔː] *n* cuñado *m*.

brotherly ['brʌðəli] *adj* fraternal.

brought [brɔːt] *pret and ptp of* **bring**.

brow [brau] *n* ceja *f*; (*forehead*) frente *f*; (*of hill*) cumbre *f*, (*of cliff*) borde *m*; **to knit one's —** fruncir las cejas.

browbeat ['braubiːt] *vt* intimidar (con amenazas) (*into doing something* para que haga algo).

brown [braun] **1** *adj* pardo, moreno; oscuro; *hair* castaño; (*tanned*) bronceado; *bread* moreno; *sugar* negro; *shoes* de color; *paper* de embalar, de estraza; **as — as a berry** con un magnífico bronceado. **2** *n* color *m* pardo (*etc*). **3** *vt* poner pardo (*or* moreno *etc*); *skin* broncear; (*Cook*) dorar; **to — someone off** (*sl*) fastidiar a uno; **to be —ed off** (*sl*) estar harto (*with* de). **4** *vi* ponerse moreno (*etc*); (*skin*) broncearse; (*Cook*) dorarse.

brownie ['brauni] *n* duende *m*; (*person*) miembro *m* joven de las Girl Guides.

brownish ['brauniʃ] *adj* pardusco, que tira a moreno.

browse [brauz] **1** *vt* grass pacer, rozar; *trees* ramonear. **2** *vi* pacer; (*fig*) leer ociosamente; **to spend an hour browsing in a bookshop** pasar una hora hojeando los libros en una librería; **to — on** pacer.

Bruges [bruːʒ] Brujas.

Bruin ['bruːin] *n* oso *m*.

bruise [bruːz] **1** *n* contusión *f*, cardenal *m*, señal *f*, morado *m*. **2** *vt* contundir, magullar; *fruit* estropear.

bruiser ['bruːzə*] *n* (*fam*) boxeador *m*.

brunch [brʌntʃ] *n* (*fam*) comida *f* ligera de media mañana.

brunette [bruː'net] **1** *adj* moreno. **2** *n* morena *f*.

brunt [brʌnt] *n*: **the — of the attack** lo más fuerte del ataque; **the — of the work** lo peor del trabajo; **to bear the — of** aguantar lo más recio de.

brush [brʌʃ] **1** *n* (**a**) (*act of brushing*) cepilladura *f*, cepillado *m*. (**b**) (*implement*) cepillo *m*; (*large*) escoba *f*; (*shaving-*) brocha *f*; (*scrubbing-*) bruza *f*; (*artist's*) pincel *m*; (*housepainter's*) brocha *f*; (*Elec*) escobilla *f*. (**c**) (*fox's*) rabo *m*, hopo *m*. (**d**) (*Bot*) broza *f*; maleza *f*, monte *m* bajo. (**e**) (*Mil*) escaramuza *f*; (*fig*) encuentro *m*; **to have a — with someone** tener un disgusto con uno. **2** *vt* (a)cepillar; *shoes etc* limpiar; (*in passing*) rozar al pasar; **to — aside** rechazar, no hacer caso de; **to — away** quitar (*con un cepillo, con la mano etc*); **to — down** (a)cepillar, limpiar; *horse* almohazar; **to — up** acicalar, (*fig*) repasar, refrescar. **3** *vi*: **to — against** rozar al pasar; **to — by, to — past** pasar muy cerca (de).

brush-off ['brʌʃɔf] *n*: **to give someone the —** desairar a uno, despedir bruscamente a uno.

brush-stroke ['brʌʃstrəuk] *n* pincelada *f*.

brush up ['brʌʃ'ʌp] *n*: **to have a —** lavarse y peinarse, arreglarse.

brushwood ['brʌʃwud] *n* maleza *f*, monte *m* bajo; (*faggots*) broza *f*, leña *f* menuda.

brusque [bruːsk] *adj* brusco, abrupto, áspero.

brusquely ['bruːskli] *adv* bruscamente, abruptamente, ásperamente.

Brussels ['brʌslz] Bruselas; **— sprouts** col *f* de Bruselas.

brutal ['bruːtl] *adj* brutal.

brutality [bruː'tæliti] *n* brutalidad *f*.

brutally ['bruːtəli] *adv* de manera brutal.

brute [bruːt] **1** *adj* brutal; (*unthinking*) bruto; **by — force** a fuerza bruta. **2** *n* bruto *m*; (*person*) bestia *f*, hombre *m* bestial; **you —!** ¡bestia!; **it's a — of a problem** es un problema de los más difíciles.

brutish ['bruːtiʃ] *adj* brutal.

Brutus ['bruːtəs] *m* Bruto.

bubble ['bʌbl] **1** *n* burbuja *f*, ampolla *f*; (*under paint etc*) ampolla *f*; **to blow —s** hacer pompas. **2** *vi* burbujear, borbotar; **to — over** desbordarse, irse; **to — over with** rebosar de.

bubble-car ['bʌblkɑː*] *n* coche-cabina *m*, huevo *m*.

bubble gum ['bʌblgʌm] *n* chicle *m* de globo, chicle *m* de burbuja.

bubbly ['bʌbli] **1** *adj* burbujeante, gaseoso. **2** *n* (*fam*) champaña *m*.

bubonic plague [bjuː'bɔnik'pleig] *n* peste *f* bubónica.

buccaneer [,bʌkə'niə*] *n* bucanero *m*. **2** *vi* piratear.

buck [bʌk] **1** *adj* (*male*) macho; (*US*) *private* raso. **2** *n* (*male*) macho *m*; (*deer*) gamo *m*; (*goat*) macho *m* cabrío; (*rabbit*) conejo *m* macho; (*US sl*) dólar *m*; **to pass the —** (*sl*) echar a uno el muerto. **3** *vi* (*horse*) corcovear, ponerse de manos; **to — up** animarse, cobrar ánimo; **— up!** ¡date prisa!, ¡espabílate!

bucket ['bʌkit] *n* cubo *m*, balde *m*; (*child's*) cubito *m*; (*of waterwheel etc*) cangilón *m*; **to kick the —** (*sl*) estirar la pata.

bucketful ['bʌkitful] *n* cubo *m* (lleno), balde *m* (lleno); **by the —** a cubos, (*fig*) a montones, en grandes cantidades.

buckle ['bʌkl] **1** *n* hebilla *f*. **2** *vt* (a) abrochar con hebilla; **to — on one's sword** ceñirse la espada. (b) (*deform*) torcer, combar, encorvar. **3** *vi* torcerse, combarse, doblarse; **to — down to** dedicarse con empeño a, emprender en serio.

buckram ['bʌkrəm] *n* bucarán *m*.

buckshee [bʌk'ʃiː] (*sl*) **1** *adj* gratuito. **2** *adv* gratis.

buckshot ['bʌkʃɔt] *n* perdigón *m* zorrero.

buckskin ['bʌkskin] *n* cuero *m* de ante.

buckthorn ['bʌkθɔːn] *n* espino *m* cerval.

buck-tooth ['bʌk'tuːθ] *n* diente *m* saliente.

buck-toothed ['bʌk'tuːθt] *adj* de dientes salientes, dentón.

buckwheat ['bʌkwiːt] *n* alforfón *m*.

bucolic [bjuː'kɔlik] **1** *adj* bucólico. **2** *n*: **the B—s** las Bucólicas.

bud [bʌd] **1** *n* brote *m*, yema *f*, (*containing flower*) capullo *m*; **in —** en brote; **to nip in the —** cortar de raíz, salir al paso a. **2** *vt* injertar de escudete. **3** *vi* brotar, echar brotes.

Buddha ['budə] *m* Buda.

Buddhism ['budizəm] *n* budismo *m*.

Buddhist ['budist] **1** *adj* budista. **2** *n* budista *mf*.

budding ['bʌdiŋ] *adj* (*fig*) en ciernes, en embrión.

buddy ['bʌdi] *n* (*esp US*) compañero *m*, compinche *m*; (*in direct address*) chico, hijo.

budge [bʌdʒ] **1** *vt* mover, hacer que se mueva; **I couldn't — him an inch** no pude hacerle cambiar de opinión en lo más mínimo. **2** *vi* moverse; bullir; **he didn't dare to —** no osaba bullir; **he won't — an inch** no nos ofrece la más pequeña concesión.

budgerigar ['bʌdʒərigɑː*] *n* periquito *m*.

budget ['bʌdʒit] **1** *n* presupuesto *m*. **2** *attr* presupuestario. **3** *vi*: **to — for** presupuestar; (*fig*) tener en cuenta, contar con.

budgetary ['bʌdʒitri] *adj* presupuestario.

buff [bʌf] **1** *adj* color de ante. **2** *n* piel *f* de ante; **in the —** en cueros.

buffalo ['bʌfələu] *n*, *pl* **buffaloes** búfalo *m*.

buffer[1] ['bʌfə*] *n* amortiguador *m* (de choques); (*Rail: on carriage*) tope *m*, (*fixed*) parachoques *m*; **— state** estado *m* tapón.

buffer[2] ['bʌfə*] *n*: **old —** mastuerzo *m*.

buffet ['bʌfit] **1** *n* bofetada *f*; (*of sea, wind etc*) golpe *m*. **2** *vt* abofetear; (*of sea, wind etc*) golpear, llevar de aquí para allá, combatir.

buffet ['bufei] n aparador m; (Rail) cantina f, cafetería f; — **supper** cena f fría.

buffet car [bufeika:*] n coche-comedor m.

buffeting ['bʌfitiŋ] n (of sea etc) el golpear; **to get a —
from** sufrir los golpes de.

buffoon [bə'fu:n] n bufón m, chocarrero m.

buffoonery [bə'fu:nəri] n bufonadas fpl.

bug [bʌg] **1** n chinche f (also freq m); (loosely) bicho m, sabandija f; (Med fam) microbio m, bacilo m; (US sl) estorbo m, traba f; **big — (fam)** señorón m, pez m gordo; **to get the travel — (fam)** entusiasmarse por los viajes, dedicarse furiosamente a viajar.
    2 vt (Tel sl) intervenir.

bugaboo ['bʌgəbu:] n (US) espantajo m.

bugbear ['bʌgbeə*] n pesadilla f.

buggy ['bʌgi] n calesa f; (US) cochecillo m (de niño).

bughouse ['bʌghaus] n, pl **—houses** [ˌhauziz] (US: sl) casa f de locos, manicomio m.

bug-hunter ['bʌghʌntə*] n (fam) entomólogo m.

bugle ['bju:gl] n corneta f, clarín m.

bugler ['bju:glə*] n corneta m.

build [bild] **1** n talle m, tipo m; **of powerful —**
fornido.
    2 (irr: pret and ptp **built**) vt **(a)** construir, edificar, hacer (in, of de); ship construir; fire preparar; nest hacer; **that's the way I'm built** yo soy así; **I'm not built that way** yo no estoy hecho para cosas así; **British-built** de construcción inglesa.
    (b) to — in empotrar, (Mech) incorporar; **to — a garage on to a house** añadir un garaje a una casa; **the garage is built on to the house** la casa tiene un garaje anexo; **to — up** (Mech etc) montar, armar; (Med) fortalecer; company etc fomentar, desarrollar; sales, numbers acrecentar; reputation crear para sí; impression crear; stocks acumular, formar.
    3 vi: **to — on** edificar sobre; **to — on a site** construir casas (etc) sobre un solar.

builder ['bildə*] n constructor m (also fig) (contracting firm) contratista m; (Archit) arquitecto m; (man on site) maestro m de obras, aparejador m.

building ['bildiŋ] n edificio m; construcción f; (at exhibition) pabellón m; **the — trade** la industria de la construcción.

building contractor ['bildiŋkən'træktə*] n contratista m.

building site ['bildiŋsait] n solar m (para edificaciones).

building society ['bildiŋsə'saiəti] n cooperativa f de construcciones, sociedad f inmobiliaria.

build-up ['bildʌp] n (make-up) composición f; (of forces) concentración f; (fig) propaganda f previa.

built [bilt] pret and ptp of **build**.

built-in ['bilt'in] adj (Archit) empotrado; (Mech, Radio etc) interior, incorporado.

built-up ['bilt'ʌp] adj area urbanizada.

bulb [bʌlb] n (Bot) bulbo m; (Elec) bombilla f; (of thermometer) ampolleta f.

bulbous ['bʌlbəs] adj bulboso.

Bulgaria [bʌl'geəriə] Bulgaria f.

Bulgarian [bʌl'geəriən] **1** adj búlgaro. **2** n búlgaro m, a f. **3** n (language) búlgaro m.

bulge [bʌldʒ] **1** n bombeo m, pandeo m; protuberancia f; **the — in the birth rate** el aumento de la natalidad.
    2 vi bombearse, pandearse; sobresalir; (pocket etc) hacer bulto; **his pockets —d with apples** sus bolsillos estaban totalmente llenos de manzanas; **their eyes —d at the sight** se le saltaron los ojos al verlo.

bulging ['bʌldʒiŋ] adj: **— eyes** ojos mpl saltones.

bulk [bʌlk] **1** n **(a)** bulto m, volumen m; masa f, mole f; grueso m; **the — of those present** la mayor parte de los que asistían; **the — of the army** el grueso del ejército; **the enormous — of the ship** la enorme mole del buque; **he set his full — down in a chair** dejó caer todo el peso de su cuerpo en un sillón.
    (b) (Comm) in — a granel; to buy in — comprar en grandes cantidades.
    2 vi: **to — large** tener un puesto importante.

bulk-buying ['bʌlk'baiiŋ] n compra f en grandes cantidades.

bulkhead ['bʌlkhed] n mamparo m.

bulkiness ['bʌlkinis] n volumen m, lo abultado.

bulky ['bʌlki] adj voluminoso, abultado, grueso; goods de gran bulto.

bull[1] [bul] **1** n (Zool) toro m; **fighting —** toro m de lidia; **to be like a — in a china shop** comportarse como un elefante en una tienda de porcelana); **to take the — by the horns** coger el toro por los cuernos.
    2 adj macho.

bull[2] [bul] **1** n (Comm) alcista m. **2** adj (Comm) alcista.

bull[3] [bul] n (Eccl) bula f.

bull[4] [bul] n (sl) tonterías fpl.

bull[5] [bul] n (Mil sl) trabajos mpl rutinarios.

bulldog ['buldɔg] n dogo m; (Univ sl) bedel m; **the — breed** los ingleses (bajo su aspecto heroico y porfiado).

bulldoze ['buldəuz] vt nivelar con motoniveladora; (fig) opposition arrollar.

bulldozer ['buldəuzə*] n motoniveladora f, aplanadora f.

bullet ['bulit] n bala f.

bulletin ['bulitin] n anuncio m, parte m; (journal) boletín m.

bulletin board ['bulitinbɔ:d] n (US) tablón m de anuncios.

bulletproof ['bulitpru:f] adj a prueba de balas.

bullet-wound ['bulitwu:nd] n balazo m.

bullfight ['bulfait] n corrida f de toros.

bullfighter ['bulfaitə*] n torero m.

bullfighting ['bulfaitiŋ] n toreo m; arte m de torear, tauromaquia f; **do you like —?** ¿le gustan los toros?

bullfinch ['bulfintʃ] n camachuelo m.

bullfrog ['bulfrɔg] n rana f toro.

bullion ['buljən] n oro m en barras, plata f en barras.

bull-necked ['bul'nekt] adj de cuello de toro.

bullock ['bulək] n novillo m, toro m joven, torete m.

bullring ['buliŋ] n plaza f de toros.

bull's-eye ['bulzai] n (of target) centro m del blanco; (lantern) linterna f sorda; (Naut) ojo m de buey; (sweet) tipo m de dulce; **to score a —** dar en el blanco, (fig) acertar.

bully[1] ['buli] **1** n matón m, valentón m. **2** vt intimidar, tiranizar; **to — someone into + ger** forzar a uno con amenazas a + infin.

bully[2] ['buli] **1** adj (sl) de primera. **2** interj: **— for you!** ¡bravo!

bully beef ['buli'bi:f] n carne f de vaca conservada en lata.

bulrush ['bulrʌʃ] n anea f, espadaña f.

bulwark ['bulwək] n (Mil and fig) baluarte m; (Naut) macarrón m.

bum[1] [bʌm] n (Anat: fam) culo m.

bum[2] [bʌm] (US) **1** n (idler) holgazán m; (tramp) vagabundo m; (scrounger) sablista m; (as term of general disapproval) vago m; **you poor —!** ¡tío tonto!; **to go on the —** vivir de gorra, vagabundear.
    2 vi holgazanear, vagabundear.

bumblebee ['bʌmblbi:] n abejorro m.

bumboat ['bʌmbəut] n bote m vivandero.

bump [bʌmp] **1** n **(a)** (blow) tope m, topetón m, choque m; (jolt of vehicle) sacudida f; (Aer) rebote m; (in falling) batacazo m.
    (b) (swelling) bollo m, abolladura f, protuberancia f; (on skin) chichón m, hinchazón f; (on road) bache m; **to have a — for** tener el don de, tener un sentido especial de.
    2 vt chocar contra, topetar; **to — one's head** darse un golpe en la cabeza; **to — one's head on a door** dar con su cabeza contra una puerta; **to — off** (sl) despenar, cargarse a.
    3 vi (vehicle) dar sacudidas; **to — against** chocar contra, topetar, dar contra; **to — along** avanzar dando sacudidas; **to — into** chocar contra, tropezar con, person topar; **fancy —ing into you!** ¡qué casualidad encontrarle a Vd!

bumper ['bʌmpə*] **1** n (Aut) parachoques m; (glass) copa f llena. **2** adj: **— crop** cosecha f abundante, cosechón m.

bumpkin ['bʌmpkin] n (gen **country —**) patán m.

bumptious ['bʌmpʃəs] adj engreído, presuntuoso.

bumpy ['bʌmpi] adj surface desigual; road lleno de baches; air agitado; journey de muchas sacudidas.

bun [bʌn] n bollo m; (hair) moño m, moño m.

bunch [bʌntʃ] **1** n manojo m, puñado m; (of flowers) ramo m, ramillete m; (of grapes) racimo m, (of bananas) piña f; (of keys) manojo m; (set of people) grupo m, (pej) pandilla f.
    2 vt agrupar, juntar; **to be —ed together** estar muy juntos unos a otros.

bundle ['bʌndl] **1** n lío m, bulto m, fardo m; (of sticks) haz f; (of papers) legajo m.
    2 vt: **to — up** liar, atar, envolver; **to — someone out** hacer que uno salga precipitadamente; **they —d him out into the street** le pusieron sin ceremonia en la calle; **— it all into the case** póngalo todo en la maleta no importa cómo.

bung [bʌŋ] **1** n bitoque m.
    2 vt tapar con bitoque; (in general) cerrar, tapar; (sl: throw) tirar, lanzar; (sl: put) poner, meter; **to be —ed up** estar obturado, estar obstruido, (eye) estar hinchado.

bungalow ['bʌŋgələu] n casa f de un solo piso, chalet m.

bunghole ['bʌŋhəul] n piquera f, boca f (de tonel).

bungle ['bʌŋgl] vt *work* chapucear, hacer con los pies; **to — it** hacerlo malísimamente; desperdiciar la ocasión.

bungler ['bʌŋglə*] n chapucero m.

bungling ['bʌŋgliŋ] adj torpe, desmañado.

bunion ['bʌnjən] n juanete m.

bunk¹ [bʌŋk] n (*bed*) tarima f; (*Naut*) litera f, camastro m; (*Aer, child's*) litera f; (*fam*) cama f.

bunk² [bʌŋk] (*sl*) **1** n: **to do a — = 2** vi huir, poner pies en polvorosa.

bunk³ [bʌŋk] n (*sl*) tonterías fpl, música f celestial; **—!** ¡tonterías!; **history is —** la historia es un absurdo.

bunk bed ['bʌŋk'bed] n litera f.

bunker ['bʌŋkə*] **1** n (*for coal*) carbonera f; (*Naut*) pañol m del carbón; (*Mil*) refugio m; (*Golf*) bunker m, hoya f de arena, arenal m. **2** vt (*Naut*) proveer de carbón; **to be —ed** (*fig*) estar en un atolladero.

bunkum ['bʌŋkəm] n (*sl*) = **bunk**³.

bunny ['bʌni] n conejito m.

Bunsen burner ['bʌnsn'bə:nə*] n mechero m Bunsen.

bunting¹ ['bʌntiŋ] n (*Orn*) escribano m.

bunting² ['bʌntiŋ] n (*decoration*) banderas fpl, empavesado m; (*cloth*) lanilla f.

buoy [bɔi] **1** n boya f. **2** vt *channel* aboyar, señalar con boyas; **to — up** *person* mantener a flote, (*fig*) animar, alentar.

buoyancy ['bɔiənsi] n lo boyante, capacidad f para flotar; (*Aer*) fuerza f ascensional; (*fig*) confianza f, optimismo m.

buoyant ['bɔiənt] adj boyante, capaz de flotar; (*fig*) ilusionado, optimista; (*Comm*) con tendencia al alza.

buoyantly ['bɔiəntli] adv de modo boyante, (*fig*) de modo ilusionado, con optimismo.

bur(r) [bə:*] n (*Bot*) erizo m.

burble ['bə:bl] vi (*bubble*) burbujear, hervir; (*talk*) parlotear.

burden ['bə:dn] **1** n (a) carga f; (*weight*) peso m; (*Naut*) arqueo m.
(b) (*fig*) carga f, fardo m; (*of speech etc*) tema m principal, (*of song*) estribillo m; **— of proof** peso m de la prueba; **to be a — to someone** ser una responsabilidad molesta para uno; **he carries a heavy —** tiene que cargar con una gran responsabilidad; **to make someone's life a —** amargar la vida a uno.
2 vt cargar (*with* de); **to be —ed with** tener que cargar con.

burdensome ['bə:dnsəm] adj gravoso, oneroso.

bureau [bjuə'rəu] n (*desk*) escritorio m, buró m; (*office*) oficina f, agencia f, departamento m; **— de change** caja f de cambio; **weather —** oficina f meteorológica.

bureaucracy [bjuə'rɔkrəsi] n burocracia f.

bureaucrat ['bjuərəukræt] n burócrata mf.

bureaucratic [,bjuərəu'krætik] adj burocrático.

burgeon ['bə:dʒən] vi (*lit*) retoñar.

burgess ['bə:dʒis] n ciudadano m, a f; (*Parl*) diputado m.

burgh ['bʌrə*] n (*Scot*) villa f.

burglar ['bə:glə*] n ladrón m, escalador m.

burglar alarm ['bə:glərə,la:m] n alarma f de ladrones.

burglarize ['bə:gləraiz] vt (*US*) = **burgle**.

burglarproof ['bə:gləpru:f] adj a prueba de ladrones.

burglary ['bə:gləri] n robo m en una casa, robo m con escalonamiento, (*Law*) allanamiento m de morada.

burgle ['bə:gl] vt robar, escalar, allanar, desvalijar.

Burgundian [bə:'gʌndiən] **1** adj borgoñón. **2** n borgoñón m, ona f.

Burgundy ['bə:gəndi] Borgoña f; **b—** vino m de Borgoña.

burial ['beriəl] n entierro m.

burial ground ['beriəlgraund] n cementerio m.

burlap ['bə:læp] n harpillera f.

burlesque [bə:'lesk] **1** adj festivo, paródico; **— show** (*US*) revista f chabacana. **2** n parodia f. **3** vt parodiar.

burly ['bə:li] adj fornido, membrudo, corpulento.

Burma ['bə:mə] Birmania f.

Burmese [bə:'mi:z] **1** adj birmano. **2** n birmano m, a f.

burn¹ [bə:n] **1** n quemadura f.
2 (*irr: pret and ptp* **burned** or **burnt**) vt (a) quemar; *house etc* incendiar; *corpse* incinerar; *plants* (*by sun*) abrasar; *almonds etc* tostar; *fuel* funcionar con, utilizar como combustible; *mouth, tongue* quemar, escaldar; **to — one's hand** quemarse la mano; **to — a hole in something** hacer un agujero en algo quemándolo; **to — something to ashes** reducir algo a cenizas; **to — a house to the ground** incendiar y arrasar una casa; **to be —ed alive** ser quemado vivo; **to be —ed to death** morir en un incendio; **with a face —ed by the sun** con una cara

tostada al sol; **it has a burnt taste** sabe a quemado.
(b) **to — away** quemar, consumir; **to — down** incendiar; **to — off** quitar quemando; **to — out** (*Elec*) fundir, quemar; **to — up** quemar, consumir; *crops* abrasar; (*fig, fam*) indignar.
3 vi (a) quemar(se), arder; (*catch fire*) incendiarse; (*light, gas*) estar encendido; (*smart*) escocer; **to — down** quedar destruido en un incendio, apagarse; (*Elec*) fundirse; **to — to death** morir quemado; **to — up** consumirse; (*burn brighter*) arder más.
(b) (*fig*) arder (*with* de, en); **to — to +** *infin* desear ardientemente + *infin*; **to — with desire for** desear ardientemente; **to — with impatience** consumirse de impaciencia.

burn² [bə:n] n (*Scot*) arroyo m.

burner ['bə:nə*] n mechero m; (*on stove etc*) quemador m, fuego m.

burning ['bə:niŋ] adj ardiente (*also fig*); **question** candente, palpitante; **it's — hot** está que quema, (*sun*) hace muchísimo calor.

burnish ['bə:niʃ] vt bruñir.

burnt [bə:nt] *pret and ptp* of **burn**¹.

burp [bə:p] (*fam*) **1** n eructo m. **2** vi eructar.

burr [bə:*] n (*Bot*) erizo m.

burrow ['bʌrəu] **1** n madriguera f; (*rabbit's*) conejera f.
2 vt hacer madrigueras en; (*and undermine*) socavar, minar; **to — one's way into** abrirse camino cavando en.
3 vi amadrigarse, hacer una madriguera; **to — into** hacer madrigueras en, horadar.

bursar ['bə:sə*] n (*Univ etc*) tesorero m.

bursary ['bə:səri] n (*Univ*) beca f.

bursitis [bə:'saitis] n bursitis f.

burst [bə:st] **1** n reventón m; (*explosion*) estallido m, explosión f; (*of shots*) serie f de tiros, ráfaga f de tiros; **a — of applause** una explosión de aplausos; **a — of speed** una escapada; **a — of activity** un frenesí repentino de actividad; **in a — of anger** en un arranque de cólera.
2 (*irr: pret and ptp* **burst**) vt *balloon etc* reventar; *bubble* deshacer; *tyre* pinchar; *banks, dam, pipe* romper; **to — open a door** abrir de golpe una puerta.
3 vi (*balloon, boil, boiler*) reventar(se); (*bubble*) deshacerse; (*tyre*) pincharse; (*dam, pipe*) romperse; (*bomb etc*) estallar; (*heart*) partirse; (*storm*) desencadenarse; **to — forth** brotar, salir a chorro; **to — in** entrar violentamente; **to — into a room** irrumpir en un cuarto; **to — into tears** deshacerse en lágrimas; **to — into song** romper a cantar; **to — into flames** estallar en llamas; **to — open** abrirse de golpe; **to — out laughing** soltar la carcajada; **"No", he — out** "¡No!" gritó violentamente; **the sun — through the clouds** el sol brilló repentinamente por entre las nubes; **he was —ing to tell me** reventaba por decírmelo; **he was —ing with impatience** reventaba de impaciencia; **to — with laughter** reventar de risa; **London is —ing with young people** Londres está que bulle de juventud; **to be full to —ing** estar lleno a reventar; estar apretado a presión.

burthen ['bə:ðən] n arqueo m.

bury ['beri] vt enterrar (*also fig*); *body* enterrar, sepultar; *memory, matter* echar tierra sobre; **to — a dagger in someone's heart** clavar un puñal en el corazón de uno; **to — one's face in one's hands** ocultar el rostro en las manos; **to — oneself in the country** enterrarse en el campo; **to be buried in thought** estar absorto en la meditación.

bus [bʌs] n autobús m; **to go by —** ir en autobús; **to miss the —** (*fam*) perder la ocasión.

bush [buʃ] n arbusto m; (*Tech*) forro m de metal; **the — ** (*Australia*) el monte, el despoblado; **to beat about the —** andarse por las ramas, ir por rodeos.

bushel ['buʃl] n medida de áridos: British = 36,36 litros, US = 35,24 litros.

bushman ['buʃmən] n, pl **—men** [mən] (*African*) bosquimano m.

bushranger ['buʃ,reindʒə*] n (*Australia*) bandido m.

bush telegraph ['buʃ'teligra:f] n (*fam*) medio m de comunicación clandestina; **I heard it on the —** lo llegué a saber, me lo dijo alguno, lo supe pero no te voy a decir cómo; **they have their own —** tienen sus propios métodos para comunicarse.

bushy ['buʃi] adj *plant* parecido a un arbusto; *ground* lleno de arbustos; *beard* poblado, espeso.

busily ['bizili] adv atareadamente, afanosamente.

business ['biznis] **1** n (a) (*commerce in general; fig*) comercio m, negocios mpl; **— is —** el comercio es una cosa seria; **— before pleasure** primero es la obligación que la devoción; **— as usual** los negocios como de costumbre; **big — comercio** *m* en gran escala; **he's in —** se dedica al comercio; **he's in — in London** trabaja en una empresa comercial de Londres; **to be on —** estar (en viaje) de negocios; **to carry on —** as tener un negocio de; **to do — with** comerciar con; **to get down to —** ir al grano, ir derecho a lo esencial; **to go into —** dedicarse al comercio; **to mean —** hablar (*etc*) en serio; **to send someone about his —** echar a uno con cajas destempladas; **to set up in —** as montar un negocio de; **to set someone up in —** proveer a uno de un capital explotable.

(b) (*firm*) empresa *f*, casa *f*; **it's a family — es** una empresa familiar.

(c) (*task, duty*) **that's my — eso** me toca únicamente a mí; **it is my — to** + *infin* me corresponde + *infin*; **it's no — of mine** yo no tengo nada que ver con eso; **you had no — to** + *infin* Vd no tuvo ningún derecho a + *infin*; **what — have you to** + *infin*? ¿qué derecho tiene Vd a + *infin*?; **I will make it my — to tell him** yo me propongo decírselo, yo les aseguro que se lo diré; **mind your own —** no se meta Vd donde no le llaman.

(d) (*one's trade, profession*) oficio *m*, ocupación *f*; **what — are you in?** ¿a qué se dedica Vd?; **he's got the biggest laugh in the —** tiene la risa más fuerte que hay por aquí.

(e) (*affair*) cosa *f*, asunto *m*, cuestión *f*; **the Suez —** aquello de Suez; **the — before the meeting** los asuntos a tratar; **I have — with the minister** tengo asuntos que tratar con el ministro; **it's a nasty —** es un asunto desagradable; **did you hear about that — yesterday?** ¿le dijeron algo de lo que pasó ayer?; **what a — this is!** ¡qué lío!; **I can't stand this — of doing nothing** no puedo con este plan de no hacer nada.

(f) (*Theat*) acción *f*.

2 *attr*: *deal, connection, quarter* comercial; *house* de comercio; *cycle* económico; *trip* de negocios; *hours* de oficina.

businesslike ['bizníslaik] *adj* formal, metódico, serio, práctico.

businessman ['biznísmæn] *n*, *pl* **—men** [men] hombre *m* de negocios.

busload ['bʌsləud] *n* autobús *m* (lleno, completo); **they came by the —** (*fig*) vinieron en masa, vinieron en tropel.

busman ['bʌsmən] *n*, *pl* **—men** [mən] conductor *m* or cobrador *m* de autobús; **—'s holiday** día de fiesta en el cual uno hace el mismo trabajo que siempre.

bus-stop ['bʌsstɔp] *n* parada *f* de autobús.

bust[1] [bʌst] *n* (*Anat: Art*) busto *m*; (*bosom*) pecho *m*, pechos *mpl*.

bust[2] [bʌst] **1** *ptp* (*fam*) *of* **burst**; **to go —** (*Comm*) quebrar. **2** *vt* romper, estropear. **3** *vi* romperse, estropearse.

bustard ['bʌstəd] *n* avutarda *f*.

bustle[1] ['bʌsl] *n* (*dress*) polisón *m*.

bustle[2] ['bʌsl] **1** *n* movimiento *m*, actividad *f*; bullicio *m*, animación *f*; (*haste*) prisa *f*. **2** *vi* menearse, apresurarse, ir y venir.

bustler ['bʌslə*] *n* bullebulle *mf*.

bustling ['bʌsliŋ] *adj* activo, hacendoso; *crowd* apresurado, animado.

bust-up ['bʌstʌp] *n* (*fam*) riña *f*.

busy ['bizi] **1** *adj* (a) *person* ocupado; atareado; activo; (*pej*) entrometido; **as — as a bee** muy activo, ocupadísimo; **are you —?** ¿está ocupado?; **to be — at** (*or* on, with) estar ocupado en; **to be — doing something** estar ocupado en hacer algo; **to get —** empezar a trabajar, (*hurry*) menearse, darse prisa; **let's get —!** ¡vamos!; **to keep —** estar siempre ocupado; **to keep someone —** ocupar a uno.

(b) *day* de muchas ocupaciones; **the busiest season is the autumn** la época de mayor actividad es el otoño.

(c) *place* (muy) concurrido, de mucho movimiento; *scene* animado, lleno de movimiento.

2 *vt* ocupar.

3 *vr*: **to — oneself at** (*or* in, with) ocuparse en, estar ocupado con; **she busied herself with the children** ella se ocupó de los niños.

busybody ['bizibɔdi] *n* entrometido *m*, a *f*.

but [bʌt] **1** *adv* (*only*) sólo, solamente, no más que; **all —** casi; **nothing —** nada más que; **he is — a servant** no es más que un criado; **he talks — little** habla muy poco; **if I could — speak to him** si solamente pudiese hablar con él; **had I — known** si lo hubiera sabido.

2 *prep and conj* (*except*) excepto, menos; **all — him** todos excepto él; **the last — one** el penúltimo; **the last — three** el tercero antes del último; **— for**

a no ser por, si no fuera por; **there is nothing for it — to pay up** no hay más remedio que pagar; **I'll do anything — sing** sing lo hago todo menos cantar.

3 *conj* (a) pero; **she was poor — she was honest** era pobre pero honrada; **— it does move!** ¡pero sí se mueve!; **it never rains — it pours** no llueve sin hacerlo en exceso; **I never go there — I think of you** nunca voy allá sin pensar en ti.

(b) (*in statements of direct contradiction*) sino, *eg* **he's not English — Irish** no es inglés sino irlandés; **he didn't sing — he shouted** no cantó sino que gritó.

4 *n* pero *m*, objeción *f*; **there are no —s about it** no hay pero que valga.

butane ['bju:tein] *n* butano *m*; **— gas** gas *m* butano.

butcher ['butʃə*] **1** *n* carnicero *m* (*also fig*);! **—'s (shop)** carnicería *f*. **2** *vt* matar; (*fig*) dar muerte a, hacer una carnicería con.

butchery ['butʃəri] *n* matanza *f*, carnicería *f*.

butler ['bʌtlə*] *n* mayordomo *m*.

butt[1] [bʌt] *n* tonel *m*; (*for rainwater*) tina *f*.

butt[2] [bʌt] *n* (*end*) cabo *m*, extremo *m*; extremo *m* más grueso; (*of gun*) culata *f*; (*of cigarette*) colilla *f*; (*US fam*) culo *m*.

butt[3] [bʌt] *n* (*target*) blanco *m*; **—s** campo *m* de tiro al blanco; **to be a — for** ser el blanco de, ser el objeto de.

butt[4] [bʌt] **1** *n* (*push with head*) cabezada *f*, topetada *f*. **2** *vt* dar cabezadas contra, topetar; **to — one's head against** dar con la cabeza contra. **3** *vi*: **to — in** interrumpir; (*meddle*) entrometerse.

butt-end ['bʌtend] *n* = **butt**[2].

butter ['bʌtə*] **1** *n* mantequilla *f*; **— wouldn't melt in his mouth** es una mosquita muerta. **2** *vt* untar con mantequilla; **to — someone up** (*fam*) dar coba a uno.

buttercup ['bʌtəkʌp] *n* ranúnculo *m*.

butter-fingered ['bʌtə.fiŋgəd] *adj* desmañado en coger la pelota (*etc*).

butterfly ['bʌtəflai] *n* mariposa *f*.

butterfly-stroke ['bʌtəflai.strəuk] *n* estilo *m* mariposa.

buttermilk ['bʌtəmilk] *n* leche *f* de manteca.

butterscotch ['bʌtəskɔtʃ] *n* dulce *de azúcar terciado con mantequilla*.

buttery ['bʌtəri] *n* despensa *f*.

buttocks ['bʌtəks] *npl* nalgas *fpl*, cachas *fpl*.

button ['bʌtn] **1** *n* (*all senses*) botón *m*; **—s** (*person*) botones *m*. **2** *vt* (*also* **to — up**) abotonar, abrochar. **3** *vi*: **—s in front** se abrocha por delante.

buttonhole ['bʌtnhəul] **1** *n* ojal *m*; (*flower*) flor *f* que se lleva en el ojal. **2** *vt* obligar a escuchar, abordar; **I was —d by X** me vi obligado a detenerme en conversación con X.

buttonhook ['bʌtnhuk] *n* abotonador *m*.

buttress ['bʌtris] **1** *n* contrafuerte *m* (*also Geog*); (*fig*) apoyo *m*, sostén *m*; **flying —** arbotante *m*. **2** *vt* poner contrafuerte a; (*fig*) apoyar, reforzar.

buxom ['bʌksəm] *adj* rollizo, frescachón.

buy [bai] **1** *n* compra *f*; **a good —** un buen negocio, una ganga.

2 (*irr*: *pret and ptp* **bought**) *vt* comprar (*from, of* a); **money couldn't — it** no se puede comprar con dinero; **all right, I'll — it** bien, dime; **to — back** volver a comprar; **to — off** comprar la benevolencia de, (*bribe*) sobornar; **to — out** *partner* comprar la parte de; **to — up** comprar todas las existencias de, acaparar.

buyer ['baiə*] *n* comprador *m*, ora *f*; (*in store*) encargado *m* de compras.

buzz [bʌz] **1** *n* zumbido *m*; (*fam*) rumor *m*. **2** *vt* (*call*) llamar; (*Aer*) avisar; (*throw, fam*) lanzar, tirar. **3** *vi* zumbar; **to — about** ser muy activo, ir por todas partes; **to — off** (*fam*) largarse, najarse.

buzzard ['bʌzəd] *n* ratonero *m* común, águila *f* ratonera.

buzzer ['bʌzə*] *n* zumbador *m*, vibrador *m*.

by [bai] **1** *adv*: **— and —** más tarde, luego; **— and large** en general, por lo general.

2 *prep* (a) (*agent, by means of*) por; **a house built — X** una casa construida por X; **— one's own efforts** por sus propios esfuerzos; **— God** por Dios; **made — hand** hecho a mano; **to divide — 5** dividir por 5; **he had 3 children — his first wife** tuvo 3 hijos con su primera mujer; **he is known — the name of** se le conoce con (*of pseudonym*) bajo) el nombre de; **he did it — himself** lo hizo por sí solo, lo hizo por sí mismo.

(b) (*manner*) **— cheque** por cheque; **— air** en avión; **— train** (*come*) en tren, (*send*) por ferrocarril; **— easy stages** en cortas etapas; **— moonlight** a la luz de la luna; — **leaps and bounds** a pasos agigantados; **to be** — **oneself** estar solo.

(c) (*rate*) **hour** — **hour** hora tras hora, cada hora; — **the dozen** a docenas; **2** — **2** de 2 en 2; **little** — **little** poco a poco; **to buy something** — **the kilo** comprar algo por kilos; **to reduce something** — **a third** reducir algo en una tercera parte; **we pay** — **the month** pagamos cada mes.

(d) (*in accordance with*) según, de acuerdo con; — **what you say** según lo que dices; **to be cautious** — **nature** ser de naturaleza cauteloso.

(e) (*time*) — **2 o'clock** para las 2; — **nightfall** antes del anochecer; — **then** para entonces, antes de eso; — **day** de día.

(f) (*place*) junto a, cerca de, al lado de; — **me** a mi lado; **north** — **west** norte por oeste; (*through, along*) por; **he came in** — **the window** entró por la ventana.

(g) (*measurement*) **6 metres** — **4** 6 metros por 4; **it's too short** — **a foot** falta un pie; **he missed** — **an inch** erró el tiro en una pulgada.

(h) (*with gerund*) — **working hard** trabajando mucho; **he ended** — **saying that** terminó diciendo que.

3 *n*: — **the** — a propósito, por cierto.

bye [bai] *n*: **to have a** — pasar a la segunda eliminatoria por sorteo.

bye-bye ['bai'bai] *interj* ¡adiós!, ¡hasta luego!

by-election ['baii,lekʃən] *n* elección *f* complementaria.

bygone ['baigɔn] **1** *adj* pasado. **2** *n*: let —s be —s olvidemos lo pasado.

by-law ['bailɔ:] *n* estatuto *m*, reglamento *m*.

by-name ['baineim] *n* sobrenombre *m*; (*nickname*) apodo *m*, mote *m*.

bypass ['baipɑːs] **1** *n* carretera *f* de circunvalación. **2** *vt* evitar, evitar el contacto con; *town* evitar entrar en.

by-play ['baiplei] *n* (*Theat*) acción *f* aparte, escena *f* muda.

by-product ['bai,prɔdəkt] *n* subproducto *m*; (*Chem*) derivado *m*.

by-road ['bairəud] *n* camino *m* vecinal.

bystander ['bai,stændə*] *n* espectador *m*, ora *f*, circunstante *mf*, curioso *m*, a *f*, mirón *m*, ona *f*.

byway ['baiwei] *n* camino *m* apartado, camino *m* poco frecuentado; **the** —**s of history** los aspectos poco conocidos de la historia.

byword ['baiwə:d] *n*: **to be a** — **for** ser conocidísimo por.

Byzantine [bai'zæntain] **1** *adj* bizantino. **2** *n* bizantino *m*, a *f*.

Byzantium [bai'zæntiəm] Bizancio *m*.

C

cab [kæb] n taxi m; (arch) cabriolé m, coche m de alquiler; (of lorry etc) cabina f, casilla f.
cabal [kə'bæl] n cábala f, cabildeo m.
cabaret ['kæbərei] n cabaret m.
cabbage ['kæbidʒ] n col f, berza f; — **white** (**butterfly**) mariposa f de la col.
cab(b)ala [kə'bɑːlə] n cábala f.
cabbalistic [,kæbə'listik] adj cabalístico.
cabby ['kæbi] n (fam), **cabdriver** ['kæbdraivə*] n taxista m; (arch) cochero m.
cabin ['kæbin] n (hut) cabaña f; (Naut) camarote m; (of lorry, plane) cabina f.
cabin boy ['kæbinbɔi] n grumete m.
cabin cruiser ['kæbin,kruːzə*] n yate m de motor, motonave f para viajes de placer.
cabinet ['kæbinit] n (a) (cupboard) armario m; (for display) vitrina f; (casing) caja f; **medicine —** botiquín m.
 (b) (Pol) consejo m de ministros; — **crisis** crisis f del gobierno; — **minister** ministro m que es miembro del consejo.
cabinetmaker ['kæbinit,meikə*] n ebanista m.
cabinetmaking ['kæbinit,meikiŋ] n ebanistería f.
cable ['keibl] 1 n (Naut, Elec, Tel) cable m; (message) cablegrama m; **overhead —** (Elec) línea f eléctrica aérea. 2 vti cablegrafiar.
cable-car ['keiblkɑː*] n coche m de teleférico.
cablegram ['keiblgræm] n cablegrama m.
cable railway ['keibl'reilwei] n teleférico m, funicular m aéreo.
cable ship ['keiblʃip] n barco m cablero.
cable stitch ['keiblstitʃ] n punto m en cruz.
cableway ['keiblwei] n teleférico m, funicular m aéreo.
cabman ['kæbmən] n, pl —**men** [mən] taxista m; (arch) cochero m.
caboodle [kə'buːdl] n (sl): **the whole —** todo el negocio.
caboose [kə'buːs] n`(US: Rail) furgón m de cola.
cabrank ['kæbræŋk] n parada f de taxis, punto m de taxis.
cabstand ['kæbstænd] n parada f de taxis, punto m de taxis.
cacao [kə'kɑːəu] n cacao m.
cache [kæʃ] n (hiding place) escondite m, escondrijo m; (stores) víveres mpl (etc) escondidos; (of contraband, arms) alijo m.
cachet ['kæʃei] n sello m, marca f de distinción.
cackle ['kækl] 1 n cacareo m; (laughter) risa f aguda; (talk) cháchara f; **cut the —!** (fam) ¡callarse!, ¡basta ya de palabras!
 2 vi cacarear; (laugh) reírse agudamente, (fam) desternillarse de risa; (talk) chacharear.
cacophony [kæ'kɔfəni] n cacofonía f.
cactus ['kæktəs] n cacto m.
cad [kæd] n sinvergüenza m, caradura m, canalla m; **you —!** ¡canalla!
cadaver [kə'deivə*] n (US) cadáver m.
cadaverous [kə'dævərəs] adj cadavérico.
caddie ['kædi] n cadi m, caddie m (el portador de los palos en el golf).
caddis fly ['kædisflai] n frígano m.
caddish ['kædiʃ] adj desvergonzado, canallesco; — **trick** canallada f.
caddy ['kædi] n cajita f para té.
cadence ['keidəns] n cadencia f; **the —s of prose** el ritmo de la prosa.
cadenza [kə'denzə] n cadencia f.
cadet [kə'det] m (Mil) cadete m; (younger son) hijo m menor.
cadge [kædʒ] 1 vt sacar de gorra, obtener mendigando.
 2 vi gorronear, vivir de gorra, sablear; **you can't — off me** es inútil pedirme cosas a mí.

cadger ['kædʒə*] n gorrón m, ona f, sablista mf.
Cadiz [kə'diz] Cádiz.
cadmium ['kædmiəm] n cadmio m.
cadre ['kædri] n cuadro m.
caecum ['siːkəm] n ciego m.
Caesar ['siːzə*] m César.
Caesarean [siː'zɛəriən] adj: — **operation,** — **section** operación f cesárea.
caesura [si'zjuərə] n cesura f.
café ['kæfei] n café m.
café au lait ['kæfeiəu'lei] n café m con leche.
café crème ['kæfei'krɛːm] n café m con nata.
café noir ['kæfei'nwɑː*] n café m solo.
café society ['kæfeisə'saiəti] n (US) (sociedad f de la) gente f que frecuenta los cafés de moda, mundo m elegante de los cafés.
cafeteria [,kæfi'tiəriə] n restaurante m económico.
caffein(e) ['kæfiːn] n cafeína f.
cage [keidʒ] 1 n jaula f. 2 vt enjaular; **a —d bird** un pájaro en jaula.
cage bird ['keidʒbɜːd] n pájaro m de jaula.
cagey ['keidʒi] adj (fam) cauteloso, reservado; **he was very — about it** en eso anduvo con pies de plomo, habló del asunto con la mayor reserva.
cahoots [kə'huːts] n (sl): **to be in — with someone** obrar de acuerdo con uno; estar asociado con uno; **to go —** entrar por partes iguales.
caiman ['keimən] n caimán m.
Cain [kein] m Caín; **to raise —** armar la gorda, protestar enérgicamente.
cairn [kɛən] n mojón m, montón m de piedras (puesto en una cumbre o sobre una sepultura, etc).
Cairo ['kaiərəu] el Cairo.
caisson [kə'keisən] n (Mech) cajón m hidráulico; (Naut) cajón m de suspensión; (of dry-dock) puerta f de dique; (Mil) cajón m.
cajole [kə'dʒəul] vt halagar, camelar; **to — someone into doing something** conseguir por medio de halagos que uno haga algo.
cajolery [kə'dʒəuləri] n halagos mpl, marrullería f, engatusamiento m.
cake [keik] 1 n (large) pastel m; tarta f; (small) pasta f, pastelillo m; (sponge) bizcocho m; (of soap) pastilla f; **birthday —** tarta f de cumpleaños; **Christmas —** tarta f de Reyes; **to go** (or **sell**) **like hot —s** venderse como pan bendito; **that takes the —!** (fam) ¡es el colmo!
 2 vt endurecer; **a tyre —d with mud** un neumático cubierto de lodo endurecido.
 3 vi endurecerse, apelmazarse.
caked [keikt] 1 pret and ptp of **cake.** 2 adj endurecido.
cake shop ['keikʃɔp] n pastelería f.
calabash ['kæləbæʃ] n calabaza f.
calaboose ['kæləbuːs] n (US fam) jaula f (fam), cárcel f.
calamine ['kæləmain] n calamina f.
calamitous [kə'læmitəs] adj calamitoso.
calamity [kə'læmiti] n calamidad f.
calcareous [kæl'kɛəriəs] adj calcáreo.
calcification [,kælsifi'keiʃən] n calcificación f.
calcify ['kælsifai] 1 vt calcificar. 2 vi calcificarse.
calcination [,kælsi'neiʃən] n calcinación f.
calcine ['kælsain] 1 vt calcinar. 2 vi calcinarse.
calcium ['kælsiəm] n calcio m; — **carbonate** carbonato m de calcio.
calculable ['kælkjuləbl] adj calculable.
calculate ['kælkjuleit] 1 vt calcular; —**d to** + infin aprestado para + infin; **this is —d to give him a jolt** esto tiene el propósito de darle una sacudida; **it is hardly —d to help us** esto apenas tendrá consecuencias beneficiosas para nosotros.
 2 vi calcular; **to — on** contar con.
calculated ['kælkjuleitid] adj insult etc intencionado.
calculating ['kælkjuleitiŋ] adj astuto.

calculating machine ['kælkjuleitiŋmə,ʃiːn] n máquina f de calcular, calculadora f.

calculation [,kælkju'leiʃən] n cálculo m, cómputo m.

calculus ['kælkjuləs] n: **differential —** cálculo m diferencial.

Calcutta [kæl'kʌtə] Calcuta.

calendar ['kæləndə*] n calendario m; (Law) lista f de pleitos; **— year** año m civil.

calf¹ [kɑːf] n, pl **calves** [kɑːvz] (Zool) ternero m, a f, becerro m, a f; (of seal etc) cría f; (skin) piel f de becerro; **to be in** (or **with**) **—** estar preñada (la vaca); **to kill the fatted —** festejar con mucho rumbo a un recién llegado, celebrar una fiesta de bienvenida.

calf² [kɑːf] n, pl **calves** [kɑːvz] (Anat) pantorrilla f.

calf love ['kɑːflʌv] n amor m juvenil.

calfskin ['kɑːfskin] n piel f de becerro.

calibrate ['kælibreit] vt calibrar.

calibre, (US) **caliber** ['kælibə*] n calibre m; (fig) capacidad f, aptitud f, carácter m, valor m; **a man of his —** un hombre que vale lo que él; **then he showed his real —** luego demostró tener un gran talento.

calico ['kælikəu] n calicó m.

calipers ['kælipəz] npl calibrador m.

caliph ['keilif] n califa m.

caliphate ['keilifeit] n califato m.

call [kɔːl] **1** n (a) (in general) llamada f (also Mil, Tel); (cry) grito m; (of bird) canto m, reclamo m; (imitating bird's cry) reclamo m, (imitating animal's cry) chilla f; (Theat) llamamiento m; (at bridge) marca f, voz f; **local —** llamada f local; **trunk —**, **long-distance —** conferencia f interurbana; **the — of the unknown** la atracción de lo desconocido; **on —** disponible, a su disposición; **money on —** dinero m a la vista; **within —** al alcance de la voz; **whose — is it?** (Bridge) ¿quién habla?; **they came at my —** acudieron a mi llamada; **please give me a — at 7** haga el favor de llamarme a las 7; **he's had a — to the Palace** le han llamado a palacio; **to have a close —** escapar por un pelo, casi haber muerto.

(b) (visit) visita f; **port of —** puerto m de escala; **the boat makes a — at Vigo** el barco hace escala en Vigo; **to pay a — on someone** hacer una visita a uno.

(c) (appeal) llamamiento m; **a — went to the fire brigade** se llamó a los bomberos; **the boat sent out a — for help** el barco emitió una llamada pidiendo socorro; **the minister sent out a — to the country to remain calm** el ministro hizo un llamamiento al país para que conservara la calma.

(d) (need etc) (Comm) demanda f (for, on de); **there isn't much — for these now** éstos tienen poca demanda ahora; **you had no — to say that** Vd no tuvo motivo alguno para decir eso; **what — was there for you to intervene?** ¿qué derecho tuvo Vd a entrometerse?

(e) (claim) **there are many —s on my attention** son muchas las cosas que reclaman mi atención.

2 vt (a) (in general) llamar; **did you —?** ¿me llamaste?; **they —ed me to see it** me llamaron para que lo viese; **please — me at 8** haga el favor de llamarme a las 8.

(b) (Tel) llamar (por or al teléfono); **London —ed you this morning** esta mañana le llamaron al teléfono desde Londres; **I'll — you again tomorrow** volveré a llamarle mañana.

(c) (name) llamar; **I'm —ed Peter** me llamo Pedro; **what are you —ed?** ¿cómo te llamas?; **what are they —ing him?** ¿qué nombre le van a poner?; **they're —ing the boy John** al niño le van a dar el nombre de Juan; **I — it an insult** yo digo que es un insulto; **I —ed him a liar** le califiqué de mentiroso; **are you —ing me a liar?** ¿dice Vd que yo soy un mentiroso?

(d) (special uses) **attention** llamar (to sobre); **meeting** convocar; **roll** pasar; **strike** declarar; (Bridge) **he —ed 3 hearts** marcó 3 corazones; **to — someone as a witness** citar a uno como testigo; **see halt, name, question** etc.

(e) **to — aside** llamar aparte; **to — back** hacer volver, (Tel) volver a llamar; **to — down blessings upon someone** pedir al cielo mil bendiciones para uno; **to — forth** sacar; **remark etc** inspirar; **protest etc** motivar, provocar; **police** llamar, pedir la ayuda de; **old notes** retirar de la circulación; **to — off** cancelar; **search etc** dar por terminado, suspender, abandonar; **dogs** llamar; **to — out workers** llamar a la huelga; **to — over** llamar; **names** pasar la lista de; **to — together** convocar; **to — up** hacer subir, (Tel) llamar; **memory** evocar; (Mil) llamar al servicio militar.

3 vi (a) (cry out) llamar, dar voces, dar gritos.

(b) (Tel) **who is it —ing?** ¿de parte de quién?; (Radio) **Madrid —ing!** ¡aquí Radio Madrid!

(c) (visit) venir, hacer una visita.

(d) **to — at house** visitar, pasar por; **port** hacer escala en; **to — back** volver (for por); **to — for** venir por, venir a recoger; (demand) pedir, exigir; **to — for help** pedir socorro a voces; **to — in** entrar, venir; **dar un vistazo; to — on** visitar, ir a ver; (for a speech) invitar a hablar; **I now — on Mr Brown** cedo la palabra al Sr Brown; **to — on someone for help** acudir a uno para pedir ayuda; **the minister —ed on the nation to help** el ministro hizo un llamamiento a la nación para que ayudase; **to — out** gritar, dar voces; **to — to** dar voces a; **heart —s to heart** los corazones se hablan.

callbox ['kɔːlbɔks] n cabina f telefónica.

callboy ['kɔːlbɔi] n (Theat) traspunte m.

caller ['kɔːlə*] n visita f; (Tel) usuario m; **the first — at the shop** el primer cliente de la tienda.

call girl ['kɔːlgəːl] n prostituta f (que hace citas por teléfono).

calligraphic [,kæli'græfik] adj caligráfico.

calligraphy [kə'ligrəfi] n caligrafía f.

calling ['kɔːliŋ] n vocación f, profesión f.

calling card ['kɔːliŋkɑːd] n (US) tarjeta f de visita.

callipers ['kælipəz] npl calibrador m; (Med) soporte m, corrector m.

callisthenics [,kælis'θeniks] n sing calistenia f.

call letters ['kɔːl,letəz] npl (US: Tel) letras fpl de identificación.

call money ['kɔːlmʌni] n dinero m a la vista.

callosity [kæ'bɔsiti] n callosidad f.

callous ['kæləs] adj insensible, cruel; (Med) calloso.

callously ['kæləsli] adv cruelmente.

callousness ['kæləsnis] n insensibilidad f, crueldad f.

callow ['kæləu] adj inexperto, novato; **youth** imberbe.

call sign ['kɔːlsain] n (Radio) indicativo m.

call-up ['kɔːlʌp] n (of reserves) movilización f; (conscription) servicio m militar obligatorio; (act of calling) llamamiento m.

callus ['kæləs] n callo m.

calm [kɑːm] **1** adj person, mind tranquilo, sosegado; weather calmoso, sin viento; sea liso, en calma; **to keep —** no emocionarse, conservar la tranquilidad; **to grow —** calmarse, sosegarse.

2 n calma f; **dead —** calma f chicha.

3 vt calmar, tranquilizar (also **to — down**).

4 vi calmarse, tranquilizarse (also **to — down**); **— down!** ¡cálmese!, (to excited child) ¡tente quieto!

5 vr: **— yourself!** ¡cálmese!

calming ['kɑːmiŋ] adj calmante.

calmly ['kɑːmli] adv con calma, tranquilamente.

calmness ['kɑːmnis] n calma f, tranquilidad f.

caloric ['kælərik] adj calórico.

calorie ['kæləri] n caloría f.

calorific [,kælə'rifik] adj calorífico.

calumniate [kə'lʌmnieit] vt calumniar.

calumny ['kæləmni] n calumnia f.

Calvary ['kælvəri] Calvario m.

calve [kɑːv] vi parir (la vaca).

calves [kɑːvz] npl of **calf**¹ and **calf**².

Calvin ['kælvin] m Calvino.

Calvinism ['kælvinizəm] n calvinismo m.

Calvinist ['kælvinist] **1** adj calvinista. **2** n calvinista mf.

Calvinistic [,kælvi'nistik] adj calvinista.

calypso [kə'lipsəu] n calipso m.

calyx ['keiliks] n, pl **calyces** ['keilisiz] cáliz m.

cam [kæm] n leva f.

camaraderie [,kæmə'rɑːdəri] n compañerismo m.

camber ['kæmbə*] **1** n combadura f; convexidad f. **2** vt combar, arquear. **3** vi combarse, arquearse.

Cambodia [kæm'bəudiə] Camboya f.

Cambodian [kæm'bəudiən] **1** adj camboyano. **2** n camboyano m, a f.

cambric ['keimbrik] n batista f.

came [keim] pret of **come**.

camel ['kæməl] n camello m.

camel hair ['kæməlheə*] n pelo m de camello.

camel's-hair ['kæməlzheə*] adj de pelo de camello.

camellia [kə'miːliə] n camelia f.

cameo ['kæmiəu] n camafeo m.

camera ['kæmərə] n máquina f (fotográfica); (Cine, TV) cámara f; **aerial —** aparato m de fotografía aérea; **colour —** cámara f para hacer fotos en color; **in —** en secreto.

cameraman ['kæmərəmæn] n, pl **-men** [men] cameraman m, cámara m.

Cameroon [,kæmə'ruːn] Camerón m.

camisole ['kæmisəul] n cubrecorsé m.

camomile ['kæməumail] n camomila f; **— tea** manzanilla f.

camouflage ['kæməflɑ:ʒ] **1** n camuflaje m. **2** vt camuflar.

camp[1] [kæmp] **1** n campamento m, campo m; (Pol etc) grupo m, facción f; **concentration** — campo m de concentración; **internment** — campo m de internamiento; **holiday** — colonia f veraniega; **labour** — campamento m de trabajo; **prison** — campamento m para prisioneros; **summer** — (for children etc) colonia f veraniega; **to pitch** — poner el campamento, armar la tienda, acampar(se); **to strike** — levantar el campamento.
　2 vi acampar(se); (fam) alojarse temporalmente; **to** — **out on the beach** pasar la noche en la playa.

camp[2] [kæmp] **1** adj (a) afectado (y divertido), (intencionadamente) teatral; sensible, elegante; (Lit etc) afectado, amanerado.
　(b) afeminado; (abiertamente) homosexual.
　2 n (a) afectación f divertida, exageración f, teatralidad f intencionada; (Lit etc) amaneramiento m.
　(b) afeminación f; homosexualidad f (abierta).
　3 vi parodiarse a sí mismo; comportarse ostentosamente de modo raro; guasearse, hacer el tonto; **stop** —**ing!** ¡déjate de bromas!

campaign [kæm'pein] **1** n campaña f; **election** — campaña f electoral.
　2 vi (Mil) luchar; servir; hacer campaña; **to** — **against** hacer campaña en contra de; **to** — **for** hacer campaña a favor de.

campaigner [kæm'peinə*] n (fig) paladín m, partidario m, a f (for de), propagandista mf (for por); **old** — (Mil) veterano m.

campanile [,kæmpə'ni:li] n campanario m.

campbed ['kæmp'bed] n cama f de campaña.

camp chair ['kæmp'tʃeə*] n silla f plegadiza.

camper ['kæmpə*] n acampador m, ora f, campista mf.

campfire ['kæmp'faiə*] n hoguera f de campamento; (of scouts) reunión f alrededor de la hoguera.

camp follower ['kæmp,fɔləuə*] n vivandero m, a f; (pej) prostituta f.

campground ['kæmpgraund] n (US) camping m.

camphor ['kæmfə*] n alcanfor m.

camphorated ['kæmfəreitid] adj alcanforado.

camping ['kæmpiŋ] n camping m; **to go** — hacer camping.

camping ground ['kæmpiŋgraund] n, **camping site** ['kæmpiŋsait] n (terreno m de) camping m.

campsite ['kæmpsait] n camping m; campamento m.

campstool ['kæmpstu:l] n taburete m plegable.

camp stove ['kæmp'stəuv] n hornillo m de campista.

campus ['kæmpəs] n (Univ) recinto m.

campy ['kæmpi] adj (sl) = **camp**[2] **1**.

camshaft ['kæmʃɑ:ft] n árbol m de levas.

can[1] [kæn] (irr: pret **could**; defective) vi (a) (be able to) poder; **if I** — si puedo; **we can't swim today** hoy no podemos ir a bañarnos.
　(b) (with verbs of perception, often not translated) **I** — **hear it** lo oigo; **I couldn't see it anywhere** no lo veía en ninguna parte; **I can't understand why** no comprendo por qué.
　(c) (of acquired skills, know how to) saber, eg — **you swim?** ¿sabes nadar?
　(d) (have permission to) poder, eg — **I go now?** ¿puedo irme ahora?

can[2] [kæn] **1** n lata f, bote m; (for petrol etc) bidón m; (US sl) wáter m; **to carry the** — (sl) pagar el pato.
　2 vt conservar en lata; enlatar, envasar; — **it!** (sl) ¡cállate!; see also **canned**.

Canada ['kænədə] el Canadá.

Canadian [kə'neidiən] **1** adj canadiense. **2** n canadiense mf.

canal [kə'næl] n canal m; **alimentary** — tubo m digestivo.

canalization [,kænəlai'zeiʃən] n canalización f.

canalize ['kænəlaiz] vt canalizar.

canapé ['kænəpei] n canapé m.

canard [kæ'nɑ:d] n filfa f, hablilla f, noticia f falsa.

Canarian [kə'neəriən] **1** adj canario. **2** n canario m, a f.

canary [kə'neəri] n canario m.

Canary Isles [kə'neəriailz] pl Islas fpl Canarias.

canasta [kə'næstə] n canasta f.

cancan ['kænkæn] n cancán m.

cancel ['kænsəl] **1** vt cancelar; suprimir; permission etc retirar; stamp matar, inutilizar; **they** — **each other out** se anulan mutuamente.
　2 vi (Math): **to** — **out** destruirse.

cancellation [,kænsə'leiʃən] n cancelación f; supresión f; el retirar; (Post: mark) matasellos m, (act) inutilización f.

cancer ['kænsə*] n cáncer m.

cancerous ['kænsərəs] adj canceroso; **to become** — cancerarse.

candelabra [,kændi'lɑ:brə] n candelabro m.

candid ['kændid] adj franco, sincero, abierto; **to be quite** — hablando con franqueza.

candidly ['kændidli] adv francamente, con franqueza.

candidness ['kændidnis] n franqueza f.

candidate ['kændideit] n (applicant) aspirante mf (for a), solicitante mf (for de); (for election, examinee, Pol, etc) candidato m, a f (for a); (in competitive exams) opositor m, ora f (for a).

candidature ['kændidətʃə*] n candidatura f.

candied ['kændid] adj azucarado.

candle ['kændl] n vela f; (esp large) candela f; (Eccl) cirio m; **to burn the** — **at both ends** consumir la vida, gastar sus fuerzas; **you can't hold a** — **to him** no llegas a la suela de su zapato.

candlelight ['kændllait] n luz f de una vela; **by** — a la luz de una vela.

Candlemas ['kændlmæs] n Candelaria f (2 febrero).

candle power ['kændl,pauə*] n bujía f.

candlestick ['kændlstik] n (single) candelero m; (low) palmatoria f; (large, ornamental) candelabro m; (processional) cirial m.

candlewick ['kændlwik] n pabilo m, mecha f (de vela).

candour, (US) **candor** ['kændə*] n franqueza f.

candy ['kændi] **1** n azúcar m cande; (US) bombón m, dulce m. **2** vt azucarar, garapiñar.

candy-floss ['kændiflɔs] n caramelo m americano.

candy store ['kændistɔ:*] n (US) bombonería f, confitería f.

cane [kein] **1** n (Bot) caña f; (sugar-) caña f de azúcar; (stick) bastón m; (for punishment) palmeta f, vara f; (in furnishings) mimbre f.
　2 vt castigar con palmeta.

canine ['kænain] **1** adj canino; — **tooth** diente m canino, colmillo m. **2** n (dog) perro m, can m; (tooth) canino m, colmillo m.

caning ['keiniŋ] n castigo m con palmeta; **to give someone a** — castigar a uno con la palmeta, (fig) cascar a uno.

canister ['kænistə*] n lata f, bote m.

canker ['kæŋkə*] **1** n (Med) llaga f gangrenosa; úlcera f en la boca; (Bot) cancro m; (fig) cáncer m.
　2 vt ulcerar; (fig) corromper.
　3 vi ulcerarse; (fig) corromperse.

cankerous ['kæŋkərəs] adj ulceroso.

cannabis ['kænəbis] n marijuana f.

canned ['kænd] **1** pret and ptp of **can**[2]. **2** adj food en lata, de lata; music (fam) en discos, grabado; person (sl) borracho.

cannery ['kænəri] n fábrica f de conservas alimenticias.

cannibal ['kænibəl] **1** adj antropófago. **2** n caníbal mf, antropófago m.

cannibalism ['kænibəlizəm] n canibalismo m.

cannibalize ['kænibəlaiz] **1** vt (a) someter al canibalismo, practicar el canibalismo en.
　(b) (fig) **to** — **an old car** desmontar un coche viejo para aprovechar sus piezas como repuestos.
　2 vi practicar el canibalismo.

canning ['kæniŋ] n enlatado m; — **industry** industria f conservera.

cannon ['kænən] **1** n cañón m; (collectively) artillería f; (Billiards) carambola f.
　2 vi (Billiards) hacer carambola; **to** — **into** chocar violentamente con; **to** — **off** rebotar contra.

cannonade [,kænə'neid] n cañoneo m.

cannonball ['kænənbɔ:l] n bala f de cañón.

cannon fodder ['kænən,fɔdə*] n carne f de cañón.

cannon-shot ['kænənʃɔt] n cañonazo m, tiro m de cañón; (ammunition) bala f de cañón; **within** — al alcance de un cañón.

cannot ['kænɔt] negative of **can**[1].

canny ['kæni] adj (Scot) astuto.

canoe [kə'nu:] **1** n canoa f; (sporting) piragua f. **2** vi ir en canoa.

canoeing [kə'nu:iŋ] n piragüismo m.

canoeist [kə'nu:ist] n piragüista mf.

canon ['kænən] n canon m; (Typ) gran canon m; (person) canónigo m; — **law** derecho m canónico.

canonical [kə'nɔnikəl] adj canónico.

canonization [,kænənai'zeiʃən] n canonización f.

canonize ['kænənaiz] vt canonizar.

canonry ['kænənri] n canonjía f.

canoodle [kə'nu:dl] vi (sl) besuquearse.

can opener ['kænəupnə*] n abrelatas m.

canopy ['kænəpi] n dosel m, toldo m; (over bed) cielo m; (Archit) baldaquín m; (over tomb) doselete m; **the** — **of heaven** la bóveda celeste.

cant[1] [kænt] **1** n (slope) inclinación f, sesgo m; (of crystal etc) bisel m. **2** vt inclinar, sesgar. **3** vi inclinarse, ladearse; **to — over** volcar.

cant² [kænt] **1** n (special language) jerga f; (hypocritical talk) hipocresías fpl, camándulas fpl, gazmoñería f. **2** vi camandulear.

can't [ka:nt] = **cannot.**

Cantabrian [kæn'tæbriən] adj cantábrico.

cantaloup ['kæntəlu:p] n cantalupo m.

cantankerous [kæn'tæŋkərəs] adj arisco, malhumorado, irritable.

cantata [kæn'ta:tə] n cantata f.

canteen [kæn'ti:n] n (bar) cantina f; (bottle) cantimplora f; (of cutlery) juego m.

canter ['kæntə*] **1** n medio galope m; **to win in a —** (fig) ganar fácilmente. **2** vi ir a medio galope.

Canterbury ['kæntəberi] Cantórbery.

cantharides [kæn'θæridi:z] npl polvo m de cantárida.

canticle ['kæntikl] n cántico m; **the C—s** el Cantar de los Cantares.

cantilever ['kæntili:və*] n viga f voladiza; **— bridge** puente m voladizo.

canting ['kæntiŋ] adj hipócrita.

canto ['kæntəu] n canto m.

canton ['kæntən] n cantón m.

cantonal ['kæntənl] adj cantonal.

Cantonese [,kæntə'ni:z] **1** adj cantonés. **2** n cantonés m, esa f. **3** n (dialect) cantonés m.

cantonment [kən'tu:nmənt] n acantonamiento m.

canvas ['kænvəs] n lona f; (Art) lienzo m; (Naut) velamen m, velas fpl; **under —** en tiendas de campaña.

canvass ['kænvəs] **1** n (inquiry) sondeo m; (for votes) solicitación f; **to make a door-to-door —** ir solicitando votos de puerta en puerta.

2 vt possibility, question discutir, hacer que se discuta, someter a una discusión pública; opinion sondear; votes solicitar; voter solicitar el voto de.

3 vi: **to — for** solicitar votos por, hacer campaña a favor de.

canvasser ['kænvəsə*] n (Pol) solicitador m, ora f (de votos).

canvassing ['kænvəsiŋ] n solicitación f (de votos).

canyon ['kænjən] n cañón m.

cap [kæp] **1** n **(a)** (hat) gorra f; (Univ) bonete m; (servant's etc) cofia f; **cloth —** gorra f de paño; **peaked —** gorra f de visera; **— and gown** toga f y bonete; **to come — in hand to someone** venir a uno con el sombrero en la mano; **if the — fits wear it** el que se pica ajos come; **to put on one's thinking —** meditarlo bien; **to set one's — at someone** proponerse conquistar a uno como novio.

(b) (lid) tapa f, tapón m; (of gun, bottle) cápsula f; (of pen) capuchón m; (on chimney) caballete m; (Mech) casquete m; **polar —** casquete m polar.

2 vt hill etc coronar; work terminar, poner remate a; (surpass) exceder, superar; **see if you can — that story** a ver si cuentas un chiste mejor que ése; **I can — that** yo sé algo mejor sobre el mismo asunto; **to — it all** para colmo de desgracias.

capability [keipə'biləti] n capacidad f, aptitud f.

capable ['keipəbl] adj capaz, competente; **to be — of** ser capaz de; **it's — of some improvement** es susceptible de ser algo mejorado.

capably ['keipəbli] adv competentemente.

capacious [kə'peiʃəs] adj room grande, extenso, espacioso; container grande, capaz; dress ancho, holgado.

capacity [kə'pæsiti] **1** n capacidad f; (Aut) cilindrada f; **carrying —** capacidad f de cargo; **effective —**, **useful —** capacidad f útil; **seating —** cabida f, número m de asientos; **filled to —** totalmente lleno; **in my —** as en mi calidad de.

2 attr: **there was a — crowd** el campo (or teatro etc) estuvo totalmente lleno.

caparison [kə'pærisn] **1** n caparazón m, gualdrapa f; (harness etc) equipo m.

2 vt engualdrapar; **gaily —ed** brillantemente enjaezado, (fig) brillantemente vestido.

cape¹ [keip] n (Geog) cabo m, promontorio m.

cape² [keip] n capa f; (short) capotillo m, esclavina f; (of fur) cuello m; (oilskin) chubasquero m.

Cape Horn ['keip'hɔ:n] Cabo m de Hornos.

Cape of Good Hope ['keipʊgud'həup] Cabo m de Buena Esperanza.

caper¹ ['keipə*] n (Bot) alcaparra f.

caper² ['keipə*] **1** n **(a)** (of horse) cabriola f; **to cut —s** hacer cabriolas.

(b) (fig) (prank) travesura f; (fam) lío m, embrollo m; **that was quite a —** eso sí que fue un lío; **how did your Spanish — go?** ¿qué tal el viajecito por España?

2 vi (horse) hacer cabriolas; (other animal) brincar, corcovear; (child) juguetear, correr y brincar; (fam) ir, correr; **to — about** brincar, juguetear; **he went —ing off to Paris** se marchó a París como si tal cosa.

capercaillie [,kæpə'keili] n urogallo m.

capeskin ['keipskin] n (US) (especie f de) cabritilla f.

Cape Town ['keiptaun] Ciudad f del Cabo.

Cape Verde Islands ['keip'və:d'ailəndz] pl Islas fpl de Cabo Verde.

capillarity [,kæpi'læriti] n capilaridad f.

capillary [kə'piləri] **1** adj capilar. **2** n vaso m capilar.

capital ['kæpitl] **1** adj capital; importance primordial; (fam) magnífico, estupendo; **—!** ¡magnífico!; **— city** capital f; **— gains** ganancias fpl (por venta de bienes) de capital; **— goods** bienes mpl de capital; **— letter** mayúscula f; **— punishment** pena f de muerte; **— ship** acorazado m; **— sum** capital m.

2 n **(a)** (money) capital m; **working —** capital m de explotación; **to make — out of** (fig) aprovechar, sacar partido de.

(b) (city) capital f.

(c) (Archit) capitel m.

(d) (letter) mayúscula f; **large —s** (Typ) versales fpl; **small —s** (Typ) versalitas fpl.

capitalism ['kæpitəlizm] n capitalismo m.

capitalist ['kæpitəlist] **1** adj capitalista. **2** n capitalista mf.

capitalistic [,kæpitə'listik] adj capitalista.

capitalization [kə,pitəlai'zeiʃən] n capitalización f.

capitalize [kə'pitəlaiz] **1** vt capitalizar; (Typ) escribir (or imprimir) con mayúscula. **2** vi: **to — on** aprovechar, sarcar partido de.

capitation [,kæpi'teiʃən] n capitación f.

Capitol ['kæpitəl] n Capitolio m.

capitulate [kə'pitjuleit] vi capitular (to ante), rendirse, entregarse (to a); (fig) ceder, conformarse.

capitulation [kə,pitju'leiʃən] n capitulación f, rendición f.

capon ['keipən] n capón m.

caprice [kə'pri:s] n capricho m.

capricious [kə'priʃəs] adj caprichoso, caprichudo.

capriciously [kə'priʃəsli] adv caprichosamente.

Capricorn ['kæprikɔ:n] Capricornio m.

capsicum ['kæpsikəm] n pimiento m.

capsize [kæp'saiz] **1** vt volcar; (Naut) hacer zozobrar, tumbar. **2** vi volcarse, dar una vuelta de campana; (Naut) zozobrar.

capstan ['kæpstən] n cabrestante m.

capsule ['kæpsju:l] n (all senses) cápsula f.

captain ['kæptin] **1** n capitán m; **— of industry** gran industrial m, magnate m.

2 vt capitanear, ser el capitán de; **a team —ed by Grace** un equipo capitaneado por Grace.

captaincy ['kæptənsi] n capitanía f.

caption ['kæpʃən] **1** n (heading) encabezamiento m, título m; (to cartoon etc) pie m; (in film) subtítulo m.

2 vt titular; poner un pie a.

captious ['kæpʃəs] adj criticón, reparón.

captivate ['kæptiveit] vt cautivar, encantar.

captivating ['kæptiveitiŋ] adj encantador, delicioso.

captive ['kæptiv] **1** adj cautivo. **2** n cautivo m, a f.

captivity [kæp'tiviti] n cautiverio m.

captor ['kæptə*] n apresador m, ora f.

capture ['kæptʃə*] **1** n **(a)** (act) apresamiento m, captura f; (of city etc) toma f, conquista f.

(b) (thing captured) presa f.

2 vt person prender; apresar; specimen etc capturar; animal coger; city etc tomar, conquistar; (fig) captar; attention llamar, atraer; interest ocupar; (Art etc) captar, reproducir, representar fielmente.

capuchin ['kæpuʃin] **(a)** (cowl) capucho m. **(b)** (Zool) mono m capuchino. **(c)** **C—** (Eccl) capuchino m.

car [ka:*] n (Aut) coche m, automóvil m; (tramcar) tranvía m; (Rail) vagón m, coche m; (of cable railway) coche m; (of lift) caja f; (of balloon etc) barquilla f; **racing —** coche m de carreras; **saloon —, touring —** turismo m.

carafe [kə'ræf] n garrafa f.

caramel ['kærəməl] n caramelo m.

carapace ['kærəpeis] n carapacho m.

carat ['kærət] n quilate m.

caravan ['kærəvæn] n (gipsies') carricoche m, carromato m; (trailer, for holidays) caravana f, remolque m, rulota f, roulotte f; (of camels) caravana f.

caravel ['kærə'vel] n carabela f.

caraway ['kærəwei] n alcaravea f.

carbide ['ka:baid] n carburo m.

carbine ['ka:bain] n carabina f.

carbohydrate ['ka:bəu'haidreit] n hidrato m de carbono; (starch in food) fécula f.

carbolic [ka:'bɔlik] adj: **— acid** ácido m carbólico.

carbon ['kɑːbən] carbono m; (Elec, — paper) carbón m; — **dioxide** bióxido m de carbono; — **monoxide** monóxido m de carbono.
carbonaceous [ˌkɑːbə'neiʃəs] adj carbonoso.
carbonate ['kɑːbənit] n carbonato m.
carbon copy ['kɑːbən'kɔpi] n copia f al carbón.
carbonic [kɑː'bɔnik] adj: — **acid** ácido m carbónico.
carboniferous [ˌkɑːbə'nifərəs] adj carbonífero.
carbonization [ˌkɑːbənai'zeiʃən] n carbonización f.
carbonize ['kɑːbənaiz] **1** vt carbonizar. **2** vi carbonizarse.
carbon paper ['kɑːbən,peipə*] n papel m carbón.
carborundum [ˌkɑːbə'rʌndəm] n carborundo m.
carboy ['kɑːbɔi] n bombona f, garrafón m.
carbuncle ['kɑːbʌŋkl] n (ruby) carbunclo m; (Med) carbunco m, grano m.
carburettor [ˌkɑːbjuˈretə*] n carburador m.
carcass ['kɑːkəs] n cadáver m de animal, res f muerta; (frame) armazón f; (fam) cuerpo m.
carcinogen [kɑː'sinədʒen] n agente m carcinogénico.
carcinogenic [ˌkɑːsinə'dʒenik] adj carcinogénico.
carcinoma ['kɑːsi'nəumə] n, pl **carcinomata** [ˌkɑːsi'nəumətə] carcinoma m.
card¹ [kɑːd] (Tech) **1** n carda f. **2** vt cardar.
card² [kɑːd] n (a) (playing-) carta f, naipe m; (Post) tarjeta f, postal f; (visiting-) tarjeta f; (index-) ficha f; (member's, press-) carnet m, carné m (Acad); (piece of cardboard) cartulina f; **to play** — s jugar a las cartas; **to lose money at** — s perder el dinero jugando a las cartas.
  (b) (idioms) **isn't he a** —? es célebre ¿no?, ¡qué tipo más salado!; **like a house of** — s como un castillo de naipes; **it is quite on the** — s **that . . .** es perfectamente posible que **. . . + subj; to have a** — **up one's sleeve** quedar a uno todavía un recurso; **to hold all the** — s tener los triunfos en la mano; **to lay one's** — s **on the table** poner las cartas boca arriba; **if you play your** — s **properly** si obras con el debido cuidado; **to speak by the** — hablar con conocimiento de causa.
cardamom ['kɑːdəməm] n cardamomo m.
cardboard ['kɑːbɔːd] n cartón m, cartulina f; — **box** caja f de cartón.
card catalogue ['kɑːd,kætəlɔg] n catálogo m de fichas, fichero m.
card game ['kɑːdgeim] n juego m de naipes.
cardiac ['kɑːdiæk] adj cardíaco.
cardigan ['kɑːdigən] n rebeca f.
cardinal ['kɑːdinl] **1** adj cardinal. **2** n cardenal m.
card index ['kɑːd,indeks] n fichero m.
cardiological [ˌkɑːdiə'lɔdʒikəl] adj cardiológico.
cardiologist [ˌkɑːdi'ɔlədʒist] n cardiólogo m.
cardiology [ˌkɑːdi'ɔlədʒi] n cardiología f.
card sharper ['kɑːd,ʃɑːpə*] n fullero m.
card table ['kɑːd,teibl] n mesa f de baraja, tapete m verde.
card trick ['kɑːd,trik] n juego m de naipes, truco m de naipes.
care [kɛə*] **1** n (a) (anxiety) cuidado m; inquietud f, solicitud f; **he has many** — s son muchas las cosas que le preocupan; **he hasn't a** — **in the world** le importa todo un rábano; **the** — s **of State** las responsabilidades de un cargo oficial, las preocupaciones y fatigas del gobierno.
  (b) (carefulness) cuidado m, esmero m, atención f; **"with —!"** "¡atención!", "¡cuidado!"; **have a** —, **sir!** ¡mire lo que está diciendo!; **to take** — tener cuidado; **take —!** ¡ten cuidado!, ¡ojo!; **to take** — **of** cuidar de, valuable object guardar, custodiar, thing to be done encargarse de; **I'll take** — **of him** (fam) yo me encargo de él; **that can take** — **of itself** eso se resolverá por sí mismo; **to take good** — **of oneself** cuidarse mucho; **to take** — **to + infin** cuidar de que + subj, asegurar que + subj; **he doesn't take enough** — **to + infin** no pone bastante cuidado en + infin; **to take** — **not to + infin** guardarse de + infin; **take** — **not to drop it!** ¡ten cuidado, no lo dejes caer!
  (c) (charge) cargo m, custodia f; (Med etc) asistencia f; — **of** (on letter) en casa de; **to be in the** — **of** estar bajo la custodia de; **he is in the** — **of Dr X** le asiste el doctor X, le atiende el doctor X.
  2 vi (a) (absolute) **what do I** —? ¿qué se me da a mí?, ¡maldito lo que me importa!; **as if I** —d! ¡cómo si eso tuviera que ver conmigo!; **I couldn't** — **less!** eso me trae sin cuidado; **for all I** — **you can take it** me resulta indiferente que lo tomes; **I don't** — me es igual, no me importa; **I don't** — **tuppence!** (or **a fig, hoot, jot, rap** etc) ¡me importa un comino!; **I don't** — **either way** me resulta indiferente; **I don't** — **what people say** me trae sin cuidado lo que diga la gente.

  (b) **to** — **about** preocuparse de (or por), tener interés en; **to** — **deeply about someone's fate** preocuparse hondamente por la suerte de uno; **that's all he** — s **about** es lo único que le interesa; **to** — **for** cuidar; person querer; **I don't** — **for the idea** no me hace gracia la idea; **I don't** — **for coffee** no me gusta el café; **would you** — **for a walk?** ¿te apetece dar un paseo?; **would you** — **for a drink?** ¿quieres tomar algo?; **the kids are being** —d **for by their aunt** los niños los está cuidando su tía; **well** —d **for** bien cuidado; **to** — **to + infin** tener ganas de + infin; **if you** — **to** si Vd quiere; **would you** — **to tell me?** ¿quiere Vd decírmelo?; **would you** — **to go for a walk?** ¿te apetece dar un paseo?, ¿te gustaría dar un paseo?; **would you** — **to take off your hat?** ¿tendría inconveniente en quitarse el sombrero?
careen [kə'riːn] vt carenar.
career [kə'riə*] **1** n carrera f; — **diplomat** (US) diplomático m de carrera. **2** vi correr a toda velocidad.
careerist [kə'riərist] n ambicioso m, a f.
carefree ['kɛəfriː] adj despreocupado, libre de preocupaciones, alegre, inconsciente.
careful ['kɛəful] adj cuidadoso; **piece of work** esmerado; (in acting) cauteloso, prudente; (with money) económico, ahorrativo, (pej) tacaño; —! ¡cuidado!, ¡ojo!; **to be** — tener cuidado; **be** —! ¡ten cuidado!; **one can't be too** — nunca se peca por demasiado cuidadoso; **we must be very** — **here** en esto conviene andar con pies de plomo; **be** — **what you say to him** ten cuidado con lo que le dices; **to be** — **of** tener cuidado con; **to be** — **to + infin** poner diligencia en + infin, asegurar cuidadosamente que + subj; **he was** — **to say that . . .** dijo de modo particular que . . .
carefully ['kɛəfəli] adv con cuidado, cuidadosamente; **we must go** — **here** en esto conviene andar con pies de plomo; **I have to spend** — tengo que pensar mucho en lo que gasto; **he replied** — contestó con cautela.
carefulness ['kɛəfulnis] n cuidado m; esmero m; prudencia f, cautela f; economía f, tacañería f.
careless ['kɛəlis] adj descuidado; (inattentive) poco atento; (thoughtless) irreflexivo, imprudente; **stroke** hecho a la ligera; **appearance** descuidado, desaliñado; (— **of others**) indiferente, insensible (**of** a); **that was very** — **of you** en eso ha sido Vd muy imprudente.
carelessly ['kɛəlisli] adv descuidadamente; a la ligera.
carelessness ['kɛəlisnis] n descuido m; falta f de atención; desaliño m; indiferencia f (**of** a); **through sheer** — por simple descuido, por simple falta de atención.
caress [kə'res] **1** n caricia f. **2** vt acariciar.
caressing [kə'resiŋ] adj acariciador, acariciante, seductor.
caret ['kærət] n signo m de intercalación (�‸).
caretaker ['kɛə,teikə*] n vigilante m; (in museum etc) guardián m; (of flats) portero m, conserje m, casero m.
careworn ['kɛəwɔːn] adj agobiado de inquietudes.
carfare ['kɑːfɛə*] n pasaje m, precio m (del billete).
car-ferry ['kɑː,feri] n transbordador m para coches.
cargo ['kɑːgəu] n cargamento m, carga f.
cargo boat ['kɑːgəubəut] n barco m de carga.
carhop ['kɑːhɔp] n (US) camarero m de motel, camarera f de motel.
Caribbean [ˌkæri'biːən] adj caribe.
Caribbean Sea [ˌkæri'biːən'siː] Mar m Caribe.
caribou ['kæribuː] n caribú m.
caricature ['kærikətjuə*] **1** n caricatura f; (in newspaper) dibujo m cómico. **2** vt caricaturizar.
caricaturist [ˌkærikə'tjuərist] n caricaturista mf, dibujante mf.
caries ['kɛəriiːz] n caries f.
carillon [kə'riljən] n carillón m.
carious ['kɛəriəs] adj cariado.
Carlism ['kɑːlizəm] n carlismo m.
Carlist ['kɑːlist] **1** adj carlista. **2** n carlista mf.
Carmelite ['kɑːməlait] **1** adj carmelita. **2** n carmelita mf.
carminative ['kɑːminətiv] **1** adj carminativo. **2** n carminativo m.
carmine ['kɑːmain] **1** adj carmíneo. **2** n carmín m.
carnage ['kɑːnidʒ] n carnicería f, mortandad f.
carnal ['kɑːnl] adj carnal.
carnation [kɑː'neiʃən] n clavel m.
carnelian [kɑː'niːliən] n cornalina f, cornerina f.
carnival ['kɑːnivəl] n carnaval m; fiesta f, feria f; — **queen** reina f de la fiesta, dama f regidora.
carnivore ['kɑːnivɔː*] n carnívoro m.
carnivorous [kɑː'nivərəs] adj carnívoro.

carol ['kærəl] **1** n vil ancico m. **2** vi cantar alegremente.

Carolingian [kærə'linʒiən] adj carolingio.

carotid [kə'rɒtid] n carótida f.

carousal [kə'rauzəl] n jarana f, parranda f.

carouse [kə'rauz] vi jaranear, estar de parranda.

carp¹ [kɑːp] n carpa f.

carp² [kɑːp] vi criticar (sin motivo); **to —** at quejarse (sin motivo) de, murmurar de.

car park ['kɑːpɑːk] n aparcamiento m, parque m.

Carpathians [kɑːˈpeiθiənz] pl Montes mpl Cárpatos.

carpenter ['kɑːpintə*] n carpintero m.

carpentry ['kɑːpintri] n carpintería f.

carpet ['kɑːpit] **1** n alfombra f; **to be on the —** (fam) tener que aguantar un rapapolvo; **to roll out the red — for someone** volcarse para festejar la llegada de uno.
2 vt alfombrar; (fig) alfombrar, cubrir, revestir (with de); **to — someone** (fam) echar un rapapolvo a uno.

carpetbagger ['kɑːpit.bægə*] n (US) aventurero m político, explotador m político (venido de fuera).

carpet slippers ['kɑːpit.slipəz] npl zapatillas fpl.

carpet sweeper ['kɑːpit.swiːpə*] n aspirador m.

carping ['kɑːpiŋ] adj criticón, reparón.

carport ['kɑːpɔːt] n garaje m abierto, cobertizo m para coche.

carriage ['kærid3] n **(a)** (Rail) vagón m, coche m; (horse-drawn) carruaje m, coche m; (of gun) cureña f; (of typewriter etc) carro m.
(b) (bearing) andares mpl, modo m de andar, porte m.
(c) (act of carrying) transporte m; (Comm) porte m; **— free** franco de porte; **— paid** porte pagado.

carriage drive ['kærid3draiv] n calzada f.

carriage trade ['kærid3.treid] n (US) clientela f de gente acaudalada.

carriageway ['kærid3wei] n carretera f; **dual —** (Aut) carretera f de dos calles, carretera f de doble calzada.

carrier ['kæriə*] n (person) trajinante m, carrero m (ordinario); (company) empresa f de transportes; (Med) portador m, ora f (de gérmenes); (on car, cycle) portaequipajes m; (Naut) portaaviones m.

carrier-bag ['kæriə'bæg] n pequeño saco m de papel (para compras).

carrion ['kæriən] n carroña f; inmundicia f.

carrion crow ['kæriən'krəu] n corneja f negra.

carrot ['kærət] n zanahoria f.

carroty ['kærəti] adj pelirrojo.

carrousel [kæru:'sel] n carusel m, tiovivo m.

carry ['kæri] **1** n alcance m.
2 vt llevar; traer; transportar, acarrear; burden, weight sostener; (on one's person) llevar encima, tener consigo; (Math) llevar; stock tener en existencia; meaning tener; interpretation encerrar, llevar implícito; (in the mind) retener; (extend) extender, prolongar; (Mil) conquistar, tomar; (Parl) seat ganar, ganar las elecciones en; proposition hacer aceptar; motion aprobar; **to — the committee with one** persuadir al comité a que apruebe lo que se le propone; **to — one's audience with one** meterse al auditorio en el bolsillo; **to — about** llevar consigo; llevar de acá para allá; **to — along** llevar; (water etc) arrastrar; **to — away** llevarse; (kidnap) secuestrar; (fig) arrebatar, inspirar, entusiasmar; **to get carried away** exaltarse, entusiasmarse (demasiado), extasiarse, hacerse inconsciente de la situación real; **to — all before one** vencer todos los obstáculos, arrollarlo todo; **to — down** bajar; **to — something too far** exagerar algo, llevar algo al exceso; **to — forward** (Comm) pasar a cuenta nueva; **carried forward** suma y sigue; **to — off** llevarse; prize alzarse con, ganar; election ganar; (kill) matar; **he carried it off splendidly** salió muy airoso de la prueba, su actuación fue brillante; **to — on** work continuar, proseguir; business poseer, tener, ser dueño de; **to — out** order, threat, promise cumplir; plan llevar a cabo, poner por obra; intention realizar; repairs hacer; test verificar; **to — over** guardar para más tarde; (Comm) pasar a cuenta nueva; **to — through** llevar a cabo; person sostener hasta el fin; **to — up** subir.
3 vi (reach) alcanzar, llegar; (sound) oírse; **to — on (a)** (continue) continuar, seguir adelante; **if you — on like that** como sigas en ese plan; **we — on somehow** vamos tirando; **— on!** ¡adelante!, ¡siga!, (in talking) ¡prosigue!
(b) (fam: complain) quejarse, protestar; murmurar (about de).
(c) (fam: insist) insistir, machacar (about en); **you do — on!** ¡dale que dale!; **don't — on so!** ¡no machaques!

(d) (fam: amorously) **to be —ing on with someone** tener un plan con uno.
4 vr: **to — oneself** andar; **to — oneself well** andar con garbo, tener buena presencia.

carryall ['kæriɔːl] n (US) cesto m grande; **= holdall**.

carrycot ['kærikɒt] n cuna f portátil, capazo m.

carrying-on ['kæriiŋ'ɒn] n **(a)** continuación f; prosecución f.
(b) (fam) plan m, relaciones fpl amorosas (ilícitas); **I don't approve of their —** no apruebo sus relaciones.

carry-on [.kæri'ɒn] n (fam) aspaviento m, conmoción f, alharaca f; lío m; riña f, pelea f; **there was a great — about the tickets** se armó un tremendo lío a causa de los billetes; **did you ever see such a —?** ¿se ha visto igual?

carry-over ['kæri'əuvə*] n (surplus) sobrante m; (Comm) suma f anterior, suma f que pasa de una página (de cuenta) a la siguiente.

cart [kɑːt] **1** n carro m, carreta f; (heavy) carretón m; (hand-) carretilla f, carro m de mano; **to be in the —** (fam) estar en un atolladero; **to put the — before the horse** trastrocar las cosas, tomar el rábano por las hojas.
2 vt llevar, acarrear, carretear; (fam) llevar (con gran dificultad).

cartage ['kɑːtid3] n acarreo m, porte m.

carte blanche ['kɑːt'blɑːnʃ] n carta f blanca; **to give someone —** dar carta blanca a uno.

cartel [kɑːˈtel] n cartel m.

carter ['kɑːtə*] n carretero m.

Cartesian [kɑːˈtiːziən] **1** adj cartesiano. **2** n cartesiano m.

Carthage ['kɑːθid3] Cartago f.

Carthaginian [.kɑːθə'd3iniən] **1** adj cartaginés. **2** n cartaginés m, esa f.

cart-horse ['kɑːthɔːs] n caballo m de tiro.

Carthusian [kɑːˈθjuːziən] **1** adj cartujano. **2** n cartujo m, cartujano m.

cartilage ['kɑːtilid3] n cartílago m.

cartilaginous [.kɑːti'læd3inəs] adj cartilaginoso.

cartload ['kɑːtləud] n carretada f (also fig); **by the —** a carretadas, a montones.

cartographer [kɑːˈtɒgrəfə*] n cartógrafo m.

cartography [kɑːˈtɒgrəfi] n cartografía f.

carton ['kɑːtən] n envase m, caja f de cartón.

cartoon [kɑːˈtuːn] n (newspaper) dibujo m cómico, caricatura f; (Art) cartón m; (film) dibujos mpl animados, película f de dibujos.

cartoonist [.kɑːˈtuːnist] n dibujante mf, caricaturista mf.

cartridge ['kɑːtrid3] n cartucho m; **blank —** cartucho m sin bala.

cartridge belt ['kɑːtrid3belt] n cartuchera f, canana f.

cartridge case ['kɑːtrid3keis] n cartucho m.

cartridge paper ['kɑːtrid3.peipə*] n papel m guarro, papel m camso.

cart-track ['kɑːttræk] n (rut) carril m, rodada f; (road) camino m (para carros).

cartulary ['kɑːtjuləri] n cartulario m.

cartwheel ['kɑːtwiːl] n rueda f de carro; (fig) salto m mortal de lado, rueda f.

cartwright ['kɑːtrait] n carretero m.

carve [kɑːv] vt meat trinchar; stone esculpir, tallar, labrar; name on tree etc grabar; **to — one's way through** abrirse a la fuerza un camino por; **to — up** country dividir, repartir entre los vencedores; person coser a puñaladas.

carver ['kɑːvə*] n (Cook) trinchador m; (Art) escultor m, ora f, tallista mf; **—s** cubierto m de trinchar.

carving ['kɑːviŋ] n (Cook) arte m de trinchar; (Art) escultura f, obra f de talla.

carving knife ['kɑːviŋnaif] n, pl **— knives** [naivz] trinchante m.

car wash ['kɑːwɒʃ] n lavado m de coches.

caryatid [.kæri'ætid] n cariátide f.

cascade [kæs'keid] **1** n cascada f, salto m de agua; (fig) chorro m; torrente m. **2** vi caer.

cascara [kæs'kɑːrə] n cáscara f sagrada.

case¹ [keis] **1** n (container) caja f; (packing-) cajón m; (suitcase) maleta f; (for jewels, spectacles etc) estuche m; (for scissors etc) vaina f; (of watch) caja f; (of window) marco m, bastidor m; (of cartridge) cartucho m, cápsula f; (showcase) vitrina f; (Typ) caja f; **lower —** caja f baja; **upper —** caja f alta.
2 vt encajonar; enfundar; **—d in concrete** revestido de hormigón.

case² [keis] n (a) caso m (also Gram, Med); asunto m; **a fever —** un caso de fiebre; **a hospital —** un caso para el hospital, un enfermo que tendrá que ser trasladado al hospital; **a — in point** un ejemplo que hace al caso; **it's a sad —** es un caso triste; **it's a hopeless —** es un caso desahuciado; **it's a — for the police** éste es asunto para la policía; **it's a clear — of murder** es un claro caso de homicidio; **he's working on the train-robbery —** está haciendo investigaciones sobre el robo del tren; **he's a —** es una persona rarísima.

(b) **there seems to be a — for reform** parece que hay razones para reformarlo; **that alters the —** eso cambia la cosa; **I understand that is not the —** tengo entendido que no es así; **if that is the —,** such being the — si las cosas son así; **as the — may be** según el caso.

(c) *(with prep)* **in — he comes** por si viene, (en) caso de que venga; **in — of** en caso de; **in your —** en el caso de Vd; **as in the —** of como en el caso de; **in most —s** en la mayoría de los casos; **in any —** en todo caso, de todas formas; **just in —** por si acaso, por si las moscas; **in such a —** en tal caso; **in that —** en ese caso.

(d) *(Law)* causa *f*, pleito *m*, proceso *m*; **the — for the defence** la defensa, el conjunto de razones alegadas por el acusado; **the — for the prosecution** la acusación, el conjunto de acusaciones alegadas por el fiscal; **the Dreyfus —** el proceso de Dreyfus, (*more loosely*) el asunto Dreyfus; **there is no — to answer** no hay acusación que merezca la pena de rechazarse; **to have a good** (*or* **strong) —** tener argumentos fuertes (*for* para); **to make out a good —** presentar argumentos convincentes (*for* para); **to put** (*or* **state) one's —** presentar sus argumentos; **to rest one's —** terminar la presentación de argumentos.

casebook ['keisbuk] *n* diario *m*, registro *m* (*de un médico, detective etc*).

case-hardened ['keis,hɑːdnd] *adj* cementado; (*fig*) insensible, poco compasivo.

case history ['keis'histəri] *n* historia *f*, historial *m*, antecedentes *mpl*; **what is the patient's —?** ¿cuál es la historia médica del enfermo?; **I'll give you the full —** le contaré la historia con todos los detalles.

casement ['keismənt] *n* ventana *f* a bisagra; (*frame*) marco *m* de ventana.

casework ['keiswɔːk] *n* asistencia *f* social individualizada, casework *m*.

caseworker ['keis,wɔːkə*] *n* asistente *m* social, caseworker *mf*.

cash [kæʃ] **1** *n* dinero *m* contante; (*fam*) dinero *m*; (*cashdesk*) caja *f*; **hard —** dinero *m* contante y sonante; **petty —** (dinero *m* para) gastos *mpl* menores; **— down, for —** al contado; **— payment, — terms** pago *m* al contado; **— price** precio *m* al contado; **— prize** premio *m* en metálico; **— in hand** efectivo *m* en caja; **— on delivery** pagar contra recepción; **in —** en metálico; **to be out of —** estar sin blanca; **to pay — for** pagar al contado.

2 *vt cheque* cobrar, hacer efectivo.

3 *vi:* **to — in on** sacar partido de, aprovechar.

cash-and-carry ['kæʃən'kæri] *attr:* **— system** sistema *m* de pago al contado con el transporte pagado por el comprador.

cashbook ['kæʃbuk] *n* libro *m* de caja.

cashbox ['kæʃbɔks] *n* caja *f*.

cash crop ['kæʃkrɔp] *n* cultivo *m* que se vende inmediatamente después de la recolección (*sin almacenar*); producción *f* agrícola que tiene una salida fácil.

cashdesk ['kæʃdesk] *n* caja *f*.

cashew [kæ'ʃuː] *n* (*also* — **nut**) anacardo *m*.

cashier [kæ'ʃiə*] **1** *n* cajero *m*, a *f*. **2** *vt* separar del servicio.

cashmere [kæʃ'miə*] *n* casimir *m*, cachemira *f*.

cash register ['kæʃ,redʒistə*] *n* caja *f* registradora.

casing ['keisiŋ] *n* caja *f*, cubierta *f*, envoltura *f*, revestimiento *m*.

casino [kə'siːnəu] *n* casino *m*.

cask [kɑːsk] *n* tonel *m*, barril *m*.

casket ['kɑːskit] *n* cajita *f*, cofrecito *m*, estuche *m*, arquilla *f*; (*US*) ataúd *m*.

Caspian Sea ['kæspiən,siː] Mar *m* Caspio.

Cassandra [kə'sændrə] *f* Casandra.

cassava [kə'sɑːvə] *n* mandioca *f*.

casserole ['kæsərəul] *n* cacerola *f*.

Cassius ['kæsiəs] *m* Casio.

cassock ['kæsək] *n* sotana *f*.

cassowary ['kæsəwɛəri] *n* casuario *m*.

cast [kɑːst] **1** *n* (*throw*) echada *f*; (*shape*) forma *f*, molde *m*; (*plaster-*) vaciado *m*; (*Metal*) pieza *f* fundida; (*Theat*) reparto *m*, personal *m*; (*in eye*) defecto *m*; **— of features** facciones *fpl*, fisonomía *f*; **— of mind** temperamento *m*; inclinación *f*.

2 (*irr: pret and ptp* **cast**) *vt* (*throw*) echar, lanzar, arrojar; *anchor, blame, glance, lots, net etc* echar; *eyes* volver (*on* a, hacia); *shadow* proyectar; *light* arrojar (*on* sobre); *skin* mudar; (*lose*) perder; *vote* dar; (*in a mould*) vaciar; (*Metal*) fundir; *horoscope* hacer; (*Theat*) *parts in a play* repartir; *part* asignar; **to — an actor in** (*or* **for) the part of** dar a un actor el papel de; **he was — as the king** le dieron el papel del rey; **to — aside** desechar; **to — away** desechar, tirar; abandonar; **to be — away** (*Naut*) naufragar; **to be — away on a desert island** naufragar y arribar a una isla desierta; **to — down** derribar; (*fig*) desanimar; *eyes* bajar; **to be — down** estar deprimido; **to — forth** despedir; **to — loose** soltar; **to — off** abandonar; *wife* repudiar; *burden* deshacerse de, quitar de encima; (*Knitting*) terminar (la última hilera de puntadas de); **to — on** (*Knitting*) montar; **to — out** arrojar, echar fuera de sí; **to — up** echar; vomitar; *account* sumar.

3 *vi* (*Fishing*) lanzar, arrojar; **to — about for** buscar, andar buscando; **to — off** soltar las amarras, desamarrar.

castanets [,kæstə'nets] *n pl* castañuelas *fpl*.

castaway ['kɑːstəwei] *n* náufrago *m*, a *f*.

caste [kɑːst] *n* casta *f*; **to lose —** desprestigiarse.

castellated ['kæstəleitid] *adj* almenado.

caster ['kɑːstə*] *n see* **castor**.

castigate ['kæstigeit] *vt* castigar.

castigation [,kæsti'geiʃən] *n* castigo *m*.

Castile [kæs'tiːl] Castilla *f*.

Castilian [kæs'tiliən] **1** *adj* castellano. **2** *n* castellano *m*, a *f*. **3** *n* (*language*) castellano *m*.

casting ['kɑːstiŋ] **1** *adj* *vote* de calidad, decisivo. **2** *n* pieza *f* fundida, pieza *f* de fundición.

castiron ['kɑːst'aiən] **1** *adj* hecho de hierro fundido; (*fig*) fuerte, duro; *will* inflexible; *case* sólido, convincente; *excuse* inatacable. **2** *n* hierro *m* colado, hierro *m* fundido.

castle ['kɑːsl] **1** *n* castillo *m*; (*Chess*) torre *f*, roque *m*; **to build —s in the air** construir castillos en el aire; **an Englishman's home is his —** la casa de un inglés es su castillo.

2 *vi* (*Chess*) enrocar.

castling ['kɑːsliŋ] *n* (*Chess*) enroque *m*.

cast-off ['kɑːstɔf] **1** *adj* *clothing etc* de desecho.

2 *n* persona *f* (*or* cosa) abandonada, persona *f* (*or* cosa) desechada, plato *m* de segunda mesa; **—s** ropa *f* de desecho.

castor[1] ['kɑːstə*] *n* (*at table*) azucarero *m*; **—s** convoy *m*, angarillas *fpl*.

castor[2] ['kɑːstə*] *n* (*wheel*) ruedecilla *f*.

castor oil ['kɑːstər'ɔil] *n* aceite *m* de ricino.

castor sugar ['kɑːstə'ʃugə*] *n* azúcar *m* extrafino.

castrate [kæs'treit] *vt* castrar.

castration [kæs'treiʃən] *n* castración *f*.

casual ['kæʒjul] *adj* **(a)** (*happening by chance*) fortuito, accidental; **a — glance** una mirada al azar; **a — stroll** un paseo sin propósito fijo; **in a — conversation I had with him** en una conversación sin trascendencia que tuve con él, en una conversación que por casualidad tuve con él; **a — remark** una observación hecha a la ligera; **a — meeting** un encuentro fortuito.

(b) (*offhand*) despreocupado; **he tried to sound —** se esforzó por parecer tan tranquilo como siempre; **to assume a —** air hacer como si nada; **he was very — about it** no daba importancia a la cosa.

(c) *clothing* de estar por casa, de sport.

(d) *labour* temporero, eventual; **— worker** jornalero *m*, temporero *m*.

casually ['kæʒjuli] *adv* **(a)** (*by chance*) por casualidad, de manera fortuita.

(b) (*offhandedly*) de manera despreocupada; **he said —** dijo con mucha tranquilidad; **I was — watching them** los miraba con aire distraído; **I said it quite —** lo dije sin darle importancia.

casualty ['kæʒjulti] *n* **(a)** (*Mil*) baja *f*; **casualties** pérdidas *fpl*; **there were heavy casualties** hubo pérdidas importantes.

(b) (*in accident*) víctima *f*, herido *m*, muerto *m*; **casualties** víctimas *fpl*; **fortunately there were no casualties** por fortuna no hubo víctimas.

casualty list ['kæʒjultilist] *n* (*Mil*) lista *f* de bajas; (*in accident*) lista *f* de víctimas.

casuist ['kæʒjuist] *n* casuista *mf*; (*pej*) sofista *mf*.

casuistry ['kæʒjuistri] *n* casuística *f*; (*pej*) sofismas *mpl*, razonamiento *m* falaz.

cat [kæt] *n* gato *m*, (*she-*) gata *f*; (*whip*) azote *m* con nueve ramales; **to be like a — on hot bricks** estar como gato sobre ascuas; **to lead a — and dog life** vivir como perros y gatos; **to let the — out of the bag** revelar el secreto; **to rain —s and dogs** llover a cántaros; **to see which way the — jumps** esperar a ver qué sesgo toma el asunto; **to set the — among the pigeons** meter los perros en danza; **there isn't room to swing a —** aquí no cabe un alfiler.

cataclysm ['kætəklizəm] n cataclismo m.

catacombs ['kætəku:mz] npl catacumbas fpl.

catafalque ['kætəfælk] n catafalco m.

Catalan ['kætəlæn] **1** adj catalán. **2** n catalán m, ana f. **3** n (language) catalán m.

catalepsy ['kætəlepsi] n catalepsia f.

cataleptic [,kætə'leptik] **1** adj cataléptico. **2** n cataléptico m, a f.

catalog (US), **catalogue** ['kætəlɔg] **1** n catálogo m; (of cards) fichero m. **2** vt catalogar, poner en un catálogo; **it is not —d** no consta en el catálogo.

Catalonia [,kætə'ləuniə] Cataluña f.

Catalonian [,kætə'ləuniən] see **Catalan**.

catalyst ['kætəlist] n catalizador m.

catamaran [,kætəmə'ræn] n catamarán m.

cat-and-mouse ['kætn'maus]: **to play a — game with someone** jugar al gato y ratón con uno.

catapult ['kætəpʌlt] **1** n (Hist and Aer) catapulta f; (boy's) tirador m. **2** vt (Aer) catapultar.

cataract ['kætərækt] n (Geog and Med) catarata f.

catarrh [kə'tɑ:*] n catarro m.

catastrophe [kə'tæstrəfi] n catástrofe f.

catastrophic [,kætə'strɔfik] adj catastrófico.

catbird ['kætbə:d] n pájaro m gato.

cat burglar ['kætbə:glə*] n balconero m.

cat call ['kætkɔ:l] **1** n silbo m, rechifla f. **2** vi silbar, rechiflar.

catch [kætʃ] **1** n (a) (act of catching) cogida f.
  (b) (quantity caught) pesca f, cantidad f de peces cogidos; **he's a good —** es un buen partido.
  (c) (of lock, on door) pestillo m; (of box, window) cerradura f; (small flange) fiador m.
  (d) (Mus) canon m.
  (e) (trick) trampa f; **there must be a — here somewhere** aquí debe haber trampa; **the — is la** dificultad es que; **a question with a — to it** una pregunta de pega.
  (f) **with a — in one's voice** con la voz entrecortada.
  2 (irr: pret and ptp **caught**) vt **(a)** (capture) coger, atrapar; (grasp) asir; (arrest) prender, detener; ball recoger, coger, parar; bus, train etc coger, tomar; (catch up with) alcanzar; **—!** ¡cógelo!, ¡toma!; **we only just caught the train** por poco perdimos el tren; **I caught my fingers in the door** me cogí los dedos en la puerta; **I caught my coat on that nail** mi chaqueta se enganchó en ese clavo; **I caught my head on that beam** di con la cabeza contra esa viga.
  (b) **to — someone a blow** dar un golpe a uno.
  (c) (surprise) sorprender, cazar, coger en una falta; **you'll not — me doing it** yo sería incapaz de hacer eso, yo nunca haría eso.
  (d) person's meaning comprender; (manage to hear) oír, llegar a oír; **I didn't quite — you** no oí lo que Vd dijo.
  (e) **the poet has caught the mood of the times** el poeta ha hecho revivir el espíritu de la época; **the painter has caught his expression** el pintor ha sabido captar su gesto.
  (f) (Med) contagiarse de, coger; habit tomar, adoptar.
  (g) breath suspender.
  (h) (fam) **to — it** merecerse un regaño (from de); **you'll — it!** ¡las vas a pagar!
  (i) **to — someone out** sorprender a uno, cazar a uno, coger a uno en una falta; **to — up** thing asir; person alcanzar, emparejar con.
  3 vi enredarse (in en), engancharse (on en); (Tech) engranar; (fire) encenderse; **to — at** tratar de coger, asir; **to — on** (see the joke) percibir lo gracioso del cuento; (tumble to something) caer en la cuenta; (get the knack) coger el tino; (song, craze etc) hacerse popular, alcanzar gran popularidad, afirmarse en el gusto del público; **it never really caught on** nunca logró establecerse; **to — on something** prender en algo, (parts of machine) rozar, ludir con; **to — on to** comprender; **to — up** ponerse al día; hacer los atrasos de trabajo (etc); ponerse al nivel de los demás; **to — up with** news ponerse al corriente de, person alcanzar.

catcher ['kætʃə*] n (Baseball) apañador m.

catching ['kætʃiŋ] adj (Med) contagioso; (fig) pegajoso.

catchment ['kætʃmənt] n: **— area** zona f de captación; **— basin** cuenca f.

catchpenny ['kætʃ,peni] adj de pacotilla, sin valor.

catch phrase ['kætʃfreiz] n tópico m; slogan m; (Radio etc) frase f típica.

catchword ['kætʃwə:d] n (Typ) reclamo m; (Theat) pie m; (catch phrase) tópico m.

catchy ['kætʃi] adj (Mus) pegajoso, pegadizo, que se pega.

catechize ['kætikaiz] vt catequizar.

catechism ['kætikizəm] n catequismo m.

categoric(al) [,kæti'gɔrik(əl)] adj categórico, terminante; refusal rotundo.

categorically [,kæti'gɔrikəli] adv state etc de modo terminante; refuse rotundamente.

categorize ['kætigəraiz] vt clasificar; **to — something** as calificar algo de.

category ['kætigəri] n categoría f.

cater ['keitə*] vi: **to — for** abastecer a, proveer comida a; (fig) atender a, proveer a; **to — for all tastes** atender a todos los gustos.

cater-cornered ['keitə'kɔ:nəd] (US) **1** adj diagonal. **2** adv diagonalmente.

caterer ['keitərə*] n abastecedor m, ora f, proveedor m, ora f.

catering ['keitəriŋ] n abastecimiento m; servicio m de comidas, servicio m de comedor.

caterpillar ['kætəpilə*] n oruga f, gusano m; **— track, — tread** rodado m de oruga; **— tractor** tractor m de oruga.

caterwaul ['kætəwɔ:l] vi chillar.

catfish ['kætfiʃ] n siluro m, bagre m.

catgut ['kætgʌt] n cuerda f de tripa; (Med) catgut m.

Catharine ['kæθərin] f Catalina.

catharsis [kə'θɑ:sis] n catarsis f.

cathartic [kə'θɑ:tik] **1** adj (Med) catártico, purgante; (Lit) catártico. **2** n purgante m.

cathedral [kə'θi:drəl] n catedral f; **— city** ciudad f episcopal; **— church** iglesia f catedral.

Catherine ['kæθərin] f Catalina; **— wheel** (firework) rueda f catalina.

catheter ['kæθitə*] n catéter m.

cathode ['kæθəud] n cátodo m; **— ray tube** tubo m de rayos catódicos.

catholic ['kæθəlik] adj católico; (fig) liberal, de amplias miras; **a person of — tastes** una persona a quien le gusta todo.

Catholic ['kæθəlik] **1** adj católico. **2** n católico m, a f.

Catholicism [kə'θɔlisizəm] n catolicismo m.

catkin ['kætkin] n amento m.

cat-lick ['kætlik] n (fam) lavado m de gato.

catlike ['kætlaik] adj felino, gatuno.

catmint ['kætmint] n, (US) **catnip** ['kætnip] n hierba f gatera.

catnap ['kætnæp] n siesta f breve.

Cato ['keitəu] m Catón.

cat-o'nine-tails ['kætə'nainteilz] n azote m con nueve ramales.

cat's-cradle ['kæts,kreidl] n cunas fpl, pata f de gallina.

cat's-paw ['kætspɔ:] n instrumento m.

catsup ['kætsəp] n (US) salsa f de tomate.

cattle ['kætl] npl ganado m, ganado m vacuno, vacas fpl.

cattleman ['kætlmæn] n, pl **—men** [men] ganadero m.

cattle raising ['kætlreiziŋ] n ganadería f.

cattle rustler ['kætlrʌslə*] n (US) ladrón m de ganado, cuatrero m.

cattle show ['kætlʃəu] n feria f de ganado.

cattle truck ['kætltrʌk] n (Aut) camión m ganadero; (Rail) vagón m para ganado.

catty ['kæti] adj malicioso, rencoroso.

Catullus [kə'tʌləs] m Catulo.

catwalk ['kætwɔ:k] n pasadizo m, pasarela f.

Caucasian [kɔ:'keiziən] **1** adj (by race) caucásico; (Geog) caucasiano. **2** n (by race) caucásico m, a f; (Geog) caucasiano m, a f.

Caucasus ['kɔ:kəsəs] Cáucaso m.

caucus ['kɔ:kəs] n camarilla f política.

caudal ['kɔ:dl] adj caudal.

caught [kɔ:t] pret and ptp of **catch**.

caul [kɔ:l] n redaño m.

cauldron ['kɔ:ldrən] n caldera f, calderón m.

cauliflower ['kɔliflauə*] n coliflor f; **— ear** (Boxing) oreja f deformada por los golpes.

caulk [kɔ:k] vt calafatear.

causal ['kɔ:zəl] adj causal.

causality [kɔ:'zæliti] n causalidad f.

causation [kɔ:'zeiʃən] n causalidad f.

causative ['kɔ:zətiv] adj causativo.

cause [kɔ:z] **1** n causa f, motivo m, razón f; (Law) causa f; lost **—** causa f perdida, causa f imposible; **with good —** con razón; **to be the — of** ser causa de, motivar; **there's no — for alarm** no hay para qué asustarse; **in the — of liberty** por la libertad; **it's all in a good —** todo esto tiene un propósito noble; **to die in a good —** morir por una causa noble; **to give — for complaint** dar motivo para que se queje uno; **you have — to be worried** Vd tiene buen motivo para inquietarse; **to make common —** with hacer un frente común con, hacer causa común con; **to show —** aducir argumentos convincentes; **to take up someone's —** apoyar la campaña de uno, acudir a la defensa de uno.

2 *vt* causar, motivar, provocar; **to — an accident** causar un accidente; **to — trouble** provocar un disturbio; armar un lío; **to — someone to do something** hacer que uno haga algo.

cause célèbre [,kɔːzei'lebr] *n* caso *m* célebre.
causeway ['kɔːzwei] *n* calzada *f*; *(in sea)* arrecife *m*.
caustic ['kɔːstik] *adj* cáustico; *(fig)* cáustico, mordaz; **— soda** sosa *f* cáustica.
cauterize ['kɔːtəraiz] *vt* cauterizar.
cautery ['kɔːtəri] *n* cauterio *m*.
caution ['kɔːʃən] **1** *n* **(a)** cautela *f*, prudencia *f*; **"—!"** "¡atención!"
    (b) *(warning)* advertencia *f*, amonestación *f*.
    (c) *(fam)* **he's a —** es un tío muy raro, *(amusing)* es un tío divertidísimo.
    2 *vt* amonestar *(against* contra).
cautionary ['kɔːʃənəri] *adj* *tale* de escarmiento, aleccionador.
cautious ['kɔːʃəs] *adj* cauteloso, prudente, precavido; **to make a — statement** hacer una declaración prudente; **to play a — game** jugar con mucha prudencia.
cautiously ['kɔːʃəsli] *adv* cautelosamente, con cautela.
cautiousness ['kɔːʃəsnis] *n* cautela *f*, prudencia *f*.
cavalcade [,kævəl'keid] *n* cabalgata *f*; *(fig)* desfile *m*.
cavalier [,kævə'liə*] **1** *adj* arrogante, desdeñoso; *treatment* sin miramientos.
    2 *n* caballero *m*; *(arch)* galán *m*; *(Hist) partidario del Rey en la Guerra Civil inglesa* (1641–49).
cavalierly [,kævə'liəli] *adv* arrogantemente, desdeñosamente; sin miramientos.
cavalry ['kævəlri] *n* caballería *f*.
cavalryman ['kævəlrimən] *n*, *pl* **-men** [mən] soldado *m* de caballería.
cave¹ [keiv] **1** *n* cueva *f*, caverna *f*. **2** *vi*: **to — in** derrumbarse, hundirse *(also fig)*.
cave² ['keivi] *interj*: **—!** ¡ojo!, ¡ahí viene!; **to keep —** estar a la mira.
caveat ['kæviæt] *n* advertencia *f*; *(Law)* advertencia *f* de suspensión; **to enter a —** hacer una advertencia.
cave dweller ['keiv,dwelə*] *n* cavernícola *mf*, troglodita *mf*.
cave-in ['keivin] *n (of roof etc)* derrumbe *m*, derrumbamiento *m*; *(of pavement etc)* socavón *m*.
caveman ['keivmæn] *n*, *pl* **-men** [men] hombre *m* de las cavernas; *(hum and iro)* machote *m*.
cave painting ['keiv,peintiŋ] *n* pintura *f* rupestre.
cavern ['kævən] *n* caverna *f*.
cavernous ['kævənəs] *adj* cavernoso.
caviar(e) ['kævia:*] *n* caviar *m*.
cavil ['kævil] **1** *n* reparo *m*. **2** *vi* sutilizar, critiquizar; **to — at** poner peros a, criticar sin motivo.
caving ['keiviŋ] *n* espeleología *f*.
cavity ['kæviti] *n* cavidad *f*, hueco *m*, hoyo *m*; **nasal cavities** fosas *fpl* nasales.
cavort [kə'vɔːt] *vi* dar cabrioladas; *(fig)* ir de juerga, divertirse ruidosamente.
cavy ['keivi] *n* conejillo *m* de Indias, cobaya *m*.
caw [kɔː] **1** *n* graznido *m*. **2** *vi* graznar.
cawing ['kɔːiŋ] *n* graznidos *mpl*, el graznar.
cayenne pepper ['keien,pepə*] *n* pimentón *m*.
cayman ['keimən] *n* caimán *m*.
cease [siːs] **1** *vt* suspender, cesar; **to — work** suspender el trabajo, terminar de trabajar.
    2 *vi* cesar; **to — (from)** + *ger*, **to — to** + *infin* dejar de + *infin*, cesar de + *infin*; **to — from strife** dejar de luchar.
ceasefire [,siːs'faiə*] *n* cese *m* de hostilidades, alto *m* el fuego; **— line** línea *f* de alto el fuego.
ceaseless ['siːslis] *adj* incesante, continuo.
ceaselessly ['siːslisli] *adv* incesantemente, sin cesar.
Cecil ['sesl] *m* Cecilio.
Cecily ['sisili] *f* Cecilia.
cecum ['siːkəm] *n (US)* = **caecum.**
cedar ['siːdə*] *n* cedro *m*.
cede [siːd] *vt* ceder *(to* a).
cedilla [si'dilə] *n* cedilla *f*.
ceiling ['siːliŋ] *n* techo *m* *(also Aer)*; *(fig)* límite *m*, punto *m* más alto; **— price** precio *m* tope; **to fix a — for, to put a — on** fijar el límite de, señalar el punto más alto de; **to hit the —** *(sl)* ponerse negro;

he has not yet reached his — se desarrollará todavía algo más, ha de ser mejor aún.
celandine ['seləndain] *n* celidonia *f*.
celebrant ['selibrənt] *n* celebrante *m*.
celebrate ['selibreit] **1** *vt* celebrar; *marriage* solemnizar; *happy event* celebrar, señalar con una fiesta; **we're celebrating his arrival** estamos celebrando su llegada; **what are you celebrating?** ¿qué motivo tiene esta fiesta?; **he —d his birthday by scoring 2 goals** celebró su cumpleaños marcando 2 goles.
    2 *vi* divertirse, estar *(or* ir) de parranda.
celebrated ['selibreitid] *adj* célebre, famoso *(for* por).
celebration [,seli'breiʃən] *n* celebración *f*; *(party)* fiesta *f*, guateque *m*; *(public rejoicing)* festividad *f*; **—s** *(of anniversary etc)* conmemoraciones *fpl*; **in —** of en conmemoración de.
celebrity [si'lebriti] *n (all senses)* celebridad *f*.
celeriac [sə'leriæk] *n* apio-nabo *m*.
celerity [si'leriti] *n* celeridad *f*.
celery ['seləri] *n* apio *m*.
celestial [si'lestiəl] *adj* celestial.
celibacy ['selibəsi] *n* celibato *m*.
celibate ['selibit] **1** *adj* célibe. **2** *n* célibe *mf*.
cell [sel] *n (of prison, monastery)* celda *f*; *(Bio, Pol)* célula *f*; *(of bees)* celda *f*; celdilla *f*; *(Elec)* elemento *m*; **condemned —** celda *f* de los condenados a muerte.
cellar ['selə*] *n* sótano *m*; *(for wine)* bodega *f*; **to keep a good —** tener buena bodega.
'cellist ['tʃelist] *n* violoncelista *mf*.
'cello ['tʃeləu] *n* violoncelo *m*.
cellophane ['seləfein] *n (Protected Trade Name)* celofán *m*.
cellular ['seljulə*] *adj* celular.
celluloid ['seljulɔid] *n* celuloide *m*.
cellulose ['seljuləus] *n* celulosa *f*.
Celt [kelt, selt] *n* celta *mf*.
Celtiberia [,keltai'biəriə] Celtiberia *f*.
Celtiberian [,keltai'biəriən] **1** *adj* celtibérico. **2** *n* celtíbero *m*, a *f*.
Celtic ['keltik, 'seltik] **1** *adj* celta, céltico. **2** *n* *(language)* céltico *m*.
cement [sə'ment] **1** *n* cemento *m*; *(Phot)* cola *f*. **2** *vt* cementar; cubrir *(or* revestir *etc)* de cemento; *(fig)* fortalecer, reforzar, consolidar.
cementation [,siːmen'teiʃən] *n* cementación *f*.
cemetery ['semitri] *n* cementerio *m*.
cenotaph ['senəta:f] *n* cenotafio *m*.
censer ['sensə*] *n* incensario *m*.
censor ['sensə*] **1** *n* censor *m*. **2** *vt* censurar; *(delete)* tachar, suprimir.
censorious [sen'sɔːriəs] *adj* hipercrítico, criticón.
censorship ['sensəʃip] *n* censura *f*.
censurable ['senʃərəbl] *adj* censurable.
censure ['senʃə*] **1** *n* censura *f*. **2** *vt* censurar.
census ['sensəs] *n* censo *m*; empadronamiento *m*; **to take a — of** levantar el censo de, empadronar.
cent [sent] *n* centavo *m*; **per —** por ciento, por cien; **I haven't a —** no tengo un céntimo.
centaur ['sentɔ:*] *n* centauro *m*.
centaury ['sentɔːri] *n* centaura *f*.
centenarian [,senti'nɛəriən] **1** *adj* centenario. **2** *n* centenario *m*, a *f*.
centenary [sen'tiːnəri] *n* centenario *m*; **the — celebrations** las festividades para celebrar el centenario de . . .
centennial [sen'teniəl] **1** *adj* centenario. **2** *n* centenario *m*.
center ['sentə*] *n (US)* = **centre.**
centesimal [sen'tesiməl] *adj* centesimal.
centigrade ['sentigreid] *adj* centígrado; **30 degrees —** 30 grados centígrados.
centigramme, *(US)* —gram ['sentigræm] *n* centigramo *m*.
centilitre, *(US)* —liter ['senti,liːtə*] *n* centilitro *m*.
centime ['sãːntiːm] *n* céntimo *m*.
centimetre, *(US)* —meter ['senti,miːtə*] *n* centímetro *m*.
centipede ['sentipiːd] *n* ciempiés *m*.
central ['sentrəl] *adj* central; *(in town etc)* céntrico.
Central America ['sentrələ'merikə] Centroamérica *f*.
Central American ['sentrələ'merikən] **1** *adj* centroamericano. **2** *n* centroamericano *m*, a *f*.
Central European ['sentrəl,juərə'piːən] **1** *adj* centroeuropeo. **2** *n* centroeuropeo *m*, a *f*.
central heating [,sentrəl'hiːtiŋ] *n* calefacción *f* central.
centralization [,sentrəlai'zeiʃən] *n* centralización *f*.
centralize ['sentrəlaiz] *vt* centralizar; concentrar, reunir en un centro.
centre, *(US)* center ['sentə*] **1** *n* centro *m*; núcleo *m*; **city —** centro *m* de la ciudad; **civic —** conjunto *m*

de edificios municipales; **community** — centro *m* social; **dead** — el mismo centro, (*Mech*) punto *m* muerto; — **of attraction** centro *m* de atracción; — **of gravity** centro *m* de gravedad; — **of intrigue** centro *m* de intrigas.

2 *attr* central; del centro.

3 *vt* centrar; *ball* pasar al centro; (*fig*) concentrar (*on* en).

4 *vi*: **to** — **in, to** — **on** concentrarse en, estar concentrado en, tener por centro, (*hopes etc*) cifrarse en.

centre-board, (*US*) **center**— ['sentəbɔːd] *n* orza *f* de deriva.

centre-forward ['sentə'fɔːwəd] *n* delantero *m* centro.

centre-half ['sentə'hɑːf] *n, pl* —**halves** [hɑːvz] medio *m* centro.

centre-piece, (*US*) **center**— ['sentəpiːs] *n* centro *m* de mesa; (*fig*) atracción *f* principal, objeto *m* (*etc*) de mayor interés.

centrifugal [sen'trifjugəl] *adj* centrífugo.

centrifuge ['sentrifjuːʒ] **1** *n* centrífuga *f*. **2** *vt* centrifugar.

centripetal [sen'tripitl] *adj* centrípeto.

centuries-old ['sentjuriz‚əuld] *adj* secular.

centurion [sen'tjuəriən] *n* centurión *m*.

century ['sentjuri] *n* siglo *m*; **in the 20th** — en el siglo veinte.

cephalic [si'fælik] *adj* cefálico.

ceramic [si'ræmik] *adj* cerámico.

ceramics [si'ræmiks] *n sing* cerámica *f*.

cereal ['siəriəl] **1** *adj* cereal. **2** *n* cereal *m*; —**s** (*crops, cornflakes*) cereales *mpl*.

cerebellum [‚seri'beləm] *n* cerebelo *m*.

cerebral ['seribrəl] *adj* cerebral.

cerebrate ['seribreit] *vi* pensar, meditar.

cerebration [‚seri'bɪeiʃən] *n* meditación *f*, actividad *f* mental.

ceremonial [‚seri'məuniəl] **1** *adj* ceremonial; de ceremonia, de gala. **2** *n* ceremonial *m*.

ceremonially [‚seri'məuniəli] *adv* con ceremonia.

ceremonious [‚seri'məuniəs] *adj* ceremonioso.

ceremoniously [‚seri'məuniəsli] *adv* ceremoniosamente.

ceremony ['seriməni] *n* ceremonia *f*; **to stand on** — hacer ceremonias, estar de cumplido; **let's not stand on** — dejémonos de cumplidos.

cerise [sə'riːz] **1** *adj* (de) color de cereza. **2** *n* cereza *f*.

cert [səːt] *n* (*sl*): **it's a** — es cosa segura.

certain ['səːtən] *adj* (**a**) (*of things*) seguro, cierto; **it is** — **that** es seguro que, es cierto que; **it is** — **death to go there** ir allí es buscarse una muerte segura.

(**b**) (*of person*) seguro; **are you** —**?** ¿estás seguro?; **I am** — **of it** estoy seguro de ello; **I am** — **that** estoy seguro de que; **we are** — **of his support** estamos seguros de tener su apoyo; **he is** — **to be there** es seguro que él estará allí; **be** — **to call on him** no dejes de visitarle; **you don't sound very** — no pareces estar muy seguro.

(**c**) (*a particular*) cierto; **to quote a** — **book** citar cierto libro; **to see a** — **man** ver a cierto hombre; **a** —**Mr Smith** un tal Sr Smith; **on a** — **day in May** cierto día de mayo.

(**d**) (*phrases*) **we don't know for** — no sabemos a ciencia cierta; **to make** — **of** asegurarse de; **I'll make** — **yo lo averiguaré; I'll make it as** — **as I can** yo lo haré todo lo seguro que pueda ser; **this should make victory** — esto ha de asegurarnos la victoria; **you should make** — **of your facts** conviene comprobar los datos.

certainly ['səːtənli] *adv* (**a**) —**!** ¡desde luego!, ¡naturalmente!; — **madam!** ¡con mucho gusto, señora!, ¡cómo Vd quiera, señora!; — **not!** ¡de ninguna manera!, ¡ni hablar!

(**b**) **it is** — **true that** desde luego es verdad que; **you may** — **take the car** desde luego que puedes tomar el coche; **I shall** — **be there** es seguro que yo asistiré, yo estaré allí sin falta; **you** — **did that well** eso sí que lo hiciste bien; **the meat is** — **tough** la carne sí es dura; **and** — **the Germans had more planes** y por cierto los alemanes tuvieron más aviones.

certainty ['səːtənti] *n* certeza *f*, certidumbre *f*; seguridad *f*; **in the** — **of being able to go** con la certeza de poder ir; **there is no** — **about it** sobre esto no hay seguridad alguna; **his** — **was alarming** su convicción era desconcertante; **faced with the** — **of disaster** ante la inevitabilidad del desastre; **it's a** — es cosa segura; **we know for a** — **that** sabemos a ciencia cierta que; **we can't know with any** — no lo podemos saber a ciencia cierta.

certifiable [‚səːti'faiəbl] *adj* certificable; (*Med*) demente, que padece tal demencia que hay que encerrarle en un manicomio.

certificate [sə'tifikit] *n* certificado *m*; (*academic etc*) título *m*; (*of birth etc*) partida *f*; **medical** — certificado *m* médico; — **of baptism** partida *f* de bautismo; — **of birth** partida *f* de nacimiento; — **of death** partida *f* de defunción; — **of marriage** partida *f* de casamiento.

certificated [sə'tifikeitid] *adj* con título, diplomado.

certify ['səːtifai] *vt* certificar; **to** — **that** declarar que; **to** — **someone insane** certificar que uno está loco.

certitude ['səːtitjuːd] *n* certidumbre *f*.

cervical ['səːvikəl] *adj* cervical.

cervix ['səːviks] *n, pl* **cervices** ['səːvisiːz] cerviz *f*.

cessation [se'seiʃən] *n* cesación *f*, suspensión *f*; — **of hostilities** cese *m* de hostilidades.

cession ['seʃən] *n* cesión *f*.

cesspool ['sespuːl] *n* pozo *m* negro; (*fig*) sentina *f*.

cetacean [si'teiʃən] **1** *adj* cetáceo. **2** *n* cetáceo *m*.

Ceylon [si'lɔn] Ceilán *m*.

Ceylonese [silə'niːz] **1** *adj* ceilanés. **2** *n* ceilanés *m*, esa *f*.

chafe [tʃeif] **1** *vt* rozar, raer; (*warm*) calentar frotando; (*fig*) irritar.

2 *vi* desgastarse (*against*, on contra); (*fig*) irritarse, impacientarse; **to** — **at, to** — **under** (*fig*) impacientarse por, irritarse debido a.

chaff [tʃɑːf] **1** *n* barcia *f*, aechaduras *fpl*; (*waste*) desperdicios *mpl*; (*fig*) zumbas *fpl*, chanzas *fpl*. **2** *vt* zumbarse de, tomar el pelo a.

chaffinch ['tʃæfintʃ] *n* pinzón *m* vulgar.

chafing dish ['tʃeifindiʃ] *n* escalfador *m*.

chagrin ['ʃægrin] **1** *n* mortificación *f*, desazón *f*, disgusto *m*; **to my** — con gran disgusto mío. **2** *vt* mortificar, disgustar.

chain [tʃein] **1** *n* cadena *f* (*also fig*); — **of mountains** cordillera *f*. **2** *vt* encadenar.

chain gang ['tʃeingæŋ] *n* (*US and Hist*) cadena *f* de presidiarios.

chain letter ['tʃein‚letə*] *n* carta *f* que circula en cadena (*con promesa de una ganancia cuantiosa para los que la hacen seguir según las indicaciones*).

chain lightning ['tʃein'laitniŋ] *n* (*US*) relámpagos *mpl* en zigzag.

chain mail ['tʃein'meil] *n* cota *f* de malla.

chain pump ['tʃeinpʌmp] *n* bomba *f* de cadena.

chain reaction ['tʃeinriː'ækʃən] *n* reacción *f* en cadena.

chain smoker ['tʃeinsməukə*] *n* fumador *m* que fuma un pitillo tras otro.

chain stitch ['tʃeinstitʃ] *n* cadeneta *f*.

chain store ['tʃeinstɔː*] *n* tienda *f* de una cadena.

chair [tʃeə*] **1** *n* silla *f*; (*Univ*) cátedra *f*; (*of meeting*) presidencia *f*; **electric** — silla *f* eléctrica; **high** — silla *f* alta; **to be in the** —, **to take the** — presidir (*at a meeting* una reunión); **won't you take a** —? ¿quiere Vd sentarse?

2 *vt* (**a**) *person* llevar a hombros; **they** —**ed him off the ground** le sacaron a hombros del campo.

(**b**) *meeting* presidir.

chairlift ['tʃeəlift] *n* telesilla *m*.

chairman ['tʃeəmən] *n, pl* —**men** [mən] presidente *m*.

chairmanship ['tʃeəmənʃip] *n* (*post*) presidencia *f*; (*art*) arte *m* de presidir reuniones.

chaise [ʃeiz] *n* calesa *f*, landó *m*.

chaise longue ['ʃeiz'lɔ̃ːŋ] *n* tumbona *f*.

chalet ['ʃælei] *n* chalet *m*, chalé *m* (*Acad*).

chalice ['tʃælis] *n* cáliz *m*.

chalk [tʃɔːk] **1** *n* (*Geol*) creta *f*; (*for writing*) tiza *f*; **French** — jaboncillo *m* de sastre, esteatita *f*; **not by a long** — ni con mucho; **it's as different as** — **from cheese** son tan diferentes como el agua y el vino.

2 *vt* marcar (*or* dibujar *etc*) con tiza; **to** — **up** apuntar.

chalkpit ['tʃɔːkpit] *n* cantera *f* de creta.

chalky ['tʃɔːki] *adj* cretoso.

challenge ['tʃælindʒ] **1** *n* (*to duel*) desafío *m*, reto *m*; (*of sentry*) quién vive *m*; (*Law*) recusación *f*; **the** — **of new ideas** el estímulo de las nuevas ideas; **the** — **of the 20th century** el incentivo (*or* estímulo) del siglo XX, las posibilidades del siglo XX; **Vigo's** — **for the league leadership** la tentativa que hace el Vigo para tomar el liderato de la liga; **this is a** — **to us all** esto nos llama a todos a la acción; **to issue a** — **to someone** desafiar a uno; **to take up a** — aceptar un desafío.

2 *vt* (*to duel*) desafiar, retar; (*sentry*) dar el quién vive a; (*Law*) recusar; *fact, point* poner en duda, expresar dudas acerca de; *speaker* hablar en contra de; **to** — **someone to** + *infin* desafiar a uno a que + *subj*.

challenger ['tʃælindʒə*] n desafiador m; (competitor) concursante mf; (opponent) contrincante mf.

challenging ['tʃælindʒiŋ] adj desafiante; tone de desafío; speech etc emocionante, estimulante, provocador; book sugestivo, lleno de sugestiones.

chamber ['tʃeimbə*] n cámara f; (arch) aposento m, sala f; (of gun) recámara f; —s (Law) despacho m; — of commerce cámara f de comercio.

chamberlain ['tʃeimbəlin] n chambelán m, gentil-hombre m de cámara.

chambermaid ['tʃeimbəmeid] n camarera f, sirvienta f.

chamber music ['tʃeimbə,mju:zik] n música f de cámara.

chamberpot ['tʃeimbəpɔt] n orinal m.

chambray ['tʃæmbrei] n (US) cambray m.

chameleon [kə'mi:liən] n camaleón m.

chamfer ['tʃæmfə*] 1 n chaflán m. 2 vt chaflanar.

chamois n (a) (Zool) ['ʃæmwɑ:] gamuza f. (b) (leather) ['ʃæmi] gamuza f.

chamois leather ['ʃæmi,leðə*] n gamuza f.

champ[1] [tʃæmp] vt morder, mordiscar; bit tascar.

champ[2] n (fam) = **champion**.

Champagne [ʃæm'pein] Champaña f.

champagne [ʃæm'pein] n champán m, champaña m.

champion ['tʃæmpiən] 1 adj campeón; a — athlete un atleta campeón.

2 n campeón m, ona f; (of a cause) defensor m, ora f, paladín m; **world** — campeón m mundial.

3 vt defender, apoyar, abogar por.

championship ['tʃæmpiənʃip] n campeonato m.

chance [tʃɑ:ns] 1 adj fortuito, casual; imprevisto; (random) aleatorio.

2 n (a) (luck, fortune, fate) casualidad f; azar m; suerte f; **game of** — juego m de azar; **the —s of war** la fortuna de la guerra; — **was against him** la suerte le fue contraria; — **ordained that** la suerte quiso que; **it cannot have been a matter of** — esto no habrá tenido nada de casual; **by** — por casualidad; **by sheer** — por pura casualidad; **do you by any** — **have a pen?** ¿tienes por casualidad una pluma?; **to leave things to** — dejar las cosas al azar; **to leave nothing to** — obrar con la mayor previsión, comprobarlo todo hasta el más pequeño detalle.

(b) (opportunity) ocasión f, oportunidad f; **now's our** —! ya nos toca el turno, nos ha llegado la vez; **this is my big** — ésta es la oportunidad que venía esperando; **you'll never get another** — **like this** la suerte nunca se deparará otra ocasión como ésta; **give me a** — **to show what I can do** déme la oportunidad de mostrar si soy capaz; **give me a** — **won't you?** ¡déjame un momento en paz!; **to give someone another** — olvidar el pasado de uno, seguir empleando a uno a pesar de su insuficiencia (etc); **he has had every** — le hemos dado todas las oportunidades posibles; **to have an eye for the main** —, **to look out for the main** — mirar por su propio provecho; **to waste one's** —s desperdiciar las ocasiones.

(c) (possibility) posibilidad f, probabilidad f; **the** —s **are that** lo más probable es que + subj; **there is no** — **of that** no existe la posibilidad de que ocurra eso; **it's a long** — eso es poco probable; **to have a fair** — **of** + ger tener buenas probabilidades de + infin; **he hasn't a** — no tiene posibilidad alguna; **I never had a** — **in life** la suerte no me ha favorecido jamás en la vida; **to stand a** — tener posibilidades; **you don't stand a** — no tienes posibilidad alguna.

(d) (risk) riesgo m; **to take a** — arriesgarse, probar fortuna; **to take no** —s obrar con la mayor previsión, comprobarlo todo hasta el más pequeño detalle; **that's a** — **we shall have to take** es un peligro que no podemos soslayar.

3 vt arriesgar; probar; **to** — **it** probarlo, aventurarse; **shall we** — **it?** ¿probaremos?

4 vi: **it** —d **that** aconteció que; **if it** —s **that** si resulta que; **I** —d **to see him** le vi por casualidad; **to** — **upon** encontrar por casualidad, tropezar con.

chancel ['tʃɑ:nsəl] n coro m y presbiterio.

chancellery ['tʃɑ:nsələri] n cancillería f.

chancellor ['tʃɑ:nsələ*] n canciller m; **C**— **of the Exchequer** Ministro m de Hacienda; **Lord C**— presidente de la Cámara de los Lores.

chancery ['tʃɑ:nsəri] n (Law) chancillería f; **ward in** — pupilo m, a f bajo la protección del tribunal.

chancre ['ʃæŋkə*] n chancro m.

chancy ['tʃɑ:nsi] adj (fam) arriesgado; dudoso.

chandelier [ʃændə'liə*] n araña f (de luces).

chandler ['tʃɑ:ndlə*] n velero m.

change [tʃeindʒ] 1 n cambio m; modificación f;

transformación f; (of skin etc) muda f; (small coins) moneda f suelta, calderilla f, suelto m; (for a larger coin) cambio m; (money returned) vuelta f; — **of address** cambio m de domicilio; — **of clothes** cambio m de ropa; — **of front** cambio m de frente; — **of heart** cambio m de sentimiento, conversión f; — **of horses** relevo m de los tiros; — **of life** menopausia f; — **of scene** (Theat) mutación f; **for a** — para variar un poco; **it's a** — **for the better** es un cambio beneficioso; **to get no** — **out of someone** no conseguir sacar nada a uno; **you may keep the** — quédese con la vuelta; **to ring the** —s **on something** hacer algo de diversas maneras.

2 vt cambiar (for por), trocar; reemplazar; modificar; transformar (into en); clothes, colour, gear, mind etc cambiar de, mudar de; **can you** — **this note for me?** ¿me hace Vd el favor de cambiar este billete?; **I find him much** —d le veo muy cambiado.

3 vi cambiar(se), mudar; (Rail etc) hacer transbordo, cambiar de tren (etc); **all** —! ¡cambio de tren!; **to** — **over** cambiar (to a); **you haven't** —d **a bit!** ¡no has cambiado en lo más mínimo!

changeability [,tʃeindʒə'biliti] n lo cambiable, mutabilidad f; inconstancia f, lo cambiadizo; **the** — **of the weather** lo cambiable del tiempo.

changeable ['tʃeindʒəbl] adj cambiable, mudable; inconstante, cambiadizo.

changeless ['tʃeindʒlis] adj inmutable.

changeling ['tʃeindʒliŋ] n niño m. cambiado por otro, niña f cambiada por otra.

changeover ['tʃeindʒ,əuvə*] n cambio m.

changing ['tʃeindʒiŋ] adj cambiante.

changing-room ['tʃeindʒiŋrum] n vestuario m.

channel ['tʃænl] 1 n canal m (also TV); (of a river) cauce m; (strait) estrecho m; (fig) conducto m, medio m; **irrigation** — acequia f, canal m de riego; **the C**— el Canal (de la Mancha).

2 vt acanalar; (fig) encauzar, dirigir (into a, por).

Channel Isles ['tʃænl,ailz] fpl Islas fpl Normandas.

chant [tʃɑ:nt] 1 n canto m llano; (fig) sonsonete m.

2 vt cantar (el canto llano); praises cantar; (fig) salmodiar, recitar en tono monótono.

chaos ['keiɔs] n caos m, desorden m.

chaotic [kei'ɔtik] adj caótico, desordenado.

chap[1] [tʃæp] 1 n grieta f, hendedura f. 2 vt agrietar. 3 vi agrietarse.

chap[2] [tʃæp] n (Anat) mandíbula f; (cheek) mejilla f.

chap[3] [tʃæp] n (fam) tío m, tipo m, pájaro m; **a** — **I know** un tío que yo conozco; **he's a nice** — es buen chico, es buena persona; **he's very deaf, poor** — es muy sordo, el pobre; **how are you, old** —? ¿qué tal, amigo?; **be a good** — **and say nothing** sé buen chico y no digas ni pío de esto.

chapbook ['tʃæpbuk] n libreta f, librito m de cuentos (etc).

chapel ['tʃæpəl] n capilla f; (Protestant etc) templo m; (Typ) personal m de una imprenta.

chaperon ['ʃæpərəun] 1 n acompañanta f (de señorita), carabina f (fam). 2 vt acompañar (a una señorita).

chaplain ['tʃæplin] n capellán m.

chaplaincy ['tʃæplənsi] n capellanía f.

chaplet ['tʃæplit] n guirnalda f, corona f de flores; (necklace) collar m; (Eccl) rosario m.

chappy ['tʃæpi] n (fam) = **chap**[3].

chaps [tʃæps] npl (US) zahones mpl, chaparreras fpl.

chapter ['tʃæptə*] n capítulo m; (Eccl) cabildo m; — **of accidents** serie f de desgracias; **with** — **and verse** con pelos y señales; **he can quote you** — **and verse** él lo sabe citar con todos sus pelos y señales.

chapter house ['tʃæptəhaus] n sala f capitular.

char[1] [tʃɑ:*] n (Fish) umbra f.

char[2] [tʃɑ:*] vt carbonizar, chamuscar.

char[3] [tʃɑ:*] n (sl) té m.

char[4] [tʃɑ:*] n (fam) = **charlady**.

char-à-banc ['ʃærəbæŋ] n (arch) autocar m.

character ['kæriktə*] n (a) (nature of thing) carácter m, naturaleza f, índole f, calidad f; (moral — of person) carácter m; **a man of** — un hombre de carácter; **to be in** — ser característico, ser conforme al tipo; **to be out of** — ser nada característico; **to bear a good** — tener una buena reputación; **to have a bad** — tener mala fama; **to give someone a good** — dar a uno una recomendación satisfactoria.

(b) (personaje in novel, play etc) personaje m; (rôle) papel m; **"Six C**—s **in Search of an Author"** "Seis personajes en busca de autor"; **the play has 8** —s la obra tiene 8 personajes; **chief** — protagonista mf; — **actor** actor m de carácter; — **actress** característica f; **in the** — **of** en el papel de; **that is more in** — eso está más en carácter.

(c) (*fam*) tipo *m*, sujeto *m*; **a — I know** un tipo que yo conozco; **he's quite a —** es un tipo pintoresco, es un original; **he's a very odd —** es un tipo muy raro.

(d) (*Bio, Typ etc*) carácter *m*.

characteristic [ˌkærɪktəˈrɪstɪk] **1** *adj* característico (*of* de). **2** *n* característica *f*, carácter *m*; distintivo *m*, señal *f* distintiva.

characteristically [ˌkærɪktəˈrɪstɪkəli] *adv* característicamente, de modo característico.

characterization [ˌkærɪktəraɪˈzeɪʃən] *n* caracterización *f*.

characterize [ˈkærɪktəraɪz] *vt* caracterizar.

characterless [ˈkærɪktəlɪs] *adj* sin carácter.

charade [ʃəˈrɑːd] *n* charada *f* (*also fig*).

charcoal [ˈtʃɑːkəʊl] *n* carbón *m* vegetal; (*Art*) carboncillo *m*; **— drawing** dibujo *m* al carbón.

charcoal burner [ˈtʃɑːkəʊl,bɜːnə*] *n* carbonero *m*.

charge [tʃɑːdʒ] **1** *n* **(a)** (*explosive, electrical*) carga *f*.

(b) (*attack*) carga *f*, ataque *m*, asalto *m*; (*of bull*) embestida *f*; (*Sport*) carga *f*; **cavalry —** carga *f* de caballería.

(c) (*Law etc*) acusación *f*, cargo *m*; **to appear on a —** of comparecer acusado de; **to bring** (*or* lay) **—s against** hacer acusaciones contra; **to give someone in —** entregar a uno a la policía; **to return to the —** volver al cargo, repetir la acusación.

(d) (*price*) precio *m*, coste *m*; **professional —s** honorarios *mpl*; **extra —** recargo *m*, suplemento *m*; **free of —** gratis; **— for admission** precio *m* de entrada; **"no — for admission"** "entrada gratis"; **to be a — upon** cargarse en cuenta a; **to make a — for something** cobrar por algo; **to reverse the —s** (*Tel*) cobrar al número llamado.

(e) responsabilidad *f*; (*office*) cargo *m*; (*task*) encargo *m*, cometido *m*; **the person in —** la persona responsable; **to be in —** mandar; **who is in — here?** ¿quién manda aquí?; **to be in — of** estar encargado de; **to be in the — of** correr a cargo de; **to take — of** hacerse cargo de, encargarse de; *men, expedition etc* asumir el mando de.

(f) (*Her*) blasón *m*.

2 *vt* **(a)** (*fill*) cargar (*also* Mil, Elec; *with* de).

(b) (*attack*) atacar, cargar; (*bull etc*) embestir; (*Sport*) cargar.

(c) (*Law etc*) acusar (*with* de).

(d) *price* pedir; *price, person* cobrar (a); **what are they charging for it?** ¿cuánto piden por él?; **what did they — you for it?** ¿cuánto te cobraron?; **to — something (up) to someone, to — something to someone's account** cargar algo en cuenta a uno.

(e) (*order*) **to — someone to do something** ordenar a uno hacer algo; **to — someone with a mission** confiar una misión a uno; **I am —d with the task of +** *ger* me han encargado el deber de + *infin*.

3 *vi* **(a)** (*Mil*) atacar, cargar; (*bull*) embestir; **to — down upon** cargar sobre, precipitarse sobre; **to — into** chocar contra.

(b) (*make pay*) cobrar, (*a lot*) cobrar mucho.

chargeable [ˈtʃɑːdʒəbl] *adj* cobradero.

charge account [ˈtʃɑːdʒə,kaʊnt] *n* (*US*) cuenta *f* corriente.

charged [tʃɑːdʒd] *adj* (*Elec*) cargado, con carga.

chargé d'affaires [ˈʃɑːʒeɪdæˈfeə*] *n* encargado *m* de negocios.

charger [ˈtʃɑːdʒə*] *n* (*horse*) corcel *m*, caballo *m* de guerra; (*Elec*) cargador *m*.

charily [ˈtʃeərɪli] *adv* cuidadosamente, cautelosamente; parcamente, con parquedad.

chariot [ˈtʃærɪət] *n* carro *m* (romano, de guerra *etc*).

charioteer [ˌtʃærɪəˈtɪə*] *n* auriga *m*.

charisma [kæˈrɪzmə] *n* carisma *m*.

charitable [ˈtʃærɪtəbl] *adj* **(a)** *person* caritativo; *remark, view* comprensivo, compasivo. **(b)** *purpose, society* benéfico.

charity [ˈtʃærɪti] *n* **(a)** caridad *f*; (*sympathy*) comprensión *f*, compasión *f*; **out of —** por caridad; **— begins at home** la caridad empieza por uno mismo; **to live on —** vivir de limosnas.

(b) (*organization*) sociedad *f* benéfica; **to raffle something for —** rifar algo para fines benéficos; **most of it goes to —** la mayor parte está destinada a obras de beneficencia.

charlady [ˈtʃɑːleɪdi] *n* asistenta *f*, mujer *f* de la limpieza.

charlatan [ˈʃɑːlətən] *n* charlatán *m*; (*Med*) curandero *m*.

Charlemagne [ˈʃɑːləmeɪn] *m* Carlomagno.

Charles [tʃɑːlz] *m* Carlos.

charleston [ˈtʃɑːlstən] *n* charlestón *m*.

charley horse [ˈtʃɑːlihɔːs] *n* (*US fam*) calambre *m*.

Charlie [ˈtʃɑːli] *m* Carlitos.

Charlotte [ˈʃɑːlət] *f* Carlota.

charm [tʃɑːm] **1** *n* (*in general*) encanto *m*, atractivo *m*, hechizo *m*; (*magic spell*) hechizo *m*; (*recited spell*) ensalmo *m*; (*trinket*) amuleto *m*, dije *m*; **—s** (*of woman*) atractivo *m*, hechizos *mpl*; **he has great —** tiene mucho encanto, tiene un fuerte atractivo; **typical Spanish —** la típica simpatía española; **to turn on the —** ponerse fino, deshacerse en finuras.

2 *vt* hechizar, encantar, seducir; **we were —ed by Granada** nos encantó Granada; **to — away** hacer desaparecer como por magia, llevarse misteriosamente.

charmer [ˈtʃɑːmə*] *n* hombre *m* (*etc*) de fuerte atractivo.

charming [ˈtʃɑːmɪŋ] *adj* encantador; *person* encantador, simpático; *present, remark etc* fino, gentil; **—!** (*iro*) ¡qué simpático!; **how — of you!** ¡qué detalle!

charmingly [ˈtʃɑːmɪŋli] *adv* de modo encantador; con finura; **a — simple dress** un vestido sencillo pero muy mono.

charnel-house [ˈtʃɑːnlhaʊs] *n* osario *m*.

chart [tʃɑːt] **1** *n* tabla *f*, cuadro *m*, esquema *m*, gráfico *m*; (*graph*) gráfica *f*; (*Naut*) carta *f* de navegación.

2 *vt* poner en una carta, (*loosely*) explorar; **to — a course** trazar un derrotero.

charter [ˈtʃɑːtə*] **1** *n* carta *f*; (*of city, bill of rights*) fuero *m*; (*of company*) carta *f* de privilegio; **royal —** cédula *f* real.

2 *vt* estatuir; *ship* fletar; *bus, plane* alquilar.

chartered [ˈtʃɑːtəd] *adj accountant etc* diplomado.

charwoman [ˈtʃɑː,wʊmən] *n, pl* **—women** [ˌwɪmɪn] *see* **charlady**.

chary [ˈtʃeəri] *adj* cuidadoso, cauteloso; **to be — of** + *n* ser avaro de + *n*, ser parco en + *n*; **to be — of** + *ger* evitar + *infin*, no prestarse de buena gana a + *infin*.

chase¹ [tʃeɪs] **1** *n* persecución *f*; (*hunt*) caza *f*; **to give — to** dar caza a, perseguir; **to join in the — for something** unirse a los que buscan algo.

2 *vt* (*follow*) perseguir; (*hunt*) cazar; *girl etc* perseguir, dar caza a; **to — away, to — off** ahuyentar; **to — out** echar fuera.

3 *vi* correr, precipitarse; **to — after** ir en pos de, (*fig*) correr tras.

4 *vr*: **go — yourself!** (*fam*) ¡vete al cuerno!

chase² [tʃeɪs] *vt* (*Tech*) grabar; *jewel* engastar.

chaser [ˈtʃeɪsə*] *n* copita *f* de licor.

chasm [ˈkæzəm] *n* (*Geog*) sima *f*, abismo *m*, grieta *f*; (*fig*) abismo *m*.

chassis [ˈʃæsi] *n* chasis *m*.

chaste [tʃeɪst] *adj* casto.

chastely [ˈtʃeɪstli] *adv* castamente.

chasten [ˈtʃeɪsn] *vt* castigar, corregir, escarmentar.

chastened [ˈtʃeɪsnd] **1** *pret and ptp of* **chasten. 2** *adj* (*by experience etc*) escarmentado; *tone etc* sumiso; **they seemed much —** parecían haberse arrepentido.

chasteness [ˈtʃeɪstnɪs] *n* castidad *f*.

chastening [ˈtʃeɪsnɪŋ] *adj experience etc* aleccionador.

chastise [tʃæsˈtaɪz] *vt* castigar.

chastisement [ˈtʃæstɪzmənt] *n* castigo *m*.

chastity [ˈtʃæstɪti] *n* castidad *f*.

chasuble [ˈtʃæzjubl] *n* casulla *f*.

chat [tʃæt] **1** *n* charla *f*; **to have a — with** charlar con; **I'll have a — with him** hablaré con él.

2 *vt*: **to — someone up** (*sl*) dar jabón a uno.

3 *vi* charlar (*to, with* con).

chatelaine [ˈʃætəleɪn] *n* (*Hist*) castellana *f*.

chattels [ˈtʃætlz] *npl* bienes *mpl* muebles; (*loosely*) cosas *fpl*, enseres *mpl*.

chatter [ˈtʃætə*] **1** *n* (*talk*) charla *f*, cháchara *f*; (*of birds*) parloteo *m*; (*of teeth*) castañeteo *m*.

2 *vi* (*person*) charlar, chacharear; (*birds*) parlotear; (*monkeys*) chillar; (*teeth*) castañetear; **she does — so** es muy habladora; **stop —ing!** ¡silencio!

chatterbox [ˈtʃætəbɒks] *n* parlanchín *m*, ina *f*, tarabilla *mf*.

chatty [ˈtʃæti] *adj person* hablador, locuaz; *style* familiar; *letter* afectuoso y lleno de noticias; *article* de tono familiar.

chauffeur [ˈʃəʊfə*] *n* chófer *m*, chofer *m* (S *Am*).

chauvinism [ˈʃəʊvɪnɪzəm] *n* chauvinismo *m*.

chauvinist [ˈʃəʊvɪnɪst] **1** *adj* chauvinista. **2** *n* chauvinista *mf*.

chauvinistic [ˌʃəʊviˈnɪstɪk] *adj* chauvinista.

chaw [tʃɔː] *vt* (*US fam*) mascar; **to — someone up** (*US sl*) poner a uno como un trapo.

cheap [tʃiːp] **1** *adj* barato; *ticket* económico; (*person selling* —) baratero; (*fig*) de mal gusto, cursi, chabacano; *trick* malo; **that's pretty —** eso es poco recto, eso se llama no jugar limpio; **on the** — barato; en plan económico; **to feel** — sentirse humillado, sentir vergüenza; **to hold** — tener en poco; **to make oneself** — hacer cosas indignas de sí, aplebeyarse; **to make a product** —er abaratar un producto. 2 *adv* barato.

cheapen ['tʃiːpən] **1** *vt* abaratar. **2** *vi* abaratarse. **3** *vr*: **to** — **oneself** hacer cosas indignas de sí, aplebeyarse.

cheaply ['tʃiːpli] *adv* barato; a precio económico; **to get off** — no tener que pagar (*etc*) lo que se calculaba.

cheapness ['tʃiːpnis] *n* lo barato, baratura *f*.

cheapskate ['tʃiːpskeit] *n* (*US: fam*) canalla *m*.

cheat [tʃiːt] **1** *n* (**a**) trampa *f*, fraude *m*; **it was a** — fue una decepción, hubo trampa; **there's a** — **in it somewhere** aquí hay trampa.
(**b**) (*person*) tramposo *m*, a *f*, petardista *mf*; (*at cards*) fullero *m*.
2 *vt person* defraudar, timar; **to** — **someone out of something** estafar algo a uno; **to** — **the gallows** suicidarse para no ser ejecutado.

cheating ['tʃiːtiŋ] *n* trampa *f*, fraude *m*; (*at cards*) fullerías *fpl*.

check¹ [tʃek] **1** *n* (**a**) (*halt*) parada *f* (súbita); (*Mil*) repulsa *f*; (*to plans*) contratiempo *m*, revés *m*; (*restraint*) restricción *f* (*on* de); (*obstacle*) impedimento *m* (*on* para), estorbo *m* (*on* a); —**s and balances in a constitution** frenos *mpl* y equilibrios de una constitución; **to act as a** — **on** (*restrain*) refrenar, (*impede*) ser un estorbo a; **to hold** (*or* **keep**) **in** — contener, tener a raya; **to suffer a** — sufrir un revés.
(**b**) (*Chess*) jaque *m*; **in** — en jaque; **continuous** — tablas *fpl* por jaque continuo.
(**c**) (*check-up*) control *m*, inspección *f*, verificación *f* (*on* de); (*Mech etc*) repaso *m*; (*Med*) reconocimiento *m* general; **they gave the rocket a final** — dieron al cohete el último repaso; **to keep a** — **on** controlar.
(**d**) (*token*) (*counterfoil*) talón *m*; (*at cloakroom*) billete *m*, boleto *m*; (*in games*) ficha *f*; (*US: invoice*) factura *f*; (*US: cheque*) cheque *m*; (*bill for food*) nota *f*, cuenta *f*; **to hand in one's** —**s** (*sl*) estirar la pata.
2 *interj* (*Chess*) ¡jaque!
3 *vt* (**a**) *motion* parar, detener; *spread etc* restringir, tener a raya, refrenar; (*be an obstacle to*) impedir, estorbar; *attack* rechazar.
(**b**) (*Chess*) dar jaque a.
(**c**) (*examine*) controlar, examinar, inspeccionar; *facts* comprobar; *document* compulsar; (*count*) llevar la cuenta de, contar; (*Mech*) revisar, repasar; *baggage* (US) facturar; **to** — **a copy against an original** cotejar una copia con el original; **to** — **items off on a list** marcar artículos en una lista.
4 *vi*: **to** — **in** inscribirse (en un hotel); **to** — **on something** comprobar algo, verificar algo; investigar algo; **to** — **on someone** investigar los antecedentes (*or* la lealtad *etc*) de uno; **to** — **out** pagar su cuenta (de hotel) y marcharse, (*loosely*) salir, marcharse; **to** — **up** comprobarlo; investigarlo; **to** — **up on** = **to** — **on**; **to** — **with someone** consultar con uno.
5 *vr*: **to** — **oneself** detenerse, refrenarse.

check² [tʃek] *n* (*in pattern*) cuadro *m*; (*cloth*) paño *m* a cuadros; — **suit** traje *m* a cuadros.

checkbook ['tʃekbuk] *n* (US) = **cheque book.**

checkerboard ['tʃekəbɔːd] *n* tablero *m* de damas.

checkers ['tʃekəz] *npl* (US) juego *m* de damas.

checking ['tʃekiŋ] *n* control *m*, comprobación *f*.

checkmate ['tʃek'meit] **1** *n* mate *m*, jaque *m* mate. **2** *vt* dar mate a; **to be** —**d** (*fig*) estar en un callejón sin salida.

checkpoint ['tʃekpɔint] *n* (punto *m* de) control *m*.

checkroom ['tʃekrum] *n* (US) guardarropa *m*; (*Rail*) consigna *f*; (*euph*) lavabo *m*.

checkup ['tʃekʌp] *n* comprobación *f*, verificación *f*; examen *m*; (*Med*) reconocimiento *m* general.

cheek [tʃiːk] **1** *n* mejilla *f*, carrillo *m*; (*fig*) descaro *m*, frescura *f*, tupé *m*; — **by jowl** lado a lado (*with* con); **what (a)** —!, **of all the** —! ¡qué cara dura!, ¡qué valor!; **to have the** — **to** + *infin* atreverse a + *infin*, tener el valor de + *infin*; **to turn the other** — volver la otra mejilla.
2 *vt* (*fig*) decir cosas descaradas a, portarse como un fresco con.

cheekbone ['tʃiːkbəun] *n* pómulo *m*.

cheekily ['tʃiːkili] *adv* descaradamente, con frescura.

cheekiness ['tʃiːkinis] *n* descaro *m*, frescura *f*.

cheeky ['tʃiːki] *adj* descarado, fresco.

cheer [tʃiə*] **1** *n* (**a**) (*applause*) grito *m* de entusiasmo; —**s** aplausos *mpl*, aclamaciones *fpl*; **there were loud** —**s at this** en esto hubo muchos aplausos; **to give**

three —**s for** vitorear a, aclamar a; **three** —**s for the general**! ¡viva el general!
(**b**) (*food*) comida *f*.
(**c**) (*state of mind*) humor *m*; **what** —? ¿qué tal?; —**s!** (*fam*) ¡salud y pesetas!; **be of good** —! ¡ánimo!
2 *vt* (**a**) (*also* **to** — **up**) alegrar, animar; **I was much** —**ed by the news** me alegró mucho la noticia.
(**b**) (*applaud*) aplaudir, aclamar, vitorear; **to** — **on** animar con aplausos.
3 *vi* aplaudir, gritar con entusiasmo; **to** — **up** cobrar ánimo, alegrarse; — **up!** ¡ánimo!, ¡anímate!

cheerful ['tʃiəful] *adj* alegre; de buen humor.

cheerfully ['tʃiəfuli] *adv* alegremente.

cheerfulness ['tʃiəfulnis] *n* alegría *f*; buen humor *m*.

cheerily ['tʃiərili] *adv* alegremente, jovialmente; de modo acogedor.

cheering ['tʃiəriŋ] **1** *adj* news etc bueno, esperanzador.
2 *n* aplausos *mpl*, aclamaciones *fpl*, gritos *mpl* de entusiasmo.

cheerio ['tʃiəri'əu] *interj* ¡hasta luego!

cheerless ['tʃiəlis] *adj* triste, sombrío.

cheery ['tʃiəri] *adj* alegre, jovial; *room etc* acogedor.

cheese [tʃiːz] **1** *n* queso *m*; **cream** — requesón *m*; **Dutch** — queso *m* de bola; **grated** — queso *m* rallado; **hard** — (*sl*) ¡mala potra!
2 *vt* (*US: sl*) dejar, poner fin a; — **it!** ¡déjalo!; ¡ojo, que viene gente!; **let's** — **it** dejémoslo; vámonos.

cheesecake ['tʃiːzkeik] *n* quesadilla *f*; (*sl*) fotos, dibujos etc de chicas atractivas en traje o actitud incitante.

cheesecloth ['tʃiːzklɔθ] *n* estopilla *f*.

cheesedish ['tʃiːzdiʃ] *n* quesera *f*.

cheeseparing ['tʃiːz,pɛəriŋ] **1** *adj* tacaño. **2** *n* economías *fpl* pequeñas.

cheesy ['tʃiːzi] *adj* (**a**) caseoso, como queso; que huele (*or* sabe) a queso. (**b**) (US: *sl*) horrible, sin valor.

cheetah ['tʃiːtə] *n* leopardo *m* cazador.

chef [ʃef] *n* jefe *m* de cocina.

cheiromancy ['kaiərəmænsi] *n* quiromancia *f*.

Chekhov ['tʃekɔf] *m* Chejof.

chemical ['kemikəl] **1** *adj* químico. **2** *n* sustancia *f* química, producto *m* químico.

chemically ['kemikəli] *adv* químicamente, por medios químicos.

chemise [ʃə'miːz] *n* camisa *f* de señora.

chemist ['kemist] *n* (*scientist*) químico *m*, a *f*; (*pharmacist*) farmacéutico *m*; —**'s (shop)** farmacia *f*; **all-night** —**'s** farmacia *f* de guardia.

chemistry ['kemistri] *n* química *f*.

chenille [ʃə'niːl] *n* felpilla *f*.

cheque [tʃek] *n* cheque *m*; **bad** —, **rubber** — (*fam*) cheque *m* sin fondos, cheque *m* sin provisión; **crossed** — cheque *m* cruzado; **open** — cheque *m* abierto; **traveller's** — cheque *m* de viajero; **blank** — cheque *m* en blanco; **to give someone a blank** — (*fig*) dar carta blanca a uno; **to pay by** — pagar mediante cheque.

cheque book ['tʃekbuk] *n* libro *m* de cheques.

chequered ['tʃekəd] *adj cloth etc* a cuadros; (*fig*) *career* accidentado, lleno de altibajos; *collection* variado.

cherish ['tʃeriʃ] *vt* querer, apreciar; cuidar, proteger; mimar; *hope etc* abrigar, acariciar.

cheroot [ʃə'ruːt] *n* cheruto *m*.

cherry ['tʃeri] **1** *adj* (de) color rojo cereza. **2** *n* (*fruit*) cereza *f*; (*tree, wood*) cerezo *m*; (*colour*) rojo *m* cereza.

cherry brandy ['tʃeri'brændi] *n* aguardiente *m* de cerezas.

cherry-red ['tʃeri'red] *adj* (de) color rojo cereza.

cherry tree ['tʃeritriː] *n* cerezo *m*.

cherub ['tʃerəb] *n* querubín *m*.

cherubic [tʃe'ruːbik] *adj* querúbico.

chervil ['tʃəːvil] *n* cerafolio *m*.

chess [tʃes] *n* ajedrez *m*.

chessboard ['tʃesbɔːd] *n* tablero *m* de ajedrez.

chessman ['tʃesmæn] *n*, *pl* —**men** [men] pieza *f*, trebejo *m*, ficha *f*.

chessplayer ['tʃespleiə*] *n* ajedrecista *mf*.

chest [tʃest] *n* (**a**) (*Anat*) pecho *m*; — **trouble** enfermedad *f* del pecho; **to get something off one's** — (*fam*) desahogarse, confesar algo de una vez; **to have a cold on the** — tener el pecho resfriado.
(**b**) (*box*) cofre *m*, arca *f*, cajón *m*; — **of drawers** cómoda *f*.

chest protector ['tʃestprə,tektə*] *n* pechera *f*.

chestnut ['tʃesnʌt] **1** *adj* castaño.
2 *n* (*fruit*) castaña *f*; (*tree, wood*) castaño *m*; (*horse*) caballo *m* castaño; (*joke*) chiste *m* viejo; **to pull the** —**s out of the fire for someone** sacar a uno las castañas del fuego.

chestnut tree ['tʃesnʌtriː] *n* castaño *m*.

chesty ['tʃesti] adj que tiene el pecho resfriado, congestionado.

cheval glass [ʃə'vælglɑːs] n psique f.

chevron ['ʃevrən] n (Mil) galón m; (Her) cheurón m.

chew [tʃuː] vt mascar, masticar; **to — something over** rumiar algo; **to — up** grass etc estropear; person (fam) dar un rapapolvo a.

chewing gum ['tʃuːiŋʌm] n chicle m.

chiaroscuro [ki,ɑːrəs'kuərəu] n claroscuro m.

chic [ʃiːk] **1** adj elegante. **2** n chic m, elegancia f.

chicanery [ʃi'keinəri] n embustes mpl, sofismas mpl; **a piece of —** un sofisma, una superchería, un subterfugio.

chick [tʃik] n pollito m, polluelo m; (fam) chica f.

chicken ['tʃikin] **1** n gallina f, pollo m; (as food) pollo m; **to be —** (sl) dejarse intimidar, acobardarse, cejar; **she's no —** ya no es una pollita; **don't count your —s before they're hatched** no hagas las cuentas de la lechera.

2 vi: **to — out** (fam) retirarse miedoso, amedrentarse; dejarse intimidar.

chicken farmer ['tʃikin,fɑːmə*] n avicultor m.

chicken farming ['tʃikin,fɑːmiŋ] n avicultura f.

chicken feed ['tʃikinfiːd] n (fig) pan m comido.

chicken-hearted ['tʃikin,hɑːtid] adj cobarde, gallina.

chickenpox ['tʃikinpɒks] n varicela f.

chicken run ['tʃikinrʌn] n corral m, gallinero m.

chickpea ['tʃikpiː] n garbanzo m.

chickweed ['tʃikwiːd] n pamplina f.

chicory ['tʃikəri] n achicoria f.

chide [tʃaid] (irr: pret **chid**, ptp **chidden** or **chid**) vt (lit) reprender.

chief [tʃiːf] **1** adj principal, primero, mayor, capital; official en jefe, mayor.

2 n jefe m (also fam); jerarca m; (of tribe) jefe m, cacique m; **— of staff** jefe m del estado mayor; **— of state** jefe m de estado; **... in ...** en jefe.

chiefly ['tʃiːfli] adv principalmente, sobre todo.

chieftain ['tʃiːftən] n jefe m, cacique m.

chiffon ['ʃifɒn] n gasa f, soplillo m.

chignon ['ʃiːnjɔːŋ] n rodete m, moño m.

chilblain ['tʃilblein] n sabañón m.

child [tʃaild] n, pl **children** ['tʃildrən] niño m, a f; (as offspring) hijo m, a f; **to be with —** estar encinta; **to get someone with —** dejar a una encinta; **I have known him from a —** le conozco desde niño.

childbearing ['tʃaild,bɛəriŋ] **1** attr: **— women** las mujeres fecundas, las mujeres que producen hijos; **women of — age** las mujeres de edad para tener hijos.

2 n (act) parto m; (as statistic) natalidad f.

childbed ['tʃaildbed] n parturición f.

childbirth ['tʃaildbɜːθ] n parto m; **to die in —** morir de sobreparto.

childhood ['tʃaildhud] n niñez f, infancia f; **to be in one's second —** chochear; **from —** desde niño.

childish ['tʃaildiʃ] adj pueril, aniñado; **don't be so —!** ¡no seas niño!

childishly ['tʃaildiʃli] adv de modo pueril; **she behaved —** se portó como una niña.

childishness ['tʃaildiʃnis] n puerilidad f.

childless ['tʃaildlis] adj sin hijos.

childlike ['tʃaildlaik] adj como de niño.

children ['tʃildrən] npl of **child**.

child's play ['tʃaildzplei] n (fig): **it's —** es cosa de coser y cantar (to para).

Chile ['tʃili] Chile m.

Chilean ['tʃilian] **1** adj chileno. **2** n chileno m, a f.

chili ['tʃili] n chile m.

chill [tʃil] **1** adj frío. **2** n frío m; (Med) escalofrío m; resfriado m; **a — of horror** un estremecimiento de horror; **to cast a — over a meeting** hacer que se enfríe el ambiente de una reunión; **to catch a —** resfriarse; **to take the — off** liquid, room calentar un poco.

3 vt enfriar; (with fear etc) helar; meat etc congelar; **to be —ed to the bone** estar helado hasta los huesos.

chill(i)ness ['tʃil(i)nis] n frío m; (fig) frialdad f.

chilly ['tʃili] adj **(a)** frío; **it is (very) —** hace (mucho) frío; **I am feeling —** tengo frío.

(b) (sensitive to cold) friolento, friolero; atmosphere frío, glacial.

chime [tʃaim] **1** n (set) juego m de campanas, carillón m; (peal) repique m, campanada f.

2 vt repicar; **to — six** dar las seis.

3 vi repicar, sonar; **to — in** hablar inesperadamente, (pej) entrometerse; **to — in with** decir inesperadamente; (harmonize) estar en armonía con.

chimera [kai'miərə] n quimera f.

chimerical [kai'merikəl] adj quimérico.

chimney ['tʃimni] n chimenea f; (of lamp) tubo m de lámpara; (Mountaineering) olla f, cañón m.

chimney pot ['tʃimnipɒt] n tubo m de chimenea.

chimney stack ['tʃimnistæk] n fuste m de chimenea.

chimney sweep ['tʃimniswiːp] n deshollinador m, limpiachimeneas m.

chimpanzee [,tʃimpæn'ziː] n chimpancé m.

chin [tʃin] **1** n barba f, barbilla f, mentón m; **double —** papada f; **to keep one's — up** no desanimarse; **keep your — up!** ¡ánimo! **2** vi (fam) charlar.

china ['tʃainə] n porcelana f, china f; (used loosely) loza f.

China ['tʃainə] China f.

china clay ['tʃainə'klei] n barro m de porcelana, arcilla f figulina.

Chinaman ['tʃainəmən] n, pl **-men** [mən] chino m.

chinatown ['tʃainətaun] n (US fam) barrio m chino.

chinch bug ['tʃintʃbʌg] n (US) chinche m or f de los cereales.

chinchilla [tʃin'tʃilə] n chinchilla f.

Chinese ['tʃai'niːz] **1** adj chino. **2** n chino m, a f. **3** n (language) chino m.

chink¹ [tʃiŋk] n (slit) grieta f, hendedura f, resquicio m; **— in one's armour** punto m débil.

chink² [tʃiŋk] **1** n (sound) sonido m metálico, tintineo m. **2** vt hacer sonar. **3** vi sonar (a metal), tintinear.

Chink [tʃiŋk] n (sl) chino m.

chintz [tʃints] n zaraza f.

chinwag ['tʃinwæg] **1** n charla f. **2** vi charlar.

chip [tʃip] **1** n (splinter) astilla f, pedacito m; (of stone) lasca f; (mark on surface) saltadura f, desportilladura f; (at poker) ficha f; **—s** patatas fpl fritas, patatas fpl a la española; **he's a — off the old block** de tal palo tal astilla; **to have a — on one's shoulder** ser un resentido.

2 vt astillar, desportillar; surface picar; sculpture cincelar; (sl) tomar el pelo a.

3 vi astillarse, desportillar; (surface) picarse, desconcharse; **to — in** cortar, interrumpir (with diciendo).

chipboard ['tʃipbɔːd] n (US) cartón m (de baja calidad).

chipmunk ['tʃipmʌŋk] n ardilla f listada.

chiropodist [ki'rɒpədist] n pedicuro m, podólogo m, callista mf.

chiropody [ki'rɒpədi] n pedicura f.

chirp [tʃɜːp] **1** n pío m, gorjeo m; (of cricket) chirrido m. **2** vi piar, gorjear; (cricket) chirriar.

chirpy ['tʃɜːpi] adj (fam) alegre.

chirrup ['tʃirəp] see **chirp**.

chisel ['tʃizl] **1** n (for wood) formón m, escoplo m; (for stone) cincel m. **2** vt escoplear; cincelar; (sl) timar.

chiseller ['tʃizlə*] n (sl) timador m.

chit¹ [tʃit] n: **a — of a girl** una muchacha no muy crecida.

chit² [tʃit] n nota f, esquela f.

chitchat ['tʃittʃæt] n chismes mpl, habladurías fpl.

chitterlings ['tʃitəliŋz] npl menudos mpl de cerdo (comestibles).

chitty ['tʃiti] n = **chit²**.

chivalresque [ʃivəl'resk] adj, **chivalric** [ʃi'vælrik] adj caballeresco.

chivalrous ['ʃivəlrəs] adj caballeroso.

chivalrously ['ʃivəlrəsli] adv caballerosamente.

chivalry ['ʃivəlri] n (institution) caballería f; (spirit) caballerosidad f.

chive [tʃaiv] n cebollino m.

chivvy ['tʃivi] vt (fam) perseguir, atormentar, acosar; **to — someone into doing something** no dejar en paz a uno hasta que haga algo.

chloral ['klɔːrəl] n cloral m.

chloride ['klɔːraid] n cloruro m; **— of lime** cloruro m de cal.

chlorinate ['klɔːrineit] vt clorinar.

chlorine ['klɔːriːn] n cloro m.

chloroform ['klɔːrəfɔːm] **1** n cloroformo m. **2** vt cloroformizar.

chlorophyl(l) ['klɔːrəfil] n clorofila f.

chock [tʃɒk] **1** n calzo m, cuña f. **2** vt calzar, acuñar, poner calzos a.

chock-a-block ['tʃɒkə'blɒk] adj, **chock-full** ['tʃɒk'ful] adj de bote en bote; **— of, — with** atestado de, totalmente lleno de.

chocolate ['tʃɒklit] n (in bar, for drinking) chocolate m; **a —** un bombón; **a box of —s** una caja de bombones.

choice [tʃɔis] **1** adj selecto, escogido; quality, wine etc fino.

2 n (act of choosing) elección f, selección f; (thing chosen) preferencia f; (range to choose from) surtido m, serie f de posibilidades; **for —** preferentemente; **he did it but not from —** lo hizo pero de mala gana; **the house of my —** mi casa predilecta; **the prince married the girl of his —** el príncipe se casó con

choir una joven que él había elegido; **it was not a free —** no estuvo libre para elegir a su gusto; **we have a wide —** (Comm) tenemos un gran surtido; **you have a wide —** Vd tiene muchas posibilidades; **to have no —** no tener alternativa; **he had no — but to go** no tuvo más remedio que ir; **to take one's —** elegir; **take your —!** ¡lo que Vd quiera!

choir ['kwaiə*] n coro m; coros mpl; orfeón m; coral f; (Archit) coro m.

choirboy ['kwaiəbɔi] n niño m de coro.

choirmaster ['kwaiə,mɑːstə*] n maestro m de coros.

choke [tʃəuk] **1** n (Mech) obturador m, cierre m; (Aut) estrangulador m, (loosely) aire m.
   2 vt pipe etc atascar, obstruir; person (to death) estrangular, ahogar, sofocar; **in a voice —d with emotion** en una voz embargada (or empañada) por la emoción; **a canal —d with weeds** un canal atascado de hierbas; **to — back** contener, ahogar; **to — someone off** (fam) echar un rapapolvo a uno.
   3 vi sofocarse (also **to — to death**); (over food) atragantarse; no poder respirar; **to — on a bone** atragantarse con un hueso; **to — with laughter** desternillarse de risa.

choker ['tʃəuk*] n (Mech) obturador m; (hum) cuello m alto.

choky ['tʃəuki] n (sl) trena f.

cholera ['kɔlərə] n cólera m.

choleric ['kɔlərik] adj colérico.

choose [tʃuːz] (irr: pret **chose**, ptp **chosen**) **1** vt elegir, escoger; team etc seleccionar; **he was chosen leader** fue elegido caudillo.
   2 vi: **to — between** elegir entre; **there is nothing to — between them** no les veo diferencia alguna; **there are 5 kinds to — from** a elegir entre 5 tipos; **to — to + infin** optar por + infin; **I'll do it when I — lo** haré cuando me dé la gana; **if I don't — to** si no quiero; **he cannot — but** (to) go no tiene más remedio que ir; **you cannot — but admire it** Vd no puede menos de admirarlo.

choos(e)y ['tʃuːzi] adj (fam) melindroso, delicado; **he's a bit — about it** en esto es algo difícil de contentar; **I'm — about whom I go out with** yo no salgo con un cualquiera.

chop [tʃɔp] **1** n (blow) golpe m cortante; (meat) chuleta f; **—s** boca f, labios mpl; **—s and changes** cambios mpl; **to get the —** (fam) ser despedido.
   2 vt cortar, tajar; (also **to — up**) desmenuzar, meat picar; **to — down** tree talar; **to — off** tronchar, separar.
   3 vi: **to — and change** (wind) virar, (person) cambiar constantemente de opinión.

chop-chop ['tʃɔp'tʃɔp] interj (sl) ¡en seguida!, ¡ya voy!

chophouse ['tʃɔphaus] n restaurante m económico.

chopper ['tʃɔpə*] n hacha f; (butcher's) tajadera f, cuchilla f; (Mil sl) helicóptero m.

chopping block ['tʃɔpiŋblɔk] n tajo m.

chopping board ['tʃɔpiŋ,bɔːd] n tajadera f.

chopping knife ['tʃɔpiŋ,naif] n tajadera f.

choppy ['tʃɔpi] adj sea picado, agitado.

chopsticks ['tʃɔpstiks] npl palillos mpl (de los chinos, para comer).

choral ['kɔːrəl] adj coral; **— society** orfeón m.

chorale [kɔ'rɑːl] n coral m.

chord [kɔːd] n (string, Anat, Math) cuerda f; (group of notes, sound) acorde m; **to strike the right —** juzgar bien el ambiente (de una reunión etc).

chore [tʃɔə*] n faena f, tarea f, tarea f necesaria pero falta de interés, trabajo m rutinario; **—s** (at home) quehaceres mpl domésticos.

choreographer [,kɔri'ɔgrəfə*] n coreógrafo m.

choreography [,kɔri'ɔgrəfi] n coreografía f.

chorister ['kɔristə*] n corista mf.

chortle ['tʃɔːtl] **1** n risa f alegre. **2** vi reírse alegremente; (pej) reírse satisfecho (over por).

chorus ['kɔːrəs] **1** n (Mus) coro m; (of chorus girls) conjunto m; (repeated words) estribillo m; **a — of praise greeted the book** el libro recibió la aprobación de todos, el libro se mereció las alabanzas de todos; **a — of shouts greeted this** todos gritaron a la vez al oír esto; **in —** en coro; **to sing in —** cantar en coro; **to join in the —** cantar el estribillo.
   2 vi cantar (etc) en coro; (answer) contestar todos a una voz.

chorus girl ['kɔːrəsgəːl] n corista f, vicetiple f.

chose [tʃəuz] pret of **choose**.

chosen ['tʃəuzn] **1** ptp of **choose**. **2** adj preferido, predilecto; **the — people** el pueblo escogido; **one of the —** uno de los elegidos.

chough [tʃʌf] n chova f piquirroja.

chow¹ [tʃau] n (dog) chao m.

chow² [tʃau] n (sl) comida f.

chowder ['tʃaudə*] n (US) pescado m con legumbres (etc); (soup) sopa f de pescado.

Christ [kraist] m Cristo; **—!** ¡Dios mío!

christen ['krisn] vt bautizar (also fig).

Christendom ['krisndəm] n cristiandad f.

christening ['krisniŋ] n bautizo m, bautismo m.

Christian ['kristiən] **1** adj cristiano; **name** de pila. **2** n cristiano m, a f.

Christianity [,kristi'æniti] n cristianismo m.

Christianize ['kristiənaiz] vt cristianizar.

Christlike ['kraistlaik] adj parecido a Jesucristo.

Christmas ['krisməs] **1** n Navidad f; (ie — period) Navidades fpl; **at —** por Navidades; **merry —!** ¡felices Pascuas!; **Father —** Padre m Noel, (Spanish equivalent bringing presents on 6 January) Reyes mpl Magos.
   2 attr navideño, de Navidad; **— Day** día m de Navidad; **— Eve** Nochebuena f.

Christmas box ['krisməsbɔks] n aguinaldo m.

Christmas card ['krisməskɑːd] n crismas m, tarjeta f de Navidad (Acad).

Christmas time ['krisməstaim] n Navidades fpl.

Christmas tree ['krisməstriː] n árbol m de Navidad.

Christopher ['kristəfə*] m Cristóbal.

chromatic [krə'mætik] adj cromático.

chrome [krəum] n cromo m; **— steel** acerocromo m; **— yellow** amarillo m de cromo.

chromium ['krəumiəm] n cromo m.

chromium-plated ['krəumiəm,pleitid] adj cromado.

chromium-plating ['krəumiəm,pleitiŋ] n cromado m.

chromosome ['krəuməsəum] n cromosoma m.

chronic ['krɔnik] adj crónico; (fig) constante, inextirpable; (fam) horrible, malísimo.

chronicle ['krɔnikl] **1** n crónica f; **C—s** (Bib) Crónicas fpl. **2** vt historiar; registrar, describir.

chronicler ['krɔniklə*] n cronista mf.

chronological [,krɔnə'lɔdʒikəl] adj cronológico.

chronologically [,krɔnə'lɔdʒikəli] adv por orden cronológico.

chronology [krə'nɔlədʒi] n cronología f.

chronometer [krə'nɔmitə*] n cronómetro m.

chrysalis ['krisəlis] n crisálida f.

chrysanthemum [kri'sænθəməm] n crisantemo m.

chub [tʃʌb] n cacho m.

chubby ['tʃʌbi] adj rechoncho, gordinflón; face mofletudo.

chuck¹ [tʃʌk] **1** n: **— under the chin** mamola f; **to get the —** (sl) ser despedido.
   2 vt (throw) lanzar, arrojar; (hand) pasar, dar; (give up) abandonar; **— it!** ¡basta ya!, ¡déjalo!; **I'm thinking of —ing it** pienso en la conveniencia de dejarlo; **so I had to — it** así que tuve que abandonarlo; **to — someone under the chin** dar la mamola a uno; **to — away** tirar, money despilfarrar, chance desperdiciar; **to — out** rubbish tirar, person poner de patitas en la calle, person from work etc despedir, dar el pasaporte a; **to — up** abandonar, renunciar a.

chuck² [tʃʌk] = **chock**.

chucker-out ['tʃʌkər'aut] n (fam) el forzudo que echa a los alborotadores de un café etc.

chuckle ['tʃʌkl] **1** n risita f, risa f sofocada; **we had a good — over that** nos reímos bastante con eso.
   2 vi reírse entre dientes, soltar una risita; **to — at, to — over** reírse con.

chuffed [tʃʌft] adj (sl) contento, alegre; **he was pretty — about it** estaba la mar de contento.

chug [tʃʌg] vi hacer ruidos explosivos repetidos; (Rail) resoplar; **to — along** (Aut) ir despacio, avanzar sin gran velocidad; (fig) ir tirando; **the train —ged past** pasó el tren resoplando.

chum [tʃʌm] **1** n compinche m, compañero m; (child) amiguito m, a f; **to be great —s** ser íntimos amigos; **to be —s with someone** ser amigo de uno.
   2 vi: **to — up** hacerse amigos; **to — up with someone** hacerse amigo de uno.

chummy ['tʃʌmi] adj familiar, muy afable; **they're very —** son muy amigos; **he's very — with the boss** es muy amigo del jefe.

chump [tʃʌmp] n (fam) **(a)** (head) cabeza f; **to be off one's —** estar chiflado. **(b)** (idiot) imbécil m, melón m; **you —!** ¡imbécil!

chunk [tʃʌŋk] n pedazo m, trozo m.

chunky ['tʃʌŋki] adj (fam) fornido.

church [tʃəːtʃ] n iglesia f; (esp non-Catholic) templo m; **C— of England** Iglesia f Anglicana; **High C—** sector de la Iglesia Anglicana de tendencia conservadora; **Low C—** sector de la Iglesia Anglicana de tendencia más protestante; **Mother C—** la santa Madre Iglesia; **mother —** iglesia f metropolitana; **to go to —** (Protestant) ir al oficio, asistir al culto,

(*Catholic*) ir a misa; **to go into the —** hacerse cura (*or* pastor *etc*).

churchgoer ['tʃɜːtʃ͵gəuə*] n fiel *mf* (que practica una religión).

churchman ['tʃɜːtʃmən] n, pl **—men** [mən] sacerdote *m*, eclesiástico *m*.

churchwarden ['tʃɜːtʃ͵wɔːdn] n capiller *m*.

churchy ['tʃɜːtʃi] adj (*fam*) beato; que va mucho a la iglesia, que toma muy en serio las cosas de la iglesia.

churchyard ['tʃɜːtʃjɑːd] n cementerio *m*, campo *m* santo.

churl [tʃɜːl] n (*fig*) patán *m*.

churlish ['tʃɜːliʃ] adj *person* poco afable, grosero, hosco; *remark* nada amistoso; **it would be — not to thank him** sería muy maleducado no darle las gracias.

churlishly ['tʃɜːliʃli] adv *behave etc* groseramente, sin educación.

churlishness ['tʃɜːliʃnis] n grosería *f*, hosquedad; conducta *f* (*etc*) poco amistosa; mala educación *f*.

churn [tʃɜːn] **1** n (*for milk*) lechera *f*; (*for butter*) mantequera *f*.

2 vt *butter* batir (*or* hacer) en una mantequera; (*fig*: *also* **to — up**) revolver, agitar.

3 vi revolverse, agitarse.

chute [ʃuːt] n (*Tech*) tolva *f*, vertedor *m*, rampa *f* de caída; (*in playground, swimming pool*) tobogán *m*; (*Aer, fam*) paracaídas *m*.

chutney ['tʃʌtni] n salsa *f* picante.

cicada [si'kɑːdə] n cigarra *f*.

Cicero ['sisərəu] m Cicerón.

cicerone [͵tʃitʃə'rəuni] n cicerone *m*.

Ciceronian [͵sisə'rəuniən] adj ciceroniano.

cider ['saidə*] n sidra *f*.

cider-press ['saidəpres] n lagar *m* para hacer sidra.

cider vinegar ['saidə'vinəgə*] n vinagre *m* de sidra.

cigar [si'gɑː*] n puro *m*.

cigar case [si'gɑːkeis] n cigarrera *f*.

cigarette [͵sigə'ret] n cigarrillo *m*, pitillo *m*, cigarro *m*.

cigarette case [͵sigə'ret͵keis] n pitillera *f*, petaca *f*.

cigarette end [͵sigə'ret͵end] n colilla *f* de cigarrillo.

cigarette holder [͵sigə'ret͵həuldə*] n boquilla *f*.

cigarette lighter [͵sigə'ret͵laitə*] n mechero *m*, encendedor *m*.

cigarette paper [͵sigə'ret͵peipə*] n papel *m* de fumar.

cinch [sintʃ] n (*sl*): **it's a —** es muy fácil; es cosa segura.

cinder ['sində*] n carbonilla *f*; **—s** cenizas *fpl*; **to be burned to a —** quedar carbonizado.

Cinderella [͵sində'relə] f la Cenicienta.

cinder track ['sindətræk] n pista *f* de ceniza.

cine-camera ['sini'kæmərə] n cámara *f* cinematográfica.

cinema ['sinəmə] n cine *m*.

Cinemascope ['sinəməskəup] n (*Protected Trade Name*) cinemascopio *m*.

cinematograph [͵sini'mætəgrɑːf] n cinematógrafo *m*.

cine-projector [͵siniprə'dʒektə*] n proyector *m* de películas.

cinerama [͵sinə'rɑːmə] n cinerama *m*.

cinerary ['sinərəri] adj cinerario.

cinnabar ['sinəbɑː*] n cinabrio *m*.

cinnamon ['sinəmən] n canela *f*.

cipher ['saifə*] **1** n (*o*) cero *m*; (*any number, initials, code*) cifra *f*; **he's a —** es un cero a la izquierda; **in —** en cifra.

2 vt (*code*) cifrar; (*Math*) calcular.

circle ['sɜːkl] **1** n (*a*) círculo *m*; (*Theat*) anfiteatro *m*; (*set of people*) grupo *m*; **turning —** dirección *f* cerrada; **vicious —** círculo *m* vicioso; **an inner —** of ministers un grupo interior de ministros; **within the family —** dentro del grupo familiar; **John and his —** Juan y sus amigos, Juan y su peña; **to be one of the charmed —** formar parte del grupo especial, ser uno de los escogidos; **the wheel has come full —** la rueda ha dado una vuelta completa.

(b) **—s** (*fig*): **in certain —s** en ciertos medios; **in business —s** en medios comerciales; **to move in fashionable —s** frecuentar la buena sociedad; **to go round in small —s** perderse en detalles nimios.

2 vt (*be round*) cercar, rodear; (*move round*) girar alrededor de, dar la vuelta a; *part of body* ceñir, rodear; **the lion —d its prey** el león se movió alrededor de la presa; **the cosmonaut —d the earth** el cosmonauta dio la vuelta al mundo; **the aircraft —d the town twice** el avión dio dos vueltas sobre la ciudad.

3 vi dar vueltas.

circlet ['sɜːklit] n anillo *m*; adorno *m* en forma de círculo.

circuit ['sɜːkit] n (*Elec etc*) circuito *m*; (*tour*) gira *f*; (*track*) pista *f*; (*lap by runner*) vuelta *f*; (*Law, approx*) distrito *m*.

circuit breaker ['sɜːkit͵breikə*] n cortacircuitos *m*.

circuitous [sɜː'kjuitəs] adj tortuoso, indirecto.

circular ['sɜːkjulə*] **1** adj circular; *tour* redondo. **2** n circular *f*.

circularize ['sɜːkjuləraiz] vt enviar circulares a.

circulate ['sɜːkjuleit] **1** vt poner en circulación; *letter, papers etc* hacer circular; *news* divulgar. **2** vi circular.

circulating ['sɜːkjuleitiŋ] adj circulante.

circulation [͵sɜːkju'leiʃən] n circulación *f*; (*number of papers printed*) tirada *f*; **— of the blood** circulación *f* sanguínea; **to put into —** poner en circulación.

circulatory [͵sɜːkju'leitəri] adj circulatorio.

circum . . . ['sɜːkəm] circun . . ., circum . . .

circumcise ['sɜːkəmsaiz] vt circuncidar.

circumcision [͵sɜːkəm'siʒən] n circuncisión *f*.

circumference [sə'kʌmfərəns] n circunferencia *f*.

circumflex ['sɜːkəmfleks] n circunflejo *m*.

circumlocution [͵sɜːkəmlə'kjuːʃən] n circunlocución *f*, circunloquio *m*, rodeo *m*.

circumnavigate [͵sɜːkəm'nævigeit] vt circunnavegar.

circumnavigation ['sɜːkəm͵nævi'geiʃən] n circunnavegación *f*.

circumscribe ['sɜːkəmskraib] vt circunscribir; limitar, restringir.

circumspect ['sɜːkəmspekt] adj circunspecto, prudente.

circumspectly ['sɜːkəmspektli] adv prudentemente.

circumspection [͵sɜːkəm'spekʃən] n circunspección *f*, prudencia *f*.

circumstance ['sɜːkəmstəns] n **(a)** circunstancia *f*; **extenuating —s** *fpl* atenuantes; **in (or under) the —s** en las circunstancias; **under no —s** de ninguna manera, bajo ningún concepto; **—s alter cases** las circunstancias cambian los casos; **were it not for the — that** si no fuera por la circunstancia de que; *see* **pomp.**

(b) —s (*ie economic situation*) **to be in easy —s** estar acomodado; **to be in narrow (or reduced) —s** vivir muy justo, vivir al borde del hambre; **what are your —s?** ¿cuál es su situación económica?; **if the family —s allow it** si lo permite la situación económica de la familia.

circumstantial [͵sɜːkəm'stænʃəl] adj *report* detallado, circunstanciado; *evidence* indiciario.

circumstantiate [͵sɜːkəm'stænʃieit] vt probar refiriendo todos los detalles.

circumvent [͵sɜːkəm'vent] vt burlar; *difficulty, obstacle* salvar.

circumvention [͵sɜːkəm'venʃən] n acción *f* de burlar (*or* salvar); **the — of this obstacle will not be easy** no va a ser fácil salvar este obstáculo.

circus ['sɜːkəs] n circo *m*; (*in town*) plaza *f* redonda, glorieta *f*.

cirrhosis [si'rəusis] n cirrosis *f*.

cirrus ['sirəs] n, pl **cirri** ['sirai] cirro *m*.

Cistercian [sis'tɜːʃən] **1** adj cisterciense; **— Order** Orden *f* del Cister. **2** n cisterciense *m*.

cistern ['sistən] n tanque *m*, depósito *m*; (*of WC*) cisterna *f*, depósito *m*; (*for hot water*) termo *m*; (*for rainwater*) aljibe *m*.

citadel ['sitədl] n ciudadela *f*; (*in Spain, freq*) alcázar *m*; (*fig*) reducto *m*.

citation [sai'teiʃən] n cita *f*; (*Law*) citación *f*; (*Mil*) mención *f*.

cite [sait] vt citar; (*Mil*) mencionar.

citizen ['sitizn] n ciudadano *m*, a *f*; (*in counting inhabitants etc*) habitante *mf*, vecino *m*, a *f*; **French —** súbdito *m* francés.

citizenry ['sitiznri] n ciudadanos *mpl*, ciudadanía *f*.

citizenship ['sitiznʃip] n ciudadanía *f*.

citrate ['sitreit] n citrato *m*.

citric ['sitrik] adj: **— acid** ácido *m* cítrico.

citron ['sitrən] n (*fruit*) cidra *f*; (*tree*) cidro *m*.

citrus ['sitrəs] n cidro *m*; **— fruits** agrios *mpl*.

city ['siti] **1** n ciudad *f*; **open —** ciudad *f* abierta; **the C—** el centro bursátil y bancario de Londres; **— editor** redactor encargado de las noticias financieras; **— page** sección de información financiera (*en un periódico*).

2 attr municipal, de la ciudad.

civet ['sivit] n algalia *f*.

civic ['sivik] adj cívico; municipal.

civics ['siviks] npl ciencia *f* de los deberes y derechos del ciudadano.

civies ['siviz] npl (*US: fam*) = **civvies.**

civil ['sivl] adj civil; *defence* pasivo; (*polite*) cortés, atento; amable; **he was very — to me** fue muy cortés conmigo; **that's very — of you** es Vd muy amable; **be more —!** ¡hable Vd con más educación!

civilian [si'viliən] **1** *adj* (de) paisano; civil. **2** *n* civil *mf*, paisano *m*, a *f*.

civility [si'viliti] *n* (a) (*politeness*) cortesía *f*; amabilidad *f*; **lack of —** falta *f* de educación. (b) (*polite remark*) cortesía *f*, cumplido *m*.

civilization [,sivilai'zeiʃən] *n* civilización *f*.

civilize ['sivilaiz] *vt* civilizar.

civilized ['sivilaizd] *adj* civilizado.

civilly ['sivili] *adv* cortésmente, atentamente.

civism ['sivizəm] *n* civismo *m*.

civvies ['siviz] *npl* (*fam*) traje *m* de paisano; **in —** vestido de paisano.

clack [klæk] *vi* (*chatter*) charlar, chismear; **this will make the tongues —** esto será tema para los chismosos.

clad [klæd] (*arch*) **1** *pret and ptp* of **clothe**. **2** *adj*: **— in** vestido de.

claim [kleim] **1** *n* (a) (*in general, demand*) reclamación *f*; (*formally stated*) petición *f*; **to have a — on someone** tener derecho a pedir algo a uno; **I think this has a — on your attention** creo que esto merece su atención; **I have many —s on my time** son muchas las cosas que ocupan el tiempo de que dispongo; **to lay — to** reclamar; **he put in a — for a rise** pidió que se le subiese el sueldo.

(b) (*Law*) demanda *f* (*for* de); **to put in a — for** entablar demanda de; **to state a —** presentar demanda; **you have no legal —** Vd no tiene derecho legal alguno.

(c) (*pretension*) pretensión *f*; (*stated*) afirmación *f*, declaración *f*; **his — turned out to be untrue** su declaración resultó ser falsa; **that's a big — to make** eso es mucho decir; **to make large —s for an invention** pretender que un invento tiene grandes ventajas.

(d) (*Min*) pertenencia *f*, concesión *f*.

2 *vt* (a) (*demand as one's due*) reclamar, exigir; **to — the right to vote** reclamar (*or* reivindicar) el derecho de votar; **to — something from someone** reclamar a uno la devolución de algo; **something else —ed her attention** otra cosa le llamó la atención; **death —ed him** se lo llevó la muerte.

(b) (*Law*) demandar; **to — damages from someone** reclamar a uno por daños.

(c) (*profess, assert*) pretender; **to — kinship with someone** pretender ser pariente de uno; **he —s to be her son** pretende ser su hijo; **he —s to have seen her** afirma haberla visto; **to — that** sostener que, afirmar que; **that's —ing a lot** eso es mucho decir.

claimant ['kleimənt] *n* (*Law*) demandante *mf*; (*to throne*) pretendiente *m*, a *f*.

clairvoyance [klɛə'vɔiəns] *n* clarividencia *f*, doble vista *f*.

clairvoyant(e) [klɛə'vɔiənt] *n* clarividente *mf*, vidente *m*.

clam [klæm] *n* almeja *f*.

clamber ['klæmbə*] *vi* trepar, subir gateando (*over* sobre, *up* a).

clammy ['klæmi] *adj* frío y húmedo.

clamorous ['klæmərəs] *adj* clamoroso.

clamour, (*US*) **clamor** ['klæmə*] **1** *n* clamor *m*, clamoreo *m*, griterío *m*. **2** *vi* clamorear, vociferar; **to — for** clamar por, pedir a voces.

clamp [klæmp] **1** *n* (*brace*) abrazadera *f*; (*eg in laboratory*) grapa *f*; (*Carpentry*) tornillo *m* de banco, cárcel *f*; (*Agr*) ensilado *m*, montón *m*.

2 *vt* afianzar (*or* sujetar *etc*) con abrazadera; **he —ed it in his hand** lo agarró con la mano; **he —ed his hand down on it** lo sujetó firmemente con la mano.

3 *vi*: **to — down on** (*fig*) tratar de acabar con, restringir, suprimir.

clan [klæn] *n* clan *m*.

clandestine [klæn'destin] *adj* clandestino.

clang [klæŋ] **1** *n* sonido *m* metálico fuerte, estruendo *m*. **2** *vt* hacer sonar. **3** *vi* sonar, hacer estruendo; **the gate —ed shut** la puerta se cerró ruidosamente.

clanger ['klæŋə*] *n* (*sl*) plancha *f*; **to drop a —** tirarse una plancha, meter la pata.

clangorous ['klæŋgərəs] *adj* estrepitoso, estruendoso.

clangour, (*US*) **clangor** ['klæŋgə*] *n* estruendo *m*.

clank ['klæŋk] **1** *n* sonido *m* metálico seco, golpeo *m* metálico.

2 *vt* hacer sonar.

3 *vi* sonar, hacer estruendo, rechinar metálico; **the train went —ing past** pasó el tren con estruendoso rechinar metálico.

clannish ['klæniʃ] *adj* exclusivista, con fuerte sentimiento de tribu.

clap¹ [klæp] **1** *n* (*on shoulder*) palmoteo *m*; (*of the hands*) palmada *f*; **— of thunder** trueno *m* seco, estampido *m* seco de trueno.

2 *vt* (a) (*with hands*) *person, play, announcement* aplaudir; **to — one's hands** batir las manos, dar palmadas, batir palmas; **to — someone on the back** dar a uno una palmada en la espalda.

(b) (*place*) poner; (*put on*) ponerse; **to — a hand over someone's mouth** tapar a uno la boca con la mano; **to — something shut** cerrar algo de golpe; **to — someone in jail** encarcelar a uno al instante.

3 *vi* aplaudir.

clap² [klæp] *n* (*Med: fam*) gonorrea *f*.

clapboard ['klæpbɔ:d] *n* (*US*) chilla *f*.

clapper ['klæpə*] *n* badajo *m*.

clapping ['klæpiŋ] *n* aplausos *mpl*.

claptrap ['klæptræp] *n* faramalla *f*, farfulla *f*.

claque [klæk] *n* claque *f*.

claret ['klærət] *n* clarete *m*.

clarification [,klærifi'keiʃən] *n* aclaración *f*.

clarify ['klærifai] *vt* aclarar.

clarinet [,klæri'net] *n* clarinete *m*.

clarion ['klæriən] *n* (*fig*) toque *m* de trompeta.

clarity ['klæriti] *n* claridad *f*.

clash [klæʃ] **1** *n* (a) (*noise*) estruendo *m*, fragor *m*.

(b) (*conflict*) choque *m*; (*Mil*) encuentro *m*; (*of opinions etc*) desacuerdo *m*, conflicto *m*; **— of dates** coincidencia *f* de fechas; **— of wills** lucha *f* de voluntades; **timetable —** incompatibilidad *f* de horas; **verbal —** choque *m* verbal.

2 *vt* batir, golpear.

3 *vi* (*Mil*) encontrarse, batirse; (*be opposed*) pugnar (con), estar en pugna, chocar; (*persons*) pelearse, reñir; (*colours*) desentonar; (*dates*) coincidir; (*opinions*) estar en desacuerdo.

clasp [klɑ:sp] **1** *n* (*fastener*) broche *m*, corchete *m*; (*of box, necklace etc*) cierre *m*; (*of book*) broche *m*, manecilla *f*; **with a — of the hand** con un apretón de manos.

2 *vt* (*fasten*) abrochar; (*embrace*) abrazar; *hand* apretar, estrechar; (*in one's hand*) tener asido, agarrar; **to — someone to one's bosom** estrechar a uno contra el pecho.

clasp knife ['klɑ:spnaif] *n* navaja *f*.

class [klɑ:s] **1** *n* (a) (*room*) *cabin* — clase *f* de cámara; **first —** primera clase *f*; **lower —es** clase *f* baja; **middle —es** clase *f* media; **upper —** clase *f* alta; **working —** clase *f* obrera; **social —** clase *f* social; **tourist —** clase *f* turista, (*as fare*) tarifa *f* turística; **a good — novel** una novela de buena calidad; **it's just not in the same —** no hay comparación entre los dos; **it's in a — by itself** tiene una neta superioridad, es único en su línea; **she's certainly got —** ella sí que tiene clase.

2 *attr* clasista, de clase(s).

3 *vt* clasificar.

class-conscious ['klɑ:s'kɔnʃəs] *adj* consciente de las distinciones de clase.

class consciousness ['klɑ:s'kɔnʃəsnis] *n* conciencia *f* de las distinciones de clase.

classic ['klæsik] **1** *adj* clásico. **2** *n* (*person*) autor *m* clásico; (*work*) obra *f* clásica; **the —s** las obras clásicas; **—s** (*Univ etc*) clásicas *fpl*.

classical ['klæsikəl] *adj* clásico; **— scholar** erudito *m* en lenguas clásicas.

classicism ['klæsisizəm] *n* clasicismo *m*.

classifiable ['klæsifaiəbl] *adj* clasificable.

classification [,klæsifi'keiʃən] *n* clasificación *f*.

classified ['klæsifaid] *adj information* secreto; **— advertisement** anuncio *m* por palabras.

classify ['klæsifai] *vt* clasificar (*in, into* en; *under letter B* en la B).

classmate ['klɑ:smeit] *n* compañero *m* de clase, compañera *f* de clase.

classroom ['klɑ:srum] *n* aula *f*, clase *f*.

class struggle ['klɑ:s'strʌgl] *n* lucha *f* de clases.

class war ['klɑ:s'wɔ:*] *n* lucha *f* de clases.

classy ['klɑ:si] *adj* (*fam*) de buen tono, muy pera.

clatter ['klætə*] **1** *n* ruido *m*, estruendo *m*; (*of plates*) choque *m*; (*of hooves*) trápala *f*; (*hammering*) martilleo *m*.

2 *vi* hacer ruido, hacer estruendo; (*hooves, feet*) trapalear; (*metal etc*) guachapear; **to come —ing down** caer ruidosamente; **to — down the stairs** bajar ruidosamente la escalera.

clause [klɔ:z] *n* cláusula *f*; (*Gram*) oración *f*; **saving —** cláusula *f* que contiene una salvedad.

claustrophobia [,klɔ:strə'fəubiə] *n* claustrofobia *f*.

claustrophobic [,klɔ:strə'fəubik] *adj person* que padece claustrofobia; *feeling* de claustrofobia; *situation* que produce claustrofobia.

clavichord ['klævikɔ:d] *n* clavicordio *m*.

clavicle ['klævikl] *n* clavícula *f*.

claw [klɔ:] **1** *n* (*Zool*) garra *f*, (*of cat*) uña *f*, (*of lobster*) pinza *f*; (*Tech*) garfio *m*, gancho *m*; **—s** (*fam*) dedos

mpl, mano f; **to get one's —s into someone** tener inquina a uno; **get your —s off that!** ¡fuera las manos!; **to show one's —s** sacar las uñas.
2 vt, also 3 vi: **to — at** arañar; (*tear*) desgarrar.
claw-hammer ['klɔː,hæmə*] n martillo m de orejas, martillo m sacaclavos.
clay [klei] n arcilla f; **potter's —** arcilla f de alfarería; **— pigeon** pichón m de barro.
clayey ['kleii] adj arcilloso.
clean [kliːn] **1** adj (*not dirty*) limpio; (*clear-cut*) neto, distinto, bien definido; (*shapely*) bien formado; (*unobstructed*) despejado; (*adroit*) diestro, elegante; (*pure*) decente; **as — as a new pin** como una plata; **to come —** (*sl*) confesarlo todo, desembuchar.
2 adv enteramente; **he cut — through it** lo cortó de un golpe; **it cuts — across tradition** esto corta netamente la tradición; **to get — away** escaparse sin dejar rastro; **the fish jumped — out of the net** el pez saltó fuera de la red.
3 n limpia f, limpiadura f; **to give the car a —** limpiar el coche.
4 vt limpiar; asear; *streets* barrer; (*dry-clean*) lavar al seco; **to — out** limpiar vaciando; **to — out a box** limpiar el interior de una caja; **it —ed us out** (*sl*) nos dejó sin blanca; **we were —ed out** quedamos limpios; **to — up** limpiar, asear; (*fig*) *play etc* suprimir los pasajes verdes de, *area of town* limpiar; **they're trying to — up television** tratan de hacer más decentes los programas de televisión; **to — up after someone** limpiar lo que ha ensuciado otro; **we —ed up £50** (*sl*) sacamos 50 libras de ganancia.
clean-cut ['kliːn'kʌt] adj (a) claro, bien definido, preciso; *outline* nítido. (b) *person* de buen parecer; de tipo elegante.
cleaner ['kliːnə*] n asistenta f, mujer f de la limpieza; **—'s** (*shop*) tintorería f.
cleaning ['kliːniŋ] n limpia f, limpiadura f.
cleanliness ['klenlinis] n limpieza f (*habitual*), aseo m.
cleanly ['klenli] adj limpio, aseado.
cleanly ['kliːnli] adv limpiamente; (*adroitly*) diestramente, con destreza.
cleanness ['kliːnnis] n limpieza f, aseo m.
cleanse [klenz] vt limpiar (*of* de).
cleanser ['klenzə*] n agente m de limpieza, producto m químico para la limpieza.
clean-shaven ['kliːn'ʃeivn] adj sin barba ni bigote, carilampiño.
cleanup ['kliːnʌp] n limpia f, limpiadura f.
clear [kliə*] **1** adj (a) (*transparent, audible, distinct, unambiguous, obvious*) claro; *sky, surface* despejado; *air* transparente; *conscience* limpio, tranquilo; *mind* penetrante, despejado; *majority* absoluto, neto; *round* (*Sport*) sin penalizaciones; **as — as crystal** más claro que el agua; **as — as day** más claro que el sol; **it is — that** está claro que; **is that —?** ¿comprende?; **I wish to make it — that** quiero subrayar que; **a — case of murder** un caso evidente de homicidio.
(b) (*certain*) **I'm not — whether** yo no sé a punto fijo si; **he was perfectly — that he did not intend to go** dijo de modo tajante que no pensaba ir; **are we — that we want this?** ¿estamos seguros de que queremos esto?
(c) (*complete*) entero, completo; **3 — days** 3 días completos; **£3 — profit** una ganancia neta de 3 libras; **to win by a — head** ganar por una cabeza larga.
(d) (*free*) **— of** libre de; **to be — of debt** estar libre de deudas.
2 adv claramente; **I can hear you loud and — le** oigo perfectamente; **to get — away** escaparse sin dejar rastro alguno; **to get — of** deshacerse de; **when we get — of London** cuando estemos fuera de Londres; **to steer — of** evitar cualquier contacto con.
3 n: **to be in the —** (*of debt*) estar libre de deudas; (*of suspicion*) quedar fuera de toda sospecha; (*of danger*) estar fuera de peligro.
4 vt (a) *place, surface, football* despejar; *site, woodland* desmontar; *debt, stock* liquidar; *court* desocupar, desalojar de público; *profit* sacar (una ganancia de); *cheque* pasar por un banco; **to — a space for** hacer un sitio para; **to — the table** levantar la mesa; **to — one's throat** carraspear, aclarar la voz; **to — a ship for action** alistar un buque para el combate; **to — a way for** abrir camino para; **to — away** quitar; **to — out** limpiar, vaciar, quitar; **to — up** (*clean*) limpiar, asear; (*arrange*) arreglar; *food* comerse; *doubt* resolver; *difficulty* aclarar.
(b) (*jump over*) salvar, saltar por encima de; **to — 2 metres** saltar 2 metros; (*avoid touching*)

pasar sin tocar; **the plane just —ed the roof** el avión por poco no tocó el tejado.
(c) *suspect* absolver, probar la inocencia de; **you will have to be —ed by Security** será necesario que le acredite la Seguridad; **the plan will have to be —ed with the chief** el proyecto tendrá que ser aprobado por el jefe.
5 vi (*liquid*) aclararse; (*weather*) despejarse; (*Sport*) despejar; **to — away** (*after meal*) quitar los platos; **to — off, to — out** irse, largarse, desaparecer; **— off!** ¡fuera de aquí!
6 vr: **to — oneself of a charge** probar su inocencia de una acusación.
clearance ['kliərəns] n (*space*) espacio m libre; (*distance above ground*) luz f libre; (*Tech*) espacio m muerto; (*Sport*) despeje m; (*by Customs*) despacho m de aduana; (*by Security*) acreditación f; **— sale** liquidación f.
clear-cut ['kliə'kʌt] adj claro, bien definido, neto.
clear-headed ['kliə'hedid] adj de mentalidad lógica, perspicaz, inteligente.
clear-headedness ['kliə'hedidnis] n mentalidad f lógica, perspicacia f, inteligencia f.
clearing ['kliəriŋ] n (*in wood*) claro m.
clearing bank ['kliəriŋ,bæŋk] n, **clearing house** ['kliəriŋhaus] n, pl **— houses** [,hauziz] cámara f de compensación.
clearly ['kliəli] adv claramente; (*at start of sentence*) desde luego; (*as answer*) sin duda, naturalmente.
clearness ['kliənis] n claridad f.
clear-sighted ['kliə'saitid] adj clarividente, perspicaz.
clear-sightedness ['kliə'saitidnis] n clarividencia f, perspicacia f.
clearway ['kliəwei] n carretera f principal (para velocidades altas), carretera f en la que está prohibido estacionar.
cleat [kliːt] n abrazadera f, listón m, fiador m.
cleavage ['kliːvidʒ] n (*fig*) escisión f, división f; (*in dress*) escote m.
cleave¹ [kliːv] (*irr*: pret **clove** or **cleft**, ptp **cloven** or **cleft**) vt partir, hender, abrir por medio; *water* surcar.
cleave² [kliːv] vi: **to — to** adherirse a, no separarse de; **to — together** ser inseparables.
cleaver ['kliːvə*] n cuchilla f de carnicero.
clef [klef] n clave f; **bass —** clave f de fa; **treble —** clave f de sol.
cleft [kleft] **1** pret and ptp of **cleave¹**. **2** n grieta f, hendedura f.
cleft palate ['kleft'pælit] n palatosquisis f.
clematis ['klemətis] n clemátide f.
clemency ['klemənsi] n clemencia f.
clement ['klemənt] adj clemente.
Clement ['klemənt] m Clemente.
clench [klentʃ] vt *teeth, fist* apretar, cerrar; **the —ed fist** el puño cerrado; *see also* **clinch**.
clergy ['klɜːdʒi] n clero m.
clergyman ['klɜːdʒimən] n, pl **-men** [mən] clérigo m; (*specifically Anglican*) sacerdote m anglicano; (*Protestant minister*) pastor m.
cleric ['klerik] n eclesiástico m.
clerical ['klerikəl] adj oficinista, oficinesco, de oficina; (*Eccl*) clerical; **— error** error m de pluma, error m de copia; **— work** trabajo m de oficina; **— worker** empleado m.
clerihew ['klerihjuː] n estrofa inglesa de 4 versos, de carácter festivo.
clerk [klɑːk, (*US*) klɜːrk] n oficinista mf, empleado m, a f; secretario m, a f; (*in hotel*) recepcionista mf; (*esp US*) dependiente m, a f, vendedor m, ora f; (*Law*) escribano m; (*Eccl, also* **— in holy orders**) clérigo m; **town —** secretario m del Ayuntamiento.
clerkship ['klɑːkʃip, (*US*) 'klɜːrkʃip] n empleo m de oficinista; (*Law*) escribanía f.
clever ['klevə*] adj inteligente, listo; *move, speech etc* hábil; *invention, parody etc* ingenioso; **to be — at** ser listo en, tener aptitud para; **he is very — with his fingers** es muy hábil con los dedos, tiene mucha destreza manual; **that was — of you** lo hiciste muy bien, ¡qué habilidad!, (*you were right*) estuviste en lo cierto; **that's —, isn't it?** ¿es ingenioso, eh?; **to be too — by half** pasarse de listo; **he was too — for us** logró embaucarnos; **he tries to be too — se** esfuerza por parecer ingenioso.
cleverly ['klevəli] adv hábilmente; ingeniosamente; con destreza.
cleverness ['klevənis] n inteligencia f; habilidad f; ingenio m; destreza f.
clew [kluː] n (*US*) = **clue**; (*Naut*) puño m.
cliché ['kliːʃei] n cliché m, tópico m, frase f hecha.

click [klik] **1** *n* golpecito *m* seco; (*of gun*) piñoneo *m*; (*of heels*) taconeo *m*; (*of tongue*) chasquido *m*.
2 *vt tongue etc* chasquear; **to — one's heels** taconear.
3 *vi* (*gun*) piñonear; sonar con un golpecito seco; (*fam*) tener suerte, lograrlo; (2 *persons*) congeniar; hacerse novios.
client ['klaiənt] *n* cliente *mf*.
clientèle [ˌkliːãːn'tel] *n* clientela *f*.
cliff [klif] *n* risco *m*, precipicio *m*; (*sea-*) acantilado *m*.
cliff-hanging ['klif,hæŋiŋ] *adj event* que produce el máximo suspense, que tiene a todos pendientes de su resultado; *drama* de suspense.
climacteric [klai'mæktərik] **1** *adj* climactérico. **2** *n* período *m* climactérico.
climactic [klai'mæktik] *adj* culminante.
climate ['klaimit] *n* clima *m*; (*fig*) ambiente *m*; **— of opinion** opinión *f* general.
climatic [klai'mætik] *adj* climático.
climatology [ˌklaimə'tɔlədʒi] *n* climatología *f*.
climax ['klaimæks] *n* punto *m* culminante, colmo *m*, apogeo *m*, crisis *f*; (*of play etc*) clímax *m*; **to reach a —** llegar a su punto álgido, alcanzar una cima de intensidad.
climb [klaim] **1** *n* subida *f*, escalada *f*, ascenso *m*; **it was a stiff —** la subida fue penosa.
2 *vt tree, wall etc* trepar a; *staircase* subir, subir por; *mountain* subir a, escalar.
3 *vi* (**a**) subir, trepar; **the path —s higher yet** la senda sigue subiendo todavía; **to — to power** subir al poder; **to — down a cliff** bajar por un precipicio; **to — into an aircraft** trepar a un aparato; **to — out of a hole** salir trepando de un socavón; **to — over a wall** franquear una tapia; **to — up a rope** trepar por una cuerda.
(**b**) (*fig*) **to — down** rendirse, desdecirse, retroceder.
climber ['klaimə*] *n* montañista *mf*, alpinista *mf*, escalador *m*, ora *f*; (*fig*) arribista *mf*; (*Bot*) trepadora *f*, enredadera *f*; **social —** arribista *mf*.
climbing ['klaimiŋ] *n* montañismo *m*, alpinismo *m*.
climbing irons ['klaimiŋaiənz] *npl* garfios *mpl*.
clinch [klintʃ] **1** *n* abrazo *m*; (*Boxing*) clincha *f*; **to go into a —** abrazarse.
2 *vt* (*secure*) afianzar; *nail* remachar, roblar; (*fig*) resolver de una vez, decidir; *argument* remachar; *deal* cerrar; **to — matters** para remacharlo todavía; **that —es it eso es concluyente**; *see also* **clench**.
cling [kliŋ] (*irr: pret and ptp* **clung**) *vi:* **to — to** adherirse a, pegarse a, quedar pegado a; *person* abrazarse a, quedar abrazado a; *person pursued* no separarse de; *opinion* seguir fiel a, sostener todavía; **they clung to one another** quedaron abrazados; **a dress that —s to the figure** un vestido que se ajuste al cuerpo.
clinging ['kliŋiŋ] *adj dress* ceñido, muy ajustado; *person* pegajoso.
clinic ['klinik] *n* clínica *f*.
clinical ['klinikəl] *adj* clínico.
clink[1] [kliŋk] **1** *n* tintín *m*, sonido *m* metálico; (*of glasses*) choque *m*. **2** *vt* hacer sonar, hacer tintinar; *glasses* chocar. **3** *vi* tintinar.
clink[2] [kliŋk] *n* (*sl*) trena *f*.
clinker ['kliŋkə*] *n* escoria *f* de hulla.
clinker-built ['kliŋkə,bilt] *adj* (*Naut*) de tingladillo.
clip[1] [klip] **1** *n* (*cut with scissors*) tijeretada *f*; (*shearing*) esquileo *m*; (*wool*) cantidad *f* de lana esquilada; (*blow*) golpe *m*.
2 *vt* (*cut*) cortar; (*cut to shorten*) acortar; *wool* trasquilar, esquilar; *coin* cercenar; *ticket* picar; *wings* cortar; *words* comerse, abreviar; (*hit*) golpear.
clip[2] [klip] **1** *n* (*clamp*) grapa *f*; (*for papers*) sujetapapeles *m*; (*of pen*) sujetador *m*; (*for hair*) prendido *m*; (*brooch*) alfiler *m* de pecho, clip *m*.
2 *vt* sujetar; **to — together** unir; **to — something on to one's dress** prender algo al traje con un alfiler.
clipper ['klipə*] *n* (*Naut*) clíper *m*.
clippers ['klipəz] *npl* (*for hair*) maquinilla *f* (para el pelo); (*Hort*) tijeras *fpl* podadoras.
clippie ['klipi] *n* (*fam*) cobradora *f*.
clipping ['klipiŋ] *n* (*from newspaper*) recorte *m*.
clique [kliːk] *n* pandilla *f*, camarilla *f*, peña *f*.
cliquish ['kliːkiʃ] *adj* exclusivista.
cliquishness ['kliːkiʃnis] *n* exclusivismo *m*.
cloak [kləuk] **1** *n* capa *f*, manto *m*; (*fig*) pretexto *m*; **under the — of piety** so capa de la piedad.
2 *vt* encapotar; (*cover*) cubrir (*in, with* de); (*fig*) encubrir, disimular.
cloak-and-dagger ['kləukən'dægə*] *adj* clandestino, propio de agente secreto; *story* de agentes secretos, de espías.

cloakroom ['kləukrum] *n* guardarropa *m*; (*Rail*) consigna *f*; (*euph*) aseos *mpl*, lavabo *m*.
clobber ['klɔbə*] (*sl*) **1** *n* (*dress*) ropa *f*, traje *m*; (*gear*) cosas *fpl*, trastos *mpl*. **2** *vt* (*defeat*) cascar; (*beat up*) aporrear.
cloche [klɔʃ] *n* campana *f* de cristal.
clock [klɔk] **1** *n* reloj *m*; (*fam*) (*dial*) esfera *f*, cuadrante *m*; (*of taxi*) taxímetro *m*; (*Aut: speedometer*) velocímetro *m*, (*milometer*) cuentakilómetros *m*; (*sl*) cara *f*; **electric —** reloj *m* eléctrico; **grandfather —** reloj *m* de pie, reloj *m* de caja; **against the —** contra (el) reloj; **to sleep round the —** dormir doce horas.
2 *vt* registrar; **we —ed 80 m.p.h.** alcanzamos una velocidad de 80 millas por hora.
3 *vi:* **to — in** fichar; (*loosely*) llegar (al trabajo *etc*).
clockwise ['klɔkwaiz] *adv* en la dirección de las agujas del reloj.
clockwork ['klɔkwə:k] **1** *n* aparato *m* de relojería; **to go like —** ir como un reloj. **2** *attr* de cuerda; **— train** tren *m* de cuerda.
clod [klɔd] *n* terrón *m*; (*person*) patán *m*; **you —!** ¡bestia!
clodhopper ['klɔd,hɔpə*] *n* patán *m*.
clog [klɔg] **1** *n* zueco *m*, chanclo *m*. **2** *vt* atascar. **3** *vi* atascarse.
cloister ['klɔistə*] *n* claustro *m*.
cloistered ['klɔistəd] *adj life* de ermitaño.
close [kləus] **1** *adv* cerca; **— by** muy cerca; **— by something**, **— to something** cerca de algo; **to be — together** estar muy juntos, estar muy cerca unos de otros; **to come —** acercarse; **that comes — to an insult** eso equivale casi a un insulto; **the runners finished very —** llegaron los atletas casi a la par; **to fit —** ajustarse al cuerpo (*etc*); **to follow — behind someone** seguir muy de cerca a uno; **to keep — to the wall** ir arrimado a la pared; **it's — on 6 o'clock** son las 6 casi; **he must be — on 50** se acercará a los 50; **according to sources — to the police** según fuentes allegadas a la comisaría.
2 *adj* (*near*) cercano, próximo; (*of objects standing — together*) apretados, arrimados unos a otros, densos; *weave* compacto, tupido; *print* compacto, *formation*, *vowel* cerrado; *connection*, *friendship* estrecho, íntimo; *friend* íntimo; *relative* cercano; *attention* concienzudo; *study, questioning, argument* detallado, minucioso; *election, finish, result* muy reñido; *scores* casi iguales; *resemblance* casi completo; *imitation* arrimado; *translation* fiel, exacto; *person's character* reservado, (*mean*) tacaño; *atmosphere* sofocante; *room* mal ventilado; *weather* pesado, bochornoso.
3 *n* recinto *m*.
close [kləuz] **1** *n* fin *m*, final *m*, conclusión *f*; **at the — al final del día; at the — of day** a la caída de la tarde; **at the — of the year** al fin del año; **to bring something to a —** terminar algo, concluir algo; **to draw to a —** tocar a su fin, estar terminando.
2 *vt* (*shut*) cerrar; (*end*) concluir, terminar; *hole etc* tapar, obstruir; *deal, list* cerrar; *ceremony, bank account* clausurar; *account* (*Comm*) saldar; *bank account* liquidar; *ranks* apretar; **"road —d"** "cerrado el paso"; **to — down** cerrar definitivamente; **to — up** cerrar (del todo).
3 *vi* (*shut*) cerrarse; (*end*) concluir(se), terminar(se); **to — down** cerrarse definitivamente; (*Radio*) cerrar la emisión; **to — in** acercarse rodeando; **the days are closing in** los días son cada vez más cortos; **night was closing in** se cerraba ya la noche; **to — in on someone** rodear a uno, cercar a uno; **the crowd —d round him** se agolpó la multitud en torno suyo; **the clouds —d round the peak** las nubes envolvieron la cumbre; **the waters —d round it** lo rodearon las aguas; **to — up** (*flower etc*) cerrarse (del todo); (*people etc*) arrimarse más, ponerse más cerca unos de otros; (*ranks*) apretarse; (*wound*) cicatrizar; (*fall silent*) callarse; **to — with someone** cerrar con uno.
close-cropped ['kləus'krɔpt] *adj* al rape.
closed [kləuzd] **1** *pret and ptp* of **close**. **2** *adj car, circuit etc* cerrado; *mind* de miras estrechas; *society* exclusivista.
closed-circuit ['kləuzd'sə:kit] *adj:* **— television** circuito *m* interno de televisión, televisión *f* por circuito cerrado.
close-down ['kləuzdaun] *n* (*Radio*) cierre *m*.
close-fisted ['kləus'fistid] *adj* tacaño.
close-fitting ['kləus'fitiŋ] *adj* ceñido, ajustado.
close-knit ['kləusnit] *adj* muy unido, bien ensamblado, homogéneo.
closely ['kləusli] *adv* (*exactly*) fielmente, exactamente; (*carefully*) atentamente; **— packed** *case* atestado,

objects apretados unos contra otros; — **printed** de impresión compacta; — **contested** muy reñido; — **guarded** rigurosamente guardado; — **connected with** en íntima relación con, estrechamente relacionado con.

closeness ['klǝusnis] *n (nearness)* proximidad *f; (of connection)* intimidad *f; (of election)* lo muy reñido; *(of translation)* fidelidad *f; (of room)* mala ventilación *f; (of weather)* pesantez *f,* lo bochornoso; *(meanness)* tacañería *f.*

closet ['klɔzit] **1** *n* wáter *m,* lavabo *m; (US: cupboard)* armario *m, (for clothes)* ropero *m.* **2** *vt:* **to be —ed with** estar encerrado con.

close-up ['klǝusʌp] *n* primer plano *m.*

closure ['klǝuʒǝ*] *n (close-down)* cierre *m; (end)* fin *m,* conclusión *f; (Parl)* clausura *f.*

clot [klɔt] **1** *n* **(a)** grumo *m,* cuajarón *m,* coágulo *m; (Med)* embolia *f;* — **on the brain** embolia *f* cerebral.
(b) *(sl)* papanatas *m;* **you** —! ¡imbécil!
2 *vi* cuajarse, coagularse.

cloth [klɔθ] *n, pl* **cloths** [klɔθs] *(material)* paño *m,* tela *f; (for cleaning)* trapo *m; (table-)* mantel *m;* **the** — *(Eccl)* el clero; **bound in** — encuadernado en tela; **American** — hule *m;* **made out of whole** — *(US)* enteramente fabuloso; **to lay the** — poner la mesa.

clothe [klǝuð] *vt* vestir *(in, with* de); *(fig)* cubrir, revestir *(in, with* de).

clothes [klǝuðz] *npl* ropa *f,* vestidos *mpl;* **in plain** — en traje de calle, de paisano.

clothes basket ['klǝuðz,bɑːskit] *n* cesto *m* de la colada.

clothes brush ['klǝuðzbrʌʃ] *n* cepillo *m* para la ropa.

clothes hanger ['klǝuðz,hæŋǝ*] *n* percha *f.*

clothes line ['klǝuðzlain] *n* cuerda *f* para tender la ropa.

clothes moth ['klǝuðzmɔθ] *n* polilla *f.*

clothes peg ['klǝuðzpeg] *n,* *(US)* **clothespin** ['klǝuðzpin] *n* pinza *f.*

clothespole ['klǝuðzpǝul] *n* palo *m* de apoyo *(para tender la ropa).*

clothesprop ['klǝuðzprɔp] *n* palo *m* de apoyo.

clothier ['klǝuðiǝ*] *n* pañero *m,* ropero *m, (tailor)* sastre *m;* —**'s (shop)** pañería *f,* ropería *f, (tailor's)* sastrería *f.*

clothing ['klǝuðiŋ] **1** *n* ropa *f,* vestidos *mpl;* **article of** — prenda *f* de vestir.
2 *attr:* — **shop** pañería *f,* ropería *f, (tailor's)* sastrería *f;* **the** — **trade** la industria del vestido.

cloud [klaud] **1** *n* nube *f (also fig); (storm-)* nubarrón *m;* **to be under a** — estar desacreditado; **to leave under a** — ser despedido bajo sospecha; **to be up in the** —s estar en las nubes; **every** — **has a silver lining** no hay mal que por bien no venga.
2 *vt* anublar *(also fig).*
3 *vi* nublarse *(also fig, also to* — **over).**

cloudberry ['klaudbǝri] *n (US)* camemoro *m.*

cloudburst ['klaudbǝːst] *n* chaparrón *m.*

cloud-capped ['klaudkæpt] *adj* coronado de nubes.

cloudiness ['klaudinis] *n* lo anublado, lo nuboso; lo turbio.

cloudless ['klaudlis] *adj* sin nubes, despejado.

cloudy ['klaudi] *adj* anublado, nuboso; *liquid* turbio; **it is** — el cielo está anublado.

clout¹ [klaut] **1** *n* tortazo *m.* **2** *vt* dar un tortazo a.

clout² [klaut] *n:* **ne'er cast a — till May be out** hasta el cuarenta de mayo no te quites el sayo.

clove¹ [klǝuv] *n* clavo *m* de especia; — **of garlic** diente *m* de ajo.

clove² [klǝuv] *pret* of **cleave¹.**

clove hitch ['klǝuvhitʃ] *n* ballestrinque *m.*

cloven ['klǝuvn] *ptp* of **cleave²;** *see* **hoof.**

clover ['klǝuvǝ*] *n* trébol *m;* **to be in** — estar en jauja.

cloverleaf ['klǝuvǝliːf] *n, pl* —**leaves** [liːvz] hoja *f* de trébol; *(Aut)* cruce *m* en trébol.

clown [klaun] **1** *n* payaso *m,* clown *m; (boor)* patán *m.*
2 *vi* hacer el payaso; **stop —ing!** ¡déjate de tonterías!

clowning ['klauniŋ] *n* payasadas *fpl.*

cloy [klɔi] *vti* empalagar.

cloying ['klɔiiŋ] *adj* empalagoso.

club [klʌb] **1** *n* **(a)** *(stick)* porra *f,* cachiporra *f; (golf-)* palo *m;* **Indian** — maza *f* (de gimnasia); *(Cards)* —**s** tréboles *mpl,* (in Spanish pack) bastones *mpl.*
(b) *(association)* club *m; (for gaming etc)* casino *m.*
2 *vt* aporrear; **to** — **someone to death** matar a uno a porrazos.
3 *vi:* **to** — **together** hacer una colecta, pagar cada uno su escote; **we** —**bed together to buy it for him** entre todos se lo compramos.

club-foot ['klʌb'fut] *n* pie *m* zopo.

clubhouse ['klʌbhaus] *n, pl* —**houses** [,hauziz] *(Golf)* chalet *m,* chalé *m (Acad).*

clubman ['klʌbmǝn] *n, pl* — **men** [mǝn] casinista *m.*

clubroom ['klʌbrum] *n* salón *m,* sala *f* de reuniones.

cluck [klʌk] *vi* cloquear.

clue [kluː] *n* indicio *m; (in a crime etc)* pista *f; (of crossword)* indicación *f;* **I haven't a** — no tengo ni idea; **he hasn't a** — es un pobre hombre, tiene un tremendo despiste; **can you give me a** —? ¿me puedes dar algún indicio?

clump¹ [klʌmp] *n (of trees)* grupo *m; (of plant)* mata *f.*

clump² [klʌmp] **1** *n (noise of feet)* pisadas *fpl* fuertes.
2 *vi* andar con pisadas fuertes.

clumsily ['klʌmzili] *adv* torpemente; pesadamente; toscamente, chapuceramente.

clumsiness ['klʌmzinis] *n* torpeza *f,* desmaña *f;* tosquedad *f.*

clumsy ['klʌmzi] *adj* torpe, desmañado; *(in movement)* desgarbado, pesado; *(inartistic)* tosco, chapucero.

clung [klʌŋ] *pret* and *ptp* of **cling.**

Cluniac ['kluːniæk] **1** *adj* cluniacense. **2** *n* cluniacense *m.*

cluster ['klʌstǝ*] **1** *n* grupo *m; (Bot)* racimo *m.* **2** *vi* agruparse, apiñarse; *(Bot)* arracimarse; **to** — **round someone** reunirse en torno de uno.

clutch¹ [klʌtʃ] **1** *n* **(a)** *(grasp)* agarro *m,* apretón *m;* **to make a** — **at something** tratar de agarrar algo.
(b) —**es: to fall into someone's** —**es** caer en las garras de uno; **to get something out of someone's** —**es** hacer que uno ceda la posesión de algo.
(c) *(Aut)* embrague *m; (pedal)* pedal *m* de embrague; **to disengage the** — desembragar; **to let in the** — embragar.
2 *vt* tener asido en la mano; sujetar, apretar, empuñar; **he** —**ed her to his heart** la estrechó contra el pecho.
3 *vi:* **to** — **at** agarrarse a, tratar de asir; **he** —**ed at my hand** trató de coger mi mano; **to** — **at a hope** aferrarse a una esperanza.

clutch² [klʌtʃ] *n (of eggs)* nidada *f.*

clutter ['klʌtǝ*] **1** *n* desorden *m,* confusión *f;* **a** — **of shoes** un montón de zapatos. **2** *vt* llenar desordenadamente, atestar; **to be** —**ed up with** estar atestado de.

coach [kǝutʃ] **1** *n* **(a)** *(in general)* coche *m; (stage-)* diligencia *f; (ceremonial)* carroza *f; (Rail)* coche *m,* vagón *m; (Aut)* autocar *m.*
(b) *(Sport)* entrenador *m,* preparador *m,* instructor *m; (tutor)* profesor *m* particular.
2 *vt* *team* entrenar, preparar; *student* enseñar, preparar; **to** — **someone in French** enseñar francés a uno; **to** — **someone in a part** hacer que uno ensaye su papel.

coachman ['kǝutʃmǝn] *n, pl* —**men** [mǝn] cochero *m.*

coachwork ['kǝutʃwǝːk] *n* carrocería *f.*

coadjutant [kǝu'ædʒutǝnt] *n* auxiliar *mf.*

coagulant [kǝu'ægjulǝnt] *n* coagulante *m.*

coagulate [kǝu'ægjuleit] **1** *vt* coagular. **2** *vi* coagularse.

coagulation [kǝu,ægju'leiʃǝn] *n* coagulación *f.*

coal [kǝul] **1** *n* carbón *m;* hulla *f;* **a** — un pedazo de carbón; **live** —, brasa *f; soft* — hulla *f* grasa; **to carry** —**s to Newcastle** ir a vendimiar y llevar uvas de postre; **to haul someone over the** —**s** echar un rapapolvo a uno; **to heap** —**s of fire on someone's head** avergonzar a uno devolviéndole bien por mal.
2 *attr:* — **industry** industria *f* hullera.
3 *vi (Naut)* tomar carbón.

coal-black ['kǝul'blæk] *adj* negro como el carbón.

coal-burning ['kǝul,bǝːniŋ] *adj* que quema carbón.

coal cellar ['kǝul,selǝ*] *n* carbonera *f.*

coal cutter ['kǝul,kʌtǝ*] *n* excavadora-zapadora *f.*

coaldust ['kǝuldʌst] *n* polvillo *m* de carbón.

coalesce [,kǝuǝ'les] *vi* fundirse; unirse, incorporarse.

coalescence [,kǝuǝ'lesǝns] *n* fusión *f;* unión *f,* incorporación *f.*

coal face ['kǝulfeis] *n* frente *m* de carbón.

coalfield ['kǝulfiːld] *n* yacimiento *m* de carbón; *(large area)* cuenca *f* minera.

coalgas ['kǝulgæs] *n* gas *m* de hulla.

coalition [,kǝuǝ'liʃǝn] *n* coalición *f.*

coalman ['kǝulmǝn] *n, pl* —**men** [mǝn], **coal merchant** ['kǝul,mǝːtʃǝnt] *n* carbonero *m.*

coalmine ['kǝulmain] *n* mina *f* de carbón.

coalminer ['kǝul,mainǝ*] *n* minero *m* de carbón.

coalmining ['kǝul,mainiŋ] *n* minería *f* de carbón.

coalpit ['kǝulpit] *n* mina *f* de carbón.

coal scuttle ['kǝul,skʌtl] *n* cubo *m* para carbón.

coal tar ['kǝul'tɑ:*] *n* alquitrán *m* mineral.

coarse [kɔːs] *adj* (*of texture*) basto, burdo; *sand etc* grueso; (*badly-made*) tosco, torpe; *hands* poco elegante, *skin* áspero, poco fino; *character*, *laugh*, *remark* ordinario, grosero; *joke* verde.

coarse-grained ['kɔːsgreind] *adj* de grano grueso; (*fig*) tosco, basto.

coarsely ['kɔːsli] *adv* toscamente; groseramente.

coarsen ['kɔːsn] **1** *vt person* embrutecer; *skin* curtir. **2** *vi* (*person*) embrutecerse; (*skin*) curtirse.

coarseness ['kɔːsnis] *n* basteza *f*; tosquedad *f*; falta *f* de finura, falta *f* de elegancia; ordinariez *f*, grosería *f*; lo verde.

coast [kəust] **1** *n* costa *f*; litoral *m*; **the — is clear** ya no hay moros en la costa.
2 *vi* (*Aut etc*) ir en punto muerto; (*on sledge*, *cycle etc*) deslizarse cuesta abajo; **to — along** avanzar sin esfuerzo.

coastal ['kəustəl] *adj* costero, costanero; **— defences** defensas *fpl* costeras; **— traffic** (*Naut*) cabotaje *m*.

coaster ['kəustə*] *n* buque *m* costero, barco *m* de cabotaje; (*US*) trineo *m*.

coastguard ['kəustgɑːd] *n* guardacostas *m*.

coastline ['kəustlain] *n* litoral *m*.

coat [kəut] **1** *n* (a) (*jacket*) chaqueta *f*, americana *f*, saco *m* (*SAm*); (*overcoat*) abrigo *m*; **white —** (*chemist's etc*) bata *f*; **— of arms** escudo *m* de armas; **— of mail** cota *f* de malla; **to cut one's — according to one's cloth** adaptarse a las circunstancias; **to turn one's —** chaquetear, cambiar de camisa.
(b) (*animal's*) pelo *m*, lana *f*.
(c) (*layer*) capa *f*; **— of paint** mano *f* de pintura.
2 *vt* cubrir, revestir (*with* de); (*with a liquid*) bañar (*with* en); **to — something with paint** dar una mano de pintura a algo.

coat hanger ['kəut,hæŋə*] *n* percha *f*.

coating ['kəutiŋ] *n* capa *f*, baño *m*.

coattails ['kəutteilz] *npl* faldón *m*.

co-author '[kəu,ɔːθə*] *n* coautor *m*, ora *f*.

coax [kəuks] *vt* engatusar; **to — something out of someone** sonsacar algo a uno; **to — someone into doing something** conseguir por medio de halagos que uno haga algo; **she likes to be —ed** ella se hace rogar; **to — someone along** mimar a uno.

coaxing ['kəuksiŋ] **1** *adj* mimoso. **2** *n* mimos *mpl*, halagos *mpl*.

coaxingly ['kəuksiŋli] *adv* mimosamente.

cob [kɔb] *n* (*swan*) cisne *m* macho; (*horse*) jaca *f* fuerte; (*loaf*) pan *m* redondo; (*nut*) avellana *f*.

cobalt ['kəubɔlt] *n* cobalto *m*; **— blue** azul *m* de cobalto.

cobber ['kɔbə*] *n* (*Australia: fam*) amigo *m*, compañero *m*; (*in direct address*) amigo, hombre.

cobble ['kɔbl] *vt shoes* remendar; *street* empedrar con guijarros.

cobbler ['kɔblə*] *n* zapatero *m* remendón.

cobbles ['kɔblz] *npl*, **cobblestones** ['kɔblstəunz] *npl* guijarros *mpl*, enguijarrado *m*.

cobra ['kəubrə] *n* cobra *f*.

cobweb ['kɔbweb] *n*.telaraña *f*; **to blow the —s away** salir a tomar el fresco.

cocaine [kə'kein] *n* cocaína *f*.

coccus ['kɔkəs] *n*, *pl* **cocci** ['kɔkai] coco *m*.

cochineal ['kɔtʃiniːl] *n* cochinilla *f*.

cock [kɔk] **1** *n* (a) (*cockerel*) gallo *m*; (*other male bird*) macho *m*; **fighting —** gallo *m* de pelea; **— of the walk** gallito *m* del lugar; **old —!** (*fam*) ¡amigo!
(b) (*tap*) grifo *m*, espita *f*; (*Anat*: *tabu*) polla *f*.
(c) (*of gun*) martillo *m*; **to go off at half —** (*plan*) ponerse por obra sin la debida preparación.
2 *vt gun* amartillar; *head* ladear; *ears* aguzar; **to — one's eye at** mirar con intención a.

cockade [kɔ'keid] *n* escarapela *f*.

cock-a-doodle-doo ['kɔkəduːdl'duː] *interj* ¡quiquiriquí!

cock-a-hoop ['kɔkə'huːp] *adj*: **to be —** estar jubiloso.

cock-and-bull ['kɔkən'bul] *adj*: **— story** cuento *m*, camelo *m*.

cockatoo [,kɔkə'tuː] *n* cacatúa *f*.

cockchafer ['kɔk,tʃeifə*] *n* abejorro *m*.

cockcrow ['kɔkkrəu] *n*: **at —** al amanecer.

cocked [kɔkt] *adj*: **— hat** sombrero *m* de tres picos; **to knock something into a — hat** ser netamente superior a, dar quince y raya a.

cocker ['kɔkə*] *n* (*also* **— spaniel**) cocker *m*.

cockerel ['kɔkrəl] *n* gallito *m*, gallo *m* joven.

cockeyed ['kɔkaid] *adj* (*fam*) incomprensible, estúpido.

cockfight ['kɔkfait] *n*, **cockfighting** ['kɔk,faitiŋ] *n* riña *f* de gallos.

cockle ['kɔkl] *n* (*Zool*) berberecho *m*; **to warm the —s of someone's heart** dar grandísimo contento a uno.

cockleshell ['kɔklʃel] *n* concha *f* de berberecho; (*boat*) cascarón *m* de nuez.

cockney ['kɔkni] *n habitante de ciertos barrios bajos de Londres; dialecto de ciertos barrios bajos de Londres*.

cockpit ['kɔkpit] *n* (*Aer*) carlinga *f*; (*for cockfight*) cancha *f*, reñidero *m* de gallos; **the — of Europe** Bélgica *f* (*escenario de muchos combates*).

cockroach ['kɔkrəutʃ] *n* cucaracha *f*.

cockscomb ['kɔkskəum] *n* cresta *f* de gallo.

cocksure ['kɔk'ʃuə*] *adj* presumido, presuntuoso.

cocktail ['kɔkteil] *n* combinado *m*, copetín *m*, coctel *or* cóctel *m*.

cocktail cabinet ['kɔkteil,kæbinit] *n* mueble-bar *m*.

cocktail party ['kɔkteil,pɑːti] *n* coctel *or* cóctel *m*.

cocktail shaker ['kɔkteil,ʃeikə*] *n* coctelera *f*.

cocky ['kɔki] *adj* (*fam*) engreído, hinchado.

cocoa ['kəukəu] *n* cacao *m*; (*drink*) chocolate *m*.

coconut ['kəukənʌt] *n* coco *m*.

coconut palm ['kəukənʌt,pɑːm] *n* cocotero *m*.

cocoon [kə'kuːn] *n* capullo *m*.

cod [kɔd] *n* bacalao *m*.

coddle ['kɔdl] *vt* mimar, hacer mimos a.

code [kəud] **1** *n* (a) (*Law etc*) código *m*; **highway —** código *m* de la circulación; **penal —** código *m* penal.
(b) (*cypher*) cifra *f*; **in —** en cifra; **Morse —** el alfabeto Morse.
2 *vt* cifrar, poner en cifra.

codeine ['kəudiːn] *n* codeína *f*.

codex ['kəudeks] *n*, *pl* **codices** ['kɔdisiːz] códice *m*.

codfish ['kɔdfiʃ] *n* bacalao *m*.

codger ['kɔdʒə*] *n*: **old —** sujeto *m*, vejete *m*.

codicil ['kɔdisil] *n* codicilo *m*.

codify ['kəudifai] *vt* codificar.

cod-liver oil ['kɔdlivər'ɔil] *n* aceite *m* de hígado de bacalao.

co-driver ['kəudraivə*] *n* copiloto *m*.

coed ['kəu'ed] **1** *adj* (*fam*) coeducacional. **2** *n* alumna *f* de un colegio coeducacional.

coeducation ['kəu,edju'keiʃən] *n* coeducación *f*.

coeducational ['kəu,edju'keiʃənl] *adj* coeducacional.

coefficient [,kəui'fiʃənt] *n* coeficiente *m*.

coerce [kəu'əːs] *vt* forzar, obligar (*into doing something* a hacer algo).

coercion [kəu'əːʃən] *n* coacción *f*, compulsión *f*; **under —** obligado a ello.

coercive [kəu'əːsiv] *adj* coactivo.

coeval [kəu'iːvəl] **1** *adj* coetáneo (*with* de), contemporáneo (*with* de). **2** *n* coetáneo *m*, a *f*, contemporáneo *m*, a *f*.

coexist ['kəuig'zist] *vi* coexistir (*with* con).

coexistence ['kəuig'zistəns] *n* coexistencia *f*; **peaceful —** coexistencia *f* pacífica.

coexistent ['kəuig'zistənt] *adj* coexistente.

coffee ['kɔfi] *n* café *m*; **black —** café *m* solo; **white —** café *m* con leche.

coffee bar ['kɔfibɑː*] *n* cafetería *f*.

coffee bean ['kɔfibiːn] *n* grano *m* de café.

coffee cup ['kɔfikʌp] *n* taza *f* para café.

coffee grounds ['kɔfigraundz] *n* heces *fpl* de café.

coffee house ['kɔfihaus] *n* café *m*.

coffee mill ['kɔfimil] *n* molinillo *m* de café.

coffeepot ['kɔfipɔt] *n* cafetera *f*.

coffer ['kɔfə*] *n* cofre *m*, arca *f*; (*Archit*) artesón *m*; **—s** (*fig*) fondos *mpl*.

cofferdam ['kɔfədæm] *n* ataguía *f*.

coffin ['kɔfin] *n* ataúd *m*.

cog [kɔg] *n* diente *m*; (*wheel*) rueda *f* dentada; **to be just a — in a machine** ser solamente una pieza de un mecanismo.

cogency ['kəudʒənsi] *n* fuerza *f*, lógica *f*, convicción *f*.

cogent ['kəudʒənt] *adj* fuerte, lógico, convincente, sólido.

cogently ['kəudʒəntli] *adv* lógicamente, de modo convincente, con argumentos sólidos.

cogitate ['kɔdʒiteit] *vti* meditar.

cogitation [,kɔdʒi'teiʃən] *n* meditación *f*.

cognac ['kɔnjæk] *n* coñac *m*.

cognate ['kɔgneit] **1** *adj* cognado (*with* con); afín. **2** *n* cognado *m*.

cognition [kɔg'niʃən] *n* cognición *f*.

cognizance ['kɔgnizəns] *n* conocimiento *m*; **to be within one's —** ser de la competencia de uno; **to take — of** tener en cuenta.

cognizant ['kɔgnizənt] *adj*: **to be — of** saber, estar enterado de.

cognomen [kɔg'nəumen] *n* apodo *m*, sobrenombre *m*.

cogwheel ['kɔgwiːl] *n* rueda *f* dentada.

cohabit [kəu'hæbit] *vi* cohabitar.

cohabitation [,kəuhæbi'teiʃən] *n* cohabitación *f*.

coheir ['kəu'eə*] *n* coheredero *m*.

coheiress ['kəu'eəris] *n* coheredera *f*.

cohere [kəu'hiə*] vi adherirse, pegarse; (ideas etc) formar un conjunto sólido, ser consecuentes.
coherence [kəu'hiərəns] n coherencia f.
coherent [kəu'hiərənt] adj coherente; lógico, comprensible.
cohesion [kəu'hi:ʒən] n cohesión f.
cohesive [kəu'hi:siv] adj cohesivo; unido.
cohort ['kəuhɔ:t] n cohorte f.
coif [kɔif] n cofia f.
coiffeur [kwɔ'fə:*] n peluquero m.
coiffure [kwɔ'fjuə*] n peinado m.
coil [kɔil] **1** n rollo m; (of rope etc) adujada f; (of snake) anillo m; (of smoke) espiral f; (of still etc) serpentín m; (Elec) bobina f, carrete m.
  2 vt arrollar, enrollar; rope (Naut) adujar.
  3 vi arrollarse, enrollarse; to — up (snake) enroscarse; (smoke) subir en espiral.
coin [kɔin] **1** n moneda f; to pay someone back in his own — pagar a uno en la misma moneda; to toss a — echar a cara o cruz.
  2 vt money acuñar; word etc inventar, idear; he must be —ing money está acuñando dinero, el negocio ha de ser un río de oro para él.
coinage ['kɔinidʒ] n (system) moneda f, sistema m monetario; (act) acuñación f; (of word etc) invención f.
coincide [,kəuin'said] vi coincidir (with con); (agree) estar de acuerdo (with con).
coincidence [kəu'insidəns] n coincidencia f; (chance) casualidad f; what a —! ¡qué casualidad!
coincidental [kəu,insi'dentl] adj coincidente; (by chance) fortuito.
coitus ['kɔitəs] n coito m.
coke¹ [kəuk] n coque m.
coke² [kəuk] n (fam) Coca-Cola f.
colander ['kʌləndə*] n colador m, escurridor m.
cold [kəuld] **1** adj frío (also fig); as — as charity más frío que el hielo; my feet are — as ice tengo los pies helados; to be — (person) tener frío, (thing) estar frío, (weather) hacer frío; to be very — (person) tener mucho frío, (thing) estar muy frío, (weather) hacer mucho frío; to get — (thing) enfriarse, (weather) empezar a hacer frío; he's got them — (audience) los tiene en el bolsillo; he's got three tricks — tiene tres bazas segurísimas; to knock someone — poner a uno fuera de combate; it leaves me — no me produce emoción alguna.
  2 n (a) frío m; to catch — tomar frío; to leave someone out in the — dejar a uno al margen.
  (b) (Med, also common —) resfriado m, catarro m; to catch a — resfriarse, acatarrarse; to have a — estar resfriado, estar acatarrado.
cold-blooded ['kəuld'blʌdid] adj (Zool) de sangre fría; (fig) insensible; (cruel) desalmado.
cold cream ['kəuld'kri:m] n colcrén m, crema f.
cold cuts ['kəuld'kʌts] npl (US) fiambres mpl.
cold-hearted ['kəuld'hɑ:tid] adj insensible, cruel.
coldly ['kəuldli] adv fríamente (also fig).
cold-shoulder ['kəuld'ʃəuldə*] vt tratar con frialdad.
cold storage ['kəuld'stɔ:ridʒ] n almacenaje m frigorífico; to put something into — dar carpetazo a algo.
coleslaw ['kəulslɔ:] n (US) ensalada f de col.
colic ['kɔlik] n cólico m.
Coliseum [,kɔli'si:əm] Coliseo m.
colitis [kɔ'laitis] n colitis f.
collaborate [kə'læbəreit] vi colaborar (in, on en; with con).
collaboration [kə,læbə'reiʃən] n colaboración f; (Pol) colaboracionismo m.
collaborator [kə'læbəreitə*] n colaborador m, ora f; (Pol) colaboracionista mf.
collage [kɔ'lɑ:ʒ] n (Art) collage m.
collapse [kə'læps] **1** n (Med) colapso m; (of building) hundimiento m, derrumbamiento m, desplome m; (of roadway etc) socavón m; (of plans) fracaso m.
  2 vi (a) (Med) sufrir colapso; (fig) to — with laughter morirse de risa.
  (b) (building) hundirse, derrumbarse, desplomarse; (fig) fracasar; hood that —s capota f plegable.
collapsible [kə'læpsəbl] adj plegable.
collar ['kɔlə*] **1** n cuello m; (of animal, Tech) collar m; soft — cuello m blando; stiff — cuello m duro, cuello m almidonado; to get hot under the — sulfurarse.
  2 vt prender por el cuello; (fam) apropiarse, pisar.
collarbone ['kɔləbəun] n clavícula f.
collate [kɔ'leit] vt cotejar.
collateral [kɔ'lætərəl] **1** adj colateral. **2** n resguardo m, seguridad f colateral.
collation [kə'leiʃən] n (meal) colación f; (of texts) cotejo m.

colleague ['kɔli:g] n colega m.
collect ['kɔlekt] n (Eccl) colecta f.
collect [kə'lekt] **1** vt reunir, acumular; people reunir; stamps etc coleccionar; fares, wages cobrar; debts, taxes recaudar; money for charity colectar; (pick up, Post) recoger; dust, water etc retener; I'll go and — the mail voy por el correo; I'll — you at 8 vengo a recogerte a las 8; I must — my bags from the station tengo que recoger mi equipaje a la estación.
  2 vi reunirse, acumularse; (people) reunirse, congregarse; (be a collector) ser coleccionista, coleccionar; (water) estancarse; (dust) acumularse; when do we —? ¿cuándo cobramos?; to — for charity hacer una colecta con fines benéficos.
  3 vr: to — oneself reponerse, sosegarse.
collected [kə'lektid] **1** pret and ptp of collect. **2** adj (cool) sosegado, tranquilo; — works obras fpl completas.
collection [kə'lekʃən] n acumulación f, montón m; (of people) grupo m; (of pictures, stamps etc) colección f; (of fares, wages) cobro m; (of debts, taxes) recaudación f; (Eccl) colecta f; (for charity) colecta f, cuestación f; (Post) recogida f; to make a — for hacer una colecta a beneficio de.
collective [kə'lektiv] adj colectivo.
collectively [kə'lektivli] adv colectivamente.
collectivize [kə'lektivaiz] vt colectivizar.
collector [kə'lektə*] n coleccionador m, ora f; (of stamps etc) coleccionista mf; (tax-) recaudador m.
colleen [kɔ'li:n] n (Ir) muchacha f.
college ['kɔlidʒ] n colegio m; (eg of Oxford) colegio m mayor; (eg of art) escuela f; commercial — escuela f para secretarias; electoral — colegio m electoral; junior — (US) colegio m que comprende los 2 primeros años universitarios.
collegiate [kə'li:dʒiit] adj (a) (Eccl) colegial, colegiado; — church iglesia f colegial. (b) (Univ) que tiene colegios, organizado a base de colegios.
collide [kə'laid] vi chocar (with con; also fig).
collie ['kɔli] n perro m pastor.
collier ['kɔliə*] n minero m de carbón; (boat) barco m carbonero.
colliery ['kɔliəri] n mina f de carbón.
collision [kə'liʒən] n choque m (also fig), colisión f; to come into — with chocar con.
colloquial [kə'ləukwiəl] adj familiar, coloquial.
colloquialism [kə'ləukwiəlizəm] n palabra f (or expresión f) familiar; (style) estilo m familiar.
colloquy ['kɔləkwi] n coloquio m.
collusion [kə'lu:ʒən] n confabulación f; connivencia f; to be in — with conspirar con, confabular con.
collywobbles ['kɔli,wɔblz] npl (fam) rugido m de tripas.
Cologne [kə'ləun] Colonia.
colon¹ ['kəulən] n (Anat) colon m.
colon² ['kəulən] n (Typ) dos puntos mpl.
colonel ['kɔ:nl] n coronel m.
colonial [kə'ləuniəl] **1** adj colonial; power colonizador. **2** n colono m.
colonialism [kə'ləuniəlizəm] n colonialismo m.
colonialist [kə'ləuniəlist] n colonialista mf.
colonist ['kɔlənist] n colonizador m, colono m.
colonization [,kɔlənai'zeiʃən] n colonización f.
colonize ['kɔlənaiz] vt colonizar.
colonnade [,kɔlə'neid] n columnata f.
colony ['kɔləni] n colonia f.
colophon ['kɔləfən] n colofón m.
Colorado [,kɔlə'rɑ:dəu]: — beetle escarabajo m de la patata.
coloration [,kʌlə'reiʃən] n colorido m, colores mpl.
colossal [kə'lɔsl] adj colosal.
colossus [kə'lɔsəs] n coloso m.
colour, (US) **color** ['kʌlə*] **1** n (a) color m; fast — color m sólido; high — color m subido; local — color m local; it's a blue —, it's blue in — es de color azul; what — is it? ¿de qué color es?; in full — a todo color; to be off — estar indispuesto; to change — mudar de color; to lend — to a story hacer que un cuento parezca más verosímil; let's see the — of your money! ¡a ver el dinero!; to take all the — out of something quitar lo pintoresco de algo, suprimir lo emocionante de algo.
  (b) —s (flag) bandera f; to call to the —s llamar a filas, llamar al servicio militar; to come out with flying —s salir con lucimiento, salir airoso de la prueba; to sail under false —s encubrir su verdadera lealtad; to show oneself in one's true —s dejar ver su verdadero carácter.
  2 vt color(e)ar; (paint) pintar, (dye) teñir (red de rojo); drawing iluminar.
  3 vi (also to — up) sonrojarse.
colour bar ['kʌləbɑ:*] n barrera f racial.
colour-blind ['kʌləblaind] adj daltoniano.

colour blindness ['kʌlə,blaindnis] n daltonismo m.
coloured ['kʌləd] 1 pret and ptp of **colour**. 2 adj person, pencil de color; **a highly — tale** un cuento de los más pintorescos.
colour film ['kʌləfilm] n película f en colores.
colourful ['kʌləful] adj lleno de color; scene vivo, animado; person etc pintoresco.
colouring ['kʌləriŋ] n colorido m; (substance) colorante m; (of complexion) colores mpl.
colourless ['kʌləlis] adj sin color, incoloro; (fig) soso.
colour television ['kʌlə,teli'viʒən] n televisión f en colores.
colt [kəult] n potro m.
coltish ['kəultiʃ] adj juguetón, retozón.
coltsfoot ['kəultsfut] n uña f de caballo, fárfara f.
columbine ['kɔləmbain] n aguileña f.
Columbine ['kɔləmbain] f Columbina.
Columbus [kə'lʌmbəs] m Colón.
column ['kɔləm] n (all senses) columna f; **advertisement —** sección f de anuncios; **armoured** columna f blindada; **fifth —** quinta columna f; **spinal —** columna f vertebral; **steering —** columna f de dirección.
columnist ['kɔləmnist] n columnista mf, articulista mf.
coma ['kəumə] n (Med) coma m.
comatose ['kəumətəus] adj comatoso.
comb [kəum] 1 n peine m; (ornamental) peineta f; (for horse) almohaza f; (cock's) cresta f; (Tech) carda f; (honey-) panal m; **to give one's hair a —** peinarse (el pelo).
2 vt peinar; wool cardar; countryside etc registrar con minuciosidad (for en busca de); **to — one's hair** peinarse.
combat ['kɔmbæt] 1 n combate m; **single —** combate m singular; **— duty** servicio m de frente. 2 vt combatir, luchar contra.
combatant ['kɔmbətənt] n combatiente m.
combative ['kɔmbətiv] adj agresivo, belicoso.
combination [,kɔmbi'neiʃən] n combinación f; **— lock** cerradura f de combinación.
combine ['kɔmbain] n (Comm) asociación f, (pej) monopolio m; (Agr) cosechadora f, segadora-trilladora f.
combine [kəm'bain] 1 vt combinar; qualities etc reunir, conjugar. 2 vi combinarse; (companies etc) asociarse, fusionarse.
combined [kəm'baind] 1 pret and ptp of **combine**. 2 adj operation coordinado.
combings ['kəumiŋz] npl peinaduras fpl.
combustible [kəm'bʌstibl] 1 adj combustible. 2 n combustible m.
combustion [kəm'bʌstʃən] n combustión f; **internal — engine** motor m de explosión interna; **spontaneous —** combustión f espontánea.
come [kʌm] (irr: pret **came**, ptp **come**) vi venir; **coming!** ¡voy!; **oh —!, — —!, — now!** ¡vamos!, ¡no es para tanto!; **the harvest —s in August** la recolección es en agosto; **it came as a great surprise to us** la cosa nos sorprendió muchísimo; **it —s in 3 sizes** se sirve en 3 tamaños; **recovery came slowly** el restablecimiento fue lento; **that's what —s of waiting** eso lo trae el esperar; **you could see that coming** eso se veía venir; **how —?** ¿cómo es eso?; **easy — easy go** los dineros del sacristán cantando se vienen y cantando se van; **to — across** person topar; thing dar con, encontrarse con; **to — across with** (fam) dar, proporcionar, sacar; **— again?** (fam) ¿cómo?; **to — along** venir también; **— along!** ¡vamos!, (hurrying) ¡date prisa!, (to runner etc) ¡ánimo!; **how is the book coming along?** ¿qué tal va el libro?; **to — at** solution llegar a, dar con; (attack) atacar, precipitarse sobre; **to — away** marcharse; salir de casa (etc); (part) separarse, desprenderse; **to — back** volver (for por); **to — back (into the game)** volver a tener posibilidades de ganar; **to — back with** responder diciendo; **to — between** interponerse entre; dividir, separar; **nothing can — between us** no hay nada que sea capaz de separarnos; **to — by** conseguir, adquirir, venir en posesión de; **how did you — by that name?** ¿con qué motivo te dieron ese nombre?; **to — down** bajar (from de); (roof etc) desplomarse; (be demolished) ser derribado, (Aer) aterrizar, (crashing) estrellarse, (in sea) amerizar; **it —s down to the knee** llega hasta la rodilla; **if it —s down heads** si sale cara; **to — down with** (Med) enfermar de; **to — for** venir por; **to — forward** avanzar, moverse hacia adelante; presentarse; (to + infin a + infin); **to — from** (stem from) venir de, proceder de; **in** entrar; (train) llegar; (tide) crecer; (fashion) ponerse de moda, imponerse; **to —**

in last (in race) llegar el último; **— in!** ¡adelante!, ¡pase Vd!; **to — into** room entrar en; estate heredar; scheme asociarse con; **to — of a good family** ser de buena familia; **to — off** (part) desprenderse, soltarse; (take place) tener lugar, verificarse; (succeed) tener éxito; **to — off badly** salir malparado, salir perdiendo; **does this lid — off?** ¿esta tapa se puede quitar?; **— off it!** ¡no me digas!; **to — on** (adv) (advance) avanzar; (grow) crecer, desarrollarse; (actor) salir a la escena; (improve) hacer progresos; **— on!** ¡vamos!, (hurrying) ¡date prisa!, (to runner etc) ¡ánimo!; **I've a cold coming on** me va a dar un catarro; **winter was coming on** entraba el invierno; **how is the book coming on?** ¿qué tal va el libro?; **to — on** (prep) encontrar, descubrir; **to — out** salir (of de), mostrarse; (book) salir a luz; (new thing) aparecer, estrenarse; (debutante) ser presentada en sociedad; (news) revelarse, traslucirse; (flower) florecer; (workers) declararse en huelga; (stain) quitarse; **to — out against something** declararse en contra de algo; **to — out for something** declararse a favor de algo; **to — out with** descolgarse con, soltar; **to — over** (visit) venir a ver a uno; **what's — over you?** ¿te pasa algo?; **I don't know what came over me** no sé lo que me pasó; **to — round** (visit) venir a ver a uno; (agree) asentir, dejarse persuadir; (Med) volver en sí; **to — to** (adv) (Naut) fachear; (Med) volver en sí; **to — to** (prep) (sum) ascender a; **it came to me suddenly** se me ocurrió de repente; **so it —s to this así** que se reduce a esto; **I came to believe it** llegué a creerlo; **what are we coming to?** ¿adónde va a parar todo esto?; **he had it coming to him** bien merecido lo tenía; **to — together** reunirse, juntarse; **to — under** person estar bajo la jurisdicción de, ser de la competencia de; heading estar comprendido en; **to — up** subir; (sun) salir; (plant) aparecer; (difficulty) surgir; (in conversation) ser mencionado; (Univ) matricularse; **to — up before the judge** comparecer ante el juez; **to — up against** problem tropezar con; enemy tener que habérselas con; **to — up to** subir a; (in height) llegar hasta; (approach) acercarse a; (in street) abordar; (fig) estar a la altura de, corresponder a; standard satisfacer; **to — up with** person alcanzar; thing proponer, sugerir; **to — within someone's jurisdiction** estar bajo la jurisdicción de uno.
comeback ['kʌmbæk] n (fam) **(a)** restablecimiento m, rehabilitación f; esfuerzo m por volver a su antigua posición; **to make a —** restablecerse, rehabilitarse.
(b) reacción f; réplica f; **witty —** respuesta f aguda.
comedian [kə'mi:diən] n cómico m.
comedienne [kə,mi:di'en] n cómica f.
comedown ['kʌmdaun] n (fam) revés m, humillación f; bajón m.
comedy ['kɔmidi] n comedia f; (humour of event) comicidad f; **C— of Errors** Comedia f de las equivocaciones; **— of manners** comedia f de costumbres; **high —** alta comedia f; **low —** farsa f; **musical —** opereta f, (in Spain) zarzuela f.
come-hither ['kʌm'hiðə*] adj look incitante, provocativo.
comely ['kʌmli] adj gentil, lindo.
comer ['kʌmə*] n: **all —s** todos los contendientes; **the first —** el primero en llegar.
comestible [kə'mestibl] 1 adj comestible. 2 **—s** npl comestibles mpl.
comet ['kɔmit] n cometa m.
comfort ['kʌmfət] 1 n **(a)** (solace) consuelo m; (from pain) alivio m; **that's cold (or small) —, that's no — at all** eso no me consuela nada; **you're a great — to me** eres un gran consuelo; **to give — to the enemy** dar aliento al enemigo.
(b) (bodily) confort m, comodidad f; bienestar m; **the —s of life** las cosas agradables de la vida diaria; **with every modern —** con todo confort; **to live in —** vivir cómodamente.
2 vt (solace) consolar; pain aliviar; (bodily) confortar; (encourage) alentar.
comfortable ['kʌmfətəbl] adj house, chair, shoes etc cómodo, confortable; income adecuado; majority suficiente, adecuado; living holgado; **to feel —** encontrarse a gusto; **I don't feel altogether — about it** la cosa me trae muy preocupado; **to have a — win over someone** vencer a uno fácilmente; **to make oneself —** acomodarse a su gusto; **make yourself —!** ¡póngase cómodamente!, ¡acomódese a su gusto!
comfortably ['kʌmfətəbli] adv sit etc cómodamente; live holgadamente; win fácilmente; **to be — off** tener una renta adecuada.

comforter ['kʌmfətə*] n (a) (person) consolador m, ora f. (b) (scarf) bufanda f; (US) colcha f, edredón m. (c) (baby's) chupete m.

comforting ['kʌmfətiŋ] adj consolador, (re)confortante.

comfortless ['kʌmfətlis] adj incómodo, sin comodidad.

comfort station ['kʌmfət,steiʃən] n (US) urinario m público.

comfy ['kʌmfi] adj (fam) = **comfortable**.

comic ['kɔmik] n (person) cómico m; (paper) tebeo m.

comic(al) ['kɔmik(əl)] adj cómico; divertido, entretenido.

comically ['kɔmikəli] adv cómicamente; divertidamente, entretenidamente.

coming ['kʌmiŋ] 1 adj year etc que viene; (future) venidero; (promising) prometedor; it's the — thing es la moda del futuro.
2 n venida f, llegada f; (of Christ) advenimiento m; — and going ir y venir m, trajín m, ajetreo m.

coming-out ['kʌmiŋ'aut] n presentación f en sociedad.

comma ['kɔmə] n coma f; inverted —s comillas fpl; in inverted —s entre comillas.

command [kə'mɑːnd] 1 n (a) (order) orden f; mandato m; at the — of, by (the) — of por orden de; by royal — por real orden; to be at the — of estar a la disposición de.
(b) (control) mando m, dominio m; — of the seas dominio m de los mares; under the — of bajo el mando de; to be in — of estar al mando de; who is in — here? ¿quién manda aquí?; to have at one's —men mandar; to have at one's —, to have a good — of language dominar; to have good resources at one's — disponer de muchos recursos; to take — of asumir el mando de.
(c) (authority, Mil, Naut, territory, fleet etc) comandancia f; high — alto mando m; second in — segundo m, subjefe m, (Naut) segundo m de a bordo; **bomber** — jefatura f de bombardeo, sección f de bombardeo.
2 vt (give an order to) mandar, ordenar (to do hacer); men mandar; ship comandar; (have at one's disposal) disponer de; attention llamar poderosamente; price venderse a (or por); respect imponer; sympathy merecerse; view tener, dominar.

commandant [,kɔmən'dænt] n comandante m.

commandeer [,kɔmən'diə*] vt stores, ship etc requisar, expropiar; men reclutar por fuerza; (fam) tomar, apropiarse.

commander [kə'mɑːndə*] n (in general) comandante m, jefe m; (rank) capitán m de fragata.

commander-in-chief [kə'mɑːdərin'tʃiːf] n jefe m supremo, generalísimo m.

commanding [kə'mɑːndiŋ] adj position dominante; appearance imponente; lead, advantage abrumador; — officer jefe m.

commandment [kə'mɑːndmənt] n mandamiento m.

commando [kə'mɑːndəu] n (man, group) comando m.

commemorate [kə'meməreit] vt conmemorar.

commemoration [kə,memə'reiʃən] n conmemoración f; in — of en conmemoración de.

commemorative [kə'memərətiv] 1 adj conmemorativo. 2 n (stamp) conmemorativo m.

commence [kə'mens] 1 vt comenzar, empezar. 2 vi to — to + infin, to — + ger empezar a + infin.

commencement [kə'mensmənt] n comienzo m, principio m; (mainly US: Univ) graduación f.

commend [kə'mend] vt (a) (praise) alabar, elogiar; to — someone for his action alabar la acción de uno.
(b) (recommend) I — him to you se lo recomiendo; I — it to your attention creo que merece su atención; the plan does not — itself to me el proyecto no me resulta aceptable; it has little to — it poco hay que decir a su favor.
(c) (entrust) encomendar (to a).

commendable [kə'mendəbl] adj recomendable, plausible, loable.

commendably [kə'mendəbli] adv de manera loable; it was — short tuvo el mérito de ser breve; you have been — prompt le felicito por la prontitud.

commendation [,kɔmen'deiʃən] n (a) (praise) elogio m, encomio m. (b) recomendación f.

commensurable [kə'menʃərəbl] adj conmensurable, comparable (with con).

commensurate [kə'menʃərit] adj proporcionado; — with equivalente a, que corresponde a.

comment ['kɔment] 1 n comentario m; observación f; no — no tengo nada que decir; it seems to call for — sobre eso conviene hacer algún comentario; to make the — that observar que.
2 vi: to — that observar que; to — on text comentar; subject etc hacer observaciones acerca de; to — unfavourably on something criticar algo.

commentary ['kɔmentəri] n comentario m.

commentator ['kɔmenteitə*] n comentador m, comentarista m (also Radio).

commerce ['kɔmə:s] n comercio m.

commercial [kə'mə:ʃəl] 1 adj comercial; law mercantil. 2 n (fam) emisión f publicitaria; (person) viajante m.

commercialism [kə'mə:ʃəlizəm] n mercantilismo m.

commercialize [kə'mə:ʃəlaiz] vt comercializar.

commiserate [kə'mizəreit] vi expresar su sentimiento; to — with compadecerse de, condolerse de.

commiseration [kə,mizə'reiʃən] n conmiseración f.

commissar ['kɔmisɑ:*] n comisario m.

commissariat [,kɔmi'sɛəriət] n comisariato m, comisaría f.

commissary ['kɔmisəri] n comisario m.

commission [kə'miʃən] 1 n (order, fee) comisión f; (act) perpetración f; (Mil) graduación f de oficial, despacho m de oficial, (warrant) nombramiento m; — agent comisionista m; Royal C— Comisión f Real; on — a comisión; to be out of — estar fuera de servicio; to put out of — inutilizar; to put into — poner en servicio activo.
2 vt officer nombrar (in a regiment a un regimiento); ship poner en servicio activo; architect etc nombrar, hacer un encargo a; picture encargar; to — someone to do something encargar a uno que haga algo.

commissionaire [kə,miʃə'nɛə*] n portero m, conserje m.

commissioner [kə'miʃənə*] m comisario m; high — alto comisario m; — for oaths notario m público; — of police jefe m de policía.

commit [kə'mit] 1 vt (a) crime cometer; error hacer, incurrir en.
(b) (involve) troops enviar a la batalla; resources empeñar.
(c) (entrust) entregar (to a); (Parl) bill someter a una comisión; to — something to someone's charge confiar algo a uno; to — something to the flames entregar algo a las llamas; to — something to memory aprender algo de memoria; to — someone to prison encarcelar a uno; to — someone for trial remitir a uno al tribunal; to — something to paper (or writing) poner algo por escrito.
2 vr: to — oneself hacer una promesa, declararse; to — oneself to comprometerse a, declararse a favor de; I can't — myself to that no puedo comprometerme a eso; without — ing myself sin compromiso por mi parte; I am —ted to help him me he comprometido a ayudarle; we are deeply —ted to this policy nos hemos declarado firmemente a favor de esta política.

commitment [kə'mitmənt] n compromiso m, obligación f, cometido m.

committal [kə'mitl] comisión f; compromiso m, cometido m; (burial) entierro m; — to prison (auto m de) prisión f.

committee [kə'miti] n comisión f, comité m; management — consejo m de administración; organizing — comité m organizador; to be on a — ser miembro de un comité.

commode [kə'məud] n sillico m.

commodious [kə'məudiəs] adj grande, espacioso.

commodity [kə'mɔditi] n artículo m (de consumo or de comercio), mercancía f, mercadería f, producto m; commodities mercancías fpl, géneros mpl.

commodore ['kɔmədɔ:*] n comodoro m.

common ['kɔmən] 1 adj (a) (belonging to many) común (also Math, Gram); law consuetudinario; it is — to all men es común a todos; A has nothing in — with B A no tiene nada de común con B; we have nothing in — no tenemos ningún interés en común; we have a lot in — tenemos muchos intereses en común; I, in — with everybody else yo, al igual que todos los demás; to work for a — aim cooperar todos a un mismo fin.
(b) (public) público.
(c) (frequent) común, frecuente; this butterfly is — in Spain esta mariposa es común en España.
(d) (usual, ordinary) corriente, usual; soldier raso; belief vulgar; the — man el hombre medio; in — use de uso corriente; it is no more than — courtesy to write no es más que una cortesía elemental escribir; it is — to see such things now ahora es frecuente ver tales cosas.
(e) (vulgar) ordinario; she's very — es muy ordinaria; as — as dirt de lo más ordinario; — or garden ordinario.

2 n (a) campo m común, ejido m.

(b) —s (Pol) estado m llano; the C—s los Comunes.

(c) short —s ración f escasa; to be on short —s comer mal.

commoner ['kɔmənə*] n plebeyo m, a f; (Univ) estudiante m que no tiene beca del colegio.

commonly ['kɔmənli] adv comúnmente, frecuentemente; generalmente; it is — believed that se cree vulgarmente que.

commonness ['kɔmənnis] n frecuencia f; (vulgarity) ordinariez f.

commonplace ['kɔmənpleis] 1 adj vulgar, trivial; it is — to see that es frecuente ver que.

2 n (a) (ordinary thing) cosa f común, cosa f corriente.

(b) (Lit etc) lugar m común, tópico m, perogrullada f.

commonroom ['kɔmənrum] n salón m (de un colegio etc).

commonsense ['kɔmən,sens] adj racional, lógico; the — thing to do is lo lógico es.

commonwealth ['kɔmənwelθ] n república f; the (British) C— la Mancomunidad (Británica).

commotion [kə'məuʃən] n tumulto m, confusión f; civil — disturbio m, perturbación f del orden público; to cause a — armar un lío; there was a — in the crowd se armó un lío entre los espectadores.

communal ['kɔmju:nl] adj comunal.

communally ['kɔmju:nəli] adv comunalmente; to act — obrar como comunidad; the property is held — la propiedad la posee la comunidad.

commune ['kɔmju:n] n (Pol) comuna f.

commune [kə'mju:n] vi (Eccl) comulgar; to — with conversar con, comunicarse con.

communicable [kə'mju:nikəbl] adj comunicable; disease transmisible.

communicant [kə'mju:nikənt] n comulgante mf.

communicate [kə'mju:nikeit] 1 vt comunicar. 2 vi (Eccl) comulgar; (buildings etc) mandarse; (speak) comunicarse (with con).

communication [kə,mju:ni'keiʃən] n comunicación f; to be in — with estar en contacto con; to get into — with ponerse en contacto con.

communication cord [kə,mju:ni'keiʃənkɔ:d] n (Rail) timbre m de alarma.

communicative [kə'mju:nikətiv] adj comunicativo.

communion [kə'mju:niən] n comunión f; to take — comulgar.

communiqué [kə'mju:nikei] n comunicado m, parte m; joint — comunicado m conjunto.

communism ['kɔmjunizəm] n comunismo m.

communist ['kɔmjunist] 1 adj comunista. 2 n comunista mf.

communistic [,kɔmju'nistik] adj comunista.

community [kə'mju:niti] n comunidad f; (people at large) colectividad f, sociedad f; (local inhabitants) vecindario m; — centre centro m social; — singing canto m colectivo.

communize ['kɔmju:naiz] vt comunizar.

commutation [,kɔmju'teiʃən] n (US) conmutación f; (Rail etc) uso m de un billete de abono; — ticket billete m de abono.

commute [kə'mju:t] 1 vt payment conmutar (into en, for por); sentence conmutar (to en, por). 2 vi viajar a diario, ir y venir regularmente (to work al trabajo).

commuter [kə'mju:tə*] n persona f que viaja a diario (al trabajo), persona f que viaja muy a menudo.

compact ['kɔmpækt] n (a) pacto m, convenio m.

(b) (powder-) polvera f.

compact [kəm'pækt] 1 adj compacto; material apretado, sólido; style breve, conciso. 2 vt material comprimir (into en); condensar; to be —ed of consistir en.

compactly [kəm'pæktli] adv de modo compacto; apretadamente, sólidamente; brevemente, concisamente.

compactness [kəm'pæktnis] n compacidad f, compresión f; (of style) concisión f.

companion [kəm'pæniən] n compañero m, a f; (lady's) señora f de compañía.

companionable [kəm'pæniənəbl] adj sociable, simpático.

companionship [kəm'pæniənʃip] n compañerismo m.

companionway [kəm'pæniənwei] n (Naut) escalera f de cámara.

company ['kʌmpəni] n (a) (in general) compañía f (also Mil, Theat); ship's — tripulación f; he's good — es un compañero divertido; present — excepted mejorando lo presente, con perdón de los presentes;

we have — tenemos visita; to join — with reunirse con; to keep someone — acompañar a uno, estar con uno; to keep — (lovers) andar en relaciones; to keep bad — tener amistades sospechosas; a man is known by the — he keeps dime con quién andas y te diré quién eres; to part — separarse (with de), (fig) desprenderse, soltarse.

(b) (Comm) sociedad f, compañía f, empresa f; Smith and C— Smith y Compañía; affiliated — sociedad f filial; holding — sociedad f de control, compañía f tenedora; joint-stock —, limited (liability) — sociedad f anónima; shipping — compañía f naviera; trust — banco m fideicomisario.

comparable ['kɔmpərəbl] adj comparable; a — case un caso análogo; they are not — no se les puede comparar.

comparative [kəm'pærətiv] 1 adj relativo; (Gram etc) comparativo; study comparado. 2 n (Gram) comparativo m.

comparatively [kəm'pærətivli] adv relativamente.

compare [kəm'pεə*] 1 n: beyond —, past —, without — sin comparación.

2 vt comparar (to, with con); (put side by side) cotejar; as —d with comparado con; they are not to be —d no se les puede comparar.

3 vi poderse comparar; he can't — with you no se le puede comparar con Vd; it —s very favourably with the other no pierde por comparación con el otro; how do they —? ¿cuáles son sus cualidades respectivas?; how do they — for speed? ¿cuál tiene mayor velocidad?

comparison [kəm'pærisn] n comparación f; cotejo m; in — with en comparación con.

compartment [kəm'pɑ:tmənt] n compartimiento m; (Rail, of case etc) departamento m.

compass ['kʌmpəs] 1 n (a) (Naut etc) brújula f.

(b) (range) alcance m, extensión f; (area) ámbito m; beyond my — fuera de mi alcance; in a small — en un espacio reducido.

(c) —es compás m; a pair of —es un compás.

2 vt (contrive) conseguir, (pej) tramar; (grasp mentally) comprender; (surround) rodear; to be —ed about by estar rodeado de.

compassion [kəm'pæʃən] n compasión f; to have — on tener piedad de; to move someone to — mover a uno a compasión.

compassionate [kəm'pæʃənit] adj compasivo; on — grounds por compasión.

compatibility [kəm,pætə'biliti] n compatibilidad f.

compatible [kəm'pætibl] adj compatible, conciliable.

compatriot [kəm'pætriət] n compatriota mf.

compel [kəm'pel] vt obligar; respect imponer; surrender exigir, hacer inevitable; to — someone to do something forzar a uno a hacer algo; I feel —led to say me veo obligado a decir.

compelling [kəm'peliŋ] adj argument convincente; curiosity etc compulsivo.

compellingly [kəm'peliŋli] adv de modo convincente.

compendious [kəm'pendiəs] adj compendioso.

compendium [kəm'pendiəm] n compendio m.

compensate ['kɔmpenseit] 1 vt compensar; (reward) recompensar; (for loss etc) indemnizar, resarcir (for de). 2 vi: to — for something compensar algo.

compensation [,kɔmpen'seiʃən] n compensación f; (reward) recompensa f; (for loss etc) indemnización f, resarcimiento m.

compensatory [kəm'pensətəri] adj compensatorio.

compère ['kɔmpεə*] n presentador m.

compete [kəm'pi:t] vi (as rivals; Comm) competir, hacer competencia (against, with con, for por); (in a race) tomar parte (in en), presentarse (in a), concurrir (in a); to — in a market concurrir a un mercado.

competence ['kɔmpitəns] n aptitud f, capacidad f, competencia f; (of court etc) competencia f, incumbencia f; that is not within my — eso está fuera de mi competencia.

competent ['kɔmpitənt] adj competente, capaz, adecuado; to be — to do something ser competente para hacer algo.

competently ['kɔmpitəntli] adv de modo adecuado, competentemente.

competition [,kɔmpi'tiʃən] n (a) (spirit) competencia f, rivalidad f; in — with en competencia con; there was keen — for the prize se disputó reñidamente el premio.

(b) (Comm) competencia f; unfair — competencia f desleal.

(c) (contest) concurso m; (eg for Civil Service posts) oposiciones fpl; 60 places to be filled by — 60 vacantes a cubrir por oposiciones.

competitive [kəm'petitiv] adj spirit competidor, de competencia; exam de concurso; price competitivo.

competitor [kəm'petitə*] n (a) (rival) competidor m, ora f, rival mf; (Comm) competidor m. (b) (in contest) concursante mf; (eg for Civil Service post) opositor m, ora f.

compilation [ˌkɔmpi'leiʃən] n compilación f, recopilación f.

compile [kəm'pail] vt compilar, recopilar.

compiler [kəm'pailə*] n compilador m, ora f, recopilador m, ora f; autor m, ora f.

complacence [kəm'pleisəns] n, **complacency** [kəm'pleisnsi] n suficiencia f, satisfacción f de sí mismo (or consigo).

complacent [kəm'pleisənt] adj suficiente, satisfecho de sí mismo (or consigo); complacido.

complacently [kəm'pleisəntli] adv suficientemente, de modo satisfecho; **he looked at me —** me miró complacido.

complain [kəm'plein] vi quejarse (about, of de, that de que, to a); **I can't —** yo no tengo motivo para quejarme.

complaint [kəm'pleint] n (a) queja f; (Law) querella f, demanda f; **to have cause for —** tener motivo para quejarse; **to lodge** (or make) **a —** formular una queja, hacer una reclamación. (b) (Med) enfermedad f, mal m, dolencia f.

complaisant [kəm'pleizənt] adj servicial, cortés; husband consentido.

complement ['kɔmplimənt] n complemento m; (Naut) dotación f, personal m.

complement ['kɔmpliment] vt complementar.

complementary [ˌkɔmpli'mentəri] adj complementario; **they are —** se complementan.

complete [kəm'pli:t] 1 adj entero, completo; total; (finished) acabado; (accomplished) consumado; **my happiness is —** mi dicha es completa; **tell me the — story** cuénteme la historia en su totalidad; **it is a — mistake to think that** es totalmente erróneo pensar que; **it's a — disaster** es un desastre total; **it was not a — success** no obtuvo un éxito rotundo que digamos; **my report is still not quite —** mi informe todavía no está terminado del todo; **are we —?** ¿estamos todos? 2 vt completar; (finish) terminar, acabar, concluir; years cumplir; form llenar; **to — my happiness** para colmo de dicha.

completely [kəm'pli:tli] adv completamente, enteramente; totalmente; por completo; a fondo.

completeness [kəm'pli:tnis] n lo completo etc; **for the sake of —** para completar.

completion [kəm'pli:ʃən] n terminación f, conclusión f; (of contract etc) realización f; **on —** en cuanto se termine; **to be nearing —** estar para terminarse.

complex ['kɔmpleks] 1 adj complejo, complicado. 2 n (a) (Psych) complejo m; **inferiority —** complejo m de inferioridad; **Oedipus —** complejo m de Edipo; **he's got a — about it** sobre eso tiene una idea fija, aquello le obsesiona. (b) (Tech) complejo m; **industrial —** complejo m industrial.

complexion [kəm'plekʃən] n tez f, cutis m; (fig) aspecto m; **that puts a different — on it** entonces la cosa cambia de aspecto.

complexity [kəm'pleksiti] n complejidad f, lo complicado.

compliance [kəm'plaiəns] n condescendencia f, sumisión f (with a); (agreement) conformidad f; **in — with** de acuerdo con, obedeciendo a.

compliant [kəm'plaiənt] adj condescendiente, sumiso.

complicate ['kɔmplikeit] vt complicar.

complicated ['kɔmplikeitid] adj complicado.

complication [ˌkɔmpli'keiʃən] n complicación f; lo complicado; **—s** dificultades fpl; **it seems there are —s** parece que han surgido dificultades.

complicity [kəm'plisiti] n complicidad f (in en).

compliment ['kɔmplimənt] n (a) (polite expression, of praise) cumplido m; (amorous) piropo m; **what a nice —!** ¡qué detalle!; **that was meant as a —** lo dije con buena intención; **to pay a —** to hacer cumplidos a, woman piropear a; **I take that as a —** agradezco la cortesía; **I take it as a — that** para mí es un honor que + subj; **they did me the — of coming along** me hicieron el honor de asistir. (b) **—s** (greetings) saludos mpl; **with the —s of Mr X** de parte del Sr X; **with the —s of the season** deseándole felices Pascuas (etc); **with the author's —s** homenaje del autor; **to send one's —s** to enviar saludos a.

compliment ['kɔmpliment] vt: **to — someone on something** felicitar a uno por algo.

complimentary [ˌkɔmpli'mentəri] adj remark etc lisonjero; ticket de favor; **he was very — about the play** habló en términos lisonjeros de la obra.

comply [kəm'plai] vi obedecer; **to — with** conformarse con, ajustarse a, order obedecer.

component [kəm'pəunənt] 1 adj componente; **its — parts** las piezas que lo integran. 2 n (Chem) componente m; (Tech) pieza f.

comport [kəm'pɔ:t] 1 vi: **to — with** concordar con. 2 vr: **to — oneself** comportarse.

comportment [kəm'pɔ:tmənt] n comportamiento m.

compose [kəm'pəuz] 1 vt componer; **to be —d of** constar de, componerse de. 2 vr: **to — oneself** tranquilizarse; **I —d myself to play** me dispuse a tocar.

composed [kəm'pəuzd] adj sosegado.

composedly [kəm'pəuzidli] adv sosegadamente.

composer [kəm'pəuzə*] n compositor m.

composite ['kɔmpəzit] adj compuesto.

composition [ˌkɔmpə'ziʃən] n composición f.

compositor [kəm'pɔzitə*] n cajista m.

compos mentis ['kɔmpɔs'mentis] adj: **to be —** estar en su juicio.

compost ['kɔmpɔst] n abono m compuesto.

compost heap ['kɔmpɔsthi:p] n montón m de abono compuesto.

composure [kəm'pəuʒə*] n serenidad f, calma f; **to recover one's —** serenarse.

compote ['kɔmpəut] n compota f.

compound¹ ['kɔmpaund] 1 adj compuesto; fracture complicado. 2 n (Chem) compuesto m; (Gram) vocablo m compuesto.

compound² ['kɔmpaund] n (enclosure) recinto m.

compound [kəm'paund] 1 vt componer, mezclar; **to — a felony** aceptar dinero para no entablar juicio. 2 vi: **to — with** capitular con.

comprehend [ˌkɔmpri'hend] vt comprender.

comprehensible [ˌkɔmpri'hensəbl] adj comprensible.

comprehension [ˌkɔmpri'henʃən] n comprensión f; **it is past —** es incomprensible; **it passes my — that** para mí resulta incomprensible que.

comprehensive [ˌkɔmpri'hensiv] adj knowledge, study extenso; report global; account, view de conjunto; insurance contra todo riesgo; school integrado.

compress ['kɔmpres] n compresa f.

compress [kəm'pres] vt comprimir (into en); text etc reducir (into a).

compressed [kəm'prest] adj comprimido; **— air** aire m comprimido.

compression [kəm'preʃən] n compresión f.

comprise [kəm'praiz] vt (include) comprender (consist of) constar de, componerse de; range abarcar; **to be —d within certain limits** estar incluido dentro de ciertos límites.

compromise ['kɔmprəmaiz] 1 n (spirit, art of —) transigencia f; (agreement) componenda f, avenencia f, arreglo m; (midway point) término m medio; **there can be no — with treason** no transigimos con la traición; **to reach a —** llegar a un arreglo. 2 vt person comprometer, thing poner en peligro. 3 vi transigir, ceder un poco para llegar a un acuerdo; **I agreed to —** consentí en que la cosa quedase en un término medio; **to — with** transigir con, avenirse con.

compromising ['kɔmprəmaiziŋ] adj situation comprometedor; mind, spirit acomodaticio.

comptroller [kən'trəulə*] n interventor m.

compulsion [kəm'pʌlʃən] n obligación f, fuerza f mayor, coacción f; **under —** por fuerza; **you are under no —** nadie le obliga a ello.

compulsive [kəm'pʌlsiv] adj compulsivo.

compulsorily [kəm'pʌlsərili] adv por fuerza, forzosamente.

compulsory [kəm'pʌlsəri] adj obligatorio; purchase forzoso.

compunction [kəm'pʌŋkʃən] n remordimiento m; **without —** sin escrúpulo.

computation [ˌkɔmpju'teiʃən] n cómputo m, cálculo m.

compute [kəm'pju:t] vt computar, calcular (at en).

computer [kəm'pju:tə*] n computador m, calculadora f; **digital —** computador m digital.

computerize [kəm'pju:təraiz] vt reorganizar (or preparar, programar) para su tratamiento por computador.

comrade ['kɔmrid] n camarada m (also Pol), compañero m, a f.

comrade-in-arms ['kɔmridin'ɑ:mz] n compañero m de armas.

comradeship ['kɔmridʃip] n compañerismo m.

con¹ [kɔn] vt estudiar, repasar (also **to — over**).

con² [kɔn] vt (sl) timar.

con³ [kɔn] n see **pro**.

concatenation [kɔnˌkæti'neiʃən] n concatenación f.

concave ['kɔn'keiv] adj cóncavo.

concavity [kɔn'kæviti] n concavidad f.

conceal [kən'siːl] *vt* ocultar (*from* a); *emotion* disimular; (*Law*) encubrir.

concealed [kən'siːld] *adj* oculto; *emotion* disimulado; *lighting* indirecto.

concealment [kən'siːlmənt] *n* encubrimiento *m* (*also* Law); (*of emotion*) disimulación *f*; **place of —** escondrijo *m*.

concede [kən'siːd] *vt* conceder; **I — that** confieso que; **to — victory to an opponent** reconocer que un rival ha ganado.

conceit [kən'siːt] *n* (a) presunción *f*, engreimiento *m*. (b) (*Lit*) concepto *m*.

conceited [kən'siːtid] *adj* presumido, engreído, vanidoso; **to be — about** envanecerse con.

conceivable [kən'siːvəbl] *adj* concebible: **is it — that ... ?** ¿es posible que ... (+ *subj*)?

conceivably [kən'siːvəbli] *adv* posiblemente; **it cannot — be true** no es posible que sea verdad.

conceive [kən'siːv] **1** *vt* (a) (*child*) concebir.
(b) (*imagine*) imaginar, formarse un concepto de; *idea* tener; *plan* idear; **I — it to be my duty** creo que es mi deber; **I cannot — why** no me explico por qué; **—d in plain terms** formulado en lenguaje sencillo.
(c) *affection, dislike etc* tomar, cobrar (*for* a).
2 *vi* concebir; **to — of** formarse un concepto de; **I cannot — of anything worse** para mí no hay nada peor.

concentrate ['kɔnsəntreit] **1** *n* (*Chem*) concentrado *m*, sustancia *f* concentrada.
2 *vt* concentrar; *troops etc* concentrar, reunir; *hopes* cifrar (*on* en).
3 *vi* concentrarse; (*troops etc*) concentrarse, reunirse; **to — on** *thing* concentrarse en, concentrar la atención en; **to — on doing something** concentrarse para hacer algo; **he can't —** no se puede concentrar.

concentration [,kɔnsən'treiʃən] *n* concentración *f*.

concentric [kən'sentrik] *adj* concéntrico.

concept ['kɔnsept] *n* concepto *m*.

conception [kən'sepʃən] *n* (a) (*of child*) concepción *f*; **the Immaculate C—** la Purísima Concepción.
(b) (*idea*) idea *f*, concepto *m*; **a bold —** un concepto grandioso; **he has not the remotest — of** no tiene la menor idea de.

conceptual [kən'septjuəl] *adj* conceptual.

concern [kən'səːn] **1** *n* (a) (*matter*) asunto *m*; **that's my —** eso es cuenta mía; **it's no — of yours** no tiene nada que ver con Vd; **that's your —!** ¡allá Vd!
(b) (*interest*) interés *m*; **it is of some — to us all** nos interesa a todos; **it's of no —** la cosa no tiene importancia.
(c) (*anxiety*) preocupación *f* (*for, with* con, por), inquietud *f*; **it is a matter for — that** es inquietante que; **he showed his —** se mostró preocupado; **with growing —** con creciente alarma.
(d) (*firm*) empresa *f*; **going —** empresa *f* en pleno funcionamiento; **the whole —** (*fam*) el asunto entero, todo el negocio.
2 *vt* tener que ver con, interesar, concernir; **as —s** respecto de; **that does not —** me eso no tiene que ver conmigo; **it —s me closely** me toca de cerca; **the book —s a family** el libro tiene por tema una familia; **my question —s money** mi pregunta se refiere al dinero; **those —ed** los interesados; **as far as I am —ed** en cuanto a mí, por lo que a mí se refiere; **to be —ed in** tomar parte en, intervenir en; **were you —ed in this?** ¿tú andabas mezclado en esto?; **to be —ed with others in a crime** estar implicado con otros en un crimen; **I am —ed to + infin** me interesa + *infin*; **we are —ed with facts** a nosotros nos interesan los hechos.
3 *vr*: **to — oneself with** interesarse por, ocuparse de.

concerned [kən'səːnd] *adj* inquieto, preocupado; **to be very —** inquietarse mucho (*about* por); **he sounded very —** parecía estar muy inquieto; **I am — about you** me traes preocupado; **I am — to find that** me inquieta descubrir que.

concerning [kən'səːniŋ] *prep* sobre, acerca de.

concert ['kɔnsət] *n* concierto *m*; **in — with** de concierto con; **to act in —** obrar de común acuerdo.

concert [kən'səːt] *vt* concertar; *policy* coordinar, armonizar.

concertgoer ['kɔnsət,gəuə*] *n* aficionado *m* a los conciertos, aficionada *f* a los conciertos; **we are regular —s** vamos con regularidad a los conciertos; **the —s are an odd lot** los que asisten al concierto son gente rara.

concert hall ['kɔnsəthɔːl] *n* sala *f* de conciertos.

concertina [,kɔnsə'tiːnə] *n* concertina *f*.

concertmaster ['kɔnsət,mɑːstə*] *n* (US) concertino *m*.

concerto [kən'tʃeətəu] *n* concierto *m*.

concession [kən'seʃən] *n* concesión *f*; privilegio *m*; **tax —** privilegio *m* fiscal.

concessionaire [kən,seʃə'nɛə*] *n* concesionario *m*.

concierge [,kɔ̃nsi'eəʒ] *n* conserje *m*.

conciliate [kən'silieit] *vt* conciliar.

conciliation [kən,sili'eiʃən] *n* conciliación *f*.

conciliatory [kən'siliətəri] *adj* conciliador.

concise [kən'sais] *adj* conciso.

concisely [kən'saisli] *adv* concisamente.

conciseness [kən'saisnis] *n*, **concision** [kən'siʒən] *n* concisión *f*.

conclave ['kɔnkleiv] *n* cónclave *m*.

conclude [kən'kluːd] **1** *vt* (a) (*end*) concluir, terminar; **"to be —d"** (*serial*) "continuará".
(b) (*arrange*) *treaty* hacer, firmar, pactar; *agreement* llegar a, concertar.
(c) (*infer*) **I — that** saco la consecuencia de que; **what are we to — from that?** ¿qué consecuencia se saca de eso?
2 *vi* terminar(se); **he —d with this remark** terminó haciendo esta observación; **he —d by saying** terminó diciendo; **the book —s poorly** el libro termina mal; **the judge —d in his favour** el juez decidió a su favor.

concluding [kən'kluːdiŋ] *adj* final.

conclusion [kən'kluːʒən] *n* (a) (*end*) conclusión *f*; terminación *f*; **in —** en conclusión, para terminar; **to bring something to a —** concluir algo.
(b) (*inference*) conclusión *f*, consecuencia *f*; **foregone —** resultado *m* inevitable; **to come to the — that** llegar a la conclusión de que; **to jump to —s** juzgar al buen tuntún; **to try —s with** participar en una contienda con.

conclusive [kən'kluːsiv] *adj* concluyente, decisivo.

conclusively [kən'kluːsivli] *adv* concluyentemente.

concoct [kən'kɔkt] *vt* confeccionar; *lie, story* inventar; *plot* tramar.

concoction [kən'kɔkʃən] *n* (*act*) confección *f*; (*of story*) invención *f*; (*substance*) mezcla *f*, (*drink*) brebaje *m*.

concomitant [kən'kɔmitənt] *adj* concomitante.

concord ['kɔŋkɔːd] *n* concordia *f*, armonía *f*; (*Mus, Gram*) concordancia *f*.

concordance [kən'kɔːdəns] *n* concordancia *f*; (*book*) concordancias *fpl*.

concordant [kən'kɔːdənt] *adj* concordante.

concordat [kɔn'kɔːdæt] *n* concordato *m*.

concourse ['kɔŋkɔːs] *n* (*of people*) concurso *m*; (*of rivers*) confluencia *f*; (*Rail*) explanada *f*.

concrete ['kɔnkriːt] **1** *adj* concreto; (*Tech*) de hormigón. **2** *n* hormigón *m*; **reinforced —** hormigón *m* armado. **3** *vt* revestir de hormigón.

concrete mixer ['kɔnkriːt,miksə*] *n* hormigonera *f*.

concretion [kən'kriːʃən] *n* concreción *f*.

concubine ['kɔŋkjubain] *n* concubina *f*.

concupiscence [kən'kjuːpisəns] *n* concupiscencia *f*.

concupiscent [kən'kjuːpisənt] *adj* concupiscente.

concur [kən'kəː*] *vi* (a) (*happen together*) concurrir.
(b) (*agree*) asentir; **to — in** convenir en; **to — with** estar de acuerdo con.

concurrent [kən'kʌrənt] *adj* concurrente.

concurrently [kən'kʌrəntli] *adv* al mismo tiempo.

concuss [kən'kʌs] *vt* producir una conmoción cerebral en.

concussion [kən'kʌʃən] *n* conmoción *f* cerebral.

condemn [kən'dem] *vt* condenar (*to* a); (*blame*) censurar; *building* declarar ruinoso; *bad food* confiscar; **the —ed man** el reo de muerte; **such conduct is to be —ed** tal conducta es censurable.

condemnation [,kɔndem'neiʃən] *n* condenación *f*; (*blaming*) censura *f*.

condensation [,kɔnden'seiʃən] *n* condensación *f*; (*of text*) forma *f* abreviada.

condense [kən'dens] **1** *vt* condensar; *text* abreviar. **2** *vi* condensarse.

condenser [kən'densə*] *n* condensador *m*.

condescend [,kɔndi'send] *vi*: **to — to + infin** dignarse + *infin*.

condescending [,kɔndi'sendiŋ] *adj* superior, lleno de superioridad; **he's very —** se cree muy superior, tiene aire de superioridad.

condescendingly [,kɔndi'sendiŋli] *adv* de modo superior, con aire de superioridad.

condescension [,kɔndi'senʃən] *n* aire *f* de superioridad, aire *m* protector, dignación *f*.

condiment ['kɔndimənt] *n* condimento *m*.

condition [kən'diʃən] **1** *n* (a) (*stipulation*) condición *f*; **on this —** con esta condición; **on no —** de ninguna manera; **on — (that)** a condición que + *subj*.

(b) (state) condición f, estado m; **physical —** estado m físico; **weather —s** estado m del tiempo; **in a bad —** en malas condiciones; **of humble —** de clase humilde; **to be in no — to +** infin no estar en condiciones de + infin; **to be out of —** estar en mal estado; **to keep oneself in —** mantenerse en forma.

(c) —s (circumstances) condiciones fpl; **living —s** condiciones fpl de vida; **working —s** condiciones fpl de trabajo; **under existing —s** en las circunstancias actuales.

2 vt condicionar, determinar; **it is —ed by the size** depende del tamaño.

conditional [kən'diʃənl] **1** adj condicional; **to be — upon** depender de. **2** n (Gram) potencial m.

conditionally [kən'diʃnəli] adv condicionalmente, con reservas.

conditioned [kən'diʃənd] adj condicionado; **— reflex** reflejo m condicionado.

condole [kən'dəul] vi: **to — with someone** condolerse de uno.

condolences [kən'dəulənsiz] npl pésame m; **please accept my —** le acompaño en el sentimiento; **to send one's —** dar el pésame.

condominium ['kɔndə'miniəm] n condominio m.

condone [kən'dəun] vt condonar.

condor ['kɔndɔː*] n cóndor m.

conduce [kən'djuːs] vi: **to — to** conducir a.

conducive [kən'djuːsiv] adj: **— to** conducente a, que conduce a, que favorece.

conduct ['kɔndʌkt] n conducta f, comportamiento m; (of business etc) manejo m, dirección f.

conduct [kən'dʌkt] **1** vt conducir (also Phys); business, negotiations, campaign etc llevar, dirigir; one's case presentar; orchestra dirigir; **to — a correspondence** with estar en correspondencia con; **we were —ed through a passage** nos hicieron pasar por un pasillo; **we were —ed round by Lord X** actuó de guía Lord X.

2 vi (Mus) llevar la batuta.

3 vr: **to — oneself** comportarse.

conducted [kən'dʌktid] adj: **— tour** (of building) visita f dirigida, (of country) viaje m dirigido.

conduction [kən'dʌkʃən] n conducción f.

conductivity [.kɔndʌk'tiviti] n conductibilidad f.

conductor [kən'dʌktə*] n (Mus) director m; (of bus) cobrador m; (US) revisor m; (lightning-) pararrayos m.

conductress [kən'dʌktris] n cobradora f.

conduit ['kɔndit] n conducto m.

cone [kəun] n (Geom, Bot) cono m; (ice cream) barquillo m.

coney ['kəuni] n conejo m.

confab ['kɔnfæb] n (fam) = **confabulation.**

confabulate [kən'fæbjuleit] vi (hum) conferenciar.

confabulation [kən.fæbju'leiʃən] n conferencia f.

confection [kən'fekʃən] n confección f, hechura f.

confectioner [kən'fekʃənə*] n pastelero m, repostero m; **—'s** (shop) pastelería f, repostería f, confitería f.

confectionery [kən'fekʃənəri] n pasteles mpl; (sweets) dulces mpl, confites mpl, confitería f.

confederacy [kən'fedərəsi] n confederación f; (plot) complot m; **the C—** (US) los Estados confederados.

confederate [kən'fedərit] **1** adj confederado. **2** n confederado m; (Law) cómplice m.

confederate [kən'fedəreit] **1** vt confederar. **2** vi confederarse.

confederation [kən.fedə'reiʃən] n confederación f.

confer [kən'fə:*] **1** vt conceder, otorgar (on a). **2** vi conferenciar (about sobre, with con).

conference ['kɔnfərəns] n (talk) conferencia f; (assembly) congreso m.

conferment [kən'fə:mənt] n concesión f, otorgamiento m (on a).

confess [kən'fes] **1** vt confesar; guilt etc reconocer; **to — that** confesar que.

2 vi (Eccl) confesarse; **to — to a crime** confesarse culpable de un crimen; **to — to a liking for** confesar tener afición a; **I was wrong, I —** me equivoqué, lo confieso.

confessed [kən'fest] adj declarado.

confessedly [kən'fesidli] adv según se reconoce.

confession [kən'feʃən] n confesión f; **— of faith** credo m; **to go to —** confesarse; **to hear someone's —** confesar a uno; **to make a full —** confesarlo todo.

confessional [kən'feʃənl] n confesonario m.

confessor [kən'fesə*] n confesor m; **father —** padre m confesor, director m espiritual.

confetti [kən'feti] n confeti m.

confidant [.kɔnfi'dænt] n confidente m.

confidante [.kɔnfi'dænt] n confidenta f.

confide [kən'faid] **1** vt confiar (to a, en).

2 vi: **to — in** confiar en, fiarse de; **please — in me**

puedes fiarte de mí; **to — to** hacer confidencias a; **he —d to me that** me dijo en confianza que.

confidence ['kɔnfidəns] n **(a)** (in general) confianza f (in en, that en que); **in —** en confianza; **"write in strict —"** "absoluta reserva"; **to be in someone's —,** to enjoy someone's **—** disfrutar de la intimidad de uno; **to gain —** adquirir confianza; **to give someone —** infundir confianza a uno; **we have every — in you** tenemos entera confianza en Vd; **I have every — that** estoy totalmente seguro de que; **to put one's — in** confiar en.

(b) (revelation) confidencia f.

confidence man ['kɔnfidənsmæn] n, pl **— men** [men] timador m.

confidence trick ['kɔnfidənstrik] n, (US) **— game** [geim] n timo m.

confident ['kɔnfidənt] adj seguro de sí mismo, lleno de confianza, (over-) confiado; **to be — about, to be — of** estar seguro de; **to be — that** estar seguro de que.

confidential [.kɔnfi'denʃəl] adj information, letter, report etc confidencial; secretary, tone de confianza.

confidentially [.kɔnfi'denʃəli] adv en confianza.

confidently ['kɔnfidəntli] adv: **he said —** dijo lleno de confianza; **we — expect that** creemos con toda confianza que.

confiding [kən'faidiŋ] adj: (too) **—** confiado; crédulo; **in a — tone** en tono de confianza.

configuration [kən.figju'reiʃən] n configuración f.

confine [kən'fain] **1** vt (enclose) encerrar (to en); (fig) limitar (to a); **to be —d** (woman) estar de parto; **to be —d to** limitarse a; **the damage is —d to this part** el daño afecta únicamente esta parte; **this bird is —d to Spain** esta ave existe únicamente en España; **to be —d to bed** tener que guardar cama; **to be —d to one's room** no poder dejar su cuarto.

2 vr: **to — oneself to** limitarse a; **please — yourself to the facts** le ruego limitarse a exponer los hechos.

confined [kən'faind] adj reducido.

confinement [kən'fainmənt] n (enclosure) encierro m (to en); (imprisonment) prisión f, reclusión f; (Med) parto m, sobreparto m; **— to barracks** arresto m en cuartel f; **to be in solitary —** estar incomunicado.

confines ['kɔnfainz] npl confines mpl.

confirm [kən'fə:m] vt confirmar.

confirmation [.kɔnfə'meiʃən] n confirmación f.

confirmed [kən'fə:md] adj inveterado.

confiscate ['kɔnfiskeit] vt confiscar, incautarse de.

confiscation [.kɔnfis'keiʃən] n confiscación f, incautación f.

conflagration [.kɔnflə'greiʃən] n conflagración f.

conflict ['kɔnflikt] n conflicto m; **to be in — with** estar en pugna con; **to come into — with** chocar con.

conflict [kən'flikt] vi estar en pugna (with con).

conflicting [kən'fliktiŋ] adj report contradictorio; interest opuesto.

confluence ['kɔnfluəns] n confluencia f.

conform [kən'fɔ:m] vi conformarse; **to — to, to — with** ajustarse a, estar de acuerdo con, cuadrar con.

conformist [kən'fɔ:mist] **1** adj conformista. **2** n conformista mf.

conformity [kən'fɔ:miti] n conformidad f; **in — with** conforme a.

confound [kən'faund] vt confundir; **— it!** ¡demonio!; **— the man!** ¡maldito sea el hombre!

confounded [kən'faundid] adj condenado.

confront [kən'frʌnt] vt (face squarely) hacer frente a, encararse con; (face defiantly) enfrentarse con; rival confrontarse con; texts confrontar; **the problems which — us** los problemas que se nos plantean; **we were —ed by the river** se nos puso delante el río; **to — someone with something** confrontar a uno con algo; **to — the accused with witnesses** confrontar a los testigos con el acusado; **to — someone with the facts** exponer delante de uno los hechos.

confrontation [.kɔnfrən'teiʃən] n confrontación f; **nuclear —** confrontación f nuclear.

Confucius [kən'fju:ʃəs] m Confucio m.

confuse [kən'fju:z] vt **(a)** (mix up) confundir (with con); issue etc entenebrecer; **to — A and B** confundir A con B, equivocar A con B.

(b) (perplex) desconcertar, dejar confuso a, aturdir; **to get —d** desorientarse, aturrullarse, desconcertarse.

confused [kən'fju:zd] adj situation etc confuso; person perplejo, despistado; **my mind is —** tengo la cabeza trastornada.

confusedly [kən'fju:zidli] adv confusamente.

confusing [kən'fju:ziŋ] adj confuso, desconcertante; **it's all very —** todo ello es muy difícil de comprender.

confusion [kən'fjuːʒən] n (a) (disorder) confusión , desorden m; **to be in —** estar en desorden; **to retire in —** retirarse en desorden.
(b) (perplexity) confusión f, perplejidad f, desorientación f, despiste m; **to be in —** estar desorientado; **to be covered in —** estar avergonzado.
confute [kən'fjuːt] vt confutar.
congeal [kən'dʒiːl] **1** vt congelar, cuajar, coagular; blood coagular. **2** vi congelarse, cuajarse, coagularse; (blood) coagularse.
congenial [kən'dʒiːniəl] adj simpático, agradable.
congenital [kən'dʒenitl] adj congénito.
conger eel ['kɔŋgər'iːl] n congrio m.
congested [kən'dʒestid] adj area superpoblado; building etc lleno, de bote en bote; **to get — with** llenarse de, atestarse de; **it's getting very — in here** aquí hay demasiada gente.
congestion [kən'dʒestʃən] n congestión f (also Med), aglomeración f.
conglomerate [kən'glɔmərit] n conglomerado m.
conglomerate [kən'glɔməreit] **1** vt conglomerar. **2** vi conglomerarse.
conglomeration [kən,glɔmə'reiʃən] n conglomeración f.
Congo ['kɔŋgəu]: **the —** el Congo.
Congolese [,kɔŋgəu'liːz] **1** adj congolés, congoleño. **2** n congolés m, esa f, congoleño m, a f.
congratulate [kən'grætjuleit] vt felicitar, dar la enhorabuena a (on por).
congratulations [kən,grætju'leiʃənz] npl felicitaciones fpl; **— !** ¡enhorabuena!
congratulatory [kən'grætjulətəri] adj de felicitación.
congregate ['kɔŋgrigeit] vi congregarse.
congregation [,kɔŋgri'geiʃən] n (assembly) reunión f; (Eccl: present in church) fieles mpl, (parishioners) feligreses mpl.
congregational [,kɔŋgri'geiʃnl] adj congregacionalista.
congress ['kɔŋgres] n congreso m; **C— (US)** Congreso m.
congressional [kɔŋ'greʃənl] adj congresional, del congreso.
congressman ['kɔŋgresmən] n, pl **—men** [mən] diputado m.
congruent ['kɔŋgruənt] adj congruente.
congruity [kɔŋ'gruːiti] n congruencia f (with con).
congruous ['kɔŋgruəs] adj congruo (with con).
conic(al) ['kɔnik(əl)] adj cónico.
conifer ['kɔnifə*] n conifera f.
coniferous [kə'nifərəs] adj conifero.
conjectural [kən'dʒektʃərəl] adj conjetural.
conjecture [kən'dʒektʃə*] **1** n conjetura f. **2** vt conjeturar (from de, por, that que).
conjoint ['kɔn'dʒɔint] adj conjunto.
conjointly ['kɔn'dʒɔintli] adv conjuntamente, en conjunto.
conjugal ['kɔndʒugəl] adj conyugal.
conjugate ['kɔndʒugeit] vt conjugar.
conjugation [,kɔndʒu'geiʃən] n conjugación f.
conjunct [kən'dʒʌŋkt] adj conjunto.
conjunction [kən'dʒʌŋkʃən] n conjunción f; **in — with this** junto con esto; **in — with others** en unión con otros.
conjunctive [kən'dʒʌŋktiv] adj (Gram) conjuntivo.
conjunctivitis [kən,dʒʌŋkti'vaitis] n conjuntivitis f.
conjuncture [kən'dʒʌŋktʃə*] n coyuntura f.
conjure [kən'dʒuə*] vt suplicar (to do something hacer algo).
conjure ['kʌndʒə*] **1** vt: **to — away** conjurar; **to — up** hacer aparecer, (fig) evocar, hacer pensar en; **a name to — with** un nombre todopoderoso.
2 vi hacer juegos de manos; **he —s with handkerchiefs** hace un truco con pañuelos.
conjurer ['kʌndʒərə*] n ilusionista m, mago m, prestidigitador m.
conjuring ['kʌndʒəriŋ] n juegos mpl de manos, ilusionismo m, arte m de los trucos.
conjuring trick ['kʌndʒəriŋ,trik] n juego m de manos.
conk¹ [kɔŋk] n (sl) (nose) narigón m; (head) cabeza f.
conk² [kɔŋk] vi (fam): **to — out** parar, tener una avería.
conker ['kɔŋkə*] n (fam) castaña f.
con man ['kɔnmæn] n, pl **— men** [men] (fam) timador m.
connect [kə'nekt] **1** vt (join) juntar, unir (to con); (Elec) conectar (to con); (relate) relacionar, asociar (with con); **to — someone with** (Tel) poner a uno en comunicación con; **are these matters —ed?** ¿tienen alguna relación entre sí estas cuestiones?; **to be well —ed** estar bien relacionado; **the Jones are —ed with the Smiths** los Jones están emparentados con los Smith; **what firm are you —ed with?** ¿con qué

empresa trabaja Vd?; **I never —ed you with that** nunca creía que Vd ver con eso.
2 vi (join) unirse, (Elec) conectarse; **to — with** (Rail etc) enlazar con.
connecting rod [kə'nektiŋrɔd] n biela f.
connection, connexion [kə'nekʃən] n (a) (joint) juntura f, unión f; (Mech, Elec) conexión f; (Rail etc) correspondencia f (with con); **our —s with the town are poor** son malas nuestras comunicaciones con la ciudad.
(b) (fig) relación f (between entre, with con); (relative) pariente m, a f; **we have —s everywhere** tenemos relaciones con todas partes; **you have to have —s** hay que tener buenas relaciones; **no — with any other firm** ésta es una firma independiente; **in — with** a propósito de; **in this —** con respecto a esto.
conning tower ['kɔniŋ,tauə*] n torreta f.
connivance [kə'naivəns] n connivencia f; (agreement) consentimiento m; **with the — of** con el consentimiento de.
connive [kə'naiv] vi: **to — at** hacer la vista gorda a; **to — with someone to do something** confabularse con uno para hacer algo.
connoisseur [,kɔnə'sə:*] n entendido m, a f (of en), experto m.
connotation [,kɔnəu'teiʃən] n connotación f.
connote [kɔ'nəut] vt connotar.
connubial [kə'njuːbiəl] adj conyugal.
conquer ['kɔŋkə*] **1** vt territory conquistar; enemy, habit etc vencer. **2** vi triunfar.
conquering ['kɔŋkəriŋ] adj victorioso.
conqueror ['kɔŋkərə*] n conquistador m; vencedor m; **William the C—** Guillermo el Conquistador.
conquest ['kɔŋkwest] n conquista f.
consanguinity [,kɔnsæŋ'gwiniti] n consanguinidad f.
conscience ['kɔnʃəns] n conciencia f; **in all —** en verdad; **with a clear —** con la conciencia limpia; **I have a clear — about it** no creo tener culpa alguna por ello; **I have a guilty — about it** me está remordiendo la conciencia por ello; **I would not have the — to** + infin no me atrevería a + infin.
conscience money ['kɔnʃəns,mʌni] n dinero que se paga para descargar la conciencia (p. ej., atrasos de contribuciones).
conscience-stricken ['kɔnʃəns,strikən] adj lleno de remordimientos.
conscientious [,kɔnʃi'enʃəs] adj concienzudo; objector de conciencia.
conscientiously [,kɔnʃi'enʃəsli] adv concienzudamente.
conscientiousness [,kɔnʃi'enʃəsnis] n diligencia f, escrupulosidad f.
conscious ['kɔnʃəs] adj (a) (aware) **to be — of** ser consciente de, saber, hacerse cargo de; **to be — that** saber perfectamente que; **to become — of** darse cuenta de; **to become — that** darse cuenta de que.
(b) (deliberate) intencional.
(c) (Med) **to be —** tener conocimiento; **to become — volver** en sí.
consciously ['kɔnʃəsli] adv conscientemente, a sabiendas.
consciousness ['kɔnʃəsnis] n (a) consciencia f.
(b) (Med) conocimiento m; **to lose —** perder el conocimiento; **to regain —** recobrar el conocimiento, volver en sí.
conscript ['kɔnskript] n recluta m, quinto m.
conscript [kən'skript] vt llamar al servicio militar.
conscription [kən'skripʃən] n servicio m militar obligatorio; (act) llamada f al servicio militar.
consecrate ['kɔnsikreit] vt consagrar.
consecration [,kɔnsi'kreiʃən] n consagración f.
consecutive [kən'sekjutiv] adj sucesivo, seguido; (Gram etc) consecutivo; **on 3 — days** 3 días seguidos.
consecutively [kən'sekjutivli] adv sucesivamente.
consensus [kən'sensəs] n consenso m; **the — of opinion** la opinión general.
consent [kən'sent] **1** n consentimiento m (to en); **by common —** según la opinión unánime; **by mutual —** de común acuerdo.
2 vi consentir (to en, to + infin en + infin).
consentient [kən'senʃiənt] adj (a) anuente. (b) acorde, unánime.
consequence ['kɔnsikwəns] n consecuencia f; resultado m; **in —** por consiguiente; **in — of** de resultas de; **it is of no —** la cosa no tiene importancia; **to put up with (or take) the —s** aceptar las consecuencias.
consequent ['kɔnsikwənt] adj consiguiente.
consequential [,kɔnsi'kwenʃəl] adj (a) (resulting) consiguiente, resultante: **the moves — upon this decision** las medidas que resultan de esta decisión.
(b) (important) importante, de consecuencia.

consequently ['kɔnsikwəntli] *adv* por consiguiente.

conservancy [kən'sə:vənsi] *n* conservación *f*; **Nature C—** (*Brit*) autoridad pública protectora de la naturaleza (*flora, fauna, terrenos de interés científico etc*).

conservation [,kɔnsə'veiʃən] *n* conservación *f* (*esp de recursos naturales*).

conservatism [kən'sə:vətizəm] *n* (*Pol*) conservatismo *m*, conservadurismo *m*.

conservative [kən'sə:vətiv] **1** *adj* (*Pol*) conservador; *estimate etc* cauteloso, moderado. **2** *n* conservador *m*, ora *f*.

conservatoire [kən'sə:vətwɑ:*] *n* conservatorio *m*.

conservatory [kən'sə:vətri] *n* invernadero *m*.

conserve [kən'sə:v] **1** *n* conserva *f*. **2** *vt* conservar; **to — one's strength** reservarse.

consider [kən'sidə*] **1** *vt* (a) (*deem*) considerar; **I — that** considero que; **I — it an honour** lo tengo a mucha honra; **I — him to be clever** le considero inteligente, creo que es inteligente; **I — the matter closed** para mí el asunto está concluido.

(b) (*realize*) **when one —s that** cuando uno se da cuenta de que.

(c) (*think over*) considerar, pensar, meditar; **— how much you owe him** considere cuánto le debe Vd; **all things —ed** después de meditarlo bien; considerando todos los puntos; **my —ed opinion is that** estoy convencido de que.

(d) (*study*) estudiar, examinar; **we are —ing the matter** estamos estudiando el asunto; **he is being —ed for the post** le están considerando para el puesto.

(e) (*entertain*) **have you ever —ed going by train?** ¿has pensado alguna vez en ir en tren?; **I wouldn't — it for a moment** ni quiero pensarlo siquiera; **he refused even to — it** se negó a pensarlo siquiera.

(f) (*take into account*) tomar en cuenta; **you must — others' feelings** hay que tomar en cuenta los sentimientos de los demás.

2 *vr*: **I — myself happy** me considero feliz; **— yourself lucky** puede creer que ha tenido suerte; **— yourself dismissed** considérese despedido.

considerable [kən'sidərəbl] *adj* considerable; *sum etc* importante; *loss* sensible; **we had — difficulty** tuvimos bastante dificultad.

considerably [kən'sidərəbli] *adv* bastante, mucho, considerablemente.

considerate [kən'sidərit] *adj* considerado.

considerately [kən'sidəritli] *adv* con consideración.

consideration [kən,sidə'reiʃən] *n* (a) consideración *f*; **as a mark of my —** en señal de mi consideración; **in — of** en consideración a; **out of — for** por respeto a; **without due —** sin reflexión; **that is a —** eso hay que tenerlo en cuenta; **it is under —** lo estamos estudiando; **we are giving the matter our —** estamos estudiando la cuestión; **to take into —** tener en cuenta.

(b) (*payment*) retribución *f*; **for a —** si se paga el servicio.

considering [kən'sidəriŋ] **1** *adv* (*fam*) teniendo en cuenta todas las circunstancias. **2** *prep* en consideración a.

consign [kən'sain] *vt* consignar (*also Comm*); (*fig*) enviar; **to — to oblivion** sepultar en el olvido.

consignee [,kɔnsai'ni:] *n* consignatario *m*.

consigner, consignor [kən'sainə*] *n* (*Comm*) consignador *m*.

consignment [kən'sainmənt] *n* consignación *f*; envío *m*, remesa *f*; **— note** talón *m* de expedición.

consist [kən'sist] *vi*: **to — of** consistir en, constar de.

consistency [kən'sistənsi] *n* (*of person, action*) consecuencia *f*, lógica *f*; (*density*) consistencia *f*.

consistent [kən'sistənt] *adj person, action, argument* consecuente, lógico; *pupil, results* constante; (*dense*) consistente; **to be — with** ser consecuente con, estar de acuerdo con.

consistently [kən'sistəntli] *adv* (*logically*) consecuentemente; (*all the time*) constantemente; **to act —** obrar con consecuencia.

consolation [,kɔnsə'leiʃən] *n* consuelo *m*; (*act*) consolación *f*; **— prize** premio *m* de consuelo, (*academic etc*) accésit *m*; **it is some — to know that** me reconforta saber que.

consolatory [kən'sɔlətəri] *adj* consolatorio.

console[1] [kən'səul] *vt* consolar.

console[2] ['kɔnsəul] *n* (*Mus, Tech etc*) consola *f*.

consolidate [kən'sɔlideit] **1** *vt* consolidar. **2** *vi* consolidarse.

consolidation [kən,sɔli'deiʃən] *n* consolidación *f*.

consoling [kən'səuliŋ] *adj* consolador, reconfortante.

consols [kən'sɔlz] *npl* consolidados *mpl*.

consommé [kən'sɔmei] *n* consomé *m*.

consonance ['kɔnsənəns] *n* consonancia *f*.

consonant ['kɔnsənənt] **1** *adj* consonante; **— with** conforme a. **2** *n* consonante *f*.

consonantal [,kɔnsə'næntl] *adj* consonántico.

consort ['kɔnsɔ:t] *n* consorte *mf*; **prince —** príncipe *m* consorte *m*.

consort [kən'sɔ:t] *vi*: **to — with** ir con, asociarse con; (*agree*) concordar con.

consortium [kən'sɔ:tiəm] *n* consorcio *m*.

conspectus [kən'spektəs] *n* vista *f* general, ojeada *f* general; sumario *m*, resumen *m*.

conspicuous [kən'spikjuəs] *adj* visible, que llama la atención; (*fig*) notable; **to be —** destacar(se); **to make oneself —** llamar la atención; *see* **absence.**

conspicuously [kən'spikjuəsli] *adv* visiblemente, claramente; de modo que llama la atención; (*fig*) notablemente.

conspiracy [kən'spirəsi] *n* conspiración *f*, conjuración *f*, complot *m*.

conspirator [kən'spirətə*] *n* conspirador *m*, ora *f*.

conspire [kən'spaiə*] *vi* conspirar (*against* contra, *with* con, *to* + *infin* a + *infin*).

constable ['kʌnstəbl] *n* policía *m*, guardia *m*; **chief —** jefe *m* de policía.

constabulary [kən'stæbjuləri] *n* policía *f*.

Constance ['kɔnstəns] *f* Constanza.

constancy ['kɔnstənsi] *n* constancia *f*; fidelidad *f*.

constant ['kɔnstənt] **1** *adj* constante; (*faithful*) fiel, leal; (*unending*) continuo, incesante; *reader* asiduo. **2** *n* constante *f*.

constantly ['kɔnstəntli] *adv* constantemente.

Constantinople [,kɔnstænti'nəupl] Constantinopla.

constellation [,kɔnstə'leiʃən] *n* constelación *f*.

consternation [,kɔnstə'neiʃən] *n* consternación *f*; **in —** consternado; **there was general —** se consternaron todos.

constipate ['kɔnstipeit] *vt* estreñir; **to be —d** estar estreñido.

constipation [,kɔnsti'peiʃən] *n* estreñimiento *m*.

constituency [kən'stitjuənsi] *n* distrito *m* electoral, circunscripción *f*.

constituent [kən'stitjuənt] **1** *adj* constitutivo, integrante; **— assembly** cortes *fpl* constituyentes. **2** *n* constitutivo *m*, componente *m*; (*Pol*) elector *m*, ora *f*.

constitute ['kɔnstitju:t] **1** *vt* constituir; (*make up*) componer, integrar. **2** *vr*: **to — oneself a judge** constituirse en juez.

constitution [,kɔnsti'tju:ʃən] *n* constitución *f*.

constitutional [,kɔnsti'tju:ʃənl] **1** *adj* constitucional. **2** *n* paseo *m*.

constitutionally [,kɔnsti'tju:ʃənəli] *adv* según la constitución.

constitutive ['kɔnstitju:tiv] *adj* constitutivo.

constrain [kən'strein] *vt*: **to — someone to do something** obligar a uno a hacer algo; **to feel —ed to do something** verse en la necesidad de hacer algo.

constraint [kən'streint] *n* (*compulsion*) fuerza *f*; (*confinement*) encierro *m*; (*restraint*) reserva *f*, (*of atmosphere*) frialdad *f*; **under —** obligado a ello; **to feel a certain —** sentirse algo cohibido.

constrict [kən'strikt] *vt* apretar, estrechar.

constriction [kən'strikʃən] *n* constricción *f*.

construct [kən'strʌkt] *vt* construir.

construction [kən'strʌkʃən] *n* construcción *f* (*also Gram*); (*fig*) interpretación *f*; **in course of —**, **under —** en construcción; **to put a wrong — on something** interpretar algo mal.

constructional [kən'strʌkʃənl] *adj* estructural; **— toy** juguete *m* con que se construyen modelos.

constructive [kən'strʌktiv] *adj* constructivo.

constructively [kən'strʌktivli] *adv* constructivamente.

constructor [kən'strʌktə*] *n* constructor *m*.

construe [kən'stru:] *vt* interpretar; (*Gram*) construir.

consul ['kɔnsəl] *n* cónsul *m*.

consular ['kɔnsjulə*] *adj* consular.

consulate ['kɔnsjulit] *n* consulado *m*.

consulship ['kɔnsəlʃip] *n* consulado *m*.

consult [kən'sʌlt] **1** *vt* consultar; **one's interests** tener en cuenta. **2** *vi*: **to — together** reunirse para consultar; **to — with** consultar con, aconsejarse con.

consultant [kən'sʌltənt] *n* asesor *m*; (*Med*) especialista *mf*; **to act as —** asesorar.

consultation [,kɔnsəl'teiʃən] *n* (*act*) consulta *f*; (*in general*) consultación *f*.

consultative [kən'sʌltətiv] *adj* consultivo.

consulting-room [kən'sʌltiŋrum] *n* consultorio *m*.

consume [kən'sju:m] *vt* (*eat*) comerse, (*drink*) beberse; (*use*) consumir, utilizar; (*by fire etc*) consumir;

the house was —**d** by fire la casa quedó arrasada por el fuego; **to be** —**d with** *envy etc* estar muerto de.

consumer [kən'sjuːmə*] *n* consumidor *m*, ora *f*; — **goods** bienes *mpl* de consumo; — **protection** protección *f* al consumidor; — **resistance** resistencia *f* por parte del consumidor.

consuming [kən'sjuːmiŋ] *adj* arrollador, apasionado.

consummate [kən'sʌmit] *adj* consumado, completo.

consummate ['kɔnsʌmeit] *vt* consumar.

consummation [,kɔnsʌ'meiʃən] *n* consumación *f*.

consumption [kən'sʌmpʃən] *n* consumo *m*; (*Med*) tisis *f*.

consumptive [kən'sʌmptiv] **1** *adj* tísico. **2** *n* tísico *m*, a *f*.

contact ['kɔntækt] **1** *n* contacto *m*; **he has a lot of** —**s** tiene muchas relaciones, (*pej*) tiene muchos enchufes, tiene buenas aldabas; **you have to have a** — **in the business** hay que tener un buen enchufe en el negocio; **to come into** — **with** tocar, (*violently*) chocar con, (*fig*) tener que ver con, tratar; **to get into** — **with** ponerse en contacto con; **I seem to make no** — **with him** me resulta imposible comunicar con él.

2 *vt* ponerse en contacto con, comunicar con.

contact lenses ['kɔntækt,lenziz] *pl* lentes *fpl* de contacto, microlentillas *fpl*.

contact man ['kɔntæktmæn] *n*, *pl* — **men** [men] intermediario *m*.

contagion [kən'teidʒən] *n* contagio *m*.

contagious [kən'teidʒəs] *adj* contagioso.

contain [kən'tein] **1** *vt* contener; (*Math*) ser exactamente divisible por. **2** *vr*: **to** — **oneself** contenerse, contener la risa (*etc*).

container [kən'teinə*] *n* recipiente *m*, continente *m*; (*box*) caja *f*; (*wrapper etc*) envase *m*.

contaminate [kən'tæmineit] *vt* contaminar; **to be** —**d by** contaminarse con (*or* de).

contamination [kən,tæmi'neiʃən] *n* contaminación *f*.

contemplate ['kɔntempleit] *vt* (**a**) (*gaze on*) contemplar; **I** — **the future with misgiving** el futuro lo veo dudoso.

(**b**) (*expect*) contar con; **we had not** —**d this** no habíamos contado con esto.

(**c**) (*intend*) pensar, intentar, proyectar; **he** —**d suicide** pensó suicidarse; **we** — **a holiday in Spain** proyectamos unas vacaciones en España; **when do you** — **doing it?** ¿cuándo se propone hacerlo?, ¿cuándo tiene intención de hacerlo?

contemplation [,kɔntem'pleiʃən] *n* contemplación *f*.

contemplative [kən'templətiv] *adj* contemplativo.

contemporaneous [kən,tempə'reiniəs] *adj* contemporáneo.

contemporary [kən'tempərəri] **1** *adj* contemporáneo, coetáneo. **2** *n* contemporáneo *m*, a *f*, coetáneo *m*, a *f*.

contempt [kən'tempt] *n* desprecio *m*; — **of court** desacato *m* al juez; **beneath** — despreciable; **to bring into** — desprestigiar, envilecer; **to hold in** — despreciar.

contemptible [kən'temptəbl] *adj* despreciable, vil.

contemptuous [kən'temptjuəs] *adj* desdeñoso, despectivo; **to be** — **of** desdeñar, menospreciar.

contemptuously [kən'temptjuəsli] *adv* desdeñosamente, con desprecio.

contend [kən'tend] **1** *vt* afirmar, sostener (*that* que).

2 *vi* contender, luchar; **to** — **with someone for something** contender con uno sobre algo; **we have many problems to** — **with** se nos plantean muchos problemas.

contender [kən'tendə*] *n* contendiente *mf*.

contending [kən'tendiŋ] *adj* rival, opuesto.

content [kən'tent] **1** *adj* contento (*with* con), satisfecho (*with* de); **to be** — estar contento; **he was** — **to stay there** estaba contento de estar allí.

2 *n* contento *m*, satisfacción *f*; **to one's heart's** — a gusto, a más no poder, cuanto quisiera.

3 *vt* contentar, satisfacer.

4 *vr*: **to** — **oneself** contentarse (*with something* con algo, *with saying* con decir).

content ['kɔntent] *n* contenido *m*; —**s** contenido *m*.

contented [kən'tentid] *adj* satisfecho, contento.

contentedly [kən'tentidli] *adv* con satisfacción, contentamente.

contentedness [kən'tentidnis] *n* contento *m*.

contention [kən'tenʃən] *n* (**a**) (*strife*) contienda *f*. (**b**) (*point*) argumento *m*, aseveración *f*, pretensión *f*; **it is our** — **that** pretendemos que, sostenemos que.

contentious [kən'tenʃəs] *adj* contencioso.

contentment [kən'tentmənt] *n* contento *m*.

contest ['kɔntest] *n* (*struggle*) contienda *f*, lucha *f*; (*competition*) concurso *m*.

contest [kən'test] **1** *vt* (*dispute*) impugnar, atacar;

legal suit defender; *election* ser candidato en; *seat* presentarse como candidato a; **I** — **your right to do that** niego que Vd tenga el derecho de hacer eso; **the seat was not** —**ed** en las elecciones se presentó un solo candidato.

2 *vi*: **to** — **against** contender con; **they are** —**ing for a big prize** se están disputando un premio importante.

contestant [kən'testənt] *n* contendiente *mf*; (*Sport etc*) concursante *mf*.

context ['kɔntekst] *n* contexto *m*.

contextual [kɔn'tekstjuəl] *adj* del contexto, relativo al contexto.

contiguous [kən'tigjuəs] *adj* contiguo (*to* a).

continence ['kɔntinəns] *n* continencia *f*.

continent [kən'tinənt] **1** *adj* continente. **2** *n* continente *m*; **the C**— el continente europeo.

continental [,kɔnti'nentl] *adj* continental.

contingency [kən'tindʒənsi] *n* contingencia *f*; **should the** — **arise** por si acaso; **to provide for every** — tener en cuenta todas las posibilidades; **with £5 for contingencies** con 5 libras para gastos extraordinarios.

contingent [kən'tindʒənt] **1** *adj* contingente, eventual; **to be** — **upon** depender de. **2** *n* contingente *m*.

continual [kən'tinjuəl] *adj* continuo.

continually [kən'tinjuəli] *adv* constantemente.

continuance [kən'tinjuəns] *n* continuación *f*; (*stay*) permanencia *f*.

continuation [kən,tinju'eiʃən] *n* continuación *f*; (*lengthening*) prolongación *f*.

continue [kən'tinjuː] **1** *vt* continuar; seguir; *story etc* proseguir; (*retain*) mantener (*in a post* en un puesto); (*lengthen*) prolongar; —**d on page 10** sigue en la página 10; **"to be** —**d"** (*serial*) "continuará".

2 *vi* continuar; seguir; (*extend*) prolongarse; **to** — **talking, to** — **to talk** seguir hablando; **to** — **on one's way** seguir su camino; **to** — **in office** seguir en su puesto; **to** — **in a place** seguir en un sitio.

continuity [,kɔnti'njuːiti] *n* continuidad *f* (*also Cine*).

continuity girl [,kɔnti'njuːiti,gəːl] *n* (*Cine*) secretaria *f* de continuidad.

continuous [kən'tinjuəs] *adj* continuo.

continuously [kən'tinjuəsli] *adj* continuamente.

continuum [kən'tinjuəm] *n* continuo *m*.

contort [kən'tɔːt] *vt* retorcer, deformar.

contortion [kən'tɔːʃən] *n* contorsión *f*.

contortionist [kən'tɔːʃənist] *n* contorsionista *mf*.

contour ['kɔntuə*] *n* contorno *m*; — **line** curva *f* de nivel.

contour map ['kɔntuə,mæp] *n* mapa *m* que indica las curvas de nivel, plano *m* acotado.

contraband ['kɔntrəbænd] **1** *n* contrabando *m*. **2** *adj and attr* de contrabando.

contraception [,kɔntrə'sepʃən] *n* anticoncepcionismo *m*.

contraceptive [,kɔntrə'septiv] **1** *adj* anticonceptivo. **2** *n* anticonceptivo *m*.

contract ['kɔntrækt] *n* contrato *m* (*for* de); contrata *f*; **marriage** — capitulaciones *fpl* matrimoniales; **to enter into a** — hacer un contrato (*with* con); **to place a** — **with** dar un contrato a.

contract [kən'trækt] **1** *vt* contraer.

2 *vi* (*become smaller*) contraerse, encogerse; **to** — **to do something** comprometerse por contrato a hacer algo; **to** — **for** contratar; **to** — **out of something** optar por no tomar parte en algo.

contracting [kən'træktiŋ] *adj*: — **party** contratante *mf*.

contraction [kən'trækʃən] *n* contracción *f* (*in, of* de).

contractor [kən'træktə*] *n* contratista *mf*.

contractual [kən'træktjuəl] *adj* contractual.

contradict [,kɔntrə'dikt] *vt* contradecir; (*deny*) desmentir; **don't** — **me!** ¡no repliques!

contradiction [,kɔntrə'dikʃən] *n* contradicción *f*; — **in terms** falta *f* de lógica.

contradictory [,kɔntrə'diktəri] *adj* contradictorio.

contradistinction [,kɔntrədis'tiŋkʃən] *n*: **in** — **to** a diferencia de.

contralto [kən'træltəu] *n* (*person*) contralto *f*; (*voice*) contralto *m*.

contraption [kən'træpʃən] *n* dispositivo *m*, ingenio *m*, artilugio *m*; (*vehicle*) armatoste *m*.

contrapuntal [,kɔntrə'pʌntl] *adj* contrapuntístico.

contrarily [kən'treərili] *adv* tercamente.

contrariness [kən'treərinis] *n* terquedad *f*.

contrariwise [kən'treəriwaiz] *adv*: **and** — y a la inversa.

contrary ['kɔntrəri] **1** *adj* contrario (*to* a); **in a** — **direction** en dirección contraria.

2 *adv*: — **to** contrario a; — **to what we had thought** contra lo que habíamos pensado.

3 n contrario m; **the — seems to be the case** parece que es al revés; **he holds the —** él sostiene lo contrario; **quite the —** muy al contrario; **on the —** al contrario; **I know nothing to the —** yo no sé nada en contrario; **unless we hear to the —** a no ser que nos digan lo contrario.

contrary [kən'trɛəri] adj terco, que siempre lleva la contraria.

contrast ['kɔntrɑːst] n contraste m (between entre, to, with con); **in —** por contraste; **in — to** a diferencia de; **to form a —** to (or with) contrastar con.

contrast [kən'trɑːst] **1** vt poner en contraste (with con), comparar. **2** vi contrastar (with con), hacer contraste (with con).

contrasting [kən'trɑːstiŋ] adj opuesto.

contravene [,kɔntrə'viːn] vt law contravenir a; (dispute) oponerse a.

contravention [,kɔntrə'venʃən] n contravención f.

contretemps ['kɔ̃ntrətɑ̃ːŋ] n contratiempo m, revés m.

contribute [kən'tribjuːt] **1** vt contribuir (to a); article escribir (to para); aid prestar; facts, information etc aportar. **2** vi contribuir (to, towards a); **to — to** + ger contribuir + infin; **to — to a journal** colaborar en una revista; **to — to a discussion** intervenir en una discusión; **it all —d to the muddle** todo sirvió para aumentar la confusión.

contribution [,kɔntri'bjuːʃən] n contribución f; (to journal) artículo m, colaboración f; (to discussion) intervención f; (of information etc) aportación f.

contributor [kən'tribjutə*] n contribuyente m; (to journal) colaborador m, ora f (to en).

contributory [kən'tribjutəri] adj contribuidor; factor, negligence que contribuye.

contrite ['kɔntrait] adj arrepentido, contrito.

contrition [kən'trifən] n arrepentimiento m, contrición f.

contrivance [kən'traivəns] n (scheme) treta f, estratagema f; (invention) invención f; (Mech) aparato m, dispositivo m, artilugio m.

contrive [kən'traiv] **1** vt (invent) inventar, idear; (bring about) efectuar; (plot) tramar. **2** vi: **to — to** + infin lograr que + subj, ingeniarse a + infin.

contrived [kən'traivd] adj artificial.

control [kən'trəul] **1** n (a) (command) control m, mando m, gobierno m, dirección f; (of car etc) manejo m, conducción f; **— of the seas** dominio m de los mares; **dual —** doble mando m; **remote —** comando m a distancia, telecontrol m; **to be in —** mandar, tener el mando; **to be out of —** estar fuera de control; **to be under —** estar bajo control; **to be under private —** estar en manos de particulares; **the circumstances are beyond our —** las circunstancias están fuera de nuestro control; **to get out of —** desmandarse; **to get under —** conseguir dominar; **she has no — over the children** no tiene autoridad sobre los niños; **causes over which the vendor has no —** causas respecto a las cuales nada puede el vendedor, causas ajenas a la voluntad del vendedor; **to lose — of** perder control de; **to lose — of oneself** perder el control, perder los estribos.

(b) (Mech) control m; **—s** (Aer etc) aparatos mpl de mando, instrumentos mpl de mando; (attr) de mando, de control.

(c) (check) freno m (on para).

(d) (self-restraint) dominio m sobre sí mismo.

(e) (in experiment) norma f de comprobación.

2 vt (command) controlar, mandar, gobernar; traffic, business dirigir; price controlar; (Mech) regular, controlar; car etc manejar; temper dominar, refrenar.

3 vr: **to — oneself** dominarse, sobreponerse; **— yourself!** ¡domínese!, ¡cálmese!

control column [kən'trəul'kɔləm] n palanca f de mando.

control knob [kən'trəul,nɔb] n botón m de control.

controller [kən'trəulə*] n director m; inspector m; (Comm) interventor m.

controlling [kən'trəuliŋ] adj interest predominante.

control panel [kən'trəul,pænl] n tablero m de instrumentos.

control point [kən'trəulpɔint] n punto m de control.

control room [kən'trəulrum] n (Radio, TV etc) sala f de control, sala f de mando.

control tower [kən'trəul,tauə*] n torre f de control.

controversial [,kɔntrə'vɜːʃəl] adj discutible.

controversy [kən'trɔvəsi] n controversia f.

controvert ['kɔntrəvɜːt] vt contradecir.

contumacious [,kɔntju'meiʃəs] adj contumaz.

contumaciously [,kɔntju'meiʃəsli] adv contumazmente.

contumacy ['kɔntjuməsi] n contumacia f.

contusion [kən'tjuːʒən] n contusión f.

contumely ['kɔntju(ː)mli] n contumelia f.

conundrum [kə'nʌndrəm] n acertijo m; (fig) problema m.

conurbation [,kɔnə'beiʃən] n conjunto m de centros urbanos.

convalesce [,kɔnvə'les] vi convalecer.

convalescence [,kɔnvə'lesəns] n convalecencia f.

convalescent [,kɔnvə'lesənt] **1** adj convaleciente. **2** n convaleciente mf; **— home** clínica f de reposo.

convection [kən'vekʃən] n convección f.

convector [kən'vektə*] m calentador m de convección.

convene [kən'viːn] **1** vt convocar. **2** vi reunirse.

convenience [kən'viːniəns] n (a) (advantage) ventaja f; **at your —** cuando le sea conveniente; **at your earliest —** con la mayor brevedad, tan pronto como le sea posible; **for your — an envelope is enclosed** para facilitar su contestación adjuntamos un sobre; **it is a great — to be so close** resulta muy práctico estar tan cerca; **to make a — of** abusar de (la amabilidad de).

(b) public **—s** mpl aseos mpl públicos; **a house with all modern —s** una casa con todas las comodidades; "**all mod. cons**" "todo confort".

convenient [kən'viːniənt] adj (a) cómodo; tool etc práctico, útil; place accesible, céntrico; **it is — to live here** resulta práctico vivir aquí; **her death was certainly — for him** es cierto que su muerte resultó provechosa para él; **we looked for a — place to stop** buscamos un sitio apropiado para detenernos; **he put it on a — chair** lo puso en una silla que estaba a mano.

(b) (of time) oportuno; **at a — moment** en un momento oportuno; **when it is — for you** cuando le sea conveniente; **would tomorrow be —?** ¿le conviene mañana?

conveniently [kən'viːniəntli] adv con comodidad, cómodamente; oportunamente; **the house is — situated** la casa está en un sitio muy práctico; **it fell — close** cayó muy cerca; **when you — can do so** cuando Vd pueda hacerlo sin inconveniente.

convent ['kɔnvənt] n convento m (de monjas).

convention [kən'venʃən] n convención f; (meeting) asamblea f, congreso m.

conventional [kən'venʃənl] adj convencional.

converge [kən'vɜːdʒ] vi convergir (on en); **to — on** (persons) dirigirse todos a.

convergence [kən'vɜːdʒəns] n convergencia f.

convergent [kən'vɜːdʒənt] adj, **converging** [kən'vɜːdʒiŋ] adj convergente.

conversant [kən'vɜːsənt] adj: **— with** versado en, enterado de; **to become — with** llegar a conocer, informarse sobre.

conversation [,kɔnvə'seiʃən] n conversación f.

conversational [,kɔnvə'seiʃənl] adj tone familiar; person locuaz, hablador; **he's not very —** no es amigo de la conversación.

conversationalist [,kɔnvə'seiʃənəlist] n: **to be a good —** brillar en la conversación, resultar simpático charlando; **he's not much of a —** tiene poco que decir, no le gusta hablar mucho en las conversaciones.

conversationally [,kɔnvə'seiʃənəli] adv en tono familiar.

conversation piece [,kɔnvə'seiʃənpiːs] n (Lit) (pasaje m de) conversación f, diálogo m.

converse ['kɔnvɜːs] **1** adj contrario, inverso. **2** n (Math, Logic) inversa f; **but the — is true** pero la verdad es al revés.

converse [kən'vɜːs] vi conversar, hablar (with con); **to — by signs** hablar por señas.

conversely [kən'vɜːsli] adv a la inversa.

conversion [kən'vɜːʃən] n conversión f (into en, to a); (industrial) reorganización f; (Law) apropiación f ilícita; (Rugby) transformación f; **— table** tabla f de conversión.

convert ['kɔnvɜːt] n converso m, a f; **to become a —** convertirse.

convert [kən'vɜːt] **1** vt convertir (also Eccl, Fin; into en, to a), transformar (into en); industry reorganizar; (Law) apropiarse ilícitamente (to one's own use para uso propio); (Rugby) transformar.

2 vi convertirse (to a).

converter [kən'vɜːtə*] n (Elec, Metal) convertidor m; (Radio) conversor m.

convertibility [kən,vɜːtə'biliti] n convertibilidad f.

convertible [kən'vɜːtəbl] **1** adj convertible; car descapotable. **2** n descapotable m.

convex ['kɔnveks] adj convexo.

convexity [kɔn'veksiti] n convexidad f.

convey [kən'vei] vt goods transportar, llevar; person llevar; sound, smell llevar; current transmitir; news comunicar; (Law) traspasar; meaning tener, expresar (to para); **I am trying to — that** quiero dar a entender que; **the name —s nothing to me** el nombre no me dice nada; **what does this music — to you?** ¿qué sentido tiene esta música para Vd?

conveyance [kən'veiəns] n (a) (act) transporte m; transmisión f (etc); (Law) traspaso m.
(b) (Law: deed) escritura f de traspaso.
(c) (vehicle) vehículo m, medio m de transporte; **public —** vehículo m de servicio público.

conveyancing [kən'veiənsiŋ] n (Law) preparación f de escrituras de traspaso.

conveyor [kən'veiə*] n portador m, transportador m; (belt) cinta f transportadora.

conveyor belt [kən'veiəbelt] n cinta f transportadora.

convict ['kɔnvikt] n presidiario m, penado m.

convict [kən'vikt] vt condenar; **a —ed murderer** un asesino condenado como tal; **to — someone of a crime** declarar a uno culpable de un crimen; **to — someone of an error** coger a uno en una falta.

conviction [kən'vikʃən] n (a) (Law) condena f; **there were 12 —s for drunkenness** hubo 12 condenas por embriaguez; **to have no previous —s** no tener antecedentes penales.
(b) (belief) creencia f, convicción f, artículo m de fe; **it is my —** that yo creo firmemente de.
(c) **I am open to —** estoy dispuesto a dejarme convencer; **it carries —** me convence.

convince [kən'vins] vt convencer (of de, that de que).

convincing [kən'vinsiŋ] adj convincente.

convincingly [kən'vinsiŋli] adv convincentemente; **to prove something —** probar algo de modo concluyente.

convivial [kən'viviəl] adj person sociable; evening alegre, festivo, atmosphere alegre.

conviviality [kən,vivi'æliti] n alegría f, buen humor m; compañerismo m alegre; **there was a certain amount of —** nos divertimos bastante, (freq) se bebió una barbaridad.

convocation [,kɔnvə'keiʃən] n (act) convocación f; (meeting) asamblea f.

convoke [kən'vəuk] vt convocar.

convolution [,kɔnvə'luːʃən] n circunvolución f.

convolvulus [kən'vɔlvjuləs] n convólvulo m.

convoy ['kɔnvɔi] 1 n convoy m. 2 vt convoyar.

convulse [kən'vʌls] vt (fig) convulsionar, sacudir; (joke etc) hacer morir de risa; **his face was —d with pain** el dolor le crispó la cara; **to be —d with laughter** estar muerto de risa.

convulsion [kən'vʌlʃən] n convulsión f; **—s of laughter** paroxismo m de risa.

convulsive [kən'vʌlsiv] adj convulsivo.

cony ['kəuni] n conejo m.

coo[1] [kuː] vi arrullar.

coo[2] [kuː] interj ¡vaya!

cooing ['kuːiŋ] n arrullos mpl.

cook [kuk] 1 n cocinero m, a f.
2 vt guisar, cocer, cocinar; meal preparar; accounts (fam) falsificar; **to — up** excuse inventar; plan tramar.
3 vi (food) cocer; (person) cocinar; **what's —ing?** (sl) ¿qué es lo que se guisa?

cookbook ['kukbuk] n (US) libro m de cocina.

cooker ['kukə*] n (a) (stove) cocina f; **electric —** cocina f eléctrica; gas **—** cocina f de (or a) gas. (b) (fruit) fruta f para cocer.

cookery ['kukəri] n arte m de cocinar; **French —** la cocina francesa.

cookery book ['kukəribuk] n libro m de cocina.

cookhouse ['kukhaus] n, pl **—houses** [,hauziz] cocina f; (Mil) cocina f móvil de campaña.

cookie ['kuki] n (US) pastelito m dulce, bizcochito m.

cooking ['kukiŋ] n cocina f.

cookout ['kukaut] n (US) comida f al aire libre.

cool [kuːl] 1 adj (a) (rather cold) fresco; (— enough to drink etc) tibio, bastante frío, it is — (weather) hace fresco, (object) está fresco; **to get —(er)** refrescarse; **"to be kept in a — place"** "guárdese en un sitio fresco".
(b) (calm) tranquilo, imperturbable; **as — as a cucumber** más fresco que una lechuga; **to keep —** no perder la calma; **keep —!** ¡no se alarme!; **to play it —** no dejarse emocionar, no exagerar.
(c) (lacking zeal) frío, indiferente; **to be — towards a plan** acoger un proyecto con poco entusiasmo; **to be — towards someone** tratar a uno con frialdad.
(d) (calmly audacious) fresco, descarado; **he's a — customer** es un caradura; **he answered me as — as you please** me contestó tan fresco.

(e) (fam) **a — £100** cien libras contantes y sonantes.
2 n fresco m; **in the — of the evening** en el aire fresco de la tarde.
3 vt (also **to — down**) enfriar; refrescar; engine refrigerar; (fig) calmar, moderar el entusiasmo (etc) de.
4 vi (also **to — down**) enfriarse; (weather etc) refrescarse; (person) tener menos calor; (fig) calmarse; **— down!** ¡cálmese!; **to — off** (fig) perder su entusiasmo, entibiarse.

cooler ['kuːlə*] n (sl) trena f.

cool-headed ['kuːl,hedid] adj imperturbable.

coolie ['kuːli] n culí m.

cooling ['kuːliŋ] 1 adj refrescante; (Tech) refrigerante. 2 n refrigeración f.

cooling tower ['kuːliŋtauə*] n torre f de refrigeración.

coolly ['kuːli] adv (calmly) con tranquilidad; (unenthusiastically) con poco entusiasmo; (boldly) descaradamente.

coolness ['kuːlnis] n (a) (coldness) frescura f, lo fresco.
(b) (calmness) tranquilidad f, imperturbabilidad f; (in battle) sangre f fría.
(c) (lack of zeal) falta f de entusiasmo; (of welcome, between persons) frialdad f.
(d) (audacity) frescura f.

coomb [kuːm] n hondonada f.

coop [kuːp] 1 n gallinero m. 2 vt: **to — up** encerrar.

co-op ['kəuɔp] n cooperativa f.

cooper ['kuːpə*] n tonelero m.

cooperage ['kuːpəridʒ] n barrilería f, tonelería f.

cooperate [kəu'ɔpəreit] vi cooperar, colaborar (in en, with con, to + infin para + infin).

cooperation [kəu,ɔpə'reiʃən] n cooperación f, colaboración f.

cooperative [kəu'ɔpərətiv] 1 adj cooperativo; person servicial, dispuesto a ayudar; **— society** cooperativa f. 2 n cooperativa f.

coopt [kəu'ɔpt] vt: **to — someone on to a committee** nombrar a uno miembro de un comité por votación extraordinaria.

coordinate [kəu'ɔːdnit] n (Math) coordenada f.

coordinate [kəu'ɔːdineit] vt coordinar.

coordination [kəu,ɔːdi'neiʃən] n coordinación f.

coordinator [kəu'ɔːdineitə*] n coordinador m.

coot [kuːt] n focha f común; (fam) bobo m, a f.

cop [kɔp] (sl) 1 n guili m, guindilla m; **—s and robbers** (game) justicias y ladrones.
2 vt (capture) coger, prender; **he —ped 6 months** le condenaron a 6 meses de prisión; **you'll — it!** ¡las vas a pagar!; **I —ped it from the head** el director me puso como un trapo; **— this!** ¡hay que ver esto!

copartner ['kəu'pɑːtnə*] n consocio m, copartícipe m.

copartnership ['kəu'pɑːtnəʃip] n asociación f, cogestión f, coparticipación f.

cope[1] [kəup] n (Eccl) capa f pluvial.

cope[2] [kəup] vi (a) **he's coping pretty well** se las está arreglando bastante bien; **we shall be able to — better next year** podremos arreglarnos mejor el año que viene; **can you —?** ¿tú puedes con esto?; **how are you coping?** ¿cómo te va esto?
(b) **to — with** poder con; problem hacer frente a; difficulty contender con; situation enfrentarse con.

Copenhagen [,kəupn'heigən] Copenhague.

Copernicus [kə'pəːnikəs] m Copérnico.

copestone ['kəupstəun] n, **coping stone** ['kəupiŋstəun] n (piedra f de) albardilla f.

co-pilot ['kəu'pailət] n copiloto m.

copious ['kəupiəs] adj copioso, abundante.

copiously ['kəupiəsli] adv copiosamente, en abundancia.

copper[1] ['kɔpə*] 1 n (material) cobre m; (utensil) caldera f de lavar; (money) calderilla f, monedas fpl de poco valor; **it costs a few —s** vale unos peniques.
2 adj and attr de cobre, cobreño; (colour) cobrizo.

copper[2] ['kɔpə*] n (sl) guili m, guindilla m.

copper beech ['kɔpə'biːtʃ] n haya f de hoja oscura.

copperplate ['kɔpəpleit] adj writing hermoso, bien formado.

coppersmith ['kɔpəsmiθ] n cobrero m.

coppery ['kɔpəri] adj cobreño; (colour) cobrizo.

coppice ['kɔpis] n, **copse** [kɔps] n soto m, bosquecillo m.

copra ['kɔprə] n copra f.

copulate ['kɔpjuleit] vi copularse (with con).

copulation [,kɔpju'leiʃən] n cópula f.

copulative ['kɔpjulətiv] adj (Gram) copulativo.

copy ['kɔpi] 1 n copia f; (of book, paper etc) ejemplar m; (Typ) material m, original m; **author's —**

ejemplar *m* autógrafo; **presentation — ejemplar** *m*
con dedicatoria del autor; **fair — copia** *f* en limpio;
to make a fair — of something sacar algo en limpio;
rough — borrador *m*; **to make** (*or* **take**) **a — of a
letter** sacar una copia de una carta.

2 *vt* copiar (*also* **to — out**); imitar; **to — from**
copiar de; "**American papers please —**" "periódicos
americanos: por favor, tomen nota".

copybook ['kɔpibuk] *n* cuaderno *m* de escritura; **to
blot one's —** tirarse una plancha.

copycat ['kɔpikæt] *n* (*fam*) imitador *m*, ora *f*.

copy editor ['kɔpi'editə*] *n* corrector *m* de ma-
nuscritos; corrector *m* de artículos, corrector *m* de
material.

copyist ['kɔpiist] *n* copista *mf*.

copyright ['kɔpirait] **1** *adj* protegido por los derechos
del autor.

2 *n* derechos *mpl* del autor; propiedad *f* literaria;
"**— reserved**" "es propiedad", "reservados todos
los derechos".

3 *vt* registrar como propiedad literaria.

copywriter ['kɔpi,raitə*] *n* escritor *m* de material
publicitario.

coquetry ['kɔkitri] *n* coquetería *f*.

coquette [kə'ket] *n* coqueta *f*.

coquettish [kə'ketiʃ] *adj* coqueta.

cor [kɔ:*] *interj* (*sl*) ¡caramba!

coracle ['kɔrəkl] *n* barquilla *f* de forma casi redonda
y hecha de cuero.

coral ['kɔrəl] **1** *n* coral *m*. **2** *adj* coralino, de coral;
— island isla *f* coralina.

cor anglais ['kɔːr'ɔ̃nglei] *n* corno *m* inglés.

cord [kɔ:d] **1** *n* (**a**) cuerda *f*; (*Elec*) cordón *m*; **spinal
—** médula *f* espinal; **umbilical —** cordón *m*
umbilical *m*; **vocal —s** cuerdas *fpl* vocales.

(**b**) (*cloth*) pana *f*; **—s** pantalones *mpl* de pana.
2 *vt* encordelar.

cordage ['kɔ:didʒ] *n* cordaje *m*, cordería *f*.

cordial ['kɔ:diəl] **1** *adj* cordial, afectuoso. **2** *n* cordial
m.

cordiality [,kɔ:di'æliti] *n* cordialidad *f*, afecto *m*.

cordially ['kɔ:diəli] *adv* cordialmente, afectuosamente; **I — detest him** le odio cordialmente.

cordon ['kɔ:dn] **1** *n* cordón *m*. **2** *vt*: **to — off**
acordonar.

cordon bleu [,kɔ:dɔ̃n'bləː] *n* cordón *m* azul; (*Cook*)
cocinero *m* de primera clase, cocinera *f* de primera
clase.

Cordova ['kɔ:dəvə] Córdoba.

Cordovan ['kɔ:dəvən] **1** *adj* cordobés. **2** *n* cordobés
m, esa *f*; (*leather*) cordobán *m*.

corduroy ['kɔ:dərɔi] *n* pana *f*; **—s** pantalones *mpl*
de pana; **— road** (*US*) camino de troncos.

core [kɔ:*] *n* centro *m*, núcleo *m*; (*of fruit*) corazón *m*;
(*of cable*) alma *f*; (*fig, of problem etc*) lo esencial,
esencia *f*; **a hard — of resistance** un núcleo endurecido de resistencia; **English to the —** inglés hasta
los tuétanos; **rotten to the —** (*fig*) corrompido hasta
la médula.

co-religionist ['kəuri'lidʒənist] *n* correligionario *m*,
a *f*.

co-respondent ['kəuris'pɔndənt] *n persona acusada de
haber cometido adulterio con uno de los esposos, en un
pleito de divorcio.*

coriander [,kɔri'ændə*] *n* culantro *m*.

Corinth ['kɔrinθ] Corinto.

Corinthian [kə'rinθiən] *adj* corintio.

Coriolanus [,kɔriə'leinəs] *m* Coriolano.

cork [kɔ:k] **1** *n* corcho *m*. **2** *attr* de corcho. **3** *vt* tapar
con corcho (*also* **to — up**); **the wine is —ed** el vino
sabe a corcho.

corkage ['kɔ:kidʒ] *n* precio *m* que se cobra en un
restaurante por el descorche de las botellas.

corking ['kɔ:kiŋ] *adj* (*fam*) pistonudo, bárbaro.

corkscrew ['kɔ:kskru:] **1** *n* sacacorchos *m*. **2** *attr
movement* en espiral. **3** *vi* subir en espiral.

cork-tipped ['kɔ:k'tipt] *adj* emboquillado.

cork tree ['kɔ:ktri:] *n* alcornoque *m*.

corm [kɔ:m] *n* bulbo *m*.

cormorant ['kɔ:mərənt] *n* cormorán *m* grande.

corn¹ [kɔ:n] (*Bot*) granos *mpl*, cereales *mpl*; (*wheat*)
trigo *m*; (*US, also* **Indian —**) maíz *m*; (*fig*) cosas *fpl*
viejas, cosas *fpl* rancias, cosas *fpl* al estilo antiguo;
— on the cob maíz *m* en la mazorca; **— in Egypt!**
¡agua de mayo!

corn² [kɔ:n] *n* (*Med*) callo *m*; **to tread on someone's
—s** herir los sentimientos de uno.

corncob ['kɔ:nkɔb] *n* (*US*) mazorca *f* de maíz.

corncrake ['kɔ:nkreik] *n* guión *m* de codornices.

cornea ['kɔ:niə] *n* córnea *f*.

corned ['kɔ:nd] *adj*: see **beef.**

cornelian [kɔ:'ni:liən] *n* cornalina *f*.

corner ['kɔ:nə*] **1** *n* ángulo *m*; (*outside* **—**) esquina *f*,
(*inside* **—**) rincón *m*; (*bend in road*) curva *f*, recodo
m; (*Sport*) córner *m*, esquina *f*; (*Comm*) monopolio *m*
(*in de*); **— house** casa *f* en una esquina; **the four —s
of the earth** las cinco partes del mundo; **out of the
— of one's eye** con el rabillo del ojo; **it's round
the —** está a la vuelta de la esquina; **to be in a
tight —** estar en un aprieto; **to cut —s** atajar; **to
drive someone into a —** (*fig*) poner a uno entre la
espada y la pared; **to go round the —** doblar la
esquina; **to rub the —s off someone** lijar a uno,
cepillar a uno; **to turn the —** doblar la esquina,
(*fig*) ir saliendo del apuro.

2 *vt* acorralar, arrinconar; *person* abordar, detener;
fugitive cazar; *market* acaparar.

3 *vi* tomar una curva.

corner flag ['kɔ:nəflæg] *n* banderola *f* de esquina.

corner kick ['kɔ:nəkik] *n* córner *m*, saque *m* de
esquina.

corner seat ['kɔ:nəsi:t] *n* asiento *m* del rincón.

cornerstone ['kɔ:nəstəun] *n* piedra *f* angular (*also
fig*).

cornerways ['kɔ:nəweiz] *adv* diagonalmente.

cornet ['kɔ:nit] *n* (*Mus*) corneta *f*; (*of paper*) cucurucho *m*; (*ice cream*) barquillo *m*, cornete *m*.

corn exchange ['kɔ:niks'tʃeindʒ] *n* bolsa *f* de granos.

cornfield ['kɔ:nfi:ld] *n* trigal *m*, campo *m* de trigo;
(*US*) maizal *m*.

cornflour ['kɔ:nflauə*] *n* harina *f* de maíz.

cornflower ['kɔ:nflauə*] *n* aciano *m*, azulina *f*.

cornice ['kɔ:nis] *n* cornisa *f*.

Cornish ['kɔ:niʃ] **1** *adj* córnico. **2** *n* córnico *m*.

cornstarch ['kɔ:nsta:tʃ] *n* (*US*) almidón *m* de maíz.

cornucopia [,kɔ:nju'kəupiə] *n* cornucopia *f*.

Cornwall ['kɔ:nwəl] Cornualles *m*.

corny ['kɔ:ni] *adj* (*fam*) viejo, gastado, rancio.

corolla [kə'rɔlə] *n* corola *f*.

corollary [kə'rɔləri] *n* corolario *m*; consecuencia *f*
natural.

coronary ['kɔrənəri] *adj*: **— thrombosis** trombosis *f*
coronaria.

coronation [,kɔrə'neiʃən] *n* coronación *f*.

coroner ['kɔrənə*] *n* (*approx*) juez *m* de primera
instancia e instrucción.

coronet ['kɔrənit] *n* corona *f* (de marqués *etc*).

corporal ['kɔ:pərəl] **1** *adj* corporal. **2** *n* cabo *m*.

corporate ['kɔ:pərit] *adj* corporativo, colectivo.

corporation [,kɔ:pə'reiʃən] *n* corporación *f*; (*esp US
Comm*) sociedad *f* anónima; (*of city*) ayuntamiento
m; (*fam*) panza *f*.

corporeal [kɔ:'pɔ:riəl] *adj* corpóreo.

corps [kɔ:*] *n, pl* **corps** [kɔ:z] cuerpo *m*; **army —**
cuerpo *m* de ejército; **— de ballet** cuerpo *m* de baile;
diplomatic — cuerpo *m* diplomático; **medical —**
cuerpo *m* de sanidad; **service —** cuerpo *m* de
intendencia.

corpse [kɔ:ps] *n* cadáver *m*.

corpulence ['kɔ:pjuləns] *n* gordura *f*.

corpulent ['kɔ:pjulənt] *adj* gordo.

corpus ['kɔ:pəs] *n* cuerpo *m*; **C— Christi** Corpus *m*.

corpuscle ['kɔ:pʌsl] *n* (*of blood*) glóbulo *m*, corpúsculo *m*.

corral [kə'ra:l] (*US*) **1** *n* corral *m*. **2** *vt* acorralar.

correct [kə'rekt] **1** *adj* (**a**) (*accurate*) correcto, exacto,
justo; **—!** ¡exacto!; **you are perfectly —** Vd tiene
perfectamente razón, Vd está en lo cierto; **am I —
in saying that . . . ?** ¿me equivoco al decir que . . . ?

(**b**) (*proper*) correcto.

2 *vt* corregir; rectificar, emendar; *exam* puntuar,
calificar; **I stand —ed** confieso que me equivoqué.

correction [kə'rekʃən] *n* corrección *f*; rectificación *f*;
(*erasure*) tachadura *f*; **I speak under —** puede que
me equivoque.

corrective [kə'rektiv] **1** *adj* correctivo; **— glasses**
gafas *fpl* correctoras. **2** *n* correctivo *m*.

correctly [kə'rektli] *adv* correctamente.

correctness [kə'rektnis] *n* (*accuracy*) exactitud *f*;
(*properness*) corrección *f*.

correlate ['kɔrileit] **1** *vt* correlacionar. **2** *vi* tener
correlación.

correlation [,kɔri'leiʃən] *n* correlación *f*.

correlative [kə'relativ] **1** *adj* correlativo. **2** *n* correlativo *m*.

correspond [,kɔris'pɔnd] *vi* (**a**) (*agree*) corresponder
(*to, with* a). (**b**) (*by letter*) escribirse; **to — with** estar
en correspondencia con, cartearse con.

correspondence [,kɔris'pɔndəns] *n* (**a**) (*agreement*)
correspondencia *f*.

(**b**) (*by letter*) correspondencia *f*; **— course** curso *m*
por correspondencia; **to be in — with someone**
estar en correspondencia con uno.

(**c**) (*collected letters*) epistolario *m*.

correspondent [ˌkɔrisˈpɔndənt] n correspondiente mf; (of paper) corresponsal mf; **special —** corresponsal m extraordinario.

corresponding [ˌkɔrisˈpɔndiŋ] adj correspondiente.

correspondingly [ˌkɔrisˈpɔndiŋli] adv igualmente, equivalentemente.

corridor [ˈkɔridɔ:*] n pasillo m (also Rail), corredor m (also Pol).

corroborate [kəˈrɔbəreit] vt corroborar, confirmar.

corroboration [kəˌrɔbəˈreiʃən] n corroboración f, confirmación f.

corroborative [kəˈrɔbərətiv] adj corroborativo, confirmatorio.

corrode [kəˈrəud] 1 vt corroer. 2 vi corroerse.

corrosion [kəˈrəuʒən] n corrosión f.

corrosive [kəˈrəuziv] adj corrosivo.

corrugated [ˈkɔrəgeitid] adj ondulado.

corrupt [kəˈrʌpt] 1 adj corrompido; text viciado; taste depravado, estragado; person venal; **—** practices corrupción f. 2 vt corromper; (bribe) sobornar.

corruption [kəˈrʌpʃən] n corrupción f.

corsage [kɔ:ˈsɑ:ʒ] n (dress) corpiño m; (flowers) ramillete m para la cintura.

corsair [ˈkɔ:sɛə*] n corsario m.

corset [ˈkɔ:sit] n faja f, (old-style) corsé m.

Corsica [ˈkɔ:sikə] Córcega f.

Corsican [ˈkɔ:sikən] 1 adj corso. 2 n corso m, a f.

cortège [kɔ:ˈteʒ] n (procession) cortejo m, desfile m; (train) séquito m; funeral **—** cortejo m fúnebre.

cortex [ˈkɔ:teks] n, pl **cortices** [ˈkɔ:tisi:z] corteza f.

cortisone [ˈkɔ:tizəun] n cortisona f.

corundum [kəˈrʌndəm] n corindón m.

Corunna [kəˈrʌnə] La Coruña.

coruscate [ˈkɔrəskeit] vi brillar, fulgurar.

corvette [kɔ:ˈvet] n corbeta f.

cosh [kɔʃ] 1 n cachiporra f. 2 vt golpear con una cachiporra.

cosignatory [ˈkəuˈsignətəri] n cosignatario m, a f.

cosine [ˈkəusain] n coseno m.

cosiness [ˈkəuzinis] n comodidad f; lo acogedor; lo holgado.

cos lettuce [ˈkɔsˈletis] n lechuga f Cos.

cosmetic [kɔzˈmetik] 1 adj cosmético. 2 n cosmético m.

cosmic [ˈkɔzmik] adj cósmico.

cosmogony [kɔzˈmɔgəni] n cosmogonía f.

cosmographer [kɔzˈmɔgrəfə*] n cosmógrafo m.

cosmography [kɔzˈmɔgrəfi] n cosmografía f.

cosmology [kɔzˈmɔlədʒi] n cosmología f.

cosmonaut [ˈkɔzmənɔ:t] n cosmonauta mf.

cosmopolitan [ˌkɔzməˈpɔlitən] 1 adj cosmopolita. 2 n cosmopolita mf.

cosmopolite [kɔzˈmɔpəlait] n cosmopolita mf.

cosmos [ˈkɔzmɔs] n cosmos m.

Cossack [ˈkɔsæk] 1 adj cosaco m. 2 n cosaco m, a f.

cosset [ˈkɔsit] vt mimar.

cost [kɔst] 1 n (a) precio m; coste m, costo m, costa f; **—s** (in industry etc) costes mpl; **— of living** costo m de vida; **at — —** a costa; **at the — of his health** a costa de su salud; **at the — of his life** pagó con la vida; **at all —s, at any —** a todo trance, a toda costa; **at great —** tras grandes esfuerzos, tras grandes pérdidas; **at little — to himself** con poco riesgo para sí mismo; **to my —** a mis expensas; **without counting the —** sin pensar en los riesgos.
   (b) (Law) **—s** costas fpl, litisexpensas fpl; **he was ordered to pay —s** se le condenó a pagar las costas.
   2 vt calcular el coste de, preparar el presupuesto de; **it has not been properly —ed** no se ha calculado detalladamente el coste de esto.
   3 (irr: pret and ptp cost) vi costar, valer; **it — £2** costó 2 libras; **how much does this —?** ¿cuánto vale esto?, ¿cuánto es?; **what does it — to go?** ¿cuánto cuesta el viaje?; **— what it may** cueste lo que cueste; **it — him his life** le costó la vida; **it — him a lot of trouble** le causó muchas molestias.

co-star [ˈkəustɑ:*] 1 n colega mf de reparto (en una producción cinematográfica).
   2 vi: **to — with someone** figurar en un papel principal en compañía con uno.

Costa Rica [ˈkɔstəˈri:kə] Costa f Rica.

Costa Rican [ˈkɔstəˈri:kən] 1 adj costarriqueño. 2 n costarriqueño m, a f.

coster [ˈkɔstə*] n, **costermonger** [ˈkɔstəˌmʌŋgə*] n vendedor m ambulante.

costing [ˈkɔstiŋ] n cálculo m del coste.

costive [ˈkɔstiv] adj estreñido.

costliness [ˈkɔstlinis] n (dearness) alto precio m; (great value) suntuosidad f.

costly [ˈkɔstli] adj (dear) costoso; (valuable) suntuoso.

cost price [ˈkɔstˈprais] 1 n precio m de coste; **at —** = 2 adv al precio de coste.

costume [ˈkɔstju:m] n traje m; (fancy-dress) disfraz m; **— jewellery** joyas fpl de fantasía.

costumier [kɔsˈtju:miə*] n sastre m de teatro.

cosy [ˈkəuzi] 1 adj cómodo, agradable; atmosphere acogedor, amistoso; life holgado. 2 n cubierta f para tetera.

cot [kɔt] n camita f de niño, cuna f.

coterie [ˈkəutəri] n grupo m; (clique) peña f, camarilla f.

cottage [ˈkɔtidʒ] n casita f de campo; (US) vivienda f campestre, quinta f; (labourer's etc) cabaña f, barraca f; **— cheese** requesón m.

cottager [ˈkɔtidʒə*] n aldeano m, a f; (US) veraneante mf que vive en una casita de campo.

cotter [ˈkɔtə*] n chaveta f.

cotton [ˈkɔtn] 1 n algodón m; (plant) algodonero m.
   2 attr de algodón; **the — industry** la industria algodonera.
   3 vi: **to — on to** (fam) entender, caer en la cuenta de.

cotton grass [ˈkɔtngrɑ:s] n algodonosa f.

cotton mill [ˈkɔtnmil] n fábrica f de algodón.

cottonseed oil [ˈkɔtnsi:dɔil] n aceite m de algodón.

cottontail [ˈkɔtnteil] n liebre f de cola blanca.

cotton wool [ˈkɔtnˈwul] n algodón m hidrófilo (en rama).

cotyledon [ˌkɔtiˈli:dən] n cotiledón m.

couch [kautʃ] 1 n canapé m, sofá m. 2 vt expresar.

couch grass [ˈkautʃgrɑ:s] n hierba f rastrera.

cougar [ˈku:gə*] n puma f.

cough [kɔf] 1 n tos f. 2 vt: **to — up** escupir, arrojar; (sl) desembolsar, pagar. 3 vi toser; (sl) cantar; **to — up** (sl) desdinerarse, pagar.

cough drop [ˈkɔfdrɔp] n pastilla f para la tos.

could [kud] pret of **can**.

couldn't [ˈkudnt] = **could not**.

council [ˈkaunsl] n consejo m, junta f; (Eccl) concilio m; **city —, town —** concejo m municipal, ayuntamiento m; **works —** consejo m de obreros; **— of war** consejo m de guerra; **Privy C—** Consejo m Privado.

council house [ˈkaunslhaus] n, pl **— houses** [ˌhauziz] vivienda f protegida.

councillor [ˈkaunsilə*] n concejal m (also **town —**).

councilman [ˈkaunslmən] n, pl **—men** [mən] (US) concejal m.

counsel [ˈkaunsəl] 1 n (a) consejo m; **a — of perfection** un ideal imposible; **to keep one's own —** guardar silencio; **to take — with** aconsejarse con.
   (b) (Law) abogado m; **— for the defence, defending —** abogado m defensor; **— for the prosecution** fiscal m.

counsellor [ˈkaunslə*] n consejero m, a f.

count[1] [kaunt] 1 n (a) (act of counting) cuenta f, cálculo m; (of words etc) recuento m; (of votes) escrutinio m; (Boxing) cuenta f; **to keep — of** contar; **to lose — of** perder la cuenta de.
   (b) (total) suma f, total m.
   (c) (Law) cargo m, acusación f.
   2 vt (a) (Math) contar; calcular; **to — out** ir contando; (Boxing) declarar vencido; **to — up** contar.
   (b) (include) incluir; **not —ing** sin contar, además de, con exclusión de; **to — out** excluir; **please — me out** por favor no cuente conmigo.
   (c) (deem) creer, considerar; **I don't — him among my friends** no le considero como amigo.
   3 vi (a) (Math) contar; **to — down** contar hacia atrás; **to — on one's fingers** contar por los dedos; **he —s as 2** él cuenta por 2.
   (b) (be valid) **that doesn't —** eso no vale, (in games) eso no puntúa.
   (c) (be important) **every second —s** cada segundo es importante; **he doesn't —** él no vale para esto; **he doesn't — for much** él apenas si vale; **ability —s for little here** aquí la aptitud sirve para muy poco.
   (d) **to — on** contar con; **to — on + ger** contar con + infin.

count[2] [kaunt] n conde m.

countable [ˈkauntəbl] adj contable.

countdown [ˈkauntdaun] n cuenta f hacia atrás.

countenance [ˈkauntinəns] 1 n semblante m, rostro m; **to be out of —** estar desconcertado; **to give (or lend) — to news** acreditar; **to keep one's —** contener la risa; **to lose —** desconcertarse; **to put someone out of —** desconcertar a uno.
   2 vt aprobar, tolerar.

counter[1] [ˈkauntə*] n (a) (of shop) mostrador m; **under the —** (fam) por la trastienda. (b) (in games) ficha f.

counter[2] [ˈkauntə*] 1 adj contrario, de sentido opuesto (to a).
   2 adv: **to run — to** oponerse a, ser contrario a.

3 *vt* contrarrestar; *blow* parar; *attack* contestar a. **4** *vi*: **to — with** contestar con.

counteract [ˌkauntə'rækt] *vt* contrarrestar.

counter-attack ['kauntərə.tæk] **1** *n* contraataque *m*. **2** *vt* contraatacar.

counter-attraction ['kauntərə.trækʃən] *n* atracción *f* rival.

counterbalance ['kauntə.bæləns] **1** *n* contrapeso *m*. **2** *vt* contrapesar.

counterblast ['kauntəblɑːst] *n* respuesta *f* vigorosa (*to* a).

countercharge ['kauntətʃɑːdʒ] *n* recriminación *f*.

countercheck ['kauntətʃek] **1** *n* segunda comprobación *f*. **2** *vt* comprobar por segunda vez.

counterclaim ['kauntəkleim] *n* contrarreclamación *f*.

counter-clockwise ['kauntə'klɔkwaiz] *adv* en sentido contrario al de las agujas del reloj.

counter-espionage ['kauntə'respiənɑːʒ] *n* contraespionaje *m*.

counterfeit ['kauntəfiːt] **1** *adj* falso, falsificado. **2** *n* falsificación *f*; (*coin*) moneda *f* falsa. **3** *vt* falsificar, contrahacer.

counterfoil ['kauntəfɔil] *n* talón *m*.

counter-gambit ['kauntə'gæmbit] *n* contragambito *m*.

counterintelligence ['kauntərin.telidʒəns] *n* contrainteligencia *f*.

counterirritant ['kauntər'iritənt] *n* contrairritante *m*.

countermand ['kauntəmɑːnd] *vt* revocar, cancelar.

counter-measure ['kauntəmeʒə*] *n* contramedida *f*.

counter-move ['kauntəmuːv] *n* contrajugada *f*.

counter-offensive ['kauntərə'fensiv] *n* contraofensiva *f*.

counter-order ['kauntər.ɔːdə*] *n* contraorden *f*.

counterpane ['kauntəpein] *n* sobrecama *m*, colcha *f*, cobertor *m*.

counterpart ['kauntəpɑːt] *n*: **his — here is Mr X** aquí la persona que le equivale es el Sr X; **this piece has no —** a esta pieza no hay nada que le corresponda.

counterpoint ['kauntəpɔint] *n* contrapunto *m*.

counterpoise ['kauntəpɔiz] **1** *n* contrapeso *m*. **2** *vt* contrapesar.

Counter-Reformation ['kauntə.refə'meiʃən] *n* Contrarreforma *f*.

counter-revolution ['kauntərevə'luːʃən] *n* contrarrevolución *f*.

counter-revolutionary ['kauntərevə'luːʃənri] **1** *adj* contrarrevolucionario. **2** *n* contrarrevolucionario *m*.

countersign ['kauntəsain] *vt* refrendar.

countersink ['kauntəsiŋk] *vt* avellanar.

counter-stroke ['kauntəstrəuk] *n* contragolpe *m*.

counter tenor ['kauntə'tenə*] *n* tenor *m* ligero.

counterweight ['kauntəweit] *n* contrapeso *m*.

countess ['kauntis] *n* condesa *f*.

counting house ['kauntiŋ'haus] *n*, *pl* **— houses** [ˌhauziz] (*arch*) despacho *m*, oficina *f*.

countless ['kauntlis] *adj* incontable, innumerable; **— times** infinitas veces.

countrified ['kʌntrifaid] *adj* rústico.

country ['kʌntri] **1** *n* (*political*) país *m*; (*regarded more sentimentally*) patria *f*; (*countryside*) campo *m*; (*region*) región *f*, tierra *f*; **love of —** amor *m* a la patria; **Black C—** *región minera e industrial de Birmingham y su comarca (Inglaterra);* **mother —** madre *f* patria; **the old —** la patria, mi país natal; **there's some good — to the north** hacia el norte de el paisaje es muy bonito; **this is good fishing —** ésta es buena tierra para la pesca; **to go to the —** (*Pol*) celebrar elecciones generales; **to live off the —** vivir del país.
2 *attr*: **— people** gente *m* del campo; **— life** vida *f* del campo; **— club** club *m* campestre; **— house** quinta *f*, finca *f*.

country dance ['kʌntri'dɑːns] *n* contradanza *f*, baile *m* campestre.

countryman ['kʌntrimən] *n*, *pl* **—men** [mən] campesino *m*; (*fellow-*) compatriota *m*.

countryside ['kʌntrisaid] *n* campo *m*.

countrywide ['kʌntriwaid] *adj* nacional.

countrywoman ['kʌntri.wumən] *n*, *pl* **—women** [ˌwimin] campesina *f*.

county ['kaunti] **1** *n* condado *m*; **the Home Counties** *los condados alrededor de Londres.* **2** *attr and adj* aristocrático; **— town** cabeza *f* de partido.

coup [kuː] *n* golpe *m*; **— d'état** golpe *m* de estado; **— de grâce** golpe *m* de gracia; **— de théâtre** golpe *m* de teatro; **to bring off a —** obtener un éxito inesperado.

coupé ['kuːpei] *n* cupé *m*.

couple ['kʌpl] **1** *n* (*of things*) par *m*; (*of persons*)

pareja *f*; **married —** matrimonio *m*; **young — matrimonio** *m* joven; **just a — of minutes** dos minutos nada más; **we had a — in a bar** (*fam*) tomamos algo en un bar; **when he's had a — he starts to shout** cuando ha bebido más de la cuenta se pone a gritar.
2 *vt names etc* unir, juntar; *ideas* asociar; (*Mech*) acoplar, enganchar.
3 *vi* (*Zool*) copularse.

couplet ['kʌplit] *n* pareado *m*.

coupling ['kʌpliŋ] *n* (*Mech*) acoplamiento *m*; (*Rail, Aut*) enganche *m*.

coupon ['kuːpɔn] *n* cupón *m*; (*football-pool —*) boleto *m*.

courage ['kʌridʒ] *n* valor *m*, valentía *f*; **—!** ¡ánimo!; **Dutch —** envalentonamiento *m* (del que ha bebido); **to have the — of one's convictions** obrar de acuerdo con su conciencia; **to pluck up one's —** hacer de tripas corazón; **to screw up one's — to + infin** cobrar bastante ánimo como para **+ infin**; **we may take — from the fact that** es alentador el hecho de que.

courageous [kə'reidʒəs] *adj* valiente, valeroso.

courageously [kə'reidʒəsli] *adv* valientemente.

courier ['kuriə*] *n* estafeta *f*, correo *m* diplomático; (*travel —*) agente *m* de turismo.

course [kɔːs] **1** *n* **(a)** (*movement, direction*) dirección *f*, ruta *f*; (*of bullet etc*) trayectoria *f*; (*of road*) dirección *f*; (*of river, star*) curso *m*; (*of illness*) desarrollo *m*; (*Naut*) rumbo *m*, derrota *f*, (*marked on chart*) derrotero *m*; **to change —** cambiar de rumbo (*also fig*); **to set — for** hacer rumbo a; **to steer a — for** ir rumbo a.

(b) (*fig*) proceder *m*, camino *m*; **— of action** línea *f* de conducta, línea *f* de acción, proceder *m*; **— of conduct** línea *f* de conducta; **— of events** marcha *f* de los acontecimientos; **in the ordinary — of events** normalmente; **— of treatment** tratamiento *m*, cura *f*; **the — of true love** el camino del verdadero amor; **your best — is** to say nothing lo mejor es no decir nada; **there was no — open to me but to go** no tuve más remedio que ir; **what — do you suggest?** ¿qué es lo que me aconsejas?; **the affair has run its —** el asunto ha terminado; **we will let things take their —** dejaremos que las cosas se desarrollen normalmente, dejaremos correr los acontecimientos; **to take a middle —** evitar los extremos.

(c) (*Golf*) campo *m*; (*for races*) pista *f*, (*for horse races*) hipódromo *m*.

(d) (*in meal*) plato *m*; **main —** plato *m* principal; **fish —** pescado *m*.

(e) (*Archit*) hilada *f*.

(f) (*series*) curso *m*; (*Univ etc*) curso *m*, asignatura *f*; **I failed the chemistry —** me suspendieron en química; **what — do you take?** ¿qué asignatura haces?; **a French —** un curso de francés; **I bought a French grammar —** compré una gramática francesa; **a — of lectures** un ciclo de conferencias; **refresher —** curso *m* de repaso; **secretarial — curso** *m* de secretaria; **to take a — with** seguir un curso con.

(g) in the — of durante, en el curso de; **in the — of construction** en vías de construcción; **it is in — of being applied** está en trance de ser aplicado; **in — of time, in due —** andando el tiempo, a su tiempo; **we shall inform you in due —** se lo comunicaremos en el momento oportuno; **of —** desde luego, naturalmente; **of —!** ¡naturalmente!, ¡claro!; **of — it's not true** claro que no es cierto; **it is of — true that** bien es verdad que; **he takes it all as a matter of —** para él todo esto no tiene nada de especial; **he took it as a matter of — that** para él era de cajón que.
2 *vt* cazar (con perros).
3 *vi* correr; **it sent the blood coursing through my veins** me hizo hervir la sangre.

coursing ['kɔːsiŋ] *n* caza *f* con perros.

court [kɔːt] **1** *n* **(a)** (*Archit*) patio *m*; (*large room*) sala *f*.

(b) (*Sport*) pista *f*, cancha *f*; **hard —** pista *f* dura.

(c) (*royal*) corte *f*; **at —** en la corte; **— circular** noticiario *m* de la corte.

(d) to pay — to hacer la corte a.

(e) (*Law*) tribunal *m*, juzgado *m*; **divorce —** tribunal *m* de pleitos matrimoniales; **high —**, **supreme —** tribunal *m* supremo; **juvenile —** tribunal *m* tutelar de menores; **police —** tribunal *m* de policía; **— of appeal** tribunal *m* de casación; **— of inquiry** comisión *f* de investigación; **— of justice** tribunal *m* de justicia; **in open —** en pleno tribunal; **to laugh something out of** — rechazar algo poniéndolo en ridículo; **to rule something out of** — no admitir algo; **to settle out of** — arreglar una disputa de modo privado; **to take someone to** — demandar a uno; recurrir a la vía judicial.

2 vt woman cortejar, hacer la corte a, (less formally) tener relaciones con; favour solicitar; danger, trouble buscar; disaster correr a.

3 vi estar en relaciones, ser novios; **they've been —ing 3 years** llevan 3 años de relaciones; **are you —ing?** ¿tienes novio?; **—ing couple** pareja f de novios.

court card ['kɔːtkɑːd] n carta f de figura.
courteous ['kəːtiəs] adj cortés, fino.
courteously ['kəːtiəsli] adv cortésmente.
courtesan [ˌkɔːti'zæn] n cortesana f.
courtesy ['kəːtisi] n cortesía f; atención f; gentileza f; **— title** título m de cortesía; **by — of** con permiso de; **to exchange courtesies** cambiar cumplidos de etiqueta; **I'll do it out of —** lo haré por cortesía; **you might have had the — to tell me** el no decírmelo es una falta de educación; **he did me the — of reading it** tuvo conmigo la amabilidad de leerlo.
courthouse ['kɔːthaus] n, pl **—houses** [ˌhauziz] palacio m de justicia.
courtier ['kɔːtiə*] n cortesano m.
courtly ['kɔːtli] adj cortés, elegante, fino; **— love** amor m cortés.
court-martial ['kɔːt'mɑːʃəl] **1** n consejo m de guerra. **2** vt someter a consejo de guerra.
court room ['kɔːtrum] n sala f de justicia.
courtship ['kɔːtʃip] n (act) cortejo m; (period) relaciones fpl, noviazgo m.
courtyard ['kɔːtjɑːd] n patio m.
cousin ['kʌzn] n primo m, a f; **first —** primo m carnal, prima f carnal; **second —** primo m segundo, prima f segunda; **country —** pariente m pueblerino, parienta f pueblerina.
cove[1] [kəuv] n (Geog) cala f, ensenada f.
cove[2] [kəuv] n (sl) tío m.
covenant ['kʌvinənt] **1** n pacto m, convenio m; (Bible) **C—** Alianza f. **2** vi: **to — with someone for something** pactar algo con uno.
covenanter ['kʌvinəntə*] n contratante mf; (Hist) covenantario m.
Coventry ['kɔvəntri]: **to send someone to —** hacer el vacío a uno.
cover ['kʌvə*] **1** n (a) (in general) cubierta f; (lid) tapa f, tapadura f; (on bed) cobertor m; (of chair, typewriter) funda f; **—s** (bedclothes) ropa f de cama, mantas fpl; **outer —** (Aut) cubierta f.
(b) (envelope) sobre m; **first-day —** sobre m de primer día; **under separate —** por separado.
(c) (of book) forro m, cubierta f; (of magazine) portada f; **to read a book from — to —** leer un libro desde el principio hasta el fin.
(d) (at table) cubierto m.
(e) (fig) protección f; (shelter) abrigo m; (insurance) cobertura f; (pretext) pretexto m; **air —** protección f aérea; **under —** al abrigo, (indoors) bajo techo; **under — of** al abrigo de, bajo, (fig) so capa de; **under the — of night** al amparo de la noche; **to break —** salir a campo raso; **to take —** abrigarse, ponerse al abrigo, (Mil) refugiarse (from de).
2 vt cubrir (with de); revestir (with de); (with lid) tapar (with con); book forrar; (hide) cubrir, ocultar; (protect) proteger, abrigar; distance recorrer, cubrir; salvar; expenses cubrir; (include) incluir, abarcar, comprender; (Mil) person amenazar (with con), place dominar, retreat cubrir, proteger; (Journalism) investigar, hacer un reportaje sobre, escribir una crónica de, dar cuenta de; points in discussion tratar, resolver, discutir; **to — one's eyes** taparse los ojos; **to be —ed in confusion** estar lleno de confusión; **to be —ed with glory** estar cubierto de gloria; **to — in** cubrir; (roof) poner un techo a; **to — over** cubrir, revestir (with de); **to — up** cubrir completamente, tapar; correr un velo sobre; (fig) ocultar, disimular.
3 vi: **to — up for someone** encubrir a uno, usar pretextos para no delatar a uno.
4 vr: **to — oneself** protegerse a sí mismo; **to — oneself with glory** cubrirse de gloria.
coveralls ['kʌvərɔːlz] npl (US) = **overalls**.
coverage ['kʌvəridʒ] n (a) alcance m; espacio m cubierto, cantidad f cubierta; **news —** alcance m del servicio de información o un periódico etc.
(b) (Fin) conjunto m de los riesgos que cubre una póliza de seguros.
cover charge ['kʌvətʃɑːdʒ] n precio m del cubierto.
covergirl ['kʌvəgəːl] n joven f cuyo retrato ha figurado en la portada de una revista.

covering ['kʌvəriŋ] n (wrapping) cubierta f, envoltura f; (dress etc) abrigo m; **a — of snow** una capa de nieve.
coverlet ['kʌvəlit] n sobrecama m, colcha f, cobertor m.
covert ['kʌvət] **1** adj secreto, disimulado. **2** n soto m.
covet ['kʌvit] vt codiciar.
covetous ['kʌvitəs] adj codicioso.
covetousness ['kʌvitəsnis] n codicia f.
covey ['kʌvi] n (Orn) nidada f (de perdices); (fig) grupo m.
cow[1] [kau] n vaca f; (of elephant etc) hembra f; **till the —s come home** hasta que la rana críe pelo.
cow[2] [kau] vt intimidar, acobardar.
coward ['kauəd] n cobarde m.
cowardice ['kauədis] n, **cowardliness** ['kauədlinis] n cobardía f.
cowardly ['kauədli] adj cobarde.
cowbell ['kaubel] n cencerro m.
cowboy ['kaubɔi] n vaquero m.
cowboy hat ['kaubɔi'hæt] n sombrero m de vaquero.
cowcatcher ['kau̯kætʃə*] n rastrillo m delantero, quitapiedras m.
cower ['kauə*] vi encogerse (de miedo), empequeñecerse (preso del terror); **the servants were —ing in a corner** los criados se habían refugiado medrosos en un rincón.
cowherd ['kauhəːd] n pastor m de ganado.
cowhide ['kauhaid] n cuero m.
cowl [kaul] n (hood) capucha f; (garment) cogulla f; (of chimney) sombrerete m.
cowling ['kauliŋ] n cubierta f.
cowman ['kaumən] n, pl **—men** [mən] pastor m de ganado.
co-worker ['kəu'wəːkə*] n colaborador m, ora f.
cowrie ['kauri] n cauri m.
cowpox ['kaupɔks] n vacuna f.
cowshed ['kauʃed] n establo m.
cowslip ['kauslip] n primavera f.
cox [kɔks] **1** n timonel m. **2** vt gobernar. **3** vi servir de timonel.
coxswain ['kɔksn] n timonel m.
coy [kɔi] adj tímido; (roguish) coquetón.
coyly ['kɔili] adv tímidamente; con coquetería.
coyness ['kɔinis] n timidez f; coquetería f.
coyote [kɔi'əuti] n coyote m.
cozy ['kəuzi] adj = **cosy**.
crab [kræb] n cangrejo m; **C—** (Astron) Cáncer m; **to catch a —** (fig) faltar con el remo.
crabapple ['kræb.æpl] n (fruit) manzana f silvestre; (tree) manzano m silvestre.
crabbed ['kræbd] adj writing apretado, indescifrable; temperament de miras estrechas, mezquino.
crabby ['kræbi] adj hosco, de mal genio; malhumorado.
crack [kræk] **1** n (a) (noise) crujido m; (of whip) chasquido m; (shot) estallido m.
(b) (blow) golpe m (on en).
(c) (fissure) grieta f, hendedura f; (slit) rendija f; **at the — of dawn** al romper el alba; **to open the window a —** abrir la ventana un poquito.
(d) (fam) chiste m, chanza f, cuchufleta f; **to make —s about** person tomar el pelo a, burlarse de, thing poner en ridículo.
(e) (fam) **to have a — at something** intentar algo, probar algo.
2 adj team etc de primera categoría; shot experto.
3 vt (a) (cause to sound) whip, fingers chasquear; knuckles etc crujir.
(b) (break) agrietar, hender, romper; nut cascar; safe forzar; bottle abrir (with para festejar a); heavy oils craquear; **to — one's head on the wall** dar con la cabeza contra la pared.
(c) joke contar.
(d) **to — up** dar bombo a; **it's not all it's —ed up to be** no es tan bueno como la gente dice.
4 vi (a) (make noise) chasquear; crujir; (shot) estallar.
(b) (break) agrietarse, henderse, rajarse, romperse; (burst) reventar; (voice) cascarse; **to — under the strain** romperse bajo el peso, (person) sufrir un colapso bajo la presión; **to — down on** castigar severamente, suprimir; **to — up** (plane) estrellarse, (machine) tener una avería, (Med) sufrir un colapso nervioso.
(c) **to get —ing** (fam) ponerse a trabajar (etc), poner manos a la obra; **let's get —ing!** ¡a ello!, ¡manos a la obra!
crack-brained ['krækbreind] adj mentecato.
cracked [krækt] adj voice cascado; (mad) chiflado.
cracker ['krækə*] n (firework) buscapiés m; (biscuit) cracker m.
crackers ['krækəz] adj (sl) lelo, chiflado.

crack-jaw ['krækdʒɔ:] *n* trabalenguas *m*.

crackle ['krækl] **1** *n* (*of wood, bacon*) crepitación *f*; (*of dry leaves*) crujido *m*; (*of shots*) traqueteo *m*. **2** *vi* crepitar; crujir; traquetear.

crackling ['kræklɪŋ] *n* (*Cook*) chicharrón *m*; (*sound*) see **crackle**.

cracknel ['kræknl] *n* coscarana *f*.

crackpot ['krækpɔt] **1** *adj* tonto, estrafalario. **2** *n* chiflado *m*.

cracksman ['kræksmən] *n*, *pl* —**men** [mən] (*fam*) ladrón *m* de cajas fuertes.

crack-up ['krækʌp] *n* (*fam*) (*Aer*) aterrizaje *m* violento; (*Mech*) avería *f*; (*Med*) colapso *m* nervioso.

cradle ['kreidl] **1** *n* cuna *f* (*also fig*); (*for painting etc*) plataforma *f* colgante.
2 *vt*: **to — a child in one's arms** mecer un niño en los brazos.

cradlesong ['kreidlsɔŋ] *n* canción *f* de cuna.

craft [krɑ:ft] *n* (a) (*skill in general*) destreza *f*, habilidad *f*; (*special skill*) arte *m*; (*craftiness*) astucia *f*; (*trade*) oficio *m*.
(b) (*Naut*) barco *m*, embarcación *f*.

craftily ['krɑ:ftili] *adv* astutamente.

craftiness ['krɑ:ftinis] *n* astucia *f*.

craftsman ['krɑ:ftsmən] *n*, *pl* —**men** [mən] artesano *m*; artífice *m*.

craftsmanship ['krɑ:ftsmənʃip] *n* artesanía *f*.

crafty ['krɑ:fti] *adj* astuto, taimado.

crag [kræg] *n* peñasco *m*, risco *m*.

craggy ['krægi] *adj* peñascoso, escarpado; *face* nudoso.

cram [kræm] **1** *vt* (a) *hen* cebar; *subject* empollar, aprender apresuradamente; *pupil* preparar apresuradamente para un examen.
(b) **to — food into one's mouth** llenarse la boca de comida; **to — things into a case** ir metiendo cosas apretadas en una maleta; **we can't — any more in** es imposible meter más.
(c) **to — something with** llenar algo de, henchir algo de; **the hall is —med** la sala está de bote en bote; **the room is —med with furniture** el cuarto está atestado de muebles; **he had his head —med with odd ideas** tenía la cabeza cargada de ideas raras.
2 *vi* (*for exam*) empollar; (*with food*) = **3** *vr*: **to — oneself with food** darse un atracón; **to — oneself with cakes** atracarse de pastas.

cram-full ['kræm'ful] *adj* completamente lleno, de bote en bote.

crammer ['kræmə*] *n* (*School: pupil*) empollón *m*, ona *f*; (*teacher*) profesor *m* que prepara rapidísimamente a sus alumnos para los exámenes.

cramp[1] [kræmp] *n* (*Med*) calambre *m*; **writer's —** calambre *m* de los escribientes.

cramp[2] [kræmp] **1** *n* (*Tech*) grapa *f*; (*Archit*) pieza *f* de unión, abrazadera *f*.
2 *vt* (*hamper*) estorbar, restringir; **to — someone's style** cortar los vuelos a uno.

cramped [kræmpt] *adj* *room etc* estrecho; *writing* menudo, apretado; *position* violento, nada cómodo; **we are very — for space** tenemos muy poco espacio.

crampon ['kræmpən] *n* garfio *m*; (*Mountaineering*) crampón *m*.

cranberry ['krænbəri] *n* arándano *m* agrio.

crane [krein] **1** *n* (*Zool*) grulla *f*; (*Tech*) grúa *f*.
2 *vt* (*also* **to — up**) levantar con grúa; **to — one's neck** estirar el cuello.
3 *vi*: **to — forward** inclinarse estirando el cuello; **to — to look at something** estirar el cuello para mirar algo.

cranefly ['kreinflai] *n* típula *f*.

crane's-bill ['kreinzbil] *n* geranio *m*, pico *m* de cigüeña.

cranium ['kreiniəm] *n* cráneo *m*.

crank[1] [kræŋk] **1** *n* manivela *f*, manubrio *m*; cigüeñal *m*. **2** *vt engine* (*also* **to — up**) dar vuelta a, hacer arrancar con la manivela.

crank[2] [kræŋk] *n* (*person*) maniático *m*, a *f*, chiflado *m*, a *f*.

crankcase ['kræŋkkeis] *n* cárter *m* del cigüeñal.

crankshaft ['kræŋkʃɑ:ft] *n* eje *m* del cigüeñal, árbol *m* del cigüeñal.

cranky ['kræŋki] *adj person* maniático, chiflado; *idea* raro, estrafalario.

cranny ['kræni] *n* grieta *f*.

crap [kræp] *n* (*sl*) mierda *f* (*also fig*).

crape [kreip] *n* crespón *m*.

craps [kræps] *npl* dados *mpl*; **to shoot —** jugar a los dados.

crash ['kræʃ] **1** *n* (a) (*noise*) estruendo *m*, estrépito *m*; (*explosion*) estallido *m*.
(b) (*collision*) accidente *m*, choque *m*, encon-

tronazo *m*; (*Aer*) accidente *m* de aviación.
(c) (*ruin*) fracaso *m*, ruina *f*; (*Comm*) quiebra *f*; **the 1929 —** la crisis económica de 1929.
2 *vt car, aircraft* estrellar (*into* contra); estropear; **he —ed the plate to the ground** echó el plato por tierra; **he —ed the plate into her face** le dio con el plato en la cara; **to — a party** (*fam*) colarse, entrar de gorra.
3 *vi* (a) (*fall noisily*) caer con estrépito (*also* **to — down, to come —ing down**); (*shatter*) romperse, hacerse añicos.
(b) (*have accident*) tener un accidente; (*2 cars etc*) chocar; (*Aer*) estrellarse, caer a tierra; **to — into** chocar con, estrellarse contra.
(c) (*fail*) fracasar, hundirse; (*Comm*) quebrar; **when the stock market —ed** cuando la bolsa tuvo su crisis.
4 *adv*: **he went — into a tree** dio de lleno contra un árbol.
5 *interj* ¡zas!, ¡pum!
6 *adj*: **— programme** programa *m* de urgencia; **— course** curso *m* acelerado, curso *m* concentrado.

crash helmet ['kræʃˌhelmit] *n* casco *m* protector.

crass [kræs] *adj* craso.

crate [kreit] *n* cajón *m* de embalaje, jaula *f*; (*fam*) armatoste *m*.

crater ['kreitə*] *n* cráter *m*.

cravat(e) [krə'væt] *n* corbata *f*.

crave [kreiv] **1** *vt* suplicar, implorar; *attention* reclamar. **2** *vi*: **to — for** ansiar, anhelar.

craven ['kreivn] *adj* cobarde.

craving ['kreivɪŋ] *n* deseo *m* vehemente, ansia *f*, sed *f* (*for* de); (*during pregnancy*) antojo *m*; **to get a — for something** encapricharse por algo.

crawfish ['krɔ:fiʃ] *n* ástaco *m*.

crawl [krɔ:l] **1** *n* (*action*) arrastramiento *m*; (*journey*) camino *m* a gatas; (*Swimming*) crol *m*; **the traffic went at a —** la circulación avanzaba a paso de tortuga; **the — to the coast** el viaje a una lentitud desesperante hacia la costa.
2 *vi* (a) (*drag oneself*) arrastrarse; avanzar a rastras; (*child*) andar a gatas, gatear; **to — in** entrar a gatas; **the fly —ed up the window** la mosca subió despacito el cristal; **the cars were —ing along** los coches avanzaban a paso de tortuga.
(b) **to — to someone** humillarse ante uno, ir humildemente a pedir perdón a uno.
(c) **to — with, to be —ing with** estar cuajado de, estar plagado de.

crayfish ['kreifiʃ] *n* ástaco *m*.

crayon ['kreiən] **1** *n* (*Art*) pastel *m*, lápiz *m* de tiza; (*child's*) lápiz *m* de color. **2** *vt* dibujar al pastel (*etc*).

craze [kreiz] *n* manía *f* (*for* por); (*fashion*) moda *f* (*for* de); **to be the —** estar muy de moda.

crazed [kreizd] *adj* loco (*with* de), demente; **half —** medio loco.

crazily ['kreizili] *adv* locamente; *lean etc* de modo peligroso.

crazy ['kreizi] *adj* (a) *person* loco, chiflado; *idea* disparatado, estrafalario; **to be — about** *person* estar chiflado por, *thing* andar loco por; **to be — with worry** estar loco de inquietud; **to drive someone —** volver loco a uno; **it's enough to drive you —** es para volverse loco; **to go —** volverse loco.
(b) *building* destartalado; **to lean at a — angle** inclinarse de modo peligroso.
(c) *paving* en mosaico.

creak [kri:k] **1** *n* (*of wood, shoe etc*) crujido *m*; (*of hinge etc*) chirrido *m*, rechinamiento *m*. **2** *vi* crujir; chirriar, rechinar.

creaky ['kri:ki] *adj* rechinador; (*fig*) poco sólido, inestable, nada firme.

cream [kri:m] **1** *n* (a) (*on milk*) nata *f*; **whipped —** nata *f* batida; **— cake** pastel *m* de nata.
(b) (*in general*) crema *f*; **foundation —** crema *f* base; **— of tartar** crémor *m* tártaro.
(c) (*fig*) flor *f* y nata, crema *f*, lo mejor y más selecto; **the — of society** la crema de la sociedad; **the — of the joke was that** lo más gracioso fue que.
2 *adj* color de crema.
3 *vt milk* desnatar; *butter* batir; (*fig*) quitar lo mejor de.
4 *vi* formar nata.

cream puff ['kri:m'pʌf] *n* bollo *m* de crema.

creamy ['kri:mi] *adj* cremoso.

crease [kri:s] **1** *n* (*fold*) pliegue *m*; (*in trousers*) raya *f*; (*wrinkle*) arruga *f*.
2 *vt* plegar, doblar; arrugar; **to — one's trousers** hacer la raya a los pantalones.
3 *vi* plegarse, doblarse; arrugarse.

create [kri:'eit] **1** vt crear; (produce) producir, motivar; character inventar; rôle encarnar; (appoint) nombrar.
  2 vi (fam) protestar, armar un lío.
creation [kri:'eiʃən] n creación f; (appointment) nombramiento m.
creative [kri:'eitiv] adj creador; original, inventivo; work original.
creativity [ˌkri:ei'tiviti] n facultad f creadora; originalidad f inventiva.
creator [kri:'eitə*] n creador m, ora f.
creature ['kri:tʃə*] n (a) (animal) criatura f; animal m, bicho m; **poor —!** ¡pobre animal!; **— comforts** bienestar m material.
  (b) (person) **to be someone's —** ser la criatura de uno; **wretched —!** ¡desgraciado!; **he's a poor —** es un infeliz; **doesn't she look a —?** ¡qué birria!
crèche [kreiʃ] n guardería f infantil.
credence ['kri:dəns] n: **to give —** to prestar fe a.
credentials [kri'denʃəlz] npl credenciales fpl.
credenza [krə'denzə] n aparador m.
credibility [ˌkredə'biləti] n credibilidad f; **— gap** margen m de confianza.
credible ['kredibl] adj creíble.
credit ['kredit] **1** n (a) (belief) crédito m; **to give — to** creer.
  (b) (reputation) buena fama f, reputación f.
  (c) (honour) honor m, mérito m; **to his —** he confessed dicho sea a su honor, confesó la verdad; **he is a great — to the family** le hace mucho honor a la familia; **to come out of something with —** salir airoso de algo; **the only people to emerge with any —** los únicos que salen con honor; **to pass a test with —** salir bien de una prueba; **it does you — Vd** puede enorgullecerse de ello; **he did himself great —** se honró mucho; **to take the —** atribuirse el mérito (for de).
  (d) (Comm) crédito m; (side of account) haber m; **"— terms available"** "ventas a plazos"; **on —** a crédito, al fiado; **on the — side** en el haber; **you have £10 to your —** Vd tiene 10 libras en el haber; **to give someone —** abrir crédito a uno; **I gave you — for more sense** le creía con más inteligencia.
  2 attr crediticio; balance positivo, acreedor.
  3 vt (a) (believe) creer, prestar fe a; **you wouldn't — it** parece mentira.
  (b) (Comm) **to — someone with £5, to — £5 to someone** abonar 5 libras en cuenta a uno.
  (c) (fig) **I —ed you with more sense** le creía con más inteligencia; **we must — him with charm at least** por lo menos hay que reconocer que tiene gran atractivo personal; **to be —ed with having done something** pasar por haber hecho algo; **he —ed them with the victory** les atribuyó el mérito de la victoria; **they had less drawing power than they were —ed with** no tenían tanta fuerza atractiva como se les suponía.
creditable ['kreditəbl] adj loable, estimable.
creditably ['kreditəbli] adv de modo loable.
credit agency ['kredit'eidʒənsi] n agencia que investiga los recursos financieros y confiabilidad de clientes que quieren abrir cuentas para compras al fiado.
credit card ['kreditkɑ:d] n tarjeta f de crédito.
creditor ['kreditə*] n acreedor m, ora f.
credit rating ['kredit,reitiŋ] n (Comm) cifra f máxima permitida para las compras al fiado, límite m de las facilidades crediticias.
credo ['kreidəu] n credo m.
credulity [kri'dju:liti] n credulidad f.
credulous ['kredjuləs] adj crédulo.
creed [kri:d] n credo m.
creek [kri:k] n (inlet) cala f, ensenada f; (stream) riachuelo m.
creel [kri:l] n cesta f (de pescador).
creep [kri:p] **1** n (a) (sl) cobista mf, pelotillero m.
  (b) it gives me the **—s** me horripila.
  2 (irr: pret and ptp **crept**) vi (a) (animal etc) arrastrarse, deslizarse, moverse muy despacio por el suelo.
  (b) (person etc) arrastrarse, andar a gatas; (stealthily) ir cautelosamente; (slowly) ir despacito, ir a paso de tortuga; **to — about on tiptoe** andar (or de) puntillas; **to — along** (traffic) avanzar a paso de tortuga; **to — in** entrar sin ser sentido; **to — out** salir silenciosamente; **to — up on someone** acercarse sigilosamente a uno.
  (c) (fig) **it's enough to make your flesh —** es para poner carne de gallina; **an error crept in se** deslizó un error; **old age is —ing on** se está acercando la vejez; **fear crept over him** le invadió el terror; **to — to someone** (sl) hacer la pelotilla a uno, dar jabón a uno.

creeper ['kri:pə*] n (Bot) enredadera f; **—s** (shoes) zapatillas fpl de goma.
creeping ['kri:piŋ] adj (Med etc) progresivo; barrage móvil.
creepy ['kri:pi] adj horripilante.
creepy-crawly ['kri:pi'krɔ:li] n (fam) bicho m.
cremate [kri'meit] vt incinerar.
cremation [kri'meiʃən] n incineración f (de cadáveres).
crematorium [ˌkremə'tɔ:riəm] n, pl **crematoria** [ˌkremə'tɔ:riə] horno m crematorio.
crenellated ['krenileitid] adj almenado.
crenellations [ˌkreni'leiʃənz] npl almenas fpl.
Creole ['kri:əul] **1** adj criollo. **2** n criollo m, a f.
creosote ['kriəsəut] n creosota f.
crêpe [kreip] n crespón m.
crept [krept] pret and ptp of **creep**.
crepuscular [kri'pʌskjulə*] adj crepuscular.
crescent ['kresnt] **1** adj creciente. **2** n (shape) media luna f; (street) calle f en forma de semicírculo.
cress [kres] n mastuerzo m, berro m.
crest [krest] n (of bird, wave) cresta f; (of turkey) moco m; (on helmet) cimera f (also Her); (of hill) cima f, cumbre f, cresta f; (Her) blasón m.
crestfallen ['krest,fɔ:lən] adj alicaído.
cretaceous [kri'teiʃəs] adj cretáceo.
Cretan ['kri:tən] **1** adj cretense. **2** n cretense mf.
Crete [kri:t] Creta f.
cretin ['kretin] n cretino m, a f.
cretinous ['kretinəs] adj cretino; (fig) imbécil.
cretonne [kre'tɔn] n cretona f.
crevasse [kri'væs] n grieta f de glaciar.
crevice ['krevis] n grieta f, hendedura f.
crew [kru:] n (Naut, Aer) tripulación f; (Mil, number of — members) dotación f; personal m, equipo m; (gang) banda f, pandilla f; **they looked a sorry —** daba lástima verlos.
crew-cut ['kru:kʌt] n corte m de pelo al rape.
crew-neck ['kru:nek] n cuello m plano; **— sweater** suéter m sin cuello.
crib [krib] **1** n (a) pesebre m.
  (b) (fam) (translation) traducción f; (thing copied) plagio m; (in exam) chuleta f.
  (c) to crack a **—** (sl) robar una casa.
  2 vt (fam) plagiar, tomar (from de).
  3 vi (fam) usar una chuleta.
crick [krik] n: **— in the neck** torticolis m.
cricket¹ ['krikit] n (Zool) grillo m.
cricket² ['krikit] n críquet m; **that's not —** eso no es jugar limpio.
cricketer ['krikitə*] n criquetero m.
crier ['kraiə*] n: **town —** pregonero m público.
crikey ['kraiki] interj (fam) ¡caramba!
crime [kraim] n crimen m, delito m.
Crimea [krai'miə] Crimea f.
Crimean War [krai'miən'wɔ:*] Guerra f de Crimea.
criminal ['kriminl] **1** adj criminal; act, intent delictivo; code, law penal; **it would be — to let her go out** sería un crimen dejarla salir.
  2 n criminal m, delincuente m; **war — criminal m** de guerra.
criminologist [ˌkrimi'nɔlədʒist] n criminalista m.
criminology [ˌkrimi'nɔlədʒi] n criminología f.
crimp [krimp] vt rizar, encrespar.
crimson ['krimzn] **1** adj carmesí. **2** n carmesí m.
cringe [krindʒ] vi agacharse, encogerse; (fig) reptar; **to — with fear** encogerse de miedo; **the servants were cringing in a corner** los criados se habían refugiado medrosos en un rincón.
cringing ['krindʒiŋ] adj servil, rastrero.
crinkle ['kriŋkl] **1** n arruga f; (sl) parné m. **2** vt arrugar. **3** vi arrugarse.
crinkly ['kriŋkli] adj arrugado; hair rizado.
crinoline ['krinəlin] n crinolina f, miriñaque m.
cripple ['kripl] **1** n lisiado m, a f, mutilado m, a f.
  2 vt lisiar, tullir, mutilar; ship inutilizar; (fig) paralizar, estropear.
crisis ['kraisis] n, pl **crises** ['kraisi:z] crisis f.
crisp [krisp] **1** adj duro pero frágil; (after cooking) curruscante, crujiente, tostado; hair crespo; air vigorizante; manner, tone resuelto, seco; style nervioso.
  2 —s npl patatas fpl a la inglesa.
criss-crossed ['kriskrɔst] adj entrelazado; **— by** surcado de.
criterion [krai'tiəriən] n, pl **criteria** [krai'tiəriə] criterio m.
critic ['kritik] n crítico m.
critical ['kritikəl] adj crítico; (hyper-) criticón; illness grave; **to be — of** criticar.

critically ['kritikəli] *adv* críticamente; **to be — ill** estar gravemente enfermo.

criticism ['kritisizəm] *n* crítica *f*.

criticize ['kritisaiz] *vt* criticar; censurar.

critique [kri'ti:k] *n* crítica *f*.

croak [krəuk] **1** *n* (*of raven*) graznido *m*; (*of frog*) canto *m*; (*of person*) gruñido *m*. **2** *vi* (*raven*) graznar; (*frog*) croar; (*person*) gruñir.

Croat ['krəuæt] *n* croata *mf*.

Croatia [krəu'eifiə] Croacia *f*.

Croatian [krəu'eifiən] **1** *adj* croata. **2** *n* croata *mf*.

crochet ['krəufei] **1** *n* croché *m*, labor *f* de ganchillo. **2** *vt* hacer en croché, hacer de ganchillo. **3** *vi* hacer croché, hacer labor de ganchillo.

crochet hook ['krəufihuk] *n* ganchillo *m*.

crock[1] [krɔk] *n* vasija *f* de barro; **old —** (*person*) carcamal *m*, (*car etc*) cacharro *m*; **old —s' race** rallye *m* de coches clásicos.

crock[2] [krɔk] *vt* lisiar, incapacitar.

crockery ['krɔkəri] *n* loza *f*, vajilla *f*, los platos.

crocodile ['krɔkədail] *n* cocodrilo *m*; **— tears** lágrimas *fpl* de cocodrilo.

crocus ['krəukəs] *n* azafrán *m*.

Croesus ['kri:səs] *m* Creso.

croft [krɔft] *n* (*Scot*) granja *f* pequeña, parcela *f*.

crofter ['krɔftə*] *n* (*Scot*) arrendatario *m* de una granja pequeña.

croissant [krwʌsã:ŋ] *n* croissant *m*, medialuna *f*.

crone [krəun] *n* vieja *f*.

crony ['krəuni] *n* compinche *mf*.

crook [kruk] **1** *n* (**a**) (*staff*) cayado *m*; (*bend*) curva *f*; **— of the arm** pliegue *m* del codo; *see* **hook**.
(**b**) (*person*) criminal *m*, estafador *m*, ladrón *m*, maleante *m*; **you —!** (*hum*) ¡animal!
2 *vt* encorvar.
3 *vi* encorvarse.

crooked ['krukid] *adj* curvo, encorvado, torcido; *path* tortuoso; (*fig*) *deal, means* poco limpio; *person* criminal, nada honrado.

croon [kru:n] *vt* canturrear, cantar en voz baja.

crooner ['kru:nə*] *n* vocalista *mf* (sentimental), canzonetista *mf*.

crop [krɔp] **1** *n* (*species grown*) cultivo *m*; (*produce*) cosecha *f*; (*Orn*) buche *m*; (*whip*) látigo *m* mocho; (*hair style*) corte *m* a lo garçon.
2 *vt* (*cut*) cortar; (*trim*) recortar; *animal's ears* desorejar, *tail* cortar; (*graze*) pacer.
3 *vi*: *a tree which* **—s** *well* un árbol que rinde bien; **to — out, to — up** (*Geol*) aflorar; **to — up** (*fig*) surgir, producirse inesperadamente; **something must have —ped up** habrán tenido alguna dificultad; **now another problem has —ped up** ahora se ha planteado otro problema.

cropper ['krɔpə*] *n* (*fam*): **to come a —** caer; (*fig*) fracasar; tirarse una plancha.

croquet ['krəukei] *n* croquet *m*.

croquette [krəu'ket] *n* croqueta *f*.

crosier ['krəuʒə*] *n* báculo *m* pastoral.

cross [krɔs] **1** *adj* (**a**) (*crossed*) cruzado; (*diagonal etc*) transversal, oblicuo.
(**b**) (*fig*) malhumorado; **to be —** estar de mal humor; **to be — with someone** estar enfadado con uno; **don't be — with me** no te vayas a enfadar conmigo; **to get —** enfadarse (*about* de, *with* con).
2 *n* cruz *f* (*also fig*); (*Bio: in general*) cruzamiento *m*, (*hybrid*) híbrido *m*; **iron —** cruz *f* de hierro; **Maltese —** cruz *f* de Malta; **Red C—** Cruz *f* Roja; **Southern —** Cruz *f* del Sur; **it's a — between A and B** es una mezcla de A y B; **to cut something on the —** cortar algo al sesgo; **to make the sign of the C—** hacer la señal de la cruz (*over* sobre).
3 *vt* (**a**) (*place crosswise*) cruzar; *screw* trasroscar; **to — one's arms** cruzarse de brazos; **to — someone's hand with silver** dar una moneda de plata a uno; **the lines are —ed** (*Tel*) hay un cruce en las líneas.
(**b**) (*draw line across*) *cheque* cruzar; **to — off, to — out** tachar.
(**c**) (*go across*) cruzar, atravesar; *river* (*as obstacle*) salvar.
(**d**) (*meet and pass*) cruzar.
(**e**) (*Bio*) cruzar.
(**f**) (*thwart*) contrariar, ir contra; **to be —ed in love** tener un fracaso sentimental.
4 *vi* (*also* **to — over**) cruzar, ir al otro lado; (*letters*) cruzarse.
5 *vr*: **to — oneself** santiguarse.

crossbar ['krɔsbɑ:*] *n* travesaño *m*; (*Sport*) larguero *m*.

crossbeam ['krɔsbi:m] *n* viga *f* transversal.

crossbencher ['krɔs'bentʃə*] *n* (*Parl*) diputado *m* independiente.

crossbow ['krɔsbəu] *n* ballesta *f*.

crossbred ['krɔsbred] *adj* híbrido.

crossbreed ['krɔsbri:d] **1** *n* híbrido *m*, a *f*. **2** *vt* cruzar.

cross-check ['krɔstfek] **1** *n* comprobación *f* hecha al revés, comprobación *f* adicional.
2 *vt* comprobar al revés, comprobar una vez más (*or* por otro sistema).

cross-country ['krɔs'kʌntri] *adj* *route, walk* a campo traviesa; **— race** cross *m*.

cross-current ['krɔs'kʌrənt] *n* contracorriente *f*.

cross-examination ['krɔsig,zæmi'neiʃən] *n* (*Law*) repregunta *f*; (*fig*) interrogatorio *m* severo.

cross-examine ['krɔsig'zæmin] *vt* (*Law*) repreguntar; (*fig*) interrogar severamente.

cross-eyed ['krɔsaid] *adj* bizco.

cross-fertilize ['krɔs'fə:tilaiz] *vt* fecundar por fertilización cruzada.

crossfire ['krɔsfaiə*] *n* fuego *m* cruzado.

crossing ['krɔsiŋ] *n* (*intersection*) cruce *m*; (*Rail*) paso *m* a nivel; (*on road*) paso *m* para peatones; (*journey*) travesía *f*; (*Bio*) cruzamiento *m*.

cross-legged ['krɔs'legd] *adj* con las piernas cruzadas.

crossly ['krɔsli] *adv* con mal humor.

crossover ['krɔsəuvə*] *n* (*Aut etc*) paso *m* superior.

crosspatch ['krɔspætʃ] *n* persona *f* malhumorada.

crosspiece ['krɔspi:s] *n* travesaño *m*.

cross-pollination ['krɔs,pɔli'neiʃən] *n* polinización *f* cruzada.

cross-purposes ['krɔs'pə:pəsiz] *npl*: **to be at —** no comprenderse uno a otro; **I think we're at —** creo que aquí hay un malentendido.

cross-question ['krɔs'kwestʃən] *vt* (*Law*) repreguntar; (*fig*) interrogar.

cross-questioning ['krɔs'kwestʃəniŋ] *n* (*Law*) repregunta *f*; (*fig*) interrogación *f*.

cross-reference ['krɔs'refərəns] *n* contrarreferencia *f*.

crossroads ['krɔsrəudz] *n* cruce *m*, encrucijada *f*; (*fig*) punto *m* crítico, momento *m* decisivo.

cross section ['krɔs'sekʃən] *n* corte *m* transversal, sección *f* transversal, perfil *m*; (*fig*) sección *f* representativa.

cross-stitch ['krɔsstitʃ] *n* puntada *f* cruzada.

crosstalk ['krɔstɔ:k] *n* réplicas *fpl* agudas.

crosswind ['krɔswind] *n* viento *m* de costado.

crosswise ['krɔswaiz] *adv* al través; en cruz.

crossword ['krɔswə:d] *n*: **— puzzle** crucigrama *m*.

crotch [krɔtʃ] *n* (*Anat*) horcajadura *f*.

crotchet ['krɔtʃit] *n* (*Mus*) negra *f*.

crotchety ['krɔtʃiti] *adj* propenso a irritarse.

crouch [krautʃ] *vi* agacharse, acurrucarse, encogerse. **men —ing in trenches** hombres agazapados en trincheras.

croup [kru:p] *n* (*Med*) crup *m*.

croupier ['kru:piei] *n* crupier *m*.

crouton ['kru:tɔ̃n] *n* cuscurro *m*.

crow [krəu] **1** *n* cuervo *m*, grajo *m*, corneja *f*; (*cry*) canto *m*, cacareo *m*; **as the — flies** en línea recta.
2 *vi* cantar, cacarear; (*child*) gorjearse; (*fig*) jactarse, exultar; **to — over someone** triunfar de uno; **to — over something** jactarse de algo, felicitarse por algo; **it's nothing to — about** no hay motivo para sentirse satisfecho.

crowbar ['krəubɑ:*] *n* palanca *f*.

crowd [kraud] **1** *n* multitud *f*; muchedumbre *f*, gentío *m*; (*esp disorderly*) tropel *m*; (*Sport etc*) público *m*, espectadores *mpl*; (*Theat*) comparsas *mpl*; (*fam*) grupo *m*, peña *f*; **the — (common herd)** el vulgo; **there was quite a —** había bastante gente; **how big was the —?** ¿cuántas personas había?; **— scene** (*Cine*) escena *f* con muchos comparsas; **in a —** en tropel, todos juntos; **to follow the —** irse tras el hilo de la gente; **to rise above the —** destacar(se).
2 *vt* (**a**) (*collect*) amontonar; apretar unos contra otros.
(**b**) **to — the streets** llenar las calles; **to — a place with** llenar un sitio de; **to — things in** ir metiendo cosas apretadamente; **to — on sail** hacer fuerza de vela; **we got —ed out** fuimos excluidos; **he was —ed off the pavement** había tanta gente que tuvo que abandonar la acera.
3 *vi* reunirse, congregarse (*into* en); **to — around, to — together** agolparse, apiñarse; **to — round someone** apiñarse (*or* agruparse) en torno de uno; **to — in** entrar en tropel; **to — into a car** entrar todos apretadamente en un coche; **memories —ed in upon me** me invadieron muchísimos recuerdos.

crowded ['kraudid] *adj* lleno, atestado (*with* de); *meeting, event etc* muy concurrido; **it's very — here** aquí hay muchísima gente; **the place was — out** el local estaba de bote en bote; **the houses are — together** las casas están apretadas unas contra otras; **one — hour** una sola hora llena de actividad; **it's a**

very — **profession** es una profesión donde sobra gente.

crowfoot ['krəufut] n ranúnculo m.

crown [kraun] **1** n corona f; (of hat) copa f; (of hill) cumbre f; (of head) coronilla f; **the — of the road** el centro de la calzada; **half a —** media corona f.
    2 attr: **— colony** colonia f; **— jewels** joyas fpl reales; **— lands** propiedad f de la corona; **— prince** príncipe m heredero.
    3 vt coronar; (sl) golpear en la cabeza; (fig) completar, rematar; **to — it all** para completarlo todo, (misfortune) para colmo de desgracias; **to — something with success** coronar algo con éxito.

crowning ['krauniŋ] adj supremo.

crow's-foot ['krəuzfut] n (in eye) pata f de gallo.

crow's-nest ['krəuznest] n torre f de vigía.

crucial ['kru:ʃəl] adj decisivo, crítico, crucial.

crucible ['kru:sibl] n crisol m (also fig).

crucifix ['kru:sifiks] n crucifijo m, cruz f.

crucifixion [,kru:si'fikʃən] n crucifixión f.

cruciform ['kru:sifɔ:m] adj cruciforme.

crucify ['kru:sifai] vt crucificar.

crude [kru:d] adj oil etc crudo, steel etc bruto; object, workmanship tosco; (vulgar) ordinario.

crudely ['kru:dli] adv toscamente; ordinariamente.

crudeness ['kru:dnis] n, **crudity** ['kru:diti] n tosquedad f; ordinariez f.

cruel ['kruəl] adj cruel.

cruelly ['kruəli] adv cruelmente.

cruelty ['kruəlti] n crueldad f; **society for the prevention of — to animals** sociedad f protectora de los animales.

cruet ['kru:it] n vinagrera f; (stand) angarillas fpl.

cruise [kru:z] **1** n crucero m, viaje m por mar. **2** vi cruzar, navegar; (fig) ir, andar; **we were cruising along at 40 m.p.h.** íbamos a 40 millas por hora.

cruiser ['kru:zə*] n crucero m.

cruiser-weight ['kru:zəweit] n peso m medio fuerte.

cruising speed ['kru:ziŋspi:d] n velocidad f de crucero; (Aut) velocidad f económica.

cruller ['krʌlə*] n (US) buñuelo m.

crumb [krʌm] n (one) migaja f; (not crust) miga f; **a — of comfort** una migaja de consolación.

crumble ['krʌmbl] **1** vt desmenuzar, desmigajar. **2** vi (material) desmenuzarse, desmigajarse; (building etc) desmoronarse, derrumbarse.

crumbly ['krʌmbli] adj desmenuzable.

crummy ['krʌmi] adj (sl) ínfimo, de bajísima categoría.

crumpet ['krʌmpit] n bollo m blando (para tostar).

crumple ['krʌmpl] **1** vt ajar, deshacer; paper estrujar; (wrinkle) arrugar; (crease) plegar.
    2 vi ajarse, deshacerse, arrugarse; plegarse; (fig, also **to — up**) hundirse, derrumbarse; (person) desplomarse.

crunch [krʌntʃ] **1** n crujido m; (fig) crisis f, punto m decisivo. **2** vt (with teeth) mascar, ronzar; ground etc hacer crujir. **3** vi crujir.

crunchy ['krʌntʃi] adj crujiente, que cruje.

crupper ['krʌpə*] n (of horse) anca f, grupa f.

crusade [kru:'seid] **1** n cruzada f. **2** vi participar en una cruzada; **to — for** hacer campaña en pro de.

crusader [kru:'seidə*] n cruzado m.

crush [krʌʃ] **1** n (a) (of people) agolpamiento m; (of cars etc) aglomeración f; **there was an awful —** hubo la mar de gente; **there's always a — in the tube** el metro va siempre atestado de gente; **I lost my handbag in the —** perdí el bolso en el tumulto; **two died in the —** dos murieron aplastados.
    (b) **to have a — on someone** (fam) perder la chaveta por uno.
    (c) orange **—** naranjada f.
    2 vt (a) aplastar; paper etc estrujar; stones triturar, moler; grapes etc prensar, exprimir; dress ajar; **to — something into a case** meter algo a la fuerza en una maleta.
    (b) (fig) country aplastar; enemy, opposition aniquilar, destruir; person in argument confundir, dejar planchado.
    3 vi: **to — in** meterse apretadamente en.

crushing ['krʌʃiŋ] adj blow, defeat, reply aplastante; grief etc abrumador; argument decisivo; burden agobiador.

crust [krʌst] n (of bread, Geol) corteza f; (old bread) mendrugo m; (on wine, Med) costra f.

crustacean [krʌs'teiʃən] n crustáceo m.

crusty ['krʌsti] adj (fig) malhumorado, irritable.

crutch [krʌtʃ] n muleta f; (crotch) horcajadura f.

crux [krʌks] n: **the — of the matter** lo esencial del caso, el punto capital.

cry [krai] n grito m; (of peddler) pregón m; **it's a far — from that** esto tiene poco que ver con aquello;

the hounds were in full **—** los perros seguían de cerca la presa; **the crowd was in full — after him** una multitud le perseguía con gritos; **to have a good —** llorar a mares.
    2 vt gritar (also **to — out**); wares pregonar; **to — down** desacreditar; see **eye** etc.
    3 vi (a) (call) gritar; **to — for** clamar por; **to — for help** pedir socorro a voces; **to — off** retirarse, rajarse; **to — out** gritar.
    (b) (weep) llorar (for, with de); **to — over** lamentarse sobre.

crybaby ['krai,beibi] n llorón m, ona f.

crying ['kraiiŋ] adj atroz, enorme.

crypt [kript] n cripta f.

cryptic ['kriptik] adj misterioso, secreto.

cryptically ['kriptikəli] adv misteriosamente.

crypto-communist ['kriptəu'kɔmjunist] n cripto-comunista mf.

cryptogram ['kriptəugræm] n criptograma m.

cryptographer [krip'tɔgrəfə*] n criptógrafo m.

cryptographic(al) [,kriptəu'græfik(əl)] adj criptográfico.

cryptography [krip'tɔgrəfi] n criptografía f.

crystal ['kristl] **1** n cristal m. **2** adj cristalino.

crystal-clear ['kristl'kliə*] adj transparente como el cristal; (fig) totalmente claro.

crystalline ['kristəlain] adj cristalino.

crystallize ['kristəlaiz] **1** vt cristalizar. **2** vi cristalizarse; (fig) cuajarse, resolverse.

crystallized ['kristəlaizd] adj fruit escarchado.

crystallography [,kristə'lɔgrəfi] n cristalografía f.

crystal set ['kristl'set] n (Radio) receptor m con detector de cristal.

cub [kʌb] n cachorro m; **— reporter** periodista m novato.

Cuba ['kju:bə] Cuba f.

Cuban ['kju:bən] **1** adj cubano. **2** n cubano m, a f.

cubbyhole ['kʌbihəul] n chiribitil m.

cube [kju:b] **1** n cubo m; (of sugar) terrón m. **2** vt cubicar.

cubic ['kju:bik] adj cúbico.

cubicle ['kju:bikəl] n cubículo m; (at swimming pool etc) caseta f.

cubism ['kju:bizəm] n cubismo m.

cubist ['kju:bist] **1** adj cubista. **2** n cubista mf.

cuckold ['kʌkəld] **1** n cornudo m. **2** vt poner los cuernos a.

cuckoo ['kuku:] **1** n cuco m, cuclillo m. **2** adj (sl) lelo.

cuckoo clock ['kuku:klɔk] n reloj m de cuclillo.

cucumber ['kju:kʌmbə*] n pepino m.

cud [kʌd] n: **to chew the —** rumiar (also fig).

cuddle ['kʌdl] **1** n abrazo m amoroso.
    2 vt abrazar amorosamente.
    3 vi (2 persons) abrazarse, estar abrazados; **to — up to someone** arrimarse amorosamente a uno.

cuddly ['kʌdli] adj mimoso; toy blando.

cudgel ['kʌdʒəl] **1** n porra f; **to take up the —s for someone** salir en defensa de uno. **2** vt aporrear.

cue [kju:] n (Billiards) taco m; (Theat) pie m, apunte m, entrada f; **that gave me my —** eso me sirvió de indicación; **to take one's — from** seguir el ejemplo de.

cuff¹ [kʌf] **1** n bofetada f. **2** vt abofetear.

cuff² [kʌf] n (of shirt) puño m; **to say something off the —** decir algo sin pensarlo, decir algo de improviso, sacar algo de la manga.

cufflinks ['kʌflinks] npl gemelos mpl.

cuisine [kwi'zi:n] n cocina f.

cul-de-sac ['kʌldə'sæk] n callejón m sin salida.

culinary ['kʌlinəri] adj culinario.

cull [kʌl] vt flowers coger; (select) entresacar.

culminate ['kʌlmineit] vi: **to — in** terminar en.

culminating ['kʌlmineitiŋ] adj culminante.

culmination [,kʌlmi'neiʃən] n (fig) culminación f, punto m culminante, colmo m; **it is the — of much effort** es la culminación de grandes esfuerzos.

culottes [kju(:)'lɔt] npl pantalón m corto (de mujer).

culpability [,kʌlpə'biliti] n culpabilidad f.

culpable ['kʌlpəbl] adj culpable.

culprit ['kʌlprit] n persona f culpable, culpado m, a f, delincuente mf.

cult [kʌlt] n culto m (of a).

cultivable ['kʌltivəbl] adj cultivable.

cultivate ['kʌltiveit] vt cultivar (also fig).

cultivated ['kʌltiveitid] adj (fig) culto.

cultivation [,kʌlti'veiʃən] n (Agr) cultivo m; (fig) cultura f.

cultivator ['kʌltiveitə*] n (Agr) cultivador m.

cultural ['kʌltʃərəl] adj cultural.

culture ['kʌltʃə*] n (Agr, Bio) cultivo m; (fig) cultura f; **physical —** cultura f física.

cultured ['kʌltʃəd] adj culto.

cultured pearl ['kʌltʃəd'pə:l] n perla f cultivada.

culture medium ['kʌltʃə,miːdiəm] n, pl — **media** [miːdiə] medio m de cultivo.

culvert ['kʌlvət] n alcantarilla f.

cumbersome ['kʌmbəsəm] adj molesto, incómodo.

cumin ['kʌmin] n comino m.

cummerbund ['kʌməbʌnd] n faja f de cintura.

cumulative ['kjuːmjulətiv] adj cumulativo.

cumulonimbus ['kjuːmələu'nimbəs] n cumulonimbo m.

cumulus ['kjuːmələs] n cúmulo m.

cuneiform ['kjuːnifɔːm] adj cuneiforme.

cunning ['kʌniŋ] 1 adj (clever), (sly) taimado; (skilfully made) artificioso, ingenioso; (fam) precioso, mono. 2 n astucia f.

cunningly ['kʌniŋli] adv astutamente; artificiosamente.

cup [kʌp] 1 n taza f; (Eccl, Bot) cáliz m; (trophy) copa f; (in ground) hoyo m, hondonada f; (in one's —s estar borracho; **his — of sorrow was full** le agobiaba el dolor; **there's many a slip twixt — and lip** de la mano a la boca desaparece la sopa; **it's not quite my — of tea** no me conviene del todo; **he's not my — of tea** no es de mi agrado, no es santo de mi devoción; **how's your —?** ¿quieres más té?
2 vt: **to — one's hands** formar bocina con las manos.

cupboard ['kʌbəd] n armario m; (on wall) alacena f.

cupboard love ['kʌbədlʌv] n amor m interesado.

cup final ['kʌpfainl] n final f de copa.

cupful ['kʌpful] n taza f, contenido m de una taza; **two —s of milk** dos tazas de leche.

Cupid ['kjuːpid] m Cupido.

cupidity [kjuː'piditi] n codicia f.

cupola ['kjuːpələ] n cúpula f.

cup-tie ['kʌptai] n partido m de copa.

cur [kɜː*] n perro m de mala raza; (person) canalla m; **you —!** ¡canalla!

curable ['kjuərəbl] adj curable.

curate ['kjuərit] n (approx) cura m.

curative ['kjuərətiv] adj curativo.

curator [kjuə'reitə*] n (of museum) director m, conservador m.

curb [kɜːb] 1 n (fig) freno m, estorbo m (on para); **to put a — on** refrenar; see **kerb**. 2 vt (fig) refrenar, reprimir, limitar; temper dominar.

curbstone ['kɜːbstəun] n (US) = **kerbstone**.

curd [kɜːd] n cuajada f.

curdle ['kɜːdl] 1 vt cuajar; **to — one's blood** helar la sangre de uno. 2 vi cuajarse.

cure [kjuə*] 1 n cura f, curación f; (Eccl) curato m. 2 vt curar (of de).

cure-all ['kjuərɔːl] n panacea f.

curfew ['kɜːfjuː] n toque m de queda.

curio ['kjuəriəu] n curiosidad f.

curiosity [,kjuəri'ɔsiti] n curiosidad f.

curious ['kjuəriəs] adj curioso; **I am — to see Granada** tengo ganas de ver Granada.

curiously ['kjuəriəsli] adv curiosamente; **— made** ingenioso, artificioso; **— enough** aunque parece mentira.

curl [kɜːl] 1 n (of hair) rizo m, bucle m; (of smoke etc) penacho m, espiral f.
2 vt hair rizar, ensortijar; paper etc arrollar; lip fruncir.
3 vi (hair) rizarse, ensortijarse, formar bucles; (paper etc) arrollarse; (leaf) abarquillarse; (waves) encresparse; **to — up** arrollarse; (smoke) subir en espiral; (animal) apelotonarse; (person) hacerse un ovillo; (fam) morirse de risa.

curler ['kɜːlə*] n (for hair) bigudí m, chincho m.

curlew ['kɜːluː] n zarapito m.

curlicue ['kɜːlikjuː] n plumada f, rasgo m.

curling iron ['kɜːliŋaiən] n, **curling tongs** ['kɜːliŋtɔŋz] npl tenacillas fpl de rizar.

curly ['kɜːli] adj rizado, ensortijado.

currant ['kʌrənt] n (dried) pasa f de Corinto; **black —** (fruit) grosella f negra, (bush) grosellero m negro; **red —** (fruit) grosella f roja, (bush) grosellero m rojo.

currency ['kʌrənsi] n (a) (money) moneda f; **hard —** moneda f dura, moneda f fuerte; **soft —** moneda f blanda, moneda f débil.
(b) (fig) uso m; **it had a certain —** se usó bastante.

current ['kʌrənt] 1 adj corriente, actual; price, account etc corriente; **the — month** el mes que corre; **the — number of a magazine** el último número de una revista; **the — opinion is that** se cree actualmente que; **it is still quite —** aún es bastante todavía; **to be in — use** estar en uso corriente; see **event** etc.
2 n (most senses) corriente f; (Elec) flúido m, corriente f; **alternating —** corriente f alterna; **direct —** corriente f continua.

currently ['kʌrəntli] adv actualmente.

curriculum [kə'rikjuləm] n, pl **curricula** [kə'rikjulə] plan m de estudios.

curriculum vitae [kə:'rikjuləm'viːtiː] n curriculum m vitae.

curry[1] ['kʌri] 1 n (spice) cari m, curry m. 2 vt preparar con cari.

curry[2] ['kʌri] vt see **favour**.

currycomb ['kʌrikəum] n almohaza f.

curry powder ['kʌri,paudə*] n polvo m de especias (para preparar el cari).

curse [kɜːs] 1 n (a) maldición f; **—s!** ¡maldición!; **a — on it!** ¡maldito sea!
(b) (oath) palabrota f.
(c) (bane) calamidad f; azote m; **the dampness is a —** here aquí la humedad es una calamidad; **drought is the — of Spain** la sequía es el azote de España; **it's been the — of my life** me ha amargado la vida, siempre me ha afligido; **the — of it is that** lo peor es que.
2 vt maldecir; echar pestes de; **to — someone with** castigar a uno con; **to be —d with** padecer de, tener que aguantar, sufrir la aflicción de; **— it!** ¡maldito sea!
3 vi blasfemar, echar pestes, soltar palabrotas.

cursed ['kɜːsid] adj maldito.

cursive ['kɜːsiv] adj cursivo.

cursorily ['kɜːsərili] adv rápidamente, de modo superficial.

cursory ['kɜːsəri] adj rápido, superficial.

curt [kɜːt] adj brusco, seco.

curtail [kɜː'teil] vt acortar, abreviar; restringir.

curtailment [kɜː'teilmənt] n acortamiento m, abreviación f; restricción f.

curtain ['kɜːtn] 1 n (also Mil); (small) visillo m; (Theat) telón m; **iron —** telón m de acero; **the iron — countries** los países detrás del telón de acero; **it was —s for him** (fam) para él fue el fin.
2 vt proveer de cortina; **to — off** separar con cortinas.

curtain call ['kɜːtnkɔːl] n salida f (de un actor a la escena para recibir aplausos).

curtain raiser ['kɜːtn,reizə*] n pieza f preliminar.

curtain ring ['kɜːtnriŋ] n anilla f.

curtain rod ['kɜːtnrɔd] n barra f de cortina.

curtly ['kɜːtli] adv bruscamente, secamente.

curtness ['kɜːtnis] n brusquedad f.

curtsy ['kɜːtsi] 1 n reverencia f; **to drop a — = 2 vi** hacer una reverencia (to a).

curvacious [kɜː'veiʃəs] adj (fam) girl de buen tipo, de tipo muy atractivo.

curvature ['kɜːvətʃə*] n curvatura f.

curve [kɜːv] 1 n curva f. 2 vt encorvar, torcer. 3 vi encorvarse, torcerse; (road etc) torcerse, hacer una curva; (through air) volar en curva.

curved [kɜːvd] adj curvo, encorvado.

cushion ['kuʃən] 1 n cojín m; (Billiards) banda f; (fig) colchón m. 2 vt blow etc amortiguar.

cushioned ['kuʃənd] adj surface acolchado, almohadillado.

cushy ['kuʃi] adj (sl) fácil, agradable.

cuss [kʌs] 1 n (fam) tipo m, tío m. 2 vt etc see **curse**.

cussed ['kʌsid] adj (fam) terco.

cussedness ['kʌsidnis] n (fam) terquedad f; **out of sheer —** de puro terco.

custard ['kʌstəd] n natillas fpl.

custard apple ['kʌstəd,æpl] n anona f; asimina f.

custodian [kʌs'təudiən] n custodio m.

custody ['kʌstədi] n custodia f; **protective —** custodia f preventiva; **to be in —** estar detenido; **to take someone into —** detener a uno.

custom ['kʌstəm] n 1 (a) costumbre f.
(b) (Comm) clientela f, parroquia f; (total sales) ventas fpl; **we've not had much — today** hoy hemos tenido pocos clientes.
(c) **—s** aduana f; (duty) derechos mpl de aduana; **to go through the —s** pasar por la aduana.
2 **—s** attr aduanero, de aduana.

customary ['kʌstəməri] adj acostumbrado, de costumbre; **it is — to + infin** es costumbre + infin, se suele + infin.

customer ['kʌstəmə*] n cliente m, a f; (fam) tipo m.

custom-made ['kʌstəm'meid] adj hecho a la medida.

customs house ['kʌstəmzhaus] n aduana f.

customs officer ['kʌstəmz,ɔfisə*] n aduanero m.

customs post ['kʌstəmzpəust] n puesto m aduanero.

cut [kʌt] 1 adj cortado; glass tallado; **— and dried** rutinario; seguro; preparado de antemano; convenido de antemano; **— off** aislado (from de).
2 n (a) (incision) corte m; (in skin) cortadura f.

(b) (*slash with sword*) tajo *m*, (*with knife*) cuchillada *f*, (*with whip*) latigazo *m*; **the — and thrust of politics** la esgrima política; **the unkindest — of all** el golpe más duro; **whose — is it?** (*Cards*) ¿quién corta?

(c) (*deletion*) corte *m*, supresión *f*, trozo *m* suprimido.

(d) short — atajo *m*; **there is no short — to success** no se alcanza el éxito por ningún camino fácil.

(e) (*of clothes*) corte *m*; **to be a — above the rest** ser algo superior a los demás.

(f) (*woodcut*) grabado *m*; (*US*) foto *f*, diagrama *m*, dibujo *m*.

(g) (*kind of meat*) clase *f* de carne; (*slice*) tajada *f*; (*share*) parte *f*, tajada *f*.

(h) (*reduction*) reducción *f*, rebaja *f* (*in* de); (*Elec*) apagón *m*.

3 (*irr: pret and ptp* **cut**) *vt* cortar; *cards, corn, communications etc* cortar; *corner* (*person*) cortar, (*car*) tomar muy cerrado; (*divide up*) partir, dividir (*into two* en dos); *line etc* cruzar; *stone etc* tallar; *disc* grabar; *hole* practicar, hacer; (*delete*) cortar, suprimir; (*reduce*) reducir (*by* 5% en un 5 por cien), *price* rebajar; *class* fumarse; *person* fingir no ver, fingir no reconocer, negar el saludo a; **he — his finger** se cortó el dedo; **he's —ting a tooth** le está saliendo un diente; **to get one's hair —** cortarse el pelo; **to — something across** cortar algo a través de; **to — across** completamente; **to — across a field** atravesar un campo, atajar por un campo; **this —s across my ideas** esto es contrario a mis ideas; **this —s across the usual categories** esto hace desaparecer las categorías establecidas; **to — away** cortar, separar cortando; **to — back** acortar, recortar; (*reduce*) reducir (*by* en); **to — down** *tree etc* derribar, cortar, talar; *price* rebajar; *costs* aminorar; *size, majority etc* reducir (*by* en); **to — off** cortar (*also Elec, Tel etc*); *leg* amputar; *troops* copar, cercar; *retreat* impedir, imposibilitar; (*disinherit*) desheredar; **to — someone's life off in its prime** tronchar la vida de uno; **we were — off by the snow** quedamos bloqueados por la nieve; **to — someone in on a deal** permitir que uno participe en un negocio (*esp* poco limpio); **to — out** recortar; *hole etc* practicar, hacer; *competitor* excluir; (*delete*) suprimir, tachar; **— it out!** ¡basta ya!, ¡déjalo!; **— out the singing!** ¡basta ya de cantar!; **we can — that out for a start** en primer lugar podemos tachar eso; **he's not — out to be a poet** no tiene condiciones para ser poeta; **he's not — out for it** no tiene talento para ello; **to — up** cortar en pedazos; dividir; desmenuzar; *meat* picar; **to be — up** afligirse (*about* por).

4 *vi* cortar; (*two lines*) cruzarse; **to — across** atajar; **to — back** volverse; **to — in** interrumpir, cortar; (*Aut*) pasar peligrosamente; **to — into one's holiday** restar una parte de las vacaciones; **to — out** (*engine*) pararse; **to — through something** abrirse camino por algo; **the argument —s both ways** el argumento tiene doble filo.

cutaneous [kjuːˈteiniəs] *adj* cutáneo.
cute [kjuːt] *adj* (*nice*) mono, lindo; (*shrewd*) astuto, listo.
cuticle [ˈkjuːtikl] *n* cutícula *f*.

cuticle remover [ˈkjuːtiklriˈmuːvə*] agente *m* químico para quitar la cutícula (de las uñas).
cutlass [ˈkʌtləs] *n* chafarote *m*.
cutler [ˈkʌtlə*] *n* cuchillero *m*.
cutlery [ˈkʌtləri] *n* cubiertos *mpl*, cuchillería *f*.
cutlet [ˈkʌtlit] *n* chuleta *f*.
cutoff [ˈkʌtɔf] *n* (*Mech*) cierre *m* de vapor, corta-vapor *m*.
cutout [ˈkʌtaut] *n* (*child's*) diseño *m* para recortar, recortable *m*; (*Elec*) portafusible *m*; (*Mech*) válvula *f* de escape.
cut-price [ˈkʌtprais] *adj* a precio reducido.
cutter [ˈkʌtə*] *n* (*Mech*) cortadora *f*; (*Naut*) cúter *m*.
cut-throat [ˈkʌtθrəut] **1** *adj* *competition* intenso. **2** *n* asesino *m*.
cutting [ˈkʌtiŋ] **1** *adj* cortante; *remark* mordaz; **— edge** filo *m*. **2** *n* (*from paper*) recorte *m*; (*Rail*) desmonte *m*, trinchera *f*; (*Bot*) esqueje *m*.
cuttlefish [ˈkʌtlfiʃ] *n* jibia *f*.
cyanide [ˈsaiənaid] *n* cianuro *m*; **— of potassium** cianuro *m* de potasio.
cybernetics [ˌsaibəˈnetiks] *n sing and pl* cibernética *f*.
cyclamen [ˈsikləmən] *n* ciclamen *m*.
cycle [ˈsaikl] **1** *n* **(a)** ciclo *m*; **life —** ciclo *m* de la vida; **menstrual —** ciclo *m* menstrual. **(b)** (*bicycle*) bicicleta *f*. **2** *vi* ir en bicicleta.
cyclic(al) [ˈsaiklik(əl)] *adj* cíclico.
cycling [ˈsaikliŋ] *n* ciclismo *m*.
cyclist [ˈsaiklist] *n* ciclista *mf*; **racing —** corredor *m* ciclista.
cyclone [ˈsaikləun] *n* ciclón *m*.
Cyclops [ˈsaiklɔps] *n* cíclope *m*.
cyclorama [ˌsaikləˈrɑːmə] *n* ciclorama *m*.
cyclostyled [ˈsaikləstaild] *adj* en ciclostil.
cyclotron [ˈsaiklətrɔn] *n* ciclotrón *m*.
cygnet [ˈsignit] *n* pollo *m* de cisne.
cylinder [ˈsilində*] *n* cilindro *m*.
cylinder block [ˈsilindəblɔk] *n* bloque *m* de cilindros.
cylinder capacity [ˈsilindəkəˈpæsiti] *n* cilindrada *f*.
cylinder head [ˈsilindəhed] *n* culata *f* de cilindro.
cylindrical [siˈlindrikəl] *adj* cilíndrico.
cymbals [ˈsimbəlz] *npl* platillos *mpl*.
cynic [ˈsinik] *n* cínico *m*; escéptico *m*.
cynical [ˈsinikəl] *adj* cínico; escéptico, despreciativo.
cynically [ˈsinikli] *adv* con cinismo.
cynicism [ˈsinisizəm] *n* cinismo *m*; escepticismo *m*, desprecio *m*.
cynosure [ˈsainəʃuə*] *n*: **— of every eye** blanco *m* de todas las miradas, miradero *m*.
cypress [ˈsaipris] *n* ciprés *m*.
Cypriot [ˈsipriət] *n* chipriota *mf*.
Cyprus [ˈsaiprəs] Chipre *f*.
cypher [ˈsaifə*] *see* **cipher**.
cyst [sist] *n* quiste *m*.
cystitis [sisˈtaitis] *n* cistitis *f*.
czar [zɑː*] *n* zar *m*.
czarina [zɑːˈriːnə] *n* zarina *f*.
Czech [tʃek] **1** *adj* checo. **2** *n* checo *m*, a . **3** *n* (*language*) checo *m*.
Czechoslovak [ˈtʃekəuˈsləuvæk] **1** *adj* checoslovaco. **2** *n* checoslovaco *m*, a *f*.
Czechoslovakia [ˈtʃekəusləˈvækiə] Checoslovaquia *f*.
Czechoslovakian [ˈtʃekəusləˈvækiən] **1** *adj* checoslovaco. **2** *n* checoslovaco *m*, a *f*.

D

dab¹ [dæb] **1** n (blow) golpe m ligero; (small amount) pequeña cantidad f; (of paint) brochazo m; (of liquid) gota f; **—s** (sl) huellas fpl dactilares.

2 vt (strike) golpear ligeramente, tocar ligeramente; (with sponge etc) tocar; (moisten) mojar ligeramente; **to — a stain off** quitar una mancha mojándola ligeramente; **to — paint on a wall** embadurnar una pared de pintura.

3 vi: **to — at one's eyes with a handkerchief** llevar repetidas veces un pañuelo a los ojos.

dab² [dæb] n (Fish) lenguado m.

dab³ [dæb] adj: **to be a — hand at** tener buena mano para.

dabble ['dæbl] **1** vt salpicar, mojar; **to — one's feet** chapotear los pies.

2 vi: **to — in something** interesarse en algo por pasatiempo, ser ligeramente aficionado a; **I only — in it** para mí es un pasatiempo nada más; **to — in politics** meterse en la política; **to — in shares** jugar a la bolsa.

dabbler ['dæblə*] n (pej) aficionado m, a f (in a), diletante mf; **he's just a —** es un simple aficionado, para él es un pasatiempo nada más.

dabchick ['dæbtʃik] n somorgujo m menor.

dabs [dæbz] npl (sl) manos fpl; huellas fpl dactilares.

dace [deis] n albur m.

dachshund ['dækshund] n perro m tejonero.

dacron ['deikrɔn] n (Protected Trade Name) dacrón m.

dactylic [dæk'tilik] adj dactílico.

dad [dæd] n, **daddy** ['dædi] n papá m.

dadaism ['dɑːdɑːizəm] n dadaísmo m.

daddy-long-legs ['dædi'lɔŋlegz] n típula f.

dado ['deidəu] n dado m; friso m.

daffodil ['dæfədil] n narciso m trompón.

daffy ['dæfi] adj (US: sl) chiflado.

daft [dɑːft] adj imbécil, estúpido.

dagger ['dægə*] n puñal m, daga f; (Typ) cruz f, obelisco m; **to be —s drawn** odiarse a muerte; **to look —s at** apuñalar con la mirada.

dago ['deigəu] n término peyorativo aplicado a españoles, portugueses e italianos.

dahlia ['deiliə] n dalia f.

Dail Eireann [dail'ɛərən] parlamento de la República de Irlanda.

daily ['deili] **1** adj diario, cotidiano; **bread** de cada día. **2** adv diario, cada día. **3** n (paper) diario m; (servant) asistenta f, sirvienta f.

daintily ['deintili] adv delicadamente; elegantemente, primorosamente; melindrosamente.

daintiness ['deintinis] n delicadeza f; elegancia f, primor m; melindres mpl.

dainty ['deinti] **1** adj (delicate) delicado, fino; (tasteful) elegante, primoroso, precioso; (fastidious) delicado, melindroso.

2 n bocado m exquisito, golosina f.

dairy ['dɛəri] **1** n (shop) lechería f; (on farm) quesería f, vaquería f. **2** attr lechero; **— cattle** vacas fpl lecheras; **— farm** granja f especializada en producción de leche; **— produce** productos mpl lácteos.

dairymaid ['dɛərimeid] n lechera f, moza f de establo.

dairyman ['dɛərimən] n, pl **-men** [mən] lechero m.

dais ['deiis] n estrado m.

daisy ['deizi] n mayo m, margarita f.

dale [deil] n valle m.

dalliance ['dæliəns] n (play) juegos mpl, diversiones fpl; (time-wasting) frivolidad f; **amorous —** coquetería f, flirteo m.

dally ['dæli] vi (delay) tardar, perder el tiempo; (amuse oneself) divertirse; **to — with** (amorously) coquetear con, entretenerse en amores con; (an idea) entretenerse con.

Dalmatia [dæl'meiʃə] Dalmacia f.

dalmatian [dæl'meiʃən] n (dog) perro m dálmata.

dam¹ [dæm] **1** n presa f; (small) dique m. **2** vt represar; construir una presa sobre; **to — up** cerrar, tapar, overflowing water contener con un dique.

dam² [dæm] adj = **damn 3, damned.**

damage ['dæmidʒ] **1** n daño m, perjuicio m; (Mech) avería f; (visible, eg on car) desperfectos mpl; **—s** (Law) daños mpl y perjuicios; **what's the —?** (fam) ¿cuánto te debo?

2 vt dañar, perjudicar; (Mech) averiar, estropear; chances, reputation perjudicar; **to be —d in a collision** sufrir daños en un choque.

damaging ['dæmidʒiŋ] adj perjudicial.

damascene ['dæməsi:n] vt damasquinar.

Damascus [də'mɑːskəs] Damasco.

damask ['dæməsk] **1** adj cloth adamascado; steel damasquino.

2 n (cloth) damasco m; (steel) acero m damasquino. **3** vt cloth adamascar; steel damasquinar.

dame [deim] n dama f, señora f; (sl) tía f.

damfool ['dæm'fu:l] adj (fam) estúpido, tonto; **some — driver** algún imbécil de conductor; **that's a — thing to say!** ¡qué tontería!

damn [dæm] **1** vt condenar (also Eccl); maldecir; **—!, — it!** ¡condenación!; **well I'm —ed!** ¡mecachis!; **I'll see him —ed first** antes le veré colgado.

2 n: **I don't give a —** maldito lo que me importa.

3 adj (fam) maldito.

damnable ['dæmnəbl] adj detestable.

damnably ['dæmnəbli] adv terriblemente.

damnation [dæm'neiʃən] n condenación f; perdición f; **—!** ¡condenación!; **to go down to —** ir a la perdición.

damned [dæmd] **1** adj condenado, maldito; (damnable) detestable, abominable; **the — book** ese maldito libro; **to do one's —est to +** infin hacer lo posible para + infin.

2 adv muy, extraordinariamente; **it's — awkward** es terriblemente difícil; **it's — hot** hace un calor terrible.

3 n: **the —** las almas en pena.

damning ['dæmiŋ] adj evidence irrecusable.

Damocles ['dæməkli:z] n Dámocles.

damp [dæmp] **1** adj húmedo; mojado.

2 n humedad f; (Min) mofeta f; **to cast a — on** hacer que se enfríe el ambiente de, introducir el desaliento en.

3 vt (also **dampen** ['dæmpən]) **(a)** (wet) mojar, humedecer.

(b) **to — down** amortiguar; fire cubrir; demand reducir.

(c) (fig) person desalentar; hopes ahogar; zeal enfriar, moderar.

damp-course ['dæmpkɔːs] n hilada f de ladrillos (etc) que impide la subida de la humedad.

damper ['dæmpə*] n (Mus) apagador m, sordina f; (of fire) regulador m de tiro.

dampish ['dæmpiʃ] adj algo húmedo.

dampness ['dæmpnis] n humedad f.

damp-proof ['dæmppru:f] adj a prueba de humedad.

damsel ['dæmzəl] n damisela f, doncella f.

damson ['dæmzən] n (fruit) ciruela f damascena; (tree) ciruelo m damasceno.

Dan [dæn] m nombre cariñoso de **Daniel.**

dance [dɑːns] **1** n baile m; **— of death** danza f de la muerte; **to lead someone a —** crear muchísimas dificultades a uno.

2 vt bailar.

3 vi bailar, danzar; (fig) danzar, saltar, brincar; **to — for joy** brincar de alegría; **shall we —?** ¿quieres bailar?

dance band ['dɑːnsbænd] n orquesta f de baile.

dance floor ['dɑːnsflɔː*] n pista f de baile.

dance hall ['dɑːnshɔːl] n salón m de baile.

dance music ['dɑːns,mjuːzik] n música f de baile.

dancer ['dɑ:nsə*] n bailador m, ora f; (professional) bailarín m, ina f.

dancing ['dɑ:nsiŋ] 1 n baile m. 2 attr de baile.

dancing-girl ['dɑ:nsiŋgə:l] n bailarina f.

dancing-partner ['dɑ:nsiŋ,pɑ:tnə*] n pareja f de baile.

dandelion ['dændilaiən] n diente m de león.

dander ['dændə*] n: to get someone's — up enojar a uno.

dandified ['dændifaid] adj guapo, acicalado.

dandle ['dændl] vt hacer saltar sobre las rodillas.

dandruff ['dændrəf] n caspa f.

dandy ['dændi] 1 n dandy m, currutaco m. 2 adj (fam) mono, de primera.

Dane [dein] n danés m, esa f; great — gran danés m.

danger ['deindʒə*] n peligro m; riesgo m; "—!" (sign) "¡peligro de muerte!"; there is a — of hay riesgo de; to be in — estar en peligro; to be in — of + ger correr riesgo de + infin; to be out of — estar fuera de peligro.

danger area ['deindʒər,ɛəriə] n zona f de peligro.

danger list ['deindʒəlist] n: to be on the — estar de cuidado.

danger money ['deindʒə,mʌni] n prima f por trabajos peligrosos.

dangerous ['deindʒrəs] adj peligroso, arriesgado; animal peligroso; substance nocivo.

dangerously ['deindʒrəsli] adv peligrosamente; arriesgadamente; to come — close to acercarse de modo peligroso a; he likes to live — le gusta arriesgar la vida.

danger signal ['deindʒə,signl] n señal f de peligro.

dangle ['dæŋgl] 1 vt colgar, dejar colgado; to — a prospect before someone ofrecer a uno la posibilidad de + infin.
2 vi estar colgado, pender; to — after ir tras de; she kept him dangling for 3 months ella le tuvo suspenso durante 3 meses.

Daniel ['dænjəl] m Daniel.

Danish ['deiniʃ] 1 adj danés, dinamarqués. 2 n (language) danés m.

dank [dæŋk] adj húmedo y malsano, liento.

Danube ['dænju:b] Danubio m.

Daphne ['dæfni] f Dafne.

dapper ['dæpə*] adj apuesto, pulcro.

dappled ['dæpld] adj moteado, salpicado de manchas; horse rodado.

Darby and Joan ['dɑ:biən'dʒəun] pl el matrimonio ideal, de ancianos que siguen viviendo en la mayor felicidad.

Dardanelles [,dɑ:də'nelz] pl Dardanelos mpl.

dare [dɛə*] 1 vt (attempt) arriesgar; someone's anger hacer frente a; gaze resistir; to — someone to do something desafiar a uno a hacer algo, provocar a uno a hacer algo.
2 vi: to — (to) do something atreverse a hacer algo, osar hacer algo; I — say quizá; I — say that no me sorprendería que + subj; how — you! ¡qué cinismo!, (more fam) ¡qué fresco!; just you —!, you wouldn't —! ¡ya te guardarás de hacerlo!

daredevil ['dɛə,devil] 1 adj temerario. 2 n temerario m, atrevido m.

daring ['dɛəriŋ] 1 adj atrevido, osado. 2 n atrevimiento m, osadía f.

daringly ['dɛəriŋli] adv atrevidamente, osadamente.

Darius [də'raiəs] m Darío.

dark [dɑ:k] 1 adj (a) (unilluminated) oscuro; tenebroso; to get — hacerse de noche, anochecer.
(b) (in colour) oscuro.
(c) complexion, hair moreno.
(d) (cheerless) triste, sombrío; — days días mpl funestos, días mpl negros.
(e) (secret) secreto, escondido; doings misterioso, sospechoso; the D— Continent el Continente Negro; to keep something — tener algo secreto; keep it —! ¡de esto no digas ni pío!
(f) (unenlightened) ignorante.
2 n oscuridad f; tinieblas fpl; after — después del anochecer; to grope about in the — ir buscando algo a oscuras; we are all in the — about it no sabemos nada en absoluto de ello; to keep someone in the — no revelar a uno cierta noticia; to be left in the — quedar sin saber nada de algo.

darken ['dɑ:kən] 1 vt oscurecer; (colour) hacer más oscuro. 2 vi oscurecerse; (sky) anublarse.

darkie ['dɑ:ki] n (fam) negro m, a f.

darkish ['dɑ:kiʃ] adj algo oscuro; hair etc algo moreno.

darkly ['dɑ:kli] adv misteriosamente.

darkness ['dɑ:knis] n oscuridad f; tinieblas fpl; the house was in — la casa estaba a oscuras; to cast someone into outer — condenar a uno a las penas infernales.

dark room ['dɑ:krum] n cuarto m oscuro.

darling ['dɑ:liŋ] 1 n querido m, a f; the — of the muses el querido de las musas; yes — sí querida; she's a little — (child) es una preciosidad.

darn¹ [dɑ:n] excl (fam) —!, — it! ¡condenación!

darn² [dɑ:n] 1 n zurcido m, zurcidura f. 2 vt zurcir.

darned [dɑ:nd] adj (fam) condenado, maldito.

darning ['dɑ:niŋ] n (act) zurcidura f; (garments) cosas fpl por zurcir.

darning needle ['dɑ:niŋ,ni:dl] n aguja f de zurcir.

dart [dɑ:t] 1 n (a) (Mil) dardo m, saeta f.
(b) (in game) rehilete m; —s juego m de rehiletes.
(c) (Sew) sisa f.
(d) (movement) movimiento m rápido; to make a — for precipitarse hacia.
2 vt look lanzar.
3 vi lanzarse, precipitarse (for, to hacia).

dartboard ['dɑ:tbɔ:d] n blanco m (en el juego de rehiletes).

Darwinian [dɑ:'winiən] adj darwiniano.

Darwinism ['dɑ:winizəm] n darwinismo m.

dash [dæʃ] 1 n (a) (small quantity) pequeña cantidad f, poquito m; a — of colour una nota de color; with a — of soda con dos gotitas de sifón.
(b) (with pen) rasgo m, plumada f; (Typ) (hyphen) guión m, (longer) raya f.
(c) (rush) carrera f; to make a — for precipitarse hacia; to make a — for it huir precipitadamente; we shall have to make a — for it tendremos que correr.
(d) to cut a — hacer gran papel, destacar.
2 vt (a) (shatter) romper, estrellar (against contra); to — something to pieces hacer algo pedazos; to — something to the ground tirar algo al suelo.
(b) hopes defraudar, acabar con.
(c) to — off a letter escribir una carta de prisa.
(d) —!, — it! ¡porras!
3 vi ir de prisa, precipitarse; we shall have to — tendremos que correr; I must — tengo que marcharme; the waves are —ing against the rock las olas se rompen contra la roca; to — away, to — off marcharse apresuradamente; to — in entrar precipitadamente; to — out salir precipitadamente; to — past pasar como un rayo; to — up llegar corriendo, (car) llegar a toda velocidad.

dashboard ['dæʃbɔ:d] n tablero m de instrumentos.

dashing ['dæʃiŋ] adj bizarro, gallardo, arrojado.

dastardly ['dæstədli] adj vil, miserable.

data ['deitə] npl datos mpl.

data processing ['deitə'prəusesiŋ] n proceso m de datos.

date¹ [deit] 1 n (a) fecha f; what's the —?, what is it today? ¿qué día es hoy?; closing —, last — fecha f tope; at an early — en fecha próxima; out of — anticuado, (person) atrasado de noticias; to go out of — quedar anticuado; to — hasta la fecha; up to — (adv) hasta la fecha; to be up to — (building etc) tener aspecto moderno; to be up to — in one's thinking tener ideas modernas; to be up to — in one's studies estar al día en los estudios; to bring something up to — modernizar algo, poner algo al día, actualizar algo; to bring someone up to — poner a uno al corriente.
(b) (of stocks etc) plazo m.
(c) (with girlfriend etc) cita f, (with friend) compromiso m; to have a — with someone tener cita con uno; have you got a — tonight? ¿tienes compromiso para esta noche?; to make a — with someone citar a uno; they made a — for 8 o'clock se citaron para las 8.
(d) (US fam) novio m, novia f.
2 vt fechar (at, to en); (US fam) citar.
3 vi ir quedando anticuado, pasar de moda; his ideas are very —d sus ideas son anticuadas ya; to — back to remontar a; to — from datar de, ser de la época de.

date² [deit] n (Bot: fruit) dátil m; (tree) palmera f datilera.

date-line ['deitlain] n línea f de cambio de fecha.

date palm ['deitpɑ:m] n palmera f datilera.

date stamp ['deitstæmp] n estampilla f para poner la fecha.

dative ['deitiv] n dativo m.

daub [dɔ:b] 1 n (smear) mancha f; (bad painting) pintarrajo m.
2 vt (smear) manchar (with de); to — a wall with paint, to — paint on to a wall embadurnar una pared de pintura.
3 vi pintarrajear.

dauber ['dɔ:bə*] n, **daubster** ['dɔ:bstə*] n pintor m de brocha gorda, mal pintor m.

daughter ['dɔ:tə*] n hija f.

daughter-in-law ['dɔ:tərinlɔ:] *n* nuera *f*, hija *f* política.

daunt [dɔ:nt] *vt* acobardar, intimidar, desalentar; **nothing** —**ed** sin inmutarse.

daunting ['dɔ:ntiŋ] *adj* desalentador, amedrentador.

dauntless ['dɔ:ntlis] *adj* impávido.

dauntlessly ['dɔ:ntlisli] *adv* impávidamente; **to carry on** — continuar impávido.

davenport ['dævnpɔ:t] *n* (*desk*) escritorio *m* pequeño; (*sofa*) sofá-cama *f*.

David ['deivid] *m* David.

davit ['dævit] *n* pescante *m*.

Davy Jones ['deivi'dʒəunz]: —' **locker** el fondo del mar (*tumba de los marineros ahogados*).

davy lamp ['deivi'læmp] *n* lámpara *f* de seguridad.

dawdle ['dɔ:dl] **1** *vt*: **to** — **away** malgastar. **2** *vi* perder el tiempo, holgazanear; (*in walking*) andar muy despacio; (*Aut etc*) ir muy despacio.

dawdler ['dɔ:dlə*] *n* holgazán *m*, ana *f*, ocioso *m*, a *f*; persona *f* que anda despacio, rezagado *m*, a *f*.

dawn [dɔ:n] **1** *n* alba *f*, amanecer *m*; (*fig*) aurora *f*, nacimiento *m*; **at** — al alba; **from** — **to dusk** de sol a sol; **to get up with the** — madrugar.

2 *vi* (a) amanecer, alborear, romper el día; **the day** —**ed rainy** el día empezó con lluvia; **a new epoch has** —**ed** ha nacido una época nueva.

(b) **it** —**ed on me that** caí en la cuenta de que, empecé a comprender que.

day [dei] *n* (a) día *m*; (*working period etc*) jornada *f*; **an 8-hour** — una jornada de 8 horas.

(b) (*with prep etc*) — **after** —, — **in** — **out** día tras día; **the** — **after** el día siguiente, al día siguiente; **the** — **after tomorrow** pasado mañana; **the** — **before** el día anterior; **the** — **before yesterday** anteayer; **two** —**s before this** dos días antes de esto; **the** — **before the coronation** la víspera de la coronación; — **by** — día por día; **by** — de día; **by the** — cada día, al día; **every other** — un día sí y otro no; **from** — **to** — de día en día; **in this** — **and age** en estos tiempos nuestros; **in my** — en mis tiempos; **in the** —**s of Queen Elizabeth, in Queen Elizabeth's** — en tiempos de la reina Isabel; **these** — **s** estos días; **to this** — hasta el día de hoy; **this** — **week** de hoy en ocho días.

(c) (*with adj etc*) **D**— **of Judgement** día *m* del Juicio Final; — **of reckoning** (*fig*) día *m* de la justicia; **it was a black** — **for the country** fué un día negro para el país; **it's early** —**s yet** todavía es pronto; **one fine** —, **one of these** —**s** el día menos pensado; **good** —! ¡buenos días!; **the good old** —**s** los buenos tiempos pasados; **working** — (*weekday*) día *m* laborable, (*number of hours*) jornada *f*.

(d) (*with verb*) **to call it a** — dejar de trabajar (*etc*), suspender el trabajo (*etc*); **let's call it a** — terminemos ya; **to carry the** — ganar la victoria; **it has had its** — ha dejado ya de ser útil, ya pasó aquello; **you don't look a** — **older** no pareces un día más viejo; **it has seen better** —**s** ya no vale lo que antes; **to take a** — **off** darse un día libre, no presentarse en el trabajo (*etc*).

daybook ['deibuk] *n* diario *m*.

day boy ['deibɔi] *n* externo *m*.

daybreak ['deibreik] *n* amanecer *m*; **at** — al amanecer.

daydream ['deidri:m] **1** *n* ensueño *m*. **2** *vi* soñar despierto.

day labourer ['dei'leibərə*] *n* jornalero *m*.

daylight ['deilait] *n* luz *f*, luz *f* del día; **in broad** — en (*or* a) pleno día; **to see** — empezar a ver el final de un trabajo (*etc*).

day nursery ['dei,nə:səri] *n* guardería *f* infantil.

day-old ['dei'əuld] *adj* **chick** de un día.

day-return ['deiri'tə:n] *n* (*also* — **ticket**) billete *m* barato de ida y vuelta en un día.

day shift ['deiʃift] *n* turno *m* de día.

daytime ['deitaim] *n* día *m*; **in the** — de día.

day-to-day ['deitə'dei] *adj* cotidiano, rutinario; **on a** — **basis** día por día.

daze [deiz] **1** *n*: **to be in a** — estar aturdido. **2** *vt* aturdir; (*dazzle*) deslumbrar.

dazed [deizd] *adj* aturdido.

dazedly ['deizidli] *adv* aturdidamente; **he said** — dijo aturdido.

dazzle ['dæzl] **1** *n* lo brillante, brillo *m*. **2** *vt* deslumbrar (*also fig*); **to be** —**d by** (*fig*) quedar deslumbrado por.

dazzling ['dæzliŋ] *adj* deslumbrante, deslumbrador.

deacon ['di:kən] *n* diácono *m*.

deaconess ['di:kənes] *n* diaconisa *f*.

dead [ded] **1** *adj* (a) muerto; **the** — **king** el difunto rey; **as** — **as the dodo, as** — **as a doornail, as** — **as mutton** más muerto que mi abuela; **to be** — estar

muerto; **he has been** — **3 years** hace 3 años que murió; **to drop** — caer muerto, morir de repente; **drop** —! (*fam*) ¡vete al cuerno!

(b) *town* muerto, desierto; *language* muerto; *leaf* marchito, seco.

(c) (*obsolete*) anticuado; **all that stuff's pretty** — **now** todo eso ya no tiene interés.

(d) (*fig*) *ball* fuera de juego; *calm* profundo, (*Naut*) chicha; *colour*, *fire* apagado; *level* exacto; *silence* profundo; *sound* sordo; *stop* en seco, repentino; *voice* monótono; **to be** — sin corriente; **the wire has gone** — (*Tel*) la línea está cortada.

2 *adv* completamente, totalmente; — **drunk** borracho como una cuba; — **slow** muy despacio; — **straight** completamente recto; — **tired** hecho polvo, muerto de cansancio; — **between the eyes** exactamente entre los ojos; — **on the target** exactamente en el blanco, en el mismo blanco; **to be** — **against something** estar totalmente opuesto a algo; **to be** — **certain** estar completamente seguro.

3 *n* (a) **the** — los muertos.

(b) **at** — **of night, in the** — **of night** en las altas horas; **in the** — **of winter** en lo más recio del invierno.

dead-and-alive ['dedənə'laiv] *adj* aburrido, monótono.

dead-beat 1 *adj* ['ded'bi:t]: **to be** — estar hecho polvo. **2** *n* ['ded] (*fam*) gorrón *m*, vagabundo *m*.

deaden ['dedn] *vt noise etc* amortiguar; *pain* aliviar.

dead end ['ded'end] *n* callejón *m* sin salida; **to reach a** — (*fig*) llegar a un punto muerto; — **kids** (*US*) chicos *mpl* de la calle.

dead heat ['ded'hi:t] **1** *n* empate *m*. **2** *vi* empatar (*with con*).

deadline ['dedlain] *n* fecha *f* tope, límite *m*, plazo *m*; **we cannot meet the government's** — no podemos terminarlo (*etc*) antes de la fecha señalada por el gobierno.

deadlock ['dedlɔk] **1** *n* (a) parálisis *f*; **the** — **is complete** la parálisis es total, no se ve salida alguna.

(b) punto *m* muerto; **to reach** — llegar a un punto muerto.

2 *vt*: **to be** —**ed** estar en un punto muerto.

deadly ['dedli] **1** *adj* mortal (*also fig*); (*very bad*) fatal; **with** — **accuracy** con la más absoluta exactitud; **it was a** — **play** la comedia fue fatal.

2 *adv*: — **dull** terriblemente aburrido, aburridísimo.

deadness ['dednis] *n* inercia *f*, falta *f* de vida.

deadnettle ['ded,netl] *n* ortiga *f* muerta.

deadpan ['ded,pæn] *adj* sin expresión.

dead reckoning ['ded'rekniŋ] *n* estima *f*.

Dead Sea ['ded'si:] Mar *m* Muerto.

dead weight ['dedweit] *n* peso *m* muerto; (*fig*) lastre *m*, carga *f* inútil.

deadwood ['ded'wud] *n* (*fig*) persona *f* inútil, gente *f* inútil, cosas *fpl* inútiles.

deaf [def] *adj* sordo (**to** a); **as** — **as a post** sordo como una tapia.

deaf-aid ['defeid] *n* aparato *m* del oído, audífono *m*.

deaf-and-dumb ['defən'dʌm] *adj* sordomudo.

deafen ['defn] *vt* ensordecer, asordar.

deafening ['defniŋ] *adj* ensordecedor.

deaf-mute ['def'mju:t] *n* sordomudo *m*, a *f*.

deafness ['defnis] *n* sordera *f*.

deal[1] [di:l] *n* madera *f* de pino (*or* abeto).

deal[2] [di:l] **1** *n* (a) (*Comm*) transacción *f*, negocio *m*, trato *m*; **business** — transacción *f* comercial; **it's a** —! ¡trato hecho!

(b) (*agreement*) pacto *m*, convenio *m*; (*secret*) pacto *m* secreto; **to do a** — **with** hacer un trato con; **we might do a** — podríamos llegar a un acuerdo; **we fear A might do a** — **with B** tememos que A pudiera ponerse de acuerdo con B.

(c) **New D**— (*US*) Nueva Política *f*, Nuevo Programa *m*, Nueva Distribución *f*; **a new** — **for the miners** un nuevo arreglo de salarios para los mineros; **Fair D**— (*US*) Política *f* Equitativa, Distribución *f* Equitativa; **raw** — injusticia *f*, trato *m* inequitativo; **he got a raw** — le trataron injustamente; **square** — justicia *f*, trato *m* equitativo; **I want a square** — yo pido justicia; **he didn't get a square** — le trataron injustamente.

(d) (*Cards*) reparto *m*; **whose** — **is it?** ¿a quién le toca dar?

(e) **a good** — bastante, mucho; **a great** — muchísimo; **a great** — **of** gran cantidad de; **to make a great** — **of** *person* estimar mucho a, *thing* dar importancia a.

2 (*irr*: *pret and ptp* **dealt**) *vt* (a) *cards* dar.

(b) *blow* dar, descargar; **to** — **a blow to** (*fig*)

destruir de un golpe; **to — a blow for freedom** librar una batalla en pro de la libertad.

(c) **to — out** repartir.

3 vi (*Cards*) ser mano; **to — in** tratar en, comerciar en; **to — with (a)** *person* tratar con, tener relaciones con; **he dealt very fairly with me** se portó muy bien conmigo; **he dealt cleverly with the ambassador** se las arregló inteligentemente con el embajador; **I'll — with him** yo me ocuparé de él; **he is used to —ing with criminals** está acostumbrado a tener que ver con criminales.

(b) *problem* ocuparse de; hacer frente a; **how should we — with this problem?** ¿qué hemos de hacer con este problema?; **the matter has been dealt with** el asunto está concluido; **how will the government — with coal?** ¿qué política tiene el gobierno para el carbón?

(c) *subject in book etc* tratar de, versar sobre, tener por tema; **he dealt with Africa in his speech** en su discurso se ocupó de África; **the book —s with war** el libro versa sobre la guerra.

(d) (*punish*) castigar; **the offenders will be dealt with** se castigará a los delincuentes; **they were dealt with severely** se les castigó de modo ejemplar.

(e) (*finish off*) *work* terminar, concluir; *person* despachar.

(f) (*in shop*) **which shop do you — with?** ¿en qué tienda compra Vd sus cosas?

dealer ['di:lə*] n comerciante m, tratante m (*in* en); (*retail*) distribuidor m (*in* de), proveedor m; (*Cards*) mano f.

dealings ['di:liŋz] npl (*Fin*) transacciones fpl; (*relations*) trato m, relaciones fpl; **to have — with** tratar con, tener relaciones con; **I wish to have no — with him** no quiero tener nada que ver con él.

dealt [delt] pret and ptp of **deal**[2].

dean [di:n] n (*Eccl*) deán m; (*Univ etc*) decano m.

dear [diə*] **1** adj (a) *person etc* querido; **yes (my) —** si querida; **a very —** friend of mine un amigo mío muy querido; **he was very — to all of us** fue querido de todos nosotros; **because your country is very — to me** por el amor que le tengo a vuestra patria.

(b) (*in letters*) **— John, — Mr White** mi querido amigo; **— Dr Green** (*from colleague*) mi querido amigo y colega; **— Sir** muy señor mío; **— Sirs** muy señores míos; **— Miss Brown** estimada Señorita, **— Madam** estimada Señora.

(c) (*expensive*) caro, costoso; *shop* carero.

2 n: **he's a —** es simpatiquísimo; **he's a little —** es un niño precioso.

3 excl: **oh —!, — me!** ¡ay!

dearie ['diəri] n (*fam*) queridito m, a f.

dearly ['diəli] adv (a) tiernamente; **to love someone — querer** muchísimo a uno; **I would — like to know why** quisiera muchísimo saber por qué.

(b) **to pay — for something** (*fig*) pagar algo caro; **it cost him —** le costó caro.

dearness ['diənis] n alto precio m, carestía f.

dearth [də:θ] n escasez f; falta f, ausencia f.

death [deθ] n muerte f; (*euph*) fallecimiento m, defunción f; **Black D—** peste f negra; **a living — una** vida peor que la muerte; **— to traitors!** ¡mueran los traidores!; **it will be the — of me** causará mi perdición; **this is — to our hopes** esto acaba con nuestras esperanzas; **it was — to the company** arruinó la sociedad; **to be in at the —** ver el final de la caza (*etc*); **to be at —'s door** estar a muerte; **to catch one's —** (*of cold*) coger un catarro de muerte; **to do** (*or* **put**) **to —** matar, dar muerte a, (*Law*) ajusticiar; **to fight to the —** luchar a muerte; **to hold on like grim —** estar firmemente agarrado, (*fig*) resistir con la mayor firmeza; **he's working himself to —** trabaja tanto que se está estropeando la salud; **he works his men to —** a sus hombres los mata trabajando.

deathbed ['deθbed] n lecho m de muerte; **— repentance** arrepentimiento m a última hora.

death-blow ['deθbləu] n golpe m mortal.

death certificate ['deθsə'tifikit] n partida f de defunción.

death duties ['deθ,dju:tiz] npl derechos mpl de herencia.

deathless ['deθlis] adj inmortal.

deathly ['deθli] adj mortal; de muerte; *silence* profundo; **— pale** pálido como la muerte.

death mask ['deθmɑːsk] n mascarilla f.

death penalty ['deθ,penəlti] n pena f de muerte.

death rate ['deθreit] n mortalidad f.

death rattle ['deθ,rætl] n estertor m.

death roll ['deθrəul] n número m de víctimas, lista f de víctimas.

death's-head ['deθshed] n calavera f.

death throes ['deθθrəuz] npl agonía f.

deathtrap ['deθtræp] n sitio m muy peligroso.

death warrant ['deθ,wɔrənt] n sentencia f de muerte.

deathwatch beetle ['deθwɔtʃ'bi:tl] n reloj m de la muerte.

deb [deb] n (*fam*) = **débutante**.

débâcle [dei'bɑ:kl] n fracaso m; (*Mil*) derrota f.

debag ['di:bæg] vt (*hum*) quitar (violentamente) los pantalones a.

debar [di'bɑ:*] vt excluir (*from* de); **to — someone from doing something** prohibir a uno hacer algo.

debase [di'beis] vt degradar, envilecer; *coinage* alterar.

debasement [di'beismənt] n degradación f, envilecimiento m; alteración f.

debatable [di'beitəbl] adj discutible.

debate [di'beit] **1** n discusión f; (*Parl etc*) debate m.

2 vt discutir, debatir.

3 vi discutir (*with* con); **to — with oneself** pensar, deliberar; **I am debating whether to do it** estoy dudando si hacerlo o no.

debater [di'beitə*] n persona f que toma parte en un debate; polemista mf; **he was a brilliant —** brillaba en los debates.

debauch [di'bɔ:tʃ] vt *youth* corromper; *woman* seducir.

debauched [di'bɔ:tʃt] adj vicioso.

debauchee [,debɔ:'tʃi:] n libertino m, disoluto f.

debauchery [di'bɔ:tʃəri] n libertinaje m, corrupción f.

debenture [di'bentʃə*] n vale m, bono m, obligación f.

debilitate [di'biliteit] vt debilitar.

debility [di'biliti] n debilidad f.

debit ['debit] **1** n debe m; **— balance** saldo m deudor, saldo m negativo; **— side** debe m. **2** vt: **to — something to someone** cargar algo en cuenta a uno.

debonair [,debə'neə*] adj elegante, gallardo.

Deborah ['debərə] f Débora.

Debrett [də'bret] n libro de referencia de la aristocracia del Reino Unido, (*loosely*) anuario m de la nobleza.

debris ['debri:] n escombros mpl; (*Geol*) rocalla f.

debt [det] n deuda f; **bad — deuda** f incobrable; **National D— Deuda** f Pública; **— of honour** deuda f de honor; **to be in — tener** deudas (*to* con); **to be £5 in — deber** 5 libras (*to* a); **to be in someone's —** (*fig*) sentirse bajo una obligación a uno; **to run into —, to run up —s** contraer deudas.

debtor ['detə*] n deudor m, ora f.

debunk ['di:'bʌŋk] vt quitar lo falso y legendario de; desacreditar, demoler; *person* desenmascarar.

début ['deibu:] n presentación f; **to make one's —** (*Theat*) hacer su presentación; (*in society*) presentarse en la sociedad, ponerse de largo.

débutante ['debju:tɑ̃:nt] n joven f que se presenta en la sociedad, debutante f.

decade ['dekeid] n decenio m.

decadence ['dekədəns] n decadencia f.

decadent ['dekədənt] adj decadente.

decagram(me) ['dekəgræm] n decagramo m.

decalitre, (*US*) **—liter** ['dekə,li:tə*] n decalitro m.

decametre, (*US*) **—meter** ['dekə,mi:tə*] n decámetro m.

decamp [di'kæmp] vi (*Mil*) decampar; (*fig*) largarse, fugarse.

decant [di'kænt] vt decantar.

decanter [di'kæntə*] n jarra f.

decapitate [di'kæpiteit] vt degollar, descabezar.

decapitation [di,kæpi'teiʃən] n degollación f.

decarbonize [di:'kɑ:bənaiz] vt descarbonizar.

decasyllable ['dekəsiləbl] n decasílabo m.

decay [di'kei] **1** n decadencia f, decaimiento m; (*rotting*) pudrición f; (*of teeth*) caries f; (*of building*) desmoronamiento m.

2 vt deteriorar, pudrir.

3 vi decaer, desmoronarse; (*rot*) pudrirse; (*teeth*) cariarse; (*building*) desmoronarse.

decayed [di'keid] adj *wood etc* podrido; *teeth* cariado; *family* venido a menos.

decease [di'si:s] **1** n fallecimiento m. **2** vi fallecer.

deceased [di'si:st] **1** adj difunto. **2** n: **the —** el difunto, la difunta.

deceit [di'si:t] n engaño m, fraude m; (*lying*) mentira f.

deceitful [di'si:tful] adj engañoso, falso, fraudulento; (*lying*) mentiroso.

deceitfully [di'si:tfəli] adv engañosamente; falsamente.

deceive [di'si:v] **1** vt engañar; *hopes* defraudar; **if my memory does not — me** si mal no recuerdo. **2** vr: **to — oneself** engañarse, equivocarse.

deceiver [di'si:və*] n impostor m, ora f, embustero m, a f; (*of woman*) seductor m.

decelerate [di:'seləreit] vt moderar la marcha de.

deceleration ['di:ˌseləˈreiʃən] n retardación f, disminución f de velocidad.
December [diˈsembə*] n diciembre m.
decency ['di:sənsi] n (a) decencia f; **offence against —** atentado m contra el pudor; **it is no more than common — to +** infin la educación exige que + subj.
(b) **decencies** buenas fpl costumbres.
(c) (kindness) bondad f.
decent ['di:sənt] adj (a) (seemly) decente.
(b) person simpático, amable, bueno; **he's a — sort** es buena persona; **he was very — to me** fue muy amable conmigo.
(c) (passable) bastante bueno; **a — sum** una cantidad considerable.
decently ['di:səntli] adv decentemente; amablemente, con amabilidad; **he very — offered it to me** muy amablemente me lo ofreció.
decentralization [di:ˌsentrəlaiˈzeiʃən] n descentralización f.
decentralize [di:ˈsentrəlaiz] vt descentralizar.
deception [diˈsepʃən] n engaño m, fraude m.
deceptive [diˈseptiv] adj engañoso.
decibel ['desibel] n decibel(io) m.
decide [diˈsaid] 1 vt decidir, determinar; **that —d me** eso me decidió.
2 vi decidir, resolver; **to — to do something** decidir hacer algo, decidirse a hacer algo, resolverse a hacer algo; **to — against something** optar por no hacer (etc) algo; **to — in favour of someone** decidir a favor de uno; **to — on something** decidir por algo, optar por algo, quedar en algo.
decided [diˈsaidid] adj person decidido, resuelto; (unquestionable) indudable.
decidedly [diˈsaididli] adv decididamente; **he said —** dijo con resolución; **it is — difficult** indudablemente es difícil.
deciding [diˈsaidiŋ] adj factor etc decisivo, concluyente; vote de calidad, decisivo.
deciduous [diˈsidjuəs] adj de hoja caduca.
decimal ['desiml] 1 adj decimal; **— fraction** fracción f decimal; **— point** coma f de decimales; **— system** sistema m métrico.
2 n decimal f; **recurring —** decimal f periódica pura.
decimate ['desimeit] vt diezmar (also fig).
decipher [diˈsaifə*] vt descifrar.
decipherable [diˈsaifərəbl] adj descifrable.
decision [diˈsiʒən] n (a) (a resolve) decisión f; (Law) fallo m; **to make** (or take) **a —** tomar una decisión.
(b) (resoluteness) resolución f, firmeza f.
decisive [diˈsaisiv] adj factor etc decisivo, concluyente; (conclusive) terminante; manner tajante.
decisively [diˈsaisivli] adv con decisión, con resolución; **to be — beaten** ser derrotado de modo decisivo.
deck [dek] 1 n (a) cubierta f; (of bus) piso m; (fam) suelo m, superficie f; **promenade —** cubierta f de paseo; **top —, upper —** (of bus) piso m de arriba; **to clear the —s** (fig) despejar la mesa (etc).
(b) (of cards) baraja f.
2 vt engalanar, adornar (with de).
deckchair ['dekˌtʃeə*] n tumbona f, hamaca f.
deck hand ['dekhænd] n marinero m de cubierta.
deckhouse ['dekhaus] n, pl **—houses** [ˌhauziz] camareta f alta.
declaim [diˈkleim] vt declamar.
declamation [ˌdekləˈmeiʃən] n declamación f.
declamatory [diˈklæmətəri] adj declamatorio.
declaration [ˌdekləˈreiʃən] n declaración f.
declare [diˈkleə*] 1 vt declarar, afirmar; dividend repartir; war declarar; **to — something to the customs** declarar algo en la aduana; **have you anything to —?** ¿tiene Vd algo que declarar?; **nothing to —** nada de pago; **to — someone to be a traitor** dar a uno por traidor.
2 vi: **to — for, to — in favour of** pronunciarse a favor de; **well I —!** ¡vaya!
3 vr: **to — oneself** declararse; **to — oneself surprised** confesar su sorpresa; **he —d himself beaten** reconoció que había sido vencido; **to — oneself against something** afirmar su oposición a algo.
declared [diˈkleəd] adj abierto, manifiesto.
declaredly [diˈkleəridli] adv declaradamente, abiertamente.
déclassé [deiˈklæsei] adj desprestigiado, empobrecido; que ha perdido su categoría social.
declension [diˈklenʃən] n declinación f.
declinable [diˈklainəbl] adj declinable.
decline [diˈklain] 1 n (lessening) declinación f, descenso m, disminución f (in de); (in price) baja f; (decay) decaimiento m, decadencia f; (of sun, empire)

ocaso m; (Med) debilitación f; **to be on the —** ir disminuyendo; **to go into a —** ir debilitándose.
2 vt rehusar, negarse a aceptar; (Gram) declinar.
3 vi (a) (go down) declinar, disminuir; (in price) bajar; (decay) decaer; (Med) debilitarse; **to — in importance** ir perdiendo importancia.
(b) (refuse) rehusar; **to — to do something** rehusar hacer algo, negarse a hacer algo.
declining [diˈklainiŋ] adj: **in my — years** en mis últimos años.
declivity [diˈkliviti] n declive m.
declutch ['di:ˈklʌtʃ] vi desembragar.
decoction [diˈkokʃən] n decocción f.
decode ['di:ˈkəud] vt descifrar.
décolletage [deiˈkolətɑːʒ] n escote m.
décolleté(e) [deiˈkoltei] adj dress escotado; woman en traje escotado.
decompose [ˌdi:kəmˈpəuz] 1 vt descomponer. 2 vi descomponerse.
decomposition [ˌdi:kompəˈziʃən] n descomposición f.
decompression [ˌdi:kəmˈpreʃən] n descompresión f; **— chamber** cámara f de descompresión.
decontaminate [ˌdi:kənˈtæmineit] vt descontaminar.
decontamination ['di:kənˌtæmiˈneiʃən] n descontaminación f.
decontrol [ˌdi:kənˈtrəul] 1 n supresión f del control 2 vt suprimir el control de.
décor ['deikɔ:*] n decoración f; (Theat) decorado m, decoraciones fpl.
decorate ['dekəreit] vt adornar, decorar (with de); room empapelar, pintar; house pintar; (Mil etc) condecorar.
decorating ['dekəreitiŋ] n: **interior —** decoración f del hogar.
decoration [ˌdekəˈreiʃən] n adorno m, ornato m; (act) decoración f; (Mil etc) condecoración f.
decorative ['dekərətiv] adj (in function) de adorno decorativo; (pleasant) hermoso, elegante.
decorator ['dekəreitə*] n pintor m decorador.
decorous ['dekərəs] adj decoroso, correcto.
decorously ['dekərəsli] adv decorosamente, correctamente.
decorum [diˈkɔ:rəm] n decoro m, corrección f.
decoy ['di:kɔi] 1 n señuelo m; (bird) cimbel m, reclamo m; (fig) señuelo m, trampa f.
2 vt atraer con señuelo; **to — someone away** lograr mediante una estratagema que uno se aparte de un sitio.
decrease [di:ˈkri:s] 1 n disminución f (in de); **to be on the —** ir disminuyendo. 2 vt disminuir, reducir. 3 vi disminuirse, reducirse.
decree [diˈkri:] 1 n decreto m. 2 vt decretar.
decree nisi [diˈkri:ˈnaisai] n orden f preliminar de divorcio.
decrepit [diˈkrepit] adj decrépito.
decrepitude [diˈkrepitju:d] n decrepitud f.
decry [diˈkrai] vt desacreditar, rebajar.
dedicate ['dedikeit] 1 vt dedicar. 2 vr: **to — oneself** to dedicarse a.
dedication [ˌdediˈkeiʃən] n dedicación f; (in book) dedicatoria f; **to work with utter —** trabajar con la más abnegada devoción.
deduce [diˈdju:s] vt deducir; **I — that** imagino que, supongo que; **what do you — from that?** ¿qué se colige de eso?
deducible [diˈdju:sibl] adj deducible (from de).
deduct [diˈdʌkt] vt restar, descontar, rebajar.
deductible [diˈdʌktəbl] adj deducible.
deduction [diˈdʌkʃən] n (a) (inference) deducción f, conclusión f; **what are your —s?** ¿cuáles son sus conclusiones? (b) (amount) descuento m, rebaja f.
deductive [diˈdʌktiv] adj deductivo.
deed [di:d] n (a) (act) hecho m, acto m, acción f; (brave etc) hazaña f. (b) (Law) escritura f.
deed-poll ['di:dˈpəul] n: **to change one's name by —** cambiar su apellido por escritura legal.
deem [di:m] vt juzgar, creer; **I — it a mistake** creo que es un error; **I — it to be true** creo que es verdad; **I — him a fool** considero que es tonto; **I — it to be my duty** considero que es mi deber.
deep [di:p] 1 adj profundo, hondo; (wide) ancho; (fig) profundo; breath profundo, a pleno pulmón; (Mus) bajo, grave; colour intenso, subido, (and dark) oscuro; tan intenso; mourning riguroso; mind penetrante; person insondable, (pej) astuto; **to be 6 metres —** tener una profundidad de 6 metros, tener 6 metros de hondo; **to be — in debt** estar lleno de deudas; **to be — in thought** estar absorto en la meditación; **he's pretty — in it** está muy metido en el asunto.
2 adv: **don't go in too —** no te metas en la parte profunda; **the miners are — underground** los

mineros están a una gran profundidad; **— in his heart** en lo más hondo del corazón; **he thrust his hand — into his pocket** metió la mano hasta el fondo del bolsillo; **— into the night** hasta las altas horas de la noche; **to form up 6 —** formarse de 6 en fondo.
3 *n*: **the —** (*lit*) el piélago.

deep-breathing ['di:p'bri:ðiŋ] *n* gimnasia *f* respiratoria.

deep-chested ['di:p'tʃestid] *adj* ancho de pecho.

deepen ['di:pən] **1** *vt hole etc* ahondar, profundizar, hacer más profundo; *voice* ahuecar; *colour, emotion* intensificar; *study* ahondar en.
2 *vi* (*water etc*) hacerse más profundo; (*colour, emotion*) intensificarse; (*gloom*) aumentarse.

deep-felt ['di:p'felt] *adj* hondamente sentido.

deep-freeze ['di:p'fri:z] **1** *n* congeladora *f*. **2** *vt* congelar.

deep-fry ['di:p'frai] *vt* freír en aceite abundante.

deep-laid ['di:p'leid] *adj plan* bien preparado.

deeply ['di:pli] *adv* profundamente, hondamente; intensamente; **to breathe —** respirar a pleno pulmón.

deep-rooted ['di:p'ru:tid] *adj* profundamente arraigado.

deep-sea ['di:p'si:] *adj* de alta mar; **— fishing** pesca *f* de altura.

deep-seated ['di:p'si:tid] *adj* profundamente arraigado.

deep-set ['di:p'set] *eyes* hundido.

deer [diə*] *n* ciervo *m*; **red —** ciervo *m* común.

deerhound ['diəhaund] *n* galgo *m* para cazar venados; galgo *m* escocés de pelo lanoso.

deerskin ['diəskin] *n* piel *f* de ciervo, gamuza *f*.

deerstalker ['diə,stɔ:kə*] *n* (a) (*person*) cazador *m* de ciervos al acecho. (b) (*hat*) gorro *m* de cazador (de ciervos).

deer-stalking ['diə,stɔ:kiŋ] *n* caza *f* de venado.

deface [di'feis] *vt* desfigurar, mutilar.

de facto [dei'fæktəu] *adj and adv* de hecho.

defamation [,defə'meiʃən] *n* difamación *f*.

defamatory [di'fæmətəri] *adj* difamatorio.

defame [di'feim] *vt* difamar, calumniar.

default [di'fɔ:lt] **1** *n*: **in — of** a falta de, en ausencia de; **judgement by —** juicio *m* en rebeldía; **he won by —** ganó por no presentarse su adversario; **we must not let it go by —** no debemos permitir que lo perdamos por descuido (*or* sin hacer nada).
2 *vi* (a) (*not pay*) no pagar, ponerse en mora; **to — on one's payments** no pagar los plazos (*etc*).
(b) (*Sport*) dejar de presentarse.

defaulter [di'fɔ:ltə*] *n* (*on payments*) moroso *m*, a *f*; (*Mil*) delincuente *m*.

defeat [di'fi:t] **1** *n* derrota *f*. **2** *vt* vencer, derrotar; *plan* estorbar, frustrar; *hopes* defraudar; **this will — its own ends** esto será contraproducente.

defeatism [di'fi:tizəm] *n* derrotismo *m*.

defeatist [di'fi:tist] **1** *adj* derrotista. **2** *n* derrotista *mf*.

defecate ['defəkeit] *vti* defecar.

defecation [,defə'keiʃən] *n* defecación *f*.

defect ['di:fekt] *n* defecto *m*.

defect [di'fekt] *vi* desertar (*from* de, *to* a).

defection [di'fekʃən] *n* deserción *f*, defección *f*.

defective [di'fektiv] **1** *adj* defectuoso; (*Gram*) defectivo; *child* anormal. **2** *n* persona *f* anormal, retrasado *m* mental.

defence [di'fens] *n* defensa *f* (*also Sport, Chess*); **civil —** defensa *f* pasiva.

defenceless [di'fenslis] *adj* indefenso; (*fig*) inocente, inofensivo.

defend [di'fend] *vt* defender (*against* contra, *from* de).

defendant [di'fendənt] *n* (*civil*) demandado *m*, a *f*; (*criminal*) acusado *m*, a *f*.

defender [di'fendə*] *n* defensor *m*.

defense [di'fens] *n* (*US*) = **defence**.

defensible [di'fensibl] *adj* defendible; *action etc* justificable.

defensive [di'fensiv] **1** *adj* defensivo. **2** *n* defensiva *f*; **to be on the —** estar a la defensiva.

defer[1] [di'fə:*] *vt* aplazar, diferir; *conscript* dar una prórroga.

defer[2] [di'fə:*] *vi*: **to — to** diferir a.

deference ['defərəns] *n* deferencia *f*, respeto *m*; **in —** **to, out of — to** por respeto a.

deferential [,defə'renʃəl] *adj* respetuoso.

deferment [di'fə:mənt] *n* aplazamiento *m*; (*Mil*) prórroga *f*.

deferred [di'fə:d] *adj payment* a plazos.

defiance [di'faiəns] *n* desafío *m* (*of* a); oposición *f* terca (*of* a); **in — of** en contra de, con infracción de; **to bid — to** desafiar a.

defiant [di'faiənt] *adj* provocativo, insolente; *tone* retador.

defiantly [di'faiəntli] *adv* de modo provocativo, insolentemente; en tono retador, en son de reto.

deficiency [di'fiʃənsi] *n* (*lack*) falta *f*; (*defect*) defecto *m*, deficiencia *f*; (*Comm*) déficit *m*, descubierto *m*; **— disease** mal *m* carencial.

deficient [di'fiʃənt] *adj* (*in quantity*) insuficiente; (*incomplete*) incompleto; (*defective*) defectuoso; (*mentally*) anormal; **to be — in** carecer de, estar falto de.

deficit ['defisit] *n* déficit *m*.

defile ['di:fail] *n* desfiladero *m*.

defile [di'fail] *vt* manchar, deshonrar; *sacred thing* profanar.

defilement [di'failmənt] *n* deshonra *f*; ensuciamiento *m*, corrupción *f*; profanación *f*.

definable [di'fainəbl] *adj* definible.

define [di'fain] *vt* definir, determinar.

definite ['definit] *adj* claro, categórico; positivo; concreto; *date etc* determinado; (*Gram*) definido; **he was very — about it** nos lo dijo sin dejar lugar a dudas; **we have no — record of it** no nos consta de manera clara; **the plan is not yet —** todavía el proyecto no se ha aprobado de modo definitivo.

definitely ['definitli] *adv* claramente, categóricamente; **oh, —!, yes, —!** si, desde luego; **he say so —?** ¿lo dijo claramente?; **we are — not going** es seguro que no vamos; **it is — impossible** es francamente imposible; **the plan is not yet — fixed** todavía el proyecto no se ha aprobado de modo definitivo.

definition [,defi'niʃən] *n* definición *f*; (*of photo*) claridad *f*; **by —** por definición.

definitive [di'finitiv] *adj* definitivo.

definitively [di'finitivli] *adv* en definitiva.

deflate [di:'fleit] *vt* desinflar; *person* quitar los humos a; *reputation* rebajar, desacreditar; (*Fin*) deflacionar.

deflation [di:'fleiʃən] *n* desinflación *f*; (*Fin*) deflación *f*.

deflationary [di:'fleiʃənəri] *adj* (*Fin*) deflacionista.

deflect [di'flekt] *vt* desviar (*from* de).

deflection [di'flekʃən] *n* desviación *f*.

defloration [,di:flɔ:'reiʃən] *n* desfloración *f*.

deflower [di:'flauə*] *vt* desflorar.

deform [di'fɔ:m] *vt* deformar.

deformation [,di:fɔ:'meiʃən] *n* deformación *f*.

deformed [di'fɔ:md] *adj* deforme, mutilado.

deformity [di'fɔ:miti] *n* deformidad *f*.

defraud [di'frɔ:d] *vt* estafar; **to — someone of something** estafar algo a uno, quitar fraudulentamente algo a uno.

defray [di'frei] *vt* sufragar, pagar.

defrost [di:'frɔst] *vt* deshelar, descongelar.

deft [deft] *adj* diestro, hábil.

deftly ['deftli] *adv* diestramente, hábilmente.

defunct [di'fʌŋkt] *adj* difunto; *company etc* que ya no existe; *idea, theory* que ya no tiene validez; *scheme* que no se realizó nunca.

defy [di'fai] *vt* (a) (*challenge*) desafiar; **to — someone to do something** desafiar a uno a hacer algo.
(b) (*resist*) oponerse tercamente a; *order* contravenir a; *bad weather* resistir a; **it defies definition** se escapa a la definición; **it defies description** resulta imposible describirlo.

degeneracy [di'dʒenərəsi] *n* degeneración *f*, depravación *f*.

degenerate [di'dʒenərit] **1** *adj* degenerado. **2** *n* degenerado *m*, a *f*.

degenerate [di'dʒenəreit] *vi* degenerar (*into* en); **to — into** (*end up being*) degenerar en, terminar siendo, terminar en; **the essay —d into jottings** el ensayo terminó siendo meros apuntes.

degeneration [di,dʒenə'reiʃən] *n* degeneración *f*.

degradation [,degrə'deiʃən] *n* degradación *f*, envilecimiento *m*.

degrade [di'greid] **1** *vt* degradar, envilecer. **2** *vr*: **to — oneself** degradarse, aplebeyarse.

degrading [di'greidiŋ] *adj* degradante.

degree [di'gri:] *n* (a) (*Math, Astron, Gram etc*) grado *m*; **10 —s below freezing** 10 grados bajo cero.
(b) (*stage in process*) etapa *f*, punto *m*; **things have reached such a — that** las cosas han llegado a tal extremo que; **by —s** poco a poco, gradualmente; **in no — de** ninguna manera; **in some —, to a certain —** hasta cierto punto; **to the highest —** en sumo grado; **he is superstitious to a —** es sumamente supersticioso.
(c) (*Univ*) grado *m*, título *m*; **first — licenciatura *f*; **doctor's — doctorado *m*; **honorary — doctorado *m* "honoris causa"; **to get a — sacar un título; **to take one's — recibir un título; **to take a — in** licenciarse en.

(d) (*social*) rango *m*, condición *f* social; **people of** — personas *fpl* de cierto rango social.

(e) **third** — interrogación *f* brutal; **to give someone the third** — interrogar a uno brutalmente.

dehumanize [diː'hjuːmənaiz] *vt* deshumanizar.

dehydrate [diː'haidreit] *vt* deshidratar.

dehydrated [,diːhai'dreitid] *adj* deshidratado.

dehydration [,diːhai'dreiʃən] *n* deshidratación *f*.

de-ice [diː'ais] *vt* deshelar, descongelar.

de-icer ['diː'aisə*] *n* (*Aer*) deshelador *m*.

deification [,diːifi'keiʃən] *n* deificación *f*.

deify ['diːifai] *vt* deificar.

deign [dein] *vi*: **to** — **to** + *infin* dignarse + *infin*.

deism ['diːizəm] *n* deísmo *m*.

deist ['diːist] *n* deísta *mf*.

deity ['diːiti] *n* deidad *f*; divinidad *f*; **the D**— Dios *m*.

dejected [di'dʒektid] *adj* abatido, desanimado.

dejection [di'dʒekʃən] *n* abatimiento *m*.

dekko ['dekəu] *n* (*sl*) vistazo *m*; **let's have a** — déjame verlo.

delay [di'lei] **1** *n* (*in general*) dilación *f*; (*a* —) retraso *m*, demora *f*; **without** — en seguida, sin más tardar.

2 *vt* (*postpone*) aplazar, demorar; (*person*) entretener; (*obstruct*) impedir; (*make slow, eg train*) retrasar, retardar; **what** —**ed you?** ¿por qué has tardado tanto?; **the train was** —**ed by fog** el tren se retrasó por la niebla; —**ed effect** efecto *m* demorado.

3 *vi* tardar, demorarse; **don't** —! (*in doing something*) ¡cuanto antes, mejor!; (*on the way*) ¡no te entretengas!

delayed-action [di'leid'ækʃən] *adj* de acción retardada.

delaying [di'leiiŋ] *adj*: — **tactics** tácticas *fpl* retardatorias.

delectable [di'lektəbl] *adj* delicioso.

delegate ['deligit] *n* delegado *m*, a *f*, diputado *m*, a *f* (*to* a).

delegate ['deligeit] *vt* delegar, diputar; **I was** —**d to do it** me dieron autoridad para hacerlo, me nombraron para hacerlo; **that task cannot be** —**d** ese cometido no se puede delegar a otro.

delegation [,deli'geiʃən] *n* (*act*) delegación *f*; (*body*) delegación *f*, diputación *f*.

delete [di'liːt] *vt* suprimir, tachar.

deleterious [,deli'tiəriəs] *adj* nocivo, perjudicial.

deletion [di'liːʃən] *n* supresión *f*.

delft [delft] *n* porcelana *f* de Delft.

deliberate [di'libərit] *adj* (*intentional*) intencionado, premeditado; (*cautious*) prudente; (*unhurried*) pausado, lento.

deliberate [di'libəreit] **1** *vt* meditar; **I** —**d what to do** medité lo que debiera hacer.

2 *vi* deliberar (*on* sobre); **I** —**d whether to do it** dudaba si hacerlo o no.

deliberately [di'libəritli] *adv* (*intentionally*) con intención, a propósito; (*cautiously*) prudentemente; (*slowly*) pausadamente.

deliberation [di,libə'reiʃən] *n* (*consideration*) reflexión *f*; (*debate*) discusión *f*; (*slowness*) lentitud *f*; **the council's** —**s** las discusiones del consejo; **after due** — después de pensarlo bien.

deliberative [di'libərətiv] *adj* deliberativo.

delicacy ['delikəsi] *n* delicadeza *f*; fragilidad *f*; (*titbit*) manjar *m* exquisito, golosina *f*.

delicate ['delikit] *adj* delicado; **workmanship** fino, exquisito; (*fragile*) frágil; **flavour, food** exquisito; **situation** difícil; **action** considerado; (*Med*) algo débil, enfermizo.

delicately ['delikitli] *adv* delicadamente; finamente, exquisitamente; frágilmente.

delicatessen [,delikə'tesn] *n* tienda que se especializa en manjares exquisitos y exóticos.

delicious [di'liʃəs] *adj* delicioso, exquisito, rico.

delight [di'lait] **1** *n* (*feeling*) placer *m*, deleite *m*; (*pleasurable thing*) encanto *m*, delicia *f*; **a** — **to the eye** un gozo para la retina; **one of the** —**s of Majorca** uno de los encantos de Mallorca; **it has been the** — **of many children** ha hecho las delicias de muchos niños; **the book is sheer** — el libro es un verdadero encanto; **to take** — **in something** deleitarse con algo; **to take** — **in** + *ger* deleitarse en + *infin*, (*pej*) gozarse en + *infin*.

2 *vt* encantar, deleitar; **the play** —**ed everyone** la obra encantó a todos; **we are** —**ed with it** estamos encantados con él; **I'm** —**ed to meet you** estoy encantado de conocerle; **we shall be** —**ed to come** tendremos muchísimo gusto en venir.

3 *vi*: **to** — **in something** deleitarse con algo; **to** — **in** + *ger* deleitarse en + *infin*, (*pej*) gozarse en + *infin*.

delightful [di'laitful] *adj* encantador, delicioso, precioso.

delightfully [di'laitfəli] *adv* deliciosamente; **to be** — **vague** tener un despiste delicioso.

delimit [diː'limit] *vt* delimitar.

delimitation [,diːlimi'teiʃən] *n* delimitación *f*.

delineate [di'linieit] *vt* delinear; (*portray*) bosquejar, pintar; (*delimit*) delimitar, definir.

delinquency [di'liŋkwənsi] *n* delincuencia *f*; (*guilt*) culpa *f*; **juvenile** — delincuencia *f* de menores.

delinquent [di'liŋkwənt] **1** *adj* delincuente.

2 *n* delincuente *mf*; **juvenile** — delincuente *mf* juvenil.

delirious [di'liriəs] *adj* delirante; **to be** — delirar, desvariar; **to be** — **with joy** estar loco de contento, estar delirante de alegría.

deliriously [di'liriəsli] *adv* con delirio; **to be** — **happy** estar loco de contento.

delirium [di'liriəm] *n* delirio *m*; — **tremens** delírium *m* tremens.

deliver [di'livə*] **1** *vt* (**a**) (*distribute*) repartir, entregar; *mail* repartir; **"we** —**"** (*Comm*) "servicio a domicilio".

(b) (*hand over*) entregar (*to* a; *also* **to** — **over**, **to** — **up**).

(c) *message* llevar, comunicar; *sermon, speech, judgement* pronunciar; *lecture* dar; *ball, missile* lanzar; *blow* dar.

(d) (*save*) librar (*from* de); — **us from evil** líbranos del mal.

(e) (*Med*) **she was** —**ed of a child** dio a luz un niño; **to** — **a woman** asistir a un parto; **the doctor** —**ed her of twins** el médico le asistió en el nacimiento de gemelos.

2 *vr*: **to** — **oneself of** *speech* pronunciar, *remark* hacer (con solemnidad), *opinion* expresar; **to** — **oneself up** entregarse (*to* a).

deliverance [di'livərəns] *n* liberación *f*, rescate *m* (*from* de).

deliverer [di'livərə*] *n* (**a**) (*Comm etc*) repartidor *m*; distribuidor *m*. (**b**) (*saviour*) libertador *m*, ora *f*, salvador *m*, ora *f*.

delivery [di'livəri] *n* (**a**) (*distribution*) distribución *f*, entrega *f*, repartido *m*; (*of mail*) reparto *m*.

(b) (*handing over*) entrega *f*; **forward** — (*Comm*) entrega *f* en fecha futura; *see* **cash**.

(c) (*of speech*) pronunciación *f*; (*manner of speaking etc*) modo *m* de leer, modo *m* de expresarse.

(d) (*saving*) liberación *f*, rescate *m* (*from* de).

(e) (*Med*) parto *m*, alumbramiento *m*.

delivery note [di'livərinəut] *n* nota *f* de entrega.

delivery room [di'livərirum] *n* sala *f* de alumbramiento.

delivery service [di'livəri,səːvis] *n* servicio *m* a domicilio.

delivery van [di'livərivæn] *n* furgoneta *f* de reparto.

dell [del] *n* vallecito *m*.

delouse ['diː'laus] *vt* despiojar, espulgar.

Delphi ['delfai] Delfos.

Delphic ['delfik] *adj* délfico.

delphinium [del'finiəm] *n* espuela *f* de caballero.

delta ['deltə] *n* (*Geog*) delta *m*; (*letter*) delta *f*.

delta-winged ['deltə'wiŋd] *adj* con alas en delta.

delude [di'luːd] **1** *vt* engañar. **2** *vr*: **to** — **oneself** engañarse.

deluded [di'luːdid] *adj* iluso, engañado.

deluge ['deljuːdʒ] **1** *n* diluvio *m*; (*fig*) diluvio *m*, inundación *f*; **a** — **of protests** un torrente de protestas.

2 *vt* inundar (*with* de); **he was** —**d with gifts** quedó inundado de regalos, le llovieron los regalos encima; **we are** —**d with work** tenemos trabajo hasta encima de las cabezas.

delusion [di'luːʒən] *n* engaño *m*, error *m*, ilusión *f*; **to labour under a** — estar equivocado.

de luxe [di'lʌks] *adj* de lujo.

delve [delv] **1** *vt* cavar. **2** *vi* cavar; (*fig*) **to** — **into** investigar, ahondar en; **we must** — **deeper** tenemos que ahondar todavía más.

demagogic [,demə'gɔgik] *adj* demagógico.

demagogue ['deməgɔg] *n* demagogo *m*.

demagoguery ['deməgɔgəri] *n* demagogismo *m*.

demagogy ['deməgɔgi] *n* demagogia *f*.

demand [di'maːnd] **1** *n* (**a**) (*request*) petición *f*, solicitud *f* (*for* de); **by popular** — a petición del público; **on** — a solicitud.

(b) (*urgent claim*) exigencia *f*; requerimiento *m*; (*for payment*) reclamación *f*, aviso *m*, intimación *f*; **the** —**s of duty** las exigencias del deber; **I have many** —**s on my time** mis asuntos me tienen ocupadísimo; **it makes great** —**s on my resources** exige mucho dinero; **he resisted the pressing** —**s made on him** resistió a los apremiantes requerimientos que se le habían dirigido.

(c) (*Comm*) demanda *f* (*for* de); **there is a — for** existe demanda de; **to be in —** tener demanda, (*fig*) ser muy solicitado, ser muy popular.
  2 *vt* **(a)** exigir (*from, of* a) reclamar, solicitar perentoriamente; **I — my rights** yo reclamo mis derechos; **the job —s care** el trabajo exige cuidado.
  (b) I —ed to know why insistí en saber por qué.
demanding [di'mɑːndiŋ] *adj* (*person*) exigente; (*task*) absorbente; **physically —** duro, agotador.
demand note [di'mɑːndnəut] *n* apremio *m* de pago.
demarcate ['diːmɑːkeit] *vt* demarcar.
demarcation [ˌdiːmɑː'keiʃən] *n* demarcación *f*.
démarche ['deimɑːʃ] *n* gestión *f*, diligencia *f*.
demean [di'miːn] *vr*: **to — oneself** degradarse.
demeanour [di'miːnə*] *n* porte *m*, conducta *f*.
demented [di'mentid] *adj* demente; (*fig*) loco.
dementedly [di'mentidli] *adv* (*fig*) como un loco.
dementia [di'menʃiə] *n* demencia *f*.
demerit [diː'merit] *n* demérito *m*.
demesne [di'mein] *n* heredad *f*; tierras *fpl* solariegas.
demi . . . ['demi] semi . . ., medio . . .
demigod ['demigɔd] *n* semidiós *m*.
demijohn ['demidʒɔn] *n* damajuana *f*.
demilitarization ['diːˌmilitəraiˈzeiʃən] *n* desmilitarización *f*.
demilitarize ['diːˈmilitəraiz] *vt* desmilitarizar.
demimonde ['demiˈmɔːnd] *n* mujeres *fpl* mundanas.
demise [di'maiz] *n* fallecimiento *m*.
demisemiquaver ['demisemiˌkweivə*] *n* fusa *f*.
demitasse [demitæs] *n* (*US*) taza *f* pequeña, tacita *f*.
demob ['diːˈmɔb] *vt* (*fam*) desmovilizar.
demobilization ['diːˌməubilaiˈzeiʃən] *n* desmovilización *f*.
demobilize [diːˈməubilaiz] *vt* desmovilizar.
democracy [di'mɔkrəsi] *n* democracia *f*.
democrat ['demokræt] *n* demócrata *mf*.
democratic [ˌdeməˈkrætik] *adj* democrático.
democratically [ˌdeməˈkrætikli] *adv* democráticamente.
democratize [di'mɔkrətaiz] *vt* democratizar.
démodé [dei'mɔdei] *adj* pasado de moda.
demography [di'mɔgrəfi] *n* demografía *f*.
demolish [di'mɔliʃ] *vt* derribar, demoler; *argument* destruir; *food* devorar, zamparse.
demolition [ˌdeməˈliʃən] *n* derribo *m*, demolición *f*.
demolition squad [ˌdeməˈliʃənskwɔd] *n* pelotón *m* de demolición.
demon ['diːmən] *n* demonio *m*.
demonetize [diːˈmʌnitaiz] *vt* desmonetizar.
demoniacal [ˌdiːməˈnaiəkəl] *adj* demoníaco.
demonstrable ['demənstrəbl] *adj* demostrable.
demonstrate ['demənstreit] **1** *vt* demostrar. **2** *vi* manifestarse, hacer una manifestación (*against* para protestar contra, *in favour of* a favor de).
demonstration [ˌdemənˈstreiʃən] *n* demostración *f*, prueba *f*; (*Pol*) manifestación *f*.
demonstrative [di'mɔnstrətiv] **1** *adj* (*Gram*) demostrativo; *person* exagerado, exaltado; **not very —** más bien reservado. **2** *n* demostrativo *m*.
demonstrator ['demənstreitə*] *n* (*Pol*) manifestante *mf*; (*Univ etc*) ayudante *mf* (en un laboratorio).
demoralize [di'mɔrəlaiz] *vt* desmoralizar.
demoralizing [di'mɔrəlaiziŋ] *adj* desmoralizador.
Demosthenes [di'mɔsθəniːz] *m* Demóstenes.
demote [di'məut] *vt* degradar.
demotic [di'mɔtik] *adj* demótico.
demotion [di'məuʃən] *n* degradación *f*.
demur [di'mɑː*] *vi* objetar, poner pegas.
demure [di'mjuə*] *adj* grave, solemne; (*modest*) recatado; (*coy*) de una coquetería disimulada; **in a — little voice** en tono dulce y algo coqueta.
demurely [di'mjuəli] *adv* gravemente, solemnemente; recatadamente; con una coquetería disimulada; en tono dulce y algo coqueta.
demureness [di'mjuənis] *n* gravedad *f*, solemnidad *f*; recato *m*; coquetería *f* disimulada.
den [den] *n* (*animal's*) madriguera *f*, guarida *f*; (*private room*) estudio *m*, gabinete *m*; **— of iniquity,** — **of vice** templo *m* del vicio; **— of thieves** ladronera *f*.
denationalization ['diːˌnæʃnəlaiˈzeiʃən] *n* desnacionalización *f*.
denationalize [diːˈnæʃnəlaiz] *vt* desnacionalizar.
denial [di'naiəl] *n* (*of request*) denegación *f*, negativa *f*; (*of report etc*) desmentimiento *m*; (*self-*) abnegación *f*.
denier ['deniə*] *n* denier *m*.
denigrate ['denigreit] *vt* denigrar.
denim ['denim] *n* dril *m* de algodón; **—s** pantalón *m* de dril.
denizen ['denizn] *n* habitante *mf*.
Denmark ['denmɑːk] Dinamarca *f*.
denominate [di'nɔmineit] *vt* denominar.

denomination [diˌnɔmi'neiʃən] *n* (*name*) denominación *f*; (*class*) clase *f*, categoría *f*; (*of coin etc*) valor *m*; (*Eccl*) secta *f*, confesión *f*.
denominational [diˌnɔmi'neiʃənl] *adj* (*Eccl*) sectario.
denominator [di'nɔmineitə*] *n*: **common —** denominador *m* común.
denote [di'nəut] *vt* denotar; indicar, significar; **what does this —?** ¿qué quiere decir esto?
dénouement [dei'nuːmɑ̃ːŋ] *n* desenlace *m*.
denounce [di'nauns] *vt* (*to police etc*) denunciar; *treaty* denunciar, abrogar; (*inveigh against*) censurar.
dense [dens] *adj* denso; espeso, compacto, tupido; *person* duro de mollera.
densely ['densli] *adv* densamente; espesamente; **— populated** con gran densidad de población.
denseness ['densnis] *n*, **density** ['densiti] *n* densidad *f*; lo espeso *etc*.
dent [dent] **1** *n* abolladura *f*; (*in edge*) mella. **2** *vt* abollar; mellar.
dental ['dentl] **1** *adj* dental; **— science** odontología *f*; **— surgeon** dentista *mf*, odontólogo *m*. **2** *n* dental *f*.
dentifrice ['dentifris] *n* dentífrico *m*.
dentist ['dentist] *n* dentista *mf*, odontólogo *m*.
dentistry ['dentistri] *n* odontología *f*.
denture ['dentʃə*] *n* dentadura *f*; (*false teeth, also* **—s**) dentadura *f* postiza.
denude [di'njuːd] *vt* (*Geol etc*) denudar; (*strip*) despojar (*of* de).
denunciation [diˌnʌnsi'eiʃən] *n* denuncia *f*, denunciación *f*; (*inveighing*) censura *f*.
deny [di'nai] **1** *vt* *possibility, truth of statement etc* negar; *request* denegar; *charge* rechazar; *report* desmentir; **he denies me his help** me niega su ayuda; **he denies that he said it, he denies having said it** niega haberlo dicho; **I don't —** it no lo niego.
  2 *vr*: **to — oneself** privarse; **to — oneself something** privarse de algo, no permitirse algo.
deodorant [diː'əudərənt] *n* desodorante *m*.
deodorize [diː'əudəraiz] *vt* desodorizar.
deoxidize [diː'ɔksidaiz] *vt* desoxidar.
depart [di'pɑːt] **1** *vt*: **to — this life** partir de esta vida.
  2 *vi* partir, irse, marcharse (*from* de); (*train etc*) salir (*at* a, *for* para, *from* de); **to — from** *custom, truth etc* apartarse de, desviarse de.
departed [di'pɑːtid] *n*: **the —** el difunto, la difunta.
department [di'pɑːtmənt] *n* departamento *m*; (*of business*) sección *f*; (*of learning, activity*) ramo *m*; (*US Pol*) ministerio *m*; **D— of State** (*US*) Ministerio *m* de Asuntos Exteriores; **in that — of the game** en ese aspecto del juego.
departmental [ˌdiːpɑːt'mentl] *adj* departamental; **— policy** política *f* del departamento; **— head** jefe *m* de sección.
department store [di'pɑːtmənt,stɔː*] *n* grandes almacenes *mpl*.
departure [di'pɑːtʃə*] *n* partida *f*, ida *f*; (*of train etc*) salida *f*; (*from norm*) desviación *f* (*from* de); **— time** hora *f* de salida; **new — rumbo** *m* nuevo; **this is a new — for us** esto es algo nuevo para nosotros; **to take one's —** marcharse.
depend [di'pend] *vi* **(a) it —s** eso depende, según; **it —s what you mean** depende de lo que Vd quiere decir.
  (b) to — on *circumstances, result etc* depender de; (*rely on*) contar con, confiar en; **can we — on you?** ¿podemos contar contigo?; **can we — on you to do it?** ¿podemos contar contigo para hacerlo?, ¿podemos confiar en que tú lo hagas?; **she — on her own resources** ella cuenta con sus propios recursos; **he has to — on his pen** tiene que vivir de su pluma; **you may — upon it** es cosa segura.
dependability [diˌpendə'biliti] *n* seguridad *f*; seriedad *f*, formalidad *f*.
dependable [di'pendəbl] *adj* *thing* seguro; *person* serio, formal.
dependant [di'pendənt] *n* familiar *mf* dependiente.
dependence [di'pendəns] *n* (*depending*) dependencio *f* (*on* de); (*reliance*) confianza *f* (*on* en); (*subordination*) subordinación *f* (*on* a).
dependency [di'pendənsi] *n* (*Pol*) posesión *f*.
dependent [di'pendənt] **1** *adj* dependiente (*on* de); (*subordinate*) subordinado (*on* a; *also Gram*); **to be — on** depender de. **2** *n* familiar *mf* dependiente.
depersonalize [diːˈpəːsənəlaiz] *vt* despersonalizar.
depict [di'pikt] *vt* representar, pintar.
depilatory [di'pilətəri] **1** *adj* depilatorio. **2** *n* depilatorio *m*.
deplete [di'pliːt] *vt* agotar; mermar, reducir.
depletion [di'pliːʃən] *n* agotamiento *m*; merma *f*, reducción *f*.
deplorable [di'plɔːrəbl] *adj* lamentable, deplorable; **it would be — if** sería lamentable que + *subj*.

deplorably [di'plɔːrəbli] *adv* lamentablemente, deplorablemente; **in — bad taste** de un mal gusto lamentable; **it has been — exaggerated** ha sido exagerado de un modo lamentable.

deplore [di'plɔː*] *vt* lamentar, deplorar; **it is to be —d** es de lamentar.

deploy [di'plɔi] **1** *vt* desplegar; (*fig*) organizar. **2** *vi* desplegarse.

deployment [di'plɔimənt] *n* despliegue *m*; (*fig*) organización *f*.

depopulate [diːˈpɔpjuleit] *vt* despoblar.

depopulation ['diːˌpɔpjuˈleiʃən] *n* despoblación *f*.

deport [di'pɔːt] **1** *vt* deportar. **2** *vr*: **to — oneself** comportarse.

deportation [ˌdiːpɔːˈteiʃən] *n* deportación *f*.

deportment [di'pɔːtmənt] *n* conducta *f*, comportamiento *m*; (*carriage*) porte *m*, modo *m* de andar.

depose [di'pəuz] **1** *vt* deponer. **2** *vi* declarar, deponer.

deposit [di'pɔzit] **1** *n* **(a)** (*Geol*) depósito *m*, yacimiento *m*; (*Chem, dregs*) poso *m*, sedimento *m*.
  (b) (*Fin etc*) depósito *m*; (*pledge*) señal *f*; (*act of —ing money in account*) imposición *f*, ingreso *m*; (*on hire purchase: on car*) depósito *m*, (*on house*) desembolso *m* inicial; **to have £50 on —** tener 50 libras en cuenta de ahorros; **to leave £50 —** hacer un desembolso inicial de 50 libras.
  2 *vt* **(a)** (*place, lay*) depositar; **eggs** poner.
  (b) (*entrust etc*) depositar (*in* en).
  (c) (*leave*) depositar (*with* en), dejar (*with* con).
  (d) (*Geol, Chem*) depositar, sedimentar.
  (e) (*Fin*) depositar; (*pledge*) dar para señal; (*money in account*) imponer, ingresar (*in* en); **to — £200 on a house** hacer un desembolso inicial de 200 libras para una casa.

deposition [ˌdiːpəˈziʃən] *n* deposición *f*; (*Law*) declaración *f*, deposición *f*.

depositor [di'pɔzitə*] *n* depositante *mf*, impositor *m*, ora *f*, imponente *mf*; cuentacorrentista *mf*.

depository [di'pɔzitəri] *n* depositaría *f*, almacén *m*; (*fig*) pozo *m*.

depot ['depəu] *n* (*storehouse*) depósito *m*, almacén *m*; (*Mil HQ*) depósito *m*; (*for vehicles*) parque *m*; (*buses, US Rail*) estación *f*.

depot ship ['depəuˈʃip] *n* buque *m* nodriza.

depravation [ˌdeprəˈveiʃən] *n* depravación *f*.

deprave [di'preiv] *vt* depravar.

depraved [di'preivd] *adj* depravado, perverso, vicioso.

depravity [di'præviti] *n* depravación *f*, perversión *f*.

deprecate ['deprikeit] *vt* desaprobar, lamentar.

deprecatingly ['deprikeitiŋli] *adv* con desaprobación.

deprecatory ['deprikətəri] *adj* de desaprobación.

depreciate [di'priːʃieit] **1** *vt* depreciar; (*fig*) desestimar. **2** *vi* depreciarse, perder valor, bajar de precio.

depreciation [diˌpriːʃiˈeiʃən] *n* depreciación *f*.

depredations [ˌdepriˈdeiʃənz] *npl* estragos *mpl*.

depress [di'pres] *vt* (*push down*) presionar, deprimir; **status** rebajar; **trade** paralizar; **price** hacer bajar; (*dispirit*) deprimir, abatir, desalentar.

depressed [di'prest] *adj* **area** deprimido, de elevado paro obrero; **person** abatido, desalentado, pesimista; **to feel — about** sentirse pesimista por.

depressing [di'presiŋ] *adj* triste, deprimente.

depressingly [di'presiŋli] *adv* tristemente, en tono pesimista; **it was a — familiar story** era la triste historia de siempre.

depression [di'preʃən] *n* (*Fin, Meteorol etc*) depresión *f*; (*slump*) crisis *f* económica, depresión *f*, bache *m*; (*in ground*) hoyo *m*; (*dejection*) depresión *f*, desaliento *m*, abatimiento *m*.

depressive [di'presiv] *adj* depresivo.

deprivation [ˌdepriˈveiʃən] *n* privación *f*; **a great —** una pérdida.

deprive [di'praiv] **1** *vt*: **to — someone of something** privar a uno de algo.
  2 *vr*: **to — oneself of something** privarse de algo; **don't — yourself!** ¡no te vayas a quedar sin nada!

deprived [di'praivd] *adj* **child** pobre.

depth [depθ] *n* **(a)** profundidad *f* (*also fig*); (*of room*) fondo *m*; (*width*) ancho *m*; (*of colour, feeling*) intensidad *f*; **defence in —** defensa *f* en profundidad; **to be 5 metres in —** tener una profundidad de 5 metros.
  (b) **—s: in the —s of the sea** en los abismos del mar; **from the —s of the mine** desde lo más hondo de la mina; (*fig*) **the —s of degradation** la mayor degradación; **the —s of despair** la mayor desesperación; **in the —s of one's heart** en lo más hondo del corazón; **in the —s of winter** en lo más recio del invierno.
  (c) he was out of his — le cubría el agua; **I'm out of my — with physics** yo no entiendo nada de

física; **to get out of one's —** meterse donde le cubre a uno, (*fig*) meterse en honduras.

depth charge ['depθtʃɑːdʒ] *n* carga *f* de profundidad.

deputation [ˌdepjuˈteiʃən] *n* diputación *f*, delegación *f*.

depute [di'pjuːt] *vt* diputar; **to — someone to do something** diputar a uno para que haga algo.

deputize ['depjutaiz] *vi*: **to — for someone** sustituir a uno, desempeñar las funciones de uno.

deputy ['depjuti] **1** *adj* suplente; **— head** subdirector *m*, ora *f*. **2** *n* sustituto *m*, suplente *m*; (*Pol*) diputado *m*; (*agent*) representante *m*.

derail [di'reil] *vt* hacer descarrilar.

derailment [di'reilmənt] *n* descarrilamiento *m*.

derange [di'reindʒ] *vt* desarreglar, descomponer; **person** volver loco; **to be —d** padecer un trastorno mental.

derangement [di'reindʒmənt] *n* desarreglo *m*; (*Med*) trastorno *m* mental.

derby ['dɑːbi] *n* (*US*) hongo *m* (*sombrero*).

derelict ['derilikt] **1** *adj* abandonado. **2** *n* (*Naut*) derrelicto *m*.

dereliction [ˌderiˈlikʃən] *n* abandono *m*; **— of duty** negligencia *f*.

deride [di'raid] *vt* ridiculizar, mofarse de.

de rigueur [dəriˈgəː*] *adv* de rigor.

derision [di'riʒən] *n* irrisión *f*, mofas *fpl*; **this was greeted with —** en esto hubo risas.

derisive [di'raisiv] *adj* burlón, mofador, irónico.

derisory [di'raisəri] *adj* **quantity etc** irrisorio, ridículo.

derivation [ˌderiˈveiʃən] *n* derivación *f*.

derivative [di'rivətiv] **1** *adj* derivado; **work** poco original. **2** *n* (*Gram, Chem*) derivado *m*.

derive [di'raiv] **1** *vt* derivar (*from* de); **profit, advantage** sacar, obtener (*from* de).
  2 *vi* derivar(se) (*from* de); **to — from, to be —d from** (*fig*) proceder de, provenir de.

dermatitis [ˌdəːməˈtaitis] *n* dermatitis *f*.

dermatologist [ˌdəːməˈtɔlədʒist] *n* dermatólogo *m*.

dermatology [ˌdəːməˈtɔlədʒi] *n* dermatología *f*.

derogatory [di'rɔgətəri] *adj* despectivo.

derrick ['derik] *n* grúa *f*; (*of oil well*) torre *f* de perforación.

dervish ['dəːviʃ] *n* derviche *m*; (*fig*) salvaje *m*.

desalinate [diːˈsælineit] *vt* desalinar, desalinizar.

desalination [diːˌsaliˈneiʃən] *n* desalación *f*, desalinización *f*.

descant ['deskænt] **1** *n* discante *m*. **2** *vi*: **to — on** disertar largamente sobre.

descend [di'send] **1** *vt* descender, bajar.
  2 *vi* descender, bajar (*from* de); **to — from ancestors etc** descender de; **to — on** caer sobre; (*as visitors*) invadir; **to — to** (*as inheritance*) pasar a; (*lower oneself*) rebajarse a; **to — to + ger** rebajarse a + *infin*.

descendant [di'sendənt] *n* descendiente *mf*; **to leave no —s** no dejar descendencia.

descent [di'sent] *n* (*Geog*) pendiente *f*, declive *m*; (*raid*) ataque *m* (*on* sobre), incursión *f*; (*coming down*) descendimiento *m* (*also Rel*), bajada *f*; (*fall*) descenso *m* (*in* de); (*origin*) descendencia *f* (*from* de).

describe [dis'kraib] *vt* describir (*also Geom*); **to — someone as** calificar a uno de.

description [dis'kripʃən] *n* descripción *f*; (*sort*) clase *f*, género *m*.

descriptive [dis'kriptiv] *adj* descriptivo.

descry [dis'krai] *vt* divisar.

desecrate ['desikreit] *vt* profanar.

desecration [ˌdesiˈkreiʃən] *n* profanación *f*.

desegregate [diːˈsegrəgeit] *vt* **school etc** abrir libremente a todas las razas; suprimir las leyes sobre la separación racial referentes a, suprimir la separación racial en.

desegregation ['diːˌsegrəˈgeiʃən] *n* acto *m* (*or* política *f etc*) de suprimir las leyes sobre la separación racial.

desensitize [diːˈsensitaiz] *vt* desensibilizar, insensibilizar; (*Phot*) hacer insensible a la luz.

desert ['dezət] **1** *adj* desierto. **2** *n* desierto *m*.

desert [di'zəːt] **1** *vt* (*Mil, Law etc*) desertar de; **person** abandonar, desamparar, dejar; **his luck —ed him** la suerte le abandonó.
  2 *vi* (*Mil*) desertar (*from* de, *to* a).

deserter [di'zəːtə*] *n* desertor *m*.

desertion [di'zəːʃən] *n* deserción *f* (*also Mil*), abandono *m*.

deserts [di'zəːts] *npl* lo merecido; **to get one's (just) —** llevar su merecido.

deserve [di'zəːv] **1** *vt* merecer, ser digno de; **he got what he —ed** llevó su merecido.
  2 *vi*: **to — well of** merecer ser bien tratado por; **to — to + infin** merecer + *infin*.

deservedly [di'zəːvidli] *adv* merecidamente.

deserving [di'zə:viŋ] *adj* meritorio; **to be — of** merecer, ser digno de.

déshabillé [,deizæ'bi:ei] *n* desabillé *m*.

desiccate ['desikeit] *vt* desecar.

desiccation [,desi'keiʃən] *n* desecación *f*.

desideratum [di,zidə'rɑ:təm] *n* desiderátum *m*.

design [di'zain] **1** *n* **(a)** (*Tech etc*) diseño *m*; (*pattern of cloth, wallpaper etc*) dibujo *m*; (*preliminary sketch*) bosquejo *m*; (*Theat, Cine*) boceto *m*; (*of building etc*) estilo *m*; (*ground plan*) distribución *f*; (*art of —*) dibujo *m*.

(b) (*aim*) intención *f*, propósito *m*; (*pej*) mala intención *f*; (*plan*) plan *m*, proyecto *m*; **grand —** plan *m* general, (*Mil*) estrategia *f* general; **by — inten-cionalmente; to have (one's) —s on** tener sus proyectos sobre, tener la mira puesta en.

2 *vt* (*contrive*) idear; (*plan*) proyectar; (*Tech*) diseñar, proyectar; *pattern* dibujar; (*sketch*) bosque-jar; **a well —ed house** una casa bien distribuida; **to be —ed to + infin** estar diseñado para + *infin*, estar proyectado para + *infin*; (*fig*) tener la intención de + *infin*, ir encaminado a + *infin*.

3 *vi*: **to — to + infin** proponerse + *infin*.

designate ['dezignit] *adj* designado, nombrado.

designate ['dezigneit] *vt* (*name*) denominar; (*appoint*) nombrar (*to + infin* para que + *subj*); (*point to*) señalar; (*destine*) designar.

designation [,dezig'neiʃən] *n* (*name*) denominación *f*; (*appointment*) nombramiento *m*.

designedly [di'zainidli] *adv* de propósito.

designer [di'zainə*] *n* (*Tech*) diseñador *m*, proyectista *m*; (*draughtsman*) delineante *m*; (*Art*) dibujante *m*; (*Theat*) escenógrafo *m*.

designing [di'zainiŋ] *adj* intrigante.

desirability [di,zaiərə'biliti] *n* lo apetecible, lo atractivo, carácter *m* atractivo; deseabilidad *f*, conveniencia *f*; **the — of the plan is not in question** nadie duda de lo atractivo que es este proyecto.

desirable [di'zaiərəbl] *adj* (*arousing desire*) apetecible, atractivo; (*proper*) deseable, conveniente; **I don't think it — to + infin** no creo que sea conveniente + *infin*.

desire [di'zaiə*] **1** *n* deseo *m* (*for* de, *to + infin* de + *infin*); **sexual —** instinto *m* sexual; **I haven't the least — to go** no tengo el menor deseo de ir; **to meet someone's —** satisfacer los deseos de uno.

2 *vt* **(a)** desear; querer tener; **to — to do** desear hacer; **what does madam —?** ¿qué manda la señora?

(b) to — someone to do something (*wish*) rogar a uno hacer algo, (*order*) mandar a uno hacer algo.

desirous [di'zaiərəs] *adj*: **— of** deseoso de; **to be — that** querer que + *subj*; **to be — to + infin** desear + *infin*.

desist [di'zist] *vi*: **to — from something** desistir de algo; **to — from + ger** dejar de + *infin*; **we begged him to —** le rogamos dejarlo, le rogamos no continuar.

desk [desk] *n* (*in office, study etc*) mesa *f* de trabajo; (*School*) pupitre *m*; (*bureau*) escritorio *m*.

desolate ['desəlit] *adj* (*lonely*) solitario; (*deserted*) desierto, deshabitado; (*ruinous*) arruinado; (*barren*) yermo, desierto; (*dreary*) triste; *person* triste, afligido.

desolate ['desəleit] *vt* asolar, arrasar; *person* afligir.

desolation [,desə'leiʃən] *n* (*act*) arrasamiento *m*; (*state*) desolación *f*, lo desierto *etc*; (*of person*) aflicción *f*.

despair [dis'pɛə*] **1** *n* desesperación *f*; **to be in —** estar desesperado.

2 *vi* perder la esperanza, desesperar(se) (*of* de); **his life is —ed of** se ha perdido la esperanza de salvarle la vida; **don't —!** ¡ánimo!

despairing [dis'pɛəriŋ] *adj* desesperado.

despairingly [dis'pɛəriŋli] *adv* desesperadamente.

despatch [dis'pætʃ] *n* = **dispatch.**

desperado [,despə'rɑ:dəu] *n* criminal *m*, bandido *m*.

desperate ['despərit] *adj* (*hopeless*) desesperado; *plight, situation* desesperado, muy grave; *urgency* apremiante; *need* extremo; *measure* arriesgado; *resistance* heroico; *effort* furioso, violento; (*reckless from despair*) dispuesto a arriesgarlo todo; **we are getting —** empezamos a perder la esperanza; **he's a — man** es un hombre peligroso.

desperately ['despəritli] *adv* desesperadamente; *fight etc* furiosamente, heroicamente; **we — need it** lo necesitamos urgentemente; **— bad** terriblemente malo; **— ill** gravemente enfermo.

desperation [,despə'reiʃən] *n* desesperación *f*; **in —** desesperado.

despicable [dis'pikəbl] *adj* vil, despreciable.

despise [dis'paiz] *vt* despreciar, desdeñar.

despite [dis'pait] *prep* a pesar de.

despoil [dis'pɔil] *vt* despojar (*of* de).

despondency [dis'pɔndənsi] *n* abatimiento *m*, desaliento *m*.

despondent [dis'pɔndənt] *adj* abatido, deprimido; *letter etc* de tono triste, pesimista; **he was very — about our chances** discutió en términos pesimistas nuestras posibilidades.

despot ['despɔt] *n* déspota *m*.

despotic [des'pɔtik] *adj* despótico.

despotically [des'pɔtikəli] *adv* despóticamente.

despotism ['despətizəm] *n* despotismo *m*.

dessert [di'zə:t] *n* postre *m*; **what is there for —?** ¿qué hay de postre?

dessertspoon [di'zə:tspu:n] *n* cuchara *f* de postre.

destination [,desti'neiʃən] *n* destino *m* (*also Rail etc*), paradero *m*.

destine ['destin] *vt* destinar (*for, to* para); **to be —d to + infin** estar llamado a + *infin*; **it was —d to fail** estuvo condenado a fracasar; **it was —d to happen this way** tuvo forzosamente que ocurrir así.

destiny ['destini] *n* destino *m*.

destitute ['destitju:t] *adj* **(a)** indigente, desamparado; **to be —** vivir en la miseria. **(b) — of** desprovisto de.

destitution [,desti'tju:ʃən] *n* indigencia *f*, miseria *f*.

destroy [dis'trɔi] *vt* destruir; (*kill*) matar; *pet* sacrificar; *vermin* exterminar; (*finish*) aniquilar, acabar con.

destroyer [dis'trɔiə*] *n* destructor *m*.

destructible [dis'trʌktəbl] *adj* destructible.

destruction [dis'trʌkʃən] *n* destrucción *f*; (*fig*) ruina *f*, perdición *f*.

destructive [dis'trʌktiv] *adj* destructivo, destructor; *animal* dañino; **to be — of** ser nocivo a, ser peligroso para, ser perjudicial para.

destructiveness [dis'trʌktivnis] *n* espíritu *m* de destrucción.

destructor [dis'trʌktə*] *n* incinerador *m* de basuras.

desuetude [di'sjuitju:d] *n* desuso *m*; **to fall into —** caer en desuso.

desultory ['desəltəri] *adj* *way of working etc* poco metódico; *fire etc* intermitente, irregular; (*dis-connected*) inconexo.

detach [di'tætʃ] *vt* separar; (*unstick*) despegar; (*Mil*) destacar.

detachable [di'tætʃəbl] *adj* separable; (*Tech*) des-montable.

detached [di'tætʃt] *adj* separado, suelto; *collar* postizo; *house* independiente; (*fig*) imparcial, objetivo; **to become —** separarse, desprenderse; **they live — from everything** viven desligados de todo; **to take a — view of something** considerar algo objetivamente.

detachment [di'tætʃmənt] *n* (*act*) separación *f*; (*Mil*) destacamento *m*; (*fig*) imparcialidad *f*, objetividad *f*.

detail ['di:teil] **1** *n* detalle *m*, pormenor *m*; (*Mil*) destacamento *m*; **in —** en detalle, detalladamente; **to go into —s** entrar en detalles, pormenorizar; **they planned it down to the last —** lo planearon todo hasta en los menores detalles.

2 *vt* detallar, referir con sus pormenores; (*Mil*) destacar (*to + infin* para + *infin*).

detailed ['di:teild] *adj* detallado, pormenorizado.

detain [di'tein] *vt* (*arrest*) detener; (*keep waiting*) retener; **I was —ed at the office** tuve que quedarme a trabajar en la oficina; **I was —ed by fog** el retraso se debe a la niebla.

detect [di'tekt] *vt* descubrir; (*perceive*) percibir; *crime* resolver, *criminal* identificar; (*Tech, by radar etc*) detectar.

detectable [di'tektəbl] *adj* perceptible.

detection [di'tekʃən] *n* descubrimiento *m*; percepción *f*; resolución *f*, identificación *f*; detección *f*.

detective [di'tektiv] *n* detective *m*.

detective story [di'tektiv,stɔ:ri] *n* novela *f* policíaca.

detector [di'tektə*] *n* (*Tech*) detector *m*.

détente ['deitã:nt] *n* detente *f*.

detention [di'tenʃən] *n* detención *f*, arresto *m*; **preventive —** arresto *m* preventivo.

deter [di'tə:*] *vt* (*discourage*) desalentar; (*dissuade*) disuadir (*from + ger* de + *infin*); (*prevent*) impedir (*from doing* hacer); *enemy etc* refrenar; **I was —red by the cost** el precio me hizo abandonar la idea; **a weapon which —s nobody** un arma que no refrena a nadie, un arma sin fuerza disuasoria; **don't let the weather — you** no dejes de hacerlo por el mal tiempo.

detergent [di'tə:dʒənt] **1** *adj* detergente. **2** *n* detergente *m*.

deteriorate [di'tiəriəreit] *vi* empeorar, deteriorarse.

deterioration [di,tiəriə'reiʃən] *n* deterioro *m*, empeoramiento *m* (*in* de).

determination [di,tə:mi'neiʃən] n (act) determinación f; (resolve) resolución f; **he set off with great —** partió muy resuelto; **in his — to do it** estando resuelto a hacerlo.

determine [di'tə:min] **1** vt (a) (ascertain, define) determinar; date etc señalar, fijar; scope, limits, boundary definir; future course, person's fate decidir; dispute determinar, resolver; (be the deciding factor in) determinar; **to — what is to be done** decidir lo que hay que hacer; **to — whether something is true** decidir si algo es verdad; **we couldn't — who it was** no podíamos decidir quién era; **demand —s supply** la demanda determina la oferta; **to be —d by** depender de.
  (b) (impel) **this —d him to go** esto le determinó a ir.
  (c) (resolve) **to — to do something** decidir hacer algo, resolverse a hacer algo.
  2 vi: **to — on** optar por.

determined [di'tə:mind] adj person resuelto; effort resuelto, enérgico; **he's very — about it** está muy empeñado en ello; **to be — to do something** estar resuelto a hacer algo.

determining [di'tə:miniŋ] adj decisivo.

determinism [di'tə:minizəm] n determinismo m.

deterrent [di'terənt] **1** adj disuasivo, disuasorio.
  2 n freno m, impedimento m (on, to para); medida f represiva; (Mil) fuerza f disuasiva, fuerza f disuasoria, amenaza f; **the nuclear —** la amenaza nuclear; **to act as a — to** servir como un freno para, ser una amenaza a, refrenar.

detest [di'test] vt detestar, aborrecer.

detestable [di'testəbl] adj detestable, aborrecible.

detestation [,di:tes'teiʃən] n detestación f, aborrecimiento m; **to hold in —** aborrecer.

dethrone [di'θrəun] vt destronar.

detonate ['detəneit] **1** vt hacer detonar. **2** vi detonar, estallar.

detonation [,detə'neiʃən] n detonación f.

detonator ['detəneitə*] n detonador m, cápsula f fulminante.

detour ['deituə*] n rodeo m, vuelta f; **to make a —** desviarse, hacer un rodeo.

detract [di'trækt] vi: **to — from** quitar mérito (or atractivo etc) a, desvirtuar, restar valor a.

detractor [di'træktə*] n detractor m, ora f.

detriment ['detrimənt] n perjuicio m; **to the — of** en perjuicio de, en detrimento de.

detrimental [,detri'mentl] adj perjudicial (to a, para).

detritus [di'traitəs] n detrito m, talud m detrítico.

de trop [də'trəu] adv: **to be —** estar de más, sobrar.

deuce [dju:s] **1** adv (Tennis) a dos.
  2 n: **a — of a row** un tremendo jaleo; **a — of a mess** una terrible confusión; **the — it is!** ¡qué demonio!; **what the ...?** ¿qué demonios ...?; **where the — ...?** ¿dónde demonios ...?; **to play the — with** arruinar, estropear.

deuced [dju:st] **1** adj maldito. **2** adv diabólicamente, terriblemente.

deuterium [dju:'tiəriəm] n deuterio m.

devaluate [di:'væljueit] vt desvalorizar, desvalorar.

devaluation [,di:vælju'eiʃən] n desvalorización f, devaluación f.

devalue ['di:'vælju:] vt desvalorizar, devaluar.

devastate ['devəsteit] vt devastar, asolar; person hundir en la tristeza; **we were simply —d** la noticia nos produjo una enorme tristeza.

devastating ['devəsteitiŋ] adj devastador; (fig) arrollador.

devastation [,devə'steiʃən] n (act) devastación f; (state) devastación f, ruinas fpl.

develop [di'veləp] **1** vt desarrollar (also Math); desenvolver; (encourage) fomentar; process perfeccionar; land urbanizar; resources, mine etc explotar; (Phot) revelar; engine trouble empezar a tener; disease coger, empezar a sufrir de, mostrar los síntomas de; tendency coger, dar en; liking mostrar, acusar; power rendir, producir.
  2 vi (a) desarrollarse; progresar, avanzar; evolucionar; **how is the book —ing?** ¿qué tal te va el libro?
  (b) (appear) aparecer, mostrarse.

developer [di'veləpə*] n (Phot) revelador m.

developing [di'veləpiŋ] adj country en vías de desarrollo.

development [di'veləpmənt] n (a) desarrollo m; progreso m; evolución f; (encouragement) fomento m; (of land) urbanización f; (of resources) explotación f; (Phot) revelado m; **— area** polo m de promoción.
  (b) **new —** cambio m, novedad f.

deviate ['di:vieit] vi desviarse (from de).

deviation [,di:vi'eiʃən] n desviación f (also Med).

deviationism [,di:vi'eiʃənizəm] n desviacionismo m.

deviationist [,di:vi'eiʃənist] **1** adj desviacionista. **2** n desviacionista mf.

device [di'vais] n (a) (Mech) aparato m, mecanismo m, dispositivo m; **nuclear —** ingenio m nuclear.
  (b) (scheme) estratagema f, recurso m.
  (c) (emblem) emblema m; (motto) lema m.
  (d) **to leave someone to his own —s** dejar a uno hacer lo que le dé la gana, dejar a uno divertirse con sus propias cosas.

devil ['devl] **1** n (a) diablo m, demonio m; (fire) arrojo m, energía f; little **—** diablillo m; printer's **—** aprendiz m de imprenta; **a poor —** un pobre diablo.
  (b) **the —!** ¡demonio!; **the — it is!** ¡qué demonio!; **what the ...?** ¿qué demonios ...?; **like the —** como el demonio.
  (c) **a — of a mess** una terrible confusión; **a — of a noise** un ruido de todos los demonios; **we had the — of a job, we had the —'s own job** nos costó muchísimo trabajo (to get obtener); **it's a — of a problem** es un problema dificilísimo.
  (d) **the — take it!** ¡que se lo lleve el diablo!; **go to the —!** ¡vete al diablo!; **to be between the — and the deep blue sea** estar entre la espada y la pared; **better the — we know** vale más lo malo conocido que lo bueno por conocer; **the — finds work for idle hands** cuando el diablo no tiene que hacer con el rabo mata moscas; **to give the — his due** a cada uno lo suyo; para ser justo hasta con los adversarios; **there'll be the — to pay** esto nos va a costar muy caro, ahí será el diablo; **to play the — with** arruinar, estropear; **to raise the —** armar la gorda; **talk of the —!** ¡hablando del ruin de Roma, por la puerta asoma!
  2 vt meat asar con mucho picante.
  3 vi: **to — for** (Law) trabajar de aprendiz para.

devilfish ['devlfiʃ] n raya f, manta f.

devilish ['devliʃ] **1** adj diabólico. **2** adv sumamente, la mar de.

devil-may-care ['devlmei'kɛə*] adj despreocupado; (rash) temerario, arriesgado.

devilment ['devlmənt] n diablura f.

devilry ['devlri] n (wickedness) maldad f, crueldad f; (mischief) diablura f.

devious ['di:viəs] adj path tortuoso; (means) intrincado, enrevesado; person taimado.

devise [di'vaiz] vt idear, inventar.

devitalize [di:'vaitəlaiz] vt debilitar, privar de vitalidad.

devoid [di'vɔid] adj: **— of** desprovisto de.

devolution [,di:və'lu:ʃən] n (Pol etc) delegación f (de poderes).

devolve [di'vɔlv] vi: **to — upon** incumbir a, corresponder a; **it —s upon me to + infin** me toca a mí + infin.

devote [di'vəut] **1** vt dedicar (to a; to + ger a + infin); **he is —d to her** la quiere con verdadera devoción; **this room is —d to Goya** esta sala está dedicada a Goya; **this chapter is —d to politics** este capítulo trata de la política.
  2 vr: **to — oneself to** dedicarse a.

devoted [di'vəutid] adj leal, fiel.

devotedly [di'vəutidli] adv con devoción.

devotee [,devəu'ti:] n devoto m, a f (of de).

devotion [di'vəuʃən] n devoción f (to a); (to studies etc) dedicación f (to a); (of friend etc) lealtad f; **—s** oraciones fpl.

devotional [di'vəuʃənl] adj piadoso, devoto.

devour [di'vauə*] vt devorar (also fig), comerse; **to be —ed with curiosity** no caber en sí de curiosidad.

devouring [di'vauəriŋ] adj (fig) absorbente.

devout [di'vaut] adj devoto, piadoso.

devoutly [di'vautli] adv con devoción, piadosamente.

dew [dju:] n rocío m.

dewdrop ['dju:drɔp] n gota f de rocío.

dewlap ['dju:læp] n papada f.

dewpond ['dju:pɔnd] n charca f formada por el rocío.

dewy ['dju:i] adj rociado; lleno de rocío; eyes húmedo.

dewy-eyed ['dju:i'aid] adj (fig) ingenuo.

dexterity [deks'teriti] n destreza f.

dextrose ['dekstrəus] n dextrosa f.

dextrous ['dekstrəs] adj diestro.

dextrously ['dekstrəsli] adv diestramente.

diabetes [,daiə'bi:ti:z] n diabetes f.

diabetic [,daiə'betik] **1** adj diabético. **2** n diabético m, a f.

diabolic [,daiə'bɔlik] adj diabólico.

diabolic(al) [,daiə'bɔlik(əl)] adj diabólico.

diacritic [,daiə'kritik] **1** adj (also —al) diacrítico. **2** nm signo m diacrítico.

diadem ['daiədem] n diadema f.

diaeresis [dai'erisis] n diéresis f.

diagnose ['daiəgnəuz] vt diagnosticar.

diagnosis [.daiəg'nəusis] n diagnóstico m.
diagnostic [.daiəg'nɔstik] adj diagnóstico.
diagonal [dai'ægənl] 1 adj diagonal 2 n diagonal f.
diagonally [dai'ægənəli] adv diagonalmente.
diagram ['daiəgræm] n diagrama m, esquema m.
diagrammatic [.daiəgrə'mætik] adj esquemático.
dial ['daiəl] 1 n esfera f, cuadrante m; (Tel) disco m; (sl) cara f. 2 vt marcar.
dialect ['daiəlekt] 1 n dialecto m. 2 attr dialectal.
dialectal [.daiə'lektl] adj dialectal.
dialectic [.daiə'lektik] 1 adj dialéctico; (Gram) dialectal. 2 n (also —s) dialéctica f.
dialectical [.daiə'lektikəl] adj dialéctico; (Gram) dialectal.
dialling tone ['daiəliŋ.təun] n tono m de marcar.
dialogue ['daiəlɔg] n diálogo m.
diameter [dai'æmitə*] n diámetro m.
diametrical [.daiə'metrikəl] adj diametral.
diametrically [.daiə'metrikəli] adv: — opposed to diametralmente opuesto a.
diamond ['daiəmənd] n diamante m; —s (Cards) diamantes mpl, carreau m, (in Spanish pack) oros mpl; rough — diamante m bruto (also fig); — cut -— tal para cual.
diamond-cutter ['daiəmənd,kʌtə*] n diamantista m.
diamond-shaped ['daiəmənd,ʃeipt] adj de forma de diamante.
Diana [dai'ænə] f Diana.
diaper ['daiəpə*] n (US) pañal m.
diaphanous [dai'æfənəs] adj diáfano.
diaphragm ['daiəfræm] n diafragma m.
diarist ['daiərist] n diarista mf.
diarrhoea [.daiə'ri:ə] n diarrea f.
diary ['daiəri] n diario m; (engagement —) agenda f, diario m.
diatonic [.daiə'tɔnik] adj diatónico.
diatribe ['daiətraib] n diatriba f.
dibble ['dibl] 1 n plantador m. 2 vt (also to — in) plantar con plantador.
dibs [dibz] n (sl) parné m.
dice [dais] 1 npl dados mpl; (shapes) cubitos mpl, cuadritos mpl. 2 vt vegetables cortar en cuadritos. 3 vi jugar a los dados; to — with death jugar con la muerte.
dicey ['daisi] adj (fam) incierto, dudoso; peligroso; difícil.
dichotomy [di'kɔtəmi] n dicotomía f.
Dick [dik] m nombre cariñoso de **Richard.**
dick [dik] n (US sl) detective m.
dickens ['dikinz] (euph) en muchas frases = **devil.**
dicker ['dikə*] vi (a) vacilar, titubear. (b) (Comm) regatear.
dickey, dicky¹ ['diki] n (fam) (a) (Zool) pajarito m. (b) (shirt front) pechera f postiza. (c) (Aut) asiento m trasero.
dicky² ['diki] adj (fam) poco firme, inestable; (Med) to feel — sentirse algo indispuesto; to have a — heart tener una debilidad cardíaca.
dictaphone ['diktəfəun] n (Protected Trade Name) dictáfono m.
dictate ['dikteit] n mandato m; —s dictados mpl.
dictate [dik'teit] 1 vt (say aloud) dictar; (order) mandar, disponer; I will not be —d to yo no estoy a las órdenes de nadie.
2 vi: to — to one's secretary dictar a su secretaria.
dictation [dik'teiʃən] n (a) dictado m; to take —, to write at the — of escribir al dictado de. (b) (order) mandato m.
dictator [dik'teitə*] n dictador m.
dictatorial [.diktə'tɔ:riəl] adj dictatorio; manner etc dictatorial, imperioso.
dictatorship [dik'teitəʃip] n dictadura f.
diction ['dikʃən] n dicción f; lengua f, lenguaje m.
dictionary ['dikʃənri] n diccionario m.
dictum ['diktəm] n, pl **dicta** ['diktə] sentencia f, aforismo m; (Law) dictamen m.
did [did] pret of **do.**
didactic [dai'dæktik] adj didáctico.
diddle ['didl] vt (fam) to — someone out of something estafar algo a uno.
didn't ['didənt] = **did not.**
die¹ [dai] vi morir (from, of de; for por); (wither) marchitarse; (disappear) desvanecerse, desaparecer; (light) palidecer, extinguirse; to — like flies morir como chinches; we nearly died! (fam) era para morirse de risa; never say —! ¡ánimo!, ¡mientras hay vida hay esperanza!; to — away acabarse gradualmente; desaparecer; (sound) cesar, dejar poco a poco de oírse; to — down (fire) apagarse (wind) perder su fuerza, amainar; (discontent etc) sosegarse; (battle etc) hacerse menos violento; the custom dies hard la costumbre tarda bastante en

desaparecer; to — off morir; to — out extinguirse, desaparecer; to be dying for something morirse por algo, perecerse por algo; to be dying to + infin morirse por + infin; to — a violent death tener una muerte violenta.
die² [dai] n (a) (pl dice [dais]) dado m; the — is cast la suerte está echada. (b) (pl dies [daiz]) cuño m, troquel m; matriz f.
die-casting ['dai'ka:stiŋ] n pieza f fundida a troquel.
diehard ['daiha:d] 1 adj intransigente, cerrado, acérrimo. 2 n incondicional m, intransigente m.
dieresis [dai'erisis] n (US) = **diaeresis.**
diesel-electric ['di:zəli'lektrik] adj dieseleléctrico.
Diesel engine ['di:zəl,endʒin] n motor m Diesel.
Diesel oil ['di:zəl,ɔil] n gas-oil m, gasóleo m (Acad).
die-sinker ['dai,siŋkə*] n grabador m de troqueles.
diet¹ ['daiət] 1 n régimen m, dieta f; to be on a — estar a dieta; to put someone on a — poner a uno a dieta. 2 vi estar a dieta.
diet² ['daiət] n (Pol) dieta f.
dietary ['daiətəri] adj dietético.
dietetic [.daii'tetik] 1 adj dietético. 2 —s n dietética f.
dietician [.daii'tiʃən] n dietético m, dieteta mf.
differ ['difə*] vi (a) they — (things) son distintos, (persons) no están de acuerdo; the texts — los textos discrepan.
(b) to — from ser distinto de, diferenciarse de, discrepar de; how does this — from that? ¿en qué se diferencia éste de aquél?
(c) (personal subject) I beg to — tengo que decir que no estoy de acuerdo; we —ed about it no estábamos de acuerdo sobre ello; I — from you no estoy de acuerdo contigo; I — from your opinion discrepo de tu opinión, no comparto tu opinión.
difference ['difrəns] n diferencia f; — of opinion desacuerdo m, (euph) controversia f, (euph: quarrel) riña f; a novel with a — una novela que tiene algo distintivo; it makes no — lo mismo da; it makes a lot of — importa mucho; what — does it make? ¿qué más da?; it will make no — to us no nos afectará en lo más mínimo; I see no — between them no les veo diferencia alguna; to split the — partir la diferencia.
different ['difrənt] adj diferente, distinto (from de).
differently ['difrəntli] adv de modo distinto, de otro modo.
differential [.difə'renʃəl] 1 adj diferencial. 2 n (Math, Aut) diferencial f.
differentiate [.difə'renʃieit] 1 vt distinguir (from de). 2 vi diferenciarse (also Bio); to — between two things distinguir entre dos cosas.
difficult ['difikəlt] adj difícil; to make life — for someone hacer la vida imposible a uno.
difficulty ['difikəlti] n dificultad f; (jam) apuro m, aprieto m; to get into difficulties hacerse un lío, meterse en apuros, (eg while swimming) encontrarse sin fuerzas para continuar, (ship) encontrarse en peligro; to have — in breathing tener la respiración penosa; he's having difficulties with his wife está a malas con su mujer; we have — in getting enough staff es difícil encontrar bastante personal; I find — in walking encuentro difícil el ir a pie; to make difficulties for someone poner estorbos a uno; I see no — in admitting that no hay dificultad para reconocer que.
diffidence ['difidəns] n timidez f, falta f de confianza en sí mismo.
diffident ['difidənt] adj tímido, falto de confianza en sí mismo.
diffidently ['difidəntli] adv tímidamente, con timidez.
diffract [di'frækt] vt difractar.
diffraction [di'frækʃən] n difracción f.
diffuse [di'fju:s] adj difuso; (long-winded) prolijo.
diffuse [di'fju:z] 1 vt difundir. 2 vi difundirse.
diffused [di'fju:zd] adj difuso.
diffusion [di'fju:ʒən] n difusión f.
dig [dig] 1 n (a) (archaeological etc) excavación f. (b) (prod) empujón m; (with elbow) codazo m. (c) (remark) indirecta f, zumba f; to have a — at aludir irónicamente a, tomar el pelo a.
2 (irr: pret and ptp dug) vt (a) cavar, excavar; (of animals) escarbar; garden cultivar, patch of earth remover con laya; coal extraer, sacar; teeth, nails hincar (into en); to — in manure añadir abonos al suelo; to — out hole excavar; (buried object) sacar cavando, extraer; thorn in flesh extraer; (fig) sacar, buscar; to — up desenterrar (also fig), descubrir; potatoes sacar; plant desarraigar; roadway etc levantar.
(b) (prod) empujar, dar un codazo a; to — someone in the ribs dar a uno un codazo en las costillas.

(c) (*sl*) **I don't — jazz** no me gusta el jazz, el jazz no me dice nada.

3 *vi* **(a)** cavar; **to — deeper into a subject** ahondar en un tema; **to — for gold** cavar en busca de oro; **to — in** (*Mil*) atrincherarse; (*fam*) empezar a comer; **to — into** *reserves etc* consumir, devorar; **he dug into his pocket** metió la mano en el bolsillo; **to — into a meal** empezar a zamparse una comida.

(b) (*fam: lodge*) alojarse, estar alojado, hospedarse.

digest ['daidʒest] *n* resumen *m*; (*Law*) digesto *m*.

digest [dai'dʒest] *vt food* digerir; (*think over*) meditar; *knowledge, territory* asimilar; *insult* tragarse; *opinion* aceptar.

digestible [di'dʒestʃbl] *adj* digerible; **easily —** fácil de digerir.

digestion [di'dʒestʃn] *n* digestión *f*.

digestive [di'dʒestiv] *adj* digestivo. ··

digger ['digə*] *n* cavador *m*; (*archaeological*) excavador *m*, ora *f*; (*fam*) australiano *m*.

diggings ['diginz] *npl* (*archaeological*) excavaciones *fpl*; (*fam*) pensión *f*, alojamiento *m*.

digit ['didʒit] *n* dígito *m*.

digital ['didʒitəl] *adj* digital.

digitalis [ˌdidʒi'teilis] *n* digital *f*.

dignified ['dignifaid] *adj* grave, solemne; *gait etc* majestuoso; *action* decoroso; **it's not — to** + *infin* no es elegante + *infin*.

dignify ['dignifai] *vt* dar un título altisonante a.

dignitary ['dignitəri] *n* dignatario *m*, dignidad *f*.

dignity ['digniti] *n* dignidad *f*; **it would be beneath my — to** + *infin* desmerecería de mi dignidad + *infin*; **to stand on one's —** ponerse en su lugar.

digress [dai'gres] *vi* hacer una digresión; **to — from** apartarse de; **but I —** pero vamos al grano.

digression [dai'greʃən] *n* digresión *f*.

digs [digz] *npl* (*fam*) pensión *f*, alojamiento *m*.

dike [daik] *n* (*embankment*) dique *m* (*also fig*); (*ditch*) canal *m*, acequia *f*.

dilapidated [di'læpideitid] *adj building etc* desmoronado, ruinoso; *vehicle etc* desvencijado.

dilapidation [di,læpi'deiʃən] *n* estado *m* ruinoso; lo desvencijado.

dilate [dai'leit] **1** *vt* dilatar. **2** *vi* dilatarse; **to — upon** dilatarse sobre.

dilation [dai'leiʃən] *n* dilatación *f*.

dilatory ['dilətəri] *adj* tardo, lento; **to be — in** **replying** tardar mucho en contestar.

dilemma [dai'lemə] *n* dilema *m*; **to be in a —** estar en un dilema.

dilettante [ˌdili'tænti] *n*, *pl* **dilettanti** [ˌdili'tænti] diletante *mf*.

diligence ['dilidʒəns] *n* diligencia *f*.

diligent ['dilidʒənt] *adj* diligente.

diligently ['dilidʒəntli] *adv* diligentemente.

dillydally ['dilidæli] *vi* (*fam*) vacilar; (*loiter*) perder el tiempo.

dilute [dai'luːt] **1** *adj* diluido. **2** *vt* diluir; (*fig*) adulterar.

dilution [dai'luːʃən] *n* dilución *f*; (*fig*) adulteración *f*.

dim [dim] **1** *adj light* débil; *sight* turbio; *room etc* oscuro, sombrío; *object, outline* indistinto, confuso; (*fam*) *opinion* poco favorable; *person* lerdo.

2 *vt light* reducir la intensidad de; *headlamps* poner a media luz; (*fig*) *splendour* ofuscar, oscurecer; *memory* borrar.

dime [daim] *n* (*US*) moneda de 10 *centavos*; **— novel** novelucha *f*.

dimension [di'menʃən] *n* dimensión *f*.

diminish [di'miniʃ] **1** *vt* disminuir. **2** *vi* disminuir(se).

diminishing [di'miniʃiŋ] *adj* menguante.

diminuendo [di,mini'uːendəu] *n* (*Mus*) diminuendo *m*.

diminution [ˌdimi'njuːʃən] *n* disminución *f*.

diminutive [di'minjutiv] **1** *adj* diminuto; (*Gram*) diminutivo. **2** *n* diminutivo *m*.

dimly ['dimli] *adv shine etc* débilmente; *see* confusamente; **one could — make out forms** se veían indistintamente unos bultos.

dimness ['dimnis] *n* debilidad *f*; lo turbio; oscuridad *f*, semioscuridad *f*, lo sombrío; lo indistinto, lo confuso; lo lerdo.

dimple ['dimpl] **1** *n* hoyuelo *m*. **2** *vt* formar hoyuelos en; *water* rizar. **3** *vi* formarse hoyuelos; (*water*) rizarse.

dimwit ['dimwit] *n* (*fam*) imbécil *mf*.

dim-witted ['dim'witid] *adj* (*fam*) lerdo, imbécil.

din [din] **1** *n* estruendo *m*, estrépito *m*.

2 *vt*: **to —'something into someone** hacer que uno se dé cuenta de algo a fuerza de repetírselo; **I had it —ned into me as a child** lo aprendí de niño a fuerza de repeticiones.

3 *vi*: **it —s in my ears** me taladra el oído.

dinar ['diːnɑː*] *n* dínar *m*.

dine [dain] **1** *vt* dar de cenar a; **they —d me very well** me dieron muy bien de cenar.

2 *vi* cenar; **to — off, to — on** cenar; **to — out** cenar fuera; **to — out on a story** ser invitado a cenar a costa de un cuento.

diner ['dainə*] *n* comensal *m*; (*Rail*) coche-comedor *m*.

dinette [di'net] *n* comedor *m* pequeño, comedorcito *m*.

ding-dong ['diŋ'dɔŋ] **1** *n*: **—!** ¡din don! **2** *adj battle* furioso, muy reñido.

dinghy ['diŋgi] *n* bote *m*; (*Aer*) **rubber —** lancha *f* neumática.

dinginess ['dindʒinis] *n* lo deslustrado, deslucimiento *m*; color *m* oscuro; lo sombrío, oscuridad *f*; lo sucio.

dingo ['diŋgəu] *n*, *pl* **dingoes** ['diŋgəuz] dingo *m*.

dingy ['dindʒi] *adj* (*dull*) deslustrado, deslucido; (*dark in colour*) de color oscuro; *room etc* sombrío, oscuro; (*dirty*) sucio.

dining car ['dainiŋkɑː*] *n* coche-comedor *m*.

dining room ['dainiŋrum] *n* comedor *m*.

dinky ['diŋki] *adj* (*fam*) (*small*) pequeñito; (*nice*) mono, precioso.

dinner ['dinə*] *n* (*evening meal*) cena *f*; (*lunch*) comida *f*; (*public feast*) cena *f*, banquete *m*; **can you come to —?** ¿puede venir a cenar?; **to have —** cenar, comer; **when he retired they gave him a —** cuando se jubiló le obsequiaron con una cena.

dinner jacket ['dinə,dʒækit] *n* smoking *m*, esmoquin *m* (*Acad*).

dinner party ['dinə,pɑːti] *n* cena *f*.

dinner service ['dinə,səːvis] *n* vajilla *f*.

dinner suit ['dinəsuːt] *n* smoking *m*, esmoquin *m* (*Acad*).

dinner table ['dinə,teibl] *n* mesa *f* de comedor.

dinner time ['dinətaim] *n* hora *f* de cenar (or comer).

dinosaur ['dainəsɔː*] *n* dinosaurio *m*.

dint [dint] **1** *n*: **by — of** a fuerza de. **2** *vt* abollar.

diocesan [dai'ɔsisən] *adj* diocesano.

diocese ['daiəsis] *n* diócesis *f*.

dip [dip] **1** *n* **(a)** (*bath, bathe*) baño *m*; **to go for a —** ir a bañarse.

(b) (*Geol*) buzamiento *m*; (*of horizon*) depresión *f*; (*slope*) pendiente *f*; inclinación *f*; (*to one side*) ladeo *m*.

(c) *lucky* —— (*approx*) tómbola *f*.

2 *vt* **(a)** (*put into liquid*) bañar, mojar (**in, into** en); *pen* mojar; *ladle, scoop etc* meter; *flag* bajar, saludar con; *headlamps* poner a media luz.

(b) **to — water out with a bucket** sacar agua con un cubo.

3 *vi* **(a)** (*slope down*) inclinarse hacia abajo; (*Geol*) buzar; **the road —s into the valley** la carretera baja hacia el valle.

(b) (*move down*) (*bird, plane*) bajar; **the sun —ped below the hill** el sol desapareció tras la colina.

(c) **to — into one's pocket** meter la mano en el bolsillo; **to — into a book** hojear un libro, leer distraídamente un libro.

diphtheria [dif'θiəriə] *n* difteria *f*.

diphthong ['difθɔŋ] *n* diptongo *m*.

diphthongize ['difθɔŋaiz] **1** *vt* diptongar. **2** *vi* diptongarse.

diploma [di'pləumə] *n* diploma *m*.

diplomacy [di'pləuməsi] *n* diplomacia *f*.

diplomat ['dipləmæt] *n* diplomático *m*.

diplomatic [ˌdiplə'mætik] *adj* diplomático.

diplomatically [ˌdiplə'mætikəli] *adv* diplomáticamente.

diplomatist [di'pləumətist] *n* diplomático *m*.

dipper[1] ['dipə*] *n* (*Orn*) mirlo *m* acuático.

dipper[2] ['dipə*] *n*: **big —** montaña *f* rusa.

dippy ['dipi] *adj* (*sl*) chiflado.

dipso ['dipsəu] (*fam*) **1** *adj* dipsomaníaco. **2** *n* dipsomaníaco *m*, a *f*, dipsómano *m*, a *f*.

dipsomania [ˌdipsəu'meiniə] *n* dipsomanía *f*.

dipsomaniac [ˌdipsəu'meiniæk] *n* dipsomaníaco *m*, a *f*, dipsómano *m*, a *f*.

dipstick ['dipstik] *n* varilla *f* para comprobar el nivel del aceite (*etc*).

dire [daiə*] *adj* horrendo, calamitoso.

direct [dai'rekt] **1** *adj* directo; *current* continuo; *answer* claro, inequívoco; *manner, character* abierto, franco.

2 *adv* (**in a — manner**) directamente; (*straight*) derecho, en línea recta.

3 *vt* **(a)** *letter, remark, gaze, attention, film etc* dirigir (**at, to** a).

(b) **can you — me to the shop?** ¿me hace el favor de decirme dónde está la tienda?, ¿podría Vd indicarme la dirección de la tienda?.

(c) (*control*) dirigir, gobernar, controlar.

(d) (*order*) mandar; **to — that** mandar que; **to**

— **someone to do something** mandar a uno hacer algo.
direction [di'rekʃən] n (a) (act of managing) dirección f.
(b) (course) dirección f; **in the — of** en la dirección de, hacia; **in the opposite —** en sentido contrario; **in all —s** por todos lados; **they ran off in different —s** salieron corriendo cada uno por su lado.
(c) —s órdenes fpl, instrucciones fpl; —s **for use** modo m de empleo.
directional [di'rekʃənl] adj direccional.
direction finder [di'rekʃən,faində*] n radiogoniómetro m.
directive [di'rektiv] n orden f, instrucción f.
directly [di'rektli] 1 adv (in a direct manner) directamente; (in a straight line) derecho, en línea recta; (at once) en seguida; — **opposite** exactamente en frente (de).
2 conj: — **you hear it** en cuanto lo oigas.
directness [dai'rektnis] n franqueza f.
director [di'rektə*] n (Comm, Cine etc) director m; **managing —** director m gerente.
directorate [dai'rektərit] n (a) (post) dirección f, cargo m de director. (b) (body) junta f directiva, consejo m de administración.
directorship [di'rektəʃip] n cargo m de director.
directory [di'rektəri] n (Tel) guía f telefónica.
dirge [də:dʒ] n endecha f.
dirigible ['diridʒəbl] 1 adj dirigible. 2 n dirigible m.
dirk [də:k] n puñal m.
dirt [də:t] n (unclean matter) suciedad f, mugre f, (litter) basura f; (earth) tierra f; (mud) lodo m; (obscenity) suciedad f, inmundicia f; (worthless stuff) porquería f; **to treat someone like —** tratar a uno como una basura.
dirt-cheap [də:t'tʃi:p] adj tirado, muy barato.
dirt road ['də:trəud] n (US) camino m sin firme.
dirt track ['də:ttræk] n pista f de ceniza.
dirty ['də:ti] 1 adj sucio; (grubby) mugriento; (stained) manchado; trick, play etc sucio; novel, story, joke verde, indecente, sucio; weather horrible.
2 n: **to do the — on someone** hacer una mala pasada a uno.
3 vt ensuciar; (stain) manchar.
disability [,disə'biliti] n (state) incapacidad f; (feature) impedimento m, estorbo m, desventaja f.
disable [dis'eibl] vt (cripple) estropear, mutilar; ship etc inutilizar; (disqualify etc) incapacitar, inhabilitar (for para).
disabled [dis'eibld] adj person mutilado.
disablement [dis'eiblmənt] n inhabilitación f.
disabuse [,disə'bju:z] vt desengañar (of de).
disadvantage [,disəd'vɑ:ntidʒ] n desventaja f, inconveniente m; **to be at a —** estar en una situación desventajosa; **to be taken at a —** encontrarse en una situación violenta.
disadvantageous [,disædvɑ:n'teidʒəs] adj desventajoso.
disaffected [,disə'fektid] adj desafecto (towards hacia).
disaffection [,disə'fekʃən] n descontento m.
disagree [,disə'gri:] vi (a) no estar de acuerdo (about, on sobre, with con), discrepar (with de); **I — with you** no estoy de acuerdo contigo, discrepo de ti, no comparto esa opinión; **their findings —** discrepan sus conclusiones.
(b) **I — with bullfighting** yo no apruebo el toreo.
(c) (quarrel) reñir.
(d) (of food etc) **to — with** sentar mal a, hacer daño a.
disagreeable [,disə'gri:əbl] adj desagradable; (bad-tempered) displicente, de mal genio; tone of voice etc malhumorado, áspero; **he was very — to me** me trató con bastante aspereza; **I'm rather — in the mornings** por la mañana estoy de bastante mal humor.
disagreement [,disə'gri:mənt] n (a) desacuerdo m, disconformidad f (with con); discrepancia f (with de).
(b) (quarrel) riña f, altercado m.
disallow ['disə'lau] vt no aceptar, no sancionar; goal anular.
disappear [,disə'piə*] vi desaparecer.
disappearance [,disə'piərəns] n desaparición f.
disappoint [,disə'pɔint] vt decepcionar, desilusionar; hopes defraudar; **we were —ed with the book** el libro nos decepcionó; **we shall be —ed if you don't come** sentiremos mucho que no vengas.
disappointing [,disə'pɔintiŋ] adj decepcionante, desilusionante; **it is — that** es triste que + subj.
disappointment [,disə'pɔintmənt] n decepción f, desilusión f; (event) contratiempo m; — **in love** fracaso m sentimental; **he is a big — to us** nos ha decepcionado muchísimo.

disapproval [,disə'pru:vəl] n desaprobación f.
disapprove [,disə'pru:v] vi: **to — of thing** desaprobar; person tener poca simpatía a; **I strongly —** yo estoy firmemente en contra; **but father —d** pero papá no quiso permitirlo.
disapproving [,disə'pru:viŋ] adj look etc de desaprobación.
disapprovingly [,disə'pru:viŋli] adv con desaprobación.
disarm [dis'ɑ:m] 1 vt desarmar. 2 vi desarmarse.
disarmament [dis'ɑ:məmənt] n desarme m.
disarming [dis'ɑ:miŋ] adj smile etc encantador; speech conciliador.
disarrange ['disə'reindʒ] vt desarreglar, descomponer.
disarray ['disə'rei] n desorden m, confusión f; **in —** desordenado.
disassemble ['disə'sembl] vt (US) desmontar.
disaster [di'zɑ:stə*] n desastre m; **to court —** correr al desastre.
disastrous [di'zɑ:strəs] adj catastrófico, desastroso.
disastrously [di'zɑ:strəsli] adv catastróficamente.
disavow ['disə'vau] vt desconocer, rechazar.
disband [dis'bænd] 1 vt army licenciar; organization disolver. 2 vi desbandarse; disolverse.
disbelief ['disbə'li:f] n incredulidad f.
disbelieve ['disbə'li:v] vt no creer, desconfiar de.
disbeliever ['disbə'li:və*] n incrédulo m, a f; (Eccl) descreído m, a f.
disburden [dis'bə:dn] 1 vt descargar. 2 vr: **to — oneself of** descargarse de.
disburse [dis'bə:s] vt desembolsar.
disbursement [dis'bə:smənt] n desembolso m.
disc [disk] n disco m.
discard ['diskɑ:d] n descarte m.
discard [dis'kɑ:d] 1 vt descartar (also Cards), rechazar, desechar; clothing dejar de llevar; unwanted thing tirar; habit renunciar a.
2 vi descartar(se).
discern [di'sə:n] vt percibir, discernir.
discernible [di'sə:nəbl] adj perceptible.
discerning [di'sə:niŋ] adj perspicaz.
discernment [di'sə:nment] n perspicacia f, discernimiento m.
discharge [dis'tʃɑ:dʒ] 1 n (of weapon, Elec) descarga f; (unloading) descargue m; (of debt) pago m, descargo m; (of duty) desempeño m, ejecución f; (Mil) licenciamiento m; (of worker) despedida f; (Med) pus m.
2 vt weapon, current, cargo, ship descargar; shot, arrow disparar; debt pagar, descargar; duty desempeñar, cumplir; task ejecutar; troops licenciar; worker despedir; person from duty dispensar, exonerar (from de); prisoner poner en libertad; patient dar de alta; **to be —d from the army** ser licenciado del ejército; **they —d him from hospital on Monday** le dieron de alta el lunes.
3 vi (river, Elec) descargar (into en); (Med) supurar.
disc harrow ['diskhærəu] n grada f de discos.
disciple [di'saipl] n discípulo m, a f.
disciplinarian [,disipli'neəriən] n ordenancista mf.
disciplinary ['disiplinəri] adj disciplinario.
discipline ['disiplin] 1 n disciplina f. 2 vt disciplinar.
disc jockey ['disk,dʒɔki] n (Radio) presentador m de discos.
disclaim [dis'kleim] vt negar, rechazar; desconocer; (Law) renunciar a; **he —ed all knowledge of it** dijo que no sabía nada en absoluto de ello.
disclaimer [dis'kleimə*] n negación f; (Law) renuncia f; **to put in a —** negarlo, rechazarlo.
disclose [dis'kləuz] vt revelar.
disclosure [dis'kləuʒə*] n revelación f.
discolour, (US) discolor [dis'kʌlə*] 1 vt descolorar. 2 vi descolorarse.
discolo(u)ration [dis,kʌlə'reiʃən] n descoloramiento m.
discomfit [dis'kʌmfit] vt desconcertar.
discomfiture [dis'kʌmfitʃə*] n desconcierto m, confusión f.
discomfort [dis'kʌmfət] n (lack of comfort) incomodidad f, falta f de comodidades; (physical) malestar m; (uneasiness) inquietud f.
discompose [,diskəm'pəuʒə*] n desconcierto m, confusión f.
disconcert [,diskən'sə:t] vt desconcertar.
disconcerting [,diskən'sə:tiŋ] adj desconcertante.
disconcertingly [,diskən'sə:tiŋli] adv de modo desconcertante; **he spoke in a — frank way** desconcertó a todos hablando con tanta franqueza.
disconnect ['diskə'nekt] vt separar, desacoplar; (Elec) desconectar.
disconnected ['diskə'nektid] adj (fig) inconexo.

disconsolate [dis'kɔnsəlit] *adj* inconsolable.
disconsolately [dis'kɔnsəlitli] *adv* inconsolablemente.
discontent ['diskən'tent] *n* descontento *m*.
discontented ['diskən'tentid] *adj* descontento, disgustado.
discontentment ['diskən'tentmənt] *n* descontento *m*.
discontinue ['diskən'tinju:] *vt* descontinuar; *payment* suspender; *newspaper etc* anular el abono de.
discontinuous ['diskən'tinjuəs] *adj* discontinuo.
discord [dis'kɔ:d] *n* discordia *f*; (*Mus*) disonancia *f*; **to sow — among** sembrar cizaña entre.
discordant [dis'kɔ:dənt] *adj* discorde; (*Mus*) disonante.
discothèque ['diskəutek] *n* discoteca *f*.
discount ['diskaunt] *n* descuento *m*, rebaja *f*; **to be at a —** (*fig*) no valorarse en su justo precio.
discount [dis'kaunt] *vt* descontar, rebajar; (*leave out of account*) dejar a un lado, descartar, desechar; *report etc* considerar exagerado.
discourage [dis'kʌridʒ] *vt person* desalentar, desanimar; *development etc* oponerse a, desaprobar; *tendency* resistir; **to — someone from doing something** disuadir a uno de hacer algo.
discouragement [dis'kʌridʒmənt] *n* desaliento *m*; oposición *f*; desaprobación *f*; disuasión *f*; (*obstacle*) estorbo *m*; **it's a real — to progress** es un verdadero estorbo para el progreso.
discouraging [dis'kʌridʒiŋ] *adj* desalentador; **he was — about it** habló de ello en tono pesimista.
discourse ['diskɔ:s] *n* discurso *m*; (*talk*) plática *f*; (*essay*) tratado *m*.
discourse [dis'kɔ:s] *vi*: **to — upon** (*converse*) platicar sobre, (*make a speech*) disertar sobre.
discourteous [dis'kə:tiəs] *adj* descortés.
discourteously [dis'kə:tiəsli] *adv* descortésmente.
discourtesy [dis'kə:tisi] *n* descortesía *f*.
discover [dis'kʌvə*] *vt* descubrir.
discoverer [dis'kʌvərə*] *n* descubridor *m*.
discovery [dis'kʌvəri] *n* descubrimiento *m*.
discredit [dis'kredit] **1** *n* descrédito *m*. **2** *vt* desacreditar, deshonrar; **that theory is now —ed** esa teoría ya está desacreditada.
discreditable [dis'kreditəbl] *adj* deshonroso, vergonzoso.
discreet [dis'kri:t] *adj* discreto, circunspecto, prudente.
discreetly [dis'kri:tli] *adv* discretamente, prudentemente.
discrepancy [dis'krepənsi] *n* discrepancia *f*, diferencia *f*.
discrete [dis'kri:t] *adj* discreto.
discretion [dis'kreʃən] *n* discreción *f*, circunspección *f*, prudencia *f*; **at one's —** a discreción; **age of —** edad *f* de discernimiento; **to use one's own —** juzgar una cosa por sí mismo, obrar como mejor le parezca a uno; **— is the better part of valour** una retirada a tiempo es una victoria.
discriminate [dis'krimineit] **1** *vt* distinguir (*from* de). **2** *vi*: **to — against** discriminar contra, hacer una distinción en perjuicio de; **to — between** distinguir entre.
discriminating [dis'krimineitiŋ] *adj* perspicaz, discernidor; *duty* diferencial; *taste etc* fino.
discrimination [dis,krimi'neiʃən] *n* (*discernment*) discernimiento *m*, perspicacia *f*; (*good taste*) buen gusto *m*, finura *f*; (*distinction*) distinción *f* (*between* entre); (*partiality*) parcialidad *f*, discriminación *f* (*against* contra); **racial —** discriminación *f* racial.
discriminatory [dis'kriminətəri] *adj duty etc* discriminatorio.
discursive [dis'kə:siv] *adj* divagador, prolijo.
discus ['diskəs] *n* disco *m*.
discuss [dis'kʌs] *vt* discutir, hablar de; *theme* tratar.
discussion [dis'kʌʃən] *n* discusión *f*; **to be under —** estar siendo discutido.
disdain [dis'dein] **1** *n* desdén *m*. **2** *vt* desdeñar. **3** *vi*: **to — to** *to* + *infin* no dignarse + *infin*.
disdainful [dis'deinful] *adj* desdeñoso.
disdainfully [dis'deinfəli] *adv* desdeñosamente.
disease [di'zi:z] *n* enfermedad *f*; (*fig*) mal *m*; **infectious —** enfermedad *f* contagiosa; **occupational —** enfermedad *f* profesional; **venereal —** enfermedad *f* venérea; **virus —** enfermedad *f* por virus.
diseased [di'zi:zd] *adj person* enfermo; *tissue* contagiado; *mind* enfermo, morboso.
disembark [,disim'ba:k] *vti* desembarcar.
disembarkation [,disemba:'keiʃən] *n* (*goods*) desembarque *m*; (*person*) desembarco *m*.
disembodied ['disim'bɔdid] *adj* incorpóreo.
disembowel [disim'bauəl] *vt* desentrañar.
disenchanted ['disin'tʃa:ntid] *adj*: **to be — with someone** quedar desencantado (*or* desengañado) con

uno; **to be — with New York** quedar desencantado (*or* desengañado) de Nueva York.
disengage [,disin'geidʒ] **1** *vt* (*free*) soltar, desasir; (*Mech*) desacoplar, desenganchar; *clutch* desembragar. **2** *vi* (*Mil*) retirarse.
disengaged [,disin'geidʒd] *adj* libre, desocupado.
disentangle ['disin'tæŋgl] **1** *vt* desenredar, desenmarañar (*also fig; from* de). **2** *vr*: **to — oneself** desenredarse (*from* de).
disestablish ['disis'tæbliʃ] *vt* (*Eccl*) separar del Estado.
disestablishment [,disis'tæbliʃmənt] *n* (*Eccl*) separación *f* del Estado.
disfavour [dis'feivə*] *n* desaprobación *f*; **to fall into —** (*custom*) dejar de usarse, caer en desuso, (*person*) caer en desgracia; **to look with — on something** desaprobar algo.
disfigure [dis'figə*] *vt* desfigurar; afear.
disfigurement [dis'figəmənt] *n* desfiguración *f*; afeamiento *m*.
disfranchise ['dis'fræntʃaiz] *vt* privar de los derechos civiles, (*esp*) privar del derecho de votar.
disgorge [dis'gɔ:dʒ] *vt* vomitar, arrojar; (*bird*) desembuchar; (*fig*) devolver, restituir.
disgrace [dis'greis] **1** *n* (**a**) (*state of shame*) ignominia *f*, deshonra *f*; **to be in —** estar desacreditado, (*pet, child*) tener que sufrir un castigo; **to bring — on** deshonrar; **to fall into —** caer en desgracia.
(**b**) (*downfall*) caída *f*.
(**c**) (*shameful thing*) vergüenza *f*; escándalo *m*; **it's a —** es una vergüenza; **what a —!** ¡qué vergüenza!
2 *vt* deshonrar, desacreditar; **he was —d and banished** le destituyeron de sus cargos y le desterraron.
3 *vr*: **to — oneself** deshonrarse.
disgraceful [dis'greisful] *adj* vergonzoso, deshonroso; *behaviour* escandaloso; **—!** ¡qué vergüenza!
disgracefully [dis'greisfəli] *adv* vergonzosamente; escandalosamente.
disgruntled [dis'grʌntld] *adj* disgustado (*at, with* de), malhumorado; **to look —** poner mala cara.
disguise [dis'gaiz] **1** *n* disfraz *m*. **2** *vt* disfrazar (*as* de). **3** *vr*: **to — oneself as** disfrazarse de.
disgust [dis'gʌst] **1** *n* repugnancia *f*, aversión *f*; **it fills me with —** me da asco.
2 *vt* repugnar, inspirar aversión a, dar asco a; (*disappointment etc*) disgustar; **the thought —s me** el pensamiento me repugna; **you — me** me das asco; **he was —ed by his failure** se enfureció contra sí mismo por su fracaso; **I am —ed with you** me das vergüenza; **I was —ed with the referee** el árbitro me dio asco.
disgusted [dis'gʌstid] *adj*: **in a — voice** en tono disgustado.
disgusting [dis'gʌstiŋ] *adj* repugnante, asqueroso; **—!** ¡qué asco!
disgustingly [dis'gʌstiŋli] *adv* asquerosamente; **they are — rich** son tan ricos que da asco.
dish [diʃ] **1** *n* (**a**) plato *m*; (*large, for serving etc*) fuente *f*; (*food*) plato *m*; **a typical Spanish —** un plato típico español; **to wash the —es** fregar los platos.
(**b**) (*fam*) chica *f* atractiva.
2 *vt* (*fig*) confundir, burlar; **to — out** repartir; **to — up** servir; **he —ed up the same old arguments** repitió los argumentos de siempre.
dishabille [,disæ'bi:l] *n* desabillé *m*.
disharmony ['dis'ha:məni] *n* discordia *f*; (*Mus*) disonancia *f*.
dish cloth ['diʃklɔθ] *n* paño *m* de cocina, bayeta *f*.
dishearten [dis'ha:tn] *vt* desalentar; **don't be —ed!** ¡ánimo!
disheartening [dis'ha:tniŋ] *adj* desalentador.
dishevelled [di'ʃevəld] *adj* despeinado, desmelenado.
dishonest [dis'ɔnist] *adj person* nada honrado, falso, tramposo; *means* fraudulento.
dishonestly [dis'ɔnistli] *adv* fraudulentamente.
dishonesty [dis'ɔnisti] *n* falta *f* de honradez, falsedad *f*; (*of means*) fraude *m*.
dishonour, (*US*) **dishonor** [dis'ɔnə*] **1** *n* deshonra *f*, deshonor *m*.
2 *vt* deshonrar; *cheque etc* negarse a aceptar, no pagar; *promise* faltar a, no cumplir.
dishonourable, (*US*) **dishonorable** [dis'ɔnərəbl] *adj* deshonroso.
dishrack ['diʃræk] *n* estante *m* para secar los platos.
dishwasher ['diʃ,wɔʃə*] *n* (*person*) friegaplatos *mf*; (*machine*) lavaplatos *m*.
dishy ['diʃi] *adj* (*fam*) atractivo, mono.
disillusion [,disi'lu:ʒən] **1** *n* desilusión *f*. **2** *vt* desilusionar; **to be —ed with someone** quedar desilusionado con uno; **to be —ed with Paris** quedar desilusionado de París.

disillusionment [,disi'lu:ʒənmənt] n desilusión f.
disincentive [,disin'sentiv] n freno m (to sobre).
disinclination [,disinkli'neiʃən] n aversión f (for a, hacia, por).
disinclined ['disin'klaind] adj: to be — to do something estar poco dispuesto a hacer algo.
disinfect [,disin'fekt] vt desinfectar.
disinfectant [,disin'fektənt] n desinfectante m.
disinfection [,disin'fekʃən] n desinfección f.
disinflation [,disin'fleiʃən] n desinflación f.
disinflationary [,disin'fleiʃənəri] adj desinflacionista.
disingenuous [,disin'dʒenjuəs] adj doble, poco sincero.
disinherit ['disin'herit] vt desheredar.
disintegrate [dis'intigreit] vi disgregarse, desagregarse, desintegrarse.
disintegration [dis,inti'greiʃən] n disgregación f, desagregación f, desintegración f.
disinter ['disin'tə:*] vt desenterrar.
disinterested [dis'intristid] adj desinteresado.
disjointed [dis'dʒɔintid] adj (fig) inconexo, descosido.
disjunctive [dis'dʒʌŋktiv] adj disyuntivo.
disk [disk] n see disc.
dislike [dis'laik] 1 n aversión f, antipatía f (for, of a, hacia); to take a — to coger antipatía a, tomar hincha a (fam).
2 vt (a) (object: person) tener aversión a, tener antipatía a; I — him me resulta antipático; it's not that I — him no es que yo le tenga aversión.
(b) (object: thing) I — that eso no me gusta; I — flying no me gusta ir en avión.
dislocate ['disləukeit] vt bone dislocarse; traffic interceptar, interrumpir; plans dar al traste con.
dislocation [,disləu'keiʃən] n dislocación f; interceptación f; confusión f.
dislodge [dis'lɔdʒ] vt enemy etc desalojar (from de); object etc hacer caer.
disloyal ['dis'lɔiəl] adj desleal.
disloyalty ['dis'lɔiəlti] n deslealtad f.
dismal ['dizməl] adj (dark) sombrío, tenebroso; (depressing) triste, tétrico; (depressed) abatido; tone lúgubre; failure catastrófico; (very bad) malísimo, fatal.
dismally ['dizməli] adv (sadly) tristemente; to fail — tener un fracaso catastrófico; the play was — bad la obra fue fatal.
dismantle [dis'mæntl] vt machine desmontar, desarmar; fort, ship desmantelar.
dismast [dis'mɑ:st] vt desarbolar.
dismay [dis'mei] 1 n consternación f; there was general — se consternaron todos; in — consternado; to fill someone with — consternar a uno. 2 vt consternar; I am —ed to hear that me da pena saber que; don't look so —ed! ¡no te aflijas!
dismember [dis'membə*] vt desmembrar.
dismemberment [dis'membəmənt] n desmembramiento m, desmembración f.
dismiss [dis'mis] 1 vt (a) (discharge) worker despedir, official destituir (from de), (Mil) licenciar; to be —ed the service ser separado del servicio.
(b) (send away) mandar ir, dar permiso a . . . para irse; parliament disolver.
(c) thought rechazar, apartar de sí; possibility descartar, desechar.
(d) to — a subject briefly hablar brevemente de un asunto; with that he —ed the matter con eso dio por concluido el asunto.
(e) (Law) appeal rechazar; the case was —ed el tribunal absolvió al acusado.
2 vi (Mil) romper filas.
dismissal [dis'misəl] n despedida f; destitución f.
dismount [dis'maunt] 1 vt desmontar. 2 vi desmontarse, apearse, bajar (from de).
disobedience [,disə'bi:diəns] n desobediencia f.
disobedient [,disə'bi:diənt] adj desobediente.
disobey [,disə'bei] vti desobedecer.
disobliging ['disə'blaidʒiŋ] adj poco servicial.
disorder [dis'ɔ:də*] 1 n (a) (confusion) desorden m; to be in — estar en desorden; to retreat in — retirarse a la desbandada.
(b) (commotion) disturbio m, tumulto m; there were —s in the streets hubo disturbios en las calles.
(c) (Med) (upset) trastorno m, (illness) enfermedad f; mental — trastorno m mental.
2 vt desordenar; (Med) trastornar.
disordered [dis'ɔ:dəd] adj desordenado; (Med) trastornado.
disorderly [dis'ɔ:dəli] adj (a) (untidy) desordenado; person poco metódico.
(b) (unruly) turbulento, indisciplinado; youth revoltoso; meeting alborotado; the meeting became — la reunión se alborotó.
(c) conduct escandaloso.

disorganization [dis,ɔ:gənai'zeiʃən] n desorganización f; confusión f, falta f de organización.
disorganize [dis'ɔ:gənaiz] vt desorganizar; communications etc interrumpir.
disorientate [dis'ɔriənteit] vt desorientar.
disown [dis'əun] vt rechazar, desconocer; belief etc renegar de.
disparage [dis'pæridʒ] vt menospreciar, denigrar, hablar mal de.
disparagement [dis'pæridʒmənt] n denigración f.
disparaging [dis'pæridʒiŋ] adj despreciativo.
disparagingly [dis'pæridʒiŋli] adv: to speak — of hablar en términos despreciativos de.
disparate ['dispərit] adj dispar.
disparity [dis'pæriti] n disparidad f.
dispassionate [dis'pæʃnit] adj desapasionado, imparcial.
dispassionately [dis'pæʃnitli] adv de modo desapasionado.
dispatch [dis'pætʃ] 1 n (a) (act of sending) (of person) envío m, (of goods) consignación f, envío m; (killing) muerte f.
(b) (speed) prontitud f.
(c) (message) mensaje m, despacho m, informe m; (Mil) parte m, comunicado m.
2 vt (a) (send) person enviar, goods consignar, enviar, remitir.
(b) (kill) despachar.
(c) (transact) despachar.
(d) food despabilar.
dispatch box [dis'pætʃbɔks] n cartera f.
dispatcher [dis'pætʃə*] n despachador m, ora f.
dispatch rider [dis'pætʃ,raidə*] n correo m.
dispel [dis'pel] vt disipar, dispersar; (fig) desvanecer.
dispensable [dis'pensəbl] adj prescindible.
dispensary [dis'pensəri] n dispensario m, farmacia f.
dispensation [,dispen'seiʃən] n (distribution, exemption) dispensación f; (of justice) administración f; (Eccl) dispensa f; (ruling) decreto m; (by Providence) designio m divino.
dispense [dis'pens] 1 vt (a) (issue) dispensar, repartir; (Pharm) preparar; justice administrar.
(b) to — someone from dispensar a uno de, eximir a uno de.
2 vi: to — with prescindir de.
dispenser [dis'pensə*] n (Pharm) farmacéutico m, a f.
dispersal [dis'pə:səl] n dispersión f; (of light) descomposición f.
disperse [dis'pə:s] 1 vt dispersar; light descomponer.
2 vi dispersarse; they —d to their homes fue cada uno a su casa.
dispersion [dis'pə:ʃən] n dispersión f.
dispirit [dis'pirit] vt desalentar.
dispirited [dis'piritid] adj abatido, deprimido.
displace [dis'pleis] vt (shift) sacar de su sitio; (remove from office) destituir; (oust) quitar el puesto a, reemplazar; (Phys, Naut) desplazar; (Chem) reemplazar.
displaced [dis'pleist] adj: — person desplazado m, a f.
displacement [dis'pleismənt] n (shift) cambio m de sitio; (removal from office) destitución f; (ousting) reemplazo m; (Phys, Naut) desplazamiento m; (Chem) reemplazo m.
display [dis'plei] 1 n (a) (act of —ing) exhibición f; (showing) exposición f; (of goods for sale) exposición f, presentación f; (of emotion) manifestación f, demostración f; (of energy) despliegue m; (Mil) alarde m, demostración f militar.
(b) (showiness) aparato m, pompa f, ostentación f.
2 vt (put on view) exponer, presentar; emotion etc acusar, manifestar, demostrar; quality revelar; energy desplegar; (show ostentatiously) hacer ostentación de, lucir.
displease [dis'pli:z] vt (be disagreeable to) desagradar; (offend) ofender; (annoy) enojar, enfadar; to be —d at (or with) estar disgustado con (or de).
displeasing [dis'pli:ziŋ] adj desagradable.
displeasure [dis'pleʒə*] n enojo m, indignación f, disgusto m; to incur someone's — ofender a uno.
disport [dis'pɔ:t] vr: to — oneself retozar, jugar, divertirse.
disposable [dis'pəuzəbl] adj napkin etc de usar y tirar.
disposal [dis'pəuzəl] n (a) (placing, arrangement) disposición f, colocación f, orden m.
(b) (sale) venta f; (of house etc) traspaso m; (of rights) enajenación f; (of rubbish) recogida f de basuras.
(c) to have at one's — disponer de, tener a su disposición; I am at your — estoy a su disposición.

dispose [dis'pəuz] **1** *vt* (a) (*place, arrange*) disponer, colocar, poner en orden.

(b) (*determine*) determinar, decidir.

(c) (*persuade*) inclinar, mover; **to — someone to help** mover a uno a ayudar; **to be —d to do something** estar dispuesto a hacer algo; **to be well —d towards something** estar bien dispuesto hacia algo.

2 *vi*: **to — of** (a) (*have at one's command*) disponer de. (b) (*get rid of*) deshacerse de; *rubbish* tirar, depositar; *rights* enajenar, ceder; (*sell*) vender; *house etc* traspasar; (*give away*) regalar; *food* comerse, despabilar; (*finish*) terminar, concluir; *problem* resolver; *business* despachar; (*kill*) matar.

disposition [,dispə'ziʃən] *n* (a) (*placing*) disposición *f*, colocación *f*; orden *m*.

(b) **—s** preparativos *mpl*; plan *m*; **to make one's —s** hacer preparativos.

(c) **to be at the — of** estar a la disposición de.

(d) (*dispensation*) disposición *f*.

(e) (*temperament*) natural *m*, temperamento *m*.

(f) (*inclination*) propensión *f* (*to* a); **I have no — to help him** no estoy dispuesto a ayudarle.

dispossess ['dispə'zes] *vt tenant* desahuciar; **to — someone of** desposeer a uno de, privar a uno de.

disproportion [,dispro'pɔ:ʃən] *n* desproporción *f*.

disproportionate [,dispro'pɔ:ʃnit] *adj* desproporcionado.

disproportionately [,dispro'pɔ:ʃnitli] *adv* desproporcionadamente.

disprove [dis'pru:v] *vt* refutar, confutar.

disputable [dis'pju:təbl] *adj* discutible.

disputation [,dispju:'teiʃən] *n* disputa *f*.

disputatious [,dispju:'teiʃəs] *adj* discutidor.

dispute [dis'pju:t] **1** *n* disputa *f*; (*spoken*) discusión *f*, altercado *m*; *labour* — conflicto *m* laboral; **beyond — indiscutible, incuestionable; it is beyond — that** es indudable que; **territory in —** territorio *m* disputado.

2 *vt* disputar; cuestionar, expresar dudas acerca de; protestar de; **a —d matter** un asunto contencioso, un asunto en litigio; **a —d decision** una decisión discutida; **I — that** yo lo dudo.

3 *vi* discutir (*about, over* sobre, *whether* si).

disqualification [dis,kwɔlifi'keiʃən] *n* (*act, effect*) inhabilitación *f*; (*Sport*) descalificación *f*; (*thing that disqualifies*) impedimento *m*, desventaja *f*.

disqualify [dis'kwɔlifai] *vt* inhabilitar, incapacitar (*for* para); (*Sport*) descalificar.

disquiet [dis'kwaiət] **1** *n* inquietud *f*. **2** *vt* inquietar.

disquieting [dis'kwaiətiŋ] *adj* inquietante.

disquisition [,diskwi'ziʃən] *n* disquisición *f*.

disregard ['disri'ga:d] **1** *n* indiferencia *f* (*for* a); (*neglect*) descuido *m* (*of* de); **with complete — for** sin atender en lo más mínimo a; **with complete — for his own safety** sin considerar un momento su propia salvación.

2 *vt* desatender, descuidar; (*ignore*) no hacer caso de.

disrepair ['disri'pɛə*] *n* mal estado *m*; **to fall into —** desmoronarse.

disreputable [dis'repjutəbl] *adj* de mala fama; (*shameful*) vergonzoso, escandaloso; *clothing etc* horrible, asqueroso.

disreputably [dis'repjutəbli] *adv* vergonzosamente.

disrepute ['disri'pju:t] *n*: **to bring something into —** desacreditar algo.

disrespect ['disris'pekt] *n* falta *f* de respeto, desacato *m*; **I mean no — no quería ofenderle.

disrespectful [,disris'pektful] *adj* irrespetuoso.

disrobe ['dis'rəub] *vi* desnudarse.

disrupt [dis'rʌpt] *vt* romper; (*fig*) *communications etc* desorganizar, interrumpir; *plans* desbaratar, dar al traste con.

disruption [dis'rʌpʃən] *n* rompimiento *m*; (*fig*) desorganización *f*, interrupción *f*; desbaratamiento *m*.

disruptive [dis'ruptiv] *adj* que tiende a romper la unidad; destructivo, subversivo, perjudicial (para la unidad).

dissatisfaction ['dis,sætis'fækʃən] *n* descontento *m*, insatisfacción *f*; disgusto *m*.

dissatisfied ['dis'sætisfaid] *adj* descontento, insatisfecho; **everyone was — with the result** el resultado no gustó a nadie, el resultado dejó insatisfechos a todos.

dissect [di'sekt] *vt* disecar; (*fig*) analizar minuciosamente.

dissection [di'sekʃən] *n* disección *f*; (*fig*) análisis *m* minucioso.

dissemble [di'sembl] **1** *vt* disimular, encubrir. **2** *vi* ser hipócrita.

disseminate [di'semineit] *vt* diseminar, difundir.

dissemination [di,semi'neiʃən] *n* diseminación *f*, difusión *f*.

dissension [di'senʃən] *n* disensión *f*, discordia *f*.

dissent [di'sent] **1** *n* disentimiento *m*; (*Eccl*) disidencia *f*. **2** *vi* disentir (*from* de); (*Eccl*) disidir.

dissenter [di'sentə*] *n* (*Eccl*) disidente *m*.

dissentient [di'senʃiənt] **1** *adj* disidente, desconforme, discrepante; **there was one — voice** hubo uno que no estaba conforme. **2** *n* disidente *m*.

dissertation [,disə'teiʃən] *n* disertación *f*; (*Univ*) tesis *f*.

disservice ['dis'sə:vis] *n* deservicio *m*; **to do a — to** perjudicar a.

dissidence ['disidəns] *n* disidencia *f*.

dissident ['disidənt] **1** *adj* disidente. **2** *n* disidente *m*.

dissimilar ['di'similə*] *adj* desemejante (*to* de).

dissimilarity [,disimi'læriti] *n* desemejanza *f*.

dissimulate [di'simjuleit] *vt* disimular.

dissimulation [di,simju'leiʃən] *n* disimulación *f*.

dissipate ['disipeit] *vt* disipar; *fear, doubt etc* desvanecer; (*waste*) derrochar, desperdiciar.

dissipated ['disipeitid] *adj* disoluto.

dissipation [,disi'peiʃən] *n* (*act*) disipación *f*; (*waste*) derroche *m*, desperdicio *m*; (*moral*) disipación *f*, disolución *f*, libertinaje *m*, vicio *m*.

dissociate [di'səuʃieit] **1** *vt* disociar (*from* de). **2** *vr*: **to — oneself from** hacerse insolidario de, separarse de, disociarse de.

dissociation [di,səusi'eiʃən] *n* disociación *f*.

dissoluble [di'sɔljubl] *adj* disoluble.

dissolute ['disəlu:t] *adj* disoluto.

dissolution [,disə'lu:ʃən] *n* disolución *f* (*also Pol*).

dissolvable [di'zɔlvəbl] *adj* soluble.

dissolve [di'zɔlv] **1** *vt* disolver (*also fig, Pol etc*). **2** *vi* disolverse; (*fade*) desvanecerse; **to — into tears** deshacerse en lágrimas.

dissonance ['disənəns] *n* disonancia *f*.

dissonant ['disənənt] *adj* disonante.

dissuade [di'sweid] *vt* disuadir (*from* de); **to — someone from doing something** disuadir a uno de hacer algo.

distaff ['dista:f] *n* rueca *f*; **on the — side** por parte de madre.

distance ['distəns] *n* distancia *f*; (*fig*) reserva *f*; (*difference*) diferencia *f*; **it's a good —** está bastante lejos, (*journey*) es mucho camino; **what — is it to London?** ¿cuánto hay de aquí a Londres?; **— race** carrera *f* de larga distancia; **focal — distancia *f* focal; **within easy —** a poca distancia, no muy lejos (*of* de); **to be within striking — of** estar al alcance de; **at a — a distancia; at a — of 60 km** a una distancia de 60 km; **at this —** a esta distancia; **at this — of time** después de tanto tiempo; **from a — desde lejos; **in the —** a lo lejos; **in the middle — en segundo término; **to keep one's — mantenerse a distancia, (*fig*) guardar las distancias; **to keep someone at a — guardar las distancias con uno.

distant ['distənt] *adj* (a) distante, lejano, remoto (*from* de); **it is 12 km — dista 12 km, está a 12 km; **is it very —? ¿está muy lejos?; **in some far — land** en algún país lejano.

(b) *relation, resemblance* lejano.

(c) (*fig*) reservado, frío; **to be — with someone** tratar a uno con frialdad.

distantly ['distəntli] *adv*: **we are — related** somos parientes lejanos; **it — resembles the one we had before** tiene una ligera semejanza con el que teníamos antes; **he treated me — me trató con frialdad.

distaste ['dis'teist] *n* aversión *f*, repugnancia *f* (*for* por).

distasteful [dis'teistful] *adj* desagradable, repugnante; *task* nada grato; **it is — to me to have to + infin** me es poco grato tener que + *infin*.

distemper¹ [dis'tempə*] **1** *n* pintura *f* al temple. **2** *vt* pintar al temple.

distemper² [dis'tempə*] *n* (*Vet*) moquillo *m*; (*fig*) mal *m*, destemplanza *f*.

distend [dis'tend] **1** *vt* dilatar, hinchar. **2** *vi* dilatarse, hincharse.

distension [dis'tenʃən] *n* distensión *f*, dilatación *f*, hinchazón *f*.

distil, (*US*) **distill** [dis'til] *vt* destilar.

distillation [,disti'leiʃən] *n* destilación *f*.

distiller [dis'tilə*] *n* destilador *m*.

distillery [dis'tiləri] *n* destilería *f*.

distinct [dis'tiŋkt] *adj* (*different*) distinto (*from* de); (*clearly perceptible*) claro, inconfundible, visible; (*unmistakable*) inequívoco; **as — from** a diferencia de; **a — French accent** un marcado acento francés; **there is a — chance that** existe una clara posibilidad de que + *subj*.

distinction [dis'tiŋkʃən] n distinción f; (exam mark) sobresaliente m, matrícula f de honor; **to draw a —between** hacer una distinción entre; **you have the —of being the first** Vd se señala por ser el primero.
distinctive [dis'tiŋktiv] adj distintivo, característico.
distinctly [dis'tiŋktli] adv claramente, inconfundiblemente; **it is — possible** bien podría ser (that que + subj); **it is — awkward** es sumamente difícil.
distinguish [dis'tiŋgwiʃ] 1 vt distinguir (between entre, from de). 2 vr: **to — oneself** distinguirse (as como); (iro) señalarse, lucirse.
distinguishable [dis'tiŋgwiʃəbl] adj distinguible.
distinguished [dis'tiŋgwiʃt] adj distinguido (for por), eminente, de categoría.
distinguishing [dis'tiŋgwiʃiŋ] adj distintivo.
distort [dis'tɔːt] vt torcer, deformar; (fig) torcer, falsear.
distortion [dis'tɔːʃən] n torcimiento m, deformación f; (of sound) distorsión f; (fig) torcimiento m, falseamiento m.
distract [dis'trækt] vt distraer; attention apartar (from de); (bewilder) aturdir, confundir.
distracted [dis'træktid] adj alocado, aturdido; **like one —** como un loco; **she is easily —** se distrae fácilmente; **to be — with anxiety** estar loco de inquietud.
distractedly [dis'træktidli] adv locamente, como un loco.
distracting [dis'træktiŋ] adj que distrae la atención, molesto.
distraction [dis'trækʃən] n (being distracted) distracción f; (bewilderment) aturdimiento m, confusión f; (amusement) diversión f; (madness) locura f; **to drive someone to —** volver loco a uno.
distrain [dis'trein] vi: **to — upon** secuestrar, embargar.
distraint [dis'treint] n secuestro m, embargo m.
distrait [dis'trei], **distraite** [dis'treit] adj distraído.
distraught [dis'trɔːt] adj muy turbado, loco de inquietud (etc); **in a — voice** en una voz embargada por la emoción.
distress [dis'tres] 1 n (pain) dolor m; (mental anguish) angustia f, pena f, aflicción f; (misfortune) desgracia f; (want) miseria f; (danger) peligro m; (Med) agotamiento m; **to be in —** estar en un apuro, (Med) estar con dolor, (ship etc) estar en peligro; **to be in financial —** pasar apuros.
2 vt (pain) doler; (cause anguish to) apenar, afligir; (Med) agotar, fatigar; **I am —ed to hear that** me da pena saber que; **I am very —ed about it** esto me inquieta muchísimo.
distressing [dis'tresiŋ] adj doloroso, penoso, que da pena.
distress signal [dis'tres,signəl] n señal f de socorro.
distribute [dis'tribjuːt] vt distribuir, repartir.
distribution [,distri'bjuːʃən] n distribución f, reparto m, repartimiento m.
distributive [dis'tribjutiv] adj distributivo; **— trade** comercio m de repartimiento.
distributor [dis'tribjutə*] n (Mech, Elec etc) distribuidor m; (Comm, Cine etc) distribuidora f.
district ['distrikt] n zona f, región f; (of town) barrio m; (of country) comarca f; (Pol) distrito m; **postal —** distrito m postal.
distrust [dis'trʌst] 1 n desconfianza f, recelo m. 2 vt desconfiar de, recelar.
distrustful [dis'trʌstful] adj desconfiado, receloso.
disturb [dis'təːb] vt peace, order, meeting etc perturbar, alterar; process, course interrumpir; balance of mind trastornar; (disarrange) desordenar; person (disquiet) perturbar, inquietar, (bother) molestar; **don't — yourself!** ¡no se moleste!; **I am seriously —ed** estoy muy preocupado.
disturbance [dis'təːbəns] n (act, state) perturbación f; (outbreak of violence) tumulto m, alboroto m, (Pol) disturbio m; (of mind) trastorno m; **there was a — in the crowd** se alborotaron algunos de los espectadores; **the —s in the Congo** los disturbios en el Congo.
disturbed [dis'təːbd] adj state alborotado, nada tranquilo; **to have a — night** dormir mal.
disturbing [dis'təːbiŋ] adj influence, thought perturbador; event inquietante; **it is — that** es inquietante que.
disunited ['disju'naitid] adj desunido.
disuse ['dis'juːs] n: **to fall into —** caer en desuso.
disused ['dis'juːzd] adj abandonado.
disyllabic [,disi'læbik] adj disílabo.
ditch [ditʃ] 1 n zanja f; (at roadside) cuneta f, arroyo m; (irrigation channel) acequia f; (defensive) foso m; **to die in the last —** luchar hasta quemar el último cartucho.

2 vt (fam) (get rid of) deshacerse de, zafarse de; plane amerizar; car estropear.
dither ['diðə*] 1 n: **to be all of a —**, **to be in a — =** 2 vi estar nerviosísimo; (be undecided) no saber qué hacer, vacilar.
dithery ['diðəri] adj nervioso; indeciso, vacilante.
ditto ['ditəu] adj idem, lo mismo; **I say —** yo digo lo mismo; **"—", he said** dijo "yo también".
ditty ['diti] n cancioneta f.
diuretic [,daijuə'retik] 1 adj diurético. 2 n diurético m.
diurnal [dai'əːnl] adj diurno.
divan [di'væn] n diván m, cama f turca.
dive [daiv] 1 n (a) zambullida f, (artistic, from board etc) salto m; **springboard —** salto m de trampolín.
(b) (by professional diver, of submarine) inmersión f.
(c) (Aer) picado m.
(d) (fam) tasca f (also **low —**).
2 vi (a) (duck etc) zambullirse; (from bank etc) tirarse al agua, saltar al agua, zambullirse; (artistically) saltar; (professional diver) bucear, sumergirse; (submarine) sumergirse; **to — into the water** tirarse al agua.
(b) (Aer) picar.
(c) **to — for cover** meterse precipitadamente en un abrigo, buscar cobijo precipitadamente; **to — into the undergrowth** meterse en la maleza; **to — into one's pocket** meter la mano en el bolsillo; **to — into a bar** entrar de prisa en un bar.
dive-bomb ['daivbɔm] vt bombardear en picado.
dive bomber ['daiv,bɔmə*] n bombardero m en picado.
dive bombing ['daiv,bɔmiŋ] n bombardeo m en picado.
diver ['daivə*] n (professional) buzo m; (sporting) saltador m, ora f; (Orn) colimbo m.
diverge [dai'vəːdʒ] vi divergir (from de); **to — from** apartarse de.
divergence [dai'vəːdʒəns] n divergencia f.
divergent [dai'vəːdʒənt] adj divergente.
divers ['daivəːz] adj pl diversos, varios.
diverse [dai'vəːs] adj diverso, variado.
diversification [dai,vəːsifi'keiʃən] n diversificación f.
diversify [dai'vəːsifai] vt diversificar, variar.
diversion [dai'vəːʃən] n (pastime, Mil) diversión f; (of route) desviación f.
diversity [dai'vəːsiti] n diversidad f.
divert [dai'vəːt] vt (amuse) divertir; (turn aside) desviar.
diverting [dai'vəːtiŋ] adj divertido.
divest [dai'vest] 1 vt: **to — someone of something** despojar a uno de algo. 2 vr: **to — oneself of something** renunciar a algo.
divide [di'vaid] 1 n (Geog) divisoria f.
2 vt dividir (by por, from de, into en); partir; separar; **to — the House** hacer que la Cámara proceda a la votación; **to — out** repartir; **to — up** dividir, partir.
3 vi dividirse (into en); separarse; (road etc) bifurcarse; **the House —d** la Cámara procedió a la votación.
dividend ['dividend] n dividendo m; (fig) beneficio m; **this should pay handsome —s** (fig) esto ha de proporcionar grandes beneficios.
dividers [di'vaidəz] npl compás m de puntas.
dividing line [di'vaidiŋlain] n línea f divisoria.
divination [,divi'neiʃən] n adivinación f.
divine [di'vain] 1 adj divino; (fig) sublime; (fam) estupendo, maravilloso. 2 n teólogo m. 3 vt adivinar.
divinely [di'vainli] adv divinamente; (fig) sublimamente; (fam) divinamente, maravillosamente.
diviner [di'vainə*] n adivinador m, ora f; (water —) zahorí m.
diving ['daiviŋ] n (professional) el bucear, buceo m; (sporting) salto m.
diving bell ['daiviŋbel] n campana f de bucear.
diving board ['daiviŋbɔːd] n trampolín m.
diving suit ['daiviŋsuːt] n escafandra f, traje m de buceo.
divining rod [di'vainiŋrɔd] n varilla f de zahorí.
divinity [di'viniti] n divinidad f; (as study) teología f.
divisible [di'vizəbl] adj divisible.
division [di'viʒən] n división f (also Math, Mil); separación f; (sharing out) repartimiento m; (within company etc) sección f; (disagreement) discordia f; (Parl) votación f; **without a —** por unanimidad; **there is a — of opinion about this** sobre esto hay diversos pareceres.
divisive [di'vaisiv] adj divisivo.
divisor [di'vaizə*] n divisor m.

divorce [di'vɔːs] **1** *n* divorcio *m*; (*fig*) separación *f* (*from* de); **to get a —** divorciarse (*from* de). **2** *vt* divorciarse de; (*fig*) divorciar, separar (*from* de).

divorcee [di͵vɔː'siː] *n* divorciado *m*, a *f*.

divulge [dai'vʌldʒ] *vt* divulgar, revelar.

dixie ['diksi] *n* (*Mil*) olla *f*.

Dixie ['diksi] el sur de los Estados Unidos.

dizzily ['dizili] *adv* vertiginosamente.

dizziness ['dizinis] *n* vértigo *m*, vértigos *mpl*.

dizzy ['dizi] *adj speed* vertiginoso; *height* que produce vértigo; *feeling* de vértigo; (*dazed*) mareado, aturdido; **to feel —, to get —** marearse, estar mareado, tener vértigos; **I'm feeling rather —** me está dando vueltas la cabeza.

do [duː] (*irr*: *pret* **did**, *ptp* **done**) **1** *vt* (a) hacer; (*Cook*) guisar, preparar; (*Theat*) *play* representar, poner, *rôle* hacer, *personage* hacer de, hacer el papel de; *duty* cumplir, hacer; *homage* rendir, tributar (*to* a); *problem* resolver; *dishes* lavar; *room* limpiar; *hair* peinar, (*wash and set*) arreglar; *subject* (*Univ etc*) estudiar, cursar; *distance* cubrir, recorrer, salvar; *speed* alcanzar, ir a; *town etc* (*fam*) hacer la visita de, visitar los monumentos de; (*sl: cheat*) estafar, timar; **they — you very well in this hotel** en este hotel la comida es muy buena; **what's to —?** ¿qué pasa?; **to have one's hair done** arreglarse el pelo.

(b) (*with adv or prep*) **to — again** rehacer, repetir, volver a hacer; **to — down** (*cheat*) estafar, (*play someone false*) hacer una mala pasada a; **to — in** (*sl*) apiolar, cargarse a; **to — a book into English** traducir un libro al inglés; **to — out** *room* pintar, renovar; **to — someone out of something** estafar algo a uno, (*chance etc*) pisar algo a uno, hacer que uno pierda algo; **to — something over** (*again*) rehacer algo; **to — up** *laces etc* liar, atar, *parcel* envolver, *room* renovar; *see also* **doing, done.**

2 *vi* (a) (*act, proceed*) hacer; obrar, actuar, proceder; **you did well** hiciste muy bien; **you would — well to draw with him** sería muy honroso lograr un empate con él; **to — better** mejorar, hacer progresos; **you can — better than that** eres capaz de hacerlo mejor; **you would — better to accept** sería aconsejable aceptar; **— as you are told!** ¡haz lo que te digo!; **— as you think best** haga lo que mejor le parezca; **— as you would be done by** trata como quieres ser tratado.

(b) (*fare*) **how is he —ing?** ¿qué tal le va esto?; **how did you — at school?** ¿qué tal le fue en el colegio?; **how do you —?** tengo mucho gusto en conocerle, (*less formally*) encantado, mucho gusto; **to — badly** sufrir reveses, ir perdiendo, fracasar, (*in exam*) salir mal; **you didn't — so badly** no le fue del todo mal; **to — well** tener éxito, prosperar, (*in exam*) salir bien; **her son's —ing well** su hijo tiene una buena posición; **business is —ing well** los negocios van bien; **the crops are —ing well** la cosecha se muestra espléndida.

(c) (*cook*) cocer.

(d) (*answer purpose*) servir; (*be suitable*) convenir, venir al caso, ser a propósito; **this one will —** me quedo con éste; **will this —?** ¿qué te parece éste?; (*suffice*) bastar; **will that —?** ¿te basta eso?; **that will — con** eso basta; está bien así; **that will —!** ¡basta ya!, ¡cállese!, ¡déjese de eso!; **that won't —** eso no vale; eso no se hace; **that will never —** eso no puede ser, eso no se puede consentir; **it would never — to** + *infin* sería inconcebible + *infin*, sería intolerable que + *subj*; **to make —** arreglárselas por su cuenta; **to make — with** contentarse con, conformarse con.

(e) (*with adv or prep*) **to — away with** suprimir, eliminar, poner fin a; *pet* sacrificar; *pest* exterminar; **to — for** (*sl*) acabar con; (*fam: as servant*) ser cocinera de, ser asistenta de, llevar la casa a; **to — with: I could — with a beer** ¡ojalá tuviera una cerveza!, ¡cuánto me gustaría beberme una cerveza!; **I could really — with another** en realidad necesito otro además; **we could — with more money** no nos vendría mal más dinero; **it can — with a wash** no le vendría mal un lavado; **to have nothing to — with** no tener (nada) que ver con; **she won't have anything to — with him** ella no quiere tener nada que ver con él; **we have nothing to — with the neighbours** no tenemos contacto alguno con los vecinos; **to — without** pasarse sin, prescindir de; **you can't — without money** es imprescindible tener dinero.

3 *v aux* (a) (*emphatic*) **— tell me** dígamelo, por favor; **I — feel better** ciertamente me encuentro mejor; **I — hope so** así lo espero; **I — so wish I could** ¡ojalá pudiera!; **but I did —** it pero yo sí lo hice.

(b) (*with inversion*) **rarely does it happen that** rara vez ocurre que.

(c) (*in questions*) **— you know him?** ¿le conoces?

(d) (*negation with* not) **you — not earn enough** Vd no gana bastante.

4 *verb substitute*: **I spoke before you did** yo hablé antes que Vd; **he talks to servants as others — to their dogs** habla a los criados como otros a sus perros; **— as I —** haga Vd como yo; **so — I** yo también, yo hago lo mismo; **did you see him? . . . I did** ¿le viste? . . . yo sí; **but I didn't** pero yo no; **he spoke as he often did** habló como lo había hecho muchas veces.

5 *vr*: **to — oneself proud** (*or* **well**) darse buena vida; permitirse cosas de lujo.

6 *n* (*fam*) (a) (*gathering*) reunión *f*; (*ceremony*) ceremonia *f*, acto *m*; (*party*) fiesta *f*, guateque *m*.

(b) (*trouble*) lío *m*; **that was quite a —** eso sí que fue un lío; **he had a — with the police** tuvo un lío con la policía.

doc [dɔk] *n* (*fam*) = **doctor.**

docile ['dəusail] *adj* dócil.

docility [dəu'siliti] *n* docilidad *f*.

dock¹ [dɔk] *n* (*Bot*) acedera *f*, ramaza *f*.

dock² [dɔk] *vt animal* descolar; *hair, tail* recortar; *pay etc* reducir, rebajar; **I've been —ed £1** me han rebajado la paga en una libra.

dock³ [dɔk] **1** *n* (*Naut*) dársena *f*, muelle *m*; (*with gates*) dique *m*; **—s** muelles *mpl*, puerto *m*; **dry — dique *m* seco; floating —** dique *m* flotante; **to be in —** (*fam: car*) estar averiado, tener averías.

2 *vt* poner en dique, hacer entrar en dique.

3 *vi* entrar en dique, atracar al muelle, (*loosely*) llegar; **we —ed at 5** llegamos a las 5, entramos en el puerto a las 5; **when we —ed at Vigo** cuando llegamos a Vigo.

dock⁴ [dɔk] *n* (*Law*) banquillo *m* de los acusados.

docker ['dɔkə*] *n* trabajador *m* portuario, estibador *m*.

docket ['dɔkit] *n* certificado *m*; (*label*) etiqueta *f*, marbete *m*.

dockyard ['dɔkjɑːd] *n* astillero *m*, (*naval*) arsenal *m*.

doctor ['dɔktə*] **1** *n* (*Med*) médico *m*, a *f*; (*Univ*) doctor *m*, ora *f* (*of* en); **family — médico *m* de cabecera; lady —, woman —** médica *f*; **to be under the —** ser atendida por el médico.

2 *vt* (*Med*) medicinar, tratar, curar; *cat etc* castrar; *drink* adulterar; *food* mezclar drogas con; **to — up** *machine etc* componer.

3 *vr*: **to — oneself** tomar medicinas, curarse.

doctorate ['dɔktərit] *n* doctorado *m*.

doctrinaire [͵dɔktri'nɛə*] **1** *adj* doctrinario. **2** *n* doctrinario *m*, a *f*.

doctrinal [dɔk'trainl] *adj* doctrinal.

doctrine ['dɔktrin] *n* doctrina *f*.

document ['dɔkjumənt] *n* documento *m*.

document ['dɔkjument] *vt* documentar.

documentary [͵dɔkju'mentəri] **1** *adj* documental. **2** *n* documental *m*.

documentation [͵dɔkjumen'teiʃən] *n* documentación *f*.

dodder ['dɔdə*] *vi* chochear.

doddering ['dɔdəriŋ] *adj*, **doddery** ['dɔdəri] *adj* chocho.

dodge [dɔdʒ] **1** *n* (*of body*) regate *m*, esguince *m*, evasión *f*; (*fig*) truco *m*, maniobra *f*; (*Mech*) dispositivo *m*.

2 *vt* (*elude*) evadir, *blow* esquivar, *pursuer* dar esquinazo a; **to — the issue** evadir el tema; **to — work** gandulear.

3 *vi* hurtar el cuerpo, dar un esguince; (*fig*) escurrir el bulto; **to — into a shop** entrar de repente en una tienda; **to — round a corner** doblar una esquina (y desaparecer); **to — behind a tree** ocultarse tras un árbol.

dodgems ['dɔdʒəmz] *npl* coches *mpl* de choque.

dodger ['dɔdʒə*] *n* gandul *mf*; **artful —** trampista *mf*.

dodo ['dəudəu] *n* dodo *m*, dodó *m*.

doe [dəu] *n* (*deer*) gama *f*; (*rabbit*) coneja *f*; (*hare*) liebre *f*.

doer ['duːə*] *n* hacedor *m*, ora *f*; agente *m*.

does [dʌz] *see* **do.**

doeskin ['dəuskin] *n* ante *m*, piel *f* de ante.

doesn't ['dʌznt] = **does not.**

doff [dɔf] *vt* quitarse.

dog [dɔg] **1** *n* (a) perro *m*; (*fox*) zorro *m*; **the —s** (*greyhounds*) carreras *fpl* de galgos, canódromo *m*.

(b) (*term of abuse*) tunante *m*, bribón *m*; **you —!** ¡canalla!, (*hum*) ¡tunante!; **gay —** tío *m* alegre; **you lucky —!** ¡qué chorra tienes!; **he's a lucky —** es un tío con suerte.

(c) **hot —** perro *m* caliente.

(d) **to be a — in the manger** ser el perro del

hortelano; **to be top** — ser el gallo del lugar, triunfar; **to go to the** —**s** echarse a perder, arruinarse; **you haven't a** —**'s chance** no tienes la más remota posibilidad; **to lead a** —**'s life** tener una vida de perros; **let sleeping** —**s lie** vale más no meneallo; **love me, love my** — quien quiere a Beltrán quiere a su can.
    2 *vt* seguir los pasos de, seguir la pista de; **he was** —**ged by ill luck** le persiguió la mala suerte.
dog biscuit ['dɔg,biskit] *n* galleta *f* de perro.
dogcart ['dɔgka:t] *n* dócar *m*.
dog collar ['dɔg,kɔlə*] *n* collar *m* de perro.
dog days ['dɔgdeiz] *npl* canícula *f*, caniculares *mpl*.
doge [dəudʒ] *n* dux *m*.
dog-eared ['dɔgiəd] *adj* sobado, muy manoseado.
dogfight ['dɔgfait] *n* (Aer) combate *m* aéreo (reñido y confuso); (*fig*) batalla *f* muy reñida.
dogfish ['dɔgfiʃ] *n* perro *m* marino, cazón *m*.
dogged ['dɔgid] *adj* tenaz, obstinado.
doggedly ['dɔgidli] *adv* tenazmente.
doggedness ['dɔgidnis] *n* tenacidad *f*.
doggerel ['dɔgərəl] *n* versos *mpl* ramplones, malos versos *mpl*, coplas *fpl* de ciego.
doggo ['dɔgəu] *adv* (*fam*): **to lie** — no bullir; estar escondido.
doggy ['dɔgi] *n* perrito *m*.
doghouse ['dɔghaus] *n*, *pl* —**houses** [,hauziz] (US) perrera *f*; **to be in the** — estar en desgracia.
dog Latin ['dɔg'lætin] *n* latín *m* macarrónico, latinajo *m*.
doglike ['dɔglaik] *adj* canino; de perro.
dogma ['dɔgmə] *n* dogma *m*.
dogmatic ['dɔg'mætik] *adj* dogmático.
dogmatically ['dɔg'mætikəli] *adv* dogmáticamente.
dogmatism ['dɔgmətizəm] *n* dogmatismo *m*.
dogmatize ['dɔgmətaiz] *vi* dogmatizar.
do-gooder ['du:'gudə*] *n* (*fam*) persona que apoya constantemente las obras benéficas etc, persona candorosa y abnegada.
dog rose ['dɔgrəuz] *n* escaramujo *m*, rosal *m* silvestre.
dogsbody ['dɔgzbɔdi] *n* (*sl*): **to be a** — cargar con la culpa de todo, ser el pagano; **to be the general** — hacer todo el trabajo rutinario, ocuparse en cosas que no quieren hacer los demás.
dog-tired ['dɔg'taiəd] *adj*: **to be** — estar rendido.
dog track ['dɔgtræk] *n* canódromo *m*.
dog-watch ['dɔgwɔtʃ] *n* (*Naut*) guardia *f* de cuartillo.
doily ['dɔili] *n* pañito *m* de adorno.
doing ['du:iŋ] **1** *pres part of* **do**; **there's not much** — hay poca animación; **nothing** —! ¡de ninguna manera!, ¡ni hablar!
    2 —**s** *npl* (**a**) (*deeds*) hechos *mpl*; (*conduct*) conducta *f*, actuación *f*; (*happenings*) sucesos *mpl*; **there were great** —**s in the house** hubo muchísima actividad en la casa.
    (**b**) (*Mech etc*) chisme *m*; **that** —**s with two knobs** aquel chisme con dos botones.
do-it-yourself ['du:itjə'self] *attr etc* hágalo Vd mismo; **a** — **kit** un equipo para hacerlo uno mismo; **he's a** — **enthusiast** le entusiasma hacer trabajos técnicos para sí mismo.
doldrums ['dɔldrəmz] *npl* (*Naut*) zona *f* de las calmas ecuatoriales; **to be in the** — (*fig: person*) estar abatido, (*business*) estar encalmado, (*stock exchange*) estar en calma.
dole [dəul] **1** *n* limosna *f*; (*of unemployed*) subsidio *m* de paro; **to be on the** — estar parado; **love on the** — el amor en la miseria.
    2 *vt*: **to** — **out** repartir, distribuir.
doleful ['dəulful] *adj* triste, lúgubre.
dolefully ['dəulfəli] *adv* tristemente.
doll [dɔl] **1** *n* muñeca *f*; (*sl*) chica *f*. **2** *vt*: **to** — **up** adornar, ataviar. **3** *vr*: **to** — **oneself up** emperejilarse, ataviarse.
dollar ['dɔlə*] *n* dólar *m*; **you can bet your bottom** — **that** es completamente seguro que.
dollop ['dɔləp] *n* porción *f*, masa *f*.
doll's house ['dɔlzhaus] *n*, *pl* — **houses** [,hauziz] casa *f* de muñecas.
dolly ['dɔli] *n* muñequita *f*.
dolomite ['dɔləmait] *n* dolomita *f*.
Dolomites ['dɔləmaits] *pl* Alpes *mpl* Dolomíticos.
dolphin ['dɔlfin] *n* delfín *m*.
dolt [dəult] *n* imbécil *m*, mastuerzo *m*; **you** —! ¡imbécil!
domain [dəu'mein] *n* (*lands*) heredad *f*, propiedad *f*; (*empire*) dominio *m*; (*sphere*) campo *m*, competencia *f*.
dome [dəum] *n* cúpula *f*; bóveda *f* (*also fig*); (*Geog*) colina *f* redonda.
domestic [də'mestik] **1** *adj* doméstico; *appliance* de uso doméstico; *industry, product* nacional; *trade*

interior; *strife* interno, intestino; (*home-loving*) casero, hogareño.
    2 *n* doméstico *m*.
domesticate [də'mestikeit] *vt* domesticar.
domesticated [də'mestikeitid] *adj* domesticado; *person* casero, hogareño.
domesticity [,dəumes'tisiti] *n* domesticidad *f*.
domicile ['dɔmisail] **1** *n* domicilio *m*. **2** *vt*: **to be** —**d in** tener su domicilio en.
domiciliary [,dɔmi'siliəri] *adj* domiciliario.
dominance ['dɔminəns] *n* dominación *f*.
dominant ['dɔminənt] *adj* dominante.
dominate ['dɔmineit] *vti* dominar.
domination [,dɔmi'neiʃən] *n* dominación *f*.
domineer [,dɔmi'niə*] *vi* dominar, tiranizar (*over someone* a alguien).
domineering [,dɔmi'niəriŋ] *adj* dominante, dominador, tiránico.
Dominica [,dɔmi'ni:kə] Dominica *f*.
Dominican [də'minikən] **1** *adj* dominicano. **2** *n* (*Pol*) dominicano *m*, a *f*; (*Eccl*) dominico *m*.
Dominican Republic [də'minikənri'pʌblik] República *f* Dominicana.
dominion [də'miniən] *n* dominio *m*.
domino ['dɔminəu] *n*, *pl* **dominoes** ['dɔminəuz] (*dress*) dominó *m*; (*in game*) ficha *f* de dominó.
dominoes ['dɔminəuz] *npl* dominó *m*s.
Domitian [də'miʃiən] *m* Domiciano.
don¹ [dɔn] *vt* ponerse.
don² [dɔn] *n* (*Univ*) catedrático *m*; (*strictly*) *socio* (*fellow*) de un colegio de las *Universidades de Oxford* y de Cambridge.
donate [dəu'neit] *vt* donar.
donation [dəu'neiʃən] *n* donativo *m*.
done [dʌn] *ptp of* **do**; (**a**) —! ¡trato hecho!; **well** —! ¡muy bien!, ¡bravo!
    (**b**) (*Cook*) **I like my meat well** — me gusta la carne muy hecha; **is it** — **yet?** ¿está hecho ya?
    (**c**) **it is not** — **to** + *infin* no es elegante + *infin*.
    (**d**) **have you** —? ¿has terminado?; **I've** — **with travelling** he terminado de viajar, he renunciado a los viajes; **I've** — **with him** he roto con él.
    (**e**) **I'm** — **for** (*tired*) estoy rendido; **if we don't leave now we shall be** — **for** si no nos vamos ahora estamos perdidos; **the car is** — **for** el coche está estropeado (para música); **as a musician he's** — **for** ya no vale para músico.
    (**f**) **to be** — **up** (*fam*) estar rendido.
Don Giovanni ['dɔndʒiəu'va:ni] *m* Don Juan.
donkey ['dɔŋki] *n* burro *m*, burra *f*; **for** —**'s years** durante tantísimos años.
donkey-engine ['dɔŋki,endʒin] *n* pequeña máquina *f* de vapor, motor *m* auxiliar.
donnish ['dɔniʃ] *adj* de erudito, de profesor; de aspecto erudito; (*pej*) pedantesco; **he looks very** — tiene aspecto de muy erudito.
donor ['dəunə*] *n* donante *mf*.
Don Quixote [dɔn'kwiksət] *m* Don Quijote.
don't [dəunt] **1** = **do not**. **2** *n* prohibición *f*, consejo *m* negativo.
doodle ['du:dl] **1** *n* garabatos *mpl* (*or* dibujos *etc*) que hace uno para distraerse. **2** *vi* hacer garabatos (*or* dibujos *etc*) para distraerse.
doom [du:m] **1** *n* (*fate*) suerte *f*, hado *m*; (*death*) perdición *f*, muerte *f*; (*Rel*) juicio *m* final.
    2 *vt* condenar (a muerte *etc*); predestinar (a la perdición *etc*); **to be** —**ed to die** ser condenado a muerte; **the plan was** —**ed to fail** el proyecto tuvo fatalmente que fracasar, el proyecto estuvo llamado a fracasar; **the** —**ed ship** el buque condenado.
doomsday ['du:mzdei] *n* día *m* del juicio final.
door [dɔ:*] *n* puerta *f*; entrada *f*; (*of vehicle*) portezuela *f*; **back** — puerta *f* de servicio; **front** — puerta *f* principal, puerta *f* de entrada; **revolving** — puerta *f* giratoria; **side** — puerta *f* accesoria; **sliding** — puerta *f* de corredera; **behind closed** —**s** a puerta cerrada; **next** — en la casa de al lado; **this is next** — **to lunacy** esto raya en la locura; **to be out of** —**s** estar al aire libre; **to be at death's** — estar a la muerte; **never darken my** — **again** no vuelva Vd nunca por aquí; **to lay the blame at someone's** — echar a uno la culpa; **to leave the** — **open for** dar libre paso a, no excluir; **to show someone to the** — acompañar a uno a la puerta; **to show someone the** — enseñar la puerta a uno; **to slam the** — dar un portazo; **to slam the** — **in someone's face** dar con la puerta en las narices de uno; **to slam the** — **on negotiations** terminar de modo concluyente las negociaciones.
doorbell ['dɔ:bel] *n* timbre *m* de llamada.
door-handle ['dɔ:,hændl] *n* tirador *m* de puerta; (*of car*) manija *f*.

doorkeeper ['dɔːˌkiːpə*] n conserje m, portero m.

door knob ['dɔːnɔb] n pomo m de puerta, tirador m de puerta.

door-knocker ['dɔːˌnɔkə*] n aldaba f, llamador m.

doorman ['dɔːmən] n, pl **-men** [mən] portero m.

doormat ['dɔːmæt] n felpudo m, estera f.

doornail ['dɔːneil] n see **dead**.

doorpost ['dɔːpəust] n jamba f (de puerta).

doorstep ['dɔːstep] n umbral m, peldaño m de la puerta.

doorway ['dɔːwei] n puerta f, entrada f; portal m.

dope [dəup] **1** n (varnish) barniz m; (drug) narcótico m, droga f; (information, sl) informes mpl, información f; (person, sl) imbécil m; **you** —! ¡imbécil! **2** vt (sl) narcotizar, drogar.

dopey ['dəupi] adj (sl) aturdido, mareado; (silly) imbécil.

doping ['dəupiŋ] n drogado m.

dormant ['dɔːmənt] adj (a) inactivo; **to be —**, **to lie —** dormir. (b) (fig) inactivo, latente, en estado latente.

dormer window ['dɔːməˈwindəu] n buhardilla f.

dormitory ['dɔːmitri] n dormitorio m.

dormouse ['dɔːmaus] n, pl **dormice** ['dɔːmais] lirón m.

Dorothy ['dɔrəθi] f Dorotea.

dorsal ['dɔːsl] adj dorsal.

dory ['dɔːri] n (Fish) gallo m, pez m de San Pedro.

dosage ['dəusidʒ] n dosificación f, dosis f.

dose [dəus] **1** n dosis f. **2** vt administrar una dosis a; medicinar; wine adulterar. **3** vr: **to — oneself** medicinarse (with de).

doss [dɔs] vi (sl) dormir; **to — down** echarse.

doss house ['dɔshaus] n, pl **— houses** [ˌhauziz] (sl) pensión f de bajísima categoría.

dossier ['dɔsiei] n expediente m; (police etc) ficha f; (fig) antecedentes mpl.

dot [dɔt] **1** n punto m; **three —s** (Typ) puntos mpl suspensivos; **—s and dashes** puntos mpl y rayas; **at 7 o'clock on the — —** a las 7 en punto; **to pay on the —** pagar puntualmente.

2 vt (a) letter poner el punto sobre; **to — the i's and cross the t's** (fig) poner los puntos sobre las íes, completar los detalles; terminar de aclarar un asunto.

(b) (speckle) puntear, motear, salpicar de puntos.

(c) (scatter; also **to — about**) esparcir, desparramar; **to be —ted with** estar salpicado de; **they are —ted about the country** se encuentran esparcidos por el país.

(d) (fam) **to — someone a blow** dar un golpe a uno; **he —ted him one** le dio un golpe.

dotage ['dəutidʒ] n chochez f; **to be in one's —** chochear.

dote [dəut] vi: **to — on** adorar, idolatrar.

doting ['dəutiŋ] adj chocho, tontamente cariñoso; **her — parents** sus padres que le querían con exceso.

dotty ['dɔti] adj (fam) chiflado; idea, scheme estrafalario, tonto.

double ['dʌbl] **1** adj doble; sense doble, ambiguo; bed de matrimonio, room para dos; **the — 6** el 6 doble; **— 9** (Tel) nueve nueve; **— the sum, a — sum** una cantidad doble, el doble; **it is — what it was** es el doble de lo que era; **my income is — that of my neighbour** mis ingresos son dobles que los de mi vecino; **to be bent —** estar encorvado.

2 adv: **— or quits** doble o nada; **to fold something —** doblar algo; **to pay —** pagar el doble; **to see —** tener doble vista.

3 n (a) doble mf, (person) doble mf, (Cine) doble mf.

(b) **—s** (Tennis) juego m de dobles; **men's —s** dobles mpl masculinos; **women's —s** dobles mpl de damas; **mixed —s** dobles mpl mixtos.

(c) (Bridge) doble m; **asking —** doble m de llamada; **penalty —** doble m de castigo.

(d) **at the —** corriendo, (Mil) a paso ligero.

4 vt doblar; money, quantity etc doblar, duplicar; efforts redoblar; (Theat, Bridge) doblar; **to be —d up with pain** retorcerse de dolor; **to be —d up with laughter** mondarse de risa.

5 vi doblarse; (quantity etc) doblarse, duplicarse; **to — back** volver sobre sus pasos; **to — for** sustituir a (also Theat), hacer las veces de; **to — up** (with pain) desplomarse, encogerse, retorcerse; (lodgers) compartir la misma habitación.

double-barrelled ['dʌblˌbærəld] adj de dos cañones; name de dos apellidos (unidos con guión).

double bass ['dʌbl'beis] n contrabajo m.

double-breasted ['dʌbl'brestid] adj cruzado, con botonadura doble.

double-cross ['dʌbl'krɔs] **1** n engaño m, trampa f, traición f. **2** vt engañar, traicionar.

double-dealing ['dʌbl'diːliŋ] n trato m doble, duplicidad f.

double-decker ['dʌbl'dekə*] n autobús m de dos pisos.

double-edged ['dʌbl'edʒd] adj de doble filo.

double entendre ['duːblɑːn'tɑːndr] n equívoco m, frase f ambigua.

double entry ['dʌbl'entri] n partida f doble.

double-jointed ['dʌbl'dʒɔintid] adj con articulaciones dobles.

double-quick ['dʌbl'kwik] adv rapidísimamente, con toda prontitud, (Mil) a paso ligero.

double-spaced ['dʌbl'speist] adv (Typ) a doble espacio.

doublet ['dʌblit] n jubón m; (Gram) doble etimología f.

double-talk ['dʌblˌtɔːk] n palabras fpl insinceras.

doubleton ['dʌbltən] n dubletón m.

doubly ['dʌbli] adv doblemente.

doubt [daut] **1** n (a —) duda f; (state) duda f, incertidumbre f; **no —!** ¡sin duda!; **beyond —**, **past all —**, **without (a) —** fuera de toda duda, indudablemente; **when in —** en caso de duda; **the matter is in some —** el caso sigue dudoso; **there is some — about it** sobre esto existen dudas; **there is no — that** es indudable que, no cabe duda de que; **to begin to have one's —s** empezar a dudar.

2 vt dudar; (distrust) dudar de; **I — it** lo dudo; **to — someone's loyalty** dudar de la lealtad de uno. **3** vi dudar; **he —ed whether to go** dudaba si iría.

doubter ['dautə*] n escéptico m, a f.

doubtful ['dautful] adj dudoso, incierto; character, place sospechoso; **I am — whether** dudo si; **he remained — about it** tenía todavía sus dudas sobre ello; **of — efficacy** de eficacia incierta.

doubtfully ['dautfəli] adv inciertamente; **he said —** dijo nada convencido.

doubtless ['dautlis] adv sin duda.

douche [duːʃ] **1** n ducha f; (Med) jeringa f. **2** vt duchar. **3** vi ducharse.

dough [dəu] n masa f, pasta f; (sl) pasta f.

doughboy ['dəubɔi] n (US fam) soldado m de infantería.

doughnut ['dəunʌt] n buñuelo m.

doughty ['dauti] adj person valiente, esforzado; deed hazañoso.

doughy ['dəui] adj pastoso.

dour [duə*] adj austero, severo; (obstinate) terco; **a — Scot** un escocés cerrado; **a — struggle** una batalla muy reñida.

Douro ['duərəu] Duero m.

douse [daus] vt light apagar; (with water) mojar, lavar (with de).

dove [dʌv] n paloma f.

dovecote ['dʌvkɔt] n palomar m.

dovetail ['dʌvteil] **1** n cola f de milano. **2** vt ensamblar a cola de milano. **3** vi (fig) encajar (con), ajustarse; **to — in with** encajar perfectamente con.

dowager ['dauədʒə*] n viuda f de un titulado; **— duchess** duquesa f viuda.

dowdy ['daudi] adj poco elegante, poco atractivo.

dowel ['dauəl] n clavija f.

down¹ [daun] n (Orn) plumón m, flojel m; (fluff) pelusa f; (on face) bozo m; (on body) vello m; (on fruit) pelusilla f; (Bot) vilano m.

down² [daun] n (Geog) colina f.

down³ [daun] **1** adv (a) (downwards) abajo, hacia abajo, para abajo; (to the ground) por tierra, en tierra; (to the south) hacia el sur; **I ran all the way —** bajé toda la distancia corriendo; **there was snow all the way —** estaba nevando durante todo el recorrido.

(b) **— below** allá abajo; **— by the river** abajo en la ribera; **— on the shore** abajo en la playa; **— to** hasta; **— under** en Australia or en Nueva Zelanda; **to go — under** ir a Australia etc.

(c) **to be —** (price, temperature, etc) haber bajado; (Aer) haber aterrizado, estar en tierra; (person) haber caído, estar en tierra; **to be — from college** haber terminado el curso universitario; **he's not — yet** todavía no ha bajado, sigue en cama; **to be — and out** no tener nada en absoluto, estar sin un cuarto, ser pobrísimo; **to be 3 goals —** tener 3 goles menos; **I'm £2 —** he perdido 2 libras, me faltan 2 libras; **to be — on someone** tener inquina a uno; **I'm — to my last cigarette** me queda un cigarrillo nada más.

2 prep: **— the hill** cuesta abajo; **— river** río abajo (from de); **to walk — the street** bajar la calle, ir po:

la calle; **the rain was running — the trunk** la lluvia corría por el tronco.

3 *interj* — **!** ¡abajo!; — **!**, — **boy!** *(to dog)* ¡quieto!; — **with the tyrant!** ¡abajo el tirano!, ¡muera el tirano!

4 *adj train, stroke* descendente; *payment* al contado.

5 *vt food* devorar; *drink* beberse (de un trago); *person* derribar, echar por los suelos; *plane* derribar, abatir; *see* **tool.**

6 *n:* **to have a — on someone** *(fam)* tener inquina a uno; *see* **up.**

down-and-out ['daunən'aut] **1** *adj* derrotado, pobrísimo. **2** *n* pobre *mf*, vagabundo *m*.

down-at-heel ['daunət'hi:l] *adj* decaído, venido a menos; *appearance* desastrado.

downcast ['daunka:st] *adj* abatido, alicaído.

downfall ['daunfɔ:l] *n* caída *f*, ruina *f*.

downgrade ['daungreid] *n:* **to be on the —** ir cuesta abajo, estar en plena decadencia.

downgrade [daun'greid] *vt* degradar, asignar a un grado más bajo.

downhearted ['daun'ha:tid] *adj* desanimado; **don't be —** no te dejes desanimar.

downhill ['daun'hil] **1** *adv* cuesta abajo; **to go —** *(fig)* ir cuesta abajo, estar en franca decadencia. **2** *adj* en declive.

downpour ['daunpɔ:*] *n* aguacero *m*, chaparrón *m*.

downright ['daunrait] **1** *adj person* franco; *lie* abierto, manifiesto; *(obvious)* notorio, evidente; *(out-and-out)* abierto, declarado. **2** *adv* completamente.

down-river ['daun'rivə*] *adv* = **downstream.**

downstairs ['daun'stɛəz] **1** *adv* abajo; *(in lower flat)* εn el piso de abajo; **to fall —** caer escaleras abajo; **he went slowly —** bajó despacio la escalera.

2 *adj* de abajo; **a — window** una ventana de la planta baja.

downstream ['daun'stri:m] *adv* aguas abajo, río abajo *(from* de); **to go —** ir río abajo; **to swim —** nadar con la corriente; **a town — from Soria** una ciudad más abajo de Soria; **about 5 km — from Zamora** unos 5 km más abajo de Zamora.

downstroke ['daunstrəuk] *n (with pen)* palote *m*, pierna *f*; *(Mech)* carrera *f* descendente.

down-to-earth ['dauntu'ə:θ] *adj* práctico, realista.

downtown ['daun'taun] **1** *adv go* hacia el centro de la ciudad, *be* en el centro de la ciudad. **2** *adj* del centro de la ciudad, céntrico.

downtrodden ['daun.trɔdn] *adj* oprimido.

downturn ['dauntə:n] *n* descenso *m*, bajada *f*, disminución *f*.

downward ['daunwəd] *adj curve, movement etc* descendente; *slope* en declive; *tendency* a la baja.

downward(s) ['daunwəd(z)] *adv* hacia abajo.

downy ['dauni] *adj* velloso; *(and soft)* blando, suave.

dowry ['dauri] *n* dote *f*.

dowse [dauz] *vt see* **douse.**

dowser ['dauzə*] *n* zahorí *m*.

doxy ['dɔksi] *n* querida *f*.

doyen ['dɔiən] *n* decano *m*.

doze [dəuz] **1** *n* sueño *m* ligero; sueño *m* breve; **to have a —** *(after meal)* echar una siestecita.

2 *vi* dormitar; **to — off** quedarse medio dormido, dormirse.

dozen ['dʌzn] *n* docena *f*; **baker's —** docena *f* del fraile; **daily —** pequeña serie *f* de ejercicios físicos para mantenerse en forma cada día; **to talk nineteen to the —** hablar más que siete.

dozy ['dəuzi] *adj (fam)* amodorrado.

drab [dræb] *adj (fig)* gris, monótono, triste.

drachm [dræm] *n,* **drachma** ['drækmə] *n* dracma *f*.

draconian [drə'kəuniən] *adj* draconiano, severo, riguroso.

draft [dra:ft] **1** *n (Comm)* giro *m*, letra *f* de cambio; *(Mil)* destacamento *m*; *(reinforcements)* refuerzos *mpl*; *(conscription)* quinta *f*; *(preliminary study)* borrador *m (also* **first —, rough —)**; **third —** tercera versión *f*; *see* **draught.**

2 *vt document* redactar; *scheme* preparar; *(rough out)* hacer un borrador de, preparar una versión de; *(Mil)* destacar, *(send)* mandar *(to* a); *(conscript)* quintar, llamar al servicio militar; *(fig)* forzar, obligar.

drag [dræg] **1** *n (net etc)* rastra *f*, red *f* barredera; *(sledge)* narria *f*; *(Aer etc)* resistencia *f* al avance; *(fig)* obstáculo *m*, estorbo *m (on* a, para); *(boring thing)* cosa *f* pesada, lata *f*; **the film is a —** la película es pesadísima.

2 *vt object* arrastrar, llevar arrastrado; *sea bed, river etc* dragar, rastrear, efectuar obras de dragado en; **to — the anchor** garrar; **to — something along** arrastrar algo tras sí, arrastrar algo con mucha

dificultad; **to — in** *reference* traer por los pelos; **to — out** *story* contar de una manera aburridísima.

3 *vi* arrastrarse por el suelo; *(go very slowly)* moverse muy despacio; *(time)* pasar lentamente; **the book begins to —** el libro empieza a perder su interés; **how that afternoon —ged!** ¡cómo nos aburrimos aquella tarde!; **to — for** rastrear en busca de; **to — on and on** continuar como si nunca fuera a acabarse, ser interminable.

4 *vr:* **to — oneself along** arrastrarse.

dragnet ['drægnet] *n* rastra *f*, red *f* barredera.

dragoman ['drægəumən] *n, pl* **—mans** [mənz] *or* **—men** [mən] dragomán *m*.

dragon ['drægən] *n* dragón *m*; *(woman)* fiera *f*.

dragonfly ['drægənflai] *n* libélula *f*, caballito *m* del diablo.

dragoon [drə'gu:n] **1** *n* dragón *m*. **2** *vt* tiranizar; **to — someone into doing something** obligar a uno por intimidación a hacer algo.

drain [drein] **1** *n (a) (outlet)* desaguadero *m*; *(in street)* boca *f* de alcantarilla, sumidero *m*; *(Agr)* zanja *f* de drenaje; **the —s** *(sewage system)* las alcantarillas, el alcantarillado.

(b) *(fig) (source of loss)* desaguadero *m*, sumidero *m*, desagüe *m*; *(loss)* pérdida *f*, disminución *f*; **to be a — on** *energies, resources* consumir, agotar; **they are a great — on our gold reserves** constituyen el gran sumidero de nuestras reservas de oro; **the brain —** la pérdida (por emigración) de gente de formación universitaria.

(c) there's just a — left quedan unas gotitas.

2 *vt (a)* desaguar; *(Agr, Med)* drenar; *(Mech)* purgar, drenar; *glass* apurar; *last drops* beberse, tragarse; *lake* desangrar, desecar; **to — away** vaciar; **to — off** desangrar.

(b) *(fig)* agotar, consumir; **the country is being —ed of wealth** el país está siendo empobrecido; **to feel —ed of energy** estar agotado, sentirse sin fuerzas.

3 *vi (washed dishes)* escurrirse; **to — away** irse; **to — into** *(river etc)* desaguar en.

drainage ['dreinidʒ] *n (a) (act)* desagüe *m*; *(Agr, Med)* drenaje *m*; *(of lake)* desecación *f*.

(b) *(sewage)* aguas *fpl* de alcantarillado; *(sewage system)* alcantarillado *m*.

drainage channel ['dreinidʒ.tʃænl] *n* zanja *f* de drenaje.

draining board ['dreinin.bɔ:d], **(US) drainboard** ['dreinbɔ:d] *n* escurreplatos *m*, escurridera *f*, escurridor *m*.

drainpipe ['dreinpaip] *n* tubo *m* de desagüe; **— trousers** pantalones *mpl* muy estrechos.

drake [dreik] *n* pato *m* macho.

dram [dræm] *n (Pharm)* dracma *f*; *(of drink)* trago *m*.

drama ['dra:mə] *n* drama *m*.

dramatic [drə'mætik] *adj* dramático.

dramatist ['dræmətist] *n* dramaturgo *m*.

dramatize ['dræmətaiz] *vt* dramatizar; **X —d by Y** X en versión dramática de Y.

drank [dræŋk] *pret of* **drink.**

drape [dreip] **1** *n* colgadura *f*, cortina *f*.

2 *vt object* adornar con colgaduras, cubrir *(in, with* de), vestir *(with* de); *cloth, clothing* arreglar los pliegues de; **— this round your shoulders** ponte esto sobre las espaldas; **he —d a towel about himself** se cubrió con una toalla; **he —d an arm about my shoulders** me ciñó el hombro con su brazo.

draper ['dreipə*] *n* pañero *m*, lencero *m*.

drapery ['dreipəri] *n (hangings)* colgaduras *fpl*, ropaje *m*; *(as merchandise)* pañería *f*.

drastic ['dræstik] *adj* drástico; enérgico, fuerte; *measure* draconiano, severo; *reduction etc* importante; *change* radical.

drastically ['dræstikəli] *adv* enérgicamente; severamente; **to be — reduced** sufrir una reducción importante; **he — revised his ideas** cambió radicalmente de ideas.

drat [dræt] *vt:* **—!**, **— it!** ¡maldición!

draught [dra:ft] **1** *n (a) (drink)* trago *m*; *(Med)* dosis *f*; **at one —** de un trago.

(b) *(Naut)* calado *m*.

(c) *(of air)* corriente *f* de aire; *(breeze)* viento *m*, brisa *f*; **to feel the —** *(fig)* tener dificultades, sufrir las consecuencias, resentirse de los efectos.

(d) **—s** *(game)* juego *m* de damas.

2 *attr horse* de tiro; *beer* de barril; *see* **draft.**

draughtboard ['dra:ftbɔ:d] *n* tablero *m* de damas.

draught excluder ['dra:ftiks'klu:də*] *n* burlete *m*.

draught horse ['dra:sthɔ:s] *n* caballo *m* de tiro.

draughtsman ['dra:ftsmən] *n, pl* **—men** [mən] delineante *m*, proyectista *m*.

draughtsmanship ['drɑ:ftsmənʃip] n arte m del delineante.

draughty ['drɑ:fti] adj room que tiene corrientes de aire, lleno de corrientes de aire; day, place de mucho viento.

draw [drɔ:] **1** n (a) (Sport) empate m, (Chess) tablas fpl.

(b) (lottery) sorteo m (for de).

(c) (attraction) atracción f; (Theat) función f taquillera, obra f de mucho éxito.

2 (irr: pret **drew**, ptp **drawn**) vt (a) (drag) arrastrar, tirar de; vehicle tirar; (attract) atraer; (take out) sacar; (extract) extraer; (pluck out) arrancar; (lengthen) alargar; attention llamar (to sobre); audience, crowd atraer; blood hacer manar, derramar; bow tender; breath tomar, aspirar; cards robar; cheque girar (on a cargo de, for por); comparison hacer; conclusion sacar; curtains correr; distinction hacer; drawing,model, scene dibujar; fowl destripar; line etc trazar, tirar; lots echar; money from bank retirar; number, prize sacarse; salary ganar, percibir, cobrar; tooth sacar, extraer; wages cobrar; water (draught) calar, tener un calado de; **to — a game** lograr el empate, empatar (with con), (Chess) entablar.

(b) **drawn: to be —n against** tener que jugar contra; **to feel —n to** subject sentir la atracción de, person tener simpatía a.

(c) **to — someone aside** apartar a uno, llamar a uno aparte; **to — back** retirar; curtain descorrer; **to — forth** hacer salir; comment motivar, suscitar; **to — in** tirar hacia dentro; atraer; **to — off** quitar; liquid vaciar, trasegar; pursuers desviar, apartar; **to — on** gloves ponerse; person engatusar; **to — out** (take out) sacar; (lengthen) alargar; wire tirar, trefilar; person hacer hablar, hacer menos reservado, (deceitfully) sonsacar; **to — together** reunir, juntar; **to — up** (raise) levantar, alzar; chair acercar; men formar; army ordenar para el combate; document redactar, preparar.

3 vi (a) (chimney) tirar (bien); (attract) atraer; (as artist) dibujar; (in game) empatar, (Chess) entablar.

(b) **to — aside** ir aparte, apartarse; **to — away** alejarse (from de); **to — back** dar un paso hacia atrás, retroceder; (fig) cejar, volverse atrás; **to — in** (evenings) hacerse más cortos; **to — near** acercarse (to a); **to — on** source inspirarse en; knowledge aprovechar; bank account retirar fondos de; supporters contar con el apoyo de; **to — out** (train etc) arrancar, ponerse en marcha, salir de la estación; **to — together** reunirse, juntarse, (fig) hacerse más unidos; **the family has —n together** la familia se ha unido más; **to — up** pararse; see close etc.

4 vr: **to — oneself up** erguirse, ponerse en su lugar.

drawback ['drɔ:bæk] n inconveniente m, desventaja f (of, to de).

drawbridge ['drɔ:bridʒ] n puente m levadizo.

drawee [drɔ:'i:] n (Comm) girado m.

drawer[1] ['drɔ:ə*] n (Comm) girador m.

drawer[2] [drɔ:*] n cajón m; **out of the top —** de primera calidad, de categoría superior.

drawers [drɔ:z] npl (man's) calzoncillos mpl, (woman's) bragas fpl.

drawing ['drɔ:iŋ] n dibujo m.

drawing board ['drɔ:iŋbɔ:d] n tablero m de delineante; (Art) tablero m de dibujo.

drawing pin ['drɔ:iŋpin] n chinche f.

drawing room ['drɔ:iŋrum] n salón m.

drawl [drɔ:l] **1** n habla f lenta y pesada. **2** vt pronunciar lenta y pesadamente, arrastrar. **3** vi hablar lenta y pesadamente.

drawn [drɔ:n] **1** ptp of **draw**. **2** adj game empatado; face cansado, ojeroso; long **— out** larguísimo, interminable; **with — sword** con la espada en la mano.

dray [drei] n carro m pesado.

dread [dred] **1** n pavor m, terror m; **to go in — of** tener miedo a; **to fill someone with —** infundir pavor a uno.

2 adj espantoso.

3 vt tener miedo a, temer; **I — what may happen when he comes** me horroriza lo que pueda pasar cuando venga; **I — to think of it** el pensamiento me horroriza.

dreadful ['dredful] **1** adj terrible, espantoso; (fig) horrible, fatal, malísimo; **how —!** ¡qué barbaridad!; **I feel —** me siento muy mal; **I feel — about it** la cosa me da vergüenza.

2 n: penny **—** novelita f (etc) de bajísima categoría.

dreadfully ['dredfəli] adv terriblemente; (fig) malísimamente; **I'm — sorry** lo siento muchísimo; **it's — difficult** es terriblemente difícil.

dreadnought ['drednɔ:t] n (Hist) acorazado m.

dream [dri:m] **1** n sueño m; (daydream) ensueño m; (ideal) ideal m; (fond hope) ilusión f; **sweet —s!** ¡duerme bien!; **the house of my —s** mi casa ideal, la casa soñada, la casa de mis ilusiones; **isn't he a —?** ¡qué despiste tiene!; **to see something in a —** ver algo en sueños; **she goes about in a —** parece que está soñando; **my fondest — is to + infin** mi mayor ilusión es + infin; **to be rich beyond one's —s** ser más rico de lo que jamás se soñara; **to succeed beyond one's wildest —s** tener muchísimo más éxito de lo que se esperaba.

2 attr ideal; **my — house** mi casa ideal; **to live in a — world** vivir en un mundo de sueños, vivir de pura fantasía.

3 (pret and ptp **dreamed** or **dreamt**) vti soñar (of con, that que); **to — away the day** pasar el día soñando; **to — up** inventar, idear; **you must have —ed it** lo habrás imaginado; **I wouldn't — of it!** ¡ni hablar!; **I wouldn't — of going** no se me ocurriría nunca ir.

dreamer ['dri:mə*] n soñador m, ora f, fantaseador m, ora f; visionario m, a f.

dreamily ['dri:mili] adv distraídamente, como si estuviera soñando.

dreamland ['dri:mlænd] n reino m del ensueño, país m de los sueños; utopía f.

dreamt [dremt] pret and ptp of **dream**.

dreamy ['dri:mi] adj character soñador, distraído, muy en las nubes; tone etc del que fantasea, distraído; music soñador, de sueño.

dreariness ['driərinis] n tristeza f, monotonía f; lo aburrido.

dreary ['driəri] adj triste, monótono; book etc aburrido.

dredge [dredʒ] **1** n draga f, rastra f. **2** vt channel dragar, limpiar (etc) con draga; mud etc dragar; **to — up** pescar (also fig).

dredger ['dredʒə*] n draga f.

dredging ['dredʒiŋ] n dragado m, obras fpl de dragado.

dregs [dregz] npl heces fpl, sedimento m; (fig) hez f; **the — of society** la hez de la sociedad; **to drain a glass to the —** apurar un vaso hasta las heces.

drench [drentʃ] **1** n (Vet) poción f. **2** vt mojar (in, with de), empapar (in, with en); **to get —ed** mojarse hasta los huesos.

drenching ['drentʃiŋ] adj torrencial.

Dresden ['drezdən] Dresde; **— china** loza f de Dresde.

dress [dres] **1** n (in general) vestido m, indumentaria f; (clothing) ropa f; (frock) vestido m; evening **—** (man's) traje m de etiqueta, (woman's) traje m de noche; full **—** traje m de etiqueta; morning **—** chaqué m.

2 vt vestir (in de, in green de verde); (Cook) aderezar, aliñar; (Agr) abonar (with de); (Mil) formar, alinear; hair peinar; skins adobar, curtir; shop window poner; Christmas tree arreglar, adornar; stone labrar; wood desbastar; wound curar, vendar; **to be —ed in** vestir, llevar, ir vestido de; **to get —ed** vestirse; **to — someone down** poner a uno como un trapo; **to — up** ataviar (in de); **to — someone up as** disfrazar a uno de.

3 vi vestirse; (Mil) alinearse; **to — well** vestir bien; **to — up** vestirse de etiqueta; **have we to get —ed up?** ¿tenemos que ir de etiqueta?; **to — up as** disfrazarse de.

dress circle ['dres'sə:kl] n principal m.

dress coat ['dres'kəut] n frac m.

dress designer ['dresdi'zainə*] n modisto m.

dresser ['dresə*] n aparador m (con estantes), rinconera f; (US) cómoda f con espejo.

dressing ['dresiŋ] n (act) el vestir(se); (Med) vendaje m; (Cook) salsa f, aliño m; (Agr) abono m.

dressing case ['dresiŋkeis] n neceser m.

dressing-down ['dresiŋ'daun] n rapapolvo m; **to give someone a —** echar un rapapolvo a uno.

dressing gown ['dresiŋgaun] n (woman's) bata f, salto m de cama; (man's) batín m.

dressing room ['dresiŋrum] n vestidor m; (Theat) camarín m, camerino m.

dressing station ['dresiŋ,steiʃən] n puesto m de socorro.

dressing table ['dresiŋ,teibl] n tocador m.

dressmaker ['dresmeikə*] n costurera f, modista f.

dressmaking ['dresmeikiŋ] n costura f.

dress rehearsal ['dresri'hə:səl] n ensayo m general.

dress shirt ['dres'ʃə:t] n camisa f de frac.

dress suit ['dres'su:t] n traje m de etiqueta.

dressy ['dresi] adj person aficionado a los trajes muy elegantes; clothing de mucho vestir, muy elegante.

drew [dru:] pret of **draw**.

dribble ['dribl] **1** n (Sport) regate m.

2 vt dejar caer gota a gota; (Sport) regatear, driblar.

3 *vi* gotear, caer gota a gota (*down* por); (*from mouth*) babear; (*Sport*) regatear, driblar.

driblet ['driblit] *n* adarme *m*; **in —s** por adarmes.

dribs [dribz] *npl:* **— and drabs** cantidades *fpl* pequeñísimas; **the money came in in — and drabs** el dinero llegó por adarmes, el dinero llegó lentamente y en pequeñas cantidades.

dried [draid] *adj* seco; *fruit* paso.

drift [drift] **1** *n* **(a)** (*Naut*) impulso *m* de la corriente, velocidad *f* de la corriente; (*amount off course*) deriva *f*; (*fig*) tendencia *f*, movimiento *m*; **the — from the land** la despoblación del campo, el éxodo rural; **the — to the city** el movimiento hacia la ciudad.
(b) (*fig: lack of drive*) inacción *f*.
(c) (*of sand, snow*) montón *m*; (*Geol*) terrenos *mpl* de acarreo.
(d) (*fig*) (*sense*) significado *m*; (*purpose*) intención *f*, propósito *m*; **to catch someone's —** caer en la cuenta de lo que uno quiere decir.
2 *vt* (*carry*) impeler, llevar; (*pile up*) amontonar.
3 *vi* (*Naut*) ir a la deriva; (*on water, in air etc*) flotar, dejarse llevar por la corriente (*or* el viento), ir arrastrado por la corriente (*or* el viento); (*be off course*) derivar; (*snow*) amontonarse; (*fig*) vivir sin rumbo, no tener propósito fijo; **to — into war** dejarse llevar a la guerra, entrar sin realmente quererlo en la guerra; **to — from job to job** cambiar a menudo de trabajo sin propósito fijo.

drifter ['driftə*] *n* trainera *f*.

drift ice ['driftais] *n* hielo *m* flotante.

drift-net ['driftnet] *n* traína *f*.

driftwood ['driftwud] *n* madera *f* de deriva.

drill [dril] **1** *n* **(a)** (*Mech*) taladro *m*; (*part of brace and bit*) broca *f*; (*bench machine*) fresadora *f*; (*dentist's*) fresa *f*; (*in mining*) perforadora *f*, barrena *f*; (*in roadmending, also* **pneumatic —**) martillo *m* picador, taladradora *f*.
(b) (*Agr: machine*) sembradora *f*.
(c) (*Agr: row*) hilera *f*, surco *m*.
(d) (*Mil etc*) instrucción; (*School*) ejercicios *mpl*, educación *f* física; **grammar —** ejercicios *mpl* de gramática; **oral —** práctica *f* oral; **you all know the —** (*fam*) todos sabéis lo que habéis de hacer; **what's the —?** (*fam*) ¿qué es lo que hemos de hacer?
2 *vt* **(a)** *metal etc* perforar, taladrar, barrenar; *hole* practicar.
(b) (*Agr*) sembrar con sembradora.
(c) (*Mil*) enseñar instrucción a; (*Sport etc*) entrenar, adiestrar; **to — a class in French** hacer ejercicios de francés con una clase; **to — someone to do something** enseñar metódicamente a uno a hacer algo.
3 *vi* **(a)** perforar (*for* en busca de).
(b) (*Mil*) hacer instrucción; (*Sport etc*) entrenarse, adiestrarse.

drilling ['driliŋ] *n* (*for oil etc*) perforación *f*.

drilling rig ['driliŋ,rig] *n* plataforma *f* de perforación submarina.

drily ['draili] *adv* secamente; **he said —** dijo guasón, dijo con su humorismo peculiar.

drink [driŋk] **1** *n* (*in general, alcohol*) bebida *f*; (*a draught*) trago *m*; **soft —** bebida *f* no alcohólica; **the —** (*sl*) el mar, el agua; **I need a — of water** necesito un trago de agua; **could I have a — of water?** ¿puede Vd darme un poco de agua?; **to have a —** tomar algo; **will you have a —?** ¿quieres tomar algo?; **we had a — or two** tomamos unas copas; **to take to —** darse a la bebida.
2 (*irr: pret* **drank**, *ptp* **drunk**) *vt* beber; tomar; **what will you —?** ¿qué quieres tomar?; **to — someone under the table** beber hasta tumbar a uno; **to — down, to — off** beber de un trago; **to — in** (*fig*) beberse, *words* estar pendiente de; **to — out of** beber de; **to — up** beberse, terminar de beber.
3 *vi* (*ie — alcohol*) beber; **thanks, I don't —** gracias, yo no bebo; **to — like a fish** beber como una esponja; **to — to someone** brindar por uno, beber a la salud de uno; **to — to the success of** brindar por el éxito de; **to — up** terminar de beber.
4 *vr:* **to — oneself to death** morir alcoholizado; **to — oneself silly** beber hasta emborracharse.

drinkable ['driŋkəbl] *adj* potable, bebible; **it's quite a —** wine es un vino nada malo.

drinker ['driŋkə*] *n* bebedor *m*, ora *f*; **hard —** bebedor *m* empedernido.

drinking bout ['driŋkiŋbaut] *n* juerga *f* de borrachera.

drinking fountain ['driŋkiŋ,fauntin] *n* fuente *f* (de agua potable).

drinking song ['driŋkiŋsɔŋ] *n* canción *f* de taberna.

drinking trough ['driŋkiŋtrɔf] *n* abrevadero *m*, camellón *m*.

drinking water ['driŋkiŋ,wɔːtə*] *n* agua *f* potable.

drip [drip] **1** *n* (*act*) goteo *m*, el gotear; (*one drop*) gota *f*; (*bore, sl*) pelmazo *m*; (*fool, sl*) tonto *m*.
2 *vt* dejar caer gota a gota.
3 *vi* gotear, caer gota a gota (*down* por).

drip-dry ['drip'drai] *adj* de lava y pon.

dripping ['dripiŋ] **1** *adj tap etc* que gotea; *clothes* chorreantes, que chorrean agua; **to be — wet** estar calado. **2** *n* pringue *m*.

drive [draiv] **1** *n* **(a)** (*outing*) paseo *m* (en coche *etc*); (*journey*) viaje *m* (en coche *etc*); **to go for a —** dar un paseo en coche; **to take someone for a —** llevar a uno de paseo en coche; **it's a long —** es mucho viaje.
(b) (*Hunting*) batida *f*; (*Mil*) ataque *m*, avance *m*; (*fig*) campaña *f* (*against, on* contra, *para* suprimir).
(c) (*stroke*) golpe *m* fuerte, golpe *m* directo; (*Tennis*) golpe *m* a ras de la red.
(d) (*energy*) energía *f*, vigor *m*; (*driving force*) impulso *m*.
(e) (*carriageway*) calzada *f*, avenida *f*.
(f) (*Mech*) mecanismo *m* de transmisión; **front-wheel —** tracción *f* delantera; **left-hand —** conducción *f* a la izquierda.
2 (*irr: pret* **drove**, *ptp* **driven**) *vt* **(a)** (*urge in a direction*) empujar, impeler; *game* batir; *cattle* guiar, llevar; **to — away** ahuyentar; *person* alejar, *cares etc* quitarse de encima, alejar; **to — back** rechazar, *defenders* obligar a ceder terreno, *crowd* obligar a retroceder; **to — off = to — away**; **to — an actor off the stage** hacer que un actor abandone la escena; **to — out** obligar a salir (*of* de); expulsar.
(b) (*urge on*) hacer trabajar, hacer sudar; **he drove us to victory** él nos condujo a la victoria.
(c) (*steer*) *car, carriage etc* conducir, pilotar, guiar; *plough* manejar.
(d) (*power*) mover, actuar; *vehicle etc* impulsar; **the wind —s the boat along** el viento empuja el barco; **a car —n by steam** un coche impulsado por vapor, un coche que funciona con vapor; **to — on** empujar, llevar adelante.
(e) *ball etc* golpear con fuerza; *furrow* hacer; *hole* perforar, practicar; *tunnel* abrir, construir; *road* construir; *nail* clavar (*into* en); *teeth etc* hincar (*into* en); *object* introducir a la fuerza (*into* en); (*fig*) *bargain* hacer; **to — a way through** abrirse paso por.
(f) (*carry*) *passenger* llevar en coche.
(g) (*force*) **to — someone to do something, to — someone into doing something** forzar a uno a hacer algo; **to — someone mad** volver a uno loco.
3 *vi* **(a)** (*steer*) conducir, manejar (*SAm*); **"drive slowly"** "marcha moderada"; **to — on the left** circular por la izquierda.
(b) (*go etc*) pasearse en coche, dar un paseo en coche; **to — to London** ir en coche a Londres; **he drove alone** hizo el viaje solo; **he drove 50 miles in an hour** recorrió 50 millas en una hora; **to — off** irse en coche, marcharse; (*car*) arrancar y alejarse; **to — on** seguir adelante; **to — past** pasar delante de; **to — up** llegar en coche; **to — up to town** ir en coche a la ciudad.
(c) **the rain is driving down** está lloviendo a chuzos.
(d) **to let — at** asestar un golpe a; (*fig*) denunciar.
(e) **to — at** insinuar, querer decir; **what are you driving at?** ¿qué quiere Vd decir?, ¿qué pretende Vd?

drive-in ['draiv,in] *n* (*US*) parador *m* (de carretera); (*cinema*) motocine *m*.

drivel ['drivl] **1** *n* tonterías *fpl*. **2** *vi* decir tonterías.

driven ['drivn] *ptp of* **drive**.

driver ['draivə*] *n* (*Aut*) conductor *m*, ora *f*; chófer *m*, chofer *m* (*SAm*); (*Rail*) maquinista *m*; (*of coach*) cochero *m*; **racing —** corredor *m* automovilista.

driveway ['draivwei] *n* calzada *f*, avenida *f*.

drive-yourself ['draivjɔːˈself] *attr:* **— service** servicio *m* de alquiler sin chófer.

driving ['draiviŋ] **1** *adj rain* torrencial. **2** *attr power motor;* (*fig*) impulsor; (*Aut*) de conducción para conductor *etc*. **3** *n* el conducir; automovilismo *m*.

driving belt ['draiviŋbelt] *n* correa *f* de transmisión.

driving instructor ['draiviŋinˈstrʌktə*] *n* instructor *m* de conducción.

driving lesson ['draiviŋ,lesn] *n* clase *f* de conducción.

driving licence ['draiviŋ,laisəns] *n* permiso *m* de conductor, carnet *m* de conductor.

driving mirror ['draiviŋ,mirə*] *n* retrovisor *m*.

driving school ['draiviŋskuːl] n autoescuela f, escuela f automovilista, academia f de conductores.
driving test ['draiviŋtest] n examen m de conducción.
drizzle ['drizl] 1 n llovizna f. 2 vi lloviznar.
droll [drəul] adj (funny) divertido, gracioso; (odd) raro.
dromedary ['drɔmidəri] n dromedario m.
drone [drəun] 1 n (a) (Ent, fig) zángano m.
(b) (noise) zumbido m; (of voice) tono m monótono.
2 vi zumbar; (voice) hablar monótonamente; he —d on and on hablaba interminablemente en tono monótono.
drool [druːl] vi babear; to — over (fig) extasiarse como un tonto ante.
droop [druːp] 1 vt inclinar; dejar caer (over por).
2 vi inclinarse; (fall) caer, colgar; (flower) marchitarse; (fig: spirit) decaer, (person) desanimarse.
drooping ['druːpiŋ] adj caído; flower marchito; ears gacho; movement lánguido, desmayado.
drop [drɔp] 1 n (a) (of liquid) gota f (also Med); (sweet) pastilla f; just a — dos gotitas nada más; there's just a — left quedan unas gotas; with a — of soda con un poquitín de sifón; I haven't touched a — no he bebido una sola gota; in 3 weeks we didn't have a — of rain no cayó ni una gota en 3 semanas; it's a — in the ocean es tan poco que no tiene importancia; he's had a — too much lleva una copa de más.
(b) (fall) caída f; (by parachute) lanzamiento m; (in price) baja f; (of temperature etc) descenso m; (in number, demand) disminución f, reducción f (in de); at the — of a hat con cualquier pretexto.
(c) (slope) bajada f, declive m, pendiente f; (cliff) precipicio m; there's a — of 6 metres esto está a una altura de 6 metros sobre el suelo; to have the — on someone (fam) llevar la delantera a uno.
(d) (Theat) telón m de boca.
2 vt (a) (let fall) dejar caer; (let go of) soltar; bomb, parachutist lanzar; anchor echar; letter in pillar box echar; note poner (to a); curtsy hacer; hint soltar; passenger dejar (at en); eyes, voice bajar; price reducir; charge retirar; (allow to drip) verter a gotas.
(b) game, enemy derribar, tumbar.
(c) (lose) perder.
(d) (lengthen) alargar, extender hacia abajo.
(e) (omit) omitir; letter H no pronunciar; syllable comerse; claim, plan renunciar a, abandonar; condition etc suprimir; habit dejar; subject dejar, cambiar de; friend romper con; — that! ¡déjese de eso!; we had to — what we were doing tuvimos que dejar lo que estábamos haciendo; they —ped him like a hot brick le abandonaron como a perro sarnoso; I've been —ped from the team ya no formo parte del equipo.
3 vi (fall) caer; caer a tierra; (terrain) bajar; (price) bajar; (temperature etc) descender; (number, demand) disminuir; (wind) calmarse, amainar; (drip) gotear; (crouch) agacharse; to — with fatigue caer rendido; I feel ready to — estoy que no me tengo; so we let the matter — así que dejamos el asunto; to — behind quedarse atrás, rezagarse; to — down caer; (crouch) agacharse; we —ped down to the coast bajamos hacia la costa; to — in entrar de sopetón, entrar de paso; to — in on someone visitar a uno inesperadamente; do — in any time ven a vernos sin ceremonias y cuando quieras; to — off (part) desprenderse, separarse; (passenger) bajar (at en); (go to sleep) quedarse dormido; to — out (part) desprenderse, separarse; (person) darse de baja; retirarse (of de); he —ped out of my life no volví a saber nada de él; see sight.
droplet ['drɔplit] n gotita f.
dropper ['drɔpə*] n (Med etc) cuentagotas m.
droppings ['drɔpiŋz] npl excremento m (de animales).
dropsical ['drɔpsikəl] adj hidrópico.
dropsy ['drɔpsi] n hidropesía f.
dross [drɔs] n escoria f (also fig).
drought [draut] n sequía f.
drove [drəuv] 1 pret of drive. 2 n (Agr) rebaño m, manada f; (of people) multitud f; people came in —s la gente acudió en tropel.
drover ['drəuvə*] n boyero m, pastor m.
drown [draun] 1 vt (kill) anegar; kittens etc ahogar; (inundate) anegar, inundar; sound apagar; cry ahogar; sorrows olvidar emborrachándose; his cries were —ed by the noise of the waves sus gritos se perdieron en el estruendo de las olas.
2 vi (also to be —ed) perecer ahogado.
3 vr: to — oneself ahogarse.
drowse [drauz] vi dormitar, quedar medio dormido; to — off adormecerse.

drowsiness ['drauzinis] n somnolencia f; (sluggishness) modorra f.
drowsy ['drauzi] adj (sleepy) soñoliento; (sluggish) amodorrado; (lulling) soporífero; to be —, to feel — tener sueño.
drub [drʌb] vt apalear, vapulear; (fig) derrotar, cascar.
drubbing ['drʌbiŋ] n paliza f; (fig) paliza f, derrota f.
drudge [drʌdʒ] 1 n esclavo m del trabajo; (in home) esclava f de la cocina. 2 vi trabajar como un esclavo.
drudgery ['drʌdʒəri] n trabajo m penoso, faena f monótona; to take the — out of work hacer el trabajo menos penoso.
drug [drʌg] 1 n (Med) droga f, medicamento m, fármaco m; (eg heroin) droga f, narcótico m, estupefaciente m; to be a — on the market ser invendible.
2 vt person narcotizar, drogar, administrar narcóticos a; wine etc echar un narcótico a; to be —ged with sleep estar muerto de sueño.
3 vr: to — oneself drogarse.
drug addict ['drʌg'ædikt] n toxicómano m, a f, morfinómano m, a f.
drug addiction ['drʌgə'dikʃən] n toxicomanía f, morfinomanía f.
druggist ['drʌgist] n farmacéutico m; —'s (shop) farmacia f.
drugstore ['drʌgstɔː*] n (US) farmacia f, droguería f.
drug traffic ['drʌg'træfik] n contrabando m de narcóticos.
druid ['druːid] n druida m.
drum [drʌm] 1 n (Mus) tambor m, (large) timbal m, bombo m; (Mech) tambor m; (for oil) bidón m; (of ear) tímpano m; —s (in band) batería f; bass — bombo m.
2 vt: to — one's fingers on the table tabalear, tamborilear con los dedos en la mesa; to — something into someone hacer que uno aprenda algo a fuerza de repetírselo; to — someone out expulsar a uno; to — up support reunir, organizar; trade fomentar.
3 vi (Mus) tocar el tambor; (with fingers) tabalear, tamborilear, teclear; (with heels) zapatear; the noise is —ming in my ears el ruido me está taladrando los oídos; his words —med in my mind sus palabras se repetían incansablemente en mi cabeza.
drumhead ['drʌmhed] n parche m de tambor; — court-martial consejo m de guerra sumarísimo.
drummer ['drʌmə*] n tambor m.
drumstick ['drʌmstik] n palillo m, baqueta f.
drunk [drʌŋk] 1 ptp of drink.
2 adj: to be — estar borracho; to get — emborracharse; to get someone — emborrachar a uno; as — as a lord más borracho que una cuba; to be — with joy estar ebrio de alegría.
3 n (fam) borracho m; to go on a — ir a emborracharse.
drunkard ['drʌŋkəd] n borracho m, a f.
drunken ['drʌŋkən] adj borracho; a — brawl una reyerta de borrachos; in a — voice en una voz turbada por el alcohol; charged with — driving acusado de conducir en estado de embriaguez.
drunkenness ['drʌŋkənnis] n embriaguez f.
dry [drai] 1 adj seco; climate árido, seco; bread sin mantequilla, (stale) viejo; measure para áridos; book, speech aburrido; wit peculiar; state (US) prohibicionista; as — as a bone completamente seco; as — as dust de lo más aburrido; I'm very — tengo mucha sed.
2 n: we are in the — estamos bajo techo.
3 vt secar (also to — off, to — up); (wipe) enjugar; tears enjugarse; to — up deshidratar.
4 vi secarse (also to — off); to — up (spring etc) secarse, agotarse; (Meteorol) dejar de llover; (fam) callarse, (in speech) atascarse; oh do — up! ¡cállese por Dios!
dry-as-dust ['draiəz'dʌst] adj de lo más seco, de lo más aburrido.
dry-clean ['drai'kliːn] vt limpiar en seco.
dry cleaner's ['drai'kliːnəz] n tintorería f.
dry cleaning ['drai'kliːniŋ] n limpieza f en seco.
dryer ['draiə*] n (for hair) secador m.
dry-eyed ['drai'aid] adj sin lágrimas.
dry goods ['draigudz] n (US): — store mercería f.
drying ['draiiŋ] adj wind secante.
drying-up ['draiiŋ'ʌp] n secamiento m; deshidratación f.
dryness ['drainis] n sequedad f, lo seco; (of climate) aridez f; (of wit) lo peculiar.
dry rot ['drai'rɔt] n putrefacción f fungoide.
dry-shod ['drai'ʃɔd] adj a pie enjuto.
dual ['djuəl] adj doble; (Gram) dual.
dualism ['djuəlizəm] n dualismo m.
duality [dju'æliti] n dualidad f.

dual-purpose ['djuəl'pəːpəs] adj que sirve para dos cosas, de doble finalidad.
dub[1] [dʌb] vt knight armar caballero a; (with name) apodar.
dub[2] [dʌb] vt film doblar.
dubbin ['dʌbin] n adobo m impermeable.
dubbing ['dʌbiŋ] n (of film) doblaje m.
dubiety [djuːˈbaiəti] n incertidumbre f.
dubious ['djuːbiəs] adj dudoso; compliment equívoco; character sospechoso; **to be — about** tener dudas sobre; **I am — whether** dudo si.
dubiously ['djuːbiəsli] adv look etc con duda; act de manera sospechosa.
Dublin ['dʌblin] Dublín.
ducal ['djuːkəl] adj ducal.
ducat ['dʌkit] n ·lucado m (moneda).
duchess ['dʌtʃis] n duquesa f.
duchy ['dʌtʃi] n ducado m (territorio).
duck[1] [dʌk] n (Orn) pato m, ánade m; (domestic) pato m; **yes, —(s)** (fam) sí, querido; **lame — persona** f incapacitada, (Comm) persona f insolvente, (US) político m derrotado; **like water off a —'s back** sin producir efecto alguno; **to play —s and drakes** hacer saltar una piedra plana sobre el agua; **to play —s and drakes with** despilfarrar; **to take to something like a — to water** aprender a hacer algo con la mayor facilidad.
duck[2] [dʌk] **1** n (a) (under water) chapuz m.
(b) (to escape) agachada f, (Boxing) esquiva f.
2 vt (a) (in water) chapuzar.
(b) (to escape) agachar (la cabeza etc), bajar.
3 vi (a) (in water) chapuzarse, sumergirse.
(b) (to escape) agachar la cabeza, agacharse, hurtar el cuerpo.
ducking ['dʌkiŋ] n chapuz m, inmersión f.
duckling ['dʌkliŋ] n patito m, anadón m.
duckweed ['dʌkwiːd] n lenteja f de agua.
ducky ['dʌki] n (fam): —! ¡querido!
duct [dʌkt] n conducto m, canal m.
ductile ['dʌktail] adj dúctil.
ductless ['dʌktlis] adj: **— gland** glándula f cerrada, glándula f de secreción interna.
dud [dʌd] **1** adj coin etc falso; shell que no estalla, que está sin estallar.
2 n (coin) moneda f falsa; (shell) obús m que no estalla, granada f que está sin estallar; (machine) filfa f; (person) persona f inútil.
dude [djuːd] n (US) petimetre m, gomoso m; **— ranch** rancho m para turistas.
dudgeon ['dʌdʒən] n: **in high —** enojadísimo.
duds [dʌdz] npl (US: fam) prendas fpl de vestir, trapos mpl; pertenencias fpl.
due [djuː] **1** adj debido; conveniente, oportuno; **to be —** (Comm) ser pagadero; **I have £5 — to me** me deben 5 libras; **our thanks are — to him** le estamos muy agradecidos; **it is — to** esto se debe a, esto se debe a; **it is — to the car breaking down** esto es debido a que el coche tuvo una avería; **the train is — at 8** el tren debe llegar a las 8; **I'm — in London tomorrow** tengo que ir a Londres mañana, mañana me esperan en Londres; **it was — to happen yesterday** esto se esperaba para ayer; **when is it — to happen?** ¿para cuándo se prevé esto?; **it is — to be demolished** se prevé su demolición; **to fall —** (Comm) vencer.
2 adv: **— to** debido a, por causa de; **to go — east** ir derecho hacia el este.
3 n (debt) deuda f; (desert) lo que merece uno; **—s** derechos mpl; **to get one's —** recibir lo que merece uno, (in bad sense) llevar su merecido; **to give him his —** hay que reconocer la razón (or las cualidades etc) que tiene; **to give him his —, I . . .** para evitar cualquier posibilidad de ser injusto con él, yo . . .
duel ['djuəl] **1** n duelo m; **to fight a — = 2** vi batirse en duelo.
duellist, (US) **duelist** ['djuəlist] n duelista m.
duet [djuːˈet] n dúo m.
duff[1] [dʌf] adj (fam) soso, insípido.
duff[2] [dʌf] vt (sl): **to — someone up** dar una paliza a uno.
duffel bag ['dʌfəlbæg] n (Mil) talego m para efectos de uso personal.
duffel coat ['dʌfəlkəut] n comando m, abrigo m tres cuartos.
duffer ['dʌfə*] n zoquete m.
dug[1] [dʌg] n (Zool) teta f, ubre f.
dug[2] [dʌg] pret and ptp of **dig.**
dugout ['dʌgaut] n refugio m subterráneo.
duke [djuːk] n duque m.
dukedom ['djuːkdəm] n ducado m (título).
dulcet ['dʌlsit] adj dulce, suave.
dulcimer ['dʌlsimə*] n dulcémele m.

dull [dʌl] **1** adj colour, gleam apagado; light sombrío, pálido; surface deslustrado, mate; sound, pain sordo; edge embotado; day, weather gris; stock market inactivo, flojo; person (slow) lerdo, torpe; (uninteresting) soso, insípido, pesado; **as — as ditchwater** de lo más aburrido; **I feel — today** hoy me siento desanimado, hoy me encuentro sin fuerzas.
2 vt edge embotar; surface deslustrar; pain aliviar; person entorpecer; enthusiasm etc enfriar.
dullard ['dʌləd] n zoquete m.
dullness ['dʌlnis] n lo deslustrado; lo sombrío; inactividad f, flojedad f; torpeza f; lo soso, insipidez f.
dully ['dʌlli] adv de modo apagado, con brillo apagado; pálidamente; sordamente, con ruido sordo.
duly ['djuːli] adv (properly) debidamente; (punctually) a su debido tiempo; **he — arrived at 3** llegó en efecto a las 3; **he — protested** protestó de la manera que se había previsto; **everybody was — shocked** se escandalizaron todos según era de esperar.
dumb [dʌm] adj mudo; (fam) estúpido, soso; **the — millions** los millones que no tienen voz; **— animal** bruto m; **to become —** quedar mudo; **to strike someone —** dejar a uno sin habla.
dumbbell ['dʌmbel] n pesa f.
dumbfound ['dʌm'faund] vt dejar sin habla, pasmar; **we were —ed** quedamos mudos de asombro.
dumbness ['dʌmnis] n mudez f; (fam) estupidez f.
dumb show ['dʌm'ʃəu] n pantomima f; **in — por** señas.
dumbwaiter ['dʌm'weitə*] n estante m giratorio; (US) montaplatos m.
dum-dum ['dʌmdʌm] adj: **— bullet** bala f dumdum.
dummy ['dʌmi] **1** adj falso, postizo.
2 n (life-size figure) muñeco m; (tailor's) maniquí m; (packet) envase m vacío; (baby's) chupete m; (Bridge) muerto m.
dump [dʌmp] **1** n (heap) montón m; (rubbish tip) basurero m, vaciadero m; (Mil) depósito m; (fam) pueblucho m, poblachón m; **to be down in the —s** (fam) tener murria.
2 vt rubbish etc descargar, verter, vaciar; (get rid of) deshacerse de, dejar; goods inundar el mercado con; **to — something down** (fam) poner algo (con mucho ruido); **can I — this here?** ¿puedo dejar esto aquí?
dumping ['dʌmpiŋ] n (Comm) dumping m.
dumpling ['dʌmpliŋ] n bola f de masa hervida.
dumpy ['dʌmpi] adj regordete, culibajo.
dun[1] [dʌn] adj pardo.
dun[2] [dʌn] vt: **to — someone** apremiar a uno para que pague lo que debe; (fig) dar la lata a uno.
dunce [dʌns] n zopenco m, a f.
dunderhead ['dʌndəhed] adj zoquete m.
dune [djuːn] n duna f.
dung [dʌŋ] n excremento m; (as manure) estiércol m.
dungarees [ˌdʌŋgəˈriːz] npl mono m.
dungeon ['dʌndʒən] n mazmorra f, calabozo m.
dunghill ['dʌŋhil] n estercolero m.
dunk [dʌŋk] vt (US) mojar, remojar.
Dunkirk [dʌn'kəːk] Dunquerque.
duo ['djuːəu] n dúo m.
duodecimal [ˌdjuːəuˈdesiməl] adj duodecimal.
duodenum [ˌdjuːəuˈdiːnəm] n duodeno m.
dupe [djuːp] **1** n primo m, inocentón m; **to be the — of** ser víctima de. **2** vt engañar, embaucar; (swindle) timar.
duplicate ['djuːplikit] **1** adj duplicado. **2** n duplicado m; (copy of letter etc) copia f, doble m; **in — por** duplicado.
duplicate ['djuːplikeit] vt duplicar; text hacer a multicopista.
duplicating machine ['djuːplikeitiŋməˈʃiːn] n multicopista m.
duplication [ˌdjuːpliˈkeiʃən] n duplicación f; pluralidad f.
duplicator ['djuːplikeitə*] n multicopista m.
duplicity [djuːˈplisiti] n duplicidad f, doblez f.
durability [ˌdjuərəˈbiliti] n lo duradero, durabilidad f.
durable ['djuərəbl] adj duradero.
duration [djuəˈreiʃən] n duración f; **for the —** (fam) mientras dure la guerra.
Dürer ['djuərə*] m Durero.
duress [djuəˈres] n compulsión f; **under — por** compulsión.
during ['djuəriŋ] prep durante.
durst [dəːst] (arch) pret of **dare.**
dusk [dʌsk] n crepúsculo m, anochecer m; **at — al** atardecer; **in the gathering —** en la oscuridad casi de la noche.
dusky ['dʌski] adj oscuro; complexion moreno.
dust [dʌst] **1** n polvo m; (sweepings) barreduras fpl;

(*rubbish*) basura *f*; (*of coal*) cisco *m*; **to bite the —** morder el polvo; **to kick up the —** levantar una polvoreda; **to raise a —** armarla; **to shake the — of a place off one's feet** salir muy ofendido de un lugar; **to throw — in someone's eyes** engañar a uno.
   2 *vt* (**a**) (*take — off*) quitar el polvo a, desempolvar, (*by beating*) sacudir el polvo a; (*clean*) limpiar.
   (**b**) **to — something with** salpicar algo de, (*Cook etc*) espolvorear algo de; **— the insecticide on the surface** espolvoree el insecticida sobre la superficie.
dustbin ['dʌstbin] *n* cubo *m* de la basura.
dustbowl ['dʌstbəul] *n* terreno *m* inutilizado por la erosión.
dustcart ['dʌstkɑːt] *n* camión *m* de la basura.
dustcloud ['dʌstklaud] *n* polvoreda *f*.
dust cover ['dʌst,kʌvə*] *n* guardapolvo *m*; (*of book*) sobrecubierta *f*, camisa *f*.
duster ['dʌstə*] *n* (*cloth*) paño *m*, trapo *m*, sacudidor *m*, bayeta *f*; (*of feathers*) plumero *m*; (*for blackboard*) borrador *m*.
dusting ['dʌstiŋ] *n* (*fam*) paliza *f*.
dust jacket ['dʌst,dʒækit] *n* sobrecubierta *f*, camisa *f*.
dustman ['dʌstmən] *n*, *pl* **—men** [mən] basurero *m*.
dustpan ['dʌstpæn] *n* cogedor *m*.
dust sheet ['dʌstʃiːt] *n* guardapolvo *m*.
dust storm ['dʌststɔːm] *n* vendaval *m* de polvo.
dustup ['dʌstʌp] *n* (*fam*) pelea *f*, reyerta *f*.
dusty ['dʌsti] *adj* polvoriento, empolvado; **to get —** cubrirse de polvo; **not so —** nada malo; **to give someone a — answer** dar a uno una respuesta equívoca.
Dutch [dʌtʃ] **1** *adj* holandés.
   2 *npl* **the —** los holandeses.
   3 *n* (*language*) holandés *m*; **double —** galimatías *m*; **to talk double —** hablar chino; **to go —** pagar cada uno su cuota, ir a escote.
Dutchman ['dʌtʃmən] *n*, *pl* **—men** [mən] holandés *m*; **it's him or I'm a —** que me maten si no es él.
Dutchwoman ['dʌtʃ,wumən] *n*, *pl* **—women** [,wimin] holandesa *f*.
dutiable ['djuːtiəbl] *adj* sujeto a derechos de aduana.
dutiful ['djuːtiful] *adj* obediente, sumiso.
dutifully ['djuːtifəli] *adv* obedientemente, sumisamente.
duty ['djuːti] *n* deber *m*, obligación *f*; (*customs —*) derechos *mpl* de aduana; **entertainments —** impuesto *m* sobre los espectáculos; **protective —** impuesto *m* proteccionista; **stamp —** impuesto *m* del timbre; **succession —** derechos *mpl* de sucesión; **— call** visita *f* molesta pero obligatoria; **out of a**

sense of — por compromiso, cumpliendo con su deber; **to be in — bound to** + *infin* estar obligado a + *infin*; **to be off —** estar libre, (*Mil*) estar libre de servicio; **to be on —** estar de servicio; **to be on sentry —** estar de guardia; **it is no part of my — to** + *infin* no me corresponde a mí + *infin*; **to do — as** servir de; **to do — for** servir en lugar de; **to do one's — cumplir** con su deber; **to do one's — by** ser justo con; **I feel it to be my —** creo que es mi deber; **to take up one's duties** entrar en funciones.
duty-free ['djuːti'friː] *adj* libre de derechos de aduana.
dwarf [dwɔːf] **1** *adj* enano; diminuto, pequeñito. **2** *n* enano *m*, a *f*. **3** *vt* achicar, empequeñecer, hacer que parezca pequeño; (*stunt*) impedir el crecimiento de.
dwell [dwel] (*irr*: *pret and ptp* **dwelt**) *vi* morar; **to — on** *subject* explicar largamente, explayarse en; *thought* meditar; *note, syllable* dar énfasis a, alargar.
dweller ['dwelə*] *n*: **— in** habitante *mf* de; inquilino *m* de, inquilina *f* de.
dwelling ['dweliŋ] *n* morada *f*, vivienda *f*.
dwelling house ['dweliŋhaus] *n*, *pl* **— houses** [,hauziz] casa *f*.
dwelt [dwelt] *pret and ptp of* **dwell**.
dwindle ['dwindl] *vi* disminuir, menguar; **to — to** quedar reducido a.
dwindling ['dwindliŋ] **1** *adj* que va disminuyendo, menguante. **2** *n* disminución *f*.
dye [dai] **1** *n* tinte *m*; (*hue*) matiz *m*, color *m*; **of deepest —** de lo más vil. **2** *vt* teñir (*green* de verde).
dyeing ['daiiŋ] *n* tinte *m*, tintura *f*.
dyer ['daiə*] *n* tintorero *m*; **—'s** tintorería *f*.
dyestuff ['daistʌf] *n* tinte *m*, materia *f* colorante.
dye works ['daiwəːks] *npl* tintorería *f*.
dying ['daiiŋ] **1** *present participle of* **die**. **2** *adj* *man* moribundo, agonizante; *moments* final; *words* último.
dyke [daik] *n* = **dike**.
dynamic [dai'næmik] **1** *adj* dinámico. **2** *n* dinámica *f*.
dynamics [dai'næmiks] *n* dinámica *f*.
dynamite ['dainəmait] **1** *n* dinamita *f*; **that issue is —** ese asunto es dinamita; **the book is —** el libro es explosivo. **2** *vt* dinamitar, volar con dinamita.
dynamo ['dainəməu] *n* dínamo *f*.
dynastic [dai'næstik] *adj* dinástico.
dynasty ['dinəsti] *n* dinastía *f*.
dysentery ['disntri] *n* disentería *f*.
dyspepsia [dis'pepsiə] *n* dispepsia *f*.
dyspeptic [dis'peptik] *adj* dispéptico.
dystrophy ['distrəfi] *n* distrofia *f*; **muscular —** distrofia *f* muscular.

E

each [i:tʃ] **1** adj cada (invariable); (— and every, any) todo.

2 pron cada uno; **they help — other** (2 persons) se ayudan (mutuamente), se ayudan uno a otro, se ayudan el uno al otro, (more than 2 persons) se ayudan unos a otros.

3 adv: **two sweets —** dos dulces por persona, dos dulces para cada uno.

eager ['i:gə*] adj impaciente; desire etc apremiante, vehemente; (hopeful) ilusionado; (ambitious) ambicioso; **to be — for** ansiar, anhelar, tener vivo deseo de; **to be — to** + infin ansiar + infin, impacientarse por + infin; **don't be so —** ¡ten paciencia!

eagerly ['i:gəli] adv con impaciencia, con ansia; con ilusión.

eagerness ['i:gənis] n impaciencia f; ansia f, deseo m (for de); (hopefulness) ilusión f; **in his — to get there first** en su ansia por llegar allí el primero.

eagle ['i:gl] n águila f; **golden —** águila f real.

eagle-eyed ['i:gl'aid] adj de ojos de lince.

ear¹ [iə*] n (Anat) oreja f; (sense, Mus) oído m; **inner —** oído m interno; **middle —** oído m medio; **to be all —s** ser todo oídos; **he could not believe his —s** no daba crédito a sus oídos; **to give —** to prestar oído a; **it goes in at one — and out at the other** por un oído le entra y por otro le sale; **to have a good —** tener buen oído; **to have the minister's —** poder contar con el interés del ministro; **to play by —** tocar de oído; **we're playing it by — (**fig) obramos por instinto, avanzamos a tientas y sin saber a dónde; **to prick up one's —s** aguzar el oído; **he set them by the —s** sembró la discordia entre ellos, hizo que se enfadasen unos con otros; **to turn a deaf — to** hacer oídos sordos a.

ear² [iə*] n (Bot) espiga f; **to come into —** espigar.

earache ['iəreik] n dolor m de oídos.

eardrum ['iədrʌm] n tímpano m.

earl [ə:l] n conde m.

earldom ['ə:ldəm] n condado m.

early ['ə:li] **1** adj temprano (also Bot); (first) primero, primitivo; age tierno; death prematuro, temprano; reply pronto; season avanzado; book, work etc juvenil, de primera época; **an — Victorian table** una mesa victoriana de primera época; **— Christian art** arte m cristiano primitivo; **to be in one's — forties** tener poco más de 40 años; see date, life etc.

2 adv (a) temprano; **as — as possible** lo más pronto posible, cuanto antes; **earlier on** antes; **— in the morning** muy de mañana, de madrugada; **— in the afternoon** a primera hora de la tarde; **— in the week** en los primeros días de la semana; **— last century** a principios del siglo pasado; **— in his life** en su juventud; **— in the twenties** en los primeros años veinte, al principio de los años veinte; **— in the book** en las primeras páginas del libro.

(b) (in good time) con tiempo, con anticipación; **to book —** reservar con mucha anticipación; **to come an hour —** llegar con una hora de anticipación; **he took his summer holiday —** anticipó el veraneo, salió en fecha temprana para veranear.

Early Bird ['ə:libə:d] n: **— (satellite)** satélite m "Pájaro del Alba".

early warning ['ə:li'wɔːniŋ] attr: **— system** sistema m de aviso inmediato (contra los ataques por misiles).

earmark ['iəma:k] vt (fig) reservar (for para), destinar (for a); **an —ed grant** una subvención destinada a fines especiales.

earn [ə:n] vt salary etc ganar(se), percibir; interest devengar; (win for oneself) merecer(se), adquirir, obtener; **it —ed him the nickname of X** le valió el apodo de X.

earnest¹ ['ə:nist] adj person, character etc serio, formal; wish etc fervoroso; **it is my — wish that** deseo con fervor que + subj; **to be in —** hablar con la mayor seriedad; **are you in —?** ¿esto va de veras?, ¿me lo dices en serio?

earnest² ['ə:nist] n prenda f, señal f; **as an — of** en señal de.

earnestly ['ə:nistli] adv speak etc con la mayor seriedad; **I — entreat you** se lo suplico de todo corazón.

earnestness ['ə:nistnis] n seriedad f, formalidad f.

earnings ['ə:niŋz] npl (of individual) sueldo m, ingresos mpl; (of company etc) ganancias fpl, beneficios mpl, utilidades fpl.

earphones ['iəfəunz] npl auriculares mpl.

earpiece ['iəpi:s] n auricular m.

earring ['iəriŋ] n (long) pendiente m; (round) arete m, zarcillo m.

earshot ['iəʃɔt] n: **to be within —** estar al alcance del oído.

ear-splitting ['iə,splitiŋ] adj que rompe el tímpano, que taladra el oído.

earth [ə:θ] **1** n (a) tierra f; **scorched —** tierra f quemada; **here on —** en este mundo; **to come down to —,** **to get back to —** volver a la realidad; **it must have cost the —** habrá costado un potosí; **to promise the —** prometer el oro y el moro.

(b) **nothing on — will stop me now** no lo dejo ahora por nada del mundo; **what on — . . .?** ¿qué demonios . . .?; **why on — do it now?** ¿por qué demonios hacerlo ahora?

(c) (Zool) madriguera f; **to run to —** encontrar finalmente.

(d) (Elec) cable m de toma de tierra.

2 vt (Elec) conectar a tierra; **to — up** (Agr) acollar.

earthen ['ə:θən] adj de tierra; pot de barro.

earthenware ['ə:θənwɛə*] **1** n loza f de barro. **2** attr de barro.

earthly ['ə:θli] adj terrenal, mundano; **to be of no — use** no servir para nada en absoluto; **there is no — reason why not** no hay la más pequeña razón en contra; **he hasn't an —** no tiene posibilidad alguna.

earthquake ['ə:θkweik] n terremoto m, seísmo m.

earthward(s) ['ə:θwəd(z)] adv hacia la tierra.

earthwork ['ə:θwə:k] n terraplén m.

earthworm ['ə:θwə:m] n lombriz f.

earthy ['ə:θi] adj terroso; character telúrico, (coarse) grosero.

ear trumpet ['iə,trʌmpit] n trompetilla f acústica.

earwax ['iəwæks] n cerumen m, cera f de los oídos.

earwig ['iəwig] n tijereta f.

ease [i:z] **1** n (a) (easiness) facilidad f; **with —** con facilidad, fácilmente.

(b) (relief from pain) alivio m.

(c) (freedom from worry) tranquilidad f; **a life of —** una vida desahogada; **to live a life of —** vivir con desahogo.

(d) (relaxed state) comodidad f; **to be at (one's) —** sentirse cómodo, encontrarse a gusto; **to be ill at —** sentirse molesto; **to put someone at his —** lograr que uno se sienta como en su casa; **to set someone's mind at —** tranquilizar el ánimo de uno; **stand at —!** en su lugar ¡descanso!; **to take one's —** descansar.

(e) (of manner) naturalidad f.

2 vt (a) task facilitar.

(b) pain aliviar; mind tranquilizar; (slacken) aflojar; pressure aflojar; weight aligerar; impact suavizar, mitigar; (free) soltar, librar; **to — a lid off** levantar una tapa poco a poco; **to — a weight up** levantar un peso con cuidado; **to — a table along** mover una mesa con cuidado.

3 vi (wind) amainar, calmarse; (rain) moderarse; **to — off,** **to — up** suavizarse, aligerarse; (at work) dejar de trabajar tanto; **to — up on someone** tratar a uno con menos rigor; **prices have —d** han bajado ligeramente los precios.

4 *vr*: **to — oneself of a burden** quitarse un peso de encima.

easel ['i:zl] *n* caballete *m*.

easily ['i:zili] *adv* fácilmente, con facilidad; **to win — ** ganar fácilmente; **it could — be** bien podría ser; **the engine is running —** el motor funciona bien; **it holds 4 litres —** caben 4 litros largos; **it's — the best** es con mucho el mejor, seguramente es el mejor; **to take life —** darse buena vida.

easiness ['i:zinis] *n* facilidad *f*.

east [i:st] **1** *n* este *m*, oriente *m*; **the E—** el Oriente; **Far E—** Extremo Oriente *m*, Lejano Oriente *m*; **Middle E—** Oriente *m* Medio; **Near E—** Próximo Oriente *m*.

2 *adj* del este, oriental; **wind** del este.

3 *adv* al este, hacia el este.

Easter ['i:stə*] *n* Pascua *f* de Resurrección; *(period, loosely)* Semana *f* Santa; **— Monday** Lunes *m* de Pascua de Resurrección; **— Sunday** Domingo *m* de Resurrección; **— egg** huevo *m* de Pascua.

easterly ['i:stəli] *adj* **point, direction** este; **wind** del este.

eastern ['i:stən] *adj* del este, oriental.

easterner ['i:stənə*] *n* habitante *mf* del este.

easternmost ['i:stənməust] *adj* (el) más oriental, situado más al este.

East Indies ['i:st'indiz] *pl* Indias *fpl* Orientales.

eastward(s) ['i:stwədz] *adv* hacia el este.

easy ['i:zi] **1** *adj* **(a)** *(simple)* fácil; sencillo; **it's — to see** why es fácil comprender por qué; **he's — to get on with** es muy simpático; **I'm — ** *(fam)* me es igual; **an — house** una casa de fácil manejo.

(b) **to feel — in one's mind** estar tranquilo; **you can rest —** puedes dormir tranquilo.

(c) **life, conditions** holgado, cómodo.

(d) *manners* natural, sin afectación; *style* llano, corriente; *movement* suelto.

(e) *money, credit* abundante; **steel is easier** el acero tiene menos demanda; **prices are easier** los precios han bajado ligeramente.

(f) *pace* lento, pausado; *woman* fácil; **to come in an — first** llegar fácilmente el primero.

2 *adv* *(fam)* fácilmente; **— there!** ¡despacio!; **to go — on someone** tratar a uno con menos rigor; **to go — with** moderar; emplear más cuidado con; economizar en; **go — with the sugar!** conviene poner menos azúcar; **to take it —** *(rest)* descansar; *(idle)* perder el tiempo; *(go slow)* ir despacio; **take it —!** ¡cálmese!, ¡no se ponga nervioso!

easy chair ['i:zi'tʃeə*] *n* butaca *f*, sillón *m*.

easy-going ['i:zi'gəuiŋ] *adj* acomodadizo, nada severo; *(morally)* de manga ancha; *(lazy)* indolente.

eat [i:t] *(irr: pret* **ate,** *ptp* **eaten) 1** *vt* comer; *meal* tomar; *(with envy etc)* consumir; **to — one's way through the menu** pedir todos los platos que figuran en la lista; **I thought he was going to — me** creía que iba a comerme vivo; **what's —ing you?** *(fam)* ¿qué mosca te ha picado?; **to — away** corroer; desgastar; **to — up** comerse, acabar; **to — up the miles** devorar los kilómetros; **the fire —s up coal** el fuego devora el carbón; **to be —en up with envy** consumirse de envidia.

2 *vi* comer; **he always —s well** siempre tiene buen apetito; **this fish —s well** este pescado es muy sabroso; **to — into** *metal* corroer; *surface etc* desgastar; *reserves etc* mermar; *leisure time etc* reducir; **to — out** comer fuera, comer en un restaurante.

eatable ['i:təbl] **1** *adj* comestible; **2** **—s** *npl* comestibles *mpl*.

eaten ['i:tn] *ptp* of **eat.**

eater ['i:tə*] *n*: **to be a big —** tener siempre buen apetito, ser comilón; **I'm not a big —** yo como bastante poco.

eating ['i:tiŋ] *n* el comer; **to be good —** ser sabroso.

eating house ['i:tiŋhaus] *n*, *pl* **— houses** [hauziz] restaurante *m*.

eats ['i:ts] *npl* *(fam)* comida *f*, comestibles *mpl*.

eau de Cologne ['əudəkə'ləun] *n* agua *f* de colonia, colonia *f*.

eaves ['i:vz] *npl* alero *m*.

eavesdrop ['i:vzdrɔp] *vi* escuchar a escondidas *(on a conversation* una conversación).

eavesdropper ['i:vz,drɔpə*] *n* escuchador *m* escondido.

ebb [eb] **1** *n* reflujo *m*; **the — and flow** el flujo y reflujo; **to be at a low —** estar decaído; **at a low — in his fortunes** en un punto bien bajo de su fortuna.

2 *vi* bajar; menguar; *(fig)* decaer; **to — and flow** fluir y refluir; **life is —ing from him** le están abandonando sus últimas fuerzas.

ebb tide ['eb'taid] *n* marea *f* menguante.

ebonite ['ebənait] *n* ebonita *f*.

ebony ['ebəni] **1** *n* ébano *m*. **2** *attr* de ébano.

ebullience [i'bʌliəns] *n* exaltación *f*, entusiasmo *m*, exuberancia *f*, animación *f*.

ebullient [i'bʌliənt] *adj* exaltado, entusiasta, exuberante, animado.

eccentric [ik'sentrik] **1** *adj* excéntrico. **2** *n* excéntrico *m*, *a f*.

eccentrically [ik'sentrikəli] *adv* de manera excéntrica.

eccentricity [,eksən'trisiti] *n* excentricidad *f*.

ecclesiastic [i,kli:zi'æstik] *n* eclesiástico *m*.

ecclesiastical [i,kli:zi'æstikəl] *adj* eclesiástico.

echelon ['eʃəlɔn] **1** *n* escalón *m*. **2** *vt* escalonar.

echo ['ekəu] **1** *n (pl* **echoes** ['ekəuz]) eco *m*; **to cheer someone to the —** aplaudir a uno repetidas veces.

2 *vt* *sound* repetir; *(imitate)* imitar; *opinion etc* hacerse eco de.

3 *vi* resonar, hacer eco; **the valley —ed with shouts** resonaban los gritos por el valle.

echo-sounder [,ekəu,saundə*] *n* sonda *f* acústica.

éclair ['eiklɛə*] *n* relámpago *m* de chocolate.

éclat ['eiklɑ:] *n* brillo *m*; *(success)* éxito *m* brillante; **with great —** brillantemente.

eclectic [i'klektik] **1** *adj* ecléctico. **2** *n* ecléctico *m*, *a f*.

eclecticism [i'klektisizəm] *n* eclecticismo *m*.

eclipse [i'klips] **1** *n* eclipse *m*. **2** *vt* eclipsar.

eclogue ['eklɔg] *n* égloga *f*.

ecological [,i:kəu'lɔdʒikəl] *adj* ecológico.

ecologist [i'kɔlədʒist] *n* ecólogo *m*.

ecology [i'kɔlədʒi] *n* ecología *f*.

econometrics [i,kɔnə'metriks] *n* econometría *f*.

economic(al) [,i:kə'nɔmik(əl)] *adj* económico; *rent* equitativo; *(— to operate, to run)* rentable.

economically [,i:kə'nɔmikəli] *adv* económicamente; de modo rentable.

economics [,i:kə'nɔmiks] *npl* economía *f* política; **home —** *(US)* economía *f* doméstica.

economist [i'kɔnəmist] *n* economista *mf*.

economize [i'kɔnəmaiz] **1** *vt* economizar, ahorrar. **2** *vi* economizar *(on* en).

economy [i'kɔnəmi] *n* economía *f*; **planned —** economía *f* dirigida; **political —** economía *f* política; **to practise —** economizar; **he writes with great —** escribe con gran economía.

ecstasy ['ekstəsi] *n* éxtasis *m*; **in an — of passion** en un arrebato de pasión, arrebatado por la pasión; **to be in ecstasies** estar en éxtasis; **to go into ecstasies over something** extasiarse ante algo.

ecstatic [eks'tætik] *adj* extático.

ecstatically [eks'tætikəli] *adv* con éxtasis.

ectoplasm ['ektəuplæzəm] *n* ectoplasma *m*.

Ecuador [,ekwə'dɔ:*] El Ecuador.

Ecuador(i)an [,ekwə'dɔ:r(i)ən] **1** *adj* ecuatoriano. **2** *n* ecuatoriano *m*, *a f*.

ecumenical [,i:kju'menikəl] *adj* ecuménico; **— council** concejo *m* ecuménico; **— movement** movimiento *m* ecuménico.

eczema ['eksimə] *n* eczema *m* (*Acad*: *f*).

Ed [ed], **Eddie** ['edi] *m* nombres cariñosos de **Edward.**

eddy ['edi] **1** *n* remolino *m*. **2** *vi* arremolinarse.

edema [i'di:mə] *n (esp US)* edema *m*.

Eden ['i:dn] Edén *m*.

edge [edʒ] **1** *n* *(cutting)* filo *m*, corte *m*; *(border: of chair, cliff, wood etc)* borde *m*; *(of paper)* margen *m*; *(of coin, table etc)* canto *m*; *(of town)* afueras *fpl*; *(of lake etc)* margen *f*, orilla *f*; *(end)* extremidad *f*; **leading —** *(Aer)* borde *m* de ataque; **milled —** cordoncillo *m*; **to be on —** estar de canto, *(fig)* tener los nervios de punta; **my nerves are on —** tengo los nervios de punta; **to be on the — of disaster** estar al borde del desastre; **to have the — on** llevar ventaja a; **to put an — on** afilar; **to set someone's teeth on —** dar dentera a uno; **to take the — off** embotar; **to take the — off one's appetite** engañar el hambre.

2 *vt* **(a)** *(Sew)* ribetear, orlar *(with* de); *path etc* poner un borde a; **—d in, —d with** ribeteado de; bordeado de.

(b) **to — something in** introducir algo de canto; **to — something along** mover algo de canto (poco a poco); **to — one's way into a room** introducirse con dificultad en un cuarto (atestado de gente).

3 *vi*: **to — along** avanzar poco a poco de lado; **to — away** alejarse poco a poco; **to — in** abrirse paso poco a poco; **to — up to someone** acercarse con cautela a uno.

edgeways ['edʒweiz] *adv* de lado, de canto; *see* **word.**

edging ['edʒiŋ] *n* *(Sew)* ribete *m*, orla *f*; *(of path etc)* borde *m*.

edgy ['edʒi] *adj* nervioso, inquieto.

edible ['edibl] *adj* comestible.

edict ['i:dikt] n edicto m.
edification [,edifi'keiʃən] n edificación f.
edifice ['edifis] n edificio m (esp grande, imponente).
edify ['edifai] vt edificar.
edifying ['edifaiiŋ] adj edificante.
Edinburgh ['edinbərə] Edimburgo.
edit ['edit] vt newspaper, magazine, series dirigir, ser director de; text, book preparar una edición de; script preparar para la imprenta, (correct) corregir; —ed by (newspaper etc) bajo la dirección de, (text, book) prólogo y notas de, a cargo de, (en) edición de.
edition [i'diʃən] n edición f; (Typ: no of copies) tirada f; **first** — edición f príncipe; **limited** — edición f limitada; **pirated** — edición f pirata.
editor ['editə*] n (of newspaper, magazine, series) director m; (staff) redactor-jefe m; (of a book) autor m de la edición; —'s note nota f de la redacción.
editorial [,edi'tɔːriəl] 1 adj editorial; de la dirección; — **staff** redacción f. 2 n artículo m de fondo, editorial m.
editor-in-chief ['editərin'tʃi:f] n jefe m de redacción.
editorship ['editəʃip] n dirección f; **under the** — **of** bajo la dirección de.
educable ['edjukəbl] adj educable.
educate ['edjukeit] vt educar; formar; instruir; **where were you** —**d?** ¿dónde cursó Vd sus estudios?; **the prince is being privately** —**d** el príncipe tiene un preceptor particular.
educated ['edjukeitid] adj culto.
education [,edju'keiʃən] n educación f; enseñanza f; instrucción f; formación f cultural, cultura f; (as Univ department etc) pedagogía f; **I never had much** — pasé poco tiempo en la escuela; **they paid for his** — le pagaron los estudios; **elementary** —, **primary** — primera enseñanza f; **secondary** — segunda enseñanza f; **higher** — enseñanza f superior; **Minister of E**— (Spain) Ministro m de Educación Nacional; **physical** — educación f física.
educational [,edju'keiʃənl] adj policy etc educacional, relativo a la educación; function etc, centre docente; film etc instructivo, educativo.
education(al)ist [,edju'keiʃən(ə)list] n especializado m en pedagogía.
educative ['edjukətiv] adj educativo.
educator ['edjukeitə*] n educador m, ora f.
educe [i'djus] vt educir, sacar.
Edward ['edwəd] m Eduardo; — **the Confessor** Eduardo el Confesor.
Edwardian [ed'wɔːdiən] adj eduardiano.
eel [i:l] n anguila f.
e'en [i:n] = **even**.
e'er [eə*] = **ever**.
eerie ['iəri] adj misterioso; sound, experience extraño, fantástico, horripilante.
efface [i'feis] 1 vt borrar. 2 vr: **to** — **oneself** retirarse modestamente, lograr pasar inadvertido.
effect [i'fekt] 1 n (result) efecto m, consecuencia f, resultado m; (impression) efecto m, impresión f; —**s** efectos mpl; **pleasing** — impresión f agradable; **side** — efecto m secundario; **striving after** — efectismo m; **just for** — sólo por impresionar; **in** — en realidad; **to be in** — (Law) estar vigente; **of no** — inútil; **to be of no** — no tener efecto, no hacer mella; **to no** — inútilmente; **to the same** — del mismo tenor, a este tenor, en el mismo sentido; **to this** — con este propósito; **or words to that** — o algo parecido; **to feel the** —(s) **of** sentir los efectos de, estar resentido de; **to give** — **to** poner en efecto, hacer efectivo; **to have an** — dejarse sentir, surtir efecto (on en); **to put into** — poner en vigor; **to take** — (remedy) surtir efecto, (law) ponerse en vigor (from a partir de). 2 vt efectuar, llevar a cabo; sale efectuar; saving hacer.
effective [i'fektiv] 1 adj eficaz; (striking) impresionante, llamativo, logrado; (real) efectivo, verdadero; capacity (Tech) útil; (Mil) útil para todos los servicios; **to become** — entrar en vigor (from, on a partir de). 2 —**s** npl efectivos mpl.
effectively [i'fektivli] adv eficazmente; (strikingly) de manera impresionante, acertadamente; (in fact) en efecto.
effectiveness [i'fektivnis] n eficacia f.
effectual [i'fektjuəl] adj eficaz.
effectuate [i'fektjueit] vt efectuar, lograr.
effeminacy [i'feminəsi] n afeminación f.
effeminate [i'feminit] adj afeminado.
effervesce [,efə'ves] vi estar en efervescencia, (begin to —) entrar en efervescencia; bullir, hervir; (fig) ser muy alegre, ser muy vivo.
effervescence [,efə'vesns] n efervescencia f.

effervescent [,efə'vesnt] adj efervescente (also fig).
effete [i'fi:t] adj decadente, cansado.
efficacious [,efi'keiʃəs] adj eficaz.
efficacy ['efikəsi] n eficacia f.
efficiency [i'fiʃənsi] n eficiencia f, eficacia f; (Mech) rendimiento m.
efficient [i'fiʃənt] adj eficiente; remedy, product eficaz; (Mech) de buen rendimiento; person eficiente, eficaz, competente, capaz.
efficiently [i'fiʃəntli] adv eficientemente, eficazmente.
effigy ['efidʒi] n efigie f; **to burn someone in** — quemar a uno en efigie.
efflorescent [,eflɔː'resnt] adj eflorescente.
effluent ['efluənt] 1 adj efluente. 2 n corriente f efluente.
effluvium [e'flu:viəm] n, pl **effluvia** [e'flu:viə] efluvio m, emanación f, tufo m.
effort ['efət] n (a) esfuerzo m; **all his** — **was directed to** todos sus esfuerzos iban dirigidos a; **to make an** — **to** + infin esforzarse por + infin, hacer un esfuerzo por + infin; **to make every** — **to** + infin, **to spare no** — **to** + infin no regatear medio para + infin.
(b) (fam) resultado m, producto m; obra f; **it was a pretty poor** — fue una exhibición pobre; **what did you think of his latest** —? ¿qué opinas de su nueva obra?; **it's not bad for a first** — siendo su primer intento no es nada malo.
effortless ['efətlis] adj sin esfuerzo alguno, fácil.
effortlessly ['efətlisli] adv sin esfuerzo alguno, fácilmente.
effrontery [i'frʌntəri] n descaro m; **what** —! ¡qué frescura!; **he had the** — **to say** llegó su cinismo hasta decir.
effusion [i'fju:ʒən] n efusión f.
effusive [i'fju:siv] adj efusivo.
effusively [i'fju:sivli] adv con efusión.
eft [eft] n tritón m.
egalitarian [i,gæli'teəriən] adj igualitario.
egg[1] [eg] n (a) huevo m; **hard-boiled** — huevo m cocido, huevo m duro; **soft-boiled** — huevo m pasado por agua; **fried** — huevo m frito, huevo m al plato; **poached** — huevo m escalfado; **scrambled** —**s** huevos mpl revueltos; **as sure as** —**s** (**is** —**s**) sin ningún género de dudas; **don't put all your** —**s in one basket** no pongas toda la carne en el asador.
(b) (fam) tío m; **bad** — sinvergüenza m.
egg[2] [eg] vt: **to** — **someone on** dar pie a uno; **to** — **someone on to do something** incitar a uno a hacer algo.
eggbeater ['eg,bi:tə*] n batidor m de huevos.
eggcup ['egkʌp] n huevera f.
egg flip ['eg'flip] n yema f mejida.
egghead ['eghed] n (fam) intelectual m.
eggnog ['eg'nɔg] n yema f mejida, ponche m de huevo.
eggplant ['egplɑːnt] n berenjena f.
egg-shaped ['egʃeipt] adj oviforme.
eggshell ['egʃel] n cáscara f de huevo.
eglantine ['egləntain] n eglantina f.
ego ['i:gəu] n el yo.
egocentric(al) [,egəu'sentrik(əl)] adj egocéntrico.
egoism ['egəuizəm] n egoísmo m.
egoist ['egəuist] n egoísta mf.
egoistical [,egəu'istikəl] adj egoísta.
egotism ['egəutizəm] n egotismo m.
egotist ['egəutist] n egotista mf.
egotistic(al) [,egəu'tistik(əl)] adj egotista.
egregious [i'gri:dʒəs] adj atroz, enorme; liar etc notorio.
egret ['i:gret] n garceta f.
Egypt ['i:dʒipt] Egipto m.
Egyptian [i'dʒipʃən] 1 adj egipcio. 2 n egipcio m, a f.
Egyptology [,i:dʒip'tɔlədʒi] n egiptología f.
eh [ei] interj (please repeat) ¿cómo?, ¿qué?; (inviting assent) ¿no?, ¿verdad?, ¿no es así?
eider ['aidə*] n, **eider duck** ['aidə'dʌk] n eider m.
eiderdown ['aidədaun] n edredón m.
eight [eit] 1 adj ocho. 2 n ocho m; (Rowing) bote m de a ocho; **to have had one over the** — llevar una copa de más.
eighteen ['ei'ti:n] adj dieciocho.
eighteenth ['ei'ti:nθ] adj decimoctavo.
eighth [eitθ] 1 adj octavo. 2 n octavo m.
eightieth ['eitiiθ] adj octogésimo.
eighty ['eiti] adj ochenta; **the eighties** (eg 1980s) los años ochenta; **to be in one's eighties** tener más de ochenta años.
Eire ['eərə] Eire m.
either ['aiðə*] 1 adj cualquier ... de los dos; **you can do it** — **way** puedes hacerlo de este modo o del otro; **on** — **side** en ambos lados; (neg sense) **I don't like**

— **book** no me gusta ninguno de los dos libros, no me gusta ni uno ni otro.
2 *pron* cualquiera de los dos, uno u otro; — **of us** cualquiera de nosotros; (*neg sense*) **I don't want** — **of them** no quiero ninguno de los dos, no quiero ni uno ni otro.
3 *conj*: — **come in or stay out** o entras o quedas fuera.
4 *adv* tampoco; **I won't go** — yo no voy tampoco.
ejaculate [i'dʒækjuleit] *vt* exclamar; proferir (de repente), lanzar; (*Med*) eyacular.
ejaculation [i,dʒækju'leiʃən] *n* exclamación *f*; (*Med*) eyaculación *f*.
eject [i'dʒekt] *vt* expulsar, echar; *tenant* desahuciar.
ejection [i'dʒekʃən] *n* expulsión *f*; desahucio *m*.
ejector [i'dʒektə*] *n* expulsor *m*; — **seat** asiento *m* proyectable.
eke [i:k] *vt*: **to** — **out** suplir las deficiencias de; *money etc* hacer que llegue; *livelihood* ganar a duras penas.
elaborate [i'læbərit] *adj* complicado; detallado; *meal* de muchos platos; *work of art* primoroso, rebuscado; *courtesy* exquisito, estudiado.
elaborate [i'læbəreit] **1** *vt* elaborar.
2 *vi* explicarse con muchos detalles; **to** — **on** ampliar, dar más explicaciones acerca de; **he refused to** — se negó a dar más detalles.
elaborately [i'læbəritli] *adv* de manera complicada; con muchos detalles; primorosamente.
elaboration [i,læbə'reiʃən] *n* elaboración *f*.
elapse [i'læps] *vi* pasar, transcurrir.
elastic [i'læstik] **1** *adj* elástico (*also fig*). **2** *n* elástico *m*; (*Sew*) goma *f*.
elastic band [i'læstik'bænd] *n* gomita *f*.
elasticity [i,i:læs'tisiti] *n* elasticidad *f*.
elated [i'leitid] *adj*: **to be** — alegrarse, regocijarse (*at, with* de).
elation [i'leiʃən] *n* alegría *f*, regocijo *m*, júbilo *m*.
elbow ['elbəu] **1** *n* codo *m*; (*of road etc*) recodo *m*; **at one's** — a la mano, muy cerca; **out at the** —**s** raído; **more power to your** —! ¡que tenga éxito en la campaña!
2 *vt* empujar con el codo; **to** — **someone aside** apartar a uno a codazos; **to** — **one's way through** abrirse paso codeando (por).
elbow grease ['elbəugri:s] *n* (*fam*) codo *m*.
elbowroom ['elbəurum] *n* espacio *m* (suficiente); espacio *m* para moverse; libertad *f* de acción.
elder[1] ['eldə*] **1** *adj* mayor; **Pliny the E—** Plinio el Viejo. **2** *n* (*Eccl*) anciano *m*; **my** — mis mayores; **the** —**s of the tribe** los jefes de la tribu.
elder[2] ['eldə*] *n* (*Bot*) saúco *m*.
elderberry ['eldə,beri] *n* baya *f* del saúco.
elderly ['eldəli] *adj* de edad, mayor; **to be getting** — ir para viejo.
eldest ['eldist] *adj* (el, la) mayor; **my** — **son** mi hijo mayor; **the** — **of the four** el mayor de los cuatro.
Eleanor ['elinə*] *f* Leonor.
elect [i'lekt] **1** *vt* elegir; **to** — **someone a member** elegir a uno socio; **to** — **to** + *infin* optar por + *infin*, decidir + *infin*.
2 *adj* electo; **president** — presidente *m* electo.
3 *n*: **the** — los elegidos.
election [i'lekʃən] *n* elección *f* (*for* a); **general** — elecciones *fpl* generales.
electioneer [i,lekʃə'niə*] *vi* hacer su campaña electoral; (*pej*) hacer propaganda a favor de su partido.
electioneering [i,lekʃə'niəriŋ] *n* campaña *f* electoral; (*pej*) maniobras *fpl* electorales.
elective [i'lektiv] *adj* electivo.
elector [i'lektə*] *n* elector *m*, ora *f*.
electoral [i'lektərəl] *adj* electoral.
electorate [i'lektərit] *n* electorado *m*; número *m* de votantes; censo *m*.
electric [i'lektrik] *adj* eléctrico; **the atmosphere was** — la atmósfera estaba cargada de electricidad.
electrical [i'lektrikəl] *adj* eléctrico.
electrically [i'lektrikəli] *adv* por electricidad.
electrician [ilek'triʃən] *n* electricista *m*.
electricity [ilek'trisiti] *n* electricidad *f*.
electrification [i'lektrifi'keiʃən] *n* electrificación *f*.
electrify [i'lektrifai] *vt* electrificar; (*fig*) electrizar.
electrifying [i'lektrifaiiŋ] *adj* electrizante.
electro . . . [i'lektrəu] electro . . .
electrocardiogram [i'lektrəu'ka:diəgræm] *n* electrocardiograma *m*.
electrocute [i'lektrəukju:t] *vt* electrocutar.
electrocution [i,lektrəu'kju:ʃən] *n* electrocución *f*.
electrode [i'lektrəud] *n* electrodo *m*.
electrodynamics [i'lektrəudai'næmiks] *n* electrodinámica *f*.

electrolysis [ilek'trɔlisis] *n* electrólisis *f*.
electromagnet [i'lektrəu'mægnit] *n* electroimán *m*.
electromagnetic [i'lektrəumæg'netik] *adj* electromagnético.
electron [i'lektrɔn] *n* electrón *m*.
electronic [ilek'trɔnik] *adj* electrónico.
electronics [ilek'trɔniks] *n* electrónica *f*.
electroplate [i'lektrəupleit] *vt* galvanizar, electrochapar.
electroplated [i'lektrəupleitid] *adj* galvanizado, electrochapado.
elegance ['eligəns] *n* elegancia *f*.
elegant ['eligənt] *adj* elegante.
elegantly ['eligəntli] *adv* elegantemente.
elegiac [,eli'dʒaiək] *adj* elegíaco.
elegy ['elidʒi] *n* elegía *f*.
element ['elimənt] *n* elemento *m* (*also Chem, Elec etc*); —**s** (*rudiments*) elementos *mpl*, primeras nociones *fpl*; **to be in one's** — estar en su elemento; **to be out of one's** — estar como pez fuera del agua; **to brave the** —**s** arrostrar la tempestad, (*go out*) salir a la intemperie; **it's the personal** — **that counts** es el factor personal el que cuenta.
elemental [,eli'mentl] *adj* elemental.
elementary [,eli'mentəri] *adj* elemental; (*primitive*) rudimentario; *school* primario, de primera enseñanza; —, **my dear Watson** es muy sencillo, querido Watson.
elephant ['elifənt] *n* elefante *m*, a *f*; **white** — maula *f*.
elephantine [,eli'fæntain] *adj* (*fig*) mastodóntico.
elevate ['eliveit] *vt* elevar; (*Eccl*) alzar; *person* exaltar; (*in rank*) ascender (*to* a).
elevated ['eliveitid] *adj* elevado, sublime.
elevation [,eli'veiʃən] *n* (*act*) elevación *f*; (*of person*) exaltación *f*; (*in rank*) ascenso *m*; (*of style*) sublimidad *f*; (*hill*) altura *f*; (*Aer etc*) altitud *f*.
elevator ['eliveitə*] *n* (*Agr*) almacén *m* de granos, elevador *m* de granos; (*Aer*) timón *m* de profundidad; (*US*) ascensor *m*, (*for goods*) montacargas *m*.
eleven [i'levn] **1** *adj* once. **2** *n* once *m*.
elevenses [i'levnziz] *npl* (*fam*): **to have** — tomar las once.
eleventh [i'levnθ] *adj* undécimo, onceno.
elf [elf] *n*, *pl* **elves** [elvz] elfo *m*, duende *m*.
elfin ['elfin] *adj* de elfo, como elfo; que tiene la magia (*or* la gracia *etc*) de los elfos; mágico.
elicit [i'lisit] *vt* sacar, (lograr) obtener.
elide [i'laid] *vt* elidir.
eligibility [,elidʒə'biliti] *n* elegibilidad *f*.
eligible ['elidʒəbl] *adj* elegible; (*desirable*) deseable, atractivo; *bachelor* de partido; **he's the most** — **bachelor in town** es el mejor partido de la ciudad; **to be** — **for** llenar los requisitos para.
eliminate [i'limineit] *vt* eliminar; suprimir; *suspect, possibility etc* descartar; *person* (*in purge*) eliminar.
elimination [i,limi'neiʃən] *n* eliminación *f*; supresión *f*.
elision [i'liʒən] *n* elisión *f*.
élite [ei'li:t] *n* élite *f*, minoría *f* selecta.
elixir [i'liksə*] *n* elixir *m*.
Elizabeth [i'lizəbəθ] *f* Isabel.
Elizabethan [i,lizə'bi:θən] **1** *adj* isabelino. **2** *n* isabelino *m*, a *f*.
elk [elk] *n* alce *m*.
ellipse [i'lips] *n* elipse *f*.
ellipsis [i'lipsis] *n*, *pl* **ellipses** [i'lipsi:z] elipsis *f*.
elliptic(al) [i'liptik(əl)] *adj* elíptico.
elm [elm] *n* olmo *m* (*also* — **tree**).
elocution [,elə'kju:ʃən] *n* elocución *f*.
elocutionist [,elə'kju:ʃənist] *n* profesor *m* de elocución.
elongate ['i:lɔŋgeit] *vt* alargar, extender.
elongated ['i:lɔŋgeitid] *adj* alargado, estirado.
elongation [,i:lɔŋ'geiʃən] *n* alargamiento *m*, estiramiento *m*.
elope [i'ləup] *vi* (1 *person*) fugarse con su amante, (2 *persons*) fugarse para casarse; **to** — **with** fugarse con.
elopement [i'ləupmənt] *n* fuga *f*.
eloquence ['eləkwəns] *n* elocuencia *f*.
eloquent ['eləkwənt] *adj* elocuente.
eloquently ['eləkwəntli] *adv* elocuentemente.
else [els] *adv* (a) (*after pron*) **all** —, **everything** — todo lo demás; **everyone** — todos los demás; **anyone** — **would do it** cualquier otra persona lo haría; **anything** — **is impossible** cualquier otra cosa es imposible; **have you anything** — **to tell me?** ¿tiene algo más que decirme?; **anything** —, **madam?** (*in shop*) ¿algo más, señora?, ¿alguna cosita más, señora?; **that was somebody** — eso fue otro; **there's somebody** —, **isn't there?** hay otro hombre ¿verdad?; **somewhere** — en otra parte.

(b) (*after pron, neg*) **I don't know anyone — here** aquí no conozco a ninguna otra persona; **nobody — knows** no lo sabe ningún otro; **there's nothing — I can do** no hay nada más que pueda hacer; **nothing —, thanks** nada más, gracias.

(c) (*adv of quantity*) **there was little — to do** apenas quedaba otra cosa que hacer; **and much — besides** y otras muchas cosas además.

(d) (*after interrog*) **how —?** ¿de qué otra manera?; **what —?** ¿qué más?; **where —?** ¿en qué otro sitio?; **where — can he have gone?** ¿a qué otro sitio habrá podido ir?; **who —?** ¿quién más?; **who — could do it as well as you?** ¿qué otra persona podría hacerlo tan bien como Vd?

(e) (*standing alone*) **how could I have done it —?** ¿de qué otro modo hubiera podido hacerlo?; **red or — black** rojo o bien negro; **or — I'll do it** si no, lo hago yo; **do this, or — . . .** hágalo, pues si no . . .

elsewhere ['els'wɛə*] *adv* en otra parte, go a otra parte.

elucidate [i'luːsideit] *vt* aclarar, elucidar.

elucidation [i‚luːsi'deiʃən] *n* aclaración *f*, elucidación *f*.

elude [i'luːd] *vt blow etc* eludir, esquivar, evitar; *grasp* escapar de; *pursuer* escaparse de, burlar, zafarse de; *obligation* zafarse de; **the name —s me** se me escapa el nombre; **the answer has so far —d us** hasta ahora no hemos encontrado la solución.

elusive [i'luːsiv] *adj* difícil de encontrar, esquivo.

elver ['elvə*] *n* anguila *f* joven.

elves [elvz] *pl of* **elf**.

Elysium [i'liziəm] Eliseo *m*.

emaciated [i'meisieitid] *adj* demacrado; **to become —** demacrarse.

emaciation [i‚meisi'eiʃən] *n* demacración *f*.

emanate ['eməneit] *vi* emanar, proceder (*from* de).

emanation [‚emə'neiʃən] *n* emanación *f*.

emancipate [i'mænsipeit] *vt* emancipar.

emancipated [i'mænsipeitid] *adj* emancipado; (*fig*) libre.

emancipation [i‚mænsi'peiʃən] *n* emancipación *f*; (*fig*) libertad *f*.

emasculate [i'mæskjuleit] *vt* (*fig*) mutilar, estropear.

emasculated [i'mæskjuleitid] *adj* mutilado, estropeado; *style* empobrecido.

embalm [im'baːm] *vt* embalsamar.

embankment [im'bæŋkmənt] *n* terraplén *m*.

embargo [im'baːgəu] *n* prohibición *f* (*on* de); **to be under an —** estar prohibido; **there is an — on arms** está prohibido comerciar en armas; **there is an — on that subject** está prohibido discutir ese asunto; **to put an — on something** prohibir el comercio de algo, (*fig*) prohibir el uso de algo.

embark [im'baːk] **1** *vt* embarcar. **2** *vi* embarcarse (*for* con rumbo a, *on* en); **to — upon** emprender, lanzarse a.

embarkation [‚embaː'keiʃən] *n* (*of persons*) embarco *m*; (*of goods*) embarque *m*.

embarrass [im'bærəs] *vt* desconcertar, turbar, azorar; (*deliberately*) poner en un aprieto; (*financially*) crear dificultades económicas a; **to be —ed** sentirse violento, sentirse molesto, estar azorado; **to be financially —ed** tener dificultades económicas; **I was —ed by the question** la pregunta me desconcertó; **I feel —ed about it** me siento algo avergonzado por eso.

embarrassing [im'bærəsiŋ] *adj experience etc* embarazoso, desconcertante; *moment, situation* violento.

embarrassment [im'bærəsmənt] *n* (**a**) (*state*) desconcierto *m*, turbación *f*, azoramiento *m*; *financial* — apuros *mpl*, dificultades *fpl* económicas; **I am in a state of some —** estoy algo perplejo.

(b) (*object*) estorbo *m*; **you are an — to us all** eres un estorbo para todos nosotros.

embassy ['embəsi] *n* embajada *f*.

embattled [im'bætld] *adj army* en orden de batalla; *city* sitiado.

embed [im'bed] **1** *vt* empotrar; *weapon, teeth etc* clavar, hincar (*in* en). **2** *vr*: **to — itself in** empotrarse *m*.

embellish [im'beliʃ] *vt* embellecer; (*fig, story etc*) adornar (*with* de).

embellishment [im'beliʃmənt] *n* embellecimiento *m*; (*fig*) adorno *m*.

embers ['embəz] *npl* rescoldo *m*, ascua *f*.

embezzle [im'bezl] *vt* malversar, desfalcar.

embezzlement [im'bezlmənt] *n* malversación *f*, desfalco *m*.

embezzler [im'bezlə*] *n* malversador *m*, desfalcador *m*.

embitter [im'bitə*] *vt* amargar; *relations etc* envenenar.

embittered [im'bitəd] *adj* resentido, rencoroso; **to be very —** estar muy amargado (*about* por, *against* contra).

emblazon [im'bleizən] *vt* engalanar (*or* esmaltar) con colores brillantes; (*fig*) escribir de modo llamativo, adornar de modo llamativo.

emblem ['embləm] *n* emblema *m*.

emblematic [‚embli'mætik] *adj* emblemático.

embodiment [im'bɔdimənt] *n* encarnación *f*, personificación *f*; **to be the very — of virtue** ser la misma virtud.

embody [im'bɔdi] *vt* (**a**) encarnar, personificar; *idea etc* expresar. (**b**) (*include*) incorporar.

embolden [im'bəuldən] *vt* envalentonar (*to* + *infin* para que + *subj*).

embolism ['embəlizəm] *n* embolia *f*.

emboss [im'bɔs] *vt* realzar; estampar en relieve; **—ed with the royal arms** con el escudo real en relieve.

embrace [im'breis] **1** *n* abrazo *m*.
2 *vt* (**a**) (*clasp*) abrazar, dar un abrazo a.
(b) (*include*) abarcar.
(c) *offer* aceptar; *opportunity* aprovechar; *course of action* adoptar; *doctrine, party* adherirse a; *profession* dedicarse a; *religion* convertirse a.
3 *vi* abrazarse.

embrasure [im'breiʒə*] *n* (*Archit*) alféizar *m*; (*Mil*) tronera *f*, cañonera *f*.

embrocation [‚embrəu'keiʃən] *n* embrocación *f*.

embroider [im'brɔidə*] *vt* bordar, recamar; (*fig*) adornar con detalles ficticios.

embroidery [im'brɔidəri] *n* bordado *m*.

embroil [im'brɔil] *vt* embrollar, enredar; **to — someone with** indisponer a uno con; **to get —ed in** enredarse en, hacerse un lío con.

embroilment [im'brɔilmənt] *n* embrollo *m*.

embryo ['embriəu] **1** *n* embrión *m*; (*fig*) germen *m*; **in —** en embrión. **2** *attr* embrionario.

embryonic [‚embri'ɔnik] *adj* embrionario.

emend [i'mend] *vt* enmendar.

emendation [‚iːmen'deiʃən] *n* enmienda *f*.

emerald ['emərəld] **1** *n* esmeralda *f*. **2** *adj* de color de esmeralda, esmeraldino; **the E— Isle** la verde Irlanda.

emerge [i'məːdʒ] *vi* salir (*from* de; *also fig*), aparecer, dejarse ver; (*problem etc*) surgir; **it —s that** resulta que; **what has —d from this inquiry?** ¿qué se saca de esta investigación?

emergence [i'məːdʒəns] *n* salida *f*, aparición *f*.

emergency [i'məːdʒənsi] **1** *n* crisis *f*; necesidad *f* urgente; situación *f* imprevista; **there is a national —** existe una crisis nacional; **in an —, in case of —** en caso de urgencia; **to provide for emergencies** tomar precauciones contra los peligros imprevisibles.
2 *attr brake* de auxilio; *exit* de urgencia, de emergencia; *landing* forzoso; *measure* de urgencia; *meeting* extraordinario.

emergent [i'məːdʒənt] *adj nation* naciente.

emeritus [i'meritəs] *adj* emeritus, honorario.

emery ['eməri] *n* esmeril *m*.

emery cloth ['eməri‚klɔθ] *n* tela *f* de esmeril.

emery paper ['eməri‚peipə*] *n* papel *m* de esmeril.

emetic [i'metik] **1** *adj* emético. **2** *n* emético *m*.

emigrant ['emigrənt] **1** *adj* emigrante. **2** *n* emigrante *mf*.

emigrate ['emigreit] *vi* emigrar.

emigration [‚emi'greiʃən] *n* emigración *f*.

émigré(e) ['emigrei] *n* emigrado *m*, a *f*.

Emily ['emili] *f* Emilia.

eminence ['eminəns] *n* eminencia *f*; **His E—** Su Eminencia; **Your E—** Vuestra Eminencia.

eminent ['eminənt] *adj* eminente.

eminently ['eminəntli] *adv* sumamente.

emir [e'miə*] *n* emir *m*.

emissary ['emisəri] *n* emisario *m*.

emission [i'miʃən] *n* emisión *f*.

emit [i'mit] *vt light, signals etc* emitir; *smoke etc* arrojar; *smell* despedir; *cry* dar; *sound* producir.

Emmanuel [i'mænjuəl] *m* Manuel.

emolument [i'mɔljumənt] *n* emolumento *m*.

emote [i'məut] *vi* (*fam*) actuar de una manera muy emocionada.

emotion [i'məuʃən] *n* emoción *f*.

emotional [i'məuʃənl] *adj* emocional; *moment* de honda emoción; *person* (*warm-hearted*) sentimental, (*taking things too hard*) demasiado sensible, (*showing excessive emotion*) exaltado, exagerado; **— tension** tensión *f* emocional.

emotionalism [i'məuʃnəlizəm] *n* sentimentalismo *m*; (*in newspaper etc*) sensacionalismo *m*.

emotionally [i'məuʃnəli] *adv* con emoción; — **unstable** poco estable en cuanto a las emociones.

emotionless [i'məuʃənlis] *adj* sin emoción.

emotive [i'məutiv] *adj* emotivo.

empanel [im'pænl] *vt jury* inscribir.

empathy [em'pæθi] *n* empatía *f*.

emperor ['empərə*] *n* emperador *m*.

emphasis ['emfəsis] *n* énfasis *m*; **to lay** (*or put*) — **on** subrayar; **the** — **is on sport** se le concede mucha importancia al deporte; **this year the** — **is on femininity** este año las modas hacen resaltar la feminidad.

emphasize ['emfəsaiz] *vt* (*Gram*) acentuar; (*fig*) subrayar, recalcar; **I must** — **that** tengo que subrayar que.

emphatic [im'fætik] *adj* enfático; *speech, condemnation etc* enérgico; *person* decidido; **he was most** — **that** dijo de modo tajante que.

emphatically [im'fætikəli] *adv* con énfasis; **yes,** — sí, sin ningún género de dudas; **the answer is** — **no** bajo ningún concepto.

empire ['empaiə*] *n* imperio *m*.

empiric(al) [em'pirik(əl)] *adj* empírico.

empiricism [em'pirisizəm] *n* empirismo *m*.

empiricist [em'pirisist] *n* empírico *m*.

emplacement [im'pleismənt] *n* (*Mil*) emplazamiento *m*.

employ [im'plɔi] **1** *n*: **to be in the** — **of** trabajar por, (*as servant etc*) estar al servicio de.
2 *vt person* emplear; *thing* emplear, usar; *time* ocupar; **to be** — **ed in** emplearse en.

employee [.emplɔi'i:] *n* empleado *m*, a *f*, dependiente *m*, a *f*.

employer [im'plɔiə*] *n* patrón *m*, ona *f*.

employment [im'plɔimənt] *n* (**a**) (*act*) empleo *m*; uso *m*.
(**b**) (*job*) empleo *m*, colocación *f*, puesto *m*; ocupación *f*; **to be in** — tener trabajo; **to give** — **to** emplear a; **to look for** — buscar colocación; — **agency** agencia *f* de colocaciones; — **exchange** bolsa *f* de trabajo.
(**c**) (*jobs collectively*) empleo *m*; **full** — pleno empleo *m*; **a high level of** — un alto nivel de trabajo.

emporium [em'pɔ:riəm] *n* emporio *m*.

empower [im'pauə*] *vt*: **to** — **someone to do something** autorizar a uno a hacer algo.

empress ['empris] *n* emperatriz *f*.

emptiness ['emptinis] *n* vacío *m*, lo vacío; (*of person's life*) vaciedad *f*, vacuidad *f*; **its** — **of moral content** su desierto de todo contenido moral.

empty ['empti] **1** *adj* vacío; *house* desocupado; *place* desierto; *vehicle* vacío, sin carga; *post* vacante; *threat, words* vano, inútil; *phrase* sin significado real; **I'm** — tengo hambre.
2 *n* (*gen pl*) botella *f* (*etc*) vacía; **returnable empties** envases *mpl* a devolver.
3 *vt contents* vaciar, verter; *container* vaciar, descargar; *place, room* dejar vacío.
4 *vi* vaciarse; (*vehicle*) quedar vacío; (*room etc*) quedar desocupado; (*place*) quedar desierto; **to** — **into** (*river*) desembocar en.

empty-handed ['empti'hændid] *adj* con las manos vacías, manivacío.

empty-headed ['empti'hedid] *adj* casquivano.

emu ['i:mju:] *n* dromeo *m*, emú *m*.

emulate ['emjuleit] *vt* emular.

emulation [.emju'leiʃən] *n* emulación *f*.

emulsify [i'mʌlsifai] *vt* emulsionar.

emulsion [i'mʌlʃən] *n* emulsión *f*.

enable [i'neibl] *vt*: **to** — **someone to do something** permitir a uno hacer algo, poner a uno en condiciones para hacer algo; **I am now** — **d to go** ahora puedo ir.

enact [i'nækt] *vt* decretar (*that que*); *law* promulgar; *play, scene* representar; *part* hacer.

enamel [i'næməl] **1** *n* esmalte *m*. **2** *vt* esmaltar, pintar al esmalte.

enamelled [i'næməld] *adj* esmaltado.

enamelware [i'næməlwɛə*] *n* utensilios *mpl* de hierro esmaltado.

enamour [i'næmə*] *vt*: **to be** — **ed of** *person* estar enamorado de, *thing* tener gran afición a, *idea* aferrarse a.

encamp [in'kæmp] *vi* acamparse.

encampment [in'kæmpmənt] *n* campamento *m*.

encase [in'keis] *vt* encerrar; **to be** — **d in** estar revestido de.

encash [in'kæʃ] *vt* cobrar, hacer efectivo.

encephalitis [.ensefə'laitis] *n* encefalitis *f*.

enchain [in'tʃein] *vt* encadenar.

enchant [in'tʃa:nt] *vt* encantar (*also fig*); **we were** — **ed with the place** el sitio nos encantó.

enchanter [in'tʃa:ntə*] *n* hechicero *m*.

enchanting [in'tʃa:ntiŋ] *adj* encantador.

enchantingly [in'tʃa:ntiŋli] *adv* de manera encantadora, deliciosamente.

enchantment [in'tʃa:ntmənt] *n* (*act*) encantamiento *m*; (*charm*) encanto *m*; **it lent** — **to the scene** aumentó el encanto de la escena.

enchantress [in'tʃa:ntris] *n* hechicera *f*.

encircle [in'sə:kl] *vt* rodear (*with de*); (*Mil*) envolver; *waist, shoulders etc* ceñir; **it is** — **d by a wall** está rodeado de una tapia.

encirclement [in'sə:klmənt] *n* (*Mil*) envolvimiento *m*.

encircling [in'sə:kliŋ] *adj movement* envolvente.

enclave ['enkleiv] *n* enclave *m*.

enclitic [in'klitik] *adj* enclítico.

enclose [in'kləuz] *vt land, garden* cercar (*with de*); (*put in a receptacle*) meter, encerrar; (*include*) encerrar; (*with letter*) remitir adjunto, adjuntar; — **d herewith please find** . . . le mandamos adjunto . . .; **the** — **d letter** la carta adjunta.

enclosure [in'kləuʒə*] *n* (*act*) cercamiento *m*; (*place*) cercado *m*, recinto *m*; (*in letter*) carta *f* adjunta, carta *f* inclusa.

encompass [in'kʌmpəs] *vt* (*surround*) cercar, rodear (*with de*); (*include*) abarcar; (*bring about*) lograr.

encore [ɔŋ'kɔ:*] **1** *interj* ¡bis!
2 *n* bis *m*, repetición *f*; **to give an** — repetir algo a petición del público; **to sing a song as an** — bisar una canción.
3 *vt song* pedir la repetición de, *person* pedir una repetición a.

encounter [in'kauntə*] **1** *n* encuentro *m*. **2** *vt* encontrar, encontrarse con; *difficulty etc* tropezar con.

encourage [in'kʌridʒ] *vt person* animar, alentar, dar aliento a; *industry* fomentar, estimular; *growth* estimular; (*in a belief*) fortalecer, reforzar; **to** — **someone to do something** animar a uno a hacer algo.

encouragement [in'kʌridʒmənt] *n* (*act*) estímulo *m*, (*of industry*) fomento *m*; (*support*) aliento *m*, aprobación *f*; **to give** — **to** infundir ánimos a, dar aliento a; **to give** — **to the enemy** ayudar al enemigo.

encouraging [in'kʌridʒiŋ] *adj* alentador, esperanzador; *favorable*, halagüeño; **it is not an** — **prospect** es una perspectiva nada halagüeña; **he was always very** — siempre me daba aliento.

encouragingly [in'kʌridʒiŋli] *adv speak etc* en tono alentador.

encroach [in'krəutʃ] *vi*: **to** — **on** *rights* usurpar; *land* (*of neighbour*) invadir, pasar los límites de; *land* (*by sea*) hurtar, comerse; *person's subject* invadir; *time* ocupar, llevar (una parte cada vez mayor de).

encroachment [in'krəutʃmənt] *n* usurpación *f* (*on* de); invasión *f* (*on* de); abuso *m* (*on* de); **this new** — **on our liberty** esta nueva usurpación de nuestra libertad.

encrusted [in'krʌstid] *adj*: — **with** incrustado de.

encumber [in'kʌmbə*] *vt person, movement* estorbar; (*with debts*) gravar, cargar; *place* llenar (*with* de); **to be** — **ed with** tener que cargar con, (*debts*) estar gravado de.

encumbrance [in'kʌmbrəns] *n* estorbo *m*; (*of debt*) carga *f*, gravamen *m*; **without** — sin familia.

encyclical [en'siklikəl] *n* encíclica *f*.

encyclopaedia, —pedia [en.saikləu'pi:diə] *n* enciclopedia *f*.

encyclopaedic, —pedic [en.saikləu'pi:dik] *adj* enciclopédico.

end [end] **1** *n* (**a**) (*in physical sense*) (*of street etc*) final *m*; (*of line, table etc*) extremo *m*; (*of rope etc*) cabo *m*; (*point*) punta *f*; (*of estate etc*) límite *m*; (*Sport*) lado *m*; (*of town*) barrio *m*; **the** — **s of the earth** las partes más remotas del mundo; **big** — (*Mech*) cabeza *f* de biela; **deep** — (*of pool*) parte *f* honda; **loose** — cabo *m* suelto; **at the** — **of**, **en the extremo de**; **al final de**; **from one** — **to the other**, **from** — **to** — de un extremo a otro; **on** — de punta, de cabeza, de canto; — **to** — juntando los dos extremos; **to be at a loose** — estar desocupado, no tener qué hacer; **to be at the** — **of one's tether** estar casi completamente agotado; estar para perder la paciencia; **to change** — **s** (*Sport*) cambiar de lado; **to get hold of the wrong** — **of the stick** tomar el rábano por las hojas; **to go off the deep** — ponerse furioso (*about* por); **to keep one's** — **up** defenderse bien; **to make both** — **s meet** hacer llegar el dinero; **to read a book to the very** — leer un libro hasta el mismo final; **to stand on** — (*hair*) erizarse, *object* poner de punta; **to start at the wrong** — empezar por el fin; **to tie up the loose** — **s** atar cabos.

(b) (*of time, process, resources*) fin *m*, final *m*; término *m*, conclusión *f*; límite *m*; (*of book etc*) desenlace *m*, conclusión *f*; **the — of the empire** el fin del imperio; **that was the — of him** así terminó él; **latter — muerte *f*; at the — of 3 months** al cabo de 3 meses; **at the — of the century** a fines del siglo; **in the —** al fin, por fin, finalmente; **no — of la mar de; no — of an expert** sumamente experto, más experto que nadie; **3 days on —** 3 días seguidos; **for days on —** durante una infinidad de días; **to the bitter —** hasta que se terminara del todo; **towards the — of** hacia el final de, *century etc* hacia fines de; **to be at an —** estar terminando, (*be all over*) haber terminado ya; **to be at the — of one's resources** haber agotado los recursos; **there's no — to it** all esto no tiene fin, esto es inacabable; **to come (or draw) to an —** terminarse; **to come to a bad —** tener mal fin, ir a acabar mal; **you'll never hear the — of it** esto no se olvidará pronto, esto no es fácil que se olvide; **to make an — of, to put an — to** acabar con, poner fin a; **to think no — of someone** tener un muy alto concepto de uno.

(c) (*aim*) fin *m*, objeto *m*, propósito *m*, intención *f*; **to this —, with this —** in view con este propósito; **to the — that** a fin de que + *subj*; **with what —?** ¿para qué?; **the — justifies the means** el fin justifica los medios; **to gain one's —s** salirse con la suya.

2 *adj* final.

3 *vt* terminar, acabar; *abuse etc* acabar con; *book* concluir.

4 *vi* terminar, acabar; **to — by saying** terminar diciendo; **to — in** terminar en; **to — up** terminar, acabar; **to — up at** ir a parar en; **to — with** terminar con.

endanger [in'deindʒə*] *vt* poner en peligro.
endear [in'diə*] **1** *vt*: **this did not — him to the public** esto no le granjeó las simpatías del público.
2 *vr*: **to — oneself to** hacerse querer de (*or* por).
endearing [in'diəriŋ] *adj* simpático, atractivo.
endearment [in'diəmənt] *n* palabra *f* cariñosa, ternura *f*.
endeavour [in'devə*] **1** *n* (*attempt*) esfuerzo *m* (*to do* por hacer), tentativa *f* (*to do* de hacer); (*striving*) empeño *m*, esfuerzos *mpl*; **to use every — to** + *infin* no regatear medio para + *infin*.
2 *vi*: **to — to do** esforzarse por hacer, procurar hacer.
endemic [en'demik] *adj* endémico.
ending ['endiŋ] *n* fin *m*, conclusión *f*; (*of book etc*) desenlace *m*; (*Gram*) terminación *f*, desinencia *f*; **the tale has a happy —** el cuento tiene un fin feliz.
endive ['endaiv] *n* escarola *f*, endibia *f*.
endless ['endlis] *adj* interminable, inacabable; *screw etc* sin fin.
endlessly ['endlisli] *adv* interminablemente, sin parar.
endocrine ['endəukrain] **1** *adj* endocrino; **— gland** glándula *f* endocrina. **2** *n* endocrina *f*.
endorse [in'dɔːs] *vt* endosar; *licence* poner nota de inhabilitación en; (*fig*) aprobar, confirmar.
endorsement [in'dɔːsmənt] *n* endoso *m*; (*in licence*) nota *f* de inhabilitación; (*fig*) aprobación *f*, confirmación *f*.
endow [in'dau] *vt* dotar (*with* con, (*fig*) de); *institution* fundar, crear; **to be —ed with** (*fig*) estar dotado de.
endowment [in'daumənt] *n* (**a**) (*act*) dotación *f*; (*creation*) fundación *f*, creación *f*. (**b**) (*amount*) dote *f*. (**c**) (*fig*) dote *f*, cualidad *f*.
endpaper ['endpeipə*] *n* hoja *f* de encuadernador.
end product ['end,prɔdəkt] *n* producto *m* final.
endue [in'djuː] *vt* dotar (*with* de).
endurable [in'djuərəbl] *adj* tolerable, soportable.
endurance [in'djuərəns] *n* resistencia *f*, aguante *m*; **beyond —, past —** intolerable; **to have great powers of —** tener gran resistencia; **— race** carrera *f* de resistencia; **— test** prueba *f* de resistencia.
endure [in'djuə*] **1** *vt* aguantar, soportar, tolerar; resistir; **I can't — him** no le puedo ver; **I can't — it a moment longer** no lo aguanto un momento más; **I can't — being corrected** no puedo sufrir que me corrijan; **I can't — being too hot** no resisto el calor excesivo.
2 *vi* (*last*) durar, perdurar; (*not give in*) resistir; sufrir sin rendirse.
enduring [in'djuəriŋ] *adj* permanente, perdurable.
endways ['endweiz] *adv* de punta; de lado, de canto.
enema ['enimə] *n* enema *f*.
enemy ['enimi] **1** *adj* enemigo. **2** *n* enemigo *m*, a *f*; **public — enemigo *m* público; to be one's own worst —** ser enemigo de sí mismo.
energetic [,enə'dʒetik] *adj* enérgico; *person etc* enérgico, activo; *protest* vigoroso.

energetically [,enə'dʒetikəli] *adv* enérgicamente; activamente; vigorosamente.
energize ['enədʒaiz] *vt* activar, dar energía a.
energy ['enədʒi] *n* energía *f*; vigor *m*; **atomic —** energía *f* atómica.
enervate ['enəːveit] *vt* enervar, debilitar.
enervating ['enəːveitiŋ] *adj* enervador; deprimente.
enfeeble [in'fiːbl] *vt* debilitar.
enfeeblement [in'fiːblmənt] *n* debilitación *f*.
enfilade [,enfi'leid] *vt* enfilar.
enfold [in'fauld] *vt* envolver; (*in arms*) abrazar, estrechar (en los brazos).
enforce [in'fɔːs] *vt* *law* hacer cumplir, (*from a date*) poner en vigor; *claim* hacer valer; *rights* hacer respetar; *demand* insistir en; *obedience, will* imponer (*on* a).
enforced [in'fɔːst] *adj* inevitable; forzoso, forzado.
enfranchise [in'fræntʃaiz] *vt* (*free*) emancipar; *voter* conceder el derecho de votar a.
enfranchisement [in'fræntʃizmənt] *n* emancipación *f* (*of* de); concesión *f* del derecho de votar (*of* a).
engage [in'geidʒ] **1** *vt* *attention* llamar, atraer; ocupar; *taxi etc* alquilar; *servant* tomar a su servicio; *person in conversation* abordar, (*and delay*) entretener; *workmen* apalabrar, ajustar; *lawyer etc* requerir los servicios de; *enemy* atacar, trabar batalla con; (*Mech*) *cog etc* engranar con, *coupling* acoplar.
2 *vi* (*Mech*) engranar; **to — in** dedicarse a, ocuparse en; *sport etc* tomar parte en; **to — to do something** comprometerse a hacer algo; **to — with** (*Mech*) engranar con.
3 *vr*: **to — oneself to do something** comprometerse a hacer algo.
engaged [in'geidʒd] **1** *ptp of* **engage**; (**a**) **to be —** (*seat*) estar ocupado; (*person*) estar ocupado; tener compromiso; no estar libre.
(b) to be — (*Tel*) estar comunicando.
(c) to be — in estar ocupado en, dedicarse a; **what are you — in?** ¿a qué se dedica Vd?
(d) to be — (to be married) estar prometido; (2 *persons*) estar prometidos, ser novios, tener relaciones formales; **they've been — for 2 years** llevan 2 años de relaciones formales; **to get —** prometerse (*to* con).
2 *adj* *writer etc* comprometido; **the — couple** los novios.
engagement [in'geidʒmənt] *n* (**a**) (*contract*) contrato *m*; obligación *f*; **to enter into an — to** + *infin* comprometerse a + *infin*.
(b) (*appointment*) compromiso *m*, cita *f*; **have you an — tonight?** ¿tienes compromiso para esta noche?; **I have an — at 10** tengo una cita a las 10; **owing to a previous —** por tener compromiso anterior.
(c) (*Mil*) combate *m*, acción *f*.
(d) (*to marry*) compromiso *m*; (*period etc*) noviazgo *m*; **they have announced their —** se han dado palabra de casamiento; **the — is announced of Miss A to Mr B** por los señores de B ha sido pedida la mano de su encantadora hija Isabel para su hijo Juan.
engagement ring [in'geidʒmənt,riŋ] *n* alianza *f*, anillo *m* de prometida, anillo *m* de compromiso.
engaging [in'geidʒiŋ] *adj* atractivo, simpático.
engender [in'dʒendə*] *vt* engendrar; (*fig*) engendrar, suscitar, motivar.
engine ['endʒin] *n* (**a**) motor *m*; **air-cooled —** motor *m* refrigerado por aire; **radial —** motor *m* radial.
(b) (*Rail*) máquina *f*, locomotora *f*; **back to the —** de espaldas a la máquina; **facing the —** de frente a la máquina.
-engined ['endʒind] *adj* de . . . motores; *eg* **four-engined** cuatrimotor, tetramotor; **petrol-engined** propulsado por gasolina.
engine driver ['endʒin,draivə*] *n* maquinista *m*.
engineer [,endʒi'niə*] **1** *n* ingeniero *m*; mecánico *m*; (*US Rail*) maquinista *m*; **civil —** ingeniero *m* civil, ingeniero *m* de caminos, canales y puentes; **electrical —** ingeniero *m* electricista; **mining —** ingeniero *m* de minas; **Royal E—s** Cuerpo *m* de Ingenieros.
2 *vt* lograr, gestionar, agenciar.
engineering [,endʒi'niəriŋ] *n* ingeniería *f*; **civil —** ingeniería *f* civil; **electrical —** electrotecnia *f*; **mechanical —** ingeniería *f* mecánica; **radio —** técnica *f* radiofónica.
engine room ['endʒinrum] *n* sala *f* de máquinas.
England ['iŋglənd] Inglaterra *f*.
English ['iŋgliʃ] **1** *adj* inglés.
2 *n*: **the —** los ingleses.
3 *n* (*language*) inglés *m*; **Old —** inglés *m* antiguo; **King's —** inglés *m* correcto; **to speak the King's —** hablar en cristiano.

English Channel ['ɪŋgliʃ'tʃænl] Canal *m* de la Mancha.

Englishman ['ɪŋgliʃmən] *n*, *pl* **—men** [mən] inglés *m*.

Englishwoman ['ɪŋgliʃ,wumən] *n*, *pl* **—women** [,wimin] inglesa *f*.

engraft [in'grɑːft] *vt* (*Agr*, *Med*) injertar; (*fig*) implantar (*on to* en).

engrave [in'greiv] *vt* grabar (*also fig: on* en); burilar.

engraver [in'greivə*] *n* grabador *m*.

engraving [in'greiviŋ] *n* grabado *m*.

engross [in'grəus] *vt* absorber; **to be —ed in** estar absorto en; **to become —ed in** dedicarse por completo a.

engrossing [in'grəusiŋ] *adj* absorbente.

engulf [in'gʌlf] *vt* tragar; sumergir, hundir; **to be —ed by** quedar sumergido bajo.

enhance [in'hɑːns] *vt* realzar, intensificar, aumentar; *price etc* aumentar.

enigma [i'nigmə] *n* enigma *m*.

enigmatic [,enig'mætik] *adj* enigmático.

enigmatically [,enig'mætikəli] *adv* enigmáticamente.

enjambement [in'dʒæmmənt] *n* encabalgamiento *m*.

enjoin [in'dʒɔin] *vt*: **to — something on someone** imponer algo a uno; **to — someone to do something** ordenar a uno hacer algo; **to — someone from doing something** (*US*) prohibir a uno hacer algo.

enjoy [in'dʒɔi] **1** *vt* (**a**) (*have use of*) *health*, *possession etc* disfrutar de, gozar de; *income*, *someone's confidence* tener; *advantage* poseer.

(**b**) (*take delight in*) *meal* comer con gusto; *pipe* fumar con fruición; **I —ed the book** me gustó el libro; **did you — the game?** ¿te gustó el partido?, ¿qué tal el partido?; **I — reading** me gusta leer, me gusta la lectura; **I hope you — your holiday** que lo pases muy bien en las vacaciones, que te diviertas mucho en las vacaciones, espero que tendrás unas vacaciones de lo más agradables; **the author did not mean his book to be —ed, exactly** el autor no quería que su libro resultase meramente divertido.

2 *vr*: **to — oneself** pasarlo bien, divertirse; **— yourselves!** ¡que lo paséis bien!; **we —ed ourselves tremendously** lo pasamos en grande, nos divertimos muchísimo; **he —ed himself chasing the girls** se divirtió persiguiendo a las chicas.

enjoyable [in'dʒɔiəbl] *adj* agradable; (*amusing*) divertido.

enjoyment [in'dʒɔimənt] *n* (**a**) (*use*) disfrute *m*; posesión *f*. (**b**) (*delight*) placer *m*, fruición *f*; **he listened with real —** escuchó con verdadera fruición.

enlarge [in'lɑːdʒ] **1** *vt* extender, aumentar, ensanchar; (*Phot*) ampliar; (*Med*) dilatar; **—d heart** dilatación *f* del corazón.

2 *vi* extenderse, aumentarse; **to — upon** tratar con más extensión, explicar con más detalles.

enlargement [in'lɑːdʒmənt] *n* extensión *f*, aumento *m*, ensanche *m*; (*Phot*) ampliación *f*.

enlarger [in'lɑːdʒə*] *n* (*Phot*) ampliadora *f*.

enlighten [in'laitn] *vt* (**a**) (*inform*) informar, instruir; **can you — me?** ¿puede Vd ayudarme?; **I was able to — him about it** pude darle informes sobre este asunto.

(**b**) (*civilize*) ilustrar, iluminar.

enlightened [in'laitnd] *adj* ilustrado, culto; bien informado; *despot* ilustrado; *attitude etc* comprensivo, inteligente.

enlightening [in'laitniŋ] *adj* informativo, lleno de datos útiles; *experience etc* instructivo.

enlightenment [in'laitnmənt] *n* ilustración *f*; *see* **age**.

enlist [in'list] **1** *vt* (*Mil*) alistar, reclutar; *support etc* conseguir. **2** *vi* alistarse (*in* en).

enlistment [in'listmənt] *n* alistamiento *m*.

enliven [in'laivn] *vt* avivar, animar.

en masse [ɑ̃ːŋ'mæs] *adv* en masa.

enmesh [in'meʃ] *vt* coger en una red; **to get —ed in** enredarse en.

enmity ['enmiti] *n* enemistad *f*.

ennoble [i'nəubl] *vt* ennoblecer.

ennui [ɑ̃ː'nwiː] *n* tedio *m*, aburrimiento *m*.

enormity [i'nɔːmiti] *n* enormidad *f*.

enormous [i'nɔːməs] *adj* enorme.

enormously [i'nɔːməsli] *adv* enormemente.

enough [i'nʌf] **1** *adv* bastante, suficientemente; **not big** — no suficientemente grande; **she sings well** — canta bastante bien; *see* **good**, **sure** *etc*.

2 *adj* bastante, suficiente; **I hadn't — money to buy it** no tuve bastante dinero para comprarlo.

3 *n*: **that's —, thanks** con eso basta, gracias; **that's — now!** ¡basta ya!; **it is — for us to know that** nos basta saber que; **there's more than — for all** hay más que suficiente para todos; **— is —** basta y sobra; **— is as good as a feast** rogar a Dios

por santos mas no por tantos; **it was — to drive you mad** era para volverse loco; **we have — to live on** tenemos bastante para vivir, tenemos con qué vivir; **one can never have — of his music** es imposible escuchar demasiado su música; **I've had — of him** estoy harto de él; **tell me when you've had —** dime en cuanto te empieces a cansar; **I had — to do to find one** me costó trabajo encontrar uno.

4 *interj*: **— of this!** ¡basta ya!, ¡concluyamos de una vez!

enquire [in'kwaiə*] *etc see* **inquire**.

enrage [in'reidʒ] *vt* enfurecer, hacer rabiar; **to be —d with pain** rabiar de dolor.

enrapture [in'ræptʃə*] *vt* encantar, embelesar.

enrich [in'ritʃ] *vt* enriquecer; *food* aumentar el valor alimenticio de; *soil* fertilizar.

enrichment [in'ritʃmənt] *n* enriquecimiento *m*; aumento *m* del valor alimenticio; fertilización *f*.

enrol [in'rəul] **1** *vt member* inscribir; *student* matricular; (*Mil*) alistar.

2 *vi* inscribirse; matricularse; alistarse; **to — for a course** matricularse para un curso.

enrolment [in'rəulmənt] *n* inscripción *f*; matrícula *f*; alistamiento *m*.

en route [ɑ̃ːn'ruːt] *adv*: **to be — for** ir camino de, ir con rumbo a, dirigirse a; **it was stolen —** lo robaron durante el viaje.

ensconce [in'skɔns] *vr*: **to — oneself** instalarse cómodamente, acomodarse; **to be —d in** estar cómodamente instalado en.

ensemble [ɑ̃ːnsɑ̃ːmbl] *n* (*whole*) conjunto *m*; (*general effect*) impresión *f* de conjunto; (*dress*) conjunto *m*; (*Mus*) conjunto *m*, agrupación *f*.

enshrine [in'ʃrain] *vt* (*fig*) encerrar.

ensign ['ensain] *n* (**a**) (*flag*) bandera *f*; **Red E—** Enseña *f* Roja (*bandera de la marina mercante británica*); **White E—** Enseña *f* Blanca (*bandera de la marina de guerra británica*).

(**b**) (*rank*) alférez *m*.

enslave [in'sleiv] *vt* esclavizar; (*fig*) dominar.

enslavement [in'sleivmənt] *n* esclavitud *f*.

ensnare [in'snɛə*] *vt* entrampar, coger en una trampa (*also fig*).

ensue [in'sjuː] *vi* (*follow*) seguirse; (*happen*) sobrevenir; (*result*) resultar (*from* de).

ensuing [in'sjuiŋ] *adj* consiguiente, subsiguiente.

ensure [in'ʃuə*] *vt* asegurar.

entail [in'teil] **1** *n* vínculo *m*.

2 *vt* (*necessitate*) imponer; (*imply*) suponer; (*bring in its train*) acarrear; (*Law*) vincular; **it —s a lot of work** supone mucho trabajo para nosotros, nos causa mucho trabajo; **it —ed buying a new car** ello nos obligó a comprar un nuevo coche.

entangle [in'tæŋgl] *vt* enredar, enmarañar; **to get —d in an affair** quedar enredado en un asunto; **to get —d with someone** meterse en un lío con uno.

entanglement [in'tæŋglmənt] *n* enredo *m*, embrollo *m*; (*love affair*) intriga *f* amorosa; (*Mil*) alambrada *f*; **to keep out of —s** no meterse en líos.

entente [ɑ̃ːn'tɑ̃ːnt] *n* entente *f*, trato *m* secreto.

enter ['entə*] **1** *vt* (**a**) (*go into*) entrar en; penetrar en; **it never —ed my head** jamás se me pasó por la cabeza.

(**b**) (*fig*) *society* ingresar en, hacerse socio de; *army* alistarse en; *college*, *school* matricularse en.

(**c**) (*write down*) *note* anotar, apuntar; *name etc* escribir; *member* inscribir, matricular; *record* asentar, anotar, dar entrada a, registrar; *order* (*Comm*) asentar; *protest* formular; **to — a horse for a race** presentar un caballo para una carrera; **to — one's son for Eton** inscribir a su hijo como futuro alumno de Eton; **to — a dog for a show** inscribir un perro en un concurso canino; **to — up** *entry* asentar; *ledger* hacer, llevar; *diary* poner al día.

2 *vi* entrar; (*Theat*) entrar en escena; **—Macbeth sale Macbeth**; **to — for** *competition*, *race* participar en, tomar parte en, presentarse para; *post* presentarse como candidato a, oponerse a; **to — into** *agreement* llegar a, firmar; *bargain* cerrar; *contract* hacer, firmar; *obligation* contraer; *explanations* dar; *argument* meterse en, tomar parte en; *conversation* entablar; *negotiations* iniciar; *relations* establecer (*with* con); *plans* formar parte de; *feelings* afectar (*en lo más mínimo*); **that doesn't — into it at all** eso no figura aquí para nada, eso no afecta la cosa en lo más mínimo; **to — upon** *career* emprender; *term of office* empezar; **to — upon** *one's 20th year* empezar.

enteric [en'terik] *adj* entérico; **— fever** fiebre *f* entérica.

enteritis [,entə'raitis] *n* enteritis *f*.

enterprise ['entəpraiz] n **(a)** *(firm, undertaking)* empresa f.
  (b) *(spirit)* iniciativa f; espíritu m emprendedor, empuje m; **free —** libre empresa f, libertad f de empresa; **private —** iniciativa f privada.

enterprising ['entəpraiziŋ] adj *person, spirit* emprendedor; **an — thing to do** una cosa que muestra mucha iniciativa; **that was — of you** en eso ha mostrado Vd tener iniciativa.

enterprisingly ['entəpraiziŋli] adv de modo emprendedor, con mucha iniciativa.

entertain [ˌentə'tein] vt **(a)** *(amuse)* divertir, entretener.
  (b) *guest (at home)* recibir, recibir en casa, alojar consigo; *(make a fuss of)* festejar, agasajar; **they — a good deal** reciben mucho en casa; **they —ed him with a dinner** le obsequiaron con una cena.
  (c) *idea, hope* abrigar, acariciar; *proposal* estudiar, considerar; **I wouldn't — it for a moment** tal idea es totalmente inconcebible para mí.

entertainer [ˌentə'teinə*] n actor m, actriz f, músico m *(etc)*.

entertaining [ˌentə'teiniŋ] adj divertido, entretenido.

entertainingly [ˌentə'teiniŋli] adv de manera divertida, graciosamente.

entertainment [ˌentə'teinmənt] n **(a)** *(amusement)* diversión f; **for your —** para divertiros.
  (b) *(show)* función f, espectáculo m, fiesta f; **musical —** concierto m; **to put on an —** organizar un espectáculo.

enthrall [in'θrɔːl] vt *(fig)* encantar, cautivar, captar la atención de; **we listened —ed** escuchamos embelesados.

enthrone [in'θrəun] vt entronizar.

enthuse [in'θuːz] vi: **to — over** entusiasmarse muchísimo por, extasiarse ante.

enthusiasm [in'θuːziæzəm] n entusiasmo m *(for por)*.

enthusiast [in'θuːziæst] n entusiasta mf *(for por)*.

enthusiastic [inˌθuːzi'æstik] adj *person* entusiasta; *cry etc* entusiástico; **to be — about** entusiasmarse por, estar lleno de entusiasmo por.

enthusiastically [inˌθuːzi'æstikəli] adv con entusiasmo; **he shouted —** gritó entusiasmado.

entice [in'tais] vt tentar, atraer (con maña); *(in bad sense)* seducir; **to — someone away from someone** persuadir mañosamente a uno a dejar a una persona; **to — someone away from a place** persuadir mañosamente a uno a abandonar un sitio; **to — someone into a room** persuadir mañosamente a uno a entrar en un cuarto; **to — someone to do something** tentar a uno a hacer algo.

enticement [in'taismənt] n **(a)** *(act)* tentación f, atracción f; seducción f; persuasión f mañosa.
  (b) *(bait)* atractivo m, aliciente m, cebo m.

enticing [in'taisiŋ] adj atractivo, tentador, seductor.

enticingly [in'taisiŋli] adv atractivamente, seductoramente.

entire [in'taiə*] adj entero, completo; total; todo; **the — world** el mundo entero; **the — trip** todo el viaje; **the — stock** todas las existencias.

entirely [in'taiəli] adv enteramente, totalmente; **that is not — true** no es del todo verdad.

entirety [in'taiərəti] n: **in its —** en su totalidad, enteramente.

entitle [in'taitl] vt **(a)** *book etc* titular; **the book is —d X** el libro se titula X.
  (b) **to — someone to do something** dar a uno el derecho a hacer algo; **to be —d to do something** tener derecho a hacer algo; **to — someone to something** dar a uno derecho a algo; **I think I am —d to some respect** creo que se me debe cierto respeto.

entity ['entiti] n entidad f, ente m; **legal —** persona f jurídica.

entomb [in'tuːm] vt sepultar.

entomologist [ˌentə'mɔlədʒist] n entomólogo m.

entomology [ˌentə'mɔlədʒi] n entomología f.

entourage [ˌɔntu'rɑːʒ] n séquito m.

entr'acte ['ɔntrækt] n descanso m; intermedio m.

entrails ['entreilz] npl entrañas fpl, tripas fpl.

entrain [in'trein] vi tomar el tren *(for a)*.

entrance ['entrəns] n *(place)* entrada f; *(act)* entrada f *(into en)*; *(into profession etc)* ingreso m; *(Theat)* entrada f en escena; **— examination** examen m de ingreso; **to make one's —** hacer su entrada.

entrance [in'trɑːns] vt encantar, hechizar; **we listened —d** escuchamos extasiados.

entrance fee ['entrənsfiː] n cuota f.

entrance hall ['entrəns,hɔːl] n hall m de entrada.

entrancing [in'trɑːnsiŋ] adj encantador, cautivador, delicioso.

entrancingly [in'trɑːnsiŋli] adv *play etc* maravillosamente, deliciosamente; **it was — beautiful** contemplamos extasiados aquella belleza.

entrant ['entrənt] n participante mf, concurrente mf.

entreat [in'triːt] vt rogar, suplicar; **to — someone to do something** suplicar a uno hacer algo.

entreatingly [in'triːtiŋli] adv de modo suplicante.

entreaty [in'triːti] n ruego m, súplica f.

entrée ['ɔntrei] n entrada f.

entrench [in'trentʃ] **1** vt atrincherar; **to be —ed** estar atrincherado *(also fig)*. **2** vr: **to — oneself** atrincherarse.

entrenchment [in'trentʃmənt] n trinchera f.

entrepôt ['ɔntrəpəu] n centro m comercial, centro m de distribución.

entrepreneur [ˌɔntrəprə'nɜː*] n *(Comm)* patrón m, dueño m; contratista m; *(Fin)* capitalista m.

entrust [in'trʌst] vt: **to — something to someone**, **to — someone with something** confiar algo a uno.

entry ['entri] n **(a)** *(place)* entrada f; *(passage)* callejuela f; *(of street)* bocacalle f; **"no —"** "prohibido el paso", *(Aut)* "dirección prohibida".
  (b) *(act)* entrada f *(into en)*; acceso m *(into a)*; *(into profession etc)* ingreso m *(into en)*; *(into office)* toma f de posesión *(into, on de)*; **— into the hall had been forbidden** se había prohibido el acceso a la sala; **to make one's —** hacer su entrada.
  (c) *(Sport etc) (total)* participación f, participantes mpl; *(competitor)* participante mf, concurrente mf.
  (d) *(in reference book)* artículo m; *(in diary)* apunte m; *(in account)* partida f; *(in record)* apunte m, apuntación f, entrada f.

entry form ['entrifɔːm] n boleto m de inscripción.

entwine [in'twain] vt entrelazar, entretejer.

enumerate [i'njuːməreit] vt enumerar.

enumeration [iˌnjuːmə'reiʃən] n enumeración f.

enunciate [i'nʌnsieit] vt *words* pronunciar, articular; *principle* enunciar.

enunciation [iˌnʌnsi'eiʃən] n pronunciación f, articulación f; enunciación f.

envelop [in'veləp] vt envolver *(in en)*.

envelop(e) ['envələup] n sobre m; *(Aer)* envoltura f.

enveloping [in'veləpiŋ] adj *movement* envolvente.

envelopment [in'veləpmənt] n envolvimiento m.

envenom [in'venəm] vt envenenar.

enviable ['enviəbl] adj envidiable.

envious ['enviəs] adj envidioso; *look etc* de envidia; **to be — of** tener envidia de; **to make someone — of something** hacer que uno tenga envidia de algo.

enviously ['enviəsli] adv con envidia.

environment [in'vaiərənmənt] n medio m ambiente, ambiente m.

environmental [inˌvaiərən'mentl] adj ambiental.

environs [in'vaiərənz] npl alrededores mpl, inmediaciones fpl.

envisage [in'vizidʒ] vt **(a)** prever; **it is —d that** se prevé que; **an increase is —d next year** está previsto que se aumentará el año que viene.
  (b) concebir, formarse una idea de, representarse; **it is hard to — such a situation** es difícil formarse una idea de tal situación.

envoy ['envɔi] n enviado m.

envy ['envi] **1** n envidia f; **it was the — of all the neighbours** nos lo envidiaban todos los vecinos; **to be green with —** estar verde de envidia. **2** vt: **to — someone** tener envidia a uno; **to — someone something** envidiar algo a uno.

enzyme ['enzaim] n enzima f.

epaulette ['epɔːlet] n charretera f.

ephemeral [i'femərəl] adj efímero.

epic ['epik] **1** adj épico. **2** n épica f, epopeya f.

epicentre ['episentə*] n epicentro m.

epicure ['epikjuə*] n gastrónomo m, sibarita m.

epicurean [ˌepikju'riːən] **1** adj epicúreo. **2** n epicúreo m.

epicureanism [ˌepikjuə'riːnizəm] n epicureísmo m.

epidemic [ˌepi'demik] **1** adj epidémico. **2** n epidemia f.

epidermis [ˌepi'dɜːmis] n epidermis f.

epiglottis [ˌepi'glɔtis] n epiglotis f.

epigram ['epigræm] n epigrama m.

epigrammatic(al) [ˌepigrə'mætik(əl)] adj epigramático.

epigraph ['epigrɑːf] n epígrafe m.

epilepsy ['epilepsi] n epilepsia f.

epileptic [ˌepi'leptik] **1** adj epiléptico. **2** n epiléptico m, a f.

epilogue ['epilɔg] n epílogo m.

Epiphany [i'pifəni] n Epifanía f.

episcopal [i'piskəpəl] adj episcopal.

episcopalian [i,piskə'peiliən] **1** *adj* episcopalista. **2** *n* episcopalista *mf*.
episode ['episəud] *n* episodio *m*.
episodic [,epi'sɔdik] *adj* episódico.
epistle [i'pisl] *n* epístola *f*.
epistolary [i'pistələri] *adj* epistolar.
epitaph ['epitɑːf] *n* epitafio *m*.
epithet ['epiθet] *n* epíteto *m*.
epitome [i'pitəmi] *n* epítome *m*, compendio *m*, resumen *m*; (*fig*) representación *f* en miniatura; **to be the — of virtue** ser la misma virtud.
epitomize [i'pitəmaiz] *vt* epitomar, compendiar, resumir; (*fig*) representar en miniatura; **he —d resistance to the enemy** se cifraba en él la resistencia al enemigo; **he —d virtue** era la misma virtud.
epoch ['iːpɔk] *n* época *f*; **to mark an —** hacer época.
epoch-making ['iːpɔk,meikiŋ] *adj* que hace época.
Epsom salts ['epsɔm,sɔːltz] *npl* sal *f* de La Higuera.
equable ['ekwəbl] *adj* climate etc uniforme, igual; *person, tone* tranquilo, afable.
equal ['iːkwəl] **1** *adj* igual (*to* a); *treatment* equitativo; **— in value** de igual valor; **with — ease** con la misma facilidad; **— sign** signo *m* de igualdad; **other things being —** si no cambian las circunstancias; **to be — to** *task* tener fuerzas para, *situation* estar a la altura de; **I don't feel — to it** no me siento con fuerzas para ello; **he is — to every demand made upon him** hace bien cuanto se le pide; **to be — to doing** something tener fuerzas para hacer algo.
  2 *n* igual *mf*; **without —** sin igual, sin par; **to treat someone as an —** tratar a uno de igual a igual.
  3 *vt* ser igual a; **to — out** igualar; **6 + 4 —s 10** 6 más 4 son 10.
equality [i'kwɔliti] *n* igualdad *f*.
equalize ['iːkwəlaiz] **1** *vt* igualar. **2** *vi* (*Sport*) lograr el empate, lograr la igualada.
equalizer ['iːkwəlaizə*] *n* (*Sport*) igualada *f*.
equally ['iːkwəli] *adv* igualmente; *share etc* por igual; *treat etc* equitativamente.
equanimity [,ekwə'nimiti] *n* ecuanimidad *f*.
equate [i'kweit] *vt* considerar equivalente (*to, with* a), comparar (*to, with* con).
equation [i'kweiʒən] *n* ecuación *f*; **quadratic —** cuadrática *f*.
equator [i'kweitə*] *n* ecuador *m*.
equatorial [,ekwə'tɔːriəl] *adj* ecuatorial.
equerry ['ekwəri] *n* caballerizo *m* del rey.
equestrian [i'kwestriən] **1** *adj* ecuestre. **2** *n* jinete *m*, a *f*.
equidistant ['iːkwi'distənt] *adj* equidistante.
equilateral ['iːkwi'lætərəl] *adj* equilátero.
equilibrium [,iːkwi'libriəm] *n* equilibrio *m*.
equine ['ekwain] *adj* equino.
equinox ['iːkwinɔks] *n* equinoccio *m*.
equip [i'kwip] *vt* equipar (*with* de); *person* proveer (*with* de); **to be —ped with** (*person*) estar provisto de, (*machine etc*) estar dotado de; **to be well —ped to + infin** estar bien dotado para + *infin*.
equipment [i'kwipmənt] *n* equipo *m*, material *m*; (*tools*) avíos *mpl*; (*mental*) aptitud *f*, dotes *fpl*.
equitable ['ekwitəbl] *adj* equitativo.
equitably ['ekwitəbli] *adv* equitativamente.
equity ['ekwiti] *n* equidad *f*; **equities** (*Comm*) acciones *fpl* de dividendo no fijo.
equivalence [i'kwivələns] *n* equivalencia *f*.
equivalent [i'kwivələnt] **1** *adj* equivalente (*to* a); **to be — to** equivaler a. **2** *n* equivalente *m*.
equivocal [i'kwivəkəl] *adj* equívoco, ambiguo.
equivocate [i'kwivəkeit] *vi* no dar una respuesta clara, soslayar el problema.
era ['iərə] *n* época *f*, era *f*; **to mark an —** hacer época.
eradicate [i'rædikeit] *vt* desarraigar, extirpar.
eradication [i,rædi'keiʃən] *n* desarraigo *m*, extirpación *f*.
erase [i'reiz] *vt* borrar (*also fig*).
eraser [i'reizə*] *n* goma *f* de borrar.
Erasmism [i'ræzmizəm] *n* erasmismo *m*.
Erasmist [i'ræzmist] **1** *adj* erasmista. **2** *n* erasmista *mf*.
Erasmus [i'ræzməs] *m* Erasmo.
erasure [i'reiʒə*] *n* borradura *f*, raspadura *f*.
ere [eə*] (*arch*) **1** *prep* antes de; **— long** dentro de poco. **2** *conj* antes de que.
erect [i'rekt] **1** *adj* erguido, derecho; vertical.
  2 *vt* (*build*) erigir, construir, levantar; (*assemble*) montar; **to — something into a principle** constituir algo en principio.
erection [i'rekʃən] *n* (*act*) erección *f*, construcción *f*; (*assembly*) montaje *m*; (*structure*) edificio *m*, construcción *f*; (*fig*) constitución *f*.
erg [əːg] *n* ergio *m*.

ergonomics [,əːgəu'nɔmiks] *n* ergonómica *f*.
ergot ['əːgət] *n* cornezuelo *m*.
Eric ['erik] *m* Erico.
Erin ['iərin] *nombre antiguo y sentimental de Irlanda*.
ermine ['əːmin] *n* armiño *m*.
Ernest ['əːnist] *m* Ernesto.
erode [i'rəud] *vt* (*Geol*) causar erosión en, erosionar; *metal* corroer, desgastar; (*fig*) erosionar, mermar, perjudicar.
erosion [i'rəuʒən] *n* (*Geol*) erosión *f*; (*of metal*) desgaste *m*.
erosive [i'rəuziv] *adj* erosivo.
erotic [i'rɔtik] *adj* erótico; (*obscene*) erotómano; (*obscene*) sicalíptico.
eroticism [i'rɔtisizəm] *n* erotomanía *f*; (*obscenity*) sicalipsis *f*.
err [əː*] *vi* errar, equivocarse; (*sin*) pecar; **to — is human** de los hombres es errar; **to — on the side of** pecar por exceso de.
errand ['erənd] *n* recado *m*, mandado *m*; misión *f*; **— of mercy** tentativa *f* de salvamento; **what — brings you here?** ¿qué le trae por aquí?; **to run an —** llevar un recado.
errand boy ['erəndbɔi] *n* recadero *m*, mandadero *m*.
errant ['erənt] *adj* errante; *knight* andante.
erratic [i'rætik] *adj* (*uncertain*) irregular, poco constante; *conduct* excéntrico; *person* voluble; *record, results etc* desigual, poco uniforme; (*Geol, Med*) errático.
erratically [i'rætikəli] *adv* de modo irregular (*etc*).
erratum [e'rɑːtəm] *n, pl* **errata** [e'rɑːtə] errata *f*.
erroneous [i'rəuniəs] *adj* erróneo.
erroneously [i'rəuniəsli] *adv* equivocadamente.
error ['erə*] *n* error *m*, equivocación *f*; **by —** por equivocación; **—s and omissions excepted** salvo error u omisión; **to be in —** estar equivocado; **to see the — of one's ways** reconocer las faltas en que uno ha incurrido.
ersatz ['eəzæts] **1** *adj* sucedáneo, sustituto. **2** *n* sucedáneo *m*, sustituto *m*.
erstwhile ['əːstwail] *adj* antiguo.
erudite ['erudait] *adj* erudito.
erudition [,eru'diʃən] *n* erudición *f*.
erupt [i'rʌpt] *vi* (*volcano*) estar en erupción, (*begin to —*) entrar en erupción; (*Med*) hacer erupción; (*anger, war etc*) estallar; **to — into a room** irrumpir en un cuarto.
eruption [i'rʌpʃən] *n* (*Geol, Med*) erupción *f*; (*fig*) explosión *f*.
erysipelas [,eri'sipiləs] *n* erisipela *f*.
Esau ['iːsɔː] *m* Esaú.
escalate ['eskəleit] **1** *vt* extender, intensificar. **2** *vi* extenderse, intensificarse.
escalation [,eskə'leiʃən] *n* extensión *f*, intensificación *f*, escalamiento *m*.
escalator ['eskəleitə*] *n* escalera *f* móvil.
escapade [,eskə'peid] *n* aventura *f*, travesura *f*.
escape [is'keip] **1** *n* escape *m*; fuga *f*, huida *f*, evasión *f*; (*leak*) fuga *f*; (*from duties etc*) escapatoria *f*; **it was a lucky — for him** tuvo suerte al poderse escapar; **to have a narrow —** escapar por los pelos; **to make one's —** escapar; **to make good one's —** escapar y desaparecer.
  2 *vt* (*avoid*) evitar, eludir; *consequences, death* escapar a; *vigilance* burlar; **the meaning —s me** se me escapa el significado; **the fact had —d me for the moment** por el momento el hecho se me escapó; **a cry —d him** no pudo contener un grito; *see* **notice**.
  3 *vi* escapar(se); evadirse, huir; (*leak*) fugarse; **to — from** *person* escaparse de, *prison* escaparse de, *clutches* librarse de; **to — to France** huir a Francia, refugiarse en Francia; **to — with a fright** escapar llevándose un susto; **he just —d being run over** por poco murió atropellado, en poco estuvo que no muriese atropellado.
escapism [is'keipizəm] *n* escapismo *m*.
escapist [is'keipist] **1** *adj* escapista. **2** *n* escapista *mf*.
escapologist [,eskə'pɔlədʒist] *n* rey *m* de la evasión.
escarpment [is'kɑːpmənt] *n* escarpa *f*.
eschatology [,eskə'tɔlədʒi] *n* escatología *f*.
eschew [is'tʃuː] *vt* evitar, renunciar a.
escort ['eskɔːt] *n* (*suite*) acompañamiento *m*; (*lady's*) acompañante *m*; (*Mil*) escolta *f*; (*Naut*) convoy *m*, buque *m* de escolta.
escort [is'kɔːt] *vt* acompañar; (*Mil*) escoltar; (*Naut*) convoyar, escoltar; **to — someone home** acompañar a uno a su casa.
escutcheon [is'kʌtʃən] *n* blasón *m*; (*fig*) honor *m*.
Eskimo ['eskiməu] **1** *adj* esquimal. **2** *n* esquimal *mf*. **3** *n* (*language*) esquimal *m*.
esoteric [,esəu'terik] *adj* esotérico.

especial [is'peʃəl] *adj* especial, particular.

especially [is'peʃəli] *adv* especialmente; sobre todo, ante todo; en particular; **it is — awkward** es especialmente difícil; **you — ought to know** Vd debiera saberlo más que nadie; **why me —?** ¿por qué yo y no otro?; **— when it rains** sobre todo cuando llueve.

Esperanto [ˌespə'ræntəu] *n* esperanto *m*.

espionage [ˌespiə'nɑːʒ] *n* espionaje *m*.

esplanade [ˌesplə'neid] *n* paseo *m*; (*by sea*) paseo *m* marítimo.

espouse [is'pauz] *vt cause* adherirse a.

espresso [es'presəu] *adj*: **— bar** café *m* donde se sirve café expreso; **— coffee** café *m* expreso.

esprit de corps ['espriːdə'kɔː*] *n* espíritu *m* de cuerpo, lealtad *f*.

espy [is'pai] *vt* divisar.

esquire [is'kwaiə*] *n*: (*on envelope*) **Colin Smith E—** Sr don Colin Smith.

essay ['esei] *n* ensayo *m*.

essay [e'sei] *vt* probar, ensayar; *task* intentar; **to — to** + *infin* intentar + *infin*.

essayist ['eseiist] *n* ensayista *mf*.

essence ['esəns] *n* esencia *f*; **the — of the matter is** lo esencial es; **speed is of the —** es esencial hacerlo con la mayor prontitud.

essential [i'senʃəl] **1** *adj* esencial; indispensable, imprescindible; **it is — to** + *infin* es imprescindible + *infin*; **it is — that** es necesario que + *subj*.
2 *n* esencial *m*; elemento *m* necesario, factor *m* imprescindible.

essentially [i'senʃəli] *adv* esencialmente, en su esencia.

establish [is'tæbliʃ] **1** *vt* establecer, fundar, crear; *facts* verificar; *proof* demostrar, probar; *relations* entablar; *precedent* crear; **we have —ed that** hemos comprobado que; **his father —ed him in business** su padre compró el negocio para él; **he —ed her in a flat** la instaló en un piso.
2 *vr*: **to — oneself** crearse una reputación, hacerse un negocio sólido; **to — itself** establecerse, consolidarse, (*custom*) arraigar.

established [is'tæbliʃt] *adj person, business* de buena reputación, sólido; *custom* arraigado; *fact* conocido; *church* oficial, del Estado; *staff* fijo, de plantilla.

establishment [is'tæbliʃmənt] *n* (**a**) (*act, body*) establecimiento *m*, fundación *f*; (*business house*) establecimiento *m*, casa *f*.
(**b**) (*Mil*) fuerzas *fpl*, efectivos *mpl*; (*servants*) servidumbre *f*; (*staff of company etc*) plantel *m*, personal *m*; **to be on the —** ser de plantilla.
(**c**) (*Britain*) **the E—** las clases directoras, el centro del poder efectivo en Gran Bretaña.

estate [is'teit] *n* (**a**) (*land*) finca *f*, hacienda *f*.
(**b**) (*property, assets*) propiedad *f*; **real —** bienes *mpl* raíces.
(**c**) (*inheritance*) bienes *mpl* relictos; herencia *f*, heredad *f*; testamentaría *f*; **he left a large —** dejó una inmensa fortuna.
(**d**) (*Pol*) estado *m*; **third — estado** *m* llano; **fourth —** la prensa.

estate agent [is'teit,eidʒənt] *n* corredor *m* de fincas, agente *m* inmobiliario.

estate car [is'teitkɑː*] *n* furgoneta *f*, rubia *f*.

estate duty [is'teit,djuːti] *n* impuesto *m* de sucesión, impuesto *m* sobre los bienes heredados.

esteem [is'tiːm] **1** *n* estima *f*, estimación *f*; consideración *f*; **to hold someone in high —** estimar en mucho a uno, tener un alto concepto de uno; **to hold someone in low —** estimar en poco a uno; **to rise in someone's —** merecer que uno le estime más.
2 *vt* estimar, apreciar.

esthete ['iːsθiːt] *n* (*etc*) = **aesthete** (*etc*).

Esthonia [es'təuniə] *n* Estonia *f*.

Esthonian [es'təuniən] **1** *adj* estonio. **2** *n* estonio *m*, a *f*. **3** *n* (*language*) estonio *m*.

estimable ['estiməbl] *adj* estimable.

estimate ['estimit] *n* (*judgement*) estimación *f*, apreciación *f*; (*approximate assessment*) tasa *f*, cálculo *m*; (*for work etc*) presupuesto *m*; **rough —** cálculo *m* aproximativo; **E—s** (*Parl*) presupuesto *m*.

estimate ['estimeit] **1** *vt* (*judge*) estimar, apreciar; (*assess*) calcular, computar, tasar (*at* en); **to — that** calcular que. **2** *vi*: **to — for** presupuestar, hacer un presupuesto de.

estimation [ˌesti'meiʃən] *n* (**a**) (*judgement*) opinión *f*; juicio *m*; **in my — a** mi juicio; **what is your — of him?** ¿qué concepto tiene Vd de él?
(**b**) (*esteem*) estima *f*, aprecio *m*.

estrange [is'treindʒ] *vt* enajenar, apartar (*from* de); **to become —d** enemistarse (*from* con).

estrangement [is'treindʒmənt] *n* enajenación *f*; separación *f*.

estuary ['estjuəri] *n* estuario *m*, ría *f*.

etcetera [it'setrə] **1** *as adv* etcétera. **2 —s** *npl* extras *mpl*, adornos *mpl*.

etch [etʃ] *vt* grabar al agua fuerte.

etching ['etʃiŋ] *n* aguafuerte *f*.

eternal [i'təːnl] *adj* eterno; sempiterno; de siempre.

eternally [i'təːnəli] *adv* eternamente; sempiternamente; siempre.

eternity [i'təːniti] *n* eternidad *f*; **it seemed like an —** parecía un siglo, parecía que no iba a acabar (*etc*) nunca.

ether ['iːθə*] *n* éter *m*.

ethereal [i'θiəriəl] *adj* etéreo (*also fig*).

ethical ['eθikəl] *adj* ético; (*honourable*) honrado.

ethics ['eθiks] *n* ética *f*; (*honourableness*) moralidad *f*.

Ethiopia [ˌiːθi'əupiə] Etiopía *f*.

Ethiopian [ˌiːθi'əupiən] **1** *adj* etíope. **2** *n* etíope *mf*.

ethnic ['eθnik] *adj* étnico.

ethnography [eθ'nɔgrəfi] *n* etnografía *f*.

ethnology [eθ'nɔlədʒi] *n* etnología *f*.

ethos ['iːθɔs] *n* genio *m*, carácter *m* (nacional), rasgo *m* distintivo (de una colectividad).

ethyl ['iːθail] *n* etilo *m*.

etiquette ['etiket] *n* etiqueta *f*; (*of profession*) honor *m* profesional; **it is not — to** + *infin* no es elegante + *infin*, está mal visto + *infin*.

Eton crop ['iːtn'krɔp] *n* corte *m* a lo garçon.

Etruscan [i'trʌskən] **1** *adj* etrusco. **2** *n* etrusco *m*, a *f*. **3** *n* (*language*) etrusco *m*.

etymological [ˌetimə'lɔdʒikəl] *adj* etimológico.

etymology [ˌeti'mɔlədʒi] *n* etimología *f*.

eucalyptus [ˌjuːkə'liptəs] *n* eucalipto *m*.

Eucharist ['juːkərist] *n* Eucaristía *f*.

Euclid ['juːklid] *m* Euclides.

Eugene [juː'ʒein] *m* Eugenio.

eugenics [juː'dʒeniks] *n* eugenismo *m*, eugenesia *f*.

eulogize ['juːlədʒaiz] *vt* elogiar, encomiar.

eulogy ['juːlədʒi] *n* elogio *m*, encomio *m*.

eunuch ['juːnək] *n* eunuco *m*.

euphemism ['juːfimizəm] *n* eufemismo *m*.

euphemistic [ˌjuːfi'mistik] *adj* eufemístico.

euphonic [juː'fɔnik] *adj*, **euphonious** [juː'fəuniəs] *adj* eufónico.

euphony ['juːfəni] *n* eufonía *f*.

euphoria [juː'fɔːriə] *n* euforia *f*.

euphoric [juː'fɔrik] *adj* eufórico.

Euphrates [juː'freitiːz] Eufrates *m*.

Eurasian [juə'reiziən] **1** *adj* eurasiano. **2** *n* eurasiano *m*, a *f*.

eureka [juə'riːkə] *interj* ¡eureka!

eurhythmics [juː'riðmiks] *n* euritmia *f*.

Euripides [juː'ripidiːz] *m* Eurípides.

Europe ['juərəp] Europa *f*.

European [ˌjuərə'piːən] **1** *adj* europeo. **2** *n* europeo *m*, a *f*.

Eurovision ['juərəviʒən] Eurovisión *f*.

Eurydice [juː'ridisiː] *f* Eurídice.

euthanasia [ˌjuːθə'neiziə] *n* eutanasia *f*.

evacuate [i'vækjueit] *vt* evacuar; *building etc* desocupar.

evacuation [iˌvækju'eiʃən] *n* evacuación *f*.

evacuee [iˌvækju'iː] *n* evacuado *m*, a *f*.

evade [i'veid] *vt* evadir, eludir; *grasp* escaparse de; **to — taxes** defraudar impuestos; *see* issue.

evaluate [i'væljueit] *vt* evaluar, calcular (el valor de); tasar; *evidence* interpretar.

evaluation [iˌvælju'eiʃən] *n* evaluación *f*, cálculo *m*; (*of evidence*) interpretación *f*.

evanescent [ˌiːvə'nesnt] *adj* efímero, evanescente.

evangelic(al) [ˌiːvæn'dʒelik(əl)] *adj* evangélico.

evangelist [i'vændʒəlist] *n* evangelizador *m*, misionero *m*; **St John the E—** San Juan Evangelista.

evangelize [i'vændʒəlaiz] *vt* evangelizar.

evaporate [i'væpəreit] **1** *vt* evaporar. **2** *vi* evaporarse; (*fig*) desvanecerse.

evaporation [iˌvæpə'reiʃən] *n* evaporación *f*.

evasion [i'veiʒən] *n* evasiva *f*, evasión *f*; **tax —** evasión *f* fiscal.

evasive [i'veiziv] *adj* evasivo; **he was very —** contestó de manera evasiva.

evasively [i'veizivli] *adv* de manera evasiva.

Eve [iːv] *f* Eva.

eve [iːv] *n* víspera *f*; **on the — of** la víspera de, (*fig*) en vísperas de.

even ['iːvən] **1** *adj* (**a**) (*level*) llano; (*smooth*) liso, igual, uniforme; (*on same level*) a nivel; *speed* uniforme; *temperature etc* uniforme, constante; *score, match, teams* igual; *number* par; *treatment* equitativo; *temper* ecuánime, apacible; *tone* imperturbable.
(**b**) **to be — with** (*at game*) tener igual número de tantos que; (*fig*) estar en paz con; **to break —** salir sin ganar ni perder; **to get — with** ajustar

cuentas con, desquitarse con; **I'll get —— with you yet!** ¡me las pagarás!; **that makes us ——** (*at game*) eso iguala el tanteo, (*fig*) tal para cual.

2 *adv* (a) **——** the priest was there hasta el cura estuvo allí; **pick them all, —— the little ones** cógelos todos incluso los pequeños; **—— on Sundays** incluso los domingos; **and he —— sings** e incluso canta.

(b) **—— more curious** aun más curioso, más curioso aun; **—— faster** aun más rápidamente.

(c) **—— I** yo también; **—— as you tricked me** del mismo modo que Vd me engañó; **—— as I went in** en el mismo momento en que yo entraba; **—— if, —— though** aunque + *subj*, aun cuando + *subj*, si bien + *indic*; **—— so** aun así; sin embargo.

(d) **not ——** ni siquiera; **not —— a look** ni una mirada siquiera; **he didn't —— kiss me** ni me besó siquiera; **without —— reading it** sin leerlo siquiera.

3 *vt* *surface* allanar, nivelar; **to —— out** *inequalities* igualar, allanar; *distribution* hacer uniforme, *thing distributed* repartir equitativamente; **to —— up = to —— out**; *score etc* igualar, nivelar.

4 *vi:* **to —— up with someone** ajustar cuentas con uno.

even-handed ['i:vən'hændid] *adj* imparcial.

evening ['i:vniŋ] **1** *n* (*early*) tarde *f*, (*at sunset*) atardecer *m*, (*after dark*) noche *f*; **—— was coming on** atardecía, anochecía; **good ——!** ¡buenas tardes!, ¡buenas noches!; **musical ——** velada *f* musical.

2 *attr* *dress* (*man's*) de etiqueta, (*woman's*) de noche; *class, institute* nocturno; *paper* de la tarde; *light, star* vespertino.

evenly ['i:vənli] *adv* (*smoothly*) lisamente; (*uniformly*) de modo uniforme; *distribute etc* igualmente, equitativamente; *speak etc* en el mismo tono, apaciblemente; *look etc* sin alterarse.

evenness ['i:vənnis] *n* lisura *f*; uniformidad *f*; igualdad *f*; (*of treatment*) imparcialidad *f*; (*of temper*) serenidad *f*, ecuanimidad *f*.

evensong ['i:vənsɔŋ] *n* vísperas *fpl*.

event [i'vent] *n* suceso *m*, acontecimiento *m*; (*in a programme*) número *m*; (*Sport*) prueba *f*; **current ——s** actualidades *fpl*; **this is quite an ——!** ¡esto sí es un acontecimiento!; **the —— will show** ya lo veremos, ello dirá, veremos qué consecuencias tendrá esto; **at all ——s, in any ——** en todo caso; **in either ——** en cualquiera de los dos casos; **in the —— tal como** resultó después; **in the —— of** en caso de; **in the —— of his dying** en caso de que muriese; **to be expecting a happy ——** estar en estado de buena esperanza; **to be wise after the ——** mostrar sabiduría cuando ya no hay remedio.

even-tempered ['i:vən'tempəd] *adj* ecuánime, apacible.

eventful [i'ventful] *adj* *life, journey etc* accidentado, azaroso; *match etc* lleno de incidentes, lleno de emoción.

eventual [i'ventʃuəl] *adj* final, definitivo; consiguiente.

eventuality [i,ventʃu'æliti] *n* eventualidad *f*; **in that ——** en esa eventualidad; **in the —— of** en la eventualidad de; **to be ready for any ——** estar dispuesto a aguantar cualquier posibilidad.

eventually [i'ventʃuəli] *adv* (*at last*) finalmente, al fin y al cabo; (*given time*) con el tiempo, a la larga.

ever ['evə*] *adv* (a) (*always*): **—— since** desde entonces, (*conj*) después de que; **as —— como** siempre; **as ——, yours ——** (*ending letter*) recibe un abrazo de tu amigo . . .; **for ——** para siempre; **for —— and ——, for —— and a day** por siempre jamás.

(b) (*at no time*) nunca, jamás; **hardly —— casi** nunca; **better than ——** mejor que nunca; **more than —— más que** nunca; **nothing —— happens** no pasa nunca nada; **not often if ——** rara vez y creo que nunca.

(c) (*at any time*) **if you —— go there** si vas allí alguna vez; **did you —— find it?** ¿lo encontraste por fin?; **did you —— meet him?** ¿llegó Vd a conocerle?; **did you ——?** (*fam*) ¿se vio jamás tal cosa?

(d) (*emphasizing question*) **what —— did he want?** ¿qué demonios quería?; **why —— did you do it?** ¿por qué demonios lo hiciste?

(e) **so: he's —— so nice** es simpatiquísimo; **it's —— so cold** hace un frío terrible; **we're —— so grateful** le estamos profundamente agradecidos; **—— so much** muchísimo; **—— so little** muy poco; **—— so many things** tantísimas cosas, la mar de cosas.

(f) (*after superl*) **the best ——** el mejor que se ha visto jamás; **the coldest night ——** la noche más fría que hemos conocido; **as soon as —— I can** en cuanto pueda.

everglade ['evəgleid] *n* (*US*) tierra *f* baja pantanosa cubierta de altas hierbas.

evergreen ['evəgri:n] **1** *adj* de hoja perenne. **2** *n* árbol *m* (*etc*) de hoja perenne.

evergreen oak ['evəgri:n,əuk] *n* encina *f*.

ever-growing ['evə'grəuiŋ] *adj* que va en continuo aumento.

everlasting [,evə'lɑ:stiŋ] *adj* eterno, perdurable, perpetuo; (*pej*) interminable.

everlastingly [,evə'lɑ:stiŋli] *adv* eternamente; (*pej*) interminablemente.

evermore ['evə'mɔ:*] *adv* eternamente; **for ——** por siempre jamás.

every ['evri] *adj* cada (*invariable*); (*each and every, any*) todo; **—— man** cada hombre, todo hombre, todos los hombres; **—— one** cada uno; **—— one of them** todos ellos; **his —— effort** todos sus esfuerzos; **I gave you —— assistance** te ayudé en lo que podía; **—— day** cada día; **—— other month** un mes sí y otro no, cada dos meses; **—— 5 years** cada 5 años; **—— now and then, —— now and again** de vez en cuando; **—— so often** cada cierto tiempo; *see bit etc.*

everybody ['evribɔdi] *pron* todos, todo el mundo.

everyday ['evridei] *adj* (*occurring daily*) diario, cotidiano, de todos los días; (*usual*) corriente, acostumbrado; (*commonplace*) vulgar; (*routine*) rutinario; **for —— (use)** de diario; **in —— use** de uso corriente; **—— clothes** ropa *f* para todos los días; **it's an —— event** es un suceso ordinario.

everything ['evriθiŋ] *pron* (a) (*as subject etc*) todo; **—— is ready** todo está dispuesto; **—— nice had been sold** se había vendido todo lo deseable; **time is —— el** tiempo lo es todo; **money isn't —— el** dinero no es la única cosa que cuenta.

(b) (*as object*) **he sold ——** lo vendió todo.

everywhere ['evriwεə*] *adv* **be —— en** todas partes, **go a** todas partes, por todas partes; **I looked —— busqué** por todas partes; **—— in Spain** en todas partes de España; **—— you go you'll find the same en** todas partes encontrarás lo mismo.

evict [i'vikt] *vt* desahuciar.

eviction [i'vikʃən] *n* desahucio *m*.

evidence ['evidəns] **1** *n* (a) (*obviousness*) evidencia *f*; **in —— bien** visible, manifiesto.

(b) (*sign*) prueba *f*, indicios *mpl*; (*testimony*) testimonio *m*; (*facts*) hechos *mpl*, datos *mpl*; **circumstantial —— prueba** *f* indiciaria; **documentary —— prueba** *f* documental; **internal —— indicios** *mpl* internos; **there is —— to show that** hay indicios que demuestran que; **what —— is there for this belief?** ¿qué hechos se alegan a favor de tal creencia?

(c) (*Law*) testimonio *m*, declaración *f*, deposición *f*; **there is no —— against him** no hay evidencia en contra suya; **to call someone in ——** llamar a uno para que deponga como testigo; **to give ——** prestar declaración, (*more formally*) deponer, dar testimonio; **to turn Queen's (or King's) ——, to turn state's ——** (*US*) delatar a los cómplices.

2 *vt* patentizar, probar; *emotion* dar muestras de; **as is ——d by the fact that** según lo demuestra el hecho de que.

evident ['evidənt] *adj* evidente, manifiesto, claro; **it is —— that** es evidente que; **to be —— in** manifestarse en; **to be —— from** quedar bien claro de.

evidently ['evidəntli] *adv*: **¡naturalmente!; it is —— difficult** por lo visto es difícil; **—— he cannot come** por lo visto no puede venir.

evil ['i:vl] **1** *adj* malo, pernicioso; *person* malo, malvado, perverso; (*unlucky*) aciago; *spirit* diabólico; *influence* funesto; *smell* horrible.

2 *n* mal *m*, maldad *f*; **the lesser of two ——s** el menor de los males; **to do ——** hacer mal; **to speak —— of** hablar mal de.

evildoer ['i:vldu:ə*] *n* malhechor *m*.

evil-minded ['i:vl'maindid] *adj* malintencionado, mal pensado.

evil-smelling ['i:vl'smeliŋ] *adj* fétido, maloliente, hediondo.

evince [i'vins] *vt* dar señales de, mostrar.

eviscerate [i'visəreit] *vt* destripar.

evocative [i'vɔkətiv] *adj* sugestivo, evocador.

evoke [i'vəuk] *vt* evocar.

evolution [,i:və'lu:ʃən] *n* evolución *f* (*also Bio*); desarrollo *m*.

evolutionary [,i:və'lu:ʃnəri] *adj* evolutivo.

evolve [i'vɔlv] **1** *vt* desarrollar, producir; *heat etc* desprender. **2** *vi* evolucionar, desarrollarse.

ewe [ju:] *n* oveja *f*.

ewer ['ju:ə*] *n* aguamanil *m*.

ex [eks] *prep* (a) **—— dividend** sin participación en el dividendo; **—— price —— factory** precio *m* en fábrica; **—— officio** de oficio.

(b) **—— leader of** antiguo jefe de; **—— ambassador**

in Moscow ex embajador en Moscú; — **minister** ex ministro.

exacerbate [eks'æsəbeit] *vt* exacerbar.

exact [ig'zækt] **1** *adj* exacto; **99, to be** — concretamente 99, en concreto 99. **2** *vt* exigir (*from* a); *obedience etc* imponer (*from* a).

exacting [ig'zæktiŋ] *adj* exigente; *conditions* severo, arduo.

exaction [ig'zækʃən] *n* exacción *f*.

exactitude [ig'zæktitjuːd] *n* exactitud *f*.

exactly [ig'zæktli] *adv* exactamente; (*of time*) en punto; —! ¡exacto!; **what did you tell him** —? ¿qué le dijiste, en concreto?; **he is not — an actor** no es un actor que digamos; **and I'm not — a dwarf** y yo tampoco soy un enano precisamente.

exactness [ig'zæktnis] *n* exactitud *f*.

exaggerate [ig'zædʒəreit] *vt* exagerar.

exaggerated [ig'zædʒəreitid] *adj* exagerado.

exaggeration [ig'zædʒəreiʃən] *n* exageración *f*.

exalt [ig'zɔːlt] *vt* (*elevate*) exaltar, elevar; (*praise*) ensalzar.

exaltation [,egzɔː'teiʃən] *n* exaltación *f*, elevación *f*; ensalzamiento *m*.

exalted [ig'zɔːltid] *adj* exaltado, elevado.

exam [ig'zæm] *n* (*fam*) = **examination**.

examination [ig,zæmi'neiʃən] *n* examen *m*; (*Law*) interrogación *f*; (*inquiry*) investigación *f* (*into* de); (*by Customs etc*) registro *m*; (*of account*) revisión *f*; **final** — examen *m* de fin de curso; **medical** — reconocimento *m* médico; **oral** — examen *m* oral; **qualifying** — examen *m* eliminatorio; **the matter is under** — el asunto está examinándose; **to enter** (*or* **go in for, sit**) **an** — presentarse a un examen; **to take an** — **in** examinarse en.

examine [ig'zæmin] *vt* examinar; inspeccionar, escudriñar; (*Law*) interrogar; *baggage etc* registrar; (*Med*) examinar, hacer un reconocimiento médico de; **we are examining whether** estamos pensando si; **we are examining the question** estamos estudiando la cuestión.

examinee [ig,zæmi'niː] *n* examinando *m*, a *f*; **to be a bad** — hacer siempre mal los exámenes.

examiner [ig'zæminə*] *n* examinador *m*, ora *f*; inspector *m*.

example [ig'zɑːmpl] *n* ejemplo *m*; (*copy, specimen*) ejemplar *m*; (*Math*) problema *m*; **for** — por ejemplo; **following the** — **of** siguiendo el ejemplo de; **to make an** — **of someone** castigar a uno de modo ejemplar; **to set an** — dar ejemplo.

exasperate [ig'zɑːspəreit] *vt* exasperar, irritar, sacar de quicio; **to get** —**d** irritarse.

exasperating [ig'zɑːspəreitiŋ] *adj* irritante, que le saca a uno de quicio; **it's so** —! es para volverse loco; **you're an** — **person** Vd es un hombre imposible.

exasperation [ig,zɑːspə'reiʃən] *n* exasperación *f*, irritación *f*.

excavate ['ekskəveit] *vt* excavar.

excavation [,ekskə'veiʃən] *n* excavación *f*.

excavator ['ekskəveitə*] *n* (*person*) excavador *m*, ora *f*; (*machine*) excavadora *f*.

exceed [ik'siːd] *vt* exceder (*by* en); *number* pasar de, exceder de; *limit* rebasar; *speed limit* sobrepasar; *rights* ir más allá de, abusar de; *powers, instructions* excederse en; *hopes, expectations* superar; **a fine not** —**ing £50** una multa que no pasa de 50 libras.

exceedingly [ik'siːdiŋli] *adv* sumamente, sobremanera.

excel [ik'sel] **1** *vt* aventajar, superar. **2** *vi* sobresalir (*at, in* en). **3** *vr*: **to** — **oneself** (*often iro*) lucirse.

excellence ['eksələns] *n* excelencia *f*.

Excellency ['eksələnsi] *n* Excelencia *f*; **His** — su Excelencia; **yes, Your** — sí, Excelencia.

excellent ['eksələnt] *adj* excelente.

except [ik'sept] **1** *vt* exceptuar, excluir.

2 *prep* (*also* — **for**) excepto, con excepción de, salvo; sin contar; menos; dejando aparte; **all** — **me** todos menos yo; — **that** salvo que.

excepting [ik'septiŋ] *prep* = **except**.

exception [ik'sepʃən] *n* excepción *f*; **with the** — **of** a excepción de; **without** — sin excepción; **to be an** — **to the rule** ser la excepción de la regla; **the** — **proves the rule** la excepción confirma la regla; **to make an** — hacer una excepción; **to take** — **to** desaprobar, (*feel offended*) ofenderse por.

exceptional [ik'sepʃənl] *adj* excepcional.

exceptionally [ik'sepʃənəli] *adv*: — **good** excepcionalmente bueno; **it happens** — **that** ocurre en casos excepcionales que.

excerpt ['eksəːpt] *n* extracto *m*.

excess [ik'ses] **1** *n* exceso *m* (*also fig*); (*Comm*)

excedente *m*; **in** — de sobra; **in** — **of** superior a; **to carry to** — llevar al exceso; **to drink to** — beber en exceso.

2 *attr* excedente, sobrante; — **fare** suplemento *m*; — **luggage** exceso *m* de equipaje; — **profits tax** impuesto *m* sobre las ganancias excesivas.

excessive [ik'sesiv] *adj* excesivo; **with** — **courtesy** con exagerada cortesía.

excessively [ik'sesivli] *adv* excesivamente; exageradamente; **you are** — **kind** es Vd amable en exceso.

exchange [iks'tʃeindʒ] **1** *n* (**a**) (*act*) cambio *m*; (*of prisoners, publications, stamps etc*) canje *m*; (*of ideas, information*) intercambio *m*; — **of shots** tiroteo *m*; **in** — **for** a cambio de.

(**b**) **foreign** — divisas *fpl*; — **control** control *m* de divisas; **rate of** — tipo *m* de cambio.

(**c**) (*building*) (*of corn, cotton etc*) lonja *f*; (*labour* —) bolsa *f* de trabajo; (*stock* —) bolsa *f*; (*Tel*) central *f* telefónica.

2 *vt* cambiar (*for* por); *prisoners, publications, stamps etc* canjear (*for* por, *with* con); *greetings, shots* cambiar; *courtesies* hacerse; *blows* darse; **we** —**d glances** nos miramos el uno al otro, cruzamos una mirada.

exchangeable [iks'tʃeindʒəbl] *adj* cambiable; canjeable.

exchequer [iks'tʃekə*] *n* hacienda *f*, tesoro *m*, erario *m*.

excise ['eksaiz] *n* impuestos *mpl* sobre artículos de comercio interior.

excise [ek'saiz] *vt* (*cut*) cortar, quitar; (*fig*) suprimir, eliminar.

exciseman ['eksaizmæn] *n*, *pl* —**men** [men] (*Hist*) recaudador *m* de impuestos interiores.

excision [ek'siʒən] *n* corte *m*; supresión *f*.

excitable [ik'saitəbl] *adj* exaltado, nervioso, excitable.

excite [ik'sait] *vt* (*move to emotion*) emocionar, llenar de emoción, entusiasmar; (*stimulate*) excitar, estimular; *provocar*; *revolt* instigar; *interest* despertar, suscitar; **to** — **someone to action** provocar a uno a la acción.

excited [ik'saitid] *adj voice etc* lleno de emoción; **to be** — (*person*) estar muy emocionado, (*and upset*) estar agitado; **I'm so** — **about the new house** la nueva casa me hace mucha ilusión; **to get** — emocionarse, entusiasmarse (*about, over* por); (*crowd etc*) alborotarse; (*discussion*) acalorarse; (*get upset*) agitarse; **don't get so** —! ¡no te emociones tanto!

excitedly [ik'saitidli] *adv* con emoción, con entusiasmo; **he said** — dijo entusiasmadísimo, dijo excitadísimo.

excitement [ik'saitmənt] *n* emoción *f*, entusiasmo *m*; excitación *f*; ilusión *f*; agitación *f*; alboroto *m*; **his arrival caused great** — su llegada produjo una enorme emoción; **why all the** —?, **what's all the** — **about?** ¿a qué se debe tanta conmoción?

exciting [ik'saitiŋ] *adj* emocionante, apasionante; excitante; **how** —! ¡qué ilusión!; **it's a most** — **film** es una película llena de emoción.

exclaim [iks'kleim] *vi* exclamar.

exclamation [,eksklə'meiʃən] *n* exclamación *f*; — **mark** punto *m* de admiración.

exclamatory [eks'klæmətəri] *adj* exclamatorio.

exclude [iks'kluːd] *vt* excluir; exceptuar; *possibility of error etc* evitar; **everything excluding coal** todo excepto el carbón.

exclusion [iks'kluːʒən] *n* exclusión *f*; **to the** — **of** con exclusión de.

exclusive [iks'kluːsiv] *adj* exclusivo; (*sole*) único; *policy* exclusivista; *shop, area, club etc* selecto; **offer of privilegio;** — **of** fuera de, sin contar; — **to** privativo de.

exclusively [iks'kluːsivli] *adv* únicamente.

excommunicate [,ekskə'mjuːnikeit] *vt* excomulgar.

excommunication ['ekskə,mjuːni'keiʃən] *n* excomunión *f*.

excrement ['ekskrimənt] *n* excremento *m*.

excrescence [iks'kresns] *n* excrecencia *f*.

excrete [eks'kriːt] *vt* excretar.

excretion [eks'kriːʃən] *n* excreción *f*.

excruciating [iks'kruːʃieitiŋ] *adj pain* agudísimo, atroz; (*very bad*) horrible, fatal.

excruciatingly [iks'kruːʃieitiŋli] *adv* atrozmente; (*very badly*) horriblemente, fatal; **it was** — **funny** era para morirse de risa.

exculpate ['ekskʌlpeit] *vt* exculpar.

excursion [iks'kəːʃən] *n* excursión *f*.

excursion ticket [iks'kəːʃən,tikit] *n* billete *m* de excursión.

excusable [iks'kjuːzəbl] *adj* perdonable, disculpable.

excuse [iks'kju:s] n disculpa f, excusa f; razón f, defensa f, justificación f; (insincere) pretexto m; **there's no — for this** esto no admite disculpa; **it's only an —** es un pretexto nada más; **to make —s for someone** presentar excusas de uno; **he's only making —s** está buscando pretextos; **he gives poverty as his —** alega su pobreza; **what's your — this time?** ¿qué razón me da Vd esta vez?

excuse [iks'kju:z] **1** vt disculpar, perdonar; **to — someone something** perdonar algo a uno; **to — someone from doing something** dispensar a uno de hacer algo, eximir a uno de hacer algo; **that does not — your conduct** eso no justifica su conducta; **— me!** (in passing someone) ¡perdón!, por favor; (on interrupting someone) perdone Vd; (on leaving table) ¡con permiso!; **if you will — me I must go** con permiso de Vds tengo que marcharme; **I must ask to be —d this time** esta vez les ruego dispensarme; **may I be —d for a moment?** ¿puedo salir un momento?

2 vr: **to — oneself from doing something** dispensarse de hacer algo; **after 10 minutes he —d himself** después de 10 minutos pidió permiso y se fue.

execrable ['eksikrəbl] adj execrable, abominable.
execrate ['eksikreit] vt execrar, abominar (de).
execration [.eksi'kreifən] n execración f, abominación f.
executant [ig'zekjutənt] n ejecutante mf.
execute ['eksikju:t] vt ejecutar (also Art, Mus); order cumplir; scheme llevar a cabo, realizar; document otorgar; man ejecutar, ajusticiar.
execution [.eksi'kju:fən] n ejecución f; cumplimiento m; realización f; otorgamiento m.
executioner [.eksi'kju:fnə*] n verdugo m.
executive [ig'zekjutiv] **1** adj ejecutivo. **2** n (power) poder m ejecutivo, autoridad f suprema; (person) gerente m, directivo m, director m, administrador m.
executor [ig'zekjutə*] n albacea m, testamentario m.
exegesis [.eksi'dʒi:sis] n exégesis f.
exemplary [ig'zempləri] adj ejemplar.
exemplify [ig'zemplifai] vt ejemplificar; ilustrar, demostrar; **as exemplified by X** según lo demuestra X.
exempt [ig'zempt] **1** adj exento, libre (from de); **to be — from paying** estar dispensado de pagar. **2** vt exentar, eximir, dispensar (from de).
exemption [ig'zempfən] n exención f (from de); inmunidad f (from de).
exercise ['eksəsaiz] **1** n ejercicio m; **to take —** hacer ejercicio; **in the — of my duties** en el ejercicio de mi cargo.

2 vt (a) (use) authority, influence, power ejercer; patience, restraint usar de, emplear; right valerse de; **to — care** tomar cuidado de, proceder con cautela; tomar precaución.

(b) mind preocupar; **I am much —d about it** esto me tiene preocupadísimo.

(c) horse, team entrenar; dog llevar de paseo; muscle ejercitar, hacer ejercicios con.

3 vi ejercitarse, hacer ejercicios.

exercise book ['eksəsaizbuk] n cuaderno m.
exert [ig'zə:t] **1** vt ejercer, emplear.

2 vr: **to — oneself** esforzarse, afanarse (to do por hacer); (overdo things) trabajar demasiado; **he doesn't — himself at all** no hace el más mínimo esfuerzo.
exertion [ig'zə:fən] n esfuerzo m; (overdoing things) esfuerzo m excesivo, trabajo m excesivo.
exeunt ['eksiʌnt] vi éxeunt.
exhale [eks'heil] **1** vt air espirar; fumes despedir. **2** vi espirar.
exhaust [ig'zɔ:st] **1** n (fumes) gases mpl de escape; **2** attr de escape. **3** vt (all senses) agotar; **to be —ed** estar agotado.
exhausting [ig'zɔ:stiŋ] adj agotador.
exhaustion [ig'zɔ:stfən] n agotamiento m; **nervous —** postración f nerviosa.
exhaustive [ig'zɔ:stiv] adj exhaustivo; inquiry minucioso.
exhaustively [ig'zɔ:stivli] adv de modo exhaustivo (or minucioso).
exhaust pipe [ig'zɔ:stpaip] n tubo m de escape.
exhibit [ig'zibit] **1** n objeto m expuesto; pieza f de museo; (painting etc) obra f expuesta; (Law) documento m; **to be on —** estar expuesto.

2 vt signs etc mostrar, manifestar; emotion acusar; exhibit exponer, presentar al público; film presentar.

3 vi (painter etc) presentar sus obras, organizar una exposición.
exhibition [.eksi'bifən] n demostración f, manifestación f; (by painter, sport etc) exposición f; (Univ)

beca f; **an — of bad temper** una demostración de mal genio; **to be on —** estar expuesto; **to make an — of oneself** ponerse en ridículo.
exhibitionism [.eksi'bifənizəm] n exhibicionismo m.
exhibitionist [.eksi'bifənist] **1** adj exhibicionista. **2** n exhibicionista mf.
exhibitor [ig'zibitə*] n expositor m, ora f.
exhilarate [ig'ziləreit] vt levantar el ánimo de, estimular, vigorizar; **to feel —d** sentirse más optimista, estar alegre.
exhilarating [ig'ziləreitiŋ] adj tónico, vigorizador, estimulador.
exhilaration [ig,zilə'reifən] n (effect) efecto m tónico, efecto m vigorizador; (mood) optimismo m, alegría f; **the — of speed** lo emocionante de la velocidad.
exhort [ig'zɔ:t] vt exhortar (to do a hacer).
exhortation [.egzɔ:'teifən] n exhortación f.
exhume [eks'hju:m] vt exhumar; (fig) desenterrar.
exigence ['eksidʒəns] n, **exigency** [ig'zidʒənsi] n (need) exigencia f, necesidad f; (emergency) caso m de urgencia.
exigent ['eksidʒənt] adj exigente; urgente.
exiguous [eg'zigjuəs] adj exiguo.
exile ['eksail] **1** n (a) (state) destierro m, exilio m.

(b) (person) exilado m, a f, exiliado m, a f (Acad), desterrado m, a f.

2 vt desterrar, poner en el exilio, exilar, exiliar (Acad).
exist [ig'zist] vi existir; vivir.
existence [ig'zistəns] n existencia f; vida f; **to be in —** existir; **to come into —** formarse, nacer, fundarse, empezar a tener existencia.
existent [ig'zistənt] adj existente, actual.
existential [.egzis'tenfəl] adj existencial.
existentialism [.egzis'tenfəlizəm] n existencialismo m.
existentialist [.egzis'tenfəlist] **1** adj existencialista. **2** n existencialista mf.
existing [ig'zistiŋ] adj existente, actual.
exit ['eksit] **1** n salida f; (Theat) mutis m; **emergency — ** salida f de urgencia; **to make one's —** salir, marcharse.

2 vi (Theat) hacer mutis; **— Hamlet** váse Hamlet.
exodus ['eksədəs] n éxodo m; **there was a general —** salieron todos.
exonerate [ig'zɔnəreit] vt exculpar, disculpar (from de).
exoneration [ig,zɔnə'reifən] n exculpación f.
exorbitant [ig'zɔ:bitənt] adj excesivo, exorbitante.
exorcise ['eksɔ:saiz] vt exorcizar, conjurar.
exorcism ['eksɔ:sizəm] n exorcismo m.
exotic [ig'zɔtik] **1** adj exótico. **2** n planta f exótica.
exoticism [eg'zɔtisizəm] n exotismo m.
expand [iks'pænd] **1** vt extender; ensanchar; dilatar; number aumentar; chest expandir; market, operations etc expandir, expansionar; wings abrir, desplegar; (Math) desarrollar.

2 vi extenderse; ensancharse; dilatarse; (number) aumentarse; (market etc) expandirse; (person) ponerse más expansivo.
expanse [iks'pæns] n extensión f; (of wings) envergadura f.
expansion [iks'pænfən] n extensión f; dilatación f; (of town etc) ensanche m; (of trade etc) expansión f; (of number) aumento m; (Math etc) desarrollo m.
expansionism [iks'pænfənizəm] n (Pol etc) expansionismo m.
expansionist [iks'pænfənist] adj (Pol etc) expansionista.
expansive [iks'pænsiv] adj expansivo (also fig).
expatiate [eks'peifieit] vi: **to — on** extenderse en un análisis de, extenderse en alabanzas (etc) de.
expatriate [eks'pætrieit] **1** adj expatriado. **2** n expatriado m, a f. **3** vt desterrar. **4** vr: **to — oneself** expatriarse.
expect [iks'pekt] **1** vt (a) (with n) storm, defeat, baby etc esperar; fun, good time prometerse; **it's not what I —ed** no es lo que yo esperaba; **I —ed as much, just what I —ed** ya me lo figuraba; **difficulties are only to be —ed** es natural que haya dificultades; **as might have been —ed, as one might —, as was to be —ed** como era de esperar, como podía esperarse; **we — your help** contamos con su ayuda; **I —ed nothing less of you** no esperaba menos de Vd; **it was not so tough as I —ed (it to be)** era menos severo de lo que yo esperaba; **when least —ed** el día menos pensado, a lo mejor; **we — you tomorrow** le esperamos mañana; **don't — to see me see me** no contéis conmigo hasta verme llegar; **you know what to —** ya sabe Vd a qué atenerse.

(b) (with verb) **I — to see him** espero verle; **we — he will come** contamos con que venga; **I — you to be punctual** cuento con que Vd sea puntual;

so you — me to pay? ¿así que esperas que pague yo?; **what do you — me to do about it?** ¿qué pretende Vd que haga yo?; **how do you — me to go out like this?** ¿cómo pretendes que salga así?; **it is —ed that** se espera que + *subj*; **it is hardly to be —ed that** apenas cabe esperar que + *subj*.

(c) (*think, suppose*) imaginar, suponer; **I — so** supongo que sí; **I — he's there by now** imagino que ya estará allí.

2 *vi*: **to be —ing** estar encinta, estar en estado (de esperanza).

expectancy [iks'pektənsi] *n* (*state*) expectación *f*; (*hope, chance*) expectativa *f* (*of* de).

expectant [iks'pektənt] *adj* expectante; (*hopeful*) ilusionado; **— mother** mujer *f* encinta, futura madre *f*.

expectantly [iks'pektəntli] *adv* con expectación; **to wait —** esperar a ver qué sale.

expectation [,ekspek'teiʃən] *n* (a) (*state*) expectación *f*; **in — of** en expectación de, esperando.

(b) (*hope*) esperanza *f*, expectativa *f*; **—s** (*in will*) esperanzas *fpl* de heredar; **— of life** probabilidades *fpl* de vida, índice *m* vital; **our — is that** esperamos que; **contrary to —** contra lo que se venía esperando; **it is beyond our —s** es mejor de lo que esperábamos; **to come up to one's —s** resultar tan bueno como se esperaba; **to exceed one's —s** sobrepasar lo que se esperaba; **to fall below one's —s** no llegar a lo que se esperaba.

expectorate [eks'pektəreit] *vt* expectorar.

expedience [iks'piːdiəns] *n*, **expediency** [iks'piːdiənsi] *n* conveniencia *f*, oportunidad *f*.

expedient [iks'piːdiənt] **1** *adj* conveniente, oportuno. **2** *n* expediente *m*, recurso *m*.

expedite ['ekspidait] *vt* (*speed up*) acelerar; *business* despachar (con prontitud); *progress* facilitar.

expedition [,ekspi'diʃən] *n* expedición *f*.

expeditionary [,ekspi'diʃnri] *adj* expedicionario.

expeditious [,ekspi'diʃəs] *adj* expeditivo, pronto.

expeditiously [,ekspi'diʃəsli] *adv* con toda prontitud.

expel [iks'pel] *vt* arrojar, expeler; *person* expulsar.

expend [iks'pend] *vt* *money* expender, gastar; *ammunition* usar; *resources* consumir, agotar; *time* pasar; *effort* dedicar (*on* a); *care* poner (*on* en).

expendable [iks'pendəbl] *adj* que se puede sacrificar, prescindible.

expenditure [iks'penditʃə*] *n* (*of money etc*) gasto *m*, desembolso *m*; **after a great — of time on it** después de haberle dedicado gran parte de su tiempo.

expense [iks'pens] *n* gasto *m*, gastos *mpl*; costa *f*; **—s** gastos *mpl*; **business —s** gastos *mpl* comerciales; **operating —s**, **working —s** gastos *mpl* de explotación; **overhead —s** gastos *mpl* generales; **travelling —s** gastos *mpl* de viaje; **at great —** gastándose muchísimo dinero; **at my —** a mi costa, corriendo yo con los gastos; **at the — of** (*fig*) a costa de, a expensas de; **regardless of —** sin parar en gastos, sin escatimar gastos; **to be a great — to someone** costar a uno mucho dinero; **to go to — meterse en gastos** (*over* por); **to pay someone's —s** pagar los gastos a uno; **to put someone to —** hacer que uno gaste dinero.

expense account [iks'pensə'kaunt] *n* cuenta *f* de gastos.

expensive [iks'pensiv] *adj* caro, costoso; *shop etc* carero.

experience [iks'piəriəns] **1** *n* experiencia *f*; **to know from bitter —** saber por amargas experiencias personales que; **to learn by —**, **to profit from —** aprender por la experiencia.

2 *vt* experimentar; *fate, loss* sufrir; *difficulty* tener, tropezar con.

experienced [iks'piəriənst] *adj* experimentado, perito, experto (*in* en).

experiment [iks'perimənt] *n* experimento *m*; prueba *f*, ensayo *m*; **as an —**, **by way of —** como experimento.

experiment [iks'periment] *vi* experimentar, hacer experimentos (*on* en, *with* con).

experimental [eks,peri'mentl] *adj* experimental.

experimentally [eks,peri'mentəli] *adv* experimentalmente, como experimento.

experimentation [eks,perimen'teiʃən] *n* experimentación *f*.

expert ['ekspəːt] **1** *adj* experto, perito (*at, in* en); *touch etc* hábil; *witness, evidence* pericial.

2 *n* experto *m*, perito *m* (*at, in* en); técnico *m*; especialista *mf*.

expertise [,ekspə'tiːz] *n* pericia *f*; (*of touch etc*) habilidad *f*.

expertly ['ekspəːtli] *adv* expertamente.

expiate ['ekspieit] *vt* expiar.

expiation [,ekspi'eiʃən] *n* expiación *f*.

expiatory ['ekspiətəri] *adj* expiatorio.

expiration [,ekspaiə'reiʃən] *n* (*ending*) terminación *f*; expiración *f*; (*Comm*) vencimiento *m*.

expire [iks'paiə*] *vi* (*end*) terminar; (*die*) expirar; (*reach its term*) expirar, cumplirse, (*Comm*) vencer, (*ticket*) caducar.

expiry [iks'paiəri] *n see* **expiration**.

explain [iks'plein] **1** *vt* explicar; *plan* exponer; *mystery* aclarar; *conduct* explicar; justificar; **that —s it** con eso todo queda aclarado; **to — something away** justificar algo hábilmente, dar razones convincentes de algo, *difficulty* salvar hábilmente; **just you — that away!** ¡a ver si logras dar razón de eso!

2 *vr*: **to — oneself** (*clearly*) hablar más claro, explicarse con más detalles; (*morally*) justificar su conducta; **kindly — yourself!** ¡explíquese Vd!

explainable [iks'pleinəbl] *adj* explicable.

explanation [,eksplə'neiʃən] *n* explicación *f*; aclaración *f*; **what is the — of this?** ¿cómo se explica esto?; **there must be some —** ha de haber alguna razón.

explanatory [iks'plænətəri] *adj* explicativo; aclaratorio.

expletive [eks'pliːtiv] *n* (*oath*) palabrota *f*.

explicable [eks'plikəbl] *adj* explicable.

explicit [iks'plisit] *adj* explícito.

explicitly [iks'plisitli] *adv* explícitamente.

explode [iks'pləud] **1** *vt* volar, hacer saltar, explotar, explosionar; *rumour* desmentir; *belief, theory* desacreditar, refutar.

2 *vi* estallar, hacer explosión, explotar, explosionar; (*with anger etc*) reventar (*with* de); **the town —d in revolt** estalló la rebelión en la ciudad; **when I said that he —d** cuando dije eso se puso furioso.

exploit ['eksplɔit] *n* hazaña *f*, proeza *f*.

exploit [iks'plɔit] *vt* explotar.

exploitation [,eksplɔi'teiʃən] *n* explotación *f*.

exploration [,eksplɔː'reiʃən] *n* exploración *f*.

exploratory [eks'plɔrətəri] *adj* exploratorio, preparatorio, de sondaje.

explore [iks'plɔː*] *vt* explorar; (*fig*) examinar, sondar, investigar.

explorer [iks'plɔːrə*] *n* explorador *m*, ora *f*.

explosion [iks'pləuʒən] *n* explosión *f* (*also fig*).

explosive [iks'pləuziv] **1** *adj* explosivo (*also fig*). **2** *n* explosivo *m*; **high —** alto explosivo *m*, explosivo *m* de gran potencia.

exponent [eks'pəunənt] *n* exponente *mf*, partidario *m*, a *f* (*of* de), intérprete *mf* (*of* de).

export ['ekspɔːt] *n* exportación *f*; **— licence** permiso *m* de exportación; **— trade** comercio *m* de exportación.

export [eks'pɔːt] *vt* exportar.

exportable [eks'pɔːtəbl] *adj* exportable.

exportation [,ekspɔː'teiʃən] *n* exportación *f*.

exporter [eks'pɔːtə*] *n* exportador *m*.

expose [iks'pəuz] **1** *vt* exponer (*also Phot*); *weakness* descubrir; *falsity* demostrar; *ignorance* revelar, descubrir; *fake, plot, impostor* desenmascarar; **to — someone to ridicule** exponer a uno al ridículo.

2 *vr*: **to — oneself** to exponerse a.

exposed [iks'pəuzd] *adj* expuesto; *position* desabrigado; *flank* desguarnecido; **to be —** (*thing normally hidden*) estar al descubierto; **to be —** to estar expuesto a.

exposition [,ekspə'ziʃən] *n* exposición *f*, explicación *f*.

expostulate [iks'pɔstjuleit] *vi* protestar; **to — with** reconvenir a, discutir con, tratar de convencer a.

expostulation [iks,pɔstju'leiʃən] *n* protesta *f*, reconvención *f*.

exposure [iks'pəuʒə*] *n* exposición *f* (*also Phot*); revelación *f*; desenmascaramiento *m*; **a house with a southerly —** una casa orientada hacia el sur; **to die from —** morir de frío, morir por estar a la intemperie.

exposure meter [iks'pəuʒə,miːtə*] *n* fotómetro *m*, exposímetro *m*.

expound [iks'paund] *vt* exponer, explicar; *text* comentar.

express [iks'pres] **1** *adj* (*clear*) expreso, explícito, categórico; *train* rápido; *letter* urgente; *service etc* rápido.

2 *n* rápido *m*.

3 *adv*: **to send something —** enviar algo por carta urgente (*etc*).

4 *vt* expresar; *juice* exprimir.

5 *vr*: **to — oneself** expresarse.

expression [iks'preʃən] *n* expresión *f*; **as an — of thanks** en señal de agradecimiento.

expressionism [eks'preʃənizəm] *n* expresionismo *m*.
expressionless [iks'preʃənlis] *adj* sin expresión.
expressive [iks'presiv] *adj* expresivo.
expressively [iks'presivli] *adv* expresivamente.
expressiveness [iks'presivnis] *n* expresividad *f*.
expressly [iks'presli] *adv* expresamente; *deny, prohibit etc* terminantemente.
expropriate [eks'prəuprieit] *vt* expropiar.
expropriation [eks,prəupri'eiʃən] *n* expropiación *f*.
expulsion [iks'pʌlʃən] *n* expulsión *f*.
expunge [iks'pʌndʒ] *vt* borrar, tachar.
expurgate [ekspə:geit] *vt* expurgar.
exquisite [eks'kwizit] **1** *adj* exquisito, primoroso; *pain etc* intenso. **2** *n* elegante *m*.
exquisitely [eks'kwizitli] *adv* primorosamente, con primor.
ex-serviceman ['eks'sə:vismən] *n, pl* **-men** [mən] excombatiente *m*.
extant [eks'tænt] *adj* existente.
extemporary [iks'tempərəri] *adj* improvisado, hecho sin preparación.
extempore [eks'tempəri] **1** *adv* de improviso, sin preparación. **2** *adj* improvisado, hecho sin preparación.
extemporize [iks'tempəraiz] *vti* improvisar.
extend [iks'tend] **1** *vt* extender; *hand* tender, alargar; *building etc* ensanchar, ampliar; *road, term etc* prolongar; *(increase)* aumentar; *thanks, welcome* dar, ofrecer; *invitation* enviar; *athlete* pedir el máximo esfuerzo a.
　2 *vi* extenderse; prolongarse; **to — over** abarcar, incluir; **to — to** extenderse a, llegar hasta, *(fig)* abarcar, incluir; **does that — to me?** ¿eso me incluye a mí?
　3 *vr*: **to — oneself** trabajar *(etc)* al máximo.
extensible [iks'tensibl] *adj* extensible.
extension [iks'tenʃən] *n* extensión *f*; *(of building etc)* ensanche *m*, ampliación *f*; *(of road, term etc)* prolongación *f*; *(Comm)* prórroga *f*; *(increase)* aumento *m*; *(Tel)* línea *f* derivada; **— ladder** escalera *f* extensible.
extensive [iks'tensiv] *adj* extenso; vasto, ancho, dilatado; *use etc* frecuente, general, común.
extensively [iks'tensivli] *adv* extensamente; **to travel —** viajar por muchos países; **he travelled — in Mexico** viajó por muchas partes de Méjico; **it is used —** se usa comúnmente.
extent [iks'tent] *n* *(space)* extensión *f*; *(scope)* alcance *m*; **to the — of** + *ger* hasta el punto de + *infin*; **to a certain —, to some —** hasta cierto punto; **to the full —** en toda su extensión; *(fig)* completamente; **to a great** *(or* **large)** **—** en gran parte, en alto grado; **to such an — that** hasta tal punto que; **to that —** hasta ahí; **to what —?** ¿hasta qué punto?
extenuate [eks'tenjueit] *vt* atenuar, mitigar, disminuir (la gravedad de).
extenuating [eks'tenjueitiŋ] *adj* circumstance atenuante.
exterior [eks'tiəriə*] **1** *adj* exterior, externo. **2** *n* exterior *m*; *(appearance)* aspecto *m*.
exterminate [eks'tə:mineit] *vt* exterminar.
extermination [eks,tə:mi'neiʃən] *n* exterminio *m*.
external [eks'tə:nl] **1** *adj* externo, exterior. **2 —s** *npl* exterioridad *f*, aspecto *m* exterior.
externally [eks'tə:nəli] *adv* externamente, exteriormente; por fuera.
extinct [iks'tiŋkt] *adj* *volcano* extinto, apagado, extinguido; *animal* extinto, desaparecido.
extinction [iks'tiŋkʃən] *n* extinción *f*.
extinguish [iks'tiŋgwiʃ] *vt* extinguir, apagar; *title etc* suprimir.
extinguisher [iks'tiŋgwiʃə*] *n* extintor *m*.
extirpate ['ekstə:peit] *vt* extirpar.
extol [iks'tɔl] *vt* ensalzar, alabar.
extort [iks'tɔ:t] *vt* obtener por fuerza *(from* de), exigir por amenazas *(from* a).
extortion [iks'tɔ:ʃən] *n* exacción *f*.
extortionate [iks'tɔ:ʃənit] *adj* *price etc* excesivo, exorbitante.
extortioner [iks'tɔ:ʃənə*] *n* desollador *m*; *(official)* concusionario *m*.
extra ['ekstrə] **1** *adj* adicional; de más, de sobra; *charge, pay etc* extraordinario; *part* de repuesto; **we need 2 — chairs** necesitamos 2 sillas más; **we seem to have 2 — men** parece que tenemos 2 hombres de sobra; **postage —** gastos de franqueo aparte; **postage and packing —** gastos de envío aparte; **5 tons — to requirements** un excedente de 5 toneladas; *see* **time** *etc*.
　2 *adv* **(a)** *(with adj, adv, verb)* especialmente, extraordinariamente; **— big** más grande que lo normal; **— smart** más elegante que de costumbre;

this is — difficult esto es extraordinariamente difícil; **to sing — loud** cantar extraordinariamente fuerte.
　(b) *(after verb, fam)* **we shall have to work —** tendremos que trabajar más.
　3 *n* **(a)** *(on bill)* extra *m*, suplemento *m*; *(Theat)* extra *mf*, comparsa *mf*; *(of paper)* edición *f* extraordinaria; *(spare part, US)* repuesto *m*.
　(b) **what shall we do with the —?** ¿qué hacemos con el exceso?, ¿qué hacemos con lo que sobra?
extract ['ekstrækt] *n* *(Lit)* cita *f*, trozo *m*; *(Pharm)* extracto *m*; *beef* — concentrado *m* de carne; **malt —** extracto *m* de malta; **—s from "Don Quijote"** *(as book)* selecciones *fpl* del "Quijote".
extract [iks'trækt] *vt* sacar *(from* de); extraer *(also Math)*; *confession etc* arrancar, sacar, obtener.
extraction [iks'trækʃən] *n* extracción *f*; obtención *f*.
extractor [iks'træktə*] *n* extractor *m*.
extraditable ['ekstrədaitəbl] *adj* sujeto a extradición.
extradite ['ekstrədait] *vt* *(holding country)* entregar, permitir la extradición de; *(claiming country)* extradicionar, obtener la extradición de.
extradition [,ekstrə'diʃən] *n* extradición *f*.
extramural ['ekstrə'mjuərəl] *adj* *jurisdiction etc* de extramuros; *activities* de carácter privado; *course* para externos.
extraneous [eks'treiniəs] *adj* extraño; **— to** ajeno a.
extraordinarily [iks'trɔ:dnrili] *adv* extraordinariamente.
extraordinary [iks'trɔ:dnri] *adj* extraordinario; *(odd)* raro; *(incredible)* increíble; **how —!** ¡qué raro!; **it is — that** es increíble que + *subj*.
extrasensory ['ekstrə'sensəri] *adj* *perception etc* extrasensorial.
extraterritorial ['ekstrə,teri'tɔ:riəl] *adj* extraterritorial.
extravagance [iks'trævəgəns] *n* prodigalidad *f*; derroche *m*; despilfarro *m*; lujo *m* desmedido; exorbitancia *f*; lo excesivo; rareza *f*.
extravagant [iks'trævəgənt] *adj* *(lavish)* pródigo; *(wasteful)* derrochador, despilfarrado; *(luxurious)* muy lujoso; *price* exorbitante; *praise* excesivo; *(odd)* raro, estrafalario.
extravagantly [iks'trævəgəntli] *adv* *spend etc* profusamente, con gran despilfarro; *(luxuriously)* muy lujosamente; *praise* excesivamente; *behave* de modo raro.
extravaganza [eks,trævə'gænzə] *n* obra *f* extravagante y fantástica.
extreme [iks'tri:m] **1** *adj* extremo; *care, poverty etc* extremado; *case* excepcional.
　2 *n* extremo *m*, extremidad *f*; **—s of temperature** temperaturas *fpl* extremas; **in the —** en sumo grado; **to go from one — to the other** pasar de un extremo a otro; **to go to —s** ir muy lejos, tomar medidas extremas.
extremely [iks'tri:mli] *adv* sumamente, extremadamente; **it is — difficult** es sumamente difícil, es dificilísimo; **we are — glad** nos alegramos muchísimo.
extremism [iks'tri:mizəm] *n* extremismo *m*.
extremist [iks'tri:mist] **1** *adj* extremista. **2** *n* extremista *mf*.
extremity [iks'tremiti] *n* **(a)** *(end)* extremidad *f*, punta *f*.
　(b) *(want)* apuro *m*, necesidad *f*; **in this —** en tal apuro; **to be driven to —** estar muy apurado.
　(c) **extremities** *(Anat)* extremidades *fpl*; *(measures)* medidas *fpl* extremas.
extricate ['ekstrikeit] **1** *vt* *(disentangle)* desenredar, soltar; *(fig)* librar, sacar *(from* de). **2** *vr*: **to — oneself from** *(fig)* lograr sacarse de.
extrinsic [eks'trinsik] *adj* extrínseco.
extrovert ['ekstrəuvə:t] **1** *adj* extrovertido. **2** *n* extrovertido *m*, a *f*.
extrude [eks'tru:d] *vt* sacar.
exuberance [ig'zu:bərəns] *n* euforia *f*; exuberancia *f*.
exuberant [ig'zu:bərənt] *adj* *person, spirit etc* eufórico; *growth, style etc* exuberante.
exude [ig'zju:d] **1** *vt* rezumar, destilar, sudar. **2** *vi* rezumarse.
exult [ig'zʌlt] *vi* exultar; **to — in, to — at** regocijarse por; **to — over** triunfar sobre; **to — to find** regocijarse al encontrar.
exultant [ig'zʌltənt] *adj* regocijado, jubiloso.
exultation [,egzʌl'teiʃən] *n* exultación *f*, júbilo *m*.
eye [ai] **1** *n* ojo *m* *(also of needle)*; *(Bot)* yema *f*; **black —** ojo *m* amoratado; **evil —** aojo *m*, mal *m* de ojo; **private —** detective *m*; **—s right!** ¡vista a la derecha!; **as far as the — can see** hasta donde alcanza la vista; **it happened before my very —s** ocurrió delante de mis propios ojos; **the grass grows before your very —s** crece la hierba a ojos

vistas; **in the —s of** a los ojos de; **with an — to + *infin*** con la intención de + *infin*; **with the naked —** a simple vista; **it's all my —!** (*fam*) ¡es puro cuento!; **to be all —s** ser todo ojos; **that's one in the — for him!** ese golpe va dirigido a él; **to be up to one's —s** (*in work*) estar hasta los ojos de trabajo; **to catch the —** llamar la atención; **to catch someone's —** atraer la atención de uno; **to clap —s on** clavar la vista en; **to cock one's — at** mirar con intención a; **to cry one's —s out** llorar a moco tendido; **to feast one's —s on something** recrear la vista mirando algo, mirar algo con fruición; **to give someone the glad —** lanzar una mirada incitante a uno; **to have an — for something** tener afición a algo, saber apreciar algo; **to have an — to something** tener algo en cuenta; **to have good —s** tener buena vista; **to have one's —s on** (*watch*) vigilar, echar una mirada a; (*covet*) echar el ojo a; **it hits you in the —** salta a la vista; **to keep an — on something** (*watch*) vigilar, echar una mirada a; (*bear in mind*) tener algo en cuenta; (*follow*) no perder algo de vista; **he couldn't keep his —s off the girl** se le fueron los ojos tras la chica; **to make —s at someone** lanzar una mirada incitante a uno; **there's more in this than meets the —** esto tiene su miga; **to open someone's —s to something** abrir los ojos de uno; **to rub one's —s** restregarse los párpados; **to run one's — over something** recorrer algo con la vista; **I don't see — to — with him over that** en eso no estoy completamente de acuerdo con él; **when I first set —s on him** la primera vez que le puse los ojos encima; **it's 5 years since I set —s on him** hace 5 años que no le veo; **to shut one's —s to something** cerrar los ojos a algo, hacer la vista gorda a (*or* ante) algo; **we must not shut our —s to this** importa que nos demos cuenta de esto; **to turn a blind — to something** fingir no ver algo, hacer la vista gorda a (*or* ante) algo.

2 *vt* ojear, mirar (detenidamente, sospechosamente *etc*).

eyeball ['aibɔːl] *n* globo *m* del ojo.

eyebath ['aibɑːθ] *n*, *pl* **—baths** [bɑːðz] ojera *f*.

eyebrow ['aibrau] *n* ceja *f*; **— pencil** lápiz *m* de cejas; **to raise one's —s** levantar las cejas; **he never raised an — at it** no se sorprendió en lo más mínimo.

eye-catcher ['ai͵kætʃə*] *n* cosa *f* que llama la atención.

eye-catching ['ai͵kætʃiŋ] *adj* llamativo, vistoso.

-eyed [aid] *adj* de ojos . . . , *eg* **green-eyed** de ojos verdes; **two-eyed** de dos ojos.

eyeful ['aiful] *n* (*fam*): **he got an — of mud** el lodo le dio de lleno en el ojo; **get an — of this!** ¡echa un vistazo a esto!, ¡mírame esto!

eyeglass ['aiglɑːs] *n* lente *m*; (*worn in the eye*) monóculo *m*.

eyelash ['ailæʃ] *n* pestaña *f*.

eyelet ['ailit] *n* (*Sew*) ojete *m*.

eyelid ['ailid] *n* párpado *m*.

eye-opener ['ai͵əupnə*] *n* revelación *f*, sorpresa *f* grande; **it was an — to me** fue una revelación para mí.

eyepiece ['aipiːs] *n* ocular *m*.

eyeshade ['aiʃeid] *n* visera *f*.

eyeshadow ['ai͵ʃædəu] *n* sombreador *m* de ojos.

eyesight ['aisait] *n* vista *f*; (*extent of —*) alcance *m* de la vista.

eyesore ['aisɔː*] *n* monstruosidad *f*, cosa *f* antiestética.

eyestrain ['aistrein] *n* vista *f* fatigada; **to get —** cansar los ojos, cansar la vista; **to suffer from —** padecer de los ojos.

eye tooth ['aituːθ] *n* colmillo *m*.

eyewash ['aiwɔʃ] *n* (*sl*) música *f* celestial; **it's a lot of —!** ¡es puro cuento!

eyewitness ['ai͵witnis] *n* testigo *mf* presencial, testigo *mf* ocular.

eyrie ['aiəri] *n* aguilera *f*.

F

fab [fæb] *adj* (*sl*) = **fabulous**.
fable ['feibl] *n* fábula *f*.
fabric ['fæbrik] *n* (*cloth*) tejido *m*, tela *f*; (*Archit*) fábrica *f*; **the upkeep of the —** la manutención de los edificios; **the — of society** la estructura de la sociedad.
fabricate ['fæbrikeit] *vt* (*fig*) inventar; *document, evidence* falsificar.
fabrication [,fæbri'keiʃən] *n* invención *f*, ficción *f*; **the whole thing is a —** todo es mentira.
fabulous ['fæbjuləs] *adj* fabuloso; (*fam*) fabuloso, estupendo, macanudo.
façade [fə'sɑːd] *n* fachada *f*; (*fig*) apariencia *f*, barniz *m*; **to keep up a — of** sostener una apariencia de, guardar las apariencias de.
face [feis] **1** *n* (**a**) (*Anat etc*) cara *f*, rostro *m*, semblante *m*; (*of dial, watch*) esfera *f*, cuadrante *m*; (*surface*) superficie *f*; (*Min*) cara *f* de trabajo; (*of building*) frente *f*, fachada *f*; **— of the earth** faz *f* de la tierra; **— downwards** boca abajo; **— upwards** boca arriba; **— to —** cara a cara; **to bring A — to — with B** confrontar A con B; **to bring two people — to —** poner a dos personas cara a cara; **in the — of** ante, en presencia de; **in the — of this threat** ante esta amenaza; **in the — of such difficulties** vistas tantas dificultades; **courage in the — of the enemy** valor en presencia del enemigo; **the wind was blowing in our —s** el viento nos daba de cara.
(**b**) **to fly in the — of reason** oponerse abiertamente a la razón; **to laugh in someone's —** reírse en la cara de uno; **he didn't dare to look me in the —** no osaba mirarme a la cara; **I could never look him in the — again** yo no tendría valor para mirarle a la cara; **to say something to someone's —** decir algo en la cara de uno; **to set one's — against something** oponerse resueltamente a algo; **to show one's —** asomar la cara, dejarse ver; **to struggle to keep a straight —** esforzarse por contener la risa.
(**c**) (*expression*) **wry —** mueca *f*; **to go about with a long —** andar cariacontecido; **to make —s, to pull —s** hacer muecas, hacer carantoñas (*at* a).
(**d**) (*effrontery*) descaro *m*, caradura *f*; **to have the — to do something** ser bastante descarado para hacer algo.
(**e**) (*dignity*) prestigio *m*; **to lose —** desprestigiarse, perder prestigio; **to save (one's) —** salvar las apariencias.
(**f**) (*outward show*) **on the — of it** a primera vista, según las apariencias; **to put a brave — on something** hacer buena cara a algo.
2 *vt* (**a**) (*look towards: of person, object*) estar de cara a; ponerse de cara a; volver la cara hacia; **— the wall!** ¡póngase de cara a la pared!; **turn it to — the fire** gírelo para que esté de cara a la lumbre; **they sat facing each other** estaban sentados uno frente al otro; **to sit facing the engine** estar sentado de frente a la máquina; **the picture facing page 19** el grabado en la página opuesta a la 19.
(**b**) (*of building*) mirar hacia, estar enfrente de, dar a; **the flat —s the Town Hall** el piso está enfrente del Ayuntamiento; **the house —s the sea** la casa tiene vistas al mar; **the house —s the south** la casa está orientada hacia el sur.
(**c**) (*fig*) *person, enemy, electorate* encararse con, enfrentarse con; *consequences, danger* arrostrar, hacer cara a; *facts* reconocer; *situation* hacer frente a; *problem* afrontar; **we — grave problems** afrontamos unos problemas graves; **we are —d with grave problems** se nos plantean graves problemas; **we will — him with the facts** le expondremos los hechos; **let's — it!** ¡seamos realistas!; **we're poor, let's — it!** ¡reconozcamos lo pobres que somos!
(**d**) **to — it out** insistir descaradamente en ello.
(**e**) (*Tech*) revestir, forrar (*with* de).

3 *vi*: **to — in a direction** estar orientado en una dirección; **which way does it —?** ¿en qué dirección está orientado?; **— this way!** ¡vuélvase hacia aquí!; **to — about** dar media vuelta, (*fig*) cambiar de postura; **to — on to** mirar hacia, dar a; **to — up to something** reconocer la realidad de algo, arrostrar algo; **she —d up to it bravely** lo aguantó con mucha resolución.
face cream ['feiskriːm] *n* crema *f* (de belleza).
-faced [feist] *adj* de cara . . ., *eg* **brown-faced** de cara morena, **long-faced** de cara larga.
face flannel ['feis,flænl] *n* manopla *f*, paño *m*.
faceless ['feislis] *adj* sin cara.
face lift ['feislift] *n* (operación *f* de) cirugía *f* estética.
face powder ['feis,paudə*] *n* polvos *mpl*.
facer ['feisə*] *n* (*fam*) problema *m* desconcertante.
face-saving ['feis,seiviŋ] **1** *adj*: **— operation** maniobra *f* para salvar las apariencias.
2 *n*: **— is important** importa salvar las apariencias; **this is a piece of blatant —** esto es una maniobra transparente para salvar las apariencias.
facet ['fæsit] *n* faceta *f* (*also fig*).
facetious [fə'siːʃəs] *adj* *person* chistoso; *remark* festivo, gracioso; *speech* divertido, lleno de chistes.
facetiously [fə'siːʃəsli] *adv* chistosamente; **he said —** dijo guasón.
face value ['feis'væljuː] *n* valor *m* nominal; (*of stamp etc*) valor *m* facial; (*fig*) valor *m* aparente, significado *m* literal; **you can't take it at its —** no se deje engañar por las apariencias; **I took his statement at its —** yo entendí su declaración en su significado literal.
facial ['feiʃəl] **1** *adj* de la cara, facial. **2** *n* masaje *m* facial.
facile ['fæsail] *adj* fácil, superficial, ligero.
facilitate [fə'siliteit] *vt* facilitar.
facility [fə'siliti] *n* facilidad *f*; **facilities** (*all senses*) facilidades *fpl*; **credit facilities** facilidades *fpl* de crédito; **they gave me every —** me ayudaron en lo posible.
facing ['feisiŋ] **1** *prep* de cara a, frente a.
2 *as adj* opuesto, de enfrente; **the houses —** las casas de enfrente.
3 *n* (*Tech*) paramento *m*, revestimiento *m*; (*Sew*) vuelta *f*, guarnición *f*; **—s** (*Sew*) vueltas *fpl*.
facsimile [fæk'simili] **1** *adj* facsímil. **2** *n* facsímil *m*.
fact [fækt] *n* hecho *m*; (*real world*) realidad *f*; **— and fiction** lo real y lo ficticio; **the —s of life** los hechos de la vida, (*esp*) los detalles de la reproducción humana; **hard —s** hechos *mpl* innegables; **a film based on —** una película que tiene una base de realidad histórica; **it has no basis in —** carece de base real; **as a matter of —, in —, in point of —** en realidad; **the — of the matter is** la pura verdad es; **the — is that** el hecho es que, ello es que; **it is a — that se ha comprobado que**; **the — that I am here** el hecho de que estoy aquí; **to bow to the —s** reconocer que las cosas son así; **I don't dispute your —s** yo no niego los hechos que alega Vd; **to know for a —** that saber a ciencia cierta que; **to stick to the —s** atenerse a los hechos; *see* **accessory**.
fact-finding ['fækt,faindiŋ] *adj* de investigación, de indagación.
faction ['fækʃən] *n* facción *f*.
factious ['fækʃəs] *adj* faccioso.
factitious [fæk'tiʃəs] *adj* facticio.
factor ['fæktə*] *n* (**a**) (*fact*) factor *m*, hecho *m*, elemento *m*; **determining —** factor *m* determinante; **human —** factor *m* humano; **safety —** factor *m* de seguridad.
(**b**) (*Math*) factor *m*; **highest common —** máximo común divisor *m*.
(**c**) (*Comm*) agente *m*.
factory ['fæktəri] *n* fábrica *f*.

factotum [fæk'təutəm] n factótum m.
factual ['fæktjuəl] adj objetivo, que consta de hechos, basado en datos; — **error** error m de hecho.
faculty ['fækəlti] n facultad f (also Univ); (US Univ) profesorado m.
fad [fæd] n manía f; novedad f; **it's just a** — es una novedad nada más, es una moda pasajera; **he has his —s** tiene sus caprichos; **the — for Italian clothes** la manía de los trajes italianos.
faddy ['fædi] adj caprichoso, dengoso, que tiene sus manías, difícil de contentar.
fade [feid] 1 vt colour, dress descolorar, desteñir; flower marchitar; **to — in, to — up** (Cine) hacer aparecer gradualmente.
2 vi (colour, dress) descolorarse, desteñirse, perder su color; (flower) marchitarse; (light) apagarse gradualmente; (sound) desvanecerse; **the daylight was fading fast** anochecía rápidamente; **he saw his chances fading** veía como se estaban acabando sus posibilidades; **guaranteed not to** — no se descolora; **to — away, to — out** (visually) desdibujarse, desvanecerse; (sound) apagarse, dejar poco a poco de oírse; **to be fading away** (dying) consumirse lentamente; (slimming) adelgazar muchísimo; **this season the team has just —d away** en esta temporada el equipo ha dejado casi de figurar; **to — to** (Cine) fundir a.
faded ['feidid] adj plant marchito, seco; colour, dress descolorido.
faeces ['fiːsiːz] npl excrementos mpl.
fag [fæg] 1 n (a) (job) faena f, trabajo m penoso; **what a —!** ¡qué faena!; **it's just too much** — es mucho trabajo.
(b) (School) alumno m joven que trabaja por otro mayor.
(c) (sl) pitillo m.
2 vt fatigar, cansar; **to be —ged out** estar rendido.
3 vi trabajar como un negro; **to — for** (School) trabajar por.
fag end ['fægend] n colilla f.
faggot, (mainly US) **fagot** ['fægət] n haz m de leña, astillas fpl.
Fahrenheit ['færənhait]: — **thermometer** termómetro m de Fahrenheit (grados Fahrenheit menos 32 × ⅝ = grados centígrados).
fail [feil] 1 n (Univ fam) suspenso m (in en); **without** — sin falta.
2 vt person faltar a, faltar en sus obligaciones a; decepcionar; exam no aprobar, salir mal en; candidate suspender; **his strength —ed him** se sintió desfallecer, le abandonaron sus fuerzas; **his heart —ed him** se encontró sin ánimo; **words — me** no encuentro palabras para expresarme; **you have —ed me** me has decepcionado.
3 vi (a) (run short: supply, strength) acabarse; (engine) fallar; (voice) desfallecer; (eyes) debilitarse; (light) acabarse; (crop) fallar; (electricity supply etc) tener una avería, averiarse; (patient) debilitarse, hacerse más débil; **the light was —ing** iba anocheciendo.
(b) (neglect) **to — to do something** dejar de hacer algo; **he —ed to appear** no se presentó, dejó de presentarse; **don't — to visit her** no deje de visitarla; **to — to keep one's word** faltar a su palabra.
(c) (be unable) **I — to see how** no veo cómo; **I — to understand why** no puedo comprender por qué.
(d) (not succeed) fracasar, no tener éxito; (remedy) no surtir efecto; (hopes) frustrarse, malograrse; (Fin) quebrar; (Univ etc) ser suspendido (in en); **a —ed painter** un pintor fracasado; **to — to be elected** no lograr ser elegido; **to — to win a prize** no obtener un premio; **to — by 5 votes** perder por 5 votos.
(e) **to — in one's duty to someone** faltar a uno, faltar en sus obligaciones a uno.
failing ['feilin] 1 prep a falta de; — **that** si eso no es posible.
2 n falta f, defecto m; (moral) flaqueza f; **the plan has numerous —s** el plan tiene muchos defectos; **it is his only** — es su único punto débil.
failure ['feiljə*] n (a) (ill success) fracaso m; (of hopes) malogro m; (failed thing) fracaso m, (person) fracasado m, a f; (Mech) fallo m, avería f; (Elec) corte m, interrupción f; (Univ etc) suspenso m (in en); **the crop was a total** — el cultivo se perdió por completo.
(b) **your — to come** el que Vd dejara de venir, el dejar de venir Vd.
faint [feint] 1 adj débil; colour pálido; line tenue; outline borroso; trace apenas perceptible;

sound casi imperceptible, débil; voice débil; smell tenue; hope nada firme; idea, memory vago; resemblance ligero; heart medroso; **to feel** — estar mareado, tener vahídos; **I haven't the —est (idea)** no tengo la más remota idea.
2 n desmayo m; **to be in a** — estar desmayado, estar sin conocimiento; **to fall down in a** — desmayarse.
3 vi desmayarse, perder conocimiento (also **to — away**); **to be —ing with tiredness** estar rendido.
fainthearted ['feint'hɑːtid] adj medroso, pusilánime.
faintly ['feintli] adv débilmente; indistintamente; vagamente; ligeramente; **she said** — dijo en voz débil.
faintness ['feintnis] n debilidad f; tenuidad f; lo indistinto; (Med) desmayo m, desfallecimiento m.
fair¹ [fɛə*] 1 adj (a) (beautiful) bello, hermoso; **the — sex** el bello sexo.
(b) (blond) hair rubio; skin blanco.
(c) (clean) copy en limpio; name honrado; reputation bueno.
(d) (just) justo, equitativo; hearing, report, summary imparcial; comment acertado; means recto; play limpio; competition leal; chance, price, warning razonable; — **enough!** ¡muy bien!; **as is only** — como es justo; **but to be** — pero en honor a la verdad; **it's not —!** ¡no hay derecho!; **it's not — on the old** afecta injustamente a los viejos.
(e) (middling) regular, mediano.
(f) (promising) prometedor, favorable, bastante bueno.
(g) (Meteorol) sky sereno, despejado; day, weather bueno; **if it's — tomorrow** si hace buen tiempo mañana.
2 adv (a) **to play** — jugar limpio.
(b) **it hit the target — and square** dio en el centro del blanco.
(c) (fam) **we were — terrified** nos asustamos bastante; **then it — rained** entonces sí que llovió.
fair² [fɛə*] n (a) feria f; **trade** — feria f de muestras; **world** — feria f mundial, exposición f internacional.
(b) (fun-) parque m de atracciones; verbena f.
fairground ['fɛəgraund] n real m (de la feria); parque m de atracciones.
fair-haired ['fɛə'hɛəd] adj, **fair-headed** ['fɛə'hedid] adj pelirrubio.
fairly ['fɛəli] adv (a) justamente, equitativamente, con imparcialidad; rectamente; limpio, limpiamente.
(b) — **good** bastante bueno.
(c) (utterly) completamente.
fair-minded ['fɛə'maindid] adj imparcial.
fairness ['fɛənis] n (a) hermosura f. (b) lo rubio; blancura f. (c) justicia f, imparcialidad f; **in all** — para ser justo (to him con él).
fair-sized ['fɛəsaizd] adj bastante grande.
fairway ['fɛəwei] n (Naut) canalizo m; (Golf) calle f.
fair-weather ['fɛə,weðə*] adj: — **friend** amigo m en la prosperidad.
fairy ['fɛəri] 1 n hada f; (sl) maricón m. 2 adj and attr feérico, mágico; story etc de hada(s).
fairyland ['fɛərilænd] n tierra f de las hadas.
fairy lights ['fɛərilaits] npl bombillas fpl de colorines.
fairy tale ['fɛəriteil] 1 n cuento m de hadas; (fig) cuento m, patraña f. 2 adj fantástico, de ensueño.
fait accompli [,feitə'kɔmpli] n hecho m consumado.
faith [feiθ] n fe f (also Eccl); (trust) confianza f (in en); (doctrine) creencia f; (sect, confession) religión f; **bad** — mala fe f; **in good** — de buena fe; **what does he belong to?** ¿qué religión tiene?; **to break** — faltar a su palabra (with dada a); **to have** — **in** tener fe en; **to keep** — cumplir su palabra (with dada a); **to pin one's** — **to** cifrar sus esperanzas en.
faithful ['feiθful] adj fiel (also Eccl); friend, servant leal; translation fiel; account exacto; **the** — los fieles.
faithfully ['feiθfəli] adv fielmente; lealmente; con exactitud; **yours** — le saluda atentamente.
faithfulness ['feiθfulnis] n fidelidad f; lealtad f; exactitud f.
faith healing ['feiθ,hiːlin] n curación f por fe.
faithless ['feiθlis] adj desleal, pérfido.
fake [feik] 1 n (thing) falsificación f, impostura f; imitación f; (person) impostor m, embustero m, (as term of abuse) farsante m.
2 adj falso, fingido, contrahecho.
3 vt (also **to — up**) contrahacer, falsificar, fingir.
fakir ['fɑːkiə*] n faquir m.
falcon ['fɔːlkən] n halcón m.
falconry ['fɔːlkənri] n halconería f, cetrería f.
Falkland Isles ['fɔːlklənd,ailz] pl Islas fpl Malvinas.
fall [fɔːl] 1 n caída f; (Fin) baja f; (decrease) disminución f; (in price, demand, temperature) descenso m (in de); (Mil) caída f, toma f, rendición f; (of

ground) declive *m*, desnivel *m*; (*of water; also* —s) salto *m* de agua, catarata *f*, cascada *f*; (*US*) otoño *m*; **the F**— la Caída; — **of earth** corrimiento *m* de tierras; — **of rocks** derrumbamiento *m* de piedras; — **of snow** nevada *f*; **to have a** — sufrir una caída; **to be riding for a** — presumir demasiado.

2 (*irr: pret* **fell**, *ptp* **fallen**) *vi* caer; caerse; (*fig:* empire, government, night, hair, drapery; morally etc) caer; (*decrease*) disminuir; (*price, level, demand, temperature* etc) bajar, descender; (*Mil*) caer, rendirse; (*ground*) estar en declive; (*wind*) amainar; **his face fell** se inmutó; **night was** —**ing** anochecía, se hacía de noche; **to** — **among thieves** ir a parar entre ladrones; **to** — **apart** romperse, deshacerse, (*empire* etc) desmoronarse; **to** — **away** (*plaster* etc) desencharse; (*cliff* etc) desmoronarse; (*ground*) estar en declive (*to* hacia); (*Med*) enflaquecer; (*Eccl* etc) ir perdiendo su fe; **to** — **back** retroceder, (*Mil*) replegarse (*on* sobre); **to** — **back on** remedy etc recurrir a; **to** — **backwards** caer de espaldas; **to** — **behind** quedarse atrás, rezagarse; **to** — **down** caer, caerse; (*person*) caerse, dar consigo en el suelo; (*building*) hundirse, derrumbarse; venirse abajo; (*fail*) fracasar, ser frustrado; **the rain was** —**ing down** llovía a cántaros; **to** — **down and worship** arrodillarse ante; **to** — **for** person enamorarse de, thing tomar afición a; trick dejarse engañar por; **he fell for it** picó; **to** — **in** (*roof*) desplomarse; (*lease*) vencer; (*Mil* etc) alinearse; — **in!** ¡en filas!; **to** — **in with** person encontrarse con, juntarse con; idea convenir en, aprobar; **to** — **into** (*river*) desembocar en; error incurrir en; conversation entablar; habit adquirir; category estar incluido en; **it** —**s into 4 parts** puede dividirse en 4 partes; **to** — **off** caerse; (*part*) desprenderse; (*leaf*) separarse; (*in quality*) empeorar; (*in quantity*) disminuir; (*zeal* etc) enfriarse; **to** — **on** (*tax burden* etc) incidir en; (*accent*) cargar sobre, caer sobre; (*Mil*) caer sobre; **to** — **on one's knees** arrodillarse; **to** — **on one's food** tirarse a la comida como un león; **my birthday** —**s on a Monday** mi cumpleaños cae en lunes; **the choice** —**s on X** la elección recae en X; **to** — **out** caer; (*quarrel*) reñir, pelearse, tener un disgusto (*with* con); (*Mil*) romper filas; **it fell out that** resultó que; **to** — **over** caer, caerse; obstacle tropezar con; **they were** —**ing over each other to buy it** se estaban pegando por comprarlo; **to** — **through** (*fig*) fracasar; **to** — **to** (*adv*) empezar a comer, ponerse a trabajar (*etc*); **to** — **to** (*prep*) (*of a duty*) corresponder a, incumbir a, tocar a; **to** — **to temptation** sucumbir a la tentación; **to** — **to** + ger empezar a + infin.

fallacious [fəˈleiʃəs] *adj* erróneo, engañoso.

fallacy [ˈfæləsi] *n* error *m*; sofisma *m*; mentira *f*; **pathetic** — patética falacia *f*, engaño *m* sentimental.

fallen [ˈfɔːlən] **1** *ptp* of **fall**; **the** — los caídos. **2** *adj* (*morally*) perdido.

fall guy [ˈfɔːlgai] *n* (*US fam*) cabeza *f* de turco.

fallibility [ˌfæliˈbiliti] *n* falibilidad *f*.

fallible [ˈfæləbl] *adj* falible.

falling-off [ˈfɔːliŋˈɔf] *n* (*in quantity*) disminución *f*; (*of price* etc) baja *f*, descenso *m*; (*in quality*) empeoramiento *m*.

falling star [ˈfɔːliŋˈstaːʳ] *n* estrella *f* fugaz.

fallout [ˈfɔːlaut] *n* polvillo *m* radiactivo, lluvia *f* radiactiva; — **shelter** refugio *m* contra ataques nucleares.

fallow [ˈfæləu] **1** *adj* barbecho; **to lie** — estar en barbecho. **2** *n* barbecho *m*.

fallow deer [ˈfæləuˈdiəʳ] *n* gamo *m*.

false [fɔːls] *adj* falso; person desleal, pérfido; hair, jewel, teeth etc postizo; bottom doble; **to be** — **to** someone, to play someone — traicionar a uno.

falsehood [ˈfɔːlshud] *n* (*falseness*) falsedad *f*; (*lie*) mentira *f*.

falsely [ˈfɔːlsli] *adv* falsamente.

falseness [ˈfɔːlsnis] *n* falsedad *f*; (*of person*) perfidia *f*.

falsification [ˌfɔːlsifiˈkeiʃən] *n* falsificación *f*.

falsify [ˈfɔːlsifai] *vt* falsificar.

falsity [ˈfɔːlsiti] *n* falsedad *f*.

falter [ˈfɔːltəʳ] **1** *vt* decir titubeando. **2** *vi* (*waver*) vacilar, titubear; (*voice*) desfallecer, empañarse; **without** —**ing** sin vacilar.

faltering [ˈfɔːltəriŋ] *adj* step vacilante; voice entrecortado.

falteringly [ˈfɔːltəriŋli] *adv* say en voz entrecortada.

fame [feim] *n* fama *f*; **ill** — mala reputación *f*; **Bader, of 1940** — Bader, famoso por lo que hizo en 1940.

famed [feimd] *adj* famoso.

familiar [fəˈmiliəʳ] *adj* familiar; (*well-known*) conocido, consabido; (*common*) corriente, común; tone of voice íntimo, de confianza; (*pej*) fresco, que

presume de amigo; **to be** — **with** estar familiarizado con, conocer, estar enterado de; **to be on** — **terms with** tener confianza con; **to make oneself** — **with** familiarizarse con; **his voice sounds** — me parece que conozco su voz; **it doesn't sound** — no me suena; **he got much too** — se tomó muchas confianzas.

familiarity [fəˌmiliˈæriti] *n* familiaridad *f*; (*knowledge*) conocimiento *m* (*with* de); (*of tone*) intimidad *f*; (*pej*) frescura *f*; **familiarities** familiaridades *fpl*; — **breeds contempt** lo conocido no se estima.

familiarize [fəˈmiliəraiz] *vr*: **to** — **oneself with** familiarizarse con.

family [ˈfæmili] **1** *n* familia *f*; **to be one of the** — ser como de la familia; **to be in the** — **way** estar en estado de buena esperanza; **to run in the** — venir de familia.

2 *attr* allowance, gathering etc familiar; butcher doméstico; doctor de cabecera; business de familia; see **tree** etc.

famine [ˈfæmin] *n* hambre *f*; (*of goods*) escasez *f*, carestía *f*.

famished [ˈfæmiʃt] *adj* hambriento, famélico; **I'm simply** — tengo un hambre canina.

famous [ˈfeiməs] *adj* famoso, célebre (*for* por).

famously [ˈfeiməsli] *adv* (*fig*) estupendamente bien, a las mil maravillas.

fan¹ [fæn] **1** *n* abanico *m* (*also fig*); (*Agr*) aventador *m*; (*machine*) ventilador *m*; **electric** — abanico *m* eléctrico, ventilador *m*.

2 *vt* face abanicar; (*mechanically*) ventilar; (*Agr*) aventar; fire soplar; (*fig*) excitar, atizar.

3 *vi*: **to** — **out** desparramarse (en abanico), avanzar separados.

4 *vr*: **to** — **oneself** abanicarse.

fan² [fæn] *n* (*fam*) aficionado *m*, a *f*, admirador *m*, ora *f*, entusiasta *mf*, partidario *m*; **radio** — radioexperimentador *m*; **the boxer's** —s los partidarios del boxeador; **thousands of Real Madrid** —s miles de hinchas del Real Madrid; **I am not one of his** —s yo no soy de sus admiradores, yo no soy de los que le admiran.

fanatic [fəˈnætik] *n* fanático *m*, a *f*.

fanatic(al) [fəˈnætik(əl)] *adj* fanático.

fanaticism [fəˈnætisizəm] *n* fanatismo *m*.

fan belt [ˈfænbelt] *n* (*Aut*) correa *f* de ventilador.

fancied [ˈfænsid] *adj* (*imaginary*) imaginario; (*preferred*) favorito; selecto.

fanciful [ˈfænsiful] *adj* temperament caprichoso; construction, explanation etc fantástico; (*unreal*) imaginario.

fan club [ˈfænklʌb] *n* club *m* de admiradores.

fancy [ˈfænsi] **1** *n* (**a**) (*delusion*) quimera *f*, suposición *f* arbitraria; **it's just your** — lo habrás soñado; **it's one of her fancies** son cosas de ella.

(**b**) (*imaginative capacity*) fantasía *f*, imaginación *f*; **in the realm of** — en el mundo de la fantasía.

(**c**) (*whim*) capricho *m*, antojo *m*; **passing** — capricho *m*; **to have a** — **for** something antojarse algo a uno; **as the** — **takes her** según su capricho.

(**d**) (*taste*) afición *f*, gusto *m*; **to take a** — **to something** tomar afición a algo, encapricharse por algo; **to take a** — **to someone** tomar cariño a uno, (*amorously*) prendarse de uno; **to take** (*or* **tickle**) **someone's** — atraer a uno, cautivar a uno, (*amuse*) caer en gracia a uno.

2 *adj* (*ornamental*) de adorno, de lujo; goods, jewels etc de fantasía; price excesivo; idea fantástico, estrafalario.

3 *vt* (**a**) (*picture to oneself*) imaginarse, figurarse.

(**b**) (*rather think*) creer, suponer; **I** — **he is away** creo que está fuera; **he fancies he knows it all** se cree un pozo de sabiduría.

(**c**) —!, — **that!**, just —! ¡fíjate!, (*doubting*) ¡parece mentira!; — **meeting you!** ¡qué casualidad encontrarle a Vd!; — **him winning!** ¡qué raro que lo ganara él!

(**d**) (*take a* — *to*) aficionarse a, encapricharse por; **I don't** — **the idea** no me gusta la idea; **what do you** —? ¿qué quieres tomar?; **do you** — **a stroll?** ¿te apetece dar un paseo?; **he fancies her** ella le interesa bastante, él se siente atraído por ella.

(**e**) (*have high opinion of*) tener un alto concepto de; **he fancies his game** cree tener muchísima habilidad; **I don't** — **his chances of winning** no creo que tenga muchas posibilidades de ganar.

4 *vr*: **to** — **oneself** (**a**) (*imagine oneself*) creerse, soñar que uno es etc; **he fancied himself in Spain** soñó que estaba en España.

(**b**) presumir; **you** — **yourself!** ¡eres un presumido!; **he fancies himself as a footballer** las echa de futbolista.

fancy dress ['fænsi'dres] n disfraz m; **fancy-dress ball** baile m de trajes.

fancy-free ['fænsi'fri:] adj libre de amores.

fancy woman ['fænsi'wumən] n, pl — **women** [,wimin] (hum) querida f.

fancy work ['fænsiwə:k] n (Sew) labor f.

fanfare ['fænfɛə*] n toque m de trompeta, fanfarria f.

fang [fæŋ] n colmillo m.

fanlight ['fænlait] n abanico m.

fanmail ['fænmeil] n cartas fpl escritas por admiradores.

fantastic [fæn'tæstik] adj fantástico.

fantastically [fæn'tæstikəli] adv fantásticamente; — **learned** enormemente erudito.

fantasy ['fæntəzi] n fantasía f.

far [fɑ:*] 1 adv (a) (distance, literal) lejos, a lo lejos (also — **away**, — **off**); not — from Dover no muy lejos de Dover; **is it** —? ¿está lejos?, ¿dista mucho?; **how** — **is it to Irún?** ¿cuánto hay de aquí a Irún?; — **and near**, — **and wide** por todas partes; **as — as** hasta; **so** — hasta aquí; **to walk** — **into the hills** penetrar profundamente en las montañas.

(b) (distance, fig) **how** — . . .? ¿hasta qué punto . . .?; **how** — **have you gone in your work?** ¿a qué punto han llegado sus trabajos?; — **into the night** hasta las altas horas de la noche; **he's not** — **off 70** tiene casi 70 años, frisa con los 70 años; **she was not** — **off** tears estaba al borde de las lágrimas; **as** — **back as we can recall** hasta donde alcanza la memoria; **so** — hasta aquí, (in time) hasta ahora; **so** — **this year** en lo que va del año; **so** — **so good** hasta aquí, bien; **so** — **and no further** hasta aquí pero ni un paso más.

(c) (fig) **as** — **as I know**, **as** — **as I can tell** que yo sepa; **I will help you as** — **as I can** te ayudaré en lo que pueda; **as** — **as I am concerned** en cuanto a mí, por lo que a mí se refiere; **in so** — **as** en tanto que.

(d) — **from approving it, I** . . . lejos de aprobarlo, yo . . .; — **from it!** ¡nada de eso!; — **be it from me to** + infin no permita Dios que yo + subj.

(e) (with adj or adv) — **better** mucho mejor; **it is** — **better not to go** más vale no ir; — **and away the best**, **the best by** — con mucho el mejor; — **superior to** muy superior a; — **faster than** mucho más rápidamente que.

(f) (with go) **to go** — (plan etc) ir lejos; **that young man will go** — ese joven irá lejos, ese joven tiene un brillante porvenir; **it doesn't go** — **enough** no va bastante lejos, no tiene todo el alcance que quisiéramos; **he's gone too** — **to back out now** ha ido demasiado lejos para retirarse ahora; **to go** — **to** + infin contribuir mucho a + infin; **to go so** — **as to** + infin llegar a + infin.

2 adj lejano, remoto; **at the** — **end** en el otro extremo, (of room) en el fondo; **at the** — **side** en el lado opuesto.

faraway ['fɑ:rəwei] adj remoto; look preocupado, distraído.

farce [fɑ:s] n (Theat) farsa f; (fig) absurdo m, tontería f; **this is a** — esto es absurdo; **what a** — **this is!** ¡qué follón!; **the trial was a** — el proceso fue una parodia de la justicia.

farcical ['fɑ:sikəl] adj absurdo, ridículo.

fare [fɛə*] 1 n (a) (cost) precio m (del viaje, del billete); (ticket) billete m; (Naut) pasaje m; —**s please!** ¡billetes, por favor!; **excess** — suplemento m.

(b) (person) pasajero m, a f.

(c) (food) comida f.

2 vi: **to** — **well** pasarlo bien, irle bien a uno; **how did you** —? ¿qué tal le fue?; **to** — **alike** correr la misma suerte.

Far East ['fɑ:r'i:st] Extremo Oriente m, Lejano Oriente m.

farewell [fɛə'wel] 1 interj ¡adiós!; **it's** — **to all that** ya se acabó todo eso; **you can say** — **to your wallet** puedes considerar tu cartera como perdida.

2 n adiós m; (ceremony) despedida f; **to bid** — **to** despedirse de.

3 attr de despedida.

far-fetched ['fɑ:'fetʃt] adj inverosímil, poco probable; comparison traído por los pelos.

far-flung ['fɑ:'flʌŋ] adj extenso.

farinaceous [,færi'neiʃəs] adj farináceo.

farm [fɑ:m] 1 n granja f; cortijo m, quinta f, estancia f (SAm); (of mink, oysters etc) criadero m; (house) cortijo m, alquería f, casa f de labranza; **collective** — granja f colectiva.

2 vt (till) cultivar, labrar; **he** —**s 300 acres** tiene una finca de 300 acres; **to** — **out** arrendar, dar en arriendo.

3 vi (till) cultivar la tierra; (as profession) ser agricultor; **he** —**s in Devon** tiene una finca (or tierras) en Devon.

farmer ['fɑ:mə*] n agricultor m, cultivador m, granjero m; (peasant —) labrador m; estanciero m (SAm).

farmhand ['fɑ:mhænd] n labriego m, mozo m de labranza, peón m.

farmhouse ['fɑ:mhaus] n, pl —**houses** [,hauziz] cortijo m, alquería f, casa f de labranza.

farming ['fɑ:miŋ] 1 n (tilling) cultivo m, labranza f; (in general) agricultura f. 2 attr agrícola; **the** — **community** los agricultores.

farmland ['fɑ:mlænd] n tierras fpl de labrantío.

farmstead ['fɑ:msted] n alquería f.

farmyard ['fɑ:mjɑ:d] n corral m.

far-off ['fɑ:r'ɔf] adj lejano, remoto.

farrago [fə'rɑ:gəu] n fárrago m.

far-reaching ['fɑ:'ri:tʃiŋ] adj trascendental, de mucho alcance, de ancha repercusión.

farrow ['færəu] 1 n lechigada f de puercos. 2 vt parir. 3 vi parir (la cerda).

far-seeing ['fɑ:'si:iŋ] adj clarividente, previsor.

far-sighted ['fɑ:'saitid] adj clarividente, previsor.

far-sightedly ['fɑ:'saitidli] adv de modo clarividente, con previsión.

far-sightedness ['fɑ:'saitidnis] n clarividencia f, previsión f.

fart [fɑ:t] (tabu) 1 n pedo m. 2 vi peer.

farther ['fɑ:ðə*] comp of **far**; see **further.**

farthest ['fɑ:ðist] superl of **far**; see **furthest.**

farthing ['fɑ:ðiŋ] n cuarto m de penique; **it's not worth a brass** — no vale un céntimo.

fascinate ['fæsineit] vt fascinar, encantar.

fascinating ['fæsineitiŋ] adj fascinador, encantador, sugestivo.

fascination [,fæsi'neiʃən] n fascinación f, encanto m, sugestión f; **his** — **with the cinema** la atracción que tuvo para él el cine.

fascism ['fæʃizəm] n fascismo m.

fascist ['fæʃist] 1 adj fascista. 2 n fascista mf.

fashion ['fæʃən] 1 n (a) (usage, manner) uso m, manera f, estilo m; **it is not my** — **to pretend** yo no acostumbro fingir; **after a** — en cierto modo; **I play after a** — toco algo; **after the** — **of** a la manera de; **in the French** — a la francesa, a lo francés, al estilo francés; **in one's own** — a su propio modo.

(b) (vogue) moda f; **it's all the** — **now** ahora está muy de moda; **it's the** — **to say that** es un tópico decir que; **to be in** — estar de moda; **to be out of** — haber pasado de moda; **to come into** — empezar a estar de moda; **to dress in the latest** — vestirse a la última moda; **to go out of** — pasar de moda; **to set the** — imponer la moda (for de).

(c) (good taste) buen tono m, buen gusto m; **what** — **demands** lo que impone el buen gusto; **a man of** — un hombre elegante.

2 vt formar, labrar, forjar (on sobre).

fashionable ['fæʃnəbl] adj dress etc de moda, elegante; place, restaurant de buen tono, elegante; **in** — **society** en la buena sociedad; **it is** — **to** + infin está de moda + infin; **he is hardly a** — **painter now** es un pintor que no está ahora muy de moda.

fashionably ['fæʃnəbli] adv: **to be** — **dressed** estar vestido muy elegantemente, ir vestido de acuerdo con la moda actual.

fashion designer ['fæʃndi'zainə*] n modisto m.

fashion model ['fæʃən,mɔdl] n modelo mf.

fashion parade ['fæʃənpə'reid] n desfile m de modelos.

fashion plate ['fæʃənpleit] n figurín m de moda.

fashion show ['fæʃənʃəu] n presentación f de modelos.

fast[1] [fɑ:st] 1 adj (a) (speedy) rápido, veloz; ligero; pitch seco y firme; **my watch is 5 minutes** — mi reloj adelanta 5 minutos; **he was too** — **for me** corrió más que yo; **to pull a** — **one on someone** jugar una mala pasada a uno, embaucar a uno.

(b) woman lanzada, cachonda, fresca; life, set disoluto.

(c) (firm) fijo, firme; friend leal; colour sólido, inalterable.

2 adv (a) (speedily) rápidamente; de prisa; **not so** —! ¡un momento!

(b) **to play** — **and loose with** jugar con.

(c) (firmly) firmemente; — **asleep** profundamente dormido; **to hold** — agarrarse bien, (fig) mantenerse firme; **hold** —! ¡agárraos!, (stop) ¡para!; **to make something** — sujetar algo; **to make a rope** — atar firmemente una cuerda; **to make a boat** — amarrar una barca; **to rain** — llover a cántaros; **to stand** — mantenerse firme; **to stick** — quedar

bien pegado; **to be stuck — in the mud** quedar
atascado en el lodo; **to be stuck — in a doorway**
estar metido por una puerta sin poderse mover.
fast² [fɑːst] **1** n ayuno m. **2** vi ayunar.
fast day ['fɑːstdei] n día m de ayuno.
fasten ['fɑːsn] **1** vt (a) asegurar, sujetar, fijar; (with
rope) atar; (with paste) pegar; box, door, window
cerrar; (with bolt) echar el cerrojo a; belt, dress
abrochar; **to — two things together** pegar dos cosas.
   (b) **to — the blame on someone** echar (or
achacar) la culpa a uno; **to — the responsibility on
someone** atribuir a uno la responsabilidad; **they're
trying to — the crime on me** tratan de demostrar
que yo fui autor del crimen.
   2 vi (box etc) cerrarse; **to — on to** agarrarse de,
pegarse a, (fig) fijarse en; **he —ed on to me at once**
se fijó en mí en seguida, (as companion) se me pegó
a mí en seguida; **to — on to a pretext** echar mano
de un pretexto.
fastener ['fɑːsnə*] n, **fastening** ['fɑːsniŋ] n (of door
etc) cerrojo m, pestillo m; (on box) cierre m; (on
dress) broche m, corchete m; (for papers) grapa f;
(zip-) cremallera f.
fastidious [fæs'tidiəs] adj delicado, quisquilloso;
(about cleanliness etc) exigente; taste fino; mind
refinado.
fastness ['fɑːstnis] n (Mil) fortaleza f; (of mountain
etc) lo más intrincado; **in their Cuban mountain —**
en las espesuras serranas de Cuba.
fat [fæt] **1** adj (a) person gordo; (thick) grueso; **to get
—** engordar.
   (b) meat poco magro, que tiene mucha grasa;
(greasy) grasiento, graso.
   (c) land fértil; living lujoso; profit pingüe;
salary muy grande.
   (d) (fam) **a — lot he knows!** ¡maldito lo que él
sabe!; **a — chance he's got** tiene poquísimas
posibilidades; **a — lot of good that is!** y eso ¿para
qué sirve?
   2 n (on person) carnes fpl; (of meat) grasa f; (for
cooking) manteca f, (lard) lardo m; **to live on the —
of the land** darse buena vida, comer lo mejor y más
rico de la tierra; **now the — is in the fire** aquí se va
a armar la gorda.
fatal ['feitl] adj fatal; consequences funesto (to para);
injury mortal; **that was —** eso fue el colmo; **it's —
to say that** es peligrosísimo decir eso.
fatalism ['feitəlizəm] n fatalismo m.
fatalist ['feitəlist] n fatalista mf.
fatalistic [,feitə'listik] adj fatalista.
fatality [fə'tæliti] n fatalidad f; (victim) víctima f,
muerto m; **luckily there were no fatalities** por
fortuna no hubo víctimas.
fatally ['feitəli] adv fatalmente; injure etc mortalmente, a muerte.
fate [feit] **1** n (a) (force) hado m, destino m, sino m;
the F—s las Parcas; **what — has in store for us** lo
que la suerte nos va a deparar.
   (b) (person's lot) suerte f; **to leave someone to
his —** dejar a uno a su suerte; **to meet one's —**
encontrar la muerte; **this sealed his —** esto acabó
de perderle.
   2 vt: **to be —d to + infin** estar predestinado a
+ infin, tener fatalmente que + infin.
fateful ['feitful] adj fatal, fatídico; decisivo.
fathead ['fæthed] n (fam) imbécil mf; **you —!**
¡imbécil!
fat-headed ['fæt,hedid] adj (fam) imbécil.
father ['fɑːðə*] **1** n padre m; **F—s of the Church**
Santos Padres mpl; **Our F—** Padre Nuestro; **Holy
F—** Santo Padre m; **city —s** concejales mpl; **my —
and mother** mis padres; **like — like son** de tal palo
tal astilla; **a — and mother of a row** una bronca
fenomenal; **to talk to someone like a —** hablar a
uno en tono paternal.
   2 vt child engendrar; (fig) inventar, producir;
to — something on someone atribuir algo a uno.
father-figure ['fɑːðə,figə*] n figura f que sirve de
padre, persona f que se finge (or cree etc) dotada de
las cualidades paternales.
fatherhood ['fɑːðəhud] n paternidad f.
father-in-law ['fɑːðərinlɔː] n suegro m.
fatherland ['fɑːðəlænd] n patria f.
fatherless ['fɑːðəlis] adj huérfano de padre.
fatherly ['fɑːðəli] adj paternal.
fathom ['fæðəm] **1** n braza f; **5 —s deep** de (or a etc)
una profundidad de 5 brazas.
   2 vt (Naut) sond(e)ar; (fig) profundizar, penetrar;
mystery desentrañar; **we couldn't — it out** no
logramos sacar nada en claro; **I can't — why** no
comprendo por qué.
fathomless ['fæðəmlis] adj insondable.

fatigue [fə'tiːg] **1** n fatiga f, cansancio m; (Mil)
faena f; **metal —** fatiga f del metal.
   2 vt fatigar, cansar.
fatigue party [fə'tiːg,pɑːti] n destacamento m de
trabajo.
fatiguing [fə'tiːgiŋ] adj fatigoso.
fatness ['fætnis] n gordura f.
fatten ['fætn] **1** vt animal engordar, cebar. **2** vi
engordar.
fatty ['fæti] **1** adj graso; tissue, degeneration etc
grasoso. **2** n (fam) gordinflón m, ona f.
fatuity [fə'tjuːiti] n fatuidad f, necedad f.
fatuous ['fætjuəs] adj fatuo, necio.
faucet ['fɔːsit] n (US) grifo m.
faugh [fɔː] interj ¡bah!
fault [fɔːlt] **1** n (a) (defect: in character) defecto m;
(in manufacture) desperfecto m, imperfección f; (in
supply, machine) avería f; **with all his —s** con todos
sus defectos; **her — is excessive shyness** peca de
demasiado reservada; **generous to a —** excesivamente generoso, generoso hasta el exceso; **to find
— with** criticar, poner peros a.
   (b) (Geol) falla f.
   (c) (blame) culpa f; **it's all your —** Vd tiene
toda la culpa; **it's not my —** yo no tengo la culpa;
whose — is it if ...? ¿quién tiene la culpa si ...?;
you were not at — Vd no tuvo la culpa; **you were
at — in not telling me** Vd hizo mal en no decírmelo;
your memory is at — Vd recuerda mal.
   (d) (mistake) falta f (also Tennis etc); **double
service —** doble falta f de saque.
   2 vt tachar, encontrar defectos en; **it cannot be
—ed** es intachable.
faultfinder ['fɔːlt,faində*] n criticón m, ona f.
faultfinding ['fɔːlt,faindiŋ] **1** adj criticón, reparón.
   2 n manía f de criticar.
faultless ['fɔːltlis] adj impecable, intachable.
faulty ['fɔːlti] adj defectuoso, imperfecto.
faun [fɔːn] n fauno m.
fauna ['fɔːnə] n fauna f.
Faust [faust] m Fausto.
faux pas ['fəu'pɑː] n (false move) paso m en falso;
(gaffe) plancha f.
favour, (US) **favor** ['feivə*] **1** n (a) (approval,
regard) favor m; aprobación f; (protection) amparo
m; **to be in — (thing)** tener mucha aceptación,
(dress etc) estar de moda; **to be in — with (person)**
tener el apoyo de, (at court etc) gozar de favor
cerca de; **to be out of — (thing)** no estimarse, (dress
etc) estar fuera de moda; **to curry —** buscar favores;
to curry — with someone tratar de congraciarse
con uno; **to find — with someone** caer en gracia a
uno; **to look with — on** favorecer; **to stand high in
someone's —** ser tenido en mucho por uno.
   (b) (kindness) favor m; **—s (of woman)** favores
mpl; **to ask a — of** pedir un favor a; **to do someone
a —** hacer un favor a uno; **please do me the — of
+ ger** haga el favor de + infin; see esteem.
   (c) (Comm) **your — of the 5th inst** su atenta
del 5 del corriente.
   (d) (partiality) parcialidad f; **by your —** con
permiso de Vd; **to show — to someone** favorecer a
uno.
   (e) (aid, support) apoyo m; **in — of** a favor de;
balance in your — saldo m a su favor; **that's a
point in his —** es un punto a su favor; **to be in — of
person** apoyar, estar por; thing aprobar, ser partidario de; **to be in — of + ger** apoyar la idea de
+ infin, ser partidario de + infin.
   (f) (token) prenda f.
   2 vt person favorecer, (unjustly) mostrar parcialidad hacia; idea, scheme aprobar, ser partidario de;
party apoyar, (choose to wear) elegir; progress ser
propicio a, ayudar; team, horse preferir; **fortune —s
the brave** la fortuna ayuda a los valientes; **he
eventually —ed us with a visit** por fin se dignó
visitarnos; **most —ed nation treatment** régimen m
de nación más favorecida.
favourable, (US) **favorable** ['feivərəbl] adj favorable; conditions etc propicio.
favourably, (US) **favorably** ['feivərəbli] adv
favorablemente.
favoured, (US) **favored** ['feivəd] adj favorecido;
(favourite) predilecto; **— by nature** dotado por la
naturaleza (with de); **one of the — few** uno de los
pocos afortunados.
favourite, (US) **favorite** ['feivərit] **1** adj favorito,
predilecto. **2** n favorito m, a f (also Sport); (at
court) valido m, privado m; (mistress) querida f.
favouritism, (US) **favoritism** ['feivəritizəm] n
favoritismo m.

fawn[1] [fɔ:n] **1** n (Zool) cervato m. **2** n (colour) color m de cervato. **3** adj color de cervato.

fawn[2] [fɔ:n] vi: **to — on** (animal) acariciar; (fig) adular, lisonjear.

fawning ['fɔ:niŋ] adj adulador, servil.

fealty ['fi:əlti] n lealtad f.

fear [fiə*] **1** n miedo m (of a, de), temor m; aprensión f; **for — of** temiendo, por miedo de; **for — that** por miedo de que + subj; **no —!** ¡ni hablar!; **there's no — of that happening** no hay peligro de que ocurra eso; **without — or favour** imparcialmente; **to go in — of one's life** temer por su vida; **to put the — of God into someone** dar un susto mortal a uno.
2 vt temer; person tener miedo a, thing tener miedo de.
3 vi: **to — for** temer por; **to — to** + infin tener miedo de + infin; **never —!** ¡no hay cuidado!

fearful ['fiəful] adj (frightened) temeroso (of de); aprensivo; (cowardly) tímido; (frightening) pavoroso, horrendo; (fam) tremendo, terrible.

fearfully ['fiəfəli] adv cower etc con miedo; say timidamente; (fam) terriblemente.

fearless ['fiəlis] adj intrépido, audaz; **— of** sin temor a.

fearlessly ['fiəlisli] adv intrépidamente, audazmente; **he went on —** siguió impertérrito.

fearlessness ['fiəlisnis] n intrepidez f.

fearsome ['fiəsəm] adj temible, espantoso.

fearsomely ['fiəsəmli] adv espantosamente.

feasibility [,fi:zə'biliti] n carácter m factible, viabilidad f; **to doubt the — of a scheme** dudar si un proyecto es factible.

feasible ['fi:zəbl] adj factible, hacedero, posible; **to make something —** posibilitar algo.

feast [fi:st] **1** n (meal) banquete m, festín m; (Eccl) fiesta f. **2** vt banquetear. **3** vi banquetear; **to — on** regalarse con.

feast day ['fi:stdei] n fiesta f.

feat [fi:t] n hazaña f, proeza f.

feather ['feðə*] **1** n pluma f; **in fine —** de excelente humor; **that is a — in his cap** es un triunfo para él; **you could have knocked me down with a —** me pasmó la noticia; **to show the white —** mostrarse cobarde.
2 vt emplumar; oar volver horizontal.

feather bed ['feðə'bed] **1** n plumón m. **2 feather-bed** vt subvencionar (demasiado), dar primas (excesivas) a.

featherbrained ['feðəbreind] adj cascabelero.

featherweight ['feðəweit] n peso m pluma.

feathery ['feðəri] adj texture plumoso; (light) ligero como pluma.

feature ['fi:tʃə*] **1** n rasgo m distintivo, característica f; (of face) facción f; (Theat) número m, (Cine) película f de largo metraje, atracción f principal; (in paper) artículo m, crónica f.
2 vt (portray) delinear, representar; (in paper etc) presentar, ofrecer (como atracción principal); actor presentar; **a film featuring Garbo as . . .** una película que presenta a Garbo en el papel de . . .
3 vi existir, constar, figurar.

featureless ['fi:tʃəlis] adj sin rasgos distintivos, monótono.

feature writer ['fi:tʃə,raitə*] n cronista mf.

febrile ['fi:brail] adj febril.

February ['februəri] n febrero m.

feces ['fi:si:z] npl (US) = **faeces**.

feckless ['feklis] adj irreflexivo; casquivano.

fecundity [fi'kʌnditi] n fecundidad f.

fed [fed] pret and ptp of **feed**.

federal ['fedərəl] adj federal.

federalism ['fedərəlizəm] n federalismo m.

federalist ['fedərəlist] n federalista mf.

federation [,fedə'reiʃən] n federación f.

fee [fi:] n (professional) derechos mpl, honorarios mpl; (to club etc) cuota f; **membership —** cuota f de socio; **registration —** derechos mpl de matrícula; **retaining —** ajuste m, anticipo m; **school —s** cuota f de enseñanza, (at boarding school) precio m de la pensión.

feeble ['fi:bl] adj débil (also Med); flojo; light, sound tenue; effort irresoluto, débil.

feeble-minded ['fi:bl'maindid] adj imbécil.

feebleness ['fi:blnis] n debilidad f (also Med); flojedad f; tenuidad f; irresolución f.

feebly ['fi:bli] adv débilmente; flojamente.

feed [fi:d] **1** n **(a)** (food) comida f; (Agr) pienso m; **to be off one's —** no tener apetito.
(b) (fam) cuchipanda f, comilona f; **to have a good —** darse un atracón.
(c) (Mech) tubo m de alimentación.
2 (irr: pret and ptp **fed**) vt (nourish) alimentar, nutrir; (give meal to) dar de comer a; baby dar el pecho a, dar de mamar a, (with bottle) dar el biberón a; fire cebar; (fig) alimentar; **they fed us well at the hotel** nos dieron bien de comer en el hotel; **to — something into a machine** ir metiendo algo en una máquina; **to — someone on something** dar algo de comer a uno; **to — up** animal cebar; **it —s me up** (fam) me fastidia, me saca de quicio; **to be fed up** estar harto (with de).
3 vi comer; (Agr) pacer; **to — on** comer, alimentarse de (also fig).

feedback ['fi:dbæk] n realimentación f.

feeder ['fi:də*] n (Mech) alimentador m, tubo m de alimentación; (Geog) afluente m; (Rail) ramal m tributario.

feeding bottle ['fi:diŋ,bɔtl] n biberón m.

feeding stuffs ['fi:diŋ,stʌfs] npl (Agr) piensos mpl.

feedpipe ['fi:dpaip] n tubo m de alimentación.

feel [fi:l] **1** n (sense of touch) tacto m; (sensation) sensación f; **at the — of his skin** al contacto con su piel; **to be rough to the —** ser áspero al tacto; **to know silk by its —** conocer la seda al tocarla; **to get the — of** acostumbrarse a, (knack) coger el tino a.
2 (irr: pret and ptp **felt**) vt **(a)** (explore) tocar, palpar, tentar; pulse tomar; (caress) acariciar, palpar; **to — out the ground** tantear el terreno, reconocer el terreno.
(b) (perceive) blow, pain, heat, need sentir; experimentar; **I felt it move** lo sentí moverse, sentí que se movió; **I felt it getting hot** sentí como se estaba calentando.
(c) (be conscious of) estar consciente de, darse cuenta de; **I — my position very much** me doy plenamente cuenta de mi situación.
(d) (experience) sentir, experimentar; (be affected by) resentirse de; **I — no interest in it** no me interesa; **we are beginning to — the effects** empezamos a resentirnos de los efectos.
(e) (think, believe) **I — that** creo que, me parece que; **I — strongly that** estoy convencido de que.
3 vi **(a)** (explore) **to — about in the dark** buscar a tientas en la oscuridad; **to — in one's pocket for a key** buscar una llave en el bolsillo.
(b) (be) sentirse; **to — bad, to — ill** sentirse mal; **to — old** sentirse viejo; **to — cold** (person) tener frío; **to — hungry** tener hambre; **how do you —?** ¿qué tal te encuentras?; **she's not —ing quite herself** no se encuentra del todo bien; **to — all the better for something** sentirse mucho mejor después de algo; **I don't — up to it** no me siento con fuerzas para ello; **I — sure** that estoy seguro de que.
(c) (think) **how do you — about this?** ¿qué opinas de esto?; **how does it — to go hungry?** ¿cómo le gusta pasar hambre?
(d) (give impression of) **it —s rough** es áspero al tacto; **it —s like silk** es como la seda al tacto, parece ser seda; **it —s cold** está frío (al tacto); **it —s colder out here** aquí fuera hace más frío; **it —s like rain** parece que va a llover.
(e) (sympathize) **I — for you** lo siento en el alma, te compadezco.
(f) **to — like doing something** tener ganas de hacer algo; **I — like an apple** me apetece una manzana; **do you — like a walk?** ¿quieres dar un paseo?, ¿te apetece dar un paseo?

feeler ['fi:lə*] n (Zool) antena f; tentáculo m; (Pol etc) sondeo m, tentativa f; **to put out a —** hacer un sondeo.

feeling ['fi:liŋ] n **(a)** (sensation) sensación f; **a cold —** una sensación de frío; **to have no — in one's arm** no tener sensibilidad en un brazo.
(b) (emotion) sentimiento m, emoción f; (tenderness) ternura f; **bad —** rencor m, envidia f, hostilidad f; **a man of —** un hombre sensible; **to speak with —** hablar con convicción, (angrily) hablar con pasión; **—s** sentimientos mpl; **you can imagine my —s** Vd puede suponer cuáles serían mis sentimientos; **to appeal to someone's finer —s** hablar a los sentimientos nobles de uno; **to hurt someone's —s** herir los sentimientos de uno; **to relieve one's —s** desahogarse.
(c) (appreciation) **he has no — for music** no sabe apreciar la música.
(d) (opinion) opinión f, parecer m; **our —s do not matter** nuestras opiniones no valen para nada; **my — is that** creo que; **what is your —?** ¿qué opina Vd?; **the general — was that** en general se creía que.
(e) (foreboding) presentimiento m; **I have a — that** presiento que, se me antoja que.

feelingly ['fi:liŋli] adv con honda emoción.

feet [fi:t] npl of **foot**.

feign [fein] vt fingir, aparentar; excuse etc inventar; **to — mad(ness)** fingirse loco; **to — sleep** fingirse dormido; **to — dead** fingirse muerto; **to — not to know** fingir no saber.

feigned [feind] adj fingido.

feint [feint] **1** n treta f, estratagema f; (Fencing) finta f. **2** vi hacer una finta.

felicitous [fi'lisitəs] adj feliz, oportuno.

felicity [fi'lisiti] n felicidad f; (phrase) ocurrencia f oportuna.

feline ['fi:lain] adj felino.

fell[1] [fel] pret of **fall**.

fell[2] [fel] vt derribar (with a blow de un golpe); tree talar, cortar; cattle acogotar.

fell[3] [fel] n (Geog: hill) montaña f; (moor) brezal m, páramo m.

fell[4] [fel] adj cruel, feroz; (fatal) funesto; **at one —** swoop de un solo golpe.

fellow ['feləu] n **(a)** (comrade) compañero m, a f; (-being) prójimo m; **one's — animals** sus prójimos los animales.
(b) (other half) pareja f; (equal) igual mf; **it has no — no tiene par.**
(c) (Univ etc) miembro de la junta de gobierno de un colegio; (of society) socio m, miembro m; **research —** becario m investigador.
(d) (chap) tipo m, sujeto m, tío m; **he's an odd —** es un tipo raro; **well, this journalist —** bueno, el tal periodista; **those journalist —s** los periodistas esos; **a — gets no peace** no le dejan a uno en paz; **my dear —!** ¡hombre!; **nice —** buen chico m, buena persona f; **old —** viejo m; **look here, old —** mira, amigo; **poor —!** ¡pobrecito!; **some poor —** algún pobre diablo; **young —** chico m; **I say, young —** oiga Vd, joven.

fellow being ['feləu'bi:iŋ] n prójimo m.

fellow citizen ['feləu'sitizən] n conciudadano m.

fellow countryman ['feləu'kʌntrimən] n, pl —men [mən] compatriota mf.

fellow creature ['feləu'kri:tʃə*] n prójimo m.

fellow feeling ['feləu'fi:liŋ] n simpatía f, afinidad f.

fellow member ['feləu'membə*] n consocio m.

fellow men ['feləu'men] n prójimos mpl.

fellow passenger ['feləu'pæsindʒə*] n compañero m de viaje.

fellowship ['feləuʃip] n (companionship) compañerismo m; (society) asociación f; (Univ) dignidad f del **fellow**; (grant) beca f.

fellow traveller ['feləu'trævlə*] n compañero m de viaje; (Pol) filocomunista mf, comunizante mf.

fellow worker ['feləu'wə:kə*] n colega m.

felon ['felən] n criminal m, delincuente mf (de mayor cuantía).

felonious [fi'ləuniəs] adj criminal, delincuente.

felony ['feləni] n crimen m, delito m (de mayor cuantía).

felspar ['felspɑ:*] n feldespato m.

felt[1] [felt] pret and ptp of **feel**.

felt[2] [felt] n fieltro m.

female ['fi:meil] **1** adj hembra; (of character) femenino. **2** n hembra f.

feminine ['feminin] adj femenino.

femininity [femi'niniti] n feminidad f.

feminism ['feminizəm] n feminismo m.

feminist ['feminist] n feminista mf.

femur ['fi:mə*] n fémur m.

fen [fen] n pantano m.

fence [fens] **1** n cerca f, cercado m, valla f; (person) receptor m de cosas robadas; **to sit on the —** ver los toros desde la barrera; no resolverse, estar a ver venir.
2 vt cercar; machinery etc cubrir, proteger; **to — in** encerrar con cerca; **to — off** separar con cerca.
3 vi (Sport) esgrimir; (fig) defenderse con evasivas.

fencer ['fensə*] n esgrimidor m, ora f.

fencing ['fensiŋ] n esgrima f.

fend [fend] **1** vt: **to — off** attack defenderse de, rechazar; blow apartar. **2** vi: **to — for oneself** apañárselas por su cuenta.

fender ['fendə*] n (round fire) guardafuego m; (US Aut) parachoques m; guardafango m; (US Rail) trompa f; (Naut) defensa f.

fennel ['fenl] n hinojo m.

Ferdinand ['fə:dinænd] m Fernando m.

ferment ['fə:ment] n (leaven) fermento m; (process) fermentación f; (fig) agitación f, conmoción f; **to be in a —** estar en conmoción.

ferment [fə'ment] **1** vt hacer fermentar. **2** vi fermentar.

fermentation [fə:men'teiʃən] n fermentación f.

fern [fə:n] n helecho m.

ferocious [fə'rəuʃəs] adj feroz.

ferociously [fə'rəuʃəsli] adv ferozmente.

ferocity [fə'rositi] n ferocidad f.

ferret ['ferit] **1** n hurón m. **2** vi: **to — about** buscar revolviéndolo todo; **to — out** person encontrar por fin; secret descubrir, lograr saber.

ferroconcrete ['ferəu'kɔŋkri:t] n ferrohormigón m.

ferrous ['ferəs] adj ferroso.

ferry ['feri] **1** n (small boat) balsa f, barca f (de pasaje); (large, for cars, trains etc) transbordador m.
2 vt: **to — someone across** llevar a uno a la otra orilla; **to — something across** transportar (or pasar) algo a través del río (etc).

ferryboat ['feribəut] n = **ferry**.

ferryman ['ferimən] n, pl —men [mən] balsero m, barquero m.

fertile ['fə:tail] adj (Agr) fértil (of, in en; also fig); (Bio) fecundo.

fertility [fə'tiliti] n fertilidad f; fecundidad f.

fertilize ['fə:tilaiz] vt fecundar, fertilizar; (Agr) abonar.

fertilizer ['fə:tilaizə*] n fertilizante m, abono m.

fervent ['fə:vənt] adj, **fervid** ['fə:vid] adj fervoroso, ardiente, apasionado.

fervour, (US) **fervor** ['fə:və*] n fervor m, ardor m, pasión f.

fester ['festə*] vi ulcerarse, enconarse; (fig) amargarse.

festival ['festivəl] n fiesta f; (Mus etc) festival m.

festive ['festiv] adj festivo, regocijado; **the — season** las Navidades; **to be in a — mood** estar muy alegre.

festivity [fes'tiviti] n (celebration) fiesta f, festividad f; (joy) regocijo m; **festivities** regocijos mpl, festejos mpl, fiestas fpl.

festoon [fes'tu:n] **1** n adorno m; (Sew) festón m. **2** vt adornar, engalanar, enguirnaldar (with de); **to be —ed with** estar adornado de.

fetch [fetʃ] **1** vt **(a)** (bring) traer; ir por, ir a buscar; (fam) atraer; **I'll go and — it for you** te lo voy a buscar; **please — my coat** ¿me trae el abrigo, por favor?; **they're —ing the doctor** han ido por el médico; **please — the doctor** llame al médico, por favor; **they —ed him all that way** le hicieron venir desde tan lejos; **to — someone back from Spain** hacer que uno vuelva de España; **to — out** sacar; **to — up** (fam) arrojar, vomitar.
(b) blow, sigh dar; price venderse por, venderse a; **how much did it —?** ¿cuánto dieron por él?
2 vi: **to — and carry** ir de acá para allá, trajinar; ocuparse en oficios humildes; **to — and carry for someone** ser como el esclavo de uno; **to — up at** ir a parar a.

fetching ['fetʃiŋ] adj atractivo.

fête [feit] **1** n fiesta f; **to be en —** estar en fiestas. **2** vt festejar.

fetid ['fetid] adj fétido.

fetish ['fi:tiʃ] n fetiche m.

fetishism ['fi:tiʃizəm] n fetichismo m.

fetishist ['fi:tiʃist] n fetichista mf.

fetlock ['fetlɔk] n (spur) espolón m; (hair) cernejas fpl.

fetter ['fetə*] vt poner grillos a, encadenar; trabar; (fig) estorbar.

fetters ['fetəz] npl grillos mpl; (fig) trabas fpl.

fettle ['fetl] n: **in fine —** en buenas condiciones; (of mood) de excelente humor.

fetus ['fi:təs] n (US) = **foetus**.

feud [fju:d] **1** n enemistad f heredada (entre dos familias etc), odio m de sangre; disputa f. **2** vi reñir, pelear.

feudal ['fju:dl] adj feudal.

feudalism ['fju:dəlizəm] n feudalismo m.

fever ['fi:və*] n (disease) fiebre f; (high temperature) fiebre f, calentura f; **scarlet —** escarlatina f; **yellow —** fiebre f amarilla; **a — of excitement** una emoción febril; **the gambling —** la fiebre del juego; **to be in a — tener fiebre.**

feverish ['fi:vəriʃ] adj **(a)** (Med) febril, calenturiento; **to be —** tener fiebre. **(b)** (fig) febril.

feverishly ['fi:vəriʃli] adv febrilmente.

few [fju:] adj pocos; algunos, unos; **a —, some —** unos pocos, unos cuantos; **a — of us** algunos de nosotros; **quite a —, not a —** no pocos, algunos; **a good —** un buen número (de); **every — minutes** cada pocos minutos; **in the next — days** un día de éstos que vienen; **the —** los pocos, la minoría; **the lucky —** los pocos afortunados; **such men are —** los hombres así son muy pocos; **they are — and far between** son poquísimos, son contadísimos.

fewer ['fju:ə*] adj comp menos; **— than 10** menos de 10; **— than I** menos que yo; **the — the better** cuantos menos mejor.

fewest ['fju:ist] *adj superl* los menos, las menos, el menor número (de).

fewness ['fju:nis] *n* corto número *m*.

fiancé [fi'ã:nsei] *n* novio *m*, prometido *m*.

fiancée [fi'ã:nsei] *n* novia *f*, prometida *f*.

fiasco [fi'æskəu] *n* fiasco *m*.

fiat ['faiæt] *n* fíat *m*, autorización *f*.

fib [fib] **1** *n* mentirilla *f*, bola *f*. **2** *vi* decir mentirillas.

fibber ['fibə*] *n* mentirosillo *m*, a *f*.

fibre, (*US*) **fiber** ['faibə*] *n* fibra *f*; (*fig*) nervio *m*, carácter *m*.

fibre-glass, (*US*) **fiberglass** ['faibəglɑ:s] *n* fibra *f* de vidrio.

fibrous ['faibrəs] *adj* fibroso.

fibula ['fibjulə] *n* (*Anat*) peroné *m*.

fickle ['fikl] *adj* inconstante, veleidoso, voluble.

fickleness ['fiklnis] *n* inconstancia *f*, veleidad *f*, volubilidad *f*.

fiction ['fikʃən] *n* (*invention*) ficción *f*, invención *f*; (*Lit*) novelas *fpl*, novelística *f*, género *m* novelístico.

fictional ['fikʃənl] *adj* novelesco; relativo a la novela (*etc*).

fictitious [fik'tiʃəs] *adj* ficticio.

fiddle ['fidl] **1** *n* (a) (*Mus*) violín *m*; **to play second —** desempeñar un papel secundario (*to* después de), ser plato de segunda mesa.
(b) (*fam*) trampa *f*, superchería *f*; **tax —** defraudación *f* fiscal, evasión *f* fiscal; **it's a —** aquí hay trampa, son unos tramposos.
2 *vt* (*fam*) *results* falsificar; *job etc* agenciarse, obtener por enchufe; **to — one's income tax** defraudar impuestos.
3 *vi* (*Mus*) tocar el violín; **to — about** perder el tiempo; **to — with** jugar con, manosear; **someone's been fiddling with it** alguno lo ha estropeado.

fiddler ['fidlə*] *n* violinista *mf*.

fiddlesticks ['fidlstiks] *interj* ¡tonterías!

fiddling ['fidliŋ] *adj* trivial, insignificante.

fidelity [fi'deliti] *n* fidelidad *f*; **high —** (*abbr*: **hi-fi**) alta fidelidad *f*.

fidget ['fidʒit] **1** *n* persona *f* inquieta, azogado *m*, a *f*; **—s** agitación *f* nerviosa; **to have the —s** tener azogue, no poder estar quieto.
2 *vt* poner nervioso.
3 *vi* tener azogue, agitarse nerviosamente; **don't —!, stop —ing!** ¡estáte quieto!; **to — about** revolverse nerviosamente; **to — with** jugar con.

fidgety ['fidʒiti] *adj* azogado, nervioso; **to be —** tener azogue.

fiduciary [fi'dju:ʃiəri] *adj* fiduciario.

fief [fi:f] *n* feudo *m*.

field [fi:ld] **1** *n* (a) (*Agr*) campo *m* (*also Elec, Her, Mil, Sport*), prado *m*; (*Geol*) yacimiento *m*; **— of battle** campo *m* de batalla; **— of vision** campo *m* visual; **magnetic —** campo *m* magnético; **to be the first in the —** ser el primero en inventar algo (*etc*); **to take the —** salir a palestra.
(b) (*fig*) esfera *f*; especialidad *f*; **— of activity** esfera *f* de actividades, ámbito *m* de acción; **what's your —?** ¿qué especialidad tiene Vd?; **it's not my —** no es de mi competencia.
(c) (*in race etc*) competidores *mpl*, (*in competition*) concurrentes *mpl*, (*for post*) opositores *mpl*, candidatos *mpl*; **is there a strong —?** ¿se ha presentado gente buena?
2 *vt ball* parar, recoger; *team* presentar.

field day ['fi:lddei] *n* (*Mil*) día *m* de maniobras; **to have a —** (*fig*) obtener un gran éxito, triunfar; divertirse muchísimo.

field glasses ['fi:ld,glɑ:siz] *npl* gemelos *mpl* (de campo), prismáticos *mpl*.

field gun ['fi:ldgʌn] *n* cañón *m* de campaña.

field kitchen ['fi:ld'kitʃin] *n* cocina *f* de campaña.

field marshal ['fi:ld'mɑ:ʃəl] *n* mariscal *m* de campo; (*Spain*) capitán *m* general del ejército.

field mouse ['fi:ldmaus] *n*, *pl* **— mice** [mais] ratón *m* de campo.

field sports ['fi:ldspɔ:ts] *npl* caza *f*.

fieldwork ['fi:ldwə:k] *n* trabajo *m* en el propio campo.

fiend [fi:nd] *n* demonio *m*, diablo *m*; (*fig*) desalmado *m*; (*for hobby etc*) fanático *m*, a *f*, entusiasta *mf* (*for* de).

fiendish ['fi:ndiʃ] *adj* diabólico.

fierce [fiəs] *adj animal etc* feroz, salvaje; cruel; *look* feroz; *attack* furioso; *wind* violento; *heat, competition* intenso; *supporter* acérrimo.

fiercely ['fiəsli] *adv* ferozmente; furiosamente; intensamente.

fierceness ['fiəsnis] *n* ferocidad *f*; furia *f*; intensidad *f*.

fiery ['faiəri] *adj* (*burning*) ardiente; (*red*) rojo; *taste*

muy picante; *temperament, speech* apasionado, vehemente; *horse* fogoso; *liquor* muy fuerte.

fife [faif] *n* pífano *m*.

fifteen [fif'ti:n] **1** *adj* quince. **2** *n* quince *m*.

fifteenth [fif'ti:nθ] *adj* decimoquinto.

fifth [fifθ] **1** *adj* quinto. **2** *n* quinta parte *f*, quinto *m*; (*Mus*) quinta *f*.

fiftieth ['fiftiiθ] *adj* quincuagésimo.

fifty ['fifti] *adj* cincuenta; **the fifties** (*eg* 1950s) los años cincuenta; **to be in one's fifties** tener más de cincuenta años; **to go fifty-fifty** ir a medias.

fiftyish ['fiftiiʃ] *adj* cincuentón.

fig [fig] *n* higo *m*; (*early*) breva *f*; (*tree*) higuera *f*.

fight [fait] **1** *n* (a) (*Mil*) combate *m*; (*between 2 persons*) pelea *f*; (*struggle, campaign*) lucha *f* (*for* por); **in fair —** en buena lid; **to make a — of it** no dejarse vencer fácilmente; **to put up a good —** dar buena cuenta de sí.
(b) (*argument*) disputa *f* (*over* sobre); (*quarrel, esp US*) riña *f*, pelea *f*; **to have a — with someone** tener una pelea con uno; **to pick a — with someone** meterse con uno.
(c) (*fighting spirit*) combatividad *f*, ánimo *m* (de pelear), brío *m*; **to show —** enseñar los dientes, mostrarse dispuesto a resistir; **there was no — left in him** no le quedaba ningún ánimo de luchar más.
2 (*irr: pret and ptp* **fought**) *vt* (*Mil*) *enemy* batirse con, luchar con (*or* contra); *battle* dar, librar; *bull* lidiar; *fire* luchar por sofocar, combatir; *proposal, urge, tendency* combatir, resistir, luchar contra; **to — a case** negar una acusación; **we shall — this case all the way** seguiremos luchando por cambiar esta decisión, no nos conformaremos nunca con esta decisión; **to — one's way out** lograr salir luchando; **to — one's way to the sea** abrirse paso luchando hacia el mar; **to — down** reprimir; **to — it out** decidirlo luchando; **to — off** *attack* rechazar, *sleep* sacudirse, *illness etc* luchar por no sucumbir ante.
3 *vi* pelear, luchar (*against* contra, *for* por, *with* con); batirse; **did you — in the war?** ¿fue Vd soldado cuando la guerra?, ¿desempeñó Vd algún papel en la guerra?; **they were —ing over it** lo estaban disputando a golpes; **we shall have to —** tendremos que luchar; **to — back** defenderse, resistir; **to go down —ing** seguir luchando hasta el fin.

fighter ['faitə*] *n* combatiente *mf*; luchador *m*, ora *f* (*for* por); (*warrior*) guerrero *m*, soldado *m*; (*boxer*) boxeador *m*; (*Aer*) caza *m*; **a bonny —** un valiente guerrero.

fighter-bomber ['faitə'bɔmə*] *n* caza-bombardero *m*.

fighter pilot ['faitə'pailət] *n* piloto *m* de caza.

fighting ['faitiŋ] **1** *n* (*in general*) el luchar, el pelear; (*battle*) combate *m*; **the street — lasted all day** se luchó todo el día en las calles; **there has been — in the colony** ha estallado la guerra en la colonia, ha habido disturbios sangrientos en la colonia; **we want no — here** aquí nada de pendencias; **the Irish are fond of —** a los irlandeses les gusta pelearse.
2 *attr*: **— man** guerrero *m*; **— forces** fuerzas *fpl* militares; **— line** frente *m* de combate; **— spirit** combatividad *f*; *see* **cock** *etc*.

fig leaf ['figli:f] *n* (*fig*) hoja *f* de parra.

figment ['figmənt] *n*: **— of the imagination** quimera *f*.

fig tree ['figtri:] *n* higuera *f*.

figurative ['figərətiv] *adj* figurado.

figure ['figə*] **1** *n* (a) (*statue*) figura *f*, estatua *f*.
(b) (*form of body*) tipo *m*, línea *f*, talle *m*, silueta *f*; **a fine — of a man** un hombre de físico imponente; **a fine — of a woman** una real hembra; **she's got a nice —** tiene buen tipo; **to keep one's —** guardar la línea.
(c) (*person*) figura *f*; **public —** figura *f* pública; **the central — in the crisis** la figura más importante de la crisis; **to cut a —** hacer papel; **to cut a sorry —** parecer ridículo, salir desairado.
(d) (*diagram*) figura *f*, dibujo *m*.
(e) (*Math*) (*numeral*) cifra *f*, número *m*, guarismo *m*; (*quantity*) cifra *f*, cantidad *f*; (*price*) precio *m*, (*sum*) suma *f*; **in round —s** en números redondos; **to be good at —s** ser fuerte en aritmética; **to have a five — income** ganar más de 10.000 libras al año; **to reach double —s** llegar a 10, **to reach 3 —s** ascender a 100.
(f) (*Geom, Dancing, Skating*) figura *f*.
(g) (*Gram*) **— of speech** figura *f*, tropo *m*.
2 *vt* (*in diagram*) representar; (*picture mentally*) representarse, figurarse; (*esp US*) imaginar; **I — it**

like this (US) yo lo veo del modo siguiente; **to —
out** problem resolver; writing descifrar; sum calcular;
I can't — it out at all no me lo explico, no lo
comprendo; **to — up** (US) calcular.
3 vi (appear) figurar (among entre, as como); constar; **it doesn't —** (US) no tiene sentido; **to — on**
(US) contar con; proyectar; esperar; **to — out at**
venir a ser.
figurehead ['figəhed] n mascarón m de proa; (fig)
figura f decorativa.
figure skating ['figə,skeitiŋ] n patinaje m de figuras.
filament ['filəmənt] n filamento m.
filch [filtʃ] vt sisar, ratear.
file[1] [fail] **1** n (tool) lima f. **2** vt limar (also **to — away,
to — down, to — off**).
file[2] [fail] **1** n (folder) carpeta f; (dossier) expediente
m; (eg loose-leaf —) archivador m, clasificador m;
(bundle of papers) legajo m; (cabinet) fichero m,
archivo m; **the —s** los archivos; **police —s** archivos
mpl policíacos; **to close the —** cerrar la carpeta;
to have something on — tener algo archivado.
2 vt archivar (also **to — away**); clasificar;
registrar; **to — a claim** presentar una reclamación;
to — a petition for divorce entablar pleito de
divorcio.
file[3] [fail] **1** n (row) fila f, hilera f; **Indian —** fila f
india; **in single —** en fila de a uno. **2** vi: **to — in**
entrar en fila; **to — past** desfilar ante.
filial ['filiəl] adj filial.
filiation [,fili'eiʃən] n filiación f.
filibuster ['filibʌstə*] **1** n (Parl: person) obstruccionista m; (act) maniobra f obstruccionista. **2** vi
usar de maniobras obstruccionistas.
filigree ['filigri:] n filigrana f.
filing cabinet ['failiŋ,kæbinit] n fichero m, archivo m.
filing clerk ['failiŋ,klɑ:k] n archivero m, a f.
filings ['failiŋz] npl limaduras fpl.
fill [fil] **1** vt llenar (with de); (stuff) rellenar; (charge,
fuel, load) cargar; space llenar completamente,
ocupar completamente; tooth obturar, empastar;
tyre inflar; sail hinchar; post, chair ocupar; vacancy
cubrir; requirement llenar; order despachar; **he —ed
the post very well** desempeñó muy bien el cargo;
to — in llenar; depression terraplenar; form llenar;
details añadir; outline completar; **to — out** (fatten)
engordar; form (US) llenar; **to — up** llenar (hasta
el borde), colmar; form llenar.
2 vi llenarse (with de; also **to — up**); (sail)
hincharse; **to — in for someone** hacer las veces de
uno, suplir a uno; **to — out** echar carnes, (face)
redondearse; **to — up with fuel** repostar combustible.
3 n: **to eat one's —** comer bastante; **to have a —
of tobacco** cargar la pipa; **I've had my — of that**
estoy harto ya de eso.
fillet ['filit] **1** n (all senses) filete m. **2** vt fish quitar la
raspa de, cortar en filetes.
filling ['filiŋ] n relleno m; (Mech) empaquetadura f;
(of tooth) obturación f, empaste m.
filling station ['filiŋ,steiʃən] n estación f de servicio.
fillip ['filip] n (fig) estímulo m; **to give a — to**
estimular.
filly ['fili] n potra f.
film [film] **1** n (thin skin) película f; (of dust) capa f;
(fig) velo m; (Phot, Cine) película f, film m, filme
m (Acad); **the —s** el cine; **silent —** película f muda;
talking — película f sonora; **to make a — of** book
hacer una película de, event filmar.
2 vt book hacer una película de, event filmar;
scene rodar (at, in en).
3 vi: **to — over** empañarse, cubrirse con película.
film fan ['filmfæn] n aficionado m, a f, al cine,
cineasta mf.
film library ['film'laibrəri] n cinemateca f.
film star ['filmstɑ:*] n astro m, estrella f (de cine).
filmstrip ['filmstrip] n tira f de película.
film studio ['film,stju:diəu] n estudio m (de cine).
filmy ['filmi] adj transparente, diáfano.
filter ['filtə*] **1** n filtro m.
2 vt filtrar.
3 vi filtrarse; **to — in, to — through** infiltrarse,
(person etc) introducirse; **to — out** (news) trascender,
llegar a saberse.
filter paper ['filtə,peipə*] n papel m de filtro.
filter tip ['filtə,tip] n boquilla f de filtro; **— cigarette**
cigarrillo m emboquillado.
filter-tipped ['filtə,tipt] adj con filtro, emboquillado.
filth [filθ] n inmundicia f, suciedad f, porquería f;
(fig) inmundicias fpl.
filthy ['filθi] adj inmundo, sucio, puerco, (fig)
inmundo, obsceno.
fin [fin] n (all senses) aleta f.

final ['fainl] **1** adj (last) último, final; (conclusive)
terminante, decisivo, definitivo; exam de fin de
curso; **and that's —** y no hay más que decir.
2 n (Sport) final f; **—s** (Univ) examen m de fin
de curso.
finale [fi'nɑ:li] n (Mus) final m; **grand —** final m
impresionante, final m triunfal.
finalist ['fainəlist] n (Sport) finalista mf.
finality [fai'næliti] n finalidad f; (decision) resolución
f; **he said with —** dijo de modo terminante.
finalize ['fainəlaiz] vt ultimar, completar, concluir,
aprobar de modo definitivo.
finally ['fainəli] adv (lastly) por último, finalmente;
(eventually) por fin; (irrevocably) de modo definitivo.
finance [fai'næns] **1** n (in general) finanzas fpl,
asuntos mpl financieros; (funds) finanzas fpl,
fondos mpl (also **—s**); **the country's —s** la situación
económica del país; **Minister of F—** Ministro m de
Hacienda; **— company** sociedad f financiera.
2 vt financiar, proveer fondos para.
financial [fai'nænʃəl] adj financiero; policy, resources, year económico.
financier [fai'nænsiə*] n financiero m.
find [faind] (irr: pret and ptp **found**) **1** vt (a) (general
sense) encontrar, hallar; descubrir; (stumble on) dar
con, tropezar con; **where did you — it?** ¿dónde lo
encontraste?; **how did you — him?** (in health)
¿qué tal le encontraste?; **it's found all over Spain**
se encuentra (or existe) en todas partes de España;
it's not to be found no se encuentra en ninguna
parte; **I now — it is not so** ahora descubro que no
es así; **it has been found that** se ha comprobado
que; **to — out** averiguar, (llegar a) saber; **to —
someone out** conocer el juego de uno, calar a uno;
his pride found him out su orgullo le traicionó.
(b) (supply, obtain) facilitar, proporcionar,
proveer; **we found him a car** le facilitamos un
coche; **if you can — the time** si Vd tiene el tiempo;
can you — the money? ¿podrás reunir el dinero?;
they found half the cost lograron hacerse con la
mitad del precio; **all found** todo incluido.
(c) (with adj) **you will not — it easy** no le será
fácil (to do hacer); **I found it impossible** me fue
imposible (to go ir); **I — the house small** la casa me
resulta pequeña; (Law) see **guilty.**
2 vi: **to — for the defendant** fallar a favor del
demandado; **to — out about** informarse sobre,
buscar detalles acerca de; **we didn't — out about
it in time** no nos enteramos a tiempo.
3 vr: **to — oneself** encontrarse; verse; **I found
myself alone** me encontré solo; **I — myself at a loss**
me encuentro perplejo; **he found himself** descubrió
su verdadera vocación (or identidad etc).
4 n hallazgo m.
finder ['faində*] n descubridor m, ora f, el (la) que
encuentra algo.
finding ['faindiŋ] n descubrimiento m; **—s** (Law etc)
fallo m; (of report etc) recomendaciones fpl.
fine[1] [fain] **1** adj (a) (delicate, small) thread fino, sutil;
particle, print menudo; line tenue; pencil, nib
delgado; edge muy afilado; distinction delicado, sutil.
(b) (good) bueno; (beautiful) bello, hermoso;
(exquisitely made) fino, delicado, primoroso; dress
elegante; (showy) vistoso; (imposing) magnífico,
imponente; (selected) escogido; (pure) refinado, puro;
ideal bello; day bueno; feeling elevado, noble;
person admirable; (accomplished) excelente, experto;
—! ¡magnífico!, ¡estupendo!; **to be —** (weather)
hacer buen tiempo; **it's a — thing to + infin** es
admirable + infin.
(c) (iro) bueno, lindo, valiente; **that's all very
—, but . . .** todo eso está muy bien, pero . . .; **a —
friend you are!** ¡valiente amigo!; **you're a — one!**
¡estás tú bueno!, ¡qué tío!
2 adv (a) (fam) muy bien; **you're doing —** lo estás
haciendo la mar de bien; **to feel —** estar como un
reloj.
(b) to chop something up — cortar algo en
trozos menudos; **to cut (or run) it —** llegar con
muy poco tiempo, dejarse muy poco tiempo.
3 vi: **to — down** adelgazar.
fine[2] [fain] **1** n multa f. **2** vt multar.
fine-drawn ['fain'drɔ:n] adj estirado en un hilo muy
delgado; wire muy delgado; distinction etc sutil, fino.
fine-grained ['fain'greind] adj de grano fino.
finely ['fainli] adv (a) sutilmente; menudamente.
(b) hermosamente; primorosamente; elegantemente;
vistosamente. **(c)** (iro) lindamente.
finery ['fainəri] n galas fpl, adornos mpl, trajes mpl
vistosos.
finesse [fi'nes] **1** n (in judgement) discriminación f
sutil, discernimiento m; (in action) diplomacia f,

tino *m*, sutileza *f*; (*cunning*) astucia *f*; (*Cards*) impase *m*. **2** *vt* hacer el impase a.

finger ['fiŋɡə*] **1** *n* dedo *m*; **first —, index —** dedo *m* índice; **little —** dedo *m* meñique; **middle —** dedo *m* del corazón; **ring —** dedo *m* anular; **his —s are all thumbs** es terriblemente desmañado; **to burn one's —s, to get one's —s burned** (*fig*) cogerse los dedos; **to have green —s** tener mucha habilidad en jardinería; **to have a — in the pie** meter su cucharada; **they never laid a — on her** no la tocaron en absoluto; **he didn't lift a — to help** no movió un dedo para ayudarnos; **to point the — of scorn at someone** señalar a uno con el dedo; **to put one's — on** (*fig*) concretar, señalar acertadamente; **to put one's — on it** (*or* **on the spot**) poner el dedo en la llaga; **there was nothing you could put your — on** no había nada concreto; **he slipped through their —s** se les escapó entre los dedos; **to snap one's —s at someone** (*fig*) tratar a uno con desprecio; **to twist someone round one's little —** hacer con uno lo que le da la gana.
  2 *vt* manosear, tocar; (*Mus*) tocar (distraídamente).

fingering ['fiŋɡəriŋ] *n* (*Mus*) digitación *f*.

fingernail ['fiŋɡəneil] *n* uña *f*.

fingerprint ['fiŋɡəprint] **1** *n* huella *f* dactilar. **2** *vt* tomar las huellas dactilares a.

fingerstall ['fiŋɡəstɔːl] *n* dedil *m*.

fingertip ['fiŋɡətip] *n* punta *f* (*or* yema *f*) del dedo; **to have something at one's —s** saber algo al dedillo.

finicky ['finiki] *adj* delicado, melindroso, superferolítico.

finish ['finiʃ] **1** *n* (a) (*end*) fin *m*, final *m*, conclusión *f*; remate *m*; (*Sport*) poste *m* de llegada; **to be in at the —** estar presente en la conclusión; **to fight to a —** seguir luchando hasta decidir la victoria.
  (b) (*of manufactured article*) acabado *m*; **gloss(y) —** acabado *m* brillo; **to have a rough —** estar sin pulir.
  2 *vt* (a) (*also* **to — off, to — up**) terminar, acabar, concluir; completar, llevar a cabo, rematar; dar la última mano a; **I'm —ed** (*tired*) estoy rendido; **he's —ed now** (*fig*) se acabó para él, ahora no vale para nada; **as a film star she's —ed** como estrella está acabada; **to — off** (*kill*) despachar, (*destroy*) acabar con; **to — up** *food* terminar de comer, *drink* terminar de beber.
  (b) (*Tech*) acabar; **—ed goods** productos *mpl* acabados.
  3 *vi* (a) terminar, acabar; **to — doing something** terminar de hacer algo; **to — up** at ir a parar a; **to — with** terminar con; **she —ed with him** rompió con él; **wait till I've —ed with him!** ¡a ver lo que le voy a hacer!
  (b) (*Sport*) llegar; **to — third** llegar el tercero.

finishing line ['finiʃiŋ‚lain] *n* línea *f* de meta.

finishing school ['finiʃiŋ‚skuːl] *n* escuela *f* particular de educación social para señoritas.

finite ['fainait] *adj* finito (*also* Gram).

Finland ['finlənd] *n* Finlandia *f*.

Finn [fin] *n* finlandés *m*, esa *f*.

Finnish ['finiʃ] **1** *adj* finlandés. **2** *n* (*language*) finlandés *m*.

fiord [fjɔːd] *n* fiordo *m*.

fir [fəː*] *n* abeto *m*.

fir cone ['fəːkəun] *n* piña *f* (de abeto).

fire [faiə*] **1** *n* (a) (*in general*) fuego *m*; (*accidental, damaging*) incendio *m*; (*in grate*) fuego *m*, lumbre *f*; **electric —** estufa *f* eléctrica; **to be on —** estar ardiendo, estar en llamas; **to catch —** encenderse; **to cook something on a slow —** cocer algo a fuego lento; **to hang —** demorarse, estar en suspenso; **to make up a —** echar carbón a la lumbre; **to play with —** jugar con fuego; **to set on —, to set — to** pegar (*or* prender) fuego a, incendiar; **to sit by** (*or* **round**) **the —** estar sentado al lado de la chimenea; **to take —** encenderse.
  (b) (*Mil*) **to open —** abrir fuego, romper el fuego; **to be under —** (*fig*) ser criticado.
  (c) (*fig*) ardor *m*, pasión *f*; entusiasmo *m*; **the — of youth** el ardor de la juventud; **men with — in their bellies** hombres llenos de celo idealista.
  2 *vt* (a) (*set — to*) encender, incendiar, pegar fuego a, quemar; *bricks, pottery* cocer.
  (b) *gun, shot, salute* disparar; *torpedo, rocket* lanzar; *person* (*fam*) despedir; **to — a question at someone** disparar una pregunta inesperada a uno.
  (c) (*fig*) *imagination* excitar, enardecer, exaltar; *interest* despertar; (*inspire*) inspirar.
  3 *vi* (a) (*catch —*) encenderse; **to — up** (*fig*) ponerse furioso.

  (b) (*Mil*) hacer fuego; **to — at, to — on** hacer fuego sobre, tirar a; **they were firing at each other all day** se estaban tiroteando todo el día; **—!** ¡fuego!; **— away!** (*fig*) ¡adelante!
  (c) (*Aut*) dar explosiones; **the engine is not firing on one cylinder** uno de los cilindros del motor no se enciende.

fire alarm ['faiərə‚lɑːm] *n* alarma *f* de incendios.

firearm ['faiərɑːm] *n* arma *f* de fuego.

fireball ['faiəbɔːl] *n* bola *f* de fuego.

firebrand ['faiəbrænd] *n* tea *f*; (*fig*) partidario *m* violento, revoltoso *m*.

firebrick ['faiəbrik] *n* ladrillo *m* refractario.

fire brigade ['faiə‚ɡeid] *n* cuerpo *m* de bomberos.

fire curtain ['faiə‚kəːtn] *n* (*Theat*) telón *m* a prueba de incendios.

firedamp ['faiədæmp] *n* grisú *m*.

fire engine ['faiər‚endʒin] *n* bomba *f* de incendios, coche *m* de bomberos.

fire escape ['faiəris‚keip] *n* escalera *f* de incendios.

fire extinguisher ['faiəriks'tiŋɡwiʃə*] *n* extintor *m*.

firefly ['faiəflai] *n* luciérnaga *f*.

fireguard ['faiəɡɑːd] *n* alambrera *f*, guardafuego *m*.

fire insurance ['faiərin‚ʃuərəns] *n* seguro *m* contra incendios.

fire irons ['faiər‚aiənz] *n* útiles *mpl* de chimenea.

firelighter ['faiə‚laitə*] *n* astillas *fpl* (para encender el fuego), tea *f*.

fireman ['faiəmən] *n*, *pl* **—men** [mən] bombero *m*; (*Rail*) fogonero *m*.

fireplace ['faiəpleis] *n* chimenea *f*; (*hearth*) hogar *m*.

fireproof ['faiəpruːf] *adj* incombustible, a prueba de fuego.

fire-raiser ['faiə‚reizə*] *n* incendiario *m*.

fire-raising ['faiə‚reiziŋ] *n* (*delito m de*) incendiar *m*, incendio *m*.

fireside ['faiəsaid] **1** *n* hogar *m*. **2** *attr* hogareño, doméstico, familiar.

fire station ['faiə‚steiʃən] *n* parque *m* de bomberos.

firewood ['faiəwud] *n* leña *f*, astillas *fpl*.

fireworks ['faiəwəːks] *npl* fuegos *mpl* artificiales; (*fig*) explosión *f* (de cólera *etc*); **there will be — at the meeting** (*fig*) en la reunión se va a armar la gorda.

firing ['faiəriŋ] *n* (*Mil*) disparo *m*, (*continuous*) tiroteo *m*, cañoneo *m*; (*Aut*) encendido *m*; (*of bricks etc*) cocción *f*.

firing line ['faiəriŋlain] *n* línea *f* de fuego.

firing squad ['faiəriŋskwɔd] *n* pelotón *m* de ejecución.

firm[1] [fəːm] *adj* firme; (*Comm*) *offer, order* en firme; **as — as a rock** tan firme como una roca; **he was very — about it** se mostró muy decidido, lo dijo de modo terminante; **to stand —** mantenerse firme.

firm[2] [fəːm] *n* firma *f*, empresa *f*, casa *f* de comercio.

firmament ['fəːməmənt] *n* firmamento *m*.

firmly ['fəːmli] *adv* firmemente; con firmeza.

firmness ['fəːmnis] *n* firmeza *f*.

first [fəːst] **1** *adj* primero; primitivo, original; *edition* príncipe.
  2 *adv* primero; (*firstly*) en primer lugar; (*for the first time*) por primera vez; **— of all, — and foremost** ante todo; **head —** de cabeza; **stern —** a la popa por delante; **ladies —** las señoras pasan primero; **women and children —!** ¡primero las mujeres y los niños!; **to get in —** (*fig*) madrugar; **to go —** entrar (*etc*) el primero, (*Rail*) viajar en primera; **you go —!** ¡Vd primero!, ¡pase Vd!
  3 *n* primero *m*, a *f*; (*Univ*) primera clase *f*, sobresaliente *m*; **at —** al principio; **I didn't see them at —** no les vi de momento; **from the —** desde el principio; **from — to last** desde el principio hasta el fin; **to be the — to do something** ser el primero en hacer algo; **he came in an easy —** llegó con mucho el primero, obtuvo fácilmente la victoria.

first aid ['fəːst'eid] **1** *n* primera curación *f*, primeros auxilios *mpl*. **2** *attr* **first-aid: — box, — kit** botiquín *m*; **— post** puesto *m* de socorro.

first-born ['fəːstbɔːn] *n* primogénito *m*, a *f*.

first-class ['fəːstklɑːs] *adj* de primera clase.

first-hand ['fəːst'hænd] *adj* de primera mano; directo, personal; **at —** directamente.

firstly ['fəːstli] *adv* en primer lugar.

first-nighter ['fəːst'naitə*] *n* estrenista *mf*.

first-rate ['fəːst'reit] *adj* de primera clase.

firth [fəːθ] *n* estuario *m*, ría *f*.

fir tree ['fəːtriː] *n* abeto *m*.

fiscal ['fiskəl] *adj* fiscal; monetario; *policy, year* económico.

fish [fiʃ] **1** *n* pez *m*, (*as food*) pescado *m*; (*fam*) tío *m*; **queer —** tipo *m* raro; **he's a poor —** es un pobre hombre; **to be like a — out of water** estar como pez fuera del agua; **to have other — to fry** tener cosas más importantes que hacer.

2 *vt river* pescar en; **to — out, to — up** sacar.

3 *vi* pescar; **to — for** (tratar de) pescar; *compliment etc* andar a la pesca de; **he —ed in his pocket for** it lo buscó en el bolsillo; **to go —ing** ir de pesca.

fishbone ['fiʃbəun] *n* raspa *f*, espina *f* de pez.

fishbowl ['fiʃbəul] *n* pecera *f*.

fisherman ['fiʃəmən] *n, pl* **-men** [mən] pescador *m*.

fishery ['fiʃəri] *n* pesquería *f*, pesquera *f*.

fish glue ['fiʃglu:] *n* cola *f* de pescado.

fish hook ['fiʃhuk] *n* anzuelo *m*.

fishing ['fiʃiŋ] *n* pesca *f*.

fishing boat ['fiʃiŋbəut] *n* barca *f* pesquera.

fishing grounds ['fiʃiŋgraundz] *npl* pesquería *f*.

fishing line ['fiʃiŋlain] *n* sedal *m*.

fishing net ['fiʃiŋnet] *n* red *f* de pesca.

fishing rod ['fiʃiŋrɔd] *n* caña *f* de pescar.

fishing tackle ['fiʃiŋ‚tækl] *n* aparejo *m* de pescar.

fish manure ['fiʃmə‚njuə*] *n* abono *m* de pescado.

fish market ['fiʃmɑːkit] *n* mercado *m* de pescado, pescadería *f*.

fishmonger ['fiʃmʌŋgə*] *n* pescadero *m*; **—'s (shop)** pescadería *f*.

fishplate ['fiʃpleit] *n* (*Rail*) eclisa *f*.

fishpond ['fiʃpɔnd] *n* piscina *f*, vivero *m*.

fish slice ['fiʃslais] *n* pala *f* para el pescado.

fishwife ['fiʃwaif] *n, pl* **-wives** [waivz] pescadera *f*; (*pej*) verdulera *f*.

fishy ['fiʃi] *adj eye* como de pez; (*of taste*) que sabe a pescado, (*of smell*) que huele a pescado; (*fam*) sospechoso; **it's —** me huele a camelo; **there's something — going on here** aquí hay gato encerrado.

fissile ['fisail] *adj* físil.

fission ['fiʃən] *n* (*Phys*) fisión *f*; (*Bio*) escisión *f*; **nuclear —** fisión *f* nuclear.

fissionable ['fiʃnəbl] *adj* fisionable.

fissure ['fiʃə*] *n* grieta *f*, hendedura *f*; (*Anat, Geol, Metal*) fisura *f*.

fissured ['fiʃəd] *adj* agrietado.

fist [fist] *n* puño *m*; (*writing*) letra *f*; **to shake one's — at someone** amenazar a uno con el puño.

fistful ['fistful] *n* puñado *m*.

fisticuffs ['fistikʌfs] *npl* puñetazos *mpl*.

fit¹ [fit] **1** *adj* (**a**) adecuado, conveniente, apto, a propósito, apropiado (*for* para); hábil, capaz; **the —test** (*Bio*) los mejores dotados; **— for duty** apto para servicio; **a meal — for a king** una comida digna de un rey; **to be — for** ser adecuado para; **he's not — for the job** no es adecuado para el puesto, no merece que se le dé el puesto; **he's not — to teach** no tiene madera de profesor; **he is not — to drive** no es apto para conducir; **— to eat** bueno de comer; **it's not — to eat** no se puede comer, es incomible; **it's not — to be seen** es indigno de que lo vean las gentes; **is this — to wear?** ¿puedo ponerme esto?; **I felt — to drop** tuve ganas de caerme rendido; **to see** (*or* **think**) **— to** + *infin* estimar conveniente + *infin*; **he saw — to** + *infin* (*iro*) se vio en el caso de + *infin*; **do as you think —** haga lo que mejor le parezca.

(**b**) (*Med*) sano, bien de salud; en buen estado físico, (*Sport*) en forma; **3 players are not —** 3 jugadores están lesionados; **come when you're — again** ven cuando te hayas repuesto del todo; **to be as — as a fiddle** andar como un reloj; **are you —?** (*fam*) ¿estás listo?, ¿vamos?; **to get —** (*Sport*) entrenarse, (*Med*) reponerse; **to keep —** mantenerse en forma, mantenerse en buen estado físico.

2 *as adv*: **to laugh — to burst** desternillarse de risa.

3 *vt* (**a**) (*make suitable*) ajustar, acomodar, adaptar (*to* a); **to — someone for a post** capacitar a uno para un puesto.

(**b**) (*suit*) *description, facts* cuadrar con, corresponder con, estar de acuerdo con; *colour scheme etc* hacer juego con; (*of dress etc*) sentar bien a, ir bien a.

(**c**) (*try on*) *clothes* probar (*on* a).

(**d**) (*fill up, exactly correspond to*) encajar en; **it —s the space perfectly** encaja perfectamente en el espacio; **the key does not — the lock** la llave no entra en la cerradura.

(**e**) (*put*) **to — two things together** unir dos cosas; **I —ted A into B** encajé A en B; **you — it in here** se encaja aquí, se coloca aquí; **to — the key into the lock** introducir la llave en la cerradura; **can you — me in?** ¿puede incluirme?; **I'll see if the director can — you in** voy a ver si el director tiene tiempo para verle; **I —ted in a trip to Ávila** logré hacer una excursión a Ávila.

(**f**) (*supply*) **to — something with** proveer algo

de; **to — someone out** (*or* **up**) **with** proveer a uno de, equipar a uno con; **—ted with a heater** provisto de un calentador, dotado de un calentador; **I'm having a new door —ted** me van a colocar una nueva portezuela; **to — out a ship** armar un buque; **to — up** montar, instalar; *see also* **fitted**.

4 *vi* (**a**) (*correspond*) corresponder, estar de acuerdo; **the facts don't —** los datos no tienen sentido; **it all —s** todo hace un conjunto lógico.

(**b**) (*of clothes etc*) entallar; **the suit —s well** el traje le sienta bien.

(**c**) (*of person*) **he —s in well here** aquí se lleva bien con todos; **I don't — in here** aquí no estoy bien.

(**d**) (*of space*) encajarse; caber; **it —s in here, it —s on here** se encaja aquí; **do they —?** ¿se encajan uno en otro?; **does it —?** ¿cabe?; **it won't — in here** aquí no cabe; **the key doesn't —** la llave no sirve; **the key —s into the lock** la llave se ajusta a la cerradura.

5 *n* ajuste *m*, corte *m*; **it's a good —** le sienta bien; **the suit is a tight —** el traje me viene bastante estrecho.

fit² [fit] *n* (*Med*) acceso *m*, ataque *m*; **— of anger** arranque *m* de cólera; **— of coughing** acceso *m* de tos; **fainting —** síncope *m*; **by —s and starts** a rachas, a empujones; **we were in —s (of laughter)** moríamos de risa; **he'd have a — if he knew** le daría un ataque si lo supiera.

fitful ['fitful] *adj* espasmódico, caprichoso.

fitfully ['fitfəli] *adv* espasmódicamente, a rachas, por intervalos.

fitment ['fitmənt] *n* mueble *m*.

fitness ['fitnis] *n* (*suitability*) conveniencia *f*, oportunidad *f*; (*for post etc*) idoneidad *f*, capacidad *f*; (*Med*) (buena) salud *f*, (buen) estado *m* físico.

fitted ['fitid] *adj suit, carpet* hecho a medida; *cupboard* empotrado; **to be — for something** tener talento para algo, ser idóneo para algo.

fitter ['fitə*] *n* (*Mech*) (mecánico *m*) ajustador *m*.

fitting ['fitiŋ] **1** *adj* (*suitable*) conveniente, adecuado; (*worthy*) digno; **it is — that** es propio que + *subj*, es justo que + *subj*; **it is not — that** no está bien que + *subj*.

2 *n* (*of dress*) prueba *f*; (*size*) medida *f*; **—s** guarniciones *fpl*; **bathroom —s** aparatos *mpl* sanitarios; **electrical —s** accesorios *mpl* eléctricos; **furniture and —s** muebles *mpl* y enseres.

fittingly ['fitiŋli] *adv* convenientemente, adecuadamente; dignamente; **—, it was he who . . .** según cabía razonablemente esperar, era él quien . . .

five [faiv] **1** *adj* cinco. **2** *n* cinco *m*.

fiver ['faivə*] *n* (*fam*) billete *m* de 5 libras.

five-year ['faiv'jiə*] *adj*: **— plan** plan *m* quinquenal.

fix [fiks] **1** *vt* (**a**) (*secure*) fijar, asegurar, sujetar; *bayonet* calar; (*Phot*) fijar; **to — something in one's memory** grabar algo en la memoria.

(**b**) (*direct*) *attention* fijar (*on* en); *eyes* clavar (*on* en); *hopes* poner (*on* en); *blame* echar (*on* a).

(**c**) **to — someone with one's eyes** fijar los ojos en uno.

(**d**) (*place*) fijar (*at* en).

(**e**) (*determine position of*) fijar, precisar.

(**f**) (*determine*) *author, date etc* fijar, señalar; *price* fijar, determinar.

(**g**) (*arrange, prepare; also* **— up**) arreglar; decidir; organizar, preparar; **it's all —ed up** todo está arreglado; **there is nothing —ed yet** todavía no se ha decidido nada.

(**h**) (*US*) dar, servir, preparar; **can I — you a drink?** ¿le traigo algo de beber?; **I'll — you some supper** te preparé una cena.

(**i**) (*repair*) componer, arreglar.

(**j**) **he —ed it with the police** se las arregló con la policía.

(**k**) **I'll — him!** ¡me lo cargaré!; **that ought to — him** eso ha de acabar con él.

(**l**) **to — someone up with something** proveer a uno de algo.

(**m**) (*Sport etc*) *game, jury* amañar; **it's been —ed!** ¡hay tongo!

(**n**) **how are we —ed for time?** ¿tenemos tiempo?; **how are we —ed for money?** ¿qué tal andamos de dinero?

2 *vi*: **to — on** escoger; *date etc* fijar, señalar; **to — up with someone** arreglarlo con uno; **to — up with someone to** + *infin* convenir con uno en + *infin*.

3 *n* (*Aer etc*) posición *f*; (*fam*) aprieto *m*; **to be in a —** estar en un aprieto.

fixation [fik'seiʃən] *n* fijación *f*.

fixative ['fiksətiv] *n* fijativo *m*.

fixed [fikst] *adj* (*all senses*) fijo.

fixedly ['fiksidli] *adv* fijamente.

fixings ['fiksiŋz] *npl* (US) accesorios *mpl*, guarniciones *fpl*.

fixture ['fikstʃə*] *n* cosa *f* fija; (*furniture etc*) mueble *m* fijo, instalación *f* fija; (*Sport*) partido *m*, encuentro *m*; (*person*) cliente *m* fijo; **lighting** —s (US) guarniciones *fpl* de alumbrado.

fizz [fiz] **1** *n* efervescencia *f*; (*noise*) ruido *m* sibilante; (*fam*) gaseosa *f*. **2** *vi* estar (*or* entrar) en efervescencia; hacer un ruido sibilante.

fizzle ['fizl] = **fizz**; (*vi*) **to** — **out** apagarse; (*fig*) no dar resultado, fracasar.

fizzy ['fizi] *adj* gaseoso, espumoso, efervescente.

flabbergast ['flæbəgɑːst] *vt* pasmar, dejar sin habla; **I was** —**ed by the news** la noticia me causó estupor.

flabby ['flæbi] *adj* flojo, fofo, blanducho; (*fat*) gordo; (*fig*) débil, soso.

flaccid ['flæksid] *adj* fláccido.

flaccidity [flæk'siditi] *n* flaccidez *f*.

flag[1] [flæg] *n* (*Bot*) lirio *m*.

flag[2] [flæg] *n* (*stone*) losa *f*.

flag[3] [flæg] **1** *n* bandera *f*, pabellón *m*; (*small, charity etc*) banderita *f*; (*small, as souvenir, also Sport*) banderín *m*; — **of convenience** bandera *f* de conveniencia; — **of truce, white** — bandera *f* de parlamento; **red** — bandera *f* roja; **to keep the** — **flying** seguir defendiéndose, resistir, no rendir la bandera; **to show the** — hacer acto de presencia.

2 *vt* hacer señales con una bandera a; **to** — **someone down** hacer señales a uno para que se detenga.

flag[4] [flæg] *vi* (*strength*) acabarse, flaquear, decaer; (*enthusiasm etc*) enfriarse; (*conversation*) languidecer.

flag day ['flægdei] *n* día *m* de la banderita.

flagellate ['flædʒəleit] *vt* flagelar.

flagellation [,flædʒə'leiʃən] *n* flagelación *f*.

flagon ['flægən] *n* (*approx*) jarro *m*; (*as measure*) botella *f* de unos 2 litros.

flagpole ['flægpəul] *n* asta *f* de bandera.

flagrant ['fleigrənt] *adj* notorio, escandaloso.

flagship ['flægʃip] *n* buque *m* insignia, buque *m* almirante, buque *m* escuadra, (*arch*) capitana *f*.

flagstaff ['flægstɑːf] *n* asta *f* de bandera.

flagstone ['flægstəun] *n* losa *f*.

flail [fleil] **1** *n* mayal *m*. **2** *vt* (*fig*) golpear, azotar. **3** *vi*: **to** — **about** debatirse.

flair [fleə*] *n* instinto *m*, aptitud *f* especial (*for* para).

flak [flæk] *n* fuego *m* antiaéreo.

flake [fleik] **1** *n* escama *f*, hojuela *f*; (*of snow*) copo *m*. **2** *vt* separar en escamas; **to be** —**d out** (*fam*) estar rendido. **3** *vi* (*also* **to** — **away, to** — **off**) desprenderse en escamas; **to** — **out** (*fam*) caer rendido.

flaky ['fleiki] *adj* escamoso; desmenuzable.

flamboyant [flæm'bɔiənt] *adj* (*Archit etc*) flameante; **dress** *etc* vistoso, llamativo; *character*, *speech* extravagante; *style* rimbombante.

flame [fleim] **1** *n* llama *f*; (*fam*) novio *m*, a *f*; **to be in** —**s** arder en llamas; **to burst into** —**s** estallar en llamas; **to commit something to the** —**s** entregar algo a las llamas; **to fan the** —**s** soplar el fuego. **2** *vi* (*burn*) llamear; (*shine*) brillar; **to** — **up** (*fig*) estallar, (*person*) inflamarse.

flamethrower ['fleim,θrəuə*] *n* lanzallamas *m*.

flaming ['fleimiŋ] *adj* (*fam*) condenado.

flamingo [flə'miŋgəu] *n* flamenco *m*.

flan [flæn] *n* tarta *f*, tarteleta *f* de fruta.

Flanders ['flɑːndəz] Flandes *m*.

flange [flændʒ] *n* pestaña *f*, reborde *m*.

flanged [flændʒd] *adj* con pestaña.

flank [flæŋk] **1** *n* (*of person*) costado *m*; (*of animal*) ijada *f*; (*of hill*) lado *m*, falda *f*; (*Mil*) flanco *m*. **2** *vt* lindar con, estar contiguo a; (*Mil etc*) flanquear; **it is** —**ed by hills** tiene unas colinas a su lado; **he was** —**ed by two policemen** iba escoltado por dos guardias.

flannel ['flænl] **1** *n* (*cloth*) franela *f*; (*face-*) manopla *f*, paño *m*; (*sl*) jabón *m*, coba *f*, (*waffle*) paja *f*; —**s** (*trousers*) pantalones *mpl* de franela, (*underclothes*) ropa *f* interior de lana. **2** *adj* de franela. **3** *vt* (*sl*) dar coba a. **4** *vi* (*sl*) llenar muchos renglones (*etc*) sin decir nada de valor.

flannelette [,flænə'let] *n* moletón *m*.

flap [flæp] **1** *n* (**a**) (*on dress*) faldilla *f*; (*of pocket*) cartera *f*; (*of envelope*) solapa *f*; (*of table*) hoja *f* plegadiza; (*of counter*) trampa *f*; (*of skin*) colgajo *m*; (*Aer*) flap *m*.
(**b**) (*of wing*) aletazo *m*, movimiento *m*.
(**c**) (*fam*) (*crisis*) crisis *f*; (*row*) lío *m*; **there's a big** — **on** hay una crisis; se ha armado un lío

imponente; **to get into a** — ponerse nervioso, inquietarse.

2 *vt* **wings** batir; (*shake*) sacudir; **arms** agitar.
3 *vi* (*wings*) aletear; (*sail*) sacudirse; (*flag etc*) ondear, agitarse; (*fam*) ponerse nervioso, inquietarse; **don't** —! ¡con calma!

flapjack ['flæpdʒæk] *n* hojuela *f*.

flare [fleə*] **1** *n* (**a**) (*blaze*) llamarada *f*; (*signal*) cohete *m* de señales, (*Mil*) bengala *f*, proyectil *m* de iluminación; **landing** — bengala *f* de aterrizaje; **solar** — erupción *f* solar.
(**b**) (*Sew*) vuelo *m*.
2 *vt* (*Sew*) abocinar, acampanar.
3 *vi* (**a**) (*blaze*) llamear, resplandecer, fulgurar; (*shine*) brillar; **to** — **up** encenderse.
(**b**) **to** — **up** (*fig: person*) encolerizarse; (*revolt etc*) estallar; (*epidemic*) declararse.
(**c**) (*skirt*) acampanarse.

flare path ['fleəpɑːθ] *n*, *pl* — **paths** [pɑːðz] baliza *f*.

flare-up ['fleərʌp] *n* (*fig: of anger*) arranque *m* de cólera; (*quarrel*) riña *f*; (*of trouble*) manifestación *f* súbita, estallido *m*.

flash [flæʃ] **1** *n* (**a**) (*of light*) relámpago *m*; destello *m*, ráfaga *f*; (*of gun*) fogonazo *m*; — **of lightning** relámpago *m*; **like a** — como un relámpago.
(**b**) (*moment*) instante *m*; **in a** — en un instante.
(**c**) — **of inspiration** ráfaga *f* de inspiración; — **of wit** rasgo *m* de ingenio; — **in the pan** esfuerzo *m* abortado, éxito *m* único; **it was just a** — **in the pan** eso fue un éxito excepcional que no se puede repetir.
(**d**) (*news-*) flash *m*, noticia *f* de última hora; mensaje *m* urgente.
(**e**) (*Phot*) flash *m*, magnesio *m*.
2 *vt* (**a**) *light* despedir, lanzar; *look* dirigir, lanzar (*rápidamente*); *message* transmitir por heliógrafo, transmitir por radio, (*fig*) transmitir rápidamente.
(**b**) (*torch*) encender; — **it this way** proyéctala por aquí; **he** —**ed the light in my eyes** hizo brillar la luz delante de mis ojos.
(**c**) **to** — **something about** sacar algo a relucir, hacer ostentación de algo.
3 *vi* relampaguear, destellar; (*window, reflection*) brillar; **to** — **past** pasar como un rayo.

flashback ['flæʃbæk] *n* escena *f* retrospectiva.

flash bulb ['flæʃbʌlb] *n* bombilla *f* fusible.

flashlight ['flæʃlait] *n* (*Phot*) flash *m*; (*torch*) linterna *f* eléctrica.

flash point ['flæʃpɔint] *n* punto *m* de inflamación.

flashy ['flæʃi] *adj* *jewel etc* de relumbrón; *car etc* ostentoso; *person* charro, chulo.

flask [flɑːsk] *n* frasco *m*; redoma *f*; (*vacuum-*) termo *m*, termos *m*; (*Chem*) matraz *m*.

flat [flæt] **1** *adj* (**a**) (*level*) *countryside etc* llano; *object* plano; horizontal; (*smooth*) liso, igual; *tyre* desinflado; *foot* plano; *nose* chato; *finish, surface* mate; *rate* uniforme, igual; **400 metres** — 400 metros lisos; **as** — **as a pancake** *countryside* totalmente llano, (*after bombing*) desnudo como la palma de la mano; **the town was just** — la ciudad quedó totalmente arrasada.
(**b**) (*downright*) terminante, categórico; **and that's** — no hay más que decir.
(**c**) (*Mus*) *voice, instrument* desafinado; *key* bemol; **E** — **major** mi bemol mayor.
(**d**) (*dull, lifeless*) *taste, style* insípido, soso; *drink* muerto; *battery* descargado; *tone* monótono; *lecture etc* aburrido, pesado; *business* flojo; *feeling of abatimiento*; **to be feeling rather** — sentirse algo deprimido.
2 *adv* (**a**) **to fall** — (*on one's face*) caer de bruces, caer de boca; **to fall** — (*joke*) caer mal, no hacer gracia a uno, (*suggestion*) caer en el vacío; **to be lying down** — estar tendido; **to put something** — **on the table** extender algo sobre la mesa.
(**b**) (*Mus*) **to sing** —, **to play** — desafinar.
(**c**) **to be** — **broke** no tener ni un céntimo; **to go** — **out** ir a máxima velocidad; **to go** — **out for something** tratar de conseguir algo por todos los medios; **to turn something down** — rechazar algo de plano.
3 *n* (*rooms*) piso *m*, apartamento *m*; (*of hand*) palma *f*; (*of sword*) plano *m*; (*Mus*) bemol *m*; (*Aut, esp US*) pinchazo *m*, neumático *m* pinchado.

flat-chested ['flæt'tʃestid] *adj* de pecho plano.

flatfish ['flætfiʃ] *n* pez *m* pleuronecto (*eg* platija, lenguado).

flatfooted ['flæt'futid] *adj* que tiene los pies planos; (*fig*) torpe, desmañado.

flatiron ['flæt,aiən] *n* plancha *f*.

flatlet ['flætlit] *n* piso *m* pequeño.

flatly ['flætli] *adv refuse etc* de plano; *deny* terminantemente; **we are — opposed to** quedamos totalmente opuestos a.

flatness ['flætnis] *n* llanura *f*, lo llano; (*fig*) insipidez *f*, monotonía *f*, aburrimiento *m*.

flatten ['flætn] **1** *vt* (*also to — out*) allanar, aplanar; (*smoothe*) alisar; *map etc* extender; *house, city* aplastar; (*fig*) desconcertar, aplastar.
2 *vi*: **to — out** (*Aer*) enderezarse.
3 *vr*: **to — oneself against a wall** aplanarse contra una pared.

flatter ['flætə*] **1** *vt* adular, lisonjear, halagar; (*photo, clothes etc*) favorecer.
2 *vr*: **to — oneself** felicitarse, congratularse (*on* de, *that* de que); **you — yourself!** ¡presumido!

flatterer ['flætərə*] *n* adulador *m*, ora *f*.

flattering ['flætəriŋ] *adj* lisonjero; halagüeño; *photo, clothes etc* que favorece.

flatteringly ['flætəriŋli] *adv speak etc* en términos lisonjeros.

flattery ['flætəri] *n* adulación *f*, lisonja *f*.

flatulence ['flætjuləns] *n* flatulencia *f*; (*fig*) hinchazón *f*.

flatulent ['flætjulənt] *adj* flatulento; (*fig*) hinchado.

flaunt [flɔ:nt] **1** *vt* ostentar, lucir; hacer gala de. **2** *vr*: **to — oneself** pavonearse.

flautist ['flɔ:tist] *n* flautista *mf*, flauta *m*.

flavour, (US) **flavor** ['fleivə*] **1** *n* sabor *m* (*of* a), gusto *m*; (*flavouring*) condimento *m*; **with a banana —** con sabor a plátano.
2 *vt* sazonar, condimentar (*with* con); (*fig*) dar un sabor característico a; **—ed with** con sabor a.

flavouring, (US) **flavoring** ['fleivəriŋ] *n* condimento *m*.

flavourless, (US) **flavorless** ['fleivəlis] *adj* insípido, soso.

flaw [flɔ:] *n* desperfecto *m*, imperfección *f*; (*crack*) grieta *f*; (*in character, scheme, case etc*) defecto *m*.

flawless ['flɔ:lis] *adj* intachable, impecable.

flax [flæks] *n* lino *m*.

flaxen ['flæksən] *adj hair* muy rubio.

flay [flei] *vt* desollar; (*fig: beat*) azotar, (*defeat*) cascar, (*criticize*) despellejar.

flea [fli:] *n* pulga *f*; **to send someone away with a — in his ear** echar a uno con cajas destempladas.

fleabite ['fli:bait] *n* picadura *f* de pulga; (*fig*) pérdida *f* insignificante.

flea-pit ['fli:pit] *n* (*fam*) cine *m* de bajísima categoría.

fleck [flek] **1** *n* punto *m*, mancha *f*. **2** *vt* puntear, salpicar (*with* de).

fled [fled] *pret and ptp of* **flee**.

fledged [fledʒd] *adj* plumado; **fully —** (*fig*) hecho y derecho.

fledgeling ['fledʒliŋ] *n* volantón *m*, pajarito *m*.

flee [fli:] (*irr: pret and ptp* **fled**) **1** *vt* (*escape from*) huir de, abandonar; (*shun*) evitar. **2** *vi* huir (*from* de), fugarse (*to* a); (*vanish*) desaparecer.

fleece [fli:s] **1** *n* vellón *m*; lana *f*; **Golden F—** Vellocino *m* de Oro. **2** *vt* esquilar; (*fig*) pelar, mondar.

fleecy ['fli:si] *adj* lanudo; *cloud* aborregado.

fleet[1] [fli:t] *n* (*Naut, Aer*) flota *f*; (*of cars*) escuadra *f*; **the British —** la armada inglesa.

fleet[2] [fli:t] *adj*, **fleet-footed** ['fli:t'futid] *adj* veloz, ligero.

fleeting ['fli:tiŋ] *adj* fugaz, efímero, pasajero; *moment* breve.

Fleming ['flemiŋ] *n* flamenco *m*, a *f*.

Flemish ['flemiʃ] **1** *adj* flamenco. **2** *n* (*language*) flamenco *m*.

flesh [fleʃ] *n* carne *f* (*also fig*); (*of fruit*) pulpa *f*; **in the — en persona**; **of — and blood** de carne y hueso; **my own — and blood** mi familia, mis parientes; **it was more than — and blood could stand** era inaguantable; **to go the way of all —** acabar como todo el género humano; **to put on —** echar carnes; *see* **creep**.

flesh colour ['fleʃ,kʌlə*] *n* color *m* de carne.

flesh-coloured ['fleʃ,kʌləd] *adj* encarnado, color de carne.

fleshpots ['fleʃpɒts] *npl* ollas *fpl*.

flesh wound ['fleʃwu:nd] *n* herida *f* superficial.

fleshy ['fleʃi] *adj* (*fat*) gordo; (*Bot etc*) carnoso.

flew [flu:] *pret of* **fly**.

flex [fleks] **1** *n* flexible *m*, hilo *m*, cordón *m* (de la luz). **2** *vt* doblar. **3** *vi* doblarse.

flexibility ['fleksi'biliti] *n* flexibilidad *f* (*also fig*).

flexible ['fleksəbl] *adj* flexible (*also fig*).

flexion ['flekʃən] *n* flexión *f*.

flibbertigibbet ['flibəti'dʒibit] *n* casquivano *m*, a *f*.

flick [flik] **1** *n* (*blow*) golpecito *m* rápido; (*with finger*) capirotazo *m*; (*of whip*) chasquido *m*; (*sl*) película *f*; **—s** (*sl*) cine *m*; **with a — of the wrist** con un movimiento rápido de la muñeca.

2 *vt* (*strike*) dar un golpecito a; (*touch in passing*) rozar levemente; (*with finger*) dar un capirotazo a; *whip* chasquear; **to — something with a whip** dar algo ligeramente con el látigo; **to — something away** quitar algo con un movimiento rápido; **to — over the pages** hojear rápidamente las páginas.

flicker ['flikə*] **1** *n* parpadeo *m*; **without a — of** sin la menor señal de.
2 *vi* (*light*) parpadear, (*on going out*) brillar con luz mortecina; (*flame*) vacilar; (*snake's tongue etc*) vibrar.

flier ['flaiə*] *n* aviador *m*, ora *f*.

flight [flait] *n* (**a**) (*flying*) vuelo *m*; (*of bullet*) trayectoria *f*; (*distance flown*) recorrido *m*; (*group of birds*) bandada *f*; (*unit*) escuadrilla *f*; **orbital —** vuelo *m* orbital; **reconnaissance —** vuelo *m* de reconocimiento; **— of fancy** sueño *m*, ilusión *f*; **to be in the first —** ser de primera categoría; **to take —** alzar el vuelo.
(**b**) (*escape*) huida *f*, fuga *f*; **— of capital** evasión *f* de capitales; **to be in full —** huir en desorden; **to put to —** ahuyentar, (*Mil*) poner en fuga; **to take to —** darse a la fuga.
(**c**) **— of steps** tramo *m*, escalera *f*; **we live 3 —s up** vivimos 3 pisos más arriba.

flight deck ['flaitdek] *n* cubierta *f* de vuelo.

flighty ['flaiti] *adj* frívolo, poco serio; caprichoso, inconstante; travieso; coqueta.

flimsily ['flimzili] *adv* débilmente; muy delgadamente, muy ligeramente; de modo diáfano; **— covered** ligeramente cubierto.

flimsiness ['flimzinis] *n* debilidad *f*, endeblez *f*; delgadez *f*, ligereza *f*; diafanidad *f*; lo baladí.

flimsy ['flimzi] *adj* (*weak*) débil, endeble; (*thin*) muy delgado, muy ligero; *cloth* diáfano; *excuse* baladí.

flinch [flintʃ] *vi* acobardarse, arredrarse, retroceder (*from* ante), encogerse de miedo; **without —ing** sin vacilar.

fling [fliŋ] **1** *n* (**a**) **to go on a —** echar una cana al aire; **to have one's —** correrla; **youth will have its —** los jóvenes se rebelan de vez en cuando; **to have a — at something** intentar algo.
(**b**) **highland —** cierto baile escocés.
2 (*irr: pret and ptp* **flung**) *vt* arrojar, tirar, lanzar; *rider* tirar al suelo; **to — someone into jail** encarcelar a uno; **to — one's arms round someone** echar los brazos encima a uno; **to — about** esparcir; **to — away** tirar, *opportunity etc* desperdiciar; **to — back** *ball* devolver, *head* echar atrás; **to — down** tirar al suelo, *building etc* derribar; **to — off** *dress* quitarse de golpe; **to — open** abrir de golpe; **to — out** echar; **to — out an arm** extender repentinamente un brazo; **to — over** tirar; **to — up** (*fig*) renunciar a.
3 *vi*: **to — out** salir muy enfadado.
4 *vr*: **to — oneself** arrojarse, precipitarse; **to — oneself down** tirarse al suelo; **to — oneself on someone** echarse sobre uno; **to — oneself over a cliff** despeñarse por un precipicio.

flint [flint] *n* pedernal *m* (*of lighter*) piedra *f*; **— axe** hacha *f* de sílex.

flinty ['flinti] *adj* (*fig*) empedernido.

flip [flip] **1** *n* capirotazo *m*; (*Aer: fam*) vuelo *m*.
2 *vt* (*with fingers*) echar de un capirotazo; (*jerk*) mover de un tirón; *coin* echar a cara o cruz; **to — open** abrir con un movimiento rápido.

flippancy ['flipənsi] *n* falta *f* de seriedad, ligereza *f*.

flippant ['flipənt] *adj* poco serio, ligero.

flippantly ['flipəntli] *adv* con poca seriedad, ligeramente.

flipper ['flipə*] *n* aleta *f* (*also sl*).

flirt [flɜ:t] **1** *n* mariposón *m*, coqueta *f*; **she's a great —** es terriblemente coqueta.
2 *vi* flirtear, coquetear (*with* con), mariposear; **to — with** (*fig*) jugar con, entretenerse con; **to — with death** jugar con la muerte; **to — with an idea** acariciar una idea con poca seriedad.

flirtation [flɜ:'teiʃən] *n* flirteo *m*; **to have a — with someone** tener un amorío con uno.

flirtatious [flɜ:'teiʃəs] *adj man* mariposón, *woman* coqueta; *glance etc* coqueta.

flit [flit] *vi* revolotear, volar con vuelo cortado; (*before eyes etc*) pasar rápidamente; (*fam*) mudarse a la chita callando.

flitch [flitʃ] *n*: **— of bacon** hoja *f* de tocino.

float [fləut] **1** *n* (*Fishing*) corcho *m*; (*of seaplane etc*) pontón *m*, flotador *m*; (*in procession*) carroza *f*.
2 *vt* hacer flotar; (*refloat*) poner a flote; *company* lanzar, fundar; *share issue, loan* emitir.
3 *vi* flotar; (*bather*) hacer la plancha; (*flag, hair*) ondear; **it —ed to the surface** salió a la superficie.

floating ['fləutiŋ] *adj object, population etc* flotante; *voter* indeciso.

flock [flɔk] **1** n (Agr etc) rebaño m; (of birds) bandada f; (Eccl) grey f; (of people) multitud f, tropel m; **they came in —s** acudieron en tropel.

2 vi congregarse, reunirse (also **to — together**); **to — about someone** reunirse en torno de uno; **to — to** acudir en tropel a.

floe [fləu] n témpano m de hielo.

flog [flɔg] vt azotar.

flogging ['flɔgiŋ] n azotaina f, paliza f.

flood [flʌd] **1** n inundación f; (in river) avenida f; (tide) pleamar f, flujo m; (fig) torrente m, diluvio m; **the F—** el Diluvio; **a — of letters** una riada de cartas; **a — of light** un torrente de luz; **to be in —** estar crecido; **to weep —s of tears** llorar a mares.

2 vt inundar, anegar; **to — the market with something** inundar el mercado de algo; **we are —ed with applications** tenemos montones de solicitudes; **ten families were —ed out** diez familias tuvieron que abandonar sus casas debido a la inundación.

3 vi desbordar; **to come —ing in** (people) entrar a raudales, (applications) llegar a montones.

floodgate ['flʌdgeit] n compuerta f, esclusa f.

flooding ['flʌdiŋ] n inundación f.

floodlight ['flʌdlait] **1** n foco m. **2** vt iluminar con focos.

floodlighting ['flʌdlaitiŋ] n iluminación f con focos.

floodtide ['flʌdtaid] n pleamar f, marea f creciente.

floor [flɔ:*] **1** n (a) suelo m; (of sea etc) fondo m; (dance-) pista f; **to cross the —** (of the House) atravesar la sala; **to have the —** tener la palabra; **to take the —** salir a bailar, (fig) salir a palestra; **to wipe the — with** (fam) cascar.

(b) (storey) piso m; **ground — planta** f baja; **first — primer** piso m, (US) planta f baja; **second — segundo** piso m, (US) primer piso m; **top — piso** m alto.

2 vt (a) room solar, entarimar (with de).

(b) person derribar; (fig) dejar sin réplica posible, confundir.

floorboard ['flɔ:bɔ:d] n tabla f (del suelo).

floorcloth ['flɔ:klɔθ] n bayeta f.

floor polish ['flɔ:.pɔliʃ] n cera f (para suelos).

floor show ['flɔ:ʃəu] n espectáculo m de cabaret, atracciones fpl (en la pista de baile).

floorwalker ['flɔ:.wɔ:kə*] n (Comm) superintendente m de división.

flop [flɔp] **1** n (fam) fracaso m; (Theat) caída f; **it was an awful —** fue un rotundo fracaso.

2 vi dejarse caer pesadamente (into en); (fam) fracasar, (Theat) venirse al foso.

flophouse ['flɔphaus] n, pl **—houses** [.hauziz] (US) pensión f de bajísima categoría.

floppy ['flɔpi] adj flojo, colgante.

flora ['flɔ:rə] n flora f.

floral ['flɔ:rəl] adj floral; tribute etc de flores.

Florence ['flɔrəns] Florencia.

Florentine ['flɔrəntain] **1** adj florentino. **2** n florentino, a f.

florescence [flə'resns] n florescencia f.

florid ['flɔrid] adj florido (also Liι etc); complexion rojizo, subido de color.

florin ['flɔrin] n florín m; (British) moneda f de 2 chelines.

florist ['flɔrist] n florista mf; **—'s (shop)** floristería f, florería f.

floss [flɔs] n (also **— silk**) cadarzo m; seda f floja.

flotilla [flə'tilə] n flotilla f.

flotsam ['flɔtsəm] n pecios mpl, restos mpl flotantes; **— and jetsam** (fig) restos mpl, desechos mpl.

flounce[1] [flauns] n (Sew) volante m.

flounce[2] [flauns] vi: **to — about** moverse violentamente; **to — away, to — off** alejarse exagerando los movimientos del cuerpo; **to — out** salir enfadado.

flounced [flaunst] adj dress guarnecido con volantes.

flounder[1] ['flaundə*] n (Fish) (especie de) platija f.

flounder[2] ['flaundə*] vi (in a speech etc) tropezar, perder el hilo, no saber qué decir; **to — about** revolcarse, debatirse, forcejear.

flour ['flauə*] **1** n harina f. **2** vt enharinar.

flour-bin ['flauəbin] n harinero m.

flourish ['flʌriʃ] **1** n (a) (with pen) rasgo m, plumada f; (on signature) rúbrica f; (of hand) movimiento m, ademán m; **to do something with a —** hacer algo con un ademán triunfal.

(b) (Mus: on guitar) floreo m, (fanfare) toque m de trompeta.

2 vt weapon etc blandir; stick etc agitar, menear; (fig) hacer gala de, mostrar orgullosamente.

3 vi florecer, prosperar; (plant etc) crecer rápidamente.

flourishing ['flʌriʃiŋ] adj floreciente, próspero; (Bot) lozano; (healthy) como un reloj.

floury ['flauəri] adj harinoso.

flout [flaut] vt mofarse de, no hacer caso de.

flow [fləu] **1** n (stream) corriente f; (jet) chorro m; (movement) flujo m, movimiento m; (quantity flowing) caudal m, cantidad f; (direction of —) curso m; (of words etc) torrente m; (of dress etc) movimiento m suave, movimiento m elegante; (of music) lo corriente, lo suave; **to have a ready — of words** hablar con soltura; **to maintain a steady —** mantener un movimiento constante.

2 vi fluir, correr (along, down por); (tide) subir, crecer; (hair) ondear (in the wind al viento); (blood, being shed) derramarse, (from wound) manar, correr; **to — away** irse; **to — back** refluir; **tears were —ing down her cheeks** le corrían las lágrimas por las mejillas; **to — from** (fig) provenir de; **money is —ing in** entra el dinero en grandes cantidades; **people are —ing in** entra la gente a raudales; **to — into** river desaguar en, desembocar en; **to — over** desbordarse; **to — past** pasar (delante de); **to — with** abundar en.

flower ['flauə*] **1** n flor f; (fig) flor f, flor f y nata; **in — en** flor; **to say something with —s** comunicar algo a uno enviando flores. **2** vi florecer.

flower bed ['flauəbed] n cuadro m, macizo m.

flowerpot ['flauəpɔt] n tiesto m, maceta f.

flower shop ['flauəʃɔp] n floristería f, florería f.

flower show ['flauəʃəu] n exposición f de flores.

flowery ['flauəri] adj florido (also fig).

flowing ['fləuiŋ] adj movement, stream corriente; hair suelto; style fluido, corriente.

flown [fləun] ptp of **fly**.

flu [flu:] n (fam) gripe f.

fluctuate ['flʌktjueit] vi fluctuar; variar.

fluctuation [.flʌktju'eiʃən] n fluctuación f; variación f.

flue [flu:] n humero m, cañón m de chimenea; (of lamp, boiler) tubo m.

fluency ['flu:ənsi] n fluidez f; elocuencia f, facundia f; **his — in Russian** su dominio del ruso.

fluent ['flu:ənt] adj style fluido, corriente; speaker elocuente, facundo; **he is — in Russian, his Russian is —** domina el ruso.

fluently ['flu:əntli] adv con fluidez, corrientemente; elocuentemente; **he speaks Russian —** domina el ruso.

fluff [flʌf] n pelusa f, lanilla f.

fluffy ['flʌfi] adj velloso, lanudo; hair encrespado; (feathered) plumoso; surface que tiene mucha pelusa.

fluid ['flu:id] **1** adj fluido, líquido; situation inestable; plan flexible. **2** n fluido m, líquido m.

fluidity [flu:'iditi] n fluidez f; inestabilidad f.

fluke[1] [flu:k] n (Zool) trematodo m; (Fish) (especie de) platija f.

fluke[2] [flu:k] n chiripa f, racha f de suerte; **to win by a —** ganar por chiripa.

fluky ['flu:ki] adj afortunado.

flummox ['flʌməks] vt (disconcert) desconcertar, confundir; (startle) asombrar; **I was completely —ed** quedé totalmente despistado.

flung [flʌŋ] pret and ptp of **fling**.

flunk [flʌŋk] (US) **1** vt student suspender; course perder; exam no aprobar, salir mal en.

2 vi ser suspendido; **I —ed me suspendieron; to — out** salir del colegio (etc) sin recibir un título.

flunk(e)y ['flʌŋki] n lacayo m (also fig).

fluorescence [fluə'resns] n fluorescencia f.

fluorescent [fluə'resnt] adj fluorescente.

fluoridation [.fluəri'deiʃən] n fluorización f.

fluoride ['fluəraid] n fluoruro m.

flurry ['flʌri] **1** n (a) (nervous haste) agitación f, estado m nervioso; **a — of activity** un frenesí de actividad; **to be in a —** estar agitado, estar aturrullado.

(b) (of snow etc) ráfaga f.

2 vt agitar, hacer nervioso; **to get flurried** aturrullarse.

flush[1] [flʌʃ] vt game levantar; **to — someone out** hacer que uno salga.

flush[2] [flʌʃ] **1** vt (also **to — out**) limpiar con un chorro de agua; WC hacer funcionar. **2** vi (WC) funcionar.

flush[3] [flʌʃ] **1** n (on face) rubor m; (in sky) arrebol m; (abundance) abundancia f repentina, plenitud f; (of fever) calor m súbito; **in the first — of success** en el momento emocionado del triunfo.

2 vt: **to be —ed with success** estar muy emocionado con el triunfo; **a face —ed with drink** una cara encendida por el alcohol.

3 vi ruborizarse, sonrojarse; (with anger) sofocarse.

flush[4] [flʌʃ] adj (a) (Tech) nivelado, igual, parejo, a ras; **to make two things —** nivelar dos cosas. (b) **to be —** (sl) tener dinero.

flush[5] [flʌʃ] n (Cards) flux m.

Flushing ['flʌʃiŋ] Flesinga.

fluster ['flʌstə*] **1** n confusión f, aturdimiento m; conmoción f; **to be in a —** estar azacaneado.
2 vt aturdir, poner nervioso, aturrullar; **to get —ed** aturrullarse.

flute [fluːt] n flauta f.

fluted ['fluːtid] adj (Archit) estriado, acanalado.

flutter ['flʌtə*] **1** n (of wings) revoloteo m, aleteo m, movimiento m; (of eyelashes) pestañeo m; (excitement) emoción f, agitación f, conmoción f; (fam) apuesta f; **to cause a —** agitar los espíritus.
2 vt agitar, menear, mover ligeramente; (fig) agitar.
3 vi (bird etc) revolotear, aletear; (butterfly) mover ligeramente las alas; (flag) ondear; (heart) palpitar; **a leaf came —ing down** cayó balanceándose una hoja.

fluty ['fluːti] adj tone aflautado.

flux [flʌks] n (flow) flujo m; **to be in a state of —** estar continuamente cambiando.

fly [flai] **1** n mosca f; (of trousers, also **flies**) bragueta f; (carriage) calesa f; **flies** (Theat) bambalinas fpl; **Spanish —** cantárida f; **there's a — in the ointment** existe una dificultad; **he's the — in the ointment** él es el estorbo; **there are no flies on him** es muy listo; **to fish with a —** pescar a mosca.
2 adj avispado, despabilado.
3 (irr: pret **flew**, ptp **flown**) vt hacer volar; plane pilotar, dirigir; passengers, goods etc transportar (en avión); ocean etc atravesar (en avión); distance recorrer (en avión); flag llevar, tener izado; danger huir (de); country abandonar, salir de.
4 vi (a) volar; (travel by air) ir en avión; (fly a plane) pilotar un avión; (flag) estar izado, ondear; **to send something —ing** echar algo a rodar; **to — into pieces** hacerse pedazos; **to — away** irse volando; **to — in** llegar (en avión); **to — into London Airport** llegar en avión al aeropuerto de Londres; **to — off** (bird, insect) alejarse volando, (in plane) partir en avión, (part) desprenderse, separarse; **to — open** abrirse de repente; **to — over Rome** sobrevolar Roma; **to let — (shoot)** tirar, disparar, hacer fuego; (emotionally) desahogarse; (verbally) empezar a proferir insultos (etc); **to let — at (shoot)** tirar sobre, disparar contra, (emotionally) desahogarse criticando, (verbally) empezar a llenar de injurias.
(b) (rush) lanzarse, precipitarse; **I must —** tengo que darme prisa; **to — at someone** lanzarse sobre uno, (fig) ponerse furioso con uno; **to — into a rage** encolerizarse; **to — to someone's help** correr a socorrer a uno; **to — to someone's side** volar hacia el lado de uno.
(c) (escape) evadirse, huir (from de); (vanish) desaparecer; **to — for one's life** salvar la vida huyendo.

fly-by-night ['flaibainait] **1** adj frívolo; poco serio, nada confiable. **2** n persona f frívola, casquivano m, a f; persona f nada confiable.

flycatcher ['flai,kætʃə*] n papamoscas m.

fly fishing ['flai,fiʃiŋ] n pesca f a mosca.

flying ['flaiiŋ] adj volante, volador; (swift) rápido, veloz; visit muy breve.

flying boat ['flaiiŋbəut] n hidroavión m.

flying bomb ['flaiiŋbɔm] n bomba f volante.

Flying Dutchman ['flaiiŋ'dʌtʃmən] el Buque fantasma.

flying fish ['flaiiŋ'fiʃ] n pez m volador.

flying machine ['flaiiŋmə,ʃiːn] n avión m.

flying time ['flaiiŋ'taim] n horas fpl de vuelo, duración f del vuelo.

flyleaf ['flailiːf] n, pl **—leaves** [liːvz] hoja f de guarda.

flyover ['flai,əuvə*] n paso m superior.

flypaper [flai,peipə*] n papel m matamoscas.

flyswat(ter) ['flaiswɔt(ə*)] n palmeta f matamoscas.

flyweight ['flaiweit] n peso m mosca.

flywheel ['flaiwiːl] n volante m (de motor).

foal [fəul] **1** n potro m, a f. **2** vi parir (la yegua).

foam [fəum] **1** n espuma f. **2** vi espumar, echar espuma; **to — at the mouth** espumajear.

foam rubber ['fəum'rʌbə*] n espuma f de caucho.

foamy ['fəumi] adj espumoso.

fob [fɔb] vt: **to — someone off** apartar a uno de un propósito con excusas; **to — someone off with something** persuadir a uno a aceptar algo (de modo fraudulento).

focal ['fəukəl] adj focal.

focus ['fəukəs] **1** n foco m; (of attention etc) centro m; **to be in —** estar enfocado; **to be out of —** estar desenfocado.
2 vt enfocar (on a); attention etc fijar, concentrar (on en); **all eyes were —sed on him** todos le miraban fijamente.
3 vi enfocar(se); **to — on** enfocar a.

fodder ['fɔdə*] n pienso m, forraje m.

foe [fəu] n (lit) enemigo m.

foetus ['fiːtəs] n feto m.

fog [fɔg] **1** n niebla f; (fig) confusión f. **2** vt (fig) matter entenebrecer; person ofuscar; (Phot) velar.

fogbound ['fɔgbaund] adj inmovilizado por la niebla.

fogey ['fəugi] n: **old —** persona f de ideas anticuadas, persona f chapada a la antigua.

foggy ['fɔgi] adj nebuloso, brumoso; day de niebla; (Phot) velado; **it is —** hay niebla; **I haven't the foggiest (idea)** no tengo la más remota idea.

foghorn ['fɔghɔːn] n sirena f (de niebla).

foible ['fɔibl] n flaco m; manía f.

foil[1] [fɔil] n (metal) hoja f, hojuela f; (fig) contraste m (to con); **to act as a — to something** servir de contraste con algo, hacer resaltar algo.

foil[2] [fɔil] vt frustrar.

foil[3] [fɔil] n (Fencing) florete m.

foist [fɔist] **1** vt: **to — something off on someone** encajar algo a uno, lograr con engaño que uno acepte algo; **the job was —ed on to me** lograron mañosamente que yo me encargara de ello.
2 vr: **to — oneself on someone** insistir en acompañar a uno, pegarse a uno.

fold[1] [fəuld] n (Agr) redil m, aprisco m; **to return to the — (Eccl)** volver al redil de la Iglesia.

fold[2] [fəuld] **1** n pliegue m, doblez m, arruga f; (Geol) pliegue m.
2 vt plegar, doblar; wings recoger; **to — one's arms** cruzar los brazos; **to — back, to — down** doblar hacia abajo; **to — someone in one's arms** abrazar a uno tiernamente, estrechar a uno contra el pecho; **to — something in a wrapper** envolver algo en una envoltura; **to — up** doblar, chair etc plegar.
3 vi plegarse, doblarse; **it —s down at night** de noche se dobla hacia abajo; **to — up** doblarse, plegarse; (fig) fracasar, terminar; (Comm) quebrar, entrar en liquidación.

folder ['fəuldə*] n (file) carpeta f; (brochure) folleto m; (of matches) carterita f.

folding ['fəuldiŋ] adj plegable, plegadizo; de tijera.

folding chair ['fəuldiŋ'tʃeə*] adj silla f de tijera.

folding doors ['fəuldiŋ'dɔːz] npl puertas fpl plegadizas.

folding table ['fəuldiŋ'teibl] n mesa f plegable.

foliage ['fəuliidʒ] n hojas fpl, follaje m.

foliation [,fəuli'eiʃən] n foliación f.

folio ['fəuliəu] n folio m; (book) infolio m, libro m en folio.

folk [fəuk] n (a) (tribe) nación f, tribu f, pueblo m.
(b) (people in general; also **—s**) gente f; **my —s** mi familia, mis parientes; **the old —s** los viejos; **hullo —s!** ¡hola, amigos!; **they're strange — here** aquí la gente es algo rara.

folk dance ['fəukdɑːns] n baile m popular, danza f tradicional.

folklore ['fəuklɔː*] n folklore m.

folk singer ['fəuk,siŋə*] n cantante mf folklorista.

folksong ['fəuksɔŋ] n canción f popular, canción f tradicional.

folksy ['fəuksi] adj (fam) afectadamente folklorista; que finge ser popular (or tradicional etc), que se esfuerza por parecer que es del pueblo.

folk tale ['fəukteil] n cuento m popular.

follow ['fɔləu] **1** vt (a) (general sense) seguir; suspect etc seguir la pista a; (pursue) perseguir; **there's someone —ing us** alguien nos viene siguiendo; **the road —s the coast** la carretera va por la costa; **to — someone into a room** entrar en una habitación detrás de uno; **they —ed this with threats** tras esto empezaron a amenazarnos; **to — someone about** seguir a uno por todas partes; **to — through, to — up** shot terminar, completar; plan llevar hasta el fin; clue investigar; matter perseguir; suggestion adoptar.
(b) advice, example seguir; person imitar el ejemplo de; instructions seguir; news estar al corriente de, estar enterado de; **do you — football?** ¿le interesa el fútbol?
(c) profession ejercer.
(d) (understand) person comprender, argument seguir el hilo de.
2 vi (a) seguir; **we'll — on behind** vendremos después.
(b) seguirse; resultar; **as —s** como sigue, a saber; **it —s that** síguese que, resulta que; **it doesn't — at all that . . .** no es lógico que . . . + subj; **it —s on from what I said** es la consecuencia lógica de lo que dije.

follower ['fɔləuə*] n (Pol etc) partidario m, a f, adherente mf; (Sport) seguidor m, hincha m; (pej) secuaz *mf*; (*Philos etc*) discípulo *m*; (*imitator*) imitador *m*, ora *f*; —s (*of prince etc*) séquito *m*; **all the** —**s of football** todos los que se interesan por el fútbol; **the** —**s of fashion** los que siguen la moda.

following ['fɔləuiŋ] **1** *adj* siguiente; *wind* en popa; **the** — lo siguiente.

2 *n* (*Pol etc*) partidarios *mpl*, (*pej*) secuaces *mpl*; (*of prince etc*) séquito *m*; **football has no** — **here** aquí nadie se interesa por el fútbol.

follow-through ['fɔləu'θru:] *n* continuación *f*.

follow-up ['fɔləu'ʌp] *adj*: — **interview** entrevista *f* complementaria; — **letter** carta *f* recordativa.

folly ['fɔli] *n* locura *f*.

foment [fəu'ment] *vt* fomentar (*also Med*); *revolt etc* provocar, instigar.

fomentation [,fəumen'teiʃən] *n* fomentación *f*; fomento *m*.

fond [fɔnd] *adj* (*loving*) cariñoso, afectuoso; (*doting*) demasiado indulgente; *hope* fervoroso; **to be** — **of** *thing* ser aficionado a, tener afición a; *person* tener mucho cariño a; **to be** — **of** + *ger* ser aficionado a + *infin*; **to become** (*or* **grow**) — **of** *thing* aficionarse a, *person* tomar cariño a.

fondle ['fɔndl] *vt* acariciar.

fondly ['fɔndli] *adv* con cariño, afectuosamente; *hope* fervorosamente; *imagine* inocentemente.

fondness ['fɔndnis] *n* cariño *m*; afición *f* (*for* a).

font [fɔnt] *n* pila *f* (*bautismal*); (*Typ*) fundición *f*.

food [fu:d] *n* alimento *m*, comida *f*; (*edible matter*) comestible *m*; (*for animals*) pasto *m*, pienso *m*; **to buy** — comprar víveres, comprar provisiones; **the** — **is good here** aquí se come bien; **the cost of** — el coste de la alimentación; **she gave him** — **le dio de comer**; **he likes plain** — le gustan las comidas sencillas; **to send** — **and clothing** enviar comestibles y ropa; **to be off one's** — no tener apetito; **to give someone** — **for thought** dar a uno en qué pensar, dar a uno un tema de meditación.

food poisoning ['fu:d,pɔizniŋ] *n* botulismo *m*, intoxicación *f* alimenticia.

foodstuffs ['fu:dstʌfs] *npl* comestibles *mpl*, artículos *mpl* alimenticios.

food value ['fu:d,vælju:] *n* valor *m* alimenticio.

fool [fu:l] **1** *n* tonto *m*, a *f*, imbécil *mf*; (*jester*) bufón *m*; **you** —! ¡imbécil!; **some** — **of a minister** algún ministro imbécil; **he's nobody's** — no se deja engañar por nadie; **to be** — **enough to** + *infin* ser bastante tonto como para + *infin*; **don't be a** —! ¡no seas tonto!, ¡déjate de tonterías!; **to act** (*or* **play**) **the** — hacer el tonto; **to live in a** —**'s paradise** vivir en un mundo de sueños, imaginarse una novela; **to make a** — **of someone** poner a uno en ridículo, engañar a uno; **to make a** — **of oneself** ponerse en ridículo; **to send someone on a** —**'s errand** enviar a uno a una misión inútil.

2 *adj* (*US*) tonto.

3 *vt* (*deceive*) engañar, embaucar; (*puzzle*) confundir, dejar perplejo; **you can't** — **me** a mí no me engaña nadie; **you had me properly** —**ed there** eso sí que me despistó; **that** —**ed nobody** no se dejó engañar nadie por eso; **to** — **away** *time* perder ociosamente, *money* despilfarrar.

4 *vi* chancear, bromear; **no** —**ing** en serio; **I was only** —**ing** lo dije en broma; **quit** —**ing**! ¡déjate de tonterías!; **to** — **about** divertirse, juguetear; hacer el tonto; **to** — **about with** jugar con, (*and damage*) estropear; **to** — **around** perder el tiempo neciamente.

foolery ['fu:ləri] *n* bufonadas *fpl*; (*nonsense*) tonterías *fpl*.

foolhardy ['fu:l,hɑ:di] *adj* temerario.

foolish ['fu:liʃ] *adj* tonto, necio; imbécil; ridículo; absurdo; estúpido; imprudente; — **thing** tontería *f*; **don't be** — no seas tonto; **that was very** — **of you** en eso fuiste muy imprudente; **I felt very** — creí haberme puesto en ridículo; **to make someone look** — hacer que uno parezca ridículo.

foolishly ['fu:liʃli] *adv* tontamente, neciamente;—, **I agreed** como un tonto consentí.

foolishness ['fu:liʃnis] *n* tontería *f*, necedad *f*; imbecilidad *f*; ridiculez *f*; estupidez *f*; imprudencia *f*.

foolproof ['fu:lpru:f] *adj* (*Tech*) a prueba de impericia; *scheme etc* de éxito seguro, infalible.

foolscap ['fu:lskæp] *n* (*approx*) papel *m* tamaño folio.

foot [fut] **1** *n*, *pl* **feet** [fi:t] pie *m*; (*of animal, furniture*) pata *f*; (*of hill, page, stairs etc*) pie *m*; (*measure*) pie *m*; **at the** — **of the hill** al pie de la colina; **he's on his feet all day long** está trajinando todo el santo día, no descansa en todo el día; **he's on his feet again** ha vuelto a levantarse y a salir; **it's wet under** — el suelo está mojado; **to come** (*or* **go**) **on** — venir (*or* ir) a pie, venir (*or* ir) andando; **to drag one's feet** (*fig*)

echarse atrás, hacerse el roncero; **to fall on one's feet** (*fig*) caer de pie; **to find one's feet** acostumbrarse al ambiente; **to get cold feet** encogerse a uno el ombligo; **to get one's** — **in the door** abrirse una brecha; **to have one** — **in the grave** estar con un pie en la sepultura; **to keep one's feet** mantenerse en pie; **to put one's** — **down** (*Aut*) acelerar, (*fig*) adoptar una actitud firme; **to put one's** — **in it** meter la pata; **to put one's best** — **forward** animarse a continuar; hacer lo posible por hacer una buena impresión; **to rise to one's feet** ponerse de pie, levantarse; **to set** — **inside someone's door** poner los pies en la casa de uno, pasar el umbral de uno; **to set something on** — promover algo, poner algo en marcha; **to set** — **on dry land** poner el pie en tierra firme; **to sit at someone's feet** ser discípulo de uno; **to stand on one's own two feet** ser independiente; **to sweep a girl off her feet** enamorar perdidamente a una chica; **to trample something under** — pisotear algo.

2 *vt* bill pagar; **to** — **it** (*walk*) ir andando, (*dance*) bailar.

foot-and-mouth (**disease**) ['futən'mauθ(di'zi:z)] *n* fiebre *f* aftosa, glosopeda *f*.

football ['futbɔ:l] *n* (*game*) fútbol *m*; (*ball*) balón *m*; **association** — fútbol *m* asociación.

footballer ['futbɔ:lə*] *n* futbolista *m*.

football pool ['futbɔ:l,pu:l] *n* quinielas *fpl*.

footboard ['futbɔ:d] *n* estribo *m*.

footbrake ['futbreik] *n* pedal *m* del freno; freno *m* de pie.

footbridge ['futbridʒ] *n* puente *m* para peatones.

-footed ['futid] *adj* de . . . patas, *eg* **four-footed** de cuatro patas; **light-footed** ligero (de pies).

footfall ['futfɔ:l] *n* paso *m*, pisada *f*.

foothills ['futhilz] *npl* estribaciones *fpl*.

foothold ['futhəuld] *n* pie *m* firme, asidero *m* para el pie; **to gain a** — ganar pie, lograr establecerse.

footing ['futiŋ] *n* (**a**) pie *m*; **to lose** (*or* **miss**) **one's** — perder el pie.

(**b**) pie *m*, posición *f*; **on an equal** — en un mismo pie de igualdad (*with* con); **on a friendly** — en relaciones amistosas; **on a war** — en pie de guerra; **to gain a** — ganar pie, lograr establecerse.

footle ['fu:tl] **1** *vt*: **to** — **away** malgastar. **2** *vi* perder el tiempo, hacer el tonto.

footlights ['futlaits] *npl* candilejas *fpl*.

footling ['fu:tliŋ] *adj* trivial, insignificante.

footloose ['futlu:s] *adj* libre; (*wandering*) andariego.

footman ['futmən] *n*, *pl* **-men** [mən] *n* lacayo *m*.

footmark ['futmɑ:k] *n* huella *f*.

footnote ['futnəut] *n* nota *f* (al pie de la página).

footpath ['futpɑ:θ] *n*, *pl* **-paths** [pɑ:ðz] senda *f*, sendero *m*; (*pavement*) acera *f*.

footplate ['futpleit] *n* plataforma *f* del maquinista.

footprint ['futprint] *n* huella *f*.

footrest ['futrest] *n* apoyapié *m*.

footslogger ['futslɔgə*] *n* (*fam*) peatón *m*; (*Mil*) soldado *m* de infantería.

footsore ['futsɔ:*] *adj*: **to be** — tener los pies cansados.

footstep ['futstep] *n* paso *m*, pisada *f*; **to follow in someone's** —**s** seguir los pasos de uno.

footstool ['futstu:l] *n* escabel *m*.

footwear ['futweə*] *n* calzado *m*.

footwork ['futwə:k] *n* (*Sport*) juego *m* de piernas.

fop [fɔp] *n* petimetre *m*, currutaco *m*.

foppish ['fɔpiʃ] *adj* currutaco.

for [fɔ:*] **1** *prep* (**a**) (*destined for*) para; **hats** — **women** sombreros para mujeres; **is this** — **me**? ¿es esto para mí?; **a job** — **next week** un trabajo para la semana que viene; **we went to Tossa** — **our holidays** fuimos a pasar nuestras vacaciones a Tossa, las vacaciones las pasamos en Tossa; **it's time** — **dinner** es hora de comer; **to write** — **the papers** escribir en los periódicos; **I have news** — **you** tengo que darle una noticia; **it was** — **your good** era para (*or* por) su bien.

(**b**) (*as, representing*) por; **member** — **Hove** diputado por Hove; **M** — **Madrid** M de Madrid; **agent** — **Ford cars** distribuidor de automóviles Ford; **will you write** — **me**? ¿quieres escribir en mi nombre?; **I'll go** — **you** yo iré en tu lugar; **if not the government will do it** — **them** si no el gobierno lo hará en su lugar; **they shot him** — **a traitor** le fusilaron por traidor.

(**c**) (*in exchange for*) por; **I'll give you this** — **that** te doy éste por ése; **I sold it** — **£5** lo vendí por 5 libras; **to exchange one's hat** — **another** cambiar el sombrero por otro; **word** — **word** palabra por palabra; **1 dead** — **every 5 injured** 1 muerto por

cada 5 lisiados; **what's the German — "hill"?**
¿cómo se dice en alemán "colina"?

(d) (*in favour of*) **I'm — the government** yo soy partidario del gobierno; **a collection — the poor** una colecta a beneficio de los pobres; **the campaign — education** la campaña pro (*or* en pro de la) enseñanza; **I'm all —** it lo apruebo sin reserva.

(e) (*because of*) por, a causa de, con motivo de, debido a; **— this reason** por esta razón; **famous — its church** famoso por su iglesia; **the reason — not doing it** la razón por no hacerlo; **we chose it — its climate** lo escogimos por su clima; **if it were not — him** si no fuera por él; **to shout — joy** gritar de alegría.

(f) (*purpose*) **what —?** ¿para qué?, ¿por qué?; **what's this —?** ¿para qué sirve esto?

(g) (*bound for*) **he left — Ohio** partió para Ohio; **the ship left — Vigo** el buque partió (con) rumbo a Vigo; **the train — Madrid** el tren de Madrid; **where are you —?** ¿adónde se dirige Vd?

(h) (*considering*) **tall — his age** alto para su edad.

(i) (*in spite of*) **he's nice — a policeman** para policía es muy simpático, a pesar de ser policía es muy simpático; *see* **all.**

(j) **oh — a horse!** ¡quién tuviera un caballo!

(k) (*distance*) **there was nothing to be seen — miles** no había nada que ver en muchos kilómetros.

(l) (*time: past*) **he was away — 2 years** estuvo ausente (durante) 2 años; **was he away — long?** ¿estuvo fuera mucho tiempo?; **it has not rained — 3 weeks** hace 3 semanas que no llueve, desde hace 3 semanas no llueve; **we went to the seaside — the day** fuimos a pasar el día en la playa; (*future*) **I'm going — 3 weeks** voy por 3 semanas; **will it be — long?** ¿será mucho tiempo?

(m) **now — it!** ¡ahora!; ¡ya viene!; **he'll be — it!** ¡le va a tocar la gorda!; **there's nothing — it** no hay más remedio; *see* **but.**

(n) (*with verb clause*) **it is — you to decide** le toca a Vd decidir; **it is best — you to go** más vale que vaya Vd; **it is right — you to go** es justo que vaya Vd; **it's bad — you to smoke so much** te hace daño fumar tanto; **— this to be possible** para que esto sea posible; **— him to fail now would be disastrous** sería terrible que fracasara ahora; **he gave orders — it to be done** mandó que se hiciera, dio instrucciones para que se hiciera.

2 *conj* pues, ya que.

forage ['fɔrɪdʒ] **1** *n* forraje *m*. **2** *vi* forrajear; **to — for** buscar.

foray ['fɔreɪ] *n* correría *f*, incursión *f* (*into* en).

forbad(e) [fɔ'bæd] *pret of* **forbid.**

forbear [fɔ:'bɛə*] (*irr: see* **bear**) *vi* contenerse; tener paciencia; **to — to + infin** abstenerse de + *infin*.

forbearance [fɔ:'bɛərəns] *n* paciencia *f*, dominio *m* sobre sí mismo.

forbears ['fɔ:bɛəz] *npl* antepasados *mpl*.

forbid [fə'bɪd] (*irr: pret* **forbad(e)**, *ptp* **forbidden**) *vt* prohibir; **to — something to someone**, **to — someone something** prohibir algo a uno; **to — someone to do something** prohibir a uno hacer algo; **that's —den** eso está prohibido; **"smoking —den"** "prohibido fumar"; *see* **God.**

forbidden [fə'bɪdn] **1** *ptp of* **forbid. 2** *adj* prohibido.

forbidding [fə'bɪdɪŋ] *adj appearance etc* formidable; (*dismal*) lúgubre; *person's manner* severo.

forbore [fɔ:'bɔ:*] *pret of* **forbear.**

forborne [fɔ:'bɔ:n] *ptp of* **forbear.**

force [fɔ:s] **1** *n* **(a)** fuerza *f*; **brute —** fuerza *f* bruta; **— of gravity** fuerza *f* de gravedad; **I can see the — of that** comprendo la fuerza de ese argumento; **to resort to —** recurrir a la fuerza; **to yield to —** rendirse a la fuerza; **by — a** la fuerza; **by — of** a fuerza de; **by — of circumstances** debido a las circunstancias; **by — of habit** por la fuerza de la costumbre; **by sheer —** por fuerza mayor; **to be in — (***Law*) ser vigente, estar en vigor, (*price*) regir, imperar; **to come in —** venir en gran número.

(b) (*persons*) personal *m*, (*Mil*) cuerpo *m*; **the — la** policía; **a strong — of police** un numeroso cuerpo de policía; **—s** (*Mil*) fuerzas *fpl* armadas; **allied —s** fuerzas *fpl* aliadas; **land —s** fuerzas *fpl* terrestres; **police — la** policía; **sales —** personal *m* de ventas; **to join —s** unir meriendas.

2 *vt* **(a)** (*compel*) forzar, obligar; *door* forzar, violentar, descerrajar; *pace* apresurar; *plant* hacer madurar temprano; (*cause*) hacer; **to — a smile** sonreír forzadamente; **to — a country into war** empujar a un país a que declare la guerra; **to — someone into a corner** arrinconar a uno, hacer que uno quede arrinconado; **to — a car off the road** hacer

que un coche salga de la calzada; **to — someone into bankruptcy** hacer que uno quiebre.

(b) **to — someone to do something** forzar a uno a hacer algo; **I am —d to say** me veo obligado a decir.

(c) **to — back** hacer retroceder; **to — down** hacer bajar; (*Aer*) obligar a aterrizar; *food* tragar por fuerza; **can you — a bit more down?** ¿cabe todavía un poco más?; **to — in** introducir por fuerza; **to — something on someone** imponer algo a uno, forzar a uno a aceptar algo; **the decision was —d on him** se le impuso la decisión; **to — open** forzar, abrir por fuerza; **to — out** hacer salir; empujar hacia fuera; *words* pronunciar con dificultad; **we —d the secret out of him** logramos por fuerza que nos dijera el secreto; **to — a bill through parliament** hacer aprobar por el parlamento un proyecto de ley.

3 *vr*: **to — oneself to + infin** hacer un esfuerzo por + *infin*.

forced [fɔ:st] *adj smile* que no le sale a uno; *laughter* forzado; *landing* forzoso; *march, sale, loan* forzado.

forceful ['fɔ:sful] *adj* enérgico, vigoroso.

forcefully ['fɔ:sfuli] *adv* enérgicamente, vigorosamente.

force majeure ['fɔ:smɑ'ʒɜ:*] *n* fuerza *f* mayor.

forcemeat ['fɔ:smi:t] *n* relleno *m* (de carne picada).

forceps ['fɔ:seps] *n sing and pl* fórceps *m*; pinzas *fpl*, tenacillas *fpl*.

forcible ['fɔ:səbl] *adj* (*done by force*) a la fuerza, a viva fuerza, por fuerza; *feeding* forzoso; (*telling*) enérgico, vigoroso.

forcibly ['fɔ:səbli] *adv* a la fuerza; enérgicamente.

ford [fɔ:d] **1** *n* vado *m*. **2** *vt* vadear.

fordable ['fɔ:dəbl] *adj* vadeable.

fore [fɔ:*] **1** *adv*: **— and aft** de popa a proa, por todas partes.

2 *adj* anterior, delantero; (*Naut*) de proa.

3 *n*: **to be at the —** ir delante; **to come to the —** empezar a destacar.

forearm ['fɔ:rɑ:m] *n* antebrazo *m*.

forebode [fɔ:'bəud] *vt* presagiar, anunciar.

foreboding [fɔ:'bəudɪŋ] *n* presagio *m*; presentimiento *m*; **to have a — that** presentir que; **to have —s** tener una corazonada.

forecast ['fɔ:kɑ:st] **1** *n* pronóstico *m*; previsión *f*; (*in betting*) acierto *m*; **according to all the —s** según todas las previsiones; **what is the — for the weather?** ¿qué pronóstico hacen del tiempo?

2 (*irr: see* **cast**) *vt* pronosticar, prever.

forecastle ['fəuksl] *n* castillo *m* de proa.

foreclose [fɔ:'kləuz] *vti* (*Law*) extinguir el derecho de redimir (una hipoteca).

foredoomed [fɔ:'du:md] *adj*: **to be — to + infin** estar condenado a + *infin*.

forefathers ['fɔ:fɑ:ðəz] *npl* antepasados *mpl*.

forefinger ['fɔ:fɪŋgə*] *n* dedo *m* índice.

forefoot ['fɔ:fut] *n*, *pl* **—feet** [fi:t] pata *f* delantera.

forefront ['fɔ:frʌnt] *n*: **to be in the —** estar en la vanguardia (*of* de).

foregoing ['fɔ:gəuɪŋ] *adj* anterior, precedente.

foregone ['fɔ:gɒn] *adj see* **conclusion.**

foreground ['fɔ:graund] *n* primer plano *m*, primer término *m*; **in the —** en primer término.

forehand ['fɔ:hænd] **1** *n* directo *m*, derechazo *m*. **2** *attr* directo.

forehead ['fɔrɪd] *n* frente *f*.

foreign ['fɔrɪn] *adj* **(a)** extranjero; *policy, trade etc* exterior; **F— Minister, F— Secretary** Ministro *m* de Asuntos Exteriores; **F— Ministry, F— Office** Ministerio *m* de Asuntos Exteriores.

(b) *body* extraño; (*belonging to someone else*) ajeno (*to* a); **deceit is — to his nature** no cabe en él el engaño.

foreigner ['fɔrɪnə*] *n* extranjero *m*, a *f*.

foreknowledge ['fɔ:'nɒlɪdʒ] *n* presciencia *f*; **to have — of something** saber algo de antemano.

foreland ['fɔ:lənd] *n* cabo *m*, promontorio *m*.

foreleg ['fɔ:leg] *n* pata *f* delantera.

forelock ['fɔ:lɒk] *n* guedeja *f*; **to take time by the —** tomar la ocasión por los cabellos.

foreman ['fɔ:mən] *n*, *pl* **—men** [mən] (*of workers*) capataz *m*; (*in building*) maestro *m* de obras; (*Law*) presidente *m* (del jurado).

foremast ['fɔ:mɑ:st] *n* trinquete *m* (*palo*).

foremost ['fɔ:məust] *adj* primero, delantero; (*outstanding*) primero, principal.

forename ['fɔ:neɪm] *n* nombre *m*, nombre *m* de pila.

forenoon ['fɔ:nu:n] *n* mañana *f*.

forensic [fə'rensɪk] *adj* forense; *medicine* legal.

forerunner ['fɔ:,rʌnə*] *n* precursor *m*, ora *f*.

foresail ['fɔ:seɪl] *n* trinquete *m* (*vela*).

foresee [fɔ:'si:] (*irr: see* **see**) *vt* prever.

foreseeable [fɔː'siːəbl] *adj* previsible; **in the — future** hasta donde se pueda ver.

foreshadow [fɔː'ʃædəu] *vt* prefigurar, anunciar; (*person*) prever.

foreshore ['fɔːʃɔː*] *n* playa *f* (entre los límites de pleamar y bajamar).

foreshorten [fɔː'ʃɔːtn] *vt* escorzar.

foreshortening [fɔː'ʃɔːtniŋ] *n* escorzo *m*.

foresight ['fɔːsait] *n* previsión *f*; **lack of —** imprevisión *f*.

foreskin ['fɔːskin] *n* prepucio *m*.

forest ['fɔrist] **1** *n* bosque *m*; (*large, dense*) selva *f*. **2** *attr* forestal, del bosque.

forestall [fɔː'stɔːl] *vt event* anticipar, prevenir, impedir; *person* anticipar (e impedir).

forester ['fɔristə*] *n* (*expert*) ingeniero *m* de montes; (*keeper*) guardabosques *m*.

forestry ['fɔristri] *n* silvicultura *f*.

foretaste ['fɔːteist] *n* anticipo *m*, muestra *f*.

foretell [fɔː'tel] (*irr: see* **tell**) *vt* (*predict*) predecir, pronosticar; (*presage*) presagiar.

forethought ['fɔːθɔːt] *n* prevención *f*, previsión *f*; (*pej*) premeditación *f*.

forewarn [fɔː'wɔːn] *vt* prevenir; **to be —ed** estar prevenido, precaverse; **—ed is forearmed** hombre prevenido vale por dos.

foreword ['fɔːwəːd] *n* prefacio *m*.

forfeit ['fɔːfit] **1** *n* (*loss*) pérdida *f*; (*fine*) multa *f*; (*penalty*) pena *f*; (*in games*) prenda *f*; **—s** juego *m* de prendas. **2** *vt* perder (el derecho a).

forfeiture ['fɔːfitʃə*] *n* pérdida *f*.

forgather [fɔː'gæðə*] *vi* reunirse.

forgave [fə'geiv] *pret of* **forgive**.

forge¹ [fɔːdʒ] **1** *n* (*fire*) fragua *f*; (*smithy*) herrería *f*; (*ironworks*) fundición *f*.
2 *vt metal* forjar, fraguar; *friendship, plan, unity etc* fraguar; (*falsify*) falsificar, falsear, contrahacer.

forge² [fɔːdʒ] *vi*: **to — ahead** avanzar constantemente; adelantarse muchísimo (*of a*).

forger ['fɔːdʒə*] *n* falsificador *m*, falsario *m*.

forgery ['fɔːdʒəri] *n* falsificación *f*.

forget [fə'get] (*irr: pret* **forgot**, *ptp* **forgotten**) **1** *vt* olvidar, olvidarse de; **I forgot my umbrella in a train** dejé el paraguas en un tren; **— it!** ¡no se preocupe!; **and don't you — it!** ¡y que no se te olvide esto!; **never to be forgotten** inolvidable.
2 *vi* olvidarse; **I —** no recuerdo, me he olvidado; **but I forgot** pero se me olvidó; **to — about** olvidarse de; **let's — about it!** ¡pelillos a la mar!; **to — to do something** olvidarse de hacer algo; **I forgot to tell you why** se me olvidó decirle por qué.
3 *vr*: **to — oneself** propasarse, olvidar los buenos modales; **you — yourself, sir!** ¡prudencia, caballero!

forgetful [fə'getful] *adj character* olvidadizo, desmemoriado; descuidado; **— of all else** olvidando todo lo demás, sin hacer caso de todo lo demás; **he's terribly —** tiene un tremendo despiste.

forgetfulness [fə'getfulnis] *n* olvido *m*, falta *f* de memoria; descuido *m*; (*absentmindedness*) despiste *m*.

forget-me-not [fə'getminɔt] *n* nomeolvides *f*.

forgivable [fə'givəbl] *adj* perdonable.

forgive [fə'giv] (*irr: see* **give**) *vt* perdonar; **to — someone (for) something** perdonar algo a uno, perdonar a uno por algo.

forgiven [fə'givn] *ptp of* **forgive**.

forgiveness [fə'givnis] *n* (*pardon*) perdón *m*; (*compassion*) misericordia *f*.

forgiving [fə'giviŋ] *adj* perdonador, misericordioso; **to feel —** estar dispuesto a perdonar.

forgo [fɔː'gəu] (*irr: see* **go**) *vt* renunciar a, privarse de.

forgot [fə'gɔt] *pret of* **forget**.

forgotten [fə'gɔtn] *ptp of* **forget**.

fork [fɔːk] **1** *n* (*at table*) tenedor *m*; (*Agr*) horca *f*, horquilla *f*; (*Mech etc*) horquilla *f*; (*in road*) bifurcación *f*; (*Anat*) horcajadura *f*, entrepierna *f*; (*in river*) horcajo *m*; (*of tree*) horcadura *f*.
2 *vt* (*also* **to — over**) cultivar con horquilla; **to — out** (*fam*) desembolsar (de mala gana); **to — over** (*fam*) entregar.
3 *vi* (*road*) bifurcarse; **— right for Oxford** tuerza a la derecha para ir a Oxford.

forked [fɔːkt] *adj* ahorquillado, bifurcado; *lightning* en zigzag; *tail* hendido.

fork-lift truck ['fɔːklift'trʌk] *n* elevadora-transportadora *f* de horquilla.

forlorn [fə'lɔːn] *adj* abandonado, desamparado; *appearance* de abandono; **to look —** (*person*) tener aspecto triste; **why so —?** ¿por qué tan triste?; **— hope** empresa *f* desesperada; esperanza *f* que tiene poca probabilidad de verse realizada.

form [fɔːm] **1** *n* (a) (*shape, style, type, method etc*; *also Lit, Gram*) forma *f*; **a new — of government** un

nuevo sistema de gobierno; **the same thing in a new —** la misma cosa bajo una nueva forma; **choose another — of words** busque otra expresión; **it took the — of a cash prize** consistió en un premio en metálico; **what — will the ceremony take?** ¿cómo se organizará la ceremonia?
(b) (*shape vaguely seen*) figura *f*, bulto *m*.
(c) (*School*) clase *f*.
(d) (*bench*) banco *m*.
(e) (*document*) hoja *f*, formulario *m*; **application —** (hoja *f* de) solicitud *f*; formulario *m* de inscripción; **to fill up a —** llenar una hoja; **has he got any —?** (*fam*) ¿tiene antecedentes penales?
(f) (*customary method*) forma *f*; **in due —** en la debida forma, en la forma reglamentaria; **that is common —** eso es muy corriente; **what's the —?** ¿qué es lo que hemos de hacer?
(g) (*formality*) **for —'s sake** por pura fórmula, para salvar las apariencias.
(h) (*behaviour*) **it's bad — to** + *infin* es de mal gusto + *infin*, es de mala educación + *infin*.
(i) (*condition*) estado *m* físico; **to be in good —** (*Sport*) estar en forma, (*be witty*) estar de vena; **to be out of —** estar desentrenado, haber perdido el tacto.
2 *vt* formar; *habit* adquirir; *company* fundar, establecer; *plan* concebir; *idea* hacerse; *impression, opinion* formarse; *queue* hacer; **to — a government** formar gobierno; **those who — the group** los que forman parte del grupo; **to — up troops** formar.
3 *vi*: **to — up** alinearse, (*Mil*) formar.

formal ['fɔːməl] *adj person's manner* ceremonioso, estirado; *person's character* etiquetero; *greeting* ceremonioso; *visit* de cumplido, oficial; *function* protocolario; *dance, dress* de etiqueta; (*relating to form*) formal; **don't be so —!** ¡no te andes con tantos cumplidos!; **there was no — agreement** no hubo contrato en forma.

formaldehyde [fɔː'mældihaid] *n* formaldehido *m*.

formalin(e) ['fɔːməlin] *n* formalina *f*.

formality [fɔː'mæliti] *n* (a) (*of occasion*) ceremonia *f*, lo ceremonioso; (*of person*) lo etiquetero; (*of dress etc*) etiqueta *f*; **with all due —** en la debida forma; **it's a mere —** es pura fórmula.
(b) **formalities** ceremonias *fpl*; formalidades *fpl*; **let's do without the formalities** prescindamos de los trámites de costumbre.

formally ['fɔːməli] *adv greet etc* ceremoniosamente; *open, visit* oficialmente; *agree etc* en forma.

format ['fɔːmæt] *n* formato *m*.

formation [fɔː'meiʃən] *n* formación *f*; **in battle —** en orden de batalla.

formative ['fɔːmətiv] *adj* formativo.

former ['fɔːmə*] *adj* (a) (*of two*) primero, anterior; **your — idea** su primera idea.
(b) (*earlier*) antiguo; **a — seat of government** una antigua sede del gobierno.
(c) (*of person*) ex, que fue; **— president** ex presidente *m*; **a — ambassador in Lima** embajador que fue en Lima.
(d) **the — (. . . the latter)** aquél *etc* (. . . éste *etc*).

formerly ['fɔːməli] *adv* antes, antiguamente.

formic ['fɔːmik] *adj*: **— acid** ácido *m* fórmico.

formidable ['fɔːmidəbl] *adj* formidable.

formless ['fɔːmlis] *adj* informe.

formula ['fɔːmjulə] *n, pl* **formulae** ['fɔːmjuliː] fórmula *f*.

formulate ['fɔːmjuleit] *vt* formular.

formulation [ˌfɔːmju'leiʃən] *n* formulación *f*.

fornicate ['fɔːnikeit] *vi* fornicar.

fornication [ˌfɔːni'keiʃən] *n* fornicación *f*.

forsake [fə'seik] (*irr: pret* **forsook**, *ptp* **forsaken**) *vt person etc* abandonar, dejar, desamparar; *plan* renunciar a; *belief* renegar de; **he forsook Seville for Madrid** abandonó Sevilla y se fue a vivir a Madrid.

forsaken [fə'seikən] *ptp of* **forsake**.

forsook [fə'suk] *pret of* **forsake**.

forswear [fɔː'sweə*] (*irr: see* **swear**) *vt* abjurar de, renunciar a.

forsythia [fɔː'saiθiə] *n* forsitia *f*.

fort [fɔːt] *n* fuerte *m*, fortín *m*; **to hold the —** (*fig*) defenderse, seguir en su puesto, encargarse del trabajo (temporalmente).

forte [fɔːt] *n* fuerte *m*.

forth [fɔːθ] *adv*: **and so —** etcétera; **y así sucesivamente; from this day —** de aquí en adelante; *see* **back** *etc*.

forthcoming [fɔːθ'kʌmiŋ] *adj* (a) (*approaching*) venidero, próximo; *book etc* de próxima aparición, en preparación.
(b) (*available*) disponible; **if help is —** si nos mandan socorros, si nos ayudan; **if funds are —** si

nos dan el dinero; **no answer was** — no hubo respuesta.

(c) *character* afable, comunicativo; **he's not very —** no dice mucho; **he's not — with strangers** tiene poca confianza con los desconocidos.

forthright ['fɔːθraɪt] *adj person* directo, franco; enérgico; *answer etc* terminante; *refusal* rotundo.

forthwith ['fɔːθ'wɪθ] *adv (then and there)* en el acto; *(without delay)* sin dilación.

fortieth ['fɔːtiɪθ] *adj* cuadragésimo.

fortification [,fɔːtifi'keiʃən] *n* fortificación *f*.

fortify ['fɔːtifai] **1** *vt (Mil)* fortificar; *(strengthen)* fortalecer; *wine* encabezar; *person* vigorizar, fortalecer; **to — someone in a belief** confirmar la opinión que tiene uno.

2 *vr:* **to — oneself** *(fig)* fortalecerse.

fortitude ['fɔːtitjuːd] *n* fortaleza *f*, estoicismo *m*, valor *m*.

fortnight ['fɔːtnait] *n* quince días *mpl*, quincena *f*; **today —** de hoy en quince (días).

fortnightly ['fɔːtnaitli] **1** *adj* que sale *(etc)* cada quince días, quincenal. **2** *adv* cada quince días, quincenalmente.

fortress ['fɔːtris] *n* fortaleza *f*, plaza *f* fuerte.

fortuitous [fɔː'tjuːitəs] *adj* fortuito, casual.

fortuitously [fɔː'tjuːitəsli] *adv* fortuitamente, por casualidad.

fortunate ['fɔːtʃənit] *adj* afortunado; *(happy)* dichoso, feliz; **to be —** *(person)* tener suerte; **that was — for you** en eso tuviste suerte.

fortunately ['fɔːtʃənitli] *adv* afortunadamente.

fortune ['fɔːtʃən] *n* (a) *(luck, fate)* fortuna *f*, suerte *f*; **by good —** por fortuna; **the —s of war** las peripecias de la guerra; **we had the good — to find him** tuvimos la suerte de encontrarle; **to tell someone's —** decir a uno la buenaventura; **to try one's —** probar fortuna.

(b) *(money)* fortuna *f*, caudal *m*; **to come into a —** heredar una fortuna; **to cost a —** valer un dineral; **to make a —** enriquecerse, hacer su pacotilla *(fam)*; **to marry a —** casarse con una mujer acaudalada.

fortuneteller ['fɔːtʃən,telə*] *n* adivina *f*.

forty ['fɔːti] *adj* cuarenta; **the forties** *(eg 1940s)* los años cuarenta; **to be in one's forties** tener más de cuarenta años.

fortyish ['fɔːtiiʃ] *adj* cuarentón.

forum ['fɔːrəm] *n* foro *m*; *(fig)* tribunal *m*.

forward ['fɔːwəd] **1** *adj* (a) *(front)* delantero; *position (Mil etc)* avanzado; *line (Sport)* delantero; *(Naut)* de proa; *movement* progresivo, de avance; *gears* de avance; *pass (Rugby)* adelantado; *delivery (Comm)* en fecha futura.

(b) *season, crop* adelantado; precoz; *person* atrevido, fresco, descarado.

2 *n (Sport)* delantero *m*.

3 *vt (send)* enviar; *(re-address)* hacer seguir; **"to be —ed", "please —"** "se ruega hacer seguir".

forward(s) ['fɔːwəd(z)] *adv* adelante, hacia adelante; *(Naut)* hacia la proa; **—!** ¡adelante!; **— march!** de frente ¡mar!; **the lever is placed well —** la palanca está colocada bastante hacia adelante; **from that day —** desde ese día en adelante; **to go —** ir hacia adelante, avanzar; *(fig)* progresar, hacer progresos.

forwardness ['fɔːwədnis] *n (of crop etc)* precocidad *f*; *(pertness)* frescura *f*, descaro *m*.

forwent [fɔː'went] *pret of* **forgo**.

fossil ['fɔsl] **1** *adj* fósil. **2** *n* fósil *m*.

fossilized ['fɔsilaizd] *adj* fosilizado.

foster ['fɔstə*] *vt (encourage)* fomentar, promover; *(aid)* favorecer; *hope* alentar; *child* criar.

foster brother ['fɔstə,brʌðə*] *n* hermano *m* de leche.

foster mother ['fɔstə,mʌðə*] *n* madre *f* adoptiva; *(wet-nurse)* ama *f* de leche.

fought [fɔːt] *pret and ptp of* **fight**.

foul [faul] **1** *adj (dirty)* sucio, puerco; *(disgusting)* asqueroso; *(of bad quality)* horrible; *(morally vile)* vil, horrible; *air* viciado; *blow, language, play* sucio; *breath* fétido; *calumny* vil; *smell* insoportable; *weather* feo, horrible; **to fall — of** indisponerse con, ponerse a malas con, *rule* infringir.

2 *n (Sport)* falta *f* (on contra).

3 *vt* (a) *(dirty)* ensuciar; *one's nest* manchar.

(b) *(block)* atascar, obstruir; *(catch up in)* enredarse en; *(hit)* chocar contra.

(c) *(Sport)* cometer una falta contra.

foulmouthed ['faul'mauðd] *adj* malhablado.

foul-smelling ['faul'smeliŋ] *adj* hediondo.

found¹ [faund] *pret and ptp of* **find**.

found² [faund] *vt* fundar, establecer; *fortune* crear; **a statement —ed on fact** una declaración basada en hechos.

found³ [faund] *vt (Tech)* fundir.

foundation [faun'deiʃən] *n* (a) *(act)* fundación *f*, establecimiento *m*; creación *f*.

(b) *(basis)* base *f*, fundamento *m*; **statement devoid of —** declaración *f* que carece de base.

(c) **—s** *(Archit)* cimientos *mpl*; **to lay the —s** echar los cimientos *(of de; also fig)*.

foundation stone [faun'deiʃənstəun] *n* primera piedra *f*; *(fig)* piedra *f* angular.

founder¹ ['faundə*] *n* fundador *m*, ora *f*.

founder² ['faundə*] *vi* irse a pique, hundirse; *(fig)* fracasar *(on* adelo a).

foundling ['faundliŋ] *n* niño *m* expósito, niña *f* expósita, inclusero *m*, a *f*; **— hospital** inclusa *f*.

foundry ['faundri] *n* fundición *f*.

fount [faunt] *n (Typ)* fundición *f*, familia *f* (de la letra).

fountain ['fauntin] *n (natural)* fuente *f*, manantial *m (also fig)*; *(artificial)* fuente *f*, surtidor *m*; *(jet)* chorro *m*.

fountainhead ['fauntinhed] *n* fuente *f*, origen *m*; **to go to the —** acudir a la propia fuente.

fountain pen ['fauntinpen] *n* estilográfica *f*, plumafuente *f (S Am)*.

four [fɔː*] **1** *adj* cuatro. **2** *n* cuatro *m*; **to be on all —s** estar en completa armonía con; **to go on all —s** ir a gatas; **to form —s** formar a cuatro.

four-door ['fɔː'dɔː*] *adj car* de cuatro puertas.

four-engined ['fɔː'rendʒind] *adj* cuatrimotor, tetramotor.

fourflusher ['fɔː'flʌʃə*] *n (US sl)* embustero *m*.

fourfold ['fɔːfəuld] **1** *adj* cuádruple. **2** *adv* cuatro veces.

fourfooted ['fɔː'futid] *adj* cuadrúpedo.

fourposter ['fɔː,pəustə*] *n (also* **— bed)** cama *f* de columnas.

fourscore ['fɔː'skɔː*] *adj* ochenta.

foursome ['fɔːsəm] *n* grupo *m* de cuatro personas.

foursquare ['fɔː'skwɛə*] **1** *adj* firme; franco, sincero. **2** *adv:* **to stand — with someone** estar en completa armonía con uno, apoyar a uno incondicionalmente.

fourteen ['fɔː'tiːn] *adj* catorce.

fourteenth ['fɔː'tiːnθ] *adj* decimocuarto.

fourth [fɔːθ] **1** *adj* cuarto. **2** *n* cuarto *m*, cuarta parte *f*; *(Mus)* cuarta *f*; **to make a —** *(Cards)* unirse a otras tres personas (para que se pueda jugar).

fourthly ['fɔːθli] *adv* en cuarto lugar.

four-wheel drive ['fɔː'wiːl'draiv] *n* tracción *f* a las cuatro ruedas.

fowl [faul] *n (bird in general)* ave *f*; *(chicken)* ave *f* de corral, gallina *f*; *(served as food)* pollo *m*; **the —s of the air** las aves.

fowlpest ['faulpest] *n* peste *f* aviar.

fox [fɔks] **1** *n* zorra *f*, *(dog-)* zorro *m*; *(fig)* zorro *m*. **2** *vt* confundir, dejar perplejo; **this will — them** esto les ha de despistar; **you had me properly —ed** there eso me tuvo completamente despistado. **3** *vi* disimular, fingir.

fox cub ['fɔkskʌb] *n* cachorro *m* (de zorro).

foxed [fɔkst] *adj* manchado.

foxglove ['fɔksglʌv] *n* dedalera *f*.

foxhole ['fɔkshəul] *n (Mil)* hoyo *m* de protección.

foxhound ['fɔkshaund] *n* perro *m* raposero.

foxhunt ['fɔkshʌnt] *n* cacería *f* de zorras.

foxhunting ['fɔks,hʌntiŋ] *n* caza *f* de zorras.

fox terrier ['fɔks'teriə*] *n* foxterrier *m*.

foxtrot ['fɔkstrɔt] *n* fox *m*.

foxy ['fɔksi] *adj* taimado, astuto.

foyer ['fɔiei] *n* hall *m*, vestíbulo *m*.

fracas ['fræka:] *n* gresca *f*, riña *f*.

fraction ['frækʃən] *n (Math)* fracción *f*, quebrado *m*; *(fig)* pequeña porción *f*, parte *f* muy pequeña.

fractional ['frækʃənl] *adj* fraccionario; *(fig)* muy pequeño.

fractious ['frækʃəs] *adj (character)* rebelón, displicente; *(mood)* malhumorado.

fracture ['fræktʃə*] **1** *n* fractura *f*; **compound —** fractura *f* complicada. **2** *vt* fracturar. **3** *vi* fracturarse.

fragile ['frædʒail] *adj* frágil, quebradizo; *person* delicado.

fragility [frə'dʒiliti] *n* fragilidad *f*.

fragment ['frægmənt] *n* fragmento *m*; trozo *m*; **to smash something to —s** hacer algo añicos.

fragmentary [fræg'mentəri] *adj* fragmentario.

fragrance ['freigrəns] *n* fragancia *f*.

fragrant ['freigrənt] *adj* fragante, oloroso; *memory* dulce.

frail [freil] *adj* frágil, quebradizo; delicado; *(Med)* débil; *(morally)* flaco, endeble.

frailty ['freilti] *n* fragilidad *f*; *(Med)* debilidad *f*; *(moral)* flaqueza *f*.

frame [freim] **1** n **(a)** (framework) estructura f, esqueleto m; (Tech) armazón f, bastidor m; (Sew) bastidor m para bordar; (of spectacles) montura f, armadura f; (of bicycle) cuadro m; (of picture, window) marco m.
(b) (body) figura f, talle m; **his large —** su cuerpo fornido; **her whole — was shaken by sobs** los sollozos sacudían su cuerpo entero.
(c) — of mind estado m de ánimo; **when you're in a better — of mind** cuando estés de mejor humor.
2 vt (construct) construir; (arrange) disponer, arreglar; picture poner un marco a, (fig) servir de marco a; (contrive) idear; sound articular; question etc formular, expresar; (fam) incriminar por medio de una estratagema.
3 vi **(a) how is it framing?** ¿qué tal se está desarrollando?; **he's framing well** hace buenos progresos, promete.
(b) to — up to someone ponerse en actitud para defenderse contra uno.
frame-up ['freimʌp] n (fam) estratagema f para incriminar a uno; **it's a —** aquí hay trampa.
framework ['freimwɔːk] n (Tech) armazón f, esqueleto m; (fig) sistema m, organización f, marco m; **within the — of the constitution** dentro del marco de la constitución.
franc [fræŋk] n franco m.
France [frɑːns] Francia f.
Frances ['frɑːnsis] f Francisca.
franchise ['fræntʃaiz] n derecho m de votar, sufragio m.
Francis ['frɑːnsis] m Francisco.
Franciscan [fræn'siskən] **1** adj franciscano. **2** n franciscano m.
francophile ['fræŋkəufail] n francófilo m, a f.
francophobe ['fræŋkəufəub] n francófobo m, a f.
Frank[1] [fræŋk] n (Hist) franco m.
Frank[2] [fræŋk] m Paco.
frank[1] [fræŋk] adj franco.
frank[2] [fræŋk] vt letter franquear.
frankfurter ['fræŋk_fəːtə*] n salchicha f.
frankincense ['fræŋkinsens] n incienso m.
Frankish ['fræŋkiʃ] **1** adj fráncico. **2** n (language) fráncico m.
frankly ['fræŋkli] adv francamente.
frankness ['fræŋknis] n franqueza f.
frantic ['fræntik] adj frenético, furioso; **to be — with worry** andar como loco de inquietud; **to drive someone —** volver a uno loco.
frantically ['fræntikəli] adv frenéticamente, con frenesí.
fraternal [frə'təːnl] adj fraternal, fraterno.
fraternity [frə'təːniti] n fraternidad f; (guild) cofradía f; (US) club m de estudiantes.
fraternization [ˌfrætənai'zeiʃən] n fraternización f.
fraternize ['frætənaiz] vi confraternizar (with con).
fratricide ['frætrisaid] n (act) fratricidio m; (person) fratricida m.
fraud [frɔːd] n fraude m; (person) impostor m, farsante m.
fraudulence ['frɔːdjuləns] n fraudulencia f, fraude m.
fraudulent ['frɔːdjulənt] adj fraudulento.
fraught [frɔːt] adj: **— with** cargado de, lleno de.
fray[1] [frei] n combate m, lucha f; **to be ready for the —** tener ganas de pelear; **to gird oneself for the —** aprestarse para la lucha.
fray[2] [frei] **1** vt desgastar, raer. **2** vi deshilacharse; **to — against, to — on** ludir con, rozar.
frayed [freid] adj raído, dishilachado; **tempers were getting —** todos estaban a punto de perder la paciencia.
frazzle ['fræzl] n (fam): **to beat someone to a —** (Sport) cascar a uno, derrotar a uno por completo; **to be worn to a —** estar rendido de cansancio.
freak [friːk] **1** n **(a)** (person) fenómeno m; (abnormal specimen) monstruo m, monstruosidad f; curiosidad f; ejemplar m anormal; (Bio) mutación f; **the result was a —** el resultado fue totalmente fortuito, fue imposible prever tal resultado.
(b) (whim) capricho m.
2 adj **= freakish**.
freakish ['friːkiʃ] adj **(a)** specimen anormal, monstruoso; result inesperado, imprevisible, fortuito.
(b) person caprichoso.
freckle ['frekl] n peca f.
freckled ['frekld] adj pecoso, lleno de pecas.
Fred [fred], **Freddie**, **Freddy** ['fredi] m nombres cariñosos de Frederick.
Frederick ['fredrik] m Federico.
free [friː] **1** adj **(a)** (at liberty etc) libre (from, of de); (not fixed) suelto, libre; (untied) libre, desatado; account, choice, translation, verse libre; port franco;

— speech libertad f de palabra; **— of duty** libro de derechos de aduana; **a surface — from dust** una superficie libre de polvo; **the fishing is —** la pesca está autorizada; **the area is — of malaria** la región es inmune contra el paludismo; **to be — to** + infin poder libremente + infin, ser libre de + infin; **he is not — to act** tiene las manos atadas; **we are — of him at last** por fin nos hemos librado de él; **to break —** soltarse; **to let someone go —** poner en libertad a uno; **to set — person** poner en libertad, libertar, librar; slave manumitir, emancipar; animal soltar.
(b) (not occupied) libre; post vacante; premises desocupado; **is this table —?** ¿está libre esta mesa?; **are you — tomorrow?** ¿estás libre mañana?
(c) language etc libre, desvergonzado; (insolent) descarado; **— and easy** despreocupado, poco ceremonioso.
(d) to be — with ser liberal con, no regatear; dar en abundancia; **to be — with one's money** ser manirroto; **he's very — in blaming others** echa libremente la culpa a otros; **he's too — with his remarks** es demasiado libre en sus comentarios; **to be — with one's hands** (stealing) ser largo de uñas, (amorously) ser un tocotón; **to make — of** (or **with**) usar como si fuera cosa propia.
(e) (for nothing) gratuito; ticket de favor; **— of charge** gratis; **admission —** entrada gratis; **catalogue — on request** el catálogo se envía gratis a petición; **— on board** franco a bordo.
2 adv gratis.
3 vt (set free) poner en libertad, libertar; slave manumitir; animal soltar; (untie) desatar, soltar; knot, tangle desenredar; place, surface etc despejar, desembarazar (of de); (rescue) librar, salvar (from de), rescatar; (from burden, tax etc) eximir, exentar (from de).
4 vr: **to — oneself** desatarse, soltarse.
freebooter ['friːbuːtə*] n filibustero m.
freedom ['friːdəm] n libertad f; exención f (from de), inmunidad f (from contra); (ease) facilidad f, soltura f; **— of a city** ciudadanía f de honor; **— of action** libertad f de acción; **— of the press** libertad f de prensa; **— of speech** libertad f de palabra; **— of worship** libertad f de cultos.
free-fight ['friː'fait] n, **free-for-all** ['friːfə'rɔːl] n sarracina f, riña f general.
freehand ['friːhænd] adj hecho a pulso.
freehold ['friːhəuld] **1** adj: **— property = 2** n feudo m franco.
freeholder ['friː_həuldə*] n poseedor m de feudo franco.
free kick ['friː'kik] n golpe m franco.
freelance ['friːlɑːns] **1** adj independiente. **2** n periodista mf (etc) independiente. **3** vi trabajar como periodista (etc) independiente.
freely ['friːli] adv libremente; (generously) liberalmente; confess, speak etc francamente; **you may come and go —** Vd puede ir y venir con toda libertad.
freeman ['friːmən] n, pl **-men** [mən] (Hist) hombre m libre; (of city) ciudadano m de honor.
freemason ['friː_meisn] n francmasón m.
freemasonry ['friː_meisnri] n francmasonería f; (fig) compañerismo m, camaradería f.
freesia ['friːziə] n fresia f.
freestyle ['friːstail] adj: **200 metres —** 200 metros libres.
freethinker ['friː'θiŋkə*] n librepensador m, ora f.
freethinking ['friː'θiŋkiŋ] n librepensamiento m.
free trade ['friː'treid] n libre cambio m.
free trader ['friː'treidə*] n librecambista m.
freewheel ['friː'wiːl] **1** n rueda f libre. **2** vi (cyclist) andar a rueda libre, (Aut) ir en punto muerto.
free will ['friː'wil] n libre albedrío m.
freeze [friːz] (irr: pret **froze**, ptp **frozen**) **1** vt helar; food, prices, wages etc congelar; **the lake is frozen over** el lago está helado; **we're simply frozen** estamos francamente helados; **we're frozen up at home** en casa las cañerías están heladas; **to — out competitor** deshacerse de (quitándole la clientela).
2 vi helarse; congelarse; (fig) quedar helado (de miedo etc); (animal) permanecer enteramente inmóvil; **I'm freezing** estoy helado; **to — to death** morir de frío; **the smile froze on his lips** se le heló la sonrisa en los labios.
3 vi (impersonal) helar; **it will — tonight** esta noche habrá helada.
4 n helada f; (of prices, wages etc) congelación f.
freezer ['friːzə*] n congelador m, heladora f.
freeze-up ['friːzʌp] n helada f.

freezing ['fri:ziŋ] **1** adj glacial (also fig), helado. **2** n (a) (of rents etc) congelación f. (b) = **freezing point**.

freezing point ['fri:ziŋpɔint] n punto m de congelación; **5 degrees below** — 5 grados bajo cero.

freight [freit] n flete m; (load) carga f; (goods) mercancías fpl.

freightage ['freitidʒ] n flete m.

freight car ['freitkɑ:*] n (US) vagón m de mercancías.

freighter ['freitə*] n buque m de carga.

French [frentʃ] **1** adj francés; **the** — los franceses. **2** n (language) francés m.

French Canadian ['frentʃkə'neidiən] **1** adj francocanadiense. **2** n francocanadiense mf.

Frenchman ['frentʃmən] n, pl **—men** [mən] francés m.

Frenchwoman ['frentʃ,wumən] n, pl **—women** [,wimin] francesa f.

frenetic [fri'netik] adj frenético.

frenzied ['frenzid] adj effort etc frenético; crowd etc enloquecido.

frenzy ['frenzi] n frenesí m, delirio m.

frequency ['fri:kwənsi] n frecuencia f (also Elec); **high** — alta frecuencia f.

frequent ['fri:kwənt] adj frecuente.

frequent [fri:'kwent] vt frecuentar.

frequently ['fri:kwəntli] adv frecuentemente, con frecuencia, a menudo.

fresco ['freskəu] n, pl **fresco(e)s** ['freskəuz] fresco m.

fresh [freʃ] adj (a) (new) nuevo; **to start a** — **life** comenzar una vida nueva; **he has had a** — **attack** ha sufrido un nuevo ataque; **it is** — **in my memory** se conserva muy fresco en mi memoria; **to put** — **courage into someone** reanimar a uno.
  (b) (newly come) — **from Spain** recién llegado (or importado etc) de España; — **from the oven** que acaba de salir del horno.
  (c) (inexperienced) nuevo.
  (d) (not stale) fruit etc fresco; air fresco, puro (and see air); water dulce; **as** — **as a daisy** tan fresco como una rosa; **to feel perfectly** — estar lleno de vigor.
  (e) (cheeky) fresco, descocado; **to get** — **with someone** ponerse fresco con uno.
  (f) (cool) fresco.
  (g) wind recio.
  (h) face, complexion de buen color.

freshen ['freʃn] **1** vt (also to — **up**) refrescar. **2** vi (temperature) refrescarse; (wind) soplar más recio; (person; also to — **up**) lavarse, arreglarse.

fresher ['freʃə*] n (fam) = **freshman**.

freshly ['freʃli] adv nuevamente; recientemente; — **made** nuevo, recién hecho, acabado de hacer.

freshman ['freʃmən] n, pl **—men** [mən] (Univ) estudiante m de primer año, pipiolo m (fam).

freshness ['freʃnis] n frescura f; (newness) novedad f; vigor m.

freshwater ['freʃ,wɔ:tə*] adj de agua dulce.

fret [fret] **1** vt (a) (wear away) corroer, raer, desgastar.
  (b) person irritar, molestar.
  (c) **to** — **the hours away** pasar las horas consumiéndose de inquietud.
  2 vi inquietarse, apurarse; impacientarse (at por); **it's** — **ting for its mother** se está apurando por la ausencia de su madre; **don't** — **!** ¡no te apuras!
  3 n: **to be in a** — estar muy inquieto, apurarse.

fretful ['fretful] adj displicente, quejoso; impaciente, inquieto.

fretfully ['fretfəli] adv impacientemente; inquietamente.

fretsaw ['fretsɔ:] n sierra f de calados.

fretwork ['fretwə:k] n calado m.

Freudian ['frɔidiən] adj freudiano.

friable ['fraiəbl] adj desmenuzable, friable.

friar ['fraiə*] n (a) fraile m; **black** — dominico m; **grey** — franciscano m; **white** — carmelita m.
  (b) (before name) fray.

fricative ['frikətiv] **1** adj fricativo. **2** n fricativa f.

friction ['frikʃən] n (Tech) fricción f, rozamiento m; (Med etc) frote m, frotamiento m; (fig) tirantez f, desavenencia f (about, over con motivo de).

Friday ['fraidi] n viernes m; **Good** — Viernes m Santo.

fridge [fridʒ] n (fam) = **refrigerator**.

fried [fraid] adj frito.

fried-fish shop ['fraid'fiʃʃɔp] n freiduría f de pescado.

friend [frend] n amigo m, a f; **F—** (Rel) cuáquero m, a f; **—s** amigos mpl, amistades fpl; — **!** (Mil) ¡gente de paz!; **a** — **of mine** un amigo mío; **he's no** — **of mine** no es de mis amigos; **he is no** — **to violence** no es partidario de la violencia; **we're the best of** — **s**

somos muy amigos; **to be** — **s with someone** ser amigo de uno; **to have a** — **at court** tener el padre alcalde; **to make** — **s with someone** hacerse amigo de uno, trabar amistad con uno; **he makes** — **s easily** le es fácil trabar amistad con las personas.

friendless ['frendlis] adj sin amigos.

friendliness ['frendlinis] n simpatía f; amabilidad f; cordialidad f; lo acogedor.

friendly ['frendli] adj (a) (of person) simpático; amable; **people here are so** — aquí la gente es muy simpática; **he's a** — **soul** es simpatiquísimo; **to be** — **with** ser amigo de; **to get** — hacerse amigos.
  (b) relationship, greeting, tone amistoso, cordial; shout jovial; atmosphere, place acogedor; match amistoso; nation amigo; society de socorro mutuo; **that wasn't a very** — **thing to do** eso no fue la acción de un amigo.

friendship ['frendʃip] n amistad f.

Friesland ['fri:zlənd] Frisia f.

frieze [fri:z] n friso m.

frigate ['frigit] n fragata f.

fright [frait] n (a) (sudden fear) susto m, sobresalto m; (state of alarm) terror m; **what a** — **you gave me!** ¡qué susto me diste!; **to have a** — tener un susto, llevarse un susto; **to take** — asustarse (at de).
  (b) (person) espantajo m; **doesn't she look a** —**?** ¡qué adefesio de mujer!

frighten ['fraitn] vt asustar, espantar, sobresaltar; alarmar; **to** — **away, to** — **off** ahuyentar, espantar; **to be** — **ed** tener miedo (of a); **don't be** — **ed !** ¡no te asustes!; **she is easily** — **ed** es asustadiza; **to** — **someone into doing something** obligar a uno a hacer algo infundiéndole miedo.

frightening ['fraitniŋ] adj espantoso, aterrador.

frightful ['fraitful] adj espantoso, horrible, horroroso; (very bad) horrible, malísimo.

frightfully ['fraitfəli] adv (fig) terriblemente, tremendamente; **it's** — **hard** es terriblemente difícil; **it's** — **good** es la mar de bueno; **I'm** — **sorry** lo siento muchísimo.

frightfulness ['fraitfulnis] n horror m; (Mil) terrorismo m.

frigid ['fridʒid] adj frío; (Med) frígido; atmosphere, look etc glacial.

frigidity [fri'dʒiditi] n frialdad f; (Med) frigidez f.

frill [fril] n lechuga f, volante m; **—s** (fig) adornos mpl.

fringe [frindʒ] **1** n (a) (Sew) franja f, orla f, borde m; (hair) flequillo m.
  (b) margen m; **the outer** —**s of the city** las partes exteriores de la ciudad; **on the** —**s of the lake** en los bordes del lago.
  (c) lunatic — elementos mpl fanáticos (y estrafalarios); **to live on the** — **of society** vivir al margen de la sociedad.
  2 attr: — **benefits** ventajas fpl supletorias, ingresos mpl accesorios.

frippery ['fripəri] n perifollos mpl, perejiles mpl.

frisk [frisk] **1** vt palpar, cachear. **2** vi (also to — **about**) retozar, juguetear, brincar.

frisky ['friski] adj retozón, juguetón; horse fogoso; **he's pretty** — **still** sigue muy activo.

fritter ['fritə*] **1** n fruta f de sartén, buñuelo m. **2** vt: **to** — **away** desperdiciar, disipar.

frivolity [fri'vɔliti] n frivolidad f, informalidad f, ligereza f.

frivolous ['frivələs] adj frívolo, poco formal, ligero.

frizz [friz] n, **frizzle** ['frizl] n rizos mpl pequeños y muy apretados.

frizz(l)y ['friz(l)i] adj muy ensortijado.

fro [frəu] adv: **to and** — de un lado a otro, de aquí para allá; **to and** — **movement** vaivén m.

frock [frɔk] n vestido m.

frock coat ['frɔk'kəut] n levita f.

frog [frɔg] n rana f; **to have a** — **in one's throat** padecer carraspera.

frogman ['frɔgmən] n, pl **—men** [mən] hombre-rana m.

frog-march ['frɔgmɑ:tʃ] vt llevar codo con codo.

frolic ['frɔlik] **1** n juego m alegre; (party) fiesta f, holgorio m; (prank) travesura f. **2** vi juguetear, retozar; divertirse (with con).

frolicsome ['frɔliksəm] adj retozón, juguetón; (mischievous) travieso.

from [frɔm] prep (a) de; — **A to Z** de A a Z, desde A hasta Z; — **door to door** de puerta en puerta; — **£2 upwards** desde 2 libras en adelante; **he had gone** — **home** se había ido de su casa; **to pick someone** — **the crowd** escoger a uno de la multitud.
  (b) (time) — **Friday** a partir del viernes; — **a child** desde niño; — **that time** desde aquel momento.
  (c) (deprivation) **to take something** — **someone**

quitar algo a uno; **he stole the book — me** me robó el libro; **I'll buy it — you** te lo compraré.

(d) (*against*) **to shelter — the rain** abrigarse de la lluvia.

(e) (*distinguishing*) **to know good — bad** saber distinguir entre el bien y el mal, saber distinguir el bien del mal.

(f) (*originating*) **the train — Madrid** el tren de Madrid, el tren procedente de Madrid; **he comes — Segovia** es de Segovia; **where are you — ?** ¿de dónde es Vd?; **a message — him** un mensaje de parte de él; **tell him that — me** dile eso de parte mía; **one of the best performances we have seen — him** uno de los mejores papeles que le hayamos visto; **to drink — a cup** beber de una taza; **we learned it — him** lo aprendimos de él; **we learned it — a book** lo aprendimos en un libro.

(g) (*because of*) **— what he says** por lo que dice, según lo que dice; **to act — conviction** obrar por convicción; **— sheer necessity** por pura necesidad; **to die — a fever** morir de una fiebre; **he is tired — overwork** está cansado por exceso de trabajo.

(h) —above desde encima; **— afar** desde lejos; **— among** de entre.

frond [frɔnd] n fronda f.

front [frʌnt] **1** adj **(a)** delantero, anterior; (*first*) primero; **door** principal, de entrada; **view** de frente.

(b) — organization organización f controlada clandestinamente por un partido político.

2 n **(a)** frente m (*also* Mil, Pol, Meteorol); (*forepart*) parte f delantera, parte f anterior; (*of house*) fachada f; (*of book, start*) principio m; (*of shirt etc*) pechera f; (*Theat*) auditorio m; (*beach*) playa f, (*promenade*) paseo m marítimo; **on Brighton —** en la playa de Brighton; **cold —** frente m frío; **popular — frente** m popular; **at** (*or* **in**) **the — of the book** al principio del libro; **in — delante; in — of** delante de; **to be in —** ir primero, ir delante, (*in race*) ir en cabeza; **to come to the — empezar** a destacar; **to push one's way to the — abrirse** camino a empujones hasta la primera fila (*etc*); **to send someone on in —** enviar a uno por delante.

(b) (*fig*) apariencias fpl; **it's all just — with him** con él no son más que apariencias; **to put on a bold — hacer** de tripas corazón.

3 vi: **to — on** (**to**) dar a, estar enfrente de.

frontage ['frʌntidʒ] n fachada f.

frontal ['frʌntl] adj frontal; **attack** de frente.

frontier ['frʌntiə*] **1** n frontera f. **2** attr fronterizo.

frontispiece ['frʌntispiːs] n (*Typ*) portada f.

front-page ['frʌnt'peidʒ] adj de primera página, de primera plana.

front room ['frʌnt'rum] n cuarto m que da a la calle, (*freq*) salón m.

front-wheel drive ['frʌntwiːl'draiv] n tracción f delantera.

frost [frɔst] **1** n helada f; (*visible, also hoar-, white —*) escarcha f; (*sl*) fracaso m; **4 degrees of —** 4 grados bajo cero.

2 vt **(a)** cubrir de escarcha; **the grass was —ed over** el césped apareció cubierto de escarcha.

(b) *plant* quemar.

frostbite ['frɔstbait] n congelación f.

frostbitten ['frɔst,bitn] adj congelado.

frosted ['frɔstid] adj *glass* deslustrado.

frosty ['frɔsti] adj **(a)** (*Meteorol*) **in — weather** en época de hielo; **on a — morning** una mañana de helada; **it was — last night** anoche heló.

(b) *surface* escarchado, cubierto de escarcha.

(c) (*fig*) glacial.

froth [frɔθ] **1** n espuma f; (*fig*) bachillerías fpl. **2** vi espumar, echar espuma; **to — at the mouth** espumajear.

frothy ['frɔθi] adj espumoso; (*fig*) superficial, de poca sustancia.

frown [fraun] **1** n ceño m; **he said with a — dijo** frunciendo el entrecejo. **2** vi fruncir el entrecejo; **to — at** mirar con ceño; **to — on** desaprobar.

frowning ['frauniŋ] adj (*fig*) ceñudo, amenazador.

frowzy ['frauzi] adj (*dirty*) sucio; (*untidy*) desaliñado; (*smelly*) fétido, maloliente.

froze [frəuz] pret of **freeze**.

frozen ['frəuzn] **1** ptp of **freeze**. **2** adj *food* congelado.

frugal ['fruːgəl] adj frugal.

frugality [fruː'gæliti] n frugalidad f.

fruit [fruːt] **1** n *sing and pl* (*on the tree etc*) fruto m (*also* Bio, fig); (*served as food*) fruta f, frutas fpl; **dried — fruta** f seca; **soft — frutas** fpl blandas; **to bear —** (*fig*) dar resultado.

2 vi frutar, dar fruto.

fruit cup ['fruːtkʌp] n sangría f.

fruit cake ['fruːtkeik] n tarta f de frutas.

fruit dish ['fruːtdiʃ] n frutera f.

fruiterer ['fruːtərə*] n frutero m; **—'s (shop)** frutería f.

fruitful ['fruːtful] adj (*fig*) fructuoso, provechoso.

fruition [fruː'iʃən] n cumplimiento m; (*of plan etc*) realización f; **to bring to — realizar; to come to —** llegar a la madurez, (*plan etc*) verse logrado, realizarse, (*hope*) cumplirse.

fruitless ['fruːtlis] adj infructuoso.

fruit machine ['fruːtmə,ʃiːn] n máquina f tragaperras.

fruit salts ['fruːtsɔlts] npl sal f de fruta(s).

fruit tree ['fruːttriː] n árbol m frutal.

fruity ['fruːti] adj que sabe a fruta; *voice* pastoso; *joke etc* verde; *style* de fuerte sabor.

frump [frʌmp] n espantajo m, estantigua f.

frustrate [frʌs'treit] vt frustrar; **to feel —d** sentirse frustrado.

frustration [frʌs'treiʃən] n frustración f.

fry¹ [frai] n (*Fish*) pececillos mpl; **small — gente** f menuda.

fry² [frai] **1** n fritada f. **2** vt freír; **fried fish** pescado m frito. **3** vi freírse.

frying pan ['fraiiŋ,pæn] n sartén f; **to jump out of the — into the fire** escaparse del trueno para dar en el relámpago.

fuchsia ['fjuːʃə] n fucsia f.

fuddled ['fʌdld] adj (*drunk*) borracho; (*confused*) aturdido; **to get — emborracharse**.

fuddy-duddy ['fʌdi,dʌdi] n (*fam*) persona f chapada a la antigua.

fuel [fjuəl] **1** n combustible m, carburante m; (*specifically coal*) carbón m, (*wood*) leña f; (*fig*) pábulo m; **to add — to the flames** echar leña al fuego.

2 vt aprovisionar de combustible.

3 vi aprovisionarse de combustible.

fuel oil ['fjuəlɔil] n aceite m combustible.

fuel tank ['fjuəltæŋk] n depósito m de combustible.

fug [fʌg] n aire m viciado (*or* confinado, cargado); **what a —!** ¡qué olor!; **there's a — in here** aquí huele a encerrado.

fuggy ['fʌgi] adj viciado, cargado; **it's — in here** aquí huele a encerrado.

fugitive ['fjuːdʒitiv] **1** adj fugitivo. **2** n fugitivo m, a f; (*refugee*) refugiado m, a f; **— from justice** prófugo m, a f.

fugue [fjuːg] n fuga f.

fulcrum ['fʌlkrəm] n fulcro m.

fulfil [ful'fil] vt *duty, promise* cumplir con; *ambition, norm, plan* realizar; *condition* satisfacer, llenar; *order* ejecutar.

fulfilment [ful'filmənt] n cumplimiento m; realización f; satisfacción f; ejecución f; (*satisfied feeling*) contento m, satisfacción f.

full [ful] **1** adj **(a)** lleno; *vehicle etc* completo (*also — up*); **— of cares** lleno de cuidados; **— of hope** lleno de esperanza, ilusionado; **— to bursting** lleno de bote en bote; **— to overflowing** lleno hasta los bordes; **to be — of food** no puedo más; **we are — up for July** no tenemos nada libre para julio; **I've had a — day** he estado ocupado todo el día; **he's had a — life** ha tenido una vida llena de actividades.

(b) (*fig*) *session* pleno, plenario; *member* de número; *authority, employment, power* pleno; **in — colour** a todo color; **in — flower** en plena floración.

(c) (*complete*) completo; *account* detallado, extenso; *measure* colmado, exacto; *meal* completo; *moon* lleno; *fare, price* íntegro, sin descuento; *speed, strength* máximo; *text* íntegro; *dress* de etiqueta; *uniform* de gala; **with — particulars** con todos los detalles; **until we have — information** hasta que tengamos todos los datos; **in the — sense of the word** en el sentido más amplio de la palabra; **a — hour** una hora entera, una hora larga; **a — 3 miles** 3 millas largas.

(d) *face* redondo; *figure* llenito; *bosom* abultado, (*euph*) importante; *lips* grueso; *skirt* amplio; *see* **name, speed** etc.

2 adv **(a) — well** perfectamente, muy bien, sobradamente.

(b) **it hit him — in the face** le dio de lleno en la cara.

3 n: **in — sin** abreviar, por extenso, sin quitar nada; **name in — nombre** m y apellidos; **text in — texto** m íntegro; **to pay in — pagar** la deuda entera; **to the — completamente**, al máximo.

fullback ['fulbæk] n defensa m.

full blast ['ful'blɑːst] adv *work* a máxima capacidad; *travel* a toda velocidad; *play etc* al máximo volumen sonoro, a toda potencia.

full-blooded ['ful'blʌdid] *adj character* viril, vigoroso; *animal* de raza.
full-blown ['ful'bləun] *adj* (*fig*) hecho y derecho.
full-bodied ['ful'bɔdid] *adj cry* fuerte; *wine* generoso.
full-dress ['ful'dres] *adj function* de etiqueta, de gala.
full-grown ['ful'grəun] *adj* crecido, maduro.
full-length ['ful'leŋθ] *adj picture* de cuerpo entero; *pool etc* de tamaño normal; — **film** cinta *f* de largo metraje.
fullness ['fulnis] *n* plenitud *f*; amplitud *f*; **in the —** **of time** a su debido tiempo.
full-scale ['ful'skeil] *adj study* amplio, extenso; *investigation* de gran alcance; *attack* en gran escala.
full-sized ['ful'saizd] *adj* de tamaño normal.
full stop ['ful'stɔp] *n* punto *m*; **to come to a —** (*fig*) pararse, paralizarse, quedar detenido en un punto muerto.
full-time ['ful'taim] **1** *adj professional man* en plena dedicación, *worker* que trabaja una jornada completa.
   2 *adv*: **to work —** trabajar en régimen de dedicación exclusiva, trabajar una jornada entera.
fully ['fuli] *adv* completamente, enteramente; **—** **dressed** completamente vestido; **I'm not — convinced** no me convenzo del todo; **he earns — as much as I do** gana sin duda tanto como yo; **it is — 3 miles** son lo menos 3 millas; **we waited — 3 hours** esperamos 3 horas largas.
fully-fashioned ['fuli'fæʃnd] *adj stocking* de costura francesa.
fully-fledged ['fuli'fledʒd] *adj* (*fig*) hecho y derecho.
fulminate ['fulmineit] *vi*: **to — against** tronar contra.
fulsome ['fulsəm] *adj* exagerado, excesivo; *person* servil.
fumble ['fʌmbl] **1** *vt* manosear, revolver (*etc*) torpemente; *ball* dejar caer; **to — one's way across a room** ir a tientas a través de un cuarto.
   2 *vi*: **to — for something** buscar algo con las manos; **to — for a word** titubear buscando una palabra; **to — in one's pockets** revolver en los bolsillos; **to — with something** manejar (*etc*) algo torpemente; **to — with a door** tratar torpemente de abrir una puerta.
fume [fju:m] *vi* humear; (*fig*) estar furioso, rabiar; echar pestes (*at thing* contra, *at person* de).
fumes [fju:mz] *npl* humo *m*, gas *m*, vapor *m*.
fumigate ['fju:migeit] *vt* fumigar.
fun [fʌn] *n* (*amusement*) diversión *f*; (*merriment*) alegría *f*; (*joke*) broma *f*; **for —, in —** en broma; **it's great —** es muy divertido; **he's great —** es una persona divertidísima; **it's not much — for us** no nos divertimos en absoluto; **it's only his —** está bromeando, te está tomando el pelo; **to do something for the — of it** hacer algo para divertirse, hacer algo sin propósito serio; **to have —** divertirse; **have —!** ¡que os divirtáis!, ¡que lo paséis bien!; **what — we had!** ¡cómo nos divertimos!; **we had — with the passports** nos armamos un lío con los pasaportes; **to make — of, to poke — at** burlarse de, ridiculizar; **to spoil the —** aguar la fiesta.
function ['fʌnkʃən] **1** *n* función *f*; **it is no part of my — to + infin** no corresponde a mi cargo + *infin*; **to exceed one's —s** excederse en sus funciones.
   2 *vi* funcionar.
functional ['fʌnkʃnəl] *adj* funcional.
functionary ['fʌnkʃənəri] *n* funcionario *m*.
fund [fʌnd] **1** *n* fondo *m*; **—s** fondos *mpl*; **to be in —s** estar en fondos; **to have a — of stories** saber un montón de chistes. **2** *vt debt* consolidar.
fundamental [.fʌndə'mentl] *adj* fundamental; **to be — to** ser esencial para.
fundamentally [.fʌndə'mentəli] *adv* fundamentalmente, esencialmente.
fundamentals [.fʌndə'mentlz] *npl* fundamentos *mpl*.
funeral ['fju:nərəl] **1** *adj* and *attr march, procession* fúnebre; *pyre* funerario; *service* de difuntos; **—** **director** director *m* de funeraria.
   2 *n* entierro *m*, funerales *mpl*; **that's your —!** (*fam*) ¡allá te las compongas!, ¡allá te las apañes!, ¡con tu pan te lo comas!
funereal [fju:'niəriəl] *adj* fúnebre, funéreo.
fun fair ['fʌnfeə*] *n* parque *m* de atracciones.
fungoid ['fʌngɔid] *adj* fungoideo.
fungous ['fʌngəs] *adj* fungoso.
fungus ['fʌngəs] *n*, *pl* **fungi** ['fʌngai] *n* hongo *m*.
funicular [fju:'nikjulə*] *n* (ferrocarril *m*) funicular *m*.
funk [fʌnk] (*fam*) **1** *n* (**a**) (*state*) canguelo *m*, jindama *f*; **to be in a** (**blue**) **—** estar muerto de miedo.
   (**b**) (*person*) gallina *mf*, mandria *mf*.
   2 *vt*: **to — it** rajarse, dejar de hacer algo por

miedo, retirarse por miedo; **to — doing something** dejar de hacer algo por miedo.
funky ['fʌnki] *adj* (*fam*) cobarde, miedoso; **you're —!** ¡cobarde!
funnel ['fʌnl] *n* embudo *m*; (*Naut, Rail etc*) chimenea *f*.
funnily ['fʌnili] *adv* de un modo divertido; **—** **enough . . .** cosa curiosa . . ., cosa más rara . . .
funny ['fʌni] *adj* (**a**) (*amusing*) divertido, gracioso, cómico; (*full of jokes*) chistoso; **I thought the film very —** la película me hizo mucha gracia; **that's not — —** eso no tiene gracia; **I find it — that, it strikes me as —** that me hace mucha gracia que; **he's trying to be —** quiere hacerse el gracioso.
   (**b**) (*odd*) raro, curioso; **a — feeling** una sensación rara; **the — thing about it is** that lo curioso es que; **he's — that way** tiene esa manía.
funny bone ['fʌnibəun] *n* hueso *m* de la alegría.
fur [fə:*] *n* piel *f*; (*on tongue*) saburra *f*; (*in kettle*) sarro *m*; **— coat** abrigo *m* de pieles.
furbish ['fə:biʃ] *vt*: **to — up** renovar, restaurar.
furious ['fjuəriəs] *adj* furioso; *effort etc* frenético, violento; *pace* vertiginoso; **to be — with someone** estar muy enfadado con uno; **to get —** ponerse furioso.
furiously ['fjuəriəsli] *adv* con furia.
furl [fə:l] *vt* (*Naut*) aferrar; *wings* recoger.
furlong ['fə:lɔŋ] *n* estadio *m* (*octava parte de una milla*).
furlough ['fə:ləu] *n* (*Mil etc*) licencia *f*.
furnace ['fə:nis] *n* horno *m*; **the town was like a —** la ciudad era un horno.
furnish ['fə:niʃ] *vt* (**a**) (*provide*) proveer, suministrar, proporcionar (*someone with something* algo a uno); *opportunity* dar, proporcionar, deparar; *proof* aducir; *information* facilitar; **we are —ed with all that is necessary** estamos equipados con todo lo necesario.
   (**b**) *room* amueblar (*with* de); **—ed flat** piso *m* amueblado.
furnishings ['fə:niʃiŋz] *npl* muebles *mpl*, mobiliario *m*.
furniture ['fə:nitʃə*] *n* muebles *mpl*, mobiliario *m*, mueblaje *m*; (*piece of —*) mueble *m*.
furniture van ['fə:nitʃə,væn] *n* camión *m* de mudanzas.
furrier ['fʌriə*] *n* peletero *m*.
furrow ['fʌrəu] **1** *n* surco *m*; (*on face*) arruga *f*; **to plough a lonely —** ser el único en estudiar (*etc*) algo. **2** *vt* surcar; arrugar.
furry ['fə:ri] *adj* peludo.
further ['fə:ðə*] *comp* of **far**: **1** *adv* (**a**) (*place*) más lejos, más allá; **move it — away** apártalo un poco más; **— back** más atrás; **— off** más lejos; **— on** más adelante; **how much — is it?** ¿cuánto camino nos queda?; **have you much — to go?** ¿le queda mucho camino por hacer?; **I got no — with him** no logré sacar más consecuencias de él; **nothing is — from my thoughts** nada más lejos de mi intención.
   (**b**) (*-more*) además; **and I — believe that** y creo además que.
   (**c**) **to go — into a matter** estudiar una cosa más detenidamente; **they questioned us —** nos hicieron más preguntas; **he heard nothing —** no le volvieron a decir nada; **don't trouble yourself any —** no se moleste más.
   2 *adj* (**a**) (*place*) más lejano, más remoto, de más allá; *end, side* opuesto; **at the — end** en el otro extremo.
   (**b**) (*additional*) nuevo, adicional; complementario, supletorio; *education* superior; **— facts** nuevos datos *mpl*, más datos *mpl*; **after — consideration** después de considerarlo más detenidamente; **till — orders** hasta nueva orden; **without — loss of time** sin más pérdida de tiempo.
   3 *vt* promover, fomentar, adelantar.
furtherance ['fə:ðərəns] *n* promoción *f*, fomento *m*.
furthermore ['fə:ðə:'mɔ:*] *adv* además.
furthermost ['fə:ðəməust] *adj* más lejano.
furthest ['fə:ðist] *superl of* **far**: **1** *adv* más lejos; **that's the — that anyone has gone** es el punto extremo a que han llegado, nadie ha ido más allá.
   2 *adj* más lejano; extremo.
furtive ['fə:tiv] *adj* furtivo.
furtively ['fə:tivli] *adv* furtivamente.
fury ['fjuəri] *n* furor *m*, furia *f*; violencia *f*; frenesí *m*; **the Furies** las Furias; **like — a** toda furia, (*of person*) hecho una furia; **to be in a —** estar furioso; **to work oneself up into a —** montar en cólera.
furze [fə:z] *n* aulaga *f*, tojo *m*.

fuse [fjuːz] **1** n (*Elec*) plomo m, fusible m; (*Mil*) mecha f, espoleta f.
2 vt fundir; (*fig*) fusionar.
3 vi fundirse; (*fig*) fusionarse; **the lights —d** se fundieron los plomos.
fuse box ['fjuːzbɔks] n caja f de fusibles.
fuselage ['fjuːzəlɑːʒ] n fuselaje m.
fusillade [ˌfjuːziˈleid] n descarga f cerrada; (*fig*) lluvia f, torrente m.
fusion ['fjuːʒən] n fusión f (*also fig*), fundición f.
fuss [fʌs] **1** n **(a)** (*noise, bustle*) conmoción f, bulla f, alharaca f.
 (b) (*dispute*) lío m; protesta f; **that — about the money** ese lío con el dinero; **to kick up** (*or* **make**) **a —** dar cuatro voces, armar un lío; **I think you were quite right to make a —** creo que hiciste bien en protestar.
 (c) (*excessive display*) aspaviento m, hazañería f; **it's a lot of — about nothing** mucho ruido y pocas nueces; **there's no need to make such a —** no es para tanto; **to make a — of** hacer mimos a, hacer fiestas a.
 (d) (*formalities*) ceremonias fpl; trámites mpl; **such a — to get a passport!** ¡tantos trámites para conseguir un pasaporte!
 2 vi agitarse, preocuparse (por bagatelas); **to —**
about andar azacaneado, andar de acá para allá; **to — over someone** mimar con exceso a uno.
fusspot ['fʌspɔt] n (*fam*) persona f que se preocupa por nimiedades, persona f tontamente exigente.
fussy ['fʌsi] adj *person* (*demanding*) exigente; (*nervous*) nervioso; *details* nimio; *dress* con muchos ringorrangos; *decoration* con muchos adornos.
fusty ['fʌsti] adj mohoso, rancio; *air*, *room* que huele a cerrado.
futile ['fjuːtail] adj inútil, vano, infructuoso.
futility [fjuːˈtiliti] n inutilidad f, lo inútil.
future ['fjuːtʃə*] **1** adj futuro; venidero; **in — years** en los años venideros.
 2 n futuro m, porvenir m; **—s** (*Comm*) futuros mpl; **in (the) —** en el futuro, en lo sucesivo; **in the near —** en fecha próxima; **there's no — in it** esto no tiene porvenir; **what does the — hold for us?** ¿qué nos tiene reservado el destino?
futurism ['fjuːtʃərizəm] n futurismo m.
futuristic [ˌfjuːtʃəˈristik] adj futurístico.
fuze [fjuːz] n (*US*) = **fuse**.
fuzz [fʌz] n tamo m, pelusa f; (*on face*) vello m.
fuzzy ['fʌzi] adj (*hairy*) velloso; *hair* muy ensortijado; (*blurred*) borroso.

G

gab [gæb] (*fam*) **1** n (*chatter*) cháchara *f*; (*chat*) charla *f*; **to have the gift of the** — tener un pico de oro. **2** *vi* parlotear, charlar, cotorrear.
gabardine [,gæbə'di:n] n gabardina *f*.
gabble ['gæbl] **1** n torrente m de palabras ininteligibles. **2** *vt* decir (*or* leer *etc*) atropelladamente, pronunciar de modo ininteligible.
3 *vi* hablar atropelladamente; parlotear, cotorrear; **they were gabbling away in French** hablaban atropelladamente en francés.
gaberdine [,gæbə'di:n] n gabardina *f*.
gable ['geibl] n aguilón m; — **roof** tejado m de dos aguas.
gad[1] [gæd] *vi*: **to** — **about** salir mucho, viajar mucho, ir a muchos sitios.
gad[2] [gæd] *interj* ¡caramba!
gadabout ['gædəbaut] n persona *f* aficionada a salir (*etc*) mucho.
gadfly ['gædflai] n tábano m.
gadget ['gædʒit] n artilugio m, chisme m, aparato m.
Gael [geil] n gaélico m, a *f*.
Gaelic ['geilik] **1** *adj* gaélico. **2** n (*language*) gaélico m.
gaff[1] [gæf] **1** n arpón m, garfio m. **2** *vt* arponear, enganchar.
gaff[2] [gæf] n (*sl*): **to blow the** — descubrir el pastel.
gaffe [gæf] n plancha *f*; **to make a** — tirarse una plancha.
gaffer ['gæfə*] n vejete m, tío m; (*foreman*) capataz m; (*boss*) jefe m.
gag [gæg] **1** n mordaza *f*; (*Parl*) clausura *f*; (*Theat*) morcilla *f*; (*joke*) chiste m; (*hoax*) broma *f*; (*gimmick*) truco m publicitario; **is this a** —? ¿es una broma esto?; **it's a** — **to raise funds** es un truco para reunir fondos.
2 *vt* amordazar; (*fig*) amordazar, hacer callar; (*Parl*) clausurar; **discussion** impedir, estorbar.
3 *vi* (*Theat*) meter morcillas; (*joke*) contar chistes, chunguear; **I was only** —**ging** lo dije en broma.
gaga ['gɑ:'gɑ:] *adj* (*sl*) lelo, chocho; **to be going** — chochear.
gaiety ['geiiti] n alegría *f*, regocijo m; (*of gathering etc*) animación *f*; **gaieties** diversiones *fpl* alegres.
gaily ['geili] *adv* alegremente.
gain [gein] **1** n (*increase*) aumento m (*in*, *of* de); (*profit*, *earning*) ganancia *f*, beneficio m; **ill-gotten** —**s** ganancias *fpl* ilícitas; **his loss is our** — su pérdida supone nuestra ganancia; **there have been** —**s of up to 3 points** ha habido alzas de hasta 3 enteros; **I lost all my** — se perdí todas mis ganancias.
2 *vt* ganar; *objective* conseguir; *possession*, *territory etc* adquirir; *approval*, *respect* merecer, captar, conquistar; (*reach*) llegar a, alcanzar; *time* ganar; **my watch has** —**ed 5 minutes** mi reloj se ha adelantado 5 minutos; **I've** —**ed 3 kilos** he engordado 3 kilos; **the shares have** —**ed 4 points** las acciones han subido 4 enteros; **what have you** —**ed by it?** ¿qué has logrado con esto?; **what do you hope to** —? ¿qué provecho vas a sacar?
3 *vi* (*shares etc*) aumentar en valor, subir; (*Med*) mejorar; (*in weight*) engordar, poner carnes; (*in advantage*) ganar terreno; **to** — **in popularity** resultar más popular, adquirir mayor popularidad; **it** —**s in contrast with the other picture** parece más atractivo al compararse con el otro cuadro; **to** — **on someone** ir ganando terreno a uno, ir alcanzando a uno, (*and outstrip*) ir dejando atrás a uno.
gainer ['geinə*] n: **to be the** — salir ganando.
gainful ['geinful] *adj* *employment* remunerado, retribuido.
gainsay [,gein'sei] (*irr*: *see* **say**) *vt* contradecir, negar; **it cannot be gainsaid** es innegable.
gait [geit] n modo m de andar, paso m.
gaiter ['geitə*] n polaina *f*.
gal [gæl] n (*fam*) = **girl**.

gala ['gɑ:lə] n fiesta *f*; **sports** — certamen m deportivo; **swimming** — gala *f* de natación.
galactic [gə'læktik] *adj* lácteo; (*Astron*) galáctico.
galaxy ['gæləksi] n galaxia *f*; (*fig*) grupo m brillante, constelación *f*, pléyade *f*.
gale [geil] n ventarrón m, vendaval m; (*storm*) tempestad *f*; **to blow a** — soplar una galerna.
Galen ['geilən] m Galeno.
Galician [gə'lifiən] **1** *adj* gallego. **2** n gallego m, a *f*. **3** n (*dialect*) gallego m.
Galilee ['gælili:] Galilea *f*.
gall[1] [gɔ:l] **1** n (*Anat*) bilis *f*, hiel *f*; (*fig*) hiel *f*; (*fam*) descaro m; **she had the** — **to say that** tuvo el descaro de decir eso. **2** *vt* mortificar.
gall[2] [gɔ:l] n (*Bot*) agalla *f*.
gallant ['gælənt] *adj* (a) (*brave*) valiente, valeroso, bizarro; (*showy*) lucido, gallardo; (*stately*) imponente; **the** — **captain** el intrépido capitán.
(b) (*attentive*: *also* [gə'lænt]) galante; cortés, atento.
gallantly ['gæləntli] *adv* (a) valientemente. (b) galantemente; cortésmente.
gallantry ['gæləntri] (a) (*bravery*) valentía *f*, valor m, heroísmo m, bizarría *f*. (b) (*courtesy*) galantería *f*, cortesía *f*; **gallantries** galanterías *fpl*.
gall-bladder ['gɔ:l,blædə*] n vesícula *f* biliar.
galleon ['gæliən] n galeón m.
gallery ['gæləri] n galería *f* (*also* Min, Theat); (*for spectators*) tribuna *f*; (**art**) — museo m de bellas artes; **a** — **of portraits** una colección de retratos; **to play to the** — actuar para la galería.
galley ['gæli] n (*ship*, Typ) galera *f*; (*kitchen*) cocina *f*, fogón m.
galley proof ['gælipru:f] n galerada *f*.
galley slave ['gælisleiv] n galeote m.
gallicism ['gælisizəm] n galicismo m.
galling ['gɔ:liŋ] *adj* mortificante.
gallivant [,gæli'vænt] *vi* = **gad**[1].
gallon ['gælən] n galón m (= 4,546 litros, US = 3,785 litros).
gallop ['gæləp] **1** n galope m; (*distance covered*) galopada *f*; **at a** —a galope; **at full** — a galope tendido; **to break into a** — echar a galopar.
2 *vt* hacer galopar.
3 *vi* galopar; **to** — **off** alejarse a galope; **to** — **past** desfilar a galope; **to** — **up** llegar a galope.
galloping ['gæləpiŋ] *adj* (*Med and fig*) galopante.
gallows ['gæləuz] n sing horca *f*.
gallstone ['gɔ:lstəun] n cálculo m biliario.
galore [gə'lɔ:*] *adv* en abundancia, a porrilla.
galosh [gə'lɔʃ] n chanclo m (de goma).
galumph [gə'lʌmf] *vi* (*hum*) saltar alegremente (por una victoria *etc*).
galvanic [gæl'vænik] *adj* galvánico.
galvanism ['gælvənizəm] n galvanismo m.
galvanize ['gælvənaiz] *vt* galvanizar; **to** — **someone into life** sacudir a uno de su abstracción; **to** — **someone into doing something** sacudir a uno para que haga algo.
galvanized ['gælvənaizd] *adj* galvanizado.
gambit ['gæmbit] n gambito m; (*fig*) táctica *f*.
gamble ['gæmbl] **1** n jugada *f* (de resultado imprevisible); empresa *f* arriesgada; **life's a** — la vida es una lotería; **I did it as a pure** — lo hice para probar suerte nada más; **the** — **came off** la tentativa tuvo éxito, la jugada nos salió bien; **to have a** — **on horse** jugar dinero a, apostar a, *company shares* especular en.
2 *vt* jugar, aventurar en el juego; **to** — **one's future** jugarse el porvenir; **to** — **away** perder en el juego.
3 *vi* jugar; (*Fin*) especular; **to** — **on the Stock Exchange** jugar a la bolsa; **to** — **on something**

happening atenerse a la probabilidad de que ocurra algo, confiar en que algo vaya a suceder; **to — with others' money** especular con el dinero ajeno.

gambler ['gæmblə*] n jugador m, ora f.

gambling ['gæmbliŋ] n juego m; **— on the Stock Exchange** especulación f en la bolsa.

gambling den ['gæmbliŋden] n garito m, casa f de juego.

gambol ['gæmbəl] vi brincar, retozar, juguetear.

game¹ [geim] **1** n (a) (in general) juego m; deporte m; (match: with ball etc) partido m, (of cards, chess etc) partida f; (at bridge) manga f; —, **set and match** juego, set y partido; — **of chance** juego m de azar; **indoor** — diversión f de salón; **it's only a —** es un juego nada más; **this isn't a —** esto no es ninguna broma, esto va de veras; **the — is not worth the candle** la cosa no vale la pena; **to be off one's —** no estar en forma, estar desentrenado; **to go to —** (Bridge) ir a manga; **to have a — of chess** echar una partida de ajedrez; **to have a — with** (tease) tomar el pelo a, hacer una broma a; **to play the —** (fig) jugar limpio; **he plays a good — of football** juega bien al fútbol, es buen futbolista; **two can play at that —** donde las dan las toman; **to play a double —** jugar doble; **to play a waiting —** estar a ver venir, esperar hasta ver qué pasa; **to put someone off his —** hacer que uno pierda su concentración.

(b) (deception) **the — is up** todo se acabó; **they saw the — was up** comprendieron que ya no había nada que hacer; **what's the —?** ¿qué hacen Vds ahí?, ¿qué pretenden Vds con eso?; **we know his little —** le hemos calado; **I wonder what his — is?** ¿qué estará tramando?

(c) (fam) lío m; **I had such a — getting here** me hice un lío al venir aquí; **what a — this is!** ¡qué faena!

(d) (business) **how long have you been in this —?** ¿cuánto tiempo lleva Vd dedicado a esto?; **what's your —?** ¿a qué se dedica Vd?

(e) (Hunting) caza f; **big —** caza f mayor; **fair —** caza f legal; (fig) objeto m legítimo; **it is fair — for criticism** es un objeto legítimo de la crítica.

2 adj animoso, valiente; **are you —?** ¿quieres?, ¿te animas?; **to be — for anything** atreverse a todo.

3 vi jugar (por dinero).

game² [geim] adj (lame) cojo.

gamebag ['geimbæg] n morral m.

game bird ['geimbə:d] n ave f de caza.

gamecock ['geimkɔk] n gallo m de pelea.

gamekeeper ['geim,ki:pə*] n guardabosque m.

gamester ['geimstə*] n jugador m, tahur m.

gamin ['gæmɛ] n golfillo m.

gamine [gæ'mi:n] n chica f provocativa, joven f picaruela; **— haircut** corte m a la garçon.

gaming ['geimiŋ] n juego m.

gaming house ['geimiŋhaus] n casa f de juego.

gammon ['gæmən] n jamón m.

gamp [gæmp] n (fam) paraguas m.

gamut ['gæmət] n gama f.

gamy ['geimi] adj meat manido.

gander ['gændə*] n ganso m (macho).

gang [gæŋ] **1** n pandilla f, cuadrilla f, grupo m; (of workmen) brigada f; (criminal) pandilla f; **he's one of the —** now ya es uno de los nuestros.

2 vi (a) (Scot) ir; **to — agley** fracasar.

(b) **to — up** conspirar, obrar de concierto (against, on contra).

ganger ['gæŋə*] n capataz m.

gangling ['gæŋgliŋ] adj larguirucho, desgarbado.

ganglion ['gæŋgliən] n ganglio m.

gangplank ['gæŋplæŋk] n (Naut) plancha f.

gangrene ['gæŋgri:n] n gangrena f.

gangster ['gæŋstə*] n pistolero m, pandillero m, gángster m.

gangsterism ['gæŋstərizəm] n gangsterismo m.

gangway ['gæŋwei] n pasillo m, pasadizo m; (Naut: on ship) escalerilla f, pasarela f; (from ship to shore) plancha f, pasadera f; **—!** ¡abran paso!

gannet ['gænit] n alcatraz m.

gantlet ['gæntlit] n (US: Rail) vía f traslapada, vía f de garganta.

gantry ['gæntri] n caballete m.

gaol [dʒeil] n see **jail**.

gap [gæp] n (natural) vacío m, hueco m; (man-made) abertura f, brecha f; (in wall etc) boquete m; (in mountains) desfiladero m; (in writing) espacio m; (in text) laguna f; (of time) intervalo m; (in traffic, trees) claro m; (crack) hendedura f, resquicio m; **he left a — which it will be hard to fill** dejó un hueco difícil de llenar; **leave a — for the name** deje un espacio para poner el nombre.

gape [geip] vi (a) abrirse (mucho), estar muy abierto; **the chasm —d before him** se abría delante de él la sima.

(b) (person) estar boquiabierto; **to — at** mirar boquiabierto, embobarse con.

gaping ['geipiŋ] adj (a) abierto. (b) person boquiabierto, embobado.

gap-toothed ['gæp'tu:θt] adj con dientes mal formados; que ha perdido un diente (or varios dientes).

garage ['gæra:ʒ] **1** n garaje m. **2** vt dejar en garaje.

garb [ga:b] **1** n traje m, vestido m; (iro) ropaje m (also fig). **2** vt vestir (in de).

garbage ['ga:bidʒ] n basuras fpl, desperdicios mpl.

garbage can ['ga:bidʒkæn] n (US) cubo m para basuras.

garble ['ga:bl] vt mutilar, falsear (por selección).

garden ['ga:dn] **1** n jardín m; **back —, kitchen —** huerto m; **front —** jardín m; **G— of Eden** Edén m. **2** attr de jardín.

3 vi cultivar un huerto, trabajar en el jardín (or huerto).

gardener ['ga:dnə*] n jardinero m, a f; (professional) hortelano m; **I'm no —** no entiendo de jardines.

gardenia [ga:'di:niə] n gardenia f.

gardening ['ga:dniŋ] n jardinería f, horticultura f.

garden party ['ga:dn,pa:ti] n recepción f (al aire libre).

gargantuan [ga:'gæntjuən] adj colosal, gigantesco.

gargle ['ga:gl] **1** n (act) gárgaras fpl; (liquid) gargarismo m. **2** vi gargarizar, hacer gárgaras.

gargoyle ['ga:gɔil] n gárgola f.

garish ['gɛəriʃ] adj chillón, llamativo, charro.

garland ['ga:lənd] **1** n guirnalda f. **2** vt enguirnaldar.

garlic ['ga:lik] n ajo m.

garment ['ga:mənt] n prenda f (de vestir).

garner ['ga:nə*] **1** n troj f, granero m; (fig) acopio m, abundancia f; provisión f. **2** vt entrojar; (fig) recoger.

garnet ['ga:nit] n granate m.

garnish ['ga:niʃ] **1** n (Cook) aderezo m. **2** vt adornar (with de); (Cook) aderezar (with de).

garnishing ['ga:niʃiŋ] n (Cook) aderezo m.

Garonne [gə'rɔn] n Garona m.

garret ['gærit] n guardilla f, desván m.

garrison ['gærisən] **1** n guarnición f. **2** vt guarnecer.

garrotte [gə'rɔt] vt agarrotar.

garrulity [gə'ru:liti] n garrulidad f.

garrulous ['gæruləs] adj gárrulo.

garter ['ga:tə*] n liga f; **Order of the G—** Orden f de la Jarretera.

garter belt ['ga:təbelt] n (US) portaligas m.

gas [gæs] **1** n gas m; (US) gasolina f; **natural —** gas m natural; **to step on the —** (fam) acelerar la marcha. **2** vt asfixiar con gas. **3** vi (fam) charlar, parlotear.

gasbag ['gæsbæg] n (Aer) bolsa f de gas; (fam) charlatán m, ana f.

gas bracket ['gæs,brækit] n brazo m de lámpara de gas.

gas burner ['gæs,bə:nə*] n mechero m de gas.

gas chamber ['gæs,tʃeimbə*] n cámara f de gas.

Gascon ['gæskən] **1** adj gascón. **2** n gascón m, ona f. **3** nm (dialect) gascón m.

Gascony ['gæskəni] n Gascuña f.

gas cooker ['gæs'kukə*] n cocina f de (or a) gas.

gaseous ['gæsiəs] adj gaseoso.

gas fire ['gæs'faiə*] n estufa f de gas.

gas fitter ['gæs,fitə*] n empleado m del gas.

gash [gæʃ] **1** n raja f, hendedura f; (wound) cuchillada f. **2** vt rajar, hender; (wound) acuchillar.

gasholder ['gæs,həuldə*] n gasómetro m.

gas jet ['gæsdʒet] n llama f de mechero de gas.

gasket ['gæskit] n (Mech) junta f.

gaslight ['gæslait] n luz f de gas, alumbrado m de gas.

gas main ['gæsmein] n cañería f maestra de gas.

gasman ['gæsmæn] n, pl **—men** [men] empleado m del gas.

gas mantle ['gæs,mæntl] n manguito m incandescente.

gasmask ['gæsma:sk] n careta f antigás.

gas meter ['gæs,mi:tə*] n contador m de gas.

gasoline ['gæsəlin] n (US) gasolina f.

gasometer [gæ'sɔmitə*] n gasómetro m.

gas oven ['gæs,ʌvn] n cocina f de (or a) gas.

gasp [ga:sp] **1** n boqueada f; (cry) grito m sofocado; **last —** boqueada f; **to be at one's last —** dar su última boqueada; **with a — of astonishment** con un grito sofocado de asombro.

2 vt: **to — (out)** decir con voz entrecortada.

3 vi boquear, anhelar, respirar con dificultad; (pant) jadear; **to — for air** (or breath) luchar por respirar; **to — with astonishment** dar un grito sofocado de asombro.

gasper ['gɑːspə*] n (sl) pito m, truja m.

gas ring ['gæsriŋ] n hornillo m de gas.

gas stove ['gæs'stəuv] n cocina f de (or a) gas.

gassy ['gæsi] adj gaseoso.

gas tank ['gæstæŋk] n (US) depósito m de gasolina.

gas tap ['gæstæp] n llave f del gas.

gastric ['gæstrik] adj gástrico.

gastritis [gæs'traitis] n gastritis f.

gastronome ['gæstrənəum] n, **gastronomist** [,gæs-'trɔnəmist] n gastrónomo m, a f.

gastronomic [,gæstrə'nɔmik] adj gastronómico.

gastronomy [gæs'trɔnəmi] n gastronomía f.

gasworks ['gæswəːks] npl fábrica f de gas.

gat [gæt] n (US sl) revólver m.

gate [geit] n puerta f (also of town); (iron) verja f; (Rail) barrera f; (of sluice) compuerta f; (Sport) entrada f.

gatecrash ['geitkræʃ] 1 vt colarse de gorra en, asistir sin ser invitado a. 2 vi colarse de gorra, asistir sin ser invitado.

gatehouse ['geithaus] n, pl **-houses** [,hauziz] casa f del guarda (or del portero etc).

gatekeeper ['geit,kiːpə*] n portero m; (Rail) guardabarrera m.

gate-legged ['geitlegd] adj: **— table** mesa f de alas abatibles.

gate money ['geit,mʌni] n ingresos mpl de entrada.

gatepost ['geitpəust] n poste m de una puerta (de cercado).

gateway ['geitwei] n = **gate**; (fig) puerta f, pórtico m (to de).

gather ['gæðə*] 1 vt (a) (assemble) reunir, recoger; acumular, acopiar; (harvest) recolectar; flowers, wood coger; (Sew) fruncir; **to — in** recoger; taxes etc recaudar; **to — together** reunir, juntar; **to — up** recoger.
(b) **to — dust** empolvarse; **to — speed** ganar velocidad, ir cada vez más rápidamente; **to — strength** cobrar fuerzas.
(c) **to — that** colegir que, sacar la consecuencia que; **I — from him that** según lo que él me dice; **what are we to — from this?** ¿qué consecuencia sacamos de esto?; **as you will have —ed** según Vd habrá comprendido; **as one —s from** según se desprende de.
2 vi (also **to — together**) reunirse, juntarse, congregarse; (clouds) amontonarse; (Med) formar pus; **to — round** someone agruparse en torno a uno; **— round!** ¡acercaos!; **the —ing storm** la tormenta que amenaza.

gathering ['gæðəriŋ] n (meeting) reunión f, asamblea f; (persons present) concurrencia f; (Med) absceso m.

gauche [gəuʃ] adj desmañado; (socially) falto de confianza, poco seguro de sí mismo.

gaudy ['gɔːdi] adj chillón, llamativo.

gauge [geidʒ] 1 n (standard measure) norma f de medida; (of gun etc) calibre m; (test) indicación f, prueba f; (instrument) indicador m, manómetro m; (Rail) ancho m, entrevía f, trocha f (SAm).
2 vt medir; calibrar; (fig) juzgar, estimar; **to — the distance with one's eye** medir la distancia con el ojo; **to — the right moment** elegir el momento propicio.

Gaul [gɔːl] 1 Galia f. 2 n (person) galo m, a f.

gaunt [gɔːnt] adj flaco, desvaído, chupado; (fig) severo, adusto.

gauntlet ['gɔːntlit] n guante m; (Hist) guantelete m; **to run the —** correr baquetas; **to run the — of** (fig) pasar por los peligros de; salir ileso de; **to throw down the —** arrojar el guante.

gauze [gɔːz] n gasa f.

gave [geiv] pret of **give**.

gavel ['gævl] n martillo m (de presidente o subastador).

gavotte [gə'vɔt] n (Hist) gavota f.

gawk [gɔːk] 1 n bobo m. 2 vi papar moscas.

gawky ['gɔːki] adj desgarbado, torpe.

gawp [gɔːp] vi (fam) papar moscas; **to — at** mirar boquiabierto.

gay [gei] adj alegre; colour, appearance brillante, vistoso; life lleno de placeres; **to have a — time** pasarlo bomba.

gaze [geiz] 1 n mirada f (fija); **his — met mine** cruzamos una mirada. 2 vi (also **to — at, to — upon**) mirar (con fijeza), contemplar.

gazelle [gə'zel] n gacela f.

gazette [gə'zet] n gaceta f.

gazetteer [,gæzi'tiə*] n diccionario m geográfico.

gear [giə*] 1 n (a) (equipment) equipo m, herramientas fpl, pertrechos mpl; (fam) cosas fpl, bártulos mpl; (clothing) ropa f, traje m.

(b) (apparatus) aparato m, mecanismo m.
(c) (Mech) engranaje m, rueda f dentada; **timing —** engranaje m de distribución; **in —** en juego, engranado; **to be in —** with engranar con; **to throw out of —** desengranar, (fig) dislocar.
(d) (Aut etc: speed) marcha f, velocidad f, cambio m; **there are 5 forward —s** hay 5 marchas adelante; **bottom —, low —** primera velocidad f; **second —** segunda velocidad f; **top —** tercera (or cuarta) velocidad f; **neutral —** punto m muerto; **reverse —** cambio m de marcha atrás; **to change —** cambiar de marcha.
2 vt (Mech) engranar (into, with con); **to — down** desmultiplicar; **to — up** multiplicar; **the programme is —ed in** with (or to) **the plan** el programa forma parte integral del plan.
3 vi engranar (into, with con); **it —s in with the plan** concuerda con el plan, se desarrolla al ritmo del plan.

gearbox ['giəbɔks] n (Aut) caja f de cambios; (Mech) caja f de engranajes; **with automatic —** con cambio de marchas automático.

gear-lever ['giə,liːvə*], (US) **gearshift** ['giə,ʃift] n palanca f de velocidades.

gearwheel ['giəwiːl] n rueda f dentada.

gee [dʒiː] interj ¡caramba!; **— up!** ¡arre!

gee-gee ['dʒiːdʒiː] n (fam) caballito m.

geese [giːs] npl of **goose**.

geezer ['giːzə*] n (sl) vejancón m, tío m.

Geiger counter ['gaigə,kauntə*] n contador m Geiger.

geisha ['geiʃə] n geisha f.

gelatin(e) ['dʒelətiːn] n gelatina f.

gelatinous [dʒi'lætinəs] adj gelatinoso.

geld [geld] vt castrar, capar.

gelding ['geldiŋ] n caballo m castrado.

gelignite ['dʒelignait] n gelignita f.

gem [dʒem] n joya f (also fig), piedra f preciosa.

Gemini ['dʒemini:] npl (Astron) Géminis m, Gemelos mpl.

gen [dʒen] n (sl) información f.

gendarme ['ʒɑ̃ːndɑːm] n gendarme m.

gender ['dʒendə*] n género m.

gene [dʒiːn] n gen m.

genealogical [,dʒiːniə'lɔdʒikəl] adj genealógico.

genealogist [,dʒiːni'ælədʒist] n genealogista mf.

genealogy [,dʒiːni'ælədʒi] n genealogía f.

genera ['dʒenərə] npl of **genus**.

general ['dʒenərəl] 1 adj general; (common) corriente, usual; cargo mixto; anaesthetic total.
2 n (Mil) general m; (servant) chica f para todo; **in —** en general, por lo general.

generality [,dʒenə'ræliti] n generalidad f.

generalization [,dʒenərəlai'zeiʃən] n generalización f.

generalize ['dʒenərəlaiz] vi generalizar.

generally ['dʒenərəli] adv generalmente, en general, por lo común; **— speaking** en términos generales.

generalship ['dʒenərəlʃip] n estrategia f, táctica f; (leadership) dirección f, don m de mando.

generate ['dʒenəreit] vt (Elec etc) generar; (fig) producir.

generating station ['dʒenəreitiŋ,steiʃən] n central f generadora.

generation [,dʒenə'reiʃən] n generación f; **the young —** los jóvenes; **the rising —** las nuevas generaciones; **the '98 —** la generación del '98.

generator ['dʒenəreitə*] n generador m.

generic [dʒi'nerik] adj genérico.

generosity [,dʒenə'rɔsiti] n generosidad f.

generous ['dʒenərəs] adj generoso; supply, quantity abundante, amplio, liberal.

generously ['dʒenərəsli] adv generosamente; abundantemente.

genesis ['dʒenisis] n génesis f; **G—** Génesis m.

genetic [dʒi'netik] adj genético, genésico.

geneticist [dʒi'netisist] n genetista mf.

genetics [dʒi'netiks] npl genética f.

Geneva [dʒi'niːvə] Ginebra f.

genial ['dʒiːniəl] adj simpático, afable.

geniality [,dʒiːni'æliti] n simpatía f, afabilidad f.

genially ['dʒiːniəli] adv afablemente.

genitals ['dʒenitlz] npl órganos mpl genitales.

genitive ['dʒenitiv] n genitivo m.

genius ['dʒiːniəs] n genio m; genialidad f; **man of —** hombre m genial; **he's a —** es un genio, es genial; **you're a —!** (iro) ¡eres un hacha!; **he has a — for propaganda** tiene genialidad para la propaganda; **you have a — for forgetting things** tienes un don especial para olvidar las cosas.

Genoa ['dʒenəuə] Génova f.

genocide ['dʒenəusaid] n genocidio m.

Genoese [,dʒenəu'iːz] **1** *adj* genovés. **2** *n* genovés *m*, esa *f*.

genre [ʒãːnr] *n* género *m*.

gent [dʒent] *n* (*fam*) = **gentleman; the —s'** el wáter (de caballeros).

genteel [dʒen'tiːl] *adj* (*iro*) fino, elegante; *school etc* de buen tono.

gentian ['dʒenʃiən] *n* genciana *f*.

gentian violet ['dʒenʃiən'vaiəlit] *n* violeta *f* de genciana.

gentile ['dʒentail] **1** *adj* no judío; (*pagan*) gentil. **2** *n* no judío *m*, a *f*; (*pagan*) gentil *mf*.

gentility [dʒen'tiliti] *n* (*iro*) finura *f*, elegancia *f*; buen tono *m*.

gentle ['dʒentl] *adj person's character* benévolo, amable; *apacible; breeze, heat, stop, progress, transition etc* suave; *rule* blando; *sound, voice* dulce; *push, touch* ligero; (*slow*) lento, pausado; *hint, reminder* discreto; *animal etc* manso, dócil, apacible; (*tender*) dulce, tierno; **of — birth** bien nacido; **— reader** amado lector; **the — sex** el sexo débil.

gentleman ['dʒentlmən] *n*, *pl* **gentlemen** ['dʒentlmən] (*man*) señor *m*; (*having gentlemanly qualities*) caballero *m*; (*at court*) gentilhombre *m*; **young —** señorito *m*; **there's a — waiting to see you** le espera un señor; **to be a perfect —** ser un cumplido caballero; **he's no —** es un mal caballero; **"gentlemen"** (*lavatory*) "caballeros".

gentlemanly ['dʒentlmənli] *adj* caballeroso; cortés, fino.

gentleness ['dʒentlnis] *n* amabilidad *f*; suavidad *f*; dulzura *f*; mansedumbre *f*; docilidad *f*; ternura *f*.

gently ['dʒentli] *adv* suavemente; dulcemente; (*slowly*) despacio, pausadamente, poco a poco; apaciblemente; tiernamente; **— !, — now !, — there !** ¡más despacio!, ¡con cuidado!

gentry ['dʒentri] *n* alta burguesía *f*, pequeña aristocracia *f*; (*pej*) familias *fpl* bien, gente *f* bien; (*set of people*) gente *f*.

genuflect ['dʒenjuflekt] *vi* doblar la rodilla.

genuflexion [,dʒenju'flekʃən] *n* genuflexión *f*.

genuine ['dʒenjuin] *adj* auténtico, legítimo, genuino; *person* sincero.

genus ['dʒenəs] *n*, *pl* **genera** ['dʒenərə] género *m*.

geodesic [,dʒi(ː)əu'desik] *adj* geodésico.

geodesy [dʒi'ɔdisi] *n* geodesia *f*.

Geoffrey ['dʒefri] *m* Geofredo, Godofredo.

geographer [dʒi'ɔgrəfə*] *n* geógrafo *m*.

geographical [dʒiə'græfikəl] *adj* geográfico.

geography [dʒi'ɔgrəfi] *n* geografía *f*.

geological [dʒiəu'lɔdʒikəl] *adj* geológico.

geologist [dʒi'ɔlədʒist] *n* geólogo *m*.

geology [dʒi'ɔlədʒi] *n* geología *f*.

geometric(al) [dʒiə'metrik(əl)] *adj* geométrico.

geometry [dʒi'ɔmitri] *n* geometría *f*; **solid — geometría** *f* del espacio.

geophysics [dʒiəu'fiziks] *n sing* geofísica *f*.

geopolitics [dʒiːəu'pɔlitiks] *n sing* geopolítica *f*.

George [dʒɔːdʒ] *m* Jorge.

Georgian ['dʒɔːdʒiən] *adj* georgiano.

geranium [dʒi'reiniəm] *n* geranio *m*.

geriatrics [,dʒeri'ætriks] *n sing* geriatría *f*.

germ [dʒəːm] *n* germen *m* (*also Med*); (*Med*) microbio *m*, bacilo *m*, bacteria *f*; (*fig*) germen *m*; **the — of an idea** el germen de una idea.

German ['dʒəːmən] **1** *adj* alemán. **2** *n* alemán *m*, ana *f*. **3** *n* (*language*) alemán *m*.

germane [dʒəː'mein] *adj* relacionado (*to* con); **not — to the issue** inoportuno.

Germanic [dʒəː'mænik] *adj* germánico.

germanophile [dʒəː'mænəfail] *n* germanófilo *m*, a *f*.

germanophobe [dʒəː'mænəfəub] *n* germanófobo *m*, a *f*.

Germany ['dʒəːməni] Alemania *f*.

germ carrier ['dʒəːm,kæriə*] *n* portador *m* de gérmenes.

germ cell ['dʒəːm'sel] *n* célula *f* germen.

germicide ['dʒəːmisaid] *n* germicida *m*, bactericida *m*.

germinate ['dʒəːmineit] *vi* germinar.

germination [,dʒəːmi'neiʃən] *n* germinación *f*.

germ-killer ['dʒəːm,kilə*] *n* germicida *m*, bactericida *m*.

germ plasm ['dʒəːm'plæzəm] *n* germen *m* plasma.

germproof ['dʒəːmpruːf] *adj* a prueba de gérmenes.

gerrymander ['dʒerimændə*] *vi* falsificar elecciones.

gerund ['dʒerənd] *n* gerundio *m*.

gerundive [dʒi'rʌndiv] *n* gerundio *m* adjetivado; (*Latin*) gerundivo *m*.

Gestapo [ges'taːpəu] *n* Gestapo *f*.

gestate [dʒes'teit] *vt* (**a**) (*Bio*) llevar en el útero. (**b**) (*fig*) *idea* meditar.

gestation [dʒes'teiʃən] *n* gestación *f*.

gesticulate [dʒes'tikjuleit] *vi* accionar, gesticular, manotear.

gesticulation [dʒes,tikju'leiʃən] *n* gesticulación *f*, manoteo *m*.

gesture ['dʒestʃə*] **1** *n* (**a**) ademán *m*, gesto *m*. (**b**) (*fig*) demostración *f*; (*small token*) muestra *f*, detalle *m*; **as a — of friendship** en señal de amistad; **as a — of support** para demostrar nuestro apoyo; **empty —** pura formalidad *f*; **what a nice —!** ¡qué detalle! **2** *vi* hacer un ademán; **he —d towards the door** con la mano indicó la puerta.

get [get] (*irr: pret* **got**, *ptp* **got**, *US* **gotten**) **1** *vt* (**a**) (*obtain*) obtener, adquirir, (*after effort*) lograr, conseguir; (*buy*) comprar; (*find*) encontrar; (*gain*) ganar; *prize* ganar, llevarse; *reputation* hacerse; *credit, glory* atribuirse; (*receive*) recibir; *radio station* captar, sintonizar; *wage* cobrar; *benefit, profit* sacar; *goals, points* marcar; **he got it for me** él me lo procuró; **he got me a job** él logró que me diesen un puesto; **that's what got him the rise** eso fue lo que le valió el aumento; **I never got an answer** no me contestaron; **— me Mr X, please** (*Tel*) póngame con el Sr X, por favor; **he got 6 months** le condenaron a 6 meses de prisión; **I don't — much from his lectures** saco poco provecho de sus clases; **we shan't — anything out of him** no lograremos sacarle nada, no nos dirá nada; **what are you —ting out of it?** ¿qué va a sacar Vd de ello?, ¿qué va a sacar Vd en beneficio propio?; **you may — some fun out of it** puede que le resulte divertido; **we got him on the subject of drugs** logramos que hablase de las drogas.

(**b**) (*arrest*) prender, detener; (*capture, kill*) cazar; **got you at last !** ¡por fin te he cazado!; **I'll — him one day !** ¡algún día me lo cargaré!; **I'll — you yet !** ¡me las pagarás!; **he got it from the teacher** el profesor le echó un rapapolvo.

(**c**) *disease* coger; **to — it bad** (*fam*) sufrir mucho; **to — religion** (*fam*) ser convertido, entusiasmarse por la religión.

(**d**) (*irritate*) **that's what —s me !** ¡eso es lo que más me fastidia!

(**e**) (*attract*) **this tune —s me** esta melodía me chifla, esta melodía me apasiona.

(**f**) (*strike*) dar en; **it got him on the head** le dio en la cabeza; **it —s me in the throat** afecta la garganta.

(**g**) (*understand*) comprender; (**do you**) **— it ?** ¿comprendes?, ¿me entiendes?

(**h**) (*move*) trasladar, pasar; **we can't — it through the door** no lo podemos pasar por la puerta; **to — something past the customs** conseguir pasar algo por la aduana; **how can we — it home ?** ¿cómo podemos llevarlo a casa?

(**i**) (*fetch*) buscar, traer, ir a buscar; *person* llamar, ir por; **I'll go and — it for you** te lo voy a buscar; **please — the doctor** por favor llame al médico; **can I — you a drink ?** ¿quieres tomar algo?, ¿te traigo algo de beber?

(**j**) *meal* preparar, hacer.

(**k**) **to have got** tener, poseer; **what have you got there ?** ¿qué tienes ahí?; **there you've got me** eso no te lo puedo decir, no sé nada de eso.

(**l**) **to have got to** + *infin* tener que + *infin*.

(**m**) **to — someone to do something** (*persuading*) conseguir que uno haga algo, persuadir a uno a hacer algo; (*ordering*) encargar a uno que haga algo.

(**n**) **to — get** + *ptp* or *adj*: **to — something done** mandar hacer algo; **to — one's hair cut** hacerse cortar el pelo, cortarse el pelo; **to — one's feet wet** mojarse los pies; (*often translated by a simple verb, eg*) **to — something ready** preparar algo.

(**o**) **to — something going** poner algo en marcha, hacer que algo empiece a funcionar; **to — a plan moving** hacer que se empiece a realizar un proyecto.

(**p**) (*with adv or prep*) **to — across** hacer entender; **to — along: we'll try to — him along** trataremos de hacerle venir; **to — away** (*remove*) quitar de en medio; separar; **to — something away from someone** quitar algo a uno; **to — someone away** ayudar a uno a escapar; **to — back** recobrar; **to — down** (*lift down*) bajar; descolgar; (*swallow*) tragar; (*note*) apuntar; (*put in writing*) poner por escrito; **it —s me down** me deprime; **don't let it — you down** no te dejes desanimar; **to — in** hacer entrar; *harvest* recoger; *word* decir; *blow* lograr dar; **to — off** quitarse de encima; *clothes* quitarse; *stain* sacar, quitar; *letter* escribir; *work* despachar, terminar; (*learn*) aprender; **to — an accused person off** lograr que se absuelva a un acusado; **to — on** poner;

clothes ponerse; **to — out** hacer salir; *(take out)* sacar; *stain* sacar, quitar; *book* publicar, *(from library)* sacar; *problem* resolver; **to — over** hacer pasar por encima de; *(put across)* hacer comprender, comunicar; *(finish)* terminar; **let's — it over!** ¡vamos a concluir de una vez!; **to — through** conseguir pasar (por); *bill* hacer que se apruebe; **to — together** reunir, juntar; **to — up** *(lift)* levantar, alzar; *(take up)* subir; *(learn)* aprender; *(revise)* repasar; *(organize)* organizar, preparar; *(dress)* ataviar (in de); *(disguise)* disfrazar *(as de).*

2 *vi* **(a)** *(become)* ponerse, volverse, hacerse *(for usage, see* **become** 2 (c); **to — +** *ptp or adj is often translated by passive, vi or vr)* **to — beaten** ser vencido; **to — run over** ser atropellado; **to — angry** enfadarse; **to — dark** hacerse de noche, anochecer; **to — drunk** emborracharse; **to — excited** emocionarse; **to — hurt** hacerse daño; **to — married** casarse; **to — old** envejecer(se); **to — wet** mojarse.

(b) *(reach)* **— from A to B** ir de A a B, trasladarse de A a B; **how did it — here?** ¿cómo llegó a encontrarse aquí?; **he got there late** llegó tarde allí.

(c) *(sl)* marcharse.

(d) to — + *ger* empezar a + *infin*; **we got talking** empezamos a charlar; **to — going, to — moving** ponerse en marcha; **— going!** ¡menearse!; **the idea never got going** la idea nunca tuvo consecuencias prácticas.

(e) *(with adv or prep)* **to — about** salir mucho, viajar mucho, ir a muchos sitios; *(after sickness)* levantarse y salir; *(report)* saberse, divulgarse; **to — above oneself** engreírse; **to — across** lograr cruzar; *(message)* surtir efecto, *(meaning)* ser comprendido; **to — across** to lograr comunicar con; **he did not — across to the audience** no logró ponerse en contacto con el público; **he got across the manager** se indispuso con el director; **to — along** seguir andando; *(depart)* irse; **we must be — ting along** es hora de irnos ya; **— along now!** ¡vete ya!; **we — along somehow** vamos tirando; **— along with you!** ¡no digas bobadas!; **to — along without something** pasarse sin algo; *(for other senses of* **to — along,** *see* **to — on);** **to — around = to — about;** **to — around to something** llegar por fin a algo; **I never seem to — around to it** parece que nunca tengo tiempo para ello; **to — at** llegar a; *facts* descubrir, averiguar; *(attack)* atacar; *(refer to)* apuntar a; *(tease)* tomar el pelo a; *(spoil)* estropear; *(bribe)* sobornar; *(intimidate)* intimidar; **what are you — ting at?** ¿qué quieres decir con esto?; **as soon as he — s at the drink** en cuanto se pone a beber; **to — away** *(leave)* conseguir marcharse; salir, ir fuera; ir de vacaciones; *(escape)* escaparse, evadirse; *(at start of race)* escapar; **— away!** ¡no digas bobadas!; **to — away from** *place, person* escaparse de; **to — away from it all** evadirse del bullicio; **to — away with** *(take, steal)* llevarse, alzarse con; *(go unpunished)* hacer impunemente, quedar sin castigo; **you shan't — away with it!** ¡me las pagarás!; **to — back** volver; **to — back at someone** desquitarse con uno; **to — behind** *(adv)* quedarse atrás; **to — behind** *(prep)* penetrar, ahondar en; **to — by** *(adv)* lograr pasar; **we'll — by** *(fig)* nos las apañaremos, nos las arreglaremos; **I can — by in Dutch** me defiendo en holandés; **to — by** *(prep)* thing lograr pasar; *person* eludir, burlar la vigilancia de; **to — down** bajar; **to — down to** llegar a; *problem* abordar, empezar a estudiar; **to — down to work** ponerse seriamente a trabajar; **to — in** *(adv)* (lograr) entrar; *(train etc)* llegar; *(arrive home)* volver a casa, regresar; *(Pol)* ser elegido; **to — in** *(prep)* (lograr) entrar en; **to — in with** congraciarse con, llegar a tener influencia con; **to — into** (lograr) entrar en; *vehicle* subir a; *club* ingresar en; *clothes* ponerse; *difficulties* meterse en; *habit* adquirir; **what's got into you?** ¿qué mosca te ha picado?; **to — off** *(adv)* *(from vehicle)* apearse, bajar; *(Aer)* despegar; *(go away)* marcharse; *(to sleep)* conciliar el sueño; **— off!** ¡suelta!; **he got off unharmed** salió indemne; **he got off with a fine** escapó con una multa; **to tell someone where he — s off** cantar a uno las cuarenta; **to — off with someone** enamorar a uno; **to — off** *(prep)* *(from vehicle)* apearse de, bajar de; *punishment* librarse de; **to — on** *(adv)* *(mount)* subir, ponerse encima; *(progress)* hacer progresos, tener éxito; *(continue)* seguir; *(depart)* irse; **— on, man!** ¡siga!; **he's — ting on for 70** anda cerca de los 70; **he's — ting on** va para viejo; **it's — ting on for 9** falta poco para las 9; **to — on with someone** llevarse bien con uno, congeniar con uno; **how are you — ting on with him?** ¿cómo te avienes con él?; **they — on well together**

se llevan bien; **I'll — on to him at once** hablaré con él en seguida; **the police have got on to him** la policía tiene una pista que le conducirá al criminal; **I can't — on with maths** no me entran las matemáticas; **to — on** *(prep)* subir a, ponerse encima de; **to — out** salir; escaparse; *(news)* saberse, hacerse público; **— out!** ¡vete!, ¡fuera de aquí!; **to — out of** *vehicle* bajar de; *duty, punishment* librarse de; *obligation* zafarse de; *habit* perder; **to — over** *(adv)* cruzar, pasar por encima; **to — over** *(prep)* vencer, superar; *illness* reponerse de; *fright* sobreponerse a; *grief* dominar; *surprise* volverse de; *resentment* olvidar; **to — round** dar la vuelta a; *difficulty* soslayar; *person* persuadir, engatusar *(see also* **to — around);** **to — through** *(adv)* lograr pasar; **to — through** *(prep)* conseguir pasar por; *time* pasar; *period, work* llegar al final de, terminar; *money* gastar; *exam* aprobar; **to — through to** comunicar con *(also Tel)*; **to — to** *place* llegar a; **to — to do something** acostumbrarse a hacer algo, aprender a hacer algo; **to — to like something** tomar afición a algo; **to — together** reunirse, verse, organizar una fiesta; **to — up** *(stand)* levantarse, ponerse de pie; *(from bed)* levantarse; *(bird etc)* alzar el vuelo; *(rise)* subir; *(wind)* empezar a soplar recio; *(fire)* avivarse; *(sea)* embravecerse; **— up!** ¡levántate!, *(to horse)* ¡arre!; **what did you — up to in London?** ¿qué diabluras hiciste en Londres?

3 *vr*: **to — oneself up** as disfrazarse de; **to — oneself arrested** hacerse detener; **to — oneself drunk** emborracharse; **to — oneself lost** extraviarse.

get-at-able [get'ætəbl] *adj* accesible.

getaway ['getəwei] *n* escape *m*, fuga *f*; **to make one's — escaparse.**

Gethsemane [geθ'semənɪ] Getsemaní *m*.

get-together ['getə,geðə*] *n* *(meeting)* reunión *f*; *(regular social gathering)* tertulia *f*; *(party)* guateque *m*.

getup ['getʌp] *n* atavío *m*.

geyser ['giːzə*] *n* *(Geog)* géiser *m*; *(heater)* calentador *m* de agua.

Ghana ['gɑːnə] Ghana.

Ghanaian [gɑː'neɪən] **1** *adj* de Ghana, ghaneano. **2** *n* natural *mf* de Ghana, ghaneano *m*, a *f*.

ghastly ['gɑːstlɪ] *adj* horrible; *(pale)* pálido; *(corpselike)* cadavérico; *(fam)* horrible, fatal, malísimo; *person* pesado.

Ghent [gent] Gante.

gherkin ['gəːkɪn] *n* pepinillo *m*.

ghetto ['getəu] *n* judería *f*.

ghost [gəust] **1** *n* fantasma *m*, espectro *m*; **Holy G—** Espíritu *m* Santo; **he hasn't the — of a chance** no tiene la más remota posibilidad; **to give up the —** entregar el alma, *(fig)* perder toda esperanza.

2 *vt book* escribir por otro; **an autobiography —ed by X** una autobiografía que escribió realmente el escritor fantasma X.

ghostly ['gəustlɪ] *adj* espectral, fantasmal.

ghost story ['gəust,stɔːrɪ] *n* cuento *m* de fantasmas.

ghost writer ['gəust,raɪtə*] *n* escritor *m* fantasma.

ghoul [guːl] *n* demonio *m* necrófago; *(fig)* persona *f* de gustos inhumanos.

ghoulish ['guːlɪʃ] *adj* espantosamente cruel, sádico.

giant ['dʒaɪənt] **1** *n* gigante *m*. **2** *adj* gigantesco, gigante.

gibber ['dʒɪbə*] *vi* farfullar, hablar atropelladamente, hablar de una manera ininteligible.

gibberish ['dʒɪbərɪʃ] *n* galimatías *m*, guirigay *m*.

gibbet ['dʒɪbɪt] *n* horca *f*.

gibbon ['gɪbən] *n* gibón *m*.

gibe [dʒaɪb] **1** *n* pulla *f*, dicterio *m*. **2** *vi* mofarse *(at* de).

giblets ['dʒɪblɪts] *npl* menudillos *mpl*.

Gibraltar [dʒɪ'brɔːltə*] Gibraltar; **Rock of —** Peñón *m* de Gibraltar; **Straits of —** Estrecho *m* de Gibraltar.

giddiness ['gɪdɪnɪs] *n* vértigo *m*.

giddy ['gɪdɪ] *adj speed* vertiginoso; *character* atolondrado, ligero de cascos; *(dizzy)* mareado; **to feel — sentirse mareado; it makes me —** me marea, me da vértigo.

gift [gɪft] *n* **(a)** *(present)* regalo *m*; obsequio *m*; *(Eccl)* ofrenda *f*; *(Law)* donación *f*; *(bargain)* ganga *f*; **the office is in the — of** la dignidad está en manos de; **it's a —!** *(fam)* ¡está tirado!; **I wouldn't have it as a —** no lo quiero ni regalado.

(b) *(faculty, talent)* don *m*, talento *m*, prenda *f*; **— of tongues** don *m* de las lenguas; **he has a — for administration** tiene talento para la administración; **he has artistic —s** tiene dotes artísticas.

gifted ['gɪftɪd] *adj* talentoso.

gig [gɪg] *n* calesín *m*; *(Naut)* lancha *f*, canoa *f*.

gigantic [dʒaɪ'gæntɪk] *adj* gigantesco.

giggle ['gigl] **1** n risilla f sofocada, risilla f tonta. **2** vi reirse con una risilla sofocada (or tonta).

gigolo ['ʒigələu] n gigoló m.

gild [gild] (irr: pret **gilded**, ptp **gilded** or **gilt**) vt dorar; metal sobredorar; (fig) embellecer, adornar; pill dorar.

gilding ['gildiŋ] n doradura f, dorado m.

Giles [dʒailz] m Gil.

gill [dʒil] n cuarta parte de una pinta (= approx ¼ litro).

gill [gil] n (Fish) agalla f, branquia f; **to look green about the —s** tener cara olivácea.

gillie ['gili] n (Scot) ayudante m de cazador (or pescador); (Scot) criado m.

gillyflower ['dʒili,flauə*] n (poet) alhelí m.

gilt [gilt] **1** ptp of **gild**. **2** adj dorado. **3** n dorado m; (fig) atractivo m.

gilt-edged ['gilt'edʒd] adj: **— securities** papel m del Estado, valores mpl de máxima confianza.

gimlet ['gimlit] n barrena f de mano.

gimmick ['gimik] n (Theat) truco m característico; (Comm) truco m publicitario; **it's just a sales —** es un truco para vender más.

gin¹ [dʒin] n (drink) ginebra f.

gin² [dʒin] n (trap) trampa f; (Mech) desmotadera f de algodón.

ginger ['dʒindʒə*] **1** n jengibre m; (fig) energía f, empuje m. **2** adj hair rojo; cat de color melado, barcino, amarillento. **3** vt: **to — up** animar, estimular.

ginger ale ['dʒindʒər'eil] n cerveza f de jengibre.

ginger beer ['dʒindʒə'biə*] n gaseosa f.

gingerbread ['dʒindʒəbred] n pan m de jengibre.

ginger group ['dʒindʒəgru:p] n grupo m de activistas.

gingerly ['dʒindʒəli] **1** adj cauteloso. **2** adv con tiento, con pies de plomo.

gipsy ['dʒipsi] **1** n gitano m, a f. **2** attr gitano.

giraffe [dʒi'rɑ:f] n jirafa f.

gird [gə:d] (irr: pret and ptp **girded** or **girt**) vt ceñir; rodear (with de); **to — on one's sword** ceñirse la espada.

girder ['gə:də*] n viga f.

girdle ['gə:dl] **1** n cinto m, ceñidor m; (belt, also fig) cinturón m; (woman's) faja f. **2** vt ceñir, rodear (also fig; with de).

girl [gə:l] n chica f, muchacha f; (small) niña f; (young woman) chica f, joven f; (servant) criada f, chica f; (girlfriend) amiguita f, novia f; **best — novia** f; **old — (of school)** antigua alumna f, (fam) vieja f.

girlfriend ['gə:lfrend] n (of girl) amiga f, amiguita f, (of boy) novia f.

girlhood ['gə:lhud] n juventud f, mocedad f.

girlish ['gə:liʃ] adj de niña; juvenil; (pej) afeminado.

girl scout ['gə:l'skaut] n (US) exploradora f, muchacha-guía f.

Gironde [dʒi'rɔnd] Gironda m.

girt [gə:t] pret and ptp of **gird**.

girth [gə:θ] n (strap) cincha f; (measure) circunferencia f; (stoutness) gordura f, obesidad f; **because of its great —** por su gran tamaño, por lo abultado.

gist [dʒist] n esencia f, lo esencial, quid m; **to get the — of a matter** entender lo esencial de una cuestión.

give [giv] (irr: pret **gave**, ptp **given**) **1** vt **(a)** (bestow free) dar; (as present) regalar; (hand over) entregar; aid prestar; life dar, sacrificar; party ofrecer, organizar (for en honor de); **to — something to someone, to — someone something** dar algo a uno; **I wouldn't want it if you gave it to me** eso no lo quiero ni regalado; **(God) — me strength!** ¡Dios me dé paciencia!; **— me the old songs!** ¡yo prefiero las canciones viejas!

(b) (deliver) entregar; regards etc dar; one's word dar, empeñar; promise hacer; **to — something into someone's hands** entregar (or confiar) algo a uno; **to — someone something to eat** dar de comer a uno.

(c) (pay) pagar, dar; **what did you — for it?** ¿cuánto pagaste por él?; **I would — a lot to know** daría un dineral por saberlo.

(d) (dedicate) energy, time etc dedicar, consagrar; **he gave his life to it** consagró su vida a ello.

(e) cry etc lanzar, proferir, dar; **to — a smile** sonreír (to a); **to — a start** sobresaltarse.

(f) (state, present, utter) particulars hacer constar; example citar; details etc dar; recitation etc ofrecer; play representar, poner; lecture dar; speech pronunciar; decision comunicar, (by judge etc) dictar; **he —s no references** no cita referencias; **he gave no name** no dijo su nombre; **it gave no sign of life** no dio señal alguna de vida; **— us a song!** ¡cántanos algo!; **I — you the Queen** brindemos por la Reina.

(g) (impart) comunicar; (pass on) transmitir; disease contagiar con; **to — someone to understand that** dar a uno a entender que; **I was given to believe that** me hicieron creer que.

(h) (allot, grant, assign) dar; conceder, otorgar; contract, job dar; task imponer; name dar, poner, (formally) imponer; punishment condenar a, castigar con.

(i) (produce) result dar por resultado, producir, arrojar; **it —s a total of 80** arroja un total de 80, suman 80; **it —s 6% a year** rinde un 6 por cien al año; **it —s an average of 4** da un promedio de 4.

(j) (cause) ocasionar, causar; **you gave me much pain** me causaste mucha pena.

(k) (allow) permitir; **I gave myself 10 minutes to do it** me permití 10 minutos para hacerlo; **he can — you 5 years** él tiene la ventaja de ser 5 años más joven que Vd; **how long would you — that marriage?** ¿cuánto tiempo crees que durará ese matrimonio?

(l) (fam) **to — it to someone** (beat) dar una paliza a uno; (verbally) poner a uno como un trapo; **I gave him what for** le dije cuatro verdades; **I'll — him what for!** ¡me lo cargaré!

(m) to — away (give free) regalar; (get rid of) deshacerse de; (sell cheap) malvender; (disclose) revelar, descubrir; (betray) traicionar; bride conducir al altar; **to — back** devolver; **to — in** entregar; **to — off** emitir, arrojar, despedir, echar; **to — out** (hand out) distribuir, repartir; (announce) anunciar; (reveal) revelar, divulgar; smoke etc emitir, arrojar; **he gave it out that** anunció que, hizo creer que; **to — over** entregar; (transfer) traspasar; **to — up** (hand over) entregar; ceder; (renounce) renunciar a; post dejar, renunciar a, dimitir de; (sacrifice) sacrificar; problem renunciar a resolver; patient desahuciar; (for lost) dar por perdido; **she gave him up** ella riñó con él; **we wish she'd give him up** estamos deseando que ella rompa con él; **he gave up smoking** dejó de fumar; **we'd —n you up** creíamos que no ibas a venir.

2 vi **(a)** (bestow) dar; **to — and take** hacer concesiones mutuas; **to — as good as one gets** devolver golpe por golpe.

(b) (stretch) dar de sí; (break) romperse; (door etc) ceder; (floor, roof etc) hundirse.

(c) to — in ceder; rendirse, darse por vencido; (agree) consentir; **to — in to person** condescender con, ceder a las súplicas de; threats etc rendirse ante, sucumbir ante; **she always —s in to him** ella hace siempre lo que él quiere; **to — on to** dar a; **to — out** (supply) agotarse, acabarse; (engine) fallar, averiarse; **to — over** cesar; **over!** ¡basta ya!; **to — up** darse por vencido; perder la esperanza; **don't — up yet!** ¡anímate!

3 vr: **to — oneself over** (or **up**) **to** entregarse a, darse a; **to — oneself up** entregarse a la policía (etc).

give-and-take ['givən'teik] n toma y daca, concesiones fpl mutuas.

giveaway ['givəwei] adj: **— price** precio m obsequio, precio m de ruina.

given ['givn] **1** ptp of **give**.

2: — money one can do anything con dinero todo es posible; **on a — day** un día determinado; **in a — time** en un tiempo dado; **— that** dado que; **to be — to** ser dado a, ser adicto a; **to be — to + ger** ser propenso a + infin.

giver ['givə*] n donador m, ora f.

gizzard ['gizəd] n molleja f; **it sticks in my —** no lo puede tragar.

glacial ['gleisiəl] adj glacial.

glaciation [,gleisi'eiʃən] n glaciación f.

glacier ['glæsiə*] n glaciar m.

glad [glæd] adj alegre; news etc bueno; **to be — about** alegrarse de; **I'm very — for you** me alegro mucho por ti; **to be — that** alegrarse de que + subj; **I am — to hear it** me alegro de saberlo; **I shall be — to come** tendré mucho gusto en venir; **he seemed — se** mostró satisfecho.

gladden ['glædn] vt alegrar, regocijar.

glade [gleid] n claro m.

gladiator ['glædieitə*] n gladiador m.

gladiolus [,glædi'əuləs] n, pl **gladioli** [,glædi'əulai] estoque m, gladiolo m.

gladly ['glædli] adv alegremente, con satisfacción; **yes, —** sí, con mucho gusto.

gladness ['glædnis] n alegría f; satisfacción f.

glamorize ['glæməraiz] vt embellecer; hacer más atractivo; **this programme —s crime** este programa presenta el crimen bajo una luz favorable, este programa nos hace ver los atractivos de la vida criminal.

glamorous ['glæmərəs] adj encantador, atractivo, hechicero.

glamour ['glæmə*] *n* encanto *m*, atractivo *m*, hechizo *m*.

glamour-girl ['glæməgə:l] *n* belleza *f*, guapa *f* (oficial).

glance [glɑ:ns] **1** *n* ojeada *f*, vistazo *m*; mirada *f*; **at a —** de un vistazo; **at first —** a primera vista; **with many a backward —** at (*fig*) pensando con mucha nostalgia en.

　　2 *vi* **(a)** (*look*) mirar; **she —d in my direction** miró hacia donde yo estaba; **to — at** *person etc* lanzar una mirada a, *object* echar un vistazo a, ojear; **to — at, to — over, to — through** *book etc* hojear, examinar de paso; **to — away** apartar los ojos.

　　(b) (*strike*) **to — off something** chocar con algo y rebotar, desviarse al chocar con algo.

glancing ['glɑ:nsiŋ] *adj* *blow* oblicuo.

gland [glænd] *n* (*Bio*) glándula *f*; (*Mech*) prensaestopas *m*.

glandular ['glændjulə*] *adj* glandular; **— fever** fiebre *f* glandular.

glare [glɛə*] **1** *n* **(a)** (*of light*) luz *f* deslumbradora, reverbero *m*, brillo *m*, luminosidad *f*; (*dazzle*) deslumbramiento *m*; **because of the — of the light in Spain** debido a lo fuerte de la luz en España.

　　(b) (*look*) mirada *f* feroz.

　　2 *vi* **(a)** relumbrar, deslumbrar.

　　(b) mirar ferozmente (*at* a), echar fuego por los ojos.

glaring ['glɛəriŋ] *adj* (*dazzling*) deslumbrador, fuerte; *colour* chillón; *mistake* manifiesto, notorio.

glass [glɑ:s] **1** *n* **(a)** (*material*) vidrio *m*, cristal *m*; (*glassware*) artículos *mpl* de vidrio, cristalería *f*; (*tumbler, also for wine*) vaso *m*; (*for beer*) caña *f*; (*for sherry, champagne etc*) copa *f*; (*for liqueur, brandy*) copita *f*; (*Meteorol*) barómetro *m*; (*spyglass*) catalejo *m*; (*mirror*) espejo *m*; **cut —** vidrio *m* tallado; **frosted —** vidrio *m* deslustrado; **under —** (*exhibit*) bajo vidrio, en una vitrina, (*plant*) en invernáculo; **to look at oneself in the —** mirarse en el espejo.

　　(b) **—es** (*spectacles*) gafas *fpl*, lentes *mpl*; (*binoculars*) gemelos *mpl*; **dark —es** gafas *fpl* negras.

　　2 *attr* de vidrio, de cristal; **— case** vitrina *f*; **— door** puerta *f* vidriera, puerta *f* de cristales; **— eye** ojo *m* de cristal.

glassful ['glɑ:sful] *n* vaso *m*.

glasshouse ['glɑ:shaus] *n*, *pl* **—houses** [‚hauziz] (*Hort*) invernáculo *m*, invernadero *m*; (*sl*) cárcel *f* (*militar*).

glassware ['glɑ:swɛə*] *n* artículos *mpl* de vidrio, cristalería *f*.

glassy ['glɑ:si] *adj* *substance* vítreo; *surface* liso; *water* espejado; *eye* vidrioso.

glaucoma [glɔ:'kəumə] *n* glaucoma *m*.

glaze [gleiz] **1** *n* vidriado *m*, barniz *m*, lustre *m*. **2** *vt* (*put glass in*) poner vidrios a, vidriar; (*fig*) lustrar.

glazed [gleizd] *adj* *surface* vidriado; *paper* satinado; *eye* vidrioso.

glazier ['gleiziə*] *n* vidriero *m*.

gleam [gli:m] **1** *n* (*of light*) rayo *m*, destello *m*; (*of colour*) viso *m*; (*in one's eye*) chispa *f*, vislumbre *f*; **there is a — of hope** hay un rayo de esperanza.

　　2 *vi* brillar (*in the sun* al sol; *with* de), relucir, destellar.

gleaming ['gli:miŋ] *adj* reluciente.

glean [gli:n] **1** *vt* espigar; (*fig*) espigar, recoger; **to — information** about recoger (con dificultad) datos sobre; **from what I have been able to —** de lo que yo he podido saber. **2** *vi* espigar.

gleaner ['gli:nə*] *n* espigador *m*, ora *f*.

gleanings ['gli:niŋs] *npl* (*fig*) fragmentos *mpl* recogidos.

glebe [gli:b] *n* (*Eccl*) terreno *m* beneficial.

glee [gli:] *n* alegría *f*, júbilo *m*, regocijo *m*.

glee club ['gli:klʌb] *n* orfeón *m*.

gleeful ['gli:ful] *adj* alegre, regocijado.

gleefully ['gli:fəli] *adv* con júbilo.

glen [glen] *n* cañada *f*, valle *m* estrecho.

glib [glib] *adj* *person* de mucha labia, poco sincero; *speech* elocuente pero poco sincero; *explanation* fácil.

glibly ['glibli] *adv* con poca sinceridad; elocuentemente pero con poca sinceridad; con una facilidad sospechosa.

glibness ['glibnis] *n* labia *f*; falta *f* de sinceridad; facilidad *f*.

glide [glaid] **1** *n* deslizamiento *m*; (*Aer*) planeo *m*, vuelo *m* sin motor; (*Mus*) ligadura *f*.

　　2 *vi* **(a)** deslizarse; **to — away, to — off** escurrirse, irse silenciosamente; **she —s to the door** se desliza hacia la puerta.

　　(b) (*Aer*) planear, volar sin motor.

glider ['glaidə*] *n* planeador *m*, velero *m*; (*towed*) avión *m* remolcado.

gliding ['glaidiŋ] *n* vuelo *m* sin motor.

glimmer ['glimə*] **1** *n* luz *f* trémula, luz *f* tenue, vislumbre *f*; **without a — of understanding** sin dar el menor indicio de comprenderme; **there is a — of hope** hay un rayo de esperanza.

　　2 *vi* brillar con luz trémula (*or* tenue).

glimpse [glimps] **1** *n* vislumbre *f*; vista *f* momentánea; **to catch a — of** vislumbrar. **2** *vt* vislumbrar, entrever, ver por un instante.

glint [glint] **1** *n* destello *m*, centelleo *m*; (*in one's eye*) chispa *f*. **2** *vi* destellar, centellear.

glisten ['glisn] *vi* relucir, brillar.

glitter ['glitə*] **1** *n* brillo *m*, resplandor *m*. **2** *vi* relucir, brillar, rutilar; **all that —s is not gold** no es oro todo lo que reluce.

glittering ['glitəriŋ] *adj* reluciente, brillante (*also fig*).

gloaming ['gləumiŋ] *n* crepúsculo *m*; **in the —** al anochecer.

gloat [gləut] *vi* relamerse; **to — over** *money etc* recrearse contemplando, *sight* saborear, *news* refocilarse con, *victory* manifestar satisfacción maligna por, *beaten enemy* triunfar jactanciosamente de.

glob [glɔb] *n* (*US*) gotita *f*, glóbulo *m*; masa *f* redonda, masa *f* pequeña; grumo *m*.

global ['gləubl] *adj* (*world-wide*) mundial; *sum etc* global.

globe [gləub] *n* globo *m*, esfera *f*; (*spherical map*) esfera *f* terrestre, globo *m* terráqueo.

globe-trotter ['gləub‚trɔtə*] *n* trotamundos *m*.

globular ['glɔbjulə*] *adj* globular.

globule ['glɔbju:l] *n* glóbulo *m*.

gloom [glu:m] *n*, **gloominess** [glu:minis] *n* oscuridad *f*, lobreguez *f*, tenebrosidad *f*; (*fig*) pesimismo *m*; melancolía *f*, tristeza *f*.

gloomily ['glu:mili] *adv* oscuramente, lóbregamente; de modo pesimista, con pesimismo; melancólicamente, tristemente.

gloomy ['glu:mi] *adj* oscuro, lóbrego, tenebroso; *atmosphere, character, forecast* pesimista; *outlook* nada prometedor; *day, tone* melancólico, triste.

glorification [‚glɔ:rifi'keiʃən] *n* glorificación *f*.

glorify ['glɔ:rifai] *vt* glorificar; (*praise*) alabar; **it was nothing but a glorified cottage** resultó ser solamente una casita con pretensiones de palacio.

glorious ['glɔ:riəs] *adj* glorioso; *day, view, stroke etc* magnífico; **it was a — muddle** la confusión era mayúscula.

glory ['glɔ:ri] **1** *n* gloria *f*; (*fig*) esplendor *m*; **Old G— bandera de EE.UU; to be in one's —** estar en sus glorias.

　　2 *vi*: **to — in** gloriarse de; **I — in the name of Briton** para mí el ser inglés es motivo de orgullo; **the café glories in the name of El Dorado** el café tiene el magnífico nombre de El Dorado.

glory hole ['glɔ:rihəul] *n* (*fam*) cuarto *m* (*or* cajón *etc*) en desorden, cuarto *m* (*etc*) que se deja sin arreglar.

gloss[1] [glɔs] (*note*) **1** *n* glosa *f*. **2** *vt* glosar, comentar.

gloss[2] [glɔs] **1** *n* lustre *m*, brillo *m*.

　　2 *attr*: **— finish** acabado *m* brillo; **— paint** pintura *f* esmalte; **— paper** papel *m* satinado.

　　3 *vt* lustrar, pulir; **to — over** (*excuse*) disculpar, (*play down*) paliar, colorear, (*cover up*) encubrir.

glossary ['glɔsəri] *n* glosario *m*.

glossy ['glɔsi] *adj* *surface* lustroso, brillante; *hair* liso; *cloth, paper* satinado; *magazine etc* de buen tono, elegante.

glove [glʌv] *n* guante *m*; **to fit someone like a —** sentar a uno como un guante.

gloved [glʌvd] *adj* *hand* enguantado.

glover ['glʌvə*] *n* guantero *m*, a *f*.

glow [gləu] **1** *n* (*of lamp, sun etc*) luz *f* (difusa); (*of jewel*) brillo *m*; (*of fire*) calor *m* vivo; (*bright colour*) color *m* vivo; (*in sky*) arrebol *m*; (*Tech*) incandescencia *f*; (*warm feeling*) sensación *f* de bienestar; (*of satisfaction etc*) sensación *f* grata, sentimiento *m* de vivo placer.

　　2 *vi* (*lamp, sun, jewel etc*) brillar (con luz difusa); (*fire*) arder vivamente; (*Tech*) estar candente; **to — with pleasure** experimentar una sensación de bienestar; **to — with health** estar rebosando de salud.

glower ['glauə*] *vi*: **to — at** mirar con ceño.

glowering ['glauəriŋ] *adj* *person, sky* ceñudo.

glowing ['gləuiŋ] *adj* candente, incandescente; *light* brillante; *fire* vivo; *cheek etc* encendido; *colour* intenso; *report etc* entusiasta.

glow-worm ['gləuwə:m] *n* luciérnaga *f*.

glucose ['glu:kəus] *n* glucosa *f*.

glue [glu:] **1** *n* cola *f*, goma *f* (de pegar). **2** *vt* encolar, pegar (*also* **to — on, to — together**); **her face was —d to the window** tenía la cara pegada a la ventana.

gluey ['glu:i] *adj* pegajoso, viscoso.

glum [glʌm] *adj* (*by nature*) taciturno, melancólico; *mood* triste, abatido; *tone* melancólico, sombrío.

glut [glʌt] **1** *n* superabundancia *f*, exceso *m*; **to be a — on the market** abarrotar el mercado.

2 *vt person* hartar, saciar; *market* abarrotar, inundar; **to be —ted with fruit** (*person*) haberse atracado de frutas.

3 *vr*: **to — oneself** atracarse (*with* de).

gluten ['glu:tən] *n* gluten *m*.

glutinous ['glu:tinəs] *adj* glutinoso.

glutton ['glʌtn] *n* glotón *m*, ona *f*; **to be a — for work** trabajar incansablemente.

gluttonous ['glʌtənəs] *adj* glotón, goloso.

gluttony ['glʌtəni] *n* glotonería *f*, gula *f*.

glycerin(e) [,glisə'ri:n] *n* glicerina *f*.

G-man ['dʒi:mæn] *n*, *pl* **-men** [men] (*US*) agente *m* secreto federal.

gnarled [nɑ:ld] *adj* nudoso, torcido.

gnash [næʃ] *vt teeth* rechinar.

gnat [næt] *n* mosquito *m*, jején *m* (*SAm*).

gnaw [nɔ:] *vt* roer.

gneiss [nais] *n* gneis *m*.

gnome [nəum] *n* gnomo *m*.

gnu [nu:] *n* ñu *m*.

go [gəu] (*irr: pret* **went**, *ptp* **gone**) **1** *vi* (a) (*general sense*) ir; viajar; andar; **to — to London** ir a Londres; **to — to England** ir a Inglaterra; **all roads — to Rome** todos los caminos van a Roma; **to — the shortest way** tomar el camino más corto; **to — (at) 30 m.p.h.** ir a 30 m.p.h.; **the numbers that — from 6 to 12** los números que van de 6 a 12; **to — to someone for something** acudir a uno a pedir (*or* buscar) algo; **there he —es!** ¡ahí va!; **here —es!** ¡vamos a ver!, ¡a ello!; **who —es there?** ¿quién va?; **there you — again!** ¡has vuelto a la misma canción!; **there —es the bell** suena el timbre; **what shall I — in?** ¿qué traje me pongo?; **it —es by seasons** esto va por temporadas; **it —es by age** varía según la edad, depende de la edad; **promotion —es by seniority** los ascensos se hacen por orden de antigüedad.

(b) (*progress*) ir; **business is —ing well** los negocios van bien; **everything went well** todo salió bien, todo resultó perfecto; **how —es it?** ¿qué tal?, ¿cómo te va esto?; **how did the exam —?** ¿qué tal el examen?; **we'll see how things —** veremos cómo se desarrolla la situación; **to make the party —** hacer que resulte alegre la fiesta, animar la fiesta; *see* **get**, **keep** *etc*.

(c) (*purpose etc*) **to — and see someone**, **to — to see someone** ir a ver a uno; **he went and bought it** lo compró, por fin se resolvió a comprarlo; (*near future*) **I am —ing to see him** voy a verle; (*emphatic*) **I am —ing to see him** sí voy a verle.

(d) (*function*) funcionar, marchar; **it won't —** no funciona; **it —es on petrol** funciona con gasolina; **it —es on wheels** marcha sobre ruedas; **to make something —** hacer funcionar algo; **to set a machine —ing** poner en marcha una máquina.

(e) (*depart*) irse, marcharse, partir; (*train etc*) partir, salir; **let's —!** ¡vamos!, ¡vámonos!; **don't — yet** no te vayas tan pronto, quédate un poco más; **be gone!**, **get you gone!** ¡váyase!; **—!** ¡ya!; **from the word —** desde el principio; **when does the train —?** ¿a qué hora sale el tren?

(f) (*disappear etc*) **my hat has gone** ha desaparecido mi sombrero; **my money is all gone** ya no me queda dinero; **the coffee is all gone** se acabó el café; **he'll have to —** (*be dismissed*) tendremos que deshacernos de él, tendremos que echarle; **luxuries will have to —** tendremos que prescindir de las cosas de lujo; **the trees have been gone for years** hace años que se quitaron los árboles; **his mind is —ing** está perdiendo la cabeza; **all my teeth have gone** he perdido todos mis dientes.

(g) (*be sold*) venderse; **it went next day** se vendió al día siguiente; **it went for £5** se vendió por 5 libras; **—ing, —ing, gone!** ¡a la una . . . a las dos . . . a las tres!

(h) (*of time*) pasar; **the day went slowly** el día pasó lentamente; **how is the time —ing?** ¿cuánto tiempo ha pasado ya?, ¿cuánto tiempo nos queda?

(i) (*of the hour*) **it has gone 3** ya dieron las 3, son las 3 y pico; **it has gone 8 already** son las 8 dadas.

(j) (*pass by descent*) pasar; **his books went to the college** sus libros pasaron al colegio.

(k) (*extend*) **the garden —es down to the lake** el jardín se extiende hasta el lago; **it's good as far as it —es** dentro de sus límites es bueno.

(l) (*be available*) estar disponible; **are there any houses —ing?** ¿hay casas en venta?; **are there any jobs —ing?** ¿están ofreciendo empleos?; **anything that's —ing** lo que haya.

(m) (*exist*) **as prices —** that's not dear considerando los precios que corren eso no es caro.

(n) (*of text*) decir, rezar; **the text —es . . .** reza el texto así . . .; **as the saying —es** como dice el refrán; **how does the song —?** ¿qué dice la canción?

(o) (*be acceptable*) **anything —es with him** se allana a todo; se amolda a todo; hace las cosas de cualquier modo; **what I say —es** aquí mando yo; **that —es for me too** yo de acuerdo, yo contigo.

(p) (*fit*) **it —es under the table** cabe debajo de la mesa; **where does this book —?** ¿dónde pongo este libro?; **this part —es here** esta pieza se coloca aquí; **3 into 12 —es 4** 12 entre 3 son 4.

(q) (*break etc*) romperse, estropearse; (*give way*) ceder, hundirse; (*fall*) caer; **a fuse went** se quemó un plomo; **it went at the seams** se deshizo por las juntas; **there —es another button** se ha descosido otro botón.

(r) (*help, contribute*) **the qualities that — to make a king** las cualidades que hacen a un rey; **it —es to show that** sirve para demostrar que; **the money —es to help the poor** el dinero se destina a ayudar a los pobres.

(s) (*with ger*) **to — fishing** ir de pesca; **to — hunting** ir de caza; **to — riding** montar a caballo.

(t) (*become*) hacerse, volverse, ponerse; (*ie bad*) pasarse, (*of milk*) cortarse; **to — black** ponerse negro; **to — mad** volverse loco; **to — communist** hacerse comunista; **to — pale** palidecer ponerse pálido; *see* **blind** *etc*.

(u) (*let*) — **let me —!** ¡suelta!, ¡déjame!; **to let — of something** soltar algo; **to let oneself —** (*emotionally*) desahogarse, (*angrily*) perder los estribos, (*on a subject*) entusiasmarse; (*physically*) abandonarse, dejar de cuidarse; **they've let the house —** han dejado de cuidar la casa; **we'll let it — at that** dejémoslo ahí.

(v) (*make a noise*) **he went "psst"** dijo "psst"; **the balloon went bang** el globo estalló.

(w) **to — about** (*move about*) andar (de un sitio para otro); (*Naut*) virar; (*undertake*) emprender, intentar; **to — about one's business** ocuparse en sus asuntos; **to — about together** salir juntos; **to — about with** salir con, alternar con; **to — after** andar tras; (*follow*) seguir; (*persecute*) perseguir; **to — against** principle *etc* ir en contra de, oponerse a, *person* oponerse a, (*result, decision*) ser desfavorable a; **to — along** (*adv*) ir; (*go away*) marcharse; **to — along with** acompañar a; **to — along with an idea** consentir en un proyecto, aprobar una idea; **we can't — along with that** no estamos de acuerdo con eso; **to — along** (*prep*) ir por, pasar por; **to — at** (*undertake*) emprender; (*attack*) lanzarse sobre, acometer; **to — away** irse, marcharse; (*vanish*) desaparecer; **to — back** (*return*) volver, regresar; (*fall back*) retroceder; **to — back on** promise faltar a, desdecirse de; **it —es back to Elizabeth I** se remonta a Isabel I; **to — before** (*adv*) ir primero; (*in order etc*) anteceder, preceder; **all that has gone before** todo lo que ha pasado (*etc*) antes; **to — before** (*prep*) (*lead*) ir a la cabeza de; (*appear before*) comparecer ante; **to — beyond** ir más allá de, (*fig*) exceder; **to — by** (*adv*) (*of place*) pasar, (*of time*) pasar, transcurrir; **to — by** (*prep*) (*place*) pasar delante de, pasar cerca de, pasar junto a; (*be guided by*) atenerse a, guiarse por; **to — by appearances** juzgar por las apariencias; **that's nothing to — by** eso no es ningún criterio seguro; **to — down** (*adv*) bajar; (*sun*) ponerse; (*ship*) hundirse; (*be defeated*) sucumbir (*before* ante); (*Univ*) salir de la universidad; (*be acceptable*) ser aceptable, poderse aguantar; gustar; (*in history*) pasar a la historia; **that will — down well with him** eso le va a gustar; **the play did not — down well** la obra no gustó; **Madrid went down 2-0 to Seville** el Madrid perdió 2-0 frente al Sevilla; **to — down** (*prep*) bajar, bajar por, descender; **to — for** (*fetch*) ir por, ir a buscar; (*attack*) atacar, acometer; **to — all out for** tratar por todos los medios de conseguir; **I really — for jazz** me entusiasma de verdad el jazz; **I don't much — for that** eso realmente no me gusta; **to — in** (*adv*) entrar; (*fit*) caber; (*compete*) presentarse (*for* a); **to — in** (*prep*) entrar en; (*fit*) caber en; (*have a place*) ponerse en, deber colocarse en; **to — in for** dedicarse a; tomar parte en; (*compete*) presentarse a; *exam* tomar, presentarse para; (*buy*) comprar, (*collect*) coleccionar; **we don't — in for such things here** aquí esas cosas no se hacen; **to — in with someone** asociarse con uno; **to — into** (*enter*) entrar en; (*fit*) caber en; (*study*) examinar, investigar; **to — off** (*adv*) (*away*) irse, marcharse; (*explode*) estallar, hacer explosión; (*gun*) dispararse; (*go bad*) pasarse, deteriorarse; *(lose the knack)* perder el tino; **it all went off well** todo salió perfecto; **how did it — off?** ¿qué tal resultó?; **to — off** *(prep)* perder el gusto por, *person* dejar de querer a; **to — on** *(travelling)* seguir, seguir adelante, seguir su camino; avanzar; *(Theat)* salir a escena; *(progress)* progresar, hacer progresos; *(last)* durar; *(narration)* continuar, decir después; **to — on** + *ger* seguir + *ger*, continuar + *ger*; **— on!** ¡vamos!, *(with narration)* ¡adelante!, *(excl of surprise)* ¡anda!; **how are you —ing on?** ¿qué tal estás?; **he does — on so** habla más que siete, no acaba nunca de hablar; **don't — on so!** ¡no machaques!; **he's always —ing on about it** siempre está con la misma cantinela; **he —es on about the government** se queja siempre del gobierno, echa pestes siempre contra el gobierno; **don't — on like that!** ¡no te pongas así! **there's nothing to — on** no hay pista que podamos seguir; **that's nothing to — on** no se puede juzgar por eso; **to be gone on someone** *(fam)* andar mochales por uno; **to — on** at reñir; **it's —ing on for 7** son casi las 7; **he's —ing on for 50** va para los 50; **to — on to** + *infin* pasar luego a *infin*; **he went on to say** dijo a continuación; **to — on with** continuar, proseguir; **to — out** salir; *(light)* apagarse; *(of fashion)* pasar de moda; **to — out with** *boyfriend etc* salir con; **to — over** *(adv)* pasar por encima; **how did it — over?** ¿qué tal lo recibió el público? *(etc)*; **to — over to the opposition** pasarse a la oposición; **to — over** *(prep)* pasar por encima de; recorrer, atravesar; *(check)* revisar, repasar; **to — round** *(adv)* dar la vuelta, hacer un rodeo; *(revolve)* girar; *(suffice)* alcanzar para todos; **to — round to John's** ir a casa de Juan; **to — round** *(prep)* dar la vuelta a, hacer un rodeo para evitar; **to — through** *(adv)* pasar a través; **your promotion has gone through se** ha aprobado su ascenso; **to — through** *(prep)* pasar por, pasar a través de; penetrar; *(undergo)* sufrir, experimentar; *(examine)* examinar, estudiar; *(spend)* gastar; **to — through with something** llevar algo a cabo; **to — to** *(bequest)* pasar a; **to — together ir** juntos; *(colours etc)* armonizar, hacer juego; ser complementarios; **to — under** *(adv)* *(ship)* hundirse; *(person)* desaparecer debajo del agua; *(fig)* fracasar; **to — under** *(prep)* *name* ser conocido por; **to — up** *(adv)* subir; *(Univ)* entrar en la universidad; *(explode)* estallar; **to — up to London** ir a Londres; **to — up to someone** acercarse a uno; **if the total —es up to 100** si el total asciende a 100; **to — with** *(with con, acompañar; *(match)* armonizar con, hacer juego con; *(in mixing drinks)* ligar con; **to — without** *(adv)* arreglárselas; **to — without** *(prep)* pasarse sin.

2 *vt*: **to — it** *(speed)* ir a toda velocidad; *(work hard)* obrar enérgicamente; *(live it up)* correrla; **— it!** ¡a ello!, ¡ánimo!; **to — it alone** obrar sin ayuda de nadie, seguir una política independiente; **to — one better** hacer mejor todavía *(than que)*; **to — 3 hearts** *(Cards)* marcar 3 corazones.

3 *n* *(mostly fam)* **(a)** *(energy)* energía *f*, empuje *m*; **there's no — about him** le falta energía.

(b) to be on the — trajinar, moverse, estar trabajando, estar viajando; **to have two novels on the —** tener dos novelas entre manos; **to keep someone on the —** hacer que uno siga trabajando, no dejar descansar a uno.

(c) *(attempt)* **at one —, in one —** de un solo golpe, de un tirón; **to have a —** hacer una tentativa, probar suerte; **have a —!** ¡a ver!; **to have a — at something** intentar algo; **to have a — at** + *ger* intentar + *infin*.

(d) *(turn)* **it's your —** te toca a ti; **whose — is it?** ¿a quién le toca?

(e) *(success)* **it's all the —** hace furor; **it's no —** es inútil, es imposible; **to make a — of something** tener éxito en algo.

(f) *(bargain)* **it's a —** ¡trato hecho!; **is it a —?** ¿hace?, ¿estamos de acuerdo?

goad [gəud] **1** *n* aguijada *f*, aguijón *m*; *(fig)* estímulo *m*. **2** *vt* aguijonear, picar; *(fig)* incitar, provocar; *(anger)* irritar, *(taunt)* provocar con insultos; **to — someone into fury** provocar a uno hasta la furia; **to — someone into doing something, to — someone to do something** incitar a uno a hacer algo.

go-ahead ['gəuəhed] **1** *adj* emprendedor, enérgico. **2** *n* permiso *m* (*or* señal *f*) para seguir adelante.

goal [gəul] *n* **(a)** *(purpose)* fin *m*, objeto *m*, meta *f*; *(ambition)* ambición *f*; **to reach one's —** llegar a la meta, realizar una ambición.

(b) *(-posts)* meta *f*, portería *f*.

(c) *(score)* gol *m*, tanto *m*; **to score a —** marcar un gol.

goal-area ['gəul,εəriə] *n* área *f* de meta.
goalie ['gəuli] *n* *(fam)* = **goalkeeper.**

goalkeeper ['gəul,ki:pə*] *n* guardameta *m*, portero *m*.
goal-kick ['gəul'kik] *n* saque *m* de portería.
goal-line ['gəullain] *n* línea *f* de portería.
goal-post ['gəulpəust] *n* poste *m* de la portería.
goat [gəut] *n* cabra *f*, macho *m* cabrío; **to get someone's —** *(fam)* sacar a uno de quicio.
goatee [gəu'ti:] *n* barba *f* de chivo.
goatherd ['gəuthə:d] *n* cabrero *m*.
goatskin ['gəutskin] *n* piel *f* de cabra.
gob [gɔb] *n* salivazo *m*; *(sl)* boca *f*.
gobble ['gɔbl] **1** *n* gluglú *m*. **2** *vt* engullir; **to — up** engullirse ávidamente. **3** *vi* *(turkey)* gluglutear.
gobbler ['gɔblə*] *n* *(Orn)* pavo *m*.
gobbledygook ['gɔbldiguːk] *n* *(fam)* jerga *f* burocrática.
go-between ['gəubi,twi:n] *n* medianero *m*, a *f*, mediador *m*, ora *f*; *(pimp)* alcahuete *m*, a *f*.
goblet ['gɔblit] *n* copa *f*.
goblin ['gɔblin] *n* duende *m*, trasgo *m*.
go-by ['gəubai] *n* *(fam)*: **to give something the —** pasar algo por alto, omitir algo; **to give a place the —** dejar de visitar un sitio; **to give someone the —** desairar a uno (no haciendo caso de él).
go-cart ['gəukɑːt] *n* cochecito *m* de niño.
god [gɔd] *n* dios *m*; **G—** Dios *m*; **—s** *(Theat)* paraíso *m*, gallinero *m*; **for G—'s sake!** ¡por Dios!; **my G—!** ¡Dios mío!, ¡santo Dios!; **G— forbid!** ¡no lo permita Dios!; **please —!** *(arch)* ¡plegue a Dios!; **G— willing** si Dios quiere, Dios mediante; **G— only knows** sólo Dios sabe; **G— helps those who help themselves** a Dios rogando y con el mazo dando.
godchild ['gɔdtʃaild] *n*, *pl* **—children** [,tʃildrən] ahijado *m*, a *f*.
goddaughter ['gɔd,dɔ:tə*] *n* ahijada *f*.
goddess ['gɔdis] *n* diosa *f*.
godfather ['gɔd,fɑːðə*] *n* padrino *m* (*to* de).
god-fearing ['gɔd,fiəriŋ] *adj* timorato.
godforsaken ['gɔdfə,seikn] *adj* *person* dejado de la mano de Dios; *place* triste, remoto, desierto.
Godfrey ['gɔdfri] *m* Godofredo.
godhead ['gɔdhed] *n* divinidad *f*.
godless ['gɔdlis] *adj* impío, descreído.
godly ['gɔdli] *adj* piadoso.
godmother ['gɔd,mʌðə*] *n* madrina *f* (*to* de); **fairy —** hada *f* madrina.
godparents ['gɔd,pεərənts] *npl* padrinos *mpl*.
godsend ['gɔdsend] *n* cosa *f* llovida del cielo; **it was a — to us** fue un regalo celestial para nosotros.
godson ['gɔdsʌn] *n* ahijado *m*.
goes [gəuz] *see* **go.**
go-getter ['gəugetə*] *n* ambicioso *m*, a *f*, egoísta *mf*.
goggle ['gɔgl] *vi* salírsele a uno los ojos de las órbitas; **to — at** mirar con ojos desorbitados, mirar sin comprender.
goggle-eyed ['gɔgl,aid] *adj* con ojos desorbitados.
goggles ['gɔglz] *npl* *(Aut etc)* anteojos *mpl*; *(of skin-diver)* gafas *fpl* submarinas; *(fam)* gafas *fpl*.
going ['gəuiŋ] *n* **(a)** *(departure)* ida *f*, partida *f*.

(b) *(pace)* **good —!** ¡bien hecho!; **that was good —** eso fue muy rápido; **it was slow —** el avance fue lento.

(c) *(state of surface etc)* estado *m* del camino, *(Sport)* estado *m* de la pista; **the path is hard —** el camino está muy malo; **let's cross while the — is good** crucemos mientras podamos; **the book was heavy —** la lectura del libro resultó pesada; **it's heavy — talking to her** exige mucho esfuerzo conversar con ella.

going-over ['gəuiŋ'əuvə*] *n* **(a)** inspección *f*; **we gave the house a thorough —** registramos la casa de arriba abajo.

(b) *(fam)* paliza *f*; **they gave him a —** le dieron una paliza.

goings-on ['gəuiŋz'ɔn] *npl* actividades *fpl* (sospechosas); conducta *f* (sospechosa).

goitre, (US) goiter ['gɔitə*] *n* bocio *m*.
gold [gəuld] **1** *n* oro *m*; **rolled —** oro *m* laminado. **2** *attr* de oro.
goldbrick ['gəuld'brik] **1** *n* *(fam)* estafa *f*. **2** *vi* *(fam)* dar gato por liebre.
Gold Coast ['gəuld'kəust] *n* Costa *f* de Oro.
goldcrest ['gəuldkrest] *n* reyezuelo *m* sencillo.
gold digger ['gəuld,digə*] *n* aventurera *f*.
golden ['gəuldən] *adj* de oro; dorado; áureo; *age, voice, wedding etc* de oro; *opportunity* excelente.
goldenrod ['gəuldən'rɔd] *n* *(Bot)* vara *f* de oro.
goldfield ['gəuldfi:ld] *n* campo *m* aurífero.
gold-filled ['gəuld,fild] *adj* lleno de oro; *(Tech)* revestido de oro, enchapado en oro; *tooth* empastado de oro.
goldfinch ['gəuldfintʃ] *n* jilguero *m*.
goldfish ['gəuldfiʃ] *n* pez *m* de colores.

goldfish bowl ['gəuldfiʃ,bəul] n pecera f.
gold mine ['gəuldmain] n mina f de oro; (fig) río m de oro, potosí m.
goldsmith ['gəuldsmiθ] n orfebre m.
gold standard ['gəuld,stændəd] n patrón m oro.
golf [gɔlf] n golf m.
golf club ['gɔlfklʌb] n (society) club m de golf; (stick) palo m (de golf).
golf course ['gɔlfkɔːs] n campo m de golf.
golfer ['gɔlfə*] n golfista mf.
golf links ['gɔlfliŋks] npl campo m de golf.
Goliath [gə'laiəθ] m Goliat.
golliwog ['gɔliwɔg] n negrito m.
golly[1] ['gɔli] n (fam) = **golliwog**.
golly[2] ['gɔli] interj (fam) ¡caramba!
golosh [gə'lɔʃ] n chanclo m, galocha f.
gonad ['gɔnæd] n gónada f.
gondola ['gɔndələ] n góndola f; (Aer) barquilla f.
gone [gɔn] ptp of **go**.
goner ['gɔnə*] n (sl): he's a — está muerto.
gong [gɔŋ] n gong m, gongo m.
gonorrhoea [,gɔnə'riə] n gonorrea f.
goo [guː] n (fam) cosa f muy pegajosa, sustancia f viscosa.
good [gud] **1** adj (comp **better**, superl **best**) (a) (general sense; also of — quality, right, morally sound, favourable etc) bueno, (before m sing n buen, eg) a — **book** un buen libro; -! ¡bueno!, ¡muy bien!; — **for you!** ¡muy bien Vd!; — **old Peter!** ¡bravo Pedro!
(b) (— enough) — **enough!** ¡muy bien!; that's — **enough for me** eso me basta; it's **just not** — **enough!** ¡esto no se puede consentir!
(c) (pleasant) it's — **to see you** me alegro de verte; **how** — **it is to know that . . .!** ¡cuánto me alegro de saber que . . .!; it's — **to be here** es agradable estar aquí; it's as — **as a holiday to me** esto me vale tanto como unas vacaciones.
(d) (beneficial) bueno, provechoso; (advantageous) ventajoso; (wholesome) sano, saludable; — **to eat** bueno de comer; it's — **for you** es cosa muy sana; it's — **for you to swim** la natación es cosa sana; **oil is** — **for burns** el aceite es bueno para las quemaduras; **spirits are not** — **for me** los licores no me sientan bien; **he eats more than is** — **for him** come más de lo razonable.
(e) (useful) bueno, útil, servible; **the only** — **chair** la única silla servible (or sana); **to be** — **for** servir para; **he's** — **for nothing** es completamente inútil; **he's** — **for 10 years yet** tiene todavía por delante 10 años de vida; **he's** — **for £5** seguramente tiene 5 libras que prestarnos; **I'm** — **for another mile** tengo fuerzas para ir otra milla más; **it'll be** — **for some years** durará todavía algunos años; **a ticket** — **for 3 months** un billete valedero para 3 meses.
(f) (clever) **to be** — **at** ser hábil en, tener aptitud para, ser fuerte en; **she's** — **with cats** entiende de gatos.
(g) (kind) bueno, amable; **he's a** — **sort** es buena persona; **he was** — **to me** fue muy amable conmigo; **he was so** — **as to** + infin tuvo la amabilidad de + infin; **please be so** — **as to** + infin ¿me hace el favor de + infin?, (more formally) **tenga la bondad de** + infin; **that's very** — **of you** es Vd muy amable.
(h) (well-behaved) de buenos modales, educado; **the child has been as** — **as gold** el niño se ha portado como un ángel; **be** — **!** (morally) ¡sé bueno!, (in behaviour) ¡pórtate bien!, (at this moment) ¡estáte formal!
(i) (at least) **a** — **3 hours** 3 horas largas; **a** — **4 miles** 4 millas largas; **a** — **£10** lo menos 10 libras.
(j) (practically) it's as — **as new** está como nuevo; it's as — **as done** está casi terminado; it's as — **as lost** puede darse por perdido; **they're as** — **as beaten** pueden darse por vencidos.
(k) **to make** — promise cumplir, accusation hacer bueno, probar, claim justificar; loss compensar, reparar; damage reparar; pagar; see **escape**.
2 adv: — **and proper** por las buenas; — **and strong** bien fuerte; **to feel** — satisfecho, creer haber hecho algo meritorio, (in health) estar como un reloj; **to give as** — **as one gets** devolver golpe por golpe; **you never had it so** — nunca habéis estado mejor; **to hold** — ser valedero, seguir verdadero (of con respecto a); **to make** — salir bien, tener éxito, demostrar tener capacidad.
3 n (a) bien m, provecho m, utilidad f; **the** — (abstract) lo bueno, (people) los buenos; — **and evil** el bien y el mal; **there is much** — **in him** tiene buenas cualidades; **there is some** — **in him** no es del todo malo; **for** — definitivamente, para siempre;

he's gone for — se ha ido para no volver; **for the** — **of** en bien de, a beneficio de; **it's for your own** — es por su propio bien; **it's no** — es inútil, no sirve para nada; **it's no** — **complaining** de nada sirve quejarse, no vale la pena de quejarse; **what's the** — **of it?** ¿para qué sirve?; **I'm no** — **at such things** yo no sirvo para tales cosas; **he's no** — (morally) es un perdido; **he's up to no** — está tramando algo malo; **he'll come to no** — tendrá mal fin; **we're £2 to the** — hemos ganado 2 libras; **we're a spoon to the** — tenemos una cuchara de sobra; **to do** — hacer bien; **he never did any** — nunca hizo nada bueno; **it can't do any** — es imposible que sea útil; **it will do him no** — esto no le aprovechará en lo más mínimo; **this medicine will do you** — esta medicina le sentará bien; **much** — **may it do him!** ¡buen provecho le haga!
(b) —**s** bienes mpl, efectos mpl; (Comm) géneros mpl, artículos mpl, mercancías fpl; **canned** —**s** conservas fpl alimenticias; **capital** —**s** bienes mpl de capital; **consumer** —**s** bienes mpl de consumo; **fancy** —**s** géneros mpl de fantasía; **knitted** —**s** géneros mpl de punto; **to deliver the** —**s** (fam) cumplir lo prometido.
4 —**s** attr de mercancías.
good-bye ['gud'bai] **1** interj ¡adiós! **2** n adiós m; **to say** — despedirse de, (fig) dar por perdido.
good-for-nothing ['gudfə'nʌθiŋ] **1** adj inútil. **2** n perdido m.
good-humoured ['gud'hjuːməd] adj person afable, jovial; remark etc jovial; discussion de tono amistoso.
good-looking ['gud'lukiŋ] adj bien parecido, guapo.
goodly ['gudli] adj (fine) agradable, excelente; sum etc importante; number crecido.
good-natured ['gud'neitʃəd] adj person afable, bonachón; discussion de tono amistoso.
goodness ['gudnis] n (virtue, kindness) bondad f; (good quality) buena calidad f; (essence) sustancia f, lo mejor; —**!**, — **gracious!**, — **me!** ¡Dios mío!; **for** —**' sake!** ¡por Dios!; — **only knows!** ¡vaya Vd a saber!
good-tempered ['gud'tempəd] adj afable, ecuánime, de natural apacible; tone afable, amistoso; discussion sereno, sin pasión.
good-time ['gud'taim] adj: — **girl** chica f alegre.
goodwill ['gud'wil] n buena voluntad f; (Comm) clientela f, buen nombre m; — **mission** misión f de buena voluntad.
goody ['gudi] (fam: esp US) **1** adj beatuco, santurrón. **2** interj (also — —) ¡qué bien!, ¡qué estupendo! **3** n golosina f.
gooey ['guːi] adj (fam) pegajoso, viscoso; sweet empalagoso.
goof [guːf] (sl) **1** n bobo m, a f. **2** vi tirarse una plancha.
goofy ['guːfi] adj (sl) bobo.
goon [guːn] n (a) imbécil mf, idiota mf. (b) (US) gorila m contratado para sembrar el terror entre los obreros.
goose [guːs] n, pl **geese** [giːs] (domestic) ganso m, a f, oca f; (wild) ánsar m; **to cook someone's** — hacer la santísima a uno.
gooseberry ['guzbəri] n uva f espina; **to play** — hacer de carabina; **I don't want to play** — yo no quiero estar de más.
gooseflesh ['guːsfleʃ] n, **goosepimples** ['guːs,pimplz] npl carne f de gallina.
goose-step ['guːsstep] **1** n paso m de ganso. **2** vi marchar a paso de ganso.
gopher ['gəufə*] n ardillón m, ardilla f de tierra; tuza f.
gore[1] [gɔː*] n sangre f (derramada).
gore[2] [gɔː*] vt cornear.
gorge [gɔːdʒ] **1** n (Geog) cañón m, barranco m, garganta f; **my** — **rises at it** me da asco.
2 vt engullir.
3 vi (also vr: **to** — **oneself**) hartarse, atracarse (on de).
gorgeous ['gɔːdʒəs] adj magnífico, brillante, vistoso; (fam) maravilloso; **hullo** —**!** (fam) ¿qué hay, ricura?
gorilla [gə'rilə] n gorila m.
gormandize ['gɔːməndaiz] vi glotonear.
gorse [gɔːs] n aulaga f, tojo m.
gory ['gɔːri] adj ensangrentado; details, story sangriento.
gosh [gɔʃ] interj (sl) ¡caray!
goshawk ['gɔshɔːk] n azor m.
gosling ['gɔzliŋ] n ansarino m.
go-slow ['gəu'sləu] **1** n huelga f de trabajo lento. **2** vi trabajar a ritmo lento, (strictly) trabajar con arreglo a las bases.

gospel ['gɔspəl] n evangelio m; **as though it were — truth** como si fuese el evangelio.

gossamer ['gɔsəmə*] n hilos mpl de telaraña; (fabric) gasa f sutil; — **thin** muy delgado.

gossip ['gɔsip] 1 n (a) (person: great talker) hablador m, ora f; (pej) chismoso m, a f, murmurador m, ora f, comadre f, mala lengua f.
(b) (conversation) charla f; **we had a good old — about it** charlamos un buen rato de ello.
(c) (scandal) chismes mpl, chismorreo m, comadreo m, habladurías fpl, murmuración f; **piece of —** chisme m, habilla f.
2 vi (talk) charlar; (talk scandal) cotillear, contar chismes.

gossip column ['gɔsip,kɔləm] n gacetilla f, notas fpl de sociedad.

gossiping ['gɔsipiŋ] 1 adj chismoso. 2 n chismorreo m.

gossipy ['gɔsipi] adj chismoso; style familiar.

got [gɔt] pret and ptp of **get**.

Goth [gɔθ] n godo m, a f.

Gothic ['gɔθik] 1 adj race godo; (Archit, Typ) gótico. 2 n (language) gótico m.

gotten ['gɔtn] (US) ptp of **get**.

gouge [gaudʒ] 1 n gubia f. 2 vt excavar con gubia; (fig) excavar; **to — someone's eyes out** sacar los ojos a uno.

gourd [guəd] n calabaza f.

gourmand ['guəmənd] n glotón m.

gourmet ['guəmei] n gastrónomo m.

gout [gaut] n (Med) gota f.

govern ['gʌvən] vt gobernar; dominar; (guide) guiar, regir; (Gram) regir; **to — one's temper** contenerse, dominarse.

governess ['gʌvənis] n institutriz f.

governing ['gʌvəniŋ] adj: — **body** junta f directiva; — **principle** principio m rector.

government ['gʌvnmənt] 1 n gobierno m; (Gram etc) régimen m; **local —** administración f local; **minority —** gobierno m minoritario.
2 attr: — **bonds** títulos mpl del Estado; — **house** palacio m del gobernador; — **policy** política f del gobierno.

governmental [,gʌvən'mentl] adj gubernamental, gubernativo.

governor ['gʌvənə*] n gobernador m; (of prison) director m, alcaide m; (Mech) regulador m; (fam: boss) jefe m, (father) progenitor m, viejo m; **thanks, —!** ¡gracias, caballero!

governor-general ['gʌvənə'dʒenərəl] n gobernador m general.

governorship ['gʌvənəʃip] n gobierno m, cargo m de gobernador.

gown [gaun] n (dress) vestido m, traje m; (Law, Univ) toga f.

grab [græb] 1 n (a) (snatch) arrebatiña f, agarro m; (fam) robo m; **to make a — at something** tratar de arrebatar algo.
(b) (Mech) cubeta f draga, cuchara f de dos mandíbulas.
2 vt asir, coger, arrebatar; (fig) arrebatarse, apropiarse.
3 vi: **to — at** (snatch) tratar de arrebatar; (in falling) tratar de asir.

grace [greis] 1 n (a) (Rel) gracia f, gracia f divina.
(b) (gracefulness) finura f, elegancia f; (of shape) armonía f; (of movement) garbo m, donaire m; (of style) elegancia f, amenidad f.
(c) **with a good —** de buen talante; **with a bad — a regañadientes; he had the — to apologize** tuvo la cortesía de pedir perdón.
(d) **it has the saving — that** tiene el único mérito de que; **to get into someone's good —s** congraciarse con uno.
(e) (delay) demora f; **3 day's —** un plazo de 3 días.
(f) (blessing) bendición f de la mesa; **to say —** bendecir la mesa.
(g) (in title: dukes) **His G— the Duke** su Excelencia; **yes, Your G—** sí, Excelencia.
(h) (in title: Eccl) **His G— Bishop X** su Ilustrísima Monseñor X; **yes, your G—** sí, Ilustrísima.
2 vt adornar (with de), embellecer; **he —d the meeting with his presence** honró a los asistentes con su presencia.

graceful ['greisful] adj gracioso, agraciado; movement airoso, elegante, garboso; compliment elegante; lines grácil.

gracefully ['greisfəli] adv elegantemente, con garbo.

graceless ['greislis] adj desgarbado; (impolite) descortés, grosero.

gracious ['greiʃəs] adj (merciful) clemente; (urbane) cortés, afable; monarch gracioso; — **(me)!** ¡Dios mío!; **he was very — to me** estuvo muy amable conmigo.

gradation [grə'deiʃən] n gradación f.

grade [greid] 1 n (degree) grado m; (quality) clase f, calidad f; (mark) nota f, clase f; (US school) clase f; (slope) pendiente f; **to make the —** alcanzar el nivel deseado, tener éxito, ser satisfactorio.
2 vt clasificar, graduar; (School, Univ) calificar, dar nota a.

grade crossing ['greid,krɔsiŋ] n (US) paso m a nivel.

grade school ['greid'sku:l] n (US) escuela f primaria.

gradient ['greidiənt] n pendiente f.

gradual ['grædjuəl] adj gradual; paulatino; progresivo.

gradually ['grædjuəli] adv gradualmente; poco a poco; paulatinamente; progresivamente.

graduate ['grædjuit] n graduado m, a f, licenciado m, a f (in en).

graduate ['grædjueit] 1 vt graduar. 2 vi (Univ) graduarse, licenciarse (in en); **to — as** recibirse de.

graduation [,grædju'eiʃən] n graduación f.

graft[1] [graːft] (Hort, Med) 1 n injerto m. 2 vt injertar (in, into, on to en).

graft[2] [graːft] n corrupción f, chanchullos mpl; **hard —** trabajo m muy duro.

graham flour ['greiəm,flauə*] n (US) harina f de trigo sin cerner.

Grail [greil] n: **Holy —** Santo Grial m.

grain [grein] n (a) (single seed) grano m; (corn) granos mpl, cereales mpl; **bread —s** granos mpl panificables.
(b) (fig) **with a — of salt** con un grano de sal; **there's not a — of truth in it** eso no tiene ni pizca de verdad.
(c) (in wood) fibra f, hebra f; (in stone) vena f, veta f; (in leather) flor f; (in cloth) granilla f; **it goes against the — with me to +** infin se me hace cuesta arriba + infin; **to saw with the —** aserrar a hebra.

grammar ['græmə*] n gramática f.

grammarian [grə'meəriən] n gramático m.

grammatical [grə'mætikəl] adj gramatical; **in — English** en buen inglés.

grammatically [grə'mætikəli] adv bien, correctamente.

gram(me) [græm] n gramo m.

gramophone ['græməfəun] n gramófono m.

gramophone record ['græməfəun,rekɔːd] n disco m de gramófono.

grampus ['græmpəs] n orca f.

granary ['grænəri] n granero m, troj f.

grand [grænd] 1 adj (fine, splendid) magnífico, imponente, grandioso; person distinguido, augusto; style elevado, sublime; staircase etc principal; (fam) magnífico, bárbaro, estupendo; **a — game** un magnífico partido; **we had a — time** lo pasamos estupendamente.
2 n (piano) piano m de cola; (US sl) mil dólares mpl.

grand(d)ad ['grændæd] n (fam) abuelito m; **yes, —** sí, abuelo.

grandchild ['græntʃaild] n, pl **—children** [,tʃildrən] nieto m, a f; **grandchildren** nietos mpl.

granddaughter ['græn,dɔːtə*] n nieta f.

grandee [,græn'diː] n grande m de España.

grandeur ['grændjə*] n magnificencia f, grandiosidad f, sublimidad f.

grandfather ['grænd,fɑːðə*] n abuelo m.

grandiloquent [græn'diləkwənt] adj altisonante, hinchado.

grandiose ['grændiəuz] adj grandioso; (pej) building etc ostentoso, hecho para impresionar; scheme, plan vasto, ambicioso; style exagerado, pomposo.

grandma ['grænmaː] n (fam) abuelita f; **yes, —** sí, abuela.

grandmother ['græn,mʌðə*] n abuela f.

grandpa ['grænpaː] n (fam) abuelito m; **yes, —** sí, abuelo.

grandparents ['græn,peərənts] npl abuelos mpl.

grandson ['grænsʌn] n nieto m.

grandstand ['grændstænd] n tribuna f.

grange [greindʒ] n (Agr) cortijo m, alquería f; (Brit) casa f solariega, casa f de señor.

granite ['grænit] n granito m.

granny ['græni] n (fam) abuelita f, nana f; **yes, —** sí, abuela.

grant [graːnt] 1 n (act) otorgamiento m, concesión f; (thing granted) concesión f; (Law) cesión f; (gift) donación f; (scholarship) beca f; (subsidy) subvención f.
2 vt (bestow, concede) otorgar, conceder; (Law) ceder; (give) donar; proposition asentir a; **—ed that**

dado que, supuesto que; **—ing this (to) be so** dado que así sea; **to take something for** —ed dar algo por sentado, suponer algo; **we may take that for** —ed eso es indudable; **he takes her for** —ed él no le hace caso alguno a ella.

grant-in-aid ['grɑ:ntin'eid] n subvención f.

granulated ['grænjuleitid] adj granulado.

granule ['grænju:l] n gránulo m.

grape [greip] n uva f; **sour** —**s**! ¡están verdes!; **it's just sour** —**s with him** es un envidioso.

grapefruit ['greipfru:t] n toronja f, pomelo m.

grape harvest ['greip,hɑ:vist] n vendimia f.

grape juice ['greipdʒu:s] n mosto m; zumo m de uva.

grapeshot ['greipʃɔt] n metralla f.

grapevine ['greipvain] n vid f; (trained against wall etc) parra f; (sl) medio m de comunicación clandestina; **I hear on the** — **that** he llegado a saber que, me ha dicho alguno que.

graph [grɑ:f] n gráfica f.

graphic ['græfik] adj gráfico.

graphite ['græfait] n grafito m.

graphology [græ'fɔlədʒi] n grafología f.

graph paper ['grɑ:f,peipə*] n papel m cuadriculado.

grapnel ['græpnəl] n rezón m, arpeo m.

grapple ['græpl] **1** vt asir, agarrar; (Naut) aferrar.
2 vi (wrestlers etc) agarrarse; **to** — **with someone** agarrar a uno, luchar a brazo partido con uno; **to** — **with a problem** esforzarse por resolver un problema, tratar de vencer un problema.

grappling iron ['græpliŋ,aiən] n arpeo m, garfio m.

grasp [grɑ:sp] **1** n (a) agarro m, asimiento m; (hand-clasp) apretón m; **to be within someone's** — estar al alcance de la mano; **he has a strong** — agarra muy fuerte; **to lose one's** — desasirse (on de).
(b) (fig) (power) garras fpl, control m; (range) alcance m; (mental hold) comprensión f, capacidad f intelectual; **it's within everyone's** — está al alcance de todos; **to have a good** — **of** dominar, conocer a fondo.
2 vt (hold firmly) asir, agarrar; hand estrechar, apretar; weapon etc empuñar; chance asir; power, territory apoderarse de; (get mental hold of) comprender.
3 vi: **to** — **at** hacer por asir, tratar de asir.

grasping ['grɑ:spiŋ] adj avaro, codicioso.

grass [grɑ:s] **1** n hierba f; (lawn) césped m; (grazing) pasto m; **"keep off the** —**"** "se prohibe pisar la hierba"; **to let the** — **grow under one's feet** dejar crecer la hierba; **to put a horse out to** — echar un caballo al pasto.
2 vt cubrir de hierba.
3 vi (sl) soplar.

grasshopper ['grɑ:s,hɔpə*] n saltamontes m.

grassland ['grɑ:slænd] n pradera f, dehesa f.

grass-roots ['grɑ:s'ru:ts] adj básico; popular; — **politics** política f donde se trata de los problemas corrientes de la gente.

grass widow ['grɑ:s'widəu] n mujer f cuyo marido está ausente.

grass widower ['grɑ:s'widəuə*] n marido m cuya mujer está ausente.

grassy ['grɑ:si] adj herboso, cubierto de hierba.

grate¹ [greit] n hogar m; (strictly) parrilla f de hogar, emparrillado m.

grate² [greit] **1** vt food rallar; teeth hacer rechinar.
2 vi (make a noise) rechinar; (rub on) rozar; **to** — **on** rozar con, (fig) molestar; **to** — **on the ear** herir el oído; **to** — **on one's nerves** destrozar los nervios a uno.

grateful ['greitful] adj agradecido, reconocido; **with** — **thanks** con mis más efusivas gracias; **I am** — **for your letter** agradezco su carta; **I am most** — **to you** te lo agradezco muchísimo; **I should be** — **if** agradecería que + subj.

gratefully ['greitfəli] adv agradecidamente, con agradecimiento; **she looked at me** — me miró agradecida.

grater ['greitə*] n rallador m.

gratification [,grætifi'keiʃən] n (a) (reward) gratificación f, recompensa f; (tip) propina f.
(b) (pleasure) placer m, satisfacción f; **to my great** — con gran satisfacción mía.

gratify ['grætifai] vt person complacer; whim etc satisfacer; **I was gratified to hear that** me alegré de saber que; **he was much gratified** estuvo muy contento.

gratifying ['grætifaiiŋ] adj satisfactorio, grato; **with** — **speed** con loable prontitud; **it is** — **to know that** me es grato saber que.

grating¹ ['greitiŋ] n reja f, enrejado m, emparrillado m.

grating² ['greitiŋ] adj tone etc áspero.

gratis ['grɑ:tis] adv gratis.

gratitude ['grætitju:d] n agradecimiento m, reconocimiento m.

gratuitous [grə'tju:itəs] adj gratuito.

gratuitously [grə'tju:itəsli] adv (free) gratis; (arbitrarily) gratuitamente.

gratuity [grə'tju:iti] n gratificación f, propina f; (at Christmas) aguinaldo m.

grave¹ [greiv] adj grave (also Gram); serio; (anxious) preocupado; solemne.

grave² [greiv] n sepultura f; (with monument) tumba f, sepulcro m.

gravedigger ['greiv,digə*] n sepulturero m.

gravel ['grævəl] n grava f, cascajo m, recebo m.

gravelled ['grævəld] adj engravado, cubierto con grava.

gravelly ['grævəli] adj arenisco, cascajoso.

gravely ['greivli] adj gravemente, seriamente; **he is** — **ill** está grave; **he spoke** — habló en tono preocupado.

graven ['greivən] adj: — **image** ídolo m; **it is** — **on my memory** lo tengo grabado en la memoria.

gravestone ['greivstəun] n lápida f sepulcral.

graveyard ['greivjɑ:d] n cementerio m (also fig), camposanto m.

graving dock ['greiviŋdɔk] n dique m de carena.

gravitate ['græviteit] vi gravitar; **to** — **towards** (fig) dejarse atraer por, tender hacia.

gravitation [,grævi'teiʃən] n gravitación f; (fig) tendencia f (towards hacia).

gravitational [,grævi'teiʃənl] adj gravitatorio.

gravity ['græviti] n gravedad f (also Phys); seriedad f; solemnidad f; **specific** — peso m específico; **the** — **of the situation** lo grave de la situación, los peligros de la situación; **he spoke with the utmost** — habló con la mayor solemnidad.

gravy ['greivi] n salsa f.

gravy boat ['greivi,bəut] n salsera f.

gray [grei] adj = **grey**.

graze¹ [greiz] (Agr) **1** vt grass pacer; cattle apacentar, pastar. **2** vi pacer.

graze² [greiz] **1** n roce m, abrasión f, desolladura f.
2 vt (touch) rozar al pasar; (scrape) raspar, raer.

grease [gri:s] **1** n grasa f; (dirt) mugre f; (of candle) sebo m. **2** vt engrasar, lubricar.

grease gun ['gri:sgʌn] n pistola f engrasadora, engrasadora f a presión.

greasepaint ['gri:speint] n maquillaje m.

greaseproof ['gri:spru:f] adj impermeable a la grasa; **paper** apergaminado.

greasiness ['gri:sinis] n lo grasiento; lo resbaladizo; mugre f; zalamería f.

greasy ['gri:si] adj substance, surface grasiento; road etc resbaladizo; pole ensebado; (grubby) mugriento; person adulón, cotista.

great [greit] adj (a) (large) grande, vasto, enorme; sum importante; care etc especial; age avanzado; time largo; **of** — **power** de gran potencia; **to my** — **surprise** con gran sorpresa mía; **what a** — **(big) dog!** ¡qué perro más grande!; **to be** — **friends** ser muy amigos; **it was a** — **joke** fue divertidísimo; **to have no** — **opinion of** tener un concepto mediocre de; see **deal, many etc**.
(b) (important) grande, importante, principal; **the** — **thing is that** lo importante es que.
(c) (outstanding) grande, famoso, destacado; **a** — **man** un gran hombre; **the** — los grandes; **he has a** — **future** tiene un brillante porvenir.
(d) (clever) **to be** — **at, to be** — **on** ser fuerte en, entender de.
(e) (keen) **he's a** — **angler** tiene gran afición a la pesca; **he's a** — **arguer** tiene la manía de discutir; **he's a** — **eater** tiene buen apetito, es muy comilón.
(f) (fam) magnífico, estupendo; —**!** ¡magnífico!; **it's** —**!** ¡es fabuloso!; **you were** —**!** ¡estuviste magnífico!

great-aunt ['greit'ɑ:nt] n tía f abuela.

Great Britain ['greit'britn] Gran Bretaña f.

greatcoat ['greitkəut] n sobretodo m, cobista.

greater ['greitə*] adj (comp of **great**) mayor.

greatest ['greitist] adj (superl of **great**) (a) el mayor, la mayor; **with the** — **difficulty** con la mayor dificultad; **the** — **writer of his age** el mayor escritor de su época; **when the heat is at its** — cuando más aprieta el calor.
(b) (fam) **it's the** —**!** ¡es el colmo!, ¡es el delirio!; **he's the** —**!** ¡es fabuloso!

great-grandchild ['greit'grænt∫aild], pl —**children** [,t∫ildrən] bisnieto m, a f.

great-grandfather ['greit'grænd,fɑ:ðə*] n bisabuelo m.

great-grandmother ['greit'græn,mʌðə*] n bisabuela f.

great-great-grandfather ['greit'greit'grænd,fɑːðə*] n tatarabuelo m.

great-great-grandson ['greit'greit'grænsʌn] n tataranieto m.

great-hearted ['greit'hɑːtid] adj valiente.

Great Lakes ['greit'leiks] pl Grandes Lagos mpl.

greatly ['greitli] adv grandemente, mucho, muy, sumamente; — **superior** muy superior; **we were —amused** nos divirtió muchísimo; **it is — to be regretted** es muy de lamentar; **not — expensive** no muy caro.

greatness ['greitnis] n grandeza f.

Great War ['greit'wɔː*] Primera Guerra f Mundial (1914-18).

grebe [griːb] n zampullín m, somormujo m.

Grecian ['griːʃən] adj griego.

Greece [griːs] Grecia f.

greed [griːd] n, **greediness** ['griːdinis] n codicia f, avaricia f; avidez f (for de); (for food) gula f, glotonería f.

greedily ['griːdili] adv con avidez; eat vorazmente.

greedy ['griːdi] adj codicioso, avaro; ávido (for de); (for food) goloso, glotón; **don't be so —!** ¡no seas glotón!

Greek [griːk] **1** adj griego.

2 n griego m, a f.

3 n (language) griego m; **ancient —** griego m antiguo; **it's — to me** para mí es chino, no entiendo ni palabra.

green [griːn] **1** adj verde; (fresh) fresco, (unripe, unseasoned) verde; (raw) crudo; complexion pálido; (inexperienced) nuevo, novato; (naïve) crédulo; **bright —** verdegay; **dark —** verdinegro; **to grow —, to look —** verdear.

2 n (a) (colour) verde m.

(b) (lawn) césped m; (field) prado m; (for bowls etc) pista f; **village —** (approx) césped m comunal.

(c) —s verduras fpl.

greenery ['griːnəri] n verdura f.

green-eyed ['griːnaid] adj de ojos verdes.

greenfinch ['griːnfintʃ] n verderón m.

greenfly ['griːnflai] n pulgón m.

greengage ['griːngeidʒ] n claudia f.

greengrocer ['griːn,grəusə*] n verdulero m, a f; —'s (shop) verdulería f.

greenhorn ['griːnhɔːn] n bisoño m, novato m.

greenhouse ['griːnhaus] n, pl —**houses** [,hauziz] invernáculo m, invernadero m.

greenish ['griːniʃ] adj verdoso.

Greenland ['griːnlənd] Groenlandia f.

Greenlander ['griːnləndə*] n groenlandés m, esa f.

greenness ['griːnnis] n verdor m, lo verde; (fig) inexperiencia f; credulidad f.

greenstuff ['griːnstʌf] n verduras fpl, legumbres fpl.

greensward ['griːnswɔːd] n césped m.

greet [griːt] vt (in general) recibir; (with words etc) saludar; (welcome) dar la bienvenida a; (meet one's eyes) presentarse a; **this was —ed by everybody** todos sintieron un gran alivio al saber la noticia; **the statement was —ed with laughter** al terminar la declaración hubo risas.

greeting ['griːtiŋ] n (with words etc) saludo m, salutación f; (welcome) bienvenida f; —**s!** ¡bienvenido!; —**s** (in letter) recuerdos mpl.

gregarious [gri'gɛəriəs] adj gregario.

Gregory ['gregəri] m Gregorio.

gremlin ['gremlin] n (Aer sl) duendecillo m.

grenade [gri'neid] n (hand-) bomba f de mano.

grenadine ['grenədiːn] n granadina f.

grew [gruː] pret of **grow**.

grey [grei] **1** adj gris; horse etc rucio. **2** n gris m; (horse) rucio m. **3** vi (hair) encanecer.

greybeard ['greibiəd] n anciano m, viejo m.

grey-haired ['grei'hɛəd] adj canoso.

greyhound ['greihaund] n galgo m, lebrel m.

greyish ['greiiʃ] adj grisáceo; hair entrecano.

grid [grid] n (with bars) reja f; (Cook etc) parrilla f; (Elec) red f; (Aut) portaequipajes m, portamaletas m; (Aut sl) armatoste m, rácano m.

gridiron ['grid,aiən] n (Cook etc) parrilla f; (US) campo m de fútbol.

grief [griːf] n dolor m, pesar m, aflicción f; **good —!** ¡demonio!; **to come to —** tener un desastre, fracasar.

grievance ['griːvəns] n motivo m de queja; agravio m, injusticia f.

grieve [griːv] **1** vt dar pena a; **you — me** me das pena; **it —s one to see . . .** da pena ver . . .

2 vi afligirse, acongojarse (about, at de, por); **to — for** llorar, llorar la pérdida (etc) de.

grievous ['griːvəs] adj loss etc cruel, doloroso, penoso; blow severo; pain fuerte; crime, offence grave; error lamentable, craso; task penoso.

griffin ['grifin] n (Myth) grifo m.

grifter ['griftə*] n (US) (a) propietario m de una caseta de feria (etc); garitero m. (b) (sl) fullero m, estafador m, timador m.

grill [gril] **1** n parrilla f; (meat) asado m a la parrilla; **mixed —** fritos mpl variados; see also **grille**. **2** vt asar a la parrilla; (fam) interrogar (sin piedad).

grille [gril] n rejilla f; (of window) reja f; (screen) verja f.

grilled [grild] adj asado a la parrilla.

grillroom ['grilruːm] n parrilla f.

grilse [grils] n salmón m joven (que sólo ha estado una vez en el mar).

grim [grim] adj (a) (stern) severo; (frowning) ceñudo; (unrelenting) inexorable, inflexible; battle porfiado, muy reñido, encarnizado; humour macabro; (frightful) horrible; **with a — smile** sonriendo inexorable; **the — truth** la verdad lisa y llana; **the — facts** los hechos inexorables.

(b) (fam) horrible, malísimo.

grimace [gri'meis] **1** n mueca f, visaje m. **2** vi hacer una mueca, hacer muecas.

grime [graim] n mugre f, suciedad f.

grimly ['grimli] adv severamente; inexorablemente; encarnizadamente; **he smiled —** sonrió inexorable; **to hang on —** resistir sin cejar.

grimy ['graimi] adj mugriento, sucio.

grin [grin] **1** n sonrisa f (abierta, bonachona, burlona etc); (grimace) mueca f.

2 vi sonreír (mostrando los dientes, bonachón, burlón etc; at a); **to — and bear it** sonreír y resignarse, poner al mal tiempo buena cara.

grind [graind] **1** n trabajo m pesado; rutina f; (boredom) lo pesado.

2 vt (irr: pret and ptp **ground**) corn etc moler; stone pulverizar; teeth hacer rechinar; (sharpen) amolar, afinar; (oppress) agobiar, oprimir; **to — down** pulverizar; (wear away) desgastar; (oppress) agobiar, oprimir; **to — down to, to — into** reducir a; **to — out** reproducir mecánicamente (or laboriosamente etc).

3 vi (machine etc) rechinar, funcionar con dificultad; **to — against** ludir ruidosamente con; **to — away** (Mus) tocar laboriosamente; **to — to a halt** pararse con gran estruendo de frenos.

grinder ['graində*] n (a) (person) molendero m; (Tech) amolador m; esmerilador m.

(b) (machine) amoladora f; esmeriladora f; (for coffee etc) molinillo m.

(c) —s (sl) muelas fpl.

grindstone ['graindstəun] n muela f, piedra f de amolar; **to keep one's nose to the —** batir el yunque.

gringo ['griŋgəu] n (US) gringo m.

grip [grip] **1** n (a) (grasp) agarre m, asimiento m; (handclasp) apretón m; **to come to —s with** luchar a brazo partido con; **to get to —s with a problem** ponerse seriamente a estudiar un problema, esforzarse por resolver un problema.

(b) (handle) asidero m, agarradero m; (of weapon) empuñadura f.

(c) (bag) maletín m, saco m de mano (con cremallera).

(d) (fig: power) garras fpl; control m, dominio m; **in the — of winter** paralizado por el invierno; **in the — of a strike** paralizado por una huelga; **to lose one's —** perder las fuerzas, decaer; **get a — on yourself!** ¡cálmese! ¡dómínese!

2 vt (a) (hold firmly) agarrar, asir; weapon empuñar; hand apretar; **the wheels — the road** las ruedas se agarran a la carretera.

(b) (fig) absorber la atención de, tener suspenso a.

3 vi (wheel) agarrarse.

gripe [graip] **1** n retortijón m de tripas (also —s). **2** vt dar cólico a. **3** vi (sl) quejarse.

gripping ['gripiŋ] adj absorbente, muy emocionante.

grisly ['grizli] adj horripilante; (fam) horrible.

grist [grist] n: **it's all — to his mill** saca agua de una piedra.

gristle ['grisl] n ternilla f, cartílago m.

gristly ['grisli] adj ternilloso, cartilaginoso.

grit [grit] **1** n (a) arena f, cascajo m; (dust) polvo m. (b) (fig: courage) valor m; (firmness of character) firmeza f; (endurance) aguante m.

2 vt teeth hacer rechinar; **to — one's teeth (and bear it)** apretar los dientes.

gritty ['griti] adj arenisco, arenoso.

grizzle ['grizl] vi gimotear.

grizzled ['grizld] adj gris, canoso.

grizzly ['grizli] **1** adj gris, canoso; — **bear =** **2** n oso m pardo.

groan [grəun] **1** n gemido m, quejido m. **2** vi gemir, quejarse; (creak) crujirse; **to — under** sufrir bajo, (weight) crujir bajo.

groats [grəuts] npl avena f a medio moler.

grocer ['grəusə*] n tendero m (de ultramarinos), mantequero m, abacero m; —'s (**shop**) tienda f de ultramarinos, tienda f de comestibles, mantequería f, abacería f.

groceries ['grəusəriz] npl comestibles mpl, provisiones fpl.

grocery ['grəusəri] n tienda f de ultramarinos, tienda f de comestibles, mantequería f, abacería f.

grog [grɔg] n grog m.

groggy ['grɔgi] adj (unsteady) poco seguro; (after blow) aturdido, turulato; (Boxing) groggy, grogui; **I still feel a bit** — no me siento del todo bien.

groin [grɔin] n (Anat) ingle f.

grommet ['grɔmit] n ojal m; (Naut) roñada f.

groom [gru:m] **1** n mozo m de caballos; (bride-)novio m.

2 vt horse almohazar, cuidar; **to be well** —ed (person) estar muy acicalado; **she's always well** —ed siempre está muy elegante; **to** — **someone for a post** preparar a uno para un puesto.

groove [gru:v] **1** n ranura f, estría f, acanaladura f; (of record) surco m. **2** vt estriar, acanalar.

grooved [gru:vd] adj estriado, acanalado.

grope [grəup] vi ir a tientas; **to** — **for** buscar a tientas (also fig); **to** — **one's way** ir a tientas; **to** — **one's way towards** (fig) avanzar a tientas hacia.

grosgrain ['grəugrein] n gro m.

gross [grəus] **1** adj (large) grueso, enorme; (fat) muy gordo; error craso; (vulgar) grosero; earnings, profit, weight etc bruto.

2 n gruesa f; **by the** — en gruesas; **in (the)** — en grueso.

3 vt: **he** —**es £4000 a year** gana en total 4000 libras al año.

grossly ['grəusli] adv groseramente; — **exaggerated** enormemente exagerado.

grossness ['grəusnis] n gordura f; grosería f.

grotesque [grəu'tesk] adj grotesco.

grotto ['grɔtəu] n gruta f.

grouch [grautʃ] vi (fam) refunfuñar, quejarse.

grouchy ['grautʃi] adj (fam) malhumorado.

ground¹ [graund] **1** n (a) (soil) suelo m, tierra f.

(**b**) (surface) suelo m, tierra f; (terrain) terreno m; above — sobre la tierra, (fig) vivo, con vida; **on the** — sobre el terreno; **to break new** — (fig) hacer algo nuevo; **to cover a lot of** — recorrer una gran distancia, (fig) tocar muchos puntos; **to cut the** — **from under someone's feet** comer el terreno a uno; **to fall to the** — caer al suelo, (fig) venirse al suelo, caer por su base; **to get off the** — (Aer) despegar, (fig) realizarse, resultar factible; **to go to** — (fox) meterse en su madriguera, (person) esconderse, refugiarse; **to raze something to the** — arrasar algo; **to run someone to** — encontrar (por fin) a uno, averiguar el paradero de uno; **it suits you down to the** — (dress) te sienta perfectamente; **it suits me down to the** — (fig) me conviene perfectamente, me viene de perilla.

(**c**) (surface, fig) **there is some common** — **between us** tenemos puntos comunes; **to be on dangerous** — pisar un terreno peligroso; **to be on firm** (or **sure**) — hablar con conocimiento de causa; **to be on one's home** — tratar materia que uno conoce a fondo; **to gain** — ganar terreno; **to give** (or **lose**) — perder terreno; **to hold** (or **stand**) **one's** — mantenerse firme; **to shift one's** — cambiar de postura.

(**d**) (pitch) terreno m, campo m; **recreation** — campo m de deportes.

(**e**) (estate, property) tierras fpl.

(**f**) —s (gardens) jardines mpl, parque m.

(**g**) —s (sediment) poso m, sedimento m.

(**h**) (Art) fondo m; primera capa f; **on a blue** — sobre un fondo azul.

(**i**) (reason) causa f, motivo m, razón f; (basis) fundamento m; —(s) **for complaint** motivo m de queja; **on the** —(s) **of** con motivo de, por causa de, debido a; **on the** —(s) **that** porque, por + infin, (pej) pretextando que; **on good** —s con razón; **what** —(s) **have you for saying so?** ¿en qué se basa Vd para decir eso?

2 vt (a) ship varar.

(**b**) (Elec) conectar con tierra.

(**c**) (Aer) **he ordered the planes to be** —**ed** ordenó que permaneciesen los aviones en tierra; **to be** —**ed by bad weather** no poder despegar por el mal tiempo.

(**d**) **to** — **someone in maths** enseñar a uno los rudimentos de las matemáticas; **to be well** —**ed in** tener un buen conocimiento de, estar versado en.

3 vi (Naut) varar, encallar; (lightly) tocar (on en).

ground² [graund] **1** pret and ptp of **grind**. **2** adj glass deslustrado; coffee molido.

ground colour ['graund,kʌlə*] n primera capa f; fondo m.

ground crew ['graundkru:] n personal m de tierra.

ground hog ['graundhɔg] n marmota f de América.

grounding ['graundiŋ] n instrucción f en los rudimentos (in de); **to give someone a** — **in** enseñar a uno los rudimentos de.

groundless ['graundlis] adj infundado.

groundnut ['graundnʌt] n cacahuete m.

ground plan ['graundplæn] n planta f, distribución f.

groundsel ['graunsl] n hierba f cana.

groundsheet ['graundʃi:t] n tela f impermeable.

ground staff ['graundstɑ:f] n (Aer) personal m de tierra.

groundswell ['graundswel] n mar m de fondo.

ground-to-air ['graundtu'eə*] adj: — **missile** proyectil m tierra-aire.

groundwork ['graundwə:k] n trabajo m preliminar; **to do the** — **for** echar las bases de.

group [gru:p] **1** n grupo m, agrupación f; (Mus) conjunto m musical.

2 attr colectivo; discussion en grupo; photo de conjunto.

3 vt agrupar (also **to** — **together**).

grouper ['gru:pə*] n (Fish) mero m.

grouse¹ [graus] n: **black** — gallo m lira; **red** — lagópodo m escocés.

grouse² [graus] (fam) **1** n queja f; motivo m de queja. **2** vi quejarse.

grout [graut] **1** n lechada f. **2** vt enlechar.

grove [grəuv] n arboleda f, bosquecillo m; — **of pines** pineda f; — **of poplars** alameda f.

grovel ['grɔvl] vi arrastrarse, (fig) humillarse (to ante).

grovelling ['grɔvliŋ] adj rastrero, servil.

grow [grəu] (irr: pret **grew**, ptp **grown**) **1** vt (Agr) cultivar; beard etc dejar crecer; **to be** —**n over with** estar cubierto de.

2 vi (a) crecer; (be cultivated) cultivarse; (increase) aumentar; (industry, market) extenderse, desarrollarse, expandirse; **that plant does not** — **in England** esa planta no se da en Inglaterra; **will it** — **here?** ¿se puede cultivar aquí?; **she grew out of her clothes** se le hizo pequeña la ropa; **to** — **out of a habit** perder una costumbre (con el tiempo); **to** — **up** (person) crecer mucho, (become adult) hacerse hombre, hacerse mujer; (custom etc) arraigar, imponerse; — **up!** ¡no seas niño!; **hatred grew up between them** nació el odio entre ellos.

(**b**) (fig) **to** — **into** hacerse, llegar a ser; **the book** —**s on one** el libro gusta cada vez más; **the habit grew on him** la costumbre arraigó en él; **to** — **out of** resultar de, originarse en; **to** — **to** + infin llegar a + infin.

(**c**) (with adj) volverse, ponerse; (often translated by vi or vr) **to** — **angry** enfadarse; **to** — **cold** (thing) enfriarse, (person) empezar a tener frío, (weather) empezar a hacer frío; **to** — **dark** ponerse oscuro, oscurecerse, (at dusk) anochecer; **to** — **old** envejecer(se).

grower ['grəuə*] n cultivador m, ora f.

growing ['grəuiŋ] adj creciente; child crecedero.

growl [graul] **1** n gruñido m. **2** vi gruñir; rezongar; (thunder) reverberar; **"yes", he** —**ed** "sí", refunfuñó.

grown [grəun] **1** ptp of **grow**. **2** adj crecido, adulto.

grown-up ['grəun'ʌp] **1** adj adulto; propio de persona mayor. **2** n persona f mayor.

growth [grəuθ] n (a) crecimiento m; aumento m; desarrollo m, expansión f; **to reach full** — llegar a la madurez, (fig) alcanzar su plenitud.

(**b**) vegetación f; (Med) tumor m; **with 3 days'** — **on his face** con barba de 3 días.

growth point ['grəuθpɔint] n polo m de desarrollo.

grub [grʌb] **1** n gusano m; (sl) comida f; — **up!** (sl) ¡la comida está servida!

2 vt: **to** — **up** arrancar, desarraigar; (discover) desenterrar.

3 vi: **to** — **about in the earth for something** remover la tierra buscando algo.

grubby ['grʌbi] adj sucio, mugriento.

grudge [grʌdʒ] **1** n motivo m de rencor; **to bear someone a** —, **to have a** — **against someone** tener inquina a uno.

2 vt (a) (give unwillingly) escatimar, dar de mala gana.

(**b**) **I don't** — **you your success** no te tengo envidia por tu éxito; **he** —**s us our pleasures** mira con malos ojos nuestros placeres.

grudging ['grʌdʒiŋ] adj praise etc poco generoso; **with** — **admiration** admirándolo a pesar de sí.

grudgingly ['grʌdʒiŋli] adv de mala gana.

gruel ['gruəl] *n* gachas *fpl*.
gruelling ['gruəliŋ] *adj* duro, penoso; *match etc* muy reñido.
gruesome ['gru:səm] *adj* horrible, horripilante.
gruff [grʌf] *adj voice* bronco; *manner* brusco, malhumorado.
grumble ['grʌmbl] **1** *n* queja *f*; *(noise)* ruido *m* sordo, estruendo *m* lejano.
    2 *vi* refunfuñar, quejarse; **to — about, to — at** quejarse de, murmurar de, protestar de; *(thunder etc)* retumbar (a lo lejos).
grumpy ['grʌmpi] *adj* gruñón, malhumorado.
grunt [grʌnt] **1** *n* gruñido *m*. **2** *vi* gruñir.
guano ['gwa:nəu] *n* guano *m*.
guarantee [.gærən'ti:] **1** *n* garantía *f*; **there is no —
that** no es seguro que + *subj*; **I give you my —** se lo aseguro.
    2 *vt* garantizar *(against* contra, *for* 3 *months* por 3 meses)*; *(ensure)* asegurar; *(make oneself responsible for)* responder de; **I — that** les aseguro que, les prometo que; **I can't — good weather** no puedo estar seguro de tener buen tiempo.
guaranteed [.gærən'ti:d] *adj* garantizado; asegurado, seguro.
guarantor [.gærən'tɔ:*] *n* garante *mf*.
guard [ga:d] **1** *n* **(a)** *(Mil duty, Fencing)* guardia *f*; *(safeguard)* resguardo *m*; **to be on —** estar de guardia; **on —!** *(Fencing)* ¡en guardia!; **to be on one's —** estar alerta, estar prevenido *(against* contra)*; **to be off one's —** estar desprevenido; **to catch someone off his —** coger a uno desprevenido; **to drop** *(or* **lower) one's —** aflojar la guardia, descuidarse; **to keep —** vigilar; **to mount —** montar (la) guardia; **to put someone on his —** poner a uno en guardia, prevenir a uno *(against* contra).
    (b) *(of sword)* guarda *f*, guarnición *f*.
    (c) *(regiment, squad of men)* guardia *f*; **changing of the —** relevo *m* de la guardia; **to change —** relevar la guardia.
    (d) *(person: soldier)* guardia *m*; *(sentry)* centinela *m*; *(escort)* escolta *f*; *(Rail)* jefe *m* de tren.
    2 *vt place etc* guardar, proteger, defender *(against, from* de)*; *person* vigilar, *(while travelling)* escoltar.
    3 *vi:* **to — against** precaverse de; *(prevent)* impedir, estorbar, evitar; **in order to — against this** para evitar esto.
guarded ['ga:did] *adj* cauteloso, circunspecto.
guardedly ['ga:didli] *adv* cautelosamente, con circunspección.
guardhouse ['ga:dhaus] *n, pl* **—houses** [.hauziz] cuartel *m* de la guardia; cárcel *f* militar.
guardian ['ga:diən] *n* protector *m*, ora *f*, guardián *m*, ana *f*; *(Law)* tutor *m*, ora *f*.
guardsman ['ga:dzmən] *n, pl* **—men** [mən] guardia *m*.
guard's van ['ga:dzvæn] *n* furgón *m*.
Guatemala [.gwa:ti'ma:lə] Guatemala *f*.
Guatemalan [.gwa:ti'ma:lən] **1** *adj* guatemalteco. **2** *n* guatemalteco, a *f*.
guava ['gwa:və] *n* guayaba *f*.
Guayana [gai'a:nə] Guayana *f*.
gubernatorial [.gu:bənə'tɔ:riəl] *adj* de(l) gobernador.
gudgeon[1] ['gʌdʒən] *n (Fish)* gobio *m*.
gudgeon[2] ['gʌdʒən] *n (Tech)* gorrón *m*; cuello *m* de eje.
Guernsey ['gə:nzi] Guernesey *m*.
guerrilla [gə'rilə] *n* guerrillero *m*, a *f*; **— warfare** guerra *f* de guerrilleros.
guess [ges] **1** *n* conjetura *f*, suposición *f*; **rough —** estimación *f* aproximada; **at a —** poco más o menos; **my — is that** yo conjeturo que, imagino que; **your — is as good as mine!** ¡vaya Vd a saber!; **have a —, I'll give you 3 —s** a ver si lo adivinas.
    2 *vti* **(a)** adivinar, conjeturar, suponer; **to — right** acertar; **— who!** ¡a ver si adivinas quién soy!, ¿me conoces?; **you'll never —** no lo adivinarás nunca; **you've —ed it!** has acertado, estás en lo cierto; **I —ed as much** ya lo supuse; **I —ed him to be about 20** conjeturé que tenía unos 20 años; **to keep someone —ing** tener a uno en suspenso; **to — at** conjeturar, (tratar de) estimar aproximadamente.
    (b) *(esp US)* creer, imaginar, suponer; **I — we'll buy it** imagino que lo compraremos; **I — so** imagino que sí; así será, sin duda.
guesswork ['geswə:k] *n* conjeturas *fpl*; **it's all —** son meras conjeturas.
guest [gest] *n* convidado *m*, a *f*, invitado *m*, a *f*; *(at hotel etc, lodger)* huésped *m*, eda *f*; **— of honour** agasajado *m*, a *f*; **paying —** pensionista *mf*; **be my —** invito yo; **we were their —s last summer** pasamos un rato en casa de ellos el verano pasado.
guest-house ['gesthaus] *n, pl* **—houses** [.hauziz] casa *f* de huéspedes.
guest room ['gestrum] *n* cuarto *m* de las visitas.

guff [gʌf] *n (sl)* música *f* celestial.
guffaw [gʌ'fɔ:] **1** *n* risotada *f*. **2** *vi* reírse a carcajadas.
Guiana [gai'a:nə] Guayana *f*.
guidance ['gaidəns] *n (control)* dirección *f*, gobierno *m*; *(advice)* consejos *mpl*; **vocational —** guía *f* vocacional.
guide [gaid] **1** *n* **(a)** *(person)* guía *mf*; **girl —** exploradora *f*. **(b)** *(book, Mech, fig)* guía *f*. **2** *vt* guiar; conducir; *(govern)* dirigir, gobernar.
guidebook ['gaidbuk] *n* guía *f* (del turista *etc*).
guided ['gaidid] *adj* **missile** teledirigido.
guide line ['gaidlain] *n* línea *f* de guía *(also fig)*.
guidepost ['gaidpəust] *n* poste *m* indicador.
guild [gild] *n* gremio *m*, cofradía *f*.
guile [gail] *n* astucia *f*, maña *f*.
guileful ['gailful] *adj* astuto, mañoso.
guileless ['gaillis] *adj* inocente, candoroso.
guillemot ['gilimot] *n* arao *m*.
guillotine [.gilə'ti:n] **1** *n* guillotina *f*. **2** *vt* guillotinar.
guilt [gilt] *n* culpabilidad *f*.
guiltless ['giltlis] *adj* inocente, libre de culpa *(of* de)*.
guilty ['gilti] *adj* **(a)** culpable *(of* de)*; **verdict of —** sentencia *f* de culpabilidad; **to find someone —** declarar culpable a uno; **to find someone not —** declarar inocente a uno; **to plead —** confesarse culpable; **to plead not —** negar la acusación; **"not —", he replied** "soy inocente", contestó.
    (b) *look* lleno de confusión; *conscience* lleno de remordimiento; *thought* pecaminoso, criminal.
Guinea ['gini] Guinea *f*.
guinea ['gini] *n* guinea *f* (= 21 *chelines*).
guinea-fowl ['ginifaul] *n* gallina *f* de Guinea.
guinea-pig ['ginipig] *n* cobayo *m*, conejillo *m* de Indias.
Guinevere ['gwinivlə*] *f* Ginebra.
guise [gaiz] *n:* **in that —** de esa manera; **under the — of** bajo el disfraz de; so capa de.
guitar [gi'ta:*] *n* guitarra *f*.
guitarist [gi'ta:rist] *n* guitarrista *mf*.
gulch [gʌlʃ] *n (US)* barranco *m*.
gulf [gʌlf] *n* golfo *m*; *(also fig)* abismo *m*, sima *f*.
Gulf Stream ['gʌlfstri:m] Corriente *f* del Golfo.
gull [gʌl] **1** *n* gaviota *f*. **2** *vt* estafar, timar.
gullet ['gʌlit] *n* esófago *m*; garganta *f*.
gullibility [.gʌli'biliti] *n* credulidad *f*, simpleza *f*.
gullible ['gʌlibl] *adj* crédulo, simplón.
gully ['gʌli] *n* barranco *m*, torrentera *f*.
gulp [gʌlp] **1** *n* trago *m*, sorbo *m*; **at one —** de un trago; **"yes", he said with a —** "sí", dijo tragando saliva.
    2 *vt (also* **to — down)** tragarse, engullir.
    3 *vi* tragar saliva.
gum[1] [gʌm] *n (Anat)* encía *f*.
gum[2] [gʌm] **1** *n (in general)* goma *f*; *(adhesive)* goma *f*, cola *f*, pegamín *m*; *(chewing)* chicle *m*; **— arabic** goma *f* arábiga.
    2 *vt* engomar, pegar con goma; **to — up** *(fig)* estropear, paralizar, parar; inutilizar.
gum[3] [gʌm] *interj:* **by —!** ¡caramba!
gumboil ['gʌmbɔil] *n* flemón *m*.
gumboots ['gʌmbu:ts] *npl* botas *fpl* altas de goma.
gumdrop ['gʌmdrɔp] *n* pastilla *f* de goma.
gummy ['gʌmi] *adj* gomoso.
gump [gʌmp] *n* **(a)** *(fam)* sentido *m* común. **(b)** tonto *m*, imbécil *mf*.
gumption ['gʌmpʃən] *n (fam)* seso *m*, sentido *m* común.
gum tree ['gʌmtri:] *n* eucalipto *m*; **to be up a —** *(fam)* estar en un aprieto.
gun [gʌn] **1** *n (in general)* arma *f* de fuego; *(artillery piece)* cañón *m*; *(shot-)* escopeta *f*; *(rifle)* fusil *m*; *(pistol)* revólver *m*, pistola *f*; **a 21-— salute** una salva de 21 cañonazos; **the —s** *(Mil)* la artillería; **big —** *(fam)* pez *m* gordo, espadón *m*; **to be going great —s** hacer grandes progresos, ir a las mil maravillas; **to jump the —** *(fig)* madrugar; **to stick to one's —s** mantenerse firme.
    2 *vt* disparar sobre, atacar.
    3 *vi:* **to — for** andar a la caza de, perseguir.
gunboat ['gʌnbəut] *n (seagoing)* cañonero *m*; *(small)* lancha *f* cañonera.
gun carriage ['gʌn.kæridʒ] *n* cureña *f*; *(at funeral)* armón *m* de artillería.
guncotton ['gʌn.kɔtn] *n* algodón *m* pólvora.
gun crew ['gʌnkru:] *n* dotación *f* de un cañón.
gunfire ['gʌnfaiə*] *n* cañoneo *m*.
gun licence ['gʌn.laisns] *n* licencia *f* de armas.
gunman ['gʌnmən] *n, pl* **—men** [mən] pistolero *m*, gángster *m*.
gunmetal ['gʌn.metl] *n* bronce *m* de cañón.
gunner ['gʌnə*] *n (Mil)* artillero *m*.
gunnery ['gʌnəri] *n* tiro *m*, puntería *f*.
gunpowder ['gʌn.paudə*] *n* pólvora *f*.

gunrunner ['gʌn,rʌnə*] n contrabandista m de armas.
gunrunning ['gʌn,rʌniŋ] n contrabando m de armas.
gunshot ['gʌnʃɔt] n (noise) cañonazo m, escopetazo m; — wound escopetazo m; **within** — a tiro de fusil.
gunsmith ['gʌnsmiθ] n escopetero m.
gun turret ['gʌn,tʌrit] n torreta f.
gunwale ['gʌnl] n borde m, regala f.
gurgle ['gə:gl] **1** n (of liquid) gorgoteo m, gluglú m; (baby's) gorjeo m. **2** vi gorgotear, hacer gluglú; gorjear.
gush [gʌʃ] **1** n (of liquid) chorro m, borbotón m; (of words) torrente m; (fig) efusión f; sentimentalismo m; afectación f.
  2 vt blood etc chorrear, derramar a borbollones.
  3 vi chorrear, borbotar, salir a borbollones (from de); (person) hacer extremos; **to — over** hablar con efusión de, extasiarse ante.
gushing ['gʌʃiŋ] adj efusivo.
gusset ['gʌsit] n escudete m.
gust [gʌst] n ráfaga f, racha f.
gusto ['gʌstəu] n entusiasmo m; **with** — con entusiasmo.
gusty ['gʌsti] adj borrascoso; wind racheado.
gut [gʌt] **1** n (a) (Anat) intestino m, tripa f; (string) cuerda f de tripa; (Naut) estrecho m.
  (b) —s (Anat) tripas fpl; (fig: content) meollo m, sustancia f; (pluck) valor m; (staying power) aguante m, resistencia f; (moral strength) carácter m; **to have —s** tener agallas.
  2 vt animal destripar; (of fire etc) destruir el interior de.
gutta-percha ['gʌtə'pə:tʃə] n gutapercha f.
gutter ['gʌtə*] n (in street) arroyo m, cuneta f; (on roof) canal m, canalón m, gotera f; **the —** (fig) los barrios bajos, (criminal) el hampa; **he rose from the** — (fig) salió de la nada.
gutter-press ['gʌtə'pres] n prensa f sensacionalista.
guttersnipe ['gʌtəsnaip] n golfillo m.
guttural ['gʌtərəl] adj gutural.
guy¹ [gai] **1** n mamarracho m; (US fam) tío m, individuo m; **wise —** sabelotodo m; **he's a nice —** es un buen chico.
  2 vt ridiculizar; (Theat etc) parodiar.
guy² [gai] n, **guy-rope** ['gairəup] n viento m, cuerda f.
Guy [gai] m Guido.
guzzle ['gʌzl] vt tragarse, engullir.
gym [dʒim] n (fam) gimnasio m.
gymkhana [dʒim'kɑ:nə] n reunión f deportiva.
gymnasium [dʒim'neiziəm] n gimnasio m.
gymnast ['dʒimnæst] n gimnasta mf.
gymnastic [dʒim'næstik] adj gimnástico.
gymnastics [dʒim'næstiks] n sing and pl gimnasia f.
gynaecologist, (US) **gynecologist** [,gaini'kɔlədʒist] n ginecólogo m, a f.
gynaecology, (US) **gynecology** [,gaini'kɔlədʒi] n ginecología f.
gyp¹ [dʒip] (sl) **1** n (a) estafa f, timo m. (b) (person) estafador m, timador m. **2** vt estafar, timar.
gyp² [dʒip] n (Univ) criado m (de colegio).
gyp³ [dʒip] n (sl): **to give someone —** echar un rapapolvo de aúpa a uno; poner a uno como un trapo; **it's giving me —** me duele una barbaridad.
gypsum ['dʒipsəm] n yeso m.
gypsy ['dʒipsi] n (esp US) = **gipsy**.
gyrate [dʒai'reit] vi girar.
gyration [,dʒai'reiʃən] n giro m, vuelta f.
gyratory [,dʒai'reitəri] adj giratorio.
gyrocompass ['dʒairəu'kʌmpəs] n girocompás m.
gyroscope ['dʒairəskəup] n giróscopo m.

H

ha [haː] *interj* ¡ah!
habeas corpus ['heibiəs'kɔːpəs] *n* hábeas corpus *m*.
haberdasher ['hæbədæʃə*] *n* mercero *m*, a *f*, (US) camisero *m*, a *f*; —'s (**shop**) mercería *f*, (US) camisería *f*.
haberdashery [,hæbə'dæʃəri] *n* mercería *f*, (US) artículos *mpl* de moda para caballeros.
habiliments [hə'bilimənts] *npl* (arch) prendas *fpl* de vestir.
habit ['hæbit] *n* (a) costumbre *f*, hábito *m*; **bad** — vicio *m*, mala costumbre *f*; **from** —, **out of sheer** — por costumbre; **to be in the** — **of** + ger acostumbrar + infin, soler + infin; **to get into the** — **of** + ger acostumbrarse a + infin; **to get out of the** — **of** + ger perder la costumbre de + infin; **to make a** — **of something** aficionarse a algo; **let's hope he doesn't make a** — **of it** esperamos que no vuelva a hacerlo; **to make a** — **of** + ger adquirir la costumbre de + infin. (b) (dress) hábito *m*.
habitable ['hæbitəbl] *adj* habitable.
habitat ['hæbitæt] *n* habitat *m*, habitación *f*.
habitation [,hæbi'teiʃən] *n* habitación *f*.
habit-forming ['hæbit,fɔːmiŋ] *adj* que conduce al hábito morboso.
habitual [hə'bitjuəl] *adj* habitual, acostumbrado, usual; *drunkard, liar etc* inveterado, empedernido.
habitually [hə'bitjuəli] *adv* por costumbre; constantemente.
habitué(e) [hə'bitjuei] *n* asiduo *m*, a *f*, parroquiano *m*, a *f*.
hacienda [,hæsi'endə] *n* (US) hacienda *f*.
hack¹ [hæk] **1** *n* (blow, cut) corte *m*, hachazo *m*, tajo *m*; (kick) puntapié *m* (en la espinilla); (dent) mella *f*.
2 *vt* (with knife etc) cortar, acuchillar, tajar; (dent) mellar; **to** — **someone on the shin** dar a uno un puntapié en la espinilla; **to** — **something to pieces** cortar algo en pedazos (violentamente, despiadadamente etc); **to** — **an army to pieces** destrozar un ejército; **to** — **one's way through something** abrirse paso por algo a fuerza de tajos; **to** — **down** derribar a hachazos etc.
3 *vi*: **to** — **at** tirar tajos a.
hack² [hæk] **1** *n* (hired horse) caballo *m* de alquiler; (bad horse) rocín *m*; (writer) escritorzuelo *m*, plumífero *m*, gacetillero *m*.
2 attr *writer* mercenario, (fig) ínfimo; *see* **hackneyed**.
hacking ['hækiŋ] *adj* cough seco.
hackle ['hækl] *n*: **with his** —**s up** encolerizado; dispuesto a luchar; **to make someone's** —**s rise** encolerizar a uno, provocar a uno.
hackman ['hækmən] *n*, *pl* —**men** [mən] (US: Hist) cochero *m* de punto.
hackney carriage ['hækni'kærid3] *n* coche *m* de alquiler.
hackneyed ['hæknid] *adj* trillado, gastado.
hacksaw ['hæksɔː] *n* sierra *f* de arco para metales.
hackwork ['hækwɔːk] *n* trabajo *m* de rutina, trabajo *m* de poca originalidad.
had [hæd] *pret and ptp of* **have**.
haddock ['hædək] *n* eglefino *m*, merlango *m*.
Hades ['heidiːz] *n* infierno *m*.
hadn't ['hædnt] = **had not**.
Hadrian ['heidriən] *m* Adriano.
haemoglobin, (US) **hemo**— [,hiːməu'gləubin] *n* hemoglobina *f*.
haemophilia, (US) **hemo**—[,hiːməu'filiə] *n* hemofilia *f*.
haemorrhage, (US) **hemo**— ['hemərid3] *n* hemorragia *f*.
haemorrhoids, (US) **hemo**— ['hemərɔidz] *npl* hemorroides *fpl*.
haft [haːft] *n* mango *m*.
hag [hæg] *n* bruja *f*.

haggard ['hægəd] *adj* ojeroso, trasnochado.
haggis ['hægis] *n* (Scot) estómago de cordero relleno con el hígado, el corazón y la lengua del animal, avena etc (plato nacional escocés).
haggish ['hægiʃ] *adj* como de bruja.
haggle ['hægl] *vi* (a) discutir, disputar; **don't** —! ¡no discutas! (b) (in selling) regatear; **to** — **about** (or **over**) **the price** regatear, regatear el precio.
haggling ['hægliŋ] *n* (a) discusión *f*, disputa *f*. (b) regateo *m*.
hagiography [,hægi'ɒgrəfi] *n* hagiografía *f*.
hag-ridden ['hægridn] *adj* atormentado por una pesadilla; (fam) dominado por una mujer.
Hague [heig]: **The** — La Haya.
ha-ha ['haː'haː] *interj* ¡ja, ja!
hail¹ [heil] (Meteorol) **1** *n* granizo *m*, pedrisco *m*; **a** — **of bullets** una lluvia de balas. **2** *vi* granizar; **to** — **down** (fig) llover.
hail² [heil] **1** *n* (shout) grito *m*; (greeting) saludo *m*; —! ¡hola!, (more formally) ¡salve!; **to be within** — estar al alcance de la voz.
2 *vt* llamar a, gritar a; saludar; aclamar (as king rey); **within** —**ing distance** al habla, al alcance de la voz.
3 *vi*: **to** — **from** ser natural de, ser de.
hail-fellow-well-met ['heil,feləu'wel'met] *adj* demasiado efusivo.
hailstone ['heilstəun] *n* piedra *f* de granizo.
hailstorm ['heilstɔːm] *n* granizada *f*, pedrusco *m*.
hair [heə*] *n* (a) (one —) pelo *m*, cabello *m*; —'s **breadth** (ancho *m* de un) pelo *m*; **to escape by a** —'s **breadth** escapar por un pelo; **to be within a** —'s **breadth of** estar a dos dedos de; **to split** —s pararse en cosas nimias, buscar tres pies al gato; **he didn't turn a** — no se inmutó.
(b) (head of —) pelo *m*, cabello *m*, cabellera *f*; (on legs etc) vello *m*; **grey** —, **white** — canas *fpl*; **long** — melena *f*; **to comb one's** —s **peinarse**; **to do one's** —, **to have one's** — **done** arreglarse el pelo; **keep your** — **on!** ¡cálmate!; **to let one's** — **down** (fig) echar una cana al aire; **to part one's** —s hacerse la raya; **it was enough to make your** — **stand on end** era espeluznante; **to tear one's** — mesarse el pelo.
hairbrush ['heəbrʌʃ] *n* cepillo *m* para el pelo.
hair cream ['heəkriːm] *n* brillantina *f*, fijapelo *m*.
hair-curler ['heə,kɔːlə*] *n* chincho *m*.
haircut ['heəkʌt] *n* corte *m* de pelo; **to get (or have) a** — hacerse cortar el pelo.
hairdo ['heəduː] *n* peinado *m*.
hairdresser ['heə,dresə*] *n* peluquero *m*, a *f*; —'s (**shop**) peluquería *f*.
hair-drier ['heədraiə*] *n* secador *m* de pelo.
-haired [heəd] *adj* de pelo . . ., *eg* **fair-haired** pelirrubio; **long**— de pelo largo, melenudo.
hairless ['heəlis] *adj* sin pelo, pelón, calvo.
hairline ['heəlain] *n* límite *m* del pelo; (in writing) rayita *f*; (Tech) estría *f* muy delgada; — **crack** grieta *f* muy fina, grieta *f* casi imperceptible.
hairnet ['heənet] *n* redecilla *f*.
hair oil ['heərɔil] *n* brillantina *f*.
hairpiece ['heəpiːs] *n* trenza *f* postiza.
hairpin ['heəpin] *n* horquilla *f*.
hair-raising ['heə,reiziŋ] *adj* espeluznante.
hair-splitting ['heə,splitiŋ] **1** *adj* nimio; *discussion* sobre detalles nimios. **2** *n* sofismas *mpl*, sofistería *f*.
hair style ['heəstail] *n* peinado *m*.
hairy ['heəri] *adj* peludo, velloso.
Haiti ['heiti] Haití *m*.
Haitian ['heiʃiən] **1** *adj* haitiano. **2** *n* haitiano *m*, haitiana *f*.
hake [heik] *n* merluza *f*.
halcyon ['hælsiən] *adj*: — **days** días *mpl* felices.
hale [heil] *adj* sano, robusto; — **and hearty** sano y fuerte.

half [hɑːf] n, pl **halves** [hɑːvz] **1** n (a) mitad f; — **and** — mitad y mitad; **my better** — mi cara mitad; **first** — (Sport) primer tiempo m; **return** — (of ticket) parte f de vuelta; **by** — con mucho; **better by** — con mucho el mejor; **to be too clever by** — pasarse de listo; **to do something by halves** hacer algo a medias; **to go halves with someone** ir a medias con uno; **to cut something in** — cortar algo en dos mitades.

(b) (Sport: person) medio m.

2 adj medio; — **an orange** media naranja; **a pound and a** —, **one and a** — **pounds** libra f y media; **3 and a** — **hours, 3 hours and a** — 3 horas y media.

3 adv (a) medio, a medias, semi . . .; casi; — **asleep** medio dormido, dormido a medias, semidormido; — **done** a medio hacer; — **laughing,** — **crying** medio riendo, medio llorando; **I only** — **read it** lo leí sólo a medias; **he** — **got up** se levantó a medias; **it cost only** — **as much** costó la mitad nada más; **there were only** — **as many people as before** había solamente la mitad de los que había antes; **they paid** — **as much again** pagaron la mitad más.

(b) (with not) **it was not** — **as bad as I had thought** no era tan malo como me lo había imaginado; **he didn't** — **run** corrió muchísimo; **it didn't** — **rain**! ¡había que ver cómo llovía!; **it wasn't** — **dear** nos resultó sumamente caro; **not** —! ¡ya lo creo!

half-back ['hɑːfbæk] n medio m.

half-baked ['hɑːf'beikt] adj a medio cocer; (fig) plan, idea incompleto, sin terminar; person soso.

half-bred ['hɑːfbred] adj mestizo.

half-breed ['hɑːfbriːd] n mestizo m, a f.

half-brother ['hɑːf,brʌðə*] n medio hermano m.

half-caste ['hɑːfkɑːst] **1** adj mestizo. **2** n mestizo m, a f.

half-circle ['hɑːf'sɜːkl] n semicírculo m.

half-cock ['hɑːf'kɔk] n posición f de medio amartillado (de la escopeta etc); **to go off at** — (fig) obrar precipitadamente, obrar antes del momento propicio; (of plan) ponerse en efecto sin la debida preparación, fracasar por falta de preparación.

half-crown ['hɑːf'kraun] n media corona f.

half-dead ['hɑːf'ded] adj medio muerto, más muerto que vivo.

half-dozen ['hɑːf'dʌzn] n media docena f.

half-empty ['hɑːf'empti] adj medio vacío; hall etc semidesierto.

half-full ['hɑːf'ful] adj a medio llenar, mediado.

half-hearted ['hɑːf'hɑːtid] adj poco entusiasta, indiferente; effort débil.

half-heartedly ['hɑːf'hɑːtidli] adv con poco entusiasmo.

half-holiday ['hɑːf'hɔlidi] n medio día m festivo.

half-hour ['hɑːf'auə*] n media hora f.

half-length ['hɑːf'leŋθ] adj de medio cuerpo.

half-mast ['hɑːf'mɑːst] n: **at** — **a** media asta.

half-measure ['hɑːf'meʒə*] n medida f poco eficaz.

half-moon ['hɑːf'muːn] n media luna f.

half-naked ['hɑːf'neikid] adj semidesnudo.

half note ['hɑːf'nəut] n (Mus) nota f blanca.

half-pay ['hɑːf'pei] n media paga f.

halfpenny ['heipni] n medio penique m.

half-price ['hɑːf'prais] adv a mitad de precio.

half-seas over ['hɑːfsiːz'əuvə*] adv: **to be** — estar entre dos velas.

half-term ['hɑːf'tɜːm] n vacación f a mediados del trimestre.

half-time ['hɑːf'taim] n (Sport) descanso m.

half-tone ['hɑːftəun] adj: — **illustration** fotograbado m a media tinta.

half-track ['hɑːf'træk] n camión m semi-oruga.

half-truth ['hɑːf'truːθ] n, pl —**truths** [truːðz] verdad f a medias, semi-verdad f.

halfway ['hɑːf'wei] **1** adv **a medio camino; we're** — **there** estamos a medio camino; — **through the film** hacia la mitad de la película; **to meet someone** — partir el camino con uno, (fig) hacer concesiones mutuas.

2 adj intermedio; — **house** (fig) punto m intermediario, término m medio.

half-witted ['hɑːf'witid] adj imbécil.

half-yearly ['hɑːf'jiəli] **1** adv semestralmente. **2** adj semestral.

halibut ['hælibət] n halibut m.

halitosis [,hæli'təusis] n halitosis f.

hall [hɔːl] n (entrance) vestíbulo m, hall m; (for concerts etc) sala f; (dining room) comedor m; (Univ: central —) paraninfo m, (hostel) residencia f, colegio m mayor; (large house) casa f solariega; **city** — palacio m municipal; **town** — ayuntamiento m.

hallelujah [,hæli'luːjə] n aleluya f.

hallmark ['hɔːlmɑːk] n marca f del contraste; (fig) sello m.

hallo [hʌ'ləu] see **hullo**.

halloo [hə'luː] **1** interj (Hunting) ¡sus! **2** n grito m. **3** vi gritar.

hallow ['hæləu] vt santificar.

Hallowe'en ['hæləu'iːn] n (Scot, US) víspera f de Todos los Santos.

hallstand ['hɔːlstænd] n perchero m.

hallucination [hə,luːsi'neiʃən] n alucinación f; ilusión f, fantasma m.

hallway ['hɔːlwei] n vestíbulo m, hall m.

halo ['heiləu] n aureola f, nimbo m; halo m.

halogen ['heiləudʒin] n (Chem) halógeno m.

halt [hɔːlt] **1** n alto m, parada f; interrupción f; (Rail) apeadero m; **10 minutes'** — parada f de 10 minutos; **to call a** — mandar hacer alto; **to call a** — **to** parar, atajar; **to come to a** — pararse, (process etc) interrumpirse.

2 vt parar, detener; interrumpir.

3 vi hacer alto; pararse; (process etc) interrumpirse; —! ¡alto!

halter ['hɔːltə*] n cabestro m, ronzal m; (noose) dogal m.

halting ['hɔːltiŋ] adj vacilante, titubeante.

halve [hɑːv] vt partir por mitad; **to** — **a game** empatar.

halves [hɑːvz] npl of **half**.

halyard ['hæljəd] n driza f.

ham [hæm] n (a) jamón m; (Anat) —s nalgas fpl.

(b) (Theat sl) comicastro m, maleta m, racionista mf; (Radio sl) radioaficionado m.

Hamburg ['hæmbɜːg] Hamburgo.

hamburger ['hæm,bɜːgə*] n hamburguesa f.

ham-handed ['hæm'hændid] adj, **ham-fisted** ['hæm'fistid] adj torpe, desmañado.

Hamitic [hæ'mitik] adj camítico.

hamlet ['hæmlit] n aldehuela f, caserío m.

hammer ['hæmə*] **1** n martillo m; (Mus) macillo m; (of firearm) percusor m; **to come under the** — ser subastado; **to go at it** — **and tongs** luchar (etc) a brazo partido.

2 vt martillar; batir; (Fin) declarar insolvente; **to** — **a point home** subrayar repetidas veces un argumento; **to** — **some sense into someone** hacer que uno vaya comprendiendo algo a fuerza de repetírselo; **to** — **down** lid asegurar con clavos; **to** — **something in** clavar algo con martillo; **to** — **something into shape** formar algo a martillo; **to** — **out** dent quitar a martillo, extender bajo el martillo; settlement etc elaborar trabajosamente.

3 vi: **to** — **at** (or **on**) **a door** dar golpes en una puerta; **to** — **away at** subject insistir con ahinco en, work trabajar asiduamente en; **to** — **away on the piano** tocar estrepitosamente el piano.

hammock ['hæmək] n hamaca f, (Naut) coy m.

hamper[1] ['hæmpə*] n cesto m, canasta f.

hamper[2] ['hæmpə*] vt estorbar, impedir.

hamster ['hæmstə*] n hámster m.

hamstring ['hæmstriŋ] (irr: see **string**) vt desjarretar; (fig) paralizar.

hand [hænd] **1** n (a) (general sense) mano f; —s off! ¡fuera las manos!; —s up! ¡arriba las manos!; **to be clever with one's** —s tener mucha destreza manual; **to go on one's** —s **and knees** ir a gatas.

(b) (phrases with verb) **A is** — **in glove with B** A y B son uña y carne, se ha confabulado A con B; **to bear a** — arrimar el hombro; **to change** —s cambiar de dueño; **to clutch at an offer with both** —s aceptar una oferta de muy buena gana; **he never does a** —'s **turn** no da golpe; **to force someone's** — obligar a uno a hacer algo contra su voluntad; **to get one's** —**s in** hacerse la mano; **to give someone a** — ayudar a uno; **to have a** — **in** tomar parte en, intervenir en; **he had no** — **in it** no tuvo arte ni parte en ello; **to hold** —s (children) ir cogidos de la mano, (lovers) hacer manitas; **to join** —s darse las manos; **to keep one's** — **in** conservar la práctica (at de), mantenerse en forma; **to keep one's** —s **off something** no tocar algo; **to lay** —s **on** echar mano a, (obtain) conseguir, (Eccl) imponer las manos a; **to lend a** — arrimar el hombro; **to lend someone a** — echar una mano a uno; **lend a** —! ¡manos a la obra!; **to make money** — **over fist** amasar una fortuna; **to put one's** — **to something** emprender algo; **to shake** —s estrecharse la mano, darse las manos; **to shake** —s **with someone** estrechar la mano a uno; **to take a** — tomar parte, intervenir (at, in en); **to throw up one's** —s **(in horror)** escandalizarse; **to turn one's** — **to** dedicarse a; **he can turn his** — **to anything** vale tanto para un barrido como para un fregado; **to wash one's —s of** desentenderse de; **to win —s down** ganar fácilmente.

(c) *(phrases with adj)* **to rule with a firm —** gobernar con firmeza; **to give someone a free —** dar carta blanca a uno; **to have a free —** tener carta blanca; **to have one's —s full** estar ocupado; **with a heavy —** cruelmente, sin piedad; **with a high —** despóticamente; **to give someone a helping —** echar una mano a uno; **to get** *(or* **gain) the upper —** empezar a dominar; **to have the upper —** tener la ventaja.

(d) *(phrases with prep before n)* (at) **at — a mano**; **to be near at —** estar a la mano; estar cerca; **winter was at —** se acercaba el invierno; **at first —** de primera mano, directamente; de buena tinta; **to suffer at the —s of** sufrir a manos de; *(by)* **by —** *make* a mano, *raise etc* a fuerza de brazos; **to send a letter by —** enviar una carta en mano; **to take someone by the —** llevar a uno de la mano; *(from)* **to live from — to mouth** vivir al día, vivir de la mano a la boca; *(in)* **gun in —** el revólver en la mano, empuñando el revólver; **to be in someone's —s** estar en manos de uno; **to have something in —** tener algo entre manos; **to have a matter in —** estar estudiando un asunto; **the situation is in —** se ha conseguido dominar la situación; **he has them well in —** los domina perfectamente; **to put something in —** emprender algo; **to take someone in —** enseñar a uno, entrenar a uno; imponer disciplina a uno; **to take something in —** hacerse cargo de algo; **I like to have something in —** me gusta tener algo en reserva; **money in —** dinero *m* contante; **how much have we in —?** ¿cuánto tenemos en el haber?; *(into)* **to fall into enemy —s** caer en manos del enemigo; **to play into someone's —s** ceder la ventaja a un contrario; **to put something into a lawyer's —s** pedir el consejo de un abogado acerca de algo; **to take justice into one's own —s** tomar la justicia por su mano; *(off)* **to get something off one's —s** deshacerse de algo; terminar de hacer algo; *(on)* **on the left —** a la izquierda, **on the right —** a la derecha; **on every —, on all —s** por todas partes; **on the one —** por una parte, **on the other —** por otra parte; **to be on —** estar a la mano; **he's on my —s all day** está conmigo todo el día; **to have work on —** tener trabajo entre manos; **the goods were left on his —s** los géneros resultaron ser invendibles; *(out)* **to condemn someone out of —** condenar a uno sin estudiar el caso; **to shoot someone out of —** fusilar a uno sin más; **to get out of —** desmandarse; *(to)* **to come to —** llegar a las manos; **your letter of the 3rd is to —** he recibido su carta del 3.

(e) *(of instrument)* aguja *f*; *(of clock)* manecilla *f*.

(f) *(measure)* palmo *m*.

(g) *(Cards)* mano *f*; **to have a — of bridge** echar una partida de bridge.

(h) *(writing)* escritura *f*, letra *f*; **in one's own —** de puño y letra de uno; **he writes a good —** tiene buena letra; **to put one's — to something** firmar algo.

(i) *(in marriage)* **to ask for someone's —** pedir la mano de una; **she gave him her —** se casó con él.

(j) *(person)* operario *m*, a *f*, obrero *m*, a *f*; (Agr etc) peón *m*; **—s** (Naut) tripulación *f*; **all —s on deck!** ¡todos a la cubierta!; **to be lost with all —s** desaparecer con toda la tripulación; **to be a good — at —** tener buena mano para, ser hábil en; **to be an old —** ser perro viejo.

(k) *(influence)* influencia *f*; **his — was everywhere** se notaba su influencia por todas partes.

(l) *(applause)* **they gave him a big —** le aplaudieron calurosamente.

2 *vt* dar, entregar, poner en manos de; alargar; pasar; **to — down** *object* bajar; *heirloom* pasar; *tradition* transmitir; *judgement* dictar; *person* ayudar a bajar; **to — in** entregar; *resignation* presentar; *person* ayudar a subir; **to — off** rechazar; **to — on** *tradition* transmitir; *news* comunicar; *object* pasar; **to — over** entregar; **to — round** pasar de mano en mano; *(distribute)* repartir; *chocolates etc* ofrecer; **you've got to — it to him** hay que reconocer que lo hace *(etc)* muy bien; **to — up** subir.

3 *vi* **to — over to** ceder su puesto a.

handbag ['hændbæg] *n* bolso *m*.
handball ['hændbɔːl] *n* balonmano *m*.
handbell ['hændbel] *n* campanilla *f*.
handbook ['hændbuk] *n* manual *m*; *(guide)* guía *f*.
handbrake ['hændbreik] *n* freno *m* de mano.
handcart ['hændkɑːt] *n* carretilla *f*, carretón *m*.
handclasp ['hændklɑːsp] *n* apretón *m* de manos.
handcuff ['hændkʌf] *vt* poner las esposas a, esposar.
handcuffs ['hændkʌfs] *npl* esposas *fpl*.

-handed ['hændid] *adj* de ... mano(s); de mano(s) ...; **four-handed game** juego *m* para cuatro personas.
handful ['hændful] *n* puñado *m*, manojo *m*; **a — of people** un puñado de gente; **he's a real —** tiene el diablo en el cuerpo.
hand grenade ['hændgri,neid] *n* bomba *f* de mano.
handgrip ['hændgrip] = **handle**; = **grip**.
handgun ['hændgʌn] *n* revólver *m*, pistola *f*.
handicap ['hændikæp] 1 *n* desventaja *f*, estorbo *m*, obstáculo *m*; *(Sport)* hándicap *m*.
2 *vt* perjudicar, estorbar; *(Sport)* handicapar; **he has always been —ped by his accent** su acento siempre ha sido una desventaja para él.
handicapped ['hændikæpt] *adj*: **mentally —** anormal, retrasado; **physically —** mutilado, tullido.
handicraft ['hændikrɑːft] *n* artesanía *f*; *(skill)* destreza *f* manual; **— teacher** profesor *m* de trabajos manuales.
handiness ['hændinis] *n* (a) proximidad *f*, lo cercano; **because of the — of the library** debido a que la biblioteca está tan cerca, porque resulta tan cómodo ir a la biblioteca.
(b) conveniencia *f*, comodidad *f*; carácter *m* manuable, facilidad *f* en el manejo.
(c) habilidad *f*, destreza *f*; **his — with a gun** su destreza con un fusil.
hand-in-hand ['hændin'hænd] *adv*: **to go —** ir cogidos de la mano; **it goes — with** está estrechamente relacionado con; **these plans should go —** estos proyectos han de realizarse al mismo ritmo.
handiwork ['hændiwɑːk] *n* obra *f*.
handkerchief ['hæŋkətʃif] *n* pañuelo *m*.
handle ['hændl] 1 *n* *(haft)* mango *m*; *(lever)* palanca *f*; *(crank)* manivela *f*; *(for winding)* manubrio *m*; *(of basket, jug etc)* asa *f*, asidero *m*; *(of door, drawer etc)* tirador *m*, manija *f*; *(fig)* pretexto *m*, asidero *m*; *(fam)* título *m*; **to have a — to one's name** *(fam)* tener título de nobleza; **to fly off the —** *(fam)* salirse de sus casillas, perder los estribos.
2 *vt* (a) *(touch)* tocar, *(improperly)* manosear; *(Sport)* tocar con la mano; *(delicately)* manejar, manipular; **"— with care"** "manéjese con cuidado"; **don't — the fruit** no manosees la fruta; **the police —d him roughly** la policía le trató brutalmente.
(b) *(fig)* situation, theme, resources etc manejar; *car* conducir, *ship* gobernar; *unruly element* saber dominar; *commodity, product* tratar en, comerciar en; **I'll — this** yo me encargo de esto; **do you — tax matters?** ¿tiene Vd que ver con las contribuciones?; **we — 2000 travellers a day** por aquí pasan 2000 viajeros cada día; **can the port — big ships?** ¿el puerto tiene capacidad para los buques grandes?
handlebar ['hændlbɑː*] *n* manillar *m*.
handler ['hændlə*] *n* (Comm) tratante *m*, comerciante *m*; *(Sport)* entrenador *m*; *(of dog)* amo *m*.
handling ['hændliŋ] *n* manejo *m*, manejar *m*; manipulación *f*; manoseo *m*; *(of car)* conducción *f*; *(of ship)* gobierno *m*; **rough —** trato *m* brutal, malos tratos *mpl*; **his — of the matter** su manejo del asunto, su modo de manejar el asunto.
hand-luggage ['hænd,lʌgidʒ] *n* bultos *mpl* de mano.
handmade ['hændmeid] *adj* hecho a mano; de artesanía.
handout ['hændaut] *n* *(act)* distribución *f*, repartimiento *m*; *(charity)* limosna *f*; *(press —)* nota *f* de prensa; *(leaflet)* folleto *m*.
hand-picked ['hænd'pikt] *adj* escogido a mano.
handrail ['hændreil] *n* pasamano *m*.
handset ['hændset] *n* (Tel) aparato *m*, microteléfono *m*.
handshake ['hændʃeik] *n* apretón *m* de manos; **golden —** dinero que se paga a los grandes industriales *(etc)* al jubilarse éstos.
handsome ['hænsəm] *adj* *(beautiful)* hermoso, bello; elegante; *man* guapo, bien parecido, distinguido; *gesture, salary, treatment etc* generoso; *fortune, profit* considerable; *victory* fácil, agobiador.
handsomely ['hænsəmli] *adv* elegantemente; generosamente; *win* fácilmente.
handspring ['hændspriŋ] *n* voltereta *f* sobre las manos.
handstand ['hændstænd] *n* farol *m*, puntal *m*; *(Gymnastics)* posición *f* de manos.
hand-to-hand ['hændtə'hænd] *adv*, *adj* cuerpo a cuerpo.
hand-to-mouth ['hændtə'mauθ] *adj* existence precario.
handwriting ['hænd,raitiŋ] *n* escritura *f*, letra *f*.
handwritten ['hænd'ritn] *adj* escrito a mano.
handy ['hændi] *adj* (a) *(near)* a mano; próximo, cercano; **the shop is —** la tienda está cerca; **to keep something —** tener algo listo para usar.

(b) (convenient) conveniente, cómodo, práctico; machine etc manuable, fácil de manejar; **a — little car** un coche práctico; **it's — living here** resulta muy práctico vivir aquí; **it's — for the shops** está muy cerca de las tiendas; **to come in —** venir bien, servir.

(c) (skilful) hábil, diestro; **to be — with one's fists** saber defenderse con los puños; **to be — with a gun** saber manejar un fusil.

handyman ['hændimən] n, pl **—men** [mən] factótum m; hombre m que tiene dotes prácticas (para hacer trabajos de carpintería en casa etc).

hang [hæŋ] (irr: pret and ptp **hung**, (Law) pret and ptp **hanged**) **1** vt **(a)** colgar, suspender; wallpaper pegar; **to — out** washing etc tender; streamers etc colgar, extender; **to — up** colgar.

(b) head bajar, inclinar.

(c) to — a room with tapestries entapizar un cuarto, adornar un cuarto con tapicerías; **balconies hung with flags** balcones mpl engalanados con banderas; **trees hung with lights** árboles mpl llenos de farolillos; **a wall hung with ivy** un muro cubierto de hiedra.

(d) criminal ahorcar; **— the fellow!** ¡qué tío!; **— it (all)!** ¡por Dios!; ¡demonio!; **— the expense!** ¡que no se hable de los gastos!; **I'll be —ed if I know** que me cuelguen si lo sé.

(e) to be hung up in the fog sufrir un retraso debido a la niebla; **to be hung up with a visitor** retrasarse por tener que atender a una visita; **we are hung up for lack of bricks** no podemos ir adelante por falta de ladrillos.

2 vi colgar, pender, estar suspendido (from de, on en); (garment, hair) caer; **a picture —ing on the wall** un cuadro colgado en la pared; **the hawk hung motionless in the sky** el halcón se mantenía inmóvil en el cielo; **he'll — for it** por este crimen le ahorcarán; **to — about, to — around** (adv) (idle) no hacer nada, haraganear, (wait) esperar; **to keep someone —ing about** hacer esperar a uno; **to — about** (prep) (frequent) frecuentar; (haunt) rondar; **to — about a woman** andar rondando a una mujer, andar detrás de una mujer; **the clouds hung about the summit** las nubes se pegaban a la cumbre; **to — back** quedarse atrás, resistirse a pasar adelante; (fig) vacilar, no resolverse; **her hair —s down her back** el pelo le cae por la espalda; **to — on** (adv) esperar; **— on!** ¡espera un momentito!; **they're still —ing on** siguen resistiendo; **to — on** (prep) colgar de; (fig) depender de; **we are all —ing on his decision** todos estamos pendientes de su decisión; **time —s heavy on him** se le hacen las horas siglos, para él no corre el tiempo; **to — on to** agarrarse a; (fam) (keep) guardar, quedarse con, (preserve) conservar; **— on to it till I see you** guárdalo hasta que nos veamos; **to — out** colgar fuera; (fam) vivir; **to — out for more** esperar a que se ofrezca más; **to — out of the window** asomarse por la ventana; **to — over** (adv) colgar por el borde, sobresalir; **to — over** (prep) cernerse sobre; **a heavy silence hung over the town** se cernía sobre la ciudad un profundo silencio; **the threat —ing over us** la amenaza que se cierne sobre nosotros; **he hung over the table** se inclinó sobre la mesa; **to — together** (person) mantenerse unidos; (argument etc) ser consistente; **to — up** (Tel) colgar.

3 vr: **to — oneself** ahorcarse.

4 n (of garment) caída f; **to get the — of something** lograr entender algo; **I can't get the — of this machine** no entiendo el modo de manejar esta máquina; see care.

hangar ['hæŋə*] n hangar m.

hangdog ['hæŋdɔg] adj avergonzado; **he had a — look** tenía cara de pocos amigos.

hanger ['hæŋə*] n percha f, colgadero m.

hanger-on ['hæŋər'ɔn] n parásito m, pegote m.

hanging ['hæŋiŋ] **1** adj pendiente, colgante; lamp de techo; garden pensil; **— committee** junta f de una exposición; **it's not a — matter** no es cosa de vida o de muerte.

2 n ahorcadura f; **—s** colgaduras fpl.

hangman ['hæŋmən] n, pl **—men** [mən] verdugo m.

hangnail ['hæŋneil] n padrastro m.

hang-out ['hæŋaut] n (fam) guarida f, nidal m.

hangover ['hæŋˌəuvə*] n (after drinking) resaca f; **it's a — from pre-war days** es algo que ha quedado de la preguerra.

hank [hæŋk] n madeja f.

hanker ['hæŋkə*] vi: **to — after** añorar; **to — for** anhelar, suspirar por.

hankering ['hæŋkəriŋ] n (feeling) añoranza f; (wish) anhelo m; **to have a — for** anhelar, suspirar por.

hankie ['hæŋki] n (fam) pañuelo m.

hanky-panky ['hæŋki'pæŋki] n trucos mpl, supercherías fpl; **there's some — going on** esto huele a camelo, aquí hay trampa; **we want no — with the girls** aquí nadie se meta en líos con las chicas.

Hannibal ['hænibəl] m Aníbal.

Hanover ['hænəvə*] Hanovre.

hansom ['hænsəm] n simón m.

haphazard ['hæp'hæzəd] **1** adj fortuito. **2** adv de cualquier modo, a troche y moche.

hapless ['hæplis] adj desventurado.

happen ['hæpən] vi **(a)** (occur) pasar, suceder, ocurrir, acontecer, acaecer; producirse; **what —ed?** ¿qué pasó?; **how did it —?** ¿cómo fue esto?; **an explosion —ed** se produjo una explosión; **these things —** son cosas que pasan; **whatever —s suceda** lo que suceda; **see it doesn't — again** y que no vuelva a ocurrir; **as it —s, it (so) —s that** da la casualidad que; **as if nothing had —ed** como si tal cosa; **how does it — that . . .?** ¿cómo es posible que . . . + subj?

(b) (take place) tener lugar, verificarse; **the match never —ed** el partido no tuvo lugar nunca.

(c) a funny thing —ed to me me pasó algo raro; **if anything should — to him** si le sobreviniera algo malo; **what —ed to him?** ¿qué fue de él?

(d) I —ed to be there me encontraba allí por casualidad; **if anyone should — to know him?** ¿le conoce Vd acaso te viste; **do you — to know him?** ¿le conoce Vd por ventura?; **I — to know that** pues me consta que; **it —s to be true** a pesar de todo es verdad.

(e) to — on something tropezar con algo; **to — on the solution** acertar, dar con la solución.

happening ['hæpniŋ] n suceso m, acontecimiento m; **there will be a beatnik "—" in the park** habrá un "acontecimiento" de los beatniks en el parque.

happenstance ['hæpənstæns] n (US) azar m, casualidad f; **by —** por casualidad.

happily ['hæpili] adv (fortunately) por fortuna, afortunadamente; (merrily) alegremente; **now they are living — in Seville** ahora viven muy contentos en Sevilla; **they lived — ever after** vivieron felices.

happiness ['hæpinis] n (contentment) felicidad f, dicha f; (merriment) alegría f.

happy ['hæpi] adj **(a)** (fortunate) feliz, dichoso, afortunado; **that — age** aquella época tan feliz.

(b) (contented) contento, satisfecho; **are you —?** ¿estás contento?; **are you — with him?** ¿eres feliz con él?; **we are not entirely — about the plan** no estamos del todo contentos con el proyecto, no nos satisface del todo el proyecto; **your success makes us all —** su éxito nos alegra a todos; **we're very — for you** nos alegramos mucho por ti; **we were — to hear it** nos alegramos de saberlo; **I am — to tell you that** tengo mucho gusto en comunicarle que.

(c) (merry, cheerful) alegre; (sl) entre dos velas; ending of book etc feliz; **to be as — as a lark** (or sandboy) estar como unas pascuas.

(d) (apt) feliz, oportuno; **it seems to be a — solution** parece ser una solución satisfactoria.

happy-go-lucky ['hæpigəu'lʌki] adj despreocupado.

Hapsburg ['hæpsbəːg] Habsburgo.

hara-kiri ['hærə'kiri] n haraquiri m.

harangue [hə'ræŋ] **1** n arenga f. **2** vt arengar.

harass ['hærəs] vt acosar, hostigar; (Mil) hostilizar, picar; person (with worries etc) atormentar, perseguir; **to be —ed by doubts** ser atormentado por las dudas.

harassed ['hærəst] adj look preocupado.

harbinger ['hɑːbindʒə*] n heraldo m, nuncio m; precursor m; presagio m; **— of doom** presagio m del desastre; **the swallow is a — of spring** la golondrina anuncia la venida de la primavera.

harbour, (US) **harbor** ['hɑːbə*] **1** n puerto m; **outer — rada f.**

2 attr portuario.

3 vt fear, hope etc abrigar; (lodge) hospedar; (conceal) esconder; **that corner —s the dust** en ese rincón se amontona el polvo.

harbour master, (US) **harbor master** ['hɑːbəˌmɑːstə*] n capitán m de puerto.

hard [hɑːd] **1** adj **(a)** (unyielding, also fig) duro; sólido, firme; mud, snow endurecido; muscle firme; court, currency, water duro; drink alcohólico; liquor espiritoso; cash contante; look fijo; **he's as — as nails** tiene muchísima resistencia.

(b) (harsh, tough) work arduo, penoso, agotador; blow duro, (fig) cruel, rudo; frost fuerte; weather, winter severo; climate áspero; fight, match muy reñido; rule severo; decision injusto; fact innegable; word nada amistoso; luck, times malo.

(c) (of person) severo, inflexible; **you're a — man** eres cruel; **to be — on someone** ser muy duro con uno; **to be — on one's clothes** destrozar la ropa.

(d) *decision (final)* definitivo, irrevocable.

(e) *(difficult)* difícil; **to be — to beat** ser difícil de vencer; **I find it — to believe that** se me hace cuesta arriba creer que; **to be — to please** ser exigente, ser quisquilloso; **he's — of hearing** es duro de oído.

2 *adv* **(a)** *(strenuously)* mucho; de firme; **to pull a rope** — tirar fuertemente de una cuerda; **he threw it — down** lo arrojó violentamente; **to hit someone** — dar un golpe recio a uno, *(fig)* ser un golpe cruel para uno; **to be — at it** trabajar *(etc)* con ahinco; **to work** — trabajar mucho; **to rain** — llover mucho; **to beg — for something** pedir algo con insistencia; **to think** — pensar mucho, meditar profundamente; **to look** — mirar fijamente; **to drink** — beber con exceso; **hold** —! ¡tente!, ¡para!; **to try one's —est to** + *infin* esforzarse mucho por + *infin*.

(b) to be — up estar a la cuarta pregunta; **to — up for books** no tener casi libros, estar muy falto de libros; **I was — put to it** estuve en un aprieto; **to be — put to it to decide** encontrar difícil decidir; **to be — done by** ser tratado injustamente; **he took it pretty** — fue un golpe bastante rudo para él.

(c) — by *(adv)* muy cerca, *(prep)* muy cerca de; **A followed — upon B** A siguió de cerca a B.

hard-and-fast ['hɑːdən'fɑːst] *adj* *rule* rígido; *decision* definitivo, irrevocable.

hard-bitten ['hɑːd'bitn] *adj* de carácter duro.

hardboard ['hɑːdbɔːd] *n* chapa *f* de madera dura.

hard-boiled ['hɑːd'bɔild] *adj* *egg* duro; *person* de carácter duro, severo.

hard-earned ['hɑːd'əːnd] *adj* ganado con el sudor de la frente.

harden ['hɑːdn] **1** *vt* endurecer *(also Comm)*, solidificar; **to — someone to adversity** acostumbrar a uno a la adversidad; **to — someone to war** aguerrir a uno; **he —ed his heart** se mostró más inflexible.

2 *vi* endurecerse *(also Comm)*, solidificarse; **his voice —ed** adoptó un tono más áspero.

hardened ['hɑːdnd] *adj* *criminal* habitual.

hardening ['hɑːdniŋ] *n* endurecimiento *m* *(also Comm)*; **— of the arteries** endurecimiento *m* de las arterias, arteriosclerosis *f*.

hard-fought ['hɑːd'fɔːt] *adj* muy reñido.

hard-headed ['hɑːd'hedid] *adj* práctico, realista, poco sentimental.

hard-hearted ['hɑːd'hɑːtid] *adj* duro de corazón, insensible.

hardly ['hɑːdli] *adv* **(a)** *(in a hard manner)* duramente; difícilmente; *(badly)* mal.

(b) *(scarcely)* apenas; **he can — read** apenas sabe leer; **that can — be true** eso difícilmente puede ser verdad; **— anyone** casi nadie; **— ever** casi nunca; **—!** ¡nada de eso!

hardness ['hɑːdnis] *n* dureza *f*; dificultad *f*; rigor *m*; severidad *f*; **— of hearing** dureza *f* de oído; **— of heart** insensibilidad *f*.

hardship ['hɑːdʃip] *n* trabajos *mpl*, penas *fpl*; infortunio *m*; prueba *f*; *(economic etc)* apuro *m*, privación *f*; **to suffer —(s)** pasar apuros; **it is no — to him to give up smoking** él con toda facilidad puede dejar de fumar.

hardtack ['hɑːdtæk] *n* *(Naut)* galleta *f*.

hardware ['hɑːdweə*] *n* ferretería *f*, quincalla *f*; **— shop** *(or* **store)** ferretería *f*, quincallería *f*; **nuclear** — *(equipo m de)* armas *fpl* nucleares.

hard-wearing ['hɑːd'weəriŋ] *adj* resistente, duradero.

hard-won ['hɑːd'wʌn] *adj* ganado a duras penas.

hardwood ['hɑːd'wud] *n* madera *f* dura; **— tree** árbol *m* de hojas caducas.

hard-working ['hɑːd'wəːkiŋ] *adj* trabajador.

hardy ['hɑːdi] *adj* fuerte, robusto; *(Bot)* resistente.

hare [heə*] **1** *n* liebre *f*; **first catch your** — no hay que empezar por el tejado. **2** *vi* *(fam)* correr, ir rápidamente; **he went haring past** pasó como un rayo.

harebell ['heəbel] *n* campánula *f*.

hare-brained ['heəbreind] *adj* casquivano.

harelip ['heə'lip] *n* labio *m* leporino.

harem [hɑː'riːm] *n* harén *m*.

haricot ['hærikəu] *n* *(also* **— bean)** alubia *f*.

hark [hɑːk] *vi* —! ¡escucha!; **— at this!** ¡oye!; **— at him!** ¡qué cosas dice!; **— at him singing!** ¡cómo canta el tío!; **to — back to** *matter* volver a, *earlier occasion* recordar; **he's always —ing back to that** siempre está con la misma canción; **to — to** escuchar.

Harlequin ['hɑːlikwin] *m* Arlequín.

harlot ['hɑːlət] *n* ramera *f*.

harm [hɑːm] **1** *n* daño *m*, mal *m*; perjuicio *m*; **to be out of —'s way** estar a salvo; **to keep out of —'s way**

evitar el peligro, permanecer lejos del sitio peligroso; **there's no — in** + *ger* no hay ningún mal en + *infin*; **I see no — in that** no veo nada en contra de eso; **to do someone** — hacer daño a uno, *(fig)* perjudicar a uno; **it does more — than good** es peor el remedio que la enfermedad; **the — is done now** el mal ya está hecho; **he means no** — tiene buenas intenciones.

2 *vt* *person* hacer daño a, hacer mal a; *crops etc* dañar, estropear; *interests etc* perjudicar.

3 *vi*: **will it — in the rain?** ¿lo estropeará la lluvia?; **it won't — for that** eso no le hará daño.

harmful ['hɑːmful] *adj* perjudicial *(to para)*, dañoso, nocivo; *pest, tobacco etc* dañino.

harmless ['hɑːmlis] *adj* inocuo, inofensivo.

harmonic [hɑː'mɔnik] *adj* armónico.

harmonica [hɑː'mɔnikə] *n* armónica *f*.

harmonious [hɑː'məuniəs] *adj* armonioso.

harmonium [hɑː'məuniəm] *n* armonio *m*.

harmonize ['hɑːmənaiz] *vti* armonizar *(with* con).

harmony ['hɑːməni] *n* armonía *f*; **close** — perfecta harmonía *f*.

harness ['hɑːnis] **1** *n* guarniciones *fpl*, arreos *mpl*; **to die in** — morir con las botas puestas; **to get back in** — volver al trabajo, volver a su puesto.

2 *vt* **(a)** *horse* poner guarniciones a, enjaezar; **to — a horse to a cart** enganchar un caballo a un carro.

(b) *resources etc* hacer trabajar, utilizar, aprovechar.

harp [hɑːp] **1** *n* arpa *f*. **2** *vi*: **to — on** hablar constantemente de; **stop —ing on it!** ¡no machaques!

harpist ['hɑːpist] *n* arpista *mf*.

harpoon [hɑː'puːn] **1** *n* arpón *m*. **2** *vt* arponear.

harpsichord ['hɑːpsikɔːd] *n* arpicordio *m*, clavicémbalo *m*.

harpy ['hɑːpi] *n* arpía *f*.

harquebus ['hɑːkwibəs] *n* *(Hist)* arcabuz *m*.

harridan ['hæridən] *n* bruja *f*.

harrow ['hærəu] **1** *n* grada *f*. **2** *vt* gradar.

harrowing ['hærəuiŋ] *adj* horrendo, horroroso, angustioso.

Harry ['hæri] *m* Enrique; **to play old — with** endiablar, estropear.

harry ['hæri] *vt* *(devastate)* asolar; *(Mil)* hostilizar; *person etc* hostigar, acosar.

harsh [hɑːʃ] *adj* *person, decision etc* severo, duro, cruel; *voice, cloth etc* áspero; *contrast* violento; *weather* severo; *colour* chillón; *taste* acerbo; *words* nada amistoso.

harshly ['hɑːʃli] *adv* severamente, duramente; ásperamente.

harshness ['hɑːʃnis] *n* severidad *f*, dureza *f*, rigor *m*; aspereza *f*.

hart [hɑːt] *n* ciervo *m*.

harum-scarum ['heərəm'skeərəm] **1** *adj* tarambana. **2** *n* tarambana *mf*.

harvest ['hɑːvist] **1** *n* cosecha *f*, recolección *f*; *(time of year)* siega *f*; *(of grape)* vendimia *f*; *(fig)* cosecha *f*. **2** *vt* cosechar *(also fig)*, recoger, recolectar.

harvester ['hɑːvistə*] *n* *(person)* segador *m*, ora *f*; *(machine)* cosechadora *f*, segadora-trilladora *f*.

harvest festival ['hɑːvist'festivəl] *n* fiesta *f* de la cosecha.

harvest time ['hɑːvist,taim] *n* siega *f*.

has [hæz] *see* **have.**

has-been ['hæzbiːn] *n* persona *f* que ya no sirve, vieja gloria *f*.

hash [hæʃ] **1** *n* picadillo *m*; *(fam)* embrollo *m*, lío *m*; **to make a — of something** armarse un lío con algo, estropear algo, hacer algo muy mal; **to settle someone's** — cargarse a uno, acabar con uno.

2 *vt*: **to — something up** rehacer algo (y presentarlo como nuevo).

hashish ['hæʃiʃ] *n* hachich *m*.

hasn't ['hæznt] = **has not.**

hasp [hɑːsp] *n* pasador *m*, sujetador *m*.

hassle ['hæsl] *n* *(US: fam)* pelea *f*, riña *f*.

hassock ['hæsək] *n* *(Eccl)* cojín *m*.

haste [heist] *n* prisa *f*, precipitación *f*; **more — less speed, make — slowly** vísteme despacio que tengo prisa; **to do something in** — hacer algo de prisa; hacer algo precipitadamente; **to make** — darse prisa; **make —!** ¡date prisa!; **to make — to** + *infin* apresurarse a + *infin*.

hasten ['heisn] **1** *vt* acelerar; **to — one's steps** apretar el paso.

2 *vi* darse prisa, apresurarse; **to — to** + *infin* apresurarse a + *infin*; **to — away, to — off** marcharse precipitadamente; **to — back** volver con toda prisa; **to — on** seguir adelante con toda prisa; **to — up** llegar apresuradamente, llegar corriendo.

hastily ['heistili] *adv* (*hurriedly*) de prisa, precipitada-mente; *speak* sin reflexión, con impaciencia; *judge* a la ligera; **I — suggested that** me apresuré a sugerir que.

hasty ['heisti] *adj* (*hurried*) apresurado, precipitado; (*rash*) imprudente; (*quick-tempered*) impaciente, que tiene genio; (*superficial*) ligero; **don't be so —** hay que tomar las cosas con más calma.

hat [hæt] *n* sombrero *m*; **my —!** ¡caramba!; **that's old** — eso es de lo más anticuado; eso lo tenemos archisabido; **I'll eat my — if . . .** que me maten si . . .; **keep it under your —** de esto no digas ni pío; **to pass the — round** pasar el platillo; **to raise** (*or* **take off**) **one's —** descubrirse; **to take one's — off to** (*fig*) quitarse el sombrero y hacer reverencia a; **to talk through one's —** decir tonterías.

hatbox ['hætbɔks] *n* sombrerera *f*.

hatch¹ [hætʃ] *n* (*hatchway*) escotilla *f*.

hatch² [hætʃ] **1** *vt* chick empollar, incubar; sacar del cascarón; (*fig*) idear; *plot* tramar.
2 *vi* (*bird*) salir del huevo; **the egg —ed** el pollo rompió el cascarón y salió; **those eggs never —ed** esos huevos resultaron ser infecundos.

hatchet ['hætʃit] *n* hacha *f* (pequeña), machado *m*; **to bury the —** echar pelillos a la mar.

hatchet-faced ['hætʃit,feist] *adj* de cara de cuchillo.

hatching¹ ['hætʃiŋ] *n* incubación *f*; salida *f* del huevo; (*fig*) ideación *f*; preparación *f*, maquinación *f*.

hatching² ['hætʃiŋ] *n* (*Art*) sombreado *m*.

hatchway ['hætʃwei] *n* escotilla *f*.

hate [heit] **1** *n* odio *m*.
2 *vt* (*a*) odiar, detestar, aborrecer; **to — someone like poison** odiar a uno a muerte.
(*b*) **I — to see that** me da asco ver aquello; **I — to say so** lamento tener que decirlo; **I — having to do it** me repugna hacerlo; **I — to trouble you** siento muchísimo molestarle; **I should — to have to sell it** me molestaría tener que venderlo; **he —s to be corrected** se indigna si se le corrige.

hateful ['heitful] *adj* odioso, repugnante.

hatless ['hætlis] *adj* sin sombrero, descubierto.

hatpin ['hætpin] *n* agujón *m*.

hatred ['heitrid] *n* odio *m* (*for* a), aborrecimiento *m* (*for* de).

hatter ['hætə*] *n* sombrerero *m*.

hat trick ['hættrik] *n* (*fig*) tres triunfos *mpl* seguidos.

haughtily ['hɔːtili] *adv* arrogantemente.

haughtiness ['hɔːtinis] *n* altanería *f*, arrogancia *f*, altivez *f*.

haughty ['hɔːti] *adj* altanero, arrogante, altivo.

haul [hɔːl] **1** *n* (*a*) (*act of pulling*) tirón *m*, estirón *m* (*on* de).
(*b*) (*distance*) recorrido *m*, trayecto *m*; **it's a good** (*or* **long**) **—** es mucho camino.
(*c*) (*amount of fish*) redada *f*; (*fig*) cantidad *f* cazada, número *m* de piezas cazadas; (*financial*) ganancia *f*; (*stolen*) botín *m*; **the thieves made a good —** los ladrones obtuvieron un cuantioso botín.
2 *vt* (*drag*) tirar, arrastrar; (*transport*) acarrear, transportar; **to — down** flag arriar; **to — in** net etc ir recogiendo; **to — up** ir levantando.
3 *vi*: **to — on**, **to — at** tirar de, (*Naut*) halar.

haulage ['hɔːlidʒ] *n* (*act*) acarreo *m*, transporte *m*; (*cost*) gastos *mpl* de acarreo.

haulage contractor ['hɔːlidʒkən'træktə*] *n*, **haulier** ['hɔːliə*] *n* contratista *m* de transportes.

haunch [hɔːntʃ] *n* anca *f*; (*of meat*) pierna *f*; **to sit on one's —es** sentarse en cuclillas.

haunt [hɔːnt] **1** *n* (*animal's*) nidal *m*, guarida *f*, querencia *f*; **I know his —s** yo conozco sus sitios favoritos, yo sé dónde suele estar; **it's a — of artists** es lugar predilecto de los artistas.
2 *vt* (*a*) (*frequent*) frecuentar, rondar; **he —s the theatres** aparece constantemente en los teatros.
(*b*) (*of ghost*) aparecer en, andar por; **the house is —ed** en la casa andan fantasmas, la casa está embrujada; **—ed house** casa *f* de fantasmas.
(*c*) *person* perseguir; obsesionar; **he is —ed by memories** le persiguen sus recuerdos, le atormentan sus recuerdos; **he is —ed by the thought that** le obsesiona el pensamiento de que.

haunted ['hɔːntid] *adj* look etc obsesionado; **— house** see **haunt**.

haunting ['hɔːntiŋ] *adj* obsesionante; *melody* inolvi-dable.

Havana [hə'vænə] La Habana.

have [hæv] (*irr*: *3rd sing present* **has**, *pret and ptp* **had**) **1** *vt* (*a*) (*possess*) tener; poseer; **all I —** todo lo que tengo; **— you any bananas?** (*in shop*) ¿hay plátanos?; **I — no words to express . . .** no encuentro palabras para expresar . . .; **I — no German** no sé

alemán; **I — it! ¡ya!; . . . and what — you . . .** et-cétera, etcétera; **the dog had him by the throat** el perro le tenía agarrado por la garganta.
(*b*) (*bear*, *carry*) tener, llevar; **the book has no name on it** el libro no lleva el nombre del dueño; **to — a hat on** llevar un sombrero (puesto); **do you — a shilling about you?** ¿llevas encima un chelín?
(*c*) *baby* parir, dar a luz; **she's going to — a baby** va a tener un niño.
(*d*) (*obtain*, *acquire*, *hand over*) **to — a letter from someone** recibir una carta de uno; **to — no news** no tener noticias; **I — it on good authority that** sé de buena tinta que; **it is to be had at the chemist's** se vende en la farmacia; **it's not to be had anywhere** no se puede conseguir en ninguna parte; **I must — £5 at once** necesito 5 libras en seguida; **you can — it for £2** te lo vendo por 2 libras; **let me — your pen** déme la pluma; **he let me — some money** me facilitó dinero; **I will let you — my reply tomorrow** les daré mi respuesta mañana.
(*e*) (*strike*) **let him — it!** ¡dale!; **then they let him — it** luego empezaron a pegarle, (*fig*) luego le dijeron cuatro verdades.
(*f*) (*eat*, *drink etc*) tomar; **I don't — anything at night** por la noche no tomo nada; **to — tea with someone** tomar el té con uno, merendar con uno; **he's having his dinner** está comiendo; **what did you — at the dinner?** ¿qué te dieron de comer en el banquete?; **will you — a drink?** ¿quieres tomar algo?; **will you — some more?** ¿quieres más?; **to — a cigarette** fumar un pitillo.
(*g*) (*for many n phrases, see the n; eg*) **to — a game** echar una partida; **to — a bath** tomar un baño; **to — a lesson** tomar lección; **to — measles** tener sarampión; **to — a good time** pasarlo bien; **did you — any trouble?** ¿tuviste alguna dificultad?; **I had a strange adventure** me pasó algo raro; **I never seem to — anything happen to me** parece que no me pasa nunca nada.
(*h*) (*wish*) **which will you —?** ¿cuál quieres?; **what more would you —?** ¿qué más quieres?; **as ill-luck would — it** desgraciadamente, como quiso la desgracia; **I would — you know that** sepa Vd que.
(*i*) (*permit*) **I won't — such behaviour** no tolero esta conducta; **I'm not having that** no puedo consentir en que se haga (*or* diga *etc*) eso; **we can't — that** eso no se puede consentir; **we don't — children here** aquí no recibimos a los matrimonios que traigan hijos.
(*j*) (*insist*, *say*) **he will — it that** sostiene que; **he will not — it that** no quiere reconocer que; **as rumour has it** según se dice; **as Keats has it** según (dice) Keats.
(*k*) (*deceive*) **you've been had** te han engañado; **I'm not to be had that way** no se me engaña así; **there you — me** de eso no sé nada en absoluto.
(*l*) (*obligation*) **to — to do something** tener que hacer algo; **it has to be done this way** ha de hacerse de este modo; **does it — to be ironed?** ¿hay que plancharlo?
(*m*) (*causative*) **to — something done** hacer hacer algo; **to — a suit made** mandar confeccionar un traje; **please — it repaired** por favor, mándelo componer; **he had his watch stolen** le robaron el reloj; **he had his arm broken** se rompió el brazo; **I won't — her insulted** no permito que se le insulte; **to — someone do something** hacer que uno haga algo; **he would — me do it** insistió en que yo lo hiciera; **what else would you — me do?** ¿qué más queréis que haga?
(*n*) **I — letters to write** tengo cartas que escribir; **haven't you anything to do?** ¿no tienes nada que hacer?
(*o*) (*auxiliary*) haber; **he has gone** ha ido; **he had spoken** había hablado; **it has been raining for 3 days** llueve desde hace 3 días; **I haven't seen him for 2 years** hace 2 años que no le veo; **"I — 2 cars" . . . "so — I"** "yo tengo 2 coches" . . . "yo también"; **"it's gone!" . . . "so it has!"** "¡ha desaparecido!" . . . "¡es verdad!"; **see just** *etc*.
(*p*) **I had better**, **sooner** *etc*: see **better**, **sooner** *etc*.
(*q*) (*with adv or prep*) **let's — him in!** ¡que pase!, ¡que entre!; **to — someone in to tea** invitar a uno a merendar; **we're having people in** tenemos invitados; **we'd better — the doctor in** será mejor llamar al médico; **to — it in for someone** tener manía a uno; **to — someone on** tomar el pelo a uno; **to — a tooth out** hacer sacar una muela; **to — it out with someone** resolver un problema discutiendo con uno, (*unfriendly*) ajustar cuentas con uno; **to — someone up** llevar a uno ante los tribunales (*for* y

acusarle de); **he was had up for larceny** le procesaron por ladrón.
2 n: **the —s and the have-nots** los ricos y los pobres.

haven ['heivn] n puerto m; (fig) refugio m, asilo m.

have-nots ['hævnɒts] npl: **the —** los pobres, los desposeídos.

haven't ['hævnt] = **have not**.

haversack ['hævəsæk] n mochila f.

havoc ['hævək] n estragos mpl, destrucción f; **to make — of, to play — with** hacer estragos en, arruinar, estropear.

haw [hɔ:] n baya f del espino.

Hawaii [hə'waii:] Islas fpl Hawai.

Hawaiian [hə'waijən] **1** adj hawaiano. **2** n hawaiano m, a f.

hawk[1] [hɔ:k] n (Orn) halcón m, gavilán m; **—s and doves** (Pol) gavilanes mpl y palomas fpl.

hawk[2] [hɔ:k] vt pregonar, vender por las calles.

hawk[3] [hɔ:k] **1** vt: **to — up** arrojar tosiendo. **2** vi carraspear.

hawker ['hɔ:kə*] n vendedor m ambulante.

hawser ['hɔ:zə*] n guindaleza f, calabrote m, maroma f.

hawthorn ['hɔ:θɔ:n] n espino m.

hay [hei] n heno m; **to hit the —** (fam) acostarse; **to make — of** enemy desbaratar, team cascar, argument destruir; **to make — while the sun shines** hacer su agosto.

haycock ['heikɔk] n montón m de heno.

hay fever ['hei,fi:və*] n fiebre f del heno.

hayloft ['heilɔft] n henil m.

haymaker ['heimeikə*] n heneador m, labrador m que trabaja en la siega (or la recolección) del heno.

haymaking ['heimeikiŋ] n henificación f; época f del heno; siega f del heno, recolección f del heno.

haystack ['heistæk] n almiar m.

haywire ['heiwaiə*] adj (fam) (confused) en desorden; (mad) loco; **to go —** (person) volverse loco, (scheme etc) embrollarse, embarrullarse; **it's all gone —** en eso existe la mayor confusión, todo está en desorden.

hazard ['hæzəd] **1** n riesgo m; **at all —s** todo riesgo. **2** vt arriesgar, poner en peligro; guess, remark atreverse a hacer, aventurar.

hazardous ['hæzədəs] adj arriesgado, peligroso.

haze [heiz] n calina f, neblina f; (fig) confusión f; **a — of tobacco smoke filled the room** el cuarto estaba lleno de humo de tabaco.

hazel ['heizl] n avellano m.

hazelnut ['heizlnʌt] n avellana f.

haziness ['heizinis] n lo calinoso, lo brumoso; (fig) confusión f, vaguedad f.

hazy ['heizi] adj calinoso, brumoso; (fig) confuso, vago; **he's — about dates** no recuerda exactamente las fechas; **I'm — about maths** tengo solamente una idea vaga de las matemáticas; **he seemed very —** parecía no tener ninguna idea clara.

H-bomb ['eitʃbɒm] m bomba f H.

he [hi:] **1** pron él; **— who** el que, quien. **2** n macho m, varón m; **to play —** (children's game) dar la despe. **3** attr macho.

head [hed] **1** n (a) (Anat) cabeza f; **— of hair** cabellera f; **— first, — foremost** de cabeza; **to go — over heels** caer patas arriba; **to fall — over heels in love with someone** enamorarse perdidamente de uno; **from — to foot** de pies a cabeza; **we are banging our —s against a brick wall** todo esto es trabajo perdido; **to bite someone's — off** echar un rapapolvo a uno; **to give a horse its —** dar rienda suelta a un caballo; **now he can hold his — up again** ahora ha recuperado la propia estimación; **to keep one's — above water** (fig) ir tirando; **to nod one's —** asentir con la cabeza, mover la cabeza afirmativamente; **to shake one's —** negar algo con la cabeza, mover la cabeza negativamente; **he stands — and shoulders above the rest** los demás no le llegan a la suela del zapato; **to talk one's — off** hablar por los codos.

(b) (with prep before n) **he is taller than his brother by a —** le saca la cabeza a su hermano; **to win by a (short) —** ganar por una cabeza (escasa); **on his own —** be it sea bajo su propia responsabilidad; **to put a price on someone's —** poner la cabeza de uno a precio; **to stand on one's —** echar el pino; **to stand an argument on its —** demostrar la falsedad de un argumento; **to give orders over someone's —** dar órdenes sin consultar a uno; **they went over my — to the mayor** hablaron con el alcalde sin hacer caso de mí; **to sell a house over someone's —** vender una casa sin decir nada a uno; **the wine goes to my —** el vino se me sube a la cabeza; **success has gone to his —** el éxito le ha hecho ser muy vanidoso.

(c) (intellect, mind) cabeza f, inteligencia f;

talento m; **two —s are better than one** cuatro ojos ven más que dos; **don't bother your — about it** no se preocupe, no se canse tratando de explicarlo (etc); **it never entered my —** jamás se me pasó por la cabeza; **to have a bad —** tener dolor de cabeza; **to have a swelled —** ser vanidoso; **to have a — for business** tener talento para los negocios; **to have a — for languages** tener aptitud para los idiomas; **to have no — for heights** no tener cabeza para las alturas; **he has a good — on him** es inteligente, tiene talento; **to keep one's —** conservar la sangre fría; **to lose one's —** perder la cabeza; **so we put our —s together** así que tratamos los dos de resolverlo; **to turn someone's —** trastornar el juicio de uno, (make vain) envanecer a uno.

(d) (as (c), with prep before n) **it was above their —s** estaba fuera de su alcance, no eran lo bastante inteligentes para comprenderlo; **to do a sum in one's —** hacer un cálculo mental; **to be soft** (or weak) **in the —** ser un poco tocado; **to get something into someone's —** meter a uno algo en la cabeza; **he has got it into his —** that cree firmemente que; **get it into your —** that dése cuenta de que; **I can't get that tune out of my —** me obsesiona esa melodía; **what put that into your —?** ¿cómo se formó Vd tal idea?, ¿de dónde colige Vd eso?; **to take it into one's — to + infin** ocurrírse a uno + infin; **to be off one's —** estar loco; **you must be off your —!** ¡estás loco?

(e) (person) (leader) jefe m, cabeza m; (of school) director m, ora f; **— of a department** jefe m de departamento; **— of state** jefe m de estado; **crowned —** testa f coronada; **£5 a —** 5 libras por persona.

(f) (on coin) cara f; **to toss —s or tails** echar a cara o cruz; **—s I win, tails you lose** cara, yo gano, cruz, usted pierde; **I couldn't make — or tail of it** no entendí palabra, no le encontré sentido alguno.

(g) **20 — of cattle** 20 reses fpl; **20 — of sheep** 20 ovejas fpl.

(h) (objects etc) (of bed) cabecera f; (of table, bridge, nail etc) cabeza f; (of arrow etc) punta f; (of stick) puño m; (of cylinder) culata f; (Naut) proa f; (Geog) punta f; (of water) altura f de caída; (on beer) espuma f; (Bot) flor f, cabezuela f; (of tree) copa f; (of corn) espigas fpl; **at the — of the valley** al final del valle; **to bring something to a —** hacer que algo llegue a su punto decisivo; **to come to a —** (abscess) supurar, (fig) llegar a la crisis.

(i) (heading) título m, encabezamiento m; (section) sección f, artículo m; **under this —** en esta sección.

(j) (front place) cabeza f; **— of the family** cabeza mf de la familia; **to be at the — of the list** encabezar la lista; **to be at the — of the league** ir en cabeza de la liga.

2 attr (a) principal, primero; **— cook** primer cocinero m; **— salesman** vendedor m en jefe.

(b) part delantero, de frente.

3 vt list etc encabezar, estar a la cabeza de; league ir en cabeza de; poll ganar; rebellion acaudillar; company dirigir; team capitanear; football cabecear; goal rematar con la cabeza; **he —ed the boat for the shore** dirigió la barca hacia la costa; **to be —ed for** ir con rumbo a; **to — off** interceptar, atajar; desviar; (fig) distraer.

4 vi: **to — for, to — towards** dirigirse a (or hacia); **to be —ing for** ir con rumbo a; **where are you —ing for?** ¿adónde se dirige Vd?; **we are —ing for ruin** vamos camino de la destrucción.

headache ['hedeik] n dolor m de cabeza; (fig) quebradero m de cabeza.

headband ['hedbænd] n cinta f (para la cabeza), venda f (para la cabeza).

headdress ['heddres] n toca f, tocado m.

-headed ['hedid] adj con cabeza . . ., de cabeza . . ., eg **small-headed** de cabeza pequeña; **fair-headed** pelirrubio.

header ['hedə*] n (fall) caída f de cabeza; (dive) salto m de cabeza; (Sport) cabezazo m.

headgear ['hedgiə*] n sombrero m; (woman's) tocado m.

headhunter ['hed,hʌntə*] n cazador m de cabezas.

heading ['hediŋ] n (title) encabezamiento m, título m; (letterhead) membrete m; (section) sección f, apartado m; **to come under the — of** clasificarse bajo, estar incluido en.

headlamp ['hedlæmp] n faro m.

headland ['hedlənd] n promontorio m.

headlight ['hedlait] n faro m.

headline ['hedlain] n titular m; **this will hit the —s** los periódicos tendrán mucho que decir sobre esto, esto es sensacional.

headlong ['hedlɔŋ] **1** adj fall de cabeza; rush etc precipitado. **2** adv de cabeza; precipitadamente.

headman ['hedmæn] n, pl —**men** [men] cacique m.

headmaster ['hed'mɑːstə*] n director m (de colegio etc).

headmistress ['hed'mistris] n directora f (de colegio etc).

head-on ['hed'ɔn] **1** adj collision de frente. **2** adv de frente.

headphones ['hedfəunz] npl auriculares mpl.

headquarters ['hed'kwɔːtəz] npl (Mil) cuartel m general; (of party, organization) sede f; (Comm) oficina f central, central f; (of revolt etc) centro m, foco m.

headrest ['hedrest] n reposa-cabezas m.

headroom ['hedrum] n espacio m para la cabeza; espacio m para estar (derecho) de pie; (under bridge etc) luz f.

headscarf ['hedskɑːf] n pañuelo m.

headship ['hedʃip] n jefatura f; dirección f; (of school) puesto m de director(a).

headsman ['hedzmən] n, pl —**men** [mən] verdugo m.

headstand ['hedstænd] n posición f de cabeza.

headstone ['hedstəun] n lápida f mortuoria.

headstrong ['hedstrɔŋ] adj voluntarioso, impetuoso.

headwaters ['hed‚wɔːtəz] npl cabecera f (de un río).

headway ['hedwei] n progreso m; **to make** — avanzar, (fig) hacer progresos; **we could make no** — **against the current** no logramos avanzar contra la corriente, la corriente nos impidió avanzar; **I didn't make much** — **with him** no he conseguido nada de él.

headwind ['hedwind] n viento m contrario.

heady ['hedi] adj wine fuerte, cabezudo; (fig) embriagador.

heal [hiːl] **1** vt curar, sanar (of de); (fig) curar, remediar. **2** vi (also **to** — **up**) cicatrizarse.

healing ['hiːliŋ] **1** adj curativo, sanativo. **2** n curación f.

health [helθ] n (a) (of person) salud f; (public —) sanidad f, higiene f; **Ministry of H**— (Spain) Dirección f General de Sanidad; **National H**— **Service** (Spain) Seguro m de Enfermedad; **to be in good (bad)** — estar bien (mal) de salud; **to restore someone to** — devolver la salud a uno.

(b) (toast) brindis m; **good** —! ¡salud y pesetas!; **here's a** — **to X!** ¡vaya por X!; **to drink (to) someone's** — beber a la salud de uno, brindar por uno.

healthful ['helθful] adj, **health-giving** ['helθ‚giviŋ] adj sano, saludable.

health officer ['helθ‚ɔfisə*] n inspector m de sanidad.

health resort ['helθri‚zɔːt] n balneario m.

healthy ['helθi] adj (a) (healthful) sano, saludable; place etc salubre. (b) **to be** — (person) tener buena salud.

heap [hiːp] **1** n montón m, pila f, rimero m; (fig) montón m; **a whole** — **of trouble** un montón de disgustos; **a whole** — **of people** muchísimas personas; —**s of times** muchísimas veces; **we have** —**s** tenemos montones; **we have** —**s of time** nos sobra tiempo, tenemos tiempo de sobra; **the news struck him all of a** — la noticia le causó estupor.

2 vt (also **to** — **up**) amontonar, apilar; plate, spoon etc colmar (with de); **to** — **together** juntar en un montón; **to** — **favours on someone** colmar a uno de favores.

3 —**s** adv (fam) muchísimo.

hear [hiə*] (irr: pret and ptp **heard**) **1** vt oír; (perceive) sentir; (listen to) escuchar; lecture asistir a; piece of news saber; (Law) case ver; **do you** — **me?** ¿me oyes?; **I** — **bad reports of him** me dan malos informes sobre él; **I never** —**d such rubbish!** ¡en mi vida he oído tantos disparates!; **I have** —**d it said that** he oído decir que; **to** — **someone speak** oír hablar a uno; **I could hardly make myself** —**d** apenas pude hacerme entender; **to** — **someone out** escuchar a uno hasta el fin; **to** — **that** oír decir que; **when I** —**d that** . . . cuando supe que . . .

2 vi oír; — —**!** ¡muy bien!; **to** — **about, to** — **of** oír hablar de, saber, enterarse de; **when I** —**d of it** cuando lo supe; **I've never** —**d of him** no le conozco en absoluto; **he won't** — **of it** no lo permite, no quiere autorizarlo; **I won't** — **of it!** ¡ni hablar!; **to** — **from** tener noticias de, recibir carta de; **you'll be** —**ing from me** te escribiré; **let's** — **from you soon!** ¡no deje de escribirnos pronto!, ¡mándenos noticias suyas!

heard [həːd] pret and ptp of **hear**.

hearer ['hiərə*] n oyente mf.

hearing ['hiəriŋ] n (sense of —) oído m; (act of —) audición f; (Law) vista f; **in my** — en mi presencia, estando yo delante; **to be out of** — estar fuera del alcance del oído; **to be within** — estar al alcance del oído; **to condemn someone without a** — condenar a uno sin escuchar su defensa.

hearing aid ['hiəriŋeid] n aparato m del oído, audífono m.

hearken ['hɑːkən] vi: **to** — escuchar.

hearsay ['hiəsei] n rumores mpl, hablillas fpl; **it's just** — son rumores; **by** — de oídas.

hearse [həːs] n coche m fúnebre.

heart [hɑːt] n (a) (Anat) corazón m; **she spoke with beating** — le palpitaba el corazón al decirlo; **to clasp someone to one's** — abrazar a uno estrechamente; **to have a weak** — ser cardíaco.

(b) (fig) (Cards) corazones mpl, (in Spanish pack) copas fpl; (of lettuce) cogollo m; (of place, earth etc) corazón m, seno m, centro m; **in the** — **of the country** en lo más retirado del campo; **in the** — **of the wood** en el centro del bosque; **the** — **of the matter** lo esencial, el quid.

(c) (symbol of love) corazón m; **with all one's** — de todo corazón, con toda el alma; **affair of the** — aventura f sentimental; **to break someone's** — (in love) partir el corazón a uno, (by behaviour etc) matar a uno a disgustos; **to break one's** — **over** partirse el corazón por; **to die of a broken** — morir de pena; **to lose one's** — **to** enamorarse de; **to wear one's** — **on one's sleeve** llevar el corazón en la mano; **to win someone's** — enamorar a uno.

(d) (seat of feeling, sympathy etc) **he's a man after my own** — es un hombre de los que me gustan; **at** — en el fondo; **to have someone's interests at** — tener presente el interés de uno; **to be sick at** — tener la muerte en el alma; **from the** — con toda sinceridad; **in his** — **of** —**s** en lo más íntimo de su corazón; **with a heavy** — con dolor, sintiéndolo; **his** — **is in the right place** tiene buenas intenciones; **to cut someone to the** — herir a uno en lo vivo; **to cry one's** — **out** llorar a mares; **it would have done your** — **good** le habría alegrado muchísimo; **to eat one's** — **out** estar muriéndose de pena; **to have no** — no tener entrañas; **have a** —! ¡ten un poco de piedad!; **he has a** — **of gold** es buenísima persona; **to set someone's** — **at rest** tranquilizar a uno; **to take something to** — tomar algo a pecho.

(e) (seat of desire, intention) **his** — **was not in it** no tenía fe en lo que estaba haciendo; **to set one's** — **on** poner el corazón en; see **content** etc.

(f) (symbol of courage) **to be in good** — estar lleno de confianza, (soil) estar en buen estado; **I could not find it in my** — **to** + infin, **I did not have the** — **to** + infin no tuve valor para + infin; **to have one's** — **in one's mouth** tener el alma en un hilo; **to lose** — descorazonarse; **to put new** — **into someone** infundir ánimo a uno; **my** — **sank** se me cayeron las alas del corazón; **to take** — cobrar ánimo; **we may take** — **from the fact that** que nos aliente el hecho de que.

(g) **by** — de memoria.

heartache ['hɑːteik] n angustia f, pena f.

heart attack ['hɑːtətæk] n ataque m cardíaco.

heartbeat ['hɑːtbiːt] n latido m del corazón.

heartbreaking ['hɑːt‚breikiŋ] adj angustioso, desgarrador; **it was** — **to see them** daba lástima verlos.

heartbroken ['hɑːt‚brəukən] adj angustiado, acongojado; **she was** — **about it** esto le partió el corazón.

heartburn ['hɑːtbəːn] n acedía f.

heartburning ['hɑːt‚bəːniŋ] n (bad feeling) envidia f, rencor m; (regret) sentimiento m.

heart complaint ['hɑːtkəm‚pleint] n, **heart disease** ['hɑːtdi‚ziːz] n enfermedad f cardíaca.

-hearted ['hɑːtid] adj de corazón . . .; **faint-hearted** medroso, pusilánime.

hearten ['hɑːtn] vt alentar, infundir ánimo a.

heart failure ['hɑːt‚feiljə*] n fallo m de corazón, colapso m cardíaco.

heartfelt ['hɑːtfelt] adj cordial, sincero; sympathy más sentido; thanks más efusivo.

hearth [hɑːθ] n hogar m (also fig), chimenea f.

heartily ['hɑːtili] adv sinceramente, cordialmente; enérgicamente, fuertemente; laugh a carcajadas; eat con buen apetito; thank con efusión; sing con entusiasmo; **to be** — **glad** alegrarse sinceramente; **to be** — **sick of** estar completamente harto de.

heartless ['hɑːtlis] adj cruel, inhumano.

heartlessly ['hɑːtlisli] adv cruelmente, despiadadamente.

heartlessness ['hɑːtlisnis] n crueldad f, inhumanidad f.

heartrending ['hɑːt‚rendiŋ] adj angustioso, desgarrador; **it was** — **to see them** daba lástima verlos.

heart-searching ['hɑːt‚səːtʃiŋ] n examen m de conciencia.

heartstrings ['hɑːtstriŋz] *npl* fibras *fpl* del corazón.
heart-throb ['hɑːtθrɔb] *n* (*fam*) novio *m*, novia *f*.
heart-to-heart ['hɑːttə'hɑːt] *adj* íntimo.

hearty ['hɑːti] *adj person* campechano, francote; *feelings* sincero, cordial; *effort* enérgico; *kick, slap etc* fuerte; *laugh* sano, franco; *appetite* bueno; *meal* abundante; *thanks* efusivo; **to be a — eater** tener buen diente.

heat [hiːt] **1** *n* (**a**) (*warmth*) calor *m*; (*heating system*) calefacción *f*; **red —** calor *m* rojo; **white —** candencia *f*; **in the — of the day** en las horas de más calor.
  (**b**) (*fig*) calor *m*, ardor *m*, vehemencia *f*, pasión *f*; **in the — of the moment** en el calor del momento; **he replied with some —** contestó bastante indignado; **to turn on the —** empezar a ejercer presiones, (*Pol*) crear un ambiente de crisis.
  (**c**) (*Sport*) (*prueba f*) eliminatoria *f*, prueba *f* clasificatoria.
  (**d**) (*Zool*) celo *m*; **to be on —** estar en celo.
2 *vt* (*also* **to — up**) calentar; (*fig*) acalorar.
3 *vi* (*also* **to — up**) calentarse; (*fig*) acalorarse.
heated ['hiːtid] *adj* acalorado; **to become —** acalorarse.
heatedly ['hiːtidli] *adv* con vehemencia, con pasión; **he replied —** contestó indignado.
heater ['hiːtə*] *n* calentador *m*.
heath [hiːθ] *n* (*place*) brezal *m*; (*plant*) brezo *m*; **native —** patria *f* chica.
heathen ['hiːðən] **1** *adj* pagano. **2** *n* pagano *m*, a *f*; (*fig*) bárbaro *m*, a *f*.
heathenish ['hiːðəniʃ] *adj* pagano, gentílico.
heathenism ['hiːðənizəm] *n* paganismo *m*.
heather ['heðə*] *n* brezo *m*.
heating ['hiːtiŋ] *n* calefacción *f*.
heatproof ['hiːtpruːf] *adj* termorresistente, a prueba de calor.
heatstroke ['hiːtstrəuk] *n* insolación *f*.
heatwave ['hiːtweiv] *n* ola *f* de calor.
heave [hiːv] **1** *n* (*lift*) esfuerzo *m* para levantar; (*pull*) tirón *m* (*on de*); (*push*) empujón *m*; (*throw*) echada *f*, tirada *f*; **with a — of his shoulders** con un fuerte movimiento de hombros; **one more — and they're out** un empujón más y los echamos fuera a todos.
2 *vt* (*irr: pret and ptp* **heaved**, (*Naut*) *pret and ptp* **hove**) (*pull*) tirar de; (*push*) empujar; (*lift*) levantar; (*drag*) arrastrar; (*carry*) llevar; (*throw*) tirar, lanzar; **sigh** exhalar.
3 *vi* (*water etc*) subir y bajar, agitarse; (*surface*) palpitar, ondular; (*feel sick*) basquear, tener náuseas; **it makes me —** me da asco; **to — at, to — on** tirar de, (*Naut*) jalar; **to — in(to) sight** aparecer; **to — to** ponerse al pairo.
heave-ho ['hiːv'həu] *interj* ¡ahora!, (*Naut*) ¡iza!
heaven ['hevn] *n* cielo *m*; **—s** cielos *mpl*; (*good*) **—s!** ¡cielos!; **thank —!** ¡gracias a Dios!; **— forbid!** ¡no lo quiera Dios!; **— forbid that I . . .** Dios me libre de + *infin*; **for —'s sake!** ¡por Dios!; **seventh —** (*fig*) paraíso *m*; **an injustice that cries out to —** una injusticia que clama al cielo; **to move — and earth** mover cielo y tierra (*to* + *infin* para + *infin*); **to stink to high —** heder a perro muerto.
heavenly ['hevnli] *adj* celestial; (*Astron*) celeste; (*fig*) maravilloso, estupendo.
heaven-sent ['hevn'sent] *adj* milagroso.
heavenward(s) ['hevnwəd(z)] *adv* hacia el cielo.
heavily ['hevili] *adv fall, move, tread* pesadamente; *rain* fuertemente, mucho; *concentrate* densamente; *sigh, sleep* profundamente; *drink* con exceso; **— underlined** subrayado con línea gruesa; **to lean —** on apoyarse mucho en; **to lose —** (*team*) sufrir una grave derrota, (*gambler*) tener pérdidas cuantiosas; **it weighs — on him** pesa mucho sobre él.
heavily-built ['hevili'bilt] *adj* corpulento.
heaviness ['hevinis] *n* peso *m*; pesadez *f* (*also fig*); lo fuerte, fuerza *f*; densidad *f*; gravedad *f*; (*drowsiness*) letargo *m*, modorra *f*; **— of heart** tristeza *f*.
heavy ['hevi] *adj* (**a**) pesado; **to be —** ser pesado, pesar mucho; **is it —?** ¿pesa mucho?; **how — are you?** ¿cuánto pesas?
  (**b**) (*fig*) *artillery, cruiser, fall, industry, tread* pesado; *cloth, features, line, sea, type* grueso; *emphasis, expense, meal, rain, scent, shower, wine* fuerte; *concentration, population, traffic* denso; (*boring*) pesado; *atmosphere* pesado, opresivo; *blow* fuerte, duro; *build of person* corpulento; *burden* (*fig*) grave, oneroso; *crop* abundante; *defeat* grave; *feeling* aletargado; *fire* (*Mil*) intenso; *food* indigesto; *heart* triste; *humour* laborioso; *liquid* espeso, viscoso; *loss* considerable, cuantioso; *movement* lento, torpe, pesado; *part* (*Theat*) serio, trágico; *responsibility* grave; *sigh, silence, sleep* profundo; *sky* encapotado; *soil* arcilloso; *surface* difícil; *task* duro, penoso; *eyes*

— with sleep ojos de sueño; **the air was — with scent** el aire estaba cargado de perfumes; **I've had a — day** he estado ocupadísimo todo el día; **to be a — drinker** (*etc*) beber (*etc*) mucho, beber (*etc*) con exceso; **to be a — sleeper** tener el sueño profundo.
heavyweight ['heviweit] *n* peso *m* pesado.
Hebrew ['hiːbruː] **1** *adj* hebreo. **2** *n* hebreo *m*, a *f*. **3** *n* (*language*) hebreo *m*.
Hebrides ['hebridiːz] *pl* Hébridas *fpl*.
heck [hek] *interj* (*euph*) = **hell**.
heckle ['hekl] *vti* interrumpir, molestar con preguntas.
heckler ['heklə*] *n* el (la) que interrumpe (*or molesta*) a un orador.
heckling ['hekliŋ] *n* interrupciones *fpl*, gritos *mpl* de protesta.
hectare ['hektɑː*] *n* hectárea *f*.
hectic ['hektik] *adj* (*fig*) febril; **we had 3 — days** tuvimos 3 días llenos de frenética actividad, tuvimos 3 días llenos de confusión (*or incertidumbre etc*); **he has a — life** tiene una vida muy agitada; **the journey was pretty —** el viaje era para volverse loco.
hectogramme, (*US*) **hectogram** ['hektəugræm] *n* hectogramo *m*.
hectolitre, (*US*) **hectoliter** ['hektəu,liːtə*] *n* hectolitro *m*.
hector ['hektə*] **1** *vt* intimidar con bravatas. **2** *vi* echar bravatas.
he'd [hiːd] = **he would; he had**.
hedge [hedʒ] **1** *n* seto *m* vivo.
  2 *vt* (**a**) cercar con un seto; **to — off** separar con un seto.
  (**b**) (*fig*) **to — something about, to — something in** rodear algo, encerrar algo; **to be —d about with** estar erizado de.
  (**c**) **to — a bet** hacer apuestas compensatorias.
  3 *vi* contestar con evasivas, no querer comprometerse a nada.
hedgehog ['hedʒhɔg] *n* erizo *m*.
hedgehop ['hedʒhɔp] *vi* volar a ras de tierra.
hedgerow ['hedʒrəu] *n* seto *m* vivo.
hedge sparrow ['hedʒ,spærəu] *n* acentor *m* común.
hedonism ['hiːdənizəm] *n* hedonismo *m*.
hedonist ['hiːdənist] *n* hedonista *mf*.
heed [hiːd] **1** *n*: **to give (*or* pay) —** to prestar atención a, hacer caso de; **to take no — of something** no hacer caso de algo, no tener algo en cuenta; **to take — to** + *infin* poner atención en + *infin*; **take —!** ¡atención!
  2 *vt* prestar atención a, hacer caso de; tener en cuenta.
heedless ['hiːdlis] *adj* desatento, descuidado; **to be — of** no hacer caso de.
heedlessly ['hiːdlisli] *adv* sin hacer caso.
heehaw ['hiːhɔː] **1** *n* rebuzno *m*. **2** *vi* rebuznar.
heel¹ [hiːl] **1** *n* (*Anat*) talón *m*, calcañar *m*; (*of shoe*) tacón *m*; (*sl*) canalla *m*; **to be at (*or* on) someone's —s** pisar los talones a uno; **to be down at —** ir mal vestido, estar desaseado; **to be under the — of** estar bajo los talones de; **to bring someone to —** sobreponerse a uno; **to cool one's —s** hacer antesala, tener que esperar; **to kick one's —s** no tener nada que hacer; **to show someone a clean pair of —s, to take to one's —s** poner pies en polvorosa; **to turn on one's —** dar media vuelta.
  2 *vt shoe* poner tacón a; *ball* talonear; **to be well —ed** (*sl*) ser un ricacho.
heel² [hiːl] *vi*: **to — over** ladearse, (*Naut*) zozobrar, escorar.
heft [heft] **1** *n* (*US fam*) influencia *f*; **the — of** la mayor parte de. **2** *vt* levantar; sopesar.
hefty ['hefti] *adj object* pesado; *person* fuerte, fornido; *dose etc* grande.
hegemony [hi'gemɔni] *n* hegemonía *f*.
hegira [he'dʒaiərə] *n* hégira *f*.
he-goat ['hiːgəut] *n* macho *m* cabrío.
heifer ['hefə*] *n* novilla *f*, vaquilla *f*.
heigh [hei] *interj* ¡oye!, ¡eh!
heigh-ho ['hei'həu] *interj* ¡ay!
height [hait] *n* (**a**) altura *f*, elevación *f*, altitud *f*; **— above sea level** altura *f* sobre el nivel del mar; **at a — of 2000 m** a una altura de 2000 m; **to be 20 m in —** medir 20 m de alto, tener una altura de 20 m; **to gain —** ganar altura.
  (**b**) (*of person*) talle *m*, estatura *f*; **of average —** de talle mediano; **he drew himself up to his full —** se irguió; **what — are you?** ¿cuánto mides de alto?
  (**c**) (*hill*) colina *f*, cerro *m*; **the —s** las cumbres.
  (**d**) (*fig*) (*of fever*) crisis *f*; **the — of absurdity** el colmo de lo absurdo; **it's the — of fashion** está muy de moda; **at the — of summer** en los días más calurosos del verano; **at the — of the battle** en los

momentos más críticos de la batalla; **his performance never reached the —s** su actuación distaba mucho de ser perfecta, su actuación nunca nos emocionó como debiera.

heighten ['haitn] vt (raise) elevar, hacer más alto; (increase) aumentar; (enhance) realzar, intensificar.

heinous ['heinəs] adj atroz, nefando.

heir [ɛə*] n heredero m; **— apparent, — at law** heredero m forzoso; **joint —** coheredero m; **universal —** heredero m único; **— to the throne** heredero m del trono; **he is — to a fortune** ha de heredar una fortuna.

heiress ['ɛəres] n heredera f; (fam) soltera f adinerada.

heirloom ['ɛəlu:m] n reliquia f de familia.

heist [haist] (US sl) 1 n robo m (en casa). 2 vt robar (de una casa).

held [held] pret and ptp of **hold**.

Helen ['helin] f Elena, Helena.

helicopter ['helikɔptə*] n helicóptero m.

heliograph ['hi:liəugrɑ:f] n heliógrafo m.

heliotrope ['hi:liətrəup] n heliotropo m.

heliport ['helipɔ:t] n helipuerto m.

helium ['hi:liəm] n helio m.

helix ['hi:liks] n, pl **helices** ['helisi:z] hélice f.

hell [hel] n infierno m; **gambling —** garito m; **—!, oh —!; demonio!; all — was let loose** se desencadenó un ruido infernal; **a — of a lot** muchísimos, la mar de, una barbaridad de; **a — of a noise** un ruido de todos los demonios; **we had a — of a time** (bad) pasamos un rato malísimo, (good) lo pasamos en grande; **who the — are you?** ¿quién demonios es Vd?; **what the — do you want?** ¿qué demonios quiere Vd?; **like —!** ¡ni hablar!; **to run like —** correr a todo correr; **to work like —** trabajar como un demonio; **come — or high water** contra viento y marea; **get the — out of here!** ¡vete al diablo!; **let's get the — out of here!** ¡vámonos!; **to give someone —** poner a uno como un trapo; **to go — for leather** ir como el demonio; **go to —!** ¡vete al diablo!; **to raise —** armar la gorda.

he'll [hi:l] = **he will; he shall.**

hellbent ['hel'bent] adj (a) totalmente resuelto; **to be — on doing something** estar totalmente resuelto a hacer algo. (b) rapidísimo, velocísimo.

Hellene ['heli:n] n heleno m, a f.

Hellenic ['he'li:nik] adj helénico.

hellfire ['hel'faiə*] n llamas fpl del infierno.

hellish ['heliʃ] 1 adj infernal, diabólico; (fam) horrible. 2 adv (fam) muy, terriblemente.

hello [hʌ'ləu] see **hullo.**

helm [helm] n timón m; **to be at the —** (fig) gobernar, estar en el mando.

helmet ['helmit] n casco m.

helmsman ['helmzmən] n, pl **—men** [mən] timonel m.

help [help] 1 n (a) ayuda f; auxilio m, socorro m; favor m, protección f; **—!** ¡socorro!; **by (or with) the — of** con la ayuda de; **without —** sin ayuda de nadie; **to call for —** pedir socorro; **to come to someone's —** acudir en auxilio de uno.

(b) **there's no — for it** no hay más remedio; **to be past —** estar desahuciado.

(c) (person: servant) criada f; (in shop etc) empleado m; **daily —** asistenta f; **mother's —** niñera f; **she has no — in the house** no tiene criada; **we're short of — in the shop** nos falta personal en la tienda; **he's a great —** me ayuda muchísimo; **you're a great —!** (iro) ¡valiente ayuda!

2 vt (a) ayudar; (esp in distress) auxiliar, socorrer; scheme etc promover; progress facilitar; pain aliviar; **so — me God!** bien lo sabe Dios; **to — someone to do something** ayudar a uno a hacer algo; **this will — to save it** esto contribuirá a salvarlo; **to — along** person ayudar, scheme etc promover, fomentar; **to — someone down** ayudar a uno a bajar; **to — someone on with a dress** ayudar a uno a ponerse un vestido; **to — someone out** ayudar a uno, (of vehicle) ayudar a uno a bajar; **to — someone out of a jam** ayudar a uno a salir de un apuro; **to — someone up** ayudar a uno a subir.

(b) (at table) servir; **to — someone to soup** servir la sopa a uno.

(c) (avoid) **he can't — coughing** no puede dejar de toser; **I couldn't — (doing) it** no pude menos de hacerlo; **it can't be —ed** no hay más remedio; **he won't if I can** — it no lo hará si puede evitarlo; **can I — it if it rains?** ¿es que yo puedo impedir que llueva?; **don't spend more than you can — no** gastes más de lo necesario.

3 vi (also **to — out**) ayudar.

4 vr: **to — oneself** (at table) servirse; **— yourself!**

(to food) ¡sírvete!, (to other things) está a su disposición, tome cuanto quiera; **to — oneself to** food servirse, (steal) alzarse con, llevarse, robar.

helper ['helpə*] n ayudante m, asistente m, a f; (co-worker) colaborador m, ora f.

helpful ['helpfu l] adj útil, provechoso; person servicial, atento; **he was very — to me** me ayudó mucho; **you have been most —** Vd ha sido muy amable.

helpfully ['helpfəli] adv amablemente.

helpfulness ['helpfulnis] n utilidad f; (of person) amabilidad f.

helping ['helpiŋ] n porción f, ración f; **will you have a second —?** ¿quiere Vd servirse más?

helpless ['helplis] adj (forsaken) desamparado; (destitute) desvalido; (powerless) impotente; (of weak character) débil, incapaz, inútil; creature indefenso; invalid que no puede hacer nada en absoluto; **we were — to do anything about it** nos veíamos imposibilitados para remediarlo; **to feel —** sentirse perplejo, estar indeciso.

helplessly ['helplisli] adv struggle en vano; **he said —** dijo indeciso.

helplessness ['helplisnis] n desamparo m; impotencia f; incapacidad f, inutilidad f; irresolución f.

helpmate ['helpmeit] n buen compañero m, buena compañera f; (spouse) esposo m, a f.

help-page ['help'peidʒ] n consultorio m.

helter-skelter ['heltə'skeltə*] 1 adv atropelladamente. 2 n desbandada f general.

hem [hem] 1 n dobladillo m, bastilla f; (edge) orilla f. 2 vt: **to — in** encerrar, cercar (also Mil).

he-man ['hi:mæn] n, pl **—men** [men] (fam) machote m.

hemiplegia [hemi'pli:dʒiə] n hemiplejía f.

hemisphere ['hemisfiə*] n hemisferio m.

hemistich ['hemistik] n hemistiquio m.

hemline ['hemlain] n (Sew) bajo m (del vestido).

hemlock ['hemlɔk] n cicuta f.

hemp [hemp] n cáñamo m; **Indian —** hachich m.

hen [hen] n gallina f; (female bird) hembra f.

henbane ['henbein] n beleño m.

hence [hens] adv (a) (place) de aquí, desde aquí; **—!** ¡fuera de aquí!

(b) (time) desde ahora; **5 years —** de aquí a 5 años.

(c) (therefore) por lo tanto, por eso; **— my letter** de aquí que le escribiera; **— the fact that** de aquí que.

henceforth ['hens'fɔ:θ] adv, **henceforward** ['hens'fɔ:wəd] adv de hoy en adelante, (of past time) en lo sucesivo.

henchman ['hentʃmən] n, pl **—men** [mən] (follower) secuaz m, partidario m; (guard) guardaespaldas m.

hendecasyllabic ['hendekəsi'læbik] adj endecasílabo.

hendecasyllable ['hendekə,siləbl] n endecasílabo m.

henhouse ['hen'haus] n gallinero m.

henna ['henə] n alheña f.

hen party ['hen,pɑ:ti] n (fam) tertulia f de mujeres.

henpecked ['henpekt] adj dominado por su mujer.

Henry ['henri] m Enrique.

hep [hep] adj: **to get —** (sl) enfrascarse en los encantos de la música, dejarse dominar por el ritmo de la música.

her [hə:*] 1 pron (acc) la; (dat) le; (after prep) ella. 2 poss adj su(s).

herald ['herəld] 1 n heraldo m; (fig) precursor m, anunciador m. 2 vt anunciar, proclamar.

heraldic [he'rældik] adj heráldico.

heraldry ['herəldri] n heráldica f.

herb [hə:b] n hierba f.

herbaceous [hə:'beifəs] adj herbáceo.

herbage ['hə:bidʒ] n herbaje m, vegetación f, plantas fpl.

herbal ['hə:bəl] adj herbario.

herbalist ['hə:bəlist] n herbolario m, a f.

herbarium [hə:'bɛəriəm] n herbario m.

herbivorous [hə:'bivərəs] adj herbívoro.

Herculean [,hə:kju'li:ən] adj hercúleo.

Hercules ['hə:kjuli:z] m Hércules.

herd [hə:d] 1 n rebaño m, hato m, manada f; (of pigs) piara f; (of people etc) multitud f, tropel m; **the common —** el vulgo; **— instinct** instinto m gregario. 2 vt (tend) guardar; (gather) reunir en manada (etc); (move) llevar en manada. 3 vi: **to — together** reunirse en manada, (in confusion) apiñarse unos contra otros; (people) reunirse, ir juntos.

herd-book ['hə:dbuk] n libro m genealógico.

herdsman ['hə:dzmən] n, pl **—men** [mən] (of cattle) vaquero m; (of sheep etc) pastor m.

here [hiə*] adv (place where) aquí; (motion to) acá; **—!** (at rollcall) ¡presente!, (offering something) ¡toma!, (interj) ¡oye!, ¡eh!; **— and now** ahora mismo; — **and there** aquí y allá; —, **there and everywhere** en todas partes; — **below** aquí abajo; **in** —, **please** por aquí, por favor; **up to** — hasta aquí; **my mate** — **will do it** este compañero mío lo hará; **and** — **he laughed** y en este punto se rió; — **is,** — **are he** aquí; — **it is** aquí lo tiene Vd; **that's neither** — **nor there** eso no viene al caso; **spring is** — ha llegado la primavera; **he's** — **at last** por fin ha llegado; —**'s to X!** ¡vaya por X!; **come** — **!** ¡ven acá!; — **he comes** ya viene; *see* **go.**

hereabouts ['hiərə,bauts] *adv* por aquí (cerca).
hereafter [hiər'ɑ:ftə*] **1** *adv* en el futuro. **2** *n* futuro *m*; **the H**— la otra vida.
hereby ['hiə'bai] *adv* por este medio; (*with reference to document*) por la presente.
hereditary [hi'reditəri] *adj* hereditario.
heredity [hi'rediti] *n* herencia *f*.
heresy ['herəsi] *n* herejía *f*.
heretic ['herətik] *n* hereje *mf*.
heretical [hi'retikəl] *adj* herético.
hereupon ['hiərə'pɔn] *adv* en seguida.
herewith ['hiə'wið] *adv* junto con esto; **I send you** — ... le mando adjunto ...
heritage ['heritidʒ] *n* herencia *f*; (*fig*) patrimonio *m*.
hermaphrodite [hə:'mæfrədait] **1** *adj* hermafrodita. **2** *n* hermafrodita *f*.
hermetic [hə:'metik] *adj* hermético.
hermetically [hə:'metikəli] *adv* herméticamente.
hermit ['hə:mit] *n* ermitaño *m*.
hermitage ['hə:mitidʒ] *n* ermita *f*.
hernia ['hə:niə] *n* hernia *f*.
hero ['hiərəu] *n*, *pl* **heroes** ['hiərəuz] héroe *m*; (*Lit etc*) protagonista *m*, personaje *m* principal.
Herod ['herəd] *m* Herodes.
heroic [hi'rəuik] *adj* heroico.
heroically [hi'rəuikəli] *adv* heroicamente.
heroin ['herəuin] *n* heroína *f*.
heroine ['herəuin] *n* heroína *f*; (*Lit etc*) protagonista *f*, personaje *m* principal.
heroism ['herəuizəm] *n* heroísmo *m*.
heron ['herən] *n* garza *f* real.
hero worship ['hiərəu,wə:ʃip] *n* culto *m* a los héroes.
herring ['heriŋ] *n* arenque *m*; **red** — pista *f* falsa, ardid *m* para apartar la atención del asunto principal.
herringbone ['heriŋbəun] *n*: — **pattern** muestra *f* espiga; — **stitch** punto *m* de escapulario.
herring-pond ['heriŋpɔnd] *n*: (*hum*) **to cross the** — cruzar el charco.
hers [hə:z] *poss pron* (el) suya, (la) suya *etc*.
herself [hə:'self] *pron* (*subject*) ella misma; (*acc, dat*) se; (*after prep*) sí (misma); *see* **oneself.**
he's [hi:z] = **he is; he has.**
hesitancy ['hezitənsi] *n* = **hesitation.**
hesitant ['hezitənt] *adj* vacilante, irresoluto, indeciso; **I am somewhat** — **about accepting it** no me resuelvo a aceptarlo.
hesitantly ['hezitəntli] *adv* con irresolución; **he said** — dijo indeciso, dijo perplejo.
hesitate ['heziteit] *vi* vacilar, mostrarse indeciso; (*in speech*) titubear; **to** — **about,** **to** — **over** no tomar una resolución sobre; **he** —**d over his reply** tardó en dar su respuesta; **to** — **to** + *infin* vacilar en + *infin*; **I** — **to condemn him outright** no me puedo persuadir a condenarlo del todo; **don't** — **to ask me** no vacile en pedírmelo.
hesitation [,hezi'teiʃən] *n* vacilación *f*, irresolución *f*, indecisión *f*; **without the slightest** — sin vacilar; **I feel a certain** — **about it** tengo algunas dudas acerca de ello.
het [het] *adj* (*fam*): **to get** — **up** acalorarse, emocionarse (*about, over* por); **don't get so** — **up!** ¡tranquilízate!
heterodox ['hetərədɔks] *adj* heterodoxo.
heterodoxy ['hetərədɔksi] *n* heterodoxia *f*.
heterogeneous ['hetərəu'dʒi:niəs] *adj* heterogéneo.
heterosexual ['hetərəu'seksjuəl] **1** *adj* heterosexual. **2** *n* heterosexual *mf*.
heterosexuality ['hetərəu,seksju'æliti] *n* heterosexualidad *f*.
hew [hju:] *vt* (*irr: pret* **hewed,** *ptp* **hewed** *or* **hewn**) cortar, tajar; (*shape*) labrar, tallar; **to** — **down** talar; **to** — **out** excavar; **career** hacerse.
hewn [hju:n] *ptp of* **hew.**
hex [heks] (*US fam*) **1** *n* bruja *f*. **2** *vt* embrujar.
hexagon ['heksəgən] *n* hexágono *m*.
hexagonal [hek'sægənəl] *adj* hexagonal.
hexameter [hek'sæmitə*] *n* hexámetro *m*.
hey [hei] *interj* ¡oye!, ¡eh!
heyday ['heidei] *n* auge *m*, apogeo *m*, buenos tiempos *mpl*; **in the** — **of the theatre** cuando el teatro estaba en su apogeo.

hi [hai] *interj* ¡oye!, ¡eh!; (*hullo*) ¡hola!
hiatus [hai'eitəs] *n* (*Gram*) hiato *m*; (*fig*) vacío *m*, laguna *f*, interrupción *f*; solución *f* de continuidad.
hibernate ['haibəneit] *vi* invernar, hibernar.
hibernation [,haibə'neiʃən] *n* invernación *f*, hibernación *f*.
hiccough ['hikʌp], **hiccup** ['hikʌp] **1** *n* hipo *m*; **to have** —**s** tener hipo. **2** *vi* hipar; **"yes", he** —**ed** "sí", dijo hipando.
hick [hik] (*US*) **1** *adj* rústico, de aldea. **2** *n* palurdo *m*.
hickory ['hikəri] *n* nuez *f* dura.
hid [hid] *pret of* **hide.**
hidden ['hidn] **1** *ptp of* **hide.** **2** *adj* escondido; (*fig*) oculto, secreto.
hide[1] [haid] *n* (*skin*) piel *f*, pellejo *m*; (*tanned*) cuero *m*; (*of person*) pellejo *m*.
hide[2] [haid] **1** *n* (*Hunting*) paranza *f*, trepa *f*.
2 *vt* (*irr: pret* **hid,** *ptp* **hidden**) esconder (*from* de); ocultar (*from* a, de); *feeling etc* ocultar, encubrir, disimular; **he's hiding something** tiene algo que no quiere revelar.
3 *vi* esconderse, ocultarse (*from* de); **he's hiding behind his chief** se está buscando la protección de su jefe.
hide-and-seek ['haidən'si:k] *n* escondite *m*; **to play** — **with** jugar al escondite con (*also fig*).
hidebound ['haidbaund] *adj* rígido, aferrado a la tradición.
hideous ['hidiəs] *adj* horrible.
hideously ['hidiəsli] *adv* horriblemente; — **ugly** feísimo.
hideout ['haidaut] *n* escondrijo *m*, guarida *f*.
hiding[1] ['haidiŋ] *n* (*beating*) paliza *f*.
hiding[2] ['haidiŋ] *n*: **to be in** — estar escondido; **he is in** — **in France** se ha refugiado en Francia; **to go into** — ocultarse, refugiarse.
hiding place ['haidiŋpleis] *n* escondrijo *m*.
hie [hai] (*arch or hum*) **1** *vt* apresurar. **2** *vi* ir, ir con prisa, correr. **3** *vr*: **to** — **oneself home** apresurarse a volver a casa.
hierarchic(al) [,haiə'rɑ:kik(əl)] *adj* jerárquico.
hierarchy ['haiərɑ:ki] *n* jerarquía *f*.
hieroglyph ['haiərəglif] *n* jeroglífico *m*.
hieroglyphic [,haiərə'glifik] **1** *adj* jeroglífico. **2** *n* jeroglífico *m*.
hi-fi ['hai'fai] (*abbr of* **high fidelity**) **1** *adj* de alta fidelidad. **2** *n* alta fidelidad *f*.
higgledy-piggledy ['higldi'pigldi] (*fam*) **1** *adv* be *etc* en desorden; *do etc* de cualquier modo. **2** *adj* revuelto, desordenado.
high [hai] **1** *adj* (**a**) alto; **it's 20 feet** — tiene 20 pies de alto; **how** — **is that tree?** ¿qué altura tiene ese árbol?, ¿cuánto mide ese árbol de alto?; **I knew him when he was so** — le conocí tamañito, le conocí de niño.
(**b**) (*fig*) *frequency, tension, temperature, treason, command etc* alto; *number, speed* grande; *price, rent, stake* elevado; *official, court* superior; *post* importante; *altar, mass, street* mayor; *priest* sumo; *quality* superior, bueno; *opinion* bueno; *note* agudo; *sea* tempestuoso; *wind* recio, fuerte; *explosive* de gran potencia; *colour* subido; *polish* brillante; (*Cook*) *game* manido; *food* pasado; — **and dry** en seco; **to leave someone** — **and dry** dejar a uno plantado; **and mighty** engreído.
2 *adv* (**a**) *fly etc* a gran altura; — **above my head** muy por encima de mi cabeza; **it rose** — **in the air** se elevó por los aires; **it sailed** — **over the house** voló por los aires muy por encima de la casa.
(**b**) **to aim** — picar muy alto; **to blow** — soplar recio; **the numbers go as** — **as 20** los números llegan hasta 20; **I had to go as** — **as £8 for it** tuve que pagar 8 libras nada menos por él; **the bidding went as** — **as £5** se ofrecieron hasta 5 libras; **it went for as** — **as £6** se vendió por 6 libras nada menos; **to hunt** — **and low for someone** buscar a uno por todas partes; **to run** — (*sea*) embravecerse, (*river*) estar crecido; (*of feelings*) encenderse, exaltarse; **feelings were running** — la gente estaba muy acalorada.
3 *n* (*Meteorol*) zona *f* de alta presión; **on** — en las alturas, en el cielo; **exports have reached a new** — las exportaciones han alcanzado cifras nunca conocidas antes.
highborn ['haibɔ:n] *adj* linajudo.
highbrow ['haibrau] **1** *adj* intelectual, culto, esotérico. **2** *n* intelectual *mf*, persona *f* culta.
high-class ['hai'klɑ:s] *adj* de clase superior.
higher ['haiə*] **1** *adj comp of* **high;** más alto; *form, study etc* superior; *price* más elevado; *number, speed* mayor; **any number** — **than 6** cualquier número superior a 6.
2 *adv comp of* **high; to fly** — **than the clouds** volar

encima de las nubes; **to fly — still** volar a mayor altura aun; **— up the hill** más arriba en la colina; **— up the road** más hacia el final de la calle.

highfalutin(g) ['haifə'luːtin] *adj* presuntuoso, pomposo.

high-flown ['haifləun] *adj* exagerado, altisonante.

high-grade ['hai'greid] *adj* de calidad superior.

high-handed ['hai'hændid] *adj* arbitrario, despótico.

high-hat ['hai'hæt] *adj* (*fam*) encopetado, esnob.

high-heeled ['hai'hiːld] *adj* shoes de tacones altos.

highjack ['haidʒæk] (*fam*) atracar.

high jump ['haidʒʌmp] *n* salto *m* de altura.

highlander ['hailəndə*] *n* montañés *m*, esa *f*.

highlands ['hailəndz] *npl* tierras *fpl* altas, montañas *fpl*; **the H—** las tierras altas de Escocia.

high-level ['hai'levl] *adj* de alto nivel.

highlight ['hailait] **1** *n* (*Art*) toque *m* de luz; (*fig*) aspecto *m* notable, aspecto *m* interesante; momento *m* culminante. **2** *vt* subrayar, destacar.

highly ['haili] *adv* (**a**) muy, muy bien, sumamente; **— amusing** divertidísimo; **— coloured** (*fig*) exagerado; **— paid** muy bien pagado, muy bien retribuido; **— placed official** oficial *m* de categoría, funcionario *m* importante; **— seasoned** muy picante; **— strung** muy excitable, hipertenso. (**b**) **to praise someone —** alabar mucho a uno; **to speak — of** decir mil bienes de; **to think — of** someone tener en mucho a uno.

high-minded ['hai'maindid] *adj* person de nobles pensamientos; act noble, altruista.

highness ['hainis] *n* altura *f*; **H—** (*as title*) Alteza *f*; **His (or Her) Royal H—** Su Alteza Real.

high-pitched ['hai'pitʃt] *adj* de tono alto, agudo; *voice* aflautado.

high-powered ['hai'pauəd] *adj* de gran potencia; *person* enérgico, dinámico.

high-pressure ['hai'preʃə*] *adj* de alta presión; (*fig*) enérgico, dinámico, apremiante.

high-ranking ['hai'ræŋkin] *adj* de categoría; *official* de alto grado, (*Mil*) de alta (graduación).

highroad ['hairəud] *n* carretera *f*; (*fig*) camino *m* real (*to* de).

high-sounding ['hai'saundin] *adj* altisonante.

high-speed ['hai'spiːd] *adj* *vehicle etc* de alta velocidad; *test etc* rápido.

high-spirited ['hai'spiritid] *adj* brioso, animoso; *horse* fogoso; (*merry*) alegre.

high-tension ['hai'tenʃən] *adj* de alta tensión.

high-test ['hai'test] *adj*: **— fuel** supercarburante *m*.

high-up ['hai'ʌp] (*fam*) **1** *adj* de categoría, importante. **2** *n* oficial *m* importante, pez *m* gordo.

highway ['haiwei] *n* carretera *f*.

highwayman ['haiweimən] *n*, *pl* **-men** [mən] salteador *m* de caminos.

hijack ['haidʒæk] *vt* (*US fam*) = **highjack**.

hike [haik] **1** *n* caminata *f*, excursión *f* a pie; **to go on a —** dar una caminata.
2 *vt*: **to — it** ir a pie.
3 *vi* dar una caminata, ir de excursión (a pie); ir a pie, ir andando.

hiker ['haikə*] *n* excursionista *mf*.

hiking ['haikin] *n* excursionismo *m* a pie.

hilarious [hi'lɛəriəs] *adj* scene etc divertido, regocijante; *laughter* alegre.

hilarity [hi'læriti] *n* regocijo *m*, alegría *f*; **it caused — in the audience** provocó las carcajadas del público.

hill [hil] *n* colina *f*, cerro *m*, otero *m*; (*high*) montaña *f*; (*slope*) cuesta *f*; **to chase someone up — and down dale** perseguir a uno por todas partes; **to curse someone up — and down dale** echar mil pestes de uno; **to take to the —s** echarse al monte.

hillbilly ['hil'bili] *n* (*US*) rústico *m* montañés.

hillock ['hilək] *n* montículo *m*, altozano *m*.

hillside ['hilsaid] *n* ladera *f*.

hilltop ['hiltɔp] *n* cumbre *f*.

hilly ['hili] *adj* montañoso, accidentado; *road* de fuertes pendientes.

hilt [hilt] *n* puño *m*, empuñadura *f*; **up to the —** hasta las cachas; **to back someone up to the —** apoyar a uno incondicionalmente; **to prove something up to the —** probar algo completamente, demostrar algo hasta la saciedad.

him [him] *pron* (*acc*) le, lo; (*dat*) le; (*after prep*) él.

Himalayas [ˌhiməˈleiəz] *pl* los montes Himalaya, el Himalaya.

himself [him'self] *pron* (*subject*) él mismo; (*acc, dat*) se; (*after prep*) sí (mismo); *see* **oneself**.

hind[1] [haind] *n* cierva *f*.

hind[2] [haind] *adj* trasero, posterior.

hinder ['hində*] *vt* person estorbar, impedir; progress etc estorbar, dificultar; trade, traffic entorpecer; **to —**

— someone from doing something impedir a uno hacer algo.

hindmost ['haindməust] *adj* postrero, último.

hindrance ['hindrəns] *n* estorbo *m*, obstáculo *m* (*to* para).

Hindu ['hin'duː] **1** *adj* hindú. **2** *n* hindú *mf*.

Hindustan [ˌhindu'staːn] Indostán *m*.

Hindustani [ˌhindu'staːni] *n* (*language*) indostánico *m*, indostaní *m*.

hinge [hindʒ] **1** *n* gozne *m*, bisagra *f*; charnela *f* (*also* *Zool*); (*for stamps*) fijasello *m*; (*fig*) eje *m*.
2 *vt* engoznar.
3 *vi* moverse sobre goznes; **to — on** moverse sobre, girar sobre; (*fig*) depender de.

hinged [hindʒd] *adj* con goznes, de bisagra.

hint [hint] **1** *n* (**a**) (*suggestion*) indirecta *f*, indicación *f*; insinuación *f*; (*advice*) consejo *m*; **broad —** indicación *f* inconfundible; **—s for purchasers** aviso *m* a los compradores; **—s on maintenance** instrucciones *fpl* para la manutención; **to drop** (*or* let fall, throw out) **a —** soltar una indirecta; **to drop a — that** insinuar que; **take a — from** me permite que te dé un consejo; **to take the —** aprovechar la indicación. (**b**) (*trace*) señal *f*, indicio *m*; **without the least — of** sin la menor señal de; **with just a — of garlic** con un ligerísimo sabor a ajo; **with a — of irony** con un dejo de ironía.
2 *vt*: **to — that** insinuar que.
3 *vi* soltar indirectas; **to — at** hacer alusión a; **what are you —ing (at)?** ¿qué pretende Vd insinuar?

hinterland ['hintəlænd] *n* interior *m*, traspaís *m*.

hip[1] [hip] *n* (*Anat*) cadera *f*.

hip[2] [hip] *n* (*Bot*) escaramujo *m*.

hip[3] [hip] *interj*: **— hurray!** ¡viva!

hipped[1] [hipt] *adj* (*Archit*) a cuatro aguas.

hipped[2] [hipt] *adj* (*US: fam*) triste; enojado, resentido; **— on** obsesionado por.

hippie ['hipi] *n* (*fam*) hippie *mf*.

hippo ['hipəu] *n* (*fam*) hipopótamo *m*.

Hippocrates [hi'pɔkrətiːz] *m* Hipócrates.

hippopotamus [ˌhipə'pɔtəməs] *n*, *pl* **hippopotamuses** [ˌhipə'pɔtəməsiz] *or* **hippopotami** [ˌhipə'pɔtəmai] hipopótamo *m*.

hire ['haiə*] **1** *n* alquiler *m*; (*of person*) salario *m*, jornal *m*; **"for —"** "se alquila"; **to be on —** estar de alquiler.
2 *vt* (*also* **to — out**) alquilar; *person* contratar, emplear.

hireling ['haiəlin] *n* mercenario *m*.

hire purchase ['haiə'pəːtʃis] *n* compra *f* a plazos.

hirsute ['həːsjuːt] *adj* hirsuto.

his [hiz] **1** *poss adj* su(s). **2** *poss pron* (el) suyo, (la) suya *etc*.

Hispanic [his'pænik] *adj* hispánico.

hispanicism [his'pænisizəm] *n* hispanismo *m*.

hispanicize [his'pænisaiz] *vt* españolizar, hispanizar.

hispanist ['hispənist] *n* hispanista *mf*.

hispanophile [his'pænəufail] *n* hispanófilo *m*, a *f*.

hispanophobe [his'pænəufaub] *n* hispanófobo *m*, a *f*.

hiss [his] **1** *n* silbido *m*, siseo *m*; (*of protest*) silbido *m*.
2 *vt* silbar; **to — an actor off the stage** abuchear a un actor hasta que abandone la escena.
3 *vi* silbar, sisear; (*in protest*) silbar.

histology [his'tɔlədʒi] *n* histología *f*.

historian [his'tɔːriən] *n* historiador *m*, ora *f*.

historic(al) [his'tɔrik(əl)] *adj* histórico.

historiography [ˌhistɔri'ɔgrəfi] *n* historiografía *f*.

history ['histəri] *n* historia *f*; **natural —** historia *f* natural; **that's ancient —** ésa es cosa vieja; **to go down in —** pasar a la historia (*as* como); **to know the inner — of an affair** conocer el secreto de un asunto.

histrionic [ˌhistri'ɔnik] *adj* histriónico; *person* exagerado.

histrionics [ˌhistri'ɔniks] *npl* histrionismo *m*.

hit [hit] **1** *n* (**a**) (*blow*) golpe *m*; (*shot*) tiro *m* certero; (*with shell etc*) impacto *m*; (*good guess*) acierto *m*; **direct —** impacto *m* directo; **we made 3 —s on the target** dimos 3 veces en el blanco; **that's a — at you** lo dijo por ti; **he made a — at the government** hizo un ataque contra el gobierno.
(**b**) (*Mus, Theat etc*) éxito *m*, sensación *f*; **to be a —** obtener un éxito, ser un triunfo; **the song was a big —** la canción se hizo popularísima; **to make a — with someone** caer en gracia a uno.
2 *attr* (*fam*) sensacional; **— songs of the twenties** las canciones más populares de los años veinte.
3 (*irr*: pret and ptp **hit**) *vt* (**a**) (*strike*) person golpear, pegar; (*wound*) herir; *target* alcanzar, hacer blanco en, acertar, dar en; **to — someone a blow** dar

un golpe a uno; **to — one's head against a wall** dar con la cabeza contra una pared; **the president was — by 3 bullets** el presidente fue alcanzado por 3 balas; **the house was — by a bomb** la casa fue blanco de una bomba; **I realized my plane had been —** me di cuenta de que mi avión había sido tocado; **his father used to — him** su padre le pegaba; **then it — me** (*of realization*) aquello fue el flechazo; en seguida me di cuenta.
(b) (*collide with*) chocar con, dar contra.
(c) (*damage*) hacer daño a, afectar; **the crops were — by the rain** las lluvias dañaron los cultivos; **the news — him hard** la noticia le afectó mucho; **the company has been hard —** la compañía ha sido afectada de mala manera, la compañía ha sufrido un rudo golpe.
(d) (*find, reach*) llegar a, alcanzar; **problem** tropezar con; **when we — the main road** cuando lleguemos a la carretera.
(e) **to — off** (*imitate*) imitar, remedar; *resemblance* coger; (*describe*) describir con gran acierto; **to — it off with someone** hacer buenas migas con uno; **they don't — it off** no se llevan bien.
4 *vi* (*collide*) chocar; **to — against** chocar con, dar contra; **to — at** asestar un golpe a, (*fig*) atacar, apuntar a, satirizar; **to — back** devolver golpe por golpe, defenderse; **to — on** dar con, tropezar con; **I — on the idea** se me ocurrió la idea; **to — out** lanzar un ataque, (*wildly*) repartir golpes; **to — out at someone** asestar un golpe a uno, (*fig*) atacar a uno; **to do something — or miss** hacer algo a la buena de Dios; **to — and run** atacar y retirarse.
hit-and-run [ˈhitənˈrʌn] *adj*: **— driver** conductor *m* que atropella y huye.
hitch [hitʃ] 1 *n* (*tug*) tirón *m*; (*knot*) cote *m*, vuelta *f* de cabo; (*fig*) obstáculo *m*, dificultad *f*; **without a —** a pedir de boca; **there was a — of 15 minutes** hubo un retraso de 15 minutos; **there's been a — ha** surgido una dificultad.
2 *vt* (a) (*shift*) mover de un tirón; **he —ed a chair over** acercó una silla a tirones; **to — up** alzar.
(b) (*fasten*) atar, amarrar (*to* a); **to — a horse to a wagon** enganchar un caballo a un carro.
(c) **to — lifts** hacer autostop; **to — a lift to Rome** lograr que un automovilista le lleve a uno a Roma.
(d) **to get —ed** (*sl*) casarse.
hitch-hike [ˈhitʃhaik] *vi* hacer autostop.
hitch-hiker [ˈhitʃhaikə*] *n* autostopista *mf*.
hitch-hiking [ˈhitʃhaikiŋ] *n* autostop *m*.
hither [ˈhiðə*] *adv* (*lit*) acá; **— and thither** acá y acullá.
hitherto [ˈhiðəˈtuː] *adv* hasta ahora.
Hittite [ˈhitait] 1 *adj* heteo, hitita. 2 *n* heteo *m*, a *f*, hitita *mf*. 3 *n* (*language*) hitita *m*.
hive [haiv] *n* colmena *f*; **a — of industry** un centro de industria, un lugar donde se trabaja muchísimo.
hoard [hɔːd] 1 *n* acumulación *f*; provisión *f*; (*money*) tesoro *m* escondido.
2 *vt* (*also* **to — up**) acumular, amontonar (en secreto); *money* atesorar; *goods in short supply* retener, acaparar.
hoarding[1] [ˈhɔːdiŋ] *n* (*act*) acumulación *f*, retención *f*; acaparamiento *m*.
hoarding[2] [ˈhɔːdiŋ] *n* (*fence*) valla *f* de construcción; (*for posters*) cartelera *f*.
hoarfrost [ˈhɔːˈfrɔst] *n* escarcha *f*.
hoarse [hɔːs] *adj* ronco; **to be —** tener la voz ronca; **to shout oneself —** enronquecer a fuerza de gritar.
hoarsely [ˈhɔːsli] *adv* en voz ronca.
hoarseness [ˈhɔːsnis] *n* (*Med*) ronquera *f*; (*hoarse quality*) ronquedad *f*.
hoary [ˈhɔːri] *adj* cano; *joke etc* viejo.
hoax [həuks] 1 *n* trampa *f*, truco *m*, mistificación *f*.
2 *vt* engañar, burlar, mistificar.
hobble [ˈhɔbl] 1 *n* (*lameness*) cojera *f*; (*rope*) maniota *f*; **to walk with a —** cojear.
2 *vt* *horse* manear.
3 *vi* (*also* **to — along**) cojear, andar cojeando; **to — to the door** ir cojeando a la puerta.
hobbledehoy [ˈhɔbldiˈhɔi] *n* gamberro *m*.
hobby [ˈhɔbi] *n* pasatiempo *m*, afición *f*; **it's just a —** es sólo un pasatiempo; **he began to paint as a —** empezó a pintar como distracción.
hobby-horse [ˈhɔbihɔːs] *n* caballito *m* (de niño), caballo *m* mecedor; (*fig*) caballo *m* de batalla, tema *f*; **he's riding his — again** ha vuelto a la misma canción.
hobgoblin [ˈhɔbˌgɔblin] *n* duende *m*, trasgo *m*.
hobnail [ˈhɔbneil] *n* clavo *m* (de botas).
hobnailed [ˈhɔbneild] *adj* *boots* con clavos, claveteado.

hobnob [ˈhɔbnɔb] *vi* tratarse con familiaridad; **to — with** codearse con, alternar con.
hobo [ˈhəubəu] *n* (*US*) vagabundo *m*.
hock[1] [hɔk] *n* (*Anat*) corvejón *m*.
hock[2] [hɔk] *n* (*wine*) vino *m* del Rin.
hock[3] [hɔk] *vt* (*fam*) empeñar.
hockey [ˈhɔki] *n* hockey *m*.
hocus-pocus [ˈhəukəsˈpaukəs] *n* (*jugglery*) abracadabra *m*, pasapasa *m*; (*deception*) trampa *f*.
hod [hɔd] *n* cuezo *m*, capacho *m*.
hodgepodge [ˈhɔdʒpɔdʒ] *n* = **hotchpotch**.
hoe [həu] 1 *n* azada *f*, azadón *m*, sacho *m*. 2 *vt* *earth* azadonar; *crop* sachar.
hog [hɔg] 1 *n* cerdo *m*, puerco *m* (*also fig*); **to go the whole —** liarse la manta a la cabeza, poner toda la carne en el asador.
2 *vt* *food* devorar; (*take for oneself*) acaparar, tragarse lo mejor de; **to — all the credit** atribuirse todo el mérito de algo.
Hogmanay [ˈhɔgmənei] *n* (*Scot*) noche *f* vieja.
hogshead [ˈhɔgzhed] *n* medida *f* de capacidad (= 52,5 galones = (*approx*) 225 litros).
hoist [hɔist] 1 *n* (*lift*) montacargas *m*; (*crane*) grúa *f*; **to give someone a — (up)** ayudar a uno a subir.
2 *vt* alzar, levantar (*also* **to — up**); *flag* enarbolar, (*Naut*) izar.
hoity-toity [ˈhɔitiˈtɔiti] 1 *adj* presumido, repipi. 2 *interj* ¡tate!
hold [həuld] 1 *n* (a) (*grasp*) agarro *m*, asimiento *m*; (*Wrestling*) presa *f*; **to catch** (*or* **get, lay, seize, take) — of** agarrar, asirse de, coger; **catch —!** ¡toma!; **to get — of** (*fig*) (*take over*) adquirir, apoderarse de, (*obtain*) procurarse, conseguir; **where did you get — of that?** ¿dónde adquirió Vd eso?; **we're trying to get — of him** tratamos de ponernos en contacto con él; **where did you get — of that idea?** ¿de dónde colige Vd eso?; **you get — of some odd ideas** te formas unas ideas muy raras; **to have — of** estar agarrado a; **to keep — of** seguir agarrado a; (*fig*) guardar para sí; **to relax one's —** desasirse (*on* de).
(b) (*place to grip*) asidero *m*.
(c) (*fig*) influencia *f*, dominio *m* (*over* sobre); arraigo *m*; **to gain a firm — over someone** llegar a dominar a uno; **to have a — (thing)** estar arraigado (*over* en); **to have a — over** (*person*) dominar a uno, ejercer gran influencia sobre uno.
(d) (*Naut*) bodega *f*.
2 (*irr: pret & ptp* **held**) *vt* (a) (*general sense*) tener; (*take — of*) agarrar, coger; (*bear weight of*) soportar; *attention* mantener; *belief* tener; *note* sostener; *road* agarrarse a; **— him or he'll fall** sostén gale que va a caer; **he held my arm** me tuvo por el brazo; **— this for a moment** coge esto un momento; **to — something tight** agarrar algo fuertemente; **to — someone tight** abrazar a uno estrechamente; **to — something in place** sujetar algo en un lugar; **to — someone to his promise** hacer que uno cumpla su promesa; **he —s the key to the mystery** él tiene la clave del misterio; **he held us spellbound** nos tuvo embelesados; **can he — an audience?** ¿sabe mantener el interés de un público? see **hand** *etc*.
(b) (*keep back*) retener, guardar; **I will — the money for you** guardaré el dinero para ti; **the police held him for 3 days** le detuvo la policía durante 3 días; **we are —ing it pending inquiries** lo guardamos mientras se hagan indagaciones.
(c) (*check, restrain*) *enemy, breath* contener; **— it!** ¡para!; **— everything!** ¡que se pare todo!; **there was no —ing him** no había manera de detenerle.
(d) (*possess*) *post, town, lands* ocupar; *shares, title* tener; *reserves* tener en reserva, tener guardado; *record* ostentar, estar en posesión de.
(e) (*contain*) contener, tener capacidad (*or* cabida) para; **this —s the money** esto contiene el dinero; **this bag won't — them** all en este saco no caben todos; **a car that —s 6** un coche de 6 plazas; **what the future — s for us** lo que el futuro guarda para nosotros.
(f) *interview, meeting, election* celebrar; *conversation* tener, (*formally*) celebrar; **the meeting will be held on Monday** se celebrará la reunión el lunes, la reunión tendrá lugar el lunes.
(g) (*consider*) **to — that** creer que, sostener que; **I — that** tengo para mí que; **it is held by some that** hay quien cree que; **to — something to be true** creer que algo es verdad; **to — someone guilty** juzgar a uno culpable; **to — someone responsible** hacer a uno responsable (*for* de); **to — someone in respect** tener respeto a uno; **to — someone dear** tener cariño a uno.
(h) **to — back** (*keep*) guardar, retener; *water etc* retener; *progress* detener, refrenar; **to — down**

sujetar; *populace* oprimir; **to — down a job** (*retain*) mantenerse en su puesto, (*be equal to*) estar a la altura de su cargo; **you can't — a good man down** los realmente buenos triunfan a la larga; **to — in** contener; **to — off** *attack, enemy* rechazar; *threat* apartar; *person* defenderse contra; **to — out** *hand* tender, alargar; *arm* extender; *object* ofrecer, alargar; *possibility* ofrecer; *hope* dar; **to — over** aplazar; **to — together** *group, company* mantener la unidad de, *2 persons* mantener unidos; **to — up** (*support*) apoyar, sostener; (*display*) mostrar, enseñar; (*delay*) atrasar; (*stop*) detener, parar; *work* interrumpir, suspender; *delivery, payments* suspender; (*rob*) atracar, asaltar; **to — something up to the light** acercar algo a la luz; **to — something up as a model** presentar algo como un modelo; **we were held up for 3 hours** no nos pudimos mover durante 3 horas; **the train was held up by fog** el tren viene con retraso debido a la niebla; **we are held up for** (*or by lack of*) **bricks** la escasez de ladrillos afecta el ritmo de las obras.

 3 *vi* (**a**) (*stick*) pegarse; (*not give way*) mantenerse firme, resistir; (*weather*) continuar, seguir bueno.

 (**b**) (*be true*) valer, ser valedero; **the objection does not —** la objeción no vale.

 (**c**) **to — back** refrenarse, (*in doubt*) vacilar; **to — forth** hablar largamente (*about, on* de); **to — off** mantenerse a distancia; (*wait*) esperar; **if the rain —s off** si no llueve; **to — on** (*grip*) agarrarse bien; (*not give way*) aguantar, defenderse, resistir; **— on!** (*wait*) ¡tente!, ¡espera!, (*Tel*) ¡no cuelgue Vd!; (*giving encouragement*) ¡ánimo!; **can you — on?** ¿te animas a continuar?; **to — on to** (*clutch*) agarrarse a; (*keep back*) guardar, quedarse con; *post* retener; **to — out** resistir; **to — out for something** no cejar hasta que se conceda algo, insistir en algo; **to — to** atenerse a; **to — together** mantenerse unidos; **to — up** (*weather*) seguir bueno; **to — up under the strain** soportar bien la presión; **to — with** estar de acuerdo con, aprobar.

 4 *vr*: **to — oneself back** contenerse, refrenarse; **to — oneself ready** (*or in readiness*) estar listo (*for* para); **to — oneself upright** mantenerse erguido.

holdall ['həuldɔːl] *n* funda *f*, neceser *m*.

holder ['həuldə*] *n* (**a**) (*person*) tenedor *m*, ora *f*, poseedor *m*, ora *f*; (*of property*) inquilino *m*, a *f*, arrendatario *m*, a *f*; (*of bonds*) tenedor *m*; (*of title, office, passport*) titular *m*; (*of record*) poseedor *m*, ora *f*, detentor *m*.

 (**b**) (*support*) soporte *m*; (*handle*) asidero *m*; (*haft*) mango *m*; (*vessel*) receptáculo *m*, (*in compounds*) porta . . ., eg **lamp-holder** portalámparas *m*.

holding ['həuldiŋ] *n* (*act*) tenencia *f*; (*thing*) posesión *f*, propiedad *f*; **—s** (*Comm*) valores *mpl* en cartera.

holdup ['həuldʌp] *n* (**a**) (*robbery*) atraco *m*; **— man** atracador *m*. (**b**) (*stoppage*) parada *f*, interrupción *f*, suspensión *f*; (*of traffic*) embotellamiento *m*.

hole [həul] 1 *n* (**a**) agujero *m*; (*in ground, also Golf*) hoyo *m*; (*hollow*) cavidad *f*, hueco *m*; (*in road*) bache *m*; (*in wall*) boquete *m*; (*in defences, dam*) brecha *f*; (*burrow*) madriguera *f*; (*in clothes*) roto *m*; **through a — in the clouds** a través de un agujero de las nubes; **to bore** (*or make*) **a —** practicar un agujero en; **this will make a — in my salary** esto ha de agotar gran parte de mi sueldo; **to pick —s in** encontrar defectos en.

 (**b**) (*fig: jam*) apuro *m*, aprieto *m*; **to be in a —** estar en un aprieto; **to get someone out of a —** sacar a uno de un aprieto.

 (**c**) (*fig: room*) cuchitril *m*; (*town*) pueblo *m* muerto, pueblo *m* sin ambiente.

 2 *vt* agujerear; *ball* meter en el hoyo.

 3 *vi*: **to — out** (*Golf*) meter la pelota en el hoyo; **to — out in 5** terminar en 5 golpes.

hole-and-corner ['həulən'kɔːnə*] *adj* furtivo.

holey ['həuli] *adj* (*fam*) lleno de rotos.

holiday ['hɔlədi] 1 *n* (*day*) día *m* de fiesta, día *m* festivo; (*period*) vacaciones *fpl*; **—s with pay** vacaciones *fpl* retribuidas; **tomorrow is a —** mañana es fiesta; **to be on** (*one's*) **—** estar de vacaciones; **to declare a day a —** declarar festivo un día; **to take a —** tomarse unas vacaciones.

 2 *attr town* de veraneo; *mood etc* alegre, festivo; *season* de las vacaciones.

 3 *vi* pasar las vacaciones, (*esp*) veranear.

holiday-maker ['hɔlədi,meikə*] *n* veraneante *mf*, excursionista *mf*, turista *mf*.

holiness ['həulinis] *n* santidad *f*; **His H—** Su Santidad.

Holland ['hɔlənd] Holanda *f*.

holler ['hɔlə*] *vti* gritar, vocear.

hollow ['hɔləu] 1 *adj* hueco, ahuecado; *eyes* hundido;

sound sordo; *voice* sepulcral, cavernoso; *laughter* irónico; *doctrine etc* vacío, falso; *victory* más aparente que real.

 2 *adv*: **to beat someone —** cascar a uno, vencer a uno fácilmente.

 3 *n* hueco *m*; concavidad *f*; (*in ground*) hoyo *m*, depresión *f*; (*small valley*) hondonada *f*; **in the — of one's back** en los riñones.

 4 *vt* (*also* **to — out**) ahuecar, excavar, vaciar.

hollow-eyed ['hɔləu'aid] *adj* de ojos hundidos; (*with fatigue etc*) ojeroso.

holly ['hɔli] *n* acebo *m* (*also* **— tree**).

hollyhock ['hɔlihɔk] *n* malva *f* loca.

holm oak ['həum'əuk] *n* encina *f*.

holocaust ['hɔləkɔːst] *n* (*fig*) incendio *m*, destrucción *f* (*causada por un incendio*).

holograph ['hɔləgrɑːf] 1 *adj* ológrafo. 2 *n* ológrafo *m*.

holster ['həulstə*] *n* pistolera *f*.

holy ['həuli] *adj* santo; sagrado; *water etc* bendito.

Holy Land ['həulilænd] Tierra *f* Santa.

Holy See ['həuli'siː] *n* Santa Sede *f*.

homage ['hɔmidʒ] *n* homenaje *m*; **to do** (*or pay*) **—** rendir homenaje.

home [həum] 1 *n* casa *f*; (*more officially*) domicilio *m*; (*more sentimentally*) hogar *m*; (*town*) ciudad *f* natal, (*region, native land*) patria *f*; (*Bio*) habitat *m*, (*environment*) ambiente *m* natural; (*Sport*) meta *f*; (*in children's games*) la madre; (*institution*) asilo *m*; **— for the aged** asilo *m* de ancianos; **mental —** manicomio *m*; **Jewish National H—** hogar *m* nacional judío; **we live in Madrid but my — is in Jaén** vivimos en Madrid pero nací en Jaén; **for some years he made his — in France** durante algunos años vivió en Francia; **refugees who made their — in Britain** los refugiados que se establecieron en Gran Bretaña; **Scotland is the — of the haggis** Escocia es la patria del haggis; **at — en casa**; **at — and abroad** dentro y fuera del país; **is Mr X at —?** ¿está (en casa) el Sr X?; **he is at — on any topic** puede hablar sobre cualquier materia; **to feel at —** sentirse como en su casa, estar a sus anchas; **make yourself at —!** ¡estás en tu casa!; **there's no place like —** no hay lugar como la propia casa; **that remark came near —** esa observación le hirió en lo vivo; **to have a — of one's own** tener casa propia; **to give someone a —** recibir a uno como si fuera de la familia, (*fig*) adoptar a uno, recibir a uno; **to leave —** salir de su casa.

 2 *attr* (**a**) casero, doméstico, de casa; de familia; **my — address** las señas de mi casa; **— cooking** cocina *f* casera; **— journey** viaje *m* a casa, viaje *m* de vuelta; **— life** vida *f* doméstica, vida *f* de familia.

 (**b**) **the — side** el equipo de casa, el equipo local.

 (**c**) **the — straight** la recta de llegada; **we're on the — stretch** ésta es la última etapa del viaje.

 (**d**) *natal*; **— area** región *f* natal; **— town** ciudad *f* natal; **— port** puerto *m* de origen.

 (**e**) *defence, industry, product* nacional; *population* metropolitano; *news* del país, doméstico; *trade* interior; **H— Office** Ministerio *m* del Interior, (*Spain*) Ministerio *m* de la Gobernación; **H— Secretary** Ministro *m* del Interior, (*Spain*) Ministro *m* de la Gobernación; *see* **rule** *etc*.

 3 *adv* (**a**) **to be —** estar en casa, (*return*) estar de vuelta; **to come —** volver a casa, (*from abroad*) volver a la patria; **to get —** llegar a casa; **to go —** ir a casa, (*from abroad*) volver a la patria; **to stay —** quedarse en casa.

 (**b**) (*fig*) **to bring something — to someone** hacer que uno se dé cuenta cabal de algo; **it came — to me** me di cuenta cabal de ello, me llegó al alma; **to screw** (*etc*) **something —** atornillar (*etc*) algo a fondo; **to strike —** (*shell etc*) hacer blanco, dar en el blanco, (*on person*) herir en lo vivo.

 4 *vi* volver a casa; (*animal*) buscar la querencia; **to — on the target** buscar al blanco.

home-baked ['həum'beikt] *adj* hecho en casa.

home-brewed ['həum'bruːd] *adj* hecho en casa.

homecoming ['həumkʌmiŋ] *n* regreso *m* al hogar.

home-grown ['həum'grəun] *adj* de cosecha propia.

homeland ['həumlænd] *n* tierra *f* natal, patria *f*.

homeless ['həumlis] *adj* sin casa ni hogar; **the storm left a hundred —** la tormenta dejó sin hogar a cien personas.

homely ['həumli] *adj* casero, doméstico, familiar; (*unpretentious*) llano, sencillo; (*US*) feo.

home-made ['həum'meid] *adj* casero, de fabricación casera.

Homer ['həumə*] *m* Homero.

Homeric [həu'merik] *adj* homérico.

home run ['həum'rʌn] *n* (*US: Baseball*) carrera *f* completa, jonrón *m* (*SAm*).

homesick ['həumsik] *adj* nostálgico; **to be —** tener morriña.
homesickness ['həumsiknis] *n* nostalgia *f*, morriña *f*.
homespun ['həumspʌn] *adj* tejido en casa, hecho en casa; (*fig*) llano.
homestead ['həumsted] *n* casa *f*, caserío *m*; (*farm*) granja *f*.
homeward(s) ['həumwəd(z)] *adv* hacia casa; (*from abroad*) hacia la patria; **— bound** (*Naut*) con rumbo al puerto de origen.
homework ['həumwə:k] *n* deberes *mpl*, ejercicios *mpl* para casa.
homicidal [,homi'saidl] *adj* homicida.
homicide ['homisaid] *n* (*act*) homicidio *m*; (*person*) homicida *mf*.
homily ['homili] *n* homilía *f*; (*fig*) sermón *m*.
homoeopath, (*US*) **homeo—** ['həumiəupæθ] *n* homeópata *m*.
homoeopathy, (*US*) **homeo—** [,həumi'ɔpəθi] *n* homeopatía *f*.
homogeneity [,homəudʒə'ni:iti] *n* homogeneidad *f*.
homogeneous [,homə'dʒi:niəs] *adj* homogéneo.
homograph ['homəugra:f] *n* homógrafo *m*.
homonym ['homənim] *n* homónimo *m*.
homosexual ['homəu'seksjuəl] **1** *adj* homosexual. **2** *n* homosexual *mf*.
homosexuality ['homəuseksju'æliti] *n* homosexualidad *f*.
Honduran [hon'djuərən] **1** *adj* hondureño. **2** *n* hondureño *m*, a *f*.
Honduras [hon'djuərəs] Honduras *f*.
hone [həun] **1** *n* piedra *f* de afilar. **2** *vt* afilar.
honest ['onist] *adj* (*upright*) honrado, recto; (*speaking openly*) franco, sincero; **by — means** por medios legales; **the — truth is** la pura verdad es; **what is your — opinion?** ¿qué piensa Vd francamente de esto?; **be —!** ¡diga la verdad!; **you were not entirely — with me** Vd no me dijo honradamente toda la verdad.
honestly ['onistli] *adv* honradamente; francamente; **I don't — know**, — **I don't know** francamente no lo sé; —? ¿de veras?
honesty ['onisti] *n* honradez *f*, rectitud *f*; franqueza *f*; **in all —** con toda franqueza.
honey ['hʌni] *n* miel *f*; **yes, —** (*US*) sí, querida; **hullo —!** (*US*) ¡oye, guapa!; **she's a —** (*US*) es un encanto.
honey-bee ['hʌnibi:] *n* abeja *f* (obrera).
honeycomb ['hʌnikəum] **1** *n* panal *m*. **2** *vt*: **the building is —ed with passages** hay un sinfín de pasillos en el edificio; **the hill is —ed with galleries** una multitud de galerías penetran por la colina.
honeyed ['hʌnid] *adj* meloso, melifluo.
honeymoon ['hʌnimu:n] **1** *n* luna *f* de miel, viaje *f* de novios. **2** *vi* pasar la luna de miel.
honeypot ['hʌnipot] *n* mielera *f*.
honeysuckle ['hʌni,sʌkl] *n* madreselva *f*.
honk [honk] **1** *n* (*Orn*) graznido *m*; (*Aut*) bocinazo *m*. **2** *vi* graznar; tocar la bocina, bocinar.
Honolulu [,honə'lu:lu:] Honolulú.
honorarium [,onə'reəriəm] *n* honorarios *mpl*.
honorary ['onərəri] *adj* honorario; *president, member* de honor; (*unpaid*) no remunerado.
honour, (*US*) **honor** ['onə*] **1** *n* (a) honor *m*; (*good name*) honra *f*; (*uprightness*) honradez *f*; **in —** of en honor de; **on my —!** ¡palabra de honor!; **it's a great — for him** es un gran honor para él; **to be on one's — to** + *infin*, **to be in — bound to** + *infin* estar moralmente obligado a + *infin*; **I consider it an — to** + *infin* tengo a mucha honra + *infin*; **I had the — to** + *infin* (*or* of + *ger*) tuve el honor de + *infin*; **to hold someone in high —** tener mucho respeto a uno.
(b) **Your H—** Señor Juez.
(c) (*medal etc*) condecoración *f*.
(d) **—s** honores *mpl*; **last —s** honras *fpl* fúnebres; **the —s are even** se ha logrado un empate; **to bury someone with full military —s** sepultar a uno con todos los honores militares; **to do the —s of the house** hacer los honores de la casa.
(e) (*Univ*) **—s degree** título *m* (*otorgado después de un curso de estudios superiores o especializados*); **to take —s in chemistry** graduarse en química (*con estudios superiores o especializados*).
(f) (*Bridge*) **—s** honores *mpl*; **3 —s tricks** 3 bazas *fpl* de honores.
2 *vt* honrar; *pledge, signature* hacer honor a; (*respect*) respetar, reverenciar; **I — you for it** te respeto más por esto; **to — someone with one's confidence** honrar a uno con su confianza; **I am deeply —ed** lo tengo a mucha honra; **I should be —ed if . . .** estimaría que . . . + *subj*.
honourable, (*US*) **honorable** ['onərəbl] *adj* (*worthy*)

honorable; (*upright*) honrado; *title, deed etc* honroso; *mention* honorífico.
honourably, (*US*) **honorably** ['onərəbli] *adv* honradamente.
hooch [hu:tʃ] *n* (*US fam*) licor *m*.
hood [hud] *n* (*of cloak, raincoat, Eccl*) capucha *f*; (*Univ*) muceta *f* (con capucha); (*of penitent, hawk*) capirote *m*; (*Aut*) capota *f*; (*US Aut*) capó *m*; (*US sl*) criminal *m*, gángster *m*.
hooded ['hudid] *adj* encapuchado; encapirotado.
hoodlum ['hu:dləm] *n* (*US fam*) gorila *m*, matón *m*.
hoodoo ['hu:du:] *n* vudú *m*; gafancia *f*, mala suerte *f*; **there's a — on it** quien lo toque (*etc*) tendrá mala suerte, eso no se puede tocar.
hoodwink ['hudwink] *vt* burlar, engañar.
hooey ['hu:i] *n* (*sl*) música *f* celestial; —! ¡tonterías!
hoof [hu:f] **1** *n*, *pl* **hoofs** *or* **hooves** [hu:vz] casco *m*, pezuña *f*; (*foot*) pata *f*; **cloven —** pata *f* hendida. **2** *vt* (*fam*): **to — it** (*walk*) ir a pie, (*depart*) liar el petate.
hoofed [hu:ft] *adj* ungulado.
hook [huk] **1** *n* gancho *m*; garfio *m*; (*Fishing*) anzuelo *m*; (*hanger*) colgadero *m*; (*Boxing*) gancho *m*, crochet *m*; **—s** (*sl*) manos *fpl*; **—s and eyes** corchetes *mpl*; **—, line and sinker** totalmente, hasta las cejas; **by — or by crook** por las buenas o por las malas; **to get someone off the —** ayudar a uno a salir de un apuro; **to let someone off the —** dejar escapar a uno, permitir que uno se salve; **to sling one's —** (*sl*) suspender el trabajo.
2 *vt* (a) (*attach*) enganchar; (*Fishing*) pescar, coger, enganchar; (*sl*) birlar; **to — something to a rope** enganchar algo a una cuerda; **to — a rope round a nail** atar una cuerda a un clavo; **she finally —ed him** (*fam*) ella por fin le pescó; **to — it** (*sl*) largarse; **to get —ed on** enviciarse con, entregarse a; **to — up** enganchar, *dress* abrochar.
(b) (*curve*) encorvar.
3 *vi* (a) engancharse (*on to* a).
(b) encorvarse.
hookah ['hukɑ:] *n* narguile *m*.
hooked [hukt] *adj* ganchudo.
hookup ['hukʌp] *n* (*Elec*) acoplamiento *m*; (*Radio*) transmisión *f* en circuito; **a — with Eurovision** una emisión conjunta con Eurovisión.
hookworm ['hukwə:m] *n* anquilostoma *m*.
hooky ['huki] *n*: **to play —** hacer novillos.
hooligan ['hu:ligən] *n* gamberro *m*.
hooliganism ['hu:ligənizəm] *n* gamberrismo *m*.
hoop [hu:p] *n* aro *m*; (*in croquet*) argolla *f*.
hoopoe ['hu:pu:] *n* abubilla *f*.
hoosegow ['hu:sgau] *n* (*US sl*) trena *f* (*sl*).
hoot [hu:t] **1** *n* (*of owl*) grito *m*, ululato *m*; (*of horn*) bocinazo *m*; (*of ship, factory*) toque *m* de sirena; (*laugh*) risotada *f*; **it was a —!** ¡era para morirse de risa!; *see* **care**.
2 *vt* (*also* **to — off**) silbar, abuchear; **to — someone off the stage** abuchear a uno hasta que abandone la escena.
3 *vi* (*owl*) ululular, gritar; (*person*) silbar; (*Aut: person*) tocar la bocina, (*car*) dar un bocinazo; (*ship*) dar un toque de sirena; **to — with laughter** morirse de risa.
hooter ['hu:tə*] *n* (*of ship, factory*) sirena *f*; (*Aut*) bocina *f*, claxon *m*.
hooves [hu:vz] *npl* of **hoof**.
hop¹ [hop] *n* (*Bot: also* **—s**) lúpulo *m*.
hop² [hop] **1** *n* salto *m*, saltito *m*, brinco *m*; (*Aer*) vuelo *m*, etapa *f* de un vuelo; (*fam*) baile *m*; **—, skip and jump** triple salto *m*; **in one —** de un salto, (*Aer*) sin hacer escala; **to catch someone on the —** coger a uno desprevenido.
2 *vt* cruzar de un salto; **to — it** (*fam*) escabullirse, largarse; **— it!** ¡lárgate!
3 *vi* saltar, brincar; saltar con un pie; (*limp*) cojear; **to — along** avanzar a saltos; **to — off** bajar (de); **to — on** subir (a); **to — out of bed** saltar de la cama.
hope [həup] **1** *n* esperanza *f*; (*trust*) confianza *f*; (*hopefulness*) ilusión *f*; (*chance*) posibilidad *f*; **some —s!** ¡de eso ni hablar!; **my —** is that yo espero que; **there is no — of that** no hay posibilidad alguna de eso; **you are my last —** tú eres mi única salvación; **to be full of —** estar lleno de ilusión, estar muy ilusionado; **to build up —s** hacerse ilusiones; **to conceive the — that** hacerse la ilusión de + *infin*; **to live in — of something** vivir con la esperanza de algo; **to lose —** perder la esperanza, desesperarse; **to place — in something** poner esperanzas en algo.
2 *vt*: **to — that** esperar que + *subj*.
3 *vi* esperar; **to — for something** esperar algo; **to — to** + *infin* esperar + *infin*; **hoping to hear from**

you en espera de sus gratas noticias; **what do you —
to gain by that?** ¿qué pretende Vd con eso?; **to —
against —** esperar desesperando; **to — in** confiar en.

hopeful ['həupful] adj person lleno de esperanzas,
optimista, (falsely) ilusionado; prospect etc
esperanzador, prometedor; **he wasn't very —** no se
mostró muy optimista; **it looks —** promete mucho;
a young — un joven ilusionado.

hopefully ['həupfəli] adv con optimismo; con ilusión.

hopeless ['həuplis] adj **(a)** person (without hope)
desesperado, sin esperanza.
(b) (impossible, useless) situation desesperado,
irremediable; task imposible; (Med) case desahuciado; drunkard etc incurable; **to give something
up as —** renunciar a algo por imposible; **I'm — at it**
yo soy inútil para eso; **it's — trying to +** infin es
inútil tratar de + infin.

hopelessly ['həuplisli] adv live etc sin esperanza; **she
looked at me —** me miró desesperada; **I'm — confused** estoy totalmente despistado; **it's — dear for
us** es excesivamente caro para nosotros.

hopper ['hɔpə*] n tolva f; (Rail) vagón m tolva.

hopscotch ['hɔpskɔtʃ] n: **to play —** jugar a la pata
coja.

Horace ['hɔris] m Horacio.

Horatian [hə'reiʃən] adj horaciano.

horde [hɔːd] n horda f; (fig) multitud f, muchedumbre
f.

horehound ['hɔːhaund] n (Bot) marrubio m.

horizon [hə'raizn] n horizonte m.

horizontal [,hɔri'zɔntl] adj horizontal.

horizontally [,hɔri'zɔntəli] adv horizontalmente.

hormone ['hɔːməun] n hormona f, hormón m (Acad).

horn [hɔːn] 1 n **(a)** (of bull etc) cuerno m; (of deer) asta
f; (of insect) antena f; (of snail) tentáculo m;
(material) cuerno m; **— of plenty** cuerno m de la
abundancia, cornucopia f; **to be on the —s of a
dilemma** estar entre la espada y la pared; **to draw
in one's —s** retroceder, volverse atrás, (with money)
hacer economías.
(b) (Mus) cuerno m, trompa f; (Aut) bocina f,
claxon m; **to blow (or sound) one's —** tocar la
bocina, tocar el claxon.
2 vi: **to — in** (fam) entrometerse (on en).

horned [hɔːnd] adj con cuernos, enastado; (in compounds) de cuernos . . .

hornet ['hɔːnit] n avispón m.

hornless ['hɔːnlis] adj sin cuernos, mocho.

hornpipe ['hɔːnpaip] n cierto baile de marineros.

horn-rimmed ['hɔːnrimd] adj spectacles de concha.

horny ['hɔːni] adj material córneo; hand calloso.

horoscope ['hɔrəskəup] n horóscopo m; **to cast a —**
sacar un horóscopo.

horrible ['hɔribl] adj horrible.

horribly ['hɔribli] adv horriblemente; **it's — difficult**
es terriblemente difícil; **he swore most —** soltó unos
tacos espantosos.

horrid ['hɔrid] adj horrible, horroroso; (fam) horrible;
person etc de lo más antipático, inaguantable; **you —
thing!** ¡bestia!; **to be — to someone** tratar a uno
muy mal, portarse muy mal con uno; **don't be —!**
¡no seas bestia!

horrendous [hɔ'rendəs] adj horrendo; (hum) horroroso.

horrific [hɔ'rifik] adj horrendo.

horrify ['hɔrifai] vt horrorizar; (shock) escandalizar,
pasmar; **they were all horrified** se escandalizaron
todos; **I was horrified to discover that** me horrorizó
descubrir que.

horrifying ['hɔrifaiiŋ] adj horroroso, horripilante.

horror ['hɔrə*] n horror m; **to have a — of** tener
horror a; **it gives me the —s** me da horror; **—s!** ¡qué
horror!; **you —!** ¡bestia!

horror-stricken ['hɔrə,strikən] adj horrorizado.

hors d'oeuvres [ɔː'dəːvr] npl entremeses mpl.

horse [hɔːs] n (Zool) caballo m; (in gymnastics) potro
m; (Tech) caballete m; (cavalry) caballería f; **dark —**
(mystery) incógnita f, figura f misteriosa, (in election)
candidato m poco conocido, (winner) ganador m
inesperado; **white —s** (waves) palomas fpl; **that's a
— of a different colour** ésa es harina de otro costal;
it's straight from the —'s mouth lo sé de buena
tinta, me lo dijo el mismo interesado; **to change —s
in midstream** cambiar de política (or personal etc) a
mitad de camino; **to eat like a —** comer como una
vaca; **to flog a dead —** machacar en hierro frío; **to
get on one's high —** darse ínfulas; **hold your —s!**
¡despacito!; **don't look a gift — in the mouth** a
caballo regalado no le mires el diente.

horse-artillery ['hɔːsaː'tiləri] n artillería f montada.

horseback ['hɔːsbæk] n: **on — adv** a caballo.

horse-box ['hɔːsbɔks] n camión m para caballerías,
(Rail) vagón m para caballerías.

horse-breaker ['hɔːs,breikə*] n domador m de
caballos.

horse chestnut ['hɔːs'tʃesnʌt] n (fruit) castaña f de
Indias; (tree) castaño m de Indias.

horse-collar ['hɔːs,kɔlə*] n collera f.

horse-dealer ['hɔːs,diːlə*] n chalán m.

horse-doctor ['hɔːs,dɔktə*] n veterinario m.

horse-drawn ['hɔːsdrɔːn] adj traído por caballo(s).

horsefly ['hɔːsflai] n tábano m.

Horse Guards ['hɔːsgaːdz] npl guardias fpl montadas.

horsehair ['hɔːshɛə*] n crin m.

horsehide ['hɔːshaid] n cuero m de caballo.

horse-laugh ['hɔːslaːf] n risotada f.

horseman ['hɔːsmən] n, pl **—men** [mən] jinete m;
caballista m.

horsemanship ['hɔːsmənʃip] n equitación f, manejo
m (del caballo).

horse opera ['hɔːs,ɔpərə] n (US) película f que se
desarrolla en el oeste de EE.UU., película f de
vaqueros.

horseplay ['hɔːsplei] n payasadas fpl, pelea f amistosa.

horsepower ['hɔːs,pauə*] n caballo m (de fuerza);
potencia f en caballos; **a 20 — engine** un motor de
20 caballos; **what is the — of this car?** ¿qué
potencia tiene este coche?

horse-race ['hɔːsreis] n carrera f de caballos.

horse-racing ['hɔːs,reisiŋ] n carreras fpl de caballos,
hipismo m.

horseradish ['hɔːs,rædiʃ] n rábano m picante.

horse-sense ['hɔːssens] n sentido m común.

horseshoe ['hɔːsʃuː] n herradura f.

horse show ['hɔːsʃəu] n concurso m hípico.

horsewhip ['hɔːswip] 1 n látigo m. 2 vt zurriagar.

horsewoman ['hɔːs,wumən] n, pl **—women** [,wimin]
amazona f, caballista f.

horsy ['hɔːsi] adj (fond of horses) aficionado a los
caballos; (fond of racing) aficionado a las carreras de
caballos, carrerista; appearance caballuno.

horticultural [,hɔːti'kʌltʃərəl] adj hortícola; **— show**
exposición f de flores y legumbres.

horticulture ['hɔːtikʌltʃə*] n horticultura f.

horticulturist [,hɔːti'kʌltʃərist] n horticultor m, ora f.

hose [həuz] 1 n **(a)** (stockings) medias fpl, (socks)
calcetines mpl; (arch) calzas fpl.
(b) (hosepipe) manga f, manguera f.
2 vt (also **to — down**) regar (or limpiar etc) con
manga.

hosepipe ['həuzpaip] n manga f, manguera f.

hosier ['həuʒə*] n calcetero m, a f.

hosiery ['həuʒəri] n calcetería f.

hospice ['hɔspis] n hospicio m.

hospitable [hɔs'pitəbl] adj hospitalario; atmosphere
etc acogedor.

hospitably [hɔs'pitəbli] adv de modo hospitalario.

hospital ['hɔspitl] n hospital m; **isolation —** hospital
m de contagiosos; **maternity —** casa f de maternidad; **mental —** manicomio m.

hospitality [,hɔspi'tæliti] n hospitalidad f.

hospitalize ['hɔspitəlaiz] vt hospitalizar.

hospital ship ['hɔspitl,ʃip] n buque m hospital.

host¹ [həust] n **(a)** (crowd) multitud f; **I have a — of
problems** tengo multitud de problemas; **for a whole
— of reasons** por muchísimas razones; **they came in
—s** acudieron a millares.
(b) (arch) hueste f, ejército m.

host² [həust] n (to guest) huésped m, eda f; (Bio)
huésped m; (at meal) anfitrión m, ona f; (of inn)
patrón m, mesonero m; **I thanked my —s** di las
gracias a los que me habían invitado; **we were —s
for a week to a Spanish boy** recibimos en casa
durante una semana a un joven español.

host³ [həust] n (Eccl) hostia f.

hostage ['hɔstidʒ] n rehén m.

hostel ['hɔstəl] n parador m; (youth —) albergue m;
(Univ) residencia f (de estudiantes).

hostelry ['hɔstəlri] n parador m, mesón m.

hostess ['həustes] n huéspeda f; anfitriona f (see
host²); (Aer) azafata f; (in night club) cabaretera f.

hostile ['hɔstail] adj (enemy) enemigo, hostil; manner,
voice etc nada amistoso; circumstances etc adverso,
desfavorable; **they were — to the plan** se opusieron
al proyecto.

hostility [hɔs'tiliti] n hostilidad f (to, towards hacia),
enemistad f, antagonismo m; **hostilities** hostilidades
fpl; **to start hostilities** romper las hostilidades; **to
call for an end to hostilities** abogar por un cese de
hostilidades.

hostler ['ɔslə*] n = ostler.

hot [hɔt] 1 adj **(a)** caliente; climate cálido; day,
summer caluroso, de calor; sun abrasador; spring
termal; **with running — and cold (water)** con agua

corriente caliente y fría; **to be —** (*person*) tener calor, (*thing*) estar caliente, (*weather*) hacer calor; **to be very —** (*person*) tener mucho calor, (*thing*) estar muy caliente, (*weather*) hacer mucho calor; **to get —** (*thing*) calentarse, (*weather*) empezar a hacer calor; **it was a very — day** fue un día de mucho calor; **it was a — and tiring walk** fue una caminata que nos hizo sudar y nos cansó mucho; **to get — and bothered** sofocarse.

(**b**) (*fig*) *taste* picante; *contest* muy reñido; *dispute* acalorado; *temper* vivo; *temperament* apasionado, ardiente, vehemente; *situation* muy difícil, apurado, de mucho peligro; *pursuit* enérgico; *supporter* acérrimo; (*sexually: fam*) cachondo; (*stolen*) robado.

(**c**) *news* **— from the press** una noticia que acaba de publicarse en la prensa; **to be — on someone's trail** seguir enérgicamente la pista de uno; **he's pretty — at maths** es un hacha para las matemáticas, es muy fuerte en matemáticas; **he's a pretty — player** es un jugador experto; **to make a place too — for someone** hacer que uno abandone un lugar; **to make things — for someone** amargar la vida a uno, hacer insoportable la vida a uno.

2 *adv*: **to blow — and cold** ser veleta, mudar a todos los vientos; **to give it to someone — and strong** no morderse la lengua; **to go at it — and strong** pelearse (*etc*) violentamente.

hotbed ['hɔtbed] *n* (*fig*) semillero *m*.
hot-blooded ['hɔt'blʌdid] *adj* apasionado, impetuoso.
hotchpotch ['hɔtʃpɔtʃ] *n* mezcolanza *f*, baturrillo *m*.
hotel [həu'tel] *n* hotel *m*.
hotfoot ['hɔt'fut] *adv* a toda prisa.
hothead ['hɔthed] *n* exaltado *m*, a *f*, fanático *m*, a *f*, extremista *mf*.
hotheaded ['hɔt'hedid] *adj* (*extreme*) exaltado, fanático, extremista; (*rash*) impetuoso.
hothouse ['hɔthaus] *n* invernáculo *m*.
hotly ['hɔtli] *adv* con pasión, con vehemencia.
hotplate ['hɔtpleit] *n* calientaplatos *m*.
hotpot ['hɔtpɔt] *n* estofado *m*.
hotrod ['hɔtrɔd] *n* (*US Aut: sl*) bólido *m*.
hotshot ['hɔtʃɔt] *adj* (*US sl*) excelente, de primera.
hot-water bottle [hɔt'wɔːtə,bɔtl] *n* bolsa *f* de agua caliente.
hound [haund] **1** *n* perro *m* (de caza), podenco *m*, sabueso *m*; (*fig*) canalla *m*.

2 *vt* acosar, perseguir; **to — someone down** perseguir a uno hasta encontrarle; **to — someone on** incitar a uno (*to + infin* a *+ infin*); **to — someone out** hacer que uno abandone su puesto (*etc*) a fuerza de darle guerra.

hour [auə*] *n* hora *f*; **30 miles an —** 30 millas por hora; **peak —s** horas *fpl* punta; **small —s** altas horas *fpl*; **visiting —s** horas *fpl* de visita; **after —s** fuera de horas; **at the eleventh —** a última hora; **by the —** por horas; **— by —** hora tras hora, cada hora; **on the —** a la hora en punto; **to keep late —s** acostarse a altas horas de la noche; **to strike the —** dar la hora; **it takes —s** es cosa de muchas horas; **we waited —s** esperamos horas y horas; **to work long —s** trabajar muchas horas cada día.
hourglass ['auəglɑːs] *n* reloj *m* de arena.
hourhand ['auəhænd] *n* horario *m*.
hourly ['auəli] **1** *adj* de cada hora; **the — rate** el sueldo por hora; **there's an — bus** hay un autobús cada hora.

2 *adv* cada hora; **we expected him —** le esperábamos de un momento a otro.

house [haus] *n*, *pl* **houses** ['hauziz] **1** *n* casa *f*; (*Comm*) casa *f*, firma *f*; (*Theat: auditorium*) sala *f*, (*audience*) público *m*, (*takings*) entrada *f*; (*Parl*) cámara *f*; (*Univ*) colegio *m*, (*part of college*) pabellón *m*; (*lineage*) casa *f*, familia *f*; **"— full"** (*Theat*) "no hay localidades"; **— and home** hogar *m*; **— of cards** castillo *m* de naipes; **H— of Commons** Cámara *f* de los Comunes; **H— of Lords** Cámara *f* de los Lores; **H—s of Parliament** Parlamento *m*, Cámara *f* de los Lores y la de los Comunes; **H— of Representatives** (*US*) Cámara *f* de Representantes; **banking —** casa *f* de banca; **the big —** la casa del mayor terrateniente (de una comarca); **business —** casa *f* de comercio; **detached —** casa *f* independiente, hotelito *m*, chalet *m*, chalé *m* (*Acad*); **disorderly —** (*euph*) burdel *m*; **full —** (*Theat*) lleno *m*; **public —** taberna *f*; **publishing —** casa *f* editorial; **it's on the —** la casa invita, está pagado (por el dueño); **to bring the — down** (*Theat*) hacer venirse abajo el teatro, (*speech*) obtener un gran éxito, ser muy aplaudido, (*joke*) hacer morir de risa a todos; **to get on like a — afire** (*progress*) avanzar rapidísimamente, (2 *persons*) hacer buenas migas; **to keep —** llevar la casa (*for* a, para); **to keep open —** recibir a todo el mundo, ser muy hospitalario; **to move —** mudarse; **to put one's — in order** arreglar los asuntos personales; **to set up —** poner casa, establecerse.

2 *attr property* inmueble; *arrest* domiciliario; *dog etc* de casa.

house [hauz] *vt person* alojar, hospedar; *population* proveer viviendas para; (*store*) guardar, almacenar; (*Mech*) encajar; **the building will not — them all** no cabrán todos en el edificio.
house agent ['haus,eidʒənt] *n* corredor *m* de casas.
house arrest ['hausə,rest] *n*: **to be under —** estar bajo arresto domiciliario.
houseboat ['hausbout] *n* habitación *f* flotante.
housebreaker ['haus,breikə*] *n* ladrón *m* de casas.
housebreaking ['haus,breikiŋ] *n* robo *m* en una casa.
housecleaning ['haus'kliːniŋ] *n* (*US*) limpieza *f* de la casa.
housecoat ['hauskəut] *n* bata *f*.
housedress ['hausdres] *n* bata *f*, mono *m*.
housefly ['hausflai] *n* mosca *f* doméstica.
household ['haushəuld] **1** *n* casa *f*, familia *f*; **royal — corte** *f*.

2 *attr*: **— accounts** cuentas *fpl* de la casa; **— chores** quehaceres *mpl* domésticos; **— gods** penates *mpl*; **— troops** guardia *f* real; **it's a — word** es un nombre conocidísimo.
householder ['haus,həuldə*] *n* cabeza *f* de familia; dueño *m* de una casa.
housekeeper ['haus,kiːpə*] *n* ama *f* de casa, ama *f* de llaves.
housekeeping ['haus,kiːpiŋ] *n* gobierno *m* de la casa, economía *f* doméstica; **— (money)** dinero *m* para gastos domésticos.
housemaid ['hausmeid] *n* criada *f*.
house painter ['haus,peintə*] *n* pintor *m* (de brocha gorda).
house party ['haus,pɑːti] *n* grupo *m* de invitados (que pasan varios días en una casa de campo).
house physician ['hausfi,ziʃən] *n* médico *m* residente.
house-proud ['hauspraud] *adj*: **she's very —** cuida muy bien su hogar, tiene la casa como una plata.
houseroom ['hausrum] *n* capacidad *f* de una casa; **to give something —** guardar algo en su casa; **I wouldn't give it —** no quisiera tenerlo en mi casa.
house surgeon ['haus,səːdʒən] *n* cirujano *m* residente (en el hospital).
house-to-house ['haustə'haus] *adj and adv* de casa en casa.
housetop ['haustɔp] *n* tejado *m*; **to shout something from the —s** pregonar algo a los cuatro vientos.
house-trained ['haustreind] *adj* bien enseñado, limpio.
housewares ['hauswɛəz] *npl* (*US*) artículos *mpl* de uso doméstico, utensilios *mpl* domésticos.
house warming ['haus,wɔːmiŋ] *n* fiesta *f* de estreno de una casa.
housewife ['hauswaif] *n*, *pl* **—wives** [waivz] ama *f* de casa; madre *f* de familia.
housewifery ['hauswifəri] *n* economía *f* doméstica.
housing ['hauziŋ] *n* (**a**) (*act*) alojamiento *m*; provisión *f* de vivienda.

(**b**) (*houses*) casas *fpl*, viviendas *fpl*; **— estate** bloque *m* de casas; **— shortage** crisis *f* de la vivienda; **there's a lot of new —** hay muchas casas nuevas.

(**c**) (*Mech*) caja *f*, cubierta *f*, tapa *f*.
hove [həuv] *pret and ptp of* **heave** (*Naut*).
hovel ['hɔvəl] *n* casucha *f*, tugurio *m*.
hover ['hɔvə*] *vi* permanecer inmóvil (en el aire), estar suspendido, flotar (en el aire); (*hawk etc*) cernerse; **to — round someone** rondar a uno, girar en torno a uno.
hovercraft ['hɔvəkrɑːft] *n* hidroala *m*, aerodeslizador *m*.
how [hau] *adv* (**a**) cómo; **— did you do it?** ¿cómo lo hiciste? **I know — you did it** yo sé cómo lo hiciste; **— are you?** ¿cómo está Vd?, ¿qué tal estás?; **— is it that . . . ?** ¿cómo resulta que . . . ?, ¿por qué . . . ?, ¿cómo es posible que . . . + *subj*?; **— can that be?** ¿cómo puede ser eso?; **I see — it is** comprendo la situación; **— was the play?** ¿qué tal la comedia?; **— do you like your steak?** ¿cómo le gusta que se le sirva el biftec?; **— do you like the steak?** ¿qué tal le parece el biftec?; **to know — to do something** saber hacer algo; **to learn — to do something** aprender a hacer algo, aprender cómo se hace algo, aprender el modo de hacer algo; **and —!** ¡ya lo creo!

(**b**) (*with adj or adv etc*) **— beautiful!** ¡qué hermoso!; **— big it is!** ¡qué grande es!; **I know — hard it is** yo sé lo difícil que esto es; **— kind of you!** es Vd muy amable; **— fast?** ¿a qué velocidad?; **— big is it?** ¿cómo es de grande?, ¿de qué tamaño es?;

— **wide is this room?** ¿cuánto tiene este cuarto de ancho?; **how wide shall I make it?** ¿con qué ancho lo hago?; — **old are you?** ¿cuántos años tienes?; — **glad I am to see you!** ¡cuánto me alegro de verte!; — **sorry I am for you!** ¡cuánto te compadezco!; — **she's changed!** ¡cuánto ha cambiado!; *see* **about, else, much** *etc.*

how-d'ye-do ['haudjə'du:] *n* lío *m*.

however [hau'evə*] **1** *adv* **(a)** (*with verb*) — **I do it como quiera que lo haga;** **he may want to do it de cualquier modo que él quiera hacerlo;** — **that may be** sea como ello fuere.

(b) (*with adj or adv*) por (muy) . . . que + *subj*; — **rough it is** por (muy) tosco que sea; — **fast he runs** por rápidamente que corra; — **hot it is** por mucho calor que haga; *see* **many, much.**

2 *conj* sin embargo, no obstante.

howitzer ['hauitsə*] *n* obús *m*.

howl [haul] **1** *n* aullido *m*, chillido *m*, grito *m*, alarido *m*; berrido *m*; bramido *m*; **with a** — **of rage** dando un alarido de furia; **to set up a** — (*fig*) poner el grito en el cielo.

2 *vt*: **to** — **someone down** hacer callar a uno abucheándole.

3 *vi* (*animal etc*) aullar, chillar; (*person*) gritar, dar alaridos; (*child*) berrear; (*with laughter*) reírse a carcajadas; (*wind*) bramar; **to** — **with rage** bramar de furia, bramar furioso.

howler ['haulə*] *n* plancha *f*, falta *f* garrafal.

howling ['haulin] *adj* **success** clamoroso.

hoy [hɔi] *interj* ¡eh!, ¡hola!

hub [hʌb] *n* cubo *m*; (*fig*) centro *m*.

hubbub ['hʌbʌb] *n* barahúnda *f*, batahola *f*; **a** — **of voices** un ruido confuso de voces; **when he finished a** — **arose** cuando terminó se armó una bronca.

hubby ['hʌbi] *n* (*fam*) marido *m*.

hub cap ['hʌbkæp] *n* tapacubos *m*.

huckster ['hʌkstə*] *n* vendedor *m* ambulante, buhonero *m*.

huddle ['hʌdl] **1** *n* (*of things*) montón *m*, grupo *m*; (*of persons*) grupo *m*, corrillo *m*; **to go into a** — ir aparte para conferenciar.

2 *vt* (*also to* — **together**) amontonar, poner muy juntos.

3 *vi* (*also to* — **together, to** — **up**) amontonarse, apretarse (unos contra otros); acurrucarse; **they were huddling together for warmth** estaban apretados unos contra otros para darse calor; **the chairs were** — **d in a corner** las sillas estaban amontonadas en un rincón; **we** — **d round the fire** nos arrimamos al fuego, nos apiñábamos junto a la lumbre.

hue[1] [hju:] *n* (*colour*) color *m*; (*shade*) matiz *m*, tono *m*; (*of opinion*) matiz *m*; **people of every political** — gente *f* de todos los matices de opinión política.

hue[2] [hju:] *n*: — **and cry** alarma *f*; (*of protest*) clamor *m*, griterío *f*; **they set up a great** — **and cry** protestaron clamorosamente; **there was a** — **and cry after him** se le persiguió enérgicamente.

huff [hʌf] *n* rabieta *f*; **to go off in a** — irse ofendido; **to get into a** — indignarse, ofenderse.

huffily ['hʌfili] *adv* malhumoradamente; **he said** — dijo malhumorado.

huffy ['hʌfi] *adj* (*of character*) enojadizo; (*in mood*) malhumorado, ofendido; **he was a bit** — **about it** se ofendió un tanto por ello.

hug [hʌg] **1** *n* abrazo *m*; **give me a** — dame un abrazo.

2 *vt* (*lovingly*) abrazar; (*of bear etc*) apretar con los brazos, apretujar; *coast* no apartarse de; *prejudice etc* acariciar; *idea* aferrarse a; *belief* afirmarse en.

3 *vr*: **to** — **oneself** felicitarse (*on* por).

huge [hju:dʒ] *adj* enorme, vasto, inmenso; (*overlarge*) descomunal.

hugely ['hju:dʒli] *adv* enormemente; **we enjoyed ourselves** — nos divertimos una barbaridad; **he laughed** — se rió muchísimo.

hugeness ['hju:dʒnis] *n* inmensidad *f*.

hugger-mugger ['hʌgə,mʌgə*] (*fam*) **1** *n* confusión *f*; **a** — **of books** un montón de libros en desorden. **2** *adv* desordenadamente.

Hugh [hju:] *m* Hugo, Ugo.

Huguenot ['hju:gənəu] **1** *adj* hugonote. **2** *n* hugonote *m*, a *f*.

hulk [hʌlk] *n* (*wreck*) barco *m* viejo; (*hull*) casco *m* (arrumbado); (*useless vessel*) carcamán *m*; (*mass*) bulto *m*, mole *f*.

hulking ['hʌlkiŋ] *adj* grueso, pesado; **a** — **great brute** un hombrón.

hull [hʌl] *n* casco *m*.

hullabaloo [,hʌləbə'lu:] *n* (*fam*) (*noise*) vocería *f*, tumulto *m*; (*fuss*) lío *m*, bronca *f*; **a great** — **broke**

out estalló un ruido espantoso; **that** — **about the money** ese lío que se armó por el dinero.

hullo [hʌ'ləu] *interj* (*greeting*) ¡hola!; (*surprise*) ¡caramba!; (*Tel: calling*) ¡oiga!, (*answering*) ¡diga!; —, **what's all this?** ¡vamos a ver!

hum [hʌm] **1** *n* zumbido *m*; tarareo *m*; (*of voices etc*) ruido *m* confuso, murmullo *m*.

2 *vt tune* tararear, canturrear.

3 *vi* **(a)** (*insect, wire etc*) zumbar; (*person*) canturrear, tararear una canción; **to** — **with activity** bullir de actividad; **to make things** — desplegar gran actividad; avivarlo, estimular la actividad; **then things began to** — entonces sí empezaron a pasar cosas, hubo luego una actividad frenética.

(b) (*fam: smell*) oler mal.

(c) to — **and haw** vacilar, no resolverse.

human ['hju:mən] **1** *adj* humano. **2** *n* humano *m*, a *f*.

humane [hju:'mein] *adj* humano, humanitario.

humanism ['hju:mənizəm] *n* humanismo *m*.

humanist ['hju:mənist] *n* humanista *mf*.

humanistic [,hju:mə'nistik] *adj* humanístico.

humanitarian [hju:,mæni'tɛəriən] **1** *adj* humanitario. **2** *n* humanitario *m*, a *f*.

humanity [hju:'mæniti] *n* humanidad *f*; **the humanities** las humanidades.

humanize ['hju:mənaiz] *vt* humanizar.

humankind ['hju:mən'kaind] *n* género *m* humano.

humanly ['hju:mənli] *adv* humanamente; **all that is** — **possible** todo lo que pueda hacer un hombre, todo lo que cabe dentro de las posibilidades humanas.

humble ['hʌmbl] **1** *adj* humilde. **2** *vt* humillar. **3** *vr*: **to** — **oneself** humillarse.

humble-bee ['hʌmblbi:] *n* abejorro *m*.

humbleness ['hʌmblnis] *n* humildad *f*.

humbly ['hʌmbli] *adv* humildemente, con humildad.

humbug ['hʌmbag] *n* **(a)** (*thing*) bola *f*, embustes *mpl*, disparates *mpl*; **utter** —! ¡tonterías!; **what** —! ¡qué cinismo!

(b) (*sweet*) caramelo *m* de menta.

(c) (*person*) farsante *mf*, cínico *m*, charlatán *m*; **he's an old** — es un farsante.

humdinger ['hʌmdiŋə*] *n* (*sl*): **it's a** —! ¡es una auténtica maravilla!; **a real** — **of a car** un coche maravilloso.

humdrum ['hʌmdrʌm] *adj* monótono, aburrido; vulgar, ordinario; rutinario; mediocre, sin interés.

humerus ['hju:mərəs] *n*, *pl* **humeri** ['hju:mərai] húmero *m*.

humid ['hju:mid] *adj* húmedo.

humidifier [hju:'midifaiə*] *n* humectador *m*.

humidify [hju:'midifai] *vt* humedecer.

humidity [hju:'miditi] *n* humedad *f*.

humidor ['hju:midɔ:*] *n* (*for tobacco*) bote *m* humectativo; (*Tech*) humectador *m*.

humiliate [hju:'milieit] *vt* humillar.

humiliating [hju:'milieitiŋ] *adj* vergonzoso, humillante.

humiliation [hju:,mili'eifən] *n* humillación *f*.

humility [hju:'militi] *n* humildad *f*.

hummingbird ['hʌmiŋbə:d] *n* colibrí *m*.

humming-top ['hʌmiŋtɔp] *n* trompa *f*.

hummock ['hʌmək] *n* montecillo *m*, morón *m*.

humorist ['hju:mərist] *n* persona *f* chistosa; (*writer*) humorista *mf*; **what a** — **you are!** ¡qué gracioso eres!

humorous ['hju:mərəs] *adj* **person** gracioso, chistoso, divertido; **writer, genre** festivo, cómico; **joke, event, book** divertido; **tone** festivo.

humorously ['hju:mərəsli] *adv* graciosamente, de manera divertida; en tono festivo.

humour, (US) **humor** ['hju:mə*] **1** *n* **(a)** (*amusingness*) humorismo *m*; (*sense of*) sentido *m* del humor; (*creative talent*) vis *f* cómica; (*of joke, event*) gracia *f*; (*of situation*) comicidad *f*; **he has no** — **no tiene sentido del humor; I see no** — **in that** no encuentro nada divertido en eso; **this is no time for** — **éste no es lugar para chistes; I don't like the** — **in** "**Macbeth**" no me gustan las escenas cómicas de "Macbeth".

(b) (*mood*) humor *m*; **to be in a good** — estar de buen humor; **to be in high good** — estar de excelente humor; **they were in no** — **for fighting** no estaban de humor para pelear; **to be out of** — estar de mal humor.

(c) (*whim*) capricho *m*.

2 *vt* complacer, seguir el humor a; (*indulge*) mimar.

-humoured, (US) **-humored** ['hju:məd] *adj* de humor . . .

humourless, (US) **humorless** ['hju:məlis] *adj* **person** sin sentido del humor; **joke** nada divertido.

hump [hʌ...] **1** *n* (*Anat*) joroba *f*, corcova *f*, giba *f*; (*camel's*) giba *f*; (*in ground*) montecillo *m*; **to give**

someone the — jorobar, fastidiar; **to have the** — estar de mal humor; **we're over the** — **now** ya hemos vencido la cuesta.
　2 vt (a) **to** — **one's back** encorvarse, corcovarse. (b) (carry) llevar, llevar al hombro.

humpbacked ['hʌmpbækt] adj corcovado, jorobado; bridge de fuerte pendiente.

humph [mm] interj ¡bah!; ¡veremos!

humpy ['hʌmpi] adj desigual.

humus ['hju:məs] n humus m.

Hun [hʌn] n (Hist) huno m; (pej) tudesco m, alemán m; a — un alemán, the — los alemanes.

hunch [hʌntʃ] 1 n (Anat) see **hump**; (fig) idea f; sospecha f; (presentiment) presentimiento m; it's **only a** — no es más que una sospecha que tengo; **I have a** — that tengo la idea de que, se me ocurre que, me da el corazón que; —**es sometimes pay off a** veces los presentimientos se cumplen.
　2 vt (also to — up) encorvar; to — one's back encorvarse; **to sit** —**ed up** estar sentado con el cuerpo doblado.

hunchback ['hʌntʃbæk] n jorobado m, a f, corcovado m, a f.

hunchbacked ['hʌntʃbækt] adj jorobado, corcovado.

hundred ['hʌndrid] 1 adj ciento, (before n) cien; a — **and one** ciento uno; **a** — **and ten** ciento diez; **a** — **thousand** cien mil; **a** — **per cent** (fig) cien por cien.
　2 n ciento m, (less exactly) centenar m, centena f; —**s of people** centenares mpl de personas; —**s of thousands of bees** centenas de miles de abejas; **in** —**s, by the** — a centenares.

hundredfold ['hʌndridfəuld] 1 adj céntuplo. 2 adv cien veces.

hundredth ['hʌndridθ] 1 adj centésimo. 2 n centésimo m, centésima parte f.

hundredweight ['hʌndridweit] n (= 112 libras = 50,8 kilogramos) approx quintal m.

Hundred Years' War ['hʌndridjiəz'wɔː*] Guerra f de los Cien Años.

hung [hʌŋ] pret and ptp of **hang**.

Hungarian [hʌŋ'gεəriən] 1 adj húngaro. 2 n húngaro m, a f. 3 n (language) húngaro m.

Hungary ['hʌŋgəri] Hungría f.

hunger ['hʌŋgə*] 1 n hambre f (also fig: for de). 2 vi tener hambre, estar hambriento; **to** — **after, to** — **for** tener hambre de, ansiar, anhelar.

hunger strike ['hʌŋgəstraik] n huelga f de hambre.

hungrily ['hʌŋgrili] adv eat etc ansiosamente, ávidamente; **to look** — **at something** mirar algo con ganas de comerlo.

hungry ['hʌŋgri] adj hambriento; land pobre, estéril; **to be** — tener hambre (for de); **to be very** — tener mucha hambre; **to go** — pasar hambre; **to make someone** — dar hambre a uno.

hunk [hʌŋk] n pedazo m, trozo m.

hunt [hʌnt] 1 n caza f, cacería f (for de); (expedition) partida f de caza; (persons) grupo m de cazadores; (search) busca f, búsqueda f (for de); (pursuit) persecución f; **the** — **for the murderer** la persecución del asesino; **to be on the** — **for** ir a la caza de; **the** — **is on, the** — **is up** ha comenzado la búsqueda; **we joined in the** — **for the missing key** ayudamos a buscar la llave perdida.
　2 vt animal cazar; (search for) buscar; (pursue) perseguir; hounds etc emplear en la caza; country recorrer de caza, cazar en; **to** — **down** person perseguir (y encontrar), thing buscar hasta dar con; **to** — **out, to** — **up** (look for) buscar, (find) encontrar.
　3 vi cazar; dedicarse a la caza; **to** — **for** buscar; **to** — **about for** buscar por todas partes; **he** —**ed for it in his pocket** lo buscó en el bolsillo; **to go** —**ing** ir de caza.

hunter ['hʌntə*] n cazador m, ora f; (horse) caballo m de caza.

hunting ['hʌntiŋ] 1 n caza f, montería f. 2 attr de caza; **the** — **fraternity** los aficionados a la caza.

hunting box ['hʌntiŋbɔks] n pabellón m de caza.

hunting ground ['hʌntiŋgraund] n cazadero m; **a happy** — **for** un buen terreno para.

huntress ['hʌntris] n cazadora f.

huntsman ['hʌntsmən] n, pl —**men** [mən] cazador m, montero m.

hurdle ['hə:dl] n zarzo m, valla f; (Sport) valla f; (fig) obstáculo m.

hurdler ['hə:dlə*] n corredor m en las carreras de vallas.

hurdle-race ['hə:dlreis] n carrera f de vallas.

hurdy-gurdy ['hə:di,gə:di] n organillo m.

hurl [hə:l] 1 vt lanzar, arrojar; **to** — **back** enemy rechazar; **to** — **insults at someone** llenar a uno de improperios.

　2 vr: **to** — **oneself at** (or upon) **someone** abalanzarse sobre uno; **to** — **oneself into the fray** lanzarse a la batalla; **to** — **oneself over a cliff** arrojarse por un precipicio.

hurly-burly ['hə:li'bə:li] n tumulto m; **the** — **of politics** la vida alborotada de la política.

hurrah [hu'rɑ:], **hurray** [hu'rei] 1 interj ¡viva!, ¡vítor!; — **for Brown!** ¡viva Brown! 2 n vítor m.

hurricane ['hʌrikən] n huracán m.

hurricane lamp ['hʌrikən'læmp] n lámpara f a prueba de viento.

hurried ['hʌrid] adj apresurado, hecho de prisa; reading etc superficial; **he had a** — **meal** comió de prisa.

hurriedly ['hʌridli] adv con prisa, apresuradamente; study etc superficialmente; write etc a vuela pluma; **I left** — me apresuré a salir.

hurry ['hʌri] 1 n prisa f; **to be in a** — tener prisa (to do por hacer), estar de prisa; **to do something in a** — hacer algo de prisa; **are you in a** — **for this?** ¿corre prisa esto?; **is there any** —? ¿corre prisa?; **what's all the** —?, **what's your** —? ¿por qué tanta prisa?; **I shan't come back here in a** — aquí no pongo los pies nunca más; **he won't do that again in a** — no volverá a hacer eso si puede evitarlo.
　2 vt work etc apresurar, dar prisa a, acelerar (also **to** — **along, to** — **on, to** — **up**); **they hurried him to a doctor** le llevaron con toda prisa a un médico; **troops were hurried to the spot** se enviaron tropas al lugar con toda prisa; **this is a plan that cannot be hurried** éste es proyecto que no se puede realizar de prisa; **to** — **the work along** acelerar el ritmo del trabajo; **to** — **someone away, to** — **someone off** hacer marchar a uno de prisa; **the policeman hurried him away** el policía se le llevó apresuradamente; **to** — **someone out** dar prisa a uno para que salga; **to** — **someone up** hacer que uno se dé prisa.
　3 vi apresurarse (to do a hacer), darse prisa (to do para hacer); —! ¡dése prisa!; **don't** —! ¡no hay prisa!; **I must** — tengo que darme prisa; **she hurried home** se dio prisa para llegar a casa; **to** — **after someone** correr detrás de uno; **to** — **along** correr, ir de prisa; **to** — **away, to** — **off** marcharse de prisa; **to** — **back** darse prisa para volver, volver de prisa; **to** — **in** entrar de prisa, entrar corriendo; **to** — **out** salir de prisa, salir corriendo; **to** — **over** place cruzar rápidamente; work concluir aprisa, hacer con precipitación; **to** — **up** darse prisa; — **up!** ¡date prisa!

hurry-scurry ['hʌri'skʌri] 1 adv precipitadamente, atropelladamente.
　2 n precipitación f, prisa f grande; carrera f precipitada.
　3 vi precipitarse, lanzarse, correr precipitadamente.

hurt [hə:t] 1 n (wound etc) herida f, lesión f; (harm) daño m, mal m, perjuicio m.
　2 (irr: pret and ptp **hurt**) vt (injure, bodily) herir, hacer mal a, hacer daño a, lastimar; (cause pain to) doler; (damage) dañar; business, interests etc perjudicar, afectar; feelings herir, ofender; (be bad for) hacer daño a; **he** — **his foot** se lastimó el pie; **where does it** — **you?** ¿dónde le duele?; **to get** — hacerse daño; **in such affairs someone's bound to get** — en estos asuntos siempre sale uno perjudicado; **wine never** — **anybody** el vino no hizo nunca daño a nadie; **she's feeling rather** — **about it** se ofendió bastante por ello.
　3 vi (feel pain) doler; (take harm) sufrir daño, estropearse, echarse a perder; **does it** — **much?** ¿duele mucho?; **it won't** — **for being left another week** no se va a estropear si lo dejamos una semana más.
　4 vr: **to** — **oneself** hacerse daño, lastimarse.
　5 adj and ptp of **hurt**; foot etc lastimado, lisiado; feelings ofendido; **with a** — **look** con cara de ofendido; **in a** — **tone** quejoso, ofendido.

hurtful ['hə:tful] adj dañoso, perjudicial; remark etc hiriente.

hurtle ['hə:tl] 1 vt arrojar violentamente.
　2 vi: **to** — **along, to** — **past** (adv) ir como un rayo; **to** — **down** caer con violencia; **the car** —**d past us** el coche cruzó como un rayo delante de nosotros; **the rock** —**d over the cliff** la roca cayó estrepitosamente por el precipicio.

husband ['hʌzbənd] 1 n marido m; esposo m; **now they're** — **and wife** ahora son marido y mujer. 2 vt economizar, ahorrar, manejar prudentemente.

husbandry ['hʌzbəndri] n (Agr) agricultura f, labranza f; (fig) buen gobierno m, manejo m prudente.

hush [hʌʃ] **1** n silencio m; **a — fell** se hizo un silencio.
2 vt hacer callar, acallar, imponer silencio a; **to —
up** affair encubrir, echar tierra a; person tapar la
boca a.
3 vi callar(se); —! ¡chitón!, ¡cállate!
hushed [hʌʃt] adj tone callado, muy bajo; silence
profundo; **all were —** se callaron todos.
hush-hush ['hʌʃ'hʌʃ] adj muy secreto.
hush money ['hʌʃ,mʌni] n dinero m con que se
compra el silencio de uno, dinero m por callar.
husk [hʌsk] **1** n cáscara f, vaina f; (of corn) cascabillo
m. **2** vt descascarar, desvainar.
huskily ['hʌskili] adv roncamente, en voz ronca.
huskiness ['hʌskinis] n ronquedad f.
husky[1] ['hʌski] adj voice, person ronco; (tough)
fornido.
husky[2] ['hʌski] n perro m esquimal.
hussar [hə'zɑ:*] n húsar m.
hussy ['hʌsi] n pícara f, sinvergonzona f; **you —!**
¡lagarta!; **she's a little —** es una fresca.
hustings ['hʌstiŋz] npl (fig) elecciones fpl.
hustle ['hʌsl] **1** n actividad f febril, bullicio m;
(pushfulness) empuje m; **— and bustle** vaivén m,
actividad f bulliciosa; **to get a — on** (fam) darse
prisa.
2 vt (jostle) empujar, codear; (hurry up) person dar
prisa a, thing acelerar; **I won't be —d into anything** yo no resuelvo las cosas de prisa; **they —d him
into a car** le llevaron apresuradamente a un coche,
le hicieron entrar sin ceremonia en un coche; **to —
someone out of a room** hacer que uno salga precipitadamente de un cuarto; **they —d the job to finish
it** se apresuraron a concluir el trabajo.
3 vi darse prisa, menearse.
hut [hʌt] n casilla f; (shed) cobertizo m; (hovel)
barraca f, cabaña f; **mountain —** albergue m de
montaña.
hutch [hʌtʃ] n conejera f.
hyacinth ['haiəsinθ] n (Bot, Min) jacinto m.
hyaena [hai'i:nə] n hiena f.
hybrid ['haibrid] **1** adj híbrido. **2** n híbrido m, a f.
hybridism ['haibridizəm] n hibridismo m.
hybridization [,haibridai'zeiʃən] n hibridación f.
hybridize ['haibridaiz] vti hibridar.
hydra ['haidrə] n hidra f; **H—** (Myth) Hidra f.
hydrangea [hai'dreindʒə] n hortensia f.
hydrant ['haidrənt] n boca f de riego; **fire —** boca f
de incendios.
hydrate ['haidreit] **1** n hidrato m. **2** vt hidratar.
hydraulic [hai'drɔlik] adj hidráulico.
hydraulics [hai'drɔliks] n hidráulica f.
hydro . . . ['haidrəu] hidro . . .
hydrocarbon ['haidrəu'kɑ:bən] n hidrocarburo m.
hydrochloric ['haidrə'klɔrik] adj: **— acid** ácido m
clorhídrico.
hydrocyanic ['haidrəsai'ænik] adj: **— acid** ácido m
cianhídrico.
hydrodynamics ['haidrəudai'næmiks] n hidrodinámica f.
hydroelectric ['haidrəui'lektrik] adj hidroeléctrico;

— power station, — power plant central f hidro-
eléctrica.
hydrogen ['haidridʒən] n hidrógeno m.
hydrography [hai'drɔgrəfi] n hidrografía f.
hydrolysis [hai'drɔlisis] n hidrólisis f.
hydrolyze ['haidrəulaiz] **1** vt hidrolizar. **2** vi hidrolizarse.
hydrometer [hai'drɔmitə*] n areómetro m.
hydrophobia [,haidrə'fəubiə] n hidrofobia f.
hydrophobic [,haidrə'fəubik] adj hidrofóbico.
hydroplane ['haidrəuplein] n hidroplano m, hidroavión m.
hydroxide [hai'drɔksaid] n hidróxido m.
hyena [hai'i:nə] n hiena f.
hygiene ['haidʒi:n] n higiene f.
hygienic [hai'dʒi:nik] adj higiénico.
hymen ['haimen] n (Anat) himen m.
hymn [him] n himno m.
hymnal ['himnəl] n, **hymn book** ['himbuk] n
himnario m.
hyperacidity ['haipərə'siditi] n hiperacidez f.
hyperbola [hai'pə:bələ] n hipérbola f.
hyperbole [hai'pə:bəli] n hipérbole f.
hyperbolic(al) [,haipə'bɔlik(əl)] adj hiperbólico.
hypercritical ['haipə'kritikəl] adj hipercrítico.
hypersensitive ['haipə'sensitiv] adj extremadamente
sensible.
hypertension ['haipə'tenʃən] n hipertensión f.
hyphen ['haifən] n guión m.
hyphenate ['haifəneit] vt escribir (or unir, separar)
con guión.
hypnosis [hip'nəusis] n hipnosis f.
hypnotic [hip'nɔtik] **1** adj hipnótico. **2** n hipnótico m.
hypnotism ['hipnətizəm] n hipnotismo m.
hypnotist ['hipnətist] n hipnotista mf.
hypnotize ['hipnətaiz] vt hipnotizar.
hypo ['haipəu] n hiposulfito m sódico.
hypochondria [,haipəu'kɔndriə] n hipocondría f.
hypochondriac [,haipəu'kɔndriæk] n hipocondríaco
m, a f.
hypocrisy [hi'pɔkrisi] n hipocresía f.
hypocrite ['hipəkrit] n hipócrita mf.
hypocritical [,hipə'kritikəl] adj hipócrita.
hypocritically [,hipə'kritikəli] adv hipócritamente.
hypodermic [,haipə'də:mik] n (also **— needle**) aguja
f hipodérmica.
hypotenuse [hai'pɔtinju:z] n hipotenusa f.
hypothesis [hai'pɔθisis] n, pl **hypotheses** [hai'pɔ-
θisi:z] hipótesis f.
hypothetic(al) [,haipəu'θetik(əl)] adj hipotético.
hypothetically [,haipəu'θetikəli] adv hipotéticamente.
hysterectomy [,histə'rektəmi] n histerectomía f.
hysteria [his'tiəriə] n histerismo m, histeria f.
hysterical [his'terikəl] adj histérico; **— laughter**
risa f histérica; **to get —** ponerse histérico, excitarse
locamente.
hysterically [his'terikəli] adv histéricamente.
hysterics [his'teriks] npl histerismo m, paroxismo m
histérico; **to go into —** ponerse histérico; **we were in
— about it** nos morimos casi de risa.

I

I [ai] *pron* yo.
iambic [ai'æmbik] *adj* yámbico.
Iberia [ai'biəriə] Iberia *f*.
Iberian [ai'biəriən] **1** *adj* ibero, ibérico. **2** *n* ibero *m*, a *f*.
Iberian Peninsula [ai'biəriənpə'ninsjulə] Península *f* Ibérica.
ibex ['aibeks] *n* íbice *m*, rebeco *m*.
ibis ['aibis] *n* ibis *f*.
ice [ais] **1** *n* hielo *m*; (*ice cream*) helado *m*; (*on cake*) alcorza *f*, garapiña *f*; **my feet are like** — tengo los pies helados; **to break the** — (*fig*) romper el hielo; **he cuts no** — no pincha ni corta; **it cuts no** — **with me** no me convence; **to keep something on** — conservar algo en frigorífico, (*fig*) tener algo en reserva; **to skate on thin** — pisar terreno peligroso.
   2 *vt* helar; *drink* enfriar, echar cubos de hielo a; *cake* alcorzar, escarchar, garapiñar.
   3 *vi* (*also* **to** — **over**, **to** — **up**) helarse.
ice age ['aiseidʒ] *n* período *m* glacial.
ice axe ['aisæks] *n* piolet *m*.
iceberg ['aisbəːg] *n* iceberg *m*.
iceboat ['aisbəut] *n* (*US Sport*) trineo *m* con vela (para deslizarse sobre el hielo).
icebound ['aisbaund] *adj* road helado, bloqueado por el hielo; *ship* preso entre los hielos.
icebox ['aisbɔks] *n* nevera *f*.
icebreaker ['ais,breikə*] *n* rompehielos *m*.
icecap ['aiskæp] *n* casquete *m* de hielo.
ice-cold ['ais'kəuld] *adj* más frío que el hielo.
ice cream ['ais'kriːm] *n* helado *m*.
ice cube ['aiskjuːb] *n* cubito *m* de hielo.
iced [aist] *adj* cake escarchado; *drink* con hielo.
ice field ['aisfiːld] *n* campo *m* de hielo, banquisa *f*.
ice floe ['aisfləu] *n* témpano *m* de hielo.
ice hockey ['ais'hɔki] *n* hockey *m* sobre hielo.
icehouse ['aishaus] *n*, *pl* —**houses** [,hauziz] (a) (*US*) nevera *f*. (b) (*of Eskimo*) iglú *m*.
Iceland ['aislənd] Islandia *f*.
Icelander ['aisləndə*] *n* islandés *m*, esa *f*.
Icelandic [ais'lændik] **1** *adj* islandés. **2** *n* islandés *m*.
iceman ['aismæn] *n*, *pl* —**men** [men] (*US*) vendedor *m* de hielo, repartidor *m* de hielo.
ice pick ['aispik] *n* piolet *m*.
ice rink ['aisriŋk] pista *f* de hielo, pista *f* de patinaje.
iceskate ['aisskeit] *n* patín *m* de hielo, patín *m* de cuchilla.
ice-skate ['aisskeit] *vi* patinar sobre hielo.
ice skating ['aisskeitiŋ] *n* patinaje *m* sobre hielo.
ichthyology [,ikθi'ɔlədʒi] *n* ictiología *f*.
icicle ['aisikl] *n* carámbano *m*.
icily ['aisili] *adv* glacialmente (*also fig*).
icing ['aisiŋ] *n* formación *f* de hielo; (*on cake*) alcorza *f*, garapiña *f*.
icing sugar ['aisiŋ'ʃugə*] *n* azúcar *m* de alcorza.
icon ['aikɔn] *n* icono *m*.
iconoclast [ai'kɔnəklæst] *n* iconoclasta *mf*.
iconoclastic [ai,kɔnə'klæstik] *adj* iconoclasta.
icy ['aisi] *adj* helado, glacial; (*fig*) glacial; **it's** — **cold** hace un frío glacial.
id [id] *n* id *m*.
I'd [aid] = **I would; I had.**
idea [ai'diə] *n* idea *f*; concepto *m*; ocurrencia *f*; **bright** — idea *f* luminosa, idea *f* genial; **what an** —!, **the very** —! ¡ni hablar!, ¡qué cosas dices!; **the** — **is to sell it** nos proponemos venderlo; **whose** — **was it to come this way?** ¿a quién se le ocurrió venir por aquí?; **it would not be a bad** — **to** hacer it no le vendría mal una mano de pintura; **that's the** —! ¡eso es!; **what's the big** —? ¿que hace Vd ahí?, ¿qué pretende Vd con esto?; **to get an** — **of something** hacerse una idea de algo; **to get an** — **for a novel** encontrar la inspiración para hacer una novela; **you're getting the** — estás empezando a comprender, (*of knack*) estás cogiendo el tino; **to get an** —

into one's head meterse una idea en la cabeza; **don't go getting** —**s** no te hagas ilusiones; **he has some** — **of French** tiene algunas nociones de francés; **I've no** —! ¡ni idea!; **I haven't the foggiest** (*or remotest etc*) — no tengo la más remota idea; **I had no** — **that . . .** no tenía la menor idea de que . . .; **he hit on the** — **of** + ger se le ocurrió + infin; **to put** —**s into someone's head** sugerir cosas a uno.
ideal [ai'diəl] **1** *adj* ideal; perfecto; soñado. **2** *n* ideal *m*.
idealism [ai'diəlizəm] *n* idealismo *m*.
idealist [ai'diəlist] *n* idealista *mf*.
idealistic [ai,diə'listik] *adj* idealista.
idealize [ai'diəlaiz] *vt* idealizar.
ideally [ai'diəli] *adv* idealmente; perfectamente; **they are** — **suited to each other** se convienen perfectamente uno a otra; —, **we should all go** en el mejor de los casos, debemos ir todos.
idée fixe ['iːdei'fiːks] *n* idea *f* fija.
identical [ai'dentikəl] *adj* idéntico.
identification [ai,dentifi'keiʃən] *n* identificación *f*; — **mark** señal *f* de identificación; — **tag** chapa *f* de identificación.
identify [ai'dentifai] **1** *vt* identificar. **2** *vr*: **to** — **oneself** identificarse, establecer su identidad; **to** — **oneself with** identificarse con.
identikit [ai'dentikit] *n*: — **picture** retrato-robot *m*.
identity [ai'dentiti] *n* identidad *f*; **mistaken** — identificación *f* errónea; — **card** cédula *f* personal, carnet *m* de identidad *m*; — **disc** chapa *f* de identidad.
ideological [,aidiə'lɔdʒikəl] *adj* ideológico.
ideologist [,aidi'ɔlədʒist] *n* ideólogo *m*.
ideology [,aidi'ɔlədʒi] *n* ideología *f*.
ides [aidz] *npl* idus *mpl*.
idiocy ['idiəsi] *n* imbecilidad *f*; estupidez *f*.
idiom ['idiəm] *n* (*phrase*) idiotismo *m*, modismo *m*, locución *f*; (*style of expression*) lenguaje *m*.
idiomatic [,idiə'mætik] *adj* idiomático.
idiosyncrasy [,idiə'siŋkrəsi] *n* idiosincrasia *f*.
idiosyncratic [,idiəsiŋ'krætik] *adj* idiosincrásico.
idiot ['idiət] *n* idiota *mf*, imbécil *mf*, tonto *m*, a *f*; **village** — tonto *m* del lugar; **you** —! ¡imbécil!
idiotic [,idi'ɔtik] *adj* idiota, imbécil, tonto, estúpido; *laughter* tonto; **that was** — **of you** has hecho el tonto.
idiotically [,idi'ɔtikəli] *adv* tontamente, estúpidamente; **to laugh** — reírse como un tonto.
idle ['aidl] **1** *adj* ocioso; (*lazy*) holgazán; (*work-shy*) vago; *student etc* gandul; (*without work*) desocupado; *fear* vano, infundado; *speculation* inútil; *question* ocioso; *talk* frívolo; *moment* de ocio, libre; **the machine is never** — la máquina no está parada jamás; **the strike made 100 workers** — la huelga dejó sin trabajo a 100 obreros.
   2 *vt*: **to** — **away** *time* perder, malgastar.
   3 *vi* haraganear, gandulear; (*Mech*) marchar en vacío; **we spent a few days idling in Paris** pasamos unos días ociosos en París; **we** —**d over our meal** no nos dimos prisa para terminar la comida.
idleness ['aidlnis] *n* ociosidad *f*, holgazanería *f*, gandulería *f*; desocupación *f*; inutilidad *f*; frivolidad *f*; **to live in** — vivir en el ocio.
idler ['aidlə*] *n* ocioso *m*, a *f*, holgazán *m*, ana *f*, vago *m*, a *f*; (*student*) gandul *m*.
idly ['aidli] *adv* ociosamente; vanamente, inútilmente; **he glanced** — **out of the window** miró distraído por la ventana.
idol ['aidl] *n* ídolo *m*.
idolater [ai'dɔlətə*] *n* idólatra *mf*.
idolatrous [ai'dɔlətrəs] *adj* idólatra, idolátrico.
idolatry [ai'dɔlətri] *n* idolatría *f*.
idolize ['aidəlaiz] *vt* idolatrar.
idyll ['idil] *n* idilio *m*.

idyllic [i'dilik] *adj* idílico.
if [if] **1** *conj* **(a)** si; *(open condition)* — **he comes I'll go** si él viene yo iré; *(past: habit)* — **it was fine we went out** si hacía buen tiempo dábamos un paseo; *(past: unfulfilled)* — **you were to say that you would be wrong** si dijese eso se equivocaría; — **you had said that you would have been wrong** si hubiera dicho eso se habría equivocado.
  (b) — **I were you** yo en tu lugar, yo que tú.
  (c) *(whether)* si; **I don't know** — **he's here** no sé si está aquí.
  (d) — **anything this one is better** hasta creo que éste es mejor; — **not** si no; — **so** si es así; **a nice film** — **rather long** una buena película pero algo larga.
  (e) — **only to see him** si solamente para verle; — **only for a few hours** si solamente durante unas pocas horas; — **only I could!** ¡ojalá pudiera!, ¡si solamente pudiera!; — **only I had known!** ¡si lo hubiese sabido!; — **only we had a car!** ¡quién tuviera coche!; *see* **as, even** *etc*.
  2 *n* hipótesis *f*; duda *f*; **there are a lot of** —**s and buts** hay muchas dudas no resueltas; **it's a big** — **es** una duda importante, es sumamente dudoso.
iffy ['ifi] *adj (US fam)* dudoso, incierto.
igloo ['iglu:] *n* iglú *m*.
Ignatius [ig'neifəs] *m* Ignacio.
igneous ['igniəs] *adj* ígneo.
ignite [ig'nait] **1** *vt* encender, incendiar, pegar fuego a. **2** *vi* encenderse, incendiarse.
ignition [ig'nifən] *n* ignición *f*; *(Aut)* encendido *m*.
ignition key [ig'nifən,ki:] *n* llave *f* de contacto.
ignoble [ig'nəubl] *adj* innoble, vil.
ignominious [,ignə'miniəs] *adj* ignominioso, oprobioso; *defeat* vergonzoso.
ignominiously [,ignə'miniəsli] *adv* ignominiosamente; **to be** — **defeated** sufrir una derrota vergonzosa.
ignominy ['ignəmini] *n* ignominia *f*, oprobio *m*, vergüenza *f*.
ignoramus [,ignə'reiməs] *n* ignorante *mf*.
ignorance ['ignərəns] *n* ignorancia *f*; **to be in** — **of something** ignorar algo, desconocer algo.
ignorant ['ignərənt] *adj* ignorante; **to be** — **of** ignorar, no saber, desconocer.
ignorantly ['ignərəntli] *adv* neciamente; **we** — **went to the next house** por ignorancia fuimos a la casa de al lado.
ignore [ig'nɔ:*] *vt* no hacer caso de, desatender; *(omit)* pasar por alto; *awkward fact* cerrar los ojos ante; **we can safely** — **that** eso lo podemos dejar a un lado; **I smiled but she** —**d me** le sonreí pero ella no me hizo caso.
iguana [i'gwɑ:nə] *n* iguana *f*.
ikon ['aikɒn] *n* icono *m*.
ilex ['aileks] *n* encina *f*.
Iliad ['iliæd] Ilíada *f*.
ilk [ilk] *n*: **and others of that** — y otros de ese jaez.
ill [il] **1** *adj* **(a)** *(Med)* enfermo, malo; **to be** — estar enfermo; **to fall** *(or* **take, be taken)** — ponerse enfermo, enfermar; **to feel** — sentirse mal.
  (b) *fame, temper, turn etc* malo.
  2 *adv* mal; **we can** — **afford to lose him** mal podemos permitir que se vaya; **to speak** — **of someone** hablar mal de uno, criticar a uno; **he took it very** — se ofendió bastante; **don't take it** — no lo tome a mal.
  3 *n* *(Med)* mal *m*; *(fig)* infortunio *m*, desgracia *f*; **the** —**s of the economy** la dolencia de la economía.
I'll [ail] = **I will, I shall.**
ill-advised ['iləd'vaizd] *adj*: **an** — **plan** un proyecto nada recomendable; **you were very** — en eso no anduvo Vd muy acertado; **you would be** — **to** + *infin* sería poco aconsejable que Vd + *subj*.
ill-at-ease ['ilət'i:z] *adj* molesto; inquieto, intranquilo.
ill-bred ['il'bred] *adj* mal educado, mal criado.
ill-considered ['ilkən'sidəd] *adj* *plan* nada recomendable; *act* irreflexivo.
ill-disposed ['ildis'pəuzd] *adj* malintencionado; **to be** — **towards someone** estar maldispuesto hacia uno; **he is** — **towards the idea** la idea no le hace gracia.
illegal [i'li:gəl] *adj* ilegal, ilícito.
illegality [,ili:'gæliti] *n* ilegalidad *f*.
illegally [i'li:gəli] *adv* ilegalmente, ilícitamente.
illegible [i'ledʒəbl] *adj* ilegible.
illegibly [i'ledʒəbli] *adv* de un modo ilegible.
illegitimacy [,ili'dʒitiməsi] *n* ilegitimidad *f*.
illegitimate [,ili'dʒitimit] *adj* ilegítimo.
illegitimately [,ili'dʒitimitli] *adv* ilegítimamente.
ill-fated ['il'feitid] *adj* malogrado, malhadado.
ill-favoured ['il'feivəd] *adj* feo, mal parecido.

ill-feeling ['il'fi:liŋ] *n* hostilidad *f*, rencor *m*.
ill-founded ['il'faundid] *adj* *claim etc* mal fundado, infundado.
ill-gotten ['il'gɒtn] *adj* mal adquirido.
ill health ['il'helθ] *n* mala salud *f*; **to be in** — no estar bien de salud.
ill humour, *(US)* —**humor** ['il'hju:mə*] *n* mal humor *m*.
ill-humoured, *(US)* —**-humored** ['il'hju:məd] *adj* malhumorado.
illiberal [i'libərəl] *adj* iliberal; intolerante.
illicit [i'lisit] *adj* ilícito.
illicitly [i'lisitli] *adv* ilícitamente.
illimitable [i'limitəbl] *adj* ilimitable, sin límites.
ill-informed ['ilin'fɔ:md] *adj* poco enterado, ignorante.
illiteracy [i'litərəsi] *n* analfabetismo *m*.
illiterate [i'litərit] **1** *adj* analfabeto; *(fig)* sin instrucción, poco instruido; iletrado; *style etc* inculto. **2** *n* analfabeto *m*, a *f*.
ill-judged ['il'dʒʌdʒd] *adj* imprudente.
ill-kempt ['il'kempt] *adj* desaliñado, desaseado.
ill luck ['il'lʌk] *n* mala suerte *f*; **as** — **would have it** desgraciadamente, como quiso la desgracia.
ill-mannered ['il'mænəd] *adj* mal educado, sin educación.
ill-natured ['il'neitʃəd] *adj* malévolo, malicioso.
illness ['ilnis] *n* enfermedad *f*, mal *m*.
illogical [i'lɒdʒikəl] *adj* ilógico.
illogicality [i'lɒdʒi'kæliti] *n* falta *f* de lógica.
ill-omened ['il'əumənd] *adj* de mal agüero; nefasto.
ill-starred ['il'stɑ:d] *adj* malhadado, malogrado.
ill-suited ['il'su:tid] *adj*: **they are** — no se convienen uno a otro; **he is** — **to the job** no conviene al puesto, no tiene las cualidades que convienen al puesto.
ill-tempered ['il'tempəd] *adj* *person* de mal genio; *remark, tone etc* malhumorado.
ill-timed ['il'taimd] *adj* inoportuno, intempestivo.
ill-treat ['il'tri:t] *vt* maltratar, tratar mal.
ill treatment ['il'tri:tmənt] *n* maltratamiento *m*, malos tratos *mpl*.
illuminate [i'lu:mineit] *vt* iluminar *(also Art)*; *(decorate with lights)* poner luminarias en; *subject* aclarar; **the castle is** —**d in summer** en el verano el castillo está iluminado.
illuminated [i'lu:mineitid] *adj* *sign etc* luminoso.
illuminating [i'lu:mineitiŋ] *adj* aclaratorio; *book, speech etc* instructivo; *remark etc* revelador, significativo.
illumination [i,lu:mi'neifən] *n* iluminación *f* *(also Art)*, alumbrado *m*; —**s** *(festive etc)* luminarias *fpl*.
illuminator [i'lu:mineitə*] *n* iluminador *m*.
illumine [i'lu:min] *vt* = **illuminate.**
ill-use ['il'ju:z] *vt* maltratar, tratar mal.
illusion [i'lu:ʒən] *n* ilusión *f*; *optical* — ilusión *f* de óptica; **to be under an** — estar equivocado; **I am under no** —**s on that score** sobre ese punto no tengo ilusiones.
illusive [i'lu:siv] *adj*, **illusory** [i'lu:səri] *adj* ilusorio.
illustrate ['iləstreit] *vt* ilustrar; *subject* aclarar; *point* ejemplificar, demostrar; *book* ilustrar; **a book** —**d by X** un libro con grabados de X; **I can best** — **this in the following way** esto quedará más claro si se explica del modo siguiente.
illustration [,iləs'treifən] *n* *(example)* ejemplo *m*; *(explanation)* explicación *f*, aclaración *f*; *(in book)* grabado *m*, lámina *f*, ilustración *f*.
illustrative ['iləstrətiv] *adj* ilustrativo, ilustrador, aclaratorio; **to be** — **of something** ejemplificar algo.
illustrator ['iləstreitə*] *n* ilustrador *m*.
illustrious [i'lʌstriəs] *adj* ilustre.
ill will ['il'wil] *n* mala voluntad *f*; *(spite)* rencor *m*; **I bear you no** — **for that** no le guardo rencor por eso.
I'm [aim] = **I am.**
image ['imidʒ] *n* **(a)** imagen *f* *(also Lit, Eccl)*; *mirror* — reflejo *m* exacto; **to be the very** *(or* **spitting)** — **of** ser el vivo retrato de; **to make someone in one's own** — hacer a uno a su imagen.
  (b) *(public face)* reputación *f*, opinión *f*; **brand** — reputación *f* de una marca; **the company's** — la reputación de la compañía; **we must improve our** — hemos de mejorar la opinión que el público tiene de nosotros.
imagery ['imidʒəri] *n* *(Lit)* imágenes *fpl*, metáforas *fpl*.
imaginable [i'mædʒinəbl] *adj* imaginable; **the biggest surprise** — la mayor sorpresa que se puede imaginar.
imaginary [i'mædʒinəri] *adj* imaginario.
imagination [i,mædʒi'neifən] *n* imaginación *f*;

(*capacity for* —) imaginativa *f*; (*inventiveness*) inventiva *f*; **it's all** —**!** ¡es pura fantasía!, ¡lo has soñado!; **have you no** —**?** ¿eres incapaz de imaginártelo?; **she lets her** — **run away with her** se deja llevar por la imaginación.

imaginative [i'mædʒinətiv] *adj* imaginativo.

imaginativeness [i'mædʒinətivnis] *n* imaginativa *f*.

imagine [i'mædʒin] *vt* imaginar, imaginarse, figurarse; **just** —**!** ¡imagínese!; **you can** — **how I felt!** ¡Vd puede suponer lo que yo sufría!; **don't** — **that** . . . no se vaya a pensar que yo + *subj*; **to fondly** — **that** . . . hacerse la ilusión de que . . ., creer inocentemente que . . .

imbalance [im'bæləns] *n* desequilibrio *m*, falta *f* de equilibrio.

imbecile ['imbəsi:l] **1** *adj* imbécil. **2** *n* imbécil *mf*; **you** —**!** ¡imbécil!

imbecility [,imbi'siliti] *n* imbecilidad *f*.

imbibe [im'baib] **1** *vt* (*drink*) beber; (*absorb*) embeber; (*fig*) embeberse de (*or* en), empaparse de. **2** *vi* beber.

imbroglio [im'brəuliəu] *n* embrollo *m*, lío *m*.

imbue [im'bju:] *vt*: **to** — **something with** imbuir algo de (*or* en); **to** —**d with** estar empapado de.

imitable ['imitəbl] *adj* imitable.

imitate ['imiteit] *vt* imitar; (*pej*) remedar; (*make another copy of*) copiar, reproducir.

imitation [,imi'teiʃən] **1** *n* imitación *f*; (*pej*) remedo *m*; (*copy*) copia *f*, reproducción *f*; **in** — **of** a imitación de; **beware of** —**s** desconfíe de las imitaciones.
   2 *attr*: — **jewels** joyas *fpl* de imitación.

imitative ['imitətiv] *adj* imitativo; imitador; **a style** — **of Joyce's** un estilo que imita el de Joyce.

imitator ['imiteitə*] *n* imitador *m*, ora *f*.

immaculate [i'mækjulit] *adj* (*spotless*) limpísimo, perfectamente limpio; *style etc* perfecto; (*Eccl*) inmaculado, purísimo.

immanent ['imənənt] *adj* inmanente.

immaterial [,imə'tiəriəl] *adj* inmaterial, incorpóreo; **it is** — **whether** . . . no importa si . . .; **that is quite** — eso no hace al caso; **that is** — **to me** eso me es indiferente.

immature [,imə'tjuə*] *adj* inmaturo, no maduro; *specimen* joven; *fruit* verde; *work* juvenil.

immaturity [,imə'tjuəriti] *n* inmadurez *f*, falta *f* de madurez; juventud *f*.

immeasurable [i'meʒərəbl] *adj* inmensurable, inconmensurable.

immeasurably [i'meʒərəbli] *adv* enormemente.

immediacy [i'mi:diəsi] *n* inmediatez *f*; urgencia *f*.

immediate [i'mi:diət] *adj* inmediato; (*pressing*) urgente, apremiante; (*prime*) primero, principal; **my** — **object** mi primer propósito; **the** — **area** las inmediaciones; **we must take** — **action** hay que obrar inmediatamente.

immediately [i'mi:diətli] **1** *adv* (**a**) (*of time*) inmediatamente, en seguida; sin demora; en el acto; — **following the dinner** luego de la cena; — **following this discussion** a raíz de esta discusión.
   (**b**) (*of place*) — **next to the wall** muy junto a la pared.
   2 *conj* así que, luego que, al instante que; **let me know** — **he comes** avíseme en cuanto venga.

immemorial [,imi'mɔ:riəl] *adj* inmemorial, inmemorable; **from time** — desde hace muchísimo tiempo.

immense [i'mens] *adj* inmenso, enorme.

immensely [i'mensli] *adv* enormemente; **we were** — **cheered** nos alegramos muchísimo; **did you enjoy yourselves?** yes, — ¿qué tal lo pasasteis? estupendamente; **it is** — **difficult** es enormemente difícil.

immensity [i'mensiti] *n* inmensidad *f*.

immerse [i'mə:s] **1** *vt* sumergir; hundir; **to be** —**d in** (*fig*) estar absorto en. **2** *vr*: **to** — **oneself in** (*fig*) sumergirse en.

immersion [i'mə:ʃən] *n* inmersión *f*, sumersión *f*.

immersion heater [i'mə:ʃən,hi:tə*] *n* calentador *m* de inmersión.

immigrant ['imigrənt] **1** *adj* inmigrante. **2** *n* inmigrante *mf*.

immigrate ['imigreit] *vi* inmigrar.

immigration [,imi'greiʃən] *n* inmigración *f*.

imminence ['iminəns] *n* inminencia *f*.

imminent ['iminənt] *adj* inminente.

immobile [i'məubail] *adj* inmóvil, inmoble.

immobility [,iməu'biliti] *n* inmovilidad *f*.

immobilize [i'məubilaiz] *vt* inmovilizar.

immoderate [i'mɔdərit] *adj* excesivo.

immoderately [i'mɔdəritli] *adv* excesivamente; **to drink** — beber en exceso.

immodest [i'mɔdist] *adj* (*indecent*) deshonesto, impúdico; (*impudent*) descarado.

immodestly [i'mɔdistli] *adv* impúdicamente; descaradamente.

immodesty [i'mɔdisti] *n* deshonestidad *f*, impudicia *f*; descaro *m*.

immolate ['iməuleit] *vt* inmolar.

immoral [i'mɔrəl] *adj* inmoral; *earnings* ilícito.

immorality [,imə'ræliti] *n* inmoralidad *f*.

immortal [i'mɔ:tl] **1** *adj* inmortal; *fame etc* imperecedero. **2** *n* inmortal *mf*.

immortality [,imɔ:'tæliti] *n* inmortalidad *f*.

immortalize [i'mɔ:təlaiz] *vt* inmortalizar.

immovable [i'mu:vəbl] *adj* inmoble, inmóvil; que no se puede mover; *feast etc* fijo; (*fig*) inalterable, inconmovible; **he was quite** — fue imposible convencerle.

immune [i'mju:n] *adj* inmune (*also Med; from*, **to** a, contra); **to be** — **from taxes** estar exento de impuestos.

immunity [i'mju:niti] *n* inmunidad *f* (*also Med; from*, **to** contra); exención *f* (*from* de); **diplomatic** — inmunidad *f* diplomática; **parliamentary** — inmunidad *f* parlamentaria.

immunization [,imjunai'zeiʃən] *n* (*Med*) inmunización *f*.

immunize ['imjunaiz] *vt* inmunizar.

immure [i'mjuə*] *vt* emparedar; (*fig*) encerrar; **to be** —**d in** estar encerrado en.

immutability [i,mju:tə'biliti] *n* inmutabilidad *f*, inalterabilidad *f*.

immutable [i'mju:təbl] *adj* inmutable, inalterable.

imp [imp] *n* diablillo *m* (*also fig*).

impact ['impækt] *n* impacto *m*, choque *m*; (*fig*) impacto *m*, efecto *m*, consecuencias *fpl*; **the book had a great** — **on its readers** el libro conmovió profundamente a sus lectores; **the** — **of our advertising campaign** el efecto de nuestra campaña publicitaria.

impair [im'peə*] *vt* perjudicar, dañar, deteriorar, debilitar.

impale [im'peil] **1** *vt* (*as punishment*) empalar; (*on sword etc*) espetar, atravesar. **2** *vr*: **to** — **oneself on** atravesarse en.

impalpable [im'pælpəbl] *adj* impalpable; (*fig*) intangible, inaprensible.

imparity [im'pæriti] *n* disparidad *f*.

impart [im'pa:t] *vt* comunicar.

impartial [im'pa:ʃəl] *adj* imparcial.

impartiality [im,pa:ʃi'æliti] *n* imparcialidad *f*.

impartially [im'pa:ʃəli] *adv* imparcialmente.

impassable [im'pa:səbl] *adj* intransitable; *river etc* invadeable; *barrier* infranqueable.

impasse [æm'pa:s] *n* callejón *m* sin salida; parálisis *f*, situación *f* sin solución; **the** — **lasted 3 months** la parálisis duró 3 meses; **the** — **is complete** la parálisis es total; **negotiations have reached an** — las negociaciones han llegado a un punto muerto, las negociaciones están en un callejón sin salida.

impassioned [im'pæʃnd] *adj* apasionado, exaltado.

impassive [im'pæsiv] *adj* impasible, imperturbable.

impassively [im'pæsivli] *adv* imperturbablemente; **he listened** — escuchó impasible.

impatience [im'peiʃəns] *n* impaciencia *f*.

impatient [im'peiʃənt] *adj* impaciente; intolerante; **to be** — **to** + *infin* impacientarse por + *infin*; **to be** — **of something** no sufrir algo con paciencia, no aguantar algo ; **to get** (*or* **become, grow**) — **about something** impacientarse ante algo, impacientarse por algo; **to get** — **with someone** perder la paciencia con uno; **to make someone** — impacientar a uno.

impatiently [im'peiʃəntli] *adv* con impaciencia, impacientemente.

impeach [im'pi:tʃ] *vt* (*accuse*) acusar (de alta traición); (*try*) procesar; (*criticize*) censurar; tachar.

impeachment [im'pi:tʃmənt] *n* acusación *f* (de alta traición); proceso *m*.

impeccable [im'pekəbl] *adj* impecable, intachable.

impecunious [,impi'kju:niəs] *adj* inope, indigente.

impede [im'pi:d] *vt person* estorbar; (*fig*) dificultar, estorbar, impedir.

impediment [im'pedimənt] *n* obstáculo *m*, estorbo *m* (*to* para); (*Law*) impedimento *m*; (*in speech*) defecto *m* del habla.

impedimenta [im,pedi'mentə] *npl* equipaje *m*; (*Mil*) impedimenta *f*.

impel [im'pel] *vt* impulsar, mover (*to* + *infin* a + *infin*); **I feel** —**led to say** . . . me veo obligado a decir . . .

impend [im'pend] *vi* amenazar, ser inminente.

impending [im'pendiŋ] *adj* inminente; (*near*) próximo; **his** — **fate** el hado que le amenazaba; **his** — **retirement** su jubilación que va a realizarse en breve; **our** — **removal** nuestra mudanza en fecha próxima.

impenetrability [im,penitrə'biliti] *n* impenetrabilidad *f*.

impenetrable [im'penitrəbl] *adj* impenetrable (*to* a); *mind etc* insondable, enigmático.
impenitence [im'penitəns] *n* impenitencia *f*.
impenitent [im'penitənt] *adj* impenitente, incorregible; **he was quite — about it** no tuvo el menor deseo de pedir perdón por ello.
imperative [im'perətiv] **1** *adj tone* imperioso, perentorio; (*Gram*) imperativo; (*necessary*) esencial, indispensable; (*pressing*) urgente, apremiante; **it is — that** es imprescindible que + *subj*.
2 *n* (*Gram*) imperativo *m*.
imperceptible [,impə'septəbl] *adj* imperceptible, insensible.
imperceptibly [,impə'septəbli] *adv* imperceptiblemente, insensiblemente.
imperfect [im'pə:fikt] **1** *adj* imperfecto (*also Gram*), defectuoso. **2** *n* (*Gram*) imperfecto *m*.
imperfection [,impə'fekʃən] *n* (*state*) imperfección *f*; (*blemish*) desperfecto *m*, tacha *f*.
imperfectly [im'pə:fiktli] *adv* defectuosamente.
imperial [im'piəriəl] *adj* imperial.
imperialism [im'piəriəlizəm] *n* imperialismo *m*.
imperialist [im'piəriəlist] *n* imperialista *mf*.
imperialistic [im,piəriə'listik] *adj* imperialista.
imperially [im'piəriəli] *adv* imperialmente.
imperil [im'peril] *vt* poner en peligro, arriesgar.
imperious [im'piəriəs] *adj* imperioso, arrogante; *need* apremiante.
imperiously [im'piəriəsli] *adv* imperiosamente.
imperishable [im'periʃəbl] *adj* imperecedero.
impermanent [im'pə:mənənt] *adj* impermanente.
impermeable [im'pə:miəbl] *adj* impermeable (*to* a).
impersonal [im'pə:snl] *adj* impersonal.
impersonality [im,pə:sə'næliti] *n* impersonalidad *f*.
impersonate [im'pə:səneit] *vt* hacerse pasar por; (*Theat*) imitar.
impersonation [im,pə:sə'neiʃən] *n* (*Theat*) imitación *f*.
impersonator [im'pə:səneitə*] *n* (*Theat*) imitador *m*, ora *f*.
impertinence [im'pə:tinəns] *n* impertinencia *f*, insolencia *f*, descaro *m*; **an —, a piece of —** una impertinencia; **it would be an — to** + *infin* sería inoportuno + *infin*; **what —!**, **the — of it!** ¡qué frescura!
impertinent [im'pə:tinənt] *adj* impertinente, insolente, descarado; **to be — to someone** decir impertinencias a uno; **don't be —!** ¡no seas fresco!
impertinently [im'pə:tinəntli] *adv* impertinentemente, descaradamente.
imperturbable [,impə'tə:bəbl] *adj* imperturbable.
impervious [im'pə:viəs] *adj* impermeable, impenetrable (*to* a); (*fig*) insensible (*to* a).
impetigo [,impi'taigəu] *n* impétigo *m*.
impetuosity [im,petju'ɔsiti] *n* impetuosidad *f*, irreflexión *f*.
impetuous [im'petjuəs] *adj* impetuoso, irreflexivo.
impetuously [im'petjuəsli] *adv* impetuosamente, irreflexivamente.
impetus ['impitəs] *n* ímpetu *m*; (*fig*) impulso *m*, incentivo *m*, fuerza *f* motriz.
impiety [im'paiəti] *n* impiedad *f*.
impinge [im'pindʒ] *vi*: **to — on** afectar a.
impious ['impiəs] *adj* impío.
impish ['impiʃ] *adj* travieso, endiablado.
implacable [im'plækəbl] *adj* implacable.
implant [im'plɑ:nt] *vt* implantar; *idea etc* inculcar.
implausible [im'plɔ:zəbl] *adj* inverosímil; poco convincente.
implement ['implimənt] *n* herramienta *f*, instrumento *m*; (*Agr*) apero *m*.
implement ['impliment] *vt* poner por obra, llevar a cabo, hacer efectivo; realizar, ejecutar.
implementation [,implimen'teiʃən] *n* realización *f*, ejecución *f*.
implicate ['implikeit] *vt* comprometer; enredar; **he —d 3 others** acusó a 3 más (de haber tomado parte en el crimen), delató a 3 cómplices suyos; **are you —d in this?** ¿anda Vd metido en esto?
implication [,impli'keiʃən] *n* (a) (*act*) comprometimiento *m*.
(b) (*in crime*) complicidad *f*.
(c) (*consequence etc*) consecuencia *f*, inferencia *f*; **—s** consecuencias *fpl*, trascendencia *f*; **by —, then...** de ahí se deduce, pues, ...; **he did not realise the full —s of his words** no se dio cuenta de la trascendencia de sus palabras; **we shall have to study all the —s** tendremos que estudiar todas las consecuencias.
implicit [im'plisit] *adj* implícito; *faith etc* incondicional, absoluto.
implicitly [im'plisitli] *adv* implícitamente; sin reservas, incondicionalmente.

implied [im'plaid] *adj* implícito, tácito; **it is not stated but it is —** no se declara abiertamente pero se sobreentiende.
implore [im'plɔ:*] *vt thing* implorar, suplicar; *person* suplicar; **I — you!** ¡se lo suplico!; **to — someone to do something** suplicar a uno hacer algo.
imploring [im'plɔ:riŋ] *adj* suplicante; *look etc* lleno de suplicación.
imploringly [im'plɔ:riŋli] *adv* de modo suplicante.
imply [im'plai] *vt* (*involve*) implicar, suponer, presuponer; (*mean*) querer decir, significar; (*state indirectly*) dar a entender; (*hint*) insinuar; **that implies some intelligence** eso supone cierta inteligencia; **are you —ing that ...?** ¿quiere Vd decir que ...?; **what do you — by that?** ¿qué quiere Vd insinuar con eso?; **he implied he would do it** dio a entender que lo haría; **it implies a lot of work for him** esto significa que tendrá mucho trabajo.
impolite [,impə'lait] *adj* descortés, mal educado.
impolitely [,impə'laitli] *adv* con descortesía.
impolitic [im'pɔlitik] *adj* impolítico.
imponderable [im'pɔndərəbl] **1** *adj* imponderable.
2 —s *npl* (elementos *mpl*) imponderables *mpl*.
import ['impɔ:t] **1** *n* (a) (*Comm*) importación *f*, artículo *m* importado.
(b) (*meaning*) significado *m*, sentido *m*; importancia *f*.
2 *attr*: **— duty** derechos *mpl* de entrada; **— licence** permiso *m* de importación; **— surcharge** sobrecarga *f* de importación; **— trade** comercio *m* importador.
import [im'pɔ:t] *vt* (a) (*Comm*) importar (*from* de, *into* en). (b) (*mean*) significar, querer decir.
importance [im'pɔ:təns] *n* importancia *f*; **of some —** de cierta importancia, importante; **a fact of the first —** un hecho primordial; **to attach great — to** something conceder mucha importancia a algo; **to be of —** tener importancia; **that's of no —** eso no importa; **to be full of one's own —** darse ínfulas.
important [im'pɔ:tənt] *adj* importante; de categoría; **it's not —** no importa, no tiene importancia; **to try to look —** tratar de hacer figura.
importantly [im'pɔ:təntli] *adv* *say etc* en tono rimbombante.
importation [,impɔ:'teiʃən] *n* importación *f*.
imported [im'pɔ:tid] *adj article* de importación.
importer [im'pɔ:tə*] *n* importador *m*, ora *f*.
importunate [im'pɔ:tjunit] *adj demand etc* importuno; *person* molesto, pesado.
importune [,impɔ:'tju:n] *vt* importunar, perseguir, fastidiar; (*prostitute*) abordar con fines inmorales.
importunity [,impɔ:'tju:niti] *n* importunidad *f*; pesadez *f*.
impose [im'pəuz] **1** *vt* imponer (*on* a); (*palm off*) hacer aceptar (*on* a).
2 *vi*: **to — upon** (*deceive*) embaucar; (*take advantage of*) *kindness etc* abusar de, *person* abusar de la amabilidad de; **I don't wish to — upon you** no quiero abusar, no quiero molestarle.
imposing [im'pəuziŋ] *adj* imponente, impresionante; majestuoso.
imposition [,impə'ziʃən] *n* (*act*) imposición *f*; (*burden*) carga *f*, molestia *f*; abuso *m*; (*tax*) impuesto *m*; **it's a bit of an —** me resulta bastante molesto; **I fear it's rather an — for you** me temo que le vaya a molestar bastante.
impossibility [im,pɔsə'biliti] *n* imposibilidad *f*.
impossible [im'pɔsəbl] *adj* imposible; *person* inaguantable, insufrible; **you're —!** ¡eres insufrible!, ¡no puedo contigo!; **to do the —** hacer lo imposible; **to make it — for someone to do something** quitar a uno la posibilidad de hacer algo, imposibilitar algo a uno.
impossibly [im'pɔsəbli] *adv* imposiblemente; **— difficult** de lo más difícil, tan difícil que resulta imposible.
impost ['impəust] *n* impuesto *m*.
impostor [im'pɔstə*] *n* impostor *m*, ora *f*, embustero *m*, a *f*.
imposture [im'pɔstʃə*] *n* impostura *f*, engaño *m*, fraude *m*.
impotence ['impətəns] *n* impotencia *f*.
impotent ['impətənt] *adj* impotente.
impound [im'paund] *vt goods* embargar, confiscar.
impoverish [im'pɔvəriʃ] *vt* empobrecer, reducir a la miseria; *land* agotar.
impoverished [im'pɔvəriʃt] *adj* necesitado, indigente; *land* agotado.
impoverishment [im'pɔvəriʃmənt] *n* empobrecimiento *m*; agotamiento *m*.
impracticability [im,præktikə'biliti] *n* impracticabilidad *f*, imposibilidad *f*.

impracticable [im'præktikəbl] *adj* impracticable, no factible, imposible de realizar.

impractical [im'præktikəl] *adj* falto de sentido práctico, poco práctico; desmañado.

imprecation [,impri'keiʃən] *n* imprecación *f*.

impregnable [im'pregnəbl] *adj* inexpugnable.

impregnate ['impregneit] *vt* impregnar, empapar (with de); (Bio) fecundar; **to become —d with** impregnarse de.

impregnation [,impreg'neiʃən] *n* impregnación *f*; (Bio) fecundación *f*.

impresario [,impre'sɑːriəu] *n* empresario *m*.

impress ['impres] *n* impresión *f*, señal *f*; (fig) sello *m*, huella *f*.

impress [im'pres] **1** *vt* (a) (mark, stamp) estampar; (fig) grabar, inculcar; **I must — upon you that . . .** tengo que subrayar que . . . ; **it —ed itself upon my mind** quedó grabado en mi memoria; **I tried to — the importance of the job on him** traté de convencerle de la importancia del puesto.

(b) (affect) impresionar; **he does it just to — people** lo hace sólo para impresionar a la gente; **he is not easily —ed** no se deja impresionar fácilmente; **I was not —ed** no me hizo buena impresión; **he —ed me quite favourably** me hizo una impresión bastante buena; **how did it — you?** ¿qué impresión te produjo?; **the play deeply —ed everyone** la obra causó honda impresión en todos.

2 *vi* hacer buena impresión.

impression [im'preʃən] *n* impresión *f*; huella *f*; señal *f*; (Typ) edición *f*, tirada *f*; (fig) impresión *f*, efecto *m*; **to be under the — that, to have the — that** tener la impresión de que; **he gives an — of knowing a lot** da la impresión de saber mucho; **to make an —** impresionar; **she's out to make an —** se dedica a impresionar, quiere causar una sensación; **to make an — on someone** impresionar a uno; **what — did it make on you?** ¿qué impresión le produjo?; **all our arguments seemed to make no — on him** todos nuestros argumentos al parecer no tuvieron efecto alguno en él; **he could make no — on his opponent's majority** no logró rebajar la mayoría de su rival.

impressionable [im'preʃnəbl] *adj* impresionable; influenciable; sensible.

impressionism [im'preʃənizəm] *n* impresionismo *m*.

impressionist [im'preʃənist] **1** *adj* impresionista. **2** *n* impresionista *mf*.

impressionistic [im,preʃə'nistik] *adj* impresionista.

impressive [im'presiv] *adj* impresionante.

impressively [im'presivli] *adv* de modo impresionante.

imprint ['imprint] *n* impresión *f*, huella *f*, señal *f*; (Typ) pie *m* de imprenta.

imprint [im'print] *vt* imprimir, estampar (on en); (fig) grabar (on the mind en la memoria).

imprison [im'prizn] *vt* encarcelar, poner en la cárcel; **the judge —ed him for 10 years** el juez le condenó a 10 años de prisión.

imprisonment [im'priznmənt] *n* encarcelamiento *m*, prisión *f*; **false —** detención *f* ilegal; **the judge sentenced him to 10 years' —** el juez le condenó a 10 años de prisión; **to escape from —** escapar de la cárcel.

improbability [im,prɔbə'biliti] *n* improbabilidad *f*; inverosimilitud *f*.

improbable [im'prɔbəbl] *adj* improbable; inverosímil; **it is — that it will happen** no es probable que ocurra eso, es poco probable que ocurra eso.

impromptu [im'prɔmptjuː] **1** *adj* performance improvisado, no preparado de antemano; utterance impremeditado.

2 *adv* perform de improviso, sin preparación; say etc de repente.

3 *n* improvisación *f*.

improper [im'prɔpə*] *adj* impropio, incorrecto, indebido; (unseemly) indecoroso; (indecent) indecente, deshonesto.

improperly [im'prɔpəli] *adv* impropiamente, incorrectamente, indebidamente; indecorosamente; indecentemente, deshonestamente.

impropriety [,imprə'praiəti] *n* inconveniencia *f*; incorrección *f*; falta *f* de decoro; indecencia *f*, deshonestidad *f*; (of language) impropiedad *f*.

improve [im'pruːv] **1** *vt* mejorar, perfeccionar; reformar; (beautify) embellecer; land abonar, bonificar; property aumentar el valor de; production, yield aumentar; mind ilustrar, edificar; opportunity aprovechar; wording etc corregir, enmendar.

2 *vi* mejorar(se); perfeccionarse; (production, yield) aumentar(se); (price) subir; (in skill, studies etc) hacer progresos; **the patient is improving** el enfermo está mejor; **to — on** mejorar, perfeccionar;

it cannot be —ed on es inmejorable; **to — on someone's offer** ofrecer más que otro.

3 *vr*: **to — oneself** (in mind) edificarse, instruirse; (in wealth etc) mejorar su situación.

improvement [im'pruːvmənt] *n* mejora *f*, mejoramiento *m*; perfeccionamiento *m*; reforma *f*; embellecimiento *m*; aumento *m*, subida *f* (in de); progreso *m*, adelantamiento *m*; (Med) mejoría *f*; enmienda *f*; **there has been some — in the patient's condition** el enfermo está algo mejor; **it's an — on the old one** es mejor que el antiguo; **to make —s in a text** enmendar un texto; **to make —s to a property** hacer reformas en un inmueble.

improvidence [im'prɔvidəns] *n* imprevisión *f*.

improvident [im'prɔvidənt] *adj* impróvido, imprevisor.

improvidently [im'prɔvidəntli] *adv* impróvidamente.

improving [im'pruːviŋ] *adj* edificante, instructivo.

improvisation [,imprəvai'zeiʃən] *n* improvisación *f*.

improvise ['imprəvaiz] *vti* improvisar.

imprudence [im'pruːdəns] *n* imprudencia *f*.

imprudent [im'pruːdənt] *adj* imprudente.

imprudently [im'pruːdəntli] *adv* imprudentemente.

impudence ['impjudəns] *n* descaro *m*, insolencia *f*, atrevimiento *m*; **what —!** ¡qué frescura!; **he had the — to say** that tuvo la cara dura de decir que.

impudent ['impjudənt] *adj* descarado, insolente, atrevido.

impudently ['impjudəntli] *adv* descaradamente, insolentemente.

impugn [im'pjuːn] *vt* impugnar.

impulse ['impʌls] *n* (Mech etc) impulso *m*; (fig) impulso *m*, impulsión *f*, estímulo *m*; incitación *f*; **to act on —** obrar por capricho, obrar sin reflexión; **my first — was to +** infin mi primera idea fue de + infin, primero intenté + infin; **to yield to a sudden —** dejarse llevar por un capricho.

impulsion [im'pʌlʃən] *n* impulsión *f*.

impulsive [im'pʌlsiv] *adj* person irreflexivo, que no reflexiona, impulsivo; act irreflexivo.

impulsively [im'pʌlsivli] *adv* por impulso; sin reflexión, sin pensar.

impulsiveness [im'pʌlsivnis] *n* irreflexión *f*; carácter *m* impulsivo.

impunity [im'pjuːniti] *n* impunidad *f*; **with —** impunemente.

impure [im'pjuə*] *adj* impuro; adulterado, mezclado; (morally) deshonesto.

impurity [im'pjuəriti] *n* impureza *f*; deshonestidad *f*.

imputation [,impju'teiʃən] *n* imputación *f*; acusación *f*.

impute [im'pjuːt] *vt* imputar, achacar, atribuir (to a); acusar.

in [in] **1** *adv* (a) dentro, adentro; **— here** aquí dentro; **— there** allí dentro; **day —, day out** día tras día; **£10 a week all —** 10 libras por semana todo incluido.

(b) **to be —** (person) estar, estar en casa, estar en la oficina (etc); **is Mr Cox —?** ¿está el Sr Cox?; **the train is —** ha llegado el tren; **he's — for 5 years** le condenaron a 5 años; **when the Tories were —** cuando los conservadores estaban en el poder; **when the sun is —** cuando el sol está escondido; **the harvest is —** ha terminado la recolección; **strawberries are —** las fresas están en sazón; **short skirts are —** la falda corta está de moda.

(c) **to be — for a post** ser candidato a un puesto, solicitar un puesto; **to be — for a competition** concurrir a un certamen, tomar parte en un concurso; **to be — for an exam** presentarse a un examen; **we're — for it now** aquí se va a armar la gorda; **you don't know what you're — for** no sabes lo que te pescas; **we're — for a hard time** vamos a pasar un mal rato.

(d) **to be — on the secret** estar en el secreto; **to be — on a plan** estar enterado de un proyecto.

(e) **to be well — with someone** estar muy metido con uno, tener mucha confianza con uno.

(f) **to be all —, to feel all —** estar rendido, no poder más.

2 *prep* (a) (place) en; dentro de; **— the house** en la casa; **— one's hand** en la mano; **— Rome** en Roma; **— Italy** en Italia; **— prison** en la cárcel; **— school** en la escuela; **— the distance** a lo lejos; **— everybody's eyes** a los ojos de todos; **it is not — him to do that** no es capaz de hacer eso, no cabe en él hacer eso; **he has it — him to succeed** es capaz de triunfar.

(b) (in respect of) better **— health** mejor de salud; strong **— maths** fuerte en matemáticas; a change **— policy** un cambio de política; a rise **— prices** una subida de los precios; 3 metres **— length**

3 metros de largo; **long — the leg** de piernas largas; **diseased — mind** de mentalidad anormal.

(c) (*ratio*) **1 — 7** 1 sobre 7, 1 de cada 7.

(d) (*time*) **— 1972** en 1972; **— the 20th century** en el siglo XX; — **May** en mayo; **— summer** en el verano; **— the past** en el pasado; **— the reign of** bajo el reinado de; **it was built — a week** fue construido en una semana; **I'll bring it back — a week** lo devolveré dentro de una semana, lo devolveré de aquí a ocho días; **a week he was back** al cabo de una semana volvió; **— the morning** por la mañana; **at 8 — the morning** a las 8 de la mañana; **— the daytime** de día, durante el día; **I haven't seen him —** years hace años que no le veo.

(e) — tears llorando; **— despair** desesperado; **any man — his senses** cualquier hombre sensato.

(f) (*clothed in*) **the girl — green** la chica vestida de verde; **he went out — his new raincoat** al salir se puso el impermeable nuevo; **she looks nice — that hat** con ese sombrero está guapísima.

(g) (*weather*) **— the rain** bajo la lluvia; **— the July sun** bajo el sol de julio.

(h) he's — the tyre business se dedica al comercio de neumáticos, tiene un negocio de neumáticos; **those — teaching** los profesores, los que se dedican a enseñar; **he travels — soap** es viajante en jabones; **she has shares — oil** tiene acciones de compañías de petróleo; **he's something — advertising** tiene un puesto en la publicidad; **the latest thing — hats** lo más nuevo en cuanto a sombreros.

(i) (*manner*) **— this way** de este modo; **— the American fashion** a la americana; **— alphabetical order** por orden alfabético; **cut — half** cortado por el medio; **— French** en francés; **written — pencil** escrito con (*or* a) lápiz; **painted — black** pintado de negro; **packed — dozens** envasados por docenas; **— hundreds** a cientos, a centenares; **— cash** en metálico; **— mourning** de luto; **— writing** por escrito; **— anger** con enojo; **lame — one foot** cojo de un pie.

(j) (*after superlative*) **the best pupil — the class** el mejor alumno de la clase; **the biggest — Europe** el mayor de Europa.

(k) (*with verb*) **— saying this** al decir esto; **— making a fortune he lost his wife** mientras se ganaba una fortuna, perdió a su mujer.

3 *n*: **—s and outs** recovecos *mpl*; (*fig*) detalles *mpl* nimios; interioridades *fpl*.

inability [,inə'biliti] *n* incapacidad *f*, falta *f* de aptitud; **my — to come** el que yo no pueda venir.

inaccessibility ['inæk,sesə'biliti] *n* inaccesibilidad *f*.

inaccessible [,inæk'sesəbl] *adj* inaccesible.

inaccuracy [in'ækjurəsi] *n* inexactitud *f*, incorrección *f*.

inaccurate [in'ækjurit] *adj* inexacto, incorrecto, erróneo.

inaccurately [in'ækjuritli] *adv* erróneamente.

inaction [in'ækʃən] *n* inacción *f*.

inactive [in'æktiv] *adj* inactivo.

inactivity [,inæk'tiviti] *n* inactividad *f*.

inadequacy [in'ædikwəsi] *n* insuficiencia *f*; (*of person*) incapacidad *f*.

inadequate [in'ædikwit] *adj* insuficiente, inadecuado; *person* incapaz.

inadequately [in'ædikwitli] *adv* de modo inadecuado.

inadmissible [,inəd'misəbl] *adj* inadmisible.

inadvertence [,inəd'və:təns] *n* inadvertencia *f*; **by —** por equivocación, por descuido.

inadvertent [,inəd'və:tənt] *adj* inadvertido; accidental.

inadvertently [,inəd'və:təntli] *adv* por equivocación, por descuido.

inadvisability ['inəd,vaizə'biliti] *n* imprudencia *f*, inconveniencia *f*.

inadvisable [,inəd'vaizəbl] *adj* no aconsejable, desaconsejable, imprudente, inconveniente.

inalienable [in'eiliənəbl] *adj* inalienable.

inamorata [in,æmə'rɑ:tə] *n* amada *f*, querida *f*.

inane [i'nein] *adj* necio, fatuo, inútil.

inanimate [in'ænimit] *adj* inanimado.

inanition [,inə'niʃən] *n* inanición *f*.

inanity [i'næniti] *n* necedad *f*, fatuidad *f*, inutilidad *f*; **inanities** estupideces *fpl*, necedades *fpl*.

inapplicable [in'æplikəbl] *adj* inaplicable.

inappropriate [,inə'prəupriit] *adj* inoportuno, inconveniente, impropio.

inappropriately [,inə'prəupriitli] *adv* inoportunamente.

inapt [in'æpt] *adj* impropio; (*lacking skill*) inhábil.

inaptitude [in'æptitju:d] *n* impropiedad *f*; inhabilidad *f*.

inarticulate [,inɑ:'tikjulit] *adj* (*of character*) incapaz de expresarse, que habla poco y mal; **an — speech** un discurso mal pronunciado; **he was — with rage** la rabia le embargó la voz.

inartistic [,inɑ:'tistik] *adj* *work* antiestético, burdo, mal hecho; *person* falto de talento artístico.

inasmuch [inəz'mʌtʃ]: **— as** *conj* puesto que, ya que.

inattention [,inə'tenʃən] *n* inatención *f*, desatención *f*, distracción *f*.

inattentive [,inə'tentiv] *adj* desatento, distraído.

inattentively [,inə'tentivli] *adv* distraídamente.

inaudible [in'ɔ:dəbl] *adj* inaudible, que no se puede oír; **he was almost —** apenas se le podía oír.

inaudibly [in'ɔ:dəbli] *adv* de modo inaudible; **he spoke almost —** habló tan bajo que apenas se le podía oír.

inaugural [i'nɔ:gjurəl] *adj* inaugural; *speech* de apertura.

inaugurate [i'nɔ:gjureit] *vt* inaugurar.

inauguration [i,nɔ:gju'reiʃən] *n* inauguración *f*; ceremonia *f* de apertura; (*US Pol*) toma *f* de posesión (*de su cargo por el presidente*).

inauspicious [,inɔ:s'piʃəs] *adj* poco propicio, desfavorable.

inauspiciously [,inɔ:s'piʃəsli] *adv* de modo poco propicio, en condiciones desfavorables.

in-between [in'bi'twi:n] *adj* intermedio; de en medio; **it's rather —** ocupa una posición más bien intermedia, no es ni lo uno ni lo otro.

inboard ['inbɔ:d] *adj* (*Naut*) *engine* interior.

inborn [in'bɔ:n] *adj* innato; instintivo.

inbred ['in'bred] *adj* *tendency etc* innato; instintivo; (*of race*) engendrado por endogamia; **people there are very —** allí la endogamia ha debilitado a la gente.

inbreeding ['in'bri:diŋ] *n* endogamia *f*.

Inca ['iŋkə] **1** *n* inca *mf*. **2** *attr* incaico, de los incas.

incalculable [in'kælkjuləbl] *adj* incalculable; *person etc* voluble, veleidoso.

Incan ['iŋkən] *adj* inca, incaico, de los incas.

incandescence [,inkæn'desns] *n* incandescencia *f*.

incandescent [,inkæn'desnt] *adj* incandescente.

incantation [,inkæn'teiʃən] *n* conjuro *m*, ensalmo *m*.

incapability [in,keipə'biliti] *n* incapacidad *f*.

incapable [in'keipəbl] *adj* incapaz (*of* de); (*physically*) imposibilitado; **to be — of speech** no poder hablar; **she is — of shame** no tiene vergüenza; **he was drunk and — estaba** totalmente borracho.

incapacitate [,inkə'pæsiteit] *vt* incapacitar, inhabilitar; (*physically*) imposibilitar.

incapacity [,inkə'pæsiti] *n* incapacidad *f*; insuficiencia *f*.

incarcerate [in'kɑ:səreit] *vt* encarcelar.

incarnate [in'kɑ:nit] *adj*: **the devil —** el mismo diablo, el diablo en persona; **to become —** encarnar.

incarnate ['inkɑ:neit] *vt* encarnar.

incarnation [,inkɑ:'neiʃən] *n* encarnación *f*; **to be the — of vice** ser el mismo vicio.

incautious [in'kɔ:ʃəs] *adj* incauto, imprudente.

incautiously [in'kɔ:ʃəsli] *adv* incautamente.

incendiary [in'sendiəri] **1** *adj* incendiario. **2** *n* (*person*) incendiario *m*; (*bomb*) bomba *f* incendiaria.

incense ['insens] *n* incienso *m*.

incense [in'sens] *vt* indignar, encolerizar.

incentive [in'sentiv] *n* incentivo *m*, estímulo *m*; **an — to harder work** un incentivo para que se trabaje más.

inception [in'sepʃən] *n* comienzo *m*, principio *m*; **from its —** desde los comienzos.

incertitude [in'sə:titju:d] *n* incertidumbre *f*.

incessant [in'sesnt] *adj* incesante, constante, continuo.

incessantly [in'sesntli] *adv* constantemente, sin cesar.

incest ['insest] *n* incesto *m*.

incestuous [in'sestjuəs] *adj* incestuoso.

inch [intʃ] **1** *n* pulgada *f* (= 2,54 cm); **—es** (*of person: height*) estatura *f*, (*of waist*) cintura *f*; **not an — from my face** a dos centímetros de mi cara; **— by —**, **by —es** palmo a palmo; **not an — of Spanish territory** ni un palmo de territorio español; **we searched every — of the room** registramos minuciosamente el cuarto; **every — of soil is used** se aprovecha la tierra hasta el último centímetro; **he's every — a man** es todo un hombre; **he's every — a soldier** es lo que se llama un soldado; **to be within an — of** estar a dos dedos de; **he didn't give an —** no nos ofreció la menor concesión; **give him an — and he'll take a yard** dale un dedo y se toma hasta el codo.

2 *vi*: **to — (one's way) forward** avanzar palmo a palmo; **prices are —ing up** los precios suben constantemente un poco.

inchoate ['inkəueit] *adj* rudimentario, incompleto, todavía no formado.

incidence ['insidəns] *n* frecuencia *f*; extensión *f*; distribución *f*; **the — of measles in children** la frecuencia del sarampión en los niños; **the — of taxation** el peso de las contribuciones.

incident ['insidənt] *n* incidente *m*, episodio *m*, suceso *m*; **the Agadir —** el episodio de Agadir; **to provoke a diplomatic —** provocar una crisis diplomática; **a life full of —** una vida azarosa, una vida llena de acontecimientos; **to arrive without —** llegar sin novedad.

incidental [,insi'dentl] **1** *adj* incidental, incidente; (*casual*) fortuito; (*inessential*) no esencial, accesorio, de importancia secundaria; **— expenses** gastos *mpl* no previsibles; **— music** música *f* de fondo; **the troubles — to any journey** las dificultades que acarrea cualquier viaje; **but that is — to my purpose** pero eso queda al margen de mi propósito. **2** *n* cosa *f* fortuita; cosa *f* accesoria, cosa *f* sin importancia.

incidentally [,insi'dentəli] *adv* incidentemente; **and — ... y** a propósito . . . ; **it was interesting only —** era interesante solamente en parte.

incinerate [in'sinəreit] *vt* incinerar.

incinerator [in'sinəreitə*] *n* incinerador *m*.

incipient [in'sipiənt] *adj* incipiente, naciente.

incise [in'saiz] *vt* cortar; (*Art*) grabar, tallar.

incision [in'siʒən] *n* incisión *f*, corte *m*.

incisive [in'saisiv] *adj* *mind* penetrante; *tone* mordaz; *words*, *criticism*, *speech* tajante.

incisively [in'saisivli] *adv* con penetración; mordazmente; de modo tajante.

incisiveness [in'saisivnis] *n* penetración *f*; mordacidad *f*; lo tajante.

incisor [in'saizə*] *n* incisivo *m*.

incite [in'sait] *vt* incitar, estimular, provocar; **to — someone to do something** incitar a uno a hacer algo.

incitement [in'saitmənt] *n* incitación *f*, instigación *f* (*to* de).

incivility [,insi'viliti] *n* descortesía *f*, incivilidad *f*.

inclemency [in'klemənsi] *n* inclemencia *f*; (*of weather*) intemperie *f*.

inclement [in'klemənt] *adj* inclemente, riguroso; *weather* malo, feo.

inclination [,inkli'neiʃən] *n* (a) (*slope*) inclinación *f*. (b) (*tendency*) inclinación *f*, tendencia *f*, propensión *f*; **my — is to +** *infin* yo prefiero la idea de *+ infin*; **what are his natural —s?** ¿cuáles son sus propensiones naturales?; **to have an — to meanness** tener tendencia a ser tacaño; **I have no — to help him** no estoy dispuesto a ayudarle, tengo pocas ganas de ayudarle; **to follow one's —s** seguir su capricho, hacer lo que le dé la gana.

incline ['inklain] *n* cuesta *f*, pendiente *f*.

incline [in'klain] **1** *vt* (a) (*slope*) inclinar, ladear, poner oblicuamente; **he —d his head** puso la cabeza de lado.
(b) (*fig*) **to — someone to adopt a plan** inducir a uno a adoptar un plan.
(c) **to be —d to +** *infin* (*of tendency*) inclinarse *+ infin*, tener tendencia a *+ infin*, ser propenso a *+ infin*; (*of person's volition*) estar dispuesto a *+ infin*, estar por *+ infin*; **it's —d to break** tiene tendencia a romperse; **I'm —d to believe you** estoy dispuesto a creerle; **the child is —d to be left-handed** el niño tiene tendencia de zurdo; **he's that way —d** él es así; **if you feel so —d** si Vd quiere.
2 *vi* (a) (*slope*, *act*) inclinarse, ladearse, (*state*) estar inclinado, estar ladeado.
(b) (*fig*) **I — to the belief that** yo prefiero creer que, yo creo más lógica la opinión de que; **yellow inclining to red** amarillo que tira a rojo.

inclined [in'klaind] *adj* *plane* inclinado.

inclose [in'kləuz] *vt* see **enclose**.

include [in'kluːd] *vt* incluir; comprender, contener, encerrar; (*with letter*) adjuntar, enviar adjunto; **your name is not —d in the list** su nombre no figura en la lista; **does that remark — me?** ¿se refiere esa observación también a mí?; **he is not —d in the team** no forma parte del equipo; **he sold the lot, books —d** lo vendió todo, incluso los libros; **everything —d** (*hotel etc*) todo comprendido.

including [in'kluːdiŋ] *as prep* incluso, inclusive, con inclusión de; **seven — this one** siete con inclusión de éste; **everyone came, — the priest** vinieron todos, incluso (*or* hasta) el cura; **terms £15, not — service** precio 15 libras, servicio no comprendido.

inclusion [in'kluːʒən] *n* inclusión *f*.

inclusive [in'kluːsiv] **1** *adj* inclusivo, completo; **— terms** todo incluido; **to be — of** incluir.

2 *adv* inclusive; **from the 10th to the 15th —** del 10 al 15 ambos inclusive.

inclusively [in'kluːsivli] *adv* = **inclusive 2**.

incognito [in'kɔgnitəu] **1** *adv* *travel etc* de incógnito. **2** *n* incógnito *m*.

incoherence [,inkəu'hiərəns] *n* incoherencia *f*; ininteligibilidad *f*.

incoherent [,inkəu'hiərənt] *adj* incoherente, inconexo; ininteligible; *argument etc* sin pies ni cabeza; **his speech became —** empezó a hablar de modo ininteligible; **he was — with rage** balbuceaba de rabia.

incoherently [,inkəu'hiərəntli] *adv* de modo incoherente; de modo ininteligible.

incombustible [,inkəm'bʌstəbl] *adj* incombustible.

income ['inkʌm] *n* ingresos *mpl*, renta *f*, entrada *f*; (*profit*) rédito *m* (*from* de); **annual —** ingresos *mpl* anuales; **family —** entradas *fpl* familiares; **gross —** renta *f* bruta; **national —** renta *f* nacional; **net —** renta *f* neta; **private —** renta *f* de fuente particular; **—s policy** política *f* de rentas; **to live up to one's —** gastarse toda la renta; **to live beyond one's —** gastar más de lo que se gana; **to live within one's —** vivir con arreglo a los ingresos; **I can't live on my —** no puedo vivir con lo que gano.

incomer ['in,kʌmə*] *n* (*US*) recién llegado *m*, recién llegada *f*; persona *f* nueva (en una sociedad *etc*); inmigrante *mf*.

income tax ['inkʌmtæks] *n* impuesto *m* sobre la renta.

incoming ['in,kʌmiŋ] *adj* entrante, nuevo; *tide* ascendente.

incomings ['in,kʌmiŋz] *npl* ingresos *mpl*.

incommensurable [,inkə'menʃərəbl] *adj* inconmensurable.

incommensurate [,inkə'menʃərit] *adj* desproporcionado; **to be — with** no guardar relación con.

incommode [,inkə'məud] *vt* incomodar, molestar.

incommodious [,inkə'məudiəs] *adj* incómodo.

incommunicado [,inkəmjuni'kɑːdəu] *adj* incomunicado.

incomparable [in'kɔmpərəbl] *adj* incomparable, sin par.

incomparably [in'kɔmpərəbli] *adv* incomparablemente; **this one is — better** éste es mejor sin ningún género de dudas.

incompatibility ['inkɔm,pætə'biliti] *n* incompatibilidad *f*.

incompatible [,inkəm'pætəbl] *adj* incompatible (*with* con).

incompetence [in'kɔmpitəns] *n* incompetencia *f*, inhabilidad *f*, incapacidad *f*.

incompetent [in'kɔmpitənt] *adj* incompetente, inhábil, incapaz.

incomplete [,inkəm'pliːt] *adj* incompleto, defectuoso; (*unfinished*) sin terminar, inacabado.

incompletely [,inkəm'pliːtli] *adv* incompletamente.

incompleteness [,inkəm'pliːtnis] *n* lo incompleto, estado *m* incompleto; **because of its —** debido a que no está terminado.

incomprehensible [in,kɔmpri'hensəbl] *adj* incomprensible.

incomprehensibly [in,kɔmpri'hensəbli] *adv* de modo incomprensible.

inconceivable [,inkən'siːvəbl] *adj* inconcebible.

inconclusive [,inkən'kluːsiv] *adj* *reasoning etc* inconcluyente, poco convincente, cuestionable; *interview*, *investigation* que no da resultados definitivos.

inconclusively [,inkən'kluːsivli] *adv* de modo inconcluyente, de modo poco convincente; **it ended —** terminó sin resultados definitivos.

incongruity [,inkɔn'gruːiti] *n* incongruencia *f*; desacuerdo *m*, falta *f* de lógica; lo absurdo.

incongruous [in'kɔngruəs] *adj* incongruo; disonante, que no concuerda, nada lógico; *appearance etc* estrafalario, absurdo; **it seems — that** parece extraño que.

inconsequent [in'kɔnsikwənt] *adj* inconsecuente.

inconsequential [in,kɔnsi'kwenʃəl] *adj* inconsecuente; (*unimportant*) sin trascendencia.

inconsiderable [,inkən'sidərəbl] *adj* insignificante.

inconsiderate [,inkən'sidərit] *adj* desconsiderado; **it was most — of you** Vd ha obrado con poca formalidad.

inconsistency [,inkən'sistənsi] *n* inconsecuencia *f*.

inconsistent [,inkən'sistənt] *adj* inconsecuente; **this is — with what you told me** esto no concuerda con lo que Vd me dijo.

inconsolable [,inkən'səuləbl] *adj* inconsolable.

inconspicuous [,inkən'spikjuəs] *adj* apenas visible, que no llama la atención; (*fig*) poco llamativo, modesto; **try to be as — as possible** procure no llamar la atención.

inconspicuously [,inkən'spikjuəsli] *adv* de modo apenas visible, sin llamar la atención; de modo poco llamativo, modestamente.

inconstancy [in'kɔnstənsi] *n* inconstancia *f*, veleidad *f*.

inconstant [in'kɔnstənt] *adj* inconstante, mudable, veleidoso.

incontestable [,inkən'testəbl] *adj* incontestable.

incontinence [in'kɔntinəns] *n* incontinencia *f* (*also Med*).

incontinent [in'kɔntinənt] *adj* incontinente.

incontrovertible [in,kɔntrə'və:təbl] *adj* incontrovertible.

inconvenience [,inkən'vi:niəns] **1** *n* incomodidad *f*, molestia *f*, inconvenientes *mpl*; **the — of living at a distance** los inconvenientes de vivir lejos; **you caused a lot of —** Vd nos creó muchas dificultades; **to put someone to —** molestar a uno.
2 *vt* incomodar, molestar, causar inconvenientes a.

inconvenient [,inkən'vi:niənt] *adj house, journey etc* incómodo, poco práctico, molesto; *time* malo, inoportuno; **it is — for me to +** *infin* me molesta tener que + *infin*; **it's all very —** es muy difícil.

inconveniently [,inkən'vi:niəntli] *adv* incómodamente, de modo poco práctico; a deshora, inoportunamente, en un momento inoportuno; **to come — early** venir tan temprano que crea dificultades.

inconvertibility ['inkən,və:ti'biliti] *n* inconvertibilidad *f*.

inconvertible [,inkən'və:təbl] *adj* inconvertible.

incorporate [in'kɔ:pəreit] *vt* incorporar (*in, into* a); incluir; comprender, contener; (*add*) agregar, añadir; **a product incorporating vitamin Q** un producto que contiene vitamina Q; **to — a company** constituir una compañía en sociedad anónima.

incorporated [in'kɔ:pəreitid] *adj* (*US Comm*): **Jones & Lloyd I—** Jones y Lloyd Sociedad Anónima (*abbr* S.A.).

incorporation [in,kɔ:pə'reiʃən] *n* incorporación *f*; inclusión *f*, adición *f*; (*Comm*) constitución *f* en sociedad anónima.

incorrect [,inkə'rekt] *adj* incorrecto, erróneo, inexacto; **that is —** eso no es cierto.

incorrectly [,inkə'rektli] *adv* incorrectamente, erróneamente; **a letter — addressed** una carta con las señas mal puestas.

incorrigible [in'kɔridʒəbl] *adj* incorregible; **you're —!** ¡eres un perdido!

incorruptible [,inkə'rʌptəbl] *adj* incorruptible; (*not open to bribery*) insobornable.

increase ['inkri:s] *n* aumento *m*, incremento *m* (*in* de); crecimiento *m*; (*in price*) subida *f*, alza *f*; **an — in pay** un aumento de sueldo; **to be on the —** ir en aumento.

increase [in'kri:s] **1** *vt* aumentar, acrecentar, incrementar. **2** *vi* aumentar(se), acrecentarse, tomar incremento; crecer; (*price*) subir.

increasing [in'kri:siŋ] *adj* creciente.

increasingly [in'kri:siŋli] *adv* de modo creciente; más y más, de más en más; **it becomes — difficult** se hace más y más difícil; **our — difficult task** nuestra labor cada vez más difícil.

incredible [in'kredəbl] *adj* increíble.

incredibly [in'kredəbli] *adv* increíblemente.

incredulity [,inkri'dju:liti] *n* incredulidad *f*.

incredulous [in'kredjuləs] *adj* incrédulo.

incredulously [in'kredjuləsli] *adv* con incredulidad.

increment ['inkrimənt] *n* aumento *m*, incremento *m* (*in* de); **an — in salary** un aumento de sueldo; **unearned —** plusvalía *f*.

incriminate [in'krimineit] *vt* acriminar, incriminar.

incrimination [in,krimi'neiʃən] *n* acriminación *f*, incriminación *f*.

incriminating [in'krimineitiŋ] *adj*, **incriminatory** [in'krimənətəri] *adj* acriminador.

incrust [in'krʌst] *vt* incrustar (*with* de).

incrustation [,inkrʌs'teiʃən] *n* incrustación *f*; costra *f*.

incubate ['inkjubeit] *vt* empollar, incubar.

incubation [,inkju'beiʃən] *n* incubación *f*; **— period** período *m* de incubación.

incubator ['inkjubeitə*] *n* incubadora *f*.

incubus ['iŋkjubəs] *n* íncubo *m*.

inculcate ['inkʌlkeit] *vt* inculcar (*in* en).

incumbent [in'kʌmbənt] **1** *adj*: **to be — on someone** incumbir a uno (*to do* hacer).
2 *n* ocupante *mf*, poseedor *m*, ora *f* (de un cargo o dignidad); (*Eccl*) beneficiado *m*.

incunable [in'kju:nəbl] *n* incunable *m*.

incunabula [,inkju'næbjulə] *npl* incunables *mpl*.

incur [in'kə:*] *vt* incurrir en; *debt, obligation* contraer; *expenditure* hacer.

incurable [in'kjuərəbl] **1** *adj* incurable; (*fig*) irremediable. **2** *n* incurable *mf*.

incurably [in'kjuərəbli] *adv* (*fig*) irremediablemente; **to be — optimistic** tener un optimismo indestructible.

incurious [in'kjuəriəs] *adj* poco curioso.

incursion [in'kə:ʃən] *n* incursión *f*, invasión *f*.

indebted [in'detid] *adj* (*fig*): **to be — to someone** estar en deuda con uno; **I am — to you for your help** agradezco su ayuda.

indebtedness [in'detidnis] *n* deuda *f*; agradecimiento *m*.

indecency [in'di:snsi] *n* indecencia *f*.

indecent [in'di:snt] *adj* indecente; *haste* nada decoroso.

indecently [in'di:sntli] *adv* indecentemente.

indecipherable [,indi'saifərəbl] *adj* indescifrable.

indecision [,indi'siʒən] *n* irresolución *f*.

indecisive [,indi'saisiv] *adj person* irresoluto, indeciso, vacilante; *result etc* inconcluyente, que no resuelve nada.

indecisively [,indi'saisivli] *adv* con irresolución, indecisamente, de modo vacilante; **it ended —** terminó sin resultados definitivos.

indeclinable [,indi'klainəbl] *adj* indeclinable.

indecorous [in'dekərəs] *adj* indecoroso.

indecorously [in'dekərəsli] *adv* indecorosamente.

indecorum [,indi'kɔ:rəm] *n* indecoro *m*, falta *f* de decoro.

indeed [in'di:d] *adv*: **—!, — yes!, yes —!** ¡claro que sí!, ¡ya lo creo!; **—?, is it —?, did you —?** ¿de veras?; **that's praise —** eso sí es una alabanza; **— you may** claro que puedes; **it is — difficult** es verdaderamente difícil, es difícil de verdad; **it is — a big house** es en efecto una casa grande, es una casa realmente grande; **I'm very glad —** me alegro muchísimo; **they're very bad —** son malísimos; **I may — be wrong** es posible que esté equivocado, claro está.

indefatigable [,indi'fætigəbl] *adj* incansable.

indefatigably [,indi'fætigəbli] *adv* incansablemente.

indefensible [,indi'fensəbl] *adj* indefendible; *theory etc* insostenible; **your conduct has been —** su conducta no tiene excusa, su conducta no admite disculpa.

indefinable [,indi'fainəbl] *adj* indefinible.

indefinite [in'definit] *adj* indefinido (*also Gram*); incierto, poco seguro; **he was very — about it all** mostró no tener ninguna idea clara sobre el asunto; **our plans are somewhat —** as yet todavía no hemos hecho ningún plan definitivo.

indefinitely [in'definitli] *adv* (**a**) indefinidamente; **it extends — into space** se prolonga indefinidamente en el espacio.
(**b**) **we can carry on —** podemos continuar hasta cuando sea (*or* por tiempo indefinido).

indelible [in'deləbl] *adj* indeleble, imborrable (*also fig*); **— pencil** lápiz *m* tinta.

indelicacy [in'delikəsi] *n* indecoro *m*, falta *f* de decoro; inoportunidad *f*.

indelicate [in'delikit] *adj* indecoroso, inoportuno.

indemnification [in,demnifi'keiʃən] *n* indemnización *f*.

indemnify [in'demnifai] *vt* indemnizar, resarcir (*against, for* de).

indemnity [in'demniti] *n* (*security*) indemnidad *f*; (*compensation*) indemnización *f*, reparación *f*.

indent ['indent] *n* (*Comm*) pedido *m*; (*Mil etc*) requisición *f*.

indent [in'dent] **1** *vt* (*cut into*) endentar, mellar; (*Typ*) sangrar.
2 *vi*: **to — for** pedir, requisar; **to — on someone for something** pedir algo a uno, requisar algo a uno.

indentation [,inden'teiʃən] *n* mella *f*, muesca *f*; (*Typ*) sangría *f*.

indenture [in'dentʃə*] *n* contrato *m* de aprendizaje.

independence [,indi'pendəns] *n* independencia *f*.

independent [,indi'pendənt] *adj* independiente (*of* de); **of — means** acomodado; **to become —** independizarse (*of* de).

independently [,indi'pendəntli] *adv* independientemente; **— of what he may decide** sin tomar en cuenta lo que él decida.

indescribable [,indis'kraibəbl] *adj* indescriptible; (*pej*) indecible, incalificable.

indescribably [,indis'kraibəbli] *adv* indescriptiblemente; (*pej*) indeciblemente, de modo incalificable; **— bad** tan malo que resulta incalificable.

indestructible [,indis'trʌktəbl] *adj* indestructible.

indeterminate [,indi'tə:minit] *adj* indeterminado.

indeterminately [,indi'tə:minitli] *adv* de modo indeterminado.

index ['indeks] **1** *n*, *pl* **indices** ['indisi:z] (*finger, of book*) índice *m*; (*Math*) exponente *m*; (*fig*) indicación *f* (*to* de); **I—** (*Eccl*) índice *m* expurgatorio; **cost-of-living —** índice *m* del coste de la vida.

2 *vt* book poner índice a; *entry* poner en un índice; **it is —ed under Smith** está clasificado bajo Smith, está clasificado en el artículo Smith.

India ['india] la India.

Indian ['indian] **1** *adj* indio. **2** *n* indio *m*, a *f*; **Red —** piel roja *mf*.

Indian Ocean ['indian'auʃən] Océano *m* Índico, Mar *m* de las Indias.

indiarubber ['india'rʌbə*] *n* caucho *m*; (*eraser*) goma *f* de borrar.

indicate ['indikeit] *vt* indicar.

indication [,indi'keiʃən] *n* indicación *f*, indicio *m*, señal *f*.

indicative [in'dikativ] **1** *adj* indicativo (*also Gram*); **to be — of** indicar. **2** *n* indicativo *m*.

indicator ['indikeitə*] *n* indicador *m*; (*Aut*) indicador *m* de dirección.

indices ['indisi:z] *npl of* **index**.

indict [in'dait] *vt* acusar (*for, on a charge of* de), encausar, procesar.

indictable [in'daitəbl] *adj* procesable, denunciable.

indictment [in'daitmənt] *n* (*charge*) acusación *f*; (*act*) procesamiento *m*; **the report is an — of our whole system** el informe critica duramente todo nuestro sistema.

Indies ['indiz] *pl* las Indias; *see* **East —** *etc*.

indifference [in'difrəns] *n* indiferencia *f* (*to* ante); **it is a matter of supreme — to me** no me importa en lo más mínimo.

indifferent [in'difrənt] *adj* indiferente; desinteresado, imparcial; (*mediocre*) ordinario, regular; **it is — to me** me es igual, me es indiferente.

indifferently [in'difrəntli] *adv* indiferentemente; de modo desinteresado, imparcialmente; regularmente; **they go — to one or the other** van sin distinción al uno o al otro; **she performed —** su actuación fue regular nada más.

indigence ['indidʒəns] *n* indigencia *f*.

indigenous [in'didʒinəs] *adj* indígena (*to* de).

indigent ['indidʒənt] *adj* indigente.

indigestible [,indi'dʒestəbl] *adj* indigesto.

indigestion [,indi'dʒestʃən] *n* indigestión *f*, empacho *m*.

indignant [in'dignənt] *adj* indignado; **to be — about something** indignarse por algo; **to get — with someone** indignarse con uno; **it's no good getting —** de nada sirve perder la paciencia; **to make someone —** indignar a uno.

indignantly [in'dignəntli] *adv* con indignación, indignado.

indignation [,indig'neiʃən] *n* indignación *f*; **— meeting** mitin *m* de protesta.

indignity [in'digniti] *n* indignidad *f*; ultraje *m*, afrenta *f*; **to suffer the — of +** *ger* sufrir la indignidad de + *infin*.

indigo ['indigəu] **1** *n* añil *m*. **2** *adj* color de añil.

indirect [,indi'rekt] *adj* indirecto.

indirectly [,indi'rektli] *adv* indirectamente.

indiscernible [,indi'sə:nəbl] *adj* imperceptible.

indiscipline [in'disiplin] *n* indisciplina *f*.

indiscreet [,indis'kri:t] *adj* indiscreto, imprudente.

indiscreetly [,indis'kri:tli] *adv* indiscretamente.

indiscretion [,indis'kreʃən] *n* indiscreción *f*, imprudencia *f*.

indiscriminate [,indis'kriminit] *adj* indistinto, sin distinción; *person* falto de discernimiento; *admirer* ciego.

indiscriminately [,indis'kriminitli] *adv* indistintamente, sin distinción; *admire* ciegamente.

indispensable [,indis'pensəbl] *adj* indispensable, imprescindible.

indisposed [,indis'pəuzd] *adj:* **to be —** estar indispuesto.

indisposition [,indispə'ziʃən] *n* indisposición *f*, enfermedad *f*.

indisputable [,indis'pju:təbl] *adj* incontestable, incuestionable.

indisputably [,indis'pju:təbli] *adv* incontestablemente; **it is — the best** es el mejor sin ningún género de dudas; **oh, — claro que sí.

indissoluble [,indi'sɔljubl] *adj* indisoluble; *link* irrompible.

indissolubly [,indi'sɔljubli] *adv* indisolublemente; **to be — linked** tener vínculos irrompibles.

indistinct [,indis'tiŋkt] *adj* indistinto; confuso.

indistinctly [,indis'tiŋktli] *adv* indistintamente; confusamente.

indistinguishable [,indis'tiŋgwiʃəbl] *adv* indistinguible (*from* de).

individual [,indi'vidjuəl] **1** *adj* individual; personal; (*for one person alone*) particular, propio. **2** *n* individuo *m*.

individualism [,indi'vidjuəlizəm] *n* individualismo *m*.

individualist [,indi'vidjuəlist] *n* individualista *mf*.

individuality [,indi,vidju'æliti] *n* individualidad *f*, personalidad *f*.

individualize [,indi'vidjuəlaiz] *vt* individuar, individualizar.

individually [,indi'vidjuəli] *adv* individualmente; particularmente; **they're all right —** cada uno de por sí es buena persona.

indivisible [,indi'vizəbl] *adj* indivisible.

Indo . . . ['indəu] indo . . .

Indo-China ['indəu'tʃainə] la Indochina.

indoctrinate [in'dɔktrineit] *vt* adoctrinar (*with* en).

indoctrination [in,dɔktri'neiʃən] *n* adoctrinamiento *m*.

Indo-European ['indəu,juərə'pi:ən] **1** *adj* indoeuropeo. **2** *n* indoeuropeo *m*, a *f*. **3** *n* (*language*) indoeuropeo *m*.

indolence ['indələns] *n* indolencia *f*, pereza *f*.

indolent ['indələnt] *adj* indolente, perezoso.

indolently ['indələntli] *adv* perezosamente.

indomitable [in'dɔmitəbl] *adj* indómito, indomable.

Indonesia [,indəu'ni:ziə] Indonesia *f*.

Indonesian [,indəu'ni:ziən] **1** *adj* indonesio. **2** *n* indonesio *m*, a *f*.

indoor ['indɔ:*] *adj* interior; de casa; de puertas adentro; *sport* en sala, bajo cubierta, en pista cubierta; *game* de salón; *aerial* de interior; *swimming pool* cubierto.

indoors [in'dɔ:z] *adv* en casa; dentro; bajo techado; **to go —** entrar en la casa; **he had to spend a week —** tuvo que estar una semana sin salir de casa; **I like the outside, but what's it like —?** me gusta lo de fuera, pero ¿qué tal está por dentro?

indubitable [in'dju:bitəbl] *adj* indudable.

indubitably [in'dju:bitəbli] *adv* indudablemente, sin duda.

induce [in'dju:s] *vt* inducir; producir, ocasionar; *sleep etc* provocar; (*Elec*) inducir; **to — someone to do something** inducir a uno a hacer algo, persuadir a uno a hacer algo; **nothing would — me to go** nada me persuadiría a ir.

inducement [in'dju:smənt] *n* incentivo *m*, aliciente *m*, estímulo *m*; **to hold out something to someone as an —** ofrecer algo a uno como aliciente; **it offers no — to harder work** no ofrece nada que estimulara a la gente a trabajar más; **as an added — it has . . .** tiene además el atractivo de . . .

induct [in'dʌkt] *vt* (*Eccl*) instalar; *new member etc* iniciar (*into* en); (*US Mil*) quintar.

induction [in'dʌkʃən] *n* (*Eccl*) instalación *f*; (*of member*) iniciación *f*; (*US Mil*) quinta *f*; (*Elec, Philos*) inducción *f*.

induction coil [in'dʌkʃənkɔil] *n* carrete *m* de inducción.

inductive [in'dʌktiv] *adj* inductivo.

indulge [in'dʌldʒ] **1** *vt* desire etc satisfacer, dar rienda suelta a; *whim* condescender con; *person* complacer, dar gusto a; *child etc* consentir, mimar.

2 *vi* (*ie drink*) beber; **to — in** darse el lujo de, permitirse; (*viciously*) darse a, abandonarse a.

3 *vr:* **to — oneself** darse gusto, permitirse un lujo.

indulgence [in'dʌldʒəns] *n* (*of desire etc*) satisfacción *f*, gratificación *f*; (*vicious*) abandono *m* (*in* a), desenfreno *m*; (*tolerance*) tolerancia *f*, complacencia *f*; (*Eccl*) indulgencia *f*.

indulgent [in'dʌldʒənt] *adj* indulgente (*towards* con).

indulgently [in'dʌldʒəntli] *adv* indulgentemente.

industrial [in'dʌstriəl] *adj* industrial; *accident* de trabajo.

industrialism [in'dʌstriəlizəm] *n* industrialismo *m*.

industrialist [in'dʌstriəlist] *n* industrial *m*.

industrialization [in,dʌstriəlai'zeiʃən] *n* industrialización *f*.

industrialize [in'dʌstriəlaiz] *vt* industrializar.

industrious [in'dʌstriəs] *adj* trabajador, laborioso; *student* aplicado, diligente.

industriously [in'dʌstriəsli] *adv* laboriosamente; con aplicación, diligentemente.

industriousness [in'dʌstriəsnis] *n* laboriosidad *f*; aplicación *f*, diligencia *f*.

industry ['indəstri] *n* (a) (*Tech*) industria *f*; **basic —** industria *f* básica; **heavy —** industria *f* pesada; **the hotel —** el comercio hotelero; **the tourist —** el turismo.

(b) (*industriousness*) laboriosidad *f*, aplicación *f*, diligencia *f*.

inebriate [i'ni:briit] *n* borracho *m*, a *f*.
inebriate [i'ni:brieit] *vt* embriagar, emborrachar.
inebriated [i'ni:brieitid] *adj* ebrio, borracho.
inebriation [i,ni:bri'eiʃən] *n* embriaguez *f*.
inedible [in'edibl] *adj* incomible, no comestible.
ineducable [in'edjukəbl] *adj* ineducable.
ineffable [in'efəbl] *adj* inefable.
ineffaceable [,ini'feisəbl] *adj* imborrable.
ineffective [,ini'fektiv] *adj*, **ineffectual** [,ini'fektjuəl] *adj remedy etc* ineficaz, inútil; *person* incapaz, inútil; **he's wholly —** es un cero a la izquierda; **the plan proved —** el proyecto no surtió efecto.
ineffectively [,ini'fektivli] *adv* ineficazmente, inútilmente.
inefficacious [,inefi'keiʃəs] *adj* ineficaz.
inefficacy [in'efikəsi] *n* ineficacia *f*.
inefficiency [,ini'fiʃənsi] *n* ineficacia *f*; incapacidad *f*, incompetencia *f*.
inefficient [,ini'fiʃənt] *adj* ineficaz, ineficiente; *person* incapaz, incompetente.
inefficiently [,ini'fiʃəntli] *adv* ineficazmente; de modo incompetente.
inelastic [,ini'læstik] *adj* inelástico; *(fig)* rígido, poco flexible.
inelegant [in'eligənt] *adj* inelegante, poco elegante.
inelegantly [in'eligəntli] *adv* inelegantemente.
inelegible [in'elidʒəbl] *adj* inelegible; **to be — to vote** no tener derecho a votar.
ineluctable [,ini'lʌktəbl] *adj* ineludible.
inept [i'nept] *adj* inepto; *person* incompetente, incapaz.
ineptitude [i'neptitju:d] *n*, **ineptness** [i'neptnis] *n* inepcia *f*, ineptitud *f*; incompetencia *f*, incapacidad *f*.
inequality [,ini'kwɔliti] *n* desigualdad *f*.
inequitable [in'ekwitəbl] *adj* injusto.
inequity [in'ekwiti] *n* injusticia *f*.
ineradicable [,ini'rædikəbl] *adj* inextirpable.
inert [i'nə:t] *adj* inerte, inactivo; *(motionless)* inmóvil; **he lay — on the floor** estuvo tumbado sin moverse en el suelo.
inertia [i'nə:ʃə] *n* inercia *f* *(also Phys)*, inacción *f*; pereza *f*.
inescapable [,inis'keipəbl] *adj* ineludible.
inessential ['ini'senʃəl] 1 *adj* no esencial. 2 *n* cosa *f* no esencial.
inestimable[in'estiməbl] *adj* inapreciable, inestimable.
inevitability [in,evitə'biliti] *n* inevitabilidad *f*.
inevitable [in'evitəbl] *adj* inevitable, ineludible; forzoso; **it was — it should happen** tuvo forzosamente *(or fatalmente)* que ocurrir.
inevitably [in'evitəbli] *adv* inevitablemente, forzosamente.
inexact [,inig'zækt] *adj* inexacto.
inexactly [,inig'zæktli] *adv* de modo inexacto.
inexcusable [,iniks'kju:zəbl] *adj* imperdonable.
inexcusably [,iniks'kju:zəbli] *adv* imperdonablemente.
inexhaustible [,inig'zɔ:stəbl] *adj* inagotable.
inexorable [in'eksərəbl] *adj* inexorable, implacable.
inexorably [in'eksərəbli] *adv* inexorablemente, implacablemente.
inexpedient [,iniks'pi:diənt] *adj* inoportuno, inconveniente, imprudente.
inexpensive [,iniks'pensiv] *adj* económico, barato.
inexperience [,iniks'piəriəns] *n* inexperiencia *f*, falta *f* de experiencia.
inexperienced [,iniks'piəriənst] *adj* inexperto, falto de experiencia.
inexpert [in'ekspə:t] *adj* imperito, inexperto, inhábil.
inexpertly [in'ekspə:tli] *adv* sin habilidad, desmañadamente.
inexplicable [,iniks'plikəbl] *adj* inexplicable.
inexplicably [,iniks'plikəbli] *adv* inexplicablemente, misteriosamente.
inexpressible [,iniks'presəbl] *adj* inefable.
inexpressive [,iniks'presiv] *adj style etc* inexpresivo; *person* reservado, callado.
inextinguishable [,iniks'tiŋgwiʃəbl] *adj* inextinguible, inapagable.
inextricable [,iniks'trikəbl] *adj* inextricable, inseparable, imposible de desenredar *(etc)*.
inextricably [,iniks'trikəbli] *adv*: **— entwined** entrelazados de modo inextricable.
infallibility [in,fælə'biliti] *n* infalibilidad *f*.
infallible [in'fæləbl] *adj* infalible; indefectible.
infallibly [in'fæləbli] *adv* infaliblemente; indefectiblemente.
infamous ['infəməs] *adj* infame.
infamy ['infəmi] *n* infamia *f*.
infancy ['infənsi] *n* infancia *f*; *(Law)* menor edad *f*; **from —** desde niño; **it is still in its —** está todavía en mantillas.

infant ['infənt] 1 *adj mortality etc* infantil; *school* de párvulos; *industry etc* naciente.
2 *n* criatura *f*, niño *m*, a *f*; *(Law)* menor *mf*; **the — Jesus** el niño Jesús.
infanta [in'fæntə] *n* infanta *f*.
infante [in'fænti] *n* infante *m*.
infanticide [in'fæntisaid] *n* *(act)* infanticidio *m*; *(person)* infanticida *mf*.
infantile ['infəntail] *adj* infantil *(also Med)*; *(pej)* aniñado, pueril; **don't be so —!** ¡no seas niño!
infantry ['infəntri] *n* infantería *f*.
infantryman ['infəntrimən] *n*, *pl* **—men** [mən] soldado *m* de infantería.
infatuated [in'fætjueitid] *adj*: **to be — with** *idea etc* encapricharse por; *person* estar chiflado por.
infatuation [in,fætju'eiʃən] *n* encaprichamiento *m*; chifladura *f*.
infect [in'fekt] *vt air, well, wound etc* infectar, inficionar; *person* contagiar *(with* con*)*; *(fig)* contagiar, comunicar; *(pej)* corromper, inficionar; **to be —ed with** *(act)* contagiarse de, *(state)* estar contagiado de; **he —s everybody with his enthusiasm** contagia a todos con su entusiasmo.
infection [in'fekʃən] *n* *(Med)* infección *f*, contagio *m*; *(fig)* contagio *m*; **she has a slight —** está ligeramente indispuesta.
infectious [in'fekʃəs] *adj* contagioso *(also fig)*, infeccioso.
infectiousness [in'fekʃəsnis] *n* contagiosidad *f*.
infelicitous [,infi'lisitəs] *adj* infeliz, impropio.
infelicity [,infi'lisiti] *n* infelicidad *f*, impropiedad *f*.
infer [in'fə:*] *vt* deducir, colegir, inferir *(from* de*)*.
inference ['infərəns] *n* deducción *f*, inferencia *f*, conclusión *f*.
inferential [,infə'renʃəl] *adj* ilativo, deductivo.
inferentially [,infə'renʃəli] *adv* por inferencia, por deducción.
inferior [in'fiəriə*] 1 *adj* inferior *(to* a*)*. 2 *n* inferior *mf*.
inferiority [in,fiəri'ɔriti] *n* inferioridad *f*.
infernal [in'fə:nl] *adj* infernal *(also fig)*.
infernally [in'fə:nəli] *adv*: **it's — awkward** es terriblemente difícil.
inferno [in'fə:nəu] *n* infierno *m*; **it's like an — in there** allí dentro hace un calor insufrible; **in a few minutes the house was a blazing —** en pocos minutos la casa estaba hecha una hoguera.
infertile [in'fə:tail] *adj* estéril, infecundo.
infertility [,infə:'tiliti] *adj* esterilidad *f*, infecundidad *f*.
infest [in'fest] *vt* infestar; **to be —ed with** estar plagado de.
infestation [,infes'teiʃən] *n* infestación *f*, plaga *f*.
infidel ['infidəl] 1 *adj* infiel, pagano, descreído. 2 *n* infiel *mf*, pagano *m*, a *f*, descreído *m*, a *f*; **the I—** los descreídos, la gente descreída.
infidelity [,infi'deliti] *n* infidelidad *f* *(to* para con*)*; **marital —** infidelidad *f* conyugal.
in-fighting ['infaitiŋ] *n* lucha *f* cuerpo a cuerpo.
infiltrate ['infiltreit] 1 *vt* infiltrarse en. 2 *vi* infiltrarse.
infiltration [,infil'treiʃən] *n* infiltración *f*.
infinite ['infinit] 1 *adj* infinito; *(fig)* infinito, inmenso, enorme; **we had — trouble finding it** nos costó muchísimo trabajo encontrarlo; **he took — pains over it** lo hizo con el mayor esmero.
2 *n*: **the —** el infinito.
infinitely ['infinitli] *adv* infinitamente; **this is — harder** esto es muchísimo más difícil; **we liked it — more the second time** la segunda vez nos gustó muchísimo más; **yes, —** sí, muchísimo.
infinitesimal [,infini'tesiməl] *adj* infinitesimal.
infinitive [in'finitiv] 1 *adj* infinitivo. 2 *n* infinitivo *m*.
infinity [in'finiti] *n* *(Math)* infinito *m*; **an — of** infinidad de, un sinfín de.
infirm [in'fə:m] *adj* enfermizo, achacoso, débil; **— of purpose** irresoluto; **the old and —** los ancianos y enfermos.
infirmary [in'fə:məri] *n* hospital *m*; *(at bullring etc)* enfermería *f*.
infirmity [in'fə:miti] *n* *(state)* debilidad *f*; *(illness)* enfermedad *f*, achaque *m*, dolencia *f*; *(moral)* flaqueza *f*.
inflame [in'fleim] *vt* inflamar *(also Med)*; **to be —d with** arder de, inflamarse de.
inflammable [in'flæməbl] *adj* inflamable; *(situation etc)* explosivo, de gran tirantez.
inflammation [,inflə'meiʃən] *n* inflamación *f* *(also Med)*.
inflammatory [in'flæmətəri] *adj* inflamatorio; *propaganda, speech* incendiario.

inflate [in'fleit] vt hinchar, inflar (with de); (fig) hinchar (with de); report etc exagerar; price inflar, aumentar de modo excesivo.

inflated [in'fleitid] adj report exagerado; price excesivo.

inflation [in'fleiʃən] n inflación f (also Fin).

inflationary [in'fleiʃnəri] adj inflacionista, inflatorio.

inflationism [in'fleiʃənizəm] n inflacionismo m.

inflect [in'flekt] vt torcer, doblar; voice modular; (Gram) noun etc declinar, verb conjugar.

inflected [in'flektid] adj language flexional.

inflection [in'flekʃən] n inflexión f.

inflexibility [in,fleksi'biliti] n inflexibilidad f; (fig) rigidez f.

inflexible [in'fleksəbl] adj inflexible; (fig) rígido.

inflexion [in'flekʃən] n inflexión f.

inflict [in'flikt] 1 vt wound etc infligir, inferir (on a); penalty, tax etc imponer (on a); grief, damage etc causar (on a).
2 vr: to — oneself on someone molestar a uno acompañándole (or visitándole etc).

infliction [in'flikʃən] n (act) imposición f; (penalty etc) pena f, castigo m.

inflow ['infləu] n afluencia f.

influence ['influəns] 1 n influencia f, influjo m (on sobre); ascendiente m (over sobre); valimiento m (with cerca de); a man of — un hombre influyente; to be under the — (of drink) estar borracho; to drive under the — conducir en estado de embriaguez; to bring every — to bear on someone ejercer todas las presiones posibles sobre uno; to have — (person) tener el padre alcalde, tener buenas aldabas; you've got to have — to get a job para conseguir un puesto hay que tener un buen enchufe; to have — over someone tener ascendiente sobre uno.
2 vt person etc influir en, influenciar; sugestionar; decision etc influir en, efectar; the novelist has been —d by Quevedo el novelista ha sufrido la influencia de Quevedo, el novelista está influido por Quevedo; what factors —d your decision? ¿qué factores influyeron en su decisión?; don't let him — you no se deje persuadir por él; to be easily —d ser influenciable.

influential [,influ'enʃəl] adj influyente, prestigioso.

influenza [,influ'enzə] n gripe f.

influx ['inflʌks] n afluencia f; (Mech etc) aflujo m, entrada f.

inform [in'fɔːm] 1 vt informar (about sobre, of de); avisar; comunicar, participar; I am happy to — you that... tengo el gusto de comunicarle que...; well —ed enterado, instruido; to be —ed about something estar enterado de algo, estar al corriente de algo; why was I not —ed? ¿por qué no me avisaron?; I should like to be —ed as soon as he comes que me avisen en cuanto llegue; to keep someone —ed about something tener a uno al corriente de algo.
2 vi soplar; to — against someone delatar a uno, denunciar a uno.
3 vr: to — oneself about something informarse sobre algo.

informal [in'fɔːməl] adj person desenvuelto, afable, poco ceremonioso; occasion sin ceremonia, sin protocolo; dance sin etiqueta; visit, gathering de confianza, íntimo; tone, manner familiar; (unofficial) extraoficial.

informality [,infɔː'mæliti] n afabilidad f; falta f de ceremonia; intimidad f; familiaridad f; we liked the — of the occasion nos gustó la función por su ausencia de ceremonia.

informally [in'fɔːməli] adv: it was organized very — se organizó sin ceremonia; the president spoke — to the journalists el presidente habló en tono de confianza con los periodistas; I have been told that... me han dicho de modo extraoficial que...

informant [in'fɔːmənt] n: my — el que me lo dijo.

information [,infə'meiʃən] n (a) (in general) información f, informes mpl, datos mpl; (news) noticias fpl; a piece of — una información, un dato, una noticia; classified — información f secreta; for your —, let me tell you... para sacarle de duda, sepa Vd que...; to ask for — pedir informes; to gather — about something tomar informes sobre algo, informarse sobre algo, reunir datos acerca de algo; we have no — on that point no tenemos información sobre ese particular.
(b) (knowledge) conocimientos mpl; he writes well but is short of — escribe bien pero tiene escasos conocimientos.
(c) (Law) denuncia f, delatación f; to lay — about a crime denunciar un crimen; to lay — against someone delatar a uno.

informative [in'fɔːmətiv] adj informativo.

informer [in'fɔːmə*] n (Law) denunciante mf, delator m, ora f; (criminal) soplón m.

infraction [in'frækʃən] n infracción f, violación f.

infra dig ['infrə'dig] adj (fam) deshonroso, indecoroso.

infrared ['infrə'red] adj infrarrojo.

infrequency [in'friːkwənsi] n infrecuencia f.

infrequent [in'friːkwənt] adj poco frecuente, infrecuente.

infrequently [in'friːkwəntli] adv rara vez.

infringe [in'frindʒ] 1 vt infringir, violar. 2 vi: to — on invadir, abusar de.

infringement [in'frindʒmənt] n infracción f, violación f; (of rights etc) invasión f, abuso m; (Sport) falta f.

infuriate [in'fjuərieit] vt enfurecer, poner rabioso; to be —d estar furioso; this kind of thing —s me estas cosas me hacen rabiar; at times you — me hay veces que me sacas de quicio.

infuriating [in'fjuərieitiŋ] adj enloquecedor; it's simply — es para volverse loco.

infuse [in'fjuːz] vt infundir (into a); to — courage into someone infundir ánimo a uno; they were —d with a new hope se les infundió una nueva esperanza.

infusion [in'fjuːʒən] n infusión f; — of tea infusión f de té.

ingenious [in'dʒiːniəs] adj ingenioso, inventivo, hábil; machine etc ingenioso; scheme etc genial.

ingeniously [in'dʒiːniəsli] adv ingeniosamente, hábilmente; con genialidad.

ingénue [,ɛ̃ːnʒei'njuː] n joven f ingenua, muchacha f candorosa.

ingenuity [,indʒi'njuːiti] n ingeniosidad f, inventiva f, habilidad f; genialidad f.

ingenuous [in'dʒenjuəs] adj ingenuo, candoroso.

ingest [in'dʒest] vt ingerir.

ingestion [in'dʒestʃən] n ingestión f.

inglenook ['iŋglnuk] n rincón m de la chimenea.

inglorious [in'glɔːriəs] adj ignominioso, vergonzoso.

ingot ['iŋgət] n lingote m, barra f; steel — acero m en lingotes.

ingrained [in'greind] adj profundamente arraigado.

ingratiate [in'greiʃieit] vr: to — oneself with someone congraciarse con uno, hacerse simpático a uno, insinuarse en el favor de uno.

ingratiating [in'greiʃieitiŋ] adj smile etc insinuante, lleno de insinuación; person congraciador, zalamero.

ingratitude [in'grætitjuːd] n ingratitud f, desagradecimiento m.

ingredient [in'griːdiənt] n ingrediente m, componente m.

ingress ['ingres] n ingreso m, entrada f.

ingrowing [in'grəuiŋ] adj: — nail uñero m.

inhabit [in'hæbit] vt habitar; vivir en; ocupar.

inhabitable [in'hæbitəbl] adj habitable.

inhabitant [in'hæbitənt] n habitante m.

inhabited [in'hæbitid] adj habitado, poblado.

inhalation [,inhə'leiʃən] n aspiración f; (Med) inhalación f.

inhalator ['inhəleitə*] n (US) inhalador m.

inhale [in'heil] vt aspirar; (Med) inhalar.

inhaler [in'heilə*] n inhalador m.

inharmonious [,inhɑː'məuniəs] adj inarmónico, disonante; (fig) discorde, poco armonioso.

inherent [in'hiərənt] adj innato, inmanente, intrínseco; — in inherente a; with all the — difficulties con todas las dificultades inevitables.

inherently [in'hiərəntli] adv intrínsecamente.

inherit [in'herit] vt heredar.

inheritance [in'heritəns] n herencia f; (fig) patrimonio m, legado m; our national — nuestro patrimonio nacional; it's an — from the last government es un legado del gobierno anterior.

inhibit [in'hibit] vt inhibir, impedir, imposibilitar; to — someone from doing something impedir a uno hacer algo; don't let my presence — the discussion no quiero que mi presencia impida la discusión; we cannot — change no podemos detener los cambios.

inhibited [in'hibitid] adj cohibido; to feel rather — sentirse algo cohibido.

inhibition [,inhi'biʃən] n inhibición f.

inhibitory [in'hibitəri] adj inhibitorio.

inhospitable [,inhɔs'pitəbl] adj person inhospitalario; country inhóspito; attitude, remark poco amistoso.

inhospitably [,inhɔs'pitəbli] adv de modo inhospitalario.

inhospitality ['in,hɔspi'tæliti] n inhospitalidad f.

inhuman [in'hjuːmən] adj inhumano.

inhumane [,inhju(ː)'mein] adj inhumano.

inhumanity [,inhju'mæniti] n inhumanidad f.

inhumation [,inhju'meiʃən] n inhumación f.

inimical [i'nimikəl] *adj:* — **to** opuesto a, contrario a, perjudicial para.

inimitable [i'nimitəbl] *adj* inimitable.

iniquitous [i'nikwitəs] *adj* inicuo; enorme; monstruoso; diabólico.

iniquity [i'nikwiti] *n* iniquidad *f;* perversidad *f;* injusticia *f;* enormidad *f;* **iniquities** (*of system*) injusticias *fpl,* (*of person*) excesos *mpl,* desmanes *mpl.*

initial [i'niʃəl] **1** *adj* inicial; primero; **in the** — **stages** al principio, en las primeras etapas; **my** — **reaction was to . . .** mi primer pensamiento era de . . .
2 *n* inicial *f,* letra *f* inicial; —**s** (*of person etc*) iniciales *fpl,* (*used as abbreviation*) siglas *fpl.*
3 *vt* marcar (*or* firmar *etc*) con las iniciales.

initially [i'niʃəli] *adv* al principio, en primer lugar.

initiate [i'niʃiit] *n* iniciado *m,* a *f.*

initiate [i'niʃieit] *vt* **(a)** (*begin*) iniciar, empezar, dar comienzo a, dar origen a; *reform etc* promover; *fashion* introducir; (*Law*) *proceedings* entablar.
   (b) to — **someone into a secret** iniciar a uno en un secreto; **to** — **someone into a society** admitir a uno a una sociedad.

initiation [i,niʃi'eiʃən] *n* iniciación *f;* principio *m,* comienzo *m;* admisión *f;* — **rite** ceremonia *f* de iniciación.

initiative [i'niʃətiv] *n* iniciativa *f;* **on one's own** — por iniciativa propia; **to take the** — tomar la iniciativa.

inject [in'dʒekt] *vt* (*Med etc*) inyectar (*into* en); (*fig*) injertar, introducir (*into* en), infundir (*into* a); **to** — **someone with something** inyectar algo en uno; **to** — **new life into a club** infundir un espíritu nuevo a un club.

injection [in'dʒekʃən] *n* inyección *f.*

injudicious [,indʒu'diʃəs] *adj* imprudente, indiscreto.

injudiciously [,indʒu'diʃəsli] *adv* imprudentemente, indiscretamente.

injunction [in'dʒʌŋkʃən] *n* mandato *m;* (*Law*) entredicho *m;* interdicto *m.*

injure [in'dʒə*] **1** *vt* **(a)** (*physically*) herir, hacer daño a, lastimar, lesionar, (*permanently*) lisiar; **he —d his arm** se lesionó el brazo.
   (b) *chances, reputation, trade etc* perjudicar; (*offend*) ofender, agraviar; *feelings* herir.
2 *vr:* **to** — **oneself** hacerse daño, lesionarse.

injured [in'dʒəd] *adj:* **with an** — **arm** con un brazo lesionado; **an** — **player** un jugador lesionado; **there were 4** — hubo 4 heridos; **in an** — **tone** en tono ofendido; **the** — **party** la persona ofendida, la persona perjudicada.

injurious [in'dʒuəriəs] *adj* (*harmful*) nocivo, dañoso, perjudicial (*to* para); (*insulting*) injurioso, ofensivo; — **to health** perjudicial para la salud.

injury [in'dʒəri] *n* **(a)** (*physical*) herida *f,* lesión *f;* **3 players have injuries** 3 jugadores están lesionados; **to do someone an** — herir a uno; **to do oneself an** — hacerse daño, lesionarse.
   (b) (*fig*) perjuicio *m,* daño *m;* **our reputation has suffered** — nuestra reputación ha sido perjudicada.

injustice [in'dʒʌstis] *n* injusticia *f;* **you do me an** — Vd me juzga mal, Vd es injusto conmigo.

ink [iŋk] **1** *n* tinta *f;* **in** — con tinta; **Indian** — tinta *f* china; **invisible** — tinta *f* simpática; **printer's** —, **printing** — tinta *f* de imprenta.
2 *vt* entintar; **to** — **in** entintar; **to** — **over** volver a escribir con tinta.

inkling [iŋkliŋ] *n* (*hint*) indicio *m;* (*suspicion*) sospecha *f;* (*vague idea*) atisbo *m;* idea *f* vaga; **I had no** — **that** no tuve la menor idea de que; **we had some** — **of it** nos habíamos formado alguna idea de ello; **there was no** — **of the disaster to come** no había indicio alguno del desastre que había de sobrevenir.

inkpad [iŋkpæd] *n* tampón *m* de entintar.

inkpot [iŋkpɔt] *n* tintero *m.*

inkstand [iŋkstænd] *n* escribanía *f.*

inkwell [iŋkwel] *n* tintero *m.*

inky [iŋki] *adj* (*stained*) manchado de tinta; (*black*) negro como la tinta.

inlaid [in'leid] **1** *pret and ptp of* **inlay. 2** *adj:* — **floor** entarimado *m;* — **work** taracea *f.*

inland [in'lænd] **1** *adj* interior; del interior; — **town** ciudad *f* del interior. **2** *adv* tierra adentro, hacia el interior. **3** *n* interior *m* (del país).

in-laws [in,lɔːz] *npl* parientes *mpl* políticos.

inlay [in'lei] *vt* (*irr: see* **lay**) taracear, embutir, incrustar; **a sword inlaid with jewels** una espada incrustada de joyas.

inlet [inlet] *n* (*Geog*) ensenada *f,* cala *f,* entrante *m;* (*Mech*) admisión *f,* entrada *f;* — **pipe** tubo *m* de entrada; — **valve** válvula *f* de entrada.

inmate [inmeit] *n* habitante *mf,* ocupante *mf,* residente *mf;* inquilino *m,* a *f;* (*of hospital*) enfermo *m,* a *f;* (*of asylum*) internado *m,* a *f;* (*of prison*) preso *m,* presidiario *m.*

inmost [inmaust] *adj* = **innermost.**

inn [in] *n* posada *f,* hostería *f,* mesón *m;* (*poor, wayside*) venta *f,* (*large, wayside*) fonda *f;* (*pub*) taberna *f;* **I—s of Court** (*London*) Colegio *m* de Abogados.

innards [inədz] *npl* (*fam*) tripas *fpl.*

innate [i'neit] *adj* innato.

inner [inə*] *adj* interior, interno; *thoughts etc* íntimo, secreto.

innermost [inəmaust] *adj* (más) interior, más central; *thoughts etc* más íntimo, más secreto.

innings [iniŋz] *n sing and pl* turno *m,* entrada *f;* (*fig*) turno *m,* oportunidad *f.*

innkeeper [inki:pə*] *n* posadero *m,* a *f,* mesonero *m,* a *f;* ventero *m,* a *f;* fondista *mf;* tabernero *m,* a *f* (*see* **inn**).

innocence [inəsns] *n* inocencia *f;* **in all** — inocentemente; sin segunda intención, sin malicia.

innocent [inəsnt] **1** *adj* inocente (*of* de); *amusement etc* honesto. **2** *n* inocente *mf.*

innocently [inəsntli] *adv* inocentemente.

innocuous [i'nɔkjuəs] *adj* innocuo, inofensivo.

innovate [inəuveit] *vi* introducir novedades.

innovation [,inəu'veiʃən] *n* innovación *f,* novedad *f.*

innovator [inəuveitə*] *n* innovador *m,* ora *f.*

innuendo [,inju'endəu] *n* indirecta *f,* insinuación *f.*

innumerable [i'nju:mərəbl] *adj* innumerable; **there are** — **reasons** hay infinidad de razones; **I've told you** — **times** te lo he dicho muchísimas veces.

inoculate [i'nɔkjuleit] *vt* inocular (*against* contra, *with* de).

inoculation [i,nɔkju'leiʃən] *n* inoculación *f.*

inoffensive [,inə'fensiv] *adj* inofensivo; *person* apacible, pacífico.

inoperable [in'ɔpərəbl] *adj* inoperable.

inoperative [in'ɔpərətiv] *adj* inoperante.

inopportune [in'ɔpətju:n] *adj* inoportuno.

inopportunely [in'ɔpətju:nli] *adv* inoportunamente, a deshora.

inordinate [i'nɔ:dinit] *adj* desmesurado, excesivo, desmedido.

inordinately [i'nɔ:dinitli] *adv* desmesuradamente, excesivamente.

inorganic [,inɔ:'gænik] *adj* inorgánico.

in-patient [in,peiʃənt] *n* paciente *m* interno, paciente *f* interna.

input [input] *n* (*Elec, Mech*) entrada *f,* potencia *f* de entrada; (*Fin*) dinero *m* invertido, inversión *f.*

inquest [inkwest] *n* **(a)** (*Law*) investigación *f,* pesquisa *f* judicial; (*coroner's*) — encuesta *f* judicial, encuesta *f* post-mortem.
   (b) (*fig*) indagación *f,* encuesta *f;* **an** — **was held on the defeat** la derrota fue objeto de una encuesta; **he likes to hold an** — **on every game** le gusta discutir cada partido hasta la saciedad.

inquire [in'kwaiə*] **1** *vt* preguntar; informarse de, pedir informes sobre; **to** — **something of someone** preguntar algo a uno; **he —d the price** preguntó cuánto costaba.
2 *vi:* **to** — **about, to** — **after, to** — **for** preguntar por, pedir informes sobre; **to** — **into** investigar, examinar, indagar; **to** — **into the truth of something** averiguar la verdad de un suceso; **to** — **of someone** preguntar a uno; **"** — **at No. 14"** "razón: núm. 14"; **"** — **within"** "se dan informaciones".

inquirer [in'kwaiərə*] *n* (*asker*) el (*or* la *etc*) que pregunta; (*researcher*) investigador *m,* ora *f* (*into* de).

inquiring [in'kwaiəriŋ] *adj mind* activo, penetrante, curioso; *look etc* interrogativo, de interrogación.

inquiringly [in'kwaiəriŋli] *adv look etc* interrogativamente.

inquiry [in'kwaiəri] *n* **(a)** (*question*) pregunta *f;* petición *f* de informes; **"Inquiries"** (*sign etc*) **"Información"; "inquiries at No. 14"** "razón: núm. 14"; **"all inquiries to the secretary"** "dirigirse al secretario"; **on** — al preguntar; **have you an** —? ¿quiere Vd preguntar algo?; **to make inquiries** pedir informes, tomar informes (*about,* on sobre; *of* a).
   (b) a look of — una mirada interrogativa.
   (c) (*Law etc*) investigación *f,* pesquisa *f,* indagación *f,* examen *m,* encuesta *f;* **there will have to be an** — esto tendrá que ser investigado; **to hold an** — **into something** investigar algo, examinar algo; **the police are making inquiries** la policía está investigando el asunto.
   (d) (*commission etc*) comisión *f* de investigación, comisión *f* investigadora; **to set up an** — **into the**

disaster nombrar una comisión para investigar el desastre.

inquiry office [in'kwaiəri‚ɔfis] n oficina f de informaciones.

inquisition [‚inkwi'ziʃən] n investigación f, inquisición f; **the I—** la Inquisición, el Santo Oficio.

inquisitive [in'kwizitiv] adj mind etc inquiridor, activo, curioso; (pej) preguntón, fisgón, curioso.

inquisitively [in'kwizitivli] adv con curiosidad f.

inquisitiveness [in'kwizitivnis] n curiosidad f.

inquisitor [in'kwizitə*] n inquisidor m.

inquisitorial [in‚kwizi'tɔːriəl] adj inquisitorial.

inroad ['inrəud] n incursión f, irrupción f (into en); (fig) invasión f, usurpación f (into de); **to make —s into someone's savings** agotar parte de los ahorros de uno.

inrush ['inrʌʃ] n irrupción f; (of tourists etc) afluencia f.

insalubrious [‚insə'luːbriəs] adj insalubre, malsano.

insane [in'sein] adj person loco, demente; act etc insensato; **you must be —!** ¿estás loco?; **to become —** volverse loco; **to drive someone —** volver loco a uno.

insanely [in'seinli] adv: **to laugh —** reírse como un loco; **to be — jealous** ser terriblemente celoso.

insanitary [in'sænitəri] adj insalubre, antihigiénico.

insanity [in'sæniti] n locura f, demencia f; (of act etc) insensatez f; **to drive someone to —** volver loco a uno.

insatiable [in'seiʃəbl] adj insaciable.

inscribe [in'skraib] vt inscribir; book dedicar.

inscription [in'skripʃən] n inscripción f; (in book) dedicatoria f; (label) rótulo m, letrero m.

inscrutability [in‚skruːtə'biliti] n inescrutabilidad f.

inscrutable [in'skruːtəbl] adj inescrutable, enigmático, insondable.

insect ['insekt] n insecto m.

insecticide [in'sektisaid] n insecticida m.

insectivorous [‚insek'tivərəs] adj insectívoro.

insecure [‚insi'kjuə*] adj inseguro.

insecurity [‚insi'kjuəriti] n inseguridad f.

inseminate [in'semineit] vt inseminar.

insemination [in‚semi'neiʃən] n fecundación f; **artificial —** fecundación f artificial, inseminación f artificial.

insensate [in'senseit] adj insensato.

insensibility [in‚sensə'biliti] n (a) insensibilidad f (to a), impasibilidad f; inconsciencia f (of de). (b) (Med) estupor m, desmayo m, pérdida f de conocimiento.

insensible [in'sensəbl] adj (a) (insensitive) insensible (to a), impasible, inconmovible; (unaware) inconsciente (of de). (b) (Med) sin conocimiento; **he fell down —** cayó sin conocimiento; **the blow knocked him —** el golpe le hizo perder el conocimiento; **to drink oneself —** beber hasta perder el conocimiento.

insensitive [in'sensitiv] adj insensible (to a).

insensitivity [in‚sensi'tiviti] n insensibilidad f.

inseparable [in'sepərəbl] adj inseparable, indisoluble; **as children they were —** cuando eran niños les unió la más estrecha amistad; **the two questions are —** los dos asuntos no se pueden considerar por separado.

inseparably [in'sepərəbli] adv inseparablemente, indisolublemente.

insert ['insəːt] n cosa f insertada; (page) hoja f suelta; (section) sección f añadida, materia f adicional.

insert [in'səːt] vt insertar, intercalar; object, finger etc introducir, meter dentro; (in newspaper) publicar; advert poner.

insertion [in'səːʃən] n inserción f; introducción f; publicación f; (new section) sección f añadida, materia f adicional.

inset ['inset] n (Typ) grabado m (or mapa, dibujo etc) que se imprime en un ángulo de otro mayor.

inshore ['in'ʃɔː] **1** adv be, fish cerca de la orilla; blow, flow, go hacia la orilla. **2** adj cercano a la orilla; fishing cercano a la costa.

inside ['in'said] **1** adv dentro; hacia dentro; por dentro; (on bus) en el piso inferior, abajo; (fam) en la cárcel; **he wouldn't come —** no quiso entrar; **please step —** pase Vd, por favor; **to pass the ball —** pasar el balón hacia dentro.
2 prep dentro de; en el interior de; **— 4 hours** en menos de 4 horas; **— the record** en tiempo inferior a la marca.
3 adj interior; interno; information secreto, confidencial; **it must be an — job** ha de ser obra de un empleado de la casa.
4 n (a) interior m, parte f interior; (lining) forro

m; **to know the — of an affair** conocer el secreto de un asunto; **to see a firm from the —** estudiar una empresa por dentro; **on the —** por dentro; **ladies walk on the — of the pavement** las señoras van en la parte de la acera más alejada de la calzada; **the car overtook on the —** (Brit) el coche pasó en el lado izquierdo.
(b) to be — out estar al revés; **to put a dress on — out** ponerse un vestido al revés; **to turn something — out** volver algo al revés; **they turned the whole place — out** lo revolvieron todo, lo registraron todo de arriba abajo; **to know a subject — out** conocer un tema a fondo.
(c) (Anat: also **—s**) estómago m, tripas fpl; **I have a pain in my —** me duele el estómago.

inside-forward ['insaid'fɔːwəd] n delantero m interior.

inside-left ['insaid'left] n interior m izquierdo.

inside-right ['insaid'rait] n interior m derecho.

insidious [in'sidiəs] adj insidioso; pernicioso; maligno; agitation etc clandestino, subversivo.

insidiously [in'sidiəsli] adv insidiosamente; perniciosamente; clandestinamente.

insight ['insait] n penetración f (psicológica), perspicacia f, intuición f; **to gain (or get etc) an — into something** formarse una idea de algo.

insignia [in'signiə] npl insignias fpl.

insignificance [‚insig'nifikəns] n insignificancia f; **A pales into — beside B** A pierde toda su importancia al compararse con B.

insignificant [‚insig'nifikənt] adj insignificante.

insincere [‚insin'siə*] adj poco sincero, nada franco, doble.

insincerity [‚insin'seriti] n falta f de sinceridad, doblez f.

insinuate [in'sinjueit] **1** vt insinuar; **what are you insinuating?** ¿qué quiere Vd insinuar?; **to — that** insinuar que, dar a entender que.
2 vr: **to — oneself into** insinuarse en, introducirse en.

insinuating [in'sinjueitiŋ] adj insinuador; remark malintencionado, con segunda intención.

insinuation [in‚sinju'eiʃən] n (act) insinuación f, introducción f; (hint) indirecta f, sugestión f; **it carries the — that** lleva implícita la noción de que; **he made certain —s** soltó ciertas indirectas.

insipid [in'sipid] adj insípido, soso, insulso.

insipidity [‚insi'piditi] n insipidez f, sosería f, insulsez f.

insist [in'sist] vi insistir; (obstinately) porfiar, empeñarse, persistir; **if you —** si Vd lo quiere de verdad; **to — on something** insistir en algo, exigir algo; **to — on doing something** insistir en hacer algo, empeñarse en hacer algo, obstinarse en hacer algo; **to — that something is so** insistir en que algo es así; **to — that something should be done** insistir en que se haga algo.

insistence [in'sistəns] n insistencia f (on en); empeño m (on en); porfía f; **I did it at his —** lo hice cediendo a sus ruegos.

insistent [in'sistənt] adj insistente; porfiado, persistente; urgente; **he was most — about it** se empeñó mucho en ello; **he said in — tones dijo en tono apremiante.

insistently [in'sistəntli] adv con insistencia; porfiadamente; urgentemente.

insole ['insəul] n plantilla f.

insolence ['insələns] n insolencia f, descaro m, atrevimiento m.

insolent ['insələnt] adj insolente, descarado, atrevido; **don't be —!** ¡qué frescura!

insolently ['insələntli] adv insolentemente, descaradamente.

insoluble [in'sɔljubl] adj insoluble.

insolvency [in'sɔlvənsi] n insolvencia f.

insolvent [in'sɔlvənt] adj insolvente.

insomnia [in'sɔmniə] n insomnio m.

insomniac [in'sɔmniæk] n insomne mf.

insomuch [‚insəu'mʌtʃ]: **— as** adv puesto que, ya que; **— that** hasta tal punto que.

insouciance [in'suːsiəns] n despreocupación f.

insouciant [in'suːsiənt] adj despreocupado.

inspect [in'spekt] vt inspeccionar, examinar; (officially) registrar, reconocer; troops pasar revista a.

inspection [in'spekʃən] n inspección f, examen m; registro m, reconocimiento m; (Mil) revista f; **customs —** revisión f aduanera; **— pit** foso m de reconocimiento.

inspector [in'spektə*] n inspector m; (Rail) revisor m; **customs —** aduanero m.

inspectorate [in'spektərit] n inspectorado m.

inspiration [,inspə'reiʃən] n inspiración f; **to find — in** inspirarse en; **you have been an — to us all** Vd nos ha inspirado a todos.
inspire [in'spaiə*] vt inspirar; **to — something in someone, to — someone with something** inspirar algo a uno, infundir algo a uno, llenar a uno de algo; **to — someone to do something** mover a uno a hacer algo.
inspired [in'spaiəd] adj genial.
inspiring [in'spaiəriŋ] adj inspirador.
instability [,instə'biliti] n inestabilidad f.
install [in'stɔːl] 1 vt instalar. 2 vr: **to — oneself** instalarse.
installation [,instə'leiʃən] n instalación f.
instalment, (US) installment [in'stɔːlmənt] n (of story etc) entrega f; (Comm) plazo m; **payment by —s** pago m a plazos; **to pay in —s** pagar a plazos; **monthly — mensualidad** f.
instance ['instəns] 1 n (a) (example) ejemplo m; caso m; **for —** por ejemplo; **in that —** en ese caso; **in many —s** en muchos casos; **let's take an actual —** tomemos un caso concreto.
   (b) **at the — of** a instancia de, a petición de.
   (c) **in the first —** en primer lugar.
   2 vt poner por caso, citar como ejemplo.
instant ['instənt] 1 adj inmediato, instantáneo; **— coffee** café m en polvo (listo para hacer); **the 3rd —** el 3 del (mes) corriente.
   2 n instante m, momento m; **in an —, on the —, this —** al instante, en seguida.
   3 as conj: **tell me the — he comes** avíseme en cuanto venga; **the — I heard it** luego que lo supe.
instantaneous [,instən'teiniəs] adj instantáneo.
instantaneously [,instən'teiniəsli] adv instantáneamente.
instantly ['instəntli] adv al instante, inmediatamente, en seguida.
instead [in'sted] adv en cambio, en lugar de eso; **— of** en lugar de, en vez de.
instep ['instep] n empeine m.
instigate ['instigeit] vt instigar.
instigation [,insti'geiʃən] n instigación f; **at the — of** a instigación de.
instigator ['instigeitə*] n instigador m, ora f.
instil [in'stil] vt infundir, inculcar; **to — something into someone** infundir algo a uno, inculcar algo en uno.
instinct [in'stiŋkt] adj: **— with** lleno de, imbuido de.
instinct ['instiŋkt] n instinto m; **by —** por instinto.
instinctive [in'stiŋktiv] adj instintivo.
instinctively [in'stiŋktivli] adv instintivamente, por instinto.
institute ['institjuːt] 1 n instituto m; (for professional training) escuela f; (of professional body) colegio m, asociación f.
   2 vt (found) instituir, establecer, fundar; inquiry etc iniciar, empezar; proceedings (Law) entablar.
institution [,insti'tjuːʃən] n (a) (act) institución f, establecimiento m, fundación f; iniciación f; entablación f.
   (b) (organization) instituto m, asociación f.
   (c) (workhouse etc) asilo m; (madhouse) manicomio m; (Med) hospital m.
   (d) (custom etc) institución f, costumbre f, tradición f; (person etc) persona f conocidísima; **it is too much of an — to abolish** es una costumbre demasiado arraigada para poder suprimirla; **tea is a British —** el té es bebida típica de los ingleses.
institutional [,insti'tjuːʃənl] adj institucional.
institutionalize [,insti'tjuːʃnəlaiz] vt reglamentar.
instruct [in'strʌkt] vt (a) (teach) instruir (about, in de, en, sobre); **to — someone in maths** enseñar matemáticas a uno.
   (b) (order) **to — someone to do something** mandar a uno hacer algo.
   (c) solicitor dar instrucciones a.
instruction [in'strʌkʃən] n (a) (teaching) instrucción f, enseñanza f; **to give someone — in fencing** enseñar esgrima a uno.
   (b) (order) orden f, mandato m; **—s instrucciones** fpl; órdenes fpl; **"— for use"** (on packet etc) "modo de empleo" m; **operating —s** (of pilot etc) órdenes fpl, consigna f; **on the —s of** por orden de.
instructive [in'strʌktiv] adj instructivo, informativo, aleccionador.
instructor [in'strʌktə*] n instructor m; profesor m; (US Univ) profesor m auxiliar.
instructress [in'strʌktris] n instructora f; profesora f.
instrument ['instrəmənt] n (all senses) instrumento m; **musical —** instrumento m músico; **stringed —** instrumento m de cuerda; **wind —** instrumento m

de viento; **scientific —s** instrumentos mpl científicos; **set of —s** instrumental m; **to fly on —s** volar por instrumentos.
instrumental [,instru'mentl] adj instrumental; **to be — in + ger** contribuir materialmente a + infin, ser instrumento eficaz para + infin.
instrumentalist [,instru'mentəlist] n instrumentista mf.
instrumentality [,instrumen'tæliti] n mediación f, agencia f; **by (or through) the — of** por medio de, gracias a.
instrumentation [,instrumen'teiʃən] n instrumentación f.
instrument panel ['instrumənt,pænl] n (Aer) tablero m de instrumentos.
insubordinate [,insə'bɔːdənit] adj insubordinado, desobediente, rebelde.
insubordination ['insə,bɔːdi'neiʃən] n insubordinación f, desobediencia f, rebeldía f.
insubstantial [,insəb'stænʃəl] adj insustancial.
insufferable [in'sʌfərəbl] adj insufrible, inaguantable.
insufferably [in'sʌfərəbli] adv de modo insufrible; **— rude** de lo más grosero.
insufficiency [,insə'fiʃənsi] n insuficiencia f.
insufficient [,insə'fiʃənt] adj insuficiente.
insufficiently [,insə'fiʃəntli] adv insuficientemente.
insular ['insjələ*] adj insular; (fig) de miras estrechas.
insularity [,insju'læriti] n insularidad f; (fig) estrechez f de miras.
insulate ['insjuleit] vt aislar (from de).
insulating tape ['insjuleitiŋ,teip] n cinta f aislante (or aisladora).
insulation [,insju'leiʃən] n aislamiento m.
insulator ['insjuleitə*] n aislante m, aislador m.
insulin ['insjulin] n insulina f.
insult ['insʌlt] n insulto m, injuria f, ultraje m, ofensa f; **they are an — to the profession** son un insulto para la profesión.
insult [in'sʌlt] vt insultar, injuriar; ofender; **he felt —ed by this offer** creyó que tal oferta era deshonrosa para él; **now don't feel —ed** pues no te vayas a ofender.
insulting [in'sʌltiŋ] adj insultante, injurioso; ofensivo; deshonroso.
insultingly [in'sʌltiŋli] adv injuriosamente, ofensivamente.
insuperable [in'suːpərəbl] adj insuperable.
insuperably [in'suːpərəbli] adv: **— difficult** dificilísimo; **A is — better than B** A es con mucho mejor que B.
insupportable [,insə'pɔːtəbl] adj insoportable.
insurable [in'ʃuərəbl] adj asegurable.
insurance [in'ʃuərəns] n (Comm) seguro m; **life —** seguro m sobre la vida; **mutual —** seguro m mutuo; **third-party —** seguro m contra tercera persona; **— agent** agente m de seguros; **— broker** corredor m de seguros; **— company** compañía f de seguros; **— policy** póliza f (de seguros); **— premium** prima f de seguros.
insure [in'ʃuə*] vt asegurar.
insured [in'ʃuəd] n: **the —** el asegurado, la asegurada.
insurer [in'ʃuərə*] n asegurador m, ora f.
insurgent [in'sɔːdʒənt] 1 adj insurrecto, insurgente.
   2 n insurrecto m, insurgente mf.
insurmountable [,insə'mauntəbl] adj insuperable.
insurrection [,insə'rekʃən] n sublevación f, insurrección f.
insurrectionary [,insə'rekʃnəri] adj rebelde, insurreccional.
intact [in'tækt] adj intacto; íntegro; ileso, entero, sano; **not a window was left —** no quedaba cristal sano (or sin romper).
intake ['inteik] n (a) (Mech) admisión f, toma f, entrada f; tubo m de admisión, válvula f de admisión; **air —** tubo m de admisión de aire.
   (b) (quantity) cantidad f admitida, número m admitido; **what is your student —?** ¿cuántos alumnos se matriculan (cada año)?
intangible [in'tændʒəbl] adj intangible.
integer ['intidʒə*] n (número m) entero m.
integral ['intigrəl] 1 adj (whole) íntegro; part, component integrante; (Math) integral; **it is an — part of the plan** es parte esencial del proyecto.
   2 n (Math) integral f.
integrate ['intigreit] 1 vt integrar (also Math); combinar en un todo, formar un conjunto con.
   2 vi integrarse (into en).
integrated ['intigreitid] adj plan de conjunto, que forma un conjunto; personality armonioso, estable, sano; population, school integrado, sin separación racial.

integration [,inti'greiʃən] n integración f; **racial —** integración f racial.

integrity [in'tegriti] n integridad f, honradez f, rectitud f.

integument [in'tegjumənt] n integumento m.

intellect ['intilekt] n intelecto m.

intellectual [,inti'lektjuəl] **1** adj intelectual. **2** n intelectual mf.

intelligence [in'telidʒəns] n **(a)** (understanding) inteligencia f; see **test** etc.

(b) (information) información f, informes mpl, noticias fpl; **— officer** oficial m de informaciones; **— service** (Mil) servicio m de información; **shipping — noticias** fpl navieras; **according to our latest —** según las últimas noticias.

intelligent [in'telidʒənt] adj inteligente.

intelligently [in'telidʒəntli] adv inteligentemente.

intelligentsia [in,teli'dʒentsiə] n intelectualidad f.

intelligibility [in,telidʒə'biliti] n inteligibilidad f.

intelligible [in'telidʒəbl] adj inteligible, comprensible; **it is scarcely — that** apenas es creíble que.

intelligibly [in'telidʒəbli] adv inteligiblemente, de modo inteligible.

intemperance [in'tempərəns] n intemperancia f, inmoderación f; (drunkenness) exceso m en la bebida.

intemperate [in'tempərit] adj intemperante, inmoderado; (drunken) dado a la bebida, que bebe con exceso.

intend [in'tend] vt **(a)** (n object) **what does he — by that?** ¿qué quiere decir con eso?; **I — it as a present** pienso darlo como regalo; **it is —ed for John** está destinado a Juan, es para Juan; **no offence was —ed, he —ed** no tenía la intención de ofender a nadie; **that remark was —ed for you** esa observación iba dirigida a Vd, eso lo dijo por Vd.

(b) (with verb) **to — to +** infin, **to — +** ger pensar + infin, proponerse + infin; **what do you — to do about it?** ¿qué piensas hacer?; **this scheme is —ed to help** este proyecto tiene la finalidad de ayudar; **I — that he should see it** pretendo que él lo vea, quiero que él lo vea; **I fully — to punish him** tengo la firme intención de castigarle.

intended [in'tendid] **1** adj deseado. **2** n prometido m, a f.

intense [in'tens] adj intenso; interest etc muy grande, sumo, enorme; person exagerado, nervioso.

intensely [in'tensli] adv intensamente; **— difficult** sumamente difícil, terriblemente difícil, dificilísimo; **she speaks so —** habla en tono tan exagerado.

intensification [in,tensifi'keiʃən] n intensificación f.

intensify [in'tensifai] **1** vt intensificar; aumentar, reforzar. **2** vi intensificarse; aumentar(se), reforzarse.

intensity [in'tensiti] n intensidad f; (of interest etc) fuerza f; (of person) exageración f, nerviosismo m, hipertensión f.

intensive [in'tensiv] adj intensivo; course intensivo, concentrado; study profundo, detenido.

intensively [in'tensivli] adv intensivamente; profundamente, detenidamente.

intent [in'tent] **1** adj (absorbed) absorto (on en), atento; **to be — on doing something** estar resuelto a hacer algo.

2 n intento m, propósito m; **with — to +** infin con el propósito de + infin; **to all —s and purposes** en realidad, en efecto.

intention [in'tenʃən] n intención f; intento m, propósito m; proyecto m; **my — is to +** infin me propongo + infin, intento + infin; **I have no — of +** ger no es mi propósito + infin; **with the best —s** con buena voluntad; **what are your —s?** ¿qué piensa hacer?, ¿qué proyectos tiene Vd?; **his —s towards the girl were strictly honourable** pensaba casarse honradamente con la joven.

intentional [in'tenʃənl] adj intencional, deliberado.

intentionally [in'tenʃnəli] adv intencionalmente, de propósito, adrede.

intently [in'tentli] adv atentamente, fijamente.

inter [in'tə:*] vt enterrar, sepultar.

inter . . . ['intə*] inter . . ., entre . . .

interact [,intər'ækt] vi obrar recíprocamente (on en); **they —** se influyen mutuamente.

interaction [,intər'ækʃən] n interacción f, acción f recíproca, influencia f mutua.

interbreed [intə'bri:d] (irr: see **breed**) **1** vt entrecruzar. **2** vi entrecruzarse.

intercalate [in'tə:kəleit] vt intercalar.

intercalation [in,tə:kə'leiʃən] n intercalación f.

intercede [,intə'si:d] vi interceder (for por, with con).

intercept [,intə'sept] vt interceptar; detener; (Math) cortar; (cut off) atajar.

interception [,intə'sepʃən] n interceptación f, detención f; atajo m.

interceptor [,intə(:)'septə*] n interceptor m.

intercession [,intə'seʃən] n intercesión f, mediación f.

interchange ['intə'tʃeindʒ] n intercambio m, cambio m; canje m; alternación f.

interchange [,intə'tʃeindʒ] vt intercambiar, cambiar; prisoners, publications etc canjear; (alternate) alternar.

interchangeable [,intə'tʃeindʒəbl] adj intercambiable.

intercollegiate ['intə(:)kə'li:dʒiit] adj interuniversitario.

intercom ['intəkɔm] n (fam) sistema m de intercomunicación.

intercommunicate [,intəkə'mju:nikeit] vi comunicarse.

intercommunication ['intəkə,mju:ni'keiʃən] n intercomunicación f.

intercommunion [,intəkə'mju:niən] n intercomunión f.

interconnect [,intəkə'nekt] vt interconectar.

intercontinental ['intə,kɔnti'nentl] adj intercontinental.

intercourse ['intəkɔ:s] n (social) trato m, relaciones fpl, comercio m; **sexual —** comercio m sexual, trato m sexual, coito m; **to have (sexual) — with** tener comercio sexual con.

interdenominational ['intədi,nɔmi'neiʃənl] adj interconfesional.

interdependence [,intədi'pendəns] n interdependencia f.

interdependent [,intədi'pendənt] adj interdependiente.

interdict ['intədikt] n entredicho m, interdicto m.

interdiction [,intə'dikʃən] n interdicción f.

interest ['intrist] **1** n **(a)** (curiosity) interés m; **of great —** de gran interés; **questions of public —** asuntos mpl que interesan a todos; **to be of — interesar**; **it is of no —** to us no nos interesa; **to do something just for —** hacer algo como pasatiempo nada más; **to have an — in** estar interesado en, interesarse en (or por); **to take an — in something** interesarse en (or por) algo; **to take no further — in something** dejar de interesarse en algo; **no participar más en algo.

(b) (profit, advantage) ventaja f, provecho m, beneficio m; **in one's own —(s)** en beneficio propio; **it is in your own —** to confess hay que confesarlo en beneficio propio; **in the —s of hygiene** en interés de la higiene; **to act in someone's —s** obrar en beneficio de uno; **to promote someone's —s** fomentar los intereses de uno; **it is not in Britain's — to leave the base** le perjudicará a Inglaterra abandonar la base.

(c) (Comm: share, stake) participación f, interés m; **—s** intereses mpl; **the coal —** la industria hullera, los propietarios de las minas de carbón; **the conservative —** los conservadores, el partido conservador; **the landed —** los terratenientes; **business —s** los negocios, el mundo de los negocios, los hombres de negocios; **vested —s** intereses mpl creados; **Switzerland is looking after British —s** Suiza se encarga de los intereses ingleses; **to have a financial — in a company** tener acciones en una compañía, ser accionista de una compañía; **to have a controlling —** tener más de la mitad de las acciones; **to give someone a joint —** admitir a uno como copartícipe.

(d) (Comm: on loan, shares etc) interés m; rédito m; **compound —** interés m compuesto; **simple — interés** m simple; **at an — of 5%** con interés de 5 por ciento; **to bear —** devengar intereses; **to bear — at 5%** producir un 5 por ciento de interés; **to lend at —** dar a interés; **to put out at —** poner a interés; **to repay with — (iro)** devolver con creces; **shares that yield a high —** acciones fpl que rinden bien.

2 vt interesar; **to be —ed in** (financially) estar interesado en, (from curiosity) interesarse en (or por); **the company is —ed in acquiring 200** la compañía está interesada en adquirir 200; **I'm not —ed in football** no me interesa el fútbol.

3 vr: **to — oneself in** interesarse en (or por).

interested ['intristid] adj: **— party, — person** interesado m, a f.

interesting ['intristin] adj interesante.

interfere [,intə'fiə*] vi intervenir, entrometerse, mezclarse (in en); **to — with** (hinder) estorbar, dificultar, impedir; (damage) manosear, estropear; (Radio etc) interferir; **who told you to —?** ¿quién le mete a Vd en esto?

interference [,intə'fiərəns] n intervención f, intromisión f, entrometimiento m; interposición f; (Radio etc) interferencia f.

interfering [,intə'fiəriŋ] adj entrometido.

interim ['intərim] 1 n interin m, intermedio m; **in the —** entretanto, en el interin, interinamente. 2 attr interino, provisional.

interior [in'tiəriə*] 1 adj interior, interno. 2 n interior m.

interject [,intə'dʒekt] vt interponer.

interjection [,intə'dʒekʃən] n interposición f; (word) interjección f, exclamación f.

interlace [,intə(:)'leis] 1 vt entrelazar. 2 vi entrelazarse.

interlard [,intə'laːd] vt: **to — with** salpicar de.

interleave [,intə'liːv] vt interfoliar.

interline [,intə(:)'lain] vt (Typ) interlinear; (Sew) entretelar.

interlinear [,intə(:)'liniə*] adj interlineal.

interlock [,intə'lɔk] 1 vt trabar, unir, entrelazar; wheels endentar, engranar.
  2 vi trabarse, unirse, entrelazarse; (wheels etc) endentarse, engranar; **the parts of the plan —** las partes del plan tienen una fuerte trabazón.

interlocutor [,intə'lɔkjutə*] n interlocutor m, ora f.

interloper ['intələupə*] n intruso m, a f; (Comm) intérlope m, comerciante m (etc) no autorizado.

interlude [,intəluːd] n intervalo m, intermedio m; (rest) descanso m; (Theat: playlet, interval) intermedio m; (Mus) interludio m.

intermarriage [,intə'mæridʒ] n matrimonio m entre parientes; matrimonio m entre personas de distintas razas.

intermarry ['intə'mæri] vi casarse (parientes or personas de distintas razas); **in this village they have intermarried for centuries** en este pueblo se vienen casando los parientes desde hace siglos.

intermediary [,intə'miːdiəri] 1 adj intermediario. 2 n intermediario m, a f.

intermediate [,intə'miːdiət] adj intermedio, medio; intermediario; **— stop** escala f.

interment [in'təːmənt] n entierro m.

interminable [in'təːminəbl] adj inacabable, interminable.

interminably [in'təːminəbli] adv: **he spoke —** habló como si nunca fuera a acabar.

intermingle [,intə'miŋgl] 1 vt entremezclar. 2 vi entremezclarse.

intermission [,intə'miʃən] n intermisión f, interrupción f, intervalo m; (Theat) descanso m; **it went on without —** continuó sin interrupción.

intermittent [,intə'mitənt] adj intermitente.

intermittently [,intə'mitəntli] adv a intervalos, a ratos.

intern [in'təːn] vt internar, recluir, encerrar.

intern ['intəːn] n (US Med) interno m de hospital.

internal [in'təːnl] adj interno, interior.

internally [in'təːnəli] adv interiormente.

international [,intə'næʃnəl] 1 adj internacional. 2 n **I—** Internacional f; (Sport: game) partido m internacional, (player) jugador m internacional.

internationalism [intə'næʃnəlizəm] n internacionalismo m.

internationalize [,intə'næʃnəlaiz] vt internacionalizar.

internecine [,intə'niːsain] adj: **— war** guerra f de aniquilación mutua.

internee [,intəː'niː] n internado m, a f.

internment [in'təːnmənt] n internamiento m.

interplanetary [,intə'plænitəri] adj interplanetario.

interplay ['intəplei] n interacción f.

interpolate [in'təːpəleit] vt interpolar.

interpolation [in,təːpə'leiʃən] n interpolación f.

interpose [,intə'pəuz] vt interponer; remark introducir, hacer de paso; **"never!", —d John** "¡jamás!", cortó Juan.

interpret [in'təːprit] vt interpretar; (translate) traducir; (understand) entender, explicar; **how are we to — that remark?** ¿cómo hemos de entender esa observación?; **if I — your wishes correctly** si entiendo bien sus deseos; **that is not how I — it** yo lo entiendo de otro modo.

interpretation [in,təːpri'teiʃən] n interpretación f; traducción f; (meaning) significado m; **what — am I to place on your conduct?** ¿cómo he de entender su conducta?; **the words bear another —** las palabras tienen otro significado, las palabras pueden entenderse de otro modo.

interpretative [in'təːpritətiv] adj interpretativo, aclaratorio, explicativo.

interpreter [in'təːpritə*] n intérprete mf.

interregnum [,intə'regnəm] n interregno m.

interrelate [,intəri'leit] vt interrelacionar.

interrelated [,intəri'leitid] adj interrelacionado.

interrelation [,intəri'leiʃən] n interrelación f.

interrogate [in'terəgeit] vt interrogar.

interrogation [in,terə'geiʃən] n interrogación f.

interrogative [,intə'rɔgətiv] 1 adj interrogativo. 2 n interrogativo m.

interrogator [in'terəgeitə*] n interrogador m, ora f.

interrogatory [,intə'rɔgətəri] adj interrogante.

interrupt [,intə'rʌpt] vti interrumpir.

interruption [intə'rʌpʃən] n interrupción f.

intersect [,intə'sekt] 1 vt cruzar, cortar. 2 vi (Geom) intersecarse; (roads etc) cruzarse.

intersection [,intə'sekʃən] n intersección f; cruce m.

intersperse [,intə'spəːs] vt esparcir, entremezclar; **dashes —d with dots** rayas con puntos a intervalos (or a ratos); **a speech —d with jokes** un discurso salpicado de chistes.

interstate [,intə'steit] adj (esp US) interestatal.

interstice [in'təːstis] n intersticio m.

intertwine [,intə'twain] 1 vt entrelazar, entretejer. 2 vi entrelazarse, entretejerse.

interurban [,intəː'əːbən] adj interurbano.

interval ['intəvl] n intervalo m; (Theat) descanso m, (more formally) entreacto m; (Sport etc) descanso m; **at —s** de vez en cuando, de trecho a trecho; **at —s of** a intervalos; **at rare —s** muy de tarde en tarde; **at regular —s** con regularidad; **bright —s** (Meteorol) períodos mpl de sol; **lucid —** intervalo m lúcido; **the work went on without an —** el trabajo continuó sin interrupción; **there was an — for meditation** se hizo una pausa para la meditación.

intervene [,intə'viːn] vi intervenir (in en); tomar parte, participar (in en); (occur) surgir, interponerse, sobrevenir; **if nothing —s to prevent it** si no surge nada que lo impida.

intervening [,intə'viːniŋ] adj intermedio.

intervention [,intə'venʃən] n intervención f.

interview ['intəvjuː] 1 n entrevista f, (for press, TV etc) interviú f; **to have an — with someone** entrevistarse con uno.
  2 vt entrevistarse con, (for press, TV etc) interviuvar; **3% of those —ed did not know that . . .** un 3 por cien de los entrevistados ignoraban que . . .

interviewer ['intəvjuːə*] n interviuvador m, ora f; (pressman) reportero m, periodista m.

interweave [,intə'wiːv] (irr: see **weave**) vt entretejer.

intestate [in'testit] adj intestado.

intestinal [,intes'tainl] adj intestinal.

intestine [in'testin] n intestino m; **large —** intestino m grueso; **small —** intestino m delgado.

intimacy ['intiməsi] n intimidad f; (euph) relaciones fpl íntimas.

intimate ['intimeit] vt dar a entender, indicar, intimar.

intimate ['intimit] 1 adj íntimo; friendship etc estrecho; knowledge profundo, detallado; **they are — friends** son íntimos amigos; **they are very —** son muy amigos; **he was — with her** (euph) tuvo relaciones íntimas con ella; **they became — se** intimaron; **A became — with B** A se intimó con B. 2 n amigo m de confianza; (pej) compinche m.

intimately ['intimitli] adv íntimamente; a fondo, profundamente.

intimation [,inti'meiʃən] n (news) indicación f, intimación f; (hint) insinuación f, indirecta f; **it was the first — we had had of it** fue la primera indicación que habíamos tenido de ello.

intimidate [in'timideit] vt intimidar, acobardar, amedrentar.

intimidation [in,timi'deiʃən] n intimidación f.

into ['intu] prep en; a; dentro de; hacia el interior de; **to put something — a box** poner algo en una caja; **to go — the wood** penetrar en el bosque; **to go off — the desert** ir hacia el interior del desierto; **to go — town** ir a la ciudad; **it got — the cage** entró en la jaula; **they got — the plane** subieron al avión; **it fell — the lake** cayó al lago, cayó en el lago; **to change something — something else** convertir algo en otra cosa; **to translate a text — Latin** traducir un texto al latín; **to grow — a man** hacerse hombre; see **far, go** etc.

intolerable [in'tɔlərəbl] adj intolerable, inaguantable, insufrible; **it is — that** no se puede consentir que + subj.

intolerably [in'tɔlərəbli] adj insufriblemente; **he is — vain** es tremendamente vanidoso.

intolerance [in'tɔlərəns] n intolerancia f.

intolerant [in'tɔlərənt] adj intolerante (of con, para).

intonation [,intəu'neiʃən] n entonación f.

intone [in'təun] vt entonar; (Eccl etc) salmodiar.

intoxicant [in'tɔksikənt] 1 adj embriagador. 2 n bebida f alcohólica.

intoxicate [in'tɔksikeit] vt embriagar (also fig); (Med) intoxicar.

intoxicated [in'tɔksikeitid] adj ebrio, borracho; **to be — with** (fig) estar ebrio de.

intoxication [in,tɔksi'keiʃən] n embriaguez f (also fig); (Med) intoxicación f.

intra . . . ['intrə] intra . . .

intractable [in'træktəbl] adj person intratable; material difícil de trabajar; problem insoluble, espinoso.

intransigence [in'trænsidʒəns] n intransigencia f.

intransigent [in'trænsidʒənt] adj intransigente.

intransitive [in'trænsitiv] adj intransitivo, neutro.

intravenous [,intrə'vi:nəs] adj intravenoso.

intrepid [in'trepid] adj intrépido.

intrepidity [,intri'piditi] n intrepidez f.

intrepidly [in'trepidli] adv intrépidamente.

intricacy ['intrikəsi] n lo intrincado; complejidad f.

intricate ['intrikit] adj intrincado; complejo.

intricately ['intrikitli] adv intrincadamente, de modo intrincado.

intrigue [in'tri:g] **1** n intriga f; (amorous) amorío m, lío m.

2 vt interesar, fascinar, despertar la curiosidad de; **she —s me** ella me fascina; **I am —d to know whether** me interesa saber si; **I am much —d by your news** me interesa muchísimo esa noticia; **we were —d by a sign** nos llamó la atención un letrero, un letrero despertó nuestra curiosidad.

3 vi intrigar, andar en intrigas, meterse en líos.

intriguer [in'tri:gə*] n intrigante mf.

intriguing [in'tri:giŋ] adj (a) (scheming) enredador.
(b) (fascinating) intrigante, fascinador, curioso, interesante; seductor; misterioso; **a most —** problem un problema interesantísimo; **an — gadget** un chisme de los más curiosos; **how very —!** ¡qué raro!, ¡muy interesante!

intrinsic [in'trinsik] adj intrínseco.

intrinsically [in'trinsikli] adv intrínsecamente.

intro . . . ['intrəu, 'intrə] intro . .

introduce [,intrə'dju:s] vt (a) (insert) introducir, meter, insertar (into en).
(b) (put forward) new thing, reform etc introducir; new fashion introducir, poner de moda, lanzar; new product, bill presentar; newcomer presentar, dar a conocer; book (preface) prologar; subject into conversation mencionar, sacar a colación; **be careful how you — the subject** hay que abordar el tema con mucho cuidado; **I was —d into a dark room** me hicieron entrar en un cuarto oscuro; **I was —d into his presence** me llevaron ante él; **I was —d to chess at 8** empecé a jugar al ajedrez a los 8 años; **I was —d to Milton too young** me hicieron leer a Milton demasiado temprano.
(c) person presentar; **may I — Mr X?** permítame presentarle al Sr X; **I don't think we've been —d** creo que no nos han presentado oficialmente.

introduction [,intrə'dʌkʃən] n introducción f, inserción f; presentación f; (to book) prólogo m; **my — to life in Cadiz** mi primera experiencia de la vida en Cádiz; **my — to maths** el comienzo de mis estudios matemáticos; **to give someone an — to a person** dar a uno una carta de recomendación para una persona; **will you make the —s?** ¿quiere Vd presentarnos?

introductory [,intrə'dʌktəri] adj preliminar.

introit ['introit] n introito m.

introspection [,intrəu'spekʃən] n introspección f.

introspective [,intrəu'spektiv] adj introspectivo.

introversion [,intrəu'və:ʃən] n introversión f.

introvert ['intrəuvə:t] **1** adj introvertido. **2** n introvertido m, a f.

intrude [in'tru:d] **1** vt introducir (sin derecho), meter (in en); imponer (upon a).
2 vi entrometerse, encajarse (upon en); estorbar, molestar; **do I —?** ¿te molesto?; **to — on someone's privacy** molestar a uno cuando quiere estar a solas; **sometimes sentimentality —s** a veces se asoma el sentimentalismo; **he lets no feelings of pity —** no deja lugar a la compasión.

intruder [in'tru:də*] n intruso m, a f.

intrusion [in'tru:ʒən] n intrusión f; invasión f; **the — of sentimentality** la aparición del sentimentalismo; **please pardon the —** siento tener que molestarle.

intrusive [in'tru:siv] adj intruso.

intuition [,intju:'iʃən] n intuición f.

intuitive [in'tju:itiv] adj intuitivo.

intuitively [in'tju:itivli] adv intuitivamente, por intuición.

inundate ['inʌndeit] vt inundar (also fig).

inundation [,inʌn'deiʃən] n inundación f.

inure [in'juə*] vt acostumbrar, habituar (to a), endurecer.

invade [in'veid] vt invadir.

invader [in'veidə*] n invasor m.

invading [in'veidiŋ] adj invasor.

invalid [in'vælid] adj inválido, nulo; **to become —** caducar.

invalid ['invəlid] **1** adj inválido, enfermo. **2** n inválido m, a f. **3** vt: **to — someone out of the army** licenciar a uno por invalidez.

invalidate [in'vælideit] vt invalidar, anular, quitar valor a; argument destruir.

invaluable [in'væljuəbl] adj inestimable, inapreciable.

invariable [in'vɛəriəbl] adj invariable, inalterable.

invariably [in'vɛəriəbli] adv invariablemente; **it — happens that** ocurre siempre que; **he is — late** siempre llega tarde.

invasion [in'veiʒən] n invasión f.

invective [in'vektiv] n invectiva f; palabras fpl fuertes, improperios mpl.

inveigh [in'vei] vi: **to — against** vituperar, hablar en contra de, condenar.

inveigle [in'vi:gl] vt: **to — someone into something** inducir (engañosamente) a uno a algo; **to — someone into doing something** persuadir (mañosamente) a uno a hacer algo; **he let himself be —d into it** se dejó engatusar para que lo hiciera.

invent [in'vent] vt inventar; idear.

invention [in'venʃən] n (gadget etc) invención f, invento m; (inventiveness) inventiva f; (falsehood) ficción f, mentira f; **it's sheer — on her part** son cosas que ella ha soñado, son cosas de ella; **it's — from start to finish** todo es mentira.

inventive [in'ventiv] adj inventivo, ingenioso.

inventiveness [in'ventivnis] n inventiva f, ingenio m.

inventor [in'ventə*] n inventor m, ora f.

inventory ['invəntri] **1** n inventario m. **2** vt inventariar.

inverse ['in'və:s] adj inverso.

inversely [in'və:sli] adv a la inversa.

inversion [in'və:ʃən] n inversión f.

invert [in'və:t] vt invertir, volver al revés, trastrocar.

invertebrate [in'və:tibrit] **1** adj invertebrado. **2** n invertebrado m.

invest [in'vest] **1** vt (a) money invertir (in en).
(b) (Mil) sitiar, cercar.
(c) **to — someone with something** investir a uno de (or con) algo; **to be —ed with a dignity** revestirse con una dignidad; **he —ed it with a certain mystery** lo revistió con cierto misterio; **he seems to — it with some importance** parece que da cierta importancia a la cosa.
2 vi: **to — in company etc** invertir dinero en; (buy) comprar, adquirir; (support) apoyar, demostrar tener confianza en; **to — with** invertir dinero en.

investigate [in'vestigeit] vt investigar; examinar, estudiar.

investigation [in,vesti'geiʃən] n investigación f; pesquisa f; examen m, estudio m (into de).

investigator [in'vestigeitə*] n investigador m, ora f.

investiture [in'vestitʃə*] n investidura f.

investment [in'vestmənt] n (Comm) inversión f; (Mil) sitio m, cerco m; (investiture) investidura f; **—s** inversiones fpl, fondos mpl invertidos, (shares) valores mpl en cartera.

investor [in'vestə*] n inversionista mf.

inveterate [in'vetərit] adj empedernido, habitual, incurable.

invidious [in'vidiəs] adj odioso, injusto.

invigilate [in'vidʒileit] vti vigilar (durante los exámenes).

invigilator [in'vidʒileitə*] n celador m, ora f.

invigorate [in'vigəreit] vt vigorizar; campaign etc avivar, estimular.

invigorating [in'vigəreitiŋ] adj vigorizante, vigorizador.

invincibility [in,vinsi'biliti] n invencibilidad f.

invincible [in'vinsəbl] adj invencible.

inviolability [in,vaiələ'biliti] n inviolabilidad f.

inviolable [in'vaiələbl] adj inviolable.

inviolate [in'vaiəlit] adj inviolado.

invisibility [in,vizə'biliti] n invisibilidad f.

invisible [in'vizəbl] adj invisible; ink simpático.

invitation [,invi'teiʃən] n invitación f; convite m.

invite [in'vait] vt (a) (general sense) invitar, (esp to food and drink) convidar; **to — someone to supper** invitar a uno a cenar; **to — someone to do something** invitar a uno a hacer algo; **to — someone to have a drink** convidar a uno a tomar algo.
(b) (request) pedir, rogar; **the chairman —d me to speak** el presidente me rogó tomar la palabra; **he —s our opinions** pide nuestras opiniones.

(c) *trouble etc* correr a, buscarse; **it's just inviting trouble** esto es crear dificultades para sí; **to do so is to — defeat** hacer esto es procurar la propia derrota.

(d) *(induce)* inducir a, sugerir; **A —s comparison with B** A nos induce a compararlo con B, se impone la comparación de A con B; **she seems to — stares** según parece le gusta que la mire la gente.

invite ['invait] n *(fam)* invitación f.
inviting [in'vaitiŋ] adj atractivo, atrayente, tentador; *look* incitante, provocativo; *food* apetitoso.
invitingly [in'vaitiŋli] adv de modo atractivo *(etc)*; de modo incitante; apetitosamente.
invocation [ˌinvəu'keiʃən] n invocación f.
invoice ['invɔis] **1** n factura f; **pro forma —** factura f simulada; **as per —** según factura; **to send an —** pasar factura, presentar factura. **2** vt facturar.
invoke [in'vəuk] vt invocar; *aid* suplicar, implorar; *law* recurrir a, acogerse a; *spirit* conjurar.
involuntarily [in'vɔləntərili] adv involuntariamente, sin querer.
involuntary [in'vɔləntəri] adj involuntario.
involve [in'vɔlv] vt **(a)** *(physically)* enredar, enmarañar; *matter* complicar, entenebrecer.

(b) *(implicate etc)* implicar, comprometer; **to — someone in a quarrel** mezclar a uno en una disputa; **the persons —d** los interesados; **the forces —d** las fuerzas en juego; **a question of principle is —d** aquí está en juego un principio; **to be —d in** estar implicado en, estar metido en, andar envuelto en; **to be —d in a plot** estar implicado en un complot; **was he —d in it?** ¿anduvo él metido en ello?, ¿tuvo él que ver con el asunto?; **how did you come to be —d?** ¿cómo llegó Vd a estar envuelto en esto?; **to get** *(or* **become)** **—d in** meterse en, enredarse en, embrollarse en; **he got —d with a girl** se armó un lío con una joven; **I don't want to get —d** no quiero dejarme ir demasiado lejos, allí no entro yo.

(c) *(imply)* suponer, implicar, traer consigo, acarrear, ocasionar; **it —s moving house** ello supone que tendremos que mudar de casa; **it —d a lot of expense** nos acarreó muchos gastos; **does it — much trouble?** ¿esto supone mucho trabajo para Vd?

involved [in'vɔlvd] adj complicado; *style* enrevesado, laberíntico.
involvement [in'vɔlvmənt] n enredo m; compromiso m; *(difficulty)* apuro m, dificultad f; **we don't know the extent of his —** no sabemos hasta qué punto se había comprometido; **his — in the plot** su participación en el complot; **we must keep out of —s** hay que evitar los enredos.
invulnerability [in,vʌlnərə'biliti] n invulnerabilidad f.
invulnerable [in'vʌlnərəbl] adj invulnerable.
inward ['inwəd] adj interior, interno; íntimo; espiritual.
inward(s) ['inwəd(z)] adv hacia dentro, para dentro.
inwardly ['inwədli] adv interiormente; *laugh etc* para sí, entre sí.
inwards ['inədz] npl *(fam)* tripas fpl, estómago m.
iodine ['aiədi:n] n yodo m.
iodoform [ai'ɔdəfɔ:m] n yodoformo m.
ion ['aiən] n ion m.
Ionic [ai'ɔnik] adj jónico.
ionize ['aiənaiz] vt ionizar.
ionosphere [ai'ɔnəsfiə*] n ionosfera f.
iota [ai'əutə] n *(letter)* iota f; *(fig)* jota f, ápice m; **there's not one — of truth in it** eso no tiene ni pizca de verdad; **if he had an — of sense** si tuviera un poquito de inteligencia.
ipecacuanha [ˌipikækju'ænə] n ipecacuana f.
Irak [i'rɑ:k] El Irak.
Iraki [i'rɑ:ki] **1** adj iraquí. **2** n iraquí mf.
Iran [i'rɑ:n] El Irán.
Iranian [i'reiniən] **1** adj iranio, iraní. **2** n iranio m, a f, iraní mf.
Iraq [i'rɑ:k] El Irak.
Iraqi [i'rɑ:ki] **1** adj iraquí. **2** n iraquí mf.
irascibility [i,ræsi'biliti] n irascibilidad f.
irascible [i'ræsibl] adj irascible, de prontos enojos.
irascibly [i'ræsibli] adv: **he said —** dijo colérico.
irate [ai'reit] adj colérico, enojado, indignado; **he got very —** se encolerizó mucho.
ire [aiə*] n ira f, cólera f; **to rouse someone's —** provocar la ira de uno; **that always rouses his —** eso siempre le saca de quicio.
Ireland ['aiələnd] Irlanda f; **Northern —** Irlanda f del Norte.
iridescence [ˌiri'desns] n iridescencia f, irisación f.
iridescent [ˌiri'desnt] adj iridescente, irisado, tornasolado.
iris ['aiəris] n *(Anat)* iris m; *(Bot)* lirio m.

Irish ['aiəriʃ] **1** adj irlandés. **2** n: **the —** los irlandeses. **3** n *(language)* irlandés m.
Irish Free State ['aiəriʃˌfri:'steit] Estado m Libre de Irlanda.
Irishman ['aiəriʃmən] n, pl **—men** [mən] irlandés m.
Irish Sea ['aiəriʃ'si:] Mar m de Irlanda.
Irishwoman ['aiəriʃˌwumən] n, pl **—women** [ˌwimin] irlandesa f.
irk [ə:k] vt fastidiar, molestar.
irksome ['ə:ksəm] adj molesto, pesado, fastidioso.
iron ['aiən] **1** n **(a)** *(Min)* hierro m; *(fig)* hierro m, acero m; *(Golf)* hierro m; *(flat-)* plancha f; **man of —** hombre m de acero; **corrugated —** hierro m ondulado; **old —** chatarra f, hierro m viejo; **wrought —** hierro m forjado, hierro m batido; **to strike while the —** is hot a hierro candente batir de repente.

(b) **—s** *(fetters)* hierros mpl, grillos mpl; *(at table: fam)* cuchillo m y tenedor m; **to have too many —s in the fire** tener demasiados asuntos entre manos; **to put someone in —s** aherrojar a uno, echar grillos a uno.

2 attr de hierro; *curtain, man etc* de acero; **will —** férreo.

3 vt *clothes* planchar; **to — out** *unevenness* allanar; *crease* quitar; *difficulties* allanar, suprimir; *differences* nivelar.
ironclad ['aiənklæd] **1** adj acorazado. **2** n acorazado m.
iron foundry ['aiənˌfaundri] n fundición f de hierro.
ironic(al) [ai'rɔnik(əl)] adj irónico.
ironically [ai'rɔnikəli] adv irónicamente; *say etc* con ironía; **— enough** paradójicamente, como quiso la suerte.
ironing ['aiəniŋ] n *(act)* planchado m; *(clothes)* ropa f por planchar, ropa f planchada; **to give a dress an —** planchar un vestido.
ironing board ['aiəniŋbɔ:d] n tabla f de planchar.
ironmonger ['aiənˌmʌŋgə*] n ferretero m, quincallero m; **—'s** *(shop)* ferretería f, quincallería f.
ironmongery ['aiənˌmʌŋgəri] n quincalla f, ferretería f *(also fig)*.
iron ore ['aiɔn:*] n mineral m de hierro.
ironwork ['aiənwə:k] n herraje m; obra f de hierro.
ironworks ['aiənwə:ks] n *sing and pl* herrería f, fundición f, fábrica f de hierro.
irony ['aiərəni] n ironía f; **the — of fate** lo irónico del destino; **the — of it is that** lo irónico es que.
irradiate [i'reidieit] vt irradiar.
irradiation [i,reidi'eiʃən] n irradiación f.
irrational [i'ræʃənl] adj irracional.
irrationally [i'ræʃnəli] adv irracionalmente.
irreconcilable [i,rekən'sailəbl] adj irreconciliable, inconciliable.
irrecoverable [ˌiri'kʌvərəbl] adj irrecuperable, incobrable.
irredeemable [ˌiri'di:məbl] adj irredimible; *(Comm)* perpetuo, no amortizable.
irreducible [ˌiri'dju:səbl] adj irreducible.
irrefutable [ˌiri'fju:təbl] adj irrefutable, irrebatible.
irregular [i'regjulə*] **1** adj irregular; anormal; *surface* desigual; *(unlawful)* ilegal, no conforme con la ley; **this is really most —** realmente esto no se debiera permitir. **2** n guerrillero m.
irregularity [i,regju'læriti] n irregularidad f; anormalidad f; desigualdad f.
irrelevance [i'reləvəns] n impertinencia f, inoportunidad f, inaplicabilidad f.
irrelevant [i'reləvənt] adj impertinente, inoportuno, inaplicable, fuera de propósito; **that's —** eso no hace al caso.
irreligious [ˌiri'lidʒəs] adj irreligioso.
irremediable [ˌiri'mi:diəbl] adj irremediable.
irremediably [ˌiri'mi:diəbli] adv irremediablemente.
irremovable [ˌiri'mu:vəbl] adj inamovible.
irreparable [i'repərəbl] adj irreparable.
irreparably [i'repərəbli] adv irreparablemente.
irreplaceable [ˌiri'pleisəbl] adj insustituible, irreemplazable.
irrepressible [ˌiri'presəbl] adj incontrolable, irrefrenable.
irreproachable [ˌiri'prəutʃəbl] adj irreprochable, intachable.
irresistible [ˌiri'zistəbl] adj irresistible.
irresistibly [ˌiri'zistəbli] adv irresistiblemente.
irresolute [i'rezəlu:t] adj irresoluto, indeciso.
irresoluteness [i'rezəlu:tnis] n irresolución f, indecisión f.
irrespective [ˌiri'spektiv]: **— of** prep aparte de, sin consideración a, con independencia de.
irresponsibility ['iris,pɔnsə'biliti] n irresponsabilidad f, falta f de seriedad.

irresponsible [ˌiris'pɔnsəbl] *adj* irresponsable, poco serio.

irretrievable [ˌiri'tri:vəbl] *adj* irrecuperable; *error* irreparable.

irretrievably [ˌiri'tri:vəbli] *adv*: — **lost** totalmente perdido, perdido sin remedio.

irreverence [i'revərəns] *n* irreverencia *f*.

irreverent [i'revərənt] *adj* irreverente, irrespetuoso.

irreverently [i'revərəntli] *adv* de modo irreverente, irrespetuosamente.

irreversible [ˌiri'və:səbl] *adj* *decision* irrevocable.

irrevocable [i'revəkəbl] *adj* irrevocable.

irrevocably [i'revəkəbli] *adv* irrevocablemente.

irrigable ['irigəbl] *adj* regadío; — **land** tierra *f* de regadío.

irrigate ['irigeit] *vt* (*Agr*) regar; (*Med*) irrigar.

irrigation [ˌiri'geiʃən] *n* (*Agr*) riego *m*; (*Med*) irrigación *f*.

irritability [ˌiritə'biliti] *n* irritabilidad *f*.

irritable ['iritəbl] *adj* (*temperament*) irritable, de prontos enojos; (*mood*) de mal humor; **to get —** ponerse nervioso.

irritably ['iritəbli] *adv*: **he said —** dijo malhumorado.

irritant ['iritənt] *n* irritante *m*.

irritate ['iriteit] *vt* irritar (*also Med*), sacar de quicio, molestar; **to get —d** irritarse, enfadarse.

irritating ['iriteitiŋ] *adj* *person etc* molesto, pesado, enojoso; *thing* molesto, fastidioso; **it's really most —** es para sacar a uno de quicio.

irritation [ˌiri'teiʃən] *n* irritación *f*, enojo *m*; (*Med*) picazón *f*, picor *m*.

irruption [i'rʌpʃən] *n* irrupción *f*.

is [iz] *see* **be**.

Isaac ['aizək] *m* Isaac.

Isabel ['izəbel] *f* Isabel.

isinglass ['aiziŋglɑ:s] *n* cola *f* de pescado.

Islam ['izlɑ:m] Islam *m*.

Islamic [iz'læmik] *adj* islámico.

island ['ailənd] **1** *n* isla *f*; (*in street*) refugio *m*. **2** *attr* isleño.

islander ['ailəndə*] *n* isleño *m*, a *f*.

isle [ail] *n* isla *f*.

islet ['ailit] *n* isleta *f*, islote *m*.

ism ['izəm] *n* ismo *m*.

isn't ['iznt] = **is not**.

iso... ['aisəu] iso...

isobar ['aisəubɑ:*] *n* isobara *f*.

isolate ['aisəuleit] *vt* aislar.

isolated ['aisəuleitid] *adj* *place etc* aislado, apartado; *case* único; **to feel —** sentirse aislado.

isolation [ˌaisəu'leiʃən] *n* aislamiento *m*.

isolationism [ˌaisəu'leiʃənizəm] *n* aislacionismo *m*.

isolationist [ˌaisəu'leiʃənist] **1** *adj* aislacionista. **2** *n* aislacionista *mf*.

Isolde [i'zɔldə] *f* Iseo, Isolda.

isosceles [ai'sɔsili:z] *adj*: — **triangle** triángulo *m* isósceles.

isotherm ['aisəuθə:m] *n* isoterma *f*.

isotope ['aisəutəup] *n* isótopo *m*.

Israel ['izreil] Israel *m*.

Israeli [iz'reili] **1** *adj* israelí. **2** *n* israelí *mf*.

Israelite ['izriəlait] **1** *adj* israelita. **2** *n* israelita *mf*.

issue ['iʃu:] **1** *n* (**a**) (*outcome*) resultado *m*, consecuencia *f*; **in the —** en fin; **until the — is decided** hasta que se sepa el resultado; **to await the —** esperar el resultado.
(**b**) (*matter*) cuestión *f*, asunto *m*, problema *m*, punto *m*; **an — of fact** una cuestión de hechos; **side —** cuestión *f* secundaria; **the point at —** el punto en cuestión, el asunto en litigio; **the — is whether...** se trata de decidir si...; **it's not a political —** no es una cuestión política; **to evade the —** evadir el tema, esquivar la pregunta; soslayar el problema; **to face the —** afrontar la situación; **to force the —** forzar una decisión; **to join** (*or* **take**) **— with someone** llevar la contraria a uno, oponerse a uno; **I feel I must take — with you over that** permítaseme disentir de esa opinión.
(**c**) (*of shares, stamps etc*) emisión *f*; (*of rations*) distribución *f*, repartimiento *m*.
(**d**) (*of book: size of —*) edición *f*, tirada *f*; (*copy*) número *m*; **back —** número *m* atrasado.
(**e**) (*offspring*) sucesión *f*, descendencia *f*; **to die without —** morir sin dejar descendencia.
(**f**) (*Med*) flujo *m*.
2 *attr* (*Mil etc*) reglamentario.
3 *vt* *shares, stamps etc* emitir; poner en circulación; *rations etc* distribuir, repartir; *book* publicar; *order* dar; *decree* promulgar; *certificate etc* expedir; *cheque* extender; *licence* facilitar; **a warrant has been —d**

for the arrest of X se ha ordenado la detención de X; **to — a rifle to each man, to — each man with a rifle** dar un fusil a cada hombre; **we were —d with 10 rounds each** nos dieron a cada uno 10 cartuchos.
4 *vi* salir (*from* de); **to — from** (*fig*) provenir de; **to — in** dar por resultado.

Istanbul [ˌistæn'bu:l] Estambul.

isthmus ['isməs] *n* istmo *m*.

it¹ [it] *pron* (**a**) (*nom*) él, ella, ello; (*acc*) lo, la; (*dat*) le; (*after prep*) él, ella, ello.
(**b**) (*nom pron referring to a specific noun, freq not translated*) **—'s on the table** está en la mesa; **where is —?** ¿dónde está?
(**c**) (*pron referring to "this affair", "that whole business"*) ello, eso, *eg* **— is difficult** es difícil, ello es difícil; **I have no money for —** no tengo dinero para ello; **he won't agree to —** no quiere consentir en eso.
(**d**) (*never translated in such cases as*) **— is true that** es verdad que; **— was raining** llovía; **— is 4 o'clock** son las 4; **— is not in him to do it** no es capaz de hacer eso; **— is said that** se dice que; **I have heard — said** that he oído decir que; **I do not think — (is) wise to go** creo que es más prudente no ir; **— is I, —'s me** soy yo; **—'s Jack** soy Juanito; **— was he who brought them** fue él quien los trajo.
(**e**) (*special uses with* **to be**) **this is —** ya llegó la hora; **ahí viene**; (*before action*) ¡vamos!, ¡a ello!; **that's —** (*agreeing*) eso es; (*adjusting machine etc*) ya está, está bien; (*on finishing something*) eso es todo, hemos terminado, está hecho, nada más; **that's — then!** ¡muy bien!; **that's just —!** ¡ahí está la dificultad!; **the worst of — is that** lo peor del caso es que; **how is — that...?** ¿cómo resulta que...? (*and see* **how** (a)).
(**f**) (*predicative*) **you're —!** (*children's games*) ¡tú te quedas!; **she thinks she's just —** se da mucho tono, se cree la mar de elegante.
(**g**) (*sexual attraction*) aquél *m*, atracción *f* sexual; **she's got —** tiene aquél, tiene tilín; *see* **with**.

it² [it] *n* (*fam*) vermut *m* italiano.

Italian [i'tæliən] **1** *adj* italiano. **2** *n* italiano *m*, a *f*. **3** *n* (*language*) italiano *m*.

italic [i'tælik] *adj* (*Typ*) en bastardilla; (*of Italy*) itálico.

italicize [i'tælisaiz] *vt* poner en bastardilla, subrayar.

italics [i'tæliks] *npl* (*letra*) bastardilla *f*, cursiva *f*; **in —** en bastardilla, en cursiva; **my —** lo subrayado es mío.

Italy ['itəli] Italia *f*.

itch [itʃ] **1** *n* (**a**) (*Med*) (*an —*) picazón *f*, comezón *f*; (*the —*) sarna *f*.
(**b**) (*fig*) prurito *m*, deseo *m* vehemente; **to have the — to do something** tener el prurito de hacer algo, rabiar por hacer algo.
2 *vi* picar, sentir comezón; **my leg —es** me pica la pierna, siento comezón en la pierna; **to — to do something** tener el prurito de hacer algo, rabiar por hacer algo.

itching ['itʃiŋ] *n* picazón *f*, comezón *f*.

itching powder ['itʃiŋˌpaudə*] *n* polvos *mpl* de pica-pica.

itchy ['itʃi] *adj*: **to feel —** sentir comezón; **to have an — leg** sentir comezón en la pierna.

it'd ['itd] = **it would; it had**.

item ['aitəm] *n* artículo *m*; (*detail*) detalle *m*; (*Comm*) partida *f*; (*in programme*) número *m*; (*on agenda*) asunto *m* a tratar; (*in newspaper*) noticia *f*, suelto *m*; **what's the next —?** ¿qué viene después?; **it's an important — in our policy** es un punto importante de nuestra política.

itemize ['aitəmaiz] *vt* detallar, particularizar, especificar.

itinerant [i'tinərənt] *adj* ambulante.

itinerary [ai'tinərəri] *n* ruta *f*, itinerario *m*; (*book, map*) guía *f*.

it'll ['itl] = **it will; it shall**.

its [its] **1** *poss adj* su(s). **2** *poss pron* (el) suyo, (la) suya *etc*.

it's [its] = **it is, it has**.

itself [it'self] *pron* (*nom*) él mismo, ella misma, ello mismo; (*acc, dat*) se; (*after prep*) sí mismo, sí misma; *see* **oneself**.

I've [aiv] = **I have**.

ivory ['aivəri] **1** *n* marfil *m*; **ivories** (*sl: teeth*) dientes *mpl*, (*Mus*) teclas *fpl*, (*Billiards*) bolas *fpl*. **2** *attr* de marfil.

Ivory Coast ['aivəri'kəust] Costa *f* de Marfil.

ivy ['aivi] *n* hiedra *f*.

J

jab [dʒæb] **1** n (poke) pinchazo m; (with elbow) codazo m; (blow) golpe m; (Boxing) golpe m rápido (dado sin extender el brazo); (prick) pinchazo m.
2 vt hurgonear; dar un codazo a; golpear, dar un golpe rápido a; pinchar; **he —bed a gun in my back** me puso un revólver en los riñones; **I —bed the knife in my arm** me pinché el brazo con el cuchillo; **he —bed the knife into the table** clavó el cuchillo en la mesa; **he —bed a finger at the map** indicó el mapa con un movimiento brusco del dedo.
3 vi: **to — at someone with a knife** tratar de acuchillar a uno; **he —bed at the map with a finger** indicó el mapa con un movimiento brusco del dedo.

jabber ['dʒæbə*] **1** n (also **jabbering** ['dʒæbəriŋ]) torrente m de palabras ininteligibles; chapurreo m, farfulla f; (of monkeys) chillidos mpl; **a — of French** un torrente de francés; **a — of voices** un ruido confuso de voces.
2 vt decir atropelladamente.
3 vi hablar atropelladamente, hablar de modo ininteligible; chapurrear, farfullar; (monkeys) chillar; **they were —ing away in Russian** hablaban atropelladamente en ruso.

jacaranda [,dʒækə'rændə] n jacaranda f.

jack [dʒæk] **1** n (Mech) gato m; (boot-) sacabotas m; (Bowls) boliche m; (Cards) valet m, (in Spanish pack) sota f; (Naut) marinero m; (Fish) lucio m joven.
2 vt: **to — up** (Mech) alzar con gato; price, production etc aumentar.

Jack [dʒæk] m Juan, Juanito; **I'm all right, —!** ¡a mí nada!; **— Frost** personificación del hielo; **— Ketch** el verdugo; **before you can say — Robinson** en un decir Jesús; **— Tar** el marinero.

jackal ['dʒækɔ:l] n chacal m; (fig) paniaguado m, secuaz m.

jackanapes ['dʒækəneips] n mequetrefe m.

jackass ['dʒækæs] n burro m (also fig).

jackboots ['dʒækbu:ts] npl botas fpl fuertes; **under the — of the Nazis** bajo el azote de los nazis.

jackdaw ['dʒækdɔ:] n grajilla f.

jacket ['dʒækit] n chaqueta f, americana f; (of boiler etc) camisa f, envoltura f; (of book) sobrecubierta f, camisa f.

jack-in-the-box ['dʒækinðəbɔks] n caja f sorpresa, caja f de resorte.

jack-knife ['dʒæknaif] n, pl **-knives** [naivz] navaja f.

jack-of-all-trades ['dʒækəv'ɔ:ltreidz] n hombre m de muchos oficios (and master of none y maestro de ninguno).

jack-of-all-work ['dʒækəv'ɔ:lwə:k] n factótum m.

jack-o'-lantern ['dʒækəu'læntən] n fuego m fatuo.

jack plane ['dʒækplein] n garlopa f.

jackpot ['dʒækpɔt] n bote m; (fig) premio m gordo; **he hit the —** sacó el premio gordo, (fig) acertó, dio en el blanco.

jack rabbit ['dʒæk,ræbit] n liebre f grande (especie norteamericana).

jackstraw ['dʒækstrɔ:] n (US) pajita f.

Jacob ['dʒeikəb] m Jacob.

Jacobean [,dʒækə'bi:ən] adj de la época de Jacobo I (de Inglaterra).

Jacobin ['dʒækəbin] **1** adj jacobino. **2** n jacobino m, a f.

Jacobite ['dʒækəbait] **1** adj jacobita. **2** n jacobita mf.

jade[1] [dʒeid] n (horse) rocín m; (woman) mujerzuela f; **you —!** ¡picarona!, ¡lagarta!

jade[2] [dʒeid] n (Min) jade m.

jaded ['dʒeidid] adj cansado, hastiado; **to feel —** estar cansado; **to get —** cansarse, perder el entusiasmo.

jade-green ['dʒeid'gri:n] adj verde jade.

jag[1] [dʒæg] n punta f, pua f.

jag[2] [dʒæg] n (fam): **to go on a —** ir de juerga.

jagged ['dʒægid] adj dentado, mellado, desigual.

jaguar ['dʒægjuə*] n jaguar m.

jail [dʒeil] **1** n cárcel f; **2 years' —** 2 años de prisión, condena f de 2 años. **2** vt encarcelar.

jailbird ['dʒeilbə:d] n presidiario m.

jailbreak ['dʒeilbreik] n fuga f de la cárcel.

jailer ['dʒeilə*] n carcelero m.

jalop(p)y [dʒə'lɔpi] n cacharro m, armatoste m.

jalousie ['ʒælu(:)zi:] n celosía f.

jam[1] [dʒæm] **1** n (food) mermelada f; (fig) lo mejor, la parte más rica; **you want — on it!** ¡y un jamón con chorreras!; **look at that for —!** ¡qué chorra tiene el tío!
2 vt hacer mermelada de.

jam[2] [dʒæm] **1** n (a) (blockage) atasco m, obstrucción f; (of people) agolpamiento m; (Aut) embotellamiento m, aglomeración f, ensalada f; **there's a — in the pipe** se ha atascado el tubo, está atascado el tubo; **there was a — in the doorway** se había agolpado la gente en la puerta; **you never saw such a —!** ¡había que ver cómo se agolpaba la gente!; **a 5-mile — of cars** una cola de coches que se extiende hasta 5 millas; **there are always —s here** aquí siempre se embotella el tráfico.
(b) (difficulty) apuro m, aprieto m; **to be in a —** estar en un aprieto; **to get into a —** meterse en un apuro; **to get into a — with a problem** armarse un lío con un problema; **to get someone out of a —** ayudar a uno a salir del paso.
2 vt pipe etc atascar, obstruir; wheel trabar; exit, road cerrar, obstruir; radio station interferir; **it's got —med** se ha atascado, no se puede mover (or quitar, retirar etc); **people —med all the exits** la gente se agolpaba en todas las salidas; **if we can — 2 more books in** si podemos introducir a la fuerza 2 libros más; **there were 15 people —med in one room** había 15 personas apretadas unas contra otras en un cuarto; **the room was —med with people** el cuarto estaba atestado de gente; **to — one's fingers in the door** cogerse los dedos en la puerta; **to — something into a box** meter algo apretadamente en una caja; **to — a hat on one's head** encasquetarse un sombrero; **with his hat —med on his head** con la cabeza encasquetada en un sombrero; **to — one's brakes on** echar los frenos con violencia, frenar de repente.
3 vi (pipe etc) atascarse, obstruirse; (nut, part, wheel etc) trabarse; **this part has —med** no se puede mover esta pieza.

Jamaica [dʒə'meikə] Jamaica f.

Jamaican [dʒə'meikən] **1** adj jamaicano. **2** n jamaicano m, a f.

jamb [dʒæm] n jamba f.

jamboree [,dʒæmbə'ri:] n (of Scouts) congreso m de niños exploradores; (fam) francachela f, juerga f.

James [dʒeimz] m Jaime, Diego; (Saint) Santiago; (British kings) Jacobo.

jam-full ['dʒæm'ful] adv de bote en bote.

jamjar ['dʒæmdʒɑ:*] n pote m para mermelada.

jamming ['dʒæmiŋ] n (Radio) interferencia f.

jam session ['dʒæmsefən] n (sl) concierto m improvisado de jazz.

Jane [dʒein] f Juana.

jangle ['dʒæŋgl] **1** n sonido m discordante (metálico), cencerreo m.
2 vt chocar, hacer sonar de manera discordante.
3 vi sonar de manera discordante, cencerrear.

jangling ['dʒæŋgliŋ] adj discordante, desapacible, ruidoso.

janitor ['dʒænitə*] n portero m, conserje m.

January ['dʒænjuəri] enero m.

Jap [dʒæp] (fam) = **Japanese**.

japan [dʒə'pæn] **1** n laca f japonesa. **2** vt charolar con laca japonesa.

Japan [dʒə'pæn] el Japón.

Japanese [,dʒæpə'niːz] **1** adj japonés. **2** n japonés m, esa f; **the —** (pl) los japoneses. **3** n (language) japonés m.

jape [dʒeip] n burla f, broma f.

japonica [dʒə'pɔnikə] n rosal m de China, rosal m japonés.

jar¹ [dʒɑ:*] n (small) tarro m, pote m; (with handles) jarra f; (large) tinaja f.

jar² [dʒɑ:*] **1** n (jolt) sacudida f, choque m; vibración f; (fig) sacudida f, sorpresa f desagradable; **it gave me a bit of a —** me chocó bastante.

2 vt (jog) tocar; mover; (shake) sacudir, hacer vibrar; **he must have —red the camera** ha debido mover ligeramente la máquina; **someone —red my elbow** alguien me hizo mover el codo.

3 vi (grate) chirriar; (shake) vibrar; (sounds) ser discorde, sonar mal; (colours) chillar; **to — on someone** poner a uno los nervios de punta, crispar los nervios a uno.

jar³ [dʒɑ:*]: **on the —** adv see **ajar.**

jargon ['dʒɑːgən] n (incomprehensible) jerigonza f; (specialist) jerga f.

jarring ['dʒɑːriŋ] adj sound discorde, desapacible; colour chillón; (fig) opuesto, adverso, discorde.

jasmin(e) ['dʒæzmin] n jazmín m.

jasper ['dʒæspə*] n jaspe m.

jaundice ['dʒɔːndis] n ictericia f.

jaundiced ['dʒɔːndist] adj (fig: envious, sour) envidioso, avinagrado, agrio; (disillusioned) desilusionado, decepcionado.

jaunt [dʒɔːnt] n excursión f (also fig); viajecito m.

jauntily ['dʒɔːntili] adv con garbo, airosamente; con confianza; **he replied —** contestó satisfecho.

jauntiness ['dʒɔːntinis] n garbo m; confianza f, satisfacción f.

jaunting car ['dʒɔːntiŋ,kɑ:*] n tílburi m (irlandés).

jaunty ['dʒɔːnti] adj garboso, airoso; alegre; desenvuelto; confiado, satisfecho.

Java ['dʒɑːvə] Java f.

Javanese [,dʒɑːvə'niːz] **1** adj javanés. **2** n javanés m, esa f.

javelin ['dʒævlin] n jabalina f; **to throw the —** lanzar la jabalina.

jaw [dʒɔː] **1** n (a) (Anat) quijada f, mandíbula f; (Mech) mordaza f, mandíbula f; **a blow on the —** un golpe en la mandíbula.

(b) —s (Anat) boca f; (fig: swallowing) boca f, fauces fpl; (holding) garras fpl; **they rode into the very —s of death** entraron por entre las mismas garras de la muerte.

(c) (fam) cháchara f; palabrería f; **we had a good old —** charlamos largo rato; **it's just a lot of —** mucho ruido y pocas nueces; **hold your —!** ¡cállate la boca!

2 vt (sl) sermonear.

3 vi (fam) charlar; hablar por los codos, hablar interminablemente.

jawbone ['dʒɔːbəun] n mandíbula f, maxilar m.

jawbreaker ['dʒɔː,breikə*] n (fam) trabalenguas m, palabra f kilométrica, terminacho m.

jay [dʒei] n arrendajo m.

jaywalker ['dʒei,wɔːkə*] n peatón m imprudente.

jazz [dʒæz] **1** n jazz m; **all that —** (sl) esas tonterías. **2** attr de jazz. **3** vt (also **to — up**) sincopar; (fig) animar, avivar.

jazzy ['dʒæzi] adj (Mus) sincopado; dress etc de colores llamativos, de colores chillones.

jealous ['dʒeləs] adj celoso; envidioso; **— husband** marido m celoso; **with — care** con el mayor celo; **to be —** tener celos (of someone de uno); **to make someone —** dar celos a uno.

jealously ['dʒeləsli] adv celosamente; envidiosamente.

jealousy ['dʒeləsi] n celos mpl; envidia f.

jeans [dʒiːnz] npl pantalones mpl vaqueros, pantalones mpl tejanos.

jeep [dʒiːp] n jeep m.

jeer [dʒiə*] **1** n (shout) grito m de sarcasmo, grito m de protesta; (insult) insulto m, dicterio m; (boo) abucheo m.

2 vt mofarse de; llenar de insultos; abuchear.

3 vi mofarse (at de), befar; gritar con sarcasmo (etc; at a), prorrumpir en gritos sarcásticos (etc).

jeering ['dʒiəriŋ] **1** adj mofador, sarcástico; **he was led through a —crowd** le hicieron pasar por una multitud que le llenó de insultos.

2 n gritos mpl de sarcasmo, protestas fpl; insultos mpl; abucheo m.

Jehovah [dʒi'həuvə] m Jehová.

jejune [dʒi'dʒuːn] adj árido; insípido, sin sustancia.

jell [dʒel] vi convertirse en jalea, cuajar; (fig) cuajar.

jelly ['dʒeli] n jalea f, gelatina f; **petroleum —** vaselina f, jalea f de petróleo.

jellyfish ['dʒelifiʃ] n medusa f.

jemmy ['dʒemi] n palanqueta f.

jeopardize ['dʒepədaiz] vt arriesgar, poner en peligro, comprometer.

jeopardy ['dʒepədi] n: **to be in —** estar en peligro, correr riesgo; **to put something in —** poner algo en peligro, hacer peligrar algo.

jeremiad [,dʒeri'maiəd] n jeremiada f.

Jeremy ['dʒeremi] m Jeremías.

Jericho ['dʒerikəu] Jericó.

jerk [dʒəːk] **1** n tirón m, sacudida f; espasmo m muscular; **physical —s** ejercicios mpl físicos, gimnasia f; **by —s** a sacudidas; **he sat up with a —** se incorporó de repente, se incorporó con un movimiento brusco; **to put a — in it** (fam) menearse.

2 vt (shake etc) sacudir, dar una sacudida a; (pull) tirar bruscamente de; (throw) arrojar con un movimiento rápido; meat (US) atasajar; **to — something along** mover algo a tirones; **to — something away from someone** quitar algo a uno de un tirón.

3 vi sacudirse, dar una sacudida; **to — along** moverse a sacudidas, avanzar a tirones.

4 vr: **to — oneself free** librarse con un movimiento brusco; **to — oneself along** moverse a sacudidas, avanzar a tirones.

jerkily ['dʒəːkili] adv move etc a tirones, a sacudidas; play, write etc de modo desigual, nerviosamente.

jerkin ['dʒəːkin] n justillo m.

jerkwater ['dʒəːk,wɔːtə*] adj (US fam) de poca monta.

jerky ['dʒəːki] adj (in movement) que se mueve a sacudidas, que avanza a tirones; movement espasmódico, nervioso; (uneven) desigual, nervioso.

Jerome [dʒə'rəum] m Jerónimo.

jerry ['dʒeri] n (sl) orinal m.

Jerry ['dʒeri] n (Mil sl): **a —** un alemán; **the —s** los alemanes.

jerry-builder ['dʒeri,bildə*] n mal constructor m, tapa(a)gujeros m.

jerry-building ['dʒeri,bildiŋ] n mala construcción f, construcción f defectuosa.

jerry-built ['dʒeribilt] adj mal construido, de pacotilla.

jersey ['dʒəːzi] n jersey m, jersé m, jersei m (Acad).

Jerusalem [dʒə'ruːsələm] Jerusalén.

jessamine ['dʒesəmin] n jazmín m.

jest [dʒest] **1** n chanza f, broma f; (verbal) chiste m; **in —** en broma, de guasa. **2** vi bromear, chancearse; **he was only —ing** lo dijo en broma nada más.

jester ['dʒestə*] n bufón m.

jesting ['dʒestiŋ] **1** adj person chistoso, guasón; tone guasón; reference burlón, en broma. **2** n chanzas fpl, bromas fpl; chistes mpl.

Jesuit ['dʒezjuit] **1** adj jesuita. **2** n jesuita m.

Jesuitical [,dʒezju'itikəl] adj jesuítico.

Jesus ['dʒiːzəs] m Jesús; **— Christ** Jesucristo.

jet¹ [dʒet] n (Min) azabache m.

jet² [dʒet] **1** n (a) (of liquid) chorro m, surtidor m; (gas burner) mechero m; **a — of flame** una llama.

(b) (Aer) avión m a reacción, avión m a chorro, reactor m; **the big —s of the future** los grandes reactores del futuro.

2 attr (Aer) a reacción, a chorro.

3 vt lanzar en chorro, echar en chorro.

4 vi chorrear, salir a chorro.

jet-black ['dʒet'blæk] adj de azabache, negro como el azabache.

jet engine ['dʒet'endʒin] n motor m a reacción, reactor m.

jet plane ['dʒet'plein] n avión m a reacción, avión m a chorro, reactor m.

jet-powered ['dʒet'pauəd] adj, **jet-propelled** ['dʒetprə'peld] adj a reacción, a chorro.

jet propulsion ['dʒetprə'pʌlʃən] n propulsión f por reacción, propulsión f a chorro.

jetsam ['dʒetsəm] n echazón f.

jettison ['dʒetisn] vt (Naut etc) echar al mar, echar por la borda; (fig) desechar, abandonar, librarse de; **we can safely — that** bien podemos prescindir de eso.

jetty ['dʒeti] n malecón m, muelle m, embarcadero m.

Jew [dʒuː] n judío m, a f.

jewel ['dʒuːəl] n joya f (also fig), alhaja f; (of watch) rubí m.

jewel case ['dʒuːəlkeis] n joyero m, estuche m de joyas.

jewelled, (esp US) **jeweled** ['dʒuːəld] adj adornado con piedras preciosas, enjoyado; watch con rubíes.

jeweller, (esp US) **jeweler** ['dʒuːələ*] n joyero m; **—'s (shop)** joyería f.

jewellery, (esp US) **jewelry** ['dʒuːəlri] n joyas fpl, alhajas fpl.
Jewess ['dʒuːis] n judía f.
Jewish ['dʒuːiʃ] adj judío.
Jewishness ['dʒuːiʃnis] n judaísmo m.
Jewry ['dʒuəri] n judería f, los judíos.
Jew's-harp ['dʒuːz'hɑːp] n birimbao m.
jib¹ [dʒib] n (Naut) foque m; (Mech) aguilón m, brazo m.
jib² [dʒib] vi (horse) plantarse; (person) rehusar; I — at that no puedo consentir en eso; he —ed at it se negó a aprobarlo (etc), no quiso permitirlo, se opuso a ello.
jib boom ['dʒib'buːm] n botalón m de foque.
jibe [dʒaib] 1 n pulla f, dicterio m. 2 vi mofarse (at de).
jiffy ['dʒifi] n (fam) instante m, momento m; I'll be with you in a — un momento y estoy con vosotros; to do something in a — hacer algo en un decir Jesús.
jig [dʒig] 1 n (dance) jiga f; (Mech) plantilla f (de guía).
 2 vi (dance) bailar la (la jiga); to — along, to — up and down vibrarse, sacudirse, (person) moverse a saltitos; to keep —ging up and down no poderse estar quieto.
jigger ['dʒigə*] n (sl) chisme m.
jiggered ['dʒigəd] adj (sl): well I'm — ! ¡caramba!; I'm — if I will que me cuelguen si lo hago.
jiggery-pokery ['dʒigəri'pəukəri] n (fam) trampas fpl, embustes mpl, maniobras mpl poco limpias; there's some — going on hay trampa; están maquinando algo.
jiggle ['dʒigl] 1 n zangoloteo m. 2 vt zangolotear. 3 vi zangolotearse.
jigsaw ['dʒigsɔː] n sierra f de vaivén; (puzzle) rompecabezas m.
jigsaw puzzle ['dʒigsɔː,pʌzl] n rompecabezas m.
jilt [dʒilt] vt dar calabazas a.
Jim [dʒim] m nombre cariñoso de James.
Jim Crow ['dʒim'krəu] 1 n el negro estadounidense. 2 attr segregado; relativo a la segregación racial; Jim-Crow law ley f racista, ley f segregacionista.
jimjams ['dʒimdʒæmz] npl (sl) delírium m tremens; it gives me the — me horripila, me da miedo.
Jimmy ['dʒimi] m nombre cariñoso de James.
jimmy ['dʒimi] n = jemmy.
jingle ['dʒingl] 1 n tintineo m, retintín m, ruido m (de campanita, monedas etc); cascabeleo m; (Lit) verso m, poemita m popular, rima f infantil.
 2 vt hacer sonar.
 3 vi tintinear, retiñir, cascabelear.
jingo ['dʒingəu] n patriotero m, a f, jingoísta mf; by — ! ¡caramba!
jingoism ['dʒingəuizəm] n patriotería f, jingoísmo m.
jingoistic [dʒingəu'istik] adj patriotero, jingoísta.
jinks [dʒinks] npl : high — jolgorio m; fiesta f animadísima; we had high — last night anoche lo pasamos bomba.
jinx [dʒinks] n (fam) cenizo m, gafe m; (gremlin) duendecillo m; there's a — on it esto está como encantado, esto está que da rabia.
jitney ['dʒitni] n (US sl) (a) taxi m. (b) moneda de 5 centavos.
jitterbug ['dʒitəbʌg] n persona f aficionada a bailar el jazz.
jitters ['dʒitəz] npl (sl) inquietud f, nerviosismo m; to get the — ponerse nervioso; to have the — estar nervioso.
jittery ['dʒitəri] adj (sl) muy inquieto, nervioso; to get — inquietarse, ponerse nervioso.
jiujitsu [dʒuː'dʒitsuː] n jiu-jitsu m.
jive [dʒaiv] vi (sl) bailar (el jazz), bailar con frenesí.
Joan [dʒəun] f Juana; — of Arc Juana de Arco.
job [dʒɔb] 1 n (a) (piece of work) trabajo m, tarea f; odd — tarea f suelta, chapuza f; odd—— man hombre m que hace de todo; to be on the — estar trabajando; he has done a good — with the book ha hecho un buen trabajo con el libro, en el libro ha realizado una labor muy meritoria; he never did a — in his life no ha trabajado nunca; to fall down on the — fracasar, demostrar no tener capacidad; he knows his — sabe su oficio; to make a good — of something hacer algo bien.
 (b) (criminal, fam) golpe m, robo m; that warehouse — ese robo en el almacén; he did his first — at 12 dio el primer golpe a los 12 años.
 (c) (piecework) destajo m; by the — a destajo.
 (d) (duty) deber m, cometido m; my — is to sell them mi deber es venderlos, yo estoy encargado de venderlos; that's not his — eso no le toca a él, eso no le cumple a él; he does his — hace lo que debe; I had the — of telling him yo tuve la tarea ingrata de decírselo.
 (e) (post, employment) empleo m, puesto m,

trabajo m; we shall create 1000 new —s vamos a crear 1000 puestos de trabajo más; to be in a — tener trabajo; to be out of a — estar sin trabajo, estar desocupado; to look for a — buscar un empleo; to lose one's — perder su empleo, ser despedido; automation has put them out of a — la automatización les ha quitado el trabajo, han sido despedidos debido a la automatización.
 (f) (fam) it's a bad — es una situación difícil; es lamentable, es terrible; to make the best of a bad — poner a mal tiempo buena cara; that's a good —!, and a good — too! ¡menos mal!; it's a good — that menos mal que; we had quite a — getting here nos costó trabajo venir aquí, nos armamos un lío al venir aquí; he has a — to express himself le cuesta expresarse.
 (g) (fam) it's just the —! ¡estupendo!; a holiday in Majorca would be just the — sería estupendo pasar unas vacaciones en Mallorca; this machine is just the — esta máquina es exactamente lo que nos hacía falta.
 2 attr (a) — evaluation apreciación f del trabajo.
 (b) — lot lote m suelto de mercancías, saldo m.
Job [dʒəub] m Job; —'s comforter el que, bajo pretexto de animar a otro, le desconsuela todavía más.
jobber ['dʒɔbə*] n (Stock Exchange) agiotista m; (agent) corredor m; (middleman) intermediario m.
jobbery ['dʒɔbəri] n intrigas fpl, chanchullos mpl; piece of — intriga f, chanchullo m; by a piece of — por enchufe.
jobbing ['dʒɔbiŋ] 1 adj que trabaja a destajo. 2 n agiotaje m; comercio m de intermediario.
jobless ['dʒɔblis] adj sin trabajo.
Jock [dʒɔk] m el escocés típico; the —s los escoceses.
jockey ['dʒɔki] 1 n jockey m, yoquey m (Acad).
 2 vt: to — someone into doing something persuadir mañosamente a uno a hacer algo; to — someone out of doing something disuadir mañosamente a uno de hacer algo; to — someone out of a post lograr mañosamente que uno renuncie a un puesto.
 3 vi : to — for a position maniobrar para conseguir una posición.
jockstrap ['dʒɔkstræp] n suspensorio m.
jocose [dʒə'kəus] adj, **jocular** ['dʒɔkjulə*] adj (merry) alegre, de buen humor; (humorous) guasón, zumbón, jocoso.
jodhpurs ['dʒɔdpəːz] npl pantalones mpl de equitación.
Joe [dʒəu] m Pepe; (US sl) tío m; a good — un buen chico.
jog [dʒɔg] 1 n (a) (push etc) empujoncito m, sacudida f (ligera), codazo m; (encouragement) estímulo m; to give someone's memory a — refrescar la memoria de uno.
 (b) (pace) trote m corto; to go at a steady — andar a trote corto.
 2 vt (push etc) empujar (ligeramente), sacudir (levemente); (encourage) estimular; memory refrescar; he —ged my arm me dio ligeramente con el codo.
 3 vi (also to — along) andar a trote corto, avanzar despacio; (fig) hacer algunos progresos, avanzar pero sin prisa; we keep —ging along vamos tirando.
joggle ['dʒɔgl] 1 n traqueo m. 2 vti traquear.
jog-trot ['dʒɔg'trɔt] n: at a — a trote corto.
John [dʒɔn] m Juan; — Bull personificación de Inglaterra; — Doe Fulano de Tal.
john [dʒɔn] n (US sl) wáter m.
Johnny ['dʒɔni] m Juanito.
johnny ['dʒɔni] n (fam) tío m, sujeto m.
joie de vivre ['ʒwɑːdə'viːvr] n goce m del vivir, alegría f vital.
join [dʒɔin] 1 n juntura f; (Sew) costura f.
 2 vt (a) two things unir, juntar, poner juntos; (Tech) unir, acoplar, ensamblar; everybody —ed hands se cogieron todos de la mano; to his genius he —s humanity a su genialidad une la humanidad.
 (b) society ingresar en, club hacerse socio de, party afiliarse a, hacerse miembro de; (Mil) alistarse en; to — one's regiment incorporarse a su regimiento; to — one's ship volver a su buque; where the track —s the road donde el camino empalma con la carretera.
 (c) person reunirse con, unirse a, juntarse con; may I — you? ¿se permite?; will you — me in a drink? ¿quieres tomar algo conmigo?; they —ed us last Friday vinieron a estar con nosotros el viernes pasado; they will — us for the holidays vendrán a pasar las vacaciones con nosotros; to — someone in doing something acompañar a uno en hacer algo, hacer algo juntamente con uno; they —ed us in protesting se hicieron eco de nuestras protestas.

3 *vi* unirse, juntarse; (*lines*) empalmar; (*rivers*) confluir; **where the paths —** donde empalman los caminos; **to — in** (*adv*) tomar parte, participar; **he doesn't — in much** apenas participa en nuestras actividades; **to — in** (*prep*) tomar parte en, participar en; *discussion* intervenir en; *chorus etc* cantar todos; **to — together** unirse; **to — up** unirse; (*Mil*) alistarse; **to — up with someone** reunirse con uno; **to — with someone in something** acompañar a uno en algo, participar juntamente con uno en algo; **we — with you in that feeling** compartimos esa opinión, nos hacemos eco de eso; **we — with you in hoping that . . .** lo mismo que Vds esperamos que . . .

Joiner ['dʒɔinə*] *n* carpintero *m* (de blanco), ensamblador *m*.

joinery ['dʒɔinəri] *n* carpintería *f*.

joint [dʒɔint] **1** *adj* (en) común; combinado; *action*, *effort*, *product etc* colectivo; *agreement* mutuo; *declaration etc* conjunto; *responsibility* solidario, que comparten todos; *committee etc* mixto; *ownership* común; *account* (*Comm*) indistinto; (*in compounds*) co . . .; *see* **company, stock** *etc*.
2 *n* (**a**) (*Tech: metal*) junta *f*, juntura *f*, unión *f*; (*wood*) ensambladura *f*; (*hinge*) bisagra *f*; (*Anat*) articulación *f*, coyuntura *f*; (*knuckle*) nudillo *m*; (*Bot*) nudo *m*; (*of meat*) cuarto *m*; **mitre —** ensambladura *f* de inglete; **universal —** junta *f* cardán, junta *f* universal; **to be out of —** (*bone*) estar descoyuntado, estar dislocado; (*fig*) estar fuera de quicio; **to put a bone out of —** dislocarse un hueso; **to put someone's nose out of —** desconcertar a uno (adelantándose a él); **to throw someone's plans out of —** estropear los planes de uno.
(**b**) (*sl*) garito *m*, tasca *f*, cafetucho *m*.
3 *vt* articular; *parts* juntar, unir; *wood etc* ensamblar.

jointed ['dʒɔintid] *adj* articulado; (*folding*) plegadizo, plegable.

jointly ['dʒɔintli] *adv* en común; colectivamente; mutuamente; conjuntamente.

joist [dʒɔist] *n* viga *f*, vigueta *f*.

joke [dʒəuk] **1** *n* (*hoax etc*) broma *f*, burla *f*; (*witticism*, *story*) chiste *m*; (*person*) hazmerreír *m*; **practical —** broma *f* pesada, mistificación *f*, trastada *f*; **he's a standing —** es un pobre hombre, es un hombre que da risa; **it's a standing — here** aquí eso siempre provoca a risa; **it's no —** no es cosa de risa, no es para reírse; **it's no — having to +** *infin* no tiene uno de divertido **+** *infin*; **the — is that** lo gracioso es que; **the — is on you** Vd es el aludido, eso lo dicen por Vd; **it's beyond a —** esto es el colmo, esto pasa de castaño oscuro; **what sort of a — is this?** ¿qué broma es ésta?; **is that your idea of a —?** ¿es que eso tiene gracia?; **to crack** (*or* **make**) **a —** hacer un chiste; **to crack —s with someone** contar chistes a uno; **they spent an evening cracking —s together** pasaron una tarde contándose chistes; **he will have his little —** le gusta tomar el pelo; **to play a — on someone** gastar una broma a uno; **I can take a —** tengo mucho aguante; **he can't take a —** no le gusta que se le tome el pelo; **to tell a —** contar un chiste; **why do you have to turn everything into a —?** ¿eres incapaz de tomar nada en serio?
2 *vi* bromear, chancearse, chunguear; hablar en broma; (*tell —s*) contar chistes; **I was only joking** lo dije en broma; **I'm not joking** esto lo digo en serio; **you must be joking!** ¡pero lo dices en serio?; **to — about something** tomar algo en chunga.

joker ['dʒəukə*] *n* (*wit*) chistoso *m*, a *f*, guasón *m*, ona *f*; (*practical*) bromista *mf*; (*Cards*) comodín *m*; (*fam*) tío *m*, sujeto *m*.

joking ['dʒəukiŋ] **1** *adj reference etc* humorístico; *tone* guasón; **I'm not in a — mood** no estoy para bromas.
2 *n* bromas *fpl*; chistes *mpl*.

jokingly ['dʒəukiŋli] *adv* humorísticamente; **he said —** dijo en broma, dijo guasón.

jollification [,dʒɔlifi'keiʃən] *n* (*merriment*) regocijo *m*, festividades *fpl*; (*party*) fiesta *f*, guateque *m*.

jollity ['dʒɔliti] *n* alegría *f*, regocijo *m*.

jolly ['dʒɔli] **1** *adj* alegre; divertido; *character* alegre, jovial; **to get —** (*fam*) achisparse; **we had a — time** lo pasamos muy bien, nos divertimos mucho; **it wasn't very — for the rest of us** los demás no nos divertimos nada.
2 *adv* (*fam*) muy, terriblemente; **it's — hard** es terriblemente difícil; **we were — glad** nos alegramos muchísimo; **you did — well** lo hiciste la mar de bien; **you've — well got to** no tienes más remedio en absoluto; **— good!** ¡estupendo!
3 *vt*: **to — someone along** engatusar a uno, seguir el humor a uno; **to — someone into doing something** persuadir mañosamente a uno a hacer algo.

jolly boat ['dʒɔlibəut] *n* esquife *m*.

jolt [dʒəult] **1** *n* sacudida *f*, choque *m*; **to give someone a —** (*fig*) dar una sacudida a uno; **it gave me a bit of a —** me dio un susto, con eso me pegué un susto.
2 *vt* sacudir; *elbow etc* empujar (ligeramente), sacudir (levemente); **to — someone into doing something** dar una sacudida a uno para animarle a hacer algo; **to — someone out of his complacency** hacer que uno se dé cuenta de la necesidad de hacer algo, destruir el optimismo de uno.
3 *vi* (*vehicle*) traquetear, dar saltos.

jolting ['dʒəultiŋ] *n* (*of vehicle*) traqueteo *m*.

jolty ['dʒəulti] *adj vehicle* que traquetea, que da saltos.

Jonah ['dʒəunə] *m* Jonás.

jonquil ['dʒɔŋkwil] *n* junquillo *m*.

Jordan ['dʒɔːdn] (*river*) Jordán *m*; (*country*) Jordania *f*.

Joseph ['dʒəuzif] *m* José.

Josephine ['dʒəuzifiːn] *f* Josefina.

josh [dʒɔʃ] *vt* (*US sl*) tomar el pelo a.

Joshua ['dʒɔʃwə] *m* Josué.

josser ['dʒɔsə*] *n* (*sl*) tío *m*, individuo *m*.

joss stick ['dʒɔsstik] *n* pebete *m*.

jostle ['dʒɔsl] **1** *n* empujón *m*, empellón *m*, codazo *m*.
2 *vt* empujar.
3 *vi* empujar, dar empellones, codear; **they were all jostling for a place** todos se estaban empujando para asegurarse un sitio.

jot [dʒɔt] **1** *n* jota *f*, pizca *f*; **there's not a — of truth in it** eso no tiene ni pizca de verdad; *see* **care. 2** *vt*: **to — down** apuntar.

jotter ['dʒɔtə*] *n* taco *m* para notas.

jottings ['dʒɔtiŋz] *npl* apuntes *mpl*.

journal ['dʒəːnl] *n* (*newspaper*) periódico *m*; (*review*, *magazine*) revista *f*; (*diary*) diario *m*; (*Naut*) diario *m* de navegación; (*Mech*) gorrón *m*, muñón *m*.

journal bearing ['dʒəːnl'beəriŋ] *n* cojinete *m*.

journalese [,dʒəːnə'liːz] *n* lenguaje *m* periodístico.

journalism ['dʒəːnəlizəm] *n* periodismo *m*.

journalist ['dʒəːnəlist] *n* periodista *mf*.

journalistic [,dʒəːnə'listik] *adj* periodístico.

journey ['dʒəːni] **1** *n* viaje *m*; trayecto *m*; camino *m*; **outward —** viaje *m* de ida; **return —** viaje *m* de regreso; **Scott's — to the Pole** la expedición de Scott al Polo; **the capsule's — through space** el trayecto de la cápsula por el espacio; **pleasant —!** ¡buen viaje!; **to be on a —** estar de viaje; **have you much — left?** ¿le queda mucho camino?
2 *vi* viajar.

journeyman ['dʒəːnimən] *n*, *pl* **—men** [mən] oficial *m*.

joust [dʒaust] **1** *n* justa *f*, torneo *m*. **2** *vi* justar.

Jove [dʒəuv] *m* Júpiter; **by —!** ¡caramba!

jovial ['dʒəuviəl] *adj* jovial.

joviality [,dʒəuvi'æliti] *n* jovialidad *f*.

jowl [dʒaul] *n* (*Anat: jaw*) quijada *f*; (*chin*) barba *f*; (*cheek*) carrillo *m*; (*Zool*) papada *f*.

joy [dʒɔi] *n* (*gladness*) alegría *f*, júbilo *m*, regocijo *m*; (*pleasant quality*) deleite *m*, encanto *m*; **the —s of opera** los encantos de la ópera; **the —s** *pl* — **to hear him** da gozo escucharle; **to be a — to the eye** ser un gozo para la retina; **to be beside oneself with —** no caber en sí de gozo; **to jump for —** saltar de alegría; **I wish you —!** ¡enhorabuena! (*also iro*).

joyful ['dʒɔiful] *adj* alegre; jubiloso, regocijado; **to be — about** alegrarse de.

joyfully ['dʒɔifəli] *adv* alegremente; con júbilo, regocijadamente.

joyfulness ['dʒɔifulnis] *n* alegría *f*; júbilo *m*, regocijo *m*.

joyless ['dʒɔilis] *adj* sin alegría, triste.

joyous ['dʒɔiəs] *adj* alegre.

joy ride ['dʒɔiraid] *n* paseo *m* en coche (*etc*), excursión *f* en coche (*etc*).

joystick ['dʒɔistik] *n* (*Aer*) palanca *f* de gobierno.

jubilant ['dʒuːbilənt] *adj* jubiloso.

jubilation [,dʒuːbi'leiʃən] *n* júbilo *m*.

jubilee ['dʒuːbiliː] *n* (*Hist, Eccl*) jubileo *m*; (*anniversary: strictly*) quincuagésimo aniversario *m*; **diamond —** sexagésimo aniversario *m*; **golden —** quincuagésimo aniversario *m*; **silver —** vigésimo quinto aniversario *m*.

Judaea [dʒuː'diə] Judea *f*.

Judah ['dʒuːdə] Judá *f*.

Judaic [dʒuː'deiik] *adj* judaico.

Judaism ['dʒuːdeiizəm] *n* judaísmo *m*.

Judaize ['dʒuːdeiaiz] *vi* judaizar.

Judas ['dʒuːdəs] *m* Judas.

judge [dʒʌdʒ] **1** *n* (*Law*) juez *m*; (*Sport*) árbitro *m*, (*in races*) juez *m* de raya; (*connoisseur*) conocedor m, ora *f* (*of* de), (*expert*) perito *m* (*of* en); — **of appeal** juez *m* de alzados; **he's a fine** — **of horses** es un excelente conocedor de caballos; **I'm no** — **of wines** yo no entiendo de vinos.

2 *vt* person, case juzgar; *question* decidir, resolver; (*Sport*) arbitrar; (*consider*) juzgar, considerar; **I** — **it to be right** lo considero acertado; **I** — **him a fool** considero que es tonto; **one has to** — **the distance** hay que conjeturar la distancia; **he** —**d the moment well** acertó escogiendo tal momento; **who can** — **this question?** ¿quién puede resolver esta cuestión?

3 *vi* juzgar; opinar, expresar una opinión; **to** — **by, judging by** a juzgar por; **to** — **of** juzgar de, opinar sobre; **who am I to** —**?** ¿es que yo soy capaz de juzgar? **only an expert can** — sólo lo puede decidir un experto; **to** — **for oneself** formar su propia opinión.

judge-advocate ['dʒʌdʒ'ædvəkit] *n* (*Mil*) auditor *m* de guerra.

judg(e)ment ['dʒʌdʒmənt] *n* (a) (*Law*) juicio *m*; sentencia *f*, fallo *m*; **Last J**— **Juicio** *m* Final; **J**— **Day** día *m* del Juicio Final; — **seat** tribunal *m*; **it's a** — **on you for lying** es un castigo por haber mentido; **to pass** (*or* **pronounce**) — (*Law*) pronunciar sentencia (**on** en, **sobre**), (*fig*) emitir un juicio crítico sobre, dictaminar sobre.

(b) (*opinion*) opinión *f*, parecer *m*; juicio *m*; **a critical** — **of Auden** un juicio crítico de Auden.

(c) (*understanding*) juicio *m*; criterio *m*, entendimiento *m*, discernimiento *m*; **in my** — en mi opinión; **to the best of my** — según mi leal saber y entender; **to have good** (*or* **sound**) — tener buen juicio, tener buen criterio.

judicature ['dʒuːdikətʃə*] *n* judicatura *f*.

judicial [dʒuː'diʃəl] *adj* judicial; *murder, separation etc* legal.

judiciary [dʒuː'diʃiəri] 1 *adj* judicial. 2 *n* judicatura *f*.

judicious [dʒuː'diʃəs] *adj* juicioso; prudente, sensato, acertado.

judiciously [dʒuː'diʃəsli] *adv* juiciosamente; prudentemente, acertadamente.

Judith ['dʒuːdiθ] *f* Judit.

judo ['dʒuːdəu] *n* judo *m*.

Judy ['dʒuːdi] *f* nombre cariñoso de **Judith**.

jug [dʒʌg] 1 *n* jarro *m*; (*sl*) chirona *f*. 2 *vt* (*sl*) encarcelar; —**ged hare** liebre *f* en estofado.

juggernaut ['dʒʌgənɔːt] *n* monstruo *m* destructor de los hombres.

juggins ['dʒʌginz] *n* (*fam*) bobo *m*, a *f*.

juggle ['dʒʌgl] *vi* hacer juegos malabares, hacer juegos de manos (*with* con); **to** — **with** (*fig*) arreglar de otro modo, (*pej*) falsear, falsificar, hacer trampa con.

juggler ['dʒʌglə*] *n* malabarista *mf*.

jugglery ['dʒʌgləri] *n*, **juggling** ['dʒʌgliŋ] *n* juegos *mpl* malabares, malabarismo *m*, juegos *mpl* de manos; (*pej*) trampas *fpl*, fraude *m*.

Jugoslav ['juːgəu'slɑːv] 1 *adj* yugo(e)slavo. 2 *n* yugo(e)slavo *m*, a *f*.

Jugoslavia ['juːgəu'slɑːviə] *n* Yugo(e)slavia *f*.

jugular ['dʒʌgjulə*] *adj*: — **vein** vena *f* yugular.

juice [dʒuːs] *n* (*fruit-*) jugo *m*, zumo *m*; (*sl*) salacidad *f*, lo verde, lo picante; (*Aut sl*) gasolina *f*, (*Elec sl*) fuerza *f*, corriente *f*; **digestive** —**s** jugos *mpl* digestivos.

juiciness ['dʒuːsinis] *n* jugosidad *f*; (*sl*) salacidad *f*, lo verde.

juicy ['dʒuːsi] *adj* jugoso, zumoso; (*sl*) salaz, verde, picante.

jujube ['dʒuːdʒuːb] *n* pastilla *f*.

jujutsu [dʒuː'dʒitsu] *n* jiu-jitsu *m*.

jukebox ['dʒuːkbɔks] *n* tocadiscos *m* automático, tocadiscos *m* tragaperras, gramola *f*.

julep ['dʒuːlep] *n* julepe *m*.

Julian ['dʒuːliən] *m* Juliano, Julián.

Juliet ['dʒuːliet] *f* Julieta.

Julius ['dʒuːliəs] *m* Julio; — **Caesar** Julio César.

July [dʒuː'lai] *n* julio *m*.

jumble ['dʒʌmbl] 1 *n* revoltijo *m*, confusión *f*; **a** — **of furniture** un montón de muebles revueltos; **a** — **of sounds** una serie de ruidos confusos.

2 *vt* (*also* **to** — **together**, **to** — **up**) mezclar, emburujar; **papers** —**d up together** papeles *mpl* revueltos; **they were just** —**d together anyhow** estaban amontonados sin orden.

jumble sale ['dʒʌmblseil] *n* venta *f* de objetos usados (con fines benéficos).

jumbo ['dʒʌmbəu] *n* elefante *m*.

jump [dʒʌmp] 1 *n* salto *m*, brinco *m*; (*fig*) ascenso *m*, aumento *m*; **to give a** — dar un saltito; **to give someone a** — dar un susto a uno; **you gave me quite a** —! ¡ay qué susto me diste!; **to have the** — **on**

someone (*fam*) llevar ventaja a uno; **the temperature took a** — subió rápidamente la temperatura; **there has been a big** — **in the reserves** las reservas han subido de golpe.

2 *vt* (a) saltar, saltar por encima de, salvar; *see* **gun, rail** etc.

(b) *horse* hacer saltar; presentar en un concurso hípico.

(c) (*omit*) pasar por alto, omitir.

3 *vi* (a) saltar, brincar, dar saltos; (*Sport*) saltar; (*Aer*) lanzarse (en paracaídas); (*vibrate*) temblar, bailar, vibrar; **to** — **about** dar saltos, brincar; moverse de un lado para otro; **to** — **across a stream** cruzar un arroyo de un salto, saltar por encima de un arroyo; **to** — **down** bajar de un salto, saltar a tierra; **to** — **in!** ¡vamos!; **to** — **into a car** entrar de prisa en un coche; **to** — **on to something** ponerse encima de algo de un salto; **we** —**ed on to the train** subimos de prisa al tren; **to** — **on someone** (*fam*) poner verde a uno; **to** — **on an abuse** (*fam*) tratar de acabar con un abuso; **to** — **out of bed** saltar de la cama; **I nearly** —**ed out of my skin!** ¡vaya susto que me pegué!; **he** —**ed out from behind a bush** salió de repente de detrás de un arbusto; **to** — **over** saltar, saltar por (encima de), salvar; — **to it!** ¡menearse!; **to** — **up** ponerse en pie de un salto; *see* **conclusion** etc.

(b) (*fig: start*) asustarse, sobresaltarse, pegar un bote; **to make someone** — dar un susto a uno; **you did make me** —! ¡ay qué susto me diste!

(c) (*fig: emotion*) **to** — **for joy** saltar de alegría, no caber en sí de gozo.

(d) **to** — **at a chance** apresurarse a aprovechar una oportunidad; **to** — **at an offer** apresurarse a aceptar una oferta.

jumped-up ['dʒʌmpt'ʌp] *adj* arribista, presuntuoso.

jumper ['dʒʌmpə*] *n* saltador *m*, ora *f*; (*dress*) suéter *m*, jersey *m*.

jumping-off place ['dʒʌmpiŋ'ɔf,pleis] *n* base *f* avanzada.

jumpy ['dʒʌmpi] *adj* nervioso, asustadizo.

junction ['dʒʌŋkʃən] *n* juntura *f*, unión *f*; (*of roads*) cruce *m*; (*Rail*) empalme *m*; (*of rivers*) confluencia *f*.

junction box ['dʒʌŋkʃənbɔks] *n* caja *f* de empalmes.

juncture ['dʒʌŋktʃə*] *n* coyuntura *f*; **at this** — en este momento, en esta coyuntura; **critical** — coyuntura *f* crítica.

June [dʒuːn] *n* junio *m*.

jungle ['dʒʌŋgl] *n* selva *f*, jungla *f*; (*fig*) maraña *f*, selva *f*.

junior ['dʒuːniə*] 1 *adj* (*in age*) menor, más joven; (*on a staff*) más nuevo; *position, rank* subalterno; *section* (*in competition etc*) juvenil, para menores; *partner* menor, menos antiguo; **Roy Smith, J**— Roy Smith, hijo.

2 *n* menor *m*, joven *mf*; (*British School*) alumno *m* (*or* alumna *f*) de 8 a 11 años; (*US Univ*) estudiante *mf* de tercer año; **he is my** — **by 3 years**, **he is 3 years my** — tiene 3 años menos que yo, le llevo 3 años.

juniper ['dʒuːnipə*] *n* enebro *m*.

junk[1] [dʒʌŋk] *n* (*Naut*) junco *m*.

junk[2] [dʒʌŋk] *n* (*lumber*) trastos *mpl* viejos; (*rubbish*) basura *f*, desperdicios *mpl*; (*iron*) chatarra *f*; (*cheap goods*) baratijas *fpl*; **the play is a lot of** — la obra es una porquería; **he talks a lot of** — no habla más que tonterías.

junket ['dʒʌŋkit] 1 *n* dulce *m* de leche cuajada. 2 *vi* ir de juerga, ir de jira, estar de fiesta.

junketing ['dʒʌŋkitiŋ] *n* (*also* —**s**) festividades *fpl*, fiestas *fpl*.

junkie ['dʒʌŋki] (*fam*) drogadicto *m*, a *f*.

junkshop ['dʒʌŋkʃɔp] *n* tienda *f* de trastos viejos.

junk yard ['dʒʌŋkjɑːd] *n* parque *m* de chatarra.

junta ['dʒʌntə] *n* junta *f*.

Jupiter ['dʒuːpitə*] *m* Júpiter.

juridical [dʒuə'ridikəl] *adj* jurídico.

jurisdiction [,dʒuəris'dikʃən] *n* jurisdicción *f*; **to come within someone's** — ser de la competencia de uno.

jurisprudence [,dʒuəris'pruːdəns] *n* jurisprudencia *f*; **medical** — medicina *f* legal.

jurist ['dʒuərist] *n* jurista *m*.

juror ['dʒuərə*] *n* jurado *m* (*persona*).

jury ['dʒuəri] *n* jurado *m* (*conjunto de jurados*); **grand** — (*US*) jurado *m* de acusación; **to be on the** — ser miembro del jurado.

jury box ['dʒuəribɔks] *n* tribuna *f* del jurado.

juryman ['dʒuərimən] *n*, *pl* —**men** [mən] (miembro *m* del) jurado *m*.

jury mast ['dʒuərimɑːst] *n* bandola *f*.

jury rig ['dʒuəririg] *n* aparejo *m* provisional.

just [dʒʌst] **1** adj (upright) justo, recto, imparcial; (accurate) exacto, correcto; (deserved) merecido, apropiado; (well grounded) justificado, lógico; **as is only** — como es justo, como es de razón; **the** — los justos.

2 adv **(a)** (exactly) exactamente, precisamente; — **here** aquí mismo; — **by the church** al lado mismo de la iglesia, muy cerca de la iglesia; — **beyond the pub** un poco más allá de la tasca; **it's** — **4 o'clock** son las 4 en punto; — **so!** ¡eso es!, ¡perfectamente!, ¡precisamente!; **that's** — **it!** ¡ahí está la dificultad!; **it's** — **the same** es exactamente igual; **it's** — **what I needed** es precisamente lo que necesitaba; **we were** — **talking about it** precisamente estábamos hablando de eso; — **when he started to sing** precisamente cuando empezaba a cantar; **I was** — **going** estaba a punto de marcharme; **now** — **what did he say?** ¿qué es lo que dijo, en concreto?; — **how many we don't know** no sabemos exactamente cuántos; **a policeman? that's** — **what I am** ¿un policía? pues yo lo soy.

(b) (with as) **you sing** — **as well as I do** Vd canta tan bien como yo; — **as you wish** como Vd quiera; — **as it started to rain** en el momento en que empezó a llover; **we left everything** — **as it was** lo dejamos todo exactamente como estaba; **it's** — **as well it's insured** menos mal que está asegurado; **it would be** — **as well if he went** más vale que se vaya él.

(c) (only) solamente, sólo; — **as a joke** en broma nada más; — **for a laugh** sólo para hacer reír; — **once** una vez nada más, solamente una vez, una vez solamente; — **the two of us** nosotros dos solamente; — **a little bit** un poquito; — **a few** unos pocos; **he's** — **a lad** no es más que un chico; — **let me get at him!** ¡que me dejen llegar a él!

(d) (merely) **I** — **told him to go away** le dije que se fuera, nada más; — **wait a moment!** ¡espere un momento!; — **imagine!** ¡imagínese!; — **listen!** ¡escucha un poco!; — **look!** ¡mira!, ¡fíjate!; — **a tick!** un momentito!

(e) (positively) **it's** — **fine!** ¡es francamente maravilloso!, ¡es sencillamente maravilloso!; **it's** — **perfect!** ¡qué maravilla!

(f) (barely) **I** — **managed to catch it** por poco lo perdí; **he was only** — **saved from drowning** en poco estuvo que muriese ahogado; **you're** — **in time** llegas justamente con tiempo; — **before it rained** momentos antes de que lloviese.

(g) (with have etc) **I have** — **seen him** acabo de verle; **I had** — **seen him** acababa de verle; **the book is** — **out** el libro acaba de publicarse; — **appointed** recién nombrado; — **received** acabado de recibir; — **cooked** recién hecho, recién salido del horno.

(h) (emphatic, fam) **don't I** —**!** ¡ya lo creo!; see **now, yet** etc.

justice ['dʒʌstis] n **(a)** justicia f; **poetic** — justicia f poética; **to bring someone to** — llevar a uno ante el tribunal, hacer que uno sea procesado; **to do someone** — hacer justicia a uno, tratar debidamente a uno; **to do oneself** — quedar bien, justificarse; **to do a mea!** — hacer los debidos honores a una comida; **this work does not do your talents** — este ensayo no está a la altura de su talento.

(b) (person) juez m, juez m municipal; — **of the peace** (approx) juez m de paz; **Lord Chief J**— Justicia m Mayor.

justifiable ['dʒʌstifaiəbl] adj justificable; justificado.

justifiably ['dʒʌstifaiəbli] adv justificadamente; **and** — **so** y con razón; — **proud** orgulloso y con razón.

justification [,dʒʌstifi'keiʃən] n justificación f.

justify ['dʒʌstifai] vt justificar, vindicar; dar motivo para; (excuse) disculpar; **the future does not** — **the slightest optimism** el futuro no autoriza el más leve optimismo; **to be justified in** + ger tener motivo para + infin, tener plenamente razón al + infin; **you were not justified in that** en eso no tuviste razón; **am I justified in thinking that . . .?** ¿hay motivo para creer que . . .?

justly ['dʒʌstli] adv justamente, con justicia; con derecho; debidamente; con razón; **it has been** — **said that** se ha dicho con razón que.

justness ['dʒʌstnis] n justicia f; rectitud f.

jut [dʒʌt] vi (also **to** — **out**) sobresalir.

Jute [dʒuːt] n juto m, a f.

jute [dʒuːt] n yute m.

juvenile ['dʒuːvənail] **1** adj juvenil; de (or para) menores; (pej) infantil; court de menores; **delinquency** de menores, **delinquent** juvenil.

2 n joven mf.

juxtapose ['dʒʌkstəpəuz] vt yuxtaponer.

juxtaposition [,dʒʌkstəpə'ziʃən] n yuxtaposición f.

K

Kaffir ['kæfə*] n cafre mf.

Kaiser ['kaizə*] n emperador m.

kale, kail [keil] n col f rizada.

kaleidoscope [kə'laidəskəup] n calidoscopio m.

kaleidoscopic [kə,laidə'skɔpik] adj calidoscópico.

kangaroo [,kæŋgə'ru:] n canguro m.

kaolin ['keiəlin] n caolín m.

kapok ['keipɔk] n capoc m.

kaput [kə'put] adj (sl): it's — está roto, está estropeado; se acabó; it went — se rompió, se estropeó.

karat ['kærət] n see **carat.**

Kashmir [kæʃ'miə*] Cachemira f.

Kate [keit] f nombre cariñoso de **Catherine** etc.

Katharine, Katherine ['kæθərin], **Kathleen** ['kæθli:n] f Catalina.

katydid ['keitidid] n saltamontes m (especie norteamericana).

kayak ['kaiæk] n kayac m.

kedge [kedʒ] n anclote m.

kedgeree [,kedʒə'ri:] n plato de pescado, huevos y arroz.

keel [ki:l] 1 n quilla f; on an even — (Naut) en iguales calados, (fig) en equilibrio, equilibrado; to keep something on an even — mantener el equilibrio de algo.
  2 vi: to — over (Naut) zozobrar, dar de quilla, (fig) volcar(se), (person) desplomarse.

keelhaul ['ki:lhɔ:l] vt pasar por debajo de la quilla (como castigo).

keen [ki:n] adj (a) edge afilado; wind penetrante, glacial; eyesight, hearing agudo; mind agudo, penetrante, perspicaz; look fijo, penetrante; price bajo, competitivo, económico; competition intenso; interest grande; emotion intenso, vivo, hondo; appetite bueno; to have a — sense of history tener un profundo sentido de la historia.
  (b) (of person) entusiasta; celoso; he's a — footballer es muy aficionado a jugar al fútbol; he's a — socialist es un socialista acérrimo; try not to seem too — procura no mostrar demasiado entusiasmo; to be as — as mustard ser extraordinariamente entusiasta; I'm terribly — about the new play la nueva obra me hace muchísima ilusión; he's very — about the programme tiene mucho entusiasmo por el programa; to be — on something ser aficionado a algo; are you — on opera? ¿le gusta la ópera?; I'm not all that — on grapes no me gustan mucho las uvas; I'm not — on the idea no me hace gracia la idea; he's — on her ella le interesa bastante; I'm not very — on him no es santo de mi devoción; to be — to + infin tener vivo deseo de + infin, tener muchas ganas de + infin, ansiar + infin; I'm not — to do it no tengo ganas de hacerlo.

keenly ['ki:nli] adv (a) de modo penetrante; agudamente; intensamente, vivamente; he felt her death — su muerte le afectó profundamente; he looked at me — me miró fijamente.
  (b) work etc con entusiasmo.

keenness ['ki:nnis] n (a) penetración f, agudeza f; intensidad f, viveza f.
  (b) entusiasmo m, ilusión f; interés m, afición f; there isn't much — here aquí hay poco interés.

keep [ki:p] (irr: pret and ptp kept) 1 vt (a) promise cumplir; rule observar, atenerse a; appointment acudir a; festivity observar, celebrar.
  (b) order mantener, imponer.
  (c) (possess etc) dog, servant tener; chicken, sheep etc criar, dedicarse a criar, ocuparse en la cría de; family mantener; shop tener; business, hotel etc ser propietario de, dirigir; diary escribir; account, record, house llevar; he —s a good cellar tiene una buena bodega; he doesn't — his garden neat no mantiene en buen estado su jardín; he —s his 3

daughters in clothes les paga los vestidos a sus 3 hijas; he has his parents to — tiene que mantener a sus padres.
  (d) (detain) detener; (in conversation etc) entretener; they kept him in prison for 6 months le tuvieron 6 meses en la cárcel; illness kept her at home se quedó en casa debido a la enfermedad, la enfermedad no le permitió salir de casa; what kept you? ¿por qué vienes tarde?, ¿a qué se debe este retraso?; I mustn't — you no le entretengo más.
  (e) (prevent) to — someone from doing something impedir a uno hacer algo, no dejar a uno hacer algo.
  (f) (save) poner aparte, tener guardado, reservar; I was —ing it for you lo tenía guardado para Vd.
  (g) (retain) guardar, retener; reservar; secret, figure etc guardar; job retener, mantenerse en; (not give back) quedarse con; (in museum etc) conservar, custodiar; — the change quédese con la vuelta; to — one's seat permanecer sentado, (Parl) retener su escaño.
  (h) (with adj, verb etc) to — something clean conservar algo limpio; "K— Spain Clean" (antilitter campaign) "Mantenga limpia España"; she always —s the house very clean tiene la casa siempre muy limpia; to — something safe tener algo seguro; to — something warm tener algo caliente, mantener el calor de algo; to — someone talking entretener a uno en conversación; to — someone waiting hacer que uno espere, hacer esperar a uno; to — one's eyes fixed on something tener los ojos puestos en algo; to — someone at it obligar a uno a seguir trabajando (etc).
  (i) (with adv or prep) to — someone away mantener a uno a distancia, alejar a uno (from de), no dejar a uno acercarse (from a); they kept him away from school no le dejaron ir a la escuela; they kept guns away from the child no le dejaron al niño jugar con pistolas; to — back (retain) guardar, retener; information ocultar; emotion contener, reprimir; enemy no dejar avanzar, tener a raya; progress estorbar, cortar el paso a; to — some money by one guardar algún dinero para un apuro; to — down (hold down) sujetar; no dejar subir; price, temperature etc mantener bajo; growth etc restringir, limitar; (oppress) oprimir; to — something from someone ocultar algo a uno, no decir algo a uno; to — in fire mantener encendido; feelings contener; person, pet etc no dejar salir, tener encerrado; (in school) hacer quedar en la escuela (como castigo); to — off tener a raya, cerrar el paso a; no dejar entrar; alejar; — the dog off! ¡que no se acerque más el perro!; to — someone off a subject hacer que uno no discuta un tema, persuadir a uno a no tocar un tema; to — one's hat on no quitarse el sombrero, seguir con el sombrero puesto; to — the light on tener la luz puesta; to — someone on in a job mantener a uno en un puesto; to — out no dejar entrar, excluir; to — something to oneself guardar algo para sí; guardar algo en secreto; to — someone to his promise obligar a uno a cumplir su promesa; to — together mantener unido(s); to — someone under tener a uno subyugado; to — up (maintain) mantener; conservar; (hold up) sostener; to — someone up (at night) hacer que uno siga sin dormir, entretener a uno hasta muy tarde; to — it up mantener el nivel, seguir como antes; no cejar; — it up! ¡ánimo!, ¡dale!
  2 vi (a) (remain) quedar(se), permanecer; seguir, continuar; to — quiet no hacer ruido; no decir nada, quedar callado, callarse; — still! ¡estáte quieto!; to — clear of evitar cualquier contacto con; seguir libre de; how are you —ing? ¿cómo está Vd?; to — well estar bien de salud.

(b) *(with ger)* **to — + ger** seguir + ger, continuar + ger; no dejar de + *infin*; **she —s talking** sigue hablando; no deja de hablar; **she —s asking me for it** me lo está pidiendo constantemente; **to — smiling** seguir con la sonrisa en los labios; **to — standing** seguir en pie; **to — going** seguir adelante, no cejar; **we — going somehow** vamos tirando; nos arreglamos para continuar; **I can — going in French** me defiendo en francés.

(c) *(continue)* seguir, continuar; **to — at work** seguir trabajando, mantenerse en su puesto; — **straight on for Madrid** para ir a Madrid vaya Vd todo seguido; **to — to the left** circular por la izquierda.

(d) *(of food)* conservarse fresco, conservarse en buen estado; **an apple that —s** una manzana que dura; **the news will — till I see you** no pierdes nada si me guardo la noticia hasta que nos veamos.

(e) *(with adv or prep)* **to — at something** trabajar sin descanso en algo, no cejar en algo, perseverar en algo; **— at it!** ¡dale!; **to — away** mantenerse alejado *(from de)*, mantenerse a distancia; *(not attend)* no venir, no acudir; no dejarse ver; **to — away from someone** no meterse en líos con uno, evitar cualquier contacto con uno; **— away from my daughter!** ¡no venga más a ver a mi hija!; **he can't — away from the subject** siempre vuelve al tema; **to — back** hacerse a un lado; **— back, please!** ¡más atrás, por favor!; **to — down** seguir acurrucado *(or* tumbado *etc)*, no levantar la cabeza; **to — from + ger** abstenerse de + *infin*, guardarse de + *infin*; **to — in with someone** mantener buenas relaciones con uno, cultivar la amistad de uno, *(pej)* asegurarse de la protección de uno; **to — off** mantenerse a distancia; **"— off"** "prohibida la entrada"; **to — off the grass** no pisar la hierba; **to — off a subject** no aludir a un tema, no discutir una cuestión; **if the rain —s off** si no llueve; **to — on** continuar; **to — on + ger** seguir + ger, continuar + ger; **he —s on talking** sigue hablando; no deja de hablar; **he —s on hoping** no renuncia a esperar, no pierde la esperanza; **don't — on so!** ¡no machaques!; **to — on at someone about something** insistir en discutir algo con uno; **to — on with something** continuar con algo; **to — out** permanecer fuera; **"— out!"** "prohibida la entrada!"; **to — out of place, organization etc** no entrar en; *affair* no meterse en; *trouble* evitar; **to — to** *direction* llevar; *path* seguir; *promise* cumplir; *instructions* seguir al pie de la letra; **to — to one's bed** guardar cama; **to — to one's room** no salir de su habitación; **they — to themselves** evitan tener contacto con otros, permanecen aislados; **to — together** mantenerse unidos; **to — up** no rezagarse; **to — up with** *(in pace)* ir al paso de; *(rival)* emular, mantenerse a la altura de; **to — up with one's work** hacer su trabajo al ritmo apropiado, mantenerse al día en su trabajo; **to — up with the times** ir con los tiempos, mantenerse al día.

3 *vr*: **to — oneself clean** mantenerse limpio, cuidar su limpieza personal; **to — oneself from + ger** abstenerse de + *infin*, guardarse de + *infin*; **they — themselves to themselves** evitan tener contacto con otros, permanecen aislados.

4 *n* (a) comida *f*, subsistencia *f*; **to earn one's —** trabajar por la comida, pagar la comida trabajando; *(fig)* producir *(etc)* bastante; **I pay £5 a week for my —** la pensión me cuesta 5 libras a la semana; **he isn't worth his —** no trabaja como debe, no merece que sigamos empleándole.

(b) *(Hist)* torreón *m*, torre *f* del homenaje.

(c) **for —s** *(fam)* permanentemente, para guardar.

keeper ['kiːpə*] *n (game-)* guardabosque *m*; *(in art gallery, museum, library)* conservador *m*; *(in record office)* archivero *m*; *(in park, zoo)* guardián *m*; **am I my brother's —?** ¿es que yo respondo por mi hermano?

keeping ['kiːpiŋ] *n* (a) **to be in — with** estar de acuerdo con, estar en armonía con; **to be out of — with** estar en desacuerdo con.

(b) **to be in the — of X** estar en manos de X, estar bajo la custodia de X; **to be in safe —** estar en un lugar seguro, estar en buenas manos; **to give something to someone for safe —** dar algo a uno para mayor seguridad.

keepsake ['kiːpseik] *n* recuerdo *m*.

keg [keg] *n* barrilete *m*, cuñete *m*.

kelp [kelp] *n* quelpo *m*.

ken [ken] 1 *n*: **to be beyond someone's —** ser incomprensible para uno; **to be within someone's —** ser comprensible para uno.

2 *vt (know)* *person etc* conocer, *fact* saber; *(recognize)* reconocer.

kennel ['kenl] *n (doghouse)* perrera *f*; *(pack)* jauría *f*; *(fig)* cuchitril *m*.

Kenya ['kenjə] Kenia *f*.

kepi ['keipi] *n* quepis *m*.

kept [kept] *pret and ptp of* **keep**.

kerb [kəːb] *n*, **kerbstone** ['kəːbstəun] *n* bordillo *m*, encintado *m*.

kerchief ['kəːtʃif] *n* pañuelo *m*, pañoleta *f*.

kernel ['kəːnl] *n* almendra *f*; *(fig)* núcleo *m*, meollo *m*; **a — of truth** una parte de verdad.

kerosene ['kerəsiːn] *n* keroseno *m*, queroseno *m* *(Acad)*; **— lamp** lámpara *f* de petróleo.

kestrel ['kestrəl] *n* cernícalo *m (vulgar)*.

ketch [ketʃ] *n* queche *m*.

ketchup ['ketʃəp] *n* salsa *f* de tomate.

kettle ['ketl] *n (approx)* hervidor *m*, olla *f* en forma de cafetera *(or* tetera), pava *f (SAm)*; **this is a pretty — of fish!** ¡en buen berenjenal nos hemos metido!

kettledrum ['ketldrʌm] *n* timbal *m*.

key [kiː] 1 *n* (a) *(door- etc)* llave *f*; *(of typewriter, piano etc)* tecla *f*; *(of wind instrument)* llave *f*, pistón *m*; *(Tel)* manipulador *m*; *(Tech)* chaveta *f*, cuña *f*; *(Elec)* llave *f*, interruptor *m*; *(Archit)* clave *f*.

(b) *(Mus)* tonalidad *f*, tono *m*; **major —** tonalidad *f* mayor; **minor —** tonalidad *f* menor; **change of —** cambio *m* de tonalidad; **to be in —** estar a tono, estar templado; **to play off —** desafinar, tocar desafinadamente.

(c) *(fig: to problem, also Bio, Chess)* clave *f (to de)*; **the — to the mystery** la clave del misterio.

2 *attr* clave; **— industry** industria *f* clave; **— point** punto *m* clave; **— man** hombre *m* clave; **— question** cuestión *f* principal, cuestión *f* madre.

3 *vt (Tech)* enchavetar, acuñar; *(Mus)* templar, afinar; **to — up** emocionar; **to be all —ed up** estar emocionadísimo, tener los nervios en punta.

keyboard ['kiːbɔːd] *n* teclado *m*.

keyhole ['kiːhəul] *n* ojo *m* (de la cerradura).

keynote ['kiːnəut] *n* tónica *f*; *(fig)* tónica *f*, piedra *f* clave, idea *f* fundamental; **— speech** discurso *m* de apertura, discurso *m* en que se sientan las bases de una política *(or* programa).

key ring ['kiːriŋ] *n* llavero *m*.

keystone ['kiːstəun] *n* piedra *f* clave; *(fig)* piedra *f* angular.

khaki ['kaːki] 1 *n* caqui *m*. 2 *attr* de caqui.

Khartoum [kɑrˈtuːm] Jartum.

kibitzer ['kibitsə*] *n (US)* mirón *m*, ona *f*.

kibosh ['kaibɔʃ] *n (sl)*: **to put the — on something** acabar con algo definitivamente.

kick [kik] 1 *n* patada *f*, puntapié *m (also Sport)*; *(by animal)* coz *f*; *(of firearm)* culatazo *m*; *(fig)* reacción *f*; **a drink with a —** te il una bebida muy fuerte; **to do something for —s** hacer algo sólo para distraerse de la emoción que ello produce, hacer algo sólo para divertirse; **I get a — out of it** esto me entusiasma, encuentro placer en esto.

2 *vt ball etc* dar un puntapié a; golpear (con el pie); *goal* marcar; *person* dar una patada a; *(animal)* dar de coces a; **to — someone's bottom** dar a uno una patada en el culo; **to — a man when he's down** dar a moro muerto gran lanzada; **to — someone downstairs** echar a uno escaleras abajo; **to — someone upstairs** hacer que un miembro de los Comunes pase a serlo de los Lores; **to — one's legs in the air** agitar las piernas; **to — a ball about** divertirse dando patadas a un balón; **to — a ball away** apartar un balón con el pie; **to — someone out** echar a uno a puntapiés, *(fig)* poner a uno de patitas en la calle, expulsar a uno; *see* **dust**, **heel** *etc*.

3 *vi (animal)* dar coces, cocear; *(gun)* dar un culatazo, recular; *(fig)* protestar, quejarse; respingar, reaccionar; **it's —ing about somewhere** estará por ahí; **to — off** hacer el saque inicial; **to — out** repartir coces; **to — out for the shore** nadar enérgicamente hacia la playa.

4 *vr*: **I could have —ed myself** me di cuenta de que había hecho el tonto.

kickback ['kikbæk] *n* (a) *(Mil)* culatazo *m*. (b) *(fig)* reacción *f*, resaca *f*, contragolpe *m*.

kick-off ['kikɔf] *n* saque *m* inicial.

kid [kid] 1 *n* (a) *(Zool)* cabrito *m*, a *f*, chivo *m*, a *f*; *(meat)* carne *f* de cabrito; *(skin)* cabritilla *f*.

(b) *(child: fam)* chiquillo *m*, a *f*, chaval *m*, ala *f*; **when I was a —** cuando yo era chaval; **that's —'s stuff** eso es para chicos, son chiquilladas.

2 *attr*: **— gloves** guantes *mpl* de cabritilla; *(fig)* trato *m* muy blando.

3 *vt (fam)* tomar el pelo a; **you can't — me** no se me engaña así.

4 *vi* bromearse, chunguear; **I was only —ding** lo decía en broma; **no —ding!** ¡en serio!; **are you —ding?** ¿lo dices en serio?; **are you —ding!** ¡ni hablar!

5 *vr*: **to — oneself** engañarse a sí mismo, vivir engañado; **he —s himself** that se hace creer que; **it's time we stopped —ding ourselves** es hora ya de desengañarnos, es hora ya de despertar a la realidad.

kiddy ['kidi] *n* (*fam*) chiquillo *m*, a *f*.

kidnap ['kidnæp] *vt* secuestrar, raptar.

kidnapper ['kidnæpə*] *n* secuestrador *m*, ora *f*, raptor *m*, ora *f*.

kidnapping ['kidnæpiŋ] *n* secuestro *m*, rapto *m*.

kidney ['kidni] *n* riñón *m*; (*fig*) índole *f*, especie *f*.

kidney machine ['kidni͵ʃiːn] *n* aparato *m* de riñón artificial.

kill [kil] **1** *vt* **(a)** matar; dar muerte a; asesinar; destruir; **he was —ed by savages** le mataron los salvajes, fue muerto por los salvajes; **thou shalt not —** no matarás; **to — off** matar, exterminar.

(b) (*fig*) *rumour, threat* acabar con; *feeling, hope etc* destruir; *flavour, taste* quitar; (*Parl*) *bill* ahogar; **this heat is —ing me** este calor acabará conmigo; **the pace is —ing him** se está matando trabajando (*etc*) a tal ritmo.

(c) (*fig*) hacer morir de risa; hacer una impresión irresistible en; **this will — you** vas a morir de risa; **to be dressed to —** ir vestida con muchísima elegancia.

2 *vr*: **to — oneself** matarse; suicidarse; **to — oneself with work** matarse trabajando.

3 *n* (*Hunting*) pieza *f*, animal *m* matado, (*collectively*) piezas *fpl*, animales *mpl* matados; (*act of —ing*) matanza *f*; **they gathered round for the —** se reunieron para dar el golpe final, cercaron el animal (*etc*) para acabar con él.

killer ['kilə*] *n* matador *m*, ora *f*; (*murderer*) asesino *m*; **diphtheria used to be a —** antes la difteria mataba a sus víctimas.

killer whale ['kiləweil] *n* orca *f*.

killing ['kiliŋ] **1** *adj disease etc* que mata, mortal; *burden* abrumador; (*ravishing*) irresistible; (*funny*) divertidísimo, muy cómico; **it was —** fue para morirse de risa.

2 *n* matanza *f*; (*murder*) asesinato *m*; (*Fin*) éxito *m* financiero; **to make a —** tener un gran éxito financiero.

killingly ['kiliŋli] *adv*: **— funny** divertidísimo; **it was — funny** fue para morirse de risa.

killjoy ['kildʒɔi] *n* aguafiestas *mf*.

kiln [kiln] *n* horno *m*.

kilo ['kiːləu] *n* kilo *m*.

kilocycle ['kiləu͵saikl] *n* kilociclo *m*.

kilogramme, (*US*) **—gram** ['kiləugræm] *n* kilo-(gramo) *m*.

kilolitre, (*US*) **—liter** ['kiləu͵liːtə*] *n* kilolitro *m*.

kilometre, (*US*) **—meter** ['kiləumiːtə*] *n* kilómetro *m*.

kilometric [͵kiləu'metrik] *adj* kilométrico.

kilowatt ['kiləuwɔt] *n* kilovatio *m*.

kilowatt-hours ['kiləuwɔt͵auəz] *npl* kilovatios-hora *mpl*.

kilt [kilt] *n* falda *f*, tonelete *m* (*de los escoceses*).

kimono [ki'məunəu] *n* quimono *m*.

kin [kin] *n* familia *f*, parientes *mpl*, parentela *f*; **next of —** parientes *mpl* más próximos.

kind [kaind] **1** *adj* **(a)** *person* bondadoso, amable, bueno; **you're very —, you're too —** es Vd muy amable; **to be — to someone** ser amable con uno; **please be so — as to + *infin*** tenga la bondad de + *infin*; **would you be so — as to + *infin*?** ¿me hace el favor de + *infin*?; **he was — enough to + *infin*** tuvo la amabilidad de + *infin*; **they were not — to the play in New York** trataron la obra algo duramente en Nueva York; **we must be — to animals** hay que tratar bien los animales.

(b) *act* bueno; *climate* bueno, benigno; *criticism, remark, word* elogioso, comprensivo, favorable; *tone of voice* cariñoso, tierno; *treatment* bueno, blando; **it's very — of you** es Vd muy amable; **that wasn't very — of you** eso me ha parecido algo injusto, en eso fuiste demasiado duro.

2 *n* **(a)** clase *f*, género *m*, especie *f*; **but not that —** pero no de ese tipo, pero no como eso; **he's the — who'll cheat you** él es de los que te engañarán; **to pay in —** pagar en especie, (*fig*) pagar en la misma moneda.

(b) (*a —of*) **a — of** uno a modo de; **he's a — of agent** es algo así como un agente; **I'm not that — of girl** yo no soy de ésas; **he's not that — of person** no es capaz de hacer eso, no es de los que hacen tales cosas; **I felt a — of pity** sentí algo parecido a la compasión, en cierto modo sentí compasión; **and all that — of thing** y otras cosas por el estilo; **that's the — of thing I mean** eso es precisamente lo que quiero decir; **I don't like that — of talk** no me gusta ese modo de hablar; **what — of book?** ¿qué clase de libro?; **what — of man is he?** ¿qué clase de hombre es?

(c) (*of a —*) **three of a —** tres de la misma especie; **books of all —s** toda clase de libros, libros de toda clase; **it's tea of a —** es té pero bastante inferior, es lo que apenas se puede llamar té; **perfect of its —** perfecto en su línea; **something of the —** algo por el estilo; **nothing of the —!** ¡nada de eso!, ¡ni hablar!

3 (*as adv*: *fam*) **it's — of awkward** es bastante difícil; **it's — of blue** es más bien azul; **it's — of finished** está más o menos terminado; **aren't you pleased?** — **of** ¿no te alegras? en cierto modo.

kindergarten ['kində͵gɑːtn] *n* jardín *m* de la infancia.

kind-hearted ['kaind'hɑːtid] *adj* bondadoso, de buen corazón.

kind-heartedness ['kaind'hɑːtidnis] *n* bondad *f*.

kindle ['kindl] **1** *vt* encender (*also fig*). **2** *vi* encenderse (*also fig*).

kindliness ['kaindlinis] *n* bondad *f*, benevolencia *f*.

kindling ['kindliŋ] *n* leña *f* menuda, astillas *fpl*.

kindly ['kaindli] **1** *adj* bondadoso, benévolo; *climate etc* bueno, benigno; *remark etc* elogioso, comprensivo, favorable; *tone of voice* cariñoso, tierno; *treatment* bueno, blando.

2 *adv* **(a)** bondadosamente, amablemente; **he very — helped me** muy amablemente me ayudó; **to take — to something** aceptar algo de buen grado; **he would take it — if you did so** lo agradecería que Vd lo hiciese.

(b) **— pass the salt** por favor, pase la sal; **— wait a moment** haga el favor de esperar un momento; **"— pay here"** "se ruega pagar aquí".

kindness ['kaindnis] *n* **(a)** bondad *f*, amabilidad *f*, benevolencia *f*; atención *f*, consideración *f*; **they treated him with every —** le trataron con todo género de consideraciones; **to show — to someone** mostrarse bondadoso con uno.

(b) (*a —*) favor *m*; **to do someone a —** hacer un favor a uno; **it would be a — to tell him** decírselo sería un favor.

kindred ['kindrid] **1** *adj* (*related by blood*) emparentado; (*fig*) afín, semejante, análogo; **— spirits** espíritus *mpl* afines.

2 *n* (*relationship*) parentesco *m*; (*relations*) familia *f*, parientes *mpl*.

kinetic [ki'netik] *adj* cinético.

king [kiŋ] *n* rey *m*, (*fig, Chess, Cards*) rey *m*; (*Draughts*) dama *f*; **an oil —** un magnate del petróleo; **the — and queen** los reyes; **the Three K—s** los Reyes, los Reyes Magos; **— of arms** rey *m* de armas; **to live like a —** vivir a cuerpo de rey.

kingcup ['kiŋkʌp] *n* botón *m* de oro.

kingdom ['kiŋdəm] *n* reino *m*; **animal —** reino *m* animal; **plant —** reino *m* vegetal; **till K— come** hasta el Día del Juicio.

kingfisher ['kiŋfiʃə*] *n* martín *m* pescador.

kingly ['kiŋli] *adj* real, regio; digno de un rey.

kingpin ['kiŋpin] *n* (*Tech*) perno *m* real, perno *m* pinzote; (*fig*) piedra *f* angular, cosa *f* fundamental, persona *f* principal.

kingship ['kiŋʃip] *n* dignidad *f* real, monarquía *f*; **they offered him the —** le ofrecieron el trono.

king-size ['kiŋsaiz] *adj* de tamaño extra.

kink [kiŋk] **1** *n* (*in rope etc*) coca *f*, enroscadura *f*; (*in hair*) rizo *m*; (*in paper etc*) arruga *f*, pliegue *m*; (*fig*) peculiaridad *f*, manía *f*, (*sexual*) perversión *f*.

2 *vi* formar cocas (*etc*).

kinky ['kiŋki] *adj* enroscado; rizado, ensortijado; arrugado; (*fig*) peculiar; pervertido.

kinsfolk ['kinzfəuk] *npl* familia *f*, parientes *mpl*.

kinship ['kinʃip] *n* (*by blood*) parentesco *m*; (*fig*) afinidad *f*, relación *f*.

kinsman ['kinzmən] *n*, *pl* **—men** [mən] pariente *m*.

kinswoman ['kinz͵wumən] *n*, *pl* **—women** [͵wimin] parienta *f*.

kiosk ['kiːɔsk] *n* quiosco *m*; (*Tel*) cabina *f*.

kip [kip] (*sl*) **1** *n* (*lodging*) alojamiento *m*; (*bed*) cama *f*; (*sleep*) sueño *m*; **to have a —** dormir un rato.

2 *vi* dormir; **to — down** echarse a dormir.

kipper ['kipə*] *n* arenque *m* ahumado.

kirk [kəːk] *n* (*Scot*) iglesia *f*; **the K—** la Iglesia (Presbiteriana) de Escocia.

kiss [kis] **1** *n* beso *m*; (*light touch*) roce *m*; **to blow**

someone a — tirar un beso a uno, dar un beso volado a uno.
  2 *vt* besar.
  3 *vi:* **they —ed** se besaron, se dieron un beso; **to — and be friends** hacer las paces.

kisser ['kisə*] *n* (*sl*) cara *f*.

kissproof ['kispru:f] *adj* indeleble.

Kit [kit] *mf nombre cariñoso de* **Catherine** *etc,* **Christopher.**

kit [kit] **1** *n* (*gear in general*) avíos *mpl*; (*baggage*) equipaje *m*; (*tools*) herramientas *fpl*, herramental *m*; (*first-aid*) botiquín *m*; (*Mil*) equipo *m*.
  2 *vt:* **to — someone out** equipar a uno (*with* de).

kitbag ['kitbæg] *n* saco *m* de viaje; (*Mil*) saco *m*.

kitchen ['kitʃin] *n* cocina *f*.

kitchenette [,kitʃi'net] *n* cocina *f* pequeña.

kitchen garden ['kitʃin'gɑːdn] *n* huerto *m*.

kitchen range ['kitʃin'reindʒ] *n* cocina *f* económica, fogón *m*.

kitchen sink ['kitʃin'siŋk] **1** *n* fregadero *m*. **2** *attr* **play** *etc* ultrarrealista, que tiene por tema la vida de los bajos fondos.

kitchenware ['kitʃinweə*] *n* batería *f* de cocina.

kite [kait] *n* (*Orn*) milano *m* real; (*toy*) cometa *f*; **to fly a —** (*fig*) lanzar una idea para sondear la opinión.

kith [kiθ] *n:* **— and kin** parientes *mpl* y amigos.

kitten ['kitn] *n* gatito *m*, a *f*.

kittenish ['kitəniʃ] *adj* (*fig*) picaruelo, coquetón.

kittiwake ['kitiweik] *n* gaviota *f* tridáctila, gavina *f*.

Kitty ['kiti] *f nombre cariñoso de* **Catherine** *etc.*

kitty ['kiti] *n* (*collection*) colecta *f*, fondo *m*; (*Cards*) puesta *f*, bote *m*, polla *f*; **how much have we in the —?** ¿cuánto tenemos en el haber?; **there's nothing in the —** no tenemos dinero alguno.

kiwi ['ki:wi:] *n* kiwi *m*.

klaxon ['klæksn] *n* claxon *m*.

kleptomania [,kleptəu'meiniə] *n* cleptomanía *f*.

kleptomaniac [,kleptəu'meiniæk] *n* cleptómano *m*, a *f*.

knack [næk] *n* tino *m*; maña *f*, destreza *f*; truco *m*; **it's just a —** es un truco que se aprende; **to get the — of doing something** aprender el modo de hacer algo; **to have the — of doing something** tener el don de hacer algo; **he has a happy — of saying the right thing** siempre acierta al escoger la palabra exacta.

knacker ['nækə*] *n* matarife *m* de caballos.

knapsack ['næpsæk] *n* mochila *f*.

knave [neiv] *n* bellaco *m*, bribón *m*; (*Cards*) valet *m*, (*in Spanish pack*) sota *f*.

knavery ['neivəri] *n* bellaquería *f*.

knavish ['neiviʃ] *adj* bellaco, bribón, ruin.

knead [ni:d] *vt* amasar, sobar; (*fig*) formar.

knee [ni:] **1** *n* rodilla *f*; **on bended —, on one's —s** de rodillas; **to bow the —** to humillarse ante, someterse a; **to bring someone to his —s** someter a uno, humillar a uno; **to fall on one's —s, to go down on one's —s** arrodillarse, caer de rodillas; **to go down on one's —s to someone** implorar a uno de rodillas.
  2 *vt* dar un rodillazo a.

knee breeches ['ni:,britʃiz] *npl* calzón *m* corto.

kneecap ['ni:kæp] *n* rótula *f*, choquezuela *f*.

knee-deep ['ni:'di:p] *adv:* **to be — in** estar metido hasta las rodillas en; **the place was — in paper** (*fig*) había montones de papeles por todos lados; **to go into the water —** avanzar hasta que el agua llegue a las rodillas.

knee-high ['ni:'hai] **1** *adv* hasta las rodillas; al nivel de las rodillas. **2** *adj:* **— grass** hierba *f* que crece hasta la altura de las rodillas.

knee joint ['ni:dʒɔint] *n* articulación *f* de la rodilla.

kneel [ni:l] (*irr: pret and ptp* **knelt**) *vi* (a) (*act*) arrodillarse, ponerse de rodillas, hincarse de rodillas (*also* **to — down**); **to — to** (*fig*) hincar la rodilla ante.
  (b) (*state*) estar de rodillas.

kneepad ['ni:pæd] *n* rodillera *f*.

knell [nel] *n* toque *m* de difuntos, doble *m*; **it sounded the — of the empire** anunció el fin del imperio, presagió el derrumbamiento del imperio.

knelt [nelt] *pret and ptp of* **kneel.**

knew [nju:] *pret of* **know.**

knickerbockers ['nikəbɔkəz] *npl* pantalones *mpl* cortos.

knickers ['nikəz] *npl* bragas *fpl*; (*old-fashioned*) pantalones *mpl* de señora.

knick-knack ['niknæk] *n* chuchería *f*, bujería *f*, baratija *f*.

knife [naif] **1** *n*, *pl* **knives** [naivz] cuchillo *m*; (*folding*) navaja *f*; (*Mech*) cuchilla *f*; **— and fork** (*at table*) cubierto *m*; **war to the —** guerra *f* a muerte; **to have one's — into someone** tener inquina a uno; **before you can say —** en un decir Jesús.
  2 *vt* acuchillar.

knife box ['naifbɔks] *n* portacubiertos *m*.

knife edge ['naifedʒ] *n* filo *m* (de cuchillo); **to be balanced on a —** (*fig*) estar pendiente de un hilo.

knife-grinder ['naif,graində*] *n* amolador *m*, afilador *m*.

knight [nait] **1** *n* caballero *m*; (*Chess*) caballo *m*. **2** *vt* (*Hist*) armar caballero; (*modern British*) dar el título de **Sir** a.

knight-errant ['nait'erənt] *n* caballero *m* andante.

knight-errantry ['nait'erəntri] *n* caballería *f* andante.

knighthood ['naithud] *n* (*order*) caballería *f*; (*title*) título *m* de caballero, (*modern British*) título *m* de **Sir.**

knightly ['naitli] *adj* caballeroso, caballeresco.

knit [nit] **1** *vt* **dress** hacer a punto de aguja; **brows** fruncir; **to — together** (*fig*) juntar, unir.
  2 *vi* hacer calceta, hacer media, hacer punto; (*bone*) soldarse; (*fig*) unirse.

knitted ['nitid] *adj* de punto; **— goods** géneros *mpl* de punto.

knitting ['nitiŋ] *n* labor *f* de punto; **plain —** punto *m* de media; **she was doing her —** estaba haciendo calceta.

knitting machine ['nitiŋmə,ʃi:n] *n* máquina *f* de tricotar, tricotosa *f*.

knitting needle ['nitiŋ,ni:dl] *n* aguja *f* de hacer calceta.

knitwear ['nitweə*] *n* géneros *mpl* de punto.

knives [naivz] *npl* of **knife.**

knob [nɔb] *n* (*natural*) protuberancia *f*, bulto *m*; (*Mech etc*) botón *m*; (*of door*) tirador *m*; (*of stick*) puño *m*; **— of sugar** terrón *m* de azúcar.

knobbly ['nɔbli] *adj*, **knobby** [nɔbi] *adj* nudoso.

knock [nɔk] **1** *n* (a) (*blow*) golpe *m*; (*in collision*) choque *m*; (*on door*) llamada *f*; (*Aut*) golpeo *m*; **there was a — on the door** se llamó a la puerta; **he got a — on the head** recibió un golpe en la cabeza; **to get the —** (*sl*) mosquearse, ofenderse; perder la paciencia, ponerse negro.
  (b) (*fig*) golpe *m*; **the team took a hard — yesterday** ayer el equipo recibió un rudo golpe; **he can take plenty of hard —s** sabe aguantar todos los reveses.
  2 *vt* (a) (*strike*) golpear; (*collide with*) chocar contra; (*fam*) criticar, denigrar, hablar mal de; (*Comm*) hacer publicidad en contra de; **to — a hole in something** abrir a la fuerza un agujero en algo; **to — the bottom out of a box** desfondar una caja; **to — the smile off someone's face** hacer que uno deje de sonreír a fuerza de golpes; **to — someone on the head** golpear a uno en la cabeza; **to — one's head on a beam** dar con la cabeza contra una viga; **to — something to the floor** tirar algo violentamente al suelo.
  (b) **to — someone about** pegar a uno, maltratar a uno, (*beat up*) aporrear a uno; **the place was badly —ed about** el lugar sufrió grandes estragos; **the car was rather —ed about** el coche sufrió algunos desperfectos; **to — back** (*sl*) *drink* beberse (de un trago); **he can certainly — them back** él sí sabe beber; **to — down** *building* derribar, demoler, echar por tierra; *person* derribar; *pedestrian* atropellar; *argument* destruir; *price* rebajar; **to — something down to someone for £5** rematar algo a uno en 5 libras; **it was —ed down to the highest bidder** se adjudicó al mejor postor; **to — in** hacer entrar a golpes; *nail* clavar; **to — off** quitar (de un golpe); (*cause to fall*) hacer caer; (*steal, sl*) birlar, limpiar; (*arrest, sl*) detener; *task* ejecutar prontamente, despachar; *work* terminar, suspender; **to — £2 off the price** rebajar el precio en 2 libras, descontar 2 libras del precio; **to — 3 minutes off the record** mejorar la marca en 3 minutos; **so we had to — it off** (*sl*) así que tuvimos que dejarlo; **— it off, will you?** (*sl*) ¡déjalo, por Dios!; **to — out** *person* (*in accident etc*) dejar sin sentido, hacer perder el conocimiento; (*Boxing*) poner fuera de combate, dejar K.O.; *teeth* romper; (*remove*) suprimir, quitar; **to — over** volcar; *pedestrian* atropellar; **to — together** construir (*or* componer *etc*) de prisa; **to — up** *building* construir de prisa, construir toscamente; (*awaken*) llamar, despertar; (*tire*) agotar; (*make pregnant, sl*) dejar encinta; **the work —ed him up** el trabajo le agotó; **he was —ed up for a month** el agotamiento le duró un mes.
  3 *vi* golpear; (*at door*) llamar a la puerta; (*Aut*) golpear, martillear; **he's —ing on 50** (*fam*) va para los 50; **to — about** vagabundear, andar vagando, rodar; **I've —ed about a bit** he visto mucho mundo; **he's —ing about somewhere** estará por ahí; **he —s about with some odd friends** tiene unas amistades rarísimas; **to — against** chocar contra, dar contra;

to — **into** chocar contra; *person* topar; **to — off** suspender el trabajo, terminar, salir del trabajo; **he —s off at 5** sale del trabajo a las 5; **to — up** (*Tennis*) pelotear; **to — up against** chocar contra; *person* topar.

knockabout ['nɔkəbaut] *adj* bullicioso, tumultuoso, confuso; **— comedy** farsa *f* bulliciosa, (*fig*) payasadas *fpl*.

knockdown ['nɔkdaun] *adj*: **— price** precio *m* obsequio.

knocker ['nɔkə*] *n* aldaba *f*; (*fam*) detractor *m*, ora *f*, crítico *m*, a *f*.

knocker-up ['nɔkə'rʌp] *n* despertador *m*.

knocking ['nɔkiŋ] **1** *adj*: **— copy** anuncio *m* destinado a denigrar el producto de otro. **2** *n* golpes *mpl*, golpeo *m*; (*at door*) llamada *f*; (*Aut*) golpeo *m*.

knock-kneed ['nɔk'ni:d] *adj* patizambo; (*fig*) débil, irresoluto.

knockout ['nɔkaut] **1** *adj*: **— blow** golpe *m* aplastante, (*Boxing*) K.O. *m*; **— competition** concurso *m* eliminatorio, eliminatoria *f*.

2 *n* (*Boxing*) knock-out *m*, K.O. *m*; (*competition*) concurso *m* eliminatorio, eliminatoria *f*; **a —** (*sl*) ¡es la monda!; **she's a —** (*sl*) es una chica estupenda; **it was a real —** (*sl*) fue una noticia (*etc*) sorprendente, la noticia nos pasmó.

knock-up ['nɔkʌp] *n* (*Tennis*) peloteo *m*.

knoll [nəul] *n* otero *m*, montículo *m*.

knot [nɔt] **1** *n* nudo *m* (*also Naut, in wood*); (*bow*) lazo *m*; (*of people*) grupo *m*, corrillo *m*; **Gordian —** nudo *m* gordiano; **to get tied up in —s** anudarse, enmarañarse, (*fig*) armarse un lío, crearse confusiones; **to tie a —** hacer un nudo.

2 *vt* anudar, atar; **get —ted!** (*sl*) ¡fastídiate!

3 *vi* anudarse.

knot-hole ['nɔthəul] *n* agujero *m* (que deja un nudo en la madera).

knotty ['nɔti] *adj* nudoso; (*fig*) difícil, complicado, espinoso.

knout [naut] *n* knut *m*.

know [nəu] (*irr: pret* **knew**, *ptp* **known**) **1** *vti* (a) (*general sense*) *fact etc* saber; **to — Japanese** saber japonés; **I —!** ¡ya sé!; **who —s?** ¿quién sabe?; **what do you —?** (*fam*) ¿qué hay de nuevo?; **well, what do you —!** ¡caramba!, ¡cosa más rara!; **how should I —?** ¿yo qué sé?; **to — what's what** saber cuántas son cinco; **it's not easy, you —** mire Vd, esto no es fácil; **there were 7% "don't knows"** un 7 por cien se abstuvo de contestar, un 7 por cien no quisieron opinar; **to — about, to — of** saber de, tener conocimiento de; **I didn't — about that** no sabía nada de eso, lo ignoraba; **oh, I don't — about that** pues eso no es cierto; ¡hombre, no tanto!; **she —s about cats** ella entiende de gatos; **did you — about John?** ¿has oído lo de Juan?; **I don't — about you!** (*despairing*) ¿qué le vamos a hacer?; **to — something** (llegar a) saber algo, enterarse de algo; **we'll let you —** le avisaremos; **why didn't you let me —?** ¿por qué no me avisó Vd?; **afterwards they just don't want to —** después "si te vi no me acuerdo".

(b) (*be acquainted with*) *person, book, subject etc* conocer; **do you — him?** ¿le conoces?; **do you — Spain?** ¿conoces España?; **to come to — someone, to get to — someone** (llegar a) conocer a uno.

(c) **to — how to** + *infin* saber + *infin*.

(d) (*recognize*) conocer, reconocer; **to — someone by sight** conocer a uno de vista; **to — someone by (or from) his walk** conocer a uno por su modo de andar; **I knew him at once** le reconocí en seguida.

(e) **don't I — it!** ¡y tú que me lo dices!; **not if I — it** no será, si puedo evitarlo; *see also* **known**.

2 *n*: **to be in the —** estar enterado, estar en el secreto.

knowable ['nəuəbl] *adj* conocible.

know-all ['nəuɔ:l] *n* sabelotodo *mf*.

know-how ['nəuhau] *n* habilidad *f*, destreza *f*; experiencia *f*; (*expertise*) pericia *f*; **a certain amount of technical —** algunos conocimientos *mpl* técnicos.

knowing ['nəuiŋ] **1** *adj* (*sharp*) astuto, avispado; *look etc* de complicidad, malicioso; **worth —** digno de saberse.

2 *n*: **there's no —** no hay modo de saberlo; **there's no — what he'll do** es imposible adivinar lo que hará.

knowingly ['nəuiŋli] *adv* (*intentionally*) a sabiendas, adrede; *look etc* maliciosamente, con malicia.

know-it-all ['nəuitɔ:l] *n* (*US*) sabelotodo *mf*.

knowledge ['nɔlidʒ] *n* (*knowing*) conocimiento *m*; (*person's range of information*) conocimientos *mpl*, saber *m*; (*learning*) erudición *f*, ciencia *f*; **the advance of —** el progreso de la ciencia; **his — will die with him** morirá su erudición con él; **to my —** según mi leal entender y saber, que yo sepa; **not to my —** que yo sepa; **without my —** sin saberlo yo; **that is common —** eso lo sabe todo el mundo; **his failure is common —** su fracaso es ya del dominio público; **it is common —** se sabe perfectamente que, es notorio que; **it has come to my — that** he llegado a saber que; **to have a — of Welsh** saber algo de galés; **to have a working —** of dominar los principios esenciales de; **to have a thorough — of** conocer a fondo.

knowledgeable ['nɔlidʒəbl] *adj person* entendido, erudito (*about* en); *remark* erudito.

known [nəun] **1** *ptp of* **know**; **X, — as Y** X, conocido por el nombre de Y; **a product — everywhere** un producto conocido en todas partes; **he is — everywhere** se le conoce en todas partes; **to become —** (*fact*) llegar a saberse, (*person*) llegar a ser conocido; **it became — that** se supo que; **to make oneself —** darse a conocer (*to* a); **to make something — to someone** anunciar algo a uno, hacer que uno se entere de algo; **to make one's wishes —** hacer que se sepa lo que uno desea.

2 *adj*: **a — thief** un ladrón conocido; **a — expert** un experto reconocido como tal; **the — facts** los hechos establecidos, los hechos ciertos.

knuckle ['nʌkl] **1** *n* nudillo *m*; **to rap someone's —s, to rap someone over the —s** echar un rapapolvo a uno.

2 *vi*: **to — down to something** ponerse a hacer algo con ahinco, dedicarse a algo en serio; **to — under** someterse.

knuckleduster ['nʌkl,dʌstə*] *n* puño *m* de hierro.

knurl [nə:l] **1** *n* nudo *m*, protuberancia *f*; (*of coin*) moleteado *m*. **2** *vt coin* moletear.

knurled [nə:ld] *adj* nudoso; *coin* moleteado.

koala [kəu'ɑ:lə] *n* coala *f*.

Koran [kɔ'rɑ:n] *n* Corán *m*, Alcorán *m*.

Koranic [kɔ'rænik] *adj* coránico, alcoránico.

Korea [kə'riə] Corea *f*.

Korean [kə'riən] **1** *adj* coreano. **2** *n* coreano *m*, a *f*.

kosher ['kəuʃə*] *adj* autorizado por la ley judía.

kowtow ['kau'tau] *vi* (*bow*) saludar humildemente; **to — to someone** humillarse ante uno.

kudos ['kju:dɔs] *n* gloria *f*, mérito *m*; **he got all the — for it** se atribuyó todo el mérito; **there's no — in it for us** esto no aumentará nuestro prestigio, esto no nos dará más renombre.

L

lab [læb] *n* (*fam*) *see* **laboratory**.
label ['leibl] **1** *n* etiqueta *f*, rótulo *m*, marbete *m*; (*on specimen etc*) letrero *m*; (*on book*) tejuelo *m*; (*fig*) calificación *f*, designación *f*, descripción *f*, clasificación *f*.
2 *vt* (**a**) poner etiqueta a; rotular, poner un letrero a; **it is not clearly** —**led** la etiqueta no es legible, no hay etiqueta (*etc*) que lo describa claramente; **every case must be** —**led** cada maleta ha de llevar una etiqueta.
(**b**) (*fig*) calificar (*as* de), designar (*as* como), describir (*as* como); **to** — **someone as** (*fig*) tachar a uno de; **he got himself** —**led a troublemaker** se hizo una reputación de turbulento.
labial ['leibiəl] **1** *adj* labial. **2** *n* labial *f*.
laboratory [lə'bɔrətəri] *n* laboratorio *m*.
Labor Day ['leibədei] *n* (*US*) Día *m* del Trabajo (*primer lunes de setiembre*).
laborious [lə'bɔːriəs] *adj* penoso; difícil, pesado.
laboriously [lə'bɔːriəsli] *adv* penosamente, con dificultad.
labour, (*US*) **labor** ['leibə*] **1** *n* (**a**) (*work in general*) trabajo *m*; **Ministry of L**— Ministerio *m* de Trabajo.
(**b**) (*task*) trabajo *m*, labor *f*, faena *f*, tarea *f*; **a** — **of love** una tarea muy grata, un trabajo agradable; —**s of Hercules** trabajos *mpl* de Hércules.
(**c**) (*toil*) pena *f*, fatiga *f*, esfuerzo *m*; **after much** — tras grandes esfuerzos.
(**d**) (*Law*) **hard** — trabajos *mpl* forzados; **5 years' hard** — 5 años de trabajos forzados.
(**e**) (*person*) obreros *mpl*, mano *f* de obra; (*as class*) clase *f* obrera; **we are short of** — nos falta mano de obra; **capital and** — el capitalismo y los obreros.
(**f**) (*Pol*) **L**— laborismo *m*, Partido *m* Laborista.
(**g**) (*Med*) parto *m*, dolores *mpl* del parto; **to be in** — estar de parto.
2 *attr* (**a**) de trabajo; **camp** de trabajo; *conflict, troubles* laboral; *exchange* del trabajo; *legislation, union* obrero, industrial.
(**b**) (*Pol*) *party* laborista; *movement* obrero.
3 *vt point etc* insistir en, machacar en, desarrollar con nimiedad; **I won't** — **the point** me abstengo de subrayar esto, no hace falta insistir en esto.
4 *vi* (**a**) (*work*) trabajar (*at* en); **to** — **in vain** trabajar de balde; **to** — **to do something** afanarse por hacer algo; **to** — **under a delusion** estar equivocado; **to** — **under difficulties** trabajar en condiciones difíciles.
(**b**) (*move etc*) moverse penosamente, avanzar con dificultad; **the engine is** —**ing** el motor no funciona bien.
laboured, (*US*) **labored** ['leibəd] *adj breathing* fatigoso; *movement* torpe, lento, penoso; *style* pesado, premioso.
labourer, (*US*) **laborer** ['leibərə*] *n* (*on roads etc*) peón *m*; (*farm* —) labriego *m*, bracero *m*, peón *m*; (*day* —) jornalero *m*; **bricklayer's** — peón *m* de albañil.
labouring, (*US*) **laboring** ['leibəriŋ] *adj class* obrero.
labourite, (*US*) **laborite** ['leibərait] *n* (*pej*) laborista *mf*.
labour-saving, (*US*) **labor-saving** ['leibə,seiviŋ] *adj* que ahorra trabajo.
laburnum [lə'bəːnəm] *n* lluvia *f* de oro, codeso *m*.
labyrinth ['læbərinθ] *n* laberinto *m*.
labyrinthine [,læbə'rinθain] *adj* laberíntico.
lac [læk] *n* laca *f*.
lace [leis] **1** *n* (*open fabric*) encaje *m*, (*as trimming*) puntilla *f*; (*of shoe, corset*) cordón *m*; (*of gold, silver*) galón *m*.
2 *vt* (*Sew*) guarnecer con encajes (*etc*); *shoe etc* atar, atar el cordón de (*also* **to** — **up**); *drink* echar licor a; **a drink** —**d with brandy** una bebida reforzada con coñac.
3 *vi*: **to** — **into someone** (*sl*) dar una paliza a uno.
lacerate ['læsəreit] *vt* lacerar; *feelings etc* herir.
laceration [,læsə'reiʃən] *n* laceración *f*.
lachrymose ['lækriməus] *adj* lacrimoso, lloroso.
lack [læk] **1** *n* falta *f*, ausencia *f*, carencia *f*; escasez *f*; **for** — **of, through** — **of** por falta de; **there is a grave** — **of water** nos hace muchísima falta el agua; **there is no** — **of money** no es que falte dinero.
2 *vt* no tener; carecer de, necesitar; **we** — **time to do it** nos falta tiempo para hacerlo; **we're** —**ing 3 players to make up a team** nos hacen falta 3 jugadores para completar el equipo; **he does not** — **talent** no carece de aptitud, es cierto que tiene aptitud; **what is it that you** —? ¿qué es lo que necesitas?; **he** —**s confidence** no tiene confianza en sí mismo.
3 *vi* (**a**) **to be** —**ing** faltar, estar ausente, no haber; **but money is** —**ing** pero no hay dinero, pero falta el dinero; **nothing was** —**ing to make the play succeed** no faltaba nada para que la obra obtuviera un éxito; **where decency is** —**ing** donde falta la decencia.
(**b**) **he is** —**ing in confidence** no tiene confianza en sí mismo, le falta confianza en sí mismo; **it's not that he's** —**ing in good qualities** no es que le falten buenas cualidades.
lackadaisical [,lækə'deizikəl] *adj* lánguido, indiferente; (*dreamy*) ensimismado, despistado, distraído; (*slow*) perezoso, tardo; (*careless*) descuidado, informal.
lackey ['læki] *n* lacayo *m*; (*fig*) secuaz *m* servil.
lacking ['lækiŋ] *as prep* sin, no teniendo, en ausencia de; desprovisto de.
lacklustre, (*US*) **lackluster** ['læk,lʌstə*] *adj surface* deslustrado, deslucido; *style etc* inexpresivo; *eyes* apagado; *person* pesado, soso.
laconic [lə'kɔnik] *adj* lacónico.
laconically [lə'kɔnikəli] *adv* lacónicamente.
lacquer ['lækə*] **1** *n* laca *f*, maque *m*, pintura *f* al duco. **2** *vt* laquear, maquear, pintar al duco.
lacquered ['lækəd] *adj* barnizado con laca, laqueado, pintado al duco.
lacrosse [lə'krɔs] *n* lacrosse *f*.
lactate ['lækteit] *vi* lactar.
lactation [læk'teiʃən] *n* lactancia *f*.
lacteal ['læktiəl] *adj* lácteo.
lactic ['læktik] *adj* láctico.
lactose ['læktəus] *n* lactosa *f*.
lacuna [lə'kjuːnə] *n*, *pl* **lacunae** [lə'kjuːniː] laguna *f*.
lacustrine [lə'kʌstrain] *adj* lacustre.
lacy ['leisi] *adj* (*of lace*) de encaje; (*like lace*) parecido a encaje; (*fig*) transparente, diáfano.
lad [læd] *n* muchacho *m*, chico *m*; (*country* —) mozo *m*, zagal *m*; (*in stable etc*) mozo *m*; **young** — muchacho *m*, mozalbete *m*; **when I was a** — cuando yo era chaval; **he's only a** — es muy joven; **don't do that,** —! ¡no hagas eso, joven!; **come on,** —**s!** ¡vamos, muchachos!; **all together,** —**s!** ¡todos juntos, muchachos!; **he's a bit of a** — es un chico poco formal; es un tipo muy divertido; **he's a bit of a** — **with the girls** le da guerra a las chicas, se bromea mucho con las chicas.
ladder ['lædə*] **1** *n* (**a**) escalera *f* (de mano), escala *f*; (*in stocking*) carrera *f*; **folding** — escala *f* plegable; **rope** — escala *f* de cuerda.
(**b**) (*fig*) camino *m*, escalón *m* (*to* de); **social** — escala *f* social; **it's a first step up the** — es el primer paso hacia el éxito; **to be at the top of the** — estar en la cumbre de su profesión (*etc*), ocupar el rango más alto.
2 *vt stocking* hacer una carrera en.
3 *vi* (*stocking*) hacerse una carrera, desmallarse.

ladderproof ['lædəpru:f] *adj stocking* indesmallable.
laddie ['lædi] *n (fam)* = **lad.**
lade [leid] *(irr: pret* **laded,** *ptp* **laden) 1** *vt* cargar *(with* de). **2** *vi* tomar cargamento.
laden ['leidn] *ptp of* **lade;** — **with** cargado de.
la-di-da ['lɑ:di'dɑ:] *(fam)* **1** *adj* afectado, repipi *(fam).*
2 *adv* talk *etc* de manera afectada, con afectación.
lading ['leidiŋ] *n* cargamento *m,* flete *m.*
ladle ['leidl] **1** *n* cucharón *m,* cazo *m.* **2** *vt (also to* — **out)** servir *(or* sacar *etc)* con cucharón; *(fig)* repartir generosamente, distribuir a manos llenas.
ladleful ['leidlful] *n* cucharón *m,* contenido *m* de un cucharón.
lady ['leidi] **1** *n* señora *f; (aged, distinguished, noble)* dama *f;* "**Ladies**" *(lavatory)* "Señoras"; **ladies and gentlemen;** — **of the house** señora *f* de la casa; **the minister and his** — el ministro y su esposa; **your good** — su esposa; **First L**— *(US)* primera dama *f;* **leading** — primera actriz *f;* **Our L**— Nuestra Señora *f;* **young** — señorita *f,* joven *f;* **his young** — su novia *f;* **she's no** — esa mujer no es lo que aparenta, es una mujer que tiene historia; **shall we join the ladies?** ¿pasamos a estar con las señoras?
2 *attr etc* **(a)** — **doctor** médica *f;* — **mayoress** alcaldesa *f;* —'**s cycle** bicicleta *f* de señora; **ladies' room** lavabo *m* de señoras.
(b) L— **Chapel** capilla *f* de la Virgen; **L**— **Day** día *m* de la Anunciación (25 *marzo).*
ladybird ['leidibə:d] *n, (US)* **ladybug** ['leidibʌg] *n* mariquita *f,* vaca *f* de San Antón.
lady-in-waiting ['leidiin'weitiŋ] *n* dama *f* de honor.
ladykiller ['leidi,kilə*] *n* tenorio *m,* ladrón *m* de corazones.
ladylike ['leidilaik] *adj* elegante, fino, distinguido, bien educado; *(pej)* afeminado.
lady-love ['leidilʌv] *n* amada *f.*
ladyship ['leidiʃip] *n:* **Her** —, **Your L**— Su Señoría.
lag¹ [læg] **1** *n* retraso *m.*
2 *vi (also to* — **behind)** retrasarse; *(in pace)* rezagarse, quedarse atrás; **Ruritania** —**s behind Slobodia** Ruritania anda a rastras detrás de Eslobodia, Ruritania no ha hecho tantos progresos como Eslobodia; **we** — **behind in space exploration** nos hemos retrasado en la exploración espacial, no destacamos en la exploración espacial.
lag² [læg] *vt (Tech)* revestir, recubrir, forrar *(with* de); *boiler* calorifugar.
lag³ [læg] *(sl)* **1** *n (also* **old** —) presidiario *m.* **2** *vt* encarcelar.
lager ['lɑ:gə*] *n* cerveza *f* tipo Pilsen.
laggard ['lægəd] *n (having fallen behind)* rezagado *m,* a *f; (idler)* holgazán *m,* ana *f.*
lagging ['lægiŋ] *n (Tech)* revestimiento *m,* forro *m.*
lagoon [lə'gu:n] *n* laguna *f.*
laicize ['leiisaiz] *vt* laicizar.
laid [leid] *pret and ptp of* **lay; to be** — **up** *(Med)* estar enfermo, tener que guardar cama *(with* a causa de); *(car etc)* estar fuera de circulación, estar en garaje.
lain [lein] *ptp of* **lie².**
lair [lɛə*] *n* cubil *m,* guarida *f.*
laird [lɛəd] *n (Scot)* señor *m;* terrateniente *m,* propietario *m.*
laissez-faire ['leisei'fɛə*] *n* laissez-faire *m.*
laity ['leiiti] *n* laicado *m,* legos *mpl.*
lake¹ [leik] *n (colour)* laca *f.*
lake² [leik] *n (Geog)* lago *m.*
Lake District ['leik,distrikt] País *m* de los Lagos.
lake dwelling ['leik,dweliŋ] *n* habitación *f* lacustre.
lam [læm] *(sl)* **1** *vt* pegar, dar una paliza a. **2** *vi:* **to** — **into someone** dar una paliza a uno.
lama ['lɑ:mə] *n* lama *m.*
lamb [læm] **1** *n* cordero *m,* a *f; (older)* borrego *m,* a *f; (meat)* carne *f* de cordero; **the L**— **of God** el Cordero de Dios; **my poor** —! ¡pobrecito!; **he took it like a** — recibió la noticia con la mayor tranquilidad, no se ofendió en lo más mínimo.
2 *vi* parir *(la oveja).*
lambast(e) [læm'beist] *vt* dar una paliza a; *(fig)* poner como un trapo.
lamb chop ['læm'tʃɔp] *n* chuleta *f* de cordero.
lamb-like ['læmlaik] *adj* manso como un cordero.
lambskin ['læmskin] *n* corderina *f,* piel *f* de cordero.
lamb's wool ['læmzwul] *n* lana *f* de cordero, añinos *mpl.*
lame [leim] **1** *adj* **(a)** cojo, lisiado; **to be** — *(permanently)* ser cojo, *(temporarily)* estar cojo; **to be** — **in one foot** ser cojo de un pie, cojear de un pie; **to go** — estropearse un pie, lisiarse un pie, empezar a cojear.

(b) *(fig)* **excuse** débil, poco convincente; *argument* flojo; *(Lit)* metre defectuoso, que cojea.
2 *vt* lisiar, hacer cojo; incapacitar.
lamely ['leimli] *adv* walk *etc* cojeando; *argue, say etc* sin convicción.
lameness ['leimnis] *n* cojera *f;* incapacidad *f; (fig)* falta *f* de convicción; flojedad *f.*
lament [lə'ment] **1** *n* lamento *m;* queja *f; (Lit etc)* elegía *f (for* por).
2 *vt* lamentar, lamentarse de; **to** — **someone** llorar a uno, llorar la pérdida de uno; **it is much to be** —**ed that . . .** es de lamentar que + *subj.*
3 *vi* lamentarse *(for, over* de).
lamentable ['læməntəbl] *adj* lamentable.
lamentably ['læməntəbli] *adv* lamentablemente.
lamentation [,læmən'teiʃən] *n* lamentación *f.*
laminated ['læmineitid] *adj* laminado; *glass* inastillable; — **wood** contrachapado *m.*
lamp [læmp] *n* lámpara *f;* linterna *f; (in street)* farol *m; (Aut, Rail etc)* faro *m; (bulb)* bombilla *f; (fig)* antorcha *f;* **desk** — lámpara *f* de escritorio; **standard** — lámpara *f* de pie; **rear** — faro *m* trasero.
lampblack ['læmpblæk] *n* negro *m* de humo.
lamp bracket ['læmp,brækit] *n* brazo *m* de lámpara.
lamp chimney ['læmp,tʃimni] *n,* **lamp glass** ['læmpglɑ:s] *n* tubo *m* de lámpara.
lampholder ['læmp,həuldə*] *n* portalámpara *m.*
lamplight ['læmplait] *n* luz *f* de (la) lámpara; **by** —, **in the** — a la luz de la lámpara.
lamplighter ['læmp,laitə*] *n* farolero *m.*
lampoon [læm'pu:n] **1** *n* pasquín *m,* sátira *f.* **2** *vt* pasquinar, satirizar.
lamppost ['læmppəust] *n (poste m* de) farol *m,* farola *f.*
lamprey ['læmpri] *n* lamprea *f.*
lampshade ['læmpʃeid] *n* pantalla *f* (de lámpara).
lance [lɑ:ns] **1** *n* lanza *f.* **2** *vt* alancear, herir con lanza; *(Med)* abrir con lanceta.
lance corporal ['lɑ:ns'kɔ:pərəl] *n* soldado *m* de primera.
Lancelot ['lɑ:nslət] *m* Lanzarote.
lancer ['lɑ:nsə*] *n* lancero *m;* —**s** *(dance)* lanceros *mpl.*
lancet ['lɑ:nsit] *n* lanceta *f;* — **arch** ojiva *f* aguda; — **window** ventana *f* ojival.
land [lænd] **1** *n (in most senses)* tierra *f; (nation)* país *m; (region)* tierra *f,* región *f; (soil)* tierra *f,* suelo *m; (as property)* tierras *fpl,* finca *f; (tract of* —) terreno *m; (Agr, fig)* campo *m,* agricultura *f,* eg **the drift from the** — la despoblación del campo, el éxodo rural; **he went on the** — se dedicó a la agricultura; **arable** — tierra *f* de labrantío; **cultivated** — tierras *fpl* cultivadas; **dry** — *(infertile)* tierra *f* de secano, *(not sea)* tierra *f* firme; **irrigated** — tierra *f* de regadío; **native** — patria *f;* — **of milk and honey** paraíso *m* terrenal, jauja *f;* — **of promise, promised** — tierra *f* de promisión; **back to the** —! ¡a cultivar la tierra! *(campaña de tiempos de guerra);* **by** — por tierra, por vía terrestre; **on** — en tierra; **to live off the** — *(army etc)* vivir sobre el país; **to see how the** — **lies** tantear el terreno, hacer un reconocimiento.
2 *attr breeze* de tierra; *defences, forces, route* terrestre; *law, question, reform* agrario; *see* **agent** *etc.*
3 *vt* **(a)** *person, goods, fish at port etc* desembarcar.
(b) *fish on hook* pescar, coger, sacar del agua, traer a la orilla; *(fig: obtain)* conseguir, lograr; *prize* obtener, ganar, sacar; *job* conseguir.
(c) *plane* poner en tierra.
(d) *blow* dar, asestar *(on* en).
(e) *(place)* **it** —**ed him in debt** le hizo contraer deudas; **it** —**ed him in jail** por ello acabó en la cárcel; **it** —**ed me in a mess** me puso en un apuro, me creó un lío; **I got** —**ed with the job** tuve que cargar con el cometido; **I got** —**ed with him for 2 hours** yo tuve que acompañarle durante 2 horas.
4 *vi* **(a)** *(from ship)* desembarcar *(at* en).
(b) *(Aer)* aterrizar, tomar tierra; *(on sea)* amerizar, amarar; *(on moon)* alunizar; *(of bird, insect)* posar(se).
(c) *(hit, strike)* dar en, hacer blanco en; **the hat** —**ed in my lap** el sombrero cayó sobre mis rodillas; **it** —**ed square on the target** dio de lleno en el blanco; **the bomb** —**ed on the building** la bomba hizo blanco en el edificio; **the blow** —**ed on his cheek** el golpe le dio en la mejilla; **to** — **on one's feet** caer de pies; **to** — **on one's head** caer de cabeza; **where did it** —? ¿dónde fue a parar?
(d) *(fig)* llegar; terminar; **to** — **up at Wigan** llegar (inesperadamente) a Wigan, ir a parar a Wigan; **to** — **up in a dreadful mess** terminar haciéndose un tremendo lío; **to** — **up with only £2** acabar con sólo 2 libras.
landau ['lændɔ:] *n* landó *m.*

landed ['lændid] *adj person* hacendado, que posee tierras; *property* que consiste en tierras; — **gentry** terratenientes *mpl*, pequeña aristocracia *f* rural; — **property** bienes *mpl* raíces.

landfall ['lændfɔ:l] *n* (*Naut*) aterrada *f*.

landholder ['lænd,həuldə*] *n* terrateniente *m*.

landing ['lændiŋ] *n* (**a**) (*Naut: of person*) desembarco *m*, (*of goods*) desembarque *m*.

(**b**) (*Aer*) aterrizaje *m*; (*on sea*) amerizaje *m*; (*on moon*) alunizaje *m*; (*descent*) descenso *m*; **crash** — aterrizaje *m* violento; **emergency** —, **forced** — aterrizaje *m* forzoso; **pancake** — aterrizaje *m* de panza; **hard** — aterrizaje *m* duro; **soft** — aterrizaje *m* suave.

(**c**) (*of stairs*) descanso *m*, rellano *m*.

landing craft ['lændiŋkrɑ:ft] *n* barcaza *f* (*or* lancha *f*) de desembarco.

landing gear ['lændiŋgiə*] *n* tren *m* de aterrizaje.

landing ground ['lændiŋgraund] *n* campo *m* de aterrizaje.

landing net ['lændiŋnet] *n* salabardo *m*, manga *f*, cuchara *f*.

landing run ['lændiŋrʌn] *n* recorrido *m* de aterrizaje.

landing stage ['lændiŋsteidʒ] *n* desembarcadero *m*.

landing strip ['lændiŋstrip] *n* pista *f* de aterrizaje.

landing wheels ['lændiŋwi:lz] *npl* ruedas *fpl* de aterrizaje.

landlady ['lænd,leidi] *n* (*owner*) dueña *f*; (*of boarding house*) patrona *f*; (*of flat*) propietaria *f*.

landless ['lændlis] *adj peasant etc* sin tierras, que no posee tierras.

landlocked ['lændlɒkt] *adj* cercado de tierra.

landlord ['lændlɔ:d] *n* (*of property, land*) propietario *m*, dueño *m*; (*of boarding house*) patrón *m*; (*of flat*) casero *m*; (*of inn*) posadero *m*, mesonero *m*; (*of pub*) patrón *m*.

landlubber ['lænd,lʌbə*] *n* marinero *m* de agua dulce, hombre *m* de tierra.

landmark ['lændmɑ:k] *n* (**a**) (*Naut*) marca *f*, señal *f* fija; (*boundary mark*) mojón *m*; (*high place*) punto *m* destacado; (*well-known thing*) lugar *m* muy conocido.

(**b**) **to be a** — (*fig*) hacer época, formar época, marcar un hito histórico.

landmine ['lændmain] *n* mina *f* terrestre.

landowner ['lænd,əunə*] *n* terrateniente *m*, hacendado *m*.

landscape ['lænskeip] **1** *n* paisaje *m*. **2** *vt park etc* reformar artísticamente, *terrain* convertir en parque.

landscape gardening ['lænskeip'gɑ:dniŋ] *n* arquitectura *f* de jardines.

landslide ['lændslaid] *n* corrimiento *m* de tierras, desprendimiento *m* de tierras; (*Pol*) victoria *f* electoral arrolladora; **the Liberal** — **of 1906** la victoria arrolladora de los liberales en 1906.

landslip ['lændslip] *see* **landslide**.

land tax ['lændtæks] *n* contribución *f* territorial.

landward ['lændwəd] *adj* de hacia tierra, de la parte de la tierra; **on the** — **side** en el lado de la tierra.

landward(s) ['lændwədz] *adv* hacia tierra; **to** — en la dirección de la tierra.

lane [lein] *n* (*in country*) camino *m* vecinal, vereda *f*; (*in town*) callejón *m*; (*between plantations*) vereda *f*; (*Sport*) calle *f*, banda *f*; (*Aut*) senda *f*, carril *m*; **shipping** — ruta *f* de navegación.

language ['læŋgwidʒ] *n* (*faculty of speech, mode of speech, style*) lenguaje *m*; (*national tongue*) lengua *f*, idioma *m*; **bad** — lenguaje *m* indecente; palabrotas *fpl*, tacos *mpl*; **to use bad** — ser mal hablado; **strong** — palabras *fpl* mayores; **that's no** — **to use to your mother!** ¡así no se habla a tu madre!

languid ['læŋgwid] *adj* lánguido.

languidly ['læŋgwidli] *adv* lánguidamente.

languidness ['læŋgwidnis] *n* languidez *f*.

languish ['læŋgwiʃ] *vi* languidecer; (*in prison*) pudrirse; (*pine*) consumirse (*for* por); (*amorously*) ponerse sentimental.

languishing ['læŋgwiʃiŋ] *adj* lánguido; *look, tone etc* amoroso, sentimental.

languor ['læŋgə*] *n* languidez *f*.

languorous ['læŋgərəs] *adj* lánguido.

lank [læŋk] *adj person* alto y flaco; *hair* lacio; *grass* largo.

lanky ['læŋki] *adj* larguirucho.

lanolin(e) ['lænəulin] *n* lanolina *f*.

lantern ['læntən] *n* linterna *f* (*also Archit*); (*Naut*) faro *m*, farol *m*; (*of lighthouse*) fanal *m*; **Chinese** — farolillo *m*.

lantern-jawed ['læntən'dʒɔ:d] *adj* chupado de cara.

lantern lecture ['læntən,lektʃə*] *n* conferencia *f* con proyecciones.

lantern slide ['læntənslaid] *n* diapositiva *f*.

lanyard ['lænjəd] *n* acollador *m*.

Laos [laus] Laos *m*.

Laotian ['lauʃiən] **1** *adj* laosiano. **2** *n* laosiano *m*, a *f*.

lap[1] [læp] **1** *n* (*Anat*) regazo *m*; (*knees*) rodillas *fpl*; (*skirt*) falda *f*; (*fig*) seno *m*; (*overlap*) traslapo *m*, solapa *f*; **to sit on someone's** — (*woman's*) estar sentado en el regazo (*or* en el halda) de una, (*man's*) estar sentado en las rodillas de uno; **it's in the** — **of the gods** está en manos de los dioses; **to live in the** — **of luxury** vivir en el mayor lujo, tener una vida muy regalada.

2 *vt* (*overlap*) traslapar; (*wrap*) envolver (*in* en; *also fig*); **to** — **something about** with cercar algo de, (*fig*) envolver algo en.

3 *vi* (*overlap*) traslaparse.

lap[2] [læp] (*Sport*) **1** *n* (*round*) vuelta *f*; (*stage*) etapa *f*, fase *f*; — **of honour** vuelta *f* de honor; **we're on the last** — **now** (*fig*) ésta es la última etapa, hemos vencido la cuesta ya.

2 *vt*: **to** — **someone** aventajar a uno en una vuelta entera.

3 *vi*: **to** — **at 90 m.p.h.** hacer una vuelta a 90 m.p.h.

lap[3] [læp] **1** *n* (*lick*) lamedura *f*, lametada *f*; (*of waves*) chapaleteo *m*.

2 *vt* (**a**) (*lick*) lamer; **to** — **up** beber con la lengua, (*swallow*) tragar; **to** — **up** (*fig*) aceptar con entusiasmo, absorber, aprender con facilidad (*etc*).

(**b**) (*of water*) estar al nivel de, correr tan alto como.

3 *vi* (*waves*) chapalear; **to** — **against** besar, tocar, lamer; **to** — **over** desbordarse, irse, salir fuera.

lapdog ['læpdɒg] *n* perro *m* faldero.

lapel [lə'pel] *n* solapa *f*.

lapis lazuli ['læpis'læzjulai] *n* lapislázuli *m*.

Lapland ['læplænd] Laponia *f*.

Laplander ['læplændə*] *n*, **Lapp** [læp] *n* lapón *m*, ona *f*.

lapping ['læpiŋ] *n* (*of water*) chapaleteo *m*.

lapse [læps] **1** *n* (**a**) (*error*) error *m*, equivocación *f*; (*moral*) desliz *m*, falta *f*; lapso *m*; (*relapse*) recaída *f* (*into* en); **a strange** — un extraño error.

(**b**) (*of time*) intervalo *m*, período *m*, lapso *m*; **after a** — **of 4 months** después de un período de 4 meses, al cabo de 4 meses.

2 *vi* (**a**) (*err*) caer en el error, equivocarse; (*morally*) cometer un desliz; (*relapse*) recaer, reincidir (*into* en); **to** — **from duty** faltar a su deber; **to** — **into one's old ways** volver a las andadas, volver a las malas costumbres; **he** —**d into the vernacular** volvió a hablar en la lengua vernácula; **he** —**d into silence** se calló, quedó callado, no dijo más.

(**b**) (*expire*) caducar; (*cease to exist*) dejar de existir, desaparecer.

(**c**) (*time*) pasar, transcurrir.

lapwing ['læpwiŋ] *n* avefría *f*.

larboard ['lɑ:bəd] **1** *adj* de babor. **2** *n* babor *m*.

larceny ['lɑ:səni] *n* latrocinio *m*; **grand** — (*US*) robo *m* de cantidad importante; **petty** — robo *m* de menor cuantía *f*.

larch [lɑ:tʃ] *n* alerce *m* (*also* **larch tree**).

lard [lɑ:d] **1** *n* manteca *f* (de cerdo), lardo *m*. **2** *vt* (*Cook*) lardear, mechar; (*fig*) **to** — **something with** adornar algo de, salpicar algo de, sembrar algo de.

larder ['lɑ:də*] *n* despensa *f*.

lardy ['lɑ:di] *adj* mantecoso.

large [lɑ:dʒ] **1** *adj* (**a**) grande; *packet etc* abultado, voluminoso; *interests* extenso; *powers* amplio, extenso; *sum* importante; *family* numeroso; (*main, chief*) principal; **as** — **as life** de tamaño natural; **there he was as** — **as life** ahí estaba en persona; **there it was as** — **as life** allí se nos apareció de modo inconfundible.

(**b**) **ambassador at** — embajador *m* volante (que no está acreditado permanentemente en ningún país); **people at** — la gente en general; **the world at** — el mundo en general; **to be at** — estar en libertad.

2 *adv see* **by**.

largely ['lɑ:dʒli] *adv* en su mayor parte, en gran parte.

largeness ['lɑ:dʒnis] *n* gran tamaño *m*; lo abultado (*etc*); extensión *f*; lo numeroso.

larger ['lɑ:dʒə*] *adj comp of* **large**; más grande, mayor; **to grow** — crecer; aumentar(se); **to make** — hacer más grande; aumentar; *premises etc* ampliar, ensanchar.

large-scale ['lɑ:dʒ'skeil] *adj* en gran escala.

large-sized ['lɑ:dʒ'saizd] *adj* de gran tamaño, de tamaño extra.

largesse [lɑ:'ʒes] *n* generosidad *f*, liberalidad *f*; (*gift*) dádiva *f* espléndida.

largo ['lɑ:gəu] *n* (*Mus*) largo *m*.

lariat ['læriət] *n* lazo *m*.

lark[1] [lɑːk] n (Orn) alondra f; **to get up with the —** levantarse con las gallinas, madrugar; see **happy**.

lark[2] [lɑːk] **1** n (a) (spree) juerga f; **to go on a —** ir de juerga.

(b) (joke etc) broma f, travesura f; **that's a —!**, **what a —!** ¡qué bien!, ¡qué risa!; **that was a —!** ¡cómo nos reímos con aquello!; **isn't he a —?** ¿es célebre, no?; **to do something for a —** hacer algo para divertirse, divertirse haciendo algo; **to have a — with someone** gastar una broma a uno, tomar el pelo a uno.

(c) (business, affair) **that ice-cream —** ese asunto de los helados; **the Suez —** la fiestecita de Suez; **this dinner-jacket —** esta costumbre tan estúpida de ponerse un smoking.

2 vi (be on a spree) andar de jarana; (amuse oneself) divertirse; **to — about** hacer travesuras, gastarse bromas, divertirse tontamente; **stop —ing about!** ¡quieto!; **to — about with something** (play) divertirse con algo, jugar con algo, (damage) estropear algo, manosear algo.

larkspur ['lɑːkspəː*] n espuela f de caballero.

larky ['lɑːki] adj (fam) guasón, bromista.

larva ['lɑːvə] n, pl **larvae** ['lɑːviː] larva f.

laryngitis [ˌlærin'dʒaitis] n laringitis f.

larynx ['læriŋks] n laringe f.

lascivious [lə'siviəs] adj lascivo.

lasciviously [lə'siviəsli] adv lascivamente.

lasciviousness [lə'siviəsnis] n lascivia f.

lash [læʃ] **1** n (a) (whip) látigo m, (used for punishment) azote m; (thong) tralla f; (Anat) pestaña f.

(b) (stroke) latigazo m, (as punishment) azote m; (of tail) coletazo m; **the — of the rain** el azote de la lluvia; **the — of the waves** el azote de las olas; **under the — of the Nazis** bajo el azote de los nazis.

2 vt (a) (beat etc) azotar, dar latigazos a, fustigar; tail agitar; (of hail, rain, waves) azotar; (fig: criticize) fustigar, dar una paliza a, increpar; **he was —ing the horse along** le daba duramente al caballo con el látigo; **the wind —ed the trees** el viento azotaba los árboles; **the wind —ed the sea into a fury** el viento levantaba enormes olas; **to — someone with one's tongue** increpar duramente a uno; **to — someone into a fury** provocar a uno hasta la furia.

(b) (tie) atar, (Naut) trincar, amarrar (to a); **to — down** sujetar, atar firmemente.

(c) (fam) **he had to — out £5** tuvo que pagar 5 libras (de mala gana), tuvo que desembolsar 5 libras; **they were —ing out the drink** estaban sirviendo las bebidas en grandes cantidades.

3 vi (a) **to — out** (with fists) repartir golpes a diestro y siniestro, dar golpes furiosos sin mirar a quién; (with feet) tirar coces.

(b) (fam) **to — out** desdinerarse, pagar; repartir dinero generosamente; **now we can really — out** ahora sí podemos gastar dinero; **he —ed out and bought himself a Rolls** dejó de economizar y se compró un Rolls.

(c) **to — out at** censurar enérgicamente, criticar duramente.

4 vr: **to — oneself into a fury** montar en cólera.

lashing ['læʃiŋ] n (a) (beating) azotamiento m, azotes mpl. (b) (tie) atadura f, (Naut) trinca f, amarradura f. (c) **—s** (fam) montones mpl.

lass [læs] n muchacha f, chica f, joven f; (country-) moza f, zagala f.

lassie ['læsi] n (fam) = **lass**.

lassitude ['læsitjuːd] n lasitud f.

lasso [læ'suː] **1** n lazo m. **2** vt lazar, coger con el lazo.

last[1] [lɑːst] **1** adj último; final; extremo; week, month etc pasado; **— Monday, on Monday —** el lunes pasado; **— night** anoche; **the night before —** anteanoche; **the year before —** el año antepasado; **the — trick but one** la penúltima baza; **the — trick but 3** la tercera baza antes de la última; **during the — 20 years** en los últimos 20 años; **it has not been seen these — 3 years** hace 3 años que no se le ve por aquí; **to be the — (one) to do something** ser el último en hacer algo; **to be the — but not least** ser el último pero no el peor; **that's the — thing to worry about** eso es lo de menos; **that was the — thing I expected** eso era lo último que yo esperaba; **you're the — person to be entrusted with it** tú eres el menos indicado para hacerse cargo de ello.

2 n último m, a f, última cosa f, lo último; (end) fin m; **each one better than the —** cada uno mejor que el anterior (or precedente); **my — mi** última carta; **at —** por fin; **at long —** al fin y al cabo; **to the —** hasta el fin; **this is the — of it** éste es el último de la serie (etc), **con éste terminamos,**

después de éste no quedan más; **that was the — we saw of him** no le volvimos a ver; **I shall be glad to see the —** of this estoy deseando que termine esto; **to breathe one's —** exhalar el último suspiro; **we shall never hear the — of it** no nos dejarán en paz nunca; **to look one's — on something** ver algo por última vez, despedirse de algo (antes de su desaparición).

3 adv por último; en último lugar; por última vez; finalmente; **to arrive —** llegar el último; **the horse came in —** el caballo llegó el último, el caballo ocupó el último puesto en la clasificación; **when I — saw him** cuando le vi por última vez.

last[2] [lɑːst] **1** vt: **it —ed me a lifetime** me duró toda la vida; **the car has —ed me 8 years** el coche sigue siéndome útil después de 8 años; **I can — you out any time** de todos modos yo resisto mejor que tú; **he —ed all his colleagues out** sobrevivió a todos sus colegas.

2 vi durar; perdurar; permanecer, resistir; sostenerse, mantenerse; (continue) continuar, seguir; (cloth etc) ser duro, ser resistente; **it —s 2 hours** dura 2 horas; **it can't —** no puede seguir así; **things are too good to —** las cosas van demasiado bien para seguir así; **will this material —?** ¿es resistente este paño?; **he won't — long in this job** no resistirá mucho tiempo en este puesto; **the previous boss —ed only a week** el jefe anterior permaneció solamente una semana en el puesto; **to — out** resistir, continuar; (money, resources) durar, llegar; **can you — out another mile?** ¿puedes hacer una milla más?; **I can't — out** no puedo más, no resisto más; **my money doesn't — out the month** el dinero no me llega para un mes entero.

last[3] [lɑːst] n horma f; **stick to your —!** ¡zapatero, a tus zapatos!

last-ditch ['lɑːst'ditʃ] adj defence de lo más terco, que continúa hasta quemar el último cartucho.

lasting ['lɑːstiŋ] adj duradero, perdurable, permanente; constante; shame etc eterno; colour sólido.

lastly ['lɑːstli] adv por último, finalmente.

last-minute ['lɑːst'minit] adj decision etc de última hora.

latch [lætʃ] **1** n picaporte m, pestillo m; **to be on the —** estar cerrado con picaporte; **to drop the —** echar el pestillo.

2 vt cerrar con picaporte; (fig) sujetar, asegurar.

3 vi: **to — on to something** fijarse en algo; **to — on to someone** pegarse a uno.

latchkey ['lætʃki] n llavín m.

late [leit] **1** adj (a) (person) **to be — for something** llegar tarde para algo; **I was too — for it** llegué tarde para ello; **I was — in getting up** tardé en levantarme; **I don't want to make you —** no quiero entretenerle.

(b) (impersonal) **it's —** es tarde; **it's — in the day to change your mind** es tarde para mudar de opinión; **it's getting —** se está haciendo tarde.

(c) tardío; hour avanzado; delivery atrasado; entry que se presenta después de la fecha señalada; **— frost** helada f tardía; **— potato** patata f tardía; **at a — hour** a una hora avanzada, a última hora; **in the — eighties** en los últimos años ochenta; **in the — spring** hacia fines de la primavera; **in the — morning** en la última parte de la mañana; **a 18th century building** un edificio de fines del siglo XVIII; **L— Stone Age** período m neolítico; **Easter is — this year** la Semana Santa cae tarde este año.

(d) (deceased) fallecido, difunto, finado; **the — king** el finado rey.

(e) (former) antiguo, ex; **— prime minister** antiguo primer ministro m, ex primer ministro m.

2 adv (a) tarde; **to come —** llegar tarde; **to arrive too —** llegar tarde (for para); **the train arrived 8 minutes —** el tren llegó con 8 minutos de retraso; **better — than never** más vale tarde que nunca; **to sit up —, to stay up —** velar, no acostarse hasta las altas horas, seguir sin acostarse; **to work — at the office** trabajar en la oficina después de la hora acostumbrada, quedarse a trabajar en la oficina hasta una hora tardía; **— at night, — in the night** ya muy entrada la noche; **— into the night** hasta muy entrada la noche; **— in the afternoon** a última hora de la tarde; **— in the year** hacia fines del año; **— in life** a una edad avanzada; **— last century** hacia fines del siglo pasado; **of — últimamente, recientemente; as — as 1900** todavía en 1900.

(b) **— of No. 13** que vivió hasta hace poco en el núm. 13; **— of the Diplomatic Service** hasta hace poco miembro del Cuerpo Diplomático, ex miembro del Cuerpo Diplomático.

latecomer ['leitkʌmə*] n recién llegado m, a f; **el**

(etc) que llega tarde; **the firm is a — to the industry** la compañía es nueva en la industria, la compañía acaba de establecerse en la industria.

late-lamented ['leitlə'mentid] *adj* malogrado, fallecido.

lately ['leitli] *adv* últimamente, recientemente; hace poco; **till — hasta** hace poco.

latency ['leitənsi] *n* estado *m* latente.

lateness ['leitnis] *n* lo tarde; lo tardío; lo reciente; *(of hour)* lo avanzado; *(delay)* retraso *m*; **he was fined for persistent —** le impusieron una multa por venir constantemente tarde.

latent ['leitənt] *adj* latente.

later ['leitə*] **1** *adj comp of* late; más tardío; *(in newness)* más reciente; *(in series)* posterior, ulterior; *hour* más avanzada; **his — symphonies** sus sinfonías más recientes, sus sinfonías posteriores; **this version is — than that one** esta versión es posterior a ésa; **it must have been painted at a — stage** debe de haberse pintado en una fase posterior; **at a — meeting** en una reunión celebrada después; **in his — years** en sus últimos años.

2 *adv comp of* late; más tarde; *(afterwards)* luego, después; **posteriormente; a moment —** un momento después; **a few years —** a los pocos años; varios años después; **yes dear, —** *(on being interrupted)* sí querida, luego; **see you —!** ¡hasta pronto!; **no — than yesterday** no más lejos que ayer, ayer sin ir más lejos; **not — than 1980** no después de 1980; **— on** más tarde, después.

lateral ['lætərəl] *adj* lateral.

laterally ['lætərəli] *adv* lateralmente.

latest ['leitist] **1** *adj superl of* late; último; más reciente; *fashion, news etc* último; **his — painting** su último cuadro, su cuadro más reciente; **to be the — to do something** ser el último en hacer algo; **what is the — date you can come?** ¿hasta qué fecha estás libre para venir?

2 *adv superl of* late; **he came —** él vino el último.

3 *n* (a) *(fam)* **have you seen John's —?** *(girl)* ¿has visto a la novia actual de Juan?; **have you heard John's —?** *(joke)* ¿has oído el último chiste de Juan?; **did you hear about John's —?** *(exploit)* ¿te han contado la última de Juan?, ¿has oído lo de Juan?

(b) at the — a lo más tarde, a más tardar, como límite.

latex ['leiteks] *n* látex *m*.

lath [læθ] *n*, *pl* **laths** [lɑːðz] listón *m*.

lathe [leið] *n* torno *m*.

lather ['læðə*] **1** *n* espuma *f* (de jabón), jabonaduras *fpl*; *(of sweat)* espuma *f*; **the horse was in a —** el caballo estaba cubierto de espuma.

2 *vt* enjabonar; *(fam)* zurrar.

3 *vi* hacer espuma.

latifundia [,læti'fundiə] *npl* latifundios *mpl*.

Latin ['lætin] **1** *adj* latino.

2 *n* *(person)* latino *m*, a *f*; **the —s** los latinos.

3 *n* *(language)* latín *m*; **Late —** latín *m* tardío; **Low —** bajo latín *m*; **Vulgar —** latín *m* vulgar.

Latin America ['lætin'merikə] América *f* Latina.

Latin-American ['lætinə'merikən] **1** *adj* latinoamericano. **2** *n* latinoamericano *m*, a *f*.

latinism ['lætinizəm] *n* latinismo *m*.

latinist ['lætinist] *n* latinista *mf*.

latinity [lə'tiniti] *n* latinidad *f*.

latinization [,lætinai'zeiʃən] *n* latinización *f*.

latinize ['lætinaiz] *vti* latinizar.

latitude ['lætitjuːd] *n* latitud *f*; *(fig)* libertad *f*.

latitudinal [,læti'tjuːdinl] *adj* latitudinal.

Latium ['leiʃiəm] Lacio *m*.

latrine [lə'triːn] *n* letrina *f*.

latter ['lætə*] *adj* (a) más reciente; posterior; último; *(of two)* segundo; **the — part of the story** la segunda mitad del cuento; **in the — part of the century** hacia fines del siglo; **the — opinion** esta (última) opinión.

(b) the former . . . the — aquél . . . éste.

latter-day ['lætə'dei] *adj* moderno, reciente.

latterly ['lætəli] *adv* últimamente, recientemente.

lattice ['lætis] *n* enrejado *m*; *(on window)* reja *f*, celosía *f*.

latticed ['lætist] *adj window* con reja.

lattice work ['lætiswɔːk] *n* enrejado *m*.

Latvia ['lætviə] Letonia *f*, Latvia *f*.

Latvian ['lætviən] **1** *adj* letón, latvio. **2** *n* letón *m*, ona *f*, latvio *m*, a *f*.

laud [lɔːd] *vt* alabar, elogiar.

laudable ['lɔːdəbl] *adj* loable; plausible.

laudably ['lɔːdəbli] *adv* de modo loable, laudablemente.

laudanum ['lɔːdnəm] *n* láudano *m*.

laudatory ['lɔːdətəri] *adj* laudatorio.

laugh [lɑːf] **1** *n* risa *f*; *(loud)* carcajada *f*, risotada *f*; **what a —!** ¡qué risa!, ¡qué bien!; **just for a —** sólo para hacer reír; **to have a good — over something** reírse mucho con algo; **to have the — over someone** llevar ventaja a uno, quedar por encima de uno; **to play something for —s** representar algo con el propósito de hacer reír al público.

2 *vt*: **to — something off** tomar algo a risa; **he —s everything off** no toma nada en serio; *see* court, scorn.

3 *vi* reír, reírse; *(loud)* reírse a carcajadas, carcajearse; **to — about something, to — over something** reírse con algo; **it's nothing to — about** no es cosa de risa; **to — at someone** reírse de uno, burlarse de uno; **are you —ing at me?** ¿se ríe Vd de mí?; **we must be able to — at ourselves** hay que ver los aspectos ridículos de nosotros mismos; **to — out loud** soltar la carcajada, reírse abiertamente; **he who —s last —s longest** el último que ríe, ríe más fuerte.

laughable ['lɑːfəbl] *adj* ridículo, absurdo; cómico, divertido; **it's — that . . .** es absurdo que + *subj*.

laughing ['lɑːfiŋ] **1** *adj* risueño, alegre; **it's no — matter** no es cosa de risa. **2** *n* risa *f*.

laughing gas ['lɑːfiŋ'gæs] *n* gas *m* hilarante.

laughingly ['lɑːfiŋli] *adv*: **he said —** dijo riendo.

laughing stock ['lɑːfiŋstɔk] *n* hazmerreír *m*.

laughter ['lɑːftə*] *n* risa *f*, risas *fpl*; **amid the — of those present** entre las risas de los asistentes; **at this there was —** en esto hubo risas; **to burst into —** soltar la carcajada.

Launcelot ['lɑːnslət] *m* Lanzarote.

launch [lɔːntʃ] **1** *n* *(act)* botadura *f*; *(vessel)* lancha *f*, falúa *f*.

2 *vt* *(throw)* lanzar; *rocket etc* lanzar; *new vessel* botar; *lifeboat* echar al agua, largar; *offensive* emprender, comenzar; *company* crear, fundar, lanzar; *new product* lanzar, introducir en el mercado; *film, play* estrenar; *idea* lanzar; *plan* poner en operación; *share issue etc* emitir; **to — someone on his way** ayudar a uno a emprender su carrera, poner a uno en camino.

3 *vi*: **to — forth, to — out** lanzarse, ponerse en marcha; **now we can afford to — out a bit** ahora nos podemos permitir algunas cosas de lujo, ahora podemos extender nuestras actividades *(etc)*; **to — out into** lanzarse a; engolfarse en; **to — out into a career** emprender una carrera; **he —ed out into a violent speech** pasó a pronunciar un discurso violento; **once he is —ed on this subject we shall never stop him** en cuanto se ponga a hablar de este tema no le haremos nunca callar.

launching ['lɔːntʃiŋ] *n* botadura *f*; lanzamiento *m*; inauguración *f*, iniciación *f*; estreno *m*; emisión *f*.

launching pad ['lɔːntʃiŋpæd] *n* plataforma *f* de lanzamiento.

launching site ['lɔːntʃiŋsait] *n* rampa *f* de lanzamiento.

launder ['lɔːndə*] **1** *vt* lavar (y planchar). **2** *vt* resistir el lavado (bien, mal *etc*).

launderette [lɔːndə'ret] *n* lavandería *f* automática.

laundress ['lɔːndris] *n* lavandera *f*.

laundry ['lɔːndri] *n* *(establishment)* lavadero *m*, lavandería *f*; *(clothes: dirty)* ropa *f* sucia, ropa *f* por lavar, *(washed)* ropa *f* lavada, colada *f*.

laureate ['lɔːriit] *n* laureado *m*.

laurel ['lɔrəl] *n* laurel *m* (cerezo); **to look to one's —s** no dormirse sobre sus laureles; **to rest on one's —s** dormirse sobre sus laureles; **to win one's —s** cargarse de laureles, laurearse.

Laurence ['lɔrəns] *m* Lorenzo.

Lausanne [ləu'zæn] Lausana *f*.

lav [læv] *n* *(fam)* = lavatory.

lava ['lɑːvə] *n* lava *f*.

lavatory ['lævətri] *n* *(utensil)* wáter *m*, excusado *m*, inodoro *m*; *(room)* lavabo *m*, aseos *mpl*; **public —** urinarios *mpl*.

lavender ['lævində*] *n*-espliego *m*, lavanda *f*, lavándula *f*.

lavish ['læviʃ] **1** *adj* *(abundant)* profuso, abundante; *(luxurious)* lujoso; *(of person, prodigal)* pródigo; *expenditure* pródigo, liberal; **to be — of** ser pródigo de, prodigar, no escatimar; **to be — with one's money** gastar libremente su dinero, derrochar su dinero.

2 *vt*: **to — something on someone** colmar a uno de algo; **to — care on something** poner la máxima atención en algo; **to — attentions on someone** colmar a uno de atenciones.

lavishly ['læviʃli] *adv* profusamente, en profusión, abundantemente; lujosamente; pródigamente; **the house is — furnished** la casa está lujosamente amueblada; **he spends money —** derrocha su dinero.

lavishness ['lævɪʃnɪs] n profusión f, abundancia f; lujo m; prodigalidad f.

law [lɔ:] n (a —, the —) ley f; (study, body of —s) derecho m, jurisprudencia f; (Sport, games) regla f; **the L—** (Jewish) la ley de Moisés, (fam) la policía; **— and order** orden m público; **the forces of — and order** las fuerzas del orden; **— of nature** ley f natural; **canon —** derecho m canónico; **civil —** derecho m civil; **commercial —** derecho m mercantil; **common —** derecho m consuetudinario; **constitutional —** derecho m político; **criminal —** derecho m penal; **international —** derecho m internacional, derecho m de gentes; **maritime —** código m marítimo; **martial —** ley f marcial, gobierno m militar; **Roman —** derecho m romano; **according to —**, **in — según** derecho; **by —** según la ley, de acuerdo con la ley; **in-law político**, eg **brother-in-law** hermano m político, cuñado m; **it's the —** es la ley; **his word is —** su palabra es ley; **is there a — against it?** ¿hay una ley que lo prohíba?; **he is above the —** está por encima de la ley; **he is outside the —** está fuera de la ley; **to be a — unto oneself** obrar por cuenta propia, no hacer caso alguno de los demás; **to go to —** pleitear, poner pleito (about sobre), recurrir a la ley; **to have the — on someone** denunciar a uno a la policía, llevar a uno ante el tribunal; **to keep within the —** obrar legalmente; **to lay down the —** hablar autoritariamente; **to practise —** ejercer de abogado; **to take the — into one's own hands** tomarse la justicia por su mano; **to take a case to —** recurrir a la vía judicial.

law-abiding ['lɔːrə,baidiŋ] adj observante de la ley, que vive conforme a la ley; decente.

lawbreaker ['lɔːr,breikə*] n transgresor m, ora f, infractor m de la ley.

law court ['lɔːkɔːt] n tribunal m (de justicia).

lawful ['lɔːful] adj legítimo, lícito.

lawfully ['lɔːfəli] adv legítimamente, lícitamente.

lawgiver ['lɔː,givə*] n legislador m, ora f.

lawless ['lɔːlis] adj act ilegal; person rebelde, violento, criminal; country sin leyes, ingobernable, desordenado.

lawlessness ['lɔːlisnis] n desorden m; violencia f; criminalidad f.

lawn¹ [lɔːn] n césped m.

lawn² [lɔːn] n linón m.

lawnmower ['lɔːn,məuə*] n cortacésped m.

lawn tennis ['lɔːn'tenis] n tenis m.

Lawrence ['lɔːrəns] m Lorenzo.

law school ['lɔːskuːl] n escuela f de derecho, facultad f de derecho.

law student ['lɔː,stjuːdənt] n estudiante mf de derecho.

lawsuit ['lɔːsuːt] n pleito m, litigio m, proceso m.

lawyer ['lɔːjə*] n abogado m.

lax [læks] adj flojo; negligente, descuidado, poco exigente; indisciplinado; (morally) laxo; **to be — in + ger** ser negligente en + infin; **things are very — at the school** en la escuela hay poca disciplina; **he is — in his approach** su actitud es poco seria.

laxative ['læksətiv] 1 adj laxante. 2 n laxante m.

laxity ['læksiti] n, **laxness** ['læksnis] n flojedad f; negligencia f, descuido m; falta f de disciplina; (moral) laxitud f, relajamiento m.

lay¹ [lei] n (Mus, Lit) trova f, canción f.

lay² [lei] adj (not in orders) laico, lego, seglar; (not expert) profano, no experto.

lay³ [lei] pret of **lie**².

lay⁴ [lei] 1 n (a) disposición f, situación f; **the — of the land** la configuración del terreno, (fig) la situación actual, el estado actual de las cosas.
(b) hen **in —** gallina f ponedora; **to come into —** empezar a poner huevos; **to go out of —** dejar de poner huevos.
(c) (US sl) **she's an easy —** es plan.
2 (irr: pret, ptp laid) vt (a) (prostrate, etc) corn abatir, encamar; dust matar; fears aquietar, acallar; ghost conjurar, exorcizar; **to — something flat** derribar algo, tirar algo al suelo; **to — a town flat** arrasar (or destruir) una ciudad.
(b) (place, put, colocar; dejar; blame echar (on a); bricks poner, colocar; cable, mains, track tender; cloth, meal, table poner; carpet, lino extender; fire preparar; foundations echar; foundation stone colocar; gun apuntar; hand etc poner (on en); mines sembrar; pipes etc (in building) instalar; plans hacer, formar, preparar; responsibility atribuir (on a); scene poner, situar; tax imponer (on a).
(c) egg poner; **to — eggs** (hen) poner huevos, (fish, insect etc) desovar.

(d) bet hacer (on a); money apostar (on a); **I — you a fiver on it!** ¡te apuesto 5 libras a que es así!
(e) accusation, charge hacer; complaint formular, presentar; information dar.
(f) (with adv or prep) **to — aside** book, pen etc dejar; work dejar, suspender; (keep in reserve) poner aparte, poner a un lado; (save) ahorrar, guardar; (cast away) desechar; plan etc arrinconar, dar carpetazo a; **to — away = to — aside**; **to — something before someone** poner algo delante de uno; idea, plan exponer ante uno; claim etc presentar a uno; **to — by = to — aside**; **to — down** book, pen etc dejar; poner a un lado; (lay flat) acostar, poner en tierra; arms deponer, rendir, dejar; burden posar, depositar en tierra; cards extender sobre el tapete; condition asentar; life dar, sacrificar; policy asentar, trazar, marcar; precedent sentar, establecer; principle afirmar; ruling dictar; ship colocar la quilla de; **to — it down that . . .** asentar que . . ., afirmar que . . .; dictaminar que . . .; **to — in supplies** proveerse de; (save) ahorrar; (amass) acumular; (buy) comprar; **to — off** workers despedir (temporalmente, por falta de trabajo); **to — on** blows descargar (sobre); paint poner, pintar; water etc instalar; duty, punishment, tax imponer (a); **a house with water laid on** una casa con agua corriente; **to — it on someone** (beat) dar una paliza a uno; **to — it on** (thick) (flatter) adular más de la cuenta, (exaggerate) recargar las tintas; **to — out** tender, extender; disponer, arreglar; corpse amortajar; garden, town trazar, hacer el trazado de; money (spend) gastar, (invest) invertir, emplear (on en); **to — someone out** derribar a uno, poner a uno fuera de combate; (with drink etc) hacer perder el conocimiento a uno, (by illness) debilitar gravemente a uno; **the house is well laid out** la casa está bien distribuida; **the town is well laid out** la ciudad tiene un trazado elegante; **to — up** (store) guardar, almacenar; (amass) acumular; (save) ahorrar, atesorar; ship desarmar; boat amarrar; car etc encerrar en el garaje, dejar de usar temporalmente; (Med) obligar a guardar cama; see also laid.
3 vi (hen) poner, poner huevos; **to — that . . .** apostar a que . . .; **to — about one** dar palos de ciego, repartir golpes a diestro y siniestro; **to — down** (Cards) poner sus cartas sobre el tapete; **to — into someone** (fam) dar una paliza a uno (also fig); **to — off** (Naut) virar de bordo; **to — off someone** (fam) dejar a uno en paz; **— off, will you?** (fam) ¡déjalo, por Dios!; **to — off something** (fam) dejar algo; **to — off + ger** (fam) dejar de + infin; **to — on** arremeter, empezar a luchar, darse golpes.
4 vr: **to — oneself down** tumbarse, echarse; **to — oneself out** hacer un gran esfuerzo (to + infin por + infin), tomarse la molestia (for someone de ayudar a uno, to + infin de + infin); **to — oneself out to please** volcarse por complacer a uno; **to — oneself out with a blow** darse un golpe y ponerse fuera de combate.

layabout ['leiəbaut] n gandul m, vago m, a f.

lay brother ['lei'brʌðə*] n donado m, lego m.

lay-by ['leibai] n (Aut) apartadero m.

layer ['leiə*] 1 n (a) capa f; (Geol) estrato m. (b) (Agr) acodo m. (c) (hen) gallina f ponedora; **the best —** la más ponedora. 2 vt (Agr) acodar.

layette [lei'et] n canastilla f, ajuar m (de niño).

lay figure ['lei'figə*] n maniquí m.

laying ['leiiŋ] n (placing) colocación f; (of cable, track etc) tendido m; (of eggs) puesta f, postura f; **— on of hands** imposición f de manos.

layman ['leimən] n, pl **—men** [mən] (Eccl) seglar m, lego m; (fig) profano m, persona f no experta, lego m.

lay-off ['leiɔf] n paro m involuntario.

layout ['leiaut] n plan m, distribución f, trazado m; disposición f; (Typ etc) composición f.

lay sister ['lei'sistə*] n donada f, lega f.

Lazarus ['læzərəs] m Lázaro.

laze [leiz] 1 n: **to have a —** descansar.
2 vi no hacer nada, darse al ocio; (pej) holgazanear, gandulear; **we —d in the sun for a week** durante una semana tomamos el sol y nada más.

lazily ['leizili] adv perezosamente; lentamente.

laziness ['leizinis] n pereza f, holgazanería f, vaguedad f, indolencia f.

lazy ['leizi] adj perezoso, holgazán, vago, indolente; movement etc lento; **we had a — holiday** pasamos las vacaciones sin hacer nada, durante las vacaciones no hicimos nada sino descansar.

lazybones ['leizi,bəunz] n gandul m, vago m, a f.

lea [li:] n (poet) prado m.

leach [li:tʃ] 1 vt lixiviar. 2 vi lixiviarse.

lead [led] n (metal) plomo m; (Naut) sonda f, escandallo m; (Typ) regleta f, interlínea f; (in pencil) mina f; **—s** chapas fpl de plomo; **red —** minio m; **white —** albayalde m; **they filled him full of —** le acribillaron a balazos; **to swing the —** (fam) fingirse enfermo, racanear, hacer el rácano.

lead [li:d] **1** n **(a)** (front position) delantera f, cabeza f; (leading position, Sport) liderato m; (distance, time ahead) ventaja f; **to be in the —** ir en cabeza, ir primero; (in league etc) ocupar el primer puesto; **to take the —** tomar la delantera, tomar el mando; **to have 2 minutes' — over someone** llevar a uno una ventaja de 2 minutos; **to have a — of half a length** tener medio cuerpo de ventaja.

(b) (example) ejemplo m; iniciativa f; **to follow someone's —** seguir el ejemplo de uno; **to give someone a —** guiar a uno, dar el ejemplo a uno, mostrar el camino a uno; **to take the —** tomar la iniciativa (in en, in doing en hacer).

(c) (clue) pista f, indicación f; **the police have a —** la policía tiene una pista; **it gave the police a — to the criminal** puso a la policía sobre la pista del criminal; **give me a —** (in guessing) ¿me puedes dar alguna indicación?

(d) (Cards) **it's my —** yo soy mano, salgo yo; **whose — is it?** ¿quién sale?; **if the — is in hearts** si la salida es a corazones.

(e) (Theat) papel m principal; **with Garbo in the —** con la Garbo en el primer papel; **to play the —** tener el papel principal; **to sing the —** llevar la voz cantante.

(f) (leash) trailla f, cuerda f.

(g) (Elec) conductor m, cable m (eléctrico).

2 (irr: pret and ptp **led**) vt **(a)** (conduct) conducir; llevar; guiar; **to — someone to a table** conducir a uno a una mesa; **to — someone along** llevar a uno (por la mano etc); **kindly — me to him** haga el favor de conducirme a su presencia (or de llevarme donde está); **each reference led me to another** cada referencia me remitió a otra; **what led you to Venice?** ¿qué le llevó a Venecia?, ¿con qué motivo fue Vd a Venecia?; **to — the way** ir primero, dar el ejemplo, mostrar el camino; **he is easily led** es muy influenciable; **to — someone into error** inducir a uno a error.

(b) (be the leader of, govern) government dirigir, encabezar; party encabezar, ser el jefe de; expedition, regiment mandar; team capitanear; movement, revolution encabezar, acaudillar; orchestra dirigir; league, procession ir a la cabeza de, encabezar.

(c) (be first in) ser el primero en, sobresalir en, ocupar el primer puesto en; **to — the field** ir el primero de todos, estar en cabeza, ganar; **they led us by 30 seconds** nos llevaban una ventaja de 30 segundos; **Britain —s the world in textiles** en la industria textil Inglaterra supera a los demás, en los textiles Inglaterra ocupa el primer puesto.

(d) card salir con.

(e) life llevar; **to — a strange life** llevar una vida muy rara; **to — someone a wretched life** amargar la vida a uno, tratar a uno como una basura; see also **dance, life**.

(f) to — someone to do something inducir (or inclinar, persuadir, mover) a uno a hacer algo; **to — someone to believe that . . .** hacer creer a uno que . . .; **I am led to the conclusion that . . .** llego a la conclusión de que . . .

(g) (with adv or prep) **to — someone away** conducir a uno a otra parte; llevarse a uno; **he was led away by the police** se lo llevaron los policías; **we must not be led away from the matter in hand** no nos apartemos del asunto que estamos tratando; **to — someone back** hacer volver a uno, conducir a uno a donde estaba; **this road —s you back to Jaca** por este camino se vuelve a Jaca; **to — someone in** hacer entrar a uno; **they led him into the king's presence** le condujeron ante el rey; **to — someone off** hacer marcharse a uno, llevarse a uno; **to — someone on** (persuade) engatusar a uno, halagar a uno; (amorously) coquetear con uno, ir dando esperanzas a uno; (morally) seducir a uno; (make someone talk) hacer hablar a uno, tirar de la lengua a uno; **to — someone out** conducir a uno fuera; **to — someone out to dance** sacar a una a bailar.

3 vi **(a)** (go in front) llevar la delantera, ir primero; **— on!** ¡adelante!; **to — by 10 metres** tener una ventaja de 10 metros; **he easily —s** sobresale, supera fácilmente a los demás.

(b) (be in command) tener el mando, ser el jefe.

(c) (Cards) ser mano, salir; **who —s?** ¿quién sale?; **South —s** Sur sale.

(d) (of street etc) **to — to** conducir a, llevar a,

salir a, desembocar en; **this street —s to the station** esta calle conduce a la estación, por esta calle se va a la estación; **where does this corridor —?** ¿adónde conduce este pasillo?; **it —s into that room** comunica con ese cuarto.

(e) (result in) dar, producir; **it led to a result** dio un resultado; **it led to a change** produjo un cambio; **it led to nothing** no dio resultado, no surtió efecto, no condujo a nada; **it led to his arrest** dio lugar a su detención; **it led to war** causó la guerra.

(f) (with adv or prep) **to — off** (begin) empezar; (Sport) abrir el juego; (Cards) salir (with con); **the streets that — off the square** las calles que salen de la plaza; **a room —ing off another** un cuarto que comunica con otro; **to — up to** conducir a; preparar el terreno para; **the events that led up to the war** los sucesos que condujeron a la guerra; **the years that led up to the war** los años que precedieron a la guerra; **what's all this —ing up to?** ¿qué propósito tiene todo esto?, ¿adónde conduce todo esto?; **he led carefully up to the proposal** preparó con cuidado el terreno antes de hacer la propuesta.

leaded ['ledid] adj: **— lights** cristales mpl emplomados.

leaden ['ledn] adj (of lead) de plomo, plúmbeo; (in colour) plomizo; (fig) pesado, triste.

leader ['li:də*] n (in general) jefe m, líder m; (Pol, of nation, union etc) dirigente m; (of party) jefe m, líder m; (esp military) caudillo m; (of gang) cuadrillero m; (of rebels) cabecilla m; (guide) guía mf, conductor m, ora f; (Sport: in league) líder m, (horse etc) caballo m (etc) delantero; (Mus: of orchestra) primer violín m, (of band) director m; (Typ) artículo m de fondo; **party —** jefe m de partido; **— of the opposition** jefe m de la oposición; **a — of the masses** un conductor de masas; **our political —s** nuestros dirigentes políticos.

leadership ['li:dəʃip] n **(a)** (persons, office) jefatura f, dirección f; mando m, liderato m; caudillaje m; **under the — of** bajo la jefatura de; **a crisis in the —** una crisis de dirección, una crisis en la dirigencia; **to resign the —** dimitir la jefatura; **to take over the —** asumir la dirección, tomar el mando.

(b) (quality) iniciativa f; (powers of —) dotes fpl de mando.

leader-writer ['li:də‚raitə*] n editorialista mf.

lead-in ['li:d'in] n introducción f; entrada f; **a useful — to a discussion** una manera útil de introducir una discusión.

leading ['li:diŋ] adj **(a)** (front) delantero; wheel delantero, conductor; edge (Aer) de ataque.

(b) part, person, idea etc principal, importante; (outstanding) sobresaliente, destacado; (in race) primero, delantero; see **article, lady** etc.

leading strings ['li:diŋstriŋz] npl andaderas fpl.

lead pencil ['led'pensl] n lápiz m.

lead poisoning ['led‚poizniŋ] n plumbismo m.

leaf [li:f] **1** n, pl **leaves** [li:vz] hoja f; **gold —** pan m de oro, oro m batido; **tobacco —** tabaco m en rama; **to come into —** echar hojas, cubrirse de hojas; **to take a — out of someone's book** seguir el ejemplo de uno; **to turn over a new —** reformarse, cambiar de modo de ser, hacer vida nueva.

2 vi: **to — through a book** hojear un libro.

leaf bud ['li:fbʌd] n yema f.

leafless ['li:flis] adj sin hojas, deshojado.

leaflet ['li:flit] n folleto m, hoja f volante; prospecto m.

leaf mould, (US) **leaf mold** ['li:fməuld] n abono m verde.

leafy ['li:fi] adj frondoso.

league¹ [li:g] n (measure) legua f.

league² [li:g] n liga f (also Sport); sociedad f, asociación f, comunidad f; **L— of Nations** Sociedad f de las Naciones; **Hanseatic L—** Liga f Hanseática; **to be in — with someone** estar de manga con uno, haberse confabulado con uno.

leak [li:k] **1** n (hole) agujero m; (Naut) vía f de agua; (in roof etc) gotera f; (of gas, liquid) escape m, fuga f, pérdida f, salida f; (of money) filtración f; **there has been a security —** se ha divulgado una noticia confidencial (or información secreta); **to spring a —** abrirse una vía de agua.

2 vt **(a)** rezumar, dejar perderse, derramar; **it's —ing acid all over the place** se está derramando el ácido por todas partes.

(b) to — information to a spy comunicar información secreta a un espía.

3 vi **(a)** (of ship) hacer agua; (of receptacle) rezumarse, tener agujeros, estar agujereado; (of pipe) tener fugas, dejar fugarse el gas (etc); (of pen) derramar tinta, derramarse.

(b) (of gas, liquid etc) escaparse, fugarse, salirse,

irse; (*ooze out*) rezumarse; (*drop by drop*) gotear; (*of money*) filtrarse; **to — away** irse, agotarse debido a una fuga; **to — out = to — away**; (*of news*) divulgarse (sin autorización), llegar a saberse, trascender; **finally it —ed out that . . .** por fin se supo que . . .

leakage ['li:kidʒ] n = **leak**; **security —** divulgación f (no autorizada) de información secreta.

leaky ['li:ki] *adj* que hace agua, que tiene vías de agua; *roof* que tiene goteras; *receptacle* agujereado, defectuoso.

lean¹ [li:n] **1** *adj* (*thin*) flaco; *face* enjuto; *meat* magro; *year* difícil, de carestía; **to grow —** enflaquecer. **2** n carne f magra.

lean² [li:n] **1** n inclinación f.
2 (*irr: pret and ptp* **leaned** *or* **leant**) *vt* ladear, inclinar, poner oblicuamente; **to — a ladder against a wall** poner (*or* apoyar) una escala contra una pared; **to — one's head on someone's shoulder** apoyar la cabeza en el hombro de uno.
3 *vi* ladearse, inclinarse, estar ladeado, estar inclinado; **to — against something** apoyarse en algo; **to — back** reclinarse, echar el cuerpo atrás; **to — forward** inclinarse; **to — on something** apoyarse en algo (*also fig*); **to — on someone for support** contar con el apoyo de uno; **to — on someone** (*fam*) ejercer presión sobre uno, amenazar a uno; **to — out** asomarse (*of* a); **to — over** inclinarse; **to — over someone** inclinarse sobre uno; **to — over backwards to help someone** volcarse por ayudar a uno, desvivirse por ayudar a uno; **we have —ed over backwards to get agreement** hemos hecho todas las concesiones posibles para llegar a un acuerdo; **to — to the Left** (*Pol*) inclinarse a la izquierda; **to — towards someone's opinion** inclinarse hacia la opinión de uno.

Leander [li:'ændə*] m Leandro.

leaning ['li:niŋ] **1** *adj* inclinado.
2 n inclinación f (*to, towards* hacia); tendencia f, propensión f (*to* a); predilección f (*to, towards* por); **what are his —s?** ¿cuál es su predilección?; **he has artistic —s** se siente atraído por una carrera artística.

leanness ['li:nnis] n flaqueza f; magrez f; carestía f, pobreza f.

leant [lent] *pret and ptp of* **lean²**.

lean-to ['li:ntu:] n colgadizo m, alpende m.

leap [li:p] **1** n salto m, brinco m; (*fig*) salto m; **the great — forward** (*China*) el gran salto hacia adelante; **— in the dark** salto m en el vacío; **by —s and bounds** a pasos agigantados; **in one —** de un salto.
2 (*irr: pret and ptp* **leaped** *or* **leapt**) *vt* saltar, saltar por encima de.
3 *vi* saltar, brincar, dar un salto; (*of fish*) saltar, bañarse; **my heart —ed** mi corazón dio un vuelco; **to — about** dar saltos, brincar; **to — at a chance** apresurarse a aprovechar una oportunidad; **to — at an offer** apresurarse a aceptar una oferta; **to — down** bajar de un salto, saltar en tierra; **to — for joy** saltar de alegría; **to — out of a car** saltar de un coche; **to — over** saltar, saltar por (encima de), salvar; **to — to one's feet** saltar en pie; **to — up** ponerse de pie de un salto, (*of flame*) subir de repente, volver a estallar, (*of figure etc*) subir de punto.

leapfrog ['li:pfrɒg] **1** n pídola f; **to play —** jugar a la pídola. **2** *vt* saltar por encima de. **3** *vi* jugar a la pídola, saltar.

leapt [lept] *pret and ptp of* **leap**.

leap year ['li:pjiə*] n año m bisiesto.

learn [lə:n] (*irr: pret and ptp* **learned** *or* **learnt**) *vti* (*in general*) aprender; *news, fact etc* saber, enterarse de; (*discover, find out*) descubrir, averiguar; **to — to do something** aprender a hacer algo; **to — how to do something** aprender a hacer algo, aprender cómo se hace algo, aprender el modo de hacer algo; **to — about something** (*hear of*) saber algo, (*instruct oneself*) informarse sobre algo, instruirse en algo; **to — from experience** aprender por experiencia; **to — of** saber, tener noticia de; **to — up** esforzarse por aprender, repasar, empollar.

learned ['lə:nid] *adj person* docto, sabio, erudito; *remark, speech, society etc* erudito; *profession* liberal; **to be — in** ser erudito en, ser muy entendido en.

learnedly ['lə:nidli] *adv* eruditamente.

learner ['lə:nə*] n principiante *mf*, aprendiz m, iza f; (*student*) estudiante *mf*, estudioso m, a f.

learner-driver ['lə:nə'draivə*] n aprendiz m de conductor, aprendiza f de conductora.

learning ['lə:niŋ] n (*act*) el aprender, estudio m; (*fund of —*) saber m, conocimientos *mpl*; (*erudition*)

saber m, erudición f; **man of —** sabio m, erudito m; **seat of —** centro m de estudios.

learnt [lə:nt] *pret and ptp of* **learn**.

lease [li:s] **1** n arriendo m, contrato m de arrendamiento; **to occupy a house on a 99-year —** ocupar una casa por un plazo de 99 años; **to let something out on —** dar algo en arriendo; **to give someone a new — of life** devolver la vitalidad a uno, servir de tónico a uno; **to take on a new — of life** (*person*) recobrar su vigor, (*thing*) renovarse.
2 *vt* (*take*) arrendar (*from de*), tomar en arriendo; (*give: also* **to — out**) arrendar, dar en arriendo.

leasehold ['li:shəuld] **1** n (*contract*) arrendamiento m; (*property*) inmueble m arrendado.
2 *attr* arrendado, alquilado; **— reform** reforma f del sistema de arriendos.

leaseholder ['li:shəuldə*] n arrendatario m, a f.

leash [li:ʃ] n trailla f, cuerda f.

least [li:st] **1** *adj* menor; más pequeño; mínimo; menos importante, menos considerable; **the — of them** el menor de ellos; **with the — possible expenditure** gastándose lo menos posible; **that's the — of my worries** eso es lo de menos.
2 *adv* menos; **the — expensive car** el coche menos costoso; **he deserves it — of all** se lo merece menos que todos los demás; **she is — able to afford it** ella es quien menos puede permitírselo; **— of all would I wish to offend him** ante todo no quiero ofenderle; *see* **expect** *etc*.
3 n lo menos; **it's the — one can ask** es lo menos que se puede pedir; **you gave yourself the —** Vd se sirvió la ración más pequeña; **at —** a lo menos, al menos, por lo menos; **at — it's fine** por lo menos hace buen tiempo; **there were 8 at —** había a lo menos 8; **we can at — try** al menos podemos probarlo; **at the very —** lo menos; **not in the —!** ¡en absoluto!, ¡de ninguna manera!; **he was not in the — upset** no se alteró en lo más mínimo; **to say the —** para no decir más.

leastways ['li:stweiz] *adv* (*fam*) de todos modos.

leather ['leðə*] **1** n cuero m; piel f; (*wash-*) gamuza f; **American —** cuero m artificial; **patent —** charol m.
2 *vt* (*fam*) zurrar.

leathern ['leðə(:)n] *adj* de cuero.

leathery ['leðəri] *adj* correoso; *skin* curtido.

leave [li:v] **1** n (a) (*permission*) permiso m; **by your —** con permiso de Vd; **without so much as a "by your —"** sin pedir permiso a nadie; **to ask — to do something** pedir permiso para hacer algo.
(b) (*permission to be absent*) permiso m; (*Mil, brief*) permiso m, (*lengthy, compassionate etc*) licencia f; **— of absence** permiso m para estar ausente; **compassionate —** permiso m especial; **to be on —** estar de permiso, estar de licencia; **to take French —** despedirse a la francesa.
(c) **to take one's —** despedirse (*of* de); **I must take my —** tengo que marcharme.
2 (*irr: pret and ptp* **left**) *vt* (a) (*allow to remain*) dejar; **to — 2 pages blank** dejar 2 páginas en blanco; **let's — it at that** dejemos las cosas así; **to — something with someone** dejar algo en manos de uno; **to — things lying about** dejar las cosas de cualquier modo; **to — one's supper** dejar la cena sin comer; **to — one's greens** no comer las verduras; **to — a good impression on someone** producir a uno una buena impresión; **it —s much to be desired** deja mucho que desear; **take it or — it** una de dos, o esto o lo otro, como Vd quiera; *see* **chance, cold** *etc*.
(b) (*person*) **I'll — you at the station** te dejo en la estación; **to — a wife and 2 children** dejar una viuda y 2 hijos; **he has left his wife** ha abandonado a su mujer; **I must — you** tengo que despedirme de vosotros, con permiso de Vds me voy; **you may — us** Vd puede retirarse; **to — someone free for the afternoon** permitir a uno disfrutar de una tarde libre.
(c) (*bequeath*) dejar, legar; **her father left her £500** su padre le legó 500 libras.
(d) (*Math*) **3 from 10 —s 7** de 3 a 10 van 7, 10 menos 3 son 7.
(e) (*remain, be over*) quedar; sobrar; **all the money I have left** todo el dinero que me queda; **how many are there left?** ¿cuántos quedan?; **nothing was left for me but to sell it** no tuve más remedio que venderlo; **there are 3 left** over sobran 3.
(f) (*entrust*) **I — it to you** le toca a Vd decidir, que lo decida Vd; **— it to me** yo me encargo de eso; **I — it to you to do lo dejo en sus manos; que lo haga Vd; I — it to you to judge** júzguelo Vd.
(g) (*depart from, quit*) salir de, abandonar; **to — a place** salir de un lugar, abandonar un lugar;

when the king left **Rome** cuando el rey abandonó Roma; **to — home** salir de su casa; **to — prison** salir de la cárcel; **to — school** salir del colegio; **to — the table** levantarse de la mesa; **to — one's post** dejar su puesto, dimitir su cargo, (*improperly*) abandonar su puesto; **to — the road** salir fuera de la carretera; **to — the rails** descarrilar.

(**h**) (*with adv or prep*) **to — aside** omitir, prescindir de, (*forgetfully*) olvidar; **to — someone behind** dejar a uno atrás; **we have left all that behind us** todo eso ha quedado a la espalda; **I left my coat behind** olvidé el abrigo; **he left the children behind** no llevó consigo a los niños, dejó allí a los niños; **to — off** *clothes* quitarse, no ponerse; *habit* renunciar a, dejar; **to — out** omitir, prescindir de; suprimir; **to — someone out in the rain** dejar a uno fuera en la lluvia; *see* **alone** *etc.*

3 *vi* irse, marcharse; salir (*for* para); (*of train etc*) salir; **to — off** terminar, cesar; suspender el trabajo; **when the rain —s off, when it —s off raining** cuando deje de llover; **to — off doing something** dejar de hacer algo, terminar de hacer algo.

leaven ['levn] **1** *n* levadura *f*; (*fig*) mezcla *f*; estímulo *m*. **2** *vt* aleudar; (*fig*) penetrar e influenciar, servir de estímulo a, ayudar a transformar.

leavening ['levniŋ] *n* levadura *f*; (*fig*) mezcla *f*, estímulo *m*.

leaves [li:vz] *npl of* **leaf**.

leave-taking ['li:v͵teikiŋ] *n* despedida *f*.

leavings ['li:viŋz] *npl* sobras *fpl*.

Lebanese [͵lebə'ni:z] **1** *adj* libanés. **2** *n* libanés *m*, esa *f*.

Lebanon ['lebənən] Líbano *m*.

lecher ['letʃə*] *n* libertino *m*.

lecherous ['letʃərəs] *adj* lascivo, lujurioso.

lecherously ['letʃərəsli] *adv* lascivamente.

lechery ['letʃəri] *n* lascivia *f*.

lectern ['lektə(:)n] *n* atril *m*; (*Eccl*) facistol *m*.

lecture ['lektʃə*] **1** *n* (*formal, by visitor etc*) conferencia *f*; (*Univ class*) clase *f*; (*fig*) sermoneo *m*; **to attend — s on** seguir un curso sobre (*or* de); **to give a —** dar una conferencia; **to read someone a —** sermonear a uno.

2 *vt* (*scold*) sermonear; **he —s us in French** nos da clases de francés.

3 *vi* dar una conferencia, dar una clase; **he —s in Law** tiene una cátedra de derecho; **he —s at 9 o'clock** da su clase a las 9; **he —s at Princeton** tiene una cátedra en Princeton; **he's lecturing at the moment** ahora está en clase; **he —s well** habla muy bien.

lecturer ['lektʃərə*] *n* (*visitor*) conferenciante *mf*, conferencista *mf*; (*Univ*) catedrático *m*; **assistant —** profesor *m* adjunto, profesora *f* adjunta.

lecture room ['lektʃə͵rum] *n* sala *f* de conferencias; (*Univ*) aula *f*.

lectureship ['lektʃəʃip] *n* cátedra *f*, cargo *m* (*or* puesto *m*) de profesor (adjunto).

led [led] *pret and ptp of* **lead**.

ledge [ledʒ] *n* repisa *f*, reborde *m*; (*along wall*) retallo *m*; (*of window*) antepecho *m*, alféizar *m*; (*shelf*) anaquel *m*; (*on mountain*) plataforma *f*, saliente *m*.

ledger ['ledʒə*] *n* libro *m* mayor.

lee [li:] **1** *adj* a sotavento, de sotavento. **2** *n* sotavento *m*; (*shelter*) socaire *m*; **in the — of** al socaire de, al abrigo de.

leech [li:tʃ] *n* sanguijuela *f* (*also fig*).

leek [li:k] *n* puerro *m*.

leer [liə*] **1** *n* mirada *f* impúdica, mirada *f* maliciosa; sonrisa *f* impúdica; **he said with a —** dijo sonriendo impúdico.

2 *vi* mirar impúdico, mirar malicioso (*at someone* a uno); sonreír impúdico (*at someone* a uno).

lees [li:z] *npl* heces *fpl*, poso *m*.

leeward ['li:wəd] **1** *adj* a sotavento, de sotavento. **2** *adv* a sotavento. **3** *n* sotavento *m*; **to — a** sotavento (*of* de).

Leeward Isles ['li:wəd͵ailz] *pl* Islas *fpl* de Sotavento.

leeway ['li:wei] *n* (*Naut*) deriva *f*; (*fig*) atraso *m*, tiempo *m* (*etc*) perdido; **to make up —** salir del atraso, recuperar el tiempo perdido; **there's a lot of — to make up** son muchas las pérdidas que tenemos que suplir.

left¹ [left] *pret and ptp of* **leave**.

left² [left] **1** *adj* izquierdo; (*Pol*) izquierdista. **2** *adv* a la izquierda, hacia la izquierda. **3** *n* (**a**) izquierda *f*; **on the —, to the —** a la izquierda; **to keep to the —** (*Aut*) circular por la izquierda. (**b**) (*Pol*) izquierda *f*, izquierdas *fpl*; **he has always been on the —** siempre ha sido de izquierdas; **he's further to the — than I am** es más izquierdista que yo.

left-hand ['lefthænd] *adj*: **— drive** conducción *f* a la izquierda; **— side** izquierda *f*; **— turn** vuelta *f* a la izquierda.

left-handed ['left'hændid] *adj* zurdo; (*fig*) *person* torpe, desmañado; *compliment* ambiguo, de doble filo; *marriage* de la mano izquierda; *tool* para zurdo.

leftist ['leftist] **1** *adj* izquierdista. **2** *n* izquierdista *mf*.

left-luggage ['left'lʌgidʒ] *attr*: **— office** consigna *f*.

left-overs ['left͵əuvəz] *npl* sobras *fpl*.

left-wing ['left͵wiŋ] *adj* izquierdista.

left-winger ['left'wiŋə*] *n* izquierdista *mf*.

leg [leg] **1** *n* pierna *f*; (*of animal, bird, furniture*) pata *f*; (*support*) pie *m*; (*of trousers*) pernera *f*; (*of stocking*) caña *f*; (*of pork*) pernil *m*; (*of lamb, veal*) pierna *f*; (*stage*) etapa *f*, fase *f*; **I've been on my —s all day** he estado trajinando todo el santo día; **to be on one's last —s** estar en las últimas; **to give someone a —** up ayudar a uno a subir (*also fig*); **he hasn't a — to stand on** no tiene razón alguna, no hay nada que hable a su favor; **to pull someone's —** tomar el pelo a uno; **to shake a —** (*fam*) bailar; **to show a —** (*fam*) despertar, levantarse; **show a —!** ¡a levantarse!; **to stand on one's own two —s** (*fig*) ser independiente; **to stretch one's —s** estirar las piernas, (*after stiffness*) desentumecerse las piernas, (*fig*) dar un paseíto; **to take to one's —s** poner pies en polvorosa, echar a correr; **to walk someone off his —s** dejar a uno rendido tras una larguísima caminata.

2 *vt*: **to — it** ir andando.

legacy ['legəsi] *n* legado *m*; (*fig*) herencia *f*, patrimonio *m*.

legal ['li:gəl] *adj* (*lawful*) lícito, legítimo; (*relating to the law*) legal; *department, entity, inquiry* jurídico; *matter* de derecho; **— profession** abogacía *f*; *see* **advice, cost** *etc.*

legality [li:'gæliti] *n* legalidad *f*.

legalization [͵li:gəlai'zeiʃən] *n* legalización *f*.

legalize ['li:gəlaiz] *vt* legalizar; autorizar, legitimar.

legally ['li:gəli] *adv* según la ley, según el derecho; legalmente.

legate ['legit] *n* legado *m*.

legatee [͵legə'ti:] *n* legatario *m*, a *f*.

legation [li'geiʃən] *n* legación *f*.

legend ['ledʒənd] *n* leyenda *f*; **the black —** la leyenda negra.

legendary ['ledʒəndəri] *adj* legendario.

legerdemain ['ledʒədə'mein] *n* juego *m* de manos; (*fig*) trapacería *f*.

-legged ['legid] *adj* de piernas . . . , *eg* **long-legged** de piernas largas, zancudo; **three-legged** de tres piernas, *stool* de tres patas.

leggings ['legiŋz] *npl* polainas *fpl*; (*baby's*) pantalones *mpl* polainas.

leggy ['legi] *adj* zanquilargo, zancudo.

Leghorn ['leg'hɔ:n] Liorna.

legibility [͵ledʒi'biliti] *n* legibilidad *f*.

legible ['ledʒəbl] *adj* legible.

legibly ['ledʒəbli] *adv* legiblemente.

legion ['li:dʒən] *n* legión *f* (*also fig*); **American L—, British L—** organizaciones de veteranos de las dos guerras mundiales; **Foreign L—** Legión *f* Extranjera; **they are —** son legión.

legionary ['li:dʒənəri] **1** *adj* legionario. **2** *n* legionario *m*.

legionnaire [͵li:dʒə'neə*] *n* legionario *m*.

legislate ['ledʒisleit] **1** *vt*: **to — something out of existence** imponer tantas restricciones legales sobre algo que no puede continuar existiendo.

2 *vi* legislar; **one cannot — for every case** es imposible legislar para todo.

legislation [͵ledʒis'leiʃən] *n* legislación *f*.

legislative ['ledʒislətiv] *adj* legislativo.

legislator ['ledʒisleitə*] *n* legislador *m*, ora *f*.

legislature ['ledʒislətʃə*] *n* cuerpo *m* legislativo, asamblea *f* legislativa.

legist ['li:dʒist] *n* legista *m*.

legit [lə'dʒit] *adj* (*sl*) = **legitimate**.

legitimacy [li'dʒitiməsi] *n* legitimidad *f*.

legitimate [li'dʒitimit] *adj* legítimo; (*proper*) admisible, justo; **the — theatre** el teatro teatro, el teatro propiamente dicho, el teatro verdadero.

legitimate [li'dʒitimeit] *vt*, **legitimize** [li'dʒitimaiz] *vt* legitimar.

leg-pull ['legpul] *n* broma *f*.

leg-puller ['legpulə*] *n* bromista *mf*.

legroom ['legrum] *n* espacio *m* para las piernas.

leg-show ['legʃəu] *n* exhibición *f* de piernas.

legume ['legju:m] *n* (*species*) legumbre *f*; (*fruit*) vaina *f*.

leguminous [le'gju:minəs] *adj* leguminoso.

leisure ['leʒə*] **1** n ocio m, tiempo m libre; **people of —** gente f acomodada, (pej) gente f bien; **a life of —** una vida regalada; **to be at —** estar desocupado, no tener nada que hacer; **do it at your —** hágalo en sus ratos libres, hágalo cuando tenga tiempo; **to have the —** to **do something** disponer de bastante tiempo para hacer algo.
2 attr: **— occupation** pasatiempo m, modo m de ocuparse durante los ratos libres; **in one's — time** en sus ratos libres, en los momentos de ocio.
leisured ['leʒəd] adj class acomodado.
leisurely ['leʒəli] **1** adj pausado, lento. **2** adv pausadamente, despacio, con calma.
lemming ['lemiŋ] n conejo m de Noruega.
lemon ['lemən] **1** n (fruit) limón m; (tree) limonero m.
2 attr, adj de limón; (colour) limonado.
lemonade [,lemə'neid] n limonada f.
lemon grove ['leməngrəuv] n limonar m.
lemon squash ['lemən'skwɔʃ] n limonada f natural, zumo m de limón.
lemon squeezer ['lemən,skwi:zə*] n exprimelimones m, exprimidor m, prensalimones m.
lemur ['li:mə*] n lémur m.
lend [lend] (irr: pret and ptp lent) **1** vt prestar; (fig) prestar, dar, añadir; **to — out** prestar.
2 vr: **to — oneself to** prestarse a; **it does not — itself to** being filmed no es apto para ser transformado en película.
lender ['lendə*] n prestador m, ora f; (professional) prestamista m.
lending ['lendiŋ] adj library circulante.
lend-lease ['lend'li:s] n: **— agreement** convenio m de préstamos y arriendos.
length [leŋθ] n **(a)** (in general) largo m, longitud f; (Naut) eslora f; **along the whole — of the river** a lo largo de todo el río; **over the — and breadth of England** por toda Inglaterra, en toda la extensión de Inglaterra; **the — of skirts** el largo de las faldas; **the — of this letter** la longitud de esta carta; **to be 4 metres in —, to have a — of 4 metres** tener 4 metros de largo; **what — is it?** ¿cuánto tiene de largo?; **what — do you want?** ¿cuánto quiere?; **to measure one's — (on the floor)** medir el suelo; **to go to any —(s)** no pararse en barras; **to go to any —(s) to + infin** hacer todo lo posible para + infin; **to go to great —s in** extremarse en; **to go to the — of + ger** llegar al extremo de + infin.
(b) (Sport) cuerpo m; **to win by half a —** ganar por medio cuerpo; **to win by 4 —s** ganar por 4 cuerpos.
(c) (section: of cloth) corte m; (of road, track etc) tramo m.
(d) (of time) espacio m, extensión f, duración f; **— of life** duración f de la vida; **— of service** duración f del servicio; **— of a syllable** cantidad f de una sílaba; **for what — of time?** ¿durante cuánto tiempo?; **at — (finally)** por fin, finalmente; **to speak at —** hablar largamente; **to discuss something at —** discutir algo detenidamente; **to explain something at —** explicar algo por extenso.
lengthen ['leŋθən] **1** vt alargar, prolongar, extender.
2 vi alargarse, prolongarse, extenderse; (days) crecer.
lengthily ['leŋθili] adv largamente, extensamente.
lengthways ['leŋθweiz], **lengthwise** ['leŋθwaiz] **1** adj longitudinal, de largo.
2 adv longitudinalmente; a lo largo; **to measure something —** medir el largo de algo.
lengthy ['leŋθi] adj largo, extenso; (pej) larguísimo; illness etc de larga duración; meeting prolongado.
lenience ['li:niəns] n, **leniency** ['li:niənsi] n lenidad f, poca severidad f; indulgencia f.
lenient ['li:niənt] adj poco severo, más blando; indulgente.
leniently ['li:niəntli] adv con poca severidad, con indulgencia.
Leningrad ['leningræd] Leningrado.
lens [lenz] n (Opt, Phot) lente f; (of camera) objetivo m; (hand-, for stamps etc) lupa f; (Anat) cristalino m.
lent [lent] pret and ptp of **lend**.
Lent [lent] n Cuaresma f.
Lenten ['lentən] adj cuaresmal.
lentil ['lentl] n lenteja f.
Leon ['li:ɔn] León m.
Leonese [li:ə'ni:z] **1** adj leonés. **2** n leonés m, esa f.
3 n (dialect) leonés m.
leonine ['li:ənain] adj leonino.
leopard ['lepəd] n leopardo m.
leper ['lepə*] n leproso m, a f.
leper colony ['lepə,kɔləni] n leprosería f.
lepidoptera [,lepi'dɔptərə] npl lepidópteros mpl.
leprechaun ['leprəkɔ:n] n (Ir) duende m.
leprosy ['leprəsi] n lepra f.

leprous ['leprəs] adj leproso.
Lesbian ['lezbiən] **1** adj lesbio; tortillera (fam). **2** n lesbiana f; tortillera f (fam).
Lesbianism ['lezbiənizəm] n lesbianismo m.
lèse-majesté, lese-majesty ['leiz'mæʒəsti] n lesa majestad f.
lesion ['li:ʒən] n lesión f.
less [les] **1** adj (a) (in size, degree etc) menor, inferior; **a sum — than £1** una cantidad inferior a 1 libra; **A or B, whichever is the —** la menor de las dos cantidades A o B; **it's nothing — than a disaster** no es sino un verdadero desastre, es un desastre y no se puede llamar de otro modo; **it's nothing — than disgraceful** es francamente vergonzoso; **St James the L—** Santiago el Menor; **no — a person than the bishop** no otro que el obispo, el obispo y no otro, el mismísimo obispo; **that was told me by the minister, no —** eso me lo dijo el mismo ministro.
(b) (in quantity) menos; **now we eat — bread** ahora comemos menos pan; **of — importance** de menos importancia; **— noise please!** ¡menos ruido, por favor!; **— of it!** ¡basta ya!; **to grow —** menguar, decrecer, disminuir.
2 adv menos; **— and —** cada vez menos; **— than 6** menos de 6; **in — than an hour** en menos de una hora; **he works — than I (do)** él trabaja menos que yo; **it's — than you think** es menos de lo que piensas; **he is — well known** es menos conocido; **the — he works the — he earns** mientras menos trabaja menos gana; **even — menos** aun; **still — menos** todavía; **none the — sin** embargo, a pesar de todo, con todo; **there will be so much the — to pay** tanto menos habrá que pagar; **can't you let me have it for —?** ¿no me lo puedes ceder en menos?; **the problem is — one of capital than of personnel** el problema más que de capitales es de personal.
3 prep menos; **the price — 10%** el precio menos 10 por ciento; **a year — 4 days** un año menos 4 días.
-less [lis] sin, eg hatless sin sombrero, **sunless** sin sol.
lessee [le'si:] n arrendatario m, a f.
lessen ['lesn] **1** vt disminuir, reducir, aminorar; cost, stature etc rebajar. **2** vt disminuir(se), reducirse, menguar.
lessening ['lesniŋ] n disminución f, reducción f.
lesser ['lesə*] adj comp of **less**; menor, más pequeño; inferior.
lesson ['lesn] n lección f; clase f; **—s** clases fpl; **a French —** una clase de francés; **to give a —** dar clase; **to have a —** tomar lección; **to learn one's — (fig)** escarmentar; **let that be a — to you!** ¡que te sirva de lección!, ¡para que lo aprendas!; **to teach someone a — (fig)** hacer que uno vaya aprendiendo.
lessor [le'sɔ:*] n arrendador m, ora f.
lest [lest] conj para que no + subj, de miedo que + subj; **— we forget** para que no olvidemos; **— he catch me unprepared** para que no me coja desprevenido; **I feared — he should fall** temía que fuera a caer; **I didn't do it — someone should object** no lo hice por miedo de que alguien pusiera peros.
let¹ [let] n (Tennis) let m; **without — or hindrance** sin estorbo ni obstáculo.
let² [let] (irr: pret and ptp **let**) **1** vt **(a)** (permit) dejar, permitir; **to — someone do something** dejar a uno hacer algo, permitir a uno hacer algo, permitir que uno haga algo; **— me help you** déjeme ayudarle.
(b) blood (surgically) sacar; **without —ting any blood** sin efusión de sangre.
(c) (hire out) alquilar; **"to —"** "se alquila"; **we can't find a house to —** no encontramos una casa que alquilar.
(d) (v aux, gen translated by subj) **— us pray** oremos; **—'s go!** ¡vamos!; **—'s get out here** bajémonos aquí; **— there be light** hágase la luz; **— there be no mistake about it** entiéndase bien que ...; **— them all come!** ¡que vengan todos!; **— their need be never so great** por muy grande que sea su necesidad; **— X be 60** supongamos que X equivale a 60.
(e) (with adv or prep) **to — someone by** dejar a uno pasar; **to — down** seat, step etc bajar; hair dejar caer, soltar; dress alargar; tyre desinflar, deshinchar; **to — something down on a rope** bajar algo con una cuerda; **to — someone down on a rope** descolgar a uno con una cuerda; **to — someone down (morally)** defraudar la confianza de uno, faltar a uno; dejar a uno plantado; desilusionar a uno; **it has never — us down yet** no nos ha fallado nunca; **the weather — us down** nos defraudó el tiempo; **to be — down** llevarse un chasco; **to — someone down gently** (fig) castigar a uno con poca severidad; **to — someone in** dejar a uno entrar, visitor hacer

a uno pasar; **shoes that — in water** zapatos *mpl* que dejan entrar el agua; **I got — in for £5** tuve que pagar 5 libras; **to — someone in for a lot of trouble** causar a uno muchas molestias, plantear a uno muchos problemas; **to — someone in on a secret** revelar a uno un secreto; **to — someone into a house** dejar a uno entrar en una casa; **to — a plaque into a wall** empotrar una lápida en una pared; **to — off** *arrow, gun* disparar; *firework* hacer estallar; *steam* dejar escapar; **to — someone off** perdonar a uno, dejar libre a uno; **to — someone off something** perdonar algo a uno; **to — someone off with a warning** dar a uno una amonestación pero sin otro castigo; **he was — off with a fine** escapó con una multa nada más; **to — on about something to someone** revelar algo a uno; **he's not —ting on** no dice nada; **don't go and — on about this** de esto no digas ni pío; **to — out** dejar salir; *prisoner* poner en libertad; *cattle etc* soltar, echar al pasto; *secret* revelar, divulgar; *fire* dejar apagarse; *dress* ensanchar; *(hire out)* alquilar; **the dog is — out at 8** se le deja salir al perro a las 8; **I'll — you out** te acompaño a la puerta; **the watchman — me out** el sereno me abrió la puerta para que saliese; **that —s me out** eso me deja libre; **to — the air out of a tyre** desinflar un neumático; **to — out a yell** dar un alarido; **to — out one's belt** aflojar un poco el cinturón; **to — someone through** dejar pasar a uno; *see* **alone, fly, go** *etc*.
2 *vi* *(be hired)* alquilarse *(at, for* en); **to — on** revelar el secreto, cantar; **he — on that . . .** reveló que . . .; **but he wouldn't — on** pero no dijo nada; **to — up** moderarse (en el uso de, en el consumo de); trabajar *(etc)* menos; **when the rain —s up** cuando deje de llover tanto; **to — up on someone** tratar a uno con menos rigor.
3 *vr:* **to — oneself be seen** dejarse ver; **to — oneself down** *(fig)* no estar a la altura de uno; **to — oneself down by a rope** descolgarse con una cuerda; **to — oneself in** abrirse la puerta; **to — oneself in for trouble** crearse molestias, plantearse problemas; **you don't know what you're —ting yourself in for** no sabes lo que te pescas.
let-down ['letdaun] *n* decepción *f*, chasco *m*.
lethal ['li:θəl] *adj* mortífero; *wound etc, dose* mortal; *weapon* mortífero.
lethargic [le'θɑ:dʒik] *adj* aletargado, letárgico.
lethargy ['leθədʒi] *n* letargo *m*.
Lethe ['li:θi:] Lete(o) *m*.
Lett [let] *see* **Latvian**.
letter ['letə*] **1** *n* **(a)** *(of alphabet)* letra *f*; **block —, capital —** mayúscula *f*; **dead —** letra *f* muerta; **small —** minúscula *f*; **the — of the law** la ley escrita; **to the —** a la letra, al pie de la letra.
(b) *(missive)* carta *f*; **covering —** carta *f* adjunta; **open —** carta *f* abierta; **registered —** carta *f* certificada; **— of credit** carta *f* de crédito; **— of introduction** carta *f* de recomendación (to para); **—s of Galdós** *(as published)* epistolario *m* de Galdós; **—s patent** patente *m* de privilegio; **by —** por carta, por escrito.
(c) **—s** *(learning)* letras *fpl*; **man of —s** hombre *m* de letras, literato *m*.
2 *vt* rotular, inscribir, estampar con letras.
letterbox ['letəbɔks] *n* buzón *m*.
letter-card ['letəkɑ:d] *n* carta-tarjeta *f*.
lettered ['letəd] *adj* *person* culto; *object* rotulado, marcado con letras; **— in gold** marcado con letras doradas.
letter file ['letəfail] *n* carpeta *f*.
letterhead ['letəhed] *n* membrete *m*.
lettering ['letəriŋ] *n* letras *fpl*, inscripción *f*, rótulo *m*.
letterpress ['letəpres] *n* *(Typ)* texto *m* impreso.
letting ['letiŋ] *n* arrendamiento *m*.
lettuce ['letis] *n* lechuga *f*.
let-up ['letʌp] *n* calma *f*, respiro *m*, tregua *f*, descanso *m*; **we worked 5 hours without a —** trabajamos 5 horas sin interrupción; **there was no —** no hubo ningún intervalo de calma; **if there is a — in the rain** si deja un momento de llover.
leukaemia, (US) **leukemia** [lu:'ki:miə] *n* leucemia *f*.
Levant [li'vænt] Levante *m*.
Levantine ['levəntain] **1** *adj* levantino. **2** *n* levantino *m*, a *f*.
levee ['levei] *n* besamanos *m*, recepción *f*.
levee ['levi] *n* ribero *m*, dique *m*.
level ['levl] **1** *adj* llano, plano, raso; a nivel, nivelado; igual, uniforme; *tone* ecuánime; *judgement, mind* juicioso; **to be dead —** estar completamente a nivel; **to be — with** estar a nivel con; **to be — with the ground** estar a ras de la tierra; **to be — with the**

water estar a flor del agua; **I'll do my — best** haré todo lo que pueda.
2 *adv* a nivel; ras con ras; **to draw — with someone** llegar a la altura de uno, alcanzar a uno, *(in league etc)* llegar a empatar con uno, colocarse en igual posición que uno.
3 *n* **(a)** *(instrument)* nivel *m*.
(b) *(altitude, degree)* nivel *m*; **dead —** superficie *f* completamente llana; **at eye —** a la altura del ojo; **at roof —** a la altura de los tejados; **speed on the —** velocidad *f* sobre superficie llana; **it's on the —** *(fam)* es un negocio honrado, es un juego perfectamente limpio; **is he on the —?** *(fam)* ¿es de fiar?, ¿es una persona honrada?; **are you telling me this on the —?** *(fam)* ¿me lo dices en serio?; **to be on a — with** estar al nivel de; **to be on a — with the ground** estar a ras de la tierra; **to be on a — with** *(fig)* estar al nivel de; ser parangonable con; **that trick is on a — with the other** esa jugada es tan vil como la otra; **to come down to someone's —** bajar al nivel en que está uno.
(c) *(flat place)* llano *m*.
4 *vt* **(a)** *ground etc* nivelar, allanar; *building* derribar; *site* desmontar, despejar; *quantities* igualar, nivelar; **to — down** rebajar al mismo nivel; **to — up** elevar al mismo nivel; **to — something to** *(or* with) **the ground** arrasar algo.
(b) *blow etc* asestar *(at* a); *weapon* apuntar *(at* a); *accusation* dirigir *(against, at* a), hacer *(against, at* contra).
5 *vi:* **to — off,** **to — out** nivelarse; *(of prices etc)* estabilizarse; *(Aer)* enderezarse.
level crossing ['levl'krɔsiŋ] *n* paso *m* a nivel.
level-headed ['levl'hedid] *adj* juicioso, sensato.
levelling ['levliŋ] *n* nivelación *f*; aplanamiento *m*.
lever ['li:və*] **1** *n* palanca *f* *(also fig)*. **2** *vt* apalancar; **to — something up** alzar algo con palanca.
leverage ['li:vəridʒ] *n* apalancamiento *m*; *(fig)* influencia *f*; fuerza *f*; ventaja *f*.
leveret ['levərit] *n* lebrato *m*.
leviathan [li'vaiəθən] *n* leviatán *m*; *(fig)* buque *m* enorme.
levitate ['leviteit] **1** *vt* elevar (por medios espiritistas). **2** *vi* elevarse (por medios espiritistas).
levitation [,levi'teiʃən] *n* elevación *f* (por medios espiritistas).
Levite ['li:vait] *n* levita *m*.
levity ['leviti] *n* frivolidad *f*, ligereza *f*, informalidad *f*; *(mirth)* risas *fpl*.
levy ['levi] **1** *n* *(act)* exacción *f* (de tributos); *(tax)* impuesto *m*; *(surcharge)* sobrecarga *f*, sobretasa *f*; *(Mil)* leva *f*.
2 *vt* *tax* exigir *(on* a), recaudar; *fine* imponer *(on* a); *(Mil)* reclutar.
lewd [lu:d] *adj* impúdico, obsceno; *song, story etc* verde.
lewdly ['lu:dli] *adv* impúdicamente, obscenamente.
lewdness ['lu:dnis] *n* impudicicia *f*, obscenidad *f*; lo verde.
lexical ['leksikəl] *adj* léxico.
lexicographer [,leksi'kɔgrəfə*] *n* lexicógrafo *m*.
lexicographical [,leksikəu'græfikəl] *adj* lexicográfico.
lexicography [,leksi'kɔgrəfi] *n* lexicografía *f*.
lexicon ['leksikən] *n* léxico *m*.
Leyden ['laidn] Leide(n), Leida.
liability [,laiə'biliti] *n* **(a)** responsabilidad *f*; riesgo *m*; tendencia *f*; *(burden)* carga *f* onerosa, lastre *m*; desventaja *f*; **one's — for tax** la cantidad que uno puede ser llamado a pagar en impuestos; **he's a real —** es un estorbo, es absolutamente inútil.
(b) **liabilities** obligaciones *fpl*, compromisos *mpl*; *(Comm)* pasivo *m*, deudas *fpl*; **to meet one's liabilities** satisfacer sus deudas; *see* **company**.
liable ['laiəbl] *adj:* **to be —** ser el responsable; **to be — for** ser responsable de; **to be — for taxes** *(thing)* estar sujeto a impuestos, *(person)* tener que pagar impuestos; **to be — to** + *infin* tener tendencia a + *infin*, ser propenso a + *infin*; **he is — not to come** es capaz de no venir, tiene tendencia a no venir; **the pond is — to freeze** el estanque tiene tendencia a helarse, el estanque bien puede helarse; **the plan is — to changes** el plan bien puede sufrir cambios; **we are — to get shot at here** aquí corremos el riesgo de que disparen sobre nosotros, aquí estamos expuestos a los tiros.
liaison [li:'eizɔn] *n* **(a)** *(coordination)* enlace *m*, conexión *f*, coordinación *f*; *(Mil)* enlace *m*. **(b)** *(affair)* lío *m*, relaciones *fpl* amorosas.
liaison officer [li:'eizɔn,ɔfisə*] *n* oficial *m* de enlace.
liar ['laiə*] *n* mentiroso *m*, a *f*, embustero *m*, a *f*; **—!** ¡mentira!
libation [lai'beiʃən] *n* libación *f*.

libel ['laibəl] **1** *n* difamación *f*, calumnia *f* (*on* de); (*written*) libelo *m*; **it's a —!** (*hum*) ¡es mentira!; **it's a — on all of us!** ¡esto nos calumnia a todos!
2 *vt* difamar, calumniar.
libellous, (US) **libelous** ['laibələs] *adj* difamatorio, calumnioso.
liberal ['libərəl] **1** *adj* liberal (*also Pol*); *offer etc* generoso; *supply* abundante; (*in views*) tolerante.
2 *n* liberal *mf*.
liberalism ['libərəlizəm] *n* liberalismo *m*.
liberality [,libə'ræliti] *n* generosidad *f*, liberalidad *f*.
liberalize ['libərəlaiz] *vt* liberalizar.
liberally ['libərəli] *adv* generosamente, liberalmente; abundantemente; con tolerancia.
liberal-minded ['libərəl'maindid] *adj* tolerante.
liberal-mindedness ['libərəl'maindidnis] *n* tolerancia *f*.
liberate ['libəreit] *vt* (*free*) libertar, librar (*from* de); *prisoner* poner en libertad; *gas etc* dejar escapar.
liberation [,libə'reiʃən] *n* liberación *f*.
liberator ['libəreitə*] *n* libertador *m*, ora *f*.
libertinage ['libətinidʒ] *n* libertinaje *m*.
libertine ['libətiːn] *n* libertino *m*.
liberty ['libəti] *n* libertad *f*; **— of conscience** libertad *f* de conciencia; **— of the press** libertad *f* de prensa; **it's a dead —!** (*fam*) ¡no hay derecho!; **to be at —** estar en libertad, (*at leisure*) estar desocupado; **to be at — to** + *infin* tener permiso para + *infin*, tener el derecho de + *infin*, estar autorizado para + *infin*; **is he at — to come?** ¿está libre para venir?; **when you are at — to study it** cuando tenga tiempo para estudiarlo; **to restore someone to —** devolver la libertad a uno; **to set someone at —** poner a uno en libertad; **I have taken the — of giving your name** me he tomado la libertad de darles su nombre; **to take liberties with a text** tomarse libertades con un texto, interpretar demasiado libremente un texto; **to take liberties with someone** tratar a uno con demasiada familiaridad, (*sexually*) propasarse con una.
libidinous [li'bidinəs] *adj* libidinoso.
libido [li'biːdəu] *n* libido *f*.
librarian [lai'breəriən] *n* bibliotecario *m*, a *f*.
librarianship [lai'breəriənʃip] *n* (**a**) profesión *f* de bibliotecario. (**b**) conocimientos *mpl* especializados del bibliotecario. (**c**) puesto *m* de bibliotecario.
library ['laibrəri] *n* biblioteca *f*; (*esp private*) librería *f*; **circulating —, lending —** biblioteca *f* circulante; **public —** biblioteca *f* pública; **reference —** biblioteca *f* de consulta; **university —** biblioteca *f* universitaria.
librettist [li'bretist] *n* libretista *mf*.
libretto [li'bretəu] *n* libreto *m*.
Libya ['libiə] Libia *f*.
Libyan ['libiən] **1** *adj* libio. **2** *n* libio *m*, a *f*.
lice [lais] *npl of* **louse**.
licence, (US) **license** ['laisəns] *n* (**a**) (*permit*) licencia *f*, permiso *m*; autorización *f*; (*Aut etc*) carnet *m*, permiso *m*; **dog —** licencia *f* para perro; **export —** permiso *m* de exportación; **import —** permiso *m* de importación; **marriage —** licencia *f* para casarse; **poetic —** licencia *f* poética; **wireless —** licencia para radio; **to manufacture something under —** fabricar algo bajo licencia.
(**b**) (*excess*) libertinaje *m*, desenfreno *m*; (*freedom*) libertad *f*; **you can allow some — in translation** Vd puede permitirse cierta libertad al traducirlo.
licence number ['laisəns,nʌmbə*] *n* (*Aut*) número *m* de matrícula.
licence plate ['laisəns,pleit] *n* (*Aut*) placa *f* de matrícula.
license ['laisəns] *vt* licenciar, autorizar, dar permiso a; *car* sacar la patente de; **to be —d to** + *infin* tener permiso para + *infin*, estar autorizado para + *infin*.
licensee [,laisən'siː] *n* concesionario *m*, a *f*, persona *f* autorizada; (*of bar*) patrón *m*.
licentiate [lai'senʃiit] *n* (*person*) licenciado *m*; (*title*) licencia *f*, licenciatura *f*.
licentious [lai'senʃəs] *adj* licencioso.
lichen ['laikən] *n* liquen *m*.
lichgate ['litʃgeit] *n* puerta *f* de cementerio.
licit ['lisit] *adj* lícito.
lick [lik] **1** *n* lamedura *f*, lengüetada *f*; **a — of paint** una mano de pintura; **a — of polish** un poquito de cera; **to go at a good —** (*fam*) ir a buen tren, correr rápidamente.
2 *vt* (*with tongue, of flames*) lamer; (*of waves*) besar; (*fam*: *tan, defeat*) dar una paliza a; *see* **dust, lip** *etc*.
licking ['likiŋ] *n* lamedura *f*; (*fam*) paliza *f*; **to give someone a —** dar una paliza a uno.
lickspittle ['likspitl] *n* lameculos *m*.
licorice ['likəris] *n* regaliz *m*.

lid [lid] *n* (*of box, case, pot etc*) tapa *f*; (*of pan etc*) cobertera *f*; (*Anat*) párpado *m*; (*sl: hat*) techo *m*; **that puts the —** *on* it se acabó, eso es el fin.
lido ['liːdəu] *n* (*bathing*) establecimiento *m* de baños; (*swimming*) centro *m* de natación, piscina *f*; (*boating*) centro *m* de balandrismo.
lie¹ [lai] **1** *n* mentira *f*; **white —** mentira *f* piadosa, mentirilla *f*; **it's a —!** ¡es mentira!; **to give the — to** *person* dar el mentís a, *report* desmentir; **to tell a —** mentir.
2 *vi* mentir.
lie² [lai] (*irr: pret* **lay**, *ptp* **lain**) **1** *vi* (**a**) (*person etc: act*) echarse, acostarse, tenderse; (*state*) estar echado, estar tumbado, estar acostado, estar tendido; (*in grave*) yacer, estar enterrado; **here —s** aquí yace; **he lay where he had fallen** estaba tumbado donde había caído; **don't — on the grass** no te eches sobre el césped; **to — asleep** estar dormido; **to — dead** yacer muerto; **to — in bed** estar en la cama, (*lazily*) seguir en la cama; **to — helpless** estar tumbado sin poder ayudarse; **to — resting** estar descansando; **to — still** quedarse inmóvil.
(**b**) (*objects etc*) estar; (*be situated*) estar, estar situado, encontrarse; (*stretch*) extenderse; **the book lay on the table** el libro estaba en la mesa; **the book lay unopened** el libro quedaba sin abrir; **the snow lay half a metre deep** había medio metro de nieve; **the snow did not —** la nieve se derritió; **the money is lying in the bank** el dinero sigue en el banco; **it —s further on** está situado más adelante; **our road lay along the river** nuestro camino seguía a lo largo del río; **the road —s over the hills** el camino cruza las colinas; **the factory lay idle** la fábrica estaba parada; **obstacles — in the way** hay obstáculos por delante; **the plain lay before us** la llanura se extendía delante de nosotros; **how does the land —?** ¿cuál es el estado actual de las cosas?; **where does the difficulty —?** ¿en qué consiste la dificultad?; **the fault —s with you** la falta es tuya, tú eres el culpable; **it —s with you to reform it** le corresponde a Vd reformarlo; **it does not — with me** no depende de mí, no me toca a mí.
(**c**) (*evidence etc*) ser admisible.
(**d**) (*with adv or prep*) **to — about** estar esparcido; estar en desorden; **he just —s about** pasa el tiempo sin hacer nada; **we lay about on our beds** quedamos tumbados en las camas; **it must be lying about somewhere** estará por aquí, debe de andar por aquí; **to — back** recostarse (*against, on* sobre); **to — down** (*act*) echarse, acostarse, tenderse; (*state*) estar echado, estar tumbado, estar acostado, estar tendido; **— down!** (*to dog*) ¡échate!; **to — down under it, to take it lying down** aceptarlo sin protestar, soportarlo sin chistar, tragarlo; **he's not one to take things lying down** no es de los que aceptan mansamente las injusticias; **to — in** seguir en la cama, no levantarse; (*at birth*) estar de parto; **to — over** quedar aplazado, quedar en suspenso; **to — to** (*Naut: act*) ponerse a la capa, (*state*) estar a la capa; **to — up** (*hide*) estar escondido; (*rest*) descansar; (*Naut*) estar amarrado.
2 *n* (*of ball etc*) posición *f*; **— of the land** configuración *f* del terreno, (*fig*) estado *m* de las cosas.
lie-abed ['laiəbed] *n* dormilón *m*, ona *f*.
lie detector ['laidi,tektə*] *n* detector *m* de mentiras.
lief [liːf] *adv* (*arch*): **I would as — + *infin*** preferiría + *infin*.
Liège [li'eiʒ] Lieja *f*.
liege [liːdʒ] *n* (*lord*) señor *m* feudal; (*vassal*) vasallo *m*; **my —** señor.
liege lord ['liːdʒ,lɔːd] *n* señor *m* feudal.
liegeman ['liːdʒmæn] *n*, *pl* **—men** [men] vasallo *m*.
lien [liən] *n* derecho *m* de retención (*on* de).
lieu [luː] *n*: **in — of** en lugar de.
lieutenant [lef'tenənt] *n* lugarteniente *m*; (*Mil*) teniente *m*; (*Naut*) teniente *m* de navío; **second —** alférez *m*.
lieutenant-colonel [lef'tenənt'kəːnl] *n* teniente *m* coronel.
lieutenant-commander [lef'tenəntkə'maːndə*] *n* capitán *m* de corbeta.
lieutenant-general [lef'tenənt'dʒenərəl] *n* teniente *m* general.
life [laif] *n*, *pl* **lives** [laivz] **1** *n* (**a**) (*in general*) vida *f*; ser *m*, existencia *f*; modo *m* de vivir; (*liveliness*) vida *f*, vivacidad *f*, animación *f*; (*of licence etc*) vigencia *f*, validez *f*; (*of battery*) vida *f*, duración *f*; **bird —** los pájaros; **plant —** vida *f* vegetal, las plantas; **there is not much insect —** here aquí hay pocos insectos.
(**b**) (*with adj*) **early —** juventud *f*, años *mpl* juveniles; **in her early —** en su juventud; **in later**

— más tarde, en los años posteriores; **the good** — una vida agradable, (*Rel*) la vida santa; **it's a good** — es una vida agradable; **high** — alta sociedad *f*, gran mundo *m*; **home** — vida *f* de familia; **low** — hampa *f*; **private** — vida *f* privada; **the private** — **of Henry VIII** la vida íntima de Enrique VIII; **X, known in private** — **as Z X**, conocido en la intimidad como Z; **my** —! ¡Dios mío!; **what a** —! ¡qué vida ésta!

(**c**) (*with* to be) **to be a matter of** — **and death** ser cosa de vida o de muerte; **to be the** — **and soul of the party** ser el alma de la fiesta; **such is** —! ¡así es la vida!; **this is the** —! ¡qué vida nos chupamos!, ¡esto es jauja!

(**d**) (*with prep*) **at my time of** — a mi edad, con los años que yo tengo; **for** — de por vida; **to be on trial for one's** — ser acusado de un crimen que pudiera castigarse con pena de muerte; **for one's** —, **for dear** — para salvarse la vida, desesperadamente, (*all out*) a más no poder; **run for your lives!** ¡sálvese el que pueda!; **for the** — **of me I can't see** why que me maten si comprendo por qué; **from** — del natural; **never in my** — en mi vida; **not on your** —! ¡ni hablar!; **to the** — al vivo; **true to** — conforme con la realidad, verdadero; **to come to** — resucitar(se), (*fig*) empezar a animarse.

(**e**) (*with verb other than* to be) **to bear a charmed** — salir milagrosamente ileso de todos los peligros; **she began** — **as a teacher** primero se dedicó a la enseñanza; — **begins at 40** la vida comienza de verdad a los 40; **to depart this** — partir de esta vida; **to lay down one's** — dar su vida, entregar su vida; **to lead a quiet** — llevar una vida tranquila; **to lead a strange** — llevar una vida muy rara; **to live the** — **of Riley** darse buena vida; **how many lives were lost?** ¿cuántas víctimas hubo?; **no lives were lost** no hubo víctimas; **to put new** — **into someone** reanimar a uno, infundir nueva vida a uno; **to see** — ver mundo; **to sell one's** — **dearly** vender muy cara la vida; **to take one's** — **in one's hands** jugarse la vida; **to take someone's** — quitar la vida a uno; **to take one's own** — suicidarse.

(**f**) (*fam*) = — **imprisonment**; **to do** — cumplir una condena de reclusión perpetua; **to get** — ser condenado a reclusión perpetua.

2 *attr* de vida; **annuity etc** vitalicio; — **president** presidente *m* de por vida; — **imprisonment** prisión *f* a perpetuidad; — **sentence** condena *f* a perpetuidad, condena *f* de reclusión perpetua; — **and death struggle** lucha *f* a muerte.

life annuity ['laifə'njuːiti] *n* renta *f* vitalicia, pensión *f* vitalicia.

life assurance ['laifə,ʃuərəns] *n* seguro *m* sobre la vida.

lifebelt ['laifbelt] *n* cinturón *m* salvavidas.

lifeblood ['laifblʌd] *n* sangre *f* vital; (*fig*) alma *f*, nervio *m*, sustento *m*.

lifeboat ['laifbəut] *n* (*from shore*) lancha *f* de socorro; (*from ship*) bote *m* salvavidas, chalupa *f*.

lifebuoy ['laifbɔi] *n* guindola *f*.

life force ['laiffɔːs] *n* fuerza *f* vital.

life-giving ['laifgiviŋ] *adj* que da vida, vivificante.

lifeguard ['laifgaːd] *n* (*on beach*) vigilante *m*; (*Mil*) guardia *m* de corps.

life interest ['laif'intərest] *n* usufructo *m* vitalicio (**in** de).

lifejacket ['laif,dʒækit] *n* chaleco *m* salvavidas.

lifeless ['laiflis] *adj* sin vida, muerto, exánime; (*fig*) soso, flojo.

lifelessness ['laiflisnis] *n* (*fig*) falta *f* de vida, sosería *f*, flojedad *f*.

lifelike ['laiflaik] *adj* natural, vivo.

lifeline ['laiflain] *n* cuerda *f* salvavidas; (*fig*) alma *f*, sustento *m*.

lifelong ['laiflɔŋ] *adj* de toda la vida.

life preserver ['laifpri,zɔːvə*] *n* cachiporra *f*.

life-saving ['laifseiviŋ] **1** *n* salvamento *m*; (*training for* —) socorrismo *m*. **2** *attr* de salvamento, salvavidas; — **raft** balsa *f* salvavidas.

life-size(d) ['laif'saiz(d)] *adj* de tamaño natural.

lifetime ['laiftaim] *n* (**a**) vida *f*; **the** — **of a horse** el término medio de vida de un caballo; **once in a** — una vez en la vida; **in my** — durante mi vida; **the chance of a** — una oportunidad única en la vida; **the work of a** — el trabajo de una vida entera.

(**b**) (*fig*) eternidad *f*, mucho tiempo *m*; **it seemed a** — parecía una eternidad.

lifework ['laif'wəːk] *n* trabajo *m* de toda la vida.

lift [lift] **1** *n* (**a**) (*act of* —*ing*) alzamiento *m*, levantamiento *m*, elevación *f*; (*effort*) esfuerzo *m* para levantar; (*upward push*) empuje *m* para arriba; (*help*) ayuda *f* (para levantar); (*Aer*) sustentación *f*, fuerza *f* de sustentación; (*Mech, of valve etc*) carrera

f, juego *m*; (*moral uplift*) exaltación *f* de ánimo, estímulo *m*; **give me a** — **with this trunk** ¿me ayudas a levantar este baúl?

(**b**) (*in car etc*) viaje *m* gratuito, viaje *m* en coche (*etc*) ajeno; **to give someone a** — llevar a uno gratis en su coche; **I can give you a** — **to Burgos** le puedo llevar a Burgos; *see* **hitch**.

(**c**) (*elevator*) ascensor *m*, (*for goods*) montacargas *m*.

2 *vt* (*raise*) alzar, levantar, elevar (*also* **to** — **up**); (*pick up*) coger, recoger; *child etc* levantar en brazos; *hat* quitarse; (*by air*) transportar en avión, transportar por puente aéreo; *restrictions etc* levantar, suprimir; (*fam: steal*) birlar, ratear, (*Lit etc*) plagiar (*from* de); (*morally uplift*) exaltar, estimular; **to** — **someone down** bajar a uno en brazos; **to** — **something down carefully** bajar algo con cuidado.

3 *vi* levantarse, alzarse; (*clouds*) disiparse.

lift attendant ['liftə,tendənt] *n*, **lift boy** ['liftbɔi] *n*, **liftman** ['liftmæn] *n*, *pl* —**men** [men] ascensorista *m*.

lift shaft ['liftʃaːft] *n* hueco *m* del ascensor.

ligament ['ligəmənt] *n* ligamento *m*.

ligature ['ligətʃə*] *n* (*Med, Mus*) ligadura *f*; (*Typ*) ligado *m*.

light¹ [lait] **1** *n* (**a**) (*in general*) luz *f*; lumbre *f*; — **and shade** luz *f* y sombra; **electric** — luz *f* eléctrica; **northern** —**s** aurora *f* boreal; **the** — **of day** la luz del día; **in the cold** — **of day** a la luz del día; **against the** — a trasluz; **at first** — al rayar el día; **by the** — **of a candle** a la luz de una vela; **in the** — **of a** la luz de; **in the** — **of what you say** por lo que Vd nos dice; **it is** — **now** ahora es de día; **to bring to** — sacar a luz, descubrir; **to come to** — salir a luz, descubrirse; **to cast** (*or* **shed, throw**) — **on** aclarar, arrojar luz sobre; **it revealed him in a strange** — le reveló bajo una luz extraña; **to see the** — (*be born*) nacer; (*understand*) comprender, caer en la cuenta; (*Rel*) convertirse, darse cuenta de su error; **I don't see things in that** — yo no veo las cosas así; **to see things in a new** — ver las cosas bajo otro aspecto, ver las cosas desde otro punto de vista; **to stand in someone's** — quitar la luz a uno.

(**b**) (*lamp*) luz *f*, lámpara *f*; (*Aut, Naut*) faro *m*; **overhead** — lámpara *f* de techo; **blinker** — luz *f* destelladora; **pilot** — (*Aut*) luz *f* de situación; **rear** —**s** luces *fpl* traseras; **reversing** —**s** faros *mpl* de marcha atrás; —**s out** hora *f* de apagar las luces; **what time is** —**s out?** ¿a qué hora se apagan las luces?; **to hide one's** — **under a bushel** darse de menos, retirarse modestamente; **to show someone a** — alumbrar a uno.

(**c**) (*signal*) **the** —**s** (*Aut*) el semáforo, las luces de tráfico; **green** — luz *f* verde; **to get the green** — **from someone** (*fig*) ser autorizado por uno para pasar adelante; **to give someone the green** — (*fig*) dar a uno la señal para pasar adelante; **she was giving me the green** — me estaba incitando a ir adelante, me daba indicios favorables; **red** — luz *f* roja, (*fig*) señal *f* de peligro, aviso *m*; **to see the red** — (*fig*) ver el peligro que hay por delante.

(**d**) (*flame*) fuego *m*, lumbre *f*; **pilot** — (*on stove*) mechero *m*, encendedor *m*; **have you a** —? ¿tienes fuego?; **to put a** — **to something, to set** — **to something** pegar fuego a algo, encender algo.

(**e**) (*Art*) toque *m* de luz.

(**f**) (*Archit*) cristal *m*, vidrio *m*; **leaded** —**s** cristales *mpl* emplomados.

(**g**) (*person*) **leading** — figura *f* principal, figura *f* más destacada (**in** de); **shining** — lumbrera *f*, figura *f* genial.

(**h**) —**s** (*intelligence*) luces *fpl*, conocimientos *mpl*; **according to his** —**s** según Dios le da a entender.

2 *adj* (**a**) (*bright*) claro; (*illuminated*) bañado de luz, con mucha luz; **to grow** — clarear, hacerse de día.

(**b**) *colour* claro; *hair* rubio; *skin* blanco; **a** — **green dress** un vestido verde claro.

3 (*irr: pret and ptp* **lit** *or* **lighted**) *vt* (**a**) (*illuminate*) alumbrar, iluminar (*also to* — **up**); **a smile lit up her face** una sonrisa le iluminó la cara; **to** — **the way for someone** alumbrar a uno.

(**b**) *cigarette, fire etc* encender.

4 *vi* (**a**) (*begin to shine; also to* — **up**) alumbrarse, iluminarse; **her face lit up** se iluminó su cara.

(**b**) (*ignite, switch on*) encenderse; **to** — **up** (*smoke*) encender un cigarrillo (*etc*), empezar a fumar.

(**c**) (*sl*) **to** — **into someone** embestir a uno, empezar a pegar a uno; **to** — **out** largarse (*for* para).

light² [lait] (*irr: pret and ptp* **lit** *or* **lighted**) *vi:* **to —
on** dar con, tropezar con, encontrar.

light³ [lait] *adj* (*in weight*) ligero; *food, gun, meal,
sleep, troops, work* ligero; *soil* poco denso; (*Naut*) en
lastre; *lorry, train* vacío, sin carga; *breeze, punishment, tax, wound etc* leve; *wine* suave; *task* fácil;
comedy, reading ameno, de puro entretenimiento;
(*morally*) ligero, liviano; (*cheerful*) alegre; **as — as
air, as — as a feather** tan ligero como la pluma;
to be — on one's feet ser ligero de pies, moverse
con agilidad; **to make — of** no dar importancia a,
restar importancia a.

light bulb ['laitbʌlb] *n* bombilla *f*.

light-coloured ['lait'kʌləd] *adj* claro, de color claro.

lighten¹ ['laitn] **1** *vt* iluminar. **2** *vi* clarear;
(*Meteorol*) relampaguear.

lighten² ['laitn] **1** *vt load* aligerar, hacer menos
pesado; *cares* aliviar; *heart* alegrar. **2** *vi* (*load*)
aligerarse, hacerse menos pesado; (*heart*) alegrarse.

lighter¹ ['laitə*] *n* encendedor *m*, mechero *m*.

lighter² ['laitə*] *n* (*Naut*) gabarra *f*, barcaza *f*.

light-fingered ['lait'fiŋgəd] *adj* largo de uñas.

light fitting ['lait.fitiŋ] *n* guarnición *f* del alumbrado.

light-footed ['lait'futid] *adj* ligero (de pies).

light-haired ['lait'hɛəd] *adj* de pelo rubio.

light-headed ['lait'hedid] *adj* (*by temperament*)
ligero de cascos, casquivano; (*dizzy*) mareado; (*with
fever*) delirante; (*with excitement*) exaltado; **wine
makes me —** el vino me hace ser muy frívolo, me
aturde el vino.

light-hearted ['lait'hɑːtid] *adj* alegre.

light-heartedly ['lait'hɑːtidli] *adv* alegremente.

lighthouse ['laithaus] *n, pl* **-houses** [.hauziz] faro *m*.

lighthouse keeper ['laithaus.kiːpə*] *n* torrero *m*,
farero *m*.

lighting ['laitiŋ] *n* (*act*) iluminación *f*; encendimiento
m; (*system*) alumbrado *m*; **— engineering** lumino-
tecnia *f*; **— fixtures** guarniciones *fpl* de alumbrado.

lighting-up ['laitiŋ'ʌp] *n:* **— time** hora *f* de encender
los faros.

lightly ['laitli] *adv* ligeramente; levemente; ágilmente; alegremente; *act etc* sin pensarlo bien, a la
ligera; **— clad** vistiendo ropa ligera, con muy poca
ropa; **— wounded** levemente herido; **to get off —**
escapar casi indemne; ser castigado con poca
severidad; **to speak — of** someone hablar de uno en
términos despreciativos; **to speak — of something**
menospreciar algo; **to touch — on something**
mencionar algo de paso.

light meter ['lait.miːtə*] *n* fotómetro *m*.

lightness ['laitnis] *n* (a) (*brightness*) claridad *f*,
luminosidad *f*; (*of colour*) claridad *f*.
 (b) (*in weight etc*) ligereza *f*, poco peso *m*; levedad
f; agilidad *f*; alegría *f*.

lightning ['laitniŋ] **1** *n* relámpago *m*, (*doing damage*)
rayo *m*; **as quick as —**, **like (greased) —** como un
relámpago; **where the — struck** donde cayó el rayo.
 2 *attr* relámpago.

lightning conductor ['laitniŋkən.dʌktə*] *n*, (US)
lightning rod [rɒd] *n* pararrayos *m*.

lights [laits] *npl* (*Anat*) bofes *mpl*, livianos *mpl*.

lightship ['laitʃip] *n* buque-faro *m*.

light wave ['laitweiv] *n* onda *f* luminosa.

lightweight ['laitweit] **1** *adj* ligero, de poco peso.
 2 *n* persona *f* de poco peso; (*Boxing*) peso *m* ligero;
(*fig*) cero *m* a la izquierda.

light-year ['laitjiə*] *n* año *m* luz.

ligneous ['ligniəs] *adj* leñoso.

lignite ['lignait] *n* lignito *m*.

lignum vitae ['lignəm'viːtai] *n* palo *m* santo; (*tree*)
guayacán *m*.

like [laik] **1** *adj* (a) parecido, semejante; igual;
mismo; **in — cases** en casos parecidos; **on this and
— subjects** sobre este tema y otros parecidos; **two
birds of — genus** dos pájaros del mismo género;
the 3 divided the work into a — number of parts
los 3 se dividieron el trabajo en otras tantas
porciones; **— father —** son de tal palo tal astilla;
they are as — as two peas se parecen como dos
gotas de agua.
 (b) **to be — someone** parecerse a uno; **they are
very — each other** se parecen mucho; **a house —
mine** una casa parecida a la mía, una casa como la
mía; **eyes — stars** ojos como estrellas; **I found one
— it** encontré otro parecido (*or* igual); **people —
that** las personas de esa clase; **the Russians are —
that** los rusos son así; **he is rather — you** tiene
bastante parecido con Vd; **who(m) is he —?** ¿a
quién se parece?; **what's he —?** ¿cómo es?, ¿qué
tal es?; **what's the coat —?** ¿cómo es el abrigo?;
she was — a sister to me fue (como) una hermana

para mí; **the portrait is not — him** el retrato no le
representa bien.
 (c) (*idioms*) **it's not — him** no es propio de él
(*to come late* venir tarde), no es característico de él;
I never saw anything — it no he visto nunca nada
igual; **isn't it — him?** ¡son cosas de él!; **that's just
— a woman!** ¡eso es muy de mujeres!; **that's more
— it!** ¡eso es mucho mejor!; **that hat's nothing —
as nice as this one** ese sombrero es muy inferior a
éste; **that's something — a fish!** ¡eso es mucho pez!;
I was thinking of something — a doll pensaba en
algo así como una muñeca, pensaba en una muñeca
o algo por el estilo; *see feel, look etc.*
 2 *prep* como; del mismo modo que, igual que;
tal como; **— a man** como un hombre; **— mad** como
un loco (*see also mad*); **— that** así; **he thinks — us**
opina lo mismo que nosotros; **just — anybody else**
igual que cualquier otro; **A, — B, thinks that . . .**
A, al igual que B, considera que . . .
 3 *adv:* **it's nothing —** no tiene parecido alguno,
no se parece ni con mucho; **very —**, **— enough**, **as
— as not** a lo mejor; **I found this money, —** (*fam*)
me encontré este dinero, sabe Vd.
 4 *conj* como, del mismo modo que; **— we used to
(do)** como hacíamos antes; **do it — I do** hágalo
como yo; **it's just — I say** es como yo lo digo.
 5 *n* (a) (*equal etc*) semejante *mf*; **we shall not see
his — again** no volveremos a ver otro tan bueno
(*etc*) como él, otro como él no le veremos nunca;
did you ever see the —? ¿se vio jamás tal cosa?;
and the —, **and such —** y otros por el estilo, y
otros de ese jaez; **I've no time for the —s of him**
(*fam*) los hombres así no los puedo ver.
 (b) (*taste*) **—s** gustos *mpl*, simpatías *fpl*, cosas
fpl predilectas; **—s and dislikes** predilecciones *fpl*
y aversiones, simpatías *fpl* y antipatías.
 6 *vt* (a) *person* querer, tener simpatía a, tener
cariño a, apreciar; **I — him** me es simpático;
I don't — him at all me resulta totalmente antipático; **don't you — me a little bit?** ¿no me quieres
un poquitín?; **how do you — him?** ¿qué te parece
él?; **he is well —d here** aquí se le quiere mucho.
 (b) (*find pleasure in*) gustar, *eg* **I — black shoes**
me gustan los zapatos negros; **I — football** me
gusta el fútbol; **I — dancing** me gusta bailar; **we —
it here** estamos contentos aquí, aquí disfrutamos;
your father won't — it esto no le va a gustar a tu
padre; **I — your nerve!** ¡qué frescura!
 (c) (*wish, wish for*) querer; **I should — more
time** quisiera tener más tiempo; **I should — to
know why** quisiera saber por qué; **I should — you
to do it** quiero que Vd lo haga; **I — to be obeyed**
quiero que me obedezcan; **whether he —s it or not**
quiera o no quiera, de buen o mal grado; **he is free
to act as he —s** está libre para hacer lo que le dé la
gana; **as you —** como quieras; **if you —** si quieres;
when you — cuando quieras; **would you — a
drink?** ¿quieres tomar algo?; **would you — to go to
Seville?** ¿te gustaría ir a Sevilla?
 (d) (*judge, find*) **how do you — Cadiz?** ¿qué te
parece Cádiz?; **how do you — it here?** ¿qué te
parece esto?, ¿estás contento aquí?; **how would
you — a walk?** ¿te apetece dar un paseo?

likeable ['laikəbl] *adj* simpático.

likeableness ['laikəblnis] *n* simpatía *f*.

likelihood ['laiklihud] *n* probabilidad *f*; **in all —**
según todas las probabilidades; **there is no — of
that** eso no es probable; **there is little — that . . .**
es poco probable que + *subj*.

likely ['laikli] **1** *adj* (a) (*probable*) probable; verosímil; **a — explanation** una razón verosímil, una
explicación razonable; **a — story!** ¡puro cuento!,
¡qué cuento más inverosímil!; **the — outcome** el
resultado más probable; **the plan most — to
succeed** el plan con mejores probabilidades de
éxito; **an incident — to cause trouble** un incidente
que pudiera dar lugar a disturbios; **he is not — to
come** no es probable que venga; **is it — that I did?**
¿es probable que lo hiciera yo?
 (b) (*suitable*) apropiado; **I asked 6 — people**
se pregunté a 6 personas apropiadas.
 (c) (*promising*) prometedor; **a — youth** un
joven prometedor, un joven que promete.
 2 *adv* probablemente; **as — as not** a lo mejor;
very — they've lost it a lo mejor lo han perdido.

like-minded ['laik'maindid] *adj* animado por los
mismos sentimientos, que piensan del mismo modo.

liken ['laikən] *vt* comparar (*to* con), asemejar (*to* a).

likeness ['laiknis] *n* parecido *m*, semejanza *f*;
(*portrait*) retrato *m*; **family —** aire *m* de familia;
speaking — retrato *m* al vivo.

likewise ['laikwaiz] *adv* asimismo, igualmente; además; lo mismo; — **it is true that** . . . asimismo es verdad que . . .; **he did** — él hizo lo mismo.

liking ['laikiŋ] *n* (**a**) (*for person*) simpatía *f* (*for* a), cariño *m* (*for* a); **to have a** — **for someone** tener simpatía a uno, tener cariño a uno; **to take a** — **to someone** tomar cariño a uno, coger cariño a uno.

(**b**) (*for thing*) gusto *m* (*for* por), afición *f* (*for* a); **to be to someone's** — ser del gusto de uno; **to have a** — **for something** ser aficionado a algo; **to take a** — **to something** tomar gusto a algo, cobrar afición a algo.

lilac ['lailək] **1** *n* lila *f*. **2** *adj* color de lila.

Lille [li:l] Lila.

Lilliputian [,lili'pju:ʃiən] **1** *adj* liliputiense. **2** *n* liliputiense *mf*.

lilt [lilt] *n* (*sound*) ritmo *m* marcado, compases *mpl*, armonía *f*; (*song*) canción *f*; **a song with a** — **to it** una canción de agradable ritmo.

lily ['lili] *n* lirio *m*, azucena *f*; — **of the valley** muguete *m*, lirio *m* de los valles.

lily-livered ['lili'livəd] *adj* cobarde, pusilánime.

lily pad ['lilipæd] *n* (*US*) hoja *f* de nenúfar.

lily-white ['liliwait] *adj* blanco como la azucena.

limb [lim] *n* (*Anat*) miembro *m*; (*Bot*) rama *f*; **to be out on a** — estar aislado; estar en una situación peligrosa; **to tear someone** — **from** — despedazar a uno.

limber¹ ['limbə*] **1** *adj* ágil; flexible.

2 *vt* hacer flexible.

3 *vi*: **to** — **up** agilitarse; (*Sport*) entrar en calor, hacer ejercicios preparatorios; (*fig*) entrenarse, prepararse.

limber² ['limbə*] *n* (*Mil*) armón *m* de artillería.

limbless ['limlis] *adj* que está falto de un brazo (*or* pierna).

limbo ['limbəu] *n* limbo *m*; **to be in** — (*fig*) estar olvidado, permanecer en la oscuridad.

lime¹ [laim] (*Geol*) **1** *n* cal *f*; (*bird-*) liga *f*; **slaked** — cal *f* muerta. **2** *vt* (*Agr*) abonar con cal.

lime² [laim] *n* (*Bot: linden*) tilo *m*.

lime³ [laim] *n* (*Bot: citrus fruit*) lima *f*; (*tree*) limero *m*.

lime juice ['laimdʒu:s] *n* jugo *m* de lima.

lime kiln ['laimkiln] *n* horno *m* de cal.

limelight ['laimlait] *n* luz *m* de calcio; **to be in the** — estar a la vista del público, ser el centro de atención; **he had long experience of the** — tuvo una larga experiencia de estar a la luz de la publicidad; **he never sought the** — no trató nunca de llamar hacia sí la atención.

limerick ['limərik] *n* especie de quintilla jocosa.

limestone ['laimstəun] *n* piedra *f* caliza.

lime tree ['laimtri:] *n* (*linden*) tilo *m*.

limey ['laimi] *adj* inglés *m*, inglesa *f*.

limit ['limit] **1** *n* límite *m*; **it's the (very)** —! ¡es el colmo!, ¡no faltaba más!; **he's the** —!, **isn't he the** —? ¿qué le vamos a hacer?, ¿qué tío!; **to be at the** — **of one's endurance** ya no poder más, estar completamente agotado; **I am at the** — **of my patience** ya no tengo más paciencia; **there is a** — **to what one can do** no es infinita la fuerza que tiene uno; **it is true within** —**s** es verdad dentro de ciertos límites; **to go to the** — **to help someone** hacer todo lo posible para ayudar a uno, volcarse por ayudar a uno; **to know no** —**s** ser infinito, no tener límites.

2 *vt* limitar, restringir (*to* a); **that plant is** —**ed to Spain** esa planta se encuentra únicamente en España; **are you** —**ed as to time?** ¿hay restricción de tiempo?

3 *vr*: **to** — **oneself to a few remarks** limitarse a hacer algunas observaciones; **I** — **myself to 10 cigarettes a day** me permito tan sólo 10 cigarrillos al día.

limitation [,limi'teiʃən] *n* limitación *f*, restricción *f*; (*Law*) prescripción *f*; **he has his** —**s** tiene sus puntos flacos; **there is no** — **on exports** no hay restricción de artículos exportados.

limited ['limitid] *adj* limitado, restringido; *edition* limitado; *intelligence* más bien mediocre; *means* escaso, reducido; *person* de cortos alcances, de miras estrechas; *see* **company**.

limitless ['limitlis] *adj* ilimitado, sin límites.

limousine ['liməzi:n] *n* limusina *f*, limosina *f*.

limp¹ [limp] **1** *n* cojera *f*; **to walk with a** — cojear.

2 *vi* cojear; **he** —**ed off** se marchó cojeando; **he** —**ed to the door** se fue cojeando a la puerta; **the ship managed to** — **to port** el buque llegó con dificultad al puerto.

limp² [limp] *adj* flojo, lacio; fláccido; flexible; *movement etc* lánguido; **I feel** — **today** hoy me

---

siento sin fuerzas; **she felt** — **all over** tenía un desmayo en todo el cuerpo; **he said in a** — **voice** dijo en tono desmayado; **let your body go** — deje que el cuerpo pierda su rigidez.

limpet ['limpit] *n* lapa *f*; (*fig*) persona *f* tenaz.

limpid ['limpid] *adj liquid* límpido, cristalino, transparente; *air* diáfano, puro; *eyes* claro.

limply ['limpli] *adv* flojamente; lánguidamente; **he said** — dijo en tono desmayado.

limpness ['limpnis] *n* flojedad *f*; languidez *f*.

limy ['laimi] *adj* calizo.

linchpin ['lintʃpin] *n* pezonera *f*; (*fig*) pivote *m*, eje *m*.

linden ['lindən] *n* tilo *m* (*also* **linden tree**).

line¹ [lain] **1** *n* (**a**) (*rope etc*) cuerda *f*; (*fishing-*) sedal *m*; **hard** —**s!** ¡mala suerte!; **it's hard** —**s on Joe** es mala suerte para Pepe.

(**b**) (*Geom etc*) línea *f*; (*on tennis court etc*) raya *f*; (*on face, palm*) arruga *f*, (*in palmistry*) raya *f*, línea *f*; **the L** — (*Geog*) el ecuador; — **of fire** línea *f* de tiro; — **of life** línea *f* de la vida; — **of vision** visual *f*; **black** — raya *f* en negro; **dotted** — línea *f* de puntos; **straight** — línea *f* recta; — **drawing** dibujo *m* de líneas; **the** —**s of a ship** las formas de un buque; **all along the** — en toda la línea, (*fig*) completamente, cien por cien; **I draw the** — **at that** yo de ahí no paso; **I draw the** — **at blasphemy** yo no tolero la blasfemia; **one must draw the** — **somewhere** hay que fijar ciertos límites; **to know where to draw the** — tener sentido de la moderación, saber dónde conviene detenerse; **to shoot a** — (*fam*) darse bombo (*fam*); **to sign on the dotted** — (*fig*) aprobar algo maquinalmente.

(**c**) (*row*) hilera *f*, línea *f*; (*of waiting cars etc*) cola *f*, (*of parked cars*) fila *f*; **forward** — línea *f* delantera; **front** — primera línea *f*; **ship of the** — navío *m* de línea; — **of battle** línea *f* de batalla; — **of traffic** cola *f* de coches; **to fall** (*or* **get**) **into** — (*abreast*) meterse en fila, (*behind one another*) formar hilera, hacer cola; **to fall into** — **with** (*fig*) conformarse con; **to keep the party in** — mantener la disciplina del partido; **to stand in** — hacer cola.

(**d**) (*in factory*) línea *f*; **production** — línea *f* de montaje.

(**e**) (*Elec*) línea *f*; **high-tension** — línea *f* de alta tensión.

(**f**) (*of aircraft, liners*) línea *f*.

(**g**) (*of descent*) línea *f*, linaje *m*; **royal** — familia *f* real, casa *f* real; **in an unbroken** — en línea directa; **in the male** — por el lado de los varones.

(**h**) (*Rail: in general*) línea *f*; (*track*) vía *f*; **down** — vía *f* descendente; **up** — vía *f* ascendente; **to cross the** — cruzar la vía; **to leave the** —**s** descarrilar; **the** — **to Palencia** el ferrocarril de Palencia, la línea de Palencia.

(**i**) (*Tel*) línea *f*; (*flex*) hilo *m*; **the hot** — el hilo rojo; **party** — línea *f* de dos (*o* más) abonados; **to be on the** — **to someone** estar al habla con uno; **hold the** —! ¡no cuelgue Vd.!, ¡espere un momento!; **can you get me a** — **to Chicago?** ¿me puede poner con Chicago?

(**j**) (*of print*) renglón *m*, línea *f*; (*Poet*) verso *m*; —**s** (*Theat*) papel *m*; **marriage** —**s** partida *f* de matrimonio; **in the very next** — a renglón seguido; **to drop someone a** — poner unas líneas a uno; **to read between the** —**s** leer entre líneas.

(**k**) (*fig: course*) — **of argument** argumento *m*; — **of conduct** línea *f* de conducta; — **of inquiry** tema *m* de investigación; pista *f*; — **of thought** hilo *m* del pensamiento; **to be on the right** —**s** ir bien, ir por buen camino; **to take a strong** — **with** someone adoptar una actitud firme con uno.

(**l**) (*fig: clue*) pista *f*; indicación *f*; **to give someone a** — **on something** poner a uno sobre la pista de algo; **can you give me a** — **on it?** ¿me puedes dar algunas indicaciones acerca de ello?; **the police have a** — **on the criminal** la policía tiene una pista que le conducirá al delincuente.

(**m**) (*fig: notions of conformity*) **party** — línea *f* de partido, política *f* del partido; **along the** —**s of**, **on the** —**s of** de acuerdo con, conforme a, a tenor de; **something along these** —**s** algo por el estilo, algo en este sentido; **to be in** — **with** estar de acuerdo con, ser conforme a; **to bring something into** — **with** alinear algo con; **to step out of** — independizarse, mostrar su disconformidad, dejar de obedecer; **to toe the** — conformarse, someterse.

(**n**) (*fig: métier, speciality*) especialidad *f*, rama *f*; profesión *f*; **the best in its** — el mejor en su línea; **what** — **are you in?** ¿a qué se dedica Vd.?; **that's not in my** — eso no es de mi especialidad; **fishing's more in my** — me interesa más la pesca, de pesca si sé algo; **we have a good — in spring hats** tenemos un buen surtido de sombreros para primavera; **that — did not sell at all** ese género resultó ser invendible.

2 *vt* **(a)** (*cross with —s*) rayar; *field etc* surcar; *face etc* arrugar.

(b) to — up *people, objects* alinear, poner en fila.

(c) to — the streets ocupar las aceras; **to — the route** alinearse a lo largo de la ruta; **the streets were —d with cheering crowds** en las calles había a cada lado multitudes que gritaban entusiastas; **portraits —d the walls** las paredes estaban llenas de cuadros.

3 *vi* **to — up** (*along street etc*) alinearse, (*in queue*) hacer cola, ponerse en fila, (*Mil*) formar(se); **the teams —d up like this . . .** los equipos formaron así . . .

line² [lain] *vt clothes etc* forrar (*with* de); (*Tech*) revestir (*with* de); *brakes* guarnecer; *see* **pocket.**

lineage ['liniidʒ] *n* linaje *m*.

lineal ['liniəl] *adj* lineal, en línea recta.

lineament ['liniəmənt] *n* lineamento *m*.

linear ['liniə*] *adj* lineal; *measure* de longitud.

lined [laind] *adj face etc* arrugado; *coat* forrado, con forro; (*Tech*) revestido; **to become —** arrugarse.

linen ['linin] **1** *n* lino *m*, hilo *m*; lienzo *m*; (*table-*) mantelería *f*; (*sheets, underclothes etc*) ropa *f* blanca; **clean —** ropa *f* limpia; **dirty —** ropa *f* sucia, ropa *f* para lavar; **to wash one's dirty — in public** (*fig*) lavar sus trapos sucios ante el mundo entero.

2 *adj* de lino.

linen closet ['linin,klɔzit] *n*, **linen cupboard** ['linin,kʌbəd] *n* armario *m* para ropa blanca.

linen draper ['linin,dreipə*] *n* lencero *m*, a *f*; **—'s** (*shop*) lencería *f*.

line-out ['lainaut] *n* (*Sport*) saque *m* de banda.

liner ['lainə*] *n* transatlántico *m*, vapor *m* de línea.

linesman ['lainzmən] *n*, *pl* **-men** [mən] (*Sport*) juez *m* de línea; (*Rail*) guardavía *m*; (*Elec*) celador *m*, recorredor *m* de la línea.

line-up ['lainʌp] *n* (*Sport*) alineación *f*, formación *f*.

ling¹ [liŋ] *n* (*Fish*) especie de abadejo *m*.

ling² [liŋ] *n* (*Bot*) brezo *m*.

linger ['liŋgə*] *vi* **(a)** (*also* **to — on**; *be unwilling to go*) tardar en marcharse, permanecer por indecisión; (*in dying*) tardar en morirse; (*of doubts etc*) persistir, quedar; **won't you — here a while?** ¿no puedes quedarte aquí un rato?

(b) (*delay on journey etc*) quedarse atrás, retardarse.

(c) to — on a subject dilatarse en un tema; **I let my eye — on the scene** seguía sin apartar los ojos de la escena; **to — over a meal** comer despacio, no darse prisa por terminar de comer; **to — over a task** hacer un trabajo despacio.

lingering ['liŋgəriŋ] *adj* lento, prolongado; *death* lento; *doubt* persistente, que no se desvanece; *look* fijo y triste.

lingerie ['lænʒəri:] *n* ropa *f* blanca, ropa *f* interior (de mujer).

lingo ['liŋgəu] *n* (*fam*) lengua *f*, idioma *m*; (*specialist jargon*) jerga *f*.

lingua franca ['liŋgwə'fræŋkə] *n* lengua *f* franca.

linguist ['liŋgwist] *n* **(a)** (*speaker of languages*) políglota *mf*; **he's a good —** domina varios idiomas, aprende los idiomas con facilidad; **I'm no —** no puedo con los idiomas.

(b) (*specialist in linguistics*) lingüista *mf*.

linguistic [liŋ'gwistik] *adj* lingüístico.

linguistics [liŋ'gwistiks] *n* lingüística *f*.

liniment ['linimənt] *n* linimento *m*.

lining ['lainiŋ] *n* (*of clothes etc*) forro *m*; (*Tech*) revestimiento *m*; (*of brake*) guarnición *f*.

link [liŋk] **1** *n* (*of chain*) eslabón *m*; (*fig: connection*) enlace *m*, conexión *f*; (*bond*) lazo *m*, vínculo *m*; **a new rail — for Teruel** nuevo enlace *m* ferroviario para Teruel; **cultural —s** relaciones *fpl* culturales; **the —s of friendship** los lazos de la amistad; **missing —** eslabón *m* perdido.

2 *vt* eslabonar; *spaceships* acoplar; (*fig*) enlazar, unir, vincular; **to — arms** cogerse del brazo; **we are —ed by telephone to . . .** tenemos conexión telefónica con . . .; **we hope to — up the two spaceships** esperamos acoplar las dos naves espaciales; **we are —ed in friendship** nos vincula la amistad; **the two companies are now —ed** ahora están unidas las dos compañías.

3 *vi*: **to — together** (*parts*) eslabonarse; **to — up** (*persons*) reunirse (*with* con); (*companies etc*) unirse; (*spaceships etc*) acoplarse; (*railway lines etc*) empalmar.

links [liŋks] *npl* campo *m* de golf.

link-up ['liŋkʌp] *n* unión *f*; (*of spaceships*) acoplamiento *m*, atraque *m*.

linnet ['linit] *n* pardillo *m* común.

lino ['lainəu] *n*, **linoleum** [li'nəuliəm] *n* linóleo *m*.

linotype ['lainəutaip] *n* linotipia *f*.

linseed ['linsi:d] *n* linaza *f*.

linseed oil ['linsi:d'ɔil] *n* aceite *m* de linaza.

lint [lint] *n* hilas *fpl*.

lintel ['lintl] *n* dintel *m*.

lion ['laiən] *n* león *m*; (*fig*) celebridad *f*; **—'s share** parte *f* del león; **to beard the — in his den** entrar en el cubil de la fiera; **to put one's head in the —'s mouth** meterse en la boca del lobo.

lioness ['laiənis] *n* leona *f*.

lionize ['laiənaiz] *vt*: **to — someone** tratar a uno como una celebridad, volcarse por agasajar a uno.

lip [lip] *n* **(a)** (*Anat and fig*) labio *m*; (*of jug*) pico *m*; (*of cup, crater*) borde *m*; **to hang on someone's —s** estar pendiente de las palabras de uno; **to keep a stiff upper —** no inmutarse, aguantarse todo sin chistar; **to lick** (*or* **smack**) **one's —s** relamerse, chuparse los dedos.

(b) (*sl: abuse*) injurias *fpl*; (*backchat*) insolencia *f*; **none of your —!** ¡cállate la boca!

lipread ['lipri:d] (*irr: see* **read**) *vi* interpretar el movimiento de los labios (de otro que habla).

lip-reading ['lip,ri:diŋ] *n* interpretación *f* del movimiento de los labios.

lip service ['lip,sə:vis] *n* jarabe *m* de pico; **to pay — to an ideal** alabar un ideal pero sin hacer nada práctico.

lipstick ['lipstik] *n* lápiz *m* labial, rojo *m* de labios, barra *f* de labios.

liquefaction [,likwi'fækʃən] *n* licuefacción *f*.

liquefy ['likwifai] **1** *vt* licuar. **2** *vi* licuarse.

liqueur [li'kjuə*] *n* licor *m*, poscafé *m*.

liquid ['likwid] **1** *adj* líquido; *measure* para líquidos; *asset* líquido, realizable; *sound* claro, puro, (*in Phonetics*) líquido; *air* diáfano.

2 *n* líquido *m*; (*Phonetics*) líquida *f*.

liquidate ['likwideit] *vt* (*all senses*) liquidar.

liquidation [,likwi'deiʃən] *n* liquidación *f*; **to go into —** entrar en liquidación.

liquidize ['likwidaiz] **1** *vt* liquidar. **2** *vi* liquidarse.

liquor ['likə*] *n* licor *m*, bebida *f* alcohólica, bebidas *fpl* alcohólicas; **hard —** licor *m* espiritoso; **to be in — estar borracho; to be the worse for —** haber bebido más de la cuenta, estar algo borracho.

liquorice ['likəris] *n* regaliz *m*.

Lisbon ['lizbən] Lisboa.

lisle [lail] *n* hilo *m* de Escocia.

lisp [lisp] **1** *n* ceceo *m*; (*of child*) balbuceo *m*; **to speak with a —** cecear. **2** *vt* decir ceceando; decir balbuceando. **3** *vi* cecear; balbucear.

lissom ['lisəm] *adj* ágil, ligero.

list¹ [list] **1** *n* lista *f*; relación *f*; catálogo *m*; (*of officials*) escalafón *m*; **to be on the active —** estar en activo.

2 *attr*: **— price** precio *m* de tarifa.

3 *vt* poner en una lista; inscribir; hacer una lista de; catalogar; (*Fin*) cotizar (*at* a); **he began to — all he had been doing** empezó a enumerar todas las cosas que había hecho; **it is not —ed** no consta (en la lista).

list² [list] (*Naut*) **1** *n* inclinación *f*, escora *f*; **to have a bad —** inclinarse de modo peligroso; **to have a — of 20°** tener una inclinación de 20 grados.

2 *vi* inclinarse (*to port* a babor), escorar; **to — badly** inclinarse de modo peligroso.

listen ['lisn] *vi* **(a)** (*hear*) escuchar, oír (*to something* algo, *to someone* a uno); (*heed*) escuchar, prestar atención, dar oídos, atender (*to* a); **—!** ¡escucha!; **— to me!** ¡escúchame!; **he wouldn't —** no quiso escuchar.

(b) to — in (*eavesdrop*) escuchar a hurtadillas (*on a conversation* una conversación); (*Radio*) escuchar la radio.

listener ['lisnə*] *n* oyente *mf*; (*Radio*) radioyente *mf*; **dear —s!** ¡queridos oyentes!; **to be a good —** tener mucha paciencia, escuchar amablemente todo lo que se le dice a uno.

listening ['lisniŋ] *n*: **good —!** ¡que se diviertan escuchando nuestros programas!; **we don't do much —** now ahora escuchamos muy poco la radio.

listening post ['lisniŋpəust] *n* puesto *m* de escucha.

listless ['listlis] *adj* lánguido, desmayado, apático, indiferente.

listlessly ['listlisli] *adv* lánguidamente, con apatía, con indiferencia.

listlessness ['listlisnis] *n* languidez *f*, desmayo *m*, apatía *f*, indiferencia *f*.

lists [lists] *npl* (*Hist*) liza *f*; **to enter the —** (*fig*) salir a la palestra.

lit [lit] *pret and ptp of* **light**; **to be — up** (*sl*) estar achispado.

litany ['litəni] *n* letanía *f*.

literacy ['litərəsi] *n* capacidad *f* de leer y escribir; **— campaign** campaña *f* de alfabetización; **— is low in Slobodia** en Eslobodia son pocos los que saben leer y escribir.

literal ['litərəl] *adj* literal.

literally ['litərəli] *adv* (*in a literal way*) literalmente; (*fig*) materialmente, *eg* **it was — impossible to work there** era materialmente imposible trabajar allí; **it had — ceased to exist** había dejado materialmente de existir.

literal-minded ['litərəl'maindid] *adj* sin imaginación, poco imaginativo.

literary ['litərəri] *adj* literario.

literate ['litərit] *adj* que sabe leer y escribir; **highly —** (*fig*) muy culto; **not very —** (*fig*) poco culto, que tiene poca cultura.

literati [,litə'rɑːti] *npl* literatos *mpl*.

literature ['litəritʃə*] *n* literatura *f*; (*fam: brochures etc*) impresos *mpl*, folletos *mpl*; información *f* impresa; (*learned studies of subject*) estudios *mpl* impresos, bibliografía *f*.

lithe [laið] *adj* ágil, ligero.

lithium ['liθiəm] *n* litio *m*.

lithograph ['liθəugrɑːf] **1** *n* litografía *f*. **2** *vt* litografiar.

lithography [li'θɔgrəfi] *n* litografía *f*.

Lithuania [,liθju'einiə] Lituania *f*.

Lithuanian [,liθju'einiən] **1** *adj* lituano. **2** *n* lituano *m*, a *f*. **3** *n* (*language*) lituano *m*.

litigant ['litigənt] *n* litigante *mf*.

litigate ['litigeit] *vi* litigar, pleitear.

litigation [,liti'geiʃən] *n* litigio *m*, litigación *f*.

litigious [li'tidʒəs] *adj* litigioso.

litmus ['litməs] *n* tornasol *m*.

litmus paper ['litməs,peipə*] *n* papel *m* de tornasol.

litre, (*US*) **liter** ['liːtə*] *n* litro *m*.

litter ['litə*] **1** *n* (**a**) (*vehicle*) litera *f*; (*Med*) camilla *f*.
(**b**) (*bedding*) lecho *m*, cama *f* de paja.
(**c**) (*Zool*) camada *f*, cría *f*, críos *mpl*.
(**d**) (*rubbish*) basura *f*, desperdicios *mpl*; (*papers*) papeles *mpl* (viejos); (*wrappings*) envases *mpl*; **a — of books** un montón de libros en desorden, un revoltijo de libros.
(**e**) (*general untidiness*) desorden *m*, confusión *f*; **in a —** en desorden.
2 *vt* (**a**) *animal* dar cama de paja a.
(**b**) (*give birth to*) parir.
(**c**) **to — papers about a room, to — a room with papers** esparcir papeles por un cuarto, dejar los papeles esparcidos por un cuarto; **a street —ed with paper** una calle llena de trozos de papel.

litter basket ['litəbɑːskit] *n*, **litter bin** ['litəbin] *n* papelera *f*.

litterbug ['litəbʌg] *n* persona *f* que esparce papeles usados (*or* envases *etc*) por las calles (*or* en el campo).

little ['litl] **1** *adj* (**a**) pequeño, chico; poco; escaso; **a — book** un libro pequeño; **a — wine** un poco de vino; **with no — trouble** con bastante dificultad, con no poca dificultad.
(**b**) (**— with noun, often translated by suffix**, *eg*) **a — house** una casita, **just a — gift** (*as charity*) una limosnita, **a very — fish** un pececillo, **a — sip** un sorbito.
2 *adv* poco; **he reads —** lee poco; **a — better** un poco mejor; **— more than a month ago** hace poco más de un mes; **we were not a — worried** nos inquietamos bastante, quedamos muy inquietos; **— does he know that . . .** no tiene la menor idea de que . . . ; **I walk as — as possible** voy a pie lo menos posible.
3 *n* poco *m*; **he knows —** sabe poco; **to spend — or nothing** gastar poco o nada; **he had — to say** poco fue lo que tenía que decir, apenas tenía nada que decir; **there was but — we could do** apenas había nada que hacer; **give me a —** dame un poco; **— by —** poco a poco; **for a —** un rato, por un rato, durante un rato; **in —** en pequeño; **to make — of something** sacar poco en claro de algo.

littleness ['litlnis] *n* pequeñez *f*; poquedad *f*.

littoral ['litərəl] **1** *adj* litoral. **2** *n* litoral *m*.

liturgical [li'təːdʒikəl] *adj* litúrgico.

liturgy ['litədʒi] *n* liturgia *f*.

livable ['livəbl] *adj* llevadero, soportable.

livable-in ['livəbl,in] *adj* (*fam*) habitable.

livable-with ['livəbl,wið] *adj* (*fam*) tratable, simpático.

live [liv] **1** *vt life* llevar, tener, pasar; *experience* vivir;

to — a happy life tener una vida feliz; **to — a part** encarnar brillantemente un papel, (*pej*) convertir un papel dramático en realidad; **to — down** lograr borrar; **to — out *period, reign*** vivir hasta el fin de, sobrevivir a, *one's own life* pasar el resto de; **to — it up** (*fam*) correr las grandes juergas (*fam*); **let's go and — it up** vamos a echar una cana al aire.
2 *vi* vivir; **long — Queen Anne!** ¡viva la reina Ana!; **to — and learn** vivir para ver; **to — and let ser** tolerante con todos; **to — from hand to mouth** vivir al día; **to — like a king** (*or* **lord**) vivir a cuerpo de rey; **as long as I —** mientras viva; **he hasn't long to —** no le queda mucho de vida; **to — again** volver a vivir; **to — by one's pen** vivir de su pluma; **to — high, to — well** darse buena vida, vivir en el lujo; **to — in** (*adv*) estar de interno, ser interno; **to — in** (*prep*) vivir en, habitar, ocupar; **a house not fit to — in** una casa no habitable; **to — off one's estate** vivir de las rentas de su finca; **to — off one's relations** vivir a costa de sus parientes; **to — on** (*adv*) vivir, seguir viviendo; **to — on eggs** alimentarse de huevos, comer (únicamente) huevos; **to — on hope** nutrirse (*or* vivir) de esperanzas; **what does he — on?** ¿de qué vive?; **to — on a private income** vivir de unas rentas particulares; **he doesn't earn enough to — on** no gana bastante para vivir; **to — through an experience** vivir una experiencia; **to — together** (*in amity*) convivir, (*in sin*) vivir juntos; **to — up to a standard** vivir con arreglo a (*or* en conformidad con) una norma; **to — up to a promise** cumplir una promesa; **to — up to one's reputation** justificar su reputación; **to — up to one's hopes** corresponder a sus esperanzas; *see* **income, means** *etc*.

live [laiv] *adj* vivo; *coal etc* encendido, ardiente; *weight* en vivo; *cartridge* con bala, *shell* cargado; *wire* con corriente, conectado; (*Radio, TV*) en vivo; *issue* candente, de actualidad; **a real — duke** un duque en persona, un duque de verdad.

livelihood ['laivlihud] *n* vida *f*; sustento *m*; **rice is their —** el arroz es su único sustento; **to earn a —** ganarse la vida.

liveliness ['laivlinis] *n* vida *f*, vivacidad *f*, viveza *f*; energía *f*; animación *f*; alegría *f*.

livelong ['livlɔŋ] *adj*: **all the — day** todo el santo día.

lively ['laivli] *adj person, imagination, account etc* vivo; *campaign, effort, speech* enérgico; *conversation* animado; *interest* grande; *pace* rápido; *party, scene etc* bullicioso, alegre; *tune* alegre; **things are getting —** esto se está animando, empiezan a pasar cosas; **to have a — time of it** pasar un rato lleno de incidentes.

liven ['laivn] **1** *vt*: **to — up** animar, estimular; alegrar. **2** *vi*: **to — up** animarse; alegrarse.

liver[1] ['livə*] *n*: **fast —** calavera *m*; **good — gastrónomo** *m*; persona *f* que se da buena vida.

liver[2] ['livə*] *n* (*Anat*) hígado *m*; **— complaint** mal *m* de hígado, afección *f* hepática.

liveried ['livərid] *adj* en librea.

liverish ['livəriʃ] *adj*: **to be —, to feel —** sentirse mal del hígado.

liverwurst ['livəwəːst] *n* embutido *m* de hígado.

livery ['livəri] *n* librea *f*; (*lit*) ropaje *m*; **— company** gremio *m* (*antiguo, de la Ciudad de Londres*).

livery stable ['livəri, steibl] *n* caballeriza *f* de alquiler.

lives [laivz] *npl of* **life**.

livestock ['laivstɔk] *n* ganado *m*, ganadería *f*.

livid ['livid] *adj* (**a**) lívido. (**b**) (*fam*) **he was — estaba** furioso; **he got —** se puso negro.

living ['liviŋ] **1** *adj* vivo, viviente; *image, language* vivo; **the — los** vivos; **or dead** vivo o muerto; **"The L— Desert"** "El desierto viviente"; **the greatest — pianist** el mejor pianista de los que ahora viven.
2 *n* (**a**) vida *f*; **gracious — vida** *f* elegante; **high — vida** *f* regalada, vida *f* de lujo; **loose — vida** *f* inmoral; **to earn** (*or* **make**) **a —** ganarse la vida; **to make a bare —** ganar lo justo para vivir; **to work for one's —** ganarse la vida trabajando.
(**b**) (*Eccl*) beneficio *m*.
3 *attr* de vida; *conditions* de vida, vital; *expenses* de mantenimiento; *wage* suficiente para vivir.

living room ['liviŋrum] *n* sala *f* de estar, living *m*.

living space ['liviŋspeis] *n* espacio *m* vital (*also fig*).

Livy ['livi] *m* Livio.

lizard ['lizəd] *n* lagarto *m*, (*small*) lagartija *f*.

llama ['lɑːmə] *n* llama *f*.

lo [ləu] *interj*: **— and behold the result!** ¡he aquí el resultado!, ¡ved aquí el resultado!; **and — and behold there it was** y por milagro ahí estaba.

loach [ləutʃ] *n* locha *f*.

load [ləud] **1** *n* (**a**) carga *f* (*also Elec, Tech, fig*); (*weight*) peso *m*; (*quantity*) cantidad *f*; (*Agr etc: as* *measure*) carretada *f*; **dead — carga** *f* **fija; under full — en** plena carga; **peak — carga** *f* **máxima; useful — carga** *f* útil.

(b) (*fig and fam*) **—s of, a — of** gran cantidad de, montones de; **thanks, we have —s** gracias, tenemos bastante; **it's a — of old rubbish** es una basura, no vale para nada; **that's a — off my mind** ¡qué alivio!, ¡se me quita un peso de encima!; **get a — of this!** ¡mírame esto!, ¡escucha esto un poco!

2 *vt* cargar (*with* con, de; *also Elec*); (*burden, weigh down*) agobiar (*with* de); **to — someone with honours** llenar a uno de honores, colmar a uno de honores; **the branch was —ed with pears** la rama estaba cargada de peras; **the whole thing is —ed with problems** el asunto está erizado de dificultades; **we're —ed with debts** estamos agobiados de deudas; **to — up** cargar (*with* de).

3 *vi* **(a)** cargar, tomar carga; **"—ing and unloading"** (*street sign*) "permitido carga y descarga".

(b) (*Mil*) cargar; **—!** ¡carguen armas!; **how does this gun —?** ¿cómo se carga esta escopeta?; **to — again** volver a cargar.

4 *vr:* **to — oneself with** cargarse de.

loaded ['ləudid] *adj* cargado; *dice, gun* cargado; *question* intencionado, que sugiere una contestación; **to be —** (*sl: drunk*) estar trompa, (*rich*) estar podrido de dinero, (*carry much money*) llevar encima mucho dinero.

loader ['ləudə*] *n* cargador *m*.

load line ['ləudlain] *n* línea *f* de flotación con carga.

loadstone ['ləudstəun] *n* piedra *f* imán.

loaf[1] [ləuf] *n, pl* **loaves** [ləuvz] pan *m*; (*large, cottage*) hogaza *f*; (*small, French*) barra *f*; (*of sugar*) pan *m*, pilón *m*; **half a — is better than no bread** vale más tener un poco que no tener nada; **use your —!** (*sl*) ¡despabílate!

loaf[2] [ləuf] *vi* haraganear, gandulear.

loafer ['ləufə*] *n.* vago *m*, gandul *m*; (*in street*) azotacalles *m*.

loam [ləum] *n* marga *f*.

loamy ['ləumi] *adj* margoso.

loan [ləun] **1** *n* (*thing lent between persons*) préstamo *m*; (*Comm, public*) empréstito *m*; **it's on —** está prestado; **I asked for the — of the book** le pedí prestado el libro; **I had it on — from the company** me lo prestó la compañía; **to raise a —** (*public*) procurar un empréstito.

2 *vt* prestar.

loan fund ['ləunfʌnd] *n* caja *f* de empréstitos.

loanword ['ləunwəːd] *n* préstamo *m*.

loath, loth [ləuθ] *adj:* **nothing — de** buena gana; **to be — to do something** estar poco dispuesto a hacer algo; **to be — for someone to do something** no querer en absoluto que uno haga algo.

loathe [ləuð] *vt thing* abominar, detestar, aborrecer; *person* odiar; **I — doing it** me repugna hacerlo; **he —s being corrected** se indigna si se le corrige.

loathing ['ləuðiŋ] *n* aversión *f* (*of* hacia, por); aborrecimiento *m* (*of* de); odio *m* (*of* hacia, por); **it fills me with —** me da asco; **the — which I felt for him** el odio que sentía hacia él.

loathsome ['ləuðsəm] *adj thing* asqueroso, repugnante; *person* odioso.

loathsomeness ['ləuðsəmnis] *n* lo asqueroso; lo odioso.

loaves [ləuvz] *npl* of **loaf**.

lob [lɔb] **1** *n* (*Tennis*) voleo *m* alto.

2 *vt ball* volear por alto; **to — something over to someone** tirar algo a uno; **— it over, will you?** ¿me lo das, por favor?

3 *vi* volear por alto.

lobby ['lɔbi] **1** *n* (*entrance hall*) vestíbulo *m*; (*corridor*) pasillo *m*; (*anteroom*) antecámara *f*; (*waiting room*) sala *f* de espera; (*Parl, fig*) organización *f* de cabildeo, camarilla *f* de cabilderos; grupo *m* de presión; **the China —** el grupo de los que apoyan a la China (nacionalista).

2 *vt:* **to — one's member of parliament** tratar de convencer a su diputado (*yendo los electores a hablar con él en el edificio del parlamento*).

3 *vi* cabildear, ejercer presiones; **to — for a reform** tratar de convencer a su diputado de la necesidad de una reforma, ejercer presiones para conseguir una reforma.

lobbying ['lɔbiiŋ] *n* cabildeo *m*.

lobbyist ['lɔbiist] *n* cabildero *m*.

lobe [ləub] *n* lóbulo *m*.

lobelia [ləu'biːliə] *n* lobelia *f*.

lobster ['lɔbstə*] *n* langosta *f*; (*large*) bogavante *m*.

lobster pot ['lɔbstəpɔt] *n* langostera *f*.

local ['ləukəl] **1** *adj* local; *authority, government, colour, anaesthetic etc* local; *radio station* comarcal,

regional; *train* de cercanías; *road* vecinal; (*in distribution, frequency*) poco común, que no se encuentra en todos los sitios, de distribución restringida; **he's a — man** es de aquí; **the — doctor** el médico del pueblo, el médico del barrio.

2 *n:* **the —** (*fam*) la taberna; **the —s** los vecinos, el vecindario, los de aquí.

locale [ləu'kɑːl] *n* lugar *m*, escenario *m*.

locality [ləu'kæliti] *n* localidad *f*.

localize ['ləukəlaiz] *vt* localizar.

locally ['ləukəli] *adv:* **houses are dear — por** aquí las casas cuestan bastante; **we deliver free — en** la ciudad y sus inmediaciones la entrega a domicilio es gratuita; **the plant is common — la** planta es común en ciertas localidades.

locate [ləu'keit] *vt* (*place*) colocar, establecer; (*find*) encontrar, localizar; **to be —d at** estar situado en, estar ubicado en, radicar en; **we —d it eventually** por fin averiguamos su paradero; **where is it —d?** ¿dónde está?

location [ləu'keiʃən] *n* **(a)** (*place*) situación *f*, posición *f*; (*placing*) colocación *f*; (*finding*) localización *f*.

(b) (*Cine*) rodaje *m* fuera del estudio; terreno *m* para rodaje de exteriores; **to be on — in Mexico** estar rodando en Méjico.

locative ['lɔkətiv] *n* locativo *m* (*also —* **case**).

loch [lɔx] *n* (*Scot*) lago *m*; (*sea-*) ría *f*, brazo *m* de mar.

lock[1] [lɔk] *n* (*of hair*) mechón *m*, guedeja *f*; (*ringlet*) bucle *m*; **—s** cabellos *mpl*.

lock[2] [lɔk] **1** *n* (*on door, box etc*) cerradura *f*; (*Mech*) traba *f*; (*stop*) retén *m*, tope *m*; (*of gun; also Wrestling*) llave *f*; (*canal-*) esclusa *f*; (*pressure chamber*) cámara *f* intermedia; **—, stock and barrel** por completo, del todo; **to put something under — and key** encerrar algo bajo llave.

2 *vt door etc* cerrar con llave; (*Mech*) trabar; **to — something away** guardar algo bajo llave; **to — someone in a room** encerrar a uno en un cuarto; **the armies were —ed in combat** los ejércitos seguían luchando encarnizadamente; **they were —ed in each other's arms** quedaban estrechamente abrazados; **to — someone out** cerrar la puerta a uno, dejar a uno en la calle; **the workers were —ed out** los obreros quedaron sin trabajo debido al cierre por los patronos; **to find oneself —ed out** estar fuera sin llave para abrir la puerta; **to — up** encerrar; (*in prison*) encarcelar; *capital* inmovilizar; **you ought to be —ed up!** ¡irás a parar a la cárcel!

3 *vi* cerrarse con llave; (*Mech*) trabarse; **to — up** echar la llave.

locker ['lɔkə*] *n* armario *m* (*particular*); cajón *m* con llave.

locket ['lɔkit] *n* medallón *m*, guardapelo *m*.

lock gate ['lɔkgeit] *n* puerta *f* de esclusa.

lockjaw ['lɔkdʒɔː] *n* trismo *m*.

lock keeper ['lɔk,kiːpə*] *n* esclusero *m*.

locknut ['lɔknʌt] *n* contratuerca *f*.

lockout ['lɔkaut] *n* cierre *m* (*or* paro *m* voluntario) por los patronos, lock-out *m*.

locksmith ['lɔksmiθ] *n* cerrajero *m*.

lock-up ['lɔkʌp] **1** *n* cárcel *f*, jaula *f*. **2** *attr* con cerradura; **— garage** jaula *f*.

loco ['ləukəu] *n* (*fam*) *see* **locomotive**.

locomotion [,ləukə'məuʃən] *n* locomoción *f*.

locomotive [,ləukə'məutiv] **1** *adj* locomotor. **2** *n* locomotora *f*, máquina *f*.

locum (tenens) ['ləukəm('tenenz)] *n* interino *m*, a *f*.

locus ['ləukəs] *n, pl* **loci** ['lɔkiː] punto *m*, sitio *m*; (*Math*) lugar *m* (geométrico).

locust ['ləukəst] *n* langosta *f*.

locust tree ['ləukəst,triː] *n* acacia *f* falsa; algarrobo *m*.

locution [lə'kjuːʃən] *n* locución *f*.

locutory ['lɔkjutəri] *n* locutorio *m*.

lode [ləud] *n* filón *m*.

lodestar ['ləudstɑː*] *n* estrella *f* polar; (*fig*) norte *m*.

lodestone ['ləudstəun] *n* piedra *f* imán.

lodge [lɔdʒ] **1** *n* (*in park*) casa *f* del guarda; (*porter's*) portería *f*; (*Univ, master's*) rectoría *f*; (*masonic*) logia *f*.

2 *vt person* alojar, hospedar; *object* (*place*) colocar, (*insert*) meter, introducir; *complaint* presentar (*with* a); **to — something with someone** dejar algo en manos de uno, entregar algo a uno; **the bullet is —d in the lung** la bala se ha alojado en el pulmón.

3 *vi* alojarse, hospedarse (*at, in* en; *with* con, en casa de); (*of object: end up*) ir a parar; (*remain*) quedarse, fijarse, quedar empotrado (*in* en); introducirse, penetrar (*in* en); **where do you —?** ¿dónde tiene Vd su pensión?, ¿en qué pensión vive Vd?; **the bullet —d in the lung** la bala se alojó en el pulmón.

lodger ['lɔdʒə*] n huésped m, eda f; **I was a — there once** hace tiempo me hospedé allí; **she takes —s** tiene una pensión.

lodging ['lɔdʒiŋ] n alojamiento m, hospedaje m; **—s** (in general) alojamiento m, pensión f; (room) habitación f; **they gave me a night's —** me recibieron en su casa esa noche; **to look for —s** buscar alojamiento, buscar una pensión; **we took —s with Mrs P** nos hospedamos en casa de la Sra de P; **are they good —s?** ¿es buena la pensión?

lodging house ['lɔdʒiŋhaus] n, pl **—houses** [ˌhauziz] casa f de huéspedes, pensión f.

loft [lɔft] n desván m; (straw-) pajar m; (Eccl) galería f.

loftily ['lɔftili] adv en alto, hacia lo alto; say etc orgullosamente, arrogantemente.

loftiness ['lɔftinis] n altura f; grandiosidad f; sublimidad f; altanería f, orgullo m.

lofty ['lɔfti] adj (high) alto, elevado, encumbrado; (grandiose) grandioso; (high-flown) noble, sublime; (haughty) altanero, orgulloso.

log[1] [lɔg] 1 n leño m, tronco m; (Naut: apparatus) corredera f; see **logbook, sleep.**
 2 vt apuntar, registrar; **we —ged 50 kilometres that day** ese día recorrimos (or cubrimos) 50 kilómetros.
 3 vi cortar (y transportar) troncos.

log[2] [lɔg] n (Math) see **logarithm.**

loganberry ['laugənbəri] n (fruit) frambuesa f norteamericana; (bush) frambueso m norteamericano.

logarithm ['lɔgəriθəm] n logaritmo m.

logbook ['lɔgbuk] n (Naut) cuaderno m de bitácora, diario m de navegación, diario m de a bordo; (Aer) libro m de vuelo; (Tech) cuaderno m de trabajo.

log cabin ['lɔg.kæbin] n cabaña f de madera.

loggerheads ['lɔgəhedz] npl: **to be at —** estar de pique (with con).

logging ['lɔgiŋ] n explotación f forestal; transporte m de troncos.

logic ['lɔdʒik] n lógica f; **in —** lógicamente.

logical ['lɔdʒikəl] adj lógico.

logically ['lɔdʒikəli] adv lógicamente.

logician [lɔ'dʒiʃən] n lógico m, a f.

logistic [lɔ'dʒistik] adj logístico.

logistics [lɔ'dʒistiks] n logística f.

log rolling ['lɔg.rəuliŋ] n intercambio m de favores políticos, sistema m de concesiones mutuas.

logy ['laugi] adj (US) torpe, lerdo.

loin [lɔin] n ijada f; (of meat) lomo m; **—s** lomos mpl; **to gird up one's —** aprestarse para la lucha.

loincloth ['lɔinklɔθ] n, pl **—cloths** [klɔðz] taparrabo m.

Loire [lwa:r] Loira m.

loiter ['lɔitə*] 1 vt: **to — away the time** perder el tiempo.
 2 vi (waste time) perder el tiempo; (idle) gandulear, holgazanear; (fall behind) rezagarse; (on the way) entretenerse; **don't — on the way!** ¡no te entretengas!; **to — with intent** rondar un edificio (etc) con fines criminales, merodear con fines criminales.

loll [lɔl] vi: **to — about** repantigarse; **to — against, to — back on** recostarse con indolencia contra; **to — back in a chair** repanchigarse en un asiento, estar repanchigado en un asiento; **the dog's tongue was —ing out** la lengua del perro colgaba hacia fuera.

lollipop ['lɔlipɔp] n pirulí m; (iced-) polo m.

lollop ['lɔləp] vi: **to — along** moverse torpemente, arrastrar los pies.

lolly ['lɔli] n (sl) parné m (sl); see **lollipop.**

Lombard ['lɔmba:d] 1 adj lombardo. 2 n lombardo m, a f.

Lombardy ['lɔmbədi] Lombardía f.

London ['lʌndən] Londres; attr londinense.

Londoner ['lʌndənə*] n londinense mf.

lone [ləun] adj solitario, único, aislado; see **lonely.**

loneliness ['ləunlinis] n soledad f; aislamiento m.

lonely ['ləunli] adj, **lonesome** ['ləunsəm] adj solitario, solo; place etc aislado, remoto; (deserted) desierto; **to feel —** sentirse muy solo; **it's a — life** es una vida solitaria; **it's terribly — out here** aquí se siente uno terriblemente solo.

loner ['ləunə*] n solitario m.

long[1] [lɔŋ] 1 adj (a) (of size) largo; mirror de cuerpo entero; suit (Cards) fuerte; person (fam) alto; **it is 6 metres —** tiene 6 metros de largo; **how — is it?** ¿cuánto tiene de largo?; **to be — in the leg** tener piernas largas.
 (b) (of time) largo; prolongado; job de muchas horas, de muchos años (etc); **to be — in + ger** tardar en + infin; **how — is the lesson?** ¿cuánto tiempo dura la clase?; **the days are getting —er** los días se están alargando.

 2 adv (a) largo tiempo, mucho tiempo; largamente; **don't be —!** ¡vuelve pronto!; **I shan't be —** (in finishing) termino pronto, en seguida concluyo, (in returning) vuelvo pronto; **we didn't stay —** no nos quedamos mucho tiempo; **he talked — about politics** habló largamente de política; **to live —** ser longevo; **women live —er than men** las mujeres son más longevas que los hombres; **— before** (adv) mucho antes, mucho tiempo antes; **you should have done it — before now** Vd debió hacerlo hace mucho tiempo ya; **— before** (conj) mucho antes de que + subj; **not — before** (adv) poco tiempo antes.
 (b) **—er** más tiempo; **we stayed —er than you** quedamos más tiempo que Vds; **how much —er can you stay?** ¿hasta cuándo podéis quedaros?; **how much —er do we have to wait?** ¿hasta cuándo tenemos que esperar?; **he no —er comes** ya no viene.
 (c) (in comparisons) **as — as** mientras; **as — as the war lasted** mientras duró la guerra; **as — as the war lasts** mientras dure la guerra; **stay as — as you like** quédate hasta cuando quieras, quédate el tiempo que quieras; **as — as, so — as** (provided that) con tal que + subj.
 (d) **so —!** ¡hasta luego!; see **ago.**
 3 n: **the — and the short of it** en resumidas cuentas; **before —** en breve, dentro de poco, (in past contexts) poco tiempo después; **are you going for —?** ¿vas a estar mucho tiempo?; **to take — to + infin** tardar en + infin.

long[2] [lɔŋ] vi: **to — for something** anhelar algo, suspirar por algo; **to — for someone** sentir la ausencia de uno, suspirar por uno; **to — to do something** anhelar hacer algo, suspirar por hacer algo.

long-armed ['lɔŋ'a:md] adj de brazos largos.

longboat ['lɔŋbəut] n lancha f.

longbow ['lɔŋbəu] n arco m.

long-dated ['lɔŋ'deitid] adj a largo plazo.

long-distance ['lɔŋ'distəns] adj bus para servicio interurbano; flight a distancia; call (Tel) interurbano; race de fondo, de larga distancia, de resistencia.

long-drawn-out ['lɔŋdrɔ:n'aut] adj muy prolongado, larguísimo, interminable.

long-eared ['lɔŋ'iəd] adj de orejas largas.

longed-for ['lɔŋdfɔ:*] adj ansiado, apetecido.

longevity [lɔn'dʒeviti] n longevidad f.

long-forgotten ['lɔŋfə'gɔtn] adj olvidado hace mucho tiempo.

long-haired ['lɔŋ'hɛəd] adj person de pelo largo, melenudo; dog etc de pelo largo.

longhand ['lɔŋhænd] 1 adj escrito a mano. 2 n escritura f normal, escritura f sin abreviaturas; **in —** en escritura normal.

longing ['lɔŋiŋ] 1 adj anhelante. 2 n anhelo m, ansia f, deseo m vehemente (for de); nostalgia f (for de); **sexual —** hambre f sexual, instinto m sexual.

longish ['lɔŋiʃ] adj bastante largo.

longitude ['lɔŋgitju:d] n longitud f.

longitudinal [ˌlɔŋgi'tju:dinl] adj longitudinal.

longitudinally [ˌlɔŋgi'tju:dinəli] adv longitudinalmente.

long jump ['lɔŋdʒʌmp] n salto m de longitud.

long-legged ['lɔŋ'legid] adj de piernas largas, zancudo.

long-lived ['lɔŋ'livd] adj longevo, de larga vida, que vive hasta una edad avanzada; **women are more —than men** las mujeres son más longevas que los hombres.

long-lost ['lɔŋ'lɔst] adj perdido hace mucho tiempo, desaparecido hace mucho tiempo.

long-playing ['lɔŋ'pleiiŋ] adj record microsurco, de larga duración.

long-range ['lɔŋ'reindʒ] adj gun de gran alcance; aircraft de gran autonomía, de largo radio de acción; weather forecast del próximo futuro, del mes (etc) que viene.

longshoreman ['lɔŋʃɔ:mən] n, pl **—men** [mən] estibador m, obrero m portuario.

long-sighted ['lɔŋ'saitid] adj présbita; (fig) previsor, clarividente.

long-sightedness ['lɔŋ'saitidnis] n presbicia f; (fig) previsión f, clarividencia f.

long-standing ['lɔŋ'stændiŋ] adj de mucho tiempo, existente desde hace mucho tiempo, viejo.

long-suffering ['lɔŋ'sʌfəriŋ] adj sufrido.

long-term ['lɔŋ'tə:m] adj a largo plazo (also fig).

long-wave ['lɔŋ'weiv] adj de onda larga.

longways ['lɔŋweiz] adv longitudinalmente, a lo largo.

long-winded ['lɔŋ'windid] adj prolijo.

long-windedly ['lɔŋ'windidli] adv prolijamente.

loo [lu:] n (fam) wáter m.

loofah ['lu:fə*] n esponja f de lufa.

look [luk] **1** n **(a)** (glance) mirada f; vistazo m, ojeada f; **he gave me a furious —** me miró furioso, me lanzó una mirada furiosa; **she gave me a dirty —** me miró recelosa, me lanzó una mirada llena de recelo; **we got some very odd —s** la gente nos miró extrañada; **to have** (or take) **a — at something** echar un vistazo a algo; **have a — at this!** ¡a ver esto!; **let's have a —** déjame verlo, a ver; **do you want a —?** ¿quieres verlo?; **to take a good — at something** mirar algo con cuidado, examinar algo detenidamente; **take a long hard — before deciding** antes de decidir conviene pensar muchísimo; **we never got** (or had) **a —** in no nos dejaron participar, (of losers) nunca tuvimos posibilidades de ganar; **to have a — for something** buscar algo; **to have a — round a house** inspeccionar una casa; **shall we have a — round the town?** ¿visitamos la ciudad?

(b) (air, appearance) aspecto m, apariencia f; aire m; traza f; **good —s** buen parecer m; **the new —** la nueva moda; **by the — of things** según parece; **by the — of him** a juzgar por su aspecto; **you can't go by —s** alone es arriesgado juzgar por las apariencias nada más; **he had the — of a sailor** tenía aire de marinero; **I don't like the — of him** no me hace buena impresión; **I don't like the — of it at all** esto tiene traza de ser peligroso (etc), no me fío de esto.

2 vt emotion expresar con la mirada; age representar; **to — someone straight in the eye** mirar directamente a los ojos de uno; **to — something out** (search) buscar algo, (choose) escoger algo; **to — over** examinar; revisar; **to — a place over** dar un vistazo a un sitio; **to — up** buscar; averiguar; person ir a ver, visitar; **to — someone up and down** mirar a uno de arriba abajo; see **last**.

3 vi **(a)** (see, glance) mirar; (search) mirar, buscar; **— here!** ¡oye!; **just —!** ¡mira!, ¡fíjate!; **— before you leap** antes de que te cases mira lo que haces.

(b) (seem) parecer; tener aire de, tener traza de; mostrarse; **he —s happy** parece estar contento; **it —s all right to me** me parece que está bien; **how does it — to you?** ¿qué te parece?; **he —ed surprised** hizo un gesto de extrañeza; **she —ed prettier than ever** estaba más guapa que nunca; **how pretty you —!** ¡qué guapa estás!; **the corn —s good** el trigo se muestra espléndido; **to — well** (person) tener buena cara; **it —s well** parece muy bien, tiene buena apariencia; **it —s well on you** te sienta bien, te cae bien.

(c) to — like parecerse a; **he —s like his brother** se parece a su hermano; **the picture doesn't — like him** el retrato no se le parece, el retrato no le representa bien; **it —s like rain** parece que va a llover; **it —s like cheese to me** me parece que es queso; **the festival —s like being lively** el festival se anuncia animado.

(d) (with adv or prep) **to — about** mirar alrededor; **to — about one** mirar a su alrededor; (fig) considerar las cosas con calma; **to — about for something** andar buscando algo; **to — after something** (attend to) ocuparse de algo, encargarse de algo, (watch over) vigilar algo; **to — after someone** cuidar de uno; **to — at** mirar; considerar, examinar; problem enfocar, estudiar; **it depends how you — at it** depende de cómo se enfoca la cuestión, depende del punto de vista de uno; **to — away** desviar los ojos, apartar la mirada (from de); **to — back** mirar hacia atrás; (fig) considerar el pasado, volverse atrás; **to — back on something** recordar algo, evocar algo; **to — down** mirar hacia abajo; bajar los ojos; **to — down on something** dominar algo, (disdain) despreciar algo, mirar algo por encima del hombro; **to — for** (seek) buscar; (wait for) esperar; **to — forward** considerar el futuro; **to — forward to something** alegrarse de antemano de algo, pensar en algo con mucha ilusión, prometerse algo bueno; **I'm so —ing forward to the trip** el viaje me hace muchísima ilusión; **we had been —ing forward to it for weeks** durante semanas enteras veníamos pensando en ello con mucha ilusión; **to — in** (visit) hacer una breve visita (on a), pasar por casa, entrar por un instante; **I'll — in on Monday** pasaré por casa el lunes; **to — in** (TV) mirar la televisión; **to — into something** investigar algo; **to — on** mirar, (pej) estar de mirón; **to — on someone as a friend** considerar a uno como un amigo; **to — on to** dar a; **to — out** tener cuidado, tener ojo; **— out!** ¡ojo!; **— out for pickpockets** ojo con los carteristas; **to — out for** (seek) buscar, (expect) estar a la expectativa de, (await) esperar; **we'll — out for you in the**

station te esperamos en la estación; **to — out of window** mirar por, asomarse a; **to — out on** dar a; **to — round** (adv) volver la cabeza; **to — round** (prep) inspeccionar, visitar; **we just want to — round** queremos verlo nada más; **to — round for someone** buscar a uno con los ojos; **to — through window** mirar por; book hojear; (search among) registrar; **to — to** ocuparse de, mirar por; (look after) cuidar de; (beware of) tener cuidado con; (rely on) contar con; acudir a; tener puestas las esperanzas en; **to — to someone to + infin** esperar que uno + subj, contar con uno para + infin; **to — up** mirar hacia arriba; levantar los ojos; (improve) mejorar, ir mejor; **to — up to someone** respetar a uno, admirar a uno; **to — upon someone** as mirar a uno como; see **alike** etc.

looked-for ['luktfɔ:*] adj esperado, deseado.

looker ['lukə*] n (US fam) guapa f.

looker-on ['lukər'ɒn] n espectador m, ora f; (pej) mirón m, ona f.

looking-glass ['lukɪŋglɑːs] n espejo m.

look-out ['lukaut] n **(a)** (tower etc) atalaya f, puesto m de observación; (viewpoint) miradero m.

(b) (person) vigía m.

(c) (act) observación f, vigilancia f; **to be on the — for, to keep a — for** estar a la mira de; **to keep a sharp —** estar ojo avizor.

(d) (prospect) perspectiva f; **it's a poor — for cotton** el algodón tiene un porvenir dudoso; **it's a grim — for us** es una perspectiva negra para nosotros, esto no nos promete nada bueno; **that's his —!** ¡allá él!

look-see ['luksiː] n (fam) vistazo m.

loom¹ [lu:m] n telar m.

loom² [lu:m] vi (also **to — up**) surgir, aparecer, asomarse; (threaten) amenazar; **dangers — ahead** se vislumbran los peligros que hay por delante; **the ship —ed up out of the mist** el buque surgió de la niebla; **to — large** ser de gran importancia, ocupar un puesto importante.

loon [lu:n] n bobo m, a f.

loony ['lu:ni] (fam) **1** adj loco; **to drive someone —** volver loco a uno; **to go —** volverse loco. **2** n loco m, a f.

loony bin ['lu:nibin] n (sl) manicomio m.

loop [lu:p] **1** n (knot) lazo m, gaza f; (bend) curva f, vuelta f, recodo m; (Elec) circuito m cerrado; (fastening) presilla f; (Aer) rizo m; **to — the —** hacer el rizo, rizar el rizo.

2 vt rope etc hacer gaza con; (fasten) asegurar con gaza (or presilla); **to — something round a post** pasar algo alrededor de un poste.

3 vi (rope etc) formar lazo; (line, road etc) serpentear.

loophole ['lu:phəul] n (Mil) aspillera f, tronera f; (fig) escapatoria f; pretexto m; (in law) rendija f.

loop line ['lu:plain] n (Rail) vía f de circunvalación.

loose [lu:s] **1** adj (free) suelto; change, end suelto; (untied) suelto, desatado; (not tight) flojo; (movable) movible, movedizo; earth poco firme; bandage, button, knot, screw flojo; (Med) suelto de vientre; tooth inseguro; dress holgado, ancho; pulley, wheel (Mech) loco, flotante; connection desconectado; (unpacked) sin envase, a granel, suelto; translation libre, aproximado, (pej) poco exacto; thinking ilógico; style impreciso, vago; morals relajado; conduct, life disoluto; woman fácil; **to become** (or **come, get, work**) **—** (part) soltarse, desprenderse, (knot) aflojarse, desatarse; **to break —** desatarse, escaparse, (fig) desencadenarse; **to cast** (or **let, set, turn**) **—** soltar; **to cut —** separarse, independizarse (from de); **to hang —** caer suelto.

2 n (fam) **to be on the —** (free) estar en libertad; **to be** (or **go**) **on the —** ir de juerga, echar una cana al aire.

3 vt (free) soltar; (untie) desatar; (slacken) aflojar; storm, abuse etc desencadenar; **to — off gun** disparar (at sobre).

4 vi: **to — off at** (fire) disparar sobre; (abuse) empezar a soltar injurias contra.

loose-leaf ['lu:sliːf] adj book de hojas sueltas, de hojas cambiables.

loose-limbed ['lu:slimd] adj de movimientos sueltos, ágil.

loose-living ['lu:slivin] adj de vida airada, de vida inmoral.

loosely ['lu:sli] adv sueltamente; flojamente; holgadamente; libremente, aproximadamente; con poca exactitud; ilógicamente; imprecisamente; disolutamente; **it is — translated as** se traduce aproximadamente por; **— dressed** con vestidos holgados.

loosen ['luːsn] 1 *vt* (*free*) soltar; (*untie*) desatar; (*slacken*) aflojar; **to — up** *muscles* desentumecer; *see* **tongue** *etc*.

2 *vi* soltarse; desatarse; aflojarse (*also* **to — up**); **to — up** (*before game*) desentumecer los músculos, entrar en calor; **to — up on someone** tratar a uno con menos severidad.

looseness ['luːsnis] *n* soltura *f*; flojedad *f*; holgura *f*; libertad *f*; imprecisión *f*; disolución *f*; relajación *f*; (*Med*) diarrea *f*.

loot [luːt] 1 *n* botín *m*, presa *f*; (*fam*) ganancias *fpl*, (*money*) dinero *m*. 2 *vt* saquear.

looter ['luːtə*] *n* saqueador *m*, ora *f*.

lop [lɔp] *vt* *tree* mochar, desmochar; *branches* podar; (*esp fig*) cercenar; **to — away, to — off** cortar.

lope [ləup] *vi* correr a paso largo (*also* **to — along**); **to — off** alejarse a paso largo.

lop-eared ['lɔp,iəd] *adj* de orejas caídas.

lop-sided ['lɔp'saidid] *adj* desproporcionado; desequilibrado; ladeado, sesgado; (*fig*) desequilibrado, falso.

loquacious [lə'kweiʃəs] *adj* locuaz.

loquacity [lə'kwæsiti] *n* locuacidad *f*.

lord [lɔːd] 1 *n* señor *m*; (*British title*) lord *m*; **the L—** (*Eccl*) el Señor; **Our L—** (*Eccl*) Nuestro Señor; **the L—s** (*Parl*) la Cámara de los Lores; **the —s of England** (*peers*) los nobles de Inglaterra; **my —** (*to bishop*) Ilustrísima, (*to noble*) señor, (*to judge*) señor juez; **my — bishop of Tooting** su Ilustrísima el obispo de Tooting; **good L—!** ¡Dios mío!; — **of the manor** señor *m* feudal; — **and master** dueño *m*; *see* **justice, live** *etc*.

2 *vt*; **to — it** hacer el señor, mandar despóticamente; **to — it over someone** dominar a uno despóticamente, mandar a uno como señor.

lordliness ['lɔːdlinis] *n* lo señorial, carácter *m* señorial; altivez *f*, arrogancia *f*.

lordly ['lɔːdli] *adj* *house, vehicle etc* señorial, señoril; *manner* altivo, arrogante; *command* imperioso.

lords-and-ladies ['lɔːdzənd'leidiz] *n* (*Bot*) aro *m*.

lordship ['lɔːdʃip] *n* (*title*) señoría *f*; (*rule*) señorío *m*; **his —** su señoría.

lore [lɔː*] *n* saber *m* popular; ciencia *f*, tradiciones *fpl*; **in local —** según la tradición local; **he knows a lot about plant —** sabe mucho de las plantas, es muy erudito en botánica.

lorgnette [lɔː'njet] *n* impertinentes *mpl*.

Lorraine [lɔ'rein] Lorena *f*.

lorry ['lɔri] *n* camión *m*.

lorry driver ['lɔri,draivə*] *n* camionero *m*, camionista *m*, conductor *m* de camión.

lose [luːz] (*irr*: *pret and ptp* **lost**) 1 *vt* (a) perder; *patient* no lograr salvar la vida de; **that lost us the war** eso nos hizo perder la guerra; **that lost us the game** eso nos costó la victoria.

(b) (*passive with* **lost**) **to be lost** perderse, quedar perdido; **to be lost at sea** (*person*) perecer en el mar, morir ahogado; **the ship was lost with all hands** se hundió el buque con toda la tripulación; **all is lost!** ¡todo está perdido!, ¡se acabó todo!; **to get lost** perderse, extraviarse, errar el camino; **get lost!** (*fam*) ¡vete a la porra! (*fam*); **to be lost in thought** estar absorto en meditación; **to be lost in wonder** quedar asombrado; **to look lost** parecer estar confuso, parecer estar desorientado, tener aire perplejo; **after his death I felt lost** después de su muerte no sabía qué hacer; **to give someone up for lost** dar a uno por perdido; **the motion was lost** se rechazó la moción; **he was lost to science** se perdió para la ciencia; **he is lost to all finer feelings** es insensible a todos los sentimientos nobles; **the joke was lost on her** no comprendió el chiste; **the remark was lost on him** la observación pasó inadvertida por él; **this modern music is lost on me** no entiendo esta música moderna.

2 *vi* perder; ser vencido; **you can't —** tienes forzosamente que salir ganando; **the story did not — in the telling** el cuento no perdió en la narración; **the clock is losing** el reloj atrasa.

3 *vr*: **to — oneself** perderse, extraviarse, errar el camino; (*in speech*) padecer una confusión, perder el hilo; **to — oneself in thought** ensimismarse.

loser ['luːzə*] *n* (*person*) perdedor *m*, ora *f*; (*Sport etc*) el que pierde, el vencido, el equipo derrotado; (*card*) carta *f* perdedora; **to be a bad —** irritarse al perder, quejarse al ser vencido; **to come off the —** salir perdiendo.

losing ['luːzɪŋ] 1 *adj* *team* vencido, derrotado; *trick etc* perdedor. 2 *n* *pl* **—s** *npl* pérdidas *fpl*.

loss [lɔs] *n* (a) pérdida *f*; — **of memory** amnesia *f*; **without — of time** sin pérdida de tiempo, sin demora; **there was a heavy — of life** hubo muchas

víctimas, perecieron muchos; **the army suffered heavy —es** el ejército sufrió pérdidas cuantiosas; **to cut one's —es** cortar por lo sano.

(b) **it's your —** Vd es el que pierde; **he's no —** no vamos a sentir su ausencia; **he's a dead —** es una calamidad; **the book is a dead —** el libro es absolutamente inútil, el libro no vale para nada en absoluto; **the ship is a total —** el buque puede considerarse como totalmente perdido.

(c) **to be at a —** estar perplejo, no saber qué hacer; **to be at a — to explain something** no saber cómo explicarse algo; **we are at a — to know why** no sabemos en absoluto por qué; **to be at a — for words** no encontrar palabras con que expresarse; **he's never at a — (for words)** tiene mucha facilidad de palabra, tiene la palabra facilísima; **to sell something at a —** vender algo con pérdida.

lost [lɔst] 1 *pret and ptp of* **lose**. 2 *adj* perdido.

lost-and-found department ['lɔstən'faunddi,paːtmənt] *n* (*US*), **lost property office** ['lɔst'prɔpəti,ɔfis] *n* oficina *f* de objetos perdidos.

lot [lɔt] *n* (a) (*random selection*) — echando suertes; **to cast —s, to draw —s** echar suertes (*for something* para decidir quién tendrá algo, *to decide something* para decidir algo); **the — fell on him** él resultó elegido, la suerte le tocó a él; **to throw in one's — with someone** unirse a la suerte de uno.

(b) (*share*) porción *f*, parte *f*; (*destiny*) suerte *f*; **his — was different** su suerte fue otra; **it fell to my —** me cayó en suerte, me cupo en suerte; **it falls to my — to + infin** me incumbe + *infin*.

(c) (*plot*) solar *m*, terreno *m*; **building —** solar *m* de construcción.

(d) (*at auction*) lote *m*; **he's a bad —** es un mal sujeto; **what a —!** ¡qué tíos!; **I'll send it in 3 —s** se lo mando en 3 paquetes.

(e) (*quantity*) cantidad *f*; grupo *m*, serie *f*, colección *f*; **a fine — of fish** una bonita serie de peces; **a fine — of students** un buen grupo de estudiantes; **a — of money** mucho dinero; **a — of books, —s of books** muchos libros; **quite a — of books** bastantes libros; **such a — of books** tantos libros; **an awful — of things to do** la mar de cosas que hacer; **we have —s of flowers** (we don't want) nos sobran flores, tenemos flores de sobra; **that's the —** eso es todo; **the whole — of them** ellos todos, todos ellos sin excepción; **he collared the —** se los llevó todos; **big ones, little ones, the —!** ¡los grandes, los pequeños, todos!

(f) (*as adv*) **I read a —** leo bastante; **we don't go out a —** no salimos mucho; **things have changed a —** las cosas han cambiado mucho; **there wasn't a — we could do** apenas había nada que pudiéramos hacer; **he drinks an awful —** bebe una barbaridad; **I'd give a — to know** me gustaría muchísimo saberlo; **I feel —s better** me encuentro mucho mejor; *see* **fat**.

lotion ['ləuʃən] *n* loción *f*.

lottery ['lɔtəri] *n* lotería *f*.

lotus ['ləutəs] *n* loto *m*.

loud [laud] 1 *adj* *voice, tone etc* alto; *shout etc* fuerte, recio; (*noisy*) ruidoso, estrepitoso; *applause* fuerte, estrepitoso; *behaviour* ruidoso, turbulento, maleducado; (*-mouthed*) gritón; *colour* chillón; (*in bad taste*) charro, cursi.

2 *adv* *see* **loudly**; **to say something out —** decir algo en alta voz.

loudhailer ['laud'heilə*] *n* megáfono *m*, bocina *f*.

loudly ['laudli] *adv* en alta voz; fuertemente; ruidosamente, estrepitosamente.

loud-mouthed ['laud'mauðd] *adj* gritón.

loudness ['laudnis] *n* lo alto; fuerza *f*; ruido *m*; lo chillón; vulgaridad *f*.

loudspeaker ['laud'spiːkə*] *n* altavoz *m*, altoparlante *m*.

Louis ['luːi] *m* Luis.

Louisiana [lu,iːzi'ænə] Luisiana *f*.

lounge [laundʒ] 1 *n* (*in house*) salón *m*, sala *f* de estar; (*on liner etc*) salón *m*.

2 *vi* (*saunter*) pasearse despacito; (*idle*) gandulear, pasar un rato sin hacer nada; **to — about** tirarse a la bartola; **to — against a wall** apoyarse distraídamente en una pared; **to — back in a chair** repanchigarse en un asiento; **we spent a week lounging in Naples** pasamos una semana en Nápoles sin hacer nada.

lounger ['laundʒə*] *n* gandul *m*, haragán *m*, ana *f*; azotacalles *mf*.

lounge suit ['laundʒ'suːt] *n* traje *m* de calle.

louse [laus] 1 *n*, *pl* **lice** [lais] piojo *m*. 2 *vt* (*sl*): **to — something up** estropear algo.

lousy ['lauzi] *adj* piojoso; (*fam: very bad*) malísimo, horrible; *trick etc* vil, asqueroso; **to be — with money** estar podrido de dinero.

lout [laut] *n* gamberro *m*; patán *m*.

loutish ['lautiʃ] *adj* grosero, maleducado.

Louvain ['lu:vein] Lovaina.

louver ['lu:və*] *n* lumbrera *f*; (*blind*) persiana *f*.

lovable ['lʌvəbl] *adj* amable, simpático.

love [lʌv] **1** *n* **(a)** amor *m* (*for, of, towards* a, de); cariño *m*; (*for hobby etc*) afición *f* (*for, of* a); **first —** primer amor *m*; **mother —** amor *m* maternal; **— in a cottage** contigo pan y cebolla; **— at first sight** amor *m* a primera vista, flechazo *m*; **for —** por amor, (*free*) gratis, (*without stakes*) sin jugarse dinero, sin apuestas; **not for — nor money** por nada del mundo; **for the — of** por el amor de; **for the — of God!** ¡por Dios!; **to marry for —** casarse por amor; **he studies history for the — of it** estudia la historia por pura afición al tema; **to be in —** estar enamorado (*with* de); **to fall in —** enamorarse (*with* de); **to make —** hacer el amor; **to make — to someone** (*court*) pretender a una, (*sexually*) hacer el amor a una, (*fig*) hacer la pelotilla a uno; **there is no — lost between them** existe entre ellos una fuerte antipatía.

(b) (*greetings, in letters etc*) **"with my —"** "besos"; **give him my —** mándale recuerdos míos; **to send one's — to someone** mandar cariñosos saludos a uno.

(c) (*person*) amado *m*, a *f*; **yes, —** sí, querida; **my —** mi amor; **the child's a little —** el niño es una monada.

(d) (*Tennis*) **—** all cero-cero; **15 —** 15 a cero.

2 *vt* *person etc* amar, querer; tener cariño a; *hobby etc* ser muy aficionado a; **she —s me, she —s me not** me quiere, no me quiere; **I — Madrid** me encanta Madrid, me gusta muchísimo Madrid; **I — this record** me encanta este disco; **he —s swimming, he —s to swim** le gusta muchísimo nadar, le entusiasma la natación; **I should — to come** me gustaría mucho venir, me encantaría venir; **— me — my dog** quien quiere a Beltrán quiere a su can.

love affair ['lʌvə,feə*] *n* amores *mpl*; aventura *f* sentimental; (*pej*) amoríos *mpl*.

lovebird ['lʌvbə:d] *n* periquito *m*; (*fig*) palomito *m*.

love child ['lʌvtʃaild] *n*, *pl* **— children** [,tʃildrən] hijo *m* del amor, hija *f* del amor.

loveless ['lʌvlis] *adj* sin amor.

love letter ['lʌv,letə*] *n* carta *f* de amor.

love life ['lʌvlaif] *n* vida *f* sentimental; vida *f* sexual.

loveliness ['lʌvlinis] *n* hermosura *f*, belleza *f*; encanto *m*.

lovelorn ['lʌvlɔ:n] *adj* suspirando de amor, herido de amor.

lovely ['lʌvli] **1** *adj* (*beautiful*) hermoso; bello; (*delightful*) encantador, precioso, delicioso; (*pleasing, of objects etc*) mono, precioso, rico; (*US*) simpático; **isn't it —?** ¿verdad que es precioso?, ¡qué rico!, ¡qué monada!; **we had a — time** lo pasamos la mar de bien; **I hope you have a — time!** ¡que os divirtáis!; **it's been — to see you** ha sido una visita encantadora.

2 *n* belleza *f*, guapa *f*.

love-making ['lʌv,meikiŋ] *n* (*courtship*) galanteo *m*; (*sexual*) trato *m* sexual.

love match ['lʌvmætʃ] *n* matrimonio *m* por amor.

love nest ['lʌvnest] *n* nido *m* de amor.

lover ['lʌvə*] *n* **(a)** amante *mf*; (*pej*) amante *m*, querida *f*; **he became her —** se hizo amante de ella; **we were —s for 2 years** durante 2 años fuimos amantes; **so she took a —** así que tomó un amante; **the —s** los amantes, los novios.

(b) a **— of** (*hobby, wine etc*) un amigo de, una amiga de, un aficionado a, una aficionada a; **he is a great — of the violin** tiene muchísima afición al violín.

(c) (*in compounds*) eg **music —** persona *f* aficionada a la música, **football —s everywhere** los aficionados al fútbol de todas partes.

lovesick ['lʌvsik] *adj* enfermo de amor, amartelado.

lovesong ['lʌvsɔŋ] *n* canción *f* de amor.

loving ['lʌviŋ] *adj* amoroso; cariñoso, tierno.

loving cup ['lʌviŋkʌp] *n* copa *f* de la amistad.

lovingly ['lʌviŋli] *adv* amorosamente; cariñosamente, tiernamente.

low[1] [ləu] **1** *adj* bajo; *number, rate, speed, temperature, tide, voice* bajo; *bow* profundo; *blow* sucio; *dress* escotado; *card* pequeño; *gear* primero; *price* bajo; reducido, módico; *stock* escaso; *diet* deficiente; *note, tone* grave; *health* débil, malo; *birth, rank* humilde; *manners* grosero; *character* vil; *opinion* malo; *joke,*

song verde; *trick* sucio, malo; *comedian* chabacano; **5 at the —est** 5 como mínimo; **activity is at its —est** las actividades están en su punto más bajo; **to feel —** estar deprimido; **stocks are getting —** las existencias escasean; **we are getting — on fuel** tenemos poco combustible, se nos está agotando el combustible.

2 *adv* *swing etc* bajo, cerca de la tierra (*etc*); *say, sing* bajo, en voz baja; **to bow —** hacer una profunda reverencia; **a dress cut — in the back** un vestido muy escotado de espalda; **to fall —** (*morally*) envilecerse, caer muy bajo; **England never fell so —** Inglaterra nunca cayó tan bajo; **to lay someone —** derribar a uno, abatir a uno, poner a uno fuera de combate; **to be laid — with 'flu** ser postrado por la gripe; **to lie —** estar escondido, no asomar la cabeza; **to play —** (*Cards*) poner pequeño; **to run —** escasear, casi agotarse; **to sink — = to fall —.**

3 *n* (*Meteorol*) área *f* de baja presión, depresión *f*; (*Aut*) primera marcha *f*; (*fig*) punto *m* más bajo; **to reach a new —** caer a su punto más bajo; **this represents a new — in deceit** ésta es la peor forma de vileza; no se ha visto cosa más vil; *see* **all-time.**

low[2] [ləu] **1** *n* mugido *m*. **2** *vi* mugir.

lowborn ['ləu'bɔ:n] *adj* de humilde cuna.

lowbrow ['ləubrau] **1** *adj* nada intelectual, poco culto. **2** *n* persona *f* nada intelectual, persona *f* de poca cultura.

low-class ['ləu,klɑ:s] *adj* de clase baja.

low-cost ['ləu'kɔst] *adj* económico.

Low Countries ['ləu'kʌntriz] *pl* Países *mpl* Bajos.

low-cut ['ləu'kʌt] *adj* *dress* escotado.

low-down[1] ['ləudaun] *adj* bajo, vil.

low-down[2] ['ləudaun] *n* (*fam*) verdad *f*; informes *mpl* confidenciales; **he gave me the — on it** me contó la verdad del caso; **come on, give us the —** ven, dinos la verdad.

lower ['ləuə*] **1** *adj* *comp of* **low**; más bajo, menos alto; *inferior; classes* bajo.

2 *adv* *comp of* **low**; más bajo.

3 *vt* bajar; *boat* lanzar; *flag, sail* arriar; (*reduce*) reducir, disminuir; *price* rebajar; *morale, resistance* debilitar; *guard* aflojar; (*in dignity*) humillar.

4 *vr*: **to — oneself** descolgarse (*by, on, with* con); (*fig*) envilecerse; **to — oneself to do something** rebajarse a hacer algo.

lower ['lauə*] *vi* (*person*) fruncir el entrecejo, mirar con ceño; (*sky*) encapotarse.

lower-class ['ləuə,klɑ:s] *adj* de la clase baja.

lowering ['lauəriŋ] *adj* ceñudo; amenazador; *sky* encapotado.

low-grade ['ləu,greid] *adj* de baja calidad.

low-heeled ['ləu'hi:ld] *adj* *shoes* de tacones bajos.

lowing ['ləuiŋ] *n* mugidos *mpl*.

lowland ['ləulənd] **1** *n* tierra *f* baja; **the L—s** las tierras bajas de Escocia. **2** *adj* de tierra baja.

lowlander ['ləuləndə*] *n* habitante *mf* de tierra baja.

low-level ['ləu'levl] *adj* de bajo nivel.

lowliness ['ləulinis] *n* humildad *f*.

lowly ['ləuli] *adj* humilde.

low-lying ['ləu,laiiŋ] *adj* bajo.

low-minded ['ləu'maindid] *adj* malpensado.

low-necked ['ləu'nekt] *adj* escotado.

lowness ['ləunis] *n* bajeza *f*, lo bajo; escasez *f*; gravedad *f*; humildad *f*; vileza *f*; lo verde; (*of spirits*) abatimiento *m*.

low-pressure ['ləu'preʃə*] *adj* de baja presión.

low-spirited ['ləu'spiritid] *adj* deprimido, abatido.

low-tension ['ləu'tenʃən] *adj* de baja tensión.

loyal ['lɔiəl] *adj* leal, fiel (*to* a).

loyalist ['lɔiəlist] *n* legitimista *mf*, gubernamental *mf*; (*Spain, 1936*) republicano *m*, a *f*.

loyally ['lɔiəli] *adv* lealmente.

loyalty ['lɔiəlti] *n* lealtad *f*, fidelidad *f* (*to* a); **one's loyalties** la lealtad de uno.

lozenge ['lɔzindʒ] (*Med*) pastilla *f*; (*Math*) rombo *m*; (*Her*) losange *m*.

lubricant ['lu:brikənt] **1** *adj* lubricante. **2** *n* lubricante *m*.

lubricate ['lu:brikeit] *vt* lubricar, engrasar.

lubrication [,lu:bri'keiʃən] *n* lubricación *f*, engrase *m*.

lubricator ['lu:brikeitə*] *n* lubricador *m*.

lubricity [lu:'brisiti] *n* lubricidad *f*.

Lucan ['lu:kən] *m* Lucano.

lucerne [lu:'sə:n] *n* alfalfa *f*.

lucid ['lu:sid] *adj* claro, lúcido.

lucidly ['lu:sidli] *adv* claramente, con claridad.

Lucifer ['lu:sifə*] *m* Lucifer.

luck [lʌk] *n* suerte *f*, fortuna *f*; azar *m*; **bad —, hard —** mala suerte *f*; **bad —!** ¡mala suerte!; **good —** suerte *f*; **good —!** ¡que tengas suerte!;

beginner's — suerte *f* del principiante; **here's** —! (*toast*) ¡salud!; **no such** —! ¡ojalá; **with any** — a lo mejor; **worse** —! ¡desgraciadamente; **better** — **next time!** ¡a la tercera va la vencida!; **and the best of** (*British*) —! (*iro*) ¡Dios te la depare buena!; **to be in** — estar de suerte, tener suerte; **to be out of** —! estar de malas; **to bring someone bad** — traer mala suerte a uno; **as** — **would have it** quiso la suerte que . . .; **to have the devil's own** —, **to have the** — **of the devil** tener chorra, tener buena pata; **to have the** — **to** + *infin* tener la suerte de + *infin*; **to keep something for** — guardar algo porque pudiera traer suerte; **take this for** — toma esto por si trae suerte; **to do something trusting to** — hacer algo a la buena de Dios; **to try one's** — probar fortuna.

luckily ['lʌkili] *adv* afortunadamente, por fortuna.
luckless ['lʌklis] *adj* desdichado, desafortunado.
lucky ['lʌki] *adj person* afortunado, feliz, que tiene suerte; *day* de buen agüero; *move, shot etc* afortunado; *charm* que trae suerte; **third time** —! ¡a la tercera va la vencida!; — **you!** ¡qué suerte!; **to be** — (*person*) tener suerte; **to be a** — **sort** tener buena sombra; **to be born** — nacer de pie; **to be** — **in that** . . . tener la suerte de que . . .; **that was very** — **for you** en eso tuviste mucha suerte; **to believe in one's** — **star** creer en su buena estrella.
lucrative ['lu:krətiv] *adj* lucrativo, provechoso.
lucre ['lu:kə*] *n*: **filthy** — el vil metal.
Lucretia [lu:'kri:ʃə] *f* Lucrecia.
Lucretius [lu:'kri:ʃəs] *m* Lucrecio.
lucubration [,lu:kju'breiʃən] *n* lucubración *f*.
ludicrous ['lu:dikrəs] *adj* absurdo, ridículo.
luff [lʌf] **1** *n* orza *f*. **2** *vi* orzar.
lug [lʌg] **1** *n* (**a**) oreja *f* (*also sl*); agarradera *f*; (*Tech*) orejeta *f*.
(**b**) (*tug*) tirón *m*.
2 *vt* (*drag*) arrastrar; llevar con dificultad; (*pull*) tirar de; **to** — **something about with one** llevar algo consigo (con dificultad); **to** — **something along** arrastrar algo; **to** — **something in** llevar algo dentro arrastrándolo, *subject* sacar en colación; **they** —**ged him off to the theatre** le llevaron contra su voluntad al teatro.
luggage ['lʌgidʒ] *n* equipaje *m*.
luggage boot ['lʌgidʒ,bu:t] *n* (*Aut*) maleta *f*, portaequipajes *m*.
luggage carrier ['lʌgidʒ,kæriə*] *n*, **luggage grid** ['lʌgidʒ,grid] *n* portaequipajes *m*, baca *f*.
luggage rack ['lʌgidʒ,ræk] *n* (*Rail etc*) rejilla *f*, redecilla *f*; (*Aut*) portaequipajes *m*, baca *f*.
luggage van ['lʌgidʒ,væn] *n* furgón *m* de equipaje.
lugger ['lʌgə*] *n* lugre *m*.
lugsail ['lʌgsl] *n* vela *f* al tercio.
lugubrious [lu:'gu:briəs] *adj* lúgubre, triste.
lugubriously [lu:'gu:briəsli] *adv* lúgubremente, tristemente.
Luke [lu:k] *m* Lucas.
lukewarm ['lu:kwɔ:m] *adj* tibio, templado; (*fig*) tibio, indiferente, poco entusiasta.
lull [lʌl] **1** *n* tregua *f*, respiro *m*, intervalo *m* de calma; (*in storm, wind*) recalmón *m*.
2 *vt person* calmar, (*to sleep*) adormecer, arrullar; *fears etc* aquietar, sosegar.
lullaby ['lʌləbai] *n* nana *f*, canción *f* de cuna.
lumbago [lʌm'beigəu] *n* lumbago *m*.
lumbar ['lʌmbə*] *adj* lumbar.
lumber[1] ['lʌmbə*] **1** *n* (*timber*) maderos *mpl*, maderas *fpl* (de sierra); (*junk*) trastos *mpl* viejos.
2 *vt space, room* obstruir (*with* de); **to** — **things together** amontonar cosas, (*fig*) juntar cosas sin orden; **to** — **someone with something** hacer que uno cargue con algo; **he got** —**ed with the job** él tuvo que cargar con el trabajo; **I got** —**ed with the girl for the evening** tuve que pasar toda la tarde con la chica.
3 *vi* cortar y aserrar árboles, explotar los bosques.
lumber[2] ['lʌmbə*] *vi*: **to** — **about**, **to** — **along** moverse pesadamente, avanzar con ruido sordo.
lumbering ['lʌmbəriŋ] *adj* pesado.
lumberjack ['lʌmbədʒæk] *n*, **lumberman** ['lʌmbəmən] *n*, *pl* —**men** [mən] maderero *m*, hachero *m*; trabajador *m* forestal.
lumber mill ['lʌmbə,mil] *n* aserradero *m*.
lumber room ['lʌmbərum] *n* trastera *f*.
lumberyard ['lʌmbəja:d] *n* (*US*) almacén *m* de madera.
luminary ['lu:minəri] *n* lumbrera *f*.
luminescence [,lu:mi'nesns] *n* luminescencia *f*.
luminosity [,lu:mi'nɔsiti] *n* luminosidad *f*.
luminous ['lu:minəs] *adj* luminoso.
lummox ['lʌməks] *n* (*US fam*) bobo *m*.

lummy ['lʌmi] *interj* (*fam*) ¡caramba!
lump [lʌmp] **1** *n* (*of earth, sugar etc*) terrón *m*; (*mass*) masa *f* informe; (*fragment*) trozo *m*, pedazo *m*; (*swelling*) bulto *m*, hinchazón *f*; (*on surface*) protuberancia *f*; (*in throat*) nudo *m*; (*person*) zoquete *m*; **with a** — **in one's throat** con un nudo en la garganta; **I get a** — **in my throat** se me anuda la garganta.
2 *adj sum etc* global.
3 *vt*: **to** — **together** *objects* amontonar; *persons, subjects* poner juntos, agrupar, mezclar; **so we** —**ed it** así que nos marchamos, así que no tomamos parte alguna en ello; **if he doesn't like it he can** — **it** si no le gusta que se fastidie.
lumpish ['lʌmpiʃ] *adj* torpe, pesado.
lump sugar ['lʌmp'ʃugə*] *n* azúcar *m* en terrón, azúcar *m* de cortadillo.
lumpy ['lʌmpi] *adj* aterronado; *liquid etc* lleno de grumos, con muchos grumos; *bed etc* desigual, nada cómodo.
lunacy ['lu:nəsi] *n* locura *f*; **it's sheer** —! ¡es una locura!
lunar ['lu:nə*] *adj* lunar.
lunatic ['lu:nətik] **1** *adj* loco, demente. **2** *n* loco *m*, a *f*.
lunch [lʌntʃ] **1** *n* (*also more formally* **luncheon** ['lʌntʃən]) almuerzo *m*, comida *f*; (*snack*) bocadillo *m*; **to have** —, **to take** — comer.
2 *vi* almorzar, comer (*on fish* pescado); tomar un bocadillo.
lunch hour ['lʌntʃauə*] *n* período *m* libre de mediodía.
lunchtime ['lʌntʃtaim] *n* hora *f* de comer.
lung [lʌŋ] *n* pulmón *m*; **iron** — pulmón *m* de acero.
lung cancer ['lʌŋ,kænsə*] *n* cáncer *m* de pulmón.
lunge [lʌndʒ] **1** *n* arremetida *f*, embestida *f*; (*Fencing*) estocada *f*.
2 *vi* arremeter (*at* contra, *with* con), embestir; dar una estocada; **to** — **at someone** abalanzarse sobre uno; **he** —**d with his right** le asestó un golpe con la mano derecha.
lupin ['lu:pin] *n* altramuz *m*, lupino *m*.
lurch[1] [lə:tʃ] *n*: **to leave someone in the** — dejar a uno plantado.
lurch[2] [lə:tʃ] **1** *n* sacudida *f*, tumbo *m*, movimiento *m* repentino; (*Naut*) bandazo *m*; **to give a** — dar un tumbo (*etc*).
2 *vi* (*vehicle etc*) dar sacudidas, dar tumbos, dar un tumbo; (*Naut*) dar un bandazo; (*person*) tambalearse; **to** — **along** (*vehicle*) ir dando tumbos, (*person*) avanzar tambaleándose; **to** — **in** entrar tambaleándose; **to** — **out** salir tambaleándose.
lure [ljuə*] **1** *n* (*bait*) cebo *m*; (*decoy*) señuelo *m*; (*fig*) aliciente *m*, atractivo *m*; encanto *m*; (*deceitful*) señuelo *m*.
2 *vt* atraer (con señuelo); *person* atraer, tentar; seducir; **to** — **someone away from** apartar a uno de; **to** — **someone into a trap** hacer que uno caiga en una trampa; **to** — **someone into a house** persuadir mañosamente a uno a entrar en una casa; **to** — **someone on to destruction** hacer que uno avance ciegamente hacia su ruina; **to** — **someone out** persuadir mañosamente a uno a salir.
lurid ['ljuərid] *adj light* misterioso, fantástico; *colour of skin* lívido, cárdeno; *dress etc* chillón; *language* fuerte, pintoresco; *account* sensacional; *detail* horripilante, espeluznante.
lurk [lə:k] *vi* estar escondido; estar en acecho.
lurking ['lə:kiŋ] *adj fear etc* vago, indefinible.
luscious ['lʌʃəs] *adj* delicioso, suculento, riquísimo, exquisito; *style* empalagoso; *girl* delicioso, apetitoso.
lush [lʌʃ] *adj* lozano, exuberante, (*fam*) *see* **luscious**.
lust [lʌst] **1** *n* (*sexual*) lujuria *f*, lascivia *f*; sensualidad *f*; (*greed*) codicia *f*, deseo *m* vehemente (*for* de).
2 *vi* lujuriar; **to** — **after**, **to** — **for** (*sexually*) apetecer contacto carnal con, (*greedily*) codiciar.
lustful ['lʌstful] *adj* lujurioso, libidinoso; *look etc* lascivo.
lustfully ['lʌstfəli] *adv* lujuriosamente, libidinosamente; lascivamente.
lustfulness ['lʌstfulnis] *n* lujuria *f*, lascivia *f*; sensualidad *f*.
lustre, (*US*) **luster** ['lʌstə*] *n* lustre *m*, brillo *m*.
lustreless, (*US*) **lusterless** ['lʌstəlis] *adj* deslustrado; *eyes* apagado.
lustrous ['lʌstrəs] *adj* lustroso, brillante.
lusty ['lʌsti] *adj person* vigoroso, fuerte, robusto; *plant* lozano; *cry* fuerte; *effort etc* grande.
lute [lu:t] *n* laúd *m*.
Luther ['lu:θə*] *m* Lutero.
Lutheran ['lu:θərən] **1** *adj* luterano. **2** *n* luterano *m*, a *f*.

Lutheranism ['luːθərənizəm] *n* luteranismo *m*.
Luxembourg ['lʌksəmbəːg] Luxemburgo *m*.
luxuriance [lʌg'zjuəriəns] *n* lozanía *f*, exuberancia *f*.
luxuriant [lʌg'zjuəriənt] *adj* lozano, exuberante.
luxuriate [lʌg'zjuərieit] *vi* (*plant*) crecer con exuberancia; (*person*) disfrutar; **to — in** disfrutar de, deleitarse con, entregarse al lujo de.
luxurious [lʌg'zjuəriəs] *adj* lujoso.
luxuriously [lʌg'zjuəriəsli] *adv* lujosamente, con lujo; **he sank back —** se recostó con fruición.
luxury ['lʌkʃəri] **1** *n* (*in general*) lujo *m*; (*article*) artículo *m* de lujo; **to live in —** vivir en el lujo. **2** *attr* de lujo; *tax* suntuario.
lyceum [lai'siːəm] *n* liceo *m*.
lychgate ['litʃgeit] *n* puerta *f* de cementerio.
lye [lai] *n* lejía *f*.
lying ['laiiŋ] **1** *adj* mentiroso, falso. **2** *n* mentiras *fpl*.
lying-in ['laiiŋ'in] *n* (*Med*) parto *m*; **— ward** sala *f* de maternidad.
lymph [limf] *n* linfa *f*.

lymphatic [lim'fætik] **1** *adj* linfático. **2** *n* vaso *m* linfático.
lynch [lintʃ] *vt* linchar.
lynching ['lintʃiŋ] *n* linchamiento *m*.
lynch law ['lintʃlɔː] *n* ley *f* de Lynch.
lynx [liŋks] *n* lince *m*.
lynx-eyed ['liŋksaid] *adj* de ojos de lince.
Lyons ['laiənz] Lyón, León de Francia.
lyre ['laiə*] *n* lira *f*.
lyrebird ['laiəbəːd] *n* ave *f* lira.
lyric ['lirik] **1** *adj* lírico. **2** *n* (*poem*) poema *m* lírico, poesía *f* lírica; (*genre*) lírica *f*; (*words of song*) letra *f* de una canción.
lyrical ['lirikəl] *adj* lírico; (*fig*) elocuente, entusiasta; **to get — about something** entusiasmarse por algo, extasiarse ante algo.
lyrically ['lirikəli] *adv* (*fig*) con entusiasmo, con éxtasis.
lyricism ['lirisizem] *n* lirismo *m*.
lysol ['laisɔl] *n* lisol *m*.

M

ma [mɑ:] *n* (*fam*) mamá *f* (*fam*).
ma'am [mæm] *n see* **madam**.
mac [mæk] *n* impermeable *m*.
macabre [mə'kɑ:br] *adj* macabro.
macadam [mə'kædəm] *n* macadán *m*.
macadamize [mə'kædəmaiz] *vt* macadamizar.
macaroni [ˌmækə'rəuni] *n* macarrones *mpl*.
macaronic [ˌmækə'rɔnik] *adj* macarrónico.
macaroon [ˌmækə'ru:n] *n* macarrón *m* (de almendras), mostachón *m*.
macaw [mə'kɔ:] *n* ararauna *f*.
mace[1] [meis] *n* (*Bot*) macis *f*.
mace[2] [meis] *n* maza *f*.
macebearer ['meis,bɛərə*] *n* macero *m*.
macerate ['mæsəreit] **1** *vt* macerar. **2** *vi* macerar(se).
machete [mə'tʃeiti] *n* machete *m*.
Machiavelli [ˌmækiə'veli] *m* Maquiavelo.
Machiavellian [ˌmækiə'veliən] *adj* maquiavélico.
machination [ˌmæki'neiʃən] *n* maquinación *f*.
machine [mə'ʃi:n] **1** *n* máquina *f* (*also fig*); aparato *m*; (*Aut*) coche *m*; (*cycle*) bicicleta *f*; (*Aer*) aparato *m*, avión *m*; (*Pol etc*) organización *f*.
2 *attr* mecánico, (hecho) a máquina.
3 *vt* (*Tech*) trabajar a máquina, acabar a máquina; (*Sew*) coser a máquina.
machine gun [mə'ʃi:ngʌn] **1** *n* ametralladora *f*. **2** *vt* ametrallar.
machine gunner [mə'ʃi:ngʌnə*] *n* ametrallador *m*.
machine-made [mə'ʃi:nmeid] *adj* hecho a máquina.
machinery [mə'ʃi:nəri] *n* (*machines*) maquinaria *f*; (*mechanism*) mecanismo *m*; (*fig*) mecanismo *m*, organización *f*, sistema *m*.
machine shop [mə'ʃi:nʃɔp] *n* taller *m* de máquinas.
machine tool [mə'ʃi:ntu:l] *n* máquina *f* herramienta.
machinist [mə'ʃi:nist] *n* (*Tech*) operario *m* de máquina, mecánico *m*; (*Sew*) costurera *f* a máquina.
mackerel ['mækrəl] *n* caballa *f*, escombro *m*; — **sky** cielo *m* aborregado.
mackintosh ['mækintɔʃ] *n* impermeable *m*.
macro . . . ['mækrəu] macro . . .
macrocosm ['mækrəukɔzəm] *n* macrocosmo *m*.
mad [mæd] **1** *adj* loco; demente; *dog* rabioso; *idea* loco, insensato, disparatado; *gallop, rush etc* loco, precipitado; (*angry*) furioso; — **as a hatter**, — **as a March hare** más loco que una cabra; **raving** —, **stark** — loco de atar; **a** — **thing** (**to do**) una locura; **are you** —? ¿estás loco?; **you must be** —! ¡qué locura!; **he's hopping** — está que bota; **to be** — **about something** (*keen*), **to be** — **on something** estar loco por algo, ser muy aficionado a algo, entusiasmarse por algo; **to be** — **about something** (*angry*) estar furioso por algo; **to be** — **about someone** (*angry*), **to be** — **at someone** estar furioso contra uno; **to be** — **about someone** (*in love*) estar locamente enamorado de uno; **I'm just** — **about you** ando loco por ti; **to be** — **with joy** estar loco de alegría; **to drive someone** — volver loco a uno; **to get** — enfadarse, ponerse furioso (*with* con); **it's no good getting** — **with me** de nada sirve ponerte furioso conmigo; **to go** — volverse loco, enloquecer; **this is patriotism gone** — esto es el patriotismo en grado ridículo.
2 *adv*: **to be** — **keen on something** entusiasmarse como un loco por algo; **to be** — **keen to do something** desear con vehemencia hacer algo; **to play** (*etc*) **like** — tocar (*etc*) como un loco; **to rain like** — llover muchísimo; **the plant grows like** — la planta crece con una rapidez asombrosa.
madam ['mædəm] *n* señora *f*; **yes** — sí señora; **little** — niña *f* precoz, niña *f* repipi; *see* **dear**.
madame ['mædəm] *n*, *pl* **mesdames** ['meidæm] **(a)** madama *f*, señora *f*; **M— Dupont** la señora de Dupont. **(b)** (*of brothel*) ama *f*, dueña *f*.

madcap ['mædkæp] **1** *adj* atolondrado. **2** *n* locuelo *m*, a *f*, tarambana *mf*.
madden ['mædn] *vt* volver loco; (*fig*) volver loco, enfurecer, sacar de quicio; **it** —**s me es para volverse loco**.
maddening ['mædniŋ] *adj* *delay etc* desesperante, exasperante; **isn't it** —? ¡es para volverse loco!
maddeningly ['mædniŋli] *adv* de modo desesperante; — **slow** terriblemente lento.
made [meid] *pret and ptp of* **make**.
Madeira [mə'diərə] Madera *f*; (*wine*) vino *m* de Madera.
made-up ['meid'ʌp] *adj* hecho; compuesto, artificial; *dress* confeccionado; *story* ficticio; *face* pintado, maquillado.
madhouse ['mædhaus] *n*, *pl* —**houses** [ˌhauziz] manicomio *m*, casa *f* de locos; **this is a** —! ¡esto es un guirigay!
madly ['mædli] *adv* locamente; furiosamente, como un loco; con rabia; **we were** — **gay** nos divertimos una barbaridad, nos divertimos de las maneras más raras; **to be** — **in love with someone** estar enamorado perdidamente de uno.
madman ['mædmən] *n*, *pl* —**men** [mən] loco *m*.
madness ['mædnis] *n* locura *f*; demencia *f*; furia *f*; rabia *f*; **it's sheer** —! ¡es una locura!; **what** —! ¡qué locura!
Madonna [mə'dɔnə] *n* Virgen *f*, Madona *f*.
Madrid [mə'drid] Madrid; (*attr*) madrileño, matritense.
madrigal ['mædrigəl] *n* madrigal *m*.
madwoman ['mædwumən] *n*, *pl* —**women** [ˌwimin] loca *f*.
maelstrom ['meilstrəum] *n* vórtice *m* (*also fig*), remolino *m*.
maestro [mɑ:'estrəu] *n* maestro *m*.
Mae West ['mei'west] *n* (*Aer*: *hum*) chaleco *m* salvavidas.
mag [mæg] *n* (*fam*) revista *f*.
magazine [ˌmægə'zi:n] *n* (*journal*) revista *f*; (*in rifle*) depósito *m* de cartuchos, recámara *f*; (*Typ*) almacén *m* de matrices; (*Mil*: *store*) almacén *m*, (*for powder*) polvorín *m*, (*Naut*) santabárbara *f*.
Magdalen ['mægdəlin] *f* Magdalena.
Magellan [mə'gelən] *m* Magallanes; — **Straits** Estrecho *m* de Magallanes.
magenta [mə'dʒentə] **1** *n* magenta *f*. **2** *adj* color magenta.
Maggie ['mægi] *f* *nombre cariñoso de* **Margaret**.
maggot ['mægət] *n* cresa *f*, gusano *m*.
maggoty ['mægəti] *adj* agusanado, lleno de gusanos.
Magi ['meidʒai] *npl*: **the** — los Reyes Magos.
magic ['mædʒik] **1** *adj* mágico. **2** *n* magia *f*; **by** — por arte de magia; **as if by** — como por ensalmo; **the** — **of that moment** la magia de ese momento.
magical ['mædʒikəl] *adj* mágico.
magically ['mædʒikəli] *adv* por arte de magia; (*fig*) como por ensalmo.
magician [mə'dʒiʃən] *n* mago *m*, mágico *m*, brujo *m*; (*conjuror*) mago *m*, prestidigitador *m*; **"Love the M—"** "El Amor brujo".
magic lantern ['mædʒik'læntən] *n* linterna *f* mágica.
magisterial [ˌmædʒis'tiəriəl] *adj* magistral.
magistracy ['mædʒistrəsi] *n* magistratura *f*.
magistrate ['mædʒistreit] *n* magistrado *m*; juez *m* (*municipal*).
Magna Charta ['mægnə'kɑ:tə] Carta *f* Magna.
magnanimity [ˌmægnə'nimiti] *n* magnanimidad *f*.
magnanimous [mæg'næniməs] *adj* magnánimo.
magnanimously [mæg'næniməsli] *adv* magnánimamente.
magnate ['mægneit] *n* magnate *m*, potentado *m*.
magnesia [mæg'ni:ʃə] *n* magnesia *f*.
magnesium [mæg'ni:ziəm] *n* magnesio *m*.

magnet ['mægnit] n imán m.
magnetic [mæg'netik] adj magnético; (fig) magnético, atractivo.
magnetically [mæg'netikəli] adv magnéticamente.
magnetism ['mægnitizəm] n magnetismo m; (fig) magnetismo m personal, don m de gentes.
magnetize ['mægnitaiz] vt magnetizar, iman(t)ar.
magneto [mæg'ni:təu] n magneto f.
magnification [,mægnifi'keiʃən] n (a) (Opt) aumento m; enfoque m; **high** — gran aumento m; **low** — pequeño aumento m. (b) (fig) exageración f.
magnificence [mæg'nifisəns] n magnificencia f.
magnificent [mæg'nifisənt] adj magnífico; —! ¡magnífico!
magnificently [mæg'nifisəntli] adv magníficamente; **you did** — lo hiciste estupendamente bien.
magnify ['mægnifai] vt (a) (Opt) aumentar; **to** — **something 7 times** aumentar algo 7 veces. (b) (fig) agrandar, exagerar; (praise) magnificar.
magnifying glass ['mægnifaiiŋ,glɑ:s] n lente f de aumento, lupa f.
magnitude ['mægnitju:d] n magnitud f; (fig) magnitud f, envergadura f; **a star of the first** — una estrella de primera magnitud; **in operations of this** — en operaciones de esta envergadura.
magnolia [mæg'nəuliə] n magnolia f.
magnum ['mægnəm] n botella f de dos litros.
magpie ['mægpai] n urraca f, marica f.
Magyar ['mægjɑ:*] 1 adj magiar. 2 n magiar mf.
maharajah [,mɑ:hə'rɑ:dʒə] n maharajá m.
mahogany [mə'hɔgəni] n caoba f.
Mahomet [mə'hɔmit] m Mahoma.
Mahometan [mə'hɔmitən] 1 adj mahometano. 2 n mahometano m, a f.
maid [meid] n (servant) criada f, doncella f; (in hotel etc) camarera f; (maiden: lit) doncella f; (young girl) muchacha f; **old** — solterona f; **she'll be an old** — quedará para vestir santos; **lady's** — doncella f; — **of honour** dama f de honor; — **of all work** criada f para todo.
maiden ['meidn] 1 n doncella f.
    2 adj virginal, intacto; soltera; name de soltera; flight, voyage etc inaugural; speech primero; — **aunt** tía f solterona.
maidenhair ['meidnhɛə*] n cabello m de Venus.
maidenhead ['meidnhed] n (Anat) himen m.
maidenhood ['meidnhud] n doncellez f.
maidenly ['meidnli] adj virginal; recatado, modesto.
maidservant ['meid,sə:vənt] n criada f, sirvienta f.
mail¹ [meil] n (Mil) malla f, cota f de malla.
mail² [meil] 1 n (in general) correo m; (letters) cartas fpl, correspondencia f; **is there any** — **for me?** ¿hay cartas para mí?
    2 vt (post off) echar al correo; (send by —) enviar por correo.
mailbag ['meilbæg] n saca f de correos.
mailboat ['meilbəut] n vapor m correo.
mailbox ['meilbɔks] n (US) buzón m.
mail car ['meilkɑ:*] n (Rail) furgón m postal, vagón-correo m.
mail coach ['meilkəutʃ] n (Hist) diligencia f, coche m correo; (Rail) furgón m postal, vagón-correo m.
mailing list ['meiliŋlist] n lista de personas a quienes se envía (por correo) propaganda comercial (etc).
mailman ['meilmæn] n, pl —**men** [men] (US) cartero m.
mail-order ['meil,ɔ:də*] n pedido m postal; — **firm**, — **house** casa f de ventas por correo.
mail train ['meiltrein] n tren-correo m, tren m postal.
mail van ['meilvæn] n (Rail) furgón m postal, vagón-correo m.
maim [meim] vt mutilar, lisiar, estropear; **to be** —**ed for life** quedar lisiado de por vida.
main [mein] 1 adj principal, más importante; mayor; beam, pipe etc maestro; floor primero, bajo; office central; course, line, road principal; **the** — **thing is to** + infin lo más importante es + infin.
    2 n (pipe) cañería f maestra, conducción f; (Elec; also —**s**) red f eléctrica; **the** — (poet) el océano; **in the** —**s** red f eléctrica; **the** — (poet) el océano; **in the** — en general, en su mayoría, en su mayor parte.
mainland ['meinlənd] n tierra f firme, continente m.
main line ['mein'lain] 1 n línea f principal. 2 **main-line** attr train principal.
mainly ['meinli] adv principalmente; en su mayoría, en su mayor parte.
mainmast ['meinmɑ:st] n palo m mayor.
mainsail ['meinsl] n vela f mayor.
mainspring ['meinspriŋ] n (Mech) muelle m real; (fig) motivo m principal, origen m.
mainstay ['meinstei] n estay m mayor; (fig) sostén m principal, pilar m.

mainstream ['meinstri:m] (fig) 1 n corriente f principal, línea f central (de evolución etc); **to be in the** — **of modern philosophy** estar en la línea central de la evolución de la filosofía moderna.
    2 attr de la corriente principal, en la línea central.
maintain [mein'tein] vt (a) attitude, order, family, justice etc mantener; silence guardar; road conservar en buen estado; student pagar los estudios de; (Mech) entretener; **if the improvement is** —**ed** si la cosa sigue mejorando.
    (b) **to** — **that**... sostener que..., afirmar que...
maintenance ['meintinəns] n mantenimiento m; conservación f; (Mech) entretenimiento m; manutención f; — **costs** gastos mpl de conservación; — **crew** personal m de conservación; — **grant** consignación f para mantenimiento.
Mainz [maints] Maguncia.
maisonette [,meizə'net] n casita f, hotelito m.
maize [meiz] n maíz m.
maize field ['meizfi:ld] n maizal m.
majestic [mə'dʒestik] adj majestuoso.
majestically [mə'dʒestikəli] adv majestuosamente.
majesty ['mædʒisti] n majestad f; **Her M**—, **His M**— Su Majestad; **Your M**— (Vuestra) Majestad.
major ['meidʒə*] 1 adj mayor (also Mus), principal; **of** — **interest** de máximo interés; **of** — **importance** de la mayor importancia; **Smith M**— Smith el mayor.
    2 n (Law) mayor mf de edad; (Mil) comandante m; (US Univ) asignatura f principal, especialidad f.
    3 vi (US Univ): **to** — **in French** estudiar el francés como asignatura principal, especializarse en francés.
Majorca [mə'dʒɔ:kə] Mallorca f.
majordomo ['meidʒə'dəuməu] n mayordomo m.
major-general ['meidʒə'dʒənərəl] n general m de división.
majority [mə'dʒɔriti] 1 n mayoría f; **a four-fifths** — una mayoría de las cuatro quintas partes; **the great** — **of lecturers** la mayor parte de los conferenciantes; **the vast** — la inmensa mayoría; **to attain one's** — llegar a mayoría de edad; **such people are in a** — tales personas son las más, predominan tales personas; **to be in a** — **of 3** formar parte de una mayoría de 3.
    2 attr: — **rule** gobierno m mayoritario, gobierno m de la mayoría.
make [meik] (irr: pret and ptp **made**) 1 vt (a) (general sense) hacer; fabricar; construir; elaborar; formar; crear; componer; bed, effort, fire, noise, peace, remark, tea, war, will hacer; dress confeccionar; meal preparar; speech pronunciar; error cometer; payment efectuar; cards barajar; face poner; sense tener; **to** — **someone a judge** constituir a uno juez, nombrar a uno juez; **to** — **someone king** elevar a uno al trono; **they've made John secretary** han puesto a Juan por secretario; **to** — **a friend of someone** trabar amistad con uno; **he's as cunning as they** — **'em** es de lo más astuto, es sumamente astuto; **I'm not made for running** yo no estoy hecho para correr; **to be made of** estar hecho de, estar compuesto de, consistir en, constar de; **it's made of gold** es de oro, está hecho de oro; **to show what one is made of** demostrar las cualidades que tiene uno; **what do you** — **of this?** ¿qué te parece esto?; **what did you** — **of the film?** ¿qué impresión te produjo la película?; **what do you** — **of him?** ¿qué piensas de él?, ¿qué impresión te has formado de él?; **I can** — **nothing of it** no lo entiendo, no saco nada en claro; **I don't know what to** — **of it** no me lo explico.
    (b) (complete, constitute) circuit cerrar; trick ganar, hacer; **2 and 2** — **4** 2 y 2 son 4; **that** —**s 20** con éste hacen veinte; **it still doesn't** — **a set** todavía no completa una serie entera; **it doesn't** — **a full course** no equivale a una asignatura completa, no es igual a una serie completa; **to** — **a contract** (Cards) cumplir un contrato; **South leads and** —**s 5 tricks** Sur sale y efectúa 5 bazas; **it made a nice surprise** fue una sorpresa agradable; **partridges** — **good eating** las perdices son buenas de comer; **it** —**s pleasant reading** da gusto leerlo; **he made a good husband** resultó ser un buen marido; **he'll** — **a good footballer** será buen futbolista, tiene madera de futbolista; **I made one of the party** yo era (uno) del grupo.
    (c) (earn etc) ganar; **he** —**s £30 a week** gana 30 libras a la semana; **how much do you** —? ¿cuánto ganas?, ¿qué sueldo cobras?; **to** — **a fortune** enriquecerse, hacer su pacotilla (fam); **what will you** — **by it?** ¿cuánto vas a ganar en

esto?; **how much do you stand to —?** ¿cuánto esperas ganar?

(d) (*assure future of*) hacer la fortuna de; asegurar el triunfo de; **this film made her** esta película fue el principio de su éxito; **he was made for life** se aseguró un porvenir brillante; **to — or break someone** hacer la fortuna o ser la ruina de uno; **to — or mar something** decidir de una vez la suerte de algo.

(e) (*with pred adj*) hacer; **to — someone happy** hacer a uno feliz; **to — someone angry** irritar a uno, provocar a uno, sacar a uno de quicio; **to — someone ashamed** dar vergüenza a uno; **to — someone sleepy** dar a uno ganas de dormirse; **to — someone rich** enriquecer a uno; **to — someone ill** sentar a uno mal; **to — something ready** preparar algo; **to — iron hot** calentar un trozo de hierro; **to — one's voice heard** hacer que se escuche la voz de uno.

(f) (*say, agree*) **let's — it 9 o'clock** citémonos para las 9, pongamos las 9.

(g) (*believe*) creer; **the situation is not so bad as you —** it la situación es menos grave de lo que Vd cree.

(h) (*calculate*) **what do you — the time?** ¿qué hora tienes?; **I —** it 7.30 yo tengo las 7 y media; **how many do you —** it? ¿cuántos dices tú?, ¿cuántos tienes en total?

(i) (*force*) **to — someone do something** forzar (*or* obligar, compeler) a uno a hacer algo; (*persuade*) inclinar (*or* inducir) a uno a hacer algo; **you can't — me** Vd no puede forzarme a hacerlo; **what —s you do it?** ¿por qué te ves obligado a hacerlo?; **what made you say that?** ¿por qué dijiste eso?; **to — someone laugh** mover a uno a risa.

(j) (*reach, attain*) **we made 15 knots** alcanzamos una velocidad de 15 nudos; **we shall never — the shore** no llegamos nunca a la playa, será imposible alcanzar la playa; **to —** it (*arrive*) llegar; (*achieve something*) conseguir lo que se deseaba; (*succeed*) tener éxito, triunfar; **eventually we made it** por fin llegamos; **we just made it in time** llegamos apenas con el tiempo justo; **can you —** it by 10? ¿puedes llegar para las 10?; **to —** it **with someone** (*sl*) conseguir acostarse con una.

(k) (*with adv or prep*) **to — into** convertir en, transformar en; **to — out** *cheque, document, receipt* extender; *list* hacer, redactar; *form* llenar; **the cheque should be made out to Pérez** el cheque será nominativo a favor de Pérez; **to — out** (*see*) distinguir, vislumbrar, divisar; *writing* descifrar; (*understand*) entender; **I can't — it out at all** no me lo explico, no lo entiendo; **he made out that . . .** dio a entender que . . ., dio la impresión de que . . ., nos hizo creer que . . .; **you — him out to be better than he is** Vd hace creer que es mejor de lo que es en realidad; **he's not as rich as people — out** es menos rico de lo que dice la gente; **how do you — that out?** ¿cómo deduces eso?, ¿de qué se infiere eso?; **to — over** ceder, traspasar; **to — up** (*make*) hacer; fabricar; *dress* confeccionar; *medicine* preparar; *collection* reunir; *parcel* empaquetar; *envolver*; *list* hacer, redactar; *print, page* hacer; **to — up** (*compose*) componer, formar, constituir; **the parts which — it up** las partes que lo componen; **the party was made up of 8 bishops** el grupo lo integraban 8 obispos; **to — up** (*invent*) inventar; **you're making it up!** ¡puro cuento!; **to — up** (*complete*) completar; *quantity, total* completar, hacer; **to — up** *loss* subsanar; *lost time etc* recuperar; *deficit* cubrir; **to —** it **up to someone** compensar a uno, indemnizar a uno; **to — up a fire** echar carbón a una lumbre; **to — up a quarrel** hacer las paces; **to —** it **up with someone** hacer las paces con uno; **to — up one's face** pintarse, maquillarse; **to — up an actor** maquillar a un actor.

2 *vi* **(a)** (*tide*) crecer, subir.

(b) he made as if to + *infin* hizo como si quisiese + *infin*, fingió que iba a + *infin*, hizo además de + *infin*.

(c) to — away, to — off largarse; huir, escaparse; **to — away with, to — off with** llevarse, alzarse con; escaparse con; **to — away with someone** matar a uno; **to — away with oneself** quitarse la vida, suicidarse.

(d) to — after someone seguir a uno, perseguir a uno; **to — for a place, to — towards a place** dirigirse a un lugar, encaminarse a un lugar; **where are you making for?** ¿adónde se dirige Vd?; **to — for someone** atacar a uno, abalanzarse sobre uno.

(e) to — for *result etc* contribuir a, conducir a;

it —s for optimism ayuda a crear el optimismo, fomenta el optimismo; **it —s for difficulties** tiende a crear dificultades.

(f) to — out arreglárselas, salir bien; **we're making out** vamos tirando; **we made out eventually** por fin nos las arreglamos; **how are you making out?** ¿cómo te va eso?

(g) to — up pintarse, maquillarse.

(h) to — up for someone's losses compensar a uno por sus pérdidas, indemnizar a uno de sus pérdidas; **to — up for a lack of** suplir una falta de; **to — up for lost time** recuperar el tiempo perdido.

(i) to — up to someone (*procurar*) congraciarse con uno, (*procurar*) ganarse la amistad de uno; halagar a uno, hacer zalamerías a uno.

3 *vr*: **(a) to — oneself an expert in** llegar a ser experto en; **to — oneself dictator** hacerse dictador, constituirse en dictador.

(b) to — oneself comfortable acomodarse a su gusto; **to — oneself ill with work** enfermar por exceso de trabajo; **to — oneself ridiculous** ponerse en ridículo; *see hear etc.*

(c) to — oneself do something obligarse a hacer algo; **I have to — myself** (do it) tengo que hacer un esfuerzo (por hacerlo).

4 *n* **(a)** (*brand*) marca *f*; (*type etc*) tipo *m*, modelo *m*; **it's a good — es** buena marca; **what — of car was it?** ¿qué tipo de coche fue?; **these are my own —** estos son según mi propia receta; **they have rifles of Belgian —** tienen fusiles de fabricación belga.

(b) to be on the — (*fam*) buscar el propio provecho, procurar a toda costa ir adelante; **the town is full of dealers on the —** la ciudad está llena de comerciantes que quieren enriquecerse.

make-believe ['meikbi,li:v] **1** *adj* fingido, simulado; *world etc* de ensueño, soñado.
2 *n* ficción *f*, invención *f*; imaginación *f*; **a world of —** un mundo de ensueño; **don't worry, it's just —** no te apures, es de mentirijillas.
3 *vi* fingir.

maker ['meikə*] *n* hacedor *m*, ora *f*, creador *m*, ora *f*; artífice *mf*; (*builder*) constructor *m*, ora *f*; (*manufacturer*) fabricante *m*; **the M—** el Hacedor.

makeshift ['meikʃift] **1** *adj* improvisado; provisional, temporal. **2** *n* improvisación *f*; expediente *m*; arreglo *m* provisional.

make-up ['meikʌp] *n* (*composition*) composición *f*; estructura *f*; (*of person etc*) carácter *m*, modo *m* de ser, naturaleza *f*; (*of clothes*) confección *f*; (*Typ*) imposición *f*; (*for face*) maquillaje *m*, cosméticos *mpl*; **— artist, — man** maquillador *m*; **— artist, — girl** maquilladora *f*.

makeweight ['meikweit] *n* contrapeso *m*; (*fig*) suplente *m*, sustituto *m*; tapa(a)gujeros *m*.

making ['meikiŋ] *n* **(a)** fabricación *f*; construcción *f*; elaboración *f*; formación *f*; creación *f*; confección *f*; preparación *f*; **in the — en** vías de formarse (*or* hacerse *etc*); **it's still in the — está** todavía en construcción, está todavía sin acabar; **while it was still in the — mientras** se estaba haciendo; **it's a civil war in the — es** una guerra civil en potencia; **it's history in the — es** la historia como proceso actual, es la historia que actualmente se está escribiendo; **the mistake was not of my — no** soy yo el responsable del error; **it was the — of him** fue la causa de su éxito, (*morally*) fue el motivo de su reforma moral.

(b) —s elementos *mpl* (necesarios); **he has the —s of an actor** es un actor que promete, tiene talento para ser actor, tiene madera de actor.

maladjusted ['mælə'dʒʌstid] *adj person* inadaptado.
maladjustment ['mælə'dʒʌstmənt] *n* inadaptación *f*.
maladministration ['mæləd,minis'treiʃən] *n* mala administración *f*.
maladroit ['mælə'drɔit] *adj* torpe.
maladroitly ['mælə'drɔitli] *adv* torpemente.
maladroitness ['mælə'drɔitnis] *n* torpeza *f*.
malady ['mælədi] *n* mal *m*, enfermedad *f*.
malaise [mæ'leiz] *n* malestar *m*.
malapropism ['mæləprɔpizəm] *n* despropósito *m* lingüístico, equivocación *f* de palabras.
malaria [mə'lɛəria] *f* paludismo *m*, malaria *f*.
malarial [mə'lɛəriəl] *adj* palúdico.
Malay [mə'lei] **1** *adj* malayo. **2** *n* malayo *m*, a *f*. **3** *n* (*language*) malayo *m*.
Malaya [mə'leiə] Malaya *f*, Malaca *f*.
Malayan [mə'leiən] **1** *adj* malayo. **2** *n* malayo *m*, a *f*.
Malaysia [mə'leiziə] Malaysia *f*.
malcontent ['mælkən'tent] **1** *adj* malcontento, revoltoso. **2** *n* malcontento *m*, a *f*, revoltoso *m*, a *f*.

male [meil] **1** adj (Bio, Mech) macho; child etc varón; sex masculino; (manly) viril, masculino; attire etc de hombres, para hombre; see nurse etc.
2 n macho m (also Bio); varón m.
malediction [ˌmæli'dikʃən] n maldición f.
malefactor ['mælifæktə*] n malhechor m, ora f.
malevolence [mə'levələns] n malevolencia f.
malevolent [mə'levələnt] adj malévolo.
malevolently [mə'levələntli] adv con malevolencia.
malformation [ˌmælfɔ:'meiʃən] n malformación f.
malfunction [mæl'fʌŋkʃən] n funcionamiento m defectuoso.
malice ['mælis] n malevolencia f, mala voluntad f; (Law) intención f delictuosa; out of — por malevolencia; with — toward none sin malevolencia para nadie; to bear someone — guardar rencor a uno; I bear him no — no le guardo rencor.
malicious [mə'liʃəs] adj malévolo, maligno; rencoroso.
maliciously [mə'liʃəsli] adv con malevolencia, con malignidad; rencorosamente.
malign [mə'lain] **1** adj maligno. **2** vt calumniar, difamar; tratar injustamente, ser injusto con; you — me eso no es justo, ésa no era mi intención.
malignancy [mə'lignənsi] n malignidad f.
malignant [mə'lignənt] adj maligno (also Med).
malignity [mə'ligniti] n malignidad f.
malinger [mə'liŋgə*] vi fingirse enfermo.
malingerer [mə'liŋgərə*] n enfermo m fingido, enferma f fingida.
mall [mæl] n alameda f, paseo m de árboles.
mallard ['mæləd] n pato m real, ánade m real.
malleability [ˌmæliə'biliti] n maleabilidad f.
malleable ['mæliəbl] adj maleable.
mallet ['mælit] n mazo m.
mallow ['mæləu] n malva f.
malnutrition ['mælnju:'triʃən] n desnutrición f.
malodorous [mæ'ləudərəs] adj maloliente, hediondo.
malpractice ['mæl'præktis] n procedimientos mpl ilegales; abuso m de autoridad; mala conducta f.
malt [mɔ:lt] **1** n malta f. **2** vt barley hacer germinar; drink etc preparar con malta; **—ed milk** harina f lacteada.
Malta ['mɔ:ltə] Malta f.
Maltese ['mɔ:l'ti:z] **1** adj maltés. **2** n maltés m esa f. **3** n (language) maltés m.
maltreat [mæl'tri:t] vt maltratar, tratar mal.
maltreatment [mæl'tri:tmənt] n maltrato m, maltratamiento m, malos tratos mpl.
mam(m)a [mə'mɑ:] n (fam) mamá f (fam).
mammal ['mæməl] n mamífero m.
mammalian [mæ'meiliən] adj mamífero.
mammary ['mæməri] adj mamario; — **gland** mama f, teta f.
Mammon ['mæmən] m (Bib) Mammón m.
mammoth ['mæməθ] **1** n mamut m. **2** adj gigantesco; (Comm) de tamaño extra.
mammy ['mæmi] n (fam) mamaíta f (fam); (US) nodriza f negra.
man [mæn] **1** n, pl **men** [men] **(a)** (general sense) hombre m; varón m; (humanity in general) el hombre, los hombres, el género humano; (servant) criado m; (workman) obrero m; (Mil) soldado m; (Naut) marinero m; (Chess etc) pieza f, ficha f, trebejo m.
(b) (with adj) **best** — padrino m de boda, testigo m del novio; **family** — padre m de familia, (home-loving) hombre m casero; — **Friday** criado m fiel; **all good men and true** todos los que merecen llamarse hombres; **her** — su marido; **the inner** — el estómago; **ladies'** — Perico entre ellas, hombre m de salón; **leading** — primer galán m; **medical** — médico m; **old** — viejo m, anciano m; **my old** — (fam) el pariente; **red** — piel roja m; **the grand old** — **of the party** el líder veterano del partido; **the strong** — **of the government** el hombre fuerte del gobierno; **young** — joven m; **her young** — su novio.
(c) (with qualifying phrase) — **about town** hombre m mundano, joven m amigo de los placeres, señorito m; — **and boy** desde pequeño; — **and wife** marido y mujer; — **in the moon** mujer f (or hombre m) de la luna; — **in the street** hombre m de la calle, hombre m medio; — **of letters** literato m; — **of means,** — **of property** hombre m acaudalado; — **of parts** hombre m de talento; — **of the world** hombre m de mundo.
(d) (used as pron etc) **men say that** . . . se dice que . . .; **when a** — **needs a wash** cuando uno necesita lavarse; **any** — cualquiera, cualquier hombre; **no** — nadie; **that** — Jones ese Jones; **as one** — unánimemente; como un sólo hombre,

todos a uno; — **to** — de hombre a hombre; **they're communists to a** — todos sin excepción son comunistas.
(e) (sort, type) **I'm not a drinking** — yo no bebo; **I'm not a football** — yo no soy aficionado al fútbol, no me gusta el fútbol; **he's a 4-pint** — es de los que se beben 4 pintas; **he's a Leeds** — es de Leeds; **it's got to be a local** — tiene que ser uno de aquí; **then I'm your** — entonces yo soy el que busca Vd.
(f) (in direct address) **you can't do that,** — hombre, no puedes hacer eso; —, **was I startled!** ¡vaya susto que me llevé!; (my) **little** —! ¡tirillas!; **my good** — buen hombre; **good** —! ¡bravo!, ¡muy bien!; **look here, old** — mire, amigo.
(g) (verb phrases) **to be odd** — **out** (different) diferenciarse de los demás, ser distinto, (left out) quedar excluido, (one too many) estar de más, sobrar; **he's not the** — **to do it** no es capaz de hacerlo; **he's not the** — **for the job** no es persona adecuada para el puesto; **to make a** — **of someone** hacer un hombre de uno; — **proposes, God disposes** el hombre propone y Dios dispone; **to reach** —'s **estate** llegar a la edad viril.
2 vt ship tripular; fortress guarnecer; guns servir; pumps acudir a, hacer funcionar; **a fully —ned ship** un buque con toda su tripulación; **the telephone is —ned all day** el telefonista está de servicio todo el día; see also **manned.**
manacle ['mænəkl] **1** n manilla f; **—s** esposas fpl, grillos mpl.
2 vt poner esposas a; **they were —d together** iban esposados juntos; **his hands were —d** llevaba esposas en las muñecas.
manage ['mænidʒ] **1** vt **(a)** tool etc manejar; manipular; car conducir; ship gobernar.
(b) company dirigir; organization regir, administrar; property administrar; affair manejar; election (pej) falsificar.
(c) person, child, animal manejar; **she can't** — **children** no puede con los niños; **I can** — **him** yo me encargo de él.
(d) £5 is the most I can — 5 libras es todo lo que puedo darte (or pagar etc); **I shall** — **it** lo haré; **you'll** — **it next time** ya harás la próxima vez; **can you** — **the cases?** ¿puedes llevar las maletas?; **thanks, I can** — **them** gracias, yo puedo con ellas; **can you** — **two more in the car?** ¿puedes llevar a dos más en el coche?; **can you** — **8 o'clock?** ¿puedes venir a las 8?; **can you** — **another cup?** ¿quieres otra taza?; **I can** — **another cake** me atrevo con otra pasta; **I couldn't** — **another thing** no podría comer ni un bocado más.
2 vi **(a)** arreglárselas, ir tirando; **can you** —? ¿tú puedes con eso?; **thanks, I can** — gracias, yo puedo; **she —s well enough** se las arregla bastante bien; **how do you** —? ¿cómo se las arregla Vd?; **to** — **without something** pasarse sin algo; **to** — **without someone** prescindir de uno.
(b) to — **to do something** lograr hacer algo; arreglárselas para hacer algo, ingeniarse para hacer algo; **how did you** — **to get it?** ¿cómo lo conseguiste?; **he —d not to get his feet wet** logró no mojarse los pies.
manageable ['mænidʒəbl] adj manejable; person, animal dócil; **of** — **size** de tamaño razonable.
management ['mænidʒmənt] n **(a)** (act) manejo m; gobierno m; dirección f; gerencia f; administración f.
(b) (persons) dirección f; junta f de directores; (as a class) clase f patronal y directorial; (Theat) empresa f; **"under new —"** "nueva dirección".
manager ['mænidʒə*] n (Comm etc) director m, gerente m; (of estate etc) administrador m; (Theat) empresario m; **sales** — gerente m de ventas; **works** — gerente m de fábrica; **business** — (for play etc) secretario m; **publicity** — agente m de publicidad; **she's a good** — es buena administradora, es muy económica.
manageress ['mænidʒə'res] n directora f; administradora f.
managerial [ˌmænə'dʒiəriəl] adj directivo, directorial; administrativo; **the** — **class** la clase patronal y directorial; **the** — **society** la sociedad patronal y directorial.
managing ['mænidʒiŋ] adj (pej) mandón; see **director.**
man-at-arms ['mænət'ɑ:mz] n, pl **men-at-arms** ['menət'ɑ:mz] hombre m de armas.
manatee [ˌmænə'ti:] n manatí m.
Manchuria [mæn'tʃuəriə] Manchuria f.
Manchurian [mæn'tʃuəriən] **1** adj manchuriano. **2** n manchuriano m, a f.

mandarin ['mændərin] *n* mandarín *m*; **M—** (*language*) mandarina *f*.

mandate ['mændeit] **1** *n* mandato *m*; (*country*) territorio *m* bajo mandato. **2** *vt* asignar como mandato (*to* a).

mandated ['mændeitid] *adj* territory bajo mandato.

mandatory ['mændətəri] *adj* obligatorio; **to be —** **upon someone to do something** incumbir a uno como obligación hacer algo.

man-day ['mæn'dei] *n*, *pl* **man-days** ['mæn'deiz] día-hombre *m*.

mandible ['mændibl] *n* mandíbula *f*.

mandolin(e) ['mændəlin] *n* mandolina *f*.

mandrake ['mændreik] *n* mandrágora *f*.

mandrill ['mændril] *n* mandril *m*.

mane [mein] *n* (*of lion, person*) melena *f*; (*of horse*) crin *f*, crines *fpl*.

man-eater ['mæn,i:tə*] *n* tigre *m* (*etc*) [cebado, tigre *m* (*etc*) devorador de hombres.

man-eating ['mæn,i:tiŋ] *adj* antropófago, peligroso para los hombres.

maneuver [mə'nu:və*] *etc* (*US*) see **manoeuvre**.

manful ['mænful] *adj* valiente, resuelto.

manfully ['mænfəli] *adv* valientemente, resueltamente.

manganese [,mæŋgə'ni:z] *n* manganeso *m*.

mange [meindʒ] *n* roña *f*, sarna *f*.

mangel(-wurzel) ['mæŋgl('wə:zl)] *n* remolacha *f* forrajera.

manger ['meindʒə*] *n* pesebre *m*.

mangle[1] ['mæŋgl] **1** *n* rodillo *m*, exprimidor *m* de la ropa. **2** *vt* pasar por el exprimidor.

mangle[2] ['mæŋgl] *vt* destrozar, mutilar, magullar; *text etc* mutilar, estropear.

mango ['mæŋgəu] *n* (*fruit and tree*) mango *m*.

mangold(-wurzel) ['mæŋgl('wə:zl)] *n* remolacha *f* forrajera.

mangrove ['mæŋgrəuv] *n* mangle *m*.

mangrove swamp ['mæŋgrəuv,swɔmp] *n* manglar *m*.

mangy ['meindʒi] *adj* roñoso, sarnoso.

manhandle ['mæn,hændl] *vt* (*Tech*) mover a brazo; (*fig*) maltratar.

manhole ['mænhəul] *n* registro *m* de inspección, pozo *m* de visita.

manhole cover ['manhəul,kʌvə*] *n* tapa *f* de registro, tapadera *f* de cloaca.

manhood ['mænhud] *n* (*state*) virilidad *f*; (*age*) edad *f* viril; (*manliness*) hombradía *f*; **to reach —** llegar a la edad viril.

man-hour ['mæn'auə*] *n*, *pl* **man-hours** ['mæn'auəz] hora-hombre *f*.

manhunt ['mænhʌnt] *n* persecución *f* de un criminal, caza *f* de hombre.

mania ['meiniə] *n* manía *f*; **persecution —** manía *f* persecutoria; **to have a — for something** tener la manía de algo; **to have a — for doing something** tener la manía de hacer algo.

maniac ['meiniæk] **1** *adj* maníaco. **2** *n* maníaco *m*, a *f*; (*fig*) maniático *m*, a *f*; **these sports —s** estos fanáticos del deporte, estos entusiastas del deporte; **he drives like a —** conduce como un loco.

maniacal [mə'naiəkəl] *adj* maníaco.

manic-depressive ['mænikdi'presiv] **1** *adj* maníacodepresivo. **2** *n* maníacodepresivo *m*, a *f*.

manicure ['mænikjuə*] **1** *n* manicura *f*. **2** *vt person* hacer manicura a; *nails* limpiar, arreglar.

manicure case ['mænikjuə,keis] *n*, **manicure set** ['mænikjuə,set] *n* estuche *m* de manicura.

manicurist ['mænikjuərist] *n* manicuro *m*, a *f*.

manifest ['mænifest] **1** *adj* manifiesto, evidente, patente; **to make something —** poner algo de manifiesto.

2 *n* (*Naut*) manifiesto *m*.

3 *vt* mostrar, revelar, patentizar.

manifestation [,mænifes'teiʃən] *n* manifestación *f*.

manifestly ['mænifestli] *adv* evidentemente.

manifesto [,mæni'festəu] *n*, *pl* **manifestoes** [,mæni'festəuz] manifiesto *m*.

manifold ['mænifəuld] **1** *adj* múltiple. **2** *n* (*Aut*) colector *m* de escape.

manikin ['mænikin] *n* (*dwarf*) enano *m*; (*Art*) maniquí *m*.

manioc ['mæniɔk] *n* mandioca *f*.

manipulate [mə'nipjuleit] *vt* manipular, manejar.

manipulation [mə,nipju'leiʃən] *n* manipulación *f*, manejo *m*.

mankind [mæn'kaind] *n* humanidad *f*, género *m* humano, los hombres.

manlike ['mænlaik] *adj* varonil.

manliness ['mænlinis] *n* virilidad *f*, masculinidad *f*, hombradía *f*.

manly ['mænli] *adj* varonil, viril, masculino; (*courageous*) valiente; (*strong*) fuerte; **to be very —** ser muy hombre, ser todo un hombre.

man-made ['mæn'meid] *adj* artificial.

manna ['mænə] maná *m*.

manned [mænd] *adj* satellite etc pilotado, habitado, tripulado.

mannequin ['mænikin] *n* (*Art*) maniquí *m*; (*fashion-*) modelo *f*.

manner ['mænə*] *n* (a) (*mode*) manera *f*, modo *m*; **— of payment** modo *m* de pago, forma *f* de pago; **after this —**, **in this —** de esta manera; **after** (*or* **in**) **the — of X** a la manera de X, en el estilo de X; **in like —** de la misma manera; **in such a — that ...** de tal manera que . . .; **a painter in the grand —** un pintor de cuadros grandiosos; **in a — of speaking** (*so to speak*) por así decirlo, como si dijéramos, (*up to a point*) hasta cierto punto, en cierto modo; **it's a — of speaking** es un modo de decir; **as if to the — born** como si fuese avezado desde la cuna.

(b) **—s** (*of society*) costumbres *fpl*; **a novel of —s** una novela de costumbres; **—s maketh man** la sociedad (*or* el medio ambiente) forma al hombre.

(c) (*behaviour etc*) conducta *f*; aire *m*, ademán *m*, porte *m*; manera *f* de ser; **his — to his parents** su modo de comportarse con sus padres; **I don't like his —** no me gusta su actitud; **he had the — of an old man** tenía aire de viejo; **there's something odd about his —** tiene un aire algo raro.

(d) **—s** (*good, bad etc*) modales *mpl*; educación *f*, crianza *f*; **bad —s** mala educación *f*; **good —s** educación *f*; **road —s** educación *f* en la carretera, conducta *f* en la carretera; **it's bad —s to yawn** es de mala educación bostezar; **good —s demand that . . .** la educación exige que . . .; **to have bad —s** ser mal criado, ser mal educado; **he has no —s** no tiene crianza, es un mal criado; **to forget one's —s** descomedirse; **to teach someone —s** enseñar crianza a uno.

(e) (*class, type*) clase *f*, especie *f*; **all — of birds** toda clase de aves, aves de toda clase; **no — of doubt** sin ningún género de duda; **by no — of means** de ningún modo; **what — of man is he?** ¿qué tipo de hombre es?

mannered ['mænəd] *adj* style amanerado; (*in compounds*) de modales . . .; see **bad-** etc.

mannerism ['mænərizəm] *n* (a) (*of style: Art, Lit*) manierismo *m*, (*pej*) amaneramiento *m*. (b) (*trick of speech, gesture*) hábito *m*, peculiaridad *f*.

mannerist ['mænərist] **1** *adj* manierista. **2** *n* manierista *mf*.

mannerliness ['mænəlinis] *n* (buena) educación *f*, crianza *f*, cortesía *f*.

mannerly ['mænəli] *adj* (bien) educado, bien criado, cortés.

mannish ['mæniʃ] *adj* hombruno.

manoeuvrability [mə,nu:vrə'biliti] *n* maniobrabilidad *f*.

manoeuvrable [mə'nu:vrəbl] *adj* maniobrable, manejable.

manoeuvre [mə'nu:və*] **1** *n* maniobra *f*.

2 *vt* hacer maniobrar; manipular, manejar; **to — a gun into position** mover un cañón a su posición; **to — someone into doing something** lograr mañosamente que uno haga algo.

3 *vi* maniobrar (*also fig*).

man-of-war ['mænəv'wɔ:*] *n*, *pl* **men-of-war** ['menəv'wɔ:*] *n* buque *m* de guerra.

manor ['mænə*] *n* (*feudal*) feudo *m*; señorío *m*; (*modern*) finca *f*; (*fam*) distrito *m*, barrio *m*; see **manor house**.

manor house ['mænəhaus] *n*, *pl* **— houses** [,hauziz] casa *f* señorial, casa *f* solariega.

manorial [mə'nɔ:riəl] *adj* señorial.

manpower ['mænpauə*] *n* mano *f* de obra.

manqué ['mɔ̃:ŋkei] *adj*: **a novelist —** uno que pudiera haber sido gran novelista.

manse [mæns] *n* (*esp Scot*) casa *f* del párroco.

manservant ['mæn,sə:vənt] *n*, *pl* **menservants** ['men,sə:vənts] criado *m*.

mansion ['mænʃən] *n* palacio *m*, hotel *m*; casa *f* grande; (*of ancient family*) casa *f* solariega; **M— House** residencia del alcalde de Londres.

man-sized ['mænsaizd] *adj* de tamaño de hombre; (*fig*) bien grande, grandote.

manslaughter ['mæn,slɔ:tə*] *n* homicidio *m* sin premeditación.

mantelpiece ['mæntlpi:s] *n*, **mantelshelf** ['mæntl-ʃelf] *n*, *pl* **—shelves** [ʃelvz] repisa *f* de chimenea.

mantilla [mæn'tilə] *n* mantilla *f*.

mantis ['mæntis] *n*: **praying —** mantis *f* religiosa.

mantle ['mæntl] **1** n manto m (also Zool), capa f (also fig); (gas-) manguito m incandescente. **2** vt cubrir, ocultar; envolver (in en).

man-to-man ['mæntə'mæn] adj, adv de hombre a hombre.

mantrap ['mæntræp] n cepo m.

manual ['mænjuəl] **1** adj manual. **2** n (book) manual m; (Mus) teclado m.

manually ['mænjuəli] adv manualmente, a mano.

manufacture [,mænju'fæktʃə*] **1** n (act) fabricación f; (product) manufactura f, producto m. **2** vt fabricar (also fig), manufacturar.

manufacturer [,mænju'fæktʃərə*] n fabricante m; industrial m.

manufacturing [,mænju'fæktʃəriŋ] **1** adj manufacturero, fabril. **2** n fabricación f.

manure [mə'njuə*] **1** n estiércol m, abono m; artificial — abono m artificial. **2** vt estercolar, abonar.

manure heap [mə'njuəhi:p] n estercolero m.

manuscript ['mænjuskript] **1** adj manuscrito. **2** n manuscrito m; (Typ, original of article) original m.

Manx [mæŋks] **1** adj de la Isla de Man; **the —** los habitantes de la Isla de Man. **2** n lengua f (celta) de la Isla de Man.

Manxman ['mæŋksmən] n, pl **—men** [mən] habitante m de la Isla de Man.

many ['meni] **1** adj muchos, muchas; **— people** muchas personas, mucha gente, muchos; **in — cases** en muchos casos; **— of them** muchos de ellos; **a time I saw him act**, **—'s the time I saw him act** muchas veces le vi representar; **he has as — as** I have tiene tantos como yo; **he has 3 times as — as** I have tiene 3 veces más que yo; **there were as — as** 20 había hasta 20; **how — were there?** ¿cuántos había?; **however —** you have por muchos que tenga Vd; **so — flies** tantas moscas; **ever so — people** la mar de gente, tantísimas personas; **too — difficulties** demasiadas dificultades; **there's one too —** hay uno de más, hay uno que sobra, sobra uno.

2 n muchos mpl, muchas fpl; gran número m; **a good — houses, a great — houses** muchísimas casas, un buen número de casas; **the —** la mayoría, las masas.

many-coloured ['meni'kʌləd] adj multicolor.

many-sided ['meni'saidid] adj figure multilátero; talent, personality polifacético; problem complicado.

map [mæp] **1** n mapa m; (of streets, town) plano m; (chart) carta f; **geological —** mapa m geológico; **relief —** mapa m en relieve; **it's right off the —** está muy aislado, está en el quinto infierno; **this will put Cheam on the —** esto ha de subrayar la importancia que tiene Cheam, ahora sí que se hablará de Cheam.

2 vt trazar el mapa (or plano) de; **to — out** (fig) proyectar; ordenar, organizar.

maple ['meipl] n arce m (also maple tree).

maple sugar ['meipl'ʃugə*] n azúcar m de arce.

maple syrup ['meipl'sirəp] n jarabe m de arce.

mapmaker ['mæp,meikə*] n cartógrafo m.

mapmaking ['mæp,meikiŋ] n, **mapping** ['mæpiŋ] n cartografía f.

mar [mɑ:*] vt estropear; desfigurar; echar a perder; happiness etc afectar; enjoyment aguar.

marathon ['mærəθən] **1** n (also — **race**) carrera f de maratón. **2** adj (fig) larguísimo, interminable.

maraud [mə'rɔ:d] vi merodear.

marauder [mə'rɔ:də*] n merodeador m; intruso m, indeseable m.

marauding [mə'rɔ:diŋ] **1** adj merodeador; intruso, indeseable. **2** n merodeo m.

marble ['mɑ:bl] **1** n (material) mármol m; (glass ball) canica f, bola f; **to play —s** jugar a las bolas. **2** adj marmóreo (also fig), de mármol.

marbled ['mɑ:bld] adj surface jaspeado.

March ['mɑ:tʃ] n marzo m.

march¹ [mɑ:tʃ] **1** n marcha f (also Mus, fig); (fig: long walk) caminata f; **dead —** marcha f fúnebre; **forced —** marcha f forzada; **to steal a — on someone** madrugar, ganar por la mano a uno, sacar la delantera a uno.

2 vt soldiers hacer marchar, llevar; distance recorrer marchando, (fig) llevar andado; **to — someone off** llevarse a uno sin ceremonia.

3 vi marchar; (fig) andar, ir a pie; (stalk) ir resueltamente, caminar con resolución; **forward —!**, **quick —!** ¡de frente ¡mar!; **to — in** entrar (resueltamente etc); **to — into a room** entrar resueltamente en un cuarto; **to — on** seguir marchando; **to — out** salir (resueltamente, airado etc); **to — past** desfilar; **to — past someone** desfilar ante uno; **to — up to**

someone abordar a uno tan fresco, acercarse resueltamente a uno.

march² [mɑ:tʃ] n (Hist) marca f; **the Welsh —es** la zona fronteriza entre Inglaterra y Gales.

marching ['mɑ:tʃiŋ] adj song etc de marcha.

marchioness ['mɑ:ʃənis] n marquesa f.

march-past ['mɑ:tʃ,pɑ:st] n desfile m.

mare [mɛə*] n yegua f.

mare's-nest ['mɛəznest] n parto m de los montes, hallazgo m ilusorio.

Margaret ['mɑ:gərit] f Margarita.

margarine [,mɑ:dʒə'ri:n] n, **marge** [mɑ:dʒ] n (fam) margarina f.

margin ['mɑ:dʒin] n margen m (also Typ); (fig) margen m; reserva f; excedente m, sobrante m; **— of error** margen m de error; **— of profit** margen m de beneficio; **— of safety** margen m de seguridad; **to write something in the —** escribir algo al margen.

marginal ['mɑ:dʒinl] adj note, profit etc marginal; land de poco valor agrícola; case etc dudoso, incierto.

marguerite [,mɑ:gə'ri:t] n margarita f.

Maria [mə'raiə] f María.

Marian ['mɛəriən] adj mariano.

Marie Antoinette [mə'ri:æntwɑ:'net] f María Antonieta.

marigold ['mærigəuld] n caléndula f, maravilla f.

marijuana [,mæri'hwɑ:nə] n marijuana f.

marina [mə'ri:nə] n centro m de deportes acuáticos, centro m de balandrismo.

marinade [,mæri'neid] **1** n escabeche m. **2** vt (also **marinate** ['mærineit]) escabechar, marinar.

marine [mə'ri:n] **1** adj marino; marítimo; **— insurance** seguro m marítimo; **— life** vida f marina. **2** n (a) (fleet) marina f; **mercantile —, merchant —** marina f mercante.

(b) (person) soldado m de marina; **—s** infantería f de marina; **tell that to the —s!** ¡a otro perro con ese hueso!

mariner ['mærinə*] n marinero m, marino m.

mariolatry [,mɛəri'ɔlətri] n mariolatría f.

marionette [,mæriə'net] n marioneta f, títere m.

marital ['mæritl] adj marital; matrimonial; **— status** estado m civil.

maritime ['mæritaim] adj marítimo.

marjoram ['mɑ:dʒərəm] n mejorana f, orégano m.

Mark [mɑ:k] m Marcos.

mark¹ [mɑ:k] n (coin) marco m.

mark² [mɑ:k] **1** n (a) (written symbol on paper etc) señal f, marca f; llamada f; (sign, indication) señal f, indicio m; (trade-) marca f; (stain) mancha f; (imprint, trace) huella f; **the —s of** violence las señales de la violencia; **he had the —s of old age** tenía los indicios de la vejez; **he left the ring without a —** on his body salió del cuadrilátero sin llevar en el cuerpo señal alguna de haber recibido golpe; **it's the — of a gentleman** así se distinguen los caballeros, es señal de caballerosidad; **printer's —** pie m de imprenta; **as a — of my disapproval** en señal de mi desaprobación; **as a — of our gratitude** en señal de nuestro agradecimiento; **it bears the — of genius** tiene el sello de la genialidad; **to leave one's —** dejar memoria de sí; **to leave one's — on something** dejar sus huellas en algo.

(b) (signature) cruz f; **to make one's —** firmar con una cruz, (fig) señalarse, distinguirse, destacar.

(c) (Sport) raya f; **to be quick off the —** ser muy listo; adelantarse a los demás; **to be slow off the —** ser lerdo; dejar que otros cojan la delantera a uno; **to be up to the —** ser satisfactorio, estar a la altura de las circunstancias; **to come up to the —** alcanzar el nivel que era de esperar; **to overstep the —** propasarse.

(d) (label) etiqueta f.

(e) **of —** de categoría, de cierta distinción.

(f) (target) blanco m; **to be wide of the —** no dar en el blanco, (fig) no acertar, ser erróneo, alejarse de la verdad; **to hit the —** dar en el blanco, (fig) acertar, dar en el clavo.

(g) (in exam; also **—s**) puntuación f; calificación f, nota f; **52 —s** 52 puntos, 52 por cien; **first-class —s** nota f de sobresaliente; **to get high —s in French** sacar buena nota en francés; **you get no —s at all as a cook** como cocinera no vales para nada; **there are no —s for guessing** las simples conjeturas no merecen punto alguno.

2 vt (a) (make a — on) señalar, marcar, poner una señal en; (stain) manchar; desfigurar; **— it with an asterisk** ponga un asterisco allí; **he was not —ed at all** no tuvo señal alguna de haber recibido golpe (or de haber sido lesionado); **a bird —ed with red** un pájaro manchado de rojo, un pájaro con manchas rojas.

(b) (*label*) rotular, poner un rótulo a; (*Comm*) poner una etiqueta a, indicar el precio de; **this exhibit is not —ed** este objeto no lleva rótulo; **the chair is —ed at £2** se indica el precio de la silla como de 2 libras.

(c) (*indicate*) señalar, marcar, indicar; **stones — the path** unas piedras señalan el camino; **this —s the frontier** esto marca la frontera; **it —s a change of policy** ello indica un cambio de política; **this —s him as a future star** esto le señala como un as futuro; **it's not —ed on the map** no está indicado en el mapa, no consta en el mapa.

(d) (*note down*) apuntar; (*notice*) advertir, observar; (*heed*) prestar atención a; **did you — where it fell?** ¿vio Vd en qué sitio cayó?; **— you, — my words** entiéndase bien que . . .; **— you, he may have been right** de todas formas, puede haber tenido razón; **what I say** escucha lo que te digo.

(e) *exam* puntuar, calificar; *candidate* dar nota a; **we —ed him (as) first class** le dimos nota de sobresaliente.

(f) **to — down** (*note*) apuntar; (*select*) escoger; (*Comm*) rebajar, rebajar el precio de; **to — off** señalar; distinguir, separar (*from* de); (*by stages etc*) jalonar; **to — out** *road etc* trazar, marcar; jalonar; **the road is —ed out by flags** el camino está jalonado de banderas; **he is —ed out for promotion** se le ha señalado para un ascenso.

marked [mɑːkt] *adj contrast etc* acusado, fuerte; *accent* marcado; *improvement etc* notable, grande; **— man** hombre m que ha llamado la atención; hombre m que se ha señalado como futura víctima; **it is becoming more —** se acusa cada vez más.

markedly ['mɑːkidli] *adv* marcadamente; fuertemente; notablemente; **it is — better than the other** es netamente superior al otro; **they are not — different** no son netamente distintos.

marker ['mɑːkə*] *n* (*Billiards etc*) marcador m, (*in other games*) ficha f; (*in book*) registro m.

market ['mɑːkit] **1** *n* mercado m; (*stock exchange*) bolsa f; **black —** estraperlo m, mercado m negro; **to buy something on the black —** comprar algo de estraperlo; **buyer's —** mercado m de signo favorable al comprador; **seller's —** mercado m de signo favorable al vendedor; **home —** mercado m nacional, mercado m interior; **overseas —** mercado m exterior; **world —** mercado m mundial; **Common M—** Mercado m Común; **open —** mercado m al aire libre; **free —** mercado m libre (*in de*); **there's no — for pink socks** los calcetines rosados no encuentran salida; **to be in the — for something** estar dispuesto a comprar algo; **to be on the —** estar de venta; **it's the dearest shirt on the —** es la camisa más cara del mercado; **to come on to the —** (empezar a) venderse, ponerse en venta, ofrecerse; **to corner the — in** *maize* acaparar el maíz; **to find a ready —** venderse fácilmente, tener fácil salida; **to flood the — with something** inundar el mercado de algo; **strawberries are flooding the —** las fresas inundan el mercado; **to play the —** jugar a la bolsa; **to rig the —** manipular la lonja.

2 *attr* **— price** precio m de mercado; **— research** análisis m de mercados; **— value** valor m en el mercado.

3 *vt* vender, poner a la venta; *new product etc* llevar al mercado.

4 *vi* ir de compras; hacer las compras.

marketable ['mɑːkitəbl] *adj* vendible, comerciable; de valor comercial.

market day ['mɑːkitdei] *n* día m de mercado.

marketeer [,mɑːki'tiə*] *n* (*Pol*) partidario m del Mercado Común; **black —** estraperlista m.

market garden ['mɑːkit,gɑːdn] *n* huerto m, (*large*) huerta f.

market gardener ['mɑːkit,gɑːdnə*] *n* hortelano m.

marketing ['mɑːkitiŋ] *n* venta f, comercialización f.

market place ['mɑːkitpleis] *n* mercado m, plaza f del mercado.

marking ['mɑːkiŋ] *n* (*mark*) señal f, marca f; (*on animal*) mancha f, pinta f; (*coloration*) coloración f; (*of exams*) puntuación f, calificación f.

marking ink ['mɑːkiŋ,iŋk] *n* tinta f de marcar, tinta f indeleble.

marksman ['mɑːksmən] *n*, *pl* **-men** [mən] tirador m, ora f.

marksmanship ['mɑːksmənʃip] *n* puntería f.

markup ['mɑːkʌp] *n* precio m; aumento m de precio.

marl [mɑːl] *n* marga f.

marlin ['mɑːlin] *n* (*Fish*) aguja f.

marlinespike ['mɑːlinspaik] *n* pasador m.

marly ['mɑːli] *adj* margoso.

marmalade ['mɑːməleid] *n* mermelada f (de naranjas amargas).

marmoreal [mɑː'mɔːriəl] *adj* marmóreo.

marmoset ['mɑːməzet] *n* tití m.

marmot ['mɑːmət] *n* marmota f.

maroon[1] [mə'ruːn] **1** *adj* marrón. **2** *n* (*colour*) marrón m; (*firework*) petardo m.

maroon[2] [mə'ruːn] *vt* abandonar (en una isla desierta); **we were —ed by floods** quedamos aislados por las inundaciones.

marquee [mɑː'kiː] *n* entoldado m.

marquess, marquis ['mɑːkwis] *n* marqués m.

marquetry ['mɑːkitri] *n* marquetería f.

marriage ['mærid3] *n* (*as institution*) matrimonio m; (*wedding*) boda f, bodas fpl; casamiento m; (*fig*) unión f; **civil —** matrimonio m civil; **shotgun —** casamiento m a la fuerza; **— of convenience** matrimonio m de conveniencia; **aunt by —** tía f política; **to be related by —** estar emparentados; **to become related by — to someone** emparentar con uno; **to give someone in —** to dar a una en matrimonio a.

marriageable ['mærid3əbl] *adj* casadero.

marriage bed ['mærid3bed] *n* lecho m nupcial, tálamo m.

marriage rate ['mærid3reit] *n* índice m de nupcialidad.

married ['mærid] *adj person* casado; *life, love, state etc* conyugal; **— man** casado m, **— woman** casada f; *see* **couple** *etc*.

marrow ['mærəu] *n* **(a)** (*Anat*) médula f, tuétano m, meollo m; (*fig*) meollo m; (*as food*) tuétano m de hueso; **a Spaniard to the —** español hasta los tuétanos; **to be frozen to the —** estar completamente helado.

(b) (*Bot*) calabacín m (*also* **vegetable —**).

marrowbone ['mærəubəun] *n* hueso m con tuétano; **—s** (*fam*) rodillas fpl.

marry ['mæri] **1** *vt* (*give or join in marriage*) casar (*to* con); (*take in marriage*) casarse con, casar con; (*fig*) unir; **he has 3 daughters to — (off)** tiene 3 hijas por casar; **to — money** casarse con uno (*or* una) que tiene una fortuna.

2 *vi* (*also* **to get married**) casarse; **to — again** volver a casarse, casarse en segundas nupcias; **to — beneath oneself** casarse con uno (*or* una) de rango inferior; **to — into a family** emparentar con una familia.

Mars [mɑːz] m Marte.

Marseillaise [,mɑːsə'leiz] *n*: **the —** la Marsellesa.

Marseilles [mɑː'seilz] Marsella.

marsh [mɑːʃ] *n* pantano m; (*salt-*) marisma f.

marshal ['mɑːʃəl] **1** *n* (*Mil*) mariscal m; (*at ceremony*) maestro m de ceremonias; (*at sports meeting etc*) oficial m; (*US*) alguacil m, oficial m de justicia.

2 *vt facts etc* ordenar, arreglar; *soldiers, procession* formar.

marshalling yard ['mɑːʃəliŋ,jɑːd] *n* playa f de clasificación.

marsh fever ['mɑːʃ,fiːvə*] *n* paludismo m.

marsh gas ['mɑːʃgæs] *n* gas m de los pantanos.

marshland ['mɑːʃlænd] *n* pantanal m.

marshmallow ['mɑːʃ'mæləu] *n* (*Bot*) malvavisco m; (*sweet*) bombón m de merengue blando.

marsh marigold ['mɑːʃ'mærigəuld] *n* calta f palustre.

marshy ['mɑːʃi] *adj* pantanoso.

marsupial [mɑː'suːpiəl] **1** *adj* marsupial. **2** *n* marsupial m.

mart [mɑːt] *n* (*trade centre*) emporio m; (*market*) mercado m; (*auction room*) martillo m; **property —** (*in newspaper*) bolsa f de la propiedad.

marten ['mɑːtin] *n* marta f.

Martial ['mɑːʃəl] m Marcial.

martial ['mɑːʃəl] *adj* marcial; castrense; *law etc* marcial, militar.

Martian ['mɑːʃiən] **1** *adj* marciano. **2** *n* marciano m, a f.

Martin ['mɑːtin] m Martín.

martin ['mɑːtin] *n* (*Orn*) avión m.

martinet [,mɑːti'net] *n* ordenancista mf, rigorista mf.

Martinique [,mɑːti'niːk] Martinica f.

Martinmas ['mɑːtinməs] *n* día m de San Martín (11 *noviembre*).

martyr ['mɑːtə*] **1** *n* mártir mf; **to be a — to arthritis** ser martirizado por la artritis, ser víctima de la artritis. **2** *vt* martirizar.

martyrdom ['mɑːtədəm] *n* martirio m.

martyrize ['mɑːtiraiz] *vt* martirizar.

marvel ['mɑːvəl] **1** *n* maravilla; prodigio m; **if he gets there it will be a —** si llega allí será maravilla;

it's a — to me how he does it no llego a comprender cómo lo hace, me asombra el que lo pueda hacer. **2** *vi* maravillarse (**at** de, con).

marvellous, (US) **marvelous** ['mɑːvələs] *adj* maravilloso; —! ¡magnífico!; **isn't it** —? ¡qué bien! (*also iro*).

marvellously, (US) **marvelously** ['mɑːvələslɪ] *adv* maravillosamente; a maravilla.

Marxism ['mɑːksɪzəm] *n* marxismo *m*.

Marxist ['mɑːksɪst] **1** *adj* marxista. **2** *n* marxista *mf*.

Mary ['mɛərɪ] *f* María; — **Stuart** María Estuardo; **Bloody** — María la Sangrienta.

marzipan [,mɑːzɪ'pæn] *n* mazapán *m*.

mascara [mæs'kɑːrə] *n* rimel *m*.

mascot ['mæskət] *n* mascota *f*.

masculine ['mæskjulɪn] **1** *adj* masculino; varonil; *woman* hombruno. **2** *n* (*Gram*) masculino *m*.

masculinity [,mæskju'lɪnɪtɪ] *n* masculinidad *f*.

mash [mæʃ] **1** *n* (*mixture*) mezcla *f*; (*pulp*) pasta *f*, amasijo *m*, batiburrillo *m*; (*potatoes*) puré *m* de patatas; (*in brewing*) malta *f* remojada; (*bran*) afrecho *m* remojado.
2 *vt* mezclar; amasar, despachurrar; *potatoes* hacer un puré de.

mashed [mæʃt] *adj*: — **potatoes** puré *m* de patatas.

masher ['mæʃə*] *n* (*fam*) pisaverde *m*.

mask [mɑːsk] **1** *n* máscara *f* (*also fig*); (*disguise*) disfraz *m*; (*protective*) antifaz *m*; (*gas- etc*) careta *f*; (*surgeon's, death-*) mascarilla *f*; *see* **masque**.
2 *vt* enmascarar; (*fig*) encubrir, ocultar.

masked [mɑːskt] *adj* enmascarado; — **ball** baile *m* de máscaras.

masochism ['mæzəʊkɪzəm] *n* masoquismo *m*.

masochist ['mæzəʊkɪst] *n* masoquista *mf*.

masochistic [,mæzəʊ'kɪstɪk] *adj* masoquista.

mason ['meɪsn] *n* (*builder*) albañil *m*; (*in quarry*) cantero *m*; (*free-*) masón *m*, francmasón *m*; **monumental** — escultor *m* de monumentos funerarios.

masonic [mə'sɒnɪk] *adj* masónico.

masonry ['meɪsnrɪ] *n* albañilería *f*; mampostería *f*; (*free-*) masonería *f*, francmasonería *f*.

masque [mɑːsk] *n* mascarada *f*.

masquerade [,mæskə'reɪd] **1** *n* baile *m* de máscaras, mascarada *f*; (*fig*) farsa *f*. **2** *vi*: **to — as** disfrazarse de, hacerse pasar por.

mass¹ [mæs] *n* (*Eccl*) misa *f*; **high** — misa *f* mayor; **low** — misa *f* rezada; **midnight** — misa *f* del gallo; **to go to** — ir a misa, oír misa; **to hear** — oír misa; **to say** — decir misa.

mass² [mæs] **1** *n* masa *f* (*also Phys*); (*vague shape*) bulto *m* informe; (*of mountains*) macizo *m*; (*great quantity*) montón *m*, gran cantidad *f*; (*of people*) muchedumbre *f*; **the —es** las masas; **a great — of people** una gran muchedumbre; **the — of** la mayoría de; **the great — of** la inmensa mayoría de; **in the —** en conjunto; **to gather in —es** acudir en masa, reunirse en tropel; **we have —es** tenemos montones; **he's a — of bruises** está cubierto de cardenales; **the garden is a — of yellow** el jardín es todo flores amarillas; **he's a — of nerves** es una madeja de nervios, tiene una tremenda tensión nerviosa.
2 *adj, attr production* en serie; *meeting* popular, público; *murders etc* en masa, en serie; *psychology* de masas; — **media** medios *mpl* de comunicación con las multitudes (*prensa, television etc*).
3 *vt* juntar en masa, reunir; *troops etc* concentrar.
4 *vi* juntarse en masa, reunirse; (*Mil*) concentrarse.

massacre ['mæsəkə*] **1** *n* matanza *f*, carnicería *f*, degollina *f*, masacre *f*. **2** *vt* hacer una carnicería de, matar despiadadamente, masacrar.

massage ['mæsɑːʒ] **1** *n* masaje *m*. **2** *vt* dar masaje a.

masseur [mæ'sɜː*] *n* masajista *m*.

masseuse [mæ'sɜːz] *n* masajista *f*.

massif [mæ'siːf] *n* (*Geog*) macizo *m*.

massive ['mæsɪv] *adj* (*solid*) macizo, sólido; *head etc* grande, abultado; (*imposing*) imponente, impresionante; *contribution, support, intervention* enérgico, fuerte, masivo, en gran escala.

massively ['mæsɪvlɪ] *adv* macizamente, sólidamente; de modo imponente; enérgicamente, fuertemente.

massiveness ['mæsɪvnɪs] *n* macicez *f*, solidez *f*; lo grande, lo abultado; energía *f*, fuerza *f*.

mass-produce ['mæsprə'djuːs] *vt* fabricar en serie.

mass production ['mæsprə'dʌkʃən] *n* fabricación *f* en serie.

mast¹ [mɑːst] *n* (*Naut*) mástil *m*, palo *m*; (*Radio etc*) torre *f*; **10 years before the —** 10 años de servicio como marinero.

mast² [mɑːst] *n* (*Bot: of oak*) bellota *f*, (*of beech*) hayuco *m*.

-masted ['mɑːstɪd] *adj* de . . . palos, *eg* **three-masted** de tres palos.

master ['mɑːstə*] **1** *n* (*of the house etc*) señor *m*, amo *m*; (*owner*) dueño *m*; (*Naut: of ship*) capitán *m*, (*of boat*) patrón *m*; (*expert, musician, painter etc*) maestro *m*; (*of Mil order*) maestre *m*; (*teacher*) maestro *m*, (*in secondary school*) profesor *m*; (*of college*) director *m*; **old — (man)** pintor *m* clásico, (*work*) obra *f* clásica, cuadro *m* de uno de los pintores clásicos; **the young —** el señorito; **— of arts** maestro *m* en artes; **— of ceremonies** maestro *m* de ceremonias; **— of foxhounds** cazador *m* mayor; **to be a past — at politics** ser maestro en política, ser un político consumado; **to be — of** poseer; **to be — of the situation** ser dueño de la situación, ser dueño del baile; **the — is not at home** el señor no está; **I am the — now** ahora mando yo; **to be — in one's own house** mandar en su propia casa; **to be one's own —** ser independiente; trabajar por cuenta propia; **to be the — of** one's fate decidir su propio destino; **to make oneself — of** apoderarse de; **to meet one's —** ser derrotado por fin, tener que sucumbir por fin.
2 *attr card, mason etc* maestro; *switch etc* principal; — **mariner** capitán *m*.
3 *vt* (*defeat*) vencer, derrotar; *difficulty etc* vencer; *situation* dominar; *one's defects* sobreponerse a; *subject* dominar; *craft* llegar a ser maestro en.

master builder ['mɑːstə'bɪldə*] *n* constructor *m*; arquitecto *m*.

masterful ['mɑːstəful] *adj* imperioso, autoritario; *personality etc* dominante.

master key ['mɑːstə,kiː] *n* llave *f* maestra.

masterly ['mɑːstəlɪ] *adj* magistral, genial.

mastermind ['mɑːstəmaind] **1** *n* inteligencia *f* genial; (*in crime etc*) mente *f* directora, figura *f* principal. **2** *vt operation* dirigir, planear.

masterpiece ['mɑːstəpiːs] *n* obra *f* maestra.

Mastersingers ['mɑːstə,sɪŋəz] *pl*: "**The —**" "Los maestros cantores".

master stroke ['mɑːstəstrəʊk] *n* golpe *m* maestro.

mastery ['mɑːstərɪ] *n* (*sway*) dominio *m*; autoridad *f*; (*skill*) maestría *f*; (*over competitors etc*) dominio *m*, superioridad *f*; **to gain the — of** (*take over*) hacerse el señor de, (*dominate*) llegar a dominar.

masthead ['mɑːsthed] *n* tope *m*.

masticate ['mæstɪkeɪt] *vti* masticar.

mastiff ['mæstɪf] *n* mastín *m*, alano *m*.

mastitis [mæs'taitɪs] *n* mastitis *f*.

mastodon ['mæstədən] *n* mastodonte *m*.

mastoid ['mæstɔid] **1** *adj* mastoides. **2** *n* mastoides *f*.

masturbate ['mæstəbeɪt] *vi* masturbarse.

masturbation [,mæstə'beɪʃən] *n* masturbación *f*.

mat¹ [mæt] **1** *n* estera *f*, (*small*) esterilla *f*; (*round*) ruedo *m*; (*at door*) felpudo *m*; (*on table*) salvamanteles *m*; (*of lace etc*) tapetito *m*; (*of hair*) greña *f*.
2 *vt* enmarañar, entretejer.
3 *vi* enmarañarse, entretejerse.

mat² [mæt] *adj* mate.

match¹ [mætʃ] *n* cerilla *f*, fósforo *m*; (*fuse*) mecha *f*.

match² [mætʃ] **1** *n* (a) (*person etc*) igual *mf*; **the two of them make a good —** los dos hacen una buena pareja; **the skirt is a good — for the jumper** la falda hace juego con el jersé; **to be a — for someone** poder competir (*etc*) con uno en pie de igualdad; **he's a — for anybody** puede dar quince y raya al más pintado; **A is no — for B** A no puede con B; **A was more than a — for B** A venció fácilmente a B; **to meet one's match** encontrar la horma de su zapato.
(b) (*marriage*) casamiento *m*, matrimonio *m*; **who thought up this —?** ¿quién ideó este matrimonio?; **she made a good —** hizo una buena boda; **he's a good —** es buen partido.
(c) (*Sport*) partido *m*, encuentro *m*; (*race*) carrera *f*; (*Boxing*) lucha *f*; (*Fencing*) asalto *m*; (*quiz etc*) concurso *m*; **return —** (partido *m* de) desquite *m*, revancha *f*; **away —** partido *m* fuera de casa; **home —** partido *m* en casa, partido *m* en casero; **they never tried to make a — of it** no se esforzaron en ningún momento por vencer; **let's make a — of it** juguemos con la intención de ganar.
2 *vt* (a) (*pair off*) emparejar, parear; **to — A against B** hacer que A compita con B; **they're well —ed** hacen una buena pareja; **the teams are well —ed** los equipos son muy iguales.
(b) (*equal*) igualar, ser igual a, valer lo que; **A doesn't quite — B in originality** en cuanto a originalidad A no vale lo que B; **the results did not — our hopes** los resultados no eran tan buenos como los habíamos esperado.
(c) (*of clothes, colours*) hacer juego con; **his tie**

—es his socks su corbata hace juego con los calcetines; **can you — this silk?** (in shop etc) ¿tiene una seda igual que ésta?
3 vi hacer juego, armonizar, ser a tono; **with a skirt to —** con una falda acompañada, con una falda a tono.

matchbox ['mætʃbɔks] n cajita f de cerillas.
matching ['mætʃiŋ] adj acompañado, a tono, del mismo estilo y color.
matchless ['mætʃlis] adj sin par, incomparable.
matchmaker ['mætʃ,meikə*] n casamentero m, a f.
matchmaking ['mætʃ,meikiŋ] **1** n actividades fpl de casamentero. **2** adj casamentero.
matchwood ['mætʃwud] n astillas fpl; **to smash something to —** hacer algo añicos; **to be smashed to —** ser convertido en un montón de astillas.
mate[1] [meit] **1** n mate m. **2** vt dar jaque mate a, matar; **white plays and —s in 2** blanco juega y mata en 2.
mate[2] [meit] **1** n (companion) compañero m, camarada m; (married) compañero m, a f; cónyuge mf, (Zool) macho m, hembra f; (assistant) ayudante m, peón m; (Naut) primer oficial m, pilota m, segundo m de a bordo; **John and his —s** Juan y sus compañeros; **first —** primer oficial m, piloto m; **plumber's —** ayudante m de fontanero, aprendiz m de fontanero; **look here, —** (fam) mire, amigo; **yes, —** (fam) sí, hombre.
2 vt (Zool) parear, acoplar; (fig) unir; **they are well —d** hacen una buena pareja.
3 vi (Zool) parearse, acoplarse; **age should not — with youth** no debe casarse el viejo con la joven.
material [mə'tiəriəl] **1** adj material; importante, esencial; well-being etc físico; loss, damage importante, considerable.
2 n (ingredient, equipment, also fig) material m; (substance) materia f; (data) datos mpl, material m; (cloth) tejido m, tela f; **—s** material m, materiales mpl; **building —s** material m de construcción; **raw —s** materias fpl primas; **war —** material m bélico; **writing —s** efectos mpl de escritorio.
materialism [mə'tiəriəlizəm] n materialismo m; **dialectical —** materialismo m dialéctico.
materialist [mə'tiəriəlist] **1** adj materialista. **2** n materialista mf.
materialistic [mə,tiəriə'listik] adj materialista.
materialize [mə'tiəriəlaiz] **1** vt materializar. **2** vi (spirit) tomar forma visible; (idea etc) realizarse, convertirse en hecho.
materially [mə'tiəriəli] adv materialmente; **that does not — alter things** eso no afecta la cosa de modo sensible; **they are not — different** no difieren en su esencia.
maternal [mə'tə:nl] adj grandfather etc materno; affection etc maternal.
maternity [mə'tə:niti] n maternidad f; **— dress** vestido m premamá; see **hospital** etc.
matey ['meiti] adj (fam) person afable, simpático; bonachón; atmosphere acogedor; gathering sin ceremonias, familiar, de ambiente acogedor.
math [mæθ] n (US fam) see **mathematics**.
mathematical [,mæθə'mætikəl] adj matemático; **he's a — genius** tiene un genio para las matemáticas.
mathematically [,mæθə'mætikəli] adv matemáticamente.
mathematician [,mæθəmə'tiʃən] n matemático m.
mathematics [,mæθə'mætiks] n matemáticas fpl; **applied —** matemáticas fpl aplicadas; **pure —** matemáticas fpl teóricas.
Mat(h)ilda [mə'tildə] f Matilde.
maths [mæθs] n (fam) see **mathematics**.
matinée ['mætinei] n función f de tarde.
mating ['meitiŋ] n (Zool) apareamiento m, acoplamiento m; (fig) unión f.
matins ['mætinz] npl maitines mpl.
matriarch ['meitriɑ:k] n matriarca f.
matriarchal [,meitri'ɑ:kl] adj matriarcal.
matriarchy ['meitriɑ:ki] n matriarcado m.
matric [mə'trik] n see **matriculation**.
matricide ['meitrisaid] n (act) matricidio m; (person) matricida mf.
matriculate [mə'trikjuleit] **1** vt matricular. **2** vi matricularse; (Brit Univ) cumplir los requisitos para entrar en la universidad.
matriculation [mə,trikju'leiʃən] n matriculación f; (Brit Univ) requisitos mpl para entrar en la universidad, (loosely) examen m para entrar en la universidad.
matrimonial [,mætri'məuniəl] adj matrimonial; conyugal.
matrimony ['mætriməni] n matrimonio m; vida f conyugal.
matrix ['meitriks] n matriz f.

matron ['meitrən] n (married woman) matrona f; (in hospital) enfermera f jefa; (in school) ama f de llaves.
matronly ['meitrənli] adj matronal, de matrona; figure etc maduro y algo corpulento.
matt [mæt] adj mate.
matted ['mætid] adj enmarañado, entretejido; espeso; **— hair** greña f.
matter ['mætə*] **1** n (a) (substance) materia f; sustancia f; (Typ) material m; **advertising —** material m de publicidad; **colouring —** colorante m; **grey —** materia f gris, seso m; **printed —** impresos mpl; **vegetable —** material f vegetal.
(b) (Med) pus m, materia f.
(c) (Lit etc) materia f, tema m; **form and —** la forma y el contenido, la forma y la materia; **the main — of his speech** el tema principal de su discurso.
(d) (question, affair) asunto m, cuestión f, cosa f; **for that —, for the — of that** si vamos a eso, en cuanto a eso; **in this —** en este asunto; **in the — of** en materia de, en asuntos de; **there's the — of my expenses** hay aquello de mis gastos; **it will be a — of a few weeks** es cosa de varias semanas; **it's a — of a couple of hours** es cosa de dos horas; **in a — of 10 minutes** en cosa de 10 minutos; **it's a — of great concern to us** es cosa que nos tiene preocupadísimos; es cosa que nos importa muchísimo; **it is no great —** es poca cosa, no importa; **that's quite another —**, that's another — altogether, that's a very different — eso es harina de otro costal; **it's an easy — to + infin** es fácil + infin; **it will be no easy —** no será fácil; **it's a serious —** es cosa seria; **it's no laughing —** no es cosa de risa; **business —s** negocios mpl; **money —s** asuntos mpl financieros; **the — in hand** el asunto de que se trata; **as —s stand** tal como están las cosas; **the — is closed** el asunto está concluido; **to make — worse** para colmo de desgracias; **he doesn't mince —s** no tiene pelos en la lengua; **he didn't mince —s with me** conmigo no se paró en barras; **well, not to mince —s** bueno, para decirlo como es; **as a — of course** por rutina; **it's a — of course with us** con nosotros es cosa de cajón (see also **course** 1 (b)); **as a — of fact . . .** en realidad . . ., el caso es que . . .; **as a — of fact we were just talking about you** precisamente estábamos hablando de Vd; **it's a — of form** es pura formalidad; **it's a — of taste** es cuestión de gusto.
(e) **no —, it makes no —** no importa; **what —?** ¿qué importa?; **no — how you do it** no importa cómo lo haga Vd; **no — what he says** diga lo que diga; **no — how big it is** por grande que sea; **no — how hot it is** por mucho calor que haga; **no — when** no importa cuándo; **no — who goes** quienquiera que vaya; **get one, no — how** procure uno, del modo que sea.
(f) **what's the —?** ¿qué hay?, ¿qué pasa?; **what's the — with you?** ¿te pasa algo?, ¿qué tienes?; **what's the — with John?** ¿qué le pasa a Juan?; **what's the — with my hat?** ¿qué tiene mi sombrero?; **what's the — with singing?** ¿es que está prohibido cantar?; **what's the — with smoking?** ¿qué inconveniente hay en fumar?; **something's the — with the lights** algo les pasa a las luces; **nothing's the — no** pasa nada; **as if nothing was the —** como si no hubiese pasado nada, como si tal cosa.
2 vi importar; **it doesn't —** no importa, lo mismo da, es igual; **what does it —?** ¿qué importa?; **does it — to you if I go?** ¿te importa que yo vaya?; **why should it — to me?** y a mí ¿qué?; **some things — more than others** algunas cosas son más importantes que otras.
matter-of-fact ['mætərəv'fækt] adj prosaico; práctico; flemático.
Matthew ['mæθju:] m Mateo.
matting ['mætiŋ] n estera f.
mattock ['mætək] n azadón m.
mattress ['mætris] n colchón m.
mature [mə'tjuə*] **1** adj maduro; (Comm) vencido; **of — years** de edad madura; **to become —** (Comm) vencer. **2** vti madurar; (Comm) vencer.
maturity [mə'tjuəriti] n madurez f; (Comm) vencimiento m.
maudlin ['mɔ:dlin] adj (sentimental) sensiblero; (weepy) llorón; **at the point of deshacerse en lágrimas.
maul [mɔ:l] vt destrozar, magullar, herir; writer, play etc maltratar; (finger) manosear; text estropear; **he got badly —ed in the press** la prensa le puso como un trapo.
Maundy ['mɔ:ndi] n: **— money** dinero que reparte el monarca a los pobres el Jueves Santo; **— Thursday** Jueves m Santo.
Maurice ['mɔris] m Mauricio.

Mauritius [məˈriʃəs] Mauricio m, Isla f de Francia.

mausoleum [ˌmɔːsəˈliːəm] n mausoleo m.

mauve [məuv] **1** adj (de) color de malva. **2** n color m de malva.

maverick [ˈmævərik] n (US Agr) res f sin marcar; (Pol etc) disidente m, inconformista mf, persona f independiente.

maw [mɔː] n (Anat) estómago m; (of cow etc) cuajar m; (of bird) molleja f, buche m; (fig) fauces fpl.

mawkish [ˈmɔːkiʃ] adj empalagoso, sensiblero, insulso.

mawkishness [ˈmɔːkiʃnis] n sensiblería f, insulsez f.

maxim [ˈmæksim] n máxima f.

maximize [ˈmæksimaiz] vt llevar al máximum; extremar.

maximum [ˈmæksiməm] **1** adj máximo. **2** n máximo m, máximum m; (up) to the — al máximo; up to a — of £8 hasta 8 libras como máximum.

maxiskirt [ˈmæksiskəːt] n maxifalda f.

May [mei] **1** n mayo m; m— (Bot: flower) flor f del espino, (tree) espino m. **2** vi: to go m—ing ir a la fiesta de mayo.

may [mei] (irr: pret **might**) vi (a) (of possibility) poder, ser posible; **it — rain** es posible que llueva, puede que llueva; **it — be that ...** puede ser que + subj, quizá + subj; **he — not be hungry** puede no tener hambre; **I — have said so** es posible que lo haya dicho, puedo haberlo dicho; **I might have said so** pudiera haberlo dicho; **yes, I —** sí, es posible; **be that as it —** sea como fuere; **that's as — be** eso puede ser.
(b) (of permission) poder, tener permiso para; **yes, you —** sí puedes; **if I —** si me lo permites; **— I?** ¿se permite?; **— I see it?** ¿me permites verlo?; **— I come in?** ¿se puede?; **— I go now?** ¿puedo irme ya?; **you — smoke** se permite fumar; **you — not smoke** se prohibe fumar; **if I — advise you** si me permite Vd ofrecer un consejo.
(c) **I hope he — succeed** espero que lo logre; **I hoped he might succeed this time** esperaba que lo lograra esta vez; **such a policy as might bring peace** una política que pudiera traernos la paz; **we — as well go** más vale irnos, bien podemos irnos; **he might have offered to help** bien pudiera habernos ofrecido su ayuda; **you might shut the door!** ¡podrías (or podías) cerrar la puerta!; **you might try Smith's** quizá valga la pena de buscarlo en la tienda de Smith; **as you might expect** como era de esperar, según cabía esperar; **run as he might** por mucho que corriese.
(d) (of wishing) **— you be lucky!** ¡que tengas suerte!; **— you be forgiven!** ¡que Dios le perdone!; **long — he reign!** ¡viva muchos años!; **or — I never eat prawns again** o que no vuelva yo nunca a comer gambas.
(e) (in questions) **who might you be?** ¿quién es Vd?; **how old might you be?** ¿cuántos años tendrá Vd?

Maya [ˈmɑːjə], **Mayan** [ˈmɑːjən] **1** adj maya. **2** n maya mf.

maybe [ˈmeibiː] **1** adv quizá, tal vez. **2** conj: **— he'll come** quizá venga.

May Day [ˈmeidei] n primero m de mayo.

mayfly [ˈmeiflai] n efímera f.

mayhem [ˈmeihem] n mutilación f criminal.

mayn't [meint] = **may not**.

mayonnaise [meiəˈneiz] n mayonesa f.

mayor [mɛə*] n alcalde m.

mayoralty [ˈmɛərəlti] n alcaldía f.

mayoress [ˈmɛəres] n alcaldesa f.

maypole [ˈmeipəul] n mayo m.

May queen [ˈmeikwiːn] n maya f.

maze [meiz] n laberinto m; **to be in a —** (fig) estar perplejo.

me [miː] pron me; (after prep) mí; **with —** conmigo; **dear —!** ¡vaya!; **it's —** (fam) soy yo; **it's —, Paul** (identifying self) soy Pablo.

mead [miːd] n aguamiel f, hidromiel m.

meadow [ˈmedəu] n prado m, pradera f; (esp water-) vega f.

meadowsweet [ˈmedəuswiːt] n reina f de los prados.

meagre, (US) **meager** [ˈmiːgə*] adj escaso, exiguo, pobre.

meal¹ [miːl] n (flour) harina f.

meal² [miːl] n comida f; square — comida f realmente buena (see also **square 1** (c)); **to have a —** comer; **to have a good —** comer bien; **to make a — of something** comer algo, contentarse con comer algo.

mealtime [ˈmiːltaim] n hora f de comer.

mealy [ˈmiːli] adj harinoso.

mealy-mouthed [ˈmiːliˈmauðd] adj excesivamente circunspecto; **let us not be — about it** hablemos claro sobre esto.

mean¹ [miːn] adj (of poor quality) inferior; birth etc humilde, pobre; (shabby, unimpressive) humilde, vil; (with money) tacaño; (petty) mezquino; **don't be —!** ¡no seas malo!; **you — thing!** ¡canalla!; **the —est citizen** el menor ciudadano; **he is no — player** es un jugador nada despreciable; **you were — to me** me has tratado muy mal; **it made me feel —** me hizo sentir vergüenza.

mean² [miːn] **1** adj medio. **2** n (a) (middle term) medio m, promedio m, término m medio; (Math) media f; **golden —**, **happy —** justo medio m.
(b) **—s** (method) medio m, manera f, método m; **—s to an end** medio m de conseguir un fin; **there is no —s of doing it** no hay modo de hacerlo; **he was the —s of sending it** él nos proporcionó un medio de enviarlo; **by all —s** por todos los medios, (fig) por cierto; **by all —s!** ¡naturalmente!, ¡claro que sí!; **by all —s take one** por favor tome uno; **by any —s** de cualquier modo, del modo que sea; **by no —s**, **not by any —s** de ningún modo; **by no —s!** ¡de ningún modo!; **it is by no —s difficult** no es nada difícil; **by —s of** por medio de, mediante; **by this —s** por este medio, de este modo; **by fair —s** por medios rectos; **by fair —s or foul** por las buenas o por las malas.
(c) **—s** (Fin) recursos mpl, medios mpl, fondos mpl, dinero m; **a man of —s** un hombre acaudalado; **we have no —s to do it** nos faltan recursos para hacerlo; **to have private —s** tener ingresos de fuente particular; **to live beyond one's —s** vivir por encima de sus posibilidades, gastar más de lo que se gana; **to live within one's —s** vivir con arreglo a los ingresos, vivir dentro de los medios.

mean³ [miːn] (irr: pret and ptp **meant**) vt (a) (intend: with noun etc) pretender, intentar; **he —s well** tiene buenas intenciones; **I — it to digo en serio**; **do you — it?** ¿lo dices en serio?; **you can't — it!** ¡vaya!; **I —t it as a joke** lo dije en broma; **he —s no harm** tiene buenas intenciones; **I —t no harm by what I said** no lo dije con mala idea; **he —t no offence** no tenía la intención de ofender a nadie.
(b) (intend: with verb) **to — to** + infin pensar + infin, proponerse + infin, pretender + infin; **what do you — to do?** ¿qué piensas hacer?; **I —t to help** tenía la intención de ayudar; **he didn't — to do it** lo hizo sin querer; **this photo is —t to be Anne** esta foto quiere ser Ana; **I — to be obeyed** insisto en que se me obedezca; **I — to have it** quiero tenerlo, me propongo obtenerlo; **if he —s to be awkward** si quiere ser difícil.
(c) (destine) destinar (for a, para); **this present was —t for you** este regalo era para ti; **do you — me?** ¿es a mí?; **was that remark —t for me?** esa observación ¿iba dirigida contra mí?; **he —t that for you** lo dijo por ti.
(d) (signify: person, statement etc) querer decir (by con); (word) significar (to para); **what does "ohm" —?** ¿qué quiere decir "ohmio"?; **what do you — by that?** ¿qué quieres decir con eso?; **"coger" —s something different in America** en América "coger" tiene otro significado, en América "coger" significa otra cosa; **the name —s nothing to me** el nombre no me suena; **it —s a lot of expense for us** nos supone unos grandes gastos; **this —s our ruin** esto es nuestra ruina, esto significa nuestra ruina; **a pound —s a lot to her** para ella una libra es mucho dinero; **the play didn't — a thing to me** poca cosa saqué en claro de la obra; **your friendship —s much to me** tu amistad es muy importante para mí; **don't I — anything to you?** ¿no significo yo nada para ti?, ¿no tengo yo siquiera un poquito de importancia para ti?

meander [miˈændə*] **1** n meandro m; **—s** (fig) meandros mpl. **2** vi (river) serpentear; (person etc) andar sin propósito fijo, vagar.

meaning [ˈmiːniŋ] **1** adj look etc significativo, lleno de intención.
2 n (a) (intention) intención f, propósito m; **a look full of —** una mirada llena de intención; **to mistake someone's —** interpretar mal la intención de uno.
(b) (sense of words etc) sentido m, significado m; (particular sense of word) acepción f; (general impact) significación f; **double —** doble sentido m; **literal —** sentido m literal; **what's the — of "hick"?** ¿qué significa "hick"?, ¿qué quiere decir "hick"?; **what's the — of this?** (as reprimand) y esto ¿qué quiere decir?

meaningful [ˈmiːniŋful] adj significativo, que tiene sentido.

meaningless [ˈmiːniŋlis] adj sin sentido; (rash, mad) insensato; **in this situation it is —** en esta situación no tiene sentido; **to write "xybj" is —** escribir "xybj" carece de sentido.

meanness ['miːnnis] *n* humildad *f*; vileza *f*, bajeza *f*; tacañería *f*; mezquindad *f*; maldad *f*.

means test ['miːnztest] *n* averiguación *f* de los recursos económicos (*del que pide o recibe asistencia pública etc*).

meant [ment] *pret and ptp of* **mean**.

meantime ['miːn'taim] *adv*, **meanwhile** ['miːn'wail] *adv* entretanto, mientras tanto; **in the meantime** mientras tanto, en el ínterin.

measles ['miːzlz] *n* sarampión *m*; **German** — rubéola *f*.

measly ['miːzli] *adj* (*fam*) miserable, cochino, malísimo.

measurable ['meʒərəbl] *adj* mensurable, que se puede medir; (*perceptible*) apreciable, perceptible.

measure ['meʒə*] 1 *n* (a) (*system of —*) medida *f*; — **of capacity** medida *f* de capacidad; **cubic** — medida *f* cúbica; **dry** — medida *f* para áridos; **full** — medida *f* exacta, cantidad *f* exacta; **liquid** — medida *f* para líquidos; **square** — medida *f* cuadrada; **standard** — medida *f* tipo; **made to** — hecho a la medida; **I think we have his** — **now** creo que le tenemos calado ya; **to take someone's** — (*fig*) tomar las medidas a uno.
(b) (*rule etc*) regla *f*; (*glass*) probeta *f* graduada.
(c) (*limit*) **beyond** — hasta no más; excesivamente; **better beyond** — incomparablemente mejor; **in full** — abundantemente, como se debe, adecuadamente; **for good** — por añadidura; **in great** —, **in large** — en gran parte; **in some** — hasta cierto punto.
(d) (*step*) medida *f*; (*Parl: bill*) proyecto *m* de ley, (*act*) ley *f*; **emergency** — medida *f* de urgencia; **preventive** — medida *f* preventiva; **to take** —**s** tomar medidas (*to* + *infin* para + *infin*); **to take extreme** —**s** tomar medidas extremas.
(e) **coal** —**s** depósitos *mpl* de carbón.
(f) (*Mus*) compás *m*.
2 *vt* (*also to* — **off, to** — **out**) medir; *person* (*for height*) tallar, (*for clothes*) tomar las medidas a; *words etc* pesar, pensar bien; **to** — **out** (*issue*) repartir, distribuir; *see* **length**.
3 *vi* medir; **it** — **s 3 metres by 2 metres** mide 3 metros por 2 metros; **what does it** —? ¿cuánto mide?; **to** — **up to something** estar a la altura de algo.

measured ['meʒəd] *adj tread etc* deliberado, rítmico; *tone* mesurado; *statement etc* moderado, circunspecto, prudente.

measureless ['meʒəlis] *adj* inmensurable, inmenso.

measurement ['meʒəmənt] *n* (*system*) medición *f*; (*measure*) medida *f*; dimensión *f*; **to take someone's** —**s** tomar las medidas a uno.

measuring ['meʒəriŋ] *n* medición *f*; **to take** —**s of** hacer mediciones de.

meat [miːt] 1 *n* carne *f*; (*fig*) sustancia *f*, meollo *m*, jugo *m*; (*of fat etc*) parte *f* gruesa; **cold** — fiambre *m*, carne *f* fiambre; **a book with some** — **in it** un libro sólido, un libro jugoso; **one man's** — **is another man's poison** lo que para uno es bueno es para otro es veneno; **it's** — **and drink to me** no puedo vivir sin él. 2 *attr* de carne; *industry etc*, *product* cárnico.

meatball ['miːt'bɔːl] *n* albóndiga *f*.

meatfly ['miːtflai] *n* mosca *f* de la carne.

meat pie ['miːt'pai] *n* pastel *m* de carne, empanada *f*.

meat safe ['miːtseif] *n* fresquera *f*.

meaty ['miːti] *adj* carnoso; (*fig*) sustancioso, jugoso, sólido.

Mecca ['mekə] La Meca.

mechanic [mi'kænik] *n* mecánico *m*; **motor** — mecánico *m* de automóviles.

mechanical [mi'kænikəl] *adj* mecánico; (*fig*) maquinal.

mechanically [mi'kænikəli] *adv* mecánicamente; (*fig*) maquinalmente.

mechanics [mi'kæniks] *n* mecánica *f*; mecanismo *m*, técnica *f*.

mechanism ['mekənizəm] *n* (*all senses*) mecanismo *m*; **defence** — mecanismo *m* de defensa.

mechanistic [,mekə'nistik] *adj* mecánico, maquinal.

mechanization [,mekənai'zeiʃən] *n* mecanización *f*.

mechanize ['mekənaiz] *vt* mecanizar.

medal ['medl] *n* medalla *f*.

medallion [mi'dæljən] *n* medallón *m*.

medallist, (*US*) **medalist** ['medəlist] *n* persona *f* condecorada con una medalla; (*Sport*) campeón *m*, ona *f*, titular *mf*.

meddle ['medl] *vi* entrometerse (*in* en); **to** — **with something** manosear algo, tocar algo, (*and damage*) estropear algo; **who asked you to** —? ¿quién le mete a Vd en esto?; **he's always meddling** es un entrometido.

meddler ['medlə*] *n* entrometido *m*, a *f*.

meddlesome ['medlsəm] *adj*, **meddling** ['medliŋ] *adj* entrometido.

meddlesomeness ['medlsəmnis] *n* entrometimiento *m*.

Mede [miːd] *n*: **the** —**s and the Persians** los medos y los persas.

mediaeval [,medi'iːvəl] *adj* (*etc*) *see* **medieval** (*etc*).

medial ['miːdiəl] *adj* medial.

median ['miːdiən] 1 *adj* mediano. 2 *n* (*US*) zona *f* central (*entre las dos calzadas de una autopista*); (*Math*) número *m* medio; punto *m* medio.

mediate ['miːdieit] *vi* mediar (*between* entre, *in* en).

mediation [,miːdi'eiʃən] *n* mediación *f*.

mediator ['miːdieitə*] *n* mediador *m*, árbitro *m*.

medic ['medik] *n* (*fam*) médico *m*; (*Univ*) estudiante *mf* de medicina.

medical ['medikəl] 1 *adj* médico; *school, student etc* de medicina. 2 *n* reconocimiento *m* médico.

medically ['medikəli] *adv* médicamente; — **speaking** desde el punto de vista médico; **to be** — **examined** tener un reconocimiento médico.

medicament [me'dikəmənt] *n* medicamento *m*.

medicate ['medikeit] *vt* medicar; impregnar (*with* de).

medication [,medi'keiʃən] *n* medicación *f*.

medicinal [me'disinl] *adj* medicinal.

medicine ['medsin, 'medisin] *n* medicina *f*; medicamento *m*; **forensic** — medicina *f* legal; **patent** — específico *m*; **preventive** — medicina *f* preventiva; **to take one's** — (*fig*) sufrir las consecuencias.

medicine box ['medsinbɔks] *n*, **medicine chest** ['medsintʃest] *n* botiquín *m*.

medicine man ['medsinmæn] *n*, *pl* — **men** [men] hechizador *m*.

medico ['medikəu] *n* (*fam*) médico *m*.

medieval [,medi'iːvəl] *adj* medieval.

medievalism [,medi'iːvəlizəm] *n* medievalismo *m*.

medievalist [,medi'iːvəlist] *n* medievalista *mf*.

mediocre [,miːdi'əukə*] *adj* mediocre, mediano.

mediocrity [,miːdi'ɔkriti] *n* mediocridad *f*, medianía *f* (*also person*).

meditate ['mediteit] 1 *vt* meditar. 2 *vi* meditar (*on something* algo), reflexionar (*on* en, *sobre*).

meditation [,medi'teiʃən] *n* meditación *f*.

meditative ['mediteitiv] *adj* meditabundo.

meditatively ['mediteitivli] *adv* reflexivamente.

Mediterranean [,meditə'reiniən] 1 *adj* mediterráneo; — **Sea** Mar *m* Mediterráneo. 2 *n* Mediterráneo *m*.

medium ['miːdiəm] 1 *adj quality etc* mediano, regular; *size* mediano, intermedio; *wave* medio; **of** — **height** de estatura regular; **of** — **difficulty** de mediana dificultad.
2 *n* (*pl in some senses* **media** ['miːdiə]) medio *m*; (*person*) médium *mf*; **happy** — justo medio *m*, término *m* medio; **advertising media** medios *mpl* de publicidad; **through the** — **of** por medio de.

medium-fine ['miːdiəm'fain] *adj* entrefino.

medium-sized ['miːdiəm'saizd] *adj* de tamaño mediano.

medlar ['medlə*] *n* (*fruit*) níspola *f*; (*tree*) níspero *m*.

medley ['medli] *n* mezcla *f*, mezcolanza *f*; miscelánea *f*; (*Mus*) popurrí *m*.

medulla [me'dʌlə] *n* medula *f*.

meek [miːk] *adj* manso, dócil, sumiso; **to be very** — **and mild** (*person*) ser como una malva.

meekly ['miːkli] *adv* mansamente, dócilmente, sumisamente.

meekness ['miːknis] *n* mansedumbre *f*, docilidad *f*.

meerschaum ['miəʃəm] *n* espuma *f* de mar; (*pipe*) pipa *f* de espuma de mar.

meet[1] [miːt] *adj* (*lit, arch*) conveniente, apropiado; **it is** — **that . . .** conviene que + *subj*; **to be** — **for** ser apto para.

meet[2] [miːt] (*irr: pret and ptp* **met**) 1 *vt* (a) *person etc* (*encounter*) encontrar; (*accidentally*) encontrarse con; (*by arrangement*) reunirse con, (*formally*) entrevistarse con; **to arrange to** — **someone** citarse con uno, dar una cita a uno.
(b) *difficulty* encontrar, tropezar con; *death* hallar, encontrar; *opponent, opposing team* enfrentarse con, (*in duel*) batirse con; **he met his death in 1800** halló la muerte en 1800; **to** — **death calmly** enfrentarse tranquilamente con la muerte; **to** — **death courageously** ir valiente y resueltamente a su muerte.
(c) (*go to* —) ir a recibir, ir a buscar, esperar, ir al encuentro de; **I'll** — **you at the garage** te espero en el garaje; **we met her at the station** fuimos a recibirla en la estación; **don't bother to** — **me** no os molestéis viniendo a buscarme; **the car will** — **the train** el coche esperará la llegada del tren; **the bus** —**s the aircraft** hay correspondencia entre el autobús y el avión.

(d) (*get to know*) conocer; **I never met him** no le conocí nunca, no le llegué a conocer; **I met my wife in 1960** conocí a mi mujer en 1960; — **Mr Jones** quiero presentarle al Sr Jones; **I am very pleased to** — **you** tengo mucho gusto en conocerle; **pleased to** — **you!** ¡tanto gusto!

(e) **what a scene met my eyes!** ¡qué cosas se presentaron a mis ojos!; **I could not** — **his eye** no podía mirarle a los ojos; *see also* **eye.**

(f) *charge* refutar; *debt* pagar, honrar, satisfacer; *deficit* cubrir; *expense* sostener, correr con, hacer frente a; *liabilities* honrar; *need* satisfacer, cubrir; *objection* responder a; *obligation* atender, cumplir; *requirement* satisfacer; *demand, wish* conformarse con, condescender con, satisfacer; *scorn* tener que aguantar; **to** — **someone halfway** partir el camino con uno; **we met each other halfway** (*fig*) nos hicimos concesiones mutuas.

2 *vi* **(a)** (*encounter each other*) encontrarse, verse; (*by arrangement*) reunirse, verse; (*meeting, society*) reunirse; **the society** —**s at 8** la sociedad se reúne a las 8, la sesión de la sociedad comienza a las 8; **let's** — **at 8** citémonos para las 8; **until we** — **again!** ¡hasta la vista!; **keep it until we** — **again** guárdalo hasta que nos veamos.

(b) (*get to know*) conocerse; **we met in Seville** nos conocimos en Sevilla; **we have met before** nos conocemos ya; **have we met?** ¿nos conocimos antes?

(c) (*fight*) batirse; **Bilbao and Valencia will** — **in the final** el Bilbao se enfrentará con el Valencia en la final, Bilbao y Valencia se disputarán la final.

(d) (*join*) encontrarse; **our eyes met** cruzamos una mirada, nos miramos el uno al otro; **where the rivers** — donde confluyen los ríos; **the roads** — **at Toledo** las carreteras empalman en Toledo.

(e) **to** — **with** (*esp US*) *person* juntarse con, reunirse con; *kindness etc* encontrar; *accident* tener, sufrir; *loss* sufrir; *shock* experimentar; *success* tener; *difficulty* tropezar con; **to** — **up with someone** reunirse con uno.

3 *n* (*Sport*) reunión *f*; (*Hunting*) cacería *f*.

meeting ['mi:tiŋ] *n* **(a)** (*between 2 persons: accidental*) encuentro *m*, (*arranged*) cita *f*, (*formal*) entrevista *f*; **the minister had a** — **with the ambassador** el ministro se entrevistó con el embajador.

(b) (*assembly*) reunión *f*; (*esp of legislative body*) sesión *f*; (*popular gathering*) mitin *m*; — **of creditors** concurso *m* de acreedores; **annual general** — junta *f* general anual; **special** (*or* **extraordinary**) **general** — junta *f* general extraordinaria; **mass** — mitin *m*, reunión *f* popular, manifestación *f* popular; **to address the** — tomar la palabra en la reunión, dirigirse a los asistentes; **to call a** — **of shareholders** convocar una junta de accionistas; **to adjourn** (*or* **close**) **the** — levantar la sesión; **to hold a** — celebrar una junta, (*Parl*) celebrar sesión; **to open the** — abrir la sesión.

(c) (*Sport: eg athletic*) concurso *m*; (*horse races*) reunión *f*; (*clash between teams*) encuentro *m*.

(d) (*of rivers*) confluencia *f*.

meeting house ['mi:tiŋ,haus] *n*, *pl* — **houses** [,hauziz] templo *m* de los cuáqueros.

meeting place ['mi:tiŋpleis] *n* (*of 2 persons*) lugar *m* de cita, (*of many*) punto *m* de reunión; **this bar was their usual** — solían citarse en este bar, acostumbraban reunirse en este bar.

megacycle ['megə,saikl] *n* megaciclo *m*.

megalith ['megəliθ] *n* megalito *m*.

megalithic [,megə'liθik] *adj* megalítico.

megalomania ['megələu'meiniə] *n* megalomanía *f*.

megalomaniac [,megələu'meiniæk] *n* megalómano *m*, a *f*.

megaphone ['megəfəun] *n* megáfono *m*.

megaton ['megətʌn] *n* megatón *m*.

megavolt ['megəvəult] *n* megavoltio *m*.

megawatt ['megəwɔt] *n* megavatio *m*.

melancholia [,melən'kəuliə] *n* melancolía *f*.

melancholic [,melən'kɔlik] *adj* melancólico.

melancholy ['melənkəli] **1** *adj* melancólico; *duty, sight etc* triste. **2** *n* melancolía *f*.

melanism ['melənizəm] *n* melanismo *m*.

melée ['melei] *n* pelea *f* confusa, refriega *f*; tumulto *m*; **there was such a** — **at the booking office** se apiñaba la gente delante de la taquilla; **it got lost in the** — se perdió en el tumulto.

mellifluous [me'lifluəs] *adj* melifluo.

mellow ['meləu] **1** *adj* *fruit etc* maduro, dulce; *wine* añejo; *colour, sound* dulce; *light* suave; *voice* suave, meloso; *instrument* melodioso; *character* maduro y tranquilo; **in** — **old age** en la vejez tranquila; **to be**

— (*fam: person*) estar entre dos luces; **to get** — (*fam*) achisparse.

2 *vt* madurar; suavizar, ablandar.

3 *vi* madurarse; suavizarse, ablandarse.

mellowing ['meləuiŋ] *n* maduración *f*.

mellowness ['meləunis] *n* madurez *f*; dulzura *f*, suavidad *f*; lo melodioso.

melodic [mi'lɔdik] *adj* melódico.

melodious [mi'ləudiəs] *adj* melodioso.

melodiously [mi'ləudiəsli] *adv* melodiosamente.

melodrama ['meləu,drɑ:mə] *n* melodrama *m*.

melodramatic [,meləudrə'mætik] *adj* melodramático.

melodramatically [,meləudrə'mætikli] *adv* melodramáticamente.

melody ['melədi] *n* melodía *f*.

melon ['melən] *n* melón *m*.

melt [melt] **1** *vt metal* fundir; *snow* derretir; *chemical disolver*; (*fig*) *heart etc* ablandar; **to** — **down** fundir.

2 *vi* fundirse; derretirse; disolverse; ablandarse, enternecerse; **to** — **away** (*money, confidence etc*) esfumarse, desvanecerse, desaparecer misteriosamente; (*crowd etc*) dispersarse; (*person*) desaparecer silenciosamente, escurrirse; **to** — **into tears** deshacerse en lágrimas.

melting ['meltiŋ] **1** *adj look etc* tierno, dulce. **2** *n* fundición *f*; derretimiento *m*; disolución *f*.

melting point ['meltiŋpɔint] *n* punto *m* de fusión.

melting pot ['meltiŋpɔt] *n* crisol *m* (*also fig*); **the plan is in the** — el plan está sobre el tapete; **it is a nation in the** — es una nación en formación.

member ['membə*] *n* **(a)** (*person*) miembro *m*; (*of company, society*) miembro *m*, socio *m*; (*Parl*) miembro *m*, diputado *m*; "—**s only**" "reservado a los socios", "sólo para socios"; — **of the family** miembro *m* de la familia; — **of parliament** diputado *m*, miembro *m* del parlamento, (*Spain*) diputado *m* a Cortes; **if any** — **of the audience . . .** si cualquiera de los asistentes . . .; **the** — **for Woodford** el diputado por Woodford; **full** — miembro *m* de número; **private** — (*Parl*) miembro *m* (*que no es ministro*); **the** — **countries** los países participantes (*of en*).

(b) (*Anat*) miembro *m*; **male** — miembro *m* viril.

membership ['membəʃip] *n* calidad *f* de miembro (*or socio*); (*numerical*) número *m* de miembros (*or socios*); **Britain's** — **of the Common Market** el ingreso de Gran Bretaña en el Mercado Común; la participación de Gran Bretaña en el Mercado Común; **when I applied for** — **of the club** cuando solicité el ingreso en el club, cuando quise hacerme socio del club; — **carries certain rights** el ser miembro da ciertos derechos; — **list** relación *f* de socios; *see* **fee** *etc*.

membrane ['membrein] *n* membrana *f*.

membranous [mem'breinəs] *adj* membranoso.

memento [mə'mentəu] *n* recuerdo *m*.

memo ['meməu] *n* (*fam*) = **memorandum.**

memoir ['memwɑ:*] *n* memoria *f*; biografía *f*, autobiografía *f*; nota *f* biográfica; —**s** memorias *fpl*.

memorable ['memərəbl] *adj* memorable.

memorably ['memərəbli] *adv* memorablemente.

memorandum [,memə'rændəm] *n*, *pl* **memoranda** [,memə'rændə] memorándum *m*, memorando *m* (*Acad*); apunte *m*, nota *f*, memoria *f*.

memorial [mi'mɔ:riəl] **1** *adj* conmemorativo. **2** *n* monumento *m* (conmemorativo); (*document*) memorial *m*; **war** — monumento *m* a los caídos.

memorize ['meməraiz] *vt* aprender de memoria.

memory ['meməri] *n* (*faculty*) memoria *f*; (*recollection*) recuerdo *m*; **"Memories of life in Slobodia"** "Recuerdos *mpl* de la vida en Eslobodia"; **to speak from** — hablar fiándose de su memoria; **in** — **of** en memoria de, en conmemoración de; **the biggest flood in living** — la mayor inundación de que hay memoria, la mayor inundación que se recuerda; **of blessed** — de feliz recuerdo; **to the best of my** — que yo recuerde; **to commit something to** — aprender algo de memoria; **I have a bad** — **for faces** recuerdo mal las caras de las personas; **to have a** — **like a sieve** tener malísima memoria; **to have happy memories of** tener agradables recuerdos de; **if my** — **serves me** si mi memoria no me falla, si tengo buena memoria.

men [men] *npl of* **man.**

menace ['menis] **1** *n* amenaza *f*; (*fam*) persona *f* peligrosa, individuo *m* pesado. **2** *vt* amenazar.

menacing ['menisiŋ] *adj* amenazador.

menacingly ['menisiŋli] *adv* de modo amenazador.

ménage [me'nɑ:ʒ] *n* casa *f*, hogar *m*, menaje *m*.

menagerie [mi'nædʒəri] *n* casa *f* de fieras, colección *f* de fieras.

mend [mend] **1** n (patch) remiendo m; (darn) zurcido m; **to be on the —** ir mejorando.
2 vt (repair) reparar, componer; (darn) zurcir; (improve) reformar, mejorar; (rectify) remediar.
3 vi mejorar, reponerse.

mendacious [men'deiʃəs] adj mendaz.

mendacity [men'dæsiti] n mendacidad f.

Mendelian [men'di:liən] adj mendeliano.

Mendelianism ['mendəlizəm] n, **Mendelism** ['mendəlizəm] n mendelismo m.

mendicant ['mendikənt] **1** adj mendicante. **2** n mendicante mf.

mendicity [men'disiti] n mendicidad f.

mending ['mendiŋ] n (act) reparación f, compostura f; zurcidura f; (clothes) ropa f de repaso, ropa f por zurcir; **invisible —** puntada f invisible.

Menelaus [,meni'leiəs] n Menelao.

menfolk ['menfəuk] npl hombres mpl.

menial ['mi:niəl] **1** adj doméstico; (pej) bajo. **2** n criado m, a f.

meningitis [,menin'dʒaitis] n meningitis f.

menopause ['menəupɔ:z] n menopausia f.

menses ['mensi:z] npl menstruo m.

menstrual ['menstruəl] adj menstrual.

menstruate ['menstrueit] vi menstruar.

menstruation [,menstru'eiʃən] n menstruación f.

mensuration [,mensjuə'reiʃən] n mensuración f.

mental ['mentl] adj mental; (fam) anormal, tocado; **see defective** etc.

mentality [men'tæliti] n mentalidad f.

mentally ['mentəli] adv mentalmente; **— ill** alienado.

menthol ['menθəl] n mentol m.

mentholated ['menθəleitid] adj mentolado.

mention ['menʃən] **1** n mención f, alusión f; **honourable —** mención f honorífica.
2 vt mencionar, aludir a; hablar de; (in dispatches) nombrar; **not to —** ... sin contar ..., además de ..., amén de ...; **too numerous to —** demasiado numerosos para mencionar por nombre; **don't — it!** ¡no hay de qué!, ¡de nada!; **if I may —** it si se me permite aludir a ello; **I need hardly — that** ... excusado es decir que ...; **I will — it to him** se lo diré; **he —ed no names** no dijo los nombres; **to — someone in one's will** mencionar a uno en su testamento, legar algo a uno.

mentor ['mentɔ:*] n mentor m.

menu ['menju:] n lista f (de platos), menú m, minuta f.

meow [mi'au] **1** n maullido m. **2** vi maullar.

Mephistopheles [,mefis'tɔfili:z] m Mefistófeles.

mercantile ['mə:kəntail] adj mercantil; **marine —** mercante.

mercantilism ['mə:kəntilizəm] n mercantilismo m.

mercenary ['mə:sinəri] **1** adj mercenario. **2** n mercenario m.

merchandise ['mə:tʃəndaiz] n mercancías fpl, géneros mpl.

merchant ['mə:tʃənt] **1** n comerciante m, negociante m; (arch) mercader m; (fam) sujeto m; **a diamond —** un comerciante en diamantes; **"The M— of Venice"** "El Mercader de Venecia".
2 attr etc marine, navy, ship mercante; **— prince** comerciante m rico; **— tailor** sastre m comerciante.

merchantman ['mə:tʃəntmən] n, pl **—men** [mən] buque m mercante.

merciful ['mə:siful] adj person misericordioso, compasivo, clemente; release etc afortunado, feliz.

mercifully ['mə:sifəli] adv act etc misericordiosamente, con compasión; **— it was short** gracias a Dios fue breve.

merciless ['mə:silis] adj despiadado.

mercilessly ['mə:silisli] adv despiadadamente, sin piedad.

mercurial [mə:'kjuəriəl] adj (Chem) mercurial; (lively) vivo; (changeable) veleidoso, voluble.

Mercury ['mə:kjuri] m Mercurio.

mercury ['mə:kjuri] n mercurio m.

mercy ['mə:si] n misericordia f, compasión f, clemencia f; **with a recommendation to —** con la recomendación de que no se aplique la sentencia en todo su rigor; **to be at the — of someone** estar a la merced de uno; **it is a — that** ... gracias a Dios que ..., menos mal que ...; **to beg for —** pedir clemencia; **to have — on someone** tener compasión de uno, apiadarse de uno; **have —!** ¡por piedad!; **to be left to the tender mercies of someone** verse abandonado en las manos nada piadosas de uno; **to show someone no —** tratar a uno con el mayor rigor; **no — was shown to the rioters** no hubo clemencia para los revoltosos; **to throw oneself on someone's —** pedir clemencia a uno (como única manera de salvarse).

mercy killing ['mə:si,kiliŋ] n eutanasia f.

mere[1] [miə*] n lago m.

mere[2] [miə*] adj mero, simple; solo, no más que; **he's a — clerk** es un simple empleado, no es más que un empleado; **it's — nonsense, it's the —st nonsense** es puro disparate; **it's — talk** son palabras al aire; **they quarrelled over a —** nothing riñeron por una friolera; **it's a — formality** es pura fórmula.

merely ['miəli] adv meramente, simplemente; sólo; **I — said that** ... sólo dije que ..., lo único que dije era que ...; **she's — a secretary** es una simple secretaria, no es más que una secretaria; **it's not — broken, it's ruined** no sólo está roto, sino que se ha estropeado del todo.

meretricious [,meri'triʃəs] adj de oropel, charro, postizo.

merge [mə:dʒ] **1** vt unir, combinar (with con); mezclar; fundir; (Comm) fusionar.
2 vi unirse, combinarse; fundirse; (Comm) fusionarse; **to — into** ir convirtiéndose en; **the bird —d into its background of leaves** el pájaro se hacía casi invisible contra el fondo de hojas; **this question —s into that bigger one** esta cuestión se pierde en aquélla mayor.

merger ['mə:dʒə*] n (Comm) fusión f.

meridian [mə'ridiən] n (Astron, Geog) meridiano m; (fig) cenit m, auge m.

meridional [mə'ridiənl] adj meridional.

meringue [mə'ræŋ] n merengue m.

merino [mə'ri:nəu] **1** adj merino. **2** n merino m.

merit ['merit] **1** n mérito m; **to treat a case on its —s** considerar un caso en relación con sus circunstancias. **2** vt merecer, ser digno de.

meritocracy [,meri'tɔkrəsi] n meritocracia f.

meritorious [,meri'tɔ:riəs] adj meritorio.

meritoriously [,meri'tɔ:riəsli] adv merecidamente.

merlin ['mə:lin] n esmerejón m.

mermaid ['mə:meid] n sirena f.

merman ['mə:mæn] n, pl **—men** [men] tritón m.

Merovingian [,merəu'vindʒiən] **1** adj merovingio. **2** n merovingio m, a f.

merrily ['merili] adv alegremente; regocijadamente, con alborozo.

merriment ['merimənt] n alegría f; regocijo m, alborozo m; (laughter) risas fpl; **at this there was much —** en esto hubo muchas risas.

merry ['meri] adj alegre; regocijado; alborozado; joke etc divertido; **to be as — as a lark** (or cricket) estar como unas pascuas; **to get — (fam)** achisparse; **to make —** divertirse, estar de juerga; **see Christmas.**

merry-go-round ['merigəu,raund] n tiovivo m, caballitos mpl.

merrymaking ['meri,meikiŋ] n festividades fpl.

mescalin ['meskəlin] n mescalina f.

mesentery ['mezəntri] n mesenterio m.

mesh [meʃ] **1** n malla f; (Mech) engrane m, engranaje m; **—es** (fig) red f, trampa f; **to be in — (Mech)** engranar, estar engranado.
2 vt: **to get —ed** enredarse (in en).
3 vi (Tech) engranar (with con).

mesmeric [mez'merik] adj mesmeriano.

mesmerism ['mezmərizəm] n mesmerismo m.

mesmerize ['mezməraiz] vt hipnotizar.

meson ['mi:zɔn] n (Phys) mesón m.

mess [mes] **1** n (a) (confusion) confusión f; (of objects) revoltijo m; (dirt) suciedad f; (bungled affair) lío m; **what a —!** ¡qué sucio está todo!; ¡qué asco!; ¡qué lío!; **to be in a —** (things) estar revuelto, (house etc) estar desarreglado, (person) estar en un aprieto; **his life is in a —** su vida es un fracaso; **to get into a —** (person) meterse en un lío, (things) desarreglarse, (accounts etc) enredarse; **to leave things in a —** dejar las cosas en confusión; **to leave a room in a —** dejar las cosas revueltas en un cuarto; **to make a — of** objects desordenar, job fracasar en, hacer muy mal, someone else's life llenar de confusión, arruinar, one's life fracasar en, (dirty) ensuciar.
(b) **— of pottage** plato m de lentejas.
(c) (Mil etc: food) rancho m, comida f; (room) comedor m del cuartel (etc); **officers' —** comedor m de oficiales.
2 vt: **to — someone about** fastidiar a uno, desorientar a uno (cambiando una cita etc con él); **to — up** (disarrange) desarreglar, desordenar; (dirty) ensuciar; (ruin) arruinar, estropear, echar a perder; affair, deal fracasar en, (deliberately) chafar.
3 vi (a) **to — about** perder el tiempo, ocuparse en fruslerías, trabajar (etc) con poca seriedad; **he enjoys —ing about in boats** le gusta entretener sus ocios navegando (etc) en bote; **we —ed about in Paris for two days** pasamos dos días en París haciendo

esto y lo otro; **they kept us —ing about for an hour** nos hicieron esperar una hora sin decirnos nada; **stop —ing about !** ¡déjate de tonterías!; **to — about with something** (*handle*) manosear algo, tocar algo, (*amuse oneself*) divertirse con algo, (*break*) romper algo, estropear algo.
   (b) (*feed*) hacer rancho, comer (juntos).

message ['mesidʒ] *n* mensaje *m*, recado *m*; (*diplomatic etc*) comunicación *f*; (*of speech, book etc*) lección *f*, tema *m*, sentido *m*; **to get the — (**fig**)** comprender, caer en la cuenta; **do you think he got the —?** (*fig*) ¿crees que comprendió?; **to leave a —** dejar un recado.

messenger ['mesindʒə*] *n* mensajero *m*, a *f*, mandadero *m*, a *f*.

Messiah [mi'saiə] Mesías *m*.

messianic [,mesi'ænik] *adj* mesiánico.

Messieurs [me'səz], *abbr* **Messrs** ['mesəz] señores *mpl* (*abbr* Sres).

messmate ['mesmeit] *n* compañero *m* de rancho, comensal *m*, (*loosely*) amigo *m*.

mess tin ['mestin] *n* plato *m* de campaña.

mess-up ['mesʌp] *n* (*fam*) fracaso *m*, enredo *m*, lío *m*; **we had a — with the trains** nos hicimos un lío con los trenes; **what a —!** ¡qué lío!

messy ['mesi] *adj* (*dirty*) sucio; (*untidy*) desaseado, desaliñado, *room etc* en desorden; (*confused*) confuso, nada claro.

met [met] *pret and ptp of* **meet**.

metabolic [,metə'bɔlik] *adj* metabólico.

metabolism [me'tæbəlizəm] *n* metabolismo *m*.

metacarpal [,metə'kɑ:pl] *n* metacarpiano *m*.

metal ['metl] **1** *n* metal *m*; (*on road*) grava *f*; (*fig*) temple *m*, ánimo *m*; **—s** (*Rail*) rieles *mpl*. **2** *adj* metálico, de metal. **3** *vt* *road* engravar.

metallic [mi'tælik] *adj* metálico.

metallurgic(al) [,metə'lɜːdʒik(əl)] *adj* metalúrgico.

metallurgist [me'tælədʒist] *n* metalúrgico *m*.

metallurgy [me'tælədʒi] *n* metalurgia *f*.

metal polish ['metl,pɔliʃ] *n* lustre *m* para metales.

metalwork ['metlwə:k] *n* metalistería *f*.

metamorphic [,metə'mɔ:fik] *adj* metamórfico.

metamorphose [,metə'mɔ:fəuz] **1** *vt* metamorfosear (*into* en). **2** *vi* metamorfosearse.

metamorphosis [,metə'mɔ:fəsis] *n*, *pl* **metamorphoses** [,metə'mɔ:fəsi:z] metamorfosis *f*.

metaphor ['metəfɔ:*] *n* metáfora *f*; **mixed —** metáfora *f* disparatada.

metaphorical [,metə'fɔrikəl] *adj* metafórico.

metaphysical [,metə'fizikəl] *adj* metafísico.

metaphysics [,metə'fiziks] *n* metafísica *f*.

metatarsal [,metə'tɑ:sl] *n* metatarsiano *m*.

metathesis [me'tæθəsis] *n* metátesis *f*.

mete [mi:t] *vt*: **to — out** repartir; *punishment etc* dar, imponer.

meteor ['mi:tiə*] *n* meteorito *m*, bólido *m*; (*esp fig*) meteoro *m*.

meteoric [,mi:ti'ɔrik] *adj* meteórico (*also fig*).

meteorite ['mi:tiarait] *n* meteorito *m*, bólido *m*.

meteoroid ['mi:tiərɔid] *n* meteoroide *m*.

meteorological [,mi:tiərə'lɔdʒikəl] *adj* meteorológico.

meteorologist [,mi:tiə'rɔlədʒist] *n* meteorologista *mf*.

meteorology [,mi:tiə'rɔlədʒi] *n* meteorología *f*.

meter ['mi:tə*] **1** *n* contador *m*; *see also* **metre**. **2** *vt* medir (con contador).

methane ['mi:θein] *n* metano *m*.

method ['meθəd] *n* método *m*; sistema *m*, procedimiento *m*; **there's — in his madness** no es tan loco como parece.

methodical [mi'θɔdikəl] *adj* metódico.

Methodism ['meθədizəm] *n* metodismo *m*.

Methodist ['meθədist] **1** *adj* metodista. **2** *n* metodista *mf*.

methodology [,meθə'dɔlədʒi] *n* metodología *f*.

meths [meθs] *n* (*fam*), **methylated spirit** ['meθileitid'spirit] *n* alcohol *m* metilado, alcohol *m* desnaturalizado.

meticulous [mi'tikjuləs] *adj* meticuloso; minucioso.

meticulously [mi'tikjuləsli] *adv* con meticulosidad; minuciosamente; **— clean** limpísimo.

métier ['meitiei] *n* (*trade*) oficio *m*; (*strong point*) fuerte *m*; (*speciality*) especialidad *f*; **it's not my —** no es de mi especialidad.

metre, (US) **meter** ['mi:tə*] *n* (*all senses*) metro *m*.

metric(al) ['metrik(əl)] *adj* métrico.

metrics ['metriks] *n* métrica *f*.

metronome ['metrənəum] *n* metrónomo *m*.

metropolis [mi'trɔpəlis] *n* metrópoli *f*.

metropolitan [,metrə'pɔlitən] **1** *adj* metropolitano. **2** *n* (*Eccl*) metropolitano *m*.

mettle ['metl] *n* temple *m*; ánimo *m*, brío *m*; valor *m*; **to be on one's —** estar dispuesto a mostrar todo lo que uno vale; **to put someone on his —** provocar a uno a mostrar cuánto vale, picar a uno en el amor propio.

mettlesome ['metlsəm] *adj* animoso, brioso, esforzado.

Meuse [mə:z] Mosa *m*.

mew [mju:] **1** *n* maullido *m*. **2** *vi* maullar.

mewl [mju:l] *vi* (*cat*) maullar; (*baby*) lloriquear.

mews [mju:z] *n* caballeriza *f*.

Mexican ['meksikən] **1** *adj* mejicano, (*in Mexico*) mexicano. **2** *n* mejicano *m*, a *f*, (*in Mexico*) mexicano *m*, a *f*.

Mexico ['meksikəu] Méjico *m*, (*in Mexico*) México *m*.

mezzanine ['mezəni:n] *n* entresuelo *m*.

mezzo-soprano ['metsəusə'prɑ:nəu] *n* mezzo-soprano *f*.

mezzotint ['metzəutint] *n* grabado *m* mezzotinto.

miaow [mi:'au] **1** *n* miau *m*. **2** *vi* maullar.

miasma [mi'æzmə] *n*, *pl* **miasmata** [mi'æzmətə] miasma *m*.

mica ['maikə] *n* mica *f*.

mice [mais] *npl of* **mouse**.

Michael ['maikl] *m* Miguel.

Michaelangelo [,maikəl'ændʒiləu] *m* Miguel Ángel.

Michaelmas ['miklməs] fiesta *f* de San Miguel (29 setiembre).

mickey ['miki] *n* (*sl*): **to take the — out of someone** tomar el pelo a uno.

micro . . . ['maikrəu] micro . . .

microbe ['maikrəub] *n* microbio *m*.

microbial [mai'krəubiəl] *adj* microbiano.

microbiologist [,maikrəubai'ɔlidʒist] *n* microbiólogo *m*.

microbiology [,maikrəubai'ɔlədʒi] *n* microbiología *f*.

microcosm ['maikrəukɔzəm] *n* microcosmo(s) *m*.

microfilm ['maikrəufilm] **1** *n* microfilm *m*, microfilme *m* (*Acad*). **2** *vt* hacer un microfilm de.

microfilm reader ['maikrəufilm,ri:də*] *n* aparato *m* lector de microfilms.

microgroove ['maikrəugru:v] *n* microsurco *m*.

micrometer [mai'krɔmitə*] *n* micrómetro *m*.

microorganism ['maikrəu'ɔ:gənizəm] *n* microorganismo *m*.

microphone ['maikrəfəun] *n* micrófono *m*.

microscope ['maikrəskəup] *n* microscopio *m*.

microscopic(al) [,maikrə'skɔpik(əl)] *adj* microscópico.

microscopy [mai'krɔskəpi] *n* microscopía *f*.

mid [mid] **1** *adj* medio, *eg* **in — journey** a medio camino; **in — June** a mediados de junio; **in — afternoon** a media tarde; **in — course** a media carrera; **in — channel** en medio del canal. **2** *prep* (*lit, poet*) *see* **amid**.

Midas ['maidəs] *m* Midas.

midday ['mid'dei] **1** *n* mediodía *m*; **at —** a mediodía. **2** *adj* de mediodía.

midden ['midn] *n* muladar *m*.

middle ['midl] **1** *adj* (*of place*) medio, central; de en medio; intermedio; (*in quality, size etc*) mediano; **class** medio.
   2 *n* medio *m*, centro *m*, mitad *f*; (*waist*) cintura *f*; **in the — of the table** en el centro de la mesa; **in the — of the field** en medio del campo; **right in the — of the room** en el mismo centro del cuarto; **in the — of nowhere** donde Cristo dio las tres voces; **in the — of summer** en pleno verano; **in (**or **about, towards) the — of May** a mediados de mayo; **in the — of the century** a mediados del siglo; **in the — of the morning** a media mañana; **I'm in the — of reading it** voy a mitad de su lectura.

middle-aged ['midl'eidʒd] *adj* de mediana edad, de edad madura.

middlebrow ['midlbrau] **1** *adj* de (*or* para) gusto medianamente culto, de gusto entre intelectual y plebeyo.
   2 *n* persona *f* de gusto medianamente culto, persona *f* de cultura mediana.

middle-class ['midl'klɑ:s] *adj* de la clase media.

middleman ['midlmæn] *n*, *pl* **—men** [men] intermediario *m*.

middle-of-the-road ['midləvðə'rəud] *adj* moderado, nada extremista.

middle-sized ['midl,saizd] *adj* de tamaño mediano; *person* de estatura mediana.

middleweight ['midlweit] *n* (*Boxing*) peso *m* medio.

middling ['midliŋ] **1** *adj* mediano, regular. **2** *adv* (**a**) regular; **how are you?** — ¿qué tal estás? . . . regular. (**b**) **— good** medianamente bueno.

middy ['midi] *n* (*fam*) *see* **midshipman**.

midge [midʒ] *n* mosca *f*, mosquito *m*.

midget ['midʒit] **1** n enano m, a f. **2** adj en miniatura, en pequeña escala; *submarine etc* de bolsillo.

midland ['midlənd] **1** adj del interior, del centro. **2** n: **the M—s** *la región central de Inglaterra.*

mid-morning ['mid'mɔːniŋ] adj: — **coffee** café m de media mañana.

midnight ['midnait] **1** n medianoche f. **2** adj, attr de medianoche.

midriff ['midrif] n diafragma m.

midsection ['midsekʃən] n sección f de en medio.

midshipman ['midʃipmən] n, pl **—men** [mən] guardia m marina.

midships ['midʃips] adv en medio del navío.

midst [midst] **1** n: **in the —** of entre, en medio de; **in our —** entre nosotros; **in the — of plenty** en medio de la abundancia. **2** prep see **amid(st).**

midstream ['mid'striːm] n: **in —** en medio de la corriente, en medio del río.

midsummer ['mid'sʌmə*] **1** n pleno verano m, (*strictly*) solsticio m estival; **M— (Day)** fiesta f de San Juan (24 *junio*); **"M— Night's Dream"** "El sueño de una noche de verano"; **at —** el día del solsticio de verano; **in —** en pleno verano. **2** adj, attr de pleno verano, estival.

midway ['mid'wei] **1** adv a mitad del camino; — **between X and Y** a mitad del camino (*or* a medio camino) entre X e Y; **we are now —** ahora estamos a medio camino. **2** adj situado a medio camino; **a — point** un punto intermedio, un punto equidistante de los dos extremos.

midweek ['mid'wiːk] **1** adv entre semana. **2** adj flight *etc* de entre semana.

Midwest ['mid'west] n medioeste m (*llanura central de EE.UU.*).

Midwestern ['mid,westən] adj del medioeste (*de EE.UU.*).

midwife ['midwaif] n, pl **—wives** [waivz] comadrona f, partera f.

midwifery ['mid,wifəri] n partería f.

midwinter ['mid'wintə*] **1** n pleno invierno m, (*strictly*) solsticio m de invierno; **at —** el día del solsticio de invierno; **in —** en pleno invierno. **2** adj, attr de pleno invierno.

mien [miːn] n aire m, porte m, semblante m.

miff [mif] (US fam) **1** n disgusto m. **2** vt disgustar, ofender.

might¹ [mait] pret of **may.**

might² [mait] n fuerza f, poder m, poderío m; — **is right** es la ley del embudo; **with — and main** a más no poder, esforzándose muchísimo; **with all one's —** con todas sus fuerzas, empleándose a fondo.

might-have-been ['maitəv,biːn] n esperanza f no cumplida.

mightily ['maitili] adv fuertemente; poderosamente; **I was — surprised** me sorprendí muchísimo.

mightiness ['maitinis] n fuerza f; poder m, poderío m.

mightn't [maitnt] = **might not.**

mighty ['maiti] **1** adj fuerte; potente, poderoso; (*fam*) enorme, inmenso. **2** adv (fam) muy, terriblemente; **it's — awkward** es terriblemente difícil; **I was — surprised** me sorprendí muchísimo.

mignonette [,minjə'net] n reseda f.

migraine ['miːgrein] n jaqueca f.

migrant ['maigrənt] **1** adj migratorio. **2** n peregrino m, nómada m; (*bird*) ave f migratoria, ave f de paso; (*insect*) insecto m migratorio.

migrate [mai'greit] vi emigrar.

migration [mai'greiʃən] n migración f.

migratory ['mai'greitəri] adj migratorio.

mike¹ [maik] n (sl): **to have a good —** no hacer nada, tirarse a la bartola; gandulear, racanear.

mike² [maik] n (sl: Radio) micro m (sl).

Mike [maik] m nombre cariñoso de **Michael;** **for the love of —!** ¡por Dios!

milady [mi'leidi] n miladi f.

Milan [mi'læn] Milán.

milch [miltʃ] n: — **cow** vaca f lechera.

mild [maild] adj (of character) apacible, pacífico; manso; rule etc blando; climate templado; day blando; medicine, effect, taste etc suave, dulce; (slight) leve, ligero; (Med) benigno.

mildew ['mildjuː] n moho m; (on wheat) añublo m; (on vine) mildeu m.

mildly ['maildli] adv apaciblemente, pacíficamente; blandamente; suavemente, dulcemente; levemente, ligeramente; **to put it —, and that's putting it —** para no decir más.

mildness ['maildnis] n apacibilidad f; blandura f; suavidad f, dulzura f; levedad f.

mile [mail] n milla f (= 1609,33 m); **nautical —** milla f marina; **square —** milla f cuadrada; **—s per gallon** equivalent to kilómetros por litro; **not a hundred —s from here** (fig) no muy lejos de aquí; **we walked —s!** ¡hemos andado kilómetros y kilómetros!; **they live —s away** viven bastante lejos de aquí; **you were —s off the target** no te acercaste ni con mucho al objetivo; **you can tell it a — off** eso se ve a la legua; **it smelled for —s around** olía a muchas leguas a la redonda.

mileage ['mailidʒ] n número m de millas, distancia f recorrida en millas; (Aut) kilometraje m; — **per gallon** equivalent to kilómetros mpl por litro; **what — has this car done?** ¿cuántos kilómetros tiene este coche?

mileage indicator ['mailidʒ,indikeitə*] n (Aut) indicador m de recorrido, cuentakilómetros m.

mileage ticket ['mailidʒ,tikit] n billete m kilométrico.

milepost ['mailpəust] n poste m miliar.

milestone ['mailstəun] n piedra f miliaria; (in Spain etc) mojón m kilométrico, hito m kilométrico; **these events are —s in our history** estos acontecimientos hacen época (or son hitos) en nuestra historia.

milieu ['miːljəː] n medio m, ambiente m, medio m ambiente.

militant ['militənt] **1** adj militante; belicoso, agresivo. **2** n militante mf, extremista mf, partidario m vehemente.

militarism ['militərizəm] n militarismo m.

militarist ['militərist] **1** adj militarista. **2** n militarista m.

militaristic [,militə'ristik] adj militarista.

militarize ['militəraiz] vt militarizar.

military ['militəri] **1** adj militar. **2** n: **the —** los militares.

militate ['militeit] vi: **to — against** militar contra.

militia [mi'liʃə] n milicia f.

militiaman [mi'liʃəmən] n, pl **—men** [mən] miliciano m.

milk [milk] **1** n leche f; **condensed —** leche f condensada; **evaporated —** leche f evaporada; **powdered —** leche f en polvo; **skim —** leche f desnatada; **whole —** leche f sin desnatar; — **of magnesia** leche f de magnesia; **the — of human kindness** la crema de la amabilidad humana, la humanidad; **it's no good crying over spilt —** ahora no sirven lamentaciones, agua pasada no mueve molino. **2** attr de leche; diet, product etc lácteo. **3** vt ordeñar; (fig) chupar. **4** vi dar leche.

milk-and-water ['milkən'wɔːtə*] adj (fig) débil, flojo.

milk bar ['milkbɑː*] n cafetería f.

milk chocolate ['milk'tʃɔklit] n chocolate m con leche.

milk churn ['milktʃəːn] n lechera f.

milk float ['milkfləut] n carro m de la leche.

milking ['milkiŋ] **1** adj lechero. **2** n ordeño m.

milking machine ['milkiŋmə,ʃiːn] n ordeñadora f mecánica.

milkmaid ['milkmeid] n lechera f.

milkman ['milkmən] n, pl **—men** [mən] lechero m, repartidor m de leche.

milk shake ['milk'ʃeik] n batido m de leche.

milksop ['milksɔp] n marica m.

milk tooth ['milktuːθ] n, pl **—teeth** [tiːθ] diente m de leche.

milkweed ['milkwiːd] n (US) algodoncillo m.

milk-white ['milk'wait] adj blanco como la leche.

milky ['milki] adj lechoso.

Milky Way ['milki'wei] Vía f Láctea.

mill [mil] **1** n (wind-) molino m; (small, for coffee etc) molinillo m; (factory) fábrica f; (spinning-) hilandería f; (weaving-) tejeduría f, fábrica f de tejidos; (steel-) acería f, fábrica f de acero; (workshop) taller m; **to go through the —** pasar por muchas cosas en la vida, sufrir mucho; aprender por experiencia práctica; (strain) entrenarse rigurosamente; **to put someone through the —** someter a uno a un entrenamiento riguroso; hacer que uno aprenda por experiencia práctica; pasar a uno por la piedra. **2** vt (grind) moler; (Mech) fresar; coin acordonar; cloth abatanar; chocolate batir. **3** vi: **to — around** circular en masa, moverse por todas partes; **people were —ing around the office** la gente se apiñaba impaciente delante de la taquilla; **stop —ing around!** ¡quietos!

milled [mild] adj grain molido; coin, edge acordonado.

millenary [mi'lenəri] **1** adj milenario. **2** n milenario m.

millennium [mi'leniəm] n milenio m, milenario m.

millennial [mi'leniəl] adj milenario.

miller ['milə*] n molinero m.

millet ['milit] n mijo m.

millhand ['milhænd] n obrero m, a f, operario m, a f.

milliard ['miliɑːd] n mil millones mpl; **a — marks** mil millones de marcos.

milligram(me) ['miligræm] n miligramo m.

millilitre, (US) **—liter** ['mili,liːtə*] n mililitro m.

millimetre, (US) **—meter** ['mili,miːtə*] n milímetro m.

milliner ['milinə*] n sombrerera f, modista f (de sombreros); **—'s (shop)** sombrerería f, tienda f de sombreros (de señora).

millinery ['milinəri] n sombrerería f, sombreros mpl de señora.

milling ['miliŋ] n (grinding) molienda f; (on coin) cordoncillo m.

milling machine ['miliŋmə,ʃiːn] n fresadora f.

million ['miljən] n millón m; **one — fleas** un millón de pulgas; **4 — dogs** 4 millones de perros; **she's one in a —** es una verdadera joya, es un mirlo blanco.

millionaire [,miljə'neə*] n millonario m, a f.

millionth ['miljənθ] **1** adj millonésimo. **2** n millonésimo m.

millipede ['milipiːd] n miriópodo m.

millpond ['milpɒnd] n represa f de molino.

millrace ['milreis] n caz m.

millstone ['milstəun] n piedra f de molino, muela f; **it's a — round his neck** representa un grandísimo estorbo para él.

millwheel ['milwiːl] n rueda f de molino.

milometer [mai'lɒmitə*] n cuentakilómetros m.

milord [mi'lɔːd] n milord m.

milt [milt] n (Fish) lecha f.

mime [maim] **1** n pantomima f, mímica f; (ancient play) mímica f, teatro m de mímica; (actor) mimo m. **2** vt hacer en pantomima, remedar; representar con gestos. **3** vi actuar de mimo.

mimeograph ['mimiəgrɑːf] **1** n mimeógrafo m. **2** vt mimeografiar.

mimic ['mimik] **1** adj mímico; (pretended) fingido, simulado. **2** n remedador m, ora f, imitador m, ora f. **3** vt remedar, imitar.

mimicry ['mimikri] n imitación f, remedo m; (Bio) mimetismo m; **protective —** mimetismo m protector.

mimosa [mi'məuzə] n mimosa f.

minaret [minə'ret] n alminar m.

minatory ['minətəri] adj (lit) amenazador.

mince [mins] **1** n carne f picada. **2** vt desmenuzar; meat picar. **3** vi (in walking) andar con pasos menuditos; (in talking) hablar remilgadamente.

mincemeat ['minsmiːt] n conserva f de picadillo de fruta; **to make — of** (fig) vencer fácilmente, hacer pedazos.

mince pie ['mins'pai] n pastel m de picadillo de fruta.

mincer ['minsə*] n máquina f de picar carne.

mincing ['minsiŋ] adj remilgado, afectado; step menudito.

mincing machine ['minsiŋmə,ʃiːn] n máquina f de picar carne.

mind [maind] **1** n mente f; (intellect) inteligencia f, entendimiento m; (memory) memoria f; (contrasted with matter) espíritu m; (cast of —) mentalidad f; (sanity, judgement) juicio m; (intention) intención f, voluntad f; (opinion) opinión f, parecer m; (leaning) inclinación f; **—'s eye** imaginación f; **state of —** estado m de ánimo; **of unsound —** mentalmente incapacitado; **time out of —** tiempo m inmemorial; **to my —** en mi opinión; **with one —** unánimemente; **with an open —** con espíritu amplio, sin prejuicios, sin ideas preconcebidas; **great —s think alike** los sabios piensan lo mismo; **to be in one's right —** estar en su cabal juicio; **to be in two —s** dudar, no saber a qué carta quedarse (about en el asunto de); **I am not clear in my — about the incident** no recuerdo el incidente con entera claridad; **I am not clear in my — about the plan** no entiendo del todo el proyecto; **to be uneasy in one's —** estar algo inquieto; **to be of one —** ser unánimes, estar de acuerdo; **I was of the same — as my brother** yo compartía el criterio de mi hermano, mi hermano y yo éramos de la misma opinión; **what's on your —?** ¿qué es lo que te preocupa?; **the child's death was much on his —** le angustiaba muchísimo la muerte del niño; **to be out of one's —** estar fuera de juicio, estar (como) loco; **you must be out of your —!** ¿se te ha vuelto el juicio?; **to bear something in —** tener algo presente; **I'll bear you in —** te acordaré de Vd, no le olvidaré; **we must bear (it) in — that ...** hemos de recordar que ...; **to call something to — recordar algo; **that calls something else to —** eso me trae otra cosa a la memoria; **to change one's —** cambiar de opinión, mudar de parecer; **it came to my — that ...** se me ocurrió que ...; **it

crossed my — se me ocurrió (that que); **yes, it had crossed my —** sí, eso se me había ocurrido; **it never crossed my —** jamás se me pasó por la cabeza; **does it ever cross your — that ...?** ¿piensas alguna vez que ...?; **I can't get it out of my —** eso no lo puedo quitar de la cabeza; **to give one's — to something** aplicarse a algo; **to give someone a piece of one's —** decir cuatro verdades a uno; **to go out of one's —** volverse loco; **I have a good — to do it, I have half a — to do it** casi estoy por hacerlo, tengo ganas de hacerlo, por poco lo hago; **to have something in —** pensar en algo, tener algo pensado; **to have it in — to + infin** pensar + infin, proponerse + infin; **whom have you in — for the job?** ¿a quién piensas dar el puesto?; **to have something on one's —** estar preocupado por algo; **to improve one's —** edificar su espíritu, educarse, instruirse; **to keep something in —** see to bear something in —; **to keep an open — on a subject** evitar tener prejuicios acerca de un asunto; estar todavía sin decidirse acerca de un asunto; **to know one's own —** saber lo que uno quiere; **to let one's — run on something** dejar que la mente se distraiga en algo; **to make up one's —** resolverse, decidirse (to + infin a + infin); tomar partido; **we can't make up our —s about the house** no nos resolvemos a vender (etc) la casa; **I can't make up my — about him** todavía tengo ciertas dudas con respecto a él; **to pass out of —** caer en el olvido; **he puts me in — of his father** recuerda a su padre, me hace pensar en su padre; **you can put that right out of your —** conviene no pensar más en eso; **to read someone's —** adivinar el pensamiento de uno; **to set one's — on something** desear algo con vehemencia, estar resuelto a conseguir (or hacer etc) algo; **it slipped my —** se me olvidó; **to speak one's —** hablar con franqueza, hablar claro; **this will take your — off it** esto servirá para distraerte.

2 vt **(a)** (pay attention to) hacer caso de; fijarse en; preocuparse de; rules etc obedecer, guiarse por; **never —!** (don't worry) ¡no se preocupe!, (pay no attention) ¡no haga Vd caso!, (it makes no odds) ¡es igual!, ¡no importa!, ¡qué más da!; **never — him!** ¡no haga Vd caso de él!; **never — that now!** ¡no se preocupe con eso ya!; ¡déjate de eso!; **buy it and never — the expense** cómpralo sin hacer caso del precio; **I don't — the cold** el frío me trae sin cuidado, no me molesta el frío; **— what you're doing!** ¡cuidado con lo que haces!; **don't — me!** ¡no se ocupe Vd de mí!, (iro) ¿y yo que estoy delante?; **— what I say!** ¡escucha lo que te digo!; **he didn't do it, — you,** pero en realidad no lo hizo, la verdad es que no lo hizo; **— you, it was raining at the time** hay que confesar que en ese momento llovía.

(b) (meddle in) see business.

(c) (be put out by) sentirse molesto por, tener inconveniente en; **I don't —** me es igual, no tengo inconveniente; **do you —?** ¿se puede?; **do you —!** (iro) ¡por Dios!; **a cigarette? I don't —** (if I do) ¿un cigarrillo? pues muchas gracias; **close the door, if you don't —** haga el favor de cerrar la puerta; **do you — the noise?** ¿le molesta el ruido?; **I don't — 4, but 6 is too many** con 4 estoy bien, pero 6 son muchos; **I shouldn't — a cup of tea** no vendría mal una taza de té; **do you — coming with me?** ¿quiere hacer el favor de venir conmigo?; **would you — opening the door?** ¿me hace el favor de abrir la puerta?; **do you — if I open the window?** ¿le molesta que abra la ventana?; **I don't — having to wait** no tengo inconveniente en esperar.

(d) (beware of) tener cuidado con (or de); **—!** ¡cuidado!; **— the stairs!** ¡cuidado con la escalera!; **— you don't get wet!** ¡ten cuidado de no mojarte!; **— you do it!** ¡hágalo sin falta!, ¡no deje de hacerlo!; **— your language!** ¡cuida tu lengua!, ¡cuidado con lo que dices!

(e) (oversee) cuidar, vigilar, estar al cuidado de; children etc cuidar; shop ocuparse de, encargarse de; machine atender.

(f) (remember) acordarse de, recordar; **I — the time when ...** me acuerdo de cuando ...

minded ['maindid] adj: **if you are so —** si estás dispuesto a hacerlo, si quieres hacerlo.

-minded ['maindid] adj de mente ..., de mentalidad ...; eg **fair-minded** imparcial; **an industrially-minded nation** una nación consciente de sus industrias, una nación que se dedica a la industria; **a romantically-minded girl** una joven de pensamientos románticos, una joven con ideas románticas.

mindful ['maindful] adj: **— of** consciente de, atento a; **we must be — of the risks** hay que tener presentes los riesgos, acordémonos de los riesgos.

mindless ['maindlis] *adj* estúpido.

mine¹ [main] *poss pron* (el) mío, (la) mía *etc*; **— and thine** lo mío y lo tuyo; **this car is —** este coche es mío, éste es mi coche; **is this —?** ¿es mío esto?; **his friends and —** sus amigos y los míos; **I have what is —** tengo lo que es mío; **a friend of —** un amigo mío, uno de mis amigos; **it's no business of —** no tiene que ver conmigo.

mine² [main] **1** *n* **(a)** (*Min*) mina *f*; **to work a —** explotar una mina.

(b) (*Mil, Naut etc*) mina *f*; **magnetic —** mina *f* magnética; **to lay —s** sembrar minas; **to sweep —s** dragar minas, barrer minas.

(c) (*fig*) tesoro *m*, pozo *m*; **the book is a — of information** el libro es un tesoro de datos útiles.

2 *vt* **(a)** *coal, metal* extraer, explotar.

(b) (*Mil, Naut*) *channel, road* sembrar minas en; proteger con minas; *ship* hundir por medio de una mina.

3 *vi* extraer minerales; dedicarse a la minería; **to — for something** buscar algo abriendo una mina; explotar los yacimientos de algo.

mine detector ['maindi,tektə*] *n* detector *m* de minas.

minefield ['mainfi:ld] *n* campo de minas.

minelayer ['main,leiə*] *n* barco *m* siembra-minas, buque *m* minador.

miner ['mainə*] *n* minero *m*.

mineral ['minərəl] **1** *adj* mineral. **2** *n* mineral *m*.

mineralogist [,minə'rælədʒist] *n* mineralogista *m*.

mineralogy [,minə'rælədʒi] *n* mineralogía *f*.

mineral water ['minərəl,wɔ:tə*] *n* agua *f* mineral, (*loosely*) gaseosa *f*.

minesweeper ['main,swi:pə*] *n* dragaminas *m*, barreminas *m*.

mingle ['mingl] **1** *vt* mezclar (*with* con).

2 *vi* mezclarse; (*become indistinguishable*) confundirse (*in, with* con); **he —d with people of all classes** se asociaba con personas de todas las clases, vivía con personas de todas las clases; **the police —d with the demonstrators** los policías se confundieron con los manifestantes.

mingy ['mindʒi] *adj* (*fam*) tacaño.

mini . . . ['mini] mini . . ., micro . . .

miniature ['minitʃə*] **1** *n* miniatura *f*; modelo *m* pequeño; **in —** en miniatura, en pequeña escala.

2 *adj* (en) miniatura; **— golf** golf *m* miniatura; **— poodle** perro *m* de lanas miniatura; **— submarine** submarino *m* de bolsillo; **— watches** relojes *mpl* miniatura.

miniaturize ['minitʃəraiz] *vt* reducir a forma miniatura.

minibus ['minibʌs] *n* microbús *m*.

minicab ['minikæb] *n* microtaxi *m*.

minim ['minim] *n* (*Mus*) blanca *f*.

minimal ['miniml] *adj* mínimo.

minimize ['minimaiz] *vt* minimizar; aminorar, minorizar, empequeñecer.

minimum ['miniməm] **1** *adj* mínimo. **2** *n* mínimo *m*, mínimum *m*; **(down) to the —** al mínimo; **down to a — of 5 degrees** hasta 5 grados como mínimum.

mining ['mainiŋ] **1** *n* minería *f*; explotación *f*, extracción *f*. **2** *attr area, industry, town* minero; *engineer* de minas.

minion ['minjən] *n* (*favourite*) favorito *m*, a *f*; (*royal favourite*) privado *m*, valido *m*; (*servant*) paniaguado *m*.

miniskirt ['miniskə:t] *n* minifalda *f*.

minister ['ministə*] **1** *n* (*Pol etc*) ministro *m* (*for, of* de); (*Eccl*) pastor *m*.

2 *vi*: **to — to someone** atender a uno; **to — to someone's needs** ayudar a uno dándole lo que necesita, satisfacer las necesidades de uno; **to — to a result** contribuir a un resultado.

ministerial [,minis'tiəriəl] *adj* ministerial, de ministro; **— crisis** crisis *f* de gobierno.

ministration [,minis'treiʃən] *n* ayuda *f*, agencia *f*, servicio *m*; (*Eccl*) ministerio *m*.

ministry ['ministri] *n* ministerio *m* (*for, of* de); (*Eccl*) sacerdocio *m*; **to enter the —** hacerse sacerdote, (*Protestant*) hacerse pastor.

minium ['miniəm] *n* minio *m*.

mink [miŋk] *n* (*Zool*) visón *m*; (*fur*) piel *f* de visón; **— coat** abrigo *m* de visón.

minnow ['minəu] *n* pececillo *m* (*de agua dulce*).

minor ['mainə*] **1** *adj* menor (*also Eccl, Mus etc*); (*under age*) menor de edad; *writer etc* de segundo orden, secundario; *operation* pequeño, sin trascendencia; *detail* sin importancia; *role, position* secundario, de categoría inferior; **Smith —** Smith el joven; **G —** (*Mus*) sol *m* menor; **— third** tercera *f* menor.

2 *n* menor *mf* de edad; (*US Univ*) asignatura *f* secundaria.

Minorca [mi'nɔ:kə] Menorca *f*.

minority [mai'nɔriti] **1** *n* minoría *f*; (*age*) minoridad *f*, menor edad *f*; **to be in a —** estar en la minoría; **you are in a — of one** Vd es el único que piensa así.

2 *attr rule etc* minoritario.

Minotaur ['mainətɔ:*] Minotauro *m*.

minster ['minstə*] *n* catedral *f*; iglesia *f* de un monasterio; **York M—** la catedral de York.

minstrel ['minstrəl] *n* juglar *m*; cantor *m*; **nigger —** cómico *m* (disfrazado de negro).

minstrelsy ['minstrəlsi] *n* (*music*) música *f*; (*song*) canto *m*; (*art of epic minstrel*) juglaría *f*, (*art of lyric minstrel*) gaya ciencia *f*.

mint¹ [mint] **1** *n* casa *f* de moneda; **Royal M—** Real Casa *f* de la Moneda; **to be worth a — (of money)** valer un dineral.

2 *adj stamp etc* nuevo, en nuevo, sin usar; **in — condition** en perfecto estado, sin estrenar.

3 *vt coin* acuñar; *phrase etc* idear, inventar.

mint² [mint] *n* (*Bot*) hierbabuena *f*, menta *f*; (*sweet*) pastilla *f* de menta.

mint julep ['mint'dʒu:lep] *n* julepe *m*.

mint sauce ['mint'sɔ:s] *n* salsa *f* de menta.

minuet [,minju'et] *n* minué *m*.

minus ['mainəs] **1** *prep* **(a)** menos; **9 — 6** 9 menos 6.

(b) (*without, deprived of*) sin, desprovisto de, falto de; **he appeared — his trousers** apareció sin pantalón.

2 *adj* menos; negativo.

3 *n* (*sign*) signo *m* menos; (*amount*) cantidad *f* negativa.

minuscule ['minəskju:l] *adj* minúsculo.

minute ['minit] **1** *n* **(a)** (*of degree, time*) minuto *m*; (*fig*) momento *m*, instante *m*; **at the last — a** última hora; **at 6 o'clock to the —** a las 6 en punto; **I'll come in a —** vengo al momento; **it was all over in a —** todo esto ocurrió en un instante; **this very —** ahora mismo; **to leave things until the last —** dejar las cosas hasta última hora; **tell me the — he comes** avíseme en cuanto venga; **I shan't be a —** vuelvo (*or* termino *etc*) muy pronto; **we expect him any —** le esperamos de un momento a otro; **it won't take 5 —s** es cosa de pocos minutos; **wait a —!** ¡un momento!

(b) (*draft*) borrador *m*, proyecto *m*, minuta *f*; (*note*) nota *f*, apuntación *f*; **—s** (*of meeting*) acta *f*, actas *fpl*; **to write up the —s of a meeting** levantar acta de una reunión.

2 *vt meeting* levantar acta de; (*draft*) hacer el borrador de, minutar.

minute [mai'nju:t] *adj* (*small*) diminuto, menudo, pequeño; *detail etc* insignificante; (*accurate, searching*) minucioso.

minute book ['minitbuk] *n* libro *m* de actas.

minute hand ['minithænd] *n* minutero *m*.

minutely [mai'nju:tli] *adv* minuciosamente, con minuciosidad; **a — detailed account** un relato completo hasta en los más pequeños detalles; **anything — resembling a fish** cualquier cosa que tuviera el más ligero parecido con un pez.

minutiae [mi'nju:ʃii:] *npl* detalles *mpl* minuciosos.

minx [miŋks] *n* picaruela *f*, mujer *f* descarada; **you —!** ¡lagarta!

miracle ['mirəkl] *n* milagro *m*; **by a —, by some —** por milagro; **it will be a — if . . .** será un milagro si . . .

miracle play ['mirəkl,plei] *n* milagro *m*, auto *m*.

miraculous [mi'rækjuləs] *adj* milagroso.

miraculously [mi'rækjuləsli] *adv* milagrosamente, por milagro.

mirage ['mira:ʒ] *n* espejismo *m* (*also fig*).

mire [maiə*] *n* fango *m*, lodo *m*.

mirror ['mirə*] **1** *n* espejo *m*; (*Aut*) retrovisor *m*; **to look at oneself in the —** mirarse al espejo. **2** *vt* reflejar.

mirth [mə:θ] *n* alegría *f*, regocijo *m*; (*laughter*) risa *f*, risas *fpl*; **at this there was —** en esto hubo risas; **there was some unseemly —** se rieron algunos descaradamente.

mirthful ['mə:θful] *adj* alegre.

mirthless ['mə:θlis] *adj* triste, sin alegría.

miry ['maiəri] *adj* fangoso, lodoso; **— place** lodazal *m*.

misadventure [,misəd'ventʃə*] *n* desgracia *f*, accidente *m*; **death by —** muerte *f* accidental.

misalliance [,misə'laiəns] n casamiento m desigual.
misanthrope ['mizənθrəup] n misántropo m.
misanthropic [,mizən'θrɔpik] adj misantrópico.
misanthropist [mi'zænθrəpist] n misántropo m.
misanthropy [mi'zænθrəpi] n misantropía f.
misapply ['misə'plai] vt aplicar mal; abusar de.
misapprehend ['mis,æpri'hend] vt comprender mal.
misapprehension ['mis,æpri'henʃən] n equivocación f, error m, concepto m erróneo; **to be under a —** estar equivocado; **there seems to be some —** parece haber algún malentendido.
misappropriate ['misə'prəuprieit] vt malversar.
misappropriation ['misə,prəupri'eiʃən] n malversación f.
misbegotten ['misbi'gɔtn] adj bastardo, ilegítimo; plan etc ineficaz, llamado a fracasar.
misbehave ['misbi'heiv] vi portarse mal; (child) ser malo.
misbehaviour, (US) **misbehavior** ['misbi'heivjə*] n mala conducta f.
miscalculate ['mis'kælkjuleit] vti calcular mal.
miscalculation ['mis,kælkju'leiʃən] n cálculo m erróneo; (fig) error m, desacierto m.
miscall ['mis'kɔ:l] vt llamar equivocadamente.
miscarriage ['mis,kæridʒ] n (Med) aborto m, malparto m; (failure) fracaso m, malogro m; (of letter, goods) extravío m; **— of justice** error m judicial.
miscarry [mis'kæri] vi (Med) malparir, abortar; (fail) fracasar, salir mal, frustrarse; (letter, goods) extraviarse.
miscegenation [,misidʒi'neiʃən] n entrecruzamiento m de razas.
miscellaneous [,misi'leiniəs] adj vario, diverso.
miscellany [mi'seləni] n miscelánea f.
mischance [mis'tʃɑ:ns] n mala suerte f; infortunio m, desgracia f; **by some —** por desgracia.
mischief ['mistʃif] n (harm) mal m, daño m; (naughtiness) travesura f, diablura f; (roguishness) malicia f; (person) diablillo m; **he's up to some —** está haciendo alguna travesura; **there's some — going on** están tramando algo mal; **there's no — in him** no es capaz de ninguna maldad; **to do someone a —** hacer un daño a uno; **to do oneself a —** hacerse daño; **he's always getting into —** anda siempre metido en alguna travesura; **to keep someone out of —** impedir a uno hacer travesuras; **to make —** armar líos; **to make — for someone** crear dificultades para uno, amargar la vida a uno.
mischief-maker ['mistʃif,meikə*] n revoltoso m, a f, persona f turbulenta, persona f que anda metida en líos.
mischievous ['mistʃivəs] adj person malo, dañoso; (playful) malicioso, juguetón; child travieso; attack etc perjudicial; glance etc malicioso, lleno de malicia.
mischievously ['mistʃivəsli] adv maliciosamente, con malicia; por travesura.
misconceive ['miskən'si:v] vt entender mal, formar un concepto erróneo de.
misconception ['miskən'sepʃən] n concepto m erróneo, idea f falsa, equivocación f.
misconduct [mis'kɔndʌkt] n mala conducta f; (sexual) adulterio m.
misconduct [,miskən'dʌkt] 1 vt manejar mal, dirigir mal. 2 vr: **to — oneself** portarse mal.
misconstruction ['miskəns'trʌkʃən] n mala interpretación f; mala traducción f; (deliberate) tergiversación f.
misconstrue ['miskən'stru:] vt interpretar mal; traducir mal; (deliberately) tergiversar.
miscount ['mis'kaunt] 1 vt contar mal, equivocarse en la cuenta de. 2 vi contar mal.
miscreant ['miskriənt] n sinvergüenza mf, bellaco m, a f.
misdeal ['mis'di:l] 1 n reparto m erróneo. 2 (irr: see deal) vt cards dar mal, repartir mal.
misdeed ['mis'di:d] n delito m, crimen m, fechoría f.
misdemeanour, (US) **misdemeanor** [,misdi'mi:nə*] n ofensa f, delito m; (Law) delito m de menor cuantía.
misdirect ['misdi'rekt] vt operation etc manejar mal, dirigir mal; letter etc poner unas señas incorrectas en; person informar mal (acerca del camino a tomar), hacer perder el camino.
misdirection ['misdi'rekʃən] n mal manejo m, mala dirección f; instrucciones fpl erróneas, información f errónea.
miser ['maizə*] n avaro m, a f, avariento m, a f, tacaño m, a f.
miserable ['mizərəbl] adj (unhappy) triste, desdichado, desgraciado; abatido; (filthy, wretched) indecente, vil; (contemptible) vil, despreciable; (valueless) sin valor; show, spectacle de pena;

weather muy feo, de perros; wage raquítico; **it was a — failure** fue un rotundo fracaso; **what are you so — about?** ¿por qué estás tan triste?; **I feel — today** hoy me siento abatido; hoy me siento sin fuerzas para nada; **to make someone —** entristecer a uno, abatir a uno; **to make someone's life —** amargar la vida a uno.
miserably ['mizərəbli] adv say etc tristemente; **it failed —** fracasó rotundamente; **they played —** jugaron terriblemente mal.
misère [mi'zɛə*] n (Cards) nulos mpl; **to go —** jugar a nulos.
miserliness ['maizəlinis] n avaricia f, tacañería f.
miserly ['maizəli] adj avariento, tacaño.
misery ['mizəri] n (suffering) sufrimiento m; (sadness) pena f, tristeza f; (wretchedness) aflicción f, desdicha f; **a — life of** — una vida desgraciada; **to make someone's life a —** amargar la vida a uno; **to put an animal out of its —** acortar la agonía a un animal; **to put someone out of his —** (fig) satisfacer por fin a uno (contándole una noticia or revelándole un secreto etc).
misfire ['mis'faiə*] vi fallar.
misfit ['misfit] n cosa f mal ajustada; (dress) traje m que no cae bien; (person) inadaptado m, a f, desplazado m, a f, persona f reñida con su ambiente; **he's always been a — here** no se ha adaptado nunca a las condiciones de aquí, en ningún momento ha estado realmente contento aquí.
misfortune [mis'fɔ:tʃən] n desgracia f, infortunio m, desventura f; **companion in —** compañero m en la desgracia, compañero m de infortunio; **it is his — that he is lame** tiene la mala suerte de ser cojo; **I had the — to meet him** tuve la mala suerte de encontrarme con él.
misgiving [mis'givin] n (mistrust) recelo m, duda f, temor m; (apprehension) presentimiento m; **not without some —** no sin cierto recelo; **I had —s about the scheme** tuve mis dudas acerca del proyecto.
misgovern ['mis'gʌvən] vti gobernar mal; administrar mal.
misgovernment ['mis'gʌvənmənt] n desgobierno m, mal gobierno m; mala administración f.
misguided ['mis'gaidid] adj equivocado.
misguidedly ['mis'gaididli] adv equivocadamente.
mishandle ['mis'hændl] vt manejar mal.
mishap ['mishæp] n desgracia f, contratiempo m, accidente m; **without —** sin novedad; **to have a —** tener un accidente.
mishear ['mis'hiə*] (irr: see **hear**) vti oír mal.
mishmash ['miʃmæʃ] n masa f informe, masa f confusa; baturrillo m, ensaladilla f.
misinform ['misin'fɔ:m] vt informar mal, dar informes erróneos a.
misinterpret ['misin'tə:prit] vt interpretar mal; traducir mal; (deliberately) tergiversar.
misinterpretation ['misin,tə:pri'teiʃən] n mala interpretación f; mala traducción f; tergiversación f.
misjudge ['mis'dʒʌdʒ] vt juzgar mal, equivocarse sobre.
misjudgement [,mis'dʒʌdʒmənt] n juicio m erróneo.
mislay [mis'lei] (irr: see **lay**) vt extraviar, perder.
mislead [mis'li:d] (irr: see **lead**) vt llevar a conclusiones erróneas, despistar; (deliberately) engañar; **I fear you have been misled** me temo que se lo hayan dicho mal.
misleading [mis'li:diŋ] adj erróneo; (deliberately) engañoso.
mismanage ['mis'mænidʒ] vt manejar mal, administrar mal.
mismanagement ['mis'mænidʒmənt] n mal manejo m, mala administración f.
mismatch ['mis'mætʃ] vt emparejar mal, hermanar mal.
misname ['mis'neim] vt llamar equivocadamente.
misnomer ['mis'nəumə*] n nombre m equivocado, nombre m inapropiado; **that is a —** ese nombre no es correcto.
misogamist [mi'sɔgəmist] n misógamo m, a f.
misogamy [mi'sɔgəmi] n misogamia f.
misogynist [mi'sɔdʒinist] n misógino m.
misogyny [mi'sɔdʒini] n misoginia f.
misplace ['mis'pleis] vt colocar mal; poner fuera de su lugar; (lose) extraviar, perder.
misplaced ['mis'pleist] adj equivocado; inoportuno; inmerecido.
misprint ['misprint] n errata f, error m de imprenta.
misprint [mis'print] vt imprimir mal.
mispronounce ['misprə'nauns] vt pronunciar mal.
mispronunciation ['misprə,nʌnsi'eiʃən] n mala pronunciación f.

misquotation ['miskwəu'teiʃən] n cita f equivocada.

misquote ['mis'kwəut] vt citar mal; **he was —d in the press** en la prensa interpretaron mal lo que había dicho, en la prensa no citaron correctamente lo que había dicho.

misread ['mis'ri:d] (irr: see **read**) vt leer mal; interpretar mal.

misrepresent ['mis,repri'zent] vt desfigurar, falsificar; describir engañosamente; tergiversar; **he was —ed in the papers** los informes de los periódicos falsificaron lo que había dicho.

misrepresentation ['mis,reprizen'teiʃən] n desfiguración f; falsificación f; descripción f engañosa; tergiversación f; **this report is a — of what I said** este informe falsifica lo que yo dije.

misrule ['mis'ru:l] 1 n desgobierno m, mal gobierno m. 2 vt desgobernar, gobernar mal.

miss[1] [mis] 1 n (shot) tiro m errado, tiro m perdido; (mistake) error m, desacierto m; (failure) fracaso m; **a — is as good as a mile** lo mismo da librarse por poco que por mucho; **it was a near —** el tiro me anduvo muy cerca; **it was a near — with that car** faltó poco para que ese coche chocara con nosotros; **to give something a —** (not go) dejar de asistir a algo, no asistir a algo, (not visit) dejar de visitar algo; **we're giving it a —** this year este año no vamos; **they voted the record a —** opinaron que el disco carecía de valor.

2 vt **(a)** (fail to hit) aim, target errar; **the shot just —ed me** por poco la bala me alcanzó, el tiro me anduvo muy cerca; **the plane just —ed the tower** faltó poco para que el avión chocara con la torre; **he narrowly —ed being run over** por poco fue atropellado, faltó poco para que se le atropellara.

(b) (fail to find, catch, use etc) vocation errar, equivocarse en la elección de; solution no acertar; thing sought no encontrar; bus, train, chance, footing etc perder; one's way equivocarse de; class, lecture perder; appointment no acudir a; meeting etc no asistir a, no poder asistir a; **you haven't —ed much!** ¡no has perdido nada!; **we —ed the tide** perdimos la pleamar; **we're afraid of —ing the market** tememos perder el momento más propicio para la venta; **she —ed her holiday last year** el año pasado no pudo tomarse las vacaciones; **I —ed you at the station** no te vi en la estación; **they —ed each other in the crowd** no lograron encontrarse entre tanta gente; **you mustn't — this film** esta película hay que verla, no dejes de ver esta película; **don't — the Prado** no dejes de visitar el Prado; **you can't — the house** es imposible equivocarse al venir a la casa.

(c) (fail to hear) **I —ed what you said** se me escapó lo que dijo Vd; **I —ed that** eso no lo entendí; **you're —ing the point** no comprendes el punto principal.

(d) (omit) omitir; (overlook) pasar por alto; **let's — the next dance** no bailemos la próxima vez; **he —ed out a word** omitió una palabra; **he was —ed out in the promotions** en los ascensos le pasaron por alto.

(e) (notice absence of, regret absence of) **—** menos; notar la falta de; **I — the old trams** echo de menos los viejos tranvías; **I — you** so te echo mucho de menos; **he is much —ed** se le echa mucho de menos; **then I —ed my wallet** luego me di cuenta de que no tenía ya cartera; **he won't be —ed** bien podemos prescindir de él; **we're —ing 8 dollars** nos faltan 8 dólares.

3 vi (shot, person) errar el blanco, errar el tiro; (motor) fallar; **he —ed** erró el tiro; **he never —es** (fam) siempre acierta; **you can't —!** ¡es imposible fallar!; **I've not —ed once in 10 years** en 10 años no he faltado ni una sola vez.

miss[2] [mis] n señorita f; (fam) niña f precoz, niña f repipi; **a modern —** una señorita moderna; **M— Jennie Smith** (la) Señorita Jennie Smith; **yes, M— Smith** sí, señorita; **M— Spain 1980** Miss España 1980.

missal ['misəl] n misal m.

misshapen ['mis'ʃeipən] adj deforme.

missile ['misail] n proyectil m; (javelin etc) arma f arrojadiza; **air-to-air —** proyectil m de aire a aire; **guided —** proyectil m teledirigido; **intercontinental ballistic —** proyectil m balístico intercontinental.

missing ['misin] adj **(a)** person ausente, (Mil etc) desaparecido; thing perdido, extraviado, que falta; **— in action** desaparecido en combate; **— person** desaparecido m; **supply the — letters** poner las letras que faltan; **the three — students** are safe los tres estudiantes desaparecidos están a salvo.

(b) to be **—** faltar; haber desaparecido; **there are 9 books —, 9 books are —** faltan 9 libros; **how many are —?** ¿cuántos faltan?; **one of our aircraft is —** uno de nuestros aviones no ha vuelto.

mission ['miʃən] n misión f; **goodwill —** misión f de buena voluntad; **trade —** misión f comercial; **her — in life is to + infin** su misión en la vida es + infin; **to send someone on a secret —** enviar a uno en misión secreta.

missionary ['miʃənri] 1 adj zeal etc misional. 2 n misionero m, a f.

missis ['misiz] n (fam) **my —, the —** la parienta; **John and his —** Juan y su costilla; **yes, —** sí, señora; **is the —?** ¿está la señora?

Mississippi [,misi'sipi] Misisipí m.

missive ['misiv] n misiva f.

Missouri [mi'zuəri] Misuri m.

misspell ['mis'spel] (irr: see **spell**) vt escribir mal.

misspelling ['mis'spelin] n error m de ortografía.

misspend ['mis'spend] (irr: see **spend**) vt malgastar, desperdiciar, perder; **a misspent youth** una juventud mal empleada, una juventud pasada en la disipación.

misstate ['mis'steit] vt declarar erróneamente; (deliberately) declarar falsamente.

misstatement ['mis'steitmənt] n declaración f errónea; declaración f falsa.

missus ['misiz] n (fam) see **missis**.

missy ['misi] n (fam) = **miss**[2].

mist [mist] 1 n (fog) niebla f; (slight) neblina f; (summery; at sea) bruma f; (fig) nube f, velo m; **morning —** bruma f del alba; **Scotch —** llovizna f; **through a — of tears** por ojos llenos de lágrimas. 2 vt (fig) empañar, velar. 3 vi (also to — over, to — up) empañarse, velarse; (eyes) llenarse de lágrimas.

mistakable [mis'teikəbl] adj confundible.

mistake [mis'teik] 1 n equivocación f, error m, falta f; **by —** por equivocación, (carelessly) por descuido, (involuntarily) sin querer; **it's finished and no —!** ¡ya lo creo que está terminado!; **he took my hat in — for his** confundió mi sombrero con el suyo; **to acknowledge one's —** confesar su error; **the — is mine** la culpa es mía, la culpa la tengo yo; **there must be some —** ha de haber algún error; **there's no — about it** está muy claro, no hay que darle vueltas; **let there be no — about it** entiéndase bien que . . .; quede perfectamente claro que . . .; **to make a —** equivocarse; **you're making a big —** te equivocas gravemente, es una decisión totalmente errónea; **make no — (about it)** y que no queden dudas sobre esto; **to make the — of asking too much** cometer el error de pedir demasiado.

2 (irr: see **take**) vt **(a)** meaning entender mal, equivocarse sobre; road etc equivocar, equivocarse de.

(b) to **— A for B** equivocar A con B, confundir A con B.

(c) to be **—n** equivocarse, estar equivocado, engañarse; **if I am not —n** si no me equivoco; **he is often —n for Peter** se le confunde muchas veces con Pedro; **it cannot possibly be —n for anything else** es imposible confundirlo con otra cosa.

mistaken [mis'teikən] 1 ptp of **mistake**. 2 adj equivocado, erróneo; incorrecto.

mistakenly [mis'teikənli] adv equivocadamente, erróneamente.

mister ['mistə*] n (gen abbr **Mr**) señor m (gen abbr Sr).

mistime ['mis'taim] vt act etc hacer (or decir etc) a deshora, hacer en momento poco oportuno; race etc cronometrar mal.

mistle thrush ['mislθrʌʃ] n zorzal m charlo.

mistletoe ['misltəu] n muérdago m.

mistranslate ['mistræns'leit] vt traducir mal.

mistranslation ['mistræns'leiʃən] n mala traducción f.

mistreat [mis'tri:t] vt maltratar, tratar mal.

mistreatment [mis'tri:tmənt] n maltrato m, maltratamiento m, malos tratos mpl.

mistress ['mistris] n (of house etc) señora f, ama f de casa; (lover) querida f, amante f; (teacher: in primary school) maestra f, (in secondary school) profesora f; (abbr **Mrs** ['misiz]) señora f de . . .

mistrial [mis'trail] n juicio m viciado de nulidad.

mistrust [mis'trʌst] 1 n desconfianza f, recelo m. 2 vt desconfiar de, dudar de.

mistrustful [mis'trʌstful] adj desconfiado, receloso; **to be — of** recelarse de.

misty ['misti] adj nebuloso, brumoso; day de niebla; (fig) nebuloso, vaporoso; glasses, window empañado; **it's getting —** se está anieblando, está bajando la niebla; **the window is getting —** la ventana se está empañando.

misunderstand ['misʌndə'stænd] (*irr: see* **stand**) *vti* entender mal, comprender mal; tomar en sentido erróneo; interpretar mal; **you — me** no me entiendes, no entiendes lo que digo.

misunderstanding ['misʌndə'stændiŋ] *n* equivocación *f*, error *m*; concepto *m* erróneo; (*disagreement*) desavenencia *f*; (*between two persons*) malentendido *m*; **there must be some —** ha de haber algún malentendido.

misunderstood ['misʌndə'stud] *adj* no comprendido; insuficientemente estimado; **a — person** una persona incomprendida.

misuse ['mis'juːs] *n* abuso *m*, mal uso *m*; (*of word*) empleo *m* erróneo; (*of funds*) malversación *f*.

misuse ['mis'juːz] *vt* abusar de; *word* emplear mal; *funds* malversar; *person etc* maltratar.

mite[1] [mait] *n* (*Zool*) ácaro *m*.

mite[2] [mait] *n* (*coin*) ardite *m*, (*as contribution*) óbolo *m*; (*small quantity*) pizca *f*, poquitín *m*; (*child*) niño *m* pequeño, niña *f* pequeña, nene *m*, a *f*; **poor little —!** ¡pobrecito!; **a — of consolation** una pizca de consuelo; **there's not a — left** no queda ni una sola gota; **well, just a — then** bueno, un poquitín; **we were a — surprised** quedamos un tanto atónitos, nos sorprendimos un poquito.

Mithraic [miθ'reiik] *adj* mitraico.

Mithraism ['miθreiizəm] *n* mitraísmo *m*.

Mithras ['miθræs] *m* Mitra.

mitigate ['mitigeit] *vt* mitigar.

mitigation [,miti'geiʃən] *n* mitigación *f*; **to say a word in —** decir algo para mitigar la ofensa (*etc*).

mitre, (*US*) **miter** ['maitə*] **1** *n* (*Eccl*) mitra *f*; (*Tech*) inglete *m*. **2** *vt* (*Tech*) ingletear.

mitt [mit] *n see* **mitten**, (*sl*) mano *f*.

mitten ['mitn] *n* mitón *m*, guante *m* con solo el pulgar separado; **—s** (*fam*) guantes *mpl* de boxeo; **to get the —** (*sl*) recibir calabazas; **to give someone the —** (*sl*) dar calabazas a uno.

mix [miks] **1** *vt* mezclar; combinar, unir; confundir; *concrete, flour, plaster etc* amasar; *drinks* preparar, mezclar; *salad* aderezar; **to — something in** añadir algo, echar algo; **to — sugar into something** añadir azúcar a algo; **to — it** (*fam*) venir a las manos, arreglar las cosas luchando; **to — up** mezclar, confundir; **don't — me up** no me confundas; **I've —ed you up with Michael** le he confundido (*or equivocado*) con Miguel; **to be —ed up in an affair** estar metido en un asunto; **are you —ed in this?** ¿tú andas metido en esto?, ¿tú tienes que ver con esto?; **to get —ed up in an affair** meterse en un asunto, mojar en un asunto.

2 *vi* mezclarse, poder mezclarse; (*ingredients etc*) ir bien juntos; (*persons: get on well*) llevarse bien; **to — (in) with others** asociarse con otros, ir con otros, alternar con otros, frecuentar la compañía de otros; **he's not keen to — (in)** tiene pocas ganas de alternar; **to — in high society** frecuentar la alta sociedad.

mixed [mikst] *adj* mixto; mezclado; (*assorted*) variado, surtido; *choir, doubles, bathing etc* mixto; **a — set of people** un grupo de personas variadas; **with — results** con resultados diversos, (*pej*) con resultados más bien mediocres; **we had — weather** el tiempo ha sido variable.

mixed-up ['mikst'ʌp] *adj things* mezclados; (*disordered*) revueltos, confusos; **I'm all —** estoy totalmente confuso; **a badly — youth** un joven de mentalidad gravemente confusa, un joven lleno de incertidumbre.

mixer ['miksə*] *n* (*Cook*) mezcladora *f*; licuadora *f*; (*Radio*) mezclador *m*; (*person*) persona *f* sociable; **to be a good —** tener don de gentes; **he's not much of a —** tiene pocas ganas de alternar, no tiene don de gentes.

mixture ['mikstʃə*] *n* mezcla *f*; (*Med*) medicina *f*; **the — as before** la misma receta que antes, (*fig*) lo de siempre; **freezing —** mezcla *f* refrigerante; **the family is an odd —** la familia muestra una extraña diversidad; **he's an odd — of poet and plumber** se reúnen en él de modo bastante raro el poeta y el fontanero.

mix-up ['miksʌp] *n* confusión *f*, lío *m*; **there was a dreadful —** hubo un tremendo lío; **we got in a — with the trains** nos hicimos un lío con los trenes.

mizzen ['mizn] *n* mesana *f*.

mizzenmast ['miznmɑːst] *n* palo *m* de mesana.

mizzle ['mizl] *vi* lloviznar.

mnemonic [ni'mɔnik] **1** *adj* mnemotécnico **2** *n* figura *f* (*or* frase *f etc*) mnemotécnica.

mnemonics [ni'mɔniks] *n* mnemotécnica *f*.

moan [məun] **1** *n* (*groan*) gemido *m*, quejido *m*; (*complaint*) queja *f*, protesta *f*.
2 *vt* lamentar.
3 *vi* gemir; quejarse, protestar; **"yes", he —ed** "sí", dijo gimiendo; **they're —ing about the food again** han vuelto a quejarse de la comida.

moaning ['məuniŋ] *n* gemidos *mpl*; quejas *fpl*, protestas *fpl*.

moat [məut] *n* foso *m*.

moated ['məutid] *adj* con foso, rodeado de un foso.

mob [mɔb] **1** *n* (**a**) multitud *f*, muchedumbre *f*, gentío *m*; (*pej*) turba *f*; (*of birds etc*) bandada *f*, multitud *f*; **the —** el populacho; **houses were burnt by the —s** unas casas fueron incendiadas por las turbas; **they went in a — to the town hall** fueron en tropel al ayuntamiento; **to join the —** echarse a las calles; **the army has become a —** el ejército se ha transformado en una turba.
(**b**) (*fam*) grupo *m*, pandilla *f*, peña *f*; **Joe and his —** Pepe y su peña, Pepe y sus amigotes; **I had nothing to do with that —** no tuve nada que ver con aquéllos; **which — were you in?** (*Mil*) ¿en qué regimiento (*etc*) estuviste?; **they're a hard-drinking —** son unos borrachos.
2 *vt* (*molest*) acosar, atropellar; (*attack*) atacar en masa; *actor etc* festejar tumultuosamente, apiñarse entusiastas en torno de; **the minister was —bed by journalists** los periodistas se apiñaban en torno del ministro; **he was —bed whenever he went out** al salir siempre se veía acosado por la gente.

mobcap ['mɔbkæp] *n* cofia *f*.

mobile ['məubail] *adj* móvil, movible; *canteen etc* ambulante; **now that we're —** (*fam*) ahora que tenemos coche.

mobility [məu'biliti] *n* movilidad *f*.

mobilization [,məubilai'zeiʃən] *n* movilización *f*.

mobilize ['məubilaiz] **1** *vt* movilizar. **2** *vi* movilizarse.

mob law ['mɔblɔː] *n* ley *f* de Lynch, ley *f* de la calle.

moccasin ['mɔkəsin] *n* mocasín *m*.

mocha ['mɔkə] *n* moca *f*.

mock [mɔk] **1** *n*: **to make a — of something** poner algo en ridículo.
2 *adj* (*sham*) fingido, simulado; (*imitated*) imitado; (*parodied*) burlesco; **in — anger** con ira simulada; **a — battle** un simulacro de combate.
3 *vt* (*ridicule*) ridiculizar; (*defy*) burlarse de; (*scoff at*) burlarse de; (*mimic*) remedar, imitar; *efforts, plans etc* frustrar, desbaratar.
4 *vi* mofarse (*at* de).

mocker ['mɔkə*] *n* mofador *m*, ora *f*.

mockery ['mɔkəri] *n* (*derision*) mofas *fpl*, burlas *fpl*; (*object*) parodia *f*, mal remedo *m*; **this is a — of justice** esto es una negación de la justicia; **it was a — of a trial** fue una parodia de un proceso; **what a — this is!** ¡esto es absurdo!, ¡qué tontería!; **he had to put up with a lot of —** tuvo que aguantar muchas burlas; **to make a — of something** hacer algo ridículo.

mock-heroic ['mɔkhi'rəuik] *adj* heroicocómico.

mocking ['mɔkiŋ] **1** *adj tone etc* burlón. **2** *n* burlas *fpl*.

mockingbird ['mɔkiŋbəːd] *n* sinsonte *m*.

mockingly ['mɔkiŋli] *adv* en tono burlón, con sorna.

mock orange ['mɔk'ɔrindʒ] *n* jeringuilla *f*.

mock-up ['mɔkʌp] *n* maqueta *f*, modelo *m* en escala natural.

modal ['məudl] *adj* modal.

modality [məu'dæliti] *n* modalidad *f*.

mode [məud] *n* modo *m* (*also Gram, Mus, Philos*), manera *f*; (*fashion*) moda *f*.

model ['mɔdl] **1** *n* (**a**) modelo *m*; (*architect's, town planner's etc*) maqueta *f*; **it is made on the — of X** está hecho a imitación de X.
(**b**) (*person: Fashion, Art*) modelo *mf*; **he is a — of good behaviour** es un modelo de buenas costumbres; **to hold someone out** (*or* up) **as a —** presentar a uno como modelo.
2 *adj* modelo; **— prison** cárcel *f* modelo; **— railway** ferrocarril *m* de juguete, ferrocarril *m* en miniatura; **— town** ciudad *f* modelo.
3 *vt* (**a**) (*make a —*) modelar; (*fig*) modelar, formar, planear; **to — something on something else** modelar algo sobre otra cosa, construir algo a imitación de otra cosa, planear algo según otra cosa.
(**b**) *dress etc* llevar, presentar.
4 *vi* servir de modelo (*for* a, para); ejercer la profesión de modelo, ser modelo.
5 *vr*: **to — oneself on** modelarse sobre.

modeller, (*US*) **modeler** ['mɔdlə*] *n* modelador *m*, ora *f*.

modelling, (*US*) **modeling** ['mɔdliŋ] *n* modelado *m*; profesión *f* de modelo.

moderate ['mɔdərit] **1** *adj* moderado (*also Pol*); (*fair, medium*) regular, mediano, mediocre; *price* módico. **2** *n* (*Pol*) moderado *m*, a *f*.

moderate ['mɔdəreit] **1** *vt* moderar; mitigar; *wind etc* calmar. **2** *vi* moderarse; mitigarse; (*wind etc*) calmarse, amainar; (*act as moderator*) arbitrar, servir de asesor.

moderately ['mɔdəritli] *adv* moderadamente; medianamente, mediocremente; módicamente; **a — expensive suit** un traje medianamente caro; **he was — successful** tuvo un razonable éxito.

moderation [,mɔdə'reiʃən] *n* moderación *f*; **in —** con moderación.

moderator ['mɔdəreitə*] *n* árbitro *m*, asesor *m*, ora *f*; **M—** (*Eccl*) *presidente de la asamblea de la Iglesia Escocesa y de otras iglesias protestantes.*

modern ['mɔdən] **1** *adj* moderno. **2** *n* moderno *m*.

modernism ['mɔdənizəm] *n* modernismo *m*.

modernist ['mɔdənist] **1** *adj* modernista. **2** *n* modernista *mf*.

modernistic [,mɔdə'nistik] *adj* modernista.

modernity [mɔ'də:niti] *n* modernidad *f*.

modernization [,mɔdənai'zeiʃən] *n* modernización *f*; actualización *f*.

modernize ['mɔdənaiz] **1** *vt* modernizar; actualizar. **2** *vi* modernizarse; actualizarse.

modest ['mɔdist] *adj* modesto; moderado; (*chaste etc*) pudoroso, púdico; **to be — about one's successes** hablar en términos modestos de sus triunfos; **to be — in one's demands** ser moderado en sus reclamaciones.

modestly ['mɔdistli] *adv* modestamente; con moderación; pudorosamente.

modesty ['mɔdisti] *n* modestia *f*; moderación *f*; pudor *m*.

modicum ['mɔdikəm] *n*: **with a — of** con una cantidad mínima de, con un poquito de.

modification [,mɔdifi'keiʃən] *n* modificación *f*.

modifier ['mɔdifaiə*] *n* (*Gram*) modificante *m*.

modify ['mɔdifai] *vt* modificar.

modish ['məudiʃ] *adj* muy de moda, sumamente elegante.

modishly ['məudiʃli] *adv* elegantemente; **to be — dressed** ir vestido con suma elegancia.

modiste [məu'di:st] *n* modista *f*.

modulate ['mɔdjuleit] *vti* modular.

modulated ['mɔdjuleitid] *adj* modulado.

modulation [,mɔdju'leiʃən] *n* modulación *f*; **frequency —** (*Radio*) modulación *f* de frecuencia.

mogul ['məugəl] *n* magnate *m*; **the Great M—** el Gran Mogol.

mohair ['məuhɛə*] *n* moer *m*.

Mohammed [məu'hæmed] *n* Mahoma.

Mohammedan [məu'hæmidən] **1** *adj* mahometano. **2** *n* mahometano *m*, a *f*.

Mohammedanism [məu'hæmidənizəm] *n* mahometanismo *m*.

moiré ['mwa:rei] *n* muaré *m*.

moist [mɔist] *adj* húmedo; mojado.

moisten ['mɔisn] **1** *vt* humedecer, mojar. **2** *vi* humedecerse, mojarse.

moistness ['mɔistnis] *n*, **moisture** ['mɔistʃə*] *n* humedad *f*.

moisturize ['mɔistʃəraiz] *vt* humedecer, mojar.

moke [məuk] *n* (*sl*) burro *m*.

molar ['məulə*] *n* muela *f*.

molasses [mə'læsiz] *n sing and pl* melaza *f*, melazas *fpl*.

mold [məuld] *n etc see* **mould**.

mole¹ [məul] *n* (*Anat*) lunar *m*.

mole² [məul] *n* (*Zool*) topo *m*.

mole³ [məul] *n* (*Naut*) malecón *m*, muelle *m*.

molecular [mə'lekjulə*] *adj* molecular.

molecule ['mɔlikju:l] *n* molécula *f*.

molehill ['məulhil] *n* topera *f*.

moleskin ['məulskin] *n* piel *f* de topo.

molest [məu'lest] *vt* faltar al respeto a, meterse con, importunar; (*euph*) abordar con propósitos deshonestos.

molestation [,məules'teiʃən] *n* importunidad *f*, vejación *f*.

moll [mɔl] *n* (*sl*) querida *f*.

mollify ['mɔlifai] *vt* apaciguar, calmar; **he was somewhat mollified by this** con esto se calmó un poco.

mollusc ['mɔləsk] *n* molusco *m*.

mollycoddle ['mɔlikɔdl] **1** *n* marica *m*, niño *m* mimado. **2** *vt* mimar.

molten ['məultən] *adj* fundido, derretido; *lava etc* líquido.

molybdenum [mɔ'libdinəm] *n* molibdeno *m*.

moment ['məumənt] *n* (**a**) (*instant*) momento *m*, instante *m*; (*juncture*) momento *m*, coyuntura *f*;

man of the — hombre *m* del momento; **odd —s** momentos *mpl* de ocio (*and see* **odd**); **psychological — momento** *m* psicológico; **at any —** de un momento a otro; **at the —** de momento, por ahora; **at the last — a última hora; at this —** en este momento, ahora mismo; **for the —** por el momento; **not for a —** ni por pienso; **in a —** en un momento; **yes, in a —!** ¡sí, en seguida!; **I'll come in a —** vengo en seguida; **it was all over in a —** todo esto ocurrió en un instante; **to leave things until the last —** dejar las cosas hasta última hora; **one —!, half a —!, wait a —!** ¡un momento!; **I shan't be a —** vuelvo muy pronto; **termino muy pronto; ahora mismo; do it this very —!** ¡hazlo al instante!; **I have just this — heard of it** acabo de saberlo; **it won't take a —** es cosa de unos pocos momentos; **tell me the —** he comes avíseme en cuanto venga.

(**b**) (*Mech*) momento *m*; **— of inertia** momento *m* de inercia.

(**c**) (*importance*) importancia *f*, momento *m*; **of little —** de poca importancia, de poco momento; **matters of —** asuntos *mpl* de importancia.

momentarily ['məuməntərili] *adv* momentáneamente; *expect etc* de un momento a otro; (*US*) en este momento.

momentary ['məuməntəri] *adj* momentáneo.

momentous [məu'mentəs] *adj* trascendental, muy crítico, de suma importancia, decisivo.

momentousness [məu'mentəsnis] *n* trascendencia *f*, suma importancia *f*, lo decisivo.

momentum [məu'mentəm] *n* momento *m*; (*fig*) ímpetu *m*; **to gather —** cobrar velocidad.

monad ['mɔnæd] *n* mónada *f*.

Mona Lisa ['məunə'li:zə] *f* la Gioconda.

monarch ['mɔnək] *n* monarca *m*.

monarchic(al) [mɔ'na:kik(əl)] *adj* monárquico.

monarchism ['mɔnəkizəm] *n* monarquismo *m*.

monarchist ['mɔnəkist] **1** *adj* monárquico. **2** *n* monárquico *m*, a *f*.

monarchy ['mɔnəki] *n* monarquía *f*.

monastery ['mɔnəstri] *n* monasterio *m*.

monastic [mə'næstik] *adj* monástico.

monasticism [mə'næstisizəm] *n* monacato *m*, vida *f* monástica.

Monday ['mʌndi] *n* lunes *m*.

monetary ['mʌnitəri] *adj* monetario.

money ['mʌni] **1** *n* dinero *m*; **paper —** papel *m* moneda, billetes *mpl* de banco; **ready —** dinero *m* contante; **your — or your life!** ¡la bolsa o la vida!; **— talks** poderoso caballero es don Dinero; **— makes — dinero** llama dinero; **there's — in it** es un buen negocio; **it's a bargain for the —** a ese precio es una verdadera ganga; **that's the team for my —!** ¡ése sí es un equipo!, ¡ése es lo que se llama un equipo!; **it's — for jam, it's — for old rope** es dinero que se gana sin el menor esfuerzo; **he must be coining —** está forrándose de dinero; **to come into —** heredar una suma de dinero; **bad — drives out good** el dinero malo echa fuera al bueno; **to earn good —** tener un buen sueldo; **he gets his — on Fridays** cobra los viernes; **when do I get my —?** ¿cuándo cobro?, ¿cuándo me vas a pagar?; **to keep someone in —** proveer a uno de dinero; **he's made of —** es de oro; **do you think I'm made of —?** ¿crees que soy millonario?; **to make —** (*person*) ganar dinero, (*business*) dar dinero, rendir bien; **to make — hand over fist** amasar una fortuna; **to be rolling in —** nadar en oro; **to throw good — after bad** echar la soga tras el caldero.

2 *attr*: **— payment** pago *m* en metálico; **— prize** premio *m* en metálico; **— matters** asuntos *mpl* financieros.

moneybag ['mʌnibæg] *n* gato *m*, talega *f*; **—s** (*fig*) talegas *fpl*, riqueza *f*.

moneybox ['mʌnibɔks] *n* hucha *f*.

moneychanger ['mʌni,tʃeindʒə*] *n* cambista *mf*.

moneyed ['mʌnid] *adj* adinerado.

moneygrubber ['mʌni,grʌbə*] *n* avaro *m*, a *f*.

moneygrubbing ['mʌni,grʌbiŋ] **1** *adj* avaro, avariento. **2** *n* esfuerzo *m* por enriquecerse, afán *m* de dinero.

moneylender ['mʌni,lendə*] *n* prestamista *mf*.

moneymaker ['mʌni,meikə*] *n* artículo *m* (*or* producto *m*) que rinde grandes beneficios.

moneymaking ['mʌni,meikiŋ] **1** *adj* provechoso, lucrativo. **2** *n* ganancia *f*, lucro *m*.

money market ['mʌni,ma:kit] *n* mercado *m* de dinero.

money order ['mʌni,ɔ:də*] *n* giro *m* postal.

money's-worth ['mʌnizwə:θ] *n*: **to get one's —** estar satisfecho, estar contento con lo que uno ha adquirido (*etc*); **to get one's — out of something** sacar todo el valor de algo.

-monger ['mʌŋgə*] n traficante m en . . ., tratante m en . . .; see fish- etc.
Mongol ['mɔŋgəl] **1** adj mogol. **2** n mogol m, ola f. **3** n (language) mogol m.
Mongolia [mɔŋ'gəuliə] la Mogolia.
Mongolian [mɔŋ'gəuliən] see **Mongol**.
mongolism ['mɔŋgəlizəm] n mogolismo m.
mongoose ['mɔŋguːs] n, pl **mongooses** ['mɔŋguːsiz] mangosta f.
mongrel ['mʌŋgrəl] **1** adj mestizo; dog mestizo, cruzado, (pej) callejero. **2** n (person) mestizo m, a f; (dog) perro m mestizo, (pej) perro m callejero.
monitor ['mɔnitə*] **1** n (School) monitor m; (Radio: person) escucha mf, monitor m; (TV set) receptor m de control. **2** vt foreign station escuchar; TV programme controlar.
monk [mʌŋk] n monje m.
monkey ['mʌŋki] **1** n mono m, a f, mico m, a f; (fig: child) diablillo m, golfillo m; (sl) 500 libras fpl; to **make a — out of someone** poner a uno en ridículo.
 2 vi: to **— about** hacer travesuras, juguetear, hacer diabluras; to **— about with something** manosear algo, (and damage) estropear algo.
monkey business ['mʌŋki,biznis] n trampas fpl, malas mañas fpl.
monkey nut ['mʌŋkinʌt] n cacahuete m.
monkey puzzle ['mʌŋki,pʌzl] n araucaria f.
monkey tricks ['mʌŋki,triks] npl travesuras fpl, diabluras fpl.
monkey wrench ['mʌŋki,rentʃ] n llave f inglesa.
monkish ['mʌŋkiʃ] adj monacal, de monje; monástico; (pej) frailuno.
monkshood ['mʌŋkshud] n (Bot) acónito m.
mono . . . ['mɔnəu] mono . . .
monochrome ['mɔnəkrəum] **1** adj monocromo m. **2** n monocromo m.
monocle ['mɔnəkl] n monóculo m.
monogamous [mɔ'nɔgəməs] adj monógamo m.
monogamy [mɔ'nɔgəmi] n monogamia f.
monogram ['mɔnəgræm] n monograma m.
monograph ['mɔnəgræf] n monografía f.
monolingual [,mɔnəu'liŋgwəl] adj monolingüe.
monolith ['mɔnəuliθ] n monolito m.
monolithic [,mɔnəu'liθik] adj monolítico.
monologue ['mɔnəlɔg] n monólogo m.
monomania [,mɔnəu'meiniə] n monomanía f.
monomial [mɔ'nəumiəl] **1** adj que consta de un solo término. **2** n monomio m.
monoplane ['mɔnəplein] n monoplano m.
monopolize [mə'nɔpəlaiz] vt monopolizar (also fig), acaparar.
monopoly [mə'nɔpəli] n monopolio m.
monorail ['mɔnəureil] n monorail m, monocarril m.
monosyllabic ['mɔnəusi'læbik] adj word monosílabo utterance monosilábico.
monosyllable ['mɔnə,siləbl] n monosílabo m.
monotheism ['mɔnəu,θiːizəm] n monoteísmo m.
monotheist ['mɔnəu,θiːist] n monoteísta mf.
monotheistic [,mɔnəuθi:'istik] adj monoteísta.
monotone ['mɔnətəun] n monotonía f; to **speak in a — hablar en un solo tono.
monotonous [mə'nɔtənəs] adj monótono.
monotony [mə'nɔtəni] n monotonía f.
monotype ['mɔnəutaip] n monotipia f; — **machine** máquina f monotipo.
monoxide [mɔ'nɔksaid] n monóxido m.
monseigneur [,mɔnsen'jə:*] n monseñor m.
monsignor [mɔn'si:njə*] n monseñor m.
monsoon [mɔn'suːn] n monzón m or f; **the — rains** las lluvias monzónicas.
monster ['mɔnstə*] **1** adj enorme, monstruoso; (hum) grandísimo.
 2 n monstruo m; **a real — of a fish** un pez verdaderamente enorme; **a — of greed** un monstruo de la avaricia.
monstrance ['mɔnstrəns] n (Eccl) custodia f.
monstrosity [mɔns'trɔsiti] n monstruosidad f.
monstrous ['mɔnstrəs] adj monstruoso, enorme; **it is — that . . .** es terriblemente injusto que + subj.
monstrously ['mɔnstrəsli] adv enormemente; — **unfair** terriblemente injusto.
montage [mɔn'tɑ:ʒ] n montaje m.
month [mʌnθ] n mes m; **30 dollars a —** 30 dólares al mes, 30 dólares mensuales; **not in a — of Sundays** jamás; **it went on for —s** duró meses y meses.
monthly ['mʌnθli] **1** adj mensual.
 2 adv cada mes, mensualmente; **40 dollars —** 40 dólares al mes, 40 dólares mensuales.
 3 n revista f mensual; **monthlies** (Med) reglas fpl.
monument ['mɔnjumənt] n monumento m (to de, que conmemora).

monumental [,mɔnju'mentl] adj monumental; ignorance terrible; error garrafal.
moo [mu:] **1** n mugido m. **2** vi mugir, hacer mu.
mooch [mu:tʃ] vi (fam): to **— about** no saber qué hacer, no tener nada que hacer, haraganear; to **— along** andar arrastrando los pies.
mood[1] [mu:d] n (Gram) modo m; **imperative —** modo m imperativo; **subjunctive —** modo m subjuntivo.
mood[2] [mu:d] n humor m; disposición f (de ánimo); capricho m; **to be in a bad —** estar de mal humor; **to be in a good —** estar de buen humor; **to be in a generous —** sentirse generoso; **to be in an ugly —** (person) estar de muy mal humor, (crowd) amenazar violencia; **to be in a forgiving —** estar dispuesto a perdonar; **to be in no laughing —, to be in no — for laughing** no tener ganas de reír; **are you in a — for chess?** ¿te apetece una partida de ajedrez?, ¿quieres jugar al ajedrez?; **to be in the — (for love)** sentirse amoroso; **I'm not in the —** no quiero; **he plays well when he's in the —** toca bien cuando está de vena; **he's in one of his —s** está en uno de sus momentos de mal humor; **that depends on his —** eso es según el humor que tenga; **he has —s** (of anger) tiene arranques de cólera, (of gloom) tiene sus rachas de melancolía.
moodily ['mu:dili] adv answer etc malhumoradamente; melancólicamente.
moodiness ['mu:dinis] n mal humor m; melancolía f; propensión f a cambiar bruscamente de humor.
moody ['mu:di] adj: to **be —** (angry) tener arranques de cólera; (gloomy) tener rachas de melancolía; (variable) ser propenso a cambiar bruscamente de humor.
moon [mu:n] **1** n luna f; (poet) mes m; **crescent — media luna f; **full — luna f llena, plenilunio m; **new — luna f nueva, novilunio m; **once in a blue — de guindas a brevas, de Pascuas a Ramos; **to ask (or cry) for the — pedir peras al olmo; **to promise the — prometer el oro y el moro, prometer la luna.
 2 vt: to **— away a couple of hours** pasar un par de horas sin hacer nada, pasar un par de horas soñando.
 3 vi: to **— about** mirar a las musarañas, pasar el tiempo sin hacer nada; parecer estar soñando despierto.
moonbeam ['mu:nbi:m] n rayo m de luna.
moonless ['mu:nlis] adj sin luna.
moonlight ['mu:nlait] **1** n luz f de la luna; **by —, in the — a la luz de la luna; **— flit** mudanza f a la chita callando; **it was — había luna.
 2 vi (US fam) tener un empleo secundario además del principal.
moonlit ['mu:nlit] adj object iluminado por la luna; night de luna.
moonrise ['mu:nraiz] n salida f de la luna.
moonshine ['mu:nʃain] n luz f de la luna; (fam: nonsense) pamplinas fpl, música f celestial; (US sl) licor m destilado ilegalmente; **that's just —!** ¡es puro cuento!
moonshiner ['mu:nʃainə*] n (US sl) fabricante m de licor ilegal.
moonstone ['mu:nstəun] n adularia f.
moonstruck ['mu:nstrʌk] adj tocado, que tiene el juicio trastornado, lunático.
Moor [muə*] n moro m, a f.
moor[1] [muə*] n páramo m, brezal m; (for game) coto m.
moor[2] [muə*] **1** vt amarrar. **2** vi echar las amarras.
moorhen ['muəhen] n polla f de agua.
moorings ['muəriŋz] npl (ropes) amarras fpl; (place) amarradero m.
Moorish ['muəriʃ] adj moro; (Archit etc) árabe; arch arábigo.
moorland ['muələnd] n páramo m, brezal m.
moose [mu:s] n alce m de América.
moot [mu:t] **1** n junta f, asamblea f.
 2 adj point, question discutible.
 3 vt proponer para la discusión; **it has been —ed whether . . . se ha discutido si . . .; **when the question was first —ed** cuando se discutió la cuestión por primera vez.
mop [mɔp] **1** n (implement) fregasuelos m, lampazo m; (hair) mata f, greña f; **— of hair** pelambrera f.
 2 vt fregar, limpiar; brow enjugar; to **— up floor, liquid** limpiar, enjugar; (absorb) absorber; (dry up) secar; (Mil) terrain limpiar, remnants acabar con; (fam) beberse.
mope [məup] vi estar deprimido, estar abatido; to **— about** andar alicaído; to **— for someone** resentirse de la ausencia de uno, estar triste por la pérdida de uno.
moped ['məuped] n ciclomotor m.
mopes [məups] npl depresión f, melancolía f.

moping ['məupiŋ] *adj*, **mopish** ['məupiʃ] *adj* abatido, melancólico.

moquette [mə'ket] *n* moqueta *f*.

moraine [mə'rein] *n* (*Geol*) morena *f*.

moral ['mɔrəl] **1** *adj* moral; *philosophy, support, victory* moral; (*chaste*) virtuoso; (*honourable*) honrado.
   2 *n* (**a**) (*of story*) moraleja *f*; sentido *m* moral; **to draw a — from** sacar una moraleja de; **to point the —** hacer resaltar la moraleja.
   (**b**) **—s** moral *f*, ética *f*; moralidad *f*; (*conduct*) costumbres *fpl*; **the —s of actors** la moralidad de los actores; **she has no —s** no tiene sentido moral, carece de toda noción de la moralidad.

morale [mə'rɑːl] *n* moral *f*.

moralist ['mɔrəlist] *n* moralizador *m*, ora *f*; (*philosopher, teacher*) moralista *mf*.

morality [mə'ræliti] *n* moralidad *f*.

morality play [mə'ræliti,plei] *n* moralidad *f*.

moralize ['mɔrəlaiz] *vti* moralizar.

moralizing ['mɔrəlaiziŋ] **1** *adj* moralizador. **2** *n* instrucción *f* moral, predicación *f* sobre la moralidad.

morally ['mɔrəli] *adv* moralmente.

morass [mə'ræs] *n* cenagal *m*, pantano *m*; **a — of problems** un laberinto de problemas; **a — of figures** un mar de cifras.

moratorium [,mɔrə'tɔːriəm] *n* moratoria *f*.

moray ['mɔrei] *n* morena *f*.

morbid ['mɔːbid] *adj* insano, malsano; *mind* enfermizo; (*Med*) mórbido; (*depressed*) pesimista, melancólico; **don't be so —!** ¡no digas esas cosas horribles!

morbidity [mɔː'biditi] *n*, **morbidness** ['mɔːbidnis] *n* lo insano, lo malsano; lo enfermizo; (*Med*) morbosidad *f*; pesimismo *m*.

morbidly ['mɔːbidli] *adv talk etc* en tono pesimista; *think etc* con pesimismo.

mordacity [mɔː'dæsiti] *n* mordacidad *f*.

mordant ['mɔːdənt] *adj* mordaz.

more [mɔː*] **1** *adj* (**a**) más; **you have — money than I** Vd tiene más dinero que yo; **— light, please** ¡más luz, por favor!; **a few — weeks** algunas semanas más; **do you want some — tea?** ¿quieres más té?; **is there any — wine in the bottle?** ¿queda vino en la botella?; **many — people** muchas más personas; **much — butter** mucha más mantequilla.
   (**b**) (*numerals*) **— than half** más de la mitad; **— than one** más de uno; **— than 15** más de 15; **not — than one** no más de uno; **not — than 15** no más de quince.
   2 *n and pron* más; **we can't afford —** no podemos pagar más; **this house cost — than ours** esta casa costó más que la nuestra; **it cost — than we had expected** costó más de lo que esperábamos; **I shall have — to say about this** volveré a hablar de esto; **and what's — . . .** y además . . .
   3 *adv* más; **— easily** más fácilmente, con mayor facilidad (*than que*); **— and —** más y más, cada vez más; **— or less** más o menos; **neither — nor less** ni más ni menos; **once —** otra vez, una vez más; **never — nunca más**; **if he comes here any —** si vuelve por aquí; **if he says that any —** si dice eso otra vez; **the house is — than half built** la casa está más que medio construida; **I had — than carried out my obligation** había cumplido con creces mi obligación; **it will — than meet the demand** satisfará ampliamente la demanda; **he was — surprised than angry** más que enfadarse se sorprendió; **it's — a short story than a novel** más que novela es un cuento.
   4 (**the —**) **the — you give him the — he wants** cuanto más se le da tanto más quiere; **the — he drank the thirstier he got** cuanto más bebía más sed tenía; **it makes me (all) the — ashamed** tanto más vergüenza me da; **all the — so because . . .** tanto más cuanto que . . .; **the — the merrier** cuantos más mejor.
   5 (*no — etc*) **I have no — pennies** no tengo más peniques; **no — singing, I can't bear it!** ¡que no se cante más, no lo aguanto!; **let's say no — about it** no se hable más de esto; **he doesn't live here any —** ya no vive aquí; **Queen Anne is no —** la reina Ana ya no existe; **we shall see her no —** no la volveremos a ver; **"I don't understand it" . . . "no — do I"** "no lo comprendo" . . . "ni yo tampoco"; **she's no — a duchess than I am** tan duquesa es como mi padre; **he no — thought of paying me than of flying to the moon** antes iría volando a la luna que pensar pagarme a mí.

moreover [mɔː'rəuvə*] *adv* además, por otra parte.

mores ['mɔːreiz] *npl* costumbres *fpl*, tradiciones *fpl*; moralidad *f*.

morganatic [,mɔːgə'nætik] *adj* morganático.

morganatically [,mɔːgə'nætikəli] *adv*: **he married her —** se casó con ella en casamiento morganático.

morgue [mɔːg] *n* depósito *m* de cadáveres.

moribund ['mɔribʌnd] *adj* moribundo (*also fig*).

Mormon ['mɔːmən] **1** *adj* mormónico. **2** *n* mormón *m*, ona *f*.

Mormonism ['mɔːmənizəm] *n* mormonismo *m*.

morn [mɔːn] *n* (*poet*) *see* **morning**; (*dawn*) alborada *f*.

morning ['mɔːniŋ] **1** *n* mañana *f*; (*before dawn*) madrugada *f*; **good —!** ¡buenos días!; **the — after** (*hum*) la mañana después de la juerga; **the next —** la mañana siguiente, a la mañana; **early in the —** muy de mañana; **in the —** por la mañana; **at 7 o'clock in the —** a las 7 de la mañana; **at 3 in the —** a las 3 de la madrugada; **— yesterday —** ayer por la mañana.
   2 *adj*, *attr* de (la) mañana; *light, star* del alba; *newspaper, train etc* de la mañana.

morning coat ['mɔːniŋ,kəut] *n* chaqué *m*.

morning-glory ['mɔːniŋ'glɔːri] *n* dondiego *m* de día.

morning sickness ['mɔːniŋ'siknis] *n* vómitos *mpl* del embarazo, achaques *mpl* mañaneros.

Moroccan [mə'rɔkən] **1** *adj* marroquí. **2** *n* marroquí *mf*.

Morocco [mə'rɔkəu] Marruecos *m*.

morocco [mə'rɔkəu] *n* (*also* **— leather**) marroquí *m*, tafilete *m*.

moron ['mɔːrɔn] *n* imbécil *mf*.

moronic [mə'rɔnik] *adj* imbécil.

morose [mə'rəus] *adj* malhumorado, hosco, taciturno.

morpheme ['mɔːfiːm] *n* morfema *m*.

morphia ['mɔːfiə] *n*, **morphine** ['mɔːfiːn] *n* morfina *f*.

morphological [,mɔːfə'lɔdʒikəl] *adj* morfológico.

morphology [mɔː'fɔlədʒi] *n* morfología *f*.

morrow ['mɔrəu] *n* (*lit*): **on the —** al día siguiente.

Morse [mɔːs] *n*: **— code** alfabeto *m* Morse.

morsel ['mɔːsl] *n* (*small piece*) pedazo *m*, fragmento *m*; (*of food*) bocado *m*.

mortal ['mɔːtl] **1** *adj* mortal. **2** *n* mortal *mf*.

mortality [mɔː'tæliti] *n* mortalidad *f*; (*number killed in war, accident*) mortandad *f*, número *m* de víctimas; **infantile —** mortalidad *f* infantil; **there was heavy —** hubo numerosas víctimas, murieron muchos.

mortally ['mɔːtəli] *adv* mortalmente; **— wounded** herido de muerte; **— offended** mortalmente ofendido.

mortar ['mɔːtə*] **1** *n* (*Tech, Mil*) mortero *m*. **2** *vt* bombardear con morteros.

mortarboard ['mɔːtəbɔːd] *n* (*Univ*) birrete *m*.

mortgage ['mɔːgidʒ] **1** *n* hipoteca *f*; **to pay off a —** redimir una hipoteca; **to raise a —, to take out a —** obtener una hipoteca (*on sobre*).
   2 *vt* hipotecar; (*fig*) vender, poner en manos ajenas.

mortgagee [,mɔːgə'dʒiː] *n* acreedor *m* hipotecario, acreedora *f* hipotecaria.

mortgagor ['mɔːgədʒə*] *n* deudor *m* hipotecario, deudora *f* hipotecaria.

mortification [,mɔːtifi'keiʃən] *n* mortificación *f*; humillación *f*; (*Med*) gangrena *f*.

mortify ['mɔːtifai] **1** *vt* mortificar; humillar; **I was mortified to find that . . .** me avergoncé al descubrir que . . . **2** *vi* (*Med*) gangrenarse.

mortifying ['mɔːtifaiiŋ] *adj* humillante.

mortise, mortice ['mɔːtis] *n* muesca *f*, mortaja *f*.

mortuary ['mɔːtjuəri] **1** *adj* mortuorio. **2** *n* depósito *m* de cadáveres.

Mosaic [məu'zeiik] *adj* mosaico.

mosaic [məu'zeiik] *n* mosaico *m*.

Moscow ['mɔskəu] Moscú *m*.

Moselle [məu'zel] Mosela *f*.

Moses ['məuzis] *m* Moisés.

Moses basket ['məuzis,bɑːskit] *n* moisés *m*.

Moslem ['mɔzlem] **1** *adj* musulmán. **2** *n* musulmán *m*, ana *f*.

mosque [mɔsk] *n* mezquita *f*.

mosquito [mɔs'kiːtəu] *n*, *pl* **—oes** [əuz] mosquito *m*.

mosquito net [mɔs'kiːtəu,net] *n* mosquitero *m*.

moss [mɔs] *n* (*Bot*) musgo *m*; (*Geog*) pantano *m*, marjal *m*.

mossy ['mɔsi] *adj* musgoso, cubierto de musgo.

most [məust] **1** *adj superl* (**a**) (*with sing*) más; **who has — money?** ¿quién tiene más dinero?
   (**b**) (*with pl*) **— men** la mayor parte de los hombres, la mayoría de los hombres, los más hombres, casi todos los hombres.
   2 *n and pron*: **do the — you can** haga todo lo que pueda; **— of them** casi todos ellos; **— of those present** la mayor parte de los asistentes; **— of the time** la mayor parte del tiempo; **at —, at the —, at the very —** a lo más, a lo sumo, todo lo más; **it's the**

—! (*sl*) ¡es fenomenal! (*fam*); **this group is the —!** (*sl*) ¡este conjunto es fabuloso! (*fam*); **the girl with the —** (*sl*) la chica más atractiva; **to make the — of an affair** sacar el mejor partido de un asunto; **to make the — of one's advantages** aprovechar bien sus ventajas; **he made the — of the story** explotó todas las posibilidades del cuento, exageró los detalles del cuento.

3 *adv* (**a**) *superl* **he spent —** él gastó más; **the — attractive girl there** la chica más atractiva allí; **the — difficult of our problems** el más difícil de nuestros problemas; **which one did it — easily?** ¿quién lo hizo con la mayor facilidad?

(**b**) (*intensive*) muy, sumamente; **— likely** muy probable; **a — expensive toy** un juguete de los más caros, un juguete carísimo; **a — interesting book** un libro de lo más interesante, un libro interesantísimo; **you have been — kind** Vd ha sido muy amable; **— holy** santísimo; **— reverend** reverendísimo; *see* **all, part** *etc*.

-most [məust] más, *eg* **centremost** más central, **furthermost** más lejano.

mostly ['məustli] *adv* en su mayor parte; principalmente; en su mayoría; en general; **they are — women** en su mayoría son mujeres, casi todas son mujeres; **— because . . .** principalmente porque . . .; **we — sell retail** en general vendemos al detalle, principalmente vendemos al por menor; **it's — finished** está casi terminado.

mote [məut] *n* átomo *m*, mota *f*; **to see the — in our neighbour's eye and not the beam in our own** ver la paja en el ojo ajeno y no la viga en el propio.

motel [məu'tel] *n* motel *m*.

motet [məu'tet] *n* motete *m*.

moth [mɔθ] *n* mariposa *f* (nocturna); (*clothes-*) polilla *f*.

mothball ['mɔθbɔːl] *n* bola *f* de naftalina; **in —s** (*Naut etc*) en la reserva.

moth-eaten ['mɔθˌiːtn] *adj* apolillado, comido de la polilla.

mother ['mʌðə*] **1** *n* madre *f*; **M— of God** Madre *f* de Dios; **M— Superior** superiora *f*, madre *f* superiora; **to be a — to someone** ser como una madre para uno.

2 *adj*, *attr* madre; *tongue etc* materno; *love etc* maternal; *see* **country** *etc*.

3 *vt* (*give birth to*) parir, dar a luz; (*act as — to*) servir de madre a; (*spoil*) mimar; *young animal* prohijar.

mothercraft ['mʌðəkrɑːft] *n* arte *m* de cuidar a los niños pequeños, arte *m* de ser madre.

motherhood ['mʌðəhud] *n* maternidad *f*; **to prepare for —** prepararse para ser madre.

mother-in-law ['mʌðərinlɔː] *n*, *pl* **mothers-in-law** ['mʌðəzinlɔː] suegra *f*.

motherland ['mʌðəlænd] *n* patria *f*, (*more sentimentally*) madre patria *f*.

motherless ['mʌðəlis] *adj* huérfano de madre, sin madre.

motherly ['mʌðəli] *adj* maternal.

mother-of-pearl ['mʌðərəv'pəːl] **1** *n* nácar *m*. **2** *adj* nacarado.

mother ship ['mʌðəʃip] *n* buque *m* nodriza.

mother-to-be ['mʌðətə'biː] *n*, *pl* **mothers-to-be** ['mʌðəztə'biː] futura madre *f*.

moth-hole ['mɔθhəul] *n* apolilladura *f*.

mothproof ['mɔθpruːf] *adj* a prueba de polillas.

motif [məu'tiːf] *n* (*Art*, *Mus*) motivo *m*; (*of speech etc*) tema *m*; (*Sew*) adorno *m*.

motion ['məuʃən] **1** *n* (**a**) (*movement*) movimiento *m*; (*of parts of machine*) marcha *f*, operación *f*, funcionamiento *m*; **perpetual —** movimiento *m* perpetuo; **to be in —** estar en movimiento; **to go through the —s** hacer algo en la debida forma, obrar de acuerdo con las reglas (pero sin creer que se vaya a conseguir nada); obrar por pura fórmula; **to set something in —** poner algo en marcha.

(**b**) (*sign*) ademán *m*, señal *f*; **he made a — with his hand** hizo una señal con la mano.

(**c**) (*Parl etc*) moción *f*, proposición *f*; **to bring forward** (*or propose*, *US* **make**) **a —** presentar una moción; **to carry a —** (*person*) hacer adoptar una moción, (*meeting*) adoptar una moción, aprobar una moción; **to vote on a —** votar una moción; **the — is carried** se ha aprobado la moción; **the — is lost** se ha rechazado la moción.

(**d**) (*Mech*, *moving part*) mecanismo *m*.

(**e**) (*Med*) movimiento *m* del vientre.

2 *vti*: **to — (to) someone to do something** hacer señas a uno para que haga algo, indicar a uno con la mano (*etc*) que haga algo; **he —ed me to a chair** indicó con la mano que me sentara.

motionless ['məuʃənlis] *adj* inmóvil.

motion picture ['məuʃənˌpiktʃə*] (*US*) **1** *n* película *f*.

2 *attr* **motion-picture** cinematográfico; **— camera** cámara *f* cinematográfica; **— industry** industria *f* del cine; **— theatre**, (*US*) **theater** cine *m*.

motivate ['məutiveit] *vt* motivar.

motivation [ˌməutiˈveiʃən] *n* motivación *f*.

motive ['məutiv] **1** *adj* motor (*f*: motora, motriz).

2 *n* motivo *m* (*for de*); móvil *m*; **profit —** afán *m* de lucro; **ulterior —** motivo *m* oculto; **what can his — have been?** ¿cuál habrá sido su motivo?, ¿qué motivo habrá tenido?; **my —s were of the purest** lo hice con la mejor intención.

motiveless ['məutivlis] *adv* sin motivo, inmotivado.

motley ['mɔtli] **1** *adj* (*many-coloured*) abigarrado, multicolor; (*diversified*) vario, compuesto de elementos muy diversos.

2 *n* botarga *f*, traje *m* de colores; **on with the —** vistámonos de payaso.

motor ['məutə*] **1** *adj* (*giving motion*) motor; (*motorized*) automóvil.

2 *n* (*engine*) motor *m*; (*car*) coche *m*, automóvil *m*.

3 *vi* ir en coche, viajar en automóvil; **we —ed down to Ascot** fuimos en coche a Ascot; **we —ed over to see them** fuimos a visitarles (en coche).

motorbike ['məutəbaik] *n* (*fam*) moto *f*.

motorboat ['məutəbəut] *n* motora *f*, motorbote *m*, lancha *f* rápida, lancha *f* automóvil.

motor bus ['məutəbʌs] *n* autobús *m*.

motorcade ['məutəkeid] *n* caravana *f* de automóviles.

motorcar ['məutəkɑː*] *n* coche *m*, automóvil *m*.

motor coach ['məutəkəutʃ] *n* autocar *m*.

motorcycle ['məutəˌsaikl] *n* motocicleta *f*; **— combination** motocicleta *f* con sidecar.

motorcycling ['məutəˌsaikliŋ] *n* motorismo *m*.

motorcyclist ['məutəˌsaiklist] *n* motorista *mf*.

motor-driven ['məutəˌdrivn] *adj* automóvil, propulsado por motor.

-motored ['məutəd] *adj*: *eg* **four-motored** cuatrimotor, tetramotor; **petrol-motored** propulsado por gasolina.

motoring ['məutəriŋ] **1** *adj* *accident etc* de automóvil, automovilístico, de carretera; **the — public** el público aficionado al automovilismo.

2 *n* automovilismo *m*.

motoring school ['məutəriŋˌskuːl] *n* autoescuela *f*, escuela *f* automovilista.

motorist ['məutərist] *n* automovilista *mf*; conductor *m*, ora *f* (*de coche*), chófer *m*; **racing —** corredor *m* automovilista.

motorization [ˌməutərai'zeiʃən] *n* motorización *f*.

motorize ['məutəraiz] *vt* motorizar; **to get —d** (*fam*) adquirir un coche; **now that we're —d** (*fam*) ahora que tenemos coche.

motorized ['məutəraizd] *adj* motorizado.

motor launch ['məutəlɔːntʃ] *n* lancha *f* automóvil, lancha *f* motora.

motor lorry ['məutəˌlɔri] *n* camión *m*.

motorman ['məutəmən] *n*, *pl* **-men** [mən] *n* conductor *m* (*de locomotora eléctrica etc*), maquinista *m*.

motor oil ['məutərˌɔil] *n* aceite *m* para motores.

motor racing ['məutəˌreisiŋ] *n* automovilismo *m* deportivo, carreras *fpl* de coches.

motor road ['məutəˌrəud] *n* autopista *f*.

motor scooter ['məutəˌskuːtə*] *n* motosilla *f*, escúter *m*, moto *f*.

motor ship ['məutəʃip] *n* motonave *f*.

motor show ['məutəˌʃəu] *n* exposición *f* de automóviles; **the Paris —** el salón del automóvil de París.

motor spirit ['məutəˌspirit] *n* bencina *f*, gasolina *f* (*de auto*).

motor vehicle ['məutəˌviːikl] *n* automóvil *m*.

motor vessel ['məutəˌvesl] *n* motonave *f*.

motorway ['məutəwei] *n* autopista *f*.

mottled ['mɔtld] *adj* abigarrado, multicolor; *marble etc* jaspeado; *complexion* con manchas; *animal*, *bird* con manchas, moteado; **— with** con manchado de, pintado de.

motto ['mɔtəu] *n*, *pl* **mottoes** ['mɔtəuz] lema *m*; (*Heraldry*) divisa *f*; (*watchword*) consigna *f*; (*in cracker: verse*) versos *mpl*, (*joke*) chiste *m*.

mould[1], (*US*) **mold** [məuld] *n* (*soil*) mantillo *m*.

mould[2], (*US*) **mold** [məuld] **1** *n* (*hollow form*) molde *m*; (*—ed object*) cosa *f* moldeada; (*fig*) carácter *m*, índole *f*, temple *m*; **cast in a heroic —** de carácter heroico.

2 *vt* (*fashion*) moldear; (*cast*) vaciar; (*Carpentry*) moldurar; (*fig*) amoldar (*on a*), formar; **it is —ed on . . .** está hecho según . . .

3 *vr*: **to — oneself on someone** amoldarse por uno, modelarse sobre uno, tomar a uno como ejemplo.

mould³, (US) **mold** [məuld] n (fungus) moho m; (iron-) mancha f de orín.

moulder¹, (US) **molder** ['məuldə*] n (Tech) moldeador m, ora f.

moulder², (US) **molder** ['məuldə*] vi (also to — away) desmoronarse, convertirse en polvo; (fig) desmoronarse, decaer.

mouldiness, (US) **moldiness** ['məuldinis] n moho m, lo mohoso, enmohecimiento m.

moulding, (US) **molding** ['məuldiŋ] n (act) amoldamiento m; (cast) vaciado m; (Archit) moldura f; (fig) amoldamiento m, formación f.

mouldy, (US) **moldy** ['məuldi] adj mohoso, enmohecido; (sl) horrible, malísimo; miserable, cochino; **the play was —** la obra fue horrible; **all he gave me was a —** old penny lo único que me dio fue un cochino penique.

moult, (US) **molt** [məult] **1** n muda f. **2** vt mudar. **3** vi (snake etc) mudar la piel, (bird) mudar la pluma.

mound [maund] n (pile) montón m; (earthwork) terraplén m; (burial-) túmulo m; (hillock) montículo m.

mount [maunt] **1** n (a) (hill) montón m, (hillock) montículo m.
   (b) (horse etc) montura f, caballería f.
   (c) (of machine etc) base f, soporte m; (of jewel) engaste m; (of photo etc) borde m, marco m: (stamp-) fijasello m.
   2 vt (a) horse montar, subir a; platform etc subir a, subir en; ladder subir; throne subir a.
   (b) machine etc montar, armar; play poner en escena; exhibition organizar; attack lanzar, hacer.
   (c) picture poner un borde a, poner un marco a; stamp pegar, fijar; jewel engastar.
   (d) guard montar.
   (e) (provide with horse) proveer de caballo.
   3 vi (climb) subir; (get on horse) montar; (of quantity, price etc; also to — up) subir, aumentar.

mountain ['mauntin] **1** n montaña f; (pile) montón m; **to make a — out of a molehill** hacer de una pulga un elefante.
   2 adj, attr montañés, de montaña; montañero, serrano.

mountain ash ['mauntin'æʃ] n serbal m.

mountaineer [,maunti'niə*] **1** n montañero m, a f, alpinista mf. **2** vi dedicarse al montañismo, hacer alpinismo.

mountaineering [,maunti'niəriŋ] **1** n montañismo m, alpinismo m. **2** adj, attr montañero, alpinista; **in — circles** en los medios montañeros.

mountainous ['mauntinəs] adj montañoso; (fig) enorme, colosal.

mountainside ['mauntin,said] n ladera f de montaña, falda f de montaña.

mountebank ['mauntibæŋk] n saltabanco m, saltimbanqui m.

mounted ['mauntid] adj montado.

mounting ['mauntiŋ] n (of machine: act) montaje m; (frame, base) armadura f, base f, soporte m; (of jewel) engaste m; (of photo etc) marco m.

mourn [mɔ:n] **1** vt llorar, llorar la muerte de, lamentar; (wear —ing for) llevar luto por.
   2 vi afligirse, lamentarse; (wear —ing) estar de luto; **to — for someone** llorar la muerte de uno; **to — for something** llorar la pérdida (or desaparición etc) de algo; **it's no good —ing over it** de nada sirve afligirse por eso.

mourner ['mɔ:nə*] n doliente mf; (hired) plañidero m, a f; **the — s** los que acompañan el féretro.

mournful ['mɔ:nful] adj person triste, afligido; tone, sound triste, lúgubre, lastimero; occasion triste, melancólico.

mournfully ['mɔ:nfəli] adv tristemente.

mournfulness ['mɔ:nfulnis] n tristeza f; aflicción f; melancolía f.

mourning ['mɔ:niŋ] **1** n (act) lamentación f; (period etc) luto m, duelo m; (dress) luto m; **deep —** luto m riguroso; **half —** medio luto m; **to be in —** estar de luto; **to be in — for** llevar luto por; **to come out of — dejar** el luto; **to go into —** ponerse de luto; **to plunge a town into —** enlutar una ciudad.
   2 attr de luto.

mouse [maus] **1** n, pl **mice** [mais] ratón m. **2** vi cazar ratones.

mousehole ['maushəul] n ratonera f.

mouser ['mausə*] n cazador m de ratones.

mousetrap ['maustræp] n ratonera f.

moustache [məs'ta:ʃ, US 'mʌstæʃ] n bigote m, bigotes mpl, mostacho m; **walrus —** bigotes mpl de foca; **to wear a —** tener bigote.

mousy ['mausi] adj person tímido, de personalidad poco fuerte; colour pardusco.

mouth [mauθ] n, pl **mouths** [mauðz] boca f; (fig, of bottle, cave etc) boca f; (of river) desembocadura f; (of channel) embocadero m; (of wind instrument) boquilla f; **to be down in the —** estar deprimido, andar alicaído; **to foam (or froth) at the —** espumajear; **to keep one's — shut** (fig) tener la boca cerrada, guardar un secreto; **he never opened his — at the meeting** en la reunión no abrió la boca; **she didn't dare to open her —** no se atrevió a decir ni pío; **to put words into someone's —** atribuir (falsamente) una declaración a uno; **to shoot off one's —** hablar inoportunamente, hablar más de la cuenta; **to stop someone's —** hacer callar a uno; see **water** etc.

mouth [mauð] **1** vt (affectedly) pronunciar con afectación, articular con rimbombancia; (soundlessly) formar con los labios.
   2 vi hablar exagerando los movimientos de la boca.

mouthed [mauðd] adj de boca . . ., que tiene la boca . . ., eg **big-mouthed** de boca grande.

mouthful ['mauθful] n bocado m; (of smoke, air) bocanada f; **the name is a proper —** es un nombre kilométrico.

mouth organ ['mauθ,ɔ:gən] n armónica f.

mouthpiece ['mauθpi:s] n (Mus) boquilla f; (of bridle) embocadura f; (Tel) micrófono m; (fig, person) portavoz m.

mouthwash ['mauθwɔʃ] n enjuague m.

mouth-watering ['mauθ'wɔ:təriŋ] adj sumamente apetitoso.

movable ['mu:vəbl] **1** adj movible; **not easily —** nada fácil de mover. **2 —s** npl muebles mpl, mobiliario m; (Law) bienes mpl muebles.

move [mu:v] **1** n (a) (movement) movimiento m; **Spain is a country on the —** España es país en marcha; **to be always on the —** estar siempre en movimiento, (travelling) estar siempre de viaje, (of animal, child) no saber estar quieto; **to get a — on** (person) menearse, darse prisa; (process etc) hacer grandes progresos, avanzar rápidamente; **get a — on!** ¡menearse!, ¡espabílate!; **they're getting a — on with the bridge now** ahora la construcción del puente avanza rápidamente; **it's time we made a — (to go)** es hora de irnos; **it was midnight and no-one had made a —** era medianoche pero nadie se había ido.
   (b) (in game) jugada f; (at chess) jugada f, movida f; **key —** movida f clave; **it's my —** yo juego; **whose — is it?** ¿a quién le toca jugar?; **he's up to every — in the game** se las sabe todas; **to have first —** empezar, salir, jugar primero; **to make a —** hacer una jugada, jugar.
   (c) (step) paso m, acción f; gestión f; maniobra f; **the government's first —** la primera gestión del gobierno; **false —** paso m en falso; **what's the next —?** ¿qué hacemos ahora?, y ahora ¿qué?; **to make a — dar** un paso; tomar medidas; **it's up to him to make the first —** le toca a él dar el primer paso; **without making the least — to** + infin sin hacer la menor intención de + infin; **to watch someone's every —** observar a uno sin perder detalle.
   (d) (of house) mudanza f; (of person to job) traslado m; **it's our third — in two years** ésta es la tercera vez en dos años que nos mudamos; **then he made a — to Buenos Aires** luego se trasladó a Buenos Aires.
   2 vt (a) (change place of) mover; cambiar de sitio, trasladar; (transport) transportar; (propel) propulsar, impeler; **he was —d to Quito** le trasladaron a Quito; **if we can — the table a few inches sí podemos mover** la mesa unos centímetros; **to — a piece** (Chess) jugar una pieza.
   (b) **to — house** mudarse; **to — one's job** cambiar de empleo.
   (c) (cause to —) remover, agitar, sacudir, menear; **the breeze —d the leaves gently** la brisa agitaba dulcemente las hojas; **to — the bowels** desocupar el vientre.
   (d) (person, from opinion) hacer cambiar de opinión; **he will not be easily —d** no será fácil hacerle cambiar de idea.
   (e) (emotionally) conmover, enternecer; impresionar; **to be easily —d** ser impresionable, ser sensible; **to — someone to do something** mover a uno a hacer algo; **when I feel so —d** cuando estoy de humor para ello; **to — someone to anger** encolerizar a uno; **to — someone to tears** hacer que uno llore; see **pity**.
   (f) (Parl) **to — a resolution** proponer una resolución, hacer una moción; **to — that . . .** proponer que + subj.
   (g) (with adv or prep) **to — something aside**

apartar algo; **to — something away** alejar algo, apartar algo; quitar algo de en medio; **to — back** mover hacia atrás; (*postpone*) aplazar; **to — forward** mover hacia adelante; (*help progress*) avanzar, adelantar, promover; *meeting etc* adelantar la fecha de; **to — people on** hacer circular la gente; **to — someone out** desalojar a uno, trasladar a uno a otra parte; **to — up troops** mover las tropas hacia el frente; **we'll — your luggage up** le subiremos el equipaje; **to — a child up a class** trasladar a un niño a una clase superior; **he was —ed up into the next grade** le ascendieron al grado superior.

3 *vi* (**a**) (*in general*) moverse; (*to a place*) trasladarse (*to* a); (*shake*) moverse, agitarse, temblar; **—!** ¡menearse!; **she —d to the next room** fue a la habitación inmediata; **let's — into the garden** vamos al jardín; **she —s beautifully** anda con garbo; **I'll not — from here** no me muevo de aquí; **to — freely** (*part, Mech*) moverse libremente, (*person, traffic*) circular libremente; **to keep the traffic moving** mantener fluida la circulación; **keep moving!** ¡circulen!, ¡vayan pasando por delante!; **to — in high society** frecuentar la buena sociedad, alternar con personas de la buena sociedad.

(**b**) (*depart*) irse, marcharse; **it's time we were moving** es hora de irnos.

(**c**) (*travel*) ir; estar en movimiento; **we —d 100 miles that day** ese día cubrimos 100 millas; **the car was not moving** el coche no estaba en movimiento; **the bus was moving at 30 mph** el autobús iba a 30 mph; **the capsule is moving at 18,000 mph** la cápsula se desplaza a 18.000 mph; **he was certainly moving!** ¡iba como el demonio!

(**d**) (*progress*) ir adelante, avanzar, hacer progresos; (*of plants*) crecer; **things are moving at last** por fin se están haciendo progresos.

(**e**) (**— house**) mudarse, mudar de casa; **the family —d to a new house** la familia se mudó a una casa nueva.

(**f**) (*in games*) jugar, hacer una jugada; **who —s next?** ¿a quién le toca jugar?; **white —s** (*Chess*) blanco juega.

(**g**) (*take steps*) dar un paso, hacer una gestión, tomar medidas; **the government must — first** el gobierno ha de dar el primer paso; **the council —d to stop the abuse** el consejo hizo gestiones para corregir el abuso.

(**h**) (*with adv or prep*) **to — about** ir y venir, ir de acá para allá, desplazarse; moverse; **to — about freely** circular libremente; **to — along** avanzar por; **to — aside** ponerse a un lado, apartarse, quitarse de en medio; **to — away** alejarse, apartarse (*from* de); (*depart*) marcharse; (**— house**) mudar de casa; **to — back** retroceder; **to — down** bajar; **to — forward** avanzar; **to — in** tomar posesión de una casa (*etc*), instalarse en una casa (*etc*); **to — in on someone** invadir a uno; **to — off** alejarse; (*depart*) marcharse, ponerse en marcha, ponerse en camino; **to — on** (*go on*) seguir, seguir andando; reanudar el viaje; (*go forward*) avanzar; (*of time*) pasar; (*depart*) marcharse; **to — out** salir, abandonar la casa (*etc*); **we are moving out tomorrow** nos vamos mañana; **when the army —d out** cuando el ejército abandonó la ciudad (*etc*); **to — up** subir; (*in rank*) ser ascendido.

movement ['mu:vmənt] *n* (**a**) (*act*) movimiento *m*; (*of part*) juego *m*, movimiento *m*; (*of traffic etc*) circulación *f*; (*on stock exchange*) actividad *f*, (*change of price*) cambio *m* de precio; (*Med*) evacuación *f*; **encircling —** movimiento *m* envolvente; **upward —** movimiento *m* ascensional; **to be in —** estar en movimiento; **there was a — towards the door** se dirigieron algunos hacia la puerta.

(**b**) (*Pol*) movimiento *m*; **he founded the M— in 1936** fundó el Movimiento en 1936.

(**c**) (*Mus*) tiempo *m*.

(**d**) (*Mech, part*) mecanismo *m*.

mover ['mu:və*] *n* (*of motion*) autor *m*, ora *f*; **prime — ** (*Mech*) máquina *f* motriz; (*Philos*) primer motor *m*; (*person*) promotor *m*, ora *f*.

movie ['mu:vi] *n* (*US*) película *f*; **the —s** el cine; **to go to the —s** ir al cine.

movie camera ['mu:vi,kæmərə] *n* (*US*) cámara *f* cinematográfica.

moviegoer ['mu:vi,gəuə*] *n* (*US*) aficionado *m* al cine, aficionada *f* al cine.

movie house ['mu:vihaus] *n*, *pl* **— houses** [,hauziz] (*US*) cine *m*.

movieland ['mu:vilænd] *n* (*US*) (*dreamworld*) mundo *m* de ensueño creado por el cine; (*eg Hollywood*) centro *m* de la industria cinematográfica.

moving ['mu:viŋ] *adj* (*that moves*) movedor; movedizo; *part, staircase etc* móvil; (*motive*) motor; (*fig*) conmovedor; emocionante.

movingly ['mu:viŋli] *adv* de modo conmovedor; **he spoke most —** conmovió profundamente a los que le escuchaban.

mow [məu] (*irr: pret* **mowed**, *ptp* **mown** *or* **mowed**) *vt corn etc* segar; *grass* cortar; **to — down** segar.

mower ['məuə*] *n* segador *m*, ora *f*; (*lawn-*) cortacésped *m*.

mowing ['məuiŋ] *n* siega *f*.

mowing machine ['məuiŋmə,ʃi:n] *n* segadora *f* (mecánica).

mown [məun] *ptp of* **mow**.

Mozarab [mɔzˈærəb] *n* mozárabe *mf*.

Mozarabic [mɔzˈærəbik] **1** *adj* mozárabe. **2** *n* (*dialect*) mozárabe *m*.

much [mʌtʃ] **1** *adj* mucho; **— money** mucho dinero; **how — money?** ¿cuánto dinero?

2 *adv* (**a**) mucho; (*before ptp*) muy; **— better** mucho mejor; **— pleased** muy satisfecho; **it doesn't — matter** no importa mucho; **he's — richer than I (am)** es mucho más rico que yo; **ever so —** muchísimo; **not —** no mucho, poco; **— to my astonishment** con gran sorpresa mía.

(**b**) (*by far*) con mucho; **— the biggest** con mucho el más grande; **I would — rather stay** prefiero con mucho quedarme.

(**c**) (*almost*) casi, más o menos; **they are — of an age** tienen casi la misma edad; **they're — the same size** tienen más o menos el mismo tamaño.

(**d**) **how — is it?** ¿cuánto es?, ¿cuánto vale?; **how — is it a kilo?** ¿cuánto vale el kilo de esto?

(**e**) **however —** he tries por mucho que se esfuerce.

3 *n*: **but — remains** pero queda mucho; **— of this is true** gran parte de esto es verdad; **we don't see — of each other** nos vemos poco; **there's not — to do** no hay mucho que hacer; **it's not up to —** no vale gran cosa; **I'm not — of a musician** yo sé muy poco de música, entiendo poco de música, como músico no sirvo para nada; **he's not — of a player** como jugador no vale mucho; **that wasn't — of a dinner** eso apenas se podía llamar cena; **to make — of someone** mimar a uno, hacer fiestas a uno; agasajar a uno; **to make — of something** dar mucha importancia a algo; subrayar la importancia de algo.

4 (*with* as, so, too) (**a**) **— as I should like to** por más que yo quisiera; **— as I would like to go** por mucho que me gustara ir; **— as I like him** aunque le quiero mucho.

(**b**) (**as —**) **as — again** otro tanto; **three times as — tea** tres veces la cantidad de té; **I thought as — ** ya me lo figuraba, lo había previsto ya.

(**c**) (**as — as, so — as**) **he has as — money as you** tiene tanto dinero como Vd; **he spends as — as he earns** gasta tanto como gana; **I have three times as — as I can eat** tengo tres veces más de lo que puedo comer; **it's as — as I can do to stand up** apenas puedo ponerme de pie; **as — as to say . . .** como si dijera . . .; **the problem is not so — one of modernization as of investment** el problema más que de modernización es de inversión; **he went without saying so — as a single word** se fue sin decir una sola palabra siquiera; **I haven't so — as a penny** no tengo ni un solo penique.

(**d**) (**so —**) **so — bad weather** tanto mal tiempo; **it has been so —** exagerated se ha exagerado tanto; **we don't go out so —** now ahora no salimos tanto; **so — the better** tanto mejor; **so — for that!** ¡allá eso!; ¡ya se acabó aquello!; **that's so — the less to pay** tanto menos habrá que pagar; **at so — a pound** a tantas pesetas (*etc*) la libra; **so — so that . . .** tanto que . . .

(**e**) (**too —**) demasiado;¿ **he talks too —** habla demasiado; **too — jam** demasiada mermelada *f*, exceso *m* de mermelada; **you gave me sixpence too — ** Vd me dio seis peniques de más; **that's too — by half** de eso sobra la mitad; **don't make too — of it** no exageres la importancia de esto.

muchness ['mʌtʃnis] *n*: **they're much of a —** son casi lo mismo.

mucilage ['mju:silidʒ] *n* mucílago *m*.

mucilaginous [,mju:si'lædʒinəs] *adj* mucilaginoso.

muck [mʌk] **1** *n* (**a**) (*dung*) estiércol *m*; (*dirt*) suciedad *f*, inmundicias *fpl*, mierda *f*; **to be in a —** estar sucio.

(**b**) (*fig*) porquería *f*; **the article is just —** el artículo es una porquería.

2 *vt* (**a**) **to — out a stable** limpiar una cuadra; **to — up** (*dirty*) ensuciar.

(**b**) **to — someone about** fastidiar a uno, desorientar a uno (cambiando una cita *etc* con él); **to —**

up (disarrange) desarreglar, desordenar; (ruin) arruinar, estropear, echar a perder; affair, deal fracasar en, (deliberately) chafar.

3 vi: **to — about** perder el tiempo, ocuparse en fruslerías, trabajar (etc) con poca seriedad; **he enjoys —ing about in boats** le gusta entretener sus ocios navegando (etc) en bote; **stop —ing about!** ¡déjate de tonterías!; **to — about with something** (handle) manosear algo, tocar algo, (amuse oneself) divertirse con algo, (break) romper algo, estropear algo.

muckiness ['mʌkinis] n suciedad f.

muckrake ['mʌkreik] vi remover el pasado; buscar y revelar cosas vergonzosas en la vida de otros, escarbar vidas ajenas.

muckraker ['mʌk,reikə*] n escarbador m de vidas ajenas, escarbadora f de vidas ajenas.

muck-up ['mʌkʌp] n (fam) lío m grande; fracaso m total; **what a —!** ¡qué faena! (fam); **that — with the timetable** ese lío que nos armamos con el horario.

mucky ['mʌki] adj sucio; puerco; asqueroso; **to get oneself all —** ensuciarse; **to get one's dress all —** ensuciar el vestido.

mucous ['mju:kəs] adj mucoso; **— membrane** mucosa f.

mucus ['mju:kəs] n moco m, mocosidad f.

mud [mʌd] **1** n lodo m, barro m, fango m; (fig) fango m; **to stick in the —** (cart) atascarse, atollarse, (ship) embarrancarse; **— in your eye!** ¡salud y pesetas!; **his name is —** tiene una reputación malísima, no se le estima en nada; **if people hear this my name will be —** si esto llega a saberse estoy perdido; **to drag someone's name through the —** llenar a uno de fango; **to sling** (or **throw**) **— at someone** vilipendiar a uno.

2 attr: **— hut** choza f de barro; **— wall** tapia f.

mudbank ['mʌdbæŋk] n banco m de arena.

mudbath ['mʌdba:θ] n, pl **-baths** [ba:ðz] baño m de lodo, lodos mpl.

muddle ['mʌdl] **1** n (a) (disorder) desorden m, confusión f; **you should have seen what a — there was in the room!** ¡había que ver el desorden que había en el cuarto!; **what a —!** ¡qué confusión!; **how did things get into such a —?** ¿cómo se produjo tanta confusión?

(b) (perplexity) perplejidad f, confusión f; **now I'm all in a —** ahora estoy totalmente confuso.

(c) (mix-up) embrollo m, lío m; **there was a — over the seats** hubo un lío con las entradas; **to get into a —** embrollarse; **to get into a — with one's accounts** armarse un lío con las cuentas; **what a —!** ¡qué lío!, ¡qué faena!

2 vt (also **to — up**) **(a)** things embrollar, confundir; introducir el desorden en; **you've —d up A and B** has confundido A con B.

(b) person aturdir, dejar perplejo, confundir; **I was properly —d** estaba totalmente confuso; **to get —d** aturdirse; armarse un lío.

3 vi: **to — along, to — through** salir del paso sin saber cómo; **I expect we shall — through** espero que lo logremos de algún modo u otro.

muddle-headed ['mʌdl,hedid] adj person atontado, de ideas nada claras; ideas confuso.

muddy ['mʌdi] **1** adj place lodoso, fangoso; hands, dress etc cubierto de lodo; liquid turbio; complexion cetrino.

2 vt enlodar; cubrir de lodo; hands, dress etc manchar de lodo; liquid enturbiar.

mud flats ['mʌdflæts] npl marisma f.

mudguard ['mʌdga:d] n guardabarros m.

mudlark ['mʌdla:k] n galopín m.

mudpack ['mʌdpæk] n mascarilla f facial de barro.

mud-slinging ['mʌd,sliŋiŋ] n injurias fpl, vilipendio m.

muezzin [mu:'ezin] n almuecín m, almuédano m.

muff¹ [mʌf] n manguito m (also Tech).

muff² [mʌf] vt ball dejar escapar; catch, stop no lograr por torpeza; shot errar; chance perder, desperdiciar; entrance, lines (Theat) estropear; **to — it** fracasar, hacerlo malísimamente, no lograrlo por torpeza.

muffin ['mʌfin] n (approx) mollete m.

muffle ['mʌfl] **1** vt **(a)** (also **to — up**) envolver; person etc embozar, tapar (with de); **—d up** in embozado de. **(b)** noise amortiguar, apagar; noisy thing amortiguar el ruido de; bells, oars envolver con tela; drum enfundar.

2 vi = **3** vr: **to — oneself up** embozarse, taparse.

muffled ['mʌfld] adj sound sordo, apagado.

muffler ['mʌflə*] n (scarf) bufanda f; (Mus) sordina f; (Mech) silenciador m.

mufti ['mʌfti] n traje m de paisano; **in —** vestido de paisano.

mug [mʌg] **1** n **(a)** (cup) taza f (alta, sin platillo); (for beer) pichel m, barro m, jarra f.

(b) (person: sl) bobo m, primo m; **what a — I've been!** ¡he sido un tonto!

(c) (face: sl) jeta f (sl), hocico m (sl); **what a — she's got!** ¡qué jeta tiene!; **he hit him in the —** le pegó un tortazo en el hocico.

2 vt (US sl) asaltar, pegar; **to — up** (sl) aprender (or estudiar etc) sin interés.

mugging ['mʌgiŋ] n (US sl) asalto m, vapuleo m.

muggins ['mʌginz] n sing (sl) tonto m, primo m; **— will pay for it** este pobre hombre lo pagará.

muggy ['mʌgi] adj húmedo y sofocante, bochornoso.

mugwump ['mʌgwʌmp] n (US Pol) votante que no es miembro de ningún partido.

mulatto [mju:'lætəu] **1** adj mulato. **2** n, pl **mulattoes** [mju:'lætəuz] mulato m, a f.

mulberry ['mʌlbəri] n (fruit) mora f; (tree) morera f, moral m.

mulch [mʌltʃ] **1** n capa f de hierba, paja, hojas (etc). **2** vt cubrir con una capa de hierba, paja, hojas (etc).

mulct [mʌlkt] vt multar; **to — someone of something** quitar algo a uno, privar a uno de algo.

mule¹ [mju:l] n mulo m, a f; (person) testarudo m, a f; (Tech) máquina f de hilar intermitente, selfactina f.

mule² [mju:l] n (slipper) babucha f.

muleteer [,mju:li'tiə*] n mulatero m, arriero m.

mule track ['mju:ltræk] n camino m de herradura.

mulish ['mju:liʃ] adj terco, testarudo.

mulishness ['mju:liʃnis] n terquedad f, testarudez f.

mull¹ [mʌl] vt wine calentar con especias.

mull² [mʌl] vt: **to — something over** meditar algo, reflexionar sobre algo.

mullet ['mʌlit] n: **grey —** mújol m; **red —** salmonete m.

mullion ['mʌliən] n parteluz m.

mullioned ['mʌliənd] adj window dividido con parteluz.

multi . . . ['mʌlti] multi . . .

multichannel ['mʌlti'tʃænl] adj (TV) multicanal.

multicoloured, (US) —colored ['mʌlti'kʌləd] adj multicolor.

multifarious [,mʌlti'fɛəriəs] adj múltiple.

multiform ['mʌltifɔ:m] adj multiforme.

multilateral ['mʌlti'lætərəl] adj multilátero.

multimillionaire ['mʌltimiljə'nɛə*] n multimillonario m, a f.

multiple ['mʌltipl] **1** adj (of many parts) múltiplo; (in pl, many and various) múltiple; firm con muchas sucursales; **— stores** cadena f de grandes almacenes.

2 n múltiplo m; **lowest common —** mínimo común múltiplo m.

multiplicand [,mʌltipli'kænd] n multiplicando m.

multiplication [,mʌltipli'keiʃən] n multiplicación f.

multiplicity [,mʌlti'plisiti] n multiplicidad f; **for a — of reasons** por múltiples razones; **a — of solutions** una gran diversidad de soluciones.

multiply ['mʌltiplai] **1** vt multiplicar; **to — 8 by 7** multiplicar 8 por 7. **2** vi multiplicarse.

multiracial ['mʌlti'reiʃəl] adj multirracial.

multitude ['mʌltitju:d] n multitud f; **the —** (pej) las masas, la plebe; **for a — of reasons** por múltiples razones; **they came in —s** acudieron en tropel.

multitudinous [,mʌlti'tju:dinəs] adj multitudinario; muy numeroso, numerosísimo.

mum¹ [mʌm] adj: **—'s the word!** ¡punto en boca!; **to keep —** callarse; **see that you keep — about it** de esto no digas ni pío; **everybody is keeping very — about it** esto lo tienen todos muy secreto.

mum² [mʌm] n (fam) mamá f (fam).

mumble ['mʌmbl] **1** n: **he said in a —** dijo refunfuñando, dijo entre dientes. **2** vt decir entre dientes. **3** vi musitar, refunfuñar, hablar entre dientes.

mumbo jumbo ['mʌmbəu'dʒʌmbəu] n (cult) fetiche m; (spell) conjuro m; (empty ritual) mistificación f, farsa f.

mummer ['mʌmə*] n máscara mf.

mummery ['mʌməri] n (fig) mistificación f; ceremonia f ridícula, farsa f.

mummification [,mʌmifi'keiʃən] n momificación f.

mummify ['mʌmifai] **1** vt momificar. **2** vi momificarse.

mummy¹ ['mʌmi] n (Hist) momia f.

mummy² ['mʌmi] n (fam) mamá f (fam).

mumps [mʌmps] n sing paperas fpl, parótidas fpl.

munch [mʌntʃ] vt mascar, ronzar.

mundane ['mʌn'dein] adj mundano; (humdrum) vulgar, trivial.

municipal [mju:'nisipəl] adj municipal.

municipality [mju:,nisi'pæliti] n municipio m.

munificence [mju:'nifisns] n munificencia f.

munificent [mju:'nifisnt] adj munífico.

muniments ['mju:nimənts] *npl* documentos *mpl* (probatorios); (*also* — **room**) archivos *mpl*.

munitions [mju:'nifənz] *npl* municiones *fpl*; — **dump** depósito *m* de municiones.

mural ['mjuərəl] **1** *adj* mural. **2** *n* pintura *f* mural, mural *m*.

murder ['mə:də*] **1** *n* (a) asesinato *m*, (*as Law term*) homicidio *m*; **accused of** — acusado de homicidio; **wilful** —, — **in the first degree** homicidio *m* premeditado.
(b) (*fam*) **it was** —! ¡un horror!; **to cry** —, **to shout blue** — protestar enérgicamente, poner el grito en el cielo; **she could get away with** — hace lo que quiere y siempre sale impune.
2 *vt* asesinar; matar, dar muerte a; *song etc* arruinar, estropear; *play* degollar.

murderer ['mə:dərə*] *n* asesino *m*, (*as Law term*) homicida *m*.

murderess ['mə:dəris] *n* asesina *f*, (*as Law term*) homicida *f*.

murderous ['mə:dərəs] *adj* homicida; (*fig*) cruel, feroz, sanguinario; (*fam*) fatal, horroroso.

murk [mə:k] *n* oscuridad *f*, tinieblas *fpl*.

murkiness ['mə:kinis] *n* oscuridad *f*, lobreguez *f*; (*fig*) lo tenebroso, lo turbio.

murky ['mə:ki] *adj* oscuro, lóbrego; (*fig*) tenebroso, turbio.

murmur ['mə:mə*] **1** *n* (*soft speech*) murmullo *m*; (*of water*) murmullo *m*, murmurio *m*; (*of leaves etc*) susurro *m*; (*of distant traffic etc*) rumor *m*; (*complaint*) queja *f*, murmurio *m*; **there were** —**s of disagreement** hubo murmurios de disconformidad.
2 *vt* murmurar, decir en voz baja.
3 *vi* murmullar, murmurar; susurrar; quejarse; **to** — **about, to** — **against** murmurar de, quejarse de.

muscatel [,mʌskə'tel] **1** *adj* moscatel. **2** *n* moscatel *m*.

muscle ['mʌsl] **1** *n* músculo *m*; (*fig*) fuerza *f* muscular; **he never moved a** — se mantuvo inmóvil, no se inmutó en absoluto; **to flex one's** —**s** preparar su musculatura.
2 *vi*: **to** — **in** (*sl*) introducirse por fuerza (**on** a deal en un negocio).

musclebound ['mʌslbaund] *adj* envarado por exceso de ejercicio, con calambre en los músculos.

Muscovite ['mʌskəvait] **1** *adj* moscovita. **2** *n* moscovita *mf*.

muscular ['mʌskjulə*] *adj* *tissue etc* muscular; (*having muscles*) musculoso; (*brawny*) fornido, membrudo.

musculature ['mʌskjulətjuə*] *n* musculatura *f*.

Muse [mju:z] *n* musa *f*; **the** —**s** las Musas.

muse [mju:z] *vi* meditar, reflexionar, rumiar; **to** — **about something, to** — **on something** meditar algo, reflexionar sobre algo; **to** — **on a scene** contemplar distraído una escena; **"yes", he** —**d "sí"**, dijo distraído.

museum [mju:'ziəm] *n* museo *m*; **archaeological** — museo *m* arqueológico; **the British M**— el Museo Británico.

museum piece [mju:'ziəm,pi:s] *n* (*fig*) cosa *f* anticuada, antigualla *f*; **the car is a real** — el coche realmente es digno de estar en un museo.

mush [mʌʃ] *n* gachas *fpl*; masa *f* blanda y espesa; (*fig*) sensiblería *f*, sentimentalismo *m*.

mushroom ['mʌʃrum] **1** *n* seta *f*, hongo *m*; (*as food*) champiñón *m*; **a great** — **of smoke** un enorme hongo de humo; **to grow like** —**s** surgir como hongos, crecer de la noche a la mañana.
2 *adj*: — **town** ciudad *f* que aparece de la noche a la mañana.
3 *vi* (*town etc*) surgir como hongos, crecer de la noche a la mañana, crecer rapidísimamente; **the cloud of smoke went** —**ing up** subió el humo en forma de hongo; **to** — **into** convertirse rapidísimamente en.

mushy ['mʌʃi] *adj* pulposo, mollar, como gachas; (*fig*) sensiblero, muy sentimental.

music ['mju:zik] *n* música *f*; — **of the spheres** música *f* mundana, armonía *f* celestial; **to face the** — pagar el pato; **to set a work to** — poner música a una obra.

musical ['mju:zikəl] **1** *adj* (a) musical; *instrument, composition etc* músico; *sound, voice* armonioso, melodioso.
(b) **he's very** — tiene mucho talento para la música; **he comes from a** — **family** es de familia de músicos.
2 *n* comedia *f* musical.

musical box ['mju:zik'bɒks] *n* caja *f* de música.

musicale [mju:zi'ka:l] *n* velada *f* musical.

musically ['mju:zikəli] *adv* armoniosamente, melodiosamente.

music hall ['mju:zikhɔ:l] *n* teatro *m* de variedades.

musician [mju:'ziʃən] *n* músico *m*, a *f*.

musicianship [mju:'ziʃənʃip] *n* maestría *f* musical.

music lover ['mju:zik,lʌvə*] *n* persona *f* aficionada a la música.

musicologist [,mju:zi'kɒlədʒist] *n* musicólogo *m*.

musicology [,mju:zi'kɒlədʒi] *n* musicología *f*.

music paper ['mju:zik,peipə*] *n* papel *m* de música.

music stand ['mju:zikstænd] *n* atril *m*.

musingly ['mju:ziŋli] *adv* *say etc* con aire distraído, pensativamente.

musk [mʌsk] *n* (*substance*) almizcle *m*; (*scent*) perfume *m* de almizcle; (*smell*) olor *m* a almizcle; (*Bot*) almizcleña *f*.

musket ['mʌskit] *n* mosquete *m*.

musketeer [,mʌski'tiə*] *n* mosquetero *m*.

musketry ['mʌskitri] *n* (*muskets*) mosquetes *mpl*; (*troops*) mosquetería *f*; (*firing*) fuego *m* de mosquetes, tiros *mpl*.

muskmelon ['mʌskmelən] *n* melón *m*.

musk ox ['mʌskɒks] *n*, *pl* — **oxen** [ɒksən] buey *m* almizclado.

muskrat ['mʌskræt] *n* rata *f* almizclera.

musk rose ['mʌskrəuz] *n* rosa *f* almizcleña.

musky ['mʌski] *adj* almizcleño, almizclado; *smell* a almizcle.

Muslim ['muslim] *see* **Moslem**; **Black** — musulmán *m* negro.

muslin ['mʌzlin] **1** *n* muselina *f*. **2** *adj*, *attr* de muselina.

musquash ['mʌskwɒʃ] *n* rata *f* almizclera; (*fur*) piel *f* de rata almizclera.

muss [mʌs] *vt* (*also* **to** — **up**) *hair* desarreglar, despeinar; *dress* ajar, chafar.

mussel ['mʌsl] *n* mejillón *m*.

mussel bed ['mʌslbed] *n* criadero *m* de mejillones.

Mussulman ['mʌslmən] *see* **Moslem**.

must[1] [mʌst] *n* (*of wine*) mosto *m*.

must[2] [mʌst] *n* *see* **mustiness**.

must[3] [mʌst] *v aux* (*present tense only*) **1** (a) (*obligation*) **I** — **do it** debo hacerlo, tengo que hacerlo, he de hacerlo; **one** — **be careful** hay que tener cuidado; **one** — **not be too hopeful** no hay que ser demasiado optimista; **the patient** — **have complete quiet** el enfermo precisa silencio absoluto; **but you** — **come** pero es imprescindible que vengas; **do it if you** — hágalo si es necesario, hágalo si no hay más remedio; **there** — **be a reason** debe haber una razón, ha de haber una razón.
(b) (*probability*) **he** — **be there by now** ya debe de estar allí, ya estará allí; **it** — **be cold up there** hará frío allá arriba; **it** — **be about 3 o'clock** serán las 3; **it** — **have been about 5** serían alrededor de las 5; **but you** — **have seen him!** ¡pero debes haberle visto!; **he** — **be a Mexican** debe de ser mejicano.
2 *n* (*fam*) **this programme is a** — **for everybody** este programa no lo ha de perder ningún oyente, es imprescindible que todos los oyentes escuchen este programa.

mustache ['mʌstæʃ] *n* (*US*) *see* **moustache**.

mustang ['mʌstæŋ] *n* potro *m* mesteño.

mustard ['mʌstəd] *n* mostaza *f*.

mustard gas ['mʌstədgæs] *n* gas *m* mostaza.

mustard plaster ['mʌstəd'pla:stə*] *n* sinapismo *m*, cataplasma *f* de mostaza.

mustard pot ['mʌstədpɒt] *n* mostacera *f*.

muster ['mʌstə*] **1** *n* (*gathering*) asamblea *f* (*also* Mil), reunión *f*; (*review*) revista *f*; (*list*) lista *f*, matrícula *f*, (Naut) lista *f*; **to pass** — pasar revista, (*fig*) ser aceptable, ser satisfactorio.
2 *vt* (*call together for inspection*) llamar a asamblea, juntar para pasar revista; (*collect*) juntar, reunir; (*also* **to** — **up**) *courage, strength* cobrar; **the club can** — **20 members** el club cuenta con 20 miembros, el club consiste en 20 miembros.
3 *vi* juntarse, reunirse.

mustiness ['mʌstinis] *n* moho *m*; ranciedad *f*; (*of room etc*) olor *m* a humedad, olor *m* a cerrado.

mustn't ['mʌsnt] = **must not**.

musty ['mʌsti] *adj* mohoso; rancio; *room etc* que huele a humedad, que huele a cerrado; *joke etc* viejo, gastado.

mutability [,mju:tə'biliti] *n* mutabilidad *f*.

mutable ['mju:təbl] *adj* mudable.

mutant ['mju:tənt] *n* mutante *m*.

mutate [mju:'teit] **1** *vt* mudar. **2** *vi* sufrir mutación.

mutation [mju:'teiʃən] *n* mutación *f*.

mute [mju:t] **1** *adj* mudo, silencioso; **with H** — con hache muda; **to become** — enmudecer.
2 *n* (*person*) mudo *m*, a *f*; (Mus) sordina *f*; (Gram) letra *f* muda.
3 *vt* (Mus) poner sordina a; *noise* amortiguar, apagar.

muted ['mju:tid] *adj noise* sordo, apagado; *criticism* callado.

mutilate ['mju:tileit] *vt* mutilar.

mutilation [ˌmjuti'leiʃən] *n* mutilación *f.*

mutineer [ˌmju:ti'niə*] *n* amotinado *m*, amotinador *m.*

mutinous ['mju:tinəs] *adj* amotinado; (*fig*) turbulento, rebelde; **we were feeling pretty —** estábamos hartos ya, estábamos dispuestos a rebelarnos.

mutiny ['mju:tini] **1** *n* motín *m*, sublevación *f.* **2** *vi* amotinarse, sublevarse.

mutt [mʌt] *n* (*sl*) bobo *m.*

mutter ['mʌtə*] **1** *n* murmullo *m*; **a — of voices** un rumor de voces.
2 *vt* murmurar, decir entre dientes; **"yes", he —ed** "sí", refunfuñó.
3 *vi* murmurar; (*guns, thunder*) retumbar a lo lejos.

mutton ['mʌtn] *n* carne *f* de cordero.

mutton chop ['mʌtn'tʃɔp] *n* chuleta *f* de cordero.

mutual ['mju:tjuəl] *adj* mutuo; (*loosely*) común; **the feeling is —** yo comparto esa opinión, lo mismo digo yo; **our — friend** nuestro amigo; **their — friend** el amigo de los dos, el amigo que tienen en común.

mutuality [ˌmju:tju'æliti] *n* mutualidad *f.*

mutually ['mju:tjuəli] *adv* mutuamente.

muzzle ['mʌzl] **1** *n* (*snout*) hocico *m*; (*for dog*) bozal *m*; (*of gun*) boca *f.* **2** *vt dog* abozalar; *criticism etc* estorbar; *critic* amordazar, imponer silencio a.

muzzle loader ['mʌzlˌləudə*] *n* arma *f* que se carga por la boca.

muzzy ['mʌzi] *adj* (*from drinking*) confuso, atontado; *outline* borroso.

my [mai, mi] **1** *poss adj* mi. **2** *interj* ¡caramba!

mycology [mai'kɔlədʒi] *n* micología *f.*

myopia [mai'əupiə] *n* miopía *f.*

myopic [mai'ɔpik] *adj* miope.

myriad ['miriəd] **1** *n* miríada *f.* **2** *adj*: **a — flies** miríadas de moscas.

myrmidon ['mə:midən] *n* secuaz *m* fiel, satélite *m*, esbirro *m.*

myrrh [mə:*] *n* mirra *f.*

myrtle ['mə:tl] *n* arrayán *m*, mirto *m.*

myself [mai'self] *pron* (*subject*) yo mismo, yo misma; (*acc, dat*) me; (*after prep*) mí (mismo, misma); *see* oneself.

mysterious [mis'tiəriəs] *adj* misterioso.

mysteriously [mis'tiəriəsli] *adv* misteriosamente.

mystery ['mistəri] *n* misterio *m*; (*Theat*) auto *m*, misterio *m*; **he's a — man** es un hombre misterioso; **there's no — about it** aquí no hay misterio; **it's a — to me where it can have gone** no tengo la menor idea de dónde se habrá metido; **to make a great — out of a matter** envolver un asunto en un ambiente de misterio.

mystery play ['mistəriˌplei] *n* auto *m*, misterio *m.*

mystic ['mistik] **1** *adj* místico. **2** *n* místico *m*, a *f.*

mystical ['mistikəl] *adj* místico.

mysticism ['mistisizəm] *n* misticismo *m*; (*doctrine, literary genre*) mística *f.*

mystification [ˌmistifi'keiʃən] *n* misterio *m*; confusión *f*, perplejidad *f*; **why all the —?** ¿por qué tanto misterio?; **my — increased** creció mi perplejidad.

mystify ['mistifai] *vt* dejar perplejo, desorientar, desconcertar; **I am mystified** estoy perplejo; **it completely mystified him** le desorientó por completo, le despistó por completo.

mystique [mis'ti:k] *n* misterio *m* (profesional *etc*), técnica *f* (al parecer) misteriosa, pericia *f* impresionante.

myth [miθ] *n* mito *m.*

mythic(al) ['miθik(ə)l] *adj* mítico.

mythological [ˌmiθə'lɔdʒikəl] *adj* mitológico.

mythology [mi'θɔlədʒi] *n* mitología *f.*

myxomatosis [ˌmiksəumə'təusis] *n* mixomatosis *f.*

N

nab [næb] *vt* coger, echar el guante a; (*arrest*) prender.
nabob ['neibɔb] *n* nabab *m*.
nacelle [næ'sel] *n* (*Aer*) barquilla *f*, góndola *f*.
nacre ['neikə*] *n* nácar *m*.
nacreous ['neikriəs] *adj* nacarino, nacarado, de nácar.
nadir ['neidiə*] *n* nadir *m*; (*fig*) punto *m* más bajo.
nag¹ [næg] *n* jaca *f*; (*pej*) rocín *m*.
nag² [næg] **1** *vt* (*scold*) regañar; (*annoy*) importunar, fastidiar; criticar; **don't — me so!** ¡no machaques!; **his conscience —ged him** le remordía la conciencia; **he was —ged by doubts** le asaltaron dudas; **she —s him all day long** ella le importuna con sus quejas todo el día.
  2 *vi* ser regañón, ser importuno, criticar, quejarse; **to — at someone** importunar a uno, criticar a uno; **don't —, woman!** ¡no machaques, mujer!
nagging ['nægiŋ] **1** *adj person* regañón, criticón; *pain* continuo; *conscience* nada tranquilo; *doubt, fear etc* persistente, que no se desvanece.
  2 *n* importunar *m*; críticas *fpl*; quejas *fpl*.
naiad ['naiæd] *n* náyade *f*.
nail [neil] **1** *n* (**a**) (*Anat*) uña *f*; (*of animal*) garra *f*; **to bite one's —s** comerse las uñas.
  (**b**) (*metal*) clavo *m*; **to hit the — on the head** dar en el clavo, acertar; **to pay on the —** pagar a toca teja.
  2 *vt* clavar, enclavar; adornar con clavos, clavetear; (*catch, get hold of*) coger; *lie* acabar con; *rumour etc* desmentir, demostrar la falsedad de; **to — something down** clavar algo, sujetar algo con clavos; **to — someone down** poner a uno entre la espada y la pared; **we —ed him down to come tomorrow** le comprometimos a que viniera mañana; **you can't — him down** es imposible hacerle concretar; **to — two things together** fijar (*or* unir) dos cosas con clavos; **to — something up** cerrar algo con clavos.
nail-biting ['neil,baitiŋ] *n* mala costumbre *f* de comerse las uñas.
nailbrush ['neilbrʌʃ] *n* cepillo *m* para las uñas.
nailfile ['neilfail] *n* lima *f* para las uñas.
nail polish ['neil,pɔliʃ] *n*, **— varnish** [,va:niʃ] *n* esmalte *m* para las uñas, laca *f* para las uñas; **— remover** quita-esmalte *m*.
nail scissors ['neil,sizəz] *npl* tijeras *fpl* para las uñas.
naïve [nai'i:v] *adj* ingenuo, cándido, sencillo.
naïvely [nai'i:vli] *adv* ingenuamente.
naïveté *n*, **naïvety** [nai'i:vti] *n* ingenuidad *f*, candor *m*, sencillez *f*.
naked ['neikid] *adj* desnudo; (*fig*) desabrigado, indefenso; *flame* expuesto al aire; *lamp* sin pantalla; *sword* desenvainado; *attempt* abierto, manifiesto; **the — truth** la verdad lisa y llana; **stark —** en cueros, en pelota, como le parió su madre; **to go —** ir desnudo; **to strip someone** —desnudar a uno completamente, dejar a uno en cueros.
nakedness ['neikidnis] *n* desnudez *f*.
namby-pamby ['næmbi'pæmbi] **1** *adj* soso, ñoño.
  2 *n* persona *f* sosa, ñoño *m*, a *f*.
name [neim] **1** *n* (**a**) nombre *m*; designación *f*; (*surname*) apellido *m*; (*nickname*) apodo *m*; (*of book etc*) título *m*; **Christian —, first —** nombre *m* de pila; **full —** (*in Spain*) nombre *m* y apellidos; **maiden —** apellido *m* de soltera; **married —** apellido *m* de casada; **pet —** nombre *m* cariñoso, (*short form*) diminutivo *m* afectuoso; **proper —** nombre *m* propio; **by — de nombre; Pérez by —** de nombre Pérez, llamado Pérez; **a lady by the — of Dulcinea** una señora llamada Dulcinea; **I know him by — only** le conozco solamente de nombre; **we know it by** (*or* **under**) **another —** lo conocemos bajo otro nombre; **to go by** (*or* **under**) **the — of** ser conocido por el nombre de, vivir bajo el nombre de; **in — de** nombre; **he was king in — only** era rey tan sólo de

nombre, de rey no tenía más que el nombre; **it exists in — only** no existe sino de nombre; **at least in —** al menos nominalmente; **in the — of peace en** nombre de la paz; **I thank you in the — of all those present** le doy las gracias en nombre de todos los asistentes; **open up, in the — of the law!** ¡abran en nombre de la ley!; **what's in a —?** ¿qué importa el nombre?; **he hasn't a penny to his —** no tiene donde caerse muerto; **what's your —?** ¿cómo se llama?; **my — is Peter** me llamo Pedro; **I'll do it, or my —'s not Bloggs!** ¡como me llamo Bloggs, que lo haré!; **to call someone —s** poner motes a uno, llenar a uno de injurias; **what — are they giving the child?** ¿qué nombre le van a poner al niño?; **they married to give the child a —** se casaron para legitimar al niño; **to mention no —s** no mencionar nombres; **to put one's — down for a car** solicitar un coche; **what — shall I say?** (*Tel*) ¿ de parte de quién?; (*announcing arrival*) ¿qué nombre quiere que diga?; **to send in one's —** presentarse; **to take someone's — and address** apuntar las señas de uno.
  (**b**) (*reputation*) nombre *m*; reputación *f*, fama *f*; **the firm has a good —** la casa tiene buena reputación; **he has a — for carelessness** es sabido que es bastante descuidado, tiene fama de poco cuidadoso; **his middle — is "lover"** le han apodado "el enamorado"; **to get (oneself) a bad —** crearse una mala reputación; **to make a — for oneself** darse a conocer, empezar a ser conocido (*as* como); **to make one's —** llegar a ser famoso.
  (**c**) (*person*) **big —** gran figura *f*, personaje *m* de relieve; **he's one of the big —s in the business** es uno de los personajes importantes en ese campo.
  2 *vt* (*call: thing*) llamar; designar, denominar; (*person*) llamar, (*at birth*) bautizar, poner de nombre a; (*surname*) apellidar; (*mention*) mencionar, mentar; (*nominate*) nombrar; (*date, price etc*) fijar, señalar; **a man —d Jack** un hombre llamado Juanito; **they —d the child Mary** a la niña le pusieron María; **you — it, we have it** cualquier cosa que pida Vd la tenemos; **he is not —d in this list** no figura en esta lista; **you were not —d in the speech** no se le mencionó a Vd en el discurso; **— the third president of the USA** diga el nombre del tercer presidente de EE.UU.; **to — someone after his grandfather** poner a uno el nombre de su abuelo; **they —d him Winston after Churchill** le pusieron (el nombre de) Winston por Churchill; **he was —d ambassador to Warsaw** le nombraron embajador en Varsovia.
name day ['neim'dei] *n* fiesta *f* onomástica.
name dropping ['neim'drɔpiŋ] *n vicio de procurar impresionar a la gente mencionando las personas importantes que uno conoce (o finge haber conocido.)*
nameless ['neimlis] *adj* anónimo, sin nombre, innominado; *vice* nefando; *dread etc* vago, indecible; **a person who shall be —** una persona cuyo nombre no digo.
namely ['neimli] *adv* a saber.
nameplate ['neimpleit] *n* letrero *m* con nombre (*del dueño etc*); placa *f* del fabricante.
namesake ['neimseik] *n* tocayo *m*, a *f*, homónimo *m*, a *f*.
nance [næns] *n*, **nancy-boy** ['nænsibɔi] *n* (*fam*) maricón *m* (*fam*).
nanny ['næni] *n* niñera *f*, chacha *f*.
nanny-goat ['nænigəut] *n* cabra *f*.
nap¹ [næp] **1** *n* sueñecito *m*, dormirela *f*; (*in afternoon*) siesta *f*; **to have a —, to take a —** descabezar un sueño, echar una siesta, dormir la siesta.
  2 *vi* dormitar; dormir la siesta; **to catch someone —ping** coger a uno desprevenido; **to be caught —ping** estar desprevenido.
nap² [næp] *n* (*on cloth*) lanilla *f*, flojel *m*.

nap³ [næp] (*Cards: game*) napolitana *f*; **to go —** jugarse el todo (*on* a).

napalm ['neipɑːm] *n* jalea *f* de gasolina.

nape [neip] *n* (*also —* **of the neck**) nuca *f*, cogote *m*.

naphtha ['næfθə] *n* nafta *f*.

naphthalene ['næfθəliːn] *n* naftalina *f*.

napkin ['næpkin] *n* (*table-*) servilleta *f*; (*baby's*) pañal *m*.

napkin ring ['næpkinriŋ] *n* servilletero *m*.

Naples ['neiplz] Nápoles.

Napoleon [nə'pəuliən] *m* Napoleón.

Napoleonic [nə,pəuli'ɔnik] *adj* napoleónico.

nappy ['næpi] *n* pañal *m*.

Narbonne [nɑː'bɔn] Narbona.

narcissism [nɑː'sisizəm] *n* narcisismo *m*.

narcissistic [,nɑːsi'sistik] *adj* narcisista.

narcissus [nɑː'sisəs] *n*, *pl* **—i** [ai] narciso *m*.

narcosis [nɑː'kəusis] *n* narcosis *f*, narcotismo *m*.

narcotic [nɑː'kɔtik] **1** *adj* narcótico. **2** *n* narcótico *m*.

narcotize ['nɑːkətaiz] *vt* narcotizar.

nard [nɑːd] *n* nardo *m*.

nark¹ [nɑːk] *n* (*sl*) soplón *m*.

nark² [nɑːk] *vt* (*sl*): **it —s me** me fastidia terriblemente; **he got properly —ed** se puso negro (*fam*); **— it!** (*stop it*) ¡déjalo!, (*go away*) ¡lárgate! (*fam*).

narrate [nə'reit] *vt* narrar, referir, contar.

narration [nə'reiʃən] *n* narración *f*, relato *m*.

narrative ['nærətiv] **1** *adj* narrativo. **2** *n* narrativa *f*, narración *f*.

narrator [nə'reitə*] *n* narrador *m*, ora *f*.

narrow ['nærəu] **1** *adj* estrecho, angosto; *trousers etc* estrecho; *advantage, majority* pequeño; *restricted* reducido, corto, restringido; *escape* de milagro, por los pelos; (*person*) de miras estrechas, intolerante; **in the — sense of the word** en el sentido estricto de la palabra; **on — resources** con escasos recursos.
  2 *vt* estrechar, angostar; reducir; **we have —ed it down to 3 possibilities** lo hemos reducido a 3 posibilidades; **the police have —ed the search down to Bristol** la policía ha podido limitar sus pesquisas a Bristol.
  3 *vi* estrecharse, angostarse, hacerse más angosto; reducirse; **the passage —s at the end** el pasillo se hace más estrecho hacia el final; **the search has now —ed to Soho** se ha podido restringir las pesquisas a Soho; **so the question —s down to this** . . . así que la cuestión se reduce a esto . . .

narrow-gauge ['nærəugeidʒ] *adj* de vía estrecha.

narrowly ['nærəuli] *adv* estrechamente; por poco; **the slate — missed him** por poco la pizarra le alcanzó, faltó poco para que la pizarra le diese; **he — missed being elected** no fué elegido por unos pocos votos.

narrow-minded ['nærəu'maindid] *adj* de miras estrechas, intolerante.

narrow-mindedness ['nærəu'maindidnis] *n* estrechez *f* de miras, intolerancia *f*.

narrows ['nærəuz] *npl* (*Naut*) estrecho *m*.

narwhal ['nɑːwəl] *n* narval *m*.

nasal ['neizəl] **1** *adj* nasal; (*twanging*) gangoso. **2** *n* nasal *f*.

nasality [nei'zæliti] *n* nasalidad *f*.

nasalize ['neizəlaiz] *vt* nasalizar; (*twangingly*) pronunciar con timbre gangoso.

nasally ['neizəli] *adv* nasalmente; con timbre nasal; **to speak —** hablar por las narices, ganguear.

nascent ['næsnt] *adj* naciente.

nastily ['nɑːstili] *adv* suciamente; horriblemente; groseramente; gravemente; peligrosamente; **he said — dijo groseramente; it was raining quite —** llovía de muy mala manera.

nastiness ['nɑːstinis] *n* suciedad *f*; cosas *fpl* horribles; indecencia *f*; lo asqueroso, lo horrible; lo malo; gravedad *f*; lo peligroso; grosería *f*; rencor *m*.

nasturtium [nəs'təːʃəm] *n* capuchina *f*.

nasty ['nɑːsti] *adj* (*a*) (*dirty*) sucio, puerco; (*obscene*) sucio, indecente, obsceno; (*disagreeable*) asqueroso, horrible, repugnante; *smell, taste* horrible; *remark* feo, horrible; (*rude*) grosero; *weather* feo, malo; *accident* grave; *wound etc* peligroso, de gravedad; *corner, turn* etc peligroso; *temper* vivo; *trick* malo; *habit* feo; **a very — film** una película asquerosa, un film de lo más horrible; **a — mess** un lío imponente; **what a — mind you have!** ¡qué mal pensado es Vd!; **to smell —** tener un olor desagradable; **to taste —** tener un sabor desagradable; **to turn —** *situation* ponerse difícil, *weather* volverse malo.
  (*b*) (*of person*) antipático; poco afable; (*rude*) grosero; (*malicious*) rencoroso, malévolo; **what a — man!** ¡qué hombre más horrible!; **to be — to someone** tratar muy mal a uno, portarse mal con uno; **they were — to her in the shop** se portaron groseramente con ella en la tienda; **don't be —!** ¡no

digas esas cosas horribles¡; ¡no seas mal pensado¡; **to turn —** ponerse negro.

natal ['neitl] *adj* natal.

natality [nə'tæliti] *n* natalidad *f*.

nation ['neiʃən] *n* nación *f*.

national ['næʃənl] **1** *adj* nacional. **2** *n* nacional *mf*.

nationalism ['næʃnəlizəm] *n* nacionalismo *m*.

nationalist ['næʃnəlist] **1** *adj* nacionalista. **2** *n* nacionalista *mf*.

nationalistic [,næʃnə'listik] *adj* nacionalista.

nationality [,næʃə'næliti] *n* nacionalidad *f*; **dual —** nacionalidad *f* doble.

nationalization [,næʃnəlai'zeiʃən] *n* estatificación *f*; nacionalización *f*.

nationalize ['næʃnəlaiz] *vt* (*bring under public ownership*) estatificar; (*foreign property etc*) nacionalizar.

nationally ['næʃnəli] *adv* en escala nacional; por toda la nación; nacionalmente, como nación; desde el punto de vista nacional.

nationhood ['neiʃənhud] *n* carácter *m* de nación; **to achieve —** llegar a constituir una nación, llegar a tener categoría de nación.

nation-wide ['neiʃənwaid] *adj* por toda la nación, a escala nacional; de toda la nación.

native ['neitiv] **1** *adj* (*a*) (*innate*) natural, innato.
  (*b*) (*artless*) sencillo.
  (*c*) (*of one's birth*) natal; *land, town* natal; *language* materno, nativo.
  (*d*) (*Min*) nativo.
  (*e*) (*indigenous*) indígena; *product, resources etc* natural, nacional, del país; **the animal is — to Africa** el animal es indígena de África, el animal es originario de África.
  (*f*) (*of natives*) indígena, nativo; **the — customs** las costumbres de los indígenas; **Minister for N— Affairs** Ministro *m* de Asuntos Indígenas; **to learn the — language** aprender el idioma de los indígenas; **to go —** vivir como los indígenas; *see* **land** *etc*.
  2 *n* (*a*) (*with reference to birth or nationality*) natural *mf*; nacional *mf*; **he was a — of Seville** nació en Sevilla, era natural de Sevilla, era sevillano; **the plant is a — of China** la planta es originaria de China; **he speaks German like a —** habla alemán como un alemán, habla alemán como si hubiera nacido allí.
  (*b*) (*primitive*) nativo *m*, a *f*, indígena *mf*.

nativity [nə'tiviti] *n* natividad *f*; **the N—** Navidad *f*; (*Art*) nacimiento *m*; (*crib etc*) belén *m*; **— play** auto *m* del nacimiento.

natter ['nætə*] (*fam*) **1** *n* charla *f*; **to have a —** charlar (*with* con).
  2 *vi* (*chat*) charlar; (*chatter*) parlotear, hablar mucho; (*keep on*) machacar; (*complain*) quejarse.

natty ['næti] *adj* (*spruce*) majo, elegante, acicalado; (*deft*) diestro; (*gadget etc*) ingenioso.

natural ['nætʃrəl] **1** *adj* (*in most senses*) natural; instintivo; *person* inafectado, sin afectación; *child* ilegítimo; **it is — that** . . . es natural que . . ., es lógico que . . .; **it seems — enough to me** me parece totalmente normal; **he's a — painter** es un pintor nato, nació para pintor.
  2 *n* (*person*) imbécil *mf*; (*Mus*) nota *f* natural; (*sign*) becuadro *m*; (*key*) tecla *f* blanca; (*fam*) cosa *f* de éxito seguro, persona *f* segura de tener éxito.

naturalism ['nætʃrəlizəm] *n* naturalismo *m*.

naturalist ['nætʃrəlist] *n* naturalista *mf*.

naturalistic [,nætʃrə'listik] *adj* naturalista.

naturalization [,nætʃrəlai'zeiʃən] *n* naturalización *f*.

naturalize ['nætʃrəlaiz] **1** *vt* (*person*) naturalizar; **to become —** naturalizarse. **2** *vi* (*person*) naturalizarse; (*plant etc*) aclimatarse, establecerse.

naturally ['nætʃrəli] *adv* (*a*) (*in a natural way*) naturalmente; sin afectación, con naturalidad; instintivamente, por instinto; **a — optimistic person** una persona optimista por naturaleza; **to write —** escribir con naturalidad.
  (*b*) (*of course*) naturalmente; desde luego . . ., claro que . . .; **—!** ¡naturalmente!; **— it is not true** desde luego no es cierto.

naturalness ['nætʃrəlnis] *n* naturalidad *f*.

nature ['neitʃə*] *n* (*a*) (*essential quality, character*) naturaleza *f*; modo *m* de ser; esencia *f*; (*of person*) natural *m*, carácter *m*, temperamento *m*, genio *m*; **good —** afabilidad *f*, amabilidad *f*; **to abuse someone's good —** abusar de la amabilidad de uno; **he has a nice —** tiene un carácter simpático; **it is not in his —** to say that no cabe en él decir tal cosa; **that's very much in his —** eso es muy de él; **the — of birds is to fly** las aves vuelan naturalmente; **outspokenness is second — with him** la franqueza le es completamente natural; **to be cautious by —** ser de naturaleza cauteloso; **it's against —**, **it's**

contrary to — es contrario a la naturaleza; **in the
— of things it's impossible** lógicamente es imposible.

(b) (*kind*) género *m*, clase *f*; **something of that** —
algo por el estilo; **of quite another** — de otra
índole; **some conclusions of a — to amaze one** unas
conclusiones de tipo sorprendente; **in the — of** del
género de, algo así como.

(c) (*Bio, Phys etc*) naturaleza *f*; **the laws of N**—
las leyes de la Naturaleza; **a keen student of** — un
estudiante entusiasta de la naturaleza (*or* de la
historia natural); **in a state of** — en su estado
natural; **to draw from** — dibujar del natural; **to
return to** — volver a su estado natural.

(d) **to relieve** — hacer del cuerpo.

natured ['neitʃəd] *adj* de carácter . . ., de condición . . .; **ill-natured** malévolo, malicioso; *see* **good-
natured** *etc*.

nature lover ['neitʃə‚lʌvə*] *n* amigo *m* de la naturaleza, amiga *f* de la naturaleza.

nature study ['neitʃə‚stʌdi] *n* historia *f* natural.

nature worship ['neitʃə‚wə:ʃip] *n* culto *m* de la
naturaleza; (*ancient*) panteísmo *m*.

naturism ['neitʃərizəm] *n* naturismo *m*.

naturist ['neitʃərist] *n* naturista *mf*.

naught [nɔ:t] *n* nada; **there's — I can do about it** no
hay nada que yo pueda hacer; **all for** — todo en
balde; **to bring to** — *attempt, plan* frustrar, *hope*
destruir; **to come to** — fracasar, malograrse, no dar
resultado; **to set at** — no hacer caso de, despreciar;
see also **nought**.

naughtily ['nɔ:tili] *adv* traviesamente, mal; escabrosamente; con picardía, con malicia.

naughtiness ['nɔ:tinis] *n* travesuras *fpl*, mala conducta *f*, picardía *f*; desobediencia *f*; lo verde, lo
escabroso; malicia *f*.

naughty ['nɔ:ti] *adj* (a) *child etc* travieso, malo,
pícaro; desobediente, revoltoso; **you've been very** —,
that was very — of you, that was a — thing to do
has sido muy malo; —! ¡malo!; **don't be** —! ¡no
seas malo!; **you — boy!** ¡pillo!, **you — girl!** ¡picaruela!

(b) *joke, song etc* verde, escabroso; **that —
jealousy of yours** esos pícaros celos tuyos; **she gave
me a — look** me miró picaruela; **what — times we
live in!** ¡qué tiempos más inmorales éstos!

nausea ['nɔ:siə] *n* náusea *f*, bascas *fpl*; (*fig*) asco *m*,
repugnancia *f*.

nauseate ['nɔ:sieit] *vt* dar náuseas a; (*fig*) dar asco a,
repugnar; **your conduct —s me** me repugna su conducta; **that cheese —s me** ese queso me da asco.

nauseating ['nɔ:sieitiŋ] *adj* repugnante, asqueroso.

nauseatingly ['nɔ:sieitiŋli] *adv* asquerosamente; —
virtuous tan virtuoso que da asco.

nauseous ['nɔ:siəs] *adj* nauseabundo.

nautical ['nɔ:tikəl] *adj* náutico, marítimo; *mile*
marino.

nautilus ['nɔ:tiləs] *n* nautilo *m*.

naval ['neivəl] *adj* naval, de marina; de la marina de
guerra; naval militar; *base, engagement* naval;
hospital, officer de marina; *forces* de la marina;
college naval militar; *power* marítimo.

Navarre [nə'vɑ:*] Navarra *f*.

Navarrese [‚nævə'ri:z] **1** *adj* navarro. **2** *n* navarro *m*,
a *f*. **3** *n* (*dialect*) navarro *m*.

nave [neiv] *n* (*Archit*) nave *f*.

navel ['neivəl] *n* ombligo *m*.

navigable ['nævigəbl] *adj river etc* navegable; (*steerable*) governable, dirigible.

navigate ['nævigeit] **1** *vt ship* marear, gobernar;
river etc navegar por; (*fig*) conducir, guiar. **2** *vi*
navegar.

navigation [‚nævi'geiʃən] *n* navegación *f*; (*science of
—*) náutica *f*.

navigator ['nævigeitə*] *n* (*Naut*) navegador *m*,
navegante *m*; (*Aer*) navegante *m*.

navvy ['nævi] *n* peón *m* caminero, peón *m* zapador,
bracero *m*.

navy ['neivi] *n* marina *f* de guerra, armada *f*, flota *f*.

navy-blue ['neivi'blu:] **1** *n* azul *m* marino. **2** *adj* azul
marino.

nay [nei] **1** *adv* (*arch or prov*) no; (*or rather*) más aun,
mejor dicho, más bien; *bad,* **— terrible** malo, mejor
dicho, horrible; **dozens, — hundreds** docenas, digo
centenares.

2 *n* (*refusal*) negativa *f*; (*in voting*) voto *m* negativo, voto *m* en contra; **to say someone —** dar una
respuesta negativa a uno.

Nazarene [‚næzə'ri:n] **1** *adj* nazareno. **2** *n* nazareno
m, a *f*.

Nazareth ['næzərəθ] Nazaret.

Nazi ['nɑ:tsi] **1** *adj* nazi, nazista. **2** *n* nazi *mf*.

Nazism ['nɑ:tsizəm] *n* nazismo *m*.

neap [ni:p] *n* (*also* **—tide**) marea *f* muerta.

Neapolitan [niə'pɔlitən] **1** *adj* napolitano. **2** *n* napolitano *m*, a *f*.

near [niə*] **1** *adv* cerca; **as — as I can recall** que yo
recuerde; **— on 30 books** (*fam*) casi 30 libros; **that's
— enough** (*fig*) está bien, basta ya; **no vale la pena
hacerlo más exacto; **to bring something —** acercar
algo; **to come —, to draw —** acercarse.

2 *prep* (*also* **— to**) (*of place*) cerca de; junto a,
próximo a, al lado de; (*of time*) cerca de, casi; (*of
numbers*) casi; **— here** aquí cerca; **to be — (to)** the
fire estar cerca del fuego; **the passage is — the end
of the book** el trozo está hacia el final del libro; **—
the end of the century** hacia fines del siglo; **she was
— her end** tocaba a su fin, estaba cerca de la muerte;
she was — to crying estaba a punto de llorar; **we
were — to being drowned** por poco nos morimos
ahogados.

3 *adj place etc* cercano; próximo, inmediato,
vecino; (*of time*) próximo; *relationship* estrecho,
íntimo; *relative* cercano; *resemblance* grande; *guess*
casi acertado; *translation etc* aproximativo; *side*
(*Aut etc: Brit*) izquierdo, (*US, Spain etc*) derecho;
the —est way el camino más corto; **work it out to
the —est pound** calcúlalo en libras enteras; **one's
—est and dearest** los más allegados y queridos.

4 *vt* acercarse a, aproximarse a; **the building is
—ing completion** el edificio está casi terminado, el
edificio se terminará dentro de poco; **he is —ing 50**
tiene casi 50 años; **the country is —ing disaster** el
país está al borde de la catástrofe.

nearby ['niə'bai] *adv* cerca.

nearby ['niəbai] *adj* cercano, próximo, inmediato.

Near East ['niər'i:st] Próximo Oriente *m*.

nearly ['niəli] *adv* (a) **it touches me —** me toca de
cerca.

(b) **it's — 3 o'clock** son casi las 3; **she's — 40** tiene
casi 40 años, frisa en los 40.

(c) (*with adj etc*) **— finished** casi terminado; **—
black** casi negro, más o menos negro; **very —!** ¡casi
casi!; **it's pretty — dead** está casi muerto; **the same
number or —** so el mismo número o casi.

(d) (*with negative*) **it's not — ready** no está listo
ni con mucho; **it's not — good enough** no es lo
suficientemente bueno (*to* + *infin* para + *infin*);
she is not — so poor as she says no es, ni con mucho,
tan pobre como ella dice.

(e) (*with verb*) **I — lost it** por loco lo perdí; **I very
— caught it** por poco lo cogí.

nearness ['niənis] *n* proximidad *f*, cercanía *f*, lo
cercano; intimidad *f*; **because of its — to the
station** por estar tan cerca de la estación.

near-sighted ['niə'saitid] *adj* corto de vista, miope.

near-sightedness ['niə'saitidnis] *n* miopía *f*.

neat [ni:t] *adj* (*of person's appearance, etc*) pulcro,
esmerado, acicalado; *figure* atractivo, esbelto;
(*shapely*) bien proporcionado; *garden, room etc* bien
cuidado, bien arreglado; *work* primoroso; *writing,
phrase* elegante; *plan* hábil, ingenioso; (*skilful*)
diestro; *drink* puro, solo, sin mezcla; **to make a —
job of something** hacer algo con esmero.

neatly ['ni:tli] *adv* pulcramente, esmeradamente, con
esmero; con primor, primorosamente; elegantemente; hábilmente, ingeniosamente; diestramente.

neatness ['ni:tnis] *n* pulcritud *f*, esmero *m*; esbeltez *f*;
buena proporción *f*; lo arreglado, lo cuidado; primor
m; elegancia *f*; habilidad *f*; destreza *f*.

Nebuchadnezzar [‚nebjukəd'nezə*] *m* Nabucodonosor.

nebula ['nebjulə] *n* nebulosa *f*.

nebulous ['nebjuləs] *adj* nebuloso; (*fig*) vago, cen-
fuso, impreciso.

necessarily ['nesisərili] *adv* necesariamente; forzosamente; **not —** cabe otra posibilidad, eso no es cierto
del todo; **it is not — true that . . .** no es necesariamente cierto que . . .

necessary ['nesisəri] *adj* necesario; preciso, esencial,
indispensable, imprescindible; **with the — enthusiasm** con el debido entusiasmo; **all the —
ceremonies** todas las ceremonias obligatorias; **if —**
si es necesario, si es preciso; **it is — that . . .** es
necesario que + *subj*, es preciso que + *subj*; **it is —
for us to go** es preciso que vayamos; **it made it —
for us to sell them** hizo inevitable que los vendiése-
mos; **I shall do everything —** haré todo lo necesario;
to do the — hacer lo que hace falta, hacer lo que hay
que hacer; **don't do more than is —** no haga más de
lo necesario.

2 *n cosa f* necesaria, requisito *m* indispensable;
(*also* **necessaries** *pl*) lo necesario; (*fam: money*)
cónquibus *m*.

necessitate [ni'sesiteit] *vt* necesitar, exigir.

necessitous [ni'sesitəs] *adj* necesitado, indigente.

necessity [ni'sesiti] *n* (**a**) necesidad *f*; inevitabilidad *f*; — **is the mother of invention** la necesidad estimula la invención, el hambre aguza el ingenio; **the — for care** la necesidad del cuidado; **of** — por necesidad, forzosamente; **out of sheer** — por fuerza; **in case of** — si fuese necesario, en caso de urgencia; **it's a case of sheer** — es un caso de la mayor necesidad; **dire — leads me to ask** la más apremiante necesidad me obliga a pedirlo; **there is no — for you to do it** no es necesario que Vd lo haga; **to be under the — of** + *ger* verse obligado a + *infin*.

(**b**) (*article*) cosa *f* necesaria, requisito *m* indispensable; **necessities** artículos *mpl* de primera necesidad; **the necessities of life** las cosas necesarias para la vida; **a fridge is a — nowadays** es indispensable ahora tener nevera.

(**c**) (*poverty*) indigencia *f*; **to be in —** estar necesitado.

neck [nek] **1** *n* (**a**) (*Anat*) cuello *m*; garganta *f*; (*of animal*) pescuezo *m*; (*of bottle*) cuello *m*, gollete *m*; (*Geog*) istmo *m*; (*Sew*) escote *m*; (*Mus: of guitar*) cuello *m*, (*of violin*) mástil *m*; **to race — and —** ir a las parejas; **— or nothing** todo o nada; **to fall — and crop** caer de cabeza; **to beat someone — and crop** vencer a uno fácilmente; **to be up to one's —** (*in work*) tener trabajo hasta por encima de las cejas; **to be in something up to one's —** estar muy metido en un asunto; **to break one's —** desnucarse; **to break someone's —** romper el pescuezo a uno; **she fell on his —** ella se colgó de su cuello; **to get it in the —** (*fam*) pagarlas, cargárselas (*fam*), (*be told off*) recibir una peluca (*fam*); **to have someone breathing down one's —** ser seguido de cerca por uno, tener a uno sobre sus talones; **to stick one's — out** arriesgarse, exponerse a un ataque posible, atreverse a expresar una opinión; **to win by a —** ganar por un cuello; **to wring a rabbit's —** torcer el pescuezo a un conejo.

(**b**) (*fam*) = **nerve** 1(d).

2 *vi* (*fam*) acariciarse, abrazarse amorosamente.

neckband ['nekbænd] *n* tirilla *f*.

neckerchief ['nekətʃiːf] *n* (*arch*) pañuelo *m* de cuello.

necking ['nekiŋ] *n* (*fam*) caricias *fpl*, abrazos *mpl* amorosos.

necklace ['neklis] *n*, **necklet** ['neklit] *n* collar *m*.

neckline ['neklain] *n* escote *m*; **plunging —** escote *m* muy bajo.

necktie ['nektai] *n* corbata *f*.

necrological [,nekrəu'lɔdʒikəl] *adj* necrológico.

necrology [ne'krɔlədʒi] *n* necrología *f*.

necromancer ['nekrəumænsə*] *n* nigromante *m*.

necromancy ['nekrəumænsi] *n* nigromancia *f*, nigromancia *f*.

necropolis [ne'krɔpəlis] *n* necrópolis *f*.

nectar ['nektə*] *n* néctar *m*.

nectarine ['nektəriːn] *n* nectarina *f*.

née [nei]: **Mary Green, — Smith** Mary Smith de Green.

need [niːd] **1** *n* (**a**) necesidad *f* (*for, of* de); **if —(s) be, in case of —** si fuera necesario, en caso de urgencia; **there is every —** es totalmente indispensable; **I see no —** no veo la necesidad; **there is no — to** + *infin* no hace falta + *infin*; **there's no — to worry** no hay para qué inquietarse; **what — is there to buy it?** ¿qué necesidad hay de comprarlo?; **no — to say that . . .** excusado es decir que . . .; **no — to tell him what to do** no hace falta decirle qué hacer; **to be in — of, to have — of, to stand in — of** necesitar; **I have no — of advice** no necesito consejos, no me hacen falta consejos; **you have no — to go** no es preciso que vayas; **when I'm in — of a drink** cuando siento la necesidad de beber algo; **a house in — of painting** una casa que hay que pintar, una casa que convendría pintar.

(**b**) (*want, lack*) adversidad *f*; apuro *m*; (*absence*) carencia *f*; falta *f*, escasez *f*; **in times of —** en tiempos de adversidad, en tiempos de carestía; **there is much — of food** hay una gran escasez de alimentos.

(**c**) (*poverty*) necesidad *f*, indigencia *f*; **my — is great** es grande mi necesidad; **to be in —** estar necesitado.

(**d**) (*thing needed*) cosa *f* necesaria, requisito *m*; **bodily —s** necesidades *fpl* corporales; **the —s of industry** las necesidades de la industria; **my —s are few** soy poco exigente; **to supply someone's —s** proveer lo que necesita uno.

2 *vt* (**a**) (*of person*) necesitar; **I — it** lo necesito, me hace falta; **it's just what I —ed** es precisamente lo que necesitaba; **I — two more to make up the series** me faltan dos para completar la serie; **he —ed no**

bidding no se hizo de rogar; **he —s watching** hay que vigilarle, conviene vigilarle.

(**b**) (*of thing*) exigir, requerir, reclamar; **it —s care** requiere cuidado, exige cuidado; **a visa is —ed** se exige visado; **the report —s no comment** el informe no tiene necesidad de comentarios; **a much —ed holiday** unas vacaciones muy necesarias; **I gave it a much —ed wash** lo lavé pues le hacía mucha falta; **this will — some explaining** no va a ser fácil explicar esto.

(**c**) (**to —** + *infin*) **I — to do it** tengo que hacerlo, debo hacerlo; **he —s to be told twice** hay que decírselo todo dos veces; **they don't — to be told all the details** no es preciso contarles todos los detalles; **you will hardly — to be reminded that . . .** apenas es necesario recordarles que . . .; **you only —ed to ask** no había sino pedir; **this room —s to be painted** hay que pintar este cuarto, conviene pintar este cuarto.

(**d**) (*v aux*) **— I go?** ¿he de ir?; **he —n't do it, — he?** ¿es esencial que lo haga?; **I — hardly add that . . .** apenas hay que añadir que . . .; **it — not be done now** no es preciso hacerlo ahora.

(**e**) (*impersonal*) **it —ed a war to alter that** fue necesaria una guerra para cambiar eso; **it doesn't — me to tell him** no hace falta que yo se lo diga.

needful ['niːdful] **1** *adj* necesario. **2** *n* (*fam*) **the —** el cónquibus (*fam*).

neediness ['niːdinis] *n* necesidad *f*, pobreza *f*.

needle ['niːdl] **1** *n* aguja *f* (*all senses*); **to look for a — in a haystack** buscar una aguja en un pajar.

2 *adj*: **— match** partido *m* importantísimo, partido *m* muy emocionante, partido *m* muy reñido.

3 *vt* (*fam*) *person* picar, provocar, fastidiar; *drink* (*US*) añadir alcohol a.

needle case ['niːdlkeis] *n* alfiletero *m*.

needlecraft ['niːdlkrɑːft] *n* arte *m* de la costura.

needless ['niːdlis] *adj* innecesario, superfluo, inútil; **— to say . . .** excusado es decir que . . ., está de más decir que . . ., huelga decir que . . .; **he was, — to say, drunk** estaba borracho, claro (está).

needlessly ['niːdlisli] *adv* innecesariamente, inútilmente, en vano; **you worry quite —** te inquietas sin motivo alguno.

needlewoman ['niːdl,wumən] *n*, *pl* **-women** [,wimin] costurera *f*; **to be a good —** coser bien.

needlework ['niːdlwəːk] *n* labor *f* de aguja, costura *f*, bordado *m*; **to do —** hacer costura, coser.

needs [niːdz] *adv* necesariamente, forzosamente; **if — must** si hace falta; **we must — walk** no tenemos más remedio que ir andando.

needy ['niːdi] *adj* necesitado, pobre, indigente.

ne'er [nɛə*] *adv* (*poet*) nunca.

ne'er-do-well ['nɛədu,wel] **1** *adj* perdido. **2** *n* perdido *m*, perdulario *m*.

nefarious [ni'fɛəriəs] *adj* nefario, vil, inicuo.

negate [ni'geit] *vt* anular, invalidar.

negation [ni'geiʃən] *n* negación *f*.

negative ['negətiv] **1** *adj* negativo.

2 *n* (*answer*) negativa *f*; (*Gram*) negación *f*; (*Phot*) negativo *m*, prueba *f* negativa; (*Elec*) polo *m* negativo; **double —** negación *f* doble; **to answer in the —** dar una respuesta negativa.

3 *vt* (*veto*) poner veto a; (*vote down*) rechazar, desaprobar; *statement* negar, desmentir; *effect* anular.

negatively ['negətivli] *adv* negativamente.

neglect [ni'glekt] **1** *n* (*carelessness*) negligencia *f*, descuido *m*; (*of rule etc*) inobservancia *f*; (*of duty*) incumplimiento *m*; (*neglected state*) abandono *m*; (*of oneself*) dejadez *f*; (*towards others*) desatención *f*; **to die in —** morir abandonado.

2 *vt* *obligations etc* descuidar, desatender; *duty etc* no cumplir, faltar a; *friends* dejar de ver; desairar; *advice etc* no hacer caso de; (*omit*) omitir, olvidar; *opportunity* no aprovechar; *garden etc* no cuidar; *wife* dejar sola; **to — to** + *infin* olvidarse de + *infin*.

neglected [ni'glektid] *adj* *appearance* descuidado, desaliñado; *garden etc* sin cuidar; *wife* abandonada.

neglectful [ni'glektful] *adj* negligente, descuidado; **to be — of** descuidar, desatender.

negligée ['negliʒei] *n* (*nightdress etc*) salto *m* de cama; (*housecoat*) bata *f*.

negligence ['neglidʒəns] *n* negligencia *f*, descuido *m*; **through —** por descuido.

negligent ['neglidʒənt] *adj* negligente, descuidado; **to be — of** descuidar, desatender.

negligently ['neglidʒəntli] *adv* negligentemente, con descuido.

negligible ['neglidʒəbl] *adj* insignificante; despreciable; **a — quantity** una cantidad insignificante; **a by no means — opponent** un adversario nada despreciable.

negotiable [ni'gəuʃiəbl] adj negociable; road etc transitable; **not —** que no puede negociarse.

negotiate [ni'gəuʃieit] **1** vt **(a)** treaty negociar; loan, deal etc negociar, gestionar, agenciar.
(b) obstacle salvar, franquear; river etc pasar, cruzar; bend tomar.
2 vi negociar; **to — for** negociar para obtener; **to — for peace** pedir la paz; **to — with someone** negociar con uno.

negotiation [ni,gəuʃi'eiʃən] n negociación f; gestión f; **to be in — with someone** estar negociando con uno; **the treaty is under —** el tratado está siendo negociado; **that will be a matter for —** eso tendrá que ser discutido, eso tendrá que someterse a discusión; **to enter into —s with someone** entrar en negociaciones con uno.

negotiator [ni'gəuʃieitə*] n negociador m, ora f.

Negress ['ni:gres] n negra f.

Negro ['ni:grəu] **1** adj negro. **2** n, pl **Negroes** ['ni:grəuz] negro m.

negroid ['ni:grɔid] adj negroide.

neigh [nei] **1** n relincho m. **2** vi relinchar.

neighbour, (US) **neighbor** ['neibə*] **1** n vecino m, a f; (fellow being) prójimo m, a f; **Good N— Policy** (US) Política f del Buen Vecino.
2 vt, also vi: **to — upon** (adjoin) colindar con, estar contiguo a; (be almost) rayar en.

neighbourhood, (US) **neighborhood** ['neibəhud] n **(a)** (area) vecindad f; barrio m, sección f, sector m; **all the girls of the —** todas las jóvenes del barrio; **not a very nice —** un barrio poco atractivo; **somewhere in the —** por allí, cerca de allí; **anyone in the — of the crime** cualquier persona que estuviera cerca del lugar del crimen; **the soil in that —** el suelo de aquel sector; **in the — of £80** alrededor de 80 libras.
(b) (surrounding area) alrededores mpl, cercanías fpl; **Málaga and its —** Málaga y su región.
(c) (persons) vecinos mpl, vecindario m.

neighbouring, (US) **neighboring** ['neibəriŋ] adj vecino; cercano, inmediato.

neighbourly, (US) **neighborly** ['neibəli] adj de buen vecino, amable, amistoso.

neighing ['neiiŋ] n relinchos mpl.

neither ['naiðə*] **1** adv and conj: **— he nor I** ni él ni yo; **he — smokes nor drinks** no bebe ni fuma.
2 conj: **if you aren't going, — am I** si tú no vas, yo tampoco; **— will he agree to sell it** ni consiente en venderlo tampoco.
3 pron: **— of them has any money** ninguno de los dos tiene dinero, ni el uno ni el otro tiene dinero; **— of them saw it** ni el uno ni el otro lo vio.
4 adj: **on — side** por ninguno de los dos lados, en ningún lado; **— car is for sale** no se vende ninguno de los dos coches.

nemesis ['nemisis] n (fig) justo castigo m, justicia f.

neoclassical ['ni:əu'klæsikəl] adj neoclásico.

neoclassicism ['ni:əu'klæsisizəm] n neoclasicismo m.

neofascism ['ni:əu'fæʃizəm] n neofascismo m.

neofascist ['ni:əu'fæʃist] **1** adj neofascista. **2** n neofascista mf.

neolithic [,ni:əu'liθik] adj neolítico.

neologism [ni'ɔlədʒizəm] n neologismo m.

neon ['ni:ɔn] n neón m, neo m; **— lamp, — light** lámpara f de neón.

neonazi ['ni:əu'nɑːtsi] **1** adj neonazi, neonazista. **2** n neonazi mf.

neophyte ['ni:əufait] n neófito m, a f.

neoplatonic ['ni:əuplə'tɔnik] adj neoplatónico.

neoplatonism ['ni:əu'pleitənizəm] n neoplatonismo m.

neoplatonist ['ni:əu'pleitənist] n neoplatonista mf.

Nepal [ni'pɔːl] Nepal m.

Nepalese [,nepɔː'liːz] **1** adj nepalés. **2** n nepalés m, esa f.

nephew ['nevjuː] n sobrino m.

nephritis [ne'fraitis] n nefritis f.

nepotism ['nepətizəm] n nepotismo m.

Neptune ['neptjuːn] n Neptuno.

nereid ['niəriid] n nereida f.

Nero ['niərəu] m Nerón.

nerve [nəːv] n **(a)** (Anat, Bot) nervio m; (Ent) nervadura f; **my —s are on edge** tengo los nervios de punta; **it gets on my —s** me pone los nervios de punta, me crispa los nervios, me saca de quicio; **he gets on my —s** me fastidia terriblemente; **to strain every — to + infin** hacer un esfuerzo supremo por + infin.
(b) **—s** nerviosidad f, nerviosismo m; excitabilidad f nerviosa; **a fit of —s** un ataque de excitabilidad nerviosa; **to be in a state of —** estar nervioso, estar

hipertenso; **she suffers from —s** padece una hipertensión nerviosa.
(c) (courage) valor m, sangre f fría; **I hadn't the — to do it** no tuve el valor de hacerlo; **to lose one's —** perder el valor; **it takes some — to do that** hacer eso exige mucha sangre fría.
(d) (cheek) descaro m, tupé m, frescura f, caradura f; **of all the —!, the — of it!, what a —!** ¡qué frescura!, ¡qué caradura!; **you've got a —!** ¡eres un caradura!, ¡eres un fresco!; **to have the — to + infin** ser bastante descarado como para + infin.
2 vt: **to — someone to do something** animar a uno a hacer algo, infundir a uno bastante ánimo para hacer algo.
3 vr: **to — oneself to do something** animarse a hacer algo, esforzarse por hacer algo.

nerve cell ['nəːvsel] n neurona f.

nerve centre, (US) **— center** ['nəːv,sentə*] n (Anat) centro m nervioso; (fig) punto m neurálgico.

nerveless ['nəːvlis] adj (fig) grasp flojo; person enervado, débil, soso.

nerve-racking ['nəːv,rækiŋ] adj que crispa los nervios; horripilante, espantoso.

nerviness ['nəːvinis] n nerviosidad f, nerviosismo m.

nervous ['nəːvəs] adj person nervioso; (by nature) tímido; miedoso, asustadizo; breakdown, system etc nervioso; **to be — of** tener miedo a; **to be — of + ger** tener miedo a + infin; **I was — on his account** estaba inquieto por él; **I was — about speaking to her** me daba miedo la noción de hablar con ella; **to get —** ponerse nervioso, sentir miedo; **I get — when I'm alone** me entra cierto miedo estando a solas; **it makes me —** me da miedo.

nervously ['nəːvəsli] adv nerviosamente; tímidamente.

nervousness ['nəːvəsnis] n nerviosidad f, nerviosismo m, timidez f, miedo m.

nervy ['nəːvi] n pajarito m.

nest [nest] **1** n (of bird) nido m; (of hen) nidal m; (of animal) madriguera f; (of wasps) avispero m; (of ants) hormiguero m; (clutch of eggs, young birds) nidada f; (person's house) casita f, hogar m; (of thieves etc) nido m, cueva f, guarida f; (of boxes, drawers) juego m; **to feather one's —** ponerse las botas, hacer su agosto; **to foul one's own —** manchar el proprio nido.
2 vi (bird) anidar, hacer su nido; (collector) buscar nidos.

nest egg ['nesteg] n nidal m; (fig) ahorros mpl, cantidad f ahorrada, buena hucha f.

nesting box ['nestiŋbɔks] n nidal m, ponedero m.

nestle ['nesl] vi **(a)** **to — among leaves** hacerse un nido entre las hojas; **to — down among the blankets** hacerse un ovillo entre las mantas; **to — up to someone** arrimarse cómodamente a uno, apretarse contra uno.
(b) **a house nestling beside a wood** una casa situada al abrigo de un bosque; **a village nestling among hills** un pueblecito protegido por las colinas.

nestling ['nesliŋ] n pajarito m.

net¹ [net] **1** n red f (also fig); (mesh) malla f; (fabric) tul m; (for hair etc) redecilla f. **2** vt coger con red.

net² [net] (Comm) **1** adj neto, líquido; income, price, weight etc neto; **at a — profit of 5%** con un beneficio neto de 5 por cien; **"terms strictly —"** "sin descuento". **2** vt ganar en limpio, producir en limpio; **he —s £3000 a year** gana una renta neta de 3000 libras al año.

nether ['neðə*] adj inferior, más bajo, de abajo; **— lip** labio m inferior; **— regions** infierno m.

Netherlands ['neðələndz] pl Países mpl Bajos.

nethermost ['neðəməust] adj superl (el etc) más bajo.

netting ['netiŋ] n red f, redes fpl; (obra f de) malla f.

nettle ['netl] **1** n ortiga f. **2** vt provocar, irritar, molestar; **somewhat —d by this** algo molesto por eso.

nettle rash ['netlræʃ] n urticaria f.

network ['netwəːk] n (fig) red f; **radio —** red f de emisoras; **the national railway —** la red nacional de ferrocarriles; **a — of spies** una red de espías.

neural ['njuərəl] adj neural.

neuralgia [njuə'rældʒə] n neuralgia f.

neurasthenia [,njuərəs'θiːniə] n neurastenia f.

neurasthenic [,njuərəs'θenik] adj neurasténico.

neuritis [njuə'raitis] n neuritis f.

neurologist [njuə'rɔlədʒist] n neurólogo m.

neurology [njuə'rɔlədʒi] n neurología f.

neuron ['njuərɔn] n neurona f.

neuropath ['njuərəpæθ] n neurópata mf.

neurosis [njuə'rəusis] n pl **neuroses** [njuə'rəusiːz] neurosis f.

neurotic [njuə'rɔtik] **1** *adj* neurótico. **2** *n* neurótico *m*, a *f*.

neuter ['nju:tə*] **1** *adj* (*Gram*) neutro; *cat etc* sin sexo, castrado.
2 *n* (*Gram*) género *m* neutro; (*cat etc*) macho *m* castrado, animal *m* sin sexo.
3 *vt cat etc* castrar, capar.

neutral ['nju:trəl] **1** *adj person, country, opinion* neutral; (*Zool, Bot, Elec, Chem etc*) neutro; *colour* indeciso, indeterminado; **to remain —** seguir siendo neutral, no tomar partido.
2 *n* neutral *mf*; país *m* neutral; **in —** (*Mech*) en punto muerto.

neutralism ['nju:trəlizəm] *n* neutralismo *m*.
neutralist ['nju:trəlist] **1** *adj* neutralista. **2** *n* neutralista *mf*.
neutrality [nju:'træliti] *n* neutralidad *f*.
neutralization [,nju:trəlai'zeifən] *n* neutralización *f*.
neutralize ['nju:trəlaiz] *vt* neutralizar.
neutron ['nju:trɔn] *n* neutrón *m*.

never ['nevə*] *adv* (**a**) nunca, jamás; **—! ¡**jamás!; **I — went** no fui nunca, no fui jamás; **you — saw anything like it** nunca se ha visto nada parecido; **I have — yet seen anything so horrible** en mi vida he visto nada más horrible; **— in all my life** jamás en la vida; **it had — been tried before** no se había intentado antes.
(**b**) (*emphatic negative*) **—!, you — did!** ¿de veras?; **— a one** ni uno siquiera; **— a word did he say** no dijo ni una sola palabra; **I — expected it** no contaba con eso de ningún modo; **surely you — bought it?** ¿pero lo has comprado de veras?; **well I —! ¡**caramba!

never-ending ['nevər'endiŋ] *adj* inacabable, interminable.
never-failing ['nevə'feiliŋ] *adj* infalible.
nevermore ['nevə'mɔ:*] *adv* nunca más.
never-never ['nevə'nevə*] *n* (*fam*): **to buy something on the —** comprar algo a plazos.
nevertheless [,nevəðə'les] *adv* sin embargo, no obstante, con todo; **it is — true that . . .** con todo es verdad que . . .
never-to-be-forgotten ['nevətəbi:,fə'gɔtn] *adj* inolvidable.

new [nju:] *adj* nuevo; reciente; (*fresh*) fresco, nuevo; *bread* tierno; (*different*) nuevo, distinto; **a — car** (*different*) un nuevo coche, (*brand new*) un coche nuevo; **the — students** los nuevos estudiantes; **the — people in No. 5** la nueva familia del núm 5, la familia que acaba de establecerse en el núm 5; **she's very —, poor girl** no está habituada, la pobre; **are you — here?** ¿eres nuevo aquí?; **are you — to this?** ¿esto es nuevo para ti?; **he came — to us last year** empezó a trabajar con nosotros el año pasado nada más; **what's —?** (*fam*) ¿qué hay de nuevo? (*fam*); **it's as good as —** está como nuevo; **there's nothing — under the sun** no hay nada nuevo bajo las estrellas.
new- [nju:] (*in compounds*) recién . . .
newborn ['nju:bɔ:n] *adj* recién nacido.
newcomer ['nju:,kʌmə*] *n* recién llegado *m*, a *f*, nuevo *m*, a *f*.
New England [,nju:'iŋglənd] la Nueva Inglaterra.
new-fangled ['nju:,fæŋgld] *adj* (*pej*) recién inventado, modernísimo; que está tan de moda.
new-found ['nju:,faund] *adj* recién descubierto; **his — zeal** el entusiasmo que acaba de mostrar.
Newfoundland [,nju:fənd'lænd] Terranova *f*; **— dog** perro *m* de Terranova.
New Guinea [,nju:'gini:] Nueva Guinea *f*.
newish ['nju:if] *adj* bastante nuevo.
new-laid ['nju:'leid] *adj egg* recién puesto, fresco.
newly ['nju:li] *adv* nuevamente, recién . . .; **— made** recién hecho, acabado de hacer; **those — arrived** los recién llegados; **those — arrived from France** los que acaban de llegar de Francia.
newly-weds ['nju:liwedz] *npl* recién casados *mpl*.
New Mexico [,nju:'meksikəu] Nuevo Méjico *m*.
new-mown ['nju:'məun] *adj* recién segado.
newness ['nju:nis] *n* novedad *f*; (*in a job etc*) inexperiencia *f*, falta *f* de práctica.
New Orleans [nju:'ɔ:liənz] Nueva Orleáns *m*.
news [nju:z] *n sing* noticias *fpl*; nuevas *fpl*; **a piece of —** una noticia, una nueva; **"N— in Brief"** (*newspaper*) "Brevedades"; **a sad piece of —** una triste noticia; **that's good —** es buena noticia; **no — is good —** falta de noticias: buena señal; **it was — to me** me cogió de nuevas; **what —?, what's the —?** ¿qué hay de nuevo?; **they're in the —** se oye hablar mucho de ellos, figuran mucho en los periódicos (*etc*); **to break the — to someone** dar una noticia a uno; **when the — broke** al saberse la noticia; **I have — for you** tengo que darte una noticia.

newsagent ['nju:z,eidʒənt] *n* vendedor *m* de periódicos.
newsboy ['nju:zbɔi] *n* chico *m* que reparte periódicos.
news bulletin ['nju:z,bulitin] *n* (*Radio*) noticiario *m*, diario *m* hablado; (TV) telediario *m*.
newscast ['nju:zkɑ:st] *n* telediario *m*.
newscaster ['nju:z'kɑ:stə*] *n* locutor *m* de telediario, locutora *f* de telediario.
newsdealer ['nju:z,di:lə*] *n* vendedor *m* de periódicos.
news flash ['nju:zflæf] *n* flash *m*, noticia *f* de última hora.
news item ['nju:z,aitəm] *n* noticia *f*.
newsletter ['nju:z,letə*] *n* hoja *f* informativa, informe *m*.
newsman ['nju:zmæn] *n, pl* **—men** [men] periodista *m*, reportero *m*.
news sheet ['nju:zfi:t] *n* hoja *f* informativa; periódico *m*.
New South Wales ['nju:sauθ'weilz] Nueva Gales *f* del Sur.
newspaper ['nju:s,peipə*] **1** *n* periódico *m*, diario *m*. **2** *attr* de periódico, periodístico.
newspaperman ['nju:s'peipəmæn] *n, pl* **—men** [men] periodista *m*.
newsprint ['nju:zprint] *n* papel *m* prensa.
newsreel ['nju:zri:l] *n* noticiario *m*, película *f* de actualidades, (*in Spain*) Nodo *m* (*noticiario m documental*).
newsroom ['nju:zrum] *n* gabinete *m* de lectura.
news stand ['nju:zstænd] *n* quiosco *m* de periódicos.
news theatre ['nju:z,θiətə*] *n* cine *m* de actualidades.
newsworthy ['nju:z,wə:ði] *adj* periodístico, sensacional.
newsy ['nju:zi] *adj* lleno de noticias.
newt [nju:t] *n* tritón *m*.
New York ['nju:'jɔ:k] Nueva York; (*attr*) neoyorquino.
New Yorker ['nju:'jɔ:kə*] *n* neoyorquino *m*, a *f*.
New Zealand [nju:'zi:lənd] Nueva Zelanda *f*, Nueva Zelandia *f*; (*attr*) neozelandés.
New Zealander [nju:'zi:ləndə*] *n* neozelandés *m*, esa *f*.

next [nekst] **1** *adj* (**a**) (*of place*) próximo, inmediato, contiguo, vecino; **the — room** la habitación al lado de ésta; **the — house** la casa vecina, la casa de al lado; **on the — page** a la vuelta, a la página siguiente; **I get out at the — stop** yo salgo en la próxima parada.
(**b**) (*of order*) próximo, siguiente; primero; **the — in order is . . .** el próximo siguiendo el orden es . . ., el primero según el orden es . . .; **in the — volume** en el tomo siguiente, en el tomo después de éste; **the — life** la próxima vez; **— time you see him** la próxima vez que le veas; **the — but one** el segundo después de éste; **"see — page"** "véase a la página siguiente"; **"continued in the — column"** "sigue en la columna inmediata"; **"to be continued in our —"** "continuará"; **he's — after me** es el primero después de mí; **— please! ¡**el siguiente!; **what —?** y ahora ¿qué?; **what —, madam?** (*in shop*) ¿algo más, señora?; **who's —?** ¿quién es el siguiente?; **whatever —! ¡**qué horror!
(**c**) (*of time*) próximo, siguiente; *week, month, year* próximo, que viene; **— year** (*looking to future*) el año que viene, (*in past time*) el año siguiente; **— day** el día siguiente; **the — day but one** el segundo día después de éste; **the — 5 days** los 5 días que vienen; **— morning** la mañana siguiente, a la mañana; **on 4th May** — el próximo 4 de mayo; **the year after —** el segundo año después de éste; **by this time —** **year** por estas fechas del año que viene.
2 *adv* (**a**) (*of place, order*) inmediatamente después; **who comes —?** ¿quién sigue?, ¿a quién le toca?; **what do we do —?** ¿qué hacemos ahora?; **the — smaller size** el tamaño más pequeño después de éste; **the — best thing would be to + infin** lo mejor después de esto sería **+ infin**; **to take the — best** tomar el segundo.
(**b**) (*of time*) luego, después; inmediatamente; **la próxima vez; we put the salt in —** luego echamos la sal; **what did he do —?** ¿qué hizo después?; **when you — see him** cuando le veas la próxima vez; **when I — saw him** cuando le volví a ver.
3 *prep* (**a**) (*also* **— to**) junto a, al lado de; **the car — to the door** el coche que está junto a la puerta; **his room is — to mine** su habitación está al lado de la mía; **to wear silk — (to) one's skin** llevar seda sobre la piel.
(**b**) (*fig*) casi; **we got it for — to nothing** lo adquirimos por casi nada; **there was — to nobody**

there no había casi nadie; **there is — to no news** apenas hay noticias, no hay noticias casi; *see* **door, kin** etc.

next-door ['neks'dɔɪ*] adj de al lado.

nexus ['neksəs] n nexo m.

Niagara [nai'ægrə] Niágara m; **— Falls** Cataratas fpl de Niágara.

nib [nib] n punta f; (of fountain pen) plumilla f, plumín m.

nibble ['nibl] **1** n mordisco m; **I never had a — all day** (Fishing) el corcho no se movió en todo el día; **at £3000 he never got a —** a las 3000 libras nadie le echó un tiento.

  2 vt mordiscar; (rat etc) roer; (horse) rozar; (fish) picar; **the cheese is all —d** el queso está lleno de roeduras.

  3 vi: **to — at** mordiscar etc (as vt); **to — at an offer** considerar una oferta, mostrar cierto interés por una oferta.

nibs [nibz] n (fam): **his —** su señoría.

Nicaragua [ˌnikə'ræguə] Nicaragua f.

Nicaraguan [ˌnikə'ræguən] **1** adj nicaragüense. **2** n nicaragüense mf.

Nice [niːs] Niza.

nice [nais] adj **(a)** (of person: likeable) simpático; **he's a — man** es un hombre simpático.

  (b) (of person: kind) amable; **he was very — about it** estuvo muy amable; **it is — of you to help** Vd es muy amable ayudándome; **try to be — to him** procura ser amable con él; **I find it hard to be — to him** encuentro difícil hablar amistosamente con él.

  (c) (of person: attractive) guapo, mono, bonito; **how — you look!** ¡qué guapa estás!

  (d) (of thing: pleasant) agradable, ameno; (attractive) mono, bonito, precioso; weather etc bueno; **a — photo** una bonita foto; **that's a — ring** ¡qué anillo más mono!; **what a — idea that was!** ¡ésa sí fue una idea genial!; **it's — here** aquí se está bien; **we had a very — holiday in Ibiza** lo pasamos muy bien en Ibiza, hemos pasado unas vacaciones excelentes en Ibiza; **it smells —** huele bien, tiene un olor agradable; **it doesn't taste at all —** tiene un sabor nada agradable; **they give you — things to do** te lo dan cosas interesantes que hacer; **they give you — things to eat** te lo dan cosas deliciosas que comer; **it's not very — to have to + infin** no es muy agradable tener que + infin.

  (e) (of things, persons: refined) fino, culto, bien; **he has — manners** tiene modales muy finos; **where are all the — girls?** ¿adónde se habrán metido todas las chicas finas?; **only — people live here** aquí no vive sino gente culta, (pej) aquí no vive sino gente bien; **a — district** un barrio elegante; **that's not — aquello** es feo, eso no es fino.

  (f) (intensive) muy, bastante, bien; **— and sweet** bien dulce; **— and early** tempranito; **it's — and warm here** aquí hace un calor agradable; **my feet are — and warm** tengo los pies a gusto y calientes; **a — long holiday** unas vacaciones bien largas; **a — cold drink** una bebida bien fría.

  (g) (fastidious) melindroso, delicado; difícil de contentar; (exacting) exigente; (precise) exacto, meticuloso; (scrupulous) escrupuloso; **he's not too — about his methods** no es demasiado escrupuloso en cuanto a sus métodos.

  (h) (requiring care etc) fino, delicado, sutil; **a — distinction** una distinción sutil; **a — point** un punto delicado; **it's a — question whether . . .** es difícil determinar si . . .

  (i) (discriminating) fino, discernidor; **he has a — ear** tiene un oído fino.

  (j) (iro) bonito, valiente; **a — friend you are!** ¡valiente amigo!; **that's a — thing to say!** ¡qué cosas más bonitas me dices!; **a — mess** ¡un lío imponente!

nice-looking ['nais'lukiŋ] adj atractivo; person mono, guapo.

nicely ['naisli] adv amablemente; agradablemente; con finura, bien; very —, thanks muy bien, gracias; **a — situated house** una casa bien situada; **that will do —** eso está muy bien; **he's getting on —** hace buenos progresos; **she thanked me very —** muy amablemente me dio las gracias; **the child behaves quite —** el niño tiene modales bastante buenos.

niceness ['naisnis] n simpatía f, lo simpático; amabilidad f; lo agradable, amenidad f; finura f, lo culto; delicadeza f; meticulosidad f; escrupulosidad f; sutileza f; discernimiento m.

nicety ['naisiti] n = **niceness**; **to judge something to a —** juzgar algo con toda precisión; **niceties detalles** mpl, puntos mpl sutiles.

niche [niːʃ] n nicho m; hornacina f; (fig) colocación f

conveniente, buena posición f; **to find a — for oneself** encontrarse una buena posición.

Nicholas ['nikələs] m Nicolás.

Nick [nik] nombre cariñoso de **Nicholas; Old — Patillas.**

nick¹ [nik] **1** n mella f, muesca f, corte m; **in the — of time** a última hora, en el momento crítico.

  2 vt **(a)** mellar, hacer muescas en, hacer cortes en; cortar; (with sword etc) pinchar.

  (b) (sl: steal) robar, birlar; (sl: arrest) trincar.

nick² [nik] n (sl: prison) jaula f.

nickel ['nikl] n níquel m; (US) moneda de 5 centavos.

nickel-plated ['nikl'pleitid] adj niquelado.

nickname ['nikneim] **1** n apodo m, mote m. **2** vt apodar; **they —d him Nobby** le dieron el apodo de Nobby; **Clark —d Nobby Clark** apodado Nobby.

nicotine ['nikətiːn] n nicotina f.

niece [niːs] n sobrina f.

niff [nif] n (sl) olorcito m (of a); tufillo m.

niffy ['nifi] adj (sl) maloliente.

nifty ['nifti] adj (fam) (smart) elegante, muy pena; (skilful) diestro, hábil, experto.

Nigeria [nai'dʒiəriə] Nigeria f.

Nigerian [nai'dʒiəriən] **1** adj nigeriano. **2** n nigeriano m, a f.

niggardliness ['nigədlinis] n tacañería f.

niggardly ['nigədli] adj person tacaño, avariento; allowance etc miserable.

nigger ['nigə*] n (pej) negro m, a f; **to be the — in the woodpile** ser el obstáculo, ser la cosa que estropea el todo.

niggle ['nigl] vi (worry) inquietarse por pequeñeces; (fuss) perder el tiempo con detalles nimios; (complain) quejarse, murmurar.

niggling ['nigliŋ] adj detail nimio, insignificante; (small-minded) de miras estrechas.

nigh [nai] (arch or prov) **1** adv cerca; casi, **it's — on finished** está casi terminado. **2** prep cerca de.

night [nait] **1** n noche f; **a Beethoven —** un concierto dedicado a la música de Beethoven; **first —** (Theat) estreno m; **good —!** ¡buenas noches!; **last — anoche; the — before last** anteanoche; **tomorrow — mañana** por la noche; **the — before the ceremony** la víspera de la ceremonia; **all — toda la noche; at —, by —, in the —** de noche, por la noche; **11 o'clock at —** las 11 de la noche; **it is — es** de noche; **it's the servant's — out** es la tarde libre de la criada; **to have a — out** salir de juerga por la noche; **to have a bad —** dormir mal, pasar una mala noche; **to have a late —** no acostarse hasta muy tarde; **she's used to late —s** ella está acostumbrada a acostarse muy tarde; **to make a — of it** estar de juerga hasta muy entrada la noche.

  2 attr nocturno, de noche; **— work** trabajo m nocturno.

night-bird ['naitbəːd] n pájaro m nocturno; (person) trasnochador m, ora f.

nightcap ['naitkæp] n gorro m de dormir; (drink) resopón m.

night club ['naitklʌb] n cabaret m.

nightdress ['naitdres] n camisón m (de noche).

nightfall ['naitfɔːl] n anochecer m; **at —** al anochecer; **by —** antes del anochecer.

night-fighter ['naitfaitə*] n (Aer) caza m nocturno.

nightgown ['naitgaun] n, **nightie** ['naiti] n (fam) camisón m (de noche).

nightingale ['naitiŋgeil] n ruiseñor m.

nightjar ['naitdʒaː*] n chotacabras m.

night life ['naitlaif] n vida f nocturna.

night light ['naitlait] n mariposa f.

nightly ['naitli] **1** adv todas las noches. **2** adj de noche, nocturno; (regular) de todas las noches.

nightmare ['naitmeə*] n pesadilla f (also fig).

nightmarish ['naitmeəriʃ] adj de pesadilla.

night school ['naitskuːl] n escuela f nocturna.

nightshade ['naitʃeid] n dulcamara f, hierba f mora; **deadly —** belladona f.

nightshift ['naitʃift] n turno m de noche.

nightshirt ['naitʃəːt] n camisa f de dormir (de caballero).

night-time ['naittaim] n noche f; **in the —** de noche, durante la noche.

night watchman ['nait'wɔtʃmən] n, pl **—men** [mən] sereno m; vigilante m de noche, vigilante m nocturno.

nihilism ['naiilizəm] n nihilismo m.

nihilist ['naiilist] n nihilista mf.

nihilistic [ˌnaii'listik] adj nihilista.

nil [nil] n cero m, nada f; **Granada beat Murcia two — el** Granada venció al Murcia dos-cero.

Nile [nail] Nilo m.

nimble ['nimbl] adj (in moving) ágil, ligero; (in wit) listo; fingers etc diestro, experto.

nimbly ['nimbli] adv ágilmente, ligeramente; diestramente.

nimbus ['nimbəs] n nimbo m.

nincompoop ['niŋkəmpu:p] n bobo m, a f, papirote m.

nine [nain] adj nueve; **to be dressed up to the —s** estar hecho un brazo de mar.

ninepins ['nainpinz] npl (objects) bolos mpl; (game) juego m de bolos; **to go down like —** caer como bolos en bolera.

nineteen ['nain'ti:n] adj diecinueve; see **dozen.**

nineteenth ['nain'ti:nθ] adj decimonoveno, decimonono.

ninetieth ['naintiiθ] adj nonagésimo.

ninety ['nainti] adj noventa; **the nineties** (eg 1990s) los años noventa; **the naughty nineties** los alegres años noventa (del siglo XIX); **to be in one's nineties** tener más de noventa años.

ninny ['nini] n bobo m, a f.

ninth [nainθ] adj noveno, nono.

nip[1] [nip] **1** n pellizco m; mordisco m; **there's a — in the air** hace un poco frío, hay helada.
2 vt (with fingers) pellizcar, pinchar; (bite) mordiscar; (cut) cortar; plant helar; (wind) picar, helar; (sl) coger, birlar; **to — one's fingers in a door** cogerse los dedos en una puerta; **to — off** cortar.
3 vi correr, ir a toda velocidad; **we were —ping along at 80 mph** corríamos a 80 mph; **to — in** entrar, entrar un momento; entrar sin ser visto; **to — in and out of the traffic** colarse por entre el tráfico; **to — off** pirarse, largarse; **I must — out for a moment** salgo un momento; **I —ped round to the shop** fui en dos patadas a la tienda.

nip[2] [nip] n (of drink) trago m.

nipper ['nipə*] n chiquillo m, a f.

nipple ['nipl] n (Anat) pezón m; (of man, bottle) tetilla f; (Mech) boquilla f roscada, manguito m de unión; (for greasing) engrasador m, pezón m de engrase.

nippy ['nipi] adj person ágil, listo; car etc rápido, veloz; **be — about it!** ¡corre!, ¡menéarse!; **we shall have to be —** tendremos que darnos prisa.

nit [nit] n (Zool) liendre f; (sl) imbécil mf, idiota m; **you —!** ¡imbécil!

nitrate ['naitreit] n nitrato m.

nitre, (US) **niter** ['naitə*] n nitro m.

nitric ['naitrik] adj: **— acid** ácido m nítrico.

nitrogen ['naitrədʒən] n nitrógeno m.

nitrogenous [nai'trɔdʒinəs] adj nitrogenado.

nitroglycerin(e) ['naitrəu'glisəri:n] n nitroglicerina f.

nitrous ['naitrəs] adj nitroso.

nitwit ['nitwit] n (sl) imbécil mf, idiota m; **you —!** ¡imbécil!

nix [niks] n (sl) nada.

no [nəu] **1** adv (a) no; **whether he comes or —** si viene o no.
(b) (comp) **I am — taller than you** yo no soy más alto que tú.
2 adj (a) ninguno, no . . . alguno; **no-one** see **nobody;** (often not translated, eg) **I have — money** no tengo dinero, no tengo dinero alguno; **he made — reply** no contestó, no dio respuesta alguna; **— two of them are alike** no hay dos iguales; **it's — distance** no está lejos; **it's — trouble** no es molestia; **— surrender!** ¡no nos rendimos! **"— smoking"** "se prohíbe fumar"; **details of little or — interest** detalles mpl de poco o ningún interés.
(b) **problems of — easy solution** problemas que no tienen soluciones fáciles, problemas que no se resolverán fácilmente; **it is — easy task** es una tarea nada fácil; **he's — poet** de poeta no tiene nada; **he was — general** no era lo que se llama un general, no merecía el nombre de general; **judge or — judge, he's a fool** no importa que sea juez, es un tonto.
(c) **there's — denying it** es imposible negarlo; **there's — getting out of it** no hay posibilidad de evitarlo; **there's — pleasing him** resulta imposible contentarle.
3 n (pl **noes** [nəuz]) (a) no m; **I won't take — for an answer** no permito que lo rechaces, no acepto una respuesta negativa.
(b) (Parl) voto m negativo, voto m en contra; **there were 7 —es** votaron 7 en contra; **the —es have it** se ha rechazado la moción.

Noah ['nəuə] m Noé.

nob[1] [nɔb] n (sl: Anat) cabeza f.

nob[2] [nɔb] n (sl: person of importance) personaje m, pájaro m de cuenta; (toff) majo m, currutaco m.

nobble ['nɔbl] vt (sl) person sobornar; ejercer presión sobre, persuadir por medios nada rectos; horse narcotizar, estropear; (arrest) coger; (steal) birlar, pisar.

nobility [nəu'biliti] n (all senses) nobleza f.

noble ['nəubl] **1** adj noble; title de nobleza. **2** n noble m, aristócrata m, (Spanish Hist) hidalgo m.

nobleman ['nəublmən] n, pl **—men** [mən] noble m, aristócrata m, (Spanish Hist) hidalgo m.

nobleness ['nəublnis] n nobleza f.

noblesse oblige [nəu'blesəu'bli:ʒ] nobleza obliga.

noblewoman ['nəublwumən] n, pl **—women** [wimin] dama f noble, aristócrata f, (Spanish Hist) hidalga f.

nobly ['nəubli] adv noblemente, con nobleza; (fig) generosamente.

nobody ['nəubədi] **1** pron nadie; **— spoke** nadie habló, no habló nadie; **who spoke? . . . —** ¿quién habló? . . . nadie; **— has more right to it than she has** no hay nadie que tenga más derecho a ello que ella; **would — buy it?** ¿no había quién lo comprara?
2 n: **a mere —** un don nadie, un cero a la izquierda; **I knew him when he was —** le conocí cuando no era nadie.

nocturnal [nɔk'tə:nl] adj nocturno.

nocturne ['nɔktə:n] n nocturno m.

nod [nɔd] **1** n (sleepy etc) cabezada f; (sign) señal f hecha con la cabeza, inclinación f de cabeza; **a — is as good as a wink** a buen entendedor con pocas palabras basta; **he gave me a —** me saludó inclinando la cabeza; **he agreed with a —** asintió con la cabeza; **to go through on the —** ser aprobado sin discusión, ser aprobado sin someterse a votación.
2 vt head inclinar, mover, hacer una señal con; **he —ded his agreement** asintió con la cabeza; **he —ded a greeting** me saludó inclinando la cabeza; **he —ded his head** (ie saying yes) asintió con la cabeza, movió la cabeza afirmativamente.
3 vi (sleepily) dar cabezadas, cabecear; (say yes) decir que sí con la cabeza, asentir con la cabeza; (trees) mecerse, inclinarse; **Homer —s** incluso Homero se duerme a veces.

noddle ['nɔdl] n (fam) mollera f.

node [nəud] n (Anat, Astron, Phys) nodo m; (Bot) nudo m.

nodular ['nɔdjulə*] adj nodular.

nodule ['nɔdju:l] n nódulo m.

noggin ['nɔgin] n (a) vaso m pequeño, (loosely) vaso m, caña f (de cerveza); **let's have a —** tomemos algo.
(b) (measure) medida de licor (= 1,42 decilitros).

no-good ['nəugud] adj (US fam) malísimo, malvado.

nohow ['nəuhau] adv (fam) de ninguna manera, por ningún medio que sea.

noise [nɔiz] **1** n (a) ruido m; estrépito m; estruendo m; clamor m; tumulto m; alboroto m; (fig) escándalo m; **to make a —** hacer ruido; **the book made a lot of — when it came out** el libro causó un escándalo cuando apareció, al aparecer se armó un escándalo en torno al libro.
(b) **big —** (person: fam) pez m gordo, pájaro m de cuenta; **he's a big —** now ahora es un personaje.
2 vt: **to — something abroad** divulgar la noticia de algo, hacer correr la voz de algo; **we don't want it —d abroad** no queremos que se publique.

noiseless ['nɔizlis] adj silenciosamente, sin ruido.

noisily ['nɔizili] adv ruidosamente, estrepitosamente, clamorosamente; escandalosamente.

noisiness ['nɔizinis] n ruido m, estrépito m; lo ruidoso, lo estrepitoso.

noisome ['nɔisəm] adj (disgusting) asqueroso; (smelly) fétido, maloliente; (harmful) nocivo.

noisy ['nɔizi] adj ruidoso, estrepitoso, clamoroso; child etc escandaloso; protest ruidoso.

nomad ['nəumæd] n nómada mf.

nomadic [nəu'mædik] adj nómada.

nomadism ['nəumædizəm] n nomadismo m.

no-man's land ['nəumænzlænd] n tierra f de nadie.

nom de plume ['nɔmdə'plu:m] n seudónimo m, nombre m artístico.

nomenclature [nəu'menklətʃə*] n nomenclatura f.

nominal ['nɔminl] adj nominal; sum, rent etc nominal; **he's only the — head** es el jefe solamente en nombre.

nominalism ['nɔminəlizəm] n nominalismo m.

nominally ['nɔminəli] adv nominalmente.

nominate ['nɔmineit] vt nombrar; **to — someone as chairman** proponer a uno como candidato a la presidencia, nombrar a uno para presidente; **to — someone for a job** nombrar a uno para un cargo.

nomination [,nɔmi'neiʃən] n nombramiento m; propuesta f.

nominative ['nɔminətiv] n nominativo m.

nominee [,nɔmi'ni:] n candidato m; **the — of someone** el candidato propuesto por uno, el candidato que apoya uno.

non . . . [nɔn] *in compounds:* no . . ., des . . ., in . . .

non-acceptance ['nɔnək'septəns] n rechazo m.

nonagenarian [ˌnɔnədʒi'nɛəriən] **1** adj nonagenario, noventón. **2** n nonagenario m, a f, noventón m, ona f.

non-aggression ['nɔnə'greʃən] n no agresión f; — **pact** pacto m de no agresión.

non-alcoholic ['nɔnælkə'hɔlik] adj no alcohólico, analcohólico.

non-aligned ['nɔnə'laind] adj neutral, no comprometido.

non-alignment ['nɔnə'lainmənt] n neutralismo m; no comprometimiento m.

non-appearance ['nɔnə'piərəns] n ausencia f; (Law) no comparecencia f.

non-arrival ['nɔnə'raivəl] n ausencia f.

non-attendance ['nɔnə'tendəns] n ausencia f, falta f de asistencia.

nonbelligerent ['nɔnbi'lidʒərənt] **1** adj no beligerante. **2** n no beligerante mf.

non-breakable ['nɔn'breikəbl] adj irrompible.

non-Catholic ['nɔn'kæθlik] **1** adj no católico, acatólico. **2** n no católico m, no católica f.

nonce [nɔns] adv: **for the —** por el momento.

nonce-word ['nɔnswəːd] n palabra f creada para un caso especial.

nonchalance ['nɔnʃələns] n indiferencia f; negligencia f; aplomo m; sangre f fría, calma f.

nonchalant ['nɔnʃələnt] adj indiferente, impasible; negligente; **to be — about something** no prestar atención a algo, no tomar algo en serio; **with — ease** con aplomo y facilidad.

nonchalantly ['nɔnʃələntli] adv con indiferencia; negligentemente; con aplomo, con calma; **a — knotted tie** una corbata negligentemente anudada.

noncom ['nɔnkəm] n (Mil fam) suboficial m.

non-combatant ['nɔn'kɔmbətənt] **1** adj no combatiente. **2** n no combatiente mf.

non-commissioned ['nɔnkə'miʃənd] adj: **— officer** suboficial m, sargento m or cabo m; **— officers** (approx) clases fpl de tropa.

non-committal ['nɔnkə'mitl] adj statement etc que no compromete a nada; (pej) evasivo, equívoco; **he was very — about it** se abstuvo de comprometerse a nada, no quiso concretar, eludió tomar una resolución definitiva.

non-compliance ['nɔnkəm'plaiəns] n incumplimiento m, infracción f (with de); desobediencia f (with de).

non-conductor ['nɔnkən'dʌktə*] n (Elec) no conductor m, mal conductor m.

nonconformism ['nɔnkən'fɔːmizəm] n inconformismo m.

nonconformist ['nɔnkən'fɔːmist] **1** adj inconformista. **2** n inconformista mf.

nonconformity ['nɔnkən'fɔːmiti] n inconformismo m, disidencia f.

non-cooperation ['nɔnkəu,ɔpə'reiʃən] n (Pol) no cooperación f.

nondescript ['nɔndiskript] adj indeterminado, inclasificable; (pej) mediocre.

none [nʌn] **1** pron (person) nadie; (person, thing) ninguno; (thing) nada; **— of them** ninguno de ellos; **— of you can tell me** ninguno de vosotros sabe decirme; **we have — of your books** no tenemos ninguno de sus libros; **— can tell** nadie lo sabe; **but he knows of this** nadie sino él está enterado de esto; **— of this is true** ninguna parte de esto es verdad; **any news? . . .** — ¿alguna noticia? . . . nada; **I'm sorry, there are —** lo siento, pero no hay; **there are — left** no queda ninguno; **— of that, now!** ¡déjese de eso!; **I want — of your lectures!** ¡basta ya de sermones!; **he is aware, — better, that . . .** se da cuenta, cómo no, de que . . .; **it was — other than the bishop** fue el obispo en persona, fue el propio obispo.

2 adj: **riches have I —** riqueza no la tengo; **reply came there —** no hubo respuesta.

3 adv de ningún modo; **I was — too comfortable** no me sentía muy cómodo; **they get on — too well** no se llevan del todo bien; **it was — too soon** ya era tiempo; **it's — the worse for that** no es peor por eso (and see worse); **he was still — the better off** aun así no había mejorado su posición en lo más mínimo.

nonentity [nɔ'nentiti] n nulidad f, cero m a la izquierda.

non-essential ['nɔni'senʃəl] **1** adj no esencial. **2** n cosa f no esencial.

non-existence ['nɔnig'zistəns] n inexistencia f.

non-existent ['nɔnig'zistənt] adj inexistente.

non-ferrous ['nɔn'ferəs] adj no ferroso, no férreo.

non-fiction ['nɔn'fikʃən] n literatura f no novelesca.

non-fulfilment ['nɔnful'filmənt] n incumplimiento m.

non-inflammable ['nɔnin'flæməbl] adj ininflamable.

non-intervention ['nɔn,intə'venʃən] n no intervención f.

non-iron ['nɔn'aiən] adj de no planchar, que no necesita planchado.

non-laddering ['nɔn'lædəriŋ] adj (stocking) indesmallable.

non-member ['nɔn,membə*] n no miembro m, visitante mf.

nonpareil ['nɔnpərəl] **1** adj sin par. **2** n persona f sin par, cosa f sin par; (Typ) nomparell m.

nonpartisan ['nɔn,pɑːti'zæn] adj independiente, imparcial.

non-party ['nɔn'pɑːti] adj (Pol) independiente.

non-payment ['nɔn'peimənt] n impago m; **sued for — of debts** demandado por no pagar sus deudas.

nonplus ['nɔn'plʌs] vt dejar perplejo, confundir; **he was completely —sed** estaba totalmente perplejo; **I confess myself —sed** confieso que estoy perplejo.

non-professional ['nɔnprə'feʃnəl] adj no profesional, aficionado.

non-profitmaking ['nɔn'prɔfitmeikiŋ] adj no lucrativo, no comercial.

non-resident ['nɔn'rezidənt] **1** adj no residente, no fijo, transeúnte. **2** n no residente mf, huésped m no fijo, transeúnte mf.

nonsectarian ['nɔnsek'tɛəriən] adj no sectario.

nonsense ['nɔnsəns] n disparates mpl, tonterías fpl, desatinos mpl; **a —, a piece of —** una tontería; **¡tonterías!; what —!** ¡qué ridículo!; **but that's —** ¡eso es absurdo!; **it is — to say that . . .** es absurdo decir que . . .; **this passage makes —** este pasaje no tiene sentido; **this makes a — of our policy** esto es volver de arriba abajo nuestra política; **to talk —** no decir más que tonterías; **it's just his —** son cosas de él; **we don't want any of your —** no queremos escuchar esas tonterías tuyas.

nonsensical [nɔn'sensikəl] adj disparatado, absurdo, tonto.

non-shrink ['nɔn'ʃriŋk] adj inencogible.

non-skid ['nɔn'skid] adj antideslizante, antirresbaladizo.

non-smoker ['nɔn'sməukə*] n (person) no fumador m; (Rail) departamento m de no fumadores; **I've always been a —** no he fumado nunca.

non-smoking ['nɔn'sməukiŋ] adj person que no fuma; (Rail) para no fumadores.

non-stop ['nɔn'stɔp] **1** adv sin parar; (Rail) directamente; (Aer etc) sin escalas; **he talks —** no para de hablar. **2** adj continuo, incesante; (Rail) directo; (Aer) sin escalas.

non-taxable ['nɔn'tæksəbl] adj no sujeto a impuestos.

non-union ['nɔn'juːnjən] adj shop etc no sindicalizado.

non-violence ['nɔn'vaiələns] n no violencia f.

non-violent ['nɔn'vaiələnt] adj no violento, pacífico.

noodle ['nuːdl] n (fam: head) cabeza f; (fool) bobo m a f.

noodles ['nuːdlz] npl tallarines mpl; **— soup** sopa f de pastas.

nook [nuk] n rincón m; escondrijo m.

noon [nuːn] n (also **noonday** ['nuːndei]) **1** n mediodía m; **at —** a mediodía; **high —** (fig) apogeo m, punto m culminante. **2** attr de mediodía.

no-one ['nəuwan] pron = **nobody**.

noose [nuːs] **1** n lazo m corredizo; (hangman's) dogal m. **2** vt coger con lazo.

nope [nəup] interj (esp US fam) ¡no!

nor [nɔː*] conj ni; **neither A — B** ni A ni B; **— I** ni yo, ni yo tampoco; **I don't know, — can I guess** no lo sé, ni puedo conjeturarlo; **— does it seem likely** ni tampoco parece probable; **— was this all** y esto no fue todo.

Nordic ['nɔːdik] adj nórdico.

norm [nɔːm] n norma f; pauta f; modelo m; (Bio etc) tipo m; **larger than the —** más grande que lo normal, (Bio) más grande que el tipo; **to exceed one's —** exceder de la norma.

normal ['nɔːməl] **1** adj normal; regular, corriente; **the child is not —** el niño es anormal; **it is perfectly — to + infin** es muy normal + infin. **2** n estado m normal; nivel m normal; normalidad f; **the — is 20 degrees** lo normal es 20 grados; **things are returning to —** la situación vuelve a la normalidad.

normalcy ['nɔːməlsi] n normalidad f.

normality [nɔː'mæliti] n normalidad f.

normalize ['nɔːməlaiz] vt normalizar.

normally ['nɔːməli] adv normalmente.

Norman ['nɔːmən] **1** adj normando; (Archit) normánico. **2** n normando m, a f.

Normandy ['nɔ:məndi] Normandía f.

Norman-French ['nɔ:mən'frentʃ] **1** adj normando francés. **2** n normando francés m.

Norse [nɔ:s] **1** adj nórdico, noruego, escandinavo. **2** n (language) nórdico m.

Norseman ['nɔ:smən] n, pl —**men** [mən] vikingo m, escandinavo m.

north [nɔ:θ] **1** n norte m. **2** adj del norte, septentrional. **3** adv al norte, hacia el norte.

North Africa ['nɔ:θ'æfrikə] África f del Norte.

North America ['nɔ:θə'merikə] América f del Norte, Norteamérica f.

North American ['nɔ:θə'merikən] **1** adj norteamericano. **2** n norteamericano m, a f.

north-east ['nɔ:θ'i:st] **1** n nor(d)este m. **2** adj point, direction nor(d)este; wind del nor(d)este.

north-easterly ['nɔ:θ'i:stəli] adj point, direction nor(d)este; wind del nor(d)este.

north-eastern ['nɔ:θ'i:stən] adj nor(d)este.

north-eastward(s) ['nɔ:θ'i:stwəd(z)] adv hacia el nor(d)este.

northerly ['nɔ:ðəli] adj point, direction norte; wind del norte; **the most — point in Europe** el punto más septentrional de Europa, el punto más nórdico de Europa.

northern ['nɔ:ðən] adj del norte, septentrional, norteño.

northerner ['nɔ:ðənə*] n habitante mf del norte; nórdico m, a f; **he's a —** es del norte; **the —s are kindly people** los nórdicos son gente amable.

Northern Ireland ['nɔ:ðən'aiələnd] Irlanda f del Norte.

northernmost ['nɔ:ðənməust] adj (el) más norte, situado más al norte; **the — town in Europe** la ciudad más septentrional de Europa.

North Korea ['nɔ:θkə'riə] Corea f del Norte.

North Korean ['nɔ:θkə'riən] **1** adj norcoreano. **2** n norcoreano m, a f.

northland ['nɔ:θlənd] n (US) región f septentrional.

Northman ['nɔ:θmən] n, pl —**men** [mən] vikingo m, escandinavo m.

North Sea ['nɔ:θ'si:] Mar m del Norte.

North Vietnam ['nɔ:θviet'næm] Vietnam m del Norte.

North Vietnamese ['nɔ:θvietnə'mi:z] **1** adj norvietnamita. **2** n norvietnamita mf.

northward(s) ['nɔ:θwəd(z)] adv hacia el norte.

north-west ['nɔ:θ'west] **1** n noroeste m. **2** adj point, direction noroeste; wind del noroeste.

north-westerly ['nɔ:θ'westəli] adj point, direction noroeste; wind del noroeste.

north-western ['nɔ:θ'westən] adj noroeste.

north-westward(s) ['nɔ:θ'westwəd(z)] adv hacia el noroeste.

Norway ['nɔ:wei] Noruega f.

Norwegian [nɔ:'wi:dʒən] **1** adj noruego. **2** n noruego m, a f. **3** n (language) noruego m.

nose [nəuz] **1** n (Anat) nariz f; (pej) narizota f, narices fpl; (of animal) hocico m; (sense of smell) olfato m; (Aer) morro m, proa f; (Naut) proa f; **flat —** nariz f chata; **snub —** nariz f respingona; **Roman —** nariz f aguileña; **right under one's —** a ojos vistas, en las barbas de uno, bajo las narices de uno; **to bleed at the —** echar sangre por las narices; **to blow one's —** sonarse (las narices); **to follow one's —** (go straight) ir todo seguido, (by instinct) dejarse guiar por el instinto; **to get one's — in front** conseguir una pequeña ventaja; **to have a good — for something** tener buen olfato para algo; **to hold one's —** taparse las narices; **to lead someone by the —** tener a uno agarrado por las narices; **to look down one's — at something** desdeñar algo, mirar algo con desprecio; **to make someone pay through the —** desollar a uno, cobrar a uno un precio elevadísimo; **to pay through the —** dejarse desollar (for something al comprar algo); **to talk through one's —** hablar por las narices; **to poke** (or **stick**) **one's — into something** meter las narices en algo; **who asked you to poke your — in?** ¿quién le manda a Vd meter su nariz en esto?; **to turn up one's — at something** hacer un gesto de desprecio al ver algo, desdeñar algo; see **grindstone**, **joint**. **2** vt: **to — something out** husmear algo, olfatear algo; secret lograr descubrir; **to — one's way forward** avanzar con precaución. **3** vi: **to — about** curiosear.

nosebag ['nəuzbæg] n morral m, cebadera f.

nosebleed ['nəuzbli:d] n hemorragia f nasal.

-nosed [nəuzd] adj de nariz . . ., eg **red-nosed** de nariz coloradota.

nose-dive ['nəuzdaiv] **1** n picado m vertical; (involuntary) caída f de narices. **2** vi descender en picado; (involuntarily) caer de morro (into en).

nosegay ['nəuzgei] n ramillete m.

nosey ['nəuzi] adj curioso, fisgón.

nosey-parker ['nəuzi'pɑ:kə*] n fisgón m, ona f.

nosh [nɔʃ] n (sl) comida f; — **up**! ¡la comida está servida!

nostalgia [nɔs'tældʒiə] nostalgia f.

nostalgic [nɔs'tældʒik] adj nostálgico.

nostril ['nɔstril] n nariz f, ventana f de la nariz; —**s** narices fpl.

nostrum ['nɔstrəm] n panacea f (also fig); remedio m secreto.

not [nɔt] adv (a) no; **he is — here** no está aquí; **fear —**! ¡no temas!; **is it — so**? ¿no es verdad?; **you owe me money, do you —**? me debes algo, ¿no es verdad?; **he is a doctor, is he —**? es (un) médico, ¿no?; **he asked me — to do it** me rogó no hacerlo.
(b) **I wish it were — so** ¡ojalá no fuera así!; **whether you go or —** vayas o no; **let me know if — avíseme en caso contrario; si no, me avisa; I think — creo que no; — thinking that . . . sin pensar que . . .; — that I don't like him** no es que me resulte antipático; **big, — to say enormous** grande, por no decir enorme; **why —**? ¿por qué no?, ¿cómo no?; — **without some regrets** no sin cierto sentimiento.
(c) **absolutely —**! ¡en absoluto!; **certainly —**!, — **likely**! ¡de ninguna manera!, ¡ni hablar!; **of course —**! ¡claro que no!
(d) (with pron etc) — **I**! ¡yo no!; — **one** ni uno; — **him either** él tampoco, ni él tampoco; — **everybody can do it** no es cosa que todos sepan hacer; — **any more** ya no.
(e) (understatement) **with — a little surprise** con no poca sorpresa; **there were — a few lions** hubo no pocos leones; see **even**, **much** etc.

notability [,nəutə'biliti] n notabilidad f; (person) notabilidad f, personaje m.

notable ['nəutəbl] **1** adj notable; señalado, memorable; **it is — that . . . es notable que . . . 2** n notabilidad f, personaje m; —**s** notables mpl.

notably ['nəutəbli] adv notablemente, señaladamente.

notarial [nəu'tɛəriəl] adj notarial.

notary ['nəutəri] n notario m (also **public —**).

notation [nəu'teifən] n notación f.

notch [nɔtʃ] **1** n muesca f, mella f, corte m. **2** vt cortar muescas en, mellar; **to — up** apuntar.

note [nəut] **1** n (a) (Mus etc) nota f; **false —** nota f falsa; **with a — of anxiety in his voice** con una nota de inquietud en la voz; **to hit the right —** (fig) acertar, elegir acertadamente el tono (de un discurso etc); **to strike quite the wrong —** (fig) desentonar, ser como perro en misa, ser como guitarra en un entierro.
(b) (sign, stigma) marca f, señal f; — **of infamy** nota f de infamia.
(c) (annotation) nota f, apunte m; apuntación f; (foot—) nota f (en pie de página); "**N—s on Lucan**" "Apuntes mpl sobre Lucano"; "**editor's —**" (in newspaper) "nota de la redacción"; **to compare —s** cambiar impresiones, discutir los resultados; **to make a — of something** apuntar algo, tomar nota de algo; **to speak from —s** pronunciar un discurso a base de apuntes; **to take a — of something** tomar nota de algo; **to take down —s** tomar apuntes.
(d) (letter etc) nota f, carta f; recado m; esquela f; **take a —, Miss Jones** tome nota, señorita.
(e) (Comm) vale m; (bank—) billete m; **promissory —** pagaré m.
(f) (eminence) **of —** notable, eminente, de importancia; **man of —** hombre m notable.
(g) (notice) **worthy of —** digno de atención; **nothing of —** nada de particular, sin novedad; **to take — of** prestar atención a, ocuparse de; **only the critics took — of the book** sólo se ocuparon del libro los críticos.
2 vt (observe) notar, observar, advertir; (write down) apuntar, anotar (also **to — down**); **we duly — that . . . nos hacemos cuenta de que . . . ; your remarks have been —d** hemos leído con atención sus observaciones.

notebook ['nəutbuk] n libro m de apuntes, libreta f; (student's etc) cuaderno m.

note-case ['nəutkeis] n cartera f, billetero m.

noted ['nəutid] adj célebre, conocido, famoso (for por).

notepaper ['nəut,peipə*] n papel m para cartas.

noteworthy ['nəut,wə:ði] adj notable, digno de notarse; **it is — that . . . es notable que . . .**

nothing ['nʌθiŋ] **1** n **(a)** nada; (nought) cero m; **I have — to give you** no tengo nada que darte, nada tengo que darte; **I see — that I like** no veo nada que me guste; **— else** nada más; **— much** poca cosa; **there's — much to be said** poco es lo que hay que decir; **next to —** casi nada; **there is — mean about him** no tiene nada de tacaño; **there's — special about it** no tiene nada de particular; **it's — to be proud of** no hay motivo para enorgullecerse; **there's — to fear** no hay de qué tener miedo.

(b) there is — in the rumours los rumores no tienen ni pizca de verdad; **there's — in it** (in race) van muy iguales; **there's — in it for us** de esto no vamos a sacar nada útil; **there's — for it but to pay** no hay más remedio que pagar; **there's — to it!** ¡es facilísimo!; **she is — to him** ella le es indiferente; **it is — to me whether he comes or not** no me importa que venga o no; **he is — if not careful** es prudente por encima de todo; **I'm — of a swimmer** yo nado bastante mal.

(c) for — (free) gratis, (unpaid) gratuitamente, sin sueldo, (in vain) en vano, en balde; **it is not for — that . . .** no es sin motivo que . . .

(d) to build up a business from — crear un negocio de la nada; **to come to —** fracasar, parar en nada, no dar resultado; **to make — of** (not understand) no entender, no sacar nada en claro de; (not use) no aprovechar; (not esteem) no dar importancia a; **to say — of** sin mencionar . . ., amén de . . .; **to think — of** tener en poco, **task** tener por fácil; **he thinks — of walking 20 miles** para él no tiene importancia recorrer 20 millas a pie; **he thinks — of borrowing a fiver** con la mayor frescura pide prestado un billete de 5 libras; **think — of it!** ¡no hay de qué!

(e) a mere — una friolera, una bagatela; **a mere —!** ¡una bagatela!; **to say sweet —s to someone** decir mil ternezas a una; see **do, doing, kind** etc.

2 adv de ninguna manera; **it's — like him** el retrato no se le parece en nada; **it was — like so big as we thought** era mucho menos grande de lo que nos imaginábamos; **pretty girl —!** ¡guapa, ni hablar! (fam); **— daunted** sin inmutarse; see **less.**

nothingness ['nʌθiŋnis] n nada f.

notice ['nəutis] **1** n **(a)** (intimation, warning) aviso m; **at short —** a corto plazo, con poco tiempo de anticipación; **at a moment's —** en el acto, inmediatamente, casi sin aviso; **you must be ready to leave at a moment's —** has de estar listo para partir luego de recibir el aviso; **until further —** hasta nuevo aviso; **without previous —** sin previo aviso; **he went without —** se fue sin avisar a nadie; **to give someone at least a week's —** avisar a uno lo menos con una semana de anticipación; **to give someone — that . . .,** **to serve — on someone that . . .** avisar a uno que . . ., hacer saber a uno que . . .; **— is hereby given that . . .** se pone en conocimiento del público que . . .; **to give someone — to do something** avisar a uno que haga algo; **I must have — es** imprescindible avisarme con anticipación; **we had no — of it** no nos habían avisado, no sabíamos nada de ello; **final —** aviso m definitivo (or final); **— to quit** aviso m de desalojo.

(b) (order to leave job etc: by employer) despido m, (by employee) dimisión f; (period) plazo m; **to be under —** estar dimitido; **to dismiss someone without —** despedir a uno sin aviso; **to get one's —** ser despedido; **to give someone —** despedir a uno; **to give someone a week's —** despedir a uno con una semana de plazo; **to give someone — to do something** avisar a uno que . . .; **to take — of someone** hacer caso a uno; **a fat lot of — he takes of me!** ¡maldito el caso que me hace!; **to take — of something** hacer caso de algo, prestar atención a algo; **to take no — of something** no hacer caso de algo; **he took no —** no hizo caso; **take no —!** ¡no haga Vd caso!, ¡no importa!; **I was not taking much — at the time** en ese momento iba yo algo distraído; **to sit up and take —** despertar y prestar atención.

2 vt **(a)** (perceive) notar, observar, reparar en, fijarse en; **I never —d** no me había fijado; **I don't — such things** no me fijo en tales cosas.

(b) (heed) hacer caso de.

(c) (recognize) ver, reconocer; **eventually he deigned to — me** por fin se dignó reconocerme.

(d) (review) reseñar, escribir una reseña de.

noticeable ['nəutisəbl] adj evidente, obvio; sensible, perceptible; notable; **it was — that . . .** era evidente que . . ., se echaba de ver que . . .; **there has been a — increase in . . .** ha habido un aumento sensible de . . .

noticeably ['nəutisəbli] adv evidentemente, obviamente; sensiblemente; notablemente; **it has — improved** ha mejorado sensiblemente.

notice board ['nəutisbɔːd] n tablón m de anuncios.

notifiable ['nəutifaiəbl] adj de declaración obligatoria.

notification [,nəutifi'keiʃən] n notificación f, aviso m.

notify ['nəutifai] vt notificar, comunicar, avisar; **to — someone of something** comunicar algo a uno, hacer saber algo a uno.

notion ['nəuʃən] n (idea) noción f, idea f; concepto m; (view) opinión f; (whim) idea f; capricho m; inclinación f; **what an odd —!** ¡qué idea más rara!; **I have a — that . . .** tengo la idea de que . . ., se me ocurre pensar que . . .; **to have no — of something** no tener concepto alguno de algo; **you have no —!** ¡no te lo puedes imaginar!; **I haven't the slightest —** no tengo la más remota idea; **it's a —** she has es un capricho suyo, son cosas de ella; **to have a — to do something** tener la intención de hacer algo, estar inclinado a hacer algo, estar dispuesto a hacer algo.

notional ['nəuʃənl] adj nocional; especulativo; imaginario; **it is purely —** existe en el pensamiento nada más, es teórico nada más.

notoriety [,nəutə'raiəti] n notoriedad f; (pej) mala fama f; escándalo m; **such was his — that . . .** tan mala fama tuvo que . . .; **to seek —** buscarse la publicidad, tratar de darse a conocer, hacer que se hable de uno.

notorious [nəu'tɔːriəs] adj muy conocido, notorio; célebre (for por); (pej) de mala fama; escandaloso; **a — crime** un crimen muy sonado; **it is — that . . .** es sabido que . . ., es voz pública que . . .; **he is — for his affairs** es archiconocido por sus amoríos.

notoriously [nəu'tɔːriəsli] adj notoriamente; **it is — difficult to** + infin se sabe perfectamente que es difícil + infin; **he is — unreliable** tiene fama de informal.

no-trumps ['nəu'trʌmps] n: **to bid 4 —** marcar 4 sin triunfo.

notwithstanding [,nɔtwið'stændiŋ] **1** adv no obstante, sin embargo; **this —** no obstante esto, a pesar de esto; **this rule —** no obstante esta regla; **I shall go —** sin embargo iré, de todas formas iré.

2 prep a pesar de.

3 conj (also — that) a pesar de que, por más que + subj.

nougat ['nuːgɑː] n (approx) turrón m.

nought [nɔːt] n nada f; (Math etc) cero m; **Murcia beat Granada two —** el Murcia venció al Granada dos-cero; see also **naught.**

noun [naun] n nombre m, sustantivo m.

nourish ['nʌriʃ] vt nutrir, alimentar, sustentar; (fig) fomentar, nutrir; **to — someone on something** alimentar a uno con algo, dar a uno algo de comer.

nourishing ['nʌriʃiŋ] adj nutritivo, rico; de gran valor alimenticio.

nourishment ['nʌriʃmənt] n alimento m, sustento m; nutrición f; **to derive — from** sustentarse de.

nouveau riche ['nuːvəu'riːʃ] n nuevo rico m.

Nova Scotia ['nəuvə'skəuʃə] Nueva Escocia f.

novel ['nɔvəl] **1** adj nuevo; original; insólito; **this is something —** esto es nuevo. **2** n novela f; **picaresque —** novela f picaresca.

novelette [,nɔvə'let] n novela f corta; (pej) novela f sentimental, novela f sin valor.

novelettish [,nɔvə'letiʃ] adj novelero; sentimental, romántico.

novelist ['nɔvəlist] n novelista mf.

novelty ['nɔvəlti] n (newness) novedad f; (new thing) novedad f, innovación f; (Comm) novedad f; **once the — has worn off** cuando deja de parecer tan nuevo.

November [nəu'vembə*] n noviembre m.
novice ['nɔvis] n principiante mf, novato m, a f;
(Eccl) novicio m, a f; **a — painter** un pintor principiante, un aspirante a pintor; **he's no — ** no es ningún principiante; **to be a — at a job** ser nuevo en un oficio.
noviciate, novitiate [nəu'viʃiit] n período m de aprendizaje; (Eccl) noviciado m.
now [nau] **1** adv (a) ahora; actualmente, al presente, hoy día; (in past time) luego, entonces; **just — (right —)** ahora mismo, (lately) hace poco; **right — ** ahora mismo; **even — ** aun ahora; **even — we have no rifles** no tenemos todavía fusiles; **not —, dear** dejémoslo para después, querido; ahora no quiero, querido; **I must be off — ** me tengo que marchar ya; **they won't be long — ** ya no tardarán en venir; **— I am committed** me he comprometido ya; **— I'm ready** ya estoy listo; (every) **— and again,** (every) **— and then** de vez en cuando.
(b) **— she dances, — she sings** ya baila, ya canta; **— in France, — in Spain** ora en Francia, ora en España.
(c) (with prep) **before — ** (already) antes, ya; (at other times) en otras ocasiones; **long before — ** hace tiempo ya, mucho tiempo ha; **between — and next Tuesday** entre hoy y el martes que viene; **by — ** ahora, ya; **they must be there by — ** habrán llegado ya allí; **by — ** everybody was tired antes de eso todos se habían cansado; **3 weeks from — ** de hoy en 3 semanas; **from — on** a partir de ahora, de aquí en adelante; **until —, up to — ** hasta ahora.
(d) (without temporal force) **—! ** ¡a ver!; **come —! ** ¡vamos!, ¡no es para tanto!; **well — ** ahora bien; **— then! ** ¡vamos a ver!; **— then, what's all this?** ¡eh! ¿qué hacéis aquí?, ¡eh! ¿qué es esto?; **— Johnny! ** (warning) ¡oye, Juanito!
2 conj (a) **— (that) you are 16** ahora que tienes 16 años; **take it, — that I've got 2** tómalo, pues tengo dos.
(b) (without temporal force) ahora bien, pues; **— as you all know . . .** pues como saben todos Vds . . .; **— Peter was a fisherman** ahora bien, Pedro era pescador.
nowadays ['nauədeiz] adv hoy día, actualmente.
noways ['nəuweiz] adv (US fam) de ninguna manera.
nowhere ['nəuweə*] adv (a) **I see it — ** no lo veo en ninguna parte; **you're going — ** no vas a ninguna parte; **— in Europe** en ninguna parte de Europa; **— else** en ninguna otra parte; **it's — you know** no es ningún sitio de los que conoce Vd; **it's — you'll ever find it** está en un sitio donde no lo encontrará Vd nunca; **they seemed to come from — ** parecían haber salido de la nada.
(b) (fig) **it's — near as good** no es tan bueno ni con mucho, dista mucho de ser tan bueno; **A is — near as big as B** A no es tan grande como B ni con mucho; **the rest of the runners came — ** los demás atletas quedaron muy atrás; **in my opinion the rest come — ** en mi opinión los demás son muy inferiores.
nowise ['nəuwaiz] adv (US) de ninguna manera.
noxious ['nɔkʃəs] adj nocivo, dañoso.
nozzle ['nɔzl] n (Mech) tobera f, inyector m; (of hose, vacuum cleaner etc) boquilla f; (of spray) pulverizador m.
nuance ['nju:ã:ns] n matiz m.
nub [nʌb] n pedazo m, trozo m; protuberancia f; (fig) lo esencial, parte f esencial; **that's the — of the question** eso es lo esencial, eso es lo que más importa.
nubile ['nju:bail] adj núbil.
nuclear ['nju:kliə*] adj nuclear.
nucleus ['nju:kliəs] n, pl **nuclei** ['nju:kliai] núcleo m; **atomic — ** núcleo m atómico; **the — of a library** el núcleo indispensable de una biblioteca; **we have the — of a crew** tenemos los elementos indispensables para formar una tripulación.
nude [nju:d] **1** adj desnudo. **2** n (Art) desnudo m; **a — of Goya** un desnudo de Goya. (b) (person) desnudo m; mujer f desnuda. (c) **in the — ** desnudo.
nudge [nʌdʒ] **1** n codazo m (ligero). **2** vt dar un codazo a; empujar (ligeramente); **to — someone's memory** refrescar la memoria de uno.
nudism ['nju:dizəm] n desnudismo m.
nudist ['nju:dist] n desnudista mf, nudista mf; **— colony** colonia f de desnudistas.
nudity ['nju:diti] n desnudez f.
nugatory ['nju:gətəri] adj (trivial) insignificante; (useless) ineficaz.
nugget ['nʌgit] n (Min) pepita f; **gold — ** pepita f de oro.
nuisance ['nju:sns] **1** n (a) molestia f, incomodidad

f; **the — of having to shave** la incomodidad de tener que afeitarse.
(b) molestia f, fastidio m, lata f; **what a —! ** ¡qué lata!, ¡qué fastidio!; **this hat is a — ** este sombrero me está fastidiando; me estoy armando un lío con este sombrero; **it's a — having to shave** es una molestia tener que afeitarse, es incómodo tener que afeitarse; **"commit no —"** "mantenga limpio este sitio", (more specifically) "prohibido hacer aguas".
(c) (person) moscón m, pelmazo m; pesado m; **what a — you are! ** ¡eres un pesado!; **you're being a — ** me estás dando la lata; **to make a — of oneself** dar la lata.
2 attr: **— value** valor m como irritante.
null [nʌl] adj nulo, inválido; **— and void** nulo y sin efecto; **to render someone's efforts — ** hacer que los esfuerzos de uno resulten infructuosos.
nullification [ˌnʌlifi'keiʃən] n anulación f, invalidación f.
nullify ['nʌlifai] vt anular, invalidar.
nullity ['nʌliti] n nulidad f.
numb [nʌm] **1** adj entumecido; (fig) insensible; **my leg has gone — ** se me ha dormido la pierna; **to be — with cold** estar entumecido de frío, (fig) estar helado; **to be — with fright** estar paralizado de temor. **2** vt entumecer, entorpecer.
number ['nʌmbə*] **1** n (a) (Math) número m; (figure) número m, cifra f; (Gram, Tel, Theat, of journal etc) número m; **—s** (Poet) versos mpl; **cardinal — ** número m cardinal; **ordinal — ** número m ordinal; **whole — ** número m entero; **round — ** número m redondo; **in round —s** en números redondos; **rational — ** número m racional; **a — of** algunos, varios, una porción de; **a — of people have protested** varias personas han protestado; **a large — of people** buen número de personas, muchísimas personas; **in a small — of cases** en unos pocos casos, en contados casos; **on a — of occasions** en diversas ocasiones, varias veces; **any — of la mar de; any — of times** muchísimas veces; **to be few in — ** ser pocos; **to be 8 in — ** ser 8; **to come in —s** venir en tropel, venir en masa; **they exist in —s in Africa** en África hay muchos, en África son frecuentes; **one of their — ** uno de ellos; **he is not of that — ** no es de ésos, no forma parte de ese grupo; **to the — of some 200** en número de unos 200; **times without — ** muchísimas veces; **his — is up** todo se acabó para él; **I've got his — now** le tengo calado ya.
(b) (of house etc) número m; **we live at No. 15** vivimos en el núm. 15; **reference — ** número m de referencia; **registration — ** (Aut etc) matrícula f; **the — one Spanish player** el jugador número uno de España; **to look after — one** mirar por sí, cuidar de sí mismo.
(c) (person) **a nice little — ** (sl) una chica monísima; **my opposite — in France** el que ocupa el puesto equivalente en Francia.
2 vt (a) (count) contar; **the library —s 30,000 books** la biblioteca cuenta con 30.000 libros, la biblioteca posee 30.000 libros; **to — someone among one's friends** contar a uno entre sus amigos; **to be —ed among** figurar entre, ser de; **his days are —ed** tiene los días contados; **his days seem to be —ed** sus días parecen contados.
(b) (amount to) ascender a, sumar; **they — 187** hay 187, ascienden a 187, suman 187; **they — several hundreds** hay varios centenares.
(c) (assign — to) numerar, poner número a; **MS pages** foliar; **the houses are not —ed** las casas no están numeradas, las casas no tienen número.
3 vi: **to — off** numerarse (from the right por la derecha).
numberless ['nʌmbəlis] adj innumerable, sin número.
number plate ['nʌmbəpleit] n (Aut etc) placa f de matrícula.
numbness ['nʌmnis] n entumecimiento m; (fig) insensibilidad f; parálisis f.
numeral ['nju:mərəl] **1** adj numeral. **2** n número m, cifra f, guarismo m; **Arabic — ** número m arábigo; **Roman — ** número m romano.
numeration [ˌnju:mə'reiʃən] n numeración f.
numerator ['nju:məreitə*] n numerador m.
numerical [nju:'merikəl] adj numérico.
numerically [nju:'merikəli] adv numéricamente; **superior to** con superioridad numérica a, superiores en cuanto a su número a.
numerous ['nju:mərəs] adj numeroso; muchos; **a — family** una familia numerosa; **in — cases** en muchos casos; **— people believe that . . .** mucha gente cree que . . .

numismatic [ˌnjuːmizˈmætik] *adj* numismático.
numismatics [ˌnjuːmizˈmætiks] *n* numismática *f*.
numismatist [njuːˈmizmətist] *n* numismático *m*.
numskull, numbskull [ˈnʌmskʌl] *n* zote *m*, majadero *m*; **you —! ¡majadero!**
nun [nʌn] *n* monja *f*, religiosa *f*; **to become a —** tomar el hábito, meterse monja.
nunciature [ˈnʌnʃiətjuə*] *n* nunciatura *f*.
nuncio [ˈnʌnʃiəu] *n* (*also* **papal —**) nuncio *m* apostólico.
nunnery [ˈnʌnəri] *n* convento *m* de monjas.
nuptial [ˈnʌpʃəl] *adj* nupcial.
nuptials [ˈnʌpʃəlz] *npl* (*hum or US*) nupcias *fpl*.
nurse [nəːs] **1** *n* (*Med*) enfermera *f*; (*wet-*) nodriza *f*, ama *f* de leche; (*children's*) niñera *f*; **male —** enfermero *m*; **practical —** (*US*) enfermera *f* práctica.
    2 *vt* *patient* cuidar, atender, asistir; (*suckle*) criar, amamantar; (*in arms*) mecer; **to — someone back to health** cuidar a uno hasta que se reponga; **to — a cold** tratar de curarse de un resfriado; **to — a constituency** (*Parl*) establecerse como candidato en un distrito electoral, hacerse conocer por los electores de un distrito; **to — a business along** fomentar un negocio, promover un negocio.
nursemaid [ˈnəːsmeid] *n* niñera *f*, chacha *f*.
nursery [ˈnəːsri] *n* (**a**) cuarto *m* de los niños; **from the —** desde la niñez, desde niño.
    (**b**) (*Agr etc*) criadero *m*, semillero *m*, plantel *m*; (*fig*) plantel *m*; **a — for new players** un plantel de jóvenes jugadores.
nurseryman [ˈnəːsrimən] *n*, *pl* **-men** [mən] horticultor *m*.
nursery rhyme [ˈnəːsriraim] *n* canción *f* infantil.
nursery school [ˈnəːsriˌskuːl] *n* jardín *m* de la infancia.
nursing [ˈnəːsiŋ] **1** *adj*: **— mother** madre *f* lactante; **— staff** enfermeras *fpl*, personal *m* del hospital.
    2 *n* (*of patient*) asistencia *f*, cuidado *m*; (*profession*) profesión *f* de enfermera; (*suckling*) lactancia *f*; **to go in for —** hacerse enfermera.
nursing home [ˈnəːsiŋˌhəum] *n* clínica *f* de reposo, clínica *f* particular.
nurture [ˈnəːtʃə*] **1** *n* (*nourishment*) nutrición *f*; (*bringing-up*) educación *f*, crianza *f*. **2** *vt* alimentar, nutrir (*on* de); educar, criar.

nut [nʌt] *n* (**a**) nuez *f*; (*Mech*) tuerca *f*; (*sl: head*) cabeza *f*; (*sl: person*) loco *m*, a *f*, bobo *m*, a *f*; excéntrico *m*; **it's a hard — to crack** es un hueso duro de roer; **to do one's —** (*sl*) echar el resto (*fam*); **to be off one's —** (*sl*) faltarle a uno un tornillo (*fam*); **you must be off your —!** (*sl*) ¿estás grillado? (*sl*).
    (**b**) **—s** (*sl*): **to be —s** estar loco; **to be —s about** (*or* **on**) **something** estar loco por algo; **I'm —s about you** estoy chalado por ti (*fam*); **to drive someone —s** volver loco a uno; **to go —s** volverse loco.
    (**c**) **—s** (*sl: Anat*) cojones *mpl*; **—s! ¡narices!** (*fam*); **he can't play for —s** no tiene talento en absoluto para el juego, como jugador no vale para nada.
nutcase [ˈnʌtkeis] *n* (*sl*) loco *m*, a *f*.
nutcrackers [ˈnʌtˌkrækəz] *npl* cascanueces *m*; **a pair of —** un cascanueces.
nuthatch [ˈnʌthætʃ] *n* trepador *m*.
nuthouse [ˈnʌthaus] *n*, *pl* **-houses** [ˌhauziz] (*sl*) manicomio *m*.
nutmeg [ˈnʌtmeg] *n* nuez *f* moscada.
nutrient [ˈnjuːtriənt] **1** *adj* nutritivo. **2** *n* nutrimento *m*.
nutriment [ˈnjuːtrimənt] *n* nutrimento *m*, alimento *m*.
nutrition [njuːˈtriʃən] *n* nutrición *f*, alimentación *f*.
nutritional [njuːˈtriʃənl] *adj* *value etc* nutritivo.
nutritious [njuːˈtriʃəs] *adj*, **nutritive** [ˈnjuːtritiv] *adj* nutritivo, rico.
nutshell [ˈnʌtʃel] *n* cáscara *f* de nuez; **in a —** en resumidas cuentas; **to put it in a —** para decirlo brevemente; **that puts it in a —** eso lo dice en pocas palabras.
nut-tree [ˈnʌttriː] *n* (*hazel*) avellano *m*, (*walnut*) nogal *m*.
nutty [ˈnʌti] *adj* (**a**) *colour* de nuez; *cake* con nueces; *taste* a nueces, que sabe a nueces.
    (**b**) (*sl*) loco; **to be — about something** estar loco por algo.
nuzzle [ˈnʌzl] **1** *vt* acariciar con el hocico. **2** *vi* = **snuggle, nestle**.
nylon [ˈnailɔn] **1** *n* nilón *m*; **—s** medias *fpl* de nilón. **2** *adj* de nilón.
nymph [nimf] *n* ninfa *f*.
nymphet [nimˈfet] *n* ninfita *f*, ninfilla *f*.
nymphomania [ˌnimfəuˈmeiniə] *n* ninfomanía *f*.
nymphomaniac [ˌnimfəuˈmeiniæk] **1** *adj* ninfómano. **2** *n* ninfómana *f*.

O

O [əu] *see* **oh**.
oaf [əuf] *n* zoquete *m*, patán *m*.
oafish ['əufiʃ] *adj* lerdo, zafio.
oak [əuk] **1** *n* roble *m*; **to sport one's —** (*Univ*) cerrar la puerta (para no recibir visitas). **2** *adj*, *attr* de roble.
oak apple ['əuk,æpl] *n* agalla *f* (de roble).
oaken ['əukən] *adj* de roble.
oakum ['əukəm] *n* estopa *f* (de calafatear).
oakwood ['əukwud] *n* robledo *m*.
oar [ɔː*] *n* (a) remo *m*; **to lie** (*or* **rest**) **on one's —s** dejar de remar, (*fig*) descansar, dormir sobre sus laureles; **to put** (*or* **shove**) **one's — in** entrometerse; **to ship the —s** desarmar los remos.
  (b) (*person*) remero *m*, a *f*; **to be a good —** ser buen remero, remar bien.
oared [ɔːd] *adj* provisto de remos; de . . . remos, *eg* **eight-oared** de ocho remos.
oarlock ['ɔːlɔk] *n* escalamera *f*.
oarsman ['ɔːzmən] *n*, *pl* **—men** [mən] remero *m*.
oarsmanship ['ɔːzmənʃip] *n* arte *m* de remar.
oasis [əu'eisis] *n*, *pl* **oases** [əu'eisiːz] oasis *m*; (*fig*) oasis *m*; remanso *m*; **an — of peace** un remanso de paz.
oast-house ['əusthaus] *n*, *pl* **—houses** [hauziz] secadero *m* para lúpulo.
oatcake ['əutkeik] *n* torta *f* de avena.
oaten ['əutn] *adj* de avena.
oatfield ['əutfiːld] *n* avenal *m*.
oath [əuθ] *n*, *pl* **oaths** [əuðz] (a) (*solemn promise etc*) juramento *m*; **under —, on —,** bajo juramento; **to administer an — to someone** tomar juramento a uno; **to break one's —** violar su juramento; **to put someone on —** hacer prestar juramento a uno; **to take the** (*or* **an**) **—** prestar juramento (*on* sobre); **to take an — that . . .** jurar que . . .; **to take the — of allegiance** (*Mil*) jurar la bandera.
  (b) (*curse*) blasfemia *f*, reniego *m*, palabrota *f*.
oatmeal ['əutmiːl] *n* harina *f* de avena.
oats [əuts] *npl* avena *f*; **rolled —** copos *mpl* de avena; **wild oat** avena *f* silvestre; **to be off one's —s** no tener ganas de comer, haber perdido el apetito; **to sow one's wild —** correrla, pasar las mocedades.
obbligato [,ɔbli'gaːtəu] *n* (*Mus*) obligado *m*.
obduracy ['ɔbdjurəsi] *n* obstinación *f*, terquedad *f*; inflexibilidad *f*.
obdurate ['ɔbdjurit] *adj* obstinado, terco; (*in refusing etc*) inflexible.
obedience [ə'biːdiəns] *n* obediencia *f*; sumisión *f*; docilidad *f*; **in — to** conforme a, de acuerdo con; **in — to your wishes** accediendo a sus deseos; **blind —** obediencia *f* ciega; **to compel —** exigir obediencia (*from* a).
obedient [ə'biːdiənt] *adj* obediente; sumiso, dócil; **to be — to** ser obediente a, obedecer a.
obediently [ə'biːdiəntli] *adv* obedientemente; sumisamente, dócilmente; **yours —** su atento servidor.
obeisance [əu'beisəns] *n* (*bow etc*) reverencia *f*; (*salutation*) saludo *m*; (*homage*) homenaje *m*; **to do** (*or* **make, pay**) **—** tributar homenaje a.
obelisk ['ɔbilisk] *n* obelisco *m*.
obese [əu'biːs] *adj* obeso.
obeseness [əu'biːsnis] *n*, **obesity** [əu'biːsiti] *n* obesidad *f*.
obey [ə'bei] *vt* (*person etc*) obedecer; (*pay heed to*) hacer caso a; *need, controls* responder; *summons* acudir a; *law* cumplir, observar, obrar de acuerdo con; *instruction* cumplir; **the machine was no longer —ing the controls** la máquina ya no respondía a los mandos; **I like to be —ed** quiero que se me obedezca.
obfuscate ['ɔbfəskeit] *vt* ofuscar.
obituary [ə'bitjuəri] **1** *adj* necrológico; **— column** sección *f* necrológica; **— notice** necrología *f*; esquela *f* de defunción. **2** *n* necrología *f*, obituario *m*.

object ['ɔbdʒikt] *n* (a) (*thing in general*) objeto *m*; cosa *f*, artículo *m*; (*pej: thing*) mamarracho *m* (*person*) espantajo *m*, estantigua *f*; **she was an — of pity to all** daba lástima a cuantos la veían; **he became an — of ridicule** se puso en ridículo.
  (b) (*aim*) objeto *m*, propósito *m*, intento *m*; **with this — in view** con este propósito; **with the — of** con el propósito de, al objeto de; **what is the — of the plan?** ¿qué finalidad tiene el plan?; **expense is no —** no importan los gastos; **salary no —** el sueldo no es de primera importancia.
  (c) (*Gram*) complemento *m*.
object [əb'dʒekt] **1** *vt*: **to — that** objetar que . . .; **to this it was —ed that . . .** a esto se objetó que . . . **2** *vi* hacer objeciones, oponerse; poner reparos; **I —!** ¡yo protesto!; **I — most strongly!** ¡yo me opongo rotundamente a ello!; **if you don't —** si Vd no tiene inconveniente; **I — to that remark!** ¡protesto contra esa observación!; **to — to someone doing something** oponerse a que uno haga algo; **do you — to my going?** ¿se opone Vd a que vaya yo?; **do you — to my smoking?** ¿le molesta que fume?; **I don't — to an occasional drink** no me opongo a que se tome algo de vez en cuando.
objection [əb'dʒekʃən] *n* objeción *f*, reparo *m*; protesta *f*; (*obstacle*) inconveniente *m*; obstáculo *m*, dificultad *f*; **—!** ¡yo protesto!; **what are the —s?** ¿qué obstáculo hay?, ¿cuáles son las dificultades?; **there is no — no** hay inconveniente; **there is no — to your going no** hay inconveniente en que vaya Vd; **I can find no — to it** no le encuentro ninguna dificultad; **I have no —** no tengo inconveniente; **if you have no —** si no tiene inconveniente; **have you any — to my smoking?** ¿le molesta que fume?; **have you any — to my going?** ¿tiene Vd algún inconveniente en que vaya yo?; **he made no —** no hizo ninguna objeción, no protestó, no se opuso a ello; **to raise —s** poner reparos (*to* a), protestar (*to* contra); **I see no —** no veo inconveniente.
objectionable [əb'dʒekʃnəbl] *adj* desagradable; *person* molesto, pesado; indeseable; *conduct etc* censurable; **a most — person** una persona inaguantable.
objective [əb'dʒektiv] **1** *adj* objetivo. **2** *n* objetivo *m*.
objectively [əb'dʒektivli] *adv* objetivamente.
objectivism [əb'dʒektivizəm] *n* objetivismo *m*.
objectivity [,ɔbdʒik'tiviti] *n* objetividad *f*.
object lens ['ɔbdʒikt,lenz] *n* objetivo *m*.
object lesson ['ɔbdʒikt,lesn] *n* lección *f* práctica, ejemplo *m*; **it was an — in good manners** fue una perfecta demostración de cortesía.
objector [əb'dʒektə*] *n* objetante *mf*; **conscientious —** objetor *m* de conciencia, pacifista *m* que se niega a tomar las armas.
objurgate ['ɔbdʒəːgeit] *vt* increpar, reprender.
objurgation [,ɔbdʒəː'geiʃən] *n* increpación *f*, reprensión *f*.
oblation [əu'bleiʃən] *n* oblación *f*; (*gift*) oblata *f*, ofrenda *f*.
obligate ['ɔbligeit] *vt*: **to — someone to do something** obligar a uno a hacer algo; **to be —d to + infin** estar obligado a + *infin*.
obligation [,ɔbli'geiʃən] *n* obligación *f*; deber *m*; compromiso *m*; **of —** (*Eccl*) de precepto; **without —** (*in advert*) sin compromiso; **it is your — to see that . . .** le cumple a Vd comprobar que . . ., es su deber comprobar que + *subj*; **to be under an — to someone** deber favores a uno; **to be under an — to + infin** deber + *infin*, haberse comprometido a + *infin*, tener obligación de + *infin*; **to lay** (*or* **put**) **someone under an —** poner a uno bajo una obligación; **to meet one's —s** (*Comm*) cumplir sus compromisos; **to fail to meet one's —s** no poder cumplir sus compromisos.

obligatory [ə'bligətəri] *adj* obligatorio; **to make it —
for someone to do something** imponer a uno la
obligación de + *infin*.
oblige [ə'blaidʒ] *vt* (a) *(force)* obligar, forzar; **to —
someone to do something** obligar a uno a hacer algo,
forzar a uno a hacer algo; **to be —d to do something**
verse obligado a hacer algo; **you are not —d to do it**
nada le obliga a hacerlo.
(b) *(gratify)* complacer, hacer un favor a; **you
would greatly — me if** . . . agradecería mucho que
+ *subj*; **anything to — a friend!** ¡lo que sea por
complacer a un amigo!; **he did it to — us** lo hizo
como favor, lo hizo para complacernos; **to — someone with a match** hacer a uno el favor de (prestarle,
darle) una cerilla.
(c) *(obliged)* **much —d!** ¡muchísimas gracias!, ¡se
agradece!; **I should be much —d if** . . . agradecería
que + *subj*; **I am —d to you for your help** agradezco su ayuda; **to be —d to someone** estar reconocido a uno, deber favores a uno.
obliging [ə'blaidʒiŋ] *adj* servicial, atento, obsequioso.
obligingly [ə'blaidʒiŋli] *adv* atentamente; **he very —
helped us** muy amablemente nos ayudó.
oblique [ə'bli:k] *adj* oblicuo; *reference etc* indirecto,
tangencial.
obliquely [ə'bli:kli] *adv* oblicuamente; indirectamente, tangencialmente.
obliqueness [ə'bli:knis] *n*, **obliquity** [ə'blikwiti] *n*
oblicuidad *f*; lo indirecto, lo tangencial.
obliterate [ə'blitəreit] *vt* borrar, eliminar, destruir
toda huella de; *town etc* arrasar, destruir; *(Med)*
obliterar.
obliteration [ə,blitə'reiʃən] *n* borradura *f*, eliminación *f*; arrasamiento *m*, destrucción *f*; *(Med)*
obliteración *f*.
oblivion [ə'bliviən] *n* olvido *m*; **to cast into —** echar
al olvido; **to fall** (*or* **sink**) **into —** sumirse en el
olvido.
oblivious [ə'bliviəs] *adj*: **to be — of, to be — to**
estar inconsciente de; **he, totally — of what was
happening** . . . él, totalmente inconsciente de lo que
pasaba . . .
oblong ['ɔblɔŋ] **1** *adj* rectangular, cuadrilongo. **2** *n*
rectángulo *m*, cuadrilongo *m*.
obloquy ['ɔbləkwi] *n* *(abuse)* injurias *fpl*, calumnia *f*;
(shame) deshonra *f*; **to cover someone with —** llenar
a uno de injurias.
obnoxious [əb'nɔkʃəs] *adj* detestable, repugnante,
odioso; *fumes etc* nocivo, desagradable; **it is — to
me to** + *infin* me repugna + *infin*, me es repugnante + *infin*.
oboe ['əubəu] *n* oboe *m*.
oboist ['əubəuist] *n* oboe *m* *(persona)*.
obscene [əb'si:n] *adj* obsceno, indecente, escabroso.
obscenely [əb'si:nli] *adv* obscenamente, escabrosamente.
obscenity [əb'seniti] *n* obscenidad *f*, indecencia *f*,
escabrosidad *f*; **to utter obscenities** proferir
obscenidades.
obscurantism [,ɔbskjuə'ræntizəm] *n* oscurantismo *m*.
obscurantist [,ɔbskjuə'ræntist] **1** *adj* oscurantista.
2 *n* oscurantista *mf*.
obscure [əb'skjuə*] **1** *adj* oscuro *(also fig)*.
2 *vt* oscurecer; *(eclipse)* eclipsar; *(hide)* esconder;
issue entenebrecer, confundir; *memory, glory etc*
oscurecer; **the house is —d by the trees** la casa está
escondida detrás de los árboles; **it served only to —
the matter further** sirvió para entenebrecer aun más
el asunto.
obscurely [əb'skjuəli] *adv* oscuramente.
obscurity [əb'skjuəriti] *n* oscuridad *f (also fig)*; **to live
in —** vivir en la oscuridad.
obsequies ['ɔbsikwiz] *npl* exequias *fpl*.
obsequious [əb'si:kwiəs] *adj* servil.
obsequiously [əb'si:kwiəsli] *adv* servilmente.
obsequiousness [əb'si:kwiəsnis] *n* servilismo *m*.
observable [əb'zə:vəbl] *adj* observable, visible; **as is
— in rabbits** según se puede apreciar en los conejos;
no — difference ninguna diferencia perceptible.
observance [əb'zə:vəns] *n* *(of rule etc)* observancia *f*
(of de), cumplimiento *m (of* con); *(rite etc)* práctica *f*,
costumbre *f*.
observant [əb'zə:vənt] *adj* observador, perspicaz;
(watchful) vigilante; *(attentive)* atento; **the child is
very —** el niño es muy observador.
observation [,ɔbzə'veiʃən] *n* *(in most senses)* observación *f*; *(of rule etc)* observancia *f*; **"O—s on
Petrarch"** "Apuntes *mpl* sobre Petrarca"; **to be
under —** estar vigilado; **we can keep the valley
under — from here** desde aquí dominamos el valle;
the police are keeping him under — la policía le
está vigilando; **he is under — in hospital** le están

examinando en el hospital; **to escape —** pasar
inadvertido.
observation car [,ɔbzə'veiʃənka:*] *n (Rail)* vagón-
mirador *m*.
observation post [,ɔbzə'veiʃənpəust] *n* puesto *m* de
observación.
observatory [əb'zə:vətri] *n* observatorio *m*.
observe [əb'zə:v] *vt* *rule etc* observar, cumplir; *(watch,
examine; also Astron)* observar; *(remark)* observar,
decir; *(care)* usar de, emplear; *Sabbath, silence etc*
guardar; *suspect etc* vigilar; **I —d to him that** . . . le
hice observar que . . .; **as Eliot has —d** . . . según ha
dicho Eliot . . .; **I —d him steal the duck** le vi robar
el pato; **now — this closely** fíjense bien en esto.
observer [əb'zə:və*] *n* observador *m*, ora *f*.
obsess [əb'ses] *vt* obsesionar, causar obsesión a; **to be
—ed by** (*or* **with**) **an idea** estar obsesionado por una
idea.
obsession [əb'seʃən] *n* obsesión *f*; idea *f* fija, manía *f*;
the — about cleanliness la obsesión de la limpieza,
la manía de la limpieza; **to have an — about an
idea** estar obsesionado por una idea; **it's an — with
him** es una manía que tiene.
obsessive [əb'sesiv] *adj* obsesionante.
obsessively [əb'sesivli] *adv* de modo obsesionante.
obsidian [əb'sidiən] *n* obsidiana *f*.
obsolescence [,ɔbsə'lesns] *n* caída *f* en desuso.
obsolescent [,ɔbsə'lesnt] *adj* algo anticuado; **to be —**
irse haciendo anticuado, estar cayendo en desuso.
obsolete ['ɔbsəli:t] *adj* anticuado, desusado; obsoleto;
(Bio) rudimentario.
obstacle ['ɔbstəkl] *n* obstáculo *m*; estorbo *m*, impedimento *m*, inconveniente *m*; **—s to independence** los
factores que dificultan la independencia; **one of the
—s is money** uno de los obstáculos es el dinero; **to
be an — to something** ser un estorbo para algo; **that
is no — to our doing it** eso no impide que lo hagamos; **to put —s in someone's way** crear dificultades
a uno, dificultar el camino a uno.
obstacle race ['ɔbstəkl,reis] *n* carrera *f* de obstáculos.
obstetric(al) [ɔb'stetrik(əl)] *adj* obstétrico.
obstetrician [,ɔbstə'triʃən] *n* obstétrico *m*.
obstetrics [ɔb'stetriks] *n* obstetricia *f*.
obstinacy ['ɔbstinəsi] *n* obstinación *f*, terquedad *f*,
porfía *f*; tenacidad *f*.
obstinate ['ɔbstinit] *adj* obstinado, terco, porfiado;
pursuit etc tenaz; **as — as a mule** tan terco como una
mula; **to be — about something** insistir con tesón en
algo.
obstinately ['ɔbstinitli] *adv* obstinadamente, tercamente, porfiadamente; tenazmente.
obstreperous [əb'strepərəs] *adj* *(noisy)* ruidoso,
estrepitoso; *(unruly)* turbulento, desmandado; **he
became —** empezó a desmandarse.
obstreperously [əb'strepərəsli] *adv* ruidosamente,
estrepitosamente; de modo turbulento.
obstruct [əb'strʌkt] **1** *vt* obstruir; *(Parl, Sport)*
obstruir; *plan, progress etc* estorbar; *person* estorbar,
impedir; *road* cerrar, bloquear, obstruir; *pipe etc*
obstruir, atascar, atorar.
2 *vi* estorbar.
obstruction [əb'strʌkʃən] *n* obstrucción *f (also Parl)*;
estorbo *m*, obstáculo *m*; **to cause an —** ser un
estorbo, *(Aut etc)* obstruir el tráfico.
obstructionism [əb'strʌkʃənizəm] *n* obstruccionismo
m.
obstructionist [əb'strʌkʃənist] **1** *adj* obstruccionista.
2 *n* obstruccionista *mf*.
obstructive [əb'strʌktiv] *adj* obstructivo, estor-
bador; **you're being —** Vd nos está estorbando.
obtain [əb'tein] **1** *vt* obtener; adquirir; lograr, conseguir; **oil can be —ed from coal** el aceite se puede
extraer del carbón; **his uncle —ed the job for him**
su tío le consiguió el puesto; **a work for which he
—ed a prize** un trabajo por el que le dieron un premio, un
trabajo por el que le valió un premio.
2 *vi* prevalecer, predominar; privar; regir; **the
price which —s now** el precio que es normal ahora;
in the conditions then —ing en las condiciones que
existían entonces; **that did not — in my day** en mis
tiempos no existía eso, en mis tiempos no era así.
obtainable [əb'teinəbl] *adj*: **to be —** ser asequible,
poderse adquirir; *(in shop)* estar a la venta; **"— at
all chemists'"** "de venta en todas las farmacias";
it is no longer — ya no se puede conseguir.
obtrude [əb'tru:d] **1** *vt tongue etc* sacar, extender; **to
— something on someone** imponer algo a uno.
2 *vi (person)* entrometerse; **he does not let his
opinions —** no hace gala de sus opiniones, no
impone sus opiniones a los demás.
obtrusion [əb'tru:ʒən] *n* imposición *f*; importunidad
f; entrometimiento *m*.

obtrusive [əb'truːsiv] *adj* importuno, molesto; indiscreto; *building etc* demasiado visible, que salta a la vista; *smell* penetrante; *person* entrometido, intruso.

obtrusively [əb'truːsivli] *adv* importunamente; indiscretamente; de modo demasiado visible; de modo penetrante.

obtuse [əb'tjuːs] *adj* (*Math etc*) obtuso; *person* obtuso, estúpido, duro de mollera; *remark* poco inteligente; **now you're just being** — te has empeñado en no comprender; **he can be very** — **at times** a veces puede ser muy obtuso.

obtuseness [əb'tjuːsnis] *n* (*fig*) estupidez *f*, torpeza *f*.

obverse ['ɔbvəːs] **1** *adj* del anverso. **2** *n* anverso *m*.

obviate ['ɔbvieit] *vt* obviar, evitar, eliminar.

obvious ['ɔbviəs] *adj* (*clear, perceptible*) evidente, obvio, manifiesto, patente; (*expected*) obvio, natural; (*unsubtle*) poco sutil, transparente; (*suitable*) indicado; **the** — **thing to do is ...** lo lógico es . . .; **he's the** — **man for the job** es el hombre más indicado para el puesto; **it's** —, **isn't it?** ¿es obvio, no?; **it's not** — **to me** para mí no está tan claro; **we must not be too** — **about it** en esto conviene ser algo astuto.

obviously ['ɔbviəsli] *adv* evidentemente; —! ¡naturalmente!; **it's** — **the best** evidentemente es el mejor; **he was not** — **drunk** no estaba tan borracho como para que no quedase lugar a dudas.

ocarina [ˌɔkə'riːnə] *n* ocarina *f*.

occasion [ə'keiʒən] **1** *n* (**a**) (*suitable juncture*) coyuntura *f*; oportunidad *f*, ocasión *f*; **he was awaiting a suitable** — aguardaba una coyuntura favorable, esperaba un momento propicio; **to take** — **to +** *infin* aprovechar la oportunidad de + *infin*.

(**b**) (*reason*) razón *f*, motivo *m*; **there is no** — **for alarm** no hay motivo para inquietarse, no hay por qué inquietarse; **there was no** — **for it** no había necesidad de ello; **to give** — **for scandal** provocar el escándalo; **he has given me no** — **for saying so** no me ha dado ocasión para decirlo; **I had** — **to reprimand him** tuve que reprenderle; **if you have** — **to use it** si se ve en el caso de usarlo.

(**c**) **to go about one's lawful** —**s** ir a sus negocios legítimos.

(**d**) (*time, occurrence*) ocasión *f*, vez *f*; **on the** — **of the cup final** cuando la final de copa; **on the** — **of his retirement** con motivo de su jubilación, para festejar su jubilación, para conmemorar su jubilación; **on** — de vez en cuando; **on one** — una vez; **on other** —**s** otras veces; **on just such an** — otra vez exactamente igual que ésta; **on that** — esa vez, en aquella ocasión; **as the** — **requires** según el caso; **if the** — **arises** si se da el caso; **should the** — **so demand** si lo exigen las circunstancias; **to rise to the** — ponerse a la altura de las circunstancias.

(**e**) (*event, function*) función *f*, acontecimiento *m*; **this is an important** — esto es un acontecimiento importante; **it will be a big** — será una función impresionante; **the three big** —**s of the university year** las tres grandes funciones del año universitario; **it was quite an** — realmente fue un acontecimiento; **music written for the** — música *f* compuesta para la función.

2 *vt* ocasionar, causar.

occasional [ə'keiʒənl] *adj* (**a**) **an** — **event** algo que pasa de vez en cuando, un acontecimiento poco frecuente; **we have an** — **visitor** recibimos de vez en cuando una visita; **we're just** — **visitors** estamos de visita nada más.

(**b**) *music etc* de circunstancia, compuesto para una función determinada.

occasionally [ə'keiʒnəli] *adv* de vez en cuando, a veces; **very** — muy de tarde en tarde.

occident ['ɔksidənt] *n* occidente *m*.

occidental [ˌɔksi'dentl] *adj* occidental.

occiput ['ɔksipʌt] *n* occipucio *m*.

occluded [ɔ'kluːdid] *adj*: — **front** oclusión *f*.

occlusion [ɔ'kluːʒən] *n* oclusión *f*.

occlusive [ɔ'kluːsiv] (*Ling*) **1** *adj* oclusivo. **2** *n* oclusiva *f*.

occult [ɔ'kʌlt] **1** *adj reason etc* oculto, misterioso; (*mystic*) oculto, sobrenatural, mágico.

2 *n*: **the** — lo oculto, lo sobrenatural; **to study the** — dedicarse al ocultismo, estudiar las ciencias ocultas.

occultism ['ɔkʌltizəm] *n* ocultismo *m*.

occultist ['ɔkəltist] *n* ocultista *mf*.

occupancy ['ɔkjupənsi] *n* ocupación *f*, tenencia *f*.

occupant ['ɔkjupənt] *n* (*of boat, car etc*) ocupante *mf*; (*of house*) habitante *mf*, inquilino *m*, a *f*; **all the** —**s were killed** perecieron todos los viajeros; **the** —**s could not be reached** resultó imposible socorrer a los que iban dentro.

occupation [ˌɔkju'peiʃən] *n* (**a**) (*of house etc*) tenencia *f*, inquilinato *m*; (*of country*) ocupación *f*; (*of office*) tenencia *f*; **military** — ocupación *f* militar; **a house unfit for** — una casa inhabitable; **to be in** — **of** ocupar; **we found them already in** — encontramos que ya se habían instalado allí.

(**b**) (*act of taking*) ocupación *f*; **the** — **of Paris in 1940** la ocupación de París en 1940; **the house is ready for** — la casa está lista para su ocupación.

(**c**) (*work*) trabajo *m*; (*employment*) empleo *m*; oficio *m*; (*calling*) oficio *m*; profesión *f*; (*pastime*) pasatiempo *m*; **a harmless enough** — un pasatiempo inocente; **a tailor by** — de oficio sastre; **what is he by** —?, **what is his** —? ¿qué oficio tiene?; **it gives** — **to 50 men** emplea a 50 hombres, da trabajo a 50 hombres; **this will give some** — **to your mind** esto le servirá para entretener la inteligencia.

occupational [ˌɔkju'peiʃənl] *adj* de oficio, relativo al oficio, profesional; *disease* profesional; *therapy* laboral; *see* **risk** *etc*.

occupier ['ɔkjupaiə*] *n* inquilino *m*, a *f*.

occupy ['ɔkjupai] *vt* ocupar (*also Mil*); *house* habitar, vivir en; *time* emplear, pasar; *attention, mind* entretener; **to be occupied in** (*or* **with**) ocuparse de (*or* en, con); **he is occupied in research** se dedica a la investigación; **he is very occupied at the moment** de momento está muy ocupado.

occur [ə'kəː*] *vi* (**a**) (*happen*) ocurrir, suceder, acontecer, pasar; **to** — **again** volver a suceder, producirse de nuevo; **if a vacancy** —**s** si se produce una vacante; **if the opportunity** —**s** si se presenta la oportunidad; **don't let it ever** — **again** y que esto no vuelva a ocurrir nunca.

(**b**) (*be found*) encontrarse, existir; **the plant** —**s all over Spain** la planta existe en todas partes en España.

(**c**) (*come to mind*) **it** —**s to me that ...** se me ocurre que . . .; **it** —**red to me to ask him** se me ocurrió preguntárselo a él; **such an idea would never have** —**red to her** tal idea no se le hubiera ocurrido nunca.

occurrence [ə'kʌrəns] *n* (**a**) (*happening*) acontecimiento *m*; incidente *m*; caso *m*; **a common** — un caso frecuente; **an everyday** — un suceso de todos los días; **that is a common** — eso sucede a menudo, ese caso se da con frecuencia.

(**b**) (*existence*) existencia *f*; aparición *f*; **its** — **in the south is well known** se sabe que existe en el sur, es conocida su existencia en el sur; **its** — **here is unexpected** su aparición aquí es inesperada.

ocean ['əuʃən] *n* océano *m*; —**s of** (*fig*) la mar de.

ocean-going ['əuʃən,gəuiŋ] *adj* de alta mar.

Oceania [ˌəuʃi'einiə] Oceanía *f*.

oceanic [ˌəuʃi'ænik] *adj* oceánico.

oceanography [ˌəuʃə'nɔgrəfi] *n* oceanografía *f*.

ocelot ['əusilɔt] *n* ocelote *m*.

ochre ['əukə*] *n* ocre *m*; **red** — ocre *m* rojo, almagre *m*; **yellow** — ocre *m* amarillo.

ochreous ['əukriəs] *adj* de color ocre.

o'clock [ə'klɔk] *adv* (= *of the clock*) **it is 1** — es la una; **it is 3** — son las 3; **at 9** — a las 9; **at exactly 9** — a las 9 en punto; **it is just after 2** — son un poco más de las 2; **it is nearly 8** — son casi las 8.

octagon ['ɔktəgən] *n* octágono *m*.

octagonal [ɔk'tægənl] *adj* octagonal.

octahedron ['ɔktə'hiːdrən] *n* octaedro *m*.

octane ['ɔktein] *n* octano *m*; **high-** — **petrol** gasolina *f* de alto octanaje.

octave ['ɔktiv] *n* (*Mus, Poet*) octava *f*.

Octavian [ɔk'teiviən] *m* Octavio.

octavo [ɔk'teivəu] **1** *adj* en octavo. **2** *n* libro *m* en octavo.

octet(te) [ɔk'tet] *n* octeto *m*.

October [ɔk'təubə*] *n* octubre *m*.

octogenarian [ˌɔktəudʒi'nɛəriən] **1** *adj* octagenario. **2** *n* octagenario *m*, a *f*.

octupus ['ɔktəpəs] *n* pulpo *m*.

octosyllabic [ˌɔktəusi'læbik] *adj* octosílabo.

octosyllable ['ɔktəu'siləbl] *n* octosílabo *m*.

ocular ['ɔkjulə*] *adj* ocular.

oculist ['ɔkjulist] *n* oculista *m*.

odalisque ['əudəlisk] *n* odalisca *f*.

odd [ɔd] *adj* (**a**) (*extra, left over*) sobrante, de más; (*isolated*) suelto; (*unpaired*) sin pareja, desparejado; **the** — **shilling** el chelín que sobra *or* el chelín que hace falta; **to be the** — **man out** estar de más, sobrar (*see also* **man 1(g)**); **we might pick up the** — **trick** pudiéramos ganar alguna baza más.

(**b**) (*Math*) impar; — **or even** par o impar.

(**c**) (*and a few more*) **30** — treinta y pico, treinta y tantos; **£20** — unas 20 libras.

(**d**) (*casual*) **at** — **moments** a ratos perdidos; **hay** veces cuando . . .; **at — times** de vez en cuando; **he has written the — article** ha escrito algún que otro artículo; **he has done the — job for us** ha trabajado para nosotros de vez en cuando.

(e) (strange) raro, extraño, singular; misterioso; estrambótico; **how —!, very —!, most —!** ¡qué raro!; **the — thing about it is . . .** lo raro es que . . .; **he's very — in his ways** tiene manías; **he's got rather — lately** recientemente se ha vuelto algo raro.

oddball ['ɔdbɔːl] (US) **1** adj raro, excéntrico. **2** n tipo m raro, excéntrico m.

oddity ['ɔditi] n (strangeness) rareza f, singularidad f, excentricidad f; (peculiar trait) rareza f, manía f; (odd person) individuo m singular; (odd thing) cosa f rara; **he has his oddities** tiene sus manías; **one of the oddities of the situation** uno de los aspectos raros que tiene la situación.

oddly ['ɔdli] singularmente, extrañamente; **they are — similar** tienen un extraño parecido; **— attractive** extrañamente atractivo; **— enough, . . .** aunque parezca mentira, . . .; **he is behaving most —** se está comportando de una manera muy rara.

oddment ['ɔdmənt] n artículo m suelto, artículo m que sobra; (pej) bagatela f, baratija f; (Comm) retal m.

oddness ['ɔdnis] n rareza f, singularidad f.

odds [ɔdz] npl (a) (difference) **what's the —?** ¿qué importa?, ¿qué más da?; **it makes no —** no importa, lo mismo da; **it makes no — to me** me es igual.

(b) (variance, strife) **to be at —** estar reñidos, estar de punta; **to be at — with someone** estar reñido con uno (about, over con motivo de); estar incomodado con uno; **to set 2 people at —** enemistar a 2 personas, hacer que riñan 2 personas.

(c) (balance of advantage) ventaja f, superioridad f; **the — are in his favour** él parece tener la ventaja; **the — are too great** nuestra desventaja es demasiado grande, los peligros son demasiado grandes; **to fight against overwhelming —s** luchar contra fuerzas abrumadoras.

(d) (equalizing allowance) ventaja f; **to give someone —** dar ventaja a uno.

(e) (in betting) puntos mpl de ventaja; **the — on the horse are 5 to 1** los puntos de ventaja del caballo son de 5 a 1; **to give — of 3 to 1** ofrecer 3 puntos de ventaja a 1; **what — will you give me?** ¿cuánta ventaja me da?

(f) (chances) probabilidades fpl; **the — are that . . .** lo más probable es que + subj; **the — are against it** es poco probable.

(g) **— and ends** (of cloth etc) retazos mpl, materiales mpl sobrantes; (trinkets) baratijas fpl, chucherías fpl; (things in disorder) cosas fpl sin arreglar; (possessions) chismes mpl; **there were — and ends of machinery** había piezas sueltas de máquinas.

odds-on ['ɔdz'ɔn] adj: **— favourite** caballo m favorito, caballo m con puntos de ventaja; **he's — favourite for the job** él tiene las mejores posibilidades de ganar el puesto.

ode [əud] n oda f.

odious ['əudiəs] adj odioso, detestable.

odium ['əudiəm] n odio m; oprobio m; **to bring — on someone** hacer que uno sea odiado; **to incur the — of having + ptp** suscitar el odio de la gente por haber + ptp.

odometer ['ɔdəmitə*] n odómetro m.

odontologist [.ɔdɔn'tɔlədʒist] n odontólogo m.

odontology [.ɔdɔn'tɔlədʒi] n odontología f.

odoriferous [.əudə'rifərəs] adj odorífero.

odorous ['əudərəs] adj oloroso.

odour, (US) **odor** ['əudə*] n olor m (of a); fragancia f, perfume m; (fig) sospecha f; **— of sanctity** olor m de santidad; **bad —** mal olor m; **to be in bad —** tener mala fama, estar bajo sospecha; **to be in bad — with someone** llevarse mal con uno.

odourless, (US) **odorless** ['əudəlis] adj inodoro.

Odysseus [ə'disjuːs] n Odiseo.

Odyssey ['ɔdisi] n Odisea f; **o—** (fig) odisea f.

oecology n etc see **ecology** etc.

oecumenical, (US) **ecumenical** [.iːkjuː'menikəl] adj ecuménico.

Oedipus ['iːdipəs] m Edipo; **— complex** complejo m de Edipo.

o'er ['əuə*] (poet) = **over.**

oesophagus, (US) **esophagus** [iː'sɔfəgəs] n esófago m.

of [ɔv, əv] prep (a) (possession) de; **the pen — my aunt** la pluma de mi tía; **a friend — mine** un amigo mío; **love — country** el amor a la patria; **the love — God** el amor de Dios; **it's no business — yours** aquí no se meta Vd, Vd no tiene que ver con esto.

(b) (partitive etc) de; **how much — this do you want?** ¿cuánto quieres de esto?; **there were 4 — us** éramos 4; **all — them** todos ellos; **the 12 two were bad** de los 12, dos estaban pasados; **most — all** más que nada; **you — all people ought to know** Vd debiera saberlo más que nadie; **the best — friends** el mejor amigo; **the book — books** el libro de los libros; **king — kings** rey de reyes.

(c) (descriptive genitive) **the city — Burgos** la ciudad de Burgos; **a boy — 8** un muchacho de 8 años; **cakes — her making** pasteles que ella había hecho; **by the name — Green** llamado Green; **bright — eye** de ojos claros; **hard — heart** duro de corazón; **that idiot — a minister** ese idiota de ministro.

(d) (origin, cause etc) **to buy something — someone** comprar algo a uno; **"— all chemists"** "De venta en todas las farmacias"; **— necessity** por necesidad, forzosamente; **— itself** de por sí; **to die — a disease** morir de una enfermedad.

(e) (material) de; **made — metal** hecho de metal.

(f) (agent) **beloved — all** querido de todos; **it was very harsh — him to + infin** ha sido durísimo en + infin; **it is kind — you** es Vd muy amable.

(g) (with certain verbs) **to dream — something** soñar con algo; **to judge — something** juzgar algo, opinar sobre algo; **to smell — something** oler a algo; **he was robbed — his watch** le robaron el reloj, se le robó el reloj.

(h) (fam) **he died — a Friday** murió un viernes; **it was fine — a morning** por la mañana hacía buen tiempo.

(i) (with hours: US) **it is 10 minutes — 4** son las 4 menos 10.

off [ɔf] **1** adv (a) (away) **a place 2 miles —** un lugar a 20 millas (de distancia); **it landed not 50 metres —** cayó a solamente 50 metros de nosotros; **noises —** ruidos mpl de fondo; **a voice —** voz de fondo, (Cine) voz en off.

(b) (of removal) **with his hat —** sin sombrero, llevando el sombrero en la mano; **with his shoes —** sin zapatos, descalzo; **hats —!** ¡descúbranse!; **with those wet socks!** ¡quítate esos calcetines mojados!; **— with his head!** ¡que le corten la cabeza!; **hands —!** ¡fuera las manos!; **the lid is —** la tapa está quitada; **— with you!** ¡fuera de aquí!, (tenderly) ¡vete ya!; **— we go!** ¡vamos!; **"10% —"** "descuento de 10 por cien"; **I'll give you 5% —** te doy un descuento de 5 por cien; **to have a day —** tomarse un día de asueto.

(c) **— and on** de vez en cuando, a intervalos; **ya bien ya mal; right —, straight —** sin parar, sin interrupción; **3 days straight —** 3 días seguidos.

2 adv (with to be) (a) (of distance, time) **it's some way —** está algo lejos, dista varios kilómetros de aquí; **the game is 3 days —** faltan 3 días para el partido.

(b) (depart) **to be —** irse; **I'm — me** voy; **I must be —** tengo que marcharme; **I'm — to Paris** voy a París, salgo para París; **be —!** ¡fuera de aquí!, ¡lárgate!; **they're —!** (race etc) ¡ya!; **he's — fishing every Sunday** todos los domingos sale a pescar, todos los domingos va de pesca.

(c) (be absent) **to be —** estar fuera, no estar; **he's — fishing** ha ido a pescar; **she's — on Tuesdays** los martes no viene (a trabajar); **are you — this weekend?** ¿vas a estar fuera este fin de semana?; **salmon is —** (on menu) no hay salmón ya, se acabó el salmón; **there are 2 buttons —** faltan 2 botones; **the game is —** se ha cancelado el partido; **sorry, but the party's —** lo siento, pero no hay guateque; **the talks are —** se han cancelado las conversaciones.

(d) (of switches etc) **to be —** estar en posición de desconectado; (apparatus, radio, TV) estar desenchufado, estar desconectado; (light) estar apagado; (tap) estar cerrado; (Mech) estar parado; (water etc) estar desapretado.

(e) (be bad) **to be —** estar pasado; (milk) estar cortado.

(f) (fig) **it's a bit —, isn't it?** esto no lo apruebo, ¿sabes?; **I thought his behaviour was rather —** me pareció que su conducta era bastante censurable.

(g) **to be well —** estar acomodado, tener dinero; **he's better — where he is** está mejor allí donde está ahora; **we should be no better —** no ganaríamos nada; **to be badly —** andar mal de dinero; **to be badly — for potatoes** andar escaso de patatas, tener escasez de patatas; see **well-off, worse 2** etc.

3 prep (a) de; **height — the ground** altura f del suelo, altura f sobre el suelo; **to fall — a table** caer de una mesa; **to fall — a cliff** caer por un precipicio; **to eat — a dish** comer en un plato; **to dine — fish**

cenar pescado; **to allow 5% — the price** rebajar el precio en un 5 por cien.

(b) a street — the square una calle que sale de la plaza; **a house — the main road** una casa algo apartada de la carretera.

(c) (*Naut*) **— Portland Bill** a la altura de Portland Bill, frente a Portland Bill.

(d) there are 2 buttons — my coat le faltan 2 botones a mi chaqueta; **to be — one's food** no tener apetito; **he was — work for 3 weeks** durante 3 semanas no pudo trabajar; **to take 3 days — work** tomarse 3 días de vacaciones.

4 *adj*: **— side** (*Aut etc*: *British*) lado *m* derecho, (*US*, *Spain etc*) lado *m* izquierdo; **to have an — day** tener un día malo; **in the — season** fuera de temporada; **in the — position** en posición de cerrado (*etc*).

offal ['ɔfəl] *n* asadura *f*, menudencias *fpl*.

offbeat ['ɔf,biːt] *adj* excéntrico, original; inconformista, nada convencional.

off-centre, (*US*) **off-center** ['ɔf'sentə*] *adj*: **to be —** estar descentrado.

off chance ['ɔftʃɑːns] *n* posibilidad *f* remota; **we'll go on the —** iremos por si acaso, iremos aunque hay poca posibilidad; **he bought it on the — that it would come in useful** lo compró pensando que tal vez resultaría útil algún día.

off-colour, (*US*) **off-color** ['ɔf'kʌlə*] *adj* fabric etc desteñido; (*ill*) indispuesto, (*of child*) pachucho; *joke etc* verde.

offence, (*US*) **offense** [ə'fens] *n* **(a)** (*insult*) ofensa *f*; **no — !, no — meant** sin ofender a Vd; **no — was intended, he intended no —** no tenía la intención de ofender a nadie; **to give —** ofender; **to take —** ofenderse (*at por*), resentirse (*at de*).

(b) (*crime*) delito *m*, crimen *m*, infracción *f* de la ley; (*moral*) transgresión *f*, pecado *m*; **first — primer delito** *m*; **indictable — delito** *m* procesable; **minor — delito** *m* de menor cuantía; **political — crimen** *m* político; **second — reincidencia** *f*; **technical — cuasidelito** *m*; **it is an — to** + *infin* la ley castiga a los que . . .; **to commit an — cometer un delito.**

offend [ə'fend] **1** *vt* ofender; **it —s my sense of justice** ello ofende mi sentido de justicia; **to be — at, by** por), tomarlo a mal; **he wasn't a bit —ed** no se ofendió en lo más mínimo; **don't be —ed** no se vaya a ofender, no lo tome a mal; **he is easily —ed** es algo picajoso; **to become —ed** ofenderse.

2 *vi*: **to — against** pecar contra.

offender [ə'fɔndə*] *n* **(a)** (*insulter*) ofensor *m*, ora *f*.

(b) (*criminal*) delincuente *mf*, culpable *mf*; (*against traffic code etc*) infractor *m*, ora *f* (*against de*); **first — delincuente** *mf* sin antecedente penal.

(c) (*moral*) transgresor *m*, ora *f*, pecador *m*, ora *f*.

offending [ə'fendiŋ] *adj* delincuente, culpable.

offensive [ə'fensiv] **1** *adj warfare etc* ofensivo; (*insulting*) ofensivo, injurioso; (*disgusting*) repugnante; **don't be — !** ¡hable con más educación; **to be — to someone** ser grosero con uno, decir injurias a uno.

2 *n* ofensiva *f*; **to go over to the —, to take the —** tomar la ofensiva.

offensively [ə'fensivli] *adv* injuriosamente; repugnantemente; groseramente.

offer ['ɔfə*] **1** *n* oferta *f*, ofrecimiento *m*; (*Comm*) oferta *f*; **— of marriage** oferta *f* de matrimonio; **peace —** ofrecimiento *m* de paz; **to be on —** estar en oferta, ofrecerse; **it was on — at £400** se ofrecía a 400 libras; **to make an — for something** hacer una oferta por algo, ofrecerse a comprar algo; **make me an — !** ¡hágame una oferta!; **it's the best —** I can make no puedo ofrecer más.

2 *vt* **(a)** *help, services etc* ofrecer; *prayers* rezar, ofrecer (*also to — up*); *opportunity, prospect etc* brindar, facilitar, deparar; **to — something to someone** ofrecer algo a uno; **to — one's flank to the enemy** exponer su flanco al enemigo; **to — resistance** oponer resistencia (*to a*); **he —ed no resistance** no se resistió.

(b) to — to do something ofrecerse a hacer algo; **he —ed to strike me** hizo ademán de pegarme, hizo como si fuera a pegarme.

(c) *comment, remark* hacer; **he —ed no comment** no dijo nada; **I wish to — two comments** quiero hacer dos observaciones.

(d) the flowers — a magnificent spectacle las flores se muestran espléndidas.

3 *vi*: **if the opportunity —s** si se me da la oportunidad, si se da el caso.

4 *vr*: **to — oneself for a mission** ofrecerse a ir a una misión; **to — oneself for a post** presentarse para un puesto.

offering ['ɔfəriŋ] *n* ofrecimiento *m*; (*Eccl*) ofrenda *f*; (*gift*) regalo *m*, don *m*; (*sacrifice*) sacrificio *m*; **burnt — holocausto** *m*; **votive — exvoto** *m*.

offertory ['ɔfətəri] *n* (*Eccl*) ofertorio *m*.

offertory box ['ɔfətri,bɔks] *n* (*Eccl*) cepillo *m*.,

offhand ['ɔf'hænd] **1** *adj* informal, brusco, descortés; poco ceremonioso; **to treat someone in an — manner** tratar a uno con bastante informalidad; **he was very — about it** lo discutió con poca seriedad.

2 *adv* de improviso, sin pensarlo; **— I couldn't tell you** así de improviso no se lo puedo decir.

offhandedly ['ɔf'hændidli] *adv* con informalidad, bruscamente, descortésmente; sin ceremonias, sin miramientos; **to treat someone —** tratar a uno con bastante informalidad; **he said —** dijo en tono brusco.

offhandedness ['ɔf'hændidnis] *n* informalidad *f*; brusquedad *f*; descortesía *f*.

office ['ɔfis] **1** *n* **(a)** (*place*) oficina *f*; (*room*) despacho *m*; (*lawyer's*) bufete *m*; (*as part of organization*) sección *f*, departamento *m*; (*ministry*) ministerio *m*; (*branch*) sucursal *f*; **head — central** *f*, sede *f*, oficina *f* principal; **manager's — dirección** *f*; **newspaper — redacción** *f*; **"usual —s" "aseos"; Foreign O— Ministerio** *m* de Asuntos Exteriores; *see* **home** *etc*.

(b) (*function*) oficio *m*; (*post*) cargo *m*; **it is my — to** + *infin* yo tengo el deber de + *infin*, me incumbe + *infin*; **to be in —, to hold — (person)** estar en funciones, desempeñar un cargo, (*govt*) estar en el poder; **he is in — for one year** ocupa el cargo durante un año; **to be out of —** no estar en el poder; **to come into —, to take — (person)** asumir un cargo, (*govt*) entrar en el poder; **to leave — (person)** dimitir un cargo, (*govt*) salir del poder; **to perform the — of someone** hacer las veces de uno.

(c) good —s buenos oficios *mpl*; **to offer one's good —s** ofrecer sus buenos oficios; **through the —s of** gracias a la mediación de.

(d) O— for the Dead (*Eccl*) oficio *m* de difuntos.

2 *attr hours, work etc* de oficina; *party* del personal de la oficina; **— supplies** materiales *mpl* de oficina.

office block ['ɔfisblɔk] *n* bloque *m* de oficinas.

office boy ['ɔfisbɔi] *n* mandadero *m*; botones *mpl*; mozo *m* de oficina.

officer ['ɔfisə*] **1** *n* (*Mil, Naut, Aer*) oficial *m*; (*of society*) dignatario *m*; (*of local govt*) magistrado *m*; funcionario *m*; (*of company*) director *m*; (*of police*) policía *m*, agente *m* de policía; (*form of address to policeman*) agente, guardia; **— of the watch** oficial *m* de guardia; **the —s of a company** los directores de una sociedad, la junta directiva de una sociedad; **commissioned — oficial** *m*; **non-commissioned — suboficial** *m*, sargento *m* or cabo *m*; **medical — médico** *m*, (*Mil*) oficial *m* médico, (*of town*) jefe *m* de sanidad municipal; **naval — oficial** *m* de marina; **orderly — oficial** *m* de día; **petty — suboficial** *m* de marina; **police — policía** *m*, agente *m* de policía; **staff — oficial** *m* del estado mayor.

2 *vt* (*command*) mandar; (*staff*) proveer de oficiales **to be well —ed** tener buena oficialidad.

office worker ['ɔfiswə:kə*] *n* oficinista *mf*.

official [ə'fiʃəl] **1** *adj* oficial; autorizado; *voice, style etc* ceremonioso, solemne; **in — circles** en círculos oficiales; **is that —?** (*fig*) ¿es cierto eso?

2 *n* oficial *m*, oficial *m* público, funcionario *m*; **high — oficial** *m* importante; **an — of the ministry** un funcionario del Ministerio.

officialdom [ə'fiʃəldəm] *n* (*pej*) burocracia *f*.

officialese [ə,fiʃə'liːz] *n* lenguaje *m* burocrático, estilo *m* oficial burocrático.

officially [ə'fiʃəli] *adv* oficialmente; de modo autorizado.

officiate [ə'fiʃieit] *vi* oficiar (*as de*).

officious [ə'fiʃəs] *adj* oficioso.

officiously [ə'fiʃəsli] *adv* oficiosamente.

officiousness [ə'fiʃəsnis] *n* oficiosidad *f*.

offing ['ɔfiŋ] *n*: **to be in the —** (*Naut*) estar cerca, (*fig*) estar en perspectiva.

off-licence ['ɔf,laisəns] *n* tienda donde se venden bebidas alcohólicas (*sin permitirse su consumo en el local*).

offprint ['ɔfprint] *n* separata *f*, tirada *f* aparte.

offset ['ɔfset] **1** *n* compensación *f*; (*Typ*) offset *m*; (*Hort: layer*) acodo *m*, (*bulb*) bulbo *m* reproductor; (*Archit*) retallo *m*; **— press** prensa *f* offset.

2 *vt* (*irr*: *see* **set**) compensar; contrarrestar, contrapesar.

offshoot ['ɔfʃuːt] *n* (*Bot*) renuevo *m*, vástago *m*; (*fig*) ramal *m* (*from de*).

offshore ['ɔf'ʃɔː*] **1** *adv* a lo largo. **2** *adj breeze* terral, que sopla de tierra; *island etc* a poca distancia de la costa.

offside [ˌɔf'said] **1** adv: **to be —** estar fuera de juego. **2** adj: **the — rule** la regla de fuera de juego. **3** interj ¡offside! (pronounced [or'sail]).

offspring ['ɔfspriŋ] n (sing) vástago m, descendiente mf; (pl) descendencia f, hijos mpl, prole f; **to die without —** morir sin dejar descendencia.

offstage ['ɔf'steidʒ] **1** adv entre bastidores. **2** adj de entre bastidores.

off-the-peg ['ɔfðə'peg] adv, adj confeccionado.

off-white ['ɔf'wait] adj de blanco algo oscuro, de un blanco que tira a gris.

oft [ɔft] adv (poet) = **often; many a time and —** muchísimas veces.

often ['ɔfən] adv muchas veces, mucho, a menudo, con frecuencia; **very —** muchísimas veces, repetidas veces, muy a menudo; **not —** pocas veces; **how —?** ¿cuántas veces?; **so —** tantas veces; **as — as** tantas veces como, siempre que; **as — as not, more — than not** las más veces; **every so — (of time)** cada cierto tiempo, (of distance, spacing) cada cierta distancia; **it is not — that . . .** no es frecuente que . . .; **it cannot be said too — that . . .** es necesario repetir que . .

oft-times ['ɔftaimz] adv (lit) a menudo.

ogival [ou'dʒaivəl] adj ojival.

ogive ['əudʒaiv] n ojiva f.

ogle ['əugl] vt echar miradas amorosas (or incitantes) a.

ogre ['əugə*] n ogro m.

oh [əu] interj (a) (vocative) — **king!** ¡oh rey! (b) (pain) ¡ay! (c) (preceding questions and excls) — **really?** ¿de veras?; — **is he?** ¿en serio?; — **what a surprise!** ¡qué sorpresa!; — **no you don't!** ¡eso no!

ohm [əum] n ohmio m.

oil [ɔil] **1** n (in most senses) aceite m, (Geol, as mineral) petróleo m; (Art, Eccl) óleo m; **an — by Rembrandt** un óleo de Rembrandt; **crude —** petróleo m bruto; **heavy —** aceite m pesado; **holy —** crisma f, santo óleo m; **lubricating —** aceite m lubricante; **sweet —** aceite m de oliva; **vegetable —** accite m vegetal; **to burn the midnight —** quemarse las cejas; **to check the —** (Aut etc) revisar el nivel del aceite; **to paint in —s** pintar al óleo; **to pour — on troubled waters** echar aceite sobre aguas turbulentas; **to strike —** encontrar un pozo de petróleo, (fig) encontrar un filón, enriquecerse de súbito.

2 attr industry etc petrolero; lamp etc de aceite.

3 vt lubricar, lubrificar, engrasar; **to be well —ed** (sl) ir a la vela.

oil-burning ['ɔil,bəːniŋ] adj que quema aceite combustible, que utiliza aceite combustible como combustible.

oilcake ['ɔilkeik] n torta f de borujo.

oilcan ['ɔilkæn] n aceitera f.

oilcloth ['ɔilklɔθ] n hule m, encerado m.

oilfield ['ɔilfiːld] n campo m petrolífero.

oil-fired ['ɔilfaiəd] adj = **oil-burning.**

oil gauge ['ɔilgeidʒ] n manómetro m de aceite; indicador m del nivel del aceite.

oiliness ['ɔilinis] n lo aceitoso, oleaginosidad f; lo grasiento; zalamería f.

oil lamp ['ɔillæmp] n velón m, quinqué m.

oil level ['ɔillevl] n nivel m del aceite.

oilman ['ɔilmæn] n, pl **-men** [men] petrolero m; magnate m del petróleo.

oil painting ['ɔil,peintiŋ] n pintura f al óleo; **she's no — ** no es tan hermosa que digamos.

oil pan ['ɔilpæn] n (US Aut) colector m de aceite.

oil refinery ['ɔilri,fainəri] n refinería f de petróleo

oilskin ['ɔilskin] n hule m, encerado m; **—s** traje m de encerado, chubasquero m.

oil stove ['ɔilstəuv] n (cooking) cocina f de petróleo, (heating) estufa f de petróleo.

oil tanker ['ɔiltæŋkə*] n petrolero m.

oil well ['ɔilwel] n pozo m de petróleo.

oily ['ɔili] adj liquid etc aceitoso, oleaginoso; meal grasiento; person zalamero.

ointment ['ɔintmənt] n ungüento m.

O.K., okay ['əu'kei] (fam) **1** interj ¡está bien!; sí!; ¡comprendido!; ¡vale! **2** adj (agreed) aprobado; (satisfactory) satisfactorio; **it's — with me** lo apruebo, estoy de acuerdo; **is it — with you if . . .?** ¿me das permiso para + infin . . .?, ¿me permites + infin . . .?; **that may have been — last year** eso puede haber estado de moda el año pasado; **the — hair-do of 1980** el peinado elegante de 1980, el peinado que está de moda en 1980. **3** n visto m bueno; **to give something one's — ** dar el visto bueno a algo, aprobar algo. **4** vt dar el visto bueno a, aprobar.

old [əuld] adj (a) (person: aged) viejo; anciano; **an — man** un viejo; **an — woman** una vieja; **the — los** viejos, los ancianos; **— and young** grandes y pequeños; **— Peter** Pedro el viejo; **— Mrs Brown** la vieja señora de Brown; **he's a good — horse** es un buen caballo aunque bastante viejo ya; **to grow — ** envejecerse; **to live to be — ** llegar a una edad avanzada; **if I live to be that — ** si llego a esa edad.

(b) (ancient) thing viejo; clothes etc viejo; usado, gastado; bread duro; wine añejo; **it's too — to be any use** es demasiado viejo para servir.

(c) (with expression of years: person) **how — are you?** ¿cuántos años tienes?, ¿qué edad tienes?; **I am 7 years — ** tengo 7 años; **she's 3 years — today** hoy cumple 3 años; **she is —er than I** tiene más años que yo; **she is the —est** es la mayor; **to be 4 years —er than someone** tener 4 años más que uno; **she's — enough to go alone** tiene bastante edad para ir sola; **he's — enough to know his own mind** tiene bastante edad para saber lo que quiere; **he's — enough to know better** a la edad que él tiene conviene obrar con más juicio.

(d) (with expression of years: thing) **the building is 300 years — ** el edificio se construyó hace 300 años; **the company is a century — ** la sociedad existe desde hace un siglo, la sociedad se fundó hace un siglo.

(e) (old-established, long-standing) viejo, antiguo; **an — friend of mine** un viejo amigo mío; **that's as — as the hills** eso es de tiempos de Maricastaña, eso es viejísimo.

(f) (former) antiguo; **an — boy of the school** un antiguo alumno del colegio; **my — school** mi antiguo colegio; **in the — days** antaño, en el pasado; **O— French** antiguo francés m; **the — country** la madre patria; **the O— World** el Viejo Mundo.

(g) (affectionate: fam) **— Lucas** el tío Lucas; **the — man** el jefe, el patrón; **my — man** el pariente, **my — woman** la parienta; **I say, — man** oye, chico; **any — thing does for me** me contento con cualquie. cosa; **any — thing you like** lo que quieras.

(h) **of — ** antiguamente, antaño; **knights of — ** los caballeros de antaño; **I know him of — ** le conozco de antiguo.

old-clothes ['əuld'kləuðz] adj: **— dealer** ropavejero m, a f; **— shop** ropavejería f.

olden ['əuldən] adj (arch or lit) antiguo; **in the — days** antaño, en el pasado.

old-established ['əuldis'tæbliʃt] adj viejo.

olde-worlde ['əuldi'wəːldi] adj (hum) viejísimo, antiquísimo; de antaño, de sabor arcaico; **with — lettering** con letras al estilo antiguo; **a very — interior** un interior pintoresco de antaño; **Stratford is terribly — ** Stratford tiene fuerte sabor arcaico.

old-fashioned ['əuld'fæʃnd] adj thing anticuado, pasado de moda; person de ideas anticuadas, chapado a la antigua.

oldish ['əuldiʃ] adj algo viejo, más bien viejo, que va para viejo.

old-line ['əuldlain] adj conservador, de mentalidad tradicionalista.

old-looking ['əuld,lukiŋ] adj de aspecto viejo.

old-maidish ['əuld'meidiʃ] adj de solterona; remilgado.

old stager ['əuld'steidʒə*] n veterano m.

oldster ['əuldstə*] n (US) viejo m, vieja f.

old-style ['əuld'stail] adj antiguo, al estilo antiguo, a la antigua.

old-timer [ˌəuld'taimə*] n veterano m.

old-world ['əuld'wəːld] adj (Bio, Geog) del Viejo Mundo; character etc antiguo, arcaico, rancio; **the — charm of Toledo** la atractiva ranciedad de Toledo, el sabor arcaico de Toledo.

oleaginous [əuli'ædʒinəs] adj oleaginoso.

oleander [ˌəuli'ændə*] n adelfa f.

oleo . . . ['əuliəu] in compounds oleo . . .

olfactory [ɔl'fæktəri] adj olfativo, olfatorio.

oligarchic(al) [ˌɔli'gaːkik(əl)] adj oligárquico.

oligarchy ['ɔligaːki] n oligarquía f.

olive ['ɔliv] **1** n (fruit) aceituna f, oliva f; (tree) olivo m. **2** adj aceitunado, oliváceo.

olive branch ['ɔlivbraːntʃ] n ramo m de olivo (also fig); **to hold out the — to someone** ofrecer el ramo de olivo a uno.

olive-green ['ɔliv'griːn] adj verde-oliva; **— uniforms** uniformes mpl verde oliva.

olive grove ['ɔlivgrəuv] n olivar m.

olive oil ['ɔliv'ɔil] n aceite m de oliva.

Oliver ['ɔlivə*] m Oliverio.

Olympiad [əu'limpiæd] n olimpíada f.

Olympian [əu'limpiən] adj olímpico.

Olympic [əu'limpik] **1** *adj* olímpico. **2 O—s** *npl* Juegos *mpl* Olímpicos.

Olympus [əu'limpəs] Olimpo *m*.

omega ['əumigə] *n* omega *f*.

omelet(te) ['ɔmlit] *n* tortilla *f*.

omen ['əumen] *n* agüero *m*, presagio *m*; **bird of ill —** ave *f* de mal agüero; **it is a good — that . . .** es buena señal que. . . .

ominous ['ɔminəs] *adj* siniestro, de mal agüero, amenazador; **the silence was —** el silencio no auguraba nada bueno; **in an — tone** en tono amenazador; **that's —** eso es mala señal.

ominously ['ɔminəsli] *adv*: **the thunder rumbled —** retumbaba amenazador el trueno; **it was — familiar to us** nos era siniestramente familiar; **he spoke —** habló en tono amenazador.

omission [əu'miʃən] *n* omisión *f*; supresión *f*; olvido *m*, descuido *m*; **it was an — on my part** fue un descuido mío.

omit [əu'mit] *vt* omitir; suprimir; olvidar, descuidar; *person, person's name* pasar por alto; **we should — all reference to . . .** debiéramos suprimir toda mención de . . .; **to — to do something** olvidar de + *infin*, dejar de + *infin*; **don't — to visit her** no dejes de visitarla.

omnibus ['ɔmnibəs] **1** *adj* general, para todo; *edition* completo. **2** *n* autobús *m*.

omnipotence [ɔm'nipətəns] *n* omnipotencia *f*.

omnipotent [ɔm'nipətənt] *adj* omnipotente.

omnipresence ['ɔmni'prezəns] *n* omnipresencia *f*.

omnipresent ['ɔmni'prezənt] *adj* omnipresente.

omniscience [ɔm'nisiəns] *n* omnisciencia *f*.

omniscient [ɔm'nisiənt] *adj* omnisciente, omniscio.

omnivorous [ɔm'nivərəs] *adj* omnívoro; **she is an — reader** lo lee todo con avidez, en su lectura muestra tener gustos muy diversos.

on [ɔn] **1** *adv see* **to put —** *etc*; *see* **further, later** *etc*. **(a) to be —** *(actor)* estar en la escena; **to have one's boots —** llevar las botas puestas; **what had he got —?** ¿qué prendas llevaba puestas?

(b) to drive —, to go —, to ride —, to walk — *etc* seguir adelante *(see also* **go** *etc)*; **to read —** seguir leyendo; **and so —** y así sucesivamente, y así los demás; etcétera; **to talk — and —** hablar sin parar, hablar incansablemente.

(c) from that time — desde entonces, a partir de entonces; **well — in June** bien entrado junio; **well — in years** entrado en años, que va para viejo.

(d) *(with to be: of switches etc)* **to be —** estar conectado; *(apparatus, Radio, TV)* estar conectado, estar puesto, estar enchufado; *(light)* estar encendido, estar puesto; *(tap)* estar abierto; *(Mech)* estar en marcha, estar funcionando; *(brake)* estar apretado.

(e) *(with to be: of shows etc)* **the show is now —** ha comenzado el espectáculo; **the show is now — in London** se ha estrenado el espectáculo en Londres; **— with the show!** ¡que empiece *(or* continúe) el espectáculo!; **— with the dancing girls !** ¡que salgan las bailarinas!; **what's — at the cinema ?** ¿qué ponen en el cine?; **what's — at the theatre ?** ¿qué representan en el teatro?; **"what's — in London"** "cartelera de los espectáculos londinenses"; **have you anything — this evening ?** ¿tienes compromiso para esta noche?; **the deal is —** se ha cerrado el trato, ya está concertado el trato; **that's not —!** ¡eso no se hace!, ¡no hay derecho!

(f) *(idioms with* to be) **to be — to something** creer haber encontrado algo, seguir una pista interesante; **he's — to something good** se ha encontrado algo bueno; **he knows he's — to a good thing** sabe que ha tenido la mar de suerte; **the police are — to the villain** la policía tiene una pista que le conducirá al criminal; **they were — to him at once** le calaron en seguida, le identificaron en el acto; **he's always — to me about it** me está majando continuamente con eso.

(g) — and off de vez en cuando, a intervalos.

2 *interj* ¡adelante!

3 *prep* **(a)** *(of place etc)* en, sobre; encima de; **— the Continent** en el continente; **— the table** en la mesa, sobre la mesa; **a meal — the train** una comida en el tren; **— all sides** por todas partes, por todos lados; **— the ceiling** sobre el techo; **— the high seas** en alta mar; **hanging — the wall** colgado de la pared; **with her hat — her head** con el sombrero puesto; **a house — the square** una casa en la plaza; **— page 2** en la página 2; **— the right** a la derecha; **— foot** a pie; **— horseback** a caballo; **I've no money — me** no llevo dinero encima, no llevo dinero; **to drift — to the shore** flotar hacia la playa; **so they came — to me** así que los hicieron pasar a mí, así que vinieron a mis manos.

(b) *(fig)* **a story based — fact** una historia basada en hechos; **the march — Rome** la marcha sobre Roma; **an attack — the government** un ataque contra el gobierno; **to swear — the Bible** prestar juramento sobre la Biblia; **all the children play — the piano** todos los chicos saben tocar el piano; **so he played it — the violin** así que lo tocó al violín; **he's — the committee** es miembro del comité; **he's — the staff** es de plantilla; **— average** por término medio; **— good authority** de buena tinta; **— his authority** con su autorización; **— my responsibility** bajo mi responsabilidad; **— a charge of murder** acusado de homicidio; **— pain of** so pena de; **— account of** a causa de; **— sale** de venta, en venta; **a student — a grant** un estudiante con beca; **I'm on £3,000** yo gano 3.000 libras (al año); **we're — irregular verbs** estamos estudiando los verbos irregulares; **I'm — a milk diet** sigo un régimen lácteo; **many live — less than** that muchos viven con menos; *(for many expressions, eg* **— duty, —hand,** *see the noun).*

(c) *(of time)* **— Friday** el viernes; **— Fridays** los viernes; **— the next day** al día siguiente; **— 14th May** el catorce de mayo; **— the evening of the 2nd July** el 2 de julio por la tarde; **— a day like this** un día como éste; **— some days it is** hay días cuando lo es; **— and after the 15th** el día 15 y a partir de la misma fecha; **— or about the 8th** el día 8 o por ahí; **— my arrival** al llegar yo.

(d) *(on + ger)* **— seeing him** al verle; **— my calling to him** al llamarle yo.

(e) *(concerning)* sobre, acerca de; **a book — physics** un libro de física, un libro sobre física; **an examination — maths** un examen de matemáticas; **Eden — the events of 1956** lo que dice Eden acerca de los acontecimientos de 1956; **Bentley — Horace** los comentarios de Bentley a Horacio; **have you heard the boss — the new tax?** ¿has oído lo que dice el jefe acerca de la nueva contribución?

(f) *(after, according to)* según; **— this model** según este modelo.

(g) *(engaged in)* **he's away — business** está fuera por negocios; **the company is — tour** la compañía está en gira; **to be — holiday** estar de vacaciones.

(h) *(at the expense of)* **this round's — me** esto corre de mi cuenta, invito yo; **it's — the house** la casa invita, está pagado *(por el dueño)*; **the tour was — the Council** la gira la pagó el Consejo, corrió el Consejo con los gastos de la gira.

(i) woe — woe dolor sobre dolor; **snow — snow** nieve y más nieve.

4 *adj*: **the — side** *(Aut etc; British)* el lado izquierdo, el lado de la izquierda, *(US, Spain etc)* el lado derecho; **in the — position** en posición de abierto *(etc).*

onanism ['əunanizəm] *n* onanismo *m*.

once [wʌns] **1** *adv* **(a)** *(on one occasion)* una vez; **— before** una vez antes, ya . . . una vez; **— or twice** algunas veces; **— a week** una vez por semana; **— only** una vez nada más; **— again, — more** otra vez, una vez más; **— in a while** de vez en cuando; **— and for all** una vez para siempre; **just this —** esta vez nada más; **for —** por una vez; **more than —** más de una vez; **not — in** ni una vez siquiera; **— a thief always a thief** los ladrones suelen ser incorregibles.

(b) *(formerly)* antes, antiguamente, en otro tiempo; **— when we were young** hace tiempo, cuando éramos jóvenes; **— upon a time** en tiempos de Maricastaña, *(as start of story)* érase una vez . . ., hubo una vez . . .; **it had — been white** antes había sido blanco; **I knew him —** le conocía hace tiempo.

(c) at — en seguida, inmediatamente; *(in one go)* de una vez; **at — a food and a tonic** alimento y tónico a la vez, juntamente alimento y tónico; **all at —** *(suddenly)* de repente, de golpe; *(in one go)* de una vez; *(all together)* todo junto, todos juntos, a un mismo tiempo.

2 *conj* una vez que . . ., si . . .; **— allow this all is lost** en cuanto esto se permita se acaba todo; **— you give him the chance** una vez que le des la oportunidad, si le das la oportunidad.

once-over ['wʌns,əuvə*] *n* *(fam)*: **to give something the —** dar un vistazo a algo, examinar algo *(rápidamente)*; **they gave the house the —** registraron superficialmente la casa.

oncoming ['ɔn,kʌmiŋ] *adj* que se acerca.

one [wʌn] **1** *adj* **(a)** *(numeral)* uno, una; *(before sing n)* un, *eg* **one man** un hombre; **— or two people** algunas personas; **— man out of two** uno de cada dos hombres; **there is only — left** queda uno solamente; **chapter —** el primer capítulo; **the last but —** el penúltimo; **that's — way of doing it** es uno de los métodos de hacerlo; *see* **number.**

(b) *(sole)* solo, único; **the — and only difficulty** la única dificultad; **the — and only Charlie Chaplin** el único Charlot; **his — care** su único cuidado; **the — way to do it** el único método de hacerlo; **no — man could do it** ningún hombre podría hacerlo por sí sólo.

(c) *(same)* mismo; **all in — direction** todos en la misma dirección; **they are — and the same** son el mismo; **it's all —** es lo mismo; **it's all — to me** me es igual; **God is —** Dios es uno; **to be — with something** formar un conjunto con algo; **to become — casarse.**

2 *n:* **— and twopence** un chelín con dos peniques; **price of —** *(Comm)* precio *m* de la unidad; **it's made all in —** está hecho en una sola pieza; **to be at — with someone** estar completamente de acuerdo con uno; **to be — up** tener la ventaja; tener un punto *(or* gol *etc)* de ventaja; haber ganado un partido más que los adversarios; **to be — up on someone** llevar ventaja a uno; **that puts us — up** eso nos da punto *(or* gol *etc)* de ventaja; **to go — better than someone** quedar por encima de uno, colocarse en posición ventajosa con relación a uno; **but John went — better** pero Juan hizo más; **he dotted her —** *(fam)* le dio un golpe; **to have a quick —** beberse un trago sin pérdida de tiempo; **to have — for the road** beberse un trago antes de partir.

3 *dem pron:* **this —** éste, ésta; **that —** ése, ésa, aquél, aquélla; **this — is better than that —** éste es mejor que ése; **— or two** algunos; **which — do you want?** ¿cuál quieres?

4 *rel pron* (a) **the — on the floor** el que está en el suelo; **the — who, the —** that el que, la que; **the —s who, the —s that** los que, las que; **they were the —s who told us** ellos eran quienes nos lo dijeron.

(b) **the white dress and the grey —** el traje blanco y el gris; **who wants these red —s?** ¿quién quiere estos colorados?; **what about this little —?** ¿y el pequeño éste?

(c) **that's a good —!** ¡ésa sí que es buena!; **to pull a fast — on someone** jugar una mala pasada a uno, embaucar a uno; **that's a difficult —** eso es un problema difícil; **our dear —s** nuestros seres queridos; **the Evil O—** el Malo; **the little —s** los pequeños, los chiquillos, la gente menuda; **he's a clever —** es un taimado; **you're a fine —!** ¡estás tú bueno!, ¡qué tío!; **he's the troublesome —** él es el elemento revoltoso; **he's a great — for chess** es estupendo para el ajedrez, es un entusiasta del ajedrez; **he's — for the ladies** es Perico entre ellas; **he's not much of a — for sweets** no le gustan mucho los dulces; **he is not the — to protest** no es de los que protestan.

5 *indef adj:* **— day** un día, cierto día; **— hot July evening** una tarde de julio de mucho calor.

6 *indef pron* (a) **have you got —?** ¿tienes uno?; **the book is — which I have never read** el libro es de los que no he leído nunca; **— of them** uno de ellos; **any — of us** cualquiera de nosotros; **he's — of the group** es del grupo, forma parte del grupo; **he's — of the family** now ya es de la familia; **I for — am not going** de todas formas yo no voy.

(b) **never a —** ni uno siquiera; **— and all** todos sin excepción; **the —...,** the other ... el uno ..., el otro ...; **you can't buy — without the other** no se puede comprar el uno sin el otro; **— after the other** uno tras otro; **for — reason or another** por alguna que otra razón; **— by —** uno a uno, uno tras otro.

(c) *(one another)* **they kissed — another** se besaron, se besaron el uno al otro; **they all kissed — another** se besaron unos a otros; **do you see — another much?** ¿os visitáis mucho?; **it's a year since we saw — another** hace un año que no nos vemos.

(d) **he looked like — who had seen a ghost** tenía el aspecto del que acababa de ver un fantasma; **— more sensitive would have fainted** una persona de mayor sensibilidad se hubiera desmayado; **to — who can read between the lines** para el que sabe leer entre líneas; **— Pérez** un tal Pérez.

(e) *(subject etc)* **— never knows** nunca se sabe; **— must wash** hay que lavarse; **— has one's pride** uno tiene cierto amor propio.

(f) *(possessive)* **—'s life is not really safe** la vida de uno no es realmente segura; **—'s opinion does not count** la opinión de uno no vale; **to cut —'s finger** cortarse el dedo.

one- [wʌn] *in compounds:* de un ..., de un solo ..., un-, *eg* **a one-line message** un mensaje de una sola línea; **a one-celled animal** un animal unicelular;

he's a one-woman man es un hombre para el que no existe más que una mujer.

one-act ['wʌn'ækt] *adj* de un solo acto.

one-armed ['wʌn'ɑːmd] *adj* manco.

one-eyed ['wʌn'aid] *adj* tuerto.

one-handed ['wʌn'hændid] **1** *adv:* **to catch the ball —** recoger la pelota con una sola mano. **2** *adj* manco.

one-horse ['wʌn'hɔːs] *adj* insignificante, de poca monta; **— town** pueblucho *m.*

one-legged ['wʌn'legid] *adj* con una sola pierna.

one-man ['wʌn'mæn] *adj* monohombre, individual.

oneness ['wʌnnis] *n* unidad *f.*

one-party ['wʌn'pɑːti] *adj* *state etc* de partido único.

one-piece ['wʌn'piːs] *adj* enterizo, de una pieza.

onerous ['ɔnərəs] *adj* oneroso.

oneself [wʌn'self] *pron (subject)* uno mismo, una misma; *(acc, dat)* ser; *(after prep)* sí (mismo, misma); **to be by —** estar solo, estar a solas; **to do something by —** hacer algo solo, hacer algo por sí mismo; **to look out for —** mirar por sí; **to come to —** volver en sí; **to say to —** decir para sí, decir entre sí; **to talk to —** hablar consigo mismo.

one-sided ['wʌn'saidid] *adj* unilateral; *(unbalanced)* desequilibrado; *contest, game* desigual; *view etc* parcial.

one-time ['wʌntaim] *adj* antiguo; **— butler to Lord Yaxley** antiguo mayordomo de Lord Yaxley; **— prime minister** ex primer ministro *m.*

one-to-one ['wʌntə'wʌn] *adj, adv* en proporción de uno a uno.

one-track ['wʌntræk] *adj* *(Rail)* de vía única; **— mind** que tiene un solo pensamiento.

one-upmanship [wʌn'ʌpmənʃip] *n (hum)* arte de establecerse en una posición superior con respecto a otra persona (logrando una ventaja táctica en una conversación etc).

one-way ['wʌnwei] *adj:* **— street** calle *f* de dirección única; **"— traffic"** "dirección única", "dirección obligatoria"; **— ticket** billete *m* sencillo.

ongoing ['ɔn,gəuiŋ] *adj* continuo, que continúa, que sigue funcionando.

onion ['ʌnjən] *n* cebolla *f;* *(sl)* cabeza *f;* **cocktail —** cebollita *f* perla; **to know one's —s** conocer a fondo su oficio.

onlooker ['ɔn,lukə*] *n* espectador *m,* ora *f;* observador *m,* ora *f;* *(esp pej)* mirón *m,* ona *f;* **I was a mere —** yo era un simple espectador.

only ['əunli] **1** *adv* sólo, solamente, únicamente; **no ... — más que;** nada más; **we have — 5** tenemos solamente 5, tenemos 5 solamente, tenemos 5 nada más; **what, — 5?** ¿cómo, 5, nada más?; **"Ladies —"** "Señoras"; **— God can tell** sólo Dios lo sabe; **— time will show** el tiempo lo dirá; **I'm — the porter** yo soy simplemente el conserje; **I — touched it** no hice más que tocarlo; **you — have to ask** no hay sino preguntar; **I will — say that ...** diré solamente que ...; **— to think of it!** ¡sólo pensar en ello!; **— too glad!** ¡con mucho gusto!; **if — I could!** ¡ojalá!, ¡ojalá pudiese ...!; **— just** apenas; **not — A but also B** no sólo A sino tambien B; *see if etc.*

2 *adj* único, solo; **their — son** su hijo único; **your — hope is to + infin** tu única posibilidad es **+ infin;** **his — response was to laugh** por toda respuesta se rió; **to be the — one to + infin** ser el único en **+ infin;** **you are not the — one** Vd no es el único en hacer *(etc)* eso.

3 *conj:* **it's very good, — rather dear** es muy bueno, pero algo caro; **I would gladly do it, — I shall be away** lo haría de buena gana sólo que voy a estar fuera.

onomastic [,ɔnəu'mæstik] *adj* onomástico.

onomatopoeia [,ɔnəumætəu'piːə] *n* onomatopeya *f.*

onomatopoeic [,ɔnəumætəu'piːik] *adj* onomatopéyico.

onrush ['ɔnrʌʃ] *n* arremetida *f,* embestida *f;* fuerza *f,* ímpetu *m.*

onset ['ɔnset] *n (attack)* ataque *m,* arremetida *f;* *(beginning)* comienzo *m;* **the — of winter** el comienzo del invierno.

onshore ['ɔnʃɔː*] **1** *adv* hacia la tierra. **2** *adj* *breeze* que sopla hacia la tierra.

onslaught ['ɔnslɔːt] *n* ataque *m* violento, embestida *f* furiosa; **to make a furious — on a critic** atacar violentamente a un crítico.

onto ['ɔntu] *prep (fam)* = **on to.**

ontological [,ɔntə'lɔdʒikəl] *adj* ontológico.

ontology [ɔn'tɔlədʒi] *n* ontología *f.*

onus ['əunəs] *n (no pl)* carga *f,* responsabilidad *f;* **the — is upon the makers** la responsabilidad es de los fabricantes; **the — is upon him to + infin** le incumbe a él **+ infin;** **the — of proof is on the prosecution** le incumbe al fiscal probar la acusación.

onward ['ɔnwəd] *adj march etc* progresivo, hacia adelante.

onward(s) ['ɔnwəd(z)] **1** *adv* adelante,'hacia adelante; **from that time** — desde entonces; **from the 12th century** — desde el siglo XII en adelante, a partir del siglo XII.
2 *interj* ¡adelante!

onyx ['ɔniks] *n* ónice *m*.

oodles ['uːdlz] *npl (fam):* **we have** — tenemos montones, tenemos muchísimo; **we have** — **of** tenemos la mar de, tenemos montones de.

oolite ['əuəlait] *n* oolito *m*.

oolitic [,əuə'litik] *adj* oolítico.

oomph [umf] *n (sl)* aquél *m*, atracción *f* sexual, sexy *m* (sl).

ooze [uːz] **1** *n* cieno *m*, lama *f*.
2 *vt* rezumar; *(fig)* rezumar, rebosar de; **he simply** —**s confidence** rebosa confianza.
3 *vi (liquid)* rezumar, rezumarse; *(blood)* manar suavemente; *(barrel etc)* rezumar; **to** — **away, to** — **out** rezumarse; agotarse poco a poco; **the wound was oozing blood** la herida sangraba lentamente.

opacity [əu'pæsiti] *n* opacidad *f*.

opal ['əupəl] *n* ópalo *m*.

opalescence [,əupə'lesns] *n* opalescencia *f*.

opalescent [,əupə'lesnt] *adj* opalescente.

opaque [əu'peik] *adj* opaco.

open ['əupən] **1** *adj* **(a)** *(not closed)* abierto; *book, grave, parcel, pores, wound etc* destapado; *bottle etc* destapado; **wide** — muy abierto, *door etc* abierto de par en par; **the door is** — la puerta está abierta; **a dress** — **at the neck** un vestido abierto por el cuello; **with his shirt** — con la camisa desabotonada; — **to the public on Mondays** se abre al público los lunes; **to break a safe** — forzar una caja fuerte; **to cut a sack** — abrir un saco cortándolo, abrir un saco de un tajo; **to fling** *(or* **throw) a door** — abrir una puerta de golpe, abrir una puerta de par en par.
(b) *(unobstructed)* abierto, sin límites, no limitado; *road* franco, abierto, no obstruido; — **country** campo *m* raso; — **sea** mar *m* abierto; **in the** — **air** al aire libre; **with** — **views** con amplias vistas, con extensas vistas; **the way to Paris lay** — ya no quedaban obstáculos en el camino de París.
(c) *(permissible)* **it is** — **to you to** + *infin* Vd puede perfectamente + *infin*, Vd tiene derecho a + *infin*; **what choices are** — **to me?** qué posibilidades hay?
(d) *(exposed)* abierto, descubierto; *town* abierto; *boat, car, carriage* descubierto; **the map was** — **on the table** el mapa estaba extendido sobre la mesa; **the book was** — **at page 7** el libro estaba abierto por la página 7; — **to every wind** expuesto a todos los vientos; — **to influence from advertisers** accesible a la influencia de los anunciantes; **it is** — **to doubt whether . . .** es discutible si . . ., es dudoso que + *subj*; **it is** — **to criticism on several counts** se le puede criticar por diversas razones, es criticable desde diversos puntos de vista; **I am** — **to persuasion** estoy dispuesto a dejarme persuadir; **I am** — **to advice** escucho de buena gana los consejos; **to lay** — abrir; *secret etc* poner al descubierto; **to lay oneself** — **to criticism** exponerse a ser criticado.
(e) *(public, unrestricted)* público; para todos; *championship, competition, race etc* abierto; *trial* público; *letter* abierto; *secret* a voces; **the competition is** — **to all** todos pueden participar en el certamen, el certamen se abre a todos; **membership is not** — **to women** la sociedad no admite a las mujeres.
(f) *(declared, frank)* abierto, franco; *admiration etc* franco; **an** — **enemy of the Church** un enemigo declarado de la Iglesia; **to be in** — **revolt** estar en franca rebeldía, estar en plena rebeldía; **he was not very** — **with us** no se portó del todo honradamente con nosotros.
(g) *(undecided)* *mind* receptivo, imparcial, sin prejuicios; *question* sin resolver, discutible, por decidir; *race* abierto, muy igual; *cheque* sin cruzar, abierto; **let's leave it** — dejémoslo sin decidir, no hace falta decidirlo ahora.
2 *n:* **to be out in the** — *(in the country)* estar en el campo; *(in bare country)* estar al raso; *(out of doors)* estar al aire libre; **to sleep in the** — dormir al raso, dormir a cielo abierto; **to bring a dispute into the** — hacer que una disputa llegue a ser del dominio público; **their true feelings came into the** — sus verdaderos sentimientos salieron a flor de piel; **why don't you come into the** — **about it?** ¿por qué no lo declara abiertamente?
3 *vt* **(a)** *(general sense)* abrir; *arms, eyes, heart, mouth, case, letter etc* abrir; *(unfold)* desplegar,

extender; *legs etc* abrir, separar; *abscess* cortar; *bottle etc* destapar; *parcel* deshacer, desenvolver; *shop* abrir, poner; *(tear)* romper; *(leave exposed)* dejar al descubierto; **to** — **a road to traffic** abrir una carretera al tráfico.
(b) *(drive)* **to** — **a hole in a wall** practicar un agujero en una pared; **to** — **a road through a forest** construir una carretera a través de un bosque.
(c) *(begin)* *conversation, debate, negotiations etc* iniciar, empezar; **to** — **an account in someone's name** abrir una cuenta a nombre de uno; **to** — **the case** *(Law)* exponer los detalles de la acusación, presentar los hechos en que se basa la acusación; **to** — **3 hearts** *(Bridge)* abrir de 3 corazones.
(d) *(declare* —, *inaugurate)* inaugurar; **the exhibition was** —**ed by the Queen** la exposición fue inaugurada por la Reina.
(e) **to** — **out** abrir; *(unfold)* desplegar, extender.
(f) **to** — **up** abrir; *secret, new vista* revelar; *new possibility* crear; *route, country* explorar; — **up!** *(police command)* ¡abran a la autoridad!; **to** — **up a market** abrirse un mercado, conquistar un mercado; **to** — **up a country for trade** ayudar al comercio a penetrar en un país; **to** — **up a country for development** fomentar el desarrollo de un país; **when the oilfield was** —**ed up** cuando se empezó a explotar el campo petrolífero; **to** — **up a blocked road** franquear una carretera obstruida, hacer transitable una carretera.
4 *vi* **(a)** *(general sense)* abrirse; *flower etc* abrirse; **the door** —**ed** se abrió la puerta; **a door that** —**s on to the garden** una puerta por la que se sale al jardín; **this room** —**s into a larger one** este cuarto comunica con otro más grande; **the shops** — **at 9** las tiendas se abren a las 9.
(b) *(begin)* empezar, comenzar, iniciarse; *(Bridge)* abrir la declaración; **the season** —**s in June** la temporada comienza en junio; **when we** —**ed in Bradford** cuando dimos la primera representación en Bradford; **the play** —**ed to great applause** el estreno de la obra fue muy aplaudido; **to** — **for the Crown** *(Law)* exponer los detalles de la acusación, presentar los hechos en que se basa la acusación; **the book** —**s with a long description** el libro comienza con una larga descripción; **to** — **with 2 hearts** *(Bridge)* abrir de 2 corazones.
(c) **to** — **out** *map etc* extenderse, desplegarse; *flower etc* abrirse; *passage, tunnel* hacerse más ancho; *car etc* acelerar; **a fine view** —**ed before us** delante de nosotros se extendía un magnífico panorama; **the team** —**ed out in the second half** en el segundo tiempo el equipo se mostró más enérgico; **the company is** —**ing out a bit now** ahora la compañía está ensanchando el campo de sus actividades.
(d) **to** — **up** *(Comm etc)* empezar, comenzar; *(Mil)* romper el fuego; *(emotionally)* franquearse, descubrir el pecho.

open-air ['əupn'ɛə*] *adj* al aire libre.

opencast ['əupn'kɑːst] *adj* a cielo abierto, de cielo abierto.

open-ended ['əupən'endid] *adj discussion etc* sin límites fijos, sin resultados previsibles, no limitado de antemano.

opener ['əupnə*] *n (tin-)* abrelatas *m*.

open-eyed ['əupn'aid] *adj* con los ojos abiertos; *(amazed)* con ojos desorbitados.

open-handed ['əupn'hændid] *adj* liberal, generoso.

open-handedness ['əupn'hændidnis] *n* liberalidad *f*, generosidad *f*.

opening ['əupniŋ] **1** *adj remark etc* primero; *speech, ceremony, price* de apertura.
2 *n (gap)* abertura *f*; *(in walls etc)* brecha *f*; *(in wood)* claro *m*; *(in clouds)* abertura *f*, claro *m*; *(beginning)* comienzo *m*, principio *m*; *(of play)* estreno *m*; *(of exhibition etc)* inauguración *f*; *(Chess)* apertura *f*; *(chance)* oportunidad *f*; *(Comm)* salida *f*; *(post)* puesto *m*, vacante *f*; **an unusual** — **occurs for . . .** se ofrece un puesto interesante de . . .; **it's a fine** — **for a young man** es una magnífica oportunidad para un joven; **to give someone an** — **for something** dar a uno la oportunidad de hacer algo.

openly ['əupənli] *adv* abiertamente, francamente; públicamente.

open-minded ['əupn'maindid] *adj* libre de prejuicios, imparcial; **I am still** — **about it** no me he decidido todavía, sigo sin resolverme.

open-mouthed ['əupn'mauðd] *adj* boquiabierto.

open-necked ['əupn'nekt] *adj* sin cuello, sin corbata.

openness ['əupnnis] *n* franqueza *f*.

openwork ['əupnwəːk] *n (Sew)* calado *m*, enrejado *m*.

opera ['ɔpərə] n ópera f; (building) teatro m de la ópera; **comic —** ópera f bufa, (in Spain) zarzuela f; **grand —** ópera f seria; **light —** opereta f, (in Spain) zarzuela f.

operable ['ɔpərəbl] adj operable.

opera glasses ['ɔpərəgla:siz] npl gemelos mpl de teatro.

opera hat ['ɔpərəhæt] n clac m.

opera house ['ɔpərəhaus] n, pl **— houses** [,hauziz] teatro m de la ópera.

opera singer ['ɔpərə,siŋə*] n cantante mf de la ópera, operista mf.

operate ['ɔpəreit] **1** vt motor etc impulsar; machine hacer funcionar, (as driver etc) manejar; company etc dirigir; eg canal explotar, administrar; **a machine —d by electricity** una máquina impulsada (or accionada) por electricidad; **can you — this tool?** ¿sabes manejar esta herramienta?; **he has been operating a clever swindle** ha estado manejando una hábil estafa.

2 vi **(a)** (person etc) obrar, actuar; (Mech) funcionar; drug etc surtir efecto (on en); (Mil etc) operar; **to — on** producir efecto en, afectar, influir.

(b) (Med) **to — on someone for something** operar a uno de algo; **to — for appendicitis** operar a uno de apendicitis; **he has still not been —d on** todavía no se le ha operado; **to — on someone's liver** operar de hígado a uno.

operatic [,ɔpə'rætik] adj de ópera, operístico.

operating ['ɔpəreitiŋ] adj operante; expenses etc de explotación.

operating theatre, (US) **— theater** ['ɔpəreitiŋ,θiətə*] n quirófano m, sala f de operaciones.

operation [,ɔpə'reiʃən] n **(a)** funcionamiento m; manejo m; dirección f; explotación f, administración f; (Mil etc) operación f; (of person) actuación f; (manoeuvre) maniobra f; **the company's —s during the year** las actividades de la compañía durante el año; **military —s** operaciones fpl militares; **combined —s** operaciones fpl conjuntas; **—s of doubtful legality** maniobras fpl de dudosa legalidad; **to be in —** (Mech) estar en funcionamiento, estar funcionando; (Law) estar en vigor, ser vigente; **to be in full —** estar en pleno funcionamiento; **to bring a machine into —** poner una máquina en funcionamiento; **to come into —** (Law) entrar en vigor; **to put into —** (Law) hacer entrar en vigor, poner en obra.

(b) (Med) operación f, intervención f quirúrgica; **a liver —** una operación de hígado; **to perform an — on someone for something** operar a uno de algo; **to undergo an —** ser operado (for something de algo).

operational [,ɔpə'reiʃənl] adj (relating to operations) de operaciones; (fit: Mil) en condiciones de servicio, operacional; (Mech) en buen estado, capaz de funcionar; **it is not — until next year** no se pondrá en funcionamiento hasta el año que viene; **when the service is fully —** cuando el servicio esté en pleno funcionamiento.

operative ['ɔpərətiv] **1** adj **(a)** (Law) **to be —** estar en vigor; **to become — from the 9th** entrar en vigor a partir del 9.

(b) (Med) operatorio.

2 n operario m, a f.

operator ['ɔpəreitə*] n (of machine) operario m, a f; maquinista mf; (Cine, Med) operador m; (Tel) telefonista mf; (Comm) agente m, corredor m de bolsa; **a big-time —** un criminal a gran escala; **he's a very clever — (pej)** es un criminal de los más hábiles.

operetta [,ɔpə'retə] n opereta f; (in Spain) zarzuela f.

Ophelia [ɔ'fi:liə] f Ofelia.

ophthalmia [ɔf'θælmiə] n oftalmía f.

ophthalmic [ɔf'θælmik] adj oftálmico.

ophthalmologist [,ɔfθæl'mɔlədʒist] n oftalmólogo m.

ophthalmology [,ɔfθæl'mɔlədʒi] n oftalmología f.

opiate ['əupiit] n opiata f, narcótico m.

opine [əu'pain] vi opinar.

opinion [ə'pinjən] n opinión f, parecer m; juicio m; concepto m; **public —** opinión f pública; **in my —** en mi opinión, a mi juicio; **in the — of those who know** en la opinión de los que saben, según los que saben; **well, that's my —** por lo menos eso digo yo; **I am of the — that . . .** soy del parecer de que; **I am entirely of your —** estoy completamente de acuerdo con Vd; **it's a matter of —** sobre eso hay diversos pareceres; **what is your — of him?** ¿qué concepto tienes de él?, ¿qué piensas de él?; **to ask someone's —** pedir el parecer de uno; **his — doesn't count** no vale su opinión; **to echo someone's —** compartir el sentir de uno; **to form an —** formarse una opinión; **to give one's —** dar su parecer; **to have a high — of someone** tener muy buen concepto de uno, tener a uno en mucho; **to have a high — of**

oneself pagarse de sí mismo; **to have a low (or poor) — of someone** tener un concepto poco favorable de uno; **I do not share your —** no comparto esa opinión.

opinionated [ə'pinjəneitid] adj porfiado, terco.

opium ['əupiəm] n opio m.

opium den ['əupiəm,den] n fumadero m de opio.

opossum [ə'pɔsəm] n zarigüeya f.

opponent [ə'pəunənt] n adversario m, a f, contrario m, a f, contrincante m.

opportune ['ɔpətju:n] adj oportuno, a propósito; **to be —** venir al caso, (of time etc) ser propicio; **at an — moment** en el momento oportuno; **his arrival was most —** su llegada fue muy oportuna.

opportunely ['ɔpətju:nli] adv oportunamente, a propósito; **this comes most —** esto viene al pelo.

opportunism [,ɔpə'tju:nizəm] n oportunismo m.

opportunist [,ɔpə'tju:nist] **1** adj oportunista. **2** n oportunista mf.

opportunity [,ɔpə'tju:niti] n oportunidad f, ocasión f; **equality of —** igualdad f de oportunidades; **to have the — to + infin** tener la oportunidad de + infin; **to make the most of one's —** aprovechar la ocasión; **to miss one's —** desperdiciar la ocasión; **I take this — to + infin** aprovecho esta ocasión para + infin.

oppose [ə'pəuz] vt oponerse a; resistir, combatir; **but he —d it** pero él se opuso a ello; **they —d the motion** ellos hablaron en contra de la moción; **we shall — this by all the means in our power** lucharemos contra esto por todos los medios.

opposed [ə'pəuzd] adj opuesto; **to be — to something** oponerse a algo, hablar en contra de algo, resistirse a aceptar algo; **it is — to all our experience** es contrario a toda nuestra experiencia; **savings as — to investments** los ahorros y no las inversiones, los ahorros en comparación con las inversiones.

opposing [ə'pəuziŋ] adj opuesto, contrario.

opposite ['ɔpəzit] **1** adv en frente; **they sat —** se sentaron uno enfrente del otro; **it is immediately —** está exactamente en frente; **they are directly —** están frente por frente.

2 prep (also **— to**) enfrente de, frente a; **a house — the school** una casa enfrente de la escuela; **— the bus stop** frente a la parada del autobús; **— the setting sun** de cara al sol que se ponía; **to sit — someone** sentarse enfrente de uno; **we were — Calais at the time** (Naut) a la sazón estábamos a la altura de Calais.

3 adj **(a) on the — page** en la página de enfrente; (of position) de enfrente; opuesto; **the house —** la casa de enfrente; **on the — bank** en la ribera opuesta; **in the — direction** en sentido contrario.

(b) (point of view etc) opuesto, contrario; (hostile) antagónico; **we take an — view** pensamos al contrario, creemos lo contrario; **of the — sex** del otro sexo; see **number**.

⊦ 4 n: **the — is true** la verdad es al contrario; **he maintains the —** él sostiene lo contrario; **it's the — of what we wanted** es totalmente distinto de lo que queríamos.

opposition [,ɔpə'ziʃən] **1** n oposición f (also Pol); resistencia f; (Comm) competencia f; **he made his — known** indicó su disconformidad; **to advance a kilometre without —** avanzar un kilómetro sin encontrar resistencia; **to act in — to the chairman** obrar de modo contrario al presidente; **the party in —** el partido de la oposición; **to be in —** (Pol) estar en la oposición; **to start up a business in — to another** montar un negocio para hacer competencia a otro.

2 attr member, party de la oposición.

oppress [ə'pres] vt oprimir; (of moral cause etc) agobiar; (heat etc) agobiar, ahogar.

oppression [ə'preʃən] n opresión f; agobio m.

oppressive [ə'presiv] adj (Pol etc) opresivo; tiránico, cruel; burden agobiante, oneroso; tax gravoso; heat etc agobiante, agobiador, sofocante.

oppressively [ə'presivli] adv opresivamente; cruelmente; de modo agobiante, de modo sofocante; **an — hot day** un día de calor agobiante.

oppressor [ə'presə*] n opresor m, ora f.

opprobrious [ə'prəubriəs] adj oprobioso.

opprobrium [ə'prəubriəm] n oprobio m.

opt [ɔpt] vi: **to — for something** elegir algo, escoger algo; **to — to + infin** optar por + infin.

optative ['ɔptətiv] (Gram) **1** adj optativo. **2** n optativo m.

optic(al) ['ɔptik(əl)] adj óptico.

optician [ɔp'tiʃən] n óptico m.

optics ['ɔptiks] n óptica f.

optimism ['ɔptimizəm] n optimismo m.

optimist ['ɔptimist] n optimista mf.

optimistic [ˌɔpti'mistik] *adj* optimista; **I am not —
about it** no lo veo tan fácil, no soy optimista
respecto de ello.
optimistically [ˌɔpti'mistikli] *adv* con optimismo;
speak etc en tono optimista.
optimum ['ɔptiməm] **1** *adj* óptimo, mejor; más
favorable; **the — number is 8** el mejor número es 8;
in — conditions en las condiciones más favorables.
2 *n* lo óptimo, lo mejor; cantidad *f* óptima, grado
m óptimo (*etc*).
option ['ɔpʃən] *n* opción *f*; **with an — on 10 more
aircraft** con opción para la compra de 10 aviones
más; **6 months without the — (of a fine)** una condena
de 6 meses sin la posibilidad de pagar una multa;
at the — of the purchaser según lo desee el comprador; **to have the — of doing something** tener la
posibilidad de hacer algo; **I have no —** no tengo otro
recurso, no tengo más remedio; **to take out an — on
another 100** suscribir una opción para la compra de
otros 100.
optional ['ɔpʃənl] *adj* discrecional, facultativo; *part,
fitting etc* opcional, de opción, optativo; **dress —**
traje de etiqueta o de calle, traje a voluntad; **the
heater is —** el calentador es de opción, el calentador
es optativo; **that is completely —** eso es según lo
desee Vd.
optometrist [ɔp'tɔmətrist] *n* optometrista *m*.
opulence ['ɔpjuləns] *n* opulencia *f*.
opulent ['ɔpjulənt] *adj* opulento.
opus ['əupəs] *n, pl* **opera** ['ɔpərə] (*Mus*) opus *m*,
obra *f*; (*hum*) obra *f*.
or [ɔː*] *conj* (a) o; (*before* o—, ho—) u, *eg* 7 — 8 siete u
ocho, **this one — another** éste u otro; **either A — B**
o A o B; **— else** o bien, si no; de otro modo; **an
hour — so** una hora más o menos; **20 — so** unos
veinte, veinte más o menos; **let me go — I'll
scream!** ¡suélteme, que voy a gritar!
(**b**) (*after negative*) ni; **without relatives — friends**
sin parientes ni amigos; **without fear — favour**
imparcialmente; **he didn't write — telephone** no
escribió ni telefoneó.
oracle ['ɔrəkl] *n* oráculo *m*; **to work the —** dirigirlo
todo entre bastidores.
oracular [ɔ'rækjulə*] *adj* profético, fatídico; sentencioso; misterioso.
oral ['ɔːrəl] **1** *adj* oral; (*Anat*) bucal; *message* verbal,
hablado. **2** *n* examen *m* oral.
orally ['ɔːrəli] *adv* oralmente; *tell etc* por boca, en
palabras; (*Anat, Med*) por vía bucal.
orange ['ɔrindʒ] **1** *n* (*fruit*) naranja *f*; (*tree*) naranjo
m; (*colour*) color *m* naranja; **bitter —, Seville —**
naranja *f* amarga.
2 *adj* anaranjado, anaranjado, color naranja.
orangeade ['ɔrindʒ'eid] *n* naranjada *f*.
orange blossom ['ɔrindʒ.blɔsəm] *n* azahar *m*.
orange-coloured ['ɔrindʒ.kʌləd] *adj* = **orange 2**.
orange grove ['ɔrindʒgrəuv] *n* naranjal *m*.
Orangeman ['ɔrindʒmən] *n, pl* **-men** [mən]
orangista *m* (*miembro del partido protestante de
Irlanda del Norte*).
orang-outang, orang-utan ['ɔːræŋ'uːtæn] *n* orangután *m*.
orate [ɔː'reit] *vi* (*hum*) perorar.
oration [ɔː'reiʃən] *n* oración *f*, discurso *m*; **funeral —**
oración *f* fúnebre.
orator ['ɔrətə*] *n* orador *m*, ora *f*.
oratorical [ˌɔrə'tɔrikəl] *adj* oratorio; retórico.
oratorio [ˌɔrə'tɔːriəu] *n* (*Mus*) oratorio *m*.
oratory[1] ['ɔrətəri] *n* oratoria *f*; **parliamentary —**
oratoria *f* parlamentaria.
oratory[2] ['ɔrətəri] *n* (*Eccl*) oratorio *m*.
orb [ɔːb] *n* orbe *m*; esfera *f*, globo *m*.
orbit ['ɔːbit] **1** *n* órbita *f* (*also fig*); **to be in —** estar en
órbita; **to go into — round the moon** entrar en
órbita alrededor de la luna.
2 *vt* orbitar, girar alrededor de.
3 *vi* orbitar, girar.
orbital ['ɔːbitl] *adj* orbital.
orchard ['ɔːtʃəd] *n* huerto *m*; (*apple —*) pomar *m*.
orchestra ['ɔːkistrə] *n* orquesta *f*; (*seating part of
theatre*) platea *f*, patio *m* de butacas.
orchestral [ɔː'kestrəl] *adj* orquestal.
orchestrate ['ɔːkistreit] *vt* orquestar, instrumentar.
orchestration [ˌɔːkis'treiʃən] *n* orquestación *f*,
instrumentación *f*.
orchid ['ɔːkid] *n*, **orchis** ['ɔːkis] *n* orquídea *f*.
ordain [ɔː'dein] *vt* **1** *vt* (*order*) ordenar, decretar; **to
— that . . .** ordenar que + *subj*; **to — someone's
exile** decretar el destierro de uno.
(**b**) (*Eccl*) ordenar; **to — someone priest** ordenar

a uno de sacerdote; **to be —ed** ordenarse de sacerdote.
2 *vi* mandar, disponer; **as God —s** según Dios
manda, como Dios manda.
ordeal [ɔː'diːl] *n* (**a**) (*Hist*) ordalías *fpl*; **— by fire**
ordalías *fpl* del fuego.
(**b**) (*fig*) prueba *f* rigurosa, experiencia *f* penosa;
sufrimiento *m*; **it was a terrible —** fue una experiencia terrible; **after such an —** después de tanto
sufrir; **exams are an — for me** para mí los exámenes
son una cosa horrible, sufro lo indecible con los
exámenes.
order ['ɔːdə*] **1** *n* (**a**) (*of society etc, Bio*) orden *m*;
clase *f*, categoría *f*; **the lower —s** la clase baja, la
plebe; **talents of the first —** talentos *mpl* de primer
orden; **of the — of 500** del orden de 500.
(**b**) (*Eccl*) **holy —s** órdenes *fpl* sagradas; **minor
—s** órdenes *fpl* menores; **to be in holy —s** estar en
órdenes sagradas, ser sacerdote; **to take (holy) —s**
ordenarse de sacerdote.
(**c**) (*society, decoration*) (*Eccl*) orden *f*; (*secular*)
orden *f*, sociedad *f*; (*worn on dress*) condecoración *f*,
insignia *f*; **Benedictine O—** Orden *f* de San Benito;
monastic — orden *f* monástica; **— of knighthood**
orden *f* de caballería; **O— of the British Empire**
Orden *f* del Imperio Británico; **O— of the Garter**
Orden *f* de la Jarretera; **to be wearing all one's —s**
vestir todas sus condecoraciones.
(**d**) (*Archit*) orden *m*; **Doric —** orden *m* dórico.
(**e**) (*succession, disposition*) orden *m*; clasificación *f*; método *m*; **in —** en orden, por orden, por su
orden; **in alphabetical —** por orden alfabético; **in
chronological —** por orden cronológico; **in — of
seniority** por orden de antigüedad; **to be out of —**
estar mal arreglados; estar fuera de serie; **to get out
of —** desarreglarse; **to put in —** poner en orden,
arreglar, ordenar; clasificar.
(**f**) (*Mil*) **in close —** en filas apretadas; **in
battle —** en orden de batalla; **in marching —** en
orden de marchar.
(**g**) (*good —*) estado *m*; **in —** en regla; **in good —**
en buen estado, en buenas condiciones; **his papers
are in —** tiene los papeles en regla; **everything is in
—** todo está en regla; **is this passport in —?** ¿este
pasaporte está en regla?; **what sort of an — is it in?**
¿en qué estado está?; **to put a matter in —** arreglar
un asunto; **a machine in working —** una máquina
en funcionamiento; **is it in — for me to go to Rome?**
¿tengo permiso para ir a Roma?; **"out of —"** "no
funciona"; **to be out of —** estar desarreglado;
(*Mech*) no funcionar, estar descompuesto; **my
liver is out of —** no estoy bien del hígado; **to get
out of —** (*Mech*) descomponerse, estropearse.
(**h**) (*Parl*) **—!** ¡orden! **to be out of —** estar fuera
de orden, estar fuera de la cuestión; **it is not in —
to discuss the Congo** el Congo está fuera de la
cuestión; **to call someone to —** llamar a uno al
orden; **to rise to a point of —** levantarse para
discutir una cuestión de procedimiento; **to rule a
matter out of —** decidir que un asunto no se puede
discutir.
(**i**) (*peace*) orden; **law and —** orden *m* público;
the forces of — las fuerzas del orden; **to keep —**
mantener el orden; **she can't keep —** es incapaz de
imponer la disciplina, no puede hacerse obedecer;
to keep children in — mantener a los niños en orden.
(**j**) **in — to** + *infin* para + *infin*; **in — that . . .**
para que + *subj*.
(**k**) (*command*) orden *f*; decreto *m*, mandato; (*of
court etc*) sentencia *f*, fallo *m*; **— of the day** orden *f*
del día; (*fig*) moda *f*, lo que es de rigor; **strikes are
the — of the day** las huelgas están a la orden del día;
O— in Council Orden *f* Real; **— of the court**
sentencia *f* del tribunal; **judge's —** mandamiento *m*
del juez; **sailing —s** últimas instrucciones *fpl* (dadas
al capitán de un buque); **sealed —s** órdenes *fpl*
secretas; **standing —s** reglamento *m*, estatuto *m*;
by — de por orden de; **by — of the king** por Real
Orden; **on the —s of** por orden de; **till further —s**
hasta nueva orden; **that's an —!** ¡es una orden!;
—s are —s las órdenes no se discuten; **to be under
the —s of** estar bajo el mando de; **to be under
starter's —s** estar listo para la salida; **to get one's
marching —s** (*fig*) ser despedido; **to give an —** dar
una orden; **to give someone —s to do something**
ordenar a uno hacer algo; **to give —s that something
should be done** mandar que se haga algo; **to obey —s**
cumplir las órdenes; **I don't take —s from anyone**
a mí no me da órdenes nadie.
(**l**) (*Comm*) pedido *m*, encargo *m*; **repeat —**
pedido *m* de repetición; **rush —** pedido *m* urgente;

unfilled —s pedidos *mpl* pendientes; **standing** — pedido *m* permanente, pedido *m* regular; **made to** — hecho por encargo especial, hecho a la orden; **to the** — **of** a la orden de; **we can't do things to** — no podemos proveer en seguida todo cuanto se nos pide; **to give an** — **for something** pedir algo, hacer un pedido de algo; **to place an** — **for something with someone** pedir algo a uno; **we have it on** — **for you** está pedido para Vd; **we will put it on** — **for you** se lo pediremos para Vd al fabricante; **that's rather a tall** — eso es much pedir.

(**m**) (*Fin*) libranza *f*; giro *m*; **banker's** — orden *f* bancaria; *see* **money**, **postal**.

2 *vt* (**a**) (*put in* —) disponer, arreglar, poner en orden; clasificar; **to** — **one's life properly** organizar bien su vida, vivir con arreglo a cierto método.

(**b**) **to** — **someone to do something** mandar a uno hacer una cosa, ordenar a uno hacer algo; **to** — **someone a new drug** recetar un nuevo fármaco para uno; **to** — **someone a complete rest** mandar a uno reposo absoluto; **to be** —**ed to pay costs** ser condenado a pagar las costas.

(**c**) (*Comm*) pedir, encargar; *meal, taxi* encargar; **to** — **a suit of clothes** mandar hacer un traje; **have you** —**ed yet?** ¿has encargado la comida ya?

(**d**) (*with adv or prep*) **to** — **someone about** mandar a uno de acá para allá, ser muy mandón con uno; **to** — **a regiment abroad** mandar un regimiento al extranjero; **to** — **someone back** mandar a uno volver; **to** — **someone in** mandar a uno entrar; **to** — **someone off** despedir a uno, echar a uno, decir a uno que se vaya; **the referee** —**ed him off (the field)** el árbitro le expulsó; **to** — **someone out** mandar a uno salir; **to** — **the troops out** llamar a las tropas, enviar a las tropas.

order book ['ɔːdəbuk] *n* libro *m* de pedidos.
order form ['ɔːdəfɔːm] *n* hoja *f* de pedido.
orderly ['ɔːdəli] 1 *adj* (*methodical*) ordenado, metódico; (*tidy*) aseado, en orden, en buen estado; (*well-behaved*) formal; *crowd etc* pacífico, obediente; disciplinado.
2 *n* (*Mil*) ordenanza *m*, asistente *m*; (*Med*) enfermero *m*.
orderly room ['ɔːdəli,rum] *n* (*Mil*) oficina *f*.
order paper ['ɔːdə,peipə*] *n* (*Parl etc*) lista *f* de asuntos a tratar.
ordinal ['ɔːdinl] 1 *adj* ordinal. 2 *n* ordinal *m*.
ordinance ['ɔːdinəns] *n* ordenanza *f*, decreto *m*.
ordinarily ['ɔːdnrili] *adv* ordinariamente, de ordinario; — **we buy 6 at a time** generalmente compramos 6 a la vez; **more than** — **polite** más cortés de lo común.
ordinary ['ɔːdnri] 1 *adj* (**a**) corriente, común, normal; **the** — **Frenchman** el francés corriente; **an** — **citizen** un simple ciudadano; **for the** — **reader** para el lector medio; **it's not what you'd call an** — **present** no es lo que se diría un regalo de todos los días.

(**b**) *seaman* simple; *share* ordinario.

(**c**) (*pej*) vulgar, ordinario; mediocre; **just an** — **man** un hombre vulgar; **they're very** — **people** son gente muy ordinaria; **neither good nor bad, just** — ni bueno ni malo, solamente mediocre.

2 *n*: **a man above the** — un hombre destacado, un hombre que no es del montón; **something out of the** — algo fuera de lo común, algo extraordinario.
ordination [,ɔːdi'neiʃən] *n* (*Eccl*) ordenación *f*.
ordnance ['ɔːdnəns] *n* (*guns*) artillería *f*, cañones *mpl*; (*supplies*) pertrechos *mpl* de guerra; **O**— **Corps** Cuerpo *m* de Armamento y Material; **O**— **Survey** *servicio oficial de topografía*; **O**— **Survey map** = mapa *m* del Estado Mayor.
ordure ['ɔːdjuə*] *n* inmundicia *f* (*also fig*).
ore [ɔː*] *n* mineral *m*, mena *f*; **copper** — mineral *m* de cobre.
organ ['ɔːgən] *n* (*all senses*) órgano *m*; **sexual** —**s** órganos *mpl* sexuales; **vocal** —**s** órganos *mpl* de la voz.
organdie ['ɔːgəndi] *n* organdí *m*.
organ-grinder ['ɔːgən,graində*] *n* organillero *m*.
organic [ɔː'gænik] *adj* orgánico.
organically [ɔː'gænikəli] *adv* orgánicamente; **there's nothing** — **wrong with you** Vd está en buen estado en cuanto a lo físico.
organism ['ɔːgənizəm] *n* organismo *m*.
organist ['ɔːgənist] *n* organista *mf*.
organization [,ɔːgənai'zeiʃən] *n* (*act*) organización *f*; (*body*) organización *f*, organismo *m*.
organize ['ɔːgənaiz] 1 *vt* organizar; (*sl*) agenciarse; **to get** —**ed** organizarse, arreglárselas; **you must give**

us time to get —**d** hay que darnos tiempo para que nos las arreglemos.
2 *vi* organizarse (*for* para).
organizer ['ɔːgənaizə*] *n* organizador *m*, ora *f*.
organ loft ['ɔːgənlɔft] *n* tribuna *f* del órgano.
organ pipe ['ɔːgənpaip] *n* cañón *m* de órgano.
organ stop ['ɔːgənstɔp] *n* registro *m* de órgano.
orgasm ['ɔːgæzəm] *n* orgasmo *m*.
orgiastic [,ɔːdʒi'æstik] *adj* orgiástico.
orgy ['ɔːdʒi] *n* orgía *f*; **an** — **of destruction** una orgía de destrucción; **the flowers were an** — **of colour** las flores eran una explosión de colores.
oriel ['ɔːriəl] *n* mirador *m*.
Orient ['ɔːriənt] Oriente *m*.
oriental [,ɔːri'entəl] 1 *adj* oriental. 2 *n* oriental *mf*.
orientate ['ɔːrienteit] 1 *vt* orientar. 2 *vr*: **to** — **oneself** orientarse.
orientation [,ɔːrien'teiʃən] *n* orientación *f*.
orifice ['ɔrifis] *n* orificio *m*.
origin ['ɔridʒin] *n* origen *m*; (*point of departure*) procedencia *f*; **country of** — pais *m* de procedencia; **to be of humble** —, **to have humble** —**s** ser de nacimiento humilde.
original [ə'ridʒinl] 1 *adj* original; *idea, meaning, sin etc* original; (*first*) primero; (*earlier*) primitivo; **the** — **sense was . . .** el sentido primitivo era . . .; **one of the** — **members** uno de los primeros miembros, uno de los socios fundadores; **its** — **inventor** su inventor primitivo.
2 *n* (*MS, painting etc*) original *m*; (*archetype*) prototipo *m*; (*person*) original *m*, excéntrico *m*; **the** — **is lost** el original está perdido; **he reads Cervantes in the** — lee a Cervantes en su idioma original, lee a Cervantes en su propia lengua.
originality [ə,ridʒi'næliti] *n* originalidad *f*.
originally [ə'ridʒənəli] *adv* (**a**) (*at first*) al principio, en sus orígenes; originariamente; **as they were** — **written** tal como fueron escritas originariamente; — **they were in Athens** al principio estuvieron an Atenas, antiguamente estuvieron en Atenas.

(**b**) (*in an original manner*) **it is quite** — **written** está escrito con bastante originalidad; **he deals with the subject** — trata el asunto con inventiva.
originate [ə'ridʒineit] 1 *vt* producir, originar, dar lugar a; (*of person*) idear, inventar, crear.
2 *vi* originarse, nacer, surgir; **to** — **from**, **to** — **in** traer su origen de; **to** — **with someone** ser invento de uno, ser invento de uno; **where did the fire** —? ¿dónde empezó el incendio?; **with whom did the idea** —? ¿quién tuvo la idea primero?
originator [ə'ridʒineitə*] *n* inventor *m*, ora *f*, autor *m*, ora *f*.
oriole ['ɔːriəul] *n*: **golden** — oropéndola *f*.
Orkney Islands ['ɔːkni,ailəndz] *pl*, **Orkneys** ['ɔːkniz] *pl* Órcadas *fpl*.
ormolu ['ɔːmɔluː] *n* oro *m* molido.
ornament ['ɔːnəmənt] *n* adorno *m*, ornato *m*, ornamento *m*; (*trinket*) chuchería *f*; (*vase etc*) objeto *m* de adorno; **he is the chief** — **of his country** es el máximo valor de su patria; —**s** (*Eccl*) ornamentos *mpl*.
ornament ['ɔːnəment] *vt* adornar, ornamentar (*with* de).
ornamental [,ɔːnə'mentl] *adj* ornamental (*also Bot*); decorativo, de adorno.
ornamentation [,ɔːnəmen'teiʃən] *n* ornamentación *f*.
ornate [ɔː'neit] *adj* muy ornado, vistoso; *style* florido.
ornately [ɔː'neitli] *adv* vistosamente; en estilo florido.
ornateness [ɔː'neitnis] *n* vistosidad *f*; estilo *m* florido *m*; lo florido.
ornithological [,ɔːniθə'lɔdʒikəl] *adj* ornitológico.
ornithologist [,ɔːni'θɔlədʒist] *n* ornitólogo *m*.
ornithology [,ɔːni'θɔlədʒi] *n* ornitología *f*.
orphan ['ɔːfən] 1 *adj* huérfano.
2 *n* huérfano *m*, a *f*.
3 *vt* dejar huérfano a; **the children were** —**ed by the accident** el accidente dejó huérfanos a los niños; **she was** —**ed at the age of 9** quedó huérfana a los 9 años.
orphanage ['ɔːfənidʒ] *n* orfanato *m*.
Orpheus ['ɔːfiuːs] *m* Orfeo.
orthodontics [,ɔːθəu'dɔntiks] *n* ortodoncia *f*.
orthodox ['ɔːθədɔks] *adj* ortodoxo.
orthodoxy ['ɔːθədɔksi] *n* ortodoxia *f*.
orthographic(al) [,ɔːθə'græfik(əl)] *adj* ortográfico.
orthography [ɔː'θɔgrəfi] *n* ortografía *f*.
orthopaedic, (*US*) —**pedic** [,ɔːθəu'piːdik] *adj* ortopédico.
orthopaedics, (*US*) —**pedics** [,ɔːθəu'piːdiks] *n* ortopedia *f*.

orthopaedist, (US) **—pedist** [.ɔ:θəu'pi:dist] n ortopedista mf.

oscillate ['ɔsileit] **1** vt hacer oscilar.

2 vi **(a)** oscilar (between entre; from A to Z de A a Z); fluctuar, variar.

(b) (person) vacilar; **he —s between boredom and keenness** pasa del aburrimiento al entusiasmo.

oscillating ['ɔsileitiŋ] adj oscilante.

oscillation [.ɔsi'leifən] n oscilación f; fluctuación f, variación f; vacilación f.

oscillator ['ɔsileitə*] n oscilador m.

oscillatory [.ɔsi'leitəri] adj oscilatorio.

osculate ['ɔskjuleit] (hum) **1** vt oscular. **2** vi oscularse.

osculation [.ɔskju'leifən] n (hum) ósculo m.

osier ['əuʒə*] n mimbre f.

osier bed ['əuʒəbed] n mimbrera f.

osmosis [ɔz'məusis] n ósmosis f.

osmotic [ɔz'mɔtik] adj osmótico.

osprey ['ɔsprei] n águila f pescadora.

osseous ['ɔsiəs] adj óseo.

ossification [.ɔsifi'keifən] n osificación f.

ossify ['ɔsifai] **1** vt osificar. **2** vi osificarse.

ossuary ['ɔsjuəri] n osario m.

Ostend [ɔs'tend] Ostende.

ostensible [ɔs'tensəbl] adj pretendido, aparente.

ostensibly [ɔs'tensəbli] adv aparentemente, en apariencia.

ostentation [.ɔsten'teifən] n ostentación f; aparato m, boato m; fausto m.

ostentatious [.ɔsten'teifəs] adj ostentoso; aparatoso; person ostentativo.

ostentatiously [.ɔsten'teifəsli] adv ostentosamente, con ostentación; aparatosamente; con boato; **he remained — silent** permaneció ostentosamente silencioso.

osteoarthritis ['ɔstiəuɑ:'θraitis] n osteoartritis f.

osteopath ['ɔstiəpæθ] n osteópata m.

osteopathy [.ɔsti'ɔpəθi] n osteopatía f.

ostler ['ɔslə*] n mozo m de cuadra.

ostracism ['ɔstrəsizəm] n ostracismo m.

ostracize ['ɔstrəsaiz] vt condenar al ostracismo, excluir de la sociedad (or del trato, del grupo etc); **he was —d** vivió en el ostracismo.

ostrich ['ɔstritʃ] n avestruz m.

Othello [ə'θeləu] m Otelo.

other ['ʌðə*] **1** adj otro; **the — one** el otro; **the — five** los otros cinco; **the — day** el otro día; **come some — day** venga otro día; **all the — books have been sold** todos los otros libros se han vendido, todos los demás libros se han vendido; **— people have done it** otros lo han hecho; **— people's property** la propiedad ajena; **— people's ideas** las ideas ajenas; **I do not wish him — than he is** no quiero que sea distinto de lo que es.

2 pron: **the —** el otro; **the —s** los otros, los demás; **one after the —** uno tras otro; **some do, —s don't** los hay que sí, otros no; **are there any —s?** ¿hay otros?; **and these 5 —s** y estos otros 5; **she and no — ella** y no otra; **some fool or — algún tonto; somebody or — alguien; one or — of us** uno de nosotros; **no — ningún otro; our happiness depends on that of —s** nuestra felicidad depende de la de otros; **we must respect —s' rights** hay que respetar los derechos ajenos; see **each**.

3 adv: **— than** de otra manera que; otra cosa que; **he could not act — than as he did** no podía hacer otra cosa que la que hizo; **I did not read it — than cursorily** no le di sino una lectura superficial.

otherwise ['ʌðəwaiz] adv **(a)** (in another way) de otra manera; **it cannot be —** no puede ser de otra manera.

(b) (in other respects) por lo demás, por otra parte; **— it's a very good car** por lo demás es un coche muy bueno, aparte de esto es un coche muy bueno.

(c) (if not) si no; **— we shall have to walk** pues si no, tendremos que ir a pie.

other-worldly ['ʌðə'wə:ldli] adj person espiritual, poco realista.

otiose ['əufiəus] adj ocioso, inútil.

otter ['ɔtə*] n nutria f.

Otto ['ɔtəu] m Otón.

Ottoman ['ɔtəmən] **1** adj otomano. **2** n otomano m, a f.

ottoman ['ɔtəmən] n otomana f.

ought[1] [ɔ:t] n = aught.

ought[2] [ɔ:t] v aux **(a)** (obligation) deber; **I — to do it** debo hacerlo, debiera hacerlo; **I — to have done it** debiera haberlo hecho; **one — not to do it** conviene no hacerlo, sería mejor no hacerlo; **to behave as one — comportarse** como se debe; **one — to be able to find it** ha de ser posible encontrarlo; **I thought I — to tell you** me creí en el deber de decírselo.

(b) (vague desirability) **you — to go and see it** vale la pena ir a verlo; **you — to have seen it!** ¡era de ver!; **you — to have seen him!** ¡había que verle!

(c) (probability) **that car — to win** ese coche tiene más probabilidades de ganar; **that — to be enough** eso ha de bastar; **he — to have arrived by now** debe de haber llegado ya.

ounce [auns] n **(a)** onza f (= 28,35 gr).

(b) (fig) pizca f; **there's not an — of truth in it** eso no tiene ni pizca de verdad; **if you had an — of common sense** si tuvieras una pizca de sentido común.

our [auə*] poss adj nuestro(s), nuestra(s).

ours [auəz] poss pron (subject) (el) nuestro, (la) nuestra etc.

ourselves [.auə'selvz] pron (subject) nosotros mismos, nosotras mismas; (acc, dat) nos; (after prep) nosotros (mismos), nosotras (mismas); see **oneself**.

oust [aust] vt desalojar; expulsar, echar; (from house etc) desahuciar; **to — someone from a post** lograr que uno renuncie a un puesto; **we —ed them from the position** les hicimos abandonar la posición; **"fabulous" has —ed "smashing"** "fabuloso" ha sustituido a "pistonudo".

out [aut] **1** adv **(a)** (general sense) fuera, afuera; hacia fuera; **"—"** (notice) "salida"; **— you go!** ¡fuera!; **with him!** ¡fuera con él!, ¡que le echen fuera!; **— with it!** ¡desembucha!; **the voyage —** el viaje de ida; **murder will —** el asesinato se descubrirá; **— here** aquí fuera; aquí, aquí en este sitio tan remoto; **— there** allí fuera; allí, allí en ese sitio tan remoto; **it carried us — to sea** nos llevó mar afuera; **to have a day —** pasar un día fuera de casa, pasar un día en el campo, pasar un día al aire libre; **it's her evening — es** su tarde libre; **to have a night —** salir de juerga por la noche.

(b) see other verbs, eg **to come —, to go —** salir; **to run —** salir corriendo.

(c) to be — (person): no estar (en casa), estar fuera; haber salido; **Mr Green is —** el Sr Green no está; **he's — a good deal** pasa bastante tiempo fuera; **to be — and about again** estar levantado y salir (después de una enfermedad etc); **now that the Liberals are —** ahora que los liberales están fuera del poder; **the railwaymen are —** los ferroviarios están en huelga; **I was — for some minutes** estuve varios minutos sin conocimiento; **he was — cold** estuvo completamente sin conocimiento; **I'm 2 shillings —** he perdido 2 chelines en el cálculo; **he was — in his reckoning** había hecho mal el cálculo, había calculado mal; **I was not far —** lo acerté casi; **and he was not far — either** y su conjetura resultó ser casi exacta.

(d) to be — (things): **when the sun is —** cuando brilla el sol; **the dahlias are —** las dalias están en flor; **the book is —** se ha publicado el libro, ha salido el libro; **the secret is —** el secreto ha salido a luz; **the ball is —** el balón está fuera del terreno; **the tide is —** la marea está baja; **long dresses are —** los vestidos largos ya no están de moda; **your watch is 15 minutes —** su reloj lleva 5 minutos de atraso (or de adelanto); **before the week is —** antes del fin de la semana; **to be — fire, light, gas** estar apagado; **"lights — at 10 pm"** "se apagan las luces a las 10"; **my pipe is —** se me ha apagado la pipa.

(e) to be — for buscar; ambicionar, aspirar a; **he's — for all he can get** quiere apoderarse de todo cuanto se le ofrezca; **we're — for a quick decision** queremos que la cosa se decida cuanto antes; **they're — for trouble** quieren armar un escándalo; **we are — after duck** salimos a cazar ánades; **she's — to find a husband** se propone pescar un marido, tiene intención de buscarse un marido, se está esforzando por encontrar un marido.

(f) the coat is — at the elbows la chaqueta está rota por los codos.

(g) (intensive) **it's the biggest swindle —** es la mayor estafa que hay; **he's the best footballer —** es el mejor futbolista que se ha visto, es el mejor futbolista que se ha conocido jamás.

(h) — **loud** en alta voz; **right —, straight — a** quemarropa, sin rodeos.

2 prep: **— of (a)** (outside, beyond) fuera de; **to be — of range** fuera de alcance; **to be — of danger** estar fuera de peligro; **to be — of sight** estar invisible, no estar a la vista, no poderse ver; **to be — of season** estar fuera de temporada; **we're well — of it** de buena nos hemos librado; **to feel — of it** sentirse aislado, no tomar parte en las actividades sociales (etc).

(b) (incompatible with) **to be — of proportion**

with no guardar proporción con; — **of measure** fuera de medida; **times** — **of number** innumerables veces; *see* **mind, sort** *etc*.

(c) (*verbs of motion etc*) **to go** — **of the house** salir de la casa; **to go** — **of the door** salir por la puerta; **to throw something** — **of a window** tirar algo por una ventana; **we looked** — **of the window** nos asomamos a la ventana, miramos por la ventana; **to turn someone** — **of the house** echar a uno de la casa.

(d) (*origin*) de; **a chapter** — **of a novel** un capítulo de una novela; **like a princess** — **of a fairy tale** como una princesa de un cuento de hadas; **to drink** — **of a glass** beber de un vaso; **to eat** — **of the same dish** comer del mismo plato; **to take something** — **of a drawer** sacar algo de un cajón; **to read** — **of a novel** leer en una novela; **to copy something** — **of a book** copiar algo de un libro; **1** — **of 10** de cada 10, 1; **1** — **of every 3 smokers** 1 de cada 3 fumadores.

(e) (*material*) de; **a box made** — **of wood** una caja hecha de madera.

(f) (*because of*) por; — **of respect for you** por el respeto que le tengo; — **of spite** por despecho; — **of necessity** por necesidad; **to do something** — **of sympathy** hacer algo movido por la compasión.

(g) (**to be** — **of**: *lacking*) **we're** — **of petrol** no hay gasolina, se acabó la gasolina, nos hemos quedado sin gasolina; **it's** — **of stock** no hay, no tenemos; **to be** — **of a suit** (*Bridge*) estar fallo; **to be** — **of hearts** tener fallo a corazones.

3 *n*: *see* **in 3**.

out-and-out ['autən'aut] *adj believer etc* firme, acérrimo, cien por cien; de tomo y lomo; *scoundrel* consumado, redomado.

outback ['autbæk] *n* (*Australia*) despoblado *m*, campo *m*.

outbid [aut'bid] (*irr: see* **bid**) *vt* licitar más que, hacer mejor oferta que; sobrepujar.

outboard ['autbɔːd] *adj* fuera de borda; — **motor** motor *m* fuera de borda, motor *m* fuera-bordo.

outbreak ['autbreik] *n* (*of spots*) erupción *f*; (*of disease*) epidemia *f*, brote *m*; (*of revolt*) estallido *m*; (*of war*) comienzo *m*, declaración *f*, (*of hostilities*) rompimiento *m*; (*of feeling, violence etc*) arranque *m*; (*of crimes etc*) ola *f*; **at the** — **of war** al declararse la guerra.

outbuilding ['aut,bildiŋ] *n* dependencia *f*, edificio *m* accesorio; (*shed*) cobertizo *m*.

outburst ['autbəːst] *n* explosión *f*; arranque *m*, acceso *m*; **an** — **of anger** una explosión de cólera; **there was an** — **of applause** estallaron ruidosos los aplausos; **forgive my** — **last week** le ruego perdonar el que perdiera los estribos la semana pasada.

outcast ['autkɑːst] *n* paria *mf*, proscrito *m*, a *f*; **he is a social** — vive desterrado de la sociedad.

outclass [aut'klɑːs] *vt* ser netamente superior a, aventajar con mucho.

outcome ['autkʌm] *n* resultado *m*.

outcrop ['autkrɔp] **1** *n* afloramiento *m*. **2** *vi* aflorar.

outcry ['autkrai] *n* grito *m*, protesta *f* ruidosa; **to raise an** — **about something** poner el grito en el cielo por motivo de algo; **there was a great** — hubo fuertes protestas, se armó la gorda.

outdated [aut'deitid] *adj* anticuado, fuera de moda.

outdistance [aut'distəns] *vt* dejar atrás.

outdo [aut'duː] (*irr: see* **do**) *vt* exceder, sobrepujar; **to** — **someone in something** exceder a uno en algo; **he was not be outdone** no se quedó en menos; **I, not to be outdone** . . . pues yo, para no quedar en menos . . .

outdoor ['autdɔː*] *adj* al aire libre.

outdoors ['aut'dɔːz] *adv* al aire libre; fuera de casa; **go and play** — id a jugar fuera.

outer ['autə*] *adj* exterior; externo.

outermost ['autəməust] *adj place* extremo, (el) más remoto; *cover etc* (el) más exterior, primero.

outfall ['autfɔːl] *n* desembocadura *f*.

outfield ['autfiːld] *n* (*Sport*) parte *f* exterior del campo, (*Baseball*) jardín *m*.

outfit ['autfit] *n* (a) (*gear*) equipo *m*; (*tools*) herramientas *fpl*, juego *m* de herramientas; (*of clothes*) traje *m*; **a complete camper's** — un equipo completo de campista; **why are you wearing that** —? ¿por qué te has trajeado así?

(b) (*fam: Mil*) cuerpo *m*, equipo *m*; grupo *m*; organización *f*; **when I joined this** — cuando vine a formar parte de esta unidad; **it's a rotten** — es una sección horrible.

outfitter ['autfitə*] *n* camisero *m*.

outflank [aut'flæŋk] *vt* (*Mil*) flanquear; (*fig*) superar en táctica, burlar.

outflow ['autfləu] *n* efusión *f*; desagüe *m*; pérdida *f*; (*Mech*) tubo *m* de salida.

outgeneral [aut'dʒenərəl] *vt* superar en estrategia.

outgo ['autgəu] *n* (US) gastos *mpl*.

outgoing ['aut,gəuiŋ] *adj* (a) *president etc* saliente; *ministry* que acaba de dimitir; *mail* que sale; *tide* que baja.

(b) (*of character*) extrovertido, vivo, bullicioso.

outgoings ['aut,gəuiŋz] *npl* gastos *mpl*.

outgrow [aut'grəu] (*irr: see* **grow**) *vt* (*person*) crecer más que; *habit etc* pasar de la edad de, ser ya viejo para; *defect, illness* curarse de . . . con la edad; *clothes* hacerse demasiado grande para; **she has** —**n her gloves** se le han quedado chicos los guantes; **we've** —**n all that** todo eso ha quedado ya a la espalda.

outhouse ['authaus] *n*, *pl* —**houses** [hauziz] = **outbuilding**.

outing ['autiŋ] *n* (*walk*) paseo *m*; (*trip*) excursión *f*, jira *f* campestre; **I took a brief** — di un pequeño paseo, di una vuelta; **everyone went on an** — **to Toledo** todos fueron de excursión a Toledo.

outlandish [aut'lændiʃ] *adj* estrafalario, extravagante.

outlast [aut'lɑːst] *vt* durar más tiempo que; (*person*) sobrevivir a.

outlaw ['autlɔː] **1** *n* proscrito *m*, forajido *m*. **2** *vt* proscribir; *practice etc* declarar ilegal, declarar fuera de la ley.

outlawry ['autlɔːri] *n* bandolerismo *m*.

outlay ['autlei] *n* desembolso *m*, inversión *f*.

outlet ['autlet] *n* salida *f* (*also fig, Comm*); (*of drain etc*) desagüe *m*, desaguadero *m*; (*of stream etc*) desembocadura *f*; (*Mech*) salida *f*, tubo *m* de salida; **to find an** — **for a product** encontrar una salida (*or un mercado*) para un producto; **it provides an** — **for his energies** es un modo de emplear útilmente su energía.

outline ['autlain] **1** *n* (*profile*) contorno *m*, perfil *m*; (*of plan*) trazado *m*; (*sketch*) esbozo *m*, bosquejo *m*; (*general idea, also* —**s**) idea *f* general, nociones *fpl* generales; **"O—s of History"** (*as title*) "Introducción a la Historia"; **in broad** — a grandes líneas, a grandes rasgos; **in broad** — **the plan is as follows** . . . el trazado general del plan es el siguiente . . .; **I'll give you a rapid** — **of the scheme** le explicaré el proyecto en términos generales.

2 *vt* (*draw profile of*) perfilar; (*sketch*) trazar, bosquejar; *policy etc* explicar en términos generales, dar una idea general de; prefigurar; **to be** —**d against** destacarse contra, dibujarse contra; **the building was** —**d in the distance** a lo lejos se dibujaba el edificio.

outlive [aut'liv] *vt* sobrevivir a; (*thing*) durar más tiempo que; (*live down*) hacer olvidar.

outlook ['autluk] *n* (a) (*view, future promise*) perspectiva *f*, perspectivas *fpl*; **the** — **for the wheat crop is good** son favorables las perspectivas de la cosecha de trigo; **it's a grim** — es una perspectiva nada halagüeña, el futuro no promete nada bueno.

(b) (*opinion*) punto *m* de vista; actitud *f*; **what is his** — **on the matter?** ¿cuál es su punto de vista en este asunto?; **his** — **is always pessimistic** su actitud siempre es pesimista; **a person with a broad** — una persona de amplias miras.

outlying ['aut,laiiŋ] *adj* (*distant*) remoto, lejano, aislado; *suburb etc* exterior.

outmanoeuvre, (US) outmaneuver [,autmə'nuːvə*] *vt* superar en la táctica.

outmatch [aut'mætʃ] *vt* superar, aventajar.

outmoded [aut'məudid] *adj* anticuado, pasado de moda.

outnumber [aut'nʌmbə*] *vt* exceder en número, ser más numeroso que; **we were** —**ed 10 to 1** ellos eran diez veces más que nosotros.

out-of-date ['autəv'deit] *adj* anticuado; *see also* **date**[1] **1**.

out-of-doors ['autəv'dɔːz] *adv*: *see* **outdoors**.

out-of-the-way ['autəvðə'wei] *adj* (*remote*) remoto, apartado, aislado, inaccesible; (*unusual*) poco común; (*recherché*) rebuscado.

outpace [aut'peis] *vt* dejar atrás.

outpatient ['aut,peiʃənt] *n* paciente *m* externo, paciente *f* externa (del hospital).

outplay [aut'plei] *vt* (*Sport*) superar en la táctica, jugar mejor que; **we were** —**ed in every department** ellos resultaron ser mejores que nosotros en todos los aspectos del juego.

outpost ['autpəust] *n* avanzada *f* (*also fig*), puesto *m* avanzado.

outpouring ['aut,pɔːriŋ] *n* efusión *f*; **the** —**s of a sick mind** la efusión de una mente enferma; **an** — **of emotion** una efusión de emoción.

output ['autput] *n* producción *f*, volumen *m* de producción; (*of machine*) rendimiento *m*; (*Elec*) potencia *f* de salida; **to raise** — aumentar la producción.

outrage ['autreidʒ] **1** *n* atrocidad *f*; atropello *m*; (*committed during riot etc*) desmán *m*, desafuero *m*; (*public scandal*) escándalo *m*; (*suffered by someone*) indignidad *f*; **bomb** — incidente *m* en que estalla una bomba; **it's an** —! ¡es un escándalo!, ¡qué barbaridad!, ¡no hay derecho!; **to commit an** — **against** (*or* **on**) **someone** cometer un desafuero contra uno.
2 *vt* ultrajar, violentar, atropellar; (*rape*) violar; **it** —**s justice** atropella la justicia.

outrageous [aut'reidʒəs] *adj* atroz, terrible; monstruoso; escandaloso; indignante; **your** — **conduct** su conducta escandalosa; **it is absolutely** — **that** ... es indignante que + *subj*; **it's** —! ¡es un escándalo!, ¡qué barbaridad!, ¡no hay derecho!

outrageously [aut'reidʒəsli] *adv* **behave** *etc* de modo escandaloso.

outrank [aut'ræŋk] *vt* ser de categoría superior a.

outré ['u:trei] *adj* extravagante, estrafalario.

outrider ['aut,raidə*] *n* motociclista *m* de escolta.

outrigger ['aut,rigə*] *n* (*beam, spar*) batanga *f*, balancín *m*; (*rowlock*) portarremos *m* exterior; (*boat*) bote *m* con batanga, bote *m* con portarremos exterior.

outright ['autrait] *adj* (*complete*) completo, entero, total; **sale** *etc* en su totalidad, definitivo; (*forthright*) franco; **supporter** *etc* incondicional, declarado; **refusal** rotundo.

outright [aut'rait] *adv* (*once and for all*) de una vez, de un golpe; (*forthrightly*) abiertamente, francamente; **to buy something** — comprar algo en su totalidad, comprar algo definitivamente; **to reject an offer** — rechazar una oferta de pleno; **to laugh** — **at something** reírse abiertamente de algo.

outrun [aut'rʌn] (*irr: see* **run**) *vt* correr más que; (*fig*) exceder, rebasar, pasar los límites de.

outset ['autset] *n* principio *m*, comienzo *m*; **at the** — al principio; **from the** — desde el principio.

outshine [aut'ʃain] (*irr: see* **shine**) *vt* brillar más que; (*fig*) eclipsar, superar en brillantez.

outside ['aut'said] **1** *adv* fuera; **to be** — estar fuera; **to leave a car** — dejar un coche fuera, (*at night etc*) dejar un coche en la calle, dejar un coche al descubierto; **to put the cat** — hacer salir al gato; **seen from** — visto desde fuera; **to ride** — (*on bus*) viajar en el piso superior; — **of** = **2**.
2 *prep* fuera de; al exterior de; (*beyond*) más allá de, al otro lado de; **he's waiting** — **the door** espera a la puerta; **one could hear everything that was said** — **the door** se oía todo cuanto se estaba diciendo al otro lado de la puerta; **it's** — **the normal range** eso cae fuera del alcance normal; **it's** — **our scheme** no forma parte de nuestro proyecto; **that's** — **our terms of reference** eso no está comprendido dentro de nuestros puntos de consulta.
3 *adj* (*outer*) exterior, externo; (*outermost*) extremo; **chance** *etc* remoto, poco prometedor; (*relating to other people*) ajeno; (*brought from* —) traído desde fuera; **TV broadcast** exterior; **forward** (*Sport*) extremo; (*seat on bus*) del piso superior; **thanks to** — **influence** gracias a la influencia de personas ajenas al asunto, gracias a influencias exteriores; **to get an** — **opinion** buscar las opiniones de personas no comprometidas, sondear la opinión independiente.
4 *n* (*outer part*) exterior *m*; (*surface*) superficie *f*; (*outward aspect*) aspecto *m* exterior, apariencia *f*; (*of bus*) piso *m* superior; **at the** — a lo sumo, cuando más; **from the** — desde fuera, desde el exterior; **to open a window from the** — abrir una ventana desde fuera; **on the** — por fuera; **to pass someone on the** — adelantar a uno por el exterior; **the window opens to the** — la ventana se abre hacia fuera.

outside-forward ['autsaid'fɔ:wəd] *n* delantero *m* extremo.

outside-left ['autsaid'left] *n* extremo *m* izquierdo.

outsider ['aut'saidə*] *n* (*stranger*) forastero *m*, a *f*, desconocido *m*, a *f*, (*pej*) intruso *m*, a *f*; (*in racing*) caballo *m* que no figura entre los favoritos, (*in election*) candidato *m* poco conocido; (*cad*) canalla *m*, persona *f* indeseable; (*independent*) persona *f* independiente, persona *f* ajena al asunto, persona *f* no comprometida.

outside-right ['autsaid'rait] *n* extremo *m* derecho.

outsize ['autsaiz] *adj* de tamaño extraordinario; (*hum*) enorme.

outskirts ['autskə:ts] *npl* afueras *fpl*; alrededores *mpl*; barrios *mpl* exteriores.

outsmart [aut'sma:t] *vt* ser más listo que, vencer en perspicacia; (*deceive*) engañar, burlar.

outspoken [aut'spəukən] *adj* franco, abierto; **to be** — no tener pelos en la lengua.

outspokenly [aut'spəukənli] *adv* francamente.

outspokenness [aut'spəukənnis] *n* franqueza *f*.

outspread ['aut'spred] *adj* extendido; desplegado.

outstanding [aut'stændiŋ] *adj* (*exceptional*) destacado; excepcional, relevante, sobresaliente; **problem** pendiente, no resuelto; **account** por pagar.

outstandingly [aut'stændiŋli] *adv* excepcionalmente, extraordinariamente.

outstay [aut'stei] *vt* **person** quedarse más tiempo que; **to** — **one's welcome** permanecer tanto tiempo que uno resulta pesado; **I don't want to outstay my welcome** no quiero ser un pesado.

outstretched ['autstretʃt] *adj* extendido; alargado.

outstrip [aut'strip] *vt* dejar atrás, aventajar, superar.

outvote [aut'vaut] *vt* **person** vencer en las elecciones; **proposal** rechazar por votación; **but I was** —**d** pero en la votación perdí.

outward ['autwəd] *adj* exterior, externo; **journey** de ida.

outward(s) ['autwəd(z)] *adv* hacia fuera; exteriormente; **to be** — **bound from Vigo** haber salido de Vigo; **to be** — **bound for Gijón** ir con rumbo a Gijón.

outwardly ['autwədli] *adv* por fuera, aparentemente.

outwear [aut'weə*] (*irr: see* **wear**) *vt* (*last longer than*) durar más tiempo que; (*wear out*) gastar.

outweigh [aut'wei] *vt* pesar más que, tener mayor peso que; (*fig*) pesar más que; **this** —**s all other considerations** éste vale más que todos los demás factores.

outwit [aut'wit] *vt* ser más listo que, burlar.

outworn [aut'wɔ:n] *adj* gastado, cansado.

oval ['əuvəl] **1** *adj* oval, ovalado. **2** *n* óvalo *m*.

ovary ['əuvəri] *n* ovario *m*.

ovate ['əuveit] *adj* ovado.

ovation [əu'veiʃən] *n* ovación *f*; **to give someone an** — ovacionar a uno; **to receive an** — ser ovacionado; **he got a standing** — **from the delegates** fue ovacionado por los delegados puestos de pie.

oven ['ʌvn] *n* horno *m*; **Huelva was like an** — Huelva era un horno; **it's like an** — **in there** allí dentro es el mismo infierno.

ovenproof ['ʌvnpru:f] *adj* refractario.

ovenware ['ʌvnweə*] *n* utensilios *mpl* para horno, utensilios *mpl* termorresistentes.

over ['əuvə*] **1** *adv* (**a**) (*of place*) encima; por encima; **this goes under and that goes** — éste pasa por debajo y ése por encima.
(**b**) (*in another place*) — **here** acá; — **there** allá; — **in France** allá en Francia; **they're** — **for the day** han venido a pasar el día; **when we were** — **in the States** cuando estábamos allá en Estados Unidos; — **against the wall** contra la pared; — **against the church** al lado de la iglesia, junto a la iglesia.
(**c**) (**all** — *etc*) **the world** — en todo el mundo; **to search the whole country** — registrar el país de arriba abajo; **embroidered all** — todo bordado; **to tremble all** — estar todo tembloroso; **I ache all** — me duele en todas partes; **I looked for you all** — te busqué por todas partes; **it happens all** — ocurre en todas partes, ocurre por doquier; **he was all** — **flour** estaba completamente cubierto de harina, estaba cubierto de harina de pies a cabeza; **that's him all** — eso es muy de él.
(**d**) (*with verbs*) **to bend** — inclinarse, encorvarse; **to bend something** — doblar algo; **to boil** — irse, rebosar; **to flow** — desbordarse; *see* **fall, lean, look** *etc*.
(**e**) (*of number, quantity*) **persons of 21 and** — las personas de 21 años para arriba; **4 into 29 goes 7 and 1** — 29 dividido entre 4 son 7 y queda 1; **we have 4 pounds and a bit** — tenemos 4 libras y algo más; **there are 3** — sobran 3, quedan 3; **I have a card** — me sobra una carta, tengo una carta de más.
(**f**) **to be** — (*finished*) estar terminado; **when this is all** — cuando esto haya terminado, cuando se acabe esto; **as soon as the war is** — en cuanto termine la guerra; — **the storm is** — ya pasó la tormenta; **it's all** —! ¡se acabó!; **it's all** — **with him** se acabó con él, (*relationship*) he roto con él.
2 *prep* (**a**) (*place:* **above**) encima de, por encima de; (**on, in contact with**) sobre; — **our heads** por encima de nuestras cabezas; **to spread a sheet** — **something** extender una sábana sobre algo; **to jump** — **something** saltar por encima de algo; **we looked** — **the wall** miramos por encima de la tapia; **with a sign**

— **the door** con un rótulo sobre la puerta; **it sticks out** — **the street** sobresale por encima de la calle; **to bend** — **a table** inclinarse sobre una mesa; **to fall** — **a cliff** caer por un precipicio; **to trip** — **something** tropezar con algo; **to sit** — **the fire** estar sentado muy junto a la lumbre; **the water came** — **her knees** el agua le cubrió las rodillas; **a change came** — **him** se operó en él un cambio.

(b) (*place: across*) **the pub** — **the road** la taberna de enfrente; **it's just** — **the road from us** está justamente enfrente de nuestra casa; **it's** — **the river** está en la otra orilla del río; **the bridge** — **the river** el puente que cruza el río.

(c) (*place: with all*) **all** — **Spain** por toda España; **known all** — **the world** conocido en el mundo entero; **he had mud all** — **himself** estaba totalmente cubierto de lodo; **they were all** — **him** le recibieron con el mayor entusiasmo, le dieron grandes testimonios de su afecto; **Zaragoza were all** — **Bilbao** (*Sport*) el Bilbao nada pudo contra el Zaragoza.

(d) (*place: fig*) **to rule** — **a people** reinar sobre un pueblo; **he's** — **me** tiene una categoría superior a la mía; **they gave me the preference** — **him** me prefirieron a él; **to have an advantage** — **someone** llevar ventaja a uno.

(e) (*numbers*) **the numbers** — **20** los números superiores a 20, los números más allá de 20; — **200** más de 200; **well** — **200** 200 y muchos más; **she's** — **21 now** tiene más de 21 años ya; **he must be** — **60** tendrá más de 60 años; — **and above last year's figure** en exceso de la cifra del año pasado; **an increase of 5%** — **last year's total** un aumento de 5 por cien en relación con el año anterior.

(f) (*time*) — **the last few years** durante los últimos años; **payments spread** — **some years** pagos que abarcan varios años; **we stayed** — **the weekend** nos quedamos a pasar el fin de semana.

(g) (*motive*) **they fell out** — **money** riñeron por cuestión de dinero; **to pause** — **a difficulty** detenerse a considerar un punto difícil.

(h) (*means*) **I heard it** — **the radio** lo supe por la radio.

over- ['əuvə*] *in compounds*: sobre . . ., super . . .; demasiado. . . .

overabundance ['əuvərə'bʌndəns] *n* sobreabundancia *f*.

overabundant ['əuvərə'bʌndənt] *adj* sobreabundante.

overact ['əuvər'ækt] *vi* exagerar el papel.

overactive ['əuvər'æktiv] *adj* demasiado activo.

overall [,əuvər'ɔ:l] *adv* en conjunto, en su totalidad.

overall [,əuvər'ɔ:l] *adj* study, view etc de conjunto; length etc total; (total) global.

overalls ['əuvərɔ:lz] *npl* guardapolvo *m*, mono *m*, bata *f*.

overambitious ['əuvəræm'biʃəs] *adj* demasiado ambicioso, superambicioso.

overanxious ['əuvər'æŋkʃəs] *adj* **(a)** (*worried*) demasiado preocupado, preocupado sin motivo. **(b)** (*eager*) demasiado deseoso (*for* de; *to do* de hacer); **I'm not** — **to go** tengo pocas ganas de ir.

overawe [,əuvər'ɔ:] *vt* intimidar; imponer respeto a; **to be** — **d by** ser fuertemente impresionado por.

overbalance [,əuvə'bæləns] **1** *vt* hacer perder el equilibrio. **2** *vi* perder el equilibrio.

overbearing [,əuvə'bɛəriŋ] *adj* imperioso, altivo; despótico.

overbid ['əuvəbid] *n* (*at auction*) mejor oferta *f*, mejor postura *f*; (*Bridge*) sobremarca *f*.

overbid [,əuvə'bid] (*irr: see* bid) **1** *vt* (*at auction*) licitar más que, hacer mejor oferta que; (*Bridge*) marcar más que.

2 *vi* (*Bridge*) hacer una sobremarca, (*foolishly*) declarar demasiado.

overblown ['əuvə'bləun] *adj* marchito, pasado.

overboard ['əuvəbɔ:d] *adv*: **man** — ! ¡hombre al agua! **to fall** — caer al agua; **to throw something** — echar algo por la borda (*also fig*).

overbold ['əuvə'bəuld] *adj* demasiado atrevido.

overburden [,əuvə'bə:dn] *vt* sobrecargar; oprimir, agobiar (*with* de); **not exactly** — **ed with worries** no precisamente agobiado de preocupaciones.

overcall [,əuvə'kɔ:l] *vti* = **overbid**.

overcast ['əuvəkɑ:st] *adj* sky encapotado, cubierto.

overcautious ['əuvə'kɔ:ʃəs] *adj* demasiado cauteloso, prudente con exceso.

overcharge ['əuvə'tʃɑ:dʒ] *vt* sobrecargar; (*Elec*) poner una carga excesiva a; person hacer pagar demasiado, cobrar un precio excesivo a.

overcoat ['əuvəkəut] *n* abrigo *m*, sobretodo *m*, gabán *m*.

overcome [,əuvə'kʌm] (*irr: see* come) **1** *vt* enemy, temptation etc vencer; difficulty salvar, superar;

sleep overcame him le rindió el sueño; **he was** — **by remorse** le remordió la conciencia; **he was** — **by grief** estaba postrado de dolor.

2 *vi* vencer, triunfar; **we shall** — venceremos.

overcompensation ['əuvə,kɔmpen'seiʃən] *n* compensación *f* excesiva.

overconfidence ['əuvə'kɔnfidəns] *n* confianza *f* excesiva, exceso *m* de confianza.

overconfident ['əuvə'kɔnfidənt] *adj* demasiado confiado (*of* en).

overconsumption ['əuvəkən'sʌmpʃən] *n* superconsumo *m*.

overcook ['əuvə'kuk] *vt* recocer, requemar.

overcrowd [,əuvə'kraud] *vt* atestar, llenar, congestionar.

overcrowded [,əuvə'kraudid] *adj* room etc atestado de gente, muy lleno; suburb etc congestionado; country superpoblado.

overcrowding [,əuvə'kraudiŋ] *n* superpoblación *f*, congestionamiento *m*; (*in tenement etc*) número *m* excesivo de inquilinos.

overdeveloped ['əuvədi'veləpt] *adj* demasiado desarrollado.

overdo [,əuvə'du:] (*irr: see* do) *vt* food recocer, requemar; (*exaggerate*) exagerar; (*use to excess*) usar demasiado; llevar a extremos, excederse en; **to** — **it, to** — **things** (*work too hard*) trabajar demasiado, fatigarse; (*exaggerate*) exagerar; (*in description, sentiment etc*) cargar la mano; **she rather** — **es the scent** se pone demasiado perfume; **see that you don't** — **it** cuidado con no fatigarte; **Espronceda** — **es the passion** Espronceda exagera la pasión.

overdone [,əuvə'dʌn] *adj* exagerado; food muy hecho, pasado.

overdose ['əuvədəus] *n* dosis *f* excesiva.

overdraft ['əuvədrɑ:ft] *n* (*Comm*) sobregiro *m*, giro *m* en descubierto; (*on account*) saldo *m* deudor; (*loan*) préstamo *m*; **to have an** — **at the bank** tener un saldo deudor con el banco, deber dinero al banco.

overdraw ['əuvə'drɔ:] (*irr: see* draw) girar en descubierto; **your account is** — **n (by £50)** su cuenta tiene un saldo deudor (de 50 libras).

overdress ['əuvə'dres] *vi* vestirse con demasiada elegancia.

overdrive ['əuvədraiv] *n* (*Aut*) sobremarcha *f*.

overdue ['əuvə'dju:] *adj* (*Comm*) vencido y no pagado; train etc atrasado; **the bus is 30 minutes** — el autobús tiene 30 minutos de atraso; **that change was long** — ese cambio debió hacerse mucho tiempo antes.

overeager ['əuvər'i:gə*] *adj* demasiado deseoso (*for* de; *to do* de hacer); demasiado entusiasta, entusiasta con exceso; **she was not** — **to help** tenía pocas ganas de ayudar.

overeat ['əuvər'i:t] (*irr: see* eat) *vi* comer con exceso; (*at 1 meal*) atracarse, darse un atracón.

overelaborate ['əuvəri'læbərit] *adj* demasiado complicado; demasiado detallado; rebuscado; courtesy etc estudiado.

overemployment ['əuvərim'plɔimənt] *n* superempleo *m*.

overenthusiastic ['əuvərin,θju:zi'æstik] *adj* demasiado entusiasta.

overestimate ['əuvər'estimit] *n* sobreestimación *f*, estimación *f* excesiva; (*Fin*) presupuesto *m* excesivo.

overestimate ['əuvər'estimeit] *vt* sobreestimar, apreciar en una cantidad (etc) excesiva; estimar en valor excesivo; person tener un concepto exagerado de; **to** — **one's strength** creerse uno más fuerte de lo que es.

overexcite ['əuvərik'sait] *vt* sobreexcitar.

overexcited ['əuvərik'saitid] *adj* sobreexcitado; **to get** — sobreexcitarse.

overexcitement ['əuvərik'saitmənt] *n* sobreexcitación *f*.

overexert ['əuvərig'zə:t] *vr*: **to** — **oneself** hacer un esfuerzo excesivo.

overexertion ['əuvərig'zə:ʃən] *n* (*effort*) esfuerzo *m* excesivo; (*weariness*) fatiga *f*.

overexpose ['əuvəriks'pəuz] *vt* (*Phot*) sobreexponer.

overexposure ['əuvəriks'pəuʒə*] *n* (*Phot*) sobreexposición *f*.

overfamiliar ['əuvəfə'miliə*] *adj* demasiado familiar.

overfeed ['əuvə'fi:d] (*irr: see* feed) **1** *vt* sobrealimentar; dar demasiado de comer a. **2** *vi* sobrealimentarse; comer demasiado, atracarse.

overflow ['əuvəfləu] *n* (*liquid*) exceso *m* de líquido, líquido *m* derramado; (*pipe etc*) rebosadero *m*, cañería *f* de desagüe.

overflow [,əuvə'fləu] *vi* (*vessel*) rebosar, desbordarse; (*river*) desbordarse, salir de madre; **to** — **with** (*fig*) rebosar de; **to fill a cup to** — **ing** llenar una taza hasta que se derrame el líquido.

overfly ['əuvə'flai] (*irr: see* **fly**) *vt* sobrevolar.

overfull ['əuvə'ful] *adj* demasiado lleno (*of* de), más que lleno.

overgenerous ['əuvə'dʒenərəs] *adj* demasiado generoso; **an — helping** una porción excesivamente grande; **they were — in their praise** le elogiaron con exceso.

overgrown ['əuvə'grəun] *adj boy etc* demasiado grande para su edad; **— with** cubierto de, revestido de; **the path is quite — now** ya no se ve senda alguna, la senda ha desaparecido bajo la vegetación.

overhand ['əuvəhænd] **1** *adj stroke* hecho (*or* dado *etc*) por lo alto. **2** *adv* por lo alto.

overhang ['əuvəhæŋ] *n* proyección *f*; (*of roof*) alero *m*; (*in rock climbing*) extraplomo m, panza *f* de burro.

overhang ['əuvə'hæŋ] (*irr: see* **hang**) **1** *vt* sobresalir por encima de; estar pendiente sobre, estar colgado sobre; (*fig*) amenazar.

2 *vi* sobresalir; estar pendiente, estar colgado.

overhanging ['əuvə'hæŋiŋ] *adj* sobresaliente, voladizo.

overhaul ['əuvəhɔːl] *n* repaso *m* general, revisión *f*.

overhaul [ˌəuvə'hɔːl] *vt* **(a)** (*check*) *machine* revisar, repasar, dar un repaso general a; *plans etc* volver a pensar, rehacer, examinar.

(b) (*overtake*) alcanzar, adelantarse a.

overhead ['əuvəhed] *adv* por lo alto, en alto, por encima de la cabeza; **a bird flew —** pasó un pájaro.

overhead ['əuvəhed] *adj* de arriba, encima de la cabeza; *cable etc* aéreo; *camshaft* en cabeza; *crane* de techo; *railway* elevado, suspendido; *expenses* general.

overheads ['əuvəhedz] *npl* gastos *mpl* generales.

overhear [ˌəuvə'hiə*] (*irr: see* **hear**) *vt* oír, oír por casualidad; acertar a oír; **she was —d complaining** se le oyó por casualidad quejarse.

overheat ['əuvə'hiːt] **1** *vt* recalentar; **to get —ed** recalentarse. **2** *vi* recalentarse.

overindulge ['əuvərin'dʌldʒ] **1** *vt child* mimar con exceso; *passion etc* dar rienda suelta a; *taste etc* satisfacer con exceso.

2 *vi* darse demasiada buena vida; **to — in something** comer (*etc*) un exceso de algo.

overindulgence ['əuvərin'dʌldʒəns] *n* **(a)** (*excess*) exceso *m* vicioso; **by his — in . . .** por su abandono vicioso a . . . **(b)** (*kindness*) exceso *m* de tolerancia (*towards* con).

overindulgent ['əuvərin'dʌldʒənt] *adj* demasiado indulgente (*towards* con).

overjoyed [ˌəuvə'dʒɔid] *adj:* **they were —** estuvieron llenos de alegría, se alegraron muchísimo; **he was — at the news** no cabía en sí de contento con la noticia; **she will be — to see you** se alegrará muchísimo de veros.

overkill ['əuvəkil] *n* contragolpe *m* más eficaz que el golpe del enemigo.

overland [ˌəuvə'lænd] *adv* por tierra, por vía terrestre.

overland ['əuvəlænd] *adj* terrestre.

overlap ['əuvəlæp] *n* traslapo *m*, solapo *m*; (*fig*) coincidencia *f* parcial.

overlap [ˌəuvə'læp] **1** *vt* traslapar. **2** *vi* traslaparse; (*fig*) coincidir en parte.

overlay ['əuvəlei] *n* capa *f* sobrepuesta; incrustación *f*.

overlay [ˌəuvə'lei] (*irr: see* **lay**) *vt* cubrir (*with* con); **to get overlaid with** formarse una capa de, cubrirse con, incrustarse de.

overleaf [ˌəuvə'liːf] *adv* a la vuelta; **"see —"** "véase al dorso".

overload ['əuvələud] *n* sobrecarga *f*.

overload [ˌəuvə'ləud] *vt* sobrecargar (*with* de); **to be —ed with** estar sobrecargado de, estar agobiado de.

overlook [ˌəuvə'luk] *vt* **(a)** (*of view: person*) dominar con la vista; (*of building*) dar a, mirar hacia, tener vista a; **the house —s the park** la casa tiene vistas al parque; **the garden is not —ed** el jardín no tiene ningún edificio al lado que lo domine.

(b) (*watch over*) vigilar; (*inspect*) inspeccionar, examinar.

(c) (*leave out*) pasar por alto; olvidar; no hacer caso de; (*tolerate*) disimular; (*forgive*) perdonar; (*wink at*) hacer la vista gorda a; **we'll — it this time** se perdona esta vez; **the plant is easily —ed** es fácil no echar de ver la planta.

overlord ['əuvəlɔːd] *n* (*feudal etc*) señor *m*; (*leader*) jefe *m* supremo.

overlordship ['əuvəlɔːdʃip] *n* señoría *f*; jefatura *f* suprema.

overmuch ['əuvə'mʌtʃ] *adv* demasiado.

overnice ['əuvə'nais] *adj* melindroso, remilgado.

overnight ['əuvə'nait] **1** *adv:* **it happened —** ocurrió durante la noche, ocurrió de la noche a la mañana; **to stay —** pasar la noche, pernoctar (*at* en); **we drove —** viajamos por la noche; **will it keep —?** ¿se conservará fresco hasta mañana? **we can't solve this one —** no podemos resolver este problema de la noche a la mañana. **2** *adj:* **— journey** viaje *m* de noche; **— stay** estancia *f* de una noche.

overparticular ['əuvəpə'tikjulə*] *adj* melindroso, remilgado; **he's not — about money** le importa poco el dinero, (*pej*) es poco escrupuloso en asuntos de dinero; **I'm not —** me da igual.

overpass ['əuvəpaːs] *n* paso *m* superior.

overpay ['əuvə'pei] (*irr: see* **pay**) *vt* pagar un sueldo excesivo a.

overpayment ['əuvə'peimənt] *n* pago *m* excesivo, sueldo *m* excesivo.

overpopulated ['əuvə'pɔpjuleitid] *adj* superpoblado.

overpower [ˌəuvə'pauə*] *vt* (*defeat*) sobreponerse a, vencer, subyugar; (*subdue physically*) dominar, asir y tener quieto; (*fig*) dominar; dejar estupefacto; *senses* embargar; **we were —ed by a sense of tragedy** se apoderó de nosotros un sentimiento de tragedia.

overpowering [ˌəuvə'pauəriŋ] *adj* abrumador, arrollador.

overpraise ['əuvə'preiz] *vt* elogiar demasiado.

overprint ['əuvə'print] **1** *n* sobrecarga *f*. **2** *vt* sobrecargar (*with* de).

overproduction ['əuvəprə'dʌkʃən] *n* superproducción *f*, exceso *m* de producción.

overrate ['əuvə'reit] *vt* exagerar el valor de; *person* tener un concepto demasiado alto de.

overreach [ˌəuvə'riːtʃ] *vr:* **to — oneself** aventurarse más allá de sus fuerzas, ir demasiado lejos.

override [ˌəuvə'raid] (*irr: see* **ride**) *vt* (*ignore*) no hacer caso de; (*invalidate*) anular, invalidar, restar valor a; (*set aside*) poner a un lado; **this fact —s all others** este hecho domina todos los demás; **our protests were overridden** no hicieron caso de nuestras protestas; **this —s what we decided before** esto anula lo que decidimos antes.

overriding [ˌəuvə'raidiŋ] *adj* predominante, decisivo; *importance* primero, primordial; *need etc* imperioso.

overripe ['əuvə'raip] *adj* demasiado maduro, pasado.

overrule [ˌəuvə'ruːl] *vt* (*override*) anular; *request etc* denegar, rechazar; **but we were —d** pero rechazaron nuestra propuesta.

overrun [ˌəuvə'rʌn] (*irr: see* **run**) **1** *vt* cubrir enteramente, invadir; *time limit etc* rebasar, exceder; **the field is — with weeds** las malas hierbas han invadido el campo; **the town is — with tourists** la ciudad ha sido invadida por los turistas.

2 *vi* rebasar el límite; **his speech overran by 15 minutes** su discurso se excedió en 15 minutos.

overscrupulous ['əuvə'skruːpjuləs] *adj* = **overparticular.**

overseas ['əuvə'siːz] **1** *adv* en ultramar, allende el mar; **to be —** estar en el extranjero; **to go —** ir al extranjero; **to travel —** viajar por el extranjero; **visitors from —** visitantes *mpl* de ultramar; **to send a regiment to fight —** enviar un regimiento a servir en el extranjero.

2 *adj* de ultramar; **— service** (*Mil etc*) servicio *m* en el extranjero; **— trade** comercio *m* exterior.

oversee ['əuvə'siː] (*irr: see* **see**) *vt* superentender, vigilar.

overseer ['əuvəsiə*] *n* superintendente *mf*; inspector *m*; (*foreman*) capataz *m*.

oversell [ˌəuvə'sel] (*irr: see* **sell**) *vt* (*Comm*) *product* hacer una propaganda excesiva a favor de.

oversensitive ['əuvə'sensitiv] *adj* demasiado sensible.

overshadow [ˌəuvə'ʃædəu] *vt* sombrear, ensombrecer; (*fig*) eclipsar; **it was —ed by greater events** fue eclipsado por sucesos de mayor trascendencia.

overshoe ['əuvəʃuː] *n* chanclo *m*.

overshoot [ˌəuvə'ʃuːt] (*irr: see* **shoot**) *vti:* **to — (the mark)** pasar de la raya, excederse; **to — (the target) by 40 tons** producir 40 toneladas más de lo provisto; **to — (the runway)** (*Aer*) ir a aterrizar más allá de la pista.

oversight ['əuvəsait] *n* **(a)** (*omission*) descuido *m*, equivocación *f*; **by an —** por descuido; **it was an —** ha sido una distracción.

(b) (*supervision*) superintendencia *f*, vigilancia *f*.

oversimplification ['əuvə,simplifi'keiʃən] *n* simplificación *f* excesiva, supersimplificación *f*.

oversimplify ['əuvə'simplifai] *vt* simplificar demasiado.

oversleep ['əuvə'sliːp] (*irr: see* **sleep**) *vi* dormir demasiado, no despertar; **I overslept** durmiendo se me pasó la hora.

overspend ['əuvə'spend] (*irr: see* **spend**) **1** *vt:* **to — one's allowance** gastar más de lo que permite la renta de uno.

2 *vi:* **we have overspent by 5 dollars** hemos gastado 5 dólares más de lo que debíamos.

overspill ['əuvəspil] n (act) desparramamiento m de población; (quantity) exceso m de población; **an — town for Manchester** una ciudad vecinal de absorción de Manchester.

overstate ['əuvə'steit] vt exagerar.

overstatement ['əuvə'steitmənt] n exageración f.

overstay ['əuvə'stei] vt: **to — one's leave** quedarse más tiempo de lo que la licencia permite.

overstep ['əuvə'step] vt exceder, pasar de, traspasar; see **mark** etc.

overstock ['əuvə'stɔk] vt: **to be —ed with** tener existencias excesivas de.

overstrain ['əuvə'strein] **1** n fatiga f excesiva; (nervous) hipertensión f. **2** vt person fatigar excesivamente; provocar una hipertensión en; metal deformar, torcer; resources exigir demasiado de, someter a exigencias excesivas.

overstrung ['əuvə'strʌŋ] adj sobreexcitado, hipertenso.

oversubscribe ['əuvəsəb'skraib] **1** vt (Fin): **the issue was —d** se pidieron más acciones de las que había; **the issue was —d 4 times** la solicitud de acciones rebasó 4 veces la cantidad de títulos ofrecidos.
  2 vi contribuir más de lo pedido.

oversupply ['əuvəsə'plai] vt proveer en exceso (with de); **we are oversupplied with cars** tenemos exceso de coches.

overt [əu'vəːt] adj abierto, público.

overtake [.əuvə'teik] (irr: see **take**) **1** vt (a) alcanzar; (Aut) adelantar; pasar, sobrepasar; **he doesn't want to be —n** no quiere dejarse adelantar; **we overtook a lorry near Burgos** cerca de Burgos pasamos un camión; **you can't — that car on the bend** no puedes adelantar ese coche en la curva; **X has —n Y in steel production** X se ha adelantado a Y en la producción de acero.
  (b) (fig) coger de improviso, sorprender; **to be —n by events** ser sorprendido por los sucesos.
  2 vi adelantar, pasar; "**no overtaking**" "prohibido adelantar".

overtaking [.əuvə'teikiŋ] n adelantamiento m, paso m.

overtax ['əuvə'tæks] **1** vt (Fin) oprimir con tributos, exigir contribuciones excesivas a; (with effort) agobiar, exigir demasiados esfuerzos a.
  2 vr: **to — oneself** fatigarse demasiado, exigirse demasiados esfuerzos a sí mismo.

overthrow ['əuvəθrəu] n derrumbamiento m, derrocamiento m.

overthrow [.əuvə'θrəu] (irr: see **throw**) echar abajo, derribar; (overturn) volcar; dictator, system, empire etc derrumbar, derrocar.

overtime ['əuvətaim] n horas fpl extraordinarias; — **pay** pago m de horas extraordinarias; **to do —, to work —** trabajar horas extraordinarias; **we shall have to work — to catch up** (fig) tendremos que esforzarnos al máximo para recuperar lo que hemos perdido.

overtly [əu'vəːtli] adv abiertamente, públicamente.

overtone ['əuvətəun] n (Mus) armónico m; (fig) sugestión f; **a speech with a hostile —** un discurso con alguna nota de hostilidad.

overtop ['əuvə'tɔp] vt descollar sobre.

overtrick ['əuvətrik] n (Cards) baza f de más.

overtrump ['əuvə'trʌmp] vt (Cards) contrafallar.

overture ['əuvətjuə*] n (Mus) obertura f; (fig) proposición f, propuesta f; sondeo m; **to make —s to someone** hacer una propuesta a uno; **to make —s for an armistice** proponer que se acuerde un armisticio.

overturn [.əuvə'təːn] **1** vt car, saucepan etc volcar; (disarrange) trastornar; government etc derrumbar, derrocar.
  2 vi car, aircraft etc volcar, capotar, dar una vuelta de campana; boat zozobrar.

overuse ['əuvə'juːz] vt usar demasiado.

overvalue ['əuvə'vælju:] vt sobrevalorar.

overweening [.əuvə'wiːniŋ] adj arrogante, presuntuoso, altivo; — **pride** desmesurado orgullo m.

overweight ['əuvə'weit] **1** adj demasiado pesado; **to be —** pesar demasiado, person ser gordo, tener exceso de carnes; **he is 8 kilos —** tiene 8 kilos de más; **the parcel is a kilo —** el paquete tiene un exceso de un kilo. **2** n exceso m de peso, sobrepeso m.

overwhelm [.əuvə'welm] vt opponent, team etc arrollar, aplastar; (in argument) aplastar; (of waves etc) fundir, inundar; (of grief etc) vencer, postrar; (of work etc) abrumar, agobiar; **he speedily —ed his opponent** arrolló a su contrincante en muy poco tiempo; **to — someone with favours** colmar a uno de favores; **to — someone with kindness** tratar a uno con excesiva amabilidad; **he was —ed with joy**

rebosaba alegría, no cabía en sí de contento; **we have been —ed with offers of help** estamos inundados por las ofertas de ayuda; **Venice just —s me** Venecia deja a uno boquiabierto, Venecia es pasmosa; **you — me!** ¡basta ya, se lo ruego!

overwhelming [.əuvə'welmiŋ] adj defeat etc arrollador, aplastante, contundente; success arrollador; majority abrumador; pressure etc irresistible; **one's — impression is of heat** la más fuerte impresión de todas es la del calor.

overwhelmingly [.əuvə'welmiŋli] adv de modo arrollador; abrumadoramente; irresistiblemente; **they voted — for X** la abrumadora mayoría de ellos votó por X; **he was — defeated** sufrió una derrota arrolladora.

overwind ['əuvə'waind] (irr: see **wind**) vt watch dar demasiada cuerda a.

overwork ['əuvə'wəːk] **1** n trabajo m excesivo; **to suffer from —** haberse cansado trabajando demasiado.
  2 vt hacer trabajar demasiado; exigir un esfuerzo excesivo a.
  3 vi trabajar demasiado, cansarse trabajando demasiado.

overwrought ['əuvə'rɔːt] adj: **to be —** estar nerviosísimo, haberse agotado por la emoción (etc), estar sobreexcitado.

overzealous ['əuvə'zeləs] adj demasiado entusiasta.

Ovid ['ɔvid] m Ovidio.

oviduct ['ɔuvidʌkt] n oviducto m.

oviform ['əuvifɔːm] adj oviforme.

ovine ['əuvain] adj ovino.

oviparous [əu'vipərəs] adj ovíparo.

ovoid ['əuvɔid] **1** adj ovoide. **2** n ovoide m.

ovulation [.əuvju'leiʃən] n ovulación f.

ovule ['əuvjuːl] n óvulo m.

ovum ['əuvəm] n, pl **ova** ['əuvə] óvulo m.

owe [əu] **1** vt deber; **to — someone £2** deber 2 libras a uno; **I'll — it to you** te lo quedo a deber; **to — allegiance to someone** deber lealtad a uno; **to — someone a grudge** guardar rencor a uno; **to — someone thanks for his help** estar agradecido a uno por su ayuda, deber las gracias a uno por su ayuda; **to — one's life to a lucky chance** deber su vida a una casualidad; **he —s his talent to his mother** le debe su talento a su madre; **to whom do I — this honour?** ¿a quién le debo este honor?; **I — it to her to confess** mi deber con ella me obliga a confesarlo; **you — it to yourself to come** venir es un deber que Vd tiene consigo mismo.
  2 vi tener deudas; **to — someone for a meal** estar en deuda con uno por una comida.

owing ['əuiŋ] **1** adj: **the £5 —** las 5 libras que debemos, las 5 libras que se nos deben; **how much is — to you now?** ¿cuanto se le debe ahora?
  2: — to prep debido a, por causa de; — **to the bad weather** debido al mal tiempo, por el mal tiempo; **it is — to lack of time** se debe a la falta de tiempo.

owl [aul] n (barn-) lechuza f; (little —) mochuelo m; (long-eared —) búho m; (tawny —) cárabo m.

owlish ['auliʃ] adj look etc de buho.

own [əun] **1** adj (a) propio; **it's all my — money** todo el dinero es el mío propio; **but his — brother said so** pero su propio hermano lo dijo; **in her — house** en su propia casa; **the house has its — garage** la casa tiene garaje propio.
  (b) (pred) **the house is her (very) —** la casa es la suya propia, la casa le pertenece únicamente a ella; **my time is my —** dispongo de mi tiempo como quiero; **the decision was his —** la decisión fue de él y no otro.
  2 n lo suyo etc; **all my —** todo lo mío; **he has a style all his —** tiene un estilo muy suyo; **may I keep it for my (very) —?** ¿me lo puedo guardar como cosa que me pertenece únicamente a mí?; **she has money of her —** tiene dinero particular; **I'll give you a copy of your —** te daré un ejemplar propio, te daré un ejemplar para guardar; **for reasons of his —** por motivos particulares; **a place of one's —** una casa propia, una casa para sí; **to come into one's —** entrar en posesión de lo suyo, (fig) justificarse, encontrar su plena justificación; obtener el éxito merecido; **to be on one's —** estar a solas, estar solo; ser independiente; **now we're on our —** ya estamos solos; **she was all on her — for a week** pasó una semana enteramente sola; **if I can get him on his —** si puedo hablar con él a solas; **to do something on one's —** hacer algo sin ayuda (de nadie); **to call something one's —** ser dueño de algo, disponer de algo como de cosa propia; **without a chair to call my —** sin una silla que pueda decir que es mía; **I am so busy I can scarcely call my time my —**

estoy tan ocupado que apenas dispongo de mi tiempo; **to get one's — back** tomar su revancha; **to hold one's —** no cejar, mantenerse firme; no ceder terreno; mantenerse al nivel de los demás; **he can hold his — with anybody** no le va a la zaga a nadie; **I can hold my — in German** me defiendo en alemán.

3 vt **(a)** (*possess*) poseer, tener; ser dueño de; **he —s 2 tractors** posee 2 tractores; **he —s 3 newspapers** es dueño de 3 periódicos; **who —s the newspaper?** ¿quién es el dueño del periódico?; **who —s this pen?** ¿a quién pertenece esta pluma?; **to come in as if one —ed the place** entrar como Pedro por su casa; **a cat nobody wants to —** un gato que no parece pertenecer a nadie.

(b) (*acknowledge, recognize*) reconocer; **he —ed the child as his** reconoció al niño como suyo; **I — my mistake** reconozco mi error.

(c) (*confess*) confesar; **I —** it lo confieso; **I — I was wrong** confieso que me equivoqué.

4 vi: **to — to a mistake** confesar un error, reconocer un error; **I —ed to debts of £47** confesé tener deudas de 47 libras; **to — up** confesar, confesar de plano; **— up!** ¡confiésalo!; **she —ed up to being 40** confesó tener 40 años; **they —ed up to having stolen the apples** confesaron haber robado las manzanas.

owner ['əunə*] n dueño m, a f, propietario m, a f, amo m, a f; poseedor m, ora f; (*Naut: fam*) capitán m; **the — of car no. NBG 999** el dueño del coche matrícula NBG 999; **is the — about?** ¿está el dueño?

ownerless ['əunəlis] adj sin dueño.

ownership ['əunəʃip] n posesión f; propiedad f;

"under new —" "nuevo propietario", "nuevo dueño"; **books in** (*or* under) **the — of . . .** libros que son de la propiedad de . . .; **under his — the business flourished** el negocio prosperó bajo su dirección.

ox [ɔks] n, pl **oxen** ['ɔksən] buey m.

oxalic [ɔk'sælik] adj: **— acid** ácido m oxálico.

oxcart ['ɔkskɑːt] n carro m de bueyes.

oxhide ['ɔkshaid] n cuero m de buey.

oxidation [,ɔksi'deiʃən] n oxidación f.

oxide ['ɔksaid] n óxido m.

oxidise ['ɔksidaiz] 1 vt oxidar. 2 vi oxidarse.

oxlip ['ɔkslip] n prímula f.

Oxonian [ɔk'səuniən] 1 adj oxoniense. 2 n oxoniense mf.

oxtail ['ɔksteil] n: **— soup** sopa f de cola de buey.

oxyacetylene ['ɔksiə'setiliːn] adj oxiacetilénico; **— burner, — torch** soplete m oxiacetilénico; **— welding** soldadura f oxiacetilénica.

oxygen ['ɔksidʒən] n oxígeno m.

oxygenate [ɔk'sidʒəneit] vt oxigenar.

oxygenation [,ɔksidʒə'neiʃən] n oxigenación f.

oxygen mask ['ɔksidʒən,mɑːsk] n máscara f de oxígeno.

oxygen tent ['ɔksidʒən,tent] n tienda f de oxígeno.

oyez [əu'jez] interj ¡oíd!

oyster ['ɔistə*] n ostra f.

oyster bed ['ɔistəbed] n criadero m de ostras, vivero m de otras.

oystercatcher ['ɔistə,kætʃə*] n ostrero m.

oyster farm ['ɔistəfɑːm] n criadero m de ostras.

oyster shell ['ɔistəʃel] n concha f de ostra.

ozone ['əuzəun] n ozono m.

P

P [pi:]: **to mind one's —s and Qs** cuidarse de no meter la pata.

pa [pɑ:] n (fam) papá m.

pace [peis] **1** n **(a)** (step) paso m; **12 —s off** a 12 pasos; **to put a horse through its —s** ejercitar un caballo, entrenar un caballo; **to put someone through his —s** poner a uno a prueba, demostrar las cualidades de uno.

(b) (speed) paso m, marcha f, velocidad f; ritmo m; **at a good —, at a smart —** rápidamente; **at a slow —** a paso lento; **at a walking —** a la velocidad del que camina a pie; **at a snail's —** a paso de tortuga; **we kept up a good — with the work** mantuvimos un buen ritmo de trabajo; **the present — of development** el actual ritmo del desarrollo; **to keep —** ir al mismo paso; **to keep — with someone** llevar el mismo paso que uno; **industry has not kept — with technology** la industria no ha avanzado al mismo paso que la tecnología; **I can't keep — with events** no puedo mantenerme al corriente de los sucesos; **to make the —, to set the —** establecer el paso, marcar el ritmo; **to quicken one's —** apretar el paso.

2 vt distance medir a pasos (also **to — out**); floor, room pasearse preocupado (etc) por; competitor marcar el paso para; **to — off 10 yards** medir 10 yardas a pasos.

3 vi: **— up and down** pasearse de un lado a otro.

pacemaker ['peis,meikə*] n el que marca el paso, el que abre carrera.

pacer ['peisə*] n (Sport) establecedor m del paso.

pachyderm ['pækidə:m] n paquidermo m.

pacific [pə'sifik] adj pacífico.

pacifically [pə'sifikəli] adv pacíficamente.

pacification [,pæsifi'keiʃən] n pacificación f.

Pacific Ocean [pə'sifik'əuʃən] Océano m Pacífico.

pacifier ['pæsifaiə*] n (US: baby's) chupete m.

pacifism ['pæsifizəm] n pacifismo m.

pacifist ['pæsifist] **1** adj pacifista. **2** n pacifista mf.

pacify ['pæsifai] vt pacificar; apaciguar, calmar; **we managed to — him eventually** por fin logramos apaciguarle.

pack [pæk] **1** n (bundle) lío m, fardo m; (on animal) carga f; (rucksack, also Mil) mochila f; (packet) paquete m; (of cigarettes: US) paquete m, cajetilla f; (wrapping) envase m; (Med) compresa f; (of cards) baraja f; (of hounds) jauría f; (of wolves) manada f; **the —** (Rugby) los delanteros; **a — of lies** un montón de mentiras; **it's a — of lies!** ¡todo es mentira!

2 vt (a) container llenar, ir llenando; case, trunk etc hacer; things in case etc poner; fish, meat in tin enlatar; (wrap) envasar; (put into parcel) empaquetar; **to — up a tent** desarmar una tienda, plegar una tienda; **articles —ed in dozens** artículos en caja de a docena; **it comes —ed in polythene** se sirve envasado en politeno.

(b) (excessively) container llenar, atestar (with de); articles meter apretadamente (also **to — in**); **to — down** apretar, comprimir; (with feet etc) apisonar; **to — earth round a plant** acollar una planta; **the place was —ed** el local estaba de bote en bote; **the Costa Brava is —ed with tourists** la Costa Brava está llena de turistas; **to — more people in** ir introduciendo más personas; **can you — two more in?** ¿caben dos más?; **they were —ed in like sardines** estaban como sardinas en banasta; **the show is —ing them in** el espectáculo tiene un lleno cada noche, el espectáculo es un éxito indiscutible.

(c) meeting llenar de partidarios; jury nombrar de modo fraudulento.

(d) to — someone off despachar a uno; despedir a uno, deshacerse de uno; **so they —ed him off to London** así que le enviaron sin más a Londres; **to — a child off to bed** mandar a un niño a la cama;

to send someone —ing despedir a uno con cajas destempladas.

(e) to — it in (fam) dejarlo; **— it in!** ¡déjalo!; **it's time we —ed it in** es hora de dejarlo ya.

3 vi **(a)** (of luggage: also **to — up**) hacer las maletas, hacer el equipaje; **a tent that —s up easily** una tienda que se desarma fácilmente.

(b) to — up (fam) terminar; (and depart) liar el petate; **then the engine —ed up** luego se averió el motor.

(c) to — round, to — together apiñarse; **they —ed round the president** se apiñaron en torno al presidente.

(d) (form a mass) endurecerse, consolidarse, formar una masa compacta; **the snow had —ed round the wheels** la nieve se había endurecido junto a las ruedas.

package ['pækidʒ] **1** n paquete m; bulto m.

2 attr: **— deal** acuerdo m que supone unas concesiones mutuas, convenio m que resuelve diversos problemas.

3 vt empaquetar, envasar.

pack animal ['pæk,æniməl] n animal m de carga.

packer ['pækə*] n embalador m, ora f, empaquetador m, ora f.

packet ['pækit] n paquete m; (of cigarettes) paquete m, cajetilla f; (of stamps) sobre m; (Naut) paquebote m; **— postal** — paquete m postal; **a whole — of trouble** la mar de disgustos; **to make a —** (fam) ganar mucho dinero; **to make one's —** (fam) hacer su pacotilla; **that must have cost a —** eso habrá costado un dineral.

packet boat ['pækitbəut] n paquebote m.

packhorse ['pækhɔ:s] n caballo m de carga.

pack ice ['pækais] n témpanos mpl flotantes.

packing ['pækiŋ] n **(a)** (act) embalaje m, envase m; **to do one's —** hacer sus maletas, arreglar el equipaje.

(b) (material: outer) envase m, (inner) relleno m, empaquetadura f.

packing case ['pækiŋkeis] n cajón m de embalaje.

packsaddle ['pæk,sædl] n albarda f.

pact [pækt] **1** n pacto m; **to make a — with someone** pactar con uno.

2 vi pactar (with con); **to — with someone to +** infin llegar a un acuerdo para + infin.

pad[1] [pæd] vi: **to — about, to — along** andar, pisar (sin hacer ruido).

pad[2] [pæd] **1** n almohadilla f, cojinete m; (of fox etc) pata f; (for inking) tampón m, almohadilla f para entintar; (of paper) bloc m, taco m; (of blotting paper) secafirmas m; (on shoulder) hombrera f; (launching) plataforma f de lanzamiento.

2 vt almohadillar; acolchar; rellenar, forrar; shoulders bombear; book etc (also **to — out**) meter paja en, hinchar con mucha paja; **the speech was —ded out with references to . . .** el discurso estaba hinchado con referencias a . . .

pad[3] [pæd] n (sl) querencia f, guarida f.

padded ['pædid] adj shoulders bombeado; dashboard etc almohadillado; armour enguatado; cell acolchonado, de aislamiento.

padding ['pædiŋ] n relleno m, almohadilla f; (material) borra f; (fig) paja f.

paddle ['pædl] **1** n **(a)** (oar) canalete m, zagual m; (blade of wheel) paleta f; (wheel) rueda f de paletas.

(b) to go for a —, to have a — ir a mojarse los pies, chapotear en el mar (etc).

2 vt **(a)** boat impulsar con canalete, remar con canalete.

(b) to — one's feet in the sea mojarse los pies en el mar, chapotear en el mar.

3 vi **(a)** (in boat) remar con canalete; **they —ed to the bank** dirigieron el bote a la orilla.

(b) (with feet) mojarse los pies, chapotear.

paddle boat ['pædlbaut] *n*, **paddle steamer** ['pædl‚sti:mə*] *n* vapor *m* de ruedas.
paddle wheel ['pædlwi:l] *n* rueda *f* de paletas.
paddling pool ['pædliŋpu:l] *n* estanque *m* para chapotear, estanque *m* de juegos.
paddock ['pædək] *n* (*field*) prado *m*; (*of racecourse*) corral *m*, explanada *f* de ensillado.
Paddy ['pædi] *nombre cariñoso de* **Patrick**; *el irlandés típico.*
paddy[1] ['pædi] *n* (*rice*) arroz *m*.
paddy[2] ['pædi] *n* (*fam*) rabieta *f*; **to get into a —** coger una rabieta.
paddywhack ['pædiwæk] *n* (*fam*) rabieta *f*.
padlock ['pædlɔk] **1** *n* candado *m*. **2** *vt* cerrar con candado.
padre ['pɑːdri] *n* (*fam*: *Mil*) capellán *m* militar; (*Univ*) capellán *m* de colegio; (*in direct address*) padre.
paean ['piːən] *n* himno *m* de alegría; **—s of praise** alabanzas *fpl*.
paediatrician, (US) ped— [‚piːdiə'trifən] *n* pediatra *mf*, médico *m* puericultor.
paediatrics, (US) ped— [‚piːdi'ætriks] *n* pediatría *f*.
pagan ['peigən] **1** *adj* pagano. **2** *n* pagano *m*, a *f*.
paganism ['peigənizəm] *n* paganismo *m*.
page[1] [peidʒ] **1** *n* (*boy-servant*) paje *m*; (*squire*) escudero *m*.
　　2 *vt*: **to — someone** buscar a uno llamando su nombre, hacer llamar a uno por el botones.
page[2] [peidʒ] **1** *n* página *f*; (*Typ*, *of newspaper*) plana *f*; **the news was on the front** — la noticia figuraba en la primera plana; **on — 14** a la página 14, en la página 14; **"see — 20"** "véase la página 20".
　　2 *vt* paginar, foliar.
pageant ['pædʒənt] *n* (*show*) espectáculo *m* brillante; (*procession*) desfile *m*; **a — of Elizabethan times** una representación de la época isabelina en una serie de cuadros; **the town held a — to mark the anniversary** la ciudad organizó una serie de fiestas públicas para celebrar el aniversario.
pageantry ['pædʒəntri] *n* pompa *f*, boato *m*; **the — of the occasion** lo espectacular del acontecimiento, lo vistoso del acontecimiento; **all the — of History** toda la magnificencia de la Historia; **it was celebrated with much —** se celebró con gran boato.
page boy ['peidʒbɔi] *n* paje *m*.
page proofs ['peidʒpruːfs] *npl* pruebas *fpl* de planas.
paginate ['pædʒineit] *vt* paginar, foliar.
pagination [‚pædʒi'neifən] *n* paginación *f*, foliación *f*; **without —** sin paginar.
pagoda [pə'gəudə] *n* pagoda *f*.
paid [peid] **1** *pret and ptp of* **pay**.
　　2 *adj* bill etc pagado; *official* asalariado, que recibe un sueldo; *work* remunerado; **to put — to something** acabar con algo.
paid-up ['peid‚ʌp], (US) **paid-in** ['peid'in] *adj share* liberado; **fully—share** acción *f* totalmente liberada.
pail [peil] *n* cubo *m*, balde *m*; (*child's*) cubito *m*.
pailful ['peilful] *n* cubo *m*, contenido *m* de un cubo.
paillasse ['pæliæs] *n* jergón *m*.
pain [pein] **1** *n* (a) dolor *m*; sufrimiento *m*; **to be in — estar con dolor; to be in great — tener mucho** dolor, sufrir mucho; **he's a — in the neck, it gives me a — in the neck** me da cien patadas; **cucumber gives me a —** el pepino me sienta mal; **I have a — in my leg** me duele la pierna; **to put a wounded animal out of its —** acortar la agonía de un animal herido, despachar un animal herido.
　　(b) —s (*efforts*) trabajos *mpl*, cuidados *mpl*, esfuerzos *mpl*; **to be at great —s over something, to take — s over something** esmerarse en algo, tomarse trabajo en algo; **all he got for his — s was** ... lo único que logró después de tantos trabajos fue . . .; **to spare no —s** no perdonar esfuerzos (*to* + *infin* por + *infin*); **to take —s to** + *infin* poner especial cuidado en + *infin*.
　　(c) (*penalty*) pena *f*; **on — of death** so pena de muerte; **with all the —s and penalties of fame** con todas las dificultades y disgustos que acarrea la fama.
　　2 *vt* (*physically*) doler, (*mentally*) dar lástima a; **Spain —s me** me duele España; **you — me!** ¡me das lástima!; **where does it — you?** ¿dónde le duele?
pained [peind] *adj expression* de disgusto, afligido; *voice* dolorido; **he looked —** hizo una mueca, torció el gesto.
painful ['peinful] *adj* (*physically*) doloroso, dolorido; (*difficult*) difícil, penoso, angustioso; *duty* desagradable, nada grato; (*fam*) horrible, malísimo; **it is my — duty to tell you that** . . ; tengo el deber nada grato de decirle que . . .; **my arm was becoming —** empezaba a dolerme el brazo; **it was — to behold**

daba lástima verlo; **—, isn't it?** ¿es horrible, no?; **she gave a — performance** hizo una malísima actuación.
painfully ['peinfəli] *adv* dolorosamente, con dolor; penosamente; (*fam*) terriblemente; **he dragged himself — along** se arrastraba penosamente por el suelo; **she's — shy** es terriblemente tímida.
painkiller ['pein‚kilə*] *n* quitadolores *m*, calmante *m*.
painless ['peinlis] *adj* indoloro, sin dolor.
painlessly ['peinlisli] *adv* sin causar dolor.
painstaking ['peinz‚teikiŋ] *adj person* laborioso, concienzudo, esmerado; *piece of work* hecho con cuidado, hecho con esmero.
painstakingly ['peinz‚teikiŋli] *adv* laboriosamente, concienzudamente, esmeradamente.
paint [peint] **1** *n* pintura *f*; (*for face*) colorete *m*; **box of —s** caja *f* de pinturas; **"wet —"** "¡ojo, que pinta!", "¡cuidado con la pintura!"
　　2 *vt* pintar; **to — something out** tachar algo con una mano de pintura; **to — something black** pintar algo de negro; **to — one's face** pintarse, ponerse colorete.
　　3 *vi* pintar; ser pintor.
paintbox ['peintbɔks] *n* caja *f* de pinturas.
paintbrush ['peintbrʌʃ] *n* (*Art*) pincel *m*; (*for decorating*) brocha *f*.
painter[1] ['peintə*] *n* (*Art*) pintor *m*, ora *f*; (*decorator*) pintor *m* de brocha gorda.
painter[2] ['peintə*] *n* amarra *f*; **to cut the —** (*fig*) cortar las amarras, independizarse.
painting ['peintiŋ] *n* (*as a whole*) pintura *f*; (*picture*) cuadro *m*, pintura *f*.
paintpot ['peintpɔt] *n* bote *m* de pintura.
paint roller ['peint‚rəulə*] *n* rodillo *m* pintor.
paint spray ['peintsprei] *n* pistola *f* rociadora de pintura.
pair [pɛə*] **1** *n* (*of gloves, shoes, etc*) par *m*; (*of people, cards, stamps*) pareja *f*; (*of oxen*) yunta *f*; **a — of trousers** un pantalón, unos pantalones; **a carriage and —** un landó con dos caballos; **a — of scissors** unas tijeras; **the happy —** la feliz pareja, los novios; **arranged in —s** arreglados (*or* colocados) de dos en dos.
　　2 *vt* aparear (*also Bio*).
　　3 *vi* aparearse (*also Bio*); **to — off** aparearse, formar pareja; **to — with** (*Bio*) aparearse con, juntarse con.
pairing ['pɛəriŋ] *n* (*Bio*) apareamiento *m*.
pajamas [pə'dʒɑːməz] *npl* pijama *m*.
Pakistan [‚pɑːkis'tɑːn] Pakistán *m*, Paquistán *m* (*Acad*).
Pakistani [‚pɑːkis'tɑːni] **1** *adj* pakistaní, paquistaní (*Acad*). **2** *n* pakistaní *mf*, paquistaní *mf* (*Acad*).
pal [pæl] (*fam*) **1** *n* camarada *mf*, compinche *m*, compañero *m*, a *f*; **be a —!** ¡vamos, pórtate como un amigo!; **you've always been a — to me** siempre has sido muy amable conmigo.
　　2 *vi*: **to — up** hacerse amigos; **to — up with someone** hacerse amigo de uno.
palace ['pælis] *n* palacio *m*; **bishop's —** palacio *m* episcopal; **royal —** palacio *m* real.
palaeo- ['pæliəu] *see* **paleo-**.
palatable ['pælətəbl] *adj* sabroso, apetitoso; comible; (*fig*) aceptable (*to* a); **it may not be — to the government** puede no ser del gusto del gobierno, puede no ser del agrado del gobierno.
palatal ['pælətl] **1** *adj* palatal. **2** *n* palatal *f*.
palatalize ['pælətəlaiz] **1** *vi* palatalizar. **2** *vi* palatalizarse.
palate ['pælit] *n* paladar *m* (*also fig*); **hard —** paladar *m*; **soft —** velo *m* del paladar; **to have a delicate —** tener un paladar delicado; **to have no — for something** (*fig*) no poder tragar algo, no encontrar nada agradable en algo.
palatial [pə'leifəl] *adj* suntuoso, espléndido.
palatinate [pə'lætinit] *n* palatinado *m*.
palaver [pə'lɑːvə*] **1** *n* (*conference*) conferencia *f*, parlamento *m*; (*fuss*) lío *m*; (*trouble*) molestias *fpl*, trámites *mpl* engorrosos; **that — about the car** aquel lío que se armó acerca del coche; **can't we do it without a lot of —?** ¿no podemos hacerlo sin tantas molestias?, ¿no podemos hacerlo sin meternos en tantos líos? **2** *vi* parlamentar.
pale[1] [peil] **1** *adj complexion, face* pálido; *colour* claro; *light* tenue; **a — blue dress** un vestido azul claro; **she was deathly —** estaba pálida como la muerte; **to go —, to grow —, to turn —** palidecer, ponerse pálido.
　　2 *vi* palidecer, ponerse pálido; **but X —s beside Y** pero X pierde al lado de Y; *see* **insignificance**.
pale[2] [peil] *n* (*stake*) estaca *f*; **to be beyond the —** estar excluido de la buena sociedad; ser inaceptable,

ser un indeseable; **to be outside the —** of quedar fuera de los límites de.

paleface ['peilfeis] n hombre m blanco, mujer f blanca.

paleness ['peilnis] n palidez f; tenuidad f.

paleo . . . ['pæliəu] paleo . . .

paleographer [,pæli'ɔgrəfə*] n paleógrafo m.

paleography [,pæli'ɔgrəfi] n paleografía f.

paleolithic [,pæliəu'liθik] adj paleolítico.

paleontology [,pæliɔn'tɔlədʒi] n paleontología f.

Palestine ['pælistain] Palestina f.

Palestinian [,pæləs'tinian] 1 adj palestino. 2 n palestino m, a f.

palette ['pælit] n paleta f.

palette knife ['pælitnaif] n, pl — **knives** [naivz] espátula f.

palfrey ['pɔːlfri] n palafré m.

palimpsest ['pælimpsest] n palimpsesto m.

palindrome ['pælindrəum] n palindromo m.

paling ['peiliŋ] n (stake) estaca f; (fence) valla f, empalizada f.

palisade [,pæli'seid] n palizada f, estacada f.

pall¹ [pɔːl] n (on coffin) paño m mortuorio; (robe, Eccl) palio m; (fig) manto m, capa f; **a —** of smoke (covering) una capa de humo, (rising in air) un penacho de humo.

pall² [pɔːl] vi perder su sabor (on para), dejar de gustar (on a); empalagar (on a); **it —s after a time** después de cierto tiempo deja de gustar; **it never —s** nunca pierde su sabor; **I found the book —ed** encontré que el libro empezaba a aburrirme.

pallbearer ['pɔːl,beərə*] n el que ayuda a llevar a hombros el féretro.

pallet ['pælit] n (bed) jergón m.

palliasse ['pæliæs] n jergón m.

palliate ['pælieit] vt paliar, mitigar.

palliative ['pæliətiv] 1 adj paliativo. 2 n paliativo m.

pallid ['pælid] adj pálido.

pallidness ['pælidnis] n, **pallor** ['pælə*] n palidez f.

pally ['pæli] adj (fam): **he's a — sort** es una persona afable; **they're very —** son muy amigos; **to be pretty — with someone** estar muy amigo de uno.

palm¹ [pɑːm] n (Bot) palma f, palmera f; (English sallow) sauce m; (as carried at Easter) ramo m; **to bear the —** llevarse la palma; **to yield the — to someone** reconocer la superioridad de uno, reconocer a uno por vencedor.

palm² [pɑːm] (Anat) 1 n palma f; **to grease someone's —** untar la mano a uno; **to have an itching —** ser muy codicioso; (be bribable) estar dispuesto a dejarse sobornar.

2 vt card escamotear; **to — something off on someone** encajar algo a uno.

palmist ['pɑːmist] n quiromántico m, a f.

palmistry ['pɑːmistri] n quiromancia f.

palm oil ['pɑːmɔil] n aceite m de palma.

palm tree ['pɑːmtriː] n palma f, palmera f.

palmy ['pɑːmi] adj floreciente; próspero, feliz; **those — days** aquellos días tan felices.

palpable ['pælpəbl] adj palpable; (fig) palpable, sensible.

palpably ['pælpəbli] adv palpablemente; sensiblemente; **a — unjust sentence** una condena manifiestamente injusta; **that is — untrue** eso es a todas luces falso.

palpitate ['pælpiteit] vi palpitar.

palpitating ['pælpiteitiŋ] adj palpitante.

palpitation [,pælpi'teiʃən] n palpitación f; **to have —s** tener vahidos.

palsied ['pɔːlzid] adj paralítico.

palsy ['pɔːlzi] n perlesía f, parálisis f; **cerebral —** parálisis f cerebral.

paltry ['pɔːltri] adj insignificante, baladí; vil; miserable; **for a few — pesetas** por unas pesetillas, por unas miserables pesetas; **for some — reason** por alguna razón insignificante.

pampas ['pæmpəs] npl pampa f, pampas fpl; **the P— (SAm)** la Pampa.

pamper ['pæmpə*] vt mimar.

pampered ['pæmpəd] adj child etc mimado, consentido; life regalado; **he was — all his life** se crió entre algodones.

pamphlet ['pæmflit] n (informative, brochure) folleto m; (literary) panfleto m; (political, handed out in street) octavilla f, hoja f de propaganda.

pamphleteer [,pæmfli'tiə*] n folletista mf.

pan [pæn] 1 n (utensil) cazuela f, cacerola f; perol m; (frying —) sartén f; (of lavatory) taza f; (of firearm) cazoleta f.

2 vt gold separar en la gamella; play (sl) dar un palo a; (camera: Cine) tomar en panorámicas; **to — out** repartir.

3 vi: **to — out** salir bien, tener éxito; **if it —s**

out as we hope si sale como nosotros lo esperamos; **it didn't — out at all well** no dio ningún resultado satisfactorio; **we must wait and see how it —s out** tenemos que esperar hasta ver que éxito tiene esto.

pan . . . [pæn] in compounds: pan . . ., eg **pan-African** panafricano.

panacea [,pænə'siə] n panacea f.

panache [pə'næʃ] n: **to do something with —** hacer algo con brío, hacer algo con aire triunfal.

Panama [,pænə'mɑː] Panamá m; — **Canal** Canal m de Panamá; — **hat** sombrero m de jipijapa, panamá m.

Panamanian [,pænə'meiniən] 1 adj panameño. 2 n panameño m, a f.

Pan-American ['pænə'merikən] adj panamericano; — **Union** Unión f Panamericana.

Pan-Americanism ['pænə'merikənizəm] n pan-americanismo m.

pancake ['pænkeik] n hojuela f, tortita f, panqueque m (SAm).

pancake day ['pænkeik,dei] n martes m de carnaval (en que en Inglaterra se sirven hojuelas).

panchromatic ['pænkrəu'mætik] adj pancromático.

pancreas ['pæŋkriəs] n páncreas m.

pancreatic [,pæŋkri'ætik] adj pancreático.

panda ['pændə] n panda mf.

pandemonium [,pændi'məuniəm] n ruido m de todos los diablos, estruendo m infernal; **it's sheer —!** ¡es la monda!; **at this there was —** en esto estallaron ruidosos los gritos (etc).

pander ['pændə*] 1 n alcahuete m. 2 vi alcahuetear; **to — to someone** ser indulgente con uno, mimar a uno, desvivirse por complacer a uno; **to — to someone's desires** tratar por todos los medios de satisfacer los deseos de uno; **this is —ing to the public's worst tastes** esto es condescender con los peores gustos del público.

Pandora [pæn'dɔːrə] : —**'s box** caja f de Pandora.

pane [pein] n cristal m, hoja f de vidrio.

panegyric [,pæni'dʒirik] n panegírico m.

panel ['pænl] 1 n (a) panel m; (of wall) panel m; (of ceiling) artesón m; (of door) entrepaño m; (Sew) paño m; (Art) tabla f; (of instruments, switches) tablero m.

(b) (Med etc) lista f de pacientes; (of judges, in a competition) jurado m.

2 vt poner paneles (etc) a, adornar con paneles (etc).

panelist ['pænəlist] n miembro m del jurado (de un concurso etc).

panelled, (US) **paneled** ['pænld] adj con paneles, adornado de paneles; artesonado.

panelling, (US) **paneling** ['pænəliŋ] n paneles mpl; artesonado m; entrepaños mpl.

pang [pæŋ] n punzada f, dolor m súbito, dolor m agudo; — **of conscience** remordimiento m; **I felt a — of conscience** me remordió la conciencia; —**s of childbirth** dolores mpl del parto; —**s of hunger** dolores mpl del hambre.

panhandle ['pænhændl] (US) 1 n faja angosta de territorio de un estado que entra en el de otro. 2 vi (sl) mendigar, pedir limosna.

panic ['pænik] 1 n terror m pánico, pánico m; **to flee in —** huir aterrado; **the country was thrown into a —** el terror cundió en el país, el país fue preso de un terror pánico.

2 vt aterrar, infundir terror a.

3 vi llenarse de terror, aterrarse, ser preso de un terror pánico; **the crew —ked** la tripulación se abandonó al terror; **don't —!** ¡con calma!

panicky ['pæniki] adj (a) person asustadizo; lleno de un terror pánico; **to get —** llenarse de terror; **don't get —!** ¡con calma!

(b) act, measure etc influido por el terror.

panic-stricken ['pænik,strikən] adj preso de un terror pánico, muerto de miedo.

panjandrum [pæn'dʒændrəm] n jefazo m, mandamás m; **he's the great —** es el mandamás.

pannier ['pæniə*] n cuévano m, serón m, banasta f.

pannier bag ['pæniə,bæg] n (on motorcycle etc) cartera f, bolsa f (para equipage); (for mule etc) alforja f.

panoply ['pænəpli] n (armour) panoplia f; (fig) pompa f, esplendor m.

panorama [,pænə'rɑːmə] n panorama m.

panoramic [,pænə'ræmik] adj panorámico.

pansy ['pænzi] n (Bot) pensamiento m; (fam) maricón m.

pant [pænt] 1 n jadeo m; resuello m.

2 vi jadear; resollar; (of heart) palpitar; **to — for water** jadear sediento; **to — for breath** jadear; **to — for** (fig) suspirar por, anhelar; **to — out a few words** decir jadeando algunas palabras; **to — with desire for something** desear algo ardientemente.

pantaloons [,pæntə'luːnz] *npl* (*Hist*) pantalones *mpl*.
pantechnicon [pæn'teknikən] *n* camión *m* de mudanzas.
pantheism ['pænθiːizəm] *n* panteísmo *m*.
pantheist ['pænθiːist] *n* panteísta *mf*.
pantheistic [,pænθiː'istik] *adj* panteísta.
pantheon ['pænθiən] *n* panteón *m*.
panther ['pænθə*] *n* pantera *f*.
panties ['pæntiz] *npl* bragas *fpl*, braguitas *fpl*; **a pair of** — unas bragas.
panting ['pæntiŋ] *n* jadeo *m*; respiración *f* difícil.
pantograph ['pæntəgrɑːf] *n* pantógrafo *m*.
pantomime ['pæntəmaim] *n* (*classical*) pantomima *f*; (*British*) revista musical en época de Navidades, a base de cuentos de hadas etc; **what a** — ! ¡qué absurdo!, ¡qué ridículo!
pantry ['pæntri] *n* despensa *f*.
pants [pænts] *npl* calzoncillos *mpl*; (*US*) pantalones *mpl*; **a pair of** — unos calzoncillos, (*US*) unos pantalones, un pantalón.
Panzer ['pæntsə*] **1** *adj* motorizado; — **division** división *f* motorizada. **2** *n*: **the** —**s** las tropas motorizadas.
pap [pæp] *n* papilla *f*, gachas *fpl*.
papa [pə'pɑː] *n* papá *m*.
papacy ['peipəsi] *n* papado *m*, pontificado *m*.
papal ['peipəl] *adj* papal, pontificio.
paper ['peipə*] **1** *n* (**a**) (*material, in general*) papel *m*; **a piece of** — un papel, una hoja de papel, un trozo de papel; **brown** — papel *m* de embalar, papel *m* de estraza; **corrugated** — papel *m* ondulado; **hand-made** — papel *m* de tina; **India** — papel *m* de China, papel *m* biblia; **rice** — papel *m* de paja de arroz; **squared** — papel *m* cuadriculado; **vellum** — papel *m* vitela; **waste** — papel *m* viejo, papeles *mpl* usados; **on** — sobre el papel, teóricamente; **to commit something to** —, **to get** (*or* **put**) **something down on** — poner algo por escrito.
(**b**) (*document*) papel *m*, documento *m*; —**s** (*identity etc*) papeles *mpl*, documentación *f*; **identity** —**s** documentación *f* personal, carnet *m* de identidad; **your** —**s**, **please** la documentación, por favor; **ship's** —**s** documentación *f* del barco; **Churchill's private** —**s** los papeles personales de Churchill.
(**c**) (*Univ etc exercise*) ejercicio *m*, ensayo *m*; (*exam*) cuestionario *m* de examen; **to do a good** — **in maths** hacer un buen examen de matemáticas; **to set a** — **in physics** poner un examen de física.
(**d**) (*learned: written*) artículo *m*, (*read aloud*) comunicación *f*, ponencia *f*; **we heard a good** — **on place-names** escuchamos una buena ponencia sobre toponimia.
(**e**) (*newspaper*) periódico *m*; **daily** —, **morning** — periódico *m*, diario *m*; **evening** — periódico *m* de la tarde; **weekly** — semanario *m*; **Sunday** — periódico *m* del domingo; **fashion** — revista *f* de modas; **illustrated** — revista *f* gráfica; **trade** — revista *f* comercial; **women's** — revista *f* para mujeres; **to write for the** —**s** colaborar en los periódicos, escribir artículos para los periódicos; **to write to the** — **about something** escribir una carta al director de un periódico.
2 *attr* de papel; **money** — papel *m* moneda, billetes *mpl* de banco.
3 *vt wall, room* empapelar.
paperback ['peipəbæk] *n* libro *m* en rústica.
paperbacked ['peipəbækt] *adj* en rústica.
paper bag ['peipə'bæg] *n* saco *m* de papel.
paperboy ['peipəbɔi] *n* repartidor *m* de periódicos.
paper chain ['peipətʃein] *n* cadeneta *f* de papel.
paper chase ['peipətʃeis] *n* rallye-paper *m*.
paper clip ['peipəklip] *n* clip *m*, sujetapapeles *m*.
paper fastener ['peipə,fɑːsnə*] *n* grapa *f*.
paperhanger ['peipə,hæŋə*] *n* empapelador *m*.
paper knife ['peipənaif] *n*, *pl* — **knives** [naivz] abrecartas *m*, plegadera *f*.
paper mill ['peipəmil] *n* fábrica *f* de papel.
paperweight ['peipəweit] *n* pisapapeles *m*.
paper work ['peipəwɜːk] *n* trabajo *m* administrativo; trabajo *m* de oficina; aspecto *m* teórico; (*pej*) papeleo *m*, trámites *mpl* burocráticos.
papery ['peipəri] *adj* parecido al papel; delgado como el papel.
papier-mâché ['pæpiei'mæʃei] **1** *adj* de cartón piedra. **2** *n* cartón *m* piedra.
papist ['peipist] *n* papista *mf*.
papistry ['peipistri] *n* papismo *m*.
paprika ['pæprikə] *n* pimienta *f* húngara.
papyrus [pə'paiərəs] *n*, *pl* **papyri** [pə'paiərai] papiro *m*.
par [pɑː*] **1** *adj value etc* nominal.
2 *n* (*Comm*) par *f*; (*Golf*) par *m*; **to be above** (*or*

over) — (*Comm*) estar por encima de la par; **to be under** (*or* **below**) — (*Comm*) estar por debajo de la par, (*Med*) estar indispuesto, sentirse mal, (*fig*) ser inferior a la calidad normal; **to get round in 6 under** — (*Golf*) hacer un recorrido con 6 por debajo del par; **to be at** — (*Comm*) estar a la par; **to be on a** — **with** ser equivalente a, correr parejas con; **to place something on a** — **with** parangonar algo con, equiparar algo con.
parable ['pærəbl] *n* parábola *f*.
parabola [pə'ræbələ] *n* (*Math*) parábola *f*.
parabolic [,pærə'bɒlik] *adj* parabólico.
parachute ['pærəʃuːt] **1** *n* paracaídas *m*.
2 *vt* lanzar en paracaídas; **to** — **food to someone** suministrar víveres a uno en paracaídas.
3 *vi* lanzarse en paracaídas; bajar en paracaídas (*also* **to** — **down**); **to** — **to safety** salvarse utilizando el paracaídas.
parachutist ['pærəʃuːtist] *n* paracaidista *m*.
parade [pə'reid] **1** *n* (*procession*) desfile *m*; (*Mil*) desfile *m*, parada *f*; (*road*) paseo *m*; (*fig*) alarde *m*; **mannequin** — desfile *m* de modelos; **to make a** — **of** hacer alarde de, hacer ostentación de.
2 *vt troops* formar, formar en parada; *streets* recorrer, desfilar por; *placard, image etc* pasear (*through the streets* por las calles); (*show off*) hacer alarde de, hacer ostentación de, lucir; **to** — **one's learning** hacer alarde de su erudición.
3 *vi* (*Mil*) formar en parada, pasar revista; (*group of people*) desfilar; (*one person*) pasearse; **the strikers** —**d through the town** los huelguistas desfilaron por la ciudad; **she** —**d up and down with the hat on** se paseó de un lado a otro con el sombrero puesto, andaba de acá para allá para lucir el sombrero.
parade ground [pə'reidgraund] *n* plaza *f* de armas.
paradigm ['pærədaim] *n* paradigma *m*.
paradise ['pærədais] *n* paraíso *m*; **an earthly** — un paraíso terrenal, un edén; **this is** —! ¡esto es jauja!; *see* **fool**.
paradox ['pærədɒks] *n* paradoja *f*.
paradoxical [,pærə'dɒksikəl] *adj* paradójico.
paradoxically [,pærə'dɒksikəli] *adv* paradójicamente.
paraffin ['pærəfin] *n* (*oil*) petróleo *m* (de alumbrado); (*wax*) parafina *f*.
paraffin lamp ['pærəfin,læmp] *n* quinqué *m* de petróleo.
paraffin oil ['pærəfin,ɔil] *n* petróleo *m* de alumbrado.
paraffin wax ['pærəfin,wæks] *n* parafina *f*.
paragon ['pærəgən] *n* dechado *m*; **a** — **of virtue** un dechado de virtudes.
paragraph ['pærəgrɑːf] **1** *n* párrafo *m*; (*Typ*) suelto *m*; **"new** —" "(punto y) aparte". **2** *vt* dividir en párrafos.
Paraguay ['pærəgwai] el Paraguay.
Paraguayan [,pærə'gwaiən] **1** *adj* paraguayo. **2** *n* paraguayo *m*, a *f*.
parakeet ['pærəkiːt] *n* perico *m*, periquito *m*.
parallel ['pærəlel] **1** *adj* paralelo; (*Elec*) en paralelo; (*fig*) semejante, análogo (*to* a); **in a** — **direction to** en dirección paralela a; **to run** — **to** ir en línea paralela a; **this is a** — **case to the last one** este caso es análogo al anterior.
2 *n* (*Geom*) paralela *f*, línea *f* paralela; (*Geog, fig*) paralelo *m*; **the 49th** — el paralelo 49; **in** — (*Elec*) en paralelo; **a case without** — un caso inaudito, un caso nunca visto; **it has no** — **as far as I know** que yo sepa es único, que yo sepa no hay nada parecido; **to draw a** — **between X and Y** establecer un paralelo entre X e Y.
3 *vt* (*fig*) ser paralelo a, ser análogo a, correr parejas con; **it is** —**led by** ... corre parejas con ..., tiene su paralelo en ...
parallelism ['pærəlelizəm] *n* paralelismo *m*.
parallelogram [,pærə'leləugræm] *n* paralelogramo *m*.
paralysis [pə'ræləsis] *n* parálisis *f*; **creeping** — parálisis *f* progresiva; **infantile** — parálisis *f* infantil.
paralytic [,pærə'litik] **1** *adj* paralítico. **2** *n* paralítico *m*, a *f*.
paralyzation [,pærəlai'zeiʃən] *n* paralización *f*.
paralyze ['pærəlaiz] *vt* paralizar (*also fig*); **to be** —**d in both legs** estar paralizado de las dos piernas; **to be** —**d with fright** estar paralizado de miedo.
paramilitary [,pærə'militəri] *adj* paramilitar.
paramount ['pærəmaunt] *adj* supremo; **of** — **importance** de la mayor importancia, primordial; **solvency must be** — la solvencia es lo más importante, ante todo la solvencia.
paramour ['pærəmuə*] *n* (*esp hum*) amante *mf*, querido *m*, a *f*.
paranoia [,pærə'nɔiə] *n* paranoia *f*.

paranoiac [,pærə'nɔiik] n paranoico m.

parapet ['pærəpit] n parapeto m; (of well etc) brocal m.

paraphernalia ['pærəfə'neiliə] n (belongings, gear) avíos mpl, chismes mpl; (adornments) arreos mpl; (fuss) molestias fpl.

paraphrase ['pærəfreiz] 1 n paráfrasis f. 2 vt parafrasear.

paraplegia [,pærə'pli:dʒə] n paraplejía f.

paraplegic [,pærə'pli:dʒik] 1 adj parapléjico. 2 n parapléjico m, a f.

parasite ['pærəsait] n parásito m (also fig: on de).

parasitic(al) [,pærə'sitik(əl)] adj parasítico, parasitario; **to be — on** ser parásito de.

parasitism ['pærəsitizəm] n parasitismo m.

parasitology [,pærəsi'tɔlədʒi] n parasitología f.

parasol [,pærə'sɔl] n sombrilla f, quitasol m.

paratrooper ['pærətru:pə*] n paracaidista m.

paratroops ['pærətru:ps] npl paracaidistas mpl.

paratyphoid ['pærə'taifɔid] n paratifoidea f.

parboil ['pɑːbɔil] vt sancochar.

Parcae ['pɑːki:] npl: **the — las** Parcas.

parcel ['pɑːsl] 1 n paquete m; (of land) parcela f. 2 vt: **to — out** repartir; dividir; land parcelar; **to — up** empaquetar, embalar.

parcel post ['pɑːslpəust] n servicio m de paquetes postales.

parch [pɑːtʃ] 1 vt secar, resecar; quemar. 2 vi secarse.

parched [pɑːtʃt] adj land etc seco; **to be — (with thirst)** morirse de sed.

parchment ['pɑːtʃmənt] n pergamino m.

parchment-like ['pɑːtʃmənt,laik] adj apergaminado.

pardon ['pɑːdn] 1 n perdón m; (Law) indulto m; **general — amnistía** f; **to beg someone's — pedir** perdón a uno; **I beg your —, but could you . . .?** perdone la molestia, pero ¿podría Vd . . .?; **I beg your —!** ¡perdone Vd!, ¡ay perdone!; **—?, I beg your —?** ¿cómo?
2 vt perdonar, dispensar; (Law) indultar; **to — someone something** perdonar algo a uno; dispensar a uno de hacer (etc) algo; **— me, but could you . . .?** perdone la molestia, pero ¿podría Vd . . .?; **— me!** ¡perdone Vd!, ¡ay perdone!; **— my mentioning it** siento tener que decirlo, perdone que se lo diga.

pardonable ['pɑːdnəbl] adj perdonable.

pardonably ['pɑːdnəbli] adv: **he was — angry** es fácil disculpar su enojo, se comprende fácilmente que se encolerizara.

pare [peə*] vt nails cortar; fruit etc mondar; stick etc adelgazar; **to — away, to — down** (fig) reducir, ir reduciendo; **to — something down to the minimum** reducir algo al mínimo.

parent ['peərənt] 1 n padre m, madre f; **—s** padres mpl. 2 adj: **the — plant** la planta madre; **the — company** la casa matriz.

parentage ['peərəntidʒ] n familia f, linaje m; of humble — de nacimiento humilde.

parental [pə'rentl] adj care etc de padre y madre, de los padres, paternal, maternal.

parenthesis [pə'renθisis] n, pl **parentheses** [pə'renθisi:z] paréntesis m.

parenthetic(al) [,pærən'θetik(əl)] adj entre paréntesis; explicativo.

parenthetically [,pærən'θetikəli] adv entre paréntesis; a modo de explicación.

parenthood ['peərənthud] n el ser padre (or madre), el tener hijos; paternidad f, maternidad f.

par excellence [pɑːr'eksəlɑːns] adv por excelencia.

pariah ['pæriə] n paria mf.

parietal [pə'raiitl] adj parietal.

pari mutuel ['pærimu:tu'el] n totalizador m.

parings ['peəriŋz] npl peladuras fpl, mondaduras fpl; desperdicios mpl.

pari passu ['pæri'pæsu:] adv a ritmo parecido, al igual; **— with** a ritmo parecido al de, al igual que.

Paris ['pæris] París m; (attr) parisiense.

parish ['pæriʃ] 1 n parroquia f. 2 attr parroquial, de la parroquia.

parishioner [pə'riʃənə*] n feligrés m, esa f.

parish-pump ['pæriʃ'pʌmp] attr (pej) de campanario, de aldea.

Parisian [pə'riziən] 1 adj parisiense, parisino, parisién. 2 n parisiense mf.

parity ['pæriti] n paridad f, igualdad f; **the — of the dollar** la paridad del dólar.

park [pɑːk] 1 n parque m; jardines mpl; (Aut) aparcamiento m, parque m (de automóviles).
2 vt (Aut: briefly) estacionar, (for longer period) aparcar; (fam) poner, dejar, depositar; **can I — my car here?** ¿puedo aparcar mi coche aquí?
3 vi (Aut: briefly) estacionarse, (for longer period) aparcar; (fam) quedarse.

parking ['pɑːkiŋ] n estacionamiento m; aparcamiento m; **"no —"** "prohibido estacionarse"; **"good — for cars"** "fácil aparcamiento de coches"; **"— for 50 cars"** "aparcamiento para 50 coches".

parking attendant ['pɑːkiŋə,tendənt] n celador m.

parking lights ['pɑːkiŋlaits] npl luces fpl de estacionamiento.

parking lot ['pɑːkiŋlɔt] n (US) aparcamiento m.

parking meter ['pɑːkiŋ,mi:tə*] n parquímetro m, contador m de aparcamiento.

parking place ['pɑːkiŋpleis] n sitio m para aparcar, aparcamiento m; **to look for a — buscar** dónde aparcar.

park keeper ['pɑːk,ki:pə*] n guardián m (de parque), guardabosque m.

parkway ['pɑːkwei] n (US) gran vía f adornada de árboles.

parky ['pɑːki] adj (sl) frío; **it's pretty — hace** un frío glacial.

parlance ['pɑːləns] n lenguaje m; **in common — en** lenguaje corriente; **in technical — en** lenguaje técnico.

parley ['pɑːli] 1 n parlamento m. 2 vi parlamentar (with con).

parliament ['pɑːləmənt] n parlamento m; (Spanish) Cortes fpl; **to get into — llegar** a ser diputado, ser elegido.

parliamentarian [,pɑːləmen'teəriən] 1 adj parlamentario. 2 n parlamentario m, a f.

parliamentary [,pɑːlə'mentəri] adj parlamentario.

parlour, (US) parlor ['pɑːlə*] n sala f de recibo, salón m; (Eccl) locutorio m.

parlour game, (US) parlor — ['pɑːləgeim] n juego m de salón.

parlourmaid, (US) parlor— ['pɑːləmeid] n camarera f.

parlous ['pɑːləs] adj state lamentable, crítico, pésimo.

Parnassus [pɑː'næsəs] Parnaso m.

parochial [pə'rəukiəl] adj (Eccl) parroquial; (fig) estrecho, limitado, restringido; de miras estrechas.

parochialism [pə'rəukiəlizəm] n (fig) estrechez f, lo limitado, lo restringido; estrechez f de miras.

parodist ['pærədist] n parodista mf.

parody ['pærədi] 1 n parodia f. 2 vt parodiar.

parole [pə'rəul] 1 n (promise) palabra f, palabra f de honor; (freedom) libertad f bajo palabra, libertad f condicional; **to be on — estar** libre bajo palabra; **to break one's — faltar** a su palabra; **to put someone on — dejar** a uno libre bajo palabra.
2 vt dejar libre bajo palabra.

paroxysm ['pærəksizəm] n paroxismo m.

parquet ['pɑːkei] n parquet m, parqué m (Acad); entarimado m de hojas quebradas.

parquetry ['pɑːkitri] n entarimado m, obra f de entarimado.

parricide ['pærisaid] n (act) parricidio m; (person) parricida mf.

parrot ['pærət] 1 n loro m, papagayo m. 2 vt words repetir como un loro, (person) imitar como un loro.

parrot fashion ['pærət,fæʃən] adv learn etc mecánicamente.

parry ['pæri] vt (Fencing) parar, quitar; blow parar, desviar; attack rechazar, defenderse de; (fig) esquivar, eludir, desviar hábilmente.

parse [pɑːz] vt (Gram) analizar.

Parsee [pɑː'si:] n parsi mf.

parsimonious [,pɑːsi'məuniəs] adj parco; escaso, corto; frugal.

parsimoniously [,pɑːsi'məuniəsli] adv parcamente; escasamente; frugalmente.

parsimony ['pɑːsiməni] n parquedad f; escasez f; frugalidad f.

parsley ['pɑːsli] n perejil m.

parsnip ['pɑːsnip] n chirivía f.

parson ['pɑːsn] n clérigo m, cura m; (esp) párroco m.

parsonage ['pɑːsnidʒ] n casa f del cura, casa f del párroco.

parsonical [pɑː'sɔnikəl] adj (hum) frailuno.

part [pɑːt] 1 n (a) (portion, fragment) parte f; porción f; trozo m; **this — is blue** esta parte es azul; **the funny — of it is that . . .** lo gracioso es que . . .; **you haven't heard the best — yet** todavía no te he dicho lo mejor; **that's the awkward — eso** es lo difícil; **private —s, privy —s** partes fpl pudendas; **it is — and parcel of the scheme** es parte esencial del proyecto, es parte integrante del proyecto; **the book is good in —s** el libro es bueno solamente en parte, hay partes del libro que son buenas; **the greater — of it is done** la mayor parte está hecha; **this is in great — due to . . .** esto se debe ante todo a . . ., más que nada esto se debe a . . .; **for the better — of the day** durante la mayor parte del día; **in the latter**

— **of the year** en los últimos meses del año; **in —** en parte; **it is ready in —** en parte está listo; **to pay a debt in —** pagar parte de una deuda; **5 —s of sand to 1 of cement** 5 partes de arena y 1 de cemento; **three —s** tres cuartos; **it's 3 —s gone** las tres cuartas partes se han usado ya.

(**b**) (*Mech*) pieza *f*; **moving —** pieza *f* móvil; **spare —** pieza *f* de recambio, recambio *m*.

(**c**) (*Gram*) parte *f*; **— of speech** parte *f* de la oración; **principal —s of a verb** partes *fpl* principales de un verbo.

(**d**) (*of journal*) fascículo *m*, número *m*; (*of series*) tomo *m*; (*of serial*) entrega *f*.

(**e**) (*share*) parte *f*; **to do one's —** cumplir con sus obligaciones; **each one did his —** cada uno colaboró perfectamente; **to have no — in something** (*not be active*) no participar en algo, (*have nothing to do with*) no tener nada que ver con algo, ser ajeno a algo, desentenderse de algo; **he had no — in stealing it** él no ayudó a robarlo, él no intervino en el robo; **to take (a) — in** tomar parte en, intervenir en, participar en; **are you taking —?** ¿vas a tomar parte?

(**f**) (*Theat and fig*) papel *m*; **bit —, small —** papel *m* pequeño; **it is not my — to + infin** no me toca a mí + *infin*; **to look the —** vestir el cargo; **to play a —** hacer un papel, (*fig*) desempeñar un papel; **what — do you play?** ¿qué papel haces?; **he's just playing a —** está haciendo un papel, nada más; **the climate has played a — in + ger** el clima ha contribuido a + *infin*.

(**g**) (*Mus*) parte *f*; **the soprano —** la parte de soprano; **to sing in —s** cantar por partes.

(**h**) **—s** (*Geog*) lugar *m*; comarca *f*, región *f*; **from all —s** de todas partes; **in these —s** por aquí; **the biggest thief in these —s** el mayor ladrón en estos contornos; **in foreign —s** en el extranjero; **what — are you from?** ¿de dónde es Vd?; **he's not from these —s** no es de aquí; **it's a lovely —** es una región hermosa.

(**i**) (*side*) parte *f*; **for my —**, **on my —** por mi parte; **a mistake on the — of . . .** un error por parte de . . ., un error debido a . . .; **on the one — . . ., on the other —** por una parte . . ., por otra . . .; **there is opposition on the — of some** hay oposición por parte de algunos; **to take someone's —** defender a uno, tomar el partido de uno.

(**j**) **to take something in good —** tomar algo en buena parte.

(**k**) **a man of —s** un hombre de talento.

2 *adv*: **— one and — the other** parte esto y parte lo otro; **it is — brass and — copper** parte es latón y parte es cobre; **it was — eaten** había sido comido en parte.

3 *adj* parcial; **co- . . ., con- . . .,** *eg* **part-author** coautor *m*, ora *f*; **part-owner** condueño *m*, a *f*; copropietario *m*, a *f*.

4 *vt* separar, dividir (*from* de); (*break*) romper, partir; **to — something in two** partir algo en dos; **he —ed the grass with his hand** con la mano apartó la hierba; **to — one's hair** hacerse la raya.

5 *vi* (**a**) (*of crowd etc*) apartarse; **the branches —ed** se apartaron las ramas; **the people —ed to let her through** la gente se hizo a un lado para dejarla pasar.

(**b**) (*of 2 persons*) separarse; **they —ed 5 years ago** se separaron hace 5 años; **the best of friends must —** los mejores amigos han de separarse alguna vez; **to — from someone** separarse de uno, despedirse de uno; **when we —ed from Seville** cuando nos despedimos de Sevilla.

(**c**) (*roads etc*) bifurcarse.

(**d**) (*snap, break*) romperse; (*fall away*) separarse, desprenderse.

(**e**) **to — with** ceder, entregar; (*money*) pagar, dar; (*get rid of*) deshacerse de; **I hate —ing with it** siento mucho tener que cederlo, me da pena perderlo.

partake [pɑːˈteik] (*irr: see* **take**) *vti* (**a**) **to — of** *food* comer, comer de, aceptar; *drink* tomar, beber; **do you —?** ¿bebes vino? (*etc*); **will you —?** ¿quieres de esto?

(**b**) **to — of a quality** tener algo de una cualidad, tener rasgos de una cualidad.

(**c**) **to — in** tomar parte en, participar en; **are you partaking?** ¿vas a tomar parte?

part exchange [ˈpɑːtiksˈtʃeindʒ] *n*: **to offer something in —** ofrecer algo como parte del pago; **"we take your old car in —"** "admitimos su coche usado a cambio".

parthenogenesis [ˌpɑːθinəuˈdʒenisis] *n* partenogénesis *f*.

partial [ˈpɑːʃəl] *adj* parcial; **to be — to something** ser aficionado a algo, tener gusto por algo.

partiality [ˌpɑːʃiˈæliti] *n* parcialidad *f*; **—, for, — to** afición *f* a, gusto *m* por.

partially [ˈpɑːʃəli] *adv* (*partly*) parcialmente, en parte; (*with bias*) con parcialidad.

participant [pɑːˈtisipənt] *n* partícipe *mf*; (*in competition*) concursante *mf*; (*in fight*) combatiente *mf*.

participate [pɑːˈtisipeit] *vi* participar, tomar parte (*in* en).

participation [pɑːˌtisiˈpeiʃən] *n* participación *f*.

participial [ˌpɑːtiˈsipiəl] *adj* participial.

participle [ˈpɑːtisipl] *n* participio *m*; **past —** participio *m* de pasado; **present —** participio *m* de presente.

particle [ˈpɑːtikl] *n* partícula *f*; (*of dust etc*) átomo *m*, grano *m*; (*fig*) pizca *f*; **there's not a — of truth in it** eso no tiene ni pizca de verdad.

parti-coloured, (*US*) **—colored** [ˈpɑːtiˌkʌləd] *adj* de diversos colores, abigarrado.

particular [pəˈtikjulə*] **1** *adj* (**a**) (*special*) particular; especial; concreto; determinado; individual; **that — person** esa persona (y no otra); **a — thing** una cosa determinada; **in — cases** en algunos casos; **en casos especiales**; **it varies according to the — case** varía según el caso individual; **in this — case** en este caso concreto; **for no — reason** por ninguna razón especial; **to take — care** tomar especial cuidado, ser especialmente cuidadoso.

(**b**) *account etc* detallado, minucioso.

(**c**) (*fastidious*) exigente, quisquilloso (*about, as to, as to what* en cuanto a, en asuntos de, para); (*scrupulous*) escrupuloso; (*about food etc*) delicado; **he's — about his food** es delicado para la comida; **he is very — about cleanliness** es muy exigente para la limpieza; **he's — about his car** cuida mucho del coche; **I'm — about my friends** escojo mis amigos con cierto cuidado; **I'm not too — (about it)** lo mismo da, me es igual; **he was most — about it** insistió mucho sobre esto; **he was very — to say that . . .** subrayó que . . ., dijo con toda claridad que . . .

2 *n* detalle *m*, pormenor *m*, dato *m*; **—s** detalles *mpl*; **in this —** en este caso particular; **correct in every —** correcto en todos los detalles; **for further —s apply to . . .** para más informes escriban a . . .; **to give —s** citar los detalles; **please give full —s** se ruega hacer constar todos los detalles, se ruega dar un informe pormenorizado.

particularity [pəˌtikjuˈlæriti] *n* particularidad *f*.

particularize [pəˈtikjuləraiz] **1** *vt* particularizar, especificar, señalar; **he did not — which one he wanted** no dijo de modo concreto cuál quería.

2 *vi* dar todos los detalles, concretar; **he did not —** no concretó.

particularly [pəˈtikjuləli] *adv*: **this is — true of . . .** esto es especialmente verdad por lo que se refiere a . . .; **notice — that . . .** observen Vds sobre todo que . . .; **he said most — not to do it** dijo de modo particular que no se hiciera; **do you want it — for tomorrow?** ¿lo necesita Vd especialmente para mañana?; **he was not — pleased** no se puso loco de contento que digamos; **not —!** ¡no mucho!

parting [ˈpɑːtiŋ] **1** *adj* de despedida; **a — present** un regalo de despedida; **his — words** sus palabras al despedirse; **he made a — threat** al separarse de nosotros pronunció una amenaza.

2 *n* separación *f*; despedida *f*; (*in hair*) raya *f*; **the — of the ways** el momento de la separación, (*fig*) el punto decisivo.

partisan [ˌpɑːtiˈzæn] **1** *adj* partidista; (*Mil*) de partisanos, de guerrilleros; **— warfare** guerra *f* de guerrilleros; **— spirit** partidismo *m*.

2 *n* partidario *m*, a *f*, (*of* de); (*Mil*) partisano *m*, guerrillero *m*.

partisanship [ˌpɑːtiˈzænʃip] *n* partidismo *m*.

partition [pɑːˈtiʃən] **1** *n* (**a**) partición *f*, división *f*; **the — of Poland** la división de Polonia.

(**b**) (*wall*) tabique *m*; **glass —** tabique *m* de vidrio; **wooden —** tabique *m* de madera.

2 *vt* (**a**) *country etc* partir, dividir; (*share*) repartir (*among* entre).

(**b**) *room etc* tabicar, dividir con tabique; **to — a part off** separar una parte con tabique.

partitive [ˈpɑːtitiv] *adj* partitivo.

partly [ˈpɑːtli] *adv* en parte; en cierto modo; **only — true** verdad sólo en parte; **it was — destroyed** quedaba destruido en parte.

partner [ˈpɑːtnə*] **1** *n* compañero *m*, a *f* (*also Cards*); (*Comm*) socio *m*, a *f*; (*in dance, at tennis etc*) pareja *f*; (*in crime*) codelincuente *mf*; (*spouse*) cónyuge *mf*; **junior —** socio *m* menos antiguo; **senior —** socio *m*

más antiguo; **sleeping —, silent —** (US) socio m comanditario.
   2 vt acompañar; **to be —ed by** ir acompañado de; tener a uno por pareja (etc).

partnership ['pɑːtnəʃip] n asociación f, (Comm) sociedad f; (of spouses) vida f conyugal, vida f en común; **to enter into —, to form a —** asociarse (with con); **to take someone into —** tomar a uno como socio.

part owner ['pɑːt'əunə*] n condueño m, a f, copropietario m, a f.

part payment ['pɑːt'peimənt] n: **to offer something in —** ofrecer algo como parte del pago.

partridge ['pɑːtridʒ] n perdiz f.

part song ['pɑːtsɔŋ] n canción f a varias voces.

part-time ['pɑːt'taim] **1** adv: **to work —** trabajar parte de la jornada. **2** adj person en dedicación parcial, que trabaja por horas; work por horas.

parturition [ˌpɑːtjuə'riʃən] n parturición f.

party ['pɑːti] **1** n **(a)** (Pol) partido m; **Communist P—** Partido m Comunista; **Conservative P—** Partido m Conservador; **Labour P—** Partido m Laborista; **Liberal P—** Partido m Liberal; **Socialist P—** Partido m Socialista; **to be a member of the —** ser miembro del partido; **to join the —** hacerse miembro del partido.
   (b) (group) grupo m; (Mil) pelotón m, destacamento m; **a — of travellers** un grupo de viajeros; **boarding —** pelotón m de abordaje; **hunting —** partida f de caza; **we were a — of 5** éramos un grupo de 5; **we were only a small —** éramos pocos; **I was one of the —** yo formaba parte del grupo; **to join someone's —** unirse al grupo de uno.
   (c) (gathering) reunión f; (tea— etc) tertulia f; (merry) fiesta f, guateque m; **birthday —** fiesta f para festejar el cumpleaños de uno; **bottle —** guateque m al que cada invitado contribuye una botella; **Christmas —** fiesta f en época de Navidades; **evening —** velada f; **private —** fiesta f particular; **that little — at El Alamein** (fam) la fiestecita de El Alamein; **that was quite a —!** ¡eso fue de miedo!; **to crash a —** (fam) colarse, entrar de gorra; **to give a —** ofrecer una fiesta, organizar una fiesta; **to go to a —** ir a una fiesta.
   (d) (Law etc) parte f; interesado m, a f; **third —** tercera persona f, tercero m; **the parties to a dispute** las partes de una disputa, los interesados; **the high contracting parties** las altas partes contratantes; **to be a — to an agreement** firmar un acuerdo; **to be a — to a crime** ser cómplice en un crimen; **were you a — to this?** ¿tuvo Vd algo que ver con esto?; **I will not be a — to any violence** no quiero tener nada que ver con la violencia; **I will not be a — to any such attempt** yo no me presto a ninguna tentativa de ese tipo.
   (e) (fam) individuo m; **a — of the name of Pérez** un individuo llamado Pérez.
   2 attr **(a)** (Pol) de partido; **— politics** política f de partidos, (pej) partidismo m, politiqueo m.
   (b) dress etc de gala, para fiestas.

parvenu ['pɑːvənjuː] n arribista mf.

pas de deux ['pɑːdə'dəː] n paso m a dos.

pasha ['pæʃə] n bajá m, pachá m.

pass¹ [pɑːs] n (Geog) puerto m; (small) desfiladero m; **the —es through the Guadarrama** los puertos del Guadarrama; **to sell the —** traicionar la causa; ceder lo que bien podría ser defendido.

pass² [pɑːs] **1** n **(a)** (permit) permiso m; (Mil etc) salvoconducto m; (of journalist, worker etc) permiso m; (Theat) entrada f de favor; (Rail etc) billete m de favor; (membership card) carnet m.
   (b) (Sport, Fencing, by conjuror, mesmerist) pase m; **forward —** pase m adelantado.
   (c) (in exams) aprobado m, nota f de aprobado; **to get a — in German** aprobar en alemán; **I need a — in physics still** todavía tengo que aprobar la física.
   (d) **things have come to a pretty —** las cosas han llegado a una situación crítica, estamos en una situación crítica; **it came to — that . . .** sucedió que.
   (e) **to make a — at someone** echar un tiento a una, requebrar de amores a una.
   2 vt **(a)** (move past) pasar; pasar por delante de; person (on street etc) cruzarse con; competitor alcanzar y dejar atrás; (Aut: overtake) pasar, adelantar a; **they —ed each other on the way** se cruzaron en el camino; **we are now —ing the Tower of London** pasamos ahora delante de la Torre de Londres.
   (b) (cross) frontier etc cruzar.
   (c) **it —es belief** es increíble (that que); **it —es**

my comprehension that . . . para mí resulta incomprensible que . . .
   (d) (Univ etc) exam aprobar, ser aprobado en.
   (e) censor ser aprobado por, critic merecer la aprobación de.
   (f) (approve) motion, plan, candidate etc aprobar; **to — someone fit** dar a uno de alta; **to — someone for the army** declarar a uno apto para el servicio militar.
   (g) ball etc pasar; **to — something from hand to hand** pasar algo de mano a mano; **— me the salt, please** ¿me hace el favor de pasar la sal?
   (h) false coin pasar.
   (i) **to — a cloth over something** limpiar algo con un paño, frotar algo con un trapo; **to — one's hand between two bars** introducir la mano entre dos rejas.
   (j) (spend) time pasar; **we —ed the weekend pleasantly** pasamos el fin de semana de modo muy agradable; **just to — the time** para pasar el rato; **I —ed the time of day with him** me detuve un rato a charlar con él, cambié algunas palabras con él.
   (k) remark hacer; opinion expresar; sentence pronunciar, dictar (on sobre, en el asunto de).
   (l) (with adv or prep) **to — along** pasar de uno a otro; **to — by** no hacer caso de, no fijarse en, pasar por alto; **to — down** pasar; **to — off** coin pasar; offence disimular; **to — something off as a joke** hacer creer que algo se había dicho (etc) para hacer reír, hacer ver el aspecto gracioso de algo; **to — on** (hand down) pasar, transmitir; message dar, decir, comunicar; **to — out** distribuir; **to — over** (omit) pasar por alto, omitir; **he was —ed over again for promotion** en los ascensos volvieron a postergarle; **I think we can — that bit over** creo que podemos excusar ese trozo; **to — round** pasar de uno a otro; **to — up** claim renunciar a, opportunity no aprovechar.
   3 vi **(a)** (come, go) pasar; **to — into a tunnel** entrar en un túnel; **to — into oblivion** ser olvidado; **to — out of sight** perderse de vista; **the funeral —ed slowly by** el entierro pasó lentamente; **— along the car please!** ¡vayan pasando por delante!; **words —ed between them** se cambiaron algunas palabras (fuertes); **no money has —ed** ningún dinero ha cambiado de dueño; **to let something —** no hacer caso de algo, no protestar contra algo; **we can't let that —!** ¡eso no lo podemos consentir!; **let it —** conviene dejarlo, conviene no protestar.
   (b) (of time) pasar (also — by); **how time —es!** ¡cómo pasa el tiempo!
   (c) (disappear) pasar; desaparecer; (clouds etc) disiparse; **it'll —** eso pasará, eso se olvidará.
   (d) (be acceptable) ser aceptable, aprobarse; **what —es in New York may not be good enough here** lo que se aprueba en Nueva York puede resultar inaceptable aquí.
   (e) (be considered as) **it —es for a restaurant** pasa por ser restaurante; **in her day she —ed for a great beauty** en sus tiempos se le consideraba una gran belleza; **or what —es nowadays for a hat** o lo que se llama sombrero hoy día.
   (f) (Univ etc) aprobar, ser aprobado; **I —ed!** ¡aprobé!; **did you — in chemistry?** ¿aprobaste en química?
   (g) (with adv or prep) **to — away** pasar, desaparecer; olvidarse; (euph: die) fallecer; **to — by** (adv) pasar de largo; **to — by** (prep) pasar delante de, pasar cerca de; **to — off** pasar, desaparecer; **to — on** pasar adelante; (euph: die) fallecer; **to — out** salir (of de); **to — out from military college** graduarse en la escuela militar; **to — out** (fam) caer rodando, perder el conocimiento; **to — through** (adv) pasar; **to — through** (prep) pasar por.
   4 vr: **to — oneself off as** hacerse pasar por.

passable ['pɑːsəbl] adj (tolerable) pasable; (usable, crossable) transitable.

passably ['pɑːsəbli] adv medianamente, pasablemente.

passage ['pæsidʒ] n **(a)** (act of passing) paso m, tránsito m; (voyage) viaje m, travesía f; (fare) pasaje m; (Parl: process) trámites mpl, (final) aprobación f; **the — of time** el paso del tiempo; **in the — of time** andando el tiempo, con el tiempo; see **work** 2 (g).
   (b) (corridor) pasillo m, galería f, pasadizo m; (alley) callejón m; (Mech) tubo m, conducto m; (Anat) tubo m; **secret —** galería f secreta.
   (c) **— of arms** combate m.
   (d) (Lit, Mus etc) pasaje m; trozo m; episodio m, sección f; **"selected —s from Caesar"** "selecciones de César"; **purple —** trozo m de estilo hinchado, trozo m demasiado sentimental.

passage money ['pæsidʒˌmʌni] n (Naut) pasaje m.
passageway ['pæsidʒwei] n pasillo m, galería f, pasadizo m.
passbook ['pɑːsbuk] n libreta f de banco.
passé ['pæsei] adj pasado de moda.
passenger ['pæsindʒə*] 1 n pasajero m, a f; viajero m, a f; **will —s please rejoin the train?** ¡señores viajeros, al tren! 2 attr aircraft, train de pasajeros.
passenger miles ['pæsindʒə'mailz] npl millas-pasajero fpl.
passe-partout ['pæspɑːtuː] n paspartú m.
passer-by ['pɑːsə'bai] n, pl **passers-by** ['pɑːsəz'bai] transeúnte mf.
passing ['pɑːsiŋ] 1 adj (fleeting) pasajero; glance etc rápido, superficial; **a — car** un coche que pasaba.
  2 n paso m; (Parl) aprobación f; (disappearance) desaparición f; (euph: death) fallecimiento m; **in —** de paso, de pasada.
passing bell ['pɑːsiŋbel] n toque m de difuntos.
passion ['pæʃən] n pasión f; (anger) cólera f, arranque m de cólera; **the P—** la Pasión; **ruling —** pasión f dominante; **he said with —** dijo con pasión; **political —s are strong here** aquí son muy fuertes las pasiones políticas; **to be in a —** estar encolerizado; **to burst (or fly) into a —** montar en cólera, encolerizarse; **to conceive a — for someone** enamorarse con verdadera pasión de uno; **I have a — for shellfish** tengo pasión por los mariscos, me apasionan los mariscos.
passionate ['pæʃənit] adj embrace, speech, temperament etc apasionado; believer, desire vehemente, ardiente; (angry) colérico.
passionately ['pæʃənitli] adv apasionadamente, con pasión; con vehemencia, ardientemente; coléricamente; **to love someone —** amar a uno con pasión.
passionflower ['pæʃənˌflauə*] n pasionaria f.
passionfruit ['pæʃənfruːt] n granadilla f.
passionless ['pæʃənlis] adj affair etc sin pasión, frío; (dispassionate) imparcial.
passion play ['pæʃənˌplei] n drama m de la Pasión.
passive ['pæsiv] 1 adj pasivo (also Gram); inactivo, inerte. 2 n (Gram) voz f pasiva.
passively ['pæsivli] adv pasivamente.
passiveness ['pæsivnis] n, **passivity** [pæ'siviti] n pasividad f; inercia f.
passkey ['pɑːskiː] n llave f maestra.
Passover ['pɑːsəuvə*] n Pascua f (de los judíos).
passport ['pɑːspɔːt] n pasaporte m.
password ['pɑːswəːd] n santo m y seña.
past [pɑːst] 1 adv por delante; **to fly —** pasar volando; **to rush —** pasar precipitadamente; **he went — without stopping** pasó sin detenerse; **she walked slowly —** pasó despacio.
  2 prep (a) (of place: in front of) por delante de; (beyond) más allá de; **just — the town hall** un poco más allá del Ayuntamiento; **to run — someone** pasar delante de uno corriendo; alcanzar y pasar a uno corriendo.
  (b) (with numbers) más de; **we're — 100 already** hemos contado más de 100 ya; **she's — 40** tiene más de 40 años.
  (c) (with time) después de; **10 — 3** las 3 y 10; **half — 4** las 4 y media; **at a quarter — 9** a las 9 y cuarto; **it's — 12** dieron las 12 ya.
  (d) (other expressions) **it is — belief** es increíble; **it is — endurance** es intolerable; **we're — caring** eso ya nos trae sin cuidado, ya no tenemos por qué preocuparnos de eso; **he's — it** ya no puede, ya no tiene fuerzas para eso; **I wouldn't put it — him** le creo capaz hasta de eso.
  3 adj pasado (also Gram); (former) antiguo, ex..., que fue; master etc consumado; **for some time —** de algún tiempo a esta parte; **in times —** en otro tiempo, antiguamente; **all that is now —** todo eso ha quedado ya a la espalda; **in — years** en otros años, en estos últimos años; **— president of...** antiguo presidente de..., ex presidente de..., presidente que fue de...
  4 n el pasado (also Gram), lo pasado; (early history) historia f, antecedentes mpl; **in the —** en el pasado, antes, antiguamente; **as we did in the —** como hacíamos antes; **it's a thing of the —** eso pertenece a la historia; **silent pictures are things of the —** las películas mudas han quedado anticuadas; **that belongs to my murky —** eso pertenece a mi turbio pasado; **what's his —?** ¿cuáles son sus antecedentes?; **a town with a —** una ciudad de abolengo histórico, una ciudad llena de historia; **she's a woman with a —** es una mujer que tiene historia.
paste [peist] 1 n (material in general) pasta f; (for sticking) engrudo m; (fish-) pasta f; (gems) diamante m de imitación, bisutería f.
  2 vt (apply — to) engrudar; engomar; (affix, stick together) pegar; (beat: sl) pegar, (Sport) cascar, dar una paliza a; **to — something to a wall** pegar algo a una pared; **to — up a notice** pegar un anuncio.
pasteboard ['peistbɔːd] 1 n cartón m, cartulina f. 2 attr de cartón, de cartulina.
pastel ['pæstəl] 1 n (material) pastel m; (drawing etc) pintura f al pastel. 2 attr: **— drawing** pintura f al pastel; **— shade** tono m pastel.
pastern ['pæstəːn] n cuartilla f (del caballo).
pasteurization [ˌpæstərai'zeiʃən] n pasteurización f.
pasteurize ['pæstəraiz] vt pasteurizar.
pasteurized ['pæstəraizd] adj pasteurizado.
pastiche [pæs'tiːʃ] n imitación f; **a Mozart —** una imitación de Mozart, una obra hecha a la manera de Mozart.
pastille ['pæstil] n pastilla f.
pastime ['pɑːstaim] n pasatiempo m.
pasting ['peistiŋ] n (sl) paliza f; **to give someone a —** dar una paliza a uno; **he got a — from the critics** los críticos le dieron una paliza.
pastor ['pɑːstə*] n pastor m.
pastoral ['pɑːstərəl] 1 adj economy pastoral; (Eccl) pastoral; (Lit) pastoril. 2 n (Eccl) pastoral f.
pastry ['peistri] n (dough) pasta f; (collectively) pastas fpl, pasteles mpl; (art) pastelería f; **pastries** pastas fpl, pasteles mpl.
pastrycook ['peistrikuk] n pastelero m, a f, repostero m, a f.
pastry shop ['peistriʃɔp] n pastelería f, repostería f.
pasturage ['pɑːstjuridʒ] n see **pasture 1**.
pasture ['pɑːstʃə*] 1 n (grass) pasto m; (land) pasto m, prado m, dehesa f. 2 vt animals apacentar, pastorear; grass comer, pacer. 3 vi pastar, pacer.
pasture land ['pɑːstʃələænd] n pasto m, prado m, dehesa f.
pasty ['peisti] adj material pastoso; colour pálido; **to look —** estar pálido.
pasty ['pæsti] n pastel m (de carne), empanada f.
pasty-faced ['peisti.feist] adj pálido, de cara pálida.
Pat [pæt] nombre cariñoso de **Patricia, Patrick**.
pat[1] [pæt] 1 n (with hand) palmadita f, golpecito m; (on shoulder) palmada f; (caress) caricia f; (of butter) pastelillo m; **to give someone a — on the back** dar a uno una palmada en la espalda, (fig) pronunciar unas palabras elogiosas para uno, felicitar a uno; **to give oneself a — on the back** felicitarse a sí mismo.
  2 vt (touch) tocar, pasar la mano por, posar la mano sobre; (tap, with hand) dar una palmadita en, shoulder dar una palmada en; dog etc acariciar; **he —ted the chair with the book** tocó la silla con el libro; **he —ted his secretary's bottom** le dio un azotito a su secretaria; **to — someone on the back** dar a uno una palmada en la espalda, (fig) pronunciar unas palabras elogiosas para uno, felicitar a uno.
  3 vr: **to — oneself on the back** (fig) felicitarse a sí mismo.
pat[2] [pæt] 1 adv: **he knows it (off) —** lo sabe al dedillo; **he always has an excuse just —** siempre le es fácil encontrar un modo convincente de disculparse; **the answer came too —** dio su respuesta con demasiada prontitud; **to stand —** mantenerse firme.
  2 adj answer etc oportuno, a propósito; pronto; convincente.
patch [pætʃ] 1 n (piece of cloth etc) pedazo m; (mend) remiendo m; (on tyre, wound) parche m; (beauty spot) lunar m postizo; (stain etc) mancha f; (small area) pedazo m, pequeña extensión f; (Agr) terreno m, parcela f; **a — of oil** una mancha de aceite; **a — of blue flowers** una masa de flores azules, una extensión de flores azules; **a — of blue sky** un pedazo de cielo azul; **purple —** trozo m de estilo hinchado, pasaje m demasiado sentimental; **the team is having a bad —** el equipo pasa por un momento difícil; **we have had our bad —es** hemos tenido nuestros momentos malos; **then we hit a bad — of road** dimos luego con un tramo de carretera bastante malo; **it's not a — on the other one** no se puede comparar con el otro, no está a la altura del otro.
  2 vt remendar, poner remiendo a; **to — something up** componer algo de modo provisional; **we'll see if we can — something up for you** trataremos de arreglarlo para Vd; **to — up a quarrel** hacer las paces (with con).
patchwork ['pætʃwəːk] n labor f de retazos; **— quilt** centón m; **a — of fields** una confusa multitud de campos.
patchy ['pætʃi] adj desigual, poco uniforme; pattern etc manchado.
pate [peit] n mollera f.

pâté ['pɑːteɪ] n pastel m (de carne etc); **— de foie gras** pastelillo m de hígado de ganso.

patella [pə'telə] n rótula f.

paten ['pætən] n patena f.

patent ['peitənt] **1** adj patente, evidente, palmario; (Comm) de patente, patentado; see **leather** etc.

  2 n patente f; **— applied for** se ha solicitado patente; **to take out a —** obtener una patente.

  3 attr de patentes; **— agent** agente m de patentes; **— office** oficina f de patentes.

  4 vt patentar.

patentee [,peitən'tiː] n poseedor m de patente.

patently ['peitəntli] adv evidentemente, a las claras; **a — untrue statement** una declaración de evidente falsedad.

pater ['peitə*] n: **the —** (fam) el páter.

paterfamilias ['peitəfə'miliæs] n padre m de familia.

paternal [pə'təːnl] adj quality paternal; relation paterno.

paternalism [pə'təːnəlizəm] n gobierno m paternal.

paternally [pə'təːnəli] adv paternalmente; **he said —** dijo paternal.

paternity [pə'təːniti] n paternidad f.

paternoster ['pætə'nɔstə*] n padrenuestro m.

path [pɑːθ] n, pl **paths** [pɑːðz] senda f, sendero m, vereda f; (fig) camino m; trayectoria f, curso m; (person's track) pista f; (of bullet) trayectoria f; (of hurricane etc) rastro m, marcha f; **the — to power** el camino del poder; **the beaten —** el camino trillado; **to cross someone's —** tropezar con uno; crear dificultades a uno; **to keep to the straight and narrow —** ir por la vereda, no apartarse del buen camino; **to lead someone up the garden —** embaucar a uno, hacer que uno se crea ilusiones; **to smoothe someone's — for him** allanarle el camino a uno.

pathetic [pə'θetik] adj (a) patético, lastimoso, conmovedor; **a — sight** una escena lastimosa; **a — creature** un infeliz, un pobre hombre; **it was — to see it** daba pena verlo.

  (b) (very bad) horrible, malísimo; **—, isn't it?** ¿es horrible, no?; **it was a — performance** fue una exhibición que daba pena.

pathetically [pə'θetikli] adv patéticamente, lastimosamente; **a — inadequate answer** una respuesta tan poco satisfactoria que daba pena.

pathfinder ['pɑːθ,faində*] n explorador m, piloto m.

pathological [,pæθə'lɔdʒikəl] adj patológico.

pathologist [pə'θɔlədʒist] n patólogo m.

pathology [pə'θɔlədʒi] n patología f.

pathos ['peiθɔs] n patetismo m, lo patético.

pathway ['pɑːθwei] n see **path**.

patience ['peiʃəns] n paciencia f; (Cards) solitario m; **my — is exhausted** se me acaba la paciencia, no tengo más paciencia; **you must have — hay que tener paciencia; I have no — with you** ya no aguanto más, estoy para desesperarme; **to lose one's —** perder la paciencia; **to possess one's soul in —** tener muchísima paciencia; **she taxes (or tries) my — very much** me cuesta no impacientarme con ella.

patient ['peiʃənt] **1** adj paciente; sufrido; **to be — with someone** ser paciente con uno; **you must be very — about it** hay que tener mucha paciencia; **we have been — long enough!** ¡ya no aguantamos más!

  2 n paciente mf, enfermo m, a f.

patiently ['peiʃəntli] adv pacientemente, con paciencia.

patina ['pætinə] n pátina f.

patio ['pætiəu] n patio m.

patois ['pætwɑː] n dialecto m.

patriarch ['peitriɑːk] n patriarca m.

patriarchal [,peitri'ɑːkəl] adj patriarcal.

patriarchy ['peitriɑːki] n patriarcado m.

Patricia [pə'triʃə] f Patricia.

patrician [pə'triʃən] **1** adj patricio. **2** n patricio m, a f.

Patrick ['pætrik] m Patricio.

patrimony ['pætriməni] n patrimonio m.

patriot ['peitriət] n patriota mf.

patriotic [,pætri'ɔtik] adj patriótico.

patriotically [,pætri'ɔtikəli] adv patrióticamente.

patriotism ['pætriətizəm] n patriotismo m.

patrol [pə'trəul] **1** n patrulla f; **to be on —** estar de patrulla, patrullar.

  2 vt (a) patrullar por; frontier etc guardar, defender; **they —ed the streets at night** patrullaban por las calles de noche; **the frontier is not —led** la frontera no tiene patrullas.

  (b) (fig) rondar, pasearse por.

  3 vi (a) patrullar.

  (b) (fig) rondar, pasearse; **he —s up and down** se pasea de un lado a otro.

patrol boat [pə'trəulbəut] n patrullero m; bote m patrullero.

patrol car [pə'trəulkɑː*] n coche m patrulla.

patrol leader [pə'trəul,liːdə*] n jefe m de patrulla.

patrolman [pə'trəulmən] n, pl **—men** [mən] (US) guardia m, policía m.

patron ['peitrən] n (Comm) parroquiano m, a f, cliente mf; (of enterprise) patrocinador m; (Lit, Art) mecenas m; (Eccl, also **— saint**) patrono m, patrona f.

patronage ['pætrənidʒ] n (of enterprise) patrocinio m; (Lit, Art) mecenazgo m, protección f; (Eccl) patronato m; **under the — of** bajo el patronato de, patrocinado por, bajo los auspicios de.

patronize ['pætrənaiz] vt shop ser parroquiano de, comprar cosas en; services etc usar, utilizar; enterprise patrocinar, favorecer, fomentar, apoyar; (treat condescendingly) tratar con aire protector; **the shop is well —d** la tienda tiene mucha parroquia, la tienda está muy acreditada.

patronizing ['pætrənaiziŋ] adj protector.

patronizingly ['pætrənaiziŋli] adv protectoramente, con aire protector.

patronymic [,pætrə'nimik] **1** adj patronímico. **2** n patronímico m.

patten ['pætn] n zueco m, chanclo m.

patter[1] ['pætə*] **1** n (jargon) jerga f; (of salesman) jerga f publicitaria; (rapid speech) parloteo m; **the fellow has some very clever —** el tío tiene unos argumentos muy hábiles, hablando el tío es muy listo.

  2 vi charlar, parlotear (also **to — on**; about de).

patter[2] ['pætə*] **1** n (of feet) pasos mpl ligeros, ruido m sordo; (taps) golpecitos mpl; golpeteo m; (of rain) tamborileo m.

  2 vi andar con pasos ligeros, pisar con ruido sordo (also **to — about**); (rain) tamborilear; **he —ed over to the door** fue con pasos ligeros a la puerta.

pattern ['pætən] **1** n modelo m; (sample) muestra f; (design) diseño m, dibujo m; (Sew) patrón m; (fig) pauta f, norma f; **on the — of** sobre el modelo de, según el diseño de; **it set a — for other conferences** estableció una pauta para otros congresos; **it is following the usual —** se está desarrollando como siempre, sigue la norma.

  2 vt modelar (on sobre), diseñar (on según).

pattern book ['pætənbuk] n libro m de muestras.

pattern maker ['pætən,meikə*] n carpintero m modelista.

patty ['pæti] n empanada f.

paucity ['pɔːsiti] n escasez f, insuficiencia f, corto número m; **there is a — of money** hay poco dinero; **because of the — of new films** debido a la escasez de películas nuevas.

Paul [pɔːl] m Pablo; (Saint) Pablo; (Pope) Paulo.

Pauline ['pɔːlain] adj: **the — Epistles** las Epístolas de San Pablo.

Pauline ['pɔːliːn] f Paulina.

paunch [pɔːntʃ] **1** n panza f, barriga f. **2** vt rabbit etc destripar.

paunchy ['pɔːntʃi] adj panzudo, barrigudo.

pauper ['pɔːpə*] n pobre mf.

pauperism ['pɔːpərizəm] n pauperismo m.

pauperization [,pɔːpərai'zeiʃən] n empobrecimiento m.

pauperize ['pɔːpəraiz] vt empobrecer, reducir a la miseria.

pause [pɔːz] **1** n pausa f (also Mus); intervalo m; interrupción f; silencio m; **there was a — while . . .** hubo un silencio mientras . . .; **we carried on without — continuamos** sin interrupción, seguíamos trabajando (etc) sin descansar; **to give someone — dar** que pensar a uno, hacer vacilar a uno.

  2 vi hacer una pausa; (speaker etc) detenerse (brevemente), callarse (momentáneamente), interrumpirse; **— before you act** reflexione antes de obrar; **he —d for breath** se calló para cobrar aliento; **he spoke for 30 minutes without once pausing** habló durante 30 minutos sin interrumpirse una sola vez; **let's — here** detengámonos aquí un rato; **it made him —** le hizo vacilar.

pave [peiv] vt pavimentar; (with flags) enlosar; (with stones) empedrar; (with bricks) enladrillar; **to — the way** preparar el terreno (for a).

paved [peivd] adj pavimentado; enlosado; empedrado; enladrillado; (US) road asfaltado, afirmado.

pavement ['peivmənt] n pavimento m; (sidewalk) acera f; (US) calzada f, camino m asfaltado; **brick — enladrillado m; stone —** empedrado m, **to leave the — (US Aut)** salir de la calzada.

pavement artist ['peivmənt,ɑːtist] n pintor m callejero.

pavilion [pə'viliən] n pabellón m; (for band etc) quiosco m; (Sport) caseta f, vestuario m.

paving ['peiviŋ] n pavimento m, pavimentación f, enlosado m, adoquinado m, enladrillado m.

paving stone ['peiviŋstəun] n losa f.

paw [pɔː] **1** n (of animal) pata f; (of cat) garra f; (of lion) zarpa f; (large hand) manaza f, manota f.

2 vt tocar con la pata; (lion) dar zarpazos a; (person: touch) tocar, manosear, (amorously) sobar, palpar; **to — the ground** piafar; **stop —ing me!** ¡fuera las manos!, ¡manos quietas!

3 vi: **to — at something** tocar algo con la pata, (to wound) dar zarpazos a algo.

pawky ['pɔːki] adj desgarbado.

pawl [pɔːl] n trinquete m.

pawn[1] [pɔːn] n (Chess) peón m; (fig) instrumento m.

pawn[2] [pɔːn] **1** n: **in —** en prenda; **to leave** (or **put**) **something in —** dejar algo en prenda; **the country is in — to foreigners** el país está en manos de extranjeros, el país está a merced de extranjeros.

2 vt empeñar, pignorar, dejar en prenda.

pawnbroker ['pɔːnbrəukə*] n prestamista m, prendero m; **—'s (shop)** casa f de empeños, prendería f, monte m de piedad.

pawnshop ['pɔːnʃɔp] n casa f de empeños, prendería f, monte m de piedad.

pawn ticket ['pɔːn,tikit] n papeleta f de empeño.

pax [pæks] n: **—!** ¡me rindo!

pay [pei] **1** n paga f; remuneración f, retribución f; (of professional man) sueldo m; (of worker) salario m, sueldo m; (of day labourer) jornal m; **equal —** igualdad f de retribución (para hombres y mujeres); **extra —** sobresueldo m; **retirement —** jubilación f, (Mil) retiro m; **to be in someone's —** ser asalariado de uno, estar al servicio de uno; **agents in the enemy's —** agentes mpl al servicio del enemigo; **to draw** (or **get**) **one's —** cobrar; **the —'s not very good** el sueldo no es muy bueno, no pagan muy bien; **it comes out of my —** se descuenta de mi sueldo; **to stop £1 out of someone's —** retener una libra del sueldo de uno; **we'll stop it out of your —** lo descontaremos de su sueldo; see **holiday** etc.

2 (irr: pret and ptp **paid**) vt (a) pagar; **to — someone £10** pagar 10 libras a uno, entregar 10 libras a uno; **to — money into an account** ingresar dinero en una cuenta; **how much is there to —?** ¿cuánto hay que pagar?; **to be** (or **get**) **paid on Fridays** cobrar los viernes; **when do you get paid?** ¿cuándo cobras?; **to — cash (down)** pagar al contado; **shares that — 5%** acciones fpl que producen un 5 por 100 de interés; **the company paid 12% last year** el año pasado la sociedad declaró un dividendo de 12 por 100; **to — someone to do a job** pagar a uno para que haga un trabajo; **I — you to prevent such mistakes** yo le pago un sueldo con el deber de impedir tales errores; **a badly paid worker** un obrero mal retribuido; **a badly paid job** un empleo mal remunerado; see also **paid**.

(b) account, debt liquidar; satisfacer; bill, duty, fee pagar; **"paid"** (on receipted bill) "pagado".

(c) (be profitable to) ser provechoso a; **it wouldn't — him to do it** no le saldría a cuenta hacerlo, (fig) no le sería aconsejable hacerlo, no le valdría la pena hacerlo; **it doesn't — you to be kind nowadays** hoy día no vale la pena mostrarse amable; **but it paid him in the long run** pero a la larga le fue provechoso.

(d) attention prestar (to a); homage rendir (to a); respects ofrecer, presentar; visit hacer; see also **address** etc.

(e) (with adv or prep) **to — away** pagar, desembolsar; **to — back** money devolver, restituir; reintegrar; reembolsar; person pagar; **to — someone back (in his own coin)** pagar a uno en la misma moneda; **to — £200 down (as cash)** pagar 200 libras al contado, (as deposit) pagar un desembolso inicial de 200 libras; **to — for** pagar por; **he paid £4 for it** pagó 4 libras por él, lo compró por 4 libras; **what did you — for it?** ¿cuánto pagaste por él?; **it's a service that has to be paid for** es un servicio que no se da gratis; **to — in a cheque** ingresar un cheque; **to — in £5** ingresar 5 libras (en una cuenta); **to — off** debt etc liquidar, saldar; mortgage etc amortizar, redimir; old scores ajustar; workmen pagar y despedir; **to — out** money pagar, desembolsar; rope ir dando; **to — someone out** pagar a uno en la misma moneda; **I'll — you out for this!** ¡me las pagarás!; **to — over** pagar, entregar; **to — up** pagar (de mala gana).

3 vi (a) pagar; **who —s?** ¿quién paga?; **to — on account** pagar a cuenta; **to — in advance** pagar por adelantado; **to — in full** pagarlo todo, pagar la cantidad íntegra; **to — in instalments** pagar a plazos; **"please — at the door"** "por favor: paguen a la entrada".

(b) (be profitable) rendir, rendir bien, ser provechoso; **it's a business that —s** es un negocio que rinde; **it's —ing at last** por fin produce ganancias; **it —s to be courteous** vale la pena mostrarse cortés; **it doesn't — to paint it** vale más no pintarlo, es mejor no pintarlo; **it —s to advertise** compensa hacer publicidad.

(c) **to — for something** pagar algo; **he paid for it** lo pagó él, lo costeó él, corrió él con los gastos; **they made him — dearly for it** le hicieron pagar muy caro; **he paid for it up to the hilt** lo pagó todo hasta el último céntimo; **she paid for it with her life** lo pagó con la vida; **he paid for his rashness with his life** su temeridad le costó la vida; **they paid for her education** le pagaron los estudios; **I'll make you — for this!** ¡me las pagarás!; **he invites people out and —s for them** invita a la gente a acompañarle sin que tengan que pagar nada; **they paid for her to go** pagaron para que fuera ella.

(d) (with other advs or preps) **to — in** ingresar dinero; **he was —ing in for 20 years** llevaba 20 años pagando contribuciones; **the ruse paid off** la estratagema tuvo éxito; **it has paid off many times over** ha demostrado su valor muchísimas veces; **to — out on a policy** pagar una póliza; **to — up** pagar, pagar lo que se debe; soltar la mosca (fam).

payable ['peiəbl] adj pagadero; **— to bearer** pagadero al portador; **— on demand** pagadero a presentación; **— at sight** pagadero a vista; **to make a cheque — to someone** extender un cheque a favor de uno.

payday ['peidei] n día m de paga.

paydesk ['peidesk] n caja f.

paydirt ['peidəːt] n (US) grava f provechosa.

payee [pei'iː] n portador m, ora f, tenedor m, ora f; (on cheque) orden f, tomador m.

payer ['peiə*] n pagador m, ora f; **slow —, bad —** moroso m, a f.

paying ['peiiŋ] adj provechoso, que rinde bien; **it's a — proposition** es un negocio provechoso.

payload ['peiləud] n carga f útil.

paymaster ['peimaːstə*] n oficial m pagador.

payment ['peimənt] n pago m; remuneración f, retribución f; **— on account** pago m a cuenta; **advance —** anticipo m; **cash —** pago m al contado; **deferred —, — by instalments** pago m a plazos; **down —** (cash) pago m al contado, (deposit) desembolso m inicial; **monthly —** mensualidad f; **yearly —** anualidad f; **gross —** íntegro m; **net —** líquido m; **as — for, in — for** en pago de; **as — for your services** en concepto de sus servicios; **on — of £5** pagando 5 libras, mediante el pago de 5 libras; **without —** sin remuneración; **to make a —** efectuar un pago; **to present something for —** presentar algo al cobro; **to stop —s** (bank) suspender los pagos; **to stop — of a cheque** detener el cobro de un cheque.

payoff ['peiɔf] n (fam) momento m decisivo, coyuntura f crítica, colmo m.

pay office ['pei,ɔfis] n caja f, pagaduría f.

pay packet ['pei,pækit] n sobre m de paga.

pay pause ['peipɔːz] n congelación f de sueldos y salarios.

payroll ['peirəul] n nómina f; **he has 1000 people on his —** tiene una nómina de 1000 personas.

paysheet ['peiʃiːt] n nómina f.

pay station ['pei,steiʃən] n (US) teléfono m público.

pay-television ['pei'teli,viʒən] n televisión f pagada.

pea [piː] n guisante m; **sweet —** guisante m de olor; see **like**.

peace [piːs] n paz f; (peacefulness) paz f, tranquilidad f, sosiego m; **— of mind** tranquilidad f de ánimo; **the (King's) —** el orden público; **—!** ¡silencio!; **to be at —** estar en paz; **to hold one's —** guardar silencio, callarse; **to keep the —** mantener la paz; **to make —** hacer las paces (with con).

peaceable ['piːsəbl] adj pacífico.

peaceably ['piːsəbli] adv pacíficamente; en paz.

peaceful ['piːsful] adj (not warlike) pacífico; (quiet) tranquilo, sosegado; coexistence pacífico; **it's very — here** aquí todo está perfectamente tranquilo; **on a — June evening** una tarde tranquila de junio.

peacefully ['piːsfəli] adv pacíficamente, en paz; tranquilamente; **to die —** morirse tranquilamente.

peacefulness ['piːsfulnis] n tranquilidad f, sosiego m, calma f; (of nation) carácter m pacífico.

peace-keeping ['piːs,kiːpiŋ] **1** adj: **— operation** operación f pacificadora; **— force** fuerzas fpl de pacificación. **2** n pacificación f; mantenimiento m de la paz.

peace-loving ['piːs,lʌviŋ] *adj nation* amante de la paz.
peacemaker ['piːs,meikə*] *n* pacificador *m*, ora *f*;
(*between 2 sides*) árbitro *m*, conciliador *m*, ora *f*.
peace offensive ['piːsə,fensiv] *n* ofensiva *f* de paz.
peace offering ['piːs,ɔfəriŋ] *n* prenda *f* de paz, ramo
m de olivo; (*to gods*) sacrificio *m* propiciatorio.
peach¹ [piːtʃ] **1** *n* (a) (*fruit*) melocotón *m*; (*tree*)
melocotonero *m*.
(b) (*fam*) **she's a** — es un bombón, es una real
moza; **it's a** — es una monada; **a** — **of a girl** una
real moza; **a** — **of a dress** un vestido monísimo.
(c) (*colour*) color *m* de melocotón.
2 *adj* color melocotón.
peach² [piːtʃ] *vi* (*sl*) soplar (*on* contra).
peach tree ['piːtʃtriː] *n* melocotonero *m*.
peacock ['piːkɔk] *n* pavo *m* real, pavón *m*.
peagreen ['piːˈgriːn] *adj* verde claro.
peahen ['piːhen] *n* pava *f* real.
pea jacket ['piːˌdʒækit] *n* chaqueta *f* de marinero.
peak [piːk] **1** *n* (*point*) punta *f*; (*of mountain*) cumbre
f, cima *f*; (*mountain*) pico *m*; (*of cap*) visera *f*; (*fig*)
cumbre *f*; apogeo *m*, punto *m* más alto; **when the
empire was at its** — cuando el imperio estaba en su
apogeo; **when demand is at its** — cuando la
demanda alcanza su punto más alto; **he was at
the** — **of his fame** estaba en la cumbre de su fama.
2 *as adj*: — **hours** horas *fpl* punta; — **load** carga
f máxima; — **season** época *f* más popular del año,
época *f* de mayor afluencia turística (*etc*); — **traffic**
movimiento *m* máximo de tráfico.
peaked [piːkt] *adj cap* con visera.
peaky ['piːki] *adj* pálido, enfermizo; **to look** — tener
la cara pálida.
peal [piːl] **1** *n* (*sound of bells*) repique *m*, campanillazo
m, toque *m* de campanas; — **of bells** (*set*) juego *m* de
campanas; — **of laughter** carcajada *f*; — **of the
organ** sonido *m* del órgano; — **of thunder** trueno *m*.
2 *vt* repicar, tocar a vuelo.
3 *vi* (*bell*) repicar, tocar a vuelo; (*organ*) sonar.
peanut ['piːnʌt] *n* cacahuete *m*; **we're not playing
for** —**s** (*fam*) esto va en serio.
peanut butter ['piːnʌt'bʌtə*] *n* manteca *f* de
cacahuete.
peapod ['piːpɔd] *n* vaina *f* de guisante.
pear [peə*] *n* (*fruit*) pera *f*; (*tree*) peral *m*.
pearl [pəːl] **1** *n* perla *f* (*also fig*); (*mother-of-pearl*)
nácar *m*; **cultivated** — perla *f* cultivada; **imitation**
—**s** perlas *fpl* de imitación; **to cast** —**s before swine**
echar margaritas a los cerdos.
2 *attr necklace etc* de perla, de perlas; (*in colour*)
color de perla.
pearl barley ['pəːl'baːli] *n* cebada *f* perlada.
pearl fishery ['pəːl'fifəri] *n* pescaduría *f* de perlas.
pearl fishing ['pəːl'fifiŋ] *n* pesca *f* de perlas.
pearl grey ['pəːl'grei] *adj* gris perla.
pearl oyster ['pəːl'ɔistə*] *n* ostra *f* perlífera.
pearly ['pəːli] *adj* (*made of pearl*) de perla, de perlas;
(*in colour*) color de perla, perlino; nacarado.
pear-shaped ['peəfeipt] *adj* de forma de pera.
pear tree ['peətriː] *n* peral *m*.
peasant ['pezənt] **1** *n* campesino *m*, a *f*; labrador *m*,
ora *f* **2** *attr* campesino; rústico.
peasantry ['pezəntri] *n* campesinos *mpl*, gente *f* del
campo.
peashooter ['piːˌʃuːtə*] *n* cerbatana *f*.
pea soup ['piːˈsuːp] *n* puré *m* de guisantes.
pea souper ['piːˈsuːpə*] *n* (*fam*) puré *m* de guisantes,
niebla *f* muy densa.
peat [piːt] *n* turba *f*.
peat bog ['piːtbɔg] *n* turbera *f*.
peaty ['piːti] *adj* turboso.
pebble ['pebl] *n* guija *f*, guijarro *m*, china *f*; **he's not
the only** — **on the beach** no es el único en tener
pretensiones, no es el único pretendiente.
pebbly ['pebli] *adj* guijarroso.
pecan [pi'kæn] *n* pacana *f*.
peccadillo [,pekə'diləu] *n* falta *f* leve, pecadillo *m*.
peccary ['pekəri] *n* pecarí *m*.
peck¹ [pek] *n* medida de áridos* (= 9,087 *litros*); (*fig*)
montón *m*; **a** — **of troubles** la mar de disgustos.
peck² [pek] **1** *n* picotazo *m*; (*kiss*) beso *m* no muy
cariñoso, beso *m* dado de mala gana.
2 *vt* picotear; (*kiss*) besar con poco cariño, besar
de mala gana.
3 *vi* picotear; **to** — **at** (*of bird*) intentar picotear,
(*in eating*) comer melindrosamente.
pecker ['pekə*] *n* (*fam*): **to keep one's** — **up** no
dejarse desanimar; **keep your** — **up**! ¡ánimo!
pecking order ['pekiŋ'ɔːdə*] *n* (*Bio*) orden *m* en que
picotean las gallinas; (*fig*) orden *m* jerárquico
establecido por los miembros de un grupo (*al
recibir algo etc*).

peckish ['pekiʃ] *adj* (*fam*) hambriento, con hambre;
I'm —, **I feel** — me anda el gusanillo.
pectin ['pektin] *n* pectina *f*.
pectoral ['pektərəl] *adj* pectoral.
peculation [,pekju'leiʃən] *n* peculado *m*.
peculiar [pi'kjuːliə*] *adj* (a) (*belong exclusively*)
peculiar; (*typical*) propio, característico; (*marked*)
particular, especial; **an animal** — **to Africa** un
animal autóctono de África, un animal que existe
únicamente en África; **it is a phrase** — **to him** es
una frase propia de él; **the region has its** — **dialect**
la región tiene su dialecto especial.
(b) (*strange*) singular, extraño, raro; **a most** —
flavour un sabor muy extraño; **he's a** — **chap** es un
tío raro; **how very** —! ¡qué raro!; **it's really most** —
es realmente extraño.
peculiarity [pi,kjuli'æriti] *n* (a) peculiaridad *f*;
particularidad *f*; rasgo *m* característico; **it has the** —
that . . . tiene la particularidad de ser . . .; "**special
peculiarities**" (*on passport etc*) "señas *fpl* particulares".
(b) singularidad *f*, rareza *f*; extravagancia *f*,
manía *f*; **there is some** — **which I cannot quite
define** hay alguna rareza que no puedo precisar; **it's
a** — **he has** es una manía que tiene; **he has his
peculiarities** tiene sus manías.
peculiarly [pi'kjuːliəli] *adv* (a) particularmente,
especialmente; **a** — **difficult work** una obra particularmente difícil.
(b) extrañamente, de modo raro; **he has been
acting very** — se ha comportado de modo rarísimo.
pecuniary [pi'kjuːniəri] *adj* pecuniario.
pedagogic(al) [,pedə'gɔdʒik(əl)] *adj* pedagógico.
pedagogue ['pedəgɔg] *n* pedagogo *m*.
pedagogy ['pedəgɔgi] *n* pedagogía *f*.
pedal ['pedl] **1** *n* pedal *m* (*also Mus*); **loud** — **pedal**
m fuerte; **soft** — **pedal** *m* piano. **2** *vt* impulsar
pedaleando. **3** *vi* pedalear.
pedant ['pedənt] *n* pedante *m*.
pedantic [pi'dæntik] *adj person* pedante; *manner etc*
pedantesco.
pedantically [pi'dæntikəli] *adv* con pedantería,
pedantescamente.
pedantry ['pedəntri] *n* pedantería *f*.
peddle ['pedl] *vt* vender como buhonero, vender por
las casas, andar vendiendo de puerta en puerta;
(*fig: scandal etc*) contar, repetir, difundir.
peddler ['pedlə*] *n* (US) *see* **pedlar**.
pederast ['pedəræst] *n* pederasta *m*.
pederasty ['pedəræsti] *n* pederastia *f*.
pedestal ['pedistl] *n* pedestal *m*, basa *f*; **to put
someone on a** — poner a uno sobre un pedestal.
pedestal lamp ['pedistl,læmp] *n* lámpara *f* de pie.
pedestrian [pi'destriən] **1** *adj* pedestre. **2** *n* peatón *m*.
3 *attr* de peatones, para peatones; — **traffic** circulación *f* de peatones.
pedestrian crossing [pi'destriən'krɔsiŋ] *n* paso *m* de
peatones.
pedicure ['pedikjuə*] *n* pedicura *f*, quiropedia *f*.
pedigree ['pedigriː] **1** *n* (*lineage*) genealogía *f*, linaje
m; (*tree*) árbol *m* genealógico; (*document*) certificado
m de genealogía. **2** *attr* de raza, de casta, de pura
sangre; (*fig*) certificado, garantizado.
pediment ['pedimənt] *n* frontón *m*.
pedlar ['pedlə*] *n* vendedor *m* ambulante, buhonero
m.
pedometer [pi'dɔmitə*] *n* podómetro *m*.
pee [piː] *see* **piss**.
peek [piːk] **1** *n* mirada *f* rápida, mirada *f* furtiva; **to
take a** — **at** echar una mirada rápida (*or* furtiva) a.
2 *vi* mirar a hurtadillas; **to** — **at** echar una mirada
rápida (*or* furtiva) a.
peel [piːl] **1** *n* piel *f*; (*after removal*) pieles *fpl*, monda
f, peladuras *fpl*; (*fragment in cocktail etc*) corteza *f*;
candied — piel *f* almibarada.
2 *vt fruit etc* pelar, mondar, quitar la piel a; *bark*
descortezar; *layer of paper etc* quitar, quitar una
capa de; **to** — **off** *dress etc* quitarse rápidamente,
quitarse lisamente.
3 *vi* (*layer of paper etc*) quitarse, despegarse,
desprenderse; (*paint etc*) desconcharse; (*bark*) des-
cortezarse; **to** — **off** (*fam*) desnudarse rápidamente.
peelings ['piːliŋz] *npl* monda *f*, peladuras *fpl*.
peep¹ [piːp] **1** *n* (*of bird etc*) pío *m*; **there hasn't been a**
— **out of them** no han hecho comunicación alguna
con nosotros; **we can't get a** — **out of them** no les
podemos hacer contestar; **I don't want a single** —
out of you de esto no digas ni pío.
2 *vi* piar.
peep² [piːp] **1** *n* mirada *f* rápida, mirada *f* furtiva,
ojeada *f*; **at** — **of day** al amanecer; **to get a** — **at
something** lograr ver algo brevemente; **let's take**

a — vamos a verlo; **take a — at this** echa una ojeada a esto.

2 *vt* asomar; **she —ed her head out** asomó la cabeza.

3 *vi* **(a)** mirar rápidamente, mirar furtivamente; **to — at something** echar una mirada rápida (*or* furtiva) a algo; **to — from behind a tree** mirar a hurtadillas desde detrás de un árbol; **to — over a wall** mirar a hurtadillas por encima de una tapia, asomar cuidadosamente la cabeza por encima de una tapia para mirar; **to — through a window** atisbar a través de una ventana.

(b) to — out asomar; **the book is —ing out of his pocket** se deja ver el libro que no cabe enteramente en su bolsillo; **a head —ed out** se asomó una cabeza; **the sun —ed out from behind the clouds** apareció el sol detrás de las nubes, el sol empezó a dejarse ver.

peepers ['pi:pəz] *npl* (*sl*) ojos *mpl*.
peephole ['pi:phəul] *n* mirilla *f*, atisbadero *m*.
peep show ['pi:pʃəu] *n* (*fam*) vistas *fpl* sicalípticas, espectáculo *m* deshonesto.
peer[1] [pɪə*] *n* (*noble*) par *m*; (*equal*) igual *mf*, par *mf*; **— of the realm** par *m* del reino; **as a musician he has no —** como músico no tiene par.
peer[2] [pɪə*] *vi* **(a)** (*person*) mirar con ojos de miope; **to — at something** mirar algo de cerca, mirar algo con ojos de miope; **to — into a room** mirar para ver lo que hay dentro de un cuarto; **to — out of a window** asomarse curioso a una ventana; **to — over a wall** asomar cuidadosamente la cabeza por encima de una tapia para mirar.

(b) (*fig*) **two eyes —ed out** aparecieron dos ojos, se asomaron dos ojos.
peerage ['pɪərɪdʒ] *n* (*person*) nobleza *f*, aristocracia *f*; (*rank*) título *m* de nobleza, dignidad *f* de par; (*book*) guía *f* de la nobleza; **to get a —** recibir un título de nobleza; **so they gave him a —** así que le dieron un título de nobleza.
peeress ['pɪərɪs] *n* paresa *f*.
peerless ['pɪəlɪs] *adj* sin par, incomparable.
peeve [pi:v] *vt* (*fam*) enojar, irritar.
peeved [pi:vd] *adj* (*fam*): **to be —** estar negro, estar enojado, estar furioso; **to get —** ponerse negro, sulfurarse; ofenderse; **he got a bit —** se puso negro; se ofendió.
peevish ['pi:vɪʃ] *adj* malhumorado, displicente, picajoso; impaciente.
peevishly ['pi:vɪʃlɪ] *adv* malhumoradamente, con mal humor; impacientemente; **he said —** dijo malhumorado.
peevishness ['pi:vɪʃnɪs] *n* mal humor *m*, displicencia *f*; impaciencia *f*.
peewee ['pi:wi:] *see* **piss**.
peewit ['pi:wɪt] *n* avefría *f*.
peg [peg] **1** *n* clavija *f*, claveta *f*; (*Mus*) clavija *f*; (*in ground*) estaca *f*, estaquilla *f*; (*tent-*) estaca *f*; (*clothes-*) pinza *f*; (*for coat*) gancho *m*, colgadero *m*; (*in barrel*) estaquilla *f*; (*fig*) pretexto *m*; (*for argument etc*) punto *m* de apoyo, punto *m* de partida; **a — of whisky** un trago de whiskey; **to be a square — in a round hole** estar como pez fuera del agua, estar en un empleo (*or* ambiente *etc*) que no conviene a uno; **to take someone down a —** bajar los humos a uno.

2 *vt* **(a)** (*fix —s to*) enclavijar; **to — down** estaquillar, fijar con estacas, sujetar con estacas; **to — out** *area* señalar con estacas; *clothes* tender (con pinzas).

(b) to — prices fijar los precios, estabilizar los precios a su nivel actual.

3 *vi*: **to — away** machacar, batir el yunque; **to — away at something** persistir en algo, afanarse por lograr algo; **to — out** (*sl*) estirar la pata (*fam*).
Pegasus ['pegəsəs] Pegaso.
pegleg ['pegleg] *n* pata *f* de palo, pierna *f* artificial.
peignoir ['peɪnwɑ:*] *n* bata *f* (de señora), peinador *m*.
pejorative [pɪ'dʒɒrɪtɪv] *adj* peyorativo (*also Gram*), despectivo.
pekinese [,pi:ki'ni:z] *n* pequinés *m*, esa *f*.
Pekin(g) [pi:'kɪŋ] Pekín.
pelagic [pɪ'lædʒɪk] *adj* pelágico.
pelican ['pelɪkən] *n* pelícano *m*.
pellet ['pelɪt] *n* bolita *f*; (*pill etc*) píldora *f*; (*shot*) perdigón *m*.
pell-mell ['pel'mel] *adv* en tropel, atropelladamente.
pellucid [pe'lu:sɪd] *adj* diáfano, cristalino.
pelmet ['pelmɪt] *n* galería *f* (para cubrir la barra de las cortinas).
pelota [pɪ'ləutə] *n* pelota *f* (vasca).
pelota player [pɪ'ləutə,pleɪə*] *n* pelotari *m*.
pelt[1] [pelt] *n* (*skin*) pellejo *m*; (*fur*) piel *f*.
pelt[2] [pelt] **1** *vt* **(a)** (*throw*) tirar, arrojar (*at* a).

(b) to — someone with eggs tirar huevos a uno;

to — someone with stones apedrear a uno; **they —ed him with questions** le hicieron muchísimas preguntas.

2 *vi* **(a)** (*of rain*) llover a cántaros (*also* **to — with rain**); **it was —ing down** llovía de verdad, diluviaba.

(b) (*fam*) ir a máxima velocidad; **to go —ing past** pasar como un rayo; **to go —ing off** partir como un rayo.

3 *n*: **to go full —** ir a todo correr, ir a máxima velocidad.
pelvic ['pelvɪk] *adj* pélvico.
pelvis ['pelvɪs] *n* pelvis *f*.
pen[1] [pen] **1** *n* (*enclosure*) corral *m*; (*sheep-*) redil *m*, aprisco *m*; (*bull-*) toril *m*; (*play-*) parque *m* de niño; (*US fam*) cárcel *f*. **2** *vi* encerrar, acorralar.
pen[2] [pen] **1** *n* pluma *f*; (*fountain —*) estilográfica *f*, plumafuente *f* (*SAm*); **to put — to paper** escribir algo; **to wield a —** menear cálamo.

2 *vt* escribir; redactar, formular.
penal ['pi:nl] *adj* **(a)** *code, colony, etc* penal; *see* **servitude** *etc*. **(b)** *taxation etc* muy gravoso, perjudicial.
penalization [,pi:nəlaɪ'zeɪʃən] *n* castigo *m*.
penalize ['pi:nəlaɪz] *vt* penar; (*accidentally, unfairly*) perjudicar; (*Sport*) castigar, penalizar; **to be —d for a foul** ser castigado por una falta; **we are —d by not having a car** somos perjudicados por no tener coche; **the decision —s those who . . .** la decisión perjudica a los que. . . .
penalty ['penəltɪ] *n* pena *f*, castigo *m*; (*fine*) multa *f*; (*Sport*) castigo *m*, (*football etc*) penalty *m*, (*golf*) penalización *f*, (*Bridge*) multa *f*, castigo *m*; "**— £5**" "la infracción se castigará con una multa de 5 libras"; **on — of** so pena de; **the — for this is death** esto se castiga con la muerte; **to pay the —** sufrir el castigo (*for* de).
penalty area ['penəltɪ,ɛərɪə] *n* área *f* de castigo.
penalty kick ['penəltɪ,kɪk] *n* golpe *m* de castigo, penálty *m*.
penalty spot ['penəltɪ,spɒt] *n* punto *m* de ejecución del penálty.
penance ['penəns] *n* penitencia *f*; **to do —** hacer penitencia (*for* por).
pence [pens] *npl* of **penny**.
penchant [,pɑ̃:ŋʃɑ̃:ŋ] *n* predilección *f* (*for* por), inclinación *f* (*for* hacia); **to have a — for** tener predilección por.
pencil ['pensl] **1** *n* lápiz *m*; (*propelling —*) lapicero *m*; (*for eyebrows*) lápiz *m* de cejas; (*of light*) rayo *m* delgado. **2** *vt* escribir con lápiz (*also* **to — in**).
pencil box ['penslbɒks] *n* cajita de lápices.
pencil mark ['penslmɑ:k] *n* señal *f* hecha con lápiz.
pencil rubber ['pensl,rʌbə*] *n* goma *f* de borrar lápiz.
pencil sharpener ['pensl,ʃɑ:pnə*] *n* sacapuntas *m*.
pendant ['pendənt] *n* pendiente *m*, medallón *m*.
pending ['pendɪŋ] **1** *adj* pendiente; **to be —** estar pendiente, estar en trámite; **and other matters — y** otros asuntos todavía por resolver.

2 *prep*: **— the arrival of . . .** antes de la llegada de . . ., hasta la llegada de . . ., hasta que llegue. . . .
pendulous ['pendjuləs] *adj* colgante.
pendulum ['pendjuləm] *n* péndulo *m*.
penetrable ['penɪtrəbl] *adj* penetrable.
penetrate ['penɪtreɪt] *vt* penetrar (por).
penetrating ['penɪtreɪtɪŋ] *adj* penetrante (*also fig*); (*sound*) que taladra los oídos.
penetratingly ['penɪtreɪtɪŋlɪ] *adv* con penetración.
penetration [,penɪ'treɪʃən] *n* penetración *f* (*also fig*).
penetrative ['penɪtrətɪv] *adj* penetrante.
penfriend ['penfrend] *n* amigo *m* por correspondencia, amiga *f* por correspondencia.
penguin ['pengwɪn] *n* pingüino *m*.
penholder ['pen,həuldə*] *n* portaplumas *m*.
penicillin [,penɪ'sɪlɪn] *n* penicilina *f*.
peninsula [pɪ'nɪnsjulə] *n* península *f*; **Iberian P—** Península *f* Ibérica.
peninsular [pɪ'nɪnsjulə*] *adj* peninsular; **the P—War** la Guerra de Independencia.
penis ['pi:nɪs] *n* pene *m*.
penitence ['penɪtəns] *n* penitencia *f*, arrepentimiento *m*.
penitent ['penɪtənt] **1** *adj* penitente (*also Eccl*); arrepentido, compungido. **2** *n* penitente *mf*.
penitential [,penɪ'tenʃəl] *adj* penitencial.
penitentiary [,penɪ'tenʃərɪ] *n* cárcel *f*, presidio *m*.
penknife ['pennaɪf] *n*, *pl* **—knives** [naɪvz] navaja *f*.
penman ['penmən] *n*, *pl* **—men** [mən] pendolista *m*.
penmanship ['penmənʃɪp] *n* caligrafía *f*.
pen name ['pen'neɪm] *n* seudónimo *m*, nombre *m* artístico.
pennant ['penənt] *n* banderola *f*; (*Naut*) gallardete *m*.

pen nib ['pennib] *n* punta *f* (de pluma); plumilla *f*, plumín *m* (de estilográfica).

penniless ['penilis] *adj* pobre; sin dinero; **to be** — no tener un céntimo; **to be left** — quedar completamente sin dinero.

pennon ['penən] *n* pendón *m*.

Pennsylvania [,pensil'veiniə] Pensilvania *f*.

penny ['peni] *n*, *pl* **pennies** ['peniz] *or* **pence** [pens] penique *m*; (*US*) centavo *m*; (*Spanish equivalent*) perra *f*; **for two pence I'd** ... por menos de nada yo ...; **in for a** —, **in for a pound** preso por mil, preso por mil quinientos; **I'm not a** — **the wiser** lo entiendo menos que antes; **that must have cost a pretty** — esa habrá costado un dineral; **to earn an honest** — emplearse en un oficio honrado; **he hasn't a** — **to his name** no tiene donde caerse muerto; **take care of the pennies and the pounds will take care of themselves** toda economía es buena por pequeña que sea; **he turns up like a bad** — aparece una y otra vez como la falsa moneda.

penny-a-liner ['penia'lainə*] *n* escritorzuelo *m*.

penny dreadful ['peni'dredful] *n* tebeo *m* (*or* revista *f* juvenil) de bajísima calidad.

penny-in-the-slot machine ['peninðə'slɔtmə,ʃiːn] *n* máquina *f* tragaperras.

pennyweight ['peniweit] *n* peso *f* de 24 gramos.

pennyworth ['penəθ] *n* valor *m* de un penique, cantidad *f* que se compra con un penique; (*fig*) pizca *f*.

penologist [piː'nɔlədʒist] *n* penalista *mf*.

penology [piː'nɔlədʒi] *n* ciencia *f* penal.

penpusher ['pen,puʃə*] *n* (*Lit*) plumífero *m*; (*clerk*) empleadillo *m*, a *f*.

pension ['penʃən] **1** *n* pensión *f*; (*Mil*) retiro *m*; (*superannuation etc*) jubilación *f*; **old age** — subsidio *m* de vejez, pensión *f*; **retirement** — jubilación *f*; **to retire on a** — jubilarse.
  2 *vt* pensionar, dar una pensión a; **to** — **someone off** jubilar a uno.

pensioner ['penʃənə*] *n* pensionado *m*, a *f*, pensionista *mf*; (*Mil*) inválido *m*; **old age** — pensionista *mf*.

pension fund ['penʃənfʌnd] *n* caja *f* de jubilaciones.

pensive ['pensiv] *adj* pensativo, meditabundo; preocupado; triste.

pensively ['pensivli] *adv* pensativamente; tristemente; **he said** — dijo pensativo.

pent [pent] *adj see* **pent-up**.

pentagon ['pentəgən] *n* pentágono *m*; **the P**— (*Washington*) el Pentágono.

pentagonal [pen'tægənl] *adj* pentagonal.

pentameter [pen'tæmitə*] *n* pentámetro *m*; **iambic** — pentámetro *m* yámbico.

Pentateuch ['pentətjuːk] *n* Pentateuco *m*.

pentathlon [pen'tæθlən] *n* pentatlón *m*.

pentatonic [,pentə'tɔnik] *adj* pentatónico; — **scale** escala *f* pentatónica.

Pentecost ['pentikɔst] *n* Pentecostés *m*.

Pentecostal [,penti'kɔstl] *adj* de Pentecostés.

penthouse ['penthaus] *n*, *pl* —**houses** [,hauziz] cobertizo *m*; (*flat*) ático *m*, casa *f* de azotea.

pent-up ['pentʌp] *adj* (a) **to be** —, **to feel** — (*of person etc*) estar encerrado, sentirse como enjaulado. (b) *emotion etc* reprimido.

penult [pi'nʌlt] *n* (*Gram*) penúltima *f*.

penultimate [pi'nʌltimit] *adj* penúltimo.

penumbra [pi'nʌmbrə] *n* penumbra *f*.

penurious [pi'njuəriəs] *adj* miserable, pobrísimo.

penury ['penjuri] *n* (a) (*poverty*) miseria *f*, pobreza *f*; **to live in** — vivir en la miseria. (b) (*lack*) falta *f*, escasez *f* (*of* de).

penwiper ['pen,waipə*] *n* limpiaplumas *m*.

peon ['piːən] *n* peón *m*.

peonage ['piːənidʒ] *n* condición *f* de peón; estado *m* en que viven los peones; (*fig*) servidumbre *f*, esclavitud *f*.

peony ['piəni] *n* peonía *f*.

people ['piːpl] **1** *n* (a) (*Pol etc*) pueblo *m*; ciudadanos *mpl*; **the** — (*pej*), **the common** — el pueblo, la plebe; **the** — **at large** el pueblo en general; **a man of the** — un hombre del pueblo; **the king and his** — el rey y su pueblo, el rey y sus súbditos; **government by the** — gobierno *m* del pueblo.
  (b) (*race*) pueblo *m*, nación *f*; **English** — los ingleses; **the English** — el pueblo inglés; **the British** — la nación británica; **the Beaker P**— (*Hist*) la tribu de las copas, el pueblo de las copas.
  (c) (*parents*) padres *mpl*; (*relatives*) parientes *mpl*, familia *f*; **my** — mis padres, mi familia; **how are all your** —? ¿cómo están los de tu casa?, ¿cómo está tu familia?; **have you met his** —? ¿conoce Vd a sus padres?

(d) (*in general*) gente *f*; **country** — gente *f* del campo; **fashionable** — gente *f* elegante, gente *f* de buen tono; **the good** —, **the little** — las hadas; **old** — los viejos; **young** — los jóvenes, la juventud; **respectable** — gente *f* de bien; **top** — la gente bien; **what do you** — **think?** y ustedes, ¿ qué opinan?; **the place was full of** — el local estaba lleno de gente; **they're strange** — son gente rara; **I like the** — **here** aquí la gente es simpática, la gente de aquí me gusta.
  (e) (*inhabitants*) habitantes *mpl*; **the** — **of London** los habitantes de Londres, los londinenses; **Madrid has over 2 million** — Madrid tiene más de 2 millones de habitantes.
  (f) (*with numerals*) **20** — 20 personas; **many** — **think that** ... muchas personas creen que ..., son muchos los que creen que ...; **some** — algunos, algunas personas.
  (g) (*vague subject use*) — **say that** ... se dice que ..., la gente dice que ...; **here** — **quarrel a lot** aquí se riñe mucho; — **get worried** la gente se inquieta; **it's enough to worry** — basta para inquietar a la gente.
  2 *vt* poblar; **the country is** —**d by** ... el país está poblado por ..., el país está habitado por ...

pep [pep] (*sl*) **1** *n* empuje *m*, dinamismo *m*, impetu *m*, energía *f*. **2** *vt*: **to** — **up** estimular, animar, hacer más dinámico; *drink etc* fortalecer.

pepper ['pepə*] **1** *n* (*spice*) pimienta *f*; (*vegetable*) pimiento *m*; (-*plant*) pimentero *m*; **green** — pimiento *m*.
  2 *vt* (*spice*) sazonar con pimienta, añadir pimienta a; **to** — **a work with quotations** salpicar una obra de citas; **to** — **someone with shot** acribillar a uno a tiros.

pepper-and-salt ['pepərən'sɔːlt] *adj* **marking** mezclado de negro y blanco.

pepperbox ['pepəbɔks] *n* pimentero *m*.

peppercorn ['pepəkɔːn] *n* grano *m* de pimienta; — **rent** (*fig*) alquiler *m* nominal.

peppermint ['pepəmint] *n* (*plant, flavour*) menta *f*; (*sweet*) pastilla *f* de menta.

pepperpot ['pepəpɔt] *n* pimentero *m*.

peppery ['pepəri] *adj taste* picante; (*fig*) enojadizo, de malas pulgas.

pep pill ['peppil] *n* píldora *f* antifatiga.

pepsin ['pepsin] *n* pepsina *f*.

peptalk ['peptɔːk] *n* (*sl*) (*speech*) discurso *m* de tono edificante, (*chat*) charla *f* que procura levantar los ánimos.

peptic ['peptik] *adj* péptico.

peptone ['peptəun] *n* peptona *f*.

per [pəː*] *prep por*; (*with year etc*) a; **£20** — **annum** 20 libras al año; **£7** — **week** 7 libras a la semana; **10/-** — **dozen** 10 chelines la docena; **60 miles** — **hour** 60 millas por hora; **30 miles** — **gallon** 30 millas por galón (*in Spain, eg* 15 km por litro); — **cent** por ciento, por cien; **20** — **cent** 20 por cien; **it has increased by 8** — **cent** ha aumentado en un 8 por cien; **there is a 10** — **cent discount** hay un descuento de un 10 por cien; — **capita**, — **person** por persona; — **se** de por sí; **as** — **invoice** según factura; *see* **usual**.

perambulate [pə'ræmbjuleit] **1** *vt* recorrer (para inspeccionar). **2** *vi* pasearse, deambular.

perambulation [pə,ræmbju'leiʃən] *n* visita *f* de inspección; (*stroll*) paseo *m*; (*journey*) viaje *m*.

perambulator ['præmbjuleitə*] *n* cochecito *m* de niño.

perceive [pə'siːv] *vt* percibir; (*see*) notar, observar; (*understand*) comprender; (*realize*) darse cuenta de; **now I** — **that** ... ahora veo que ...; **do you** — **anything strange?** ¿notas algo raro?; **I do not** — **how it can be done** no comprendo cómo se puede hacer.

percentage [pə'sentidʒ] **1** *n* porcentaje *m*, tanto *m* por ciento; proporción *f*; (*rake-off*: *sl*) tajada *f*; (*commission*) comisión *f* porcentual; **the figure is expressed as a** — la cifra está expresada como un tanto por ciento; **a high** — **are girls** un elevado porcentaje son chicas; **to get a** — **on all sales** recibir un tanto por ciento sobre todas las ventas.
  2 *attr* porcentual; **on a** — **basis** según un sistema porcentual; — **sign** signo *m* del tanto por ciento.

perceptible [pə'septəbl] *adj* perceptible; sensible.

perceptibly [pə'septəbli] *adv* perceptiblemente; sensiblemente; **it has improved** — ha mejorado sensiblemente.

perception [pə'sepʃən] *adj* perspicaz; penetrante, agudo.

perceptive [pə'septiv] *adj* perspicaz; penetrante, agudo; *function* perceptivo.

perch[1] [pəːtʃ] *n* (*Fish*) perca *f*.

perch² [pɜːtʃ] **1** n **(a)** *medida de longitud* = 5,029 m.
(b) (*of bird*) percha f; (*fig*) posición f elevada; posición f peligrosa, posición f poco segura; **to knock someone off his** — destronar a uno, acabar con el dominio ejercido por uno.
2 vt colocar (en una posición elevada, poco segura *etc*); **he** —ed **his hat on his head** se puso el sombrero de modo no muy firme; **we** —ed **the child on the wall** pusimos al niño en lo alto de la tapia.
3 vi (*bird*) posarse (**on** en); (*person etc*) sentarse (en un sitio elevado, poco seguro *etc*); colocarse en una posición elevada; **we** —ed **in a tree to see the procession** nos subimos a un árbol para ver el desfile; **she** —ed **on the arm of my chair** se acomodó en el brazo de mi butaca.
perchance [pəˈtʃɑːns] adv (*lit*) por ventura, acaso.
percipient [pəˈsɪpɪənt] adj perspicaz; penetrante, agudo.
percolate [ˈpɜːkəleɪt] **1** vt filtrar, colar; (*fig*) filtrarse en, filtrarse por; *coffee* preparar.
2 vi **(a)** filtrarse, colarse; **to** — **down to** penetrar hasta; **to** — **through** penetrar por.
(b) (*coffee*) prepararse.
percolator [ˈpɜːkəleɪtə*] n cafetera f filtradora.
percussion [pəˈkʌʃən] **1** n percusión f. **2** attr *instrument etc* de percusión.
percussion cap [pəˈkʌʃən͵kæp] n cápsula f fulminante.
perdition [pəˈdɪʃən] perdición f.
peregrination [͵perɪɡrɪˈneɪʃən] n peregrinación f; —s (*hum*) vagabundeo m, periplo m.
peregrine [ˈperɪɡrɪn] n halcón m común, neblí m.
peremptorily [pəˈremptərɪlɪ] adv perentoriamente; imperiosamente, autoritariamente.
peremptory [pəˈremptərɪ] adj perentorio; *person* imperioso, autoritario.
perennial [pəˈrenɪəl] **1** adj perenne (*also Bot*); eterno, perpetuo; **it's a** — **complaint** es una queja constante. **2** n (*Bot*) perenne m, planta f vivaz.
perennially [pəˈrenɪəlɪ] adv perennemente; perpetuamente, constantemente.
perfect [ˈpɜːfɪkt] **1** adj perfecto (*also Gram*); **it's just** —! ¡qué maravilla!; **with** — **assurance** con la más completa confianza; **she's a** — **terror** es una bruja, es una arpía; **he's a** — **stranger to me** me es completamente desconocido; **his Spanish is far from** — su español dista mucho de ser perfecto.
2 n (*Gram*) perfecto m.
perfect [pəˈfekt] vt perfeccionar.
perfectibility [pə͵fektɪˈbɪlɪtɪ] n perfectibilidad f.
perfectible [pəˈfektəbl] adj perfectible.
perfection [pəˈfekʃən] n perfección f; **she does it to** — lo hace a la perfección, lo hace a las mil maravillas.
perfectionist [pəˈfekʃənɪst] n perfeccionista mf, persona f que lo quiere tener todo perfecto, persona f que cuida hasta los detalles más nimios.
perfectly [ˈpɜːfɪktlɪ] adv **(a)** perfectamente; **she does it** — lo hace perfectamente.
(b) it's — **marvellous** es de lo más maravilloso; **it's** — **ridiculous** es completamente absurdo; **we're** — **happy about it** estamos completamente contentos con esto.
perfidious [pəˈfɪdɪəs] adj pérfido.
perfidiously [pəˈfɪdɪəslɪ] adv pérfidamente.
perfidy [ˈpɜːfɪdɪ] n perfidia f.
perforate [ˈpɜːfəreɪt] vt perforar, horadar, agujerear; **to** — **holes in something** practicar agujeros en algo.
perforated [ˈpɜːfəreɪtɪd] adj *stamp* dentado.
perforation [͵pɜːfəˈreɪʃən] n perforación f; agujero m; (*of stamp*) trepado m.
perforce [pəˈfɔːs] adv (*lit*) forzosamente.
perform [pəˈfɔːm] **1** vt *task etc* hacer, cumplir, realizar; *duty* cumplir; *function* desempeñar; ejercer; (*Theat*) *play* representar, dar, poner, *part* interpretar, hacer; (*Mus*) ejecutar, interpretar.
2 vi (*Mus: play*) tocar, (*sing*) cantar, (*Theat*) representar, actuar, trabajar; hacer un papel, tener un papel; (*Mech etc*) funcionar, comportarse; (*trained animal*) hacer trucos; **to** — **on the violin** tocar el violín, interpretar una obra al violín; **how did he** —? ¿qué tal lo hizo?; **he** —ed **brilliantly as Hamlet** interpretó brillantemente el papel de Hamlet, en el papel de Hamlet se lució; **when we** —ed **in Seville** cuando dimos una representación en Sevilla; **I'm not** —**ing this time** esta vez no hago ningún papel, esta vez no tomo parte; **the car is not** —**ing properly** el coche no funciona bien; **how does the metal** — **under pressure?** ¿cómo se comporta el metal bajo presión?
performance [pəˈfɔːməns] n **(a)** (*of task etc*) cumplimiento m, ejecución f, realización f; (*of function*)

desempeño m; ejercicio m; acción f, actuación f; **in the** — **of his duties** en el ejercicio de su cargo.
(b) (*Theat: of play*) representación f, (*by actor, of a part*) actuación f, desempeño m; interpretación f; (*sitting: Theat*) función f, (*cinema*) sesión f; **"continuous** —" "sesión f continua"; **the late** —la función de la noche, la sesión de la noche; **"no** — **tonight"** "no hay representación esta noche"; **first** — estreno m; **we didn't like his** — **as Don Juan** no nos gustó su interpretación del papel de don Juan, su modo de entender el papel de don Juan no nos gustó; **he gave a splendid** — su actuación fue estupenda; **the play had 300** —s la obra tuvo 300 representaciones, la obra siguió en la cartelera durante 300 representaciones; **it has not had a** — **since 1950** no se ha representado desde 1950.
(c) (*Mus*) ejecución f; interpretación f; **a fine** — **of the Ninth Symphony** una magnífica interpretación de la Novena Sinfonía.
(d) (*Mech etc*) comportamiento m; funcionamiento m; (*by motor*) rendimiento m; (*of team in match*) actuación f, desempeño m; (*of car in race*) performance f; **the team gave a poor** — el equipo tuvo una actuación nada satisfactoria; **they eventually put up a good** — por fin estuvieron a su altura; **it's a series of cars with outstanding** —s es una serie de coches con unas performances notables; **what a** —! (*iro*) ¡qué lío!, ¡vaya lío que se han armado!
performer [pəˈfɔːmə*] n (*Theat*) actor m, actriz f; artista mf; (*Mus*) intérprete mf, ejecutante mf, músico m; **a skilled** — **on the piano** un pianista experto.
performing [pəˈfɔːmɪŋ] adj *animal* amaestrado, sabio.
perfume [ˈpɜːfjuːm] n perfume m.
perfume [pəˈfjuːm] vt perfumar.
perfumery [pəˈfjuːmərɪ] n (*perfumes*) perfumes mpl; (*factory*) perfumería f.
perfunctorily [pəˈfʌŋktərɪlɪ] adv superficialmente, someramente, a la ligera.
perfunctory [pəˈfʌŋktərɪ] adj superficial, somero, hecho (*etc*) a la ligera.
pergola [ˈpɜːɡələ] n pérgola f.
perhaps [pəˈhæps, præps] adv tal vez, quizá(s), puede que; — ¡quizá!; — **not** puede que no; — **so** quizá, quizá sea así; — **he did it** quizá lo hizo él; **he's in Segovia** puede que esté en Segovia; — **he'll come** quizá venga, puede que venga.
peril [ˈperɪl] n peligro m, riesgo m; **to be in** — estar en peligro; **to be in** — **of one's life** correr riesgo de perder la vida; **do it at your** — hágalo a su riesgo.
perilous [ˈperɪləs] adj peligroso, arriesgado; **it would be** — **to** + *infin* sería arriesgado + *infin*.
perilously [ˈperɪləslɪ] adv peligrosamente; **to come** — **close to . . .** acercarse de modo peligroso a . . ., (*fig*) rayar en . . . .
perimeter [pəˈrɪmɪtə*] n perímetro m.
period [ˈpɪərɪəd] **1** n período m; época f, edad f; (*time limit*) plazo m; (*Gram*) período m; (*full stop*) punto m; (*School*) hora f, clase f; (*Sport*) tiempo m; (*Med*), —s período m, reglas fpl; **at that** — en aquel entonces; **within a 3 month** — en 3 meses; **dentro de un plazo de 3 meses; this is a bad** — **for . . .** ésta es una mala época para . . .; **a painting of his early** — un cuadro de su primera época, un cuadro de su juventud; **the postwar** — la posguerra.
2 attr: **in** — **dress** en trajes de la época; — **furniture** muebles mpl de época, muebles mpl clásicos; — **piece** mueble m (*etc*) clásico.
periodic [͵pɪərɪˈɒdɪk] adj periódico.
periodical [͵pɪərɪˈɒdɪkəl] **1** adj periódico. **2** n revista f, publicación f periódica.
periodically [͵pɪərɪˈɒdɪkəlɪ] adv periódicamente; (*from time to time*) de vez en cuando, cada cierto tiempo.
periodicity [͵pɪərɪəˈdɪsɪtɪ] n periodicidad f.
peripatetic [͵perɪpəˈtetɪk] adj ambulante, que no tiene residencia fija; (*Philos*) peripatético; **to lead a** — **existence** cambiar mucho de domicilio, no tener residencia fija.
peripheral [pəˈrɪfərəl] adj periférico.
periphery [pəˈrɪfərɪ] n periferia f.
periphrasis [pəˈrɪfrəsɪs] n, pl **periphrases** [pəˈrɪfrəsiːz] perífrasis f.
periphrastic [͵perɪˈfræstɪk] adj perifrástico.
periscope [ˈperɪskəʊp] n periscopio m.
perish [ˈperɪʃ] **1** vt deteriorar, estropear, echar a perder; **to be** —ed (**with cold**) estar helado.
2 vi (*person*) *etc* perecer; (*material*) deteriorarse, estropearse, echarse a perder; **we shall do it or** — **in the attempt** lo conseguiremos o moriremos intentándolo; **he** —ed **at sea** murió en el mar; — **the thought!** ¡ni por pensamiento!

perishable ['periʃəbl] **1** *adj* perecedero; *fruit etc* que no se conserva bien, sujeto a putrefacción, corruptible. **2** —s *npl* mercancías *fpl* corruptibles, artículos *mpl* que no se conservan bien.

perisher ['periʃə*] *n* (*sl*) tío *m*; **little** — tunante *m*; **you little** —! ¡tunante!

perishing ['periʃiŋ] *adj* (*fam*): **it's** — (**cold**) hace un frío glacial; **I'm** — estoy helado.

peristyle ['peristail] *n* peristilo *m*.

peritoneum [,peritə'niːəm] *n* peritoneo *m*.

peritonitis [,peritə'naitis] *n* peritonitis *f*.

periwig ['periwig] *n* peluca *f*.

periwinkle ['peri,wiŋkl] *n* (*Bot*) vincapervinca *f*; (*Zool*) litorina *f*.

perjure ['pəːdʒə*] *vt*: **to** — **oneself** perjurar, perjurarse.

perjured ['pəːdʒed] *adj evidence* falso.

perjurer ['pəːdʒərə*] *n* perjuro *m*.

perjury ['pəːdʒəri] *n* perjurio *m*; **to commit** — jurar en falso, perjurar.

perk [pəːk] **1** *vt*: **to** — **someone up** reanimar a uno, infundir nuevo vigor a uno; **this will** — **you up**; ¡anímate con esto!, ¡esto servirá para reanimarte!; **to** — **one's ears up** aguzar las orejas; **to** — **one's head up** levantar la cabeza.
　　2 *vi*: **to** — **up** (*person*) reanimarse, cobrar ánimo; (*in health*) sentirse mejor; **business is** —**ing up** los negocios van mejor.

perkily ['pəːkili] *adv* alegremente; de modo despabilado; con frescura.

perkiness ['pəːkinis] *n* alegría *f*, buen humor *m*; despejo *m*; frescura *f*.

perks [pəːks] *npl* (*sl*) *see* **perquisite**.

perky ['pəːki] *adj* (*gay*) alegre, de excelente humor; (*wide-awake*) despabilado; (*pert*) fresco; **to feel** — estar alegre, estar de buen humor.

perm [pəːm] (*fam*) **1** *n* permanente *f*; **to have a** — hacerse una permanente. **2** *vt*: **to** — **someone's hair** hacer una permanente a una; **to have one's hair** —**ed** hacerse una permanente.

permanence ['pəːmənəns] *n* permanencia *f*.

permanency ['pəːmənənsi] *n* (*permanence*) permanencia *f*; (*permanent arrangement*) arreglo *m* permanente, cosa *f* fija; **the post is not a** — no es un puesto permanente; **I hope this is now a** — espero que esto sea un arreglo definitivo.

permanent ['pəːmənənt] *adj* permanente; estable, fijo; *finish on steel etc* inalterable; *wave* permanente; **I'm not** — **here** yo no ocupo aquí un puesto permanente; **we cannot make any** — **arrangements** no podemos arreglar las cosas de modo definitivo.

permanently ['pəːmənəntli] *adv* permanentemente; de modo estable, de modo definitivo; **we seem to be** — **stuck here** parece que nos vamos a quedar aquí para siempre; **he is** — **drunk** está borracho todo el tiempo.

permanganate [pəː'mæŋgənit] *n* permanganato *m*; — **of potash** permanganato *m* de potasio.

permeability [,pəːmiə'biliti] *n* permeabilidad *f*.

permeable ['pəːmiəbl] *adj* permeable.

permeate ['pəːmieit] *vt* penetrar; saturar, impregnar (*with* de); **to be** —**d with** estar impregnado de.

permissible [pə'misəbl] *adj* permisible, lícito; **it is not** — **to** + *infin* no se permite + *infin*; **would it be** — **to say that . . .?** ¿podemos decir que . . .?, ¿sería lícito decir que . . .?

permission [pə'miʃən] *n* permiso *m*; licencia *f*; autorización *f*; **with your** — con permiso de Vds; **without** — sin licencia; **"by kind** — **of Pérez Ltd"** "con permiso de la Cía. Pérez"; **to give someone** — **to** + *infin* autorizar a uno para que + *subj*; **no** — **is needed** no hay que pedir permiso; **to withhold one's** — negar su permiso.

permissive [pə'misiv] *adj* permisivo; (*optional*) facultativo, opcional; **modern society is very** — la sociedad moderna lo permite todo, la sociedad moderna no pone su veto a casi nada.

permit ['pəːmit] *n* permiso *m*, licencia *f*; (*allowing free entry etc*) pase *m*; **entry** — permiso *m* de entrada; **exit** — permiso *m* de salida; **export** — permiso *m* de exportación; **import** — permiso *m* de importación.

permit [pə'mit] **1** *vt* permitir; autorizar; tolerar; sufrir; **to** — **someone to do something** permitir a uno hacer algo; **is it** —**ted to smoke?** ¿se puede fumar?; **whoever** —**ted this was a fool** el que dio permiso para eso fue un tonto; **we could never** — **it to happen** no podríamos nunca tolerar eso; — **me!** ¡permítame ayudarle a Vd!
　　2 *vi* (**a**) permitir; **weather** —**ing** si el tiempo no lo impide.
　　　(**b**) **to** — **of** permitir; dar lugar a; posibilitar; **it** —**s of certain changes** nos permite hacer varios

cambios; **it does not** — **of doubt** no deja lugar a dudas.

permutation [,pəːmjuː'teiʃən] *n* permutación *f*.

permute [pə'mjuːt] *vt* permutar.

pernicious [pəː'niʃəs] *adj* pernicioso (*also Med*); nocivo, dañoso; peligroso; funesto; **the** — **custom of . . .** la funesta costumbre de . . .

pernickety [pə'nikiti] *adj* (*fam*) quisquilloso, remirado; **he's very** — **about clocks** tiene ideas raras sobre los relojes; **he's terribly** — **about punctuality** tiene la manía de la puntualidad.

peroration [,perə'reiʃən] *n* peroración *f*.

peroxide [pə'rɔksaid] *n* peróxido *m*; **hydrogen** — peróxido *m* de hidrógeno; — **blonde** rubia *f* de bote, rubia *f* de frasco.

perpendicular [,pəːpən'dikjulə*] **1** *adj* perpendicular. **2** *n* perpendicular *f*; **to be out of the** — salir de la perpendicular.

perpendicularly [,pəːpən'dikjuləli] *adv* perpendicularmente.

perpetrate ['pəːpitreit] *vt* cometer; (*Law*) perpetrar.

perpetration [,pəːpi'treiʃən] *n* comisión *f*; (*Law*) perpetración *f*.

perpetrator ['pəːpitreitə*] *n* autor *m*, ora *f*; responsable *mf*; (*Law*) perpetrador *m*, ora *f*.

perpetual [pə'petjuəl] *adj* perpetuo; incesante, constante, continuo; *motion etc* perpetuo, continuo; **these** — **complaints** este continuo quejarse.

perpetually [pə'petjuəli] *adv* perpetuamente; constantemente, continuamente; **we were** — **hungry** teníamos hambre siempre; **they complain** — se quejan constantemente.

perpetuate [pə'petjueit] *vt* perpetuar.

perpetuation [pə,petju'eiʃən] *n* perpetuación *f*.

perpetuity [,pəːpi'tjuːiti] *n* perpetuidad *f*; **in** — para siempre.

Perpignan ['pəːpiːnjɔ̃] Perpiñán.

perplex [pə'pleks] *vt* dejar perplejo, confundir.

perplexed [pə'plekst] *adj* perplejo; confuso; **to look** — parecer estar confuso.

perplexedly [pə'pleksidli] *adv* perplejamente.

perplexing [pə'pleksiŋ] *adj* confuso, que causa perplejidad; complicado; misterioso; **it's all very** — no entiendo nada; **it's a** — **situation** es una situación complicada, es una situación que deja a todos perplejos.

perplexity [pə'pleksiti] *n* perplejidad *f*, confusión *f*; **to be in some** — estar algo perplejo.

perquisite ['pəːkwizit] *n* gaje *m*; —**s** gajes *mpl*, (*tips*) propinas *fpl*; **a salary and** —**s** un sueldo y lo que cae, un sueldo y otras cosillas; **there are no** —**s in this job** en este empleo no hay nada aparte del sueldo.

perry ['peri] *n* sidra *f* de peras.

persecute ['pəːsikjuːt] *vt* perseguir; importunar, molestar, acosar; **is this man persecuting you?** ¿le molesta este hombre?; **under the Nazis they were** —**d** bajo los nazis se les persiguió, bajo los nazis sufrieron la persecución.

persecution [,pəːsi'kjuːʃən] *n* persecución *f*.

persecutor ['pəːsikjuːtə*] *n* perseguidor *m*, ora *f*.

perseverance [,pəːsi'viərəns] *n* perseverancia *f*.

persevere [,pəːsi'viə*] *vi* perseverar, persistir (*in* en); **to** — **with** continuar con, no abandonar.

persevering [,pəːsi'viəriŋ] *adj* perseverante.

perseveringly [,pəːsi'viəriŋli] *adv* con perseverancia, perseverantemente.

Persia ['pəːʃə] Persia *f*.

Persian ['pəːʃən] **1** *adj* persa; — **cat** gato *m* de Angora, gata *f* de Angora; — **lamb** (*animal*) oveja *f* caracul, (*skin*) caracul *m*. **2** *n* persa *mf*. **3** *n* (*language*) persa *m*.

Persian Gulf ['pəːʃən'gʌlf] Golfo *m* Pérsico.

persiflage [,pəːsi'flɑːʒ] *n* burlas *fpl*, zumba *f*.

persimmon [pəː'simən] *n* placaminero *m*.

persist [pə'sist] *vi* (**a**) persistir; continuar; **we must** — hay que persistir, tenemos que mantenernos firmes; **we shall** — **in our efforts to** + *infin* seguiremos esforzándonos por + *infin*; **it will** — **some time yet** durará todavía algún tiempo.
　　(**b**) (*insist*) porfiar, empeñarse, obstinarse; **if he** —**s** si se empeña en ello, si se obstina; **to** — **in doing something** empeñarse en hacer algo, obstinarse en hacer algo.

persistence [pə'sistəns] *n*, **persistency** [pə'sistənsi] *n* persistencia *f*; porfía *f*, empeño *m*; (*of disease etc*) pertinacia *f*; **as a reward for her** — en premio a sus esfuerzos.

persistent [pə'sistənt] *adj* persistente; continuo; porfiado; *disease etc* pertinaz; **he is most** — es muy porfiado, se porfía mucho; **despite our** — **warnings** a pesar de nuestras continuas advertencias.

persistently [pə'sistəntli] *adv* con persistencia, persistentemente; constantemente; **he — refuses to help** se niega constantemente a prestar su ayuda.

person ['pə:sn] *n* persona *f*; **private —** particular *m*; **in —** en persona; **in the — of** en la persona de; **he is neat in his —** es aseado en cuanto a su persona; **in the first —** (*Gram*) en primera persona; **per —** por persona; **murder by — or —s unknown** homicidio *m* por mano desconocida.

persona [pə:'səunə] *n*, *pl* **personae** [pə:'səunai] persona *f*; **— grata** persona *f* grata; **— non grata** persona *f* no grata.

personable ['pə:snəbl] *adj* bien parecido, atractivo.

personage ['pə:snidʒ] *n* personaje *m*.

personal ['pə:snl] **1** *adj* personal; (*private*) privado, íntimo, particular; (*for one's sole use*) de uso personal; *cleanliness etc* corporal; *liberty etc* individual; *appearance, interview* en persona; **call** (*Tel*) de persona a persona; **column** de anuncios personales, de anuncios por palabras; **to ask — questions** hacer preguntas sobre asuntos íntimos; **don't be —!** ¡Vd es un maleducado!; **to become —** pasar a hacer crítica personal, empezar a hacer referencias de tipo personal; **I have no — knowledge of it** no lo conozco directamente; **my — view is that . . .** yo creo para mí que . . .; **to make a — application for something** solicitar algo en persona.

2 *n* (*US fam*) nota *f* de sociedad.

personality [,pə:sə'næliti] *n* (*character*) personalidad *f*; (*person, figure*) personaje *m*; figura *f*; (*personal reference, insult*) personalismo *m*; **dual —** conciencia *f* doble; **split —** personalidad *f* desdoblada; **a well-known radio —** conocida figura *f* de la radio; **to indulge in personalities** hacer crítica personal, cambiar personalismos, hacer referencias de tipo personal.

personality cult [,pə:sə'nælitikʌlt] *n* culto *m* a la personalidad.

personally ['pə:snəli] *adv* **(a)** personalmente; **— I think that . . .** creo personalmente que . . ., yo creo para mí que . . .; **— I am willing, but others . . .** en cuanto a mí digo que sí, pero otros . . .; **don't take it too —** no vaya Vd a creer que lo digo contra Vd, no se vaya Vd a ofender de modo personal.

(b) to hand something over — entregar algo en persona; **the manager saw her —** el gerente habló con ella en persona.

personalty ['pə:snlti] *n* (*Law*) bienes *mpl* muebles.

personate ['pə:səneit] *vt* (*impersonate*) hacerse pasar por; (*Theat*) hacer el papel de.

personification [pə:,sɔnifi'keiʃən] *n* personificación *f*; **he is the — of good taste** es el buen gusto en persona, es el mismo buen gusto, tiene un gusto exquisito.

personify [pə:'sɔnifai] *vt* personificar; representar; **he personified the spirit of resistance** encarnó el espíritu de la resistencia; **he is greed personified** es la codicia en persona, es la misma codicia.

personnel [,pə:sə'nel] **1** *n* personal *m*. **2** *attr*: **— management** relaciones *fpl* humanas; **— manager,** **— officer** jefe *m* del personal.

perspective [pə'spektiv] *n* perspectiva *f*; **in —** en perspectiva; **let's get things in —** pongamos las cosas en su sitio; **to see things in their proper —** apreciar debidamente las cosas, apreciar las cosas en su justo valor.

Perspex ['pə:speks] (*Protected Trade Name*) *n* plexiglás *m*.

perspicacious [,pə:spi'keiʃəs] *adj* perspicaz.

perspicacity [,pə:spi'kæsiti] *n* perspicacia *f*.

perspicuous [,pə'spikjuəs] *adj* perspicuo.

perspicuity [,pə:spi'kju(:)iti] *n* perspicuidad *f*.

perspiration [,pə:spə'reiʃən] *n* transpiración *f*; sudor *m*; **beads of —** gotitas *fpl* de sudor; **to be bathed in —** estar bañado en sudor, estar todo sudoroso.

perspire [pəs'paiə*] *vi* transpirar, sudar; **to — freely** sudar mucho.

perspiring [pəs'paiəriŋ] *adj* sudoroso.

persuadable [pə'sweidəbl] *adj* influenciable, persuasible; **he may be —** quizá le podamos persuadir.

persuade [pə'sweid] *vt* persuadir; **to — someone to do something** persuadir a uno a hacer algo, inducir a uno a hacer algo; **but they —d me not to** pero ellos me disuadieron, pero ellos me persuadieron a dejarlo; **to — someone that something is true** convencer a uno de que algo es verdad; **I am —d that . . .** estoy convencido de que . . .; **to — someone of the truth of a theory** convencer a uno de que una teoría es verdadera; **she is easily —d** se deja convencer fácilmente; **it does not take much to — him** exige poco esfuerzo convencerle.

persuasion [pə'sweiʒən] *n* **(a)** (*act*) persuasión *f*. **(b)** (*persuasiveness*) persuasiva *f*; **he needed a lot of —** había que ejercer mucha persuasiva; **I don't need much — to stop working** me cuesta poco dejar el trabajo.

(c) (*creed*) creencia *f*, secta *f*; opinión *f*; **I am not of that —** no es ésa mi opinión, yo lo veo de otro modo; **the Methodist —** la secta metodista; **and others of that —** y otros que creen así.

persuasive [pə'sweisiv] *adj* persuasivo; **I had to be very —** tuve que ejercer mucha persuasión.

persuasively [pə'sweisivli] *adv* de modo persuasivo.

persuasiveness [pə'sweisivnis] *n* persuasiva *f*.

pert [pə:t] *adj* impertinente, respondón, fresco.

pertain [pə:'tein] *vi*: **to — to** (*concern*) tener que ver con, estar relacionado con; (*belong to*) pertenecer a; (*be the province of*) incumbir a; **and other matters —ing to it** y otros asuntos relacionados con eso.

pertinacious [,pə:ti'neiʃəs] *adj* pertinaz.

pertinaciously [,pə:ti'neiʃəsli] *adv* con pertinacia.

pertinacity [,pə:ti'næsiti] *n* pertinacia *f*.

pertinence ['pə:tinəns] *n* pertinencia *f*, oportunidad *f*.

pertinent ['pə:tinənt] *adj* pertinente, oportuno, a propósito; **not very —** poco oportuno, no muy a propósito.

pertinently ['pə:tinəntli] *adv* oportunamente, a propósito, atinadamente.

pertly ['pə:tli] *adv* de modo impertinente, descaradamente, con frescura.

pertness ['pə:tnis] *n* impertinencia, *f*, frescura *f*.

perturb [pə'tə:b] *vt* perturbar, inquietar; **we are all very —ed** todos estamos muy inquietos.

perturbation [,pə:tə:'beiʃən] *n* perturbación *f*, inquietud *f*; **she asked in some —** preguntó algo perturbada.

perturbing [pə'tə:biŋ] *adj* perturbador, inquietante.

Peru [pə'ru:] *n* el Perú.

perusal [pə'ru:zəl] *n* lectura *f* (cuidadosa), examen *m* (detenido).

peruse [pə'ru:z] *vt* leer (con atención), examinar (con detenimiento).

Peruvian [pə'ru:viən] **1** *adj* peruano. **2** *n* peruano *m*, a *f*.

pervade [pə:'veid] *vt* extenderse por, difundirse por, impregnar, saturar; **to be —d with** estar impregnado de, estar saturado de.

pervasive [pə:'veisiv] *adj* penetrante; omnipresente.

perverse [pə'və:s] *adj* (*wicked*) perverso; (*obstinate*) terco, contumaz; (*wayward*) travieso, díscolo.

perversely [pə'və:sli] *adv* perversamente; tercamente; traviesamente.

perverseness [pə'və:snis] *n* perversidad *f*; terquedad *f*, contumacia *f*; lo travieso.

perversion [pə'və:ʃən] *n* perversión *f* (*also Med*); **sexual —** perversión *f* sexual.

perversity [pə'və:siti] *n see* **perverseness**.

pervert ['pə:və:t] *n* (*Med*) pervertido *m*, a *f*.

pervert [pə'və:t] *vt* pervertir (*also Med*); *taste etc* estragar, estropear; *words* torcer, forzar; *talent* emplear mal.

pervious ['pə:viəs] *adj* permeable (*to* a).

peseta [pə'setə] *n* peseta *f*.

pesky ['peski] *adj* (*US fam*) molesto, fastidioso.

pessary ['pesəri] *n* pesario *m*.

pessimism ['pesimizəm] *n* pesimismo *m*.

pessimist ['pesimist] *n* pesimista *mf*.

pessimistic [,pesi'mistik] *adj* pesimista.

pessimistically [,pesi'mistikəli] *adv* con pesimismo.

pest [pest] *n* **(a)** (*Zool*) plaga *f*; insecto *m* nocivo, animal *m* dañino; **the moth is a — of pinewoods** la mariposa es una plaga de los pinares; **rabbits are a — in Australia** el conejo es muy dañino en Australia; **this will kill the —s on your roses** esto matará los insectos nocivos de sus rosas.

(b) (*fig: person*) machaca *f*, mosca *f*, pelma *m*; (*thing*) molestia *f*, lata *f*; **what a — that child is!** ¡cómo me fastidia ese niño!; **it's a — having to go** es una lata tener que ir.

pest control ['pestkən,trəul] *n* lucha *f* contra los insectos nocivos, lucha *f* contra las plagas.

pester ['pestə*] *vt* molestar, acosar, importunar; **he —s me no me deja a sol ni a sombra; is this man —ing you?** ¿le molesta este hombre?; **she —ed me for the book** me pidió el libro repetidas veces; **she —s me with questions** me molesta con sus preguntas, me fastidia haciendo tantas preguntas; **stop —ing!** ¡no machaques!; **to — someone to do something** insistir constantemente en que uno haga algo, rogar repetidas veces que uno haga algo.

pesticide ['pestisaid] *n* pesticida *m*.

pestilence ['pestiləns] *n* pestilencia *f*, peste *f*.

pestilent ['pestilənt] *adj* pestilente.

pestilential [ˌpestiˈlenʃəl] *adj* pestilente; *(fam)* engorroso, latoso.

pestle ['pesl] *n* mano *f* de mortero.

pet[1] [pet] **1** *adj* animal doméstico, domesticado, de casa, familiar; *(favourite)* favorito; *name etc* cariñoso; **a — lion** un león domesticado; **her two — dogs** sus dos perros de casa; **it's my — subject** es mi tema predilecto; *see* **aversion** *etc*.

2 (a) *(animal)* animal *m* doméstico, animal *m* de casa; perro *m*, gato *m* *(etc)*; **no —s are allowed in school** no se permite llevar animales a la escuela.

(b) *(person)* favorito *m*, a *f*; persona *f* querida; persona *f* muy mimada; **yes, my —** sí, mi cielo; **she's teacher's —** es la favorita de la maestra; **he's rather a —** es simpatiquísimo, es un ángel.

3 *vt* acariciar; *(amorously)* acariciar, tocar, sobar; *(spoil)* mimar.

4 *vi* acariciarse, besuquearse, sobarse, hacerse arrumacos; **—ting can go too far** las caricias pueden resultar peligrosas.

pet[2] [pet] *n*: **to be in a —** estar de mal humor, estar enojado.

petal ['petl] *n* pétalo *m*.

petard [pe'taːd] *n* petardo *m*; **he was hoist with his own —** le salió el tiro por la culata.

Pete [piːt] *m* Perico.

Peter ['piːtə*] *m* Pedro; **—'s pence** los diezmos de San Pedro; **to rob — to pay Paul** desnudar a un santo para vestir a otro; **the — the Great** Pedro el Grande.

peter ['piːtə*] *vi*: **to — out** *(supply)* agotarse, acabarse; *(vein of metal etc)* desaparecer; *(plan etc)* parar en nada, no dar resultado.

petite [pə'tiːt] *adj* chiquita.

petition [pə'tiʃən] **1** *n* petición *f*, memorial *m*; súplica *f*; **— for divorce** petición *f* de divorcio; **to file a —** presentar una petición.

2 *vt person* dirigir una instancia a; **to — for something** pedir algo, solicitar algo; **to — someone to do something** rogar a uno hacer algo, pedir que uno haga algo.

petitioner [pə'tiʃnə*] *n* suplicante *mf*.

Petrarch ['petraːk] *m* Petrarca.

Petrarchan [pe'traːkən] *adj* petrarquista.

Petrarchism ['petraːkizəm] *n* petrarquismo *m*.

petrel ['petrəl] *n* petrel *m*, paíño *m*.

petrifaction [ˌpetri'fækʃən] *n* petrificación *f*.

petrified ['petrifaid] *adj* petrificado; *see* **petrify**.

petrify ['petrifai] **1** *vt* (a) petrificar; **to become petrified** petrificarse.

(b) *(fig)* pasmar, horrorizar; **I was simply petrified!** ¡vaya susto que me pegué!; **to be petrified with fear** estar muerto de miedo.

2 *vi* petrificarse.

petrol ['petrəl] *n* gasolina *f*; *(for lighter)* bencina *f*; **to run out of —** quedarse sin gasolina.

petrol can ['petrəlkæn] *n* bidón *m* de gasolina.

petrol engine ['petrəl.endʒin] *n* motor *m* de gasolina.

petroleum [pi'trəuliəm] *n* petróleo *m*.

petrol gauge ['petrəlgeidʒ] *n* indicador *m* de nivel de gasolina.

petroliferous [ˌpetrə'lifərəs] *adj* petrolífero.

petrology [pe'trɔlidʒi] *n* petrología *f*.

petrol pump ['petrəlpʌmp] *n* *(in engine)* bomba *f* de gasolina; *(at garage)* surtidor *m* de gasolina.

petrol station ['petrəl.steiʃən] *n* estación *f* de gasolina, gasolinera *f*.

petrol tank ['petrəltæŋk] *n* depósito *m* de gasolina.

petticoat ['petikəut] **1** *n* enaguas *fpl*; *(slip)* combinación *f*; *(stiff)* falda *f* can-can.

2 *attr*: **— government** gobierno *m* de mujeres, dominación *f* de la mujer.

pettifogging ['petifɔgiŋ] *adj detail etc* insignificante, pequeño, nimio; *lawyer etc* pedante, charlatán; *suggestion etc* hecho para entenebrecer el asunto.

pettiness ['petinis] *n* (a) insignificancia *f*, pequeñez *f*; nimiedad *f*, frivolidad *f*.

(b) mezquindad *f*; estrechez *f* de miras; rencor *m*; manía *f* de criticar; intolerancia *f*.

pettish ['petiʃ] *adj* malhumorado.

petty ['peti] *adj* (a) *detail etc* insignificante, pequeño, nimio; de poca monta; *excuse* frívolo, baladí; **the — wars of the time** las pequeñas guerras de la época; **the — kings of Moslem Spain** los reyezuelos de la España musulmana; **some — chieftain** algún jefe sin importancia.

(b) *(small-minded)* mezquino; de miras estrechas; *(preoccupied with detail)* que se para en menudencias, que se interesa por los detalles nimios; *(spiteful)* rencoroso; *(faultfinding)* reparón, criticón; *(intolerant)* intolerante; **you're being very — about it** en esto te estás mostrando poco comprensivo, en

esto muestras que guardas rencor; *see* **cash, officer** *etc*.

petulance ['petjuləns] *n* mal humor *m*.

petulant ['petjulənt] *adj* malhumorado.

petulantly ['petjuləntli] *adv* malhumoradamente, con mal humor.

petunia [pi'tjuːniə] *n* petunia *f*.

pew [pjuː] *n* *(Eccl)* banco *m* (de iglesia, de los fieles); *(fam)* asiento *m*; **take a —!** ¡siéntate!; **can you find a —?** ¿puedes buscarte un asiento?

pewter ['pjuːtə*] **1** *n* peltre *m*. **2** *attr* de peltre.

phalange ['fælændʒ] *n* falange; **P— *(Spain)*** Falange *f*.

phalangist [fæ'lændʒist] **1** *adj* falangista. **2** *n* falangista *mf*.

phalanx ['fælæŋks] *n* falange *f*.

phalarope ['fælərəup] *n* falaropo *m*.

phallic ['fælik] *adj* fálico.

phallus ['fæləs] *n* falo *m*.

phantasm ['fæntæzəm] *n* fantasma *m*.

phantasmagoria [ˌfæntæzmə'gɔːriə] *n* fantasmagoría *f*.

phantasmagoric [ˌfæntæzmə'gɔrik] *adj* fantasmagórico.

phantasmal [fæn'tæzməl] *adj* fantasmal.

phantom ['fæntəm] **1** *n* fantasma *m*. **2** *adj* fantasmal; **the — ship** el buque fantasma.

Pharaoh ['feərəu] *m* Faraón.

Pharaonic [feə'rɔnik] *adj* faraónico.

Pharisaic(al) [ˌfæri'seiik(əl)] *adj* farisaico.

Pharisee ['færisiː] *n* fariseo *m*.

pharmaceutical [ˌfaːmə'sjuːtikəl] *adj* farmacéutico.

pharmacist ['faːməsist] *n* farmacéutico *m*.

pharmacological [ˌfaːməkə'lɔdʒikəl] *adj* farmacológico.

pharmacologist [ˌfaːmə'kɔlədʒist] *n* farmacólogo *m*.

pharmacology [ˌfaːmə'kɔlədʒi] *n* farmacología *f*.

pharmacopoeia [ˌfaːməkə'piːə] *n* farmacopea *f*.

pharmacy ['faːməsi] *n* farmacia *f*.

pharyngitis [ˌfærin'dʒaitis] *n* faringitis *f*.

pharynx ['færiŋks] *n* faringe *f*.

phase [feiz] **1** *n* fase *f* *(also Astron)*; etapa *f*; **to be out of —** estar fuera de fase.

2 *vt plan etc* proyectar en una serie de etapas; arreglar, organizar; **we must — this carefully** hay que organizar esto con cuidado; **a —d withdrawal** una retirada progresiva, una retirada por etapas.

pheasant ['feznt] *n* faisán *m*.

phenobarbitone ['fiːnəu'baːbitəun] *n* fenobarbitona *f*.

phenol ['fiːnɔl] *n* fenol *m*.

phenomenal [fi'nɔminl] *adj* fenomenal.

phenomenally [fi'nɔminəli] *adv* de modo fenomenal; **— rich** rico en un grado fenomenal.

phenomenon [fi'nɔminən] *n*, *pl* **phenomena** [fi'nɔminə] fenómeno *m*.

phew [fjuː] *interj* ¡puf!; ¡caramba!

phial ['faiəl] *n* ampolla *f*, redoma *f*, frasco *m*.

Philadelphia [ˌfilə'delfiə] Filadelfia.

philander [fi'lændə*] *vi* flirtear, mariposear *(with con)*.

philanderer [fi'lændərə*] *n* tenorio *m*, mariposón *m*.

philandering [fi'lændəriŋ] **1** *adj* mariposón. **2** *n* flirteo *m*.

philanthropic [ˌfilən'θrɔpik] *adj* filantrópico.

philanthropist [fi'lænθrəpist] *n* filántropo *m*, a *f*.

philanthropy [fi'lænθrəpi] *n* filantropía *f*.

philatelic [ˌfilə'telik] *adj* filatélico.

philatelist [fi'lætəlist] *n* filatelista *mf*.

philately [fi'lætəli] *n* filatelia *f*.

—phile [fail] **—filo**, *eg* **francophile** francófilo *m*, a *f*.

philharmonic [ˌfilaː'mɔnik] *adj* filarmónico.

Philip ['filip] *m* Felipe.

philippic [fi'lipik] *n* filípica *f*.

Philippine ['filipiːn] **1** *adj* filipino. **2** *n* filipino *m*, a *f*.

Philippines ['filipiːnz] *pl*, **Philippine Islands** ['filipiːn,ailəndz] *pl* Islas *fpl* Filipinas.

Philistine ['filistain] **1** *adj* filisteo. **2** *n* filisteo *m*, a *f*.

philistinism ['filistinizəm] *n* filisteísmo *m*.

philological [ˌfilə'lɔdʒikəl] *adj* filológico.

philologist [fi'lɔlədʒist] *n* filólogo *m*.

philology [fi'lɔlədʒi] *n* filología *f*.

philosopher [fi'lɔsəfə*] *n* filósofo *m*.

philosophic(al) [ˌfilə'sɔfik(əl)] *adj* filosófico.

philosophize [fi'lɔsəfaiz] *vi* filosofar.

philosophy [fi'lɔsəfi] *n* filosofía *f*; **— of life** filosofía *f* de la vida; **moral —** filosofía *f* moral; **natural —** filosofía *f* natural.

philtre, *(US)* **philter** ['filtə*] *n* filtro *m*.

phiz [fiz] *n* *(fam)* jeta *f*.

phlebitis [fli'baitis] *n* flebitis *f*.

phlegm [flem] *n* flema *f* *(also fig)*.

phlegmatic [fleg'mætik] *adj* flemático.
phlegmatically [fleg'mætikəli] *adv* con flema; **he said** — dijo flemático.
phlox [floks] *n* flox *m*.
—phobe [fəub] —fobo, *eg* **francophobe** francófobo *m*, a *f*.
phobia ['fəubiə] *n* fobia *f*.
—phobia ['fəubiə] —fobia, *eg* **anglophobia** anglofobia *f*.
Phoebus ['fi:bəs] *m* Febo.
Phoenicia [fi'niʃiə] Fenicia *f*.
Phoenician [fi'niʃiən] **1** *adj* fenicio. **2** *n* fenicio *m*, a *f*.
phoenix ['fi:niks] *n* fénix *m*.
'phone [fəun] *see* **telephone**.
phoneme ['fəuni:m] *n* fonema *m*.
phonemic [fəu'ni:mik] *adj* fonémico.
phonetic [fəu'netik] *adj* fonético.
phonetician [ˌfəuni'tiʃən] *n* fonetista *mf*.
phonetics [fəu'netiks] *n* fonética *f*.
phoney ['fəuni] (*fam*) **1** *adj* falso, postizo; sospechoso; insincero; **the** — **war** la extraña guerra; **it's completely** — no es lo que parece ser en absoluto; **there's something** — **about it** esto huele a camelo.
    2 *n* (*person*) farsante *mf*; (*thing*) cosa *f* falsa, cosa *f* postiza; **it's a** — no tiene nada de auténtico.
phonic ['fonik] *adj* fónico.
phonograph ['fəunəgrɑ:f] *n* (*US*) gramófono *m*, fonógrafo *m*.
phonological [ˌfəunə'lɔdʒikəl] *adj* fonológico.
phonology [fəu'nɔlədʒi] *n* fonología *f*.
phosgene ['fɔzdʒi:n] *n* fosgeno *m*.
phosphate ['fɔsfeit] *n* fosfato *m*.
phosphoresce [ˌfɔsfə'res] *vi* fosforecer.
phosphorescence [ˌfɔsfə'resns] *n* fosforescencia *f*.
phosphorescent [ˌfɔsfə'resnt] *adj* fosforescente.
phosphoric [fɔs'fɔrik] *adj* fosfórico.
phosphorous ['fɔsfərəs] *adj* fosforoso.
phosphorus ['fɔsfərəs] *n* fósforo *m*.
photo ['fəutəu] *n* foto *f*; *see* **photograph**.
photocopier ['fəutəu'kɔpiə*] *n* fotocopiador *m*.
photocopy ['fəutəu,kɔpi] **1** *n* fotocopia *f*. **2** *vt* fotocopiar.
photoelectric ['fəutəui'lektrik] *adj* fotoeléctrico; — **cell** célula *f* fotoeléctrica.
photoengraving ['fəutəuen'greiviŋ] *n* fotograbado *m*.
photo finish ['fəutəu'finiʃ] *n* resultado *m* comprobado por fotocontrol; (*fig*) final *m* muy reñido.
photoflash ['fəutəuflæʃ] *n* flash *m*, magnesio *m*.
photogenic ['fəutəu'dʒenik] *adj* fotogénico.
photograph ['fəutəgræf] **1** *n* fotografía *f* (*foto*); **aerial** — aerofoto *f*; **colour** — fotografía *f* en colores; **to take a** — sacar una foto.
    2 *vt* fotografiar, hacer una fotografía de, sacar una foto de; **"—ed by X"** "fotografía de X".
    3 *vi*: **to** — **well** ser fotogénico, sacar buena foto.
photographer [fə'tɔgrəfə*] *n* fotógrafo *m*, a *f*.
photographic [ˌfəutə'græfik] *adj* fotográfico.
photographically [ˌfəutə'græfikəli] *adv*: **to record something** — registrar algo por medio de fotografías, hacer una historia fotográfica de algo.
photography [fə'tɔgrəfi] *n* fotografía *f* (*arte*); **aerial** — fotografía *f* aérea; **colour** — fotografía *f* en colores; **trick** — trucaje *m*.
photogravure [ˌfəutəgrə'vjuə*] *n* fotograbado *m*.
photometer [fə'tɔmətə*] *n* fotómetro *m*.
photon ['fəutɔn] *n* fotón *m*.
photostat ['fəutəustæt] (*Protected Trade Name in US*) **1** *n* fotóstato *m*. **2** *vt* fotostatar.
photosynthesis [ˌfəutəu'sinθəsis] *n* fotosíntesis *f*.
phototropism ['fəutəu'trəupizəm] *n* fototropismo *m*.
phrase [freiz] **1** *n* frase *f* (*also* Mus), expresión *f*, locución *f*; **set** — frase *f* hecha.
    2 *vt* expresar; **a carefully** —**d letter** una carta redactada con cuidado; **can we** — **that differently?** ¿podemos poner eso de otro modo?
phrasebook ['freizbuk] *n* libro *m* de frases.
phraseology [ˌfreizi'ɔlədʒi] *n* fraseología *f*.
phrasing ['freiziŋ] *n* (*act*) redacción *f*; (*style*) estilo *m*, fraseología *f*, términos *mpl*; (*Mus*) fraseo *m*; **the** — **is rather unfortunate** los términos empleados se han escogido bastante mal.
phrenetic [fri'netik] *adj* frenético.
phrenologist [fri'nɔlədʒist] *n* frenólogo *m*.
phrenology [fri'nɔlədʒi] *n* frenología *f*.
phthisis ['θaisis] *n* tisis *f*.
phut [fʌt] *adj* (*fam*): **to go** — estropearse, romperse, averiarse; (*fig*) fracasar, acabarse.
phylactery [fi'læktəri] *n* filacteria *f*.
phylloxera [ˌfilɔk'siərə] *n* filoxera *f*.

phylum ['failum] *n*, *pl* **phyla** ['failə] filo *m*, filum *m*.
physic ['fizik] *n* (*arch*) medicina *f*.
physical ['fizikəl] *adj* físico.
physically ['fizikəli] *adv* físicamente.
physician [fi'ziʃən] *n* médico *m*.
physicist ['fizisist] *n* físico *m*.
physics ['fiziks] *n* física *f*; **nuclear** — física *f* nuclear.
physiognomy [ˌfizi'ɔnəmi] *n* fisonomía *f*.
physiological ['fiziə'lɔdʒikəl] *adj* fisiológico.
physiologist [ˌfizi'ɔlədʒist] *n* fisiólogo *m*.
physiology [ˌfizi'ɔlədʒi] *n* fisiología *f*.
physiotherapist [ˌfiziə'θerəpist] *n* fisioterapeuta *mf*.
physiotherapy [ˌfiziə'θerəpi] *n* fisioterapia *f*.
physique [fi'zi:k] *n* físico *m*.
pi [pai] *adj* (*sl*) piadoso, devoto.
pianist ['piənist] *n* pianista *mf*.
piano ['pjɑ:nəu] *n*, **pianoforte** [ˌpjɑ:nəu'fɔ:ti] *n* piano *m*; **baby grand** — piano *m* de media cola; **grand** — piano *m* de cola; **upright** — piano *m* vertical.
piano-accordion ['pjɑ:nəuə'kɔ:diən] *n* acordeón-piano *m*.
pianola [piə'nəulə] *n* piano *m* mecánico, aristón *m*.
piano stool ['pjɑ:nəu,stu:l] *n* taburete *m* de piano.
piano tuner ['pjɑ:nəu,tju:nə*] *n* afinador *m* de pianos.
piastre, (*US*) **piaster** [pi'æstə*] *n* piastra *f*.
piazza [pi'ætsə] *n* (*US*) pórtico *m*, galería *f*.
pica ['paikə] *n* (*Med*, *Vet*) pica *f*; (*Typ*) cícero *m*.
Picardy ['pikədi] Picardía *f*.
picaresque [ˌpikə'resk] *adj* picaresco.
picayune [ˌpikə'ju:n] (*US*) **1** *adj* de poca monta. **2** *n* (*person*) persona *f* insignificante; (*thing*) bagatela *f*.
piccalilli ['pikə,lili] *n* legumbres *fpl* en escabeche.
piccaninny ['pikə,nini] *n* negrito *m*, a *f*.
piccolo ['pikələu] *n* flautín *m*, píccolo *m*.
pick [pik] **1** *n* (a) (*tool*) pico *m*, zapapico *m*, piqueta *f*.
    (b) (*choice, right to choose*) derecho *m* de elección; **it's your** — a ti te toca elegir; **whose** — **is it?** ¿a quién le toca elegir?; **take your** —**!** ¡escoja el que quiera!
    (c) (*best*) lo mejor, lo más escogido; flor *f* y nata; **it's the** — **of the bunch** es el mejor del grupo.
    2 *vt* (a) *hole etc* picar, hacer; *teeth* mondarse, limpiarse; *nose* hurgarse; *bone* roer; *bird* desplumar; *lock* forzar, abrir con ganzúa.
    (b) (*choose*) escoger, elegir; escoger con cuidado; *team* seleccionar; (*pluck*) *flowers* coger, *fruit* coger, recoger; **to** — **one's way** andar con mucho tiento (*across* por), abrirse camino (*among* entre, *through* por).
    (c) **to** — **pockets** ratear, dedicarse a ser carterista; **to** — **someone's pocket** robar algo del bolsillo de uno.
    (d) (*with adv or prep*) **to** — **off** *paint etc* arrancar, separar; (*shoot*) matar de un tiro, matar con tiros sucesivos; **to** — **out** (*choose*) escoger; entresacar; (*identify*) conocer, identificar; (*discern*) lograr ver, alcanzar a ver; **to** — **out a tune on the piano** tocar de oído una melodía al piano; **to** — **out a colour** hacer resaltar un color; **to** — **out letters in gold** hacer resaltar unas letras pintándolas de oro; **to** — **some books over** ir revolviendo y examinando unos libros; **to** — **up** *object on floor etc* recoger; *telephone* descolgar; (*acquire*) adquirir, (*buy*) comprar, (*find*) encontrar; *prisoner* detener; *girl* conocer, encontrar; (*learn*) aprender, (*come to hear of*) saber, saber por casualidad; *radio message* interceptar, *radio station* captar; (*recover*) recobrar; **to** — **up a child in one's arms** levantar a un niño en los brazos; **to** — **up a trick** aprender un truco; **to** — **up some words of a language** aprender algunas palabras de un idioma; **I** —**ed it up cheap** lo adquirí por muy poco dinero; **the car** —**ed up speed** el coche se aceleró, el coche cobró velocidad; **we** —**ed them up at the station** fuimos a recogerles a la estación; **he** —**ed her up at a café** la conoció en un café; **he** —**s up a living selling firewood** se gana la vida vendiendo astillas; **I** —**ed that bit of news up yesterday** esa noticia la supe ayer.
    3 *vi*: **to** — **and choose** tardar en decidirse; hacer melindres al escoger, mostrarse difícil; **I like to** — **and choose** me gusta elegir con cuidado; **to** — **at one's food** comer con poco apetito, comer con poca gana; **to** — **at someone** (*US*), **to** — **on someone** perseguir a uno, criticar mucho a uno; **why** — **on me?** ¿por qué me lo dice a mí y no a otro?; **you're always** —**ing on me** me tiene manía; **to** — **up** (*Med etc*) reponerse; **business is** —**ing up** los negocios van mejor; **the team** —**ed up towards the end** hacia el final el equipo jugó mejor.

pickaback ['pikəbæk] *adv*: **to carry someone —** llevar a uno sobre los hombros.

pickaxe ['pikæks] *n* pico *m*, zapapico *m*, piqueta *f*.

picked [pikt] *adj* escogido, selecto.

picker ['pikə*] *n* (*of fruit etc*) recogedor *m*, ora *f*.

picket ['pikit] **1** *n* (**a**) (*stake*) estaca *f*.
(**b**) (*Mil*) piquete *m*; (*band of strikers*) guardia *f* de vigilantes huelguistas, piquete *m*; (*striker*) vigilante *m* huelguista, piquetero *m*.
2 *vt factory* piquetear, cercar con un cordón de huelguistas.
3 *vi* estar de guardia (los vigilantes huelguistas).

picket line ['pikitlain] *n* línea *f* de vigilantes huelguistas.

picking ['pikiŋ] *n* (**a**) (*of fruit etc*) recolección *f*, cosecha *f*; (*act of choosing*) elección *f*, selección *f*.
(**b**) **—s** (*leftovers*) sobras *fpl*, desperdicios *mpl*; (*profits*) ganancias *fpl*; (*stolen goods*) artículos *mpl* robados.

pickle ['pikl] **1** *n* (**a**) (*as condiment*) encurtido *m* (*also* **—s**); (*of fish, olives*) escabeche *m*; (*of meat*) adobo *m*; (*in salt solution*) salmuera *f*.
(**b**) (*plight*) apuro *m*; **to be in a** (*person*) **—** estar en un apuro, (*room*) estar en desorden, estar revuelto; **to get into a —** meterse en líos; **what a —!** ¡qué lío!
(**c**) (*child*) diablillo *m*, pillo *m*.
2 *vt* encurtir; escabechar; adobar; conservar, conservar en vinagre; (*Bio*) conservar en alcohol, conservar en formalina.

pickled ['pikld] *adj* (**a**) escabechado, encurtido, en conserva; **— onions** cebollas *fpl* en vinagre; **— herrings** arenques *mpl* en escabeche.
(**b**) **to be —** (*sl*) estar jumado (*sl*).

picklock ['piklɔk] *n* ganzúa *f*.

pick-me-up ['pikmi:ʌp] *n* (*drink*) reconstituyente *m*; (*Med*) tónico *m*.

pickpocket ['pik,pɔkit] *n* carterista *m*, ratero *m*.

pickup ['pikʌp] *n* (*of gramophone*) pick-up *m*, fonocaptor *m* (*Acad*).

picnic ['piknik] **1** *n* (**a**) jira *f*, excursión *f* campestre, merienda *f* en el campo, picnic *m*; **to go for a —**, **to go on a —** ir de jira, merendar en el campo; **we found a nice place for a —** encontramos un buen sitio para merendar.
(**b**) (*fam*) **it was no —** no tenía nada de fácil, no tenía nada de agradable.
2 *vi* ir de jira, merendar en el campo; llevar la merienda al campo; **we —ked by the river** merendamos junto al río; **we go —king every Sunday** todos los domingos vamos de jira.

picnicker ['piknikə*] *n* excursionista *mf*.

Pict [pikt] *n* picto *m*, a *f*.

Pictish ['piktiʃ] **1** *adj* picto. **2** *n* picto *m*.

pictorial [pik'tɔ:riəl] **1** *adj* pictórico; *magazine* gráfico, ilustrado. **2** *n* revista *f* ilustrada.

pictorially [pik'tɔ:riəli] *adv* pictóricamente; *represent etc* gráficamente, por imágenes.

picture ['piktʃə*] **1** *n* (**a**) (*Art*) cuadro *m*, pintura *f*; (*portrait*) retrato *m*; (*photo*) fotografía *f*; (*in book*) lámina *f*, estampa *f*, grabado *m*.
(**b**) (*TV*) cuadro *m*, imagen *f*; **we had a good —** la imagen era buena.
(**c**) (*Cine*) película *f*, film *m*; **the —s** el cine; **silent —** película *f* muda; **talking —** película *f* sonora; **to go to a —** ir a ver una película; **to go to the —s** ir al cine.
(**d**) (*spoken etc*) descripción *f*; (*mental*) imagen *f*; idea *f*; recuerdo *m*; (*outlook*) perspectiva *f*; (*overall view*) visión *f* de conjunto; **the other side of the —** el reverso de la medalla; **she looked a —!** ¡estaba guapísima!; **the garden is a —** in June en junio el jardín es de lo más hermoso; **his face was a —!** ¡había que ver la cara que puso!; **she looked a — of health** era la salud personificada; **he gave us a grim —** nos hizo una descripción horrorosa; **he painted a black — of the future** nos hizo un cuadro muy negro del porvenir; **I have no very clear — of it** no lo recuerdo con claridad; **these figures give the general —** estas cifras ofrecen una visión de conjunto; **are you in the —?** ¿estás enterado?; **to put someone in the —** poner a uno al corriente de algo.
2 *attr* de pinturas, de cuadros; *paper* gráfico, ilustrado; *hat* de ala ancha.
3 *vt* (*paint*) pintar; (*describe*) pintar, describir; **to — something to oneself** imaginarse algo, representarse algo en la imaginación; **the scene figuraos la escena: — if you can a winkle** imaginaos, si podéis, una litorina.

picture book ['piktʃəbuk] *n* libro *m* de imágenes.

picture frame ['piktʃəfreim] *n* marco *m* (para cuadro).

picture gallery ['piktʃə'gæləri] *n* museo *m* de pintura, museo *m* de bellas artes; **the Prado —** el Museo del Prado.

picturegoer ['piktʃə,gəuə*] *n* aficionado *m* al cine, aficionada *f* al cine.

picture palace ['piktʃə,pælis] *n* cine *m*.

picture postcard ['piktʃə'pəustka:d] *n* postal *f* ilustrada.

picture rail ['piktʃəreil] *n* moldura *f* (*pegada a la pared para colgar cuadros*).

picturesque [,piktʃə'resk] *adj* pintoresco; (*quaint, of tourist interest*) típico.

picturesquely [,piktʃə'reskli] *adv* de modo pintoresco.

picture window ['piktʃə,windəu] *n* ventana *f* grande (de una sola hoja de vidrio).

piddle ['pidl] *see* piss.

piddling ['pidliŋ] *adj* (*fam*) de poca monta, insignificante.

pidgin ['pidʒin] *n* (*also* **— English**) lengua franca (*inglés–chino*) comercial del Lejano Oriente.

pie [pai] *n* (*of fruit etc*) pastel *m*, tarta *f*; (*of meat*) empanada *f*, pastel *m*; **it's — in the sky** es como prometer la luna; **to eat humble —** humillarse y pedir perdón.

piebald ['paibɔ:ld] *adj* pío, de varios colores.

piece [pi:s] **1** *n* (**a**) (*fragment*) pedazo *m*, trozo *m*, fragmento *m*; (*Mech, Mil*) pieza *f*; (*coin*) moneda *f*; (*Lit, Theat, Mus*) obra *f*, pieza *f*; (*Chess*) pieza *f*, ficha *f*; **a two-shilling —** una moneda de dos chelines; **set —** (*of fireworks etc*) cuadro *m*, (*Art*) grupo *m*, (*Lit etc*) escena *f* importante, episodio *m* central; **that nice — in the third movement** aquel pasaje tan bonito del tercer tiempo; **to buy something by the —** comprar algo por piezas; **it is made all in one —** está hecho de una pieza, forma pieza única, las partes no son separables; **the back is all of a — with the seat** el respaldo forma pieza única con el asiento; **to get back all in one —** volver sano y salvo; **we got it back all in one —** nos lo devolvieron en buen estado; **this is of a — with the other** éste es de la misma clase que el otro, éste se parece al otro; **this is of a — with what he told us** esto es conforme con lo que él nos dijo, esto concuerda con lo que él nos dijo.
(**b**) (*girl: sl*) **a nice little —** una pizpireta, una chica muy mona.
(**c**) (*examples of* **a —** *of*) **a — of paper** un trozo de papel, una hoja de papel, un papel; **a — of bread** un pedazo de pan; **a — of cake** una porción de tarta; **another — of cake?** ¿quieres más tarta?; **a — of my work** una de mis obras, una muestra de mi trabajo; **a — out of a book** un trozo de un libro; **a — of advice** un consejo; **a — of carelessness** un descuido, un acto de imprudencia; **a — of clothing** una prenda (de vestir); **a — of folly** una locura, un acto de locura; **a — of furniture** un mueble; **a — of ground** un terreno, (*for building*) un solar; **by a — of good luck** por suerte; **a — of luggage** un bulto; **3 —s of luggage** 3 bultos; **a — of news** una noticia, una nueva; **a — of poetry** una poesía; *see* mind *etc*.
(**d**) **to be in —s** (*taken apart*) estar desmontado, (*broken*) estar hecho pedazos, estar roto; **to break something to (*or* in) —s** hacer algo pedazos; **to break (*vi*) in —s** hacerse pedazos; **to come to —s**, **to fall to —s** hacerse pedazos, romperse; **it comes to —s** se desmonta, es desmontable; **to go to —s** (*person*) sufrir un ataque de nervios, (*Med*) perder la salud, (*team etc*) desanimarse por completo; **to hack something to —s** cortar algo en pedazos (*violentamente, despiadadamente etc*); **to pull to —s** deshacer, despedazar, hacer pedazos, *argument* deshacer, *person* criticar duramente; **to smash something to —s** destrozar algo violentamente, romper algo a golpes; **the boat was smashed to —s on the rocks** el barco se estrelló contra las rocas y se hizo pedazos; **to take something to —s** desmontar algo; **it takes to —s** se desmonta, es desmontable; **to tear something to —s** romper algo violentamente, (*prey etc*) desgarrar algo; **the crowd will tear him to —s** la gente le hará pedazos; **he tore the theory to —s** deshizo rápidamente la teoría.
2 *vt*: **to — together** juntar, juntar las partes de; (*Mech*) montar, ir montando; (*fig*) atar cabos e ir comprendiendo; **we eventually —d the story together** por fin logramos saber toda la historia, por fin logramos atar todos los cabos.

pièce de résistance [,pjesdərezis'tã:s] *n* lo principal, lo más importante; (*on menu*) plato *m* principal; (*in programme*) atracción *f* principal, número *m* más importante.

piecemeal ['pi:smi:l] **1** *adv* (*bit by bit*) poco a poco, a trozos, por etapas; (*haphazard*) sin sistema fijo. **2** *adj* poco sistemático.

piecework ['pi:swə:k] *n* trabajo *m* a destajo; **to be on —, to do —** trabajar a destajo.

pieceworker ['pi:swə:kə*] *n* destajista *mf*.

piecrust ['paikrʌst] *n* pasta *f* de pastel.

pied [paid] *adj animal* pío, de varios colores; *bird* manchado.

pied-à-terre [ˌpieidæ'teə*] *n* apeadero *m*.

Piedmont ['pi:dmɔnt] Piamonte *m*.

Piedmontese [ˌpi:dmən'ti:z] **1** *adj* piamontés. **2** *n* piamontés *m*, esa *f*.

pie-eyed ['pai'aid] *adj* (*fam*) jumado (*fam*).

pier [piə*] *n* (*Archit*) pilar *m*, columna *f*; (*of bridge*) estribo *m*, pila *f*; (*Naut*) dique *m*, malecón *m*, embarcadero *m*, (*with amusements*) muelle *m*.

pierce [piəs] *vt* penetrar; atravesar; (*hole*) agujerear; (*bore*) horadar, perforar; (*punch*) taladrar; (*puncture*) pinchar; **the bullet —d the armour** la bala penetró en la coraza; **the bullet —d his lung** la bala le atravesó el pulmón, la bala entró en el pulmón; **to have one's ears —d** hacerse taladrar las orejas; **the rock is —d by numerous holes** la roca está agujereada (*or* horadada) en muchos sitios; **a nail —d the tyre** un clavo pinchó el neumático; **the dam had been —d in various places** se habían abierto brechas en distintas partes de la presa; **a wall —d with loopholes** un muro en el que se abrían aspilleras; **to — something through and through** perforar algo una y otra vez; **a cry —d the silence** un grito desgarró el silencio; **a light —d the darkness** una luz empezó súbitamente a brillar en la oscuridad; **the news —d him to the heart** la noticia le hirió en el alma.

piercing ['piəsiŋ] *adj wind* cortante; *cry* agudo, penetrante; *look* penetrante.

piercingly ['piəsiŋli] *adv blow* de modo cortante; *cry* agudamente, en tono penetrante.

pier glass ['piəglɑ:s] *n* espejo *m* de cuerpo entero.

pierhead ['piəhed] *n* punta *f* del muelle.

pierrot ['piərəu] *n* pierrot *m*.

pietism ['paiətizəm] *n* piedad *f*, devoción *f*; (*pej*) beatería *f*, mojigatería *f*.

pietistic [paiə'tistik] *adj* (*pej*) beato, mojigato.

piety ['paiəti] *n* piedad *f*, devoción *f*; **affected —** beatería *f*.

piffle ['pifl] *n* disparates *mpl*, tonterías *fpl*; **—!** ¡tonterías!

piffling ['pifliŋ] *adj* de poca monta, insignificante.

pig [pig] **1** *n* (a) cerdo *m*, puerco *m*, cochino *m*; **roast —** cochinillo *m* asado, lechón *m* asado; **to buy a — in a poke** cerrar un trato a ciegas; **to sell someone a — in a poke** dar gato por liebre.
(b) (*fig: person*) cochino *m*, marrano *m*; **you —!** (*hum*) ¡bandido!; **the boss is a —** el jefe es un bruto; **you're a —, sir!** ¡Vd es un maleducado!; **to make a — of oneself** comer demasiado; darse un atracón (*over de*).
(c) (*Metal*) lingote *m*.
2 *vt*: **to —** it vivir como cerdos.

pigeon ['pidʒən] *n* paloma *f*, palomo *m*; (*young*) palomino *m*, pichón *m*; (*as food*) pichón *m*; **carrier —, homing —** paloma *f* mensajera; **clay —** pichón *m* de barro.

pigeonhole ['pidʒənhəul] **1** *n* casilla *f*; **set of —s** casillas *fpl*, casillero *m*.
2 *vt* (*classify*) encasillar, clasificar; (*store away*) archivar; archivar en la memoria; (*shelve*) dar carpetazo a.

pigeon house ['pidʒənhaus] *n*, *pl* **— houses** [hauziz], **pigeon loft** ['pidʒənlɔft] *n* palomar *m*.

pigeon shooting ['pidʒənˌʃu:tiŋ] *n* tiro *m* de pichón.

pigeon-toed ['pidʒən'təud] *adj* patituerto.

piggery ['pigəri] *n* pocilga *f*, porqueriza *f*, cochiquera *f*.

piggy ['pigi] *n* cerdito *m*, cochinillo *m*, lechón *m*.

piggy bank ['pigibæŋk] *n* hucha *f* en forma de cerdito.

pigheaded ['pig'hedid] *adj person* terco, testarudo; *attitude etc* obstinado; **it was a — thing to do** fue un acto que reveló su terquedad.

pigheadedly ['pig'hedidli] *adv* tercamente, obstinadamente.

pigheadedness ['pig'hedidnis] *n* terquedad *f*, testarudez *f*; obstinación *f*.

pig iron ['pigˌaiən] *n* hierro *m* en lingotes.

piglet ['piglit] *n* cerdito *m*, cochinillo *m*, lechón *m*.

pigman ['pigmæn] *n*, *pl* **—men** [men] porquerizo *m*, porquero *m*.

pigment ['pigmənt] *n* pigmento *m*.

pigmentation [ˌpigmən'teifən] *n* pigmentación *f*.

pigmented [pig'mentid] *adj* pigmentado.

pigmy ['pigmi] **1** *adj* pigmeo; (*fig*) enano; miniatura; pequeñito. **2** *n* pigmeo *m*, a *f*, enano *m*, a *f*.

pigskin ['pigskin] *n* piel *f* de cerdo.

pigsty ['pigstai] *n* pocilga *f*, porqueriza *f*, cochiquera *f* (*also fig*).

pigtail ['pigteil] *n* (*of Chinese, bullfighter etc*) coleta *f*; (*girl's*) trenza *f*.

pigswill ['pigswil] *n* bazofia *f* (*also fig*).

pike[1] [paik] *n* (*Mil*) pica *f*, chuzo *m*.

pike[2] [paik] *n* (*Fish*) lucio *m*, sollo *m*.

pike[3] [paik] *n* (*Geog*) pico *m*.

pikeman ['paikmən] *n*, *pl* **—men** [mən] piquero *m*.

piker ['paikə*] *n* (*US sl*) (*mean person*) cicatero *m*; (*unimportant person*) persona *f* de poco fuste; (*coward*) cobarde *m*.

pikestaff ['paikstɑ:f] *n see* **plain 1**.

pilaster [pi'læstə*] *n* pilastra *f*.

Pilate ['pailət] *m* Pilatos *m*.

pilchard ['piltʃəd] *n* sardina *f* arenque.

pile[1] [pail] *n* (*Archit*) pilote *m*.

pile[2] [pail] **1** *n* (a) (*heap*) montón *m*, pila *f*, rimero *m*; **to make a — of things, to put things in a —** amontonar cosas, juntar cosas en un montón.
(b) (*fam*) fortuna *f*; **to make one's —** hacer su agosto; **he made his — in oil** se hizo una fortuna en el negocio del petróleo.
(c) (*of buildings*) mole *f*, masa *f* imponente, conjunto *m* grandioso; **the Escorial, that noble —** El Escorial, aquel edificio tan imponente.
(d) (*Phys etc*) pila *f*; **atomic —** pila *f* atómica.
2 *vt* (*also to — up*) amontonar, apilar, juntar en un montón; acumular: **we —d it all up high** hicimos un montón tan alto como podía ser; **a table —d high with books** una mesa cargada de libros; **he went on piling up the evidence** fue acumulando los datos, fue amontonando las pruebas; **to — on the pressure** ir aumentando la presión, (*fig*) presionar cada vez más fuerte; **to — on the agony** aumentar el dolor, añadir dolor sobre dolor; **to — coal on the fire, to — the fire up with coal** echar carbón al fuego; **to — it on** exagerar; **he does rather — it on** es un exagerado.
3 *vi* (a) (*also to — up*) amontonarse, apilarse; acumularse; **the evidence is piling up** las pruebas van acumulándose.
(b) **the car —d up against the wall** el coche se estrelló contra el muro; **the ship —d up on the rocks** el buque se estrelló contra las rocas.
(c) **we all —d into the car** entramos todos en el coche; **— in!** ¡dentro todos, que nos vamos!

pile[3] [pail] *n* (*of carpet*) pelo *m*; (*of cloth*) pelillo *m*.

pile driver ['pailˌdraivə*] *n* martinete *m*.

piles [pailz] *npl* (*Med*) almorranas *fpl*, hemorroides *fpl*.

pileup ['pailʌp] *n* (*Aut etc*) accidente *m* múltiple; **there was a — at the corner** chocaron varios coches en la esquina, hubo un accidente múltiple en la esquina.

pilfer ['pilfə*] **1** *vt article* ratear; **the crate had been —ed** algunos artículos habían sido robados del cajón; **they often — the trucks** con frecuencia roban cosas de los vagones.
2 *vi* ratear, robar cosas.

pilferer ['pilfərə*] *n* ratero *m*, a *f*.

pilfering ['pilfəriŋ] *n* ratería *f*.

pilgrim ['pilgrim] *n* peregrino *m*, a *f*, romero *m*, a *f*; **the —s to Compostela** los que van en peregrinación a Compostela; **the P— Fathers** los padres peregrinos.

pilgrimage ['pilgrimidʒ] *n* peregrinación *f*, romería *f*; **to go on a —, to make a —** ir en peregrinación, ir en romería (*to a*).

pill [pil] *n* píldora *f*; (*sl*) pelota *f*; **birth-control —** píldora *f* anticonceptiva; **it was a bitter — (to swallow)** fue una píldora amarga, fue un trago amargo; **to sugar the —** dorar la píldora.

pillage ['pilidʒ] **1** *n* pillaje *m*, saqueo *m*. **2** *vt* pillar, saquear.

pillar ['pilə*] *n* pilar *m*, columna *f*; (*fig*) sostén *m*, pilar *m*; **— of salt** estatua *f* de sal; **the P—s of Hercules** las Columnas de Hércules; **to be a — of strength** ser una roca, ser una columna de sostén; **to chase someone from — to post** no dejar a uno a sol ni a sombra.

pillar box ['piləbɔks] *n* buzón *m*.

pillbox ['pilbɔks] *n* (*Med*) cajita *f* de píldoras; (*Mil*) fortín *m*.

pillion ['piljən] *n*: **— seat** asiento *m* de atrás, asiento *m* de pasajero; **to ride —** ir en el asiento de atrás.

pillory ['piləri] **1** *n* picota *f*. **2** *vt* (*fig*) poner en ridículo, satirizar; censurar duramente.

pillow ['piləu] **1** n almohada f.
  2 vt apoyar sobre una almohada; apoyar, servir de almohada a; **she —ed her head on my shoulder** apoyó la cabeza en mi hombro.

pillowcase ['piləukeis] n funda f de almohada.

pilot ['pailət] **1** n (Aer) piloto m; (Naut) práctico m, piloto m; **automatic —** piloto m automático.
  2 adj piloto, experimental; see **plant**.
  3 vt pilotar; (fig) guiar, conducir; dirigir; **a plane —ed by . . .** un avión pilotado por . . .; **he —ed the negotiations through** él dirigió las negociaciones, él condujo las negociaciones a buen fin; **to — a bill through the House** encargarse de un proyecto de ley durante los debates parlamentarios sobre éste.

pilot boat ['pailətbəut] n bote m del práctico.

pilot house ['pailəthaus] n, pl **— houses** [hauziz] (Naut) timonera f.

pilot officer ['pailət‚ɔfisə*] n oficial m de aviación.

pimento [pi'mentəu] n pimienta f.

pimp [pimp] **1** n alcahuete m; coime m, chulo m de putas. **2** vi alcahuetear; ser coime, ser chulo de putas;
  to — for somone servir de alcahuete a uno.

pimpernel ['pimpənel] n murajes mpl, pimpinela f; **the Scarlet P—** el Pimpinela escarlata.

pimple ['pimpl] n grano m; **she came out in —s** le salieron granos.

pimply ['pimpli] adj lleno de granos, cubierto de granos; **— youth** (fig) mocoso m, mozalbete m.

pin [pin] **1** n (Sew etc) alfiler m; (Mech: bolt) perno m, (cotter) chaveta f; (wooden) clavija f; **—s** (sl) piernas fpl; **split —** chaveta f; **—s and needles** hormiguillo m, hormigueo m; **like a new —** como una patena; **for two —s I'd knock his head off** le daría una paliza por menos de nada; **you could have heard a — drop** se hizo un profundo silencio.
  2 vt **(a)** prender con alfiler, prender con alfileres; (with bolt) sujetar con (perno etc); **to — a notice up** fijar un anuncio con chinches; **to — a medal to someone's uniform** prender una medalla al uniforme de uno; **to — papers together** unir unos papeles con una grapa; **to — someone's arms to his side** sujetar los brazos de uno; **to — someone against a wall** apretar a uno contra una pared; **the battalion was —ned against the river** el batallón estaba copado junto al río, el batallón quedó inmovilizado junto al río.
  (b) (fig) **to — someone down** obligar a uno a que concrete; **it's impossible to — him down** es imposible hacerle concretar; **you can't — him down to a date** es imposible lograr que nos diga una fecha concreta; **there's something odd I can't quite — down** hay alguna rareza que no puedo precisar; **the idea is rather hard to — down** es un concepto inaprehensible.
  (c) (fam) **to — something on someone** acusar (falsamente) a uno de algo; **you can't — it on me** no podéis lograr que yo cargue con la culpa, es imposible probar que yo lo hiciera; **they —ned a number of robberies on him** le acusaron (falsamente) de haber participado en una serie de robos.

pinafore ['pinəfɔ:*] n delantal m (de niña); **— dress** mandil m.

pince-nez ['pɛ̃:nsnei] npl quevedos mpl.

pincer ['pinsə*] adj: **— movement** (Mil) movimiento m de pinza.

pincers ['pinsəz] npl tenazas fpl, pinzas fpl; **a pair of —** unas tenazas.

pinch [pintʃ] **1** n **(a)** (with fingers) pellizco m; **to give someone a — on the arm** pellizcar el brazo a uno.
  (b) (small quantity) pizca f; pellizcada f; **a — of salt** (Cook) una pizca de sal; **to take something with a — of salt** tomar algo con un grano de sal; **a — of snuff** un polvo de rapé.
  (c) apuro m; **to feel the —** (empezar a) pasar apuros; **to feel the — of hunger** empezar a tener hambre; **to feel the — of poverty** saber lo que significa ser pobre; **at a —** si es realmente necesario, en caso de necesidad.
  2 vt **(a)** (with fingers) pellizcar, dar un pellizcón a; (squeeze, crush) apretar, estrujar, aplastar; (of shoe) apretar; **to — one's finger in the door** cogerse el dedo al cerrar la puerta; **to — off a bud** quitar un brote con los dedos, separar un brote con la uña.
  (b) (fam: steal) birlar (fam), guindar (fam), pisar (fam); (arrest) detener, coger, pescar (fam); (charge) acusar; **I had my pen —ed** me guindaron la pluma; **he —ed that idea from Shaw** esa idea la tomó de Shaw; **A —ed B's girl** A le pisó la novia a B; **the po̱lice —ed him with the stuff on him** los policías le detuvieron llevando todavía encima los géneros robados; **he got —ed for a parking offence** le pescaron en una infracción de aparcamiento.

3 vi **(a)** (shoe) apretar; **to know where the shoe —es** saber dónde aprieta el zapato.
  (b) (economize) economizar; privarse de lo necesario; **we had to — and scrape** tuvimos que hacer muchas economías; **they —ed and scraped to send her to college** se privaron de muchas cosas a fin de poder enviarla a la universidad.

pinchbeck ['pintʃbek] **1** n similor m. **2** attr de similor.

pinched ['pintʃt] adj: **to look —** tener la cara pálida; **to look — with cold** estar aterido, estar chupado.

pinch-hit ['pintʃhit] vi (US) batear de suplente; (fig) sustituir a otro en un apuro.

pinchpenny ['pintʃpeni] adj tacaño.

pincushion ['pin‚kuʃən] n acerico m.

Pindar ['pində*] m Píndaro.

Pindaric [pin'dærik] adj pindárico.

pine[1] [pain] n pino m.

pine[2] [pain] vi (also **to — away**) languidecer, consumirse; **to — for** suspirar por, perecer por, consumirse pensando en.

pineapple ['pain‚æpl] n piña f (de las Indias), ananás m.

pinecone ['painkəun] n piña f.

pine grove ['paingrəuv] n pinar m.

pine kernel ['pain‚kə:nl] n piñón m.

pine marten ['pain‚mɑ:tin] n marta f.

pine needle ['pain‚ni:dl] n aguja f de pino.

pine tree ['paintri:] n pino m.

pinewood ['painwud] n pinar m.

ping [piŋ] **1** n (of bullet: through air) silbido m, (on striking) sonido m metálico; (of bell) tintín m.
  2 vi silbar (como una bala); hacer un sonido metálico (como una bala); tintinear, hacer tintín.

ping-pong ['piŋpɔŋ] (Protected Trade Name in US) n ping-pong m.

pinion ['pinjən] **1** n (Mech) piñón m; (wing: poet) ala f. **2** vt bird cortar las alas a; person atar los brazos a; **he was —ed against the wall** estaba contra la pared sin poderse mover.

pink[1] [piŋk] **1** n **(a)** (Bot) clavel m, clavellina f.
  (b) (colour) color m de rosa.
  (c) hunting — levitín m rojo de caza.
  (d) (Pol) rojillo m, a f.
  (e) **to be in the —** estar en perfecta salud, estar como un reloj; **to be in the — of condition** estar en perfecto estado, estar en el mejor estado posible.
  2 adj (colour) rosado, color m de rosa; (Pol) rojillo; **strike me —!** (fam) ¡caray!; **to be tickled — about something** (fam) encontrar algo divertidísimo, reírse mucho con algo.

pink[2] [piŋk] vt (Sew) ondear, picar; **to — someone with a sword** herir a uno levemente con un florete.

pink[3] [piŋk] vi (US) picar (por autoencendido).

pinkie ['piŋki] n (Pol fam) rojillo m, a f; (fam) dedo m meñique.

pinking shears ['piŋkiŋ‚ʃiəz] npl tijeras fpl grandes (de costura) de corte ondulado.

pinkish ['piŋkiʃ] adj rosáceo; (sl) rojillo.

pin money ['pin‚mʌni] n alfileres mpl.

pinnace ['pinis] n pinaza f.

pinnacle ['pinəkl] n (Archit) pináculo m, remate m; chapitel m; (of rock etc) punta f; (of mountain) cumbre f; **the — of fame** la cumbre de la fama.

pinny ['pini] n (fam) = **pinafore**.

pinpoint ['pinpɔint] **1** n punta f de alfiler; (fig) punto m muy pequeño. **2** vt indicar con toda precisión; concretar; poner el dedo en.

pinprick ['pinprik] n alfilerazo m; (fig) alfilerazo m, molestia f pequeña.

pinstripe ['pinstraip] **1** adj a rayas, rayado; **— suit** traje m a rayas. **2** n traje m (etc) a rayas.

pint [paint] n **(a)** pinta f (= 0,57 litros, US = 0,47 litros).
  (b) (loosely) vaso m grande de cerveza, caña f de cerveza; **we had a — together** tomamos una caña; **he likes his —** le gusta la cerveza, es algo aficionado a la cerveza; **we had a few —s** bebimos cierta cantidad.

pin table ['pinteibl] n billar m romano, billar m automático.

pintail ['pinteil] n ánade m rabudo.

pinup ['pinʌp] n pin-up mf, foto f de muchacha guapa (or de hombre bien parecido etc); **she's my —** es mi mujer ideal.

pioneer [‚paiə'niə*] **1** n (explorer) explorador m; (early settler) colonizador m; (Mil) zapador m; (of scheme, in study) iniciador m, promotor m; **he was one of the —s** él es de los iniciadores; **he was a — in the study of bats** fue uno de los primeros en estudiar los murciélagos.
  2 vt settlement etc preparar el terreno para, hacer

los preparativos para; *scheme, study* iniciar, promover; echar los cimientos de, sentar las bases de.

3 *vi* explorar, abrir nuevos caminos.

pious ['paiəs] *adj* piadoso, devoto.

piously ['paiəsli] *adv* piadosamente, devotamente.

pip[1] [pip] *n* (*Med*) pepita *f*; **it gives me the —** me fastidia terriblemente; **it's enough to give you the —** es para volverse loco; **he's got the —** está de muy mal humor.

pip[2] [pip] *n* (*Bot*) pepita *f*; (*on card, dice*) punto *m*, pinta *f*; (*on uniform*) estrella *f*.

pip[3] [pip] **1** *vt* (*wound*) herir (levemente); (*defeat*) vencer; *exam* no aprobar, ser suspendido en; **A —ped B at the post** A alcanzó a B a la altura del mismo poste de llegada, (*fig*) A venció a B pero con muy pequeño margen; **I —ped French again** volvieron a suspenderme en francés.

2 *vi* (*lose*) perder; (*fail*) fracasar; (*in exam*) ser suspendido.

pipe [paip] **1** *n* (**a**) (*tube*) tubo *m*, caño *m*, conducto *m*; (*also* **—s**) tubería *f*, cañería *f*; (*of a hose etc*) manga *f*; (*of wine*) pipa *f*.

(**b**) (*Mus: of organ*) cañón *m*, tubo *m*; (*instrument*) caramillo *m*, (*boatswain's*) pito *m*; **—s** (*Scot*) gaita *f*, (*Pan's*) flauta *f*.

(**c**) (*smoker's*) pipa *f*; **— of peace** pipa *f* de la paz; **to fill one's —** cargar la pipa; **put that in your — and smoke it!** (*fam*) ¡chúpate eso!

2 *vt* (**a**) *water etc* conducir en cañerías; **water is —d to the farm** se conduce el agua a la granja por unas cañerías; **the oil is —d across the desert** el petroleo es conducido a través del desierto en un oleoducto.

(**b**) (*Mus*) *tune* tocar; **to — the admiral aboard** tocar el pito al llegar el almirante a bordo.

3 *vi* (*Mus*) tocar el caramillo, tocar la flauta; tocar la gaita; (*bird*) trinar; **to — down** (*fam*) callarse; **to — up** decir (inesperadamente), comenzar a hablar (inesperadamente).

pipeclay ['paipklei] **1** *n* albero *m*. **2** *vt* blanquear con albero.

pipe cleaner ['paip,kli:nə*] *n* limpiapipas *m*, limpiador *m* de pipa.

pipe dream ['paipdri:m] *n* esperanza *f* imposible, sueño *m* imposible.

pipeful ['paipful] *n* pipa *f*; **a — of tobacco** una pipa de tabaco.

pipeline ['paiplain] *n* tubería *f*, cañería *f*; tubería *f* de distribución; (*for oil*) oleoducto *m*; (*for gas*) gasoducto *m*; **it is in the —** (*fig*) está en trámite, se está tramitando.

piper ['paipə*] *n* flautista *mf*; (*Scot*) gaitero *m*; **the Pied P— of Hamelin** el flautista de Hamelin; **to pay the —** cargar con los gastos; **he who pays the — calls the tune** el que paga tiene derecho a escoger.

pipe tobacco ['paiptə,bækəu] *n* tabaco *m* de pipa.

pipette [pi'pet] *n* pipeta *f*.

piping[1] ['paipiŋ] *n* (**a**) tubería *f*, cañería *f*; (*Sew*) ribete *m*, cordoncillo *m*.

(**b**) (*Mus*) sonido *m* del caramillo, música *f* de flauta; (*of bird*) trinar *m*, trinos *mpl*.

piping[2] ['paipiŋ] **1** *adv*: **— hot** bien caliente, que casi quema. **2** *adj* voice agudo.

pipistrelle [,pipi'strel] *n* murciélago *m* pequeño.

pipit ['pipit] *n* bisbita *f*.

pipkin ['pipkin] *n* ollita *f* de barro.

pippin ['pipin] *n* camuesa *f*, manzana *f* reineta.

pipsqueak ['pipskwi:k] *n* (*fam*) persona *f* insignificante, cosa *f* trivial.

piquancy ['pi:kənsi] *n* picante *m*, lo picante.

piquant ['pi:kənt] *adj* picante.

piquantly ['pi:kəntli] *adv* de modo picante.

pique [pi:k] **1** *n* pique *m*, resentimiento *m*; **to be in a —** estar resentido; **to do something in a fit of —**, **to do something out of —** hacer algo motivado por el rencor.

2 *vt* picar, herir; **to be —d at** ofenderse por.

3 *vr*: **to — oneself on something** preciarse de algo, enorgullecerse de algo.

piquet [pi'ket] *n* séptimo *m*, juego *m* de los cientos.

piracy ['paiərəsi] *n* piratería *f*; (*of book*) publicación *f* desautorizada.

piranha [pi'rɑːnjə] *n* piraña *f*.

pirate ['paiərit] **1** *n* pirata *m*. **2** *adj*: **— radio** emisora *f* ilegal. **3** *vt* book publicar en una edición furtiva.

pirated ['paiəritid] *adj*: **— edition** edición *f* furtiva, edición *f* desautorizada.

piratical [pai'rætikəl] *adj* pirático.

pirouette [,piru'et] **1** *n* pirueta *f*. **2** *vi* piruetear.

piss [pis] (*tabu*) **1** *n* orina *f*, meados *mpl*; **to have a —** mear. **2** *vti* mear; **to be —ed** (*sl*) estar ajumado (*sl*).

pistachio [pis'tɑːʃiəu] *n* pistacho *m*.

pistil ['pistil] *n* pistilo *m*.

pistol ['pistl] *n* pistola *f*, revólver *m*.

pistol shot ['pistl,ʃɔt] *n* pistoletazo *m*; **to be within —** estar a tiro de pistola.

piston ['pistən] *n* pistón *m*, émbolo *m*.

piston engine ['pistən,endʒin] *n* motor *m* de pistón.

piston-engined ['pistən,endʒind] *adj* con motor de pistón.

piston ring ['pistən,riŋ] *n* aro *m* de pistón, segmento *m* de pistón.

piston rod ['pistən,rɔd] *n* vástago *m* de émbolo.

piston stroke ['pistən,strəuk] *n* carrera *f* del émbolo.

pit[1] [pit] **1** *n* (*hole in ground*) hoyo *m*, hoya *f*, foso *m*; (*small depression in surface*) hoyo *m*; (*as trap*) trampa *f*; (*at garage*) foso *m* de inspección, foso *m* de reparación; (*for cockfighting*) cancha *f*, reñidero *m*; (*in motor racing*) box *m*; (*of stomach*) boca *f*; (*Theat*) platea *f*; (*Min*) mina *f*, (*quarry*) cantera *f*; (*fig*) abismo *m*; (*fig: hell*) el infierno; **the — of hell** lo más profundo del infierno; **the —s** (*motor racing*) los boxes.

2 *vt* (**a**) *surface* hacer hoyos en, marcar con hoyos; (*with smallpox*) marcar con viruelas; **the surface was —ted with . . .** en la superficie había hoyos formados por . . .

(**b**) **to — A against B** oponer A a B; **we —ted all our strength against him** nos opusimos a él con todas nuestras fuerzas; **he found himself —ted against the champion** encontró que tenía que habérselas con el campeón.

pit[2] [pit] (*US*) **1** *n* (*Bot*) hueso *m*. **2** *vt* deshuesar, quitar el hueso a.

pitapat ['pitə'pæt] *adv*: **my heart went —** mi corazón latía rápidamente, mi corazón hacía tictac.

pitch[1] [pitʃ] **1** *n* pez *f*, brea *f*. **2** *vt* embrear.

pitch[2] [pitʃ] **1** *n* (**a**) (*throw*) lanzamiento *m*; echada *f*; **it came full —** llegó a mis manos sin tocar el suelo; **it fell full — into the garden** cayó de plano en el jardín.

(**b**) (*Naut*) cabezada *f*.

(**c**) (*Sport*) campo *m*, terreno *m*; **the — is under water** el campo está inundado; **the supporters poured on to the —** los hinchas invadieron el campo.

(**d**) (*place in market etc*) puesto *m*; (*fig*) terreno *m*; **this is my usual —** éste es mi puesto habitual; **keep off our —!** ¡cuidado con no meteros en lo nuestro!; **to queer someone's —** crear dificultades a uno, chafar la guitarra a uno.

(**e**) (*slope*) grado *m* de inclinación; (*of roof*) pendiente *f*.

(**f**) (*height, degree*) punto *m*, extremo *m*; (*Mus*) tono *m*; (*height*) elevación *f*; (*of propeller etc*) paso *m*; **to such a — that . . .** a tal punto que . . .; **excitement is at fever —** la emoción está al rojo vivo; **matters reached such a — that . . .** las cosas llegaron a tal extremo que . . .; **to adjust the — of an instrument** ajustar el tono de un instrumento; **concert —, standard —** diapasón *m* normal.

2 *vt* (**a**) (*throw*) arrojar, lanzar, tirar; (*Baseball etc*) lanzar; **to — someone off** quitar a uno de encima; **he was —ed off his horse** cayó del caballo; **— it over here!** ¡tíramelo!; **to — something out** tirar algo; **to — someone out** echar a uno, expulsar a uno; **they —ed him out into the street** le pusieron de patitas en la calle.

(**b**) (*Mus*) *note* dar, producir, entonar; (*play*) tocar, (*sing*) cantar; *instrument* graduar el tono de; **she can't — a note properly** es incapaz de producir una nota buena; **I'll — you a note** os doy la nota para empezar; **you're —ing it too high for me** lo tocas demasiado alto para mí; **to — one's aspirations too high** picar muy alto; **it is —ed in rather high-flown terms** está redactado en términos algo retóricos; **it must be —ed at the right level for the audience** el tono ha de ajustarse al público.

(**c**) *tent* armar.

(**d**) **to — it strong** exagerar, no perdonar detalle; **to — someone a story** contar a uno un cuento (inverosímil); **he —ed me this hard-luck story** me contó esta historia tan trágica.

3 *vi* (**a**) (*fall*) caer, caerse; **to — forward** caer de cabeza; **he —ed off his horse** cayó del caballo; **the ball —ed in front of him** la pelota cayó delante de él, la pelota vino a parar a sus pies; **after —ing it bounced high** después de tocar el suelo rebotó muy alto; **the aircraft —ed into the sea** el avión cayó al mar.

(**b**) (*Naut*) cabecear.

(**c**) **to — on something** (*choose*) elegir algo; (*find*) encontrar algo, dar con algo; **we —ed on it by accident** dimos con él por pura casualidad.

(d) to — in empezar a hacer algo, (esp) empezar a comer; — in! ¡a ello!, ¡manos a la obra!; so we all —ed in together así que todos nos pusimos a trabajar juntos; to — into someone (attack) atacar a uno (vigorosamente), (verbally etc) arremeter contra uno, (scold) dar un rapapolvo a uno; to — into the work emprender enérgicamente el trabajo, ponerse enérgicamente a trabajar; they —ed into the food empezaron a comer con buen apetito.

pitch-and-toss ['pitʃən'tɔs] n juego m de cara o cruz.
pitch-black ['pitʃ'blæk] adj negro como boca de lobo.
pitchblende ['pitʃblend] n pechblenda f.
pitch-dark ['pitʃ'dɑːk] adj negro como boca de lobo.
pitched [pitʃt] adj: — battle batalla f campal.
pitcher[1] ['pitʃə*] n cántaro m, jarro m.
pitcher[2] ['pitʃə*] n (Baseball) lanzador m.
pitchfork ['pitʃfɔːk] 1 n horca f, bielda f.
 2 vt (fig): to — someone into a job imponer inesperadamente a uno una tarea, hacer que uno se encargue de algo de buena o mala gana; I was —ed into it no me dieron la oportunidad de decir que no.
pitch pine ['pitʃpain] n pino m de tea.
piteous ['pitiəs] adj lastimero, lastimoso.
piteously ['pitiəsli] adv lastimosamente.
pitfall ['pitfɔːl] n escollo m, peligro m; trampa f; it's a — for the unwary es una trampa para los imprudentes; "P—s of English" "Escollos mpl del inglés"; there are many —s ahead hay muchos peligros por delante.
pith [piθ] n (Bot) médula f; (fig) meollo m, jugo m, esencia f.
pithead ['pithed] n bocamina f.
pithiness ['piθinis] n jugosidad f; lo sentencioso, lo expresivo, lo sucinto, lo lacónico.
pithy ['piθi] adj (full of sense) jugoso; sentencioso, expresivo, (terse) sucinto, lacónico; — saying dicho m sentencioso.
pitiable ['pitiəbl] adj lastimoso, digno de compasión; in a — state en un estado que da lástima; it was most — to see daba lástima verlo.
pitiful ['pitiful] adj (a) (moving to pity) lastimero, lastimoso; conmovedor. (b) (contemptible) lamentable, miserable, despreciable; a — display una exhibición lamentable; it was just — daba lástima.
pitifully ['pitifəli] adv (a) lastimosamente; de modo conmovedor; she was crying most — lloraba que daba lástima. (b) lamentablemente; a — bad play una comedia tan mala que da lástima.
pitiless ['pitilis] adj despiadado, implacable.
pitilessly ['pitilisli] adv despiadadamente, implacablemente.
pit prop ['pitprɔp] n puntal m, peón m.
pittance ['pitəns] n miseria f, renta f miserable; a mere —! ¡una miseria!; to live on a — vivir de una renta miserable.
pitted ['pitid] adj (US) fruit deshuesado, sin hueso.
pitter-patter ['pitə'pætə*] n etc = **patter**[2].
pituitary [pi'tjuːitəri] 1 adj pituitario; — gland = 2 n glándula f pituitaria.
pity ['piti] 1 n (a) compasión f, piedad f; for —'s sake! ¡por piedad!, (less seriously) ¡por Dios!; to do something out of — for someone hacer algo movido por la compasión que se tiene a uno; to feel no — for someone no sentir compasión por uno; to move someone to — mover a uno a compasión, dar lástima a uno; to take — on someone tener piedad de uno, apiadarse de uno.
 (b) lástima f; what a —! ¡qué lástima!, ¡qué pena!; more's the —! ¡desgraciadamente!; it is a — that . . . es una lástima que . . . , una pena que + subj, es de lástima que + subj; the — of it was that . . . lo lamentable fue que . . . , lo peor del caso fue que . . . ; it is a thousand pities that . . . es muy de lamentar que + subj.
 2 vt compadecer(se de), tener lástima a; apiadarse de.
pitying ['pitiiŋ] adj glance etc de lástima, lleno de compasión, compasivo.
pityingly ['pitiiŋli] adv con lástima, compasivamente.
Pius ['paiəs] m Pío.
pivot ['pivət] 1 n pivote m; (fig) eje m, punto m central.
 2 vt montar sobre un pivote; he —ed it on his hand lo hizo girar sobre la mano, lo mantuvo en equilibrio sobre la mano.
 3 vi girar (on sobre); to — on (fig) depender de.
pivotal ['pivətl] adj (fig) central, fundamental.
pixie ['piksi] n duende m.
pixie hood ['piksihud] n caperucita f.
placard ['plækɑːd] 1 n (on wall etc) cartel m; (sign, announcement) letrero m; (carried in procession etc) pancarta f.

 2 vt: the wall is —ed all over la pared está llena de carteles; the town is —ed with slogans en todas partes de la ciudad se ven carteles con slogans.
placate [plə'keit] vt aplacar, apaciguar.
place [pleis] 1 n (a) (in general) sitio m, lugar m; this is the — éste es el lugar; we came to a — where . . . llegamos a un sitio donde . . . ; any — will do cualquier lugar será conveniente; I don't see it any — (US) no lo veo en ninguna parte; it must be some — else (US) estará en otra parte; it's a pretty low sort of — es un lugar no muy decente; this is no — for you éste no es sitio conveniente para Vd; from — to — de lugar en lugar; in another — en otra parte, (Parl) en la otra cámara; in high —s allá arriba, en las altas esferas, en el gobierno (etc); the furniture was all over the — los muebles estaban en desorden; we're all over the — vivimos en la mayor confusión; your work is all over the — Vd hace su trabajo de cualquier modo; to find one's — in a book encontrar en un libro el pasaje que uno quiere leer; to lose one's — perder el hilo, padecer confusión al querer seguir su lectura (etc); to laugh at the right — reírse en el momento oportuno; to go —s (travel) viajar, visitar muchos países (etc); we like to go —s at weekends durante los fines de semana nos gusta salir de excursión; he's going —s es un ambicioso; tiene una carrera brillante por delante; es un hombre de empuje; we're going —s at last por fin empezamos a hacer progresos.
 (b) (specific) sitio m, local m; — amusement lugar m de diversión; — of business oficina f, (shop) comercio m; — of refuge refugio m, asilo m; — of residence residencia f, domicilio m; — of worship templo m, edificio m de culto.
 (c) (town etc) lugar m; ciudad f (etc); fortified — plaza f, fortaleza f; find a native of the — busque a uno nacido aquí, busque a uno que sea realmente de aquí; it's a small — es un pueblo pequeño; it's just a small country — no es más que un pequeño pueblo rural.
 (d) (house) casa f; his — in the country su casa de campo; they have a new — now tienen una nueva casa ya; it's a vast great — es una casa inmensa; we were at Peter's — estuvimos en casa de Pedro; come to our — ven a visitarnos a casa.
 (e) (in street names) plaza f.
 (f) (— in relation to owner etc) sitio m, lugar m, puesto m; does this have a —? ¿tiene esto un sitio determinado?; to be in — estar en su lugar; to put something back in its — devolver algo a su sitio; to hold something in — sujetar algo en un lugar; in — of en lugar de, en vez de; if I were in your — yo en tu lugar, yo que tú; to be out of — estar fuera de lugar; estar fuera de serie; haberse equivocado de sitio; that remark was quite out of — esa observación estaba fuera de propósito, no cabía tal observación; it looks out of — here aquí no está bien, aquí parece que está fuera de su lugar; I feel rather out of — here aquí me siento algo desplazado; to change —s cambiar de sitio; to change —s with someone trocarse con uno; to give — to ceder el paso a; to take — tener lugar, verificarse; (meeting etc) celebrarse; the marriage will not now take — la boda no se celebrará.
 (g) (seat) plaza f, asiento m; (at table) cubierto m; a theatre with 2000 —s un teatro de 2000 asientos, un teatro que tiene un aforo de 2000; are there any —s left? ¿quedan plazas?; is this — taken? ¿está ocupado este asiento?; to lay an extra — for someone poner otro cubierto para uno.
 (h) (post) puesto m, empleo m; colocación f; —s for 500 workers 500 puestos mpl de trabajo; school — puesto m escolar; it is not my — to + infin no me cumple a mí + infin; he found a — for his nephew in the firm le dio un puesto en la compañía a su sobrino; to seek a — in publishing buscar una colocación en una casa editorial.
 (i) (in series, as rank etc) lugar m, puesto m; (in exam) calificación f; (rank) posición f, rango m; in the first — en primer lugar; in the second — en segundo lugar; in the next — luego, después; to three —s of decimals en milésimas; to work something out to three —s of decimals calcular algo hasta las milésimas; P won, with Q in second — ganó P, con Q en segunda posición; to attain a high — llegar muy alto, alcanzar un rango alto; to back a horse for a — apostar algo a un caballo para colocado; to give up one's — (in a queue) ceder la vez, ceder su turno; to keep one's — mantenerse en la misma posición, lograr seguir como antes; to know one's — ser respetuoso, guardar las distancias; to put someone in his — bajar los humos a uno; if he gets

fresh put him in his — si se pone fresco vuélvele a su sitio; **that properly put him in his** — eso sí le hizo sentirse humilde.

2 *vt* **(a)** (*in general*) poner, colocar; fijar; situar, emplazar; — **it on the table** ponlo en la mesa; **it is** —**d rather high up** está en una posición más bien alta, se ha fijado un poco alto; **the house is well** —**d** la casa está bien situada; **the shop is awkwardly** —**d** la tienda está en una posición de difícil acceso; **the town is** —**d on a hill** la ciudad está emplazada en una colina; **to** — **confidence in someone** poner confianza en uno, confiar a uno; **we should** — **no trust in that** no hay que fiarse de eso.

(b) (*of orders etc*) **to** — **a book with a publisher** lograr que un editor acepte un libro para publicarlo; **I shall** — **the book elsewhere** ofreceré el libro a otra editorial; **to** — **a contract for machinery with a French firm** firmar un contrato con una compañía francesa para adquirir unas máquinas; **to** — **money** invertir dinero; **to** — **money at interest** colocar dinero a interés; **to** — **an order** colocar un pedido (*for* de), pedir; **goods that are difficult to** — unos géneros que no se encuentran salida; **Cuba was trying to** — **her sugar** Cuba trataba de colocar su azúcar.

(c) (*of jobs*) dar un puesto a, emplear, colocar; **we could** — **200 men if we had them** podríamos colocar a 200 hombres si los tuviera.

(d) (*of series, rank etc*) **to be** —**d** (*in race*) colocarse; **to be** —**d second** colocarse en segundo lugar; **Vigo is well** —**d in the League** Vigo tiene un buen puesto en la Liga; **he is well** —**d to see it all** está en una buena posición para observarlo todo; **we are better** —**d than a month ago** hemos mejorado de posición en relación con la que ocupábamos hace un mes; **we are well** —**d to attack** estamos en una buena posición para pasar a la ofensiva.

(e) (*recall etc*) recordar, traer a la memoria; (*recognize*) reconocer; (*identify*) identificar; **I can't** — **him** no le recuerdo; **I can't quite** — **it** no puedo identificarlo con precisión; **she** —**d him at once** le reconoció en seguida.

place card ['pleiskɑːd] *n* tarjeta que indica el puesto que uno ha de ocupar en la mesa.

place kick ['pleiskik] *n* puntapié *m* colocado.

place mat ['pleismæt] *n* salvamantel *m*, reposaplatos *m*.

placement ['pleismənt] *n* colocación *f*.

place-name ['pleisneim] *n* topónimo *m*; —**s** (*as study, in general*) toponimia *f*; **the** —**s of Aragon** la toponimia aragonesa.

placenta [plə'sentə] *n* placenta *f*.

placid ['plæsid] *adj* plácido; apacible; tranquilo, sosegado.

placidity [plə'siditi] *n* placidez *f*; apacibilidad *f*; tranquilidad *f*; sosiego *m*.

placing ['pleisiŋ] *n* (*act*) colocación *f*; (— *in table, rank*) puesto *m*, calificación *f*.

plagiarism ['pleidʒiərizəm] *n* plagio *m*.

plagiarist ['pleidʒiərist] *n* plagiario *m*, a *f*.

plagiarize ['pleidʒiəraiz] *vt* plagiar.

plague [pleig] **1** *n* (*Med*) peste *f*; (*fig*) plaga *f*; **what a** — **he is!** ¡es un pesado!; **to avoid something like the** — huir de algo como de la peste, evitar algo a toda costa; **to hate something like the** — detestar algo.

2 *vt* plagar, infestar; (*fig*) acosar, atormentar; fastidiar; **a thought is plaguing me** me atormenta una idea; **to** — **the life out of someone** fastidiar a uno terriblemente, amargar la vida a uno; **to** — **someone with questions** importunar a uno con preguntas.

plaguey ['pleigi] *adj* (*fam*) latoso, engorroso.

plaice [pleis] *n* platija *f*.

plaid [plæd] *n* (*cloth*) tela *f* a cuadros; (*cloak*) manta *f* escocesa, plaid *m*.

plain [plein] **1** *adj* **(a)** (*clear*) claro, evidente; **a** — **case of jealousy** un caso evidente de celos; **it is** — **that . . .** es evidente que . . ., está claro que . . .; **it must be** — **to all that . . .** ha de ser obvio para todos que . . .; **it's as** — **as a pikestaff** está claro como la luz del día; **to make something** — **to someone** explicar algo a uno con toda claridad; decir algo a uno de modo que no quede lugar a dudas; **I must make it** — **that . . .** conste que . . ., quede bien claro que . . ., tengo que subrayar que . . .; **to make one's meaning** — explicar lo que uno quiere decir; **do I make myself** —? ¿me entiendes?

(b) (*outspoken*) franco, abierto; **to be** — **with someone** hablar claro a uno; **let me be** — **with you** dejémonos de rodeos, pongamos las cosas en su sitio.

(c) (*unadorned*) sencillo, llano; sin adornos; *answer* franco; *dealing* honrado; *language, style*

llano; *living* sin lujo; *knitting* de media; *cooking* corriente, casero; *truth* liso y llano; **in** — **language** hablando sin rodeos; para decirlo como ello es, para llamar las cosas por su nombre; **they're very** — **people** son gente muy sencilla; **I'm a** — **man** yo soy un hombre llano; **they used to be called** — **Smith** antes se llamaban Smith sin más.

(d) (*unmixed*) natural, puro, sin mezcla; **I like** — **whisky** me gusta el whiskey sin añadidura, me gusta el whiskey sin mezcla.

(e) (*of appearance*) sin atractivo, algo feo, ordinario; **she's terribly** —, **poor girl** no tiene atractivo alguno, la pobre; **pretty girls and** — **ones** las guapas y las feas; *see* **clothes**, **English** etc.

2 *adv* claro, claramente; **so I told him pretty** —, así que se lo dije con toda claridad; **I can't say it any** —**er** no lo puedo decir de modo más claro.

3 *n* llano *m*, llanura *f*; **the Great P**—**s** (*USA*) la Pradera.

plain-clothes ['plein'kləʊðz] *adj*: — **man** agente *m* de policía que lleva traje de calle.

plainly ['pleinli] *adv* **(a)** claramente, evidentemente; — **I was not welcome** evidentemente no iban a recibirme con placer; **to put something** — explicar algo con claridad; **to speak** — **to someone** hablar claro a uno.

(b) francamente, con franqueza.

(c) sencillamente, claramente.

plainness ['pleinnis] *n* **(a)** claridad *f*; evidencia *f*.

(b) franqueza *f*.

(c) sencillez *f*, llaneza *f*.

(d) (*of face*) falta *f* de atractivo, fealdad *f*, ordinariez *f*.

plainsman ['pleinzmən] *n*, *pl* —**men** [mən] llanero *m*.

plainsong ['pleinsɔŋ] *n* canto *m* llano.

plain speaking ['plein'spiːkiŋ] *n* franqueza *f*.

plain-spoken ['plein'spəʊkən] *adj* franco, llano.

plaintiff ['pleintif] *n* demandante *mf*, querellante *mf*.

plaintive ['pleintiv] *adj* lastimero, dolorido.

plaintively ['pleintivli] *adv* lastimeramente, con dolor.

plait [plæt] **1** *n* trenza *f*; **in** —**s** trenzado, en trenzas. **2** *vt* trenzar.

plan [plæn] **1** *n* **(a)** (*Archit*) plano *m*; **to make a** — **of** trazar el plano de.

(b) (*schedule etc*) programa *m*; (*system*) sistema *m*; (*tariff, in hotel etc*) tarifa *f*; **American** — (*in hotel: US*) cuarto *m* con comidas, pensión *f* completa; **European** — (*in hotel: US*) cuarto *m* sólo; **if everything goes according to** — si todo se realiza tal como se prevé; **everything went according to** — todo salió bien, todo resultó como se había previsto.

(c) (*Pol, Econ etc*) plan *m*; — **of campaign** plan *m* de campaña; **the Badajoz P**— el Plan Badajoz; **development** — plan *m* de desarrollo; **five-year** — plan *m* quinquenal; **the Marshall P**— el Plan Marshall; **to draw up a** — hacer un plan, redactar un plan.

(d) (*personal project etc*) proyecto *m*; **the** — **is to come back later** pensamos volver más tarde, tenemos la idea de volver más tarde; **the best** — **is to** + *infin* la mejor idea es + *infin*; **to change one's** — cambiar de proyecto, cambiar de idea; **what** —**s have you for the holiday?** ¿qué proyectos tienes para las vacaciones?; **have you any** —**s for tonight?** ¿tienes compromiso para esta noche?; **I have no fixed** —**s** no he arreglado nada en definitivo; **what** —**s have you for Jim?** ¿qué proyectos hay para Jaimito?, ¿qué ideas tienes sobre el porvenir de Jaimito?; **to make a** —**s** hacer proyectos; **to upset someone's** —**s** dar al traste con los proyectos de uno.

2 *vt* planear, planificar; proyectar; idear; **to** — **a robbery** planear un robo; **to** — **the future of an industry** planificar el porvenir de una industria; **the mania of** —**ning everything** la manía de planificarlo todo; **this trip was** —**ned by him** este viaje lo ideó él, fue él quien hizo los proyectos para este viaje.

3 *vi*: **to** — **for months** hacer proyectos durante meses enteros; **we are** —**ning for next April** hacemos proyectos para el abril que viene; **one has to** — **months ahead** hay que hacer los proyectos con varios meses de antelación; **to** — **to do something** proponerse hacer algo, pensar hacer algo; proyectar hacer algo; **we weren't** —**ning to** no teníamos tal intención; no se nos había ocurrido; **how long do you** — **to stay?** ¿cuánto tiempo piensas quedarte?

planchette [plɑːn'ʃet] *n* tabla *f* de escritura espiritista.

plane¹ [plein] *n* (*Bot*) plátano *m*.

plane² [plein] **1** *adj* plano; **— geometry** geometría *f* plana.

2 *n* **(a)** (*Math*) plano *m*; **focal —** plano *m* focal; **inclined —** plano *m* inclinado.

(b) (*fig*) nivel *m*, esfera *f*; **he seems to exist on another —** parece existir en una esfera distinta; **on this —** en este nivel, a esta altura.

(c) (*tool*) cepillo *m* (de carpintero).

(d) (*Aer*) avión *m*; **to go by —** ir en avión; **to send goods by —** enviar artículos por avión.

3 *vt* acepillar; **to — down** acepillar, desbastar, alisar.

planet ['plænit] *n* planeta *m*.
plane table ['pleinteibl] *n* plancheta *f*.
planetarium [,plæni'tɛəriəm] *n* planetario *m*.
planetary ['plænitəri] *adj* planetario.
plangent ['plændʒənt] *adj* plañidero.
planish ['plæniʃ] *vt* aplanar.
plank [plæŋk] **1** *n* tabla *f* (gruesa), tablón *m*; **—s** (*planking*) tablaje *m*; **deck —s** (*Naut*) tablazón *f* de la cubierta; (*fig: Pol*) principio *m*, artículo *m* (de un programa político).

2 *vt* entablar, entarimar; **to — something down** tirar algo violentamente, arrojar algo violentamente.

3 *vr*: **to — oneself down** sentarse (*etc*) de modo agresivo.

planking ['plæŋkiŋ] *n* tablas *fpl*, tablaje *m*; (*Naut*) tablazón *f* de la cubierta.
plankton ['plæŋktən] *n* plankton *m*.
planned [plænd] *adj economy* dirigido.
planner ['plænə*] *n* planificador *m*.
planning ['plæniŋ] *n* (*Pol, Econ etc*) planificación *f*; (*personal projects*) proyectos *mpl*; **family —** control *m* de natalidad.

planning board ['plæniŋ,bɔːd] *n* comisión *f* planificadora.

plant [plɑːnt] **1** *n* **(a)** (*Bot*) planta *f*.

(b) (*Tech: machinery*) equipo *m*, maquinaria *f*, instalación *f*; (*factory*) fábrica *f*; **we need new —** necesitamos un nuevo equipo, hace falta renovar la instalación; **pilot —** planta *f* piloto, fábrica *f* experimental.

(c) (*sl*) estratagema *f* para incriminar a uno; **it's a —** aquí hay trampa.

2 *attr* vegetal; **— life** vida *f* vegetal, las plantas; **— kingdom** reino *m* vegetal.

3 *vt* **(a)** *plant* plantar; *seed* sembrar; **to — a field with turnips** sembrar un campo de nabos; **the field is —ed with wheat** el campo está sembrado de trigo.

(b) (*place*) poner, colocar; fijar; *people* establecer; *blow* plantar, asestar; *idea etc* inculcar (*in* en), imbuir (*in* con); **to — something on someone** ocultar algo en la ropa (*or* en la habitación *etc*) de uno para incriminarle.

4 *vr*: **to — oneself in the middle of the road** ponerse en medio de la calle.

plantain ['plæntin] *n* llantén *m*.
plantation [plæn'teiʃən] *n* (*of tea, sugar etc*) plantación *f*; (*large estate*) hacienda *f*; (*of trees*) arboleda *f*; (*of young trees*) plantel *m*; **coffee —** cafetal *m*; **rubber —** cauchal *m*.

planter ['plɑːntə*] *n* plantador *m*; (*loosely*) colono *m*.
plantpot ['plɑːntpɔt] *n* tiesto *m*, maceta *f*.
plaque [plæk] *n* placa *f*.
plash [plæʃ] *see* splash.
plasm ['plæzəm], **plasma** ['plæzmə] *n* plasma *m*.
plaster ['plɑːstə*] **1** *n* (*lime material*) yeso *m*; (*in building*) argamasa *f*, (*layer on wall*) enlucido *m*; (*Med: applied to wound*) emplasto *m*, parche *m*, (*for eg injured arm*) escayola *f*, tablilla *f* de yeso; **adhesive —** esparadrapo *m*; **— of Paris** yeso *m* mate; **with his leg in —** con la pierna escayolada; **to have one's neck in —** tener el cuello escayolado.

2 *vt* **(a)** *wall* enyesar, enlucir; (*Med*) emplastar, aplicar un emplasto a; **to — a wall with posters** llenar (*or* cubrir) una pared de carteles; **to — posters on a wall** pegar carteles a una pared; **to — over a hole** llenar un hoyo de argamasa; **the children came back —ed with mud** los niños volvieron cubiertos de lodo. **(b)** (*fam*) dar una paliza a, pegar.

plasterboard ['plɑːstəbɔːd] *n* cartón *m* de yeso y fieltro.

plaster cast ['plɑːstə,kɑːst] *n* vaciado *m*; (*death mask*) mascarilla *f* mortuoria.

plastered ['plɑːstəd] *adj* (*sl*): **to be —** estar ajumado (*fam*).

plasterer ['plɑːstərə*] *n* yesero *m*, enlucidor *m*.
plastering ['plɑːstəriŋ] *n* enlucido *m*.
plastic ['plæstik] **1** *adj* plástico. **2** *n* plástico *m*.
Plasticine ['plæstisiːn] *n* (*Protected Trade Name*) plasticina *f*.
plasticity [plæs'tisiti] *n* plasticidad *f*.

plate [pleit] **1** *n* (*dish*) plato *m*; (*of metal etc*) lámina *f*, chapa *f*, plancha *f*; (*plaque*) placa *f*; (*silver*) vajilla *f* de plata; (*for taking collection*) platillo *m*; (*Typ*) lámina *f*; (*Phot*) placa *f*; (*prize, in racing*) premio *m*; (*also dental —*) placa *f* de la dentadura postiza; **gold —** vajilla *f* de oro; **to hand someone something on a —** (*fig*) servir algo a uno en bandeja de plata; **to have a lot on one's —** estar muy ocupado, tener muchos asuntos entre manos, tener grandes responsabilidades.

2 *vt* (*with metal*) planchear, chapear; (*with armour*) blindar; (*with silver*) platear; (*with nickel*) niquelar.

plate armour, (*US*) **— armor** ['pleit,ɑːmə*] *n* blindaje *m*.
plateau ['plætəu] *n*, *pl* **plateaux** [plæ'təuz] meseta *f*, altiplanicie *f*.
plated ['pleitid] *adj* chapeado (*with* de); (*armoured*) blindado.
plateful ['pleitful] *n* plato *m*.
plate glass ['pleit'glɑːs] *n* vidrio *m* cilindrado.
plateholder ['pleit,həuldə*] *n* (*Phot*) portaplacas *m*.
platelayer ['pleit,leiə*] *n* obrero *m* de ferrocarriles.
platform ['plætfɔːm] *n* **(a)** plataforma *f*; (*at meeting*) tribuna *f*; (*for band etc*) estrado *m*; (*roughly-built*) tablado *m*; (*Pol*) programa *m* electoral, política *f*; **the — speakers** los oradores de la tribuna.

(b) (*Rail*) andén *m*; (*with number mentioned*) vía *f*; **arrival —** andén *m* de vacío; **departure —** andén *m* de salida; **the 5.15 is at** (*or* **on**) **— 8** el tren de las 5.15 está en la vía número 8.

platform ticket ['plætfɔːm,tikit] *n* billete *m* de andén.
plating ['pleitiŋ] *n* enchapado *m*; capa *f* metálica; (*armour-*) blindaje *m*; (*of nickel*) niquelado *m*.
platinum ['plætinəm] *n* platino *m*.
platitude ['plætitjuːd] *n* lugar *m* común, tópico *m*, perogrullada *f*; **it is a — to say that . . .** es un tópico decir que . . .
platitudinous [,plæti'tjuːdinəs] *adj speech* lleno de lugares comunes (*etc*); *speaker* aficionado a los lugares comunes (*etc*), que peca por exceso de tópicos.
Plato ['pleitəu] *m* Platón.
Platonic [plə'tɔnik] *adj* platónico.
Platonist ['pleitənist] *n* platonista *mf*.
Platonism ['pleitənizəm] *n* platonismo *m*.
platoon [plə'tuːn] *n* pelotón *m*, sección *f*.
platter ['plætə*] *n* fuente *f*.
platypus ['plætipəs] *n* ornitorrinco *m*.
plaudits ['plɔːdits] *npl* aplausos *mpl*.
plausibility [,plɔːzə'biliti] *n* verosimilitud *f*, admisibilidad *f*, credibilidad *f*; **his — is such that . . .** habla tan bien que . . .
plausible ['plɔːzəbl] *adj argument etc* verosímil, admisible, creíble; *person* bien hablado pero no del todo confiable, que convence casi; **he's a — sort** tiene mucho cuento.
plausibly ['plɔːzəbli] *adv* de modo verosímil, creíblemente; **he tells it most —** lo cuenta de modo que convence casi.
play [plei] **1** *n* **(a)** (*amusement etc*) juego *m*, recreo *m*, diversión *f*; **— on words** juego *m* de palabras; **to be at —** estar jugando; **to make — of** burlarse de; **to say something in —** decir algo en broma.

(b) (*act of —ing*) jugada *f*; **neat —** una bonita jugada; **a clever piece of —** una hábil jugada; **fair —** juego *m* limpio; **foul —** juego *m* sucio; **to be in —** estar en juego; **to be out of —** estar fuera de juego; **— began at 3 o'clock** el partido comenzó a las 3, empezó a jugar a las 3.

(c) (*activity etc*) juego *m*, actividad *f*; **to bring into —** poner en juego; **to come into —** entrar en juego; **to give full — to one's imagination** dar rienda suelta a la imaginación; **to make great — with something** recalcar algo, insistir en algo.

(d) (*Mech*) juego *m*, holgura *f*, movimiento *m* libre.

(e) **the — of light on the water** el rielar de la luz sobre el agua; **the — of light and dark in this picture** el efecto de luz y sombra en este cuadro.

(f) (*Theat*) obra *f*, obra *f* dramática, comedia *f*; **radio —** comedia *f* radiofónica; **the —s of Lope** las obras dramáticas de Lope, el teatro de Lope; **to go to the —** ir al teatro.

2 *vt* **(a)** (*Theat etc*) *play* representar, poner, dar; *part* hacer, hacer el papel de, (*fig*) desempeñar; **when we —ed "Hamlet"** cuando representamos "Hamlet"; **when I —ed Hamlet** cuando hice el papel de Hamlet; **what did you —?** ¿qué papel tuvo Vd?; **we shall be —ing the West End** pondremos la obra en el West End; **when we last —ed Blackpool** cuando representamos la última vez en Blackpool; **we —ed "Lear" as a comedy** representamos "Lear" como comedia; **we —ed "Charley's Aunt" straight** representamos "Charley's Aunt" como obra seria; **let's — it for laughs** hagámoslo en versión burlesca; **he likes to — the soldier** se las echa de soldado, se da aires de militar; *see fool etc*.

(b) to — a joke on someone gastar una broma a uno; **to — a dirty trick on someone** hacer una mala pasada a uno.

(c) *card* jugar; *ball* golpear; *chess piece etc* mover; *fish* dejar que se canse, agotar; **to — the market** jugar a la bolsa.

(d) *cards, game etc* jugar a; **to — a game of tennis** jugar un partido de tenis; **to — a game of cards with someone** echar una partida de cartas con uno; **do you — football?** ¿juegas al fútbol?

(e) *opponent* jugar con, jugar contra; **I —ed him at chess** jugué contra él al ajedrez; **I —ed him twice** jugué contra él dos veces; **I'll — you for the drinks** el que pierda el juego que pague la cuenta.

(f) *(make member of team)* incluir, incluir en el equipo; **are they —ing Gento?** ¿juega Gento?, ¿van a incluir a Gento?

(g) to — someone false traicionar a uno.

(h) *(direct)* dirigir *(on* hacia, sobre); **to — hoses on a fire** utilizar unas mangueras para sofocar un incendio; **— the hose this way a bit** dirija la manguera más hacia este lado; **to — a searchlight on an aircraft** dirigir un reflector hacia un avión, hacer de un avión el blanco de un reflector.

(i) *(Mus) instrument, record* tocar; **to learn to — the piano** aprender a tocar el piano; **they —ed the 5th Symphony** tocaron la Quinta Sinfonía, interpretaron la Quinta Sinfonía.

(j) *(with adv or prep)* **to — a record back** repetir un disco; **to — a tape back** repetir lo grabado en una cinta; **to — an event down** quitar importancia a un suceso, tratar de minimizar un suceso; **to — off A against B** oponer A a B, contraponer A a B; **to — a match off** jugar el partido de desquite; **to — a work out to the end** seguir representando una obra hasta el fin; **to — out time** seguir jugando hasta el fin (sin hacer ningún esfuerzo para marcar otro gol *etc*); **the organ —ed the congregation out** tocaba el órgano mientras salían los fieles; **the vein is —ed out** la veta está agotada; **I'm —ed out** estoy agotado, estoy rendido; **that joke is —ed out now** ese chiste ya no vale; **to — someone up** burlarse de la autoridad de uno; **the kids — the teacher up** los pequeños le dan guerra a la maestra.

3 *vi* **(a)** *(amuse oneself)* jugar; divertirse; *(frolic)* jugar, juguetear; *(gambol)* retozar; **run away and —!** ¡idos a jugar!; **to — with a stick** jugar con un palo; **to — with fire** jugar con fuego; **he's just —ing with you** se está burlando de ti; **to — with an idea** acariciar una idea; **this is not a question to be —ed with** éste no es asunto para reírse, éste no es asunto para tomar en broma; *see fast etc*.

(b) *(at a game etc)* **to — at chess** jugar al ajedrez; **he just —s at it** lo hace con poca seriedad; **the little girl —s at being a woman** la niña juega a ser mujer; **he's —ing at being a soldier** se las echa de militar; no toma en serio la profesión militar; **—!** ¡listo!; **who —s first?** ¿quién juega primero?; **are you —ing today?** ¿tú juegas hoy?; **I've not —ed for a long time** hace mucho tiempo que no juego; **to — fair** jugar limpio; **to — for time** tratar de ganar tiempo; **to — into someone's hands** ceder la ventaja a un contrario.

(c) *(Mus)* tocar; **to — on the piano** tocar el piano; **do you —?** ¿sabe tocar?; **to be —ed on two pianos** tocar para tocar en dos pianos; **to — to someone** tocar para uno; **I —ed it specially for you** lo toqué para ti sólo; **the band was —ing rather loudly** tocaba la orquestra algo fuerte; **when the organ —s** cuando suena el órgano.

(d) *(light)* rielar; **the sun was —ing on the water** rielaba el sol sobre el agua.

(e) *(fountain)* correr; funcionar.

(f) *(act)* **to — in a film** tener *(or* hacer) un papel en una película; **we have —ed all over the South** hemos representado en todas partes del Sur; **to — ill** fingirse enfermo.

(g) to — on someone's credulity explotar la credulidad de uno; **to — on someone's feelings** aprovecharse de los sentimientos de uno; **we must — on their nerves** les hemos de hacer una guerra de nervios.

(h) *(with adv or prep)* **to — off** jugar el partido de desempate; **to — on** seguir jugando; **— on!** ¡adelante!; **to — up** *(play better)* jugar con más ánimo,

reanimarse; *(be naughty)* dar guerra; **— up!** ¡ánimo!, ¡aúpa!; **to — up to someone** hacer la pelotilla a uno.

playact ['pleiækt] *vi* hacer la comedia.

playacting ['plei,æktɪŋ] *n* comedia *f*, farsa *f*; **this is mere —** esto es puro teatro, no es más que una comedia.

playbill ['pleibil] *n* cartel *m* (de teatro).

playboy ['pleibɔi] *n* señorito *m*, córrelas *m*, joven *m* rico y amante de los placeres; **"The P— of the Western World"** "El córrelas del mundo occidental".

played-out ['pleid'aut] *adj* agotado.

player ['pleiə*] *n* *(Theat)* actor *m*, actriz *f*, representante *mf*; *(Mus)* músico *m*, a *f*; *(Sport)* jugador *m*, ora *f*; *(not amateur)* jugador *m* profesional; **gentlemen versus —s** los aficionados contra los profesionales.

playfellow ['plei,felou] *n* compañero *m* de juego, compañera *f* de juego.

playful ['pleiful] *adj person* juguetón; *mood* alegre; *remark* dicho en broma.

playfully ['pleifəli] *adv* jugando, en juego; alegremente; en broma; **he said —** dijo guasón.

playfulness ['pleifulnis] *n* carácter *m* juguetón; alegría *f*; tono *m* guasón.

playgoer ['plei,gəuə*] *n* aficionado *m* al teatro, aficionado *f* al teatro; **we are regular —s** vamos con regularidad al teatro.

playground ['pleigraund] *n* patio *m* de recreo.

playhouse ['pleihaus] *n*, *pl* **—houses** [hauziz] teatro *m*; *(US)* casita *f* de muñecas.

playing card ['pleiɪŋkɑ:d] *n* carta *f*.

playing field ['pleiɪŋfi:ld] *n* campo *m* de deportes.

playmate ['pleimeit] *n* camarada *mf*, compañero *m* de juego, compañera *f* de juego.

play-off ['pleiɔf] *n* partido *m* de desempate.

playpen ['pleipen] *n* parque *m* de jugar, corral *m* (de niño).

playroom ['pleirum] *n* cuarto *m* de los niños.

plaything ['pleiθɪŋ] *n* juguete *m* *(also fig)*.

playtime ['pleitaim] *n* hora *f* de recreo.

playwright ['pleirait] *n* dramaturgo *m*.

plea [pli:] *n* *(excuse)* pretexto *m*, disculpa *f*; *(entreaty)* súplica *f*, petición *f*; *(Law)* alegato *m*, defensa *f*; contestación *f* a la demanda, declaración *f*; **he made a — for mercy** pidió clemencia; **a — of insanity** un alegato de desequilibrio mental.

plead [pli:d] **1** *vt*: **to — someone's cause** hablar po uno, interceder por uno, *(Law)* defender a uno en juicio; **to — ignorance** pretender ignorancia, pretextar que uno no sabe; **he —ed certain difficulties** alegó ciertas dificultades.

2 *vi* **(a)** suplicar, rogar; **to — with someone** suplicar a uno; **to — with someone for something** rogar a uno que conceda *(or* permita *etc)* algo; **I —ed and —ed but it was no use** le supliqué mil veces pero de nada sirvió; **the village has —ed for a new bridge for 10 years** durante 10 años el pueblo viene reclamando un nuevo puente.

(b) *(Law: as barrister)* abogar.

(c) *(Law: as defendant)* declarar; **what do you —?** ¿qué contestación hace Vd a la demanda?; **to — guilty** confesarse culpable; **to — not guilty** negar la acusación.

pleading ['pli:dɪŋ] *n* súplicas *fpl*; *(Law)* alegatos *mpl*; **special —** argumentos *mpl* especiosos.

pleasant ['pleznt] *adj* agradable; *surprise etc* grato; *manner, style* ameno; *person* simpático, afable, amable; **we had a — time** lo pasamos muy bien; **it made a — change from our usual holiday** fueron unas vacaciones distintas de las acostumbradas y muy agradables; **it's a — surprise to find that . . .** es una grata sorpresa descubrir que . . .; **it did not make — reading** su lectura no fue nada agradable; **to make oneself — to someone** procurar ser amable con uno.

pleasantly ['plezntli] *adv* agradablemente; gratamente; en estilo ameno; afablemente, amablemente; **I am — surprised that . . .** para mí es una grata sorpresa que + *subj*; **it is — warm** hace un calor agradable.

pleasantness ['plezntnis] *n* agrado *m*, lo agradable; amenidad *f*; simpatía *f*, amabilidad *f*.

pleasantry ['plezntri] *n* chiste *m*, dicho *m* gracioso.

please [pli:z] **1** *vti* **(a)** *(give pleasure to)* dar gusto a, dar satisfacción a, agradar, contentar; caer en gracia a; **I did it just to — you** lo hice únicamente para darte gusto; **there's no pleasing him** es imposible contentarle; **he is easily —d** se contenta con cualquier cosa; **she's hard to —** es muy exigente; **the joke —d him** el chiste le cayó en gracia; **he is anxious to —** procura dar satisfacción; **a gift that is**

sure to — un regalo que siempre agrada; **music that —s the ear** una música grata para el oído; **to lay oneself out to — someone** desvivirse por contentar a uno; **it —d him to order that . . .** tuvo a bien ordenar que + *subj*.

(b) (*impers*) — **God!** (*arch*) ¡plegue a Dios!; **— God that . . .!** ¡plegue a Dios que + *subj*!

(c) (*expressing wish*) **—!** ¡por favor!, (*as protest*) ¡por Dios!; **my bill,** — la cuenta, por favor; **two pints —!** ¡dos cañas, por favor!; **two to Victoria,** — a Victoria, dos, por favor; **— pass the salt, pass the salt** — ¿me hace el favor de pasar la sal?; **— tell me** haga el favor de decírmelo, dígamelo por favor; **— be seated** siéntense; **— sit down!** ¡hagan el favor de sentarse!; **— accept this book** le ruego acepte este libro; **"— not to open this door"** "se ruega no abrir esta puerta"; **— don't cry!** ¡no llores, te lo suplico!; **now — do let me know if . . .** no dejes de decirme si . . .; **may I? . . . — do!** ¿se puede? . . . ¡naturalmente!

(d) (*think fit*) **if you —** si te parece; con tu permiso; **he wanted 10, if you —!** ¡quería llevarse 10, fíjate!; **to do as one —s** hacer lo que le da la gana; **I shall do what I —** haré lo que me parezca bien; **as you —** como Vd quiera; **do as you —** haga lo que quiera.

2 *vr*: **to — oneself** hacer lo que le da la gana; **— yourself!** ¡como Vd quiera!; **he has always —d himself about holidays** en asunto de vacaciones siempre ha hecho únicamente lo que ha querido.

pleased [pli:zd] *adj* (a) (*happy*) alegre, contento; **to be — estar** contento; **to be as — as Punch** estar como unas pascuas; **to look —** estar alegre, parece estar contento; tener aire satisfecho.

(b) **to be — with something** estar satisfecho de algo; **to be — with someone** mostrarse satisfecho con uno; **to be — with oneself** estar satisfecho de sí mismo; **they were anything but — with the news** la noticia no fue de su agrado, antes todo lo contrario; **I am — at the decision** me alegro de la decisión; **I am — to hear it** me alegro de saberlo; **I am — to meet you** tengo mucho gusto en conocerle; **I am — to be able to announce that . . .** me es grato poderles anunciar que . . .; **we are — to inform you that . . .** (*Comm*) nos complacemos en comunicarles que . . ., nos es grato informarles que . . .

(c) (*royal usage*) **Her Majesty has been graciously — to accept . . .** su Majestad aceptó sumamente complacida . . .

pleasing ['pli:ziŋ] *adj* agradable; grato; halagüeño; **— with — results** con resultados halagüeños; **a most — piece of news** una noticia muy grata.

pleasingly ['pli:ziŋli] *adv* agradablemente; gratamente.

pleasurable ['pleʒərəbl] *adj* agradable, deleitoso.

pleasurably ['pleʒərəbli] *adv* agradablemente, deleitosamente; **we were — surprised** para nosotros fue una grata sorpresa.

pleasure ['pleʒə*] 1 *n* (a) (*in general*) placer *m*, gusto *m*, satisfacción *f*; **with —** con mucho gusto; **it's a — to see him** da gusto verle; **it's a — to know that . . .** es un motivo de satisfacción saber que . . .; **it's a real —** es un verdadero placer; **—!, the — is mine!** (*returning thanks*) ¡no hay de qué!; **to find — in chess** divertirse jugando al ajedrez; **what — can you find in shooting partridges?** ¿qué placer encuentras en matar perdices?; **to give someone —** dar gusto a uno; **if it gives you any —** si Vd quiere; **I have much — in informing you that . . .** me es grato informarle que . . .; **may I have the —?** (*at dance*) ¿quiere Vd bailar?; **to take — in books** disfrutar leyendo; **I take great — in watching them grow** disfruto muchísimo viéndolos crecer; **to take — in doing damage** complacerse en hacer daño; **Mr and Mrs X request the — of Y's company** los señores de X solicitan el placer de su compañía.

(b) (*amusements*) placeres *mpl*; diversión *f*, recreo *m*; **all the —s of London** todos los placeres de Londres, todas las diversiones de Londres; **sexual —** placer *m* sexual; **to be fond of —** ser amante de los placeres.

(c) (*will*) voluntad *f*; **at — a** voluntad; **do it at your —** hágalo Vd cuando quiera, hágalo Vd cuando tenga tiempo; **during the royal —** todo el tiempo que quiera el monarca; **what is your —, sir?** ¿en qué puedo servirle, señor?, ¿qué manda Vd, señor?

2 *attr* de recreo, *eg* **— trip** viaje *m* de recreo.

pleasure boat ['pleʒəbəut] *n* barco *m* de recreo.
pleasure cruise ['pleʒəkru:z] *n* crucero *m* de recreo.
pleasure ground ['pleʒəgraund] *n* parque *m* de atracciones.

pleasure-loving ['pleʒə,lʌviŋ] *adj* amante de los placeres.
pleasure steamer ['pleʒə,sti:mə*] *n* vapor *m* de recreo.
pleat [pli:t] 1 *n* pliegue *m*. 2 *vt* plegar, plisar.
pleb [pleb] *n* (*fam*) plebeyo *m*, a *f*, persona *f* ordinaria; **the —s** la plebe.
plebeian [pli'bi:ən] 1 *adj* plebeyo. 2 *n* plebeyo *m*, a *f*.
plebiscite ['plebisit] *n* plebiscito *m*.
plectrum ['plektrəm] *n* plectro *m*.
pled [pled] (*US, Scot*) *irr: pret, ptp* of **plead**.
pledge [pledʒ] 1 *n* (*given as security*) prenda *f*; (*promise*) promesa *f*, voto *m*; garantía *f*; (*between governments etc*) compromiso *m*; (*toast*) brindis *m*; **as a —** en señal de, como garantía de; **I give you this —** os hago esta promesa; **the government will honour its —** el gobierno hará honor a sus compromisos; **to sign the —** jurar abstenerse del alcohol.

2 *vt* (a) (*pawn*) empeñar, pignorar, dejar en prenda.

(b) (*promise*) prometer; **to — support for someone** prometer su apoyo a uno, prometer apoyar a uno; **to — one's allegiance to someone** jurar ser fiel a uno; **I am —d to secrecy** he jurado guardarlo secreto; **we are —d to go to their aid** hemos prometido ir a ayudarles, nos hemos comprometido a ayudarles.

(c) (*toast*) brindar por.

3 *vr*: **to — oneself to** + *infin* comprometerse a + *infin*.

plenary ['pli:nəri] *adj* plenario.
plenipotentiary [,plenipə'tenʃəri] *n* plenipotenciario *m*.
plenitude ['plenitju:d] *n* plenitud *f*.
plenteous ['plentiəs] *adj*, **plentiful** ['plentiful] *adj* copioso, abundante; **a — supply of . . .** una buena provisión de . . ., un buen surtido de . . .; **eggs are now —** hay abundancia de huevos, abundan los huevos.
plentifully ['plentifəli] *adv* copiosamente, abundantemente.
plenty ['plenti] 1 *n* (a) abundancia *f*; cantidad *f* suficiente; **land of —** tierra *f* de la abundancia; **in —** en abundancia; **it rained in —** llovió copiosamente; **it grows here in —** por aquí existe en abundancia; **to live in —** vivir en el lujo; **that's —, thanks!** ¡basta, gracias!; **we have —** tenemos bastante; **there's — to go on** hay suficientes datos, son muchas las pruebas; **we know — about you** sabemos mucho acerca de Vd.

(b) **— of** bastante; muchos, muchísimos; una cantidad suficiente de; **we have — of money** tenemos bastante dinero; **they have — of money** tienen mucho dinero; **we have — of tea** tenemos una cantidad suficiente de té; **we have — of time** tenemos tiempo de sobra; **it takes — of courage** exige bastante valor; **— of people do** hay muchos que lo hacen, son muchos los que lo hacen.

2 *adv* (*fam*): **it's — big enough** claro que es bastante grande; **they're — rich enough to pay for two** desde luego son lo bastante ricos para pagar dos de ellos; **it rained — (US)** y ¡cómo llovió!; **we like it — (US)** nos gusta muchísimo.

pleonasm ['pli:ənæzəm] *n* pleonasmo *m*.
pleonastic [plia'næstik] *adj* pleonástico.
plethora ['pleθərə] *n* plétora *f*.
plethoric [ple'θɔrik] *adj* pletórico.
pleurisy ['pluərisi] *n* pleuresía *f*.
plexus ['pleksəs] *n* plexo *m*; **solar —** plexo *m* solar.
pliability [,plaiə'biliti] *n* flexibilidad *f*; (*fig*) docilidad *f*.
pliable ['plaiəbl] *adj*, **pliant** ['plaiənt] *adj* flexible; plegable; (*fig*) dócil, manejable.
pliers ['plaiəz] *npl* alicates *mpl*, tenazas *fpl*; **a pair of —, some —** unos alicates, unas tenazas.
plight[1] [plait] *vt word* dar, empeñar; **to — one's troth** (*arch or hum*) prometerse, dar su palabra de casamiento (*to* a).
plight[2] [plait] *n* condición *f* (inquietante), situación *f* (difícil); **the — of the shellfish industry** la situación difícil de la industria marisquera; **the country's economic —** la situación económica del país; los apuros económicos del país; **to be in a sad (or sorry) —** estar en un estado lamentable.
plimsolls ['plimsəlz] *npl* zapatillas *fpl* de goma.
plinth [plinθ] *n* plinto *m*.
Pliny ['plini] *m* Plinio; **— the Elder** Plinio el Viejo; **— the Younger** Plinio el Joven.
plod [plɔd] 1 *n* (a) **to go at a steady —** caminar despacio pero sin desanimarse.

(b) **it's a long — to the village** queda mucho camino para llegar al pueblo.

2 *vt* recorrer despacio; **we —ded the road for another hour** seguimos andando penosamente durante una hora más; **we —ded our way homeward** volvimos penosamente hacia casa.

3 *vi* (a) caminar despacio, andar penosamente, avanzar con dificultad (*also* **to — along, to — on**); **keep —ding!** ¡ánimo!, ¡no os dejéis desanimar!

(b) (*at work etc*) trabajar laboriosamente, trabajar lentamente pero sin desanimarse; **to — away at a task** dedicarse laboriosamente a un trabajo, seguir trabajando a pesar de las dificultades.

plodder ['plɔdə*] *n* estudiante *mf* más aplicado que brillante, persona *f* que trabaja con más aplicación que talento.

plodding ['plɔdiŋ] *adj* perseverante, laborioso; *student, worker* más aplicado que brillante.

plonk [plɔŋk] (*fam*) 1 *n* golpe *m* seco, ruido *m* seco; **it fell with a — to the floor** cayó al suelo con un ruido seco.

2 *adv*: **he went — into the stream** cayó aparatosamente al arroyo; **it landed — on his cheek** le dio de lleno en la mejilla.

3 *vt* (a) (*Mus*) puntear.

(b) **to — something down** arrojar algo con fuerza, dejar caer algo pesadamente.

4 *vr*: **to — oneself down in a chair** dejarse caer pesadamente en una silla; sentarse sin tener intención de levantarse.

plop [plɔp] 1 *n* paf *m*; **—!** ¡paf! 2 *vt* (*also* **to — down**) arrojar dejando oír un paf. 3 *vi* caer dejando oír un paf.

plosive ['pləusiv] (*Ling*) 1 *adj* oclusivo. 2 *n* oclusiva *f*.

plot[1] [plɔt] *n* (*Agr*) terreno *m*; parcela *f*; (*of vegetables, flowers etc*) cuadro *m*; (*for building*) solar *m*.

plot[2] [plɔt] 1 *n* (a) (*conspiracy*) complot *m*, conspiración *f*, conjura *f*.

(b) (*Lit, Theat*) argumento *m*; trama *f*, intriga *f*; **the — thickens** el argumento se complica, (*fig*) la cosa se complica.

2 *vt* (a) *course* (*on graph etc*) trazar; **to — A against Z** trazar A como función de Z.

(b) *downfall etc* urdir, tramar, maquinar.

3 *vi* conspirar, conjurarse; intrigar; **to — to do something** conspirar para hacer algo, conjurarse para hacer algo.

plotter ['plɔtə*] *n* conspirador *m*, ora *f*, conjurado *m*, a *f*.

plotting ['plɔtiŋ] *n* conspiración *f*, intrigas *fpl*, maquinaciones *fpl*.

plough, (US) plow [plau] 1 *n* arado *m*; **the P— (**Astron**)** el Carro, la Osa Mayor.

2 *vt* arar; (*fig*) surcar; (*Univ sl*) cargar, dar calabazas a; **I was —ed in French** me cargaron en francés; **to — back** (*Comm*) reinvertir; **to — in to — under** cubrir arando, enterrar arando; **to — up** *new ground* roturar, *bushes etc* arrancar con el arado, *pathway* hacer desaparecer arando; **the train —ed up the track for 100 metres** el tren destrozó unos 100 metros de la vía; **to — one's way through snow** abrirse con dificultad paso por la nieve; **to — one's way through a book** leer un libro con dificultad; **I —ed my way through it eventually** por fin acabé de leerlo pero resultó pesadísimo.

3 *vi* (a) arar; **to — through** *see vt* (**to — one's way**).

(b) (*sl*) **I —ed again** volvieron a suspenderme.

ploughing, (US) plowing ['plauiŋ] *n* arada *f*.

ploughing back, (US) plowing — ['plauiŋˌbæk] *n* (*Comm*) reinversión *f*.

ploughland, (US) plow— ['plaulænd] *n* tierra *f* de labrantío.

ploughman, (US) plow— ['plaumən] *n*, *pl* **—men** [mən] arador *m*, labrador *m*.

ploughshare, (US) plow— ['plauʃɛə*] *n* reja *f* del arado.

plover ['plʌvə*] *n* chorlito *m*.

plow [plau] (*US*) *see* **plough**.

ploy [plɔi] *n* (*fam*) truco *m*, estratagema *f*.

pluck[1] [plʌk] *n* (*courage*) valor *m*, ánimo *m*; (*guts*) agallas *fpl*; **it takes — to do that** hace falta tener agallas para conseguir eso; **he's got plenty of —** sí tiene agallas; **I didn't have the — to confess** no tuve bastante ánimo para confesar.

pluck[2] [plʌk] 1 *n* (*tug*) tirón *m*.

2 *vt* *fruit, flower* coger; *bird* desplumar; *guitar* puntear; **to — one's eyebrows** depilarse las cejas; **to — off, to — out, to — up** arrancar con los dedos, arrancar de un tirón; quitar de un tirón; **he —ed it up off the table** lo recogió de la mesa con un movimiento brusco; *see* **courage**.

3 *vi*: **to — at** tirar de, dar un tirón a; **to — at someone's sleeve** tirar de la manga de uno.

pluckily ['plʌkili] *adv* valientemente; con resolución.

pluckiness ['plʌkinis] *n* valor *m*, ánimo *m*; resolución *f*.

plucky ['plʌki] *adj* valiente, valeroso; resuelto.

plug [plʌg] 1 *n* (a) (*bung*) tapón *m*, taco *m*; (*in bath etc*) tapón *m*; (*Med, of cotton wool etc*) tampón *m*; (*of tobacco*) rollo *m*, tableta *f*; (*Aut*) bujía *f*; (*Elec: free, on wire, on apparatus*) clavija *f*, enchufe *m*, (*in wall*) toma *f*; (*Tel*) clavija *f*; **two-pin —** clavija *f* bipolar; **three-pin —** clavija *f* de 3 polos.

(b) (*sl*) anuncio *m* incidental, publicidad *f* incidental; **to give someone a —** permitir que uno se beneficie de la publicidad; **to put in a — for a product** lograr anunciar un producto de modo solapado.

2 *vt* (a) *hole etc* tapar, llenar, obturar; (*Archit*) rellenar; *tooth* empastar; **to — in a radio** conectar una radio; **to — a lead into a socket** enchufar un hilo en una toma; **to — up** tapar, obturar; **to — the drain on the reserves** acabar con las pérdidas de divisas.

(b) (*sl: hit*) pegar, (*shoot*) pegar un tiro a.

(c) (*Comm sl*) anunciar de modo solapado, dar publicidad incidental a; (*repeat*) repetir, machacar en; **he's been —ging that line for years** hace años que viene diciendo lo mismo.

3 *vi*: **to — away** seguir trabajando (*etc*) a pesar de todo, batir el yunque; no dejarse desanimar.

plughole ['plʌghəul] *n* tubo *m* de salida, salida *f*.

plug-in ['plʌgin] *adj* (*Elec*) enchufable.

plum [plʌm] *n* (*fruit*) ciruela *f*; (*tree*) ciruelo *m*; (*fig: the best*) lo mejor; (*post*) pingüe destino *m*, turrón *m*, breva *f*.

plumage ['plu:midʒ] *n* plumaje *m*.

plumb [plʌm] 1 *n* plomada *f*.

2 *adj* vertical, a plomo.

3 *adv* verticalmente, a plomo.

(b) (*fam*) totalmente, completamente; **— crazy** completamente loco; **— in the middle** exactamente en el centro; **it hit him — on the nose** le dio de lleno en las narices.

4 *vt* sondar, sondear (*also fig*).

plumbago [plʌmˈbeigəu] *n* plombagina *f*.

plumber ['plʌmə*] *n* fontanero *m*.

plumbic ['plʌmbik] *adj* plúmbico, plúmbeo.

plumbing ['plʌmiŋ] *n* (*craft*) fontanería *f*; (*piping*) instalación *f* de cañerías; (*bathroom fittings*) aparatos *mpl* sanitarios.

plumbline ['plʌmlain] *n* cuerda *f* de plomada.

plume [plu:m] 1 *n* pluma *f*; (*on helmet*) penacho *m*; (*of smoke etc*) penacho *m*, hilo *m*.

2 *vr*: **the bird —s itself** el ave se limpia las plumas, el ave se arregla las plumas.

plumed [plu:md] *adj* plumado; con plumas; *helmet* empenachado.

plummet ['plʌmit] 1 *n* plomada *f*. 2 *vi*: **to — down, to come —ing down** caer a plomo.

plummy ['plʌmi] *adj* (*fam*) *voice* pastoso.

plump[1] [plʌmp] 1 *adj* *body* rechoncho, rollizo; *face* mofletudo; *chicken etc* gordo. 2 *vt* (*fatten*) engordar; (*swell*) hinchar. 3 *vi* engordar; hincharse.

plump[2] [plʌmp] 1 *adv* de lleno; **to fall — on to something** caer de lleno en algo.

2 *vt*: **to — something down** arrojar algo pesadamente, dejar caer algo pesadamente en el suelo.

3 *vi* (a) (*fall*) caer pesadamente, dejarse caer pesadamente; **to — down on to a chair** dejarse caer pesadamente en un sillón.

(b) **to — for** optar por; (*vote*) votar por.

4 *vr*: **to — oneself down** dejarse caer pesadamente.

plumpness ['plʌmpnis] *n* gordura *f*; lo rollizo.

plum pudding ['plʌm'pudiŋ] *n* especie de *pudín inglés de ciruela (esp de Navidad)*.

plum tree ['plʌmtri:] *n* ciruelo *m*.

plunder ['plʌndə*] 1 *n* (*act*) pillaje *m*, saqueo *m*; (*loot*) botín *m*.

2 *vt* saquear, pillar; *tomb* robar; *safe* robar el contenido de, robar (las alhajas de); **they —ed my cellar** saquearon mi bodega.

plunderer ['plʌndərə*] *n* saqueador *m*.

plundering ['plʌndəriŋ] *n* saqueo *m*.

plunge [plʌndʒ] 1 *n* (a) (*dive from bank etc*) salto *m*; (*submersion by swimmer, bird etc*) zambullida *f*; (*by professional diver*) inmersión *f*; (*bathe*) baño *m*; **the diver rested after each —** el buzo descansó después de cada inmersión; **he had a — before breakfast** se fue a bañar antes de desayunar.

(b) (*bath*) baño *m*; (*pool*) piscina *f*; **cold —** baño *m* frío.

(c) (*fig*) **to take the —** dar el paso decisivo, resolverse; jugarse el todo; **we are about to take the —** estamos al punto de dar el paso decisivo;

I took the — and bought it por fin me resolví a comprarlo.
  2 vt **(a)** (immerse) sumergir; hundir (into en); **he —d his hands into the water** hundió las manos en el agua; **he —d his hand into his pocket** metió la mano en el bolsillo.
  (b) to — a dagger into someone's chest hundir (or clavar) un puñal en el pecho de uno.
  (c) to — a room into darkness sumir un cuarto en la oscuridad; **New York was suddenly —d into darkness** Nueva York se vio de repente sumida en la oscuridad.
  (d) to — someone into sadness hundir (or sumir, abismar) a uno en la tristeza; **we were —d into gloom by the news** la noticia nos sumió en la tristeza.
  3 vi **(a)** (dive) saltar; zambullirse; sumergirse; (sink) hundirse; **then the submarine —d** luego se sumergió el submarino; **she —d into 10 metres of water** se zambulló en 10 metros de agua.
  (b) (fall) caer; **he —d to his death** tuvo una caída mortal; **he —d from a 5th storey window** se arrojó desde una ventana del 5° piso; **the aircraft —d into the sea off Dover** el avión cayó al mar a la altura de Dover.
  (c) (dress: fam) tener mucho escote, ser muy escotado.
  (d) (ship) cabecear; (horse) corcovear.
  (e) (person: rush) arrojarse, lanzarse, precipitarse; **to — forward** precipitarse hacia adelante; **to — into one's work** emprender resuelto su trabajo, engolfarse en el trabajo; **to — heedlessly into danger** meterse en los peligros sin hacer caso de ellos; **he —d into a discussion of Plato** se lanzó a una discusión de Platón.
  (f) (fam: gamble) apostar el todo; (Comm) arriesgar mucho dinero.
  (g) (fam: decide) resolverse, dar el paso decisivo.
plunger ['plʌndʒə*] n émbolo m.
plunging ['plʌndʒiŋ] adj (fam) **neckline** muy bajo.
plunk [plʌŋk] n etc (US) = **plonk**.
pluperfect [plu:'pə:fikt] n pluscuamperfecto m.
plural ['pluərəl] **1** adj plural; **the — form of the noun** la forma del sustantivo en plural. **2** n plural m; **in the — en el plural**.
plurality [ˌpluə'ræliti] n pluralidad f.
plus [plʌs] **1** prep más, y; además de; juntamente con; **3 – 4** 3 más 4; **— what I have to do already** además de lo que tengo que hacer ya.
  2 adj **(a)** (Math, quantity, Elec) positivo, de signo positivo.
  (b) two pounds — dos libras y algo más, más de dos libras; **twenty —** veinte y pico, veintitantos.
  3 n (Math: sign) signo m más; (amount) cantidad f positiva.
plus fours ['plʌs'fɔ:z] npl pantalones mpl de golf. pantalones mpl holgados de media pierna.
plush [plʌʃ] **1** n felpa f. **2** adj de felpa; (fam) see **plushy.**
plushy ['plʌʃi] adj (fam) lujoso, elegante, de buen tono.
Plutarch ['plu:ta:k] m Plutarco.
Pluto ['plu:təu] m Plutón.
plutocracy [ˌplu:'tɔkrəsi] n plutocracia f.
plutocrat ['plu:təukræt] n plutócrata mf.
plutocratic [ˌplu:təu'krætik] adj plutocrático.
plutonium [plu:'təuniəm] n plutonio m.
pluviometer [ˌplu:vi'ɔmitə*] n pluviómetro m.
ply¹ [plai] n: eg **three —** (wood) de tres capas, (wool) de tres cordones.
ply² [plai] **1** vt needle, tool etc manejar, menear (vigorosamente); oars etc emplear; trade ejercer; seas, river navegar por; person no dejar descansar a; **to — someone with questions** importunar a uno haciéndole muchas preguntas; **to — someone for information** importunar a uno pidiéndole informes; **to — someone with drink** dar a uno repetidas veces de beber, emborrachar a uno; **to — someone with cakes** ofrecer repetidas veces los pastelitos a uno.
  2 vi: **to — between** hacer el servicio entre, ir y venir entre; **to — for hire** ofrecerse para alquilar.
plywood ['plaiwud] n madera f contrachapada, madera f multilaminar, panel m.
pneumatic [nju:'mætik] adj neumático.
pneumatically [nju:'mætikəli] adv neumáticamente.
pneumonia [nju:'məuniə] n pulmonía f; **double —** pulmonía f doble.
po [pəu] n (fam) orinal m; wáter m.
poach¹ [pəutʃ] vt egg escalfar.
poach² [pəutʃ] **1** vt cazar (or pescar etc) en vedado; cazar (or pescar etc) ilegalmente; (fig: steal) robar, advantage etc pisar, tomar.

  2 vi cazar (or pescar etc) en finca ajena; **to — on someone's preserves** (fig) cazar en finca ajena, meterse en los asuntos ajenos.
poached [pəutʃt] adj egg escalfado.
poacher ['pəutʃə*] n cazador m furtivo.
poaching ['pəutʃiŋ] n caza f furtiva, pesca f furtiva.
pochard ['pəutʃəd] n (Zool) porrón m.
pock [pɔk] n pústula f.
pocket ['pɔkit] **1** n bolsillo m; (Billiards) tronera f; (fig, Geol, Mil etc) bolsa f; hoyo m, cavidad f, hueco m; (Aer) bolsa f de aire; **trouser —** bolsillo m del pantalón; **— of resistance** bolsa f de resistencia; **to be in —** salir ganando; **to be £5 in —** haber ganado 5 libras; **to be out of —** salir perdiendo; **to be £5 out of —** haber perdido 5 libras; **he has the game in his —** domina el partido, está seguro de ganar el partido; **to have someone in one's —** haberse cazado la voluntad de uno; **to line one's —s** ponerse las botas; see **pick**.
  2 attr de bolsillo; **— battleship** acorazado m de bolsillo; **— edition** edición f de bolsillo.
  3 vt meter en el bolsillo, guardar en el bolsillo; (Billiards) entronerar; (earn, make) ganar; (pej) apropiarse, alzarse con, embolsar; **he —ed half the takings** se embolsó la mitad de la recaudación; see **pride** etc.
pocketbook ['pɔkitbuk] n cartera f, portamonedas m.
pocketful ['pɔkitful] n bolsillo m; cantidad f que cabe en el bolsillo; **a — of nuts** un bolsillo lleno de nueces.
pocket-handkerchief [ˌpɔkit'hæŋkətʃif] n pañuelo m.
pocket knife ['pɔkitnaif] n, pl **— knives** [naivz] navaja f.
pocket money ['pɔkitˌmʌni] n dinero m para pequeños gastos personales.
pocket-size ['pɔkitsaiz] adj de bolsillo.
pockmark ['pɔkma:k] n hoyo m.
pockmarked ['pɔkma:kt] adj face picado de viruelas; surface marcado de hoyos; **to be — with** estar marcado de, estar acribillado de.
pod [pɔd] n vaina f.
podgy ['pɔdʒi] adj gordinflón; face mofletudo.
podiatry [pɔ'diətri] n podiatría f.
podium ['pəudiəm] n podio m.
poem ['pəuim] n poesía f; (long, narrative) poema m; **P— of the Cid** Poema m de mío Cid, Cantar m de mío Cid; **Lorca's —s** las poesías de Lorca, la obra poética de Lorca, las obras en verso de Lorca.
poet ['pəuit] n poeta m; **— laureate** poeta m laureado.
poetaster [ˌpəui'tæstə*] n poetastro m.
poetess ['pəuites] n poetisa f.
poetic(al) [pəu'etik(əl)] adj poético.
poetically [pəu'etikəli] adv poéticamente.
poeticize [pəu'etisaiz] vt (enhance) poetizar, adornar con detalles poéticos; (translate into verse) hacer un poema de, hacer una versión poética de.
poetics [pəu'etiks] n poética f.
poetry ['pəuitri] n poesía f; see also **poem**.
pogrom ['pɔgrəm] n pogrom m, pogromo m, persecución f antisemítica.
poignancy ['pɔinjənsi] n patetismo m; intensidad f, profundidad f.
poignant ['pɔinjənt] adj (moving) conmovedor, patético; (profound) intenso, agudo, profundo.
poignantly ['pɔinjəntli] adv de modo conmovedor, patéticamente; intensamente, agudamente.
poinsettia [pɔin'setiə] n flor f de la Pascua.
point [pɔint] **1** n **(a)** (Typ etc) punto m; **decimal —** punto m decimal, coma f; **7.6** 7,6 (siete enteros y seis décimos).
  (b) (on scale; place, time) punto m; **— of the compass** cuarta f; **— of departure** punto m de partida; **angular —** vértice m; **cardinal —s** puntos mpl cardinales; **focal —** punto m focal; **reference —** punto m de referencia; see **boiling —** etc; **Slough and all —s west** Slough y las estaciones más hacia el oeste; **at the — where the road forks** donde se bifurca el camino; **at this —** en esto, llegado a este punto; **at that — in time** en aquel momento; **at all —s** por todas partes, en todos los sitios; **matters are at such a — that . . .** las cosas han llegado a tal punto que . . .; **to be on the — of + ger** estar a punto de + infin; **delivered free to all —s in Spain** se entrega a porte pagado en toda España; **he is severe to the — of cruelty** es tan severo que hasta se puede decir que es cruel; **up to a —** hasta cierto punto; **up to a —, Lord Copper** en cierto modo, Lord Copper.
  (c) (aspect) punto m, aspecto m; **— of interest** punto m interesante, aspecto m interesante; **— of honour** cuestión f de honor, punto m de honor; **— of order** cuestión f de procedimiento; **in — of en**

cuanto a, por lo que se refiere a; **in — of fact** en realidad; **in — of numbers** en cuanto al número; **in — of sheer strength** en cuanto a la fuerza sola.

(**d**) **— of view** punto *m* de vista; **from the — of view of** desde el punto de vista de; **to come round to someone's — of view** adoptar el criterio de uno, compartir la opinión de uno; **to look at a matter from all —s of view** considerar una cuestión bajo todos sus aspectos; **to see** (*or* **understand**) **someone's — of view** comprender el punto de vista de uno.

(**e**) (*of argument etc*) punto *m*; **the — at issue** el punto en cuestión, el asunto en litigio; **the —s to remember are . . .** los puntos a retener son los siguientes . . .; **to be beside the —** no venir al caso; **it is beside the — that . . .** no importa que + *subj*; **it's off the —** está fuera de propósito; **to get off the —**, **to wander off the —** salirse del tema, apartarse del tema; **on this —** sobre este punto; **on that —** en cuanto a eso; **on that — we agree** sobre eso estamos de acuerdo; **to differ on a —** no estar de acuerdo en un particular; **an argument very much to the —** un argumento muy a propósito; **that is hardly to the —** eso apenas hace al caso; **to come to the —** ir al grano; **let's come to the —!** ¡vamos al grano!, ¡dejémonos de historias!; **to get back to the —** volver al tema; **to keep to the —** no salirse del tema; **to carry one's — salirse** con la suya; **it gave — to the argument** hizo ver la importancia del argumento; **to make a — **establecer un punto, hacer aceptar una opinión; **he made the following —** dijo lo siguiente; **to make the — that . . .** hacer ver que . . ., hacer comprender que . . .; **to make a — of** + *ger* no dejar de + *infin*, insistir en + *infin*; **to press the —** insistir (*that* en que); **to pursue one's —** seguir su tema; **to stretch a — **hacer una excepción, hacer una concesión.

(**f**) (*significant part, important thing*) lo significativo, lo importante; **this is the —** esto es lo importante; **the — is, . . .** lo importante es . . .; **the whole — is . . .** lo único que importa es . . .; **the — is that . . .** lo importante es que . . .; **that's just the —!** ¡sí eso es lo más importante!; **that's not the —** no es eso; **the — of the joke is that . . .** la gracia del chiste consiste en que . . .; **to get the —** comprender; **to miss the —** no ver lo esencial.

(**g**) (*purpose*) fin *m*, finalidad *f*, objeto *m*; (*usefulness*) utilidad *f*; **what's the — of railways?** ¿qué utilidad tienen los ferrocarriles?, ¿de qué sirven los ferrocarriles?; **what's the — of trying?** ¿de qué sirve esforzarse?; **there is no — in** + *ger* no vale la pena + *infin*, no hay para qué + *infin*; **I don't see the — of doing it** no entiendo por qué sea necesario hacerlo, no creo que sea necesario hacerlo.

(**h**) (*of character*) rasgo *m*, característica *f*; cualidad *f*; **weak —** flaco *m*, punto *m* débil; **—s of a horse** características *fpl* de un caballo; **he has his —s** tiene algunas cualidades buenas; **it was always his strong —** siempre ha sido su punto fuerte; **maths is not a strong — of mine** nunca he entendido gran cosa en matemáticas; **what —s should I look for?** ¿qué puntos debo examinar?

(**i**) (*Games*) punto *m*, tanto *m*; **—s against** puntos *mpl* en contra; **—s for** puntos *mpl* a favor; **to give someone —s** dar una ventaja a uno; **to score 10 —s** marcar 10 puntos; **to win on —s** ganar por puntos.

(**j**) (*unit*) **the thermometer went up 3 —s** el termómetro subió 3 grados; **the shares went down 2 —s** las acciones bajaron 2 enteros.

(**k**) (*sharp end: of needle etc*) punta *f*; (*of pen*) puntilla *f*; (*Geog*) punta *f*, promontorio *m*, cabo *m*; (*Elec*) enchufe *m*, toma *m*; **—s** (*Rail*) agujas *fpl*; **a five-point star** una estrella de cinco puntas; **to put a — on a pencil** sacar punta a un lápiz; **to put too fine a — on it** para decirlo como ello es, hablando sin rodeos.

2 *vt* (**a**) (*sharpen*) afilar, aguzar; *pencil* sacar punta a.

(**b**) **to — a moral** inculcar una lección, subrayar una moraleja.

(**c**) *gun, telescope etc* apuntar (*at* a); **to — a gun at someone** apuntar a uno con un fusil; **to — a finger at someone** señalar a uno con el dedo.

(**d**) *path, way* indicar.

(**e**) *wall* rejuntar.

(**f**) *text* puntuar; *Hebrew etc* puntar.

(**g**) **to — out** indicar, señalar; **to — out something to someone** señalar algo a uno, enseñar algo a uno; (*in speaking*) hacer ver algo a uno, indicar algo a uno; **to — out someone's mistakes** señalar los errores de uno; **to — out to someone the advantages of a car** explicar a uno las ventajas de tener coche; **to — out that . . .** indicar que . . ., advertir que . . .;

may I — out that . . . permítaseme observar que . . .

(**h**) **to — up** destacar, poner de relieve.

3 *vi* (**a**) **to — at someone** señalar (*or* indicar) a uno con el dedo.

(**b**) (*of dog*) mostrar la caza, pararse.

(**c**) **it —s north** está orientado hacia el norte; **the hand —ed to midnight** la aguja marcaba las 12; **this —s to the fact that . . .** esto indica que . . .; **everything —s that way** todo parece indicarlo; **everything —s to his success** todo anuncia su éxito; **everything —s to the festival being a lively one** el festival se anuncia animado; **the evidence —s to her** las pruebas indican que ella es la culpable.

point-blank ['pɔint'blæŋk] **1** *adv* a quemarropa (*also fig*); **to ask someone something —** preguntar algo a uno a quemarropa; **to refuse —** dar una negativa rotunda.

2 *adj question, shot* hecho a quemarropa.

point duty ['pɔint,djuːti] *n* control *m* de la circulación.

pointed ['pɔintid] *adj shape* puntiagudo; (*sharp*) afilado, agudo; (*Archit*) *window* ojival; *remark etc* lleno de intención; inequívoco, directo; enfático.

pointedly ['pɔintidli] *adv say etc* con intención; inequívocamente, directamente; enfáticamente.

pointer ['pɔintə*] *n* (*needle*) indicador *m*, aguja *f*; (*of balance*) fiel *m*; (*long stick*) puntero *m*; (*dog*) perro *m* de muestra; (*fig*) indicación *f*; pista *f*; **it is a — to a possible solution** es una indicación de una solución posible; **there is at present no — to the outcome** por ahora nada indica qué resultado tendrá; **this is a — to the guilty man** es una pista que conducirá al criminal.

pointillism ['pwæntilizəm] *n* puntillismo *m*.

pointless ['pɔintlis] *adj* (*useless*) inútil; (*motiveless*) sin motivo, inmotivado; (*meaningless*) sin sentido; insensato; **it is — to complain** es inútil quejarse, de nada sirve quejarse; **an apparently — crime** un crimen que parece carecer de motivo; **a — existence** una vida sin sentido, una vida que carece de propósito.

pointlessly ['pɔintlisli] *adv* inútilmente; sin motivo.

pointlessness ['pɔintlisnis] *n* inutilidad *f*; falta *f* de motivo; falta *f* de sentido; **the — of war** la insensatez *f* de la guerra.

point-to-point ['pɔinttə'pɔint] *n* (*also* **— race**) carrera de caballos a través del campo.

poise [pɔiz] **1** *n* (**a**) (*balance*) equilibrio *m*.

(**b**) (*fig: of body*) aire *m*, porte *m*; elegancia *f*; **she dances with such —** baila con tanta elegancia, baila con tal aplomo.

(**c**) (*of mind*) serenidad *f*; aplomo *m*; confianza *f* en sí mismo; **she does it with great —** lo hace con el mayor aplomo; **he lacks —** le falta confianza en sí mismo.

2 *vt* equilibrar; balancear; **he —d it on his hand** lo puso en equilibrio sobre la mano; **to be —d** estar suspendido; (*hover*) cernerse, estar inmóvil (en el aire *etc*); **they are —d to attack, they are —d for the attack** están listos para atacar, están en condiciones de lanzarse al ataque.

poised [pɔizd] *adj* (*in temperament*) sereno, ecuánime, confiado en sí mismo; *see* **poise 2**.

poison ['pɔizn] **1** *n* veneno *m*; tóxico *m*; (*fig*) ponzoña *f*, veneno *m*; **to die of —** morir envenenado; **to take — envenenarse**.

2 *vt* envenenar; (*fig*) envenenar, emponzoñar; corromper.

poisoner ['pɔizənə*] *n* envenenador *m*, ora *f*.

poison gas ['pɔizn'gæs] *n* gas *m* tóxico, gas *m* asfixiante.

poisoning ['pɔizniŋ] *n* envenenamiento *m*.

poisonous ['pɔiznəs] *adj snake etc* venenoso; *substance, fumes etc* tóxico; (*fig: damaging*) pernicioso, (*very bad*) horrible, malísimo; **this — propaganda** esta propaganda perniciosa; **the play was —** la obra fue horrible; **he's a — individual** es una persona horrible.

poison-pen ['pɔizn'pen] *adj*: **— letter** carta *f* anónima con injurias.

poke¹ [pəuk] *n* (*sack*) saco *m*, bolsa *f*.

poke² [pəuk] **1** *n* (*push*) empuje *m*, empujón *m*; (*with elbow*) codazo *m*; (*jab*) pinchazo *m*; hurgonazo *m*; (*with poker*) hurgonada *f*, hurgonazo *m*; **to give the fire a —** atizar la lumbre, remover la lumbre; **to give someone a — in the ribs** dar a uno un codazo en las costillas; **to give someone a — with a bayonet** dar a uno un pinchazo con la bayoneta.

2 *vt* (*push*) empujar; *fire* hurgar, atizar, remover; **to — someone in the ribs** dar a uno un codazo en las costillas; **to — someone in the ribs with a stick** dar a uno un pinchazo con un palo en las costillas; **to —**

a stick into a crack introducir un palo en una grieta; **to — a rag into a tube** introducir un trapo en un tubo; **to — a stick into the ground** clavar un palo en el suelo; **to — someone's eye out** saltar el ojo a uno, quebrar el ojo a uno; **to — a hole in a picture** hacer un agujero en un cuadro; **to — one's head out** sacar la cabeza, asomar la cabeza; *see* **fun**, **nose**, *and compare* **jab**.

3 *vi* **(a) to — at something with a stick** tratar de remover *(etc)* algo con un bastón.

(b) to — about, to — around andar buscando (algo); *(pej)* fisgar, hacer indagaciones a hurtadillas; **we spent a day poking about in the shops** pasamos un día curioseando en las tiendas; **and now you come poking about!** ¡y ahora Vd se mete a husmear!; **to — into someone's business** meterse en los asuntos de uno.

poker¹ ['pəukə*] *n* atizador *m*, badila *f*.

poker² ['pəukə*] *n* (*Cards*) póquer *m*; **to have a — face** tener una cara impasible.

poker-faced ['pəukə'feist] *adj* de cara impasible; **they looked on —** miraron impasibles, miraron sin expresión.

poky ['pəuki] *adj room* estrecho, muy pequeño; **a — little room** un cuartucho.

Poland ['pəulənd] Polonia *f*.

polar ['pəulə*] *adj* polar.

polar bear ['pəulə'bɛə*] *n* oso *m* blanco.

polarity [pəu'læriti] *n* polaridad *f*.

polarization [,pəulərai'zeiʃən] *n* polarización *f*.

polarize ['pəuləraiz] **1** *vt* polarizar. **2** *vi* polarizarse.

Pole [pəul] *n* polaco *m*, a *f*.

pole¹ [pəul] **1** *n* **(a)** *medida de longitud* = 5,029 m.

(b) palo *m*, palo *m* largo, vara *f* larga; (*flag*—) asta *f*; (*tent*—) mástil *m*; (*for fencing*) estaca *f*; (*Tel*) poste *m*; (*for gymnastics*) percha *f*; (*for vaulting*) pértiga *f*; (*for punting*) pértiga *f*; (*of cart*) vara *f*, lanza *f*; **greasy —** cucaña *f*, palo *m* ensebado; **to be up the —** (*sl*) estar chiflado (*fam*).

2 *vt punt etc* impeler con pértiga.

pole² [pəul] *n* (*Elec, Geog etc*) polo *m*; **negative —** polo *m* negativo; **positive —** polo *m* positivo; **North P— Polo** *m* Norte; **South P— Polo** *m* Sur; **from — to — de polo a polo.**

poleaxe ['pəulæks] *vt* desnucar.

polecat ['pəulkæt] *n* turón *m*; (US) mofeta *f*.

polemic [pə'lemik] **1** *adj* polémico. **2** *n* polémica *f*; **—s** polémica *f*.

polemical [pə'lemikəl] *adj* polémico.

pole star ['pəulsta:*] *n* estrella *f* polar.

pole vault ['pəulvɔ:lt] *n* salto *m* con pértiga.

police [pə'li:s] **1** *n* policía *f*; **mounted —** policía *f* montada; **river —** brigada *f* fluvial; **traffic —** policía *f* de tráfico.

2 *vt frontier* vigilar, patrullar por; *area* mantener servicio de policía en, mantener el orden público en; **the frontier is —d by UNO patrols** la frontera la vigilan las patrullas de la ONU; **the area used to be —d by Britain** antes Gran Bretaña mantenía la paz en la región.

police car [pə'li:ska:*] *n* coche *m* de policía, coche-patrulla *m*.

police constable [pə'li:s'kʌnstəbl] *n* policía *m*, guardia *m*.

police dog [pə'li:sdɔg] *n* perro *m* policía.

policeman [pə'li:smən] *n*, *pl* **—men** [mən] policía *m*, guardia *m*; **what the — are you doing?** (*sl*) ¿qué demonios haces ahí?

police state [pə'li:s'steit] *n* estado *m* policiaco.

police station [pə'li:s,steiʃən] *n* comisaría *f*.

policewoman [pə'li:s,wumən] *n*, *pl* **—women** [,wimin] policía *m* femenino, mujer *f* policía.

policy¹ ['pɔlisi] *n* **(a)** política *f*; (*loosely*) principios *mpl*; actitud *f*; sistema *m*; (*of party, at election*) programa *m* político; (*of newspaper*) normas *fpl* de conducta; **economic —** política *f* económica; **foreign —** política *f* exterior; **prices and incomes —** política *f* de ingresos y precios; **that's not my —** eso no es mi sistema; **to change one's —** cambiar de actitud; **it would be contrary to public — to +** *infin* no sería conforme con el interés nacional + *infin*.

(b) (*wisdom*) prudencia *f*; **it is — to +** *infin* es prudente + *infin*.

policy² ['pɔlisi] *n* póliza *f*; **insurance —** póliza *f* de seguros; **to take out a —** hacerse un seguro, asegurar algo.

policyholder ['pɔlisi,həuldə*] *n* tenedor *m* de una póliza, tenedora *f* de una póliza, asegurado *m*, a *f*.

polio ['pəuliəu] *n* polio *f*.

poliomyelitis ['pəuliəumaiə'laitis] *n* poliomielitis *f*.

Polish ['pəuliʃ] **1** *adj* polaco. **2** *n* polaco *m* (*idioma*).

polish ['pɔliʃ] **1** *n* **(a)** (*material*) (*shoe* —) betún *m*; (*floor* —, *furniture* —) cera *f* de lustrar; (*metal* —) líquido *m* para limpiar metales; (*nail* —) esmalte *m* para las uñas, laca *f* para las uñas.

(b) (*act*) pulimento *m*; **to give something a —** sacar brillo a algo, pulir algo; **my shoes need a —** hace falta limpiar mis zapatos.

(c) (*shine*) brillo *m*, bruñido *m*, lustre *m*; **high —** lustre *m* brillante; **the buttons have lost their —** los botones han perdido su brillo, los botones se han deslustrado; **to put a — on something** sacar brillo a algo; **the water takes the — off** el agua quita el brillo.

(d) (*fig: refinement*) finura *f*, cultura *f*, urbanidad *f*; (*of artistry etc*) elegancia *f*; perfección *f*; **his style needs —** le hace falta limar el estilo; **he lacks —** le falta finura.

2 *vt* **(a)** *shoes* limpiar; *floor, furniture* encerar, sacar brillo a; *pans etc* abrillantar; *metal* limpiar, *silver* pulir; (*mechanically, industrially*) pulimentar.

(b) (*also* **to — up**) *person* civilizar; *manners* refinar; *style etc* pulir, limar; **one's French etc** repasar, refrescar.

(c) to — off *work* terminar, despachar; *person etc* acabar con; *food, drink* despachar, dar cuenta de.

polished ['pɔliʃt] *adj* pulido; *style etc* limado, elegante; *person* culto, distinguido, fino; *manners* fino.

polisher ['pɔliʃə*] *n* (*person*) pulidor *m*, ora *f*; (*machine*) enceradora *f*.

polishing machine ['pɔliʃinmə,ʃi:n] *n* enceradora *f*.

polite [pə'lait] *adj* cortés, atento, fino; correcto; **that's not very —** eso no es fino; **he was very — to me** estuvo muy correcto conmigo; **in — society** en la buena sociedad.

politely [pə'laitli] *adv* cortésmente, atentamente; correctamente.

politeness [pə'laitnis] *n* cortesía *f*, finura *f*; corrección *f*; **with exquisite —** con la mayor finura; **to do something out of —** hacer algo por cortesía.

politic ['pɔlitik] *adj* prudente.

political [pə'litikəl] *adj* político.

politically [pə'litikəli] *adv* políticamente.

politician [,pɔli'tiʃən] *n* político *m*; (*pej*) politiquero *m*.

politics ['pɔlitiks] *npl* política *f*; **to go into —** dedicarse a la política; **to talk —** hablar de política; *see* **party 2 (a).**

polity ['pɔliti] *n* gobierno *m*, forma *f* de gobierno; estado *m*.

polka ['pɔlkə] *n* polca *f*.

polka dot ['pɔlkədɔt] *n* punto *m*; diseño *m* de puntos.

poll [pəul] **1** *n* **(a)** (*election*) votación *f*; elección *f*; **in the — of 1945, at the —s in 1945** en las elecciones de 1945; **a — was demanded** se pidió que el asunto se sometiera a votación; **to go to the —s** acudir a las urnas; **to head the —** obtener la mayoría de los votos, ser elegido, ocupar el primer puesto en la elección; **to take a —** someter un asunto a votación; **a — was taken among those present** votaron los asistentes sobre el asunto.

(b) (*total votes*) votos *mpl*; **the candidate achieved a — of 5000 votes** el candidato obtuvo 5000 votos; **there was a — of 84%** votaron el 84 por cien; **the — has been a heavy one** ha votado un elevado porcentaje del electorado.

(c) (*public-opinion organization*) organismo *m* de sondaje; (*inquiry*) encuesta *f*, sondeo *m*; **the Gallup —** el Instituto Gallup, el sondeo Gallup; **to take a —** hacer una encuesta.

2 *vt* **(a)** *cattle* descornar.

(b) *votes* obtener, recibir; **he —ed only 50 votes** obtuvo solamente 50 votos.

3 *vi*: **he —ed badly** recibió pocos votos, tuvo escaso apoyo; **we shall — heavily** obtendremos muchos votos.

pollard ['pɔləd] **1** *n* árbol *m* desmochado. **2** *vt* desmochar.

pollen ['pɔlən] *n* polen *m*.

pollinate ['pɔlineit] *vt* fecundar (con polen).

pollination [,pɔli'neiʃən] *n* polinización *f*, fecundación *f*.

polling ['pɔulin] *n* votación *f*; **— will be on Thursday** las elecciones se celebrarán el jueves, se votará el jueves; **— has been heavy** ha votado un elevado porcentaje de los electores.

polling booth ['pɔulin,bu:ð] *n* cabina *f* de votar.

polling day ['pɔulin,dei] *n* día *m* de elecciones.

polling station ['pɔulin,steiʃən] *n* colegio *m* electoral, urnas *fpl* electorales.

pollster ['pəulstə*] *n* encuestador *m*, ora *f*.

poll tax ['pəultæks] *n* capitación *f*.

pollute [pə'luːt] vt contaminar; ensuciar; (fig) corromper; **to become —d** contaminarse (with de).

pollution [pə'luːʃən] n contaminación f; polución f; (fig) corrupción f; **air —** contaminación f del aire, polución f de la atmósfera.

polo ['pəuləu] n polo m.

polonaise [,pɔlə'neiz] n polonesa f.

poltergeist ['pɔːltəgaist] n espíritu m chocante.

poltroon [pɔl'truːn] n cobarde m.

poly . . . ['pɔli] poli . . .

polyandrous [,pɔli'ændrəs] adj poliándrico.

polyandry ['pɔliændri] n poliandria f.

polyanthus [,pɔli'ænθəs] n hierba f de San Pablo mayor.

polychromatic [,pɔlikrəu'mætik] adj policromo.

polyethylene [,pɔli'eθəliːn] n (US) polietileno m.

polygamist [pɔ'ligəmist] n polígamo m.

polygamous [pɔ'ligəməs] adj polígamo.

polygamy [pɔ'ligəmi] n poligamia f.

polyglot ['pɔliglɔt] 1 adj poligloto. 2 n poligloto m, a f.

polygon ['pɔligən] n polígono m.

polygonal [pɔ'ligənl] adj poligonal.

polymer ['pɔlimə*] n polímero m.

polymerization ['pɔliməraizei'ʃən] n polimerización f.

polymorphic [,pɔli'mɔːfik] adj polimorfo.

polymorphism [,pɔli'mɔːfizəm] n polimorfismo m.

Polynesia [,pɔli'niːziə] la Polinesia.

Polynesian [,pɔli'niːziən] 1 adj polinesio. 2 n polinesio m, a f.

polyp ['pɔlip] n pólipo m.

Polyphemus [,pɔli'fiːməs] m Polifemo.

polyphonic [,pɔli'fɔnik] adj polifónico.

polyphony [pɔ'lifəni] n polifonía f.

polypus ['pɔlipəs] n pólipo m.

polysyllabic ['pɔlisi'læbik] adj polisílabo.

polysyllable ['pɔli,siləbl] n polisílabo m.

polytechnic [,pɔli'teknik] n escuela f de formación profesional.

polytheism ['pɔliθiːizəm] n politeísmo m.

polytheistic [,pɔliθiː'istik] adj politeísta.

polythene ['pɔliθiːn] n politene m, politeno m.

pom¹ [pɔm] n (sl) see **pommy**.

pom² [pɔm] n (fam) perro m de Pomerania.

pomade [pə'maːd] n pomada f.

pomegranate ['pɔməgrænit] n (fruit) granada f; (tree) granado m.

pommel ['pʌml] 1 n pomo m. 2 vt apuñear, dar de puñetazos; aporrear.

pommy ['pɔmi] n (sl, pej) inglés m, esa f (inmigrante en Australia o Nueva Zelanda).

pomp [pɔmp] n pompa f; fausto m, boato m, ostentación f; **— and circumstance** pompa f y solemnidad.

pompadour ['pɔmpəduə*] n (Hist) copete m.

Pompeii [pɔm'peii] Pompeya.

Pompey ['pɔmpi] m Pompeyo.

pompom ['pɔmpɔm] n borla f.

pomposity [pɔm'pɔsiti] n pomposidad f; fausto m, ostentación f; ampulosidad f, hinchazón f.

pompous ['pɔmpəs] adj pomposo; fastuoso, ostentoso; (language) ampuloso, hinchado.

pompously ['pɔmpəsli] adv pomposamente; ampulosamente, hinchadamente.

ponce [pɔns] n coime m, chulo m de putas.

pond [pɔnd] n (natural) charca f; (artificial) estanque m; (fish-) vivero m.

ponder ['pɔndə*] 1 vt ponderar, meditar, considerar con especial cuidado.
2 vi reflexionar, pensar; **to — on something, to — over something** meditar algo.

ponderous ['pɔndərəs] adj (all senses) pesado.

ponderously ['pɔndərəsli] adv pesadamente; say etc en tono pesado, lentamente y con énfasis.

pondlife ['pɔndlaif] n fauna f de las charcas.

pondweed ['pɔndwiːd] n planta f acuática.

pone [pəun] n (US) pan m de maíz.

poniard ['pɔnjəd] n (lit) puñal m.

pontiff ['pɔntif] n pontífice m.

pontifical [pɔn'tifikəl] adj pontificio, pontifical.

pontificate [pɔn'tifikit]n pontificado m.

pontificate [pɔn'tifikeit] vi pontificar (also fig).

Pontius Pilate ['pɔnʃəs'pailət] m Poncio Pilato.

pontoon¹ [pɔn'tuːn] n pontón m.

pontoon² [pɔn'tuːn] n (Cards) veintiuna f.

pontoon bridge [pɔn'tuːn'bridʒ] n puente m de pontones.

pony ['pəuni] n caballito m, jaca f, poney m; (sl) 25 libras; (US sl) chuleta f; see **shank**.

ponytail ['pəuniteil] n trenza f, (peinado m de) cola f de caballo.

pooch [puːtʃ] n (US sl) perro m.

poodle ['puːdl] n perro m de lanas, caniche m.

pooh [puː] interj ¡bah!, ¡qué va!

pooh-pooh [puː'puː] vt proposal etc rechazar con desdén; danger etc negar la importancia de.

pool¹ [puːl] n (natural) charca f; (artificial) estanque m; (swimming —) piscina f; (in river) pozo m, remanso m; (of spilt liquid) charco m.

pool² [puːl] 1 n (a) (Billiards) trucos mpl; (Cards) polla f; (football —) quinielas fpl; (Comm) consorcio m, asociación f; mancomunidad f; fusión f de intereses; **coal and steel —** comunidad f de carbón y acero.
(b) (reserve) reserva f; (source) fuente f; **an untapped — of ability** una reserva de inteligencia no utilizada aún.
2 vt juntar, mancomunar.

poop [puːp] n popa f.

poor [puə*] adj (a) (not rich) pobre; soil etc pobre, estéril; **a — man** un pobre; **a — woman** una mujer pobre; **the —** los pobres; **an ore — in metal** un mineral de escaso contenido metálico; **a food — in vitamins** un alimento pobre en vitaminas; **to be as — as a church-mouse** ser más pobre que las ratas, ser pobre de solemnidad.
(b) (bad) malo; de baja calidad; (in spirit) apocado, mezquino; **my — memory** mi mala memoria; **it's — stuff** es malo; **the game was pretty —** el partido fue bastante malo; **to be in — health** estar mal (de salud); **to be — at maths** ser malo en matemáticas; **to have a — opinion of someone** tener un concepto poco favorable de uno.
(c) (pitying) pobre; **— me!** ¡pobre de mí!; **— you!, — old you!, you — old thing!** ¡pobrecito!; **— Mary!** ¡pobre María!; **— Mary's lost all her money** la pobre de María ha perdido todo su dinero; **he's very ill, — old chap** está grave el pobre.

poorbox ['puəbɔks] n cepillo m para los pobres.

poorhouse ['puəhaus] n, pl **—houses** [hauziz] asilo m de los pobres.

poor law ['puələ:] n ley f de asistencia pública.

poorly ['puəli] 1 adv (a) pobremente; **they live very —** viven en la mayor pobreza.
(b) (badly) mal; **the team is doing —** el equipo juega mal; **exports are doing —** las exportaciones no van bien; **I used to do — at chemistry** tenía malas notas en química.
2 adj (ill) mal, enfermo; **to be —, to look —** estar malo.

poorness ['puənis] n (a) pobreza f. (b) mala calidad f; **— of spirit** apocamiento m, mezquindad f.

poor-spirited ['puə'spiritid] adj apocado, mezquino.

pop¹ [pɔp] 1 n (a) ligera detonación f; (of cork) taponazo m; (of fastener etc) ruido m seco; (imitative sound) ¡pum!
(b) (fam: drink) gaseosa f.
2 vt (a) balloon hacer reventar; pinchar.
(b) (place) poner, poner rápidamente; **to — something into a drawer** poner algo (rápidamente, sin ser visto etc) en un cajón; **I'll just — my hat on** voy a ponerme el sombrero; **she —ped her head out** asomó de repente la cabeza.
(c) (sl: pawn) empeñar.
3 vi (a) (burst etc) estallar, reventar (con ligera detonación); pincharse; **there were corks —ping all over** por todas partes saltaban los tapones.
(b) **to — in** entrar de sopetón, dar un vistazo; **to — in to see someone** ir a saludar a uno, pasar por la casa de uno; **I just —ped in** entré a veros; no tuve la intención de quedarme; **to — out** salir un momento; **he —ped out for some cigarettes** fue a comprar cigarillos; **he —ped out from his hiding place** salió de repente de su escondite; **we —ped over to see them** fuimos a hacerles una breve visita; **let's — round to Joe's** vamos a casa de Pepe; **to — up** aparecer inesperadamente.

pop² [pɔp] adj (fam, abbr of **popular**) popular; moderno; **— music** música f de baile moderna, música f de ritmo moderno; **— concert** concierto m de música popular.

pop³ [pɔp] n (fam, esp US) papá m.

popcorn ['pɔpkɔːn] n rosetas fpl, palomitas fpl (de maíz).

pope [pəup] n papa m; **P— John XXIII** el Papa Juan XXIII.

popery ['pəupəri] n papismo m; **no —!** ¡abajo el papa!, ¡papa . . . no!

popeyed ['pɔp'aid] adj (permanently) de ojos saltones; **they were — with amazement** se les desorbitaron los ojos con el asombro; **they looked at me —** me miraron con los ojos desorbitados.

popgun ['pɔpgʌn] n fusil m de juguete, taco m.

popinjay ['pɔpindʒei] n pisaverde m.

popish ['pəupiʃ] adj (pej) papista, católico.

poplar ['pɒplə*] n (black) chopo m, álamo m; (white) álamo m blanco; **Lombardy —** chopo m lombardo.

poplin ['pɒplin] n popelina f.

poppet ['pɒpit] n: yes, **my —** sí, hija; sí, querida; **hullo, —!** ¡oye, ricura!; **isn't she a —?** ¡qué preciosidad!

poppy ['pɒpi] n amapola f, adormidera f.

poppycock ['pɒpikɔk] n tonterías fpl; **—!** ¡tonterías!

popsy ['pɒpsi] n (sl) chica f.

populace ['pɒpjuləs] n pueblo m, plebe f, populacho m.

popular ['pɒpjulə*] adj (a) popular; **to be —** (enjoy wide esteem) ser popular, (be in fashion) estar de moda; **it's a — work** (well-liked) es una obra popular; (for the layman) es una obra de vulgarización; **the show is proving very —** el espectáculo está muy concurrido.

(b) (fam) **he's — with the girls** tiene mucho éxito con las chicas; **I'm not very — in the office just now** ahora no me quieren mucho en la oficina.

popularity [,pɒpju'læriti] n popularidad f.

popularization ['pɒpjularai'zeiʃən] n popularización f; vulgarización f.

popularize ['pɒpjuləraiz] vt (make popular) popularizar; (make available to laymen) vulgarizar.

popularly ['pɒpjuləli] adv: **X — known as Y** X conocido por regla general como Y, X al que se llama vulgarmente Y.

populate ['pɒpjuleit] vt poblar.

population [,pɒpju'leiʃən] n población f; (in numbering inhabitants) habitantes mpl; **the — explosion** la explosión demográfica.

populous ['pɒpjuləs] adj populoso; **the most — city in the world** la ciudad más poblada del mundo.

porcelain ['pɔːslin] n porcelana f.

porch [pɔːtʃ] n pórtico m; entrada f; (of house, church) portal m.

porcine ['pɔːsain] adj porcino, porcuno.

porcupine ['pɔːkjupain] n puerco m espín.

pore¹ [pɔː*] n poro m.

pore² [pɔː*] vi: **to — over something** estar absorto en el estudio de algo, estudiar algo larga y detenidamente; **we —d over it for hours** lo estudiamos durante horas y horas.

pork [pɔːk] n carne f de cerdo, carne f de puerco.

porker ['pɔːkə*] n cerdo m, cochino m.

porkpie ['pɔːk'pai] n pastel m de carne de cerdo.

porky ['pɔːki] adj (fam) gordo, gordinflón.

pornographic [,pɔːnə'græfik] adj pornográfico.

pornography [pɔː'nɒgrəfi] n pornografía f.

porosity [pɔː'rɒsiti] n porosidad f.

porous ['pɔːrəs] adj poroso.

porousness ['pɔːrəsnis] n porosidad f.

porphyry ['pɔːfiri] n pórfido m.

porpoise ['pɔːpəs] n marsopa f.

porridge ['pɒridʒ] n (approx) gachas fpl de avena; (baby's) papilla f.

port¹ [pɔːt] 1 n (Naut: harbour) puerto m; **— of call** puerto m de escala; **— of entry** puerto m de entrada; **home —** puerto m de origen; **naval —** puerto m naval; **trading —** puerto m comercial; **any — in a storm** en el peligro cualquier refugio es bueno; **to come into —, to put into —** entrar a puerto; **to leave —** hacerse a la mar, zarpar.

2 attr de puerto, portuario; **— authority** autoridad f portuaria; **— dues** derechos mpl de puerto; **— facilities** facilidades fpl portuarias.

port² [pɔːt] n (Naut: —hole) portilla f; (Mech) lumbrera f; (Mil Hist) tronera f.

port³ [pɔːt] (Naut: side) 1 n babor m; **on the — side a** babor; **the sea to —** la mar a babor; **land to —!** ¡tierra a babor!

2 vt: **to — the helm** poner el timón a babor, virar a babor.

port⁴ [pɔːt] n vino m de Oporto, oporto m.

portable ['pɔːtəbl] adj portátil.

portage ['pɔːtidʒ] n porteo m.

portal ['pɔːtl] n puerta f (grande, imponente).

portcullis [pɔːt'kʌlis] n rastrillo m.

portend [pɔː'tend] vt presagiar, anunciar; **what does this —?** ¿qué quiere decir esto?

portent ['pɔːtent] n presagio m, augurio m, señal f; **a — of doom** un presagio de la catástrofe.

portentous [pɔː'tentəs] adj portentoso.

portentously [pɔː'tentəsli] adv portentosamente.

porter ['pɔːtə*] n (a) (of hotel, office etc) portero m, conserje m; (Rail: uniformed employee) mozo m de estación, (touting for custom) mozo m de cuerda; (eg Sherpa) porteador m; **—'s lodge** portería f, conserjería f.

(b) (beer) cerveza f negra.

porterage ['pɔːtəridʒ] n porte m.

porterhouse ['pɔːtəhaus] n (arch) mesón m; **— steak** biftec m de filete.

portfolio [pɔːt'fəuliəu] n cartera f, carpeta f; (Pol) cartera f; **— of shares** cartera f de acciones; **minister without —** ministro m sin cartera.

porthole ['pɔːthəul] n portilla f.

Portia ['pɔːʃə] f Porcia.

portico ['pɔːtikəu] n pórtico m.

portion ['pɔːʃən] 1 n porción f, parte f; (helping) ración f; (also marriage —) dote f; (quantity, in relation to a whole) porción f; sección f; porcentaje m.

2 vt (also to — out) repartir, dividir.

portliness ['pɔːtlinis] n gordura f.

portly ['pɔːtli] adj gordo.

portmanteau [pɔːt'mæntəu] n baúl m de viaje; **— word** palabra f híbrida.

Porto Rico [,pɔːtəu'riːkəu] etc see **Puerto Rico** etc.

portrait ['pɔːtrit] n retrato m; **full-length —** retrato m de cuerpo entero; **half-length —** retrato m de medio cuerpo; **to have one's — painted, to sit for one's —** retratarse, hacerse retratar.

portraitist ['pɔːtritist] n, **portrait painter** ['pɔːtrit,peintə*] n retratista mf.

portraiture ['pɔːtritʃə*] n (portrait) retrato m; (portraits collectively) retratos mpl; (art of —) arte m de retratar; **Spanish — in the 16th century** retratos mpl españoles del siglo XVI.

portray [pɔː'trei] vt (Art) retratar; (fig) pintar, describir; representar.

portrayal [pɔː'treiəl] n (Art) retrato m; (fig) descripción f, descripción f gráfica, representación f; **a most unflattering —** una representación nada halagüeña.

portress ['pɔːtris] n portera f.

Portugal ['pɔːtjugəl] Portugal m.

Portuguese [,pɔːtju'giːz] 1 adj portugués. 2 n portugués m, esa f. 3 n (language) portugués m.

pose [pəuz] 1 n (of body) postura f, actitud f; (fig) afectación f, pose f; **it's just a big —** todo esto no es más que afectación.

2 vt (a) (place) colocar; **he —d the model in the position he wanted** hizo que la modelo adoptara la postura que él quería.

(b) problem plantear; question hacer, formular.

3 vi (a) (place oneself) colocarse; (as model) posar; **she once —d for Picasso** una vez posó para Picasso.

(b) (affectedly) darse tono; tomar una postura afectada; **to — as** hacerse pasar por, echárselas de.

poser ['pəuzə*] n pregunta f difícil, problema m difícil.

poseur [pəu'zɜː*] n persona f afectada.

posh [pɒʃ] (fam) 1 adj elegante, de lujo, lujoso; (— but in bad taste) cursi; wedding etc de mucho rumbo; accent afectado; school de buen tono; **— people** gente f bien; **a — car** un coche de lujo; **it's a very — neighbourhood** es un barrio de lo más elegante.

2 adv: **to talk —** hablar con acento afectado.

3 vt: **to — a place up** procurar que un local parezca más elegante, renovar la pintura (etc) de un local; **it's all —ed up** está totalmente renovado, se ha reformado por completo.

4 vr: **to — oneself up** procurar parecer más elegante; asearse, vestir mucho mejor.

posit ['pɒzit] vt proponer como principio (that que), postular.

position [pə'ziʃən] 1 n (a) (place, in physical sense) posición f, situación f; (of body, posture) posición f, postura f, actitud f; **the — of the shop on the high street** la posición de la tienda en la calle mayor; **to be in —** estar en posición, estar en su lugar; **to be in a dangerous —** estar en una posición peligrosa; **what — was the body in?** ¿cuál era la postura del cadáver?; **you are in the best — to see it** Vd está en la mejor posición para verlo, Vd está en el mejor sitio para verlo; **to place something in —** colocar algo, poner algo en su lugar; **put yourself in my —** póngase Vd en mi lugar; **to be out of —** estar fuera de su lugar, estar desplazado.

(b) (Naut) posición f; **to fix one's —** determinar su posición, averiguar su posición; **to take up an astern —** ponerse a popa.

(c) (Mil) posición f; (post) puesto m; (for gun) emplazamiento m; **our —s before the attack** nuestras posiciones antes del ataque; **to manoeuvre for —** hacer maniobras para mejorar de posición; **to storm an enemy —** tomar una posición enemiga al asalto.

(d) (rank) posición f; (social) posición f, rango m, categoría f; (in class, league etc) puesto m; **of good social —** de buena posición social, de categoría; **to have a high social —** ocupar una posición social elevada; **to lose one's — at the top of the league** perder su puesto a la cabeza de la liga.

(e) (*post*) puesto *m*, empleo *m*; colocación *f*; cargo *m*; **the — of ambassador in Bogotá** el puesto de embajador en Bogotá; **to have a good — in a bank** tener un buen puesto en un banco; **to look for a —** buscar una colocación; **he took up a — in the South** se trasladó a un puesto en el Sur.

(f) (*state*) situación *f*; **the country's economic —** la situación económica del país; **the — is that . . .** es que **. . .**, el hecho es que **. . .**; **our — is improving** estamos mejorando de situación; **to be in a — to +** *infin* estar en condiciones de + *infin*; **to be in no — to +** *infin* no estar en condiciones de + *infin*.

(g) (*opinion*) opinión *f*; actitud *f*; **what is our — on Greece?** ¿cuál es nuestra actitud hacia Grecia?, ¿cuál es nuestra política con Grecia?; **to take up a — on a matter** adoptar una actitud en un asunto; **to change one's —** cambiar de opinión, cambiar de idea.

2 *vt* colocar, disponer.

positive ['pɒzitiv] **1** *adj* **(a)** (*definite*) positivo; definitivo; real, verdadero; **proof —** la prueba definitiva; **there are some — results at last** por fin hay unos resultados positivos; **it's a — miracle !** ¡es un auténtico milagro!; **he's a — nuisance** realmente es un pesado.

(b) (*of person: sure*) seguro; **he is — of it** está seguro de ello; **I'm quite — on that point** estoy completamente convencido de ello; **you don't sound very —** no pareces estar muy seguro.

(c) (*of things: sure*) enfático, categórico; **in a — tone of voice** con énfasis.

(d) (*of character*) de fuerte personalidad, enérgico, activo; **she's a very — sort of person** es una persona enérgica, es una persona que impresiona.

(e) (*Gram*) *degree* positivo; (*affirmative*) afirmativo.

(f) (*Elec, Math, Phot*) positivo.

2 *n* (*Phot*) positiva *f*.

positively ['pɒzitivli] *adv* **(a)** positivamente; definitivamente; verdaderamente; **it's — marvellous !** ¡es realmente maravilloso!

(b) con énfasis, categóricamente.

(c) con energía, enérgicamente.

positivism ['pɒzitivizəm] *n* positivismo *m*.

positivist ['pɒzitivist] **1** *adj* positivista. **2** *n* positivista *mf*.

positron ['pɒzitrɒn] *n* positrón *m*.

posse ['pɒsi] *n* (*US*) pelotón *m*, grupo *m* (*esp fuerza civil armada bajo el mando del Sheriff*).

possess [pə'zes] **1** *vt* **(a)** (*have, own, also* **to be —ed of**) poseer; **it —es many advantages** posee muchas ventajas; **they — a fortune** poseen una fortuna, tienen una fortuna.

(b) *see* **possessed**.

(c) to be —ed by demons estar poseído por los demonios; **to be —ed by an idea** estar dominado por una idea; **we are —ed by many doubts** son muchas las dudas que tenemos; **whatever can have —ed you?** ¿cómo lo has podido hacer?; **what can have —ed you to think like that?** ¿cómo has podido pensar así?

2 *vr* **(a) to — oneself of** tomar posesión de, (*violently*) apoderarse de.

(b) to — oneself in patience tener paciencia, esperar con calma.

possessed [pə'zest] *adj* poseso, poseído; **like one —** como un poseso.

possession [pə'zeʃən] *n* **(a)** (*act, state*) posesión *f*; **to get — of** adquirir, (*improperly*) apoderarse de; **to take — of** tomar posesión de; *house etc* ocupar, entrar en; (*improperly*) apoderarse de, hacerse dueño de; (*confiscate*) incautarse de; **to be in — of** poseer, tener; **to be in full — of one's faculties** poseer todas sus facultades; **to be in the — of** estar en manos de, ser de la propiedad de, pertenecer a; **to come into — of** adquirir; **to come (or pass) into the — of** pasar a manos de; **to have something in one's —** poseer algo; **a house with vacant —** una casa desocupada, una casa lista para ocupar.

(b) (*object*) posesión *f*; **—s** posesiones *fpl*, (*as legal term*) bienes *mpl*.

possessive [pə'zesiv] **1** *adj* (*Gram*) posesivo; *love etc* dominante, tiránico, absorbente; **to be — towards someone** ser absorbente con uno.

2 *n* (*Gram*) posesivo *m*.

possessively [pə'zesivli] *adv* tiránicamente; de modo absorbente.

possessor [pə'zesə*] *n* poseedor *m*, ora *f*; dueño *m*, a *f*; **he was the proud — of . . .** se enorgullecía de poseer **. . .**

possibility [,pɒsə'biliti] *n* **(a)** (*chance*) posibilidad *f*; (*outlook*) perspectiva *f*; **the — of severe losses** la posibilidad de sufrir pérdidas cuantiosas; **there is no — of his agreeing to it** no existe posibilidad alguna de que él consienta en ello; **if by any — . . .** si por casualidad **. . .**; **it is within the bounds of —** cabe dentro de lo posible; **it's a grim —** es una perspectiva aterradora.

(b) (*event etc*) acontecimiento *m* posible; posibilidad *f*; **to allow for the — that it may happen** tener en cuenta la posibilidad de que una cosa ocurra; **to foresee all the possibilities** prever todos los resultados posibles.

(c) (*promise*) **he has possibilities** promete, es prometedor; **the subject has possibilities** es un tema prometedor, es un tema de gran potencial.

possible ['pɒsəbl] *adj* **(a)** posible; **a — defeat** una posible derrota; **all — concessions** todas las concesiones posibles; **one has to foresee all — outcomes** hay que prever todos los resultados posibles; **to make something —** hacer algo posible, posibilitar algo.

(b) (*with verb* **to be** *or etc*) **if — si** es posible, de ser posible; **it is just —** existe una pequeña posibilidad (*that* de que + *subj*); **it is — that . . .** es posible que + *subj*, puede que + *subj*; **it is — to +** *infin* es posible + *infin*; **it is not — to do more** no se puede hacer más; **it will be — for you to return the same day** le será posible volver el mismo día.

(c) (*with* **as**) **we will help as far as —** ayudaremos en lo posible, ayudaremos en cuanto podamos; **as often as —** lo más frecuentemente posible; **as soon as —** cuanto antes, lo antes posible, lo más pronto posible; **as heavy as —** lo más pesado que pueda ser, todo lo pesado que pueda ser; el más pesado que haya; *see* **much** *etc*.

possibly ['pɒsəbli] *adv* posiblemente; tal vez; **— sí**, es posible; **if I — can** si me es posible; **— they've gone already** es posible que hayan ido ya, puede que hayan ido ya, han ido ya quizá; **he did all he — could** hizo todo lo que pudo; **I come as often as I can** vengo todas las veces que puedo, vengo lo más frecuentemente posible; **I cannot — allow it** no lo puedo permitir de ninguna manera, me es totalmente imposible autorizarlo.

possum ['pɒsəm] *n* zarigüeya *f*; **to play — (sleeping)** fingir estar dormido, (*dead*) hacerse el muerto.

post¹ [pəust] **1** *n* (*of timber etc*) poste *m*; (*for fencing, marking*) estaca *f*; **the — (starting)** poste *m* de salida, (*finishing*) poste *m* de llegada, meta *f*; **to be left at the —** quedar muy atrasado (*also fig*); **to win on the —** ganar junto al mismo poste de llegada.

2 *vt* (*announce*) anunciar; *bills etc* (*also* **to — up**) fijar, pegar; **"— no bills"** "prohibido fijar carteles"; **to — someone missing** anunciar que uno es considerado como desaparecido.

post² [pəust] **1** *n* (*mail*) correo *m*; (*office*) casa *f* de correos, correos *mpl*; (*numbered: collection*) recogida *f*, (*delivery*) entrega *f*; **first —** primera recogida *f*; **last —** última recogida *f*, última entrega *f*; **registered —** correo *m* certificado; **by —** por correo; **by return of —** a vuelta de correo; **the — has come** ha llegado el correo; **it came with the —** vino con el correo; **to drop a card in the —** echar una postal al buzón; **to go to the —** ir a correos, ir al buzón; **to open one's —** abrir sus cartas; **to sort the —** clasificar las cartas; **to take a parcel to the —** llevar un paquete a correos.

(b) there has been a general — among the staff muchos miembros del personal han intercambiado sus puestos.

2 *vt* **(a)** echar al buzón, llevar a correos; **this was —ed on Monday** esto se echó al buzón el lunes; **to — something to someone** mandar algo a uno por correo.

(b) to keep someone —ed tener a uno al corriente; **please keep me —ed** no dejes de decirme las noticias.

3 *vi* (*arch*) viajar en posta; **he went —ing off to India** se fue (inesperadamente, a toda prisa *etc*) a la India.

post³ [pəust] **1** *n* **(a)** (*job*) puesto *m*, empleo *m*; destino *m*; cargo *m*; **to look for a —** buscar un puesto; **there are 10 —s for women** hay 10 puestos para mujeres; **the duties of the —** las funciones del cargo; **to take up one's —** ocupar el puesto, entrar en funciones.

(b) (*Mil*) puesto *m*; **advanced —** puesto *m* avanzado, avanzada *f*; **to die at one's —** morir en su puesto.

2 *vt* **(a)** situar, apostar; **to — sentries** apostar centinelas; **to — a man at the gate** apostar un hombre a la puerta.

(b) to — someone to Buenos Aires enviar a uno

a Buenos Aires, nombrar a uno en Buenos Aires, destinar a uno para Buenos Aires; **to be —ed to a regiment** ser ordenado a incorporarse a un regimiento; **he was —ed first to a destroyer** se le mandó primero a un destructor; **to be —ed captain** ser ascendido a capitán.

post⁴ [pəust] post . . ., pos . . .

postage ['pəustidʒ] n porte m, franqueo m; **—s** (in account) gastos mpl de correo; **— due** a pagar; **— paid** porte pagado, franco de porte.

postage stamp ['pəustidʒˌstæmp] n sello m (de correo), estampilla f (SAm)

postal ['pəustəl] adj postal, de correos.

postal order ['pəustlˌɔːdə*] n giro m postal.

postbox ['pəustbɔks] n buzón m.

postcard ['pəustkaːd] n tarjeta f postal, postal f; **reply —** tarjeta f de porte pagado.

postdate ['pəust'deit] vt poner fecha adelantada a, posfechar.

postdated ['pəust'deitid] adj cheque con fecha adelantada.

poster ['pəustə*] n cartel m.

poste restante ['pəust'restãːnt] n lista f de correos.

posterior [pɔs'tiəriə*] **1** adj posterior. **2** n (fam) culo m, trasero m.

posterity [pɔs'teriti] n posteridad f.

postern ['pəustəːn] n postigo m.

post-free ['pəust'friː] adv porte pagado, franco de porte.

postglacial ['pəust'gleisiəl] adj postglacial.

postgraduate ['pəust'grædʒuit] **1** adj postgraduado; **— course** curso m para postgraduados. **2** n postgraduado m, a f.

posthaste ['pəust'heist] adv a toda prisa, con toda urgencia.

post hole ['pəusthəul] n agujero m de poste.

posthumous ['pɔstjuməs] adj póstumo.

posthumously ['pɔstjuməsli] adv después de la muerte.

postilion [pəs'tiliən] n postillón m.

post-impressionism ['pəustim'preʃənizəm] n post-impresionismo m.

post-impressionist ['pəustim'preʃənist] **1** adj post-impresionista. **2** n postimpresionista mf.

postlude ['pəustluːd] n postludio m.

postman ['pəustmən] n, pl **—men** [mən] cartero m.

postmark ['pəustmaːk] **1** n matasellos m. **2** vt matar (el sello de), timbrar; **it is —ed "León"** lleva el matasellos de León.

postmaster ['pəustˌmaːstə*] n administrador m de correos; **P— General** Director m General de Correos.

postmeridian ['pəustməˈridiən] adj postmeridiano.

postmistress ['pəustˌmistris] n administradora f de correos.

post-mortem ['pəust'mɔːtem] n autopsia f.

postnatal ['pəust'neitl] adj postnatal.

post office ['pəustˌɔfis] n (oficina f, casa f de) correos; **General P—** Administración f General de Correos; **I was in the —** estaba en correos; **I'm going to the —** voy a correos; see **box, saving.**

post-paid ['pəust'peid] adv porte pagado, franco de porte.

postpone ['pəust'pəun] vt aplazar; **to — something for a month** aplazar algo por un mes; **it has been —d till Tuesday** ha sido aplazado hasta el martes.

postponement ['pəust'pəunmənt] n aplazamiento m.

postposition ['pəustpəˈziʃən] n posposición f.

postprandial ['pəust'prændiəl] adj speech, talk etc de sobremesa; walk etc que se da después de comer.

postscript ['pəusskript] n posdata f.

postulant ['pɔstjulənt] n postulante m, a f.

postulate ['pɔstjulit] n postulado m.

postulate ['pɔstjuleit] vt postular.

postulation [ˌpɔstjuˈleiʃən] n postulación f.

posture ['pɔstʃə*] **1** n postura f, actitud f. **2** vi tomar una postura, adoptar una actitud; (pej) adoptar una actitud afectada.

postwar ['pəust'wɔː*] adj de pos(t)guerra, de la pos(t)guerra, posbélico; **the — period** la pos(t)guerra.

posy ['pəuzi] n ramillete m de flores.

pot [pɔt] **1** n (for cooking) olla f, puchero m, marmita f; (for preserving) tarro m, pote m; (fam: cup) copa f; (flower—) tiesto m, maceta f; (chamber—) orinal m; (sl) marijuana f; big **—** (fam) pez m gordo, personaje m; **—s and kettles, the — calls the kettle black** el puchero dijo a la sartén "apártate de mí que me tiznas"; **—s and pans** cacharros mpl, (modern) batería f de cocina; **we have —s of it** tenemos montones; **to have —s of money** ser muy rico; **to go to — echarse a perder, arruinarse; to keep the —**

boiling (earn living) ganarse la vida, (make things progress) mantener las cosas en marcha.

2 vt food conservar (en botes etc); plant poner en tiesto; game derribar; abatir (a tiros); person herir, matar (a tiros).

3 vi: **to — at someone** disparar sobre uno; **to — away** seguir disparando.

potable ['pəutəbl] adj potable.

potash ['pɔtæʃ] n potasa f.

potassium [pə'tæsiəm] n potasio m; **— cyanide** cianuro m de potasio; **— nitrate** nitrato m de potasio.

potations [pəu'teiʃənz] npl libaciones fpl.

potato [pə'teitəu] n, pl **potatoes** [pə'teitəuz] patata f, papa f (SAm); **—es in their jackets** patatas fpl enteras, patatas fpl con su piel; **baked —es** patatas fpl al horno; **boiled —es** patatas fpl cocidas al agua; **chip(ped) —es, French fried —es** patatas fpl fritas, patatas fpl a la española; **mashed —es** puré m de patatas; **sweet —** batata f.

potato field [pə'teitəuˌfiːld] n patatal m.

potbellied ['pɔtˌbelid] adj barrigón, tripudo.

potboiler ['pɔtˌbɔilə*] n obra f (mediocre) compuesta para ganar dinero.

poteen [pɔ'tiːn] n whiskey m (irlandés, destilado ilegalmente).

potency ['pəutənsi] n potencia f; fuerza f; eficacia f.

potent ['pəutənt] adj potente, poderoso; drink fuerte; remedy eficaz.

potentate ['pəutənteit] n potentado m.

potential [pəu'tenʃəl] **1** adj potencial; posible, en potencia; futuro; **a — prime minister** un futuro primer ministro, un primer ministro en potencia; **— threat** una posible amenaza.

2 n potencial m (also Elec, Math, Phys); potencialidad f, capacidad f; **the war — of Ruritania** el potencial bélico de Ruritania.

potentiality [pəuˌtenʃiˈæliti] n potencialidad f.

potentially [pəu'tenʃəli] adv potencialmente, en potencia.

pother ['pɔðə*] n alharaca f, aspaviento m; lío m; **all this —!** ¡qué lío!; **to make a — about something** armar un lío a causa de algo.

pothole ['pɔthəul] **1** n (in road) bache m; (Geol) sima f, marmita f de gigante, (loosely) cueva f, caverna f profunda.

2 vi: **to —, to go potholing** dedicarse a la espeleología; ir a explorar una caverna.

potholer ['pɔthəulə*] n espeleólogo m.

potholing ['pɔthəuliŋ] n espeleología f.

pothunter ['pɔthʌntə*] n persona que toma parte en torneos (etc) con el solo propósito de ganar premios.

potion ['pəuʃən] n poción f, pócima f.

potluck ['pɔt'lʌk] n: **to take —** comer lo que haya; (fig) tomar lo que haya, contentarse con lo que haya.

potpourri [pəu'puri] n (Mus) popurrí m; (Lit etc) mezcla f, centón m.

potsherd ['pɔtˌʃəːd] n tiesto m, casco m.

potshot ['pɔtˌʃɔt] n tiro m sin apuntar, tiro m al azar; **to take a — at something** tirar a algo sin apuntar.

potted ['pɔtid] adj food en conserva, cocido y conservado en bote; plant en tiesto, en maceta.

potter¹ ['pɔtə*] n alfarero m; (artistic) ceramista mf.

potter² ['pɔtə*] vi ocuparse en fruslerías; no hacer nada de particular (also **— about**); **he likes —ing about in the garden** le gusta pasar el tiempo haciendo pequeños trabajos en el jardín; **we —along** vamos tirando; **I —ed round the house all day** hice bagatelas en casa todo el día.

pottery ['pɔtəri] n (workshop) alfar m, alfarería f; (craft) alfarería f, (art) cerámica f; (pots) cacharros mpl, (of fine quality) loza f; (archaeological remains) cerámicas fpl.

potty¹ ['pɔti] n (fam) orinal m de niño, orinal m pequeño.

potty² ['pɔti] adj (fam) (a) (small) insignificante, miserable.

(b) (mad) chiflado; **you must be —!** ¿has perdido el juicio?; **to drive someone —** volver loco a uno; **it's enough to drive you —** es para volverse loco.

pouch [pautʃ] n bolsa f (also Anat, Zool); (hunter's) morral m, zurrón m; (tobacco-) petaca f; (Mil) cartuchera f.

pouf(fe) [puːf] n pouf m.

poulterer ['pəultərə*] n pollero m; **—'s** (shop) pollería f.

poultice ['pəultis] **1** n cataplasma f, emplasto m. **2** vt poner una cataplasma a, emplastar (with con).

poultry ['pəultri] n (alive) aves fpl de corral; (dead) pollos mpl, volatería f.

poultry dealer ['pəultriˌdiːlə*] n recovero m; pollero m.

poultry farm ['pəultrifɑ:m] n granja f avícola.

poultry house ['pəultrihaus] n, pl — **houses** [hauziz] gallinero m.

poultry keeper ['pəultri,ki:pə*] n avicultor m.

poultry keeping ['pəultri,ki:piŋ] n avicultura f.

pounce [pauns] 1 n salto m; ataque m súbito; (swoop by bird) calada f.

2 vi atacar súbitamente; saltar, precipitarse; (by bird) calarse; **to — on something** saltar sobre algo, precipitarse sobre algo, arrojarse sobre algo; **to — on someone's mistake** saltar sobre el error de uno.

pound[1] [paund] n (a) (weight) libra f (=453,6 gr); **half a —** media libra f; **two shillings a —** dos chelines la libra; **they sell it by the —** lo venden por libras.

(b) (money) libra f; **— sterling** libra f esterlina; **it must have cost —s** habrá costado un potosí.

pound[2] [paund] n corral m de concejo; (police —, for cars) depósito m.

pound[3] [paund] 1 vt (crush etc) machacar, majar; (with hammer) martillar; (grind) moler; (beat) golpear, aporrear; (of sea) azotar, batir; (Mil) bombardear; **he —ed the table with his fists** aporreaba la mesa con los puños, daba golpes en la mesa con los puños; **to — someone with one's fists** dar de puñetazos a uno; **he was —ing the piano** aporreaba el piano; **he was —ing out a tune on the piano** a golpes violentos tocaba una melodía al piano; **to — something to pieces** romper algo a martillazos; **to — a fort into surrender** bombardear una fortaleza hasta que se rinda.

2 vi: **to — at, to — on** aporrear, dar golpes en, descargar golpes sobre; **to — away at** machacar en, seguir machacando en (also fig); **the sea was —ing against the rocks** las olas se rompían contra las rocas, el mar azotaba las rocas; **he was —ing along the road** corría pesadamente por la carretera; **the train —ed past us** el tren pasó estrepitosamente delante de nosotros.

poundage ['paundidʒ] n impuesto m (or comisión f etc) que se exige por cada libra.

-pounder ['paundə*] n: eg **four-pounder** (pez m etc) de cuatro libras; **twenty-five pounder** (Mil) cañón m del veinticinco.

pounding ['paundiŋ] n (noise) martilleo m, golpeo m, el aporrear etc; (of sea) azote m, embate m; (Mil) bombardeo m; **the ship took a — from the waves** el barco tuvo que aguantar la violencia de las olas; **the city took a — last night** la ciudad sufrió terriblemente en el bombardeo de anoche.

pour [pɔ:*] 1 vt (a) verter, echar; derramar; a drink, tea etc servir, echar; preparar; **he —ed me a drink** me sirvió un vaso; **shall I — the tea?** ¿sirvo el té?, ¿echo el té?; **he —ed himself some coffee** se sirvió café; **to — money into a project** invertir muchísimo dinero en un proyecto, proveer abundantes fondos para un proyecto; **he has —ed good ideas into the book** ha llenado el libro de excelentes ideas.

(b) (of rain) **to — cats and dogs, to — torrents** llover a cántaros.

(c) **to — in a broadside** hacer fuego con todos los cañones.

(d) **to — away, to — off** vaciar, verter; **to — out** coffee etc servir, echar; unwanted remainder vaciar; smoke arrojar; **to — out one's feelings** expresar tumultuosamente sus sentimientos; **to — out one's thanks** expresar efusivamente sus gracias; **to — out threats against someone** desatarse en amenazas contra uno; **to — out one's heart to someone** abrir su pecho a uno.

2 vi (a) (of rain) llover mucho, diluviar, llover a cántaros; (of water etc) correr, fluir (abundantemente); **it's —ing, it's —ing with rain** está lloviendo a cántaros; **it —ed for 4 days** llovió mucho durante 4 días; **water came —ing into the room** el agua entraba a raudales en el cuarto; **water —ed from the broken pipe** el agua salía a raudales del tubo roto; **blood —ed from the wound** la sangre salía a borbotones de la herida, la herida sangraba muchísimo.

(b) (of persons etc) **to — in** entrar a raudales, entrar en tropel; **tourists are —ing in from all sides** acuden los turistas en tropel de todas partes; **they came —ing into the shop** entraban a raudales en la tienda; **to — out** salir a raudales, salir en tropel; **they —ed out into the streets** invadieron las calles.

pouring ['pɔ:riŋ] adj: **rain** lluvia f torrencial.

pout [paut] 1 n puchero m, mala cara f; **to say with a —** decir poniendo mala cara. 2 vt: **to — one's lips** = 3 vi hacer pucheros, poner mala cara.

poverty ['pɔvəti] n pobreza f, miseria f; (of ideas etc)

falta f, escasez f; **— is no crime** pobreza no es vileza; **to live in —** vivir en la miseria.

poverty-stricken ['pɔvəti,strikn] adj menesteroso, necesitado.

powder ['paudə*] 1 n polvo m; (face —) polvos mpl; (gun-) pólvora f; **to keep one's — dry** reservarse para mejor ocasión; **to reduce something to —** reducir algo a polvo, pulverizar algo.

2 vt (a) (reduce to —) reducir a polvo, pulverizar.

(b) (apply — to) polvorear, (Cook etc) espolvorear (with de); **to — one's face, to — one's nose** ponerse polvos, empolvarse.

3 vi (a) pulverizarse, hacerse polvo.

(b) (person) ponerse polvos, empolvarse.

4 vr: **to — oneself** ponerse polvos, empolvarse.

powder blue ['paudə'blu:] 1 adj azul pálido. 2 n azul m pálido.

powder compact ['paudə,kɔmpækt] n polvera f.

powdered ['paudəd] adj milk etc en polvo.

powder keg ['paudəkeg] n (fig) polvorín m; **the country is a —** el país es un polvorín.

powder magazine ['paudəmægə,zi:n] n (Naut) santabárbara f.

powder puff ['paudəpʌf] n borla f (para empolvarse).

powder room ['paudərum] n (euph) aseos mpl.

powdery ['paudəri] adj substance en polvo, polvoriento; snow polvoriento; surface polvoriento, empolvado.

power ['pauə*] 1 n (a) (in general) poder m; (physical strength) fuerza f, energía f, vigor m; **more — to your elbow!** ¡qué tenga Vd éxito!; **it is beyond his — to save her** no está dentro de sus posibilidades salvarla, él no puede hacer nada para salvarla; **to be in the — of** estar en manos de; **to do all in one's — to + infin** hacer lo posible por + infin; **to have someone in one's —** tener a uno en su poder; **to fall into someone's —** caer en manos de uno; **it does not lie within my —** no está dentro de mis posibilidades, eso no es de mi competencia; **as far as lies within my —** en cuanto me sea posible; **to the utmost of one's —** hasta más no poder.

(b) (mental) facultad f (of de); (drive) empuje m, energía f; **mental —s** facultades fpl mentales; **his —s are failing** decaen sus facultades; **to lose the — of speech** perder el habla.

(c) (Mech etc) potencia f; energía f; (output) rendimiento m; **attractive —** fuerza f atractiva; **effective —** potencia f real; **magnifying —** fuerza f de aumento; **motive —** fuerza f motriz; **engines at half —** motores mpl a medio rendimiento; **the ship returned to port under her own —** el buque volvió al puerto impulsado por sus propios motores.

(d) (Elec) fuerza f, energía f, fluido m; **electric —** fuerza f eléctrica, energía f eléctrica; **— consumption** consumo m de energía; **— unit** (Elec) grupo m electrógeno; **they cut off the —** cortaron el fluido.

(e) (Pol etc) poder m; autoridad f; influencia f; **absolute —** poder m absoluto; **executive —** poder m ejecutivo; **— of life and death** poder m de vida y de muerte; **the —s of darkness** las fuerzas del mal; **the —s that be** los que mandan, las autoridades (actuales); **he's a — in the land** es de los que mandan en el país; **to be at the height of one's —** estar en la cumbre de su poder; **to be in —** estar en el poder; **to come to —** subir al poder, empezar a gobernar, tomar el mando; **to raise someone to —** alzar a uno al poder.

(f) (specific —) **— of attorney** poder m; **full —s** plenos poderes mpl; **to exceed one's —s** excederse, ir demasiado lejos.

(g) (nation) potencia f; **atomic —** potencia f atómica; **colonial —** poder m colonial; **world —** potencia f mundial; **the Great P—s** las Grandes Potencias.

(h) **a — of people** muchísima gente; **to make a — of money** ganar muchísimo dinero; **that did me a — of good!** ¡con eso me siento mucho mejor!, ¡ahora estoy mucho mejor!; **beer does you a — of good** la cerveza fortalece.

(i) (Math) potencia f; **7 to the — of 3** 7 elevado al cubo, 7 elevado a la 3ª potencia; **to the nth —** a la enésima potencia.

2 vt accionar, impulsar; **a car —ed by electricity** un coche impulsado por electricidad; **a plane —ed by 4 jets** un avión impulsado por 4 motores a reacción.

power cable ['pauəkeibl] n cable m de energía eléctrica.

power cut ['pauəkʌt] n corte m de corriente, apagón m.

power drill ['pauədril] n taladradora f de fuerza.

power-driven ['pauədrivn] *adj* con motor; *tool, saw etc* mecánico.

powered ['pauəd] *adj* con motor; mecánico.

powerful ['pauəful] *adj* *person, government etc* poderoso; *engine etc* potente; *build* fuerte, fornido; *emotion* intenso, profundo; *argument* convincente; **a — lot of people** (*fam*) muchísima gente; **it is a — film** es una película muy emocionante; **he gave a — performance** su actuación fue brillante.

powerfully ['pauəfəli] *adv* poderosamente; fuertemente; intensamente; profundamente; de modo convincente; **to be — built** ser fornido; **I was — affected by the book** el libro me conmovió profundamente.

power hammer ['pauə,hæmə*] *n* martillo *m* mecánico.

powerhouse ['pauəhaus] *n, pl* **—houses** [hauziz] central *f* eléctrica.

powerless ['pauəlis] *adj* impotente, ineficaz; **to be — to resist** no tener fuerzas para resistir, no poder resistir; **we are — to help you** estamos sin fuerzas para ayudarle, somos incapaces de prestarle ayuda; **they are — in the matter** no tienen autoridad para intervenir en el asunto, el asunto no es de su competencia.

power line ['pauəlain] *n* línea *f* de conducción eléctrica.

power loader ['pauə,ləudə*] *n* (*Min*) rompedora-cargadora *f*.

power plant ['pauəplɑːnt] *n* grupo *m* electrógeno.

power saw ['pauəsɔː] *n* motosierra *f*, sierra *f* mecánica.

power shovel ['pauə,ʃʌvl] *n* excavadora *f*.

power station ['pauə,steiʃən] *n* central *f* eléctrica.

power tool ['pauətuːl] *n* herramienta *f* mecánica.

powwow ['pauwau] **1** *n* conferencia *f*. **2** *vi* conferenciar.

pox [pɔks] *n* (*fam*) sífilis *f*, enfermedad *f* venérea; **a — on . . . !** (*arch*) ¡maldito sea . . . !

practicability [,præktikə'biliti] *n* factibilidad *f*.

practicable ['præktikəbl] *adj* factible, practicable, hacedero.

practical ['præktikəl] *adj* práctico; *see* **joke**.

practicality [,prækti'kæliti] *n* (*of temperament*) espíritu *m* práctico; (*of scheme etc*) factibilidad *f*; (*thing*) cosa *f* práctica.

practically ['præktikli] *adv* (*in a practical way*) prácticamente; (*almost*) prácticamente, casi; **— everybody** casi todos; **— nothing** casi nada; **there has been — no rain** no ha llovida casi.

practice ['præktis] *n* (a) (*habit*) costumbre *f*, uso *m*; **corrupt —s** corrupción *f*; **restrictive —s** normas *fpl* restrictivas, prácticas *fpl* restrictivas; **sharp —** trampa *f*, maña *f*; **according to his usual —** según su costumbre; **it is not our — to — + infin** no acostumbramos **+ infin**; **to make a — of + ger** acostumbrar **+ infin**; **to make it a — to + infin** acostumbrar **+ infin**.
(b) (*exercise*) ejercicio *m*; (*training*) adiestramiento *m*, (*period*) periodo *m* de entrenamiento; clase *f* práctica; (*Sport*) entrenamiento *m*; **to be in —** estar entrenado, estar en forma; **to be out of —** estar desentrenado, no estar en forma; **to learn by —** aprender por la práctica, aprender por la experiencia; **— makes perfect** la práctica hace maestro; **it needs a lot of —** hace falta bastante experiencia.
(c) (*reality*) práctica *f*; **in —** en la práctica; **to put something into —** poner algo en obra.
(d) (*of profession etc*) práctica *f*, ejercicio *m*; **the — of medicine** el ejercicio de la medicina; **he was in — in Bilbao** ejercía en Bilbao; **he is no longer in —** ya no ejerce la profesión; **to set up in —** (*Law*) poner su bufete; (*Med*) empezar a ejercer de médico, (*fig*) poner tienda; **to set up in — as** empezar a trabajar como.
(e) (*Med: no. of patients*) clientela *f*.

practise, (*US*) **practice** ['præktis] **1** *vt* (a) (*carry out in action*) practicar; tener por costumbre; **we — this method** nosotros empleamos (*or* seguimos) este método; **to — charity** ejercitar la caridad; **to — patience** tener paciencia; **to — what one preaches** predicar con el ejemplo.
(b) *profession* ejercer; **to — medicine** practicar la medicina, ejercer de médico.
(c) (*train oneself at*) hacer ejercicios de, hacer prácticas de; **to — the piano** hacer ejercicios en el piano, estudiar el piano; **to — football** entrenarse en el fútbol; **to — a shot at golf** ensayar un golpe de golf; **to — + ger** ensayarse **+ infin**.
2 *vi* (a) (*Mus*) tocar, estudiar, hacer ejercicios;

(*Sport*) ejercitarse, entrenarse, adiestrarse; ensayarse; **to — every day** hacer ejercicios todos los días; **one has to — a lot** hace falta estudiar mucho.
(b) **to — as a doctor** ejercer de médico, practicar la medicina.

practised, (*US*) **practiced** ['præktist] *adj* *eye etc* experto.

practising, (*US*) **practicing** ['præktisiŋ] *adj* activo, que ejerce, practicante; **a — Christian** un cristiano practicante.

practitioner [præk'tiʃənə*] *n* (*of an art*) practicante *mf*; (*Med*) médico *m*, **a f** (*also* **medical —**); **general —** médico *m* general, médica *f* general.

pr(a)esidium [pri'sidiəm] *n* (*Pol*) presidio *m*.

pragmatic [præg'mætik] *adj* pragmático.

pragmatism ['prægmətizəm] *n* pragmatismo *m*.

pragmatist ['prægmətist] *n* pragmatista *mf*.

Prague [prɑːg] Praga.

prairie ['preəri] *n* pradera *f*, llanura *f*, pampa *f* (*SAm*).

praise [preiz] **1** *n* alabanza *f*, elogio *m*; alabanzas *fpl*, elogios *mpl*; **in — of** en alabanza de; **all — to him!** ¡enhorabuena!; **— be!**, **— be to God!** ¡gracias a Dios!; **it's beyond —** queda por encima de todo elogio; **to be loud** (*or* **warm**) **in one's —s of something** alabar algo sinceramente, elogiar algo con entusiasmo; **he is not much given to —** no acostumbra pronunciar palabras de elogio; **I have nothing but — for him** merece todos mis elogios; **to heap —s on someone** amontonar alabanzas sobre uno; **to sing the —s of someone** cantar las alabanzas de uno, elogiar con efusión a uno; **to sound one's own —s** cantar sus propias alabanzas.
2 *vt* alabar, elogiar; **to — God** glorificar a Dios; **to — something up** poner algo por las nubes.

praiseworthily ['preiz,wəːðili] *adv* loablemente, plausiblemente, de modo digno de elogio.

praiseworthiness ['preiz,wəːðinis] *n* lo loable, lo plausible, mérito *m*.

praiseworthy ['preiz,wəːði] *adj* loable, plausible, digno de elogio.

pram [præm] *n* cochecito *m* de niño.

prance [prɑːns] *vi* (*horse*) hacer cabriolas, encabritarse; (*person*) saltar, bailar; andar con cierta afectación; **he came prancing into the room** entró haciendo cabriolas en la habitación; **to — with rage** enfurecerse.

prang [præŋ] *vt* (*sl*) (a) *town etc* bombardear, destruir.
(b) *plane* estrellar; *car etc* estropear.

prank [præŋk] *n* travesura *f*; broma *f*; **a childish —** una travesura, una diablura; **a student —** una broma estudiantil; **to play a — on someone** gastar una broma a uno.

prankish ['præŋkiʃ] *adj* travieso, pícaro.

prankster ['præŋkstə*] *n* bromista *mf*.

prate [preit] *vi* parlotear, charlar; **to — of** hablar interminablemente de.

prating ['preitiŋ] *adj* parlanchín.

prattle ['prætl] **1** *n* parloteo *m*; (*child's*) balbuceo *m*. **2** *vi* parlotear; balbucear.

prawn [prɔːn] *n* gamba *f*; (*small*) quisquilla *f*.

pray [prei] **1** *vt* rogar, suplicar; **I — you so lo suplico; I — you tell me . . .** le ruego decirme . . .; **to — someone to do something** rogar a uno hacer algo, rogar a uno que haga algo.
2 *vi* (a) (*say prayers*) rezar, orar; **to — to God** rogar a Dios; **to — for something** rogar algo, orar por algo; **to — for someone's soul** orar por el alma de uno; **to — for someone** orar por uno, rezar por uno; **to — that something may not happen** hacer votos para que algo no ocurra, hacer rogativas para que algo no ocurra; **he's past —ing for** ya no le valen oraciones.
(b) **— tell me . . .** dígame por favor . . ., le ruego decirme . . .; **— take a seat** siéntese por favor, haga el favor de sentarse; **what good is that, —?** ¿de qué sirve eso, pues?

prayer [preə*] *n* (a) (*to God*) oración *f*, rezo *m*; **—s** (*as service*) rezo *m*, oficio *m*; **—s for peace** oraciones *fpl* por la paz; **evening —s** vísperas *fpl*; **Lord's P—** padrenuestro *m*; **morning —s** maitines *mpl*; **Book of Common P—** liturgia de la Iglesia Anglicana; **to be at one's —s** estar en oración; **to offer up —s for** orar por, rezar por; **to say one's —s** orar, rezar.
(b) (*entreaty*) ruego *m*, súplica *f*; (*Law*) petición *f*.

prayer book ['preəbuk] *n* devocionario *m*, misal *m*.

prayer meeting ['preə,miːtiŋ] *n* reunión *f* para rezar.

pre . . . [priː] pre . . .; ante . . .

preach [priːtʃ] **1** *vt* (a) predicar; **to — a sermon** predicar un sermón; **to — the gospel** predicar el Evangelio.
(b) *advantages etc* celebrar; *patience etc* aconsejar.

2 *vt* predicar; **to — at someone** predicar a uno, dar un sermón a uno; **to — to a congregation** predicar a los fieles.

preacher ['priːtʃə*] *n* predicador *m*; (*US*) pastor *m*.

preachify ['priːtʃifai] *vi* sermonear largamente; (*fig*) disertar largamente.

preaching ['priːtʃiŋ] *n* predicación *f*; (*pej*) sermoneo *m*.

preachy ['priːtʃi] *adj* (*fam*) dado a sermonear.

preamble [priː'æmbl] *n* preámbulo *m*.

prearrange ['priːə'reindʒ] *vt* arreglar de antemano.

prebend ['prebənd] *n* (*stipend*) prebenda *f*; (*person*) prebendado *m*.

prebendary ['prebəndəri] *n* prebendado *m*.

precarious [pri'kɛəriəs] *adj* precario.

precariously [pri'kɛəriəsli] *adj* precariamente.

precaution [pri'kɔːʃən] *n* precaución *f*; **by way of —** como precaución, para mayor seguridad; **to take —s** tomar precauciones; **to take the — of + ger** tomar la cautela de + *infin*.

precautionary [pri'kɔːʃənəri] *adj* de precaución, preventivo.

precede [pri'siːd] *vti* preceder; **for a month preceding this** durante un mes antes de esto; **to — a lecture with a joke** empezar una conferencia contando un chiste.

precedence ['presidəns] *n* precedencia *f*; prioridad *f*; primacía *f*; **to take — over someone** preceder a uno, primar sobre uno.

precedent ['presidənt] *n* precedente *m*; **according to —** de acuerdo con el precedente; **against all the —s** contra todos los precedentes; **without — sin** precedentes; **to establish (or lay down, set up) a —** establecer un precedente, sentar un precedente (*for* a).

preceding [pri'siːdiŋ] *adj* precedente.

precentor [pri'sentə*] *n* chantre *m*.

precept ['priːsept] *n* precepto *m*.

preceptor [pri'septə*] *n* preceptor *m*.

precinct ['priːsiŋkt] *n* recinto *m*; (*US*: *area*) barrio *m*, (*US Pol*) distrito *m* electoral, circunscripción *f*; **—s** contornos *mpl*; **within the —s of** dentro de los límites de; **pedestrian —** calles *fpl* exclusivas para el tránsito de peatones.

preciosity [.presi'ɔsiti] *n* preciosidad *f*.

precious ['preʃəs] **1** *adj* (a) precioso; *metal, stone* precioso; *person etc* amado, querido; **my —!** ¡querida!; **the book is very — to me** para mí el libro tiene gran valor.

(b) *style etc* preciosista, afectado, rebuscado.

2 *adv* (*fam*) muy; **there are — few left** quedan muy pocos; **to take — good care to see that . . .** velar de modo muy particular para que + *subj*.

precipice ['presipis] *n* precipicio *m*, despeñadero *m*.

precipitancy [pri'sipitənsi] *n* precipitación *f*.

precipitate [pri'sipiteit] **1** *n* (*Chem*) precipitado *m*. **2** *vt* precipitar (*also Chem*); (*hasten*) acelerar; *trouble etc* causar, motivar, producir.

precipitate [pri'sipitit] *adj* precipitado, apresurado.

precipitately [pri'sipititli] *adv* precipitadamente.

precipitation [pri.sipi'teiʃən] *n* precipitación *f* (*also Chem, Meteorol*); **to act with —** obrar con precipitación.

precipitous [pri'sipitəs] *adj* escarpado, cortado a pico.

precipitously [pri'sipitəsli] *adv* en escarpa, en precipicio.

précis ['preisiː] *n* resumen *m*; **to make a — of** hacer un resumen de, resumir.

precise [pri'sais] *adj* *thing* preciso, exacto; (*clearly-stated*) claro; *person* meticuloso, puntual, escrupuloso; (*over-*) afectado, pedante; **at that — moment** en ese mismo momento; **they gave me the — book** me dieron el libro exacto; **he's very — in his ways** es meticuloso en todo; **in that — voice of hers** en ese tono suyo un tanto afectado; **let's be — about this** pongamos las cosas en su punto, concretemos; **well, to be — . . .** bueno, en rigor . . .; **there were 6, to be —** había 6, para ser exacto.

precisely [pri'saisli] *adv* precisamente, con precisión, exactamente; claramente; puntualmente, escrupulosamente; afectadamente, con pedantería; **he said very —** dijo con énfasis; **—!** ¡perfectamente!, ¡eso es!; **at — 7 o'clock** a las 7 en punto.

preciseness [pri'saisnis] *n* precisión *f*, exactitud *f*; puntualidad *f*, escrupulosidad *f*; afectación *f*, pedantería *f*.

precision [pri'siʒən] **1** *n* see **preciseness**. **2** *attr* de precisión; **— instrument** instrumento *m* de precisión.

preclude [pri'kluːd] *vt* excluir; imposibilitar; **this does not — the possibility of . . .** esto no excluye la posibilidad de . . .; **so as to — all doubt** para disipar cualquier duda; **we are —d from + ger** nos vemos

imposibilitados para + *infin*; **nos está vedado + infin**.

precocious [pri'kəuʃəs] *adj* precoz.

precociously [pri'kəuʃəsli] *adv* de modo precoz, con precocidad.

precociousness [pri'kəuʃəsnis] *n* precocidad *f*.

precocity [prə'kɔsiti] *n* precocidad *f*.

precognition [.priːkɔg'niʃən] *n* precognición *f*.

pre-Columbian [priːkə'lʌmbiən] *a* precolombino.

preconceived ['priːkən'siːvd] *adj* preconcebido.

preconception ['priːkən'sepʃən] *n* preconcepción *f*, idea *f* preconcebida.

precondition ['priːkən'diʃən] *n* condición *f* preliminar, estipulación *f* hecha de antemano.

precool ['priː'kuːl] *vt* preenfriar.

precursor [priː'kəːsə*] *n* precursor *m*, ora *f*.

predate ['priː'deit] *vt* preceder, ser anterior a.

predator ['predətə*] *n* predador *m*, animal *m* (*etc*) de rapiña.

predatory ['predətəri] *adj* *animal* rapaz, de rapiña.

predecease ['priːdi'siːs] *vt* morir antes que.

predecessor ['priːdisesə*] *n* predecesor *m*, ora *f*, antecesor *m*, ora *f*.

predestination [pri.desti'neiʃən] *n* predestinación *f*.

predestine [pri'destin] *vt* predestinar; **to be —d to + infin** ser predestinado a + *infin*.

predetermination ['priːdi.təːmi'neiʃən] *n* predeterminación *f*.

predetermine ['priːdi'təːmin] *vt* predeterminar.

predicament [pri'dikəmənt] *n* apuro *m*, situación *f* difícil; **to be in a —** estar en un apuro; **what a — to be in!** ¡qué lío!

predicate ['predikit] *n* predicado *m*.

predicative [pri'dikətiv] *adj* predicativo.

predict [pri'dikt] *vt* pronosticar, profetizar, predecir.

prediction [pri'dikʃən] *n* pronóstico *m*, profecía *f*, predicción *f*.

predictive [pri'diktiv] *adj* profético, que vale como pronóstico.

predilection [.priːdi'lekʃən] *n* predilección *f*; **to have a — for** tener predilección por.

predispose ['priːdis'pəuz] *vt* predisponer.

predisposition ['priː.dispə'ziʃən] *n* predisposición *f*.

predominance [pri'dɔminəns] *n* predominio *m*.

predominant [pri'dɔminənt] *adj* predominante.

predominantly [pri'dɔminəntli] *adv* de modo predominante, en un grado predominante; en su mayor parte.

predominate [pri'dɔmineit] *vi* predominar.

pre-eminence [priː'eminəns] *n* preeminencia *f*.

pre-eminent [priː'eminənt] *adj* preeminente.

pre-eminently [priː'eminəntli] *adv* preeminentemente; por excelencia; sobre todo.

pre-empt [priː'empt] *vt*: **to — something** asegurarse de algo antes que nadie, hacer valer sus derechos sobre algo, apropiarse algo.

pre-emption [priː'empʃən] *n* preempción *f*.

pre-emptive [priː(ː)'emptiv] *adj* *claim etc* por derecho de prioridad.

preen [priːn] **1** *vt* *feather* limpiar, arreglar con el pico.

2 *vr*: **to — oneself** (*bird*) limpiarse, arreglarse las plumas con el pico; (*person*) pavonearse, atildarse; **to — oneself on** enorgullecerse de, jactarse de.

pre-established ['priːis'tæbliʃt] *adj* establecido de antemano.

pre-exist ['priːig'zist] *vi* preexistir.

pre-existence ['priːig'zistəns] *n* preexistencia *f*.

pre-existent ['priːig'zistənt] *adj* preexistente.

prefab ['priːfæb] *n* (*fam*) casa *f* prefabricada.

prefabricate ['priː'fæbrikeit] *vt* prefabricar.

prefabricated ['priː'fæbrikeitid] *adj* prefabricado.

preface ['prefis] **1** *n* prólogo *m*, prefacio *m*.

2 *vt*: **he —d this by saying that . . .** a modo de prólogo a esto dijo que . . ., introdujo este tema diciendo que . . .; **the book is —d by an essay** el libro tiene un ensayo a modo de prólogo.

prefatory ['prefətəri] *adj* preliminar, a modo de prólogo.

prefect ['priːfekt] *n* prefecto *m*; (*School*) tutor *m*, monitor *m*.

prefecture ['priːfektjuə*] *n* prefectura *f*.

prefer [pri'fəː*] *vt* (a) preferir; **to — coffee to tea** preferir el café al té; **to — walking to going by car** preferir ir a pie a ir en coche; **to — to + infin** preferir + *infin*; **I — not to say** me parece preferible no decirlo; **which do you —?** ¿cuál prefieres?, ¿cuál te gusta más?

(b) (*promote*) ascender, promover; (*appoint*) nombrar; **he was —red to the see of Toledo** le nombraron al arzobispado de Toledo.

(c) (*charge*) hacer, presentar; **to — a charge against someone** poner a uno un juicio, acusar a uno.

preferable ['prefərəbl] *adj* preferible (*to* a).
preferably ['prefərəbli] *adv* preferentemente, más bien.
preference ['prefərəns] **1** *n* preferencia *f*, prioridad *f*; **for** — de preferencia; **A in** — **to B** A más que B, A antes que B; **to give something** — preferir algo, tener preferencia por algo; **to give something** — **over something else** anteponer algo a otra cosa; **what is your** —? ¿cuál le gusta más?; **I have no** — **no** prefiero ni el uno ni el otro.
2 *attr* share preferente.
preferential [,prefə'renʃəl] *adj* preferente.
preferment [pri'fə:mənt] *n* ascenso *m*, promoción *f*; nombramiento *m* (*to* a); **to get** — ser ascendido.
prefiguration [,pri:figə'reiʃən] *n* prefiguración *f*.
prefigure [pri:'figə*] *vt* prefigurar.
prefix ['pri:fiks] *n* prefijo *m*.
prefix [pri:'fiks] *vt* prefijar.
pregnancy ['pregnənsi] *n* embarazo *m*.
pregnant ['pregnənt] *adj* (a) embarazada; **to be** — estar embarazada, estar en estado, estar encinta.
  (b) — **with** cargado de, preñado de; **a** — **silence** un silencio cargado de emoción; **a** — **pause** una pausa llena de expectación.
preheat ['pri:'hi:t] *vt* precalentar.
prehensile [pri'hensail] *adj* prensil.
prehistoric ['pri:his'tɔrik] *adj* prehistórico.
prehistory ['pri:'histəri] *n* prehistoria *f*.
preignition ['pri:ig'niʃən] *n* preignición *f*.
prejudge ['pri:'dʒʌdʒ] *vt* prejuzgar.
prejudice ['predʒudis] **1** *n* (a) (*bias*) parcialidad *f*; (*biassed view*) prejuicio *m*; (*hostility*) mala voluntad *f*, prevención *f*; **there are many** —**s about this** sobre esto existen muchos prejuicios; **to have a** — **against someone** tener mala voluntad contra uno, tener prevención contra uno, estar predispuesto contra uno.
  (b) (*injury, detriment*) perjuicio *m*; **to the** — **of** con perjuicio de; **without** — (*Law*) sin detrimento de sus propios derechos; **without** — **to** sin perjuicio de.
2 *vt* (a) (*predispose, bias*) prevenir, predisponer (*against* contra).
  (b) (*damage*) perjudicar; **to** — **one's chances** perjudicar las posibilidades de uno.
prejudiced ['predʒudist] *adj* (a) *view etc* parcial, interesado; **he's very** — tiene muchos prejuicios.
  (b) **to be** —**d against someone** tener mala voluntad contra uno, tener prevención contra uno, estar predispuesto contra uno.
prejudicial [,predʒu'diʃəl] *adj* perjudicial (*to* para).
prelacy ['preləsi] *n* (*office*) obispado *m*; (*bishops collectively*) episcopado *m*.
prelate ['prelit] *n* prelado *m*.
preliminary [pri'liminəri] **1** *adj* preliminar. **2** *n* preliminar *m*; **preliminaries** preliminares *mpl*, preparativos *mpl*.
prelude ['prelju:d] *n* preludio *m* (*also Mus*; *to* de).
premarital ['pri:'mæritl] *adj* premarital.
premature ['premətʃuə*] *adj* prematuro; *baldness etc* precoz; **it seems** — **to think of it** parece prematuro pensar en ello.
prematurely ['premətʃuəli] *adv* prematuramente; antes de su debido tiempo; — **bald** con calvicie precoz.
premedical ['pri:'medikəl] *adj* premédico.
premeditate [pri:'mediteit] *vt* premeditar.
premeditated [pri:'mediteitid] *adj* premeditado.
premeditation [pri:,medi'teiʃən] *n* premeditación *f*.
premier ['premiə*] **1** *adj* primero, principal. **2** *n* primer ministro *m*.
première [,premi'εə*] *n* estreno *m*; **world** — estreno *m* mundial; **the film had its** — se estrenó la película.
premiership ['premiəʃip] *n* cargo *m* del primer ministro; puesto *m* de primer ministro.
premise ['premis] *n* premisa *f*; — **s** local *m*; (*house*) casa *f*; (*building*) edificio *m*; (*shop etc*) tienda *f*, establecimiento *m*; (*as property*) local *m*, propiedad *f*; **on the** —**s** en el local (*etc*).
premium ['pri:miəm] *n* (*prize*) premio *m*; (*Comm, insurance*) prima *f*; **to be at a** — (*Comm*) estar sobre la par, (*fig*) tener mucha demanda, ser muy solicitado; **to put a** — **on something** estimular algo, fomentar algo; hacer que suba el valor de algo (*debido a su escasez*); **to sell something at a** — (*debido a su escasez*); **to sell something at a** — vender algo en más de su valor nominal.
premium bond ['pri:miəm'bɔnd] *n bono de la caja de ahorros que participa en una especie de lotería nacional.*
premonition [,pri:mə'niʃən] *n* presentimiento *m*; **to have a** — **that** ... presentir que ...
prenatal ['pri:'neitl] *adj* prenatal.

preoccupation [pri:,ɔkju'peiʃən] *n* preocupación *f*.
preoccupied [pri:'ɔkjupaid] *adj* preocupado; absorto; **to be** — **about** estar preocupado por, inquietarse por; **to be** — **with something** estar absorto en algo; **he was too** — **to notice** estaba demasiado absorto para darse cuenta.
preoccupy [pri:'ɔkjupai] *vt* preocupar.
preordain ['pri:ɔ:'dein] *vt* predestinar.
prep [prep] (*fam*) see **preparation, preparatory.**
prepackaged ['pri:'pækidʒd] *adj* precintado.
prepaid ['pri:'peid] *adj* porte pagado, franco de porte.
preparation [,prepə'reiʃən] *n* preparación *f*; —**s** preparativos *mpl* (*for* para); **to be in** — (*book*) estar en preparación; **to do something without** — hacer algo sin preparación; **to make one's** —**s** hacer sus preparativos (*to* + *infin* para + *infin*); **Latin is a good** — **for Greek** saber latín es un buen método para iniciarse en el estudio del griego, el latín es buena preparación para el griego.
preparatory [pri'pærətəri] **1** *adj* preparatorio, preliminar. **2** — **to** *as prep* como preparación para; con miras a, antes de.
prepare [pri'pεə*] **1** *vt* preparar; disponer; aparejar; **how is it** —**d?** ¿cómo se prepara?; ¿cómo se hace?; **to** — **a surprise for someone** preparar una sorpresa para uno; **to** — **the way for a treaty** preparar el terreno para un tratado; **to** — **someone for bad news** prevenir a uno para recibir una mala noticia.
2 *vi* prepararse; disponerse; hacer preparativos; prevenirse; **to** — **for someone's arrival** hacer preparativos para recibir a uno; **to** — **for a storm** hacer preparativos para aguantar una tempestad; **to** — **for an examination** estudiar para un examen; **to** — **to** + *infin* disponerse a + *infin*, hacer preparativos para + *infin*.
prepared [pri'pεəd] *adj* (a) listo; "**be** —" "siempre listos", "listos para todo".
  (b) **to be** — **for anything** estar dispuesto a aguantarlo todo; no dejarse sorprender por nada; **we were not** — **for this** esto no lo esperábamos, no contábamos con esto; **we were** — **for it** lo habíamos previsto; **to be** — **to** + *infin* estar dispuesto a + *infin*; **he was not** — **to listen to us** no estaba dispuesto a escucharnos.
preparedness [pri'pεəridnis] *n* preparación *f*, estado *m* de preparación; *military* — preparación *f* militar.
prepay ['pri:'pei] (*irr: see* **pay**) *vt* pagar por adelantado.
prepayment ['pri:'peimənt] *n* pago *m* adelantado.
preponderance [pri'pɔndərəns] *n* preponderancia *f*, predominio *m*.
preponderant [pri'pɔndərənt] *adj* preponderante, predominante.
preponderantly [pri'pɔndərəntli] *adv* de modo predominante, en un grado predominante; en su mayor parte.
preponderate [pri'pɔndəreit] *vi* preponderar, predominar.
preposition [,prepə'ziʃən] *n* preposición *f*.
prepositional [,prepə'ziʃənl] *adj* preposicional.
prepossessing [,pri:pə'zesin] *adj* atractivo, agradable.
preposterous [pri'pɔstərəs] *adj* absurdo, ridículo.
preposterously [pri'pɔstərəsli] *adv* absurdamente.
preposterousness [pri'pɔstərəsnis] *n* lo absurdo.
prepuce ['pri:pju:s] *n* prepucio *m*.
pre-Raphaelite ['pri:'ræfəlait] **1** *adj* prerrafaelista. **2** *n* prerrafaelista *mf*.
prerecord ['pri:ri(:)'kɔ:d] *vt* grabar (*or* registrar) de antemano.
prerequisite ['pri:'rekwizit] *n* requisito *m* previo; cosa *f* necesaria, esencial *m*; —**s for success** las cosas necesarias para asegurar el éxito.
prerogative [pri'rɔgətiv] *n* prerrogativa *f*.
presage ['presidʒ] **1** *n* presagio *m*. **2** *vt* presagiar.
presbyopia [,prezbi'əupiə] *n* presbiopía *f*.
Presbyterian [,prezbi'tiəriən] **1** *adj* presbiteriano. **2** *n* presbiteriano *m*, a *f*.
presbytery ['prezbitəri] *n* presbiterio *m*.
preschool ['pri:'sku:l] *adj*: — **years** los años que preceden a la entrada del niño en la escuela; — **training** enseñanza *f* recibida por el niño antes de entrar en la escuela.
prescience ['presiəns] *n* presciencia *f*.
prescient ['presiənt] *adj* presciente.
prescribe [pris'kraib] *vti* (a) prescribir (*also Law*); ordenar; **in the** —**d way** en el modo que ordena la ley; **in the** —**d time** dentro del plazo que fija la ley.
  (b) (*Med*) recetar; **to** — **a medicine for someone** recetar una medicina para uno; **to** — **for boils** recetar una medicina para curar los diviesos; **he** —**d complete rest** recomendó el reposo completo; **what do you** —? ¿qué me recomienda Vd?

prescription [pris'kripʃən] n prescripción f (also Law); precepto m; (Med) receta f.

prescriptive [pris'kriptiv] adj legal; sancionado por la costumbre.

presealed ['pri:'si:ld] adj precintado.

presence ['prezns] n presencia f; (attendance) asistencia f (at a); — of mind presencia f de ánimo, serenidad f, sangre f fría; saving your — con perdón de los presentes; in the — of en presencia de, (fig) ante; to be admitted to the P— ser conducido ante el rey (etc); to make one's — felt imponerse, hacer que todos se den cuenta de lo que vale uno; your — is requested se ruega asista ...

present ['preznt] 1 adj (a) (in attendance) presente; —! ¡presente!; those — los presentes, los asistentes; to be — asistir (at a); all were — to hear it todos asistieron para oírlo, acudieron todos a oírlo; he was — at the accident fue testigo del accidente; he was — at the foundation presenció la fundación; nobody else was — no había nadie más; how many others were —? ¿cuántos más había?

(b) (actual) actual; presente; month etc corriente; (Gram) tense presente, participle de presente; — methods include ... los métodos actuales incluyen ..., los métodos en uso incluyen ...; the — Queen of England la actual Reina de Inglaterra; the — letter la presente; the — writer el que esto escribe; its — value su valor actual; in the — year en el año que corre.

2 n (a) (actuality) presente m, actualidad f; the — el presente; at — al presente, actualmente; for the — por ahora, por el momento; up to the — hasta ahora.

(b) (gift) regalo m, presente m; Christmas — regalo m de Navidad; to make someone a — of something regalar algo a uno, (fig) dar algo a uno medio regalado.

(c) (Gram) (tiempo m) presente m; — perfect pretérito m perfecto.

present [pri'zent] 1 vt (a) (introduce) presentar; to — X to Y presentar a X a Y; may I — Miss Blandish? permítame presentarle a la señorita Blandish; to be —ed at court ser presentado a la corte.

(b) (Theat) to — a play representar una obra; "—ing Garbo as Mimi" "con Garbo en el papel de Mimí".

(c) (expound) case etc exponer; to — a plan to a meeting exponer (or explicar) un proyecto a una reunión.

(d) (give) presentar, ofrecer, dar; to — something to someone, to — someone with something regalar algo a uno, (more formally) obsequiar a uno con algo; to — an account (Comm) pasar factura; to — a report presentar un informe; to — one's compliments to someone cumplimentar a uno.

(e) (provide) ofrecer; it —s a magnificent sight ofrece un espectáculo maravilloso; the case —s some odd features el caso tiene ciertas características algo raras; it —s some difficulties nos plantea algunas dificultades; the boy —s a problem el chico nos plantea un problema.

(f) (Mil) to — arms presentar las armas; — arms! ¡presenten armas!

2 vr: to — oneself presentarse (at a time a una hora, at a place en un sitio); to — oneself for examination examinarse (in de); when the chance —s itself cuando se ofrece la ocasión; a problem has —ed itself ha surgido un problema.

presentable [pri'zentəbl] adj presentable.

presentation [,prezən'teiʃən] n (a) (act) presentación f; (of case etc) exposición f; (Theat) representación f; on — of the voucher al presentarse el vale.

(b) (present) obsequio m; (ceremony) entrega f ceremoniosa de un regalo; to make someone a — on his retirement hacer un obsequio a uno en su jubilación.

present-day ['preznt'dei] adj actual.

presentiment [pri'zentimənt] n presentimiento m, corazonada f; to have a — about something tener un presentimiento acerca de algo; to have a — that ... presentir que ...

presently ['prezntli] adv luego, dentro de poco; (US) ahora, actualmente.

preservation [,prezə'veiʃən] n conservación f; preservación f; in a good state of —, in good — bien conservado, en buen estado.

preservative [pri'zə:vətiv] 1 adj preservativo. 2 n preservativo m.

preserve [pri'zə:v] 1 n (a) (Cook) conserva f; confitura f; compota f.

(b) (Hunting) coto m, vedado m; game — coto m de caza.

2 vt (a) (keep) conservar; mantener en buen estado; (keep from harm) preservar (against, from contra), guardar, proteger (against, from de); may God — you que Dios os guarde.

(b) (Cook) hacer una conserva de; (in syrup) almibarar, (in salt) salar, salpresar.

preserved [pri'zə:vd] adj food en conserva.

preshrunk ['pri:'ʃrʌŋk] adj encogido de antemano.

preside [pri'zaid] vi presidir; to — at (or over) a meeting presidir una reunión.

presidency ['prezidənsi] n presidencia f.

president ['prezidənt] n (Pol etc) presidente m; (US Comm) director m; (US Univ) rector m.

presidential [,prezi'denʃəl] adj presidencial.

press [pres] 1 n (a) (pressure) presión f; (of hand etc) apretón m, presión f; (Sport) presa f; give it a — here presione aquí.

(b) (crush etc of people) apiñamiento m, agolpamiento m; (of affairs) urgencia f; there was such a — of people había tal multitud de gente, era tal el apiñamiento; in the — of the battle en lo más reñido de la batalla.

(c) (Mech) prensa f; hydraulic — prensa f hidráulica; linen — prensa f de ropa.

(d) (Typ) (printing press, publishing firm) imprenta f; (newspapers in general) prensa f; the P— la Prensa; rotary — prensa f rotativa; yellow — periódicos mpl sensacionales; to be in — estar en prensa; to get (or have) a bad — tener mala prensa; to get (or have) a good — tener buena prensa; to go to — entrar en prensa, entrar en máquina; to pass something for the — aprobar algo para la prensa.

2 vt (a) button, switch, doorbell etc apretar, pulsar, presionar, empujar; hand, trigger apretar; hand (painfully) apretujar; grapes pisar, prensar; metal, olives etc (Tech) prensar; suit planchar; (crush, squeeze) estrujar; to — someone's hand apretar la mano a uno; to — the juice out of an orange exprimir el zumo de una naranja; it —es me here me aprieta aquí; he —ed his face to the window pegó la cara al cristal; to — someone to one's heart abrazar a uno estrechamente; to — something down comprimir algo; to — books into a case meter libros apretadamente en una maleta.

(b) (put pressure on enemy) acosar, hostigar, (in game) apretar, (in pursuit) seguir muy de cerca, pisar los talones de; to — someone hard apretar mucho a uno; to — someone for payment insistir en que uno pague algo, exigir un pago a uno; to — someone for an answer pedir insistentemente que uno conteste a algo; to — a claim insistir en una demanda; to — a point insistir en su punto de vista; to — home an advantage aprovecharse todo lo posible de una ventaja; to — a gift on someone insistir en que uno acepte un regalo; to — someone to do something instar a uno a que haga algo; to — someone to do something apremiar a uno para que haga algo, hacer presión sobre uno para que haga algo; he didn't need much —ing no hacía falta persuadirle; he was being —ed by creditors le acosaban los acreedores; to be —ed for money andar muy escaso de dinero; to be —ed for time tener poco tiempo, tener mucha prisa; see service etc.

3 vi (a) (in physical sense) apretar; ejercer presión, hacer presión; to — hard apretar mucho; to — close up to someone arrimarse a uno; to — down on something apretar algo (comprimiéndolo); pesar sobre algo; to — on one's pen escribir haciendo más presión con la pluma; the people —ed round him la gente se apiñó en torno a él.

(b) (fig) ejercer presión, hacer presión; presionar; time —es el tiempo apremia; responsibilities — hard on him las responsabilidades pesan sobre él; to — forward, to — on avanzar; seguir su camino; (hasten) apretar el paso; — on! ¡adelante!

(c) to — for something presionar por algo, presionar para conseguir algo; reclamar algo, exigir algo, pedir algo con urgencia; hacer propaganda a favor de algo.

press agency ['pres,eidʒənsi] n agencia f de información.

press agent ['pres,eidʒənt] n agente m de publicidad.

press baron ['pres,bærən] n magnate m de la prensa.

press box ['presbɔks] n tribuna f de la prensa.

press button ['pres'bʌtn] 1 n botón m (de control). 2 press-button attr mandado por botón.

press conference ['pres,kɔnfərəns] n rueda f de prensa.

press cutting ['pres,kʌtiŋ] n recorte m de periódico.

press gallery ['pres,gæləri] n tribuna f de la prensa (esp de la cámara, del parlamento).

press-gang ['presgæŋ] **1** n ronda f de enganche.
2 vt: **to — someone into something** obligar a uno muy contra su voluntad a hacer algo.
pressing ['presiŋ] adj urgente, apremiante, acuciante.
pressman ['presmæn] n, pl **-men** [men] periodista m.
pressmark ['presmɑːk] n signatura f.
press photographer ['presfə'tɔgrəfə*] n fotógrafo m de prensa.
press stud ['prestʌd] n botón m de presión.
pressure [preʃə*] n (a) (Meteorol, Phys, Tech) presión f; (weight) peso m; (strength) fuerza f; **barometric —** presión f barométrica; **tyre —** presión f de los neumáticos; **a — of X pounds to the square inch** una presión de X kilogramos al cm².
  (b) (urgency) urgencia f, apremio m; (influence) influencia f, persuasión f; (Med) tensión f nerviosa; **because of the — of business** (Comm) debido a la cantidad de negocios, (at meeting etc) por el número de los asuntos a tratar; **to act under —** obrar bajo persuasión; **to do something under — from the bankers** hacer algo presionado por los banqueros; **to bring — to bear on someone** hacer presión sobre uno (to do something para que haga algo); **to live at high —** tener una vida muy activa; **to work under —** trabajar con urgencia.
pressure cooker ['preʃə,kukə*] n olla f a presión.
pressure-feed ['preʃəfiːd] n tubo m de alimentación a presión.
pressure gauge ['preʃəgeidʒ] n manómetro m.
pressure group ['preʃəgruːp] n grupo m de presión.
pressure pan ['preʃəpæn] n (US) olla f a presión.
pressurized ['preʃəraizd] adj cabin a presión, altimático.
press view ['presvjuː] n preestreno m.
prestidigitation ['presti,didʒi'teiʃən] n prestidigitación f.
prestige [pres'tiːʒ] n prestigio m.
prestigious [pres'tidʒəs] adj prestigioso.
presto ['prestəu] adv: **hey —!** ¡abracadabra!
prestressed ['priː'strest] adj: **— concrete** hormigón m pretensado.
presumably [pri'zjuːməbli] adv probablemente, según cabe presumir; **— he will come** imagino que vendrá; **— he did** cabe presumir que lo hizo.
presume [pri'zjuːm] vti (a) presumir; supomer; **his death must be —d** hay que presumir que ha muerto, es de suponer que murió; **to — that . . .** suponer que . . .; **it may be —d that . . .** es de suponer que . . .; **to — someone to be innocent** suponer que uno es inocente; **Dr Livingstone, I — Dr** Livingstone según creo, cabe conjeturar que Vd es el Dr Livingstone.
  (b) **to — to + infin** atreverse a + infin; pretender + infin, tomarse la libertad de + infin; **if I may — to advise you** si se me permite ofrecerle un consejo.
  (c) **to — on someone's friendship** abusar de la amistad de uno; **you — too much** Vd no sabe lo que pide, eso es mucho pedir.
presumption [pri'zʌmpʃən] n (a) (arrogance) presunción f; atrevimiento m; **pardon my —** le ruego perdonar mi atrevimiento.
  (b) (thing presumed) suposición f; pretensión f; **the — is that . . .** es de suponer que . . ., puede presumirse que . . .
presumptive [pri'zʌmptiv] adj heir presunto.
presumptuous [pri'zʌmptjuəs] adj presumido, presuntuoso; atrevido; **in that I was rather — en** eso fui algo atrevido; **it would be — of me to + infin** sería atrevido + infin.
presumptuously [pri'zʌmptjuəsli] adv con presunción, presuntuosamente.
presumptuousness [pri'zʌmptjuəsnis] n presunción f, atrevimiento m.
presuppose [,priːsə'pəuz] vt presuponer.
presupposition [,priːsʌpə'ziʃən] n presuposición f.
pretence [pri'tens] n (a) (claim) pretensión f; **to make no — to learning** no pretender ser erudito.
  (b) (display) ostentación f; afectación f; **without —, devoid of all —** sin ostentación, sin afectación.
  (c) (pretext) pretexto m; **false —s** fraude m; **by false —s** fraudulentamente, con engaño; **on the — of, under the —** of so pretexto de.
  (d) (make-believe) fingimiento m; **it's all a —** todo es fingido; **to make a — of something** fingir algo.
pretend [pri'tend] **1** vt (a) (feign) fingir, aparentar, simular; **to — ignorance** fingir ignorar, aparentar no saber; **to — to + infin** fingir + infin, aparentar + infin; **to — to go away** fingir marcharse; **to — to be mad** fingirse loco; **to — to be asleep, to — to sleep** fingir dormir, fingirse dormido, hacerse el dormido; **he —s to be a poet** se dice poeta, se hace el poeta,

las echa de poeta; **to — not to be listening** hacerse el distraído; **to — not to understand** hacerse el desentendido.
  (b) (claim) pretender; **I do not — to know the answer** no pretendo saber qué solución pueda haber; **I don't — to understand art** no pretendo entender de arte.
  2 vi (a) (feign) fingir; **it's just —, we're only —ing** (to child etc) es de mentirijillas; **let's — imaginémoslo; let's not — to each other** no nos engañemos uno a otro.
  (b) (claim) **to — to the throne** pretender al trono; **to — to intelligence** afirmar tener inteligencia, pretender ser inteligente.
pretended [pri'tendid] adj pretendido.
pretender [pri'tendə*] n pretendiente mf; **the Young P—** el joven Pretendiente.
pretense [pri'tens] (US) see **pretence**.
pretension [pri'tenʃən] n (a) (claim) pretensión f; **to have —s to culture** tener pretensiones de cultura, pretender ser culto.
  (b) (pretentiousness) presunción f; afectación f.
pretentious [pri'tenʃəs] adj pretencioso; person presumido, (ostentatious) ostentoso, aparatoso, ambicioso; (and vulgar) cursi.
pretentiously [pri'tenʃəsli] adv con presunción; ostentosamente, aparatosamente.
pretentiousness [pri'tenʃəsnis] n lo pretencioso; presunción f; lo ostentoso, lo aparatoso; cursilería f.
preterite ['pretərit] n pretérito m.
preternatural [,priːtə'nætʃrəl] adj preternatural.
pretext ['priːtekst] n pretexto m; **under — of so** pretexto de; **it's just a —** es sólo un pretexto.
prettify ['pritifai] vt (pej) embellecer, adornar de modo ridículo; representar bajo una forma demasiado hermosa.
prettily ['pritili] adv con gracia, elegantemente; preciosamente; **— adorned with** con adornos elegantes de.
pretty ['priti] **1** adj (a) person guapo, bonito; dress, object etc precioso, mono; scene hermoso; **a — girl** una muchacha guapa; **a — little house** una casita preciosa; **what a — hat!** ¡qué sombrero más mono!, ¡qué monada de sombrero!; **yes, my — sí, ricura; she's as — as a picture** es guapísima; **he has a — wit** tiene un ingenio muy vivo, tiene mucha chispa.
  (b) sum etc importante, considerable.
  (c) (iro) bueno; **a — mess we're in!** ¡vaya lío!
  2 adv bastante; casi; **— good** bastante bueno, muy bueno; **— hard** bastante difícil; **it's — much the same** es lo mismo más o menos; **he got — cross** se enfadó bastante; **it's — near ruined** está casi arruinado; **— well, thanks!** ¡regular, gracias!; **to be sitting —** estar bien, estar en una posición ventajosa.
pretzel ['pretsl] n (US) galleta tostada en forma de rosquilla, polvoreada con sal.
prevail [pri'veil] vi (a) (gain mastery) prevalecer, imponerse; **to — against** (or over) **one's enemies** triunfar sobre los enemigos; **finally good sense —ed** por fin se impuso el buen sentido; **eventually peace —ed** por fin se restableció la paz.
  (b) (be current) reinar, imperar; predominar; (be in fashion) estar de moda, estar en boga; **the conditions that now —** las condiciones que ahora imperan.
  (c) (persuade) **to — upon someone to do something** persuadir a uno a hacer algo, inducir a uno a hacer algo; **he was eventually —ed upon to + infin** por fin se dejó persuadir a + infin; **he could not be —ed upon** era imposible persuadirle, no se convenció.
prevailing [pri'veiliŋ] adj reinante, imperante; predominante; usual, corriente; **the — fashion** la moda actual, la moda reinante; **under — conditions** bajo las condiciones actuales; **the — wind** el viento predominante.
prevalence ['prevələns] n predominio m; frecuencia f; uso m corriente, costumbre f.
prevalent ['prevələnt] adj predominante; frecuente, común, corriente; (fashionable) en boga, de moda; custom etc extendido; (present-day) actual.
prevaricate [pri'værikeit] vi buscar evasivas, usar sofismas, tergiversar.
prevarication [pri,væri'keiʃən] n evasivas fpl, sofismas mpl, tergiversación f.
prevent [pri'vent] vt person impedir, estorbar; event etc impedir, evitar; impedir; illness etc evitar; **it was impossible to — it** fue imposible impedirlo; **to — someone + ger, to — someone from + ger** impedir a uno + infin.
preventable [pri'ventəbl] adj evitable.
preventative [pri'ventətiv] adj see **preventive**.

prevention [pri'venʃən] n prevención f; el impedir, el evitar; **the — of errors is not easy** no es fácil evitar los errores; **for the — of accidents** para evitar los accidentes; **a society for the — of cruelty to animals** una sociedad protectora de animales.

preventive [pri'ventiv] adj preventivo, impeditivo; (Med) profiláctico; **measure, medicine** preventivo.

preview ['pri:vju:] n preestreno m; (fig) anticipo m, vista f anticipada; **to have a — of something** ver algo con anticipación, lograr ver algo antes que otros.

previous ['pri:viəs] **1** adj **(a)** previo, anterior; **in — years** en años anteriores; **no — experience necessary** no es necesario tener conocimientos del oficio; **because of a — engagement** por tener compromiso anterior.

(b) (hasty) prematuro; **this seems somewhat —** esto parece ser algo prematuro; **you have been rather —** Vd ha obrado con cierta prisa, Vd ha obrado antes del momento justo.

2 prep: **— to** antes de; **— to doing this** antes de hacer esto.

previously ['pri:viəsli] adv (already) previamente, con anticipación, anteriormente; (in early times) antes.

prewar ['pri:'wɔ:*] adj de preguerra, de la preguerra, prebélico; **the — period** la preguerra.

prey [prei] **1** n presa f, víctima f; **bird of —** ave f de rapiña; **to be a —** to ser víctima de.

2 vi **(a) to — on** (feed on) atacar, alimentarse de, comer, devorar; (plunder) robar, pillar; (sponge on) vivir a costa de; **rabbits are —ed on by foxes** los conejos son presa de los zorros.

(b) to — on (mind) agobiar, remorder, preocupar; **doubts —ed on him** le obsesionaban las dudas; **the tragedy so —ed on his mind that . . .** la tragedia le afectó de tal modo que . . .

price [prais] **1** n precio m; (quotation, Fin) cotización f; **asking —** precio m a que se ofrece; **cash —** precio m al contado; **closing — (Fin)** cotización f de cierre, cotización f de clausura; **cost —** precio m de coste; **fixed —** precio m fijo; **list —** precio m de lista; **market —** precio m de mercado; **net —** precio m neto; **opening — (Fin)** cotización f de apertura; **reserve —** precio m mínimo; **at a — of £500** a un precio de 500 libras; **at a reduced —** a un precio reducido, con descuento; **at any — (fig)** a toda costa; **peace at any —** paz a ultranza; **you can buy it at a —** se puede comprar pero cuesta bastante; **not at any —!** de ningún modo; **I don't want that at any —** eso no lo quiero ni regalado; **what — these pigs?** ¿cuánto se me ofrece por estos cerdos?; **what — liberty?** y la libertad, ¿qué?; **what — Joe Soap now?** ¿qué me dicen ahora sobre Joe Soap?; **what's the — of this?** ¿cuánto vale esto?; **to pay top — for something** pagar algo al precio máximo; **to rise in — subir de precio; houses have risen in —** ha aumentado el valor de las casas; see head.

2 vt **(a)** estimar, valuar, valorar (at en); tasar (at en), fijar el precio de; **it is —d rather high at £80** está valorado en 80 libras, lo cual es mucho; **it's not —d in the window** en el escaparate no le han puesto el precio.

(b) to be —d out of the market (article) alcanzar tal precio de coste que no puede concurrir a los mercados (internacionales), (producer, nation) señalar precios tan elevados a los artículos producidos que el productor (or el país) no puede concurrir a los mercados (internacionales).

price control ['praiskən,trəul] n control m de precios.

priceless ['praislis] adj **(a)** inapreciable, que no tiene precio. **(b)** (amusing) divertidísimo; **it was —!** ¡fue para morirse de risa!

price list ['praislist] n lista f de precios.

price range ['praisreindʒ] n gama f de precios, escala f de precios.

prick [prik] **1** n **(a)** pinchazo m, punzada f; (sting etc) picadura f; (with pin) alfilerazo m; (of spur) espolada f; (with goad) aguijonazo m; **— of conscience** escrúpulo m de conciencia, remordimiento m; **to kick against the —s** dar coces contra el aguijón.

(b) (Anat, tabu) polla f.

2 vt **(a)** pinchar, punzar, picar; (sting) picar; (with spur) dar con las espuelas; (goad) aguijar; (make hole in) agujerear; (mark with holes) marcar con agujerillos; **to — out** (Hort) plantar; **to — up one's ears** aguzar el oído.

(b) it —ed his conscience le remordió la conciencia, le dio un escrúpulo de conciencia.

3 vi: **to — up** aguzar el oído, empezar a prestar atención.

prickings ['prikiŋz] npl: **— of conscience** remordimientos mpl.

prickle ['prikl] n **(a)** (Bot) espina f; (Zool) púa f. **(b)** (on skin etc) escozor m.

prickly ['prikli] adj espinoso, lleno de espinas; lleno de púas; person poco afable, malhumorado, difícil; **he's rather — about that** sobre ese tema es algo quisquilloso.

prickly heat ['prikli'hi:t] n salpullido m causado por exceso de calor.

prickly pear ['prikli'pɛə*] n higo m chumbo, chumbera f.

pride [praid] **1** n orgullo m; (pej) orgullo m, soberbia f, arrogancia f; **it's the — of Navarre** es el orgullo de Navarra; **he's the — of the family** es el orgullo de la familia; **— comes before a fall, — must have a fall** el orgullo excesivo conduce a la caída; **it is a source of — to us that . . .** es para nosotros un motivo de orgullo el que . . .; **to pocket one's —** olvidarse de su amor propio; tragar una afrenta; **to take (a) — in something** enorgullecerse de algo, ufanarse de algo; **to take — of place** venir primero, ocupar el primer puesto.

2 vr: **to — oneself on something** enorgullecerse de algo, ufanarse de algo; **to — oneself on + ger** enorgullecerse de + infin.

priest [pri:st] n (in general, pagan) sacerdote m; (Christian) sacerdote m, cura m; **high —** sumo sacerdote m; **parish —** párroco m.

priestess ['pri:stis] n sacerdotisa f.

priesthood ['pri:sthud] n (function) sacerdocio m; (priests collectively) clero m; **to enter the —** ordenarse de sacerdote.

priestly ['pri:stli] adj sacerdotal.

priest-ridden ['pri:st,ridn] adj dominado por el clero.

prig [prig] n presumido m, a f; pedante mf; mojigato m, a f, gazmoño m, a f; **don't be such a —!** ¡no presumas!

priggish ['prigiʃ] adj presumido; pedante; mojigato, gazmoño.

priggishness ['prigiʃnis] n presunción f; pedantería f; mojigatería f, gazmoñería f.

prim [prim] adj (formal) etiquetero, estirado; (affected) remilgado; (prudish) gazmoño.

primacy ['praiməsi] n primacía f.

prima donna ['pri:mə'dɔnə] n primadonna f, diva f.

prima facie ['praimə'feiʃi] **1** adv a primera vista. **2** adj (Law) suficiente para justificar la presunción del hecho; **there are — reasons why . . .** hay suficientes razones que justifican el que + subj; **he has a — case** a primera vista parece que tiene razón.

primarily ['praimərili] adv ante todo; en primer lugar; principalmente.

primary ['praiməri] **1** adj primario; principal; colour, education primario; **that is not the — reason** ésa no es la razón principal; see school.

2 n (US) elección preliminar para nombrar candidatos.

primate ['praimit] n (Eccl) primado m.

primate ['praimeit] n (Zool) primate m.

prime [praim] **1** adj **(a)** (Math) primo.

(b) (chief) primero, principal; fundamental; **the — reason** la razón principal; **of — importance** de primera importancia; **of — necessity** de primera necesidad.

(c) (excellent) selecto, de primera clase; **quality beef** carne f de vaca de primera calidad; **in — condition** en excelente estado.

2 n **(a)** flor f, lo mejor; **the — of life** la flor de la vida, la edad viril; **to be in one's —** estar en la flor de la vida; **to be past one's —** haber dado lo mejor de sí, estar en decadencia; **to be cut off in one's —** morir en la flor de la vida.

(b) (Eccl) prima f.

3 vt gun, pump cebar; surface et preparar, aprestar; **to — someone** informar a uno de antemano, hacer que uno se entere de algo clandestinamente; **they —d him about what he should say . . .** le dieron instrucciones acerca de lo que había de decir; **to — someone with drink** emborrachar a uno, hacer que uno beba; **he arrived well —d** llegó ya a medio borracho.

prime minister [,praim'ministə*] n primer ministro m.

primer ['praimə*] n cartilla f, libro m de texto elemental; **a French —** un libro elemental de francés.

primeval [prai'mi:vəl] adj primitivo.

priming ['praimiŋ] n preparación f; (of pump etc) cebo m; (Art) primera capa f.

primitive ['primitiv] 1 adj (early; original, primary) primitivo; (old-fashioned) anticuado; (simple, rude) rudimentario, sencillo; (uncivilized) inculto; (sordid) sucio, miserable, asqueroso; (Art) primitivo.
2 n (Art) primitivo.

primly ['primli] adv remilgadamente; con gazmoñería.

primness ['primnis] n lo etiquetero, lo estirado; remilgo m; gazmoñería f.

primogeniture [,praiməu'dʒenitʃə*] n primogenitura f.

primordial [prai'mɔ:diəl] adj primordial.

primus (stove) ['praiməs(stəuv)] (Protected Trade Name) n cocinilla f de alcohol, cocinilla f de camping, infiernillo m campestre.

primrose ['primrəuz] 1 n (Bot) primavera f; (colour) color m amarillo pálido. 2 adj amarillo pálido. 3 attr: — **path** caminito m de rosas.

primula ['primjulə] n oreja f de oso.

prince [prins] n príncipe m; **P— Charming** el príncipe encantador; **the — of darkness** el príncipe de las tinieblas; **— consort** príncipe m consorte; **— regent** príncipe m regente; **P— of Wales** Príncipe m de Gales (heredero del trono del Reino Unido, equivalente al Príncipe de Asturias en España).

princely ['prinsli] adj principesco; magnífico, noble; **the — sum of two shillings** la bonita cantidad de dos chelines.

princess [prin'ses] n princesa f.

principal ['prinsipəl] 1 adj principal; mayor. 2 n principal m, jefe m; (of school, college) director m, ora f; (Fin) principal m, capital m.

principality [,prinsi'pæliti] n principado m.

principally ['prinsipəli] adv principalmente.

principle ['prinsəpl] n principio m; **in —** en principio; **on —** por principio; **to argue from first —**s construir su argumento sobre los principios fundamentales; **to go back to first —**s volver a los principios fundamentales; **to have high —**s tener principios nobles; **to lay it down as a — that . . .** sentar el principio de que . . .; **I make it a — never to + infin** me hago una regla de nunca + infin.

prink [priŋk] 1 vt acicalar, ataviar; arreglar elegantemente. 2 vi acicalarse, ataviarse; arreglarse elegantemente.

print [print] 1 n (mark, imprint) marca f, señal f, impresión f; (Typ) tipo m, letra f de molde; (printed matter) impreso m; (fabric, dress) estampado m; (picture) estampa f, grabado m; (Phot) positiva f, copia f; **large —** tipo m grande; **small —** tipo m menudo; **in (cold) —** en letras de molde; **to be in —** (be published as book etc) estar impreso, (be available) estar disponible, estar en existencia; **to be out of —** estar agotado; **he likes to see himself in —** se enorgullece de que se impriman sus artículos (etc); le agrada que le mencionen en los periódicos; **to get into —** imprimirse, publicarse; **we don't want that to get into —** no queremos que se publique la noticia en los periódicos; **I've got into — at last!** ¡por fin me van a publicar el artículo! (etc); **to rush into —** publicar una obra sin reflexionar.
2 attr dress estampado.
3 vt imprimir; (on the mind etc) grabar; book etc imprimir; sacar a luz, dar a la estampa, publicar; (Phot) imprimir; (write plainly) escribir en caracteres de imprenta, escribir en letras de molde; **—ed by** impreso por; **they —ed 300 copies** (Typ) tiraron 300 ejemplares, hicieron una tirada de 300 ejemplares.

printed ['printid] adj impreso; dress estampado; **— matter** impresos mpl.

printer ['printə*] n impresor m.

printing ['printiŋ] n (art) tipografía f, imprenta f; (act) impresión f; (quantity printed) tirada f; **4th —** 4ª impresión; **a — of 500 copies** una tirada de 500 ejemplares; **"16th century — in Toledo"** "la imprenta en Toledo en el siglo XVI".

printing frame ['printiŋ,freim] n prensa f de copiar.

printing machine ['printiŋmə,ʃi:n] n máquina f tipográfica.

printing office ['printiŋ,ɔfis] n imprenta f.

printing press ['printiŋ,pres] n prensa f de imprenta.

printing works ['printiŋ,wə:ks] n imprenta f.

prior ['praiə*] 1 adj anterior, previo; claim etc preferente.
2 adv: **— to** antes de; hasta; **— to this discovery** antes de este descubrimiento.
3 n (Eccl) prior m.

prioress ['praiəris] n priora f.

priority [prai'ɔriti] n prioridad f; (in time) antelación f, precedencia f; **to have —** tener prioridad (over someone sobre uno); **they will be given out in strict order of —** serán distribuidos con arreglo a un riguroso criterio de prioridades; **we must get our priorities right** hemos de establecer un justo orden de prioridades.

priory ['praiəri] n priorato m.

prise [praiz] vt: **to — open** abrir por fuerza, abrir con una palanca; **to — a lid up** levantar una tapa con una palanca; **to — someone out of his post** lograr que uno renuncie a su puesto, desahuciar a uno.

prism ['prizəm] n prisma m.

prismatic [priz'mætik] adj prismático.

prison ['prizn] 1 n cárcel f, prisión f; **to be in —** estar en la cárcel; **to go to — for 5 years** ser condenado a 5 años de prisión; pasar 5 años en la cárcel; **to put someone in —, to send someone to —** encarcelar a uno; **to send someone to — for 2 years** condenar a uno a 2 años de prisión.
2 attr carcelario; **— life** vida f en la cárcel; **— population** población f reclusa; **— camp** campamento m para prisioneros.

prisoner ['priznə*] n (under arrest) detenido m, a f; (facing charge, — at the bar) acusado m, a f; (convicted) preso m, a f; (Mil) prisionero m; **to hold someone —** detener a uno; **to take someone —** hacer prisionero a uno.

prison van ['priznvæn] n coche m celular.

prison yard ['priznja:d] n patio m de la cárcel.

prissy ['prisi] adj (fam) remilgado, repipi.

pristine ['pristain] adj prístino.

privacy ['privəsi] n soledad f, retiro m, aislamiento m; intimidad f; (secrecy) secreto m, reserva f; **desire for —** deseo m de estar a solas; **in search of some —** en busca de soledad; **there is no — in these flats** en estos pisos no se puede estar en privado; **in the — of one's home** en la intimidad de su casa; **in the strictest —** en el mayor secreto; **to invade someone's —** invadir la soledad de uno.

private ['praivit] 1 adj privado; particular; (for use) propio, personal; (confidential) secreto, reservado, confidencial; enterprise privado; life privado, íntimo; conversation, letter íntimo, entre los dos; opinion personal; arrangement, car, company, entrance, house, income, interview, lesson, room, school, secretary etc particular; hearing, sitting secreto, a puertas cerradas; report secreto, confidencial; **"—"** "propiedad particular"; **"— and confidential"** "privado y confidencial"; **— person** particular mf; **my — opinion is that . . .** creo para mí que . . ., mi opinión personal es que . . .; **the wedding was —** la ceremonia se celebró en la intimidad; **to keep something —** guardar el secreto de algo; **they want to be —** quieren estar a solas; see life, member, view etc.
2 n (a) (Mil) soldado m raso; **P— Jones** el soldado Jones; **P— Jones!** ¡Jones!
(b) **in —** en privado; en secreto; de persona a persona, entre los dos; confidencialmente; **I have been told in — that . . .** me han dicho confidencialmente que . . .; **the committee sat in —** la comisión se reunió a puerta cerrada; **the wedding was held in —** la ceremonia se celebró en la intimidad.
(c) **—s** (Anat) partes fpl pudendas.

privateer [,praivə'tiə*] n corsario m.

privately ['praivitli] adv privadamente, en privado; en secreto; particularmente; **the meeting was held —** la reunión fue a puerta cerrada; **the wedding took place —** la ceremonia se celebró en la intimidad; **— I think that . . .** personalmente creo que . . .; **I have been told — that . . .** me han dicho confidencialmente que . . .; **but — he was very upset** pero en su corazón se sintió muy molesto; **so he spoke — to me** así que me habló de persona a persona; **he is being — educated** está en un colegio particular; tiene un profesor particular.

privation [prai'veiʃən] n (a) (state) miseria f, estrechez f; **to live in —** vivir en la miseria. (b) (difficulty) apuro m; **to suffer many —s** pasar muchos apuros.

privative ['privətiv] adj privativo.

privet ['privit] n ligustro m, alheña f.

privilege ['privilidʒ] 1 n privilegio m; prerrogativa f; (Law, Parl) inmunidad f; **to have parliamentary —** gozar de la inmunidad parlamentaria.
2 vt: **to be —d to + infin** tener el privilegio de + infin.

privileged ['privilidʒd] adj privilegiado; speech que goza de la inmunidad parlamentaria (etc); **for a —** few para unos pocos afortunados.

privily ['privili] adv privadamente, en privado; tell etc confidencialmente.

privy ['privi] 1 adj: **to be — to something** estar enterado secretamente de algo; see council etc. 2 n retrete m.

prize[1] [praiz] **1** n **(a)** premio m; **cash** — premio m en metálico; **first** — primer premio m, (in lottery) premio m gordo; **Nobel P**— Premio m Nobel; **to carry off the** —, **to win the** — ganar el premio.

(b) (Naut) presa f.

2 adj entry, rose etc premiado; (fig) digno de premio; excelente, de primera clase; **he's a** — **idiot** es un tonto de capirote; **what a** — **idiot you are!** ¡imbécil!

3 vt apreciar, estimar; **to** — **something highly** estimar algo en mucho.

prize[2] [praiz] vt see **prise**.

prize court ['praizkɔːt] n tribunal m de presas marítimas.

prize fight ['praizfait] n partido m de boxeo profesional.

prize fighter ['praizfaitə*] n boxeador m profesional.

prize fighting ['praiz,faitiŋ] n boxeo m profesional.

prize giving ['praiz,giviŋ] n distribución f de premios.

prize money ['praiz,mʌni] n (Naut) parte f de presa; (cash) premio m en metálico; (Boxing) bolsa f.

prizewinner ['praiz,winə*] n premiado m, a f.

prize winning ['praiz,winiŋ] adj premiado.

pro[1] [prəu] prep **(a)** pro; en pro de.

(b) (in compounds) pro-, eg **pro-Soviet** prosoviético; **pro-Spanish** hispanófilo; **they were terribly pro-Franco** eran unos franquistas furibundos, eran partidarios acérrimos de Franco.

(c) the —**s and the cons** los pros y los contras; **we weigh up the** —**s and the cons** estudiamos los argumentos a favor y en contra.

(d) — **forma**, — **forma invoice** factura f simulada; — **rata** a prorrateo; **the money will be shared out** — **rata** el dinero será repartido a prorrateo, se prorrateará el dinero; — **tempore**, — **tem** (fam) por ahora, por el momento, interinamente.

pro[2] [prəu] n (fam) profesional mf.

probability [,prɔbə'biliti] n probabilidad f; **in all** — según toda probabilidad; **the** — **is that** . . . es probable que + subj.

probable ['prɔbəbl] adj probable; verosímil; **it is** — **that** . . . es probable que + subj.

probably ['prɔbəbli] adv probablemente; **he will** — **come**, — **he will come** es probable que venga; **he** — **forgot** lo habrá olvidado, a lo mejor lo olvidó.

probate ['prəubit] n verificación f oficial de los testamentos; — **court** tribunal m de testamentarías; **to value something for** — evaluar algo para la verificación oficial de testamentos.

probation [prə'beiʃən] **1** n (Law) libertad f condicional, libertad f vigilada; **to be on** — estar en libertad condicional; **to take something on** — tomar algo a prueba.

2 attr: — **officer** oficial que vigila las personas que están en libertad condicional.

probationary [prə'beiʃnəri] adj de prueba; — **period** (Law) período m de libertad condicional.

probationer [prə'beiʃnə*] n (Law) persona f en libertad condicional; (Med) aprendiza f de enfermera; (Eccl) novicio m, a f.

probe [prəub] **1** n **(a)** (Med) sonda f, tienta f; (rocket) cohete m, proyectil m; **space** — vehículo m espacial, vehículo m de exploración espacial.

(b) (inquiry) investigación f, indagación f, encuesta f; **a** — **into the drug traffic** una investigación del tráfico de narcóticos.

2 vt (Med) sondar, tentar; (ground etc sondar; (explore) explorar; (search) registrar; (investigate) investigar, indagar; **to** — **a mystery** investigar un misterio.

3 vi investigar; **to** — **into someone's past** investigar el pasado de uno; **you should have** —**d more deeply** convenía hacer una investigación más a fondo.

probing ['prəubiŋ] n sondeo m; investigación f; exploración f.

probity ['prəubiti] n probidad f.

problem ['prɔbləm] **1** n problema m; **the housing** — el problema de la vivienda; **it's a real** — realmente es un problema.

2 attr: — **child** niño m difícil; — **play** drama m de tesis.

problematic [,prɔbli'mætik] adj problemático, dudoso; **it is** — **whether** . . . es dudoso si . . .

problem page ['prɔbləm,peidʒ] n consultorio m.

proboscis [prəu'bɔsis] n probóscide f, trompa f.

procedural [prə'siːdjurəl] adj procesal; relativo al procedimiento; **a** — **question** una cuestión de procedimiento.

procedure [prə'siːdʒə*] n procedimiento m; proceder m; trámites mpl, tramitación f; **the usual** — **is to** +

infin lo que se hace por lo general es + infin; **the correct** — **would be to** + infin lo correcto sería + infin.

proceed [prə'siːd] vi **(a)** (go) proceder; ir; **before we** — **any further** antes de ir más lejos; **to** — **on one's way** seguir adelante, seguir su camino; **we** —**ed to London** fuimos a Londres; **we** —**ed to the bar** nos trasladamos al bar; **the ship** —**ed at 10 knots** el barco iba a una velocidad de 10 nudos, el barco reanudó el viaje a una velocidad de 10 nudos; **cars should** — **slowly** los automóviles deberán ir despacio; **let us** — **with caution** avancemos con precaución.

(b) (go on to) how should we —? ¿cómo hemos de proceder?; **to** — **to blows** llegar a las manos; **to** — **to business** pasar a discutir los asuntos a tratar; **let us** — **to the next item** pasemos al asunto siguiente; **to** — **to do something** pasar a hacer algo, ponerse a hacer algo, empezar a hacer algo; **he** —**ed to drink the lot** en seguida se lo bebió todo; **he** —**ed to say that** . . . dijo a continuación que . . .

(c) (continue) continuar, seguir; **the text** —**s thus** el texto sigue así; **things are** —**ing according to plan** las cosas se están desarrollando tal como se había previsto; **how does the story** — **after that?** ¿cómo se desarrolla el argumento después de eso?; **they** —**ed with their plan** prosiguieron su proyecto; —**!** ¡siga!

(d) (Law etc) **to** — **against someone** proceder contra uno, procesar a uno.

(e) (emerge) **to** — **from** salir de; (fig) proceder de, provenir de; **sounds** —**ed from the box** unos ruidos salían de la caja; **this** —**s from ignorance** esto proviene de la ignorancia.

proceeding [prə'siːdiŋ] n **(a)** (way) procedimiento m, modo m de proceder; proceder m; **the best** — el mejor modo de proceder; **a somewhat dubious** — un proceder sospechoso.

(b) —**s** (function) acto m, actos mpl, función f; **the** —**s began at 7 o'clock** el acto comenzó a las 7; **the** —**s were orderly** en estos actos no sufrió alteración el orden público.

(c) —**s** (of learned society) actas fpl, transacciones fpl; **P**—**s of the Royal Society** Actas fpl de la Real Sociedad.

(d) —**s** (measures) medidas fpl; **to take** —**s** tomar medidas; **to take** —**s against someone** (Law) proceder contra uno, procesar a uno; **to take legal** —**s** entablar demanda, instruir causa.

proceeds ['prəusiːdz] npl ganancias fpl, ingresos mpl, producto m.

process ['prəuses] **1** n **(a)** (proceeding) procedimiento m; proceso m; **the** —**es of government** los trámites gubernamentales; **the** —**es of the mind** los procedimientos de la mente; **it's a very slow** — es un proceso muy lento.

(b) (course) **in** — **of construction** bajo construcción, en construcción; **it is in** — **of reform** está siendo reformado; **it is in** — **of demolition** está siendo derribado; **in the** — **of time** con el tiempo, andando el tiempo; **we are in** — **of removal to** . . . estamos en vía de trasladarnos a . . .

(c) (method) método m, sistema m; (Tech) proceso m; **the Bessemer** — el proceso de Bessemer.

(d) (Law) proceso m.

(e) (Anat, Bot etc) proceso m.

2 vt (Tech) preparar; tratar; someter a un tratamiento especial; elaborar.

process [prə'ses] vi (fam) desfilar.

processing ['prəusesiŋ] n preparación f; tratamiento m; elaboración f.

procession [prə'seʃən] n desfile m; (Eccl) procesión f; **funeral** — cortejo m fúnebre, comitiva f fúnebre; **to go** (or walk) **in** — desfilar, (Eccl) ir en procesión.

processional [prə'seʃənl] adj procesional.

proclaim [prə'kleim] **1** vt **(a)** proclamar; **to** — **someone king** proclamar a uno rey.

(b) (reveal) revelar, anunciar; **his tone** —**ed his confidence** su tono declaraba su optimismo; **their faces** —**ed their guilt** su culpabilidad se revelaba en las caras.

2 vr: **to** — **oneself king** proclamarse rey.

proclamation [,prɔklə'meiʃən] n (act) proclamación f; (document) proclama f.

proclivity [prə'kliviti] n propensión f, inclinación f.

procrastinate [prəu'kræstineit] vi aplazar una decisión, no resolverse; hablar (etc) con el propósito de aplazar una decisión.

procrastination [prəu,kræsti'neiʃən] n dilación f, falta f de resolución.

procreate ['prəukrieit] vt procrear.

procreation [,prəukri'eiʃən] n procreación f.

Procrustean [prəu'krʌstiən] *adj* de Procusto; — **bed** lecho *m* de Procusto.

Procrustes [prəu'krʌstiːz] *m* Procustes, Procusto.

proctor ['prɔktə*] *n* (*Law*) procurador *m*; (*Univ*) censor *m*, *oficial que cuida de la disciplina*.

procurable [prə'kjuərəbl] *adj* asequible; **easily —** muy asequible.

procurator ['prɔkjureitə*] *n* procurador *m*.

procure [prə'kjuə*] **1** *vt* obtener, conseguir; lograr; gestionar; **to — someone something, to — something for someone** obtener algo para uno; **to — some relief** conseguir cierto alivio; **to — a girl** obtener una joven para una casa de prostitución.
2 *vi* alcahuetear.

procurement [prə'kjuəmənt] *n* obtención *f*, consecución *f*.

procurer [prə'kjuərə*] *n* alcahuete *m*.

procuress [prə'kjuəris] *n* alcahueta *f*.

prod [prɔd] **1** *n* (*push*) empuje *m*; (*with elbow*) codazo *m*; (*jab*) pinchazo *m*; **to give someone a —** dar un pinchazo a uno (*also fig*); **he needs an occasional —** hay que pincharle de vez en cuando.
2 *vt* (*push*) empujar; (*with elbow*) codear, dar un codazo a; (*jab*) pinchar, punzar; (*with goad*) aguijar; **he has to be —ded along** hay que empujarle constantemente hacia adelante; **he needs to be —ded** hay que pincharle; **to — someone to do something** instar a uno a hacer algo.
3 *vi*: **he —ded at the picture with a finger** indicó el cuadro con un movimiento brusco del dedo.

prodigal ['prɔdigəl] **1** *adj* pródigo; **— of** pródigo de, pródigo en; **the — son** el hijo pródigo.
2 *n* pródigo *m*, a *f*.

prodigality [,prɔdi'gæliti] *n* prodigalidad *f*.

prodigally ['prɔdigəli] *adv* pródigamente.

prodigious [prə'didʒəs] *adj* prodigioso; enorme, vasto, ingente.

prodigiously [prə'didʒəsli] *adv* prodigiosamente, maravillosamente.

prodigy ['prɔdidʒi] *n* prodigio *m*; **child —, infant —** niño *m* prodigio.

produce ['prɔdjuːs] *n* producto *m*; (*Agr*) productos *mpl* agrícolas; **home —** productos *mpl* agrícolas nacionales.

produce [prə'djuːs] *vt* (**a**) (*bring forward, show*) presentar, mostrar; *proof* aducir, presentar; **he —d it from his pocket** lo sacó del bolsillo; **he seemed to — it out of thin air** parece que lo sacó de la nada; **how can I — £100?** ¿dónde voy yo a buscar 100 libras?; **"please — your tickets"** "se ruega mostrar los billetes"; **he could — no witnesses** no pudo nombrar ningún testigo.
(**b**) (*Theat*) *play* presentar, poner en escena; representar, dar; *actors* dirigir; **when we last —d "Hamlet"** cuando representamos "Hamlet" la última vez.
(**c**) *line* prolongar.
(**d**) (*manufacture*) producir, fabricar; (*yield*) producir; *crop, fruit* dar; *interest, profit* rendir; *offspring* dar a luz, tener; **he —s 3 novels a year** escribe (*or* publica) 3 novelas al año; **it —s 200 watts** da 200 vatios, produce 200 vatios; **the mine —s 20 tons of lead** la mina produce 20 toneladas de plomo; **Ireland does not — atomic bombs** Irlanda no fabrica bombas atómicas.
(**e**) (*cause*) causar, motivar, ocasionar, producir; acarrear; **it —d great alarm** causó mucha alarma; **this —d a sensation** esto causó una sensación; **what impression does it — on you?** ¿qué impresión te produce?

producer [prə'djuːsə*] *n* productor *m*, ora *f*; (*Theat*) director *m* de escena; (*Cine*) productor *m*; (*TV*) realizador *m*, ora *f*.

product ['prɔdʌkt] *n* (*thing produced*) producto *m*; (*result*) fruto *m*, resultado *m*, consecuencia *f*; (*Math*) producto *m*; **finished —** producto *m* terminado; **gross national —** producto *m* nacional bruto; **milk —s** productos *mpl* lácteos; **waste —s** (*Bio*) desperdicios *mpl*.

production [prə'dʌkʃən] *n* (*act*) producción *f*; (*thing produced*) producto *m*; (*Art, Lit etc*) obra *f*; (*Theat: performance*) presentación *f*; representación *f*; (*of actor*) dirección *f*; **the country's steel —** la producción nacional de acero; **"Peribáñez: a new — by..."** "Peribáñez: nueva presentación a cargo de...";
the — lacked vigour la representación carecía de vigor.

production line [prə'dʌkʃən,lain] *n* línea *f* de montaje.

productive [prə'dʌktiv] *adj* (**a**) productivo; **the factory is not yet fully —** la fábrica todavía no trabaja a plena capacidad.

(**b**) **— of** fértil en, prolífico en; **to be — of error** tener fuerte tendencia a causar errores; **it is — of nothing but trouble** no produce sino disgustos.

productivity [,prɔdʌk'tiviti] *n* productividad *f*; **when it is in full —** cuando esté trabajando a plena capacidad.

prof [prɔf] *n* (*fam*) profe *m* (*profesor*).

profanation [,prɔfə'neiʃən] *n* profanación *f*.

profane [prə'fein] **1** *adj* (**a**) (*secular, uninitiated, lay*) profano; (*irreverent*) profano, sacrílego, blasfemo.
(**b**) *language etc* fuerte, indecente; **he's very —** es un malhablado; **don't be —!** ¡no digas palabrotas!; **he became —** empezó a jurar.
2 *vt* profanar.

profanity [prə'fæniti] *n* (**a**) profanidad *f*; blasfemia *f*, impiedad *f*.
(**b**) lenguaje *m* indecente, palabrotas *fpl*; **to utter a string of profanities** soltar una serie de palabrotas.

profess [prə'fes] **1** *vt faith, belief etc* profesar; (*assent*) afirmar, declarar; *regret etc* manifestar; *ignorance etc* confesar; **I do not — to be an expert** no pretendo ser un experto; **he —es to know all about it** dice estar enterado de ello; **she —es to be 25** dice tener 25 años, afirma tener 25 años.
2 *vr*: **to — oneself satisfied** declararse satisfecho; **to — oneself unable to** + *infin* declararse incapaz de + *infin*.

professed [prə'fest] *adj* declarado; (*pej*) supuesto, ostensible; (*Eccl*) profeso.

professedly [prə'fesidli] *adv* declaradamente; (*pej*) supuestamente.

profession [prə'feʃən] *n* (**a**) (*declaration*) profesión *f*, declaración *f*; **— of faith** profesión *f* de fe.
(**b**) (*calling*) profesión *f*; oficio *m*; carrera *f*; **by — he is an engineer** es ingeniero de oficio.

professional [prə'feʃənl] **1** *adj* (**a**) profesional; de profesión, de oficio; **— man** hombre *m* profesional, hombre *m* de carrera liberal; **— diplomat** diplomático *m* de carrera; **he's a — thug** es un matón de oficio.
(**b**) (*competent*) experto, perito.
2 *n* profesional *mf*.

professionalism [prə'feʃnəlizəm] *n* (**a**) profesionalismo *m*. (**b**) pericia *f*.

professionally [prə'feʃnəli] *adv* (**a**) profesionalmente; **I never met him —** no le conocí nunca en su cargo profesional; **X, known — as Y** X conocido por Y en la profesión.
(**b**) expertamente, con pericia; **they did it most —** lo hicieron expertamente.

professor [prə'fesə*] *n* profesor *m* (universitario), profesora *f* (universitaria), catedrático *m*, a *f*; **assistant —** (*US*) profesor *m* agregado; **associate —** (*US*) profesor *m* adjunto; **full —** profesor *m* numerario, profesor *m* titular; **visiting —** profesor *m* visitante.

professorial [,prɔfə'sɔːriəl] *adj* de profesor, de catedrático; profesoral.

professorship [prə'fesəʃip] *n* cátedra *f*; **to be appointed to a —** obtener una cátedra.

proffer ['prɔfə*] *vt* ofrecer.

proficiency [prə'fiʃənsi] *n* pericia *f*, habilidad *f*.

proficient [prə'fiʃənt] *adj* perito, hábil (*at, in* en).

profile ['prəufail] *n* perfil *m*; **in —** de perfil.

profit ['prɔfit] **1** *n* (*Comm*) ganancia *f*; (*fig*) provecho *m*, beneficio *m*; utilidad *f*, ventaja *f*; **—s** ganancias *fpl*, beneficios *mpl*; **— and loss** ganancias *fpl* y pérdidas; **gross —** ganancia *f* bruta; **net —** ganancia *f* neta; **to make a — of two millions** ganar dos millones, sacar una ganancia de dos millones; **to make a — on a deal** salir ganando en un negocio; **to show (*or* yield) a —** dar dinero, rendir una ganancia; **to sell something at a —** vender algo con ganancia; **to turn something to —** aprovecharse de algo.
2 *vt* servir a, aprovechar a, ser de utilidad a; **what will it — him to** + *infin*? ¿qué le aprovechará + *infin*?
3 *vi* ganar; (*Comm*) sacar ganancia; **he does not seem to have —** no parece haber sacado provecho de ello; **to — by, to — from** aprovechar, beneficiarse de, sacar partido de; **to — by the mistakes of others** escarmentar en cabeza ajena.

profitability [,prɔfitə'biliti] *n* rentabilidad *f*.

profitable ['prɔfitəbl] *adj* provechoso, útil; ventajoso; (*Comm*) lucrativo; (*economic to run etc*) rentable; **a most — trip** un viaje sumamente provechoso; **a — investment** una inversión lucrativa; **the line is no longer —** la línea ya no es rentable; **it would be — to you to read this** Vd se beneficiará de leer esto, le sería útil leer esto.

profitably ['prɔfitəbli] *adv* con provecho, provechosamente; (*Comm*) lucrativamente, con lucro.

profiteer [,prɔfi'tiə*] **1** n acaparador m, el que hace ganancias excesivas, (*black marketeer*) estraperlista m. **2** vi hacer ganancias excesivas, cobrar más de lo justo.

profiteering [,prɔfi'tiəriŋ] n ganancias fpl excesivas.

profitless ['prɔfitlis] *adj* inútil.

profitlessly ['prɔfitlisli] *adv* inútilmente.

profit-sharing ['prɔfit,ʃeəriŋ] n (*by workers*) participación f directa en los beneficios, (*by company*) reparto m de los beneficios.

profit taking ['prɔfit,teikiŋ] n (*Fin*) realización f de plusvalías.

profligacy ['prɔfligəsi] n libertinaje m; prodigalidad f.

profligate ['prɔfligit] **1** *adj* (*dissolute*) libertino, disoluto; (*extravagant*) manirroto, pródigo. **2** n libertino m; manirroto m.

profound [prə'faund] *adj* profundo.

profoundly [prə'faundli] *adv* profundamente.

profundity [prə'fʌnditi] n profundidad f.

profuse [prə'fjuːs] *adj* profuso; pródigo (en en); **to be — in one's apologies** disculparse con efusión.

profusely [prə'fjuːsli] *adv* profusamente; pródigamente; **he apologized —** se disculpó con efusión; **to sweat —** sudar muchísimo.

profusion [prə'fjuːʒən] n profusión f, abundancia f; prodigalidad f; **a — of flowers** una abundancia de flores; **trees in —** árboles mpl abundantes, muchísimos árboles mpl.

progenitor [prəu'dʒenitə*] n progenitor m.

progeny ['prɔdʒini] n progenie f, prole f.

prognosis [prɔg'nəusis] n, pl **prognoses** [prɔg'nəusiːz] (*Med*) pronóstico m.

prognostic [prɔg'nɔstik] n pronóstico m.

prognosticate [prɔg'nɔstikeit] vt pronosticar.

prognostication [prɔg,nɔsti'keiʃən] n (*act, art*) pronosticación f; (*forecast*) pronóstico m.

programme, (US) program ['prəugræm] **1** n programa m. **2** vt *computer* programar.

programmed ['prəugræmd] *adj* programado; **— learning** enseñanza f programada.

programmer, (US) programer ['prəugræmə*] n programador m, ora f.

programme music, (US) program ['prəugræm,mjuːzik] n música f de programa.

programming, (US) programing ['prəugræmiŋ] n programación f.

progress ['prəugres] n progreso m· progresos mpl; (*of events etc*) marcha f, desarrollo m; **the — of events** la marcha de los acontecimientos; **the — of a student** los progresos de un estudiante; **it is in —** está en vía de realizarse (*etc*); **harvesting is in full —** la cosecha está en plena marcha; **the game was already in —** había comenzado ya el partido; **to make (some) —** hacer progresos, progresar; **to make slow —** avanzar despacio.

progress [prə'gres] vi hacer progresos, progresar; avanzar; desarrollarse; **as the game —ed** a medida que iba desarrollándose el partido; **matters are —ing slowly** las cosas avanzan lentamente; **how is the student —ing?** ¿qué progresos hace el estudiante?; **the patient is —ing favourably** el enfermo está mejorando de modo satisfactorio.

progression [prə'greʃən] n progresión f; **arithmetical —** progresión f aritmética; **geometric —** progresión f geométrica.

progressive [prə'gresiv] **1** *adj* progresivo; (*Pol*) progresista. **2** n (*Pol*) progresista mf.

progressively [prə'gresivli] *adv* progresivamente; (*Pol*) de modo progresista; **it diminishes —** disminuye progresivamente; **it's getting — better** se va haciendo cada vez mejor.

progressiveness [prə'gresivnis] n carácter m progresista.

prohibit [prə'hibit] vt (**a**) (*forbid*) prohibir; **to — someone from doing something** prohibir a uno hacer algo; **"it is —ed to feed the animals"** "se prohíbe dar de comer a los animales"; **"smoking —ed"** "se prohíbe fumar", "prohibido fumar".
(**b**) (*prevent*) impedir; **to — someone from doing something** impedir a uno hacer algo; **his health —s him from swimming** su salud le impide nadar.

prohibition [,prəui'biʃən] n prohibición f; (*US*) prohibicionismo m.

prohibitionism [,prəui'biʃnizəm] n prohibicionismo m.

prohibitionist [,prəui'biʃnist] **1** *adj* prohibicionista. **2** n prohibicionista mf.

prohibitive [prə'hibitiv] *adj* prohibitivo; *price etc* excesivo.

prohibitory [prə'hibitəri] *adj* prohibitorio.

project ['prɔdʒekt] n proyecto m.

project [prə'dʒekt] **1** vt proyectar. **2** vi salir, sobresalir, resaltar; **to — beyond** sobresalir más allá de; **to — over** sobresalir por encima de.

projectile [prə'dʒektail] n proyectil m.

projecting [prə'dʒektiŋ] *adj* saliente.

projection [prə'dʒekʃən] n proyección f; (*overhang etc*) saliente m, resalto m; (*knob etc*) protuberancia f; (*Fin*) proyección f.

projectionist [prə'dʒekʃnist] n operador m, ora f (de proyector).

projection room [prə'dʒekʃən,rum] n cabina f (de proyección).

projector [prə'dʒektə*] n proyector m (de películas).

prolapse ['prəulæps] n prolapso m.

proletarian [,prəulə'teəriən] **1** *adj* proletario. **2** n proletario m, a f.

proletarianism [,prəulə'teəriənizəm] n proletarismo m.

proletarianize [,prəulə'teəriənaiz] vt proletariar.

proletariat [,prəulə'teəriət] n proletariado m.

proliferate [prə'lifəreit] **1** vt multiplicar; extender. **2** vi proliferar, multiplicarse; extenderse.

proliferation [prə,lifə'reiʃən] n proliferación f, multiplicación f; extensión f; **— of nuclear weapons** proliferación f de armas nucleares.

prolific [prə'lifik] *adj* prolífico (*of* en).

prolix ['prəuliks] *adj* prolijo.

prolixity [prəu'liksiti] n prolijidad f.

prologue ['prəulɔg] n prólogo m (*to* de).

prolong [prə'lɔŋ] vt (*in space*) prolongar, extender; (*in time*) alargar, extender.

prolongation [,prəulɔŋ'geiʃən] n prolongación f, alargamiento m, extensión f.

prom [prɔm] n (*fam*) (**a**) = **promenade concert**.
(**b**) (*US*) baile de gala bajo los auspicios de los alumnos de una clase universitaria.

promenade [,prɔmi'naːd] **1** n (*act*) paseo m; (*avenue*) paseo m, avenida f; (*at seaside*) paseo m marítimo; **— concert** concierto m en el que una parte del público permanece de pie.
2 vt pasear.
3 vi pasearse.

Prometheus [prə'miːθjuːs] m Prometeo.

prominence ['prɔminəns] n prominencia f; (*fig*) eminencia f, importancia f; **to bring something into —** hacer que algo destaque; **he came into — in the Cuba affair** empezó a destacar cuando lo de Cuba; **that aspect is coming into —** ese aspecto está adquiriendo importancia.

prominent ['prɔminənt] *adj* (*jutting out*) prominente; *cheekbone, tooth etc* saliente; *eye* saltón; (*fig*) eminente, importante, notable, destacado; **the most — article in the window** el objeto que más salta a la vista en el escaparate; **the most — feature of this theory** el aspecto más notable de esta teoría; **put it in a — position** ponlo muy a la vista; **to be — in a deal** desempeñar un papel importante en un negocio; **she is — in London society** es una figura destacada de la buena sociedad londinense.

prominently ['prɔminəntli] *adv*: **to display something —** exponer algo muy a la vista, poner algo en un sitio donde resulta perfectamente visible; **he figured — in the case** desempeñó un papel importante en el proceso.

promiscuity [,prɔmis'kjuːiti] n (**a**) libertad f en las relaciones sexuales, inmoralidad f, libertinaje m.
(**b**) promiscuidad f.

promiscuous [prə'miskjuəs] *adj* (**a**) *person* libre en las relaciones sexuales, inmoral, libertino; *relationship* ilícito; *conduct* inmoral, libre.
(**b**) (*mixed*) promiscuo.

promiscuously [prə'miskjuəsli] *adv* (**a**) libremente, de modo inmoral; ilícitamente. (**b**) promiscuamente.

promise ['prɔmis] **1** n (**a**) (*pledge*) promesa f; **— of marriage** palabra f de matrimonio; **under — of** bajo palabra de; **to break one's —** faltar a su palabra; **to hold (or keep) someone to his —** obligar a uno a cumplir su promesa, hacer que uno cumpla su promesa; **to keep one's —** cumplir su promesa; **to release someone from his —** absolver a uno de su promesa.
(**b**) (*hope*) promesa f; esperanza f; porvenir m; **a young man of —** un joven que promete, un joven de porvenir; **to hold out a — of** dar esperanzas de; **to show —** prometer, demostrar tener aptitudes.
2 vti prometer; augurar, pronosticar; **no, I — you** no, se lo aseguro; **to — to do something** prometer hacer algo; **to — someone something, to — something to someone** prometer dar algo a uno; **it —s trouble** nos augura algo malo; **they — us rain tomorrow** nos pronostican lluvia

para mañana; **the crop —es well** la cosecha se anuncia espléndida, la cosecha se muestra buena; **this does not — to be easy** esto me parece que no va a ser fácil.

3 *vr:* **to — oneself something** prometerse algo.

promised ['prɔmist] *adj* prometido; **land** de promisión.

promising ['prɔmisiŋ] *adj* prometedor, que promete; *future prospect* halagüeño; **a — young man** un joven que promete, un joven de porvenir; **two — candidates** dos candidatos buenos; **it doesn't look very —** no parece muy halagüeño, es una perspectiva poco atractiva.

promisingly ['prɔmisiŋli] *adv:* **it's going quite —** va bastante bien; **she plays —** toca lo bastante bien para demostrar que tiene aptitudes.

promissory ['prɔmisəri] *adj:* **— note** pagaré *m*.

promontory ['prɔmɔntri] *n* promontorio *m*.

promote [prə'məut] *vt* **(a)** *trade etc* promover, fomentar; *good feeling* fomentar; *campaign* apoyar; *(Comm) business* gestionar; *product (advertise)* dar publicidad a, hacer propaganda por, *(sell)* promover, aumentar las ventas de; *discussion etc* estimular, favorecer, facilitar; *(Parl) bill* presentar; *company* fundar, crear, financiar.

(b) *(in rank)* ascender; **to be —d** ser ascendido *(to the rank of colonel* a coronel); **Tarifa was —d to the first division** Tarifa fue promovida a primera división, Tarifa ascendió a primera división.

promoter [prə'məutə*] *n* promotor *m;* *(of company)* fundador *m;* *(Boxing)* empresario *m,* promotor *m;* **sales —** promotor *m* de ventas.

promotion [prə'məuʃən] *n* **(a)** promoción *f,* fomento *m;* apoyo *m;* gestión *f;* facilitación *f;* presentación *f;* fundación *f,* creación *f;* **sales —** promoción *f* de ventas; **"a — by Bloggs Enterprises"** "presentación de la Empresa Bloggs".

(b) *(in rank)* ascenso *m;* promoción *f;* **to get —** ser ascendido *(to* a); **to win —** *(Sport)* ser promovido, ganar la promoción, ascender.

prompt [prɔmpt] **1** *adj* pronto; *action, delivery, reply etc* pronto, inmediato; *service* rápido; *payment* puntual; *person's character* puntual; **they're very —** son muy puntuales; **"please be —"** "se ruega mucha puntualidad".

2 *adv* puntualmente; **at 6 o'clock —** a las 6 en punto.

3 *vt* **(a)** **to — someone to do something** mover a uno a hacer algo, incitar a uno a hacer algo; **I felt —ed to protest** me encontré en la necesidad de protestar; **what —ed you to do it?** ¿qué te movió a hacerlo?

(b) **a poem —ed by a memory** una poesía inspirada por un recuerdo; **it —s the thought that . . .** sugiere la noción de que . . ., hacer pensar que . . .

(c) *(Theat)* apuntar; **don't — her!** ¡no la ayudes a recordar!, ¡no le soples cosas al oído!; **the witness had to be —ed** fue necesario recordar unos hechos al testigo, hubo que traer ciertas cosas a la memoria del testigo.

4 *vi (Theat)* apuntar.

5 *n (Theat)* apuntador *m,* ora *f.*

prompt box ['prɔmptbɔks] *n* concha *f* (del apuntador).

prompter ['prɔmptə*] *n* apuntador *m,* ora *f.*

prompting ['prɔmptiŋ] *n:* **without —** sin ayuda de nadie, sin tener que consultar el texto *(etc);* **the —s of conscience** los escrúpulos de la conciencia; **the —s of love** los dictados del amor.

promptitude ['prɔmptitjuːd] *n see* **promptness.**

promptly ['prɔmptli] *adv* puntualmente, con prontitud; inmediatamente; rápidamente; **they do it very —** lo hacen con toda prontitud; **they left — at 6** partieron a las 6 en punto.

promptness ['prɔmptnis] *n* prontitud *f,* puntualidad *f;* rapidez *f.*

promulgate ['prɔmǝlgeit] *vt* promulgar.

promulgation [,prɔmǝl'geiʃǝn] *n* promulgación *f.*

prone [prǝun] *adj* **(a)** **to be —** estar postrado (boca abajo).

(b) **to be — to** + *n* ser propenso a + *n,* estar inclinado a + *n;* **to be — to** + *infin* ser propenso a + *infin.*

proneness ['prǝunnis] *n* propensión *f (to* a).

prong [prɔŋ] *n* punta *f,* púa *f,* diente *m.*

-pronged [prɔŋd] *adj:* **eg three-pronged** de tres puntas.

pronominal [prǝu'nɔminl] *adj* pronominal.

pronoun ['prǝunaun] *n* pronombre *m;* **personal —** pronombre *m* personal; **possessive —** pronombre *m* posesivo; **reflexive —** pronombre *m* reflexivo.

pronounce [prǝ'nauns] **1** *vt (Gram, Law)* pronunciar; *(with adj)* declarar; **they —d him unfit to** + *infin* le declararon incapaz de + *infin.*

2 *vi:* **to — in favour of something** pronunciarse en favor de algo; **to — on something** expresar una opinión sobre algo, juzgar algo.

pronounced [prǝ'naunst] *adj* marcado, fuerte; decidido.

pronouncement [prǝ'naunsmǝnt] *n* declaración *f;* opinión *f;* **to make a —** pronunciarse, hacer una declaración *(about* sobre).

pronto ['prɔntǝu] *adv (US fam)* pronto.

pronunciation [prǝ,nʌnsi'eiʃǝn] *n* pronunciación *f.*

proof [pruːf] **1** *n* **(a)** prueba *f (also Math etc);* comprobación *f;* **positive —, — positive** prueba *f* concluyente; **. . ., — positive that . . . . . .,** lo cual es prueba concluyente de que . . .; **in — of** en prueba de, en comprobación de; **as señal de; in — whereof** en fe de lo cual; **it is — that he is poor** es prueba de su pobreza; **to adduce — to the contrary** aducir hechos que prueban lo contrario; **to give (or show) — of** dar prueba de; **the onus of — lies with the accuser** le cumple al acusador probar lo que dice.

(b) *(Typ)* prueba *f;* **—s** pruebas *fpl;* **to read the —s** corregir las pruebas.

(c) *(of alcohol)* graduación *f* normal; **this drink is 70% —** esta bebida tiene una graduación de 70 por 100.

2 *adj* **(a)** *drink* de graduación normal.

(b) **to be — against something** ser (or estar) a prueba de algo; **it is — against moisture** está a prueba de la humedad; **I'm not — against temptation** yo no soy insensible a la tentación.

(c) *eg* **bullet-proof** a prueba de balas.

3 *vt* impermeabilizar.

proofread ['pruːfriːd] *(irr: see* **read***) vt* corregir las pruebas de.

proofreader ['pruːf,riːdǝ*] *n* corrector *m* de pruebas.

proofreading ['pruːf,riːdiŋ] *n* corrección *f* de pruebas.

proof sheets ['pruːfʃiːts] *npl* pruebas *fpl.*

proof spirit ['pruːf'spirit] *n* licor *m* de prueba.

prop [prɔp] **1** *n* apoyo *m;* *(Archit)* puntal *m;* *(Agr)* horca *f,* rodrigón *m;* *(Min)* peón *m,* entibo *m;* *(Naut)* escora *f;* *(fig)* sostén *m.*

2 *vt (also* **to — up***)* apoyar; apuntalar; apoyar con rodrigón *(etc);* *(fig)* apoyar, sostener; **to — a ladder against a wall** apoyar una escalera contra una pared; **the company was —ped up by a big loan** la compañía recibió el apoyo de un préstamo cuantioso.

3 *vr:* **to — oneself against a tree** apoyarse contra un árbol.

propaganda [,prɔpǝ'gændǝ] *n* propaganda *f.*

propagandist [,prɔpǝ'gændist] *n* propagandista *mf.*

propagate ['prɔpǝgeit] **1** *vt* propagar. **2** *vi* propagarse.

propagation [,prɔpǝ'geiʃǝn] *n* propagación *f.*

propel [prǝ'pel] *vt* impulsar, propulsar; *(push)* empujar; **it is —led by turbines** está propulsado por turbinas.

propellent [prǝ'pelǝnt] *n* propulsor *m.*

propeller [prǝ'pelǝ*] *n* hélice *f.*

propeller shaft [prǝ'pelǝʃɑːft] *n* árbol *m* de la hélice.

propelling pencil [prǝ'peliŋ'pensl] *n* lapicero *m,* portaminas *m.*

propensity [prǝ'pensiti] *n* propensión *f (to* a).

proper ['prɔpǝ*] **1** *adj* **(a)** *(peculiar, characteristic)* propio, peculiar; característico; *name* propio; **the qualities which are — to it** las cualidades que le son propias, las cualidades que son propias de él.

(b) *(correct)* verdadero, exacto, apropiado; **physics — la** física propiamente dicha; **in the — sense of the word** en el sentido estricto de la palabra.

(c) *(fam)* **he's a — rogue** es un verdadero pillo; **it's a — nuisance** es una verdadera molestia; **he's a — gentleman now** ya es un caballero hecho y derecho; **we got a — beating** nos dieron una paliza de las buenas; **there was a — row** hubo un lío de todos los diablos.

(d) *(right, suitable)* apropiado, conveniente; oportuno; debido; justo, exacto; **in — condition** en buen estado; **at the — time** en el momento oportuno; **in the — way** convenientemente, del modo conveniente; **as you think —** según le parezca; **do as you think —** haga lo que le parezca bien; **to do the — thing by someone** tratar a uno con justicia; **to say the — thing** decir lo que piden las circunstancias; **it was the — thing to say** fue lo que había que decir; **in a style — to his station** en un estilo que conviene a su rango; **I think it — to** + *infin* creo hacer bien en + *infin.*

(e) (*seemly*) decente; correcto; — **behaviour** conducta *f* correcta; **what is** — lo que está bien; **it is not** — **for you to** + *infin* no está bien que Vd + *subj*; **it's not** — **with children about** no es decente si hay niños delante.
　　(f) (*prim and* —) etiquetero, relamido; formal.
　　(g) (*Her*) natural.
　　2 *adv* (*fam*) **it's** — **difficult** es realmente difícil, es dificilísimo; **we were** — **puzzled** quedamos totalmente perplejos.

properly ['prɔpǝli] *adv* **(a)** (*correctly etc*) correctamente, apropiadamente, debidamente; **a word** — **used** una palabra correctamente empleada; — **speaking** propiamente dicho; en el sentido estricto de la palabra; **it is not** — **so called** no es correcto llamarlo así, no se llama así en propiedad, en propiedad no se dice así; **she very** — **refused** se negó a ello e hizo bien; **to do something** — hacer algo bien, hacer algo como se debe, hacer algo como Dios manda.
　　(b) (*in seemly fashion*) decentemente; correctamente; **not** — **dressed** incorrectamente vestido; **to behave** — portarse correctamente; **behave** —! ¡estáte formal!
　　(c) (*intensive*) **we were** — **ashamed** nos avergonzamos de verdad; **we got** — **beaten** nos dieron una paliza de las buenas; **we were** — **puzzled** quedamos totalmente perplejos.

propertied ['prɔpǝtid] *adj* adinerado, acaudalado.

property ['prɔpǝti] *n* **(a)** (*quality*) propiedad *f*; **the properties of this substance** las propiedades de esta sustancia.
　　(b) (*thing owned*) propiedad *f*; bienes *mpl*; (*estate*) hacienda *f*, finca *f*, propiedad *f*; **personal** — bienes *mpl* muebles; cosas *fpl* personales; **real** — (*US*) bienes *mpl* raíces; **that's my** — eso es mío; **whose** — **is this?** ¿de quién es esto?; **it doesn't seem to be anyone's** — no parece que tenga dueño, no parece que pertenezca a nadie; **that news is common** — eso lo saben todos ya, esa noticia es ya del dominio público; **it is common** — **that** . . . todos saben que . . .; **it became the** — **of Mr Jones** pasó a ser propiedad del Sr Jones; **she left her** — **to X** dejó sus bienes a X.
　　(c) **properties** (*Theat*) accesorios *mpl*.

property owner ['prɔpǝti,ǝunǝ*] *n* dueño *m* de una finca, dueña *f* de una finca; (*landed gentry*) terrateniente *mf*.

property tax ['prɔpǝti,tæks] *n* impuesto *m* sobre la propiedad.

prophecy ['prɔfisi] *n* profecía *f*.

prophesy ['prɔfisai] *vt* profetizar; (*fig*) predecir, prever, augurar (*that* que).

prophet ['prɔfit] *n* profeta *m*.

prophetess ['prɔfitis] *n* profetisa *f*.

prophetic [prǝ'fetik] *adj* profético.

prophetically [prǝ'fetikǝli] *adv* proféticamente.

prophylactic [,prɔfi'læktik] **1** *adj* profiláctico. **2** *n* profiláctico *m*.

prophylaxis [,prɔfi'læksis] *n* profilaxis *f*.

propinquity [prǝ'piŋkwiti] *n* propincuidad *f*; (*kinship*) consanguinidad *f*, parentesco *m*.

propitiate [prǝ'piʃieit] *vt* propiciar.

propitiation [prǝ,piʃi'eiʃǝn] *n* propiciación *f*.

propitiatory [prǝ'piʃiǝtǝri] *adj* propiciatorio, conciliatorio.

propitious [prǝ'piʃǝs] *adj* propicio, favorable.

propitiously [prǝ'piʃǝsli] *adv* de modo propicio, bajo signo propicio, favorablemente.

proportion [prǝ'pɔːʃǝn] *n* **(a)** proporción *f* (*also* *Math*); parte *f*, porción *f*, porcentaje *m*; **the** — **of blacks to whites** la proporción entre negros y blancos; **what** — **is in private hands?** ¿qué porción queda en manos de particulares?; **in equal** —**s** por partes iguales; **in due** — en su justa medida; **in** — **as** a medida que; **in** — **to** en proporción con, a medida de; **and the rest in** — y lo demás en proporción, (*Comm*) y lo demás a prorrateo; **to be out of** — ser desproporcionado; **to be out of** — **with** (*or* to) no guardar proporción con.
　　(b) **sense of** — sentido *m* de la medida.
　　(c) —**s** dimensiones *fpl*.

proportional [prǝ'pɔːʃǝnl] *adj* proporcional; (*representation etc*) proporcional; — **to** en proporción con, a medida de; **X is not** — **to Y** X no guarda proporción con Y.

proportionally [prǝ'pɔːʃǝli] *adv* proporcionalmente, en proporción.

proportionate [prǝ'pɔːʃnit] *adj* proporcionado.

proportionately [prǝ'pɔːʃnitli] *adv* proporcionadamente, en proporción.

proportioned [prǝ'pɔːʃnd] *adj*: **well** — bien proporcionado, de forma elegante; **person** de talle elegante.

proposal [prǝ'pǝuzl] *n* **(a)** propuesta *f*, proposición *f*; oferta *f*; (*to girl*) declaración *f* (de amor); — **of marriage** oferta *f* de matrimonio, (*formally*) petición *f* de mano; **to make a** — hacer una propuesta; **to make the** — **that** . . . proponer que . . .
　　(b) (*plan*) proyecto *m*; (*notion*) idea *f*; (*suggestion*) sugerencia *f*; **my** — **was to** + *infin* mi idea era de + *infin*; **it is a new** — **to reform the currency** es un nuevo proyecto para reformar la moneda.

propose [prǝ'pǝuz] **1** *vt* **(a)** proponer; ofrecer; **motion** proponer; **candidate** proponer, nombrar; **to** — **marriage to someone** hacer una oferta de matrimonio a una, (*formally*) pedir la mano de una a su padre; **to** — **someone for membership of a club** nombrar a uno como socio de un club; **what course do you** — **?** ¿qué línea de acción nos recomienda Vd?
　　(b) to — **someone's health** brindar por uno.
　　2 *vi* **(a) to** — **to** + *infin* proponerse + *infin*; pensar + *infin*, tener la intención de + *infin*; **what do you** — **doing?** ¿qué piensas hacer?
　　(b) Man —**s, God disposes** el hombre propone y Dios dispone.
　　(c) (*to girl*) declararse (*to* a); **to** — **to someone** (*formally*) hacer una oferta de matrimonio a una, pedir la mano de una a su padre.

proposer [prǝ'pǝuzǝ*] *n* (*Parl etc*) proponente *mf*.

proposition [,prɔpǝ'ziʃǝn] *n* **(a)** (*statement, Math, Logic etc*) proposición *f*; (*proposal*) propuesta *f*, proposición *f*; oferta *f*; (*plan*) proyecto *m*.
　　(b) (*job*) tarea *f*; (*enterprise*) empresa *f*, cosa *f*; (*problem*) problema *m*; (*objective*) propósito *m*; (*opponent*) adversario *m*, a *f*; (*prospect*) perspectiva *f*; **it's a tough** — es mucho pedir; **he's a tough** — es un adversario fuerte; **the journey alone is quite a** — sólo el viaje pide grandes esfuerzos; **it will be a paying** — dará dinero; **it's not an economic** — no es rentable.

propound [prǝ'paund] *vt* proponer, exponer, presentar.

proprietary [prǝ'praiǝtǝri] *adj* propietario; **article** patentado.

proprietor [prǝ'praiǝtǝ*] *n* propietario *m*, dueño *m*.

proprietorship [prǝ'praiǝtǝʃip] *n* propiedad *f*, posesión *f*.

proprietress [prǝ'praiǝtris] *n* propietaria *f*, dueña *f*.

propriety [prǝ'praiǝti] *n* (*seemliness*) decoro *m*, decencia *f*, corrección *f*; (*fitness*) conveniencia *f*; **the proprieties** las convenciones, los cánones sociales, el decoro; **breach of** — ofensa *f* contra el decoro; **to observe the proprieties** atenerse a los cánones sociales; **to throw** — **to the winds** abandonar totalmente el decoro.

props [prɔps] *npl* (*Theat: fam*) accesorios *mpl*.

propulsion [prǝ'pʌlʃǝn] *n* propulsión *f*.

prorate ['prǝureit] (*US*) **1** *n* prorrata *f*. **2** *vt* prorratear.

prorogation [,prǝurǝ'geiʃǝn] *n* prorrogación *f*.

prorogue [prǝ'rǝug] *vt* prorrogar.

prosaic [prǝu'zeiik] *adj* prosaico.

prosaically [prǝu'zeiikǝli] *adv* prosaicamente.

proscenium [prǝu'siːniǝm] *n* proscenio *m*.

proscribe [prǝus'kraib] *vt* proscribir.

proscription [prǝus'kripʃǝn] *n* proscripción *f*.

prose [prǝuz] **1** *n* prosa *f*. **2** *attr* de prosa; en prosa.

prosecute ['prɔsikjuːt] *vt* **(a)** (*Law*) procesar; **claim** demandar en juicio; **to** — **someone for theft** procesar a uno por ladrón; **to be** —**d for a traffic offence** ser procesado por una infracción del código; **"trespassers will be** —**d"** "se procederá contra los intrusos".
　　(b) (*follow up*) proseguir, continuar, llevar adelante.

prosecution [,prɔsi'kjuːʃǝn] *n* **(a)** (*Law: case*) proceso *m*, causa *f*, juicio *m*; (*act*) acusación *f*, procesamiento *m*; (*side*) parte *f* actora; **counsel for the** — fiscal *m*; **to start a** — **against someone** entablar juicio contra uno.
　　(b) prosecución *f*; **in the** — **of his duty** en el cumplimiento de su deber.

prosecutor ['prɔsikjuːtǝ*] *n* acusador *m*; (*also* **public** —) fiscal *m*.

proselyte ['prɔsilait] *n* prosélito *m* a *f*.

proselytism ['prɔsilitizǝm] *n* proselitismo *m*.

proselytize ['prɔsilitaiz] *vi* ganar prosélitos, convertir a las personas a la secta de uno.

prose writer ['prǝuz,raitǝ*] *n* prosista *mf*.

prosody ['prɔsǝdi] *n* métrica *f*.

prospect ['prɔspekt] n (a) (view) vista f, panorama m; **the — from the window** la vista desde la ventana; **a — of Toledo** una vista de Toledo; **where every — pleases** donde todo deleita la vista.

(b) (outlook) perspectiva f; (hope) esperanza f; (future) porvenir m; **what a —!** (iro) ¡qué perspectiva más halagüeña!; **future —s** perspectivas fpl del futuro; **—s are really good** las perspectivas son francamente buenas; **"good —s"** (advert for job) "buenas perspectivas de mejora"; **it's a grim —** es una perspectiva nada atractiva; **there are —s of a fine day** el día se presenta muy bueno; **—s for the harvest are poor** la cosecha se anuncia más bien mediocre; **his —s are outstandingly good** le espera un gran porvenir; **he has no —s** no tiene porvenir; **this — cheered him up** se alegró con esta perspectiva; **we are faced with the — of +** nos encontramos ante la perspectiva de + infin; **to have something in —** esperar algo; **to hold out a — of** dar esperanzas de.

(c) (chance) probabilidad f, posibilidad f; **the — of an early peace** la posibilidad de una pronta paz; **there is little —** of his coming hay pocas posibilidades de que venga; **to dangle a — before someone** ofrecer a uno la posibilidad de + infin, tentar a uno con la posibilidad de + infin; **I see no — of that** eso no lo creo probable.

(d) (person) persona f en perspectiva; (Comm) cliente m posible, comprador m (etc) probable; **is he a — for the team?** ¿vale considerarle como posible miembro del equipo?; **he's not much of a — for her** no vale gran cosa como posible marido de ella.

prospect [prəs'pekt] 1 vt explorar. 2 vi: **to — for** buscar.

prospecting [prəs'pektiŋ] n (Min) prospección f.

prospective [prəs'pektiv] adj anticipado, esperado, probable; **son-in-law** etc futuro; **heir** presunto; **legislation** etc en perspectiva.

prospector [prəs'pektə*] n explorador m; **gold —** buscador m de oro.

prospectus [prəs'pektəs] n prospecto m; programa m; folleto m informativo.

prosper ['prɔspə*] 1 vt favorecer, fomentar. 2 vi prosperar; medrar; florecer.

prosperity [prəs'periti] n prosperidad f.

prosperous ['prɔspərəs] adj próspero.

prosperously ['prɔspərəsli] adv prósperamente.

prostate ['prɔsteit] n próstata f.

prosthetic [prɔs'θetik] adj (Ling, Med) prostético.

prostitute ['prɔstitjuːt] 1 n prostituta f. 2 vt prostituir (also fig).

prostitution [ˌprɔsti'tjuːʃən] n prostitución f.

prostrate ['prɔstreit] adj postrado; (fig) postrado, abatido (with por).

prostrate [prɔs'treit] 1 vt postrar; (fig) postrar, abatir; **to be —d by grief** ser postrado por el dolor. 2 vr: **to — oneself** postrarse.

prostration [prɔs'treiʃən] n postración f; (fig) postración f, abatimiento m.

prosy ['prəuzi] adj prosaico, aburrido.

protagonist [prəu'tægənist] n protagonista mf.

protean ['prəutiən] adj proteico.

protect [prə'tekt] vt proteger (against, from contra, de).

protection [prə'tekʃən] n protección f; (Comm) protección f, proteccionismo m; **to be under someone's —** estar bajo la protección de alguien.

protectionism [prə'tekʃənizəm] n proteccionismo m.

protectionist [prə'tekʃənist] 1 adj proteccionista. 2 n proteccionista mf.

protective [prə'tektiv] adj protector; **custody** preventivo; (Comm) **duty, policy** proteccionista.

protectively [prə'tektivli] adv protectoramente, de modo protector.

protector [prə'tektə*] n protector m.

protectorate [prə'tektərit] n protectorado m.

protégé ['prɔteʒei] n protegido m, ahijado m.

protégée ['prɔteʒei] n protegida f, ahijada f.

protein ['prəutiːn] n proteína f.

protest ['prəutest] n protesta f; **under —** bajo protesta, haciendo objeciones; **I'll do it but under —** lo haré pero que conste mi protesta; **to make a —** hacer una protesta.

protest [prə'test] 1 vt (a) (complain) protestar; **to — that** protestar de que.

(b) (affirm) afirmar, declarar (enérgicamente, solemnemente etc).

2 vi protestar; **to — against** protestar de, protestar contra.

Protestant ['prɔtistənt] 1 adj protestante. 2 n protestante mf.

Protestantism ['prɔtistəntizəm] n protestantismo m.

protestation [ˌprɔtes'teiʃən] n (a) protesta f. (b) afirmación f, declaración f (enérgica, solemne etc).

proto . . . ['prəutəu] proto . . .

protocol ['prəutəkɔl] n protocolo m.

proton ['prəutɔn] n protón m.

protoplasm ['prəutəuplæzəm] n protoplasma m.

prototype ['prəutəutaip] n prototipo m.

protract [prə'trækt] vt prolongar; extender, alargar.

protracted [prə'træktid] adj largo, prolongado.

protraction [prə'trækʃən] n prolongación f; extensión f, alargamiento m.

protractor [prə'træktə*] n transportador m.

protrude [prə'truːd] 1 vt sacar fuera. 2 vi salir (fuera), sobresalir.

protruding [prə'truːdiŋ] adj saliente; eye, tooth salton.

protrusion [prə'truːʒən] n saliente m, protuberancia f.

protuberance [prə'tjuːbərəns] n protuberancia f, saliente m.

protuberant [prə'tjuːbərənt] adj protuberante, saliente; prominente; (tooth) salton.

proud [praud] adj (a) (of person etc) orgulloso; (pej) soberbio, arrogante, altanero; **as — as a peacock** más orgulloso que un pavo real; **to be — of** estar orgulloso de, enorgullecerse de, preciarse de, ufanarse de; **to be — that . . .** estar orgulloso de que . . .; **to be — to +** infin tener el honor de + infin, estar orgulloso de + infin; **to do oneself —** (fam) darse buena vida; permitirse cosas de lujo; **to do someone —** hacer muchas fiestas a uno, tratar a uno con toda clase de atenciones, (with food) dar muy bien de comer a uno.

(b) (imposing) espléndido, imponente; (glorious) glorioso; **it is a — day for us** es un día glorioso para nosotros; **a — ship** un magnífico buque.

proudly ['praudli] adv (a) orgullosamente; say etc con orgullo; arrogantemente. (b) de modo imponente.

prove [pruːv] 1 vt probar; (verify) comprobar; (show) demostrar; (confirm) confirmar; **will** verificar; **this —s that . . .** esto prueba que . . .; **the exception —s the rule** la excepción confirma la regla; **can you — it?** ¿tiene Vd prueba de ello?; **you can't — anything against me** Vd no puede demostrarme nada; **it remains to be —d whether . . .** queda por demostrar si . . .; **it all goes to — that . . .** todo sirve para demostrar que . . .; **he was —d right in the end** por fin quedó demostrado que había tenido razón; **to — someone innocent** demostrar la inocencia de uno.

2 vi resultar; **if it —s useful** si resulta ser útil; **the news —d false** resultó que la noticia era falsa; **she —d unequal to the job** resultó que ella no estaba al nivel del puesto; **if it —s otherwise** si sale al contrario, si resulta que no es así.

3 vr: **to — oneself** ponerse a prueba.

provenance ['prɔvinəns] n origen m, punto m de origen.

Provençal [ˌprɔvã:n'sɑːl] 1 adj provenzal. 2 n provenzal mf. 3 n (language) provenzal m.

Provence [prɔ'vã:ns] Provenza f.

provender ['prɔvində*] n forraje m; (hum) provisiones fpl, comida f.

proverb ['prɔvəːb] n refrán m, proverbio m.

proverbial [prə'vəːbiəl] adj proverbial.

proverbially [prə'vəːbiəli] adv proverbialmente.

provide [prə'vaid] 1 vt (a) (supply, furnish) suministrar, surtir; dar, proporcionar; **to — someone with something** (supply) proveer a uno de algo, suministrar algo a uno; (give) proporcionar algo a uno; **the car is —d with a heater** el coche está provisto de un calentador; **can you — a substitute?** ¿pueden encontrar un suplente?; **the government —d half the money** el gobierno proporcionó la mitad del dinero; **the plant will — an output of . . .** la fábrica permitirá una producción de . . .; **it —s shade for the cows** da sombra para las vacas.

(b) **to — that . . .** estipular que . . ., disponer que . . . .

2 vi (a) **God will —** Dios proveerá; **a husband who —s well** un marido que mantiene debidamente a su familia.

(b) **to — against** precaverse de, tomar precauciones contra; **to — for someone** mantener a uno, proporcionar medios de vida a uno, (with an allowance) señalar una pensión a uno; **they are well —d for** tienen medios adecuados; **to — for one's dependents** asegurar el porvenir de su familia; **to — for every contingency** prevenir cualquier posibilidad; **we have —d for that** eso lo hemos previsto.

(c) **the treaty —s for . . .** el tratado estipula . . .; **as —d for in the 1970 contract** de acuerdo con lo estipulado en el contrato de 1970.

3 vr: **to — oneself with something** proveerse de algo.

provided [prə'vaidid] *conj*: —, — **that** con tal que + *subj*, siempre que + *subj*; a condición de que + *subj*.

providence ['prɔvidəns] *n* (*all senses*) providencia *f*; P— Divina Providencia *f*.

provident ['prɔvidənt] *adj* providente, previsor, próvido.

providential [,prɔvi'denʃəl] *adj* providencial; (*lucky*) afortunado, milagroso.

providentially [,prɔvi'denʃəli] *adv* providencialmente; afortunadamente, milagrosamente.

providently ['prɔvidəntli] *adv* próvidamente.

provider [prə'vaidə*] *n* proveedor *m*, ora *f*.

providing [prə'vaidiŋ] *conj* = **provided**.

province ['prɔvins] *n* (**a**) provincia *f*; **they live in the** —**s** viven en provincia.
(**b**) (*fig: field*) esfera *f*; especialidad *f*; (*jurisdiction etc*) competencia *f*; **it's not within my** — no es de mi competencia.

provincial [prə'vinʃəl] **1** *adj* provincial, de provincia; (*pej*) provinciano. **2** *n* provinciano *m*, a *f*.

provincialism [prə'vinʃəlizəm] *n* provincialismo *m*.

provision [prə'viʒən] **1** *n* (**a**) (*in general*) provisión *f*; (*supply*) provisión *f*, suministro *m*; abastecimiento *m*; **the** — **of new capital** la provisión de nuevos capitales; **the** — **of new housing** la provisión de nuevas viviendas; **to make** — **for** prevenir, prever; **to make** — **for one's family** asegurar el porvenir de su familia.
(**b**) —**s** (*food*) provisiones *fpl*, comestibles *mpl*, víveres *mpl*.
(**c**) (*stipulation*) estipulación *f*, disposición *f*; **according to the** —**s of the treaty** de acuerdo con lo estipulado en el tratado; **there is no** — **to the contrary** no hay estipulación que lo prohiba; **it comes within the** —**s of this law** está comprendido dentro de lo estipulado por esta ley.
2 *vt* aprovisionar, abastecer.

provisional [prə'viʒənl] *adj* provisional; interino.

provisionally [prə'viʒnəli] *adv* provisionalmente; con carácter provisional; interinamente.

proviso [prə'vaizəu] *n* condición *f*, estipulación *f*; **with the** — **that ...** con la condición de que + *subj*.

provocation [,prɔvə'keiʃən] *n* provocación *f*; **to act under** — obrar bajo provocación; **to suffer great** — sufrir una gran provocación.

provocative [prə'vɔkətiv] *adj remark etc* provocador, provocativo; *title* provocador; *book etc* sugestivo, que invita a pensar; **she's a very** — **woman** es una mujer muy provocativa; **now you're trying to be** — ahora intentas hacerme perder los estribos.

provocatively [prə'vɔkətivli] *adv* de modo provocador, de modo provocativo.

provoke [prə'vəuk] *vt* (*cause*) causar, producir, motivar; facilitar; (*rouse, move*) provocar, incitar, mover (*to* a); (*anger*) provocar; irritar; **it** —**d us to action** nos incitó a obrar; **it** —**d the town to revolt** incitó la ciudad a sublevarse; **he is easily** —**d** se irrita con cualquier cosa.

provoking [prə'vəukiŋ] *adj* provocativo; irritante, fastidioso; **how very** —**!** ¡qué lata!

provost ['prɔvəst] *n* (*Univ*) rector *m*; director *m*; (*Scot*) alcalde *m*.

provost marshal [prə'vəu'mɑːʃəl] *n* capitán *m* preboste.

prow [prau] *n* proa *f*.

prowess ['prauis] *n* (*skill*) destreza *f*, habilidad *f*; (*courage*) valor *m*.

prowl [praul] **1** *n* ronda *f* (en busca de presa, botín *etc*).
2 *vt*: **to** — **the streets** rondar las calles, vagar por las calles.
3 *vi* rondar (en busca de presa, botín *etc*); **he** —**s round the house at night** (*outside*) ronda la casa de noche, (*inside*) se pasea por la casa de noche.

prowler ['praulə*] *n* rondador *m*, hombre *m* que ronda en busca de presa (*or* mujeres *etc*); ladrón *m*.

proximity [prɔk'simiti] *n* proximidad *f*; **in** — **to** cerca de, junto a.

proximo ['prɔksiməu] *n* (*Comm*) del mes próximo.

proxy ['prɔksi] *n* (*power*) poder *m*, procuración *f*; (*person*) apoderado, a *m*, *f*; sustituto *m*, a *f*; **by** — por poder, por poderes; **to be married by** — casarse por poderes.

prude [pruːd] *n* remilgada *f*, gazmoña *f*.

prudence ['pruːdəns] *n* prudencia *f*.

prudent ['pruːdənt] *adj* prudente.

prudential [pru(:)'denʃəl] *adj* prudencial.

prudently ['pruːdəntli] *adv* prudentemente, con prudencia.

prudery ['pruːdəri] *n* remilgo *m*, gazmoñería *f*.

prudish ['pruːdiʃ] *adj* remilgado, gazmoño.

prudishness ['pruːdiʃnis] *n see* **prudery**.

prune[1] [pruːn] *n* ciruela *f* pasa.

prune[2] [pruːn] *vt* podar; (*fig*) reducir, escamondar.

pruning ['pruːniŋ] *n* poda *f*.

pruning hook ['pruːniŋhuk] *n*, **pruning knife** ['pruːniŋnaif] *n*, **pruning shears** ['pruːniŋʃiəz] *npl* podadera *f*.

prurience ['pruəriəns] *n* salacidad *f*.

prurient ['pruəriənt] *adj* salaz.

Prussia ['prʌʃə] Prusia *f*.

Prussian ['prʌʃən] **1** *adj* prusiano. **2** *n* prusiano *m*, a *f*.

prussic ['prʌsik] *adj*: — **acid** ácido *m* prúsico.

pry[1] [prai] *vi* (*watch*) fisgonear, curiosear; (*meddle*) entrometerse; **to** — **into someone's affairs** entrometerse en lo ajeno; **to** — **into someone's secrets** tratar de saber los secretos de uno.

pry[2] [prai] *vt* (*US*) *see* **prise**.

prying ['praiiŋ] *adj* fisgón, curioso; entrometido.

psalm [sɑːm] *n* salmo *m*.

psalmist ['sɑːmist] *n* salmista *m*.

psalmody ['sælmədi] *n* salmodia *f*.

psalter ['sɔːltə*] *n* salterio *m*.

psephologist [se'fɔlədʒist] *n* psefólogo *m* (se— *Acad*).

psephology [se'fɔlədʒi] *n* psefología *f* (se— *Acad*).

pseudo . . . ['sjuːdəu] seudo . . .; falso, fingido, *eg* **a pseudo-artist** un falso artista.

pseudo ['sjuːdəu] *adj* (*fam*) falso, fraudulento; *person* fingido; (*of person's character*) artificial, afectado.

pseudonym ['sjuːdənim] *n* seudónimo *m*.

pseudonymous [sjuː'dɔniməs] *adj* seudónimo.

pshaw [pʃɔː] *interj* ¡bah!

psittacosis [,psitə'kəusis] *n* psitacosis *f*.

psych . . . [saik] psic . . ., psiqu . . .; *the Academy recommends the spelling* sic . . ., siqu . . .

Psyche ['saiki] *f* Psique *f*.

psyche ['saiki] *n* psique *f*.

psychedelic [,saiki'delik] *adj* psiquedélico.

psychiatric [,saiki'ætrik] *adj* psiquiátrico.

psychiatrist [sai'kaiətrist] *n* psiquiatra *mf*.

psychiatry [sai'kaiətri] *n* psiquiatría *f*.

psychic(al) ['saikik(əl)] *adj* psíquico.

psycho ['saikəu] *n* (*US fam*) caso *m* psicológico, persona *f* anormal.

psychoanalyse, (*US*) **psychoanalyze** [,saikəu'ænəlaiz] *vt* psicoanalizar.

psychoanalysis [,saikəuə'nælisis] *n* psicoanálisis *m*.

psychoanalyst [,saikəu'ænəlist] *n* psicoanalista *mf*.

psychological [,saikə'lɔdʒikəl] *adj* psicológico.

psychologically [,saikə'lɔdʒikəli] *adv* psicológicamente.

psychologist [sai'kɔlədʒist] *n* psicólogo *m*.

psychology [sai'kɔlədʒi] *n* psicología *f*.

psychoneurosis ['saikəunjuə'rəusis] *n*, *pl* **psychoneuroses** ['saikəunjuə'rəusiːz] psiconeurosis *f*.

psychopath ['saikəupæθ] *n* psicópata *m*.

psychopathic [,saikəu'pæθik] *adj* psicopático.

psychopathology ['saikəupə'θɔlədʒi] *n* psicopatología *f*.

psychosis [sai'kəusis] *n* psicosis *f*.

psychosomatic ['saikəusəu'mætik] *adj* psicosomático.

psychotherapy ['saikəu'θerəpi] *n* psicoterapia *f*.

psychotic [sai'kɔtik] **1** *adj* psicótico. **2** *n* psicótico *m*, a *f*.

ptarmigan ['tɑːmigən] *n* perdiz *f* blanca, perdiz *f* nival.

pterodactyl [,terəu'dæktil] *n* pterodáctilo *m*.

Ptolemaic [,tɔlə'meiik] *adj*: — **system** sistema *m* de Tolomeo.

Ptolemy ['tɔləmi] *m* Tolomeo.

ptomaine ['təumein] *n* ptomaína *f*; — **poisoning** envenenamiento *m* ptomaínico.

pub [pʌb] *n* (*fam*) taberna *f*, tasca *f*, bar *m*.

pub crawl ['pʌbkrɔːl] (*fam*) **1** *n* chateo *m* (de tasca en tasca); **to go on a** — — **= 2 pub-crawl** *vi* ir de chateo, copear, alternar.

puberty ['pjuːbəti] *n* pubertad *f*.

pubescence [pjuː'besəns] *n* pubescencia *f*.

pubescent [pjuː'besənt] *adj* pubescente.

pubic ['pjuːbik] *adj* púbico.

pubis ['pjuːbis] *n* pubis *m*.

public ['pʌblik] **1** *adj* público; **to make something** — publicar algo.
2 *n* público *m*; **in** — en público; **the general** — el gran público; **the sporting** — los aficionados al deporte; **the great British** — (*hum*) los ingleses, los súbditos de su Majestad.

publican ['pʌblikən] *n* tabernero *m*.

publication [,pʌbli'keiʃən] *n* publicación *f*.

publicist ['pʌblisist] *n* publicista *mf*.

publicity [pʌb'lisiti] *n* publicidad *f*.

publicize ['pʌblisaiz] *vt* publicar, dar publicidad a, anunciar.

publicly ['pʌblikli] *adv* públicamente, en público.

public-spirited ['pʌblik'spiritid] *adj act* de buen ciudadano; *person* lleno de civismo, consciente del bien público.
publish ['pʌbliʃ] *vt* publicar; *banns* correr.
publisher ['pʌbliʃə*] *n* editor *m*.
publishing ['pʌbliʃiŋ] *n* publicación *f* (de libros).
puce [pjuːs] **1** *n* color *m* castaño rojizo. **2** *adj* de color castaño rojizo; (*with shame etc*) colorado.
puck[1] [pʌk] *n* duende *m* (malicioso).
puck[2] [pʌk] *n* (*Sport*) disco *m* de caucho.
pucker ['pʌkə*] **1** *n* arruga *f*; (*Sew*) frunce *m*, fruncido *m*; (*accidentally formed*) buche *m*.
  2 *vt* (*also to — up*) arrugar; (*brow, Sew*) fruncir.
  3 *vi* (*also to — up*) arrugarse, formar buches.
puckish ['pʌkiʃ] *adj* malicioso, juguetón.
pud [pud] *n* (*fam*) (a) (*Cook*) = **pudding**. (b) niño *m* rollizo, niña *f* rolliza.
pudding ['pudiŋ] *n* pudín *m*; **black —** morcilla *f*.
puddingstone ['pudiŋstəun] *n* pudinga *f*.
puddle ['pʌdl] **1** *n* charco *m*. **2** *vt* (*Tech*) pudelar.
pudenda [puː'dendə] *npl* partes *fpl* pudendas.
pudgy ['pʌdʒi] *adj* = **podgy**.
puerile ['pjuərail] *adj* pueril.
puerility [pjuə'riliti] *n* puerilidad *f*.
puerperal [pjuː(ː)'əːpərəl] *adj* puerperal; **— fever** fiebre *f* puerperal.
Puerto Rican ['pwəːtəu'riːkən] **1** *adj* puertorriqueño. **2** *n* puertorriqueño *m*, a *f*.
Puerto Rico ['pwəːtəu'riːkəu] Puerto *m* Rico.
puff [pʌf] **1** *n* (a) (*of air*) soplo *m*, (*of wind*) soplo *m*, racha *f*; (*of smoke*) humareda *f*, (*from mouth*) bocanada *f*; (*sound: of breathing, of engine*) resoplido *m*, resuello *m*, bufido *m*.
  (b) (*powder —*) borla *f*; (*Cook*) pastelillo *m* de crema.
  (c) (*advert*) bombo *m*.
  2 *vt* (*blow*) soplar; *pipe etc* chupar; **to — out** *smoke etc* echar, arrojar, despedir; **to — out one's cheeks** hinchar los carrillos; **to — up** hinchar, inflar; (*fig*) dar bombo a.
  3 *vi* (*blow*) soplar; (*— and blow*) jadear, resollar, acezar; **to — (away) at one's pipe** chupar su pipa; **the train —ed out** el tren salió bufando, el tren salió echando humo.
  4 *vr*: **to — oneself up** darse bombo, engreírse.
puff adder ['pʌf͵ædə*] *n* víbora *f* puff.
puffball ['pʌfbɔːl] *n* bejín *m*, cuezco *m* de lobo.
puffed [pʌft] *adj eye* hinchado; **to be — (out of breath)** estar sin aliento, estar acezando; **to be — up** (*with pride*) estar engreído.
puffer [pʌfə*] *n* (*fam*) locomotora *f*.
puffin ['pʌfin] *n* frailecillo *m*.
puff pastry ['pʌf'peistri] *n*, (US) **— paste** [peist] *n* hojaldre *m*.
puffy ['pʌfi] *adj eye etc* hinchado.
pug [pʌg] *n* doguillo *m*.
pugilism ['pjuːdʒilizəm] *n* pugilato *m*.
pugilist ['pjuːdʒilist] *n* púgil *m*.
pugnacious [pʌg'neiʃəs] *adj* pugnaz, belicoso, agresivo.
pugnaciously [pʌg'neiʃəsli] *adv* con pugnacidad, agresivamente.
pugnacity [pʌg'næsiti] *n* pugnacidad *f*, belicosidad *f*, agresividad *f*.
pug-nosed ['pʌg'nəuzd] *adj* chato, braco.
puke [pjuːk] *vti* vomitar; (*fam*) **it makes me —** me da asco.
pukka [pʌkə] *adj* (*fam*) auténtico, genuino; elegante, lujoso.
pulchritude ['pʌlkritjuːd] *n* belleza *f*.
pull [pul] **1** *n* (a) (*tug*) tirón *m*; (*with oar etc*) golpe *m*; (*of a magnet, also fig*) atracción *f*, fuerza *f* atractiva; **the — of the south** la atracción del Sur, lo atractivo del Sur; **it was a long —** fue mucho camino; **we had a long — up the hill** nos costó mucho trabajo subir la cuesta; **give the rope a —** tira de la cuerda; **suddenly it gave a —** de repente dio un tirón.
  (b) (*advantage*) ventaja *f*; (*influence*) influencia *f*, poder *m*; **they have a — over us now** ahora nos llevan ventaja; **he has a slight —** tiene una pequeña ventaja; **he has — in the right places** tiene influencia donde hace falta tenerla.
  (c) (*at one's pipe*) chupada *f*; (*drink*) trago *m*; **he took a — at his pipe** chupó la pipa.
  (d) (*handle of drawer etc*) tirador *m*; (*of bell*) cuerda *f*.
  (e) (*Typ*) primeras pruebas *fpl*.
  2 *vt* (a) (*tug at*) *bell rope, hair etc* tirar de; *trigger* apretar; *oar* tirar de; *boat* remar; (*Naut*) *rope* halar, jalar; *weeds* arrancar; *muscle* torcerse, dislocarse.
  (b) (*extract, take out*) sacar.

  (c) (*draw along*) tirar, arrastrar; **the engine —s 6 coaches** la locomotora arrastra 6 vagones; **— your chair over** acerca la silla.
  (d) (*Typ*) imprimir.
  (e) *ball* (*at golf, etc*) golpear oblicuamente, *shot* ejecutar mal.
  (f) *see* **face, fast** *etc*.
  (g) (*with adv or prep*) **to — about** manosear, estropear; **to — along** arrastrar; **to — apart** (*separate*) separar; despegar, desunir; (*break*) romper en dos; (*take to pieces*) desmontar; **to — something away from someone** arrancar algo a uno, quitar algo a uno arrancándoselo; **to — something back** tirar algo hacia atrás; **to — down** *person etc* hacer caer, hacer bajar; (*take down*) bajar; *blinds etc* bajar; *house, fortifications* derribar, demoler; *government* derribar; *grade, price etc* rebajar; **he —ed his hat well down** se caló el sombrero, se encasquetó el sombrero; **the mark in chemistry —s her down** la nota de química es la causa de que salga mal; **to — in** tirar hacia sí; *rope* cobrar; *horse* enfrenar; *suspect* detener; **the film —s the people in** la película atrae un numeroso público; **to — off** arrancar, separar; quitar de un tirón; *clothes* quitarse (de prisa); *deal* cerrar, concluir con éxito (algo inesperadamente); *game* ganar (algo inesperadamente); **to — it off** lograrlo, llevarlo a cabo (algo inesperadamente); vencer (algo inesperadamente); **to — on** *clothes* ponerse (de prisa); **to — out** (*take out*) sacar; *teeth etc* sacar, arrancar; (*stretch*) estirar; **to — someone out of a hole** ayudar a uno a salir de un hoyo tirando de sus brazos (*etc*); **to — someone out of a river** sacar a uno de un río; **to — a car over** volcar un coche; **to — someone round** ayudar a uno a reponerse; **to — someone through** sacar a uno de un apuro (*or enfermedad etc*); **to — a team together** hacer que los jugadores recuperen su espíritu de equipo; **to — up** *plants* arrancar, desarraigar; *socks etc* alzar; *car* parar; *horse* refrenar; **to — someone up for shoddy work** reprender a uno por la baja calidad de su trabajo; **his mark in maths —ed him up a bit** su nota en matemáticas le ayudó a salir mejor.
  3 *vi* (a) tirar (*at* de); dar un tirón; **to — at a rope** tirar de una cuerda.
  (b) (*vehicle*) ir; (*oarsmen etc*) remar; **we —ed for the shore** remamos con el propósito de llegar a la orilla; **the car —ed slowly up the hill** el coche subía despacio la cuesta; **it —ed to a stop** se paró, se detuvo.
  (c) **to — at one's pipe** dar chupadas a la pipa; **to — at a bottle** echar un trago de una botella.
  (d) (*with adv or prep*) **they — apart easily** se separan fácilmente; **to — away from someone** apartarse bruscamente de uno; (*outdistance*) dejar a uno atrás; **to — in** (*Rail*) llegar, llegar al andén, (*Aut*) parar, parar junto a la acera; **to — on something** tirar de algo; **to — out** irse, marcharse (*from* de), (*Mil*) retirarse (*from* de); (*Rail*) salir de la estación; **we're —ing out** nos marchamos ya; **the red car —ed out from behind that black one** el coche rojo salió detrás del negro; **to — over to one side** (*Aut etc*) desviarse hacia un lado; **to — round** reponerse; **to — through** salir de un apuro, (*Med*) recobrar la salud; **to — together** trabajar con un propósito común, obrar de común acuerdo; **to — up** (*stop*) pararse, detenerse; (*restrain oneself*) contenerse; (*stop talking etc*) interrumpirse; (*improve*) mejorar su posición; **please — up at the corner** pare en la esquina, por favor; **the car —ed up suddenly** el coche se paró en seco.
  4 *vr*: **to — oneself along** arrastrarse; **to — oneself in** apretarse el cinturón; **to — oneself together** sobreponerse, serenarse, recobrar la calma; reanimarse; **— yourself together!** ¡anímese!
pullet ['pulit] *n* polla *f*, pollita *f*.
pulley ['puli] *n* polea *f*.
pull-in ['pul͵in] *n* (*Aut: lay-by*) apartadero *m*; (*for food*) café *m* de carretera, restaurante *m* de carretera.
Pullman ['pulmən] (*Protected Trade Name*): **— car** *n* coche *m* Pullman.
pullover ['puləuvə*] *n* jersey *m*, jersé *m*, jersei *m* (*Acad*).
pullulate ['pʌljuleit] *vi* pulular.
pulmonary ['pʌlmənəri] *adj* pulmonar.
pulp [pʌlp] **1** *n* pulpa *f*; (*Bot*) pulpa *f*, carne *f*; (*paper —, wood—*) pasta *f*; **a leg crushed to —** una pierna hecha trizas; **to beat someone to a —** dar a uno una tremenda paliza; **to reduce something to —** hacer algo pulpa, reducir algo a pulpa.
  2 *vt* hacer pulpa, reducir a pulpa.
pulpit ['pulpit] *n* púlpito *m*.
pulpy ['pʌlpi] *adj* pulposo.

pulsate [pʌl'seit] *vi* pulsar, latir.
pulsation [pʌl'seiʃən] *n* pulsación *f*, latido *m*.
pulse¹ [pʌls] **1** *n* (*Anat*) pulso *m*; (*throb*) pulsación *f*, latido *m*; **to feel** (*or* **take**) **someone's —** tomar el pulso a uno. **2** *vi* pulsar, latir.
pulse² [pʌls] *n* (*Bot*) legumbre *f*, legumbres *fpl*.
pulsebeat ['pʌlsbi:t] *n* latido *m* del pulso.
pulverization [,pʌlvərai'zeiʃən] *n* pulverización *f*.
pulverize ['pʌlvəraiz] **1** *vt* pulverizar; (*fig*) hacer polvo; anonadar; (*fam*) cascar. **2** *vi* pulverizarse.
puma ['pju:mə] *n* puma *f*.
pumice ['pʌmis] *n*, **pumice stone** ['pʌmisstəun] *n* piedra *f* pómez.
pummel ['pʌml] *see* **pommel**.
pump¹ [pʌmp] **1** *n* bomba *f*; (*Naut*) pompa *f*. **2** *vt* sacar (*or* elevar, llevar *etc*) con una bomba; **arm** mover rápidamente de arriba para abajo; **person** (*fam*) **to — air along a tube** hacer que pase el aire por un tubo por medio de una bomba; **to — a tank dry** secar (*or* vaciar) un tanque con una bomba; **to — out liquid** sacar líquido con una bomba; **to — up a tyre** inflar un neumático con una bomba; **it's no good —ing me** es inútil tratar de sonsacarme.
pump² [pʌmp] *n* (*shoe*) zapatilla *f*.
pumpernickel ['pʌmpənikl] *n* (*US*) pan *m* de centeno entero.
pump house ['pʌmphaus] *n*, *pl* **— houses** [hauziz] casa *f* de bombas.
pumping station ['pʌmpiŋ,steiʃən] *n* estación *f* de bombeo.
pumpkin ['pʌmpkin] *n* (*vegetable*) calabaza *f*; (*plant*) calabacera *f*.
pump room ['pʌmprum] *n* pabellón *m* de hidroterapia.
pun [pʌn] **1** *n* juego *m* de palabras (*on* sobre). **2** *vi* hacer un juego de palabras (*on* sobre), jugar del vocablo.
Punch [pʌntʃ] *m* Polichinela; **—-and-Judy show** teatro *m* de polichinelas.
punch¹ [pʌntʃ] **1** *n* (**a**) (*tool*) punzón *m*; (*for tickets*) taladro *m*.
 (**b**) (*blow*) puñetazo *m*, golpe *m*; **rabbit —** golpe *m* de nuca; **he packs a —** tiene mucha fuerza en los puños; **to pull one's —es** no emplear toda su fuerza; **he didn't pull any —es** (*fig*) no se mordió la lengua.
 (**c**) (*fig*) empuje *m*, vigor *m*, fuerza *f*; **he has —es** hombre de empuje; **he's a speaker with some —** es un orador de tono enérgico; **think of a phrase that's got some —** to **it** dame una frase que tenga fuerza.
 2 *vt* (**a**) (*with tool*) punzar, taladrar; agujerear; perforar; **ticket** picar; **to — holes in a sheet** practicar agujeros en una lámina.
 (**b**) (*with fist*) dar un puñetazo a, pegar con los puños, golpear.
punch² [pʌntʃ] *n* (*drink*) ponche *m*.
punchball ['pʌntʃbɔ:l] *n* saco *m* de arena, punching *m*.
punch bowl ['pʌntʃbəul] *n* ponchera *f*.
punch card ['pʌntʃkɑ:d] *n* tarjeta *f* perforada.
punch-drunk ['pʌntʃdrʌŋk] *adj*: **to be —** estar aturdido (a causa de los muchos golpes recibidos).
punched tape ['pʌntʃt'teip] *n* cinta *f* perforada.
punch line ['pʌntʃlain] *n* (*of joke*) palabras *fpl* que contienen la esencia del chiste; (*of speech etc*) palabras *fpl* más significativas, declaración *f* impresionante.
punch-up ['pʌntʃʌp] *n* (*fam*) riña *f*, pendencia *f*.
punctilio [pʌŋk'tiliəu] *n* puntillo *m*, etiqueta *f*; puntualidad *f*.
punctilious [pʌŋk'tiliəs] *adj* puntilloso, etiquetero, puntual.
punctiliously [pʌŋk'tiliəsli] *adv* de modo puntilloso; puntualmente.
punctual ['pʌŋktjuəl] *adj* puntual; **"please be —"** "se ruega la mayor puntualidad"; **will the train be —?** ¿llegará el tren a la hora exacta?
punctuality [,pʌŋktju'æliti] *n* puntualidad *f*.
punctually ['pʌŋktjuəli] *adv* puntualmente; **— at 6 o'clock** a las 6 en punto; **the bus arrived —** el autobús llegó a la hora exacta.
punctuate ['pʌŋktjueit] *vt* puntuar; (*fig*) interrumpir; **his speech was —d by bursts of applause** su discurso fue interrumpido por salvas de aplausos.
punctuation [,pʌŋktju'eiʃən] *n* puntuación *f*.
punctuation mark [,pʌŋktju'eiʃənmɑ:k] *n* signo *m* de puntuación.
puncture ['pʌŋktʃə*] **1** *n* perforación *f*; (*of skin etc*) puntura *f*, punzada *f*; (*Aut*) pinchazo *m*; (*Med*) punción *f*; **I have a —** tengo un neumático pinchado, se me ha reventado un neumático. **2** *vt* perforar; punzar, pinchar; *tyre* pinchar.

pundit ['pʌndit] *n* (*iro*) erudito *m*, sabio *m*.
pungency ['pʌndʒənsi] *n* lo acre; picante *m*; mordacidad *f*, acerbidad *f*.
pungent ['pʌndʒənt] *adj* **smell** acre; (*piquant*) picante; *satire etc* mordaz, acerbo.
pungently ['pʌndʒəntli] *adv* acremente; de modo picante; mordazmente, acerbamente.
Punic ['pju:nik] *adj* púnico. **2** *n* púnico *m*.
punish ['pʌniʃ] *vt* (**a**) castigar; **to — someone for something**, **to — someone for doing something** castigar a uno por haber hecho algo.
 (**b**) (*fig*: *maltreat*) maltratar; (*tax*) exigir esfuerzos sobrehumanos a; (*take advantage of*) aprovecharse al máximo de; **food** devorar, no perdonar.
punishable ['pʌniʃəbl] *adj* punible, castigable; **a — offence** una infracción que castiga la ley.
punishment ['pʌniʃmənt] *n* (**a**) castigo *m*; **capital —** pena *f* de muerte; **corporal —** castigo *m* corporal; **to make the — fit the crime** señalar un castigo de acuerdo con el crimen; **to take one's — like a man** sufrir el castigo sin quejarse.
 (**b**) malos tratos *mpl*, tratamiento *m* severo.
punitive ['pju:nitiv] *adj* punitivo.
punk [pʌŋk] (*US sl*) **1** *n* pobre hombre *m*; novato *m*; bobo *m*. **2** *attr* malo, baladí, de baja calidad.
punster ['pʌnstə*] *n* persona *f* aficionada a los juegos de palabras.
punt¹ [pʌnt] **1** *n* batea *f*. **2** *vt* impulsar con percha. **3** *vi* ir en batea, pasearse en batea.
punt² [pʌnt] *vt* **ball** dar un puntapié a.
punt³ [pʌnt] *vi* (*bet*) jugar, hacer apuestas.
punter ['pʌntə*] *n* jugador *m*.
punt pole ['pʌntpəul] *n* percha *f*, pértiga *f* (de batea).
puny ['pju:ni] *adj* **person etc** débil, encanijado; **effort** débil, flojo; (*petty*) insignificante.
pup [pʌp] **1** *n* cachorro *m*, a *f*; **to sell someone a —** dar a uno gato por liebre. **2** *vi* parir (*la perra*).
pupa ['pju:pə] *n*, *pl* **pupae** ['pju:pi:] crisálida *f*.
pupate ['pju:peit] *vi* crisalidar.
pupil ['pju:pl] *n* alumno *m*, a *f*; (*Anat*) pupila *f*.
puppet ['pʌpit] **1** *n* títere *m*; (*fig*) títere *m*, marioneta *mf*. **2** *attr*: **— régime** gobierno *m* títere, régimen *m* marioneta.
puppetry ['pʌpitri] *n* títeres *mpl*, arte *m* del titiritero.
puppet show ['pʌpitʃəu] *n* títeres *mpl*, teatro *m* de títeres.
puppy ['pʌpi] *n* cachorro *m*, a *f*, perrito *m*, a *f*.
purblind ['pə:blaind] *adj* cegato; (*fig*) ciego, falto de comprensión.
purchase ['pə:tʃis] **1** *n* (**a**) (*act*) compra *f*; (*thing purchased*) adquisición *f*; **to make a —** hacer una compra.
 (**b**) (*on rock etc*) agarre *m* firme, pie *m* firme; (*Mech*) apalancamiento *m*; **to get a — on the surface** tener donde agarrarse a la superficie, lograr pegarse a la superficie.
 2 *vt* comprar, adquirir.
purchaser ['pə:tʃisə*] *n* comprador *m*, ora *f*.
purchase tax ['pə:tʃistæks] *n* impuesto *m* de venta.
purchasing power ['pə:tʃisiŋ,pauə*] *n* poder *m* de compra, poder *m* adquisitivo.
pure [pjuə*] *adj* puro.
purebred ['pjuə'bred] *adj* de pura sangre, de raza.
purée ['pjuərei] *n* puré *m*.
purely ['pjuəli] *adv* puramente.
pure-minded ['pjuə'maindid] *adj* de mente pura.
pureness ['pjuənis] *n* pureza *f*.
purgation [pə:'geiʃən] *n* purgación *f*.
purgative ['pə:gətiv] **1** *adj* purgativo, purgante. **2** *n* purgante *m*.
purgatory ['pə:gətəri] *n* purgatorio *m*; **it was —!** ¡fue un purgatorio!
purge [pə:dʒ] **1** *n* (*act*) purga *f*; (*medicine*) purga *f*, purgante *m*; (*Pol*) purga *f*, depuración *f*. **2** *vt* purgar; purificar, depurar; **offence, sin** purgar; (*Pol*) **party** purgar, depurar, **member** liquidar.
purification [,pjuərifi'keiʃən] *n* purificación *f*, depuración *f*.
purifier ['pjuərifaiə*] *n* depurador *m*.
purify ['pjuərifai] *vt* purificar, depurar; **metal** acrisolar, refinar; **town etc** depurar.
purist ['pjuərist] *n* purista *mf*, casticista *mf*.
puritan ['pjuəritən] **1** *adj* puritano. **2** *n* puritano *m*, a *f*.
puritanical [,pjuəri'tænikəl] *adj* puritano.
puritanism ['pjuəritənizəm] *m* puritanismo *m*.
purity ['pjuəriti] *n* pureza *f*.
purl [pə:l] **1** *n* puntada *f* invertida. **2** *vt* hacer a puntadas invertidas; **"— two"** "dos puntadas invertidas".
purler ['pə:lə*] *n* (*fam*): **to come a —** caer pesadamente, caer aparatosamente; (*fig*) fracasar rotundamente.

purlieus ['pə:lju:z] *npl* alrededores *mpl*, inmediaciones *fpl*.
purloin [pə:'lɔin] *vt* robar, hurtar.
purple ['pə:pl] **1** *adj* purpúreo; *bruise etc* morado; **to go —** (in the face) ponerse negro. **2** *n* púrpura *f*. **3** *vt* purpurar.
purplish ['pə:pliʃ] *adj* purpurino, algo purpúreo.
purport ['pə:pət] *n* (*meaning*) significado *m*, sentido *m*; (*purpose*) intención *f*.
purport [pə:'pɔ:t] *vt* (*mean*) significar; (*convey meaning*) dar a entender (*that* que); (*profess*) pretender (*to be* ser); **this —s to be a statement of . . .** esto pretende ser una declaración de . . .
purpose ['pə:pəs] **1** *n* (a) (*intention*) propósito *m*, intención *f*, objeto *m*; **novel with a —** novela *f* de tesis, novela *f* de intención seria; **my —** in doing this mi propósito al hacer esto; **for the —** al efecto; **for this —** para este fin; **for our —s** we may disregard this para nuestros fines podemos hacer caso omiso de esto; **for the — of** + *ger* con el fin de + *infin*, al efecto de + *infin*; **for the —s of this meeting** por lo que toca a esta reunión; **on —** de propósito, adrede; **to good —, to some —** con buenos resultados, provechosamente; **to no —** inútilmente, en vano; **to answer** (*or* **serve**) someone's **—** servir para el caso, servir para lo que quiere uno; **it serves no useful —** no tiene prácticamente utilidad; **it serves a variety of —s** sirve para diversos efectos.
(b) (*sense of* **—**) resolución *f*; **infirmity of —** falta *f* de resolución; **strength of —** resolución *f*, firmeza *f*.
2 *vt* proponerse, proyectar, intentar; **to — to do something** proponerse hacer algo.
purposeful ['pə:pəsful] *adj* resuelto, determinado.
purposefully ['pə:pəsfəli] *adv* resueltamente.
purposefulness ['pə:pəsfulnis] *n* resolución *f*.
purposeless ['pə:pəslis] *adj* person's *character* irresoluto; *person's state* indeciso; *act* sin propósito fijo, sin finalidad concreta.
purposely ['pə:pəsli] *adv* de propósito, adrede, expresamente; **a — vague statement** una declaración hecha adrede en términos vagos.
purr [pə:*] **1** *n* ronroneo *m*. **2** *vt* (*say*) decir suavemente, susurrar. **3** *vi* (cat, engine) ronronear; (*person*) estar satisfecho.
purse [pə:s] **1** *n* bolsa *f*; (*handbag: US*) bolso *m*; (*prize*) premio *m*; (*collection*) colecta *f*; **privy —** gastos *mpl* personales del monarca; **a well-lined —** una bolsa llena; **it is beyond my —** mis recursos no llegan a tanto, es demasiado costoso para mí. **2** *vt*: **to — one's lips** fruncir los labios.
purser ['pə:sə*] *n* contador *m* de navío.
purse strings ['pə:sstriŋz] *npl*: **to hold the —** tener las llaves de la caja.
pursuance [pə'sju:əns] *n* prosecución *f*, cumplimiento *m*; **in — of** con arreglo a, en cumplimiento de.
pursuant [pə'sju:ənt] *adv*: **— to** de acuerdo con.
pursue [pə'sju:] *vt* (*hunt*) seguir, seguir la pista de, perseguir, cazar, dar caza a; (*chase, molest*) acosar, dar caza a, asediar; *line of conduct, inquiry* seguir; *study* proseguir; *profession* dedicarse a, ejercer; *plan* proceder de acuerdo con, obrar con arreglo a; *pleasures etc* dedicarse a; **they —d the fox into the wood** siguieron la zorra al entrar ésta en el bosque; **he —d the girl home** siguió a la chica hasta casa; **he won't stop pursuing me!** ¡no me deja a sol ni a sombra!
pursuer [pə'sju:ə*] *n* perseguidor *m*, ora *f*.
pursuit [pə'sju:t] *n* (a) (*chase*) caza *f*; perseguimiento *m*, persecución *f*; (*search*) busca *f*; **in — of** en busca de, en pos de; **with two policemen in hot —** con dos policías que le seguían muy de cerca; **to go in — of someone** ir en pos de uno; **to set out in — of someone** salir a buscar a uno.
(b) **the — of happiness** la busca de la felicidad; **the — of wealth** el afán de riqueza.
(c) (*occupation*) ocupación *f*, carrera *f*, empleo *m*; (*pastime*) pasatiempo *m*; **her favourite —** su pasatiempo predilecto; **literary —s** intereses *mpl* literarios, actividades *fpl* literarias.
pursuit plane [pə'sju:tplein] *n* avión *m* de caza.
purulence ['pjuəruləns] *n* purulencia *f*.
purulent ['pjuərulənt] *adj* purulento.
purvey [pə:'vei] *vt* proveer, suministrar, abastecer.
purveyance [pə:'veiəns] *n* provisión *f*, suministro *m*, abastecimiento *m*.
purveyor [pə:'veiə*] *n* proveedor *m*, ora *f*.
purview ['pə:vju:] *n* alcance *m*, esfera *f*; **it comes within the — of the law** está comprendido dentro de los límites de la ley.
pus [pʌs] *n* pus *m*.

push [puʃ] **1** *n* (a) (*shove*) empuje *m*, empujón *m*; (*Mil*) ataque *m*, ofensiva *f*; avance *m*; **with one —** de un empuje; **to give someone a —** dar un empujón a uno; **to give someone a helping —** ayudar a uno empujando su coche (*etc*).
(b) (*fam*) **to get the —** ser despedido; **to give someone the —** despedir a uno.
(c) (*pushfulness*) empuje *m*, energía *f*; **he's got no —** no tiene empuje, le falta energía; **he's a man with plenty of —** es hombre de empuje.
(d) (*fam*) **at a —** si es necesario, en caso de necesidad; **when it comes to the —** en el momento decisivo, llegado el punto crítico.
2 *vt* (a) (*press*) empujar; (*down, with foot*) pisar, apretar; *button etc* apretar, pulsar, presionar; **to — a car into the garage** hacer que un coche entre en el garaje empujándolo; **to — one's finger into a hole** introducir el dedo en un agujero; **he —ed his finger into my eye** me clavó el dedo en el ojo; **to — one's way through a crowd** abrirse paso empujando a través de una multitud.
(b) *person* empujar; **don't — me!** ¡no me empuje!; **to — someone off the pavement** hacer que uno abandone la acera a fuerza de empujones; **they —ed me off the ball** me quitaron el balón a empujones.
(c) (*press*) *advantage* aprovecharse de; *claim* proseguir, insistir en; *enterprise* promover, fomentar; *person* proteger, ayudar, ayudar en su carrera; *product etc* hacer una campaña publicitaria a favor de; **to — an attack home** esforzarse por asegurar el éxito de un ataque; **don't — your luck** no te fíes demasiado de tu buena suerte.
(d) (*force*) **to — someone to do something** obligar a uno a hacer algo; incitar a uno a hacer algo; **I was —ed into it** me obligaron a ello; **to — someone for payment** ejercer presión sobre uno para que pague; **we are —ed for time** tenemos poco tiempo, tenemos mucha prisa; **to be —ed for money** andar muy escaso de dinero; **I'm rather —ed for boxes just now** ahora tengo pocas cajas disponibles.
(e) (*with adv or prep*) **to — something against something else** poner algo apretadamente contra otra cosa; **to — something aside** apartar algo con la mano; **to — someone aside** apartar a uno empujándole, (*fig*) arrinconar a uno; **to — one's plate away** apartar el plato con la mano; **to — back hair etc** echar hacia atrás; *enemy* echar atrás, rechazar; *crowd* hacer retroceder; **to — down** (*press down*) comprimir; (*make fall*) hacer caer; (*lower*) hacer bajar; **to — someone forward** empujar a uno hacia adelante; **to — a plan forward** llevar adelante un proyecto; **to — in** introducir a la fuerza; empujar; clavar, hincar; **to — a lid on** quitar una tapa a la fuerza; **to — the work on** hacer que se trabaje a un ritmo acelerado; **to — a door open** abrir una puerta empujándola; **to — out** empujar hacia fuera; expulsar, hacer salir; **to — a boat out** desatracar un barco; **the snail —ed out its horns** el caracol sacó los cuernos; **to — through** *business* despachar rápidamente; (*Parl*) *bill* hacer aceptar a la fuerza; **to — up** *window etc* levantar; (*make rise*) empujar hacia arriba; *total, thermometer etc* hacer subir.
3 *vi* (a) empujar; dar un empujón, dar empujones; **"—"** (*on doors*) "empujad"; **don't —!** ¡no empujen!
(b) (*fig*) hacer esfuerzos, obrar con energía.
(c) (*with adv or prep*) **to — in** introducirse a la fuerza, entrar a empujones; **to — off** (*Naut*) desatracar; apartarse de la orilla; (*fam*) largarse, marcharse; **— off!** ¡lárgate!; **it's time to — off** es hora de marcharnos; **to — off from** (*Naut*) apartarse de, alejarse de; **to — on** seguir adelante, continuar (a pesar de todo); **they —ed on 5 miles** avanzaron 5 millas; **so we —ed on to the camp** así que seguimos hasta el campamento; **it's time to — on** es hora de ponernos otra vez en camino; **the pier —es out into the sea** el muelle se extiende sobre el mar; **to — past someone** pasar delante de uno empujándole; **to — through a crowd** abrirse camino a empujones por entre una multitud; **the plants are —ing through** están apareciendo las plantas.
4 *vr*: **to — oneself forward** ofrecer sus servicios, ofrecerse; (*pej*) darse demasiada importancia.
push-bike ['puʃbaik] *n* (*fam*) bici *f*.
push-button ['puʃˌbʌtn] **1** *n* pulsador *m*, botón *m* (de control *etc*).
2 *attr* dotado de pulsador, con botón (de mando *etc*); **with — control** con mando por botón.
pushcart ['puʃkɑ:t] *n* carretilla *f* de mano.
push chair ['puʃtʃeə*] *n* sillita *f* de ruedas.
pusher ['puʃə*] *n* persona *f* emprendedora; (*pej*) persona *f* de ambición desmesurada.

pushful ['puʃful] *adj* emprendedor, vigoroso, enérgico; ambicioso; (*pej*) agresivo.

pushfully ['puʃfəli] *adv* de modo emprendedor, enérgicamente; ambiciosamente; (*pej*) agresivamente.

pushfulness ['puʃfulnis] *n* empuje *m*, pujanza *f*, espíritu *m* emprendedor; ambición *f*; (*pej*) espíritu *m* agresivo.

pushing ['puʃiŋ] *adj see* **pushful**.

pushover ['puʃ‚əuvə*] *n* (*fam*) cosa *f* muy fácil; persona *f* muy fácil de vencer (*or* convencer *etc*); **it's a —** es facilísimo.

pusillanimity [‚pju:silə'nimiti] *n* pusilanimidad *f*.

pusillanimous [‚pju:si'læniməs] *adj* pusilánime.

puss [pus] *n* minino *m*, micho *m*; (*sl*) cara *f*; **—, —!** ¡miz, miz!; **P—in Boots** el gato con botas.

pussy ['pusi] *n see* **puss.**

pussyfoot ['pusifut] *vi* (*US fam*) moverse a paso de gato; andar a tientas; (*fig*) no decidirse, no declararse.

pustule ['pʌstju:l] *n* pústula *f*.

put [put] (*irr: pret and ptp* **put**) **1** *vt* (a) (*place*) poner; colocar; (*esp into, inside*) meter; **— it here** póngalo aqui; **to — milk in one's coffee** echar (*or* añadir) leche a su café; **to — something to one's ear** acercar algo al oído; **to — one's signature to something** poner su firma en algo, firmar algo; **to — a field under oats** sembrar un campo de avena; **to — someone under an obligation** poner a uno bajo una obligación; **to — virtue before success** anteponer la virtud al éxito, preferir la virtud al éxito; **he —s the Italians before the Spaniards** estima a los italianos más que a los españoles.

(b) (*of versions*) **to — a text into verse** poner un texto en verso, versificar un texto; **to — a passage into Greek** traducir un pasaje al griego.

(c) (*invest etc*) **to — money into a company** invertir dinero en una sociedad; **to — money into shares** comprar acciones con su dinero; **to — one's savings into marks** cambiar sus ahorros en marcos; **to — money on a horse** apostar dinero a un caballo.

(d) (*state etc*) declarar; (*express*) expresar; (*in writing*) redactar; (*plan etc*) exponer, explicar (*to a*); *problem* plantear; **as Lope —s it** como lo expresa Lope; **if I may —** it so por así decirlo; **all that can be — in 2 sentences** todo eso se puede expresar en 2 frases; **as the Portuguese — it** como dicen los portugueses; **to — it bluntly** para decirlo como es, hablando sin rodeos; **— it to him nicely** díselo lo más amablemente que puedas; **how will you — it to him?** ¿cómo se lo vas a explicar?; **he —s a convincing case** se explica con argumentos convincentes; **I — it to you that . . .** les sugiero que . . ., me veo en el caso de decirles que . . .; **to — a question to someone** hacer una pregunta a uno; **I should like to — a resolution** quiero proponer una moción; **the chairman — it to the committee** el presidente lo sometió a votación en el comité.

(e) (*estimate*) calcular; computar, estimar (*at en*); **the population is — at 2500** se calcula la población en 2500; **what would you — it at?** ¿en cuánto lo estima Vd?

(f) (*with personal object*) **to — someone to bed** acostar a uno; **to — the enemy to flight** derrotar al enemigo, hacer huir al enemigo; **they — the lad to a trade** le pusieron al muchacho de aprendiz en un oficio; **to — someone to a new kind of work** poner a uno a trabajar en un nuevo oficio; **to — someone through his paces** poner a uno a prueba, demostrar las cualidades de uno; **they really — him through it** le sometieron a las pruebas más rigurosas; **to — a horse at a fence** hacer que un caballo salte una valla.

(g) (*direct*) **to — a bullet through someone** atravesar a uno de una bala; **to — one's pen through a word** tachar una palabra con la pluma; **to — the weight** lanzar el peso.

(h) (*ptp*) **to stay —** no moverse, seguir en el mismo sitio.

2 *vt* (*with adv or prep*) (a) **to — about** *news, rumour etc* diseminar; **to — it about that . . .** dar a entender que . . ., hacer creer que . . ., hacer correr el rumor de que . . .; **to — someone about** (*anger*) enojar a uno; (*trouble*) molestar a uno, incomodar a uno; **she was much — about by it** se enfadó mucho con ello; **to — a ship about** hacer que un barco cambie de bordada.

(b) **to — across** *idea, product* hacer aceptar; *meaning* comunicar, hacer entender; *deal* cerrar; **he knows his stuff but he can't — it across** domina su material pero es incapaz de comunicarlo a otros; **to — it across someone** (*deceive*) engañar a uno, embaucar a uno; (*defeat*) dar una paliza a uno;

they properly — it across us nos dieron una paliza de verdad.

(c) **to — aside** (*reject*) rechazar; (*save*) poner aparte; *fears* desechar.

(d) **to — away** (*replace*) devolver a su lugar; (*in pocket, drawer etc*) guardar; *thought* desechar, descartar; *car* poner en el garaje; *food* zampar; *lunatic* poner en un manicomio; *wife* repudiar; *prisoner* encarcelar; (*banish*) alejar; **to — money away** ahorrar dinero, poner el dinero aparte.

(e) **to — back** (*replace*) devolver a su lugar; restituir, volver a poner; (*in pocket, drawer etc*) guardar; (*postpone*) aplazar; **— that back!** ¡déjalo!; **to — a clock back an hour** retrasar un reloj una hora; **this will — us back 10 years** esto nos retrasará 10 años.

(f) **to — by** poner aparte; (*save*) ahorrar; (*keep*) guardar; **to have money — by** tener dinero ahorrado, tener ahorros; **I had it — by for you** lo tenía guardado para Vd.

(g) **to — down** (*on ground*) poner en tierra, poner en el suelo, deponer; *blinds etc* bajar; *umbrella* cerrar; (*let go*) soltar, dejar; (*preserve*) conservar; (*put to sleep*) sacrificar; (*in rank*) degradar; *passengers* dejar apearse; *revolt* sofocar, dominar; *abuse* suprimir; (*note*) apuntar; **— it down!** ¡déjalo!, ¡suéltalo!; **I couldn't — the book down** me era imposible dejar el libro de la mano; **— it down in writing** póngalo por escrito; **did you — the names down?** ¿apuntó Vd los nombres?; **you may — my name down on the list** puede poner (*or* inscribir) mi nombre en la lista; **we — it down to his account** lo hemos sentado en su cuenta; **we — £50 down** pagamos un desembolso inicial de 50 libras; **I — him down as useless** yo le creí una calamidad; **I — him down as a troublemaker** le califiqué como un revoltoso; **I should — her down as about 30** creo que tendría unos 30 años; **we — it down to nerves** lo atribuimos a los nervios; **it can be — down to his childhood** se puede achacar a su niñez.

(h) **to — forth** *hand* alargar; *arm* extender; *leaves etc* echar; *effort etc* emplear, desplegar.

(i) **to — forward** *candidate* proponer; *idea* adelantar; *case, theory* presentar, proponer, exponer; *suggestion* hacer; (*date, function etc*) adelantar; **to — a clock forward 1 hour** adelantar un reloj una hora.

(j) **to — in** meter, introducir, insertar; *claim* presentar; *evidence* aducir; (*say*) decir; *remark etc* interponer; **to — in a good day's work** hacer bien el trabajo del día; **I — in 2 hours reading** pasé 2 horas leyendo, leí durante 2 horas; **to — in time on a project** invertir tiempo en un proyecto, dedicar tiempo a un proyecto; **they — the liberals in** votaron a los liberales, eligieron un gobierno liberal.

(k) **to — off** quitar; (*postpone*) aplazar, dejar para después; (*get rid of*) desembarazarse de; (*confuse*) desconcertar; (*discourage*) desanimar; **he keeps —ting it off** lo aplaza siempre; **you can't — off doing it for ever** no puedes evitar hacerlo siempre, no será siempre posible dejar de hacerlo; **we shall have to — the guests off** tendremos que decir a los invitados que no vengan, tendremos que ofrecer nuestras excusas a los invitados; **to — someone off with a promise** dar a uno largas con una promesa; **he's not easily — off** no es fácil apartarle de su propósito; **he tried to — me off my stroke** se esforzó por distraerme en el golpe, trató de hacerme errar el golpe; **her face is enough to — anyone off** su cara basta para desanimar al más fuerte; **you quite — me off my meal** me has quitado todo el apetito; **what you say —s me off prawns** lo que dices me quita las ganas de las gambas; **it almost — me off opera for good** casi me hizo perder permanentemente el sabor de la ópera; **we managed to — them off the scent** logramos desviarlos de la pista.

(l) **to — on** *clothes* ponerse; *shoes* ponerse, calzarse; *brake* echar, aplicar; *light, radio etc* poner, encender; *play* representar, poner en escena; (*add*) añadir; *speed* aumentar; **— the coffeepot on** pon la cafetera; **so we — on lettuce instead** así que pusimos lechuga en su lugar; **to — a clock on 1 hour** adelantar un reloj 1 hora; **to — on weight** echar carnes, engordar; **to — on an extra train** poner un tren de más; **she's —ting it on** (*pretending*) está exagerando, (*overacting*) está exagerando el papel, se emociona demasiado, (*affectedly*) se da mucho tono; **she —s the accent on** habla con un acento afectado; **to — on an innocent air** adoptar una postura de inocencia; **Jack — us on to you** Jack nos dio su nombre; **what — you on to it?** ¿qué le hizo pensar en esto?; ¿qué le dio la pista?; **one of the thieves — the police on to the others** uno de los ladrones denunció a los otros a la policía.

(m) to — out *hand* alargar, *(Aut)* sacar; *arm* extender; *tongue* sacar; *head* asomar, sacar; *horns* sacar; *leaves etc* echar; *(dislocate)* dislocarse; *(publish)* publicar, sacar a luz; *rumour* diseminar, hacer correr; *announcement* hacer; *(eject)* echar, expulsar; poner en la calle; *tenant* desahuciar; *cat* mandar a pasearse; *fire, light* apagar; **to — clothes out to dry** tender la ropa, poner la ropa a secar; **to — out a boat** echar un bote al mar; **to — money out at interest** poner el dinero a interés; **to — someone out** *(anger)* enojar a uno, irritar a uno, *(inconvenience)* molestar a uno, *(confound)* desconcertar a uno; **I don't want to — you out at all** no quiero molestarle en lo más mínimo; **she was very — out** estaba muy enfadada; **she never seems to be — out** no parece alterarse por nada.

(n) to — over = to — across; to — one over on someone *(forestall)* ganar por la mano a uno, *(deceive)* engañar a uno.

(o) to — through *task* concluir, llevar a cabo; *proposal* hacer aprobar; *business* despachar; **— me through to Sr Negro** póngame con el Sr Negro.

(p) to — together *(place together)* poner juntos, juntar; *(add)* añadir; *(Sew)* confeccionar; *(Tech)* montar, armar; *collection* reunir, juntar, formar; **more than all the rest — together** más que todos los demás reunidos; **if all the cigars in the world are — together end to end** si se ponen uno tras otro todos los puros del mundo.

(q) to — up *hand etc* poner en alto, levantar, alzar; *window etc* levantar; *umbrella* abrir; *collar* alzar; *ladder* montar, poner; *flag, sail* izar; *picture* colgar; *poster* pegar; *notice* fijar, poner; *game* levantar; *building* construir; *sword* envainar; *price* aumentar; *petition* presentar; *prayer, prize* ofrecer; *candidate* nombrar, proponer *(for* a); *lunch, prescription* preparar; **to — one's hair up** hacerse un peinado alto; **to — something up for sale** poner algo en venta; **to — up the money for something** poner el dinero para algo; **to — someone up** hospedar a uno, alojar a uno; **can you — me up for the night?** ¿me pueden dar una habitación para esta noche?; **to — someone up free** alojar a uno gratis; **to — someone up to something** incitar a uno a hacer algo; **someone must have — him up to it** alguien ha debido sugerírselo.

3 vi (a) *(Naut)* **to — about** virar, cambiar de bordada, cambiar de rumbo; **to — back to harbour** volver a puerto; **to — in at a port, to — into a port** entrar a puerto; **the boat — s in at Vigo** el barco hace escala en Vigo; **to — off, to — out** hacerse a la mar; **we — out from Cadiz** salimos del puerto de Cádiz.

(b) to — in for a post presentarse a un puesto, solicitar un puesto; **are you — ting in?** ¿te vas a presentar?; **to — up for president** ser candidato a la presidencia; **to — up for the socialists** ser candidato socialista; **to — up for East Hull** ser candidato en el distrito electoral de East Hull.

(c) to — up at an hotel hospedarse en un hotel.

(d) to — up with someone aguantar a uno; **to — up with something** resignarse a algo; **I can't — up with her** no la puedo ver; **I can't — up with it any longer** no aguanto más; **she — s up with a lot** tiene mucho aguante.

(e) to — upon someone molestar a uno, incomodar a uno; abusar de la amabilidad de uno.

4 vr: to — oneself forward ofrecerse (con poca modestia), ponerse en evidencia; llamar sobre sí la atención; **to — oneself out** tomarse la molestia, molestarse; **don't — yourself out!** ¡no se moleste!; **to — oneself over** impresionar con su personalidad; comunicar eficazmente lo que uno quiere decir.

putative ['pjuːtətiv] *adj* supuesto; *relation* putativo.
putrefaction [.pjuːtri'fækʃən] *n* putrefacción *f*.
putrefy ['pjuːtrifai] **1** *vt* pudrir. **2** *vi* pudrirse.
putrescence [pjuː'tresns] *n* pudrición *f*.
putrescent [pjuː'tresnt] *adj* putrescente, podrido.
putrid ['pjuːtrid] *adj* podrido, putrefacto; *(fam)* horrible, malísimo.
putsch [putʃ] *n* golpe *m* de estado.
putt [pʌt] **1** *n* put *m*, golpe *m* corto, tiro *m* al hoyo. **2** *vt* golpear con poca fuerza, tirar hacia el hoyo.
puttee ['pʌtiː] *n* polaina *f*.
putter ['pʌtə*] *n* putter *m*.
putting ['putiŋ] *n:* **— the weight** lanzamiento *m* del peso.
putting green ['pʌtiŋgriːn] *n* campo *m* de golf en miniatura.
putty ['pʌti] *n* masilla *f*.
putty knife ['pʌtinaif] *n*, *pl* **— knives** [naivz] espátula *f* para masilla.
put-up ['putʌp] *adj:* **— job** cosa *f* proyectada y preparada de antemano; asunto *m* fraudulento; **it was a — job to give him the post** habían decidido antes darle el puesto.
puzzle ['pʌzl] **1** *n* **(a)** *(game)* rompecabezas *m*; *(riddle)* acertijo *m*; *(crossword)* crucigrama *m*; *(jigsaw)* rompecabezas *m*.
(b) *(mystery)* problema *m*, enigma *m*, misterio *m*; **it's a real —** es un verdadero problema; **the — of their origin** el enigma de su origen; **your friends are —s to me** no comprendo en lo más mínimo a tus amigos.
2 *vt* dejar perplejo, confundir; **that properly —d him** eso le dejó totalmente perplejo; **I am —d to know why** no comprendo por qué; **I was —d to know what to answer** no sabía en absoluto lo que debía contestar; **to — something out** resolver algo, descifrar algo.
3 *vi:* **to — over something** esforzarse por resolver algo, devanarse los sesos para descifrar algo.
puzzled ['pʌzld] *adj* perplejo.
puzzlement ['pʌzlmənt] *n* perplejidad *f*, confusión *f*.
puzzler ['pʌzlə*] *n* problema *m*, enigma *m*, misterio *m*.
puzzling ['pʌzliŋ] *adj* enigmático, misterioso; **it is — that . . .** es curioso que . . .
pygmy ['pigmi] **1** *adj* pigmeo; *(fig)* miniatura, minúsculo. **2** *n* pigmeo *m*.
pyjamas [pi'dʒaːməz] *npl* pijama *m*.
pylon ['pailən] *n* pilón *m*, poste *m*; *(Elec)* torre *f* de conducción eléctrica.
pyorrhoea [.paiə'riə] *n* piorrea *f*.
pyramid ['pirəmid] *n* pirámide *f*.
pyramidal [pi'ræmidl] *adj* piramidal.
pyre ['paiə*] *n* pira *f*; *(fig)* hoguera *f*.
Pyrenean [.pirə'niːən] *adj* pirenaico, pirineo.
Pyrenees [.pirə'niːz] *pl* Pirineo *m*, Pirineos *mpl*.
pyrethrum [pai'riːθrəm] *n* piretro *m*.
pyretic [pai'retik] *adj* pirético.
pyrites [pai'raitiːz] *n* piritas *fpl*.
pyro- ['paiərəu] piro . . .
pyromaniac ['paiərəu'meiniæk] *n* incendiario *m*, a *f*.
pyrotechnic [.paiərəu'teknik] *adj* pirotécnico.
pyrotechnics [.paiərəu'tekniks] *npl* pirotecnia *f*.
Pyrrhic ['pirik] *adj:* **— victory** victoria *f* pírrica.
Pythagoras [pai'θægərəs] *m* Pitágoras *f*.
python ['paiθən] *n* pitón *m*.
pyx [piks] *n* píxide *f*.

Q

qua [kwei] *prep* como, en cuanto.
quack[1] [kwæk] **1** *n* graznido *m* (del pato). **2** *vi* graznar.
quack[2] [kwæk] **1** *n* charlatán *m*; (*Med*) curandero *m*. **2** *adj* falso, fingido; (*remedy*) de curandero; **— doctor** curandero *m*.
quackery ['kwækəri] *n* charlatanismo *m*.
quad [kwɔd] *n* (*fam*) *see* **quadrangle.**
Quadragesima [‚kwɔdrə'dʒesimə] *n* Cuadragésima *f*.
quadrangle ['kwɔdræŋgl] *n* cuadrángulo *m*; (*court*) patio *m*.
quadrangular [kwɔ'dræŋgjulə*] *adj* cuadrangular.
quadrant ['kwɔdrənt] *n* cuadrante *m*.
quadratic [kwɔ'drætik] *adj equation* de segundo grado.
quadrature ['kwɔdrətʃə*] *n* cuadratura *f*.
quadrilateral [‚kwɔdri'lætərəl] **1** *adj* cuadrilátero. **2** *n* cuadrilátero *m*.
quadrille [kwa'dril] *n* cuadrilla *f*.
quadripartite ['kwɔdri'pɑːtait] *adj* cuadripartido.
quadrivium [kwɔ'driviəm] *n* cuadrivio *m*.
quadroon [kwɔ'druːn] *n* cuarterón *m*.
quadruped ['kwɔdruped] *n* cuadrúpedo *m*.
quadruple ['kwɔdrupl] **1** *adj* cuádruple. **2** *n* cuádruplo *m*.
quadruple ['kwɔ'druːpl] **1** *vt* cuadruplicar. **2** *vi* cuadruplicarse.
quadruplets [kwɔ'druːplits] *npl* cuatrillizos *mpl*, cuatrillizas *fpl*.
quadruplicate [kwɔ'druːplikit] **1** *adj* cuadruplicado. **2** *n*: **in —** por cuadruplicado.
quadruplicate [kwɔ'druːplikeit] *vt* cuadruplicar.
quads [kwɔdz] *npl* (*fam*) *see* **quadruplets.**
quaestor ['kwiːstə*] *n* cuestor *m*.
quaff [kwɔf] *vt* (*arch or hum*) beber.
quagmire ['kwægmaiə*] *n* tremedal *m*, cenegal *m*; (*fig*) atolladero *m*.
quail[1] [kweil] *n* codorniz *f*.
quail[2] [kweil] *vi* acobardarse, amedrentarse (*before* ante).
quaint [kweint] *adj* (*odd*) curioso, original, singular; *workmanship etc* rebuscado; *person* singular; (*picturesque, of tourist interest etc*) típico, pintoresco.
quaintly ['kweintli] *adv* curiosamente; singularmente; típicamente; **he described it — as . . .** le dio la calificación curiosa de . . .
quaintness ['kweintnis] *n* curiosidad *f*, originalidad *f*, singularidad *f*; lo rebuscado; tipismo *m*, lo pintoresco.
quake [kweik] *vi* temblar, estremecerse; **to — at the knees** temblarle a uno las rodillas; **to — at the sight** estremecerse viendo tal cosa; **to — with fright** temblar de miedo; **the earth —d 3 times** la tierra tembló 3 veces.
Quaker ['kweikə*] **1** *adj* cuáquero. **2** *n* cuáquero *m*, a *f*.
Quakerism ['kweikərizəm] *n* cuaquerismo *m*.
qualification [‚kwɔlifi'keiʃən] *n* (a) (*reservation*) reserva *f*; modificación *f*, restricción *f*; **to accept something without —** aceptar algo sin reserva.
 (b) (*for a post etc*) requisito *m*; **the —s for the post are . . .** los requisitos del puesto son . . .; **the —s for membership** lo que se requiere para ser socio.
 (c) (*of person*) **—s** aptitud *f*, capacidad *f*; (*paper* **—s**) títulos *mpl*; **to have the —s for a post** llenar los requisitos de un puesto, estar capacitado para ocupar un puesto; **what are his —s?** ¿qué títulos tiene?
 (d) (*act*) calificación *f*; **the — of his work as useless** la calificación de su obra de inútil.
qualified ['kwɔlifaid] *adj* **(a)** *person* (*fit*) apto, competente (*to + infin* para + *infin*); (*trained*) capacitado, cualificado, habilitado; (*professionally*) titulado, que tiene título, con título; **a — engineer** un ingeniero titulado; **to be — to do something** estar capacitado para hacer algo; ser competente para hacer algo; **to be — to vote** tener los requisitos para votar; **I don't feel — to judge that** no me creo lo bastante experto para juzgar eso.
 (b) (*limited*) modificado, limitado; **he gave it his — approval** lo aprobó pero con reservas; **it was a — success** obtuvo un éxito moderado.
qualify ['kwɔlifai] **1** *vt* **(a)** (*describe*) calificar (*as* de); (*Gram*) calificar a.
 (b) (*make competent*) habilitar, capacitar; **this should — you for the post** esto ha de darle los requisitos para el puesto; **to — someone to do something** habilitar a uno para hacer algo; **that doesn't — him to speak on this** eso no le da derecho para hablar sobre este asunto.
 (c) (*modify*) modificar; restringir; **I think you should — that** creo que le conviene modificar eso.
 (d) (*diminish*) atenuar, moderar, disminuir.
 2 *vi* habilitarse, capacitarse; (*professionally*) cursar los estudios profesionales, estudiar; (*graduate*) obtener el título, graduarse; **to — as an engineer** estudiar para ingeniero, (*finally*) obtener el título de ingeniero; **to — for a post** llenar los requisitos para un puesto; **does he —?** ¿tiene los requisitos?; **I qualified in 1968** yo saqué el título en 1968; **we shall marry when he qualifies** nos casaremos en cuanto él termine la carrera; **he hardly qualifies as a poet** apenas se le puede calificar de poeta.
qualifying ['kwɔlifaiiŋ] *adj* (*Gram*) calificativo; *exam, round* eliminatorio.
qualitative ['kwɔlitətiv] *adj* cualitativo.
qualitatively ['kwɔlitətivli] *adv* bajo el aspecto cualitativo.
quality ['kwɔliti] **1** *n* **(a)** (*nature, kind*) calidad *f*; categoría *f*, clase *f*; **of the best —** de la mejor calidad; **of good —, of high —** de buena calidad; **of low —** de baja calidad; **fibres of —** fibras *fpl* de calidad; **he's a man of some —** es hombre de cierta categoría; **he has real —** tiene verdadera excelencia.
 (b) (*characteristic, moral — etc*) cualidad *f*; **among her qualities** entre sus cualidades; **he has many good qualities** tiene muchas buenas cualidades.
 (c) the — la aristocracia; **people of —** la gente bien nacida, las personas cultas.
 (d) (*of sound*) timbre *m*, tono *m*.
 2 *adj*: **a — carpet** una alfombra de calidad.
qualm [kwɑːm] *n* **(a)** (*Med*) bascas *fpl*, náusea *f*; mareo *m*.
 (b) (*scruple*) escrúpulo *m*, duda *f*; **to have —s about doing something** sentir escrúpulo al hacer algo; **now she's having —s about it** ahora se le está remordiendo la conciencia por ello, ahora le están asaltando las dudas; **to have no —s about doing something** no dudar en hacer algo, hacer algo sin escrúpulos, hacer algo sin remordimientos.
quandary ['kwɔndəri] *n* dilema *m*, apuro *m*; **to be in a —** estar perplejo, estar en un dilema; **to get someone out of a —** sacar a uno de un apuro.
quantitative ['kwɔntitətiv] *adj* cuantitativo.
quantitatively ['kwɔntitətivli] *adv* bajo el aspecto cuantitativo.
quantity ['kwɔntiti] *n* cantidad *f*; **unknown —** incógnita *f*; **in large quantities, in —** en grandes cantidades; **what — do you want?** ¿cuánto quiere?
quantity surveyor ['kwɔntiti‚sə'veiə*] *n* aparejador *m*.
quantum ['kwɔntəm] *n*: **— theory** teoría *f* cuántica, teoría *f* de los cuanta.
quarantine ['kwɔrəntiːn] **1** *n* cuarentena *f*; **to be in —** estar en cuarentena; **to place a dog in —** poner un perro en cuarentena. **2** *vt* poner en cuarentena.

quarrel ['kwɔrəl] **1** n (argument) riña f, disputa f; (with blows) reyerta f, pendencia f, pelea f; **to have a — with** someone reñir con uno; **we had a —** reñimos; **I have no — with you** yo no tengo nada en contra de Vd, yo no tengo queja de Vd; **to pick a —** buscar camorra; **to pick a — with** someone armar pleito con uno; **to take up someone's —** ponerse de la parte de uno.

2 vi reñir; disputar; **they —led about** (or over) **money** riñeron por cuestión de dinero; **to — with** someone reñir con uno, pelearse con uno; **we —led and I never saw him again** reñimos y no volví a verle; **to — with someone for having done something** reñir a uno por haber hecho algo; **you can't — with that** es imposible quejarse de eso; **what we — with is** . . . nuestro motivo de queja es . . .

quarrelling, (US) **quarreling** ['kwɔrəliŋ] n disputas fpl, altercados mpl; **there was constant —** se reñía constantemente.

quarrelsome ['kwɔrəlsəm] adj pendenciero, peleador.

quarrelsomeness ['kwɔrəlsəmnis] n espíritu m pendenciero.

quarry¹ ['kwɔri] n (Hunting) presa f; (fig) presa f, víctima f.

quarry² ['kwɔri] **1** n cantera f; (fig) mina f, cantera f. **2** vt sacar, extraer.
3 vi explotar una cantera, extraer piedra (etc) de una cantera.

quarryman ['kwɔrimən] n, pl **—men** [mən] cantero m, picapedrero m.

quart [kwɔːt] n cuarto de galón (= 1,136 litros); **we drank —s** bebimos una gran cantidad.

quarter ['kwɔːtə*] **1** n **(a)** (fourth part) cuarto m, cuarta parte f; (weight) = 28 libras (= 12,7 kg, approx = arroba f); (Fin US) moneda de 25 centavos; (Her) cuartel m; **—s** (of horse) anca f; **hind—s** cuartos mpl traseros, (hum, of person) culo m; **a — mile** un cuarto de milla; **a — of a century** un cuarto de siglo; **for a — of the price** por la cuarta parte del precio; **it's a — gone already** ya ha desaparecido la cuarta parte; **it's only a — as long** tiene solamente la cuarta parte de largo; **to divide something into —s** dividir algo en cuartos.

(b) (of moon) cuarto m; (3 months) trimestre m; **to pay by the —** pagar cada 3 meses, pagar trimestralmente.

(c) (time) **a — of an hour** un cuarto de hora; **it's a — to 3, it's a — of 3** (US) son las 3 menos cuarto; **it's a — past 3, it's a — after 3** (US) son las 3 y cuarto.

(d) (of compass) cuarta f; (region) región f; (fig) fuente f, origen m; procedencia f; dirección f; **the 4 —s of the globe** las 4 partes del mundo; **from all —s** de todas partes; **at close —s** de cerca, (fight) casi cuerpo a cuerpo; **from an unknown —** de procedencia desconocida, de origen desconocido; **we may expect trouble in that —** podemos tener dificultades en esa región; **the wind is in the right —** el viento sopla en dirección favorable; **what — is the wind in?** ¿qué dirección lleva el viento?

(e) (of town) barrio m; **the business —** el barrio comercial.

(f) **—s** vivienda f; alojamiento m; (Mil) alojamiento m; (barracks) cuartel m; **to have free —s** tener alojamiento gratis; **to live in cramped —s** tener un cuarto (etc) muy estrecho; **to shift one's —s** cambiar de alojamiento; **to take up one's —s** ocupar su cuarto (etc); establecerse, alojarse.

(g) to give no — no dar cuartel.

2 vt **(a)** (divide into 4) cuartear, dividir en cuartos; meat descuartizar; (Her) cuartelar.

(b) (Mil) acuartelar, alojar; **to be —ed on** someone estar alojado en casa de uno.

quarter day ['kwɔːtədei] n primer día m del trimestre; (Fin) día m en que se paga un trimestre.

quarter-deck ['kwɔːtədek] n alcázar m.

quarter final ['kwɔːtə,fainl] n cuarto m de final; **—s** cuartos mpl de final.

quartering ['kwɔːtəriŋ] n (Her) cantón m.

quarterly ['kwɔːtəli] **1** adv cada tres meses, trimestralmente, por trimestres. **2** adj trimestral. **3** n publicación f trimestral.

quartermaster ['kwɔːtə,mɑːstə*] n (approx) furriel m, comisario m.

quartermaster sergeant ['kwɔːtə,mɑːstə'sɑːdʒənt] n (approx) brigada m.

quartern ['kwɔːtən] n cuarta f; **— loaf** pan m de 4 libras.

quarterstaff ['kwɔːtəstɑːf] n (Hist) barra f.

quarter tone ['kwɔːtətəun] n cuarto m de tono.

quartet(te) [kwɔː'tet] n (Mus) cuarteto m; (set of 4) grupo m de cuatro.

quarto ['kwɔːtəu] **1** adj en cuarto; (paper size) tamaño m holandesa. **2** n libro m en cuarto.

quartz ['kwɔːts] n cuarzo m.

quartzite ['kwɔːtsait] n cuarcita f.

quash ['kwɔʃ] vt anular, invalidar.

quasi ['kwɑːzi] adv cuasi.

quatercentenary [,kwɔtəsen'tiːnəri] n cuarto centenario m.

quaternary [kwə'təːnəri] **1** adj cuaternario. **2** n cuaternario m.

quatrain ['kwɔtrein] n cuarteto m, estrofa f de cuatro versos.

quaver ['kweivə*] **1** n temblor m; vibración f; (Mus: trill) trémolo m, (note) corchea f; **with a — in her voice** con voz trémula.
2 vi temblar; vibrar; (Mus) trinar.
3 vt decir con voz temblorosa; **"yes", she —ed** "sí", dijo temblorosa.

quavering ['kweivəriŋ] adj tembloroso, trémulo; **in — tones** en tono tembloroso.

quaveringly ['kweivəriŋli] adv: **to say something —** decir algo con voz temblorosa.

quavery ['kweivəri] adj see **quavering**.

quay [kiː] n, **quayside** ['kiːsaid] n muelle m; **on the —** en el muelle.

queasiness ['kwiːzinis] n bascas fpl; propensión f a la náusea; delicadeza f, escrupulosidad f.

queasy ['kwiːzi] adj (Med) bascoso; stomach delicado; conscience delicado, escrupuloso; **I feel —** me siento mal.

queen [kwiːn] **1** n reina f; (Chess) reina f; (Cards) dama f, (in Spanish pack) caballo m; (Zool: bee) abeja f reina, (ant) hormiga f reina; **she was — to Charles II** era la reina de Carlos II.
2 vt pawn coronar; **to — it** conducirse como una reina, (fig) pavonearse.
3 vi (Chess) ser coronado.

queen bee ['kwiːn'biː] n abeja f reina.

queenly ['kwiːnli] adj regio, de reina.

queen mother ['kwiːn'mʌðə*] n reina f madre.

queer [kwiə*] **1** adj **(a)** (odd) raro, extraño, singular; misterioso; excéntrico; sospechoso; **it's very —** es muy raro; **there's something — going on** pasa algo raro; **what's — about it?** ¿qué tiene esto de raro?
(b) (fam: homosexual) maricón.
(c) (Med) enfermo; **he was — for 2 months** estuvo enfermo durante 2 meses; **to come over —**, **to feel —** tener vahídos, sentirse mal, sentirse indispuesto.
2 n (fam) maricón m.
3 vt estropear; see **pitch**.

queerly ['kwiəli] adv de modo raro, extrañamente; misteriosamente; **to behave —** comportarse de modo raro.

queerness ['kwiənis] n rareza f, singularidad f; lo misterioso; lo excéntrico.

quell [kwel] vt passion etc reprimir; calmar; revolt sofocar, dominar; opposition sobreponerse a; fears desechar.

quench [kwentʃ] vt (all senses) apagar.

quenchless ['kwentʃlis] adj inapagable.

quern [kwəːn] n molinillo m de mano.

querulous ['kweruləs] adj quejumbroso.

querulously ['kweruləsli] adv quejumbrosamente; en tono quejumbroso.

query ['kwiəri] **1** n (question) pregunta f; (doubt) duda f; (?) punto m de interrogación, (fig) interrogante f; **there are many queries about it** hay muchas interrogantes acerca de esto; **did you have a —?** ¿quería preguntar algo?; **—: who killed Cock Robin?** pregunta: ¿quién mató a Cock Robin?
2 vti (ask) preguntar; (doubt) dudar de, expresar dudas acerca de; (disagree with) no estar conforme con; **to — whether** . . . dudar si . . .; **I — that** dudo si eso es cierto, tengo mis dudas acerca de eso; **do you — the evidence?** ¿tiene Vd dudas acerca del testimonio?

quest [kwest] **1** n busca f, búsqueda f (for de); (Hist) demanda f (for de); **to go in — of** ir en busca de.
2 vti buscar (for something algo).

question ['kwestʃən] **1** n **(a)** (interrogative) pregunta f; **—s and answers** preguntas fpl y respuestas; **indirect —** (Gram) pregunta f indirecta; **leading —** (Law) pregunta f capciosa, pregunta f que sugiere la respuesta; **rhetorical —** pregunta f a la que no se espera contestación, comunicación f; **trick —** pregunta f de pega; **to ask someone a —, to put a — to someone** hacer una pregunta a uno; **many —s were left unanswered** muchas preguntas quedaron sin contestar; **to pop the —** declararse.

(b) (*matter*) asunto *m*, cuestión *f*; problema *m*; **the German** — el problema alemán; **burning** — cuestión *f* candente, cuestión *f* palpitante; **vexed** — cuestión *f* batallona; **open** — cuestión *f* pendiente, cuestión *f* sin resolver; **it is an open** — **whether** . . .; queda por resolver si . . ., el tiempo dirá si . . .; **the** — **is,** . . . el caso es, . . .; **it is a** — of se trata de . . .; **it is a** — **of whether** . . . se trata de saber si . . .; **that is the** — ahí está la dificultad; **that is not the** — no se trata de eso; **it is not simply a** — **of money** no se trata simplemente de dinero, no es cuestión de dinero y nada más; **there is no** — **of outside help** no se trata de la ayuda exterior; **there can be no** — **of your resigning** no se puede consentir en que Vd dimita; **there was some** — **of John coming** se hablaba de que pudiera venir Juan; **it's out of the** — es imposible; **that begs the** — eso es una petición de principio.

(c) (*at meeting*) asunto *m*; —! ¡que se vuelva al tema de la discusión!; **to move the previous** — pedir pareceres sobre si se ha de someter la moción a votación; **to put the** — someter la moción a votación.

(d) (*doubt etc*) **beyond** —, **past** — fuera de toda duda; **in** — en cuestión; **without** — sin duda, indudablemente; **there is no** — **about it** no existen dudas sobre ello; **to bring** (*or* **call**) **something in** — poner algo en duda; **to come into** — empezar a discutirse; **I make no** — **but that it is so** yo no dudo que es así.

2 *vt* **(a)** (*interrogate*) hacer preguntas a; (*by police etc*) interrogar; (*by examiner etc*) examinar; **we** —**ed him closely to find out whether** . . . le interrogamos del modo más apremiante para saber si . . .; **I will not be** —**ed about it** no permito que se me interrogue sobre eso.

(b) (*doubt*) poner en duda; dudar de, desconfiar de; **I** — **whether it is worthwhile** me pregunto si vale la pena; **I don't** — **your honesty** no dudo de su honradez.

questionable ['kwestʃənəbl] *adj* cuestionable, dudoso, discutible; **it is** — **whether** . . . es dudoso si . . .; **in** — **taste** de gusto dudoso.

questionary ['kwestʃənəri] *n* cuestionario *m*.

questioner ['kwestʃənə*] *n* interrogador *m*, ora *f*.

questioning ['kwestʃəniŋ] **1** *adj* interrogativo. **2** *n* preguntas *fpl*; (*by police etc*) interrogatorio *m*.

question mark ['kwestʃənmɑ:k] *n* punto *m* de interrogación; (*fig*) interrogante *f*; **a big** — **hangs over him** sobre él pende una interrogante mayúscula.

questionnaire [,kwestʃə'neə*] *n* cuestionario *m*.

queue [kju:] **1** *n* cola *f*; **to form a** —, **to stand in a** — hacer cola; **to jump the** — salirse de una cola.

2 *vi* (*also* **to** — **up**) hacer cola; **to** — **for something** hacer cola para comprar (*etc*) algo; **to** — **for 3 hours** pasar 3 horas haciendo cola.

quibble ['kwibl] **1** *n* sofistería *f*, sutileza *f*; objeción *f* de poca monta; **that's just a** — eso es pura sofistería, eso es extremar demasiado en el vocablo.

2 *vi* usar sofisterías, sutilizar, buscar evasivas; hacer objeciones de poca monta; **he always** —**s es** un sofista; **you can't** — **about that** no puedes hacer objeciones acerca de eso.

quibbler ['kwiblə*] *n* sofista *mf*.

quibbling ['kwibliŋ] *n* sofistería *f*, sofismas *mpl*; sutilezas *fpl*; objeciones *fpl* de poca monta.

quick [kwik] **1** *adj* (*speedy*) rápido; veloz; (*early*) pronto; (*of foot*) ligero, veloz; (*agile*) ágil; (*in mind*) listo, inteligente; *ear* fino; *eye*, *wit etc* agudo; *temper* vivo; **a** — **train** un tren rápido; **the** —**est method** el método más rápido; **a** — **reply** una pronta contestación; **for a** — **sale** para poder venderlo pronto; **as** — **as a flash, as** — **as lightning** como un relámpago; **be** —! ¡pronto! ¡date prisa!; **and just be** — **about it!** ¡no te entretengas!; **you have been very** — **about it** lo has hecho con la mayor prontitud; **he's too** — **for me** (*in speech*) habla demasiado de prisa para mí, (*in escaping*) corre más que yo, (*in intelligence*) es demasiado listo para mí; **to be** — **to act** obrar con prontitud; **to be** — **to take offence** ofenderse por poca cosa; **to be** — **to anger** tener repentinos enojos; **to be** — **to pity** tener repentina compasión; **to have a** — **one** beberse un trago sin pérdida de tiempo; **let's have a** — **one** entremos a tomar algo.

2 *n* **(a)** (*Anat*) carne *f* viva; **to cut someone to the** — herir a uno en lo vivo.

(b) the — (*living*) los vivos; **the** — **and the dead** los vivos y los muertos.

3 *adv* see **quickly**.

quick-acting ['kwik'æktiŋ] *adj* extrarrápido.

quick-change ['kwik'tʃeindʒ] *adj*: — **actor** transformista *m*.

quick-eared ['kwik'iəd] *adj* de oído fino.

quicken ['kwikən] **1** *vt* acelerar, apresurar; avivar; **to** — **one's pace** apretar el paso. **2** *vi* acelerarse, apresurarse; avivarse; (*embryo*) empezar a moverse.

quick-eyed ['kwik'aid] *adj* de vista aguda.

quick-fire ['kwikfaiə*] *adj* de tiro rápido; *question etc* rápido, hecho a quemarropa.

quick-firing ['kwik,faiəriŋ] *adj* de tiro rápido.

quick-freeze ['kwikfri:z] *adj* de congelación rápida.

quickie ['kwiki] *n* (*fam*) pregunta *f* relámpago.

quicklime ['kwiklaim] *n* cal *f* viva.

quickly ['kwikli] *adv* rápidamente; de prisa; pronto; —! ¡pronto!; **they answered** — contestaron pronto; **the next phase followed** — la etapa siguiente empezó inmediatamente; **he talks too** — **for me to understand** habla demasiado rápidamente para que yo pueda entenderle; **come as** — **as you can** ven cuanto antes, ven lo más pronto que puedas; **the firemen were** — **on the spot** los bomberos se presentaron sin pérdida de tiempo.

quickness ['kwiknis] *n* rapidez *f*, velocidad *f*; prontitud *f*, presteza *f*; agilidad *f*; inteligencia *f*; penetración *f*; finura *f*; agudeza *f*; viveza *f*.

quicksand ['kwiksænd] *n* arena *f* movediza.

quickset ['kwikset] **1** *adj* compuesto de plantas vivas, (*esp*) de espinos. **2** *n* (*slip*) plantón *m*; (*hawthorn*) espino *m*; (*hedge*) seto *m* vivo (*esp* de espinos).

quick-sighted ['kwik'saitid] *adj* de vista aguda.

quicksilver ['kwik,silvə*] **1** *n* azogue *m*, mercurio *m*. **2** *adj* azogado; (*fig*) inconstante, caprichoso. **3** *vt* azogar.

quick-tempered ['kwik'tempəd] *adj* de genio vivo, de prontos enojos.

quick-witted ['kwik'witid] *adj* agudo, perspicaz; **that was very** — **of you** en eso has sido muy perspicaz.

quid[1] [kwid] *n* (*sl*) libra *f* esterlina; **3** — 3 libras.

quid[2] [kwid] *n* mascada *f* (de tabaco).

quiddity ['kwiditi] *n* (*Philos*) esencia *f*; (*quibble*) sutileza *f*, sofistería *f*.

quid pro quo ['kwidprəu'kwəu] *n* compensación *f*, recompensa *f* (*for de*).

quiescence [kwai'esns] *n* quietud *f*, inactividad *f*; reposo *m*.

quiescent [kwai'esnt] *adj* quieto, inactivo; reposado.

quiet ['kwaiət] **1** *adj* **(a)** (*silent*) silencioso, callado; *person* (*by nature*) callado, reservado; *place, town etc* tranquilo; (*pej: of town life etc*) aburrido; (*of engine etc*) sin ruido, que no hace ruido, silencioso; (*not excited*) tranquilo, reposado; —!, **be** —! (*to people*) ¡silencio!, (*more forcefully*) ¡a callar!, (*to 1 person*) ¡cállate!; **to be** —(*person: after speaking*) callarse, (*in moving about*) no hacer ruido; **isn't it** —? ¡qué silencio!; **it was as** — **as the grave** había un silencio sepulcral; **to keep** — no hacer ruido; no decir nada, quedar callado, callarse; **keep those bottles** —! ¡no haga tanto ruido con esas botellas!; **they paid £100 to keep him** — pagaron 100 libras para tenerle callado.

(b) *temperament* tranquilo, sosegado; *animal* manso.

(c) *dress etc* no llamativo, discreto; *colour* suave.

(d) (*not overt*) discreto; (*private*) más bien privado; íntimo, que se celebra en la intimidad; (*informal*) íntimo, sin ceremonias; **with** — **humour he said** . . . ligeramente guasón dijo . . .; **all** — **here** aquí sin novedad; **all** — **on the Western Front** sin novedad en el frente del oeste; **it was a** — **wedding** la boda se celebró en la intimidad; **we had a** — **supper** cenamos en la intimidad; **business is very** — el negocio está muy flojo; **to have a** — **dig at someone** burlarse discretamente de uno; **they lead a** — **life** llevan una vida tranquila

2 *n* silencio *m*; paz *f*; tranquilidad *f*; reposo *m*; **an hour of blessed** — una hora de paz bendita; **on the** — a la sordina, a hurtadillas; **let's have complete** — quiero que se callen completamente todos.

3 *vt* calmar; see **quieten**.

quieten ['kwaiətn] **1** *vt* (*also* **to** — **down**) (*calm*) calmar, tranquilizar; (*silence*) hacer callar; **he managed to** — **the crowd** logró tranquilizar a la multitud.

2 *vi* (*also* **to** — **down**) calmarse, tranquilizarse; callarse; (*after unruly youth etc*) sentar los cascos, hacerse más juicioso.

quietism ['kwaiitizəm] *n* quietismo *m*.

quietist ['kwaiitist] *n* quietista *mf*.

quietly ['kwaiətli] *adv* **(a)** silenciosamente, en silencio, calladamente; tranquilamente; sin hacer ruido; **he said —** dijo dulcemente, dijo en tono bajo; **please play more —** procure tocar con menos ruido, por favor; **she came in —** entró sin hacer ruido.

(b) sosegadamente; mansamente.

(c) discretamente; **to be — dressed** ir vestido con discreción.

(d) discretamente; en la intimidad, en privado; sin ceremonias; **let's get married —** casémonos sin ceremonias; **we dined — at home** cenamos en la intimidad del hogar.

quietness ['kwaiətnis] n (a) silencio m; paz f; tranquilidad f; reposo m; **the — of her voice** lo dulce de su voz.

(b) sosiego m, lo sosegado; mansedumbre f.

(c) discreción f.

(d) discreción f; intimidad f.

quietude ['kwaiətjuːd] n quietud f.

quietus [kwaiˈiːtəs] n golpe m de gracia; (death) muerte f.

quiff [kwif] n copete m.

quill [kwil] n (Zool) pluma f de ave; (part of feather) cañón m de pluma; (pen) pluma f (de ganso); (in fishing) cañón m de pluma; (spine) púa f; (bobbin) canilla f.

quill-pen ['kwil'pen] n pluma f (de ganso).

quilt [kwilt] 1 n colcha f, edredón m. 2 vt acolchar.

quilting ['kwiltiŋ] n colchadura f.

quince [kwins] n (fruit, tree) membrillo m.

quince cheese ['kwins'tʃiːz] n carne f de membrillo.

quince jelly ['kwins'dʒeli] n conserva f de membrillo.

quincentenary [ˌkwinsen'tiːnəri] n quinto centenario m.

quinine [kwi'niːn] n quinina f.

Quinquagesima [ˌkwiŋkwə'dʒesimə] n Quincuagésima f.

quinquennial [kwiŋ'kweniəl] adj quinquenal.

quinquennium [kwiŋ'kweniəm] n quinquenio m.

quins [kwinz] npl (fam) see **quintuplets.**

quinsy ['kwinzi] n angina f.

quint [kwint] n (US fam) quintillizo m, a f.

quintessence [kwin'tesns] n quinta esencia f.

quintet(te) [kwin'tet] n quinteto m.

quintuple ['kwintjupl] 1 adj quíntuplo. 2 n quíntuplo m.

quintuple ['kwin'tjuːpl] 1 vt quintuplicar. 2 vi quintuplicarse.

quintuplets [kwin'tjuːplits] npl quintillizos mpl, quintillizas fpl.

quip [kwip] 1 n chiste m, agudeza f, pulla f. 2 vi hacer un chiste; "—", he —ped "—", dijo humorísticamente.

quire ['kwaiə*] n mano f de papel.

quirk [kwəːk] n (oddity) peculiaridad f, rasgo m peculiar; capricho m; (flourish) rasgo m; (Archit) avivador m; **by some — of fate** por algún capricho de la suerte; **it's just a — he has** son cosas suyas, es un rasgo peculiar suyo.

quisling ['kwizliŋ] n quisling m, colaboracionista m.

quit [kwit] (irr: pret and ptp quit or quitted) 1 vt dejar, abandonar; place abandonar, salir de; premises etc desocupar; **to — one's job** abandonar su puesto, dimitir; **to — work** suspender el trabajo; **to — + ger** (esp US) dejar de + infin, desistir de + infin; **— fooling!** ¡déjate de tonterías!; **it's time to — dreaming** es hora de renunciar a los sueños.

2 vi (go away) irse, marcharse; (withdraw) retirarse; (resign) dimitir; (give up, in game etc) abandonar; (stop work) suspender el trabajo; (be a quitter) renunciar a una empresa, abandonar, rajarse; **I —!** ¡me rajo!

3 adj: **to be — of someone** estar libre de algo, haberse librado de uno.

quite [kwait] adv (a) (completely) totalmente, completamente; **— new** completamente nuevo; **— a hero** todo un héroe (also iro); **— so!** ¡se comprende!,

¡así es!, perfectamente; **oh, — that!** ¡lo menos eso!; **that's — enough** eso basta y sobra; **that's — enough for me** eso me basta a mí; **not — as many as last time** no tantos como la última vez; **I — understand** lo comprendo perfectamente; **that's not — right** eso no está del todo bien; **he has not — recovered yet** no se ha repuesto todavía del todo; **it was — 3 months** era lo menos 3 meses; **it's not — what we wanted** no es exactamente lo que buscábamos; **we don't — know** no sabemos exactamente; **he's — grown up now** ahora está hecho un hombre; es todo un hombre.

(b) (rather) bastante; **it's — good** es bastante bueno; **it was — a surprise** me sorprendió bastante; **I — believe that . . .** casi tengo la certeza de que . . .

quits [kwits] adv: **to be — with someone** estar en paz con uno; **now we're —!** ¡ahora no nos debemos nada!; **let's call it —** hagamos las paces; **to cry —** (querer) hacer las paces.

quitter ['kwitə*] n remolón m, persona f que deja fácilmente lo empezado; cobarde mf.

quiver[1] ['kwivə*] n carcaj m, aljaba f.

quiver[2] ['kwivə*] 1 n temblor m, estremecimiento m. 2 vi temblar, estremecerse (with de).

qui vive [kiːˈviːv]: **to be on the —** estar alerta.

Quixote ['kwiksət] m Quijote.

quixotic [kwik'sɔtik] adj quijotesco.

quixotically [kwik'sɔtikəli] adv quijotescamente.

quixotism ['kwiksətizəm] n quijotismo m.

quiz [kwiz] 1 n (interrogation) interrogatorio m; examen m; (inquiry) encuesta f; (Radio etc; also **— programme**) concurso m (radiofónico etc).

2 vt (stare at) mirar con curiosidad; (question) interrogar (about sobre).

quizzical ['kwizikəl] adj burlón.

quizzically ['kwizikəli] adv: **he looked at me —** me miró burlón.

quod [kwɔd] n (sl) chirona f.

quoin [kwɔin] n (angle) esquina f, ángulo m; (stone) piedra f angular; (Typ) cuña f.

quoit [kwɔit] n aro m, tejo m; **—s** juego m de aros, juego m de tejos.

quondam ['kwɔndæm] adj antiguo.

Quonset ['kwɔnsit] n (Protected Trade Name in US) cobertizo m de metal semicilíndrico.

quorum ['kwɔːrəm] n quórum m; **to constitute a —** constituir un quórum; **what number constitutes a —?** ¿cuántos constituyen un quórum?

quota ['kwəutə] n cuota f; (Comm etc) contingente m, cupo m; **import —** cupo m de importación.

quotable ['kwəutəbl] adj citable; digno de citarse; (Fin) cotizable.

quotation [kwəu'teiʃən] n (words) cita f; (act) citación f; (Fin) cotización f.

quotation marks [kwəu'teiʃən,maːks] npl comillas fpl.

quote [kwəut] 1 vt (a) citar; reference number etc expresar; example dar, aducir; **he —d Góngora** citó a Góngora; **he can — Góngora all day long** es capaz de seguir recitando versos de Góngora hasta cuando sea; **please — the number of the postal order** por favor exprese el número del giro postal; **can you — me an example?** ¿puede darme un ejemplo?

(b) (Fin) cotizar (at en); **it is not —d on the Stock Exchange** no se cotiza en la Bolsa.

2 vi citar; **to — from an author** citar versos (etc) de un autor; **and I — y** aquí cito sus propias palabras.

3 n cita f; **—s** (inverted commas) comillas fpl; **"—"** "comienza la cita"; **"close the —",** "end of —"** "fin de la cita".

quoth [kwəuθ] vi (arch): **— I** dije yo; **— he** dijo él.

quotient ['kwəuʃənt] n cociente m; **intelligence —** cociente m intelectual.

R

rabbi ['ræbai] n rabino m; (before name) rabí m; **chief —** gran rabino m.

rabbinical [rə'binikəl] adj rabínico.

rabbit ['ræbit] **1** n conejo m; (Sport, fam) jugador m inhábil; **Peter R—** el Conejo Peter; **Welsh —** pan m con queso tostado.
2 vi: **to go —ing** (ir a) cazar conejos.

rabbit hole ['ræbithəul] n hura f de conejos.

rabbit hutch ['ræbithʌtʃ] n conejera f.

rabbit warren ['ræbit,wɔrən] n madriguera f de conejos.

rabble ['ræbl] n (the —) canalla f, chusma f; **a — of** una multitud turbulenta de.

rabble-rouser ['ræbl,rauzə*] n agitador m, demagogo m.

rabble-rousing ['ræbl'rauziŋ] n agitación f, demagogia f.

Rabelaisian [,ræbə'leiziən] adj rabelasiano.

rabid ['ræbid] adj (Med) rabioso; (fig) rabioso, fanático.

rabies ['reibiːz] n rabia f.

raccoon [rə'kuːn] n mapache m.

race[1] [reis] **1** n (a) (contest) carrera f, (on water) regata f; **—s** carreras fpl; **the — for the moon** la carrera hacia la luna; **— against the clock** carrera f contra reloj; **arms —** carrera f de armamentos; **flat —** carrera f lisa; **long-distance —** carrera f de fondo; **relay —** carrera f de relevos; **walking —** carrera f pedestre; **to go to the —s** ir a las carreras; **to run a —** tomar parte en una carrera; **you ran a good —** corriste muy bien.
(b) (rush) carrera f, corrida f; **— to the bus** la carrera precipitada para coger el autobús; **it was a — to finish it in time** nos dimos prisa para terminarlo a tiempo.
(c) (current) corriente f fuerte; (of mill) caz m, saetín m.
2 vt (a) horse etc hacer correr, (at race meeting) presentar.
(b) **to — someone** competir con uno en una carrera (or regata); **I'll — you!** ¡te echo una carrera!, ¡a ver quién corre más!; **I'll — you home!** ¡a ver quién llega primero a casa!
(c) (Aut etc) **to — an engine** acelerar un motor al máximo, hacer funcionar un motor a velocidad excesiva.
(d) **to — a plan through** hacer que se apruebe un proyecto de prisa; no permitir que se discuta debidamente un proyecto.
3 vi (a) (go fast) correr de prisa, (Aut etc) ir a máxima velocidad; **to — along** ir corriendo; **to — down a hill** ir cuesta abajo a máxima velocidad; **he —d past us** pasó delante de nosotros corriendo como un demonio.
(b) (pulse) latir a ritmo acelerado; (engine) girar a velocidad excesiva.
(c) (in contest) competir; presentarse; **they will — at 3 o'clock** empezarán la carrera a las 3; **we're not racing today** no tomamos parte hoy; **when did you last —?** ¿cuándo corriste (etc) la última vez?

race[2] [reis] n raza f; casta f, estirpe f, familia f; (pej) ralea f; (Bio) raza f; **human —** género m humano; **the white —** la raza blanca; **he comes from a — of smugglers** es de linaje de contrabandistas.

race card ['reiskaːd] n programa m de carreras.

racecourse ['reiskɔːs] n hipódromo m, cancha f (S Am).

racegoer [reisgəuə*] n el m (or la f) que asiste a las carreras, aficionado m a las carreras (de caballos).

race hatred ['reis'heitrid] n odio m racial.

racehorse ['reishɔːs] n caballo m de carreras.

raceme ['ræsiːm] n racimo m.

race meeting ['reis,miːtiŋ] n reunión f; concurso m hípico.

racer ['reisə*] n corredor m; (horse) caballo m de carreras; (Aut) coche m de carreras.

race riot ['reis,raiət] n disturbio m provocado por odios raciales, motín m de carácter racista.

racetrack ['reistræk] n (horses) pista f, cancha f (SAm), hipódromo m; (Aut etc) autódromo m.

Rachel ['reitʃəl] f Raquel.

rachitic [ræ'kitik] adj raquítico.

racial ['reiʃəl] adj racial; racista.

racialism ['reiʃəlizəm] n racismo m.

racialist ['reiʃəlist] **1** adj racista. **2** n racista mf.

raciness ['reisinis] n picante m, sal f, vivacidad f.

racing ['reisiŋ] **1** n carreras fpl.
2 attr de carreras; **— calendar** calendario m de carreras (de caballos); **— car** coche m de carreras; **— driver, — motorist** corredor m automovilista.

racism ['reisizəm] n racismo m.

rack[1] [ræk] **1** n (shelf) estante m, estantería f, anaquel m; (for clothes etc) percha f, perchero m, cuelgacapas m; (Rail) rejilla f; (Mech) cremallera f; (for torture) potro m; (for arms) armero m; (for billiard cues) taquera f; **— and pinion** cremallera f y piñón.
2 vt atormentar; **to be —ed by pains** tener dolores atroces por todas partes; **to be —ed by remorse** ser atormentado por el remordimiento; see **brain.**

rack[2] [ræk] vt wine (also **to — off**) trasegar.

rack[3] [ræk] n: **to go to — and ruin** arruinarse, echarse a perder.

racket[1] ['rækit] n, **racquet** ['rækit] n raqueta f; **—s** (game) especie de tenis jugado contra frontón.

racket[2] ['rækit] **1** n (a) (din) ruido m, estrépito m; (confused noise) barahúnda f, jaleo m; **you never heard such a —!** ¡no se había oído nunca tal ruido!; **to kick up** (or **make**) **a —** armar un jaleo, meter ruido.
(b) (trick) trampa f, trapacería f; (criminal) estafa f, timo m; (blackmail, protection) chantaje m; **the drug —** el negocio ilegal de los narcóticos; **the car —** (hum) el negocio del automóvil; **it's a —!** ¡aquí hay trampa!; **what — are you in?** ¿a qué se dedica Vd?; **to stand the —** pagar los platos rotos.
2 vi (make noise) hacer ruido, armar un jaleo (also **to — about**); (celebrate) jaranear.

racketeer [,ræki'tiə*] n (esp US) estafador m, timador m; chantajista m.

racketeering [,ræki'tiəriŋ] n (esp US) chantaje m sistematizado, crimen m organizado.

racking ['rækiŋ] adj pain atroz.

rack railway ['ræk'reilwei] n ferrocarril m de cremallera.

rack-rent ['rækrent] n alquiler m exorbitante.

raconteur [,rækɔn'tə:*] n narrador m, (esp) el que cuenta con gracia los chistes.

racoon [rə'kuːn] n mapache m.

racquet ['rækit] n see **racket**[1].

racy ['reisi] adj picante, salado, vivo.

radar ['reidaː*] n radar m.

radar screen ['reidaːskriːn] n pantalla f de radar.

radar station ['reidaː,steiʃən] n estación f de radar.

raddle ['rædl] **1** n almagre m. **2** vt almagrar.

radial ['reidiəl] adj radial.

radiance ['reidiəns] n brillantez f, resplandor m.

radiant ['reidiənt] adj radiante, brillante, resplandeciente; **a — smile** una sonrisa radiante; **the bride was —** la novia estaba hermosísima; **to be — with happiness** estar radiante de felicidad.

radiantly ['reidiəntli] adv brillantemente; **to be — happy** irradiar felicidad; **to smile — at someone** echar una sonrisa radiante a uno.

radiate[1] ['reidieit] adj radiado.

radiate² ['reidieit] *vt* radiar, irradiar; *happiness etc* difundir; **lines that — from the centre** líneas *fpl* que se extienden desde el centro.

radiation [,reidi'eiʃən] *n* radiación *f*.

radiation sickness [,reidi'eiʃən,siknis] *n* enfermedad *f* de radiación.

radiator ['reidieitə*] *n* radiador *m*.

radiator cap ['reidieitə,kæp] *n* (*Aut*) tapón *m* de radiador.

radical ['rædikəl] **1** *adj* radical. **2** *n* (*all senses*) radical *m*.

radicalism ['rædikəlizəm] *n* radicalismo *m*.

radically ['rædikəli] *adv* radicalmente.

radicle ['rædikl] *n* (*Bot*) radícula *f*.

radio ['reidiəu] **1** *n* (*as science etc*) radio *f*, radiofonía *f*; (*set*) radio *f*, receptor *m* de radio, radiorreceptor *m*; **by —, on the —, over the —** por radio; **to talk on the —** hablar por radio.
  2 *attr*: **— announcer** locutor *m* de radio, locutora *f* de radio; **— play** comedia *f* radiofónica; **— programme** programa *m* de radio.
  3 *vt* radiar, transmitir por radio.
  4 *vi*: **to — to someone** enviar un mensaje a uno por radio.

radioactive ['reidiəu'æktiv] *adj* radiactivo.

radioactivity ['reidiəuæk'tiviti] *n* radiactividad *f*.

radio astronomy ['reidiəuəs'trɔnəmi] *n* radioastronomía *f*.

radio beacon ['reidiəu,bi:kən] *n* radiofaro *m*.

radiobiology [,reidiəubai'ɔlədʒi] *n* radiobiología *f*.

radio-controlled ['reidiəukən'trəuld] *adj* teledirigido.

radiogram ['reidiəugræm] *n* (*set*) radiogramola *f*; (*message*) radiograma *m*.

radiograph ['reidiəugrɑ:f] **1** *n* radiografía *f*. **2** *vt* radiografiar.

radiographer [,reidi'ɔgrəfə*] *n* ayudante *mf* radiólogo.

radiography [,reidi'ɔgrəfi] *n* radiografía *f*.

radioisotope ['reidiəu'aisətəup] *n* radioisótopo *m*.

radiologist [,reidi'ɔlədʒist] *n* radiólogo *m*.

radiology [,reidi'ɔlədʒi] *n* radiología *f*.

radioscopy [,reidi'ɔskəpi] *n* radioscopia *f*.

radio set ['reidiəu,set] *n* radio *f*, receptor *m* de radio, radiorreceptor *m*.

radio station ['reidiəu,steiʃən] *n* emisora *f*.

radiotelephone ['reidiəu'telifəun] *n* radioteléfono *m*.

radiotelephony [,reidiəutə'lefəni] *n* radiotelefonía *f*.

radio telescope ['reidiəu'teliskəup] *n* radiotelescopia *m*.

radiotherapy ['reidiəu'θerəpi] *n* radioterapia *f*.

radish ['rædiʃ] *n* rábano *m*.

radium ['reidiəm] *n* radio *m*.

radius ['reidiəs] *n*, *pl* **radii** ['reidiai] (*all senses*) radio *m*; **within a — of 50 miles** en un radio de 50 millas.

radix ['reidiks] *n*, *pl* **radices** ['reidisi:z] (*Bot*, *Gram*) raíz *f*; (*Math*) base *f*.

raffia ['ræfiə] *n* rafia *f*.

raffish ['ræfiʃ] *adj* disipado, disoluto.

raffle ['ræfl] **1** *n* rifa *f*, sorteo *m*. **2** *vt* rifar, sortear; **10 bottles will be —d for charity** se sortearán 10 botellas con fines benéficos.

raft [rɑːft] *n* balsa *f*, almadía *f*; **life-saving —** balsa *f* salvavidas; **rubber —** balsa *f* neumática.

rafter ['rɑːftə*] *n* viga *f*, cabrio *m*.

rag¹ [ræg] *n* (**a**) (*piece of cloth*) trapo; (*for cleaning*) trapo *m*, paño *m*; (*shred of clothing*) andrajo *m*, harapo *m*; **—s** (*clothes: fam*) trapos *mpl*; **to be in —s** estar harapiento, estar en andrajos; **to chew the —** (US: *chat*) charlar, pasar el rato, (*argue*) discutir; **to feel like a —** estar hecho cisco; **she hasn't a — to her back** no tiene con qué vestirse; **to put on one's glad —s** endomingarse; **it's like a red — to a bull** es lo que más le provoca a cólera, no hay nada que más le enfurezca.
  (**b**) (*newspaper: fam*) periodicucho *m* (*fam*).

rag² [ræg] **1** *n* (**a**) (*practical joke*) broma *f* pesada; (*Univ*) broma *f* estudiantil, (*for charity*) función *f* estudiantil benéfica; **we did it just for a —** lo hicimos en broma nada más.
  2 *vt* dar guerra a, tomar el pelo a; **they were —ging him about his new tie** le estaban tomando el pelo con motivo de la nueva corbata.
  3 *vi* guasearse, bromearse; **I was only —ging** lo dije en broma.

ragamuffin ['rægə,mʌfin] *n* granuja *m*, galopín *m*.

rag-and-bone man [,rægən'bəunmæn] *n*, *pl* **— men** [men] trapero *m*.

ragbag ['rægbæg] *n* talego *m* de recortes; (*fig*)

mezcolanza *f*, cajón *m* de sastre; **it's a — of a book** es un libro hecho de muchos trozos insertos sin orden.

rag doll ['ræg'dɔl] *n* muñeca *f* de trapo.

rage [reidʒ] **1** *n* (**a**) (*anger*) rabia *f*, furor *m*, ira *f*; (*of wind etc*) furia *f*; **to be in a —** estar furioso (*about* por, *with someone* contra uno); **to fly into a —** encolerizarse; **to vent one's — on someone** descargar su indignación sobre uno.
  (**b**) (*fashion*) boga *f*, moda *f* (*for* de); (*craze*) manía *f* (*for* de); **it's all the —** es la moda, es la última; **his dresses are all the — in New York** sus vestidos hacen furor en Nueva York.
  2 *vi* (**a**) (*be angry*) estar furioso, rabiar; **to — against someone** estar furioso contra uno; culpar amargamente a uno; **to — against something** protestar furiosamente contra algo.
  (**b**) (*of pain*) doler atrozmente; (*sea etc*) enfurecerse; (*wind*) bramar; (*fire, plague etc*) desencadenarse; continuar con pleno vigor; **fire —d in the building for 3 hours** durante 3 horas no se pudo apagar el incendio que consumía el edificio.

rag fair ['rægfeə*] *n* rastro *m*, feria *f* de objetos usados.

ragged ['rægid] *adj* dress roto; *person* andrajoso, harapiento; *edge* desigual, mellado; *coastline etc* accidentado; *line, procession* confuso, desordenado, sin orden; *style* descuidado; (*Mus*) *note* poco suave.

ragged robin ['rægid'rɔbin] *n* (*Bot*) cuclillo *m*.

raging ['reidʒiŋ] *adj* rabioso, furioso; *storm etc* violento; *pain* atroz, agudo; **to be in a — temper** estar furiosísimo.

raglan ['ræglən] *n* raglán *m*.

ragman ['rægmæn] *n*, *pl* **—men** [men] trapero *m*.

ragout ['rægu:] *n* guisado *m*.

ragpicker ['rægpikə*] *n* trapero *m*.

rag tag ['rægtæg] *n* (*fam*) chusma *f* (*also* **— and bobtail**).

ragtime ['rægtaim] *n* (*Mus*) tiempo *m* sincopado; **in —** sincopado.

rag trade ['rægtreid] *n* (*fam*) industria *f* del vestido, comercio *m* del vestido.

ragwort ['rægwə:t] *n* hierba *f* lombriguera.

raid [reid] **1** *n* (*into territory across border etc*) incursión *f*, correría *f*; (*Aer*) ataque *m* (*on* contra), bombardeo *m* (*on* de); (*sweep by police*) redada *f*; (*by criminals*) asalto *m* (*on* a); **the men are away on a —** los hombres están fuera en una correría; **only 5 aircraft returned from the —** solamente 5 aviones regresaron después del ataque; **there was a — on the jeweller's last night** anoche fue asaltada la joyería.
  2 *vt* (*by land*) invadir, atacar, hacer una incursión en; (*Aer*) atacar, bombardear; (*by criminals*) asaltar; **the boys —ed the orchard** los muchachos invadieron el huerto; **the police —ed the club** la policía registró el club; **shall we — the larder?** ¿asaltamos la despensa?, ¿vamos a coger algo en la despensa?; **the king's tomb had already been —ed** la tumba del rey había sido ya saqueada.

raider ['reidə*] *n* (*across frontier*) invasor *m*, incursor *m*; (*Aer*) bombardero *m*; (*Naut*) buque *m* corsario; (*criminal*) criminal *m*, asaltante *m*, ladrón *m*; **the —s got away with some diamonds** los ladrones se llevaron varios diamantes.

rail¹ [reil] **1** *n* (**a**) (*hand—*) baranda *f*, barandilla *f*, pasamanos *m*; (*Naut*) barandilla *f*; borda *f*; (*of bar*) apoyo *m* para los pies; **—s** (*fence*) cerca *f*, palizada *f*.
  (**b**) (*Rail*) carril *m*, riel *m*; **—s** (*freq*) vía *f*; **—s** (*Fin*) acciones *fpl* de sociedades ferroviarias; **to come off** (*or* **run off, jump, leave**) **the —s** descarrilar; **to run off the —s** (*fig*) extraviarse; **by —** por ferrocarril.
  2 *vt* (**a**) (*also* **to — in, to — off**) cercar con una barandilla, poner barandilla a.
  (**b**) (*Rail*) transportar por ferrocarril, mandar por ferrocarril.

rail² [reil] *n* (*Orn*) rascón *m*.

rail³ [reil] *vi*: **to — at, to — against** protestar amargamente contra, quejarse amargamente de.

railhead ['reilhed] *n* estación *f* terminal.

railing ['reiliŋ] *n* baranda *f*, barandilla *f*, pasamanos *m*; **—s** verja *f*, enrejado *m*.

raillery ['reiləri] *n* burlas *fpl*, chanzas *fpl*.

railroad ['reilrəud] **1** *n* (US) see **railway**.
  2 *vt person* (*sl*) encarcelar falsamente; **to — something through** llevar algo a cabo muy precipitadamente; **to — a bill through** hacer que se apruebe un decreto de ley sin discutirse.

railway ['reilwei] **1** *n* ferrocarril *m*; (*as track*) vía *f*, vía *f* férrea; (*as route*) línea *f* (de ferrocarril);

aerial — funicular *m* aéreo; **elevated** —, **overhead** — ferrocarril *m* elevado; **narrow-gauge** — ferrocarril *m* de vía estrecha; **scenic** — montaña *f* rusa; **underground** — ferrocarril *m* subterráneo. **2** *attr* ferroviario.

railway carriage ['reilwei,kærid3] *n* vagón *m*, coche *m* (de ferrocarril).

railway engine ['reilwei,end3in] *n* máquina *f*, locomotora *f*.

railway line ['reilwei,lain] *n* (*track*) vía *f*, vía *f* férrea; (*route*) línea *f* (de ferrocarril).

railwayman ['reilweimən] *n*, *pl* **—men** [mən] ferroviario *m*.

railway station ['reilwei,steiʃən] *n* estación *f* (de ferrocarril).

railway ticket ['reilwei,tikit] *n* billete *m* de ferrocarril.

raiment ['reimənt] *n* (*lit*) hábitos *mpl*, vestimenta *f*.

rain [rein] **1** *n* lluvia *f* (*also fig*); **the —s** la época de las lluvias; **a — of gifts** una lluvia de regalos; **a walk in the —** un paseo bajo la lluvia; **to be out in the —** estar fuera aguantando la lluvia; **come in out of the —!** ¡entra, que te vas a mojar!; **come — or shine** (*fig*) contra viento y marea; **if the — keeps off** si no llueve; **it looks like —** parece que va a llover.
  2 *vti* llover; **to — blows on someone** llover golpes sobre uno; **to — gifts on someone** colmar a uno de regalos; **hereabouts it —s soot** por aquí llueve hollín; **to — cats and dogs** llover a cántaros; **blows —ed upon him** llovieron sobre él los golpes; **gifts —ed upon him** le llovieron regalos encima; **it —s on the just as well as on the unjust** la lluvia cae sobre los buenos como sobre los malos; **it never —s but it pours** (*fig*) llueve sobre mojado, una desgracia nunca viene sola.

rain belt ['reinbelt] *n* zona *f* de lluvias.

rainbow ['reinbəu] *n* arco *m* iris.

rainbow trout ['reinbəu'traut] *n* trucha *f* arco iris.

raincoat ['reinkəut] *n* impermeable *m*.

raincloud ['reinklaud] *n* nubarrón *m*.

raindrop ['reindrɔp] *n* gota *f* de agua.

rainfall ['reinfɔ:l] *n* (*act*) precipitación *f*; (*quantity*) lluvia *f*, cantidad *f* de lluvia; **the region has 3" of — a year** la región tiene 3 pulgadas de lluvia al año.

rain gauge ['reingeid3] *n* pluviómetro *m*.

raininess ['reininis] *n* lo lluvioso.

rainless ['reinlis] *adj* sin lluvia, seco.

rainproof ['reinpru:f] *adj* impermeable, a prueba de lluvia.

rainstorm ['reinstɔ:m] *n* tempestad *f* de lluvia.

rainwater ['reinwɔ:tə*] *n* agua *f* llovediza, agua *f* de lluvia.

rainy ['reini] *adj* *climate*, *region* lluvioso; **— day** día *m* de lluvia, (*fig*) tiempo *m* de escasez; **— season** estación *f* de las lluvias; **it was so — yesterday** llovió tanto ayer.

raise [reiz] **1** *n* (*esp US*) aumento *m*, subida *f*; (*of salary*) aumento *m* de sueldo; (*Cards*) sobremarca *f*.
  2 *vt* (*in some senses also* **to — up**) **(a)** (*lift*) *fallen object*, *weight*, *arm*, *eyes etc* levantar, alzar, elevar; *hat* quitarse; *flag* izar, enarbolar; *dust* levantar; *dough* fermentar; *sunken ship* sacar a flote; *camp*, *siege* levantar; *spirits* evocar; (*from the dead*) resucitar; (*Math*) elevar (a una potencia); **to — one's glass** alzar el vaso; **to — someone to power** alzar a uno al poder; **to — the standard of revolt** pronunciarse, sublevarse; **to — tribesmen in revolt** sublevar las tribus; **to — the people against a tyrant** hacer que el pueblo se subleve contra un tirano; **to — someone's hopes excessively** hacer a uno concebir esperanzas desmesuradas; **to — someone's spirits** infundir ánimo a uno; **to — someone up from poverty** ayudar a uno a salir de la miseria.
  (b) (*erect*) *building* erigir, edificar; *statue* erigir.
  (c) (*increase*) *price*, *salary* aumentar, subir; *production* aumentar; *person* (*in rank*) ascender (*to* a); *voice* levantar; **don't — your voice!** ¡no levantes la voz!
  (d) (*bring up etc*) *family*, *livestock* criar; *crop* cultivar.
  (e) (*produce*) *causar*, producir; dar lugar a; *bump etc* causar; *laughter* suscitar, provocar; *doubts* suscitar; *problem*, *question* plantear; *objection* poner, hacer; *cry etc* poner; *outcry* armar; **I'll — the point with them** se lo mencionaré; **it —s many problems for us** nos plantea muchos problemas; **this —s the question of whether . . .**

esto plantea el problema de si . . .; **can't you — a smile?** ¿no guardas una sonrisa para mí?
  (f) (*get together*) *army* reclutar; *funds* reunir; *loan* lograr, obtener; *new taxes* imponer; **to — money on an estate** obtener dinero hipotecando una propiedad.
  3 *vr*: **to — oneself** alzarse, levantarse; **he —d himself up on one elbow** se apoyó en un codo; **he has —d himself up from nothing** ha salido de la nada.

raised [reizd] *adj* (*in relief*) en relieve; (*embossed*) de realce.

raisin ['reizən] *n* pasa *f* de Corinto.

raison d'être ['reiz3:n'deːtr] *n* razón *f* de ser.

raj [rɑːd3] *n*: **the British —** el imperio británico (en la India); la soberanía británica.

rajah ['rɑːd3ə] *n* rajá *m*.

rake¹ [reik] **1** *n* (*garden* —) rastrillo *m*; (*Agr*) rastro *m*; (*fire* —) hurgón *m*.
  2 *vt* (*Agr etc*) rastrillar; *fire* hurgar; (*with shots etc*) barrer; (*with eyes*) examinar, escudriñar; (*search*, *ransack*) registrar, buscar por; **to — in** *gambling chips* recoger; **they —d in a profit of £100** se sacaron 100 libras de ganancia limpia; **he —s in £5 on every deal** se toma una tajada de 5 libras de cada negocio; **he must be raking it in** está acuñando dinero; **to — off** quitar con el rastrillo; **to — together** reunir (*or* recoger) con el rastrillo; **to — together** (*fig*) reunir (con dificultad); **we managed to — a team together** por fin logramos formar un equipo; **to — up** *subject* sacar a relucir; *the past etc* remover; **why did you have to — that up?** ¿con qué motivo has vuelto a mencionar eso?

rake² [reik] *n* (*person*) libertino *m*, calavera *m*; **old — viejo** *m* verde.

rake³ [reik] **1** *n* (*Naut*) inclinación *f*. **2** *vt* inclinar.

rake-off ['reikɔf] *n* (*fam*) tajada *f*.

rakish¹ ['reikiʃ] *adj* (*person*) libertino, disoluto.

rakish² ['reikiʃ] *adj* *ship* de palos inclinados; (*fast-looking*) veloz, ligero; (*smart*) elegante, gallardo; **with his hat at a — angle** con el sombrero echado de lado, con el sombrero a lo chulo.

rakishly ['reikiʃli] *adv* (*of hat etc*) echado al lado, a lo chulo; elegantemente.

rally¹ ['ræli] **1** *n* (*Pol etc*) reunión *f*, mitin *m*, manifestación *f*; (*of scouts etc*) reunión *f*, congreso *m*; (*Aut*) rallye *m*; (*Tennis*) peloteo *m*; (*Mil*) repliegue *m*; (*Med*, *Fin etc*) recuperación *f*.
  2 *vt* (*gather*) reunir; (*Mil*) rehacer; *faculties* concentrar; (*encourage*) reanimar, infundir ánimo a, fortalecer.
  3 *vi* (*gather*) reunirse (*around someone*, *to someone* en torno a uno); (*demonstrate*) manifestarse; (*Mil*) replegarse, rehacerse; (*Med*, *Fin etc*) recuperarse, mejorar; **they rallied to him** se reunieron en torno a él, afirmaron su adhesión, acudieron a su lado; **to — to the call** responder a la llamada; **everyone must — round** todos hemos de afirmar nuestra unidad; **they have all rallied round nobly** todos han hecho maravillas en un esfuerzo común.

rally² ['ræli] *vt* tomar el pelo a.

rallying point ['ræliiŋ,pɔint] *n* punto *m* de reunión.

ram [ræm] **1** *n* (*Zool*) carnero *m*, morueco *m*, (*Astron*) Aries *m*; (*Mil*) ariete *m*; (*Naut*) espolón *m*; (*Tech*: *rammer*) pisón *m*, (*pile driver*) martillo *m* pilón.
  2 *vt* **(a)** (*tread down*) apisonar; (*squeeze*) apretar; (*fill*) rellenar (*with* de); **to — a charge home** introducir una carga a fondo; **they —med it down his throat** se lo hicieron tragar a la fuerza; **to — clothes into a case** poner la ropa apretadamente en una maleta; **to — something into a hole** meter algo apretadamente en un agujero, introducir algo apretadamente en un agujero; **we had Campoamor —med into us at school** nos dimos un atracón de Campoamor en el colegio.
  (b) (*collide with*) chocar con, dar contra; (*Naut*: *deliberately*) atacar con el espolón; **the car —med the lamppost** el coche chocó con el farol.

Ramadan [,ræmə'dæn] *n* ramadán *m*.

ramble ['ræmbl] **1** *n* paseo *m* por el campo, excursión *f* a pie, caminata *f*; **to go for a —** salir de excursión a pie, dar una caminata.
  2 *vi* **(a)** (*walk*) salir de excursión a pie, dar una caminata; **we spent a week rambling in the hills** pasamos una semana explorando la montaña a pie.
  (b) (*in speech*) divagar; (*lose thread*) perder el hilo, salirse del tema; (*of river etc*) serpentear; (*of plant*) extenderse como una enredadera; **he just —d on and on** siguió hablando confusamente.

rambler ['ræmblə*] *n* (*person*) excursionista *mf* (a pie); **— rose** rosal *m* trepador.

rambling ['ræmbliŋ] **1** *adj* *plant* trepador; *speech* divagador, prolijo y confuso, enmarañado; *house* laberíntico, construido sobre un plano poco lógico. **2** *n* (a) excursionismo *m* a pie; excursiones *fpl* a pie.
(b) (*also* —s) desvaríos *mpl*.

ramification [ˌræmifi'keiʃən] *n* ramificación *f*; **in all its** —s en toda su complejidad; **with numerous** —s con innumerables ramificaciones; **we don't yet know all the** —s no conocemos todavía todos los recovecos.

ramify ['ræmifai] *vi* ramificarse.

ramjet ['ræmˌdʒet] *n* postquemador *m*, tubo *m* de propulsión; — **plane** avión *m* de retropropulsión.

rammer ['ræmə*] *n* pisón *m*.

ramp¹ [ræmp] *n* (*incline*) rampa *f*.

ramp² [ræmp] *n* (*fam*) estafa *f*, timo *m*; **the housing** — el escándalo (del precio) de la vivienda; **it's a** —! ¡no hay derecho!, ¡esto no se puede consentir!

rampage [ræm'peidʒ] **1** *n*: **to be on the** — = **2** *vi* desbocarse, desmandarse; comportarse como un loco; **the crowd** —d **through the market** la multitud corrió alocada por el mercado.

rampancy ['ræmpənsi] *n* exuberancia *f*, lozanía *f*; furia *f*, desenfreno *m*; agresividad *f*, predominio *m*.

rampant ['ræmpənt] *adj* (*Her*) rampante; (*Bot*) exuberante, lozano; *person* furioso, desenfrenado; agresivo; **to be** — (*prevail*) cundir, predominar; **he's a** — **anarchist** es un anarquista furibundo; **anarchism is** — **here** aquí el anarquismo está muy extendido, aquí ha cundido mucho el anarquismo.

rampart ['ræmpɑːt] *n* terraplén *m*, defensa *f*; (*city wall*) muralla *f*; **the** —s **of York** la muralla de York.

ramrod ['ræmrɔd] *n* baqueta *f*, atacador *m*.

ramshackle ['ræmˌʃækl] *adj* desvencijado, destartalado.

ram's horn ['ræmzhɔːn] *n* cuerno *m* de carnero.

ran [ræn] *pret of* **run**; *also*— caballo *m* (*etc*) que no logró colocarse, (*fig*) fracasado *m*.

ranch [rɑːntʃ] *n* (US) hacienda *f*; estancia *f*, rancho *m* (*SAm*).

rancher ['rɑːntʃə*] *n* (US) ganadero *m*.

rancid ['rænsid] *adj* rancio.

rancidity [ræn'siditi] *n*, **rancidness** ['rænsidnis] *n* rancidez *f*, ranciedad *f*.

rancorous ['ræŋkərəs] *adj* rencoroso.

rancour, (US) **rancor** ['ræŋkə*] *n* rencor *m*; **with** — **towards none** sin rencor para nadie.

randiness ['rændinis] *n* cachondez *f*.

random ['rændəm] **1** *adj* fortuito, casual; hecho al azar, hecho sin pensar; sin orden ni concierto; *distribution* (*Math*) aleatorio; *sample* seleccionado al azar; *shot* sin apuntar.
2 *n*: **at** — al azar; sin pensar; **to choose something at** — escoger algo sin pensar; **to hit out at** — repartir golpes por todos lados; **to talk at** — hablar sin pesar las palabras.

randy ['rændi] *adj* cachondo; **to feel** — estar cachondo.

rang [ræŋ] *pret of* **ring**².

range [reindʒ] **1** *n* (a) (*row*) línea *f*, hilera *f*; (*of buildings*) grupo *m*; (*of mountains*) sierra *f*, cadena *f*, cordillera *f*.
(b) (*mostly US Agr*) dehesa *f*, terreno *m* de pasto.
(c) (*for shooting: in open*) campo *m* de tiro, (*at fair*) galería *f* de tiro, barraca *f* de tiro.
(d) (*extent*) extensión *f*; (*of voice*) extensión *f*, alcance *m*, compás *m*; (*series*) serie *f*; escala *f*, gama *f*; (*Comm*) surtido *m*; — **of action** esfera *f* de acción; — **of vision** campo *m* visual; **the present** — **of knowledge** la extensión de los conocimientos actuales; — **of variation** amplitud *f* de variación; — **of colours** gama *f* de colores; — **of prices** escala *f* de precios; — **of speeds** escala *f* de velocidades; — **of frequencies** gama *f* de frecuencias; **the** — **of someone's mind** el alcance de la inteligencia de uno; **over the whole** — **of politics** sobre todo el campo de la política; **that's outside my** — eso no pertenece a mi esfera de actividades; no sé nada de eso; **to go outside one's normal** — salir de su acostumbrada esfera de actividades; **she has a wide** — **of interests** tiene una extensa gama de intereses; **they have a new** — **of models** tienen una nueva gama de modelos.
(e) (*Bio*) distribución *f*, zona *f* de distribución; **the plant has a limited** — la planta tiene una distribución restringida; **this is outside its normal** — este sitio queda fuera de su zona acostumbrada; **its** — **extends to León** alcanza la provincia de León.

(f) (*distance attainable*: Mil) alcance *m*, alcance *m* de tiro; distancia *f*; **a gun with a** — **of 3 miles** un cañón con un alcance de 3 millas; **at a** — **of 5 miles** a una distancia de 5 millas; **at close** — de cerca, (*point-blank*) a quemarropa; **within** — al alcance, a tiro, a tiro de fusil (*etc*); **the plane is out of** — el avión está fuera de alcance; **to correct the** — corregir la puntería; **to take the** — averiguar la distancia.
(g) (*of plane, ship*) autonomía *f*, radio *m* de acción; **the** — **is 3,000 miles** la autonomía es de 3.000 millas.
(h) (*kitchen* —) cocina *f* económica, fogón *m*.
2 *vt* (a) (*arrange*) arreglar, ordenar; clasificar; (*line up*) alinear; (*place*) colocar; **he** —d **them along the wall** los colocó a lo largo de la pared.
(b) (*go about*) recorrer; **they** —d **the countryside** recorrieron el campo; **his eye** —d **the horizon** escudriñó el horizonte.
(c) **to** — **a gun** apuntar un cañón.
3 *vi* (a) (*extend*) extenderse; (*wander over*) recorrer; vagar por; **the insect** —s **from Andalusia to Burgos** el insecto se extiende desde Andalucía hasta Burgos; **research ranging over a wide field** investigaciones *fpl* que se extienden sobre un ancho campo; investigaciones *fpl* de gran alcance; **his mind** —s **widely** tiene una mentalidad de gran alcance; **the troops** —d **over the whole province** las tropas recorrieron toda la provincia.
(b) (*of numbers etc*) oscilar, variar, fluctuar; **temperatures** — **from 5 to 30 degrees** las temperaturas oscilan entre los 5 y 30 grados; **they** — **as high as 40 degrees at times** a veces suben hasta los 40 grados.
4 *vr*: **to** — **oneself with someone** ponerse al lado de uno; **to** — **oneself with a group** sumarse a un grupo.

rangefinder ['reindʒˌfaində*] *n* telémetro *m*.

ranger ['reindʒə*] *n* guardabosques *m*.

Rangoon [ræŋ'guːn] Rangún.

rangy ['reindʒi] *adj* ágil, enérgico; fuerte, robusto.

rank¹ [ræŋk] **1** *n* (a) (*row*) fila *f*, hilera *f*, línea *f*; (Mil) fila *f*; **the** —s **of poplars** las hileras de álamos; **in serried** —s en filas apretadas; **the** —s, **the** — **and file** las masas, la gente común, (*of club*) los socios ordinarios, (Mil) los soldados rasos; **in the** —s **of the party** en las filas del partido; **to break** —s romper filas; **to close the** —s apretar las filas; **to join the** —s **of** (*fig*) unirse con, llegar a ser uno de; **to reduce someone to the** —s degradar a uno; **to rise from the** —s ascender desde soldado raso, llegar a oficial.
(b) (*status*) posición *f*, categoría *f*, dignidad *f*, calidad *f*; (Mil) graduación *f*, grado *m*, rango *m*; **persons of** — gente *f* de calidad; **a writer of the first** — un escritor de primera categoría; **4 officers of high** — 4 oficiales de alta graduación; **their** —s **range from lieutenant to colonel** sus graduaciones van de teniente a coronel; **to attain the** — **of major** ser ascendido a comandante, llegar a comandante.
(c) (*taxi* —) punto *m*.
2 *vt* clasificar, ordenar; **I** — **him 6th** yo le pongo en 6ª posición; **to** — **A with B** considerar iguales A y B, poner A y B en el mismo nivel; **where would you** — **him?** ¿qué posición le daría Vd?
3 *vi* clasificarse; figurar; **to** — **4th** ocupar el 4° puesto; **to** — **2nd to someone else** tener el segundo lugar después de otra persona; **to** — **high** ocupar una alta posición; **where does she** —? ¿qué posición ocupa?; **the shares will** — **for dividend** se pagará el dividendo que corresponda a estas acciones; **to** — **above** ser superior a; **to** — **among** figurar entre; estar al nivel de; **to** — **as** equivaler a, figurar como; **to** — **with** ser igual a, equipararse con, estar al nivel de.

rank² [ræŋk] *adj* (a) (*Bot*) lozano, exuberante; *soil* fértil; (*thick*) espeso, tupido.
(b) (*smelly*) maloliente, fétido, rancio; **to smell** — oler mal.
(c) (*fig*) **that's** — **nonsense!** ¡puras tonterías!; **it's a** — **bad play** es una obra francamente mala; **it's** — **injustice** es una injusticia manifiesta; **he's a** — **liar** es un mentiroso redomado.

ranker ['ræŋkə*] *n* (Mil) oficial *m* que ha sido ascendido de soldado raso.

ranking ['ræŋkiŋ] *n* categoría *f*, clase *f*, posición *f*; (Mil) graduación *f*.

rankle ['ræŋkl] *vi*: **to** — **with someone** afligir a uno, roer a uno, amargar la vida a uno; **it still** —s **duele todavía.**

rankly ['ræŋkli] *adv* lozanamente, con exuberancia; espesamente.

rankness ['ræŋknis] n lozanía f, exuberancia f; fertilidad f; espesura f; mal olor m, fetidez f, ranciedad f; (of injustice etc) enormidad f.

ransack ['rænsæk] vt (search) registrar (de arriba abajo); escudriñar (minuciosamente); (pillage) saquear; they —ed the house for arms registraron toda la casa buscando armas; the place had been —ed el local había sido saqueado.

ransom ['rænsəm] 1 n rescate m; (Rel) redención f; to hold someone to — pedir un rescate por uno, (fig) poner a uno entre la espada y la pared; the public is·being held to — by these strikers estos huelguistas amenazan al público de una manera intolerable.
2 vt rescatar; (Rel) redimir.

ransoming ['rænsəmiŋ] n rescate m; redención f.

rant [rænt] 1 n lenguaje m campanudo, lenguaje m declamatorio.
2 vi vociferar, despotricar; hablar en tono violento, hablar en un estilo hinchado; he —ed on about the Pope siguió vociferando injurias contra el papa.

ranter ['ræntə*] n fanfarrón m; orador m campanudo, orador m populachero.

ranting ['ræntiŋ] 1 adj fanfarrón; campanudo, vociferador, chillón.
2 n lenguaje m campanudo, lenguaje m declamatorio; vociferación f; for all his — por más que hable de ese modo fanfarrón.

ranunculus [rə'nʌŋkjuləs] n ranúnculo m.

rap [ræp] 1 n golpecito m, golpe m seco; (at door) llamada f, aldabada f; there was a — at the door se llamó a la puerta; to take the — pagar el pato; to take the — for something sufrir las consecuencias de algo; cargar con la culpa de algo; see care, knuckle.
2 vt golpear, dar un golpecito en, tocar; (fam) criticar severamente; to — out an order espetar una orden.
3 vi: to — at the door llamar a la puerta.

rapacious [rə'peiʃəs] adj rapaz.

rapaciously [rə'peiʃəsli] adv con rapacidad.

rapacity [rə'pæsiti] n rapacidad f.

rape¹ [reip] 1 n violación f, estupro m; (fig) destrucción f, ruina f; attempted — intento m de violación; the — of Poland la destrucción de Polonia.
2 vt violar, estuprar, forzar.

rape² [reip] n (Bio) colza f.

rape oil ['reipɔil] n aceite m de colza.

rapeseed ['reipsi:d] n rabina f.

Raphael ['ræfeiel] n Rafael.

rapid ['ræpid] adj rápido.

rapidity [rə'piditi] n rapidez f.

rapidly ['ræpidli] adv rápidamente.

rapids ['ræpidz] npl rápidos mpl, rabiones mpl.

rapier ['reipiə*] n estoque m.

rapine ['ræpain] n rapiña f.

rapist ['reipist] n (esp US) violador m.

rapping ['ræpiŋ] n golpecitos mpl, golpes mpl secos; llamadas fpl, aldabadas fpl.

rapport [ræ'pɔ:*] n (a) relación f. (b) conformidad f; to be in — with estar conforme con, estar de acuerdo con.

rapprochement [ræ'prɔʃmã:ŋ] n acercamiento m, aproximación f.

rapscallion [ræp'skæliən] n bribón m.

rapt [ræpt] adj arrebatado; (absorbed) absorto, ensimismado; (enraptured) extático, extasiado; with — attention con atención fija; to be — in contemplation estar absorto en la contemplación.

rapture ['ræptʃə*] n éxtasis m, rapto m, arrobamiento m; to be in —s estar extasiado, extasiarse; to go into —s extasiarse (over, about ante, con).

rapturous ['ræptʃərəs] adj extático; applause etc entusiasta.

rapturously ['ræptʃərəsli] adv extáticamente; con entusiasmo.

rare¹ [rɛə*] adj raro, poco común, nada frecuente; (Phys) ralo; at — intervals muy de tarde en tarde; in a moment of — generosity en un momento de generosidad poco frecuente en él; it is — to find that . . . es poco frecuente encontrar que . . .; the plant is — in Wales la planta es poco común en Gales; you gave me a — old fright! (fam) ¡qué susto me diste!

rare² [rɛə*] adj meat poco hecho.

rarebit ['rɛəbit] n: Welsh — pan m con queso tostado.

rarefaction [ˌrɛəri'fækʃən] n rarefacción f.

rarefied ['rɛərifaid] adj atmosphere (also fig) enrarecido.

rarefy ['rɛərifai] 1 vt enrarecer. 2 vi enrarecerse.

rarely ['rɛəli] adv raramente, con poca frecuencia; rara vez, pocas veces, casi nunca; it is — found here aquí se encuentra con poca frecuencia; that·method is — satisfactory ese método no es satisfactorio casi nunca.

rareness ['rɛənis] n, **rarity** ['rɛəriti] n rareza f; it's a rarity here aquí es una rareza.

rascal ['rɑːskəl] n pillo m, pícaro m.

rascality [rɑːs'kæliti] n picardía f.

rascally ['rɑːskəli] adj pícaro, truhanesco.

rash¹ [ræʃ] n (Med) erupción f (cutánea).

rash² [ræʃ] adj temerario; imprudente; precipitado; that was very — of you en eso has sido muy imprudente.

rasher ['ræʃə*] n lonja f, loncha f.

rashly ['ræʃli] adv temerariamente; imprudentemente; precipitadamente.

rashness ['ræʃnis] n temeridad f; imprudencia f; precipitación f.

rasp [rɑːsp] 1 n escofia f. 2 vt (a) escofinar, raspar. (b) (say) decir con voz áspera. 3 vi hacer un sonido desapacible.

raspberry ['rɑːzbəri] n (a) (fruit) frambuesa f; (bush) frambueso m.
(b) (fam: sound) sonido m grosero, sonido m despectivo, sonido m ofensivo; to blow someone a — hacer un gesto grosero a uno; to get the — recibir una bronca, sufrir una repulsa.

raspberry bush ['rɑːzbəribuʃ] n, **raspberry cane** ['rɑːzbərikein] n frambueso m.

rasper ['rɑːspə*] n escofina f, raspador m.

rasping ['rɑːspiŋ] adj voice etc áspero, desapacible.

rat [ræt] 1 n rata f; (fam: rotter) canalla m, (deserter) desertor m; —s! ¡narices!; you —! ¡bestia!; to smell a — oler el poste; I smell a — aquí hay gato encerrado, esto es sospechoso.
2 vi (a) cazar ratas, matar ratas.
(b) (fam) chaquetear, desertar; to — on someone chivarse de uno, soplar contra uno.

ratable ['reitəbl] adj (property) sujeto a contribución municipal; — value valor m (de una propiedad) sobre el que se calcula la contribución municipal.

ratcatcher ['ræt,kætʃə*] n cazarratas m.

ratchet ['rætʃit] n trinquete m.

ratchet wheel ['rætʃit,wi:l] n rueda f de trinquete.

rate¹ [reit] 1 n (a) (proportion, ratio) proporción f, relación f, razón f; tanto m por ciento; — of births (índice m de) natalidad f; at a — of 5% a un 5 por ciento; at a — of 5 in every 30 a razón de 5 por cada 30; at the — of 3 per person a razón de 3 por persona; at any — de todas formas, de todos modos; at that — de ese modo; if things go on at this — de seguir las cosas así.
(b) (price etc) precio m, tasa f; (of interest etc) tipo m; (of hotel etc) tarifa f; at a cheap — a un precio reducido; the — for the job el sueldo que corresponde al trabajo, el sueldo justo; advertising —s tarifa f de anuncios; see bank — etc; insurance —s tipo m de seguro; market —s precios mpl del mercado, (Fin) cotizaciones fpl; postage —s tarifa f de correo; — of exchange (tipo m de) cambio m; — of interest tipo m de interés; —s of pay tipos mpl de sueldo; — of taxation nivel m de impuestos.
(c) —s (local tax) contribución f municipal; —s and taxes contribuciones fpl e impuestos; we pay £90 in —s pagamos 90 libras de contribuciones.
(d) eg first-rate de primera clase; some third-rate author algún autor de baja categoría.
(e) (speed) velocidad f; (of work etc) ritmo m; — of climb (Aer) velocidad f de subida; — of flow velocidad f de flujo; — of growth ritmo m de expansión; a high — of growth un elevado ritmo de crecimiento; at a great — rápidamente, (of vehicle) a gran velocidad; at a — of 20 knots a una velocidad de 20 nudos.
2 vt (a) (estimate) estimar; (estimate value) tasar, valorar (at en); (classify) clasificar; I — it at £2 yo lo valoro en 2 libras; I — the book highly yo estimo el libro en mucho; I — him highly tengo un muy buen concepto de él; how do you — her? ¿qué opinas de ella?; I — him among my best 3 pupils le pongo entre mis 3 mejores alumnos.
(b) (Fin) imponer contribución municipal a; we are highly —d here aquí nos exigen una contribución elevada; the house is —d at £84 per annum se impone una contribución de 84 libras al año a esta casa, pagamos por esta casa una contribución de 84 libras al año.
3 vi: to — as ser considerado como, ser tenido por; to — for a grant ser de la clase que recibe un subsidio; he just doesn't — no cuenta para nada, no vale para nada.

rate² [reit] vt regañar, reñir.

ratepayer ['reitpeiə*] n contribuyente mf.

rather ['rɑːðə*] **1** adv (a) (used alone) antes, más bien; mejor dicho; **or** — mejor dicho; — **it is a matter of money** antes es cuestión de dinero, es al contrario cuestión de dinero.

(b) (somewhat) algo, un poco, bastante; — **good** bastante bueno; — **difficult** algo difícil; **it's** — **wet** está un poco mojado; **I'm** — **tired** estoy un poco cansado; **there's** — **a lot** hay bastante; **I** — **think he won't come** me inclino a creer que no vendrá; **I** — **expected as much** ya lo preveía; **are you keen to go?** ... **yes, I am** — ¿quieres ir en efecto? ... sí quiero; **isn't she pretty?** ... **yes, she is** — ¿es guapa, eh? ... sí, lo es bastante.

(c) **A** — **than B** A antes que B, más bien A que B; **this** — **than that** esto antes que eso; **anything** — **than that!** ¡todo menos eso!; **play anything** — **than that** toca cualquier cosa que no sea eso; **I would** — **not say** prefiero no decirlo; **I would** — **have sherry than beer** más bien tomo un jerez; **I would** — **not** más bien no quiero hacerlo (etc).

2 interj ['rɑːˈðəː*] **would you like some?** ... —! ¿quieres algo de esto? ... ¡ya lo creo!

ratification [ˌrætifiˈkeiʃən] n ratificación f.

ratify ['rætifai] vt ratificar.

rating¹ ['reitiŋ] n (a) (act of valuing) tasación f, valuación f; (value) valor m; (local tax) contribución f.

(b) (standing) clasificación f; puesto m, posición f; (of ship) clase f; **what's his** —? ¿qué puesto ocupa?; ¿qué opinión hay de él?

(c) (Naut: person) marinero m.

rating² ['reitiŋ] n reprensión f.

ratio ['reiʃiəu] n razón f, relación f, proporción f; **in direct** — **to** en razón directa con; **in the** — **of 5 to 2** a razón de 5 a 2; **the** — **of wages to raw materials** la relación entre los sueldos y las materias primas.

ratiocinate [rætiˈɔsineit] vi raciocinar.

ratiocination [ˌrætiɔsiˈneiʃən] n raciocinación f.

ration ['ræʃən] **1** n ración f; —s (Mil etc) víveres mpl, suministro m; **emergency** —, **iron** — ración f de reserva; **it's off the** — no está racionado; **to be on short** —s andar escaso de víveres, tener poco que comer; **to draw one's** —s recibir los víveres; **when they put bread on the** — cuando racionaron el pan.

2 vt racionar (also to — out).

rational ['ræʃənl] adj racional; lógico, razonable; (sane, of person) sensato, cuerdo; **the** — **thing to do would be** ... lo lógico sería ...; **he seemed quite** — parecía estar completamente cuerdo; **a long skirt is hardly** — **dress for the beach** una falda larga es poco práctica en la playa; **let's be** — **about this** seamos razonables.

rationale [ræʃəˈnɑːl] n razón f fundamental, base f lógica.

rationalism ['ræʃnəlizəm] n racionalismo m.

rationalist ['ræʃnəlist] **1** adj racionalista. **2** n racionalista mf.

rationality [ˌræʃəˈnæliti] n racionalidad f; lógica f.

rationalization [ˌræʃnəlaiˈzeiʃən] n racionalización f.

rationalize ['ræʃnəlaiz] vt hacer racional; organizar lógicamente, introducir un sistema lógico en; (Math) quitar los radicales a, racionalizar.

rationally ['ræʃnəli] adv racionalmente; lógicamente, razonablemente; **he spoke quite** — habló cuerdamente, habló de modo juicioso.

ration book ['ræʃənbuk] n, **ration card** ['ræʃənkɑːd] n cartilla f de racionamiento.

rationing ['ræʃniŋ] n racionamiento m.

Ratisbon ['rætizbɔn] Ratisbona.

rat poison ['rætˈpɔizn] n matarratas m.

rat race ['rætreis] n lucha f del hombre por ir adelante en su profesión, competencia f entre los miembros de una profesión (or sociedad etc) para aventajarse unos a otros; **it's just a** — es una lucha constante por subir.

rat-tat-tat ['rætəˈtæt] interj ¡pum!, ¡pum! (sonido de la aldaba).

rattle ['rætl] **1** n (a) (noise: banging) golpeteo m; (of cart, train etc) traqueteo m; (of machine gun etc) traqueteo m, tableteo m; (eg of stone in tin) ruido m, sonsonete m; (of hail, rain) tamborileo m; (of window etc) crujido m; (of teeth) castañeteo m; (in throat) estertor m.

(b) (instrument) carraca f, matraca f; (child's) sonajero m; (snake's) cascabel m.

2 vt (a) (shake) agitar, sacudir; (play) hacer sonar; (vibrate) hacer vibrar; (jolt) traquetear; **the**

wind —**d the window** el viento hacía crujir la ventana; **he** —**d the tin** agitó la lata.

(b) **to** — **off** enumerar rápidamente.

(c) (person) desconcertar, confundir; poner nervioso; **he was badly** —**d** quedó muy desconcertado; **that** —**d him badly** eso le desconcertó de mala manera; **to get** —**d** ponerse nervioso; **he never gets** —**d** nunca pierda la calma.

3 vi (a) golpear; traquetear, tabletear; sonar, hacer ruido; tamborilear; crujir; castañetear.

(b) **we were rattling along at 50** íbamos a 50 (kilómetros por hora); **she** —**d on** seguía parloteando; **she was rattling on about the war** seguía hablando incansablemente de la guerra.

rattlebrained ['rætlbreind] adj ligero de cascos.

rattlesnake ['rætlsneik] n serpiente f de cascabel.

rattletrap ['rætltræp] **1** adj desvencijado. **2** n armatoste m.

rattling ['rætliŋ] **1** adj: **at a** — **pace** muy rápidamente, a gran velocidad. **2** adv: — **good** realmente estupendo.

rattrap ['rættræp] n trampa f para ratas.

ratty ['ræti] adj (fam): **he was pretty** — **about it** se picó mucho por ello; **to get** — ponerse negro.

raucous ['rɔːkəs] adj estridente, ronco, chillón.

raucously ['rɔːkəsli] adv de modo estridente, roncamente, en tono chillón.

ravage ['rævidʒ] **1** n estrago m, destrozo m; —**s** destrucción f, estragos mpl; **the** —**s of time** los estragos del tiempo.

2 vt estragar, destruir, destrozar; (plunder) pillar; **the region was** —**d by floods** la región fue asolada por las inundaciones; **a picture** —**d by time** un cuadro deteriorado por el tiempo.

rave [reiv] **1** n (sl) (a) **it's a** — es lo último, es la monda.

(b) (Mus etc) concierto m de música popular, m; fiesta f animadísima.

2 adj: **the play got** — **notices** la obra fue reseñada con el mayor entusiasmo, se escribieron reseñas entusiastas de la obra.

3 vi delirar, desvariar; **to** — **about someone** pirrarse por uno, hablar en términos entusiastas de uno; **to** — **about something** entusiasmarse por algo; **to** — **at someone** insultar frenéticamente a uno de palabra.

ravel ['rævl] vt enredar, enmarañar (also fig).

raven ['reivn] **1** n cuervo m. **2** adj hair negro como el azabache.

ravening ['rævniŋ] adj rapaz, salvaje.

ravenous ['rævənəs] adj (starving) famélico, hambriento; (voracious) voraz; **I'm** —! ¡me comería un toro!; **he was** — tenía una hambre canina.

ravenously ['rævənəsli] adv vorazmente; **to be** — **hungry** tener una hambre canina.

ravine [rəˈviːn] n barranco m, garganta f.

raving ['reiviŋ] adj: — **lunatic** loco m de atar.

ravings ['reiviŋz] npl delirio m, desvarío m.

ravioli [ˌræviˈəuli] npl canalones mpl.

ravish ['ræviʃ] vt (a) (charm) encantar, embelesar. (b) (lit: carry off) raptar, robar; (rape) violar.

ravisher ['ræviʃə*] n raptor m; violador m.

ravishing ['ræviʃiŋ] adj encantador, embelesador.

ravishingly ['ræviʃiŋli] adv: — **beautiful** extremadamente hermoso.

ravishment ['ræviʃmənt] n embeleso m, éxtasis m; rapto m, robo m; violación f.

raw [rɔː] **1** adj food crudo; spirit puro, sin mezcla; weather crudo, áspero; silk, leather etc bruto, sin refinar; cotton en rama; (inexperienced) novato, inexperto; (socially coarse) tosco, grosero; **that's pretty** — eso es injusto, no hay derecho a eso; **in the** — **flesh** en la carne viva; see deal, material etc.

2 n carne f viva; **it got him on the** — le hirió en lo más vivo.

rawboned ['rɔːˈbəund] adj huesudo.

rawhide ['rɔːhaid] adj de cuero crudo.

rawness ['rɔːnis] n crudeza f; inexperiencia f; tosquedad f.

ray¹ [rei] n rayo m; (Bot) bráctea f; **cathode** —**s** rayos mpl catódicos; **cosmic** —**s** rayos mpl cósmicos; **gamma** —**s** rayos mpl gama; — **of light** rayo m de luz; **without a** — **of hope** sin esperanza alguna; **I see a** — **of hope** (or light) hay un rayo de esperanza.

ray² [rei] n (Fish) raya f.

Raymond ['reimənd] m Raimundo, Ramón.

rayon ['reiɔn] n rayón m.

raze [reiz] vt (also to — to the ground) arrasar, asolar.

razor ['reizə*] n (open) navaja f; (safety —) maquinilla f de afeitar; (electric-) maquinilla f eléctrica, rasuradora f.

razorbill ['reizəbil] n alca f (común).

razor blade ['reizəbleid] n noja f de afeitar, cuchilla f de afeitar.

razor-sharp ['reizə'ʃɑːp] adj afiladísimo; mind agudísimo, de lo más penetrante.

razor strop ['reizəstrɔp] n suavizador m.

razzle ['ræzl] n (sl) borrachera f; to go on the — ir de juerga, ir de borrachera.

razzle-dazzle ['ræzl,dæzl] n = razzle.

re [riː] prep respecto a, con referencia a; — yours of the 8th me refiero a su carta del día 8.

reabsorb ['riːəb'zɔːb] vt resorber.

reabsorption ['riːəb'zɔːpʃən] n resorción f.

reach [riːtʃ] 1 n (a) alcance m; extensión f; distancia f; (Boxing etc) envergadura f; to have a long — tener brazos largos; to be beyond someone's —, to be out of someone's — estar fuera del alcance de uno; to be within — of the hand estar al alcance de la mano; to be within (easy) — estar al alcance, estar a la mano; cars within the — of all families coches mpl al alcance de todas las familias; a house within easy — of the station una casa a corta distancia de la estación; it's within easy — by bus es fácilmente accesible en autobús.

(b) (of river) extensión f entre dos recodos; (of canal) extensión f entre dos compuertas; the upper —es of the Seine la parte alta del Sena.

2 vt (a) (stretch out) alargar, extender; he —ed out a hand alargó la mano.

(b) (pass) pasar, dar; please — me down that case por favor bájeme la maleta esa; can you — me (over) the oil? ¿me da el aceite, por favor?

(c) (arrive at, attain) alcanzar; llegar a, llegar hasta; lograr; extenderse a, abarcar; to — home llegar a casa; it doesn't — the bottom no llega al fondo; the child hardly —ed my waist el niño apenas me llegaba a la cintura; the door is —ed by a long staircase se sube a la puerta por una larga escalera; your letter —ed me this morning su carta llegó a mis manos esta mañana; when this news —ed my ears cuando supe esta noticia; to — 21 cumplir los 21 años; to — perfection lograr la perfección; to — a compromise llegar a un arreglo; production now —es 3.400 megawatts la producción actual alcanza 3.400 megavatios; the law does not — such cases la ley no se extiende a tales casos.

(d) person ponerse en contacto con; to — someone by telephone hablar con uno por teléfono; you can always — me at the office me puedes llamar en todo momento en la oficina.

3 vi (a) to — out (with one's hand) for something alargar (or tender) la mano para tomar algo; don't — over people no alargues la mano para tomar cosas delante de otros; to — for the sky aspirar al cielo; — for the sky! (sl) ¡arriba las manos!

(b) (stretch) alcanzar; extenderse; llegar; it won't — no llega; it —es to the sea se extiende hasta el mar; as far as the eye could — hasta donde alcanzaba la vista; the beer won't — till Friday la cerveza no llega al viernes.

reachable ['riːtʃəbl] adj alcanzadizo; accesible.

reach-me-downs ['riːtʃmi,daunz] npl ropa f hecha, traje m (etc) hecho.

react [riːˈækt] vi reaccionar (against contra; on sobre; to a, ante); how did she —? ¿cómo reaccionó?

reaction [riːˈækʃən] n reacción f; what was your —? ¿cómo reaccionó Vd?, ¿qué impresión le produjo?; it produced no — no surtió efecto.

reactionary [riːˈækʃənri] 1 adj reaccionario. 2 n reaccionario m, a f.

reactive [riːˈæktiv] adj reactivo.

reactor [riːˈæktə*] n reactor m; nuclear — reactor m nuclear.

read [riːd] (irr: pret and ptp read [red]) 1 vt (a) leer; (with difficulty) lograr leer, interpretar, descifrar; do you — Russian? ¿sabes leer el ruso?; I — it differently yo lo entiendo de otro modo.

(b) to — something aloud leer algo en voz alta; to — the news leer las noticias; to — a report to a meeting leer un informe a una reunión.

(c) to — someone to sleep leer un libro (etc) para dormir a uno.

(d) (Univ) estudiar, cursar; to — Romance languages estudiar lenguas románicas; what are you —ing? ¿qué asignatura estudias?

(e) to — music leer música; to — someone's hand leer la mano a uno; she can — me like a book me conoce a fondo; to — the future adivinar el porvenir; to — someone's thoughts adivinar el pensamiento de uno.

(f) (take a reading from) consultar; when I — the thermometer cuando consulté el termómetro; they come to — the meter once a month vienen una vez al mes a comprobar lo que marca el contador; he wants to — the gas meter quiere ver el contador de gas.

(g) you're —ing too much into it le atribuyes una importancia que realmente no tiene; crees ver cosas escondidas que en realidad no hay; to — into a sentence what is not there ver en una frase un significado que no tiene.

(h) (with adv or prep) to — something out leer algo en alta voz, leer algo para que lo oigan todos (etc); please — it out por favor léanoslo; to — something over, to — something through repasar algo, volver a leer algo; to — up a subject estudiar un tema; repasar un tema.

2 vi (a) leer; to — aloud leer en alta voz; I — about it in the papers lo leí en los periódicos; I'm —ing about Napoleon me estoy documentando sobre Napoleón; leo un libro sobre Napoleón; to — between the lines leer entre líneas; to — on seguir leyendo; "now — on" "prosigue el cuento"; to — to someone leer un libro (etc) a uno.

(b) (notice etc) decir, rezar; (of thermometer etc) indicar, marcar; it should — "Urraca" debiera decir "Urraca".

(c) how does the letter — now? ¿qué tal te parece la carta ahora?; it would — better if you said ... causaría mejor impresión si pusieras ..., sería más elegante si escribieras ... ; the play acts better than it —s la obra es mejor representada que leída.

3 n: I was having a quiet — in the garden leía tranquilamente un libro en el jardín; I like a good — me gusta la lectura; it's a good solid — el libro dará muchas horas de lectura amena.

read [red] pret and ptp of read; well — leído, culto, instruido; to take the minutes as — dar las actas por leídas; we can take that as — (fig) eso lo podemos dar por sentado.

readability [,riːdəˈbiliti] n legibilidad f; amenidad f, interés m.

readable ['riːdəbl] adj writing legible; book etc digno de leerse, ameno, interesante.

readdress ['riːəˈdres] vt letter poner señas nuevas (or correctas) en; to — a letter to someone volver a dirigir una carta a uno.

reader ['riːdə*] n lector m, ora f; (Typ) corrector m; (book) libro m de lectura; (Univ) profesor que ocupa una cátedra sólo inferior a la del jefe de departamento; he's a great — lee mucho, es muy aficionado a la lectura; I'm not much of a — leo poco, no me interesan mucho los libros.

readership ['riːdəʃip] n número m total de lectores (de un periódico); (Univ) puesto del reader.

readily ['redili] adv (quickly) en seguida, pronto; (willingly) de buena gana; (easily) fácilmente.

readiness ['redinis] n prontitud f; disponibilidad f; buena disposición f, buena voluntad f; (preparedness) preparación f; — of wit viveza f de ingenio; everything is in — todo está listo, todo está preparado; to hold oneself in — for something estar listo para algo; hold yourself in — for . . . prepárese para . . .

reading ['riːdiŋ] 1 n (in general) lectura f; (aloud) lectura f, recitación f; (understanding) interpretación f; (of thermometer etc) indicación f, lectura f; (Parl) lectura f, (in text) lección f; second — (Parl) segunda lectura f; to give a bill a second — leer un proyecto de ley por segunda vez.

2 adj: the — public el público que lee; he's a great — man es un hombre que lee mucho, hombre muy aficionado a la lectura.

3 attr de lectura.

reading glass ['riːdiŋglɑːs] n lente m para leer.

reading lamp ['riːdiŋlæmp] n lámpara f para leer (en la cama etc).

reading matter ['riːdiŋ,mætə*] n lectura f.

reading room ['riːdiŋrum] n sala f de lectura.

readjust ['riːəˈdʒʌst] 1 vt reajustar; reorientar. 2 vi reajustarse; reorientarse.

readjustment ['riːəˈdʒʌstmənt] n reajuste m; reorientación f.

readmit ['riːədˈmit] vt readmitir.

ready ['redi] 1 adj (a) (prepared) listo, preparado; pronto; (available) disponible; —?, are you —? ¿estás listo?, ¿vamos?; —, steady, go! ¡preparados, listos, ya! — for action dispuesto para el combate, (*fig*) lanza en ristre; — **for use** listo para usar; — **money** dinero *m* contante; **to be — to hand** estar a la mano, estar disponible; **to be — to do something** estar listo para hacer algo; **the aircraft will be — to fly in 6 months** el avión estará listo para volar en 6 meses; **I am — to face him now** le he cobrado bastante ánimo para entrar a verle ahora; — **to serve** preparado; — **to use** listo para usar; **to get —, to make —** prepararse; disponerse (*to + infin a + infin*); **to get something —, to make something —** preparar algo, disponer algo; **to hold oneself —** estar listo (*for* para); **hold yourselves — to leave at any moment** prepárense para partir en cualquier momento.

(b) (*willing*) dispuesto (*to + infin a + infin*); **he's a — helper** presta su ayuda de buena gana.

(c) (*about*) **I was — to die of hunger** estaba para morirme de hambre; **we were — to give up there and then** estábamos a punto de abandonarlo sin más.

(d) **answer** fácil, pronto; *wit* agudo, vivo; **to have a — wit** ser ingenioso, tener chispa; **to have a — pen** escribir con soltura; **to have a — tongue** no morderse la lengua; **to find a — sale** venderse fácilmente, tener una salida fácil.

2 *n* (a) **with rifles at the —** con los fusiles listos para tirar, con los fusiles apercibidos; **pen at the —** pluma en ristre.

(b) **some of the —** (*fam*) algún dinero *m* contante.

ready-cooked ['redi'kukt] *adj* listo para comer.
ready-made ['redi'meid] *adj* hecho, confeccionado.
ready reckoner ['redi'reknə*] *n* libro *m* de cálculos hechos.
ready-to-wear ['reditə'weə*] *adj* hecho, confeccionado.
reaffirm ['ri:ə'fə:m] *vt* reafirmar, reiterar.
reaffirmation ['ri:æfə'meiʃən] *n* reafirmación *f*, reiteración *f*.
reafforest ['ri:ə'fɔrist] *vt* repoblar de árboles.
reafforestation ['ri:ə‚fɔris'teiʃən] *n* repoblación *f* forestal.
reagent [ri:'eidʒənt] *n* reactivo *m*.
real [riəl] *adj* real; verdadero; auténtico; legítimo; **the — world** el mundo real; **you're a — friend** eres un verdadero amigo; **the — power is in the hands of X** el poder efectivo está en manos de X; **this is — coffee** esto es auténtico café, esto es lo que se llama café; **we have had days of — heat** hemos tenido días de auténtico calor; **is he the — king?** ¿él es el rey legítimo?; **this is the — thing at last** por fin lo tenemos sin trampa ni cartón; *see* **estate**.
realism ['riəlizəm] *n* realismo *m*; autenticidad *f*.
realist ['riəlist] *n* realista *mf*.
realistic [riə'listik] *adj* realista; auténtico.
realistically [riə'listikəli] *adv* de modo realista; auténticamente.
reality [ri:'æliti] *n* realidad *f*; **in —** en realidad; **the realities of power** la realidad del poder; **let's get back to —** volvamos a la realidad; **let's stick to realities** atengámonos a la realidad.
realizable ['riəlaizəbl] *adj* realizable.
realization [‚riəlai'zeiʃən] *n* comprensión *f*; (*Comm etc*) realización *f*; **this — came too late** esto lo comprendió tarde; **it was a sudden —** cayó de repente en la cuenta.
realize ['riəlaiz] *vt* (a) (*comprehend*) darse cuenta de, hacerse cargo de, comprender; **without realizing it** sin darse cuenta; **I — that . . .** me doy cuenta de que . . . , comprendo que . . . ; **I — how it was done** reconozco que . . . ; **once I —d how it was done** tan pronto como caí en la cuenta de cómo se hacía; **do you — what you've done?** ¿te das cuenta de lo que has hecho?

(b) (*carry out*) realizar, llevar a cabo, poner por obra.

(c) (*Comm*) **assets etc** realizar.
really ['riəli] *adv* (a) (*used alone*) **—?** ¿de veras?, ¿ah sí?; **not —?** ¿lo dices en serio?; **—!** ¡ca!; ¡eh!; ¡mire Vd!;ⁿ—, **whatever next!** ¡qué cosas pasan!

(b) (*with adj*) verdaderamente, realmente, francamente; **a — good film** una película realmente buena, una película francamente buena; **I'm — very cross with you** estoy francamente disgustado contigo; **now it's — true** ahora sí es verdad; **this time we're — done for** esta vez hemos pringado de verdad.

(c) (*with verb*) en realidad; realmente; **I don't — know** en realidad no lo sé; **you — must see it** realmente tienes que verlo; **can it — be expected that . . . ?** ¿cabe realmente esperar que . . . ?; **has he — gone?** ¿es cierto que se ha ido?; **how a gentleman**

who is — a gentleman lives cómo vive un señor señor; **as for — talking Chinese, I can't** hablar chino, lo que se dice hablar chino, no sé.
realm [relm] *n* reino *m*; (*fig*) esfera *f*, campo *m*; **in the — of speculation** en la esfera de la especulación; **in the —s of fantasy** en el país de la fantasía.
realtor ['riəltɔ:*] *n* (US) corredor *m* de bienes raíces, corredor *m* de fincas.
realty ['riəlti] *n* bienes *mpl* raíces.
ream[1] [ri:m] *n* resma *f*; (*fig*) montón *m*, gran cantidad *f*.
ream[2] [ri:m] *vt* escariar (*also* **to — out**).
reamer ['ri:mə*] *n* escariador *m*.
reanimate ['ri:'ænimeit] *vt* reanimar.
reap [ri:p] *vt* segar; (*fig*) cosechar, recoger; **to — what one has sown** cosechar lo que ha sembrado uno; **to — no profit from something** no obtener ganancia alguna de algo, (*fig*) no sacarse ventaja alguna de algo; **who —s the reward?** ¿quién saca el premio?
reaper ['ri:pə*] *n* (*person*) segador *m*, ora *f*; (*machine*) segadora *f*, agavilladora *f*.
reaping ['ri:piŋ] *n* siega *f*.
reaping hook ['ri:piŋhuk] *n* hoz *f*.
reappear ['ri:ə'piə*] *vi* reaparecer.
reappearance ['ri:ə'piərəns] *n* reaparición *f*.
reapply ['ri:ə'plai] **1** *vt* aplicar de nuevo; *paint etc* dar otra capa de. **2** *vi* volver a presentarse, mandar una nueva solicitud (*for* pidiendo).
reappoint ['ri:ə'pɔint] *vt* volver a nombrar.
reappointment ['ri:ə'pɔintmənt] *n* nuevo nombramiento *m*.
reapportion ['ri:ə'pɔ:ʃən] *vt* volver a repartir (*among* entre).
reappraisal ['ri:ə'preizəl] *n* nueva estimación *f*, nueva apreciación *f*; **agonizing —** reajuste *m* agonizante (*or* doloroso).
rear[1] [riə*] **1** *adj* trasero, posterior; de cola; (*Mil*) de retaguardia; **— wheel** rueda *f* trasera.

2 *n* parte *f* trasera, parte *f* posterior; cola *f*; (*Anat: fam*) culo *m*; (*Mil: row*) última fila *f*, (*rearguard*) retaguardia *f*; (*fam:* WC) wáter *m*; **at the — of, in (the) — of** detrás de; **in the —** (*Mil*) a retaguardia; **3 miles to the —** 3 millas a retaguardia; **to be well to the —** quedar muy atrasado; **to bring up the —** cerrar la marcha; **to take the enemy in the —** atacar al enemigo por detrás.
rear[2] [riə*] **1** *vt* (*build*) erigir; (*raise*) levantar, alzar; (*bring up*) criar. **2** *vi* encabritarse, ponerse de manos.
rear admiral ['riər'ædmərəl] *n* contraalmirante *m*.
rear-engined ['riər‚endʒind] *adj* con motor trasero.
rearguard ['riəgɑ:d] **1** *n* retaguardia *f*. **2** *attr*: **— action** combate *m* para cubrir una retirada.
rearm ['ri:'ɑ:m] **1** *vt* rearmar. **2** *vi* rearmarse.
rearmament ['ri:'ɑ:məmənt] *n* rearme *m*.
rearmost ['riəməust] *adj* trasero, último de todos.
rear-mounted ['riə'mauntid] *adj*: **— engine** motor *m* trasero, motor *m* posterior.
rearrange ['ri:ə'reindʒ] *vt* volver a arreglar; ordenar de nuevo, arreglar de otro modo; (*Lit*) refundir; (*Mus*) volver a adaptar; **—d by Rossini** en versión de Rossini.
rearrangement ['ri:ə'reindʒmənt] *n* nuevo arreglo *m*, nueva disposición *f*; (*Lit*) refundición *f*; (*Mus*) nueva adaptación *f*, versión *f*.
rear-view ['riə‚vju:] *attr* retrovisor; **— mirror** espejo *m* retrovisor.
rearward ['riəwəd] *adj* trasero, de atrás, posterior.
rearward(s) ['riəwəd(z)] *adv* hacia atrás.
reason ['ri:zn] **1** *n* (a) (*motive*) razón *f*; motivo *m*; causa *f*; **the — for my departure** el motivo de mi ida; **the — for my going** la razón por la que me marcho; **the — why** la razón por qué, el por qué; **—s of state** razón *f* de estado; **by — of** a causa de; en virtud de; **for this —** por eso, por esta razón; **for that very —** por esa misma razón; **for no good —, for no — at all** sin motivo; **for —s best known to himself** por motivos que se sabe él; **with good —** con razón; **all the more — why you should not sell it** tanto más lógico me parece no venderlo; **what — can there be for it?** ¿qué razón puede haber?; **you had — to complain** Vd tuvo motivo de queja; **we have — to believe that . . .** tenemos motivo para creer que . . . ; **as I have good — to know** según ciertos indicios que tengo.

(b) (*faculty*) razón *f*; **to lose one's —** perder la razón.

(c) (*good sense*) sensatez *f*; moderación *f*; **everything in —** todo con moderación; **we cannot in — agree** no podemos razonablemente consentir;

it's out of all — está fuera de razón; **to listen to** — meterse en razón; **it stands to** — es evidente, es lógico (*that* que); **within** — dentro de lo razonable.
2 *vt* **(a) to** — **that** razonar que; calcular que, estimar que; **ours not to** — **why** no nos cumple a nosotros averiguar por qué.
(b) to — **out a problem** resolver un problema meditándolo.
(c) to — **someone out of something** disuadir a uno de algo alegando razones en contra.
3 *vi* razonar, discurrir; **to** — **about the universe** especular acerca del universo; **to** — **from data** razonar partiendo de ciertos datos; **to** — **with someone** alegar razones para convencer a uno.
reasonable ['riːznəbl] *adj* (*in most senses*) razonable; *person* sensato, juicioso; tolerante; **be** —! ¡sé razonable!
reasonableness ['riːznəblnis] *n* lo razonable; sensatez *f*; juicio *m*; tolerancia *f*; **in an atmosphere of sweet** — en un ambiente de moderación, en un ambiente de tolerancia.
reasonably ['riːznəbli] *adv* razonablemente; **a** — **good price** un precio razonable; **a** — **accurate report** un informe bastante exacto; **he acted very** — obró con mucho tino.
reasoned ['riːznd] *adj* razonado.
reasoning ['riːznɪŋ] **1** *adj* racional. **2** *n* razonamiento *m*; argumentos *mpl*; **I don't follow your** — no comprendo sus argumentos.
reassemble ['riːə'sembl] **1** *vt* volver a reunir; (*Tech*) montar de nuevo. **2** *vi* volver a reunirse.
reassert ['riːə'sɜːt] *vt* reafirmar, reiterar.
reassess ['riːə'ses] *vt* (*Fin*) tasar de nuevo, valorar de nuevo (*at* en); *amount of tax* fijar de nuevo (*at* en); (*Lit etc*) hacer una nueva apreciación de; **we shall have to** — **the situation** tendremos que estudiar la situación de nuevo.
reassurance ['riːə'ʃuərəns] *n* noticia *f* tranquilizadora, promesa *f* tranquilizadora.
reassure ['riːə'ʃuə*] *vt* tranquilizar; alentar; **to feel** —d estar más tranquilo.
reassuring ['riːə'ʃuərɪŋ] *adj* tranquilizador; alentador.
reassuringly ['riːə'ʃuərɪŋli] *adv* de modo tranquilizador; **he spoke** — nos alentó con sus palabras; **a** — **strong performance** una actuación cuya fuerza nos alentó.
reawaken ['riːə'weikən] **1** *vt* volver a despertar. **2** *vi* (volver a) despertarse.
reawakening ['riːə'weikənɪŋ] *n* despertar *m*.
rebarbative [ri'bɑːbətiv] *adj* repugnante.
rebate ['riːbeit] **1** *n* rebaja *f*, descuento *m*. **2** *vt* rebajar, descontar.
Rebecca [ri'bekə] *f* Rebeca.
rebel ['rebl] **1** *adj* rebelde; **the** — **government** el gobierno rebelde; — **leader** cabecilla *m*. **2** *n* rebelde *mf*.
rebel [ri'bel] *vi* rebelarse, sublevarse.
rebellion [ri'beliən] *n* rebelión *f*, sublevación *f*.
rebellious [ri'beliəs] *adj* rebelde; *child etc* revoltoso, díscolo.
rebelliousness [ri'beliəsnis] *n* rebeldía *f*; carácter *m* revoltoso, naturaleza *f* díscola.
rebind ['riː'baind] (*irr: see* **bind**) *vt* volver a atar; *book* reencuadernar.
rebirth ['riː'bɜːθ] *n* renacimiento *m*.
rebore ['riː'bɔː*] **1** *n* rectificado *m*. **2** *vt* rectificar.
reborn ['riː'bɔːn] *ptp*: **to be** — renacer.
rebound ['riːbaund] *n* rebote *m*; **on the** — de rebote, de rechazo; **she married him on the** — se casó con él a consecuencia del chasco que acababa de llevarse con el otro.
rebound [ri'baund] *vi* rebotar (*off* después de chocar con), dar un rebote.
rebroadcast ['riː'brɔːdkɑːst] **1** *n* retransmisión *f*. **2** *vt* retransmitir.
rebuff [ri'bʌf] **1** *n* repulsa *f*, desaire *m*; **to meet with a** — ser repulsado, aguantar un desaire. **2** *vt* rechazar; desairar.
rebuild ['riː'bild] (*irr: see* **build**) *vt* reconstruir, reedificar.
rebuilding ['riː'bildɪŋ] *n* reconstrucción *f*, reedificación *f*.
rebuke [ri'bjuːk] **1** *n* reprensión *f*; reprimenda *f*. **2** *vt* reprender, censurar; **to** — **someone for having done something** reprender a uno por haber hecho algo.
rebus ['riːbəs] *n* jeroglífico *m*.
rebut [ri'bʌt] *vt* rebatir, refutar, rechazar.
rebuttal [ri'bʌtl] *n* refutación *f*.
recalcitrance [ri'kælsitrəns] *n* obstinación *f*, terquedad *f*.

recalcitrant [ri'kælsitrənt] *adj* reacio, refractorio, recalcitrante.
recall [ri'kɔːl] **1** *n* aviso *m*, llamada *f* (para hacer volver a uno); retirada *f*; destitución *f*; **to be beyond** (*or* **past**) — ser irrevocable; (*person*) haberse ido definitivamente; **those days are gone beyond** — aquellos días pertenecen al pasado, aquellos días quedan ya a la espalda.
2 *vt* **(a)** (*call back*) *person* llamar, hacer volver; *ambassador, capital* retirar; (*dismiss*) destituir; **to** — **someone to his duty** recordar a uno su deber, hacer que uno se acuerde de su deber.
(b) (*remember*) recordar, traer a la memoria; **I can't quite** — **whether** ... no recuerdo del todo si ... ; **it** —**s the time when** ... hace pensar en aquella ocasión cuando ...
recant [ri'kænt] **1** *vt* retractar, desdecirse de; renunciar a. **2** *vi* retractarse, desdecirse; confesar su error.
recantation [ˌriːkæn'teiʃən] *n* retractación *f*; confesión *f* de error.
recap ['riːkæp] (*fam*) **1** *n* recapitulación *f*, resumen *m*. **2** *vti* recapitular, resumir.
recapitulate [ˌriːkə'pitjuleit] *vti* recapitular, resumir.
recapitulation ['riːkəˌpitju'leiʃən] *n* recapitulación *f*, resumen *m*.
recapture [riː'kæptʃə*] **1** *n* recobro *m*; reconquista *f*.
2 *vt* *prisoner etc* recobrar, volver a prender; *town* reconquistar, volver a tomar; *memory, scene* hacer revivir, recordar (*en su totalidad*).
recast ['riː'kɑːst] (*irr: see* **cast**) *vt* (*Tech, Lit etc*) refundir.
recede [ri'siːd] *vi* retroceder, retirarse; (*floods, price*) bajar; (*danger etc*) alejarse, disminuir.
receding [ri'siːdɪŋ] *adj prospect* que va disminuyendo; *tide* que está bajando; *forehead* huidizo.
receipt [ri'siːt] **1** *n* **(a)** (*act of receiving*) recepción *f*, recibo *m*; **to acknowledge** — of acusar recibo de; **I am in** — **of your letter** he recibido su carta, (*more formally*) obra su carta en mi poder; **on** — **of** al recibo de; **on** — **of this news** al saber esta noticia, al recibir esta noticia.
(b) (*document*) recibo *m*; **please give me a** — haga el favor de darme un recibo.
(c) —s ingresos *mpl*; (*of function, game etc*) entrada *f*.
2 *vt goods* dar recibo por; *bill* poner el "recibí" en.
receipt book [ri'siːtbuk] *n* libro *m* talonario.
receivable [ri'siːvəbl] *adj* recibidero; (*Comm*) por cobrar.
receive [ri'siːv] **1** *vt* recibir; *money* recibir, (*as payment*) cobrar, (*as salary*) percibir; (*accept*) aceptar, admitir; *guests* acoger, (*to stay*) hospedar, alojar; *stolen goods* receptar; *wound* sufrir; (*stand weight of*) sufrir, apoyar; *ball* restar; (*approve*) aprobar; "—d with thanks" "recibí"; **to** — **someone into the Academy** recibir a uno en la Academia; **to** — **someone as a partner** admitir a uno como socio; **to** — **someone into the Church** bautizar a uno, recibir a uno en el seno de la Iglesia; **to** — **someone into one's home** hospedar a uno en su casa; **the idea was well** —**d** la idea tuvo buena acogida; **the book was not well** —**d** el libro tuvo una acogida poco entusiasta; **he** —**d a wound in the leg** sufrió una herida en la pierna; **to** — **a blank refusal** encontrar una negativa rotunda; **what treatment did you** —? ¿qué tratamiento le dieron?
2 *vi* (*Law*) receptar, ser receptador; (*Sport*) ser restador.
received [ri'siːvd] *adj pronunciation etc* admitido, aprobado, normal.
receiver [ri'siːvə*] *n* recibidor *m*, ora *f*; (*addressee*) destinatario *m*, a *f*; (*of stolen goods*) receptador *m*, ora *f*; (*in bankruptcy, also* **official** —) síndico *m*; (*Sport*) restador *m*; (*Radio*) receptor *m*, radiorreceptor *m*; (*Tel*) auricular *m*; (*Chem etc*) recipiente *m*.
receiving [ri'siːvɪŋ] *n* recepción *f*; (*of stolen goods*) receptar *m*.
receiving set [ri'siːvɪŋset] *n* (*Radio*) receptor *m*, radiorreceptor *m*.
recension [ri'senʃən] *n* recensión *f*.
recent ['riːsnt] *adj* reciente; nuevo; **in** — **years** en estos últimos años; **in the** — **past** en el pasado próximo.
recently ['riːsntli] *adv* recientemente; (*before ptps*) recién, *eg* — **arrived** recién llegado; **as** — **as 1970** todavía en 1970; **until** — hasta hace poco.
receptacle [ri'septəkl] *n* receptáculo *m*.
reception [ri'sepʃən] *n* (*act*) recepción *f*, recibimiento *m*; (*welcome*) acogida *f*; (*social function*) recepción *f*; (*Radio etc*) recepción *f*; **to get a warm** — tener buena acogida, ser recibido con entusiasmo; **they'll get a warm** — **if they come here** (*iro*) estamos listos para recibirles si se presentan aquí.

reception centre, (US) — **center** [ri'sepʃən,sentə*] n centro m de recepción.
receptionist [ri'sepʃənist] n (hotel) recepcionista f; (dentist's etc) chica f, chica f enfermera; (other) secretaria f.
reception room [ri'sepʃən,rum] n sala f de recibo.
receptive [ri'septiv] adj receptivo.
receptiveness [ri'septivnis] n, **receptivity** [risep'tiviti] n receptividad f.
recess [ri'ses] 1 n (a) (vacation) vacaciones fpl; (short rest) descanso m; (in school) recreo m; (Parl) suspensión f, (between sittings) intermedio m; **parliament is in** — la sesión del parlamento está suspendida.
(b) (Tech) rebajo m; (Archit) hueco m; nicho m; (hiding place) escondrijo m.
(c) —es (fig) seno m; lo más hondo, lo más recóndito m.
2 vi (Parl) prorrogarse, suspenderse la sesión.
recession [ri'seʃən] n retroceso m, retirada f; (fall) baja f; (lessening) disminución f; (Fin, Comm) recesión f.
recessional [ri'seʃənl] n himno m de fin de oficio.
recessive [ri'sesiv] adj (Bio) recesivo.
recharge [ˌriː'tʃɑːdʒ] vt recargar, volver a cargar.
recherché [rə'ʃɛəʃei] adj rebuscado.
rechristen [ˈriː'krisn] vt (Eccl) rebautizar; (rename) poner nuevo nombre a; **they have —ed the machine "Fido"** han puesto a la máquina el nuevo nombre de "Fido".
recidivist [ri'sidivist] n reincidente mf.
recipe ['resipi] n receta f (for de).
recipient [ri'sipiənt] n recibidor m, ora f, recipiente mf; (addressee) destinatario m a f.
reciprocal [ri'siprəkəl] 1 adj recíproco, mutuo. 2 n (Math) recíproca f.
reciprocally [ri'siprəkəli] adv recíprocamente, mutuamente.
reciprocate [ri'siprəkeit] 1 vt good wishes etc intercambiar, devolver; corresponder a; **and this feeling is —d** y por nuestra parte nos hacemos eco de tal sentimiento; **her kindness was not —d** no correspondieron a su amabilidad.
2 vi (Mech) oscilar, alternar; (fig) usar de reciprocidad, corresponder; **but they did not** — pero ellos no correspondieron a esto; **he —d with a short speech** pronunció un breve discurso a modo de contestación; **it is up to us to** — nos incumbe usar de reciprocidad.
reciprocation [ri,siprə'keiʃən] n reciprocación f; reciprocidad f, correspondencia f.
reciprocity [ˌresi'prɔsiti] n reciprocidad f.
recital [ri'saitl] n relación f, narración f; (Mus) recital m.
recitation [ˌresi'teiʃən] n (act) recitación f; (text, piece for —) recitado m; **with humorous —s** con recitados humorísticos.
recitative [ˌresitə'tiːv] n recitativo m.
recite [ri'sait] 1 vt narrar, referir; enumerar; recitation recitar; **she —d her troubles all over again** volvió a enumerar todas sus dificultades.
2 vi dar un recitado.
reckless ['reklis] adj person temerario, imprudente; act imprudente; speed etc excesivo, peligroso; statement inconsiderado; **a — youth** un joven atolondrado.
recklessly ['reklisli] adv temerariamente, imprudentemente; **to drive** — conducir sin cuidado, conducir de modo peligroso; **to spend** — derrochar dinero.
recklessness ['reklisnis] n temeridad f, imprudencia f; inconsideración f; **the** — **of youth** la temeridad de la juventud; **the** — **of her driving** su modo peligroso de conducir.
reckon ['rekən] 1 vt (count number) contar, calcular; computar; (ascertain quantity) calcular, estimar; (believe) considerar, estimar; **to — someone among one's friends** contar a uno entre los amigos; **to — someone as** considerar a uno como; **to — something in** incluir algo en; **to — that** ... estimar que ..., considerar que ..., creer que ...; **I — he's worth more** considero que vale más; **to — up** calcular, computar; **to — up one's losses** calcular sus pérdidas.
2 vi (do sum) calcular; hacer cálculos; (think) calcular, creer; **to learn to** — aprender a calcular; **—ing from today** contando desde hoy; **she'll come, I** — según creo vendrá, calculo que vendrá; **I —** so así lo creo; cierto; **to — on** contar con; **to — on** + ger contar con + infin; **to — with** tener en cuenta, contar con; **we didn't —** with that no contábamos con eso; **we hadn't —ed with having to walk** no habíamos tenido en cuenta la posibilidad de tener que ir a pie; **to — without someone** hacer caso omiso de uno.

reckoning ['rekniŋ] n (calculation) cálculo m, cuenta f; (bill) cuenta f; **day of** — (fig) día m de la justicia; día m del juicio final; día m decisivo; **by any** — a todas luces; en opinión de todos; **according to my** — según mis cálculos; **to be out in one's** — hacer mal el cálculo, calcular mal; **see dead** —.
reclaim [ri'kleim] 1 n: **to be beyond** (or past) — ser irremediable, no tener remedio; estar definitivamente perdido.
2 vt (claim back) reclamar; sinner etc reformar; (tame) amansar, domesticar; land recuperar, hacer utilizable; (from sea) ganar, rescatar; swamp entarquinar; rubber etc utilizar, regenerar.
reclaimable [ri'kleiməbl] adj reclamable; utilizable.
reclamation [ˌreklə'meiʃən] n reclamación f; reformación f; domesticación f; recuperación f; utilización f; **land** — rescate m de terrenos, entarquinamiento m.
recline [ri'klain] 1 vt (lean) apoyar; (lay) recostar; (rest) descansar. 2 vi reclinarse, recostarse; apoyarse; descansar; **to — upon** (fig) contar con, fiarse de.
reclining [ri'klainiŋ] adj acostado; tumbado; figure, statue yacente; — **chair** sillón m reclinable, poltrona f, (Med) silla f de extensión.
recluse [ri'kluːs] n solitario m, a f, recluso m, a f.
recognition [ˌrekəg'niʃən] n reconocimiento m; **a smile of** — una sonrisa de reconocimiento; **in** — **of** en reconocimiento de, en premio de; en señal de; **in** — **of this fact** reconociendo este hecho; **to change something beyond** — cambiar algo de modo que resulta irreconocible.
recognizable ['rekəgnaizəbl] adj reconocible; identificable; **it is** — **as** se puede reconocer como, se puede identificar como.
recognizance [ri'kɔgnizəns] n reconocimiento m; obligación f contraída; (sum) fianza f; **to enter into** —s **to** + infin comprometerse legalmente a + infin.
recognize ['rekəgnaiz] vt (a) (know again) reconocer, identificar; conocer; **you don't** — **me** no me reconoce; **I —d him by his walk** le reconocí por su modo de andar; **his own mother would not have —d him** su propia madre no le hubiera reconocido; **he was —d by 2 policemen** le reconocieron 2 policías; **do you** — **this handbag?** ¿reconoce Vd este bolso?
(b) (acknowledge) admitir, confesar; reconocer; **we** — **that** ... reconocemos que ..., confesamos que ...; **we do not** — **the government of Ruritania** no reconocemos al gobierno de Ruritania; **does the Academy** — **the word?** ¿admite la Academia la palabra?; **we do not** — **your claim** no admitimos (or aceptamos) su pretensión; **to** — **someone as king** reconocer a uno por rey.
recognized ['rekəgnaizd] adj expert etc reconocido como tal; feature conocido; agent etc acreditado, oficial; **it's the** — **method** es el sistema normal.
recoil [ri'kɔil] 1 n retroceso m; (of gun) retroceso m, rebufo m, culatazo m.
2 vi recular, retroceder; (Mil) retroceder, rebufar; **to** — **in fear** retroceder espantado; **to** — **from something** retroceder ante algo, cejar ante la perspectiva de algo; **to** — **from doing something** sentir repugnancia por hacer algo, no animarse a hacer algo; **it —ed on him** recayó sobre él, resultó contraproducente para él.
recollect [ˌrekə'lekt] vt recordar, acordarse de.
recollection [ˌrekə'lekʃən] n recuerdo m; **to the best of my** — que yo recuerde.
recommence [ˌriːkə'mens] vti recomenzar.
recommend [ˌrekə'mend] vt recomendar; **to** — **a candidate for a post** recomendar a un candidato para un puesto; **I** — **him to you most warmly** se lo recomiendo a Vd con la mayor confianza; **to** — **someone to do something** recomendar a uno que haga algo, aconsejar a uno hacer algo.
recommendable [ˌrekə'mendəbl] adj recomendable.
recommendation [ˌrekəmen'deiʃən] n recomendación f; **the —s of a report** las recomendaciones de un informe.
recommendatory [ˌrekə'mendətəri] adj recomendatorio.
recompense ['rekəmpens] 1 n recompensa f. 2 vt recompensar (for por).
reconcilable ['rekənsailəbl] adj conciliable, reconciliable.
reconcile ['rekənsail] 1 vt persons reconciliar; theories etc conciliar; quarrel componer; **to become —d to something** resignarse a algo, acomodarse con algo; **what —d him to the place was the weather** lo que hizo que se conformara con vivir en el lugar fue el tiempo.
2 vr: **to** — **oneself to something** resignarse a algo, acomodarse con algo, conformarse con algo.

reconciliation [,rekənsili'eiʃən] n reconciliación f; conciliación f; composición f.

recondite [ri'kɔndait] adj recóndito.

recondition ['ri:kən'diʃən] vt reacondicionar.·

reconnaissance [ri'kɔnisəns] n reconocimiento m; — flight vuelo m de reconocimiento; to make a — reconocer el terreno, explorar el terreno.

reconnoitre, (US) **reconnoiter** [,rekə'nɔitə*] vti reconocer, explorar.

reconquer ['ri:'kɔnkə*] vt reconquistar.

reconquest ['ri:'kɔnkwest] n reconquista f; the R— (of Spain) la Reconquista.

reconsider ['ri:kən'sidə*] vti reconsiderar, repensar.

reconsideration ['ri:kən,sidə'reiʃən] n reconsideración f; on — después de repensarlo.

reconstitute ['ri:'kɔnstitju:t] vt reconstituir.

reconstitution ['ri:,kɔnsti'tju:ʃən] n reconstitución f.

reconstruct ['ri:kən'strʌkt] vt reconstruir; reedificar; crime etc reconstituir.

reconstruction ['ri:kən'strʌkʃən] n reconstrucción f; reedificación f; reconstitución f.

reconvert ['ri:kən'və:t] vt reconvertir (to en); reorganizar.

record ['rekɔ:d] 1 n (a) (document, report etc) documento m; registro m, partida f; relación f; (Law) acta f; (note) nota f, apunte m; — of attendances registro m de asistencias; — of a case acta f de un proceso; off the — (adj) no oficial, confidencial, (adv) de modo no oficial, confidencialmente; it is on — that..., it is a matter of — that... consta que...; the fact is on — consta el hecho; there is no — of it no hay constancia de ello, no consta en los documentos; to keep (or make) a — of apuntar, tomar nota de; he left no — of it no dejó relación de ello; to place (or put) something on — hacer constar algo, dejar constancia de algo; to write something into the — añadir algo a la relación escrita.

(b) —s archivos mpl; the —s of a society los archivos de una sociedad; Public R— Office Archivo m Nacional; I will have the —s searched buscaré en los archivos; the —s (police department) archivo m del servicio de identificación.

(c) (person's past in general) historia f; reputación f; antecedentes mpl; (as dossier) expediente m; (written with application for post) carrera f, curriculum m vitae; (of person, organization etc) historial m; (Mil) hoja f de servicios; criminal — antecedentes mpl penales; her past — su historia, su historial; Iberia's splendid — el brillante historial de Iberia; his — is against him su historial obra en perjuicio suyo; has he a —? ¿tiene antecedentes penales?; he has a clean — no hay nada en su historial que le perjudique; he left behind a splendid — of achievements dejó una magnífica historia de éxitos.

(d) (Sport etc) récord m, marca f; the — for this distance is 4 minutes el tiempo mínimo para esta distancia es de 4 minutos; is this a —? ¿es esto un récord?; ¿es excepcional esto?; to beat (or break) the — batir el récord, superar la marca; to establish (or set up) a — establecer un récord; to hold the — for the 100 metres ostentar el récord de los 100 metros.

(e) (Mus etc) disco m; long-playing — disco m microsurco, disco m de larga duración; to make a — grabar un disco.

2 adj sin precedentes, máximo, nuevo; a — output una producción sin precedentes; in a — time en un tiempo récord; in the — time of 12 seconds en el tiempo récord de 12 segundos

record [ri'kɔ:d] vt (a) (set down) registrar; inscribir; apuntar; hacer constar, dejar constancia de, consignar; it is not —ed anywhere no consta en ninguna parte; I will — your order apuntaré su pedido.

(b) (on dial etc) indicar, marcar.

(c) (Mus etc) grabar, registrar; she —ed the song in 1969 grabó la canción en 1969; to have one's voice —ed hacer grabar su voz.

record breaker ['rekɔ:d,breikə*] n recordman m, plusmarquista mf.

record-breaking ['rekɔ:d,breikiŋ] adj person, team brillante, excepcional; que tantos récords ostenta; effort, run récord.

record cabinet ['rekɔ:d,kæbinit] n armario m para discos, discoteca f.

record card ['rekɔ:d,kɑ:d] n ficha f.

record changer ['rekɔ:d,tʃeindʒə*] n cambiadiscos m.

recorded [ri'kɔ:did] adj: — music música f grabada; never in — history nunca en la historia escrita; it is a — fact that... consta el hecho de que...

recorder [ri'kɔ:də*] n (a) (person) registrador m,

archivero m; he was a faithful — of the facts registró puntualmente los hechos.

(b) (Law) juez m municipal.

(c) (Mus) flauta f dulce, flauta f de pico.

(d) (Mech) contador m, indicador m.

record holder ['rekɔ:d,həuldə*] n recordman m; the 100 metres — el que ostenta el récord de los 100 metros.

recording [ri'kɔ:diŋ] n grabación f; registro m; this — of "Ave Maria" esta grabación del "Ave María"; it's a good — el registro es bueno, tiene buen registro.

recording tape [ri'kɔ:diŋ,teip] n cinta f de grabación, cinta f magnetofónica.

recording van [ri'kɔ:diŋ,væn] n camión m de grabación.

record library ['rekɔ:d,laibrəri] n discoteca f.

record player ['rekɔ:d,pleiə*] n tocadiscos m.

recount [ri'kaunt] vt contar, referir.

re-count ['ri:'kaunt] 1 n (Parl) segundo escrutinio m; to have a — someter los votos a un segundo escrutinio. 2 vt volver a contar.

recoup [ri'ku:p] vt recobrar, recuperar; indemnizarse por.

recourse [ri'kɔ:s] n recurso m; to have — to recurrir a.

recover [ri'kʌvə*] 1 vt recobrar, recuperar; money reembolsarse; stolen property recuperar; (rescue) rescatar; to — lost time recuperar el tiempo perdido; to — consciousness recobrar el conocimiento, volver en sí; to — one's health recobrar la salud, reponerse; to — something from someone hacer que uno devuelva algo; to — one's property (Law) reivindicar su propiedad; to — damages from someone ser indemnizado por daños y perjuicios por uno.

2 vi (Med, Fin etc) restablecerse, reponerse; to — from an illness reponerse de una enfermedad; has she quite —ed? ¿se ha curado del todo?; shares have —ed las acciones han vuelto a subir; when I had —ed from my astonishment cuando me hube sobrepuesto a mi asombro.

3 vr: to — oneself reponerse, sobreponerse.

re-cover ['ri:'kʌvə*] vt recubrir.

recoverable [ri'kʌvərəbl] adj recuperable; (at law) reivindicable.

recovery [ri'kʌvəri] n recobro m, recuperación f; (rescue) rescate m; (Med etc) restablecimiento m, mejoría f; (Law) reivindicación f; an action for — of damages una demanda del pago de daños y perjuicios; to be past — haberse perdido definitivamente, ser irrecuperable, (Med) estar desahuciado; to make a rapid — restablecerse rápidamente; to make a slow — restablecerse lentamente; prices made a slow — las cotizaciones tardaron en restablecerse.

recreate ['rekrieit] vt recrear.

re-create ['ri:kri'eit] vt (create again) recrear.

recreation [,rekri'eiʃən] n (act) recreación f; (play, amusement) recreo m; (School) recreo m, hora f de recreo.

recreational [,rekri'eiʃənəl] adj: — facilities facilidades fpl de recreo; this is only — esto es sólo un pasatiempo.

recreation room [,rekri'eiʃənrum] n salón m de recreo.

recreative ['rekri,eitiv] adj recreativo.

recriminate [ri'krimineit] vi recriminar.

recrimination [ri,krimi'neiʃən] n recriminación f; mutual — recriminación f mutua.

recross ['ri:'krɔs] vti volver a cruzar.

recrudesce [,ri:kru'des] vi recrudecer.

recrudescence [,ri:kru'desns] n recrudescencia f, recrudecimiento m.

recrudescent [,ri:kru'desnt] adj recrudescente.

recruit [ri'kru:t] 1 n recluta m; raw — (Mil) soldado m bisoño, quinto m, (fig) novicio m. 2 vt (Mil) reclutar; strength etc restablecer. 3 vi alistar reclutas.

recruiting [ri'kru:tiŋ] n reclutamiento m.

recruiting office [ri'kru:tiŋ,ɔfis] n caja f de reclutas.

recruitment [ri'kru:tmənt] n reclutamiento m.

rectal ['rektəl] adj rectal.

rectangle ['rek,tæŋgl] n rectángulo m.

rectangular [rek'tæŋgjulə*] adj rectangular.

rectifiable ['rektifaiəbl] adj rectificable.

rectification [,rektifi'keiʃən] n rectificación f.

rectifier ['rektifaiə*] n (Elec, Chem etc) rectificador m; (Mech) rectificadora f.

rectify ['rektifai] vt (all senses) rectificar.

rectilinear [,rekti'liniə*] adj rectilíneo.

rectitude ['rektitju:d] n rectitud f.

rector ['rektə*] n (Eccl) párroco m; (Univ etc) rector m.

rectorship ['rektəʃip] n rectorado m.

rectory ['rektəri] n (Eccl) casa f del cura.

rectum ['rektəm] n recto m.

recumbent [ri'kʌmbənt] *adj* recostado, acostado; *statue* yacente.
recuperate [ri'ku:pəreit] **1** *vt* recuperar. **2** *vi* restablecerse, reponerse; **to — after an illness** reponerse de una enfermedad.
recuperation [ri,ku:pə'reiʃən] *n* recuperación *f*; (*Med*) restablecimiento *m*.
recuperative [ri'ku:pərətiv] *adj* recuperativo.
recur [ri'kə:*] *vi* repetirse, producirse de nuevo, volver a producirse (*revert to*) volver a; (*come to mind again*) volver a la mente; **the idea —s constantly in his work** la idea se repite constantemente en su obra.
recurrence [ri'kʌrəns] *n* repetición *f*, reaparición *f*.
recurrent [ri'kʌrənt] *adj* repetido; constante; (*Anat, Med*) recurrente; **it is a — theme** es un tema constante, es un tema que se repite a menudo.
recurring [ri'kə:riŋ] *adj see* **decimal**.
recusant ['rekjuzənt] **1** *adj* recusante. **2** *n* recusante *mf*.
red [red] **1** *adj* rojo, colorado; *face* (*high-coloured*) encarnado, (*with anger*) encendido, (*with shame*) ruboroso; *hair* rojo; *wine* tinto; *ink* colorado; (*Pol*) rojo; **to be — in the face** tener la cara encendida, tener el rostro sofocado; **was my face — !** ¡cómo me avergoncé!; **to go** (*or* **turn**) **as — as a beetroot** (*or* **lobster, tomato**) ponerse como un tomate; **to go** (*or* **turn**) **— with shame** ponerse colorado, ruborizarse.
2 *n* rojo *m*, color *m* rojo; (*Pol*) rojo *m*, a *f*; **to be in the —** deber dinero, estar en el libro de los morosos; **to be £1000 in the —** deber 1000 libras; **to get into the —** contraer deudas; **to get out of the —** pagar las deudas; **to see —** sulfurarse, salirse de sus casillas; **this makes me see —** esto me saca de quicio.
redact [ri'dækt] *vt* redactar.
redaction [ri'dækʃən] *n* redacción *f*.
Red Army ['red'ɑ:mi] *n* Ejército *m* Rojo.
red-berried ['red'berid] *adj* con bayas rojas.
red-blooded ['red'blʌdid] *adj* viril, vigoroso, enérgico.
redbreast ['redbrest] *n* (*also* **robin —**) petirrojo *m*.
redcap ['redkæp] *n* (*Mil sl*) policía *m* militar; (*US*) mozo *m* de estación.
redcoat ['redkout] *n* soldado *m* inglés (del siglo XVIII *etc*).
redden ['redn] **1** *vt* enrojecer, teñir de rojo. **2** *vi* enrojecerse, ponerse rojo; (*person: with anger*) enrojecerse, (*with shame*) ponerse colorado, ruborizarse.
reddish ['rediʃ] *adj* rojizo.
redecorate [ri:'dekəreit] *vt room* renovar, pintar de nuevo, volver a decorar.
redecoration [ri:,dekə'reiʃən] *n* renovación *f*.
redeem [ri'di:m] **1** *vt* redimir (*also Rel*), rescatar; *mortgage, bonds* amortizar; (*from pawn*) desempeñar; *promise* cumplir; *fault* expiar. **2** *vr*: **to — oneself** salvarse, expiar su falta.
redeemable [ri'di:məbl] *adj* redimible; (*Fin*) amortizable.
Redeemer [ri'di:mə*] *n* Redentor *m*.
redeeming [ri'di:miŋ] *adj*: **— feature** rasgo *m* bueno, (*fig*) punto *m* favorable; **— virtue** virtud *f* compensadora; **I see no — feature in it** no le encuentro ningún aspecto bueno.
redemption [ri'dempʃən] *n* redención *f* (*also Rel*), rescate *m*; (*Fin*) amortización *f*; desempeño *m*; cumplimiento *m*; expiación *f*; **to be beyond** (*or* **past**) **—** no tener remedio, ser irremediable.
redemptive [ri'demptiv] *adj* redentor.
redeploy [ri:di'plɔi] *vt resources, men* disponer de otro modo, reorganizar; utilizar de modo distinto.
redeployment ['ri:di'plɔimənt] *n* nueva disposición *f*, reorganización *f*; utilización *f* más económica (*or* lógica).
red-eyed ['red'aid] *adj* con los ojos inyectados en sangre, con los ojos en sangre.
red-faced ['red'feist] *adj* (*with anger*) con la cara encendida; (*with shame*) colorado, ruboroso, avergonzado.
red-haired ['red'hɛəd] *adj* pelirrojo.
red-handed ['red'hændid] *adj*: **to catch someone —** coger a uno con las manos en la masa, coger a uno en flagrante delito.
redhead ['redhed] *n* pelirroja *f*.
red-headed ['red'hedid] *adj* pelirrojo.
red-hot ['red'hɔt] *adj* candente; (*fig*) *news* de última hora; *issue* peligrosísimo; de máxima importancia, de la mayor actualidad; *supporter etc* vehemente, acérrimo.
redirect [ri:dai'rekt] *vt letter* reexpedir.
rediscover ['ri:dis'kʌvə*] *vt* volver a descubrir.

rediscovery ['ri:dis'kʌvəri] *n* segundo descubrimiento *m*; **its — was the work of ...** el que se haya vuelto a descubrir se debe a ...
redistribute ['ri:dis'tribju:t] *vt* distribuir de nuevo, hacer una nueva distribución de.
redistribution ['ri:,distri'bju:ʃən] *n* nueva distribución *f*.
red-letter ['red'letə*] *adj*: **— day** día *m* señalado, día *m* especial.
red-light ['red'lait] *adj*: **— district** barrio *m* chino.
redness ['rednis] *n* rojez *f*, lo rojo, lo encarnado.
redo ['ri:'du:] (*irr: see* **do**) *vt* rehacer, volver a hacer.
redolence ['redəuləns] *n* fragancia *f*, perfume *m*.
redolent ['redəulənt] *adj*: **— of** recordando como, con perfume como el de; **to be — of** (*fig*) recordar, hacer pensar en.
redouble [ri'dʌbl] **1** *vt* redoblar, intensificar; (*Bridge*) redoblar. **2** *vi* redoblarse, intensificarse; (*Bridge*) redoblar.
redoubt [ri'daut] *n* reducto *m*; **the last — of ...** el último reducto de ...
redoubtable [ri'dautəbl] *adj* terrible, formidable.
redound [ri'daund] *vi*: **to — to** redundar en, redundar en beneficio de.
redraft ['ri:'drɑ:ft] *vt* volver a redactar, hacer un nuevo borrador de, rehacer.
redraw ['ri:'drɔ:] (*irr: see* **draw**) *vt* volver a dibujar; *map, plan* volver a trazar.
redress [ri'dres] **1** *n* reparación *f*, compensación *f*; remedio *m* (legal), derecho *m* a satisfacción; **in such a case you have no —** en tal caso Vd no tiene ningún derecho a satisfacción.
2 *vt* (*readjust*) reajustar; *balance etc* rectificar, corregir; (*make up for*) reparar, compensar; *fault* remediar; *offence* desagraviar, enmendar.
Red Riding Hood ['red'raidiŋhud] *f* Caperucita Roja.
Red Sea ['red'si:] Mar *m* Rojo.
redshank ['redʃæŋk] *n* archibebe *m*.
redskin ['redskin] *n* piel roja *mf*.
redstart ['redstɑ:t] *n* colirrojo *m* real.
reduce [ri'dju:s] **1** *vt* reducir (*to* a; *also Math etc*), disminuir; *price* rebajar; (*in rank*) degradar; (*Mil*) reducir, tomar, conquistar; **to — an article by a quarter** abreviar un artículo en la cuarta parte; **to — everything to simple terms** expresarlo todo en términos sencillos; **to — something to ashes** hacer algo cenizas, convertir algo en cenizas; **to — speed** reducir la velocidad; **this —d him to silence** esto le hizo callar; **we were —d to begging in the streets** nos vimos sin otro recurso que el de pedir por las calles.
2 *vi* reducirse, disminuir; (*slim*) adelgazar.
reduced [ri'dju:st] *adj*: **a — income** una renta mermada, unos ingresos disminuidos; **at a — price** con rebaja, con descuento; **"greatly — prices"** "grandes rebajas"; *see* **circumstance**.
reducible [ri'dju:səbl] *adj* reducible.
reduction [ri'dʌkʃən] *n* reducción *f* (*in, of* de), disminución *f*; (*in price*) rebaja *f*; (*in rank*) degradación *f*; (*Mil*) reducción *f*, toma *f*, conquista *f*; (*shortening*) abreviación *f*; **"great —s"** (*Comm*) "grandes rebajas"; **there has been no — in demand** no ha disminuido la demanda.
redundance [ri'dʌndəns] *n* (*Gram*) redundancia *f*.
redundancy [ri'dʌndənsi] *n* exceso *m*, superfluidad *f*; (*among workers*) desempleo *m*; **the problems of —** los problemas del exceso de mano de obra.
redundant [ri'dʌndənt] *adj* excesivo, superfluo; (*Gram*) redundante; **to be —** estar de más; **the workers now made —** los obreros que quedan ahora sin trabajo; **automation may make some workers —** la automatización puede hacer que varios obreros pierdan sus puestos.
reduplicate [ri'dju:plikeit] *vt* reduplicar.
reduplication [ri,dju:pli'keiʃən] *n* reduplicación *f*.
redwood ['redwud] *n* secoya *f*.
redye ['ri:'dai] *vt* reteñir.
re-echo [ri:'ekəu] **1** *vt* repetir, resonar con. **2** *vi* resonar, repercutirse.
reed [ri:d] *n* (*Bot*) carrizo *m*, junco *m*, caña *f*; (*Mus: in mouthpiece*) lengüeta *f*, (*pipe*) caramillo *m*; **broken —** persona *f* (*or* cosa *f*) que no es de fiar, persona *f* débil.
redbed ['ri:dbed] *n* carrizal *m*, juncal *m*, cañaveral *m*.
re-edit ['ri:'edit] *vt* reeditar.
reedmace ['ri:dmeis] *n* anea *f*, enea *f*.
re-educate ['ri:'edjukeit] *vt* reeducar.
re-education ['ri:,edju'keiʃən] *n* reeducación *f*.
reedy ['ri:di] *adj place* lleno de cañas, cubierto de carrizos (*etc*); (*Mus*) agudo, alto y delgado.

reef[1] [riːf] (*Naut*) **1** *n* rizo *m*; **to let out a —** largar rizos, (*fig*) aflojar el cinturón (*etc*); **to take in a —** tomar rizos, (*fig*) apretar el cinturón (*etc*).
2 *vt* arrizar.
reef[2] [riːf] *n* (*Geog*) escollo *m*, arrecife *m*; **coral —** barrera *f* coralina.
reefer[1] ['riːfə*] *n* chaquetón *m*.
reefer[2] ['riːfə*] *n* (*sl*) pitillo *m* de marijuana.
reef knot ['riːfnɔt] *n* nudo *m* de marino.
reek [riːk] **1** *n* mal olor *m*, hedor *m* (*of* a).
2 *vi* (*smoke*) humear, vahear; (*smell*) oler, heder (*of* a); trascender (*of* a); **this —s of treachery** esto huele a traición; **she —s with affectation** su afectación es inaguantable; **he comes home simply —ing** vuelve a casa oliendo a vino de muy mala manera.
reel [riːl] **1** *n* (*in fishing etc*) carrete *m*; (*for tape recorder etc*) carrete *m*, bobina *f*; (*Sew*) broca *f*, devanadera *f*; (*Phot: for small camera*) carrete *f*, película *f*, rollo *m*, (*of cine film*) bobina *f*, cinta *f*; (*Mus*) baile escocés muy vivo; **about 20 right off the —** unos 20 seguidos, unos 20 sin parar.
2 *vt* (*Sew*) devanar; **to — in one's line** ir cobrando el sedal; **to — in a fish** tirar de un pez haciendo girar el carrete; **to — off** enumerar rápidamente, recitar de una tirada, ensartar.
3 *vi* tambalear, tambalearse; (*retreat*) cejar, retroceder; **he was —ing about drunkenly** andaba haciendo eses; **the boxer —ed to his corner** el boxeador se fué tambaleando a su rincón; **the mind —s** la mente queda atolondrada; **to make someone's mind —** atolondrar a uno; **my head is —ing** mi cabeza está dando vueltas.
re-elect ['riːi'lekt] *vt* reelegir.
re-election ['riːi'lekʃən] *n* reelección *f*.
re-eligible ['riː'elidʒəbl] *adj* reelegible.
re-emerge ['riːiˈməːdʒ] *vi* volver a salir, reaparecer.
re-enact ['riːi'nækt] *vt* (*Parl*) volver a promulgar; decretar de nuevo; (*Theat etc*) volver a representar; *crime* reconstituir.
re-engage ['riːin'geidʒ] *vt* contratar de nuevo.
re-enlist ['riːin'list] *vi* reengancharse, alistarse de nuevo.
re-enter ['riː'entə*] *vt* reingresar en, volver a entrar en.
re-entry ['riː'entri] *n* reingreso *m*, segunda entrada *f*; (*of spacecraft*) reentrada *f*, reingreso *m*.
re-equip ['riːi'kwip] *vt* equipar de nuevo (*with* con).
re-establish ['riːis'tæbliʃ] *vt* restablecer.
re-establishment ['riːis'tæbliʃmənt] *n* restablecimiento *m*.
reeve [riːv] *vt* (*Naut*) asegurar (con cabo); pasar por un ojal.
re-examination ['riːig.zæmi'neiʃən] *n* reexaminación *f*.
re-examine ['riːig'zæmin] *vt* reexaminar.
re-export ['riː'ekspɔːt] *vt* reexportar.
ref [ref] *n* (*fam*) árbitro *m*.
reface ['riː'feis] *vt* revestir de nuevo, forrar de nuevo (*with* de), poner un nuevo revestimiento a.
refashion ['riː'fæʃən] *vt* formar de nuevo.
refection [ri'fekʃən] *n* refacción *f*.
refectory [ri'fektəri] *n* refectorio *m*.
refer [ri'fəː*] **1** *vt* (a) (*send, direct*) remitir; **to — something to someone** remitir algo a uno; **to — someone to something** remitir a uno a algo; **the reader is —red to page 15** remito al lector a la página 15; **it is —red to us for decision** se remite a nosotros para que decidamos; **to — a matter to a lawyer** entregar un asunto a un abogado; **a cheque —red to drawer** (*R/D*) un cheque protestado por falta de fondos.
(b) (*ascribe*) atribuir, referir (*to* a); relacionar (*to* con); **he —s his mistake to tiredness** el error lo achaca a su cansancio; **he —s the painting to the 14th century** atribuye el cuadro al siglo XIV; **this insect is to be —red to the genus Pieris** este insecto ha de clasificarse en el género Pieris.
2 *vi*: **to — to** referirse a, aludir a, mencionar, hacer referencia a; **I — to our worthy president** me refiero a nuestro benemérito presidente; **we will not — to it again** no lo volveremos a mencionar; **—ring to yours of the 5th** me refiero a su carta del 5; **please — to section 3** véase la sección 3; **you must — to the original** hay que recurrir al original.
referable [ri'fəːrəbl] *adj*: **— to** referible a; atribuible a; que ha de clasificarse a.
referee [.refə'riː] **1** *n* (*in dispute, Sport etc*) árbitro *m*; (*for application, post*) persona *f* a quien se puede acudir para una recomendación. **2** *vti* arbitrar.

reference ['refrəns] **1** *n* (a) (*act of referring*) remisión *f*; **terms of —** puntos *mpl* de consulta; **it was agreed without — to me** se acordó sin consultarme, se decidió sin que se pidiera mi parecer.
(b) (*bearing*) relación *f* (*to* con); **with — to en** cuanto a, respecto de; **with — to yours of the 8th** me refiero a su carta del 8; **without — to any particular case** sin referirme (*etc*) a ningún caso concreto; **what — has A to B?** ¿qué tiene que ver A con B?; **it has no — to what I asked** no tiene que ver con lo que yo pregunté.
(c) (*allusion*) referencia *f*, alusión *f*, mención *f*; **he spoke without any — to you** habló sin mencionar para nada a Vd; **to make — to** referirse a, hacer referencia de.
(d) (*directive*) referencia *f*; sigla *f*; (*Typ: also — mark*) llamada *f*; **" — XYZ2"** "número de referencia: XYZ2"; **a — in the margin** una referencia al margen.
(e) (*testimonial*) referencia *f*; (*person*) persona *f* a quien se puede acudir para pedir una referencia; **to have good —s** tener buenas referencias; **to take up someone's —s** pedir referencias (*or* informes) acerca de uno.
2 *attr* number, point de referencia; book, library de consulta.
referendum [.refə'rendəm] *n* referéndum *m*.
refill ['riːfil] *n* repuesto *m*, recambio *m*; (*for pencil*) mina *f*.
refill ['riː'fil] *vt* rellenar, volver a llenar.
refine [ri'fain] **1** *vt* refinar; purificar; *society etc* refinar, educar, hacer más culto; *methods* refinar; *style* limar, purificar; *oil etc* refinar; *metal* acrisolar, acendrar; *fats* clarificar.
2 *vi*: **to — upon something** refinar algo, mejorar algo; (*discuss*) discutir algo con mucha sutileza.
refined [ri'faind] *adj* refinado; *society, person* fino, culto; (*pej: often pronounced* [ri'fiːnd]) redicho, afectado; *style* elegante, pulido.
refinement [ri'fainmənt] *n* refinamiento *m*; (*act, Tech*) refinación *f*; purificación *f*; (*of society, person*) finura *f*, cultura *f*, educación *f*; (*pej*) afectación *f*; (*of style*) elegancia *f*, urbanidad *f*; **a person of some —** una persona fina; **that is a — of cruelty** eso es ser más cruel todavía; **with every possible — of cruelty** con las formas más sutiles de la crueldad.
refiner [ri'fainə*] *n* refinador *m*.
refinery [ri'fainəri] *n* refinería *f*.
refit ['riː'fit] **1** *n* reparación *f*, compostura *f*; (*Naut*) embonada *f*.
2 *vt* reparar, componer; (*Naut*) reparar, embonar; **to — something with a device** volver a equipar algo con un dispositivo.
3 *vi* (*Naut*) repararse, embonarse.
refitting ['riː'fitiŋ] *n*, **refitment** ['riː'fitmənt] *n* reparación *f*, compostura *f*; (*Naut*) embonada *f*.
reflect [ri'flekt] **1** *vt* (a) reflejar; **plants —ed in the water** plantas *fpl* reflejadas en el agua; **the difficulties are —ed in his report** el informe se hace eco de las dificultades, las dificultades se reflejan en su informe.
(b) **the speech —s credit on him** el discurso le hace honor.
2 *vi* (a) (*think*) reflexionar, pensar; meditar; **— before you act** reflexione antes de obrar; **if we but — a moment** sí sólo reflexionamos un instante; **I —ed that . . .** pensé que . . .; **— on it!** ¡medítelo!
(b) **that —s well on him** eso le hace honor; **that —s ill on him** eso le muestra bajo una luz poco favorable; **it —s on all of us** eso tiende a perjudicarnos (*or* desprestigiarnos) a todos; **it —s on her reputation** eso pone en tela de duda su fama.
reflection [ri'flekʃən] *n* (a) (*of light: act*) reflexión *f*, (*image*) reflejo *m*; **the — of the light in the mirror** el reflejo de la luz en el espejo; **a pale — of former glories** un pálido reflejo de glorias pretéritas; **to see one's — in a shop window** verse reflejado en una vitrina.
(b) (*aspersion*) reproche *m* (*on* a), crítica *f*; **this is no — on your honesty** esto no dice nada en contra de su honradez, esto no es ningún reproche a su honradez; **to cast —s on someone** reprochar a uno.
(c) (*reconsideration*) **on —** después de volver a pensarlo, pensándolo bien; **without due —** sin pensarlo bastante; **mature —s suggests that . . .** una meditación más profunda indica que . . .
(d) (*idea*) pensamiento *m*, idea *f*; **"R—s on Ortega"** "Meditación *f* sobre Ortega".
reflective [ri'flektiv] *adj* pensativo, meditabundo.
reflectively [ri'flektivli] *adv* pensativamente; **he said —** dijo pensativo; **she looked at me —** me miró pensativa.

reflector [ri'flektə*] n reflector m; (Aut: also **rear —**) captafaros m, placa f de captafaros.
reflex ['ri:fleks] 1 adj reflejo. 2 n reflejo m.
reflexive [ri'fleksiv] adj reflexivo.
refloat ['ri:'fləut] vt sacar a flote.
reforestation ['ri:,fɔris'teiʃən] n repoblación f forestal.
reform [ri'fɔ:m] 1 n reforma f; **agrarian —, land —** reforma f agraria; **monetary —** reforma f monetaria. 2 vt reformar. 3 vi reformarse.
re-form ['ri:'fɔ:m] 1 vt formar de nuevo; reorganizar, reconstituir. 2 vi formarse de nuevo; reconstituirse; (Mil) rehacerse.
reformation [,refə'meiʃən] n reformación f; **R—** (Eccl) Reforma f.
reformatory [ri'fɔ:mətəri] n reformatorio m.
reformed [ri'fɔ:md] adj reformado.
reformer [ri'fɔ:mə*] n reformador m, ora f.
reformist [ri'fɔ:mist] 1 adj reformista. 2 n reformista mf.
refract [ri'frækt] vt refractar.
refracting [ri'fræktiŋ] adj: **— telescope** telescopio m de refracción.
refraction [ri'frækʃən] n refracción f.
refractive [ri'fræktiv] adj refractivo.
refractor [ri'fræktə*] n refractor m.
refractoriness [ri'fræktərinis] n obstinacia f.
refractory [ri'fræktəri] adj refractario, obstinado; (Tech) refractario.
refrain[1] [ri'frein] n estribillo m; **his constant — is . . .** siempre está con la misma canción . . .
refrain[2] [ri'frein] vi: **to — from something** abstenerse de algo; **to — from +** ger abstenerse de **+** infin; **I couldn't — from laughing** no pude menos de reír, no pude contener la risa.
refresh [ri'freʃ] vt refrescar.
refresher [ri'freʃə*] 1 n (fam) refresco m. 2 attr course de repaso.
refreshing [ri'freʃiŋ] adj refrescante; (fig) interesante, estimulante; **it's a — change to find this es** interesante encontrar esta novedad, es alentador encontrar esto; **it's — to hear some new ideas** escuchar nuevas ideas estimula la imaginación.
refreshment [ri'freʃmənt] n refresco m; **"R—s"** "Refrescos"; **to take some —** tomar algo, comer (or beber etc).
refreshment room [ri'freʃmənt,rum] n (Rail etc) cantina f.
refreshment stall [ri'freʃmənt,stɔ:l] n puesto m de refrescos.
refrigerant [ri'fridʒərənt] n refrigerante m.
refrigerate [ri'fridʒəreit] vt refrigerar.
refrigeration [ri,fridʒə'reiʃən] n refrigeración f.
refrigerator [ri'fridʒəreitə*] n nevera f, frigorífico m, refrigerador m.
refrigerator lorry [ri'fridʒəreitə,lɔri] n camión m frigorífico.
refrigerator ship [ri'fridʒəreitə,ʃip] n buque m frigorífico.
refuel [ri:'fjuəl] 1 vt reabastecer (or rellenar) de combustible. 2 vi repostar, repostar combustible.
refuelling ['ri:'fjuəliŋ] n reabastecimiento m (or rellenado m) de combustible.
refuge ['refju:dʒ] n refugio m, asilo m; (resort) recurso m; (hut) albergue m; **God is my —** Dios es mi amparo; **to seek —** buscar dónde guarecerse; **to take —** ponerse al abrigo, guarecerse; **to take — in** refugiarse en, (fig) acogerse a, recurrir a.
refugee [,refju'dʒi:] n refugiado m, a f.
refulgence [ri'fʌldʒəns] n refulgencia f.
refulgent [ri'fʌldʒənt] adj refulgente.
refund ['ri:fʌnd] n (act) devolución f; (amount) reembolso m.
refund [ri'fʌnd] vt devolver, reintegrar, reembolsar.
refurbish ['ri:'fɔ:biʃ] vt restaurar; (decorate) renovar; literary work refundir.
refurnish ['ri:'fɔ:niʃ] vt amueblar de nuevo.
refusal [ri'fju:zəl] n (a) negativa f, denegación f; **a blank (or flat) —** una rotunda negativa; **the offer met a flat —** rechazaron la oferta de plano.
(b) (Comm etc) opción f, opción f exclusiva; **you have first —** Vd tiene opción al artículo, lo ofreceré primero a Vd.
refuse ['refju:s] n basura f, desperdicios mpl, desecho m; **household —** basura f doméstica; **garden —** basura f de jardín.
refuse [ri'fju:z] 1 vt rehusar, rechazar, denegar; no querer aceptar; negar; **to — someone something** negar algo a uno; **they can — her nothing** son incapaces de privarla de nada; **I have never been —d here** aquí no se han negado nunca a servirme; **she —d my offer** rechazó mi oferta; **I regret to**

have to — your invitation siento no poder aceptar su invitación.
2 vi (a) **he —d se** negó a hacerlo; **to — to do something** negarse a hacer algo, rehusar hacer algo.
(b) (of horse) rehusar, plantarse, resistirse a saltar.
3 vr: **to — oneself something** privarse de algo.
refuse bin ['refju:sbin] n cubo m de la basura.
refuse dump ['refju:sdʌmp] n vertidero m, basurero m.
refuse lorry ['refju:s,lɔri] n camión m de la basura.
refutable [ri'fju:təbl] adj refutable.
refutation [,refju'teiʃən] n refutación f.
refute [ri'fju:t] vt refutar, rebatir.
regain [ri'gein] vt cobrar, recobrar, recuperar; (breath) cobrar; **to — consciousness** recobrar el conocimiento, volver en sí.
regal ['ri:gəl] adj regio, real.
regale [ri'geil] 1 vt agasajar, festejar; **to — someone on oysters** agasajar a uno dándole ostras de comer; **he —d the company with a funny story** para divertirles les contó a los comensales un chiste.
2 vr: **to — oneself on something** regalarse con algo.
regalia [ri'geiliə] n insignias fpl (esp reales).
regally ['ri:gəli] adv regiamente; con pompa (etc) regia.
regard [ri'gɑ:d] 1 n (a) (gaze) mirada f.
(b) (aspect, point) respecto m; aspecto m; **in — to, with —** con respecto a, en cuanto a, por lo que se refiere a; **in this —** con respecto a esto.
(c) (attention, care) atención f; **without — to** sin hacer caso de, sin considerar; **having — to** en atención a, considerando, teniendo en cuenta; **to have no — to** (of person) no prestar atención a, no tener en cuenta; (of relationship) no guardar relación con, no tener que ver con; **— must be had to this matter** hay que tener en cuenta este asunto.
(d) (esteem) respeto m, consideración f, estimación f; **my — for him** el respeto que le tengo; **out of — for** por respeto a; **to have a high — for someone, to hold someone in high —** tener buen concepto de uno, respetar mucho a uno; **to show — for someone** mostrar tener respeto a uno; **he shows little — for their feelings** le importan poco sus susceptibilidades.
(e) **—s** recuerdos mpl; **—s to X, please give my —s to X** recuerdos a X, salude de mi parte a X; **with kind —s** con muchos recuerdos.
2 vt (a) (look at) mirar; observar; **she —ed me with astonishment** me miró atónita.
(b) (consider) considerar; **we — it as worth doing** consideramos que vale la pena hacerlo; **we don't — it as necessary** no creemos que sea necesario; **they — it with horror** lo ven con horror; **to — someone with suspicion** recelarse de uno.
(c) **as —s** en cuanto a, por lo que se refiere a.
regardful [ri'gɑ:dful] adj: **— of** atento a.
regarding [ri'gɑ:diŋ] prep en cuanto a, por lo que se refiere a; **and other things — money** y otras cosas relativas al dinero.
regardless [ri'gɑ:dlis] 1 adj: **— of** indiferente a, insensible a; sin hacer caso de, sin pensar para nada en, sin miramientos de; **buy it — of the cost** cómpralo a no importa qué precio; **they shot them all — of rank** los fusilaron a todos sin miramientos a su graduación; **we did it — of the consequences** lo hicimos sin inquietarnos por las consecuencias.
2 adv (fam) a pesar de todo; pese a quien pese; **he went on —** continuó sin prestar atención a esto, a pesar de esto siguió adelante; **press on —!** ¡adelante sin contemplaciones!, ¡adelante pase lo que pase!
regatta [ri'gætə] n regata f.
regency ['ri:dʒənsi] n regencia f.
regenerate [ri'dʒenərit] adj regenerado.
regenerate [ri'dʒenəreit] vt regenerar.
regeneration [ri,dʒenə'reiʃən] n regeneración f.
regenerative [ri'dʒenərətiv] adj regenerador.
regent ['ri:dʒənt] 1 adj: **prince —** príncipe m regente. 2 n regente mf.
regicide ['redʒisaid] n (act) regicidio m; (person) regicida mf.
régime [rei'ʒi:m] n régimen m; **ancien —** antiguo régimen m; **under the Nazi —** bajo el régimen de los nazis.
regimen ['redʒimen] n régimen m.
regiment ['redʒimənt] n (Mil) regimiento m; **a whole — of mice** todo un ejército de ratones.
regiment ['redʒiment] vt organizar muy estrictamente; reglamentar; **we are very —ed at the college** en el colegio nuestra vida está organizada muy estrictamente.

regimental [,redʒi'mentl] *adj* de regimiento, del regimiento; (*fig*) militar; **with — precision** con precisión militar.

regimentals [,redʒi'mentlz] *npl* uniforme *m*.

regimentation [,redʒimen'teiʃən] regimentación *f*, organización *f* estricta.

Reginald ['redʒinld] *m* Reinaldos, Reginaldo.

region ['ri:dʒən] *n* región *f*; comarca *f*; zona *f*; **a fertile —** una región fértil; **the lower —s** (*fig*) el infierno; **in the — of 40** alrededor de 40, unos 40; **I felt a pain in the kidney —** sentí un dolor de riñones.

regional ['ri:dʒənl] *adj* regional; **— development** desarrollo *m* regional.

regionalism ['ri:dʒənəlizəm] *n* regionalismo *m*.

regionalist ['ri:dʒənəlist] **1** *adj* regionalista. **2** *n* regionalista *mf*.

register ['redʒistə*] **1** *n* registro *m*; (*Mus, Typ, of hotel*) registro *m*; (*in school*) lista *f*; (*of members*) lista *f*, padrón *m*; (*Univ, Naut*) matrícula *f*; (*Tech*) indicador *m*; **parish —** libro *m* parroquial, registro *m* parroquial; **— of births** registro *m* de nacimientos; **— of deaths** registro *m* de defunciones; **— of marriages** registro *m* de casamientos; **— of voters, voting —** registro *m* electoral; **to be in —** (*Typ*) estar en registro; **to call the —** (*School*) pasar lista; **to sign the —** (*in hotel*) firmar el registro; *see* ton.

2 *vt* (a) registrar; *birth etc* declarar; *trademark etc* registrar; (*record*) apuntar, registrar, hacer constar; (*Univ, Naut*) matricular; (*by post*) certificar, (*by rail*) facturar.

(b) (*of instruments*) marcar, indicar; *emotion* acusar, mostrar, manifestar; **the thermometer —s 40 degrees** el termómetro marca 40 grados; **he —d no surprise** no acusó sorpresa alguna; **the patient has —d a marked improvement** el enfermo ha acusado una notable mejoría; **production has —d a big fall** la producción ha experimentado un descenso considerable.

3 *vi* (a) (*sign on etc*) inscribirse, matricularse; **to — at an hotel** registrarse en un hotel; **to — for a course** matricularse en un curso.

(b) (*Typ*) estar en registro.

(c) producir impresión (*with* en); **it doesn't seem to have —ed with her** parece no haber producido impresión en ella; **when it finally —ed** cuando se dio cuenta de ello, cuando por fin comprendió; **things like that just don't —** las cosas así pasan inadvertidas.

registered ['redʒistəd] *adj letter* certificado, *baggage* facturado; *design, trademark etc* registrado; *student etc* matriculado.

register office ['redʒistər,ɔfis] *n see* **registry office**.

registrar [,redʒis'tra:*] *n* registrador *m*, archivero *m*; (*of society*) secretario *m*; (*Univ*) secretario *m* general; (*of births etc*) secretario *m* del registro civil.

registration [,redʒis'treiʃən] *n* (*act*) registro *m*; inscripción *f*; matrícula *f*; declaración *f*; certificación *f*, facturación *f*; (*number*: *Aut, Naut, Univ etc*) matrícula *f*; **the ship's Panamanian — has been withdrawn** se ha cancelado la matrícula panameña del buque.

registration fee [,redʒis'treiʃənfi:] *n* derechos *mpl* de matrícula.

registration tag [,redʒis'treiʃəntæg] *n* (*US Aut*) placa *f* de matrícula, matrícula *f*.

registry ['redʒistri] *n* registro *m*, archivo *m*; (*Univ etc*) secretaría *f* general; **servants' —** agencia *f* de colocaciones.

registry office ['redʒistri,ɔfis] *n* (*approx*) juzgado *m* municipal, registro *m* civil; **to get married at a —** casarse por lo civil, casarse por el juzgado.

regression [ri'greʃən] *n* regresión *f*.

regressive [ri'gresiv] *adj* regresivo.

regret [ri'gret] **1** *n* (a) sentimiento *m*, pesar *m*; remordimiento *m*; **much to my —, to my great —** con gran pesar mío; **to express one's — to someone** (*for act*) expresar su sentimiento a uno, disculparse con uno, (*for death etc*) enviar el pésame a uno; **to feel —** sentirlo, sentir pesar; **I have no —s** no me arrepiento de ello; **I say it with —** lo digo con pesar.

(b) **—s** (*excuses*) excusas *fpl*; **to send one's —s for not being able to come** mandar sus excusas por no poder venir.

2 *vt* sentir, lamentar; arrepentirse de; **I — the error** lamento el error; **it is to be —ted** es de sentir, es de lamentar; **to — that . . .** sentir que + *subj*, lamentar que + *subj*; **we — to inform you that . . .** lamentamos tener que informarle que . . .; **he — having said it** lamenta haberlo dicho, se arrepiente de haberlo dicho.

regretful [ri'gretful] *adj* pesaroso; arrepentido; **to be — that . . .** lamentar que + *subj*; **he was most — about it** lo lamentó profundamente; **we are not — about leaving** no nos pesa tener que partir.

regretfully [ri'gretfəli] *adv* con pesar, sentidamente; **she spoke —** habló con sentimiento; **— I have to tell you that . . .** siento tener que decirles que . . .

regrettable [ri'gretəbl] *adj* lamentable, deplorable; *loss etc* sensible.

regrettably [ri'gretəbli] *adv* lamentablemente; sensiblemente.

regroup ['ri:'gru:p] **1** *vt* reagrupar; (*Mil etc*) reorganizar. **2** *vi* reagruparse; (*Mil etc*) reorganizarse.

regrouping ['ri:'gru:piŋ] *n* reagrupación *f*; reorganización *f*.

regular ['regjulə*] **1** *adj* (a) regular; (*Eccl, Mil, Gram etc*) regular; uniforme; normal, corriente, constante; *attender, customer, reader etc* habitual, asiduo; **our — waiter** el camarero que suele servirnos; **the — travellers on a train** los que siempre viajan en un tren; **the — staff** los empleados permanentes; **— troops** tropas *fpl* regulares; **as a — reader of your journal, may I . . .** como lector habitual de su revista, me permito . . .; **as — as clockwork** con la regularidad de una máquina; **to have a — time for doing something** hacer algo siempre a la misma hora; **to make — use of something** usar algo con regularidad.

(b) (*systematic*) sistemático, regular; (*consistent*) constante; **— features** facciones *fpl* correctas; **a man of — habits** un hombre ordenado (en sus costumbres).

(c) (*normal*) normal, corriente; **the — word is "looking glass"** la palabra corriente es "espejo"; **it's perfectly —** es completamente normal; **it's quite — to see deer here** es corriente ver ciervos por aquí.

(d) (*intensive*) cabal, verdadero; **a — feast** un verdadero banquete; **there was a — quarrel** se riñó de verdad; **he's a — guy** es buen chico, es un verdadero amigo.

2 *n* (*Eccl*) regular *m*; (*Mil*) soldado *m* de línea; (*client etc*) parroquiano *m*, cliente *m* habitual; **one of the café —s** un asiduo del café; **we keep the best goods for our —s** guardamos lo mejor para nuestros clientes habituales.

regularity [,regju'læriti] *n* regularidad *f*; **with great —** con la mayor regularidad.

regularize ['regjuləraiz] *vt* regularizar; arreglar, poner en orden; **in order to — your position** para arreglar su situación.

regularly ['regjuləli] *adv* regularmente, con regularidad; **"use brand X —"** "use la marca X con regularidad"; **he's — late** siempre llega con retraso; **a — declined noun** un sustantivo de declinación regular; **this ground has been — fought over** sobre este terreno se ha luchado constantemente.

regulate ['regjuleit] *vt* regular (*also Mech etc*); arreglar, ajustar; (*make regulations for*) reglamentar; **to — one's life by . . .** vivir según las normas establecidas por . . ., vivir con arreglo a . . .; **to — prices** regular los precios.

regulation [,regju'leiʃən] **1** *n* (*act*) regulación *f*; arreglo *m*; (*rule*) regla *f*; reglamento *m*; **the —s are very strict** los reglamentos son muy estrictos; **to introduce new traffic —s** introducir un nuevo reglamento de la circulación.

2 *adj, attr* reglamentario, de reglamento; normal; **it's — wear in school** es el uniforme del reglamento en la escuela.

regulator ['regjuleitə*] *n* regulador *m*.

regurgitate [ri'gə:dʒiteit] **1** *vt* volver a arrojar, vomitar (sin esfuerzo); (*fig*) reproducir maquinalmente. **2** *vi* regurgitar.

regurgitation [ri'gə:dʒi'teiʃən] *n* regurgitación *f*; (*fig*) reproducción *f* maquinal.

rehabilitate [,ri:ə'biliteit] *vt* rehabilitar.

rehabilitation ['ri:ə,bili'teiʃən] *n* rehabilitación *f*.

rehash ['ri:'hæʃ] **1** *n* refundición *f*. **2** *vt* refundir.

rehearsal [ri'hə:səl] *n* enumeración *f*, repetición *f*; (*Mus, Theat etc*) ensayo *m*; **it was just a — for bigger things to come** fue a modo de ensayo para las empresas mayores que habían de venir después.

rehearse [ri'hə:s] *vt* enumerar, repetir; (*Mus, Theat etc*) ensayar.

rehouse ['ri:'hauz] *vt family* dar nueva vivienda a, proveer de vivienda nueva; trasladar a otra casa; **200 families have been —d** 200 familias tienen vivienda nueva ya.

reign [rein] **1** *n* reinado *m*; (*fig*) dominio *m*, predominio *m*; **the — of the miniskirt** la moda de la minifalda; **in** (*or* **under**) **the — of** bajo el reinado de. **2** *vi* reinar; (*fig*) predominar, imperar, prevalecer.

reigning ['reiniŋ] *adj monarch* reinante, actual; *(fig)* predominante, que impera.

reimburse [ˌriːim'bəːs] *vt* reembolsar; **to — someone for something** pagar *(or* reembolsar) a uno por algo.

reimbursement [ˌriːim'bəːsmənt] *n* reembolso *m*.

reimpose ['riːim'pəuz] *vt* volver a imponer, reimponer.

rein [rein] **1** *n* rienda *f*; **to draw** — detenerse *(also fig)*; **to give** — **to** dar rienda suelta a; **to keep a tight** — **on someone** vigilar mucho a uno, mantener una estrecha vigilancia sobre uno.
2 *vt*: **to — back, to — in** refrenar.
3 *vi*: **to — in** detenerse.

reincarnate [ˌriːin'kɑːneit] *vt* reencarnar; **to be —d** reencarnar, volver a encarnar.

reincarnation ['riːinkɑː'neiʃən] *n* reencarnación *f*.

reindeer ['reindiə*] *n* reno *m*.

reinforce [ˌriːin'fɔːs] *vt* reforzar *(also fig)*; *concrete etc* armar.

reinforced [ˌriːin'fɔːst] *adj* reforzado; *concrete* armado.

reinforcement [ˌriːin'fɔːsmənt] *n (act)* reforzamiento *m*; **—s** refuerzos *mpl*.

reinsert ['riːin'səːt] *vt* volver a insertar; volver a introducir.

reinstate ['riːin'steit] *vt suppressed passage etc* reintegrar *(in* a), volver a incluir; *(rehabilitate)* rehabilitar; *dismissed worker* volver a emplear; *dismissed official* restituir a su puesto.

reinstatement ['riːin'steitmənt] *n* reintegración *f (in* a); rehabilitación *f*; vuelta *f* a su empleo; restitución *f* a su puesto.

reinsurance ['riːin'ʃuərəns] *n* reaseguro *m*.

reinsure ['riːin'ʃuə*] *vt* reasegurar.

reintegrate ['riː'intigreit] *vt* reintegrar.

reintegration ['riːˌinti'greiʃən] *n* reintegración *f*.

reinter ['riːin'təː*] *vt* enterrar de nuevo.

reinvest ['riːin'vest] *vt* reinvertir.

reinvestment ['riːin'vestmənt] *n* reinversión *f*.

reinvigorate ['riːin'vigəreit] *vt* infundir nuevo vigor a; **to feel —d** sentirse con nuevas fuerzas.

reissue ['riː'iʃjuː] **1** *n* nueva emisión *f*; reimpresión *f*; reexpedición *f*; reestreno *m*.
2 *vt stamp* volver a emitir; *book* reimprimir; *patent etc* reexpedir; *film* reestrenar.

reiterate [riː'itəreit] *vt* reiterar, repetir; subrayar; **I must** — **that** . . . tengo que subrayar que . . .

reiteration [riːˌitə'reiʃən] *n* reiteración *f*, repetición *f*.

reiterative [riː'itərətiv] *adj* reiterativo.

reject ['riːdʒekt] *n* cosa *f* rechazada, cosa *f* defectuosa; persona *f* rechazada.

reject [ri'dʒekt] *vt offer etc* rechazar; *application* denegar; *motion* rechazar, desestimar; *plan etc* desechar; *solution* descartar; *advance* repulsar; *(of stomach etc)* arrojar.

rejection [ri'dʒekʃən] *n* rechazamiento *m*; denegación *f*; desestimación *f*; **to meet with a** — sufrir una repulsa; **the novel has already had 3** —**s** la novela ya ha sido rechazada 3 veces.

rejoice [ri'dʒɔis] **1** *vt* alegrar, regocijar, causar alegría a.
2 *vi* **(a)** alegrarse, regocijarse *(at, about, over* de); **let us not** — **too soon** es aconsejable no alegrarse demasiado pronto; **I** — **that it should be so me** alegro de que sea así.
(b) to — **in the name of Anastasius** ser el afortunado poseedor del nombre de Anastasio.

rejoicings [ri'dʒɔisiŋz] *npl* regocijo *m*, júbilo *m*, alegría *f*; fiestas *fpl*; **the** — **lasted far into the night** continuaron las fiestas hasta una hora avanzada.

rejoin [ri'dʒɔin] *vt* replicar, contestar.

rejoin ['riː'dʒɔin] *vt* reunirse con, volver a juntarse con; *regiment etc* reincorporarse a.

rejoinder [ri'dʒɔində*] *n* réplica *f*; **as a** — **to** . . . como contestación a.

rejuvenate [ri'dʒuːvineit] *vt* rejuvenecer.

rekindle ['riː'kindl] *vt* reencender; *(fig)* despertar, reavivar.

relapse [ri'læps] **1** *n (Med)* recaída *f*, recidiva *f*; *(into crime, error)* reincidencia *f*; **to have a** — *(Med)* recaer, tener una recaída.
2 *vi (Med)* recaer; *(into crime, error)* reincidir *(into* en).

relate [ri'leit] **1** *vt* **(a)** *(tell)* contar, narrar, relatar; **strange to** — aunque parece mentira, por raro que parezca.
(b) *(establish relation between)* relacionar *(to, with* con), establecer una conexión entre.
2 *vi*: **to** — **to** relacionarse con, tener que ver con, referirse a; **this** —**s to what I said yesterday** esto se refiere a lo que dije ayer.

related [ri'leitid] *adj* **(a)** *subject* afín, conexo; **they are** — **subjects** son temas afines; **this murder is not** — **to the other** este asesinato no tiene que ver con el otro, no hay relación entre este asesinato y el otro.
(b) *person* emparentado; **they are** — son parientes, están emparentados; **they are closely** — entre ellos hay un estrecho parentesco; **we are** — **but only distantly** somos parientes pero lejanos; **are you** — **to the prisoner?** ¿es Vd pariente del acusado?; **they became** — **by marriage to the Borgias** emparentaron con los Borja.

relating [ri'leitiŋ] *as prep*: **details** — **to X** detalles *mpl* acerca de X; **and other matters** — **to Y** y otros asuntos concernientes a Y.

relation [ri'leiʃən] *n* **(a)** *(narration)* narración *f*; relato *m*, relación *f*.
(b) *(relationship)* conexión *f*, relación *f (to, with* con); *(between persons)* parentesco *m*; **the** — **between A and B** la relación entre A y B; **in** — **to** respecto de, con relación a; **Proust in** — **to the French novel** Proust en relación con la novela francesa; **to bear a certain** — **to** . . . guardar cierta relación con . . .; **it bears no** — **to the facts** no tiene que ver con los hechos, se desentiende por completo de los hechos.
(c) *(correspondence)* —**s** relaciones *fpl*; **good** —**s** buenas relaciones *fpl*; **public** —**s** relaciones *fpl* públicas; **public** —**s officer** (PRO) encargado *m* de relaciones públicas; —**s are rather strained** las relaciones están algo tirantes; **to break off** —**s with someone** romper con uno; **we have broken off** —**s with Ruritania** hemos roto las relaciones con Ruritania; **to enter into** —**s with someone** establecer relaciones con uno; **we have business** —**s with them** tenemos relaciones comerciales con ellos; **to have sexual** —**s with someone** tener relaciones carnales con uno.
(d) *(relative)* pariente *m*, a *f*, familiar *mf*; **friends and** — amigos *mpl* y familiares; **close** — pariente *m* cercano, parienta *f* cercana; **two distant** —**s** dos parientes lejanos; **all my** —**s** todos mis parientes, toda mi familia; **what** — **is she to you?** ¿qué parentesco hay entre ella y Vd?; **she's no** — no es parienta mía.

relationship [ri'leiʃənʃip] *n* relación *f*, conexión *f (to, with* con); afinidad *f*; *(kinship)* parentesco *m*; *(between persons)* relaciones *fpl*; amistad *f*; trato *m*; — **by marriage** parentesco *m* por enlace matrimonial; **blood** — lazo *m* de parentesco; **our** — **lasted 5 years** nuestras relaciones continuaron durante 5 años; **they have a beautiful** — (US) les unen los lazos de la más fina amistad; **what is your** — **to the prisoner?** ¿qué parentesco hay entre Vd y el acusado?; **the** — **of A to B, the** — **between A and B** la relación entre A y B.

relative ['relətiv] **1** *adj* relativo *(to* a); **with** — **ease** con relativa facilidad.
2 *n* **(a)** *(Gram)* relativo *m*.
(b) *(person)* pariente *m*, a *f*, familiar *mf*; *see* **relation (d)**.

relatively ['relətivli] *adv* relativamente; **there are** — **few** hay relativamente pocos.

relativism ['relətivizəm] *n* relativismo *m*.

relativist ['relətivist] *n* relativista *mf*.

relativistic [ˌrelətiv'istik] *adj* relativista.

relativity [ˌrelə'tiviti] *n* relatividad *f*.

relax [ri'læks] **1** *vt grip etc* relajar, aflojar; *restrictions, severity* mitigar, suavizar; **to** — **one's muscles** aflojar los músculos; **to** — **one's hold on something** dejar de agarrarse de *(or* a) algo tan apretadamente, soltar algo.
2 *vi* **(a)** *(grip etc)* relajarse, aflojarse; *(restrictions, severity)* mitigarse, suavizarse; **his face** —**ed into a smile** se le aflojaron los músculos de la cara y empezó a sonreír; **we must not** — **in our efforts** es necesario no renunciar en lo más mínimo a nuestros esfuerzos *(to + infin* por + *infin)*.
(b) *(rest)* descansar; *(amuse oneself)* esparcirse, expansionarse; —**!** ¡cálmate! ¡no te apures!; **now there is time to** — **a little** ahora hay tiempo para esparcirse un poco; **we** —**ed in the sun of Majorca** nos expansionamos bajo el sol de Mallorca.

relaxant [ri'læksənt] *n* relajante *m*.

relaxation [ˌriːlæk'seiʃən] *n* **(a)** *(act)* relajación *f*, aflojamiento *m*; mitigación *f*.
(b) *(rest)* descanso *m*; *(amusement)* esparcimiento *m*, recreo *m*; **to seek** — **in painting** esparcirse dedicándose a la pintura; **to take some** — esparcirse, expansionarse.
(c) *(pastime)* pasatiempo *m*, recreo *m*, diversión *f*; **a favourite** — **of the wealthy** un pasatiempo favorito de los ricos.

relaxed [ri'lækst] *adj* tranquilo, sosegado, ecuánime; **he always seems so** — siempre parece tan sosegado; **try to be more** — procure ser más tranquilo.

relaxing [ri'læksiŋ] *adj climate etc* enervante.

relay [ri:lei] **1** *n* (**a**) (*of workmen*) tanda *f*; (*of horses*) parada *f*, posta *f*; (*Elec*) relai *m*, relais *m*, relé *m* (*Acad*); **to work in** —s trabajar por tandas.
   (**b**) (*Sport*) — **race** carrera *f* de relevos; **the 400 metres** — los 400 metros relevos.
   2 *vt* (*Radio etc*) retransmitir; **to** — **a message to someone** pasar un mensaje a uno, hacer llegar un mensaje a uno.

re-lay ['ri:'lei] *vt* volver a colocar; *cable, rail etc* volver a tender.

relay station ['ri:lei,steifən] *n* transmisora *f*.

release [ri'li:s] **1** *n* (**a**) liberación *f*; excarcelación *f*; libertad *f*; emisión *f*; lanzamiento *m*; disparo *m*; aflojamiento *m*; descargo *m*, absolución *f*; estreno *m*; publicación *f*; divulgación *f*; **a sudden** — **of gas** un súbito escape de gas; **a sudden** — **of creative energy** un repentino estallar de energía creadora; **death came as a merciful** — la muerte fue una liberación piadosa; **a film on general** — una película que se está estrenando en muchas partes; **his** — **came through on Monday** se aprobó su excarcelación el lunes.
   (**b**) (*Mech, Phot etc*) disparador *m*.
   2 *vt* (*set free*) soltar, libertar; *prisoner* poner en libertad, *convict* excarcelar; *gas, smoke etc* despedir, arrojar, emitir; *bomb* lanzar; *brake* soltar; (*Mech*) desenganchar, disparar; (*Phot*) disparar; *grip, hold* soltar, aflojar; *pressure* aflojar; *person from obligation* descargar, absolver (*from* de); *film* estrenar; *report etc* publicar, dar a conocer; *news* divulgar; — **me, sir!** ¡suélteme, señor!; **to** — **someone on bail** poner a uno en libertad bajo fianza; **they** —**d him to go to a new post** permitieron que se fuera a ocupar un nuevo puesto; **can you** — **him for a few hours each week?** ¿nos lo ceden para trabajar con nosotros algunas horas cada semana?

relegate ['religeit] *vt* relegar (*to* a); **Mérida is** —**d to the second division** (*Sport*) Mérida pasa a la segunda división, Mérida desciende a la segunda división.

relegation [,reli'geiʃən] *n* relegación *f*; (*Sport*) descenso *m*.

relent [ri'lent] *vi* ablandarse, apiadarse, ceder.

relentless [ri'lentlis] *adj* implacable, inexorable; despiadado; **with** — **severity** con implacable severidad; **he is quite** — **about it** en esto se muestra totalmente implacable.

relentlessly [ri'lentlisli] *adv* implacablemente, inexorablemente; **he presses on** — avanza implacable.

relet ['ri:'let] *vt* realquilar.

relevance ['reləvəns] *n* pertinencia *f*; conexión *f*, relación *f*; aplicabilidad *f*; **matters of doubtful** — asuntos *mpl* de dudosa pertinencia; **what is the** — **of that?** y eso ¿tiene que ver con lo que estamos discutiendo?

relevant ['reləvənt] *adj* (**a**) (*related*) pertinente; conexo, relacionado (*to* con); aplicable; **details** — **to this affair** detalles *mpl* relacionados con este asunto, detalles *mpl* concernientes a este asunto; **that is hardly** — eso apenas tiene que ver con lo que estamos discutiendo.
   (**b**) (*fitting*) apropiado, oportuno, adecuado; **bring the** — **papers** traiga los documentos oportunos; **we have all the** — **data** tenemos todos los datos que hacen al caso.

reliability [ri,laiə'biliti] *n* exactitud *f*, veracidad *f*; seguridad *f*; confianza *f*; confiabilidad *f*; formalidad *f*, seriedad *f*.

reliable [ri'laiəbl] *adj news etc* fidedigno, fehaciente, digno de crédito; *account* exacto, veraz; *machine etc* seguro; (*person: trustworthy*) de confianza, de fiar, confiable, (*businesslike*) formal, serio; **it's a most** — **firm** es una casa perfectamente seria; **I have it from a** — **source** lo sé de fuente fidedigna; **he's not very** — no es de fiar, no hay que fiarse de él; **I've always found him very** — siempre me ha parecido de mucha formalidad.

reliably [ri'laiəbli] *adv*: **I am** — **informed that . . .** sé de fuente fidedigna que . . .

reliance [ri'laiəns] *n* confianza *f* (*on* en); dependencia *f* (*on* de); **our excessive** — **on him** nuestra excesiva dependencia de él, el que dependamos tanto de él; **you can place no** — **on that** eso no es de fiar, no hay que tener confianza en eso.

reliant [ri'laiənt] *adj* confiado; **to be** — **on something** confiar en algo, tener confianza en algo.

relic ['relik] *n* reliquia *f*, vestigio *m*; (*Eccl*) reliquia *f*.

relict ['relikt] *n* viuda *f*.

relief [ri'li:f] **1** *n* (**a**) (*alleviation*) alivio *m*; desahogo *m*; consuelo *m*; aligeramiento *m*; (*of taxation*) desgravación *f*; **by way of light** — a modo de diversión; **there is a comic scene by way of** — para aliviar la tensión sigue una escena cómica; **that's a** —! ¡menos mal!; **it is a** — **to find that . . .** me consuela encontrar que . . . , me alegro de encontrar que . . . ; **the medicine brings** — la medicina alivia; **it came as a** — **when they left** se aliviaron todos cuando ellos se marcharon; **to heave a sigh of** — dar un suspiro de alivio.
   (**b**) (*aid*) socorro *m*, ayuda *f*; **poor** — socorro *m*, beneficencia *f*; **to go on** — vivir de la beneficencia; **to go to someone's** — acudir a socorrer a uno.
   (**c**) (*Mil: of town*) descerco *m*, socorro *m*; (*party*) relevo *m*.
   (**d**) (*Law*) satisfacción *f*, remedio *m*.
   (**e**) (*Art*) relieve *m*, realce *m*; **high** — alto relieve *m*; **low** — bajo relieve *m*; **to stand out in** — destacar; **to throw something into** — hacer resaltar algo, (*fig*) servir para destacar (*or* subrayar) algo.
   2 *attr* (**a**) — **work** trabajos *mpl* de socorro; — **works** obras *fpl* públicas; — **party**, — **troops** relevo *m*; — **train** tren *m* suplementario.
   (**b**) — **map** mapa *m* en relieve.

relieve [ri'li:v] **1** *vt* (**a**) *sufferings etc* aliviar, mitigar; *person's mind* tranquilizar; *feelings* desahogar; *burden* aligerar; *pain, headache etc* quitar, suprimir, aliviar; **to** — **one's feelings** desahogarse; **I** —**ed my feelings in a letter** me desahogué escribiendo una carta; **to** — **nature** hacer del cuerpo; **to** — **the boredom of the journey** para aliviar el aburrimiento del viaje; **the plain is** —**d by an occasional hill** de vez en cuando una colina alivia la monotonía de la llanura.
   (**b**) **to** — **the poor** socorrer a los pobres.
   (**c**) **to** — **someone from doing something** librar a uno de la necesidad de hacer algo; **to** — **someone of anxiety** tranquilizar a uno; **this** —**s us of financial worries** esto acaba con nuestras preocupaciones económicas; **to** — **someone of a duty** exonerar a uno de un deber; **to** — **someone of a post** destituir a uno; **he was** —**d of his command** fue relevado de su mando; **to** — **someone of his wallet** quitar la cartera a uno, robar la cartera a uno; **let me** — **you of your coat** permítame tomarle el abrigo.
   (**d**) (*Mil*) *city* descercar, socorrer; *troops* relevar.
   2 *vr* (**a**) **to** — **oneself** hacer del cuerpo.
   (**b**) **to** — **oneself of a burden** quitarse un peso de encima.

relievo [ri'li:vəu] *n* relieve *m*.

religion [ri'lidʒən] *n* religión *f*; **to get** — (*fam*) darse a la religión.

religiosity [ri,lidʒi'ositi] *n* religiosidad *f*.

religious [ri'lidʒəs] **1** *adj* religioso; (*fig*) puntual, exacto, fiel; — **instruction** enseñanza *f* religiosa; — **toleration** libertad *f* de cultos.
   2 *n* religioso *m*, a *f*.

religiously [ri'lidʒəsli] *adv* religiosamente; (*fig*) puntualmente, exactamente, fielmente.

religiousness [ri'lidʒəsnis] *n* religiosidad *f*.

reline ['ri:'lain] *vt* reforzar, poner nuevo forro a.

relinquish [ri'liŋkwiʃ] *vt* abandonar, renunciar a; *grip* soltar; *post* renunciar a, dimitir de.

relinquishment [ri'liŋkwiʃmənt] *n* abandono *m*, renuncia *f*; dimisión *f*.

reliquary ['relikwəri] *n* relicario *m*.

relish ['reliʃ] **1** *n* (*flavour*) sabor *m*, gusto *m*; (*smack*) dejo *m* (*of* de), sabor *m* (*of* a); (*attractive quality*) apetencia *f*; (*appetite*) apetito *m*; (*zest*) entusiasmo *m*; (*liking*) afición *f*; (*sauce*) salsa *f*, condimento *m*; **to eat something with** — comer algo con apetito; **to do something with** — hacer algo de buena gana, hacer algo con entusiasmo; **to have a** — **for something** apetecer algo, gustar de algo, ser aficionado a algo; **hunting has no** — **for me now** ya no me apetece la caza; **the** — **for hunting does not seem to be so strong** no parece que la caza atraiga tanto, parece que hay menos afición a la caza.
   2 *vt taste, savour* paladear, saborear; (*like*) gustar de, tener buen apetito para; **I don't** — **the idea** no me gusta la idea; **I** — **a day's fishing** apetece salir de pesca un día, me gusta pasar el día pescando; **do you** — **some fishing?** ¿quieres ir a pescar?; **I don't** — **the idea of staying up all night** no me hace gracia la idea de estar levantado toda la noche.

relive ['ri:'liv] *vt* vivir de nuevo, volver a vivir.

reload ['ri:'ləud] *vt* recargar, volver a cargar.

relocate ['ri:ləu'keit] *vt* volver a colocar, volver a situar.

reluctance [ri'lʌktəns] n desgana f, renuencia f, repugnancia f; **with — a** desgana, de mala gana; **to affect —** aparentar no querer.
reluctant [ri'lʌktənt] adj (a) **he was —** no quiso, se mostró poco dispuesto a hacerlo; **to be — to do something** estar poco dispuesto a hacer algo, tener pocas ganas de hacer algo; **he was — to decide** vaciló en decidirse; **I should be most — to let you go** me resistiría a permitirle ir, no consentiría de buena gana en que fuera Vd.
(b) **it had his — agreement** consintió pero de mala gana; **the — dragon** el dragón que no quiso; **I should make a — secretary** no quiero en absoluto ser secretario.
reluctantly [ri'lʌktəntli] adv de mala gana, a regañadientes; **she went —** se fue pero de mala gana; **I — agree** consiento pero contra mi voluntad.
rely [ri'lai] vi: **to — on** confiar en, fiarse de, contar con; **you can't — on the trains** es imposible fiarse de los trenes; **one can't — on the weather** no puede uno fiarse del tiempo; **we are —ing on you to do it** contamos con Vd para hacerlo, confiamos en que Vd lo haga.
remain [ri'mein] vi (a) (be left over) sobrar; (survive) quedar; **if any —** si sobra alguno; **few — quedan pocos**; **the few pleasures that — to me** los pocos placeres que me quedan; **nothing —s but to sell up** no queda otro remedio sino venderlo todo; **it —s to be done** queda por hacer; **it —s to be seen whether . . .** queda por descubrir si . . .; **more than half —s to be built** queda por construir más de la mitad.
(b) (continue) quedar, quedarse, permanecer; seguir, continuar; **we —ed there 3 weeks** nos quedamos allí 3 semanas; **how long do you expect to —?** ¿cuánto tiempo piensa quedarse aquí?; **that objection —s** queda (en pie) esa objeción; **it will — in my memory** quedará grabado en mi memoria; **the fact —s that . . .** sigue siendo un hecho que . . ., no es menos cierto que . . .; **to — behind** quedarse; **to — seated, to — sitting** permanecer sentado; **to — standing** permanecer de pie.
(c) (with adj complement) **to — faithful to** seguir fiel a; **the problem —s unsolved** el problema sigue sin solucionar; **it —s true that . . .** no es menos cierto que . . .; **it —s the same** sigue siendo lo mismo; **if the weather —s fine** si el tiempo sigue bueno.
(d) (in letters) **I — yours faithfully** le saluda atentamente.
remainder [ri'meində*] 1 n resto m; **the —** lo que sobra, lo que queda; los (etc) demás; (Math) residuo m, resta f; (books) restos mpl de edición; **the — of the debt** el resto de la deuda; **during the — of the day** durante el resto del día; **the — would not come** los otros (or los demás) no quisieron venir.
2 vt books etc saldar.
remaining [ri'meiniŋ] adj que queda; **the 3 — possibilities** las 3 posibilidades que quedan; **the — passengers** los otros pasajeros, los demás pasajeros.
remains [ri'meinz] npl (human, archaeological etc) restos mpl; (left-overs) sobras fpl, desperdicios mpl; **human — restos** humanos; **literary — obras** fpl póstumas; **mortal — restos** mpl mortales.
remake ['riː'meik] (irr: see **make**) vt rehacer.
remand [ri'maːnd] 1 n: **to be on —** estar detenido (mientras se investiga una acusación or se prepara el proceso).
2 vt reencarcelar (para que se investigue una acusación or se prepare el proceso); **to — someone for a week** reencarcelar a uno durante una semana; **he was —ed to Brixton** volvieron a encarcelarle en Brixton.
remand home [ri'maːnd,həum] n reformatorio m de menores.
remark [ri'maːk] 1 n (a) (notice) **worthy of —** notable, digno de notar; **to let something pass without —** dejar pasar algo sin hacer ningún comentario acerca de ello.
(b) (comment) observación f; comentario m; **"R—s on the Press"** "Observaciones fpl sobre la Prensa"; **after some introductory —s** después de hacer algunas observaciones a modo de prefacio; **to make a —** hacer una observación; **to make the — that . . .** observar que . . .; **to pass —s on someone** hacer observaciones acerca de uno, (freq) hacer un comentario desfavorable sobre uno.
2 vt observar, notar.
3 vi: **to — on something** hacer una observación sobre algo, comentar algo.

remarkable [ri'maːkəbl] adj notable, singular; extraordinario; **—!, most —!** ¡qué raro!; **with — skill** con singular habilidad; **it is in no way —** no tiene nada que sea digno de notar; **what's — about that?** ¿es que eso le parece singular?; **he's a most — man** es un hombre extraordinario.
remarkably [ri'maːkəbli] adv extraordinariamente.
remarriage ['riː'mærid3] n segundas nupcias fpl, segundo casamiento m.
remarry ['riː'mæri] vi volver a casarse, casarse en segundas nupcias.
remediable [ri'miːdiəbl] adj remediable.
remedial [ri'miːdiəl] adj remediador; (Med) curativo, terapéutico; **— teaching** enseñanza f de los niños (etc) atrasados; **— exercises** gimnasia f terapéutica.
remedy ['remədi] 1 n remedio m (for para curar); (Law etc) recurso m; **there's no — for that** eso no tiene remedio; **the best — for that is to protest** eso se remedia protestando; **to have no — at law** no tener recurso legal.
2 vt remediar; curar; **that's soon remedied** eso es fácil remediarlo, eso fácilmente queda arreglado.
remember [ri'membə*] 1 vt (a) (recall) acordarse de, recordar; **I — seeing it, I — having seen it** recuerdo haberlo visto; **she —ed to do it** se acordó de hacerlo; **don't you — me?** ¿no se acuerda Vd de mí?; **it is worth —ing that . . .** vale la pena recordar que . . .; **give me something to — you by** dame algún recuerdo tuyo; **so I gave him something to — me by** (fig) así que le di algo para que no me olvidara; **to — someone in one's will** mencionar a uno en su testamento.
(b) (bear in mind) tener presente, no olvidar; **— that he carries a gun** tenga presente que lleva revólver; **— what happened before** no se olvide de lo que pasó antes, acuérdese de lo que pasó antes; **— to turn out the light** no te olvides de apagar la luz; **— who you're with!** ¡piensa con quién estás!
(c) (with wishes) **— me to him!** ¡dale recuerdos míos!; **she asks to be —ed to you all** ella les manda recuerdos para todos.
2 vi: **yes, I —** sí, me acuerdo; **if I — aright** si bien me acuerdo; **as far as I can —** que yo recuerde.
remembrance [ri'membrəns] n (remembering) recordación f; memoria f; (souvenir) recuerdo m; **—s recuerdos** mpl; **in — of** en conmemoración de, para conmemorar; **I have no — of** it no lo recuerdo en absoluto; **R— Day** conmemoración del fin de la guerra en 1918 (y de las dos guerras mundiales), 11 de noviembre.
remind [ri'maind] 1 vt recordar; **to — someone of something** recordar algo a uno; **that —s me of last time** eso me recuerda la vez pasada; **she —s me of Anne** me recuerda a Ana, me hace pensar en Ana, tiene mucho parecido con Ana; **that —s me!** y a propósito . . .; **to — someone to do something** recordar a uno que haga algo; **you have to keep —ing him to do it** hay que traérselo constantemente a la memoria.
2 vr: **to — oneself that . . .** recordarse que . . .; **I — myself about it all the time** me lo recuerdo constantemente.
reminder [ri'maində*] n (a) recordatorio m; advertencia f; **it's a gentle —** es una advertencia amistosa; **we will send a —** le enviaremos un recordatorio.
(b) (memento) recuerdo m; **it's a — of the good old days** recuerda los buenos tiempos pasados.
reminisce [,remi'nis] vi contar los recuerdos, recordar viejas historias (about de).
reminiscence [,remi'nisəns] n reminiscencia f, recuerdo m; **"R—s of life in the Congo"** "Recuerdos mpl de la vida en el Congo"; **the symphony has —s of Mozart** la sinfonía tiene reminiscencias de Mozart.
reminiscent [,remi'nisənt] adj (a) **it's a — work** es una obra sugestiva; **to be in a — mood** estar de humor para contar los recuerdos, estar de humor para evocar el pasado.
(b) **to be — of something** recordar algo, (pej) oler a algo, sonar a algo; **that bit is — of Rossini** ese trozo recuerda a Rossini, ese trozo tiene reminiscencia de Rossini; **that's — of another old joke** eso suena a otro chiste viejo.
reminiscently [,remi'nisəntli] adv: **he spoke —** habló pensando en el pasado.
remiss [ri'mis] adj negligente, descuidado; **I have been very — about it** he sido muy descuidado en eso; **you have been — in not attending to it** Vd merece que se le censure por no atenderlo, el no atenderlo ha sido por descuido suyo.

remission [ri'miʃən] n remisión f; — **of sins** remisión f de los pecados; **to earn 6 months'** — merecer que se le perdonen 6 meses de la condena.

remissness [ri'misnis] n negligencia f, descuido m.

remit [ri'mit] vt (a) (send) remitir, enviar. (b) (excuse) perdonar; **3 months of the sentence were** —**ted** se le perdonaron 3 meses de la condena.

remittance [ri'mitəns] n remesa f, envío m.

remittance man [ri'mitənsmæn] n, pl — **men** [men] persona f a quien se paga una pensión a condición de que viva alejado de la patria.

remittee [remi'tiː] n consignatario m, a f.

remittent [ri'mitənt] adj fever etc remitente.

remitter [ri'mitə*] n remitente mf.

remnant ['remnənt] n (remainder) resto m, residuo m; (of cloth) retazo m; (relic) vestigio m, resto m.

remodel ['riː'mɔdl] vt modelar de nuevo, remodelar; rehacer; reorganizar; (Lit etc) refundir.

remonstrance [ri'mɔnstrəns] n protesta f, reconvención f.

remonstrate ['remənstreit] vi protestar, objetar; **to** — **about something** protestar contra algo, poner reparos a algo; **to** — **with someone** reconvenir a uno.

remorse [ri'mɔːs] n remordimiento m; **to feel** — arrepentirse, compungirse.

remorseful [ri'mɔːsful] adj arrepentido, compungido; **now he's** — ahora está lleno de remordimientos, ahora le remuerde la conciencia.

remorsefully [ri'mɔːsfəli] adv con remordimiento; **he said** — dijo compungido.

remorsefulness [ri'mɔːsfulnis] n remordimiento m.

remorseless [ri'mɔːslis] adj implacable, despiadado, inexorable.

remorselessly [ri'mɔːslisli] adv implacablemente, despiadadamente, inexorablemente.

remorselessness [ri'mɔːslisnis] n inexorabilidad f.

remote [ri'məut] adj (a) remoto; distante, lejano; aislado; (slight) ligero, leve; **in a** — **spot** en un lugar remoto; **in a** — **farmstead** en una alquería aislada, en una alquería apartada; **it's** — **from the town** está lejos de la ciudad; **she is** — **from such things** queda alejada de tales cosas, tales cosas le son ajenas; **in some** — **future** en un futuro lejano; **it's a** — **prospect** es poco probable, de eso existe poca probabilidad; **there is a** — **resemblance** hay un ligero parecido; **he hasn't the** —**st chance** no tiene la más remota posibilidad; **I haven't the** —**st idea** no tengo la más remota idea.
(b) — **control** comando m a distancia, telecontrol m.

remote-controlled [ri'məutkən'trəuld] adj dirigido a distancia, teledirigido.

remotely [ri'məutli] adv remotamente; **it is** — **situated** está situado en un lugar remoto; **they are** — **related** hay un parentesco lejano entre ellos; **it's not even** — **likely** de eso no hay la más remota posibilidad.

remoteness [ri'məutnis] n distancia f; aislamiento m, alejamiento m; **her** — **from everyday life** su alejamiento de la vida diaria.

remould, (US) **remold** ['riː'məuld] vt tyre recauchutar.

remount [ri'maunt] **1** n (Mil etc) remonta f. **2** vt volver a subir (a), subir de nuevo (a); (on horse) montar de nuevo. **3** vi subir de nuevo.

removable [ri'muːvəbl] adj separable, amovible; collar etc de quita y pon.

removal [ri'muːvəl] n remoción f, el quitar (etc); supresión f; separación f; eliminación f; extirpación f; destitución f; el tachar; solución f; disipación f; apartamiento m, alejamiento m; (of house) mudanza f; **his** — **to a new post** su traslado a un nuevo puesto; **the** — **of this threat** la eliminación de esta amenaza.

removal van [ri'muːvəlvæn] n camión m de mudanzas.

remove [ri'muːv] **1** n: **this is but one** — **from disaster** esto raya en la catástrofe; **this is several** —**s from our official policy** en esto nos apartamos bastante de nuestra política oficial.
2 vt (take away) quitar; llevarse; (take off) quitar, clothes etc quitarse; (steal) llevarse, robar; (get out of the way) quitar de en medio; letter, passage, tax etc suprimir; name from list tachar, borrar (from de); (Mech) part etc separar, retirar, quitar; obstacle, threat, waste eliminar; (Med) appendix etc extirpar; person from post destituir; problem solucionar; doubt disipar; fear acabar con; (do away with) person quitar de en medio, eliminar; competitor apartar, alejar, deshacerse de; — **hats on entering** se ruega descubrirse al entrar; **he** —**d his hat** se descubrió, se quitó el sombrero; **first** — **the lid** primero quite la tapa; — **that bauble** que se

quite esa chuchería de en medio; **this effectively** —**d him from the scene** esto terminó de alejarle de allí; **illness** —**d him from politics** una enfermedad le hizo abandonar la política; **to** — **something to another place** trasladar algo a otro sitio, cambiar algo de sitio.
3 vi mudarse, trasladarse (to a).
4 vr: **to** — **oneself** irse, marcharse; quitarse de en medio; **kindly** — **yourself** at once haga el favor de irse inmediatamente; **to** — **oneself to another place** irse a otro sitio; **I must** — **myself** tengo que marcharme.

remover [ri'muːvə*] n (owner) agente m de mudanzas; (workman) carrero m.

remunerate [ri'mjuːnəreit] vt remunerar.

remuneration [ri,mjuːnə'reiʃən] n remuneración f.

remunerative [ri'mjuːnərətiv] adj remunerador.

Renaissance [rə'nesɑːns] **1** n Renacimiento m; **the 12th century** — el Renacimiento del siglo XII.
2 adj, attr renacentista, del Renacimiento.

renal ['riːnl] adj renal.

rename ['riː'neim] vt poner nuevo nombre a; **they have** —**d it "Mon Repos"** le han puesto el nuevo nombre de "Mon Repos".

renascence [ri'næsns] n renacimiento m; **a spiritual** — un renacimiento espiritual, un despertar espiritual.

renascent [ri'næsnt] adj renaciente, que renace.

renationalization ['riː,næʃnəlai'zeiʃən] n reestatificación f.

renationalize ['riː'næʃnəlaiz] vt reestatificar.

rend [rend] (irr: pret and ptp **rent**) vt (lit) (tear) rasgar, desgarrar; (split) hender, rajar; **to** — **something in twain** partir algo por medio, hender algo; **to** — **one's dress** rasgar su ropa; **to turn and** — **someone** perder por fin la paciencia y arremeter contra uno; **a cry rent the air** un grito desgarró los aires; **the air was rent with cries** los aires se llenaron súbitamente de gritos.

render ['rendə*] vt (a) (return) **to** — **good for evil** devolver bien por mal; **to** — **thanks to someone** dar las gracias a uno.
(b) (hand over) entregar; **to** — **up** ceder, entregar; **the earth** —**s up its treasures** la tierra rinde sus tesoros; — **unto Caesar . . .** a Dios lo que es de Dios y al César lo que es del César.
(c) (give) service hacer, prestar; assistance dar, prestar; honour dar.
(d) (send in) **to** — **an account** (Comm) pasar factura; **to account** —**ed** según factura anterior; **to** — **an account of one's stewardship** dar cuenta de su gobierno, justificar su conducta durante su mando; **to** — **an account to God** dar cuenta de sí ante Dios.
(e) (reproduce) reproducir, representar; (Mus) interpretar, ejecutar; (translate) traducir, vertir (into a); **no photograph could adequately** — **the scene** ninguna fotografía pudiera representar adecuadamente la escena; **how does one** — **"cursi"**? ¿cómo se traduce "cursi"?
(f) (make) hacer, volver; **this** —**s it impossible** esto lo hace imposible, esto lo imposibilita; **you have** —**d our efforts useless** Vd ha hecho inútiles nuestros esfuerzos.
(g) fat (also to — **down**) derretir.

rendering ['rendəriŋ] n reproducción f, representación f; (Mus) interpretación f; traducción f, versión f; **her** — **of the sonata** su interpretación de la sonata; **an elegant** — **of Machado** una elegante versión de Machado.

rendez-vous ['rɔndivuː] **1** n cita f; lugar m de una cita; — **in space** cita f espacial; **to have a** — **with someone** tener cita con uno; **to make a** — **with another ship at sea** efectuar un enlace con otro buque en el mar.
2 vi reunirse, verse; **we will** — **at 8** nos reuniremos a las 8; **the ships will** — **off Vigo** los buques efectuarán el enlace a la altura de Vigo.

rendition [ren'diʃən] n (Mus) interpretación f, ejecución f.

renegade ['renigeid] **1** adj renegado. **2** n renegado m, a f.

renew [ri'njuː] vt renovar; (resume) reanudar; lease, loan etc extender, prorrogar; subscription renovar; promise reafirmar; attack etc volver a; effort etc volver a hacer, redoblar; **to** — **an acquaintance with someone** volver a trabar amistad con uno; **to** — **the attack on someone** volver a arremeter contra uno; **to** — **the attack on a town** volver a atacar una ciudad; **to** — **one's strength** restablecer sus fuerzas, cobrar nuevo vigor.

renewable [ri'njuːəbl] adj renovable.

renewal [ri'njuːəl] n renovación f; reanudación f; extensión f; prorrogación f; reafirmación f; — of **subscriptions** renovación f de suscripciones; **the — of the attack** el nuevo ataque; **a spiritual —** una renovación espiritual.

renewed [ri'njuːd] adj renovado; nuevo; **with — vigour** con nuevo vigor, con redoblado vigor; **to feel spiritually —** sentirse con nuevas fuerzas espirituales.

rennet ['renit] n cuajo m.

renounce [ri'nauns] **1** vt right, inheritance, offer etc renunciar; plan, post, the world etc renunciar a. **2** vi (Cards) renunciar.

renouncement [ri'naunsmənt] n renuncia f.

renovate ['renəuveit] vt renovar.

renovation [,renəu'veiʃən] n renovación f.

renown [ri'naun] n renombre m, nombradía f.

renowned [ri'naund] adj renombrado; **it is — for . . .** es famoso por . . . , es célebre por . . .

rent[1] [rent] **1** pret and ptp of **rend**. **2** n (tear) rasgón m, rasgadura f; (split) abertura f, raja f, hendedura f; (fig) escisión f, cisma m.

rent[2] [rent] **1** n alquiler m, arriendo m; **we pay £3 in —** pagamos 3 libras de alquiler; **to build flats for —** construir pisos para alquilarlos; **"for —"** (US) **"se alquila"**.
  2 vt: **to — a flat from someone** alquilar un piso de uno; **to — a house (out) to someone** alquilar una casa a uno; **it is —ed out at £4 a week** está alquilado a 4 libras por semana.

rental ['rentl] n alquiler m, arriendo m; **fixed —** alquiler m fijo; **yearly —** alquiler m anual.

rent collector ['rentkə,lektə*] n recaudador m de alquileres.

rent control ['rentkən,trəul] n control m de alquileres.

rent-controlled ['rentkən,trəuld] adj: **a — flat** un piso de alquiler controlado.

rent-free ['rent'friː] **1** adj house etc exento de alquiler, gratuito. **2** adv: **to live —** ocupar una casa (etc) sin pagar alquiler.

rentier ['rɔntiei] n rentista m.

rent-roll ['rentrəul] n lista f de alquileres.

renumber ['riː'nʌmbə*] vt volver a numerar; corregir la numeración f.

renunciation [ri,nʌnsi'eiʃən] n renuncia f.

reoccupy ['riː'ɔkjupai] vt volver a ocupar.

reopen ['riː'əupən] **1** vt volver a abrir, reabrir; **to — a case** (Law) rever un pleito, rever un proceso, (fig) reconsiderar un asunto.
  2 vi volver a abrirse, reabrirse; **school —s on the 8th** el nuevo curso comienza el día 8.

reopening ['riː'əupniŋ] n reapertura f; (Law) revisión f; reconsideración f.

reorder ['riː'ɔːdə*] vt **(a)** objects ordenar (or arreglar etc) de nuevo, volver a poner en orden. **(b)** (Comm) volver a pedir, repetir el pedido de.

reorganization ['riː,ɔːgənai'zeiʃən] n reorganización f.

reorganize ['riː'ɔːgənaiz] **1** vt reorganizar. **2** vt reorganizarse.

rep[1] [rep] n (fabric) reps m.

rep[2] [rep] n (Comm, fam) viajante m, agente m.

rep[3] [rep] n (fam) = **repertory**.

repack ['riː'pæk] vt object reembalar, reenvasar, devolver a su caja (etc); case volver a hacer.

repaint ['riː'peint] vt repintar; **to — something blue** repintar algo de azul.

repair[1] [ri'pɛə*] vi: **to — to** (move to) trasladarse a, dirigirse a; (go regularly to) acudir a, reunirse en.

repair[2] [ri'pɛə*] **1** n (act) reparación f, compostura f; (patch etc) remiendo m; **—s** reparaciones fpl; (Archit) obras fpl, reformas fpl; **"closed for —s"** "cerrado por reformas"; **cost of —s** coste m de las reparaciones; **to be in (good) —** estar en buen estado; **to keep a house in (good) —** mantener una casa en buen estado; **to be under —** estar siendo reparado, (Archit) estar en obras; **it is beyond —** es irreparable, no se puede reparar, (fig) no tiene remedio; **it is damaged beyond —** ha sufrido tantos desperfectos que no se puede reparar.
  2 vt reparar, componer; shoes etc remendar.

repairable [ri'pɛərəbl] adj que se puede reparar.

repair kit [ri'pɛəkit] n caja f de herramientas para reparaciones.

repairman [ri'pɛəmæn] n, pl **-men** [men] (US) reparador m, mecánico m.

repair shop [ri'pɛəʃɔp] n taller m de reparaciones.

repaper ['riː'peipə*] vt empapelar de nuevo.

reparable ['repərəbl] adj reparable.

reparation [,repə'reiʃən] n reparación f; satisfacción f; **—s** (Fin) indemnizaciones fpl; **to make —s** dar satisfacción (for por).

repartee [,repɑː'tiː] n réplicas fpl agudas; (between 2 persons) dimes mpl y diretes.

repass ['riː'pɑːs] vt repasar.

repast [ri'pɑːst] n comida f.

repatriate [riː'pætriət] n repatriado m, a f.

repatriate [riː'pætrieit] vt repatriar.

repatriation [riː,pætri'eiʃən] n repatriación f.

repay [riː'pei] (irr: see **pay**) vt money devolver, reembolsar; person pagar; debt pagar, liquidar; person (in compensation) resarcir, compensar; person (pej) pagar en la misma moneda; kindness etc devolver, corresponder a; visit pagar; **to — someone in full** pagar a uno todo lo que se le debe, devolver a uno la suma entera; **how can I — you?** ¿cómo podré corresponder dignamente a tanta amabilidad?; **it —s a visit** vale la pena visitarlo; **it —s study** merece que se le estudie; **it —s reading** vale la pena leerlo.

repayable [riː'peiəbl] adj reembolsable; **£5 deposit, not —** desembolso m inicial de 5 libras, no reembolsable; **— on demand** reembolsable a petición; **the money is — on the 5th of June** el dinero ha de ser devuelto el 5 de junio.

repayment [riː'peimənt] n devolución f, reembolso m; pago m; **now he asks for —** ahora pide que se le devuelva el dinero; **in 6 —s of £8** en 6 plazos de 8 libras cada uno.

repeal [ri'piːl] **1** n revocación f, abrogación f. **2** vt revocar, abrogar.

repeat [ri'piːt] **1** n repetición f; (Radio etc) retransmisión f.
  2 vt repetir; thanks etc reiterar, volver a dar; (aloud) recitar; **she went and —ed it to the boss** fue a contárselo al jefe; **don't — it to anybody** no se lo digas a nadie; **this offer cannot be —ed** no se volverá a ofrecer nada igual; **can you — the design of this house?** ¿puede Vd construir otra casa igual que ésta?
  3 vi repetirse; (clock, rifle, taste) repetir; **the radish —s on me** vuelvo a percibir el sabor del rábano.

repeated [ri'piːtid] adj repetido; reiterado; **in spite of — reminders** a pesar de habérselo recordado infinitas veces.

repeatedly [ri'piːtidli] adv repetidamente, repetidas veces; reiteradamente; **I have told you so —** te lo he dicho repetidas veces.

repeater [ri'piːtə*] n reloj m de repetición; rifle m de repetición.

repel [ri'pel] vt rechazar, repeler; (fig) repugnar; **he —s me** me da asco; **it —s me to have to +** infin me repugna tener que + infin.

repellent [ri'pelənt] **1** adj repugnante; **it is — to insects** ahuyenta los insectos. **2** n: **insect —** loción f para ahuyentar los insectos.

repent [ri'pent] **1** vt arrepentirse de. **2** vi arrepentirse.

repentance [ri'pentəns] n arrepentimiento m.

repentant [ri'pentənt] adj arrepentido; contrito, compungido.

repeople ['riː'piːpl] vt repoblar.

repercussion [,riːpə'kʌʃən] n repercusión f; **—s** (fig) repercusiones fpl; resonancia f; **as for the political —s** en cuanto a las repercusiones políticas; **it had great —s in Ruritania** tuvo gran resonancia en Ruritania.

repertoire ['repətwɑː*] n, **repertory** ['repətəri] n **1** repertorio m; **he has an immense — of jokes** tiene un inmenso repertorio de chistes.
  2 attr: **— theatre**, **— company** teatro m de repertorio.

repetition [,repi'tiʃən] n repetición f; recitación f.

repetitious [,repi'tiʃəs] adj repetidor, que se repite; monótono.

repetitive [ri'petitiv] adj reiterativo; **the book is a bit —** los incidentes del libro tienen cierta tendencia a repetirse, se repite el autor varias veces en el libro.

repine [ri'pain] vi apurarse, quejarse (at de), afligirse (at por).

repining [ri'painiŋ] n quejas fpl, aflicción f, descontento m.

replace [ri'pleis] vt **(a)** (put back) reponer, poner en su lugar, devolver a su sitio, colocar nuevamente; **kindly — the receiver** se ruega reponer el auricular.
  (b) (take the place of) reemplazar, sustituir; **to — something by (or with) something else** sustituir a algo por otra cosa; **the Matisse was —d by a Klee** el cuadro de Matisse fue sustituido por uno de Klee, un cuadro de Klee sustituyó al de Matisse; **nobody could ever — him in my heart** sería imposible que nadie llenara el hueco que él dejó en

mi corazón; **he asked to be —d** rogó que se le sustituyera; **he had to be —d** tuvo que ser destituido; **we will — the broken glasses** nosotros pagaremos los vasos rotos.

replaceable [ri'pleisəbl] *adj* reemplazable, sustituible; **it will not easily be —** no será fácil encontrar un repuesto; **he will not easily be —** no será fácil encontrar un sustituto.

replacement [ri'pleismənt] *n (act)* reposición *f*; devolución *f*; reemplazo *m*, sustitución *f*; *(substitute: thing)* reemplazo *m*, repuesto *m*, *(person)* sustituto *m*, suplente *mf*; **his — has still not arrived** el que le sustituye no ha llegado todavía; **it took 3 days to find a —** se tardó 3 días en encontrar un repuesto.

replant ['ri:'plɑ:nt] *vt* replantar.

replay ['ri:'plei] *vti* volver a jugar.

replenish [ri'pleniʃ] *vt (refill)* rellenar; *(with supplies)* reaprovisionar *(with* de); *stocks* reponer; *(with fuel)* repostar.

replenishment [ri'pleniʃmənt] *n* rellenado *m*; reaprovisionamiento *m*; reposición *f*.

replete [ri'pli:t] *adj* repleto, totalmente lleno *(with* de).

repletion [ri'pli:ʃən] *n* repleción *f*; **to eat to —** darse un atracón, comer realmente bien.

replica ['replikə] *n (Art etc)* copia *f*, reproducción *f* (exacta); *(fig: person etc)* segunda edición *f*.

reply [ri'plai] **1** *n* respuesta *f*, contestación *f*; **— coupon** cupón-respuesta *m*; **" — paid"** "porte pagado"; **in — he said** ... contestando a esto dijo que ...; **what is your — to this?** ¿qué contesta Vd a esto?; **we await your —** *(ending letter)* en espera de sus noticias.
2 *vi* responder, contestar; **to — to someone** contestar a uno; **to — to a letter** contestar una carta.

repopulate ['ri:'pɔpjuleit] *vt* repoblar.

repopulation ['ri:ˌpɔpju'leiʃən] *n* repoblación *f*.

report [ri'pɔːt] **1** *n (a) (account)* relato *m*, relación *f*; *(Mil etc)* parte *m*; *(official)* informe *m*; *(piece of news)* noticia *f*; *(in newspaper)* reportaje *m*, crónica *f*, información *f*; *(school)* papeleta *f*, nota *f*, certificado *m* escolar; **annual —** memoria *f* anual; **chairman's —** informe *m* del presidente; **law —s** actas *fpl* de procesos; **weather —** boletín *m* meteorológico; **the Robbins R—** el Informe Robbins; **"R— on the Motor Industry"** "Informe *m* sobre la Industria del Automóvil"; **the — of his death** upset us la noticia de su muerte nos causó pesar; **to present a —** presentar un informe; **we are drawing up the — now** ahora estamos redactando el informe.
(b) (rumour) rumor *m*, voz *f*; **there is a — that** ... corre la voz de que ..., se rumorea que ...; **I only know of it by —** lo sé de oídas nada más.
(c) (reputation) reputación *f*, fama *f*; **a person of good —** una persona de buena fama; **such things as are of good —** las cosas que sean estimables.
(d) (bang) estampido *m*, estallido *m*; explosión *f*; **there was a —** se oyó una explosión.
2 *vt (recount)* relatar, narrar, dar cuenta de; *(Mil)* dar parte de; *event etc* informar acerca de; *crime etc* denunciar *(to* a); *meeting (as secretary)* levantar las actas de, *(as reporter)* escribir la crónica de; **to — that ...** informar que ..., **comunicar que ...; it is —ed from Berlin that ...** se informa desde Berlín que ..., comunican desde Berlín que ...; **what have you to —?** ¿qué tiene Vd que decirnos?; **nothing to —** sin novedad; **nothing to — from the front** sin novedad en el frente; **to — progress** dar cuenta de los progresos; **I shall have to — this** tendré que denunciar esto; **you have been —ed for idleness** Vd ha sido denunciado por vago, le han acusado de ser holgazán; **he was —ed for swearing at the referee** se le denunció por dirigir palabrotas al árbitro.
3 *vi (a) (make report)* hacer un informe, presentar un informe *(on* acerca de); **to — back to someone** rendir cuentas a uno; pedir consejos a uno; **a committee was set up to — on the pill** se creó una comisión para investigar la píldora; **Professor X —s on his discovery in the next issue** el Profesor X informará de su descubrimiento en el próximo número; **the committee will — to the cabinet** la comisión elevará su informe al consejo de ministros.
(b) (as reporter) ser reportero; **he —ed for the "Daily Echo" for 40 years** durante 40 años fue reportero del "Daily Echo".
(c) (present oneself) presentarse; **to — at a place at 18.00 hours** presentarse en un sitio a las 18.00 horas; **— to me when you are better** venga a

verme cuando se haya repuesto; **to — sick** darse de baja por enfermo; **to — fit** darse de alta.

reportage [ˌrepɔ'tɑ:ʒ] *n* reportaje *m*.

reporter [ri'pɔːtə*] *n* reportero *m*.

repose [ri'pəuz] **1** *n* reposo *m*.
2 *vt (lay etc)* reposar, descansar; recostar; **to — confidence in someone** poner confianza en uno.
3 *vi* reposar, descansar; **to — on** descansar sobre, *(fig)* estribar en, estar basado en.

repository [ri'pɔzitəri] *n* depósito *m*, almacén *m*; *(furniture —)* guardamuebles *m*; *(person)* depositario *m*, a *f*.

repossess ['ri:pə'zes] *vr:* **to — oneself of something** recobrar algo, volver a tomar algo.

reprehend [ˌrepri'hend] *vt* reprender.

reprehensible [ˌrepri'hensibl] *adj* reprensible, censurable.

reprehensibly [ˌrepri'hensibli] *adv* de modo reprensible, de modo censurable.

reprehension [ˌrepri'henʃən] *n* reprensión *f*.

represent [ˌrepri'zent] *vt* representar; *(Law)* ser apoderado de, *(fig)* hablar en nombre de; *(Comm)* ser agente de; **the goods are not as —ed** las mercancías no son las que se nos describieron; **you —ed it falsely to us** Vd nos lo describió falsamente; **it has been —ed to us that ...** se ha pretendido que ..., se nos ha dicho que ...; **he —s nobody but himself** no representa a nadie sino a sí mismo.

re-present ['ri:pri'zent] *vt* volver a presentar.

representation [ˌreprizen'teiʃən] *n (a)* representación *f*; **proportional —** representación *f* proporcional; **they have no — in Parliament** no tienen representante en el parlamento.
(b) petición *f*; **to make —s to someone** presentar una petición a uno, dirigir un memorial a uno, *(complain)* quejarse ante uno; **to make —s about something** quejarse de algo.
(c) **to make false —s** describir algo falsamente.

representational [ˌreprizen'teiʃənəl] *adj (Art)* figurativo.

representative [ˌrepri'zentətiv] **1** *adj* representativo; **these figures are more —** estas cifras son más representativas; **a person not fully — of the group** una persona que no representa adecuadamente el grupo.
2 *n* representante *mf (also Comm, US Pol)*; *(Law)* apoderado *m*.

repress [ri'pres] *vt* reprimir.

repressed [ri'prest] *adj* reprimido.

repression [ri'preʃən] *n* represión *f*.

repressive [ri'presiv] *adj* represivo.

reprieve [ri'pri:v] **1** *n (breathing space)* respiro *m*, alivio *m* temporal; *(Law)* indulto *m*, suspensión *f* *(esp* de la pena de muerte); **to win a last-minute —** ser indultado a última hora; **the wood got a —** se retiró la orden de talar el bosque.
2 *vt* indultar, suspender la pena de; **to — someone from death** indultar a uno de muerte, suspender la pena de muerte de uno.

reprimand ['reprimɑ:nd] **1** *n* reprimenda *f*, reprensión *f*. **2** *vt* reprender, reconvenir.

reprint ['ri:print] *n* reimpresión *f*; *(offprint)* tirada *f* aparte, separata *f*.

reprint ['ri:'print] *vt* reimprimir; **"—ed from the Transactions of ..."** "tirada aparte de las Actas de ..."

reprisal [ri'praizəl] *n* represalia *f*; **as a — for** como represalia por; **to take —s** tomar represalias.

reproach [ri'prəutʃ] **1** *n (spoken etc)* reproche *m*, censura *f*; *(stain, disgrace)* tacha *f*, baldón *m*, aprobio *m*; **beyond —** por encima de toda crítica, intachable; **term of —** término *m* oprobioso; **this is a — to us all** esto es deshonroso para todos nosotros; **poverty is a — to civilization** la pobreza es una vergüenza para la civilización.
2 *vt:* **to — someone for something**, **to — someone with something** reprochar algo a uno, censurar algo a uno, echar algo en cara a uno.
3 *vr:* **to — oneself for something** atribuirse la culpa de algo; **you have no reason to — yourself** Vd no tiene motivo para creerse culpable, la culpa no ha sido de Vd.

reproachful [ri'prəutʃful] *adj look etc* acusador, lleno de reproches; **next day she was —** el día siguiente me reprochó.

reproachfully [ri'prəutʃfəli] *adv look etc* con reproche; *speak etc* en tono acusador.

reprobate ['reprəubeit] *n* réprobo *m*, a *f*.

reprobation [ˌreprəu'beiʃən] *n* reprobación *f*.

reproduce [ˌri:prə'dju:s] **1** *vt* reproducir. **2** *vi* reproducirse.

reproduction [ˌri:prə'dʌkʃən] *n* reproducción *f*.

reproductive [ˌriːprəˈdʌktiv] *adj* reproductor.

reproof [riˈpruːf] *n* reprensión *f*, reconvención *f*; **to administer a —** to someone reprender a uno.

reproval [riˈpruːvəl] *n* reprobación *f*.

reprove [riˈpruːv] *vt* reprender, reconvenir; **to — someone for something** reprender algo a uno.

reproving [riˈpruːviŋ] *adj* reprobador, lleno de reproches.

reprovingly [riˈpruːviŋli] *adv* en tono reprobador, reprobadoramente, con reprobación; **she looked at me —** me miró severa, me reprendió con la mirada.

reptile [ˈreptail] *n* reptil *m*.

reptilian [repˈtiliən] **1** *adj* reptil. **2** *n* reptil *m*.

republic [riˈpʌblik] *n* república *f*.

republican [riˈpʌblikən] **1** *adj* republicano. **2** *n* republicano *m*, a *f*.

republicanism [riˈpʌblikənizəm] *n* republicanismo *m*.

republication [ˈriːˌpʌbliˈkeiʃən] *n* reedición *f*.

republish [ˈriːˈpʌbliʃ] *vt* reeditar.

repudiate [riˈpjuːdieit] *vt charge etc* rechazar, negar, desechar; *possibility* descartar; *obligation etc* rechazar, desconocer; *wife* repudiar; *debt, treaty* anular, cancelar.

repudiation [riˌpjuːdiˈeiʃən] *n* rechazamiento *m*; desconocimiento *m*; repudio *m*; anulación *f*, cancelación *f*.

repugnance [riˈpʌgnəns] *n* repugnancia *f*.

repugnant [riˈpʌgnənt] *adj* repugnante; **it is — to me** me repugna.

repulse [riˈpʌls] **1** *n* repulsa *f*, repulsión *f*; rechazo *m*; **to suffer a —** ser repulsado, ser rechazado. **2** *vt* rechazar, repulsar.

repulsion [riˈpʌlʃən] *n* repulsión *f*, repugnancia *f*; (*Phys*) repulsión *f*.

repulsive [riˈpʌlsiv] *adj* repulsivo, repelente.

repulsively [riˈpʌlsivli] *adv* de modo repulsivo; **— ugly** terriblemente feo.

repulsiveness [riˈpʌlsivnis] *n* lo repulsivo; lo repelente; **of such —** tan repelente.

repurchase [ˈriːˈpəːtʃis] *vt* readquirir, volver a comprar.

reputable [ˈrepjutəbl] *adj firm, brand etc* acreditado, de toda confianza; *person* honroso, formal, estimable.

reputation [ˌrepjuˈteiʃən] *n* reputación *f*, fama *f*; **of good —** de buena fama; **to have a bad —** tener mala fama; **to have a — for meanness** tener fama de tacaño; **the hotel has a — for good food** el hotel es célebre por su buena comida; **he has the — of being awkward** se dice que es difícil, tiene fama de difícil; **to ruin a girl's —** acabar con la buena fama de una joven.

repute [riˈpjuːt] **1** *n* reputación *f*, fama *f*; **by —** según la opinión común, según se dice; **a firm of good —** una casa acreditada; **a café of ill —** un café de mala fama; **a house of ill — (***euph***)** una casa de prostitución; **to hold someone in high —** estimar a uno en mucho; **to know someone by —** only conocer a uno sólo por su reputación, conocer a uno de oídas nada más.

2 *vt* reputar; **to be —d as** tener fama de, pasar por; **to be —d to be clever** tener fama de inteligente, pasar por ser inteligente; **he is —d to be a millionaire** se dice que es millonario.

reputed [riˈpjuːtid] *adj* supuesto.

reputedly [riˈpjuːtidli] *adv* según se dice, según la opinión común.

request [riˈkwest] **1** *n* ruego *m*, petición *f*; instancia *f*; (*formal*) solicitud *f*; (*Comm*) demanda *f*; **a — for help** una petición de socorro; **at the — of** a petición de, a instancia de; **at the urgent — of X I have decided to +** *infin* accediendo al ruego insistente de X he decidido + *infin*; **by —** a petición; **to play a record by —** tocar un disco a petición de un oyente; **it is much in —** tiene mucha demanda, está muy solicitado; **on —** a solicitud; **to grant someone's —** acceder al ruego de uno; **to make a — for something** pedir algo, hacer una petición de algo.

2 *attr programme* a petición de los radioyentes; *stop* discrecional.

3 *vt* pedir, rogar; solicitar; **to — something of someone** pedir algo a uno; **to — someone to do something** rogar a uno hacer algo, pedir que uno haga algo; **"visitors are —ed not to talk"** "se ruega a los visitantes respetar el silencio."

requiem [ˈrekwiem] *n* réquiem *m*.

require [riˈkwaiə*] *vt* **(a)** necesitar; exigir; pedir, requerir; **we — another chair** necesitamos otra silla más; **it —s great care** exige mucho cuidado; **the lock —s attention** hace falta reparar la cerradura; **the battery —s regular attention** hay que comprobar la pila con regularidad; **no maintenance —d**

no necesita manutención alguna; **it —d all his strength to lift it** hacía falta que emplease todas sus fuerzas para levantarlo; **this plant —s watering frequently** esta planta hay que regarla con frecuencia; **is my presence —d?** ¿es necesario que asista yo?; **your presence is —d** se exige que asista Vd; **if —d** en caso de necesidad, si es necesario; **as the situation may —** según lo exija la situación; **we will do all that is —d** haremos todo lo que haga falta; **what qualifications are —d?** ¿qué títulos se requieren?

(b) to — something of someone pedir algo a uno; **what do you — of me?** ¿qué piden Vds que haga?

(c) to — that . . . exigir que + *subj*, requerir que + *subj*, insistir en que + *subj*; **the law —s that it should be done** la ley exige que se haga.

required [riˈkwaiəd] *adj* necesario, obligatorio, que hace falta; **a pipe of the — length** un tubo del largo que hace falta; **by the — date** antes de la fecha tope; **within the — time** dentro de los límites de tiempo que se han señalado; **has he got the — qualities?** ¿tiene las cualidades necesarias?; **the qualities — for the job** las cualidades que se requieren para el puesto; **it is a — course for the degree** es una asignatura obligatoria para el grado.

requirement [riˈkwaiəmənt] *n* requisito *m*; estipulación *f*; necesidad *f*; **—s** requisitos *mpl*, requerimientos *mpl*; **our —s are few** nuestras necesidades son pocas, necesitamos poco; **Latin is a — for the course** para este curso se exige un dominio del latín; **it is one of the —s of the contract** es una de las estipulaciones del contrato; **to meet all the —s for something** llenar todos los requisitos para algo.

requisite [ˈrekwizit] **1** *adj* preciso, indispensable, imprescindible. **2** *n* requisito *m*; **office —s** material *m* de oficina; **toilet —s** artículos *mpl* de limpieza.

requisition [ˌrekwiˈziʃən] **1** *n* pedido *m*, solicitud *f* (*for* de); (*Mil*) requisa *f*, requisición *f*. **2** *vt* (*Mil*) requisar.

requital [riˈkwaitl] *n* compensación *f*, satisfacción *f*; desquite *m*.

requite [riˈkwait] *vt* (*make return for*) compensar, recompensar, pagar; (*get even with*) desquitarse con; **to — someone's love** corresponder al amor de uno; **that love was not —d** ese amor no fue correspondido.

reread [ˈriːˈriːd] (*irr: see* **read**) *vt* releer, volver a leer.

reredos [ˈriədɔs] *n* retablo *m*.

reroute [ˈriːˈruːt] *vt* desviar; **the train was —ed through Burgos** el tren se desvió de la ruta normal y pasó por Burgos.

rerun [ˈriːˈrʌn] (*irr: see* **run**) *vt race* correr de nuevo.

resale [ˈriːˈseil] *n* reventa *f*.

rescind [riˈsind] *vt* rescindir.

rescission [riˈsiʒən] *n* rescisión *f*.

rescue [ˈreskjuː] **1** *n* salvamento *m*, rescate *m*; liberación *f* (*from* de); **the hero of the — was . . .** el héroe del salvamento fue . . .; **to come (***or* go***) to the — of** ir al socorro de, acudir al rescate de; **to the —!** ¡al socorro!; **Batman to the —!** ¡Batman acude a la llamada!

2 *attr:* **— operations** operaciones *fpl* de salvamento, operaciones *fpl* de rescate; **the — vessel** el buque de salvamento.

3 *vt* salvar, rescatar; librar, libertar (*from* de); **three men were —d** tres hombres fueron salvados; **they waited 3 days to be —d** esperaron 3 días su rescate; **to — someone from death** librar a uno de la muerte; **the —d man is in hospital** el hombre rescatado está en el hospital.

rescuer [ˈreskjuə*] *n* salvador *m*, ora *f*.

rescue party [ˈreskjuːˌpɑːti] *n* expedición *f* de salvamento.

rescue work [ˈreskjuːwəːk] *n* trabajos *mpl* de salvamento, trabajos *mpl* de rescate.

research [riˈsəːtʃ] **1** *n* investigación *f*, investigaciones *fpl* (*in, into* de); **atomic —** investigaciones *fpl* atómicas; **our — shows that . . .** nuestras investigaciones demuestran que . . .; **a piece of —** una investigación.

2 *attr:* **— establishment** instituto *m* de investigaciones; **— work** investigaciones *fpl*, trabajos *mpl* de investigación; **— worker** investigador *m*, ora *f*.

3 *vi* investigar; **to — into something** investigar algo, hacer investigaciones de algo.

4 *vt* (*US*) investigar; **to — an article** preparar el material para un estudio, reunir datos para escribir un artículo.

researcher [riˈsəːtʃə*] *n* investigador *m*, ora *f*.

reseat [ˈriːˈsiːt] *vt valves* reasentar.

resection [riːˈsekʃən] *n* resección *f*.

resell ['ri:'sel] (*irr: see* **sell**) *vt* revender, volver a vender.

resemblance [ri'zemblǝns] *n* semejanza *f*, parecido *m*; **to bear a strong —** **to someone** parecerse mucho a uno; **to bear no —** **to someone** no parecerse en absoluto a uno; **there is no —** **between them** los dos no se parecen en absoluto; **there is hardly any —** **between this version and the one I gave you** apenas existe relación entre esta versión y la que le di.

resemble [ri'zembl] *vt* parecerse a; **he doesn't —** **his father** no se parece a su padre; **they do —** **one another** sí se parecen uno a otro.

resent [ri'zent] *vt* ofenderse por, tomar a mal, resentirse de (*or* por); **I —** **that!** ¡protesto contra esa observación!, ¡no permito que se diga eso!, ¡eso no!; **he —s my being here** se ofende por mi presencia aquí, no está conforme con mi presencia aquí; **I don't —** **your saying it** no me ofende que Vd lo diga.

resentful [ri'zentfʊl] *adj* (a) *person* resentido, ofendido, agraviado; **to be** (*or* **feel**) **— of** ofenderse por, resentirse agraviado por; **no wonder she feels —** no me extraña que se sienta ofendida; **he is still — about it** todavía guarda rencor por ello.
(b) *tone etc* resentido, ofendido.

resentfully [ri'zentfǝli] *adv* con resentimiento; **he said —** dijo resentido.

resentment [ri'zentmǝnt] *n* resentimiento *m* (*about, at* por).

reservation [rezǝ'veiʃǝn] *n* (*act*) reservación *f*, reserva *f*; (*mental*) reserva *f*, (*in contract etc*) salvedad, *f* (*in argument*) distingo *m*; (*reserved seat*) plaza *f* reservada; (*US*) reserva *f* (de indios *etc*); **with certain —s** con ciertas reservas; **to accept something without —** aceptar algo sin reserva; **I had —s about it** tenía ciertas dudas sobre ese punto; **did you make the —s?** ¿has reservado las plazas?

reserve [ri'zǝ:v] **1** *n* (a) (*of money etc*) reserva *f*; **cash —s** *fpl* en metálico; **gold —** reserva *f* de oro; **to have something in —** tener algo de reserva; **to have a —** **of strength** tener una reserva de fuerzas; **there are untapped —s of energy** hay reservas de energía que quedan sin explotar; **Spain possesses half the world's —s of pyrites** España tiene la mitad de las reservas mundiales de piritas.
(b) (*Mil*) **the —** la reserva.
(c) (*Sport etc*) suplente *mf*.
(d) (*land*) reserva *f*; **game —** coto *m*, (*large*) parque *m*; **nature —** reserva *f* natural.
(e) **without —** sin reserva.
(f) (*shyness*) reserva *f*.
2 *adj, attr*: **— fund** fondo *m* de reserva; **— petrol tank** depósito *m* de gasolina de reserva; **— price** precio *m* mínimo (fijado en una subasta).
3 *vt* (a) reservar; **that's being —d for me** eso está reservado para mí; **did you — the seats?** ¿has reservado las plazas?
(b) (*Law*) aplazar, diferir; **the judge —d sentence** el juez difirió la sentencia.
4 *vr*: **I'm reserving myself for later** me reservo para más tarde.

reserved [ri'zǝ:vd] *adj* (*all senses*) reservado.

reservedly [ri'zǝ:vidli] *adv* con reserva.

reservist [ri'zǝ:vist] *n* reservista *m*.

reservoir ['rezǝvwɑ:*] *n* (*small*) depósito *m*, represa *f*; (*tank*) depósito *m*, cisterna *f*; (*large, for irrigation, hydroelectric power*) pantano *m*, embalse *m*.

reset ['ri:'set] (*irr: see* **set**) *vt machine etc* reajustar; (*Typ*) recomponer; *bone* volver a encajar; *jewel* reengastar.

resettle ['ri:'setl] **1** *vt persons* restablecer; *land* volver a colonizar, volver a poblar; **the lands were —d by the Poles** las tierras fueron nuevamente colonizadas por los polacos.
2 *vi* restablecerse.

resettlement ['ri:'setlmǝnt] *n* restablecimiento *m*; nueva colonización *f*, repoblación *f*.

reshape ['ri:'ʃeip] *vt* reformar, formar de nuevo, rehacer; reorganizar.

reshuffle ['ri:'ʃʌfl] **1** *n* (*Pol*) reconstrucción *f*. **2** *vt cards* volver a barajar; (*Pol*) reconstruir.

reside [ri'zaid] *vi* residir, vivir; **to — in** (*fig*) residir en.

residence ['rezidǝns] **1** *n* residencia *f*; (*stay, in official parlance*) permanencia *f*; (*home, in official parlance*) domicilio *m*; (*Univ, also* **hall of —**) residencia *f*; **after 6 months' —** después de 6 meses de permanencia; **it is the prime minister's official —** es la residencia oficial del primer ministro; **"town and country —s for sale"** "se ofrecen fincas urbanas y rurales"; **to take up one's —** establecerse.
2 *attr*: **— permit** visado *m* de permanencia.

residency ['rezidǝnsi] *n* residencia *f*.

resident ['rezidǝnt] **1** *adj* residente; *population etc* fijo, permanente; *doctor etc* interno; *servant* que duerme en casa; *bird* no migratorio; **to be — in a town** residir en una ciudad, tener domicilio fijo en una ciudad; **we were — there for some years** residimos allí durante varios años.
2 *n* residente *mf*; vecino *m*, a *f*; (*in hotel etc*) huésped *m*, a *f*; **the —s got together to protest** los vecinos se reunieron para protestar.

residential [rezi'denʃǝl] *adj* residencial; **— area** barrio *m* residencial.

residual [ri'zidjuǝl] *adj* residual.

residuary [ri'zidjuǝri] *adj* restante, remanente, residual; **— legatee** legatario *m* universal, legataria *f* universal.

residue ['rezidju:] *n* resto *m*, residuo *m*; (*Fin etc*) saldo *m*, superávit *m*; **a — of bad feeling** un residuo de rencor, el rencor que queda.

residuum [ri'zidjuǝm] *n* residuo *m*.

resign [ri'zain] **1** *vt office etc* dimitir, renunciar a; *claim, task etc* renunciar a; **to — a task to others** ceder un cometido a otros; **when he —ed the leadership** cuando dimitió la jefatura.
2 *vi* dimitir; renunciar; **to — in favour of someone else** renunciar en favor de otro.
3 *vr*: **to — oneself** resignarse; **to — oneself to** resignarse a, conformarse con; **I —ed myself to never seeing her again** me resigné a no volverla a ver jamás.

resignation [rezig'neiʃǝn] *n* (a) (*act*) dimisión *f* (*from* de), renuncia *f*; **to offer** (*or* **send in, submit, tender**) **one's —** dimitir, presentar su dimisión.
(b) (*state*) resignación *f* (*to* a), conformidad *f* (*to* con); **to await something with —** esperar algo resignado, esperar algo con resignación.

resigned [ri'zaind] *adj* resignado.

resignedly [ri'zainidli] *adv* con resignación.

resilience [ri'ziliǝns] *n* elasticidad *f*; (*fig*) resistencia *f*; poder *m* de recuperación; capacidad *f* para adaptarse.

resilient [ri'ziliǝnt] *adj* elástico; (*fig*) resistente; que tiene poder de recuperación; que tiene capacidad para adaptarse.

resin ['rezin] *n* resina *f*.

resinous ['rezinǝs] *adj* resinoso.

resist [ri'zist] **1** *vt* resistir (a); oponerse a; oponer resistencia a; **to — temptation** resistir la tentación; **they —ed the attack vigorously** resistieron vigorosamente el ataque; **we — this change** nos oponemos a este cambio; **I can't — squid** me apasionan los calamares; **I couldn't — buying it** no me resistí a comprarlo, no pude menos de comprarlo, me fue imposible dejar de comprarlo; **I can't — saying that ...** no resisto al impulso de decir que ...
2 *vi* resistirse, oponer resistencia.

resistance [ri'zistǝns] *n* (*all senses*) resistencia *f*; **the R—** (*Pol*) la Resistencia; **passive —** resistencia *f* pasiva; **to offer —** oponer resistencia (*to* a); **to have good — to disease** tener mucha resistencia a la enfermedad; **to take the line of least —** optar por no resistirse, allanarse a todo; adoptar una actitud realista.

resistant [ri'zistǝnt] *adj* resistente.

resistible [ri'zistibl] *adj* resistible.

resole ['ri:'sǝul] *vt* solar, sobresolar.

resolute ['rezǝlu:t] *adj* resuelto.

resolutely ['rezǝlu:tli] *adv* resueltamente.

resoluteness ['rezǝlu:tnis] *n* resolución *f*.

resolution [rezǝ'lu:ʃǝn] *n* (a) (*resoluteness*) resolución *f*; **to show —** mostrarse resuelto.
(b) (*separation, solving*) resolución *f*.
(c) (*motion*) resolución *f*, proposición *f*; (*Parl*) acuerdo *m*; **to pass a —** tomar un acuerdo; **to put a — to a meeting** someter una moción a votación.
(d) (*resolve*) propósito *m*; **good —s** buenos propósitos *mpl*; **New Year —s** buenos propósitos *mpl* de fin de año.

resolvable [ri'zɔlvǝbl] *adj* soluble.

resolve [ri'zɔlv] **1** *n* (a) (*resoluteness*) resolución *f*; **unshakeable —** resolución *f* inquebrantable.
(b) (*decision*) propósito *m*; **to make a — to +** *infin* resolverse a + *infin*.
2 *vt* (*all senses*) resolver (*into* en); **this will — your doubts** esto ha de resolver sus dudas; **the problem is still not —d** el problema queda por resolver.
3 *vi* (a) (*separate*) resolverse (*into* en); **the question —s into 4 parts** la cuestión se resuelve en 4 partes.
(b) **to — on something** optar por algo, resolverse por algo; **to — on + ger** acordar + *infin*; **to — to +** *infin* resolverse a + *infin*; **to — that ...** acordar que ...; **it was —d that ...** se acordó que ...

resolved [ri'zɔlvd] *adj* resuelto; **to be — to** + *infin* estar resuelto a + *infin.*

resonance ['rezənəns] *n* resonancia *f.*

resonant ['rezənənt] *adj* resonante.

resonator ['rezəneitə*] *n* resonador *m.*

resorption [ri'zɔ:pfən] *n* resorción *f.*

resort [ri'zɔ:t] **1** *n* **(a)** *(recourse)* recurso *m*; **as a last —, in the last —** en último caso; **without — to force** sin recurrir a la fuerza.

(b) *(place)* punto *m* de reunión, lugar *m* de reunión; **it is a — of thieves** es lugar frecuentado por los ladrones, es donde se reúnen los ladrones; **holiday —** punto *m* de veraneo; **seaside —** playa *f*, punto *m* marítimo de veraneo; **summer —** punto *m* de veraneo; **winter-sports —** punto *m* donde se practican los deportes de invierno.

2 *vi:* **to — to (a)** *place* frecuentar, concurrir a, acudir a.

(b) *(have recourse to)* recurrir a; acudir a; hacer uso de; **to — to violence** recurrir a la violencia; **then they —ed to throwing stones** pasaron luego a tirar piedras; **then you — to me for help** así que acudes a mí a pedir ayuda.

resound [ri'zaund] *vi* resonar, retumbar; **the valley —ed with shouts** resonaron los gritos por el valle; **the whole house —s with laughter** resuenan las risas por toda la casa.

resounding [ri'zaundiŋ] *adj* sonoro; *(fig)* clamoroso, resonante.

resoundingly [ri'zaundiŋli] *adv:* **to defeat someone —** obtener una victoria resonante sobre uno.

resource [ri'sɔ:s] *n* *(expedient)* recurso *m*, expediente *m*; *(—fulness)* inventiva *f*; **—s** recursos *mpl*; **financial —s** recursos *mpl* financieros; **natural —s** recursos *mpl* naturales; **to be at the end of one's —s** haber agotado sus recursos; **he has great —s of energy** tiene una gran reserva de energía; **those —s are as yet untapped** esos recursos quedan todavía sin explotar.

resourceful [ri'sɔ:sful] *adj* inventivo, ingenioso.

resourcefully [ri'sɔ:sfəli] *adv* ingeniosamente, mostrando tener inventiva.

resourcefulness [ri'sɔ:sfulnis] *n* inventiva *f*, iniciativa *f*, ingeniosidad *f.*

respect [ris'pekt] **1** *n* **(a)** *(relation)* respecto *m*; **in every —** desde todos los puntos de vista; **in many —s** desde muchos puntos de vista; en cierto modo; **in other —s** por lo demás; **in some —s** desde varios puntos de vista; **in this —** por lo que se refiere a esto; en cuanto a esto; **in — of** respecto a, respecto de; **with — to** con respecto a; **with — to possible candidates, there are 3** en cuanto al número de candidatos que se pueden presentar, son 3.

(b) without — of persons sin distinción de personas.

(c) *(consideration)* respeto *m*, consideración *f*; **— for one's parents** respeto *m* a sus padres; **— for the truth** respeto *m* por la verdad; **out of — for someone** por consideración a uno; **out of — for the truth** en atención a la verdad; **with all — to you** sin menoscabo del respeto que se le debe a Vd; **if I may say so with —** si puedo decirlo con el mayor respeto; **worthy of —** digno de respeto, respetable; **to command —** imponer respeto, hacerse respetar; **to have — for someone, to hold someone in —** tener respeto a uno, respetar a uno; **we have the greatest — for him** le respetamos muchísimo; **to pay — to someone** respetar a uno; **to show no — to someone** faltar al respeto debido a uno; **he shows scant — for our opinions** desprecia nuestras opiniones; **to win someone's —** ganarse el respeto de uno.

(d) —s recuerdos *mpl*, saludos *mpl*; **to pay one's —s to someone** cumplimentar a uno; **to send one's —s to someone** mandar recuerdos a uno.

2 *vt* respetar; **to — someone's opinions** respetar las opiniones de uno; **to — someone's wishes** atenerse a los deseos de uno; **to make oneself —ed** hacerse respetar.

respectability [ris,pektə'biliti] *n* respetabilidad *f.*

respectable [ris'pektəbl] *adj* **(a)** *(deserving respect)* respetable; **for perfectly — reasons** por motivos perfectamente respetables.

(b) *(of fair social standing, decent)* respetable, decente, honrado; **in — society** en la buena sociedad, entre personas educadas; **that's not —** eso no se hace, eso no es decente, eso es de mala educación; **that skirt isn't —** esa falda no es decente.

(c) *amount etc* respetable, apreciable, importante; **at a — distance** a respetable distancia; **she lost a — sum** perdió una cantidad importante.

(d) *(passable)* pasable, tolerable; **we made a —**

showing lo hicimos pasablemente; **his work is — but not brilliant** su obra es pasable pero no brillante.

respectably [ris'pektəbli] *adv* respetablemente; decentemente; pasablemente.

respected [ris'pektid] *adj* respetado, estimado; **a much — person** una persona muy respetada.

respecter [ris'pektə*] *n:* **to be no — of persons** no hacer distinción de personas.

respectful [ris'pektful] *adj* respetuoso.

respectfully [ris'pektfəli] *adv* respetuosamente; **Yours —** le saluda atentamente.

respectfulness [ris'pektfulnis] *n* respetuosidad *f*, acatamiento *m.*

respecting [ris'pektiŋ] *prep* con respecto a; en cuanto a; por lo que se refiere a.

respective [ris'pektiv] *adj* respectivo.

respectively [ris'pektivli] *adv* respectivamente.

respiration [,respi'reifən] *n* respiración *f.*

respirator ['respireitə*] *n* careta *f* antigás.

respiratory [ris'paiərətəri] *adj* respiratorio.

respire [ris'paiə*] *vti* respirar.

respite ['respait] *n* respiro *m*, respiradero *m*; *(Law)* plazo *m*, prórroga *f*; **without —** sin tregua, sin respirar; **to get no —** no tener alivio, no poder descansar; **we got no — from the heat** el calor apenas nos dejó respirar ni de día ni de noche; **they gave us no —** nos hicieron trabajar *(etc)* sin tregua, no nos dejaron respirar.

resplendence [ris'plendəns] *n* resplandor *m*, refulgencia *f.*

resplendent [ris'plendənt] *adj* resplandeciente, refulgente; **to be —** resplandecer, refulgir; **to be — in a new dress** lucir un nuevo vestido; **the car is — in green** luce el coche su pintura verde.

respond [ris'pɔnd] *vi* *(answer)* responder; *(be responsive)* reaccionar, ser sensible *(to* a); **it —s to sunlight** reacciona a la luz solar, es sensible a la luz solar; **it is —ing to treatment** está mejorando con el tratamiento; **it does not seem to — to treatment** no parece que el tratamiento efectúe ningún cambio; **the cat —s to kindness** el gato es sensible a los buenos tratos.

respondent [ris'pɔndənt] *n* *(Law)* demandado *m*, a *f.*

response [ris'pɔns] *n* *(answer)* respuesta *f*, *(Eccl)* responsorio *m*; *(reaction)* reacción *f*, correspondencia *f* *(to* a); **in — to many requests ...** accediendo a muchos ruegos ...; **the — was not favourable** la reacción no fue favorable; **his only — was to yawn** por toda respuesta dio un bostezo; **we had hoped for a bigger —** habíamos esperado más correspondencia; **it found no —** no tuvo correspondencia alguna, no encontró eco alguno; **it met with a generous —** tuvo una generosa acogida.

responsibility [ris,pɔnsə'biliti] *n* **(a)** responsabilidad *f* *(for* de); **joint —** responsabilidad *f* solidaria; **on one's own —** bajo su propia responsabilidad; **to accept — for something** hacerse responsable de algo; **that's his —** eso le incumbe a él, eso le toca a él; **it is my — to decide** me toca a mí decidir.

(b) seriedad *f*; formalidad *f*; **try to show some —** procure tener un poco de seriedad.

responsible [ris'pɔnsəbl] *adj* **(a)** responsable *(for* de); **to be — to someone for something** ser responsable ante uno de algo; **those — will be punished** se castigará a las personas responsables, se castigará a los autores del crimen; **who was — for the delay?** ¿a quién se debe el retraso?; **the fog was not — this time** la niebla no tuvo la culpa esta vez; **she is — for 40 children** tiene a su cargo a 40 niños; **the committee is — to the council** la comisión depende del consejo; **he is not — for his actions** no responde de sus actos; **to hold someone — for an accident** echar a uno la culpa de un accidente, hacer a uno responsable de un accidente; **to make oneself —** responsabilizarse, tomar sobre sí la responsabilidad.

(b) *(of character)* serio, formal; **he is a fully — person** es una persona de toda formalidad; **to act in a — fashion** obrar con seriedad.

(c) *post etc* de confianza, de gran responsabilidad.

responsibly [ris'pɔnsəbli] *adv:* **to act —** obrar con seriedad.

responsive [ris'pɔnsiv] *adj:* **he was not very —** apenas dio indicio de interés, apenas parecía interesarle la cosa; **to be — to something** ser sensible a algo.

responsiveness [ris'pɔnsivnis] *n* interés *m*; sensibilidad *f* *(to* a).

rest¹ [rest] **1** *n* **(a)** *(repose)* descanso *m*, reposo *m*; *(fig)* paz *f*; **day of —** día *m* de descanso, asueto *m*, *(as calendar item)* día *m* festivo; **to be at —** estar en reposo, descansar, *(of insect etc)* estar posado, *(of* *the dead*) estar en paz; **to come to —** (*vehicle*) pararse, detenerse, (*machine*) pararse, (*insect etc*) posarse; **to go to (one's) —** ir a acostarse; **to have a 10-minute —** descansar durante 10 minutos; **to have a good night's —** dormir profundamente; **to lay someone to —** enterrar a uno; **to set someone's mind at —** tranquilizar a uno; **to take a —** descansar, descansar un rato.

(b) (*Mus*) silencio *m*, pausa *f*.

(c) (*support*) apoyo *m*, soporte *m*; (*base*) base *f*; (*Tel*) horquilla *f*; (*for lance etc*) ristre *m*.

2 *vt* **(a)** (*give — to*) descansar; dejar descansar; **to — one's men** dejar descansar a sus hombres; **horses have to be —ed** hay que dejar descansar a los caballos; **these colours — your eyes** estos colores descansan la vista; **God — his soul!** ¡Dios le acoja en su seno!

(b) (*support*) descansar, apoyar (*against* contra, *on* sobre); **— your head on the pillow** apoye la cabeza en la almohada; **— the ladder against the tree** apoya la escalera contra el árbol; **she —ed her eyes on the picture** clavó la vista en el cuadro; **to — one's case** terminar la presentación de argumentos.

3 *vi* **(a)** (*repose*) descansar (*from* de), reposar; (*stop*) detenerse, pararse; (*Theat: euph*) no tener trabajo, estar sin trabajo; **where my caravan has —ed** donde se ha detenido mi carricoche; **he never —s** no descansa nunca; **the waves never —** las olas están en continuo movimiento; **may he — in peace** descanse en paz; **we shall never — until it is settled** no nos tranquilizaremos hasta que se arregle el asunto; **let us not — until he is avenged** no descansemos hasta vengarle; **and there the matter —s** así que ahí queda el asunto; **we cannot let the matter — there** no podemos permitir que las cosas sigan en ese punto, no podemos dejar el asunto sin resolver.

(b) to — on (*perch*) posar en, posarse en; (*be supported*) descansar sobre, apoyarse en; (*fig*) estribar en, estar basado en; **her arm —ed on my chair** su brazo estaba apoyado en mi silla; **her head —ed on her hand** su cabeza se apoyaba en la mano; **the case —s on the following facts** la teoría está basada en los siguientes datos; **his eye —ed on me** su mirada se clavó en mí, clavó su mirada en mí; **a heavy responsibility —s on him** pesa sobre él una grave responsabilidad; **please — assured that . . .** tenga Vd la seguridad de que . . .

(c) to — with depender de; residir en; **it does not — with me** no depende de mí; **the authority —s with him** la autoridad reside en él.

rest² [rest] *n* resto *m*; **the —** el resto, lo demás, los demás (*etc*); **for the —** por lo demás; **the — stayed outside** los demás quedaron fuera; **what shall we give the — of them?** ¿qué daremos a los otros?; **the — of them couldn't care less** a los otros les trae sin cuidado; **the — of the soldiers** los otros soldados, los demás soldados.

restart ['riː'staːt] *vt* empezar de nuevo, volver a empezar; (*engine*) volver a arrancar.

restate ['riː'steit] *vt* repetir, reafirmar; *case* volver a exponer; *problem* volver a plantear.

restatement ['riː'steitmənt] *n* repetición *f*, reafirmación *f*; nueva exposición *f*; nuevo planteamiento *m*.

restaurant ['restərɔːŋ] *n* restaurante *m*, restorán *m*.

restaurant car ['restərɔːŋ,kaː*] *n* (*Rail*) coche-comedor *m*.

restaurateur [,restərə'təː*] *n* propietario *m* de un restaurante.

rest cure ['restkjuə*] *n* cura *f* de reposo.

restful ['restfʊl] *adj* descansado, reposado, sosegado.

restfully ['restfəli] *adv* reposadamente, sosegadamente.

rest home ['resthəum] *n* residencia *f* para jubilados.

resting place ['restiŋpleis] *n* (*also* **last —**) última morada *f*.

restitution [,resti'tjuːʃən] *n* restitución *f*; **to make — for something** indemnizar a uno por algo.

restive ['restiv] *adj* inquieto, intranquilo; *horse* rebelón; **to get —** agitarse, impacientarse.

restiveness ['restivnis] *n* inquietud *f*, intranquilidad *f*; agitación *f*, impaciencia *f*.

restless ['restlis] *adj* inquieto, intranquilo, desasosegado; descontentadizo; (*sleepless*) insomne, desvelado; (*Pol etc*) turbulento; (*roving*) andariego, de mal asiento; **the poet's — genius** el genio inquieto del poeta; **he's the — sort** es una persona de mal asiento; **he is — to be gone** se impacienta por partir; **he's been — in the job** no ha estado contento en el puesto; **the spectators were getting —** los

espectadores se estaban impacientando; **the unions are getting —** se están agitando los sindicatos; **I had a — night** pasé una mala noche, me quedé la mayor parte de la noche sin dormir.

restlessly ['restlisli] *adv* inquietamente, desasosegadamente; turbulentamente; **she moved — in her sleep** se movió inquieta mientras dormía.

restlessness ['restlisnis] *n* inquietud *f*, intranquilidad *f*, desasosiego *m*; agitación *f*, impaciencia *f*; descontento *m*; insomnio *m*, desvelo *m*; turbulencia *f*; lo andariego; **there is much — in the provinces** existe gran descontento en las provincias.

restock ['riː'stɔk] *vt larder etc* reaprovisionar; *pond etc* repoblar (*with* de); **we —ed with Brand X** renovamos las existencias de Marca X.

restoration [,restə'reiʃən] *n* restauración *f*; devolución *f*; restablecimiento *m*; **the R—** (*Hist*) la Restauración.

restorative [ris'tɔːrətiv] **1** *adj* reconstituyente. **2** *n* reconstituyente *m*.

restore [ris'tɔː*] *vt building etc* restaurar; *object to owner etc* devolver (*to* a); *strength etc* restablecer; **to — something to someone** devolver algo a uno; **to — something to its place** devolver algo a su lugar; **to — someone to health** devolver la salud a uno; **to — someone to liberty** devolver la libertad a uno; **to — someone's sight** devolver la vista a uno; **to — someone's strength** restaurar las fuerzas a uno, reconstituir las fuerzas de uno; **to — the strength of the pound** restablecer el valor de la libra; **they —d the king to his throne** volvieron a poner al rey sobre su trono; **order was soon —d** pronto se restableció el orden, se volvió pronto a la normalidad.

restorer [ris'tɔːrə*] *n* restaurador *m*, ora *f*; **hair —** loción *f* capilar.

restrain [ris'trein] **1** *vt* contener, refrenar, reprimir; moderar; tener a raya; **to — someone from +** *ger* disuadir a uno de **+** *infin*, (*physically etc*) impedir a uno **+** *infin*; **kindly — your friend** haga el favor de refrenar a su amigo; **I managed to — my anger** logré contener mi enojo.

2 *vr*: **to — oneself** contenerse, dominarse; **but I —ed myself** pero me contuve, pero me dominé; **please — yourself!** ¡por favor, cálmese!; **to restrain oneself from +** *ger* dominarse para que no **+** *subj*.

restrained [ris'treind] *adj* moderado, comedido; *style etc* refrenado, moderado; **he was very — about it** estuvo muy comedido.

restraint [ris'treint] *n* **(a)** (*check, control*) freno *m*, control *m*; restricción *f*, limitación *f*; **a — on trade** una restricción del comercio, (*on free enterprise*) una limitación de la libre competencia; **without —** sin restricción, libremente; **to be under a —** estar cohibido; **to fret under a —** impacientarse por una restricción; **to put someone under a —** refrenar a uno, (*Law*) imponer una restricción legal a uno.

(b) (*constraint: of manner*) reserva *f*, (*of character*) moderación *f*, comedimiento *m*; (*self-control*) autodominio *m*; **to cast aside all —** abandonar toda moderación, abandonar toda reserva; **he showed great —** mostró poseer gran autodominio, se mostró muy comedido.

restrict [ris'trikt] **1** *vt* restringir, limitar (*to* a).

2 *vr*: **I — myself to the facts** me limito a exponer los hechos; **nowadays I — myself to a litre a day** hoy día me limito a beber un litro diario.

restricted [ris'triktid] *adj area, circulation etc* reducido; *distribution etc* restringido; *horizon* limitado; **he has rather a — outlook** tiene miras más bien estrechas; **the plant is — to Andalusia** la planta está restringida a Andalucía; **his output is —d to novels** su producción consiste únicamente en novelas.

restriction [ris'trikʃən] *n* restricción *f*, limitación *f*; **without — as to . . .** sin restricción de . . .; **to place — on the sale of a drug** restringir la venta de una droga; **to place —s on someone's liberty** restringir la libertad de uno.

restrictive [ris'triktiv] *adj* restrictivo.

rest room ['restrum] *n* cuarto *m* de descanso; (*US euph*) aseos *mpl*.

result [ri'zʌlt] **1** *n* resultado *m*; **—s** (*of election, exam etc*) resultados *mpl*; **as a —** por consiguiente; **as a — of** de resultas de, a consecuencia de; **as a — of a misunderstanding** debido a un malentendido; **in the —** finalmente; **with the — that . . .** resultando que . . .; **without —** sin resultado; **the — is that . . .** el resultado es que . . .; **what will be the — of it all?** ¿en qué va a parar todo esto?

2 *vi*: **to — from** resultar de; **to — in** producir, motivar, terminar en, dar por resultado; **it —ed in his death** causó su muerte, condujo a su muerte;

it —ed in a large increase produjo un aumento apreciable; it didn't — in anything useful no produjo nada útil, no dio ningún resultado útil.

resultant [ri'zʌltənt] adj consiguiente, resultante.

resume [ri'zju:m] 1 vt (continue) reanudar, continuar; office etc reasumir; (summarize) resumir; to — one's seat volver a sentarse; to — one's work reanudar su trabajo; "Now then", he —d "Ahora bien", dijo reanudando la conversación.
2 vi continuar; comenzar de nuevo.

résumé ['reizju:mei] n resumen m.

resumption [ri'zʌmpʃən] n reanudación f, continuación f; reasunción f; on the — of the sitting al reanudarse la sesión.

resurface ['ri:'sə:fis] 1 vt poner nueva superficie a; volver a allanar; road rehacer el firme de.
2 vi (of submarine) volver a emerger, volver a salir a la superficie.

resurgence [ri'sə:dʒəns] n resurgimiento m.

resurgent [ri'sə:dʒənt] adj renaciente, que está en trance de renacer.

resurrect [,rezə'rekt] vt resucitar.

resurrection [,rezə'rekʃən] n resurrección f.

resuscitate [ri'sʌsiteit] vti resucitar.

resuscitation [ri,sʌsi'teiʃən] n resucitación f.

retail ['ri:teil] 1 n venta f al por menor, venta f al detalle.
2 attr, adj: — dealer, — trader comerciante mf al por menor, detallista mf; — price precio m al por menor, precio m al detalle; — trade comercio m al por menor, comercio m detallista.
3 adv: to sell something — vender algo al por menor, vender algo al detalle.

retail [ri:'teil] 1 vt (Comm) vender al por menor, vender al detalle; gossip repetir, story contar. 2 vi venderse al por menor (at a).

retailer [ri:'teilə*] n comerciante mf al por menor, detallista mf.

retain [ri'tein] vt retener; conservar; (keep in one's possession) guardar, quedarse con; (in memory) retener; (sign up) lawyer ajustar, player contratar, fichar; the sponge —s the water la esponja retiene el agua; it —s something of its past glories conserva una parte de sus viejas glorias; the customer —s that part el cliente se queda con esa porción.

retainer [ri'teinə*] n (a) (follower) secuaz m; adherente m, partidario m, a f; (servant) criado m; family —, old — viejo criado m (que lleva muchos años sirviendo en la misma familia).
(b) (Law) ajuste m, anticipo m.

retake [ri:'teik] (irr: see take) vt volver a tomar, reconquistar.

retaliate [ri'tælieit] vi desquitarse, tomar represalias, tomar su revancha; to — by — ger vengarse + ger; to — on someone tomar represalias contra uno; vengarse de uno.

retaliation [ri,tæli'eiʃən] n desquite m, represalias fpl, revancha f; venganza f; by way of —, in — para desquitarse, para vengarse.

retaliatory [ri'tæliətəri] adj: — raid ataque m vengativo, ataque m de desquite; to take — measures tomar medidas para desquitarse, tomar represalias.

retard [ri'ta:d] vt retardar, retrasar.

retarded [ri'ta:did] adj retardado, retrasado.

retch [retʃ] vi vomitar; esforzarse por vomitar.

retching ['retʃiŋ] n esfuerzo m por vomitar; náusea f, bascas fpl.

retell ['ri:'tel] (irr: see tell) vt recontar, volver a contar.

retention [ri'tenʃən] n retención f (also Med); conservación f.

retentive [ri'tentiv] adj retentivo.

retentiveness [ri'tentivnis] n retentiva f, poder m de retención.

rethink ['ri:'θiŋk] (irr: see think) vt repensar.

reticence ['retisəns] n reticencia f, reserva f.

reticent ['retisənt] adj reticente, reservado; he has been very — about it no ha querido decirnos nada acerca de ello, ha tratado el asunto con la mayor reserva.

reticently ['retisəntli] adv con reserva.

reticle ['retikl] n retículo m.

reticulate [ri'tikjulit] adj, **reticulated** [ri'tikjuleitid] adj reticular.

reticule ['retikju:l] n (Opt etc) retículo m; (bag) ridículo m.

retina ['retinə] n retina f.

retinue ['retinju:] n séquito m, comitiva f.

retire [ri'taiə*] 1 vt jubilar; he was compulsorily —d le obligaron a jubilarse.
2 vi (a) (withdraw) retirarse; to — to bed, to

— for the night ir a dormir, ir a acostarse, recogerse; to — from the world retirarse del mundo; to — into oneself encerrarse en sus pensamientos, huir del mundo exterior.
(b) (of age limit) jubilarse, (Mil) retirarse; to — from business dejar los negocios; to — from a post dimitir un cargo, renunciar a un puesto; to — on a pension jubilarse; they —d to the countryside se jubiló él y fueron a vivir en el campo.
(c) (Mil) retirarse; to — to prepared positions retirarse a ocupar posiciones preparadas de antemano.
(d) (Sport) abandonar; he had to — in the 5th lap tuvo que abandonar en la 5ª vuelta.

retired [ri'taiəd] adj jubilado, (Mil) retirado; a — person un jubilado; to place someone on the — list (Mil) dar el retiro a uno.

retirement [ri'taiəmənt] n (a) (state of being retired) retiro m; to live in — vivir en el retiro; to spend one's — growing roses ocuparse después de la jubilación cultivando rosas; how will you spend your —? ¿qué piensa Vd hacer después de jubilarse?
(b) (act of retiring) jubilación f, (Mil) retiro m; compulsory — jubilación f forzosa; see pay etc.
(c) (Mil: withdrawal) retirada f.

retiring [ri'taiəriŋ] adj (a) member etc saliente, dimitente; the — members of staff los miembros que se jubilan.
(b) (of character) reservado, retraído.

retort [ri'tɔ:t] 1 n (answer) réplica f; (Chem) retorta f. 2 vt (insult etc) devolver; he —ed that . . . contestó secamente que . . ., contestó ásperamente que . . .

retouch ['ri:'tʌtʃ] vt retocar.

retrace [ri'treis] vt volver a trazar; (in memory) recordar, rememorar; someone's journey etc seguir las huellas de.

retract [ri'trækt] 1 vt retractar, retirar; (draw in) retraer, encoger; (Tech) replegar.
2 vi retractarse; (be drawn in) retraerse; (Tech) replegarse; he refuses to — se niega a retractarse.

retractable [ri'træktəbl] adj retractable; (Aer etc) replegable, retráctil.

retractation [,ri:træk'teiʃən] n, **retraction** [ri'trækʃən] n retractación f, retracción f.

retrain ['ri:'trein] vt workers reeducar, enseñar una nueva técnica a.

retraining ['ri:'treiniŋ] n reeducación f profesional, readaptación f profesional.

retransmit ['ri:trænz'mit] n retransmitir.

retread ['ri:'tred] vt tyre recauchutar.

retreat [ri'tri:t] 1 (n) (a) (place) retiro m (also Eccl); refugio m, asilo m; (state) retraimiento m, apartamiento m.
(b) (Mil) retirada f; the — from Mons la retirada de Mons; to beat the — (Mil) dar el toque de retreta; to beat a — (Mil) retirarse, batirse en retirada; (fig) emprender la retirada; to beat a hasty — retirarse con toda prisa; to be in full — retirarse en masa, retirarse en todo el frente.
2 vi retirarse, batirse en retirada; they —ed to Dunkirk se retiraron a Dunquerque; the waters are —ing las aguas están bajando.

retrench [ri'trentʃ] 1 vt reducir, cercenar. 2 vi economizar, hacer economías.

retrenchment [ri'trentʃmənt] n reducción f, cercenadura f; economías fpl.

retrial ['ri:'traiəl] n (of person) nuevo proceso m; (of case) revisión f.

retribution [,retri'bju:ʃən] n justo castigo m, pena f merecida; desquite m.

retributive [ri'tribjutiv] adj castigador, de castigo.

retrievable [ri'tri:vəbl] adj recuperable; reparable.

retrieval [ri'tri:vəl] n recuperación f; (Hunting) cobra f; resarcimiento m; reparación f; subsanación f; rescate m.

retrieve [ri'tri:v] vt (recover) cobrar, recobrar, recuperar; (Hunting) cobrar; loss recuperar, resarcirse de; fortunes reparar; error subsanar; to — something from the water rescatar algo del agua; she —d her handkerchief recogió su pañuelo, volvió a tomar su pañuelo; we shall — nothing from this disaster no salvaremos nada de esta catástrofe.

retriever [ri'tri:və*] n perro m cobrador, perdiguero m.

retro . . . ['retrəu] retro . . .

retroactive [,retrəu'æktiv] adj retroactivo.

retroflex ['retrəufleks] adj vuelto hacia atrás.

retrograde ['retrəu'greid] *adj* retrógrado; **a — step** un paso hacia atrás, una medida reaccionaria.

retrogress [,retrəu'gres] *vi* retroceder; (*fig*) empeorar, degenerar, decaer.

retrogression [,retrəu'greʃən] *n* retrogradación *f*.

retrogressive [,retrəu'gresiv] *adj* retrógrado.

retrorocket ['retrəu'rɔkit] *n* retrocohete *m*.

retrospect ['retrəuspekt] *n*: **in —** retrospectivamente; mirando hacia atrás, volviendo a considerar el pasado; **in — it seems a happy time** visto desde esta altura parece haber sido un período feliz.

retrospection [,retrəu'spekʃən] *n* retrospección *f*, consideración *f* del pasado.

retrospective [,retrəu'spektiv] *adj* retrospectivo; *law etc* retroactivo.

retrospectively [,retrəu'spektivli] *adv* retrospectivamente; de modo retroactivo.

retroussé [rə'truːsei] *adj* *nose* respingado.

retry ['riː'trai] *vt* *person* procesar de nuevo, volver a procesar; *case* rever.

return [ri'tɜːn] **1** *n* (**a**) (*going back*) vuelta *f*, regreso *m*; (*Med etc*) reaparición *f*; **the — home** la vuelta a casa; **the — to school** la vuelta al colegio; **the — of King Kong** la vuelta de King Kong; **by —** (**of post**) a vuelta de correo; **on my —** al volver yo, a la vuelta; **many happy —s (of the day)!** ¡que los cumplas muy felices!, ¡feliz cumpleaños!

(**b**) (*Comm*) ganancia *f*; ingresos *mpl*; (*interest*) rédito *m*; **the — on investments is only 2%** las inversiones rinden sólo el 2 por ciento; **law of diminishing —s** ley *f* de rendimientos decrecientes; **to bring in a good —** rendir bien, dar un buen rédito.

(**c**) (*of thing borrowed, of merchandise*) devolución *f*; restitución *f*; **3 dozen on a sale or — basis** 3 docenas a devolver si no se venden.

(**d**) (*Tennis etc*) golpe *m* con que se resta la pelota.

(**e**) (*reward*) recompensa *f*; **in —** en cambio; **in — for** en cambio de, en recompensa de; **in — you . . .** en cambio Vd . . .; **in — for this service** en recompensa de este servicio.

(**f**) (*report*) informe *m*, relación *f*; (*answer*) respuesta *f*; (*figures*) estadística *f*; **—s** tablas *fpl* de estadísticas (*for* de); **quarterly —** informe *m* trimestral; declaración *f* trimestral; **— of income** declaración *f* de renta.

(**g**) (*Parl etc*: *of member*) elección *f*; (*voting*) resultado *m* (del escrutinio).

2 *attr* (**a**) **— flight** vuelo *m* de regreso, **— journey** viaje *m* de regreso; **— ticket** billete *m* de ida y vuelta.

(**b**) **— match** (partido *m* de) desquite *m*, revancha *f*.

(**c**) **— address** señas *fpl* del remitente.

3 *vt* (**a**) (*give back*) devolver; restituir; (*send back*) *light* reflejar; *ball* restar; *suit of cards* devolver; *answer, thanks* dar; *favour, kindness, love* corresponder a; *visit* pagar; **to — something to its place** devolver algo a su lugar; **to — partner's lead** devolver el palo que sirvió el compañero; **"— to sender"** "devuélvase al remitente"; **to — blow for blow** devolver golpe por golpe; **to — like for like** pagar a uno en la misma moneda; **I hope to — your kindness** espero poder corresponder a su amabilidad; **her love was not —ed** su amor no fue correspondido.

(**b**) (*declare*) declarar; **to — an income of £3,000** declarar tener una renta de 3.000 libras; **to — a verdict** pronunciar una sentencia, dar un fallo; **to — a verdict of guilty on someone** declarar culpable a uno.

(**c**) (*Parl etc*) elegir, votar a; **he was —ed by an overwhelming majority** resultó elegido por una abrumadora mayoría; **Old Sarum used to — two members to Parliament** Old Sarum tenía antes el derecho a dos escaños en el Parlamento.

4 *vi* (**a**) (*go back*) volver, regresar (*to* a); (*Law*) revertir (*to* a); **to — home** volver a casa; **to — from town** volver de la ciudad; **to — from a journey** volver de un viaje, regresar después de un viaje; **his good spirits —ed** renació su alegría, se restableció su buen humor.

(**b**) **to — to a task** volver a una tarea, emprender de nuevo una tarea; **to — to a theme** volver a un asunto.

(**c**) (*Med*: *of symptoms etc*) reaparecer.

returnable [ri'tɜːnəbl] *adj* restituible; (*Law*) devolutivo; (*on approval*) a prueba; **— empties** envases *mpl* a devolver; **the book is — on the 14th** el libro ha de ser devuelto el 14; **the deposit is not —** no se reembolsa el depósito.

returning officer [ri'tɜːniŋ'ɔfisə*] *n* escudriñador *m*.

reunification ['riː,juːnifi'keiʃən] *n* reunificación *f*.

reunify ['riː'juːnifai] *vt* reunificar.

reunion [riː'juːnjən] *n* reunión *f*.

reunite ['riːjuː'nait] **1** *vt* reunir; (*in friendship etc*) reconciliar; **eventually the family was —d** por fin la familia volvió a verse unida; **she was —d with her husband** volvió a verse al lado de su marido.

2 *vi* reunirse; reconciliarse; volver a verse unido.

rev [rev] (*Aut etc*, *fam*) **1** *n* revolución *f*.

2 *vt* (*also* **to — up**) girar (el motor de); acelerar (la marcha de).

3 *vi* (*also* **to — up**) girar (rápidamente); acelerarse; **the plane was —ving up** giraban los motores del avión.

revaluation [riː,væljuː'eiʃən] *n* revaloración *f*, revalorización *f*.

revalue ['riː'væljuː] *vt* revalorizar.

revamp ['riː'væmp] *vt* *shoe* poner nueva empella a; remendar; *engine* volver a componer; (*fig*) rehacer, renovar.

reveal [ri'viːl] *vt* revelar.

revealing [ri'viːliŋ] *adj* revelador.

revealingly [ri'viːliŋli] *adv* de modo revelador.

reveille [ri'væli] *n* diana *f*, toque *m* de diana.

revel ['revl] *vi* jaranear, estar de parranda, divertirse tumultuosamente; **to — in** deleitarse en, deleitarse con; **to — in + ger** deleitarse en + *infin*.

revelation [,revə'leiʃən] *n* revelación *f*; (**Book of) R—s** el Apocalipsis; **it was a — to me** fue una revelación para mí.

reveller ['revlə*] *n* jaranero *m*, juerguista *mf*; (*drunk*) borracho *m*; (*guest*) convidado *m*, a *f*.

revelry ['revlri] *n* jolgorio *m*, jarana *f*, diversión *f* tumultuosa; (*organized*) fiestas *fpl*, festividades *fpl*; **the spirit of —** el espíritu de carnaval.

revels ['revlz] *npl* jolgorio *m*, jarana *f*, diversión *f* tumultuosa; (*organized*) fiestas *fpl*, festividades *fpl*; **let the — begin!** ¡que comience la fiesta!; **the — lasted for 3 days** continuaron las fiestas durante 3 días.

revenge [ri'vendʒ] **1** *n* venganza *f*; **in —** para vengarse; **in — for something** para vengarse de algo; **to have one's —** vengarse; **to take — on someone for something** vengarse de algo en uno.

2 *vt* vengar; **to be —d on someone** vengarse en uno.

3 *vi*: **to — oneself** vengarse (*on someone* en uno, *for something* de algo).

revengeful [ri'vendʒful] *adj* vengativo.

revengefully [ri'vendʒfəli] *adv* vengativamente.

revenger [ri'vendʒə*] *n* vengador *m*, ora *f*.

revenue ['revənjuː] *n* (**a**) (*income*: *also* **—s**) ingresos *mpl*; renta *f*; (*on investments*) rédito *m*; (*profit*) ganancia *f*, beneficio *m* (*from* de).

(**b**) (*of state*) rentas *fpl* públicas; **Inland R—**, (US) **Internal R—** Delegación *f* de Contribuciones.

revenue cutter ['revənjuː,kʌtə*] *n* guardacostas *m*.

revenue officer ['revənjuː,ɔfisə*] *n* agente *m* fiscal.

revenue stamp ['revənjuː,stæmp] *n* sello *m* fiscal.

reverberate [ri'vɜːbəreit] *vi* (**a**) (*of sound*) resonar, retumbar; **the sound —d in the distance** el sonido retumbaba a lo lejos; **the valley —d with the sound** el ruido resonaba por el valle.

(**b**) (*Tech*: *of light*) reverberar.

reverberation [ri,vɜːbə'reiʃən] *n* (**a**) retumbo *m*, el retumbar, eco *m*. (**b**) reverberación *f*.

reverberator [ri'vɜːbəreitə*] *n* reverberador *m*.

revere [ri'viə*] *vt* reverenciar, venerar.

reverence ['revərəns] **1** *n* reverencia *f*; **Your R—** Reverencia. **2** *vt* reverenciar.

reverend ['revərənd] **1** *adj* reverendo; **right —** reverendísimo. **2** *n* (*fam*: *Catholic*) padre *m*, cura *m*; (*Protestant*) pastor *m*.

reverent ['revərənt] *adj* reverente.

reverential [,revə'renʃəl] *adj* reverencial.

reverently ['revərəntli] *adv* reverentemente, con reverencia.

reverie ['revəri] *n* ensueño *m*; **to be lost in —** estar absorto, estar ensimismado.

revers [ri'viə*] *n* (*Sew*) solapa *f*.

reversal [ri'vɜːsəl] *n* (*of order*) inversión *f*; (*of direction, policy*) cambio *m* completo; (*of decision*) revocación *f*.

reverse [ri'vɜːs] **1** *adj* (**a**) (*of order*) inverso, invertido; (*of direction*) contrario, opuesto; **in the — order** en orden inverso, al revés; **in the — direction** en sentido contrario; **— turn** vuelta *f* al revés.

(**b**) (*Mech*) **gear** de marcha atrás.

2 *n* (**a**) (*opposite*) **the —** lo contrario; **quite the —** todo lo contrario; **but the — is true** pero es al contrario; **it was the — of what we had expected**

fue todo lo contrario de lo que habíamos esperado; **his remarks were the — of flattering** sus observaciones eran poco halagüeñas, todo lo contrario.

(b) (face: of coin) reverso m; (of cloth) revés m; (of paper etc) dorso m.

(c) (Mech) marcha f atrás, contramarcha f; **to go into —** dar marcha atrás; **to put a car into — dar** marcha atrás a un coche.

3 vt **(a)** (invert order of) invertir, invertir el orden de; trastrocar; (turn other way round) volver al revés; **arms** llevar a la funerala; **to — A and B** invertir el orden de A y B, anteponer B a A.

(b) (change) opinion cambiar completamente de; decision revocar, anular, cancelar.

(c) (Mech) poner en marcha atrás; invertir la marcha de; (Tel) **to — the charges** cobrar al número llamado; **he —d the car into the garage** dio marcha atrás al coche y entró en el garaje; **she —d the car into a pillarbox** al dar marcha atrás al coche chocó con un buzón.

4 vi dar marcha atrás; **I —d into a van** al dar marcha atrás choqué con una furgoneta.

reversible [ri'vəːsəbl] adj reversible.

reversion [ri'vəːʃən] n reversión f (also Bio, Law); **— to type** reversión f al tipo, salto m atrás.

reversionary [ri'vəːʃnəri] adj reversionario, reversible.

revert [ri'vəːt] vi (Law) revertir (to a); (Bio) saltar atrás; **to — to a subject** volver a un tema; **—ing to the matter under discussion . . .** volviendo al tema de la discusión . . .; **to — to type** saltar atrás en la cadena natural.

revetment [ri'vetmənt] n revestimiento m.

revictual ['riː'vitl] **1** vt reabastecer. **2** vi reabastecerse.

review [ri'vjuː] **1** n **(a)** (revision: Law) revisión f; (examination) repaso m; examen m; análisis m; **the annual — of expenditure** el examen anual de los gastos; **the sentence is subject to — in the high court** la sentencia volverá a ser vista en el tribunal supremo.

(b) (Mil etc) revista f; **the Spithead R—** la revista de Spithead; **the general passed the troops in —** el general pasó revista a las tropas; **the troops passed in — before the general** las tropas desfilaron en revista ante el general.

(c) (critique) reseña f; **— copy** ejemplar m para reseñar.

(d) (journal) revista f; **weekly —** revista f semanal; **literary —** revista f literaria.

(e) (show) revista f.

2 vt **(a)** (Law) rever; (take stock of) repasar; examinar, analizar, estudiar; **we will — the position in a month** volveremos a estudiar la situación dentro de un mes; **we shall have to — our policy** tendremos que reconsiderar nuestra política.

(b) (Mil etc) pasar revista a, revistar.

(c) (write — of) reseñar; **he —ed it for the "Journal"** él lo reseñó en el "Boletín".

reviewer [ri'vjuːə*] n crítico m, a f.

revile [ri'vail] vt injuriar, llenar de injurias, vilipendiar.

revise [ri'vaiz] **1** vt (look over) revisar, volver a examinar, volver a estudiar; lesson etc repasar; (amend) modificar, corregir; proofs corregir; text refundir; decision modificar.

2 vi: **to — for exams** repasar los libros (etc) para los exámenes.

revised [ri'vaizd] adj text refundido; **R— Version** (of Bible) Versión f Enmendada.

reviser [ri'vaizə*] n revisor m, ora f; refundidor m, ora f; (Typ) corrector m.

revision [ri'viʒən] n revisión f; repaso m; modificación f, corrección f; refundición f; **I need 2 weeks for —** necesito 2 semanas para repasar mis libros (etc).

revisionism [ri'viʒənizəm] n revisionismo m.

revisionist [ri'viʒənist] **1** adj revisionista. **2** n revisionista mf.

revisit ['riː'vizit] vt volver a visitar; **"Brideshead R—ed"** "Retorno m a Brideshead".

revitalize ['riː'vaitəlaiz] vt revivificar; vigorizar; infundir fuerzas a.

revival [ri'vaivəl] n resucitación f; reanimación f; restablecimiento m; despertamiento m; (Theat) reposición f, reestreno m; (of learning, art) renacimiento m; (Pol etc) resurgimiento m; **the R— of Learning** el Renacimiento.

revivalist [ri'vaivəlist] n predicador m evangelista.

revive [ri'vaiv] **1** vt (restore to life) resucitar; (fig) reanimar; restablecer; fire avivar; accusation volver a, volver a hacer; hopes despertar; suspicion hacer revivir; play reponer, reestrenar; **this will — you**

esto te reanimará; **to — someone's courage** infundir nuevo ánimo a uno.

2 vi (come back to life) resucitar; (recover) reponerse, restablecerse; cobrar fuerzas; (after unconsciousness) revivir; **the pound has —d** la libra se ha repuesto; **interest in Gongora has —d** ha renacido el interés por Góngora; **his courage —d** se sintió con nuevo ánimo.

revivify [riː'vivifai] vt revivificar.

revocation [ˌrevə'keiʃən] n revocación f.

revoke [ri'vəuk] **1** n (Cards) renuncio m. **2** vt revocar. **3** vi (Cards) renunciar.

revolt [ri'vəult] **1** n rebelión f, sublevación f; **to be in open —** estar en franca (or plena) rebeldía; **to rise in —** rebelarse, sublevarse.

2 vt repugnar, dar asco a; **the book —ed me** el libro me dio asco.

3 vi rebelarse, sublevarse (against contra).

revolting [ri'vəultiŋ] adj asqueroso, repugnante.

revoltingly [ri'vəultiŋli] adv asquerosamente, de modo repugnante; **they're — rich** son tan ricos que da asco.

revolution [ˌrevə'luːʃən] n **(a)** (Pol) revolución f; **the Russian R—** la Revolución rusa.

(b) (turn) revolución f; vuelta f, rotación f; **600 —s per minute** 600 revoluciones por minuto.

revolutionary [ˌrevə'luːʃnəri] **1** adj revolucionario. **2** n revolucionario m, a f.

revolutionize [ˌrevə'luːʃnaiz] vt revolucionar.

revolve [ri'vɔlv] **1** vt girar, hacer girar; (in the mind) revolver, meditar.

2 vi **(a)** (Mech etc) girar (on sobre, round alrededor de); dar vueltas; (Astron) revolverse.

(b) (fig) **everything —s round him** todo depende de él, todo se centra en él.

revolver [ri'vɔlvə*] n revólver m.

revolving [ri'vɔlviŋ] adj giratorio.

revue [ri'vjuː] n (Theat) revista f.

revulsion [ri'vʌlʃən] n (disgust) asco m, repugnancia f; (Med) revulsión f; (change) reacción f, cambio m repentino.

reward [ri'wɔːd] **1** n recompensa f, premio m; (for finding something) hallazgo m; **as a — for** en recompensa de, como premio a; **"£50 —"** "50 libras de recompensa"; **"a — will be paid for information etc . . ."** "se recompensará al que dé informes acerca de . . ."

2 vt recompensar, premiar; **to — someone for his services** recompensar a uno por sus servicios; **she —ed me with a smile** me premió con una sonrisa.

rewarding [ri'wɔːdiŋ] adj remunerador; (fig) provechoso, útil, valioso.

rewind ['riː'waind] (irr: see **wind**) vt watch dar cuerda a; wool etc devanar; (Elec) rebobinar.

rewinding ['riː'waindiŋ] n (Elec) rebobinado m.

rewire ['riː'waiə*] vt house renovar completamente el alambrado de.

reword ['riː'wɔːd] vt expresar en otras palabras.

rewrite ['riː'rait] (irr: see **write**) vt volver a escribir, escribir de nuevo; text rehacer, refundir; redactar en otras palabras.

rhapsodic [ræp'sɔdik] adj rapsódico; (fig) extático, locamente entusiasmado, delirante.

rhapsodize ['ræpsədaiz] vi: **to — over something** extasiarse ante algo, entusiasmarse por algo; discutir algo en términos elogiosos.

rhapsody ['ræpsədi] n rapsodia f; (fig) transporte m de admiración (etc); **to be in rhapsodies** estar extasiado; **to go into rhapsodies over something** extasiarse ante algo, entusiasmarse por algo; discutir algo en términos elogiosos.

rhea ['riːə] n avestruz m de la pampa.

Rhenish ['reniʃ] **1** adj renano. **2** n vino m del Rin.

rheostat ['riːəustæt] n reóstato m.

rhesus ['riːsəs] n macaco m de la India.

rhetoric ['retərik] n retórica f.

rhetorical [ri'tɔrikəl] adj retórico.

rhetorically [ri'tɔrikəli] adv retóricamente; **I speak —** hablo en metáfora.

rhetorician [ˌretə'riʃən] n retórico m.

rheumatic [ruː'mætik] adj reumático.

rheumatics [ruː'mætiks] npl (fam), **rheumatism** ['ruːmətizəm] n reumatismo m.

rheumatoid ['ruːmətɔid] adj reumatoideo; **— arthritis** artritis f reumatoidea.

rheumy ['ruːmi] adj eyes legañoso, pitañoso.

Rhine [rain] Rin m.

Rhineland ['rainlənd] Renania f.

rhino ['rainəu] n (fam), **rhinoceros** [rai'nɔsərəs] n rinoceronte m.

rhizome ['raizəum] n rizoma m.

Rhodes [rəudz] Rodas f.

Rhodesia [rəu'diːʒə] Rodesia f.

Rhodesian [rəu'diːʒən] **1** adj rodesiano. **2** n rodesiano m, a f.
rhododendron [,rəudə'dendrən] n rododendro m.
rhomb [rɔm] n rombo m.
rhombic ['rɔmbik] adj (Geom) rombal.
rhomboid ['rɔmbɔid] **1** adj romboidal. **2** n romboide m.
rhombus ['rɔmbəs] n rombo m.
Rhône [rəun] Ródano m.
rhubarb ['ruːbaːb] n ruibarbo m.
rhyme [raim] **1** n rima f; (poem) poesía f, versos mpl; **in — en** verso; **without — or reason** sin ton ni son. **2** vti rimar.
rhymer ['raimə*] n, **rhymester** ['raimstə*] n rimador m, ora f.
rhythm ['riðəm] n ritmo m; **— method** (Med) método m de continencia periódica.
rhythmic(al) ['riðmik(əl)] adj rítmico.
rhythmically ['riðmikəli] adv rítmicamente, de modo rítmico.
rib [rib] **1** n (Anat) costilla f; (Bot) nervio m, nervadura f; (Archit) nervadura f; (of umbrella) varilla f; (Naut) costilla f, cuaderna f.
2 vt (fam): **to — someone** tomar el pelo a uno (fam).
ribald ['ribəld] adj verde, obsceno, escabroso; irreverente y regocijado.
ribaldry ['ribəldri] n (character) lo verde, obscenidad f, escabrosidad f; (jokes etc) cosas fpl verdes, cosas fpl obscenas.
riband ['ribənd] n = **ribbon**.
ribbed [ribd] adj (Bot) nervudo, con nervaduras.
ribbon ['ribən] **1** n cinta f; (Mil) galón m; **type-writer — cinta** f para máquina de escribir; **to tear something to —s** hacer algo trizas; **with his jacket torn to —s** con su chaqueta hecha trizas.
2 attr: **— development** desarrollo m en línea.
rice [rais] n arroz m.
ricefield ['raisfiːld] n arrozal m.
rice pudding ['rais'pudiŋ] n arroz m con leche.
rich [ritʃ] adj rico; (in price, workmanship) costoso, precioso, exquisito; colour vivo, brillante; profit pingüe; soil fértil; voice sonoro; banquet suntuoso, opíparo; food sabroso, suculento, (pej) pesado, fuerte, muy dulce, empalagoso; wine generoso; style copioso; (funny: fam) muy divertido; **that's —!** ¡qué gracioso!; **the —** los ricos; **to be — in** abundar de, abundar en; **a gallery — in im-pressionists** un museo que posee gran caudal de impresionistas; **a style — in metaphors** un estilo en el que abundan las metáforas; **the soil is — in nitrates** el suelo tiene abundantes nitratos; **to become** (or **get, grow**) **— enriquecerse** (on con); **to get — quick** enriquecerse pronto.
Richard ['ritʃəd] m Ricardo.
riches ['ritʃiz] npl riqueza f, riquezas fpl.
richly ['ritʃli] adv ricamente; preciosamente, ex-quisitamente; suntuosamente; sabrosamente; copio-samente; **a — adorned chair** una silla de exquisitos adornos; **a — humorous situation** una situación divertidísima; **she — deserves it** muy bien merecido lo tiene.
richness ['ritʃnis] n riqueza f; preciosidad f, exquisitez f; viveza f, brillantez f; fertilidad f; sonoridad f; suntuosidad f; suculencia f; lo pesado, lo fuerte; copia f; abundancia f.
rick¹ [rik] **1** n niara f, almiar m, montón m de paja (or heno, trigo etc). **2** vt recoger en niaras (etc), amontonar.
rick² [rik] vt see **wrick**.
rickets ['rikits] n raquitismo m, raquitis f.
rickety ['rikiti] adj (a) (Med) raquítico. (b) des-vencijado; (unsteady) tambaleante, inseguro.
rickshaw ['rikʃɔː] n jinrikisha f, rikisha f.
ricochet ['rikəʃei] **1** n rebote m. **2** vi rebotar (off de).
rid [rid] (irr: pret rid, ridded, ptp rid) vt (a) **to — a place of rats** librar un lugar de ratas, eliminar las ratas de un lugar; **to — someone of a difficulty** librar a uno de una dificultad; **the medicine — me of the cough** la medicina me curó la tos.
(b) **to be — of estar** libre de; **we're — of him at last!** ¡por fin nos vemos libres de él!
(c) **to get — of deshacerse** de, desembarazarse de; **the body gets — of waste** el cuerpo elimina los desechos; **to get — of someone** deshacerse de uno, (euph) eliminar a uno matándole.
2 vr: **to — oneself of librarse** de, desembarazarse de; **to — oneself of evil thoughts** librarse de los malos pensamientos.
riddance ['ridəns] n: **good —!** (iro) ¡enhoramala!; ¡vete con viento fresco!; **it was a good — de** buena nos libramos; **and good — to him** que se pudra.
ridden ['ridn] ptp of **ride**; **a horse — by . . .** un caballo montado por . . .

riddle¹ ['ridl] n (conundrum) acertijo m, adivinanza f; (mystery) enigma m, misterio m; (person etc) enigma m; **the — of the assassination** el misterio del asesinato; **to ask someone a — proponer** un acertijo a uno; **to speak in —s** hablar en términos nada claros.
riddle² ['ridl] **1** n (sieve) criba f, criba f gruesa; (potato sorter etc) escogedor m.
2 vt (sieve) cribar; potatoes etc pasar por el escogedor; **to — a door with bullets** acribillar una puerta a balazos; **the organization is —d with communists** el organismo está plagado de comunistas; **the army is —d with subversion** el ejército está lleno de subversionismo.
ride [raid] **1** n (a) (on horse) cabalgata f, paseo m a caballo; (in car etc) paseo m en coche, viaje m en coche (or bicicleta etc); (distance ridden) viaje m, recorrido m; **the — of the Valkyries** la cabalgata de las valquirias; **"2 shillings a —"** "2 chelines por persona", "2 chelines la vuelta"; **it was a rough — fue** un viaje nada cómodo; **it's only a short — es** poco camino, es poca distancia; **it's a 10-minute — by bus** el viaje dura 10 minutos en autobús; **it's a 7d — from the station** el viaje desde la estación cuesta 7 peniques; **they gave me a — into town** me llevaron en coche a la ciudad; **I got a — all the way to Bordeaux** un automovilista me llevó hasta Burdeos; **to go for a — over the fields** pasearse a caballo por los campos; **to go for a — in a car** dar un paseo en coche; **it's my first — in a Rolls** es la primera vez que viajo en un Rolls; **to take a — in a helicopter** dar un paseo en helicóptero; **to take someone for a — (fam)** engañar a uno, embaucar a uno, (US sl) dar el paseo a uno (sl).
(b) (in a wood) vereda f.
2 (irr: pret rode, ptp ridden) vt (a) **to — a horse** montar a caballo; **to — a bicycle** ir en bicicleta; **to — an elephant** ir montado en un elefante; **he rode his horse up the stairs** hizo que el caballo subiese la escalera; **he rode his horse into the shop** entró a caballo en la tienda; **it has never been ridden** hasta ahora nadie ha montado en él; **he rode it in two races** lo hizo correr en dos carreras; **to — a horse hard** castigar mucho a un caballo; **can you — a bicycle?** ¿sabes montar en bicicleta?
(b) (fig) **to — someone** tiranizar a uno, dominar a uno; **don't — him too hard** no seas demasiado severo con él; **to — an idea to death** explotar una idea con demasiado entusiasmo, acabar con una idea a fuerza de repetirla demasiado.
(c) (Naut) waves hender, surcar.
(d) **to — a good race** hacer bien una carrera, dar buena cuenta de sí en una carrera; ser adversario digno de estimación.
(e) **to — someone down** atropellar a uno; **to — out a storm** capear un temporal, hacer frente a un temporal.
3 vi (a) (an animal) montar, cabalgar; (on a bicycle, in a car) ir; pasearse; viajar; **to — on an elephant** ir montado en un elefante; **to — in a car** ir en coche; **some rode but I had to walk** algunos fueron en coche pero yo tuve que ir a pie; **to — astride** montar a horcajadas; **to — like mad** correr como el demonio; **to — home on someone's shoulders** ser llevado a casa en los hombros de uno; **she —s every day** monta a diario; **he —s for a different stable** monta para otra cuadra.
(b) (with expressions of distance and time, often not translated) **to — to Jaén** ir (a caballo) a Jaén; **we'll — over to see you** vendremos a verle; **he rode straight at me** arremetió contra mí; **he rode 12 miles** recorrió 12 millas, hizo 12 millas.
(c) (fig) **to — at anchor** estar al ancla, estar anclado; **the moon was riding high in the sky** la luna estaba en lo alto del cielo; **to be riding high** (person) estar alegre, estar en la cumbre de la felicidad; **when I'm riding high** cuando mis cosas van bien, cuando todo me va bien.
(d) (with adv or prep) **to — away, to — off** alejarse, irse; **to — back** volver (a caballo); volver (en bicicleta, en coche etc); **to — behind** ir después, caminar a la zaga; (in rear seat) ir en el asiento de atrás; (on same horse) cabalgar a la grupa; **to — by** pasar (a caballo); **to — on** seguir adelante; **to — up** llegar, acercarse; (of dress etc) subir.
rider ['raidə*] n (a) (horse-) jinete m, a f; caballero m; (cyclist) ciclista mf; (motorcyclist) motociclista mf; **I'm not much of a — apenas** sé montar; **he's a fine —** es un jinete destacado.
(b) (clause) aditamento m; corolario m; **I must add the — that . . .** tengo que añadir que . . .

ridge [ridʒ] n (of hills) cadena f, sierra f; (of hill) cresta f; (of nose, roof) caballete m; (on cloth etc) cordoncillo m; (wrinkle) arruga f; (Agr) caballón m, camellón m; **Vimy R—** la cresta de Vimy.

ridge pole ['ridʒpəul] n parhilera f, cumbrera f.

ridge tile ['ridʒtail] n teja f de caballete.

ridicule ['ridikju:l] **1** n irrisión f; burlas fpl, mofa f; **to expose someone to public —** exponer a uno a la mofa pública; **to hold someone up to —** ridiculizar a uno, mofarse de uno; **to lay oneself open to —** exponerse al ridículo.
2 vt ridiculizar, poner en ridículo, mofarse de.

ridiculous [ri'dikjuləs] adj ridículo, absurdo; **—!, how —!** ¡qué ridículo!; **to make oneself —** ponerse en ridículo.

ridiculously [ri'dikjuləsli] adv ridículamente, absurdamente; de modo ridículo; **it is — easy** es ridículamente fácil.

riding ['raidiŋ] **1** n equitación f, montar m a caballo.
2 attr de montar; de equitación.

riding boots ['raidiŋbu:ts] npl botas fpl de montar.

riding breeches ['raidiŋ,britʃiz] npl pantalones mpl de montar.

riding habit ['raidiŋ,hæbit] n traje m de montar.

riding master ['raidiŋ,mɑ:stə*] n profesor m de equitación.

riding school ['raidiŋsku:l] n picadero m, escuela f de equitación.

riding whip ['raidiŋwip] n látigo m de montar.

rife [raif] adj **(a) to be —** abundar, ser muy común; ser endémico; **corruption is —** la corrupción existe en todas partes; **measles is —** hay mucho sarampión; **the abuse has become — of late** recientemente ha cundido el abuso, recientemente se ha extendido mucho el abuso.
(b) to be — with estar lleno de, abundar de (or en).

riffraff ['rifræf] n gentuza f, chusma f; **and all the — of the neighbourhood** y todos los sinvergüenzas del barrio.

rifle[1] ['raifl] vt robar, saquear; desvalijar; **to — a case** desvalijar una maleta; **the house had been —d** habían saqueado la casa; **they —d the house in search of money** saquearon la casa buscando dinero.

rifle[2] ['raifl] **1** n rifle m, fusil m; **—s** (as regiment etc) rifleros mpl. **2** vt rayar.

rifle butt ['raiflbʌt] n culata f de rifle.

rifled ['raifld] adj (Tech) rayado.

rifleman ['raiflmən] n, pl **-men** [mən] riflero m.

rifle range ['raiflreindʒ] n campo m de tiro; (at fair) barraca f de tiro al blanco.

rifle shot ['raiflʃɔt] n tiro m de fusil; **within — a** tiro de fusil.

rifling ['raifliŋ] n (Tech) rayado m.

rift [rift] n hendedura f, grieta f, rendija f; (in clouds etc) claro m, abertura f; (in relations etc) grieta f; (between friends) desavenencia f; (in party) escisión f.

rig[1] [rig] **1** n (Naut) aparejo m; (dress, fam) atuendo m.
2 vt (Naut) aparejar, enjarciar; **to — out** (Naut) proveer (with de), equipar (with con); **to — someone out in something** ataviar a uno de algo; **to be —ed out in a new dress** lucir un vestido nuevo; **to — up** (fam: build) armar, construir; (arrange) arreglar; (improvise) improvisar; **we'll see what we can — up** veremos si podemos arreglar algo.

rig[2] [rig] vt: **to — an election** falsificar los resultados de unas elecciones; **the government had got it all —ged** el gobierno lo había arreglado de modo fraudulento; **to — the market** (Comm) manipular la lonja; **it's been —ged!** ¡aquí hay tongo!

rigger ['rigə*] n (Naut) aparejador m; (Aer) mecánico m.

rigging ['rigiŋ] n jarcia f, cordaje m, aparejo m.

right [rait] **1** adj **(a)** (just) justo; equitativo; (suitable) debido, indicado; (proper) apropiado, propio, conveniente; (reasonable) razonable; **it is — that . . .** es justo que . . .; **it is only — to add that . . .** es de justicia añadir que . . .; **it is only — and proper to** + infin la justicia exige que + subj; **it cannot be — for you to** + infin no puede ser justo que Vd + subj; **would it be — for me to ask him?** ¿convendría que yo se lo preguntase?; **it's not —!** ¡no hay derecho!; **I thought it — to** + infin me pareció conveniente + infin; **to do the — thing** hacer lo que hay que hacer.
(b) (correct) correcto, exacto; (true) verdadero; conditions etc favorable, propicio; thing sought etc que hace falta, que se busca; **Mr R—** el novio soñado, el marido ideal; **—!** ¡conforme!, ¡bueno!; **(US)** sí, eso es; ¡justo!; (answering call) ¡voy!; **— you are!** ¡bueno!; **quite —!** ¡perfectamente!; **that's —** eso es; **the —** answer la respuesta correcta, (Math: to problem etc) la solución correcta; **the — word** la palabra exacta, la palabra apropiada; **the — time** la hora exacta; **have you the — time?** ¿tiene Vd la hora exacta?; **— side of cloth** el lado derecho m de un paño, haz f de un paño; **to choose the — moment** elegir el momento oportuno (or favorable); **is this the — house?** ¿es ésta la casa? **is this the — road for Segovia?** ¿es éste el camino de Segovia?, ¿por aquí se va a Segovia? ¿**are we on the — road?** ¿vamos por buen camino?; **am I — for the station?** ¿por aquí se va a la estación?; **he's the — man for the job** es el hombre más indicado para el cargo, es el hombre que hace falta para el puesto; **it's not the — length de** largo no mide lo que debiera; **he's one of the — sort** es buen chico, es un tío simpático; **he's clever but not the — sort for us** es inteligente pero no nos conviene; **to say the — thing** decir lo que conviene, decir lo que se debe decir; **to put a clock —** poner un reloj en hora; **to put** (or set) **something —** arreglar algo, poner algo en orden; **that's soon put —** eso se corrige fácilmente; **to put a mistake —** corregir un error, rectificar un error; **to put someone —** corregir a uno, señalar a uno su error, (unpleasantly) enmendar la plana a uno.
(c) to be — (person) tener razón; **you're dead —,** **you're quite —** estás en lo cierto; **to be — to** + infin hacer bien en + infin; **am I — in thinking that . . . ?** ¿me equivoco al afirmar que . . . ?
(d) (in mind) cuerdo; **to be in one's — mind** estar en su cabal juicio; **she's not — in the head** le falta un tornillo.
(e) (in order, settled) **all's — with the world** todo le va bien al mundo; **to be as — as rain** estar perfectamente bien, estar en su estado normal; **I'm as — as rain,** thanks gracias, estoy perfectamente bien; **she'll be as — as rain in a few days** en unos pocos días se repondrá completamente de esto; **it all came — in the end** al fin todo se arregló, al fin todo salió bien; **it will all come — in the end** todo se arreglará.
(f) (all — etc) **all —!** ¡bueno!; ¡conforme!, ¡está bien!; (that's enough) ¡basta ya!; **it's all —** está bien; **yes, that's all —** sí, de acuerdo; sí, vale; **it's all — for you** Vd no tiene de qué quejarse; **it's all — for you to smile** Vd bien puede sonreír; **is it all — for me to go at 4?** ¿me da su permiso para irme a las 4?; **is it all — for me to smoke?** ¿se puede fumar?; **it will be all — on the night** todo estará listo para el estreno; **I made it all — with the cabby** lo arreglé con el taxista, quedé bien con el taxista; **to be all —** (person) estar bien (de salud); **I'm all —** now ahora estoy bien, ahora me siento mejor; **Joe's all —!** ¡te digo que Pepe es persona de toda confianza!; **is he all — with the girls?** ¿se comporta bien con respecto a las chicas?
(g) (not left) derecho; (Pol) derechista.
(h) (Math) angle recto.
(i) (fam) **he's a — idiot** es un puro idiota; **a — twit I should feel if . . .** bien tonto me creería si . . .
2 adv **(a)** (straight etc) derecho; directamente; **— away** en seguida; **— away!** (Rail etc) ¡en marcha!; **— here** aquí mismo; **— now** ahora mismo; **to go — on** ir adelante; **he just went — on talking** siguió hablando sin hacerme caso, siguió hablando tan fresco; **to speak — out** hablar con toda franqueza, hablar enteramente sin rodeos.
(b) (quite, exactly) completamente; exactamente; **— in the middle** exactamente en el centro; **— at the top** en lo alto del todo, en el punto más alto de todos; **it hit him — on the chest** le dio de lleno en el pecho; **the wind is — behind us** sopla el viento precisamente detrás de nosotros; **— at the end of his speech** precisamente al fin de su discurso; **there is a fence — round the house** hay una valla que rodea la casa por completo; **it goes — to the end** llega hasta el final (sin dejar espacio etc); **he put his hand in — to the bottom** introdujo la mano hasta el mismo fondo.
(c) (rightly) bien; correctamente; **to do —** obrar bien, obrar correctamente; **you did —** hiciste bien; **if I remember —** si bien me acuerdo; **nothing goes — with them** nada les sale bien; **it was him all —** fue él sin sombra de duda; **it's a big one all —** ya lo creo que es grande; **— enough!** ¡muy bien!; **it was there — enough** sí estaba allí; see serve.

(d) (*not left*) a la derecha, hacia la derecha; — **turn**! ¡media vuelta a la derecha!; **to turn** — torcer a la derecha; **he looked neither** — **nor left** no miró a ningún lado; **they owe money** — **and left** deben dinero a todos, tienen deudas por doquier.

3 n (a) (*what is lawful*) derecho m; (*what is just*) justicia f; (*what is morally* —) bien m; — **and wrong** el bien y el mal; **might and** — la fuerza y el derecho; **to be in the** — tener razón; **to fight for the** — luchar por la justicia; **to have** — **on one's side** tener la razón de su parte; **to know** — **from wrong** saber distinguir el bien del mal.

(b) (*title, claim*) derecho m; título m; privilegio m; — **of assembly** derecho m de reunión; —s **of the citizen** derechos mpl del ciudadano; —s **of man** derechos mpl del hombre; — **of way** derecho m de paso, (*Law*) servidumbre f de paso, (*Aut etc*) prioridad f; **divine** — derecho m divino; **sole** — (*Comm*) exclusiva f; **by** —s según derecho, en justicia; **by** — **of** por razón de; **by what** —? ¿con qué derecho . . .?; **to be within one's** —s estar en su derecho; **to exercise one's** — usar de su derecho (*to* + *infin* de + *infin*); **to have a** — **to something** tener derecho a algo; **to have the** — **to** + *infin* tener el derecho de + *infin*; **you had no** — **to** + *infin* no le correspondía a Vd + *infin*; **to own something in one's own** — poseer algo por derecho propio.

(c) (*of authorship etc*) derechos mpl; propiedad f; **film** —s derechos mpl cinematográficos; "**all** —s **reserved**" "es propiedad", "reservados todos los derechos".

(d) —s: **I don't know the** —s **of the matter** no sé quién tiene razón en el asunto; **to set something to** —s arreglar algo; componer algo.

(e) (*not left*) derecha f (*also Pol*); (*blow*) derechazo m; **on the** —, **to the** — a la derecha; **to keep to the** — (*Aut*) circular por la derecha; **reading from** — **to left** leyendo de derecha a izquierda; **he is of the** — es de derechas; **he's further to the** — **than I am** él es más derechista que yo.

4 vt (*set upright etc*) enderezar; (*correct*) corregir, rectificar; **to** — **a wrong** deshacer un agravio, acabar con un abuso.

right angle ['rait,æŋgl] n ángulo m recto.
right-angled ['rait,æŋgld] adj rectangular; **triangle** rectángulo; **bend etc** en ángulo recto.
righteous ['raitʃəs] adj justo, honrado, recto; **indignation etc** virtuoso, justificado.
righteously ['raitʃəsli] adv honradamente, rectamente; virtuosamente; con justicia.
righteousness ['raitʃəsnis] n honradez f, rectitud f; virtud f; justicia f.
rightful ['raitful] adj legítimo; verdadero.
rightfully ['raitfəli] adv legítimamente; verdaderamente.
right-hand ['raithænd] adj: — **drive** conducción f por la derecha; — **man** brazo m derecho, hombre m de confianza; — **side** derecha f; — **turn** vuelta f a la derecha.
right-handed ['rait'hændid] adj que usa la mano derecha; **tool** para persona que usa la mano derecha.
rightist ['raitist] **1** adj derechista. **2** n derechista mf.
rightly ['raitli] adv correctamente; debidamente; bien; — **or wrongly** mal que bien; **and** — **so** y con razón, a justo título; **to act** — obrar correctamente, obrar bien; **as he** — **believed** según creía correctamente; **he was** — **dismissed** con toda corrección le despidieron.
right-minded ['rait'maindid] adj (*sensible*) prudente; (*decent*) honrado.
rightness ['raitnis] n (*correctness*) exactitud f; (*justice*) justicia f.
right-thinking ['rait'θiŋkiŋ] adj juicioso, sensato.
right-wing ['rait'wiŋ] adj derechista.
right-winger ['rait'wiŋə*] n derechista mf.
rigid ['ridʒid] adj rígido; yerto; (*in attitude*) inflexible, severo; **he is quite** — **about it** es inflexible sobre ese punto; **we were** — **with fear** quedamos helados de miedo; **to shake someone** — sorprender muchísimo a uno, sobresaltar a uno.
rigidity [ri'dʒiditi] n rigidez f; inflexibilidad f, severidad f.
rigidly ['ridʒidli] adv rígidamente; inflexiblemente, severamente; **he is** — **opposed to it** está totalmente en contra de esto.
rigmarole ['rigmərəul] n galimatías m, relación f disparatada.
rigor mortis ['rigə'mɔ:tis] n rigidez f cadavérica.
rigorous ['rigərəs] adj riguroso.
rigorously ['rigərəsli] adv rigurosamente.

rigour, (*US*) **rigor** ['rigə*] n rigor m, severidad f; **the full** — **of the law** el máximo rigor de la ley; **the** —s **of the climate** los rigores del clima.
rig-out ['rigaut] n (*fam*) atuendo m.
rile [rail] vt (*fam*) sulfurar, reventar, sacar de quicio a; **it** —s **me terribly** me irrita muchísimo; **there's nothing that** —s **me more** no hay nada que me reviente más.
rill [ril] n arroyo m, riachuelo m.
rim [rim] n (*of cup etc*) borde m, canto m; (*of wheel*) llanta f, (*of car wheel*) aro m; (*of spectacles*) aro m; **the** — **of the sun** el borde del sol.
rime[1] [raim] n (*poet*) rima f.
rime[2] [raim] n (*frost*) escarcha f.
rimless ['rimlis] adj **glasses** sin aros.
rimmed [rimd] adj: — **with** . . . con un borde de . . ., bordeado de . . .; **glasses** — **with gold** gafas fpl con aros de oro.
rind [raind] n (*of fruit etc*) corteza f, cáscara f, piel f; (*of cheese*) costra f; (*of bacon*) piel f.
ring[1] [riŋ] **1** n (a) (*circle: of metal etc*) aro m; argolla f; (*on finger*) anillo m, sortija f; (*on table, for curtain*) anilla f; (*ear*—) arete m; —s (*Gymnastics*) anillas fpl; — **of smoke** anillo m de humo, (*from mouth*) bocanada f de humo; —s **of Saturn** anillos mpl de Saturno; **annual** — (*Bot*) cerco m; **to have** —s **round one's eyes** tener ojeras.

(b) (*of people*) círculo m, grupo m; (*of children, gossips etc*) corro m; (*coterie*) camarilla f; (*gang*) pandilla f; (*Comm*) confabulación f, (*on large scale*) cartel m; **there was a** — **of children round her** los niños estaban reunidos en torno suyo, ella estaba rodeada de niños; **they were sitting in a** — estaban sentados en círculo; **to make** (*or* **run**) —s **round someone** vencer fácilmente a uno.

(c) (*arena etc: Boxing*) cuadrilátero m; (*at circus*) pista f; (*bull*—) ruedo m, redondel m, plaza f; (*at horse race*) cercado m; **the** — (*fig*) el boxeo.

2 vt cercar, rodear (*by, with* de); **bird** anillar, poner anilla a; **the town is** —**ed by hills** la ciudad está rodeada de colinas; **we are** —**ed by enemies** estamos rodeados de enemigos, nos cercan los enemigos.

ring[2] [riŋ] **1** n (a) (*metallic sound*) sonido m metálico; (*resonance*) resonancia f; (*tinkle*) retintín m; (*of voice*) timbre m; (*tone*) tono m, entonación f; (*of large bell*) repique m, tañido m; (*of handbell*) campanilleo m; (*of electric bell*) toque m de timbre; (*at door*) llamada f; **there was a** — **at the door** llamaron a la puerta; **with a** — **of defiance** en son de reto; **with a sarcastic** — **in his voice** con retintín, con énfasis sarcástico; **that has the** — **of truth about it** eso tiene traza de ser verdad.

(b) (*set*) **a** — **of bells** un juego de campanas.

(c) (*Tel*) llamada f telefónica, telefonazo m; **I'll give you a** — te llamaré por teléfono.

2 (*irr: pret* **rang**, *ptp* **rung**) vt (a) (*strike, make sound*) hacer sonar; **large bell** repicar, tañer; **electric bell** tocar; — **the bell, please** por favor toque el timbre.

(b) (*Tel*) **to** — **someone** (**up**) llamar a uno al (*or por*) teléfono, telefonear a uno.

(c) **to** — **down the curtain** bajar el telón; **to** — **up the curtain** levantar el telón; **to** — **up the curtain on something** (*fig*) dar comienzo a algo; **to** — **out the old year** tañer las campanas para señalar el fin del año.

3 vi (*sound*) sonar; resonar (*with* con); (*large bell*) repicar; (*small bell*) sonar; (*tinkle*) campanillear, tintinear; (*at door*) llamar; (*ears*) zumbar; **the telephone rang** sonó el teléfono; **the valley rang with cries** resonaron los gritos por el valle; **you rang, madam?** ¿me llama Vd, señora?; **we'll** — **for some sugar** llamaremos para pedir azúcar; **to** — **off** (*Tel*) colgar; **a cry rang out** se oyó un grito; **a shot rang out** se oyó un tiro; **to** — **up** (*Tel*) llamar (al teléfono).

ring-a-ring-a-roses ['riŋə'riŋə'rəuziz] n corro m; **to play** — jugar al corro.
ring binder ['riŋbaində*] n carpeta f de anillos.
ringbolt ['riŋbəult] n perno m con anillo, (*Naut*) cáncamo m.
ringdove ['riŋdʌv] n paloma f torcaz.
ringer ['riŋə*] n campanero m.
ringing ['riŋiŋ] **1** adj resonante, sonoro; **in** — **tones** en tono vibrante, en tono enérgico.

2 n (*of large bell*) repique m, tañido m; (*of handbell*) campanilleo m; (*of electric bell*) toque m de timbre; (*in ears*) zumbido m.
ringleader ['riŋ,li:də*] n cabecilla m.
ringlet ['riŋlit] n rizo m, bucle m, tirabuzón m.

ringmaster ['riŋˌmɑːstə*] n director m de circo; (trainer) domador m.

ring road ['riŋˈrəud] n carretera f de circunvalación, carretera f perimetral.

ringside ['riŋsaid] n: **to be at the —** estar junto al cuadrilátero; **a — seat** una butaca de primera fila (en el boxeo); **to have a — seat** (fig) verlo todo desde muy cerca.

ring spanner ['riŋˌspænə*] n llave f dentada.

ringworm ['riŋwəːm] n tiña f.

rink [riŋk] n pista f.

rinse [rins] **1** n (of dishes etc) enjuague m; (of clothes) aclarado m; (hair-colouring) reflejo m; **to give one's stockings a —** aclarar las medias; **to give one's hair a blue —** dar reflejos azules a su pelo.
2 vt enjuagar; aclarar; dar reflejos a.

riot ['raiət] **1** n motín m, disturbio m; tumulto m; (fig) orgía f; **the —s** in Harlem los disturbios de Harlem; **it was a — of colour** había una exhibición brillante de colores; **there was nearly a —** hubo casi un motín; **it was a —!** (fig) ¡fue divertidísimo!, ¡fue la monda!; **to read the — act** mandar que cese el disturbio, imponer la paz; **to read the — act to someone** reprender severamente a uno; **to run —** desmandarse, cometer excesos, librarse de toda traba; (spread) extenderse por todas partes; cubrirlo todo; **to let one's imagination run —** dejar volar la imaginación.
2 vi amotinarse.

rioter ['raiətə*] n amotinado m, a f, manifestante mf, revoltoso m.

riotous ['raiətəs] adj person, populace amotinado; assembly desordenado, alborotado; party bullicioso, ruidoso; life desenfrenado; **it was a — success** obtuvo un tremendo éxito; **we had a — time** nos divertimos una barbaridad.

riotously ['raiətəsli] adv con desorden, alborotadamente; bulliciosamente, ruidosamente; desenfrenadamente; **a — funny play** una comedia tremendamente divertida.

rip[1] [rip] n calavera m; (young rascal) tunante m; **you young —!** ¡tunante!; **he's a bit of a —** es algo cascabelero.

rip[2] [rip] **1** n rasgón m, rasgadura f.
2 vt rasgar, desgarrar; **to — off** arrancar, quitar (de un tirón); **to — a box open** abrir una caja rompiéndola, quitar violentamente la tapa de una caja; **to — an envelope open** abrir un sobre rompiéndolo; **to — out** arrancar; **to — up** (tear) desgarrar, romper; **the train —ped up 100 metres of track** el tren destrozó 100 metros de la vía.
3 vi (fig) **to — along** correr rápidamente, ir a buen tren; **let her —!** ¡más rápido!, ¡acelera!

riparian [rai'pɛəriən] adj ribereño.

ripcord ['ripkɔːd] n (Aer) cabo m de desgarre.

ripe [raip] adj (a) fruit etc maduro; **to be — for picking** estar bastante maduro para poderse coger; **to grow —** madurar.
(b) (fig) listo; perfecto, en su punto; **a plan — for execution** un plan listo para ponerse en obra; **to be — for mischief** estar dispuesto a emprender cualquier diablura; **that's pretty —!** ¡eso no se puede consentir!; **to live to a — old age** llegar a muy viejo; **when the time is —** cuando se nos depare la oportunidad, cuando llegue el momento propicio.

ripen ['raipən] vti madurar.

ripeness ['raipnis] n madurez f.

riposte [ri'pɔst] **1** n (Fencing) estocada f; (reply) respuesta f aguda, réplica f. **2** vi replicar, responder con viveza.

ripper ['ripə*] n: **Jack the R—** Juanito el Destripador.

ripping ['ripiŋ] adj (fam) estupendo, bárbaro.

ripple ['ripl] **1** n (wave) rizo m, onda f; (sound) murmullo m; **a — of excitement** un susurro de emoción; **a — of applause** unos cuantos aplausos.
2 vt rizar.
3 vi rizarse; correr con rizos; murmurar; **the crowd —d with excitement** el público se estremeció emocionado.

rip-roaring ['ripˌrɔːriŋ] adj party etc bullicioso, animadísimo, de lo más ruidoso; speech apasionado, violento; success apoteósico.

rise [raiz] **1** n (a) (act of rising) subida f, ascensión f, elevación f; (of sun, moon) salida f; (of river) crecida f; **a — in the voice** una elevación de tono; **— and fall** (of water etc) subida f y bajada; (of music, voice) cadencia f.
(b) (act of rising, fig) **the — of the middle class** el desarrollo de la clase media; **the — of Bristol** el crecimiento de Bristol; **Napoleon's — to power** la subida de Napoleón al poder; **the — and fall**

of the Roman Empire la grandeza y decadencia del imperio romano; **to take a — out of someone** burlarse de uno; poner a uno en ridículo; **nobody takes a — out of me** a mí nadie me tose.
(c) (in price, temperature) subida f, alza f; (in value) aumento m; (in salary) aumento m, subida f; (promotion) ascenso m; **to ask for a —** pedir un aumento de sueldo; **they got a — of 50 pesetas** les aumentaron el sueldo en 50 pesetas; **a — of 5 degrees in temperature** una subida de temperatura de 5 grados.
(d) (of spring, river) nacimiento m; (fig) origen m; **the river takes its — in the mountains** el río nace en las montañas; **to give — to** dar origen a, motivar, ocasionar, (doubts etc) suscitar, dar lugar a.
(e) (high ground) altura f, eminencia f; (slope) cuesta f, pendiente f.
2 (irr: pret **rose**, ptp **risen**) vi (a) (of person: to one's feet etc) levantarse, ponerse en pie; **he rose to greet us** se levantó para recibirnos; **to — from table** levantarse de la mesa; **to — at 6** levantarse a las 6; **to — early** levantarse temprano, madrugar; **to — (again) from the dead** resucitar; **France shall — again** Francia renacerá; **when the House —s** cuando se suspenda la sesión.
(b) **to — (in revolt)** sublevarse, rebelarse (against contra); **to — (up) in arms** alzarse en armas.
(c) (of sun, moon) salir; (smoke etc) subir, elevarse, alzarse; (building, mountain) elevarse; **it rose 3 metres off the ground** se elevó 3 metros sobre el suelo; **the mountain —s to 3,500 metres** la montaña alcanza 3.500 metros, la montaña se eleva a 3.500 metros; **to — to the surface** salir a la superficie; **the partridge rose** se levantó la perdiz, la perdiz alzó el vuelo; **to —** (of fish) picar; **to — to the bait** picar, morder el anzuelo (also fig); **he wouldn't — (to the bait)** no quería picar.
(d) (of ground) subir (en pendiente); (dough) leudarse; (of barometer, temperature, sea etc) subir; (of river) crecer; (of wind) hacerse más fuerte, soplar más fuerte; (swell) hincharse, crecer; (of price) subir, avanzar; (Stock Exchange) estar en alza, cotizarse en alza; (of number) subir, aumentar; **prices are rising** suben los precios; **it has risen 20% in price** su precio ha subido en un 20 por cien; **a thought rose in my mind** se me ocurrió algo; **our spirits rose** volvimos a animarnos, nos reanimamos.
(e) **to — above petty rancour** mostrarse superior a los pequeños rencores; **to — to the occasion** ponerse a la altura de las circunstancias.
(f) (in rank) ascender, avanzar; **he rose to colonel** ascendió a coronel; **he rose from nothing** salió de la nada; **to — in the world** hacer carrera, avanzar en su carrera; **to — in someone's opinion** ganar en la opinión de uno.
(g) (river) nacer.

risen ['rizn] ptp of **rise**.

riser ['raizə*] n: **to be an early —** madrugar, ser madrugador; **to be a late —** levantarse tarde.

risibility [ˌrizi'biliti] n risibilidad f.

risible ['rizibl] adj risible.

rising ['raiziŋ] **1** adj number, quantity creciente; tide creciente; sun etc naciente; ground en pendiente, que sube; generation nuevo; (promising) prometedor, que promete, de porvenir; **the — numbers of murders** el creciente número de homicidios; **with — alarm** con creciente alarma.
2 n (rebellion) sublevación f, rebelión f; (of river) nacimiento m; (of sun etc) salida f; **on the — of the House** al suspenderse la sesión.

risk [risk] **1** n riesgo m, peligro m; **occupational —s** gajes mpl del oficio; **security —** (person) persona f de dudosa lealtad, persona f no enteramente confiable (desde el punto de vista de la seguridad nacional etc); **at the — of a riesgo de; at the — of one's life** con peligro de la vida, arriesgando la vida; **at one's own —** bajo su propia responsabilidad; **at owner's —** bajo la responsabilidad del dueño; **there is a fire —** hay peligro de provocar un incendio; **it's not worth the —** no vale la pena correr tanto peligro; **to run the — of defeat** correr riesgo de ser derrotado; **to run the — of + ger** correr el riesgo de + infin; **to take —s** arriesgarse; **he takes a lot of —s** se arriesga mucho; **will you take the —?** ¿te atreves?; **I can't take the —** no me puedo exponer a eso.
2 vt arriesgar; atreverse a, exponerse a; **I'll — it** lo acepto; **I can't — it** no me puedo exponer a eso; **shall we — it?** ¿nos atrevemos?; **to — defeat** correr riesgo de ser derrotado, exponerse a una posible derrota; **to — + ger** arriesgarse a + infin;

I can't — **going alone** no puedo arriesgarme a ir solo, no me atrevo a ir solo.

riskiness ['riskinis] n peligro m, lo peligroso, lo arriesgado; **in view of the — of the plan** visto lo peligroso del plan.

risky ['riski] adj (a) peligroso, arriesgado, aventurado; **a — enterprise** una empresa arriesgada; **it is — to suppose that ...** es arriesgado suponer que ... (b) = **risqué**.

risqué ['riːskei] adj verde, indecente, escabroso.

rissole ['risəul] n (approx) croqueta f, albóndiga f.

rite [rait] n rito m; **funeral —s, last —s** exequias fpl; **"The R— of Spring"** (Mus) "La Consagración de la Primavera".

ritual ['ritjuəl] **1** adj ritual; (fig) consagrado; **in the — phrase** en la expresión consagrada. **2** n ritual m, ceremonia f.

ritualism ['ritjuəlizəm] n ritualismo m.

ritualist ['ritjuəlist] n ritualista mf.

ritualistic [,ritjuə'listik] adj ritualista; (fig) consagrado, sacramental.

ritzy ['ritsi] adj (US sl) muy pera, lujoso.

rival ['raivəl] **1** adj rival, opuesto; **a — firm** una firma competidora. **2** n rival mf, competidor m, ora f. **3** vt rivalizar con, competir con.

rivalry ['raivəlri] n rivalidad f; competencia f; **to enter into — with someone** empezar a competir con uno.

riven ['rivən] adj rajado, hendido.

river ['rivə*] **1** n río m; **down — río abajo; up — río arriba; up — from Toledo** aguas arriba de Toledo. **2** attr de río, del río; fluvial; **— fish** pez m de río; **— police** brigada f fluvial.

riverbank ['rivəbæŋk] n orilla f del río, margen f del río.

riverbasin ['rivə,beisn] n cuenca f de río.

riverbed ['rivəbed] n lecho m, cauce m (del río).

rivermouth ['rivəmauθ] n, pl **—mouths** [mauðz] estuario m, ría f.

riverside ['rivəsaid] **1** n ribera f, orilla f (del río). **2** attr ribereño.

rivet ['rivit] **1** n roblón m, remache m. **2** vt remachar; (fig) clavar (on, to en); **to — one's eyes on something** clavar la vista en algo; **it —ed our attention** nos llamó fuertemente la atención.

riveter ['rivitə*] n remachador m.

Riviera [,rivi'eərə] Costa f Azul.

rivulet ['rivjulit] n riachuelo m, arroyuelo m.

roach [rəutʃ] n (Fish) escarcho m; (US) cucaracha f.

road [rəud] **1** n camino m (to de; also fig); (main —) carretera f; (in town) calle f; **—s** (Naut) rada f; **"— up"** "cerrado por obras"; **the — to Teruel** el camino de Teruel; **at the 23rd kilometre on the Valencia —** en el kilómetro 23 de la carretera de Valencia; **the — to success** el camino del éxito; **arterial —, trunk —** carretera f principal, autopista f; **country — camino** m vecinal; **main — carretera** f; **across the — al** otro lado de la calle, enfrente; **she lives across the — from us** vive en frente de nosotros; **by — por carretera; to be on the — estar** en camino; (Comm) ser viajante; **to be on the right — ir** por buen camino (also fig); **to get out of the — (fig)** quitarse de en medio; **to hold the — (Aut)** agarrarse al camino; **to take the — ponerse** en camino (to X para ir a X). **2** attr: **— accident** accidente m de carretera; **— construction** construcción f de carreteras; **— traffic** tránsito m rodado; **— transport** transportes mpl por carretera; **— vehicle** vehículo m carretero.

roadbed ['rəudbed] n (US) firme m; (Rail) capa f de balasto.

roadblock ['rəudblɔk] n barricada f.

road book ['rəudbuk] n (Aut) libro m de mapas e itinerarios (etc).

roadbridge ['rəudbridʒ] n puente m de carretera.

roadhog ['rəudhɔg] n conductor m poco considerado, criminal m de carretera.

roadhouse ['rəudhaus] n, pl **—houses** [hauziz] albergue m de carretera.

roadmaking ['rəud,meikiŋ] n construcción f de carreteras.

roadman ['rəudmæn] n, pl **—men** [men], **roadmender** ['rəud,mendə*] n peón m caminero.

roadmap ['rəudmæp] n mapa m de carreteras.

road metal ['rəudmetl] n grava f.

roadrace ['rəudreis] n carrera f sobre carretera.

roadroller ['rəud,rəulə*] n apisonadora f.

roadsense ['rəudsens] n instinto m del automovilista.

roadside ['rəudsaid] **1** n borde m del camino, borde m de la carretera. **2** attr de camino, de carretera.

roadsign ['rəudsain] n señal f de carretera, indicador m.

roadstead ['rəudsted] n (Naut) rada f.

roadster ['rəudstə*] n (car) coche m de turismo; (cycle) bicicleta f de turismo.

roadsweeper ['rəud,swiːpə*] n barrendero m.

roadtrial ['rəudtraiəl] n prueba f por carretera.

roaduser ['rəud,juːzə*] n usuario m de la vía pública.

roadway ['rəudwei] n calzada f.

roam [rəum] **1** vt vagar por, errar por, recorrer. **2** vi vagar; **to — about** andar sin propósito fijo.

roamer ['rəumə*] n hombre m errante, andariego m; (tramp) vagabundo m.

roaming ['rəumiŋ] n vagabundeo m; (as tourist etc) excursiones fpl, paseos mpl.

roan [rəun] **1** adj ruano. **2** n caballo m ruano.

roar [rɔː*] **1** n (of animal) rugido m, bramido m; (of person) rugido m; (loud noise) estruendo m, fragor m; (of fire) crepitación f; (of river, storm etc) estruendo m; (of laughter) carcajada f; **with great —s of laughter** con grandes carcajadas; **he said with a —** dijo rugiendo; **to set the room in a —** hacer reír a todo el mundo a carcajadas. **2** vt rugir, decir a gritos; **to — one's disapproval** manifestar su disconformidad a gritos; **he —ed out an order** lanzó una orden a voz en grito. **3** vi rugir, bramar; hacer estruendo; (of guns, thunder) retumbar; (with laughter) reírse a carcajadas; **to — with pain** rugir de dolor; **the lorry —ed past** el camión pasó ruidosamente; **this will make you —** esto os hará moriros de risa. **4** vr: **to — oneself hoarse** ponerse ronco gritando.

roaring ['rɔːriŋ] adj: **in front of a — fire** junto a la lumbre que arde furiosamente; **it was a — success** fue un tremendo éxito; **to do a — trade** hacer un buen negocio.

roast [rəust] **1** n carne f asada, asado m. **2** adj asado; coffee tostado. **3** vt meat asar; coffee tostar; **the sun which was —ing the city** el sol que achicharraba la ciudad; **to — one's feet by the fire** calentarse los pies junto al fuego; **to — someone** (mock) mofarse de uno, (scold) desollar vivo a uno. **4** vi asarse; tostarse; **we —ed there for a whole month** nos asamos allí durante un mes entero.

roaster ['rəustə*] n (implement) asador m; (bird) pollo m para asar.

roasting jack ['rəustiŋdʒæk] n, **roasting spit** ['rəustinspit] n asador m.

rob [rɔb] vt robar; **to — someone of something** robar algo a uno; **I've been —bed!** ¡me han robado!

robber ['rɔbə*] n ladrón m; (footpad) salteador m (de caminos); (brigand) bandido m.

robbery ['rɔbəri] n robo m; **— with violence** robo m a mano armada; **highway — salteamiento** m; **it's daylight —!** ¡es un robo descarado!

robe [rəub] **1** n (arch) manto m, túnica f; (monk's) hábito m; (priest's) sotana f; (lawyer's, Univ) toga f, traje m talar; (bath—) albornoz m; (christening —) mantillas fpl; **—s** traje m de ceremonia, traje m talar. **2** vt: **to — someone in something** vestir a uno de algo; **to appear —d in something** aparecer vestido de algo. **3** vi and vr: **to — oneself** vestirse.

Robert ['rɔbət] m Roberto.

robin[1] ['rɔbin] n (Orn) petirrojo m.

robin[2] ['rɔbin] n: **round — petición** f (or protesta f) firmada en rueda.

robot ['rəubɔt] n robot m, autómata m.

robust [rəu'bʌst] adj robusto; fuerte, vigoroso; **a — defence** una defensa vigorosa, una defensa enérgica; **a — sense of humour** un fuerte sentido del humor.

robustness [rəu'bʌstnis] n robustez f; fuerza f, vigor m, energía f.

rock[1] [rɔk] n roca f; (standing stone, —face) peña f, peñasco m; (Naut) escollo m; (sl) diamante m; **the R— (of Gibraltar)** el Peñón (de Gibraltar); **whisky on the —s** (fam) whisky m con cubitos de hielo; **to be on the —s** (broke) no tener un céntimo; **their marriage is on the —s** su matrimonio corre riesgo de fracasar; **to run on to the —s** (Naut) dar en un escollo, (fig) peligrar, estar en peligro.

rock[2] [rɔk] **1** vt (gently) mecer, balancear; (violently) sacudir; **to — a child to sleep** arrullar a un niño, adormecer a un niño meciéndole en la cuna (etc). **2** vi mecerse, balancearse; sacudirse; **the ship —ed gently on the waves** el buque se balanceaba en las olas; **the train —ed violently** el tren se sacudió violentamente; **we just —ed (with laughter)** nos morimos de risa; **the theatre —ed with laughter** las risas estremecieron el teatro.

rock-bottom ['rɔk'bɔtəm] **1** n fondo m, parte f más profunda; (fig) punto m más bajo; **prices are at —** los precios están por los suelos; **to reach** (or **touch**) **—** (fig) llegar a su punto más bajo.
2 attr price más bajo, mínimo.
rock carving ['rɔk,kɑːviŋ] n grabado m rupestre.
rock climber ['rɔk,klaimə*] n escalador m (de rocas).
rock climbing ['rɔk,klaimiŋ] n escalada f en rocas.
rock crystal ['rɔk,kristl] n cristal m de roca, cuarzo m.
rocker ['rɔkə*] n (Mech) balancín m, eje m de balancín; (sl) cabeza f; **he's off his —** (sl) le falta un tornillo; **you must be off your —!** (sl) ¡estás majareta! (sl).
rockery ['rɔkəri] n jardincito m rocoso, cuadro m alpino.
rocket¹ ['rɔkit] n (Bot) oruga f.
rocket² ['rɔkit] **1** n (a) cohete m; **distress —** cohete m de señales; **homing —** cohete m autodirigido buscador del blanco; **space —** cohete m espacial.
(b) (sl) peluca f (fam); **to get a —** from some-one recibir una peluca de uno; **to give someone a —** echar un rapapolvo a uno (for something por motivo de algo).
2 vi: **to — upwards** subir como un cohete; **to — to the moon** ir en cohete a la luna; **to — to fame** hacerse famoso de la noche a la mañana, llegar repentinamente a ser conocidísimo; **prices have —ed** los precios se han puesto por las nubes.
rocket launcher ['rɔkit,lɔːntʃə*] n lanzacohetes m.
rocket plane ['rɔkitplein] n avión m cohete.
rocket-propelled ['rɔkitprə,peld] adj propulsado por cohete(s).
rocket propulsion ['rɔkitprə,pʌlʃən] n propulsión f a cohete.
rocketry ['rɔkitri] n cohetería f.
rocket ship ['rɔkitʃip] n aeronave f cohete.
rock face ['rɔkfeis] n pared f de roca.
rock fall ['rɔkfɔːl] n deslizamiento m de montaña.
rock garden ['rɔk,gɑːdn] n jardincito m rocoso, cuadro m alpino.
rocking chair ['rɔkiŋtʃɛə*] n mecedora f.
rocking horse ['rɔkiŋhɔːs] n caballo m de balancín.
rock painting ['rɔk,peintiŋ] n pintura f rupestre.
rock plant ['rɔkplɑːnt] n planta f alpestre.
rock rose ['rɔkrəuz] n heliantemo m.
rock salt ['rɔksɔːlt] n sal f gema.
rocky¹ ['rɔki] adj substance de roca, parecido a roca; slope etc rocoso; fragoso, escabroso.
rocky² ['rɔki] adj que se bambolea, inestable; government etc débil, flojo, nada firme.
Rocky Mountains ['rɔki'mauntinz] pl Montañas fpl Rocosas.
rococo [rəu'kəukəu] **1** adj rococó. **2** n rococó m.
rod [rɔd] n (Mech etc) vara f, varilla, f, barra f; (stick, of authority) vara f; (fishing —) caña f; (Surveying) jalón m; (curtain —) barra f; (connecting —) biela f; (measure) medida de longitud = 5,029 metros; (US sl) revólver m, pistola f; **to have a — in pickle for someone** tener en reserva un medio de ajustar cuentas con uno; **to make a — for one's own back** hacer algo que después resultará contraproducente; **to rule with a — of iron** gobernar con mano de hierro, ser un gobernador muy severo; **to spare the —** excusar la vara; **this is to spare the — and spoil the child** esto es excusar el castigo cuando conviene darlo.
rode [rəud] pret de **ride**.
rodent ['rəudənt] n roedor m.
rodeo ['rəudiəu] n (US) rodeo m.
Roderick ['rɔdərik] m Rodrigo; **—, the last of the Goths** Rodrigo el último godo.
rodomontade [,rɔdəmɔn'teid] n fanfarronada f.
roe¹ [rəu] n (Zool) corzo m, a f.
roe² [rəu] n (Fish): **hard —** hueva f; **soft —** lecha f.
roebuck ['rəubʌk] n corzo m.
roe deer ['rəudiə*] n corzo m, a f.
rogations [rəu'geiʃənz] npl (Eccl) rogativas fpl.
Roger ['rɔdʒə*] m Rogelio; **Jolly R—** pabellón m negro de los piratas.
rogue [rəug] n pícaro m, pillo m; (hum) picaruelo m; **you —!** ¡canalla!; **—s' gallery** fichero m de delincuentes.
roguery ['rəugəri] n picardía f, truhanería f; (mischief) travesuras fpl, diabluras fpl; **they're up to some —** están haciendo alguna diablura.
roguish ['rəugiʃ] adj picaresco; (mischievous) travieso; look, smile etc picaruelo, malicioso.
roguishly ['rəugiʃli] adv look, smile etc con malicia; **she looked at me —** me miró picaruela.
roil [rɔil] vt (US) = **rile**.
roister ['rɔistə*] vi jaranear.

roisterer ['rɔistərə*] n jaranero m.
Roland ['rəulənd] m Roldán, Rolando.
role [rəul] n (Theat and fig) papel m; **leading —** papel m principal; **supporting —** papel m secundario; **to play** (or **take**) **a —** (Theat) hacer un papel, (fig) desempeñar un papel.
roll [rəul] **1** n (a) (of paper, tobacco, film etc) rollo m; (of cloth) pieza f; (of fat on body) rodete m; (of banknotes: US) fajo m; (of bread) panecillo m, (breakfast —) suizo m.
(b) (list) lista f; rol m, nómina f; **—s** (Hist) archivos mpl; **— of honour** lista f de honor; **electoral —** censo m, lista f electoral; **to call the —** pasar lista; **to have 500 pupils on the —** tener inscritos 500 alumnos; **to strike someone off the —** tachar a uno de la lista.
(c) (sound: of thunder) retumbo m; (of drum) redoble m.
(d) (of gait) bamboleo m; (of ship) balanceo m; **to walk with a —** andar bamboleándose; **the ship gave a sudden —** el buque se balanceó de repente.
2 vt vehicle, furniture etc hacer rodar; (move) mover; (push) empujar; soil allanar; lawn, pitch apisonar; pastry aplanar; metal laminar; cigarette liar, hacer; tongue vibrar; **letter R** pronunciar con énfasis, exagerar; **to — a car to the side of the road** empujar un coche al borde de la carretera; **to — a ball along the pavement** hacer rodar una pelota sobre la acera; **to — a stone downhill** hacer rodar una piedra cuesta abajo; **to — a stone over** remover una piedra, volver una piedra; **to — up** map, umbrella arrollar, enrollar; sleeves arremangar; **to — something up in paper** envolver algo en papel; **he was —ed up in the blankets** estaba envuelto en las mantas.
3 vi (a) (go —ing) rodar, ir rodando, dar vueltas; (on ground, in pain etc) revolcarse; (land) ondular; **it —ed under the chair** desapareció debajo de la silla; **it went —ing downhill** fue rodando cuesta abajo; **to be —ing in plenty** nadar en la abundancia; **they're —ing in money**, they're —ing in it nadan en oro.
(b) (sound: thunder) retumbar; (drum) redoblar; (organ) sonar.
(c) (in walking) bambolearse; (Naut) balancearse; **he —ed from side to side as he walked** iba bamboleándose de un lado para otro.
(d) (with adv or prep) **to — by** (cart, time) pasar; **to — down** rodar por, bajar rodando por; **tears —ed down her cheeks** las lágrimas le corrieron por las mejillas; **the waves came —ing in** llegaban grandes olas a la playa; **the money is —ing in** nos entra el dinero a raudales; **to — on** (vehicle) seguir su marcha; (river) correr, seguir su curso; (offensive, time) avanzar; **to — over** dar una vuelta, volverse al otro lado; **to — up** (car etc) llegar; (person) aparecer, presentarse, llegar (como si tal cosa); (hedgehog) enroscarse, arrollarse, hacerse un ovillo.
4 vr: **to — oneself up into a ball** arrollarse, hacerse un ovillo; **to — oneself up in a blanket** envolverse en una manta.
rollaway ['rəuləwei] n (US) (also **— bed**) cama f desmontable, cama f abatible.
roll call ['rəulkɔːl] n lista f, acto m de pasar lista.
rolled [rəuld] adj umbrella etc arrollado; metal laminado; **— oats** copos mpl de avena.
roller ['rəulə*] n (Agr, Tech) rodillo m; (castor) rueda f; (steam—) apisonadora f; (Naut) ola f larga, ola f grande.
roller bandage ['rəulə'bændidʒ] n venda f enrollada.
roller coaster ['rəulə'kəustə*] n montaña f rusa.
roller skate ['rəulə,skeit] n patín m de ruedas.
roller-skating ['rəulə,skeitiŋ] n patinaje m de ruedas.
roller towel ['rəulə'tauəl] n toalla f de rodillo.
roll film ['rəulfilm] n película f en rollo.
rollick ['rɔlik] vi jugar, divertirse; jaranear.
rollicking ['rɔlikiŋ] adj alegre, divertido; **we had a — time** nos divertimos una barbaridad; **it was a — party** fue una fiesta animadísima; **it's — non-sense** son disparates de los más divertidos; **it's a — farce** es una farsa de lo más divertido.
rolling ['rəuliŋ] **1** adj rodante; countryside ondulado. **2** n (Naut) balanceo m.
rolling mill ['rəuliŋmil] n tren m de laminación.
rolling pin ['rəuliŋpin] n rodillo m (de cocina).
rolling stock ['rəuliŋstɔk] n material m rodante, material m móvil.
roll-on ['rəulɔn] **1** n faja f elástica, tubular m. **2** adj elástico.
roll-top ['rəultɔp] adj: **— desk** buró m, escritorio m de tapa rodadera.

roly-poly ['rəuli'pəuli] **1** n pudín en forma de rollo. **2** adj regordete.

Roman ['rəumən] **1** adj romano. **2** n romano m, a f; **r—** (Typ) tipo m romano.

romance [rəu'mæns] **1** n (a) (tale) novela f (sentimental), cuento m (de amor); (medieval) libro m de caballerías, poema m caballeresco; (Mus) romanza f.

(b) (love affair) amores mpl, amorío m, aventura f sentimental; **their — lasted exactly 6 months** sus amores duraron exactamente 6 meses; **a young girl waiting for —** una joven que espera su primer amor; **I've finished with —** para mí no más amores.

(c) (romantic character) lo romántico, lo pintoresco, lo poético; **the — of the sea** el encanto del mar; **the — of travel** lo romántico del viajar; **the — of history** lo atractivo de la historia, lo poético de la historia.

(d) (language) romance m.

2 adj language romance, románico, neolatino.

3 vi soñar, inventar fábulas; exagerar; fantasear.

Romanesque [,rəumə'nesk] adj, **Romanic** [rəu'mænik] adj románico.

romanize ['rəumənaiz] vt romanizar.

romantic [rəu'mæntik] **1** adj romántico. **2** n romántico m, a f.

romantically [rəu'mæntikəli] adv románticamente, de modo romántico.

romanticism [rəu'mæntisizəm] n romanticismo m.

romanticize [rəu'mæntisaiz] **1** vt hacer romántico; añadir detalles románticos (or ambiente romántico) a. **2** vi hablar (or escribir etc) de modo romántico; soñar, fantasear.

Romany ['rɔməni] **1** adj gitano. **2** n gitano m, a f. **3** n (language) lengua f gitana, (in Spain) caló m.

Rome [rəum] (a) Roma; **— was not built in a day** no se ganó Zamora en una hora, Roma no se construyó en su solo día; **all roads lead to —** por todas partes se va a Roma; **when in —, do as the Romans do** allí donde fueres, haz lo que vieres.

(b) (Eccl) la Iglesia, el catolicismo; **Manning turned to —** Manning se convirtió al catolicismo.

Romish ['rəumiʃ] adj (pej) católico.

romp [rɔmp] **1** n retozo m, juego m; **to have a —** **in the hay** retozar en el heno; **the play was just a —** la obra era una farsa alegre nada más.

2 vi retozar, jugar, divertirse; (lambs etc) brincar, correr alegremente; **the horse —ed home to win by 19 lengths** el caballo ganó fácilmente por 19 cuerpos; **she —ed through the examination** encontró que el examen era muy fácil.

rompers ['rɔmpəz] npl pelele m, mono m.

Romulus ['rɔmjuləs] m Rómulo.

rondeau ['rɔndəu] n rondó m.

rondo ['rɔndəu] n (Mus) rondó m.

rood [ru:d] n cruz f, crucifijo m.

rood screen ['ru:dskri:n] n pantalla f de separación rematada por un crucifijo.

roof [ru:f] **1** n, pl **roofs** [ru:fs or ru:vz] techo m, tejado m; (of car etc) baca f, (of coach) imperial f; (of heaven) bóveda f celeste; **— of the mouth** paladar m, cielo m de la boca; **flat —** azotea f; **sliding —**, **sunshine —** techo m corredizo, techo m de corredera; **tiled —** tejado m; **they haven't a — over their heads** no tienen casa; **to raise the —** (protest) poner el grito en el cielo; (sing etc) cantar (etc) bastante fuerte como para hacer venir el techo abajo.

2 vt techar (also **to — in**, **to — over**), poner techo a; **it is —ed in wood** tiene techo de madera; **to — a hut in wood** (or with wood) poner techo de madera a una caseta.

roof garden ['ru:f,ga:dn] n azotea f con flores y plantas.

roofing ['ru:fiŋ] **1** n techumbre f. **2** attr felt etc para techos.

rook¹ [ruk] **1** n (Orn) graja f.

2 vt engañar, estafar; **you've been —ed** te han cobrado demasiado, te han desollado; **they always — the customer in that shop** en esa tienda siempre le cobran un precio excesivo al cliente.

rook² [ruk] n (Chess) torre f.

rookery ['rukəri] n nidada f de grajas, colonia f de grajas.

rookie ['ruki] n (Mil fam) bisoño m.

room [rum] **1** n (a) (in house) cuarto m, habitación f; pieza f; (large, public) sala f; **—s** (lodging) alojamiento m, (flat) piso m; **double —** habitación f para dos personas; **single —** habitación f individual; **furnished —** cuarto m amueblado; **ladies' —** (US: euph) lavabo m de señoras; **men's —** (US: euph) lavabo m de caballeros; **in room 504** (hotel)

en la habitación número 504; **in the professor's —** en el cuarto del profesor; **he has —s in college** tiene un cuarto en el colegio; **they've always lived in —s** han vivido siempre en pisos alquilados.

(b) (space) sitio m, espacio m; cabida f; **is there —?** ¿hay sitio?; **is there — for this?** ¿cabe esto?; **there is no — for that** eso no cabe; **there's no — for anything else** no cabe más; **is there — for me?** ¿quepo yo?, ¿hay sitio para mí?; **there is plenty of —** queda mucho espacio libre; **there is still — on Tuesday** quedan todavía localidades para la función del martes; **to be cramped for —** tener poco espacio; **to make — for someone** hacer sitio para uno, hacer lugar; **make —!** ¡abran paso!

(c) (fig) **there is no — for doubt** no queda lugar a dudas; **there is — for improvement** esto se puede mejorar todavía; **to leave — for imponderables** dar cabida a un margen de imponderables.

2 vi: **to — with a landlady** alojarse en casa de una patrona; **to — with 3 other students** estar en una pensión con otros 3 estudiantes, compartir un piso con otros 3 estudiantes.

room divider ['rumdi'vaidə*] n biombo m; tabique m.

-roomed [rumd] adj de ... piezas, eg **seven-roomed** de siete piezas.

roomer ['rumə*] n (US) (subtenant) subinquilino m, a f; (lodger) huésped m, a f.

roomful ['rumful] n: **a — of priests** un cuarto lleno de curas; **they have Picassos by the —** tienen salas enteras llenas de cuadros de Picasso.

roominess ['ruminis] adj espaciosidad f, amplitud f; holgura f.

rooming house ['rumiŋhaus] n, pl **— houses** [hauziz] (US) casa f donde se alquilan cuartos; pensión f.

roommate ['rummeit] n compañero m de cuarto, compañera f de cuarto.

room service ['rum,sə:vis] n servicio m de restaurante en los cuartos de un hotel.

roomy ['rumi] adj room espacioso, amplio; garment holgado.

roost [ru:st] **1** n percha f; (hen—) gallinero m; **to rule the —** mandar.

2 vi dormir (or descansar) en una percha; (fig) pasar la noche; **the birds — in that tree** los pájaros pasan la noche en ese árbol; **now his policies have come home to —** ahora su política produce su fruto amargo, ahora se están viendo los malos resultados de su política.

rooster ['ru:stə*] n gallo m.

root [ru:t] **1** n raíz f (also fig); (Gram) radical m; **cube —** raíz f cúbica; **square —** raíz f cuadrada; **— and branch** completamente, del todo; **money is the — of all evil** el dinero es el origen de todos nuestros males; **the — of the problem is that ...** lo fundamental del problema es que ..., la esencia del problema es que ...; **what lies at the — of his attitude?** ¿qué razón fundamental tiene su actitud?; **to put down one's —s in a country** radicarse en un país, establecerse de modo permanente en un país; **to strike** (or **take**) **—** echar raíces, arraigar; **to strike at the — of something** afectar la parte fundamental de algo, atacar la misma esencia de algo.

2 adj: **— idea** idea f fundamental, idea f esencial.

3 vt (a) (plant) hacer arraigar; **to — out** arrancar, desarraigar; (fig) desarraigar, extirpar; suprimir del todo.

(b) **to be —ed to the spot** quedar helado (de miedo etc), quedar inmovilizado, estar sin poderse mover; **it is firmly —ed in all minds that ...** está grabado en la mente de todos que ..., todos creen firmemente que ...; **a —ed prejudice** un prejuicio muy arraigado.

4 vi (Bot) echar raíces, arraigar(se); **to — about** (pig) hozar, hocicar, (fig) andar buscando por todas partes (for something algo); **to — for** (fig) gritar por el éxito de; hacer propaganda por, apoyar a.

root beer ['ru:t'biə*] n (US) bebida analcohólica hecha de extractos de diversas raíces.

rootless ['ru:tlis] adj person etc desarraigado.

rootstock ['ru:tstɔk] n rizoma m.

root word ['ru:twə:d] n palabra f radical.

rope [rəup] **1** n cuerda f; soga f; (Naut: hawser) maroma f, cable m, (in rigging) cabo m; (hangman's) dogal m; (of pearls) collar m; (of onions etc) ristra f; **the —s** (Boxing) las cuerdas; **to give someone more —** dar a uno mayor libertad de acción; **if you give him enough —** he'll hang himself sin que tú hagas nada él se condenará a sí mismo; **to know the** —s conocer un negocio a fondo, saber cuántas son dos y dos; **there were 3 of us on the —** (*Mountaineering*) los tres estábamos encordados.

2 *vt* (a) atar con una cuerda, amarrar con una cuerda; *animal* coger con lazo; **to — off a space** cercar un espacio con cuerdas; **to — two things together** atar dos cosas con una cuerda.

(b) **to — someone in** persuadir a uno a tomar parte (*for something* en algo), entruchar a uno.

3 *vr*: **they are roping themselves together** (*Mountaineering*) se están encordando; **there were 4 —d together** había 4 que iban encordados.

ropemaker ['rəup,meikə*] *n* cordelero *m*.
rope trick ['rəuptrik] *n* truco *m* de la cuerda.
ropewalk ['rəupwɔːk] *n* (*Naut*) cordelería *f*.
ropy ['rəupi] *adj liquid* viscoso; (*fam*) deteriorado, desvencijado; inestable; *plan*, *argument etc* nada convincente, flojo.
rosary ['rəuzəri] *n* rosario *m*; **to say one's —** rezar el rosario.
Rose [rəuz] *f* Rosa.
rose[1] [rəuz] 1 *n* (*Bot*) rosa *f*; (*colour*) color *m* de rosa; (*of can*) roseta *f*; (*Archit*) rosetón *m*; **wild —** rosal *m* silvestre; **there's no — without a thorn** no hay rosa sin espina.
2 *adj* color de rosa, rosado, rosáceo.
rose[2] [rəuz] *pret* of **rise**.
rosé ['rəuzei] 1 *adj* rosado. 2 *n* rosado *m*, clarete *m*.
roseate ['rəuziit] *adj* róseo, rosado.
rosebay ['rəuzbei] *n* adelfa *f*.
rosebed ['rəuzbed] *n* rosaleda *f*.
rosebud ['rəuzbʌd] *n* capullo *m* de rosa.
rosebush ['rəuzbuʃ] *n* rosal *m*.
rose-coloured, (US) **-colored** ['rəuz,kʌləd] *adj* color de rosa, rosado, rosáceo; **to see everything through — spectacles** verlo todo color de rosa.
rose garden ['rəuz,gɑːdn] *n* rosaleda *f*.
rose grower ['rəuz,grəuə*] *n* cultivador *m* de rosas, cultivadora *f* de rosas.
rose hip ['rəuzhip] *n* escaramujo *m*.
rosemary ['rəuzməri] *n* romero *m*.
Rosenkavalier ['rəuzənkævə'liə*] (*Mus*) el Caballero de la Rosa.
rose-red ['rəuz'red] *adj* color de rosa.
rose tree ['rəuztriː] *n* rosal *m*.
rosette [rəu'zet] *n* (*emblem*, *Archit*) rosetón *m*.
rose water ['rəuz,wɔːtə*] *n* agua *f* de rosas.
rose window ['rəuz'windəu] *n* rosetón *m*.
rosewood ['rəuzwud] *n* palo *m* de rosa.
rosin ['rɔzin] 1 *n* colofonia *f*. 2 *vt* aplicar colofonia a, frotar con colofonia.
roster ['rɔstə*] *n* lista *f*.
rostrum ['rɔstrəm] *n* (*speaker's*) tribuna *f*; (*Mus*) atril *m*.
rosy ['rəuzi] *adj* rosado, sonrosado; *future*, *prospect* prometedor, halagüeño; **with — cheeks** con mejillas sonrosadas.
rot [rɔt] 1 *n* (a) putrefacción *f*, podredumbre *f*; **it has — está** podrido.

(b) (*fig*) decadencia *f*; **a — set in** comenzó un período de decadencia, todo empezó a decaer; **to stop the —** acabar con la decadencia, impedir que la situación vaya de mal en peor, reformarlo todo.

(c) (*fam*) tonterías *fpl*, bobadas *fpl*; **oh —!**, **what —!** ¡tonterías!; **don't talk —!** ¡no digas bobadas!; **it is utter — to say that . . .** carece de sentido decir que . . .

2 *vt* pudrir, corromper (*also fig*), descomponer.
3 *vi* pudrirse, corromperse, descomponerse; **to — in jail** pudrirse en la cárcel; **it had —ted away with the passage of time** con el tiempo se había descompuesto; **it had quite —ted away** se había descompuesto y desaparecido del todo; **you can — for all I care!** ¡que te pudras!
rota ['rəutə] *n* lista *f* (de tandas *etc*).
Rotarian [rəu'teəriən] 1 *adj* rotario. 2 *n* rotario *m*.
rotary ['rəutəri] *adj* rotativo; giratorio.
Rotary Club ['rəutəri'klʌb] *n* Sociedad *f* Rotaria.
rotate [rəu'teit] 1 *vt* hacer girar; dar vueltas a; (*crops*) cultivar en rotación; (*vary*) alternar; **to — A and B** alternar A con B.
2 *vi* girar; dar vueltas; alternarse.
rotating [rəu'teitiŋ] *adj* rotativo; giratorio.
rotation [rəu'teiʃən] *n* rotación *f* (*also Agr*, *Astron*); alternación *f*; **— of crops** rotación *f* de cultivos; **in —** por turno; **A and B in —** A y B alternadamente; **orders are dealt with in strict —** los pedidos se sirven por riguroso orden.
rotatory ['rəuteitəri] *adj* rotativo; giratorio.

rote [rəut] *n*: **to learn something by —** aprender algo maquinalmente, aprender algo a fuerza de repetirlo (en coro).
rotogravure [,rəutəugrə'vjuə*] *n* rotograbado *m*.
rotor ['rəutə*] *n* rotor *m*.
rotproof ['rɔtpruːf] *adj* a prueba de putrefacción.
rotten ['rɔtn] *adj* (a) podrido, putrefacto, corrompido; *tooth* cariado; *wood* carcomido; (*fig*) corrompido; **to smell —** oler a podredumbre.

(b) (*fam: morally*) vil, despreciable; (*of bad quality*) malísimo, lamentable, fatal; (*Med*) malo; **what a — thing to do!** ¡qué cosa más vil!; **what a — thing to happen!** ¡que mala suerte!; **how — for you!** ¡cuánto te compadezco!, ¡lo que habrás sufrido!; **his English is —** tiene un inglés fatal; **it's a — novel** es una novela horrible, es una novela lamentable; **I feel —** estoy muy malo; **beer always makes me feel —** la cerveza siempre me pone malo; **to be — with money** (*fam*) estar podrido de dinero.
rottenness ['rɔtnnis] *n* podredumbre *f*, putrefacción *f*; (*fig*) corrupción *f*.
rotter ['rɔtə*] *n* caradura *m*, sinvergüenza *m*; **you —!** ¡canalla!
rotting ['rɔtiŋ] *adj* podrido, que se está pudriendo.
rotund [rəu'tʌnd] *adj* rotundo; (*fat*) gordo.
rotunda [rəu'tʌndə] *n* (*Archit*) rotonda *f*.
rotundity [rəu'tʌnditi] *n* rotundidad *f*; gordura *f*.
rouble ['ruːbl] *n* rublo *m*.
roué ['ruːei] *n* libertino *m*.
Rouen ['ruːɑ̃ːŋ] Ruán.
rouge [ruːʒ] 1 *n* colorete *m*, carmín *m*. 2 *vr*: **to — oneself** ponerse colorete, ponerse carmín.
rough [rʌf] 1 *adj* (a) *surface*, *skin etc* áspero; *ground* quebrado, fragoso, escabroso; *road* desigual, lleno de baches; *cloth* basto; *hand* calloso; *hair* despeinado; *edge* desigual; **— to the touch** áspero al tacto.

(b) *treatment*, *behaviour etc* brutal; *person* inculto, sin educación; *sea* bravo; encrespado, picado; *weather* borrascoso, tormentoso; *wind* violento; *play*, *sport* duro; **to be — with someone** tratar a uno de modo brutal; **to get — (sea)** embravecerse; **to get — with someone** empezar a pegar a uno; **he got a — handling in the press** le dieron una paliza en la prensa.

(c) *manners* tosco, grosero; *voice* bronco, áspero; *speech* rudo; *style* tosco; *work* chapucero; *workman* torpe, desmañado; *material* crudo, bruto; *diamond etc* bruto.

(d) *calculation*, *estimate* aproximado; *guess* aproximativo; *plan*, *sketch* a grandes rasgos; *draft* primero; *work* de preparación, preliminar; *translation* más o menos exacto; no completamente fiel.
2 *adv*: **to cut up —** ofenderse, ponerse negro; **to live —** vivir sin comodidades, vivir como un vagabundo; **to play —** jugar duro; **to sleep —** pasar la noche al raso, echarse a dormir (en el suelo *etc*).
3 *n* (*ground etc*) terreno *m* quebrado, superficie *f* áspera; (*person*) matón *m*; **in the —** en bruto; (*plan etc*) a grandes rasgos; **to take the — with the smooth** tomar las duras con las maduras, aceptar la vida como es.
4 *vt*: **to — it** pasar apuros, luchar contra dificultades, vivir sin comodidades; **to — out a plan** esbozar un plan, bosquejar un plan, trazar un plan a grandes rasgos; **to — someone up** (*fam*) dar una paliza a uno.
roughage ['rʌfidʒ] *n* alimento *m* poco digerible.
rough-and-ready ['rʌfən'redi] *adj* tosco pero eficaz; improvisado; provisional; (*person*) inculto pero estimable.
rough-and-tumble ['rʌfən'tʌmbl] *n* (*quarrel*, *fight*) riña *f*, pendencia *f*; (*activity etc*) actividad *f* frenética; **the — of life** la confusión y violencia de la vida.
roughcast ['rʌfkɑːst] *n* mezcla *f* gruesa.
roughen ['rʌfn] 1 *vt* poner áspero; hacer más tosco. 2 *vi* ponerse áspero; hacerse más tosco; (*sea*) embravecerse.
rough-hewn ['rʌf'hjuːn] *adj* toscamente labrado; desbastado; (*fig*) tosco, inculto.
roughhouse ['rʌfhaus] *n*, *pl* **—houses** [hauziz] (*fam*) trifulca *f*, riña *f* general.
roughly ['rʌfli] *adv* ásperamente; brutalmente, incultamente; violentamente; duramente; toscamente; groseramente; broncamente; torpemente; aproximadamente, más o menos; de modo preliminar; **a — made table** una mesa toscamente hecha; **I put it at — 250** yo lo calculo en 250 aproximadamente.
roughneck ['rʌfnek] *n* (*sl*) matón *m*.
roughness ['rʌfnis] *n* aspereza *f*; lo quebrado, fragosidad *f*; desigualdad *f*; callosidad *f*; brutalidad

f; incultura *f*; falta *f* de educación; braveza *f*; violencia *f*; dureza *f*; tosquedad *f*; rudeza *f*; lo chapucero; torpeza *f*, desmaña *f*.

roughrider ['rʌf̩͵raidə*] *n* domador *m* de caballos.

roughshod ['rʌfʃɔd] *adv*: **to ride — over someone** tratar a uno sin miramientos, no hacer caso alguno de uno.

rough-spoken ['rʌf'spəukən] *adj* inculto, de habla inculta.

roulette [ruːˈlet] *n* ruleta *f*.

Roumania [ruːˈmeiniə] *etc see* **Rumania** *etc*.

round [raund] **1** *adj* redondo; *number, sum* redondo; *denial etc* rotundo, terminante; *trip* de ida y vuelta, completo; *dance* en ruedo; **a — dozen** una buena docena.

2 *adv* alrededor; **all — por todos lados; all the year**—durante todo el año; **it has a fence all**—tiene una cerca que lo rodea completamente; **taking it all** —considerándolo en su totalidad, considerándolo desde todos los puntos de vista; **it is 200 metres —** tiene 200 metros en redondo; **for 5 miles — about** en 5 millas a la redonda, en 5 millas en torno; **it's a long way —** es el camino menos directo; **when you're — this way** cuando pases por aquí; **we were — at John's** estábamos en casa de Juan; **we shall be — at the pub** estaremos en el bar.

3 *prep* alrededor de; *(fig)* cerca de, cosa de; **a trip — the world** un viaje alrededor del mundo; **the wall — the town** la muralla que rodea la ciudad; **a walk — the town** un paseo por la ciudad; **it's just — the corner** está precisamente a la vuelta de la esquina; **we were sitting — the table** estábamos sentados alrededor de la mesa; **we were sitting — the fire** estábamos sentados junto a la lumbre; **it's written — the Suez episode** tiene por tema principal el episodio de Suez; **she's 36 inches — the bust** mide de pecho 36 pulgadas; **to sing hymns — the pubs** cantar himnos de bar en bar; **to deliver papers — the houses** llevar periódicos por las casas; **— 2 o'clock** a eso de las 2; **— about £50** cerca de 50 libras, cosa de 50 libras, 50 libras más o menos; **somewhere — that sum** esa cantidad más o menos.

4 *n* (a) *(circle)* círculo *m*; esfera *f*; *(slice)* rodaja *f*; **a — of toast** una tostada.

(b) **the daily —** la rutina cotidiana, la rutina de siempre; **one long — of pleasures** una sucesión de placeres, una serie sin fin de placeres.

(c) *(beat: of watchman etc)* ronda *f*, *(of postman, milkman etc)* recorrido *m*; *(of golf etc)* recorrido *m*, partido *m*; *(of doctor)* visitas *fpl*; **a — of talks** una serie de conferencias; **the first — of negotiations** la primera ronda de negociaciones; **he's out on his —s** está fuera visitando sus enfermos; **to go the —s** *(watchman etc)* estar de ronda, hacer su ronda de inspección; **the story is going the —s that . . .** se dice que . . ., se rumorea que . . .; **the story went the —s of the club** el chiste se contó en todos los corrillos del club.

(d) *(Boxing)* asalto *m*; *(in tournament)* vuelta *f*, rueda *f*; *(of election)* vuelta *f*; *(lap)* circuito *m*; *(in show jumping)* recorrido *m*; **to have a clear —** hacer un recorrido sin penalizaciones.

(e) **— of drinks** ronda *f* de bebidas; **— of applause** salva *f* de aplausos; **— of ammunition** tiro *m*, cartucho *m*, bala *f*; **who bought the last —?** ¿quién pagó la última vez?; **whose — is it?** ¿a quién le toca (pagar)?

5 *vt* (a) **to — a corner** doblar una esquina; **the ship —ed the headland** el buque dobló el promontorio.

(b) **to — off, to — out** redondear; acabar, perfeccionar; terminar; **to — the series off** para completar la serie; **to — up** acorralar, rodear *(S Am)*; **we —ed up a few friends to help** logramos que nos ayudasen unos amigos.

6 *vi*: **to — on someone** volverse contra uno.

roundabout ['raundəbaut] **1** *adj* indirecto; **by a — way** dando un rodeo, por una ruta indirecta; **to speak in a — way** ir con rodeos, hablar con circunloquios.

2 *n* *(at fair)* tiovivo *m*; *(Aut)* cruce *m* giratorio, glorieta *f*, redondel *m*.

rounded ['raundid] *adj end* redondeado; esférico; *end of boat* redondo; *style* maduro, expresivo.

roundelay ['raundilei] *n (Hist)* canción *f* que se canta en rueda; baile *m* en círculo.

round-eyed ['raund'aid] *adj, adv*: **to look at someone — mirar** a uno con los ojos desorbitados.

round-faced ['raund'feist] *adj* de cara redonda.

roundhead ['raundhed] *n (Hist)* cabeza *f* pelada.

roundhouse ['raundhaus] *n, pl* **—houses** [hauziz] *(Rail)* cocherón *m* circular, rotonda *f* para locomotoras; *(Naut)* chupeta *f*.

roundly ['raundli] *adv (fig)* rotundamente, terminantemente.

roundness ['raundnis] *n* redondez *f*.

round-shouldered ['raund'ʃəuldəd] *adj* cargado de espaldas.

roundsman ['raundzmən] *n, pl* **—men** [mən] repartidor *m*, proveedor *m* casero.

roundup ['raundʌp] *n (Agr)* rodeo *m*; *(of suspects etc)* detención *f*; *(by police)* redada *f*; investigación *f* en gran escala; **— of the latest news** vista *f* de conjunto con las últimas noticias.

rouse [rauz] **1** *vt (wake)* despertar; *emotion* excitar, suscitar, despertar; *(from torpor)* animar, reanimar; *game* levantar; **to — someone from sleep** despertar a uno; **to — someone to action** mover a uno a hacer algo; **to — someone to fury** provocar a uno a la furia; **it —ed the whole house** despertó a todo el mundo.

2 *vi* despertar(se).

3 *vr*: **to — oneself** despertarse; *(to act etc)* animarse a hacer algo.

rousing ['rauziŋ] *adj welcome etc* emocionado, entusiasta; *song etc* vivo, lleno de vigor; *speech* conmovedor.

Roussillon ['ruːsijɔ̃] Rosellón *m*.

rout[1] [raut] **1** *n (defeat)* derrota *f* (completa); *(flight)* fuga *f* desordenada. **2** *vt* derrotar (completamente).

rout[2] [raut] *vt*: **to — someone out** hacer salir a uno; **to — someone out of bed** hacer que uno se levante apresuradamente, hacer que uno abandone la cama.

route [ruːt] *n* ruta *f*, camino *m*; itinerario *m*; *(Naut)* rumbo *m*, derrota *f*; **to go by a new —** seguir una nueva ruta; **the — to the coast** el camino de la costa.

route map ['ruːtmæp] *n* mapa *m* de carreteras.

route march ['ruːtmaːtʃ] *n* marcha *f* de entrenamiento, marcha *f* de maniobras.

routine [ruːˈtiːn] **1** *n* rutina *f*; **the daily —** la rutina de todos los días; **as a matter of —** por rutina.

2 *adj* rutinario, de rutina; **a — inspection** una inspección rutinaria; **it's just —** es cosa de rutina.

rove [rəuv] **1** *vt* vagar por, errar por, recorrer.

2 *vi* vagar; **to — about** andar sin propósito fijo; **his eye —d over the room** registró rápidamente el cuarto con los ojos.

rover ['rəuvə*] *n* vagabundo *m*, andariego *m*; *(Naut)* pirata *m*; *(scout)* escultista *m*.

roving ['rəuviŋ] *adj (wandering)* errante; *salesman etc* ambulante; *ambassador* volante; *disposition* andariego; **to have a — commission** no tener puesto fijo, tener el cometido de hacer investigaciones *(etc)* donde le parezca a uno; **he has a — eye** se le van los ojos tras las mujeres.

row[1] [rəu] *n* fila *f*, hilera *f*; *(Theat etc)* fila *f*; *(of books, houses etc)* hilera *f*; *(in knitting)* pasada *f*; **in the front —** en primera fila; **in the fourth —** en la fila cuarta; **he killed four in a —** mató cuatro seguidos, mató cuatro uno tras otro; **for 5 days in a —** durante 5 días seguidos.

row[2] [rəu] **1** *n* (a) *(trip)* paseo *m* en bote de remos; **to go for a —** pasearse en bote, hacer una excursión en bote.

(b) **it was a hard — to the shore** nos costó llegar a la playa remando; **you'll have a hard — upstream** les costará trabajo remar contra la corriente.

2 *vt boat* conducir remando; **to — a race** tomar parte en una regata (de botes de remos); **you —ed a good race** habéis remado muy bien en la regata; **to — someone across a river** llevar a uno en bote a través de un río; **can you — me out to the yacht?** ¿me lleva Vd en bote al yate?

3 *vi* remar, bogar; **to — hard** esforzarse remando, hacer fuerza de remos; **to — against someone** competir con uno en una regata a remo; **we —ed for the shore** remamos para llegar a la playa; **to — round an island** dar la vuelta a una isla en bote de remos.

row [rau] **1** *n* (a) *(noise)* ruido *m*, estrépito *m*, estruendo *m*; **hold your —!, stop your —!** ¡cállate!; **the — from the engine** el ruido del motor; **it makes a devil of a —** hace un ruido de todos los demonios.

(b) *(dispute)* bronca *f*, pelea *f*; **the — about wages** la disputa acerca de los salarios; **now don't let's start a —** no riñamos.

(c) *(fuss, disturbance, incident)* jaleo *m*, lío *m*, follón *m*; escándalo *m*; **what's the — about?** ¿a qué se debe el lío?; **there was a devil of a — about it** sobre esto se armó un tremendo follón; **to kick up** a —, to make a — armar un jaleo, armar un follón; (protest) poner el grito en el cielo; he makes a — about nothing se queja por nada; make a — with your member of parliament quéjese a su diputado.

(d) (scolding) regaño m; to get into a — merecerse un regaño (for something por algo).

2 vt: to — someone echar un rapapolvo a uno.

3 vi reñir, refñirse; they're always —ing siempre están riñendo; to — with someone pelearse con uno.

rowan ['rauən] n serbal m (also — tree).

rowboat ['raubaut] n bote m de remos.

rowdiness ['raudinis] n lo ruidoso, ruido m; carácter m pendenciero; alboroto m, desorden m.

rowdy ['raudi] 1 adj person (noisy) ruidoso; (quarrelsome) pendenciero, quimerista; meeting etc alborotado, desordenado. 2 n quimerista mf.

rowdyism ['raudiizəm] n disturbios mpl, pendencias fpl; gamberrismo m.

rower ['rəuə*] n remero m, a f.

rowing ['rəuin] n remo m.

rowing boat ['rəuinbəut] n bote m de remos.

rowing club ['rəuinklʌb] n club m de remo.

rowlock ['rɔlək] n chumacera f, escalamera f.

royal ['rɔiəl] 1 adj (a) real; (esp fig) regio; — palace palacio m real; R— Academy Real Academia f.

(b) (splendid) magnífico, espléndido, suntuoso; a — feast un banquete suntuoso; to have a right — time pasarlo en grande.

2 n (fam) personaje m real, miembro m de la familia real; the —s la realeza.

royalism ['rɔiəlizəm] n sentimiento m monárquico, monarquismo m.

royalist ['rɔiəlist] 1 adj monárquico. 2 n monárquico m, a f.

royally ['rɔiəli] adv (fig) magníficamente, espléndidamente.

royalty ['rɔiəlti] n (a) realeza f; personajes mpl reales, familia f real; in the presence of — estando presente un miembro de la familia real; a shop patronized by — una tienda que visita la familia real, una tienda donde la familia real hace compras.

(b) (payment; also royalties) derechos mpl de autor; the royalties on oil los derechos del petróleo.

rozzer ['rozə*] n (sl) guili m, guindilla m (sl).

rub [rʌb] 1 n (a) frotamiento m; (accidental friction) roce m, rozadura f; to give someone's back a — frotar las espaldas de uno; to give one's shoes a — (up) limpiar los zapatos; to give the silver a — sacar brillo a la plata.

(b) there's the — ahí está el problema, ésa es la dificultad; to come to the — tropezar con la dificultad; the — is that . . . la dificultad es que . . .

2 vt (apply friction) frotar, (Med etc) friccionar; (hard) estregar, restregar; (to clean) limpiar frotando; (polish) sacar brillo a; to — something dry secar algo frotándolo; to — a surface bare alisar una superficie a fuerza de frotarla; to — away quitar frotando; to — down body secar frotando, horse almohazar, wall etc alisar frotando; to — an ointment in dar fricciones con un ungüento en la piel frotándola; to — an idea in reiterar una idea (desagradable), insistir en una idea; the lesson has to be —bed in que la lección se aprenda a fuerza de repetirla; don't — it in! ¡no machaques!, ¡no insistas!; to — off quitar frotando; to — out borrar; to — someone out (sl) cargarse a uno, despenar a uno; to — one's hands together frotarse las manos; to — up limpiar; pulir, sacar brillo a; (fig) refrescar; see way 1 (h).

3 vi: to — against something, to — on something rozar algo; to — along (fam) ir tirando; I can — along in Arabic me defiendo en árabe; ¡to — down (person) secarse frotándose con una toalla; to — off borrarse debido al roce; some of their opinions have —bed off on him una parte de sus opiniones ha influido en él, él ha hecho suyas algunas de las opiniones de ellos; to — out borrarse; it —s out easily es fácil borrarlo.

rub-a-dub ['rʌbə'dʌb] n rataplán m.

rubber[1] ['rʌbə*] 1 n (material) caucho m, goma f; (eraser) goma f de borrar; (Mech etc) paño m de pulir; synthetic — caucho m artificial; —s (shoes) chanclos mpl, zapatos mpl de goma.

2 adj, attr de caucho, de goma; — goods artículos mpl de goma, (euph) gomas fpl higiénicas; — industry industria f gomera; see band, cheque etc.

rubber[2] ['rʌbə*] n (Bridge etc) juego m.

rubberized ['rʌbəraizd] adj engomado, cubierto de goma.

rubberneck ['rʌbənek] (US fam) 1 n mirón m, ona f. 2 vi curiosear.

rubber solution ['rʌbəsə'lu:ʃən] n disolución f de goma.

rubber stamp ['rʌbə'stæmp] 1 n estampilla f de goma, sello m de caucho.

2 rubber-stamp vt (fig) aprobar maquinalmente; aprobar con carácter oficial; poner su firma a.

rubber tree ['rʌbətri:] n árbol m gomero, árbol m de caucho.

rubbery ['rʌbəri] adj elástico, parecido a la goma.

rubbish ['rʌbiʃ] n (a) basura f; desperdicios mpl, desecho m, desechos mpl.

(b) (fig: goods) pacotilla f; (production, work of art etc) basura f, porquería f; (spoken, written) tonterías fpl, bobadas fpl; —!, what —! ¡tonterías!; he talks a lot of — no dice más que tonterías; it's all — todo son bobadas; the novel is — la novela es una basura.

rubbish bin ['rʌbiʃbin] n cubo m de la basura.

rubbish dump ['rʌbiʃdʌmp] n, **rubbish heap** ['rʌbiʃhi:p] n vertedero m, basurero m.

rubbishy ['rʌbiʃi] adj goods de pacotilla; production, work of art etc que no vale para nada, de bajísima calidad.

rubble ['rʌbl] n escombros mpl, cascote m; (filling) cascajo m.

rubdown ['rʌbdaun] n masaje m; acción f de secarse con una toalla (etc).

rube [ru:b] n (US fam) patán m, palurdo m.

Rubicon ['ru:bikən] Rubicón m; to cross the — pasar el Rubicón.

rubicund ['ru:bikənd] adj rubicundo.

rubric ['ru:brik] n rúbrica f.

ruby ['ru:bi] 1 n rubí m. 2 adj necklace etc de rubíes; ring de rubí, con un rubí; colour color de rubí.

ruck[1] [rʌk] n (Racing) grueso m del pelotón; (Rugby) mêlée f; (fig) gente f común, personas fpl corrientes; to get out of the — empezar a destacar, adelantarse a los demás.

ruck[2] [rʌk], **ruckle** ['rʌkl] (esp to — up) 1 vt arrugar. 2 vi arrugarse.

rucksack ['rʌksæk] n mochila f.

ruckus ['rʌkəs] n (US) = **ruction**.

ruction ['rʌkʃən] n (fam) lío m, jaleo m; there will be —s se va a armar la gorda.

rudder ['rʌdə*] n (Naut) timón m, gobernalle m; (Aer) timón m de dirección.

rudderless ['rʌdəlis] adj sin timón.

ruddiness ['rʌdinis] n rubicundez f; lo rojizo; lo frescote, frescura f.

ruddy[1] ['rʌdi] adj rubicundo; rojizo; complexion frescote.

ruddy[2] ['rʌdi] adj (euph) condenado, puñetero.

rude [ru:d] adj (a) (offensive) grosero, descortés, ofensivo; don't be —! ¡Vd es un maleducado!, ¡Vd es un fresco!; you were very — to me once Vd estuvo muy descortés conmigo una vez; it's — to eat noisily es de mala educación hacer ruido al comer; would it be — of me to ask if . . .? ¿puedo sin ser descortés preguntar si . . .?; how —! ¡qué ordinario!

(b) (indecent) verde, indecente; they sing — songs cantan canciones verdes; there's nothing — about that picture ese cuadro no tiene nada de indecente.

(c) (uncivilized etc) rudo, grosero, tosco; inculto.

(d) (sudden) repentino; (violent) violento; a — shock un golpe inesperado; a — awakening una sorpresa desagradable.

(e) to be in — health estar muy bien de salud.

rudely ['ru:dli] adv groseramente, con descortesía, de modo ofensivo; toscamente; a — made table una mesa toscamente labrada; to answer someone — contestar a uno descortésmente.

rudeness ['ru:dnis] n grosería f, descortesía f; indecencia f; rudeza f, tosquedad f; violencia f.

rudiment ['ru:dimənt] n (Bio) rudimento m; —s rudimentos mpl, primeras nociones f.

rudimentary [,ru:di'mentəri] adj (Bio) rudimental; (fig) rudimentario; he has — Latin tiene las primeras nociones de latín, sabe un poquito de latín.

rue[1] [ru:] vt arrepentirse de, lamentar; you shall — it te arrepentirás de haberlo hecho; I — the day when I did it ojalá no lo hubiera hecho nunca; he lived to — it después se arrepintió de ello.

rue[2] [ru:] n (Bot) ruda f.

rueful ['ru:ful] adj triste; arrepentido; lamentable.

ruefully ['ru:fəli] adv tristemente.

ruefulness ['ru:fulnis] n tristeza f.

ruff[1] [rʌf] n gorguera f, gola f; (Zool, Orn) collarín m.

ruff[2] [rʌf] (Cards) 1 n fallada f. 2 vt fallar.

ruffian ['rʌfiən] n matón m, criminal m; you —! ¡canalla!

ruffianly ['rʌfiənli] *adj* brutal, criminal.
ruffle ['rʌfl] **1** *n* arruga *f*; (*Sew*) volante *m* fruncido; (*ripple*) rizo *m*.
　2 *vt* (*wrinkle*) arrugar; *surface* agitar, rizar; (*Sew*) fruncir; *hair* despeinar; *feathers* encrespar; *someone's composure* descomponer, perturbar; **to — someone's feelings** ofender a uno, herir los sentimientos de uno, irritar a uno; **nothing —s him** no se altera por nada.
　3 *vi* arrugarse; agitarse, rizarse.
rug [rʌg] *n* (*on floor*) alfombra *f*, alfombrilla *f*; (*travelling —*) manta *f* (de viaje).
rugby ['rʌgbi] *n* rugby *m*.
rugged ['rʌgid] *adj* *terrain* escabroso, áspero, accidentado, bravo; (*harsh*) duro, severo; *character* robusto; *features* fuerte, acentuado; *workmanship* tosco; *independence etc* vigoroso; *style* desigual.
ruggedness ['rʌgidnis] *n* escabrosidad *f*, aspereza *f*, lo accidentado; severidad *f*; robustez *f*; lo fuerte; tosquedad *f*; vigor *m*; desigualdad *f*.
rugger ['rʌgə*] *n* (*fam*) rugby *m*.
ruin ['ruːin] **1** *n* (**a**) ruina *f*; **—s** ruinas *fpl*; restos *mpl*; **to lay a town in —s** asolar una ciudad; **the city rose from the —s** la ciudad volvió a nacer sobre las ruinas.
　(**b**) (*act*) arruinamiento *m*.
　(**c**) (*fig*) ruina *f*; perdición *f*; **the — of someone's hopes** la destrucción de las esperanzas de uno; **it will be the — of him** será su ruina; **drink will be his —** el alcohol le perderá, el alcohol será su perdición; **to bring someone to —** arruinar a uno; **— stared us in the face** nos amenazó un desastre total.
　2 *vt* arruinar; (*spoil*) estropear; *taste etc* estragar; (*morally*) perder; **her extravagance —ed him** sus despilfarros le arruinaron; **what —ed him was gambling** fue el juego el que le perdió; **he —ed my new car** estropeó mi nuevo coche.
ruination [ˌruːi'neiʃən] *n* arruinamiento *m*, perdición *f*.
ruinous ['ruːinəs] *adj* (*all senses*) ruinoso.
ruinously ['ruːinəsli] *adv* de modo ruinoso; **— expensive** carísimo, de lo más caro.
rule [ruːl] **1** *n* (**a**) (*ruling*) regla *f*; norma *f*; costumbre *f*; **— of the road** reglamento *m* del tráfico; **— of three** (*Math*) regla *f* de tres; **— of thumb** regla *f* empírica; **by — of thumb** por experiencia, por rutina; mediante una prueba práctica; **standing —** estatuto *m*; **—s and regulations** reglamento *m*; **it's the —** es de regla; **it's against the —s** eso infringe las reglas, eso no se permite; **our — is . . .** nuestro principio es . . .; **the golden —** is . . . la regla principal es . . .; **there is no hard-and-fast — about it** sobre eso no existe ninguna regla terminante; **to do everything by —** obrar siempre de acuerdo con las reglas; **to make it a — to +** *infin* hacerse una regla de **+** *infin*; **I make it a — never to drink** yo por sistema nunca bebo.
　(**b**) (*Law*) fallo *m*, decisión *f*.
　(**c**) (*dominion etc*) dominio *m*, imperio *m*; autoridad *f*; mando *m*; **home —** autonomía *f*; **under British —** bajo la autoridad británica; **under the — of Louis XV** bajo el reinado de Luis XV; **under the — of law** bajo el imperio de la justicia; **under the — of fear** bajo el imperio del miedo.
　(**d**) (*ruler*) metro *m*; **folding —** metro *m* plegable.
　(**e**) (*Eccl*) regla *f*; **the Benedictine —** la regla benedictina.
　2 *vt* (**a**) (*govern*) gobernar, mandar, regir (*also* **to — over**); **to — an empire** gobernar un imperio; **he —d the company for 40 years** durante 40 años rigió la compañía; **he's —d by his wife** le domina su mujer; **be —d by my advice** déjese guiar por mis consejos, guíese por mí.
　(**b**) (*Law*) decidir; (*of chairman etc*) disponer, determinar; **to — that . . .** decidir que . . ., decretar que . . .; **to — something out of order** decidir que un asunto no se puede discutir.
　(**c**) (*draw*) *line* trazar, tirar; *paper* rayar, reglar.
　(**d**) **to — something out** excluir algo; **we can't — out the possibility that . . .** no podemos excluir la posibilidad de que **+** *subj*; **you are not —d out because of that** Vd no queda excluido por eso.
　3 *vi* (**a**) (*govern*) gobernar; (*of monarch*) reinar.
　(**b**) **to — against something** fallar en contra de algo; **to — in favour of someone** decidir a favor de uno.
　(**c**) (*of price*) regir.
ruled [ruːld] *adj* *paper* rayado.
ruler ['ruːlə*] *n* (*person*) gobernante *mf*, gobernador *m*, ora *f*; soberano *m*, a *f*; (*rule*) regla *f*.
ruling ['ruːliŋ] **1** *adj* *passion* predominante; *price* que

rige; **the — classes** la clase que gobierna, la clase que manda.
　2 *n* fallo *m*, decisión *f*; **to give a —** fallar, decidir; **to give a — on a dispute** pronunciar un fallo sobre una disputa.
rum[1] [rʌm] *n* ron *m*; (*US*) aguardiente *m*, bebida *f* alcohólica.
rum[2] [rʌm] *adj* (*fam*) extraño, ráro.
Rumania [ruː'meiniə] Rumania *f*.
Rumanian [ruː'meiniən] **1** *adj* rumano. **2** *n* rumano *m*, a *f*. **3** *n* (*language*) rumano *m*.
rumba ['rʌmbə] *n* rumba *f*.
rumble[1] ['rʌmbl] **1** *n* retumbo *m*, ruido *m* sordo, rumor *m*; (*of thunder etc*) redoble *m*; (*of tank etc*) rodar *m*.
　2 *vi* retumbar; hacer un ruido sordo; redoblar; rodar; (*stomach*) sonar; **the train —d past** el tren pasó con estruendo.
rumble[2] ['rʌmbl] *vt* (*fam*) calar (*fam*); **he's —d us** nos ha calado; **I soon —d what was going on** pronto descubrí lo que estaban haciendo.
rumble seat ['rʌmbl'siːt] *n* asiento *m* .trasero descubierto.
rumbling ['rʌmbliŋ] *n* *see* **rumble**[1].
rumbustious [rʌm'bʌstʃəs] *adj* bullicioso, ruidoso.
ruminant ['ruːminənt] **1** *adj* rumiante. **2** *n* rumiante *m*.
ruminate ['ruːmineit] *vti* rumiar (*also fig*).
rumination [ˌruːmi'neiʃən] *n* (*act*) rumia *f*, rumiación *f*; (*thought*) meditación *f*, reflexión *f*.
ruminative ['ruːminətiv] *adj* (*Bio*) rumiante; (*fig*) pensativo, meditabundo.
ruminatively ['ruːminətivli] *adv* pensativamente; **" —", he said — ": — "**, dijo pensativo.
rummage ['rʌmidʒ] *vi*: **to — about** revolverlo todo, buscar revolviéndolo todo; **to — about in a case** revolver en una maleta; **he —d in his pocket and produced a ticket** revolvió en el bolsillo y sacó un billete.
rummage sale ['rʌmidʒseil] *n* venta *f* de prendas usadas.
rummy[1] ['rʌmi] *adj* (*fam*) extraño, raro.
rummy[2] ['rʌmi] *n* (*Cards*) rummy *m*.
rumour, (*US*) **rumor** ['ruːmə*] **1** *n* rumor *m*; **as — has it** según se dice; **— has it that . . .** se rumorea que . . .; **2** *vt*: **it is —ed that . . .** se rumorea que . . ., se dice que . . .; **he is —ed to be rich** se dice que es rico.
rump [rʌmp] *n* (*Anat*: *of horse etc*) ancas *fpl*, grupa *f*; (*of bird*) rabadilla *f*; (*of person*) culo *m*, trasero *m*; (*Cook*) cuarto *m* trasero, cadera *f*.
rumple ['rʌmpl] *vt* ajar, arrugar, chafar.
rumpsteak ['rʌmp'steik] *n* filete *m* de lomo de vaca.
rumpus ['rʌmpəs] *n* (*fam*) lío *m*, jaleo *m*; batahála *f*, revuelo *m*; **to have a — with someone** pelearse con uno; **to kick up a —** armar un lío.
rumpus room ['rʌmpəs͵rum] *n* (*US*) cuarto *m* de los niños, cuarto *m* de juegos.
rumrunner ['rʌm͵rʌnə*] *n* (*US*) contrabandista *m* de bebidas alcohólicas.
run [rʌn] **1** *n* (**a**) (*act of running*) corrida *f*, carrera *f*; (*Sport*) carrera *f*; (*in stocking*) carrera *f*; (*of fish*) migración *f*; **at a —** corriendo; **to go at a steady —** correr a un paso regular; **to break into a —** echar a correr, empezar a correr; **a prisoner on the —** un preso fugado, un preso evadido; **he's on the — from prison** escapó de la cárcel; **he was on the — for 6 weeks** estuvo libre durante 6 semanas; **he's on the — from his creditors** se está escapando de sus acreedores; **to keep someone on the —** hacer que uno corra de acá para allá; mantener a uno en constante actividad; **we soon had the enemy on the —** pronto pusimos al enemigo en fuga; **we've got them on the —** now ya están casi vencidos; **it came down with a —** bajó repentinamente, cayó todo junto; **prices came down with a —** los precios bajaron de golpe; **I had a — to catch it** tuvé que correr bastante para cogerlo; **I have a — before breakfast** me entreno corriendo antes del desayuno; **to make a — for it** huir precipitadamente; **we shall have to make a — for it** tendremos que correr; **to give someone a — for his money** dar a uno alguna satisfacción por sus esfuerzos; hacer que uno se esfuerce para lograr lo que quiere; **to have a — for one's money** dar buena cuenta de sí, darse alguna satisfacción por sus esfuerzos.
　(**b**) (*outing*, *Aut etc*) paseo *m* (en coche), excursión *f* (en coche); **trial —** prueba *f*, viaje *m* de ensayo; **it was a very pleasant —** fue un viaje muy agradable; **to go for a —**, **to have a —** dar un paseo (en coche); **we'll have a — down to the coast** iremos de excursión a la costa.

(c) (*distance travelled: Rail etc*) trayecto *m*, recorrido *m*; **day's —** (*Naut*) singladura *f*.

(d) (*Typ*) tirada *f*; **a — of 5,000 copies** una tirada de 5.000 ejemplares.

(e) (*tendency*) tendencia *f*; **the — of the market** la tendencia del mercado; **the — of the play was favourable to us** el partido se desarrolló de modo favorable para nosotros; **they scored against the — of play** marcaron un gol durante el tiempo en el que dominaron los adversarios.

(f) (*series*) serie *f*; **a — of four** (*Cards*) una serie de cuatro; **a — of luck** una racha de suerte; **a — of bad luck** una temporada de mala suerte; **to have a long —** (*fashion*) estar en boga mucho tiempo, conservar su popularidad durante mucho tiempo; **the play had a long —** la obra se mantuvo mucho tiempo en la cartelera; **when the London — was over** al terminarse la serie de representaciones en Londres; **in the long —** a la larga.

(g) (*Comm*) **on a bank** asedio *m* de un banco; **there is a — on soap** hay una gran demanda de jabón, el jabón tiene mucha demanda.

(h) the common — of people el común de las gentes; **the common — of books** la generalidad de los libros; **it's above the common —** es superior al nivel general.

(i) to have the — of someone's house poder entrar libremente en la casa de uno; **to have the — of someone's library** tener libre uso de la biblioteca de uno, poder usar a discreción la biblioteca de uno.

(j) (*Agr etc*) terreno *m* de pasto; (*hen—*) corral *m*, gallinero *m*; (*ski—*) pista *f* de esquí.

(k) (*Mus*) glisado *m*, fermata *f*.

2 (*irr: pret* **ran**, *ptp* **run**) *vt* **(a) to — a race** tomar parte en una carrera; **you ran a good race** corriste muy bien; **they're not —ning the race this year** este año no hay carrera; **the race is — over 4 miles** la distancia de la carrera es de 4 millas.

(b) to — a risk correr un riesgo.

(c) to — someone off his legs correr hasta cansar al compañero; **to — someone close, to — someone hard** casi alcanzar a uno, ir pisándole los talones a uno (*also fig*); **to — it close, to — it fine** llegar con muy poco tiempo, dejarse muy poco tiempo; *see* **earth** *etc*.

(d) to — sheep in a field pacer las ovejas en un campo.

(e) (*move etc*) **to — a car into a garage** poner un coche en un garaje; **I'll — you up to town** te llevo a la ciudad; **to — a boat ashore** varar una embarcación; **to — guns across a frontier** pasar fusiles de contrabando a través de una frontera; **to — messages** llevar recados; **to — a new bus service** establecer un nuevo servicio de autobuses; **they're —ning an extra train** ponen un tren suplementario; **they don't — that bus on Sundays** no ponen ese autobús los domingos.

(f) to — the blockade forzar el bloqueo, burlar el bloqueo.

(g) (*have, possess*) tener, poseer; **he —s two mistresses** tiene dos queridas; **we don't — a car** no tenemos coche; **to — a (high) temperature** tener fiebre; **to — a temperature of 104°** tener una temperatura de 104 grados.

(h) (*direct etc*) *business* dirigir; controlar, gobernar, regir; administrar; organizar; *machine* manejar; *campaign* dirigir, organizar; **to — the house for someone** llevar la casa a uno; **a house which is easy to —** (*or easily —*) una casa de fácil manejo; **she's the one who really —s everything** la que en realidad lo dirige todo es ella.

(i) to — a horse correr un caballo; **he ran 3 horses last season** en la última temporada corrió 3 caballos; **to — a candidate** proponer un candidato, apoyar un candidato; **the liberals are not —ning anybody this time** esta vez los liberales no tienen candidato.

(j) (*pass*) pasar; (*pierce*) traspasar; (*introduce*) introducir; **to — one's hand over a chair** pasar la mano por un sillón, recorrer un sillón con la mano; **to — one's eye over a text** examinar rápidamente un texto; **— your eye over this** mira esto un poco; **to — a line round something** trazar una línea alrededor de algo; **we'll — a fence round it** pondremos un cerco alrededor de él; **to — a pipe through a wall** pasar un tubo a través de una pared; **to — someone through with a sword, to — a sword through someone** traspasar a uno con una espada; **I ran a thorn into my finger** me clavé una espina en el dedo.

(k) (*with adv or prep*) **to — down** *ship* hundir, echar a pique; *pedestrian* atropellar; (*find*) encontrar; (*capture*) coger, cazar, acorralar; (*catch up*

with) alcanzar; (*denigrate*) hablar mal de, vilipendiar, desacreditar; **to be — down** (*battery*) estar descargado, (*clock*) estar parado, (*person, Med*) estar agotado, estar debilitado, no estar bien de salud; **I ran that reference down** encontré esa referencia; **we ran him down in a café** por fin lo encontramos en un café; **the police will — him down** la policía le cazará; **to — someone in** (*fam*) detener a uno, meter a uno en la cárcel; **he got — in for being drunk** le detuvieron por borracho; **to — a car in** rodar un coche; **"running in"** "en rodaje"; **she ran the car into a lamppost** dio con el coche contra un farol; **this will — you into debt** esto le hará contraer una deuda; **to — off** (*recite*) enumerar rápidamente; (*Typ*) imprimir, tirar; (*Sport*) *heat* decidir; *water etc* vaciar; dejar correr; **the servant ran the water off** la criada dejó salir el agua; **to — on** (*Typ*) continuar sin dejar espacio, unir al párrafo anterior; **to — over** *pedestrian* atropellar; **to — up** *debt* incurrir en, contraer; *flag* izar; *dress etc* hacer de prisa; *building* construir.

3 *vi* **(a)** (*general sense*) correr; (*hasten*) correr, darse prisa, apresurarse; (*in race*) competir, tomar parte; **to — for all one is worth, to — like the devil** correr a todo correr; **to — downstairs** bajar la escalera corriendo; **to — down the garden** correr por el jardín; **to — for a bus** correr para coger un autobús; **to — to meet someone** correr al encuentro de uno, acudir corriendo para recibir a uno; **to — to help someone** acudir corriendo a socorrer a uno.

(b) (*flee*) huir; **we shall have to — for it** tendremos que correr; **— for your lives!** ¡sálvese el que pueda!

(c) to — for office ser candidato para un puesto, presentarse como candidato para un puesto; **are you —ning?** ¿te vas a presentar?

(d) (*Naut*) **to — before the wind** navegar con viento a popa; **to — aground** encallar, embarrancar.

(e) (*function: engine etc*) funcionar, marchar, andar; estar en marcha; **the lift isn't —ning** el ascensor no funciona; **the car —s smoothly** el coche marcha bien; **things did not — smoothly for them** las cosas no les fueron bien; **it —s on petrol** funciona con gasolina, tiene motor de gasolina; **it —s off the mains** funciona con corriente de la red.

(f) (*function: of service etc*) circular, ir; **the trains —ning between Madrid and Ávila** los trenes que circulan entre Madrid y Ávila, los trenes que hacen el servicio entre Madrid y Ávila; **there are no trains —ning to Toboso** no hay servicio de trenes a Toboso; **that train does not — on Sundays** ese tren no circula los domingos; **the buses — every 10 minutes** los autobuses salen cada 10 minutos; **steamers — daily between X and Y** hay servicio diario de vapores entre X e Y.

(g) (*pass*) **a rumour ran round the school** un rumor corrió por la escuela; **a ripple ran through the crowd** la multitud se estremeció (de emoción *etc*); **it —s through the whole history of art** afecta toda la historia del arte, se observa en toda la historia del arte; **it —s in the family** viene de familia; **the thought ran through my head that . . .** se me ocurrió pensar que . . .; **that tune keeps —ning in my head** esa melodía la tengo metida en la cabeza; **the conversation ran on wine** el tema de la conversación era el vino; **my thoughts ran on Mary** mi pensamiento se concentró en María.

(h) (*go, continue*) seguir; **the contract ran for 7 years** el contrato fue válido durante 7 años; **the play ran for 40 performances** la obra tuvo 40 representaciones seguidas; **the play — for 3 months** la obra se mantuvo en la cartelera durante 3 meses; **things must — their course** las cosas han de desarrollarse normalmente; **the affair has — its course** el asunto ha terminado; **where his writ does not —** donde su autoridad no vale, donde él no tiene jurisdicción.

(i) to — to (*extend*) extenderse a; (*of amounts*) subir a, ascender a, sumar; **the book has — into 20 editions** el libro ha alcanzado 20 ediciones; **the talk ran to 2 hours** la charla se extendió a 2 horas; **the book will — to 700 pages** el libro tendrá 700 páginas en total; **my salary won't — to a second car** mi sueldo no me permite adquirir un segundo coche; **we can't possibly — to a grand piano** nos es imposible comprar un piano de cola.

(j) (*colour*) desteñirse; (*melt*) derretirse; (*Med: sore*) supurar; **colours that will not —** colores *mpl* sólidos, colores *mpl* inalterables; **my ice is —ning** mi helado se está derritiendo.

(k) (*flow*) correr, fluir; (*tears*) correr; (*drip*) gotear; **the milk ran all over the floor** la leche se derramó por todo el suelo; **tears ran down her cheeks** las lágrimas le corrían por las mejillas; **my pen —s** mi pluma gotea; **the streets were running with water** el agua corría por las calles; **we were running with sweat** chorreábamos de sudor; **a land —ning with milk and honey** una tierra que abunda en leche y miel; **to leave a tap —ning** dejar abierto un grifo; **the Tagus —s past Toledo** el Tajo pasa por Toledo; **the river —s for 300 miles** el río corre 300 millas; **it —s into the sea at Lisbon** desemboca en el mar en Lisboa; **the street —s into the square** la calle desemboca en la plaza; **blood ran from the wound** la sangre manaba de la herida, la herida manaba sangre; **the stream ran blood** el arroyo iba tinto de sangre; **a heavy sea was —ning** el mar estaba muy picado; había una fuerte corriente; **when the tide is —ning strongly** cuando sube la marea rápidamente; **to — dry** secarse.

(l) (go, pass) ir; **a balcony —s round the hall** una galería se extiende a lo largo del interior de toda la sala; **a fence —s round the field** el campo está rodeado por una cerca; **York has walls that — right round it** York tiene una muralla que la rodea completamente; **the road —s by our house** la carretera pasa junto a nuestra casa; **it —s north and south** va de norte a sur.

(m) **so the story —s** así dice el cuento; **the text —s like this** el texto dice así, el texto reza así.

(n) **to — to seed** granar; **to — to fat** engordar; tener tendencia a engordar; see **high, low** etc.

(o) (with adv or prep) **to — about** correr por todas partes; divertirse corriendo; **to — across the road** cruzar la calle corriendo; **to — across someone** toparse con uno; **to — across something** encontrar algo; **to — after a girl** correr detrás de una chica, dar caza a una chica, perseguir a una chica; **to — along** (prep) correr por; **the road —s along the river** la carretera sigue el río, la carretera va a lo largo del río; **a fence —s along that side** hay un cerco por ese lado; **— along!** ¡anda ya!; **to — at someone** lanzarse sobre uno, precipitarse sobre uno; **to — away** evadirse, huir, escaparse; (horse) dispararse; **to — away from home** huir de casa; **to — away from prison** evadirse de la cárcel; **to — away from the facts** no prestar atención a los hechos, no hacer caso de los hechos; **to — away from one's responsibilities** no cumplir con los deberes de uno; **to — away with someone** fugarse con uno; **to — away with the cash** alzarse con el dinero; **to — away with the race** ganar fácilmente la carrera; **don't — away with the idea that . . .** no te imagines que . . ., no te dejes arrastrar por la idea de que . . .; **it simply —s away with the money** es que devora el dinero; **to — back** volver corriendo; **to — down** bajar corriendo; **the rain ran down the window pane** la lluvia corría por el cristal de la ventana; **to — down** (adv: clock) parar; **the spring has — down** se ha acabado la cuerda; **to — in** entrar corriendo; **to — into** (collide with) chocar con, dar contra; **the two cars ran into each other** chocaron los dos coches; **to — into someone** topar a uno, tropezar con uno; **to — into debt** contraer deudas; **to — into trouble** tropezar con dificultades; **to — off** huir corriendo, alejarse corriendo; **to — off with someone** fugarse con uno; **to — on** continuar, continuar sin interrupción; **it ran on for 4 hours** continuó durante 4 horas; **she does — on** so es tan habladora, no termina de hablar; **to — out** (person etc) salir corriendo; (of liquid) irse; (of time) acabarse; (of lease, term) expirar; (of contract, permit etc) vencer, caducar; (of stock etc) agotarse, acabarse; **when the money —s out** cuando se acabe el dinero; **the tide is —ning out** la marea está bajando; **the tide is —ning out** (fig), **the sands are —ning out** queda poco tiempo; **we ran out of petrol** nos quedamos sin gasolina; **to — over** (adv: water) desbordar, rebosar; **we're —ning over** hemos rebasado el límite; **the show ran over by 12 minutes** la función duró 12 minutos más de lo debido; **to — over** (prep) text etc repasar, leer por encima; (rehearse) volver a hacer, volver a ensayar; **shall we — over that bit again?** ¿hacemos ese trozo otra vez?; **to — through** book hojear, leer a la ligera; instructions etc repasar; money gastar; consumir; **to — up** (adv) acudir corriendo; stairs etc subir corriendo; **to — up** (prep) plant etc trepar por; **to — up against someone** tener que habérselas con uno; **to — up against difficulties** tropezar con dificultades.

runabout ['rʌnəbaut] n (Aut) coche m pequeño.
runaway ['rʌnəwei] **1** adj prisoner, slave fugitivo; soldier desertor; horse desbocado; lorry que está en movimiento sin conductor, con frenos inservibles;

victory fácil; marriage clandestino, no aprobado por los padres de los novios.
2 n (person) fugitivo m, a f; (horse) caballo m desbocado.
run-down ['rʌn'daun] adj en decadencia, debilitado.
rundown ['rʌndaun] n (of industry etc) cierre m gradual; (of activity) disminución f, reducción f.
rune [ruːn] n runa f.
rung[1] [rʌŋ] n escalón m, peldaño m.
rung[2] [rʌŋ] ptp of **ring**.
runic ['ruːnik] adj rúnico.
run-in ['rʌnin] n (Typ) palabras fpl insertadas en un párrafo.
runlet ['rʌnlit] n, **runnel** ['rʌnl] n arroyuelo m.
runner ['rʌnə*] n (athlete) corredor m, ora f, atleta mf; (horse) caballo m; (messenger) mensajero m, (Mil) ordenanza m; (ring) anillo m movible; (wheel) ruedecilla f; (of sledge, aircraft) patín m; (table—) tapete m; (Bot) tallo m rastrero, estolón m.
runner-up ['rʌnər'ʌp] n subcampeón m, ona f.
running ['rʌniŋ] **1** adj water corriente; knot corredizo; writing cursivo; sore supurante, purulento; commentary continuo; start lanzado; **— costs** gastos mpl corrientes; **— fight** acción f de retirada, combate m continuo; **— kick** puntapié m dado mientras corre el jugador (etc); **in — order** en buen estado; **5 days —** 5 días seguidos; **for the sixth time —** por sexta vez consecutiva.
2 n (of business etc) dirección f; control m; gobierno m; administración f; organización f; manejo m; (of machine) funcionamiento m, marcha f; **to be in the —** tener posibilidades de ganar; **to be in the — for a chair** tener posibilidades de ganar una cátedra; **to be out of the —** no tener posibilidad alguna de ganar; **to make (all) the —** ir a la cabeza, ir delante.
running board ['rʌniŋbɔːd] n (Aut etc) estribo m.
running in ['rʌniŋ'in] n (Aut) rodaje m.
running mate ['rʌniŋ'meit] n (US Pol) candidato m a la vicepresidencia.
runny ['rʌni] adj líquido; derretido.
run-off ['rʌnɔf] n (Sport) carrera f final; carrera f de desempate.
run-of-the-mill ['rʌnəvðə'mil] adj corriente y moliente.
runt [rʌnt] n redrojo m, enano m; (fig) enano m; **you little —!** ¡canalla!
run-through ['rʌnθruː] n prueba f preliminar, ensayo m.
runway ['rʌnwei] n (Aer) pista f de aterrizaje.
rupee [ruːˈpiː] n rupia f.
rupture ['rʌptʃə*] **1** n (Med) hernia f, quebradura f; (fig) ruptura f, rompimiento m.
2 vt causar una hernia en, quebrarse.
3 vr: **to — oneself** causarse una hernia, quebrarse.
rural ['ruərəl] adj rural.
ruse [ruːz] n ardid m, treta f, estratagema f.
rush[1] [rʌʃ] n (Bot) junco m.
rush[2] [rʌʃ] **1** n **(a)** (act of —ing) ímpetu m; (Mil) ataque m; acometida f; asalto m; **general —** desbandada f general; **the gold —** la carrera del oro; **there was a — to the door** se precipitaron todos hacia la puerta; **there was a — for safety** todos hicieron lo posible por ponerse a salvo; **to make a — at someone** arremeter contra uno, precipitarse sobre uno; **it got lost in the —** se perdió en la confusión; **2 were injured in the —** al precipitarse todos 2 resultaron heridos.
(b) (haste) prisa f, precipitación f; (tumult) bullicio m, ajetreo m; **the — of modern life** el ajetreo de la vida moderna; **the — of London** la prisa que tiene todo el mundo en Londres; **what's all the — about?** ¿por qué tanta prisa?; **is there any — for this?** ¿le corre prisa esto?; **we're in a —** tenemos prisa, llevamos prisa; **we're in a — to finish it** tenemos prisa por terminarlo; **I did it in a —** lo hice de prisa; **we had a — to get it ready** nos dimos prisa para tenerlo listo; **everything happened with a —** todo ocurrió de repente; **it came down with a —** cayó de repente.
(c) (Comm) demanda f (for, on de); **there has been a — on matches** ha habido una demanda extraordinaria de cerillas.
(d) (current) **a — of air** una fuerte corriente de aire, una ráfaga de aire; **a — of water** un torrente de agua; **a — of words** un torrente de palabras; **a — of people** un tropel m; **we've had a — of orders** estamos inundados de pedidos; **he had a — of blood to the head** (fig) le pasó algo totalmente inesperado; tuvo un momento de locura.
2 adj: **— hours** horas fpl punta, horas fpl de máximo tránsito; **Barcelona in the — hour**

Barcelona a la hora punta; — **order** pedido *m* urgente; — **work** trabajo *m* hecho de prisa.
3 *vt* (a) (*person*) dar prisa a, apresurar; **I hate being —ed** no permito que me metan prisa, no aguanto a los que piden que vaya más de prisa.
(b) (*work*) hacer de prisa, ejecutar de prisa; **to — a bill through** hacer aprobar de prisa un proyecto de ley.
(c) (*carry etc*) llevar rápidamente; **to — medicine to someone** llevar con toda prisa medicina a uno; **he was —ed to hospital** le llevaron al hospital con la mayor urgencia.
(d) (*Mil*) *position etc* asaltar, tomar al asalto; *troops* atacar repentinamente; **the crowd —ed the barriers** el público asaltó las barreras.
(e) (*sl*) **how much did they — you?** ¿cuánto te cobraron?; **they —ed me £2** me hicieron pagar 2 libras.
4 *vi* precipitarse, lanzarse (*at* hacia, sobre); correr (*etc*) rápidamente, ir de prisa, ir a máxima velocidad; **to — across a road** cruzar una calle a toda prisa; **you mustn't — across roads like that** es peligroso cruzar las calles con tanta precipitación; **everyone —ed to the windows** se precipitaron todos hacia las ventanas; **the rocket was —ing through space** el cohete iba a gran velocidad por el espacio; **don't — !** ¡con calma!; **to — at someone** arremeter contra uno, abalanzarse sobre uno; **to — by, to — past** pasar como un rayo; **to — in** entrar precipitadamente; **to — into the fray** lanzarse a la batalla; **to — off** partir como un rayo; **to — out** salir precipitadamente; **I —ed to her side** me di prisa por ponerme a su lado; **I was —ing to finish it** me daba prisa por terminarlo.
rushlight ['rʌʃlait] *n* vela *f* de junco.
rushy ['rʌʃi] *adj* juncoso.
rusk [rʌsk] *n* bizcocho *m* tostado.
russet ['rʌsit] **1** *n* color *m* bermejo, color *m* rojizo. **2** *adj* bermejo, rojizo.
Russia ['rʌʃə] Rusia *f*.
Russian ['rʌʃən] **1** *adj* ruso. **2** *n* ruso *m*, rusa *f*. **3** *n* (*language*) ruso *m*.
rust [rʌst] **1** *n* (*action*) oxidación *f*, corrosión *f*; (*visible*) orín *m*, herrumbre *f*, moho *m*; (*colour*) color *m* de orín; (*Agr*) roya *f*.

2 *vt* oxidar, corroer; aherrumbrar.
3 *vi* oxidarse, corroerse; aherrumbrarse, tomarse de orín.
rustic ['rʌstik] **1** *adj* rústico; aldeano; (*pej*) rústico; (*person*) palurdo. **2** *n* rústico *m*, palurdo *m*.
rusticate ['rʌstikeit] **1** *vt* (*Univ*) suspender temporalmente. **2** *vi* rusticar.
rustication [,rʌsti'keiʃən] *n* (*Univ*) suspensión *f* temporal.
rusticity [rʌs'tisiti] *n* rusticidad *f*.
rustiness ['rʌstinis] *n* herrumbre *f*, lo aherrumbrado; (*fig*) falta *f* de práctica, torpeza *f*.
rustle[1] ['rʌsl] **1** *n* (*of leaves, wind*) susurro *m*; (*of paper*) crujido *m*; (*of silk, dress*) frufrú *m*.
2 *vt* hacer susurrar, mover ligeramente; hacer crujir.
3 *vi* susurrar; crujir; hacer frufrú.
rustle[2] ['rʌsl] *vt* (*US fam*) robar, hurtar.
rustless ['rʌstlis] *adj* inoxidable.
rustproof ['rʌstpru:f] *adj*, **rust-resistant** ['rʌstri,zistənt] *adj* a prueba de herrumbre.
rusty ['rʌsti] *adj* oxidado, herrumbroso, aherrumbrado, mohoso; *colour* color de orín; (*fig*) falto de práctica, torpe; **my Catalan is pretty —** ya no hablo apenas catalán, mi catalán es bastante defectuoso.
rut[1] [rʌt] *n* rodera *f*, rodada *f*, carril *m*; bache *m*; (*fig*) rutina *f*, sendero *m* trillado; **to be in a —** estar sin poder salir de la rutina, ir encarrilado; **you've got into a —** te has hecho esclavo de la rutina; **to get out of the —** salir del bache.
rut[2] [rʌt] (*Bio*) **1** *n* celo *m*; **to be in —** estar en celo. **2** *vi* (*be*) estar en celo; (*begin to —*) caer en celo.
ruthless ['ru:θlis] *adj* despiadado; implacable, inexorable.
ruthlessly ['ru:θlisli] *adv* despiadadamente; implacablemente, inexorablemente.
ruthlessness ['ru:θlisnis] *n* crueldad *f*; implacabilidad *f*.
rutting ['rʌtiŋ] *adj* (*Bio*) en celo; — **season** época *f* de celo.
rutty ['rʌti] *adj* lleno de baches.
rye [rai] *n* centeno *m*.
rye bread ['rai'bred] *n* pan *m* de centeno.
ryegrass ['raigrɑ:s] *n* cizaña *f*, joyo *m*.

S

Saar [zɑ:*] Sarre m.
sabbatarian [ˌsæbəˈtɛəriən] **1** adj sabatario. **2** n sabatario m, a f, partidario m de guardar santamente el domingo.
sabbath [ˈsæbəθ] n (Christian) domingo m; (Jewish) sábado m.
sabbatical [səˈbætikəl] adj (Rel) sabático; dominical; — year (Univ) año m de licencia.
sable [ˈseibl] **1** n (animal, fur) cebellina f; (colour) negro m; (Her) sable m. **2** adj negro.
sabot [ˈsæbəu] n zueco m.
sabotage [ˈsæbətɑ:ʒ] **1** n sabotaje m. **2** vt sabotear (also fig).
saboteur [ˌsæbəˈtə:*] n saboteador m.
sabre, (US) **saber** [ˈseibə*] **1** n sable m. **2** vt herir (or matar etc) a sablazos.
sabre rattler, (US) **saber — ** [ˈseibəˌrætlə*] n patriotero m, jingoísta m.
sabre rattling, (US) **saber — ** [ˈseibəˌrætliŋ] n patriotería f, jingoísmo m.
sac [sæk] n (Anat etc) saco m.
saccharin(e) [ˈsækərin] n sacarina f.
saccharine [ˈsækəri:n] adj sacarino; (fig) azucarado, empalagoso.
sacerdotal [ˌsæsəˈdəutl] adj sacerdotal.
sachet [ˈsæfei] n saquito m, bolsita f.
sack[1] [sæk] **1** n (a) saco m, costal m.
(b) (fam) despido m; to get the — ser despedido; to give someone the — despedir a uno.
2 vt (a) ensacar, meter en sacos.
(b) (fam) despedir.
sack[2] [sæk] **1** n saqueo m. **2** vt saquear.
sackbut [ˈsækbʌt] n sacabuche m.
sackcloth [ˈsækklɔθ] n (h)arpillera f; to wear — and ashes ponerse el hábito de penitencia, ponerse cenizas en la cabeza.
sackful [ˈsækful] n saco m, contenido m de un saco.
sacking[1] [ˈsækiŋ] n (material) (h)arpillera f.
sacking[2] [ˈsækiŋ] n (fam) despido m.
sack race [ˈsækreis] n carrera f de sacos.
sacrament [ˈsækrəmənt] n sacramento m; Eucaristía f; the Blessed S— el Santísimo Sacramento; to receive the Holy S— comulgar; to receive the last —s recibir los últimos sacramentos.
sacramental [ˌsækrəˈmentl] adj sacramental.
sacred [ˈseikrid] adj sagrado; santo; consagrado; S— History Historia f Sagrada; — to the memory of ... consagrado a la memoria de ...; is nothing —? ¿no hay nada sagrado para Vd?, ¿no respeta Vd nada?
sacrifice [ˈsækrifais] **1** n sacrificio m; (person etc) víctima f; the — of the mass el sacrificio de la misa; to make —s privarse de algo, renunciar a algo; to sell something at a — vender algo con pérdida.
2 vt sacrificar; (Comm) vender con pérdida, vender a no importa qué precio.
3 vr: to — oneself sacrificarse.
sacrificial [ˌsækriˈfifəl] adj de sacrificio.
sacrilege [ˈsækrilidʒ] n sacrilegio m.
sacrilegious [ˌsækriˈlidʒəs] adj sacrílego.
sacrist [ˈsækrist] n, **sacristan** [ˈsækristən] n sacristán m.
sacristy [ˈsækristri] n sacristía f.
sacrosanct [ˈsækrəusæŋkt] adj sacrosanto.
sacrum [ˈseikrəm] n (Anat) sacro m.
sad [sæd] adj (a) (sorrowful) triste; melancólico; how — ! ¡qué triste!; to be — at heart estar profundamente triste; to grow — entristecerse, ponerse triste; to make someone — entristecer a uno, poner triste a uno; he left a —der and a wiser man partió habiendo aprendido una dura lección.
(b) (deplorable) lamentable; a — mistake un error lamentable; it's a — business es un asunto lamentable.

sadden [ˈsædn] vt entristecer; afligir.
saddle [ˈsædl] **1** n silla f (de montar); (cycle —) sillín m; (hill) collado m; (of meat) cuarto m trasero; to be in the — (fig) estar en el poder, mandar; to leap into the — saltar a la silla.
2 vt horse (also to — up) ensillar; to — someone with something echar algo a cuestas a uno, echar a uno la responsabilidad de algo; now we're —d with it ahora tenemos que cargar con ello; to get —d with something cargar con algo.
3 vr: to — oneself with something cargar con algo.
saddle-backed [ˈsædlbækt] adj ensillado.
saddlebag [ˈsædlbæg] n alforja f.
saddlebow [ˈsædlbəu] n arzón m delantero.
saddlecloth [ˈsædlklɔθ] n sudadero m.
saddler [ˈsædlə*] n talabartero m, guarnicionero m.
saddlery [ˈsædləri] n talabartería f, guarnicionería f.
sadism [ˈseidizəm] n sadismo m.
sadist [ˈseidist] n sadista mf.
sadistic [səˈdistik] adj sádico.
sadly [ˈsædli] adv (a) tristemente. (b) muy; — lacking in muy deficiente en; a — incompetent headmaster un director (de colegio) de lo más ineficaz.
sadness [ˈsædnis] n tristeza f, melancolía f.
safari [səˈfɑ:ri] n safari m; to be on — estar de safari.
safe [seif] **1** adj seguro; salvo, fuera de peligro; (from injury) ileso, incólume; bet etc seguro, cierto; person (trustworthy) digno de confianza, formal; (sound) prudente, sensato; — and sound sano y salvo; — from a salvo de, al abrigo de; as — as houses completamente seguro; the —st thing is to + infin lo más seguro es + infin; just to be — por precaución, para mayor seguridad; all the passengers are — todos los pasajeros están ilesos, no ha habido víctimas entre los pasajeros; these stairs are not very — esta escalera no es muy segura; it's a — beach es una playa sin peligro; no girl is — with him ninguna joven está sin peligro estando con él; is that dog — ? ¿es peligroso ese perro?; he's — with children es muy manso con los niños; your reputation is — su reputación está a salvo; the secret is — with me el secreto seguirá siéndolo conmigo; the book is — now ahora el libro está en buenas manos; you'll be perfectly — here aquí está Vd fuera de todo peligro; his life was not — no estaba seguro de su vida; is it — to go out? ¿se puede salir sin peligro?; it is — to say that ... se puede decir con confianza que ...; to come — home volver a casa sin novedad; to keep something — tener algo seguro; he plays a — game es un jugador prudente.
2 n caja f de caudales; (for meat) fresquera f.
safe-blower [ˈseifˌbləuə*] n ladrón m de cajas de caudales.
safe-conduct [ˈseifˈkɔndəkt] n salvoconducto m.
safe deposit [ˈseifdiˌpozit] n cámara f acorazada.
safeguard [ˈseifgɑ:d] **1** n protección f, garantía f; as a — por precaución; as a — against ... como defensa contra ..., para evitar ...
2 vt salvaguardar, proteger, defender.
safely [ˈseifli] adv seguramente, con seguridad; sin peligro; arrive, travel etc sin novedad, sin accidente; you may — do it now ahora puedes hacerlo sin peligro; to put something away — poner algo en un lugar seguro.
safeness [ˈseifnis] n seguridad f.
safety [ˈseifti] **1** n seguridad f; road — seguridad f en la carretera; in a place of — en un lugar seguro; for —'s sake por precaución, para mayor seguridad, en interés de la seguridad; with complete — con la mayor seguridad; to play for — obrar prudentemente; to reach — ponerse a salvo; to seek — in flight salvarse huyendo.
2 attr de seguridad.

safety belt ['seiftibelt] n cinturón m de seguridad.
safety catch ['seiftikætʃ] n fiador m; dispositivo m de seguridad; (on gun) seguro m.
safety curtain ['seifti‚kəːtn] n (Theat) telón m de seguridad.
safety first ['seifti'fəːst] attr: — **campaign** campaña f pro seguridad; **to believe in** — poner la seguridad en primer lugar, creer en la seguridad ante todo; "—" (as slogan) "¡precaución!", "¡prudencia!"
safety glass ['seiftiglɑːs] n vidrio m inastillable.
safety lamp ['seiftilæmp] n lámpara f de seguridad.
safety measure ['seifti‚meʒə*] n prevención f; **to take —s** tomar prevenciones.
safety net ['seiftinet] n red f de seguridad.
safety pin ['seiftipin] n imperdible m.
safety razor ['seifti‚reizə*] n maquinilla f de afeitar.
safety valve ['seiftivalv] n válvula f de seguridad.
saffron ['sæfrən] **1** n azafrán m. **2** adj azafranado, color azafrán.
sag [sæg] **1** n comba f. **2** vi (bulge, warp) combarse, hundirse, pandear; (slacken) aflojarse, ceder; (price etc) bajar; (spirit) flaquear.
saga ['sɑːgə] n saga f. (fig) saga f, epopeya f.
sagacious [sə'geiʃəs] adj sagaz.
sagaciously [sə'geiʃəsli] adv sagazmente.
sagacity [sə'gæsiti] n sagacidad f.
sage¹ [seidʒ] n (Bot) salvia f.
sage² [seidʒ] **1** adj sabio. **2** n sabio m.
sagebrush ['seidʒbrʌʃ] n (Bot) artemisa f.
sagely ['seidʒli] adv sabiamente.
sago ['seigəu] n sagú m.
Sahara [sə'hɑːrə] Sahara m.
sahib ['sɑːhib] n (India) **(a)** señor m; **Smith S—** (el) señor Smith. **(b)** (hum) caballero m; **pukka** — caballero m de verdad.
said [sed] **1** pret and ptp of **say. 2** adj dicho, antedicho; **the** — **animals** dichos animales, los cuales animales; **the** — **general** tal general.
sail [seil] **1** n (a) (cloth) vela f; **in full** —, **under full** —, **with all** —**s set** a toda vela, a vela llena; **to set** — hacerse a la vela, zarpar (for con rumbo a); **to lower the** —**s** arriar las velas; **to take in the** —**s** amainar.
  (b) (of mill) aspa f.
  (c) (trip) paseo m en barco (de vela), paseo m en balandro (etc); **it is 3 days'** — **from here** desde aquí es un viaje de 3 días en barco; **to go for a** — dar un paseo en barco (de vela), salir en balandro (etc).
  (d) (boat) barco m de vela, velero m; **20** — 20 barcos.
  2 vt **(a)** ship (steer) gobernar; **they** —**ed the ship to Cadiz** fueron con el barco a Cádiz, fueron en el barco a Cádiz.
  (b) to — **the seas** navegar los mares.
  3 vi **(a)** (Naut) navegar; **to** — **at 12 knots** navegar a 12 nudos, ir a 12 nudos; **we** —**ed into Lisbon** llegamos a Lisboa; **we** —**ed into harbour** entramos a puerto; **to** — **round the world** dar la vuelta al mundo; **to** — **round a headland** doblar un cabo; **to** — **up the Tagus** entrar en el Tajo, subir el Tajo.
  (b) (leave: Naut) hacerse a la vela, zarpar (for con rumbo a); (general sense) salir, partir; **she** —**s on Monday** sale el lunes; **we** — **for Australia** partimos para Australia, nos embarcamos para Australia.
  (c) (fig: swan etc) deslizarse; (cloud) flotar; (object) volar; **she** —**ed into the room** entró majestuosamente en la sala; **it** —**ed over my head** voló por encima de mi cabeza; **it** —**ed over into the next garden** voló por los aires y cayó en el jardín de al lado.
  (d) to — **into someone** (fam) arremeter contra uno, atacar a uno.
sailboat ['seilbəut] n (US) barco m de vela.
sailcloth ['seilklɔθ] n lona f.
sailfish ['seilfiʃ] n aguja f de mar, pez m vela.
sailing ['seiliŋ] n navegación f; (departure) salida f, partida f; — **date** fecha f de salida; **now it's all plain** — ahora es muy sencillo, ahora es cosa de coser y cantar; **it's not exactly plain** — no es sencillo que digamos.
sailing ship ['seiliŋʃip] n velero m, buque m de vela.
sail maker ['seil‚meikə*] n velero m.
sailor ['seilə*] n marinero m, marino m; **to be a bad** — marearse fácilmente; **to be a good** — no marearse.
sailor suit ['seiləsuːt] n traje m de marinero (de niño).
sailplane ['seilplein] n velero m, planeador m.
sainfoin ['sænfɔin] n pipirigallo m.
saint [seint] n **(a)** santo m, a f.
  (b) before m names abbreviated to San, eg **St John** San Juan; except **St Dominic** Santo Domingo, **St Thomas** Santo Tomás.

  (c) (as name of church) **at St Mark's** en San Marcos, en la iglesia de San Marcos; **the church is dedicated to St Luke** la iglesia está bajo la advocación de San Lucas.
  (d) St Andrew (patrón de Escocia) San Andrés; **St Bernard** (dog) perro m de San Bernardo; **St George** (patrón de Inglaterra) San Jorge; **St James** (patrón de España) Santiago; **St John the Baptist** San Juan Bautista; **St Kitts** (W.I.) San Cristóbal; **St Patrick** (patrón de Irlanda) San Patricio; **St Theresa** Santa Teresa; **St Valentine's Day** día m de San Valentín (14 febrero, día de los enamorados); **St Vitus' dance** baile m de San Vito.
sainted ['seintid] adj santo; bendito; (of dead) que en santa gloria esté.
sainthood ['seinthud] n santidad f.
saintliness ['seintlinis] n santidad f.
saintly ['seintli] adj santo.
sake [seik] n: **for the** — **of** por; por motivo de; en consideración a, en atención a; **for God's** — por el amor de Dios; **for God's** —!, **for heaven's** —! ¡por Dios!; **for my** — por mí; **for your own** — por su propio bien, en interés propio; **for old times'** — por respeto al pasado, en atención a los recuerdos del pasado; **for the** — **of peace** por amor a la paz, en interés de la paz; para obtener la paz; **Art for Art's** — el arte por el arte; **to talk for talking's** — hablar por hablar.
salaam [sə'lɑːm] **1** n zalema f. **2** vt hacer zalema a. **3** vi hacer zalema.
salable ['seiləbl] adj (US) = **saleable.**
salacious [sə'leiʃəs] adj salaz.
salaciousness [sə'leiʃəsnis] n salacidad f.
salad ['sæləd] n ensalada f; **fruit** — macedonia f de frutas.
salad bowl ['sælədbəul] n ensaladera f.
salad days ['sæləddeiz] npl juventud f; ingenuidad f juvenil.
salad dish ['sælədiʃ] n ensaladera f.
salad dressing ['sæləd‚dresiŋ] n mayonesa f, aliño m.
salad oil ['sælədɔil] n aceite m para ensaladas.
salamander ['sælə‚mændə*] n salamandra f.
salami [sə'lɑːmi] n salami m.
sal ammoniac [‚sælə'məuniæk] n sal f amoníaca.
salaried ['sælərid] adj: — **post** puesto m retribuido; — **person** persona f que gana un sueldo, persona f que cobra cada mes; — **staff** personal m a sueldo, (freq) empleados mpl de oficina.
salary ['sæləri] n sueldo m.
salary earner ['sæləri‚əːnə*] n persona f que gana un sueldo, persona f que cobra cada mes.
sale [seil] **1** n venta f; (clearance —) liquidación f; (annual —, spring — etc) saldo m; (auction —, public —) subasta f; "—" (in shop window) "grandes rebajas"; **I bought it at a** — lo compré en un saldo, lo compré en una subasta; "**for** —" "se vende"; "**horse for** —" "se vende (un) caballo"; **is it for** —? ¿se vende?; "**not for** —" "no se vende"; **it's going cheap for a quick** — se ofrece a un precio módico para poder venderlo pronto; **to put a house up for** — ofrecer una casa en venta; **to be on** — estar en venta; "**on** — **at all fishmongers**" "de venta en todas las pescaderías"; **the** —**s are on** es la temporada de los saldos.
  2 attr: — **price** precio m de venta; — **value** valor m en el mercado.
saleable ['seiləbl] adj vendible.
saleroom ['seilrum] n sala f de subastas.
salesman ['seilzmən] n, pl —**men** [mən] (in shop) dependiente m, vendedor m; (traveller) viajante m; "**Death of a S—**" "La muerte de un viajante".
salesmanship ['seilzmənʃip] n arte m de vender.
sales resistance ['seilzri‚zistəns] n resistencia f a comprar, resistencia f de parte del comprador.
sales tax ['seilztæks] n impuesto m sobre las ventas.
saleswoman ['seilzwumən] n, pl —**women** [wimin] dependienta f, vendedora f.
salient ['seiliənt] **1** adj saliente; (fig) sobresaliente, destacado, notable; **the most** — **feature** el aspecto más notable. **2** n saliente m.
saline ['seilain] adj salino.
salinity [sə'liniti] n salinidad f.
saliva [sə'laivə] n saliva f.
salivary ['sælivəri] adj salival.
salivate ['sæliveit] vi salivar.
salivation [‚sæli'veiʃən] n salivación f.
sallow¹ ['sæləu] n (Bot) sauce m cabruno.
sallow² ['sæləu] adj cetrino, amarillento.
sallowness ['sæləunis] n lo cetrino, amarillez f.
Sallust ['sæləst] m Salustio.
Sally ['sæli] f nombre cariñoso de **Sarah.**

sally ['sæli] **1** n (all senses) salida f; **to make a —** hacer una salida. **2** vi hacer una salida; **to — forth, to — out** salir resueltamente.

salmon ['sæmən] **1** n salmón m; (colour) color m salmón. **2** adj color salmón.

salmon trout ['sæmən,traut] n trucha f asalmonada.

salon ['sælɔːŋ] n salón m.

saloon [sə'luːn] n salón m; (Naut) cámara f, salón m; (Aut) turismo m; (US) bar m; taberna f; **billiard —** salón m de billar; **hairdressing —** salón m de peluquería.

saloon car [sə'luːnkɑːʳ] n (Rail) coche-salón m.

salsify ['sælsifi] n (Bot) salsifi m.

salt [sɔːlt] **1** n sal f; **—s** sales fpl medicinales; **kitchen — sal** f de cocina; **table — sal** f de mesa; **old — lobo** m de mar; **— of the earth sal** f de la tierra; **to be worth one's — merecer** el pan que se come; see pinch.
2 adj meat, water etc salado; taste salobre; **it's very — está** muy salado.
3 vt (cure) salar; (flavour) poner sal en, añadir sal a; **to — a dig** (Archaeology) poner objetos en una excavación para que se encuentren después; **to — away** (fig) ocultar para uso futuro.

saltcellar ['sɔːlt,selaʳ] n salero m.

saltings ['sɔːltiŋz] npl saladar m.

salt lake ['sɔːltleik] n lago m de agua salada.

salt marsh ['sɔːltmɑːʃ] n saladar m.

salt mine ['sɔːltmain] n mina f de sal.

saltness ['sɔːltnis] n salinidad f; sabor m de sal; salobridad f.

salt pan ['sɔːltpæn] n salina f.

saltpetre, (US) saltpeter ['sɔːlt,piːtəʳ] n salitre m.

salt spoon ['sɔːltspuːn] n cucharita f de sal.

saltwater ['sɔːlt,wɔːtəʳ] attr fish etc de mar, de agua salada.

saltworks ['sɔːltwəːks] n salinas fpl.

salty ['sɔːlti] adj salado (also fig); salobre.

salubrious [sə'luːbriəs] adj salubre, sano.

salubrity [sə'luːbriti] n salubridad f.

salutary ['sæljutəri] adj saludable.

salutation [,sælju'teiʃən] n salutación f, saludo m.

salutatory [,sælju'teitəri] adj de salutación.

salute [sə'luːt] **1** n (with hand etc) saludo m; (kiss) beso m; (of guns) salva f; **to fire a — of 21 guns for someone** saludar a uno con una salva de 21 cañonazos; **to take the — tomar** el saludo.
2 vti saludar.

Salvadoran [,sælvə'dɔːrən] **1** adj salvadoreño. **2** n salvadoreño m, a f.

salvage ['sælvidʒ] **1** n (act) salvamento m; recuperación f; (objects) objetos mpl salvados; (material) material m utilizable.
2 vt salvar; recuperar; **to — something from the wreckage** salvar algo de las ruinas.

salvation [sæl'veiʃən] n salvación f; **S— Army** Ejército m de Salvación.

salvationist [sæl'veiʃnist] n miembro m del Ejército de Salvación.

salve[1] [sælv] vt (Naut etc) salvar; recuperar.

salve[2] [sælv] **1** n (fig) ungüento m, bálsamo m. **2** vt curar (con ungüento); **to — one's conscience** tranquilizar la conciencia.

salver ['sælvəʳ] n bandeja f.

salvo[1] ['sælvəu] n salvedad f, reserva f.

salvo[2] ['sælvəu] n (Mil) salva f; **a — of applause** una salva de aplausos.

sal volatile [,sælvə'lætəli] n sal f volátil.

Sam [sæm] m nombre cariñoso de **Samuel**.

Samaritan [sə'mæritn] **1** adj samaritano. **2** n samaritano m, a f; **good — buen** samaritano m.

sambo ['sæmbəu] n (pej) mestizo m; negro m.

same [seim] adj mismo; igual; idéntico; **"Mr Jones?"** ... **"the —"** **"¿Señor Jones?"** ... **"el mismo";** **— here!** ¡yo también!; **it's the — with us** es igual para nosotros, nosotros tenemos lo mismo; **and I did the — y** yo hice lo mismo; **I'd do the — again** yo volvería a hacer lo mismo; **and the — to you!** ¡igualmente!; ¡a Vd!; **all the — con** todo, de todas formas; a pesar de todo; **it's all the — es** lo mismo, es todo uno; **it's all the — to me** me es igual, lo mismo me da; **if it's all the — to you** si a Vd le da lo mismo; **it's just the — es** exactamente igual; **things go on just the — eso** continúa como siempre; **they are much the — son** más o menos idénticos; **it's much about the — sigue** más o menos en el mismo estado; **it's the — old complaint** es lo de siempre; **I still feel the — about you** mis sentimientos respecto a ti siguen siendo los mismos; **the — as** ... el mismo que ...

sameness ['seimnis] n igualdad f; identidad f; (pej) monotonía f.

samovar [,sæməu'vɑːʳ] n samovar m.

sampan ['sæmpæn] n sampán m.

sample ['sɑːmpl] **1** n (all senses) muestra f; **free — muestra** f gratuita. **2** vt probar; (in blending) catar; (Math) muestrear.

sample book ['sɑːmplbuk] n muestrario m.

sampler ['sɑːmpləʳ] n (person) catador m; (Sew) dechado m.

sampling ['sɑːmpliŋ] n (Math) muestreo m; **— technique** método m de muestreo.

Samson ['sæmsn] m Sansón.

Samuel ['sæmjuəl] m Samuel.

sanatorium [,sænə'tɔːriəm] n, pl **sanatoria** [,sænə'tɔːriə] sanatorio m.

sanctification [,sæŋktifi'keiʃən] n santificación f.

sanctify ['sæŋktifai] vt santificar.

sanctimonious [,sæŋkti'məuniəs] adj mojigato, santurrón, beato.

sanctimoniously [,sæŋkti'məuniəsli] adv con mojigatería; **she said —** dijo mojigata.

sanctimoniousness [,sæŋkti'məuniəsnis] n mojigatería f, santurronería f, beatería f.

sanction ['sæŋkʃən] **1** n sanción f.
2 vt sancionar.

sanctity ['sæŋktiti] n santidad f; inviolabilidad f; **— of the mails** secreto m de correspondencia.

sanctuary ['sæŋktjuəri] n santuario m; (high altar) sagrario m; (place of refuge: Hist) sagrado m, (modern) refugio m, asilo m; **to seek — acogerse** a lo sagrado; **to seek — in** refugiarse en; **to seek — with** acogerse a.

sanctum ['sæŋktəm] n lugar m sagrado; (fig, study) despacho m particular.

sand [sænd] **1** n arena f; **—s** (of desert) arenas fpl, (beach) playa f (arenosa); **shifting —s** arenas fpl movedizas; **the —s are running out** queda poco tiempo.
2 vt enarenar.

sandal ['sændl] n sandalia f.

sandal(wood) ['sændl(wud)] n sándalo m.

sandbag ['sændbæg] **1** n saco m de arena. **2** vt proteger con sacos de arena.

sandbank ['sændbæŋk] n banco m de arena.

sand bar ['sændbɑːʳ] n barra f de arena, banco m de arena.

sandblast ['sændblɑːst] n (Tech) chorro m de arena.

sandcastle ['sænd,kɑːsl] n castillo m de arena.

sand dune ['sænddjuːn] n duna f.

sand fly ['sændflai] n jijene m.

sandglass ['sændglɑːs] n reloj m de arena.

sandlot ['sændlɔt] n (US) terreno en una ciudad que se usa para el béisbol (etc).

sandman ['sændmæn] n genio fabuloso que les trae el sueño a los niños.

sandpaper ['sænd,peipəʳ] **1** n papel m de lija. **2** vt lijar.

sandpiper ['sænd,paipəʳ] n (Orn) andarríos m, lavandera f.

sandpit ['sændpit] n arenal m; (in garden) cuadro m de arena.

sand shoes ['sændʃuːz] npl playeras fpl.

sandstone ['sændstəun] n piedra f arenisca.

sandstorm ['sændstɔːm] n simún m, tempestad f de arena.

sandwich ['sænwidʒ] **1** n sándwich m, bocadillo m.
2 vt insertar; intercalar; (Sport) apretujar; **to — something between two things** poner algo (apretadamente) entre dos cosas; **the house is —ed between two big hotels** la casa se encuentra entre dos grandes hoteles, la casa ocupa un espacio estrecho entre los dos grandes hoteles; **I was —ed between two fat ladies** me tocó estar apretujado entre dos señoras gordas.

sandwich board ['sænwidʒbɔːd] n cartelón m (que lleva el hombre-anuncio).

sandwich man ['sænwidʒmæn] n, pl **— men** [men] hombre-anuncio m.

sandy ['sændi] adj arenoso; (in colour) rojizo, dorado; hair rojo.

sane [sein] adj person cuerdo, sensato, de juicio sano; policy etc prudente; **a very — person** una persona muy sensata.

Sanforize ['sænfəraiz] (Protected Trade Name) vt sanforizar.

sang [sæŋ] pret of **sing**.

sangfroid ['sɑːŋ'frwɑː] n sangre f fría.

sanguinary ['sæŋgwinəri] adj sanguinario; sangriento.

sanguine ['sæŋgwin] adj (fig) optimista.

sanguineous [sæŋ'gwiniəs] adj sanguíneo.

sanitarium [,sæni'tɛəriəm] n (US) sanatorio m.

sanitary ['sænitəri] adj sanitario; higiénico; **— inspector** inspector m de sanidad.

sanitary towel ['sænitəri,tauəl], (US) — **napkin** [,næpkin] n paño m higiénico, compresa f higiénica.

sanitation [,sæni'teiʃən] n sanidad f; higiene f; (domestic —) instalación f sanitaria, saneamiento m, (euph) servicios mpl.

sanity ['sæniti] n cordura f, sensatez f, juicio m sano; prudencia f; **to be restored to** — recobrar su juicio; — **demands that** ... la razón exige que ...; **to return to** — ponerse en razón, volver a la razón.

sank [sæŋk] pret of **sink¹**.

Sanskrit ['sænskrit] 1 adj sánscrito. 2 n sánscrito m.

Santa Claus [,sæntə'klɔːz] San Nicolás (que en los países del norte trae regalos para los niños, el día de Navidad; equivale a los Reyes Magos).

sap¹ [sæp] n (Bot) savia f; (fig) jugo m (vital), vitalidad f.

sap² [sæp] (Mil) 1 n zapa f. 2 vt zapar; socavar; strength etc minar, agotar.

sap³ [sæp] n (sl) bobo m; **you** —! ¡bobo!

sapling ['sæpliŋ] n pimpollo m, árbol m nuevo, arbolito m.

sapper ['sæpə*] n zapador m.

sapphire ['sæfaiə*] n zafiro m.

sappy¹ ['sæpi] adj (Bot) lleno de savia, jugoso.

sappy² ['sæpi] adj (sl) bobo.

saraband ['særəbænd] n zarabanda f.

Saracen ['særəsn] 1 adj sarraceno. 2 n sarraceno m, a f.

Saragossa [,særə'gɔsə] Zaragoza.

Sarah ['sɛərə] f Sara.

sarcasm ['sɑːkæzm] n sarcasmo m.

sarcastic [sɑː'kæstik] adj sarcástico.

sarcastically [sɑː'kæstikəli] adv con sarcasmo, sarcásticamente.

sarcophagus [sɑː'kɔfəgəs] n, pl **sarcophagi** [sɑː-'kɔfəgai] sarcófago m.

sardine [sɑː'diːn] n sardina f.

Sardinia [sɑː'diniə] Cerdeña f.

Sardinian [sɑː'diniən] 1 adj sardo. 2 n sardo m, a f.

sardonic [sɑː'dɔnik] adj burlón, irónico, sarcástico.

sardonically [sɑː'dɔnikəli] adv con aire burlón, irónicamente, con sarcasmo.

sari ['sɑːri] n sari m.

sarsaparilla [,sɑːsəpə'rilə] n zarzaparrilla f.

sartorial [sɑː'tɔːriəl] adj relativo al vestido; — **elegance** elegancia f en el vestido; — **taste** gusto m en vestidos.

sash¹ [sæʃ] n faja f; (Mil: of order) fajín m.

sash² [sæʃ] n (window —) marco m corredizo de ventana.

sash cord ['sæʃkɔːd] n cuerda f de ventana (de guillotina).

sash window ['sæʃ,windəu] n ventana f de guillotina.

sass [sæs] (US) 1 n réplicas fpl. 2 vt: **to** — **someone** replicar a uno.

sassafras ['sæsəfræs] n sasafrás m.

Sassenach ['sæsənæx] n (Scot: pej) inglés m, esa f.

sassy ['sæsi] adj (US) fresco, descarado.

sat [sæt] pret and ptp of **sit**.

Satan ['seitn] m Satanás.

satanic [sə'tænik] adj satánico.

satchel ['sætʃl] n bolsa f, cartera f; (schoolboy's) cabás m.

sate [seit] vt saciar, hartar.

sateen [sæ'tiːn] n satén m.

satellite ['sætəlait] 1 n satélite m. 2 attr: — **country** país m satélite; — **town** ciudad f satélite.

satiate ['seiʃieit] vt saciar, hartar.

satiation [,seiʃi'eiʃən] n, **satiety** [sə'taiəti] n saciedad f, hartura f; **to** — hasta la saciedad.

satin ['sætin] 1 n raso m. 2 adj (also **satiny** ['sætini]) terso, liso; lustroso.

satinwood ['sætinwud] n madera f satinada de las Indias.

satire ['sætaiə*] n sátira f.

satiric(al) [sə'tirik(əl)] adj satírico.

satirically [sə'tirikəli] adv satíricamente.

satirist ['sætərist] n escritor m satírico.

satirize ['sætəraiz] vt satirizar.

satisfaction [,sætis'fækʃən] n satisfacción f; (of debt) pago m, liquidación f; **to the general** — con la satisfacción de todos; **has it been done to your** —? ¿se ha hecho a su satisfacción? **to demand** — pedir satisfacción; **to express one's** — **at a result** expresar su satisfacción con un resultado, declararse satisfecho con un resultado; **it gives every** (or full) — es completamente satisfactorio; **it gives me much** — **to introduce** ... es para mí un verdadero placer presentar a ...

satisfactorily [,sætis'fæktərili] adv satisfactoria-mente, de modo satisfactorio.

satisfactory [,sætis'fæktəri] adj satisfactorio.

satisfy ['sætisfai] 1 vt satisfacer; debt pagar, liquidar; (convince) convencer; **it completely satisfies me** me satisface completamente; **to** — **someone that** ... convencer a uno de que ...; **I am not satisfied that** ... no estoy convencido de que ...; **to** — **the requirements** llenar los requisitos; **you'll have to be satisfied with that** Vd tendrá que contentarse con eso; **we are very satisfied with it** estamos perfectamente satisfechos con él, nos satisface completamente.

2 vr: **to** — **oneself about something** satisfacerse con algo; **to** — **oneself that** ... convencerse de que ...

satisfying ['sætisfaiiŋ] adj satisfactorio, que satisface; food, meal bueno.

saturate ['sætʃəreit] 1 vt saturar, empapar (with de); **to be** —**d with** (fig) estar empapado de. 2 vr: **to** — **oneself in** (fig) empaparse en.

saturation [,sætʃə'reiʃən] n saturación f.

saturation point [,sætʃə'reiʃənpɔint] n punto m de saturación.

Saturday ['sætədi] n sábado m.

Saturn ['sætən] m Saturno.

Saturnalia [,sætə'neiliə] npl saturnales fpl.

saturnine ['sætənain] adj saturnino.

satyr ['sætə*] n sátiro m.

sauce [sɔːs] n (a) salsa f; (sweet) crema f; (of fruit) compota f; **what's** — **for the goose is** — **for the gander** lo que es bueno para uno es bueno para el otro.

(b) (fig) frescura f; **what** —! ¡qué fresco!; **none of your** —! ¡Vd es un fresco!

sauceboat ['sɔːsbəut] n salsera f.

saucepan ['sɔːspən] n cacerola f, cazo m.

saucer ['sɔːsə*] n platillo m; **flying** — platillo m volante.

saucily ['sɔːsili] adv reply etc con frescura; con coquetería.

sauciness ['sɔːsinis] n frescura f, descaro m, desfachatez f; coquetería f.

saucy ['sɔːsi] adj fresco, descarado, desfachatado; girl coqueta; hat etc coquetón; **don't be** —! ¡qué fresco!

Saudi Arabia ['saudiə'reibiə] Arabia f Saudita.

sauerkraut ['sauəkraut] n chucruta f.

Saul [sɔːl] m Saúl.

sauna ['sɔːnə] n sauna f.

saunter ['sɔːntə*] 1 n paseo m lento y tranquilo; **to have a** — **in the park** dar un paseo tranquilo en el parque.

2 vi pasearse despacio y tranquilamente; **to** — **up and down** deambular, pasearse despacio de acá para allá; **he** —**ed up to me** se acercó a mí con mucha calma.

saurian ['sɔːriən] n saurio m.

sausage ['sɔsidʒ] n (general term) embutido m; (small) salchicha f; **cocktail** — salchichita f de aperitivo; **pork** — salchicha f de cerdo.

sausage machine ['sɔsidʒmə,ʃiːn] n embutidora f.

sausage meat ['sɔsidʒmiːt] n masa f del embutido.

sausage roll ['sɔsidʒ'rəul] n pequeña empanada de salchicha (en forma cilíndrica).

sauté ['səutei] 1 adj salteado. 2 vt saltear.

savage ['sævidʒ] 1 adj salvaje; attack feroz, furioso, violento; **to be** — (fam) estar rabioso; **to get** — (fam) ponerse negro (fam).

2 n salvaje mf.

3 vt (of animal) embestir, atacar, morder.

savagely ['sævidʒli] adv de modo salvaje; ferozmente, furiosamente, violentamente; **he said** — dijo furioso.

savageness ['sævidʒnis] n, **savagery** ['sævidʒri] n salvajismo m, salvajería f; ferocidad f, furia f, violencia f.

savannah [sə'vænə] n sabana f.

savant ['sævənt] n sabio m, erudito m, intelectual m.

save¹ [seiv] 1 vt (a) (rescue) salvar; rescatar; **to** — **someone's life** salvar la vida a uno; **to** — **someone from death** salvar a uno de la muerte, rescatar a uno de la muerte; **to** — **someone from falling** impedir que caiga uno, agarrar a uno para que no se caiga; **to** — **appearances** salvar las apariencias; **to** — **the situation** estar al nivel de las circunstancias; **to** — **one's soul** salvar su alma; **God the Queen** Dios guarde a la Reina, Dios salve a la Reina; **God** — **us all!** ¡que Dios nos ayude!; **to** — **a building for posterity** lograr conservar un edificio para la posteridad; **to** — **one's eyes** cuidarse la vista; **to** — **something from the wreck** salvar algo de las ruinas.

(b) (put by) guardar, reservar; (preserve) conservar; money etc ahorrar; stamps etc coleccionar;

I —d this for you guardé esto para ti; — me a seat resérvame un asiento; **she has £200** —d sus ahorros suman 200 libras.

(c) (*avoid using up*) *time etc* ahorrar; **to — time** . . . para ahorrar tiempo . . ., para ganar tiempo . . .; **this way you — £8** por este sistema te ahorras 8 libras; **this way you — 4 miles** por esta ruta te ahorras 4 millas; **it —s fuel** economiza combustible; **he's saving his strength for tomorrow** se reserva para mañana.

(d) (*prevent*) evitar, impedir; **to — a goal** parar un tiro, impedir que se marque un gol; **it —d a lot of trouble** evitó muchas molestias, evitó muchos disgustos; **to — someone trouble** evitar molestias a uno.

2 *vi* ahorrar, economizar, hacer economías; **to — up for a new bicycle** ahorrar dinero para comprar una bicicleta.

3 *vr:* **to — oneself for** reservarse para.

save² [seiv] *prep and conj* (*esp lit*) salvo, excepto, con excepción de; **all — one** todos excepto uno, todos menos uno; **— for** excepto; si no fuera por; **— that** excepto que.

saveloy ['sævələi] *n* salchicha seca muy sazonada.

saving ['seiviŋ] **1** *adj* **(a)** económico; (*pej*) tacaño; **she's not the — sort** no es de las que economizan.

(b) *see* **clause** *etc*.

2 *n* (*act: rescue*) salvamento *m*, rescate *m*; (*Eccl*) salvación *f*; (*of money etc*) ahorro *m*; (*of cost etc*) economía *f*; **—s** ahorros *mpl*; **she has —s of £300** sus ahorros suman 300 libras; **we must make —s** tenemos que economizar.

savings bank ['seiviŋzbæŋk] *n* caja *f* de ahorros; **post office —** caja *f* postal de ahorros.

saviour ['seivjə*] *n* salvador *m*, ora *f*; **S—** Salvador *m*.

savoir-faire ['sævwɑ:'feə*] *n* desparpajo *m*; habilidad *f* práctica; sentido *m* común.

savory ['seivəri] *n* (*Bot*) tomillo *m* salsero.

savour, (*US*) **savor** ['seivə*] **1** *n* sabor *m*, gusto *m*; (*aftertaste*) dejo *m*; (*fig*) sabor *m* (*of a*); **it has lost its —** ha perdido su sabor.

2 *vt* saborear, paladear: (*fig*) saborear.

3 *vi:* **to — of** saber a, oler a (*also fig*).

savouriness, (*US*) **savoriness** ['seivərinis] *n* sabor *m*, buen sabor *m*, lo sabroso; (*fig*) respetabilidad *f*.

savourless, (*US*) **savorless** ['seivəlis] *adj* soso, insípido.

savoury, (*US*) **savory** ['seivəri] **1** *adj* (*appetizing*) sabroso, apetitoso; (*not sweet*) no dulce; (*salted*) salado; **not very —** (*fig*) no muy respetable, poco decente; **it's not a very — district** es un barrio de mala fama.

2 *n* entremés *m* salado.

Savoy [sə'vɔi] Saboya *f*.

savoy [sə'vɔi] *n* berza *f* de Saboya.

savvy ['sævi] (*sl*) **1** *n* inteligencia *f*; desparpajo *m*.

2 *vt* comprender; **—?** ¿comprende?

saw¹ [sɔ:] **1** *n* sierra *f*; **circular —** sierra *f* circular.

2 (*irr:* pret **sawed**, ptp **sawed** or **sawn**) *vt* serrar.

saw² [sɔ:] *n* refrán *m*, dicho *m*.

saw³ [sɔ:] pret of **see**.

sawbuck ['sɔ:bʌk] *n* (*US*) caballete *m* para aserrar.

sawdust ['sɔ:dʌst] *n* serrín *m*.

sawfish ['sɔ:fiʃ] *n* pez *m* sierra.

sawhorse ['sɔ:hɔ:s] *n* caballete *m* para serrar.

sawmill ['sɔ:mil] *n* aserradero *m*.

sawn [sɔ:n] ptp of **saw**.

sawyer ['sɔ:jə*] *n* aserrador *m*.

sax [sæks] *n* (*fam*) saxofón *m*, saxo *m* (*fam*).

saxifrage ['sæksifridʒ] *n* saxífraga *f*.

Saxon ['sæksn] **1** *adj* sajón. **2** *n* sajón *m*, ona *f*.

Saxony ['sæksəni] Sajonia *f*.

saxophone ['sæksəfəun] *n* saxofón *m*.

say [sei] **1** *n:* **to have a** (*or* **some**) **— in something** tener voz y voto; **to have no — in something** no tener voz en capítulo; **I had no — in it** no tuve nada que ver con ello, no pidieron mi parecer acerca de ello; **if I had had a — in it** si hubieran pedido mi parecer; **I have had my —** he dicho lo que quería; **to let someone have his —** dejar hablar a uno; **let him have his —!** ¡que hable él!

2 (*irr:* pret and ptp **said**) *vt* **(a)** decir; (*text*) decir, rezar; *mass* decir; *prayer* rezar; *lesson* recitar; **to — yes** decir que sí; **to — no** decir que no; **to — yes to an invitation** aceptar una invitación; **to — no to a proposal** rechazar una propuesta; **to — good-bye to someone** despedirse de uno; **to — good morning to someone** dar los buenos días a uno; **my watch —s 3 o'clock** mi reloj marca las 3; **it —s 30 degrees** marca 30 grados; **they — se** dice, dicen; **I must — that** . . . tengo que confesar que . . .; **to — to**

oneself decir para sí; **who shall I —?** ¿qué nombre digo?

(b) (*idioms*) **that is to —** es decir, esto es; **to — nothing of the rest** y no digamos de los demás; **to — nothing of swearing** sin mencionar lo de decir palabrotas (*and see* **nothing 1** (d)); **to — the least** para no decir más; **as one might —** como si dijéramos; **that's —ing a lot** ya es decir; **would you really — so?** ¿lo cree Vd de veras?; **what would you —?** ¿qué dice Vd?; **what would you — to that?** ¿qué contesta Vd a eso?; **what would you — to a cup of tea?** ¿le apetece una taza de té?; **she hasn't much to — for herself** es muy reservada, no es nada habladora; **that doesn't — much for her** eso no dice mucho en su favor; **it doesn't — much for his intelligence** eso no dice mucho a favor de su inteligencia; **it —s much for his courage that he stayed** el que permaneciera allí demuestra su valor; **it goes without —ing that** . . . ni que decir tiene que . . .; **that goes without —ing** eso cae de su peso.

(c) (*exclamatory idioms*) **—!** (*US*), **I —!** (*calling attention*) ¡oiga!, (*in surprise*) ¡caramba!; **you don't — (so)!** ¡parece mentira!, ¿de veras?; **I should — so!**, **you can — that again!** ¡ya lo creo!; **you've said it!** ¡eso es!; **so you — !** ¡es Vd quien lo dice!; **— no more!** ¡basta!, ¡ni una palabra más!

(d) (*phrases with ptp* **said**) **it is said that** . . . se dice que . . .; **he is said to be worth a million** se dice que es millonario; **there is something to be said for it** hay algunas razones a favor de esa opinión (*etc*); **there is a lot to be said for doing it now** hay buenas razones por las que conviene hacerlo ahora; **there is something to be said on both sides** hay mucho que decir a favor de ambos; **when all is said and done there's no money for it** total que no hay dinero para ello, a fin de cuentas no hay dinero para ello; **it's easier said than done** es más fácil hablar de esto que hacerlo; **no sooner said than done** dicho y hecho; **enough said!** al buen entendedor pocas palabras le bastan.

(e) (*suppose*) **— it is worth £20** pongamos por caso que vale 20 libras; **we sell it at — £25** pongamos que lo vendemos por 25 libras; **we were going at — 50 mph** íbamos a 50 mph más o menos; **shall we — £5?** ¿convenimos en 5 libras?; **shall we — Tuesday?** ¿para el martes, pues?

saying ['seiiŋ] *n* dicho *m*, refrán *m*; **as the — goes** como dice el refrán; **it's just a —** es un refrán, es un decir.

say-so ['seisəu] *n* **(a)** (*rumour*) rumor *m* (infundado).

(b) (*authority*) autoridad *f*; aprobación *f*; decisión *f*; **it depends on his —** tiene que aprobarlo él.

scab [skæb] *n* (*Med*) costra *f*; (*Vet*) roña *f*; (*fam*) esquirol *m*.

scabbard ['skæbəd] *n* vaina *f* (de espada).

scabby ['skæbi] *adj* costroso; lleno de costras; (*Vet*) roñoso.

scabies ['skeibii:z] *n* sarna *f*.

scabious ['skeibiəs] *n* escabiosa *f*.

scabrous ['skeibrəs] *adj* escabroso.

scads [skædz] *npl* (*fam*) montones *mpl*; **we have — of it** lo tenemos a montones, tenemos montones de eso.

scaffold ['skæfəld] *n* (*Archit*) andamio *m*; (*for execution*) cadalso *m*, patíbulo *m*.

scaffolding ['skæfəldiŋ] *n* andamio *m*, andamiaje *m*.

scalawag ['skæləwæg] *n* (*US*) = **scallywag**.

scald [skɔ:ld] **1** *n* escaldadura *f*.

2 *vt* *oneself*, *skin etc* escaldar, quemar con agua caliente; *milk* calentar; *instruments* esterilizar con agua caliente; **to — out a saucepan** limpiar una cacerola con agua caliente.

scalding ['skɔ:ldiŋ] *adj:* **— hot** hirviendo.

scale¹ [skeil] **1** *n* (*of fish etc*) escama *f*; (*flake*) hojuela *f*; laminita *f*; (*of skin*) costra *f*.

2 *vt* *fish* escamar; (*Tech*) raspar; *teeth* quitar el sarro a.

3 *vi* (*also* **to — off**) descamarse; desconcharse.

scale² [skeil] **1** *n* (*of balance*) platillo *m*; **—s** balanza *f*, (*for heavy weights*) báscula *f*; **the S—** (*Astron*) Libra *f*; **to turn** (*or* **tip**) **the —s** (*fig*) inclinar la balanza, decidirlo; **he turns the —s at 80 kilos** pesa 80 kilos.

2 *vi* pesar; **it —s 4 kilos** pesa 4 kilos.

scale³ [skeil] **1** *n* escala *f* (*also Math, Mus*); (*of salaries*) escalafón *m*; **— of charges** tarifa *f*, lista *f* de precios; **Fahrenheit —** escala *f* de Fahrenheit; **sliding —** escala *f* móvil; **the social —** la escala social; **on a — of 5 km to the centimetre** a escala de 5 km al centímetro; **on a big** (*or* **large**) **—** a gran escala, a grande escala; **on a small —** a pequeña escala; **on a national —** a escala nacional; **to draw something to —** dibujar algo a escala.

  2 attr: **— drawing** dibujo m a escala.

  3 vt mountain etc escalar; tree etc trepar a; **to — down** reducir a escala; **to — up** aumentar a escala.

scallion ['skæliən] n cebolleta f.

scallop ['skɔləp] **1** n (Zool) venera f; (Sew) festón m. **2** vt (Cook) guisar en conchas; (Sew) festonear.

scallop shell ['skɔləpʃel] n venera f.

scallywag ['skæliwæg] n see **scamp**¹.

scalp [skælp] **1** n cuero m cabelludo, cabellera f; (Anat) pericráneo m; (fig) trofeo m. **2** vt escalpar, quitar el cuero cabelludo a.

scalpel ['skælpəl] n escalpelo m.

scaly ['skeili] adj escamoso.

scamp¹ [skæmp] n tunante mf, bribón m, ona f; (child) diablillo m; **you little —** ! ¡pícaro!

scamp² [skæmp] vt chapucear, frangollar.

scamper ['skæmpə*] **1** n carrera f rápida; huida f precipitada.

  2 vi correr, darse prisa; **to — along** ir corriendo; **to — for the bus** correr para coger el autobús; **to — past** pasar corriendo; **to — away, to — off** escabullirse, escaparse corriendo.

scan [skæn] **1** vt (examine) escudriñar, examinar; (glance at) dar un vistazo a; horizon etc explorar con la vista; (by radar etc) explorar, registrar; verse medir, escandir.

  2 vi estar bien medido; **it does not —** no está bien medido.

scandal ['skændl] n (a) escándalo m; (Law) difamación f; **the groundnuts —** el escándalo de los cacahuetes; **to cause a —, to create a —** hacer un escándalo, armar un lío; **what a —!, it's a —!** ¡qué vergüenza!; **it is a — that** ... es una vergüenza que . . .

  (b) (gossip) chismorreo m, murmuración f; (pieces of gossip) habladurías fpl, chismes mpl; **the local —** los chismes del pueblo (or del barrio etc); **have you heard the latest —?** ¿te han contado los chismes del momento?; **there's a lot of — going round about the vicar** se cuentan muchos chismes acerca del pastor; **to talk —** murmurar, contar chismes.

scandalize ['skændəlaiz] vt escandalizar; **she was —d** se escandalizó.

scandalmonger ['skændl,mʌngə*] n chismoso m, a f.

scandalous ['skændələs] adj escandaloso; (libellous) calumnioso; **— talk** habladurías fpl, chismes mpl; **it's simply —!** ¡es una vergüenza! ¡no hay derecho!

scandalously ['skændələsli] adv escandalosamente.

Scandinavia [,skændi'neiviə] Escandinavia f.

Scandinavian [,skændi'neiviən] **1** adj escandinavo. **2** n escandinavo m, a f.

scanner ['skænə*] n (Radar) antena f direccional giratoria; (TV) dispositivo m explorador.

scansion ['skænʃən] n escansión f; medida f.

scant [skænt] adj escaso.

scantily ['skæntili] adv insuficientemente; **— provided with** ... con escasa provisión de ...; **— dressed** ligeramente vestido.

scantiness ['skæntinis] n escasez f, cortedad f, insuficiencia f.

scanty ['skænti] adj escaso, corto, insuficiente; clothing ligero.

scapegoat ['skeipgəut] n cabeza f de turco, víctima f propiciatoria; **to be a — for** pagar el pato por.

scapegrace ['skeipgreis] n pícaro m, bribón m.

scapula ['skæpjulə] n (Anat) escápula f.

scar¹ [ska:*] **1** n (Med) cicatriz f, señal f; (fig) señal f; **it left a deep — on his mind** dejó una profunda señal en su espíritu.

  2 vt dejar una cicatriz en; marcar con una cicatriz, marcar con cicatrices; (fig) señalar, dejar señales en; **he was —red with many wounds** llevaba las cicatrices de muchas heridas; **the walls are —red with bullets** las balas han dejado señales en las paredes.

  3 vi (also **to — over**) cicatrizarse.

scar² [ska:*] n (Geog) paraje m rocoso, pendiente f rocosa.

scarab ['skærəb] n escarabajo m.

scarce [skeəs] **1** adj escaso; poco común, poco frecuente; **money is —** hay poco dinero; **such people are —** tales personas son poco frecuentes; **the plant is — in the north** en el norte la planta es poco común; **to grow —** escasear; **to make oneself —** largarse, esfumarse.

  2 adv see **scarcely**.

scarcely ['skeəsli] adv apenas; **— 200** apenas 200; **— anybody** casi nadie; **— ever** casi nunca; **I could —**

stand up apenas pude levantarme; **I — know what to say** en realidad no sé qué decir.

scarceness ['skeəsnis] n escasez f; poca frecuencia f; **the — of the plant** la poca frecuencia de la planta.

scarcity ['skeəsiti] **1** n escasez f; poca frecuencia f; (shortage) carestía f; **in years of —** en años de carestía; **due to the — of money** debido a la escasez de dinero.

  2 attr: **— value** valor m excesivo debido a la poca frecuencia (de un artículo).

scare [skeə*] **1** n susto m, sobresalto m; **the devaluation —** el pánico de la desvalorización; **to create (or raise) a —** infundir miedo a la gente, alarmar a las personas; **to give someone a —** dar un susto a uno; **what a — you gave me!** ¡qué susto me diste!

  2 vt asustar, espantar, infundir miedo a; **to — away, to — off** ahuyentar; **to be —d to death, to be —d stiff** estar muerto de miedo; **she was too —d to talk** estaba demasiado asustada para poder hablar.

  3 vi: **he doesn't — easily** no se asusta por poca cosa.

scarecrow ['skeəkrəu] n espantapájaros m; (fig) espantajo m.

scarehead ['skeəhed] n (US Typ) titulares mpl grandes y sensacionales.

scaremonger ['skeəmʌngə*] n alarmista mf.

scarf [ska:f] n, pl **scarves** [ska:vz] bufanda f; (head-) pañuelo m.

scarface ['ska:feis] n (as nickname) caracortada mf.

scarify ['skeərifai] vt (Med, Agr) escarificar; (fig) criticar severamente.

scarifying ['skeərifaiiŋ] adj attack etc mordaz, severo.

scarlatina [,ska:lə'ti:nə] n escarlatina f.

scarlet ['ska:lit] **1** n escarlata f. **2** adj color escarlata; **to turn —** enrojecer, ponerse escarlata; **he was — with rage** se puso escarlata de furia.

scarp [ska:p] n escarpa f, declive m.

scarves [ska:vz] npl of **scarf**.

scary ['skeəri] adj (fam) asustadizo.

scat [skæt] interj ¡zape!

scathing ['skeiðiŋ] adj attack, criticism mordaz, duro; **he was — about our trains** criticó duramente nuestros trenes; **he was pretty —** tuvo cosas bastante duras que decir.

scathingly ['skeiðiŋli] adv mordazmente, duramente; **he spoke — of** ... criticó duramente ...

scatter ['skætə*] **1** n (Math, Tech) dispersión f; **a — of houses** unas casas dispersas; **a — of raindrops** unas cuantas gotas de lluvia aquí y allá.

  2 vt (dot about) esparcir, desparramar; benefits etc derramar aquí y allá (also **to — about**); (put to flight) dispersar; clouds etc disipar; **the flowers were —ed about on the floor** las flores estaban desparramadas por el suelo; **the floor was —ed with flowers** el suelo estaba sembrado de flores dispersas.

  3 vi desparramarse; dispersarse; **the family —ed to distant parts** los miembros de la familia se desparramaron por sitios lejanos; **the crowd —ed** la multitud se dispersó.

scatterbrain ['skætəbrein] n cabeza mf de chorlito.

scatterbrained ['skætəbreind] adj ligero de cascos.

scattering ['skætəriŋ] n: **a — of books** unos cuantos libros aquí y allá.

scavenge ['skævindʒ] **1** vt limpiar las calles (etc), recoger la basura. **2** vi: **to — for food** andar buscando cosas que comer (entre la basura).

scavenger ['skævindʒə*] n basurero m, barrendero m; (Zool) animal m (or ave f etc) que se alimenta de carroña.

scenario [si'na:riəu] n guión m.

scenarist ['si:nərist] n guionista mf.

scene [si:n] n (a) (Theat) escena f; **the bedroom —** la escena del dormitorio; **the big — in the film** la principal escena de la película; **behind the —s** entre bastidores; **the — is set in a castle** la acción se desarrolla en un castillo, la escena es en un castillo; **to set the — for a love affair** (fig) crear el ambiente adecuado para una aventura sentimental; **now let our reporter set the — for you** ahora permitan que nuestro reportero les describa la escena; **there were unhappy —s at the meeting** en la reunión pasaron cosas nada agradables.

  (b) (place in general) escenario m, teatro m, lugar m; **the — of operations** el teatro de las operaciones; **the — of the disaster** el lugar de la catástrofe; **the — of the crime** el escenario del crimen; **the —s of one's early life** los lugares frecuentados por uno en su juventud; **the political — in Italy** el escenario político italiano; **to appear** (or come etc) **on the —** presentarse, llegar; **when I came on the —** cuando yo llegué; **he appeared unexpectedly on the —** se presentó inesperadamente; **to disappear from the political —** desaparecer del escenario político.

(c) (*sight, vision*) vista *f*, perspectiva *f*, panorama *m*; (*landscape*) paisaje *m*; **the — from the top is marvellous** desde la cumbre se abarca un panorama maravilloso; **the — spread out before you** el panorama que se extiende delante de uno; **it was a — of utter destruction** fue una perspectiva de destrucción total; **it is a lonely —** es un paisaje solitario; **a change of — would do you good** le vendría bien un cambio de aire.

(d) (*fuss*) escándalo *m*, lío *m*, jaleo *m*; **try to avoid a —** procurar no armar un lío; **I hate —s** detesto los jaleos; **to make a —** armar un lío, armar un escándalo; **she had a — with her husband** riñó con su marido.

scene painter ['siːn,peintə*] *n* (*designer*) escenógrafo *m*, (*workman*) pintor *m* de decoraciones.

scenery ['siːnəri] *n* (*landscape*) paisaje *m*; (*Theat*) decoraciones *fpl*, decorado *m*.

scene shifter ['siːn,ʃiftə*] *n* tramoyista *mf*.

scenic ['siːnik] *adj* (*Theat*) escénico, dramático; (*picturesque*) pintoresco.

scenography [siː'nɔgrəfi] *n* escenografía *f*.

scent [sent] **1** *n* (*smell*) olor *m*; (*pleasant smell*) perfume *m*, aroma *m*, fragancia *f*; (*Hunting*) rastro *m*, pista *f*; (*sense of smell*) olfato *m*; **to be on the —** seguir la pista (*also fig; of* de); **to lose the —** perder la pista; **to throw someone off the —** despistar a uno.

2 *vt* (*add — to*) perfumar (*with* de); (*smell*) oler; *danger etc* percibir, sospechar; **to — something out** olfatear algo, husmear algo.

scent bottle ['sent,bɔtl] *n* frasco *m* de perfume.

scented ['sentid] *adj* perfumado.

scentless ['sentlis] *adj* inodoro.

scent spray ['sentsprei] *n* atomizador *m* (de perfume), pulverizador *m* (de perfume).

sceptic, (*US*) **skeptic** ['skeptik] *n* escéptico *m*, a *f*.

sceptical, (*US*) **skeptical** ['skeptikəl] *adj* escéptico; **he was — about it** se mostró escéptico acerca de ello, tenía dudas sobre ello.

scepticism, (*US*) **skepticism** ['skeptisizəm] *n* escepticismo *m*.

sceptre, (*US*) **scepter** ['septə*] *n* cetro *m*.

schedule ['ʃedjuːl, *US* 'skedjuːl] **1** *n* (*list*) lista *f*; (*timetable*) horario *m*; (*of events etc*) programa *m*; (*of questions*) cuestionario *m*; (*legal document*) inventario *m*, apéndice *m*; (*of work to be done etc*) plan *m*; **the train is behind —** el tren sufre un retraso; **the bus was on —** el autobús llegó a la hora debida, el autobús llegó sin retraso; **the work is up to —** los trabajos llevan el ritmo adecuado, los trabajos no sufren retraso; **we are working to a very tight —** trabajamos de acuerdo con un plan riguroso; **our — did not include the Prado** nuestro programa de visitas no incluía el Museo del Prado.

2 *vt* (*list*) poner en una lista, hacer una lista de; catalogar, inventariar; (*plan*) proyectar, redactar el plan de; *trains etc* establecer el horario de; *visit, lecture etc* fijar la hora de; **this stop is not —d** esta parada no es oficial; **the plane is —d for 2 o'clock, the plane is —d to land at 2 o'clock** el avión debe llegar a las 2; **you are —d to speak for 20 minutes** según el programa Vd hablará durante 20 minutos; **this building is —d for demolition** se prevé la demolición de este edificio.

Scheldt [ʃelt] Escalda *m*.

schema ['skiːmə] *n* (*Eccl etc*) esquema *m*.

schematic [ski'mætik] *adj* esquemático.

scheme [skiːm] **1** *n* (a) (*arrangement*) disposición *f*; combinación *f*; **colour —** combinación *f* de colores; **rhyme —** esquema *f* de la rima.

(b) (*systematic table*) plan *m*, esquema *m*; (*diagram*) diagrama *m*; (*summary*) resumen *m*.

(c) (*plan*) plan *m*, proyecto *m*; (*idea*) idea *f*; **the — for the new bridge** el proyecto del nuevo puente; **it's some crazy —** es una idea estrafalaria de las suyas; **it's not a bad —** no es mala idea.

(d) (*plot*) intriga *f*; (*ruse*) treta *f*, ardid *m*; **it's a — to get him out of the way** es un ardid para quitarle de ʌŋ medio.

2 *vt* (*plan*) proyectar; (*pej*) tramar, urdir.

3 *vi* (*plan*) hacer proyectos, formar planes; (*pej*) intrigar; **they're scheming to get me out** están intrigando para expulsarme.

schemer ['skiːmə*] *n* intrigante *mf*.

scheming ['skiːmiŋ] *adj* (*pej*) intrigante; astuto, mañoso.

schism ['sizəm] *n* cisma *m*.

schismatic [siz'mætik] **1** *adj* cismático. **2** *n* cismático *m*.

schismatical [siz'mætikəl] *adj* cismático.

schist [ʃist] *n* esquisto *m*.

schizo ['skitsəu] (*fam*) *see* **schizophrenic**.

schizoid ['skitsɔid] **1** *adj* esquizoide. **2** *n* esquizoide *mf*.

schizophrenia [,skitsəu'friːniə] *n* esquizofrenia *f*.

schizophrenic [,skitsəu'frenik] **1** *adj* esquizofrénico. **2** *n* esquizofrénico *m*, a *f*.

schmaltz [ʃmɔːlts] *n* (*US*) sentimentalismo *m*, sensiblería *f*.

scholar ['skɔlə*] *n* (*pupil*) colegial *m*, ala *f*, alumno *m*, a *f*, escolar *mf*; (*learned person*) erudito *m*, a *f*; sabio *m*, a *f*; (*scholarship holder*) becario *m*, a *f*; **he's a Tirso —** es especialista en Tirso; **the famous Cervantes —** el docto cervantista; **I'm no —** apenas sé nada, no soy nada intelectual.

scholarly ['skɔləli] *adj* erudito.

scholarship ['skɔləʃip] *n* erudición *f*; (*money award*) beca *f*.

scholarship holder ['skɔləʃip,həuldə*] *n* becario *m*, a *f*.

scholastic [skə'læstik] **1** *adj* (*relative to school*) escolar; (*relative to scholasticism*) escolástico; **— books** libros *mpl* escolares; **the — year** el año escolar; **the — profession** el magisterio.

2 *n* escolástico *m*.

scholasticism [skə'læstisizəm] *n* escolasticismo *m*.

school¹ [skuːl] **1** *n* (a) (*in general*) escuela *f*; (*primary, specialist, military etc*) escuela *f*; colegio *m*; academia *f*; **to be at —** estar en la escuela; **we have to be at — by 9** tenemos que estar en la clase para las 9; **you weren't at — yesterday** ayer faltaste a la clase; **which — were you at?** ¿dónde cursó Vd los estudios (del bachillerato)?; **we were at — together** fuimos al mismo instituto (*etc*); **to go to —** ir a la escuela; **to learn in a tough —** formarse en una escuela dura.

(b) **— of art** escuela *f* de bellas artes; **— of dancing** escuela *f* de baile, escuela *f* de ballet; **— of music** academia *f* de música, conservatorio *m*; **comprehensive —** instituto *m* integrado; **grammar — (state)** instituto *m*, (*private, independent, religious*) academia *f* (*or* colegio *m*) de segunda enseñanza; **high — (US, Scot)** instituto *m*; **infant —, infants' —** escuela *f* de párvulos; **junior high — (US)** colegio *m* de bachillerato elemental; **preparatory —** escuela privada para los muchachos de 8 a 12 años (*que pasan después a una* public school); **primary —** escuela *f* primaria; **private —** escuela *f* privada, escuela *f* particular; **public — (Brit, approx)** internado *m* privado, (*US, Scot*) escuela *f* pública; **secondary —** instituto *m* de segunda enseñanza; **Sunday —** escuela en que se da instrucción religiosa los domingos; **technical —, trade —** escuela *f* de artes y oficios, universidad *f* laboral; **upper —** cursos *mpl* superiores (de un instituto *etc*); *see* **driving —, night —, nursery —** etc.

(c) (*Univ*) departamento *m*, facultad *f*; **in the History —** en el departamento de Historia; **S— of Arabic Studies** Escuela *f* de Estudios Árabes.

(d) (*of thought etc*) escuela *f*; **Plato and his —** Platón y su escuela, Platón y sus discípulos; **the Dutch —** la escuela holandesa; **I am not of that —** yo no sigo esa opinión; **I am not of the — that ...** yo no soy de los que . . .; **people of the old —** gente *f* de la vieja escuela, gente *f* chapada a la antigua.

2 *attr*: **— age** edad *f* escolar; **— book** libro *m* para uso escolar; **the — population is high** el porcentaje de escolaridad es elevado; **— year** año *m* escolar; *see* **fee** etc.

3 *vt* instruir, enseñar; disciplinar; **to — someone in a technique** instruir a uno en una técnica; **to — someone to do something** enseñar a uno a hacer algo; **he has been well —ed** ha sido bien instruido.

school² [skuːl] *n* (*Fish*) banco *m*, cardumen *m*.

schoolbook ['skuːlbuk] *n* libro *m* escolar.

schoolboy ['skuːlbɔi] *n* colegial *m*, escolar *m*.

schooldays ['skuːldeiz] *npl* años *mpl* de colegio.

schoolfellow ['skuːl,feləu] *n* compañero *m* de clase, compañera *f* de clase.

schoolgirl ['skuːlgəːl] *n* colegiala *f*, escolar *f*.

schooling ['skuːliŋ] *n* (*teaching etc*) instrucción *f*, enseñanza *f*; disciplina *f*; **compulsory — up to 16** escolaridad *f* obligatoria hasta los 16 años; **— is free** la enseñanza es gratuita.

schoolman ['skuːlmən] *n*, *pl* **—men** [mən] escolástico *m*.

schoolmaster ['skuːl,mɑːstə*] *n* (*grammar school*) profesor *m* (de instituto); (*other*) maestro *m*.

schoolmistress ['sku:l,mistris] n (grammar school) profesora f (de instituto); (other) maestra f.

schoolroom ['sku:lrum] n clase f.

schoolteacher ['sku:l,ti:tʃə*] n maestro m, a f.

schooner ['sku:nə*] n goleta f.

sciatic [sai'ætik] adj ciático.

sciatica [sai'ætikə] n ciática f.

science ['saiəns] n ciencia f; **domestic** — ciencia f del hogar; **natural** —s ciencias fpl naturales; **physical** —s ciencias fpl físicas; **social** — ciencia f social; **to blind someone with** — impresionar a uno citándole muchos datos científicos; lucir sus conocimientos para impresionar a uno.

science fiction ['saiəns,fikʃən] n ciencia-ficción f.

scientific [,saiən'tifik] adj científico.

scientifically [,saiən'tifikəli] adv científicamente.

scientist ['saiəntist] n científico m, científica f.

Scillies ['siliz] pl, **Scilly Isles** ['siliailz] pl Islas fpl Sorlingues.

scimitar ['simitə*] n cimitarra f.

scintillate ['sintileit] vi centellear, chispear; (fig) brillar.

scintillating ['sintileitiŋ] adj (fig) brillante; ingenioso; de lo más vivo, animadísimo.

scion ['saiən] n (Bot, fig) vástago m; — **of a noble family** vástago m de una familia noble.

Scipio ['skipiou] m Escipión.

scissors ['sizəz] npl tijeras fpl; **a pair of** — unas tijeras.

sclerosis [skli'rəusis] n esclerosis f; **multiple** — esclerosis f múltiple.

scoff[1] [skɔf] vi mofarse, burlarse (at de).

scoff[2] [skɔf] (fam) **1** n comida f; — **up!** ¡la comida está servida! **2** vt zamparse, engullir; **she** —**ed the lot** se lo comió todo.

scoffer ['skɔfə*] n mofador m, ora f.

scoffing ['skɔfiŋ] n mofas fpl, burlas fpl.

scold [skəuld] **1** n virago f. **2** vt reprender, regañar (for por).

scolding ['skəuldiŋ] n reprensión f, regaño m; **to give someone a** — reprender a uno.

scollop ['skɔləp] see **scallop**.

sconce [skɔns] n candelabro m de pared.

scone [skɔn] n bollo m.

scoop [sku:p] **1** n (a) (instrument) pala f, paleta f, cuchara f; (for bailing) achicador m; (carpenter's) gubia f; (of dredger) cuchara f (de draga), cangilón m; (Med) espátula f.
(b) (profit) ganancia f grande; golpe m financiero; (by newspaper) primera publicación f de una noticia sensacional, exclusiva f, pisotón m; **it was a** — **for the paper** fue un gran éxito para el periódico; **we brought off the** — logramos un triunfo adelantándonos a los demás en la publicación de la noticia (etc).
2 vt (a) grain, liquid etc (also **to** — **out, to** — **up**) sacar con pala, sacar con cuchara; sacar con achicador; **to** — **up** cards etc recoger rápidamente.
(b) **to** — **out** (hollow) excavar, ahuecar; hacer.
(c) **to** — **the pool** llevar las diez de últimas; ganar todas las bazas; **we** —**ed the other papers** nos adelantamos a los demás periódicos publicando la noticia.

scoot [sku:t] vi (fam) escabullirse, largarse (fam); correr precipitadamente; **I must** — tengo que marcharme.

scooter ['sku:tə*] n (child's) patinete m; (adult's) motosilla f, escúter m, moto f.

scope [skəup] n alcance m; envergadura f; esfera f de acción; ámbito m; campo m, campo m de aplicación; **there is** — **for** hay campo para; **a programme of considerable** — un programa de gran alcance, un programa de ancha envergadura; **the** — **of the new measures must be defined** conviene delimitar el campo de aplicación de las nuevas medidas; **to give someone full** — dar carta blanca a uno; **this should give you plenty of** — **for your talents** esto te ha de darle grandes posibilidades para explotar sus talentos; **it is outside my** — eso está fuera de mi alcance; **it is well within his** — está dentro de su alcance, está bien dentro de sus posibilidades.

scorbutic [skɔ:'bju:tik] adj escorbútico.

scorch [skɔ:tʃ] **1** vt chamuscar; (of sun, wind) abrasar; plants etc quemar, secar; **to** — **the earth** (Mil) quemar la tierra, destruir todo lo útil; arrasarlo todo.
2 vi chamuscarse; quemarse, secarse; (fam) ir volando, correr a gran velocidad.

scorcher ['skɔ:tʃə*] n día m de mucho calor.

scorching ['skɔ:tʃiŋ] adj sun etc abrasador; day de mucho calor; speed grande, excesivo; **it's** — **hot**

hace un tremendo calor; **a few** — **remarks** algunas observaciones mordaces.

score [skɔ:*] **1** n (a) (notch) muesca f, entalladura f; señal f; (line) raya f, línea f.
(b) (reckoning) cuenta f; **to pay one's** — pagar la cuenta; **to pay off old** —s ajustar cuentas viejas; **to settle an old** — **with someone** desquitarse con uno; **I have a** — **to settle with him** tengo cuentas pendientes con él.
(c) (in exam, test) puntuación f; (Sport) tanteo m; tantos mpl, puntos mpl (etc); **what's the** —? ¿cómo estamos?, ¿cómo va esto?; **the** — **was Toboso 9, Barataria 1** el resultado fue Toboso 9, Barataria 1; **there was no** — **at half-time** en el primer tiempo no hubo goles; **to keep the** — tantear; **do you know the** —? ¿sabe Vd cuántos goles han marcado?; **he doesn't know the** — (fig) no está al tanto, (pej) es un despistado, es un pobre hombre; **to make a** — marcar un tanto, marcar un gol (etc).
(d) (Mus) partitura f; **full** — partitura f de orquesta.
(e) (20) veinte, veintena f; **a** — **of people** veinte personas, una veintena de personas; **3** — **years and 10** 70 años; **there were** —**s of mistakes** había muchísimas erratas, había erratas a granel; **actresses by the** — muchísimas actrices.
(f) **on the** — **of illness** por enfermedad, con motivo de su enfermedad; **on that** — a ese respecto, por lo que se refiere a eso; **on what** —? ¿con qué motivo?
2 vt (a) (notch) hacer muescas en, hacer cortes en; señalar; (line) rayar; **the wall is heavily** —**d with lines** las paredes están profundamente rayadas; **the plane** —**d the runway as it landed** al aterrizar el avión hizo rayas en la pista; **to** — **something out, to** — **something through** tachar algo.
(b) — **it up to me** apúntelo en mi cuenta.
(c) (in exam, test) obtener una puntuación . . .; obtener una nota . . .; ser calificado de . . .; (Sport) goal, points ganar, runs hacer; **to** — **70% obtener una puntuación de 70 por ciento; **to** — **well in a test** obtener buena nota en un test; **to** — **a goal** marcar un gol; **they went 5 games without scoring a point** en 5 partidos no ganaron un solo punto; **they had 14 goals** —**d against them** sus adversarios metieron 14 goles a costa suya; **to** — **a great success** obtener un gran triunfo.
(d) (Mus) instrumentar, orquestar; **it is** —**d for 5 bassoons** está instrumentado para 5 bajones.
3 vi (a) (Sport etc) marcar un tanto, marcar un gol, ganar puntos (etc); **to fail to** — no marcar ningún gol; **that's where he** —**s** en eso es donde tiene más ventajas, es en ese aspecto donde sobresale; **to** — **off someone** triunfar a costa de uno, (with witty remark) hacer un chiste a costa de uno; **she's easy to** — **off** es fácil hacer chistes a costa suya.
(b) (keep —) tantear, llevar el tanteo.
(c) (count) puntuar; **that doesn't** — eso no puntúa, eso no vale.

scoreboard ['skɔ:bɔ:d] n tanteador m, marcador m.

scorecard ['skɔ:ka:d] n tarjeta f en que se lleva el tanteo.

scorer ['skɔ:rə*] n (player) marcador m; (recorder) tanteador m; **he is top** — **in the league** es el principal goleador en la liga, ha marcado más goles que ningún otro en la liga; **the** —**s were A and B** marcaron los goles A y B.

scoring ['skɔ:riŋ] n tanteo m; **rules for** — reglas fpl para el tanteo; **a low** — **match** un partido en el que se marcan pocos goles (etc); **all the** — **was in the second half** todos los goles se marcaron en el segundo tiempo.

scorn [skɔ:n] **1** n desprecio m, desdén m (for de); **to laugh something to** — hacer ver lo absurdo que es algo, tomar algo a broma.
2 vt despreciar, desdeñar; **to** — **to do something** desdeñarse de hacer algo, no dignarse hacer algo.

scornful ['skɔ:nful] adj desdeñoso; **to be** — **about something** desdeñar algo.

scornfully ['skɔ:nfəli] adv desdeñosamente, con desprecio.

Scorpio ['skɔ:piəu] n Escorpión m.

scorpion ['skɔ:piən] n escorpión m, alacrán m.

Scot [skɔt] n escocés m, esa f.

Scotch [skɔtʃ] **1** adj escocés. **2** n (fam) whisky m escocés; **the** — los escoceses.

scotch [skɔtʃ] **1** n calza f, cuña f. **2** vt wheel calzar, engalgar; rumour desmentir; idea hacer abandonar; plan etc frustrar.

Scotch broth ['skɔtʃ'brɔθ] n caldo muy sustancioso con legumbres, cebada perlada, carne de cordero etc.

scot-free ['skɔt'friː] *adj* impune; **to get off** — salir impune; quedar sin castigo.

Scotland ['skɔtlənd] Escocia *f*; — **Yard** oficina central de la policía de Londres.

Scots [skɔts] **1** *adj* escocés. **2** *n* (*dialect*) escocés *m*.

Scotsman ['skɔtsmən] *n*, *pl* —**men** [mən] escocés *m*.

Scotswoman ['skɔts,wumən] *n*, *pl* —**women** [,wimin] escocesa *f*.

scottie ['skɔti] *n* (*fam*) terrier *m* escocés.

Scottish ['skɔtiʃ] *adj* escocés.

scoundrel ['skaundrəl] *n* canalla *m*, sinvergüenza *m*.

scoundrelly ['skaundrəli] *adj* canallesco, vil.

scour[1] ['skauə*] *vt pan etc* fregar, estregar, limpiar fregando (*also* to — **out**); *channel* limpiar; (*Med*) purgar; **the river had** —**ed out part of the bank** el río se había llevado una parte de la orilla.

scour[2] ['skauə*] **1** *vt area* recorrer, registrar; **we are** —**ing the countryside for him** recorremos el campo buscándole.
2 *vi*: **to** — **about for something** buscar algo por todas partes.

scourer ['skauərə*] *n* estropajo *m*.

scourge [skəːdʒ] **1** *n* azote *m* (*also fig*); **the** — **of malaria** el azote del paludismo; **Attila, the** — **of God** Atila, azote de Dios; **it is the** — **of our times** es la calamidad de nuestros tiempos; **God sent it as a** — Dios lo envió como castigo.
2 *vt* azotar, flagelar; (*fig*) hostigar.

scout[1] [skaut] **1** *n* (a) (*person: Mil*) explorador *m*, escucha *m*; (*Univ*) criado *m*; **boy** — muchacho *m* explorador, explorador *m*.
(b) (*reconnaissance*) reconocimiento *m*; (*search*) búsqueda *f*; **to have a** — **round** reconocer el terreno; **we'll have a** — **for it** lo buscaremos.
2 *vi* explorar; reconocer el terreno; **to** — **for something** buscar algo.

scout[2] [skaut] *vt proposal* rechazar con desdén; *rumour etc* desmentir.

scouting ['skautiŋ] *n* organización *f* de los exploradores; actividades *fpl* de los exploradores.

scoutmaster ['skaut,maːstə*] *n* jefe *m* de sección de exploradores.

scow [skau] *n* gabarra *f*.

scowl [skaul] **1** *n* ceño *m*; **he said with a** — dijo ceñudo. **2** *vi* fruncir el ceño, poner mal gesto; **to** — **at someone** mirar con ceño a uno.

scowling ['skauliŋ] *adj* ceñudo.

scrabble ['skræbl] *vi* (*in writing*) garrapatear; **to** — **about** escarbar; revolverlo todo al buscar algo; **she was scrabbling about in the coal** iba revolviendo el carbón mientras buscaba algo.

scrag [skræg] **1** *n* pescuezo *m*. **2** *vt animal* torcer el pescuezo a; *person* dar una paliza a.

scragginess ['skræginis] *n* flaqueza *f*.

scraggy ['skrægi] *adj* flaco, descarnado, escuálido.

scram [skræm] *vi* (*sl*) largarse (*fam*), dar un zarpazo (*fam*); —**!** ¡lárgate!

scramble ['skræmbl] **1** *n* (a) (*climb*) subida *f*; (*outing*) excursión *f* (de montaña, sobre terreno escabroso *etc*).
(b) (*fight etc*) arrebatiña *f*, pelea *f* (*for* por).
2 *vt eggs* revolver, hacer un revoltillo de; *message* cifrar, poner en cifra.
3 *vi* (a) **to** — **out** salir de prisa, salir con dificultad, salir a gatas; **to** — **through the hedge** abrirse paso con dificultad a través de un seto; **to** — **up** trepar a, subir gateando a.
(b) **to** — **for coins** andar a la rebatiña por unas monedas, disputarse unas monedas a gritos, luchar entre sí para recoger unas monedas.

scrap[1] [skræp] **1** *n* (a) (*small piece*) pedacito *m*, fragmento *m*; **a** — **of paper** (*iro*) un papel mojado.
(b) (*fig*) pizca *f*; **a few** —**s of news** algunas noticias de escasa importancia; **it's a** — **of comfort** es una migaja de consolación; **I overheard a** — **of conversation** logré escuchar algunas palabras de la conversación; **there is not a** — **of truth in it** eso no tiene ni pizca de verdad; **not a** —**!** ¡ni pizca!, ¡en absoluto!
(c) —**s** (*left-overs*) sobras *fpl*, desperdicios *mpl*; **the dog feeds on** —**s** el perro come las sobras de la mesa.
(d) (—*iron*) chatarra *f*, hierro *m* viejo; **to sell a ship for** — vender un barco para chatarra; **what is it worth as** —**?** ¿cuánto vale como chatarra?
2 *attr iron etc* viejo; **its** — **value is £30** como chatarra vale 30 libras.
3 *vt car, ship etc* reducir a chatarra; vender para chatarra; *plan etc* desechar, descartar; **we had to** — **that idea** tuvimos que renunciar a esa idea.

scrap[2] [skræp] (*fam*) **1** *n* riña *f*, camorra *f*, bronca *f*; **to get into** (*or* **have**) **a** — **with someone** armar una bronca con uno; **there was a tremendous** — **over the steel bill** se armó una bronca fenomenal por cuestión del proyecto de ley del acero.
2 *vi* reñir, armar una bronca, pelearse; **they were** —**ping in the street** se estaban peleando en la calle.

scrapbook ['skræpbuk] *n* álbum *m* de recortes.

scrap dealer ['skræp,diːlə*] *n* chatarrero *m*.

scrape [skreip] **1** *n* (a) (*act*) raspadura *f*; **to give something a** — raspar algo, limpiar algo raspándolo; **to give one's knee a** — rasguñarse la rodilla.
(b) (*fig*) lío *m*; apuro *m*; **to get into a** — armarse un lío; **to get someone out of a** — ayudar a uno a salir de un apuro.
2 *vt* raspar, raer; (*flesh etc*) rasguñar, raer; (— *against*) rozar; (*Mus, hum*) rascar; *shoes* restregar; **the lorry** —**d the wall** el camión rozó la pared; **the ship** —**d the bottom** el barco tocó el fondo; **to** — **one's boots** limpiarse las botas; **to** — **one's feet across the floor** arrastrar los pies por el suelo; **to** — **away**, **to** — **off** raspar, quitar raspando; **to** — **together**, **to** — **up** arañar, (*fig*) reunir poco a poco, rebañar.
3 *vi* (a) **to** — **along** rozar; **to** — **past** pasar rozando; **we just managed to** — **through the gap** pudimos con dificultad pasar por la abertura sin tocar las paredes.
(b) (*fig*) **to** — **along** ir tirando; **I can** — **along in Arabic** me defiendo en árabe; **to** — **through an exam** aprobar un examen por los pelos; **I just** —**d through** aprobé por los pelos.

scraper ['skreipə*] *n* (*tool*) rascador *m*, raspador *m*; (*in roadmaking*) niveladora *f*; (*at door*) limpiabarros *m*.

scrap heap ['skræphiːp] *n* montón *m* de desechos.

scrapings ['skreipiŋz] *npl* raspaduras *fpl*; — **of the gutter** (*fig*) hez *f* de la sociedad.

scrap iron ['skræp'aiən] *n* chatarra *f*, hierro *m* viejo.

scrap merchant ['skræp,məːtʃənt] *n* chatarrero *m*.

scrappy ['skræpi] *adj meal etc* pobre, escaso; *text etc* fragmentario; *speech* inconexo, descosido; *knowledge* superficial.

scratch ['skrætʃ] **1** *n* (a) (*from claw, on flesh etc*) rasguño *m*, arañazo *m*; (*on surface*) raya *f*, marca *f*; **it's just a** — sólo es un rasguño; **the cat gave her a** — el gato la arañó; **he hadn't a** — **on him** no tuvo la más leve herida.
(b) (*Sport*) línea *f* de salida; **to be** (*or* **come**) **up to** — (*thing*) estar en buen estado, llenar los requisitos, ser de buena calidad, (*person*) estar a la altura de las circunstancias; **to start from** — (*with no resources*) empezar sin nada, empezar sin ventaja alguna, (*from beginning*) empezar desde el principio; **we shall have to start from** — **again** tendremos que partir nuevamente de cero, tendremos que comenzar desde el principio otra vez.
2 *adj competitor* sin ventaja; *team* improvisado, sin experiencia, reunido de prisa.
3 *vt* (a) (*with claw etc*) rasguñar, arañar; (*to relieve itch*) rascar; *hard surface* rayar, marcar; (*of chicken etc*) escarbar; **to** — **a hole in something** hacer un agujero en algo rascándolo; **she** —**ed the dog's ear** le rascó la oreja al perro; **he** —**ed his head** se rascó la cabeza; **the glass of this watch cannot be** —**ed** el cristal de este reloj no puede rayarse; **we** —**ed our names on the wood** grabamos nuestros nombres en la madera; **to** — **someone's eyes out** sacar los ojos a uno con las uñas; **to** — **someone off a list** tachar el nombre de uno de una lista.
(b) (*Sport*) retirar (tachando el nombre de); **that horse has been** —**ed** ese caballo ha sido retirado; *see* **back, surface.**
4 *vi* (a) rasguñar; (*to relieve itch*) rascarse; (*of chicken etc*) escarbar; (*pen*) raspear; **the dog** —**ed at the door** el perro arañó la puerta.
(b) (*Sport*) retirarse.

scratch pad ['skrætʃpæd] *n* cuadernillo *m* de apuntes.

scratchy ['skrætʃi] *adj pen* que raspea; *tone* áspero; *writing* flojo, irregular.

scrawl [skrɔːl] **1** *n* garabatos *mpl*, garrapatos *mpl*; **the word finished in a** — la palabra terminó en un garabato; **I can't read her** — no soy capaz de leer su pésima escritura.
2 *vt*: **to** — **a note to someone** escribir con mucha prisa una nota para uno; **a wall** —**ed all over with rude words** una pared llena de palabrotas mal escritas.
3 *vi* garrapatear, hacer garabatos.

scrawny ['skrɔːni] *adj* descarnado, escuálido.

scream [skri:m] **1** n (a) chillido m, grito m (agudo); **there were —s of laughter** hubo grandes carcajadas; **to give a —** chillar, dar un grito.
    (b) (fig) **it was a —** fue para morirse de risa; **he's a —** es célebre, es un chistoso.
    2 vt abuse etc vociferar (at contra).
    3 vi chillar, gritar, **to — with pain** lanzar gritos de dolor; **to — with laughter** reírse a carcajadas.
    4 vr: **to — oneself hoarse** enronquecer a fuerza de gritar.

screamingly ['skri:miŋli] adv: **a — funny joke** un chiste de lo más divertido; **it was — funny** fue para morirse de risa.

scree ['skri:] n ladera de montaña cubierta de cantos rodados.

screech [skri:tʃ] see scream (in most senses); vi (of brakes, wheels etc) chirriar.

screech owl ['skri:tʃaul] n lechuza f.

screed [skri:d] n escrito m largo y pesado, documento m aburrido.

screen [skri:n] **1** n (a) (protective) pantalla f; (folding) biombo m; (Mil etc) cortina f; (Phot) retícula f; (sieve) tamiz m, criba f; **focusing —** placa f esmerilada; **safety —** pantalla f de seguridad.
    (b) (Cine, TV) pantalla f; **the small —** la pequeña pantalla; **stars of the —** estrellas fpl de la pantalla, estrellas fpl del cine; **to write for the —** escribir para el cine.
    2 vt (hide) ocultar, esconder; (protect) proteger (con una pantalla), abrigar; (sift) tamizar, pasar por una criba; suspects etc investigar; novel etc adaptar para el cine, hacer una película de, hacer una versión cinematográfica de; film proyectar; **the house is —ed by trees** la casa se oculta detrás de unos árboles; **in order to — our movements from the enemy** para impedir que el enemigo observara nuestros movimientos; **the film will be —ed next year** la película se estrenará el año que viene.

screen test ['skri:ntest] n prueba f de pantalla (a que se somete el actor etc que quiere hacer cine).

screw [skru:] **1** n (Mech) tornillo m; (thread of —) rosca f; (Aer, Naut) hélice f; (sl) sueldo m; **he's got a — loose** (fam) le falta un tornillo (fam); **to put the —s on someone** (fam) apretar los tornillos a uno (fam).
    2 vt screw atornillar; nut apretar; **to — something down** fijar algo con tornillos; **to — something on to a board** fijar algo en un tablón con tornillos; **to — money out of someone** arrancar dinero a uno; **to — the truth out of someone** arrancar la verdad a uno; **to — up** screw atornillar, nut apretar; paper arrugar; **to — up one's eyes** entornar los ojos; **to — up one's face** arrugar la cara, hacer visajes; see courage.
    3 vi (of ball) torcerse; **it —s on here** se fija aquí con tornillos; **it will — up tighter than that** se puede apretar todavía más.
    4 vr: **to — oneself up to do something** obligarse a hacer algo; cobrar bastante ánimo para hacer algo.

screwball ['skru:bɔ:l] (US sl) **1** adj excéntrico, estrafalario. **2** n excéntrico m, tipo m estrafalario.

screwdriver ['skru:,draivə*] n destornillador m.

screwy ['skru:i] adj (sl) chiflado (fam).

scribble ['skribl] **1** n garabatos mpl; **I can't read her —** no soy capaz de leer su pésima escritura; **a wall covered in —s** una pared llena de garabatos.
    2 vt: **to — one's signature** escribir con mucha prisa su firma; **a word —d on a wall** una palabra mal escrita en una pared; **a sheet of paper —d (over) with notes** una hoja de papel emborronada de notas.
    3 vi garrapatear, hacer garabatos; escribir con mucha prisa; (pej, hum) ser escritor, ser periodista.

scribbler ['skriblə*] n (pej, hum) escritorzuelo m, periodista m de baja categoría.

scribbling pad ['skribliŋ,pæd] n borrador m.

scribe [skraib] n (professional letter-writer etc) escribiente m; amanuense m; (of MS) copista m; (Bible) escriba m; (pej, hum) escritorzuelo m, periodista m de baja categoría.

scrimmage ['skrimidʒ] n arrebatiña f, pelea f.

scrimp [skrimp] **1** vt escatimar. **2** vi economizar, hacer economías; **to — and save** pasar grandes economías, vivir muy justo.

scrimpy ['skrimpi] adj person tacaño; supply etc escaso.

scrimshank ['skrɪ,mʃæŋk] vi (Mil sl) racanear, hacer el rácano.

scrimshanker ['skrim,ʃæŋkə*] n (Mil sl) rácano m.

scrip [skrip] n (Fin) vale m, abonaré m.

script [skript] n (writing) escritura f, letra f (cursiva); (MS) manuscrito m; (School, Univ) examen m escrito; (Cine) guión m.

script girl ['skriptgə:l] n script-girl f, secretaria f de dirección, anotadora f (Acad).

scriptural ['skriptʃərəl] adj escriturario, bíblico.

Scripture ['skriptʃə*] n (also **Holy —**) Sagrada Escritura f; (as school subject, lesson) Historia f Sagrada.

scriptwriter ['skript,raitə*] n guionista mf.

scrofula ['skrɔfjulə] n escrófula f.

scrofulous ['skrɔfjuləs] adj escrofuloso.

scroll [skrəul] n rollo m; (ancient) rollo m de escritura; rollo m de pergamino; (Art, Archit) voluta f; **— of fame** lista f de la fama; **the Dead Sea —s** los pergaminos del Mar Muerto.

Scrooge [skru:dʒ] el avariento típico (personaje del "Christmas Carol", de Dickens).

scrotum ['skrəutəm] n escroto m.

scrounge [skraundʒ] (fam) **1** n: **to be on the —** ir de gorra (fam); tratar de adquirir cosas sin pagar; tratar de pedir algo prestado; **to have a — round for something** buscar algo.
    2 vt obtener por medio de gorronería, obtener sin pagar, agenciarse; **I —d a ticket** me agencié una entrada.
    3 vi ir de gorra, gorronear, sablear; **to — around for something** buscar algo.

scrounger ['skraundʒə*] n (fam) gorrón m (fam), sablista mf (fam).

scrub¹ [skrʌb] n (Bot) maleza f, monte m bajo, matas fpl.

scrub² [skrʌb] **1** n fregado m, fregadura f; **to give something a —** limpiar algo fregándolo; **it needs a hard —** hay que fregarlo con fuerza.
    2 vt fregar, restregar; limpiar fregando.
    3 vi: **let's — round it** (fam) pasemos la esponja, borrón y cuenta nueva.

scrubbing brush ['skrʌbiŋ,brʌʃ] n bruza f, estregadera f.

scrubby ['skrʌbi] adj achaparrado, enano.

scrubwoman ['skrʌb,wumən] n, pl **—women** [,wimin] (US) fregona f.

scruff [skrʌf] n: **— of the neck** pescuezo m; **to take someone by the — of the neck** agarrar a uno por el pescuezo.

scruffy ['skrʌfi] adj sucio, piojoso.

scrum [skrʌm] n, **scrummage** ['skrʌmidʒ] n (Rugby) mêlée f; **loose —** melée f abierta; **set —** melée f cerrada.

scrumptious ['skrʌmpʃəs] adj (fam) de rechupete (fam), riquísimo.

scrunch [skrʌntʃ] vt ronzar.

scruple ['skru:pl] **1** n (a) (weight) escrúpulo m (Pharm = 20 granos = 1,296 gramos).
    (b) (fig) escrúpulo m; **a person of no —s** una persona sin escrúpulos; **he is entirely without —** no tiene conciencia en absoluto; **to have no —s about . . .** no tener escrúpulos acerca de . . .; **to make no — to + infin** no vacilar en + infin.
    2 vi: **not to — to + infin** no vacilar en + infin.

scrupulous ['skru:pjuləs] adj escrupuloso (about en cuanto a).

scrupulously ['skru:pjuləsli] adv escrupulosamente; **a — fair decision** una decisión completamente justa; **a — clean room** un cuarto completamente limpio.

scrupulousness ['skru:pjuləsnis] n escrupulosidad f.

scrutineer [,skru:ti'niə*] n escudriñador m.

scrutinize ['skru:tinaiz] vt escudriñar, examinar; votes escrutar.

scrutiny ['skru:tini] n escrutinio m, examen m; **it does not stand up to —** no resiste al examen; **to submit something to a close —** someter algo a un cuidadoso examen.

scud [skʌd] vi: **to — along** correr (llevado por el viento), deslizarse rápidamente; **the clouds were —ding across the sky** las nubes pasaron rápidamente a través del cielo; **the ship —ded before the wind** el barco iba viento en popa.

scuff [skʌf] **1** vt shoes desgastar, restregar; feet arrastrar. **2** vi andar arrastrando los pies.

scuffle ['skʌfl] **1** n refriega f, pelea f. **2** vi pelearse; **to — with the police** pelearse con la policía.

scull [skʌl] **1** n espadilla f. **2** vti remar (con espadilla).

scullery ['skʌləri] n trascocina f, fregadero m, office m, antecocina f (Acad).

scullery maid ['skʌlərimeid] n fregona f.

sculp [skʌlp] vt, **sculpt** [skʌlpt] vt esculpir.

sculptor ['skʌlptə*] n escultor m; (woman) escultora f.

sculptress ['skʌlptris] n escultora f.

sculptural ['skʌlptʃərəl] adj escultural.

sculpture ['skʌlptʃə*] **1** n (art, object) escultura f. **2** vt esculpir.

scum [skʌm] *n* (*on liquid*) espuma *f*, nata *f*; (*on pond*) verdín *m*; (*on metal*) escoria *f*; (*fig*) heces *fpl*; **the — of the earth** las heces de la sociedad; **you —!** ¡canalla!

scummy ['skʌmi] *adj* lleno de espuma; cubierto de verdín; (*fig*) canallesco, vil.

scupper ['skʌpə*] 1 *n* imbornal *m*. 2 *vt* (*Naut*) abrir los imbornales de, (*loosely*) hundir; (*fig*) arruinar, destruir, acabar con.

scurf [skə:f] *n* caspa *f*.

scurfy ['skə:fi] *adj* casposo.

scurrility [skʌ'riliti] *n* grosería *f*, procacidad *f*, chocarrería *f*; lo difamatorio.

scurrilous ['skʌriləs] *adj* grosero, procaz, chocarrero; difamatorio; **a — journal** una revista chocarrera; **to make a — attack on someone** atacar a uno de modo grosero.

scurrilously ['skʌriləsli] *adv* groseramente, con procacidad; de modo difamatorio.

scurry ['skʌri] *vi* correr, ir a toda prisa; **to — along** ir corriendo; **to — away, to — off** escabullirse; **to — for shelter** correr para ponerse al abrigo.

scurvy[1] ['skə:vi] *adj* vil, canallesco; ruin.

scurvy[2] ['skə:vi] *n* escorbuto *m*.

scut [skʌt] *n* rabito *m* (*esp de conejo*).

scutcheon ['skʌtʃən] *n see* escutcheon.

scuttle[1] ['skʌtl] *n* cubo *m*, carbonera *f*.

scuttle[2] ['skʌtl] 1 *vt* barrenar, poner un barreno a, echar a pique.
2 *vi* (*fig*) abandonar, renunciar; **a policy of —** una política de renunciar a todo.

scuttle[3] ['skʌtl] 1 *n* huida *f* precipitada, retirada *f* precipitada.
2 *vi*: **to — along** correr, ir a toda prisa; **to — away, to — off** escabullirse; **we must — tenemos** que marcharnos.

Scylla ['silə]: **— and Charybdis** Escila y Caribdis.

scythe [saið] 1 *n* guadaña *f*. 2 *vt* segar con guadaña.

sea [si:] 1 *n* (a) mar *m or f*; **calm —** mar *f* calma; **rough —** mar *f* alta; **high —s** alta mar *f*; **on the high —s** en alta mar; **inland —** mar *m* interior; **open —** mar *m* abierto; **the seven —s** todos los mares del mundo; **in Spanish —s** en aguas españolas; **at — en el mar; **beyond the —s** allende el mar; **from beyond the —s** desde allende el mar; **by — por mar, por vía marítima; **by the —** a la orilla del mar, junto al mar; **out at — en alta mar; **to be all at — estar despistado, estar perplejo; **to be all at — about something** (*or* **with something**) no saber nada en absoluto de algo; **to follow the —,** **to go to — hacerse marinero; **to put to — hacerse a la mar; **to remain 2 months at — estar navegando durante 2 meses, pasar 2 meses en el mar; **to stand out to — apartarse de la costa.
(b) (*state of the —*) **heavy —, strong — oleada *f*, marejada *f*; **to ship a green** (*or* **heavy**) **— ser inundado por una ola grande.
(c) (*fig*) **a — of faces** una multitud de caras; **a — of corn** un mar de espigas; **—s of flame** una vasta extensión de llamas; **—s of blood** ríos *mpl* de sangre.
2 *adj, attr* de mar; marino, marítimo; **— battle** batalla *f* naval; **— transport** transporte *m* por mar, transporte *m* marítimo; **— trip** viaje *m* por mar; **— air** aire *m* de mar.

sea anemone ['si:ə'neməni] *n* anémona *f* de mar.

sea bathing ['si:,beiðiŋ] *n* baños *mpl* de mar.

sea bird ['si:bə:d] *n* ave *f* marina.

seaboard ['si:bɔ:d] *n* litoral *m*.

sea boots ['si:bu:ts] *npl* botas *fpl* de marinero.

seaborne ['si:bɔ:n] *adj* transportado por mar.

sea bream ['si:'bri:m] *n* besugo *m*.

sea breeze ['si:'bri:z] *n* brisa *f* de mar.

sea captain ['si:'kæptin] *n* capitán *m* de mar.

sea coast ['si:'kəust] *n* litoral *m*, costa *f* marítima, orilla *f* del mar.

sea cow ['si:'kau] *n* manatí *m*.

sea dog ['si:dɔg] *n* lobo *m* de mar.

seafarer ['si:,fɛərə*] *n* marinero *m*.

seafaring ['si:,fɛəriŋ] 1 *adj* marinero. 2 *n* marinería *f*; vida *f* del marinero.

sea fight ['si:fait] *n* combate *m* naval.

sea fish ['si:fiʃ] *n* pez *m* de mar.

seafood ['si:fu:d] *n* mariscos *mpl*; **— restaurant** marisquería *f*.

sea front ['si:frʌnt] *n* (*beach*) playa *f*; (*promenade*) paseo *m* marítimo; **on Santander —** en la playa de Santander.

seagirt ['si:gə:t] *adj* rodeado por el mar.

seagoing ['si:,gəuiŋ] *adj* de alta mar, de altura.

sea-green ['si:gri:n] *adj* verdemar.

seagull ['si:gʌl] *n* gaviota *f*.

sea horse ['si:hɔ:s] *n* caballito *m* de mar, hipocampo *m*.

sea kale ['si:keil] *n* col *f* marina.

seal[1] [si:l] 1 *n* (*Zool*) foca *f*. 2 *vi*: **to go —ing** ir a cazar focas.

seal[2] [si:l] 1 *n* sello *m*; **lead — sello *m* de plomo; **wax — sello *m* de lacre; **great — sello *m* real; **official — sello *m* oficial; **under the — of secrecy** bajo promesa de guardar el secreto; **under my hand and — firmado y sellado por mí; **to set one's — to something** sellar algo, poner su sello en algo.
2 *vt* sellar; cerrar, cerrar herméticamente; (*with wax*) lacrar; (*with lead*) emplomar; (*fig*) *fate etc* decidir; **to — off** obturar; separar, aislar; **to — up** cerrar; (*Comm*) *packet* precintar; **to — a letter** cerrar una carta; **my lips are —ed** he prometido no decir nada, me he resuelto a no decir nada; **this —ed his fate** esto acabó de perderle; **the ship's fate is —ed** la suerte del barco está decidida.

sea legs ['si:legz] *npl* pie *m* marino; **to get one's —** acostumbrarse a la vida de a bordo.

sea level ['si:,levl] *n* nivel *m* del mar; **800 metres above — 800 metros sobre el nivel del mar.

sealing ['si:liŋ] *n* caza *f* de focas.

sealing wax ['si:liŋwæks] *n* lacre *m*.

sea lion ['si:laiən] *n* león *m* marino.

sealskin ['si:lskin] *n* piel *f* de foca.

seam [si:m] 1 *n* (*Sew*) costura *f*; (*Tech*) juntura *f*; (*line on skin*) arruga *f*; (*Anat*) sutura *f*; (*Naut*) costura *f* de los tablones; (*Geol*) filón *m*, veta *f*; **to burst** (*or* **come apart**) **at the —s** descoserse; **we're bursting at the —s in the office** en la oficina ya no cabemos más.
2 *vt* (*Sew*) coser; (*Tech*) juntar; *face* arrugar.

seaman ['si:mən] *n, pl* **—men** [mən] marinero *m*; **able-bodied — marinero *m* de primera; **ordinary — simple marinero *m*.

seamanlike ['si:mənlaik] *adj* de buen marinero.

seamanship ['si:mənʃip] *n* náutica *f*, marinería *f*.

sea mist ['si:mist] *n* bruma *f*.

seamless ['si:mlis] *adj* sin costura.

seamstress ['semstris] *n* costurera *f*.

seamy ['si:mi] *adj* miserable, vil; asqueroso; **the — side** (*fig*) el revés de la medalla.

séance ['seiã:ns] *n* sesión *f* de espiritismo.

sea piece ['si:pi:s] *n* (*Art*) marina *f*.

seaplane ['si:plein] *n* hidroavión *m*.

seaport ['si:pɔ:t] *n* puerto *m* de mar.

sea power ['si:,pauə*] *n* potencia *f* naval.

sear [siə*] *vt* (*wither*) secar, marchitar; (*Med*) cauterizar; (*of pain etc*) punzar; (*of sun, wind*) abrasar; (*scorch*) chamuscar, quemar.

search [sə:tʃ] 1 *n* (*quest*) busca *f*, búsqueda *f* (*for* de); (*of person, of house etc*) registro *m*; (*inspection*) reconocimiento *m*; **right of — derecho *m* de visita; **in — of** en busca de; en demanda de; **to make a — in a house** practicar un registro en una casa; **a — is being made for the missing child** se está buscando al niño desaparecido; **I am having a — made in the archives** estoy organizando un registro de los archivos.
2 *vt* (*scan*) examinar, escudriñar; *place* explorar, registrar; buscar en; *conscience* examinar; *house, luggage etc* registrar; *person* registrar, (*for weapon*) cachear; **we have —ed the library for it** lo hemos buscado en todas partes de la biblioteca, hemos registrado la biblioteca de arriba abajo; **the police are —ing the woods** la policía está explorando el bosque; **— me!** (*fam*) ¡yo qué sé!, ¡ni idea!; **to — someone out** buscar a uno, (*and find*) descubrir a uno tras una búsqueda; **it —es out the weak spots** identifica los puntos débiles.
3 *vi* buscar; (*Med*) tentar, sondar; **to — after, to — for** buscar; **to — into** investigar.

searcher ['sə:tʃə*] *n* buscador *m*, ora *f*.

searching ['sə:tʃiŋ] *adj look* penetrante; *question* agudo, perspicaz.

searchingly ['sə:tʃiŋli] *adv* con penetración; agudamente, con perspicacia.

searchlight ['sə:tʃlait] *n* reflector *m*, proyector *m*.

search party ['sə:tʃ,pa:ti] *n* pelotón *m* de salvamento.

search warrant ['sə:tʃ,wɔrənt] *n* mandamiento *m* judicial de registro, auto *m* de registro domiciliario.

searing ['siəriŋ] *adj heat etc* abrasador; *pain* punzante.

sea room ['si:rum] *n* espacio *m* para hacer maniobras sin peligro.

seascape ['si:skeip] *n* marina *f*.

sea serpent ['si:,sə:pənt] *n* serpiente *f* de mar.

sea shanty ['si:,ʃænti] *n* saloma *f*.

sea shell ['siːʃel] n concha f marina, caracol m marino.
seashore ['siːʃɔː*] n playa f; orilla f del mar.
seasick ['siːsik] adj mareado; **to be —** estar mareado; **to get —** marearse.
seasickness ['siːsiknis] n mareo m.
seaside ['siːsaid] **1** n playa f; orilla f del mar; **to go to the —** ir a una playa (a veranear); **to take the family to the —** for a day llevar a la familia a pasar un día junto al mar.
2 attr: **— resort** playa f, punto m marítimo de veraneo; **we like — holidays** nos gusta pasar las vacaciones en alguna playa, nos gusta veranear junto al mar.
season ['siːzn] **1** n (of the year) estación f; (indefinite) época f, período m; (eg social —, sporting —) temporada f; (opportune time) sazón f; **close — veda** f; **the dead —, the off —** la estación muerta, la parte muerta del año; **football —** temporada f de fútbol; **holiday —** época f de vacaciones; **hunting —** época f de caza; **mating —, rutting —** época f de celo; **monsoon —** época f de los monzones; **peak —** época f más popular del año; **rainy —** estación f de las lluvias; **silly —** época f de la serpiente de mar; **tourist —** temporada f de turismo; **at this —** en esta época del año; **at that —** a la sazón; **at the height of the —** en plena temporada; **for a —** durante una temporada; **in due —** a su tiempo; **a word in —** una palabra a propósito; **in — and out of —** a todo tiempo, en todo momento; **to be in —** (fruit) estar en sazón; **to be out of —** estar fuera de temporada; **the London —** la temporada social de Londres; **it was not the — for jokes** no era el momento oportuno para chistes; **we did a — at La Scala** representamos en la Scala durante una temporada; **did you have a good —?** ¿qué tal la temporada?
2 vt food sazonar, condimentar; wood curar; (moderate) moderar, templar; person etc acostumbrar (to a); ejercitar (to en); **a speech —ed with wit** un discurso salpicado de agudezas.
seasonable ['siːznəbl] adj (suitable) oportuno; weather etc propio de la estación.
seasonal ['siːznl] adj unemployment etc estacional; dress etc apropiado a la estación; **it's very —** varía mucho según la estación.
seasoned ['siːznd] adj food sazonado; timber curado, maduro; person experto, perito, (Mil) veterano, aguerrido; **highly —** muy picante, con muchas especias.
sea song ['siːsɔŋ] n saloma f.
seasoning ['siːzniŋ] n (Cook) condimento m; (of timber) cura f; (fig) salsa f, sal f; **with a — of jokes** con una salpicadura de chistes.
season ticket ['siːzn'tikit] n (Rail) billete m de abono; (Theat etc) abono m (de temporada); **season-ticket holder** abonado m, a f.
seat [siːt] **1** n (a) (chair) asiento m, silla f; (in counting numbers of —s in bus, plane etc) plaza f, asiento m; (Theat etc) localidad f, (as ticket) localidad f, entrada f; (of cycle) sillín m; **an aircraft with 250 —s** un avión de 250 plazas; **are there any —s left?** ¿quedan entradas?; **driver's —, driving — asiento** m del conductor; **folding — asiento** m plegadizo; **front — asiento** m delantero; **reserved — plaza** f reservada; **sliding — bancada** f corrediza; **tip-up — asiento** m abatible; **to keep one's — permanecer sentado; to take a — sentarse, tomar asiento; please take your —s for supper** la cena está servida; **do take a — siéntese por favor; see back—.**
(b) (Parl) escaño m; **a majority of 50 —s** una mayoría de 50 (miembros, votos etc); **to gain a — for the liberals** ganar un escaño para los liberales; **to keep one's — retener su escaño; to win 4 —s from the nationalists** ganar 4 escaños a los nacionalistas; **to take one's — prestar juramento como diputado.**
(c) (of chair) fondo m; (of trousers) fondillos mpl; (Anat) culo m, trasero m; **to get a bump on one's — darse un golpe en el trasero.**
(d) (centre: of government etc) sede f; (of governor etc) residencia f; (of infection, fire, trouble) foco m; **— of learning** centro m de estudios; **country — casa** f solariega; finca f.
(e) (of rider) **to have a good — montar** bien, caer bien a caballo; **to keep one's — seguir** en la silla; **to lose one's — caer** del caballo.
2 vt (a) person etc sentar; **to be —ed** estar sentado; **please be —ed** siéntese por favor; **where shall we — the bishop?** ¿dónde ponemos al obispo?; **to remain —ed** permanecer sentado, no levantarse; **when you are comfortably —ed** cuando estén sentados cómodamente.

(b) (of capacity) tener asientos para; **the car —s 5** el coche tiene 5 asientos, el coche tiene asientos para 5; **the table —s 12** hay sitio para 12 en esta mesa; **the theatre —s 900** el teatro tiene un aforo de 900.
(c) **to — a valve** asentar una válvula, ajustar una válvula.
3 vr: **to — oneself** sentarse.
seat back ['siːtbæk] n respaldo m.
seat belt ['siːtbelt] n cinturón m de seguridad.
-seater ['siːtə*]: eg **a 10-seater plane** un avión de 10 plazas, un avión con capacidad para 10 plazas; **see single-** etc.
seating ['siːtiŋ] n asientos mpl; **— capacity** cabida f, número m de asientos.
sea trout ['siːtraut] n trucha f marina.
sea urchin ['siːˌəːtʃin] n erizo m de mar.
sea wall ['siːwɔːl] n dique m marítimo.
seaward ['siːwəd] adj de hacia el mar, de la parte del mar; **on the — side** en el lado del mar.
seaward(s) ['siːwəd(z)] adv hacia el mar; **to —** en la dirección del mar.
sea water ['siːˌwɔːtə*] n agua f de mar.
seaway ['siːwei] n vía f marítima.
seaweed ['siːwiːd] n alga f (marina).
seaworthy ['siːˌwəːði] adj marinero, en condiciones de navegar.
secant ['siːkənt] n secante f.
secateurs [ˌsekə'təːz] n podadera f; **a pair of —** una podadera.
secede [si'siːd] vi separarse (from de).
secession [si'seʃən] n secesión f, separación f.
secessionist [si'seʃnist] **1** adj secesionista, separatista.
2 n secesionista m, separatista m.
secluded [si'kluːdid] adj retirado, apartado.
seclusion [si'kluːʒən] n retiro m, apartamiento m; **to live in —** vivir en el retiro, vivir lejos del tumulto.
second ['sekənd] **1** adj segundo; otro; **a — Manolete** otro Manolete; **every — post** cada dos postes, un poste sí y otro no; **the — largest fish** el mayor pez después del primero; **to be — to none** no ser inferior a nadie; no ir a la zaga a nadie (in en); **to be — in command** ser el segundo después del jefe, (fig) ser el segundo de a bordo; **will you have a — cup?** ¿quieres otra taza?; **you won't get a — chance** no tendrás otra oportunidad; **see fiddle** etc.
2 adv en segundo lugar; **to come —** (in race) ocupar el segundo puesto; **to go —, to travel —** (Rail) viajar en segunda.
3 n (a) (time) segundo m; **just a —!** ¡un momento!; **it won't take a —** es cosa de unos momentos; **at that very —** en ese mismo instante; **in a split —** en un instante, en un abrir y cerrar de ojos; **the operation is timed to a split —** la operación está concebida con la mayor precisión en cuanto al tiempo.
(b) (Mus) segunda f.
(c) (Univ) segunda clase f.
(d) (Boxing) segundo m, cuidador m; (in duel) padrino m.
(e) **to come in —** llegar el segundo, ocupar el segundo puesto; **to come a poor —** resultar ser muy inferior al que gana.
(f) **—s** (Comm) artículos mpl de segunda calidad, artículos mpl con algún desperfecto.
4 vt secundar, apoyar; ayudar; motion apoyar.
second [si'kɔnd] vt trasladar temporalmente (to a).
secondary ['sekəndəri] adj secundario.
second-best ['sekənd'best] **1** adj segundo; (el) mejor después del primero; **our — car** nuestro coche número dos.
2 adv: **to come off —** quedarse en segundo lugar.
3 n expediente m; sustituto m; **it's a —** es un sustituto, no es todo lo que hubiéramos deseado, sabemos que es inferior.
second-class ['sekənd'klɑːs] adj de segunda clase; inferior, más bien mediocre; **— citizens** ciudadanos mpl de segunda clase.
seconder ['sekəndə*] n el (la) que apoya una moción; **there was no —** nadie apoyó la moción.
second hand ['sekəndhænd] n (of watch) segundero m.
secondhand ['sekənd'hænd] adj de segunda mano, de lance; usado, no nuevo; **— bookseller** librero m de viejo; **— bookshop** librería f de viejo; **— clothes** ropa f usada; **— car** coche m de segunda mano; **— information** información f que viene indirectamente.
secondly ['sekəndli] adv en segundo lugar.
second-rate ['sekənd'reit] adj de segunda categoría; inferior, más bien mediocre; **some — writer** algún escritor de segunda categoría.

secrecy ['si:krəsi] *n* secreto *m*; reserva *f*, discreción *f*; **in** — en secreto; **in strict** — en el mayor secreto; **to swear someone to** — hacer que uno jure no revelar algo.

secret ['si:krit] **1** *adj* secreto; *information etc* secreto, confidencial; (*secretive*) reservado; (*hidden*) oculto, encubierto; — **agent** agente *m* de la policía secreta; — **drawer** secreto *m*; **to keep something** — tener algo secreto, no revelar algo; **it's all highly** — todo es de lo más secreto.

2 *n* secreto *m*; **open** — secreto *m* a voces; **in** — en secreto; clandestinamente; **to be in on the** — estar en el secreto; **there's no** — **about it** esto no tiene nada de secreto; **to keep a** — guardar un secreto, no revelar un secreto; **he can keep a** — es como una tumba; **to let someone into a** — revelar a uno un secreto; **shall I let you into a** —? ¿quieres que te revele un secreto?; **to make no** — **of something** no tratar de tener algo secreto; **he made no** — **that** . . . no trató de negar que . . .; **to tell someone something as a** — contar algo a uno como un secreto, decir algo a uno en confianza.

secretarial [,sekrə'təəriəl] *adj* de secretario; *college, course* de secretaria, comercial.

secretariat [,sekrə'təəriət] *n* secretaría *f*.

secretary ['sekrətri] *n* secretario *m*, a *f*; **private** — secretario *m* particular, secretaria *f* particular; **S— of State** (*Brit*) Ministro *m* (*for* de), (*US*) Ministro *m* de Asuntos Exteriores.

secretary-general ['sekrətri'dʒenərəl] *n* secretario *m* general.

secretaryship ['sekrətriʃip] *n* secretaría *f*, secretariado *m*.

secrete [si'kri:t] *vt* (*hide*) esconder, ocultar; (*Med*) secretar, segregar.

secretion [si'kri:ʃən] *n* escondimiento *m*, ocultación *f*; (*Med*) secreción *f*, segregación *f*.

secretive ['si:krətiv] *adj* reservado, callado; sigiloso; **to be** — **about something** hacer un secreto de algo, hacer algo con secreto.

secretively ['si:krətivli] *adv* calladamente; sigilosamente.

secretiveness ['si:krətivnis] *n* reserva *f*; sigilo *m*.

secretly ['si:kritli] *adv* secretamente, en secreto; a escondidas; **to be** — **pleased about something** alegrarse en el fondo de su corazón de algo.

sect [sekt] *n* secta *f*.

sectarian [sek'təəriən] **1** *adj* sectario. **2** *n* sectario *m*, a *f*.

sectarianism [sek'təəriənizəm] *n* sectarismo *m*.

section ['sekʃən] *n* sección *f*; parte *f*, porción *f*; (*of city*) barrio *m*; (*of country*) región *f*; (*of code, document, law etc*) artículo *m*; (*of pipeline, road etc*) tramo *m*; (*of opinion*) sector *m*; **conic** — sección *f* cónica; **longitudinal** — sección *f* longitudinal, corte *m* longitudinal; **vertical** — sección *f* vertical, corte *m* vertical; **passports** — sección *f* de pasaportes; **in all** —**s of the public** en todos los sectores del público.

sectional ['sekʃənl] *adj* seccional; relativo a una sección; regional, local; *furniture* combinado, desmontable, fabricado en secciones.

section mark ['sekʃənmɑːk] *n* párrafo *m*.

sector ['sektə*] *n* sector *m*; **private** — (*Comm*) sector *m* privado; **public** — (*Comm*) sector *m* público.

secular ['sekjulə*] *adj* secular, seglar.

secularization ['sekjuləraiˈzeiʃən] *n* secularización *f*.

secularize ['sekjuləraiz] *vt* secularizar.

secure [si'kjuə*] **1** *adj* (*safe, certain*) seguro; (*firm*) firme, fijo, estable; — **in the knowledge that** . . . sabiendo perfectamente que . . .; **to be** — **against**, **to be** — **from** estar asegurado contra, estar protegido contra; **to feel** — sentirse seguro; **to make a door** — cerrar firmemente una puerta; **to make a tile** — asegurar una teja.

2 *vt* (**a**) (*make firm*) asegurar, fijar, afianzar; cerrar.

(**b**) (*obtain*) obtener, conseguir; **to** — **the services of someone** obtener los servicios de uno; **I** —**d two fine specimens** obtuve dos bellos ejemplares; **he** —**d it for £900** lo adquirió por 900 libras.

securely [si'kjuəli] *adv* seguramente; firmemente, fijamente; **it is** — **fastened** está bien sujetado; **we are now** — **established** ahora estamos firmemente establecidos.

security [si'kjuəriti] **1** *n* (**a**) seguridad *f*; protección *f*; (*Fin: on loan*) fianza *f*, (*on small loan*) prenda *f*; (*person*) fiador *m*, ora *f*; **collective** — seguridad *f* colectiva; **social** — seguridad *f* social, seguro *m* social; **up to £100 without** — hasta 100 libras sin fianza; **to lend money on** — prestar dinero sobre

fianza; **to stand** — **for someone** (*Fin*) salir fiador de uno, (*fig*) salir por uno.

(**b**) **securities** (*Fin*) títulos *mpl*, valores *mpl*, obligaciones *fpl*.

2 *attr*: **S— Council** Consejo *m* de Seguridad.

sedan [si'dæn] *n* (*also* — **chair**) silla *f* de manos; (*US Aut*) sedán *m*.

sedate [si'deit] *adj* tranquilo, sosegado; serio.

sedately [si'deitli] *adv* tranquilamente, sosegadamente; seriamente.

sedateness [si'deitnis] *n* tranquilidad *f*, sosiego *m*; seriedad *f*.

sedation [si'deiʃən] *n* tratamiento *m* con calmantes.

sedative ['sedətiv] **1** *adj* sedante, calmante. **2** *n* sedante *m*, calmante *m*.

sedentary ['sedntri] *adj* sedentario.

sedge [sedʒ] *n* junco *m*, juncia *f*.

sediment ['sedimənt] *n* sedimento *m* (*also Geol*); poso *m*.

sedimentary [,sedi'mentəri] *adj* sedimentario.

sedimentation [,sedimen'teiʃən] *n* sedimentación *f*.

sedition [sə'diʃən] *n* sedición *f*.

seditious [sə'diʃəs] *adj* sedicioso.

seduce [si'djuːs] *vt* seducir; **to** — **someone from his duty** apartar a uno de su deber.

seducer [si'djuːsə*] *n* seductor *m*.

seduction [si'dʌkʃən] *n* seducción *f*.

seductive [si'dʌktiv] *adj* seductor.

seductively [si'dʌktivli] *adv* de modo seductor; en tono seductor.

sedulous ['sedjuləs] *adj* asiduo, diligente.

sedulously ['sedjuləsli] *adv* asiduamente, diligentemente.

see[1] [siː] (*irr*: *pret* **saw**, *ptp* **seen**) **1** *vt* (**a**) (*general sense*) ver; **let me** —, **let's** — a ver, vamos a ver; **I'll go and** — voy a ver; "— **page 8**" "véase la página 8"; **he's** —**n a lot of the world** ha visto mucho mundo; **she'll not** — **40 again** no volverá a tener 40 años; **I can** — **to read** veo bastante bien para poder leerlo; **as far as the eye can** — hasta donde alcanza la vista; **to** — **someone do something** ver a uno hacer algo; **I saw him coming** lo vi venir; **he was** —**n to fall** se le vio caer; **I saw it done in 1968** lo vi hacer en 1968; **I'll** — **him damned first** antes le veré colgado; **there was not a house to be** —**n** no se veía ni una sola casa; **this dress is not fit to be** —**n** este vestido es indigno de que lo vea la gente; **he's not fit to be** —**n in public** no se le puede presentar a los ojos del público.

(**b**) (*accompany*) acompañar; **to** — **someone to the door** acompañar a uno a la puerta; **to** — **a girl home** acompañar a una chica a su casa; **may I** — **you home?** ¿quieres que te acompañe?; **he was so drunk we had to** — **him to bed** estaba tan borracho que tuvimos que llevarle a la cama.

(**c**) (*understand*) comprender, entender, ver; **I** — . . . **lo veo** . . .; **I** —**!** ¡ya!, ¡ya comprendo!; **it's all over,** —**?** (*fam*) se acabó, ¿comprendes?; **he's dead, don't you** —**?** está muerto, ¿me entiendes?; **I don't** — **why** no veo por qué, no comprendo por qué; **I fail to** — **how** no comprendo cómo; **as far as I can** — según mi modo de entender las cosas; a mi ver; **this is how I** — **it** éste es mi modo de entenderlo, yo lo entiendo así; **the Russians** — **it differently** los rusos lo miran desde otro punto de vista, el criterio de los rusos es distinto; **I don't** — **you as a future minister** no puedo imaginarte como ministro; **I don't** — **it** (*fig*) no creo que sea posible; *see* **fit**.

(**d**) (*look, perceive*) mirar; observar; percibir; **now** — **here!** ¡mírel; **so I** — lo veo, lo estoy viendo; **I saw only too clearly that** . . . percibí con toda claridad que . . .; — **for yourself** véalo Vd; **I** — **in the paper that** . . . veo en el periódico que . . .; **did you** — **that Queen Anne is dead?** ¿has oído que ha muerto la reina Ana?; **I** — **nothing wrong in it** no le encuentro nada digno de represión; **I don't know what she** —**s in him** no sé lo que ella le encuentra.

(**e**) (*ensure*) **to** — **(to it) that** . . . procurar que + *subj*, asegurar que + *subj*; — **that he has all he needs** cuide que tenga todo lo que necesita; — **that it does not happen again** y que no vuelva a ocurrir; — **that you have it ready for Monday** procure tenerlo listo para el lunes; **to** — **that something is done** velar por que algo se haga.

(**f**) (*visit, frequent*) ver, visitar; **to** — **the doctor** consultar al médico; **I want to** — **you about my daughter** quiero hablar con Vd acerca de mi hija; **what did he want to** — **you about?** ¿qué asunto quería discutir con Vd?, ¿qué motivo tuvo su visita?; **we don't** — **much of them nowadays** ahora les vemos bastante poco; **we shall be** —ing **them for dinner** vamos a cenar con ellos; **to call** (or **go) and** — **someone** ir a visitar a uno; **the minister saw the Queen yesterday** el ministro se entrevistó con la Reina ayer; **I'm afraid I can't** — **you to-morrow** lamento no poder verle mañana; — **you soon!**, — **you later!** ¡hasta pronto!; — **you on Sunday!** ¡hasta el domingo!

(g) (with adv or prep) **to** — **the New Year in** celebrar el Año Nuevo; **to** — **someone off at the station** ir a despedirse de uno en la estación; **the policeman saw him off** el policía la acompañó a la puerta (etc), el policía le dijo que se fuera; **to** — **someone out** acompañar a uno a la puerta; **to** — **a play out** quedarse hasta el fin de una comedia, permanecer sentado hasta que termine una comedia; **to** — **someone through** ayudar a uno a salir de un apuro, ayudar a uno en un trance difícil; **to** — **a deal through** llevar a cabo un negocio; **don't worry, we'll** — **it through** no te preocupes, nosotros lo haremos todo.

2 vi: **to** — **about something** atender a algo; encargarse de algo; **I'll** — **about it** lo haré, me encargo de eso; (non-committally) lo pensaré; **he came to** — **about our television set** vino a ver nuestro televisor; vino a reparar nuestro televisor; **to** — **into something** investigar algo, examinar algo; **to** — **over a factory** visitar una fábrica; **to** — **through someone** calar a uno, conocer el juego de uno; **to** — **through a mystery** penetrar en un misterio; **that trick is easily** —n **through** ese truco se explica fácilmente; **to** — **to something** atender a algo; encargarse de algo; (repair) reparar, componer; **he** —s **to everything** se encarga de todo, lo hace todo; **the rats saw to that** las ratas se encargaron de eso; **it must be** —n **to at once** hay que investigar esto en seguida; **to** — **to it that ...** procurar que + subj, asegurar que + subj.

see² [si:] n sede f; **Holy S**— Santa Sede f.

seed [si:d] **1** n (Bot; for sowing) semilla f, simiente f; (within fruit) pepita f; (grain) grano m; (sperm) simiente f; (offspring) descendencia f; (fig, of idea etc) germen m; **to go to** —, **to run to** — granar, dar en grana, (fig) echarse a perder; ir a menos; **to sow** —s **of doubt in someone's mind** hacer que uno empiece a tener dudas.
2 vt land sembrar (with de); (extract —s from) despepitar; (Sport) preseleccionar.
3 vi granar, dar en grana; dejar caer semillas.

seedbed ['si:dbed] n semillero m.
seedcake ['si:dkeik] n torta f de semillas aromáticas.
seed corn ['si:dkɔːn] n trigo m de siembra.
seed drill ['si:ddril] n sembradora f.
seedling ['si:dliŋ] n planta f de semillero; planta f joven, plantón m.
seed pearl ['si:dpəːl] n aljófar m.
seed potato ['si:dpə,teitəu] n patata f de siembra.
seedsman ['si:dzmən] n, pl —**men** [mən] vendedor m de semillas.
seedtime ['si:dtaim] n siembra f.
seedy ['si:di] adj (Med) enfermo, indispuesto; ojeroso; appearance desaseado; clothing raído; place pobre, sórdido.
seeing ['si:iŋ] **1** n vista f, visión f; — **is believing** ver es creer; **a film worth** — una película que vale la pena de verse.
2 conj: — **that** visto que, puesto que.
seek [si:k] (irr: pret and ptp **sought**) **1** vt buscar; post pretender, solicitar; honour ambicionar; (search) registrar, recorrer buscando; **to** —/ **death** buscar la muerte; **to** — **shelter** buscar dónde cobijarse; **to** — **advice from someone** pedir consejos a uno; **it is much sought after** se le busca por todas partes; tiene mucha demanda; **the reason is not far to** — no es difícil indicar la causa; **he has been sought in many countries** se le ha buscado en muchos países.
2 vi buscar; **to** — **after, to** — **for** buscar; **to** — **to** + infin intentar + infin, procurar + infin; esforzarse por + infin.
seeker ['si:kə*] n buscador m, ora f.
seem [si:m] vi parecer; **so it** —s así parece; **how does it** — **to you?** ¿qué le parece?; **it** —s **that ...** parece que ...; **it does not** — **that ...** no parece que + subj; **he** —s **honest** parece honrado; **he** —ed **absorbed in ...** parecía estar absorto en ...; **she** —s **not to want to go** parece que no quiere ir; **I** — **to have heard that before** me parece que ya me contaron eso antes; **what** —s **to be the trouble?** ¿pasa algo?
seeming ['si:miŋ] **1** adj aparente. **2** n apariencia f; **to all** — según todas las apariencias.

seemingly ['si:miŋli] adv aparentemente, según parece; **it is** — **finished** parece que está terminado.
seemliness ['si:mlinis] n decoro m, decencia f, corrección f.
seemly ['si:mli] adj decoroso, decente, correcto.
seen [si:n] ptp of **see¹**.
seep [si:p] vi filtrarse, rezumarse.
seepage ['si:pidʒ] n filtración f.
seer [siə*] n vidente mf, profeta mf.
seersucker ['siə,sʌkə*] n sirsaca f.
seesaw ['si:sɔ:] **1** n balancín m, columpio m de tabla; (fig) vaivén m. **2** adj movement de vaivén, oscilante. **3** vi columpiarse; (fig) oscilar.
seethe [si:ð] vi hervir; **to** — **with** hervir de; **he's seething** está furioso; **to** — **with anger** indignarse muchísimo, estar furioso.
see-through ['si:θru:] adj dress diáfano, transparente.
segment ['segmənt] n segmento m.
segregate ['segrigeit] vt segregar, separar (from de); **to be** —d **from** estar separado de.
segregation [,segri'geiʃən] n segregación f, separación f; (esp) separación f racial.
segregationist [,segri'geiʃnist] n segregacionista mf.
Seine [sein] Sena m.
seine [sein] n jábega f.
seismic ['saizmik] adj sísmico.
seismograph ['saizməgrɑ:f] n sismógrafo m.
seismography [saiz'mɔgrəfi] n sismografía f.
seismology [saiz'mɔlədʒi] n sismología f.
seize [si:z] **1** vt (clutch) agarrar, asir, coger; (Law) person detener, prender, property embargar, secuestrar; contraband etc incautarse de; territory etc apoderarse de; opportunity aprovechar sin vacilar; **to** — **someone by the arm** asir a uno por el brazo; **to be** —d **with fear** sobrecogerse, ser preso del miedo; **he was** —d **with a desire to** + infin le entró un súbito deseo de + infin.
2 vi: **to** — **on** fijarse en; pretext etc valerse de; **to** — **up** (Mech) agarrotarse.
seizure ['si:ʒə*] n asimiento m; detención f; prendimiento m; embargo m, secuestro m; incautación f; (Med) ataque m; **the** — **of Slobodia** el acto de apoderarse de Eslobodia; **to have a** — (Med) sufrir un ataque (esp cardíaco).
seldom ['seldəm] adv rara vez, raramente.
select [si'lekt] **1** vt escoger, elegir; (Sport) seleccionar.
2 adj selecto, escogido; exclusivista; tobacco etc fino; **a very** — **neighbourhood** un barrio de muy buen tono; **a** — **group of people** un grupo selecto de personas.
selection [si'lekʃən] n selección f; elección f; (Comm) surtido m; **"**—s **from Rossini"** "selecciones fpl de Rossini"; **"**—s **from Cervantes"** "páginas fpl escogidas de Cervantes"; —s **for the big race** pronósticos mpl para la carrera principal; **natural** — selección f natural; **one has to make a** — hay que escoger, hay que tomar unos y dejar otros.
selective [si'lektiv] adj selectivo; **one has to be** — hay que escoger, hay que tomar unos y dejar otros.
selectivity [silek'tiviti] n selectividad f.
selector [si'lektə*] n (Tech) selector m; (person) seleccionador m.
self [self] **1** reflexive pron se (etc); (after prep) sí mismo (etc); (Comm, hum, or fam) = **myself** etc; **a room reserved for wife and** — una habitación reservada para mi esposa y yo.
2 adj (esp Bot) unicolor.
3 n, pl **selves** [selvz] uno mismo, una misma; **the** — el yo; **my better** — mi mejor parte; **my former** — mi ser anterior; **one's other** — su otro yo; **if your good** — **could possibly ...** si Vd tuviera tanta amabilidad como para ...; **my humble** — este servidor; **he's quite his old** — **again** se ha repuesto completamente; **he thinks of nothing but** — no piensa sino en sí mismo.
self- [self] in compounds: auto ...; ... de sí mismo.
self-abasement ['selfə'beismənt] n rebajamiento m de sí mismo, autodegradación f.
self-abuse ['selfə'bju:s] n (euph) masturbación f.
self-acting ['self'æktiŋ] adj automático.
self-addressed ['selfə'drest] adj: — **envelope** sobre m con el nombre y dirección de uno mismo.
self-adhesive ['selfəd'hi:ziv] adj autoadhesivo.
self-advertisement ['selfəd'və:tismənt] n auto-bombo m.
self-apparent ['selfə'pærənt] adj evidente, patente.
self-appointed ['selfə'pɔintid] adj que se ha nombrado a sí mismo.
self-assertion ['selfə'sə:ʃən] n presunción f; agresividad f.
self-assertive ['selfə'sə:tiv] adj presumido; agresivo.

self-assurance ['selfə'ʃuərəns] n confianza f en sí mismo.

self-assured ['selfə'ʃuəd] adj seguro de sí mismo.

self-centred, (US) — centered ['self'sentəd] adj egocéntrico.

self-coloured, (US) — colored ['self'kʌləd] adj de color uniforme; de color natural.

self-command ['selfkə'mɑːnd] n dominio m sobre sí mismo.

self-complacent ['selfkəm'pleisənt] adj satisfecho de sí mismo.

self-composed ['selfkəm'pəuzd] adj ecuánime, sereno.

self-composure ['selfkəm'pəuʒə*] n ecuanimidad f, serenidad f.

self-conceit ['selfkən'siːt] n presunción f, vanidad f, engreimiento m.

self-conceited ['selfkən'siːtid] adj presumido, vanidoso, engreído.

self-confidence ['self'kɔnfidəns] n confianza f en sí mismo.

self-confident ['self'kɔnfidənt] adj seguro de sí mismo, lleno de confianza en sí mismo.

self-conscious ['self'kɔnʃəs] adj cohibido, tímido.

self-consciousness ['self'kɔnʃəsnis] n timidez f.

self-contained ['selfkən'teind] adj independiente; que tiene sus propios recursos, que no necesita ayuda de afuera; flat, apartment completo en sí mismo, con entrada particular; person independiente; reservado, poco comunicativo.

self-contradiction ['self,kɔntrə'dikʃən] n proposición f que lleva implícita una contradicción.

self-contradictory ['self,kɔntrə'diktəri] adj que se contradice a sí mismo, que lleva implícita una contradicción.

self-control ['selfkən'trəul] n autodominio m, dominio m sobre sí mismo, control m de sí mismo; **to exercise one's —** contenerse, dominarse; **to lose one's —** perder la calma, ponerse nervioso.

self-controlled ['selfkən'trəuld] adj ecuánime, sereno.

self-criticism ['self'kritisizəm] n autocrítica f.

self-deception ['selfdi'sepʃən] n engaño m de sí mismo; **this is mere —** son ilusiones, esto es engañarse a sí mismo.

self-defeating ['selfdi'fiːtiŋ] adj contraproducente.

self-defence ['selfdi'fens] n defensa f propia; **to act in —** obrar en defensa propia.

self-denial ['selfdi'naiəl] n abnegación f.

self-denying ['selfdi'naiiŋ] adj abnegado.

self-destruction ['selfdis'trakʃən] n suicidio m.

self-determination ['selfdi,təːmi'neiʃən] n autodeterminación f.

self-discipline ['self'disiplin] n autodisciplina f.

self-educated ['self'edjukeitid] adj autodidacta.

self-effacement ['selfi'feismənt] n modestia f, humildad f.

self-effacing ['selfi'feisiŋ] adj modesto, humilde.

self-employed ['selfim'plɔid] adj que trabaja por cuenta propia.

self-esteem ['selfis'tiːm] n amor m propio.

self-evident ['self'evidənt] adj evidente, patente.

self-explanatory ['selfiks'plænitəri] adj que se explica por sí mismo.

self-expression ['selfiks'preʃən] n autoexpresión f.

self-filling ['self'filiŋ] adj de relleno automático.

self-fulfilling ['selfful'filiŋ] adj: — prophecy profecía f que por su propia naturaleza contribuye a cumplirse.

self-fulfilment ['selfful'filmənt] n realización f de los más íntimos deseos de uno, realización f completa de la potencialidad de uno.

self-governing ['self'gavəniŋ] adj autónomo.

self-government ['self'gavnmənt] n autonomía f, autogobierno m.

self-help ['self'help] n ayuda f propia.

self-importance ['selfim'pɔːtəns] n presunción f, vanidad f, engreimiento m.

self-important ['selfim'pɔːtənt] adj presumido, vanidoso, engreído.

self-imposed ['selfim'pəuzd] adj punishment etc que uno se impone a sí mismo.

self-incriminating ['selfin'krimineitiŋ] adj autoacusador, que se acusa a sí mismo.

self-indulgence ['selfin'daldʒəns] n falta f de moderación, excesos mpl (en el comer etc).

self-indulgent ['selfin'daldʒənt] adj inmoderado, que se permite excesos (en el comer etc).

self-inflicted ['selfin'fliktid] adj wound que uno se infiere a sí mismo.

self-interest ['self'intrist] n egoísmo m.

selfish ['selfiʃ] adj egoísta; interesado.

selfishly ['selfiʃli] adv con egoísmo, de modo egoísta.

selfishness ['selfiʃnis] n egoísmo m.

self-knowledge ['self'nɔlidʒ] n conocimiento m de sí mismo.

selfless ['selflis] adj desinteresado.

selflessly ['selflisli] adv desinteresadamente.

selflessness ['selflisnis] n desinterés m.

self-locking ['self'lɔkiŋ] adj de cierre automático.

self-love ['self'lav] n egoísmo m, egolatría f.

self-made ['self'meid] adj: — man hombre m que ha llegado a su posición actual por sus propios esfuerzos, hijo m de sus propias obras.

self-opinionated ['selfə'pinjəneitid] adj terco.

self-pity ['self'piti] n compasión f de sí mismo.

self-pollination ['self,pɔli'neiʃən] n autopolinización f.

self-portrait ['self'pɔːtrit] n autorretrato m.

self-possessed ['selfpə'zest] adj sereno, dueño de sí mismo.

self-possession ['selfpə'zeʃən] n serenidad f, dominio m sobre sí mismo.

self-praise ['self'preiz] n autoadulación f, autobombo m.

self-preservation ['self,prezə'veiʃən] n propia conservación f.

self-propelled ['selfprə'peld] adj autopropulsado, automotor (f: automotriz).

self-regulating ['self'regjuleitiŋ] adj de regulación automática.

self-reliance ['selfri'laiəns] n confianza f en sí mismo; independencia f.

self-reliant ['selfri'laiənt] adj seguro de sí mismo; independiente.

self-reproach ['selfri'prəutʃ] n remordimiento m.

self-respect ['selfris'pekt] n amor m propio, dignidad f.

self-respecting ['selfris'pektiŋ] adj que tiene amor propio, consciente de su dignidad personal.

self-restraint ['selfris'treint] n see self-control.

self-righteous ['self'raitʃəs] adj santurrón.

self-sacrifice ['self'sækrifais] n (act) sacrificio m de sí mismo; (spirit) abnegación f.

self-sacrificing ['self'sækrifaisiŋ] adj abnegado.

selfsame ['selfseim] adj mismo, mismísimo.

self-satisfaction ['self,sætis'fækʃən] n satisfacción f de sí mismo; suficiencia f.

self-satisfied ['self'sætisfaid] adj satisfecho de sí mismo, pagado de sí mismo; suficiente.

self-sealing ['self'siːliŋ] adj tank que tapa automáticamente cualquier abertura.

self-seeking ['self'siːkiŋ] **1** adj egoísta. **2** n egoísmo m.

self-service ['self'səːvis] adj: — restaurant autoservicio m.

self-starter ['self'stɑːtə*] n (Aut) arranque m automático.

self-styled ['self'staild] adj supuesto, sediente.

self-sufficiency ['selfsə'fiʃənsi] n independencia f; (economic) autosuficiencia f; (of person) confianza f en sí mismo.

self-sufficient ['selfsə'fiʃənt] adj independiente; (economically) autosuficiente; person seguro de sí mismo.

self-supporting ['selfsə'pɔːtiŋ] adj independiente; que vive de sus propios recursos (económicos); que vive de su propio trabajo; **you can marry her when you are —** te puedes casar con ella cuando ganes un sueldo adecuado.

self-taught ['self'tɔːt] adj autodidacta.

self-willed ['self'wild] adj terco, voluntarioso.

self-winding ['self'waindiŋ] adj: — watch reloj m de cuerda automática.

sell [sel] (irr: pret and ptp **sold**) **1** vt (a) vender (at a, for por); "car to —" "se vende coche"; "to be sold" "se vende"; **to — one's life dearly** vender cara la vida; **I was sold this in Valencia** esto me lo vendieron en Valencia; **to — something back to someone** revender algo a uno; **to — someone for a slave, to — someone into slavery** vender a uno como esclavo; **to — off, to — out** vender (todas las existencias de); liquidar, saldar; **we are sold out of bananas** hemos agotado las existencias de plátanos; **stocks of umbrellas are sold out** las existencias de paraguas están agotadas; see auction, loss etc.

(b) (fig: put over) comunicar, hacer aceptar; **if we can — coexistence to Ruritania** si podemos hacer aceptar en Ruritania la idea de la coexistencia; **he doesn't manage to — his personality** no consigue comunicar su personalidad.

(c) (fig: betray) vender, traicionar; **sold again!** ¡la estafa de siempre!; **you've been sold** le han dado gato por liebre.

(d) to be sold on estar cautivado por; **I'm not exactly sold on the idea** estoy lejos de dejarme cautivar por la idea.

2 *vi* **(a)** venderse (*at* a, *for* por); estar de venta; **it —s well** tiene buena venta, tiene una salida fácil, tiene mucha demanda; **that line doesn't —** ese género no tiene demanda; **to — out, to — up** venderlo todo, vender todas las existencias; realizar.

(b) (*fig*) ser aceptable; **the idea didn't —** la idea no resultó aceptable.

(c) to — out (*fig*) abandonar, renunciar; **to — out to the Russians** abandonar y dejar el paso libre a los rusos.

3 *vr*: **to — oneself** venderse; (*fig*) comunicar con el público, comunicar su personalidad.

4 *n* **(a)** (*fam*) decepción *f*; engaño *m*, estafa *f*; **what a —!** ¡cómo nos han decepcionado!; ¡todo ha sido engaño!

(b) (*Comm*) **to be a hard —** tener una salida difícil; **to be a soft —** tener una salida fácil.

seller ['selə*] *n* (*person who sells*) vendedor *m*, ora *f*; (*dealer*) comerciante *m* (*of* en); **good —** (*Comm*) artículo *m* que tiene mucha demanda; **—'s market** mercado *m* de signo favorable al vendedor.

selling price ['seliŋprais] *n* precio *m* de venta.

sellout ['selaut] *n* **(a)** (*betrayal*) traición *f*; abandono *m*, renuncia *f*. **(b)** (*Theat, Sport etc*) lleno *m*, función *f* para la que se venden todas las localidades.

seltzer (water) ['seltsə*,(wɔːtə*)] *n* agua *f* de seltz.

selvage, selvedge ['selvidʒ] *n* orillo *m*, borde *m*.

selves [selvz] *pl of* **self**.

semantic [si'mæntik] *adj* semántico.

semantics [si'mæntiks] *n* semántica *f*.

semaphore ['seməfɔː*] **1** *n* semáforo *m*. **2** *vt* comunicar por semáforo.

semblance ['sembləns] *n* apariencia *f*; **without a — of regret** sin mostrar remordimiento; **without a — of fear** sin dar señal alguna de miedo; **to put on a — of gaiety** procurar parecer alegre.

semen ['siːmən] *n* semen *m*.

semester [si'mestə*] *n* semestre *m*.

semi . . . ['semi] semi . . .; medio . . .

semibasement ['semi'beismənt] *n* semisótano *m*.

semibreve ['semibriːv] *n* semibreve *f*.

semicircle ['semi,səːkl] *n* semicírculo *m*.

semicircular ['semi'səːkjulə*] *adj* semicircular; *archway* de medio punto.

semicolon ['semi'kəulən] *n* punto *m* y coma.

semiconscious ['semi'kɔnʃəs] *adj* semiconsciente.

semiconsonant ['semi'kɔnsənənt] *n* semiconsonante *f*.

semidarkness ['semi'dɑːknis] *n*: **in the —** en la casi oscuridad.

semidetached ['semidi'tætʃt] *adj* semiseparado; **a pair of — houses** una casa doble.

semifinal ['semi'fainl] *n* semifinal *f*.

semifinalist ['semi'fainəlist] *n* semifinalista *mf*.

seminal ['seminl] *adj* seminal.

seminar ['seminɑː*] *n* (*Univ: class*) seminario *m*, clase *f* de discusión; (*group*) grupo *m* de investigadores; (*conference*) congreso *m*; reunión *f*; (*institute*) instituto *m*.

seminarist ['seminərist] *n* seminarista *m*.

seminary ['seminəri] *n* seminario *m*.

semiofficial ['semiə'fiʃl] *adj* semioficial.

semiprecious ['semi,preʃəs] *adj* semiprecioso.

semiquaver ['semikweivə*] *n* semicorchea *f*.

semiskilled ['semi'skild] *adj* semiexperto, semi-cualificado.

Semite ['siːmait] *n* semita *mf*.

Semitic [si'mitik] *adj* semítico.

semitone ['semitəun] *n* semitono *m*.

semivowel ['semi'vauəl] *n* semivocal *f*.

semolina [,semə'liːnə] *n* sémola *f*.

sempiternal [,sempi'təːnl] *adj* sempiterno.

sempstress ['sempstris] *n* costurera *f*.

senate ['senit] *n* senado *m*; (*Univ: approx*) claustro *m*; **the S—** (*US*) el Senado.

senator ['senitə*] *n* senador *m*.

senatorial [,senə'tɔːriəl] *adj* senatorial.

send [send] (*irr: pret and ptp* **sent**) **1** *vt* **(a)** (*general sense*) enviar, mandar; despachar; remitir; *telegram* poner; (*Radio*) *programme* transmitir; **the gods — it as a punishment** los dioses nos lo envían como castigo; **to — a child to school** poner a un niño en la escuela; **in Britain children are sent to school at 5** en Gran Bretaña los niños van a la escuela a los 5 años; **some children are sent to school without breakfast** hay niños que van a la escuela sin desayunar; **I wrote the letter but didn't — it** escribí la carta pero no la eché al correo;

to — someone for something enviar a uno a buscar algo; enviar a uno a comprar algo.

(b) (*propel*) *ball etc* lanzar; *arrow* enviar, lanzar, arrojar; **he sent everything flying** lo echó todo a rodar; **the blow sent him sprawling** el golpe le hizo caer redondo; *see* **shiver** *etc*.

(c) (*with adj*) hacer, volver, poner; **it —s the wool green** vuelve la lana verde; **it's enough to — you barmy** (*sl*) es para volverse loco.

(d) (*fam*) entusiasmar, llenar de emoción, embelesar; **that tune —s me** esa melodía me apasiona; **he —s me** me vuelve loca; **it doesn't — me** me trae sin cuidado.

(e) (*with adv or prep*) **to — away** despachar; (*by post etc*) enviar fuera; (*dismiss*) despedir; **to — back** devolver; *person* hacer volver; **to — down** hacer bajar; (*Univ*) expulsar; *criminal* encarcelar; **he was sent down for 6 months** le condenaron a 6 meses de prisión; **to — forth** *smoke etc* arrojar; *sparks* lanzar; **to — forth into the world** enviar a uno a vivir en el mundo; **to — in** *person* hacer entrar; hacer pasar; *bill, name, resignation* presentar; **— him in!** ¡que pase!; **to — off** *goods* despachar, expedir; (*by post*) enviar por correo, echar al correo; *player* expulsar; **to — on** *letter* hacer seguir; *application etc* dar curso a; *instructions* dar, transmitir; **to — out** *smoke etc* arrojar, despedir; *signal, programme* emitir; *invitations* mandar; *shoot* echar; **to — round** *letter etc* hacer circular; distribuir; **to — someone round to the pub** enviar a uno a la taberna; **I'll — the car round at 8** envío el coche a buscarle a las 8; **to — up** hacer subir; *one's name etc* enviar, presentar; *balloon* lanzar; *price, temperature* aumentar, hacer subir; (*parody*) parodiar, satirizar; **— him up!** ¡que suba!; **please — up two cups of tea** por favor, que me suban dos tazas de té.

2 *vi*: **if you don't —** si no me lo dices, si no me lo haces saber; **she sent to say that . . .** envió un recado diciendo que . . .; **to — away for spares** encargar unos repuestos por correo; **we shall have to — away for it** tendremos que pedirlo por correo; **to — for someone** enviar por uno; enviar a uno a buscar algo; **to — for the doctor** llamar al médico; **a doctor was sent for** se llamó a un médico; **she sent for her glasses** requirió sus gafas.

sender ['sendə*] *n* remitente *mf*; (*Elec*) transmisor *m*.

send-off ['sendɔf] *n* (*farewell*) despedida *f*; (*start*) principio *m*; **to give a project a good —** inaugurar felizmente un proyecto, hacer que un proyecto comience felizmente.

send-up ['sendʌp] *n* parodia *f*, sátira *f*.

Seneca ['senikə] *m* Séneca.

Senegal [,seni'gɔːl] el Senegal.

Senegalese [,senigə'liːz] **1** *adj* senegalés. **2** *n* senegalés *m*, esa *f*.

senile ['siːnail] *adj* senil; **to get —** (*Med*) padecer debilidad senil.

senility [si'niliti] *n* senilidad *f*; (*Med*) debilidad *f* senil.

senior ['siːniə*] **1** *adj* (*in age*) mayor (de edad), más viejo; (*on a staff*) más antiguo (*to* que); *position, rank* superior, de categoría superior; *section* (*in competition etc*) para mayores; *partner* más antiguo, principal; **Joe Bloggs, S—** Joe Bloggs, padre; **he is — to me** (*in age*) tiene más años que yo, es más viejo que yo, (*in rank*) tiene categoría superior a la mía.

2 *n* mayor *mf*; (*in group*) miembro *m* más antiguo; decano *m*; (*in company etc*) socio *m* más antiguo; (*Univ*) alumno *m* del último año, alumna *f* del último año; **he is my —** (*in age*) tiene más años que yo, es más viejo que yo, (*in rank*) tiene categoría superior a la mía; **he is 2 years my —, he is my — by 2 years** tiene 2 años más que yo, él me lleva 2 años.

seniority [,siːni'ɔriti] *n* antigüedad *f*.

senna ['senə] *n* sena *f*.

sensation [sen'seiʃn] *n* sensación *f*; **to be a —, to cause a —, to create a —** causar sensación; **it was a — in New York** en Nueva York causó sensación; **it's a —!** ¡es formidable!

sensational [sen'seiʃənl] *adj* sensacional.

sensationalism [sen'seiʃnəlizəm] *n* sensacionalismo *m*.

sense [sens] **1** *n* **(a)** (*bodily*) sentido *m*; **the 5 —s** los 5 sentidos; **— of hearing** oído *m*; **— of sight** vista *f*; **— of smell** olfato *m*; **— of taste** gusto *m*; **— of touch** tacto *m*; **to have a keen — of smell** tener buen olfato; **sixth —** sexto sentido *m*.

(b) **—s** (*right mind*) juicio *m*; **any man in his —s** cualquier hombre sensato; **to be out of one's —s** haber perdido el juicio, no estar en sus cabales; **to bring someone to his —s** obligar a uno a sentar la cabeza, (*Med*) hacer a uno volver en sí; **to come**

to one's —s sentar la cabeza, (Med) volver en sí; **to take leave of one's —s** perder el juicio; **have you taken leave of your —s?** ¿estás loco?, ¿has perdido el juicio?

(c) (good —) buen sentido m, juicio m; inteligencia f; **common —, good —, sound —** sentido m común; **a man of —** un hombre sensato, un hombre juicioso; **there is no —** in that eso no sirve para nada, eso es inútil; **there is no —** in + ger es inútil + infin; **what is the — of** + ger? ¿de qué sirve + infin?; **he had the — to call the doctor** tuvo bastante inteligencia como para llamar al médico; **didn't you have the — to shout?** ¿no se te ocurrió gritar?; **it doesn't make —** no tiene sentido; **it doesn't make — to me** para mí no tiene sentido; **can you make any — of it?** ¿has logrado descifrar el misterio?; **to make someone see —** hacer que uno entre en razón; **to talk —** hablar con juicio, hablar razonablemente; **now you're talking —** esto es más razonable.

(d) (feeling) sensación f; **a — of pleasure** una sensación de placer; **the picture conveys a — of occasion** el cuadro comunica una sensación del gran acontecimiento; **to labour under a — of injustice** creer que uno ha sido tratado injustamente.

(e) (instinct, insight) sentido m; **— of colour** sentido m del color; **— of humour** sentido m del humor; **she lacks all — of humour** no tiene sentido del humor en absoluto; **— of proportion** sentido m de la medida; **business —** aptitud f para los negocios.

(f) (sentiment) opinión f; **to take the — of the meeting** interpretar la opinión colectiva de la reunión.

(g) (meaning) sentido m, significado m; acepción f; significación f; **in a —** hasta cierto punto; **in the broad —** en el sentido amplio; **in the full — of that word** en toda la extensión de la palabra; **in the strict —** en el sentido estricto; **in what — do you use the word?** ¿qué significado le das a la palabra?; **it has various —s** tiene diversas acepciones; **there are —s in which that may be true** desde algunos puntos de vista eso puede ser cierto; **he's an amateur in the best —** es un aficionado en el buen sentido de la palabra.

2 vt sentir, percibir; **to — that . . .** percibir que . . ., darse cuenta de que . . ., formarse la impresión de que . . .

senseless ['senslis] adj estúpido, insensato; (Med) sin sentido, sin conocimiento; **to fall —** caer sin sentido; **to knock someone —** derribar a uno y dejarle sin sentido.

senselessly ['senslisli] adv estúpidamente, insensatamente.

senselessness ['senslisnis] n insensatez f.

sense organ ['sens͵ɔ:gən] n órgano m sensorio.

sensibility [͵sensi'biliti] n sensibilidad f (to a); **sensibilities** delicadeza f, sentimientos mpl delicados.

sensible ['sensəbl] adj **(a)** (having good sense) juicioso, sensato; prudente, discreto; inteligente; **he's a — sort** es una persona sensata, es una persona de buen criterio; **try to be — about it** procura ser razonable.

(b) (reasonable) act, decision etc prudente; razonable, lógico; reply, taste acertado; clothing etc práctico; **that's a — thing to do** eso me parece razonable; **the — course would be to** + infin lo más prudente sería + infin; **that is very — of you** en eso haces muy bien, me parece muy lógico.

(c) (appreciable) apreciable, perceptible.

(d) (aware) **to be — of** ser consciente de, darse cuenta de; **I am — of the honour you do me** agradezco el honor que se me hace.

sensibleness ['sensəblnis] n juicio m, sensatez f; prudencia f, discreción f; inteligencia f; lo razonable, lógica f; lo práctico.

sensibly ['sensəbli] adv sensatamente; prudentemente; discretamente; inteligentemente; razonablemente; lógicamente; acertadamente; **she acted very —** obró muy prudentemente; **he — answered that . . .** contestó acertadamente que . . .; **try to behave —** procura ser más formal.

sensitive ['sensitiv] adj (impressionable) impresionable, susceptible, sensible, delicado; (touchy) susceptible; (Phot: paper etc) sensibilizado; (of instruments etc) delicado; (relating to the senses) sensitivo, sensorio; **to be — to** ser sensible a; **to be — about one's hair** preocuparse mucho por su pelo, tener vergüenza de su pelo, no sentirse cómodo por lo del pelo; **you're too — about your suit** la gente no presta tanta atención a tu traje como tú te crees.

sensitiveness ['sensitivnis] n, **sensitivity** [͵sensi'tiviti] n lo impresionable, susceptibilidad f; delicadeza f; sensibilidad f (to a).

sensitize ['sensitaiz] vt sensibilizar.

sensitized ['sensitaizd] adj sensibilizado.

sensory ['sensəri] adj sensorio.

sensual ['sensjuəl] adj sensual.

sensualism ['sensjuəlizəm] n sensualismo m.

sensualist ['sensjuəlist] n sensualista mf.

sensuality [͵sensju'æliti] n sensualidad f.

sensuous ['sensjuəs] adj sensual, sensorio.

sensuousness ['sensjuəsnis] n sensualidad f.

sent [sent] pret and ptp of **send.**

sentence ['sentəns] **1** n **(a)** (Gram) frase f; oración f; **compound —** oración f compuesta; **simple —** oración f simple; **he writes very long —s** escribe frases larguísimas.

(b) (Law) sentencia f, fallo m; (with expression of time etc) condena f; **death —** condena f a la pena de muerte; **to be under — of death** estar condenado a muerte; **life —** condena f a perpetuidad, condena f de reclusión perpetua; **the judge gave him a 6-month —** el juez le condenó a 6 meses de prisión; **he got a 5-year —** se le condenó a 5 años de prisión; **to pass —** pronunciar sentencia, fallar (on someone en el proceso de uno); **to serve one's —** cumplir su condena.

2 vt condenar (to a).

sententious [sen'tenʃəs] adj sentencioso.

sententiously [sen'tenʃəsli] adv sentenciosamente.

sententiousness [sen'tenʃəsnis] n sentenciosidad f, estilo m sentencioso.

sentient ['senʃənt] adj sensitivo, sensible.

sentiment ['sentimənt] n sentimiento m; (opinion) opinión f, sentir m; (sentimentality) sentimentalismo m, sensiblería f; **those are my —s too** ése es mi criterio también, así lo pienso yo también; **to wallow in —** nadar en el sentimentalismo.

sentimental [͵senti'mentl] adj sentimental; (pej) sentimental, sensiblero; romántico.

sentimentalism [͵senti'mentəlizəm] n sentimentalismo m.

sentimentalist [͵senti'mentəlist] n persona f sentimental, romántico m, a f.

sentimentality [͵sentimen'tæliti] n sentimentalismo m, sensiblería f.

sentimentally [͵senti'mentəli] adv de modo sentimental; say en tono sentimental.

sentinel ['sentinl] n centinela m.

sentry ['sentri] n centinela m, guardia m; **to be on — duty** estar de guardia.

sentry box ['sentribɔks] n garita f de centinela.

sentry-go ['sentrigəu] n turno m de centinela; **to be on —** estar de guardia.

sepal ['sepəl] n sépalo m.

separable ['sepərəbl] adj separable.

separate ['seprit] adj separado (from de); distinto; suelto; independiente (from de); **I wrote it on a — sheet** lo escribí en otra hoja; **take a — sheet for the next part** tome una nueva hoja para lo que viene después; **everybody has a — cup** cada uno tiene su taza particular (or individual); **to sign a — peace** firmar un tratado de paz por separado; **"with — toilet"** "con inodoro aislado"; **this is quite — from his profession** esto no tiene nada que ver con su profesión.

separate ['sepəreit] **1** vt separar (from de); dividir, desunir; **to — truth from error** separar lo falso de lo verdadero, distinguir entre lo falso y lo verdadero; **he is —d from his wife** está separado de su mujer.

2 vi separarse; **they —d in 1970** se separaron en 1970.

separately ['sepritli] adv separadamente; por separado.

separation [͵sepə'reiʃən] n separación f.

separatism ['sepərətizəm] n separatismo m.

separatist ['sepərətist] **1** adj separatista. **2** n separatista mf.

separator ['sepəreitə*] n separador m.

Sephardic [se'fɑ:dik] adj sefardí.

Sephardim [se'fɑ:dim] npl sefardíes mpl.

sepia ['si:piə] n (colour, fish) sepia f.

sepoy ['si:pɔi] n cipayo m.

sepsis ['sepsis] n sepsis f.

September [sep'tembə*] n se(p)tiembre m.

septic ['septik] adj séptico.

septicaemia, (US) **septicemia** [͵septi'si:miə] n septicemia f.

septuagenarian [͵septjuədʒi'nɛəriən] **1** adj septuagenario. **2** n septuagenario m, a f.

Septuagint ['septjuədʒint] n versión f de los setenta.

sepulchral [si'pʌlkrəl] adj sepulcral (also fig).

sepulchre, (US) **sepulcher** ['sepəlkə*] n (lit) sepulcro m; **whited** — sepulcro m blanqueado.

sequel ['si:kwəl] n consecuencia f, resultado m; (of story) continuación f; **in the** — como consecuencia; **it had a tragic** — tuvo un resultado trágico, la cosa terminó trágicamente.

sequence ['si:kwəns] n sucesión f, orden m de sucesión; serie f; (Cards) serie f, escalera f; (Cine) secuencia f; — **of tenses** sucesión f de tiempos.

sequestered [si'kwestəd] adj aislado, remoto.

sequestrate [si'kwestreit] vt secuestrar.

sequestration [,si:kwes'treiʃən] n secuestración f.

sequin ['si:kwin] n lentejuela f.

sequoia [si'kwɔiə] n secoya f.

seraglio [se'rɑ:liəu] n serallo m.

seraph ['serəf] n, pl **seraphim** ['serəfim] serafín m.

seraphic [sə'ræfik] adj seráfico.

Serb [sə:b] n servio m, a f.

Serbia ['sə:biə] n Servia f.

Serbian ['sə:biən] 1 adj servio. 2 n servio m, a f.

Serbo-Croat ['sə:bəu'krəuæt] n (language) servocroata m.

Serbo-Croatian ['sə:bəukrəu'eiʃən] 1 adj servocroata. 2 n servocroata mf.

sere [siə*] adj seco, marchito.

serenade [,serə'neid] 1 n serenata f. 2 vt dar serenata a.

serene [sə'ri:n] adj sereno, tranquilo; **all** —! ¡sin novedad!

serenely [sə'ri:nli] adv serenamente, tranquilamente; — **indifferent to the noise** sin molestarse en lo más mínimo por el ruido; **"No" he said** — "No" dijo con mucha tranquilidad.

serenity [si'reniti] n serenidad f, tranquilidad f.

serf [sə:f] n siervo m, a f (de la gleba).

serfdom ['sə:fdəm] n servidumbre f (de la gleba); (fig) servidumbre f.

serge [sə:dʒ] n estameña f.

sergeant ['sɑ:dʒənt] n sargento m; — **at arms** oficial m de orden; — **first class, top** — (US) primer sargento m; **yes,** — sí, mi sargento.

sergeant-major ['sɑ:dʒənt'meidʒə*] n (approx) brigada m.

serial ['siəriəl] 1 adj consecutivo, en serie; **number** de serie; story por entregas. 2 n serial m, novela f por entregas; **radio** — serial m radiofónico.

serialize ['siəriəlaiz] vt publicar como serial, publicar por entregas; **it has been** —**d in the papers** ha aparecido en una serie de entregas en los periódicos.

serially ['siəriəli] adv en serie.

seriatim [,siəri'eitim] adv en serie.

sericulture ['seri'kʌltʃə*] n sericultura f.

series ['siəriz] n, pl **series** serie f; sucesión f; (Math) serie f, progresión f; (of lectures etc) ciclo m; **World S—** (US) Serie f Mundial; **to connect in** — (Elec) conectar en serie.

series-wound ['siəri:'waund] adj arrollado en serie.

serious ['siəriəs] adj serio; condition, mistake, news etc grave; character serio, formal; **the injury is not** — la lesión no es de gravedad; **are you** — (about it)?, **you can't be** —! ¿lo dices en serio?; **gentlemen, let's be** — señores, un poco de formalidad; **he's** — **about her** está enamorado de verdad de ella; **when we're alone he gets** — cuando estamos a solas se pone muy serio; **things are getting** — las cosas están graves.

seriously ['siəriəsli] adv seriamente; en serio; gravemente; —, **though . . .** pero en serio . . .; — **wounded** herido de gravedad; **he is** — **ill** está grave; **do you say so** —? ¿me lo dices en serio?; **we are** — **worried** estamos gravemente preocupados; **I can't take Campoamor** — no puedo tomar a Campoamor en serio; **he takes himself** — se toma muy en serio.

seriousness ['siəriəsnis] n seriedad f; gravedad f; **in all** — en serio, seriamente; **the** — **of the situation** la gravedad de la situación.

sermon ['sə:mən] n sermón m (also fig); **the S—** on **the Mount** el Sermón de la Montaña.

sermonize ['sə:mənaiz] vti sermonear.

serous ['siərəs] adj seroso.

serpent ['sə:pənt] n serpiente f, sierpe f; (fig) serpiente f.

serpentine ['sə:pəntain] 1 adj serpentino. 2 n (Min) serpentina f.

serrated [se'reitid] adj serrado, dentellado.

serration [se'reiʃən] n endentadura f.

serried ['serid] adj apretado; **in** — **ranks** en filas apretadas.

serum ['siərəm] n suero m.

servant ['sə:vənt] n (domestic) criado m, a f; (of company etc) empleado m, a f; (general fig sense) servidor m, ora f; **civil** — funcionario m del Estado, funcionaria f del Estado; **your devoted** —, **your humble** — un servidor, servidor de Vd; **your obedient** — (in letters) suyo afmo, att. y s.s. (= atento y seguro servidor); **the** —**s** (collectively) la servidumbre; **the** — **problem** el problema del servicio.

serve [sə:v] 1 vt (a) (of person) servir; estar al servicio de; apprenticeship hacer; sentence cumplir; **to** — **the Queen** servir a la Reina; **he** —**d his country well** sirvió dignamente a la patria, prestó valiosos servicios a la patria.

(b) (of thing) servir; ser útil a; **if my memory** —**s me** si mi memoria no me falla, si tengo buena memoria; see purpose.

(c) (Rail etc) **in towns** —**d by this line** en las ciudades por donde pasa esta línea; **the villages used to be** —**d by buses** antes en estos pueblos había servicio de autobuses.

(d) (in shop) goods vender; despachar; customer servir, atender; food, meal servir; **to** — **someone with 5 kilos of potatoes** vender 5 kilos de patatas a uno; **to** — **someone with hors d'oeuvres** servir los entremeses a uno; **dinner is** —**d** la cena está servida; **are you being** —**d, madam?** ¿están despachando su pedido, señora?; **they** —**d cod as halibut** hicieron pasar bacalao por halibut, sirvieron bacalao e hicieron creer que era halibut.

(e) (Tennis etc) sacar.

(f) writ entregar; see notice.

(g) (treat) tratar; **he** —**d me very ill** me trató muy mal; **it** —**s you right!** ¡bien merecido lo tienes!; **it** —**d him right for being so greedy** lo mereció por ser tan glotón; **it would have** —**d them right if he had** bien merecido lo hubieran tenido ellos si lo hubiese hecho él.

(h) (of stallion etc) cubrir.

(i) (with adv or prep) **to** — **out** repartir, distribuir; food servir; **to** — **someone out** ajustar cuentas con uno; **I'll** — **you out for this!** ¡me las pagarás!; **to** — **up** food servir; **he** —**d that up as an excuse** eso lo ofreció como excusa.

2 vi (a) servir; **to** — **10 years in the army** servir 10 años en el ejército; **to** — **at table** servir a la mesa; **to** — **on the jury** formar parte del jurado; **to** — **on the council** ser concejal; **to** — **in parliament** ser diputado; **he is not willing to** — no quiere servir, no está dispuesto a ofrecer sus servicios.

(b) **to** — **as, to** — **for** servir de; servir para; **it will** — servirá para el caso; **when the occasion** —**s** cuando se presente una ocasión propicia.

(c) (Tennis etc) sacar.

3 n (Tennis etc) saque m; **whose** — **is it?** ¿quién saca?

server ['sə:və*] n (Tennis) saque mf; (for fish etc) pala f; (Eccl) acólito m.

service ['sə:vis] 1 n (a) (in general) servicio m; **active** — servicio m activo; **to be on active** — estar en activo; **to die on active** — morir en acto de servicio; **military** — servicio m militar; **to do one's military** — hacer el servicio militar; **he has 10 years'** — lleva 10 años en el servicio, sirve desde hace 10 años; **he saw long** — sirvió durante muchos años; **to see** — as prestar servicio de.

(b) (branch, department etc) servicio m; **after-sales** — servicio m de asistencia post-venta; **civil** — burocracia f oficial; **customs** — servicio m aduanero, aduana f; **diplomatic** — cuerpo m diplomático; **intelligence** — (Mil) servicio m de información; **"all main** —**s"** "todos servicios"; **medical** — servicio m médico; **postal** —**s** servicios mpl postales; **public** —**s** servicios mpl públicos; **secret** — servicio m secreto; servicio m de contraespionaje; **the Senior S—** (British) la marina; **social** —**s** servicios mpl sociales; **the S—** (Mil) el ejército, (Aer) la aviación, (Naut) la marina; **the (three) S—s** las fuerzas armadas; **the train** — **to Pamplona** el servicio de trenes a Pamplona; **the number 13 bus** — el servicio de autobuses número 13; **to be on government** — estar al servicio del gobierno; see health etc.

(c) (domestic) **to be in** — ser criado, ser criada; servir; **she was in** — **at Lord Copper's** era criada en la casa de Lord Copper; **to go into** — entrar a servir (with a).

(d) (act of serving etc) servicio m; **for** —**s to education** en premio a sus servicios a la educación; **his** —**s to industry were most valuable** prestó valiosísimos servicios a la industria; **the** — **is really poor in this hotel** en este hotel el servicio es francamente malo; **to dispense with someone's** —

despedir a uno; **to do someone a** — prestar un servicio a uno; **to do good** — servir bien, ser muy útil; **Tristram Shandy, at your** — Tristram Shandy, para servirle (or a su disposición): **I am at your** — estoy a su disposición; **Brand X is always at your** — la marca X está siempre lista para servirle; **to bring into** — empezar a usar, introducir; **to come into** — entrar en servicio; **to press into** — thing utilizar; echar mano de; person hacer trabajar, hacer prestar servicio; **to be of** — servir, ayudar; **can I be of** —? ¿puedo ayudarle?; **it's of no** — **in an emergency** en caso de urgencia no sirve para nada; **to be out of** — (Mech) no funcionar.

(e) (Eccl: Catholic) misa f; (other) culto m, oficio m divino.

(f) (Tennis) saque m.

(g) (Law) entrega f.

(h) (set) vajilla f, juego m, servicio m de mesa; **coffee** — juego m de café; **toilet** — juego m de tocador.

2 vt (Mech) atender, mantener; reparar; **to send a car to be** —d mandar un coche al garaje para engrase y mantenimiento.

serviceable ['sə:visəbl] adj servible, utilizable, útil; práctico; (lasting) duradero.

service flat ['sə:visflæt] n piso m con servicio de comida, criada etc.

service lift ['sə:vislift], (US) — **elevator** [,eləveitə*] n montacargas m.

service line ['sə:vislain] n (Tennis etc) línea f de saque.

serviceman ['sə:vismən] n, pl —**men** [mən] militar m.

service station ['sə:vis,steiʃən] n estación f de servicio.

service tree ['sə:vistri:] n serbal m.

serviette [,sə:vi'et] n servilleta f.

serviette ring [,sə:vi'etriŋ] n servilletero m.

servile ['sə:vail] adj servil.

servility [sə:'viliti] n servilismo m.

servitude ['sə:vitju:d] n servidumbre f; **penal** — trabajos mpl forzados.

sesame ['sesəmi] n (Bot) sésamo m; **open** —! ¡sésamo ábrete!

sesquipedalian [,seskwipi'deiliən] adj sesquipedal; — **word** palabra f kilométrica.

sessile ['sesail] adj sésil.

session ['seʃən] n sesión f; (School, Univ) curso m; **petty** —**s** tribunal m de primera instancia; **to be in** — (Parl) estar celebrando sesión, sesionar; **to go into secret** — celebrar una sesión secreta.

sessional ['seʃənl] adj de una sesión; **exam** de fin de curso.

sestet [ses'tet] n sesteto m.

set [set] **1** n (a) (group: of tools, cups, golf clubs etc) juego m; (of kitchen utensils) batería f; (of cutlery) cubierto m; (of turbines etc) equipo m; (of gears) tren m; (of stamps) serie f; (of rooms) grupo m; (of books, works) colección f; — **of teeth** dentadura f; **coffee** — juego m de café; **dinner** — vajilla f, servicio m de mesa; **toilet** — juego m de tocador; **a complete** — **of Galdós novels** una colección completa de las novelas de Galdós, las obras completas de Galdós; **that one makes up the** — ése completa la serie; **it makes a** — **with those over there** hace juego con los que Vd ve allá; **I need two to make up the** — me faltan dos para completar la serie (or colección).

(b) (Tennis) set m.

(c) (Elec etc) aparato m; (Radio) aparato m de radio, radiorreceptor m; (TV) televisor m; **battery** — radio f de batería; **portable** — radio f portátil; **generating** — grupo m electrógeno.

(d) (of persons) grupo m; clase f; (pej) pandilla f, camarilla f; **the fast** — la gente de vida airada; **the literary** — los literatos, la gente literaria; **the smart** — el mundo elegante, los elegantes; **they're a** — **of thieves** son unos ladrones; **they form a** — **by themselves** forman un grupo aparte.

(e) (School) clase f; **the mathematics** — la clase de matemáticas.

(f) **to make a dead** — **at someone** (pick on) emprenderla resueltamente con uno, escoger a uno como víctima; (amorously) proponerse conquistar a uno.

(g) (hair) **to have a shampoo and** — hacerse lavar y marcar el pelo.

(h) (of fabric) caída f; (of dress) corte m, ajuste m; (of head) porte m, manera f de llevar; (of saw) triscamiento m; (of tide, wind) dirección f; (of person's mind etc) inclinación f, sesgo m, tendencia f.

(i) (Hort) planta f de transplantar; esqueje m; **onion** —**s** cebollitas fpl de transplantar.

(j) (Theat) decorado m, decorados mpl; (Cine) plató m; **to be on the** — estar en plató.

2 adj and ptp (a) (rigid) rígido, inflexible; face rígido, sin expresión; smile forzado; permanente; (in belief) inflexible; **the fruit is** — el fruto está formado.

(b) (ready) listo; **all** —?, **are we all** —? ¿estamos?, ¿estamos listos?; **to be all** — **for** estar listo para; **with their cameras all** — **to shoot** con las máquinas a punto para disparar.

(c) (fixed, decided in advance) fijo; decidido de antemano; price, purpose fijo; phrase hecho; task asignado; subject prescrito, establecido; time señalado; (usual) reglamentario; (customary) acostumbrado; **at a** — **time** a la hora señalada; **there is no** — **time for it** para eso no hay hora fija; — **books** autores mpl del programa; **with no** — **limits** sin límites determinados; **he gave us a** — **speech** pronunció un discurso preparado de antemano; **he has a** — **speech for these occasions** para estas ocasiones tiene un discurso invariable.

(d) (resolved) resuelto, decidido; **to be** — **in one's purpose** tener un propósito firme, mantenerse firme en su propósito; **to be** — **in one's ways** tener costumbres profundamente arraigadas; **to be** — **on something** estar empeñado en algo; **to be** — **on** + ger estar resuelto a + infin; **since you are so** — **on it** puesto que te empeñas en ello; **to be dead** — **against something** estar completamente opuesto a algo.

3 (irr: pret and ptp **set**) vt (a) (place) poner, colocar; situar; jewel engastar, montar; **bricks** — **in concrete** ladrillos puestos en hormigón; **to** — **places for 14** poner cubiertos para 14 personas; **to** — **the table** poner la mesa; — **the chairs by the window** ponga las sillas junto a la ventana; **to** — **a poem to music** poner música a un poema; **she** — **the dish before me** puso el plato delante de mí; **to** — **a plan before a committee** exponer un plan ante una comisión; **I** — **him above Greene** le creo superior a Greene; **what value do you** — **on it?** ¿en cuánto lo valoras?, (fig) ¿qué valor tiene para Vd?; **the ruins are** — **in a valley** las ruinas están enclavadas en un valle; **the scene is** — **in Rome** la escena tiene lugar en Roma, la acción pasa en Roma; **his stories,** — **in the society of 1890** . . . sus cuentos, ambientados en la sociedad de 1890 . . .

(b) (adjust) ajustar, arreglar; clock poner en hora; alarm clock regular; bone reducir, encasar, componer; specimen montar; hair marcar, fijar; sail desplegar; saw triscar; trap armar; snare tender (also fig); type componer; cement etc solidificar, endurecer; jelly cuajar; teeth apretar; **the alarm clock is** — **for 7** el despertador está puesto para las 7; **he** —**s his watch by Big Ben** pone su reloj por el Big Ben.

(c) (fix) fijar, señalar; **to** — **a time for a meeting** fijar una hora para una reunión; **to** — **limits to something** señalar límites a algo; **to** — **a period of 3 months** señalar un plazo de 3 meses; **to** — **the fashion** imponer la moda (for de); **to** — **a record of 10 seconds** establecer un récord de 10 segundos; **to** — **course** hacer rumbo a.

(d) (give) example dar; task imponer, asignar; problem plantear, (as test etc) poner; **to** — **Lorca for 1980** poner una obra de Lorca en el programa de estudios para 1980; **Cela is not** — **this year** este año Cela no figura en el programa; **to** — **an exam paper in German** poner un examen en alemán.

(e) **to** — **a dog on someone** azuzar un perro contra uno; **I was** — **on by 3 dogs** me atacaron 3 perros; **we** — **the police on to him** le denunciamos a la policía; **what** — **the police on the trail?** ¿qué puso a la policía sobre la pista?

(f) **the noise** — **the dogs barking** el ruido hizo ladrar a los perros; **to** — **something going** poner algo en marcha; **to** — **someone laughing** hacer reír a uno; **to** — **everyone talking** dar que hablar a todos; **this** — **me thinking** esto me hizo meditar; **to** — **someone to work** poner a uno a trabajar.

(g) (with adv or prep) **to** — **someone against someone else** indisponer a uno con otra persona, enemistar a uno con otra persona; **one has to** — **A against B** hay que pesar A contra B, hay que contraponer A a B; **to** — **aside** poner aparte; reservar, guardar; proposal desechar, rechazar; petition desatender, desestimar; law, will anular; **to** — **back** progress detener, entorpecer; poner obstáculos a; clock retrasar; **the house is** — **back from the road** la casa está algo apartada de la carretera; **this has** — **us back some years** esto representa una pérdida de varios años, esto nos ha costado varios años de progreso; **the dinner** — **me** back £7 la cena me costó 7 libras; **to — down** (*put down*) poner en tierra, poner en el suelo, depositar; **the taxi — us down here** el taxi nos dejó aquí; **the train —s down passengers at** . . . los viajeros se apean en . . .; **to — down** (*in writing*) poner por escrito; apuntar, consignar, registrar; **it is not — down here** no consta aquí; **we — it down to** . . . lo atribuimos a . . ., lo achacamos a . . .; **I — him down as a liar** le tomé por un embustero, le juzgué de mentiroso; **to — forth** (*display*) mostrar, exhibir; *theory etc* exponer, explicar; **to — off** (*explode*) hacer estallar; **to — someone off** hacer reír a uno; dar a uno la oportunidad de hablar; **that really — him off** con eso sí se puso furioso; **to — off profits against losses** contraponer las ganancias a las pérdidas; **the black —s off the red** el negro hace resaltar el rojo, el negro pone de relieve el rojo; **her dress —s off her figure** su vestido le acentúa el tipo; **to — out** (*arrange*) arreglar; sacar y disponer; clasificar; (*state*) exponer, explicar; **it's very clearly — out here** aquí se explica con toda claridad; **the material is well — out on the page** el material está bien dispuesto en la página; **to — up** *monument* erigir, levantar; *institution, company etc* crear, fundar, establecer; *committee* constituir; *fund* crear; (*Typ*) componer; (*Tech*) armar, montar; *house* poner; *government* establecer, instaurar; *record* establecer; *precedent* sentar; *cry* levantar, lanzar, dar; *protest* levantar; **to — up a fashion for** . . . crear una moda de . . ., imponer la moda de . . .; **UNO was — up in 1945** se fundó la ONU en 1945; **he — her up in a flat** la instaló en un piso; **to — someone up in business** establecer a uno en un negocio, ayudar a uno a establecerse en un negocio; **to — someone up as a model** poner a uno como modelo; **to — someone up as a judge** erigir a uno como juez; **the medicine — me up again** la medicina me fortaleció; **now he's — up for life** ahora tiene una carrera (*or* recursos, renta *etc*) que le durará(n) toda la vida; **to be well — up for** estar bien provisto de, tener buena provisión de.

4 *vi* (**a**) (*of sun etc*) ponerse.

(**b**) (*of bone*) componerse.

(**c**) (*of jelly etc*) cuajarse; (*of blood*) coagularse; (*of cement*) fraguar; (*of gum, mud*) endurecerse, solidificarse.

(**d**) (*of dog*) estar de muestra; **the tide is — in our favour** la marea fluye para llevarnos adelante, (*fig*) la tendencia actual nos favorece, llevamos el viento en popa; **the wind is — strong from the north** el viento sopla recio del norte.

(**e**) **to — to work** ponerse a trabajar; poner manos a la obra.

(**f**) (*with adv or prep*) **to — about a job** emprender una tarea, comenzar una tarea; **to — about doing something** ponerse a hacer algo; **to — about someone** atacar a uno, agredir a uno; empezar a pegar a uno; **they — about each other** llegaron a las manos; **to — forth** partir, ponerse en camino; **to — in** (*begin*) comenzar; (*breakout*) declararse; (*of night, winter*) cerrar; (*of tide*) fluir; **reaction — in after the war** la reacción se afianzó después de la guerra; **the rain has — in for the night** parece que la lluvia continuará toda la noche; **the rain has really — in** ahora está lloviendo de verdad; **to — off** partir, ponerse en camino; **to — out** partir, ponerse en camino; **to — out for** partir para, salir para; **to — out in search of someone** partir en busca de uno; **to — out to +** *infin* (*begin*) ponerse a + *infin*; **this book —s out to prove that** . . . este libro se propone demostrar que . . .; **we didn't — out to do that** no teníamos esa intención al principio; **to — to** (*start*) empezar; (*start work*) ponerse resueltamente a trabajar, aplicarse con vigor; (*start eating*) empezar a comer; **they — to with their fists** empezaron a pegarse con los puños; **to — to** ¡a ello!; **to — up as a judge** erigirse en juez, constituirse en juez; **to — up in business** establecerse en un negocio.

5 *vr*: **to — oneself against something** oponerse rotundamente a algo; **to — oneself up as a judge** erigirse en juez, constituirse en juez; **he —s himself up as a critic** se las da de crítico, hace creer que es crítico.

setback ['setbæk] *n* revés *m*, contratiempo *m*; **to suffer a —** sufrir un revés.

setscrew ['setskru:] *n* tornillo *m* de presión.

set square ['setskweə*] *n* cartabón *m*, escuadra *f*.

settee [se'ti:] *n* canapé *m*, sofá *m*.

settee-bed [se'ti:'bed] *n* sofá-cama *m*.

setter ['setə*] *n* (*of puzzle etc*) autor *m*, ora *f*; (*dog*) perro *m* de muestra inglés, setter *m*.

setting ['setiŋ] *n* (*of sun*) puesta *f*; (*act of placing*) colocación *f*; (*of jewel*) engaste *m*, montadura *f*; (*Theat etc*) escena *f*, escenario *m*; (*of action etc*) marco *m*; (*natural —, landscape etc*) marco *m*; alrededores *mpl*; (*of bone*) reducción *f*, composición *f*; (*of machine etc*) ajuste *m*; (*Typ*) composición *f*; (*Mus*) arreglo *m*, versión *f*; **a — for 2 violins** un arreglo para 2 violines.

setting lotion ['setiŋ.ləuʃən] *n* fijador *m* (para el pelo).

setting-up ['setiŋ'ʌp] *n* (*of monument*) erección *f*; (*of institution, company*) creación *f*, fundación *f*, establecimiento *m*; (*Typ*) composición *f*.

settle¹ ['setl] *n* banco *m*.

settle² ['setl] **1** *vt* (**a**) (*place*) colocar; (*place firmly*) asentar; (*fix*) asegurar, fijar, afirmar; **to — one's feet in the stirrups** afirmarse en los estribos.

(**b**) *persons* establecer; *land* colonizar, poblar (*with de*); **it was first — d by the French** los primeros colonos fueron los franceses; **he —d her in a little flat** la instaló en un modesto piso.

(**c**) **to — an income on someone** asignar (*or* señalar) una renta a uno.

(**d**) **to — one's affairs** arreglar sus asuntos; **to — an invalid for the night** poner a un enfermo cómodamente para la noche.

(**e**) (*calm*) *nerves* calmar, sosegar; *doubts* disipar, desvanecer; *stomach* asentar.

(**f**) *account* ajustar, liquidar, saldar; *claim* satisfacer; *differences, quarrel* componer; *date etc* fijar, acordar; *deal* firmar; *problem* resolver, solucionar; **several points remain to be —d** quedan varios puntos por resolver; **the terms were —d by negotiation** se acordaron las condiciones mediante una negociación; **to — an affair out of court** arreglar una disputa de modo privado; **the result was —d in the first half** se decidió el resultado en el primer tiempo; **it's all —d** todo está resuelto; ya no hay problema; **so that's —d** then así que todo está arreglado; **that —s it!** ¡ya no hay más que decir!; **— it among yourselves!** ¡allá vosotros!

(**g**) (*fam*) **I'll soon — him** me lo cargaré; **that —d him** ya no hay problema con él, ya no volverá a molestarnos.

2 *vi* (*in many cases also* **to — down**) (**a**) (*establish oneself: in a house etc*) establecerse, instalarse; (*in a country*) arraigarse; (*of bird, insect*) posarse; **to — comfortably in an armchair** sentarse cómodamente en una butaca; **the snow is settling** la nieve no se derrite; **the wind —d in the east** el viento siguió soplando del este.

(**b**) **to — down** (*after wild period etc*) sentar la cabeza; **to marry and — down** casarse y empezar a tomar las cosas en serio; **to — down to a new life** adaptarse a una vida nueva; **he's settling down at school** se está acostumbrando a la escuela; **things are beginning to — down** las cosas empiezan a volver a la normalidad; **he —d down with two mistresses** se las arregló para vivir con dos queridas; **he can't — down anywhere** es un culo de mal asiento; **to — down to work** aplicarse al trabajo, dedicarse a trabajar (en serio).

(**c**) (*of building*) asentarse; (*of liquid*) clarificarse; (*of sediment*) depositarse, sedimentarse; (*of ship*) hundirse lentamente; **things are settling into shape** las cosas empiezan a adquirir una forma.

(**d**) (*of passion etc*) calmarse; (*of weather*) serenarse; (*of conditions*) normalizarse, volver a la normalidad.

(**e**) **to — on something** decidir algo, resolver algo; (*choose*) escoger algo, optar por algo; **to — on a date** fijar una fecha.

(**f**) **to — for £250** convenir en aceptar 250 libras; **will you — for a draw?** ¿quedamos en empate?; **to — out of court** arreglar una disputa de modo privado.

(**g**) **to — up** ajustar cuentas (*with someone* con uno; *also fig*).

3 *vr*: **to — oneself down in an armchair** sentarse cómodamente en una butaca; **to — oneself down for the night** arreglarse para pasar la noche.

settlement ['setlmənt] *n* (**a**) (*of account*) ajuste *m*, liquidación *f*; (*of claim*) satisfacción *f*; (*of difference, quarrel*) arreglo *m*; (*of problem*) solución *f*.

(**b**) (*agreement*) acuerdo *m*, convenio *m*; **marriage —** contrato *m* matrimonial, capitulaciones *fpl*; **to reach a —** llegar a un acuerdo.

(**c**) (*act of settling persons*) establecimiento *m*; (*of land*) colonización *f*.

(**d**) (*colony*) colonia *f*; (*village*) pueblo *m*; núcleo *m* rural; (*homestead*) caserío *m*.

settler ['setlə*] *n* colono *m*, a *f*; (*pioneer*) colonizador *m*.

set-to ['set'tu:] n (fam) bronca f, pelea f; **to have a —
with someone** pelearse con uno.
setup ['setʌp] n tinglado m, sistema m, organización
f; estructura f; plan m; **it's an odd — here** aquí
tienen un extraño sistema; **you have to know the —**
hay que conocer el tinglado.
seven ['sevn] **1** adj siete. **2** n siete m.
sevenfold ['sevnfəuld] **1** adj séptuplo. **2** adv siete veces.
seventeen ['sevn'ti:n] adj diecisiete; **she was sweet —**
estaba en la flor de sus 17 abriles.
seventeenth ['sevn'ti:nθ] adj decimoséptimo.
seventh ['sevnθ] **1** adj séptimo. **2** n séptimo m.
seventieth ['sevntiiθ] adj septuagésimo.
seventy ['sevnti] adj setenta; **the seventies** (eg 1970s)
los años setenta; **to be in one's seventies** tener más
de setenta años.
sever ['sevə*] vt cortar; separar, dividir; relations
romper.
several ['sevrəl] **1** adj **(a)** (of number) varios, algunos;
diversos; **— times already** varias veces ya; **I bought
— books** compré algunos libros.
(b) (respective) respectivos, distintos; **they have
their — colours** tienen sus respectivos colores; **they
went their — ways** se fueron cada uno por su lado;
joint and — (Law) solidario.
2 pron algunos; **— of them wore hats** algunos de
ellos llevaban sombrero; **— were dead** algunos
estaban muertos.
severally ['sevrəli] adv respectivamente; (one by one)
por separado, individualmente.
severance ['sevərəns] n corte m; separación f,
división f; (of relations) ruptura f; **— pay** cantidad
f que se paga a un empleado al despedirle.
severe [si'viə*] adj severo; riguroso, fuerte; duro;
weather, winter, critic, restriction etc riguroso; illness,
loss, wound grave; pain intenso, agudo; storm
violento; reprimand áspero; blow duro; style adusto,
austero; **to be — on someone** tratar a uno con rigor;
to be too — on someone cargar la mano.
severely [si'viəli] adv severamente; rigurosamente,
fuertemente; duramente; gravemente; intensamente;
agudamente; ásperamente; austeramente; **—
wounded** herido de gravedad; **a — plain style** un
estilo de lo más austero; **to leave something —
alone** no tener nada en absoluto que ver con algo.
severity [si'veriti] n severidad f; rigor m; gravedad f;
intensidad f, agudeza f; aspereza f; austeridad f.
Seville [sə'vil] Sevilla.
Sevillian [sə'viliən] **1** adj sevillano. **2** n sevillano m,
a f.
sew [səu] (irr: pret sewed, ptp sewn) vti coser; **to —
on** coser, pegar; **to — up** coser, zurcir; **to get a
matter all —n up** arreglar un asunto de modo
definitivo; **we've got the game all —n up now** ya
estamos seguros de ganar este partido.
sewage ['sju:idʒ] n aguas fpl residuales.
sewage disposal ['sju:idʒdis,pəuzəl] n depuración f
de aguas residuales.
sewage farm ['sju:idʒfɑ:m] n, **sewage works**
['sju:idʒwə:ks] n estación f depuradora (de aguas
residuales).
sewer ['sjuə*] n albañal m, alcantarilla f, cloaca f;
(fig) letrina f, sentina f.
sewerage ['sjuəridʒ] n alcantarillado m; (as service on
estate etc) saneamiento m.
sewing ['səuiŋ] **1** n costura f; labor f de costura. **2**
attr de coser.
sewing basket ['səuiŋˌbɑ:skit] n cesta f de costura.
sewing machine ['səuiŋməˌʃi:n] n máquina f de coser.
sewing silk ['səuiŋsilk] n torzal m, seda f de coser.
sewn [səun] ptp of **sew.**
sex [seks] **1** n sexo m; **the female —** el sexo femenino;
the male — el sexo masculino; **the fair —** el bello
sexo; **the weaker —** el sexo débil; **of both —es** de
ambos sexos.
2 attr sexual; **— act** coito m; **— education**
instrucción f sobre el sexo; **— hygiene** higiene f
sexual.
3 vt chicks sexar, determinar el sexo de.
sexagenarian [ˌseksədʒi'neəriən] **1** adj sexagenario.
2 n sexagenario m, a f.
sex appeal ['seksə,pi:l] n atractivo m sexual, gancho
m (fam).
sexless ['sekslis] adj desprovisto de instinto sexual;
desprovisto de atractivo sexual; (Bio) sin sexo,
asexual.
sex-linked ['seks'liŋkt] adj (Bio) ligado al sexo.
sex maniac ['seks'meiniæk] n maníaco m sexual.
sexologist [sek'sɒlədʒist] n sexólogo m.
sexology [sek'sɒlədʒi] n sexología f.
sextant ['sekstənt] n sextante m.
sextet(te) [seks'tet] n sexteto m.

sexton ['sekstən] n sacristán m; (gravedigger)
sepulturero m.
sexual ['seksjuəl] adj sexual.
sexuality [ˌseksju'æliti] n sexualidad f.
sexually ['seksjuəli] adv sexualmente.
sexy ['seksi] adj person de gran atractivo sexual,
cachondo (fam); joke, film etc verde, escabroso;
dress etc que realza el atractivo sexual, provocativo.
sh [ʃ] interj ¡chitón!
shabbily ['ʃæbili] adv pobremente; injustamente;
a — dressed duke un duque pobremente vestido;
he was very — treated le trataron con suma
injusticia.
shabbiness ['ʃæbinis] n pobreza f, lo desharrapado;
lo raído, lo viejo; mal estado m; injusticia f; vileza f.
shabby ['ʃæbi] adj person pobremente vestido,
desharrapado; garment raído, gastado, viejo; area
pobre; building etc de aspecto pobre, en mal estado;
treatment injusto; trick vil, malo; **to feel —** creer ir
mal vestido; **to look —** tener aspecto pobre, tener
aspecto poco elegante.
shabby-looking ['ʃæbi,lukiŋ] adj de aspecto pobre.
shack [ʃæk] **1** n chabola f, choza f. **2** vi: **to — up
with someone** (fam) ir a vivir con uno; **to — up
together** (fam) vivir juntos.
shackle ['ʃækl] vt encadenar; poner grilletes a; (fig)
poner trabas a, estorbar; **we are —d by tradition**
las trabas de la tradición nos tienen presos.
shackles ['ʃæklz] npl grillos mpl, grilletes mpl;
(fig) trabas fpl; **the — of convention** las trabas de la
convención.
shad [ʃæd] n sábalo m.
shade [ʃeid] **1** n **(a)** (shadow) sombra f; **—s of night**
tinieblas fpl, oscuridad f; **the —s of night were
falling fast** se hacía rápidamente de noche; **in the
— a la sombra** (of de); **temperature in the —**
temperatura f a la sombra; **35° in the —** 35 grados a
la sombra; **to put something in the —** (fig) oscurecer
(la fama de) algo, eclipsar algo, dejar algo chico.
(b) (lamp-) pantalla f; (eye-) visera f; (window-,
US) persiana.
(c) (of colour) matiz m; tonalidad f, tono m;
(of meaning, opinion) matiz m, modalidad f; **a new
— of lipstick** una nueva tonalidad de lápiz labial;
have you a lighter —? ¿tiene una tonalidad más
clara?; **all —s of opinion are represented** todas las
modalidades de la opinión están representadas;
there is a further — of meaning here en el significado de esto hay todavía un matiz más.
(d) (small quantity) poquito m; **just a — more**
un poquito más; **he's a — better** está un poquito
mejor; **it's a — awkward** es un tanto difícil.
(e) (ghost) fantasma m; **the S—s** el infierno;
—s of Professor X! ¡qué diría el profesor X si
resucitara!
2 vt **(a)** dar sombra a; face etc proteger contra el
sol (etc); resguardar de la luz; **to — one's eyes with
one's hand** llevar la mano a los ojos para protegerlos
contra el sol; **to — a light** poner pantalla a una
lámpara; **her face was —d by a big hat** un sombrero
ancho le daba sombra a la cara.
(b) (Art) sombrear, esfumar; **to — away, to
— off colours** degradar; **to — one's eyes with
mascara** ponerse sombreador en los ojos.
3 vi: **to — away, to — off** cambiar poco a poco (into
hasta hacerse), transformarse gradualmente (into
en); **blue that —s off into black** azul que se trans-
forma gradualmente en negro.
shadeless ['ʃeidlis] adj sin sombra, privado de
sombra.
shadiness ['ʃeidinis] n sombra f, lo umbroso.
shading ['ʃeidiŋ] n (for eyes) sombreado m; (of
colours) degradación f; transformación f gradual
(into en).
shadow ['ʃædəu] **1** n **(a)** sombra f; **the —s** la oscuridad,
las tinieblas; **the — of death** la sombra de la
muerte; **in the — of** dentro de la sombra de, (fig)
amenazado por; **under the — of serious charges**
amenazado por unas acusaciones graves; **without a
— of doubt** sin sombra de duda, sin la menor duda;
without a — of truth sin tener la más pequeña
parte de verdad; **he is but a — of his former self**
es apenas una sombra de lo que fue; **to cast a —**
proyectar una sombra; **to cast a — over the
festivities** ser una nota triste en la fiesta; **to wear
oneself to a —** adelgazar peligrosamente por exceso
de trabajo, debilitarse trabajando con exceso.
(b) (person) policía m (or detective m etc) que
sigue a un sospechoso.
2 adj: **— factory** fábrica f secreta; **— cabinet**
consejo de los diputados de la oposición que esperan

tener carteras en un gobierno futuro; **the — Foreign Secretary** el portavoz de la oposición sobre asuntos exteriores, el diputado de la oposición que espera tener la cartera de asuntos exteriores en un gobierno futuro.
3 vt **(a)** (darken) oscurecer; (Art) sombrear; **to — forth** anunciar, indicar vagamente, simbolizar.
(b) (follow) seguir y vigilar; **have that man —ed** que se vigile a ese hombre; **I was —ed all the way home** me siguieron todo el camino hasta mi casa.
shadow boxing ['ʃædəu,bɔksiŋ] n boxeo m con un adversario imaginario; (fig) disputa f con un adversario imaginario.
shadowy ['ʃædəui] adj oscuro; (fig) oscuro; indistinto, indefinido; **a — form** un bulto, una forma indistinta; **the company leads a — existence** la compañía tiene una existencia misteriosa.
shady ['ʃeidi] adj **(a)** place sombreado, umbroso, de sombra; **a la sombra; a — tree** un árbol que da sombra; **it's — here** aquí hay sombra.
(b) (fig) person sospechoso; deal turbio; **the — side of politics** el aspecto turbio de la política; **to be on the — side of 40** tener más de 40 años.
shaft [ʃɑːft] n (arrow etc) flecha f, dardo m, saeta f; (part of arrow) astil m; (of column) caña f, fuste m; (of tool, golf club etc) mango m; (of cart, carriage) vara f; (Mech) eje m, árbol m; (Min) pozo m; (of light) rayo m; **the —s of Cupid** las flechas de Cupido; **— of wit** agudeza f; **driving —** (Mech) árbol m motor; **ventilating —** pozo m de ventilación.
shag[1] [ʃæg] n tabaco m picado.
shag[2] [ʃæg] n (Orn) cormorán m moñudo.
shaggy ['ʃægi] adj velludo, peludo, lanudo; **— dog story** chiste m goma.
shagreen [ʃæ'griːn] n chagrén m, zapa f.
Shah [ʃɑː] n cha m, chah m.
shake [ʃeik] **1** n **(a)** sacudida f, sacudimiento m; (quiver) temblor m; (of vehicle etc) vibración f; (Mus) trino m; (of head) movimiento m; **with a — in his voice** le tembló la voz al decir esto; **with a — of her head** moviendo la cabeza negativamente, con un movimiento negativo de la cabeza; **to be all of a —** estar todo tembloroso; **to give someone a good —** sacudir violentamente a uno; **to give a rug a good —** sacudir bien una alfombrilla.
(b) (milk —) batido m.
(c) **—s: he's no great —s at swimming** en natación es poco extraordinario; **he's no great —s as a swimmer** como nadador no vale mucho; **in a brace of —s, in two —s** en un decir Jesús, en un abrir y cerrar de ojos.
2 (irr: pret **shook**, ptp **shaken**) vt **(a)** sacudir; building etc hacer temblar, hacer retemblar; head mover, menear; hand estrechar; bottle agitar; cocktail etc agitar, remover; **" — the bottle"** "agite la botella"; **" — well before using"** "agítese bien antes de usarlo"; **we had to — him to rouse him** tuvimos que sacudirle para despertarle; **to — one's finger at someone** negar con el dedo lo que dice (etc) uno; **to — one's fist at someone** amenazar a uno con el puño; **to — hands** estrecharse la mano, darse las manos; **to — hands with someone** estrechar la mano a uno; **to — one's head** negar algo con la cabeza, mover la cabeza negativamente.
(b) (fig) (weaken) debilitar; hacer flaquear; (impair) perjudicar, afectar; **it has —n his health** ha afectado su salud; **nothing will — our resolve** nada hará flaquear nuestra resolución; **the firm's credit has been badly —n** ha sido perjudicada la reputación de la casa; **the prosecutor could not — his evidence** el fiscal no logró persuadirle a modificar su testimonio; el fiscal no pudo desacreditar su testimonio.
(c) (fig: alarm) inquietar, perturbar; (amaze) sorprender, pasmar, dejar estupefacto; (upset composure of) desconcertar; (shock) dar una sacudida a; **the news shook me** la noticia me pasmó; **that shook him** eso le desconcertó; **7 days which shook the world** 7 días que estremecieron el mundo; **it shook me rigid** (or **solid**; fam) me sorprendió muchísimo, me chocó bastante; **he needs to be —n out of his smugness** hay que darle una sacudida para que deje de estar tan pagado de sí mismo.
(d) (with adv or prep) **to — down** fruit etc hacer caer, sacudir; bajar sacudiendo; **to — someone down** (fam: for money) sacar dinero a uno por chantaje; **to — someone down for £50** exigir que uno pague 50 libras; **to — someone down (for arms)** palpar a uno (para comprobar si lleva armas); **to — off** dust, yoke etc sacudirse; (get rid of) quitarse de encima, deshacerse de, librarse de; pursuer zafarse de, dar esquinazo a; **I can't — off this cold** no logro quitarme este catarro; **to — out** (unfurl) desplegar;

blanket etc abrir y sacudir; **to — dust out** sacudir el polvo; **to — up** liquid, bottle agitar, remover; (fig) dar una sacudida a, dar un pinchazo a; reorganizar; estimular, reanimar; infundir nueva energía a.
3 vi estremecerse; temblar, retemblar (at, with de); (of voice) temblar; (Mus) trinar; **to — like a leaf** temblar como un azogado; **to — with fear** temblar de miedo; **to — with laughter** desternillarse de risa; **the house shook with merry singing** la casa retemblaba con alegres canciones; **the walls shook at the sound** se estremecían las paredes con el ruido; **it shook in the wind** bamboleaba al viento; **his voice shook** le tembló la voz; **—!, — on it!** ¡chócala!; **to — down** acostarse, echarse a dormir; **I can — down anywhere** yo me duermo en cualquier sitio.
4 vr: **to — oneself free** librarse de una sacudida.
shakedown ['ʃeikdaun] n (bed) cama f improvisada; (fam) exacción f de dinero; chantaje m.
shaken ['ʃeikən] ptp of **shake**.
shaker ['ʃeikə*] n (cocktail —) coctelera f.
Shakespearian [ʃeiks'piəriən] adj shakespeariano.
shake-up ['ʃeikʌp] n conmoción f; reorganización f; sacudida f, pinchazo m; infusión f de nueva energía; **the company needs a big —** la compañía necesita una reorganización completa.
shakily ['ʃeikili] adv de modo inestable; con poca firmeza; **he said —** dijo en voz trémula; **to walk —** andar con paso vacilante.
shakiness ['ʃeikinis] n inestabilidad f, falta f de firmeza; temblor m; debilidad f; (of knowledge) deficiencia f, mala calidad f.
shaking ['ʃeikiŋ] **1** adj: **a — experience** una experiencia desconcertante.
2 n: **to give someone a good —** sacudir violentamente a uno; **he needs a good —** (fig) hay que darle un pinchazo.
shako ['ʃækəu] n chacó m.
shaky ['ʃeiki] adj (unstable) inestable, poco firme, poco sólido; movedizo; hands etc tembloroso; voice trémula, débil; writing poco firme; **his Spanish is rather —** su español es algo defectuoso; **to be — on one's legs** tener las piernas débiles, andar con paso vacilante.
shale [ʃeil] n esquisto m.
shale oil ['ʃeilɔil] n aceite m esquistoso.
shall [ʃæl] (irr: see also **should**) v aux **(a)** (used to form future tense) **I — go** iré; **no I — not, no I shan't** no, yo no; **it — be done** así se hará; **— I hear from you soon?** ¿me escribirás pronto?
(b) (emphatic) **you — pay for this!** ¡me las pagarás!; **they — not pass!** ¡no pasarán!
(c) (in commands, of duty etc) **passengers — not cross the line** se prohíbe a los señores viajeros cruzar la vía; **it — be done this way** ha de hacerse de este modo; **you — do it!** ¡sí lo harás!; **thou shalt not kill** no matarás.
(d) (in questions) **— I go now?** ¿me voy ahora?, ¿quiere Vd que me vaya ahora?; **I'll buy 3, — I?** compro 3, ¿no te parece?; **let's go in, — we?** ¿entramos?; **— we let him?** ¿se lo permitimos?
shallot [ʃə'lɔt] n chalote m.
shallow ['ʃæləu] **1** adj **(a)** water etc poco profundo, no muy profundo, bajo; dish etc llano.
(b) person superficial, frívolo, sin carácter; knowledge etc superficial, somero.
2 —s npl bajos mpl, bajío m.
3 vi hacerse menos profundo.
shallowness ['ʃæləunis] n **(a)** poca profundidad f.
(b) superficialidad f, frivolidad f, falta f de carácter.
shalt [ʃælt] (arch) see **shall**; **thou — not kill** no matarás.
sham [ʃæm] **1** adj falso, fingido, simulado; **— fight** simulacro m de combate; **she's terribly —** es la mar de afectada; **with — politeness** con fingida cortesía.
2 n **(a)** (imposture) impostura f, fraude m, engaño m; imitación f; **it's all a —** todo es engaño; **the — of these elections** el fraude de estas elecciones; **the declaration was a mere —** la declaración no fue sino una impostura.
(b) (person) impostor m; **he's just a big —** es un grandísimo farsante.
3 vt fingir, simular; **to — illness** fingirse enfermo.
4 vi fingir, fingirse; **he's just —ming** lo está fingiendo; **to — dead** fingir estar muerto; **to — ill** fingirse enfermo.
shamble ['ʃæmbl] vi andar arrastrando los pies (also **to — along**); **he —d across to the window** fue arrastrando los pies a la ventana.
shambles ['ʃæmblz] n sing (scene of carnage) lugar m de gran matanza; (carnage) matanza f, carnicería

f; (*ruined place*) ruina *f*, escombrera *f*; (*muddle*) confusión *f*; **the place was a —** el sitio era todo escombros; **this room is a —!** ¡has visto qué desorden en este cuarto!; **the game was a —** el partido fue una catástrofe.

shame [ʃeim] **1** *n* **(a)** (*feeling, humiliation*) vergüenza *f*; deshonra *f*; **the — of that defeat** la vergüenza de esa derrota; **the street is the — of the town** la calle es la vergüenza (*or* el baldón) de la ciudad; **—!, for —!, — on you!, the — of it!** ¡qué vergüenza!; **to my eternal** (*or* **lasting**) **— I did nothing** me avergüenzo siempre de no haber hecho nada, siempre será para mí motivo de vergüenza el no haber hecho nada; **to be without —, to be lost to all sense of —** no tener vergüenza; **to bring — upon someone** deshonrar a uno; **have you no —?** ¡qué cinismo!; **to put someone to —** avergonzar a uno, (*fig*) superar con mucho a uno, dejar chico a uno.

(b) (*pity*) lástima *f*; **it's a — that . . .** es una lástima que + *subj*, es una pena que + *subj*; **it's a — to** + *infin* es una pena tener que + *infin*; **what a —!** ¡qué lástima!, ¡qué pena!

2 *vt* avergonzar; deshonrar; **to — someone into doing something** avergonzar a uno de tal modo que se vea obligado a hacer algo.

shamefaced [ˈʃeimfeist] *adj* avergonzado; vergonzoso, tímido.

shamefacedly [ˈʃeimfeisidli] *adv* con vergüenza, avergonzado; tímidamente.

shamefacedness [ˈʃeimfeistnis] *n* vergüenza *f*; timidez *f*.

shameful [ˈʃeimful] *adj* vergonzoso; **how —!** ¡qué vergüenza!

shamefully [ˈʃeimfəli] *adv* vergonzosamente; **— ignorant** tan ignorante que da vergüenza; **they are — underpaid** se les paga terriblemente mal.

shamefulness [ˈʃeimfulnis] *n* vergüenza *f*; ignominia *f*.

shameless [ˈʃeimlis] *adj* desvergonzado, descarado, descocado; impúdico; cínico; **— person** sinvergüenza *mf*; **are you completely —?** ¡qué cinismo!

shamelessly [ˈʃeimlisli] *adv* desvergonzadamente, descaradamente; impúdicamente; cínicamente.

shamelessness [ˈʃeimlisnis] *n* desvergüenza *f*, descaro *m*, descoco *m*; impudor *m*; cinismo *m*.

shaming [ˈʃeimiŋ] *adj* vergonzoso; **this is too —!** ¡qué vergüenza!

shammy [ˈʃæmi] *n* gamuza *f*.

shampoo [ʃæmˈpuː] **1** *n* champú *m*; **to give oneself a —** lavarse la cabeza.

2 *vt person* lavar la cabeza a; *hair* lavar; **to have one's hair —ed and set** hacerse lavar y marcar el pelo.

shamrock [ˈʃæmrɔk] *n* trébol *m* (*emblema nacional irlandés*).

shandy [ˈʃændi] *n* bebida mezclada de cerveza y limonada (*etc*).

shanghai [ʃæŋˈhai] *vt* (*Naut sl*): **to — someone** narcotizar (*or* emborrachar) a uno y embarcarle.

Shangri-la [ˈʃæŋriˈlɑː] *n* jauja *f*, país m maravilloso.

shank [ʃæŋk] *n* (*part of leg*) caña *f*; (*bird's leg*) zanca *f*; (*Bot*) tallo *m*; (*handle*) mango *m*; **—s** (*fam*) piernas *fpl*; **to go on S—s' pony** ir en el coche de San Fernando, ir a golpe de calcetín.

shan't [ʃɑːnt] = **shall not.**

shanty[1] [ˈʃænti] *n* choza *f*, chabola *f*.

shanty[2] [ˈʃænti] *n* (*Mus*) saloma *f*.

shantytown [ˈʃæntiˌtaun] *n* barrio *m* de chabolas, suburbio *m*.

shape [ʃeip] **1** *n* forma *f*; figura *f*; configuración *f*; (*of garment*) corte *m*; (*of person*) talle *m*, tipo *m*; (*for jelly etc*) molde *m*; (*thing dimly seen*) bulto *m*, forma *f*; **the — of things to come** la configuración del futuro; **not in any — or form** de ningún modo, en absoluto; **stamps of all —s** sellos *mpl* de todas las formas; **it is rectangular in —** es de forma rectangular, tiene forma rectangular; **what — is it?** ¿de qué forma es?; **to be in good —** estar en buenas condiciones, (*person*) estar bien de salud, estar en forma; **to be in bad —** estar en mal estado, (*person*) estar enfermo, estar en malas condiciones físicas; **to beat something into —** dar forma a algo a martillazos; **to knock** (*or* **lick**) **someone into —** desbastar a uno; disciplinar a uno; adiestrar a uno; **to lick a team into —** ir entrenando a un equipo; **to put an essay into —** corregir un ensayo, preparar un ensayo para publicarlo (*etc*); **to get out of —,** **to lose —** perder la forma; **to take — tomar** forma, irse formando, (*fig*) irse perfilando.

2 *vt* formar, dar forma a; *stone* labrar; *wood* tallar; *jug etc* modelar, hacer; *course etc* determinar;

plasmar, amoldar; **Plato helped to — his ideas** Platón ayudó a formar sus ideas; **the factors which — one's life** los factores que determinan el desarrollo de la vida de uno; **he did not — the course of events** él no influyó en la marcha de los acontecimientos; **there is a destiny which —s our ends** hay un destino que gobierna nuestra vida.

3 *vi* formarse, tomar forma; **to — well** desarrollarse de modo esperanzador, prometer; **he is shaping nicely as a goalkeeper** como guardameta promete, es un guardameta que promete; **how are things shaping?** ¿cómo van las cosas?; **to — up to someone** adoptar una postura para defenderse contra uno.

-shaped [ʃeipt] *adj* en forma de, *eg* **heart-shaped** en forma de corazón; **U-shaped** en forma de U.

shapeless [ˈʃeiplis] *adj* informe, sin forma definida.

shapeliness [ˈʃeiplinis] *n* proporción *f*; elegancia *f*.

shapely [ˈʃeipli] *adj* bien formado, bien proporcionado; *person* de buen talle; **— columns** columnas *fpl* elegantes; **the — Miss Galicia** la atractiva Miss Galicia.

shard [ʃɑːd] *n* tiesto *m*, casco *m*, fragmento *m* (de loza *etc*).

share[1] [ʃeə*] **1** *n* **(a)** (*thing received*) parte *f*, porción *f*; **— in the profits** participación *f* en los beneficios; **the lion's —** la parte del león; **fair —s for all** la equidad para todos, un trato equitativo para todos; **in equal —s** por partes iguales; **your — is £5** le tocan a Vd 5 libras; **how much will my — be?** ¿cuánto me corresponderá a mí?; **to come in for one's full — of work** tener que trabajar tanto como los otros o más; **the minister came in for a full — of criticism** se le criticó al ministro tanto como a cualquiera; **it fell to my —** me tocó a mí, me correspondió a mí; **to go —s** dividir lo recibido; **to go half —s with someone** dividir lo recibido con otro por partes iguales.

(b) (*contribution*) contribución *f*; cuota *f*; parte *f*; **to bear one's — of the cost** pagar la parte del coste que le corresponde a uno; **to do one's —** cumplir con su obligación; **he doesn't do his —** no hace todo lo que debiera, no hace todo lo que le cumple; **to have a — in something** participar en algo; **I had no — in that** yo no tuve nada que ver con eso; **to go —s** ir a escote, escotar cada uno lo suyo; **to pay one's —** pagar su cuota.

(c) (*Fin*) acción *f*; **ordinary —** acción *f* ordinaria; **paid-up —** acción *f* liberada; **preference —** acción *f* preferente; **to hold 1000 —s in a company** tener 1000 acciones en una compañía, poseer 1000 acciones de una compañía.

2 *vt* (*divide*) partir, dividir; (*have in common*) compartir, poseer en común; usar juntos de; **to — something with someone** compartir algo con uno; **they — a room** comparten un cuarto; **to — certain characteristics** poseer en común ciertas características; **I do not — that view** no comparto ese criterio; **to — out** repartir, distribuir.

3 *vi*: **to — and — alike** participar por partes iguales; **children have to learn to —** los niños tienen que aprender a hacerse concesiones mutuas (*or* a ser tolerantes); **there were no rooms free so I had to —** no había habitación libre y por tanto tuve que compartir una con otra persona; **to — in** tener parte en, participar en, (*fig*) participar de; **to — in someone's success** contribuir al éxito de uno.

share[2] [ʃeə*] *n* (*Agr*) reja *f*.

share certificate [ˈʃeəsəˌtifikit] *n* acción *f*.

sharecropper [ˈʃeəˌkrɔpə*] *n* aparcero *m*.

sharecropping [ˈʃeəˌkrɔpiŋ] *n* aparcería *f*.

shareholder [ˈʃeəˌhəuldə*] *n* accionista *mf*.

share-out [ˈʃeəraut] *n* reparto *m*.

shark [ʃɑːk] *n* (*Fish*) tiburón *m*; (*fam: swindler*) estafador *m*, (*expert*) perito *m*, as *m* (*fam*).

sharkskin [ˈʃɑːkskin] *n* zapa *f*.

sharp [ʃɑːp] **1** *adj* **(a)** (*cutting*) afilado, cortante; *point* puntiagudo; *angle* agudo; *curve, bend* cerrado, fuerte; *turn by car* repentino, brusco; *feature* bien marcado, anguloso; *outline* definido; *photo* nítido; *contrast* neto, marcado.

(b) (*of person*) *mind* listo, vivo, inteligente; *hearing* fino; *sight* agudo, penetrante; *glance* penetrante; **the child is quite —** el niño es bastante listo; **he's as — as they come** es de lo más avispado; **that was pretty — of you** en eso has estado muy perspicaz.

(c) (*of person: pej*) astuto, mañoso; poco escrupuloso; *practice, trick* poco honrado; **he's too — for me** es demasiado astuto para mi gusto, yo no aguanto sus malas mañas.

(d) (*fig*) *shower, storm* fuerte, repentino; *frost*

fuerte; *wind* penetrante; *pain* agudo, intenso; *fight* encarnizado; *pace* rápido, vivo; *walk* rápido; *fall in price etc* brusco; *temper* áspero, vivo; *retort* áspero; *tongue* mordaz; *rebuke* severo; *tone* acerbo, áspero, severo.

(e) *taste* acerbo, acre; *wine* ácido.

(f) *sound* agudo, penetrante; (*Mus*) sostenido.

2 *adv* (a) (*Mus*) desafinadamente.

(b) **at 5 o'clock —** a las 5 en punto; **and be — about it** y date prisa; **look —!** ¡pronto!; **look — about it!** ¡menearse!; **if you don't look —** si no te meneas; **to pull up —** frenar en seco; **to turn — left** torcer repentinamente a la izquierda.

3 *n* (*Mus*) sostenido *m*; (*person*) estafador *m*, (*card—*) fullero *m*.

sharp-edged ['ʃɑːp'edʒd] *adj* afilado, de filo cortante.

sharpen ['ʃɑːpən] 1 *vt tool* afilar, aguzar; amolar; *pencil* sacar punta a; *appetite* abrir; *wits* despabilar; *conflict, emotion, sensation* agudizar.

2 *vi* (*fig*) agudizarse.

sharpener ['ʃɑːpnə*] *n* afilador *m*, máquina *f* de afilar.

sharpening ['ʃɑːpnɪŋ] *n* (*fig*) agudización *f*.

sharper ['ʃɑːpə*] *n* estafador *m*, (*card—*) fullero *m*.

sharp-eyed ['ʃɑːp'aid] *adj* de vista aguda, de ojos de lince.

sharp-faced ['ʃɑːp'feist] *adj* de facciones angulosas.

sharpness ['ʃɑːpnis] *n* (a) lo afilado, lo cortante; lo puntiagudo; lo cerrado; lo repentino, brusquedad *f*; definición *f*; nitidez *f*; lo marcado.

(b) viveza *f*, inteligencia *f*, finura *f*; agudeza *f*.

(c) fuerza *f*; lo fuerte, lo repentino; agudeza *f*, intensidad *f*; brusquedad *f*, aspereza *f*; mordacidad *f*; severidad *f*; **there was a note of —** in his voice se notaba cierta aspereza en su tono; **there is a — in the air** empieza a notarse el frío.

sharpshooter ['ʃɑːp.ʃuːtə*] *n* tirador *m* apostado.

sharp-sighted ['ʃɑːp'saitid] *adj* de vista aguda, de ojos de lince.

sharp-tongued ['ʃɑːp'tʌŋd] *adj* de lengua mordaz.

sharp-witted ['ʃɑːp'witid] *adj* listo, perspicaz.

shatter ['ʃætə*] 1 *vt* romper, hacer añicos, hacer pedazos; *health* quebrantar; *nerves* destrozar; *hopes etc* destruir, acabar con; **to — something against a wall** estrellar algo contra una pared; **I was —ed to hear it** al saberlo quedé estupefacto; **this will — you** tengo que decirte algo pasmoso; **she was —ed by his death** su muerte la anonadó.

2 *vi* romperse, hacerse añicos; hacerse pedazos; estrellarse (*against* contra); **the windscreen —ed** el parabrisas estalló en pedazos.

shattered ['ʃætəd] *adj street etc* destrozado.

shattering ['ʃætərɪŋ] *adj attack* demoledor; *news etc* pasmoso, fulgurante; *defeat* contundente; *experience* profundamente conmovedor.

shatterproof ['ʃætəpruːf] *adj* inastillable.

shave [ʃeiv] 1 *n* (a) afeitado *m*, rasurado *m*; **to have a —** afeitarse.

(b) (*fig*) **to have a close** (*or* narrow) **—** escaparse por un pelo; **that was a close —** eso fue cosa de milagro.

2 (*irr: pret* **shaved**, *ptp* **shaved** *or* **shaven**) *vt face* afeitar, rasurar; *wood* acepillar; (*skim*) casi tocar, pasar rozando; **to — one's legs** afeitarse las piernas, depilarse las piernas; **to — off one's beard** afeitarse la barba, quitar la barba.

3 *vi* (*person*) afeitarse, rasurarse; **that razor —s** well esa navaja afeita bien.

shaven ['ʃeivn] 1 *ptp of* **shave**. 2 *adj head etc* rapado.

shaver ['ʃeivə*] *n* (a) **electric —** máquina *f* de afeitar eléctrica, afeitadora *f* eléctrica. (b) **young —** (*fam*) muchacho *m*, rapaz *m*.

Shavian ['ʃeiviən] *adj* shaviano.

shaving ['ʃeivɪŋ] 1 *n* (a) afeitado *m*, el afeitarse, rasurado *m*; **— is a nuisance** es una pesadez tener que afeitarse.

(b) **—s** virutas *pl*, acepilladuras *fpl*; **wood —s** virutas *fpl* de madera.

2 *attr* de afeitar.

shaving brush ['ʃeivɪŋbrʌʃ] *n* brocha *f* (de afeitar).

shaving cream ['ʃeivɪŋkriːm] *n* crema *f* de afeitar.

shaving lotion ['ʃeivɪŋ.ləuʃən] *n* loción *f* para el afeitado.

shaving soap ['ʃeivɪŋsəup] *n* jabón *m* de afeitar.

shaving stick ['ʃeivɪŋstik] *n* barra *f* de jabón de afeitar.

shawl [ʃɔːl] *n* chal *m*.

she [ʃiː] 1 *pron* ella; **— who** la que, quien.

2 *n* hembra *f*.

3 *attr* hembra, eg **the she-hedgehog** el erizo hembra, la hembra del erizo; **she-bear** osa *f*; **she-cat** gata *f*.

sheaf [ʃiːf] *n*, *pl* **sheaves** [ʃiːvz] (*Agr*) gavilla *f*; (*of arrows etc*) haz *m*; (*of papers*) fajo *m*, lío *m*.

shear [ʃiə*] (*irr: pret* **sheared**, *ptp* **shorn**) 1 *vt sheep* esquilar, trasquilar; *cloth* tundir; **to — off** cortar, quitar cortando; **the machine —ed off two fingers** la máquina cercenó dos dedos; **the ship had its bows shorn off in the collision** en la colisión el buque quedó con la proa destrozada.

2 *vi*: **to — through** cortar, hender.

shearer ['ʃiərə*] *n* esquilador *m*.

shearing ['ʃiərɪŋ] *n* esquileo *m*; **—s** lana *f* esquilada.

shearing machine ['ʃiərɪŋmə.ʃiːn] *n* esquiladora *f*.

shears ['ʃiəz] *npl* tijeras *fpl* grandes; (*Hort*) tijeras *fpl* de jardín; (*for metals*) cizalla *f*.

shearwater ['ʃiəwɔːtə*] *n* pardela *f*.

sheath [ʃiːθ] *n* vaina *f*; funda *f*, cubierta *f*; (*Bot etc*) vaina *f*.

sheathe [ʃiːð] *vt sword* envainar; enfundar; **to — something in metal** revestir algo de metal, poner cubierta metálica a algo.

sheathing ['ʃiːðɪŋ] *n* revestimiento *m*, cubierta *f*.

sheath knife ['ʃiːθnaif] *n*, *pl* **— knives** [naivz] cuchillo *m* de monte.

sheaves [ʃiːvz] *pl of* **sheaf**.

Sheba ['ʃiːbə] Sabá; **Queen of —** reina *f* de Sabá.

shebang [ʃə'bæŋ] *n* (*sl*): **the whole —** todo ello, todo el negocio.

shebeen [ʃi'biːn] *n* (*Ir, Scot*) taberna *f* ilícita.

shed¹ [ʃed] (*irr: pret and ptp* **shed**) *vt clothes, leaves etc* despojarse de; *skin* mudar; *unwanted thing* deshacerse de; desprenderse de, quitarse; *tears* verter; *blood* verter, derramar; *light* dar, (*fig*) echar, arrojar; **the party tried to — its leader** el partido intentó deshacerse de su jefe; **I'm trying to — 5 kilos** me esfuerzo por perder 5 kilos; **much blood has been —** se ha vertido mucha sangre; **that lamp doesn't — much light** esa lámpara no da mucha luz; **she —s happiness all around** ella irradia su felicidad por todas partes.

shed² [ʃed] *n* (*garden — etc*) cobertizo *m*, alpende *m*; (*workmen's*) barraca *f*; (*industrial*) nave *f*.

she'd [ʃiːd] = **she would**; **she had**.

sheen [ʃiːn] *n* lustre *m*; brillo *m*; **to take the — off something** deslustrar algo.

sheeny ['ʃiːni] *adj* lustroso, brillante.

sheep [ʃiːp] *n*, *pl* **sheep** [ʃiːp] oveja *f*; (*ram*) carnero *m*; (*pl, collectively*) ganado *m* lanar; **to be the black —** (*of the family*) ser la oveja negra, ser el garbanzo negro; **to count —** fingir contar ovejas (para dormirse); **to separate the — from the goats** (*fig*) apartar las ovejas de los cabritos.

sheep-dip ['ʃiːpdip] *n* desinfectante *m* para ovejas.

sheepdog ['ʃiːpdɔg] *n* perro *m* pastor; **— trials** concurso *m* de pastoreo.

sheep farmer ['ʃiːp.fɑːmə*] *n* dueño *m* de ganado lanar.

sheep farming ['ʃiːp.fɑːmɪŋ] *n* pastoreo *m*, industria *f* del ganado lanar.

sheepfold ['ʃiːpfəuld] *n* redil *m*, aprisco *m*.

sheepish ['ʃiːpiʃ] *adj* tímido, vergonzoso.

sheepishly ['ʃiːpiʃli] *adv* tímidamente.

sheepishness ['ʃiːpiʃnis] *n* timidez *f*, vergüenza *f*.

sheep-run ['ʃiːprʌn] *n* pasto *m* de ovejas, dehesa *f* de ovejas.

sheepshearing ['ʃiːp.ʃiərɪŋ] *n* esquileo *m*.

sheepskin ['ʃiːpskin] *n* piel *f* de carnero; zamarra *f*, badana *f*; **— jacket** zamarra *f*.

sheepwalk ['ʃiːpwɔːk] *n see* **sheep-run**.

sheer¹ [ʃiə*] 1 *adj* (a) (*absolute*) puro, completo, absoluto; **the — impossibility of . . .** la total imposibilidad de . . .; **— nonsense!** ¡puro disparate!; **this is — robbery** esto no puede llamarse sino robo.

(b) (*steep*) escarpado, cortado a pico; perpendicular; **there is a — fall of 200 metres** hay un descenso de 200 metros sin obstáculo alguno.

(c) (*of cloth etc*) diáfano.

2 *adv*: **it falls — to the sea** baja sin obstáculo alguno hacia el mar; **it rises — above the town** está cortado a pico por encima de la ciudad; **it rises — for 100 metres** se levanta verticalmente unos 100 metros.

sheer² [ʃiə*] *vi*: **to — off** (*Naut*) desviarse; (*fig*) largarse; **to — away from a topic** desviarse de un tema, evitar hablar de un tema.

sheet [ʃiːt] 1 *n* (*bed—*) sábana *f*; (*shroud*) mortaja *f*; (*of paper*) hoja *f*; (*newspaper*) periódico *m*, hoja *f*; (*of tin*) hoja *f*, (*of other metal*) chapa *f*, lámina *f*; (*of glass*) lámina *f*; (*of water etc*) extensión *f*; (*Naut*) escota *f*; (*cover*) cubierta *f*, (*tarpaulin*) alquitranado *m*.

2 *attr*: **— glass** vidrio *m* plano; **— steel** chapa

de acero; láminas *fpl* de acero, acero *m* en láminas.
3 *vt*: **to — something in, to — something over** cubrir algo con un alquitranado.
sheet anchor ['ʃiːtˌæŋkə*] *n* ancla *f* de la esperanza.
sheeting ['ʃiːtiŋ] *n* (*cloth*) lencería *f* para sábanas; (*metal*) placas *fpl* de metal, laminado *m*, cobertura *f* metálica.
sheet lightning ['ʃiːtˈlaitniŋ] *n* relámpago *m* difuso.
sheik(h) [ʃeik] *n* jeque *m*.
shekel ['ʃekl] *n* siclo *m*; —**s** (*fam*) pasta *f* (*sl*), parné *m* (*sl*).
shelf [ʃelf] *n*, *pl* **shelves** [ʃelvz] estante *m*, anaquel *m*; (*Naut*) banco *m* de arena, bajo *m*; (*on rock face*) repisa *f*; **continental —** (*Geog*) plataforma *f* submarina superior, schelf *m*; **shelves** (*collectively*) estantería *f*; **to be on the —** (*girl*) quedarse para vestir santos.
she'll [ʃiːl] = **she will, she shall.**
shell [ʃel] **1** *n* (**a**) (*Zool*: *of egg*) cáscara *f*, cascarón *m*; (*of nut*) cáscara *f*; (*of mollusc*) concha *f*; (*of tortoise, turtle*) caparazón *m*; (*of insect, lobster etc*) caparazón *m*, carapacho *m*; (*of pea*) vaina *f*; **to come out of one's —** salir del carapacho; **to retire into one's —** meterse en su carapacho.
(**b**) (*Tech*: *framework*) armazón *f*, esqueleto *m*; (*of house, after bombardment etc*) casco *m*; (*Naut*) casco *m*; (*outer covering*) cubierta *f*, exterior *m*.
(**c**) (*boat*) bote *m* de construcción lisa.
(**d**) (*Mil*) proyectil *m*, obús *m*, granada *f*; **dud —** obús *m* que no estalla; **live —** obús *m* con carga explosiva.
2 *vt* (**a**) *peas* desenvainar; *eggs, nuts* descascarar, quitar la cáscara a.
(**b**) **to — out** *money* (*sl*) desembolsar, pagar (de mala gana).
(**c**) (*Mil*) bombardear.
3 *vi* (*sl*) **to — out** desembolsar dinero (*for something* para pagar algo).
shellac [ʃəˈlæk] *n* laca *f*, goma *f* laca.
shelled [ʃeld] *adj*: — **nuts** nueces *fpl* sin cáscara.
shellfire ['ʃelfaiə*] *n* cañoneo *m*, fuego *m* de artillería, bombardeo *m*; **to be under —** sufrir un bombardeo; **the — lasted all night** el cañoneo duró toda la noche.
shellfish ['ʃelfiʃ] *n* (*Zool*) crustáceo *m*; (*as food*) mariscos *mpl*.
shell-hole ['ʃelhəul] *n* hoyo *m* que forma un obús al explotar.
shelling ['ʃeliŋ] *n* bombardeo *m*.
shellproof ['ʃelpruːf] *adj* a prueba de granadas.
shell shock ['ʃelʃɒk] *n* neurosis *f* de guerra.
shell-shocked ['ʃelʃɒkt] *adj* que padece neurosis de guerra.
shelter ['ʃeltə*] **1** *n* abrigo *m*, asilo *m*, refugio *m*; (*air-raid —* etc) refugio *m*; (*bus —*) refugio *m* (de espera); (*mountain —*) albergue *m*; (*fig*) protección *f*, resguardo *m*; **under —** al abrigo; **under the — of the mountain** al abrigo de la montaña; **to seek —** buscar dónde cobijarse; **to seek — for the night** buscar dónde pasar la noche; **to take —** ponerse al abrigo (*from* de), cobijarse (*from* de).
2 *vt* abrigar (*from* de); (*aid*) amparar, proteger (*from* de); (*hide*) esconder, ocultar; **to — a criminal** proteger a un criminal.
3 *vi* abrigarse, ponerse al abrigo, cobijarse (*from* de); refugiarse; **to — from the rain** ponerse al abrigo de la lluvia.
sheltered ['ʃeltəd] *adj place* abrigado; *industry* protegido contra la competencia extranjera; **she has led a very — life** se ha criado bajo las faldas de mamá, se ha criado en la inocencia; **a spot — from the wind** un sitio al abrigo del viento.
shelve¹ [ʃelv] *vt* (*fig*) dar carpetazo a, arrinconar, aplazar indefinidamente.
shelve² [ʃelv] *vi* formar declive, estar en declive; **the beach —s rapidly** el fondo está en fuerte declive; **it —s down to the sea** baja hacia el mar.
shelves [ʃelvz] *pl* of **shelf.**
shelving ['ʃelviŋ] *n* estantería *f*.
shemozzle [ʃəˈmɒzl] *n* (*sl*) lío *m*; bronca *f*, follón *m* (*fam*).
shenanigans [ʃəˈnænigənz] *npl* (*sl*) embustes *mpl*.
shepherd ['ʃepəd] **1** *n* pastor *m*; **the Good S—** el Buen Pastor.
2 *vt* guiar, conducir; **to — children across a road** conducir niños a través de una calle.
shepherd boy ['ʃepədbɔi] *n* zagal *m*.
shepherdess ['ʃepədis] *n* pastora *f*, zagala *f*.
sherbet ['ʃɜːbət] *n* sorbete *m*.
sherd [ʃɑːd] *see* **shard.**

sheriff ['ʃerif] *n* sheriff *m* (*oficial de justicia inglés, escocés, o norteamericano*).
sherry ['ʃeri] *n* jerez *m*.
she's [ʃiːz] = **she is; she has.**
Shetland Islands ['ʃetlənd͵ailəndz] *pl*, **Shetlands** ['ʃetləndz] *pl* Islas *fpl* de Zetlandia.
shew [ʃəu] *vti* (*arch*) *see* **show.**
shewn [ʃəun] *ptp* (*arch*) of **show.**
shibboleth ['ʃibələθ] *n* (*Bible*) lema *m*, santo *m* y seña; (*fig*) dogma *m* hoy desacreditado, doctrina *f* que ha quedado anticuada.
shield [ʃiːld] **1** *n* escudo *m* (*also Her*); (*round*) rodela *f*; (*Tech*) blindaje *m*, capa *f* protectora; (*fig*) escudo *m*, defensa *f*.
2 *vt* proteger, resguardar, amparar; *criminal* proteger; (*Tech*) blindar, revestir de una capa protectora; **to — one's eyes from the sun** proteger los ojos contra el sol.
shieling ['ʃiːliŋ] *n* (*Scot*) (*pasture*) pasto *m*, prado *m*; (*hut*) choza *f*, cabaña *f*; albergue *m*; (*sheepfold*) aprisco *m*.
shift [ʃift] **1** *n* (**a**) (*change*) cambio *m* (*in, of* de); cambio *m* de sitio, traslado *m*, movimiento *m*; **— of wind** cambio *m* (de dirección) del viento; **consonant —** cambio *m* consonántico; **there has been a — in policy** ha habido un cambio de política; **one notes a — of emphasis** se nota un cambio de énfasis; **the — from north to south is increasing** el movimiento de norte a sur se acelera; **to make a —** cambiar de sitio, (*of person*) irse, largarse; **it's time we made a —** ya es hora de marcharnos.
(**b**) (*at work*) turno *m*; (*of workers*) tanda *f*; **an 8-hour —** un turno de 8 horas; **three-shift system** sistema *m* de tres turnos; **to work in —s** trabajar por turnos.
(**c**) (*expedient*) recurso *m*, expediente *m*; (*pej*) maña *f*, astucia *f*; **to make — with** ayudarse con, contentarse con; **to make — without** pasarse sin; **to make — to + infin** arreglárselas para + *infin*, ingeniarse por + *infin*.
(**d**) (*arch*) camisa *f* (de mujer).
2 *vt* cambiar; (*move*) cambiar de sitio, trasladar a otro sitio, mover; (*budge*) mover; (*get rid of*) quitarse de encima, librarse de; **to — scenery** cambiar el decorado; **— it over to the wall** póngalo contra la pared; **we could not — him from his opinion** no logramos hacerle cambiar de opinión; **I can't — this cold** no me quito este catarro; **they —ed him to Valencia** le trasladaron a Valencia; **we shall have to — 20 tons** hará falta mover 20 toneladas; **to — the blame on to someone else** echar la culpa a otro.
3 *vi* (**a**) (*move*) moverse; cambiar; cambiar de sitio; (*person*) cambiar de puesto, trasladarse a otro sitio; (*move house*) mudar; (*of ballast, cargo*) correrse; (*of wind*) cambiar; **to — about, to — around** cambiar (mucho) de sitio, (*in job*) cambiar de empleo; **the government has not —ed from its earlier position** el gobierno no ha modificado en lo más mínimo su actitud anterior; **to — into second gear** cambiar a la segunda velocidad; **the scene —s to Burgos** la escena cambia a Burgos; **he —ed to Lima** se trasladó a Lima.
(**b**) (*fam: car etc*) ir a gran velocidad, correr; (*person*) darse prisa, menearse; —! ¡menearse!
(**c**) **to — for oneself** valerse por sí mismo, ayudarse a sí mismo.
shiftily ['ʃiftili] *adv* astutamente; furtivamente; **to behave —** comportarse de modo sospechoso.
shiftiness ['ʃiftinis] *n* lo tramposo, lo taimado, astucia *f*; lo sospechoso; lo furtivo.
shifting ['ʃiftiŋ] *adj sand etc* movedizo.
shift key ['ʃiftkiː] *n* tecla *f* de mayúsculas.
shiftless ['ʃiftlis] *adj* (*lazy*) vago, holgazán; (*useless*) inútil; (*untrustworthy*) informal.
shiftlessness ['ʃiftlisnis] *n* holgazanería *f*; inutilidad *f*; informalidad *f*.
shift work ['ʃiftwɜːk] *n* trabajo *m* por turno.
shifty ['ʃifti] *adj* tramposo, taimado, astuto; *conduct* sospechoso; *glance etc* furtivo.
shifty-eyed ['ʃiftiˈaid] *adj* de mirada furtiva.
shillelagh [ʃəˈleilə] *n* (*Ir*) cachiporra *f*.
shilling ['ʃiliŋ] *n* chelín *m*; **6 —s in the pound** 6 chelines por libra; **to cut someone off with a —** desheredar a uno.
shilly-shally ['ʃili͵ʃæli] *vi* vacilar, no resolverse, no saber qué hacer; **you've shilly-shallied long enough** has estado bastante tiempo ya sin resolverte.
shimmer ['ʃimə*] **1** *n* reflejo *m* trémulo, resplandor *m* trémulo. **2** *vi* rielar, relucir.
shimmering ['ʃiməriŋ] *adj*, **shimmery** ['ʃiməri] *adj* reluciente; *light* trémulo.

shimmy ['ʃimi] n (fam) camisa f (de mujer).

shin [ʃin] **1** n espinilla f; (of meat) jarrete m, corvejón m. **2** vi: to — **up** trepar; to — **up a tree** trepar a un árbol.

shinbone ['ʃinbəun] n espinilla f.

shindig ['ʃindig] n (sl) fiesta f, juerga f.

shindy ['ʃindi] n (noise) ruido m grande, conmoción f; (dispute) lío m, bronca f; **to kick up a** — meter ruido; armar un lío.

shine [ʃain] **1** n (a) (brilliance) brillo m, lustre m; **to give one's shoes a** — sacar brillo a los zapatos, limpiar los zapatos; **to take the** — **off something** deslustrar algo, hacer que algo pierda su lustre; **to take the** — **off something** hacer que algo pierda su interés, hacer que algo resulte soso; **to take a** — **to** tomar simpatía por.
(b) (Meteorol) buen tiempo m, tiempo m de sol; **we'll go rain or** — iremos no importa el tiempo que haga.
2 (irr: pret and ptp **shone**) vt (a) shoes sacar brillo a, limpiar; silver etc pulir.
(b) **to** — **a light on something** proyectar una luz sobre algo; — **the torch this way** dirige la linterna hacia este lado.
3 vi (a) brillar; relucir, resplandecer; **a lamp was shining** brillaba una lámpara; **the sun is shining** hay sol; **the metal shone in the sun** el metal relucía al sol; **her face shone with happiness** su cara irradiaba felicidad; **a certain quiet confidence** —**s through** trasciende cierta serenidad.
(b) (fig) brillar, lucirse, distinguirse; **he doesn't exactly** — **at his work** no brilla en sus estudios que digamos; **he shone as a footballer** se distinguió como futbolista.

shiner [ʃainə*] n (person) limpiabotas m; (sl: eye) ojo m; (hum) ojo m morado; (Fin) moneda antigua (inglesa) de una libra.

shingle¹ ['ʃiŋgl] **1** n (Archit) ripia f; (hair style) corte m a lo garçon. **2** vt hair cortar a lo garçon.

shingle² ['ʃiŋgl] n (pebbles) guijos mpl, guijarral m; (beach) playa f guijarrosa.

shingles ['ʃiŋglz] npl (Med) herpes mpl or fpl.

shingly ['ʃiŋgli] adj guijarroso.

shining ['ʃainiŋ] adj brillante, lustroso; face etc radiante; example notable.

shin pad ['ʃinpæd] n, (US) — **guard** [gɑːd] n espinillera f.

Shintoism ['ʃintəuizəm] n sintoísmo m.

shinty ['ʃinti] n (Scot) especie de hockey sobre hierba.

shiny ['ʃaini] adj brillante, lustroso.

ship [ʃip] **1** n (a) buque m, barco m, navío m; **capital** — acorazado m; **the good** — **Venus** el buque Venus, el Venus; **Her** (or **His**) **Majesty's S**— (abbr **HMS**) buque m de guerra inglés; **to serve on HMS Warspite** servir en el Warspite; **merchant** — mercante m; **the** — **of the desert** el camello; — **of the line** buque m de línea; **on board** — a bordo; **to abandon** — abandonar el barco; **to clear a** — **for action** alistar un buque para el combate; **when my** — **comes home** cuando me haga rico, cuando la suerte me favorezca; **to jump** — desertar del buque; **to take** — **for** embarcarse para.
(b) —**'s boat** lancha f, bote m salvavidas; —**'s company** tripulación f; —**'s doctor** médico m de a bordo; —**'s papers** documentación f del buque.
2 vt (a) (put on board) goods embarcar; mast izar; oars desarmar; **to** — **a sea** embarcar agua.
(b) (transport) transportar (por vía marítima), enviar, expedir; **a new engine had to be** —**ped out to them** hubo que enviarles un nuevo motor.
3 vi embarcarse (on en).

shipboard ['ʃipbɔːd] n: **on** — a bordo.

shipbreaker ['ʃip‚breikə*] n desguazador m.

shipbuilder ['ʃip‚bildə*] n constructor m de buques, arquitecto m naval.

shipbuilding ['ʃip‚bildiŋ] n construcción f de buques, construcción f naval.

ship canal ['ʃipkə‚næl] n canal m de navegación.

ship chandler ['ʃip‚tʃɑːndlə*] n abastecedor m de buques.

shipload ['ʃipləud] n cargamento m (entero) de un buque; (loosely) envío m, cantidad f enviada; (fam) montón m; **we have jam by the** — tenemos mermelada a montones; **the tourists are arriving by the** — los turistas vienen en masa.

shipmate ['ʃipmeit] n camarada m de a bordo.

shipment ['ʃipmənt] n (act) embarque m; transporte m; (quantity) envío m, remesa f.

shipowner ['ʃipəunə*] n naviero m.

shipper ['ʃipə*] n exportador m; (sender) remitente m.

shipping ['ʃipiŋ] **1** n (act) embarque m; transporte m (por vía marítima); (ships) buques mpl, barcos mpl; (ships of a country) flota f, marina f; **losses in 1942** cantidad f (or tonelaje m) de buques perdidos en 1942; **the canal is closed to British** — el canal está cerrado para la marina británica.
2 attr agent marítimo; company naviero; office de compañía de navegación; — **intelligence** noticias fpl navieras.

shipshape ['ʃipʃeip] adv, adj en buen orden, en regla; **to get everything** — ponerlo todo en orden.

shipwreck ['ʃiprek] **1** n naufragio m (also fig).
2 vt: **to be** —**ed** naufragar.

shipwrecked ['ʃiprekt] adj: — **person** náufrago m, a f.

shipwright ['ʃiprait] n (worker) carpintero m de navío; (owner) naviero m.

shipyard ['ʃipjɑːd] n astillero m, varadero m.

shire [ʃaiə*] n condado m; **the S**—**s** los condados centrales de Inglaterra.

-shire [ʃiə*] n in compounds: condado m.

shirk [ʃəːk] **1** vt eludir, esquivar; obligation faltar a; work no hacer, rehuir; difficulty, issue escamotear; **to** — **doing something** esquivar el deber de hacer algo.
2 vi faltar al deber; escamotear; (not work) gandulear; **you're** —**ing!** ¡eres un gandul!

shirker ['ʃəːkə*] n gandul m.

shirr [ʃəː*] vt (Sew) fruncir.

shirt [ʃəːt] n camisa f; **boiled** — camisa f de pechera dura; **soft** — camisa f sin almidonar; **to keep one's** — **on** (fam) quedarse sereno; **to put one's** — **on a horse** apostar todo lo que tiene uno a un caballo.

shirt collar ['ʃəːt‚kɔlə*] n cuello m de camisa.

shirt front ['ʃəːtfrʌnt] n pechera f.

shirtless ['ʃəːtlis] adj sin camisa, descamisado.

shirt sleeves ['ʃəːtsliːvz] npl: **to be in** — estar en mangas de camisa.

shirttail ['ʃəːtteil] n faldón m (de camisa).

shirtwaist ['ʃəːtweist] n (US) blusa f.

shirty ['ʃəːti] adj (sl): **he was pretty** — **about it** la cosa no le gustó en absoluto, la cosa no le cayó en gracia; **to get** — ponerse negro (fam).

shiver¹ ['ʃivə*] **1** n (a) temblor m, estremecimiento m; (with cold) tiritón m; (of horror etc) escalofrío m; **to give a** — estremecerse; **it sent** —**s down my back** me dio escalofríos.
(b) **the** —**s** (fig) dentera f, grima f; **it gives me the** —**s** (of fear) me da miedo, (of taste etc) me da dentera.
2 vi temblar, estremecerse; vibrar; (with fear) temblar, dar diente con diente; (with cold) tiritar.

shiver² ['ʃivə*] **1** vt (break) romper, hacer añicos.
2 vi romperse, hacerse añicos.

shivery ['ʃivəri] adj estremecido; (sensitive to cold) friolento; **to feel** — tener frío, tener escalofríos.

shoal¹ [ʃəul] **1** n (sandbank etc) banco m de arena, bajío m, bajo m. **2** vi disminuir en profundidad, hacerse menos profundo.

shoal² [ʃəul] n (of fish) banco m, cardumen m; (of people etc) multitud f; muchedumbre f; **to come in** —**s** venir en tropel; **we have** —**s of applications** tenemos montones de solicitudes.

shock¹ [ʃɔk] **1** n (a) (Elec) descarga f (eléctrica); (collision) choque m, colisión f; (jolt) sacudida f; (of earthquake) seísmo m, temblor m de tierra; **she got a** — **from the refrigerator** la nevera le dio una descarga; **the** — **of the explosion was felt 5 miles away** se apreció el choque de la explosión a una distancia de 5 millas; **the house collapsed at the first** — al primer seísmo se hundió la casa.
(b) (emotional) conmoción f (desagradable); (start) sobresalto m, susto m; **our feeling is one of** — lo que sentimos es un enorme disgusto; **the** — **was too much for him** la conmoción que le produjo la noticia le anonadó; **the** — **killed him** el disgusto le mató; **it comes as a** — **to hear that . . .** nos asombramos al saber que . . .; **to give someone a** — sobresaltar a uno; asombrar a uno; **it gave me a nasty** — me produjo una conmoción desagradable; **the news gave me quite a** — la noticia me afectó muchísimo, la noticia me disgustó bastante; **what a** — **you gave me!** ¡qué susto me diste!
(c) (Med) shock m, postración f nerviosa; **to be suffering from** — padecer una postración nerviosa.
2 adj, attr: — **tactics** táctica f de ataque repentino; — **treatment** (Med) tratamiento m de choque eléctrico; — **troops** tropas fpl de asalto; — **worker** trabajador m que se distingue superando la norma de producción.
3 vt (startle) sobresaltar, dar un susto a; (affect

emotionally) dar un disgusto a, producir una conmoción desagradable a; (*make indignant*) indignar; (*because of impropriety*) escandalizar; ofender; **she is easily —ed** se ofende por cualquier cosa, se escandaliza por poca cosa; **I was —ed to hear the news** la noticia me dio un enorme disgusto, la noticia me asombró; **now don't be —ed at what I'm going to say** no se escandalice de lo que le voy a decir; **you can't — me** yo no me asombro de nada; **to — someone into doing something** dar una sacudida a uno para animarle a hacer algo; **to — someone out of his complacency** hacer que uno se dé cuenta de la necesidad de hacer algo, destruir el optimismo de uno.

shock² [ʃɔk] (*Agr*) **1** *n* tresnal *m*, garbera *f*. **2** *vt* poner en tresnales.

shock³ [ʃɔk] *n*: **— of hair** greña *f*; melena *f*.

shock absorber [ˈʃɔkəb,zɔːbə*] *n* amortiguador *m*, parachoques *m*.

shocker [ˈʃɔkə*] *n* (a) (*Lit*) novelucha *f*. (b) **it's a —** es horrible; es de lo más vil; **he's a —** es un sinvergüenza, es un canalla; **you —!** (*hum*) ¡canalla!

shockheaded [ˈʃɔkˈhedid] *adj* greñudo; melenudo.

shocking [ˈʃɔkiŋ] **1** *adj* (*appalling*) espantoso, horrible; (*morally improper*) escandaloso, vergonzoso, ofensivo; **how —!** ¡qué horror!; **isn't it —?** ¿es espantoso, eh?; **it was a — sight** fue un espectáculo horrible; **she has — taste** tiene un pésimo gusto; **the book is not all that —** el libro es menos escandaloso de lo que se dice.

2 *adv* (*fam*): **a — bad film** una película de bajísima calidad; **it was — awful** fue de lo más horrible.

shockingly [ˈʃɔkiŋli] *adv* horriblemente; escandalosamente; **— dear** terriblemente caro; **a — bad film** una película de bajísima calidad; **to behave —** comportarse de modo escandaloso.

shockproof [ˈʃɔkpruːf] *adj* a prueba de choques; *person* imperturbable.

shock therapy [ˈʃɔk,θerəpi] *n* shockterapia *f*.

shock wave [ˈʃɔkweiv] *n* onda *f* de choque.

shod [ʃɔd] *pret and ptp of* **shoe**; **— with** calzado de.

shoddiness [ˈʃɔdinis] *n* baja calidad *f*; mala hechura *f*; cursilería *f*.

shoddy [ˈʃɔdi] **1** *adj* de pacotilla, de bajísima calidad; muy mal hecho; cursi.

2 *n* (*cloth*) paño *m* burdo de lana; (*wool*) lana *f* regenerada; (*as waste, fertilizer*) desechos *mpl* de lana.

shoe [ʃuː] **1** *n* zapato *m*; (*horse—*) herradura *f*; (*brake—*) zapata *f*; **I wouldn't like to be in his —s** no quisiera estar en su pellejo; **to cast a —** (*horse*) perder una herradura; **to put on one's —s** calzarse; **to take off one's —s** quitarse los zapatos, descalzarse; **to step into someone's —s** pasar a ocupar el puesto de uno; **to be waiting for dead men's —s** esperar a que muera uno (para pasar luego a ocupar su puesto).

2 (*irr: pret and ptp* **shod**) *vt* calzar (*with* de); *horse* herrar.

shoeblack [ˈʃuːblæk] *n* limpiabotas *m*.

shoeblacking [ˈʃuː,blækiŋ] *n* betún *m*.

shoebrush [ˈʃuːbrʌʃ] *n* cepillo *m* para zapatos.

shoehorn [ˈʃuːhɔːn] *n* calzador *m*.

shoelace [ˈʃuːleis] *n* cordón *m*.

shoe leather [ˈʃuː,leðə*] *n* cuero *m* para zapatos; **to wear out one's —** gastarse el calzado (andando de acá para allá).

shoemaker [ˈʃuː,meikə*] *n* zapatero *m*; **—'s (shop)** zapatería *f*.

shoemender [ˈʃuː,mendə*] *n* zapatero *m* remendón.

shoeshine [ˈʃuːʃain] *n* (*US*): **to have a —** hacerse limpiar los zapatos; **— boy** limpiabotas *m*.

shoeshop [ˈʃuːʃɔp] *n* zapatería *f*, tienda *f* de calzado.

shoestring [ˈʃuːstriŋ] *n* (*US*) cordón *m*; **to do something on a —** hacer algo con muy poco dinero; **to live on a —** vivir con escasos recursos.

shoetree [ˈʃuːtriː] *n* horma *f*.

shone [ʃɔn] *pret and ptp of* **shine**.

shoo [ʃuː] **1** *interj* ¡zape!, ¡ox!; (*to child*) ¡vete!, ¡fuera de aquí!

2 *vt* ahuyentar; **I had to — the children away** tuve que decirles a los niños que se fueran a otra parte; **somebody —ed us away** alguien nos mandó ir a otra parte.

shook [ʃuk] *pret of* **shake**.

shoot [ʃuːt] **1** *n* (a) (*Bot*) renuevo *m*, retoño *m*, vástago *m*.

(b) (*inclined plane*) conducto *m* inclinado; (*on ice*) resbaladero *m*; *see* **chute**.

(c) (*shooting party, hunt*) partida *f* de caza, cacería *f*; (*competition*) certamen *m* de tiro al blanco.

(d) (*preserve*) coto *m*, vedado *m*.

2 (*irr: pret and ptp* **shot**) *vt* (a) (*Mil etc*) *bullet* disparar, tirar; *arrow etc* disparar; *gun* disparar, descargar.

(b) *person, animal* matar con arma de fuego, herir con arma de fuego; (*execute*) fusilar; **to — someone dead, to — someone to death** matar a uno a tiros; **he was shot dead by a policeman** fue muerto a tiros por un policía; **he was shot in the leg** una bala le hirió en la pierna; **he had been shot through the heart** la bala le había atravesado el corazón; **I'll — you a rabbit** te cazaré un conejo; **he shot his wife** pegó un tiro a su mujer; **he was shot as a spy** le fusilaron por espía; **you'll get me shot** (*fig*) si hago esto para ti me despiden; **people have been shot for less** han fusilado a muchos por menos motivos.

(c) (*fig*) *film* rodar; *film scene* fotografiar, filmar; *subject of snapshot* tomar, sacar una instantánea de; *goal* marcar, meter; *bridge* pasar por debajo de; *rapids* salvar, atravesar; *coal, rubbish etc* verter, vaciar; *dice* echar; *net* echar; *ray of light* echar; *glance* echar, lanzar; **"— no rubbish"** "prohibido verter basuras"; **to — the sun** tomar la altura del sol; **to — a question at someone** disparar una pregunta inesperada a uno.

(d) (*with adv or prep*) **to — away all one's ammunition** quemar todos sus cartuchos; **he had a leg shot away** un disparo le cercenó una pierna; **they shot the idea back to the committee** devolvieron la idea rápidamente al comité; **to — down** *aeroplane* derribar, abatir; *person* matar de un tiro; *argument* rebatir; **he was shot down over Italy** fue derribado sobre Italia; **he had a finger shot off** una bala le cercenó un dedo; **to — out** *sparks etc* arrojar; *hand* extender rápidamente, extender inesperadamente; *tongue* sacar rápidamente; **we were literally shot out of bed by the noise** nos vimos materialmente arrancados de nuestras camas por el estruendo; **they shot it out in the saloon** lo resolvieron a tiros en el bar; **to — up** *aerodrome* destrozar a tiros, *town* asaltar a tiros.

3 *vi* (a) (*with gun: as sport*) practicar el deporte del tiro al blanco, (*as hunter*) ser cazador de escopeta; **do you —?** ¿le gusta cazar con escopeta?; **I haven't shot for years** hace tiempo que no manejo la escopeta; **he —s for Oxford** forma parte del equipo de tiro de Oxford; **we can — over Lord Emsworth's ground** podemos cazar en la finca de Lord Emsworth; **if they attack you, —** si os atacan, disparad; **— to kill** tirad a matar; **don't —!** ¡no dispare!; **to — at someone** tirar a uno, pegar un tiro a uno; **he shot at me but missed** disparó contra mí pero erró el tiro; **to — back** devolver el tiro; **to — wide of the mark** errar el tiro.

(b) **—!** (*in conversation: fam*) ¡adelante!, ¡bien, dígame!

(c) (*Football etc*) chutar, tirar; **—!** ¡chuta!; **to — at goal** tirar a gol.

(d) (*of pain*) punzar, dar punzadas.

(e) (*Bot*) brotar; **to — up** crecer, espigar (*also fig, of person*).

(f) (*move rapidly: of person*) lanzarse, precipitarse; **he shot to the door** se lanzó hacia la puerta; **to — ahead** adelantarse mucho (*of* a); **we were —ing along** íbamos a gran velocidad; **to — by, to — past** pasar como un meteoro; **to — in** entrar como una bala; **he shot into space** se lanzó al espacio; **to — off, to — out** (*person etc*) salir como una bala, salir disparado; **flames were —ing out of the window** las llamas salían de la ventana; **the car shot past us** el coche pasó como un rayo; **prices are —ing up** los precios suben vertiginosamente.

shooting [ˈʃuːtiŋ] **1** *n* (a) (*shots*) tiros *mpl*, disparos *mpl*; (*continuous —*) tiroteo *m*; (*by artillery*) cañoneo *m*, bombardeo *m*.

(b) (*act: murder*) asesinato *m*; (*execution*) fusilamiento *m*; (*of film*) rodaje *m*.

(c) (*Hunting*) caza *f* con escopeta; **he comes each year for the —** viene cada año para la caza; **there is good — in Asturias** Asturias es buen terreno para la caza; **to go —** ir de caza, ir a cazar; **good —!** ¡buen tiro!; ¡bravo!

2 *adj, attr de* caza; *pain* punzante; **— war** guerra *f* a tiros; **— affray** refriega *f* con tiros.

shooting box [ˈʃuːtiŋbɔks] *n*, **— lodge** [lɔdʒ] *n* pabellón *m* de caza.

shooting brake [ˈʃuːtiŋbreik] *n* (*Aut*) rubia *f*, furgoneta *f*.

shooting gallery [ˈʃuːtiŋ,gæləri] *n* galería *f* de tiro al blanco.

shooting jacket [ˈʃuːtiŋ,dʒækit] *n* chaquetón *m*.

shooting match ['ʃuːtiŋmætʃ] n certamen m de tiro al blanco; **the whole —** (fam) el todo, todo el negocio.

shooting party ['ʃuːtiŋ,pɑːti] n partida f de caza.

shooting range ['ʃuːtiŋreindʒ] n campo m de tiro.

shooting star ['ʃuːtiŋ'stɑː*] n estrella f fugaz.

shooting stick ['ʃuːtiŋstik] n bastón m taburete.

shop [ʃɔp] **1** n **(a)** (Comm) tienda f; (large store) almacén m; **—!** ¿quién despacha?; **to keep a —** poseer un negocio; **to set up —** poner una tienda; **to shut up —** (fig) cerrar; dar por terminado un asunto; desistir de una empresa; **to talk —** hablar del propio trabajo, hablar de asuntos profesionales; **it's all over the —** (fam) está en el mayor desorden; **she leaves things all over the —** (fam) — deja sus cosas de cualquier modo; **they're all over the —** (fam) — no tienen ni idea, carecen de todo sentido del buen orden.

(b) (Tech) taller m; **closed —** coto m cerrado. **2** vt (fam): **to — someone** traicionar a uno, delatar a uno; denunciar a uno a la policía.

3 vi comprar, hacer compras; **to go —ping** ir de compras, ir de tiendas; **to send someone —ping** enviar a uno a hacer compras; **to — at Joe's** hacer sus compras en la tienda de Joe; **to — for fish** ir a buscar pescado en las tiendas.

shop front ['ʃɔpfrʌnt] n escaparate m.

shopgirl ['ʃɔpgəːl] n dependienta f.

shop hours ['ʃɔpauəz] npl horas fpl durante las que está abierta una tienda.

shopkeeper ['ʃɔp,kiːpə*] n tendero m, a f.

shoplifter ['ʃɔp,liftə*] n mechera f, ratero m de tiendas.

shoplifting ['ʃɔp,liftiŋ] n ratería f de tiendas.

shopper ['ʃɔpə*] n comprador m, ora f.

shopping ['ʃɔpiŋ] n (act) el comprar en tiendas; (goods bought) compras fpl.

shopping bag [ʃɔpiŋbæg] n bolsa f de compras.

shopping centre, (US) **— center** ['ʃɔpiŋ,sentə*] n zona f de tiendas.

shop-soiled ['ʃɔpsɔild] adj deteriorado.

shop steward ['ʃɔp'stjuəd] n enlace m sindical.

shopwalker ['ʃɔp,wɔːkə*] n vigilante m, a f.

shop window ['ʃɔp'windəu] n escaparate m.

shore¹ [ʃɔː*] **1** n playa f; orilla f, ribera f; **these —s** (fig) estas tierras, esta parte; **on —** en tierra. **2** attr; **— leave** licencia f para ir a tierra.

shore² [ʃɔː*] **1** n puntal m; (Min) entibo m. **2** vt apuntalar; entibar; **to — up** (fig) apoyar, reforzar, sostener.

shoreline ['ʃɔːlain] n línea f de la playa.

shoreward(s) ['ʃɔːwəd(z)] adv hacia la playa.

shoring ['ʃɔːriŋ] n puntales mpl; entibos mpl.

shorn [ʃɔːn] ptp of **shear; — of sin,** desprovisto de; **— of its verbiage, this means . . .** quitando la palabrería, esto quiere decir . . .; **— of outside aid we cannot go on** sin la ayuda exterior no podemos continuar.

short [ʃɔːt] **1** adj **(a)** (in length, distance) corto; message etc corto, breve, sucinto; person bajo; radio wave corto; **the —est route** la ruta más corta; **a — way off** a poca distancia, no muy lejos; **by a — head** por una cabeza escasa; **to be — in the leg** tener las piernas cortas; **these trousers are a bit — in the leg** estos pantalones tienen la pierna algo pequeña; **the —answer is that . . .** en pocas palabras la razón es que . . .; **to take — steps** dar pequeños pasos; **to take a — walk** dar un paseíto.

(b) "Pat" is — for "Patricia" "Pat" es forma abreviada de "Patricia"; "living" is — for "living room" "living" es apócope de "living room".

(c) (in time) corto, breve; de poca duración; vowel breve; memory flaco, malo; **for a — time** por poco tiempo; **February is a — month** febrero es un mes corto; **the days are getting —er** los días se hacen más breves; **time is getting —er** nos queda poco tiempo.

(d) reply brusco, seco; manner brusco; temper vivo; **to be — with someone** tratar a uno con sequedad.

(e) (insufficient) insuficiente; **5 — faltan 5, 5 de menos; I'm £3 — me faltan 3 libras; it's 2 kilos — faltan 2 kilos; we were — last week** la semana pasada nos faltó algo; **to give — weight** vender algo con peso insuficiente; **to give someone — change** no devolver a uno toda la vuelta que se le debe; **to be on — time** trabajar en jornadas reducidas; **not far — of £100** poco menos de 100 libras; **nothing — of total surrender** nada menos que la rendición incondicional; **it's little — of madness** falta poco para que esto se llame una locura;

nothing — of a bomb would stop him fuera de una bomba nada le impediría.

(f) to be — of estar falto de, andar escaso de; **we are — of petrol** tenemos poca gasolina, casi no tenemos gasolina; **we're not — of volunteers** se han ofrecido muchos voluntarios, no andamos escasos de voluntarios; **I was — of clubs** (Cards) tenía poco trébol; **bananas are very —** escasean los plátanos, casi no hay plátanos; **to go — of** pasarse sin; **no one goes — in this house** en esta casa nadie padece hambre; **to run —** escasear; **we ran — of petrol** se nos acabó la gasolina, quedamos sin gasolina.

(g) pastry quebradizo.

2 adv **(a) to cut —** acortar, abreviar; interrumpir; terminar inesperadamente; **they had to cut — their holiday** tuvieron que interrumpir sus vacaciones; **to fall —** resultar ser insuficiente, no alcanzar el nivel previsto; **production has fallen — by 100 tons** la producción arroja un déficit de 100 toneladas; **to fall — of the target** no alcanzar el blanco, no llegar al blanco; **to fall — of expectations** no cumplir las esperanzas; **it falls far — of what we require** queda muy lejos de satisfacer nuestras exigencias; **to sell —** (Fin) vender al descubierto; **to sell someone —** (fig) engañar a uno en un negocio; **to stop —** parar en seco; parar de repente; **to stop — of** detenerse antes de a; **to be taken —** necesitar urgentemente ir al wáter.

(b) — of blowing it up a menos que lo volemos, a no ser que lo volemos; **— of murder I'll do anything** lo haré todo menos matar.

4 vt (Elec) poner en cortocircuito.

5 vi ponerse en cortocircuito.

shortage ['ʃɔːtidʒ] n escasez f, falta f; insuficiencia f; penuria f; **the housing —** la crisis de la vivienda; **— of staff** insuficiencia f de personal; **in times of —** en las épocas de penuria; **there is no — of advice** no es que falten los consejos.

shortbread ['ʃɔːtbred] n torta dulce seca y quebradiza.

shortcake ['ʃɔːtkeik] n torta f de frutas.

short-change ['ʃɔːt'tʃeindʒ] vt: **to — someone** no devolver a uno toda la vuelta que se le debe; (fig) estafar a uno, engañar a uno.

short-circuit ['ʃɔːt'səːkit] **1** n cortocircuito m. **2** vt poner en cortocircuito. **3** vi ponerse en cortocircuito.

shortcoming ['ʃɔːtkʌmiŋ] n defecto m, deficiencia f.

short-dated ['ʃɔːt'deitid] adj a corto plazo.

shorten ['ʃɔːtn] **1** vt acortar; abreviar; reducir; holiday, journey etc acortar.

2 vi acortarse; abreviarse; reducirse; **the odds have —ed** los puntos de ventaja se han reducido.

shortening ['ʃɔːtniŋ] n acortamiento m; abreviación f; reducción f.

shortfall ['ʃɔːtfɔːl] n déficit m.

short-haired ['ʃɔːt'hɛəd] adj pelicorto.

shorthand ['ʃɔːthænd] n taquigrafía f; **— note** nota f taquigráfica; **to take —** escribir al dictado; **to take something down in —** apuntar algo taquigráficamente.

short-handed ['ʃɔːt'hændid] adj falto de personal, falto de mano de obra.

shorthand typist ['ʃɔːthænd'taipist] n taquimeca f, taquimecanógrafa f.

shorthand writer ['ʃɔːthænd,raitə*] n taquígrafo m, a f.

shortish ['ʃɔːtiʃ] adj algo pequeño, más bien bajo.

short list ['ʃɔːt'list] **1** n lista f de candidatos escogidos.

2 vt: **to short-list someone** poner a uno en la lista de candidatos escogidos (quienes pasan después a otras pruebas para que se nombre a uno de ellos a un puesto); **he has not been —ed** no figura en la lista de los candidatos escogidos.

short-lived ['ʃɔːt'livd] adj efímero.

shortly ['ʃɔːtli] adv **(a)** en breve, dentro de poco; luego; **— after** poco después; **— before** this poco tiempo antes de esto; **you shall see it very —** lo va a ver muy pronto.

(b) (curtly) bruscamente, secamente.

shortness ['ʃɔːtnis] n (in length, distance) cortedad f; (of message etc) brevedad f; (of person) pequeñez f; (in time) brevedad f, poca duración f; (of manner) brusquedad f; **because of the — of my memory** debido a mi mala memoria; **— of sight** miopía f; **— of breath** falta f de aliento, respiración f difícil.

short-range ['ʃɔːt'reindʒ] adj gun de corto alcance; aircraft de autonomía limitada, de corto radio de acción.

short-sighted ['ʃɔːt'saitid] adj miope, corto de vista; (fig) person falto de previsión, imprevisor; measure etc imprudente, sin eficacia a la larga.

short-sightedly ['ʃɔːt'saitidli] *adv* con ojos de miope; (*fig*) imprudentemente.

short-sightedness ['ʃɔːt'saitidnis] *n* miopía *f*; cortedad *f* de vista; (*fig*) falta *f* de previsión, imprevisión *f*; imprudencia *f*, ineficacia *f* a la larga.

short-tempered ['ʃɔːt'tempəd] *adj* de genio vivo, enojadizo.

short-term ['ʃɔːttəːm] *adj* a plazo corto.

short-time ['ʃɔːt'taim] **1** *adj*: — **working** sistema *m* de jornadas reducidas, sistema *m* de jornada limitada; **to be on** — **working** trabajar en jornadas reducidas.
2 *adv*: **to work** — trabajar en jornadas reducidas.

shortwave ['ʃɔːt,weiv] *adj* de onda corta.

short-winded ['ʃɔːt'windid] *adj* corto de resuello.

shorty ['ʃɔːti] *n* (*fam*) persona *f* bajita.

shot [ʃɔt] **1** *n* (a) (*missile*) bala *f*; proyectil *m*; (*sound of* —) tiro *m*, disparo *m*; (*causing wound*) balazo *m*; (*pellets*) perdigones *mpl*; (*weight*, *Sport*) peso *m*; — **across the bows, warning** — cañonazo *m* de advertencia; **good** —! ¡muy bien!; **Parthian** — flecha *f* del parto; **parting** — última observación *f*; **palabra** *f* dicha al despedirse; **random** — disparo *m* hecho sin apuntar; **not by a long** — ni con mucho; **to fire a** — **at someone** disparar sobre uno, tirar a uno; **who fired that** —? ¿quién disparó?; **it surrendered without firing a** — (*or* **without a** — **being fired**) se rindió sin resistencia alguna; **we captured it without firing a** — lo tomamos sin disparar una sola vez; **to exchange** —**s** tirotearse; **to take a** — **at someone** tirar a uno.
(b) (*person*) tirador *m*, ora *f*; **big** — (*fam*) pez *m* gordo (*fam*), personaje *m* importante; **to be a crack** — ser un tirador experto.
(c) (*of space exploration*) lanzamiento *m*; cohete *m*, vehículo *m* espacial; **moon** — lanzamiento *m* de un cohete hacia la luna; *see* **space** —.
(d) (*Sport: with club etc*) golpe *m*; (*throw*) tirada *f*, echada *f*; (*at goal*) tiro *m*.
(e) **I'll do it like a** — lo haré de muy buena gana; **he did it like a** — lo hizo de buena gana; **he was off like a** — partió como una bala.
(f) (*attempt*) tentativa *f*; (*guess*) conjetura *f*; **it's your** — te toca a ti; **to have a** — probar suerte; **to have a** — **at** + *ger* hacer una tentativa de + *infin*; **will you have a** — **at it?** ¿quieres probarlo?
(g) (*injection*) inyección *f*; (*dose*) dosis *f*; **a** — **of rum** un trago de ron; **it's a** — **in the arm for . . .** es un estímulo para . . ., es una ayuda a . . .; **the industry needs a** — **in the arm** la industria necesita una ayuda económica.
(h) (*Phot*) foto *f*, instantánea *f*; (*in film*) fotograma *m*, toma *f*, plano *m*; **a series of** —**s of Venice** una serie de fotos de Venecia.
2 *pret and ptp of* **shoot**; — **silk** seda *f* tornasolada; **to get** — **of** (*fam*) deshacerse de, quitarse de encima.

-shot [ʃɔt]: *eg* **within ear**— al alcance del oído.

shot firer ['ʃɔtfaiərə*] *n* pegador *m*.

shotgun ['ʃɔtgʌn] *n* escopeta *f*; *see* **marriage**.

should [ʃud] (*irr*: *pret and conditional of* **shall**) *v aux*
(a) (*used to form conditional tense*) **I** — **go if they sent for me** iría si me llamasen; — **I be out at the time** si estoy fuera en aquel momento; **I** —**n't be surprised if . . .** no me sorprendería si . . .; **I** —**n't if I were you** yo en tu lugar no lo haría; **he ordered that it** — **be done** mandó que se hiciera así; **thanks, I** — **like to** gracias, me gustaría; **I** —**n't like to say** prefiero no decirlo.
(b) (*statements of duty and command*) **all cars** — **carry lights** todos los coches han de llevar luces, conviene que todos los coches lleven luces; **you** —**n't do that** es aconsejable no hacer eso, es mejor no hacer eso; **all is as it** — **be** todo está en regla; . . ., **which is as it** — **be**, . . ., como es razonable; **why** — **you want to know?** ¿por qué has de saberlo tú?; **he** — **know that . . .** debiera saber que . . .; **he** — **have paid it** debiera haberlo pagado.
(c) (*statements of probability*) **he** — **be there by now** ha de estar allí ya; **they** — **arrive tomorrow** han de llegar mañana; **this** — **be good** esto promete ser bueno.

shoulder ['ʃəuldə*] **1** *n* hombro *m*; espaldas *fpl*; (*of meat*) espalda *f*; (*of hill*) lomo *m*; (*of motorway*) andén *m*; **to carry something on one's** —**s** llevar algo a hombros; **he was carried out on their** —**s** le sacaron a hombros; **to give someone the cold** — volver la espalda a uno; **to give someone something straight from the** — decir algo a uno sin rodeos; **to put one's** — **to the wheel** arrimar el hombro; **to rub** —**s with someone** codearse con uno; **to stand** — **to** — estar hombro con hombro.

2 *vt* (*carry*) llevar al hombro; (*pick up*) poner al hombro; (*fig*) *responsibilities etc* cargar con; — **arms!** ¡armas al hombro!; **to** — **someone aside** apartar a uno con el hombro; abrirse paso empujando a uno con el hombro; (*fig*) dejar a uno al lado; **to** — **one's way through** abrirse paso empujando con el hombro.

shoulder blade ['ʃəuldəbleid] *n* omóplato *m*.

shoulder flash ['ʃəuldə,flæʃ] *n* (*Mil etc*) emblema *m* de hombrera, charretera *f*.

shoulder knot ['ʃəuldənɔt] *n* dragona *f*.

shoulder pad ['ʃəuldəpæd] *n* hombrera *f*.

shoulder strap ['ʃəuldəstræp] *n* (*Mil*) dragona *f*; (*of dress*) tirante *m*; (*of satchel etc*) correa *f*.

shouldn't ['ʃudnt] = **should not**.

shout [ʃaut] **1** *n* grito *m*, voz *f*; **a** — **of protest** un grito de protesta; **there were** —**s of applause** hubo grandes aplausos; **there were** —**s of laughter** hubo grandes carcajadas; **to give someone a** — llamar a uno.
2 *vt* gritar; **to** — **abuse at someone** lanzar improperios contra uno a voz en grito; **to** — **a protest** protestar en alta voz; **to** — **someone down** protestar hasta hacer callar a uno; **to** — **a play down** hundir una obra a gritos; **to** — **out** gritar, decir a voz en grito.
3 *vi* gritar; dar voces; (*talk loudly*) hablar a voz en grito; **to** — **for help** dar voces para pedir socorro, pedir socorro a voces; **to** — **with laughter** reírse a grandes carcajadas; **to** — **out** gritar, dar gritos.
4 *vr*: **to** — **oneself hoarse** enronquecer a fuerza de gritar.

shouting ['ʃautiŋ] *n* gritos *mpl*, vocerío *m*, clamoreo *m*.

shove [ʃʌv] **1** *n* empujón *m*; **to give someone a** — empujar a uno; **can you give me a** —, **please?** (*Aut*) ¿por favor, me ayuda a arrancar empujándolo?; **one more** — **and we're there** empujad una vez más y ya está.
2 *vt* empujar; **to** — **someone aside** apartar a uno empujándole, apartar a uno a codazos; **to** — **someone back** hacer retroceder a uno empujándole; **his friends** —**d him forward** sus amigos le empujaron hacia adelante; **to** — **a boat off** (*or* **out**) echar afuera un bote; **they** —**d him out** le empujaron fuera, (*fig*) le obligaron a salir de su puesto (*etc*).
3 *vi* empujar, dar empujones; **stop shoving!** ¡dejen de empujar!; **to** — **off** (*Naut*) alejarse del muelle (*etc*); (*fig, fam*) largarse (*fam*), marcharse.

shovel ['ʃʌvl] **1** *n* pala *f*; (*mechanical*) excavadora *f* con pala.
2 *vt* traspalar, mover con pala; **to** — **earth into a pile** amontonar tierra con una pala; **he was** —**ling food into his mouth** iba llenando la boca con la mayor rapidez; **to** — **coal on to a fire** añadir carbón a la lumbre con pala; **they were** —**ling out the mud** estaban sacando el lodo con palas.

shovelboard ['ʃʌvlbɔːd] *n* juego *m* de tejo.

show [ʃəu] **1** *n* (a) (*showing*) demostración *f*; — **of hands** votación *f* por manos levantadas; **an impressive** — **of power** una impresionante exhibición de poder; **the garden is a splendid** — el jardín es un encanto; **the dahlias make a fine** — las dalias se muestran espléndidas.
(b) (*exhibition*) exposición *f*; **agricultural** — feria *f* de campo; **dog** — exposición *f* canina; **horticultural** — exposición *f* de horticultura; **trade** — feria *f* de muestras; **to be on** — estar expuesto; **he's holding his first London** — está organizando su primera exposición en Londres; *see* **horse** —, **motor** — *etc*.
(c) (*Theat etc*) función *f*, espectáculo *m*; **the last** — **starts at 11** la última función empieza a las 11; **there is no** — **on Sundays** el domingo no hay función; **to go to a** — ir a un teatro, ir a un espectáculo; **variety** — espectáculo *m* de variedades, revista *f*; **wild-beast** — espectáculo *m* de fieras; **Lord Mayor's S**— desfile *m* patrocinado por el alcalde de Londres el día de su inauguración.
(d) (*fam: undertaking, organization*) negocio *m*, empresa *f*, cosa *f*, organización *f*; **who's in charge of this** —? ¿quién manda aquí?; **he runs the** — manda él, él es el amo.
(e) (*fam*) **bad** —! ¡malo!; **good** —! ¡muy bien!, ¡bravo!; **to put up a good** — hacer un buen papel, dar buena cuenta de sí; **it's a pretty poor** —, **isn't it?** esto es un desastre, ¿no?; **to give the** — **away** tirar de la manta, (*involuntarily*) clarearse.
(f) (*outward* —) apariencia *f*; (*pomp*) boato *m*, aparato *m*, pompa *f*; **it's just for** — es sólo para

impresionar; **it's all — with him** todo lo hace para impresionar; es un farsante; **to do something for —** hacer algo para impresionar; **to make a — of resistance** aparentar resistir, fingir resistir; **to make a — of unwillingness** fingir no querer; **to make a great — of sympathy** desvivirse por mostrar compasión, llevar su compasión al exceso.

2 (*irr:* pret **showed,** ptp **shown;** (*arch*) **shewed, shewn**) vt **(a)** (*manifest*) mostrar, enseñar; *film* proyectar, poner; *slides* proyectar; *picture* exhibir; *goods* exponer; **to — someone something, to — something to someone** mostrar (*or* enseñar) algo a uno; **to — one's passport** mostrar su pasaporte, presentar su pasaporte; **what can I — you, madam?** ¿qué artículos quiere que le traiga, señora?; **to — a picture at the Academy** exhibir un cuadro en la Academia; **to — a film at Cannes** proyectar una película en Cannes; **the film was first —n in 1968** la película se estrenó en 1968; **to — someone a light** alumbrar a uno, dar luz a uno; **he had nothing to — for his trouble** se quedó sin nada después de tantos trabajos, no sacó provecho alguno de tantos trabajos.

(b) (*indicate*) indicar; (*Comm*) arrojar; **it —s 200°** indica 200°, marca 200°; **it —s a speed of . . .** indica una velocidad de . . .; **as —n in the illustration** según se indica en la lámina, como lo indica la lámina; **the roads are —n in red** las carreteras están marcadas en rojo; **to — a loss** dejar una pérdida; **to — a profit** arrojar un saldo positivo; **the figures — a rise** las cifras arrojan un aumento.

(c) (*demonstrate*) mostrar, manifestar; acusar; (*prove*) probar, demostrar; **to — intelligence** mostrar tener inteligencia, mostrar ser inteligente; **to — his disagreement, he . . .** para mostrar su disconformidad, él . . .; **she —ed no reaction** no acusó reacción alguna; **her face —ed her happiness** su felicidad se acusaba en la cara; **to — one's affection** demostrar su cariño; **a big crowd turned up to — its feeling for him** una gran multitud acudió para testimoniarle su simpatía; **the choice of dishes —s excellent taste** la selección de platos demuestra un gusto muy fino; **she's beginning to — her age** empiezan a verse en la cara las señales de su edad; **to — that . . .** demostrar que . . .; **hacer ver que . . .;** **I —ed him that this could not be true** le hice ver que esto no podía ser cierto.

(d) (*reveal*) revelar; **the gap —s her legs** el espacio deja ver sus piernas; **she likes to — her legs** le gusta hacer exhibición de sus piernas; **a dress which —s the figure** un vestido que deja ver la línea; **this —s him to be a swindler** esto le revela como estafador, esto demuestra que es estafador.

(e) (*direct*) **to — someone the way** enseñar a uno el camino; **let me — you** se lo voy a enseñar; **to — someone into a room** hacer que pase uno, hacer entrar a uno en un cuarto; **I was —n into a large hall** me hicieron pasar a un vestíbulo grande; **to — someone to his seat** enseñar a uno su asiento, acompañar a uno a su asiento.

(f) (*with adv or prep*) **to — someone in** hacer pasar a uno; **— him in at once, have him —n in at once** que pase ahora mismo; **to — off** (*display*) hacer gala de, lucir; *beauty etc* hacer resaltar, destacar; **to — someone out** acompañar a uno a la puerta; **to — up** *work etc* presentar; *beauty etc* hacer resaltar, destacar; *fraud etc* descubrir; *person* desenmascarar; *defect etc* revelar; **to — someone up** (*upstairs*) hacer subir a uno; **— him up!** ¡que suba!

3 vi **(a)** mostrarse, verse, revelarse; aparecer; (*film*) proyectarse; **your slip's —ing, madam** señora, se le ve la combinación; **it doesn't —** no se nota; **don't worry, it won't —** no te preocupes, no se notará; **the tulips are beginning to —** están apareciendo los tulipanes; **a little colour is beginning to —** now ahora se empieza a verles un poco de color; **it just goes to —!** ¡hay que ver!; **it all goes to — that . . .** todo sirve para demostrar que . . .

(b) (*with adv*) **to — off** lucirse; (*pej*) darse importancia, presumir; fachendear; **to — off in front of one's friends** presumir ante las amistades; **to — through** verse; transparentarse, trascender; **to — up** (*stand out*) destacar; (*appear*) acudir, presentarse; **he never —ed up** dejó de acudir a la cita.

4 vr: **to — oneself** presentarse; hacer acto de presencia; **to — oneself incompetent** descubrir su incompetencia, mostrarse incompetente; **it —s itself in his speech** se revela en su forma de hablar, se le nota en el habla.

show biz ['ʃəubɪz] n (sl) *see* **show business.**

showboat ['ʃəubəut] n barco-teatro m.

show business ['ʃəubɪznɪs] n los espectáculos, el mundo del espectáculo, el negocio del espectáculo; la vida de actor.

showcase ['ʃəukeɪs] n vitrina f (de exposición).

showdown ['ʃəudaun] n confrontación f; conflicto m; crisis f, momento m decisivo; **the Suez —** la crisis de Suez; **if it comes to a —** si llega a un conflicto, si llega al momento decisivo; **to have a — with someone** enfrentarse con uno, confrontarse con uno; **I'm going to have a — with the boss** le voy a decir cuatro verdades al jefe.

shower ['ʃauə*] **1** n **(a)** chaparrón m, chubasco m, aguacero m; **a day of sun and —s** un día en el cual los chubascos alternan con el sol.

(b) (*fig: of arrows, stones etc*) lluvia f.

(c) (*fig, sl*) gentuza f; **they were an utter —** eran horribles, eran unos pesados; **what a —!** ¡qué pesados!

(d) (*— bath*) ducha f; **to take a —** ducharse, tomar una ducha.

2 vt (*fig*) llover, derramar (*also to — down*); **to — someone with honours, to — honours on someone** colmar a uno de honores; **he was —ed with invitations** le llovieron encima las invitaciones, le abrumaron de invitaciones.

3 vi llover, caer un chaparrón.

shower bath ['ʃauəbɑ:θ] n, pl — **baths** [bɑ:ðz] ducha f; **to take a —** ducharse, tomar una ducha.

showerproof ['ʃauəpru:f] adj impermeable, a prueba de lluvia.

showery ['ʃauərɪ] adj day etc de chaparrones; weather lluvioso; **it will be — tomorrow** mañana habrá chaparrones.

show girl ['ʃəugɜ:l] n corista f.

showground ['ʃəugraund] n real m.

showily ['ʃəuɪlɪ] adv vistosamente, llamativamente; aparatosamente; de modo espectacular; ostentosamente.

showiness ['ʃəuɪnɪs] n vistosidad f, lo llamativo; espectacularidad f, ostentación f; boato m.

showing ['ʃəuɪŋ] n **(a)** (*of pictures etc*) exposición f; (*of film*) proyección f; **a second — of "The Blue Angel"** un reestreno de "El Ángel Azul".

(b) (*performance*) actuación f; **the team's — this season** la actuación del equipo durante la temporada actual; **the poor — of the team** la pobre actuación del equipo; **to make a good —** hacer un buen papel, dar buena cuenta de sí.

(c) on his own — según él mismo confiesa.

show jumping ['ʃəuˌdʒʌmpɪŋ] n concurso m de saltos y de hipismo.

showman ['ʃəumən] n, pl —**men** [mən] empresario m, director m de espectáculos; (*fig*) persona f ostentosa, persona f que hace gala de sus talentos, (*pej*) charlatán m; **the prime minister is a consummate —** el primer ministro es un brillante actor.

showmanship ['ʃəumənʃɪp] n instinto m del buen actor; teatralidad f; talento m para organizar grandes espectáculos.

shown [ʃəun] ptp of **show.**

show-off ['ʃəuɒf] n (*fam*) persona f ostentosa; presumido m, a f.

showpiece ['ʃəupi:s] n objeto m de valor (*or* interés etc) excepcional; **the — of the exhibition is . . .** el cuadro (*etc*) más interesante de la exposición es . . .; **this vase is a real —** este florero es realmente excepcional.

showplace ['ʃəupleɪs] n lugar m de gran atractivo, centro m turístico, monumento m; **Granada is a —** Granada es una ciudad de gran atractivo, Granada es un monumento artístico e histórico; **the new school is not typical but is a —** el nuevo colegio no es un colegio corriente, es más bien una cosa excepcional para mostrar a los visitantes.

showroom ['ʃəurum] n salón m de demostraciones; (*Art*) sala f de exposición.

show window ['ʃəuˌwɪndəu] n escaparate m.

showy ['ʃəuɪ] adj vistoso, llamativo; aparatoso, espectacular; person ostentoso.

shrank [ʃræŋk] pret of **shrink.**

shrapnel ['ʃræpnl] n metralla f.

shred [ʃred] **1** n (*bit*) fragmento m, pedazo m; (*of cloth*) triza f, jirón m; (*narrow strip*) tira f; **there isn't a — of truth in it** eso no tiene ni pizca de verdad; **if you had a — of decency** si Vd tuviese una parte mínima de honradez; **without a — of clothing on** sin cubrirle el cuerpo vestido alguno; **to be in —s** estar roto, estar destrozado; **her dress hung in —s** su vestido estaba hecho jirones; **to tear something to —s** hacer algo trizas; **to tear an argument to —s** hacer un argumento pedazos.

2 *vt* hacer trizas, hacer tiras; *food etc* desmenuzar; *meat* deshilar.

shrew [ʃruː] *n* (*Zool*) musaraña *f*; (*fig*) arpía *f*, fiera *f*; "The Taming of the S—" "La fierecilla domada".

shrewd [ʃruːd] *adj person* sagaz, perspicaz; listo; *plan etc* prudente, astuto; **— reasoning** razonamiento *m* inteligente; **that is a — thing to do** eso es lo más prudente; **that is very — of you** en eso has sido muy perspicaz; **I have a — idea that . . .** se me ocurre pensar que . . ., me parece razonable suponer que . . .

shrewdly ['ʃruːdli] *adv* sagazmente, con perspicacia; prudentemente, astutamente.

shrewdness ['ʃruːdnis] *n* sagacidad *f*, perspicacia *f*; inteligencia *f*; prudencia *f*, astucia *f*.

shrewish ['ʃruːiʃ] *adj* regañón.

shriek [ʃriːk] **1** *n* chillido *m*, grito *m* agudo; **a — of pain** un grito de dolor; **with —s of laughter** con grandes carcajadas.
2 *vt* gritar; **to — abuse at someone** lanzar improperios contra uno a voz en grito.
3 *vi* chillar, gritar; **to — with pain** chillar de dolor; **to — with laughter** reírse a grandes carcajadas; **the colour simply —s at one** es un color de lo más chillón.

shrieking ['ʃriːkiŋ] **1** *adj child, colour* chillón. **2** *n* chillidos *mpl*, gritos *mpl*.

shrift [ʃrift] *n*: **to give someone short —** echar a uno con cajas destempladas; **he gave that idea short —** mostró su completa disconformidad con tal idea, desechó muy pronto tal posibilidad; **he got short — from the boss** el jefe se mostró poco compasivo con él; **he'll get short — from me!** ¡que no venga a a pedir compasión!

shrike [ʃraik] *n* alcaudón *m*.

shrill [ʃril] **1** *adj* chillón, agudo, estridente. **2** *vi* chillar.

shrillness ['ʃrilnis] *n* lo chillón, estridencia *f*.

shrilly ['ʃrili] *adv* agudamente, de modo estridente.

shrimp [ʃrimp] **1** *n* (*Zool*) camarón *m*; (*fig*) enano *m*, renacuajo *m*. **2** *vi* (*also* **to go —ing**) pescar camarones.

shrine [ʃrain] *n* (*tomb*) sepulcro *m* (de santo), santuario *m*; relicario *m*; (*chapel*) capilla *f*; (*altar*) altar *m*; (*fig*) lugar *m* sagrado.

shrink [ʃriŋk] (*irr: pret* **shrank**, *ptp* **shrunk**) **1** *vt* encoger; contraer; *quality* reducir, disminuir; **to — a part on** (*Tech*) montar una pieza en caliente.
2 *vi* (a) encogerse; contraerse; (*quantity*) reducirse, disminuir, mermar; **to — in the wash** encogerse al lavar; **"will not —"** "no se encoge", "inencogible"; **to — away to nothing** reducirse a nada, desaparecer.
(b) **to — away, to — back** retroceder (*from* ante); acobardarse, retirarse (*from, at* ante); **I — from doing it** no me atrevo a hacerlo, me repugna hacerlo.

shrinkage ['ʃriŋkidʒ] *n* encogimiento *m*; contracción *f*; reducción *f*, disminución *f*.

shrivel ['ʃrivl] **1** *vt* (*also* **to — up**) secar, marchitar; *skin* arrugar.
2 *vi* (*also* **to — up**) secarse, marchitarse; (*skin etc*) arrugarse, avellanarse, apergaminarse; consumirse.

shrivelled, (*US*) **shriveled** ['ʃrivld] *adj plant etc* seco, marchito; *skin* arrugado, apergaminado.

shroud [ʃraud] **1** *n* sudario *m*, mortaja *f*; (*fig*) velo *m*; **—s** (*Naut*) obenques *mpl*; **a — of mystery** un velo de misterio.
2 *vt* amortajar; (*fig*) velar, cubrir; **the castle was —ed in mist** el castillo estaba envuelto en niebla; **the whole thing is —ed in mystery** el asunto entero está envuelto en un velo de misterio.

Shrovetide ['ʃrauvtaid] *n* carnestolendas *fpl*.

Shrove Tuesday ['ʃrauv'tjuːzdi] *n* martes *m* de carnaval.

shrub [ʃrʌb] *n* arbusto *m*.

shrubbery ['ʃrʌbəri] *n* arbustos *mpl*, plantío *m* de arbustos.

shrug [ʃrʌg] **1** *n* encogimiento *m* de hombros; **he said with a —** dijo encogiéndose de hombros.
2 *vt*: **to — something off** negar importancia a algo, minimizar algo; **you can't just — that off** no puedes negar la importancia de eso; **to — one's shoulders = 3** *vi* encogerse de hombros.

shrunk [ʃrʌŋk] *ptp of* **shrink**.

shrunken ['ʃrʌŋkən] *adj* encogido; (*shrivelled*) seco, marchito; apergaminado; *head* reducido; *quantity* reducido, mermado.

shuck [ʃʌk] **1** *n* vaina *f*, hollejo *m*. **2** *vt* desenvainar.

shudder ['ʃʌdə*] **1** *n* estremecimiento *m*, escalofrío *m*; (*vehicle etc*) vibración *f*, sacudida *f*; **a — ran through her** se estremeció; **she realized with a — that . . .** se estremeció al darse cuenta de que . . .
2 *vi* estremecerse (*with* de); vibrar, sacudirse.

shuffle ['ʃʌfl] **1** *n* (a) **to walk with a —** caminar arrastrando los pies.
(b) (*Cards*) barajadura *f*; **to give the cards a —** barajar las cartas; **whose — is it?** ¿a quién le toca barajar?
2 *vt* (a) *feet* arrastrar.
(b) (*mix up*) mezclar, revolver; *cards* barajar.
(c) **to — someone aside** apartar a uno, relegar a uno a un puesto menos importante; **to — something off** deshacerse de algo.
3 *vi* (a) (*walk*) arrastrar los pies; caminar (*or* bailar etc) arrastrando los pies; **he —d across to the door** fue hacia la puerta arrastrando los pies.
(b) (*Cards*) barajar.

shuffleboard ['ʃʌflbɔːd] *n* juego *m* de tejo.

shun [ʃʌn] *vt* evitar, esquivar, rehuir; volver la espalda a; **to — doing something** evitar hacer algo; **to feel —ned by the world** creer que la gente le vuelve la espalda a uno.

shunt [ʃʌnt] *vt* (*Rail*) maniobrar; **to — someone aside** apartar a uno, relegar a uno a un puesto menos importante; **to — someone off** apartar a uno de su propósito; **he was —ed into retirement** mediante una hábil maniobra entró en la vía muerta de la jubilación, lograron con maña que se jubilase; **to — someone to and fro** mandar a uno de acá para allá.

shunter ['ʃʌntə*] *n* guarda(a)gujas *m*, obrero *m* del servicio de maniobras.

shunting ['ʃʌntiŋ] *n* maniobras *fpl*.

shunting engine ['ʃʌntiŋ,endʒin] *n* locomotora *f* de maniobras.

shunting yard ['ʃʌntiŋjaːd] *n* estación *f* de maniobras, playa *f* de clasificación *f*.

shush [ʃuʃ] *interj* ¡chitón!

shut [ʃʌt] (*irr: pret and ptp* **shut**) **1** *vt* (a) cerrar; **to find the door —** encontrar que la puerta está cerrada; **he had the door — in his face** le cerraron la puerta en sus narices; **to — one's fingers in the door** cogerse los dedos en la puerta.
(b) **to — down** *factory etc* cerrar; *machine* parar; **to — in** *person* encerrar; (*surround*) cercar, rodear; **to feel — in** sentirse muy encerrado; **to get — of** (*fam*) deshacerse de, quitarse de encima; **to — off** *supply* interrumpir, cortar; *water etc* cortar; *engine* parar; (*separate*) aislar, separar (*from* de); **to be — off from** estar aislado de; **to — out** excluir; *person* excluir, negar la entrada a; **the factory —s out the view** la fábrica impide ver el paisaje (*etc*); **to — up** (*close*) cerrar; (*enclose*) encerrar; (*block*) obturar; (*silence*) hacer callar, reducir al silencio; **to — someone up in prison** recluir a uno en la cárcel.
2 *vi* cerrarse; **the lid doesn't —** la tapa no cierra bien; **to — down** cerrar, cerrarse; **to — to** (*door*) cerrarse; **to — up** callarse; **— up!** ¡cállate!; **it's best to — up and get on with it** es aconsejable callarse y seguir trabajando.
3 *vr*: **to — oneself away** (*or* **up**) encerrarse; recluirse; **he —s himself up all day in his study** permanece encerrado en su cuarto todo el día.

shutdown ['ʃʌtdaun] *n* cierre *m*.

shut-eye ['ʃʌtai] *n* (*sl*) sueño *m*; **to get some —** ir a dormir, acostarse.

shut-in ['ʃʌtin] *adj* encerrado.

shutoff ['ʃʌtɔf] *n* interruptor *m*.

shut-out ['ʃʌtaut] *n* cierre *m* (para impedir la entrada); (*Sport: US*) triunfo *m* en que el contrario no gana un solo tanto; **— bid** (*Cards*) declaración *f* aplastante.

shutter ['ʃʌtə*] *n* contraventana *f*; (*Phot*) obturador *m*; **to put up the —s** (*fig*) cerrar del todo, abandonar, (*Sport etc*) resolverse a no correr riesgo alguno.

shuttle ['ʃʌtl] **1** *n* lanzadera *f*.
2 *vt*: **to — someone about** mandar a uno de acá para allá; **the form was —d about between different departments** la solicitud fue enviada de departamento a departamento (sin que nadie la atendiese).

shuttlecock ['ʃʌtlkɔk] *n* volante *m*, zoquetillo *m*.

shuttle service ['ʃʌtl,səːvis] *n* servicio *m* de trenes (*etc*) que hacen viajes cortos entre dos puntos.

shy[1] [ʃai] **1** *adj* tímido, (*bashful*) vergonzoso; (*reserved*) reservado; (*unsociable*) huraño; *animal* huraño, asustadizo; **to be — of**, **to fight — of** procurar evitar; **to be — of +** *ger* procurar evitar **+** *infin*, no atreverse a **+** *infin*; **don't be —** no tengas miedo; **I'm £2 —** (*fam*) me faltan 2 libras, he perdido 2 libras; **he makes me —** él me hace sentirme miedoso.
2 *vi* (*of horse*) espantarse, respingar (*at something* al ver algo); **to — at a fence** negarse a saltar una valla; **to — away from something** alejarse asustado

de algo; **they shied away from the idea** se asustaron de la idea; **to — away from** + *ger* asustarse y negarse a + *infin*.

shy² [ʃai] *n* (*throw*) tirada *f*; (*fig*) tentativa *f*; **to have a — at something** probar algo, intentar algo; **to have a — at** + *ger* hacer una tentativa de + *infin*; "**5 pesetas a —**" "5 pesetas la tirada".

shyly [ˈʃaili] *adv* tímidamente; con vergüenza, vergonzosamente.

shyness [ˈʃainis] *n* timidez *f*; vergüenza *f*; reserva *f*; lo huraño, lo asustadizo.

shyster [ˈʃaistə*] *n* (*US sl*) abogado *m* trampista.

Siam [saiˈæm] Siam *m*.

Siamese [ˌsaiəˈmiːz] **1** *adj* siamés. **2** *n* siamés *m*, esa *f*. **3** *n* (*language*) siamés *m*.

Siberia [saiˈbiəriə] Siberia *f*.

Siberian [saiˈbiəriən] **1** *adj* siberiano. **2** *n* siberiano *m*, a *f*.

sibilant [ˈsibilənt] **1** *adj* sibilante. **2** *n* sibilante *f*.

sibling [ˈsibliŋ] *n* (*Bio*) hermano *m*, hermana *f*.

Sibyl [ˈsibil] *f* Sibila.

sibyl [ˈsibil] *n* sibila *f*.

sibylline [ˈsibilain] *adj* sibilino.

Sicilian [siˈsiliən] **1** *adj* siciliano. **2** *n* siciliano *m*, a *f*. **3** *n* (*dialect*) siciliano *m*.

Sicily [ˈsisili] Sicilia *f*.

sick [sik] **1** *adj* **(a)** (*ill*) enfermo; **the —** los enfermos; **to be** (**off**) **—** estar enfermo; **to go —**, **to take —** caer enfermo, enfermar; (*be absent*) ausentarse debido a enfermedad; **the cow took — and died** la vaca cayó enferma y murió; **to report —** darse de baja por enfermo.
(b) (*dizzy, about to vomit*) mareado; **to be —** vomitar; arrojar; **to feel —** estar mareado; **I get — in aeroplanes** me mareo en los aviones; **too much beer makes me —** un exceso de cerveza me da ganas de vomitar.
(c) (*fig*) **to be — at heart** tener la muerte en el alma; **to be — (and tired) of** estar harto de; **I get — of that** eso se me hace pesado, cojo asco a eso; **he just did look —!** ¡estaba la mar de abatido!; estaba furioso consigo mismo; **you make me —!** ¡me das asco!; **it makes me — to think that . . .** me da asco pensar que . . .
(d) *humour* negro, malsano.
2 *vt* (*fam*): **to — up** arrojar, devolver.

sick bay [ˈsikbei] *n* enfermería *f*.

sickbed [ˈsikbed] *n* lecho *m* de enfermo.

sick benefit [ˈsikˌbenifit] *n* subsidio *m* de enfermedad.

sicken [ˈsikn] **1** *vt* dar asco a (*also fig*); **it —s me** me da asco, me repugna.
2 *vi* caer enfermo, enfermar; **to — at something** sentir náuseas ante algo; **I — at the sight of blood** el ver sangre me da náuseas; **to — for, to be —ing for** (*Med*) mostrar síntomas de; **to — for want of something** añorar algo; enfermar debido a la falta de algo.

sickening [ˈsiknin] *adj* nauseabundo; (*fig*) asqueroso, repugnante.

sickeningly [ˈsikninli] *adv* (*fig*) asquerosamente; **— sentimental** tan sensiblero que da asco.

sickle [ˈsikl] *n* hoz *f*.

sick leave [ˈsikliːv] *n* permiso *m* de convalecencia.

sickliness [ˈsiklinis] *n* lo enfermizo, lo achacoso; palidez *f*; lo nauseabundo; debilidad *f*; lo empalagoso.

sick list [ˈsiklist] *n* lista *f* de enfermos; **to be on the — estar enfermo.

sickly [ˈsikli] *adj person* enfermizo, achacoso; *appearance* pálido; *smell* nauseabundo; *smile* débil, forzado; *taste* empalagoso.

sick-making [ˈsikmeikin] *adj* (*fam*) asqueroso.

sickness [ˈsiknis] *n* (*Med*) enfermedad *f*, mal *m*; (*fig*) mal *m*, malestar *m*; **mountain —** mal *m* de montaña; **there is — on board** hay epidemia a bordo, hay una enfermedad contagiosa a bordo.

sick pay [ˈsikpei] *n* subsidio *m* de enfermedad.

sickroom [ˈsikrum] *n* cuarto *m* del enfermo.

side [said] **1** *n* **(a)** (*Anat etc*) costado *m*, lado *m*; (*of animal*) flanco *m*, ijada *f*; **— of bacon** hoja *f* de tocino; **by the —** of al lado de; **to sit by someone's —** estar sentado al lado de uno; **to sit — by — with someone** estar sentado al lado de uno; **to sleep on one's —** dormir de costado; **to split one's —s** desternillarse de risa.
(b) (*flank etc, fig*) lado *m*, flanco *m*; (*of triangle*) lado *m*; (*of car, ship*) costado *m*; (*of hill*) falda *f*, ladera *f*; (*of lake*) orilla *f*; (*of small pond etc*) borde *m*; (*of wood*) límite *m*, borde *m*; **weather —** costado *m* de barlovento; **near —** (*Aut etc: Brit*) lado *m* izquierdo, (*US, Spain etc*) lado *m* derecho; **off —**

(*Aut etc: Brit*) lado *m* derecho, (*US, Spain etc*) lado *m* izquierdo.
(c) (*face, surface*) lado *m*, superficie *f*; (*of record, slice of bread, solid etc*) cara *f*; **flip —** (*of record: fam*) cara *f* secundaria; **right —** (*of cloth*) derecho *m*, haz *f*; **to be right —** out estar bien puesto; **wrong —** revés *m*, envés *m*; **to be wrong —** out estar al revés; **what's on the other —?** (*of record*) ¿qué hay a la vuelta?
(d) (*part, region*) lado *m*; **left-hand —** izquierda *f*; **right-hand —** derecha *f*; **to be on the left-hand —** estar a la izquierda; **on one —**..., **on the other —**... por una parte..., por otra...; **on this —** por este lado; **on all —s** por todas partes, por todos lados; **on both —s** por ambos lados; **on the mother's — por parte de madre; **to come up on the blind —** acercarse por el lado donde el conductor (*etc*) tiene la vista impedida; **on the —** (*as adv*) incidentalmente; de paso; (*unofficially*) de modo extraoficial; **to make a bit on the —** ganarse un poco de dinero con algún negocio extraoficial; **to be on the right — of 40** no haber cumplido todavía los 40 años; **to put something on one —** poner algo aparte, guardarse algo; ahorrar; **I'll put it on one — for you** se lo guardaré; **to move to one —** apartarse, hacerse a un lado; **it's this — of Segovia** está más acá de Segovia; **it's the other — of Illescas** está más allá de Illescas.
(e) (*aspect*) aspecto *m*, lado *m*; **the other — (of the picture), the seamy —** el revés de la medalla; **to be on the safe —** para mayor seguridad..., por precaución...; **let's be on the safe —** atengámonos a lo más seguro; **to hear both —s of the question** escuchar los argumentos en pro y en contra; **to see only one — of the question** sólo ver un aspecto de la cuestión; **to get on the good — of someone** procurar congraciarse con uno; **to get on the wrong — of someone** ponerse a malas con uno; **to look on the bright —** ser optimista, ver el lado optimista de las cosas.
(f) **it's on the large —** es algo grande; **the results are on the poor —** los resultados son bastante mediocres; **the weather's on the cold —** el tiempo es algo frío.
(g) (*superiority: fam*) tono *m*, postín *m*; **there's no — about** (*or to*) **him** no presume, no se da aires de superioridad; **to put on —** darse tono.
(h) (*party*) partido *m*; (*team*) equipo *m*; (*Bridge etc*) bando *m*, campo *m*; **our —** nuestro campo (*etc*), los nuestros; **the home —** el equipo de casa, el equipo local; **the science — of the school** los estudios científicos del instituto; **he went on the science —** optó por estudiar ciencias; **to change —s** pasar al otro bando, cambiar de partido; cambiar de opinión; **to let the — down** hacer algo indigno de su colegio (*etc*), hacer algo que desmerece de su partido (*etc*); **to pick a —** seleccionar un equipo; **to take —s** tomar partido; **he's on our —** es de los nuestros, es partidario nuestro; **whose — are you on?** ¿a quiénes apoya Vd?; **you have tradition on your —** la tradición está de parte de los suyos, la tradición apoya su idea; **with a few concessions on the government —** con algunas concesiones por parte del gobierno.
2 *adj, attr* lateral, de lado; *door, entrance* accesorio; *elevation* lateral; *glance* de soslayo; *issue etc* secundario.
3 *vi*: **to — with someone** declararse por uno, tomar el partido de uno; **I'm siding with nobody** yo no tomo partido.

side arms [ˈsaidɑːmz] *npl* armas *fpl* de cinto.

sideboard [ˈsaidbɔːd] *n* aparador *m*.

sideboards [ˈsaidbɔːdz] *npl* (*fam: whiskers*), **sideburns** [ˈsaidbɜːnz] *npl* patillas *fpl*.

sidecar [ˈsaidkɑː*] *n* sidecar *m*.

-sided [ˈsaidid] *adj* de . . . lados, eg **six-sided** de seis lados.

side dish [ˈsaididʃ] *n* entremés *m*.

side face [ˈsaidfeis] **1** *n* perfil *m*. **2** *attr, adv* de perfil.

side glance [ˈsaidglɑːns] *n* mirada *f* de soslayo.

sidekick [ˈsaidkik] *n* compañero *m* (de trabajo *etc*), compinche *m*.

sidelight [ˈsaidlait] *n* (*Aut etc*) luz *f* lateral; (*fig*) detalle *m* incidental, información *f* incidental (*on* relativo a).

sideline [ˈsaidlain] *n* (*Rail*) apartadero *m*, vía *f* secundaria; (*Sport, Football etc*) línea *f* lateral, (*Tennis etc*) línea *f* de banda; (*fig*) empleo *m* suplementario, negocio *m* suplementario; **it's just a — es solamente una cosa secundaria; **he breeds parrots as a —** como negocio suplementario se dedica a criar loros.

sidelong ['saidlɒŋ] **1** *adv* de lado, lateralmente; oblicuamente; *glance* de soslayo. **2** *adj* lateral; oblicuo; *glance* de soslayo.

sidereal [sai'diːriəl] *adj* sidéreo.

side road ['saidrəud] *n* calle *f* lateral; calle *f* secundaria.

sidesaddle ['said,sædl] **1** *n* silla *f* de mujer. **2** *adv*: **to ride** — montar a mujeriegas, montar a la inglesa.

side show ['saidʃəu] *n* (*at fair*) barraca *f*, caseta *f* (de feria); (*fig*) función *f* secundaria.

side slip ['saidslip] *n* (*Aer*) deslizamiento *m* lateral.

sidesman ['saidzmən] *n*, *pl* **-men** [mən] acólito *m*.

side-splitting ['said,splitiŋ] *adj* joke divertidísimo.

side-step ['saidstep] **1** *n* paso *m* hacia un lado; (*dodge*) esquivada *f* lateral. **2** *vt* (*fig*) evitar, esquivar; **he neatly —ped the question** esquivó hábilmente la pregunta.

side street ['saidstriːt] *n* calle *f* lateral; calle *f* secundaria.

sidestroke ['saidstrəuk] *n* natación *f* de costado.

sidetable ['said,teibl] *n* trinchero *m*.

sidetrack ['saidtræk] **1** *n* (*Rail*) apartadero *m*, vía *f* muerta; (*fig*) cuestión *f* secundaria.
2 *vt* *person* apartar de su propósito, desviar del asunto principal; *discussion* conducir por cuestiones de poca importancia; **I got —ed** me aparté del asunto principal, me despisté.

side view ['saidvjuː] *n* perfil *m*.

sidewalk ['saidwɔːk] *n* (*US*) acera *f*.

sidewards ['saidwədz] *adv*, **sideways** ['saidweiz] *adv* de lado; hacia un lado; oblicuamente; **it goes in —** se mete de lado.

side whiskers ['said,wiskəz] *npl* patillas *fpl*.

side wind ['saidwind] *n* viento *m* lateral.

siding ['saidiŋ] *n* (*Rail*) apartadero *m*, vía *f* muerta.

sidle ['saidl] *vi*: **to — up** acercarse cautelosamente (*or* sigilosamente, servilmente; *to* a).

siege [siːdʒ] *n* cerco *m*, sitio *m*; **to lay —** to poner sitio a, sitiar, cercar; *person* asediar; **to raise the —** levantar el cerco.

sienna [si'enə] *n* siena *f*.

Sierra Leone [si'erəli'əun] Sierra *f* Leona.

siesta [si'estə] *n* siesta *f*; **to have a —** dormir la siesta.

sieve [siv] **1** *n* tamiz *m*, cedazo *m*, criba *f*; (*Cook*) coladera *f*. **2** *vt* *see* **sift**.

sift [sift] *vt* tamizar, cerner, cribar; (*fig*) escudriñar, examinar.

sifter ['siftə*] *n* cedazo *m*, criba *f*.

sigh [sai] **1** *n* suspiro *m*; (*of wind*) susurro *m*; **to breathe a — of relief** suspirar, suspirar aliviado; **to heave a —** dar un suspiro. **2** *vi* suspirar; (*wind*) susurrar; **to — for** suspirar por.

sighing ['saiiŋ] *n* suspiros *mpl*; (*of wind*) susurro *m*.

sight [sait] **1** *n* (a) (*faculty, act of seeing*) vista *f*; visión *f*; **second —** doble vista *f*; **long —** presbicia *f*; **to have long —** ser présbita; **short —** miopía *f*; **to have short —** ser miope, ser corto de vista; **30 days' —** (*Comm*) (a) 30 días vista; **at —, at first —** a primera vista; **to hate someone at first —** detestar a uno desde el principio, odiar a uno desde el primer momento; **payable at —** (*Comm*) pagadero a la vista; **to shoot at —** disparar inmediatamente; **to translate at —** traducir sin preparación, traducir sin estudiar el texto (*etc*); **it was love at first —** fue un flechazo; **to know someone by —** conocer a uno de vista; **land in —!** ¡tierra a la vista!; **to be in** (*or within*) **—** estar a la vista (*of* de); **our goal is in —** ya vemos la meta; **we are in — of victory** estamos a las puertas de la victoria; **to keep someone in —** no perder a uno de vista; **to find favour in someone's —** (*plan etc*) ser aceptable a uno, (*person*) merecerse la aprobación de uno; **to come into —** aparecer, asomarse; **to heave in(to) —** aparecer; **on — = at —; to be out of —** estar invisible, no estar a la vista, no poderse ver; **to drop out of —** desaparecer; **not to let someone out of one's —** no perder a uno de vista, vigilar constantemente a uno; **out of —, out of mind** ojos que no ven, corazón que no siente; **to be lost to —** desaparecer, perderse de vista; **I can't bear the — of blood** ver sangre me da asco; **I can't bear the — of him** no le puedo ver; **to catch — of** (*glimpse*) vislumbrar; (*happen to see*) ver por casualidad; (*on appearance of object*) alcanzar a ver; **to get a — of something** lograr ver algo; **I hate the — of him** no le puedo ver; **to lose — of someone** perder a uno de vista; **to lose — of the fact that . . .** no tener presente el hecho de que . . .; **to lose one's —** perder la vista, quedar ciego; **to regain one's —** recobrar la vista.
(b) (*on gun*) mira *f*, alza *f*, guión *m* de mira; **to set one's —s too high** (*fig*) ser demasiado ambicioso,

pedir demasiado; **to set one's —s on something** resolverse a adquirir (*or* obtener *etc*) algo.
(c) (*scene, spectacle*) vista *f*, escena *f*, espectáculo *m*; **it is a — to see** es cosa digna de verse; **it's a sad —** es una cosa triste; **it's not a pretty —** no es muy agradable para la vista; **it was a — for sore eyes** daba gusto verlo; **his face was a —!** ¡había que ver la mueca que hizo!, (*after injury etc*) ¡había que ver el estado en que quedaba su cara!
(d) (*spectacle: of person*) **I must look a —** debo parecer horroroso, ¿no?; **doesn't she look a — in that hat!** ¡con ese sombrero parece un espantajo!; **what a — you are!** ¡qué adefesio!
(e) **—s** monumentos *npl*, cosas *fpl* de interés (turístico), curiosidades *fpl*; **the —s of Córdoba** los monumentos de Córdoba; **to see the —s** visitar los monumentos, visitar los puntos de interés.
2 *as adv* (*fam*): **it's a (long) — better than the other one** es muchísimo mejor que el otro; **it's a — dearer** es mucho más caro.
3 *vt* (a) (*see*) ver, divisar, avistar; **to — land** ver tierra; **we —ed him coming down the street** le vimos bajar la calle.
(b) **to — a gun** apuntar un cañón.

sighted ['saitid] *adj* que ve, de vista normal; **a blind man and a — companion** un ciego y su compañero de vista normal.

-sighted ['saitid] *adj*: *eg* **weak-sighted** corto de vista, miope.

sighting ['saitiŋ] *n* observación *f*.

sightless ['saitlis] *adj* ciego.

sightly ['saitli] *adj*: **not very —** no muy agradable para la vista.

sight-read ['saitriːd] (*irr: see* **read**) *vti* leer sin preparación; (*Mus*) ejecutar a la primera lectura.

sight-reading ['sait,riːdiŋ] *n* lectura *f* sin preparación; (*Mus*) ejecución *f* a la primera vista.

sightseeing ['sait,siːiŋ] *n* excursionismo *m*, turismo *m*, visita *f* de puntos de interés; **"S— in Ruritania"** "Monumentos *mpl* de Ruritania"; **to go —** visitar los monumentos.

sightseer ['sait,siə*] *n* excursionista *mf*, turista *mf*; visitante *mf*.

sight-singing ['sait,siŋiŋ] *n* (*Mus*) ejecución *f* a la primera lectura.

sign [sain] **1** *n* (a) (*with hand etc*) señal *f*, seña *f*; **— of recognition** señal *f* de reconocimiento *m*; **to communicate by —s** hablar por señas; **to make a — to someone** hacer una señal a uno; **to make a rude —** hacer una señal grosera; **to make the — of the Cross** hacer la señal de la cruz; **to make the — of the Cross over something** santiguar algo.
(b) (*indication*) señal *f*, indicio *m*; asomo *m*; (*Med*) síntoma *m*; **the —s of measles are . . .** los síntomas del sarampión son . . .; **at the slightest — of disagreement** ante cualquier asomo de discrepancia; **it's a — of rain** es indicio de lluvia; **it's a sure —** es un indicio inconfundible; **it's a — of the true expert** esto indica el verdadero experto; **it's a — of the times** así son los tiempos actuales; **it's a good —** es buena señal; **to show —s of** dar muestras de, dar indicios de; **as a — of, in — of** en señal de.
(c) (*trace*) huella *f*, vestigio *m*, rastro *m*; **there was no — of it** no quedaba rastro de él; **there was no — of him anywhere** no se le veía en ninguna parte; **there was no — of the former inhabitants** no quedaba huella de los antiguos habitantes; **there is no — of their agreeing** no hay indicio alguno de que se vayan a poner de acuerdo; **there was no — of life in the village** no había vestigio de ser viviente en el pueblo.
(d) (*road —*) señal *f* de carretera; indicador *m*; (*inn —*) letrero *m*; (*shop —*) rótulo *m*; neon **—** letrero *m* de neón; **there was a big — which said "Danger"** había un grande letrero que decía "Peligro de muerte".
(e) (*written symbol*) signo *m*; símbolo *m*; (*Astron, Math, Mus, Zodiac*) signo *m*; **plus —** signo *m* de más, signo de sumar; **positive —** signo *m* positivo.
2 *vt* firmar; **—ed and sealed** firmado y lacrado, firmado y sellado; **to — away** firmar la cesión de, (*fig*) ceder, abandonar; **to — someone on, to — someone up** contratar a uno; **to — something over to someone** firmar el traspaso de algo a uno.
3 *vi* (a) **to — to someone to do something** hacer señas a uno para que haga algo, decir a uno por medio de señas que haga algo.
(b) (*with signature*) firmar, firmar su nombre; **to — off** terminar; (*Radio*) terminar el programa, terminar la transmisión; (*Bridge*) terminar la

declaración; **to — on, to — up** contratarse, (*Sport etc*) fichar (*for* por); **to — on at an hotel** firmar el registro.
4 *vt*: **he —s himself Joe Soap** usa la firma Joe Soap, firma con el nombre Joe Soap.
signal ['signl] **1** *n* (**a**) (*sign*) señal *f*, seña *f*; **calling —** (*Tel*) señal *f* de llamada; **engaged —, busy —** (*US*) señal *f* de ocupado; **at a pre-arranged —** al hacerse una señal predeterminada; **it was the — for revolt** fue la señal para la sublevación; **to give the — for** dar la señal de (*or* para); **to make a — to someone** hacer una señal a uno.
(**b**) (*apparatus*) señal *f*; **the — is at red** la señal está en rojo.
(**c**) **S—s** (*Mil*) transmisiones *fpl*, cuerpo *m* de transmisiones.
2 *adj* notable, señalado, insigne.
3 *vt*: **to — someone to do something** hacer señas a uno para que haga algo; **to — someone on** hacer señas a uno para que avance; **to — that . . .** comunicar por señales que . . . ; **to — a turn to the right** hacer una señal para hacer saber que uno va a torcer a la derecha; **to — a train** anunciar por señales la llegada de un tren; **the train is —led** la señal indica la llegada del tren.
4 *vi* hacer una señal, hacer señales; (*Aut*) señalizar; **to — before stopping** hacer una señal antes de parar.
signal box ['signlbɔks] *n* garita *f* de señales.
signal flag ['signlflæg] *n* bandera *f* de señales.
signalize ['signəlaiz] *vt* distinguir, señalar.
signal lamp ['signllæmp] *n* reflector *m* de señales, lámpara *f* de señales.
signally ['signəli] *adv* notablemente, señaladamente; **he has — failed to do it** ha sufrido un notable fracaso al tratar de hacerlo.
signalman ['signlmən] *n, pl* **—men** [mən] (*Rail*) guardavía *m*.
signatory ['signətəri] **1** *adj* firmante, signatario; **the — powers to an agreement** las potencias firmantes de un acuerdo. **2** *n* firmante *mf*, signatario *m*, a *f*.
signature ['signətʃə*] *n* firma *f*; (*Mus*, *Typ*) signatura *f*; **key —** (*Mus*) armadura *f*.
signature tune ['signətʃə,tju:n] *n* sintonía *f*.
signboard ['sainbɔ:d] *n* letrero *m*, muestra *f*.
signer ['sainə*] *n* firmante *mf*.
signet ['signit] *n* sello *m*.
signet ring ['signitriŋ] *n* anillo *m* de sello.
significance [sig'nifikəns] *n* significación *f*, significado *m*; trascendencia *f*.
significant [sig'nifikənt] *adj* significativo; trascendente, importante; *improvement etc* sensible; **look —** expresivo; **it is — that . . .** es significativo que . . .
significantly [sig'nifikəntli] *adv* significativamente; expresivamente; **it has improved —** ha mejorado sensiblemente; **it is not — different** no hay diferencia importante; **she looked at me —** me lanzó una mirada expresiva.
signify ['signifai] **1** *vt* significar, querer decir; **it signifies that . . .** significa que . . . ; **what does it —?** ¿qué quiere decir?
2 *vi*: **it does not —** no importa; **in the wider context it does not —** en el contexto más amplio no tiene importancia.
sign language ['sain,læŋgwidʒ] *n* lenguaje *m* mímico, mímica *f*; **to talk in —** hablar por señas.
sign painter ['sain,peintə*] *n* rotulista *m*.
signpost ['sainpəust] **1** *n* poste *m* indicador, indicador *m* de dirección. **2** *vt* señalizar.
signposting ['sainpəustiŋ] *n* señalización *f*.
sign writer ['sain,raitə*] *n* rotulista *m*.
silage ['sailidʒ] *n* ensilaje *m*.
silence ['sailəns] **1** *n* silencio *m*; **—!** ¡silencio!; **in dead —** en el silencio más absoluto; **there was —** hubo un silencio; **— gives consent** quien calla otorga; **to keep radio —** mantener el silencio radiofónico; **to pass over something in —** silenciar algo; pasar algo por alto; **to reduce someone to —** hacer callar a uno; **to reduce guns to —** reducir los cañones al silencio.
2 *vt* hacer callar, acallar; *guns etc* reducir al silencio; (*Tech*) silenciar; *critic* imponer silencio a.
silencer ['sailənsə*] *n* silenciador *m*.
silent ['sailənt] *adj* silencioso; callado; *film, letter* mudo; **to be —, to keep —, to remain —** callarse, guardar silencio, permanecer silencioso; **to become —** callarse, enmudecer; **it was as — as the grave** había un silencio profundo.
silently ['sailəntli] *adv* silenciosamente, en silencio.

silhouette [,silu:'et] **1** *n* silueta *f*. **2** *vt* destacar, hacer aparecer en silueta; **to be —d against** destacarse contra, destacarse sobre.
silica ['silikə] *n* sílice *f*.
silicate ['silikit] *n* silicato *m*.
siliceous [si'lifəs] *adj* silíceo.
silicon ['silikən] *n* silicio *m*.
silicosis [,sili'kəusis] *n* silicosis *f*.
silk [silk] **1** *n* seda *f*; **artificial —** seda *f* artificial; **raw —** seda *f* en rama; **to take —** (*approx*) tomar la toga, empezar a ejercer de abogado. **2** *adj, attr* de seda; **— industry** industria *f* sedera.
silken ['silkən] *adj* (*of silk*) de seda; (*like silk*) sedoso, sedeño; *manner, voice* suave, mimoso.
silkiness ['silkinis] *n* sedosidad *f*, lo sedoso; suavidad *f*, lo mimoso.
silk moth ['silkmɔθ] *n* mariposa *f* de seda.
silk raising ['silk,reiziŋ] *n* sericultura *f*.
silk-stocking ['silk'stɔkiŋ] *adj* (*US*) aristocrático.
silkworm ['silkwə:m] *n* gusano *m* de seda.
silky ['silki] *adj* sedoso.
sill [sil] *n* antepecho *m*; (*window—*) alféizar *m*; (*door—*) umbral *m*.
silliness ['silinis] *n* tontería *f*, estupidez *f*; insensatez *f*; lo absurdo.
silly ['sili] *adj person* tonto, bobo, estúpido; *act* tonto, insensato; *idea etc* absurdo; **you — child!, you big — !** ¡bobo!; **don't be —** no seas bobo; **that was — of you, that was a — thing to do** eso fue una estupidez; **I've done a — thing** he hecho una tontería, he sido un tonto; **I feel — in this hat** temo hacer el ridículo con este sombrero; **you look — carrying that fish** pareces un tonto llevando ese pez; **to knock someone —** (*fam: beat up*) dar una paliza a uno; **the blow knocked him —** el golpe le dejó sin sentido; **to make someone look —** poner a uno en ridículo.
silo ['sailəu] *n* silo *m*, ensiladora *f*.
silt [silt] **1** *n* sedimento *m*, aluvión *m*. **2** *vt* (*also to — up*) obstruir con sedimentos. **3** *vi* (*also to — up*) obstruirse con sedimentos.
silver ['silvə*] **1** *n* plata *f*. **2** *adj, attr* de plata, plateado. **3** *vt metal* platear (*also fig*); *mirror* azogar; *hair* blanquear.
silver birch ['silvə'bə:tʃ] *n* abedul *m* (plateado).
silver fir ['silvə'fə:*] *n* pinabete *m*.
silverfish ['silvəfiʃ] *n* pescadito *m* de plata, lepisma *f*.
silver foil ['silvə'fɔil] *n* hoja *f* de plata; (*paper*) papel *m* de plata.
silver fox ['silvə'fɔks] *n* zorro *m* plateado.
silver gilt ['silvə'gilt] *n* plata *f* dorada.
silver-grey ['silvə'grei] *adj* gris perla.
silver-haired ['silvə'heəd] *adj* de pelo entrecano.
silver paper ['silvə'peipə*] *n* papel *m* de plata.
silver-plate ['silvə'pleit] *vt* platear.
silver plating ['silvə'pleitiŋ] *n* plateado *m*.
silversmith ['silvəsmiθ] *n* platero *m*; **—'s (shop)** platería *f*.
silver-tongued ['silvə'tʌŋd] *adj* elocuente, con el pico de oro.
silverware ['silvəwεə*] *n* plata *f*, vajilla *f* de plata.
silvery ['silvəri] *adj* plateado; *voice etc* argentino.
simian ['simiən] *adj* símico.
similar ['similə*] *adj* parecido, semejante; **A and B are —, A is — to B** A y B se parecen; **this is — to what happened before** esto es parecido a lo que pasó antes.
similarity [,simi'læriti] *n* parecido *m*, semejanza *f*; **there is a certain —** hay cierto parecido.
similarly ['similəli] *adv* de un modo parecido; **and —, . . .** y asimismo, . . .
simile ['simili] *n* símil *m*.
similitude [si'militju:d] *n* similitud *f*.
simmer ['simə*] **1** *n*: **to be on the —, to keep on the —** hervir a fuego lento.
2 *vt* cocer a fuego lento.
3 *vi* hervir a fuego lento; (*fig*) estar hirviendo, estar a punto de estallar; **to — down** (*fig*) calmarse poco a poco, tranquilizarse lentamente; **— down!** ¡cálmate!; **to — over** irse, desbordarse, (*fig*) estallar.
Simon ['saimən] *m* Simón; **simple —** simple *m*, simplón *m*.
simony ['saiməni] *n* simonía *f*.
simp [simp] *n* (*US sl*) bobo *m*, a *f*.
simper ['simpə*] **1** *n* sonrisa *f* afectada, sonrisa *f* boba. **2** *vi* sonreírse afectadamente, sonreírse bobamente; **"Yes", she —ed** "Sí", dijo sonriendo afectada.
simpering ['simpəriŋ] *adj* afectado; bobo.
simperingly ['simpəriŋli] *adv* afectadamente; bobamente.
simple ['simpl] *adj* (**a**) (*uncomplicated, easy, plain*) sencillo; **it's as — as ABC** es de lo más sencillo;

the — life la vida sencilla; **I'm a — soul** soy un hombre sencillo; **it's very —** es muy sencillo; **it's — madness** es una locura ni más ni menos; **he's a — craftsman** es un simple artesano.

(b) (*not compound*) *interest, sentence etc* simple.

(c) (*foolish*) simple; imbécil; (*innocent*) ingenuo, inocente; crédulo; **he's a bit —** es muy bobo, está algo tocado; **I am not so — as to believe that . . .** yo no soy lo bastante ingenuo como para creer que . . .

simple-hearted ['simpl'hɑ:tid] *adj* candoroso, ingenuo.

simple-minded ['simpl'maindid] *adj* candoroso, ingenuo; (*pej*) estúpido; **I am not so —** no soy tan ingenuo; **in their —** way en su modo ingenuo.

simple-mindedness ['simpl'maindidnis] *n* candor *m*, ingenuidad *f*; (*pej*) estupidez *f*.

simpleton ['simpltən] *n* inocentón *m*.

simplicity [sim'plisiti] *n* sencillez *f*; simpleza *f*, ingenuidad *f*, credulidad *f*; **it's — itself** es de lo más sencillo.

simplifiable ['simplifaiəbl] *adj* simplificable.

simplification [ˌsimplifi'keiʃən] *n* simplificación *f*.

simplify ['simplifai] *vt* simplificar.

simply ['simpli] *adv* sencillamente; simplemente; **a — furnished room** un cuarto amueblado sencillamente; **I — said that . . .** dije sencillamente que . . .; **it's — impossible!** ¡es sencillamente imposible!; **but you — must!** ¡pero no tienes más remedio que hacerlo!; **I was — amazed** me quedé completamente asombrado.

simulacrum [ˌsimju'leikrəm] *n* simulacro *m*.

simulate ['simjuleit] *vt* simular.

simulation [ˌsimju'leiʃən] *n* simulación *f*.

simultaneity [ˌsiməltə'niəti] *n* simultaneidad *f*.

simultaneous [ˌsiməl'teiniəs] *adj* simultáneo.

simultaneously [ˌsiməl'teiniəsli] *adv* simultáneamente.

sin [sin] **1** *n* pecado *m*; **the seven deadly —s** los siete pecados capitales; **mortal —** pecado *m* mortal; **original —** pecado *m* original; **like — con** vehemencia; **for my —s** por mis pecados; **his besetting —** is . . . su mayor defecto es . . ., tiene la manía de . . .; **it would be a — to +** *infin* sería un crimen + *infin*, sería lamentable que + *subj*; **to fall into —** caer en el pecado; **to live in —** vivir juntos, vivir como marido y mujer sin serlo.

2 *vi* pecar; **he was more —ned against than —ning** era más bien el ofendido y no el ofensor.

Sinbad ['sinbæd] *m* Simbad; **— the Sailor** Simbad el marinero.

since [sins] **1** *adv* desde entonces, después; **ever —** desde entonces; **a long time —** hace mucho (tiempo); **not long —, a short time —** hace poco.

2 *prep* desde; a partir de, después de; **— Monday** desde el lunes; **ever — 1900** siempre desde 1900; todo el tiempo de 1900 acá; **how long is it — the accident?** ¿cuánto tiempo ha pasado desde el accidente?; **ever then**.

3 *conj* (a) (*time*) desde que; **I arrived** desde que llegué; **it is a week — he left** hace una semana que salió, salió hace una semana.

(b) (*because*) ya que, puesto que; **— you can't come** puesto que Vd no puede venir; **— he is Spanish** como él es español, siendo él español.

sincere [sin'siə*] *adj* sincero.

sincerely [sin'siəli] *adv* sinceramente; **Yours — le** saluda afectuosamente.

sincerity [sin'seriti] *n* sinceridad *f*; **in all — con** toda sinceridad, con toda franqueza.

sine [sain] *n* (*Math*) seno *m*.

sinecure ['sainikjuə*] *n* sinecura *f*.

sinew ['sinju:] *n* tendón *m*; **—s** (*fig*) nervio *m*, fibra *f*; recursos *mpl*; **the —s of war** los pertrechos de guerra.

sinewy ['sinju:i] *adj* nervudo, nervioso, vigoroso.

sinful ['sinful] *adj person* pecador; *act, thought* pecaminoso; *town etc* lleno de pecados, inmundo.

sinfully ['sinfəli] *adv* de modo pecaminoso.

sinfulness ['sinfulnis] *n* maldad *f*; lo pecaminoso.

sing [siŋ] (*irr*: *pret* **sang**, *ptp* **sung**) **1** *vt* cantar; **— us a song!** ¡cántanos algo!; **to — a child to sleep** arrullar a un niño, adormecer a un niño cantando.

2 *vi* cantar; (*of bird*) trinar, gorjear; (*of ears*) zumbar; (*of wind*) susurrar; (*of kettle*) silbar (al hervir); **to — flat, to — out of tune** desafinar, cantar mal; **to — small** achantarse, ser más humilde; **to — out** cantar más fuerte; (*fig*) vocear, gritar; **if you want anything — out** si necesitas algo me llamas; **to — up** cantar más fuerte; **— up!** ¡más fuerte!

Singapore [ˌsiŋgə'pɔ:*] Singapur.

singe [sindʒ] *vt* chamuscar; *hair* quemar las puntas de.

singer ['siŋə*] *n* cantor *m*, ora *f*; (*professional*) cantante *mf*; (*in cabaret etc*) vocalista *mf*.

Singhalese [ˌsiŋgə'li:z] **1** *adj* cingalés *m*, esa *f*. **2** *n* cingalés *m*, esa *f*.

singing ['siŋiŋ] *n* canto *m*; cantos *mpl*, canciones *fpl*; (*in the ears*) zumbido *m*.

single ['siŋgl] **1** *adj* único, solo; (*not double*) simple, sencillo; *bed, room* individual; *ticket, spacing* sencillo; *combat* singular; (*unmarried*) soltero; **every — day** todos los días sin excepción; **every — book I looked at** todos los libros que miré sin excepción; **not a — one spoke up** no habló ni uno solo; **there was a — rose in the garden** en el jardín había una rosa única; **she's a — woman** es soltera; **she remained —** siguió sin casarse.

2 **—s** *npl* (*Tennis*) juego *m* de individuales; **ladies' —s** individual *m* femenino; **men's —s** individual *m* masculino.

3 *vt*: **to — out** (*choose*) escoger; (*distinguish*) distinguir, singularizar; **he was —d out to lead the team** se le escogió para ser capitán del equipo; **to — (out) plants** entresacar plantas.

single-barrelled ['siŋgl'bærəld] *adj gun* de cañón único.

single-breasted ['siŋgl'brestid] *adj jacket* sin cruzar.

single-cell(ed) ['siŋgl'sel(d)] *adj* (*Bio*) unicelular.

single-chamber ['siŋgl'tʃeimbə*] *adj* (*Pol*) unicameral.

single-engined ['siŋgl'endʒind] *adj* monomotor.

single-entry ['siŋgl'entri] *n* partida *f* simple.

single-handed ['siŋgl'hændid] *adj, adv* sin ayuda (de nadie).

single-hearted ['siŋgl'hɑ:tid] *adj* resuelto, firme.

single-masted ['siŋgl'mɑ:stid] *adj* de palo único.

single-minded ['siŋgl'maindid] *adj* resuelto, firme.

singleness ['siŋglnis] *n*: **— of purpose** resolución *f*, firmeza *f*.

single-party ['siŋgl'pɑ:ti] *adj state etc* de partido único.

single-seater ['siŋgl'si:tə*] *n* (*Aer*) monoplaza *m*.

singlet ['siŋglit] *n* camiseta *f*.

singleton ['siŋgltən] *n* (*Bridge*): **to have a —** tener un semi-fallo (*in hearts* a corazones); **to play one's —** jugar la única carta que tiene uno de un palo.

single-track ['siŋgl'træk] *adj* (*Rail*) de vía única.

singly ['siŋgli] *adv* uno a uno, individualmente, separadamente.

singsong ['siŋˌsɔŋ] **1** *adj tone* monótono, cantarín.

2 *n* (*tone*) salmodia *f*, sonsonete *m*; (*songs*) concierto *m* improvisado; **to get together for a —** reunirse para cantar (canciones populares, folklóricas *etc*).

singular ['siŋgjulə*] **1** *adj* (a) (*Gram*) singular; **a — noun** un sustantivo en singular.

(b) (*odd*) raro, extraño, singular; **a most — occurrence** un acontecimiento muy extraño; **how very —!** ¡qué raro!

2 *n* singular; **in the —** en singular.

singularity [ˌsiŋgju'læriti] *n* singularidad *f*.

singularly ['siŋgjuləli] *adv* singularmente; **a — inappropriate remark** una observación de lo más inoportuno.

Sinhalese [ˌsinə'li:z] *see* **Singhalese**.

sinister ['sinistə*] *adj* siniestro.

sink¹ [siŋk] (*irr*: *pret* **sank**, *ptp* **sunk**) **1** *vt* (a) *ship* hundir, echar a pique; sumergir; (*fig*) *theory* destruir, acabar con; *person* acabar con.

(b) *mine* abrir, excavar; *hole* hacer, excavar; *well* perforar; *drink* beberse; **to — a post 2 metres in the ground** fijar un poste 2 metros bajo tierra; **to — one's teeth into something** hincar los dientes en algo; **he can — a glass of beer in 12 seconds** se bebe una caña de cerveza en 12 segundos.

(c) *differences* suprimir, olvidar; **to — one's identity in that of a group** olvidar su individualidad en la solidaridad de un grupo.

(d) **to — money in an enterprise** invertir dinero en una empresa.

(e) (*sunk*) **to be sunk in thought** estar absorto en la meditación, estar ensimismado; **to be sunk in depression** estar sumido en el abatimiento; **to be sunk in debt** estar agobiado por las deudas; **now we're sunk!** (*fam*) ¡estamos perdidos!

2 *vi* (a) (*of ship etc*) hundirse; irse a pique, naufragar; sumergirse; **to — by the bow** hundirse de proa; **to — to the bottom** ir al fondo; **it —s instead of floating** se hunde en lugar de flotar; **he was left to — or swim** (*fig*) dejaron de prestarle ayuda, dejaron de interesarse por su suerte.

(b) **to — in** (*fig*) penetrar, calar; **to let the paint — in** dejar que penetre la pintura; **the water —s in** en in time con el tiempo va penetrando el agua; his words seem to have sunk in sus palabras parecen haber surtido efecto, parece que sus palabras han hecho mella. (c) (*subside*) hundirse; (*building, land etc*) hundirse; (*fire*) estarse apagando, morir; (*person*) debilitarse, morirse; (*sun*) ponerse; he sank in the mud up to his knees se hundió en el lodo hasta las rodillas; to — (down) into a chair dejarse caer pesadamente en una silla; to — into insignificance perder su importancia; to — deeper into degradation hundirse cada vez más en la degradación, envilecerse más y más; to — into poverty caer en la miseria; to — to one's knees caer de rodillas; his voice sank to a whisper pasó a hablar en tono muy bajo; my spirits sank, my heart sank se me cayeron las alas del corazón; to — out of sight desaparecer. (d) (*in quantity*) disminuir; (*in value*) perder su valor; (*decline*) declinar, menguar; he has sunk in my estimation ha perdido mi estima; the shares have sunk to 3 dollars las acciones han bajado a 3 dólares.

sink² [siŋk] *n* fregadero *m*, pila *f*; (*Tech*) sumidero *m*; (*fig*) sentina *f*; — of iniquity sentina *f*, lugar *m* de todos los vicios; *see* **kitchen** —.

sinker ['siŋkə*] *n* (*in fishing*) plomo *m*.

sinking ['siŋkiŋ] **1** *adj*: that — feeling esa sensación de que todo se está acabando, esa sensación del desastre inminente; with — heart con la muerte en el alma. **2** *n* hundimiento *m*.

sinking fund ['siŋkiŋfʌnd] *n* fondo *m* de amortización.

sink unit ['siŋk'juːnit] *n* lavadero *m*, fregadero *m* (de cocina).

sinner ['sinə*] *n* pecador *m*, ora *f*.

Sino ... ['sainəu] *adj* sino ..., chino ...

sinuosity [‚sinju'ɔsiti] *n* sinuosidad *f*.

sinuous ['sinjuəs] *adj* sinuoso.

sinus ['sainəs] *n* (*Anat*) seno *m*.

sinusitis [‚sainə'saitis] *n* sinusitis *f*.

sip [sip] **1** *n* sorbo *m*. **2** *vt* sorber, beber a sorbitos.

siphon ['saifən] **1** *n* sifón *m*. **2** *vt* (*also* to — off, to — out) sacar con sifón; to — off (*fig*) quitar poco a poco, reducir gradualmente.

sir [sə*] *n* (*in direct address*) señor *m*; (*as title*) sir *m*; yes, — (*Mil*) sí, mi capitán (*etc*); S— (*to editor of paper*) señor director; Dear S— muy señor mío; my dear —!, my good —! ¡pero amigo . . .!

sire ['saiə*] **1** *n* (*Zool*) padre *m*; (*stallion*) semental *m*, caballo *m* padre; S— (*to monarch: arch*) Señor *m*. **2** *vt* ser el padre de; engendrar; he —d 49 children tuvo 49 hijos; the horse A, —d by B el caballo A, cuyo padre fue B.

siren ['saiərən] *n* (*all senses*) sirena *f*.

Sirius ['siriəs] *m* Sirio.

sirloin ['səːlɔin] *n* solomillo *m*.

sirocco [si'rɔkəu] *n* siroco *m*.

sisal ['saisəl] *n* henequén *m*, fique *m*, pita *f*.

sissy ['sisi] *n* marica *m*, mariquita *m*.

sister ['sistə*] *n* hermana *f*; (*Eccl*) hermana *f*, (*before name*) Sor; (*Med*) enfermera *f*, hermana *f* enfermera, (*of higher rank*) enfermera *f* jefa.

sisterhood ['sistəhud] *n* hermandad *f*.

sister-in-law ['sistərinlɔ:] *n* cuñada *f*.

sisterly ['sistəli] *adj* de hermana, como hermana.

sister ship ['sistəʃip] *n* buque *m* gemelo; X is the — of Z X es hermano gemelo de Z.

Sisyphus ['sisifəs] *m* Sísifo.

sit [sit] (*irr: pret* and *ptp* sat) **1** *vt* (a) sentar; to — someone in a chair sentar a uno en una silla; to — a child on one's knees sentar a un niño sobre las rodillas; to — an invalid up ayudar a un enfermo a incorporarse en la cama. (b) to — a horse well montar bien (a caballo). (c) to — an examination presentarse a un examen; to — an examination in French examinarse de francés. (d) to — out a dance no bailar; let's — this one out no bailemos esta vez; to — a lecture out aguantar hasta el fin de una conferencia, quedarse hasta el fin de una conferencia; to — someone out resistir durante más tiempo que uno, demostrar tener más aguante que uno. **2** *vi* (a) (*general sense: act*) sentarse, (*state*) estar sentado; — here siéntate aquí; I was —ting there estaba sentado allí; — by me siéntate a mi lado, siéntate conmigo; to — at home all day pasar todo el día en casa (sin hacer nada); to — at table sentarse a la mesa; to — with someone estar con uno; to — still permanecer sentado sin moverse;

— still! ¡quieto!; to — tight no moverse, (*fig*) no hacer nada. (b) (*of assembly*) reunirse; celebrar junta, celebrar sesión; the House sat all night la sesión de la Cámara duró toda la noche; the House sat for 22 hours la Cámara tuvo una sesión de 22 horas. (c) (*of bird, insect*) posarse; (*of hen*) empollar, incubar; the hen is —ting on 12 eggs la gallina empolla 12 huevos; the pheasant —s pretty close el faisán queda inmóvil y casi invisible. (d) (*fig: of dress*) caer, sentar (*on someone* a uno); that pie —s heavy on the stomach la empanada esa no me sienta; how —s the wind? ¿de dónde sopla el viento? (e) (*with adv or prep*) to — back sentarse cómodamente; to — back (and do nothing) cruzarse de brazos; to — down sentarse; do — down! ¡siéntese, por favor!; to — down to table sentarse a la mesa; to — down to a big supper sentarse a comer una cena fuerte; to — down under an insult aguantar un insulto; to — for a painter posar para un pintor, servir de modelo a un pintor; she sat for Reynolds se hizo retratar por Reynolds; to — for one's portrait hacerse retratar, hacerse un retrato; to — for an examination presentarse a un examen; to — for Bury (*Pol*) representar a Bury, ser diputado por Bury; to — in Parliament ser diputado (*in Spain*: a Cortes), ser miembro del parlamento; to — in on talks asistir a una conferencia (sin ser delegado oficial); to — on (*adv*) permanecer sentado; to — on a committee ser miembro de un comité, formar parte de un comité; to — on a matter dar carpetazo a un asunto; considerar un asunto; to — on someone (*fam: silence*) hacer callar a uno, (*suppress*) reprimir a uno, (*be hard on*) ser severo con uno; to — over one's work trabajar tenazmente; seguir trabajando sin descansar; to — up (*after lying*) incorporarse; to — up in bed incorporarse en la cama; to — up with a start incorporarse sobresaltado; to — up (*straighten oneself*) ponerse derecho, erguirse en la silla; so I sat up and took notice así ya empecé a prestar atención; to make someone — up dar en qué pensar a uno; impresionar fuertemente a uno; sorprender a uno; to — up to the table sentarse a la mesa; to — up (late) velar, estar sin acostarse; to — up for someone esperar a que vuelva uno, estar sin acostarse hasta que vuelva uno; to — up with a child velar a un niño. **3** *vr*: to — oneself down sentarse.

sit-down ['sitdaun] *n* (*fam*) culo *m*, trasero *m*; — strike huelga *f* de brazos caídos.

site [sait] **1** *n* sitio *m*, local *m*; (*for building*) solar *m*; the — of the battle el lugar de la batalla; a late Roman — un lugar de ocupación romana tardía; the only — for the plant in Spain la única localidad de la planta en España. **2** *vt* situar; localizar; a badly —d building un edificio mal situado.

sit-in ['sitin] *n* (*fam*) manifestación *f* de brazos caídos.

siting ['saitiŋ] *n* situación *f*, localidad *f*; the — of new industries la localización de las nuevas industrias.

sitter ['sitə*] *n* (*Art*) modelo *mf* de pintor; (*sl*) cosa *f* fácil; it was a — (*Sport*) fue un gol (*etc*) que se canta; you missed a — erraste un tiro de lo más fácil.

sitting ['sitiŋ] **1** *adj* sentado; a — bird una ave que está posada, una ave que está inmóvil; a — hen una gallina clueca. **2** *n* (*Pol etc*) sesión *f*; (*of eggs*) nidada *f*; — and standing room sitio *m* para sentarse y para estar de pie; at one — en una sesión; de una vez, de un tirón; second — for lunch segundo turno *m* de comedor.

sitting room ['sitiŋrum] *n* sala *f* de estar.

situate ['sitjueit] *vt* situar.

situated ['sitjueitid] *adj* situado; it is — in the High Street está situado en la Calle Mayor; how are you —? ¿cuál es su situación actual?; a pleasantly — house una casa bien situada.

situation [‚sitju'eiʃən] *n* situación *f*; (*job*) puesto *m*, colocación *f*, empleo *m*; "S—s wanted" "se busca trabajo"; to save the — estar a la altura de las circunstancias.

six [siks] **1** *adj* seis; it's — of one and half-a-dozen of the other lo mismo da; es tanto lo uno como lo otro. **2** *n* seis *m*; to be at —es and sevens (*things*) estar en confusión, estar en desorden, (*persons*) estar reñidos.

sixfold ['siksfəuld] **1** *adj* séxtuplo. **2** *adv* seis veces.

six-footer ['siks'futə*] *n* hombre *m* que mide 6 pies.

sixpence ['sikspəns] *n* 6 peniques *mpl*.

sixpenny ['sikspəni] *adj* de 6 peniques; (*pej*) insignificante, inútil.

six-shooter ['siks'ʃuːtə*] *n* revólver *m* de 6 tiros.

sixteen ['siks'tiːn] *adj* dieciséis.

sixteenth ['siks'tiːnθ] *adj* decimosexto.

sixth [siksθ] **1** *adj* sexto. **2** *n* sexto *m*, sexta parte *f*.

sixtieth ['sikstiiθ] *adj* sexagésimo.

sixty ['siksti] *adj* sesenta; **the sixties** (*eg* 1960s) los años sesenta; **to be in one's sixties** tener más de sesenta años.

sixtyish ['sikstiiʃ] *adj* sesentón.

size¹ [saiz] **1** *n* tamaño *m*; dimensiones *fpl*; extensión *f*; envergadura *f*, magnitud *f*; (*of person*) talla *f*, estatura *f*; (*measurement: of gloves, shoes etc*) número *m*; (*of dress, shirt etc*) talla *f*; **a hall of immense —** una sala de vastas dimensiones; **the — of the problem daunted him** la magnitud del problema le asombró; **the great — of the operation** la gran envergadura de la operación; **it's the — of a brick** es del tamaño de un ladrillo; **what — is it?** ¿de qué tamaño es?, ¿cómo es de grande?; **it's quite a —** es bastante grande; **it's 2 —s too big** yo lo quisiera 2 números más pequeño; **he's about your —** tiene más o menos la talla de Vd; **that's about the — of it** eso es lo que puedo decirle acerca del asunto, (*as answer*) así es; **to be of a —** ser del mismo tamaño, tener el mismo tamaño; **they're all of a —** tienen todos el mismo tamaño; **to cut something to —** cortar algo del tamaño preciso que se necesita; **to cut someone down to —** bajarle los humos a uno, hacer a uno darse cuenta de su escasa importancia; **it is drawn to natural —** está dibujado a tamaño natural; **what — shoe do you take?** ¿qué número calza Vd?; **I take — 9** uso el número 9; **what — shirt do you take?** ¿qué talla de camisa es la de Vd?

2 *vt* clasificar según el tamaño; **to — someone up** medir a uno con la vista; **to — up a problem** formarse una idea de un problema, hacer un estudio preliminar de un problema; **I can't quite — him up** no le entiendo del todo.

size² [saiz] **1** *n* cola *f*, apresto *m*. **2** *vt* encolar, aprestar.

sizeable ['saizəbl] *adj* bastante grande, considerable, importante; **a — sum** una cantidad importante; **it's quite a — house** es una casa bastante grande.

sizzle ['sizl] *vi* chisporrotear, churruscar, crepitar; (*in frying*) crepitar al freírse.

sizzling ['sizliŋ] **1** *adj* attack, shot etc fulminante. **2** *n* chisporroteo *m*, crepitación *f*.

skate¹ [skeit] *n* (*Fish*) raya *f*.

skate² [skeit] **1** *n* patín *m*. **2** *vi* patinar; **it went skating across the floor** se deslizó velozmente sobre el suelo; **I —d into a tree** di contra un árbol.

skater ['skeitə*] *n* patinador *m*, ora *f*.

skating ['skeitiŋ] *n* patinaje *m*.

skating rink ['skeitiŋriŋk] *n* pista *f* de patinaje.

skedaddle [ski'dædl] *vi* (*fam*) largarse (*fam*), marcharse; **they —d in all directions** huyeron por todos lados.

skein [skein] *n* madeja *f*; **a tangled —** (*fig*) un asunto enmarañado.

skeletal ['skelitl] *adj* esquelético.

skeleton ['skelitn] **1** *n* (*Anat*) esqueleto *m*; (*fig*) esquema *m*, plan *m*; (*Tech*) armazón *f*, armadura *f*; **the — at the feast** el aguafiestas; **— in the cupboard** secreto *m* vergonzoso de la familia, parte *f* de la historia familiar que se oculta a los de fuera.

2 *vt staff etc* reducido; *outline* esquemático.

skeleton key ['skelitn,kiː] *n* llave *f* maestra, ganzúa *f*.

skeptic ['skeptik] (*US*) *see* **sceptic**.

sketch [sketʃ] **1** *n* (*rough draft*) esbozo *m*, boceto *m*, bosquejo *m*, croquis *m* (*for* de); (*drawing*) dibujo *m*, diseño *m*; (*Theat*) pieza *f* corta (*esp* satírica, jocosa); **— for a costume** diseño *m* de un traje.

2 *vt* (*outline*) esbozar, trazar a grandes líneas; (*draw*) bosquejar, dibujar; **hacer un dibujo de; he —ed in the details for me** me explicó los detalles.

sketchbook ['sketʃbuk] *n* libro *m* de dibujos.

sketchily ['sketʃili] *adv* incompletamente, superficialmente.

sketching ['sketʃiŋ] *n* dibujo *m*, arte *m* de dibujar.

sketching pad ['sketʃiŋ,pæd] *n* bloc *m* de dibujo.

sketchy ['sketʃi] *adj* incompleto, superficial.

skew [skjuː] **1** *n*: **to be on the —** estar desviado, estar sesgado; estar puesto mal.

2 *adj* sesgado, oblicuo, torcido.

3 *vt* sesgar, desviar; poner mal.

4 *vi* (*also* **to — round**) desviarse, ponerse al sesgo, torcerse.

skewer ['skjuə*] **1** *n* broqueta *f*, espetón *m*. **2** *vt* espetar; pasar una broqueta por.

skew-whiff [,skjuː'wif] *adj* (*fam*) sesgado, oblicuo, torcido; **to be on —** estar puesto mal.

ski [skiː] **1** *n* esquí *m*; (*Aer*) patín *m*. **2** *vi* esquiar.

ski boot ['skiː buːt] *n* bota *f* de esquí.

skid [skid] **1** *n* (*Aut etc*) patinazo *m*, derrape *m*, deslizamiento *m*; (*Aer*) patín *m*; **to put the —s under someone** (*fam*) deshacerse de uno con maña, lograr con maña que uno abandone un puesto (*etc*).

2 *vi* (*Aut etc*) patinar, derrapar; (*of person*) resbalar; **it went —ding across the floor** se deslizó velozmente sobre el suelo; **I —ded into a tree** di contra un árbol.

skiddoo [ski'duː] *vi* (*US sl*) largarse (*fam*).

skidmark ['skidmaːk] *n* huella *f* del patinazo.

skidproof ['skidpruːf] *adv* a prueba de patinazos.

skid row ['skid'rəu] *n* (*US*) barrio *m* de mala vida; *calles donde se refugian los borrachos, drogadictos incurables etc.*

skier ['skiːə*] *n* esquiador *m*, ora *f*.

skiff [skif] *n* esquife *m*.

skiing ['skiːiŋ] *n* esquí *m*; **to go —** ir a esquiar.

skijump ['skiːdʒʌmp] *n* pista *f* para saltos de esquí.

skijumping ['skiː,dʒʌmpiŋ] *n* salto *m* de esquí.

skilift ['skiː,lift] *n* telesquí *m*, telesilla *m*.

skilful ['skilful] *adj* hábil, diestro, experto (*at, in* en).

skilfully ['skilfəli] *adv* hábilmente, diestramente.

skilfulness ['skilfulnis] *n* habilidad *f*, destreza *f*.

skill [skil] *n* habilidad *f*, destreza *f*; pericia *f*; (*technique*) arte *m*, técnica *f*; **his — at billiards** su habilidad en el billar; **he shows no small —** muestra tener no poca habilidad; **we could make good use of his —** podríamos utilizar su pericia; **it's a — that has to be acquired** es una técnica que se aprende.

skilled [skild] *adj* (*skilful*) hábil, diestro; *man* cualificado, especializado; *work* especializado, que requiere técnicas especiales; **to be — in a craft** ser perito en una artesanía; **a man — in diplomacy** un hombre de gran habilidad diplomática.

skillet ['skilit] *n* sartén *f*; cacerola *f* de mango largo.

skim [skim] **1** *vt* espumar; *milk* desnatar, quitar la nata a; (*graze*) rozar, rasar, casi tocar al pasar.

2 *vi*: **to — over** pasar rasando, pasar casi tocando; **to — through** examinar superficialmente, hojear.

skimp [skimp] **1** *vt* escatimar; *work* chapucear, frangollar.

2 *vi* economizar, ahorrar lo que puede.

skimpy ['skimpi] *adj* allowance etc escaso, pequeño; *skirt etc* muy abreviado, muy corto; *person* tacaño.

skin [skin] **1** *n* (a) piel *f*; (*with reference to texture etc*) cutis *m*; **by the — of one's teeth** por los pelos; **he's nothing but — and bone** está en los huesos; **to have a thick —** ser bastante insensible, poderlo aguantar todo; **to have a thin —** ser muy susceptible; **I've got you under my —** el recuerdo de ti no se me quita de la cabeza; **to save one's —** salvar el pellejo; **to wear wool next to one's —** llevar prenda de lana sobre la piel.

(b) (*Zool*) piel *f*, pellejo *m*; (*as hide*) piel *f*, cuero *m*; (*for wine*) odre *m*.

(c) (*Bot*) piel *f*, pellejo *m*; corteza *f*.

(d) (*fig: on milk*) capa *f* de nata; (*for duplicating*) clisé *m*; (*Aer, Naut*) revestimiento *m*.

2 *attr* de la piel; **— disease** enfermedad *f* cutánea, enfermedad *f* dérmica.

3 *vt animal* despellejar, desollar; *fruit* pelar, quitar la piel a; *tree* descortezar; **to — someone** (*fam*) despellejar a uno, esquilmar a uno; **to — someone alive** desollar vivo a uno; **to — one's knee** despellejarse la rodilla.

4 *vi*: **to — over** (*Med*) cicatrizarse.

skin-deep ['skin'diːp] *adj* superficial; **beauty is only —** la hermosura es cosa pasajera, la hermosura atañe a lo superficial.

skin diving ['skin,daiviŋ] *n* natación *f* submarina, exploración *f* submarina, pesca *f* submarina.

skinflint ['skinflint] *n* tacaño *m*, cicatero *m*.

skinful ['skinful] *n* (*fam*): **to have had a —** llevar una copa de más, haber bebido más de la cuenta.

skin game ['skingeim] *n* estafa *f*.

skin grafting ['skin,graːftiŋ] *n* injerto *m* de piel.

-skinned [skind] *adj* de piel . . ., *eg* **dark-skinned** de piel morena; **rough-skinned** de piel áspera.

skinner ['skinə*] *n* peletero *m*.

skinny ['skini] *adj* flaco, magro, escuálido, descarnado.

skint [skint] *adj* (*sl*): **to be —** no tener un céntimo.

skintight ['skintait] *adj* muy ajustado.

skip¹ [skip] **1** *n* brinco *m*, salto *m* (*pequeño*).

2 *vt passage* (*in reading etc*) omitir, pasar por alto; **to — lunch** saltarse el almuerzo, no almorzar;

— **it!** ¡déjalo!, ¡no te preocupes más de eso!; **oh, — it!** bueno, ¡no importa!

3 *vi* (a) brincar, saltar; (*with rope*) saltar a la comba; **to — with joy** brincar de alegría; **to — from one subject to another** saltar de un tema a otro; **the book —s about a lot** el libro da muchos saltos; **to — over something** saltar por encima de algo; (*omit*) omitir algo, pasar algo por alto.

(b) (*fam*) largarse (*fam*), escabullirse.

skip² [skip] *n* (*cage*) jaula *f*; (*bucket*) cuba *f*; (*basket*) cesta *f*, canasta *f*.

ski pants ['ski:'pænts] *npl* pantalones *mpl* de esquí.

skipper ['skipə*] *n* capitán *m* (*also Sport*); (*Naut*) patrón *m*; **well, you're the — bueno**, tú eres el jefe.

skipping rope ['skipiŋrəup] *n* cuerda *f* (de saltar), comba *f*.

skirl [skə:l] *n* (*Scot*): **the — of the pipes** el son de la gaita, la música de la gaita.

skirmish ['skə:miʃ] **1** *n* escaramuza *f*. **2** *vi* escaramuzar.

skirmisher ['skə:miʃə*] *n* escaramuzador *m*.

skirt [skə:t] **1** *n* falda *f*; (*of coat etc*) faldón *m*; (*sl*) falda *f*.

2 *vt* (*surround*) ceñir, rodear; (*go round*) orillar, ladear, seguir el borde (*or* la orilla) de; (*avoid*) evitar entrar en, mantenerse a distancia de; **we —ed Seville to the north** pasamos al norte de Sevilla.

skirting (board) ['skə:tiŋ(bɔ:d)] *n* rodapié *m*.

ski run ['ski:rʌn] *n* pista *f* de esquí.

skit [skit] *n* sátira *f*, parodia *f* (*on* de); (*Theat*) número *m* corto satírico.

ski tow ['ski:'təu] *n* = **skilift**.

skittish ['skitiʃ] *adj horse etc* nervioso, asustadizo; *playful* juguetón; *girl* coqueta; caprichoso.

skittishly ['skitiʃli] *adv* nerviosamente; de modo juguetón; con coquetería; caprichosamente.

skittle ['skitl] *n* bolo *m*; **—s** juego *m* de bolos, boliche *m*.

skittle alley ['skitl,æli] *n* bolera *f*.

skive [skaiv] (*sl*) **1** *n*: **to have a good — gandulear**, no hacer nada. **2** *vi* gandulear, no hacer nada.

skivvy ['skivi] *n* (*fam*) fregona *f*.

skua ['skju:ə] *n* págalo *m*.

skulduggery [skʌl'dʌgəri] *n* (*fam*) trampas *fpl*, embustes *mpl*; **piece of —** trampa *f*, embuste *m*.

skulk [skʌlk] *vi* estar escondido, permanecer oculto; acechar sin ser visto, procurar no ser visto.

skull [skʌl] *n* calavera *f*; (*Anat*) cráneo *m*; **— and crossbones** calavera *f* y dos huesos cruzados (*bandera de los piratas*).

skullcap ['skʌlkæp] *n* casquete *m*.

skunk [skʌŋk] *n* (*Zool*) mofeta *f*; (*fam*) canalla *m*; **you —!** ¡canalla!

sky [skai] *n* cielo *m*; **under blue skies** bajo un cielo azul; **the skies over England** el cielo sobre Inglaterra; **to praise someone to the skies** poner a uno por las nubes.

sky blue ['skai'blu:] **1** *n* azul *m* celeste. **2 sky-blue** *adj* azul celeste.

sky-high ['skai'hai] *adv* hasta las nubes; por las nubes; **the smoke rose —** el humo se elevaba hasta las nubes; **to blow something —** destruir algo completamente con una carga explosiva; **to blow a theory —** refutar completamente una teoría.

skylark ['skailɑ:k] **1** *n* alondra *f*. **2** *vi* (*fam*) jaranear, juguetear.

skylarking ['skailɑ:kiŋ] *n* (*fam*) jarana *f*; bromas *fpl*; pelea *f* amistosa.

skylight ['skailait] *n* tragaluz *m*, claraboya *f*.

skyline ['skailain] *n* horizonte *m*, línea *f* del horizonte; (*of building*) silueta *f*, perfil *m*; (*of city*) perfil *m*.

sky pilot ['skai'pailət] *n* (*sl*) sacerdote *m*, cura *m*.

skyrocket ['skai,rɔkit] **1** *n* cohete *m*. **2** *vi* subir (como un cohete), (*fig, of price etc*) ponerse por las nubes, subir vertiginosamente.

skyscraper ['skai,skreipə*] *n* rascacielos *m*.

skyward(s) ['skaiwəd(z)] *adv* hacia el cielo.

skywriting ['skai,raitiŋ] *n* escritura *f* aérea, publicidad *f* aérea.

slab [slæb] *n* bloque *m*; (*of wood etc*) plancha *f*, tabla *f*; (*of stone*) bloque *m*, (*flat*) losa *f*; (*of meat etc*) tajada *f* (gruesa); (*of cake*) porción *f* gruesa; (*of chocolate*) tableta *f*.

slack [slæk] **1** *adj* (*not tight*) flojo; (*lax*) descuidado, negligente; (*lazy*) vago, perezoso; *student* desaplicado, inerte, poco serio; (*Comm*) *market* flojo, encalmado; *period* de inactividad; *season* muerto; **to be —** (*of student etc*) gandulear racanear (*fam*); **business is —** el mercado está flojo, hay poca

actividad en el mercado; **to be — about one's work** desatender su trabajo, ser negligente en su trabajo; **to be — about** (*or* **in**) **doing something** dejar de hacer algo por negligencia.

2 *n* (a) (*part of rope etc*) lo flojo, parte *f* floja; **to take up the —** quitar la parte floja, tensar la cuerda (*etc*); **to take up the — in the economy** utilizar toda la capacidad productiva de la economía.

(b) (*period*) período *m* de inactividad; (*season*) estación *f* muerta.

(c) (*Min*) cisco *m*.

(d) **—s** pantalones *mpl* (de mujer).

3 *vt* (a) *see* **slacken**. (b) *see* **slake**.

4 *vi* gandulear, racanear (*fam*); **he's been —ing** ha sido muy gandul.

slacken ['slækn] **1** *vt* (*also* **to — off**) aflojar; (*reduce*) disminuir; **to — speed** (*person*) aflojar el paso, ir más despacio, (*of car etc*) disminuir la velocidad, moderar la marcha.

2 *vi* aflojarse; disminuir, reducirse; (*of wind*) amainar; (*of activity etc*) hacerse menos intenso; (*Comm*) aflojarse; **to — off** dejar de trabajar (*etc*) tanto; **to — up** (*person*) aflojar el paso, ir más despacio.

slackening ['slækniŋ] *n* aflojamiento *m*; disminución *f*.

slacker ['slækə*] *n* vago *m*, a *f*, gandul *m*, rácano *m*.

slackness ['slæknis] *n* flojedad *f*, lo flojo; descuido *m*, negligencia *f*; vaguedad *f*, pereza *f*; desaplicación *f*, inercia *f*, falta *f* de seriedad; inactividad *f*; (*Comm*) flojedad *f*, inactividad *f*.

slag [slæg] *n* escoria *f*; **basic —** escoria *f* básica.

slag heap ['slæghi:p] *n* escorial *m*, escombrera *f*.

slain [slein] *ptp of* **slay**.

slake [sleik] *vt* lime, *thirst* apagar.

slam [slæm] **1** *n* (a) golpe *m*; (*of door*) portazo *m*; **to close the door with a —** dar un portazo, cerrar la puerta ruidosamente.

(b) (*Cards*) bola *f*, capote *m*; slam *m*; **grand —** gran slam *m*; **small —** pequeño slam *m*.

2 *vt* (*strike*) golpear; **to — something down on the table** arrojar violentamente algo sobre la mesa; **to — the door** dar un portazo, cerrar la puerta ruidosamente (*see also* **door**); **Ruritania —s Slobodia** Ruritania derrota fácilmente a Eslobodia (*en un partido de fútbol etc*); **Ruritania —med in 5 goals** Ruritania marcó 5 goles.

3 *vi* (*of door*) cerrarse de golpe; **the door —med shut** la puerta se cerró de golpe.

slander ['slɑ:ndə*] **1** *n* calumnia *f*, difamación *f*; **to sue someone for —** demandar a uno por calumnia.

2 *vt* calumniar, difamar; decir mal de, hablar mal de.

slanderer ['slɑ:ndərə*] *n* calumniador *m*, ora *f*.

slanderous ['slɑ:ndərəs] *adj* calumnioso, difamatorio.

slanderously ['slɑ:ndərəsli] *adv* calumniosamente.

slang [slæŋ] **1** *n* argot *m*; (*of a group, trade etc*) jerga *f*; (*thieves' —*) germanía *f*; (*gipsy —*) caló *m*; **that word is —** esa palabra es del argot; **to talk —** hablar en argot.

2 *adj*: **— word** palabra *f* del argot, vulgarismo *m*.

3 *vt* (*insult*) llenar de insultos; (*criticize*) criticar duramente, poner como un trapo, emprenderla con.

slangily ['slæŋili] *adv*: **to talk —** hablar con mucho argot.

slangy ['slæŋi] *adj person* que emplea muchos vulgarismos, que habla en argot; *style etc* lleno de vulgarismos.

slant [slɑ:nt] **1** *n* (a) inclinación *f*, sesgo *m*; **to be on the —** estar inclinado, estar sesgado.

(b) (*fig*) punto *m* de vista; modo *m* de ver una cosa, modo *m* de enfocar un problema; **what is your — on this?** ¿cuál es su punto de vista en esto?; **to get a — on a topic** pedir pareceres sobre un asunto.

2 *vt* inclinar, sesgar; **to — a report** escribir un informe parcial, escribir un informe desde un punto de vista particular.

3 *vi* inclinarse, sesgarse; **the light —ed in at the window** la luz entraba oblicuamente por la ventana.

slant-eyed ['slɑ:nt'aid] *adj* de ojos almendrados.

slanting ['slɑ:ntiŋ] *adj* inclinado, oblicuo, sesgado.

slantwise ['slɑ:ntwaiz] *adv* oblicuamente, al sesgo.

slap [slæp] **1** *n* palmada *f*, manotada *f*; **— in the face** bofetada *f*, (*fig*) palmetazo *m*, golpe *m* rudo, desaire *m*; **— on the back** espaldarazo *m*.

2 *interj* ¡zas!

3 *adv* de lleno, de plano; directamente; **it fell — in the middle** cayó exactamente en el centro; **he ran — into a tree** dio de lleno contra un árbol.

4 vt (**a**) dar una palmada (or bofetada) a; pegar, golpear; **to — someone's face, to — someone on the face** dar una bofetada a uno, pegar un tortazo a uno; **to — someone on the back** dar un espaldarazo a uno; **to ← one's knees** palmotearse las rodillas; **to — someone down** derribar a uno de una bofetada, (fig) aplastar a uno, apabullar a uno.

(**b**) **he —ped the book on the table** arrojó el libro violentamente sobre la mesa; **they've —ped another storey on the house** han añadido un piso a la casa (como si tal cosa); **the judge —ped £100 on the fine** el juez aumentó la multa en 100 libras; **— a coat of paint on it** dale una mano de pintura.

slap-bang ['slæp'bæŋ] adv ruidosamente, violentamente; directamente, exactamente.

slapdash ['slæpdæʃ] adv person descuidado; despreocupado; work de brocha gorda, descuidado, chapucero.

slap-happy ['slæp'hæpi] adj alegre y despreocupado; totalmente inconsciente.

slapstick ['slæpstik] n payasadas fpl; **— comedy** comedia f de payasadas, comedia f de golpe y porrazo.

slap-up ['slæpʌp] adj (fam): **— meal** banquetazo m (fam), comilona f (fam); **it was —** fue un banquetazo.

slash [slæʃ] **1** n cuchillada f; (with whip) latigazo m.

2 vt (with knife etc) acuchillar; rasgar; (Sew) acuchillar; (with whip) azotar; price machacar, quemar; estimate etc reducir radicalmente; speech, text abreviar sensiblemente; (attack) atacar, criticar severamente.

3 vi: **to — at someone** tirar tajos a uno, tratar de acuchillar a uno.

slashing ['slæʃiŋ] adj attack etc fulminante.

slat [slæt] n tablilla f, hoja f.

slate[1] [sleit] **1** n pizarra f; (US Pol) lista f de candidatos; **to wipe the — clean** borrar lo escrito y empezar de nuevo.

2 adj de pizarra; color pizarra; **— roof** empizarrado m.

3 vt (**a**) cubrir de pizarras.

(**b**) (US) **it is —d to start at 9** según el programa comienza a las 9, deberá comenzar a las 9.

slate[2] [sleit] vt (fam) censurar, criticar severamente; **it got —d in the press** tuvo unas reseñas muy desfavorables en la prensa.

slate-blue ['sleit'blu:] adj color azul pizarra.

slate-coloured ['sleit,kʌləd] adj color pizarra.

slate pencil ['sleit'pensl] n pizarrín m.

slate quarry ['sleit,kwɔri] n pizarral m.

slater ['sleitə*] n pizarrero m.

slattern ['slætən] n mujer f dejada, mujer f sucia.

slatternly ['slætənli] adj sucio, puerco, desaseado.

slaty ['sleiti] adj (of material) parecido a pizarra; (in colour) color pizarra.

slaughter ['slɔ:tə*] **1** n (of animals) matanza f, sacrificio m; (of persons) carnicería f, mortandad f; **the — on the roads** la carnicería en las carreteras; **the S— of the Innocents** la Degollación de los Inocentes; **like a lamb to the —** como un cordero al sacrificio; **there was great —** hubo gran mortandad.

2 vt animals matar, sacrificar, carnear (SAm); persons matar (brutalmente), hacer una carnicería de.

slaughterer ['slɔ:tərə*] n jifero m, matarife m.

slaughterhouse ['slɔ:təhaus] n, pl **—houses** [hauziz] matadero m.

slaughterman ['slɔ:təmən] n, pl **—men** [mən] jifero m, matarife m.

Slav [slɑ:v] **1** adj eslavo. **2** n eslavo m, a f.

slave [sleiv] **1** n esclavo m, a f; **white —** esclava f blanca, prostituta f; **to be a — to tobacco** ser esclavo del tabaco; **to be a — to duty** ser esclavo del deber.

2 vi trabajar como un negro (at en), sudar tinta (also **to — away**).

slave driver ['sleiv,draivə*] n negrero m; (fig) amo m severo, jefe m despótico.

slave labour ['sleiv'leibə*] n (work) trabajo m de esclavos; (persons) trabajadores mpl forzados; **— camp** campamento m de trabajos forzados.

slaver ['sleivə*] n (ship) barco m negrero; (person) negrero m.

slaver ['slævə*] **1** n baba f. **2** vi babear.

slavery ['sleivəri] n esclavitud f; **his — to tobacco** la esclavitud en que el tabaco le tiene; **to sell someone into —** vender a uno como esclavo.

slave trade ['sleivtreid] n comercio m de esclavos, tráfico m de esclavos; **white —** trata f de blancas.

slave trader ['sleiv,treidə*] n traficante m en esclavos; negrero m.

slavey ['sleivi] n fregona f.

Slavic ['slævik] **1** adj eslavo. **2** n eslavo m.

slavish ['sleiviʃ] adj servil.

slavishly ['sleiviʃli] adv servilmente.

slavishness ['sleiviʃnis] n servilismo m.

Slavonic [slə'vɔnik] **1** adj eslavo. **2** n eslavo m.

slaw [slɔ:] n (US) ensalada f de col.

slay [slei] (irr: pret **slew**, ptp **slain**) vt matar, asesinar; (fam) hacer morir de risa; **this will — you** esto os hará morir de risa; **you — me!** (iro) ¡qué divertido!

slayer ['sleiə*] n asesino m.

sleazy ['sli:zi] adj person desaseado, desaliñado; place asqueroso; de mala fama.

sled [sled], **sledge**[1] [sledʒ] **1** n trineo m. **2** vt transportar por trineo, llevar en trineo. **3** vi ir en trineo.

sledge[2] ['sledʒ] n, **sledgehammer** ['sledʒ,hæmə*] n macho m, acotillo m, mazo m.

sleek [sli:k] **1** adj liso y brillante, lustroso; (of general appearance) pulcro, muy aseado; animal gordo y de buen aspecto.

2 vt alisar, pulir; **to — one's hair down** alisar y arreglarse el pelo.

sleekness ['sli:knis] n lisura f y brillantez, lustre m; pulcritud f, aseo m; gordura f.

sleep [sli:p] **1** n sueño m; **deep —, heavy —** sueño m pesado, sueño m profundo; **winter —** (Zool) sueño m invernal, hibernación f; **to drop off to —**, **to go to —** dormirse, quedarse dormido; **to go to —** (limb) dormirse; **to have a — dormir**, (briefly) descabezar un sueño; **to have a good night's —** dormir bien durante la noche; **to put someone to —** acostar a uno; dormir a uno, adormecer a uno; **to put an animal to —** sacrificar un animal; **to send someone to —** dormir a uno; **to sleep the — of the just** dormir con la conciencia tranquila; **dormir a pierna suelta; to walk in one's —** ser sonámbulo, pasearse dormido; **she walked downstairs in her —** estando dormida bajó la escalera.

2 (irr: pret and ptp **slept**) vt (**a**) **to — the hours away** pasar las horas durmiendo; **to — something off** dormir algo; **to — it off**, **to — off a hangover** dormir la mona (fam); **she's —ing off the effects of the drug** duerme hasta que desaparezcan los efectos del fármaco.

(**b**) **we can — 4** tenemos camas para 4; **can you — all of us?** ¿hay camas para nosotros?

3 vi dormir; **to — like a log** (or top) dormir como un lirón; **to — heavily, to — soundly** dormir profundamente; **he was —ing soundly** estaba profundamente dormido; **to — around** acostarse con todo el mundo, acostarse con cualquiera; **to — in,** **to —** (late) dormir tarde, seguir dormido; **to — in** (in house) dormir en casa; **to — on something** (fig) consultar algo con la almohada; **to — out** (not at home) dormir fuera de casa, (in open air) dormir al aire libre, pasar la noche al raso; **to — with someone** acostarse con uno; **to get to —** conciliar el sueño.

sleeper ['sli:pə*] n (**a**) (person) durmiente mf, persona f dormida; **to be a heavy —** tener el sueño pesado; **to be a light —** tener el sueño ligero.

(**b**) (Rail: tie) traviesa f; (coach) coche-cama m.

sleepily ['sli:pili] adv soñolientamente; **she said —** dijo soñolienta.

sleepiness ['sli:pinis] n somnolencia f; (fig) letargo m, carácter m soporífero.

sleeping ['sli:piŋ] **1** adj, attr durmiente, dormido; pill etc para dormir; partner comanditario; **S— Beauty** la Bella Durmiente (del Bosque).

2 n sueño m, el dormir; **between — and waking** entre duerme y vela.

sleeping bag ['sli:piŋbæg] n saco-manta m, saco m de dormir; (baby's) camiseta f de dormir.

sleeping car ['sli:piŋka:*] n coche-cama m.

sleeping draught ['sli:piŋdra:ft] n soporífero m.

sleeping pill ['sli:piŋpil] n comprimido m para dormir, somnífero m.

sleeping quarters ['sli:piŋ,kwɔ:təz] npl dormitorio m; espacio m para dormir.

sleeping sickness ['sli:piŋ,siknis] n enfermedad f del sueño, encefalitis f letárgica.

sleeping tablet ['sli:piŋ,tæblit] n comprimido m para dormir, somnífero m.

sleepless ['sli:plis] adj person insomne, desvelado; night pasado en vela, sin dormir.

sleeplessness ['sli:plisnis] n insomnio m.

sleepwalker ['sli:p,wɔ:kə*] n sonámbulo m, a f.

sleepwalking ['sli:p,wɔ:kiŋ] n sonambulismo m.

sleepy ['sli:pi] adj person, voice etc soñoliento; place soporífero; pear fofo; **to be —** (person) tener sueño;

I feel very — at midnight a medianoche empiezo
a tener mucho sueño.

sleepyhead ['sli:pihed] n dormilón m, ona f.

sleet [sli:t] 1 n nevisca f, nieve f granulada, aguanieve
f. 2 vi: it was —ing caía aguanieve, neviscaba.

sleeve [sli:v] n manga f; (Mech) manguito m, enchufe
m; to have something up one's — guardar algo
como en secreto, tener algo en reserva; to laugh
up one's — reírse con disimulo.

sleeved [sli:vd] adj con mangas.

-sleeved [sli:vd] adj con mangas . . ., eg long-sleeved
con mangas largas.

sleeveless ['sli:vlis] adj sin mangas.

sleeve links ['sli:vliŋks] npl gemelos mpl.

sleigh [slei] see sled.

sleight [slait] n: — of hand escamoteo m, prestidigitación f; destreza f; by — of hand (fig) con
maña, mañosamente.

slender ['slendə*] adj (not thick) delgado, tenue;
hand, waist etc delgado; figure esbelto; resources etc
escaso, limitado, reducido; chance pequeño, escaso;
hope remoto; excuse poco convincente.

slenderize ['slendəraiz] vt (US) adelgazar.

slenderly ['slendəli] adv: — built (person) delgado;
de talle esbelto; — made de construcción delicada.

slenderness ['slendənis] n delgadez f, tenuidad f;
esbeltez f; escasez f, lo limitado; lo remoto.

slept [slept] pret and ptp of sleep.

sleuth [slu:θ] n detective m.

slew[1] [slu:] 1 vt torcer (also to — round); to —
something to the left torcer algo a la izquierda.
2 vi torcerse (also to — round).

slew[2] [slu:] pret of slay.

slice [slais] 1 n (of meat etc) tajada f, lonja f; (of
sausage) raja f; (of bread) rebanada f, trozo m;
(of lemon, cucumber etc) rodaja f; (portion) parte f,
porción f; (tool) estrelladera f, pala f; a — of life
un trozo de la vida tal como es; it took quite a —
of our profits nos quitó una buena parte de nuestras
ganancias; it affects a large — of the population
afecta a buena parte de la población.
2 vt cortar, tajar; cortar en rodajas; bread rebanar;
ball cortar, torcer; to — off cercenar; to — something in two cortar algo en dos; —d lemon limón
m en rodajas.

slicer ['slaisə*] n rebanadora f, máquina f de cortar.

slick [slik] 1 adj (skilful) hábil, diestro; (quick)
rápido; (pej) person astuto, mañoso; meloso,
zalamero; he's the — sort es un astuto; he's too
— for me no me gusta por lo zalamero; be — about
it! ¡date prisa!
2 n (of oil etc) extensión f; masa f flotante.
3 vt see sleek 2.

slicker ['slikə*] n (US) embaucador m, tramposo
m; city — hombre m urbano y astuto procedente
de la ciudad.

slickly ['slikli] adv hábilmente, diestramente,
rápidamente; astutamente, mañosamente.

slickness ['sliknis] n habilidad f, destreza f; rapidez
f; maña f; melosidad f, zalamería f.

slid [slid] pret and ptp of slide.

slide [slaid] 1 n (on ice, mud etc) resbaladero m;
(for logs etc) deslizadero m; (in playground, swimming
pool) tobogán m.
(b) (Tech: part) corredera f, cursor m; (for hair)
pasador m; (Mus) vara f, corredera f.
(c) (microscope —) platina f, portaobjeto m;
(Phot) diapositiva f; colour — diapositiva f en color;
a lecture with —s una conferencia con diapositivas,
una conferencia con proyecciones.
(d) (act) resbalón m; (of land) desprendimiento
m; the — in share prices la baja de las cotizaciones;
the — in temperature el descenso de la temperatura.
2 (irr: pret and ptp slid) vt correr, pasar, deslizar;
to — furniture across the floor deslizar un mueble
sobre el suelo; to — the top on when you've finished
pon la tapa cuando termines.
3 vi (slip) resbalar; (glide) deslizarse; they were
sliding across the floor se deslizaban sobre el
suelo; to — down the banisters bajar deslizándose
por la barandilla; the ring —s down this rope el
anillo corre por esta cuerda; it ought to — gently
into place debiera correr suavemente a su lugar;
to — into a habit caer en un hábito (sin darse
cuenta); to let things — no ocuparse de las cosas,
no prestar atención a lo que pasa, dejar rodar la
bola; these last months he's let everything —
estos últimos meses se ha desatendido de todo.

slide holder ['slaid,həuldə*] n (Phot) portadiapositiva
m.

slide projector ['slaidprə,dʒektə*] n (Phot) proyector
m de diapositivas.

slide rule ['slaidru:l] n regla f de cálculo.

sliding ['slaidiŋ] adj part corredizo; seat corredizo;
door, roof de corredera; scale móvil.

slight [slait] 1 adj (a) figure delgado, fino; stature
pequeño, bajo; (of weak appearance) débil, frágil,
delicado.
(b) (trivial) leve; insignificante, de poca
importancia; a — pain in the arm un leve dolor de
brazo; the wound is only — la herida es más bien
leve, la herida no es de consideración; of — importance de escasa importancia.
(c) (small) leve; pequeño, escaso; a — improvement una pequeña mejora; of — intelligence
de escasa inteligencia; to a — extent en un grado
pequeño; he showed some — optimism mostró
cierto optimismo; the future does not justify the
—est optimism el futuro no autoriza el más leve
optimismo; there's not the —est possibility of that
de eso no existe la más remota posibilidad; not
in the —est en absoluto, ni en lo más mínimo.
2 n desaire m, insulto m (on a, para); this is a —
on all of us esto es un insulto para todos nosotros.
3 vt desairar, ofender, insultar.

slighting ['slaitiŋ] adj despreciativo, menospreciativo,
despectivo.

slightingly ['slaitiŋli] adv con desprecio, despectivamente.

slightly ['slaitli] adv un poco; yes, — sí, un poco;
— better un poco mejor; — built de talle delgado;
to know someone — conocer a uno ligeramente,
conocer a uno un poco.

slightness ['slaitnis] n delgadez f, finura f; pequeñez
f; fragilidad f; insignificancia f, poca importancia f.

slim [slim] 1 adj (a) (of figure) delgado, esbelto;
to get — adelgazar.
(b) resources etc escaso, insuficiente; his chances
are pretty — tiene muy pocas posibilidades.
2 vi adelgazar.

slime [slaim] n limo m, légamo m, cieno m; (of
snail) baba f; (fig) lodo m.

sliminess ['slaiminis] n lo limoso: lo baboso;
viscosidad f; lo rastrero; zalamería f.

slimming ['slimiŋ] n adelgazamiento m; to be on a
— diet seguir un régimen para adelgazar; to eat
only — foods comer solamente cosas que no
engordan a uno.

slimness ['slimnis] n delgadez f.

slimy ['slaimi] adj limoso, legamoso; snail baboso;
viscoso; person rastrero; zalamero; odioso.

sling [sliŋ] 1 n (weapon) honda f; (Med) cabestrillo
m; (for rifle etc) portafusil m; (Naut) eslinga f;
tirador m; to have one's arm in a — llevar el
brazo en cabestrillo.
2 (irr: pret and ptp slung) (throw) lanzar, tirar,
arrojar; (hoist) colgar, suspender; alzar; (Naut)
eslingar; to — something away tirar algo; to —
something over to someone tirar algo a uno, pasar
algo a uno.

slingshot ['sliŋʃɔt] n (weapon) honda f, tirador m;
(shot) hondazo m.

slink [sliŋk] (irr: pret and ptp slunk) vi: to — along
andar furtivamente; to — away, to — off largarse,
irse cabizbajo.

slinky ['sliŋki] adj (fam) seductor, provocativo.

slip[1] [slip] 1 n (a) (slide) resbalón m; (trip) traspié
m, tropezón m; (of earth) caída f, corriente m; (Geol)
dislocación f.
(b) (mistake) falta f, error m, equivocación f;
(moral) desliz m; (by neglect) descuido m; — of the
pen lapsus m calami; — of the tongue lapsus m
linguae; it was a bad — fue una grave equivocación;
there's many a — 'twixt cup and lip del plato a la
boca se pierde la sopa.
(c) (pillow—) funda f; (undergarment) combinación f; gym — túnica f de gimnasia.
(d) (Naut) —s grada f, gradas fpl.
2 vt (a) (slide) deslizar; to — a coin into a slot
introducir una moneda en una ranura; — that nut
on here pon esa tuerca aquí; to — something
across to someone pasar algo (furtivamente) a uno;
would you — the salt across, please? ¿me das la sal,
por favor?; to — an arm round someone's waist
pasar el brazo por la cintura de una; to — one over
on someone jugar una mala pasada a uno; ganar
por la mano a uno; to — someone a fiver pasar a
uno un billete de 5 libras (como propina o para
comprar su ayuda).
(b) (escape from) eludir, escaparse de; to —
a bone dislocarse un hueso; to — a cable (Naut)
soltar una amarra; the dog —ped its chain el
perro soltó la cadena; it —ped my memory se me

olvidó; **to — someone's notice** no ser advertido por uno, pasar inadvertido ante uno.

(c) (*with adv or prep*) **to — something in** introducir algo (suavemente, sin ruido *etc*); **I managed to — in a word about . . .** logré insinuar algunas palabras acerca de . . .; **to — off a dress** quitarse (rápidamente) un vestido; **to — on a jumper** ponerse (rápidamente) un jersey; **to — a dress over one's head** pasar un vestido por la cabeza.

3 *vi* **(a)** (*glide*) deslizarse (*along por, sobre*); (*stumble*) tropezar, resbalar; (*of bone etc*) dislocarse; (*of earth*) caer, correrse; **I —ped on the ice** resbalé en el hielo; **my foot —ed** se me fue el pie; **it —s easily along the wire** se desliza suavemente por el hilo; **the knot has —ped** el nudo se ha desatado; **it —ped from her hand** se le escapó de entre las manos; **the clutch —s** el embrague patina.

(b) (*move quickly*) ir (rápidamente); **I'll — round to the shop** voy a la tienda; **to — into bed** meterse en la cama; **she —ped into the room** entró (sin ser vista) en el cuarto, se introdujo (sin llamar la atención) en el cuarto; **the motorcycle —s through the traffic** la moto se cuela por entre la circulación.

(c) (*with let*) **to let it — that . . .** revelar inadvertidamente que . . .; **to let a secret —** revelar inadvertidamente un secreto; **to let a chance —** perder una oportunidad, no aprovechar una oportunidad.

(d) (*decline*) declinar, decaer; **you're —ping** no eres lo que eras antes; se te nota un ir a menos.

(e) (*with adv or prep*) **to — away, to — off** marcharse desapercibido; largarse, escabullirse; **time is —ping away** se nos escapa el tiempo, nos queda poco tiempo; **to — back** regresar con sigilo; **to — by** pasar inadvertido; **to — out for a moment** salir un instante; **it —ped out** se me escapó; lo dije sin querer; **to — through** colarse por; **to — up** (*fig*) equivocarse, cometer un error.

slip² [slip] *n* estaca *f*, plantón *m*; **— of paper** papeleta *f*, papelito *m*; (*in filing system etc*) ficha *f*; **a — of a girl** una jovenzuela.

slipcase ['slipkeis] *n* estuche *m*.

slipknot ['slipnɔt] *n* nudo *m* corredizo.

slip-on ['slipɔn] **1** *adj* que se pone por la cabeza; de quitaipón. **2** *n* prenda *f* (de vestir) que se pone por la cabeza; vestido *m* (*etc*) de estar por casa.

slipper ['slipə*] *n* zapatilla *f*; babucha *f*.

slippery ['slipəri] *adj surface* resbaladizo; *skin etc* viscoso; *person* astuto, escurridizo, evasivo, (*pej*) nada confiable, informal; **he's as — as they come** (*or as an eel*) es de lo más informal.

slippy ['slipi] *adv* (*fam*): **to be —, to look — about it** darse prisa, menearse; **look —!** ¡menearse! **we shall have to look —** tendremos que darnos prisa.

slipshod ['slipʃɔd] *adj* descuidado, poco correcto.

slipstream ['slipstriːm] *n* (*Aer*) viento *m* de la hélice.

slip-up ['slipʌp] *n* (*mistake*) falta *f*, error *m*, equivocación *f*; (*moral*) desliz *m*; (*by neglect*) descuido *m*.

slipway ['slipwei] *n* (*Naut*) grada *f*, gradas *fpl*.

slit [slit] **1** *n* hendedura *f*, raja *f*; resquicio *m*; corte *m* largo; **to make a — in something** hacer un corte en algo.

2 (*irr: pret and ptp* slit) *vt* hender, rajar; cortar; **to — a sack open** abrir un saco cortándolo con un cuchillo (*etc*); **to — someone's throat** degollar a uno.

slither ['sliðə*] *vi* deslizarse (*down a rope* por una cuerda); ir rodando (*down a slope* por una pendiente); **to — about on ice** ir resbalando sobre el hielo.

sliver ['slivə*] *n* raja *f*; (*of wood etc*) astilla *f*.

slob [slɔb] *n* (*sl*) tipo *m* odioso, sujeto *m* detestable; **you —!** ¡bestia!

slobber ['slɔbə*] **1** *n* baba *f*.

2 *vi* babear; **to — over something** extremar el sentimentalismo por algo, entusiasmarse de un modo ridículo por algo.

sloe [sləu] *n* (*fruit*) endrina *f*; (*tree*) endrino *m*.

slog [slɔg] **1** *n*: **it was a — me** costó trabajo; **it's a hard — to the top** cuesta mucho trabajo llegar a la cumbre.

2 *vt ball* golpear (sin arte).

3 *vi* **(a)** afanarse, sudar tinta; **to — away at something** afanarse por hacer algo, trabajar como un negro para terminar algo.

(b) (*walk etc*) caminar penosamente; **we —ged on for 8 kilometres** caminamos con dificultad 8 kilómetros más.

slogan ['sləugən] *n* slogan *m*.

sloop [sluːp] *n* balandra *f*; corbeta *f*.

slop [slɔp] **1** *vt* derramar, verter.

2 *vi* (*also* **to — over**) derramarse; desbordarse; **to — about in the mud** chapotear en el lodo; **the water was —ping about in the bucket** el agua chapoteaba en el cubo.

slop basin ['slɔp,beisn] *n* recipiente *m* para agua sucia; (*at table*) taza *f* para las hojas de té de desecho.

slope [sləup] **1** *n* inclinación *f*; (*up*) cuesta *f*, pendiente *f*; (*down*) declive *m*; (*of hill*) falda *f*; vertiente *f*, ladera *f*; **the —s of Mulacén** las laderas de Mulacén; **the southern — of the Guadarrama** la vertiente sur del Guadarrama; **the car got stuck on a —** el coche se quedó parado en una cuesta; **there is a — down to the town** la tierra está en declive hacia la ciudad.

2 *vt* inclinar; sesgar; **— arms!** ¡armas al hombro!

3 *vi* **(a)** inclinarse, estar inclinado; declinar, estar en declive; **to — down** estar en declive; **the garden —s down to the sea** el jardín baja hacia el mar; **to — forwards** estar inclinado hacia delante; **to — up** estar en pendiente.

(b) to — off (*fam*) largarse (*fam*).

sloping ['sləupiŋ] *adj* inclinado; (*up*) en pendiente, (*down*) en declive.

slop pail ['slɔppeil] *n* cubeta *f* para agua sucia.

sloppily ['slɔpili] *adv* descuidadamente, de modo poco sistemático; de modo sentimental, con sensiblería; **to dress —** vestir con poca elegancia.

sloppiness ['slɔpinis] *n* descuido *m*, lo descuidado, falta *f* de sistema; falta *f* de elegancia, desaseo *m*; sentimentalismo *m*, sensiblería *f*.

sloppy ['slɔpi] *adj* (*in consistency*) poco sólido, casi líquido; *road etc* lleno de charcos, lleno de barro; (*wet*) mojado; *work etc* descuidado, poco sistemático; *dress* desgalichado; *appearance* nada elegante, desaseado; (*sentimental*) sentimental, sensiblero.

slops [slɔps] *npl* (*food*) gachas *fpl*; (*waste*) agua *f* sucia, lavazas *fpl*.

slop shop ['slɔpʃɔp] *n* (*US sl*) bazar *m* de ropa barata, tienda *f* de pacotilla.

slosh [slɔʃ] (*fam*) **1** *vt person* pegar; **to — some water over something** echar agua sobre algo.

2 *vi*: **to — about in the puddles** chapotear en los charcos; **the water was —ing about in the pail** el agua chapoteaba en el cubo.

sloshed [slɔʃt] *adj* (*sl*): **to be —** estar ajumado (*fam*); **to get —** ajumarse.

slot [slɔt] **1** *n* muesca *f*, ranura *f*; **to put a coin in the —** meter una moneda en la ranura.

2 *vt*: **to — a part into another part** encajar una pieza en la ranura de otra pieza.

3 *vi*: **it —s in here** entra en esta ranura, encaja en esta ranura.

sloth [sləuθ] *n* pereza *f*; (*Zool*) perezoso *m*.

slothful ['sləuθful] *adj* perezoso.

slothfully ['sləuθfəli] *adv* perezosamente.

slot machine ['slɔtmə,ʃiːn] *n* aparato *m* vendedor automático; (*in fun fair etc*) máquina *f* tragaperras.

slouch [slautʃ] **1** *n*: **to walk with a —** andar con un aire gacho, caminar arrastrando los pies.

2 *vi*: **to — about, to — along** andar con un aire gacho, caminar arrastrando los pies; **to — about** (*fig*) gandulear, golfear; **to — off** irse cabizbajo, alejarse con un aire gacho; **to sit —ed in a chair** repanchigarse en un sillón; **he was —ed over his desk** estaba inclinado sobre su mesa de trabajo en postura desgarbada.

slouch hat ['slautʃhæt] *n* sombrero *m* gacho.

slough [slau] *n* fangal *m*, cenegal *m*; (*fig*) abismo *m*; **the S— of Despond** el abatimiento más profundo, el abismo de la desesperación.

slough [slʌf] **1** *n* (*Zool*) camisa *f*, piel *f* vieja (que muda la serpiente); (*Med*) escara *f*.

2 *vt* (*also* **to — off**) mudar, echar de sí; **to — off** (*fig*) deshacerse de, desechar.

3 *vi* (*also* **to — off**) desprenderse, caerse.

Slovak ['sləuvæk] **1** *adj* eslovaco. **2** *n* eslovaco *m*, a *f*.

Slovakian [sləu'vækiən] *adj* eslovaco.

sloven ['slʌvn] *n* (*in appearance*) persona *f* desgarbada, persona *f* desaseada; (*at work*) vago *m*, a *f*.

Slovene ['sləuviːn] **1** *adj* esloveno. **2** *n* esloveno *m*, a *f*.

slovenliness ['slʌvnlinis] *n* desaseo *m*; despreocupación *f*, dejadez *f*; descuido *m*, chapucería *f*.

slovenly ['slʌvnli] *adj appearance* desgarbado, desaseado; *person* despreocupado, dejado, descuidado; *work* descuidado, chapucero.

slow [sləu] **1** *adj* **(a)** lento; pausado; **— but sure!** ¡despacio pero seguro!; **it's — work** es un trabajo lento; **he's a — worker** trabaja despacio; **this car is —er than my old one** este coche no es tan potente como el que tenía antes; **business is very —** el negocio está muy flojo; **life here is —** aquí se vive a un ritmo lento; *see* **train.**

(b) to be — to do something tardar en hacer algo; **they were — to act** tardaron en obrar; **he was not — to notice that . . .** no tardó en observar que . . .; **to be — to anger** ser ecuánime, tener mucho aguante.

(c) (*of clock*) atrasado; **my watch is —** mi reloj se atrasa; **my watch is 20 minutes —** mi reloj se atrasa 20 minutos, mi reloj lleva 20 minutos de atraso.

(d) (*of character; phlegmatic*) flemático, cachazudo; (*stupid*) torpe, lerdo.

(e) (*boring*) aburrido; **the game is very —** el partido es la mar de aburrido.

(f) *surface, pitch* poco elástico.

2 *adv* despacio, lentamente; **to go —** ir despacio, (*in industrial dispute*) trabajar a ritmo lento, hacer trabajo lento.

3 *vt* (*also to* **— down, to — up**) retardar; *engine, machine* reducir la velocidad de, moderar la marcha de; **that car —s up the traffic** ese coche entorpece la circulación.

4 *vi* (*also to* **— down, to — up**) ir más despacio; (*in walking etc*) aflojar el paso; (*Aut*) moderar la marcha, reducir la velocidad; **"S— down"** (*road sign*) "Disminuir velocidad"; **the car —ed to a stop** el coche moderó su marcha y paró; **production has —ed to almost nothing** la producción se ha reducido casi a cero.

slow-burning ['sləu'bə:niŋ] *adj* que se quema lentamente.

slowcoach ['sləukəutʃ] *n* (*fam: idler*) perezoso *m*, a *f*, vago *m*, a *f*; (*stupid person*) torpe *mf*.

slowly ['sləuli] *adv* despacio, lentamente; poco a poco.

slow match ['sləumætʃ] *n* mecha *f* tardía.

slow motion ['sləu'məuʃən] *adj, n*: **slow-motion film** película *f* a cámara lenta; **to show a film in —** pasar una película a cámara lenta.

slowness ['sləunis] *n* lentitud *f*; flema *f*; torpeza *f*; aburrimiento *m*; falta *f* de elasticidad.

slow-witted ['sləu'witid] *adj* torpe, lerdo.

slow worm ['sləuwə:m] *n* lución *m*.

sludge [slʌdʒ] *n* (*mud*) lodo *m*, fango *m*; (*sediment*) sedimento *m* fangoso; (*sewage*) aguas *fpl* de albañal.

slug[1] [slʌg] *n* (*Zool*) babosa *f*; (*bullet*) posta *f*; (*Typ*) lingote *m*.

slug[2] [slʌg] *vt* (*sl*) pegar, aporrear.

sluggard ['slʌgəd] *n* haragán *m*, ana *f*.

sluggish ['slʌgiʃ] *adj* (*indolent*) perezoso; (*slow-moving*) lento; *animal etc* inactivo, inerte, perezoso; *business, market* flojo; *person's temperament* flemático, cachazudo.

sluggishly ['slʌgiʃli] *adv* perezosamente; lentamente; inactivamente; flojamente; con flema.

sluggishness ['slʌgiʃnis] *n* pereza *f*; lentitud *f*; inactividad *f*, inercia *f*; flojedad *f*; flema *f*.

sluice [slu:s] **1** *n* **(a)** (*gate*) compuerta *f*, esclusa *f*; (*barrier*) dique *m* de contención; (*waterway*) canal *m*. **(b) to give something a — down** echar agua sobre algo (para lavarlo); **to — someone down** dar una ducha a uno.

2 *vt*: **to — something down** echar agua sobre algo (para lavarlo), regar algo con agua; **to — something with water** regar algo con agua.

3 *vi*: **to — out** salir a borbotones.

sluice gate ['slu:sgeit] *n* compuerta *f*.

sluiceway ['slu:swei] *n* canal *m*.

slum [slʌm] **1** *n* (*area*) barrio *m* bajo, barrio *m* pobre; (*house*) casucha *f*, tugurio *m*; **the —s** los barrios bajos, los tugurios; **they live in a —** viven en una casucha; **this house will be a — in 10 years** dentro de 10 años esta casa será una ruina; **—clearance programme** programa *m* de reforma de viviendas en los barrios pobres.

2 *vi* **to —, to go —ming** visitar los barrios bajos; investigar los bajos fondos sociales, conocer los lugares de la baja vida.

slumber ['slʌmbə*] **1** *n* sueño *m* (*esp* tranquilo, profundo); (*fig*) inactividad *f*, inercia *f*; **—s** sueño *m* (*esp* tranquilo, profundo); **my —s were rudely interrupted** estando profundamente dormido me despertaron de modo brutal.

2 *vi* dormir; estar (profundamente) dormido; (*fig*) permanecer inactivo, estar inerte.

slumb(e)rous ['slʌmbərəs] *adj* soñoliento; (*fig*) inactivo, inerte.

slump [slʌmp] **1** *n* (*economic*) depresión *f*, declive *m* económico, retroceso *m*; **the 1929 —** la depresión de 1929, la crisis económica de 1929; **the — in the**

price of copper la baja repentina del precio del cobre; **— in morale** bajón *m* en la moral.

2 *vi* **(a)** (*price etc*) hundirse, bajar repentinamente; (*production*) bajar catastróficamente; (*morale etc*) sufrir un bajón, decaer gravemente.

(b) to — into a chair dejarse caer pesadamente en un sillón; **he was —ed over the wheel** se había desplomado sobre el volante; **he was —ed on the floor** estaba tumbado en el suelo.

slung [slʌŋ] *pret and ptp of* **sling.**

slunk [slʌŋk] *pret and ptp of* **slink.**

slur [slə:*] **1** *n* **(a)** (*stigma*) borrón *m*, mancha *f*, nota *f* infamante; calumnia *f*; **to cast a — on someone** calumniar a uno, hacer un reparo (injustificado) a uno; **it is no — on him to say that . . .** no es hacer un reparo a él decir que . . .

(b) (*Mus*) ligado *m*.

2 *vti* (*also to* **— over**) pasar por alto de, omitir, suprimir; (*hide*) ocultar; *word* pronunciar con poca corrección, *syllable* comerse; (*Mus*) ligar.

slurred [slə:d] *adj* *pronunciation* indistinto, poco correcto.

slush [slʌʃ] *n* (*watery snow*) nieve *f* a medio derretir; (*mud*) fango *m*, lodo *m* (líquido); (*fam*) sentimentalismo *m*, tonterías *fpl* sentimentales, cursilería *f*.

slushy ['slʌʃi] *adj* *snow* a medio derretir, casi líquido; *mud* casi líquido; *path etc* lleno de lodo, fangoso; (*fam*) tontamente sentimental, sensiblero, cursi.

slut [slʌt] *n* pazpuerca *f*, marrana *f*.

sluttish ['slʌtiʃ] *adj* puerco, desaliñado.

sly [slai] **1** *adj* (*wily*) astuto; (*hypocritical*) taimado; (*secretive*) furtivo, disimulado, sigiloso; (*arch*) malicioso; (*bantering*) guasón; (*insinuating*) intencionado.

2 *n*: **on the —** a hurtadillas; disimuladamente, sigilosamente.

slyly ['slaili] *adv* astutamente; furtivamente, disimuladamente, sigilosamente; maliciosamente; con intención.

slyness ['slainis] *n* astucia *f*; lo taimado, carácter *m* taimado; disimulo *m*, sigilo *m*; malicia *f*; guasa *f*; intención *f*.

smack[1] [smæk] **1** *n* (*taste*) sabor *m*, saborcillo *m*, dejo *m* (*of* a).

2 *vi* tener un saborcillo un poco raro; saber mal; **to — of** saber a, tener un saborcillo a; (*fig, pej*) tener resabios de; oler a; **the whole thing —s of bribery** el asunto entero huele a corrupción.

smack[2] [smæk] **1** *n* (*slap*) manotada *f*, palmada *f*; (*blow, stroke*) golpe *m*; (*sound*) ruido *m* de un golpe, chasquido *m*; **it hit the wall with a great —** dio contra la pared con mucho ruido; **to give a child a —** dar una manotada a un niño; **stop it or you'll get a —** déjalo o te pego.

2 *vt* (*slap*) dar una manotada a, pegar (con la mano); **he —ed it on to the table** lo arrojó ruidosamente sobre la mesa; **to — one's lips** relamerse, chuparse los dedos.

3 *adv*: **it fell — in the middle** cayó exactamente en el centro; **he went — into a tree** dio de golpe contra un árbol, dio de lleno contra un árbol.

4 *interj* ¡zas!

smack[3] [smæk] *n* (*Naut*) queche *m*, barco *m* de pesca.

smacker ['smækə*] *n* (*sl: kiss*) beso *m* sonado; (*blow*) golpe *m* ruidoso; (*US*) dólar *m*.

smacking ['smækiŋ] *n* zurra *f*, paliza *f*; **to give someone a —** dar una paliza a uno.

small [smɔ:l] **1** *adj* pequeño; chico; menudo; (*person*) pequeño, bajo (de estatura); *stock, supply* escaso, corto, exiguo; (*lesser*) menor; (*unimportant*) insignificante; *letter, print* menudo, minúsculo; *voice* humilde; (*the idea of — is often expressed by a diminutive, eg*) **a — house** una casita, **a — book** un librillo; **I'm sorry it's so —** siento que sea tan chiquito; **the fish here are very —** aquí los peces son chiquitines; **when we were —** cuando éramos pequeños; **to be a — eater** comer poco; **to feel —** sentirse humillado, tener vergüenza; **it made me feel pretty —** me dio vergüenza; **to make someone look —** humillar a uno, dar vergüenza a uno; **this house makes the other one look —** esta casa hace que la otra quede pequeña; **to make oneself —** hacerse chiquito, agacharse; **the —er of the two** el menor (de los dos); **the Earth is 75 times —er than Uranus** la Tierra es 75 veces menor que Urano; *see* **beer, letter** *etc.*

2 *n*: **— of the back** parte *f* más estrecha de la espalda; **—s** (*fam*) paños *mpl* menores.

small-arms ['smɔ:l'ɑ:mz] *npl* armas *fpl* cortas.

smallholding ['smɔ:l,həuldiŋ] *n* parcela *f*, granja *f* pequeña; minifundio *m*.

smallish ['smɔ:liʃ] *adj* más bien pequeño.

small-minded ['smɔːl'maindid] *adj* de miras estrechas; intolerante.
small-mindedness ['smɔːl'maindidnis] *n* estrechez *f* de miras; intolerancia *f*.
smallness ['smɔːlnis] *n* pequeñez *f*, pequeño tamaño *m*, tamaño *m* reducido; escasez *f*; insignificancia *f*.
smallpox ['smɔːlpɒks] *n* viruela *f*, viruelas *fpl*.
small-scale ['smɔːl'skeil] *adj* en pequeña escala.
small talk ['smɔːltɔːk] *n* vulgaridades *fpl*, banalidades *fpl*; cháchara *f*; **she has no —** es incapaz de charlar sobre las cosas corrientes de la vida; **to swap —** **with someone** intercambiar banalidades con uno.
small-time ['smɔːl'taim] *adj* (*fam*) de poca monta; de escasa importancia; en pequeña escala.
small-town ['smɔːl'taun] *adj* pueblerino.
smarm [smɑːm] *vt*: **to — one's hair down** alisarse y fijarse el pelo.
smarmy ['smɑːmi] *adj* (*fam*) cobista (*fam*); **he's a — sort** es un cobista.
smart [smɑːt] **1** *adj* (a) (*elegant*) elegante; pulcro, distinguido; (*not shabby*) aseado; *society* elegante, de buen tono; **that's a — car** qué coche más distinguido; **in a — shop on Serrano** en una tienda elegante de Serrano; **you're looking very —!** ¡qué elegante estás!, ¡qué guapo estás!
(b) (*bright*) listo, vivo, inteligente; (*pej*) ladino, astuto, cuco; **he's a — one** es un cuco; **he was too — for me** logró embaucarme; **that's a — trick** es un truco hábil; **he think's it's — to + infin** él se cree la mar de listo al **+ infin**; **that was pretty — of you** en eso has mostrado ser muy inteligente.
(c) (*quick*) pronto, rápido, vivo; *pace* vivo; *attack etc* repentino; **that's — work** lo has hecho con toda rapidez; **— work by the police led to ...** una pronta acción de parte de la policía condujo a ...; **and look — about it!** ¡y dáte prisa!, ¡menearse!
2 *n* escozor *m*; (*fig*) dolor *m*, resentimiento *m*.
3 *vi* (a) (*Med*) escocer, picar; **it makes my mouth —** escuece en la boca; **my eyes are —ing** me duelen los ojos; **it —s for a few minutes** escuece durante algunos minutos.
(b) (*fig*) **to — under, to — with** sufrir bajo, resentirse de; **to — under criticism** resentirse de una crítica; **you shall — for this!** ¡me las pagarás!
smart-aleck ['smɑːtˌælik] *n see* **Alec.**
smarten ['smɑːtn] **1** *vt* (*also* **to — up**) arreglar, mejorar el aspecto de; hermosear; **we'll — the house up for the summer** arreglaremos la casa para el verano.
2 *vi* (*also* **to — up**) = **3** *vr*: **to — oneself up** arreglarse; mejorarse de aspecto; **I must go and — myself up** tengo que ir a arreglarme un poco; **she has —ed herself up a lot in the last year** durante el año pasado ha mejorado mucho de aspecto.
smartly ['smɑːtli] *adv* (a) elegantemente; pulcramente, de modo distinguido; **she dresses very —** viste con mucha elegancia.
(b) inteligentemente; (*pej*) astutamente.
(c) pronto, rápidamente; a paso vivo; de repente, repentinamente; **they marched him — off to the police station** le llevaron con toda rapidez a la comisaría; **she snatched it — from me** me lo arrebató de repente.
smartness ['smɑːtnis] *n* (a) elegancia *f*; pulcritud *f*, distinción *f*; aseo *m*; buen tono *m*.
(b) viveza *f*, inteligencia *f*; (*pej*) astucia *f*, cuquería *f*.
(c) viveza *f*, rapidez *f*.
smarty ['smɑːti] *n* (*fam*) sabelotodo *m*.
smash [smæʃ] **1** *n* (*collision*) choque *m* (violento), colisión *f*, encontronazo *m*; accidente *m*; (*breakage*) rotura *f*; (*Fin*) quiebra *f*; depresión *f*, crisis *f* económica; (*Tennis etc*) smash *m*, golpe *m* violento; (*noise of* —) estruendo *m*; **he died in a car —** murió en accidente de automóvil; **the 1969 rail —** el accidente de ferrocarril de 1969; **the 1929 —** la crisis económica de 1929; **to go to — destrozarse**, quedar hecho pedazos.
2 *adj*: **— hit** éxito *m* fulminante, exitazo *m*; **the — hit of 1920** el mayor éxito de 1920.
3 *adv*: **to go — into something** dar de lleno contra algo, dar violentamente contra algo.
4 *vt* (*break*) romper; (*shatter*) hacer pedazos; (*annihilate*) destruir; *ball* golpear violentamente; *attack, opponent* aplastar; **when they —ed the atom** cuando desintegraron el átomo; **he —ed it against the wall** lo estrelló contra la pared; **the waves threatened to — the boat on the rocks** las olas amenazaban con estrellar el barco contra las rocas; **I've —ed my watch** he estropeado mi reloj;

we will — this crime ring acabaremos con esta confabulación; **A —ed his fist into B's face** A dio a B un puñetazo violento en la cara; **the gang —ed the place up** la pandilla destrozó el local; **he was all —ed up in the accident** sufrió grandes lesiones en el accidente.
5 *vi* (*break*) romperse; hacerse pedazos; estropearse; (*collide*) chocar (*against, into* con, contra), estrellarse (*against, into* contra); (*Fin*) quebrar.
smash-and-grab raid ['smæʃən'græb,reid] *n* robo *m* relámpago (en joyería *etc*).
smasher ['smæʃə*] *n* (*sl*) cosa *f* estupenda, (*esp girl*) bombón *m* (*fam*), guayabo *m* (*fam*); **it's a —!** ¡es estupendo!
smashing ['smæʃiŋ] *adj* (*sl*) imponente, bárbaro (*fam*), pistonudo (*fam*); **a — dress** un vestido monísimo; **we had a — time** lo pasamos en grande; **isn't it —?** ¿es estupendo, no?
smash-up ['smæʃʌp] *n* choque *m* violento, colisión *f* violenta, accidente *m*.
smattering ['smætəriŋ] *n* conocimientos *mpl* elementales, conocimiento *m* superficial, nociones *fpl*; **I have a — of Catalan** tengo algunas nociones de catalán.
smear [smiə*] **1** *n* mancha *f*; (*fig*) calumnia *f*, mancha *f*; (*Med*) frotis *m*.
2 *vt* (a) manchar (*with* de), untar (*with* de); **to — one's face with blood** untarse la cara de sangre; **to — wet paint** manchar la pintura fresca.
(b) (*fig*) calumniar, difamar; **to — someone as a traitor** calumniar a uno alegando que es traidor, tachar a uno de traidor; **to — someone because of his past** tachar a uno por su pasado.
smeary ['smiəri] *adj* manchado.
smell [smel] **1** *n* (a) (*sense of* —) olfato *m*; **to have a keen sense of —** tener buen olfato.
(b) (*odour*) olor *m* (*of* a); **bad —** mal olor *m*, hedor *m*; **it has a nice —** tiene un olor agradable.
(c) **let's have a —** déjame olerlo.
2 (*irr*: *pret and ptp* **smelled** *or* **smelt**) *vt* oler; (*of dog*) olfatear; **to — out** olfatear, husmear; **it's —ing the room out** hace oler mal todo el cuarto, apesta el cuarto.
3 *vi* oler (*of* a); **it —s good** huele bien; **it —s bad** huele mal, tiene mal olor; **that flower doesn't —** esa flor no tiene olor; **it's a gas which doesn't —** es un gas inodoro; **it —s damp in here** aquí dentro huele a húmedo; **the dog —ed at my shoes** el perro olió mis zapatos.
smelling bottle ['smeliŋˌbɒtl] *n* frasco *m* de sales.
smelling salts ['smeliŋzɔːlts] *npl* sales *fpl* (aromáticas).
smelly ['smeli] *adj* que huele mal, de mal olor, hediondo; **it's — in here** aquí dentro huele mal.
smelt[1] [smelt] *pret and ptp of* **smell.**
smelt[2] [smelt] *vt* fundir.
smelt[3] [smelt] *n* (*Fish*) eperlano *m*.
smelting ['smeltiŋ] *n* fundición *f*.
smelting furnace ['smeltiŋˌfɔːnis] *n* horno *m* de fundición.
smile [smail] **1** *n* sonrisa *f*; **with a — on one's lips** con una sonrisa en los labios; **a face wreathed in —s** una cara con una sonrisa radiante; **to give someone a —** sonreír a uno; **come on, give me a —!** ¡vamos, una sonrisa!; **to knock the — off someone's face** hacer que uno deje de sonreír a fuerza de golpes; **to raise a —** forzar una sonrisa; **can't you even raise a —?** ¿no sonríes siquiera?
2 *vt emotion* expresar con una sonrisa; **she —d her thanks** dio las gracias con una sonrisa; **to — a bitter —** sonreír amargamente.
3 *vi* sonreír, sonreírse (*at* de); **to keep smiling** seguir con la sonrisa en los labios; **to — at danger** reírse del peligro; **fortune —d on him** le favoreció la fortuna; **if she —s on me** si me mira con buenos ojos.
smiling ['smailiŋ] *adj* sonriente, risueño.
smilingly ['smailiŋli] *adv* sonriendo, con cara risueña, con una sonrisa.
smirch [smɜːtʃ] *vt* (*lit*) mancillar, desdorar.
smirk [smɜːk] **1** *n* sonrisa *f* satisfecha; sonrisa *f* afectada. **2** *vi* sonreírse satisfecho; sonreírse afectadamente.
smirkingly ['smɜːkiŋli] *adv* con una sonrisa satisfecha (*or* afectada).
smite [smait] (*irr*: *pret* **smote**, *ptp* **smitten**) *vt* (*strike*) golpear; (*punish*) castigar; (*pain*) doler, afligir; (*of light, sound etc*) herir; **an idea smote me** se me ocurrió una idea; **my conscience smote me** me remordió la conciencia; **he smote the ball hard** golpeó la pelota con violencia; *see also* **smitten.**
smith [smiθ] *n* herrero *m*.

smithereens ['smɪðə'riːnz] *npl*: **to smash something to —** hacer algo añicos; **it was in —** estaba hecho añicos.

smithy ['smɪðɪ] *n* herrería *f*.

smitten ['smɪtn] *ptp of* **smite**; **to be — with the plague** sufrir el azote de la peste, ser afligido por la peste; **to be — with an idea** entusiasmarse por una idea; **to be — with someone** estar chalado por uno; **I was — by the urge to +** *infin* me entraron deseos vehementes de + *infin*.

smock [smɔk] **1** *n* (*artist's, labourer's*) blusa *f*; (*child's*) delantal *m*; (*expectant mother's*) bata *f* corta, tontón *m*. **2** *vt* fruncir, adornar con frunces.

smocking ['smɔkɪŋ] *n* adorno *m* de frunces.

smog [smɔg] *n* niebla *f* espesa con humo.

smoke [sməuk] **1** *n* (a) humo *m*; **holy —!** ¡caramba!; **there's no — without fire** cuando el río suena agua lleva, lo que hace humo es porque está ardiendo; **to go up in —** quedar destruido en un incendio, quemarse, (*person: fam*) subirse por las paredes.
　(b) (*cigarette etc*) pitillo *m*, tabaco *m*; **to have a —** echar un pitillo, fumar un cigarrillo; **I like to have a — after meals** me gusta fumar después de comer; **will you have a —?** ¿quieres fumar?; **I've no —s** no tengo tabaco.
　2 *vt* (a) *tobacco* fumar; *bacon, glass etc* ahumar; **he —s a pipe** fuma en pipa; **he's smoking his pipe** está fumando su pipa.
　(b) **to — insects out** ahuyentar insectos con humo; **to — a gang out** hacer que salga una pandilla de su escondite pegándole fuego; **that lamp is smoking the room out** esa lámpara está llenando el cuarto de humo.
　3 *vi* (a) (*of chimney etc*) humear, echar humo.
　(b) (*of smoker*) fumar; **do you —?** ¿fuma Vd?; **will you —?** ¿quieres fumar?; **do you mind if I —?** ¿le molesta que fume?; **he —s like a chimney** fuma como un carretero.

smoke bomb ['sməukbɔm] *n* bomba *f* de humo.

smoked [sməukt] *adj bacon, glass etc* ahumado.

smoke-dried ['sməukdraid] *adj* ahumado, curado al humo.

smokeless ['sməuklis] *adj* sin humo; **— fuel** combustible *m* sin humo; **— zone** zona *f* libre de humo.

smoker ['sməukə*] *n* (a) (*person*) fumador *m*, ora *f*; **to be a heavy —** fumar mucho. (b) (*Rail*) coche *m* fumador.

smokeroom ['sməukrum] *n* salón *m* de fumar.

smoke screen ['sməukskriːn] *n* cortina *f* de humo; **to put up a —** (*fig*) entenebrecer un asunto, enmarañar un asunto (para despistar a la gente).

smoke signal ['sməuk,sɪgnl] *n* ahumada *f*.

smokestack ['sməukstæk] *n* chimenea *f*.

smoking ['sməukɪŋ] **1** *adj* humeante, que humea.
　2 *n* el fumar; **— is bad for you** el fumar te hace daño; **"no —"** "se prohíbe fumar".
　3 *attr* de fumar; de (*or* para) fumador.

smoking compartment ['sməukɪŋkəm,pɑːtmənt] *n*, (*US*) **— car** [,kɑː*] *n* (*Rail*) departamento *m* de fumadores, coche *m* fumador.

smoking jacket ['sməukɪŋ,dʒækit] *n* chaqueta *f* casera, medio batín *m*.

smoking room ['sməukɪŋ,rum] *n* salón *m* de fumar.

smoky ['sməukɪ] *adj chimney, fire* humeante, que humea; *room* lleno de humo; *flavour, surface etc* ahumado; **it's — in here** aquí hay mucho humo.

smolder ['sməuldə*] (*US*) *see* **smoulder**.

smooch [smuːtʃ] *vi* (*sl*) acariciarse, abrazarse amorosamente.

smooth [smuːð] **1** *adj* (a) *surface* liso, terso; suave; llano, igual, uniforme; *skin etc* liso, suave; *brow* sin arrugas; *sea* tranquilo, en calma.
　(b) (*in consistency*) *paste etc* liso, sin grumos; *running of engine, take-off etc* suave; *voice* suave; *style* fluido, suave; *passage, trip* tranquilo, sin novedad; *person's manner* afable.
　(c) *person* afable, culto; (*pej*) zalamero, meloso.
　2 *vt* (*often* **to — out, to — down**) *hair etc* alisar; *surface* allanar, igualar; *dress etc* arreglar; *wood* desbastar; *style etc* suavizar; **to — the way for someone** allanar el camino para uno, preparar el terreno para uno; **to — away** (*or over*) **difficulties** allanar dificultades, zanjar dificultades; **to — someone down** calmar a uno.

smooth-chinned ['smuːð'tʃind] *adj*, **smooth-faced** ['smuːð'feist] *adj* barbilampiño; bien afeitado; **some — youth** algún joven imberbe.

smoothing iron ['smuːðɪŋ,aiən] *n* plancha *f*.

smoothly ['smuːðli] *adv* lisamente; suavemente; de modo uniforme; tranquilamente; afablemente; **he said —** dijo sin alterarse; **everything went —** todo fue sobre ruedas, todo fue viento en popa.

smoothness ['smuːðnis] *n* lisura *f*, tersura *f*; suavidad *f*; igualdad *f*, uniformidad *f*; tranquilidad *f*, calma *f*; fluidez *f*; afabilidad *f*; (*pej*) zalamería *f*.

smooth-running ['smuːð'rʌnɪŋ] *adj engine etc* que funciona suavemente.

smooth-spoken ['smuːð'spəukən] *adj* afable, culto; (*pej*) zalamero, meloso.

smooth-tongued ['smuːð'tʌŋgd] *adj* (*pej*) zalamero, meloso.

smote [sməut] *pret of* **smite**.

smother ['smʌðə*] **1** *vt* (*stifle*) ahogar, sofocar; *fire* apagar; *yawn* contener; *criticism, doubt etc* ahogar, suprimir; **fruit —ed in cream** fruta *f* cubierta de crema; **a book —ed in dust** un libro cubierto de polvo; **the child was —ed in dirt** el niño estaba todo sucio. **2** *vi* ahogarse, sofocarse.

smoulder, *US* **smolder** ['sməuldə*] *vi* arder sin llama, arder lentamente; (*fig*) estar latente, estar sin apagarse.

smouldering, *US* **smoldering** ['sməuldərɪŋ] *adj* que arde lentamente; (*fig*) latente; **she gave me a — look** me miró provocativa.

smudge [smʌdʒ] **1** *n* mancha *f*, tiznón *m*. **2** *vt* manchar; tiznar (*with* de). **3** *vi* mancharse.

smudgy ['smʌdʒi] *adj* manchado; lleno de manchas; *outline etc* borroso.

smug [smʌg] *adj* pagado de sí mismo, suficiente; presumido; **he said with — satisfaction** dijo muy pagado de sí; **don't be so —!** ¡no presumas!

smuggle ['smʌgl] **1** *vt* pasar de contrabando; **to — goods in** introducir artículos de contrabando; **to — something past** (*or* **through**) **the customs** pasar algo por la aduana sin declararlo; **to — someone out in disguise** hacer que uno pase inadvertido gracias a su disfraz.
　2 *vi* hacer contrabando, dedicarse a pasar cosas de contrabando.

smuggled ['smʌgld] *adj goods* de contrabando.

smuggler ['smʌglə*] *n* contrabandista *mf*.

smuggling ['smʌglɪŋ] *n* contrabando *m*.

smugly ['smʌgli] *adv* con un aire satisfecho, con aire de suficiencia; con presunción.

smugness ['smʌgnis] *n* satisfacción *f* de sí mismo, suficiencia *f*; presunción *f*.

smut [smʌt] *n* (*piece of dirt*) tizne *m*; (*in eye*) mota *f* de carbonilla; (*on paper*) tiznón *m*, mancha *f*; (*Bot*) tizón *m*; (*fig*) obscenidades *fpl*, cosas *fpl* verdes; **to talk —** contar cosas verdes.

smuttiness ['smʌtinis] *n* (*fig*) obscenidad *f*.

smutty ['smʌti] *adj* obsceno, verde; (*Bot*) atizonado; (*fig*) obsceno, verde; **a lot of — talk** muchos cuentos verdes.

Smyrna ['smɜːnə] Esmirna *f*.

snack [snæk] *n* bocadillo *m*, tentempié *m*, piscolabis *m*; **to have a —** tomar un bocadillo, comer algo.

snack bar ['snækbɑː*] *n* cafetería *f*, bar *m*.

snaffle[1] ['snæfl] *n* bridón *m*.

snaffle[2] ['snæfl] *vt* (*sl*) afanar (*fam*), guindar (*fam*).

snafu [snæ'fuː] (*US*) **1** *adj* confuso; complicadísimo; arruinado, estropeado.
　2 *n* (*mistake*) equivocación *f* monumental; (*confusion*) confusionismo *m*; (*mess*) situación *f* confusa, situación *f* complicadísima; asunto *m* enmarañado; lío *m*.

snag [snæg] *n* (*in wood*) nudo *m*; (*of tree*) tocón *m*; (*of tooth*) raigón *m*; (*fig*) dificultad *f*, obstáculo *m*, estorbo *m*, pero *m*; **there's a —** hay una dificultad; **the — is that . . .** la dificultad es que . . .; **that's the — ahí** está el problema; **what's the —?** ¿qué obstáculo hay?; **to hit** (*or* **run into**) **a —** encontrar un pero, tropezar con una dificultad.

snail [sneil] *n* caracol *m*; **edible —** caracol *m* comestible; **at a —'s pace** a paso de tortuga.

snake [sneik] **1** *n* culebra *f*, serpiente *f*; **he's the — in the grass** él es el traidor, él es el enemigo oculto, él es el peligro oculto.
　2 *vi*: **to — about, to — along** serpentear; **a hand —d out** se extendió de repente una mano.

snakebite ['sneikbait] *n* mordedura *f* de serpiente.

snake charmer ['sneik,tʃɑːmə*] *n* encantador *m* de serpientes.

snaky ['sneiki] *adj* serpentino, tortuoso.

snap [snæp] **1** *n* (a) (*sound: of fingers*) castañetazo *m*; (*of whip etc*) chasquido *m*; (*report*) estallido *m*; (*click*) golpe *m* seco, ruido *m* seco; **it shut with a —** se cerró de golpe, se cerró con un ruido seco.
　(b) (*point of breakage*) rotura *f*.
　(c) **cold —** ola *f* de frío, período *m* breve de frío.
　(d) (*fam*) vigor *m*, energía *f*; **put some — into it!** ¡menearse!
　(e) (*fastener*) cierre *m*.
　(f) (*Phot*) foto *f*, instantánea *f*; **to take a — of**

someone tomar una foto de uno; **these are our holiday**—s éstas son las fotos de nuestras vacaciones.

2 *adj* repentino; — **decision** decisión *f* tomada de repente; — **vote** votación *f* apenas discutida de antemano.

3 *adv:* —! ¡crac!; **to go** — hacer crac.

4 *vt* (a) *fingers* castañetear (*see also* **finger**); *whip* chasquear; **to** — **a box shut** cerrar una caja de golpe; **to** — **something into place** meter algo en su lugar con un golpe seco.

(b) (*break*) romper, quebrar, hacer saltar.

(c) **to** — **out an order** espetar una orden, dar una orden en tono brusco.

(d) **to** — **someone** (*Phot*) tomar una foto de uno.

(e) **to** — **off** romper, separar; (*of dog etc*) morder y separar, separar con los dientes; **to** — **someone's head off** echar un rapapolvo a uno; interrumpir bruscamente a uno; **to** — **up a bargain** comprar algo con avidez; **our stock was** —**ped up at once** nuestras existencias quedaron agotadas al instante.

5 *vi* (a) **to** — **at someone** (*of dog*) querer morder a uno, tratar de morder a uno; (*of person*) contestar (*or* hablar *etc*) bruscamente a uno; **don't** — **at me!** ¡habla con más educación!

(b) (*whip etc*) chasquear; (*fastener etc*) hacer un ruido seco; **it** —**ped shut** se cerró de golpe.

(c) (*break*) romperse, quebrarse; separarse, desprenderse; saltar; **it** —**ped off** se rompió y se separó.

(d) (*fig*) **to** — **into something** emprender algo con entusiasmo; **to** — **out of something** dejarse de algo, quitarse algo de encima; — **out of it!** ¡déjate de eso!, ¡ánimo!

snapdragon ['snæp,drægən] *n* (*Bot*) cabeza *f* de dragón.

snap fastener ['snæp'faːsnə*] *n* corchete *m* de presión.

snappish ['snæpiʃ] *adj* brusco, abrupto; irritable.

snappishness ['snæpiʃnis] *n* brusquedad *f*; irritabilidad *f*.

snappy ['snæpi] *adj* (*fam*) rápido; enérgico, vigoroso; **to be** — **about something** hacer algo con toda rapidez; **and be** — **about it!** ¡y date prisa!; **make it** —! ¡rápido!

snapshot ['snæpʃɔt] *n* (*Phot*) foto *f*, instantánea *f*.

snare [snɛə*] **1** *n* lazo *m*, trampa *f*; (*fig*) trampa *f*, engaño *m*; **it's a** — **and delusion** es una trampa.

2 *vt* coger con trampas; (*fig*) hacer caer en el lazo, engañar.

snarl¹ [snaːl] **1** *n* gruñido *m*; **he said with a** — dijo gruñendo. **2** *vi* gruñir; **to** — **at someone** decir algo a uno gruñendo.

snarl² [snaːl] **1** *vt* (*also* **to** — **up**) enmarañar, enredar; **it's got all** —**ed up** (*fig*) ha quedado en la mayor confusión.

2 *vi* (*also* **to** — **up**) enmarañarse, enredarse.

snatch [snætʃ] **1** *n* (a) (*act*) arrebatamiento *m*; **to make a** — **at something** tratar de arrebatar algo.

(b) (*fam: robbery*) robo *m*; (*kidnapping*) secuestro *m*; **jewellery** — robo *m* de joyas.

(c) (*Mus etc*) trocito *m*; **to whistle** —**es of** **Mozart** silbar trocitos de Mozart.

2 *vt* (a) (*pick up*) asir, coger, agarrar; (*from someone's hold*) arrebatar (*from* a); (*out of the air*) coger al vuelo; **to** — **a meal** comer algo a toda prisa; **to** — **an opportunity** aprovechar una oportunidad; **to** — **an hour of happiness** procurarse (a pesar de todo) una hora de felicidad; **to** — **something away** arrebatar algo (*from* a); **to** — **up a knife** asir un cuchillo; **to** — **up a child** coger a un niño en brazos.

(b) (*fam: steal*) robar, (*kidnap*) secuestrar.

3 *vi:* **don't** —! ¡no me arrebates las cosas de manera tan grosera!; **to** — **at something** tratar de arrebatar algo; tratar de coger algo al vuelo; **to** — **at an opportunity** aprovechar una oportunidad.

snazzy ['snæzi] *adj* (*sl*) de lo más elegante.

sneak [sniːk] **1** *n* soplón *m*, ona *f*.

2 *vt* robar a hurtadillas, afanar, birlar.

3 *vi* (a) **to** — **about** ir a hurtadillas, moverse furtivamente; **to** — **away**, **to** — **off** escabullirse; **to** — **in** entrar a hurtadillas, entrar sin ser visto; **to** — **off with something** alzarse con algo.

(b) **to** — **on someone** soplarse de uno.

sneakers ['sniːkəz] *npl* (*fam*) zapatos *mpl* ligeros de goma.

sneaking ['sniːkiŋ] *adj* *manner* furtivo, sigiloso; **to have a** — **regard for someone** respetar a uno a pesar de todo, respetar a uno sin querer confesarlo abiertamente.

sneak thief ['sniːkθiːf] *n* ratero *m*, garduño *m*.

sneaky ['sniːki] *adj* *manner* furtivo, sigiloso; (*of character*) soplón.

sneer [sniə*] **1** *n* (*expression*) visaje *m* de burla y desprecio, sonrisa *f* de desprecio; (*remark*) burla *f*, mofa *f*; comentario *m* despreciativo; **he said with a** — dijo con desprecio; **the book is full of** —**s about . . .** el libro se mofa constantemente de . . .

2 *vi* hacer un visaje de burla y desprecio; **to** — **at someone** mofarse de uno, hablar con desprecio de uno.

sneerer ['sniərə*] *n* mofador *m*, ora *f*.

sneering ['sniəriŋ] *adj* *tone etc* burlador y despreciativo, lleno de desprecio.

sneeringly ['sniəriŋli] *adv* en tono burlador y despreciativo; con una sonrisa de desprecio.

sneeze [sniːz] **1** *n* estornudo *m*. **2** *vi* estornudar; **an offer not to be** —**d at** una oferta que no es de despreciar.

snick [snik] **1** *n* corte *m*, tijeretada *f*.

2 *vt* (a) cortar (un poco), tijeretear; **to** — **something off** cortar algo con un movimiento rápido.

(b) *ball* desviar ligeramente.

snicker ['snikə*] = **snigger**.

snide [snaid] *adj* (*esp US*) despreciativo, sarcástico.

sniff [snif] **1** *n* sorbo *m* por las narices; (*of dog etc*) husmeo *m*; **to go out for a** — **of air** salir a tomar el fresco; **we never got a** — **of the vodka** no llegamos siquiera a oler el vodka.

2 *vt* sorber por las narices; (*of dog etc, also* **to** — **out**) husmear, olfatear; **just** — **these flowers** huele un poco estas flores; **you can** — **the sea air here** aquí se huele ese aire de mar; — **the gas deeply** aspire profundamente el gas.

3 *vi* (a) (*person*) sorber por las narices; **to** — **at** oler; **don't** —! ¡no hagas ese ruido con las narices!

(b) (*dog etc*) oler, husmear, olfatear; **the dog** —**ed at my shoes** el perro olió mis zapatos.

(c) **to** — **at something** (*fig*) despreciar algo, tratar algo con desdén; **an offer not to be** —**ed at** una oferta que no es de despreciar.

sniffle ['snifl] = **snuffle**.

sniffy ['snifi] *adj* (*fam*) estirado, desdeñoso; **he was pretty** — **about it** trató el asunto con bastante desdén.

snifter ['sniftə*] *n* (*sl*) trago *m* (*esp* de whiskey); **to have a** — echarse un trago.

snigger ['snigə*] **1** *n* risa *f* disimulada. **2** *vi* reírse con disimulo (*at* de).

snip [snip] **1** *n* (*cut*) tijeretada *f*, tijeretazo *m*; (*incision*) tijeretada *f*; (*piece of material etc*) recorte *m*; (*sl: bargain*) ganga *f*.

2 *vti* tijeretear; **to** — **off** recortar.

snipe [snaip] **1** *n* (*Orn*) agachadiza *f*.

2 *vi:* **to** — **at someone** tirar a uno desde un escondite; **to** — **from the shelter of . . .** tirar desde la protección de . . .; **to** — **at one's critics** contestar (con precaución) a los críticos de uno; **he was really sniping at the Minister** (*fig*) en realidad sus ataques iban dirigidos contra el Ministro.

sniper ['snaipə*] *n* tirador *m* escondido, francotirador *m*.

snippet ['snipit] *n* (*of cloth*) retazo *m*, retal *m*; (*of information etc*) retazo *m*; —**s** retazos *mpl*; "**S**—**s**" (*heading in press etc*) "Breverías".

snitch [snitʃ] (*sl*) **1** *n* (*nose*) napias *fpl* (*sl*). **2** *vi* soplarse (*on someone* de uno).

snivel ['snivl] *vi* lloriquear.

snivelling ['snivliŋ] **1** *adj* llorón. **2** *n* lloriqueo *m*.

snob [snɔb] *n* (e)snob *mf*.

snobbery ['snɔbəri] *n* (e)snobismo *m*.

snobbish ['snɔbiʃ] *adj* (e)snob.

snobbishness ['snɔbiʃnis] *n* (e)snobismo *m*.

snood [snuːd] *n* (*band*) cintillo *m*; (*net*) redecilla *f*.

snook [snuːk] *n* (*sl*): **to cock a** — **at someone** sacar la lengua a uno, hacer una señal grosera a uno; (*fig*) mofarse abiertamente a uno.

snooker ['snuːkə*] **1** *n* especie de billar.

2 *vt:* **to** — **someone** poner a uno en un aprieto; **now we're properly** —**ed** ahora no hay nada que hacer, en buen lío nos hemos metido.

snoop [snuːp] **1** *n* (a) (*person*) fisgón *m*, ona *f*.

(b) (*act*) **I'll have a** — **round** voy a reconocer el terreno, a ver si encuentro algo; **I had a** — **round the kitchen** registré la cocina (sin que nadie me viese).

2 *vi* (*also* **to** — **about**, **to** — **around**) curiosear, fisgonear; practicar un registro furtivo, hacer una investigación furtiva; **he comes** —**ing around here** viene aquí a fisgonear.

snooper ['snuːpə*] *n* investigador *m* encubierto, inspector *m* que no anuncia públicamente sus visitas.

snooty ['snuːti] *adj* (*fam*) fachendoso, presumido; **people hereabouts are very —** por aquí la gente se da mucho tono; **there's no call to be — about it** Vd no tiene motivo para presumir.

snooze [snuːz] **1** *n* siestecita *f*, sueñecillo *m*; **to have a — 2** *vi* dormitar, echar una siestecita.

snore [snɔː*] **1** *n* ronquido *m*. **2** *vi* roncar.

snoring ['snɔːriŋ] *n* ronquidos *mpl*.

snorkel ['snɔːkl] *n* tubo *m* snorkel, tubo *m* de respiración.

snort [snɔːt] **1** *n* bufido *m*; **with a — of rage** con un bufido de enojo. **2** *vi* bufar; **"No!" he —ed** "¡No!" dijo bufando.

snorter ['snɔːtə*] *n* (*sl*): **a real — of a song** una canción estupenda; **it was a — of a game** fue un partido maravilloso.

snot [snɔt] *n* (*fam*) mocarro *m*.

snotty ['snɔti] *adj* (*fam*) mocoso; (*fig: snooty*) fachendoso, presumido; (*angry*) enojado.

snout [snaut] *n* hocico *m*, morro *m*.

snow [snəu] **1** *n* nieve *f*; (*sl*) cocaína *f*.
   2 *vi* nevar; **to be —ed in, to be —ed up** estar encerrado (*or* aprisionado) por la nieve; **to be —ed under** (*fig*) estar inundado (**by, with** por).

snowball ['snəubɔːl] **1** *n* bola *f* de nieve.
   2 *vt* lanzar bolas de nieve a.
   3 *vi* (*fig*) aumentar progresivamente, aumentar rápidamente.

snow-blind ['snəublaind] *adj* cegado por los reflejos de la nieve.

snow blindness ['snəu,blaindnis] *n* ceguera *f* causada por los reflejos de la nieve.

snowbound ['snəubaund] *adj* aprisionado por la nieve.

snow-capped ['snəukæpt] *adj* coronado de nieve.

snow-covered ['snəu'kʌvəd] *adj* cubierto de nieve, nevado.

snowdrift ['snəudrift] *n* ventisquero *m*, montón *m* de nieve, nieve *f* amontonada.

snowdrop ['snəudrɔp] *n* campanilla *f* de febrero, campanilla *f* blanca.

snowfall ['snəufɔːl] *n* nevada *f*.

snow fence ['snəufens] *n* valla *f* paranieves.

snowfield ['snəufiːld] *n* campo *m* de nieve.

snowflake ['snəufleik] *n* copo *m* de nieve.

snow line ['snəulain] *n* límite *m* de las nieves perpetuas.

snowman ['snəumæn] *n*, *pl* **—men** [men] figura *f* de nieve; **the abominable —** el abominable hombre de las nieves.

snowplough, (*US*) **snow plow** ['snəuplau] *n* quitanieves *m*.

snowshoe ['snəuʃuː] *n* raqueta *f* de nieve.

snowslide ['snəuslaid] *n* (*US*) alud *m* de nieve, caída *f* de nieve.

snowstorm ['snəustɔːm] *n* nevada *f*, nevasca *f*.

Snow White ['snəuwait] Blancanieves *f*; **"— and the Seven Dwarfs"** "Blancanieves y los siete enanitos".

snow-white ['snəu'wait] *adj* blanco como la nieve; (*poet*) níveo, cándido.

snowy ['snəui] *adj* (**a**) (*Meteorol*) *climate, region* de mucha nieve, que tiene mucha nieve; *countryside etc* cubierto de nieve; **— day** día *m* de nieve; **— season** estación *f* de las nieves; **it was very — yesterday** ayer nevó mucho, ayer cayó mucha nieve.
   (**b**) (*fig*) blanco como la nieve, (*poet*) níveo, cándido.

snub [snʌb] **1** *n* desaire *m*; repulsa *f*. **2** *vt person* desairar, ofender; repulsar; *offer etc* rechazar con desdén.

snub-nosed ['snʌb'nəuzd] *adj* chato.

snuff [snʌf] **1** *n* rapé *m*, tabaco *m* en polvo; **to take —** tomar rapé.
   2 *vt* (*breathe in*) aspirar, sorber por la nariz; *candle* despabilar; **to — out** apagar; (*fig*) extinguir; **to — it** (*fam*) estirar la pata (*fam*).

snuffbox ['snʌfbɔks] *n* tabaquera *f*.

snuffers ['snʌfəz] *npl* despabiladeras *fpl*; **a pair of —** unas despabiladeras.

snuffle ['snʌfl] **1** *n* ruido *m* de la nariz; (*twang*) gangueo *m*.
   2 *vi* respirar con ruido, hacer ruido con la nariz; (*in speaking*) ganguear.

snug [snʌg] *adj* (*cosy*) cómodo y bien caliente; (*sheltered*) abrigado, al abrigo; (*of dress*) ajustado; *income etc* respetable, nada despreciable; **to be — in bed** estar cómodamente acostado.

snuggery ['snʌgəri] *n* cuarto *m* cómodo; despacho *m*, cuarto *m* particular.

snuggle ['snʌgl] *vi*: **to — down in bed** acomodarse en la cama; **they'll — down together** se las

arreglarán para estar juntos; **to — up to someone** arrimarse (amorosamente *etc*) a uno, apretarse contra uno; **— up to me** arrímate a mí; **I like to — up with a book** me gusta ponerme cómodamente y leer.

snugly ['snʌgli] *adv* cómodamente; al abrigo; **it fits —** se ajusta perfectamente.

so [səu] **1** *adv* (**a**) (*in comparisons: before adj and adv*) tan; **— quick** tan rápido, **— quickly** tan rápidamente; **it is — big that . . .** es tan grande que . . .; **it's not — very difficult** no es tan difícil, la dificultad no es tan grande; **he's not — silly as to do that** no es tan tonto como para hacer eso, no es tan tonto para hacer eso; **— many flies** tantas moscas; **— much tea** tanto té (*and* **see many, much**); **we spent — much** gastamos tanto; **I love you —** te quiero tanto; **he who — loved Spain** él que amó tanto a España; **see kind, sure** *etc*.
   (**b**) (*thus*) así; (*in this way*) de este modo, de esta manera; **he does it —** él lo hace de este modo; **if — si** es así; **only more —** pero en mayor grado; **how —?** ¿cómo eso?; **why —?** ¿por qué?, ¿cómo?; **just —!** ¡eso es!, ¡perfectamente!, ¡precisamente!; **he likes things just —** quiere tener cada cosa en su lugar, le gusta una vida bien ordenada; **not —!** ¡nada de eso!; **— would I** yo también; **— do I** yo también, yo hago lo mismo; **he's wrong and — are you** él se equivoca y Vd también; **and — forth, and — on** y así sucesivamente, y así los demás; etcétera; **it is —** es así; **it is!**, **it does!** ¡es verdad!; **that's —** eso es; **is that —?** ¿de veras?, ¿es cierto eso?; **— be it así sea**; **— it was that . . .** así fue que . . .; **we — arranged things that . . .** lo arreglamos de modo que . . .; **and he did —** y lo hizo; **by — doing** haciéndolo así; **it — happens that . . .** da la casualidad que . . .; **I hope —** espero que sí; **— saying, he walked out** diciendo esto, se marchó; **— to speak** para decirlo así; **I think —** creo que sí, lo creo; **I told you —** te lo dije ya; **I tell you it is —** te digo que es así.
   (**c**) **— that** (*purpose*) para que + *subj*, a fin de que + *subj*; **I brought it — that you should see it** lo traje para que lo vieras.
   (**d**) **— that** (*result*) de modo que + *indic*; **he stood — that nobody could get past** estaba en tal posición que nadie podía pasar.
   (**e**) **— as to** + *infin* para + *infin*, a fin de + *infin*; **we hurried — as not to be late** nos dimos prisa para no llegar tarde.
   2 *conj* (**a**) **it rained and — we could not go out** llovió y por tanto (*or* por consiguiente) no pudimos salir.
   (**b**) **— you're Spanish?** ¿conque Vd es español?; **— you're not selling?** ¿de modo que Vd no lo vende?, ¿así que Vd no lo vende?; **see there** *etc*.

soak [səuk] **1** *vt* (**a**) **— something in a liquid** remojar algo en un líquido, empapar algo en un líquido; **to be —ed (to the skin)** estar calado hasta los huesos; **to get —ed (to the skin)** calarse hasta los huesos.
   (**b**) **to — up** absorber, embeber.
   (**c**) **to — someone** (*fam*) desplumar a uno, clavar un precio excesivo a uno (*fam*); **to — someone for a loan** pedir prestado dinero a uno; **to — the rich** imponer contribuciones gravosas a los ricos.
   2 *vi* (**a**) remojarse, estar a remojo; **to leave something to —** dejar algo a remojo.
   (**b**) **to — in, to — through** calar, penetrar; **to — in** (*fig*) penetrar; hacer mella, tener efecto.
   (**c**) (*fam*) beber mucho; emborracharse.
   3 *vr*: **to — oneself** calarse hasta los huesos; **to — oneself in** (*fig*) empaparse en.
   4 *n* (*rain*) diluvio *m*; (*person: fam*) borrachín *m*.

soaking ['səukiŋ] **1** *adj*: **to be — wet** (*person*) estar hecho una sopa, (*object*) estar totalmente mojado; **a — wet day** un día de muchísima lluvia.
   2 *n* remojo *m*; **to get a —** calarse hasta los huesos.

so-and-so ['səuənsəu] *n* (**a**) **Mr —** don Fulano (de Tal); **old — up at the shop** fulano el de la tienda; **any — could pinch it** (*fam*) cualquiera pudiera guindarlo (*fam*).
   (**b**) **he's a —** es un tío.

soap [səup] **1** *n* jabón *m*; **soft —** (*sl*) coba *f* (*fam*). **2** *vt* jabonar, enjabonar.

soapbox ['səupbɔks] *n* caja *f* vacía empleada como tribuna (en la calle); **— orator** orador *m* de barricada; **he has a — manner** habla como un orador de barricada.

soapdish ['səupdiʃ] *n* jabonera *f*.

soapflakes ['səupfleiks] *npl* escamas *fpl* de jabón.

soap opera ['səup,ɔpərə] *n* (*US fam*) serial *m* radiofónico de bajísima categoría.

soap powder ['səup,paudə*] *n* jabón *m* en polvo.

soapstone ['səupstəun] *n* esteatita *f*.

soapsuds ['səupsʌdz] *npl* jabonaduras *fpl*.

soapy ['səupi] *adj* jabonoso; cubierto de jabón; (*like soap*) parecido a jabón, jabonoso; (*person: pej*) zalamero, cobista.

soar [sɔ:*] *vi* (a) (*rise*) remontarse, encumbrarse, subir muy alto; (*hover*) cernerse.
(b) (*fig: of tower etc*) elevarse mucho sobre el suelo, elevarse hacia el cielo; (*of price etc*) subir vertiginosamente, ponerse por las nubes; **after this his ambition —ed** después de esto se extendió mucho más su ambición; **our spirits —ed** nos reanimamos de golpe; renació nuestra esperanza.

soaring ['sɔ:riŋ] *adj flight* encumbrado, por lo alto; *building* altísimo; *ambition* inmenso; *price* que va subiendo vertiginosamente.

sob [sɔb] **1** *n* sollozo *m*; **she said with a —** dijo sollozando.
2 *attr:* **— stuff** (*fam*) sentimentalismo *m*, sensiblería *f*.
3 *vti* sollozar; **"No", she —bed** "no", dijo sollozando; **to — one's heart out** llorar a mares.

sobbing ['sɔbiŋ] *n* sollozos *mpl*.

sober ['səubə*] **1** *adj* (a) (*moderate, sedate*) sobrio, serio, moderado; (*sensible*) sensato, juicioso; *colour* discreto; **a — assessment of the facts** una seria valoración de los hechos; **a — statement** una declaración razonada.
(b) (*not drunk*) no embriagado, que no ha bebido, sereno; **to be as — as a judge, to be stone-cold —** estar totalmente sereno; **I'm perfectly —** yo no he bebido en absoluto, tengo la cabeza perfectamente despejada; **one has to be — to drive** para conducir es necesario no haber bebido nada; **tomorrow, when you're —** mañana, cuando te hayas despejado de la borrachera.
2 *vt:* **to — someone down** calmar a uno; **to — someone up** quitar la sopa a uno; **this will — you up** esto te quitará la merluza.
3 *vi:* **to — down** calmarse; **he's —ed down recently** recientemente ha sentado la cabeza; **to — up** espabilar la borrachera.

soberly ['səubəli] *adv* sobriamente, seriamente, moderadamente; sensatamente; discretamente; **— dressed** discretamente vestido.

sober-minded ['səubə'maindid] *adj* serio, formal.

sobersides ['səubəsaidz] *n* (*fam*) persona *f* reservada.

sobriety [səu'braiəti] *n* (a) sobriedad *f*, seriedad *f*, moderación *f*; sensatez *f*, juicio *m*; discreción *f*. (b) serenidad *f*; moderación *f* en beber.

sobriquet ['səubrikei] *n* apodo *m*, mote *m*.

so-called ['səu'kɔ:ld] *adj* llamado, denominado; supuesto, presunto; **in the — rush hours** en las llamadas horas punta; **all these — journalists** todos estos presuntos periodistas.

soccer ['sɔkə*] *n* fútbol *m*.

sociability [,səuʃə'biliti] *n* sociabilidad *f*; afabilidad *f*.

sociable ['səuʃəbl] *adj* sociable; afable; amistoso; **I'm not feeling very —** no me siento con ganas de estar con las personas.

sociably ['səuʃəbli] *adv* sociablemente; afablemente; amistosamente; **to live — together** vivir juntos amistosamente.

social ['səuʃəl] **1** *adj* social; sociable; **a — outcast** una persona desterrada de la sociedad; **the — column** las notas de sociedad; **man is a — animal** el hombre es un animal sociable.
2 *n* velada *f*, tertulia *f*.

Social Democrat ['səuʃəl'deməkræt] *n* socialdemócrata *mf*.

Social-Democratic ['səuʃəl,demə'krætik] *adj* socialdemocrático.

socialism ['səuʃəlizəm] *n* socialismo *m*.

socialist ['səuʃəlist] **1** *adj* socialista. **2** *n* socialista *mf*.

socialistic [,səuʃə'listik] *adj* socialista.

socialite ['səuʃəlait] *n* persona *f* mundana, persona *f* conocidísima en la buena sociedad.

socialization [,səuʃəlai'zeiʃən] *n* socialización *f*.

socialize ['səuʃəlaiz] *vt* socializar.

socially ['səuʃəli] *adv* socialmente; sociablemente; **we meet —** nos vemos en las reuniones de tipo social.

social worker ['səuʃəl,wə:kə*] *n* asistente *m* social, asistenta *f* social.

society [sə'saiəti] **1** *n* sociedad *f*; asociación *f*; (*high —*) buena sociedad *f*, mundo *m* elegante; **charitable —** asociación *f* benéfica; **cooperative —** cooperativa *f*;

friendly —, provident — sociedad *f* de socorro mutuo, mutualidad *f*, montepío *m*; **the Great S— (US)** la Gran Sociedad; **high —** buena sociedad *f*; **learned —** sociedad *f* científica, academia *f*; **Royal S— Real Sociedad *f*; **S— of Friends** los cuáqueros; **S— of Jesus** Compañía *f* de Jesús; **to try to get into —** intentar penetrar en la buena sociedad; **to go into —** (*girl*) ponerse de largo.
2 *attr:* **— news** (*in press*) notas *fpl* de sociedad; **— woman** mujer *f* mundana, mujer *f* conocida en la buena sociedad.

socioeconomic ['səusiəu,i:kə'nɔmik] *adj* socioeconómico.

sociological [,səusiə'lɔdʒikəl] *adj* sociológico.

sociologist [,səusi'ɔlədʒist] *n* sociólogo *m*.

sociology [,səusi'ɔlədʒi] *n* sociología *f*.

sock¹ [sɔk] *n* calcetín *m*; (*worn inside shoe*) plantilla *f*; **to pull one's —s up** (*fig*) hacer un esfuerzo, procurar hacer mejor.

sock² [sɔk] (*fam*) **1** *n* tortazo *m* (*fam*); **to give someone —s** (*defeat*) cascar a uno (*fam*). **2** *vt* pegar; **— him one!** ¡pégale!

socket ['sɔkit] **1** *n* (*of eye*) cuenca *f*, órbita *f*; (*of tooth*) alvéolo *m*; (*of joint*) fosa *f*; (*Elec*) enchufe *m*; (*Mech*) encaje *m*, cubo *m*.

Socrates ['sɔkrati:z] *n* Sócrates.

Socratic [sɔ'krætik] *adj* socrático.

sod¹ [sɔd] *n* césped *m*.

sod² [sɔd] *n* (*fam*) sodomita *m*; (*as term of abuse*) bestia *f*, bruto *m*; **you —!** ¡cabrón!

soda ['səudə] *n* (a) (*Chem*) sosa *f*, soda *f*; **caustic —** sosa *f* cáustica; **common —, washing —** sosa *f*; **cooking —** bicarbonato *m* sódico.
(b) (*drink*) agua *f* de seltz, gaseosa *f*; **gin and —** ginebra *f* con sifón; **do you like — with it?** ¿le echo un poco de sifón?

soda biscuit ['səudə,biskit] *n* (*US*), **soda cracker** ['səudə,krækə*] *n* (*US*) galletita *f* salada.

soda fountain ['səudə,fauntin] *n* sifón *m*.

sodality [səu'dæliti] *n* (*Eccl*) hermandad *n*, cofradía *f*.

soda water ['səudə,wɔ:tə*] *n* agua *f* de seltz, gaseosa *f*; **... with ... —** con sifón.

sodden ['sɔdn] *adj* empapado, mojado, saturado; **to be — with drink** estar borracho; estar embrutecido por el alcohol.

sodium ['səudiəm] *n* sodio *m*; **— carbonate** carbonato *m* sódico.

sodomite ['sɔdəmait] *n* sodomita *m*.

sodomy ['sɔdəmi] *n* sodomía *f*.

sofa ['səufə] *n* sofá *m*.

sofa bed ['səufəbed] *n* sofá-cama *m*.

soft [sɔft] *adj* (a) (*of material etc*) blando; muelle; (*flabby*) flojo; *skin* suave, terso, fino; *metal* dúctil; *hat* flexible; *fruit* blando; **— to the touch** blando al tacto; **as — as silk, as — as velvet** tan suave como la seda; **to go —** ablandarse, ponerse blando; **his muscles have gone —** sus músculos han perdido su fuerza.
(b) (*fig*) *air, sound* suave; *voice* dulce; *step* suave; *water* blando; *rain* suave; *landing* suave; *colour* delicado; *drink* no alcohólico, analcohólico; *heart, words* tierno, compasivo; *job* fácil; *character* débil; muelle, afeminado; (*lenient*) indulgente, tolerante; **to be — on someone** tratar a uno con demasiada indulgencia; **he's soft on communism** es demasiado tolerante para con el comunismo.
(c) (*foolish*) estúpido, tonto; **you must be —!** ¿has perdido el juicio?; **he's — (in the head)** es un poco tocado; **he's going — (in the head)** está perdiendo el juicio.

softball ['sɔftbɔ:l] *n* (*US*) *especie de béisbol sobre un terreno mas pequeño que el normal, con pelota grande y blanda*.

soft-boiled ['sɔft,bɔild] *adj egg* pasado por agua.

soften ['sɔfn] **1** *vt* ablandar, reblandecer; (*weaken*) debilitar; (*mitigate*) mitigar, suavizar, templar; **to — up resistance** debilitar la resistencia.
2 *vi* ablandarse, reblandecerse; debilitarse, aflojarse; suavizarse, templarse; **to — up on someone** hacerse menos severo con uno, mitigar su severidad con uno; **we must not — up on communism** tenemos que seguir tan opuestos como siempre al comunismo.

softening ['sɔfniŋ] *n* reblandecimiento *m*; debilitación *f*; mitigación *f*, suavización *f*; **— of the brain** reblandecimiento *m* cerebral; **there has been a — of his attitude** se ha suavizado su actitud.

soft-footed ['sɔft'futid] *adj* (*Anat*) de pies blandos; (*soundless*) que pisa sin ruido, que anda sin hacer ruido.

soft-headed ['sɔft,hedid] *adj* bobo, tonto.

soft-hearted ['sɔft'hɑ:tid] *adj* compasivo, bondadoso.

soft-heartedness ['sɔft'hɑ:tidnis] *n* bondad *f*.

softly ['sɔftli] *adv* blandamente; suavemente; dulcemente; delicadamente; **she said** — dijo dulcemente; **to move** — moverse silenciosamente, moverse sin ruido.

softness ['sɔftnis] *n* blandura *f*; flojedad *f*; suavidad *f*, tersura *f*; ductilidad *f*; dulzura *f*; delicadeza *f*; ternura *f*; debilidad *f*; indulgencia *f*, tolerancia *f*; estupidez *f*.

soft-pedal ['sɔft'pedl] *vt* (*fig*) no dar tanto énfasis a, dejar de insistir en, conceder menos importancia a.

soft-spoken ['sɔft'spəukən] *adj* de voz suave, de tono sereno.

softy ['sɔfti] *n* (*fam*) mollejón *m*, ona *f*.

soggy ['sɔgi] *adj* empapado, saturado; esponjoso.

soi-disant ['swɑː'diːsɔːŋ] *adj* supuesto, presunto, sediciente.

soigné ['swɑːnjei] *adj* pulcro, acicalado.

soil[1] [sɔil] *n* tierra *f*, suelo *m*; **one's native** — su tierra, su patria.

soil[2] [sɔil] 1 *vt* ensuciar; manchar (*also fig*).
　2 *vi* ensuciarse.
　3 *vr*: **to** — **oneself** ensuciarse; **I would not** — **myself by contact with** ... no me rebajaría a tener contacto con ...

soiled [sɔild] *adj* sucio.

soil pipe ['sɔilpaip] *n* tubo *m* de desagüe sanitario.

soirée ['swɑːrei] *n* velada *f*.

sojourn ['sɔdʒəːn] 1 *n* permanencia *f*, estancia *f*. 2 *vi* permanecer, residir, morar; pasar una temporada.

solace ['sɔlis] 1 *n* consuelo *m*; **to seek** — **with** ... procurar consolarse con ...
　2 *vt* consolar.
　3 *vr*: **to** — **oneself** consolarse (*with* con).

solar ['səulə*] *adj* solar, del sol; — **plexus** plexo *m* solar; — **system** sistema *m* solar.

solarium [səu'lɛəriəm] *n*, *pl* **solaria** [səu'lɛəriə] solana *f*.

sold [səuld] *pret and ptp* of **sell**.

solder ['səuldə*] 1 *n* soldadura *f*. 2 *vt* soldar.

soldering iron ['səuldəriŋ aiən] *n* soldador *m*.

soldier ['səuldʒə*] 1 *n* soldado *m*; militar *m*; — **of fortune** aventurero *m* militar; **common** — soldado *m* raso; **old** — veterano *m*, excombatiente *m*; **to come the old** — **with someone** (*fam*) creerse superior a uno, darse aires de superioridad con respecto a uno; **private** — soldado *m* raso; **tin** — soldado *m* de plomo.
　2 *vi* militar, ser soldado; servir; **he** —**ed for 10 years in the East** sirvió durante 10 años en el Oriente; **to** — **on** continuar a pesar de todo.

soldierly ['səuldʒəli] *adj* militar.

soldiery ['səuldʒəri] *n* soldadesca *f*; **a brutal and licentious** — la soldadesca indisciplinada.

sole[1] [səul] 1 *n* (*Anat*) planta *f*; (*of shoe*) suela *f*, piso *m*. 2 *vt* poner suela a, poner piso a.

sole[2] [səul] *n* (*Fish*) lenguado *m*.

sole[3] [səul] *adj* único, solo; exclusivo; **the** — **reason is that** ... la única razón es que ...; *see* **agent, right.**

solecism ['sɔləsizəm] *n* solecismo *m*.

solely ['səulli] *adv* únicamente, solamente, sólo.

solemn ['sɔləm] *adj* solemne.

solemnity [sə'lemniti] *n* solemnidad *f*.

solemnization ['sɔləmnai'zeiʃən] *n* solemnización *f*.

solemnize ['sɔləmnaiz] *vt* solemnizar.

solemnly ['sɔləmli] *adv* solemnemente.

solenoid ['səulənɔid] *n* solenoide *m*.

solfa ['sɔl'fɑː] *n* solfa *f*.

solicit [sə'lisit] *vti* (*request*) solicitar; implorar, pedir insistentemente; (*importune*) importunar; (*of prostitute*) abordar, importunar; **to** — **someone for something, to** — **something of someone** solicitar algo a uno.

solicitation [sə,lisi'teiʃən] *n* solicitación *f*.

solicitor [sə'lisitə*] *n* (a) (*US*) representante *mf*, agente *mf*.
　(b) (*Law*) procurador *m*, abogado *m*; (*for oaths, wills etc*) notario *m*; **S— General** (*British*) subfiscal *m* de la Corona, (*US*) procurador *m* general del Estado.

solicitous [sə'lisitəs] *adj* solícito (*about, for* por); preocupado, ansioso; atento.

solicitude [sə'lisitjuːd] *n* solicitud *f*; preocupación *f*, ansiedad *f*; atención *f*.

solid ['sɔlid] 1 *adj* sólido; *gold, silver, oak etc* macizo; *tyre* macizo, sin cámara; (*of consistency of soup etc*) sustancioso; *meal* fuerte; *crowd* denso, apretado; *vote* unánime; *person's character* enteramente serio, muy formal; **a** — **argument** un argumento sólido; **the** — **South** (*US Pol*) el bloque sólido constituido por los estados del Sur (que apoyan siempre al

Partido Democrático); **Slobodia is** — **for Smith** Eslobodia apoya unánimemente a Smith; **the house is** — **enough** la casa es perfectamente sólida; **the square was** — **with cars** la plaza estaba totalmente llena de coches, la plaza estaba repleta de coches; **to be frozen** — estar completamente helado; **it was cut into** — **rock** se excavó en peña viva; **to have** — **grounds for thinking that** ... tener buenos motivos para creer que ...; **it makes good** — **sense** hace muy buen sentido; **we walked 14** — **miles** anduvimos 14 millas largas; **we waited 2** — **hours** esperamos dos horas enteras.
　2 *n* sólido *m*.

solidarity [,sɔli'dæriti] *n* solidaridad *f*; — **strike** huelga *f* por solidaridad; **out of** — **with the workers** por solidaridad con los obreros.

solidification [sə,lidifi'keiʃən] *n* solidificación *f*.

solidify [sə'lidifai] 1 *vt* solidificar. 2 *vi* solidificarse.

solidity [sə'liditi] *n* solidez *f*; unanimidad *f*.

solidly ['sɔlidli] *adv* sólidamente; densamente, apretadamente; unánimemente; **a** — **reasoned argument** un argumento sólidamente razonado; **to vote** — **for someone** votar unánimemente por uno; **we were** — **for Smith** apoyamos unánimemente a Smith; **a** —**built house** una casa de sólida construcción.

solid-state ['sɔlid,steit] *adj*: — **physics** física *f* del estado sólido.

soliloquize [sə'liləkwaiz] *vi* soliloquiar; "—", **he** —**d** "—" dijo para sí.

soliloquy [sə'liləkwi] *n* soliloquio *m*.

solipsism ['sɔulipsizəm] *n* solipsismo *m*.

solitaire [,sɔli'tɛə*] *n* (*game, gem*) solitario *m*.

solitary ['sɔlitəri] 1 *adj* (*living alone*) solitario, solo; (*secluded*) retirado, apartado; (*sole*) único, solo; **not a** — **one** ni uno; **there has been one** — **case** ha habido un caso único; **there has not been one** — **case** no ha habido ni un solo caso; **to take a** — **walk** dar un paseo solo, pasearse sin compañía; **to feel rather** — sentirse solo, sentirse aislado; *see* **confinement.**
　2 *n* solitario *m*, a *f*.

solitude ['sɔlitjuːd] *n* soledad *f*.

solo ['səuləu] 1 *n*, *pl* **solos** ['səuləuz] (*Cards, Mus*) solo *m*; **to sing a** — cantar un solo; **a tenor solo** un solo para tenor.
　2 *adj*: — **flight** vuelo *m* a solas; **passage for** — **violin** pasaje *m* para violín solo.
　3 *adv*: **to fly** —volar a solas; **to sing** —cantar solo.

soloist ['səuləuist] *n* solista *mf*.

Solomon ['sɔləmən] *m* Salomón.

solstice ['sɔlstis] *n* solsticio *m*; **summer** — solsticio *m* de verano; **winter** — solsticio *m* de invierno.

solubility [,sɔlju'biliti] *n* solubilidad *f*.

soluble ['sɔljubl] *adj* soluble; — **in water** soluble en agua.

solution [sə'luːʃən] *n* (*all senses*) solución *f* (*to a problem* de un problema).

solvable ['sɔlvəbl] *adj* soluble, que se puede resolver.

solve [sɔlv] *vt* resolver, solucionar; *riddle* adivinar.

solvency ['sɔlvənsi] *n* solvencia *f*.

solvent ['sɔlvənt] 1 *adj* solvente. 2 *n* (*Chem*) solvente *m*.

solver ['sɔlvə*] *n* solucionista *mf*.

Somali [səu'mɑːli] 1 *adj* somalí. 2 *n* somalí *mf*.

Somalia [səu'mɑːliə] Somalia *f*.

sombre, (*US*) **somber** ['sɔmbə*] *adj* sombrío; pesimista; **in** — **hues** en colores sombríos; **a** — **prospect** una perspectiva sombría; **he was** — **about our chances** se mostró pesimista acerca de nuestras posibilidades.

sombrely ['sɔmbəli] *adv* sombríamente; con pesimismo, en tono pesimista.

sombreness ['sɔmbənis] *n* lo sombrío; pesimismo *m*.

some [sʌm] 1 *adj* (a) alguno, (*before m sing n*) algún, *eg* — **man** algún hombre; unos, unos cuantos; — **day** algún día; — **people** algunos, algunas personas; — **very big cars** algunos coches muy grandes, unos coches muy grandes; — **distance away** a cierta distancia; **after** — **time** después de cierto tiempo; — **books I could name** ciertos libros que pudiera mencionar; — **days ago** hace unos días; **in** — **form or other** en alguna que otra forma; **for** — **reason or other** por alguna que otra razón; — **politician or other** algún que otro político; — **other time** otro día; — **idiot of a driver** algún imbécil de conductor.
　(b) (*partitive*) un poco de, algo de; (*freq not translated, eg*) **have you** — **money?** ¿tienes dinero?, **will you have** — **tea?** ¿quieres té?; **all I have left is** — **chocolate** solamente me queda un poco de chocolate; **here is** — **water for you** te he traído un poco de agua; —, **water, please** agua, por favor.

(c) (*intensive*) that's — fish! ¡eso es lo que se llama un pez!; ¡eso es un pez de verdad!; — expert! (*iro*) ¡valiente experto!; that's — woman es mucha mujer; it was — party ya lo creo que fue una fiesta divertida.

2 *pron* (a) algunos; — went this way and — that algunos fueron por aquí y otros por allá; — say yes and — say no algunos dicen que sí y otros que no; — believe that... algunos creen que..., hay quien cree que...

(b) algunos; algo, un poco; do take — (*pl*) toma algunos, (*sing*) toma algo, toma un poco; thanks, I have — gracias, ya tengo; could I have — of that cheese? ¿me puede servir un poco de ese queso?; — of them are crazy algunos de ellos están locos; I like — of what you said in the speech me gusta una parte de lo que Vd dijo en el discurso; — of what you say is true parte de lo que dice Vd es cierto.

(c) and then — (*fam*) y luego un poco más, y más todavía.

3 *adv* (a) — 20 people unas 20 personas, aproximadamente 20 personas, una veintena de personas; — £30 unas 30 libras, más o menos 30 libras; — few difficulties unas pocas dificultades.

(b) (*US fam*) mucho; we laughed — nos reímos mucho; it sure bothered us — ya lo creo que nos preocupó bastante; he's travelling — lleva gran velocidad.

—some [səm] *in compounds*: grupo *m* de..., *eg* threesome grupo *m* de tres personas; we'll go in a threesome iremos los tres, iremos como grupo de tres; have we a foursome for bridge? ¿tenemos cuatro para jugar al bridge?; to make up a foursome formar un grupo de cuatro.

somebody ['sʌmbədi] 1 *pron* alguien; — else algún otro, otra persona; — told me so alguien me lo dijo, me lo dijo alguno; — or other must have taken it alguien se lo habrá llevado.

2 *n*: to be — ser un personaje; he thinks he's — now ahora se cree un personaje.

someday ['sʌmdei] *adv* algún día.

somehow ['sʌmhau] *adv* (a) de algún modo, de un modo u otro; it must be done — or other de un modo u otro tiene que hacerse; — or other I never liked him por alguna que otra razón no me era simpático.

(b) it seems — odd, it seems odd — no sé por qué, pero me parece extraño.

someone ['sʌmwʌn] *pron see* somebody.

someplace ['sʌmpleis] *adv* (*US*) = somewhere.

somersault ['sʌməsɔːlt] 1 *n* (*by person*) salto *m* mortal; (*by car etc*) vuelco *m*, vuelta *f* de campana; back — salto *m* mortal hacia atrás; to turn a — dar un salto mortal; volcar; to turn —s dar saltos mortales; dar vueltas de campana.

2 *vi* dar un salto mortal; dar una vuelta de campana.

something ['sʌmθiŋ] 1 *n pron* (a) algo; alguna cosa; — else otra cosa; — or other is bothering him algo le trae preocupado; there's — the matter pasa algo; did you say —? ¿dijiste algo?; there's — odd here aquí hay algo raro; — of the kind algo por el estilo; there's — in what you say hay gran parte de verdad en lo que Vd dice; well, that's — eso ya es algo; she has a certain — tiene un no sé qué de atractivo; that certain — that makes all the difference no sé qué que importa tanto; he's called John — se llama Juan y no sé qué más; there were 30 — había treinta y algunos más; will you have — to drink? ¿quieres tomar algo?; I need — to eat necesito comer; I gave him — for himself le di una propina; it gives her — to live for le da un motivo para vivir; do you want to make — of it? ¿quién le mete a Vd en esto?; y a Vd ¿qué le importa?

(b) it's — of a problem es un problema bastante difícil; he's — of a musician es en cierto modo un músico, tiene cierto talento para la música; let's see — of you soon ven a vernos pronto.

2 *adv* (a) — over 200 más de 200, 200 y más; he left — over £10,000 dejó más de 10.000 libras; he left — like £10,000 dejó algo así como 10.000 libras; now that's — like a rose! ¡eso es lo que se llama una rosa!

(b) (*fam*) it's — chronic es horrible; the weather was — shocking el tiempo fue asqueroso.

sometime ['sʌmtaim] 1 *adv* algún día; alguna vez; — or other it will have to be done tarde o temprano tendrá que hacerse; write to me — soon escríbeme pronto, escríbeme algún día de éstos; — before tomorrow antes de mañana; — last century durante el siglo pasado; — next year el año que viene (no se sabe exactamente cuándo).

2 *adj* ex..., antiguo; — mayor of Wapping ex alcalde de Wapping.

sometimes ['sʌmtaimz] *adv* algunas veces; a veces.

somewhat ['sʌmwɔt] *adv* algo, algún tanto; we are — worried estamos algo inquietos; it was done — hastily se hizo con demasiada prisa.

somewhere ['sʌmwɛə*] *adv* (b) en alguna parte; (*go*) a alguna parte; — else (*be*) en otra parte, (*go*) a otra parte; I left it — or other lo dejé en alguna parte, lo dejé por ahí; — near Huesca cerca de Huesca; the temperature was — about 40° la temperatura era de 40 grados más o menos; he paid — about £12 pagó alrededor de 12 libras; — in Aragón en alguna parte de Aragón; to broadcast from — in Europe emitir de algún lugar de Europa.

somnambulism [sɔm'næmbjulizəm] *n* somnambulismo *m*.

somnambulist [sɔm'næmbjulist] *n* somnámbulo *m*, a *f*.

somniferous [sɔm'nifərəs] *adj* somnífero.

somnolence ['sɔmnələns] *n* somnolencia *f*.

somnolent ['sɔmnələnt] *adj* soñoliento.

son [sʌn] *n* hijo *m*; — of a bitch (*fam*) hijo *m* de puta; S— of God Hijo *m* de Dios; S— of Man Hijo *m* del Hombre.

sonata [sə'nɑːtə] *n* sonata *f*.

son et lumière [ˌsɔ̃elym'jeːr] *n* (espectáculo *m* de) luz *f* y sonido.

song [sɔŋ] *n* canción *f*; (*art of singing*) canto *m*; (*epic*) cantar *m*; festival of Spanish — festival *m* de la canción española; "A S— for Europe" "Canción *f* para Europa"; S— of Roland Cantar *m* de Roldán; S— of Solomon, S— of S—s Cantar *m* de los Cantares; to burst into — romper a cantar; give us a —! ¡cántanos algo!; to make a great — and dance about something hacer algo a bombo y platillos; he made a — and dance about the carpet armó la gorda por lo de la alfombra; there's no need to make a — and dance no es para tanto; to sell something for a (mere) — vender algo medio regalado; I got it for a — lo adquirí muy barato; to sing another — (*fig*) bajar el tono, desdecirse.

songbird ['sɔŋbəːd] *n* pájaro *m* cantor.

songbook ['sɔŋbuk] *n* cancionero *m*.

song cycle ['sɔŋ'saikl] *n* ciclo *m* de canciones.

song hit ['sɔŋhit] *n* canción *f* de moda, canción *f* popular del momento.

songster ['sɔŋstə*] *n* pájaro *m* cantor.

song thrush ['sɔŋθrʌʃ] *n* tordo *m* cantor, tordo *m* melodioso.

song writer ['sɔŋˌraitə*] *n* compositor *m* de canciones.

sonic ['sɔnik] 1 *adj* sónico. 2 —s sónica *f*.

son-in-law ['sʌninlɔː] *n* yerno *m*, hijo *m* político.

sonnet ['sɔnit] *n* soneto *m*.

sonny ['sʌni] *n* (*fam*) hijito *m*; (*in direct address*) hijo.

sonority [sə'nɔriti] *n* sonoridad *f*.

sonorous ['sɔnərəs] *adj* sonoro.

sonorousness ['sɔnərəsnis] *n* sonoridad *f*.

soon [suːn] *adv* (a) pronto, dentro de poco; (*early*) temprano; come back — vuelve pronto; — afterwards poco después; how — can you come? ¿cuándo puedes venir?; how — can you be ready? ¿para cuándo estarás listo?; we got there too — llegamos demasiado pronto; Friday is too — el viernes es muy pronto; all too — it was over la función terminó muy pronto; we were none too — llegamos en el momento oportuno; menos mal que en ese momento llegamos nosotros.

(b) (*with as*) as — as en cuanto, tan pronto como, así que; as — as you've seen him en cuanto le veas, en cuanto le hayas visto; as — as it was finished en cuanto se terminó; as — as possible cuanto antes, lo antes posible, lo más pronto posible; I would as — not go igual me daría no ir, estaría tan contento de no ir; *see also* sooner.

sooner ['suːnə*] *adv* (a) (*of time*) más temprano; we got there — nosotros llegamos antes; — or later tarde o temprano; the — the better cuanto antes, mejor; no — had we arrived, than... apenas habíamos llegado, cuando..., no bien llegamos, cuando...; no — said than done dicho y hecho; in 5 years or at his death, whichever is the — al cabo de 5 años o a su muerte, lo que suceda antes; the — we start the — we finish cuanto más pronto empecemos, más pronto podremos concluir.

(b) (*of preference*) I had — not do it, I would — not do it preferiría no hacerlo; which would you —? ¿cuál prefieres?

soot [sut] *n* hollín *m*.

sooth [suːθ] *n*: in — en realidad.

soothe [suːð] *vt* tranquilizar, calmar; *pain* aliviar.

soothing ['suːðiŋ] *adj* tranquilizador, calmante; (*pain-killing*) quitadolores; *tone, words etc* dulce, consolador.

soothingly ['su:ðiŋli] *adv speak etc* dulcemente, con dulzura, en tono consolador.

soothsayer ['su:θˌseiə*] *n* adivino *m*, a *f*.

soothsaying ['su:θˌseiiŋ] *n* adivinación *f*.

sooty ['suti] *adj* hollinoso, cubierto de hollín; *(fig)* negro como el hollín.

sop [sɔp] **1** *n (food)* sopa *f*; *(fig)* regalo *m*, dádiva *f*; compensación *f*; *(sl)* tonto *m*, a *f*; **as a — to his pride** para ayudarle a salvar las apariencias, como compensación a su amor propio; **this is a — to Cerberus** esto es para comprar la benevolencia de ...
2 *vt*: **to — up** absorber.

Sophia [sɔu'faiə] *f* Sofía.

sophism ['sɔfizəm] *n* sofisma *m*.

sophist ['sɔfist] *n* sofista *m*.

sophistical [sə'fistikəl] *adj* sofístico.

sophisticated [sə'fistikeitid] *adj* sofisticado.

sophistication [səˌfisti'keiʃən] *n* sofisticación *f*.

sophistry ['sɔfistri] *n* sofistería *f*.

Sophocles ['sɔfəkli:z] *m* Sófocles.

sophomore ['sɔfəmɔ:*] *n* (US) estudiante *mf* de segundo año.

soporific [ˌsɔpə'rifik] *adj* soporífero.

sopping ['sɔpiŋ] *adj*: **it's — (wet)** está totalmente mojado; **he was — wet** estaba hecho una sopa.

soppy ['sɔpi] *adj* (*sl: foolish*) bobo, tonto; (*mushy*) sentimental, sensiblero.

soprano [sə'prɑːnəu] **1** *n*, *pl* **sopranos** [sə'prɑːnəuz] *n* (*person*) soprano *f*, tiple *f*; (*voice and part*) soprano *m*. **2** *adj part etc* de soprano, para soprano; *voice* de soprano.

sorcerer ['sɔːsərə*] *n* hechicero *m*, brujo *m*.

sorceress ['sɔːsəres] *n* hechicera *f*, bruja *f*.

sorcery ['sɔːsəri] *n* hechicería *f*, brujería *f*.

sordid ['sɔːdid] *adj* (*squalid, dirty*) asqueroso, sucio; *place, room* miserable; *deal, motive etc* vil; **it's a pretty — business** es un asunto de lo más desagradable.

sordidness ['sɔːdidnis] *n* lo asqueroso, suciedad *f*; lo miserable; vileza *f*.

sore [sɔː*] **1** *adj* (a) (*Med*) inflamado, dolorido, que duele; **— throat** dolor *m* de garganta; **my eyes are —, I have — eyes** me duelen los ojos; **I'm — all over** me duele todo el cuerpo; **where are you —?** ¿dónde te duele?
(b) (*fig*) **to be — at heart** tener la muerte en el alma; **to be — about something** estar resentido por algo; **to be — about someone** estar enojado con uno; **what are you so — about?** ¿por qué estás tan ofendido?; **now don't get —** no te vayas a ofender; **it's a — point** es un asunto delicado; *see* **spot**.
2 *n* (*Med*) llaga *f*, úlcera *f*; (*caused by harness etc*) matadura *f*; (*fig*) llaga *f*, herida *f*; **recuerdo** *m* doloroso; **running —** úlcera *f*, llaga *f*; **to open an old —** (*fig*) renovar la herida.

sorehead ['sɔːhed] *n* (US fam) persona *f* resentida, resentido *m*.

sorely ['sɔːli] *adv*: **— wounded** herido de gravedad, gravemente herido; **I am — tempted** tengo grandes tentaciones; **I am — tempted to +** *infin* casi estoy por + *infin*; **he has been — tried** ha sufrido lo indecible.

soreness ['sɔːnis] *n* (*Med*) inflamación *f*, dolor *m*.

sorghum ['sɔːgəm] *n* sorgo *m*.

sorority [sə'rɔriti] *n* (US Univ) hermandad *f* de estudiantes.

sorrel[1] ['sɔrəl] *n* (*Bot*) acedera *f*.

sorrel[2] ['sɔrəl] **1** *adj* alazán. **2** *n* alazán *m*, caballo *m* alazán.

sorrow ['sɔrəu] **1** *n* pesar *m*, pena *f*, dolor *m*; tristeza *f*; **more in — than in anger** con más pesar que enojo; **to my (great) —** con gran pesar mío, con gran sentimiento mío; **this was a great — to me** esto me causó mucha pena; **the —s of their race** las aflicciones de su raza; **to drown one's —s** olvidar su tristeza emborrachándose, ahogar sus penas en alcohol.
2 *vi* apenarse, afligirse (*at, for, over* de, por) dolerse (*at, for, over* de).

sorrowful ['sɔrəful] *adj* afligido, triste, pesaroso.

sorrowfully ['sɔrəfli] *adv* con pena, tristemente.

sorrowing ['sɔrəuiŋ] *adj* afligido.

sorry ['sɔri] *adj* (a) (*regretful*) arrepentido; (*sad*) triste, afligido, apenado; **—!** ¡perdón!, ¡perdone!; **awfully —!, so —!, very —!** lo siento mucho, lo siento en el alma, ¡cuánto lo siento!; **to be —** sentirlo; **I am very —** lo siento mucho; **I can't say I'm —** no es que me pese la noticia, el hecho no me causa ningún sentimiento; **he wasn't in the least bit —** no se arrepintió en lo más mínimo; no pidió perdón a nadie; **to be — about something** afligirse

por algo; **I'm — about that vase** te pido perdón por lo del florero; me da pena el florero ese; **to be — for someone** compadecer a uno, tener lástima a uno; **I feel — for the child** el niño me da lástima; **there's no need to be — for him** no hace falta compadecerle; **you'll be — for this!** ¡me las pagarás!; **to be** (*or* **look**) **— for oneself** estar muy abatido; **to be — that . . .** sentir que + *subj*; **to be — to +** *infin* sentir + *infin*, lamentar + *infin*.
(b) (*bad*) *condition, plight* lastimoso; *sight* triste; *figure* ridículo; *excuse* nada convincente; *joke* pobre; **it was a — tale of defeat** fue una triste narración de derrotas.

sort [sɔːt] **1** *n* (a) clase *f*, género *m*, especie *f*; tipo *m*; **what — do you want?** ¿qué clase quiere Vd?; **the — you gave me last time** el mismo que Vd me dio la última vez; **but not that —** pero no de ese tipo, pero no como eso; **I know his —** ésos me los conozco, conozco el paño; **he's the — who will cheat you** es de los que te engañarán; **books of all —s** toda clase de libros, libros de toda clase; **he's a painter of a —,** **he's a painter of —s** es en cierto modo pintor; **it's coffee of a —** es café pero bastante inferior, es lo que apenas se puede llamar café; **perfect of its —** perfecto en su línea; **something of the —** algo por el estilo; **nothing of the —!** ¡nada de eso!, ¡ni hablar!; **I shall do nothing of the —** no haré eso bajo ningún concepto; **in some —** algo, en cierta medida; **it takes all —s (to make a world)** de todo hay en la viña del Señor.
(b) (**— of**): **what — of car?** ¿qué clase de coche?; **what — of man is he?** ¿qué tipo de hombre es?; **this — of house** una casa de este tipo; **an odd — of novel** una novela rara, una novela de tipo extraño; **all —s of dogs** toda clase de perros, perros de toda clase; **he's a — of agent** es algo así como un agente; **he's some — of painter** es pintor pero no sé de qué género; **I felt a — of shame** sentí algo parecido a la vergüenza, en cierto modo sentí vergüenza; **it's a — of dance** es una especie de baile; **I have a — of idea that . . .** tengo cierta idea de que . . .; **that's the — of thing I need** eso es lo que me hace falta; **that's the — of thing I mean** eso es precisamente lo que quiero decir; **and all that — of thing** y otras cosas por el estilo; **that's the — of person I am** yo soy así; **he's not that — of person** no es capaz de hacer eso, no es de los que hacen tales cosas; **I'm not that — of girl** yo no soy de ésas.
(c) (**— of**, *as adv: fam*) **it's — of awkward** es bastante difícil; **it's — of blue** es más bien azul; **it's — of finished** está más o menos terminado; **I — of feel that . . .** en cierto modo creo que . . .; **it — of made me laugh** no sé por qué pero me hizo reír; **aren't you pleased? . . . — of** ¿no te alegras? . . . en cierto modo.
(d) (*person*) **he's a good —** es buena persona, es un buen chico; **she sounds a good —** da la impresión de ser buena persona; **he's an odd —** es un tipo extraño; **your — never did any good** las personas como Vd nunca hicieron nada bueno.
(e) **to be out of —s** (*Med*) estar indispuesto, no estar del todo bien; (*in mood*) estar molesto, sentirse incómodo.
2 *vt* (a) (*also* **to — out**) clasificar; **to — out the bad ones** separar los malos, quitar los malos.
(b) **to — out** (*fig*) *problem etc* arreglar; solucionar; **we've got it —ed out** ya lo hemos arreglado ya; **can you — this out for me?** ¿puede Vd ayudarme con esto?; **to — someone out** (*sl*) ajustar cuentas con uno; **I'll come down there and — you out!** si bajo allá te pego una paliza.

sorter ['sɔːtə*] *n* clasificador *m*, ora *f*; (*Post*) distribuidor *m*, oficial *m* de correos.

sortie ['sɔːti] *n* salida *f*; **they flew 400 —s** realizaron un total de 400 salidas; **to make a —** hacer una salida.

sorting office ['sɔːtiŋˌɔfis] *n* oficina *f* de distribución del correo.

so-so ['səu'səu] *adv* regular, así así.

sot [sɔt] *n* borrachín *m*.

sottish ['sɔtiʃ] *adj* embrutecido (por el alcohol).

sotto voce ['sɔtəu'vəutʃi] *adv* en voz baja.

Soudan [su'dɑːn] *n* Sudán *m*.

Soudanese [ˌsuːdə'niːz] **1** *adj* sudanés. **2** *n* sudanés *m*, esa *f*.

soufflé ['suːflei] *n* suflé *m*.

sough [sau] **1** *n* susurro *m*. **2** *vi* susurrar.

sought [sɔːt] *pret and pp of* **seek**.

sought-after ['sɔːtˌɑːftə*] *adj* codiciado; solicitado, que tiene mucha demanda; **this much — title** este codiciado título.

soul [səul] n (a) alma f; **upon my —!, (God) bless my —!** ¡caramba!; ¡Dios me valga!; **with all one's —** con toda el alma; **God rest his —!** ¡Dios le acoja en su seno!; **to possess one's — in patience** tener muchísima paciencia.

(b) (fig: person) alma f; **3,000 —s** 3.000 almas; **poor —!** ¡pobrecito!; **the poor — had nowhere to sleep** el pobre no tenía dónde dormir; **he's a good —** es un bendito; **she's a simple —** es una alma de Dios; **without seeing a —** sin ver bicho viviente; **every living —** todo ser viviente; **the ship was lost with all —s** el buque se hundió con toda la tripulación (y pasajeros).

soul-destroying ['səuldis'trɔiiŋ] adj (fig) de lo más aburrido (or monótono etc); totalmente desprovisto de interés, de nulo interés intelectual (or estético etc).

soulful ['səulful] adj sentimental; conmovedor.

soulfully ['səulfəli] adv de modo sentimental; de modo conmovedor.

soulless ['səullis] adj person sin alma, desalmado; work etc mecánico, monótono, sin interés humano.

soul mate ['səulmeit] n perfecto compañero m espiritual, perfecta compañera f espiritual.

soul-stirring ['səul‚stə:riŋ] adj conmovedor, inspirador.

sound¹ [saund] **1** adj sano; firme, sólido; constitution robusto; (Comm) solvente; person formal, digno de confianza; argument, idea, opinion razonable, lógico, bien fundado; ortodoxo; policy prudente; investment bueno, seguro; move acertado, lógico; rule bueno; training etc sólido; sleep profundo; **in — condition** en buenas condiciones; **to be as — as a bell** estar en perfecta salud; **to be — in wind and limb** estar en buen estado físico; **to be — in mind and body** ser sano de cuerpo y de espíritu; **he's a very — man** es persona de la mayor confianza; **he's a — worker** es buen trabajador, trabaja con toda seriedad; **he is — enough on the theory** tiene una preparación sólida en cuanto a la teoría; tiene opiniones ortodoxas acerca de la teoría.

2 adv: **to be — asleep** estar profundamente dormido; **I shall sleep the —er for it** por eso dormiré más tranquilamente.

sound² [saund] **1** n sonido m, son m; ruido m; **to the —(s) of the national anthem** a los sones del himno nacional; **within — of** al alcance de; **not a — was heard** no hubo ruido alguno; **there came the — of breaking glass** se oyó el ruido de cristales que se rompían; **I don't like the — of it** esto no nos promete nada bueno, me inquieta la noticia, no me gusta la idea.

2 vt sonar; alarm, bell, horn, trumpet tocar; praises cantar, entonar; **to — the "d" in "hablado"** pronunciar la "d" en "hablado"; **to — the charge** tocar a carga; **to — the retreat** tocar a retirada.

3 vi (a) sonar, resonar; **the bell —ed** sonó el timbre; **it —s hollow** suena a hueco; **it —s like Dutch to me** me suena a holandés; **a gun —ed a long way off** se oyó un cañón a lo lejos.

(b) (seem) sonar, parecer; **that —s very odd** eso parece muy raro; **he —s like a good sort** parece que es buena persona, da la impresión de ser buena persona; **how does it — to you?** ¿a ti que le parece?

(c) **to — off** (fam) hablar en tono autoritario; (complain) quejarse; (protest) protestar, poner el grito en el cielo.

sound³ [saund] **1** n (Med) sonda f.

2 vt (Med, Naut) sondar; chest auscultar; **to — out** person, intentions, opinions sondear, tantear; **to — someone out about something** tratar de averiguar lo que piensa uno acerca de un asunto; **to — out one's conscience** consultar su conciencia.

sound⁴ [saund] n (Geog) estrecho m, brazo m de mar.

sound barrier ['saund‚bæriə*] n barrera f del sonido.

sound effects ['saundi‚fekts] npl efectos mpl sonoros.

sounding ['saundiŋ] n (Naut) sondeo m; **—s** (for oil etc) sondeos mpl; **to take —s** (fig) sondear la opinión, pulsar las opiniones.

sounding board ['saundiŋbɔːd] n (Mus) secreto m, caja f de resonancia; (fig) caja f de resonancia.

soundless ['saundlis] adj silencioso, sin ruido.

soundlessly ['saundlisli] adv silenciosamente, sin ruido.

soundly ['saundli] adv sólidamente; razonablemente, lógicamente, prudentemente; **to beat someone —** derrotar a uno completamente; **to thrash someone —** dar a uno una paliza de verdad; **to sleep —** dormir bien, dormir profundamente.

soundness ['saundnis] n firmeza f, solidez f; robustez f; solvencia f; formalidad f; lo razonable, lógica f, sólida fundación f; ortodoxia f; prudencia f;

seguridad f; **the — of someone's health** el buen estado físico de uno; **the — of a proposal** la solidez de una proposición.

soundproof ['saundpruːf] **1** adj insonorizado, a prueba de ruidos. **2** vt insonorizar.

soundproofing ['saundpruːfiŋ] n insonorización f.

sound recording ['saundri‚kɔːdiŋ] n grabación f sonora.

sound track ['saundtræk] n banda f sonora.

sound wave ['saundweiv] n onda f sonora.

soup¹ [suːp] n (clear, thin) caldo m, consomé m; (thick) puré m, sopa f; fish — sopa f de pescado; **vegetable —** sopa f de hortelano; **to be in the —** (fam) estar en apuros; **now we're properly in the —** (fam) ahora le hemos pringado de verdad.

soup² [suːp] vt (sl): **to — up** sobrealimentar.

soupçon ['suːpsɔ̃] n pizca f; **with a — of ginger** con una pizca de jengibre; **there is just a — of a rigged game** hay cierto olorcillo a tongo.

souped-up ['suːpt‚ʌp] adj (sl) sobrealimentado.

soup kitchen ['suːp‚kitʃin] n comedor m de beneficencia, comedor m gratuito para los pobres.

soup plate ['suːppleit] n plato m sopero.

soupspoon ['suːpspuːn] n cuchara f sopera.

soup tureen ['suːptə‚riːn] n sopera f.

soupy ['suːpi] adj liquid espeso, turbio; atmosphere pesado, espeso; viciado.

sour ['sauə*] **1** adj agrio, acre; milk cortado; land maleado; person agrio, desabrido, poco afable; **to go — (milk)** cortarse; **to turn —** agriarse, volverse agrio.

2 vt agriar; land malear; person agriar, amargar.

3 vi agriarse, volverse agrio; (land) malearse.

source [sɔːs] n (of river) fuente f, nacimiento m; (fig) fuente f, origen m; ¦procedencia f¦; (Lit etc) fuente f; (of infection) foco m; **what is the — of this information?** ¿de dónde proceden estos informes?; **I have it from a good — that...** sé de fuente fidedigna que...; **we have other —s of supply** tenemos otras fuentes de suministro.

sour-faced ['sauəfeist] adj con cara de pocos amigos.

sourish ['sauəriʃ] adj agrete.

sourly ['sauəli] adv (fig) agriamente; **to answer —** contestar en tono áspero.

sourness ['sauənis] n agrura f, acidez f; (fig) agrura f, aspereza f.

sourpuss ['sauəpus] n (US sl) persona f desabrida, persona f poco afable.

souse [saus] **1** n (pickle) escabeche m; **to have a —** (fam) lavarse, ducharse.

2 vt (pickle) escabechar; (plunge) zambullir (into en); (soak) mojar (with de); **to — someone with soup** mojar a uno derramando la sopa sobre él; **to be —ed** (sl) estar ajumado (fam); **to get —d** mojarse, calarse.

south [sauθ] **1** n sur m; mediodía m; **the Deep S—** el Profundo Sur. **2** adj del sur, meridional. **3** adv al sur, hacia el sur.

South Africa [sauθ'æfrikə] África f del Sur.

South African [sauθ'æfrikən] **1** adj sudafricano. **2** n sudafricano m, a f.

South America [‚sauθə'merikə] América f del Sur, Sudamérica f.

South American [‚sauθə'merikən] **1** adj sudamericano. **2** n sudamericano m, a f.

south-east ['sauθ'iːst] **1** n sudeste m. **2** adj point, direction sudeste; wind del sudeste.

south-easterly [sauθ'iːstəli] adj point, direction sudeste; wind del sudeste.

south-eastern [sauθ'iːstən] adj sudeste.

south-eastward(s) [sauθ'iːstwəd(z)] adv hacia el sudeste.

southerly ['sʌðəli] adj point, direction sur; wind del sur; **the most — point in Europe** el punto más meridional de Europa.

southern ['sʌðən] adj del sur, meridional.

southerner ['sʌðənə*] n habitante mf del sur; meridional mf; **she's a —** es del Sur; **—s are shorter than northerners** los meridionales son menos altos que los septentrionales.

southernmost ['sʌðənməust] adj (el) más meridional, situado más al sur; **the — town in Europe** la ciudad más meridional de Europa.

South Korea ['sauθkə'riə] Corea f del Sur.

South Korean ['sauθkə'riən] **1** adj surcoreano. **2** n surcoreano m, a f.

southpaw ['sauθpɔː] n (esp US) jugador m zurdo, boxeador m zurdo.

South Seas ['sauθ'siːz] pl mares mpl del Sur.

South Vietnam ['sauθ‚vjet'næm] Vietnam m del Sur.

South Vietnamese ['sauθ‚vjetnə'miːz] **1** adj survietnamita. **2** n survietnamita mf.

southward(s) ['sauθwəd(z)] *adv* hacia el sur.
south-west ['sauθ'west] **1** *n* suroeste *m*. **2** *adj point, direction* suroeste; *wind* del suroeste.
south-wester [sauθ'westə*] *n* (*wind*) suroeste *m*; (*hat*) sueste *m*.
south-westerly [sauθ'westəli] *adj point, direction* suroeste; *wind* del suroeste.
south-western [sauθ'westən] *adj* suroeste.
south-westward(s) [sauθ'westwəd(z)] *adv* hacia el suroeste.
souvenir [,suːvə'niə*] *n* recuerdo *m*.
sou'wester [sau'westə*] *n* sueste *m*.
sovereign ['sɔvrin] **1** *adj* soberano. **2** *n* soberano *m*, a *f*; (*coin*) soberano *m*.
sovereignty ['sɔvrənti] *n* soberanía *f*.
soviet ['səuviət] **1** *n* soviet *m*. **2** *adj, attr* soviético.
Soviet Russia ['səuviət'rʌʃə] *n* la Rusia Soviética.
Soviet Union ['səuviət'juːnjən] *n* Unión *f* Soviética.
sow [səu] (*irr: pret* sowed, *ptp* sown) *vt* sembrar (*with* de; *also fig*); esparcir; to — **mines in a strait, to — a strait with mines** plagar un estrecho de minas; to — **doubt in someone's mind** suscitar dudas en uno.
sow [sau] *n* cerda *f*, puerca *f*, marrana *f*; (*of wild boar*) jabalina *f*; (*of badger*) tejón *m* hembra; (*Tech*) galápago *m*.
sower ['səuə*] *n* sembrador *m*, ora *f*.
sowing ['səuiŋ] *n* siembra *f*.
sowing machine ['səuiŋmə,ʃiːn] *n* sembradora *f*.
sowing time ['səuiŋ,taim] *n* época *f* de la siembra, sementera *f*.
sown [səun] *ptp* of **sow**.
soya ['sɔiə] *n* soja *f*.
soya bean ['sɔiə'biːn] *n* semilla *f* de soja.
sozzled ['sɔzld] *adj* (*sl*): **to be —** estar ajumado (*fam*); **to get —** ajumarse.
spa [spɑː] *n* balneario *m*.
space [speis] **1** *n* espacio *m*; **blank —** espacio *m* en blanco; **outer —** espacio *m* exterior; **for a —** durante cierta distancia, durante cierto tiempo; **in a confined —** en un espacio restringido; **in the — of one hour** en el espacio de una hora; **in the — of 3 generations** en el espacio de 3 generaciones; **to clear a —** for hacer un sitio para; **to leave — for** dejar un sitio para; **leave a — for the name** deje un espacio para poner el nombre; **to stare into —** mirar al vacío; mirar distraído; **it takes up a lot of —** ocupa bastante espacio.
2 *attr* espacial; — **research** investigaciones *fpl* espaciales; — **programme** programa *m* de investigaciones espaciales.
3 *vt* (*also* **to — out**) espaciar (*also Typ*); **well —d out** bastante distanciados.
space capsule ['speis,kæpsjuːl] *n* cápsula *f* espacial.
spacecraft ['speiskrɑːft] *n* nave *f* espacial, astronave *f*.
space flight ['speisflait] *n* vuelo *m* espacial.
space helmet ['speis,helmit] *n* casco *m* espacial.
spaceman ['speismæn] *n*, *pl* —**men** [men] astronauta *m*, cosmonauta *m*.
spaceship ['speisʃip] *n* nave *f* espacial, astronave *f*.
space shot ['speisʃɔt] *n* (lanzamiento *m* de un) vehículo *m* espacial.
space station ['speis,steiʃən] *n* estación *f* espacial.
spacesuit ['speissuːt] *n* traje *m* espacial.
space vehicle ['speis,viːikl] *n* vehículo *m* espacial.
spacing ['speisiŋ] *n* espaciamiento *m*; **with double —** (*Typ*) a doble espacio.
spacing bar ['speisiŋbɑː*] *n* (*Typ*) barra *f* espaciadora.
spacious ['speiʃəs] *adj* espacioso, amplio; extenso; *living* holgado, lujoso.
spaciousness ['speiʃəsnis] *n* espaciosidad *f*, amplitud *f*; extensión *f*.
spade [speid] *n* (a) (*tool*) pala *f*, laya *f*; **to call a — a —** llamar al pan pan y al vino vino. (b) —**s** (*Cards*) picos *mpl*, (*in Spanish pack*) espadas *fpl*.
spadeful ['speidful] *n* pala *f*; **by the —** (*fig*) en grandes cantidades.
spadework ['speidwəːk] *n* (*fig*) trabajo *m* preliminar.
spaghetti [spə'geti] *n* espaguetis *mpl*; fideos *mpl*.
Spain [spein] *n* España *f*.
spake [speik] *pret* (*arch*) of **speak**.
span¹ [spæn] **1** *n* (*of hand, as measure*) palmo *m*; (*of time*) lapso *m*, espacio *m*; duración *f*; (*of horses*) pareja *f*, (*of oxen*) yunta *f*; (*of wing*) envergadura *f*; (*of bridge: referring to space*) ojo *m*, luz *f*, (*referring to structure*) arcada *f*, entramado *m*; (*of roof*) vano *m*; **a — of 50 metres** (*bridge*) una luz de 50 metros; **a bridge with 7 —s** un puente de 7 arcadas, un puente de 7 ojos; **the longest single-span bridge in the world** el puente más largo del mundo de una sola arcada, el puente que tiene el entramado continuo más largo del mundo; **the average — of**

life la duración media de la vida; **for a brief —** durante una breve temporada; **the whole — of world affairs** toda la extensión de los asuntos mundiales, los asuntos mundiales en toda su amplitud.
2 *vt* (*measure*) medir (a palmos); (*of bridge*) extenderse sobre, cruzar; (*of builder*) tender un puente sobre; (*in time etc*) abarcar; **his life —ned 4 reigns** su vida abarcó 4 reinados.
span² [spæn] *pret* of **spin**.
spangle ['spæŋgl] **1** *n* lentejuela *f*. **2** *vt* adornar con lentejuelas; —**d with** (*fig*) sembrado de.
Spaniard ['spænjəd] *n* español *m*, ola *f*.
spaniel ['spænjəl] *n* perro *m* de aguas.
Spanish ['spæniʃ] **1** *adj* español; **the —** los españoles.
2 *n* (*language*) español *m*, castellano *m*; **Medieval —** español *m* medieval; **Modern —** español *m* moderno; **Old —** español *m* antiguo.
Spanish-American ['spæniʃə'merikən] **1** *adj* hispanoamericano. **2** *n* hispanoamericano *m*, a *f*.
Spanishness ['spæniʃnis] *n* españolidad *f*, españolismo *m*.
Spanish-speaking ['spæniʃ'spiːkiŋ] *adj* hispanohablante, de habla española.
spank [spæŋk] **1** *n* azote *m*, manotada *f* (en las nalgas); **to give someone a —** dar un azote a uno (en las nalgas).
2 *vt* zurrar, manotear; **I'll — you!** ¡te voy a pegar!
3 *vi*: **to — along** correr, ir volando.
spanker ['spæŋkə*] *n* (*Naut*) mesana *f*.
spanking ['spæŋkiŋ] **1** *adj pace* grande, rápido; *breeze* fuerte; **we had a — (good) time** lo pasamos en grande.
2 *n* zurra *f*; **to give someone a —** zurrar a uno.
spanner ['spænə*] *n* llave *f* (inglesa), llave *f* de tuercas; **to throw a — in the works** meter un palo en la rueda.
spar¹ [spɑː*] *n* (*Naut*) palo *m*, verga *f*.
spar² [spɑː*] *vi* (*Boxing*) hacer fintas, fintar; entrenarse en el boxeo, hacer ejercicios de boxeo; **to — at someone** amagar a uno; **to — with someone about something** (*fig*) disputar algo amistosamente con uno; **he's only —ring with the problem** no intenta seriamente resolver el problema.
spar³ [spɑː*] *n* (*Min*) espato *m*; **Iceland —** espato *m* de Islandia.
spare [speə*] **1** *adj* (a) (*left over*) sobrante, que sobra, de más; (*available*) disponible; *room* para convidados; *time* libre, desocupado; *part* (*Mech*) de repuesto, de recambio; — **collar** cuello *m* de repuesto; **in my — time** en mis ratos libres, en mis ratos de ocio; **if you have any — time** si Vd dispone de tiempo, si Vd tiene tiempo; **there are 2 going — spare** 2, quedan 2; **if you have any — bottles** si Vd dispone de algunas botellas; **it's all the — cash I have** es todo el dinero contante que tengo.
(b) (*of build etc*) enjuto.
2 *n* pieza *f* de repuesto, repuesto *m*, recambio *m*; **we stock —s** tenemos existencia de repuestos.
3 *vt* (a) (*be grudging with*) excusar; escatimar; **to — no expense** no escatimar dinero; **to — no pains to do something** no perdonar esfuerzos por hacer algo.
(b) (*do without*) pasarse sin; ahorrar; economizar; **we can't — him now** ahora no podemos estar sin él, ahora no podemos permitir que se vaya; **can you — this for a moment?** ¿me puedo llevar esto un momento?, ¿me permite llevarme esto un momento?; **if you can — it** si Vd puede pasarse sin él, si Vd puede cedérmelo; **can you — the time?** ¿puede Vd dedicar su tiempo a esto?; **I can — you 5 minutes** estoy libre para verle durante 5 minutos, le puedo dedicar 5 minutos.
(c) **to — de** sobra; **there is none to —** apenas queda nada; no tenemos nada de sobra, no nos sobra nada; **we have 9 bottles to —** nos sobran 9 botellas; **there's enough and to —** no sólo hay bastante sino que sobra algo, hay más que suficiente para todos.
(d) *life* perdonar; **the fire —d nothing** el incendio no perdonó nada; **he was —d another 3 years** tuvo otros 3 años de vida; **he —s nobody** hace trabajar a todos como demonios; es severo con todos sin excepción; **to — someone's feelings** procurar no herir los sentimientos de uno; **to — someone the trouble of doing something** evitar a uno la molestia de hacer algo; — **my blushes!** ¡considere mi modestia!, ¡qué cosas me dices!
sparerib ['speə'rib] *n* (*US*) costilla *f* de cerdo (con poca carne).
sparing ['speəriŋ] *adj* escaso; (*thrift*) económico; controlado, limitado; **his — use of colour** su

parquedad con los colores; **to be — of, to be —
with** ser parco en, ser avaro de; **to be — of praise**
escatimar los elogios; **to be — of words** ser persona
de pocas palabras; ser parco en hablar.
sparingly ['speəriŋli] *adv* escasamente; económicamente; **we used water** — empleamos el agua
bastante poco; **he uses colour** — es parco en el uso
de los colores; **use it very** — úselo en pequeñas
cantidades, úselo con moderación; **to eat** — comer
poco, comer frugalmente.
sparingness ['speəriŋnis] *n* parquedad *f*; economía *f*,
moderación *f*.
spark [spɑːk] **1** *n* chispa *f*; (*of wit*) chispazo *m*; **—s**
(*Tel, fam*) telegrafista *m*; **bright** — (*fam*) tipo *m*
muy listo; **there's not a — of life about it** no tiene ni
un átomo de vida; **the book hasn't a — of interest**
el libro no tiene ni pizca de interés.
2 *vt*: **to — off** hacer estallar; (*fig*) hacer estallar,
precipitar, provocar.
3 *vi* chispear, echar chispas.
sparking plug ['spɑːkiŋplʌg] *n*, (*US*) **spark plug**
['spɑːkplʌg] *n* bujía *f*.
sparkle ['spɑːkl] **1** *n* centelleo *m*, destello *m*; (*fig*)
brillo *m*, viveza *f*, vida *f*; **a person without** — una
persona sin viveza.
2 *vi* centellear, destellar, chispear; (*shine*) brillar,
relucir; **she doesn't exactly** — no tiene mucha
viveza que digamos; **the conversation —d** la
conversación fue animadísima, en la conversación
hubo muchas salidas ingeniosas.
sparkling ['spɑːkliŋ] *adj* centelleante; brillante,
reluciente; *wine* espumoso; *eyes, wit, conversation*
chispeante.
sparring partner ['spɑːriŋ,pɑːtnə*] *n* sparring *m*.
sparrow ['spærəu] *n* gorrión *m*.
sparrowhawk ['spærəuhɔːk] *n* gavilán *m*.
sparse [spɑːs] *adj* disperso, esparcido; poco denso;
escaso; *hair* ralo; — **population** población *f* poco
densa; — **furnishings** muebles *mpl* escasos.
sparsely ['spɑːsli] *adv* de modo poco denso; escasamente; **a — furnished room** un cuarto con pocos
muebles; **a — inhabited area** una región de
población poco densa.
Sparta ['spɑːtə] Esparta *f*.
Spartan ['spɑːtən] **1** *adj* espartano (*also fig*). **2** *n*
espartano *m*, a *f*.
spasm ['spæzəm] *n* (*Med*) espasmo *m*; (*fig*) acceso *m*,
arranque *m*; **in a — of fear** en un acceso de miedo;
a sudden — of activity un arranque repentino de
actividad; **to work in —s** trabajar a rachas.
spasmodic [spæz'mɒdik] *adj* espasmódico; irregular,
intermitente.
spasmodically [spæz'mɒdikəli] *adv* de modo
espasmódico; de modo irregular, de modo intermitente; **a rachas.**
spastic ['spæstik] **1** *adj* espástico. **2** *n* espástico *m*, a *f*.
spasticity [spæs'tisiti] *n* espasticidad *f*.
spat¹ [spæt] *n* (*Fish*) freza *f*; (*of oysters*) masa *f* de
ostras jóvenes.
spat² [spæt] *n* (*gaiter*) polaina *f* corta, botón *m*.
spat³ [spæt] *n* (*US fam*) riña *f*, disputa *f* (sin trascendencia).
spat⁴ [spæt] *pret and ptp of* **spit.**
spate [speit] *n* avenida *f*, crecida *f*; (*fig*) torrente *m*;
to be in — estar crecido.
spatial ['speiʃəl] *adj* espacial.
spatter ['spætə*] *vt* salpicar, rociar (*with* de); **a dress
—ed with mud** un vestido manchado de lodo; **a
wall —ed with blood** una pared salpicada de sangre.
spatula ['spætjulə] *n* espátula *f*.
spavin ['spævin] *n* esparaván *m*.
spawn [spɔːn] **1** *n* (*Fish*) freza *f*, huevas *fpl*; (*of frog
etc*) huevas *fpl*; (*of mushroom*) semillas *fpl*; (*fig*)
prole *f*.
2 *vt* (*pej*) engendrar, producir.
3 *vi* desovar, frezar.
spawning ['spɔːniŋ] *n* desove *m*, freza *f*.
spay [spei] *vt animal* sacar los ovarios a.
speak [spiːk] (*irr: pret* **spoke,** *ptp* **spoken**) **1** *vt* (**a**) (*in
general*) decir, hablar; **to — the truth** decir la
verdad; **to — one's mind** hablar con franqueza,
hablar claro; **nobody spoke a word** nadie habló,
nadie dijo palabra.
(**b**) *language* hablar; **do you — Arabic?** ¿hablas
árabe?; **"English spoken here"** "se habla inglés".
2 *vi* (**a**) (*general sense*) hablar; **did you —?** ¿dijiste
algo?; **since they quarrelled they don't** — desde
que riñeron no se hablan; **to — to someone** hablar
con uno; **she never spoke to me again** no volvió a
dirigirme la palabra; **I'll — to him about it** se lo
diré; discutiré el asunto con él; **to — harshly to
someone** hablar a uno en tono severo; **I don't**

know him to — to no le conozco bastante como
para hablar con él; **I know him to — to** le conozco
bastante bien para cambiar algunas palabras con
él; **so to** — por decirlo así; **roughly —ing** más o
menos, aproximadamente.
(**b**) **to — for someone** hablar por uno; hablar en
nombre de uno; interceder por uno; **he —s for the
miners** habla por los mineros, representa a los
mineros; **—ing for myself** en cuanto a mí, yo por mi
parte; **it —s for itself** es evidente, habla por sí
mismo; **the facts — for themselves** los datos hablan
por sí solos; **that —s well for him** eso demuestra
su mérito; eso es un punto a su favor; **that is
already spoken for** eso está reservado ya.
(**c**) (*of gun*) oírse, sonar; (*of dog*) ladrar; **the gun
spoke** se oyó un tiro.
(**d**) (*formally, in assembly*) hablar; pronunciar
un discurso; intervenir (en un debate); (*begin to —*)
tomar la palabra, hacer uso de la palabra; **are you
—ing in the debate?** ¿interviene Vd en el debate?;
it's years since he spoke hace años que no pronuncia
ningún discurso; **the member rose to** — el diputado
se levantó para tomar la palabra; **the speaker asked
Mr X to** — el presidente le concedió la palabra al
Sr X.
(**e**) (*Tel*) **—ing!** ¡al habla!; **John —ing!** ¡soy
Juan!; **who is that —ing?** ¿quién habla?
(**f**) (*with adv or prep*) **to — of** hablar de; **—ing
of tractors . . .** a propósito de los tractores . . . ; **it's
nothing to — of** no tiene importancia; no es nada;
there are no trees to — of no hay árboles que
digamos; **everything —s of hatred** por todas partes
late el odio; **everything —s of luxury** todo indica el
lujo; **to — well of someone** decir mil bienes de uno,
poner a uno por las nubes; **to — out** hablar claro;
hablar francamente; osar hablar; **— out!** ¡más
fuerte!; **to — to the point** hablar acertadamente,
hablar con tino; **to — up** hablar alto; **— up!** ¡más
fuerte!; **to — up for someone** hablar en favor de uno.
speakeasy ['spiːk,izi] *n* taberna *f* (clandestina).
speaker ['spiːkə*] *n* (*general sense*) el (*or* la) que
habla; (*of language*) hablante *mf*; (*public —*) orador
m, ora *f*; (*lecturer*) conferenciante *mf*; (*Parl*)
presidente *m*; (*loud—*) altavoz *m*; **after-dinner** —
orador *m* de sobremesa; **as the last — said** como
dijo el señor que acaba de hablar; **he's a good —**
es buen orador, habla bien; **are you a Welsh —?**
¿habla Vd galés?; **all —s of Spanish** todos los que
hablan español, todos los hispanohablantes; **Catalan
has several million —s** el catalán es hablado por
varios millones.
speaking ['spiːkiŋ] *adj* hablante; *likeness* perfecto,
expresivo; **to be within — distance** estar al habla;
see **term.**
speaking trumpet ['spiːkiŋ,trʌmpit] *n* bocina *f*.
speaking tube ['spiːkiŋtjuːb] *n* tubo *m* acústico.
spear [spiə*] **1** *n* lanza *f*; (*fishing —*) arpón *m*.
2 *vt* alancear, herir (*or* matar) con lanza; *fish*
arponear; (*fig*) pasar, atravesar, pinchar; **he —ed
the paper on his fork** atravesó el papel en su tenedor.
spearhead ['spiəhed] *n* punta *f* de lanza (*also fig*).
spearmint ['spiəmint] *n* (*Bot etc*) menta *f* verde,
menta *f* romana.
spear thrust ['spiəθrʌst] *n* lanzada *f*.
spec [spek] *n* (*Comm*) **to buy something on** —
comprar algo como especulación; **to go along on** —
ir a ver lo que sale, ir a probar fortuna.
special ['speʃəl] **1** *adj* especial, particular; *correspondent, edition etc* extraordinario; *delivery* (*Post*)
urgente; **my — friend** mi mejor amigo, uno de mis
amigos más íntimos; **what happened? . . . nothing —**
¿qué tal? . . . sin novedad, nada de particular; **what's
so — about this house?** ¿qué tiene de particular
esta casa?; **what's so — about that?** y eso ¿qué
importa?
2 *n* (*constable*) guardia *m* auxiliar; (*edition*)
número *m* extraordinario; (*train*) tren *m* extraordinario, tren *m* especial; (*US Comm*) oferta *f* extraordinaria, ganga *f*; (*US Cook*) plato *m* del día.
specialist ['speʃəlist] *n* especialista *mf*.
speciality [,speʃi'æliti] *n*, **specialty** ['speʃəlti] *n*
especialidad *f*; **it's a — of the house** es un plato
especial de la casa; **to make a — of something**
especializarse en algo, dedicarse a algo de modo
especial.
specialization [,speʃəlai'zeiʃən] *n* especialización *f*.
specialize ['speʃəlaiz] *vi* especializarse (*in, US on* en).
specially ['speʃəli] *adv* especialmente, particularmente; sobre todo, ante todo; **a — difficult task** un
cometido especialmente difícil; **we asked for it** —
lo pedimos especialmente; **— the yellow ones** sobre
todo los amarillos.

specie ['spiːʃiː] *n* metálico *m*, efectivo *m*; **in** — en metálico.

species ['spiːʃiːz] *n*, *pl* **species** especie *f*.

specific [spə'sifik] **1** *adj* específico; expreso, explícito. **2** *n* específico *m*.

specifically [spə'sifikəli] *adv* específicamente; expresamente, explícitamente.

specification [,spesifi'keiʃən] *n* especificación *f*; —s (*plan*) presupuesto *m*, plan *m* detallado.

specify ['spesifai] *vti* especificar; designar (en un plan); mencionar de modo especial; **he did not** — no concretó, no mencionó nada concreto; **unless otherwise specified** a no ser que se especifique lo contrario.

specimen ['spesimin] *n* **1** ejemplar *m*, espécimen *m*; muestra *f*; **a fine** — **of trout** un bello ejemplar de trucha; **he's an odd** — es un tipo extraño; **you're a pretty poor** — Vd no vale para mucho.
    2 *attr*: — **copy** ejemplar *m* de muestra; — **page** página *f* que sirve de muestra; — **signature** espécimen *m* de firma.

specious ['spiːʃəs] *adj* especioso.

speciousness ['spiːʃəsnis] *n* lo especioso.

speck [spek] **1** *n* (*of dirt*) pequeña mancha *f*, manchita *f*; (*of dust*) grano *m*; (*smut*) mota *f* (de carbonilla *etc*); (*small portion*) partícula *f*, pizca *f*; (*dot, point*) punto *m*; **just a** — **on the horizon** solamente un punto en el horizonte; **just a —, thanks** (*of drink etc*) un poquitín, gracias; **there's not a** — **of truth in it** no tiene ni pizca de verdad.
    2 *vt* = **speckle**.

speckle ['spekl] **1** *n* punto *m*, mota *f*. **2** *vt* salpicar, motear (*with* de); salpicar de manchitas.

speckled ['spekld] *adj* con puntos, con manchas, moteado.

specs [speks] *npl* (*fam*) gafas *fpl*.

spectacle ['spektəkl] *n* **(a)** espectáculo *m*; **a sad** — un triste espectáculo.
    (b) —**s** gafas *fpl*, anteojos *mpl*; **a pair of** —**s** unas gafas; **to see everything through rose-coloured** —**s** verlo todo color de rosa.

spectacle case ['spektəkl,keis] *n* estuche *m* de gafas.

spectacled ['spektəkld] *adj* con gafas.

spectacular [spek'tækjulə*] *adj* espectacular; *fall etc* aparatoso; *success etc* impresionante.

spectator [spek'teitə*] *n* espectador *m*, ora *f*; —**s** (*collectively, at game etc*) público *m*.

spectral ['spektrəl] *adj* espectral.

spectre, (US) **specter** ['spektə*] *n* espectro *m*, fantasma *m*.

spectroscope ['spektrəskəup] *n* espectroscopio *m*.

spectrum ['spektrəm] *n* espectro *m*.

speculate ['spekjuleit] *vi* especular (*also Fin*; *in*, *on* en); **to** — **about** especular sobre, hacer conjeturas acerca de, formular teorías acerca de.

speculation [,spekju'leiʃən] *n* especulación *f*; **it is the subject of much** — es tema de muchas conjeturas, sobre esto existen muchas teorías; **to buy something on** — comprar algo como especulación; **it's a good** — vale como especulación.

speculative ['spekjulətiv] *adj* especulativo.

speculator ['spekjuleitə*] *n* especulador *m*, ora *f*.

speculum ['spekjuləm] *n* (*Med*) espéculo *m*; (*fig*) espejo *m*.

sped [sped] *pret and ptp of* **speed**.

speech [spiːtʃ] *n* **(a)** (*faculty of* —) habla *f*; palabra *f*; **free** — libertad *f* de palabra; — **defect** defecto *m* de la palabra; **to be slow of** — hablar lentamente, ser torpe de palabra; **to lose the power of** — perder el habla; **to recover one's** — recobrar el habla.
    (b) (*words*) palabras *fpl*; **fair** — palabras *fpl* afables; **without further** — sin decir más; **to have** — **with someone** hablar con uno.
    (c) (*language: national*) idioma *m*, (*of class etc*) lenguaje *m*, (*of region*) dialecto *m*, habla *f* regional; **in dockers'** — en el lenguaje de los portuarios; **in the** — **of Leon** en el dialecto de León.
    (d) (*oration*) discurso *m*, oración *f*; (*Law, Theat*) parlamento *m*; **closing** — discurso *m* de clausura; **keynote** — (US), **opening** — discurso *m* de apertura; **after-dinner** — discurso *m* de sobremesa; **set** — discurso *m* preparado de antemano; **to deliver a** —, **to make a** — pronunciar un discurso.
    (e) (*Gram*) oración *f*; **direct** — oración *f* directa; **indirect** — oración *f* indirecta; *see* **figure**, **part**.

speech day ['spiːtʃdei] *n* distribución *f* de premios.

speechify ['spiːtʃifai] *vi* (*pej*) disertar prolijamente, dar un tostón.

speechifying ['spiːtʃfaiiŋ] *n* (*pej*) disertaciones *fpl* prolijas, rollos *mpl*, tostones *mpl*.

speechless ['spiːtʃlis] *adj* mudo, estupefacto; **everybody was** — **at this** con esto todos quedaron estupefactos; **to be** — **with rage** enmudecer de rabia.

speechmaking ['spiːtʃ,meikiŋ] *n* pronunciación *f* de discursos; (*speeches collectively*) discursos *mpl*; (*pej*) = **speechifying**.

speech therapy ['spiːtʃ'θerəpi] *n* terapia *f* de la palabra.

speed [spiːd] **1** *n* **(a)** velocidad *f*; rapidez *f*; (*haste*) prisa *f*, (*promptness*) prontitud *f*; **at** — a gran velocidad; **at full** —, **at top** — a máxima velocidad, a toda máquina, a toda correr; **full** — **ahead!** ¡adelante a toda máquina!; **with all possible** — con toda prontitud; **the maximum** — **is 90 mph** la velocidad máxima es de 90 mph; **what** — **were you doing?** ¿a qué velocidad ibas?; **to pick up** — acelerar, cobrar velocidad.
    (b) (*gear*) velocidad *f*; **four forward** —**s** cuatro velocidades hacia adelante; **five-speed gearbox** caja *f* de cambios de cinco velocidades.
    (c) **good** —! (*arch*) ¡buen viaje!
    2 *vt* (*regular*) **(a)** **to** — **someone on his way** despedir a uno, desear un feliz viaje a uno; **God** — **you!** (*arch*) ¡vaya Vd con Dios!
    (b) **to** — **up** *engine* acelerar; *process* acelerar, activar; fomentar; *person* dar prisa a.
    3 *vi* (*irr*: *pret and ptp* **sped**) **(a)** (*of person etc*) darse prisa, apresurarse; **to** — **along** ir a gran velocidad, ir a toda rapidez; **he sped down the street** corrió a toda prisa por la calle; **to** — **off** irse a toda prisa.
    (b) (*Aut*) exceder la velocidad permitida.

speedboat ['spiːd,bəut] *n* motora *f*, lancha *f* rápida.

speed cop ['spiːdkɔp] *n* (*sl*) policía *m* de tráfico.

speedily ['spiːdili] *adv* rápidamente; prontamente, con toda prontitud; **it** — **became obvious that ...** pronto se hizo manifiesto que ...; **as** — **as possible** lo más pronto posible.

speediness ['spiːdinis] *n* velocidad *f*, rapidez *f*; prontitud *f*.

speeding ['spiːdiŋ] *n* (*Aut*) exceso *m* de velocidad; **he was fined for** — se le impuso una multa por exceso de velocidad.

speed limit ['spiːd,limit] *n* velocidad *f* máxima permitida, límite *m* de velocidad; **to exceed the** — exceder la velocidad permitida.

speedometer [spi'dɔmitə*] *n* velocímetro *m*, cuentakilómetros *m*.

speed-up ['spiːdʌp] *n* aceleración *f*.

speedway ['spiːdwei] *n* (*track*) pista *f* de ceniza, carretera *f* para carreras; (*motor-cycle racing*) carreras *fpl* de motocicleta; (US) autopista *f*.

speedwell ['spiːdwel] *n* (*Bot*) verónica *f*.

speedy ['spiːdi] *adj* veloz, rápido; *answer etc* pronto; *service etc* rápido.

spelaeologist, (US) **speleologist** [,spiːli'ɔlədʒist] *n* espeleólogo *m*.

spelaeology, (US) **speleology** [,spiːli'ɔlədʒi] *n* espeleología *f*.

spell¹ [spel] *n* encanto *m*, hechizo *m*; ensalmo *m*; **to be under a** — estar hechizado; **to cast a** — **over someone, to put someone under a** — hechizar a uno (*also fig*); **Seville casts its** — **over the tourists** Sevilla hechiza a los turistas.

spell² [spel] (*irr*: *pret and ptp* **spelled** *or* **spelt**) *vti* **(a)** escribir; **she can't** — no sabe escribir correctamente las palabras, sabe poco de ortografía; **how do you** — **"onyx"?** ¿cómo se escribe "ónice"?; **what do these letters** —? ¿qué palabra se forma con estas letras?; **to** — **out** deletrear; **to** — **something out for someone** (*fig*) explicar algo a uno de un modo muy sencillo, explicar algo a uno detalladamente.
    (b) (*denote*) anunciar, presagiar; significar; **it** —**s disaster for us** representa un desastre para nosotros; **it** —**s ruin** significa la ruina.

spell³ [spel] *n* **(a)** (*at work*) tanda *f*, turno *m*; **to take a** — **with the saw** trabajar su turno con la sierra.
    (b) (*period in general*) rato *m*; temporada *f*, período *m*; **by** —**s** a rachas, a ratos; **cold** — período *m* de frío; **a prolonged** — **of bad weather** una larga temporada de mal tiempo; **we had a** — **in Chile** pasamos una temporada en Chile; **I had a** — **as a traveller** durante cierto tiempo trabajé como viajante; **they're going through a bad** — atraviesan un mal momento.

spellbinder ['spel,baində*] *n* orador *m* fascinante.

spellbound ['spelbaund] *adj* embelesado, hechizado; **to hold one's audience** — tener a sus oyentes embelesados.

speller ['spelə*] *n*: **to be a bad** — no saber escribir correctamente las palabras.

spelling ['speliŋ] *n* ortografía *f*; **the correct** — **is ...** la buena ortografía es ...; **reformed** — nueva ortografía *f*.

spelling bee ['speliŋ,biː] n certamen m de ortografía.
spelling book ['speliŋ,buk] n abecedario m.
spelt¹ [spelt] n (Bot) espelta f.
spelt² [spelt] pret and ptp of **spell**².
spend [spend] (irr: pret and ptp **spent**) **1** vt money, effort gastar; time pasar; time (on a journey, project etc) invertir (on en) dedicar (on a); anger, emotion etc agotar, consumir; **she spent 20 pesetas on sweets** gastó 20 pesetas en bombones; **where are you —ing your holiday?** ¿dónde pasa Vd sus vacaciones?; **the storm has spent its fury** la tempestad ha agotado su violencia.
  2 vi gastar dinero; **he —s freely** gasta muchísimo dinero.
spender ['spendə*] n gastador m, ora f; **to be a free —** gastar libremente su dinero, ser derrochador.
spending money ['spendiŋ,mʌni] n dinero m para gastos personales.
spending power ['spendiŋ,pauə*] n poder m de compra, poder m adquisitivo.
spendthrift ['spendθrift] **1** adj derrochador, pródigo.
  2 n derrochador m, ora f, pródigo m, a f.
spent [spent] **1** pret and ptp of **spend**. **2** adj agotado; bullet frío; **he's a — force** es una vieja gloria, ya no vale lo que antes.
sperm [spɜːm] n (Bio) esperma f.
spermaceti [,spɜːmə'seti] n espermaceti m.
spermatozoon [,spɜːmətəu'zəuɒn] n, pl **—zoa** ['zəuə] espermatozoo m.
sperm whale ['spɜːmweil] n cachalote m.
spew [spjuː] vt vomitar; (fig) vomitar, arrojar, echar fuera (also **to — forth, to — out**); **it makes me —** (fig: fam) me da asco.
sphagnum ['sfægnəm] n esfágnea f.
sphere [sfiə*] n esfera f; (fig) esfera f, campo m; competencia f; **— of influence** esfera f de influencia; **— of activity** campo m de actividad; **in the — of music** en la esfera de la música, en el mundo de la música; **that's outside my —** eso no es de mi competencia.
spherical ['sferikəl] adj esférico.
spheroid ['sfiərɔid] n esferoide m.
sphincter ['sfiŋktə*] n esfínter m.
sphinx [sfiŋks] n esfinge f.
spice [spais] **1** n especia f; (fig) sabor m, picante m; **the detail added — to the story** el detalle dio más sabor a la narración; **the papers like stories with some —** a los periódicos les gusta reportajes con cierto picante.
  2 vt especiar, condimentar; (fig) dar picante a; **gossip —d with scandal** unos chismes con el sabor adicional de detalles escandalosos; **a highly —d account** un relato de mucho picante.
spiciness ['spaisinis] n picante m, sabor m (also fig).
spick-and-span ['spikən'spæn] adj impecablemente limpio; house etc como una tacita de plata; person pulcro, aseado, acicalado.
spicy ['spaisi] adj especiado; condimentado, picante; (fig) picante, sabroso.
spider ['spaidə*] n araña f.
spiderman ['spaidəmæn] n, pl **—men** [men] obrero m que trabaja en la construcción de edificios altos.
spidery ['spaidəri] adj delgado; writing de patas de araña.
spiel [spiːl] n (sl) arenga f, discurso m; material m publicitario; relato m con que uno procura convencer a otro.
spigot ['spigət] n (of cask) espita f, grifo m; (Tech) espiga f.
spike [spaik] **1** n (point) punta f; (tool) escarpia f; (on shoes, for letters etc) clavo m; (Zool etc) pincho m, púa f; (Bot) espiga f.
  2 vt atravesar con un pincho; sujetar con un clavo (etc); gun clavar, (fig) inutilizar, hacer inútil; drink (US) echar licor a, fortalecer.
spiked [spaikt] adj shoe claveteado.
spikenard ['spaiknɑːd] n nardo m.
spiky ['spaiki] adj puntiagudo; armado de púas, cubierto de púas, erizado.
spill¹ [spil] **1** n caída f; vuelco m; **to have a —** sufrir una caída, tener un accidente.
  2 (irr: pret and ptp **spilled** or **spilt**) vt derramar, verter; rider hacer caer, desarzonar.
  3 vi derramarse, verterse; **to — over** irse, desbordarse; (fig) desbordarse.
spill² [spil] n alegrador m, pajuela f.
spillway ['spilwei] n derramadero m.
spilt [spilt] pret and ptp of **spill**.
spin [spin] **1** n (a) (revolution) vuelta f, revolución f; **to give a wheel a —** poner una rueda en movimiento, hacer que una rueda gire.

  (b) (trip) paseo m (en coche etc); **to go for a —** dar un paseo (en coche), salir de excursión en coche.
  (c) (Aer) barrena f; **to go into a —** entrar en barrena; **to be in a flat —** (fam) estar completamente confuso, estar totalmente despistado.
  (d) (on ball) torcimiento; **to put a — on a ball** dar efecto a una pelota, torcer una pelota.
  2 (irr: pret **spun** or **span**, ptp **spun**) vt (a) thread hilar; cocoon devanar, hacer.
  (b) (turn) girar, hacer girar; dar una vuelta a; top hacer bailar; ball dar efecto a, torcer; coin echar a cara o cruz.
  (c) **to — out** alargar, prolongar; yarn.
  3 vi (resolve) girar, dar vueltas (also **to — round**); (top) bailar; (Aer) entrar en barrena; descender en barrena; **to — along** correr rápidamente, ir a buen tren; **my head is —ning** estoy mareado; **it makes my head —** me marea; **to send something —ning** echar algo a rodar; **the blow sent him —ning** el golpe le echó a rodar por los suelos.
spinach ['spinidʒ] n (plant) espinaca f; (dish) espinacas fpl.
spinal ['spainl] adj espinal; column vertebral.
spindle ['spindl] n (for spinning) huso m; (Mech) eje m.
spindleshanks ['spindlʃæŋks] n zanquivano m, a f.
spindly ['spindli] adj largo y delgado; leg zanquivano.
spin-drier ['spin'draiə*] n secador m centrífugo.
spindrift ['spindrift] n rocío m.
spine [spain] n (Anat) espinazo m, columna f vertebral; (Zool) púa f; (Bot) espina f; (of book) lomo m.
spineless ['spainlis] adj débil, flojo, falto de voluntad.
spinelessly ['spainlisli] adv débilmente, flojamente.
spinet [spi'net] n (Hist) espineta f.
spinnaker ['spinəkə*] n (Naut) balón m.
spinner ['spinə*] n hilandero m, a f.
spinneret [,spinə'ret] n (Zool) pezón m hilador.
spinney ['spini] n bosquecillo m.
spinning ['spiniŋ] n (act) hilado m; (art) hilandería f; arte m de hilar.
spinning jenny ['spiniŋ'dʒeni] n máquina f de hilar de husos múltiples.
spinning machine ['spiniŋmə'ʃiːn] n máquina f de hilar.
spinning mill ['spiniŋmil] n hilandería f.
spinning top ['spiniŋtɒp] n peonza f.
spinning wheel ['spiniŋwiːl] n torno m de hilar, rueca f.
spinster ['spinstə*] n soltera f; (pej) solterona f.
spiny ['spaini] adj con púas, erizado de púas; espinoso.
spiracle ['spirəkl] n espiráculo m.
spiral ['spaiərəl] **1** adj espiral, helicoidal; en espiral; **— staircase** escalera f de caracol.
  2 n espiral f; hélice f; **the inflationary —** la espiral inflacionista.
  3 vi dar vueltas en espiral; **the plane —led down** el avión bajó en espiral; **the smoke —led up, the smoke went —ling up** el humo subió en espiral; **prices have —led up** los precios han subido vertiginosamente.
spirally ['spaiərəli] adv en espiral.
spire [spaiə*] n aguja f, chapitel m.
spirit ['spirit] **1** n (a) (soul) espíritu m, alma f; ánima f; **an unquiet —** un alma inquieta; **to be vexed in —** sentirlo en el alma.
  (b) (ghost) aparecido m, fantasma m; **evil —** espíritu m maligno; **Holy S—** Espíritu m Santo; **"Blithe S—"** "Un espíritu burlón"; **to believe in —s** creer en fantasmas.
  (c) (person) alma f; **the leading (or moving) — in the party** el alma del partido, la figura más destacada del partido; **a few restless —s** algunas personas descontentadizas.
  (d) (humour, mood) espíritu m; temple m, humor m; **community —**, **public —** civismo m; **fighting —** espíritu m de lucha; **the — of the age** el espíritu de la época; **in a — of mischief** estando de humor para hacer alguna travesura; **everyone is in a party —** todo el mundo quiere divertirse; **it's in the — of the book** representa bien el espíritu del libro; **that's the —!** ¡muy bien!; **to enter into the — of something** dejarse emocionar por algo; empaparse en el ambiente de algo; **to take something in the wrong —** interpretar mal el espíritu con que se ha hecho algo; **it depends on the — in which it is done** depende del humor con que se hace.
  (e) (courage) valor m; (energy) energía f; (panache) brío m, ánimo m; **a man of some —** un

hombre de cierta energía; **to catch someone's —** ser influido por el valor de uno; **they lack —** carecen de energía, no tienen carácter; **to show some —** mostrar algún brío; **to sing with —** cantar con brío.

(f) —s ánimo m; humor m; **animal —s** vitalidad f; **high —s** optimismo m; alegría f; **to be in high —s** estar animadísimo, estar muy alegre; **low —s** pesimismo m, abatimiento m; **to be in low —s** estar abatido; **to keep up one's —s** no dejarse desanimar, no perder su optimismo; **we kept our —s up by singing** para no caer en el abatimiento nos dedicamos a cantar; **to raise someone's —s** dar aliento a uno, reanimar a uno; **to recover one's —s** volver a estar alegre, reanimarse; **my —s rose somewhat** me sentí algo más alegre, me sentí un poco más optimista.

(g) (*Chem*) alcohol m; (*Aut*) gasolina f (*also* **motor —**); **raw —s** licores mpl de baja calidad; **—s of wine** espíritu m de vino; **I keep off —s** yo no bebo licores.

2 vt: **to — away, to — off** llevarse misteriosamente, volatilizar, hacer desaparecer.

spirited ['spiritid] *adj person* animoso, brioso; *attack etc* enérgico, vigoroso; *horse* fogoso; *other animal* bravo.

spirit lamp ['spiritlæmp] n lamparilla f de alcohol.

spiritless ['spiritlis] *adj* apocado, sin ánimo.

spirit level ['spirit,levl] n nivel m de aire.

spirit stove ['spiritstəuv] n infiernillo m de alcohol.

spiritual ['spiritjuəl] **1** *adj* espiritual. **2** n (*Mus*) canción f religiosa (*esp* de los negros de EE.UU.).

spiritualism ['spiritjuəlizəm] n espiritismo m.

spiritualist ['spiritjuəlist] n espiritista mf.

spirituality [,spiritju'æliti] n espiritualidad f.

spiritually ['spiritjuəli] *adv* espiritualmente.

spirituous ['spiritjuəs] *adj* espirituoso.

spirt [spə:t] **1** n chorro m, chorretada f.

2 vt hacer salir en chorro, arrojar un chorro de.

3 vi (*also* **to — out, to — up**) salir en chorro, salir a chorros; brotar a borbotones; *see also* **spurt**.

spit¹ [spit] **1** n (*Cook*) asador m, espetón m; (*of land*) lengua f; (*sandbank*) banco m de arena. **2** vt espetar.

spit² [spit] **1** n saliva f; esputo m; **to be the dead** (*or* **very**) **— of someone** (*fam*) ser la segunda edición de uno, ser la viva imagen de uno.

2 (*irr: pret and ptp* **spat**) vt escupir; **to — forth, to — out** escupir (*also fig*); **— it out!** ¡dilo!, ¡desembucha!

3 vi escupir (*at a, on* en); (*of cat*) bufar; **to — in someone's face** escupir a la cara a uno; **the fish is —ting in the pan** chisporrotea el pescado en la sartén; **it is —ting with rain** caen algunas gotas de lluvia, empieza a llover.

spit³ [spit] n (*Agr*) azadada f; **to dig 3 —s deep** excavar a una profundidad de 3 azadadas.

spite [spait] **1** n rencor m, ojeriza f, despecho m; **in — of** a pesar de, a despecho de; **in — of all he says** a pesar de todo lo que dice; **to do something out of (or from) —** hacer algo por despecho.

2 vt mortificar, herir, causar pena a; **she just does it to — me** lo hace solamente para causarme pena.

spiteful ['spaitful] *adj* rencoroso, malévolo; **to be — to someone** tratar a uno con malevolencia.

spitefully ['spaitfəli] *adv* con rencor, malévolamente; por despecho; **she said —** dijo malévola.

spitefulness ['spaitfulnis] n rencor m, malevolencia f.

spitfire ['spit,faiə*] n fierabrás m.

spittle ['spitl] n saliva f, baba f.

spittoon [spi'tu:n] n escupidera f.

spiv [spiv] n (*sl: approx*) chanchullero m, caballero m de industria; (*slacker*) gandul m; (*black marketeer*) estraperlista m.

splash [splæʃ] **1** n (*spray*) salpicadura f, rociada f; (*—ing noise*) chapoteo m; (*of colour*) mancha f; **whisky with a — of water** whisky m con un poquitín de agua; **it fell with a great — into the water** cayó ruidosamente al agua, cayó al agua levantando mucha espuma; **to make a —** causar una sensación, impresionar; hacer algo en grande.

2 vt salpicar (*with* de); **to — water about** hacer que el agua salpique; **to — one's money about** derrochar su dinero por todas partes.

3 vi (*of liquid*) esparcirse, rociarse; (*of person in water*; *also* **to — about**) chapotear; **to — about in the water** chapotear en el agua; **to — out** (*fam*) derrochar dinero; **so we —ed out and bought it** así que nos resolvimos de una vez a comprarlo.

splashboard ['splæʃbɔ:d] n guardabarros m, alero m.

splashdown ['splæʃdaun] n amerizaje m, chapuzón m.

splashy ['splæʃi] *adj* líquido; fangoso.

splay [splei] vt extender (sin gracia); (*Tech*) biselar, achaflanar.

splayfoot ['spleifut] n pie m aplastado y torcido.

splayfooted ['splei'futid] *adj* zancajoso.

spleen [spli:n] n (*Anat*) bazo m; (*fig*) spleen m, esplín m, rencor m; **to vent one's —** descargar la bilis (*on* contra).

splendid ['splendid] *adj* espléndido; **—!** ¡magnífico!; **that's simply —!** ¡pero qué bien!; **but how — for you!** ¡cuánto me alegro por ti!; **a — joke** un chiste excelente; **he has done — work** ha hecho una magnífica labor.

splendidly ['splendidli] *adv* espléndidamente; magníficamente; **a — dressed man** un hombre brillantemente vestido; **you did —** hiciste muy bien, lo has hecho rebién; **everything went —** todo fue a las mil maravillas; **we get along —** nos llevamos muy bien.

splendiferous [splen'difərəs] *adj* (*fam*) *see* **splendid**.

splendour, (*US*) splendor ['splendə*] n esplendor m; magnificencia f; (*of achievement etc*) brillo m, gloria f.

splenetic [spli'netik] *adj* (*Anat*) esplénico; (*fig*) enojadizo, de genio vivo; malhumorado.

splice [splais] **1** n empalme m, junta f. **2** vt empalmar, juntar; (*sl*) casar; **to get —d** (*sl*) casarse.

splint [splint] **1** n tablilla f; **to put someone's arm in —s** entablillar el brazo a uno. **2** vt entablillar.

splinter ['splintə*] **1** n astilla f; (*in finger*) espigón m.

2 *attr*: **— group** grupo m disidente, facción f; **— party** partido m nuevo formado a raíz de la escisión de otro.

3 vt astillar, hacer astillas.

4 vi astillarse, hacerse astillas; **to — off** separarse.

splinterbone ['splintəbəun] n peroné m.

splinterless ['splintəlis] *adj* inastillable.

split [split] **1** n (*crack*) hendedura f, raja f, grieta f; (*fig*) división f; cisma m; (*Pol*) escisión f; (*quarrel*) ruptura f; **a three-way —** una división en tres partes; **there are threats of a — in the progressive party** hay amenazas de escisión en el partido progresista; **to do the —s** esparrancarse.

2 *adj* partido, hendido; *pea* majado; *personality* desdoblado; *party etc* escindido, dividido; **the party was —** el partido estaba escindido; **the party is — 3 ways** el partido está escindido en 3 grupos; *see* **second**.

3 (*irr: pret and ptp* **split**) vt (*cleave*) partir, hender, rajar; dividir; **to — the atom** disgregar el átomo; **to — the difference** partir la diferencia; **the sea had — the ship in two** el mar había partido el barco en dos; **the blow — his head open** el golpe le abrió la cabeza; **the dispute — the party** la disputa escindió el partido; **to — off** separar; **to — up** partir, dividir; *estate* parcelar; **we'll — the work up among us** dividiremos el trabajo entre nosotros.

4 vi (**a**) partirse, henderse, rajarse; dividirse; (*of party*) escindirse; **the ship — on the rocks** el buque se estrelló contra las rocas; **my head is —ting** me duele terriblemente la cabeza; **to — off** separarse, desprenderse, (*Pol*) escindirse.

(b) (*of persons*) separarse; **let's — up for safety** separémonos para mayor seguridad; **they were married 14 years but then they — up** estuvieron casados durante 14 años pero por fin se separaron.

(c) (*fam*) soplar, chivatear (*on someone* contra uno); **don't — on me** de mí no digas ni pío.

split-level ['split,levl] *adj house* construido sobre dos niveles, con planta baja de dos niveles, a desnivel.

split pin ['split'pin] n pasador m.

splitting ['splitiŋ] *adj headache* terrible, enloquecedor.

splodge [splɔdʒ] n, **splotch** [splɔtʃ] n mancha f, borrón m.

splurge [splə:dʒ] n (*fam*) fachenda f, ostentación f.

splutter ['splʌtə*] **1** n chisporroteo m; (*of speech*) farfulla f. **2** vi chisporrotear; farfullar, balbucear; **"Yes", he —ed "Sí"**, balbuceó.

spoil [spɔil] **1** n (*also* **—s**) despojo m, botín m; trofeo m; (*US Pol*) empleos mpl (*etc*) que se reparten los del partido victorioso; **the —s of war** el botín de la guerra, los trofeos de la guerra.

2 (*irr: pret and ptp* **spoiled** *or* **spoilt**) vt echar a perder, estropear, malograr, arruinar; deteriorar; *child* mimar, consentir; **to — someone's fun** aguar la fiesta a uno; **it quite —ed our holiday** arruinó completamente nuestras vacaciones; **the coast has been —ed by development** la costa ha sido arruinada por la urbanización; **to get —ed** echarse a perder, estropearse.

3 vi echarse a perder, estropearse; arruinarse; dañarse, deteriorarse; **if we leave it here it will —**

si lo dejamos aquí se estropeará; **to be —ing for a fight** querer de todos modos luchar, tener ganas de pelearse.

spoilsport ['spɔilspɔːt] n aguafiestas m; **to be a —** aguar la fiesta.

spoilt [spɔilt] **1** pret and ptp of **spoil**. **2** adj estropeado; dañado, deteriorado; child consentido, muy mimado.

spoke[1] [spəuk] n rayo m, radio m; **to put a — in someone's wheel** estorbar a uno, poner obstáculos a uno.

spoke[2] [spəuk] pret of **speak**.

spoken ['spəukən] **1** ptp of **speak**. **2** adj hablado; **the — language** la lengua hablada, la lengua oral.

spokesman ['spəuksmən] n, pl **—men** [mən] portavoz m; **to act as — for** hablar en nombre de; **they made him —** le eligieron para hablar en su nombre.

spokeshave ['spəuk.ʃeiv] n raedera f.

spoliation [.spəuli'eiʃən] n despojo m.

spondee ['spɔndiː] n espondeo m.

spondulicks [spɔn'djuːliks] npl (sl) parné m.

sponge [spʌndʒ] **1** n esponja f; (Cook) bizcocho m; **to throw up the —** darse por vencido, arriar velas. **2** vt (wash) lavar con esponja, limpiar con esponja (also **to — down**); **to — a stain off** quitar una mancha con una esponja; **to — up** absorber.

3 vi (fam) dar sablazos, vivir de gorra; **to — on someone** vivir a costa de uno; **to — on someone for something** pedir algo a uno sin ofrecerse a pagar.

sponge bag ['spʌndʒbæg] n esponjera f.

sponge cake ['spʌndʒkeik] n bizcocho m.

sponger ['spʌndʒə*] n (fam) gorrón m, sablista mf.

sponginess ['spʌndʒinis] n esponjosidad f.

sponging ['spʌndʒiŋ] n (fam) gorronería f.

spongy ['spʌndʒi] adj esponjoso.

sponsor ['spɔnsə*] **1** n patrocinador m (also Radio, TV); (godparent) padrino m, madrina f; (of membership etc) padrino m; (Comm) fiador m, garante m.

2 vt patrocinar; (Radio, TV) patrocinar, costear, presentar; idea, plan etc fomentar, promover; (as godparent, for membership etc) apadrinar, actuar de padrino a.

sponsorship ['spɔnsəʃip] n patrocinio m; **under the — of** patrocinado por, bajo los auspicios de.

spontaneity [.spɔntə'neiiti] n espontaneidad f.

spontaneous [spɔn'teiniəs] adj espontáneo.

spontaneously [spɔn'teiniəsli] adv espontáneamente.

spoof [spuːf] (fam) **1** n trampa f, truco m, mistificación f. **2** vt engañar, burlar, mistificar. **3** vi bromear.

spook [spuːk] n (fam) espectro m.

spooky ['spuːki] adj (fam) (like a ghost) fantasmal, espectral; (mysterious) misterioso; (frightening) horripilante; **a thoroughly — place** un sitio envuelto en misterio.

spool [spuːl] n (Sew, Phot) carrete m; (of sewing machine) canilla f; (fishing) cucharilla f.

spoon [spuːn] **1** n cuchara f; **to be born with a silver — in one's mouth** nacer en buena cuna, criarse en buenos pañales.

2 vt (also **to — out**) cucharear, sacar con cuchara; (fig) sacar como en cuchara; **to — up** recoger con cuchara.

3 vi (fam) acariciarse amorosamente, besuquearse.

spoonbill ['spuːnbil] n espátula f.

spoonerism ['spuːnərizəm] n juego de palabras (o error divertido) que consiste en trastrocar las letras iniciales de dos o más vocablos.

spoon-feed ['spuːnfiːd] (irr: see feed) vt dar de comer con cuchara a; (fig) tratar como un niño a, ayudar hasta con las cosas más sencillas a.

spoon-fed ['spuːnfed] adj muy mimado.

spoonful ['spuːnful] n cucharada f.

spoony ['spuːni] adj (fam) sobón; sentimental; **to be — on someone** estar tontamente enamorado de uno.

spoor [spuə*] n pista f, rastro m.

sporadic [spə'rædik] adj esporádico.

sporadically [spə'rædikəli] adv esporádicamente.

spore [spɔː*] n espora f.

sporran ['spɔrən] n (Scot) escarcela f.

sport [spɔːt] **1** n (a) (games in general) deporte m; (hunting) caza f; deporte m; (amusement) juego m, diversión f; (plaything) juguete m; **athletic —s** juegos mpl atléticos; **the — of kings** el deporte de los reyes (el hipismo); **in —** en broma; **to have some good —** tener éxito en la caza, lograr unas cuantas piezas hermosas; **the trout here give good —** aquí las truchas no se rinden fácilmente; **to make — with someone** burlarse de uno.

(b) (person) buen chico m; buen perdedor m; **be a —!** ¡como amigo!; **he's a real —** es una persona realmente buena.

(c) (Bio) mutación f.

2 vt llevar; gastar; lucir, ostentar; see oak.

3 vi divertirse; jugar, juguetear.

sporting ['spɔːtiŋ] adj deportivo; conduct, spirit etc deportivo, caballeroso; chance, offer que da cierta posibilidad de éxito; dog, gun de caza; **I'm a — man** me gusta hacer apuestas arriesgadas.

sportive ['spɔːtiv] adj juguetón.

sports car ['spɔːtskɑː*] n coche m deportivo, deportivo m, coche m sport.

sports coat ['spɔːtskəut] n chaqueta f sport.

sports commentator ['spɔːts.kɔmenteitə*] n comentarista m deportivo.

sports ground ['spɔːtsgraund] n campo m de recreo, terreno m de deporte; pista f para juegos atléticos.

sports jacket ['spɔːts.dʒækit] n chaqueta f sport.

sportsman ['spɔːtsmən] n, pl **—men** [mən] (player, hunter) deportista m; (honourable person) persona f honrada, caballero m; (betting man) persona f a quien le gusta hacer apuestas arriesgadas; **the — of the year** el mejor deportista del año.

sportsmanlike ['spɔːtsmənlaik] adj deportivo; honrado, caballeroso.

sportsmanship ['spɔːtsmənʃip] n deportividad f.

sports page ['spɔːtspeidʒ] n página f deportiva.

sportswear ['spɔːtsweə*] n trajes mpl de deporte.

sportswoman ['spɔːtswumən] n, pl **—women** [wimin] deportista f.

sporty ['spɔːti] adj (fam) (a) deportivo; aficionado a los deportes.

(b) (fig) alegre; guasón, jovial.

(c) (US) disipado, libertino; elegante, guapo.

spot [spɔt] **1** n (a) (place in general) sitio m, lugar m; **a pleasant —** un lugar agradable; **a good — for trout** un buen lugar para las truchas; **blind —** (Anat) punto m ciego, (fig) debilidad f, punto m flojo; **at the — where it happened** en el lugar donde ocurrió; **on this very —** en este mismo sitio; **to be in a (tight) —** estar en un aprieto; **to have a soft — for someone** tener una debilidad por uno; **to know someone's weak —s** saber de qué pie cojea uno; **to put one's finger on the weak —** poner el dedo en la llaga.

(b) (phrases with on) **our man on the —** nuestro hombre sobre el terreno; **the reporter was on the —** el reportero estaba allí mismo; **the firemen were on the — in 3 minutes** los bomberos llegaron al cabo de 3 minutos, acudieron los bomberos a los 3 minutos; **I always have to be on the —** yo estoy de servicio siempre; **to do something on the —** hacer algo en el acto, hacer algo acto seguido; hacer algo sin demora; **to put someone on the —** poner a uno en un aprieto; **now I'm really on the —** ahora me veo de verdad entre la espada y la pared.

(c) (Med etc) grano m, lunar m; (freckle) peca f; (stain) mancha f; (measles) **—s** manchas fpl de sarampión; **to break (or come) out in —s** salir a uno granos en la piel; **I have a — that itches** tengo un grano que me pica; **it made a — on the table** hizo una mancha en la mesa.

(d) (of colour) punto m; pinta f, mancha f; **a cloth with blue —s** un paño con puntos azules; **a dog with black —s** un perro con manchas negras; **black —** (fig) lunar m; **there are black —s in this prosperity** en esta prosperidad hay lunares; **it's a black — for accidents** es un sitio donde hay muchos accidentes; **there are black —s in his record** hay malas notas en su historial; **to knock —s off someone** vencer a uno fácilmente; **this can knock —s off yours any time** éste supera al tuyo en cualquier momento.

(e) (small quantity) poquito m, poquitín m; (of rain) gota f; **just a —, thanks** un poquitín, gracias; **we had a few —s** tuvimos algunas gotitas; **a — of bother** cierto disgusto, un poco de dificultad; **he had a — of bother with the police** se armó un lío con la policía; **we're in a — of trouble** tenemos cierta dificultad; **without a — of trouble** sin dificultad alguna.

(f) (Radio, TV) espacio m radiofónico (publicitario).

(g) **—s** (Comm) géneros mpl vendidos al contado; géneros mpl para entrega inmediata.

2 attr (a) **— goods** géneros mpl vendidos al contado; géneros mpl para entrega inmediata; **— cash** dinero m contante.

(b) **— check** comprobación f en el acto, reconocimiento m rápido; **— test** prueba f superficial.

3 *vt* (a) (*speckle*) manchar, motear, salpicar (*with* de); **to — someone with mud** salpicar a uno de lodo.

(b) (*notice, see*) notar, observar; encontrar; descubrir; (*recognize*) reconocer; (*select*) elegir, escoger; **I —ted him at once** le reconocí en seguida; **did you — the winner?** ¿escogiste el ganador?

4 *vi*: **to —** (*with rain*) chispear.

spotless ['spɔtlis] *adj* nítido; sin manchas, inmaculado; (*clean*) perfectamente limpio, como una tacita de plata.

spotlessly ['spɔtlisli] *adv*: **— clean** perfectamente limpio, como una tacita.

spotlessness ['spɔtlisnis] *n* nitidez *f*; perfecta limpieza *f*.

spotlight ['spɔtlait] **1** *n* (*Theat lamp*) foco *m*, reflector *m*, proyector *m*, (*light*) luz *f* del foco; (*Aut*) faro *m* auxiliar orientable; (*fig*) luz *f* concentrada; **to turn the — on someone** (*fig*) volver sobre uno la luz concentrada de la publicidad (*or* de la atención pública *etc*).

2 *vt* iluminar; destacar, subrayar.

spotted ['spɔtid] *adj* manchado; moteado; **a dress — with blue** un vestido con puntos azules; **a dress — with mud** un vestido manchado de lodo.

spotted fever ['spɔtid'fiːvə*] *n* tifus *m* exantemático.

spotter ['spɔtə*] *n* (*Aer etc*) observador *m*; (*Rail*) coleccionista *m* de números de locomotoras.

spotty ['spɔti] *adj* manchado, lleno de manchas; (*Med: pimply*) con granos, (*of infection*) con manchas; **to be all —** estar cubierto de manchas.

spouse [spauz] *n* cónyuge *mf*.

spout [spaut] **1** *n* (*of jar*) pico *m*; (*of teapot, wine jug*) pitón *m*, pitorro *m*; (*of guttering*) canalón *m*; (*pipe*) caño *m*, conducto *m*; (*jet of water*) chorro *m*; (*column of water*) surtidor *m*; **it's up the —** (*fam*) está empeñado, (*fig*) se acabó todo.

2 *vt* arrojar en chorro; levantar un surtidor de; (*fig*) declamar, recitar; **he can — figures about it** es capaz de recitar incansablemente las cifras referentes a ello.

3 *vi* chorrear; (*fig*) recitar, hablar incansablemente; **he was still —ing when we left** seguía hablando incansablemente cuando salimos.

sprain [sprein] **1** *n* torcedura *f*. **2** *vt* torcer; **to — one's wrist** torcerse la muñeca.

sprang [spræŋ] *pret of* **spring**.

sprat [spræt] *n* arenque *m* pequeño, sardineta *f*.

sprawl [sprɔːl] *vi* arrellanarse, repanchigarse; extenderse (en postura desgarbada), tumbarse (de modo poco elegante); (*of plant, town*) extenderse; **he was —ed in a chair** estaba tumbado de modo poco elegante en un sillón; **the body was —ed on the floor** el cadáver estaba tumbado en el suelo; **to send someone —ing** (**with a blow**) derribar a uno por el suelo; **the jolt sent him —ing** la sacudida le hizo ir rodando por el suelo.

spray¹ [sprei] *n* (*Bot*) ramita *f*.

spray² [sprei] **1** *n* (a) (*liquid*) rociada *f*; (*of sea*) espuma *f*; (*as irrigation*) riego *m* por aspersión; (*of insecticide etc*) pulverización *f*.

(b) (*implement: scent—*) atomizador *m*; (*paint—*) pistola *f* rociadora de pintura; (*Med*) rociador *m*; (*insecticide —*) pulverizador *m*.

2 *vt* rociar, regar (*with* de); atomizar, pulverizar; **to — the roses with insecticide** rociar las rosas de insecticida; **to — paint on to a car** pintar un coche con una pistola rociadora; **to — a house with bullets** rociar una casa de balas.

sprayer ['spreiə*] *n see* **spray 1** (b).

spray gun ['spreigʌn] *n* pistola *f* rociadora; pulverizador *m*.

spraying machine ['spreiiŋməˌʃiːn] *n* (*Agr*) pulverizador *m*.

spread [spred] **1** *n* (a) (*act*) extensión *f*; propagación *f*, diseminación *f*, difusión *f*; generalización *f*; proliferación *f*; **the — of education** la extensión de la educación; **the — of nuclear weapons** la proliferación de armas nucleares.

(b) (*of wings*) envergadura *f*; (*of figures, marks etc*) extensión *f*; gama *f*, escala *f*; **middle-aged —** gordura *f* de la mediana edad.

(c) (*fam*) comilona *f*, banquetazo *m*.

2 (*irr: pret and ptp* **spread**) *vt* extender, tender; *intangible things* propagar, diseminar, difundir; divulgar; generalizar; *butter etc* untar; *banner, sails, wings* desplegar; *net* tender; *table* poner; (*scatter*) esparcir, desparramar; **to — butter on one's bread** untar el pan con mantequilla, extender mantequilla sobre el pan; **to — cream on one's face** extender crema sobre el rostro; **to — oil on the sea** tender una capa de aceite sobre el mar; **to — the sea with**

oil cubrir el mar con una capa de aceite; **meadows — with flowers** prados *mpl* cubiertos de flores; **the peacock —s its tail** el pavo real hace la rueda; **repayments will be — over 18 months** los pagos se efectuarán durante 18 meses; **to — news about** divulgar una noticia; **the book —s error** el libro disemina el error; **to — out** separar; abrir, extender, desplegar; **to — a map out on a table** extender un mapa sobre una mesa.

3 *vi* extenderse; propagarse, difundirse; divulgarse; generalizarse; desplegarse; (*scatter*) esparcirse, desparramarse; **the fire — rapidly** el incendio se extendió rápidamente; **a knowledge of this — widely** el conocimiento de esto se divulgó a muchas partes; **the disease —** la enfermedad se propagó; **to — out** (*persons*) separarse; desparramarse.

4 *vr*: **to — oneself** (a) (*physically*) arrellanarse; ponerse a sus anchas, tomar una postura cómoda; **I like to — myself** me gusta tener mucho espacio (para trabajar cómodamente *etc*).

(b) (*in speech: fam*) explayarse, hablar prolijamente.

spread-eagle ['spred'iːgl] *vt* extender (completamente), extender los miembros de.

spread-eagled ['spred'iːgld] *adj* con los miembros extendidos (sin poderse ayudar).

spree [spriː] *n* (*fam*) juerga *f*, parranda *f*; excursión *f*; **spending —** expedición *f* (*or* jira *f etc*) en la que se gasta mucho dinero; **to be (out) on a —** estar de juerga; **to go on a —** ir de juerga; **let's have a —** echemos una cana al aire.

sprig [sprig] *n* (*Bot*) ramita *f*; (*of heather etc*) espiga *f*; (*Tech*) puntilla *f*.

sprightliness ['spraitlinis] *n* viveza *f*, energía *f*, animación *f*.

sprightly ['spraitli] *adj* vivo, enérgico, animado.

spring [spriŋ] **1** *n* (a) (*of water*) fuente *f*, manantial *f*; **hot —** fuente *f* termal.

(b) (*season*) primavera *f*; **in —, in the —** en la primavera; **— is in the air** se nota la llegada de la primavera.

(c) (*leap*) salto *m*, brinco *m*; **in one —** de un salto; **to take a — into the air** dar un salto.

(d) (*bounciness*) elasticidad *f*.

(e) (*Mech: of watch etc*) resorte *m*, (*of mattress, seat etc*) muelle *m*; **—s** (*Aut*) ballestas *fpl*.

2 *attr water* de fuente; (*of season*) primaveral, de primavera.

3 (*irr: pret* **sprang**, *ptp* **sprung**) *vt* (a) (*leap*) saltar, saltar por encima de.

(b) (*warp*) torcer, combar.

(c) (*mine*) volar; *trap* hacer saltar; **to — a leak** abrirse una vía de agua; **to — a piece of news on someone** comunicar una noticia imprevista a uno; **to — a surprise on someone** coger a uno de improviso; **to — an idea on someone** espetar una idea a uno, sugerir una idea a uno de buenas a primeras.

4 *vi* (a) (*of water etc*) brotar, nacer; salir en chorro; (*Bot*) brotar; **to — into existence** nacer de la noche a la mañana, aparecer repentinamente; **to — from** (*fig*) nacer de, proceder de, provenir de; *family* ser de, nacer de; **a man sprung from the people** un hombre surgido de la plebe; **to — up** (*plant*) brotar; crecer rápidamente; (*problem*) surgir, presentarse; (*friendship etc*) nacer; **the weeds — up all over** las malas hierbas aparecen por todas partes.

(b) (*leap*) saltar, brincar; **the lid sprang open** la tapa se abrió de golpe; **to — aside** hacerse de prisa a un lado; **to — at someone** abalanzarse sobre uno; **to — back** dar un paso rápidamente hacia atrás, retroceder con toda prisa; **the branch sprang back** la rama volvió a su posición como un látigo; **where on earth did you — from?** ¿de dónde diablos ha salido Vd?; **to — into the air** dar un salto; **to — into the saddle** saltar a la silla; **to — out of bed** saltar de la cama; **to — to one's feet** levantarse de un salto; **to — to someone's aid** acudir con toda rapidez a ayudar a uno; **to — up** levantarse de un salto; (*of breeze etc*) levantarse de pronto.

(c) (*warp*) torcerse, combarse.

spring balance ['spriŋ'bæləns] *n* peso *m* de muelle.

springboard ['spriŋbɔːd] *n* trampolín *m*.

springbok ['spriŋbɔk] *n especie de gacela* (*del sur de África*).

spring bolt ['spriŋbəult] *n* pestillo *m* de golpe.

spring-clean ['spriŋ'kliːn] **1** *vt* limpiar completamente. **2** *vi* limpiarlo todo, limpiar toda la casa.

spring-cleaning ['spriŋ'kliːniŋ] *n* limpieza *f* general; **to do the —** limpiar toda la casa.

spring fever ['spriŋ'fiːvə*] *n* desasosiego *m*, sentimiento *m* de malestar (*or* intranquilidad *etc*);

deseo *m* fuerte de cambiar de estilo de vida; (*hum*) celo *m* amoroso.

springe ['sprindʒ] *n* lazo *m*.

spring gun ['spriŋgʌn] *n* trampa *f* de alambre y escopeta.

springiness ['spriŋinis] *n* elasticidad *f*.

spring-like ['spriŋlaik] *adj day, weather* primaveral.

spring mattress ['spriŋ'mætris] *n* colchón *m* de muelles, somier *m*.

spring tide ['spriŋ'taid] *n* marea *f* viva.

springtime ['spriŋtaim] *n* primavera *f*.

springy ['spriŋi] *adj* elástico; *turf etc* muelle, muy molido.

sprinkle ['spriŋkl] **1** *n* rociada *f*; salpicadura *f*; **a — of rain** unas gotitas de lluvia; **a — of salt** un poquito de sal.

2 *vt* salpicar, rociar (*with* de); sembrar (*with* de); (*with holy water*) asperjar; esparcir; **to — water on a plant, to — a plant with water** rociar una planta de agua; **a rose —d with dew** una rosa cubierta de rocío; **they are —d about here and there** están esparcidos aquí y allá.

3 *vi* (*with rain*) lloviznar.

sprinkler ['spriŋklə*] *n* rociadera *f*, aparato *m* de lluvia artificial; (*of watering can etc*) regadera *f*; (*in fire fighting*) aparato *m* de rociadura automática; (*Eccl*) hisopo *m*.

sprinkling ['spriŋkliŋ] *n* rociada *f*, salpicadura *f*; aspersión *f*; **a — of knowledge** unos pocos conocimientos; **there was a — of young people** había unos cuantos jóvenes.

sprint [sprint] **1** *n* (*in race*) (e)sprint *m*; (*dash*) carrera *f*.

2 *vi* (*in race*) (e)sprintar; (*dash*) correr a todo correr, precipitarse; **he —ed for the bus** corrió a toda prisa para coger el autobús; **we shall have to —** tendremos que correr.

sprinter ['sprintə*] *n* (e)sprínter *m*, corredor *m* de cortas distancias.

sprit [sprit] *n* botavara *f*, verga *f* de abanico.

sprite [sprait] *n* duende *m*, trasgo *m*; hada *f*.

spritsail ['spritseil, *Naut* 'spritsl] *n* cebadera *f*, vela *f* de abanico.

sprocket wheel ['sprɔkitwi:l] *n* rueda *f* de cadena.

sprout [spraut] **1** *n* brote *m*, retoño *m*; **—s** col *f* de Bruselas.

2 *vt* echar, hacerse; **to — new leaves** echar nuevas hojas; **the calf is —ing horns** le salen los cuernos al ternero; **the town is —ing new buildings** en la ciudad surgen nuevos edificios.

3 *vi* brotar, retoñar, echar retoños; (*shoot up*) crecer rápidamente; **skyscrapers are —ing up** se levantan rápidamente los rascacielos.

spruce¹ [spru:s] **1** *adj* aseado, apuesto, pulcro. **2** *vt*: **to — up** arreglar, componer; **all —d up** muy acicalado. **3** *vr*: **to — oneself up** arreglarse; ataviarse; mejorar de aspecto, hacerse más elegante.

spruce² [spru:s] *n* (*Bot*) pícea *f* (*also* **— tree**).

spruceness ['spru:snis] *n* aseo *m*, pulcritud *f*; elegancia *f*.

sprung [sprʌŋ] **1** *ptp of* **spring**. **2** *adj*: **— bed** cama *f* mullida; **interior — mattress** somier *m*, colchón *m* de muelles; **— seat** asiento *m* de ballesta.

spry [sprai] *adj* ágil, activo.

spud [spʌd] *n* (*Agr*) escarda *f*; (*potato: fam*) patata *f*.

spume [spju:m] *n* espuma *f*.

spun [spʌn] **1** *pret and ptp of* **spin**. **2** *adj*: **— glass** lana *f* de vidrio; **— silk** seda *f* hilada.

spunk [spʌŋk] *n* (*fam*) ánimo *m*, valor *m*, agallas *fpl*.

spur [spə:*] **1** *n* espuela *f*; (*Zool*) espolón *m*; (*Geog*) espolón *m*; (*fig*) estímulo *m*, aguijón *m*; (*Rail*) ramal *m* corto; **the — of hunger** el estímulo del hambre; **it will be a — to further progress** estimulará a progresos ulteriores; **on the — of the moment** sin reflexión, impulsivamente, de improviso; **to win one's —s** distinguirse, demostrar de modo concluyente lo que vale uno.

2 *vt* espolear, picar con las espuelas (*also* **— on**); **to — on** (*fig*) estimular, incitar; **to — someone on to do something** incitar a uno a hacer algo, dar a uno aliento para que haga algo; **this —red him on to greater efforts** esto le incitó a hacer mayores esfuerzos; **—red on by greed** bajo el aguijón de la codicia, incitado a ello por la codicia.

3 *vi*: **to — on** picar el caballo con las espuelas; apretar el paso.

spurge [spə:dʒ] *n* euforbio *m*.

spur gear ['spə:giə*] *n* rueda *f* dentada recta.

spurge laurel ['spə:dʒ,lɔrəl] *n* lauréola *f*, torvisco *m*.

spurious ['spjuəriəs] *adj* falso.

spuriously ['spjuəriəsli] *adv* falsamente.

spuriousness ['spjuəriəsnis] *n* falsedad *f*.

spurn [spə:n] *vt* desdeñar, rechazar.

spurt [spə:t] **1** *n* esfuerzo *m* supremo; **final —** esfuerzo *m* final (para ganar una carrera); **to put in** (*or* **on**) **a —** hacer un esfuerzo supremo, acelerar.

2 *vi* hacer un esfuerzo supremo, acelerar.

sputnik ['sputnik] *n* satélite *m* artificial.

sputter ['spʌtə*] *see* **splutter**.

sputum ['spju:təm] *n* esputo *m*.

spy [spai] **1** *n* espía *mf*; **— story** novela *f* de espionaje.

2 *vt* divisar, columbrar; lograr ver; observar; descubrir; **to — out the land** reconocer el terreno; **finally I spied him coming** por fin le vi venir.

3 *vi* espiar, ser espía: **he spied for Slobodia** fue espía al servicio de Eslobodia; **to — on someone** espiar a uno, observar a uno clandestinamente; seguir los pasos a uno.

spyglass ['spaiglɑ:s] *n* catalejo *m*.

spyhole ['spaihəul] *n* mirilla *f*.

spying ['spaiiŋ] *n* espionaje *m*.

squab [skwɔb] *n* (**a**) (*Orn*) pichón *m*; pollito *m*, polluelo *m*; (*fig*) persona *f* regordeta. (**b**) (*cushion*) cojín *m*; (*sofa*) sofá *m*, canapé *m*.

squabble ['skwɔbl] **1** *n* riña *f*, disputa *f*. **2** *vi* reñir (*about, over* por cuestión de), disputar, pelearse.

squabbler ['skwɔblə*] *n* pendenciero *m*, a *f*.

squabbling ['skwɔbliŋ] *n* riñas *fpl*, disputas *fpl*.

squad [skwɔd] *n* (*Mil*) pelotón *m*; escuadra *f*; (*of police*) brigada *f*; **flying —** brigada *f* móvil.

squad car ['skwɔd,kɑ:*] *n* coche *m* patrulla.

squadron ['skwɔdrən] *n* (*Mil*) escuadrón *m*; (*Naut*) escuadra *f*; (*Aer*) escuadrilla *f*, escuadrón *m*.

squadron leader ['skwɔdrən'li:də*] *n* (*Aer*) comandante *m* (de aviación).

squalid ['skwɔlid] *adj* (*dirty*) miserable, vil, asqueroso; *motive etc* vil; *affair* asqueroso.

squall¹ [skwɔ:l] **1** *n* (*cry*) chillido *m*, grito *m*, berrido *m*. **2** *vi* chillar, gritar, berrear.

squall² [skwɔ:l] *n* (*Naut: gust*) ráfaga *f*; (*brief storm*) chubasco *m*, turbión *m*; (*fig*) tempestad *f*; **there are —s ahead** (*fig*) el futuro se anuncia no muy tranquilo.

squalling ['skwɔ:liŋ] *adj child* chillón; revoltoso.

squally ['skwɔ:li] *adj wind* que viene a ráfagas; *day* de chubascos; (*fig*) nada tranquilo, lleno de dificultades.

squalor ['skwɔlə*] *n* miseria *f*; suciedad *f*; **to live in —** vivir en la miseria, vivir en la suciedad.

squander ['skwɔndə*] *vt money* malgastar, derrochar, despilfarrar; disipar (*on* en); *opportunity* desperdiciar; *time, resources* emplear mal.

square [skwɛə*] **1** *adj* (**a**) (*in shape*) cuadrado; *corner* en ángulo recto; *edge* escuadrado; *build* robusto, fornido; *jaw, shoulder* cuadrado; **— brackets** corchetes *mpl*, paréntesis *mpl* rectos.

(**b**) (*Math*) cuadrado; **— kilometre** kilómetro *m* cuadrado; **2 metres —** 2 metros en cuadro.

(**c**) (*fig*) *deal etc* justo, equitativo; *person* honrado, formal; *meal* abundante, bueno; *refusal* rotundo; **it's 3 days since I had a — meal** hace 3 días que no tengo una comida decente; **it met with a — refusal** fue rechazado de plano.

(**d**) **to be —** **with someone** estar en paz con uno, no deber nada a uno; (*Sport*) ir iguales; **now we're all —** ahora vamos iguales; **we can start again all —** podemos volver a comenzar en pie de igualdad; **if you pay me a pound we'll call it —** si me pagas una libra diremos que no hay más deuda; **to get — with someone** ajustar cuentas con uno, desquitarse con uno; **I'll get — with him yet!** ¡me lo cargaré!

(**e**) (*fam*) idea, *taste etc* anticuado, pasado de moda; *person* de ideas anticuadas, que no se conforma con las tendencias actuales, que no comprende las actitudes de las nuevas generaciones; **he's —** es un carca.

2 *adv*: **— to, — with** en ángulo recto con; **it fell — in the middle** cayó de lleno en el centro, cayó exactamente en el centro.

3 *n* (**a**) (*shape*) cuadrado *m*; cuadro *m* (*also* Mil); (*of chessboard, graph paper*) casilla *f*; **a 6-metre —** un cuadrado de 6 metros de lado; **to divide something into —s** dividir algo en cuadrados.

(**b**) (*of town*) plaza *f*.

(**c**) (*Math*) cuadrado *m*; **4 is the — of 2** 4 es el cuadrado de 2.

(**d**) (*Archit, Tech*) escuadra *f*.

(**e**) (*Univ, fam*) birrete *m*; (*kerchief*) pañuelo *m*.

(**f**) (*fam*) persona *f* de ideas anticuadas, persona *f* que no se conforma con las tendencias actuales, persona *f* que no comprende las actitudes de las nuevas generaciones; **to be a —** ser un carca.

3 *vt* (*make —*; *also Math*) cuadrar; (*Archit, Tech*) escuadrar; (*arrange*) arreglar; (*reconcile*) ajustar, acomodar; (*bribe*) sobornar, comprar el silencio (*or* la ayuda *etc*) de; **can you — it with your conscience?** ¿lo puede acomodar con su conciencia?; **I'll — the porter, I'll — it with the porter** yo lo arreglaré con el conserje.

4 *vi* **(a)** cuadrar, conformarse (*with* con); **it doesn't — with what you said before** esto no cuadra con lo que dijiste antes; **it doesn't — with the facts** esto no cuadra con los hechos.

(b) to — up to someone ponerse en actitud para defenderse contra uno, mostrarse resuelto a defenderse contra uno.

(c) to — up with someone ajustar cuentas con uno, pagar a uno.

squared [skwɛəd] *adj* **paper** cuadriculado.

square dance ['skwɛə‚dɑːns] *n* danza *f* de figuras.

squarely ['skwɛəli] *adv* en cuadro; rotundamente; honradamente; de lleno, directamente; **we must face this —** tenemos que hacer frente a esto sin pestañear; **it hit — in the middle** dio de lleno en el centro.

squash¹ [skwɔʃ] **1** *n* **(a)** (*drink*) zumo *m*; **orange —** naranjada *f* natural, zumo *m* de naranja.

(b) (*crowd*) apiñamiento *m*, agolpamiento *m*; **there was such a — in the doorway** había tantísima gente en la puerta, se apiñaba tanto la gente en la puerta.

2 *vt* (*flatten*) aplastar; (*to — in, to — together*) apretar; apiñar; *argument* confutar; *person* apabullar, reducir a silencio; **can you — my shoes in?** ¿puedes poner mis zapatos? (aunque esté muy llena la maleta *etc*); **can you — 2 more in the car?** ¿caben 2 más en el coche?

3 *vi* aplastarse; **to — in** entrar (apretadamente, a pesar de la muchedumbre *etc*); **we all —ed in** entramos todos aunque con dificultad.

squash² [skwɔʃ] *n*, **squash rackets** ['skwɔʃ‚rækits] *n especie de tenis jugado contra frontón.*

squashy ['skwɔʃi] *adj* blando y algo líquido, muelle y húmedo.

squat [skwɔt] **1** *adj* **person** rechoncho, achaparrado; *building* desproporcionadamente bajo.

2 *vi* agacharse, sentarse en cuclillas (*also* **to — down**); (*fam*) sentarse; (*on property*) establecerse sin derecho, apropiarse sin derecho.

squatter ['skwɔtə*] *n* colono *m* usurpador, intruso *m*, persona *f* que se establece en un terreno público para crear un derecho.

squaw [skwɔː] *n* india *f* norteamericana, piel roja *f*.

squawk [skwɔːk] **1** *n* graznido *m*, chillido *m*. **2** *vi* graznar, chillar.

squeak [skwiːk] **1** *n* (*of hinge, wheel etc*) chirrido *m*, rechinamiento *m*; (*of shoe*) crujido *m*; (*of mouse etc*) chillido *m*, grito *m* agudo; (*of pen*) raspear *m*; **to have a narrow —** escaparse por un pelo; **we don't want a — out of you about this** de esto no digas ni pío.

2 *vi* chirriar, rechinar; crujir; chillar, dar chillidos, dar gritos agudos; raspear.

squeaky ['skwiːki] *adj* chirriador; que cruje; chillón; que raspea.

squeal [skwiːl] **1** *n* chillido *m*, grito *m* agudo; **with a — of pain** con un chillido de dolor.

2 *vi* chillar, dar gritos agudos; (*sl: inform*) cantar; (*complain*) quejarse; **someone —ed to the police** alguien cantó a la policía; **don't come —ing to me** no vengas a quejarte a mí; **to — for help** dar gritos agudos pidiendo socorro; **I'll make them —** (*suffer*) yo les haré sufrir, (*confess*) yo les haré cantar.

squeamish ['skwiːmiʃ] *adj* remilgado, delicado, susceptible; aprensivo; **I'm not —** yo no tengo esa delicadeza, eso me trae sin cuidado; **I'm — about spiders** tengo horror a las arañas; **don't be so —** no seas tan aprensivo, quítate esos remilgos.

squeamishness ['skwiːmiʃnis] *n* remilgos *mpl*, delicadeza *f*, susceptibilidad *f*; aprensión *f*; **to feel a certain —** sentir cierta repugnancia.

squeegee ['skwiːˈdʒiː] *n* enjugador *m* de goma.

squeeze [skwiːz] **1** *n* estrujón *m*, estrujadura *f*; presión *f*; (*of hand*) apretón *m*; (*in bus etc*) apiñamiento *m*, apretura *f*; (*at Bridge*) tenaza *f* (*in diamonds* a diamantes); (*of credit*) restricción *f*; (*fig, difficulty*) aprieto *m*; **it was a tight — in the bus** íbamos muy apretados en el autobús; **it was a tight — to get through** había muy poco espacio para pasar; **the 1966 —** las restricciones económicas de 1966; **to give someone's hand a little —** apretar dulcemente la mano a uno.

2 *vt* (*painfully*) estrujar, apretar; *hand etc* apretar; presionar; **to — out** *juice* exprimir, *person* excluir; **3 were —d to death** 3 murieron estrujados; **I —d my finger in the door** me cogí el dedo en la puerta;

to — a lemon, to — the juice out of a lemon exprimir el zumo de un limón; **to — money out of someone** arrancar dinero a uno; **to — clothes into a case** meter ropa apretadamente en una maleta; **can you — 2 more in?** ¿caben 2 más?; **I'll see if we can — you in for Thursday** (*Theat etc*) veremos si quedan por casualidad entradas para el jueves, (*for appointment*) veremos si es posible ofrecerles una hora el jueves; **to — someone in hearts** (*Bridge*) atenazar a uno a corazones.

3 *vi*: **to — in** introducirse con dificultad en, deslizarse en; **to — through a crowd** abrirse paso a codazos por entre una multitud; **to — through a hole** pasar por un agujero a pesar del poco espacio que hay.

squeezer ['skwiːzə*] *n* exprimelimones *m*, exprimidor *m*.

squelch [skweltʃ] **1** *vt* aplastar, despachurrar; **to — one's way through mud** ir chapoteando por el lodo.

2 *vi* chapotear, ir chapoteando; **to — through the mud** ir chapoteando por el lodo.

squib [skwib] *n* buscapiés *m*.

squid [skwid] *n* calamar *m*.

squiffy ['skwifi] *adj* (*sl*): **to be —** estar achispado.

squint [skwint] **1** *n* (*Med*) estrabismo *m*; (*—ing look*) mirada *f* bizca; (*sidelong glance*) mirada *f* de soslayo, mirada *f* furtiva; (*fam*) vistazo *m*; **he has a terrible —** tiene un marcado estrabismo; **let's have a —** dame un vistazo, déjame verle.

2 *vi* (*Med*) bizquear, ser bizco; (*look sidelong*) mirar de soslayo, torcer la vista; (*narrow eyes*) cerrar casi los ojos; **to — at something** mirar algo de soslayo, (*fam*) mirar algo, echar un vistazo a algo; **he —ed in the sunlight** casi cerró los ojos en el sol.

squint-eyed ['skwint'aid] *adj* bizco.

squire ['skwaiə*] **1** *n* (*landowner*) propietario *m*, hacendado *m*; (*Hist*) escudero *m*; **the —** (*in relation to villagers etc*) el señor; **the — of Ambridge** el señor de Ambridge, el mayor terrateniente de Ambridge.

2 *vt* **lady** acompañar.

squirearchy ['skwaiərɑːki] *n* aristocracia *f* rural.

squirm [skwəːm] *vi* retorcerse, revolverse; **to — with embarrassment** sentirse violento, avergonzarse mucho; **I'll make him —** yo le haré sufrir.

squirrel ['skwirəl] *n* ardilla *f*.

squirt [skwəːt] **1** *n* (*jet*) chorro *m*, jeringazo *m*; (*implement*) jeringa *f*; (*fam*) farolero *m*, farsante *m*.

2 *vt* arrojar un chorro de, arrojar a chorros; jeringar; **to — water at someone** lanzar un chorro de agua hacia uno.

3 *vi* salir a chorros; **the water —ed into my eye** salió un chorro de agua que me dio en los ojos.

stab [stæb] **1** *n* **(a)** (*with knife etc*) puñalada *f*; (*wound in general*) herida *f*; (*of pain*) pinchazo *m*, dolor *m* agudo; **— in the back** (*fig*) puñalada *f* por la espalda, puñalada *f* encubierta.

(b) (*fam*) tentativa *f*; **to have a — at something** intentar algo, probar a hacer algo.

2 *vt* apuñalar, dar de puñaladas a; **to — someone with a knife** herir a uno con un cuchillo; **to — someone in the back** (*fig*) apuñalar a uno por la espalda, apuñalar a uno encubiertamente; **to — someone to death** matar a uno a puñaladas.

3 *vi*: **to — at someone** tratar de apuñalar a uno; **he —bed at the picture with his finger** indicó el cuadro con un movimiento brusco del dedo.

stabbing ['stæbiŋ] *n* puñalada *f*, el apuñalar; **muerte** *f* a puñaladas.

stability [stə'biliti] *n* estabilidad *f*.

stabilization [‚steibəlai'zeiʃən] *n* estabilización *f*.

stabilize ['steibəlaiz] **1** *vt* estabilizar. **2** *vi* estabilizarse.

stabilizer ['steibəlaizə*] *n* (*Naut etc*) estabilizador *m*.

stable¹ ['steibl] *adj* estable, firme.

stable² ['steibl] **1** *n* cuadra *f*, caballeriza *f*; (*group of racehorses*) cuadra *f*; **to clean out the Augean —s** limpiar los establos de Augias.

2 *vt* poner en una cuadra, guardar en una cuadra.

stableboy ['steiblbɔi] *n* mozo *m* de cuadra.

stableman ['steiblmən] *n*, *pl* **—men** [mən] mozo *m* de cuadra.

stack [stæk] **1** *n* montón *m*, rimero *m*, pila *f*; (*Agr*) niara *f*, hacina *f*; (*Mil*) pabellón *m* de fusiles; (*chimney*—) cañón *m* de chimenea; fuste *m* de chimenea; (*book*—) estantería *f* de libros; (*fam*) montón *m*; **we have —s, thanks** gracias, tenemos montones; **we have —s of time** nos sobra tiempo; **I have —s of work to do** tengo un montón de trabajo que hacer.

2 *vt* amontonar, apilar; recoger en un montón, formar una pila de; (*Agr*) hacinar; **the cards are —ed against us** tenemos una gran desventaja.

stadium ['steidiəm] *n* estadio *m*.

staff [stɑːf] **1** n (a) (stick) palo m; (walking stick) bastón m, (pilgrim's) bordón m; (symbol of authority) bastón m de mando; (Eccl) báculo m; (of flag, lance etc) asta f; (fig) sostén m, apoyo m.

(b) (persons) personal m; (establishment) plantilla f de personal; (Mil) estado m mayor; **administrative** — personal m de administración; **domestic** — servidumbre f, criados mpl; **editorial** — redacción f; **teaching** — profesorado m, cuerpo m docente; **general** — estado m mayor general; **to be on the** — ser de plantilla; tener un puesto (permanente); **to join the** — entrar a formar parte del personal; **to leave the** — dimitir; **they keep a** — **of 5** (servants) tienen 5 criados.

(c) (Mus: pl **staves**) pentagrama m.

2 vt proveer de personal; **to be well** —ed tener un buen personal; **to be over** —ed tener un personal demasiado grande.

stag [stæg] n (Zool) ciervo m, venado m; (Fin) especulador m; (fam) soltero m.

stag beetle ['stæg,biːtl] n ciervo m volante.

stage [steidʒ] **1** n (a) (platform) plataforma f, estrado m, tablado m; (of microscope) portaobjeto m; (of rocket) escalón m, piso m; **a 4-stage rocket** un cohete de 4 pisos; **the second** — **fell away** se separó el segundo escalón.

(b) (Theat) escena f; (fig) escenario m, teatro m; **to go on the** — hacerse actor, hacerse actriz; **to put a play on the** — poner una obra; **to put a novel on the** — hacer una versión dramática de una novela; **don't put your daughter on the** — no permita que su hija se haga actriz; **to write for the** — escribir para el teatro.

(c) (of journey) etapa f, jornada f; (of road, pipeline etc) tramo m; (fig) fase f, etapa f; grado m; **in** —s por etapas; **in** (or **by**) **easy** — en cortas etapas; gradualmente, poco a poco; **at this** — **in the negotiations** en esta fase de las negociaciones; **what** — **have we reached?** ¿a qué punto hemos llegado?; **to go through a difficult** — pasar por una fase difícil.

2 vt play representar, poner (en escena); (bring about) efectuar, lograr, llevar a cabo; recovery efectuar; (arrange) arreglar; organizar; **that was no accident, it was** —**d** eso no fue accidente, fue una cosa que se organizó; **to** — **a comeback** restablecerse, rehabilitarse; **to** — **a demonstration** organizar una manifestación.

stage box ['steidʒ,bɒks] n palco m de proscenio.
stagecoach ['steidʒkəʊtʃ] n diligencia f.
stagecraft ['steidʒkrɑːft] n arte m teatral.
stage direction ['steidʒdi,rekʃən] n acotación f.
stage door ['steidʒ'dɔː*] n entrada f de artistas.
stage fright ['steidʒfrait] n miedo m al público.
stagehand ['steidʒhænd] n tramoyista m.
stage manager ['steidʒ,mænidʒə*] n director m de escena.
stage name ['steidʒ,neim] n nombre m en el teatro, nombre m profesional.
stage-struck ['steidʒstrʌk] adj loco por el teatro.
stage whisper ['steidʒ'wispə*] n susurro m en voz bastante alta.
stagey ['steidʒi] adj teatral, dramático.
stagger ['stægə*] **1** n tambaleo m; —**s** (Vet) modorra f.

2 vt (a) (amaze) asombrar, sorprender; (cause to waver) hacer dudar, hacer vacilar; **you** — **me!** ¡me asombras!, ¡me asustas!

(b) hours, spokes etc escalonar.

3 vi tambalear, titubear, hacer eses; **he** —**ed to the door** fue tambaleando a la puerta; **he was** —**ing about** iba tambaleando.

staggered ['stægəd] adj (a) (amazed) asombrado; **I am** — **to hear that . . .** me asombra saber que . . .; **he seemed completely** — parecía estar totalmente asombrado.

(b) hours, spokes etc escalonado.

staggering ['stægəriŋ] adj asombroso, pasmoso.
staghound ['stæghaund] n perro m de caza, sabueso m.
staghunt ['stæghʌnt] n cacería f de venado.
staghunting ['stæg,hʌntiŋ] n caza f de venado.
stagnancy ['stægnənsi] n estancamiento m.
stagnant ['stægnənt] adj estancado; (fig) estancado, paralizado, inmóvil; (Fin) inactivo.
stagnate [stæg'neit] vi estancarse; estar estancado, quedar estancado (also fig); (fig) estar paralizado.
stagnation [stæg'neiʃən] n estancamiento m; (fig) estancamiento m, paralización f, inmovilismo m; inactividad f.
stag party ['stæg,pɑːti] n (fam) tertulia f (etc) de hombres solos (or de solteros).
stagy ['steidʒi] adj teatral, dramático.
staid [steid] adj serio, formal.

staidness ['steidnis] n seriedad f, formalidad f.
stain [stein] **1** n (mark) mancha f; (dye) tinte m, tintura f; (paint) pintura f; (fig) mancha f; **without a** — **on one's character** sin la menor nota infamante, sin que haya nada en contra de la buena fama de uno.

2 vt manchar; (dye) teñir, colorar; (paint) pintar; **her hands were** —**ed with blood** sus manos estaban manchadas de sangre.

3 vi mancharse.

stained glass ['steind'glɑːs] n vidrio m de color; **stained-glass window** vidriera f de colores.
stainless ['steinlis] adj inmanchable; steel inoxidable.
stain remover ['steinri,muːvə*] n quitamanchas m.
stair [steə*] n peldaño m, escalón m; (stairway) escalera f; —**s** escalera f; **flight of** —**s** tramo m de escalera.
stair carpet ['steə,kɑːpit] n alfombra f de escalera.
staircase ['steəkeis] n escalera f, caja f de escalera; **moving** — escalera f móvil, escalera f mecánica; **spiral** —, **winding** — escalera f de caracol.
stair rod ['steərɒd] n varilla f sujetadora (de alfombra de escalera).
stairway ['steəwei] n see **staircase**.
stairwell ['steəwel] n hueco m de escalera.
stake [steik] **1** n (a) (post) estaca f, poste m; (for plant) rodrigón m.

(b) (for execution) hoguera f; **to die at the** — morir en la hoguera; **to be condemned to the** — ser condenado a morir en la hoguera.

(c) (bet) puesta f, apuesta f, parada f; —**s** (prize) premio m, (race) carrera f; **the issue at** — la cuestión de que se trata; **to be at** — estar en juego, estar en litigio; estar en peligro; **there is a lot at** — here esto nos importa muchísimo, esto nos interesa muchísimo; **to have a** — in tener interés en; **Britain had a big** — **in Rhodesia** Gran Bretaña tuvo muchos intereses en Rodesia.

2 vt (a) (also **to** — **off, to** — **out**) estacar; cercar con estacas, señalar con estacas; plant rodrigar.

(b) (bet) apostar (on a); (Fin) aventurar, arriesgar; invertir (on en); **to** — **one's all** jugar el todo por el todo; aventurarlo todo; **to** — **one's reputation on something** afirmar que algo es lo que uno dice, jurar como hombre honrado que algo es así; **to** — **a claim** hacer una reclamación; **to** — **one's claim to a job** afirmar su derecho a ser considerado para un puesto.

stakeholder ['steik,həʊldə*] n persona que guarda las apuestas hechas por otros (y paga al ganador).
stalactite ['stæləktait] n estalactita f.
stalagmite ['stæləgmait] n estalagmita f.
stale [steil] adj food no fresco, pasado, rancio; bread duro; air viciado; news viejo; joke viejo, mohoso; (old-fashioned) anticuado, pasado de moda; person cansado; **I'm getting** — me estoy cansando; ya no tengo la inventiva de antes.
stalemate ['steilmeit] **1** n (Chess) tablas fpl por ahogado; (fig) paralización f, estancamiento m; **the** — **is complete** la paralización es completa; **to reach** — llegar a un punto muerto; **there is** — **between the two powers** las relaciones entre las dos potencias están en un punto muerto.

2 vt (Chess) dar tablas por ahogado a; (fig) paralizar.

staleness ['steilnis] n rancidez f; dureza f; lo viciado; lo viejo, lo mohoso; lo anticuado; cansancio m, falta f de inventiva.
stalk¹ [stɔːk] **1** vt game cazar al acecho, acechar; person seguir los pasos a.

2 vi andar con paso majestuoso (also **to** — **along**); **to** — **away, to** — **off** irse con paso airado; **to** — **out** salir ofendido, salir con paso airado.

stalk² [stɔːk] n (Bot) tallo m, caña f; (cabbage —) troncho m; (of glass) pie m.
stalking-horse ['stɔːkiŋhɔːs] n pretexto m.
stall [stɔːl] **1** n (a) (Agr: stable) establo m, (part of stable) casilla f de establo, (manger) pesebre m; (in market etc) puesto m, caseta f; (Theat) butaca f; (Eccl) silla f de coro; **orchestra** — (Theat) butaca f de platea.

2 vt (a) (Agr) encerrar en establo, guardar en establo (para engordar).

(b) (Aut etc) parar, cortar accidentalmente, atascar.

(c) **to** — **someone off** deshacerse de uno mediante algún pretexto, tener a uno a raya.

3 vi (a) (Aut etc) pararse, atascarse; (Aer) perder velocidad; **we** —**ed on a steep hill** quedamos parados en una cuesta abrupta, se nos atascó el motor en una cuesta abrupta.

(b) (fig) buscar evasivas, evitar contestar

directamente, ir con rodeos; **stop** —**ing**! ¡déjese de evasivas!; **the minister** —**ed for 20 minutes** durante 20 minutos el ministro evitó contestar directamente.

stall-fed ['stɔːlfed] *adj* engordado en establo.

stallholder ['stɔːl,həuldə*] *n* dueño *m* de un puesto (de mercado *etc*).

stallion ['stæliən] *n* caballo *m* padre, semental *m*.

stalwart ['stɔːlwət] **1** *adj* (*in build*) fornido, robusto; (*in spirit*) leal; valiente; cien por cien, incondicional; **a** — **supporter of** . . . partidario incondicional de . . . **2** *n* partidario *m* leal.

stamen ['steimen] *n* estambre *m*.

stamina ['stæminə] *n* resistencia *f*, nervio *m*, vigor *m*; **intellectual** — dotes *fpl* intelectuales; **has he enough** — **for the job?** ¿tiene bastante resistencia para el puesto?; **you need** — hace falta tener carácter.

stammer ['stæmə*] **1** *n* tartamudeo *m*, balbuceo *m*; **he has a bad** — tartamudea terriblemente.
  2 *vt* balbucir, decir tartamudeando (*also* **to** — **out**).
  3 *vi* tartamudear; balbucir.

stammerer ['stæmərə*] *n* tartamudo *m*, a *f*.

stammering ['stæməriŋ] **1** *adj* tartamudo. **2** *n* tartamudeo *m*.

stammeringly ['stæməriŋli] *adv*: **he said** — dijo tartamudeando.

stamp [stæmp] **1** *n* (a) (*with foot*) patada *f*; **with a** — **of her foot** dando una patada.
  (b) (*rubber* —) estampilla *f*; (*die*) cuño *m*, troquel *m*.
  (c) (*mark*) marca *f*, huella *f*, impresión *f*; **a man of his** — un hombre de su temple, (*pej*) un hombre de esa calaña; **it bears the** — **of genius** lleva el sello de la genialidad.
  (d) (*postage* —) sello *m* (de correos), estampilla *f* (SAm); (*fiscal* —, *revenue* —) timbre *m*, póliza *f*; (*trading* —) cupón *m*; **airmail** — sello *m* para correo aéreo; **commemorative** — conmemorativo *m*; **mint** — sello *m* en nuevo; **unused** — sello *m* sin usar; **used** — sello *m* usado.
  2 *vt* (a) **to** — **one's foot** patear, golpear con el pie; (*in dancing*) zapatear; (*of horse*) piafar; **they** —**ed out the rhythm** marcaron el ritmo con los pies; **to** — **something down** apisonar algo, comprimir algo con los pies.
  (b) (*impress mark etc on*) estampar, imprimir; (*fig*) marcar, señalar; sellar; **paper** —**ed with one's name** papel *m* con el nombre de uno impreso; **to** — **something on one's memory** grabar algo en la memoria de uno; **his manners** — **him a gentleman** sus modales aseguran que es un caballero.
  (c) (*mark with rubber* —) marcar con estampilla; (*mark with fiscal* —) timbrar; *letter* pegar un sello a, poner un sello en; franquear; **the letter is insufficiently** —**ed** la carta no lleva suficiente franqueo; **they** —**ed my passport at the frontier** sellaron mi pasaporte en la frontera.
  (d) **to** — **out** *fire* apagar pateando; (*fig*) extirpar, acabar con, desarraigar; **we must** — **out this abuse** tenemos que acabar con esta injusticia; **the doctors** —**ed out the epidemic** los médicos dominaron la epidemia.
  3 *vi* patear, golpear con los pies; pisar muy fuerte; (*disapprovingly*) patalear; (*of horse*) piafar; **he** —**s about the house** anda por la casa pisando muy fuerte; **to** — **on** pisotear, hollar; **someone** —**ed on my foot** alguien me pisoteó el pie.

stamp album ['stæmp,ælbəm] *n* álbum *m* para sellos.

stamp collecting ['stæmpkə,lektiŋ] *n* filatelia *f*.

stamp collector ['stæmpkə,lektə*] *n* filatelista *mf*.

stamp dealer ['stæmp,diːlə*] *n* comerciante *mf* en sellos (de correo).

stamped [stæmpt] *adj* *paper* sellado, timbrado; *envelope* con sello, que lleva sello.

stampede [stæm'piːd] **1** *n* estampida *f*; fuga *f* precipitada; movimiento *m* precipitado y unánime; **there was a sudden** — **for the door** de repente se precipitaron todos hacia la puerta; **the exodus turned into a** — el éxodo se transformó en una fuga precipitada.
  2 *vt* hacer huir en desorden; infundir un terror pánico a, causar terror en; **to** — **someone into doing something** infundir terror a uno para que haga algo; hacer que uno haga algo sin la debida reflexión; **let's not be** —**d** no obremos precipitadamente.
  3 *vi* huir en desorden, huir precipitadamente; **the horses suddenly** —**d** de repente los caballos se precipitaron hacia adelante presos de un terror pánico.

stamping ground ['stæmpiŋ,graund] *n* (*fam*) guarida *f*; **this is his private** — éste es terreno particular suyo, éste es coto cerrado de su propiedad; **to keep off someone's** — no invadir el territorio de uno.

stamp machine ['stæmpmə,ʃiːn] *n* expendedor *m* automático de sellos (de correo).

stance [stæns] *n* postura *f*; **to take up a** — adoptar una postura.

stanch [staːntʃ] *vt* *blood* restañar.

stanchion ['staːnʃən] *n* puntal *m*, montante *m*.

stand [stænd] **1** *n* (a) (*position*) posición *f*, postura *f*; **to take up one's** — **by the door** ponerse cerca de la puerta; **to take one's** — **on a principle** aferrarse a un principio, sentar cátedra sobre un principio; **to take a firm** — adoptar una actitud firme.
  (b) (*Mil*) parada *f*, alto *m*; resistencia *f*; **the** — **of the Australians at Tobruk** la resistencia de los australianos en Tobruk; **they turned and made a** — hicieron alto para resistir de nuevo al enemigo; **to make a** — **against something** oponer resistencia a algo, hacer frente a algo.
  (c) (*for taxis*) punto *m*, parada *f*.
  (d) (*Theat*) función *f*, representación *f*; **one-night** — función *f* de una sola noche, representación *f* única.
  (e) (*for lamp etc*) sostén *m*; pie *m*, pedestal *m*; (*for display*) mesilla *f*; (*hall*—) perchero *m*; (*Mus*) atril *m*.
  (f) (*in market etc*) puesto *m*; barraca *f*, caseta *f*; (*news*—) quiosco *m*; (*band*—) quiosco *m*; (*at exhibition*) stand *m*; (*Sport*) tribuna *f*; **to take the** — (*Law*) subir a la tribuna de los testigos, (*fig*) prestar declaración.
  2 (*irr: pret and ptp* **stood**) *vt* (a) (*place*) poner, colocar (de pie); **to** — **something (up) against a wall** poner algo contra una pared; **to** — **a vase on a table** poner un florero sobre una mesa.
  (b) **to** — **one's ground** mantenerse firme.
  (c) (*tolerate*) tolerar, aguantar, soportar; *examination* resistir a; *test* salir muy bien de; *cost* pagar, sufragar, correr con; **it won't** — **the cold** no resiste al frío; **it won't** — **serious examination** no resiste al examen cuidadoso; **his heart couldn't** — **the shock** su corazón no resistió al choque; **the company will have to** — **the loss** la compañía tendrá que encargarse de las pérdidas; **I can't** — **him** no le puedo ver; **I can't** — **Debussy** para mí Debussy es inaguantable; **I can** — **anything but that** lo aguanto todo menos eso; **I can't** — **it any longer!** ¡no aguanto más!, ¡no puedo más!; *see* **chance**.
  (d) **to** — **someone a drink** invitar a uno a beber, pagar la bebida de uno; **he stood beers all round** invitó a todos a tomar cerveza.
  (e) **to** — **workers off** suspender (temporalmente) a obreros (por falta de trabajo); **to** — **someone up** (*fam*) dar plantón a uno, dejar a uno plantado.
  3 *vi* (a) (*be upright*) estar de pie; (*get up*) levantarse, ponerse de pie; **all** —! (*Law*) ¡levántense!; — **at ease!** en su lugar ¡descanso!; **he could hardly** — apenas podía estar de pie; **to** — **at the bar** estar junto al bar; **to** — **in the doorway** estar en la puerta; **to** — **talking** seguir hablando; quedarse a hablar; **we stood chatting for half an hour** charlamos durante media hora, pasamos media hora charlando; **he left everybody else** —**ing** (*fig*) dejó a todos muy atrás; superó fácilmente a los demás; *see* **end**, **leg** *etc*.
  (b) (*of measurement*) medir; **the tree** —**s 30 metres high** el árbol mide 30 metros, el árbol tiene 30 metros de alto; **he** —**s a good 6 feet** mide 6 pies largos; **the mountain** —**s 3000 metres high** la montaña tiene una altura de 3000 metros.
  (c) (*be, be placed*) estar, estar situado, encontrarse; **it** —**s beside the town hall** está junto al ayuntamiento; **to buy a house as it** —**s** comprar una casa tal como está; **to let something** — **in the sun** poner algo al sol, dejar algo al sol; **the car has been** —**ing in the sun** el coche ha estado expuesto al sol; **nothing now** —**s between us** ya no existe ningún estorbo entre nosotros.
  (d) (*remain*) quedar en pie, mantenerse en vigor; (*last*) perdurar, durar; **the record** —**s at 10 minutes** el record está en 10 minutos, el tiempo récord sigue siendo de 10 minutos; **the objection** —**s** la objeción es válida, la objeción vale; **the contract** —**s** el contrato sigue en vigor; **the theory** —**s or falls by this** con esto o se confirma o se destruye la teoría; **it has stood for 600 years** ha durado 600 años ya, lleva ya 600 años de vida; *see* **fast**, **firm** *etc*.

(e) (*of temporary conditions*) **as things —, as it —s** tal como están las cosas; **how do we —?** ¿cómo estamos?; **I like to know where I —** me gusta estar enterado de mi situación (con relación a otras personas); **where do you — with him?** ¿cuáles son sus relaciones con él?; **to — well with someone** llevarse bien con uno, ser tenido en mucho por uno.

(f) (*remain undisturbed*) estar; sedimentar; **to allow a liquid to —** dejar estar un líquido; **let it — for 3 days** dejarlo así durante 3 días; **don't let the tea —** no dejes que se pase el té.

(g) (*special cases*) **to — as a candidate** presentarse como candidato; **to — (as) security for someone** (*Fin*) salir fiador de uno, (*fig*) salir por uno; **the thermometer —s at 40°** el termómetro marca 40 grados; **there is £50 —ing to your credit** Vd tiene 50 libras en el haber; **sales — at 5% more than last year** las ventas han aumentado en un 5 por cien en relación con el año pasado; **we — to lose a lot** para nosotros supondría una pérdida importante, estamos en peligro de perder bastante; **what do we — to gain by it?** ¿qué posibilidades hay para nosotros de ganar algo?, ¿qué ventaja nos daría esto?; **he —s to win £5** tiene la posibilidad de ganar 5 libras; *see need etc.*

(h) (*with adv or prep*) **to — about** estar, esperar, seguir en un sitio sin propósito fijo; **they just — about all day** pasan todo el día por ahí sin hacer nada; **they kept us —ing about for hours** nos hicieron esperar de pie durante horas enteras; **to — aside** apartarse, quitarse de en medio, hacerse a un lado; **to — back** (*person*) retroceder, moverse hacia atrás; (*be placed further back*) estar algo apartado; **the house —s back from the road** la casa está algo apartada de la carretera; **— back, please!** ¡más atrás, por favor!; **to — by** (*adv*) estar cerca; estar presente (sin intervenir); (*Mil etc*) estar alerta, mantenerse listo, estar dispuesto para el combate (*etc*); estar a la expectativa; **— by for further news** estén listos para recibir más noticias; **the Navy is —ing by to help** unidades de la Flota están dispuestas a prestar ayuda; **to — by** (*prep*) **person** apoyar, sostener, defender; no abandonar; **promise** cumplir, atenerse a; **we — by what we said** nos atenemos a lo dicho; **the Minister stood by his decision** el Ministro reafirmó su decisión; **to — down** (*withdraw*) retirarse; **the candidate is —ing down to let a younger man in** el candidato se retira y cede su puesto a otro más joven; **someone has to — down** alguien tiene que ceder su puesto; **you may — down** (*to withdraw*) Vd puede retirarse; **to — for** (*defend*) apoyar; hablar por; creer en; afirmar su adhesión a; (*be instead of*) representar; (*mean*) significar; **post** proponerse para, presentarse como candidato a; (*permit, tolerate*) aguantar, permitir, consentir; **"A —s for apple"** "M es de manzana"; **here a dash —s for a word** aquí una raya representa una palabra; **I'll not — for that** eso no lo permito, eso no se ha de consentir; **I'll not — for your whims any longer** no aguanto tus caprichos un momento más; **he stood for Parliament in 1906** se presentó como candidato en las elecciones parlamentarias de 1906; **he stood for Bristol** fue uno de los candidatos de Bristol; **he stood for Labour** fue candidato laborista; **to — in to the shore** acercarse a la playa; **to — in for someone** suplir a uno; **to — in with someone** declararse por uno, apoyar a uno, (*financially*) contribuir lo mismo que uno; **to — off** (*Naut*) apartarse, alejarse; **to — on ceremony** hacer ceremonias, estar de cumplido; **let's not — on ceremony** dejémonos de cumplidos; **to — out** destacarse (*against* contra, sobre); (*fig*) destacarse, descollar, sobresalir; **to — out against something** oponerse a algo; **to — out for something** insistir en algo, no ceder hasta obtener algo; **to — out in relief** aparecer en relieve; **to — out to sea** hacerse a la mar; **to — over** (*adv*) quedar en suspenso; **to let an item — over** dejar un asunto para la próxima vez; **to — over someone to see that he studies** vigilar a uno para asegurarse de que estudie; **to — to** (*Mil*) estar alerta, estar sobre las armas; **to — up** levantarse, ponerse de pie; **a brew so strong that a spoon could — up in it** un brebaje en el cual se podría mantener de pie una cuchara; **to — up for someone** defender a uno; **to — up for oneself** defenderse a sí mismo; **to — up to someone** resistir resueltamente a uno, hacer frente a uno; **to — up to a test** salir muy bien de una prueba; **it —s up to hard wear** es muy resistente; **it won't — up to close examination** no resiste al examen cuidadoso.

standard ['stændəd] **1** n **(a)** (*flag*) estandarte m, bandera f; **to raise the — of revolt** encabezar una sublevación, sublevarse.

(b) (*measure etc used as norm*) patrón m; pauta f, norma f; (*fig*) modelo m, regla f; **gold —** patrón m oro; **bureau of —s** (*US*) oficina f de pesos y medidas.

(c) (*moral*) criterio m; **—s** valores mpl morales; **he has good —s** tiene buen criterio; **she has no —s** carece de valores morales; **to apply a double —** aplicar un doble criterio; **to judge by that — ...** si lo juzgamos desde ese criterio ...

(d) (*degree of excellence*) nivel m, grado m; **— of living** nivel m de vida; **— of culture** nivel m de cultura; **at first-year university —** al nivel del primer año universitario; **of low —** de baja calidad; inferior; **to be below —** estar por debajo del nivel correcto, ser inferior; **to be up to —** estar conforme con el debido nivel; **to set a good —** establecer un buen nivel.

(e) (*Bot*) árbol m (*etc*) de tronco derecho; (*of small lamp*) pie m; (*of street lamp*) poste m.

2 adj, attr normal, corriente; standard, estándar; uniforme, estereotipado; **— measure** medida f tipo; **— model** modelo m standard; **— work of reference** obra f clásica de consulta; **S— English** inglés m correcto, buen inglés m; **— nomenclature** nomenclatura f oficial; **— price** precio m oficial, precio m normal; **— weight** peso m legal; **that word is hardly —** esa palabra apenas pertenece al léxico oficial; **the practice became — in the 1940s** la práctica llegó a ser corriente en los años 40.

standard bearer ['stændəd,bɛərə*] n abanderado m; (*fig*) jefe m, adalid m.

standard gauge ['stændəd'geidʒ] **1** n vía f normal. **2** adj **standard-gauge de** vía normal.

standardization [,stændədai'zeiʃən] n normalización f, estandar(d)ización f.

standardize ['stændədaiz] vt normalizar, regularizar, estandar(d)izar, uniformar.

stand-by ['stændbai] n **(a)** (*person*) persona f de toda confianza, persona f siempre dispuesta a prestar su ayuda; paño m de lágrimas; (*thing*) recurso m seguro, artículo m de toda confianza.

(b) alerta m; aviso m (para partir); **to be on 24-hours —** estar listo para partir dentro de 24 horas; **to put someone on 3-day —** avisar a uno para que esté listo para partir dentro de 3 días.

standee [stæn'di:] n (*US*) espectador m que asiste de pie.

stand-in ['stændin] n suplente mf (*for* de); (*Cine*) doble mf (*for* de).

standing ['stændiŋ] **1** adj **(a)** (*upright*) derecho; (*on foot*) de pie, en pie; **stone** derecho, vertical; **crop** que sigue creciendo, que está sin segar; **start** parado; **water** estancado, encharcado; **to leave someone —** dejar a uno muy atrás, (*fig*) aventajar a uno con mucho, resultar ser muy superior a uno.

(b) *army, committee, rule etc* permanente; *custom* arraigado; *grievance, joke* constante, eterno; *see* **order.**

2 n **(a)** (*position*) posición f, situación f; (*repute*) reputación f; categoría f; importancia f; **social —** posición f social; **of high —** de categoría; **the restaurant has a high —** el restaurante tiene una buena reputación; **a man of some —** un hombre de cierta categoría; **the relative — of these problems** la relativa importancia de estos problemas; **to be in good —** gozar de buen crédito; tener buena reputación; **what is his — locally?** ¿qué reputación tiene en la ciudad? (*etc*); **he has no — in this matter** no tiene voz ni voto en este asunto.

(b) (*duration*) duración f; existencia f; (*seniority*) antigüedad f; **of only 6 months' —** que existe desde hace 6 meses solamente; **a captain of only a month's —** un capitán que lleva solamente un mes en el puesto (*or* en tal graduación); **of long —** de mucho tiempo, existente desde hace mucho tiempo, viejo.

standing room ['stændiŋrum] n sitio m para estar de pie.

stand-offish ['stænd'ɔfiʃ] adj reservado, endiosado, que se da aires de superioridad; poco amable, frío.

stand-offishly ['stænd'ɔfiʃli] adv con poca amabilidad, fríamente.

stand-offishness ['stænd'ɔfiʃnis] n reserva f; endiosamiento m, superioridad f; falta f de amabilidad, frialdad f.

standpipe ['stændpaip] n columna f de alimentación; (*in street*) tubo m vertical.

standpoint ['stændpɔint] n punto m de vista; **from the — of ...** desde el punto de vista de ...

standstill ['stændstil] n parada f; paro m; alto m; paralización f; **to be at a** — estar parado; estar paralizado; **to bring a car to a** — parar un coche; **to bring an industry to a** — paralizar una industria; **to come to a** — (persons) pararse, hacer alto, (vehicle) pararse, (industry etc) quedar paralizado.

stand-up ['stændʌp] adj: — **buffet** cantina f donde se bebe y se come de pie; — **collar** cuello m alto; — **fight** pelea f violenta, riña f a puñetazos, (fig) altercado m violento.

stank [stæŋk] pret of **stink.**

stannic ['stænik] adj estánnico.

stanza ['stænzə] n estrofa f, estancia f.

staphylococcus [ˌstæfilə'kɔkəs] n, pl —cocci [kɔkai] estafilococo m.

staple[1] ['steipl] **1** n (fastener) grapa f. **2** vt (also to — together) unir con grapa.

staple[2] ['steipl] **1** adj principal; establecido; corriente; **their** — **food** su comida corriente.
   2 n (chief product) producto m principal; (raw material) materia f prima; (of wool) fibra f (textil); (of conversation etc) asunto m principal, elemento m esencial.

stapler ['steiplə*] n, **stapling machine** ['steipliŋˌmaʃiːn] n máquina f cosepapeles, máquina f grapadora.

star [stɑː*] **1** n **(a)** (Astron) estrella f, astro m; (Typ) asterisco m; **S—s and Stripes** (bandera f de) las barras y las estrellas; **evening** — estrella f vespertina; **fixed** — estrella f fija; **guiding** — estrella f de guía; **morning** — lucero m del alba; **north** — estrella f del norte; **polar** — estrella f polar; **to be born under a lucky** — nacer con estrella; **to believe in one's lucky** — creer en su buena estrella; **you can thank your lucky** —**s that** ... puedes dar las gracias a Dios porque . . .; **to see** —**s** (fig) ver las estrellas.
   (b) (person) figura f destacada, figura f más brillante; (Cine etc) astro m, estrella f, vedette f; **the** — **of the team was X** la figura más destacada del equipo fue X.
   2 adj, attr principal; destacado, más brillante; **their** — **player** su jugador más destacado, su jugador más brillante; — **role** cargo m estelar; — **show** programa m estelar; — **turn** atracción f especial, número m más destacado.
   3 vt **(a)** (adorn with —s) estrellar, adornar con estrellas, sembrar de estrellas; (mark with —) señalar con asterisco.
   (b) (Cine etc) presentar como estrella; **a film —ring Greta Garbo** una película que presenta a Greta Garbo en el papel principal.
   4 vi (Cine etc) ser el astro, ser la estrella; tener el papel principal; (be outstanding) destacar, descollar, actuar brillantemente; **the 3 films in which James Dean —red** las 3 películas que protagonizó James Dean; **he didn't exactly — in that game** en ese partido no destacó que digamos.

starboard ['stɑːbəd] **1** n estribor m; **on the** — **side** a estribor; **the sea to** — la mar a estribor; **land to** —! ¡tierra a estribor!
   2 vt: **to** — **the helm** poner el timón a estribor, virar a estribor.

starch [stɑːtʃ] **1** n almidón m; (in food) fécula f, cosas fpl feculentas. **2** vt almidonar.

starched [stɑːtʃt] adj almidonado.

starchy ['stɑːtʃi] adj feculento; (fig) estirado, entonado, etiquetero.

star-crossed ['stɑːˌkrɔst] adj malhadado, desventurado.

stardom ['stɑːdəm] n estrellato m; **to reach** — alcanzar el estrellato.

stare [steə*] **1** n mirada f fija; **stony** — mirada f dura; **vacant** — mirada f distraída; **to give someone a** — mirar fijamente a uno.
   2 vt: **to** — **someone out of countenance** desconcertar a uno mirándole fijamente; **it's staring you in the face** salta a la vista.
   3 vi mirar fijamente; **don't** —! ¡no mires tan fijo!; **it's rude to** — es de mala educación mostrar tanta curiosidad; **to** — **at someone** mirar fijamente a uno, clavar la vista en uno, (in surprise) mirar a uno con sorpresa; **to** — **into the distance, to** — **into space** mirar las telarañas.

starfish ['stɑːfiʃ] n estrella f de mar.

stargaze ['stɑːgeiz] vi mirar las estrellas; (fig) distraerse, mirar las telarañas.

stargazer ['stɑːˌgeizə*] n astrónomo m.

stargazing ['stɑːˌgeiziŋ] n estudio m de las estrellas; astronomía f; (fig) distracción f.

staring ['steəriŋ] adj que mira fijamente, curioso; eyes saltón, (in fear) lleno de espanto.

stark [stɑːk] **1** adj (stiff) rígido; (utter) completo,

puro; (unadorned) escueto, severo; cliff etc espantoso, ceñudo.
   2 adv: — **(staring) mad** loco de atar; — **naked** en cueros, en pelota, como le parió su madre.

starless ['stɑːlis] adj sin estrellas.

starlet ['stɑːlit] n estrella f joven, estrella f en ciernes, aspirante f a estrella.

starlight ['stɑːlait] n luz f de las estrellas; **by** — a la luz de las estrellas.

starling ['stɑːliŋ] n estornino m.

starlit ['stɑːlit] adj iluminado por las estrellas.

starry ['stɑːri] adj estrellado, sembrado de estrellas.

starry-eyed ['stɑːri'aid] adj inocentón, ingenuo; idealista, poco práctico; lleno de amor (or entusiasmo etc) candoroso.

star shell ['stɑːʃel] n cohete m luminoso, bengala f iluminadora.

star-spangled ['stɑːˌspæŋgld] adj estrellado.

start [stɑːt] **1** n **(a)** (fright etc) susto m, sobresalto m; (of horse) respingo m; **to give a sudden** — sobresaltarse; **to give someone a** — asustar a uno, dar un susto a uno; **what a** — **you gave me!** ¡qué susto me diste!; **to wake with a** — despertarse sobresaltado; see **fit.**
   (b) (beginning) principio m, comienzo m; (departure) salida f, partida f; (of race) salida f; **false** — falso comienzo m; **flying** —, **running** — salida f lanzada; **standing** — salida f parada; **at the** — al principio; **at the very** — muy al principio, en los mismos comienzos; **at the** — **of the century** a principios del siglo; **we are at the** — **of something big** estamos en los comienzos de algo grandioso; **for a** — en primer lugar, para empezar; **from the** — desde el principio; **from** — **to finish** desde el principio hasta el fin, de cabo a rabo; **to get off to a good (or flying)** — empezar bien, (fig) comenzar felizmente, entrar con buen pie; **to give someone a** — **in life** ayudar a uno a situarse en la vida; **the review gave the book a good** — la reseña ayudó al libro a venderse bien desde el principio; **to make a** — empezar; **to make an early** — ponerse en camino sin perder tiempo; **to make a fresh (or new)** — **in life** hacer vida nueva, empezar de nuevo; **to make a good** — **(in life)** emprender felizmente su carrera.
   (c) (advantage) ventaja f; **to give someone a 5 minute** — dar a uno una ventaja de 5 minutos.
   2 vt **(a)** (begin) comenzar, empezar; iniciar; principiar; discussion etc abrir, iniciar; (undertake) emprender; **to** — **negotiations** iniciar las negociaciones; **to** — **a new life** comenzar una vida nueva; **to** — **a novel** empezar a escribir (or leer) una novela; **don't** — **that again!** ¡no vuelvas a eso!
   (b) to — **a race** dar la señal de salida para una carrera.
   (c) to — **a partridge** levantar una perdiz.
   (d) (cause) causar, provocar; **to** — **a fire** causar un incendio; **it** —**ed the collapse of the empire** causó el derrumbamiento del imperio.
   (e) (found) fundar, crear; **to** — **an enterprise** fundar una empresa; **to** — **a newspaper** fundar un periódico.
   (f) (Mech) poner en marcha, hacer funcionar; car, engine arrancar; clock poner en marcha.
   (g) (with personal object) **to** — **someone reminiscing** hacer que uno empiece a contar sus recuerdos; **once you** — **him on that** en cuanto le pones a hablar de eso; **to** — **someone on a career** ayudar a uno a emprender una carrera.
   (h) (with adv or prep) **to** — **off, to** — **up** see **2 (a)** etc.
   3 vi **(a)** (in fright) asustarse, sobresaltarse, sobrecogerse (at a, with de); **to** — **back** retroceder; **to** — **back in horror** retroceder horrorizado; **to** — **from one's chair** levantarse asustado de su silla; **to** — **out of one's sleep** despertarse sobresaltado; **his eyes** — **ing out of his head** se le saltaban los ojos de la cabeza; **to** — **up** incorporarse bruscamente, ponerse de pie de un salto.
   (b) (of timber etc) combarse, torcerse; (of rivets etc) soltarse.
   (c) (begin) comenzar, empezar; principiar; iniciarse; (on journey) partir, ponerse en camino; (of bus, train) salir; (in race) salir; (car, engine etc) arrancar, ponerse en marchar; empezar a funcionar; —**ing from Tuesday** a partir del martes; **the route** —**s from here** la ruta sale de aquí; **to** — **afresh** volver a empezar, comenzar de nuevo; **to** — **at the beginning** empezar desde el principio; **to** — **with a prayer** empezar con una oración; **what shall we** — **with?** ¿con qué empezamos?; **to** — **with** (as adv phrase) en primer lugar, para empezar.

(d) *(with verb constructions)* **to — to** + *infin* comenzar *(or* empezar*)* a + *infin;* **to — talking** empezar a hablar; **to — by saying** comenzar diciendo.
(e) *(with adv or prep)* **to — after someone** ir en busca de uno; ir en pos de uno; **to — back** emprender el viaje de regreso; **to — off, to — out** *(begin)* comenzar; empezar; *(on journey)* partir, ponerse en camino, *(of bus, train)* salir; **it —s off with a murder** comienza con un asesinato; **it —ed out as a play** empezó como una obra dramática; **to — on a task** emprender una tarea; **to — on something new** emprender algo nuevo; **to — up** comenzar, empezar; **then the band —ed up** luego empezó a tocar la orquesta; **when I —ed up in business** cuando yo monté el negocio; cuando empecé mi carrera en los negocios.
starter ['stɑːtə*] *n* **(a)** *(person)* *(judge)* juez *m* de salida; *(competitor)* corredor *m*, ora *f*; caballo *m* *(etc)*. **(b)** *(Aut etc: motor)* motor *m* de arranque; *(button)* botón *m* de arranque.
starting gate ['stɑːtɪŋgeit] *n* barrera *f* que se levanta para dar la salida.
starting handle ['stɑːtɪŋˌhændl] *n* manivela *f* de arranque.
starting line ['stɑːtɪŋlain] *n* línea *f* de salida.
starting motor ['stɑːtɪŋˌməutə*] *n* motor *m* de arranque.
starting point ['stɑːtɪŋpɔint] *n* punto *m* de partida, punto *m* de arranque.
starting post ['stɑːtɪŋpəust] *n* poste *m* de salida.
starting price ['stɑːtɪŋprais] *n* puntos *mpl* de ventaja al empezar la carrera.
starting switch ['stɑːtɪŋswitʃ] *n* botón *m* de arranque.
startle ['stɑːtl] *vt* asustar, sobrecoger; alarmar; **to — someone out of his serenity** asustar tanto a uno que sale de su tranquilidad.
startling ['stɑːtlɪŋ] *adj* asombroso, sorprendente; alarmante; sobrecogedor; *colour etc* chillón; *dress etc* llamativo, exagerado.
starvation [stɑː'veiʃən] **1** *n* hambre *f*, *(Med)* inanición *f*; *(fig)* privación *f*; **to die of —** morir de hambre.
2 *attr:* **— diet** régimen *m* de hambre; **— wages** sueldo *m* miserable.
starve [stɑːv] **1** *vt* **(a)** *(kill)* hacer morir de hambre; *(deprive of food)* privar de comida, hacer pasar hambre; **to — someone to death** hacer a uno morir de hambre; **to — a town into surrender** hacer que una ciudad se rinda por hambre; **to — a garrison out** hacer que una guarnición se rinda por hambre.
(b) *(fig)* **to — someone of something** privar a uno de algo; **to be —d of affection** estar privado de cariño *(paternal etc)*.
2 *vi* **(a)** *(die)* morir de hambre; *(lack food)* pasar hambre, padecer hambre; **to — to death** morir de hambre.
(b) *(fig)* morir de hambre; **I'm simply starving!** ¡estoy muerto de hambre!, ¡qué hambre tengo!
starving ['stɑːvɪŋ] *adj* hambriento, famélico.
stash [stæʃ] *vt* *(fam):* **to — away** ir acumulando; ocultar para uso futuro.
state [steit] **1** *n* **(a)** *(condition)* estado *m*, condición *f*; **— of emergency** estado *m* de emergencia; **to declare a — of emergency** declarar el estado de emergencia; **— of health** salud *f*, estado *m* físico; **— of mind** estado *m* de ánimo; **— of siege** estado *m* de sitio; **— of war** estado *m* de guerra; **— of weightlessness** estado *m* de ingravidez; **the married —** el estado matrimonial; **the single —** el estado célibe; **in a comatose —** en estado comatoso; **races still in a savage —** razas *fpl* todavía en estado de salvajismo; **to be in a bad —** estar en mal estado; **to be in a good —** estar en buenas condiciones; **he's not in a (fit) — to do it** no está en condiciones para hacerlo; **he arrived home in a shocking —** llegó a casa en un estado espantoso.
(b) *(anxiety)* agitación *f*; estado *m* nervioso; **to be in a great —** estar muy agitado, estar aturrulado; **now don't get into a — about it** no te pongas nervioso.
(c) *(rank)* rango *m*, dignidad *f*; **he attained the — of bishop** llegó a la dignidad de obispo.
(d) *(pomp)* pompa *f*, fausto *m*; ceremonia *f*; **in —** con gran pompa; **to dine in —** cenar con mucha ceremonia; **to live in —** vivir lujosamente; **to travel in —** viajar con gran pompa; **to lie in —** estar de cuerpo presente, estar expuesto en capilla ardiente.
(e) *(Pol)* estado *m*; **the S—** el Estado; **the S—s** *(US)* Estados *mpl* Unidos; **a — within a —** un estado dentro del estado; **affairs of —** asuntos *mpl* de Estado; **Church and S—** Iglesia y Estado;

Secretary of S— *(US)* Ministro *m* de Asuntos Exteriores; **Secretary of S— for . . .** Ministro *m* de . . .
2 *adj, attr* *(Pol etc)* estatal, del Estado; público; **— control** control *m* público; **S— Department** *(US)* Ministerio *m* de Asuntos Exteriores; **— education** enseñanza *f* pública; **— papers** documentos *mpl* de Estado; **— secret** secreto *m* de Estado.
(b) *apartment, banquet, coach etc* de gala.
3 *vt* **(a)** declarar, afirmar, decir; manifestar; consignar, hacer constar; **as —d above** como se ha dicho arriba; **it is nowhere —d that . . .** no se dice en ninguna parte que . . .; **I have seen it —d that . . .** he visto afirmarse que . . .; **he is —d to have been there** se afirma que él estuvo allí; **— your name** escriba su nombre; **cheques must — the amount clearly** los cheques han de consignar claramente la cantidad; **it must be —d in the records** ha de hacerse constar en los archivos.
(b) *case* exponer, explicar; *law* formular; *problem* plantear, exponer; **to — the case for the prosecution** explicar los hechos en que se basa la acusación.
statecraft ['steitkrɑːft] *n* arte *m* de gobernar.
stated ['steitid] *adj* dicho; indicado; fijo, establecido; **the sum —** la cantidad dicha; **on the — date** en la fecha indicada; **within — limits** dentro de límites fijos.
statehood ['steithud] *n* categoría *f* de estado, dignidad *f* de estado; **when the country achieves —** cuando el país alcance la categoría de estado.
stateless ['steitlis] *adj* desnacionalizado, sin patria.
stateliness ['steitlinis] *n* majestad *f*, majestuosidad *f*.
stately ['steitli] *adj* majestuoso; imponente; augusto; **— home** casa *f* solariega.
statement ['steitmənt] *n* declaración *f*, afirmación *f*, manifestación *f*; informe *m*, relación *f*; exposición *f*; *(Law)* declaración *f*; **— of account** estado *m* de cuenta; **official —** informe *m* oficial, nota *f* oficial; **according to his own —** según su propia declaración; **to make a —** *(Law)* prestar declaración.
stateroom ['steitrum] *n* *(Naut)* camarote *m*.
statesman ['steitsmən] *n, pl* **—men** [mən] estadista *m*, hombre *m* de estado; **elder —** viejo estadista *m*; *(fig)* consejero *m* de máxima autoridad; figura *f* muy respetada.
statesmanlike ['steitsmənlaik] *adj* (digno) de estadista.
statesmanship ['steitsmənʃip] *n* arte *m* de gobernar; habilidad *f* de estadista; **that showed true —** eso demostró su verdadera capacidad de estadista; **— alone will not solve the problem** la habilidad de los estadistas no resolverá el problema por sí sola.
static ['stætik] *adj* inactivo, inmóvil, estancado; *(Phys)* estático.
statics ['stætiks] *npl* *(Phys)* estática *f*; *(Radio)* parásitos *mpl*.
station ['steiʃən] **1** *n* **(a)** *(place)* puesto *m*, sitio *m*; situación *f*; **Roman —** sitio *m* ocupado por los romanos; **the only — for this rare plant** el único sitio donde existe esta planta tan poco frecuente; **action —s!** ¡a los puestos de combate!; **from my — by the window** desde el sitio donde yo estaba junto a la ventana; **to take up one's —** colocarse, ir a su puesto.
(b) *(— in life)* posición *f* social; puesto *m* en la sociedad; **of humble —** de baja posición social, de condición humilde; **a man of exalted —** un hombre de rango elevado; **to marry below one's —** casarse con un hombre *(or* una mujer*)* de posición social inferior; **to get ideas above one's —** darse aires de superioridad, darse tono.
(c) *(specific)* estación *f*; *(Radio)* emisora *f*; *(Rail)* estación *f* (de ferrocarril); **coaling —** estación *f* carbonera; **frontier —** puesto *m* de frontera; **goods —** estación *f* de mercancías; **naval —** apostadero *m* naval; **pumping —** estación *f* de bombeo; **S—s of the Cross** Estaciones *fpl* del vía Crucis.
2 *vt* colocar, situar; *(Mil)* estacionar, apostar.
3 *vr:* **to — oneself** colocarse, situarse.
stationary ['steiʃənəri] *adj* estacionario; inmóvil; *engine etc* estacionario, fijo; **to remain —** *(person)* quedar inmóvil, estar sin moverse.
stationer ['steiʃənə*] *n* papelero *m*, a *f*; **—'s (shop)** papelería *f*.
stationery ['steiʃənəri] *n* papelería *f*, papel *m* de escribir, efectos *mpl* de escritorio.
station house ['steiʃənˌhaus] *n, pl* **— houses** [ˌhauziz] *(US: Rail)* estación *f* de ferrocarril; *(police)* cuartel *m* de policía.
station master ['steiʃənˌmɑːstə*] *n* jefe *m* de estación.

station wagon ['steiʃən,wægən] n combinable f, rubia f.
statistic [stə'tistik] n estadística f, número m.
statistical [stə'tistikəl] adj estadístico.
statistically [stə'tistikəli] adv: **to prove something** — probar algo por medios estadísticos; — **that may be true** en cuanto a la estadística eso puede ser cierto.
statistician [,stætis'tiʃən] n estadístico m.
statistics [stə'tistiks] n (subject) estadística f; (numbers) estadísticas fpl; **vital** — estadísticas fpl demográficas, (hum) medidas fpl vitales.
stator ['steitə*] n (Elec, Math) estator m.
statuary ['stætjuəri] **1** adj estatuario. **2** n (art) estatuaria f; (statues) estatuas fpl; (person) estatuario m.
statue ['stætju:] n estatua f.
statuesque [,stætju'esk] adj estatuario, escultural.
statuette [,stætju'et] n figurilla f.
stature ['stætʃə*] n (a) estatura f, talla f; **to be of short** — ser de estatura baja, tener poca talla.
    (b) (fig) talla f; valor m, carácter m; **to have sufficient** — **for a post** estar a la altura de un cargo; **he lacks moral** — le falta carácter.
status ['steitəs] n posición f, condición f; rango m, categoría f; prestigio m; reputación f; (Law) estado m; **civil** —, **marital** — estado m civil; **social** — posición f social; **the** — **of the Negro population** la posición social de la población negra; **what is his** — **in the profession?** ¿qué rango ocupa en la profesión?, ¿cómo se le considera en la profesión?; **he has not sufficient** — **for the job** no tiene categoría bastante alta para ocupar este cargo.
status quo ['steitəs'kwəu] n statu m quo.
status symbol ['steitəs,simbəl] n símbolo m de prestigio.
statute ['stætju:t] n ley f, estatuto m; — **law** ley f escrita; **by** — según la ley, de acuerdo con la ley.
statute book ['stætju:tbuk] n código m de leyes.
statutory ['stætjutəri] adj estatutario; legal.
staunch[1] [stɔ:ntʃ] adj leal, firme, incondicional.
staunch[2] [stɔ:ntʃ] vt see stanch.
staunchly ['stɔ:ntʃli] adv lealmente, firmemente, incondicionalmente.
staunchness ['stɔ:ntʃnis] n lealtad f, firmeza f.
stave [steiv] **1** n (of barrel) duela f; (of ladder) peldaño m; (Mus) pentagrama m; (Lit) estrofa f.
    2 (irr: pret and ptp stove or staved) vt: **to** — **in** romper, quebrar a golpes; abrir a golpes; desfondar; **to** — **off** attack rechazar; apartar, mantener a distancia; threat etc evitar, conjurar; (delay) diferir; aplazar.
staves [steivz] npl of staff.
stay[1] [stei] **1** n **(a)** estancia f, permanencia f; visita f; **a** — **of 10 days** una estancia de 10 días; **our second** — **in Murcia** nuestra segunda visita a Murcia; **come for a longer** — **next year** ven a estar más tiempo el año que viene.
    (b) (Law) suspensión f, prórroga f; — **of execution** aplazamiento m de una sentencia; — **of proceedings** sobreseimiento m.
    2 vt **(a)** detener; controlar; poner freno a; epidemic etc tener a raya; hunger matar, engañar; **to** — **one's hand** contenerse, detenerse; **to** — **someone's hand** parar la mano a uno.
    (b) (Law) suspender, prorrogar; aplazar.
    3 vi **(a)** (wait) esperar; —! ¡espera!
    (b) (remain) quedar, quedarse, permanecer; (as guest etc) hospedarse, estar, vivir; **you** — **right there** tú te quedas ahí, no te muevas de ahí; **to** — **at home** quedarse en casa; **to** — **in bed** guardar cama; **how long can you** —? ¿hasta cuándo te puedes quedar?; **what? you** —**ed for the Debussy?** ¿cómo? ¿os quedasteis a escuchar lo de Debussy?; **to** — **for supper, to** — **to supper** quedarse a cenar; **to** — **at an hotel** hospedarse en un hotel; **to** — **with friends** hospedarse con unos amigos; **where are you** —**ing?** ¿dónde vives?; **she came for a weekend and** —**ed 3 years** vino a pasar el fin de semana y permaneció 3 años.
    (c) (remain, with adj) **it** —**s red** sigue tan rojo como antes; **if it** —**s fine** si continúa el buen tiempo, si el tiempo sigue bueno; **it** —**s motionless for hours** sigue durante horas enteras sin moverse.
    (d) (last out) resistir; **the horse doesn't** — el caballo no resiste esa distancia, el caballo no tiene bastante resistencia; **can he** — **3 miles?** ¿aguanta 3 millas?; **to** — **the course** terminar la carrera, (fig) continuar hasta el final.
    (e) (with adv or prep) **to** — **away** ausentarse (from de), no asistir (from a); **you** — **away from my daughter!** ¡no venga por aquí a molestar a mi hija!; — **away from that switch** no to acerques a

ese interruptor, no toques ese interruptor; **to** — **behind** quedarse; quedarse en casa, no salir; (in race) rezagarse; **to make someone** — **behind after school** hacer que uno se quede en la escuela después de las clases; **to** — **in** quedarse en casa, no salir; (School) quedarse después de las clases (como castigo); **the cork won't** — **in** el corcho no quiere entrar (en la botella etc); **to** — **on** quedarse; permanecer, continuar en su lugar; **he** —**ed on as manager** pasó a ser gerente en la misma compañía; **they** —**ed on after everyone else had left** se quedaron después de que todos los demás se habían marchado; **the lid won't** — **on** la tapa no quiere estar en su lugar; **to** — **out** quedarse fuera, no volver a casa; **to** — **out of something** no tomar parte en algo; **you** — **out of this!** ¡Vd no se meta en esto!; **she** —**s out till midnight** no vuelve a casa hasta medianoche; **to** — **over** pasar la noche, pernoctar; quedarse un poco; see **put 1 (h)**; **to** — **up** velar, no acostarse, seguir sin acostarse; **Spanish children** — **up later than English ones** los niños españoles se acuestan más tarde que los ingleses; **they** —**ed up for me** estuvieron esperándome sin acostarse.
stay[2] [stei] **1** n (Mech) sostén m, soporte m, puntal m; (Naut) estay m; (fig) sostén m, apoyo m; —**s** corsé m; **the** — **of one's old age** el sostén de su vejez.
    2 vt sostener, apoyar, apuntalar; **this will** — **you till lunchtime** esto te ayudará a resistir hasta la comida, esto engañará el hambre hasta la comida.
stay-at-home ['steiəthəum] **1** adj casero, hogareño. **2** n persona f casera, persona f que apenas tiene ganas de salir de su casa.
stayer ['steiə*] n (horse) caballo m apto para carreras de distancia; (person) persona f de carácter firme, persona f de mucho aguante.
staying power ['steiiŋ,pauə*] n resistencia f, aguante m.
staysail ['steiseil, Naut 'steisl] n vela f de estay.
stead [sted] n: **in his** — en su lugar; **to stand someone in good** — ser útil a uno, aprovechar a uno.
steadfast ['stedfəst] adj firme, resuelto; constante; tenaz; gaze fijo; — **in adversity** firme en el infortunio; — **in danger** impertérrito; — **in love** constante en el amor.
steadfastly ['stedfəstli] adv firmemente, resueltamente; con constancia; tenazmente; fijamente.
steadfastness ['stedfəstnis] n firmeza f, resolución f; constancia f; tenacidad f; fijeza f.
steadily ['stedili] adv firmemente, fijamente; de modo estable; regularmente, constantemente, uniformemente; continuamente; sin parar, ininterrumpidamente; sensatamente; seriamente; diligentemente; tranquilamente; resueltamente; imperturbablemente; **it gets** — **worse** se hace cada vez peor; **the temperature goes** — **up** la temperatura sube constantemente, la temperatura no deja de subir; **to work** — trabajar ininterrumpidamente; **she looked at me** — me miró sin pestañear.
steadiness ['stedinis] n firmeza f, fijeza f; estabilidad f; regularidad f, constancia f, uniformidad f; sensatez f, juicio m; seriedad f, formalidad f; diligencia f; serenidad f, ecuanimidad f; sangre f fría; imperturbabilidad f.
steady ['stedi] **1** adj firme, fijo; estable; regular, constante, uniforme; continuo, ininterrumpido; (in character) sensato, juicioso; serio, formal; (at work) diligente, trabajador; aplicado; boyfriend etc formal; (not nervous) sereno, tranquilo, ecuánime; resuelto; imperturbable; — **demand** demanda f constante; — **temperature** temperatura f constante, temperatura f uniforme; — **progress** progreso m ininterrumpido; — **job** empleo m seguro, empleo m fijo; **with a** — **hand** con mano firme; **at a** — **pace** a paso regular; **the car is very** — **at corners** el coche es muy estable en las curvas; **there was a** — **downpour for 3 hours** llovió sin interrupción durante 3 horas; **we were going at a** — **70 kph** íbamos a una velocidad uniforme de 70 kph; **he plays a very** — **game** juega muy sensatamente.
    2 adv: —! ¡con calma!, despacio!; **they are going** — **now** (fam) son novios formales ya; **they've been going** — **for 6 months** (fam) llevan 6 meses de relaciones; **is he going** — **with her?** (fam) ¿es novio formal de ella?
    3 n (fam) novio m formal, novia f formal.
    4 vt (hold) mantener firme, sujetar en posición firme; (stabilize) estabilizar, hacer más estable; uniformar, regularizar; nerves calmar; nervous person tranquilizar, wild person hacer que siente la cabeza (also **to** — **down, to** — **up**).

5 *vi* estabilizarse, hacerse más estable; uniformarse, regularizarse; calmarse; tranquilizarse; sentar la cabeza (*also* **to — down, to — up**).

6 *vr:* **to — oneself** afirmarse, recobrar el equilibrio; **to — oneself against something** apoyarse en algo.

steak [steik] *n* biftec *m*; filete *m*; (*of meat other than beef*) tajada *f*; **underdone** — filete *m* poco hecho; **— and kidney pie** pastel *m* de biftec y riñones.

steakhouse ['steikhaus] *n*, *pl* **—houses** [ˌhauziz] restaurante especializado en servir biftecs.

steak knife ['steiknaif] *n*, *pl* **— knives**[naivz] cuchillo *m* para el biftec.

steal [sti:l] (*irr: pret* **stole**, *ptp* **stolen**) **1** *vt* robar, hurtar; (*fig*) robar; **to — a glance at someone** mirar de soslayo a uno, mirar rápidamente a uno.

2 *vi:* **— away, to — off** marcharse sigilosamente, escabullirse; **to — into a room** deslizarse en un cuarto, entrar en un cuarto sin ruido; **to — up on someone** acercarse a uno sin ruido.

stealth [stelθ] *n* cautela *f*, sigilo *m*; **by —** a escondidas, a hurtadillas.

stealthily ['stelθili] *adv* clandestinamente, a hurtadillas.

stealthiness ['stelθinis] *n* cautela *f*, sigilo *m*; cáracter *m* furtivo.

stealthy ['stelθi] *adj* cauteloso, sigiloso, furtivo; clandestino.

steam [sti:m] **1** *n* vapor *m*; vaho *m*, humo *m*; **waste —** vapor *m* de escape; **wet —** vapor *m* húmedo; **full — ahead!** ¡todo avante!; **to get up —** acumular vapor, dar presión; **to let off —** descargar vapor, (*fig*) desahogarse; **the ship went on under its own —** el buque siguió adelante con sus propios motores.

2 *attr* de vapor.

3 *vt* (a) (*Cook*) cocer al vapor.

(b) *window* empañar (*also* **to — up**); **the windows quickly get —ed up** las ventanas se empañan pronto.

(c) **to — open an envelope** abrir un sobre por medio de vapor; **to — a stamp off** separar un sello por medio de vapor.

4 *vi* (a) (*give out —*) echar vapor; **the bowl was —ing on the table** la cacerola humeaba en la mesa.

(b) (*move etc, function*) **to — ahead** avanzar, (*fig*) adelantarse mucho; **to — along** ir, avanzar (echando vapor); **we were —ing at 12 knots** íbamos a 12 nudos; **the ship —ed into harbour** el buque entró al puerto (echando humo); **the train —ed out** salió el tren (echando humo).

(c) **to — up** (*of window*) empañarse.

steamboat ['sti:mbǝut] *n* vapor *m*, buque *m* de vapor.

steam-driven ['sti:mˌdrivn] *adj* impulsado por vapor, a vapor.

steam engine ['sti:mˌendʒin] *n* máquina *f* de vapor.

steam hammer ['sti:mˌhæmǝ*] *n* maza *f* de fragua.

steamer ['sti:mǝ*] *n* vapor *m*, buque *m* de vapor.

steamroller ['sti:mˌrǝulǝ*] **1** *n* apisonadora *f*.

2 *vt* allanar con apisonadora; (*fig*) aplastar, arrollar; **to — a bill through parliament** hacer aprobar un proyecto de ley sin tener en cuenta los derechos de la oposición.

steamship ['sti:mˌʃip] *n* vapor *m*, buque *m* de vapor; **— company** compañía *f* naviera; **— line** línea *f* de vapores.

steam shovel ['sti:mˌʃʌvl] *n* pala *f* mecánica de vapor, excavadora *f*.

steam turbine ['sti:mˌtǝ:bain] *n* turbina *f* de vapor.

steamy ['sti:mi] *adj* vaporoso; *room etc* lleno de vapor; *atmosphere* húmedo y de mucho calor; *window* empañado.

steed [sti:d] *n* (*lit*) corcel *m*.

steel [sti:l] **1** *n* acero *m*; (*sharpener*) acero *m*, eslabón *m*; (*for striking spark*) eslabón *m*; **stainless —** acero *m* inoxidable; **to be made of —** (*fig*) ser de bronce; **to fight with cold —** luchar con armas blancas.

2 *adj*, *attr* de acero; acerado; **— industry** industria *f* siderúrgica.

3 *vt* acerar; revestir de acero; **to — one's heart** hacerse duro de corazón; **to — one's men** infundir valor a los suyos.

4 *vr:* **to — oneself** fortalecerse (*against* contra); **to — oneself to do something** cobrar bastante ánimo para hacer algo, persuadirse a hacer algo.

steel-clad ['sti:lklæd] *adj* revestido de acero, acorazado.

steel mill ['sti:lmil] *n* acería *f*, fábrica *f* de acero; fábrica *f* siderúrgica.

steel wool ['sti:l'wul] *n* virutillas *fpl* de acero.

steelworks ['sti:lwǝ:ks] *n* acería *f*, fábrica *f* de acero, fábrica *f* siderúrgica.

steely ['sti:li] *adj* acerado; (*fig*) inflexible, duro; *gaze* duro.

steelyard ['sti:ljɑːd] *n* romana *f*.

steep[1] [sti:p] *adj* (a) escarpado, abrupto; *cliff etc* cortado a pico, precipitoso; *stairs etc* empinado; **a — slope** una fuerte pendiente; **it's too — for the tractor** es demasiado fuerte para el tractor; **it's a — climb** la subida es difícil.

(b) (*fig*) *price etc* exorbitante, excesivo; *story etc* difícil de creer, increíble; **that's pretty —!** ¡eso es demasiado!, ¡no hay derecho!; **it seems a bit — that ...** no parece razonable que + *subj*.

steep[2] [sti:p] **1** *vt* empapar, remojar (*in* en); **—ed in** (*fig*) saturado de, impregnado de, empapado en; **a town —ed in history** una ciudad saturada de historia.

2 *vi:* **to leave something to —** dejar algo en remojo.

steeple ['sti:pl] *n* aguja *f*, campanario *m*, torre *f*.

steeplechase ['sti:plˌtʃeis] *n* carrera *f* de obstáculos.

steeplechasing ['sti:plˌtʃeisiŋ] *n* deporte *m* de las carreras de obstáculos.

steeplejack ['sti:pldʒæk] *n* reparador *m* de chimeneas, torres *etc*.

steeply ['sti:pli] *adv*: **the mountain rises —** la montaña está cortada a pico; **the road climbs —** la carretera sube en fuerte pendiente; **prices have risen —** los precios han subido muchísimo.

steepness ['sti:pnis] *n* lo escarpado, lo abrupto; lo precipitoso; lo fuerte.

steer[1] [stiǝ*] **1** *vt* guiar, dirigir; *car etc* conducir; *ship* gobernar; **to — one's way through a crowd** abrirse paso por entre una multitud; **you nearly —ed us into that rock** por poco dimos con aquella roca; **I —ed her across to the bar** la llevé hacia el bar.

2 *vi* conducir; gobernar; **who's going to —?** ¿quién manejará el volante (*or* timón *etc*)?; **can you —?** ¿sabes gobernar el barco (*etc*)?; **to — for** dirigirse a, dirigirse hacia, ir con rumbo a; **to — clear of** evitar cualquier contacto con.

steer[2] [stiǝ*] *n* buey *m*; novillo *m*.

steerage ['stiǝridʒ] *n* entrepuente *m*; **to go —** viajar en tercera clase.

steering ['stiǝriŋ] *n* (*Aut etc*) dirección *f*, conducción *f*; (*Naut*) gobierno *m*.

steering arm ['stiǝriŋɑːm] *n* brazo *m* de dirección.

steering column ['stiǝriŋˌkɔlǝm] *n* columna *f* de dirección.

steering committee ['stiǝriŋkǝ'miti] *n* comisión *f* de iniciativas, comisión *f* planificadora.

steering gear ['stiǝriŋ'giǝ*] *n* mecanismo *m* de dirección.

steering wheel ['stiǝriŋwi:l] *n* volante *m* (de dirección).

steersman ['stiǝzmǝn] *n*, *pl* **—men** [mǝn] timonero *m*.

stellar ['stelǝ*] *adj* estelar.

stem [stem] **1** *n* (*of plant*) tallo *m*, (*of tree*) tronco *m*, (*of leaf etc*) pedúnculo *m*; (*of glass*) pie *m*; (*of pipe*) cañón *m*, tubo *m*; (*Mech*) vástago *m*; (*of word*) tema *m*; (*Naut*) roda *f*, tajamar *m*; **from — to stern** de proa a popa.

2 *vt* (*check, stop*) refrenar, detener; *flood* represar; *attack* rechazar; *flow of blood* restañar.

3 *vi:* **to — from** provenir de, proceder de, resultar de.

stench [stentʃ] *n* hedor *m*.

stencil ['stensl] **1** *n* (*Tech*) patrón *m* picado, estarcido *m*; (*for lettering*) plantilla *f*; (*for typing*) cliché *m*, clisé *m*.

2 *vt* estarcir; (*in typing*) hacer un cliché de.

stenographer [ste'nɔgrǝfǝ*] *n* taquígrafo *m*, a *f*.

stenography [ste'nɔgrǝfi] *n* taquigrafía *f*.

stentorian [sten'tɔːriǝn] *adj* estentóreo.

step [step] **1** *n* (a) (*pace*) paso *m*; (*sound*) paso *m*, pisada *f*; (*footprint*) huella *f*; **at every —** a cada paso; **— by —** paso a paso, poco a poco; **it's a good —** es bastante camino, está algo lejos; **it's quite a — to the village** el pueblo queda algo lejos, hay mucho camino para ir al pueblo; **to be in — with** llevar el paso con, (*fig*) estar conforme a, estar de acuerdo con; **to be out of — with** no ir al paso de, no llevar el paso con, (*fig*) estar en desacuerdo con; estar desfasado de; **to break —** romper el paso; **to fall into —** empezar a llevar el paso, (*fig*) conformarse; **to keep in —** llevar el paso; **to retrace one's —s** desandar su camino, volver sobre sus pasos; **to take a —** dar un paso; **to turn one's —s towards** dirigirse hacia; **to watch one's —** ir con tiento.

(b) (*measure*) paso *m*; medida *f*, gestión *f*; **—s to deal with the problem** medidas *fpl* para resolver el problema; **the first — is to ...** la primera medida a tomar es ...; **it's a great — forward** esto significa un gran avance; **it's a — in the right direction** es una medida plausible; **to take —s to + infin** tomar medidas para + infin; **one can't take a single — without** . . . no se puede dar un solo paso sin . . .

(c) (*stair*) peldaño m, escalón m, grada f; (*of vehicle*) estribo m.

(d) —s (*stairs*) escalera f; (*outside building*) escalinata f; **folding —s, pair of —s** escalera f de tijera, escalera f doble.

2 vt (a) (*place at intervals*) escalonar, colocar de trecho en trecho.

(b) (*also* **to — out**) *distance* medir a pasos; **to — it out** apretar el paso, andar más rápidamente.

(c) **to — down** reducir, disminuir; **to — up** aumentar, elevar; **we shall have to — up our campaign** tendremos que reforzar nuestra campaña; **to — up production** aumentar la producción.

3 vi dar un paso; (*walk*) ir, andar, caminar; (*with care, heavily etc*) pisar; **— this way** haga el favor de pasar por aquí; **to — aside** hacerse a un lado, apartarse; **to — back** retroceder, dar un paso hacia atrás; **we — back into the 18th century** volvemos al siglo XVIII; **to — down** bajar (*from de*); (*fig*) ceder su puesto, retirarse, renunciar a sus pretensiones; **to — down for someone else** retirarse en favor de otro; **to — in** (*enter*); (*fig*) intervenir; **— in!** ¡adelante!; **— inside!** ¡pase!; **to — on something** pisar algo; **— on it!** ¡date prisa!; **to — on board** ir a bordo; **to — out** apretar el paso, andar más rápidamente; **just — outside a moment** pues salga un momento; **to — over something** evitar pisar algo, evitar chocar con algo; **he —ped carefully over the cable** miró con cuidado para no pisar el cable; **to — up** subir; **to — up to someone** acercarse a uno; **to — up to receive a prize** ir a recibir un premio.

stepbrother ['step,brʌðə*] n hermanastro m.

stepchild ['steptʃaild] n, pl **—children** [,tʃildrən] hijastro m, a f, alnado m, a f.

stepdaughter ['step,dɔːtə*] n hijastra f.

stepfather ['step,fɑːðə*] n padrastro m.

Stephen ['stiːvn] m Esteban.

stepladder ['step,lædə*] n escalera f de tijera, escalera f doble.

stepmother ['step,mʌðə*] n madrastra f.

steppe [step] n estepa f.

stepping stone ['stepiŋstəun] n pasadera f; (*fig*) escalón m (*to* para llegar a).

stepsister ['step,sistə*] n hermanastra f.

stepson ['stepsʌn] n hijastro m.

stepped-up ['stept'ʌp] adj elevado; aumentado.

step-up ['stepʌp] n elevación f; aumento m; aceleración f; refuerzo m; (*promotion*) ascenso m.

stereo . . . ['stiəriəu] estereo . . .

stereophonic [,stiəriə'fɒnik] adj estereofónico.

stereophony [steri'ɒfəni] n estereofonía f.

stereoscope ['stiəriəskəup] n estereoscopio m.

stereoscopic [,stiəriəs'kɒpik] adj estereoscópico; *film* tridimensional, en relieve; *screen* ancho.

stereotype ['stiəriətaip] **1** n clisé m, estereotipo m. **2** vt clisar, estereotipar; (*fig*) estereotipar.

sterile ['sterail] adj estéril.

sterility [ste'riliti] n esterilidad f.

sterilization [,sterilai'zeiʃən] n esterilización f.

sterilize ['sterilaiz] vt esterilizar.

sterling ['stəːliŋ] **1** adj (a) (*fig*) verdadero, excelente; **a — character** una persona de toda confianza; **a person of — worth** una persona de grandes méritos.

(b) **pound —** libra f esterlina; **— area** zona f de la libra esterlina.

2 n libras fpl esterlinas.

stern[1] [stəːn] adj severo; duro; austero; **a — glance** una mirada severa; **a — warning** un aviso terminante; **he was very — with me** fue muy duro conmigo; **but he was made of —er stuff** pero él tenía más carácter.

stern[2] [stəːn] n popa f.

sternly ['stəːnli] adv severamente; duramente; austeramente; terminantemente; **she looked at me — me** miró severamente.

sternness ['stəːnnis] n severidad f; dureza f; austeridad f; lo terminante.

sternum ['stəːnəm] n esternón m.

stertorous ['stəːtərəs] adj estertoroso.

stet [stet] vi (*Typ*) suprímase la cancelación, déjese tal como estaba en el original.

stethoscope ['steθəskəup] n estetoscopio m.

stevedore ['stiːvidɔː*] n estibador m.

Steven ['stiːvn] m Esteban.

stew[1] [stjuː] n (*also the* **—s**) lupanar m.

stew[2] [stjuː] **1** n (a) cocido m; estofado m; **Irish —** estofado m irlandés.

(b) (*fig*) **to be in a —** pasar apuros, sudar la gota gorda.

2 vt estofar; guisar; *fruit* cocer, hacer una compota de; **—ed fruit** compota f de frutas.

3 vi (*of tea*) pasarse; **to let someone — in his own juice** dejar a uno cocer en su propia salsa.

steward ['stjuːəd] n (*on estate etc*) administrador m; (*butler*) mayordomo m; (*Aer, Naut, in club etc*) camarero.

stewardess ['stjuːədes] n (*Naut*) camarera f; (*Aer*) azafata f.

stewardship ['stjuːədʃip] n administración f.

stewpan ['stjuːpæn] n, **stewpot** ['stjuːpɒt] n cazuela f, cacerola f, puchero m.

stick[1] [stik] **1** n (a) palo m, vara f; (*as weapon*) palo m, porra f; (*walking —*) bastón m; (*Aer*) palanca f de mando; (*of wax, soap etc*) barra f; (*of celery*) tallo m; **—s** (*for the fire*) astillas fpl, leña f; **— of furniture** mueble m; **policy of the big —** política f del palo grueso; **to use the big —** emplear la política del palo grueso; **to be in a cleft —** estar entre la espada y la pared; **to give someone the —, to take the — to someone** dar palo a uno.

(b) **old —** (*fam*) tío m; **he's a funny old —** es un tío raro (*or* divertido).

2 vt (*Agr etc*) apoyar con rodrigón.

stick[2] [stik] (*irr: pret and ptp* **stuck**) **1** vt (a) (*gum*) pegar, encolar; **to — a stamp on** pegar un sello; **to — something down** pegar algo; **to — two things together** pegar dos cosas, unir dos cosas con cola; **to — up a notice** fijar un anuncio.

(b) (*thrust*) clavar, hincar; **to — a knife into a table** clavar un cuchillo en una mesa; **to — out** asomar, sacar; **to — someone up** (*sl*) atracar a uno, encañonar a uno; **to — up a bank** (*sl*) asaltar un banco.

(c) (*place, put*) poner, meter; **— it on the shelf** ponlo en el estante; **— it in your case** métlo en la maleta; **to — one's hat on** ponerse el sombrero.

(d) (*pierce*) picar; **to — someone with a bayonet** herir a uno con bayoneta, clavar la bayoneta a uno; **a cork stuck all over with pins** un corcho lleno de alfileres, un corcho todo cubierto de alfileres.

(e) (*tolerate*) resistir, aguantar; **I can't — him at any price** no le puedo ver de ninguna manera; **I can't — it any longer** no aguanto más, no resisto más; **to — it out** aguantar hasta el final.

2 vi (a) (*of gum etc*) pegarse, adherirse; **this stamp won't —** este sello no se pega.

(b) (*in mud*) atascarse, quedar atascado; (*of mechanism etc*) bloquearse, trabarse, no poder moverse; (*of pin etc*) prender, estar prendido; **it stuck to the wall** quedó pegado a la pared; **to — fast in the mud** quedar clavado en el barro; **to get stuck in the snow** quedar sin poderse mover en la nieve; **the mechanism was stuck** el mecanismo estaba bloqueado; **the lift is stuck at the 9th floor** el ascensor está sin poderse mover en el piso 9; **the door —s in wet weather** en tiempo de lluvia la puerta no se mueve libremente.

(c) (*remain*) pararse, quedarse parado; (*stay*) quedarse, permanecer; **here I am and here I — aquí** estoy y aquí me quedo; **the name stuck to him** el apodo se le pegó; **the charge seems to have stuck** la acusación no ha sido olvidada nunca; **to make a charge —** hacer que una acusación tenga efecto; **to get stuck into something** (*fam*) emprender algo en serio, dedicarse seriamente a algo; **to be stuck with something** tener que cargar con algo; **and now we're stuck with it** y ahora no lo podemos quitar de encima, y ahora no hay manera de deshacernos de él; **I was stuck with him for 2 hours** tuve que soportar su compañía durante 2 horas; **the problem had them all stuck** el problema les tenía a todos perplejos; **we're stuck at No. 13** no logramos pasar más allá del núm. 13.

(d) (*with adv or prep*) **to — around** esperar por ahí; **to — at something** (*not give up*) persistir en algo, no abandonar algo, seguir trabajando en algo; (*have qualms*) sentir escrúpulo por algo; **to — at nothing** no tener escrúpulos, no pararse en barras; **to — by someone** (*follow*) pegarse a uno, pisar los talones a uno; (*support*) apoyar a uno, defender a uno; ser fiel a uno; **to — out** (*project*) salir, sobresalir; asomarse; (*fig*) ser evidente; **it —s out a mile** es completamente obvio; se nota fácilmente; **to — out for something** insistir en algo, no ceder hasta obtener algo; **they're —ing out for an extra pound** porfían en reclamar una libra más; **to — to someone** = **to — by someone**; **to — to one's principles** seguir

fiel a sus principios, aferrarse a sus principios; **to —
to a promise** cumplir una promesa; **to — to it**
persistir, no cejar, seguir trabajando (*etc*); **— to it!**
¡ánimo!; **let's — to the matter in hand** ciñámonos
al asunto, no perdamos de vista el tema principal,
volvamos al grano; **to — together** mantenerse
unidos; no separarse; **to — up** salir, sobresalir (por
encima), asomarse por encima; (*hair etc*) estar de
punta; **to — up for someone** defender a uno,
sacar la cara por uno.

sticker ['stikə*] n (*person*) persona *f* aplicada,
persona *f* perseverante; (*label*) etiqueta *f* engomada,
letrero *m* engomado (con slogan publicitario,
político *etc*).

stickiness ['stikinis] n pegajosidad *f*; viscosidad *f*;
humedad *f* con calor; lo difícil.

sticking plaster ['stikiŋ,plɑ:stə*] n esparadrapo m.

stick-in-the-mud ['stikinðəmʌd] n persona *f*
pesada; persona *f* rutinaria; reaccionario m, a *f*,
persona *f* chapada a la antigua, retrógrado m.

stickleback ['stiklbæk] n espinoso m.

stickler ['stiklə*] n rigorista *mf* (*for* en cuanto a),
persona *f* etiquetera; **he's a real — for correct
spelling** insiste terminantemente en la correcta
ortografía.

stick-up ['stikʌp] n (*sl*) atraco m, asalto m.

sticky ['stiki] adj pegajoso; viscoso; *label* engomado;
atmosphere húmedo y con mucho calor; (*fig*) *problem,
person* difícil; *situation* difícil, violento; **to come to
a — end** tener mal fin, ir a acabar mal.

stiff [stif] **1** adj (**a**) (*unbending*) rígido, inflexible,
tieso; *door, joint* duro, tieso; *collar, shirt front* duro,
(*starched*) almidonado; *brush* duro; *paste, soil*
espeso, consistente; **to be — in the legs** tener las
piernas entumecidas; **to be — with cold** estar
aterido; **you'll feel — tomorrow** mañana te van a
doler los músculos, mañana tendrás agujetas.

(**b**) (*fig*) *breeze* fuerte; *climb, examination, task,
test etc* difícil; *resistance* tenaz; *price* exorbitante,
subido; *bow* frío; *person* etiquetero, ceremonioso;
manner estirado.

2 n (*sl*) cadáver m.

stiffen ['stifn] **1** vt hacer más rígido, atiesar; endurecer;
hacer más espeso; *limb* entumecer; *morale, resistance
etc* fortalecer.

2 vi hacerse más rígido, atiesarse; endurecerse;
hacerse más espeso, espesarse; entumecerse;
fortalecerse, robustecerse; hacerse más tenaz; **when
I said this she —ed** al decir yo esto, se volvió menos
cordial; **the breeze —ed** refrescó el viento; **resistance
to the idea seems to have —ed** parece que ha
aumentado la oposición a esta idea.

stiffly ['stifli] adv rígidamente, tiesamente; **to move
—** moverse con dificultad, moverse despacio con los
miembros entumecidos; **she said —** dijo fríamente,
dijo estirada; **this was — resisted** a esto opusieron
una tenaz resistencia.

stiff-necked ['stif'nekt] adj (*fig*) terco, obstinado;
estirado.

stiffness ['stifnis] n rigidez *f*, inflexibilidad *f*, tiesura
f; dureza *f*; espesura *f*, consistencia *f*; entumecimiento
m; fuerza *f*; dificultad *f*, lo difícil; tenacidad *f*; lo
exorbitante; frialdad *f*, carácter *m* etiquetero,
carácter *m* estirado.

stifle ['staifl] **1** vt ahogar, sofocar; (*fig*) suprimir; **to
— a yawn** ahogar un bostezo; **to — opposition**
suprimir la oposición.

2 vi ahogarse, sofocarse.

stifling ['staifliŋ] adj sofocante (*also fig*), bochornoso;
it's — in here aquí dentro hay un calor sofocante;
the atmosphere in the company is — en la compañía
hay una atmósfera sofocante.

stigma ['stigmə] n, in some senses pl **stigmata**
[stig'mɑ:tə] estigma m; (*moral stain*) estigma m,
tacha *f*, baldón m.

stigmatize ['stigmətaiz] vt estigmatizar; **to —
someone as** calificar a uno de, tachar a uno de.

stile [stail] n escalera *f* para pasar una cerca.

stiletto [sti'letəu] ⸢estilete m; **— heel** tacón m de
aguja.

still¹ [stil] **1** adj (*motionless*) inmóvil; quieto; (*and
quiet*) tranquilo, silencioso; *wine* no espumoso; **— !**
(*US*) ¡cállate!; **to keep —** estar inmóvil, no moverse;
keep — ! ¡estáte quieto!; **he fell and lay —** cayó y
permaneció inmóvil; **to sit —** estarse quieto en su
silla; **to stand —** estarse quieto; **my heart stood —**
se me paró el corazón.

2 n (**a**) silencio m, calma *f*; **in the — of the night**
en el silencio de la noche.

(**b**) (*Cine*) vista *f* fija.

3 adv todavía, aún; **— more** aun más, más aun;

there are — 2 more quedan 2 más; **he — hasn't
come** no ha venido todavía; **I can — recall it**
todavía lo recuerdo, lo recuerdo aún; **I — play a bit**
sigo jugando un poco; **do you — believe that?**
¿sigues creyendo eso?

4 conj sin embargo, con todo, a pesar de todo;
—, it was worth it sin embargo, valió la pena.

5 vt calmar, tranquilizar; aquietar; (*silence*) acallar.

still² [stil] n alambique m.

stillbirth ['stil,bə:θ] n nacimiento m de un niño
muerto.

stillborn ['stil,bɔ:n] adj (**a**) nacido muerto; **the child
was —** el niño nació muerto. (**b**) (*fig*) fracasado,
malogrado.

still life ['stil'laif] n bodegón m, naturaleza *f* muerta.

stillness ['stilnis] n inmovilidad *f*; quietud *f*;
tranquilidad *f*, silencio m.

stilt [stilt] n zanco m; (*Archit*) pilar m, soporte m;
pilote m.

stilted ['stiltid] adj afectado, hinchado, artificial.

stimulant ['stimjulənt] **1** adj estimulante. **2** n
estimulante m, excitante m.

stimulate ['stimjuleit] vt estimular; **to — someone to
do something** estimular a uno a hacer algo, incitar
a uno a hacer algo.

stimulating ['stimjuleitiŋ] adj (*Med etc*) estimulador,
estimulante; *experience, book etc* sugestivo; alentador;
inspirador.

stimulation [,stimju'leiʃən] n (*stimulus*) estímulo m;
(*state*) excitación *f*.

stimulus ['stimjuləs] n, pl **stimuli** ['stimjulai]
estímulo m, incentivo m.

stimy ['staimi] vt (*fam*): **to — someone** poner obstáculos infranqueables delante de uno; **now we're
properly stimied !** ¡estamos jodidos!

sting [stiŋ] **1** n (*Zool, Bot: organ*) aguijón m; (*act,
wound*) picadura *f*; (*pain*) escozor m; picazón m;
(*pain, fig*) punzada *f*; **a — of remorse** un remordimiento; **the — of the rain in one's face** el azote de
la lluvia en la cara; **I felt the — of his irony** su
ironía me hirió en lo vivo.

2 (*irr: pret and ptp* **stung**) (**a**) picar; punzar;
(*make smart*) picar, escocer en; (*of hot dishes*)
resquemar; (*of hail etc*) azotar; **the bee stung him**
la abeja le picó; **my conscience stung me** me
remordió la conciencia; **the reply stung him to the
quick** la respuesta le hirió en lo vivo.

(**b**) **to — someone to do something** incitar a
uno a hacer algo, provocar a uno a hacer algo.

(**c**) (*fam*) **they stung me for £4** me clavaron 4
libras; **how much did they — you (for)?** ¿cuánto te
clavaron?

3 vi picar; escocer; **moths don't —** las mariposas
no pican; **my eyes —** me pican los ojos; **that
mouthful stung** me quemó la lengua; **that
blow really stung** ese golpe me dolió de verdad.

stingily ['stindʒili] adv con tacañería.

stinginess ['stindʒinis] n tacañería *f*.

stinging nettle ['stiŋiŋ,netl] n ortiga *f*.

stingray ['stiŋrei] n (*Fish*) pastinaca *f*.

stingy ['stindʒi] adj tacaño; **to be — with something**
ser tacaño con algo.

stink [stiŋk] **1** n hedor m, mal olor m; tufo m; **a —
of ...** un hedor a ...; **the — of corruption** el olor a
corrupción.

2 (*irr: pret* **stank**, *ptp* **stunk**) vt: **to — out** *room*
apestar, hacer oler mal; **to — someone out** ahuyen-
tar a uno con un mal olor.

3 vi (**a**) heder, oler mal (*of* a); **it —s in here** aquí
huele muy mal.

(**b**) (*fig*) **the idea —s** es una idea horrible; **I think
the plan —s** creo que es un proyecto abominable;
as a headmaster he —s como director es un asco;
they are —ing with money son unos ricachos,
tienen tanto dinero que da asco.

stink bomb ['stiŋk'bɔm] n bomba *f* de gas hediondo.

stinker ['stiŋkə*] n (*fam: person*) mal bicho m,
canalla m; **you — !** ¡bestia!; **this problem is a —**
este problema es terriblemente difícil.

stinking ['stiŋkiŋ] adj hediondo, fétido; (*fig*) horrible,
bestial, asqueroso.

stint [stint] **1** n (**a**) (*amount of work*) destajo m; tarea
f; **to do one's —** hacer la parte que le corresponde a
uno, trabajar (*etc*) como se debe, (*fig*) cumplir con
las obligaciones que uno tiene, hacer su contribución;
to finish one's — terminar el trabajo que le
corresponde a uno.

(**b**) **without —** libremente, generosamente; sin
restricción.

2 vt limitar, restringir; escatimar; **he did not —
his praises** no escatimó sus elogios, prodigó sus
elogios; **to — someone of something** privar a uno de

algo, dar a uno menor cantidad de algo de la que pide (*or* necesita).

3 *vr*: **to — oneself** estrecharse, privarse de cosas; **don't — yourself!** ¡no te prives de nada!, ¡sírvete (*etc*) cuanto quieras!; **to — oneself of something** privarse de algo, negarse algo, no permitirse algo.

stipend ['staipend] *n* estipendio *m*, sueldo *m*.

stipendiary [stai'pendiəri] **1** *adj* estipendiario. **2** *n* estipendiario *m*.

stipple ['stipl] *vt* puntear, granear.

stipulate ['stipjuleit] **1** *vt* estipular, poner como condición; especificar. **2** *vi*: **to — for something** estipular algo, poner algo como condición.

stipulation [,stipju'leiʃən] *n* estipulación *f*, condición *f*.

stir[1] [stə:*] **1** *n* (**a**) acto *m* de agitar (*etc*); hurgonada *f*; **to give one's tea a —** remover su té; **give the fire a —** remueve un poco la lumbre.

(**b**) (*fig*) conmoción *f*, revuelo *m*; sensación *f*; agitación *f*; **to cause a —** causar una sensación, armar gran revuelo; provocar mucho interés; **it didn't make much of a —** apenas despertó interés alguno; **there was a great — in parliament** hubo una gran conmoción en el parlamento.

2 *vt* (**a**) *liquid etc* (*also* **to — up**) remover, agitar, revolver, menear; *fire* atizar, hurgar; **to — sugar into coffee** añadir azúcar a su café y removerlo; **"— before using"** "agítese antes de usar".

(**b**) (*move*) mover, agitar; **a breeze —red the leaves** una brisa movió las hojas; **he never —ed a foot all day** no movió el pie en todo el día.

(**c**) (*fig*) *emotions* conmover, despertar; *imagination* estimular; **to — up** *passions* excitar; *revolt* fomentar; *trouble* armar; **to — up the past** remover el pasado; **to — someone to do something** incitar a uno a hacer algo; **to — someone to pity** provocar a uno a lástima, hacer que uno sienta compasión; **to feel deeply —red** conmoverse profundamente, estar muy emocionado; **we were all —red by the speech** el discurso nos conmovió a todos.

3 *vi* moverse, menearse; **she hasn't —red all day** no se ha movido en todo el día; **he never —red from the spot** no abandonó el sitio ni un solo momento; **don't you — from here** no te muevas de aquí; **nobody is —ring yet** están todavía en cama.

stir[2] [stə:*] *n* (*sl*) chirona *f*.

stirring ['stə:riŋ] *adj* *speech etc* emocionante, conmovedor; inspirador; *period etc* turbulento, agitado.

stirrup ['stirəp] *n* estribo *m*.

stirrup pump ['stirəppʌmp] *n* bomba *f* pequeña de mano.

stitch [stitʃ] **1** *n* (*Sew*) puntada *f*, punto *m*; (*Med*: *in surgery*) punto *m* de sutura, (*pain*) punzada *f*; **a — in time saves 9** es mejor hacerlo ahora para evitar mayores dificultades después; **she hadn't a — on** estaba en pelota; **he hadn't a dry — on him** estaba mojado hasta los huesos; **we were in —es** nos moríamos de risa; **to put —es in a wound** suturar una herida.

2 *vt* coser (*also* **to — together, to — up**); (*Med*) suturar.

stoat [stəut] *n* armiño *m*.

stock [stɔk] **1** *n* (**a**) (*of tree*) tronco *m*, (*of vine*) cepa *f*, (*for grafting*) patrón *m*.

(**b**) (*Bot*: *species*) alhelí *m*.

(**c**) (*family*) estirpe *f*, linaje *m*, raza *f*; **of good —** de buen linaje; **of good Castilian —** de buena cepa castellana.

(**d**) (*handle*) mango *m*; (*of gun*) caja *f*, culata *f*.

(**e**) **—s** (*punishment*) cepo *m*.

(**f**) **—s** (*Naut*) astillero *m*, grada *f* de construcción; **to be on the —s** (*ship*) estar en vía de construcción, (*book etc*) estar en preparación; **he has 3 plays on the —s** tiene 3 obras entre manos.

(**g**) (*supply*) provisión *f*, (*Comm*) surtido *m*, existencias *fpl*, stock *m*; **— of spares** stock *m* de recambios; **surplus —** artículos *mpl* sobrantes; **to be in —** estar en existencia, estar en almacén; **to be out of —** estar agotado; **we are out of — of umbrellas** no nos quedan paraguas, están agotados los paraguas; **to have something in —** tener algo en existencia; **to lay in a — of** proveerse de, hacer provisión de; **to take — of** hacer inventario (*of* de); **to take — of** (*fig*) asesorarse de, considerar, calcular las posibilidades de.

(**h**) (*Agr*: **live —**) ganado *m*, ganadería *f*; **dead —** aperos *mpl*; see **rolling** *etc*.

(**i**) (*Cook*) caldo *m*.

(**j**) (*Fin*: *of company*) capital *m* (comercial); (*shares*) acciones *fpl*, valores *mpl*; **government —**

papel *m* del Estado; **joint — fondo** *m* social; **joint-stock company** sociedad *f* anónima; **his — is going up** su reputación crece, su crédito aumenta.

2 *adj*, *attr* (*Comm*) de surtido, en existencia; *size etc* corriente, normal; (*Theat*) de repertorio; *phrase* hecho; *remark* banal, vulgar; *response etc* que se espera, acostumbrado, consagrado.

3 *vt* (*supply*) surtir, proveer, abastecer (*with* de); (*of shop*) tener existencias de, tener en almacén; **to — up with** proveerse de, adquirir existencias de, (*fig*) ir acumulando; **to — a pond with fish** poblar un charco de peces; **we don't — that brand** no tenemos esa marca; **do you — bananas?** ¿vende Vd plátanos?

stockade [stɔ'keid] *n* estacada *f*.

stockbreeder ['stɔk,bri:də*] *n* ganadero *m*.

stockbreeding ['stɔk,bri:diŋ] *n* ganadería *f*.

stockbroker ['stɔk,brəukə*] *n* bolsista *m*, agente *m* de bolsa, corredor *m* de bolsa.

stockbroking ['stɔk,brəukiŋ] *n* correduría *f* de bolsa.

stock exchange ['stɔkiks,tʃeindʒ] **1** *n* bolsa *f*; **to be on the —** ser bolsista, ser miembro de la bolsa, dedicarse a negocios de bolsa; **prices on the —** cotizaciones *fpl* de bolsa.

2 *attr* bursátil.

stockholder ['stɔk,həuldə*] *n* accionista *mf*.

Stockholm ['stɔkhəum] Estocolmo.

stockinet [,stɔki'net] *n* tela *f* de punto.

stocking ['stɔkiŋ] *n* media *f*; (*knee-length*) calceta *f*; **a pair of —s** un par de medias; **nylon —s** medias *fpl* de nilón.

stock-in-trade ['stɔkin'treid] *n* (*Comm*) capital *m*; existencias *fpl*; (*fig*) repertorio *m*; **that joke is part of his —** es un chiste de su repertorio.

stockist ['stɔkist] *n* distribuidor *m*.

stockjobber ['stɔk,dʒɔbə*] *n* agiotista *m*.

stockjobbing ['stɔk,dʒɔbiŋ] *n* agiotaje *m*.

stock market ['stɔk,mɑ:kit] *n see* **stock exchange**.

stockpile ['stɔkpail] **1** *n* reserva *f* (de materias primas). **2** *vt* acumular, poner en reserva, formar una reserva de.

stock raising ['stɔk,reiziŋ] *n* ganadería *f*.

stockroom ['stɔkrum] *n* almacén *m*.

stock-still ['stɔk'stil] *adv*: **to be (or stand) —** estar completamente inmóvil.

stocktaking ['stɔk,teikiŋ] *n* inventario *m*, balance *m*; **— sale** venta *f* por balance.

stocky ['stɔki] *adj* rechoncho, bajo pero fuerte.

stockyard ['stɔkjɑ:d] *n* corral *m* de ganado.

stodge [stɔdʒ] *n* (*fam*) comida *f* indigesta, cosas *fpl* indigestas.

stodgy ['stɔdʒi] *adj* *food* indigesto, pesado; *book, style etc* pesado.

stoic ['stəuik] **1** *adj* estoico. **2** *n* estoico *m*.

stoical ['stəuikəl] *adj* estoico.

stoicism ['stəuisizəm] *n* estoicismo *m*.

stoke [stəuk] **1** *vt* *furnace* cargar, cebar; *fire* echar carbón a; (*fig*) cebar; (*hum*) comer.

2 *vi* (*also* **to — up**) cebar el hogar, echar carbón a la lumbre; (*hum*) comer.

stoker ['stəukə*] *n* fogonero *m*.

stokehold ['stəukhəuld] *n* (*Naut*) cuarto *m* de calderas.

stokehole ['stəukhəul] *n* boca *f* del horno.

stole[1] [stəul] *n* estola *f*.

stole[2] [stəul] *pret* of **steal**.

stolen ['stəulən] *ptp* of **steal**; **— goods** géneros *mpl* robados.

stolid ['stɔlid] *adj* impasible, imperturbable; flemático; (*pej*) terco.

stolidity [stɔ'liditi] *n* impasibilidad *f*, imperturbabilidad *f*; flema *f*; terquedad *f*.

stomach ['stʌmək] **1** *n* estómago *m*; vientre *m*; (*fig*) deseo *m*, apetito *m* (*for* de); **they have no — for the fight** no tienen ganas de pelear; **it turns my — me** da asco.

2 *attr* estomacal, del estómago; **— upset** trastorno *m* estomacal.

3 *vt* (*fig*) tragar, aguantar.

stomach ache ['stʌməkeik] *n* dolor *m* de estómago.

stomach pump ['stʌməkpʌmp] *n* bomba *f* estomacal.

stomach tube ['stʌməktju:b] *n* sonda *f* gástrica.

stomp [stɔmp] *vi* pisar muy fuerte.

stone [stəun] **1** *n* piedra *f*; (*of fruit*) hueso *m*; (*commemorative*) lápida *f*; (*Med*) cálculo *m*, piedra *f*, (*as complaint*) mal *m* de piedra; (*weight*) = 14 libras = 6,348 kg; **philosopher's —** piedra *f* filosofal; **precious —** piedra *f* preciosa; **within a —'s throw** a tiro de piedra, a dos pasos; **to cast the first —** lanzar la primera piedra; **which of you shall cast the first stone?** ¿quién se atreve a lanzar la primera piedra?; **to leave no — unturned** no

dejar piedra sin remover, revolver Roma con Santiago.
2 *adj* de piedra.
3 *vt* **(a)** apedrear, lapidar; *fruit* deshuesar.
　(b) *(sl)* **to be —d** estar ajumado.
stone-blind ['stəun'blaind] *adj* completamente ciego.
stone-broke ['stəun'brəuk] *adj* (US) = **stony-broke.**
stonecrop ['stəunkrɔp] *n* pan *m* de cuco.
stone-dead ['stəun'ded] *adj* más muerto que una piedra.
stone-deaf ['stəun'def] *adj* completamente sordo.
stonemason ['stəun'meisn] *n* albañil *m*; *(in quarry)* cantero *m*.
stone pit ['stəunpit] *n*, **— quarry** [,kwɔri] *n* cantera *f*.
stonewall ['stəun'wɔ:l] *vi* (Sport) emplear la táctica de cerrojo; *(in answering questions)* evitar contestar directamente.
stonewalling ['stəun'wɔ:liŋ] *n* táctica *f* de cerrojo; el evitar contestar directamente.
stoneware ['stəunwɛə*] *n* gres *m*.
stonework ['stəunwə:k] *n* cantería *f*, obra *f* de sillería; piedras *fpl*.
stonily ['stəunili] *adv* (fig) glacialmente, fríamente.
stony ['stəuni] *adj* material pétreo; como piedra, parecido a piedra; *ground* pedregoso, cubierto de piedras; *glance* glacial, frío; *heart* empedernido.
stony-broke ['stəuni'brəuk] *adj* (fam): **to be —** no tener un céntimo.
stony-hearted ['stəuni'ha:tid] *adj* de corazón empedernido.
stood [stud] *pret and ptp of* **stand.**
stooge [stu:dʒ] *n* (sl) hombre *m* de paja; secuaz *m*, partidario *m*; paniaguado *m*; *(of comedian)* compañero *m*.
stook [stu:k] **1** *n* tresnal *m*, garbera *f*. **2** *vt* poner en tresnales.
stool [stu:l] *n* taburete *m*, escabel *m*; *(folding)* silla *f* de tijera; (Bot) planta *f* madre; (Med) cámaras *fpl*; **to fall between two —s** fracasar por no saber a qué carta quedarse, terminar sin conseguir ni lo uno ni lo otro.
stool pigeon ['stu:l,pidʒən] *n* (fam) soplón *m*, espía *m*.
stoop[1] [stu:p] **1** *n* inclinación *f*; *(defect)* cargazón *f* de espaldas; **to walk with a —** andar encorvado.
2 *vt* inclinar, bajar.
3 *vi* inclinarse, encorvarse; *(permanently, as defect)* ser cargado de espaldas, anda encorvado; **to — to pick something up** inclinarse para recoger algo; **to — to +** *infin* (fig) rebajarse a + *infin*.
stoop[2] [stu:p] *n* (US) escalinata *f* de entrada.
stooping ['stu:piŋ] *adj* inclinado, encorvado; cargado de espaldas.
stop [stɔp] **1** *n* (a) *(in general)* parada *f*; alto *m*; pausa *f*, interrupción *f*; **a 20-minute — for coffee** un alto de 20 minutos para tomar café; **to be at a —** estar parado; quedar paralizado; **to bring a car to a —** parar un coche; **to come to a —** venir a parar, pararse; **to come to a dead** (*or* **sudden) —** pararse en seco, detenerse repentinamente; **to come to a full —** quedar completamente parado; quedar paralizado; llegar a un punto muerto; **to go on for 2 hours without a —** continuar durante 2 horas sin parar (*or* sin interrupción); **to put a — to something** poner fin a algo, acabar con algo.
　(b) *(stay)* estancia *f*; **a — of a few days** una estancia de unos días.
　(c) *(of bus, tram etc)* parada *f*; (Aer, Naut) escala *f*; **intermediate —** escala *f*; **request —** parada *f* discrecional; **to make a — at Bordeaux** hacer escala en Burdeos.
　(d) *(Typ: also* **full —)** punto *m*.
　(e) (Mus: *of organ)* registro *m*; *(of other instrument)* llave *f*; **to pull out all the —s** (fig) desplegar todos sus recursos, emplear toda su fuerza.
　(f) (Mech) tope *m*, retén *m*.
　(g) (Gram) consonante *f* oclusiva.
2 *vt* **(a)** *(block: also* **to — up)** *leak, hole etc* tapar; cegar; *road etc* cerrar, obstruir, bloquear; *tooth* empastar; *flow of blood* restañar; **to — one's ears** taparse los oídos; **to — a gap** tapar un agujero, (fig) llenar un vacío; **"road —ped"** "cerrado por obras".
　(b) *(arrest progress of)* parar, detener; *ball, bullet, engine, car, charge, traffic etc* parar; *blow* rechazar, parar; *aggression* rechazar, contener; *danger, threat* evitar, estorbar; *process* terminar; *abuse* poner fin a, acabar con; *(forbid)* prohibir, poner fin a; **— thief!** ¡al ladrón!; **and there is nothing to — him** y no hay nada que se lo impida; **the walls — some of the noise** las paredes suprimen una parte del ruido; **the curtains — the light** las cortinas impiden la entrada de la luz; **this should —**

any further trouble esto habrá de evitar cualquier dificultad en el futuro; **to — someone (from) doing something** *(prevent)* impedir a uno hacer algo, *(forbid)* prohibir a uno hacer algo; **to — something being done** impedir que algo se haga; **to — something happening** evitar que algo ocurra.
　(c) *(cease)* terminar; **— it!** ¡basta!, ¡basta ya!; **— that noise!** ¡basta ya de ruido!; **— the nonsense!** ¡déjate de tonterías!
　(d) *(suspend)* *payments etc* suspender; *supply* contar, interrumpir; **to — someone's electricity** cortar la electricidad de uno; **to — someone's wages** suspender el pago del sueldo de uno; **to — a pound of someone's wages** retener una libra del sueldo de uno; **all leave is —ped** han sido cancelados todos los permisos; **to — the milk for a fortnight** cancelar el encargo de la leche durante quince días.
3 *vi* **(a)** *(cease motion)* parar, pararse; detenerse; hacer alto; *(finish, run out)* terminarse, acabarse; *(of supply etc)* cortarse, interrumpirse; *(of process, rain etc)* cesar; **the car —ped** se paró el coche; **the clock has —ped** el reloj se ha parado; **—!** ¡pare!, ¡alto!; **when the programme —s** cuando termine el programa; **payments have —ped** *(temporarily)* se han suspendido los pagos, *(permanently)* han terminado los pagos; **the rain has —ped** la lluvia ha cesado, ha dejado de llover.
　(b) *(stay)* hospedarse, alojarse *(at* en, *with* con); quedarse; **she's —ping with her aunt** se hospeda en casa de su tía; vive con su tía; **did you — till the end?** ¿te quedaste hasta el fin?
　(c) *(with verb constructions)* **to — doing something** dejar de hacer algo; **she never —s talking** habla incansablemente, no termina de hablar; **it has —ped raining** ha dejado de llover, ya no llueve.
　(d) *(with adv or prep)* **to — at nothing** no pararse en barras; **to — at nothing to +** *infin* emplear sin escrúpulo todos los medios; para + *infin*; **to — away** ausentarse *(from* de), no asistir *(from* a); **you — away from my sister!** ¡no venga más por aquí a molestar a mi hermana!; **to — behind** quedarse; quedarse en casa, no salir; **to make someone — behind after school** hacer que uno quede en la escuela después de las clases; **to — by** *(adv)* detenerse brevemente hacer una breve visita; **to — by** *(prep)* pasar por; **to — dead** pararse en seco; **to — in** quedarse en casa, no salir; **to — off** interrumpir el viaje *(at* en); **to — out** quedarse fuera; no volver a casa; **to — over** pasar la noche, pernoctar; quedarse un poco; **to — to do something** *(cease motion)* detenerse a hacer algo, *(stay)* quedarse a hacer algo; **to — up** velar, no acostarse, seguir sin acostarse; **don't — up for me** no os quedéis esperándome hasta muy tarde; *see short etc.*
4 *vr*: **I —ped myself in time** me detuve a tiempo; **to — oneself doing something** abstenerse de hacer algo, guardarse de hacer algo; **I can't seem to — myself doing it** parece que me es imposible no hacerlo.
stop-and-go ['stɔpən'gəu] *n* (US) *see* **stop-go.**
stopcock ['stɔpkɔk] *n* llave *f* de cierre.
stopgap ['stɔpgæp] *n* *(thing)* recurso *m* provisional, expediente *m*; *(person)* tapaagujeros *m*, sustituto *m*.
stop-go ['stɔp'gəu] *n*: **period of —** período *m* cuando una política de expansión económica alterna con otra de restricción.
stoplights ['stɔplaits] *npl* (Aut) luces *fpl* de detención.
stopover ['stɔpəuvə*] *n* parada *f* intermedia; interrupción *f* de un viaje.
stoppage ['stɔpidʒ] *n* parada *f*, cesación *f*, detención *f*; interrupción *f*; *(of work)* paro *m*, suspensión *f*; *(in game)* detención *f*; *(strike)* huelga *f*; *(blockage)* obstrucción *f*.
stopper ['stɔpə*] **1** *n* tapón *m*; (Tech) taco *m*, tarugo *m*. **2** *vt* tapar, taponar.
stopping ['stɔpiŋ] *n* parada *f*; suspensión *f*; *(of tooth)* empaste *m*.
stopping place ['stɔpiŋpleis] *n* paradero *m*; *(of bus etc)* parada *f*.
stop-press ['stɔp'pres] *n* *(also* **— news)** noticias *fpl* de última hora; **"—"** *(as heading)* "al cerrar la edición".
stopwatch ['stɔpwɔtʃ] *n* cronómetro *m*.
storage ['stɔ:ridʒ] *n* almacenaje *m*, depósito *m*; **— charges** derechos *mpl* de almacenaje; **to put something into —** poner algo en almacén; *see* **cold —.**
storage battery ['stɔ:ridʒ,bætəri] *n* acumulador *m*.
store [stɔ:*] **1** *n* (a) *(stock)* provisión *f*; *(reserve)* reserva *f*; repuesto *m*; *(storehouse)* almacén *m*, depósito *m*; **to be in —** estar en almacén, estar en depósito; **what is in — for someone** lo que le espera a uno, lo que la suerte tiene guardado para

uno; **what has the future in — for us?** ¿qué guarda el futuro para nosotros?; **that is a treat in** — eso es un placer que nos guarda el futuro; **to have** (or **keep**) **something in** — tener algo en reserva; **to lay in a** — of hacer provisión de, proveerse de; **to put** (or **set**) **great** — **by something** conceder mucha importancia a algo, estimar algo en mucho; **to set little** — **by something** conceder poca importancia a algo, estimar algo en poco.

(**b**) (quantity) abundancia f; tesoro m; **a great** — **of expertise** gran pericia f; **he has a** — **of knowledge about . . .** tiene grandes conocimientos de . . .

(**c**) —s (Mil etc: food) víveres mpl, provisiones fpl, (equipment) pertrechos mpl; **war** —s material m bélico.

(**d**) (shop: esp US) tienda f; —s (large shop), **departmental** —s almacén m, almacenes mpl; **multiple** — cadena f de almacenes; **village** — tienda f de pueblo; **Bloggs' S**—s Almacenes mpl Bloggs.

2 vt almacenar; poner en reserva, tener en reserva, guardar (also **to** — **away**); documents archivar; **to** — **up** acumular, ir acumulando, amontonar; **a hatred** —**d up over centuries** un odio almacenado durante siglos.

storehouse ['stɔːhaus] n, pl —**houses** [ˌhauziz] almacén m, depósito m; (fig) mina f, tesoro m.

storekeeper ['stɔːˌkiːpə*] n almacenero m; (US) tendero m; (Naut) pañolero m.

storeroom ['stɔːrum] n despensa f; (Naut) pañol m.

storey ['stɔːri] n piso m; **a 9-storey building** un edificio de 9 pisos.

storeyed ['stɔːrid] adj: **an 8-storeyed building** un edificio de 8 pisos.

stork [stɔːk] n cigüeña f.

storm [stɔːm] **1** n (**a**) (Meteorol) tormenta f, tempestad f, temporal m; (Naut) borrasca f; (of wind) vendaval m, huracán m; **to brave the** — aguantar la tempestad; **to ride out a** — capear un temporal, hacer frente a un temporal.

(**b**) (fig) tempestad f, borrasca f; **a** — **in a teacup** una tempestad en un vaso de agua; — **of abuse** torrente m de injurias; — **of criticism** vendaval m de críticas, nube f de críticas; **there were** —**s of applause** sonaron fuertes aplausos, hubo grandes aplausos; **there was a political** — hubo un gran revuelo político; **it caused an international** — levantó una polvareda internacional; **to bring a** — **about one's ears** atraer sobre sí una lluvia de protestas.

(**c**) (Mil) **to take a town by** — tomar una ciudad por asalto; **the play took Paris by** — la obra cautivó a todo París, la obra obtuvo un tremendo éxito en París.

2 vt (Mil) asaltar, tomar por asalto.

3 vi rabiar, bramar; **to** — **at someone** tronar contra uno, enfurecerse con uno; **he came** —**ing into my office** entró furioso en mi oficina; **he** —**ed on for an hour about the government** pasó una hora lanzando improperios contra el gobierno.

stormbound ['stɔːmbaund] adj inmovilizado por el mal tiempo.

storm centre, (US) — **center** ['stɔːmˌsentə*] n centro m de la tempestad; (fig) centro m de los disturbios, centro m de la agitación.

storm cloud ['stɔːmklaud] n nubarrón m.

storm door ['stɔːmdɔː*] n contrapuerta f.

storm signal ['stɔːmˌsignl] n señal f de temporal.

storm-tossed ['stɔːmtɔst] adj sacudido por la tempestad.

storm troops ['stɔːmtruːps] npl tropas fpl de asalto.

stormy ['stɔːmi] adj tempestuoso, borrascoso (also fig).

stormy petrel ['stɔːmi'petrəl] n (Orn) petrel m de la tempestad; (fig) persona f pendenciera, persona f de vida borrascosa.

story[1] ['stɔːri] n (**a**) (account) historia f, relación f, relato m; (Lit) cuento m, historieta f; (joke) cuento m, chiste m; **dirty** —, **rude** — chiste m verde; **funny** — chiste m; **short** — cuento m; **tall** — cuento m exagerado, cuento m increíble; **true** — historia f verídica, **the** — **of her life** la historia de su vida; **the** — **of their travels** la relación de sus viajes; **his** — **is that . . .** según él dice . . ., según lo que él cuenta . . .; **that's another** — eso es harina de otro costal; **that's not the whole** — no te lo han contado en su totalidad, hay una parte que no te han contado; **it's the** (**same**) **old** — es lo de siempre; **it's a long** — es muy largo de contar; **to cut a long** — **short** para abreviar; **to tell a** — contar un cuento, narrar una historia; **the marks tell their own** — las señales hablan por sí solas, las señales no necesitan interpretación; **the full** — **has still to be told** todavía no se ha hecho pública toda la historia;

what a — **this house could tell!** ¡cuántas cosas nos diría esta casa!

(**b**) (plot) argumento m, trama f.

(**c**) (fig) cuento m, mentira f; embuste m; **a likely** —! ¡puro cuento!, ¡qué cuento más inverosímil!; **to tell stories** contar embustes; **don't tell stories!** ¡no me vengas con tus embustes!

story[2] ['stɔːri] n (Archit) see **storey**.

storybook ['stɔːribuk] n libro m de cuentos.

storyteller ['stɔːriˌtelə*] n cuentista mf; (fibber) cuentista mf, embustero m, a f.

stoup [stuːp] n copa f, frasco m; (Eccl) pila f.

stout [staut] **1** adj (solid) sólido, robusto, macizo, fuerte; (person) gordo, corpulento; (brave) valiente; (sturdy) fornido; (resolute) resuelto; **resistance etc** terco, tenaz; — **fellow!** ¡muy bien!; **he's a** — **fellow** es un buen chico; **with** — **hearts** resueltamente.

2 n: especie de cerveza negra.

stout-hearted ['staut'hɑːtid] adj valiente, resuelto.

stoutly ['stautli] adv: — **built** de construcción sólida, fuerte; **to resist** — resistir tenazmente; **he** — **maintains that . . .** sostiene resueltamente que . . .

stoutness ['stautnis] n gordura f, corpulencia f.

stove[1] [stəuv] n (for heating) estufa f; (for cooking) hornillo m, cocina f (de gas etc); **electric** — cocina f eléctrica.

stove[2] [stəuv] pret and ptp of **stave**.

stovepipe ['stəuvpaip] n tubo m de estufa.

stow [stəu] **1** vt (**a**) (place, poner, colocar; (Naut) estibar, arrumar; (and hide) esconder (also **to** — **away**); **where can I** — **this?** ¿esto dónde lo pongo?; **to** — **food away** (fam) despachar rápidamente una comida, zamparse una comida.

(**b**) (sl) — **it!** ¡déjate de eso!, ¡cállate!, ¡basta ya!

2 vi: **to** — **away** viajar de polizón (on a ship en un buque), viajar sin pagar y clandestinamente.

stowage ['stəuidʒ] n (act) estiba f, arrumaje m; (place) bodega f.

stowaway ['stəuəwei] n polizón m, llovido m, pasajero m clandestino.

strabismus [strə'bizməs] n estrabismo m.

straddle ['strædl] vt esparrancarse encima de, estar con una pierna a cada lado de; horse montar a horcajadas; target cubrir, caer a ambos lados de.

strafe [strɑːf] vt bombardear, cañonear, atacar; destrozar a tiros.

straggle ['strægl] vi (lag) rezagarse; (get lost) extraviarse; (spread) extenderse, estar esparcido; (wander) vagar, vagar en desorden; (Bot) lozanear; **the village** —**s on for miles** el pueblo se extiende varios kilómetros (sin tener un plano fijo); **the guests** —**d out into the night** los invitados salieron poco a poco y desaparecieron en la noche; **her hair** —**s over her face** el pelo le cae en desorden por la cara.

straggler ['stræglə*] n rezagado m; (Mil) extraviado m.

straggling ['stræglin] adj disperso; rezagado; extendido; desordenado.

straight [streit] **1** adj (**a**) (not bent) derecho, recto; line recto; back erguido; hair lacio; **as** — **as a die** más derecho que una vela; **he carries himself as** — **as a ramrod** se mantiene perfectamente erguido; see **face**.

(**b**) (honest) honrado; answer franco, directo; **is he** —? ¿es de fiar?; **let me be** — **with you** te digo esto con toda franqueza, no hagamos confusiones; **he's always dealt very** — **with me** en los negocios siempre se ha comportado como hombre honrado, siempre me ha tratado con justicia.

(**c**) (plain, uncomplicated) sencillo; drink sin mezcla, puro; fight (Pol) sencillo, de dos candidatos solamente; part, play (Theat) serio.

(**d**) (in order) en orden; **it's all** — **now** todo está en regla ya; **your tie isn't** — tu corbata no está bien; **let's get this** — no hagamos confusiones, digámoslo claramente; **to put things** — arreglar cosas, poner las cosas en orden; **are your affairs** — **at last?** ¿por fin has arreglado tus cosas?

2 adv (**a**) (in a — line) derecho, directamente, en línea recta; **to fly** — volar en línea recta; — **above us** directamente encima de nosotros; **it's** — **across the road from us** está exactamente enfrente de nosotros; — **ahead**, — **on** todo seguido; **keep** — **on for Toledo** vayan Vds todo seguido para Toledo; **I went** — **home** fui derecho a mi casa; **I went** — **to my room** fui derecho a mi cuarto, fui a mi cuarto sin detenerme para nada; **to look someone** — **in the eye** mirar directamente a los ojos de uno.

(**b**) (immediately, without diversion) directamente; inmediatamente; — **after this** inmediatamente después de esto; — **away** en seguida, inmediatamente; **— off** sin parar, sin interrupción; de un tirón; sin vacilar; **for 3 days — off** durante 3 días seguidos; **he read the whole of Proust — off** leyó toda la obra de Proust de un tirón; **she just went — off** se fue sin vacilar; **he said — off that . . .** dijo sin vacilar que . . .; **to come — to the point** ir directamente al grano; **to drink — from the bottle** beber de la misma botella.

(**c**) (*frankly*) francamente, con franqueza; **I tell you —, I'll give it to you —** te lo digo con toda franqueza; **— out** francamente, sin rodeos.

(**d**) (*pure*) sin mezcla; **we drink it —** lo bebemos sin mezcla.

(**e**) **to go — (***fam***)** enmendarse, hacer nueva vida, vivir dentro de la ley; **he's been going — for a year now** lleva un año sin tener nada que ver con el crimen.

3 n: **the — (***Racing, Rail***)** la recta; **out of (the) —** fuera de la plomada, no vertical.

straightaway ['streitə'wei] *adv* en seguida, inmediatamente.

straightedge ['streitedʒ] n regla f de borde recto.

straighten ['streitn] **1** vt (*also* **to — out**) enderezar, poner derecho; (*fig*) arreglar, poner en orden; *problem* resolver; *confused situation* desenmarañar.

2 vi (*freq* **to — up**; *also* vr **to — oneself up**) enderezarse, ponerse derecho; (*person*) erguirse.

straight-faced ['streit'feist] **1** *adj* serio, grave, solemne; **a — attitude** una actitud seria.

2 *adv*: **he told the joke very —** contó el chiste con cara muy seria.

straightforward [,streit'fɔːwəd] *adj* (*honest*) honrado; (*plain-spoken*) franco; (*simple*) sencillo.

straightforwardly [,streit'fɔːwədli] *adv* honradamente; francamente; sencillamente.

straightforwardness [,streit'fɔːwədnis] n honradez f; franqueza f; sencillez f.

strain¹ [strein] **1** n **(a)** (*Mech*) tensión f; esfuerzo m; (*damage*) deformación f; **the — on a rope** la tensión de una cuerda; **breaking —** esfuerzo m de ruptura; **to take the — off a beam** disminuir la presión sobre una viga; **can you take some of the —?** ¿me puedes ayudar a sostener (*etc*) esto?

(**b**) (*fig*) tensión f, tirantez f; esfuerzo m (grande, excesivo); **mental —** agotamiento m nervioso, postración f nerviosa; **the —s of international politics** las tensiones de la política internacional; **the —s on the economy** las presiones sobre la economía; **the —s of modern life** las tensiones de la vida moderna; **the — of 6 hours at the wheel** el agotamiento nervioso que producen 6 horas al volante; **to write without —** escribir sin esfuerzo; **to put a great — on someone** someter a uno a gran esfuerzo; exigir un gran esfuerzo a uno.

(**c**) (*Med*) torcedura f.

(**d**) **—s** (*Mus*) son m, compases mpl; **the —s of a waltz** los compases de un vals; **the bride came in to the —s of the wedding march** la novia entró a los acordes (*or* compases) de la marcha nupcial.

(**e**) (*tenor*) tenor m, estilo m, sentido m; **there was a lot else in the same —** hubo mucho más a este tenor.

2 vt **(a)** (*stretch*) estirar, poner tirante, tender con fuerza.

(**b**) (*overtax: Med*) deformar, dañar por esfuerzo excesivo; *back, muscle etc* torcerse; *eyes* cansar; *heart* cansar (exigiendo un esfuerzo excesivo a); *patience etc* cansar, abusar de; *meaning, word* forzar, hacer violencia a; *friendship, relationship* pedir demasiado a; crear tensiones en, crear tirantez en; **to — one's ears to hear** esforzarse por oír; **to — the law to help someone** hacer violencia a una ley para ayudar a uno.

(**c**) **to — someone to one's breast** abrazar a uno estrechamente.

(**d**) (*filter*) filtrar; (*Cook*) colar; **to — the water off** separar el agua.

3 vi: **to — at something** esforzarse tirando de algo, tirar con fuerza de algo; **don't — at it** no te esfuerces tanto, no te hagas daño tirando tanto; **they —ed at the crate** manipulaban el cajón con gran esfuerzo; **to — after something** esforzarse por conseguir algo; **to — to do something** esforzarse por hacer algo, hacer grandes esfuerzos por hacer algo.

strain² [strein] n (*breed*) raza f, linaje m; (*tendency*) tendencia f; **a — of weakness** un rasgo de debilidad; **a — of madness** una vena de locura.

strained [streind] *adj muscle etc* torcido; *laugh, smile etc* forzado; *relations* tenso, tirante; *style* que muestra esfuerzo, afectado.

strainer ['streinə*] n (*Cook*) colador m; (*Tech*) filtro m, coladero m.

strait [streit] n **(a)** (*Geog: also* **—s**) estrecho m; **the S— of Gibraltar** el Estrecho de Gibraltar.

(**b**) **—s** (*fig*) estrecheces fpl; situación f apurada, apuro m; **to be in dire —s** estar muy apurado; **the economic —s we are in** la difícil situación económica en que nos encontramos.

straitened ['streitnd] *adj*: **in — circumstances** en apuro, en la necesidad.

strait jacket ['streit,dʒækit] n camisa f de fuerza.

strait-laced ['streit'leist] *adj* gazmoño; remilgado.

strand¹ [strænd] (*Naut*) **1** n (*lit*) playa f, ribera f.

2 vt *ship* varar, encallar; **to — someone without money in London** dejar a uno sin dinero ni recursos en Londres; **to be —ed** (*person*) quedar solo, estar sin poderse ayudar, estar abandonado, (*by missing train etc*) quedarse colgado; (*car etc*) quedar inmovilizado; **to leave someone —ed** dejar a uno desamparado, dejar a uno plantado.

3 vi varar, encallar.

strand² [strænd] n (*of rope*) ramal m; (*of thread*) hebra f, filamento m; (*of hair*) trenza f; (*of plant*) brizna f; **to tie up the loose —s** (*fig*) atar cabos.

strange [streindʒ] *adj* (*unknown*) desconocido (*to* de); (*new*) nuevo (*to* para), no acostumbrado; (*odd*) extraño, raro, curioso; (*exotic*) exótico, peregrino; **how —!** ¡qué raro!; **it is — that . . . es** raro que + *subj*; **I find it — that . . .** me extraña que + *subj*; **I felt rather — at first** al principio no me sentí cómodo, me sentí algo molesto al principio; **I am — to the work** soy nuevo en el oficio, el trabajo es nuevo para mí; **— to say . . .** aunque parece mentira . . .

strangely ['streindʒli] *adv* extrañamente; de un modo raro; **it was — familiar to me** me era extrañamente familiar; **she acts somewhat —** se comporta de un modo bastante raro.

strangeness ['streindʒnis] n novedad f; extrañeza f, rareza f; lo exótico.

stranger ['streindʒə*] n desconocido m, a f; (*from another area etc*) forastero m, a f; **he's a — to me** es nn desconocido para mí; **I'm a — here** yo no soy de aquí, yo soy nuevo aquí; **he is no — to vice** conoce bien los vicios.

strangle ['stræŋgl] vt estrangular; (*fig*) *abuse, sob etc* ahogar.

stranglehold ['stræŋglhəuld] n (*Sport*) collar m de fuerza; (*fig*) dominio m completo; **to have a — on something** (*fig*) dominar algo completamente.

strangler ['stræŋglə*] n estrangulador m.

strangling ['stræŋgliŋ] n estrangulación f.

strangulated ['stræŋgjuleitid] *adj* (*Med*) estrangulado.

strangulation [,stræŋgju'leiʃən] n estrangulación f (*also Med*).

strap [stræp] **1** n correa f; (*Sew etc*) tira f, banda f; (*shoulder —*) tirante m, hombrera f; **to give someone the —** azotar a uno con una correa (como castigo).

2 vt (*tie*) atar con correa; **to — someone down** sujetar a uno con correa; **to — someone (***as punishment***)** azotar a uno con una correa.

straphang ['stræphæŋ] vi (*fam*) viajar de pie (agarrado a la correa).

straphanger ['stræphæŋə*] n pasajero m que va de pie (agarrado a la correa).

strapless ['stræplis] *adj dress* sin tirantes.

strapping ['stræpiŋ] *adj* robusto, fornido.

Strasbourg ['stræzbəːg] Estrasburgo.

stratagem ['strætidʒəm] n estratagema f.

strategic(al) [strə'tiːdʒik(əl)] *adj* estratégico.

strategist ['strætidʒist] n estratega m.

strategy ['strætidʒi] n estrategia f.

stratification [,strætifi'keiʃən] n estratificación f.

stratified ['strætifaid] *adj* estratificado.

stratify ['strætifai] **1** vt estratificar. **2** vi estratificarse.

stratocruiser ['strætəu,kruːzə*] n avión m estratosférico.

stratosphere ['strætəusfiə*] n estratosfera f.

stratospheric [,strætəus'ferik] *adj* estratosférico.

stratum ['strɑːtəm] n, pl **strata** ['strɑːtə] estrato m; (*fig*) estrato m, capa f.

straw [strɔː] **1** n paja f; (*drinking —*) pajita f; **to drink through a —** sorber con una pajita; **it's the last —!** ¡es el colmo!; **it's a — in the wind** es un indicio de cómo van las cosas; **to clutch at —s** echar mano de cualquier expediente.

2 *adj, attr* de paja; (*colour*) pajizo, color paja.

strawberry ['strɔːbəri] n (*fruit and plant*) fresa f; (*large, cultivated*) fresón m.

strawberry bed ['strɔːbəribed] n fresal m.

straw-coloured ['strɔː,kʌləd] *adj* pajizo, color paja.

straw hat ['strɔː'hæt] n sombrero m de paja.

straw loft ['strɔːlɒft] n pajar m, pajera f.

straw vote ['strɔː'vəut] n votación f de tanteo.
stray [strei] **1** adj animal etc extraviado; bullet
perdido; (isolated) aislado; (scattered) disperso;
(sporadic) esporádico; a — cat un gato extraviado,
un gato errante; in a few — cases en algunos casos
aislados; a few — thoughts unos cuantos pensamientos inconexos.

2 n (animal) animal m extraviado m; (child) niño
m sin hogar, niño m desamparado, niña f sin hogar,
niña f desamparada; —s (Radio) parásitos mpl.

3 vi (lose oneself) extraviarse, perderse; (wander)
vagar, errar; to — from apartarse de (also fig);
we had —ed 2 kilometres from the path nos
habíamos desviado 2 kilómetros del camino; they
—ed into the enemy camp erraron el camino y
se encontraron en el campamento enemigo; if the
gate is left open the cattle — si se deja abierta la
puerta las vacas se escapan.

streak ['striːk] **1** n (of) raya f, lista f, línea f delgada; (of
mineral) veta f, vena f; (fig: of madness etc) vena f;
(of luck) racha f; — of lightning rayo m (also fig);
there is a — of Spanish blood in her tiene una
pequeña parte de sangre española; he had a yellow
— era un tanto cobarde; he went past like a —
(of lightning) pasó como un rayo.

2 vt rayar, listar (with de).

3 vi: to — along correr a gran velocidad; to —
past pasar como un rayo.

streaky ['striːki] adj rayado, listado; bacon entreverado; shot con suerte, afortunado.

stream [striːm] **1** n (brook) arroyo m, riachuelo m;
(river) río m; (current) corriente f; (jet etc) chorro
m, flujo m; (fig) torrente m; lluvia f, oleada f;
(of cars etc) caravana f, riada f; —s of abuse torrente
m de injurias; —s of people multitud f de gente;
an unbroken — of cars una riada de coches; the
B — (School) el grupo B; people were coming out
in —s la gente salía en tropel; in one continuous
— ininterrumpidamente; against the — contra la
corriente; with the — con la corriente.

2 vt (a) water etc derramar, dejar correr; blood
manar; his face —ed blood la sangre le corría por
la cara.

(b) (School) clasificar, poner en grupos.

3 vi (liquid) correr, fluir; (blood) manar, correr;
(in wind etc) ondear, flotar; her eyes were —ing
lloraba a mares; the gas made my eyes — el gas
me hizo lagrimear; her cheeks were —ing with
tears las lágrimas le corrían por las mejillas, tenía
las mejillas bañadas en lágrimas; to — out (of
liquid) brotar, chorrear, salir a borbotones; people
came —ing out la gente salía en tropel; the cars
kept —ing past los coches pasaban ininterrumpidamente; her hair —ed in the wind su pelo le ondeaba
al viento.

streamer ['striːmə*] n flámula f; (Naut) gallardete
m; (of paper, at parties etc) serpentina f.

streamline ['striːmlain] vt aerodinamizar; (fig)
coordinar, perfeccionar, hacer más eficiente.

streamlined ['striːmlaind] adj aerodinámico.

street [striːt] **1** n calle f; the back —s (quiet) las
calles tranquilas, (poor) las calles de los barrios
bajos; he came from the —s of Seville salió
de los barrios bajos de Sevilla; to be on easy —
tener una vida fácil, vivir en el lujo; main —
calle f mayor, calle f principal; one-way — calle
f de dirección única; it's right up my — de eso sí
sé algo; eso viene pintiparado para mí; to be —s
ahead of someone llevar mucha ventaja a uno,
haberse adelantado mucho a uno; we are —s ahead
of them in design les somos muy superiores en el
diseño; they're not in the same — as us no están a
nuestra altura, quedan muy inferiores a nosotros.

2 attr callejero, de la calle; — accident accidente
m de circulación; — incident incidente m callejero;
— musician músico m ambulante; at — level en el
nivel de la calle.

street arab ['striːt.ærəb] n golfo m, chiquillo m de la
calle.

streetcar ['striːtkɑː*] n (US) tranvía m.

street cleaner ['striːt.kliːnə*] n barrendero m.

street cries ['striːt.kraiz] npl pregones mpl, gritos
mpl de los vendedores ambulantes.

street door ['striːt'dɔː*] n puerta f de la calle.

street fighting ['striːt.faitiŋ] n luchas fpl en las calles.

street lamp ['striːtlæmp] n farol m.

street lighting ['striːt.laitiŋ] n alumbrado m
público.

street sweeper ['striːt.swiːpə*] n barrendero m.

street urchin ['striːt.əːtʃin] n golfo m, chiquillo m
de la calle.

streetwalker ['striːt.wɔːkə*] n prostituta f callejera.

strength [streŋθ] n (a) fuerza f; (toughness) resistencia f; (of person) fuerzas fpl, vigor m; (of colour,
feeling etc) intensidad f; (of drink) fuerza f; the
— of the pound el valor de la libra; — of character
carácter m, firmeza f de carácter; — of will
resolución f; tensile — resistencia f a la tensión;
on the — of fundándose en, confiando en; his —
failed him se sintió desfallecer, le abandonaron sus
fuerzas; give me —! ¡Dios me dé paciencia!;
to save (or reserve) one's — reservarse.

(b) (Mil etc) número m; complemento m; efectivos
mpl; fighting — número m de soldados (listos para
el combate); to be at full — tener todo su complemento; to be on the — ser miembro del regimiento
(etc); ser de plantilla; to come in — venir en gran
número; to take someone on to the — dar a uno un
puesto en el regimiento (etc).

strengthen ['streŋθən] **1** vt fortalecer, reforzar, hacer
más fuerte; consolidar. **2** vi fortalecerse, reforzarse,
hacerse más fuerte; consolidarse.

strengthening ['streŋθəniŋ] **1** adj (Med etc) fortifi-
cante, tonificante. **2** n fortalecimiento m, refuerzo
m; consolidación f.

strenuous ['strenjuəs] adj (energetic) enérgico,
vigoroso; (tough) arduo; (exhausting) agotador;
opposition etc tenaz; exercise fuerte; to make —
efforts to + infin esforzarse a más no poder por +
infin.

strenuously ['strenjuəsli] adv enérgicamente, vigorosamente; tenazmente; to try — to + infin
procurar por todos los medios + infin.

streptococcus [.streptəu'kɔkəs] n, pl —cocci
['kɔkai] estreptococo m.

streptomycin [.streptəu'maisin] n estreptomicina f.

stress [stres] **1** n (a) (constraining force) fuerza f,
compulsión f; presión f; under — of bajo la compulsión de, impulsado por.

(b) (strain) tensión f; the —es and strains of
modern life las presiones y tensiones de la vida
moderna; mental —, nervous — tensión f nerviosa;
times of — tiempos mpl difíciles; to be under —
sufrir una tensión nerviosa; to subject someone to
great — someter a uno a grandes tensiones.

(c) (emphasis) énfasis m; (accent) acento m;
— system sistema m de acentos, acentuación f;
the — is on the second syllable el acento cae en la
segunda sílaba, la segunda sílaba está acentuada;
to lay great — on something insistir mucho en algo,
subrayar algo, recalcar la importancia de algo.

(d) (Mech) tensión f, carga f; esfuerzo m;
tensile — esfuerzo m de tensión.

stressed [strest] adj acentuado.

stressful ['stresful] adj lleno de tensión (nerviosa),
que produce tensión (nerviosa).

stretch [stretʃ] **1** n (a) (act of —ing) extensión f;
estirón m; for hours at a — durante horas enteras;
3 days at a — 3 días seguidos; he read the lot at one
— los leyó todos de un tirón; to be at full —, to go
at full — esforzarse al máximo, emplear todas sus
fuerzas (físicas etc); when the engine is at full —
cuando el motor rinde su potencia máxima; with
arms at full — con los brazos completamente
extendidos; by a — of the imagination con un
esfuerzo de imaginación.

(b) (amount of —) elasticidad f; capacidad f
para ser estirado (or extendido).

(c) (distance) trecho m; extensión f; (of road
etc) tramo m; (scope) alcance m; (of time) período
m; home — recta f de llegada, (fig) última etapa f;
in that — of the river en aquella parte del río;
a splendid — of countryside un magnífico paisaje;
for a long — it runs between . . . una extensión
considerable corre entre . . .; for a long — of time
durante mucho tiempo; to do a — (sl) cumplir una
condena (en la cárcel).

2 vt (a) (also to — out) (pull out) extender, estirar,
alargar; (widen) ensanchar, dilatar; arm extender;
hand etc tender, alargar; (spread on ground etc)
extender; to — one's legs estirar las piernas, (after
stiffness) desentumecerse las piernas, (fig) dar un
paseíto; the blow —ed him (out) cold on the floor
el golpe lo tumbó sin sentido en el suelo.

(b) money, resources estirar, hacer llegar.

(c) meaning forzar, violentar; to — a point
hacer una excepción, hacer una concesión; that's
—ing it too far eso va demasiado lejos.

(d) athlete, student etc exigir el máximo esfuerzo
a; the course does not — the student enough
el curso no exige bastante esfuerzo a los estudiantes.

3 vi (also to — out) extenderse, estirarse, alargarse;
ensancharse, dilatarse; (after sleep etc) estirar los
brazos (etc), desentumecerse las piernas; this cloth

won't — esta tela no se estira; **will it —?** (*le reach*) ¿llega?; **how far will it —?** ¿hasta dónde llega?; ¿hasta dónde se extiende?; **it —es for miles along the river** se extiende varios kilómetros a lo largo del río; **he —ed out on the ground** se tendió en el suelo; **to — out to reach something** alargar el brazo (*etc*) para tomar algo.

4 *vr:* **to — oneself** (**a**) (*after sleep etc*) estirarse, estirarse los brazos.

(**b**) (*make effort*) esforzarse al máximo; **he doesn't — himself** no se esfuerza bastante, no se exige bastante esfuerzo a sí mismo.

stretcher ['stretʃə*] *n* (*Tech*) ensanchador *m*; (*for canvas*) bastidor *m*; (*Archit*) soga *f*; (*Med*) camilla *f*.

stretcher-bearer ['stretʃə‚beərə*] *n* camillero *m*.

stretcher case ['stretʃəkeis] *n* enfermo *m* (*or* herido *m*) que tiene que ser llevado en camilla.

stretcher party ['stretʃə‚paːti] *n* equipo *m* de camilleros.

strew [struː] (*irr:* pret **strewed** *or* **strewn**) *vt* (*scatter*) derramar, esparcir; (*cover*) cubrir, sembrar (*with* de); **to — one's belongings about the room** dejar sus cosas en desorden por todo el cuarto; **there were fragments —n about everywhere** había fragmentos desparramados por todas partes; **to — sand on the floor** cubrir el suelo de arena, esparcir arena sobre el suelo; **the floors are —n with rushes** los suelos están cubiertos de juncos.

striated [straiˈeitid] *adj* estriado.

stricken ['strikən] *adj* (*and in some senses* ptp *of* **strike**) (*wounded*) herido; (*doomed*) condenado; (*damaged*) destrozado; (*ill*) enfermo; **the — city** la ciudad condenada, la ciudad destrozada; **the — families** las familias afligidas; **to be — with** estar afligido por; **to be — with grief** estar agobiado por el dolor; **she was — with remorse** le remordió la conciencia.

strict [strikt] *adj* (**a**) (*precise*) estricto; exacto, preciso; riguroso; **in the — sense of the word** en el sentido estricto de la palabra; **we need — accuracy here** aquí es necesario emplear la más rigurosa exactitud; **— neutrality** neutralidad *f* rigurosa; **in — confidence** en la más absoluta confianza (*and see* **confidence**).

(**b**) *order, ban etc* terminante; *discipline* severo, riguroso.

(**c**) (*of person*) severo, riguroso; escrupuloso; **they're terribly — here** aquí son terriblemente rigurosos; **to be — with someone** ser severo con uno, tratar a uno con severidad.

strictly ['striktli] *adv* (**a**) estrictamente; exactamente; rigurosamente; **— speaking** en rigor; **not — true** no del todo verdad; **— between ourselves . . .** en confianza entre los dos . . .; **to be — accurate . . .** para decirlo con toda precisión . . .; **to remain — neutral** guardar la más rigurosa neutralidad.

(**b**) terminantemente; severamente; **it is — forbidden to** + *infin* se prohibe terminantemente + *infin.*

(**c**) severamente, rigurosamente; **to treat someone very —** tratar a uno con mucha severidad; **she was — brought up** se la educó estrictamente.

strictness ['striktnis] *n* exactitud *f*; rigor *m*, severidad *f*; lo terminante.

stricture ['striktʃə*] *n* (**a**) (*Med*) constricción *f*. (**b**) (*fig*) censura *f*, crítica *f*, reparo *m*; **to pass —s on someone** censurar a uno, poner reparos a uno.

stridden ['stridn] ptp *of* **stride.**

stride [straid] **1** *n* zancada *f*, tranco *m*, paso *m* largo; (*in measuring*) paso *m*; **he set off with big —s** partió a grandes zancadas; **to get into one's —** alcanzar el ritmo acostumbrado; **to make great —s** hacer grandes progresos; **to take it in one's —** sabérselo tomar bien, hacerlo sin esfuerzo, estar a la altura de las circunstancias.

2 (*irr:* pret **strode** ptp **stridden**) *vt horse* montar a horcajadas; poner una pierna a cada lado de; (*cross*) cruzar de un tranco.

3 *vi* (*also* **to — along**) andar a trancos, andar a pasos largos, dar zancadas; **to — away, to — off** alejarse a grandes zancadas; **to — up to someone** acercarse resueltamente a uno; **to — up and down** andar de aquí para allá a pasos largos.

stridency ['straidənsi] *n* estridencia *f*, estridor *m*; lo chillón; lo estrepitoso.

strident ['straidənt] *adj* estridente; *colour, person* chillón; *protest* fuerte, estrepitoso.

stridently ['straidəntli] *adv* ruidosamente, de modo estridente; estrepitosamente.

strife [straif] *n* lucha *f*; (*not armed*) lucha *f*, contienda *f*; disensión *f*; **party —** lucha *f* de partidos; **internal —** disensión *f* interna; **to cease from —** deponer las armas.

strike [straik] **1** *n* (**a**) (*of labour*) huelga *f*; **general —** huelga *f* general; **sympathy —** huelga *f* por solidaridad; **to be on —** estar en huelga; **to come out on —, to go on —** ponerse en huelga, declarar la huelga; *see* **hunger** *etc.*

(**b**) (*discovery*) descubrimiento *m* (repentino); **a big oil —** un descubrimiento de petróleo en gran cantidad; **to make a —** hacer un descubrimiento.

(**c**) (*Sport*) golpe *m.*

(**d**) (*Mil*) ataque *m*; **air —** ataque *m* aéreo, bombardeo *m.*

2 (*irr:* pret **struck,** ptp **struck** and in some senses **stricken**) *vt* (**a**) (*hit*) golpear; (*with fist etc*) pegar, dar una bofetada a; (*wound*) herir; (*Tech*) percutir; (*with bullet etc*) alcanzar; *ball* golpear; *blow* asestar (*at* a); *chord* tocar; *instrument* herir, pulsar; tocar; **never — a woman** no pegar nunca a una mujer; **to — one's fist on the table, to — the table with one's fist** golpear la mesa con el puño; **the president was struck by two bullets** el presidente fue alcanzado por dos balas; **the tower was struck by lightning** cayó un rayo en la torre; **a fisherman was struck by lightning** un rayo mató a un pescador; **the light —s the window** la luz hiere la ventana.

(**b**) (*produce, make*) *coin, medal* acuñar; *a light, match* frotar, encender; **to — sparks from something** hacer que algo eche chispas; **to — a cutting** hacer que un esqueje arranque; **to — root** echar raíces, arraigar; **to — someone blind** cegar a uno; **to — someone deaf** ensordecer a uno; **to — someone dumb** (*fig*) dejar a uno sin habla; **to — terror into someone** infundir terror a uno.

(**c**) (*collide with, meet*) dar con; *rocks etc* chocar contra, estrellarse contra; *mine* chocar con; *difficulty, obstacle* encontrar, topar con; **a sound struck my ear** un ruido hirió mi oído; **his head struck the beam** dio con la cabeza contra la viga.

(**d**) (*of thoughts, impressions*) **it —s me that . . . ,** **the thought —s me that . . .** se me ocurre que . . .; **has it ever struck you that . . .?** ¿has pensado alguna vez que . . .?; **it —s me as being most unlikely** creo que es muy poco probable; **at least that's how it —s me** por lo menos eso es lo que pienso yo; **how does she — you?** ¿qué te parece (ella)?, ¿qué impresión te hace ella?; **I was much struck by his sincerity** su sinceridad me impresionó mucho; **I'm not much struck (with him)** no me hace buena impresión.

(**e**) (*find*) descubrir, encontrar; **to — oil** descubrir un yacimiento de petróleo; **he struck it rich** descubrió un buen filón, tuvo mucha suerte.

(**f**) **to — camp** levantar el campamento; **to — the flag** arriar la bandera.

(**g**) **to — work** abandonar el trabajo, declarar la huelga.

(**h**) *attitude* tomar, adoptar.

(**i**) **to — an average** calcular el promedio; **to — a balance** (*Comm*) hacer balance, (*fig*) establecer un equilibrio (*between* entre); **to — a bargain** cerrar un trato.

(**j**) (*with adv or prep*) **to — down** derribar; **he was struck down by paralysis** tuvo una parálisis, le acometió una parálisis; **he was struck down in his prime** se le llevó la muerte en la flor de la vida; **to — off** (*cut off*) cortar; cercenar, quitar de golpe; (*from list*) borrar, tachar; (*print*) tirar, imprimir; (*deduct*) rebajar; **to — out** borrar, tachar; **to — through** (*cross out*) tachar; (*penetrate*) penetrar; **to — up** *music* iniciar, empezar a tocar; *conversation* entablar; *friendship* trabar.

3 *vi* (**a**) (*attack, Mil etc*) atacar; **now is the time to —** éste es el momento en que conviene atacar; **to — against something** dar con algo, dar contra algo, chocar contra algo; **to — at someone** asestar un golpe a uno, tratar de golpear a uno; acometer a uno; (*Mil*) atacar a uno; **this —s at our very existence** esto amenaza con destruir nuestra misma existencia; **to — out** empezar a repartir golpes; **to — out wildly** dar golpes sin mirar a quién; *see* **home, iron** *etc.*

(**b**) (*of clock*) dar la hora; **the clock has struck** ha dado la hora ya; **when one's hour —s** cuando llega la hora de uno.

(**c**) (*of labour*) abandonar el trabajo, declarar la huelga; estar en huelga; **to — for higher wages** hacer una huelga para conseguir un aumento de los sueldos.

(**d**) (*of match*) encenderse.

(**e**) (*Naut: run aground*) encallar; tocar el fondo, dar contra las rocas.

(**f**) (*Naut: surrender*) arriar la bandera.

(**g**) (*Bot*) echar raíces, arraigar.

(h) to — on an idea ocurrírsele a uno una idea. **(i) the band struck up** la orquesta empezó a tocar.
(j) (*of movement, with adv or prep*) **to — across country** ir a campo traviesa; **to — into the woods** ir por el bosque, penetrar en el bosque; **the road —s off to the right** el camino se desvía hacia la derecha; **to — out for the shore** (empezar a) nadar (resueltamente) hacia la playa; **to — out for oneself, to — out on one's own** (*fig*) hacerse independiente, hacer rancho aparte, obrar por cuenta propia; **the sun —s through the mist** el sol penetra por entre la niebla.

strikebreaker ['straik,breikə*] *n* esquirol *m*.
strike fund ['straikfʌnd] *n* fondo *m* de huelga, caja *f* de resistencia.
strike pay ['straikpei] *n* subsidio *m* de huelga.
striker ['straikə*] *n* huelguista *mf*.
striking ['straikiŋ] *adj* notable, impresionante; chocante, sorprendente; *contrast etc* acusado, hiriente; *colour etc* llamativo; **of — appearance** de aspecto impresionante; **a — woman** una mujer imponente; **it is — that** . . . es chocante que . . .
strikingly ['straikiŋli] *adv* notablemente; de modo sorprendente; **a — beautiful woman** una mujer de notable hermosura, una mujer extraordinariamente hermosa.
string [striŋ] **1** *n* **(a)** (*cord*) cuerda *f*; cordel *m*, bramante *m*; guita *f*; (*of beads*) hilo *m*, sarta *f*, collar *m*; (*of onions, garlic*) ristra *f*; (*of horses etc*) reata *f*; (*of lies*) sarta *f*; (*of curses*) serie *f*, retahíla *f*; (*row*) fila *f*, hilera *f*; (*of people*) hilera *f*, desfile *m*; (*of vehicles*) caravana *f*; **to have someone on a —** dominar completamente la voluntad de uno, mover a uno como una marioneta; **to pull —s** tocar resortes, mover palancas.
(b) (*Mus*) cuerda *f*; **—s** instrumentos *mpl* de cuerda; **to have two —s to one's bow** tener dos cuerdas en su arco; **— instrument** instrumento *m* de cuerda; **— quartet** cuarteto *m* de cuerdas.
(c) (*Bot*) fibra *f*, nervio *m*.
(d) (*fig*) condición *f*; **without —s** sin condiciones; **there are no —s attached** no hay condiciones impuestas.
2 (*irr: pret and ptp* **strung**) *vt* **(a)** *pearls etc* ensartar (*also* **to — together**); *bow, violin* encordar; **to — sentences together** ir ensartando frases; **they are just stray thoughts strung together** son pensamientos aislados que se han ensartado sin propósito; **to — someone up** (*fam*) ahorcar a uno.
(b) *beans etc* quitar las fibras de.
3 *vi*: **to — along with someone** pegarse a uno, acompañar a uno; **to — out along a road** extenderse por una carretera; **they were strung out for miles** se extendían sobre varios kilómetros; **the posts are strung out across the desert** hay una serie de puestos aislados a través del desierto; **his plays are strung out from 1940 to 1965** aparecieron sus obras una a una desde 1940 hasta 1965; **they are too strung out to form a series** están demasiado aislados unos de otros para formar una serie.
4 *vr*: **to — oneself up to do something** resolverse a hacer algo, cobrar ánimo para hacer algo.
string bean ['striŋ'biːn] *n* (*US*) habichuela *f*, judía *f*.
stringed [striŋd] *adj instrument* de cuerda(s); **4-stringed** de 4 cuerdas.
stringency ['strindʒənsi] *n* **(a)** rigor *m*, severidad *f*. **(b)** tirantez *f*, dificultad *f*; **economic —** situación *f* económica apurada, estrechez *f*.
stringent ['strindʒənt] *adj* **(a)** riguroso, severo; **— rules** reglas *fpl* rigurosas; **we shall have to be — about it** tendremos que obrar con rigor.
(b) (*Comm etc*) tirante, difícil.
stringently ['strindʒəntli] *adv* severamente, rigurosamente.
stringy ['striŋi] *adj* fibroso, lleno de fibras.
strip [strip] **1** *n* tira *f*; banda *f*, faja *f*; (*of land*) zona *f*, franja *f*; (*of metal*) cinta *f*, lámina *f*; **comic —** tira *f* cómica, banda *f* de dibujos.
2 *vt* **(a)** (*denude*) desnudar, quitar la ropa (*etc*) a; **to — someone naked** desnudar a uno completamente, dejar a uno en cueros; **to — off one's clothes** quitarse (rápidamente) la ropa, despojarse de la ropa; **the wind —ped the leaves off the trees** el viento arrancó las hojas de los árboles; **to — someone of something** despojar a uno de algo; **to — a house of its furniture** dejar una casa sin muebles; **—ped of all the verbiage, this means** . . . sin palabrería, esto quiere decir . . .; **to — someone to the skin** dejar a uno en cueros.
(b) (*Tech*) desmontar, desmantelar; *gears* estropear.

3 *vi* desnudarse, quitarse la ropa; **to — off** desnudarse; (*of paint etc*) desprenderse; separarse; **to — to the skin** quitarse toda la ropa; **to — to the waist** desnudarse hasta la cintura.
strip cartoon ['stripkaː'tuːn] *n* tira *f* cómica, banda *f* de dibujos.
stripe [straip] **1** *n* raya *f*, lista *f*, banda *f*; (*Mil*) galón *m*; (*lash*) azote *m*, (*weal*) cardenal *m*. **2** *vt* rayar, listar (*with* de).
striped [straipt] *adj* listado, rayado; *trousers etc* a rayas.
strip lighting ['strip,laitiŋ] *n* alumbrado *m* de banda.
stripling ['stripliŋ] *n* mozuelo *m*, joven *m* imberbe.
stripper ['stripə*] *n* (*fam*) artista *f* de striptise.
striptease ['striptiːz] *n* estriptise *f* (*espectáculo en el cual la artista se va despojando progresivamente de la ropa*).
strive [straiv] (*irr: pret* **strove**, *ptp* **striven**) *vi* esforzarse, afanarse, luchar; **to — after something, to — for something** luchar por conseguir algo, afanarse por conseguir algo; **to — against something** luchar contra algo; **to — to do something** esforzarse por hacer algo, luchar por hacer algo.
striven ['strivn] *ptp* of **strive**.
strode [strəud] *pret* of **stride**.
stroke¹ [strəuk] **1** *n* **(a)** (*blow*) golpe *m*; **10 —s of the lash** 10 azotes; **— of lightning** rayo *m*; **at a —**, at **one —** de un golpe; **with one — of his knife** de un cuchillazo; **with one fell —** de un solo golpe fatal.
(b) (*Sport etc: Cricket, Golf*) golpe *m*; jugada *f*; (*Billiards*) tacada *f*; (*Rowing*) remada *f*, golpe *m*; (*Swimming: movement*) brazada *f*, (*type of —*) estilo *m*; **with a total of 281 —s** con un total de 281 golpes; **good —!** ¡muy bien!; **he went ahead at every —** se adelantaba con cada brazada; **they are rowing a fast —** reman a ritmo rápido; **he hasn't done a — of work** no ha hecho absolutamente nada; **he doesn't do a —** no da golpe; **— of diplomacy** éxito *m* diplomático; **— of genius** rasgo *m* de ingenio, genialidad *f*; **the idea was a — of genius** la idea ha sido genial; **— of luck** racha *f* de suerte; **by a — of luck** por suerte; **then we had a — of luck** luego nos favoreció la suerte; **a good — of business** un buen negocio; **his greatest — was to** . . . su golpe maestro fue . . .; *see* **master —**.
(c) (*of bell, clock*) campanada *f*; **on the — of 12** al acabar de dar las 12, a las 12 en punto; **to arrive on the —** (*of time*) llegar a la hora justa.
(d) (*of piston*) carrera *f*; **two-stroke engine** motor *m* de dos tiempos.
(e) (*Med*) ataque *m* fulminante, apoplejía *f*; **to have a —** tener una apoplejía; *see* **heat —**.
(f) (*of pen*) trazo *m*; rasgo *m*, plumada *f*, plumazo *m*; (*of pencil*) trazo *m*; (*of brush*) pincelada *f*; **at a — of the pen, with one — of the pen** de un plumazo; **with a thick — of the pen** con un trazo grueso de la pluma.
(g) (*Rowing: person*) primer remero *m*; **to row —** ser el primer remero, remar en el primer puesto.
2 *vt*: **to — a boat** ser el primer remero; **to — a boat to victory** ser el primer remero en el bote vencedor.
stroke² [strəuk] **1** *n* (*caress*) caricia *f*; **with a light — of the hand** con un suave movimiento de la mano.
2 *vt* acariciar; frotar suavemente; *eg chin* pasar la mano sobre, pasar la mano por.
stroll [strəul] **1** *n* paseo *m*, vuelta *f*; **to go for a —**, **to have a —** dar un paseo; **to take a —** dar un paseo.
2 *vi* pasear(se), dar un paseo, deambular, callejear; **to — up and down** pasearse de acá para allá; **to — up to someone** acercarse tranquilamente a uno.
stroller ['strəulə*] *n* paseante *mf*; (*US*) cochecito *m*.
strolling ['strəuliŋ] *adj actor etc* ambulante.
strong [strɔŋ] **1** *adj* fuerte; recio, robusto; enérgico; vigoroso; sólido; (*Fin*) firme; *accent* marcado; *believer* fervoroso; *candidate* que tiene buenas posibilidades, respetable; *characteristic* acusado; *coffee* fuerte, cargado; *colour* intenso; *constitution* robusto; *conviction* profundo, sincero; *drink* fuerte, alcohólico; *emotion* fuerte, intenso; *evidence* fehaciente; *feature* acusado; *flavour* fuerte; *language* fuerte, indecente; *measure* enérgico; *personality* acusado; *protest* enérgico; *reason* convincente; *situation* dramático, lleno de emoción; *smell* fuerte, penetrante, punzante; *solution* concentrado; *suit* (*Cards*) largo; *supporter* acérrimo; *tea* fuerte, cargado; *terms* enfático; *verb* irregular, fuerte; *voice* fuerte; *wind* fuerte, recio, violento; **to be as — as a horse** ser tan fuerte como un león; **to be — in the arm** tener los brazos fuertes; **to be — in chemistry** estar fuerte en química; **we are — in**

forwards tenemos una buena línea delantera; **the gallery is — in Goya** el museo tiene muchas obras de Goya; **he's getting —er every day** se va reponiendo poco a poco; **when you are — again** cuando te hayas repuesto del todo; **a group 20 —** un grupo de 20 (miembros *etc*); **they were 50 —** eran 50, contaban 50.

2 *adv*: **the market closed —** el mercado se cerró en situación firme; **he was going — still at the tape** al llegar a la recta corría todavía con pleno vigor; **he pitches it pretty —** exagera mucho, es un exagerado.

strong-arm ['strɔŋɑːm] *adj policy, methods* de mano dura.

strong-armed ['strɔŋ'ɑːmd] *adj* de brazos fuertes.

strongbox ['strɔŋbɔks] *n* caja *f* de caudales, caja *f* fuerte.

stronghold ['strɔŋhəuld] *n* fortaleza *f*, plaza *f* fuerte; (*fig*) baluarte *m*, centro *m*; **the last — of . . .** el último reducto de . . .

strongly ['strɔŋli] *adv* fuertemente; enérgicamente, vigorosamente; firmemente; fervorosamente; intensamente; **I — believe that . . .** creo firmemente que . . .; **he smelled — of beer** despedía fuerte olor a cerveza; **— marked** acusado, acentuado; **a — worded letter** una carta de tono enérgico.

strong-minded ['strɔŋ'maindid] *adj* resuelto; de carácter.

strong-mindedness ['strɔŋ'maindidnis] *n* resolución *f*; carácter *m*.

strongpoint ['strɔŋpɔint] *n* fuerte *m*, puesto *m* fortificado.

strongroom ['strɔŋrum] *n* cámara *f* acorazada.

strong-willed ['strɔŋ'wild] *adj* resuelto, de voluntad firme; (*pej*) obstinado.

strontium ['strɔntiəm] *n* estroncio *m*; **— 90** estroncio *m* 90.

strop [strɔp] 1 *n* suavizador *m*. 2 *vt* suavizar.

strophe ['strəufi] *n* estrofa *f*.

strove [strəuv] *pret of* **strive**.

struck [strʌk] *pret and ptp of* **strike**.

structural ['strʌktʃərəl] *adj* estructural.

structurally ['strʌktʃərəli] *adv* estructuralmente, desde el punto de vista de la estructura; **— sound** de estructura sólida.

structure ['strʌktʃə*] *n* estructura *f*; construcción *f*.

struggle ['strʌgl] 1 *n* lucha *f*; contienda *f*, conflicto *m*; (*effort*) esfuerzo *m*; **without a —** sin luchar, (*bloodlessly*) sin efusión de sangre; **the — for survival** la lucha por la vida; **the — to find a flat** la lucha por encontrarse un piso.

2 *vi* luchar; esforzarse; **to — to do something** luchar por hacer algo, esforzarse por hacer algo; **to — in vain** luchar en vano; **to — to one's feet** luchar por levantarse; levantarse con esfuerzo; **we —d on another kilometre** avanzamos con dificultad un kilómetro más; **he —d up the rock** subió penosamente por la roca; **the light tries to — through the panes** la luz se esfuerza por penetrar por los cristales.

strum [strʌm] 1 *vt guitar etc* rasguear; tocar distraídamente; tocar mal. 2 *vi* cencerrear.

strumpet ['strʌmpit] *n* ramera *f*.

strung [strʌŋ] *pret and ptp of* **string**; *see* **highly —**.

strut[1] [strʌt] *vi* (*also* **to — about**, **to — along**) pavonearse, contonearse; **to — into a room** entrar pavoneándose en un cuarto; **to — past someone** pasar delante de uno con paso majestuoso.

strut[2] [strʌt] *n* puntal *m*, riostra *f*, tornapunta *f*.

strychnine ['strikniːn] *n* estricnina *f*.

Stuart ['stjuːət] *m* Estuardo.

stub [stʌb] 1 *n* (*of tree*) tocón *m*; (*of cigarette*) colilla *f*; (*of candle, pencil etc*) cabo *m*; (*of cheque, receipt*) talón *m*.

2 *vt*: **to — one's toe** dar con el dedo del pie contra algo, dar un tropezón; **to — out** *cigarette* apagar; **to — up** *tree trunks* desarraigar, quitar.

stubble ['stʌbl] *n* rastrojo *m*; (*on chin*) barba *f* de tres días.

stubble field ['stʌblfiːld] *n* rastrojera *f*.

stubbly ['stʌbli] *adj chin* cerdoso, con barba de tres días; *beard* de tres días.

stubborn ['stʌbən] *adj* 'tenaz; *refusal* resuelto; inquebrantable; (*pej*) terco, testarudo, porfiado.

stubbornly ['stʌbənli] *adv* tenazmente; tercamente, con porfía; **he — refused to +** *infin* se negó resueltamente a + *infin*.

stubbornness ['stʌbənnis] *n* tenacidad *f*; terquedad *f*, testarudez *f*, porfía *f*.

stubby ['stʌbi] *adj* achaparrado.

stucco ['stʌkəu] 1 *n* estuco *m*. 2 *adj* de estuco. 3 *vt* estucar.

stuck [stʌk] *pret and ptp of* **stick**.

stuck-up ['stʌk'ʌp] *adj* (*fam*) engreído, presumido; **to be very — about something** presumir mucho a causa de algo.

stud[1] [stʌd] 1 *n* (*Mil*) tachón *m*; (*boot—*) taco *m*; (*decorative*) clavo *m* (de adorno); (*collar—*, *shirt—*) botón *m* de camisa.

2 *vt* tachonar; adornar con clavos; (*fig*) sembrar (*with* de).

stud[2] [stʌd] *n* caballeriza *f*, yeguada *f*.

studbook ['stʌdbuk] *n* registro *m* genealógico de caballos.

student ['stjuːdənt] 1 *n* (*pupil*) alumno *m*, a *f*; (*Univ*) estudiante *mf*; (*researcher*) investigador *m*, ora *f*; **French —** (*by nationality*) estudiante *m* francés, (*by subject*) estudiante *m* de francés; **medical —** estudiante *mf* de medicina; **old —'s association** asociación *f* de antiguos alumnos.

2 *attr* estudiantil.

studentship ['stjuːdəntʃip] *n* beca *f*.

stud farm ['stʌdfɑːm] *n* caballeriza *f*, yeguada *f*.

studhorse ['stʌdhɔːs] *n* caballo *m* padre.

studied ['stʌdid] *adj calm etc* calculado, deliberado; *insult* premeditado; *pose, style* afectado.

studio ['stjuːdiəu] *n* (*in most senses*) estudio *m*; (*sculptor's*) taller *m*; **television —** estudio *m* de televisión; **in our Barcelona —** en nuestro estudio de Barcelona.

studio couch ['stjuːdiəu,kautʃ] *n* sofá-cama *m*.

studious ['stjuːdiəs] *adj* estudioso; aplicado, asiduo; *see* **studied**.

studiously ['stjuːdiəsli] *adv* con aplicación; **he — avoided mentioning the matter** evitó cuidadosamente aludir al asunto, se guardó de aludir al asunto.

studiousness ['stjuːdiəsnis] *n* aplicación *f*.

stud mare ['stʌd,mɛə*] *n* yegua *f* de cría.

study ['stʌdi] 1 *n* (*in most senses*) estudio *m*; (*room*) despacho *m*, cuarto *m* de trabajo, estudio *m*; **to be in a brown —** estar absorto en la meditación, estar en Babia; **to make a — of something** estudiar algo, investigar algo; **my studies show that . . .** mis estudios demuestran que . . .

2 *vt* estudiar; investigar; examinar, mirar detenidamente; escudriñar.

3 *vi* estudiar; **to — under someone** estudiar con uno, trabajar bajo la dirección de uno; **to — for an exam** prepararse para un examen; **to — to be an agronomist** estudiar para agrónomo.

study group ['stʌdi'gruːp] *n grupo que se propone* (*o al que se le encarga*) *investigar un problema*.

stuff [stʌf] 1 *n* (a) (*material in general*) materia *f*; material *m*, sustancia *f*; **it's strange —** es una sustancia singular; **there is some good — in that book** ese libro tiene cosas buenas; **there's good — in him** tiene buenas cualidades; **it's poor —** no vale para nada; **do you call this — beer?** ¿llamas a esto cerveza?; **I can't read his —** no alcanzo a leer sus libros; **I can't listen to his —** no aguanto su música; **that's the —!** ¡muy bien!; **have you brought the —?** ¿lo has traído?, ¿has traído aquello?; **he is of the — that heroes are made of** tiene madera de héroe; **show him what — you are made of** demuéstrale tus cualidades, muéstrale si puedes o no.

(b) (*material, cloth*) tela *f*, paño *m*.

(c) (*possessions: fam*) cosas *fpl*, chismes *mpl*; **he leaves his — scattered about** deja sus cosas de cualquier modo; **is this your —?** ¿es tuyo esto?

(d) (*nonsense*) tonterías *fpl*; **all that — about Cervantes** todas esas tonterías acerca de Cervantes; **— and nonsense!** ¡ni hablar!, ¡narices!

(e) **hot —** (*sl*) cosa *f* maravillosa, persona *f* estupenda; **she's hot —** es cachonda, es de plan; **he's hot — at chess** es un hacha para el ajedrez.

(f) **to do one's —** (*fam*) actuar, trabajar *etc*; **you do your —** next tú eres el próximo; **he doesn't do his —** no trabaja (*etc*) como debiera; **he certainly knows his —** conoce perfectamente su oficio, domina su especialidad.

2 *vt* (*fill*) *container* llenar, hinchar, atiborrar (*with* de); (*stow*) *contents* meter sin orden, meter de prisa (*into* en); *hole, leak etc* tapar, atascar; (*Cook*) rellenar; *animal* (*for exhibition*) disecar; **to — away** *food* zampar, devorar; **he —ed it into his pocket** lo metió de prisa en el bolsillo; **can we — any more in?** ¿cabe más?; **her head is —ed with formulae** tiene la cabeza atiborrada de fórmulas; **two centuries —ed with history** dos siglos prietos (*or* llenos) de historia; **to be —ed up with** (a) *cold* estar fuertemente acatarrado; **get —ed!** (*sl*) ¡vete a la porra!

3 *vi* atracarse, comer a dos carrillos.

4 *vr*: **to — oneself with food** darse un atracón, atiborrarse de comida; **I have to — myself with sedatives** me veo obligado a embutirme de calmantes.

stuffed shirt ['stʌft'ʃəːt] *n* (*fam*) tragavirotes *m*.

stuffiness ['stʌfinis] *n* mala ventilación *f*, falta *f* de aire; (*fig*) estrechez *f* de miras; lo estirado; lo remilgado, pesadez *f*.

stuffing ['stʌfiŋ] *n* (*of furniture, animal*) relleno *m*, borra *f*; (*Cook*) relleno *m*; **he's got no —** no tiene carácter, no tiene agallas; **he had the — knocked out of him by the blow** el golpe le dejó sin fuerzas ni ánimo.

stuffy ['stʌfi] *adj* (**a**) *room* mal ventilado, donde falta el aire; *atmosphere* cargado, sofocante; **it's — in here** aquí falta el aire, aquí huele a encerrado.
(**b**) (*narrow-minded*) de miras estrechas; (*stiff*) estirado; (*prudish*) remilgado; (*of book etc*) pesado, poco interesante.

stultify ['stʌltifai] *vt* hacer inútil, quitar valor a, anular; hacer (parecer) ridículo.

stumble ['stʌmbl] **1** *n* tropezón *m*, traspié *m*.
2 *vi* tropezar, dar un traspié; **to — against** tropezar contra; **to — on** (*fig*) tropezar con, encontrar por casualidad; **to — on, to go stumbling on** avanzar dando traspiés; **to — through a speech** pronunciar muy mal un discurso.

stumbling block ['stʌmbliŋblɔk] *n* (*fig*) tropiezo *m*, obstáculo *m*.

stump [stʌmp] **1** *n* cabo *m*, fragmento *m*, último pedazo *m*; (*of tree etc*) tocón *m*; (*of limb*) muñón *m*; (*of tooth*) raigón *m*; (*Cricket*) palo *m*; (*Art*) esfumino *m*; (*fam*) pierna *f*; **to stir one's —s** (*fam*) menearse, moverse.
2 *vt* (**a**) desconcertar, dejar perplejo, dejar confuso; **I'm properly —ed** estoy totalmente perplejo; no sé qué hacer (*or* decir *etc*); no sé qué consejo darte; **he was —ed for an answer** no sabía qué contestar.
(**b**) **to — the country** (*Pol*) recorrer el país pronunciando discursos.
(**c**) (*fam*) **to — up £5** pagar 5 libras (de mala gana), desembolsar 5 libras (*for* para comprar algo, por algo).
3 *vi* (**a**) **to — about, to — along** andar pisando muy fuerte; (*lamely*) andar cojeando.
(**b**) **to — up** pagar (de mala gana; *for something* algo), soltar la guita.

stumpy ['stʌmpi] *adj person etc* achaparrado; *pencil etc* reducido a casi nada, muy gastado.

stun [stʌn] *vt* (*Med*) dejar sin sentido; aturdir de un golpe; (*fig*) aturdir, pasmar, dejar pasmado; **the news —ned everybody** la noticia aturdió a todos; **this will — you** esto será una gran sorpresa para ti; **the family were —ned by his death** la familia quedó anonadada a raíz de su muerte.

stung [stʌŋ] *pret and ptp of* **sting**.

stunk [stʌŋk] *ptp of* **stink**.

stunner ['stʌnə*] *n* (*fam*) persona *f* maravillosa, cosa *f* estupenda; **the picture is a —** el cuadro es maravilloso; **she's a real —** es francamente estupenda.

stunning ['stʌniŋ] *adj blow* que aturde; *news etc* pasmoso; *dress, girl etc* estupendo, maravilloso.

stunt¹ [stʌnt] *vt* atrofiar, impedir el desarrollo de.

stunt² [stʌnt] **1** *n* (*Aer*) vuelo m acrobático, ejercicio *m* acrobático; (*display*) proeza *f* excepcional; maniobra *f* sensacional; (*Comm*) truco *m* publicitario, treta *f* publicitaria; **it's just a — to get your money** es solamente un truco para sacarte dinero.
2 *vi* lucirse haciendo vuelos acrobáticos (*or* maniobras sensacionales *etc*).

stunted ['stʌntid] *adj* enano, achaparrado, mal desarrollado.

stuntman ['stʌntmæn] *n*, *pl* **—men** [men] *persona que se dedica a desempeñar los papeles peligrosos en el cine y otros espectáculos*.

stupefaction [ˌstjuːpi'fækʃən] *n* estupefacción *f*.

stupefy ['stjuːpifai] *vt* (**a**) (*Med*) causar estupor a, dejar sin conocimiento; **stupefied by drink** en estado de estupor después de haber bebido, (*permanently*) embrutecido por el alcohol.
(**b**) (*fig*) pasar, causar estupor a, dejar estupefacto.

stupefying ['stjuːpifaiiŋ] *adj* (*fig*) pasmoso.

stupendous [stjuː'pendəs] *adj* estupendo, asombroso.

stupendously [stjuː(ː)'pendəsli] *adv* estupendamente.

stupid ['stjuːpid] *adj* (*with sleep etc*) en estado de estupor, atontado; (*silly*) estúpido; **you — child!** ¡bobo!; **don't be —** no seas bobo; **that was — of you, that was a — thing to do** eso fue una estupidez;

I've done a — thing he hecho algo tonto; **to drink oneself —** beber tanto que uno queda en estado de estupor.

stupidly ['stjuːpidli] *adv* estúpidamente.

stupor ['stjuːpə*] *n* estupor *m* (*also fig*).

sturdily ['stəːdili] *adv* fuertemente; vigorosamente; enérgicamente; tenazmente; **— built** de construcción sólida, *person* robusto.

sturdiness ['stəːdinis] *n* robustez *f*, fuerza *f*; energía *f*; tenacidad *f*.

sturdy ['stəːdi] *adj* robusto, fuerte; vigoroso; *opposition etc* enérgico; *resistance* tenaz; **— independence** espíritu m fuerte de independencia.

sturgeon ['stəːdʒən] *n* esturión *m*.

stutter ['stʌtə*] **1** *n* tartamudeo *m*; **he has a bad —** tartamudea terriblemente; **to say something with a —** decir algo tartamudeando. **2** *vt* balbucir, decir tartamudeando (*also* **to — out**). **3** *vi* tartamudear; balbucir.

stutterer ['stʌtərə*] *n* tartamudo *m*, a *f*.

stuttering ['stʌtəriŋ] **1** *adj* tartamudo. **2** *n* tartamudeo *m*.

stutteringly ['stʌtəriŋli] *adv*: **he said —** dijo tartamudeando.

sty [stai] *n* pocilga *f*, zahurda *f*.

stye [stai] *n* (*Med*) orzuelo *m*.

Stygian ['stidʒiən] *adj* estigio.

style [stail] **1** *n* (**a**) estilo *m*; (*Art, Lit etc*) estilo *m*; (*fashion*) estilo *m*; moda *f*; (*elegance*) elegancia *f*; **— of living** estilo m de vida; **the Norman —** el estilo románico; **in the Italian —** al estilo italiano, a la italiana; **that's the —!** ¡bravo!, ¡muy bien!; **there's no — about him** no tiene elegancia en absoluto; **she has —** tiene garbo, tiene aquél; lo hace todo con elegancia; **to cramp someone's —** cortar los vuelos a uno; **to be in —** estar de moda; **to do something in —** hacer algo lo mejor posible, hacer algo realmente bien; **to travel in —** viajar con todo confort; **to live in —** vivir en el lujo; **he won in fine —** ganó de modo concluyente.
(**b**) (*of address*) tratamiento m; título m.
2 *vt* (**a**) *dress* cortar a la moda, estilizar.
(**b**) (*entitle*) intitular, nombrar.
3 *vr*: **to — oneself** intitularse, darse el título de.

style sheet ['stail.ʃiːt] *n hoja en que se explican las normas de ortografía y sistema de referencias (etc) que han de seguirse en las colaboraciones a una revista*.

styling ['stailiŋ] *n* estilización *f*.

stylish ['stailiʃ] *adj* elegante; a la moda.

stylishly ['stailiʃli] *adv* elegantemente.

stylishness ['stailiʃnis] *n* elegancia *f*.

stylist ['stailist] *n* estilista *mf*.

stylistic [stai'listik] *adj* estilístico.

stylistics [stai'listiks] *n* estilística *f*.

stylized ['stailaizd] *adj* estilizado.

stylus ['stailəs] *n* (*pen*) estilo *m*; (*of gramophone*) aguja *f*.

stymie ['staimi] *vt see* **stimy**.

styptic ['stiptik] **1** *adj* estíptico. **2** *n* estíptico *m*.

suasion ['sweiʒən] *n* (*lit*) persuasión *f*.

suave [swɑːv] *adj* afable, cortés, fino; (*pej*) zalamero.

suavely ['swɑːvli] *adv* afablemente, cortésmente, con finura; con zalamería.

suavity ['swɑːviti] *n* afabilidad *f*, cortesía *f*, finura *f*; zalamería *f*.

sub [sʌb] *n abbr of* **subaltern; submarine; subordinate; subscription; substitute**.

sub . . . [sʌb] sub . . .

subalpine ['sʌb'ælpain] *adj* subalpino.

subaltern ['sʌbltən] *n* (*Mil*) alférez *m*.

subarctic ['sʌb'ɑːktik] *adj* subártico.

subcommittee ['sʌbkəˌmiti] *n* subcomisión *f*.

subconscious ['sʌb'kɔnʃəs] **1** *adj* subconsciente. **2** *n*: **the —** el subconsciente, la subconsciencia; **in one's —** en el subconsciente.

subconsciously ['sʌb'kɔnʃəsli] *adv* de modo subconsciente.

subcontinent ['sʌb'kɔntinənt] *n* subcontinente *m*.

subcontract ['sʌb'kɔntrækt] *n* subcontrato *m*.

subcontract [ˌsʌbkən'trækt] *vt* subcontratar.

subcontractor ['sʌbkən'træktə*] *n* subcontratista *mf*.

subcutaneous ['sʌbkjuː'teiniəs] *adj* subcutáneo.

subdivide ['sʌbdi'vaid] **1** *vt* subdividir. **2** *vi* subdividirse.

subdivision ['sʌbdiˌviʒən] *n* subdivisión *f*.

subdue [səb'djuː] *vt* (*conquer*) sojuzgar, dominar, avasallar; (*diminish*) mitigar; *passions etc* dominar; *colour, voice etc* suavizar.

subdued [səb'djuːd] *adj emotion etc* templado, suave; *voice* bajo; *colour* suave, apagado; *light* tenue;

person (*docile*) sumiso, manso, (*depressed*) deprimido; **you were very — last night** anoche has mostrado poca animación, anoche estabas bastante callado; **he's very — these days** ahora es muy serio.

sub-edit ['sʌb'edit] *vt article* corregir, preparar para la prensa.

sub-editor ['sʌb'editə*] *n* redactor *m*.

subheading ['sʌb,hediŋ] *n* subtítulo *m*.

subhuman ['sʌb'hjuːmən] *adj* infrahumano.

subject ['sʌbdʒikt] **1** *adj* (a) *people* subyugado, esclavizado.

(b) **to be — to** (*obedient to*) estar sujeto a; (*liable to*) estar propenso a, (*exposed to*) estar expuesto a; **to be — to natural laws** estar sujeto a las leyes naturales.

2 — to *as prep*: **— to anything he may say** esto depende de lo que diga él; **— to the approval of** sujeto a la aprobación de; **— to change without notice** sujeto a cambio sin previo aviso; **— to correction** bajo corrección.

3 *n* (a) (*Pol*) súbdito *m*, a *f*; **British —** súbdito *m* británico; **liberty of the —** libertad *f* del ciudadano; libertad *f* del individuo.

(b) (*Gram*) sujeto *m*.

(c) (*theme*) tema *m*, materia *f*; asunto *m*, cuestión *f*; (*School, Univ*) asignatura *f*; (*Art, Lit, Mus*) tema *m*; **on the — of ...** a propósito de ...; **it's a delicate —** es un asunto delicado; **to change the —** volver la hoja, cambiar de conversación; **to keep off a —** no aludir a un tema, no discutir una cuestión; **to raise the — of the war** (*in conversation*) introducir el tema de la guerra, empezar a hablar de la guerra; **this raises the whole — of money** esto plantea el problema general del dinero.

(d) (*Med etc*) caso *m*; **he's a nervous —** es un caso nervioso; **guinea pigs make excellent —s** los conejillos son materia excelente (para los experimentos *etc*).

subject [səb'dʒekt] *vt* (a) (*conquer*) sojuzgar, dominar.

(b) someter (*to* a); **to — someone to a test** poner a uno a prueba; **to — a book to criticism** someter un libro a la crítica; **to be —ed to inquiry** ser sometido a la investigación; **I will not be —ed to this questioning** no tolero esta interrogación; **she was —ed to much indignity** tuvo que aguantar muchas afrentas.

subjection [səb'dʒekʃən] *n* (a) sujeción *f*; sometimiento *m*; **to bring a people into —** subyugar a un pueblo; **to hold a people in —** tener subyugado a un pueblo; **to be in — to someone** estar sometido a uno; **to be in a state of complete —** estar completamente sumiso.

(b) (*act*) sometimiento *m*, el someter.

subjective [səb'dʒektiv] *adj* subjetivo.

subjectively [səb'dʒektivli] *adv* subjetivamente.

subjectivism [səb'dʒektivizəm] *n* subjetivismo *m*.

subjectivity [,sʌbdʒek'tiviti] *n* subjetividad *f*.

subject matter ['sʌbdʒikt,mætə*] *n* materia *f*; (*of letter etc*) contenido *m*.

subjoin ['sʌb'dʒoin] *vt* adjuntar.

sub judice [sʌb'dʒuːdisi] *adj*: **the matter is —** el asunto está en manos del tribunal (y por lo tanto hay que abstenerse de hacer comentarios sobre él); (*loosely*) el asunto está pendiente todavía, el asunto está siendo estudiado.

subjugate ['sʌbdʒugeit] *vt* subyugar.

subjugation [,sʌbdʒu'geiʃən] *n* subyugación *f*; **to live in —** vivir subyugado.

subjunctive [səb'dʒʌŋktiv] **1** *adj* subjuntivo. **2** *n* subjuntivo *m*.

sublease ['sʌb'liːs] *vt*, **sublet** ['sʌb'let] (*irr: see* let) *vt* realquilar, subarrendar.

sub-librarian ['sʌblai'breəriən] *n* subdirector *m* de biblioteca, subdirectora *f* de biblioteca.

sub-lieutenant ['sʌblef'tenənt] *n* (*Naut*) alférez *m* de fragata; (*Mil*) subteniente *m*.

sublimate ['sʌblimit] *n* (*Chem*) sublimado *m*.

sublimate ['sʌblimeit] *vt* (*all senses*) sublimar.

sublimation [,sʌbli'meiʃən] *n* sublimación *f*.

sublime [sə'blaim] **1** *adj* sublime; **the —** lo sublime. **2** *vt* sublimar.

sublimely [sə'blaimli] *adv* sublimemente; **— unaware of ...** completamente inconsciente de ..., demasiado exaltado para darse cuenta de ...

subliminal [sʌb'liminl] *adj* subliminal.

sublimity [sə'blimiti] *n* sublimidad *f*.

submachine gun ['sʌbmə'ʃiːngʌn] *n* pistola *f* ametralladora, metralleta *f*.

submarine [,sʌbmə'riːn] **1** *adj* submarino. **2** *n* submarino *m*.

submarine chaser [,sʌbmə'riːn,tʃeisə*] *n* cazasubmarinos *m*.

submariner [sʌb'mærinə*] *n* miembro *m* de la tripulación de un submarino, marinero *m* de submarino.

submerge [səb'məːdʒ] **1** *vt* sumergir; (*flood*) inundar, cubrir. **2** *vi* sumergirse.

submerged [səb'məːdʒd] *adj* sumergido.

submersible [səb'məːsəbl] *adj* sumergible.

submersion [səb'məːʃən] *n* sumersión *f*.

submicroscopic ['sʌb,maikrəs'kɔpik] *adj* submicroscópico.

submission [səb'miʃən] *n* sumisión *f*.

submissive [səb'misiv] *adj* sumiso.

submissively [səb'misivli] *adv* sumisamente.

submissiveness [səb'misivnis] *n* sumisión *f*.

submit [səb'mit] **1** *vt* someter; *evidence* presentar, aducir; *report* presentar, rendir; **to — that ...** proponer que ..., sugerir que ...; **I — that ...** me permito decir que ...; **to — a play to the censor** someter una obra al censor; **to — a dispute to arbitration** someter una disputa a arbitraje.

2 *vi* someterse, rendirse; **to — to** someterse a; resignarse a, conformarse con; **he had to — to this indignity** tuvo que aguantar esta afrenta.

subnormal ['sʌb'nɔːməl] *adj* anormal; (*educationally*) **— child** niño *m* retrasado.

subordinate [sə'bɔːdnit] **1** *adj* subordinado (*also Gram*); secundario, de importancia secundaria, menos importante; **A is — to B** A queda subordinado a B; A no tiene tanta importancia como B; A depende de B.

2 *n* subordinado *m*, a *f*.

subordinate [sə'bɔːdineit] *vt* subordinar (*to* a).

subordination [sə,bɔːdi'neiʃən] *n* subordinación *f*.

suborn [sʌ'bɔːn] *vt* sobornar.

subplot ['sʌb,plɔt] *n* intriga *f* secundaria.

subpoena [səb'piːnə] **1** *n* comparendo *m*, citación *f*. **2** *vt* mandar comparecer, citar a uno para estrados.

sub rosa ['sʌb'rəuzə] **1** *adj* secreto, de confianza; **it's all very —** todo es de lo más secreto. **2** *adv* en secreto, en confianza.

subscribe [səb'skraib] **1** *vt money* suscribir, contribuir, dar; *signature* poner; *document etc* firmar, poner su firma en.

2 *vi* suscribir; **to — for something** contribuir dinero para algo; **to — to a paper** suscribirse a un periódico, abonarse a un periódico; **to — to an opinion** suscribir una opinión, aprobar una opinión.

subscriber [səb'skraibə*] *n* suscriptor *m*, ora *f*, abonado *m*, a *f*.

subscription [səb'skripʃən] *n* suscripción *f*, abono *m*; (*to club*) cuota *f*; **— rate** tarifa *f* de suscripción.

subsection ['sʌb,sekʃən] *n* subsección *f*, subdivisión *f*.

subsequent ['sʌbsikwənt] *adj* subsiguiente; posterior, ulterior; **— to** posterior a; **— to this** (*as prep*) después de esto, a raíz de esto.

subsequently ['sʌbsikwəntli] *adv* después, más tarde, con posterioridad.

subserve [səb'səːv] *vt* ayudar, favorecer.

subservience [səb'səːviəns] *n* subordinación *f* (*to* a); servilismo *m*.

subservient [səb'səːviənt] *adj* (*secondary*) subordinado (*to* a); (*cringing*) servil.

subside [səb'said] *vi* (*water*) bajar; (*ground, pavement etc*) hundirse; (*foundations*) asentarse; (*wind*) amainar, hacerse menos violento; (*threat etc*) disminuir, alejarse; (*excitement etc*) calmarse; **to — into a chair** dejarse caer en una silla.

subsidence [səb'saidəns] *n* bajada *f*; hundimiento *m*, (*of pavement, road*) socavón *m*; asentamiento *m*; amaine *m*; disminución *f*; apaciguamiento *m*.

subsidiary [səb'sidiəri] **1** *adj* subsidiario; secundario; auxiliar; (*Fin*) afiliado, filial. **2** *n* (*Fin*) filial *f*, sucursal *f*.

subsidize ['sʌbsidaiz] *vt* subvencionar.

subsidy ['sʌbsidi] *n* subvención *f*, subsidio *m*; **state —** subvención *f* estatal; **export —** subsidio *m* de exportación; **agricultural subsidies** subvenciones *fpl* agrícolas.

subsist [səb'sist] *vi* subsistir; sustentarse (*on a food* con una comida).

subsistence [səb'sistəns] *n* subsistencia *f*; sustentación *f*; (*allowance*) dietas *fpl*.

subsoil ['sʌbsɔil] *n* subsuelo *m*.

subsonic ['sʌb'sɔnik] *adj* subsónico.

subspecies ['sʌb'spiːʃiːz] *n* subespecie *f*.

substance ['sʌbstəns] *n* sustancia *f*; esencia *f*, parte *f*, parte *f* esencial; **an argument of —** un argumento sólido; **man of —** hombre *m* acaudalado; **the — is good but the style poor** la materia es buena pero el estilo malo.

substandard ['sʌb'stændəd] *adj* inferior, inferior al nivel normal, no del todo satisfactorio.

substantial [səb'stænʃəl] adj sustancial, sustancioso; part, proportion importante; sum considerable; loss importante; build etc sólido, fuerte; person acomodado; acaudalado; **to be in — agreement** estar de acuerdo en sustancia.

substantially [səb'stænʃəli] adv sustancialmente; **— true** en gran parte verdadero; **— built** de construcción sólida; **it contributed — to our success** contribuyó materialmente a nuestro éxito.

substantiate [səb'stænʃieit] vt establecer, comprobar, justificar.

substantiation [səb,stænʃi'eiʃən] n comprobación f, justificación f.

substantival [,sʌbstən'taivəl] adj sustantivo.

substantive ['sʌbstəntiv] **1** adj sustantivo. **2** n sustantivo m.

substation ['sʌb,steiʃən] n (Elec) subestación f.

substitute ['sʌbstitjuːt] **1** n (person) sustituto m, a f, suplente mf (for de); (thing) sustituto m, sucedáneo m; artículo m de reemplazo; **there is no — for petrol** la gasolina es insustituible.

2 adj sucedáneo; de reemplazo; person suplente.

3 vt sustituir (A for B B por A); reemplazar (A for B A por B).

4 vi: **to — for someone** suplir a uno, hacer las veces de uno.

substitution [,sʌbsti'tjuːʃən] n sustitución f; reemplazo m.

substratum ['sʌb'strɑːtəm] n, pl **substrata** ['sʌb'strɑːtə] sustrato m.

substructure ['sʌb,strʌktʃə*] n infraestructura f.

subsume [səb'sjuːm] vt subsumir.

subtenancy ['sʌb'tenənsi] n subarriendo m.

subtenant ['sʌb'tenənt] n subarrendador m, ora f.

subterfuge ['sʌbtəfjuːdʒ] n subterfugio m.

subterranean [,sʌbtə'reiniən] adj subterráneo.

subtilize ['sʌtilaiz] vt sutilizar.

subtitle ['sʌb,taitl] **1** n subtítulo m. **2** vt subtitular.

subtle ['sʌtl] adj sutil; fino, delicado; charm misterioso; perfume delicado, sutil, tenue; irony etc fino; (crafty) astuto.

subtlety ['sʌtlti] n sutileza f; finura f, delicadeza f; lo misterioso; astucia f.

subtly ['sʌtli] adv sutilmente; finamente, delicadamente; misteriosamente; astutamente.

subtract [səb'trækt] vt sustraer, restar; **to — 5 from 9** restar 5 a 9.

subtraction [səb'trækʃən] n sustracción f, resta f.

subtropical ['sʌb'trɒpikəl] adj subtropical.

suburb ['sʌbəːb] n barrio m, barrio m exterior; **new —** barrio m nuevo, ensanche m; **a London —** un barrio londinense, un distrito en las afueras de Londres; **the (outer) —s** los barrios exteriores, las afueras.

suburban [sə'bəːbən] adj suburbano; train de cercanías.

suburbanite [sə'bəːbənait] **1** adj surburbano. **2** n habitante mf de los barrios exteriores.

suburbia [sə'bəːbiə] n (freq pej) los barrios exteriores, las afueras; manera f de vivir de los barrios exteriores.

subvention [səb'venʃən] n subvención f.

subversion [səb'vəːʃən] n subversión f.

subversive [səb'vəːsiv] **1** adj subversivo. **2** n subversor m; elemento m subversivo, persona f de dudosa lealtad política.

subvert [sʌb'vəːt] vt subvertir, trastornar.

subway ['sʌbwei] n paso m subterráneo, paso m inferior; (US Rail) metro m.

sub-zero ['sʌb'ziərəu] adj: **in — temperatures** a una temperatura de varios grados bajo cero.

succeed [sək'siːd] vi (a) (be successful: of person) tener éxito, triunfar; (of plan etc) salir bien; **but he did not —** (in this) pero no tuvo éxito (con esto), pero no lo consiguió; **to — in life** triunfar en la vida; **to — in one's hopes** ver logradas sus esperanzas; **to — in one's plan** llevar a cabo su proyecto; **to — in doing something** lograr hacer algo, conseguir hacer algo.

(b) (follow) suceder; seguir; heredar; **who —s?** ¿quién hereda?; **to — to the crown** suceder a la corona, heredar la corona; **to — to the throne** subir al trono; **to — to an estate** heredar una finca; **to — someone in a post** suceder a uno en un puesto; **spring is —ed by summer** a la primavera le sigue el verano.

succeeding [sək'siːdiŋ] adj futuro; subsiguiente; sucesivo; **on 3 — Saturdays** tres sábados seguidos; **in the — chaos** en la confusión subsiguiente; **— generations will do better** las generaciones futuras harán mejor.

success [sək'ses] **1** n éxito m, buen éxito m; triunfo m; prosperidad f; **another — for our team** nuevo éxito m para nuestro equipo; **without —** sin éxito, sin resultado; **he was a great —** tuvo mucho éxito; **he was not a — as Segismundo** no estuvo bien en el papel de Segismundo; **the play was a — in New York** la obra obtuvo un éxito en Nueva York; **the new car is not a —** el nuevo coche no es satisfactorio; **the plan was a —** el proyecto salió muy bien; **she had no —** no tuvo éxito; **to make a — of something** tener éxito en algo; **to meet with —** tener éxito, prosperar.

2 attr: **— story** historia f de un triunfo.

successful [sək'sesful] adj person afortunado, feliz, que tiene éxito; attempt, plan etc logrado; business etc próspero; effort fructuoso; candidate elegido, afortunado; **to be —** (person) tener éxito, triunfar; (business etc) prosperar; **to be entirely —** tener un éxito completo; **to be — in doing something** lograr hacer algo; **he was not — last time** no lo logró la última vez.

successfully [sək'sesfəli] adv con éxito; afortunadamente; prósperamente.

succession [sək'seʃən] n (a) (series) sucesión f, serie f; **in —** sucesivamente; **4 times in —** 4 veces seguidas; **in quick —** en rápida sucesión; rápidamente uno tras otro; **after a — of disasters** después de una serie de catástrofes.

(b) (to post etc) sucesión f (to a); **in — to someone** sucediendo a uno; como sucesor de uno; **Princess Rebecca is 7th in — to the throne** la princesa Rebeca ocupa el 7° puesto en la línea de sucesión a la corona.

(c) (descendants) descendencia f.

successive [sək'sesiv] adj sucesivo; consecutivo; **4 — days** 4 días seguidos.

successively [sək'sesivli] adv sucesivamente.

successor [sək'sesə*] n sucesor m, ora f.

succinct [sək'siŋkt] adj sucinto.

succinctly [sək'siŋktli] adv sucintamente.

succour ['sʌkə*] **1** n socorro m. **2** vt socorrer.

succulence ['sʌkjuləns] n suculencia f.

succulent ['sʌkjulənt] adj suculento.

succumb [sə'kʌm] vi sucumbir (to a).

such [sʌtʃ] **1** adj (a) tal; semejante; parecido; tanto; **— a book** tal libro; **— books** tales libros; **in — cases** en tales casos, en semejantes casos; **we had — a case last year** tuvimos un caso parecido el año pasado; **on just — a day in June** un día exactamente parecido de junio; **no — thing!** ¡no hay tal!, ¡ni hablar!; **there's no — thing** no hay tal cosa; **did you ever see — a thing?** ¿se vio jamás tal cosa?; **some — idea** alguna idea de este tipo, alguna idea por el estilo; **— a plan is most unwise** un proyecto así es poco aconsejable, un proyecto de ese tipo no es aconsejable; **no — book exists** no existe tal libro; **X was — a one X** era así, X era de este tipo; **— is life** así es la vida; **— is not the case** esto no es así; **I am in — a hurry** tengo tanta prisa, estoy tan de prisa; **— an honour!** ¡tanto honor!; **it caused — trouble that ...** dio lugar a tantos disgustos que ...

(b) **— as** tal como; **— a man as Ganivet** un hombre tal como Ganivet; **— writers as Quevedo** los escritores tales como Quevedo; **there are no — things as giants** los gigantes no existen; **it is not — as to cause worry** no es tal que haya de causar inquietud; **it made — a stir as had not been known before** tuvo una repercusión como no se había conocido hasta entonces.

2 adv tan; **— good food** comida f tan buena; **— a clever girl** muchacha f tan inteligente; **it's — a long time ago** hace tanto tiempo ya.

3 pron los que, las que; **we took — as we wanted** tomamos los que queríamos; **I will send you — as I receive** te mandaré los que reciba; **and as — he was promoted** y como tal le ascendieron; **we know of no — no** tenemos noticias de ninguno así; **there are no — trees as —** no hay árboles propiamente dichos, no hay árboles que digamos, no hay árboles árboles; **rabbits and hares and —** conejos mpl y liebres y tal; **may all — perish!** ¡mueran cuantos hay como él!; **this is my car — as it is** éste es mi coche con todas sus imperfecciones.

such-and-such ['sʌtʃənsʌtʃ] adj: **she lives in — a street** vive en tal o cual calle; **on — a day in May** a tantos de mayo.

suchlike ['sʌtʃlaik] **1** adj tal, semejante; **sheep and — animals** ovejas fpl y otros tales animales, ovejas fpl y otros animales de la misma clase.

2 pron: **thieves and —** ladrones mpl y gente de esa calaña, ladrones mpl y otras tales personas; **buses and lorries and —** autobuses mpl y camiones y tal.

suck [sʌk] **1** n chupada f; sorbo m; (at breast) mamada f; **to give — (to)** amamantar.
2 vt chupar; sorber; breast mamar; **to — one's fingers** chuparse los dedos; **to — down** tragar; **to — in** liquid sorber; air, dust etc aspirar; **to — up** aspirar; absorber.
3 vi chupar; mamar; **to — at something** chupar algo; **to — up to someone** (fam) dar coba a uno, hacer la pelotilla a uno.
sucker ['sʌkə*] n **(a)** (Zool) ventosa f; (Bot) serpollo m, mamón m; (sl) dulce m, bombón m.
(b) (esp US sl) primo m, bobo m; **some —** algún pobre hombre; **to be a — for something** no poder resistir algo; sucumbir pronto a los encantos de algo.
sucking-pig ['sʌkiŋpig] n lechoncillo m.
suckle ['sʌkl] **1** vt amamantar, dar el pecho a; (fig) criar.
2 vi lactar.
suckling ['sʌkliŋ] n mamón m, ona f.
sucrose ['su:krəuz] n sucrosa f.
suction ['sʌkʃən] n succión f.
suction pump ['sʌkʃənpʌmp] n bomba f aspirante, bomba f de succión.
Sudan [su'dɑ:n] Sudán m.
Sudanese [,su:də'ni:z] **1** adj sudanés. **2** n sudanés m, esa f.
sudden ['sʌdn] adj (rapid, hurried) repentino, súbito; (unexpected) imprevisto, impensado; change of temperature, curve etc brusco; **all of a —** de repente.
suddenly ['sʌdnli] adv de repente, de pronto; inesperadamente; bruscamente.
suddenness ['sʌdnnis] n lo repentino; lo imprevisto; brusquedad f.
suds [sʌdz] npl jabonaduras fpl.
sue [su:] **1** vti: **to — someone** demandar a uno (for something por algo); **to — someone for damages** demandar a uno por daños y perjuicios; **to — for divorce** presentar demanda de divorcio, solicitar el divorcio; **to be —d for libel** ser demandado por calumnia.
2 vi: **to — for peace** pedir la paz.
suède [sweid] n suecia f, ante m; **— shoes** zapatos mpl de ante; **— gloves** guantes mpl de ante.
suet [suit] n sebo m.
Suetonius [swi'təuniəs] m Suetonio.
suety ['suiti] adj seboso.
Suez Canal ['su:izkə'næl] Canal m de Suez.
suffer ['sʌfə*] **1** vt **(a)** (painfully) sufrir, padecer; (bear) aguantar, sufrir; (undergo) sufrir, experimentar; **I can't — it a moment longer** no lo aguanto un momento más; **it has —ed a sharp decline** ha experimentado un brusco descenso; **to — a defeat** sufrir una derrota; **to — death** morir, ser muerto.
(b) (allow) permitir, tolerar; **to — someone to do something** permitir a uno hacer algo; autorizar a uno para que haga algo; **to — something to be done** permitir que se haga algo.
2 vi **(a)** sufrir, padecer; **did you — much?** ¿sufriste mucho?; **how I —ed!** ¡lo que sufrí!; **the army —ed badly** el ejército tuvo pérdidas importantes; **the town —ed in the raids** la ciudad sufrió grandes daños en los bombardeos; **we will see that you do not — by the changes** aseguraremos que Vd no pierda nada a consecuencia de estos cambios.
(b) to — for one's sins sufrir las consecuencias de sus pecados; **you will — for it** lo pagarás después.
(c) to — from sufrir, padecer (de), estar afligido por; (fig) adolecer de; ser la víctima de; **to — from boils** tener diviesos; **to — from rheumatism** padecer reumatismo; **to — from the effects of something** resentirse de algo, estar resentido de algo; **she —s from her environment** es la víctima de su ambiente; **the house is —ing from neglect** la casa padece abandono; **your style —s from overelaboration** su estilo adolece de una excesiva complicación.
sufferance ['sʌfərəns] n tolerancia f; **on —** por tolerancia.
sufferer ['sʌfərə*] n (Med) enfermo m, a f (from de); víctima f; **—s from diabetes** los enfermos de diabetes, los diabéticos; **the —s from the earthquake** las víctimas del terremoto; **fellow —** persona f que tiene la misma enfermedad que uno; compañero m en la desgracia.
suffering ['sʌfəriŋ] **1** adj que sufre; (Med) doliente, enfermo.
2 n sufrimiento m, padecimiento m; (grief etc) dolor m; **after months of —** después de sufrir durante varios meses; **the —s of the soldiers** los padecimientos de los soldados.
suffice [sə'fais] **1** vt satisfacer; ser bastante para. **2** vi bastar, ser suficiente.

sufficiency [sə'fiʃənsi] n (state) suficiencia f; (quantity) cantidad f suficiente; **to have a —** estar acomodado.
sufficient [sə'fiʃənt] adj suficiente, bastante; **to be —** ser suficiente, bastar.
sufficiently [sə'fiʃəntli] adv suficientemente, bastante; **— good** bastante bueno.
suffix ['sʌfiks] **1** n sufijo m. **2** vt añadir como sufijo (to a).
suffocate ['sʌfəkeit] **1** vt ahogar, asfixiar. **2** vi ahogarse, asfixiarse, quedar asfixiado.
suffocating ['sʌfəkeitiŋ] adj sofocante, asfixiante; **— heat** calor m sofocante.
suffocation [,sʌfə'keiʃən] n sofocación f, asfixia f.
suffragan ['sʌfrəgən] **1** adj sufragáneo. **2** n obispo m sufragáneo.
suffrage ['sʌfridʒ] n **(a)** sufragio m; derecho m de votar; **universal —** sufragio m universal; **to get the —** obtener el derecho de votar.
(b) voto m; aprobación f.
suffragette [,sʌfrə'dʒet] n sufragista f.
suffuse [sə'fju:z] vt bañar, cubrir (with de); difundirse por; **—d with light** inundado de luz, bañado de luz; **eyes —d with tears** ojos mpl bañados de lágrimas.
suffusion [sə'fju:ʒən] n difusión f.
sugar ['ʃugə*] **1** n azúcar m and f; **brown —** azúcar m negro; **cane —** azúcar m de caña; see castor **—**, lump **—**.
2 vt azucarar; echar azúcar a, añadir azúcar a.
sugar basin ['ʃugə,beisn] n azucarero m.
sugar beet ['ʃugəbi:t] n remolacha f azucarera.
sugar bowl ['ʃugəbəul] n azucarero m.
sugar candy ['ʃugə,kændi] n azúcar m candi.
sugar cane ['ʃugəkein] n caña f de azúcar.
sugar-coat ['ʃugəkəut] vt (Cook) azucarar, poner una capa de azúcar a.
sugar daddy ['ʃugə,dædi] n (US fam) viejo m adinerado amante de una joven, protector m (de una joven).
sugar loaf ['ʃugələuf] n pan m de azúcar.
sugarplum ['ʃugəplʌm] n confite m.
sugar plantation ['ʃugəplæn,teiʃən] n plantación f de caña de azúcar.
sugar refinery ['ʃugəri,fainəri] n refinería f de azúcar.
sugar tongs ['ʃugətɔŋz] npl tenacillas fpl para azúcar.
sugary ['ʃugəri] adj azucarado; (fig) style etc meloso, almibarado; (sentimental) sensiblero, sentimental; romántico.
suggest [sə'dʒest] **1** vt sugerir; (point to) indicar; (advise) aconsejar, indicar; (hint) insinuar; (evoke) evocar, hacer pensar en; **to — that . . .** (of person) sugerir que . . ., proponer que . . .; **this —s that . . .** esto hace pensar que . . ., esto lleva a pensar que . . .; **I — to you that . . .** (in law speeches) ¿no es cierto que . . .?; **it doesn't exactly — a careful man** no parece indicar un hombre prudente; **the coins — a Roman building** las monedas indican un edificio romano; **the symptoms — an operation** los síntomas aconsejan una operación; **prudence —s a retreat** la prudencia nos aconseja retirarnos; **what are you —ing?** ¿qué es lo que insinúa Vd?, ¿qué es lo que pretende Vd?
2 vr: **an idea —s itself** se me ocurre una idea; **nothing —s itself** no se me ocurre nada.
suggestible [sə'dʒestibl] adj **(a)** person sugestionable.
(b) thing sugerible, que se puede sugerir.
suggestion [sə'dʒestʃən] n **(a)** sugerencia f; indicación f; insinuación f; **if I may make (or offer) a —** si se me permite proponer algo; **my — is that . . .** yo propongo que . . .; **that is an immoral —** ésa es una idea inmoral; **following your — . . .** siguiendo sus indicaciones . . .
(b) (hypnotic) sugestión f.
(c) (trace) sombra f, traza f; **with just a — of garlic** con un poquitín de ajo; **with a — of irony in his voice** con un punto de ironía en la voz.
suggestive [sə'dʒestiv] adj sugestivo; (pej) indecente, sicalíptico; **— of** que evoca, que hace pensar en; que trasciende a.
suggestively [sə'dʒestivli] adj (pej) indecentemente.
suggestiveness [sə'dʒestivnis] n (pej) indecencia f, sicalipsis f.
suicidal [,sui'saidl] adj suicida; **to have a — tendency** tener tendencia al suicidio; **I feel — this morning** esta mañana estoy por desesperarme; **he drives in a — way** es un suicida conduciendo; **it would be —** sería peligrosísimo.
suicide ['suisaid] n (act) suicidio m; (person) suicida mf; **to commit —** suicidarse; **it would be — to say so** sería peligrosísimo decirlo.

suit [suːt] **1** n (a) traje m (also — of clothes); — of armour armadura f; ready-made — traje m hecho; two-piece — (woman's) conjunto m.
(b) (Law) pleito m, litigio m, proceso m; to bring a — poner pleito; to bring a — against someone entablar demanda contra uno (for something por algo).
(c) (request) petición f; at the — of a petición de.
(d) (in marriage) petición f de mano, oferta f de matrimonio; to press one's — hacer una oferta de matrimonio.
(e) (Cards) palo m; long —, strong — palo m largo; to have nothing in that — tener fallo a ese palo; to follow — servir del palo, (fig) hacer lo mismo.
2 vt (a) (adapt) adaptar, ajustar, acomodar (to a); to — one's style to one's audience adaptar su estilo al público; —ing the action to the word uniendo la acción a la palabra; the coat and hat are well —ed el abrigo y el sombrero van bien juntos; they are well —ed to each other están hechos el uno para el otro; he is not —ed for (or to be) a doctor no es apto para ser médico.
(b) (be suitable: of clothes) sentar a, ir bien a, caer bien a; (in general) convenir; gustar; the coat —s you el abrigo te sienta, el abrigo te va bien; the climate does not — me el clima no me sienta bien; the job —s me nicely el puesto me conviene perfectamente; does this — you? ¿te gusta esto?; come when it —s you ven cuando quieras, ven cuando te convenga; I know what —s me best sé lo que me conviene; I shall do it when it —s me lo haré cuando me dé la gana.
3 vr: he —s himself hace lo que le da la gana, hace lo que quiere; — yourself! ¡haz lo que quieras!, ¡como quieras!
suitability [ˌsuːtəˈbiliti] n conveniencia f; idoneidad f (for para).
suitable [ˈsuːtəbl] adj conveniente, apropiado; adecuado, idóneo; indicado; the most — man for the job el hombre más indicado para el puesto; is this hat —? ¿me conviene este sombrero?; the film is not — for children la película no es apta para menores; we didn't find anything at all — no encontramos nada a propósito, no encontramos nada que nos conviniera; Tuesday is the most — day el martes nos conviene más.
suitably [ˈsuːtəbli] adv convenientemente; apropiadamente; — dressed for tennis convenientemente vestido para el tenis.
suitcase [ˈsuːtkeis] n maleta f.
suite [swiːt] n (of retainers) séquito m, comitiva f; (of furniture) juego m, mobiliario m; (rooms) serie f de habitaciones, grupo m de habitaciones; (Mus) suite f; bedroom — (juego m de muebles para) alcoba f; dining-room — comedor m.
suited [ˈsuːtid] adj: see suit 2 (a).
suiting [ˈsuːtiŋ] n (Comm) tela f para trajes.
suitor [ˈsuːtə*] n pretendiente m; (Law) demandante mf.
sulfa [ˈsʌlfə] etc: see sulpha etc.
sulk [sʌlk] vi estar mohino, estar amohinado, estar de mal humor.
sulkily [ˈsʌlkili] adv con mohino; answer etc con mal humor, de mala gana.
sulkiness [ˈsʌlkinis] n mohina f, murria f, mal humor m.
sulks [sʌlks] npl mohina f, murria f, mal humor m; to have the — estar mohino, estar de mal humor; to get the — amohinarse.
sulky [ˈsʌlki] adj mohino; malhumorado; resentido; to be — estar mohino, estar de mal humor.
sullen [ˈsʌlən] adj hosco, malhumorado; resentido; taciturno; countryside triste; sky plomizo.
sullenly [ˈsʌlənli] adv hoscamente; answer con mal humor; look con resentimiento.
sullenness [ˈsʌlənnis] n hosquedad f, mal humor m; resentimiento m; taciturnidad f.
sully [ˈsʌli] vt (lit) manchar.
sulpha drugs [ˈsʌlfəˈdrʌgz] npl fármacos mpl sulfa.
sulphate [ˈsʌlfeit] n sulfato m; copper — sulfato m de cobre.
sulphide [ˈsʌlfaid] n sulfuro m.
sulphonamide [sʌlˈfɔnəmaid] n sulfonamida f.
sulphur [ˈsʌlfə*] n azufre m.
sulphureous [sʌlˈfjuəriəs] adj sulfúreo.
sulphuric [sʌlˈfjuərik] adj sulfúrico; — acid ácido m sulfúrico.
sulphurous [ˈsʌlfərəs] adj sulfuroso, sulfúreo.
sultan [ˈsʌltən] n sultán m.
sultana [sʌlˈtɑːnə] n (person) sultana f; (fruit) pasa f de Esmirna.

sultanate [ˈsʌltənit] n sultanato m.
sultriness [ˈsʌltrinis] n bochorno m; calor m sofocante.
sultry [ˈsʌltri] adj weather bochornoso; heat, atmosphere sofocante; (fig) apasionado; seductor, provocativo.
sum [sʌm] **1** n (total) suma f, total m; (quantity) suma f, cantidad f; (Math) problema m de aritmética; the — total of my ambitions is ... la meta de mis ambiciones es ..., lo único que ambiciono es ...; lump — suma f global; in — en suma, en resumen; to do —s in one's head hacer un cálculo mental; I was very bad at —s era muy malo en aritmética.
2 vt: to — up (tot up) sumar; (review) resumir; (evaluate rapidly) tomar las medidas a, evaluar (rápidamente), justipreciar; to — up an argument resumir un argumento, recapitular un argumento; to — up a debate recapitular los argumentos empleados en un debate; she —med me up at a glance me tomó las medidas con una sola mirada; he —med up the situation quickly se dio cuenta rápidamente de la situación.
3 vi: to — up recapitular, hacer un resumen; to — up ... en resumen ...
sumac(h) [ˈsuːmæk] n zumaque m.
summarily [ˈsʌmərili] adv sumariamente.
summarize [ˈsʌməraiz] vt resumir.
summary [ˈsʌməri] **1** adj sumario. **2** n resumen m, sumario m.
summation [sʌˈmeiʃən] n (act) adición f; recapitulación f, resumen m; (total) suma f, total m.
summer [ˈsʌmə*] **1** n verano m, estío m; Indian —, St Martin's — veranillo m de San Martín; a girl of 17 —s una joven de 17 abriles; a —'s day un día de verano; to spend the — veranear, pasar el verano.
2 attr day, clothing, residence de verano; season veraniego; resort de veraneo; weather, heat estival.
3 vi veranear, pasar el verano.
summerhouse [ˈsʌməhaus] n, pl —houses [ˌhauziz] cenador m, glorieta f.
summertime [ˈsʌmətaim] n (season) verano m; (hour) hora f de verano.
summery [ˈsʌməri] adj veraniego, estival.
summing-up [ˈsʌmiŋˈʌp] n resumen m, recapitulación f.
summit [ˈsʌmit] **1** n cima f, cumbre f (also fig). **2** attr: — conference conferencia f cumbre, conferencia f en la cumbre.
summon [ˈsʌmən] vt servant etc llamar; meeting convocar; aid pedir, requerir; (Law) citar, emplazar; to — up courage cobrar; memory evocar; to be —ed to someone's presence ser llamado a la presencia de uno; they —ed me to advise them me llamaron para que les diera consejos; to — a town to surrender hacer una llamada a una ciudad para que se rinda.
summons [ˈsʌmənz] **1** n llamamiento m, llamada f; requerimiento m; (Law) citación f; to serve a — on someone entregar una citación a uno; to take out a — against someone entablar demanda contra uno, citar a uno para estrados.
2 vt citar, emplazar.
sump [sʌmp] n (Aut etc) cárter m, colector m de aceite; (Min etc) sumidero m; (fig) letrina f.
sumptuary [ˈsʌmptjuəri] adj suntuario.
sumptuous [ˈsʌmptjuəs] adj suntuoso.
sumptuously [ˈsʌmptjuəsli] adv suntuosamente.
sumptuousness [ˈsʌmptjuəsnis] n suntuosidad f.
sun [sʌn] **1** n sol m; in the July — bajo el sol de julio; to be out in the — estar al sol; the milk stood in the — all day la leche estuvo al sol todo el día; they have everything under the — tienen de todo como en botica; there's no reason under the — no hay razón alguna; to bask in the — tomar el sol, estar tumbado al sol; the sun is shining hace sol, el sol brilla.
2 attr de sol; solar.
3 vt asolear.
4 vr: to — oneself asolearse, tomar el sol.
sunbaked [ˈsʌnbeikt] adj endurecido al sol.
sunbath [ˈsʌnbɑːθ] n, pl —baths [bɑːðz] baño m de sol.
sunbathe [ˈsʌnbeið] **1** n baño m de sol. **2** vi tomar el sol.
sunbather [ˈsʌnbeiðə*] n persona f que toma el sol.
sunbathing [ˈsʌnbeiðiŋ] n baños mpl de sol.
sunbeam [ˈsʌnbiːm] n rayo m de sol.
sunblind [ˈsʌnblaind] n toldo m, store m.
sunburn [ˈsʌnbəːn] n (tan) bronceado m; (painful) quemadura f del sol.
sunburnt [ˈsʌnbəːnt] adj (tanned) tostado por el sol, bronceado; (painfully) quemado por el sol; to get — broncearse; sufrir quemaduras del sol.

sunburst ['sʌnbəːst] n (US) resplandor m repentino del sol (entre las nubes).

sun deck ['sʌndek] n cubierta f de sol.

sundae ['sʌndei] n helado con frutas, nueces etc.

Sunday ['sʌndi] **1** n domingo m; **Easter** — Domingo m de Resurrección; **Palm** — Domingo m de Ramos. **2** attr paper, school, sermon etc dominical, de domingo; see **best**.

sunder ['sʌndə*] vt (lit) romper, dividir, hender; separar.

sundew ['sʌndjuː] n rocío m de sol, rosolí m.

sundial ['sʌndaiəl] n reloj m de sol.

sundown ['sʌndaun] n puesta f del sol; anochecer m; **at** — al anochecer; **before** — antes del anochecer.

sundowner ['sʌndaunə*] n (fam) trago de licor que se toma al anochecer.

sun-dried ['sʌndraid] adj secado al sol.

sundry ['sʌndri] **1** adj varios, diversos; **all and** — todos y cada uno. **2** sundries npl (Comm) géneros mpl diversos.

sunflower ['sʌn‚flauə*] n girasol m.

sung [sʌŋ] ptp of **sing**.

sunglasses ['sʌn‚glaːsiz] npl gafas fpl de sol.

sun-god ['sʌŋgɔd] n dios m del sol, divinidad f solar.

sun hat ['sʌnhæt] n sombrero m ancho.

sunk [sʌŋk] ptp of **sink**.

sunken ['sʌŋkən] adj hundido.

sun lamp ['sʌnlæmp] n lámpara f solar ultravioleta.

sunless ['sʌnlis] adj sin sol.

sunlight ['sʌnlait] n sol m, luz f del sol, luz f solar; **in the** — al sol; **the** — **is strong** el sol es fuerte; **hours of** — (Meteorol) horas fpl de insolación.

sunlit ['sʌnlit] adj iluminado por el sol.

sun lounge ['sʌnlaundʒ] n solana f.

sunny ['sʌni] adj **(a)** place, room etc soleado; expuesto al sol; bañado de sol, iluminado por el sol; day de sol; **it is** — hace sol; **June is a** — **month** junio tiene mucho sol; **Málaga is sunnier than Manchester** Málaga tiene más sol que Manchester.
(b) (fig) face risueño; smile, disposition alegre; **to be on the** — **side of 40** tener menos de 40 años.

sunray ['sʌnrei] attr: — **lamp** lámpara f solar ultravioleta; — **treatment** helioterapia f, tratamiento m con lámpara solar ultravioleta.

sunrise ['sʌnraiz] n salida f del sol; **from** — **to sunset** de sol a sol.

sunset ['sʌnset] n puesta f del sol, ocaso m.

sunshade ['sʌnʃeid] n (portable) quitasol m; (over table) sombrilla f; (awning) toldo m.

sunshine ['sʌnʃain] n sol m, luz f del sol; **in the** — al sol; **hours of** — (Meteorol) horas fpl de insolación; **daily average** — insolación f media diaria.

sunspot ['sʌnspɔt] n mancha f solar.

sunstroke ['sʌnstrəuk] n insolación f; **to have** — sufrir una insolación.

sunsuit ['sʌnsuːt] n traje m de playa.

suntrap ['sʌntræp] n solana f, lugar m muy soleado.

sunup ['sʌnʌp] n salida f del sol.

sup [sʌp] **1** vt (also to — up) sorber, beber a sorbos. **2** vi cenar; **to** — **off something, to** — **on something** cenar algo.

super ['suːpə*] **1** adj (fam) estupendo, bárbaro; **how** —! ¡qué bien!; **the new car is** — el nuevo coche es estupendo; **we had a** — **time** lo pasamos la mar de bien.
2 n (abbr: Theat, Cine) figurante m, a f; comparsa mf; (superintendent: Tech) superintendente m, (of police) subjefe m.

super ... ['suːpə*] super ..., sobre ...; eg **super-salesman** supervendedor m.

superabound [‚suːpərə'baund] vi sobreabundar (in, with en).

superabundance [‚suːpərə'bʌndəns] n sobreabundancia f, superabundancia f.

superabundant [‚suːpərə'bʌndənt] adj sobreabundante, superabundante.

superannuate [‚suːpə'rænjueit] vt jubilar.

superannuated [‚suːpə'rænjueitid] adj jubilado; (fig) anticuado.

superannuation [‚suːpə‚rænju'eiʃən] n jubilación f; — **contribution** cuota f de jubilación.

superb [suː'pəːb] adj magnífico, espléndido.

superbly [suː'pəːbli] adv magníficamente; **a** — **painted picture** un cuadro de la mayor excelencia técnica; **a** — **fit man** un hombre en magnífico estado físico.

supercargo ['suːpə‚kɑːgəu] n sobrecargo m.

supercharged ['suːpətʃɑːdʒd] adj sobrealimentado.

supercharger ['suːpətʃɑːdʒə*] n sobrealimentador m.

supercilious [‚suːpə'siliəs] adj desdeñoso, arrogante; suficiente.

superciliously [‚suːpə'siliəsli] adv desdeñosamente, con desdén; con aire de suficiencia.

superciliousness [‚suːpə'siliəsnis] n desdén m, arrogancia f; suficiencia f.

supererogation [‚suːpər‚erə'geiʃən] n supererogación f.

superficial [‚suːpə'fiʃəl] adj superficial.

superficiality [‚suːpə‚fiʃi'æliti] n superficialidad f.

superficially [‚suːpə'fiʃəli] adv superficialmente; en la superficie; — **this may be true** a primera vista esto puede ser verdad.

superfine ['suːpəfain] adj (Comm) extrafino.

superfluity [‚suːpə'fluiti] n superfluidad f.

superfluous [su'pəːfluəs] adj superfluo; sobrante, que sobra, que está de más.

superfluously [su'pəːfluəsli] adv superfluamente; **he added** — añadió fuera de propósito.

superhighway ['suːpə'haiwei] n supercarretera f, autopista f.

superhuman [‚suːpə'hjuːmən] adj sobrehumano.

superimpose ['suːpərim'pəuz] vt sobreponer (on en).

superinduce ['suːpərin'djuːs] vt sobreañadir.

superintend [‚suːpərin'tend] vt vigilar; supervisar, dirigir.

superintendence [‚suːpərin'tendəns] n superintendencia f; supervisión f, dirección f.

superintendent [‚suːpərin'tendənt] n superintendente mf; inspector m; supervisor m; (eg in swimming pool) vigilante m; — **of police** subjefe m de policía.

superior [su'piəriə*] **1** adj superior (to a); (smug) desdeñoso; satisfecho, suficiente; **she thinks herself very** — se da aires de suficiencia; **he said in that** — **tone** dijo en ese tono suficiente. **2** n superior m; (Eccl) superior m, ora f; **Mother S**— (madre f) superiora f.

superiority [su‚piəri'ɔriti] n superioridad f (to a); desdén m; suficiencia f.

superlative [suː'pəːlətiv] **1** adj superlativo (also Gram), extremo. **2** n superlativo m.

superlatively [suː'pəːlətivli] adv en sumo grado, extremadamente; — **fit** en óptimo estado físico.

superman ['suːpəmæn] n, pl —**men** [men] superhombre m.

supermarket ['suːpə‚mɑːkit] n supermercado m.

supernatural [‚suːpə'nætʃərəl] adj sobrenatural; **the** — lo sobrenatural.

supernumerary [‚suːpə'njuːmərəri] **1** adj supernumerario. **2** n supernumerario m, a f; (Theat, Cine) figurante m, a f, comparsa mf.

superphosphate ['suːpə'fɔsfeit] n superfosfato m.

superpose ['suːpəpəuz] vt sobreponer, superponer.

superposition ['suːpə‚pə'ziʃən] n superposición f.

superpower ['suːpə‚pauə*] n superpotencia f.

superscription [‚suːpə'skripʃən] n sobrescrito m.

supersede [‚suːpə'siːd] vt reemplazar, sustituir; suplantar.

supersensitive ['suːpə'sensitiv] adj extremadamente sensible (to a).

supersonic ['suːpə'sɔnik] adj supersónico.

supersonically ['suːpə'sɔnikəli] adv fly etc a velocidad superior a la del sonido.

superstition [‚suːpə'stiʃən] n superstición f.

superstitious [‚suːpə'stiʃəs] adj supersticioso.

superstitiously [‚suːpə'stiʃəsli] adv supersticiosamente.

superstructure ['suːpə‚strʌktʃə*] n superestructura f.

supertanker ['suːpə‚tæŋkə*] n superpetrolero m.

supertax ['suːpətæks] n impuesto m adicional (sobre los ingresos elevados de particulares).

supervene [‚suːpə'viːn] vi sobrevenir.

supervise ['suːpəvaiz] vt supervisar.

supervision [‚suːpə'viʒən] n supervisión f.

supervisor ['suːpəvaizə*] n supervisor m.

supervisory ['suːpəvaizəri] adj: **in a** — **post** en un cargo de supervisor; **in his** — **capacity** en su función de supervisor.

supine ['suːpain] **1** adj supino; (fig) flojo, sin carácter, débil. **2** n (Gram) supino m.

supper ['sʌpə*] n cena f; **the Last S**— la Última Cena; **to stay to** — quedarse a cenar; **to have** — cenar.

suppertime ['sʌpətaim] n hora f de cenar.

supplant [sə'plɑːnt] vt suplantar.

supple ['sʌpl] adj flexible.

supplement ['sʌplimənt] n suplemento m; apéndice m.

supplement [sʌpli'ment] vt suplir, complementar; **to** — **one's income by writing** aumentar sus ingresos escribiendo artículos (etc).

supplementary [‚sʌpli'mentəri] adj suplementario; adicional; question (Parl) secundario.

suppleness ['sʌplnis] n flexibilidad f.

suppliant ['sʌpliənt] **1** adj suplicante. **2** n suplicante mf.

supplicant ['sʌplikənt] n suplicante mf.

supplicate ['sʌplikeit] vti suplicar.

supplication [ˌsʌpli'keiʃən] n súplica f.

supplier [sə'plaiə*] n suministrador m, ora f; (Comm) proveedor m, ora f; distribuidor m, ora f; **from your usual** — de su proveedor habitual.

supply [sə'plai] **1** n (a) suministro m, provisión f, abastecimiento m; (stock: Comm) surtido m, existencias fpl; **electricity** — suministro m de electricidad; **the** — **of fuel to the engine** el suministro de combustible al motor; — **and demand** oferta f y demanda; **new cars are in short** — hay pocos coches nuevos, hay escasez de coches nuevos; **we need a fresh** — **of something** hace falta proveernos de algo; **to lay in a** — **of** proveerse de, hacer provisión de.

(b) **supplies** (food) provisiones fpl, víveres mpl; (Mil) pertrechos mpl; **electrical supplies** artículos mpl eléctricos; **office supplies** material m para oficina; **supplies are running low** escasean las provisiones; se están agotando las existencias.

(c) (Parl) provisión f financiera; **Committee on S—** Comisión f del Presupuesto; **Ministry of S—** Ministerio m de Aprovisionamientos; **to vote supplies** votar créditos.

2 vt material etc suministrar, facilitar, proporcionar; (Comm) surtir; army, city etc aprovisionar; want suplir; **the tradesmen who** — **us** nuestros proveedores; **can you** — **this spare part?** ¿pueden facilitarme este repuesto?; **she supplied the vital clue** ella nos dio la pista esencial; **to** — **someone with something** (of supplies) abastecer a uno de algo, proveer a uno de algo; **he supplied us with some facts** nos facilitó (or proporcionó) varios datos; **this supplied me with the chance** esto me brindó la oportunidad; **we are not supplied with a radio** no estamos provistos de radio.

supply ship [sə'plaiʃip] n buque m de abastecimiento.

supply teacher [sə'plai'tiːtʃə*] n maestro m suplente, maestra f suplente.

support [sə'pɔːt] **1** n (a) (Tech) soporte m, apoyo m; pilar m.

(b) (fig) apoyo m; (person) sostén m; **moral** — apoyo m moral; **financial** — ayuda f económica; **in** — **of** en apoyo de; **documents in** — **of an allegation** documentos mpl que confirman una alegación; **to speak in** — **of a candidate** apoyar la candidatura de uno; **I will give you every** — le apoyaré todo lo que pueda; **the proposal got no** — la propuesta no recibió apoyo alguno; **to lean on someone for** — apoyarse en uno; **they depend on him for financial** — dependen de él para mantenerse, reciben ayuda económica de él; **our** — **comes from the workers** nos apoyan los obreros, los obreros son partidarios nuestros; **liberal** — **got him elected** los votos de los liberales aseguraron su elección.

2 vt (a) (Tech) apoyar, sostener; **it is** —**ed on 4 columns** descansa sobre 4 columnas, está apoyado en 4 columnas.

(b) (fig) apoyar; sostener, mantener; campaign apoyar, respaldar; (financially) mantener; motion aprobar, votar por; (corroborate) confirmar; **I cannot** — **what you are doing** no apruebo lo que Vd está haciendo; **the liberals will** — **it** los liberales votarán por esto.

3 vr: **to** — **oneself** (physically) apoyarse (on en); (financially) mantenerse; ganarse la vida.

supportable [sə'pɔːtəbl] adj soportable.

supporter [sə'pɔːtə*] n (Tech) soporte m, sostén m; (Her) tenante m, soporte m; (person) defensor m, ora f; (Pol etc) partidario m, a f; (Sport) seguidor m, hincha mf; —**s' club** peña f deportiva; **after the match** —**s flooded on to the pitch** al terminar el partido los hinchas invadieron el campo de juego.

supporting [sə'pɔːtiŋ] adj film, programme, role secundario.

suppose [sə'pəuz] vti (a) (assume as hypothesis) suponer; figurarse, imaginarse; **let us** — **that X equals 3** supongamos que X vale 3; **let us** — **that . . .** pongamos por caso que . . .; **let us** — **we are living in the 8th century** figurémonos que vivimos en el siglo VIII; **even supposing it were true** aun en el caso de que fuera verdad; **always supposing he comes** en el caso de que venga.

(b) (imperative, = if) — **he comes, supposing (that) he comes** y ¿si viene?; — **we have a go** ¿probamos?; — **we buy it?** ¿qué te parece si lo compramos?; — **you have a wash?** ¿no crees que conviene ir a lavarte?; — **they could see us now!** ¡si solamente pudieran vernos ahora!

(c) (presuppose) suponer, presuponer; **that** —**s unlimited resources** eso supone unos recursos ilimitados.

(d) (take for granted, assume) suponer, presumir; creer; **I** — **so** supongo que sí, creo que sí, (unwillingly) no hay más remedio, no cabe otra explicación; **it is not to be** —**d that . . .** no se ha de suponer que . . ., no se imagine nadie que . . .; **I** — **you are right** me parece que tienes razón; **I don't** — **he really means it** no creo que lo diga en serio; **do you** — **that . . .?** ¿crees en serio que . . .?; **he's rich, I** — me imagino que es rico; **I** — **you know that . . .** me imagino que sabes que . . .; **I don't** — **you could lend me a pound?** ¿podrías por casualidad prestarme una libra?; **he is** —**d to be coming** se cree que va a venir, se supone que va a venir; **and he's** —**d to be an expert!** ¡y él que tiene fama de experto!; **he's** —**d to be in Wales** dicen que está en Gales.

(e) (of obligation) deber; **he's the one who's** —**d to do it** él debe hacerlo, le toca a él hacerlo; **you're** —**d to be in bed** tú deberías estar en la cama.

supposed [sə'pəuzd] adj supuesto, pretendido.

supposedly [sə'pauzidli] adv según cabe suponer; **he had** — **gone to Scotland** cabía suponer que había ido a Escocia; **the** — **brave James Bond** el James Bond que se suponía tan valiente; el supuesto valiente James Bond.

supposing [sə'pəuziŋ] as conj si, en el caso de que; see **suppose** (a) and (b).

supposition [ˌsʌpə'ziʃən] n suposición f, hipótesis f; **that is pure** — eso es una hipótesis nada más.

suppositious [ˌsʌpə'ziʃəs] adj fingido, espurio.

suppository [sə'pozitəri] n supositorio m.

suppress [sə'pres] vt (in most senses) suprimir; yawn etc ahogar; emotion contener; heckler etc reprimir, hacer callar; scandal etc disimular.

suppressed [sə'prest] adj book etc suprimido; **with** — **emotion** con emoción contenida; **a half** — **laugh** una risa disimulada a medias.

suppression [sə'preʃən] n supresión f; represión f; disimulación f.

suppressive [sə'presiv] adj supresivo.

suppressor [sə'presə*] n (Elec) supresor m.

suppurate ['sʌpjuəreit] vi supurar.

suppuration [ˌsʌpjuə'reiʃən] n supuración f.

supra . . . ['suːprə] supra . . ., eg **supranormal** supranormal.

supranational ['suːprə'næʃənl] adj supranacional.

supremacy [su'preməsi] n supremacía f.

supreme [su'priːm] adj supremo; court etc supremo; sumo, eg **with** — **indifference** con suma indiferencia; **to reign** — ser el único soberano; (fig) estar en la cumbre (de su profesión etc), no tener rival alguno.

sura ['suərə] n sura m.

surcharge ['sɜːtʃɑːdʒ] n sobrecarga f, sobretasa f; **import** — sobrecarga f de importación.

surcharge [sɜː'tʃɑːdʒ] vt sobrecargar.

surd [sɜːd] n número m sordo.

sure [ʃuə*] **1** adj (a) seguro; cierto; aim etc certero; hand, touch firme; **as** — **as fate, as** — **as eggs** con toda seguridad.

(b) (with to be) **to be** —**!** ¡claro!; **and there he was, to be** — y ahí estaba, efectivamente; **are you quite** —**?** ¿estás seguro del todo? ¡**I'm perfectly** — estoy perfectamente seguro; **to be** — **about something** estar seguro de algo; **I'm not so** — **about that** no estoy del todo seguro, no diría yo tanto; **to be** — **of oneself** estar seguro de sí mismo; **to be** — **that . . .** estar seguro de que . . .; **it is** — **that he will come** es seguro que vendrá; **I'm** — **I don't know** yo me maten si lo sé; **it is** — **to rain** seguramente lloverá; **he is** — **to come** seguramente vendrá; **be** — **to turn the gas off** ten cuidado de cortar el gas; **be** — **to go and see her** no dejes de ir a verla.

(c) **I don't know for** — no sé con seguridad, no sé a punto fijo; **that's for** — eso es seguro; **he'll come next time for** — vendrá la próxima vez sin falta.

(d) **to make** — **of** facts verificar, comprobar; **to make** — **of someone** asegurarse del apoyo de uno, asegurarse de poder contar con uno; (in order) **to make quite** — para asegurarse del todo; **it's best to make** — vale más estar seguro.

2 adv (a) —**!** (esp US) sí; ¡claro!; ¡naturalmente!; ¡ya lo creo!; — **enough** efectivamente, en efecto; **he'll come** — **enough** seguramente vendrá; **it's petrol** — **enough** en efecto es gasolina.

(b) (US) **he** — **was rich** ése sí que era rico; **that meat was** — **tough** la carne esa fue verdaderamente dura.

sure-fire ['ʃuə'faiə*] adj de éxito seguro, seguro.

sure-footed ['ʃuə'futid] **1** *adj* de pie firme. **2** *adv* con pie firme.

surely ['ʃuəli] *adv* seguramente; ciertamente; por supuesto; —! (*gladly*) con mucho gusto; — **you don't mean it?** ¿seguramente no lo dices en serio?; **it will** — **happen** seguramente pasará; — **he's come (hasn't he?)** ¿será posible que no haya venido?; — **he hasn't come (has he?)** ¿será posible que haya venido?

sureness ['ʃuənis] *n* seguridad *f*; certeza *f*; lo certero; firmeza *f*.

surety ['ʃuərəti] *n* (*sum*) garantía *f*; fianza *f*; (*person*) fiador *m*, ora *f*; garante *mf*; **to go** (*or* **stand**) — **for someone** ser fiador de uno, salir garante por uno; **in his own** — **of £50** bajo su propia fianza de 50 libras.

surf [sə:f] *n* (*foam*) espuma *f*; (*waves*) olas *fpl*, rompientes *mpl*; (*swell*) oleaje *m*.

surface ['sə:fis] **1** *n* superficie *f*; exterior *m*; (*of road*) firme *m*; **temporary** — **firme** *m* provisional; **we haven't done more than scratch the** — **yet** todavía no hemos ido al fondo de este problema (*etc*); **on the** — **it seems that . . .** a primera vista parece que . . .

2 *attr* de la superficie; **by** — **mail** por vía terrestre *or* por vía marítima; — **workers** (*Min*) personal *m* del exterior.

3 *vt* poner superficie a; recubrir, revestir; (*smoothe*) alisar.

4 *vi* (*submarine etc*) salir a la superficie, emerger; **he** —**s in London occasionally** de vez en cuando asoma la cara en Londres.

surface-air ['sə:fis'ɛə*] *attr*: — **missile** proyectil *m* tierra-aire.

surface tension ['sə:fis'tenʃən] *n* tensión *f* superficial.

surfboard ['sə:fbɔːd] *n* plancha *f* de deslizamiento, acuaplano *m*.

surfeit ['sə:fit] **1** *n* (*satiety*) hartura *f*, saciedad *f*; (*indigestion*) empacho *m*; (*excess*) exceso *m*; superabundancia *f*; **there is a** — **of** hay exceso de; **he died of a** — **of lampreys** murió después de hartarse de lampreas.

2 *vt* hartar, saciar (*on*, *with* de).

3 *vr*: **to** — **oneself** hartarse, saciarse (*on*, *with* de).

surfing ['sə:fiŋ] *n*, **surfriding** ['sə:f,raidiŋ] *n* esquí *m* acuático, patinaje *m* sobre las olas.

surge [sə:dʒ] **1** *n* (*Naut*) oleaje *m*, oleada *f*; (*fig*) oleada *f*, ola *f*; **a** — **of people** una oleada de gente; **there was a** — **of sympathy for him** hubo una oleada de compasión por él.

2 *vi* (*water*) agitarse, hervir; **the crowd** —**d into the building** la multitud entró a tropel en el edificio; **people** —**d down the street** una oleada de gente avanzó por la calle; **blood** —**d into her face** se le subió la sangre a la cara; **they** —**d round him** se apiñaban en torno suyo.

surgeon ['sə:dʒən] *n* cirujano *m*; (*Mil, Naut*) médico *m*, oficial *m* médico; **dental** — **dentista** *mf*, odontólogo *m*; **house** — **médico** *m* interno (de hospital); **veterinary** — **veterinario** *m*.

surgery ['sə:dʒəri] *n* (*art, operation*) cirugía *f*; (*room*) consultorio *m*, gabinete *m* de consulta; — **hours horas** *fpl* de consulta; **plastic** — **cirugía** *f* estética, cirugía *f* plástica.

surgical ['sə:dʒikəl] *adj* quirúrgico; — **dressing** vendaje *m* quirúrgico.

surging ['sə:dʒiŋ] *adj water* agitado, bravo; *crowd* que se mueve en desorden, que avanza furioso (*or* indignado etc).

surliness ['sə:linis] *n* hosquedad *f*, mal humor *m*; falta *f* de educación; aspereza *f*.

surly ['sə:li] *adj* hosco, malhumorado; maleducado; **of a** — **disposition** de genio áspero; **he gave me a** — **answer** contestó malhumorado.

surmise ['sə:maiz] *n* conjetura *f*, suposición *f*; **my** — **is that . . .** yo supongo que . . .

surmise [sə:'maiz] *vt* conjeturar, suponer; **I** —**d as much** ya lo suponía; **as one could** — **from his book** según cabía entender en su libro.

surmount [sə:'maunt] *vt* (a) *difficulty* superar, vencer. (b) —**ed by** coronado de.

surmountable [sə:'mauntəbl] *adj* superable.

surname ['sə:neim] **1** *n* apellido *m*. **2** *vt* apellidar.

surpass [sə:'pɑːs] **1** *vt* superar, exceder; eclipsar; **it** —**es anything we have seen before** supera a cuanto hemos visto antes.

2 *vr*: **to** — **oneself** excederse a sí mismo.

surpassing [sə:'pɑːsiŋ] *adj* incomparable, sin par; **of** — **beauty** de hermosura sin par.

surplice ['sə:pləs] *n* sobrepelliz *f*.

surplus ['sə:pləs] **1** *n* excedente *m*, sobrante *m*, exceso *m*; (*Fin, Comm*) superávit *m*; **the 1975 wheat** — **el excedente de trigo de 1975.**

2 *adj* excedente, sobrante; de sobra; **my** — **socks** los calcetines que me sobran, los calcetines que no necesito; **American** — **wheat** el excedente de trigo norteamericano; **sale of** — **stock** liquidación *f* de saldos; **have you any** — **sheets?** ¿tenéis sábanas que os sobren?

surprise [sə'praiz] **1** *n* sorpresa *f*; asombro *m*, extrañeza *f*; **much to my** —, **to my great** — **con gran sorpresa mía; with a look of** — **con un gesto de extrañeza; it was a** — **to find that . . .** fue una sorpresa encontrar que . . .; **imagine my** — **imaginaos cuál sería mi asombro; it came as a** — **to us** nos cogió de nuevas; **to give someone a** — **dar una sorpresa a uno; to take someone by** — **sorprender a uno, coger a uno desprevenido.**

2 *attr*: — **attack** sorpresa *f*; ataque *m* imprevisto; — **package** sorpresa *f*.

3 *vt* sorprender; asombrar, extrañar; (*Mil*) coger por sorpresa; **to** — **someone in the act** coger a uno en el acto; **you** — **me!** ¡me asombras!; **it** —**s me to learn that . . .** me asombra saber que . . .; **to be** —**d** quedar asombrado; **to be** —**d to see someone** asombrarse de ver a uno; **I should not be** —**d if . . .** no me sorprendería que + *subj*; **to look** —**d** hacer un gesto de extrañeza.

surprising [sə'praiziŋ] *adj* sorprendente, asombroso.

surprisingly [sə'praiziŋli] *adv* de modo sorprendente; asombrosamente; **he is** — **young** se asombra uno de descubrir que es tan joven; **and then** — **he left** y luego con asombro de todos partió.

surrealism [sə'riəlizəm] *n* surrealismo *m*.

surrealist [sə'riəlist] **1** *adj* surrealista. **2** *n* surrealista *mf*.

surrealistic [sə,riə'listik] *adj* surrealista.

surrender [sə'rendə*] **1** *n* rendición *f*, capitulación *f*; entrega *f*; renuncia *f*; abandono *m*; **unconditional** — **rendición** *f* sin condiciones; **the** — **of Breda** la rendición de Breda; — **of property** (*Law*) cesión *f* de bienes; **no** —! ¡no nos rendimos!; **to make a** — **of one's principles** transigir con sus principios.

2 *attr*: — **value** valor *m* de rescate.

3 *vt* (*Mil*) rendir, entregar; *goods* entregar; *claim, right* renunciar a; *hope* renunciar a, abandonar.

4 *vi* rendirse, entregarse; **to** — **to the police** entregarse a la policía; **I** —! ¡me rindo!

5 *vr*: **to** — **oneself to remorse** abandonarse al remordimiento.

surreptitious [,sʌrəp'tiʃəs] *adj* subrepticio, clandestino.

surreptitiously [,sʌrəp'tiʃəsli] *adv* subrepticiamente, clandestinamente; a hurtadillas.

surrogate ['sʌrəgeit] *n* sustituto *m*, suplente *m*; (*Eccl*) vicario *m*.

surround [sə'raund] **1** *n* marco *m*; borde *m*.

2 *vt* rodear, cercar, circundar; (*Mil*) copar, cercar; sitiar; **a town** —**ed by hills** una ciudad rodeada de colinas; **she was** —**ed by children** estaba rodeada de niños.

surrounding [sə'raundiŋ] *adj* circundante; **in the** — **hills** en las colinas vecinas, en las colinas de alrededor; **in the** — **darkness** en la oscuridad que le (*etc*) cercaba por todos lados.

surroundings [sə'raundiŋz] *npl* (*of place*) alrededores *mpl*, cercanías *fpl*, contornos *mpl*; (*environment*) ambiente *m*.

surtax ['sə:tæks] *n* impuesto *m* adicional (sobre los ingresos elevados de particulares).

surveillance [sə:'veiləns] *n* vigilancia *f*; **to be under** — **estar vigilado, estar bajo vigilancia; to keep someone under** — **vigilar a uno.**

survey ['sə:vei] *n* inspección *f*, examen *m*; estudio *m*; reconocimiento *m*; (*of land*) apeo *m*, medición *f*; (*general view*) vista *f* de conjunto; (*as published report*) informe *m*; **he gave a general** — **of the situation** hizo un informe general sobre la situación; **to make a** — **of housing in a town** estudiar la situación de la vivienda en una ciudad.

survey [sə:'vei] *vt* (*look at*) mirar, contemplar; (*inspect*) inspeccionar, examinar; (*study*) estudiar, hacer un estudio de; *ground before battle etc* reconocer; *land* apear, medir; *town etc* levantar el plano de; (*take general view of*) pasar en revista; obtener una vista de conjunto de; **he** —**ed the desolate scene** miró detenidamente la triste escena; **monarch of all he** —**s** monarca *m* de todo cuanto domina con la vista; **the report** —**s housing in Slobodia** el informe estudia la situación de la vivienda en Eslobodia; **the book** —**s events up to 1972** el libro pasa revista de los sucesos hasta 1972.

surveying [sə:'veiiŋ] *n* agrimensura *f*; planimetría *f*; topografía *f*.

surveyor [sə'veiə*] *n* agrimensor *m*; topógrafo *m*.

survival [sə'vaivəl] *n* (a) (*act*) supervivencia *f*; — **of the fittest** supervivencia *f* de los mejor dotados.
(b) (*relic*) supervivencia *f*; vestigio *m*, reliquia *f*.
survival kit [sə:'vaivəl'kit] *n* equipo *m* de emergencia.
survive [sə'vaiv] **1** *vt* (*all senses*) sobrevivir a. **2** *vi* sobrevivir; (*remain, persist*) durar, perdurar, subsistir.
survivor [sə'vaivə*] *n* superviviente *mf*.
Susan ['su:zn] *f* Susana.
susceptibility [sə,septə'biliti] *n* susceptibilidad *f*, sensibilidad *f* (*to* a); **to offend someone's susceptibilities** ofender las susceptibilidades (*or* la delicadeza) de uno.
susceptible [sə'septəbl] *adj* susceptible, sensible (*to* a); (*easily moved*) impresionable; (*to women*) enamoradizo; **to be** — **of** admitir, dar lugar a.
suspect ['sʌspekt] **1** *adj* sospechoso; **they are all** — todos están bajo sospecha; **his fitness is** — es sospechoso de no estar en buen estado físico, su estado físico deja lugar a dudas.
2 *n* sospechoso *m*, a *f*; **the chief** — **is the butler** el más sospechoso es el mayordomo.
suspect [sə'spekt] **1** *vt* (*accusingly*) sospechar; (*fear*) recelar, recelarse de; (*believe*) imaginar, figurar, creer; **to** — **someone of a crime** hacer a uno sospechoso de un crimen, sospechar a uno de haber cometido un crimen; **I** — **her of having stolen it** sospecho que ella lo ha robado; **I** — **him of being the author** sospecho que él es el autor; **are you** —**ed?** ¿estás tú bajo sospecha?; **he never** —**ed her** él nunca sospechó de ella; **he** — **s nothing** no se recela de nada; **I** — **all Irishmen** me recelo de todos los irlandeses; **I** — **it may be true** tengo la sospecha de que puede ser verdad, creo que puede ser verdad; **it's not paid for, I** — sospecho que no está pagado; **I** —**ed as much as you** ya me lo figuraba.
2 *vi* sospechar, tener sospechas.
suspend [sə'spend] *vt* (*all senses*) suspender; **he was** —**ed for 6 months** (*Aut*) le retiraron el carnet de conducir durante 6 meses.
suspender [sə'spendə*] *n* liga *f*; —**s** ligas *fpl*, (*US*) tirantes *mpl*.
suspender belt [sə'spendəbelt] *n* portaligas *m*.
suspense [sə'spens] *n* incertidumbre *f*, duda *f*; ansiedad *f*; (*Lit, Theat, Cine etc*) suspense *m*, suspensión *f* (*Acad*), tensión *f*; **it is in** — está en suspenso; **the question is in** — la cuestión está pendiente; **to keep someone in** — dejar a uno en la incertidumbre; **the** — **became unbearable** la tensión se hizo inaguantable.
suspension [sə'spenʃən] *n* (*most senses, also Tech*) suspensión *f*; **independent** — (*Aut*) suspensión *f* independiente; — **of payments** suspensión *f* de pagos; — **of driving licence** privación *f* del carnet de conducir.
suspensory [sə'spensəri] **1** *adj* suspensorio. **2** *n* (*also* — **bandage**) suspensorio *m*.
suspicion [sə'piʃən] *n* (a) sospecha *f*; recelo *m*; **my** — **is that . . .** yo sospecho que . . .; **to be above** — estar por encima de toda sospecha; **to be under** — ser sospechoso, estar bajo sospecha; **to arouse** — despertar recelos; **to arouse someone's** —**s** despertar los recelos de uno; **to arrest someone on** — detener a uno como sospechoso; **to cast** —**s on someone's honesty** hacer que se dude de la honradez de uno; **to have one's** —**s about something** tener sospechas acerca de algo; **I had no** — **that . . .** no sospechaba que . . .; **to lay oneself open to** — hacerse sospechoso: **I was right in my** —**s** resultaron ser ciertas mis sospechas; — **fell on him** se empezó a sospechar de él.
(b) (*trace*) traza *f* ligera, sombra *f*, pizca *f*; (*aftertaste*) dejo *m*; **there is a** — **of corruption about it** esto tiene un dejo de corrupción, esto huele un poquito a corrupción.
suspicious [sə'piʃəs] *adj* (a) (*feeling suspicion*) receloso; **to be** — **about something** recelarse de algo, tener sospechas acerca de algo; **that made him** — eso le hizo sospechar.
(b) (*causing suspicion*) sospechoso; **it's highly** — es sumamente sospechoso; **it looks very** — **to me** me parece muy sospechoso.
suspiciously [sə'piʃəsli] *adv* (a) *look etc* con recelo, desconfiadamente.
(b) *behave etc* de modo sospechoso; **it looks** — **like measles to me** para mí tiene toda la apariencia de ser sarampión.
suspiciousness [sə'piʃəsnis] *n* (a) recelo *m*. (b) lo sospechoso, carácter *m* sospechoso.
sustain [sə'stein] *vt* (a) (*bear weight of*) sostener, apoyar; *body, life* sustentar; (*Mus*) sostener; *part* (*Theat*) estar al nivel de; hacer dignamente; *pretence*

continuar; *effort* sostener, continuar; *assertion* sostener; *objection* (*Law*) confirmar la validez de; *charge, theory* confirmar, corroborar.
(b) (*receive*) *attack* sufrir (y rechazar); *damage* sufrir; *injury* sufrir, tener, recibir; *loss* sufrir, tener.
sustained [sə'steind] *adj* *effort etc* sostenido, ininterrumpido, continuo; *note* sostenido; *applause* prolongado.
sustenance ['sʌstinəns] *n* sustento *m*; **they depend for their** — **on, they get their** — **from** se sustentan de, se alimentan de.
suture ['su:tʃə*] **1** *n* sutura *f*. **2** *vt* suturar, coser.
suzerain ['su:zərein] *n* soberano *m*, a *f*.
suzerainty ['su:zəreinti] *n* soberanía *f*.
svelte [svelt] *adj* esbelto.
swab [swɔb] **1** *n* (*cloth, mop*) estropajo *m*, trapo *m*, (*Naut*) lampazo *m*; (*Mil*) escobillón *m*; (*Med*) algodón *m*, torunda *f*.
2 *vt* (*also to* — **down**) limpiar (con estropajo *etc*), fregar.
swaddle ['swɔdl] *vt* envolver (*in* en); *baby* empañar, fajar; **he came out** —**d in bandages** salió envuelto en vendas.
swaddling clothes ['swɔdliŋklauðz] *npl* pañales *mpl*; **to be still in** — (*fig*) estar todavía en mantillas.
swag [swæg] *n* (*fam*) botín *m*.
swagger ['swægə*] **1** *n* contoneo *m*, pavoneo *m*; **to walk with a** — andar contoneándose, andar con paso jactancioso.
2 *adj* (*fam*) muy elegante, muy pera.
3 *vi* (*also to* — **about, to** — **along**) contonearse, pavonearse, andar pavoneándose; **he** —**ed over to our table** se acercó a nuestra mesa con aire fanfarrón; **with that he** —**ed out** con eso salió con paso jactancioso.
swagger cane ['swægəkein] *n* bastón *m* ligero de paseo.
swaggering ['swægəriŋ] *adj* *person* fanfarrón, jactancioso; *gait* importante, jactancioso.
swain [swein] *n* (*arch or hum: lad*) zagal *m*; (*suitor*) pretendiente *m*, amante *m*.
swallow[1] ['swɔləu] **1** *n* trago *m*; **at one** —, **with one** — de un trago.
2 *vt* (a) tragar; engullir, deglutir; *bait* tragarse; **he** —**ed the lot** se lo tragó todo; **just** — **this pill** tómate esta píldora; **to** — **up** tragar; acabar de comer.
(b) (*fig*) tragar; **to** — **an insult** tragar un insulto; **to** — **one's pride** humillarse, olvidarse de su amor propio; **he** —**ed the story** se tragó la bola; **to** — **one's words** desdecirse, retractarse; **to** — **up** *savings etc* agotar, consumir; (*of the sea*) tragar; **the mist** —**ed them up** la niebla les envolvió; **they were soon** —**ed up in the darkness** desaparecieron pronto en la oscuridad.
3 *vi*: **to** —, **to** — **hard** (*fig*) tragar saliva.
swallow[2] ['swɔləu] *n* (*Orn*) golondrina *f*; **one** — **doesn't make a summer** una golondrina no hace verano.
swallowtail ['swɔləuteil] *n* (*butterfly*) macaón *m*.
swallow-tailed ['swɔləuteild] *adj*: — **coat** frac *m*.
swam [swæm] *pret of* **swim**.
swamp [swɔmp] **1** *n* pantano *m*, marisma *f*, ciénaga *f*.
2 *vt* (a) (*submerge*) sumergir, cubrir de agua (*etc*); (*flood*) inundar, llenar de agua; (*sink*) hundir.
(b) abrumar (*with* de), agobiar (*with* de); **towards the end of the game they** —**ed us** hacia el fin del partido nos arrollaron completamente; **they have** —**ed us with applications** nos han abrumado de solicitudes; **we are** —**ed with work** estamos agobiados de trabajo, tenemos trabajo hasta encima de las cejas.
3 *vi* (*of field etc*) inundarse, quedar inundado, empantanarse.
swampy ['swɔmpi] *adj* pantanoso; **to become** — empantanarse.
swan [swɔn] **1** *n* cisne *m*; **the Swan of Avon** el Cisne del Avon (*Shakespeare*). **2** *vi* (*fam*) pavonearse; darse mucho tono.
swank [swæŋk] (*fam*) **1** *n* (a) (*vanity, boastfulness*) fachenda *f*; ostentación *f*; **it's just a lot of** — no es sino fachenda; **he does it for** — lo hace para darse tono.
(b) (*person*) currutaco *m*; fachendón *m*, ona *f*; **he's a terrible** — es terriblemente fachendón.
2 *vi* darse tono, darse humos, fachendear; **to** — **about** (*adv*) pavonearse; **to** — **about something** fachendear a causa de algo, darse humos con motivo de algo.
swanky ['swæŋki] *adj* (*fam*) *person* ostentoso, fachendoso, fachendón; *car etc* la mar de elegante, muy pera.

swannery ['swɔnəri] n colonia f de cisnes.

swan song ['swɔnsɔŋ] n canto m del cisne.

swan-upping ['swɔn‚ʌpiŋ] n censo m anual de los cisnes (del Támesis).

swap [swɔp] **1** n intercambio m, canje m; **—s** (stamps) duplicados mpl; **it's a fair —** es un trato equitativo.
2 vt intercambiar, canjear; **to — stories (with someone)** contarse chistes; **we sat —ing reminiscences** estábamos contando nuestros recuerdos; **will you — your hat for my jacket?** ¿quieres cambiar tu sombrero por mi chaqueta?; **to — places with someone** cambiar de silla (etc) con uno.
3 vi hacer un intercambio; cambiar con uno; **I wouldn't — with anyone** no cambio lo que tengo con nadie; **shall we —?** ¿cambiamos?

sward [swɔːd] n césped m.

swarm¹ [swɔːm] **1** n (of bees etc) enjambre m; (fig) multitud f, muchedumbre f; **a — of mosquitoes** un enjambre de mosquitos; **a — of creditors** un enjambre de acreedores; **they came in —s** vinieron en tropel; **there were —s of women** hubo una multitud de mujeres, hubo millares de mujeres.
2 vi (of bees) enjambrar; (of other insects, people etc) hormiguear, pulular; **to — with** (of place) hervir de, pulular de, estar plagado de; **the tourists — everywhere** en todas partes pululan los turistas; **Stratford —s with Americans** Stratford hierve de americanos; **children —ed all over the car** los niños subían y bajaban por todas partes del coche.

swarm² [swɔːm] vi: **to — up a tree** trepar (rápidamente) a un árbol.

swarthiness ['swɔːðinis] n tez f morena, color m moreno; lo atezado.

swarthy ['swɔːði] adj moreno, atezado.

swashbuckler ['swɔʃ‚bʌklə*] n espadachín m, matón m.

swashbuckling ['swɔʃ‚bʌkliŋ] adj valentón, fanfarrón.

swastika ['swɔstikə] n esvástica f, cruz f gamada.

swat [swɔt] **1** vt fly aplastar, matar. **2** vi: **to — at a fly** tratar de aplastar una mosca (con palmeta).

swath [swɔːθ] n, pl **swaths** [swɔːðs] guadaña f, ringlera f (de heno segado etc); **to cut corn in —s** segar el trigo y dejarlo en ringleras; **to cut —s through something** avanzar por algo a guadañadas.

swathe [sweið] vt envolver; fajar; (with bandage) vendar; **—d in sheets** envuelto en sábanas.

swatter ['swɔtə*] m palmeta f matamoscas.

sway [swei] **1** n (a) (movement) balanceo m, oscilación f; (violent jerk) sacudimiento m; vaivén m.
(b) (rule) imperio m, dominio m; (influence) influencia f, ascendiente m; (power) poder m; **his — over the party** su influencia con el partido, su dominio del partido; **to bring a people under one's —** sojuzgar un pueblo, hacer que un pueblo reconozca el dominio de uno; **to hold — over a nation** gobernar una nación, dominar una nación.
2 vt (a) (move) balancear, hacer oscilar; sacudir; hacer tambalear.
(b) (influence) mover, influir en; inclinar; **these factors finally —ed me** estos factores terminaron de convencerme; **he is not —ed by any such considerations** tales cosas no influyen en él en absoluto; **I allowed myself to be —ed** me dejé persuadir.
3 vi balancearse, oscilar (in the wind al viento); mecerse; bambolearse; tambalearse; **she —s as she walks** se cimbrea al andar; **he was —ing with drink** estaba tan borracho que se tambaleaba; **the train —ed from side to side** el tren se bamboleaba de un lado para otro.

swear [sweə*] (irr: pret **swore**, ptp **sworn**) **1** vt (a) oath prestar, jurar; fidelity jurar; **I — it!** ¡lo juro!; **I — (that) I did not steal it** juro que no lo robé; **I could have sworn that was Lulu** juraría que ésa fue Lulú, que me maten si aquélla no fue Lulú; **to — something on the Bible** jurar algo sobre la Biblia.
(b) **to — someone in** tomar juramento a uno, juramentar a uno, hacer prestar juramento a uno; **to be sworn in** prestar juramento; **to — someone to secrecy** hacer que uno jure no revelar algo.
(c) **to — one's fortune away** hacer voto de renunciar a su fortuna.
2 vi (a) (solemnly) jurar; (with swearwords) jurar, decir tacos, soltar palabrotas, (blasphemously) blasfemar; **don't — in front of the children** no digas palabrotas estando los pequeños delante; **to — black and blue** echar sapos y culebras; **to — like a trooper** jurar como un carretero; **he swore most horribly** soltó unos tremendos tacos; **it's enough to make a bishop —** esto bastaría para hacer blasfemar a un obispo; **to — to do something** jurar hacer algo.

(b) (with adv or prep) **to — at someone** maldecir a uno, echar pestes de uno; **to — by something** (solemnly) jurar por algo; (fig) tener entera confianza en algo, creer ciegamente en algo; **to — off alcohol** jurar renunciar al alcohol; **to — to something** declarar algo bajo juramento; **I would — to it** juraría que fue así; **I can't — to it** no lo sé a punto fijo, no puedo afirmarlo con entera confianza.
3 n (fam): **to have a good —** desahogarse soltando palabrotas.

swearword ['sweəwəːd] n taco m, palabrota f.

sweat [swet] **1** n (a) sudor m; **by the — of one's brow** con el sudor de su frente, a pulso sudando; **to be in a —** estar sudando, estar todo sudoroso, (fig) estar en un apuro, apurarse; **to be in a — about something** estar muy preocupado por algo; **to get into a — empezar a sudar; to get into a — about something** apurarse por algo.
(b) (piece of work etc) trabajo m difícil, trabajo m pesado; **what a — that was!** eso ¡cómo nos hizo sudar!; **we had such a — to do it** nos costó hacerlo.
(c) **old —** (fam) veterano m.
2 vt (a) sudar; **to — blood** (fig) sudar la gota gorda.
(b) workers explotar.
3 vi sudar; **to — a lot, to — like a bull** (or pig etc) sudar la gota gorda.

sweatband ['swetbænd] n badana f del forro del sombrero, tafilete m.

sweated ['swetid] adj: **— labour** trabajo m muy mal pagado.

sweater ['swetə*] n suéter m.

sweater girl ['swetə'gəːl] n muchacha f vestida de suéter.

sweat gland ['swetglænd] n glándula f sudorípara.

sweating ['swetiŋ] **1** adj sudoroso. **2** n transpiración f; (of workers) explotación f.

sweat shirt ['wetʃəːt] n camisa f floja (de deporte etc).

sweat shop ['wetʃɔp] n fábrica f donde se explota al obrero.

sweaty ['sweti] adj sudoroso; cubierto de sudor, mojado de sudor; **to be all —** estar todo sudoroso.

Swede [swiːd] n sueco m, a f.

swede [swiːd] n (Bot) nabo m sueco.

Sweden ['swiːdn] Suecia f.

Swedish ['swiːdiʃ] **1** adj sueco. **2** n sueco m.

sweep [swiːp] **1** n (a) (act of —ing) barredura f, escobada f; (of scythe) golpe m, guadañada f; (of net) redada f; (of arm) gesto m, movimiento m; **at one —** de un solo golpe; **with a wide — of his arm** con un ancho movimiento del brazo; **this room could do with a —** hace falta limpiar esta habitación; **we gave it a —** lo limpiamos, lo barrimos; **to make a clean —** (Sport) ganar todos los puntos, (Cards) copar, ganar todas las bazas; **to make a clean — of** cambiar completamente, hacer tabla rasa de.
(b) (by police etc) redada f; **they made a — for hidden arms** hicieron una redada buscando armas clandestinas.
(c) (person) deshollinador m.
(d) (area) extensión f; (of wings) envergadura f; (range) alcance m; (curve) curva f; **the whole — of the Thames at Putney** toda la extensión del Támesis en Putney; **a wide — of country** una ancha extensión de paisaje, un paisaje extenso; **the — of her lines** (Naut etc) su línea, su perfil (aerodinámico etc).
(e) see sweepstake.
2 (irr: pret and ptp **swept**) vt (a) room, surface barrer; chimney deshollinar; channel etc dragar; **to — a room clean** limpiar un cuarto barriéndolo; **to — a channel clear of mines** hacer navegable un canal barriendo las minas de él; **the beach was swept by great waves** la playa fue barrida (or azotada) por olas gigantescas; **to — a road with bullets** barrer una carretera con balas; **to — the horizon with a telescope** examinar toda la extensión del horizonte con un telescopio; see board etc.
(b) dust barrer, quitar barriendo; mines rastrear, barrer; person, obstacle etc arrastrar, llevarse; **a wave swept him overboard** fue arrastrado por una ola y cayó al mar; **he was swept off his feet by the water** fue arrastrado por la corriente; **to — a girl off her feet** enamorar a una chica; **they swept him off to lunch** se lo llevaron con toda prisa a comer.
(c) (with adv or prep) **the crowd swept him along** le arrastró la multitud, desapareció arrastrado por la multitud; **to — aside** apartar bruscamente con la mano; protest desatender, no hacer caso alguno de; suggestion desechar bruscamente; **to — away**

barrer; (snatch) arrebatar, arrastrar; (remove) quitar, eliminar, suprimir; vestiges etc borrar; **the current —s logs down with it** la corriente arrastra (or lleva) consigo los troncos; **to — out** room barrer; **to — up** barrer, recoger.

3 vi (a) (with broom) barrer; **to — up after someone** recoger la basura que ha dejado uno; **to — up after a party** recoger la basura que ha resultado de un guateque.

(b) (extend) extenderse (along, down etc por); **the river —s away to the east** el río hace una gran curva hacia el este; **the hills — down to the sea** las colinas bajan (majestuosamente) hacia el mar; **the road —s up to the house** la carretera llega hasta la casa (de modo impresionante).

(c) (of movement) **to — into a room** entrar en una sala con paso majestuoso; **she swept past me angrily** pasó enfadada delante de mí; **the car swept along** el coche avanzó a gran velocidad; **it swept round the corner** dobló velozmente la esquina.

(d) (with adv or prep) **to — by** pasar rápidamente; pasar majestuosamente; (nearly touch) rozar; **they swept down the slope** se lanzaron cuesta abajo; descendieron precipitadamente por la cuesta; **to — down on someone** abalanzarse sobre uno; **to — on** seguir su avance inexorable (to hasta); **to — past** = **to — by**.

sweeper ['swiːpə*] n (person) barrendero m, a f; (machine) barredera f.

sweeping ['swiːpiŋ] adj (a) gesture dramático; bow profundo; flight majestuoso.

(b) statement etc comprensivo pero infundado, comprensivo pero que no tiene en cuenta las excepciones; change radical, fundamental; **that's pretty —** eso es mucho decir.

sweepings ['swiːpiŋz] npl barreduras fpl; (fig, of society etc) heces fpl.

sweepstake ['swiːpsteik] n lotería en la cual una persona gana todas las apuestas.

sweet [swiːt] **1** adj (a) (of taste) dulce; azucarado; **this coffee is too —** este café tiene demasiado azúcar; **is it — enough for you?** ¿le he puesto bastante azúcar?

(b) (fresh, pleasant) food fresco, nuevo; smell fragante, agradable, bueno; breath sano; land fértil; en buen estado; **to smell —** tener buen olor, oler bien.

(c) (of sounds) dulce, melodioso.

(d) (of person's character) dulce, amable, simpático; **isn't he —?** ¡es un ángel!; **that's very — of you** eres muy amable; **to be — on someone** estar un poco enamorado de uno; **to keep someone —** asegurarse de la amistad de uno, asegurarse de la buena voluntad de uno (mediante un regalo, propina etc).

(e) (generally agreeable, charming) memory, revenge etc dulce; face lindo; dress etc mono, majo, precioso; **it is — to be able to...** es agradable poder...; **you look so — in that hat** con ese sombrero eres un encanto; **what a — little hat!** ¡qué sombrerito más mono!

(f) (of running of car, machine etc) suave.

2 n (a) dulce m, caramelo m; **—s** dulces mpl, bombones mpl, golosinas fpl; **the —s of solitude** las dulzuras de la soledad; **the —s of office** (Pol) las ventajas materiales de estar en el poder, los premios que brinda el triunfo político.

(b) (course) postre m.

(c) **yes, my —** sí, mi amor.

sweet-and-sour ['swiːtən'sauə*] n (Cook) plato agridulce (especialmente en la comida china).

sweetbreads ['swiːtbredz] npl lechecillas fpl.

sweet corn ['swiːtkɔːn] n (US) maíz m tierno.

sweeten ['swiːtn] vt endulzar (also fig); azucarar, poner azúcar a.

sweetening ['swiːtniŋ] n (Cook) dulcificante m.

sweetheart ['swiːthɑːt] n novio m, a f; **yes, —** sí, mi amor.

sweetie ['swiːti] n (fam) chica f, gachí f (sl); novia f; **she's a —** es un encanto, es muy mona; **isn't she a —?** ¡qué chica más mona!

sweetish ['swiːtiʃ] adj algo dulce.

sweetly ['swiːtli] adv dulcemente; amablemente; suavemente.

sweetmeats ['swiːtmiːts] npl dulces mpl, confites mpl.

sweetness ['swiːtnis] n dulzura f; lo dulce, lo azucarado; fragancia f; buen olor m; fertilidad f; amabilidad f; suavidad f; **now all is — and light** reina ahora la más perfecta armonía; **to go around spreading — and light** ir por el mundo con una sonrisa amable para todos.

sweet-scented ['swiːt'sentid] adj perfumado, fragante, de olor agradable.

sweetshop ['swiːtʃɔp] n bombonería f, confitería f.

sweet-smelling ['swiːt'smeliŋ] adj see **sweet-scented**.

sweet-tempered ['swiːt'tempəd] adj de carácter dulce, amable; **she's always —** es siempre tan amable, no se altera nunca.

sweet-toothed ['swiːt'tuːθd] adj goloso.

sweet william ['swiːt'wiliəm] n minutisa f.

swell [swel] **1** n (a) (Naut) mar m de fondo, marejada f, oleaje m.

(b) (fam: toff) guapo m, majo m; (important person) pez m gordo, espadón m; **the —s** la gente bien, la gente de buen tono.

2 adj (fam: in dress etc) elegantísimo; (fine, good) estupendo, bárbaro, de órdago; (esp US) **we had a — time** lo pasamos en grande; **it's a — place** es un sitio estupendo; **that's mighty — of you** es Vd muy amable.

3 (irr: pret **swelled**, ptp **swollen**) vt (a) (physically) hinchar; abultar; inflar; (Med) hinchar; **to have a swollen hand** tener la mano hinchada; **eyes swollen with tears** ojos mpl hinchados de lágrimas; **the rains had swollen the river** las lluvias habían hecho crecer el río; **the river is swollen** el río está crecido.

(b) numbers etc aumentar; engrosar; **this will go to — the numbers of...** esto vendrá a aumentar el número de...

4 vi (physically: also **to — up**) hincharse; abultarse; inflarse; (in size, numbers) crecer, aumentar(se); (of river etc) crecer; **her arm —ed up** se le hinchó el brazo; **to — with pride** envanecerse, (justifiably) sentirse lleno de orgullo; **numbers have swollen greatly** el número se ha aumentado muchísimo; **the debt had swollen to...** la deuda había aumentado mucho hasta alcanzar la cifra de...

swellhead ['swelhed] n (US) vanidoso m, a f.

swellheaded ['swel'hedid] adj (US) vanidoso, engreído.

swelling ['sweliŋ] n hinchazón f; protuberancia f; (Med) tumefacción f; (bruise) chichón m, bulto m; (of gland etc) ganglio m.

swelter ['sweltə*] vi abrasarse, sofocarse de calor; chorrear de sudor; **we —ed in 40°** nos sofocábamos a una temperatura de 40 grados.

sweltering ['sweltəriŋ] adj day de muchísimo calor; heat sofocante, abrasador; **it's — in here** aquí se sofoca uno de calor.

swept [swept] pret and ptp of **sweep**.

sweptback ['swept'bæk] adj wing en flecha.

swerve [swəːv] **1** n (a) (dodge, turn) desvío m brusco, viraje m repentino; (of body, in sport etc) esguince m, regate m.

(b) (spin on ball) efecto m; **to put a — on a ball** lanzar una pelota con efecto.

2 vt (a) desviar bruscamente, torcer (a un lado).

(b) dar efecto a, lanzar con efecto, cortar.

3 vi (a) desviarse bruscamente; hurtar el cuerpo; **to — to the right** torcer repentinamente a la derecha.

(b) torcerse.

swift [swift] **1** adj rápido, veloz; repentino; pronto; **— of foot** de pies ligeros; **to be — to anger** tener prontos enojos; **we must be — to act** hemos de obrar con toda prontitud.

2 n vencejo m.

swift-flowing ['swift'fləuiŋ] adj current rápido; river de corriente rápida.

swift-footed ['swift'futid] adj de pies ligeros, veloz.

swiftly ['swiftli] adv rápidamente, velozmente; repentinamente; pronto.

swiftness ['swiftnis] n rapidez f, velocidad f; lo repentino; prontitud f.

swig [swig] (fam) **1** n trago m, tragantada f; **have a — of this** bébete un poco de esto; **he took a — at his flask** se echó un trago de la botella.

2 vt beber; beber a grandes tragos.

swill [swil] **1** n (a) bazofia f; (pej) bazofia f, aguachirle f; **how can you drink this —?** ¿cómo te es posible beber esta basura?

(b) **to give something a — (out)** limpiar algo con agua.

2 vt (a) (clean: also **to — out**) lavar, limpiar con agua.

(b) (drink) beber (a grandes tragos).

3 vi emborracharse.

swim [swim] **1** n (a) nadada f (SAm); **after a 2-kilometre —** después de cubrir 2 kilómetros nadando; **it's a long — back to the shore** nos costará llegar nadando a la playa; **that was a**

long — **for a child** eso fue mucho nadar para un niño; **that was a nice** —! ¡cuánto me gusta nadar así!; **I like a** — me gusta nadar, me gusta la natación; **to go for a** —, **to have a** — ir a nadar.

(b) **to be in the** — estar al corriente; **to keep in the** — mantenerse al día.

2 (*irr: pret* **swam**, *ptp* **swum**) *vt* (a) *river etc* pasar a nado, cruzar a nado; **it was first swum in 1900** un hombre lo cruzó a nado por primera vez en 1900; **it has not been swum before** hasta ahora nadie lo ha cruzado a nado.

(b) **she can't** — **a stroke** no sabe nadar en absoluto; **before I had swum 10 strokes** antes de haber dado 10 brazadas.

3 *vi* (a) nadar; **to** — **across a river** pasar un río a nado; **to** — **out to sea** alejarse nadando de la playa; **to** — **under water** nadar debajo del agua, bucear; **then we swam back** luego volvimos (nadando); **we shall have to** — **for it** tendremos que echarnos al agua, tendremos que salvarnos nadando; **to go** —**ming** ir a nadar, ir a bañarse.

(b) **the meat was** —**ing in gravy** la carne estaba inundada de salsa, la carne flotaba en salsa.

(c) (*of head*) dar vueltas; **everything swam before my eyes** todo parecía estar girando alrededor de mí, todo parecía bailar ante mis ojos.

swimmer ['swimə*] *n* nadador *m*, ora *f*.

swimming ['swimiŋ] *n* natación *f*.

swimming bath ['swimiŋbɑ:θ] *n*, *pl* — **baths** [bɑ:ðz] piscina *f*; **indoor** — piscina *f* cubierta.

swimming cap ['swimiŋkæp] *n* gorro *m* de baño.

swimming costume ['swimiŋˌkɔstju:m] *n* traje *m* de baño.

swimmingly ['swimiŋli] *adv*: **to go** — ir a las mil maravillas.

swimming pool ['swimiŋpu:l] *n see* **swimming bath**.

swimsuit ['swimsu:t] *n* traje *m* de baño.

swindle ['swindl] 1 *n* estafa *f*, timo *m*; **it's a** —! ¡nos han robado!

2 *vt* estafar, timar; **to** — **someone out of something** estafar algo a uno, quitar algo a uno por estafa.

swindler ['swindlə*] *n* estafador *m*, timador *m*.

swine [swain] *n* (a) *pl* (*Zool*) cerdos *mpl*, puercos *mpl*.

(b) *sing* (*fig*) canalla *m*, cochino *m*; **you** —! ¡canalla!; **what a** — **he is!** ¡es un canalla!; **they're a lot of** — son unos cochinos.

swineherd ['swainhə:d] *n* (*arch*) porquero *m*.

swing [swiŋ] 1 *n* (a) (*movement*) balanceo *m*, oscilación *f*, vaivén *m*; (*of pendulum*) oscilación *f*; (*Boxing*) golpe *m* lateral, balanceado *m*; **it has a** — **of 2 metres** tiene un recorrido de 2 metros; **to give the starting handle a** — girar la manivela; **to give a hammock a** — empujar una hamaca; **to give a child a** — empujar a un niño en un columpio; balancear a un niño colgado de los brazos (*etc*); **he took a** — **at me** me asestó un golpe (lateral); **he took a** — **at me with the axe** trató de golpearme con el hacha.

(b) (*Pol, in votes etc*) movimiento *m*, desplazamiento *m*, viraje *m*; **a sudden** — **in opinion** un viraje repentino de la opinión; **the** — **of the pendulum** (*fig*) el flujo y reflujo de la popularidad de los partidos; **there was a strong** — **in the election** en las elecciones se registró un fuerte viraje; **a** — **of 5%** **would give the opposition the majority** un 5 por 100 de desplazamiento de los votos daría a la oposición la mayoría.

(c) (*seat*) columpio *m*.

(d) (*rhythm*) ritmo *m* (fuerte, agradable); (*kind of music*) swing *m*; **a tune that goes with a** — una melodía que tiene un ritmo agradable; **it all went with a** — todo fue sobre ruedas; **to walk with a** — andar rítmicamente; **to be in full** — estar en plena marcha, estar en plena actividad; **to get with the** — **of things** acostumbrarse al ritmo de las cosas.

2 (*irr: pret and ptp* **swung**) *vt* (a) (*to and fro*) balancear; hacer oscilar; (*on a swing*) columpiar; (*brandish*) blandir, menear; *arms* menear; *propeller* girar; **to** — **a child** empujar a un niño en un columpio; balancear a un niño colgado de los brazos (*etc*); **he sat on the table** —**ing his legs** estaba sentado sobre la mesa balanceando las piernas; **to** — **one's fist at someone** asestar un golpe (lateral) a uno con el puño; **he swung the case up on to his shoulders** haciendo un esfuerzo se echó la maleta sobre los hombros.

(b) **he swung the car round** hizo un viraje brusco; **they swung the gun barrel round** hicieron girar el cañón.

(c) (*sl*) **to** — **it** fingirse enfermo, racanear, hacer el rácano; **to** — **it on someone** embaucar a uno.

3 *vi* (a) (*to and fro*) balancearse; oscilar; (*on a swing*) columpiarse; (*hang*) colgar, pender; (*door etc*) girar; **to** — **at anchor** estar anclado; **the door** —**s on its hinges** la puerta gira sobre sus goznes; **it swung open de pronto se abrió; **it** —**s in the wind** se balancea al viento; **a revolver swung from his belt** un revólver colgaba de su cinturón; **he'll** — **for it** le ahorcarán por ello.

(b) (*change direction*) cambiar de dirección; **he swung round** giró sobre los talones, se volvió bruscamente; **the car swung into the square** el coche viró y entró en la plaza; **it swung right round** dio una vuelta completa; **to** — **into action** ponerse en marcha; empezar a ponerse por obra; **the country has swung to the right** el país ha virado a la derecha.

4 *vr*: **to** — **oneself into the saddle** subir a la silla con un solo movimiento enérgico; **to** — **oneself round** girar sobre los talones.

swing bridge ['swiŋˈbridʒ] *n* puente *m* giratorio.

swing door ['swiŋˈdɔ:*] *n* puerta *f* giratoria.

swingeing ['swindʒiŋ] *adj* abrumador.

swinging ['swiŋiŋ] *adj* (*fam*) *city etc* alegre, de vida alegre, lleno de diversiones.

swinish ['swainiʃ] *adj* (*fig*) cochino, canallesco; brutal.

swipe [swaip] 1 *n* golpe *m* fuerte; **to take a** — **at someone** asestar un golpe a uno.

2 *vt* (a) golpear fuertemente; pegar; **he** —**s her** la pega.

(b) (*sl*) apandar, guindar.

3 *vi*: **to** — **at someone** asestar un golpe a uno.

swirl [swə:l] 1 *n* remolino *m*, torbellino *m*; **it disappeared in a** — **of water** desapareció en el agua arremolinada; **the** — **of the dancers' skirts** el girar de las faldas de las bailadoras.

2 *vi* arremolinarse; girar, girar confusamente.

swish [swiʃ] 1 *n* silbar, (*of dress etc*) crujir.

2 *adj* (*sl: smart*) elegantísimo; (*posh*) de buen tono.

3 *vt* *cane* agitar (*or* blandir) produciendo un silbido; *tail* agitar, menear; (*thrash*) azotar.

4 *vi* silbar; sonar, crujir.

Swiss [swis] 1 *adj* suizo. 2 *n* suizo *m*, a *f*.

switch [switʃ] 1 *n* (a) (*stick*) vara *f*, varilla *f*; (*whip*) látigo *m*.

(b) (*of hair*) trenza *f* postiza, trenza *f*, postizo *m*.

(c) (*Rail: points*) aguja *f*; (*change of line*) desviación *f*.

(d) (*Elec etc*) interruptor *m*, conmutador *m*, llave *f*, botón *m*.

(e) (*change*) cambio *m*; **a rapid** — **of plan** un cambio repentino de idea; **to do a** —, **to make a** — hacer un cambio.

2 *vt* (a) *tail* agitar, menear.

(b) (*Rail*) desviar, cambiar de vía; **to** — **a train to another line** cambiar un tren a otra vía.

(c) (*change*) *position etc* cambiar; *policy etc* cambiar de; **so we** —**ed hats** así que cambiamos los sombreros; **to** — **over A and B** cambiar A con B.

(d) (*Elec etc*) **to** — **on** (*Elec*) encender, conectar, poner; (*Aut etc*) arrancar, poner en marcha; **please** — **the radio on** por favor, encienda la radio; **to leave the television** —**ed on** dejar puesta la televisión; **to** — **off** (*Elec*) desconectar, quitar; *light* apagar; *engine* parar.

3 *vi* (a) (*change*) cambiar; **to** — **(over) from Y to Z** cambiar de Y a Z, cambiar Y para tomar Z; **to** — **over to another station** cambiar a otra emisora; **we've** —**ed over altogether to gas** lo hemos cambiado todo a gas; **to** — **round** cambiar de sitio; cambiar de idea.

(b) **to** — **on** encender la radio, poner la televisión (*etc*); arrancar el motor; **to** — **off** desconectar la televisión (*etc*).

switchback ['switʃbæk] *n* (*at fair etc*) montaña *f* rusa, tobogán *m*; (*road*) camino *m* muy desigual, carretera *f* llena de baches.

switchboard ['switʃbɔ:d] *n* (*Tech*) cuadro *m* de mandos; (*Elec*) tablero *m* de conmutadores, cuadro *m* de distribución; (*Tel: at exchange*) cuadro *m* de conexión manual, (*in office etc*) centralita *f*.

switchman ['switʃmən] *n*, *pl* —**men** [mən] (*Rail*) guardagujas *m*.

switchyard ['switʃjɑ:d] *n* (*US Rail*) patio *m* de maniobras.

Switzerland ['switsələnd] Suiza *f*.

swivel ['swivl] 1 *n* eslabón *m* giratorio; pivote *m*.

2 *attr* giratorio, movil.

3 *vt* (*also* **to** — **round**) girar.

4 *vi* (*also* **to — round**) girar; (*of person*) volverse, girar sobre los talones.

swivel seat ['swɪvlsiːt] *n* silla *f* giratoria.

swizz [swɪz] *n*, **swizzle** ['swɪzl] *n* (*fam*) *see* **swindle**.

swollen ['swəulən] *ptp of* **swell**.

swoon [swuːn] **1** *n* desmayo *m*, desvanecimiento *m*; **to fall in a —** desmayarse.

2 *vi* desmayarse, desvanecerse (*also* **to — away**); **she —ed at the news** al saber la noticia se desmayó.

swoop [swuːp] **1** *n* calada *f*, descenso *m* súbito; arremetida *f*; (*by police*) redada *f*; visita *f* de inspección; **at one fell —, in one** — de un solo golpe.

2 *vi* (*also* **to — down**; *of bird*) calarse; precipitarse, lanzarse (*on sobre*); **the plane —ed low over the village** el avión picó y voló muy bajo sobre el pueblo; **the police —ed on 8 suspects** la policía detuvo a 8 sospechosos; **he —ed on this mistake** saltó sobre este error.

swoosh [swu(ː)ʃ] = **swish**.

swop [swɒp] *see* **swap**.

sword [sɔːd] *n* espada *f*; **to cross —s with someone** habérselas con uno; reñir con uno; **to measure —s with someone** cruzar espadas con uno; **to put people to the —** pasar a cuchillo a unas gentes; **those that live by the — die by the —** el que a hierro mata a hierro muere.

sword dance ['sɔːddɑːns] *n* danza *f* de espadas.

swordfish ['sɔːdfiʃ] *n* pez *m* espada.

swordplay ['sɔːdplei] *n* esgrima *f*; manejo *m* de la espada; **the film has 5 minutes of —** en la película se combate a espada durante 5 minutos.

swordsman ['sɔːdzmən] *n*, *pl* **—men** [mən] espadachín *m*; (*fencer*) esgrimidor *m*.

swordsmanship ['sɔːdzmənʃip] *n* esgrima *f*, manejo *m* de la espada.

swordstick ['sɔːdstik] *n* bastón *m* de estoque.

sword-swallower ['sɔːd,swɒləuə*] *n* tragasables *m*.

sword thrust ['sɔːdθrʌst] *n* estocada *f*.

swore [swɔː*] *pret of* **swear**.

sworn [swɔːn] **1** *ptp of* **swear**. **2** *adj* **enemy** implacable; **evidence** dado bajo juramento.

swot [swɒt] (*fam*) **1** *n* empollón *m*, ona *f*. **2** *vt* empollar; **to — up one's maths** empollar matemáticas. **3** *vi* empollar; **to — at something** empollar algo.

swum [swʌm] *ptp of* **swim**.

swung [swʌŋ] *pret and ptp of* **swing**.

sybarite ['sibərait] *n* sibarita *mf*.

sybaritic [,sibə'ritik] *adj* sibarita, sibarítico.

sycamore ['sikəmɔː*] *n* sicomoro *m* (*also* **— tree**).

sycophancy ['sikəfənsi] *n* adulación *f*; servilismo *m*.

sycophant ['sikəfənt] *n* sicofante *m*, adulador *m*; persona *f* servil; sobón *m*.

sycophantic [,sikə'fæntik] *adj person* servil, sobón; **speech etc** adulatorio; **manner** servil.

syllabic [si'læbik] *adj* silábico.

syllabicate [si'læbikeit] *vt* silabear, dividir en sílabas.

syllabication [si,læbi'keiʃən] *n* silabeo *m*, división *f* en sílabas.

syllable ['siləbl] *n* sílaba *f*.

syllabus ['siləbəs] *n* programa *m* (*esp* de estudios).

syllogism ['silədʒizəm] *n* silogismo *m*.

syllogistic [,silə'dʒistik] *adj* silogístico.

sylph [silf] *n* (*Myth*) silfo *m*, sílfide *f*; (*woman*) sílfide *f*.

sylphlike ['silflaik] *adj* **figure etc** de sílfide.

sylvan ['silvən] *adj* selvático, silvestre; rústico.

symbiosis [,simbi'əusis] *n* simbiosis *f*.

symbol ['simbəl] *n* símbolo *m*.

symbolic(al) [sim'bɒlik(əl)] *adj* simbólico.

symbolically [sim'bɒlikəli] *adv* simbólicamente.

symbolism ['simbəlizəm] *n* simbolismo *m*.

symbolist ['simbəlist] **1** *adj* simbolista. **2** *n* simbolista *mf*.

symbolize ['simbəlaiz] *vt* simbolizar.

symmetrical [si'metrikəl] *adj* simétrico.

symmetrically [si'metrikəli] *adv* simétricamente.

symmetry ['simitri] *n* simetría *f*.

sympathetic [,simpə'θetik] *adj* **(a)** (*showing pity*) compasivo (*to con*), compadecido; (*kind*) amable, benévolo; **we found a — policeman** encontramos a un policía que amablemente nos ayudó (*etc*); **they were — but could not help se** compadecieron de nosotros pero no podían hacer nada para ayudarnos; **they are — to actors** están bien dispuestos hacia los actores.

(b) (*understanding*) comprensivo; **with a — smile** con una sonrisa comprensiva.

(c) **ink, nerve, pain etc** simpático.

sympathetically [,simpə'θetikəli] *adv* con compasión; amablemente, benévolamente; con comprensión; **she looked at me —** me miró compasiva.

sympathize ['simpəθaiz] *vi* **(a)** (*in sorrow etc*) compadecerse, condolerse; **I really do —** lo siento de

verdad; **to — with someone** compadecerse de uno, condolerse de uno; **to — with someone in his bereavement** dar el pésame a uno por la muerte de . . .; **they called to —** vinieron a dar el pésame.

(b) (*understand*) comprender; **I — with what you say, but . . .** comprendo el punto de vista de Vd, pero . . .

sympathizer ['simpəθaizə*] *n* simpatizante *mf*, partidario *m*, a *f* (*with de*).

sympathy ['simpəθi] **1** *n* **(a)** (*fellow feeling*) simpatía *f*; solidaridad *f*; **I am not in — with him** yo no comparto su criterio, yo no lo entiendo así; **the sympathies of the crowd were with him** la multitud estaba de lado de él, la multitud le apoyaba; **to strike in — with someone** declararse en huelga por solidaridad con uno.

(b) (*pity*) compasión *f*, condolencia *f*; sentimiento *m*; (*kindness*) amabilidad *f*, benevolencia *f*; **he has my —** yo le compadezco; **my sympathies are with her family** yo lo siento por la familia de ella; **have you no —?** ¿no tiene compasión?; **to express one's —** dar el pésame (*on the death of por la muerte de*); **his — for the underdog** su compasión por los desvalidos.

2 *attr* **— strike** huelga *f* por solidaridad.

symphonic [sim'fɒnik] *adj* sinfónico.

symphony ['simfəni] *n* sinfonía *f*; **— orchestra** orquesta *f* sinfónica.

symposium [sim'pəuziəm] *n*, *pl* **symposia** [sim'pəuziə] simposio *m*.

symptom ['simptəm] *n* síntoma *m*; indicio *m*.

symptomatic [,simptə'mætik] *adj* sintomático (*of de*).

synagogue ['sinəgɔg] *n* sinagoga *f*.

synchromesh ['siŋkrəu'meʃ] *n* (*also* **— gear**) cambio *m* de velocidades sincronizado.

synchronism ['siŋkrənizəm] *n* sincronismo *m*.

synchronization [,siŋkrənai'zeiʃən] *n* sincronización *f*.

synchronize ['siŋkrənaiz] **1** *vt* sincronizar (*with con*). **2** *vi* sincronizarse, ser sincrónico (*with con*); coincidir (*with con*).

synchronous ['siŋkrənəs] *adj* sincrónico, síncrono.

syncopate ['siŋkəpeit] *vt* sincopar.

syncopation [,siŋkə'peiʃən] *n* síncopa *f*.

syncope ['siŋkəpi] *n* (*Mus*) síncopa *f*; (*Ling, Med*) síncope *m*.

syndicalism ['sindikəlizəm] *n* sindicalismo *m*.

syndicalist ['sindikəlist] **1** *adj* sindicalista. **2** *n* sindicalista *mf*.

syndicate ['sindikit] *n* sindicato *m*.

syndicate ['sindikeit] *vt* sindicar.

syndrome ['sindrəum] *n* síndrome *m*.

synecdoche [si'nekdəki] *n* sinécdoque *f*.

synod ['sinəd] *n* sínodo *m*.

synonym ['sinənim] *n* sinónimo *m*.

synonymous [si'nɒniməs] *adj* sinónimo (*with con*).

synonymy [si'nɒnəmi] *n* sinonimia *f*.

synopsis [si'nɒpsis] *n*, *pl* **synopses** [si'nɒpsiːz] sinopsis *f*.

synoptic(al) [si'nɒptik(əl)] *adj* sinóptico.

syntactic(al) [sin'tæktik(əl)] *adj* sintáctico.

syntax ['sintæks] *n* sintaxis *f*.

synthesis ['sinθəsis] *n*, *pl* **syntheses** ['sinθəsiːz] síntesis *f*.

synthesize ['sinθəsaiz] *vt* sintetizar.

synthetic [sin'θetik] *adj* sintético.

synthetically [sin'θetikəli] *adv* sintéticamente.

syphilis ['sifilis] *n* sífilis *f*.

syphilitic [,sifi'litik] **1** *adj* sifilítico. **2** *n* sifilítico *m*, a *f*.

syphon ['saifən] *see* **siphon**.

Syracuse ['saiərəkjuːz] Siracusa.

Syria ['siriə] Siria *f*.

Syrian ['siriən] **1** *adj* sirio. **2** *n* sirio *m*, a *f*.

syringe [si'rindʒ] **1** *n* jeringa *f*. **2** *vt* jeringar.

syrup ['sirəp] *n* jarabe *m*; almíbar *m*.

syrupy ['sirəpi] *adj* parecido a jarabe, espeso como jarabe.

system ['sistəm] *n* sistema *m*; método *m*; (*Med*) organismo *m*, constitución *f*; (*Elec*) circuito *m*, instalación *f*; **feudal —** feudalismo *m*; **metric —** sistema *m* métrico; **nervous —** sistema *m* nervioso; **a shock to the —** una sacudida para el organismo; **to get something out of one's —** (*fig*) quitarse algo de encima.

systematic [,sistə'mætik] *adj* sistemático, metódico.

systematically [,sistə'mætikəli] *adv* sistemáticamente, metódicamente.

systematize ['sistəmətaiz] *vt* sistematizar.

systematization ['sistəmətai'zeiʃən] *n* sistematización *f*.

T

T [tiː]: **to a —** (*fam*) de perlas, de maravilla, al pelo;
it fits you to a — te sienta perfectamente; **it suits
me to a —** me va de perlas.

ta [tɑː] *interj* (*fam*) ¡gracias!; **— very much!** ¡muchas
gracias!

tab [tæb] *n* oreja *f*, lengüeta *f*; (*label*) etiqueta *f*;
(*Theat*) cortina *f*; **to keep —s on** someone echar
un ojo sobre uno, vigilar a uno; **to keep —s on
something** tener algo a la vista, tener cuenta de
algo.

tabard ['tæbəd] *n* tabardo *m*.

tabby ['tæbi] **1** *adj* atigrado. **2** *n* (*also* **— cat**) gato *m*
atigrado, gata *f* atigrada.

tabernacle ['tæbənækl] *n* tabernáculo *m*.

table ['teibl] **1** *n* (**a**) (*furniture*) mesa *f*; (*Archit*)
tablero *m*; (*of land*) meseta *f*; **bedside —** mesita *f*
de noche; **occasional —, small —** mesita *f*; **operating
—** mesa *f* de operaciones; **round —** mesa *f* redonda;
round-— conference conferencia *f* de mesa redonda;
water — (*Geog*) nivel *m* de agua freática; **to keep
a good —** tener buena mesa; **to clear the —** levantar
la mesa; **to lay the —, to set the —** poner la mesa;
to rise from the — levantarse de la mesa; **to sit
down to —** sentarse a la mesa; **to turn the —s on
someone** devolver la pelota a uno, vencer a uno
empleando sus propias armas.

(**b**) (*Math etc*) tabla *f*; (*statistical etc*) tabla *f*,
cuadro *m*; (*of prices*) lista *f*, tarifa *f*; (*league* **—**)
liga *f*, clasificación *f*, escalafón *m*; **— of contents**
índice *m* de materias; **multiplication —** tabla *f* de
multiplicar; **log —s** tablas *fpl* de logaritmos;
we are in fourth place in the — ocupamos el cuarto
lugar en la clasificación.

2 *vt* (*Parl etc*) *motion* presentar, poner sobre la
mesa; (*set out*) poner en una tabla, disponer en un
cuadro; ordenar sistemáticamente; (*US*) *bill* dar
carpetazo a.

tableau ['tæbləu] *n* cuadro *m* (vivo).

tablecloth ['teiblklɔθ] *n*, *pl* **—cloths** [klɔθs] mantel *m*.

table d'hôte ['tɑːbl'dəut] *n* mesa *f* redonda.

table lamp ['teibllæmp] *n* lámpara *f* de mesa.

tableland ['teibllænd] *n* meseta *f*.

table leg ['teiblleg] *n* pata *f* de mesa.

table linen ['teibl,linin] *n* mantelería *f*.

tablemat ['teiblmæt] *n* salvaplatos *m*, salvamanteles
m.

Table Mountain ['teibl'mauntin] Monte *m* de la
Mesa.

table napkin ['teibl,næpkin] *n* servilleta *f*.

table runner ['teibl,rʌnə*] *n* mantelillo *m*, camino
m de mesa.

tablespoon ['teiblspuːn] *n* cuchara *f* grande, cuchara
f para servir.

tablespoonful ['teibl,spuːnful] *n* cucharada *f*.

tablet ['tæblit] *n* tabla *f*; tableta *f*; (*Med*) tableta *f*,
comprimido *m*; (*of soap etc*) pastilla *f*; (*stone,
inscribed*) lápida *f*; (*writing* **—**) bloc *m*, taco *m*
(de papel).

table talk ['teibltɔːk] *n* conversación *f* de sobremesa.

table tennis ['teibl,tenis] *n* tenis *m* de mesa.

tableware ['teiblwɛə*] *n* artículos *mpl* de mesa.

table water ['teibl,wɔːtə*] *n* agua *f* mineral.

table wine ['teiblwain] *n* vino *m* de mesa.

tabloid ['tæblɔid] *n* (*Med*) tableta *f*, comprimido
m; (*newspaper*) periódico *m* de formato reducido,
tabloide *m*.

taboo [tə'buː] **1** *adj* tabú, prohibido. **2** tabú *m*;
all kinds of —s toda clase de tabúes. **3** *vt* declarar
tabú, prohibir.

tabular ['tæbjulə*] *adj* tabular.

tabulate ['tæbjuleit] *vt* disponer en tablas, exponer
en forma de tabla; resumir en tablas.

tabulation [,tæbju'leiʃən] *n* disposición *f* en tablas,
exposición *f* en forma de tabla.

tachometer [tæ'kɔmitə*] *n* tacómetro *m*.

tachymeter [tæ'kimitə*] *n* taquímetro *m*.

tacit ['tæsit] *adj* tácito.

tacitly ['tæsitli] *adv* tácitamente.

taciturn ['tæsitɜːn] *adj* taciturno.

taciturnity [,tæsi'tɜːniti] *n* taciturnidad *f*.

Tacitus ['tæsitəs] *m* Tácito.

tack [tæk] **1** *n* (**a**) (*nail*) tachuela *f*; **to get down to
brass —s** ir al grano.

(**b**) (*Sew*) hilván *m*.

(**c**) (*Naut: rope*) amura *f*; (*course*) virada *f*,
bordada *f*; (*fig*) rumbo *m*, dirección *f*; línea *f* de
conducta, política *f*; **to be on the right —** (*fig*) ir
por buen camino; **to be on the wrong —** estar
equivocado; **to try another —** abordar un problema
desde otro punto de partida; cambiar de política.

2 *vt* (**a**) (*nail*) clavar con tachuelas; **to — something
down** afirmar algo con tachuelas, sujetar algo con
tachuelas.

(**b**) (*Sew*) hilvanar; **to — something on to a
letter** añadir algo a una carta; **somehow it got —ed
on** de algún modo u otro quedó unido a lo principal,
de algún modo u otro llegó a ser añadido a la parte
principal.

3 *vi* (**a**) (*Naut*) virar, cambiar de bordada; **the
ship —ed this way and that** el buque cambió
constantemente de bordada.

(**b**) **to — on to someone** (*fig*) unirse a uno,
pegarse a uno.

tackle ['tækl] **1** *n* (**a**) (*esp Naut: pulley*) aparejo *m*;
polea *f*; (*ropes*) jarcia *f*; cordaje *m*.

(**b**) (*gear, equipment*) equipo *m*, avíos *mpl*,
aperos *mpl*; (*fig*) cosas *fpl*, enseres *mpl*; (*fishing* **—**)
aparejo *m* de pescar.

(**c**) (*Sport*) carga *f*, atajo *m*, blocaje *m*; **rough —**
atajo *m* duro.

2 *vt* (*grapple with*) agarrar, asir; atacar; (*Sport*)
atajar, blocar; *problem* abordar, atacar; *task*
emprender; **he had to — 3 intruders** tuvo que hacer
frente a 3 intrusos; **he —d Greek on his own**
emprendió el estudio del griego sin ayuda de nadie;
did you ever — Mulacén? ¿os atrevisteis alguna
vez a escalar el Mulacén?; **can you — another
helping?** ¿puedes comerte otra porción?; **I'll —
him about it at once** lo discutiré con él en seguida
(quiera o no quiera).

tacky ['tæki] *adj* pegajoso.

tact [tækt] *n* tacto *m*, discreción *f*.

tactful ['tæktful] *adj* discreto, diplomático; **be as —
as you can** use la mayor discreción; **that was not
very — of you** pudieras haberlo hecho con más tacto.

tactfully ['tæktfəli] *adv* discretamente, diplomáticamente.

tactfulness ['tæktfulnis] *n* tacto *m*, discreción *f*.

tactic ['tæktik] *n* (**a**) táctica *f*; maniobra *f*. (**b**) **—s**
(*collectively*) táctica *f*.

tactical ['tæktikəl] *adj* táctico.

tactically ['tæktikəli] *adv* tácticamente.

tactician [tæk'tiʃən] *n* táctico *m*.

tactile ['tæktail] *adj* táctil.

tactless ['tæktlis] *adj* indiscreto, falto de tacto, poco
diplomático.

tactlessly ['tæktlisli] *adv* indiscretamente, de modo
poco diplomático.

tadpole ['tædpəul] *n* renacuajo *m*.

taffeta ['tæfitə] *n* tafetán *m*.

taffrail ['tæfreil] *n* coronamiento *m*, pasamano *m* de
la borda.

taffy ['tæfi] *n* (*US*) (**a**) = **toffee**. (**b**) (*fam*) coba *f*
(*fam*).

Taffy ['tæfi] (= **David**) *el galés típico*.

tag[1] [tæg] *n* (*loose end*) cabo *m*, rabito *m*; (*rag*)
pingajo *m*; (*metal tip*) herrete *m*; (*label*) etiqueta *f*,
marbete *m*; (*commonplace*) dicho *m*, lugar *m* común;

(*quotation*) cita *f*; **identification** — chapa *f* de identificación; **price** — etiqueta *f* que lleva el precio.

2 *vt* (*follow*) seguir de cerca, pisar los talones a; (*label*) poner una etiqueta a, pegar una etiqueta a; **to** — **something on to an article** pegar algo a un artículo; **can we** — **this on?** ¿podemos añadir esto?

3 *vi*: **to** — **along** (*jog along*) seguir despacio su camino; proceder con calma; (*accompany*) ir también, venir después; **to** — **on to someone** unirse a uno, (insistir en) acompañar a uno.

tag² [tæg] *n*: **to play** — dar la despedida, jugar al tócame tú.

Tagus ['teigəs] Tajo *m*.

Tahiti [taːˈhiːti] Tahití *m*.

tail [teil] **1** *n* (*Anat*) cola *f*, rabo *m*; (*loose end*) cabo *m*; (*of hair*) trenza *f*; (*of comet*) cabellera *f*; (*Aer*) cola *f*; (*of procession etc*) cola *f*, parte *f* final; (*of coat*) faldón *m*, faldillas *fpl*; (*of shirt*) faldón *m*; **—s** (*coat*) frac *m*; (*of coin*) cruz *f*; **with its** — **between its legs** con el rabo entre las patas; **—s you lose** cruz y pierde Vd; **but there's a sting in the** — pero lo malo viene al final; **to turn** — volver la espalda, huir.

2 *vt* (a) (*follow*) seguir de cerca, pisar los talones a; vigilar.

(b) *animal* descolar; *fruit* quitar el tallo a.

3 *vi* (a) **to** — **away, to** — **off** ir disminuyendo (*into* hasta, hasta no ser más que), desaparecer poco a poco; **his voice —ed away** su voz se fue debilitando; **after that the book —s away** después de eso el libro ya no es tan bueno, después de eso el libro no tiene tantas cosas buenas.

(b) **to** — **after someone** seguir a uno (de mala gana).

tailboard ['teilbɔːd] *n* escalera *f*, tablero *m* posterior.

tail coat ['teilkəut] *n* frac *m*.

-tailed [teild] *adj* con rabo . . ., *eg* **long-tailed** con rabo largo, rabilargo.

tail end ['teil'end] *n* cola *f*; extremo *m*; parte *f* de atrás, parte *f* posterior; (*fig*) parte *f* que queda, porción *f* inservible.

tail gunner ['teil‚gʌnə*] *n* (*Aer*) artillero *m* de cola.

tail lamp ['teillæmp] *n* faro *m* trasero.

tailless ['teillis] *adj* sin rabo.

taillight ['teillait] *n* faro *m* trasero.

tailor ['teilə*] **1** *n* sastre *m*; **—'s** (**shop**) sastrería *f*.
2 *vt suit* hacer, confeccionar; (*fig*) adaptar.

tailored ['teiləd] *adj*: — **dress** vestido *m* sastre; **a well- — suit** un traje bien hecho, un traje que entalla bien.

tailoring ['teiləriŋ] *n* (*craft*) sastrería *f*; (*cut*) corte *m*, hechura *f*.

tailor-made ['teiləmeid] *adj* (a) hecho por sastre, de sastre; — **costume** traje *m* hechura sastre.

(b) (*fig*) — **for you** especial para Vd, creado especialmente para Vd.

tailpiece ['teilpiːs] *n* (*Typ*) florón *m*; (*addition*) apéndice *m*, añadidura *f*.

tailpipe ['teilpaip] *n* (*US: Aut*) tubo *m* de escape.

tailplane ['teilplein] *n* (*Aer*) cola *f*, plano *m* de cola.

tail skid ['teilskid] *n* (*Aer*) patín *m* de cola.

tailspin ['teilspin] *n* (*Aer*) barrena *f* picada.

tail unit ['teil‚juːnit] *n* conjunto *m* de cola.

tail wheel ['teil'wiːl] *n* rueda *f* de cola.

tailwind ['teilwind] *n* viento *m* de cola.

taint [teint] **1** *n* infección *f*; (*fig*) mancha *f*, tacha *f*; olor *m* (*of* a); **the** — **of sin** la mancha del pecado; **not free from the** — **of corruption** no sin cierto olor a corrupción.

2 *vt* corromper, inficionar, viciar.

3 *vi* corromperse, inficionarse, viciarse.

tainted ['teintid] *adj* viciado, corrompido; *meat etc* pasado; **a belief** — **with heresy** una creencia no exenta de herejía.

take [teik] (*irr: pret* **took**, *ptp* **taken**) **1** *vt* (a) (*general sense*) tomar; (*by force*) coger, asir, arrebatar; (*steal*) robar; (*keep*) quedarse con; **to** — **something from someone** tomar algo a uno; **who took my beer?** ¿quién se ha llevado mi cerveza?; **to** — **a book from a shelf** sacar un libro de un estante; **to** — **a passage from an author** tomar un pasaje de un autor; **to** — **someone's arm** tomar del brazo a uno; **to** — **someone in one's arms** abrazar a uno, rodear a uno con los brazos.

(b) (*capture*) *city etc* tomar, conquistar; *specimen, fish etc* coger; (*Chess*) comer; *prisoner* hacer; *suspect, wanted man* coger, detener; **to** — **someone alive or dead** coger a uno vivo o muerto; **the devil** — **it!** ¡maldición!, ¡que se lo lleve el diablo!; **to be —n ill** ponerse enfermo, enfermar; **we were very —n with him** le encontramos simpatiquísimo; **I'm not at all**

—n with the idea la idea no me gusta nada, la idea no me hace gracia.

(c) (*win*) *prize* ganar; *trick* ganar, hacer; **to** — **one's degree** recibir un título; **to** — **a degree in** licenciarse en; **to** — **£30 a day** cobrar 30 libras al día; **last year we took £30,000** el año pasado los ingresos sumaron 30.000 libras.

(d) (*rent*) alquilar; **we shall** — **a house for the summer** alquilaremos una casa para el verano; **we took rooms at Torquay** alquilamos un piso en Torquay.

(e) (*occupy*) ocupar; **is that seat —n?** ¿está ocupada esa plaza?; **please** — **your seats!** ¡siéntense, por favor!

(f) (*go by*) *bus, train etc* coger; *road* tomar, ir por; *fence* saltar, saltar por encima de; — **the first on the right** vaya por la primera calle a la derecha; **we took the wrong road** nos equivocamos de camino; **we** — **the golden road to Samarkand** vamos por el camino dorado de Samarkand.

(g) (*ingest*) *drink, food* tomar; **to** — **a meal** comer; **he took no food for 4 days** durante 4 días no comió; **how much alcohol had he —n?** ¿cuánto alcohol había ingerido?; **"not to be —n"** (*Med*) "para uso externo"; **will you** — **something before you go?** ¿quieres tomar algo antes de irte?

(h) (*have, make, undertake etc*) *bath, bend, breath, decision, exercise, holiday, liberty, possession* tomar; *step, walk,* dar; *photo* sacar, tomar; *ticket* sacar; *trip* hacer; *oath* prestar; *census* levantar, efectuar; *examination* presentarse para, sufrir; *opportunity* aprovechar; *see* **effect, stock** *etc*.

(i) (*receive*) recibir, tomar; *advice* seguir; *bet* aceptar, hacer; *responsibility* asumir; *guests* recibir; *pupils* tomar; *course of study* seguir, cursar; *subject* estudiar; *newspaper etc* leer, abonarse a; — **that!** ¡toma!; — **it from me!** ¡escucha lo que te digo!; **you can** — **it from me that . . .** puedes tener la seguridad de que . . .; **to** — **the service** (*Tennis*) restar la pelota, ser restador; **he took the ball in the chest** el balón le dio de lleno en el pecho; **what will you** — **for it?** ¿cuánto pides por él?; **to** — **a wife** casarse; **to** — **someone into partnership** tomar a uno como socio; **to** — **(holy) orders** ordenarse de sacerdote; *see* **badly, ill** *etc*.

(j) (*tolerate*) aguantar, sufrir; **we can** — **it** lo aguantamos todo; **he took a lot of punishment** sufrió mucho, llevó un duro castigo; **London took a battering in 1941** Londres recibió una paliza en 1941, Londres sufrió terriblemente en 1941; **I won't** — **no for an answer** no permito que digas no, no permito que me des una respuesta negativa; **I won't** — **that from you** no permito que digas eso; no tolero semejante cosa de Vd.

(k) (*consider*) tomar, considerar; **now** — **Ireland** consideren el caso de Irlanda, pongamos por caso Irlanda; **taking one thing with another . . .** considerándolo todo junto . . ., considerándolo en conjunto . . .; **taking one year with another . . .** tomando un año con otro . . .

(l) (*contain*) tener cabida para; **a car that —s 6 passengers** un coche con cabida para 6 personas, un coche donde caben 6 personas; **can you** — **2 more?** ¿puedes llevar 2 más?, ¿caben otros 2?; **it won't** — **any more** no cabe(n) más; **it —s weights up to 8 tons** soporta pesos hasta de 8 toneladas.

(m) (*experience*) experimentar; *illness* coger; **to** — **cold** tomar frío; coger un resfriado, resfriarse; **to** — **fright** asustarse (*at* de); **to** — **a dislike to someone** coger antipatía a uno, tomar hincha a uno (*fam*); *see* **liking** *etc*.

(n) (*suppose*) suponer; **I** — **it that . . .** supongo que . . ., imagino que . . .; **I** — **her to be about 30** supongo que tiene unos 30 años; **I took him for a foreigner** creí que era extranjero, le tomé por extranjero; **what do you** — **me for?** ¿por quién me ha tomado Vd?, ¿crees que soy un tonto?; **we took A for B** equivocamos A con B.

(o) (*require*) necesitar; hacer falta; **a recipe that —s 10 eggs** una receta en la que hacen falta 10 huevos; **it** — **s a lot of courage** exige gran valor; **it —s a brave man to do that** hace falta que un hombre tenga mucho valor para hacer eso; **he's got what it —s** tiene las cualidades precisas; **it —s 4 days** es cosa de 4 días; **it —s 4 days to get there** tarda 4 días en llegar allá; **it won't** — **long** no tarda mucho; **it —s 3 policemen to hold him down** se necesitó de 3 policías para sujetarle; **that verb —s the dative** ese verbo rige el dativo; *see* **size** *etc*.

(p) (*lead, transport*) llevar; **to** — **something to someone** llevar algo a uno; **to** — **someone some-**

where llevar a uno a un sitio; **we took her to the doctor** la llevamos al médico; **an ambulance took him to hospital** una ambulancia le llevó al hospital; **they took me over the factory** me mostraron la fábrica, me acompañaron en una visita a la fábrica; **to — someone for a walk** llevar a uno de paseo; **it took us out of our way** nos hizo desviarnos de nuestra ruta; **whatever took you to Miami?** ¿con qué propósito fuiste a Miami?, ¿qué propósito tuvo su viaje a Miami?

(q) (with adv or prep) **to — aback** see **aback**; **to — along** llevar, traer; person llevar; **to — apart** desmontar; **to — away** quitar; llevarse; person llevarse; (Math) restar; **7 — away 4 is 3** 7 menos 4 son 3; **to — back** (return) devolver; (receive back) object recibir devuelto, person recibir otra vez (como amigo or novio etc); words retractar, promise desdecirse de; **they gave it to me but then they took it back again** me lo dieron pero volvieron luego a quitármelo; **the company took him back** la compañía volvió a emplearle, la compañía le restituyó a su puesto; **to — down** (get down) bajar; descolgar; (Tech) desmontar, desarmar; note apuntar; poner por escrito; **to — someone down** quitar los humos a uno; **to — in** work aceptar, admitir; person acoger, recibir (en su casa); food tomar, ingerir; (include) abarcar; clothes achicar, belt apretarse; sail desmontar; paper abonarse a, leer; (understand) entender, comprender; **to — someone in** (fam) embaucar a uno, estafar a uno, dar a uno gato por liebre; **I was properly —n in by the disguise** el disfraz me despistó completamente; **don't let yourself be —n in by appearances** no te dejes engañar por las apariencias; **to — off** clothes, hat quitarse; limb amputar; lid, wrapping, etc quitar; (unstick) despegar; discount descontar, rebajar; (imitate) imitar; contrahacer, parodiar; **they took him off to lunch** se le llevaron a comer; **to — on** (assume) asumir, tomar; work emprender; aceptar; duties tomar sobre sí, cargar con, encargarse de; workmen contratar; cargo cargar, tomar; **to — someone on** (as challenge) desafiar a uno, atreverse a competir con uno; (Sport) jugar contra uno, luchar contra uno; **he's —n on more than he bargained for** le está resultando peor de lo que él se creía, él no contaba con tener que esforzarse tanto; **to — out** (from pocket etc) sacar; (extract) extraer, sacar; (remove) quitar; stain sacar; (outside house etc) llevar fuera; children, dog llevar de paseo; girl invitar; escoltar; salir con; pretender; patent obtener; **to — it out of someone** cansar a uno, rendir a uno; **to — it out on someone** desahogarse riñendo a uno; vengarse de uno; **to — over** responsibility asumir, encargarse de; leadership, office etc asumir; tomar posesión de; **the army has —n over power** el ejército se ha hecho cargo del poder, el ejército ha ocupado el poder; **the tourists have —n over the museums** los turistas han acaparado los museos; **to — up** (carry up) subir; (pick up) coger, recoger; arms empuñar; water etc absorber; dress etc acortar; carpet quitar; passengers tomar; case emprender investigaciones acerca de; post tomar posesión de; residence establecer, fijar; room, time ocupar, llenar; story empezar a contar, (after break) continuar, reanudar; study empezar; dedicarse a; challenge, offer aceptar; **the bus —s up and sets down passengers** el autobús toma y deja pasajeros; **it —s up a lot of my time** me quita mucho tiempo; **to — someone up on something** censurar algo a uno; expresar dudas acerca de algo que ha dicho uno; **I feel I must — you up on that** creo que es mi deber criticar esto que ha dicho Vd; **to — something upon oneself** tomar algo sobre sí, encargarse de algo; **to — it upon oneself to +** infin atreverse a + infin, (pej) tener bastante caradura como para + infin.

2 vi **(a)** (stick) pegar; (set) cuajar; (of vaccination) prender; (of plant) arraigar; (succeed) tener éxito; resultar ser eficaz.
(b) (Phot) **he —s well** saca buen retrato, saca buenas fotos.
(c) (with adv or prep) **to — after** (in looks) salir a, parecerse a; (in conduct) seguir el ejemplo de; **to — off** salir (for para); (Aer) despegar (for con rumbo a); **to — on** (fam) apurarse, excitarse, ponerse nervioso; quejarse; **don't — on so!** ¡no te apures!, ¡cálmate!; **to — over** tomar posesión; entrar en funciones; **to — to someone** coger simpatía a uno, tomar cariño a uno; **to — to something** aficionarse a algo, cobrar afición a algo; **to — to +** ger empezar a + ger; dedicarse a + infin, aficionarse a + infin; **to — up with someone**

relacionarse con uno, estrechar amistad con uno; **he took up with the wrong set** empezó a alternar con gente que no valía para nada.
3 n (Phot) toma f, vista f.

taken ['teikən] ptp of **take**.

takeoff ['teikɔf] n **(a)** (Aer) despegue m. **(b)** (imitation) imitación f; parodia f; sátira f; **(c)** (Mech) **power —** toma f de fuerza.

takeover ['teik,əuvə*] n toma f de posesión; entrada f en funciones; **the — of company A by company Z** la absorción de la compañía A por la compañía Z, la compra de la compañía A en su totalidad por la compañía Z; **— bid** oferta f para comprar la totalidad (de una compañía etc).

taker ['teikə*] n **—s of snuff** los que acostumbran tomar rapé; **—s of drink in moderation** los que beben con moderación; **at £5 there were no —s** a un precio de 5 libras nadie se ofreció a comprarlo; **this challenge found no —s** no hubo nadie que quisiera aceptar este desafío.

taking ['teikiŋ] **1** adj atractivo, encantador.
2 n toma f, conquista f; **—s** (Fin) ingresos mpl; (at show etc) taquilla f, entrada f, recaudación f; **this year's —s were only half last year's** este año se ha embolsado la mitad de la recaudación del año pasado.

talc [tælk] n talco m.
talcum powder ['tælkəm,paudə*] n (polvo m de) talco m.

tale [teil] n cuento m; historia f, relación f; (pej) cuento m, patraña f; **"T—s of King Arthur"** "Leyendas fpl del Rey Artús"; **old wives' —** cuento m de viejas, patraña f; **I hear —s about you** me cuentan cosas acerca de Vd; **to tell —s** (out of school) soplar, chismear, contar cuentos; **he told the — of his life** contó la historia de su vida; **he had quite a — to tell** tuvo cosas bastante interesantes que contar.

talebearer ['teil,bεərə*] n soplón m, ona f, chismoso m, a f.

talent ['tælənt] n talento m (for para); **man of —** hombre m de talento; **all the local —** toda la gente de talento de la comarca; **he watches for — at away matches** busca jugadores de talento en los partidos fuera de casa.

talented ['tæləntid] adj talentoso, de talento.

talent scout ['tælənt,skaut] n, **talent spotter** ['tælənt,spɔtə*] n cazatalentos m.

talisman ['tælizmən] n talismán m.

talk [tɔːk] **1** n (conversation) conversación f, (chat) charla f; (informal lecture) charla f; (gossip) chismes mpl, habladurías fpl; **idle —** charla f insustancial; **it's just —** son cosas que se dicen, son rumores; **with him it's all —** no hace más que hablar; **she's the — of the town** todos hablan de ella, es la comidilla de la ciudad; **there is (some) — of** se habla de; **there has been some — of his going** se ha hablado de que va él; **to give a —** dar una charla (about sobre); **to have a — to (or with) someone** hablar con uno; **we must have a — sometime** tenemos que citarnos un día para hablar.
2 vt **(a)** (speak); **to — Arabic** hablar árabe; **— some Arabic to me** díme algo en árabe, díme unas palabras de árabe; **to — business** hablar de negocios; **to — nonsense** no decir más que tonterías; **to — sense** hablar con juicio, hablar razonablemente; see **shop** etc.
(b) (with adv or prep) **to — away an hour** pasar una hora charlando; **to — someone down** no dejar meter baza a uno; **to — a plane down** controlar el aterrizaje de un avión desde tierra; **to — someone into something** persuadir a uno para que haga algo, convencer a uno de la conveniencia de hacer algo; **to — someone out of something** disuadir a uno de algo; **to — something over** hablar de algo, discutir algo; pasar revista a algo; **to — someone round** convencer a uno.
3 vi hablar (about, of de; to con, a); charlar; **now you're —ing!** ¡eso es más razonable!; **to keep someone —ing** entretener a uno en conversación; **to — through one's hat** decir tonterías; **— about fleas!** ¡y las pulgas!; ¡Dios mío, qué pulgas!; **what shall we — about?** ¿de qué vamos a hablar?; **it is much —ed about** se habla mucho de ello; **to get oneself —ed about in the papers** lograr que los periódicos hablen de uno; **he knows what he's —ing about** habla con conocimiento de causa; **he doesn't know what he's —ing about** no tiene la menor idea; **to — away** seguir hablando; seguir hablando más que siete; **to — back to someone** contestar con frescura a uno; **to — down to someone** darse aires de superioridad con uno; **—ing of bats, we . . . a**

propósito de los murciélagos, nosotros ...; to — to oneself hablar consigo mismo; see big.

4 vr: to — oneself hoarse enronquecer a fuerza de hablar; he —ed himself into it se autosugestionó, se convenció a sí mismo; he —ed himself out of the job hizo tan mala impresión hablando que no le dieron el puesto.

talkative ['tɔːkətiv] adj locuaz, hablador.

talkativeness ['tɔːkətivnis] n locuacidad f.

talked-of ['tɔːktɔv] adj: a much — event un suceso muy sonado.

talker ['tɔːkə*] n hablador m, ora f; to be a good — hablar bien; tener una conversación amena; he's just a — habla mucho pero no hace nada.

talkie ['tɔːki] n (Cine) película f sonora.

talking ['tɔːkiŋ] 1 adj parlante; film etc sonoro, hablado; bird parlero.

2 n conversación f; palabras fpl; "no —" "prohibido hablar"; no —, please, ¡silencio, por favor!; she does all the — ella es quien habla.

talking point ['tɔːkiŋpɔint] n tema m de conversación.

talking-to ['tɔːkiŋtuː] n: to give someone a — echar un rapapolvo a uno.

tall [tɔːl] adj alto; grande; story exagerado, increíble; that's pretty —! ¡eso no puede ser!; ¡es increíble! a building 30 metres — un edificio que tiene 30 metros de alto; how — you've got! ¡qué grande estás!; ¡cómo has crecido!; how — are you? ¿cuánto mides?; I'm 6 feet — mido 6 pies.

tallboy ['tɔːlbɔi] n cómoda f alta.

tallness ['tɔːlnis] n altura f; talla f.

tallow ['tæləu] n sebo m.

tallowy ['tæləui] adj seboso.

tally ['tæli] 1 n (stick) tarja f; (account) cuenta f; (fig) número m, total m; to keep a — of llevar la cuenta de.

2 vi concordar, corresponder, cuadrar (with con).

tally clerk ['tælikluːk] n medidor m.

tallyho ['tæli'hɔu] interj, n grito del cazador. (de zorras).

Talmud ['tælmud] n Talmud m.

Talmudic [tæl'mudik] adj talmúdico.

talon ['tælən] n garra f.

tamable ['teiməbl] adj domable, domesticable.

tamarind ['tæmərind] n tamarindo m.

tamarisk ['tæmərisk] n tamarisco m.

Tamberlane ['tæmbəlein] m Tamerlán.

tambour ['tæmbuə*] n (Archit, Mus etc) tambor m.

tambourine [ˌtæmbə'riːn] n pandereta f.

tame [teim] 1 adj (tamed) domesticado; (by nature) manso, dócil; (spiritless) insípido, soso; inocuo; (boring, flat) soso, aburrido; we have a — rabbit tenemos un conejo doméstico; the birds grow — los pájaros se acostumbran a la presencia de personas, los pájaros pierden su temor a las personas.

2 vt animal domar, domesticar; amansar; passion etc reprimir, contener.

tameness ['teimnis] n mansedumbre f; insipidez f, sosería f; falta f de temor.

tamer ['teimə*] n domador m, ora f.

taming ['teimiŋ] n domadura f; "The T— of the Shrew" "La fierecilla domada".

tam o' shanter [ˌtæmə'ʃæntə*] n boina f escocesa.

tamp [tæmp] vt (also to — down, to — in) apisonar, afirmar; (Min) atacar.

tamper ['tæmpə*] vi: to — with (mess up) estropear, descomponer; ajar; lock tratar de forzar; document falsificar; interpolar; witness sobornar; (meddle in) entrometerse en; my car had been —ed with alguien había tratado de forzar la puerta de mi coche; they are —ing with our plans están estropeando nuestros planes.

tampon ['tæmpən] n tapón m; (Med) tampón m.

tan [tæn] 1 n (sun) bronceado m, tostado m; (bark) casca f; (colour) color m café claro, color m canela; to acquire a —, to get a — broncearse.

2 adj color café claro, color canela, color marrón; shoes de color.

3 vt (of sun) broncear, tostar; leather curtir, adobar; to — someone, to — the hide off someone (fam) zurrar a uno.

4 vi broncearse, tostarse.

tandem ['tændəm] 1 n tándem m. 2 adj, adv en tándem.

tang [tæŋ] n (of knife) espiga f; (taste) sabor m, sabor m fuerte y picante; it has the — of the soil tiene fuerte sabor a tierra.

tangent ['tændʒənt] n tangente f; to fly off at a —, to go off at a — (fig) salirse por la tangente.

tangential [tæn'dʒenʃəl] adj tangencial.

tangerine [ˌtændʒə'riːn] n mandarina f.

tangibility [ˌtændʒi'biliti] n tangibilidad f.

tangible ['tændʒəbl] adj tangible; (fig) palpable, concreto, sensible.

tangibly ['tændʒəbli] adv de modo palpable, concretamente.

Tangier(s) [tæn'dʒiə(z)] Tánger.

tangle ['tæŋgl] 1 n nudo m; enredo m, maraña f; (of streets etc) laberinto m; (fig) enredo m, lío m; confusión f; to be in a — estar enmarañado, haberse formado un nudo; (fig) estar en confusión; I'm in a — with the accounts me he hecho un lío con las cuentas; to get into a — hacerse un nudo, anudarse; (fig) enredarse, enmarañarse; I got into a — with the police me hice un lío con la policía.

2 vt enredar, enmarañar (also to — up).

3 vi enredarse, enmarañarse (also to — up); to — with someone pelearse con uno, meterse con uno; habérselas con uno.

tango ['tæŋgəu] 1 n, pl tangos ['tæŋgəuz] tango m; 2 vi bailar el tango.

tank [tæŋk] 1 n tanque m, depósito m; (large, water) cisterna f, aljibe m; (Mil) tanque m, carro m (de combate).

2 vt: to get —ed up (sl) emborracharse (on beer bebiendo cerveza).

tankard ['tæŋkəd] n bock m, pichel m.

tank car ['tæŋkkuː*] n (Rail) vagón m cisterna.

tank engine ['tæŋk,endʒin] n (Rail) locomotora f ténder.

tanker ['tæŋkə*] n (Naut) petrolero m; (Aut) camión-tanque m.

tankful ['tæŋkful] n contenido m (or capacidad f) de un depósito (esp de gasolina); to get a — of petrol llenar el depósito de gasolina; a — is 25 litres la capacidad del depósito es de 25 litros.

tank wagon ['tæŋk,wægən] n (Rail) vagón m cisterna; (Aut) carro m cuba.

tanned [tænd] adj bronceado.

tanner[1] ['tænə*] n curtidor m.

tanner[2] ['tænə*] n (sl) seis peniques mpl, moneda f de seis peniques.

tannery ['tænəri] n curtiduría f.

tannic ['tænik] adj: — acid ácido m tánico.

tannin ['tænin] n tanino m.

tanning ['tæniŋ] n curtido m; (fam) zurra f (fam); to give someone a — (fam) zurrar a uno (fam).

tansy ['tænzi] n tanaceto m, atanasia f.

tantalize ['tæntəlaiz] vti atormentar (mostrando or prometiendo lo que no se puede conseguir), tentar (con cosas imposibles).

tantalizing ['tæntəlaiziŋ] adj atormentador, tentador; it is — to think that ... es tentador pensar que ...; with — slowness con desesperada lentitud; a most — offer una oferta de lo más tentador.

tantalizingly ['tæntəlaiziŋli] adv de modo atormentador, de modo tentador.

tantamount ['tæntəmaunt] adj: — to equivalente a; this is — to esto equivale a.

tantrum ['tæntrəm] n (fam) rabieta f.

Tanzania [ˌtænzə'niə] Tanzanía f.

tap[1] [tæp] 1 n (water—) grifo m; (gas—) llave f; (of barrel) espita f; (tool) macho m de terraja; (Elec) derivación f; beer on — cerveza f (sacada) de barril, cerveza f servida al grifo; to be on — (fig) estar a mano, estar disponible, estar listo.

2 vt barrel espitar; tree sangrar; (Med) hacer una puntura en; wire (Elec) hacer una derivación en, (Tel) intervenir, escuchar clandestinamente; resources explotar, utilizar.

tap[2] [tæp] 1 n palmadita f; golpecito m, golpe m ligero; (on typewriter etc) pulsación f; there was a — on the door llamaron suavemente a la puerta; I felt a — on my shoulder sentí que alguien me daba una palmadita en el hombro.

2 vt dar una palmadita a (or en); golpear suavemente, golpear ligeramente; typewriter etc pulsar; to — in a nail hacer que entre un clavo golpeándolo ligeramente; to — out a message enviar un mensaje en Morse; to — out one's pipe vaciar la pipa golpeándola ligeramente.

3 vi dar golpecitos; to — at a door llamar suavemente a una puerta; he —ped on the table several times dio varios golpecitos en la mesa.

tap-dance ['tæpdɑːns] 1 n zapateado m. 2 vi zapatear.

tap-dancer ['tæp,dɑːnsə*] n bailarín m de zapateado, bailarina f de zapateado.

tape [teip] 1 n (Sew etc) cinta f; (Sport) cinta f; (ceremonial) cinta f simbólica; (sticking —) cinta f adhesiva, (Med) esparadrapo m; (recording —) cinta f de grabación, cinta f magnetofónica; (— measure) cinta f métrica; red — (fig) (rules) reglas *fpl*; (*formalities*) formulismo *m*, formalidades *fpl* burocráticas; trámites *mpl*; papeleo *m*.

2 *vt* (*seal*) poner una cinta a, cerrar con una cinta; (*record*) grabar en cinta, registrar en un magnetofón; **I've got him —d** (*fam*) le tengo calado; **we've got it all —d** (*fam*) lo tenemos todo organizado, todo funciona perfectamente; **we have the game —d** (*fam*) hemos hecho nuestros preparativos para dominar el partido.

tape measure ['teip‚meʒə*] *n* cinta *f* métrica.

taper ['teipə*] **1** *n* bujía *f*, cerilla *f*; (*Eccl*) cirio *m*. 2 *vt* afilar, ahusar. 3 *vi* ahusarse, rematar en punta; **to — away, to — off** (*fig*) ir disminuyendo.

tape-record ['teipri‚kɔːd] *vt* grabar en cinta, registrar en un magnetofón.

tape recorder ['teipri‚kɔːdə*] *n* magnetofón *m*, magnetófono *m*.

tape recording ['teipri‚kɔːdiŋ] *n* grabación *f* en cinta.

tapered ['teipəd] *adj*, **tapering** ['teipəriŋ] *adj* ahusado, que termina en punta; (*Mech*) cónico; **finger** afilado.

tapestry ['tæpistri] *n* (*object*) tapiz *m*; (*art*) tapicería *f*.

tapeworm ['teipwəːm] *n* tenia *f*, solitaria *f*.

tapioca [‚tæpi'əukə] *n* tapioca *f*.

tapir ['teipə*] *n* tapir *m*.

tapper ['tæpə*] *n* (*Elec, Tel*) manipulador *m*.

tappet ['tæpit] *n* alzaválvulas *m*.

taproom ['tæprum] *n* bodegón *m*.

taproot ['tæpruːt] *n* raíz *f* central.

tapster ['tæpstə*] *n* mozo *m* de taberna.

tap water ['tæp‚wɔːtə*] *n* agua *f* corriente, agua *f* de grifo.

tar[1] [taː*] **1** *n* alquitrán *m*, brea *f*.
2 *vt* alquitranar, embrear; **to — and feather someone** embrear y emplumar a uno; **a newly —red road** una carretera recién alquitranada; **he's —red with the same brush** él es otro que tal, él es un ídem de lienzo.

tar[2] [taː*] *n* (*also* **Jack T—**) marinero *m*.

tarantella [‚tærən'telə] *n* tarantela *f*.

tarantula [tə'ræntjulə] *n* tarántula *f*.

tardily ['taːdili] *adv* tardíamente; lentamente.

tardiness ['taːdinis] *n* tardanza *f*; lentitud *f*.

tardy ['taːdi] *adj* (*late*) tardío; (*slow*) lento.

tare[1] [teə*] *n* (*Bot; also* **—s**) arveja *f*; (*Bib*) cizaña *f*.

tare[2] [teə*] *n* (*Comm*) tara *f*.

target ['taːgit] *n* (*Mil*) blanco *m*; (*fig*) blanco *m*, objetivo *m*; **the — vehicle** (*space research*) el vehículo blanco; **our — is £10** nuestro objetivo es reunir (*etc*) 10 libras, nos proponemos reunir (*etc*) 10 libras; **the —s for production in 1980** los objetivos previstos para la producción en 1980; **to be the — for criticism** ser el blanco de la crítica; **to be on —** (*rocket etc*) llevar la dirección que se había previsto, ir hacia el blanco.

target practice ['taːgit‚præktis] *n* tiro *m* al blanco.

tariff ['tærif] **1** *n* tarifa *f*, arancel *m*. 2 *attr* arancelario; **— reform** reforma *f* arancelaria.

tarmac ['taːmæk] *n* alquitranado *m*.

tarn [taːn] *n* lago *m* pequeño de montaña.

tarnish ['taːniʃ] **1** *vt* deslustrar, quitar el brillo a; (*fig*) deslustrar, empañar. 2 *vi* deslustrarse, perder su brillo, empañarse.

tarot ['tærəu] *n* *naipe de dibujos alegóricos*.

tarpaulin [taː'pɔːlin] *n* alquitranado *m*, encerado *m*.

tarpon ['taːpɒn] *n* tarpón *m*.

tarragon ['tærəgən] *n* (*Bot*) dragoncillo *m*, estragón *m*.

tarry ['taːri] *adj* alquitranado, embreado; cubierto (*or* manchado *etc*) de alquitrán; **to taste —** saber a alquitrán.

tarry ['tæri] *vi* (*lit*) (*stay*) quedarse; (*dally*) entretenerse, quedarse atrás; (*be late*) tardar (en venir).

tarsus ['taːsəs] *n*, *pl* **tarsi** ['taːsai] tarso *m*.

tart[1] [taːt] *adj* ácido, agrio; (*fig*) áspero.

tart[2] [taːt] *n* tarta *f*; pastelillo *m* de fruta, pastelillo *m* de mermelada; (*sl*) furcia *f* (*sl*), fulana *f* (*sl*).

tartan ['taːtən] *n* tartán *m*.

tartar ['taːtə*] *n* (*Chem*) tártaro *m*; sarro *m*.

tartar(e) ['taːtə*] *attr*: **— sauce** salsa *f* tártara; **— steak** biftec crudo, picado *y* condimentado con sal, pimiento, cebolla *etc*.

Tartar ['taːtə*] **1** *adj* tártaro. **2** *n* tártaro *m*, a *f*; (*fig*) arpía *f*, fiera *f*; **to catch a —** meterse con uno que resulta tener fuerzas superiores.

tartaric [taː'tærik] *adj*: **— acid** ácido *m* tártarico.

Tartary ['taːtəri] Tartaria *f*.

tartly ['taːtli] *adv* (*fig*) ásperamente.

tartness ['taːtnis] *n* acidez *f*, agrura *f*; (*fig*) aspereza *f*.

task [taːsk] *n* tarea *f*, labor *f*; empresa *f*, cometido *m*, deber *m*; **it's an uphill —** es una labor difícil; **to set someone the — of doing something** dar a uno el encargo de hacer algo; **to take someone to —** reprender a uno (*for something* algo), llamar a uno a capítulo.

task force ['taːskfɔːs] *n* (*Mil*) agrupación *f* de fuerzas (para una operación especial).

taskmaster ['taːsk‚maːstə*] *n* amo *m*; capataz *m*; **he's a hard —** es un amo severo.

Tasmania [tæz'meiniə] Tasmania *f*.

Tasmanian [tæz'meiniən] **1** *adj* tasmanio. **2** *n* tasmanio *m*, a *f*.

tassel ['tæsəl] *n* borla *f*.

taste [teist] **1** *n* (a) (*flavour*) sabor *m* (*of* a); dejo *m* (*of* de); **it has an odd —** tiene un sabor raro, sabe algo raro; **it has no —** no sabe a nada, es insípido.
(b) (*sample*) muestra *f*; (*sip*) sorbo *m*, trago *m*; **just a —, then** pues un sorbito nada más, pues sólo un poquitín; **add a — of salt** añadir una pizca de sal; **may I have a —?** ¿me permites probarlo?; **we got a — of what was to come** tuvimos una muestra de lo que había de venir después, se nos proporcionó un anticipo de lo que se estaba preparando; **we had a — of his bad temper** tuvimos una muestra de su mal humor.
(c) (*liking*) afición *f*, inclinación *f*, gusto *m*; **one's —s in music** las inclinaciones de uno en asuntos de música; **to acquire** (*or* **develop**) **a — for** tomar gusto a, cobrar afición a; **to have a — for** gustar de, ser aficionado a; **with sugar to —** con azúcar al gusto, con azúcar a discreción; **it is to my —** me gusta; **Wagner is not to my —** no me gusta Wagner; **—s differ, each to his own —** entre gustos no hay disputa.
(d) (*good — etc*) good **— buen gusto** *m*; **people of — gente** *f* de buen gusto; **they certainly have — es** cierto que tienen buen gusto; **to be in bad —, to be in poor —** ser de mal gusto.
2 *vt* (a) (*sample*) probar; probar un bocado de, tomarse un trago de; (*professionally*) catar; **just — this** prueba un poco de esto; **I haven't —ed salmon for years** hace años que no como salmón; **he hadn't —ed food for 3 days** desde hacía 3 días no comía.
(b) (*perceive flavour of*) percibir un sabor de; **I fancy I — garlic** creo notar un sabor a ajos; **I can't — anything when I have a cold** cuando estoy resfriado no noto sabor alguno.
(c) (*experience*) experimentar, conocer; **at last we —ed happiness** por fin conocimos la felicidad; **when he first —ed power** cuando conoció por primera vez las delicias del poder.
3 *vi*: **it doesn't — at all** no se nota sabor alguno; **it —s good** es muy sabroso, está sabrosísimo, está muy rico; **it —s all right to me** para mi gusto está bien; **to — of** saber a, tener sabor a; **it doesn't — of anything in particular** no sabe a nada en particular.

taste bud ['teistbʌd] *n* papila *f* del gusto.

tasteful ['teistful] *adj* elegante, de buen gusto.

tastefully ['teistfəli] *adv* elegantemente, con buen gusto; **a — furnished flat** un piso amueblado con buen gusto, un piso con muebles elegantes.

tastefulness ['teistfulnis] *n* elegancia *f*, buen gusto *m*.

tasteless ['teistlis] *adj* (*flat*) insípido, soso, insulso; (*in bad taste*) de mal gusto.

tastelessly ['teistlisli] *adv* insípidamente; con mal gusto.

tastelessness ['teistlisnis] *n* insipidez *f*; mal gusto *m*.

taster ['teistə*] *n* catador *m*.

tastily ['teistili] *adv* sabrosamente, apetitosamente.

tastiness ['teistinis] *n* sabor *m*, lo sabroso, lo apetitoso.

tasty ['teisti] *adj* sabroso, apetitoso.

tat [tæt] *vi* (*Sew*) hacer frivolité.

tata ['tæ'taː] *interj* (*fam*) adiós, adiosito (*fam*).

tattered ['tætəd] *adj* *person* andrajoso, harapiento; *dress, flag etc* en jirones.

tatters ['tætəz] *npl* andrajos *mpl*; jirones *mpl*; **a tramp in —** un vagabundo andrajoso; **his jacket hung in —** su chaqueta estaba hecha jirones.

tatting ['tætiŋ] *n* (*Sew*) trabajo *m* de frivolité.

tattle ['tætl] **1** *n* (*chat*) charla *f*; (*gossip*) chismes *mpl*, habladurías *fpl*. **2** *vi* (*chat*) charlar, parlotear; (*gossip*) chismear, contar chismes.

tattler ['tætlə*] *n* charlatán *m*, ana *f*; chismoso *m*, a *f*.

tattoo[1] [tə'tuː] *n* (*Mil*) retreta *f*; (*pageant*) gran espectáculo *m* militar, exhibición *f* del arte militar; **to beat a — with one's fingers** tamborilear con los dedos.

tattoo[2] [tə'tuː] **1** *n* tatuaje *m*. **2** *vt* tatuar.

tatty ['tæti] *adj (fam)* raído, desaseado; poco elegante; en mal estado.
taught [tɔːt] *pret and ptp of* **teach.**
taunt [tɔːnt] **1** *n* mofa *f*, pulla *f*, dicterio *m*; sarcasmo *m*, dicho *m* sarcástico.
　2 *vt* mofarse de; insultar, reprochar con insultos; **to — someone with something** reprochar algo a uno en tono de mofa, echar algo en cara a uno.
taunting ['tɔːntiŋ] *adj* insultante, mofador, burlón.
tauntingly ['tɔːntiŋli] *adv* burlonamente, en son de burla.
tauromachy ['tɔːrəmæki] *n* tauromaquia *f*.
taut [tɔːt] *adj* tieso, tenso, tirante; *(fig)* tirante.
tauten ['tɔːtn] **1** *vt* tesar, tensar. **2** *vi* tensarse, ponerse tieso.
tautness ['tɔːtnis] *n* tiesura *f*, tirantez *f*.
tautological [ˌtɔːtə'lɔdʒikəl] *adj* tautológico.
tautology [tɔː'tɔlədʒi] *n* tautología *f*.
tavern ['tævən] *n* taberna *f*.
tawdriness ['tɔːdrinis] *n* lo charro; lo cursi; lo indigno.
tawdry ['tɔːdri] *adj* charro; de oropel, de relumbrón, cursi; *motive etc* indigno, vergonzoso.
tawny ['tɔːni] *adj* leonado.
tax [tæks] **1** *n* **(a)** impuesto *m* (*on* sobre), contribución *f*; tributo *m*; derechos *mpl*; **betting —** impuesto *m* sobre apuestas; **capital gains —** impuesto *m* de plusvalía; **direct —** contribución *f* directa; **indirect —** contribución *f* indirecta; **petrol —** impuesto *m* sobre gasolina; **free of —** exento de contribuciones, no imponible; **to collect a —** recaudar contribuciones; **to levy a — on something** imponer contribución sobre algo.
　(b) *(fig)* carga *f* (*on* sobre), esfuerzo *m* (*on* para); **it is a — on his energies** exige un esfuerzo de él.
　2 *attr*: **— matters** asuntos *mpl* tributarios; **— system** sistema *m* tributario, tributación *f*; **— privileges** privilegios *mpl* tributarios; **— evasion** evasión *f* fiscal; **to declare something for — purposes** declarar algo al fisco.
　3 *vt* **(a)** *(Fin)* *person* imponer contribuciones a, *thing* imponer contribución sobre, gravar con un impuesto; **they are heavily —ed** pagan unas fuertes contribuciones; **the rich are being —ed out of existence** los ricos pagan tantas contribuciones que dejarán pronto de existir.
　(b) *(Law) costs* tasar.
　(c) *(fig)* cargar, abrumar (*with* de); *resources etc* exigir un esfuerzo excesivo a, someter a un esfuerzo excesivo; *patience* agotar; *tolerance* abusar de.
　(d) *(fig: accuse)* acusar (*with* de); interrogar (*with* acerca de); **to — someone with a fault** censurar una falta a uno.
taxable ['tæksəbl] *adj* imponible, sujeto a impuesto; **— income** renta *f* imponible.
taxation [tæk'seiʃən] **1** *n* impuestos *mpl*, contribuciones *fpl*; *(system)* sistema *m* tributario, tributación *f*; **direct —** contribuciones *fpl* directas; **indirect —** contribuciones *fpl* indirectas; **— is too heavy** las contribuciones son demasiado fuertes.
　2 *attr* tributario; **— system** sistema *m* tributario, tributación *f*.
tax-collecting ['tækskəˌlektiŋ] *n* recaudación *f* de contribuciones.
tax collector ['tækskəˌlektə*] *n* recaudador *m* de contribuciones.
tax-exempt ['tæksigˈzempt] *adj (US)* exento de contribuciones; exento de impuesto.
tax-free ['tæks'friː] **1** *adj* exento de contribuciones, no imponible. **2** *adv*: **to live —** vivir sin pagar contribuciones.
taxi ['tæksi] **1** *n* taxi *m*. **2** *vi (Aut)* ir en taxi; *(Aer)* carretear, rodar de suelo.
taxicab ['tæksikæb] *n* taxi *m*.
taxidermist ['tæksidəːmist] *n* taxidermista *mf*.
taxidermy ['tæksidəːmi] *n* taxidermia *f*.
taxi driver ['tæksiˌdraivə*] *n* taxista *mf*.
taxi man ['tæksimæn] *n*, *pl* **— men** [men] taxista *mf*.
taximeter ['tæksiˌmiːtə*] *n* taxímetro *m*, contador *m* de taxi.
taxi rank ['tæksiræŋk] *n*, **taxi stand** ['tæksistænd] *n* parada *f* de taxis.
taxonomist [tæk'sɔnəmist] *n* taxonomista *mf*.
taxonomy [tæk'sɔnəmi] *n* taxonomía *f*.
taxpayer ['tæksˌpeiə*] *n* contribuyente *mf*.
tax return ['tæksri'təːn] *n* declaración *f* de ingresos.
tea [tiː] *n* **(a)** *(drink)* té *m*; **not for all the — in China** por nada del mundo. **(b)** *(meal)* merienda *f*; **high —** merienda-cena *f*; **to have —** merendar.
tea bag ['tiːbæg] *n* sobre *m* de té.
tea break ['tiːbreik] *n* descanso *m* para el té.
tea caddy ['tiːˌkædi] *n* bote *m* para té.

teacake ['tiːkeik] *n* bollo *pequeño con trocitos de frutas que se toma tostado en la merienda.*
teach [tiːtʃ] *(irr: pret and ptp* **taught) 1** *vt* enseñar; **to — someone how to do something** enseñar a uno a hacer algo; **to — someone a language** enseñar una lengua a uno, instruir a uno en una lengua; **to — someone a lesson** *(fig)* hacer que uno vaya aprendiendo; **that will — him!** ¡así irá aprendiendo!; **he taught me a thing or two** él me enseñó cosas de gran utilidad; **I'll — you to leave the gas on!** ¡así aprenderás a no dejar encendido el gas!
　2 *vi* enseñar; ser profesor(a), dedicarse a la enseñanza.
teachability [ˌtiːtʃə'biliti] *n* capacidad *f* para aprender.
teachable ['tiːtʃəbl] *adj* educable.
teacher ['tiːtʃə*] *n (in general)* preceptor *m*, profesor *m*, ora *f*; *(grammar school)* profesor *m* (de instituto), profesora *f* (de instituto); *(in other school)* maestro *m*, a *f*; **our French —** nuestro profesor de francés.
teacher training ['tiːtʃə'treiniŋ] *n* formación *f* pedagógica.
tea chest ['tiːtʃest] *n* caja *f* para té.
teach-in ['tiːtʃin] *n* reunión *f* general en la que se escuchan conferencias y se organizan discusiones sobre un tema concreto.
teaching ['tiːtʃiŋ] **1** *n* *(act)* enseñanza *f*; *(belief)* enseñanza *f*, doctrina.
　2 *attr* docente; **— centre** centro *m* docente; **— hospital** hospital *m* utilizado para la enseñanza de la medicina; **— profession** magisterio *m*; **— staff** personal *m* docente, profesorado *m*.
teaching machine ['tiːtʃiŋməˌʃiːn] *n* autoprofesor *m*, profesor *m* robot.
teacloth ['tiːklɔθ] *n*, *pl* **—cloths** [klɔθs] paño *m* de cocina.
tea cosy ['tiːkəuzi] *n* cubretetera *f*, guardacalor *m* de la tetera.
teacup ['tiːkʌp] *n* taza *f* para té.
tea dance ['tiːdɑːns] *n* té *m* bailable, té-baile *m*.
tea garden ['tiːˌgɑːdn] *n* café *m* al aire libre; *(Agr)* plantación *f* de té.
teahouse ['tiːhaus] *n*, *pl* **—houses** [hauziz] salón *m* de té.
teak [tiːk] *n* teca *f*, madera *f* de teca.
teakettle ['tiːketl] *n (US)* tetera *f*.
teal [tiːl] *n* cerceta *f*.
tea leaf ['tiːliːf] *n*, *pl* **— leaves** [liːvz] hoja *f* de té.
team [tiːm] **1** *n* *(of persons)* equipo *m*, grupo *m*; *(Sport)* equipo *m*; *(of horses)* tiro *m*; *(of oxen)* yunta *f*; **away —** equipo *m* de fuera; **home —** equipo *m* de casa; **our research —** nuestro equipo de investigadores.
　2 *attr*: **— tournament** torneo *m* por equipos.
　3 *vt*: **a film which —s A with Z** una película que asocia A con Z, una película que ofrece juntamente A y Z.
　4 *vi*: **to — up** asociarse, formar un equipo (*with* con).
team mate ['tiːmmeit] *n* compañero *m* de equipo.
team spirit ['tiːm'spirit] *n* compañerismo *m*, espíritu *m* de equipo.
teamster ['tiːmstə*] *n (US)* camionero *m*, camionista *m*.
teamwork ['tiːmwəːk] *n* labor *f* de equipo, trabajo *m* en equipo; cooperación *f*, colaboración *f*.
tea party ['tiːˌpɑːti] *n* tertulia *f* donde se toma el té.
teapot ['tiːpɔt] *n* tetera *f*.
tear [tɛə*] **1** *n* rasgón *m*, desgarrón *m*; **it has a — in it** está roto.
　2 *(irr: pret* **tore**, *ptp* **torn)** *vt* **(a)** *(rip)* rasgar, desgarrar; *flesh* lacerar, romper; *(to pieces)* romper, despedazar, hacer pedazos; **to — a hole in a cloth** rasgar un paño; **to — one's hair** arrancarse los pelos, mesarse los pelos; **to — a muscle** desgarrarse un músculo.
　(b) *(snatch)* arrancar; **to — something from someone** arrancar algo a uno, quitar algo a uno violentamente.
　(c) **the country was torn by civil war** el país fue desgarrado por una guerra civil; **she was torn by conflicting emotions** estaba atormentada por dos emociones opuestas, le desgarraban dos emociones opuestas; **I am very much torn** sigo sin saber a qué carta quedarme.
　(d) **to — away** arrancar, quitar violentamente; **the wind tore the flag away** el viento arrancó la bandera; **we tore him away from the party** le sacamos del guateque; **to — down** *flag, hangings etc* quitar (arrancando), arrancar (de las paredes *etc*); *building* derribar, echar abajo; **to — off** arrancar; **to — open** abrir apresuradamente, abrir violenta-

mente; **to — out** arrancar; **to — up** *paper etc* romper; (*by roots*) desarraigar (violentamente), arrancar.

3 *vi* (**a**) rasgarse, romperse; **it —s easily** se rasga fácilmente.

(**b**) **to — at the earth with one's hands** tratar frenéticamente de remover la tierra con las manos; **she tore at my eyes** trató de arrancarme los ojos; **he tore at the paper wrapping** luchó violentamente por quitar la envoltura.

(**c**) **to — along** correr precipitadamente, precipitarse; ir a máxima velocidad; **to — along the street** correr a todo correr por la calle; **to — away** marcharse apresuradamente; **to — into a room** entrar precipitadamente en un cuarto; **to — off** irse apresuradamente; **to — past** pasar como un rayo; **he tore up in a car** llegó a toda prisa en un automóvil.

4 *vr*: **to — oneself away** irse de mala gana; **I could not — myself away** fui incapaz de moverme de allí, me fue imposible partir; **if you can — yourself away from that book** si puedes dejar ese libro de las manos un momento.

tear [tiə*] *n* lágrima *f*; **to be in —s** estar llorando; **to burst into —s, to dissolve** (*or* melt) **into —s** deshacerse en lágrimas; **to shed bitter —s** llorar amargamente; **to wipe away one's —s** secarse las lágrimas.

teardrop ['tiədrɔp] *n* lágrima *f*.

tearful ['tiəful] *adj* lloroso, llorón; lacrimoso; **to say in a — voice** decir llorando.

tearfully ['tiəfəli] *adv*: **to say —** decir lloroso, decir llorando.

teargas ['tiəgæs] *n* gas *m* lacrimógeno; **— bomb** bomba *f* lacrimógena.

tearing ['tɛəriŋ] *adj* (**a**) **with a — noise** con un ruido de tela que se rasga. (**b**) **at a — speed** a una velocidad vertiginosa, a una velocidad frenética.

tear-jerker ['tiə,dʒə:kə*] *n* (*song*) canción *f* lacrimógena; (*play*) obra *f* lacrimógena, comedia *f* muy sentimental; **a real —** una cosa realmente lacrimógena.

tear-jerking ['tiə,dʒə:kiŋ] *adj* lagrimógeno, muy sentimental.

tear-off ['tɛərɔf] *adj*: **— calendar** calendario *m* de taco.

tearoom ['tiːrum] *n* salón *m* de té.

tear-stained ['tiəsteind] *adj* manchado de lágrimas.

tease [tiːz] **1** *n* (**a**) (*person*) embromador *m*, ora *f*, guasón *m*, ona *f*; **he's a dreadful —** es terriblemente guasón, le gusta atormentar a las personas.

(**b**) **to do something for a —** hacer algo para divertirse.

2 *vt* (**a**) (*annoy*) jorobar, fastidiar, molestar; (*banter*) embromar, tomar el pelo a, guasearse con, (*cruelly*) atormentar; **they tease her about her hair** la molestan con chistes acerca de su pelo, la atormentan por lo de su pelo; **I don't like being —d** no me gusta que se me tome el pelo.

(**b**) (*Tech*) cardar.

teasel ['tiːzl] *n* (*Bot*) cardencha *f*; (*Tech*) carda *f*.

teaser ['tiːzə*] *n* rompecabezas *m*.

tea service ['tiː,sə:vis] *n*, **tea set** ['tiːset] *n* servicio *m* de té.

teashop ['tiːʃɔp] *n* café *m*, cafetería *f*, (*strictly*) salón *m* de té.

teasing ['tiːziŋ] **1** *adj* guasón, burlón. **2** *n* guasa *f*, burlas *fpl*.

teaspoon ['tiːspuːn] *n* cucharilla *f*, cucharita *f*.

teaspoonful ['tiːspunful] *n* cucharadita *f*.

tea strainer ['tiː,streinə*] *n* colador *m* de té.

teat [tiːt] *n* (*of human*) pezón *m*; (*of animal*) teta *f*; (*of bottle*) chupador *m*, tetilla *f*, pezón *m* de goma.

tea table ['tiː,teibl] *n* mesita *f* de té.

teatime ['tiːtaim] *n* hora *f* del té, hora *f* de la merienda.

tea towel ['tiː,tauəl] *n* paño *m* de cocina.

tea tray ['tiːtrei] *n* bandeja *f* en que se sirve el té.

tea trolley ['tiː,trɔli] *n* carrito *m* para servir el té.

tea urn ['tiːə:n] *n* tetera *f* grande.

tea waggon ['tiː'wægən] *n* carrito *m* para servir el té (*en fábricas, oficinas etc*).

technical ['teknikəl] *adj* técnico; *college, school* de artes y oficios; *laboral*; **— offence** (*Law*) cuasidelito *m*.

technicality [,tekni'kæliti] *n* tecnicidad *f*, carácter *m* técnico; cosa *f* técnica; (*word*) tecnicismo *m*; **I don't understand all the technicalities** no entiendo todos los detalles técnicos; **it failed because of a —** fracasó debido a una dificultad técnica.

technically ['teknikəli] *adv* técnicamente.

technician [tek'niʃən] *n* técnico *m*; (*Univ etc*) ayudante *m* de laboratorio.

Technicolor ['tekni,kʌlə*] (*Protected Trade Name*) **1** *n* tecnicolor *m*; **in —** en tecnicolor. **2** *adj* en tecnicolor; de tecnicolor.

technique [tek'niːk] *n* técnica *f*.

technological [,teknə'lɔdʒikəl] *adj* tecnológico.

technologist [tek'nɔlədʒist] *n* tecnólogo *m*.

technology [tek'nɔlədʒi] *n* tecnología *f*.

techy ['tetʃi] *adj* enojadizo, malhumorado.

Ted [ted] *nombre cariñoso de* **Edward**.

tedder ['tedə*] *n* heneador *m*.

Teddy ['tedi] *nombre cariñoso de* **Edward**.

teddy (bear) ['tedi(bɛə*)] *n* osito *m* de felpa.

teddy-boy ['tedibɔi] *n* joven *m* de atuendo ultramoderno; (*pej*) gamberro *m*.

tedious ['tiːdiəs] *adj* aburrido, pesado.

tediously ['tiːdiəsli] *n* aburridamente, de modo pesado.

tediousness ['tiːdiəsnis] *n*, **tedium** ['tiːdiəm] *n* tedio *m*, aburrimiento *m*, pesadez *f*.

tee [tiː] **1** *n* tee *m*. **2** *vti* golpear desde el tee.

tee-hee ['tiː'hiː] **1** *n* risita *f* (tonta); **—!** ¡ja, ja! **2** *vi* reírse con una risita tonta, reírse un poquito.

teem [tiːm] *vi* abundar, pulular; **to — with** abundar en, hervir de; estar lleno de; **the book —s with errors** el libro está plagado de errores; **to — with rain** diluviar.

teeming ['tiːmiŋ] *adj* numerosísimo; **the — millions** los muchos millones; **a lake — with fish** un lago donde abundan los peces; **through streets — with people** por calles llenas de gente.

teenage ['tiːneidʒ] *adj, attr fashion etc* de los jóvenes (de 13 a 19 años); **he has — daughters already** tiene hijas ya de más de 13 años.

teenager ['tiːn,eidʒə*] *n* joven *mf* de 13 a 19 años; **a club for —s** un club para jóvenes (de 13 a 19 años).

teens [tiːnz] *npl* edad *f* de 13 a 19 años; **to be in one's —** tener de 13 a 19 años; **to be still in one's —** no haber cumplido aún los 20.

teeny(weeny) ['tiːni'wiːni] *adj* (*fam*) chiquito, chiquitín.

teeter ['tiːtə*] *vi* balancearse, oscilar; **to — on the edge of something** balancearse en el borde de algo, (*fig*) estar sin resolverse sobre algo.

teeth [tiːθ] *npl of* **tooth**.

teethe [tiːð] *vi* endentecer, echar los dientes.

teething ['tiːðiŋ] *n* dentición *f*.

teething ring ['tiːðiŋriŋ] *n* chupador *m*.

teetotal ['tiː'təutl] *adj* abstemio; *propaganda etc* antialcohólico.

teetotalism ['tiː'təutəlizəm] *n* abstinencia *f* (de bebidas alcohólicas).

teetotaller, (US) **teetotaler** ['tiː'təutlə*] *n* abstemio *m*, a *f*, persona *f* que no bebe alcohol.

tegument ['tegjumənt] *n* tegumento *m*.

telecast ['telikaːst] *n* teledifusión *f*.

telecommunication ['telikə,mjuːni'keiʃən] *n* telecomunicación *f*.

telefilm ['telifilm] *n* telefilm *m*, telefilme *n* (*Acad*).

telegram ['teligræm] *n* telegrama *m*; **to send someone a —** poner un telegrama a uno.

telegraph ['teligraːf] **1** *n* telégrafo *m*. **2** *attr* telegráfico. **3** *vti* telegrafiar.

telegraphic [,teli'græfik] *adj* telegráfico.

telegraphese ['teligraːfiːz] *n* estilo *m* telegráfico.

telegraphist [ti'legrəfist] *n* telegrafista *mf*.

telegraph pole ['teligraːfpəul] *n* poste *m* telegráfico.

telegraph wire ['teligraːfwaiə*] *n* hilo *m* telegráfico.

telegraphy [ti'legrəfi] *n* telegrafía *f*.

teleology [,teli'ɔlədʒi] *n* teleología *f*.

telepathic [,teli'pæθik] *adj* telepático.

telepathist [ti'lepəθist] *n* telépata *mf*.

telepathy [ti'lepəθi] *n* telepatía *f*.

telephone ['telifəun] **1** *n* teléfono *m*; **to be on the —** (*subscriber*) tener teléfono, (*be speaking*) estar hablando por teléfono; **you're wanted on the —** quieren hablar con Vd por teléfono, le llaman al teléfono.

2 *attr* telefónico.

3 *vti* llamar por teléfono, llamar al teléfono, telefonear.

telephone booth ['telifəunbuːð] *n*, **telephone box** ['telifəunbɔks] *n* locutorio *m*, cabina *f* de teléfono.

telephone call ['telifəunkɔːl] *n* llamada *f* (telefónica).

telephone directory ['telifəundi,rektəri] *n* guía *f* telefónica.

telephone exchange ['telifəuniks,tʃeindʒ] *n* central *f* telefónica.

telephone kiosk ['telifəun,kiɔsk] *n* locutorio *m*, cabina *f* de teléfono.

telephone number ['telifəun,nʌmbə*] n número m de teléfono.

telephone operator ['telifəun,ɔpəreitə*] n telefonista mf.

telephonic [,teli'fɔnik] adj telefónico.

telephonist [ti'lefənist] n telefonista mf.

telephony [ti'lefəni] n telefonía f.

telephoto ['teli'fəutəu] adj telefotográfico; **— lens** objetivo m telefotográfico, teleobjetivo m.

teleprinter ['teli,printə*] n teletipo m.

telescope ['teliskəup] 1 n telescopio m. 2 vt telescopar; enchufar; **to — something into something else** meter algo dentro de otra cosa. 3 vi telescoparse; enchufarse; **A —s into B** A se mete dentro de B.

telescopic [,telis'kɔpik] adj telescópico; enchufable, de enchufe.

teletype ['telitaip] n teletipo m.

teletypist ['teli,taipist] n teletipista mf.

televiewer ['teli,vjuːə*] n televidente mf, telespectador m, ora f.

televise ['telivaiz] vt televisar.

television ['teli,viʒən] 1 n televisión f; **colour —** televisión f en colores; **to be on —** estar en la televisión; **to watch —** mirar la televisión. 2 attr de televisión.

television screen ['teli,viʒənskriːn] n pantalla f de televisión.

television set ['teli,viʒən'set] n televisor m, aparato m de televisión.

tell [tel] (irr: pret and ptp **told**) 1 vt (a) (general sense) decir; adventure, story etc contar; (formally) comunicar, informar; **to — a lie** mentir; **to — someone the news** comunicar las noticias a uno, contar novedades a uno; **to — the truth** decir la verdad (see also truth); **to — someone something** decir algo a uno; **I have been told that...** me han dicho que..., se me ha dicho que...; **I hear — that...** dicen que...; **I am glad to — you that...** (formal letter) me es grato comunicarle que...; **— me all about it** cuéntame todo; **I'll — you all about it** te diré todo; **I told him about the missing money** le informé acerca del dinero perdido, le dije lo del dinero desaparecido; **I cannot — you how pleased I am** no encuentro palabras para expresar mi contento; **so much happened that I can't begin to — you** pasaron tantas cosas que no sé cómo empezar a contarlas; **I — you no!**, **I — you it isn't!** ¡te digo que no!; **I told you so!**, didn't **I — you so?** ¿no te lo dije ya?

(b) (general sense: idiomatic uses) **— me another!** ¡vaya!; **— that to the marines!** ¡a otro perro con ese hueso!; **you're —ing me!** ¡a quién se lo cuentas!; **he's no saint, let me — you!** ¡no es ningún santo, se lo aseguro!; **he won't like it, I can — you** esto seguramente no le va a caer en gracia; **I could — you a thing or two about him** hay cosas de él que yo me sé; **I — you what!** ¡se me ocurre una idea!; **it hurt more than words can —** dolió una barbaridad, dolió lo indecible.

(c) (announce) decir, anunciar; (of clock, dial etc) indicar, marcar; **the sign —s us which way to go** la señal nos dice qué ruta conviene seguir; **the clock —s the quarter hours** el reloj da los cuartos de hora; **to — somebody's fortune** decir a uno la buenaventura.

(d) (order) **to — someone to do something** decir a uno que haga algo, mandar a uno hacer algo; **I told you not to** te dije que no lo hicieras; **do as you are told!** ¡haz lo que te digo!; **he won't be told** no acepta las órdenes de nadie; no quiere hacer caso de ningún consejo; **to — someone off to do something** mandar a uno hacer algo.

(e) (distinguish) distinguir; (recognize) conocer, reconocer; **to — A from B** distinguir A de B; **to — right from wrong** (saber) distinguir el bien del mal; **one can — he's a German** se conoce que es alemán; **you can — him in any disguise** se conoce bajo cualquier disfraz; **can you — the time?** ¿sabes decir la hora?; see **apart**.

(f) (know) saber; decidir, determinar; **how can I —?** ¿yo qué sé?; **who can —?** ¿quién sabe?; **we cannot —** nos es imposible saberlo; **it's impossible for anyone to —** es imposible que nadie lo sepa; **you can't — much from this** de esto no es posible deducir gran cosa; **you never can —** no se puede saber con certeza; podría pasar cualquier cosa; podría ser tanto lo uno como lo otro.

(g) (count) contar; **to — one's beads** rezar el rosario; **30 pigs all told** en total 30 cerdos.

(h) (reprimand) **to — someone off** reñir a uno, echar un rapapolvo a uno.

2 vi (a) **to — of** hablar de; **I hear — of a disaster** oigo hablar de una catástrofe, tengo noticias de una catástrofe; **I have never heard —** of it no he oído nunca hablar de eso; **the ruins told of a sad history** las ruinas hablaban de una triste historia.

(b) **to — on someone** (fam) soplarse de uno, chivatear contra uno; **don't — on us** de esto no digas ni pío.

(c) (have an effect) tener efecto, hacer mella; **blood will —** los lazos de parentesco resultan ser bastante fuertes; **words that — que impresionan**; **every blow told** cada golpe tuvo su efecto; **it told on his health** afectó su salud, se dejó ver en su salud; **the effort was beginning to — (on him)** el esfuerzo empezaba a afectarle de mala manera; **everything —s against him** todo obra en contra de él; **stamina —s in the long run** a la larga importa más la resistencia, a la larga vale más la resistencia.

teller ['telə*] n (of story) narrador m, ora f; (Parl) escrutador m; (in bank) cajero m.

telling ['teliŋ] 1 adj eficaz; fuerte, enérgico; **a — argument** un argumento eficaz.
2 n narración f; **there is no —** no se sabe, es imposible saberlo; **there is no — what he will do** es imposible saber qué va a hacer; **the story did not lose in the —** el cuento no perdió en la narración.

telltale ['telteil] 1 adj revelador; indicador. 2 n (person) soplón m, ona f; (Naut) aciómetro m.

telly ['teli] n (fam) tele f.

temblor ['temblə*] n (US) temblor m de tierra.

temerity [ti'meriti] n temeridad f; **to have the — to + infin** ser bastante atrevido como para + infin; **and you have the — to say...!** ¡y Vd se atreve a decir que...!, ¡y Vd me dice tan fresco que...!

temper ['tempə*] 1 n (a) (disposition f, natural m; humor m, genio m; (bad) genio m, mal genio m; **—!** ¡qué mal genio!; **bad —, hot —, quick —** genio m, mal genio m, genio m vivo; **good —** buen humor m; **to be in a good —** estar de buen humor; **he has a —** tiene genio; **he has a foul** (or vile etc) **—** es un hombre de malas pulgas; **to have a quick —** tener genio, tener prontos de enojo; **to keep one's —** contenerse, no alterarse; **to lose one's —** perder la paciencia, enojarse (with con); **to try someone's —** provocar a uno.

(b) (of metal) temple m.
2 vt metal templar; (fig) templar, moderar, mitigar; **to — justice with mercy** templar la justicia con la compasión.

tempera ['tempərə] n (Art) pintura f al temple.

temperament ['tempərəmənt] n temperamento m, disposición f; (moodiness, difficult —) excitabilidad f, tendencia f a cambiar repentinamente de humor; genio m; **he has a —** tiene genio, tiene sus caprichos.

temperamental [,tempərə'mentl] adj (relating to temperament) complexional, relativo al temperamento; (moody, difficult) excitable, caprichoso, sujeto a impulsos repentinos, con tendencia a cambiar repentinamente de humor.

temperance ['tempərəns] 1 n templanza f; moderación f; abstinencia f (del alcohol).
2 attr: **— movement** campaña f antialcohólica; **— hotel** hotel m donde no se sirven bebidas alcohólicas.

temperate ['tempərit] adj templado; moderado; (in drinking) abstemio; climate, zone templado; **to be — in one's demands** ser moderado en sus exigencias.

temperature ['tempritʃə*] n temperatura f; (Med) **high —)** calentura f, fiebre f; **to have a —, to run a —** tener calentura.

temperature chart ['tempritʃətʃaːt] n gráfica f de temperaturas.

tempered ['tempəd] adj templado.

tempest ['tempist] n tempestad f; **"The T—"** (Shakespeare) "La Tempestad".

tempestuous [tem'pestjuəs] adj tempestuoso; (fig) tempestuoso, borrascoso.

Templar ['templə*] n templario m.

template, (US) **templet** ['templit] n plantilla f.

temple¹ ['templ] n templo m; **the T— (London)** Colegio m de Abogados.

temple² ['templ] n (Anat) sien f.

tempo ['tempəu] n, pl **tempi** ['tempiː] (Mus) tempo m, tiempo m; (fig) ritmo m.

temporal ['tempərəl] adj temporal.

temporarily ['tempərərili] adv temporalmente.

temporary ['tempərəri] adj temporáneo, provisional; transitorio, poco duradero, de poca duración; official interino; worker temporero; **these arrangements are purely —** este arreglo es provisional nada más; **there was a — improvement** durante cierto tiempo las cosas mejoraron.

temporize ['tempəraiz] *vi* contemporizar.

tempt [tempt] *vt* **(a)** tentar; atraer; seducir; **to — someone to do something** tentar a uno a hacer algo, inducir a uno a hacer algo; **to be —ed to do something** (*fig*) estar tentado de hacer algo; **there was a time when he was —ed to resign** hubo un momento en que estuvo tentado de dimitir; **to allow oneself to be —ed** ceder a la tentación; **I am greatly —ed** es una oferta atractiva, es una perspectiva agradable; **doesn't the idea — you at all?** ¿la idea no te interesa siquiera un poquitín?; **can I — you to another cup?** ¿quieres otra taza?

(b) (*Bib etc*) poner a prueba; tentar; **one must not — fate** no hay que tentar a la suerte.

temptation [temp'teiʃən] *n* tentación *f*; atractivo *m*, aliciente *m*; **there is a — to + infin** es tentador + *infin*; hay tendencia a + *infin*; **to give way** (*or* **yield**) **to —** ceder a la tentación; **to lead someone into —** hacer que uno caiga en el pecado; **lead us not into —** guárdanos del pecado; **to resist —** resistir **(a)** la tentación (*of + ger de + infin*); **to put — in someone's way** exponer a uno a la tentación.

tempter ['temptə*] *n* tentador *m*.

tempting ['temptiŋ] *adj* tentador; atractivo; *meal* apetitoso, rico; *theory etc* seductor; **a — offer** una oferta tentadora; **it is — to think so** estamos tentados de considerarlo así; es fácil asentir a ello.

temptingly ['temptiŋli] *adv* de modo tentador; de modo seductor; apetitosamente.

temptress ['temptris] *n* tentadora *f*.

ten [ten] **1** *adj* diez. **2** *n* diez *m*; (*as round number*) decena *f*; **some — people** una decena de personas; **—s of thousands of Spaniards** decenas de miles de españoles.

tenable ['tenəbl] *adj* defendible, sostenible.

tenacious [ti'neiʃəs] *adj* tenaz; porfiado; **to be — of life** estar muy apegado a la vida.

tenaciously [ti'neiʃəsli] *adv* tenazmente; porfiadamente.

tenacity [ti'næsiti] *n* tenacidad *f*; porfía *f*.

tenancy ['tenənsi] *n* tenencia *f*; (*of house*) inquilinato *m*, ocupación *f*; (*lease*) arriendo *m*.

tenant ['tenənt] **1** *adj*: **— farmer** agricultor *m* que tiene sus tierras en arriendo.

2 *n* (*inhabitant*) habitante *mf*, morador *m*, ora *f*; (*paying rent*) inquilino *m*, a *f*, arrendatario *m*, a *f*.

tenantry ['tenəntri] *n* inquilinos *mpl*; (*Agr*) agricultores *mpl* que tienen sus tierras en arriendo.

tench [tentʃ] *n* tenca *f*.

tend[1] [tend] *vi* tender; **to — to, to — towards** tender a, inclinarse a, tener tendencia a; **we — to think that...** nos inclinamos a pensar que...; **I rather — to agree with you** casi estoy por compartir ese criterio; **anything that —s to help solve the problem** cualquier cosa que contribuya a resolver el problema, todo lo que conduzca a resolver el problema; **it is a blue —ing to green** es un azul que tira a verde; **these clothes — to shrink** estas prendas tienen tendencia a encogerse; **which way is it —ing?** ¿hacia qué lado se inclina?

tend[2] [tend] *vt* *sick etc* cuidar, atender; *cattle* guardar; *machine* manejar, operar, servir; mantener.

tendency ['tendənsi] *n* tendencia *f*, inclinación *f*, propensión *f*; proclividad *f*; **he has a — to say too much** tiene tendencia a decir demasiado; **there is a — for the ponds to dry up** los estanques tienen tendencia a secarse; **the present — to the left** la actual tendencia hacia la izquierda.

tendentious [ten'denʃəs] *adj* tendencioso.

tendentiously [ten'denʃəsli] *adv* de modo tendencioso.

tendentiousness [ten'denʃəsnis] *n* tendenciosidad *f*.

tender[1] ['tendə*] *n* (*Rail*) ténder *m*; (*Naut*) gabarra *f*, embarcación *f* auxiliar.

tender[2] ['tendə*] **1** *n* **(a)** (*Comm*) oferta *f*, proposición *f*; **to make a —, to put in a —** hacer una oferta (*for* para la construcción (*etc*) de), ofertar; **to put something out to —** solicitar ofertas para hacer algo.

(b) legal — moneda *f* corriente, moneda *f* de curso legal.

2 *vt* ofrecer; *resignation etc* presentar; *thanks* dar. **3** *vi* (*Comm*) ofertar, hacer una oferta (*for* para).

tender[3] ['tendə*] *adj* (*soft*) tierno, blando; *spot* delicado, sensible; (*painful*) dolorido; *age etc* tierno; *conscience* escrupuloso; *problem*, *subject* espinoso, delicado, difícil; (*affectionate*) tierno, afectuoso; compasivo; **I still feel — there** ese sitio me duele todavía; **it is — to the touch** es sensible al tacto; **I have — memories of her** la recuerdo con mucha ternura; **those of — years** los de tierna edad.

tenderfoot ['tendəfut] *n* (*esp US*) recién llegado *m*; principiante *m*, novato *m*.

tender-hearted ['tendə'hɑːtid] *adj* compasivo, tierno de corazón.

tender-heartedness ['tendə'hɑːtidnis] *n* compasión *f*, ternura *f*.

tenderize ['tendəraiz] *vt* ablandar.

tenderloin ['tendələin] *n* (*meat*) filete *m*.

tenderly ['tendəli] *adj* tiernamente, con ternura.

tenderness ['tendənis] *n* ternura *f*; delicadez *f*, sensibilidad *f*.

tendon ['tendən] *n* tendón *m*.

tendril ['tendril] *n* zarcillo *m*.

tenement ['tenimənt] *n* vivienda *f*; habitación *f*; **— house, —s** casa *f* de pisos, casa *f* de vecindad.

tenet ['tenət] *n* principio *m*, dogma *m*.

tenfold ['tenfəuld] **1** *adj* décuplo, diez veces mayor. **2** *adv* diez veces.

tenner ['tenə*] *n* (*fam*) billete *m* de diez libras.

tennis ['tenis] *n* tenis *m*.

tennis ball ['tenisbɔːl] *n* pelota *f* de tenis.

tennis court ['teniskɔːt] *n* pista *f* de tenis, cancha *f* de tenis (*SAm*).

tennis elbow ['tenis'elbəu] *n* sinovitis *f* del codo.

tennis player ['tenis,pleiə*] *n* tenista *mf*.

tennis racquet ['tenis,rækit] *n* raqueta *f* de tenis.

tennis shoe ['tenisʃuː] *n* zapatilla *f* de tenis.

tenon ['tenən] *n* espiga *f*, almilla *f*.

tenon saw ['tenənsɔː] *n* serrucho *m*, sierra *f* de espigas.

tenor ['tenə*] **1** *adj* *instrument*, *part*, *voice* de tenor; *aria* para tenor. **2** *n* (*Mus*) tenor *m*; (*purport*) tenor *m*, tendencia *f*; curso *m*.

tenpin bowling ['tenpin'bəuliŋ] *n* juego *m* de los bolos.

tense[1] [tens] *n* (*Gram*) tiempo *m*; **present —** tiempo *m* presente; **in the perfect —** en tiempo perfecto.

tense[2] [tens] **1** *adj* (*stretched*) tirante, estirado, tieso; (*stiff*) rígido, tieso; *moment*, *nerves*, *situation etc* tenso; **it has been a — day** la jornada ha sido muy tensa; **we waited with — expectancy** aguardamos con tensa expectación; **he looked rather —** parecía estar algo tenso; **in a — voice** en tono entrecortado.

2 *vt* tensar, tesar; estirar.

tensely ['tensli] *adv* tensamente, con tensión.

tenseness ['tensnis] *n* tirantez *f*; tensión *f*.

tensile ['tensail] *adj* tensor; extensible; de tensión, relativo a la tensión.

tension ['tenʃən] *n* tirantez *f*; tensión *f*; **there is a great racial —** existe gran tensión racial; **— is being relaxed** la tensión está disminuyendo.

tent [tent] *n* tienda *f* (de campaña).

tentacle ['tentəkl] *n* tentáculo *m*.

tentative ['tentətiv] *adj* provisional; experimental; de prueba, de ensayo; **these are — conclusions** son conclusiones provisionales; **everything is very — at the moment** por el momento todo está en vía de prueba; **she's a rather — person** es una persona que no tiene confianza en sí misma.

tentatively ['tentətivli] *adv* provisionalmente; en vía de prueba, con tanteo; **"yes", he said — "sí"**, dijo sin gran confianza.

tenterhooks ['tentəhuks] *npl*: **to be on —** estar sobre ascuas; **to keep someone on —** tener a uno sobre ascuas.

tenth [tenθ] **1** *adj* décimo. **2** *n* décimo *m*; (*part*) décima parte *f*, décima *f*.

tent peg ['tent,peg] *n* estaquilla *f* (de tienda).

tent pole ['tentpəul] *n* mástil *m* de tienda, poste *m* de tienda.

tenuity [te'njuiti] *n* tenuidad *f*; raridad *f*.

tenuous ['tenjuəs] *adj* tenue; sutil; *connection* poco fuerte; *argument* poco sólido; *air* raro.

tenure ['tenjuə*] *n* posesión *f*, tenencia *f*, ocupación *f*.

tepee ['tiːpiː] *n* (*US*) tipi *m*.

tepid ['tepid] *adj* tibio.

tepidity [te'piditi] *n*, **tepidness** ['tepidnis] *n* tibieza *f*.

tercentenary [,təːsen'tiːnəri] *n* tricentenario *m*.

tercet ['təːsit] *n* terceto *m*.

Terence ['terəns] *m* Terencio.

term [təːm] **1** *n* **(a)** (*limit*) término *m*, límite *m*, fin *m*; (*Comm*) plazo *m*; **to put** (*or* **set**) **a — to** señalar un límite a; fijar un plazo para.

(b) (*period*) período *m*; duración *f*; plazo *m*; (*of president etc*) mandato *m*; **during his — of office** durante su posesión del puesto, durante su mandato; **for a — of 6 years** durante un período de 6 años; **in the long —** a la larga; **in the short —** en el futuro próximo.

(c) (*School, Univ*) trimestre *m*; **during —, in —** durante el curso; **out of —** fuera del curso; **to keep —s** residir, estar de interno, cumplir su período de residencia.

(d) (*Math, Logic*) término *m*; **A expressed in —s of B** A expresado en términos de B; **in —s of production we are doing well** por lo que se refiere a la producción vamos bien; **he sees novels in —s of sociology** considera la novela en su función sociológica, se explica la novela desde el punto de vista sociológico.

(e) (*word*) término *m*; vocablo *m*, voz *f*, expresión *f*; **in plain —s, in simple —s** en términos sencillos, en lenguaje sencillo; **to choose one's —s carefully** elegir sus palabras con cuidado.

(f) **—s** (*conditions*) condiciones *fpl*; **—s of reference** puntos *mpl* de consulta; **—s of sale** condiciones *fpl* de venta; **—s of surrender** capitulaciones *fpl*, condiciones *fpl* de la rendición; **—s of trade** relación *f* real de intercambio; **according to the —s of the contract** según las condiciones del contrato, conforme a lo estipulado en el contrato; **not on any —s** bajo ningún concepto; **what are your —s?** ¿cuáles son sus condiciones?; **to accept someone on his own —s** aceptar a uno sabiendo lo que es, aceptar a uno sin esperar cambiar su naturaleza; **to come to —s** llegar a un acuerdo, ponerse de acuerdo; **to come to —s with a situation** adaptarse a una situación, conformarse con una situación; **to dictate —s** dictar las condiciones; **you may name your own —s** Vd puede estipular todo lo que quiera.

(g) **—s** (*Comm, Fin*) precio *m*, tarifa *f*; **our —s for full board** nuestro precio para la pensión completa; **"inclusive —s: £12"** "12 libras todo incluido", "pensión completa: 12 libras"; **we bought it on advantageous —s** lo compramos a buen precio; **we offer easy —s** ofrecemos facilidades de pago.

(h) **—s** (*relationship*) relaciones *fpl*; **to be on easy** (*or* **familiar**) **—s with someone** tener confianza con uno; **to be on bad —s with someone** llevarse mal con uno, estar en malas relaciones con uno; **to be on good —s with someone** estar en buenas relaciones con uno; **we are on the best of —s** somos muy amigos; **we're not on speaking —s** no nos hablamos; **what —s are they on?** ¿cuáles son sus relaciones?; **to fight someone on equal —s** luchar con uno en iguales condiciones.

2 *vt* nombrar, denominar; calificar de; **he —s himself a businessman** se llama hombre de negocios; **I — it a disgrace** yo lo llamo una vergüenza, yo digo que es una vergüenza.

termagant ['tɔːməgənt] *n* arpía *f*, fiera *f*.

terminal ['tɔːminl] **1** *adj* terminal, final; (*School, Univ*) trimestral.

2 *n* (*Elec*) borne *m*; polo *m*; (*Aer, Naut*) terminal *f*; (*Rail*) estación *f* terminal, término *m*.

terminate ['tɔːmineit] **1** *vt* terminar. **2** *vi* terminar(se).

termination [,tɔːmi'neiʃən] *n* terminación *f* (*also Gram*).

terminological [,tɔːminə'lɔdʒikəl] *adj* terminológico.

terminology [,tɔːmi'nɔlədʒi] *n* terminología *f*.

terminus ['tɔːminəs] *n, pl* **termini** ['tɔːminiː] término *m*; (*Rail*) estación *f* terminal término *m*.

termite ['tɔːmait] *n* termita *f*, termite *m*, comején *m*.

tern [tɔːn] *n* golondrina *f* de mar; **common —** charrán *m* común.

ternary ['tɔːnəri] *adj* ternario.

Terpsichore [tɔːp'sikəri] *f* Terpsícore.

terpsichorean [,tɔːpsikə'riːən] *adj* de Terpsícore.

terrace ['terəs] **1** *n* (*Agr*) terraza *f*; (*raised bank*) terraplén *m*; (*of houses*) hilera *f* de casas sin división entre sí; (*roof*) azotea *f*; **—s** (*Sport*) gradas *fpl*.

2 *vt* formar terrazas en; terraplenar.

terraced ['terəst] *adj* en terrazas; terraplenado.

terracotta ['terə'kɔtə] *n* terracota *f*.

terrain [te'rein] *n* terreno *m*.

terrapin ['terəpin] *n* tortuga *f* de agua dulce.

terrazzo [te'rætsəu] *n* (*US*) piso *m* veneciano.

terrestrial [ti'restriəl] *adj* terrestre.

terrible ['terəbl] *adj* terrible; (*fam*) horrible (*fam*), malísimo, fatal (*fam*); **it was just —** fue sencillamente horrible; **his Spanish is —** su español es fatal.

terribly ['terəbli] *adv* terriblemente, espantosamente; (*fam*) terriblemente; **— dangerous** tremendamente peligroso; **I think he's — nice** para mi gusto es simpatiquísimo; **she plays —** toca malísimamente.

terrier ['teriə*] *n* terrier *m*.

terrific [tə'rifik] *adj* tremendo; (*fam*) tremendo (*fam*), bárbaro (*fam*), fabuloso (*fam*); **what — news!** ¡qué noticia más estupenda!; **isn't he —?** ¿es fabuloso, no?

terrifically [tə'rifikəli] *adv* tremendamente; (*fam*) tremendamente, fabulosamente.

terrify ['terifai] *vt* aterrar, aterrorizar.

terrifying ['terifaiiŋ] *adj* aterrador, espantoso.

terrifyingly ['terifaiiŋli] *adv* espantosamente.

territorial [,teri'tɔːriəl] **1** *adj* territorial; *see* **water**. **2** *n* (*Mil*) reservista *m*.

territoriality [,teri'tɔːri'æliti] *n* territorialidad *f*.

territory ['teritəri] *n* territorio *m*; **mandated —** territorio *m* bajo mandato.

terror ['terə*] *n* terror *m*, espanto *m*.

terrorism ['terərizəm] *n* terrorismo *m*.

terrorist ['terərist] **1** *adj* terrorista. **2** *n* terrorista *m*.

terrorize ['terəraiz] *vt* aterrorizar.

terror-stricken ['terə,strikən] *adj* espantado, preso de un terror pánico.

Terry ['teri] *nombre cariñoso de* **Terence, Theresa**.

terry cloth ['teri,klɔθ] *n* (*US*) albornoz *m*.

terse [tɔːs] *adj* breve, conciso, lacónico; brusco.

tersely ['tɔːsli] *adv* concisamente, lacónicamente; bruscamente.

terseness ['tɔːsnis] *n* brevedad *f*, concisión *f*, laconismo *m*; brusquedad *f*.

tertiary ['tɔːʃəri] *adj* terciario.

Tertullian [tɔː'tʌliən] *m* Tertuliano.

Terylene ['terəliːn] *n* (*Protected Trade Name*) terylene *m*.

tesselated ['tesileitid] *adj* formado con teselas; **— pavement** mosaico *m*.

tesselation [,tesi'leiʃən] *n* mosaico *m*.

test [test] **1** *n* prueba *f*; ensayo *m*; (*School, Univ etc*) examen *m*, test *m*; (*Chem*) prueba *f*, análisis *m*; (*standard of judgement*) criterio *m*; **a weekly French —** un examen semanal de francés; **acid —** (*fig*) prueba *f* de fuego; piedra *f* de toque; **endurance —** prueba *f* de resistencia; **eye —** examen *m* para graduar la vista; **intelligence —** test *m* de inteligencia, prueba *f* de inteligencia; **nuclear —** prueba *f* nuclear; **oral —** examen *m* oral; **structural —** prueba *f* estructural; **Wasserman —** (*Med*) prueba *f* de Wasserman; **if we apply the — of visual appeal to it** si lo sometemos a la prueba de la atracción visual; **to put something to the —** poner algo a prueba, someter algo a prueba; **to stand the —** soportar la prueba; **it has stood the — of time** ha resistido el paso del tiempo; *see* **blood —**, **driving —**, **high —**.

2 *attr* de prueba.

3 *vt* probar, poner a prueba, someter a prueba; examinar; *sight* graduar; (*Chem etc*) ensayar; *new drug etc* experimentar; **it severely —ed our nerves** puso nuestros nervios a toda prueba; **the new weapon is being —ed** se está sometiendo a prueba la nueva arma.

testament ['testəmənt] *n* testamento *m*; **New T—** Nuevo Testamento *m*; **Old T—** Antiguo Testamento *m*.

testamentary [,testə'mentəri] *adj* testamentario.

testator [tes'teitə*] *n* testador *m*.

testatrix [tes'teitriks] *n* testadora *f*.

test bench ['testbentʃ] *n* banco *m* de pruebas.

test card ['testkaːd] *n* (*TV*) carta *f* de ajuste.

test case ['testkeis] *n* (*Law*) pleito *m* de ensayo (*para determinar la interpretación de una nueva ley*).

tester[1] ['testə*] *n* (*person*) ensayador *m*, ora *f*.

tester[2] ['testə*] *n* (*arch*) baldaquín *m*.

testes ['testiːz] *npl* testes *mpl*.

test flight ['testflait] *n* vuelo *m* de ensayo.

testicle ['testikl] *n* testículo *m*.

testification [,testifi'keiʃən] *n* testificación *f*.

testify ['testifai] **1** *vt* atestiguar, dar fe de; **to — that . . .** testificar que . . .; declarar que . . .

2 *vi* (a) (*Law*) prestar declaración, declarar.

(b) to — to something atestiguar algo, atestar algo; (*fig*) atestiguar algo, dar fe de algo.

testily ['testili] *adv answer etc* con enojo, malhumoradamente.

testimonial [,testi'məuniəl] *n* (a) certificado *m*; (*reference about person*) recomendación *f*, carta *f* de recomendación; **as a — to** como testimonio a, en homenaje a.

(b) (*gift*) regalo *m*, obsequio *m* (de jubilación etc).

testimony ['testiməni] *n* testimonio *m*, declaración *f*; **in — whereof . . .** en fe de lo cual . . .; **to bear — to something** atestar algo.

testing ground ['testingraund] *n* zona *f* de pruebas.

test match ['testmætʃ] *n* partido *m* internacional.

test paper ['test,peipə*] *n* (*School etc*) test *m*, examen *m*; (*Chem*) papel *m* reactivo.

test piece ['testpiːs] *n* (*Mus*) obra *f* elegida para un certamen de piano (etc).

test pilot ['test,pailət] n piloto m de pruebas.
test print ['testprint] n (Phot) copia f de prueba.
test tube ['testtju:b] n probeta f.
testy ['testi] adj enojadizo, malhumorado.
tetanus ['tetənəs] n tétanos m.
tetchy ['tetʃi] adj = **testy.**
tête-à-tête ['teitɑ:'teit] n conversación f íntima.
tether ['teðə*] **1** n atadura f, traba f, cuerda f; see end.
2 vt atar, atar con una cuerda (to a).
tetragon ['tetrəgən] n tetrágono m.
tetrahedron [,tetrə'hi:drən] n tetraedro m.
tetrameter [te'træmitə*] n tetrámetro m.
Teuton ['tju:tən] n teutón m, ona f.
Teutonic [tju'tɔnik] adj teutónico.
Texan ['teksən] **1** adj tejano. **2** n tejano m, a f.
Texas ['teksəs] Tejas m.
text [tekst] n texto m; (subject) tema m; **to stick to one's** — no apartarse de su tema; **to preach on a** — predicar un sermón valiéndose de un pasaje de la Sagrada Escritura.
textbook ['tekstbuk] n libro m de texto.
textile ['tekstail] adj textil; — **industry** industria f textil.
textiles ['tekstailz] npl textiles mpl, tejidos mpl.
textual ['tekstjuəl] adj textual; — **criticism** crítica f textual.
textually ['tekstjuəli] adv textualmente.
texture ['tekstʃə*] n textura f (also fig).
Thai [tai] **1** adj tailandés. **2** n tailandés m, esa f.
Thailand ['tailænd] Tailandia f.
thalidomide [θə'lidəumaid] n talidomida m.
Thames [temz] Támesis m; **it won't set the** — **on fire** no llamará la atención, no tiene nada de particular.
than [ðæn] conj (a) que; **I have more** — **you** yo tengo más que tú; **he swears less** — **her** él jura menos que ella; **nobody is more sorry** — **I (am)** nadie lo siente más que yo; **he has more money** — **brains** tiene más dinero que inteligencia; **clothes come out whiter** — **white** sale la ropa más que blanca; **it is better to phone** — **to write** más vale telefonear que escribir; **I'll do anything rather** — **that** haré cualquier cosa que no sea ésa, lo haré todo menos eso.
(b) (with numerals) de; **more** — **90** más de 90; — **than half** más de la mitad; **not less** — **8** no menos de 8; **more** — **once** más de una vez; **it doesn't happen more** — **once** no ocurre más que una sola vez.
(c) (with following clause) **they have more money** — **we have** tienen más dinero del que nosotros tenemos; **we have more chips** — **you have** nosotros tenemos más patatas fritas de las que Vds tienen; **it was an even sillier play** — **we had thought** la obra fue aun más estúpida de lo que habíamos pensado; **the car went faster** — **we had expected** el coche fue más rápidamente de lo que habíamos esperado.
thank [θæŋk] vt (a) **to** — **someone** dar las gracias a uno; — **you** gracias; — **you!** (emphatic, reciprocating thanks) ¡a usted!; **no** — **you** no gracias; **I cannot** — **you enough!** ¡cuánto se lo agradezco!; see **goodness** etc.
(b) **to** — **someone for something** agradecer algo a uno; — **you for the present** muchas gracias por el regalo; **did you** — **him for the flowers?** ¿le diste las gracias por las flores?; **you have him to** — **for that** eso tienes que agradecérselo a él, ese favor se lo debes a él; **he has himself to** — **for that** él mismo tiene la culpa de eso; **which he could never properly** — **you for** que él no agradecería nunca lo bastante.
(c) **I'll** — **you not to do it** agradecería no lo hiciera; **I'll** — **you to be more polite!** ¡conviene hablar con más educación!
(d) **without so much as a "**— **you"** sin la menor señal de agradecimiento.
thankful ['θæŋkful] adj agradecido; **to be** — **to** + infin alegrarse de + infin; **let us be** — **that . . .** agradezcamos que + subj; **how** — **we were for that umbrella!** ¡cuánto nos ayudó ese paraguas!, ¡cómo bendecimos ese paraguas!
thankfully ['θæŋkfəli] adv con gratitud, con agradecimiento; **he said** — dijo agradecido; dijo con alivio.
thankfulness ['θæŋkfulnis] n gratitud f, agradecimiento m.
thankless ['θæŋklis] adj person ingrato; task ímprobo, ingrato.
thanks [θæŋks] npl gracias fpl; **many** —! ¡muchas gracias!, ¡muchísimas gracias!; **my warmest** —

for your help mis gracias más efusivas por su ayuda; **vote of** — voto m de gracias; **that's all the** — **I get!** ¡cómo se me agradece!; — **to you** gracias a ti; **it's all** — **to brand X** todo es gracias a la marca X, todo lo debo a la marca X; — **be to God** gracias a Dios; **no** — **to you** no le debo nada a Vd.
thanksgiving ['θæŋks,givin] n acción f de gracias; **T**— **Day** (US) día m de Acción de Gracias.
that [ðæt] **1** dem adj (pl those) m: ese, (more remote) aquel; f: esa, (more remote) aquella; — **book** ese libro; — **hill over there** aquella colina; — **one** ése, aquél; — **lad of yours** ese chico suyo; **what about** — **cheque?** ¿y el cheque ese?
2 dem pron (pl those) m: ese, (more remote) aquél; f: ésa, (more remote) aquélla; "neuter": eso, aquello; **this car is new but** — **is old** este coche es nuevo pero ése es viejo; — **is true** eso es verdad; — **is all I can tell you** eso es todo lo que puedo decirle; —'**s what I say** eso digo yo, lo mismo digo yo; **they all say** — todos dicen lo mismo; **what is** —**?** ¿qué es?, ¿eso qué es?; **who is** —**?** ¿quién es?; — **is Joe** es Pepe; — **is . . .** esto es . . .; es decir . . .; **and** —'**s** —**!** y eso es todo; **you can't go and** —'**s** — no puedes ir y no hay más qué decir; **so** — **was** — y no había más que hacer, y ahí terminó la cosa; —'**s odd!** ¡qué raro!, ¡qué cosa más rara!; **will he come?** . . . — **he will!** ¡sí vendrá? . . . ¡ya lo creo!; **after** — después de eso; **at** — acto seguido, sin más; con eso, con lo cual; **and it was broken at** — y además estaba roto; **do it like** — hazlo de esa manera, hazlo de la manera que ves; **with** — con eso; **if it comes to** — en tal caso; si vamos a eso; **how do you like** —**?** ¿qué te parece?, (iro) ¡vaya!; see **all 1, 2; as (f); it (e).**
3 rel pron (a) que; **the book** — **I read** el libro que leí; **the houses** — **I painted** las casas que pinté; **all** — **I have** todo lo que tengo.
(b) (with prep) que, el cual, la cual etc; **the box** — **I put it in** la caja en la cual lo puse, la caja donde lo puse; **the house** — **we're speaking of** la casa de que hablamos; **not** — **I know of** no que yo sepa.
4 adv tan; — **far** tan lejos; — **high** tan alto, así de alto; — **many frogs** tantas ranas; — **much money** tanto dinero; **it is** — **much better** es tanto mejor; **he can't be** — **clever** no puede ser tan inteligente como tú dices; **nobody can be** — **rich** nadie puede ser tan rico como eso; **I didn't know he was** — **ill** no sabía que estuviera tan enfermo; **he was** — **wild** (fam) estaba tan furioso.
5 conj (a) que; **I believe** — **he exists** creo que existe; — **he should behave like this!** ¡que se comporte así!; — **he should behave like this is incredible** que se comporte así es increíble; — **he refuses is natural** el que rehuse es natural; **oh** — **we could!** ¡ojalá pudiéramos!, ¡ojalá!; see **would** etc.
(b) (in order that) para que + subj, eg **it was done (so)** — **he might sleep** se hizo para que él pudiera dormir; see **so.**
(c) **in** — **en que, por cuanto.**
thatch [θætʃ] **1** n (straw) paja f; (roof) techo m de paja; (over wall etc) barda f. **2** vt poner techo de paja a; bardar.
thatched [θætʃt] adj: — **roof** techo m de paja; **the roof is** — el techo es de paja.
thaw [θɔ:] **1** n deshielo m.
2 vt deshelar, derretir; (fig) ablandar, hacer menos severo; **to** — **out** meat etc deshelar.
3 vi deshelarse, derretirse; (fig) ablandarse, hacerse menos severo; (of person) hacerse más afable, ir perdiendo su reserva; **to** — **out** (meat, frozen fingers etc) deshelarse; **it is** —**ing** deshiela.
the [ði:, ðə] **1** def art (a) el, la, (pl) los, las (masculine singular a + el = al, eg **to the man** al hombre; masculine singular de + el = del, eg **of the cat** del gato).
(b) ("neuter") lo; — **good and** — **beautiful** lo bueno y lo bello; **within the realms of** — **possible** dentro de lo posible; **it is** — **unusual which counts** es lo insólito lo que importa.
(c) (special uses) **Charles** — **Fifth** Carlos Quinto; **Philip** — **Second** Felipe Segundo; — **Browns los Brown;** — **cheek of it!** ¡qué frescura!; **oh** — **pain!** ¡ay qué dolor!; **he hasn't** — **sense to understand** no tiene bastante inteligencia para comprender; **the child has** — **measles** el niño tiene sarampión; **2 dollars** — **pound** 2 dólares la libra.
(d) (emphatic) **he's** — **man for the job** es el hombre ideal para el puesto; es él hombre más indicado para el puesto; **you don't mean** —

Professor Bloggs? ¿quieres decir el célebre profesor Bloggs?, ¿quieres decir el profesor Bloggs de que se habla tanto?; it was — colour of 1971 fue el color que estaba tan de moda en 1971.

2 *adv*: — more he works the more he earns cuanto más trabaja (tanto) más gana; — sooner — better cuanto antes mejor; it will be all — better será tanto mejor.

theatre, (US) **theater** ['θiətə*] *n* teatro *m* (*also fig, Mil etc*); (*lecture*) — aula *f*; variety — teatro *m* de variedades; to go to the — ir al teatro.

theatregoer, (US) **theatergoer** ['θiətə,gəuə*] *n* aficionado *m* al teatro, aficionada *f* al teatro.

theatrical [θi'ætrikəl] *adj* teatral; *company etc* de teatro; *person's manner* exagerado.

theatrically [θi'ætrikəli] *adv* teatralmente, de modo teatral; de modo exagerado.

theatricals [θi'ætrikəlz] *npl* funciones *fpl* teatrales; amateur — teatro *m* de aficionados.

Thebes [θiːbz] Tebas.

thee [ðiː] *pron* (*arch or poet*) te; (*after prep*) ti; with — contigo.

theft [θeft] *n* hurto *m*, robo *m*.

their [ðeə*] *poss adj* su(s).

theirs [ðeəz] *poss pron* (el) suyo, (la) suya *etc*.

theism ['θiːizəm] *n* teísmo *m*.

theist ['θiːist] *n* teísta *mf*.

theistic [θiː'istik] *adj* teísta.

them [ðem, ðəm] *pron* (*acc*) los, las; (*dat*) les; (*after prep*) ellos, ellas.

thematic [θi'mætik] *adj* temático.

theme [θiːm] *n* tema *m*.

theme song ['θiːmsɔŋ] *n* motivo *m* principal.

themselves [ðəm'selvz] *pron* (*subject*) ellos mismos, ellas mismas; (*acc, dat*) se; (*after prep*) sí (mismos, mismas); *see* oneself.

then [ðen] **1** *adv* (*at that time*) entonces; por entonces; en ese momento; a la sazón, en aquella época; (*afterwards, next*) luego, después; it was — 8 o'clock eran las 8, eran las 8 ya; — we went to Madrid luego fuimos a Madrid; he was — a little-known writer en aquella época era un escritor poco conocido; and — again his's a red y además es un rojo; first this — that primero esto y luego aquello; by — para entonces, antes de eso; from — on, since — desde entonces, desde aquel momento, a partir de entonces; until — hasta entonces; what —? ¿qué pasó después?; (*so what*) ¿y qué?, ¿qué más?; *see* now 1 (a).

2 *conj* pues, en ese caso; por tanto; entonces; what do you want me to do —? ¿pues qué quieres que haga yo?; — you don't want it? ¿así que no lo quieres?, ¿con qué no lo quieres?; well — ahora bien, pues; *see* now 1 (d).

3 *adv* entonces, de entonces; the — King of Slobodia el entonces rey de Eslobodia, el rey de Eslobodia de entonces; the — existing government el gobierno que existía en esa época, el gobierno de entonces.

thence [ðens] *adv* (*lit*) (a) (*from that place*) de allí, desde allí. (b) (*therefore*) por eso, por consiguiente.

thenceforth ['ðens'fɔːθ] *adv*, **thenceforward** [,ðens-'fɔːwəd] *adv* (*lit*) desde entonces, de allí en adelante, a partir de entonces.

theocracy [θi'ɔkrəsi] *n* teocracia *f*.

theocratic [θiə'krætik] *adj* teocrático.

theodolite [θi'ɔdəlait] *n* teodolito *m*.

theologian [θiə'ləudʒiən] *n* teólogo *m*.

theological [θiə'lɔdʒikəl] *adj* teológico.

theologist [θi'ɔlədʒist] *n* teólogo *m*.

theology [θi'ɔlədʒi] *n* teología *f*.

theorem ['θiərəm] *m* teorema *m*.

theoretic(al) [θiə'retik(əl)] *adj* teórico.

theoretically [θiə'retikəli] *adv* teóricamente, en teoría.

theoretician [,θiərə'tiʃən] *n*, **theorist** ['θiərist] *n* teórico *m*, teorizante *m*.

theorize ['θiəraiz] *vi* teorizar.

theorizer ['θiəraizə*] *n* teorizante *m*.

theory ['θiəri] *n* teoría *f*; in — teóricamente, en teoría.

theosophical [θiə'sɔfikəl] *adj* teosófico.

theosophist [θi'ɔsəfist] *n* teósofo *m*.

theosophy [θi'ɔsəfi] *n* teosofía *f*.

therapeutic(al) [,θerə'pjuːtik(əl)] *adj* terapéutico.

therapeutics [,θerə'pjuːtiks] *n* terapéutica *f*.

therapist ['θerəpist] *n* terapeuta *mf*.

therapy ['θerəpi] *n* terapia *f*, terapéutica *f*; occupational — terapia *f* laboral.

there [ðeə*] **1** *adv* (a) allí; allá; (— *near you*) ahí; back —, down —, over — allá; 12 kilometres — and back 12 kilómetros ida y vuelta; it's in —

está allí dentro; when we left — cuando partimos de allí.

(b) (*less precisely*) mind out —! ¡ojo!, ¡cuidado!; make way —! ¡abran paso!, ¡atención!; hurry up —! ¡despabílense!; ¡menearse!; you —! ¡eh, usted!; — we differ en ese punto discrepamos; — you are wrong en eso te equivocas; —'s the bus ya viene el autobús; — she comes ya viene; — we were, stuck así que nos encontramos allí sin podernos mover.

(c) — is, — are hay; — will be habrá; — were 10 había 10, hubo 10; how many are —? ¿cuántos hay?; — was laughter at this en esto hubo risas; — was singing and dancing se cantó y se bailó; — is a pound missing falta una libra; — is no wine left no hay vino, no queda vino; are — any bananas? ¿hay plátanos?

(d) he's all — es la mar de listo; he's not all — le falta un tornillo.

2 *interj* ¡vaya!; —, — (*comforting*) ¡cálmate!, ¡no es nada!, ¡no te preocupes!; —, drink this bebe esto; but —, what's the use? pero ¡vamos!, es inútil.

thereabouts ['ðeərəbauts] *adv* por ahí, allí cerca; 12 or — 12 más o menos, alrededor de 12; £5 or — 5 libras o así.

thereafter [ðeər'ɑːftə*] *adv* después, después de eso.

thereat [ðeər'æt] *adv* (*thereupon*) con eso, acto seguido; (*for that reason*) por eso, por esa razón.

thereby ['ðeə'bai] *adv* por eso, de ese modo; por esa razón; it does not — become easier no por eso se hace más fácil; — hangs a tale sobre eso hay mucho que decir.

therefore ['ðeəfɔː*] *adv* por tanto, por lo tanto, por consiguiente; por esta razón.

therefrom [ðeə'frɔm] *adv* de ahí, de allí.

therein [ðeər'in] *adv* (*inside*) allí dentro; (*in this regard*) en eso, en esto, en este respecto; — lies the danger en eso consiste el peligro.

thereof [ðeər'ɔv] *adv* de eso, de esto; de lo mismo.

thereon [ðeər'ɔn] *adv* = **thereupon**.

there's [ðeəz] = there is; there has.

Theresa [ti'riːzə] *f* Teresa.

thereto [ðeə'tuː] *adv* a eso, a ello.

thereupon ['ðeərə'pɔn] *adv* (*at that point*) en eso, con eso; acto seguido, en seguida; (*consequently*) por tanto; por consiguiente.

therewith [ðeə'wið] *adv* con eso, con lo mismo.

therm [θəːm] *n* unidad *f* térmica.

thermal ['θəːməl] *adj* termal.

thermic ['θəːmik] *adj* térmico.

thermionic [,θəːmi'ɔnik] *adj* termoiónico; — valve lámpara *f* termoiónica.

thermocouple ['θəːməu,kʌpl] *n* termopar *m*, par *m* térmico.

thermodynamic ['θəːməudai'næmik] *adj* termodinámico.

thermodynamics ['θəːməudai'næmiks] *n* termodinámica *f*.

thermoelectric ['θəːməui'lektrik] *adj* termoeléctrico; — couple par *m* termoeléctrico.

thermometer [θə'mɔmitə*] *n* termómetro *m*; clinical — termómetro *m* clínico.

thermonuclear ['θəːməu'njuːkliə*] *adj* termonuclear.

thermopile ['θəːməupail] *n* termopila *f*.

Thermopylae [θəː'mɔpiliː] Termópilas *fpl*.

Thermos ['θəːməs] *n* (*Protected Trade Name*) (*also* — bottle, — flask) termos *m*, termo *m*.

thermostat ['θəːməstæt] *n* termostato *m*.

thermostatic [,θəːməs'tætik] *adj* termostático.

thesaurus [θi'sɔːrəs] *n* tesoro *m*.

these [ðiːz] (*pl of* this) **1** *dem adj m*: estos; *f*: estas. **2** *dem pron m*: éstos; *f*: éstas; *see also* this.

Theseus ['θiːsjuːs] *m* Teseo.

thesis ['θiːsis] *n*, *pl* theses ['θiːsiːz] tesis *f*.

Thespian ['θespiən] **1** *adj* de Tespis; (*fig*) dramático, trágico. **2** *n* actor *m*, actriz *f*.

Thespis ['θespis] *m* Tespis.

Thessaly ['θesəli] *m* Tesalia *f*.

Thetis ['θiːtis] *f* Tetis.

they [ðei] *pron* ellos, ellas; — who los que, quienes.

they'd [ðeid] = they would; they had.

they'll [ðeil] = they will, they shall.

they're [ðeə*] = they are.

they've [ðeiv] = they have.

thiamine ['θaiəmiːn] *n* tiamina *f*.

thick [θik] **1** *adj* (a) (*of solid*) espeso; *book, thread, stroke etc* grueso; it is 2 metres — tiene 2 metros de espesor; on ice only 4 centimetres — sobre hielo de solamente 4 centímetros de espesor.

(b) (*dense*) *forest, vegetation etc* espeso, denso; *growth* tupido; *eyebrows, beard* poblado; the leaves

were — on the ground había una capa espesa de hojas en el suelo; **bodies lay — on the road** había cadáveres por toda la carretera; **the field is — with strawberries** el campo abunda en fresas; **the place will be — with tourists** el sitio estará atestado de turistas.
(c) (*of liquid: cloudy*) turbio, (*stiff*) viscoso; *cream, gravy etc* espeso; *fog, smoke* denso, espeso; *air* viciado; *voice* velado, apagado, poco distinto; *accent* cerrado; **the air is pretty — in here** aquí huele a encerrado, aquí se respira con dificultad; **the air was — with insults** el aire estaba lleno de insultos.
(d) (*stupid*) estúpido, lerdo.
(e) (*of relationship*) íntimo; **they're very —** son íntimos amigos; intiman mucho; **they're as — as thieves** son uña y carne; **A is — with B** A tiene mucha intimidad con B.
(f) (*fam*) **it's a bit —!** ¡no hay derecho!, ¡esto es injusto!; **it's a bit — to have to** + *infin* es injusto tener que + *infin*.
2 *adv*: **to spread butter —** poner mucha mantequilla; **put the paint on —** ponga una buena capa de pintura; **they cut the bread very —** sirven el pan en trozos muy gruesos; **the blows fell — and fast upon him** le llovieron los golpes espesos.
3 *n* (a) **in the — of battle** en lo más reñido de la batalla; **he likes to be in the — of things** le gusta tener una vida muy activa, le gusta estar en el centro de las actividades, le gusta estar muy metido en todo.
(b) **to stick to someone through — and thin** seguir completamente fiel a uno, apoyar a uno incondicionalmente.
thicken ['θikən] **1** *vt* espesar, hacer más espeso.
2 *vi* espesarse, hacerse más espeso; hacerse más denso; (*Cook*) espesarse; (*of plot*) complicarse, enmarañarse más.
thicket ['θikit] *n* matorral *m*, espesura *f*.
thickheaded ['θik'hedid] *adj* estúpido, lerdo; terco.
thickheadedness ['θik'hedidnis] *n* estupidez *f*; terquedad *f*.
thick-lipped ['θik'lipt] *adj* de labios gruesos, bezudo.
thickly ['θikli] *adv* espesamente; gruesamente; *speak* con voz apagada, indistintamente; **— populated areas** regiones *fpl* densamente pobladas; **bread — spread with butter** pan *m* con mucha mantequilla, pan *m* con una buena capa de mantequilla; **the snow was falling —** nevaba muchísimo.
thickness ['θiknis] *n* espesura *f*; densidad *f*; grueso *m*; (*in measuring*) espesor *m*; grosor *m*; **what is the — of the snow?** ¿cuánta nieve hay?; **boards of the same —** tablas *fpl* del mismo espesor.
thickset ['θik'set] *adj* rechoncho, grueso.
thickskinned ['θik'skind] *adj* (*fig*) insensible, duro.
thief [θi:f] *n*, *pl* **thieves** [θi:vz] ladrón *m*, ona *f*; **stop —!** ¡al ladrón!; **to set a — to catch a —** poner al ladrón de ladrón y medio.
thieve [θi:v] *vti* hurtar, robar.
thievery ['θi:vəri] *n* robo *m*, latrocinio *m*.
thieving ['θi:viŋ] **1** *adj* ladrón, largo de uñas. **2** *n* robo *m*, latrocinio *m*.
thievish ['θi:viʃ] *adj* ladrón; **to have — tendencies** ser largo de uñas.
thievishness ['θi:viʃnis] *n* propensión *f* a ser ladrón.
thigh [θai] *n* muslo *m*.
thighbone ['θaibəun] *n* fémur *m*.
thimble ['θimbl] *n* dedal *m*; (*Naut*) guardacabo *m*.
thimbleful ['θimblful] *n* dedada *f*; **just a —** unas gotas nada más.
thin [θin] **1** *adj* (a) (*of materials*) delgado; *clothing, covering* ligero; *veil etc* transparente; diáfano; *layer* tenue, fino, delgado; *person* flaco; **with — legs** con piernas flacas; **to be as — as a rake** (*or lath*) estar en los huesos; **to get —ner, to grow —ner** enflaquecer.
(b) *hair* ralo, escaso; *crop, crowd, population* poco denso, escaso; **doctors are — on the ground** hay pocos médicos, escasean los médicos; **the wheat is — this year** este año hay poco trigo; **he's getting — on top** le escasea el pelo por encima.
(c) *liquid* poco denso; *soup, wine* aguado; que más bien parece ser agua; *scent, sound* tenue; *air, light* tenue, sutil; *voice* delgado; **at 20,000 metres the air is —** a los 20.000 metros el aire está enrarecido.
(d) *excuse etc* poco convincente, flojo; **to have a — time** pasarlo mal, pasar por un período difícil; **they gave him a — time of it** hicieron sufrir al pobre, le hicieron sudar la gota gorda.

2 *adv*: **to spread butter —** poner poca mantequilla; **they cut the bread very —** sirven el pan en trozos muy delgados.
3 *vt*: **to — someone down** adelgazar a uno, hacer que uno enflaquezca; **to — paint (down)** desleír la pintura, diluir la pintura; **to — soup (down)** aguar la sopa; **to — out** *plants etc* entresacar, aclarar; *crowd, number, army etc* reducir, mermar.
4 *vi* (*slim*) adelgazar(se), (*and weaken*) enflaquecer; (*of crowd etc*) hacerse menos denso, aclararse; (*of number etc*) reducirse; **the forest starts to — out here** aquí el bosque empieza a ser menos denso.
thine [ðain] *poss pron* (*arch*) (el) tuyo, (la) tuya *etc*; **mine and —** lo mío y lo tuyo; **for thee and —** para ti y los tuyos; **what is mine is —** lo que es mío también es tuyo.
thing [θiŋ] *n* (a) (*object*) cosa *f*; objeto *m*; artículo *m*; **—s** (*belongings*) cosas *fpl*, efectos *mpl*; (*equipment*) avíos *mpl*, equipo *m*; (*clothes*) ropa *f*, trapos *mpl*; (*luggage*) equipaje *m*; **—s of value** objetos *mpl* de valor; **a — of beauty** una cosa estética, una cosa bella; **my painting —s** mis avíos de pintar; **tea —s** servicio *m* de té; **to wash up the tea —s** lavar la vajilla; **where shall I put my —s?** ¿dónde pongo mis cosas?; **to pack up one's —s** hacer las maletas; **to take off one's —s** desnudarse, quitarse la ropa.
(b) (*person*) ser *m*, criatura *f*; (*pej*) sujeto *m*; **you poor —!, poor old —!** ¡pobrecito!; **he's a poor old — now** ahora no vale para nada; **you beastly (or horrid, rotten etc) —!** ¡canalla!; **how are you, old —?** ¿qué tal, hijo?
(c) (*matter, circumstance etc*) cosa *f*; asunto *m*; **the main —** lo más importante, lo esencial; **above all —s** ante todo, sobre todo; **for one —** en primer lugar; **and for another — . . .** y además . . ., y por otra parte . . .; **no such —** ¡no hay tal!; ¡ni hablar!; **what with one — and another** entre unas cosas y otras; **one — or the other . . .** una de dos . . .; **it's neither one — nor the other** no es ni lo uno ni lo otro; **first — (in the morning)** a primera hora (de la mañana); **last — (at night)** a última hora (de la noche); **the first — to do is . . .** lo primero que hay que hacer es . . .; **that's the last — we want** eso es lo que queremos menos; **the best — would be to** + *infin* lo mejor sería + *infin*; **the next best —** lo mejor después de eso; **it's a good — that . . .** menos mal que . . .; **the good — about it is that . . .** lo bueno es que . . .; **it's finished and a good — too** se acabó y me alegro de ello; **it was a close —, it was a near — escape** (*etc*) por un pelo; **this is the real — at last** por fin lo tenemos sin trampa ni cartón; **it's the very —!, it's just the —!** ¡es exactamente lo que necesitábamos!; **that's the — for me** eso es lo que me hace falta; **the — is . . .** el caso es que . . ., es que . . .; **the — is this . . .** la dificultad es que . . .; se trata de saber si . . .; **the — is to sell your car first** conviene vender primero tu coche; **the only — is to paint it** no hay más remedio que pintarlo; **the play's the —** lo que importa es la representación; **this is too much of a good —** esto es demasiado; **as —s are** tal como están las cosas; **how are —s?** ¿qué tal?; **how are —s with you?** ¿qué tal te va?; ¿cómo te va eso?; **—s are going badly** las cosas van mal; **that's how —s are** así están las cosas; **I've done a silly —** he hecho algo tonto; **we had hoped for better —s** habíamos esperado algo mejor; **I don't know a — about cars** no sé nada en absoluto de coches; **I didn't know a — for that exam** para ese examen yo estaba pez; **he knows a — or two** él sabe cuántos son cinco; **he makes a good — out of it** sabe sacar provecho de ello, con eso tiene un buen negocio; **to make a mess of —s** hacerlo todo mal; **did you ever see such a —?** ¿se vio jamás tal cosa?
(d) (*fashion*) **the latest — in hats** la última moda del sombrero, el sombrero según la moda actual; **it's quite the —** está muy de moda.
(e) (*socially acceptable —*) **it's not the (done) —** eso no se hace, eso no está bien visto; **to do the right —** obrar bien, obrar honradamente.
(f) (*obsession*) obsesión *f*; manía *f*; **she has a — about snakes** está obsesionada por las culebras, le obsesionan las culebras; **he's got a — about me** me tiene manía.
thingumabob ['θiŋəmibɔb] *n*, **thingamajig** ['θiŋə-midʒig] *n*, **thingummy** ['θiŋəmi] *n* (*fam*) cosa *f*, chisme *m*.
think [θiŋk] (*irr: pret and ptp* **thought**) **1** *vt* (a) pensar; **to — great thoughts** pensar cosas profundas, tener pensamientos profundos.

(b) to — out *plan etc* imaginar, idear; *answer* descubrir (después de pensarlo mucho); *problem* resolver (después de pensarlo mucho); **this wants —ing out** hay que pensar esto mucho; hay que estudiar esto detenidamente; **a well thought out answer** una respuesta estudiada; una contestación razonada; **he —s things out for himself** piensa por sí mismo.

(c) to — something over considerar algo detenidamente; reflexionar sobre algo; consultar algo con la almohada; **I'll — it over** lo pensaré; **you — it over!** ¡medítelo!

(d) to — up imaginar, idear; *excuse* inventar; **who thought this one up?** ¿quién ideó esto?, ¿a quién se le ocurrió esto?

2 *vti* **(a)** (*general sense, absolute sense*) pensar; meditar; **to — hard** pensar mucho; **he says little but —s a lot** dice poco pero piensa mucho, la procesión le va por dentro; **to act without —ing** obrar sin reflexionar; **— before you reply** reflexione antes de contestar; **give me time to —** déme tiempo para reflexionar; **now let me —** déjame pensarlo; **to — again** volver a pensarlo, reflexionar; **— again!** ¡medítelo!; **to — twice** pensar dos veces, reflexionar; **to — aloud** pensar en alta voz, expresar lo que uno piensa; **to — about something** pensar algo bien, considerar algo detenidamente, reflexionar sobre algo; consultar algo con la almohada; **I'll — about it** lo pensaré; **you — about it!** ¡medítelo!; **you — about money too much** le das demasiada importancia al dinero; **to — for oneself** pensar por sí mismo.

(b) (*imagine*) pensar, creer, imaginar; **who do you — you are?** ¿quién se cree Vd que es?; **who do you — you are to come marching in?** y usted ¿qué derecho cree tener para entrar aquí tan fresco?; **— of me in a bathing costume!** ¡imaginadme en traje de baño!; **just —!** ¡fíjate!, ¡imagínate!; **to — that . . .!** ¡y pensar que . . .!; **to — she once slept here!** ¡pensar que ella durmió aquí una vez!; **I can't — what you mean** no entiendo lo que Vd quiere decir; **I can't — what he can want** no llego a comprender su motivo; **I would have thought that . . .** hubiera creído que . . .; **I never thought that . . .** nunca pensé que . . .; **one might — that . . .** podría creerse que . . .; **anyone would — he was dying** cualquiera diría que se estaba muriendo; **who'd have thought it!** ¿quién lo diría?

(c) (*of ideas occurring*) **I was —ing that . . .** se me ocurrió pensar que . . .; **to — of doing something** pensar hacer algo, ocurrírsele a uno hacer algo; **don't you ever — of washing?** ¿no se te ocurre alguna vez lavarte?; **had you ever thought of going to Spain?** ¿has pensado alguna vez ir a España?

(d) (*intend*) pensar; **to — to +** *infin* pensar + *infin*; **I came here —ing to find you** vine aquí con la intención de buscarte.

(e) (*expect*) esperar; **I never thought to hear that from you** no esperaba nunca escuchar tales cosas de boca de Vd; **I thought as much ya** me lo figuraba, lo había previsto ya; **we little thought that . . .** estábamos lejos de pensar que . . .

(f) (*believe, consider*) creer, pensar: considerar; opinar; **I — so** creo que sí; **I shouldn't — so** no creo; **I — not** creo que no; **I should — so too!** ¡haces muy bien!; ¡ya era hora!; ¡buena falta te hacía!; **and it was free, I don't —!** ¡ya lo creo que me lo dieron gratis!; **I — (that) it is true** creo que es verdad, me parece que es verdad; **I don't — it can be done** no creo que se pueda hacer, no creo que sea factible; **so you — that . . .?** ¿así que Vd cree que . . .?; **what do you — I should do?** ¿qué crees tú que debiera hacer?, ¿qué me aconsejas hacer?; **to — oneself very clever** creerse la mar de listo, creerse muy astuto; *see* **better 1, 2** *etc.*

(g) (*believe, consider: with pred adj*) creer; **I — it very difficult** lo creo muy difícil, lo veo muy difícil, creo que es muy difícil; **I don't — it at all likely** lo creo muy poco probable; **everyone thought him mad** todos le tenían por loco; **they are thought to be poor** se cree que son pobres, tienen fama de ser pobres; *see* **fit, proper.**

(h) (*opine*) pensar; **she didn't know what to —** no sabía a qué carta quedarse; le fue imposible decidir; **now I don't know what to —** ahora tengo dudas, ahora estoy en duda; **what do you —?** ¿qué te parece?; **what do you — about it?** ¿qué te parece (de esto)?; *see* **what you — about it and let me know** estúdielo y dígame luego su opinión; **what do you — of him?** ¿qué piensas de él?, ¿qué

te parece él?, ¿qué concepto tienes de él?; **to — highly of someone** tener en mucho a uno; **to — well of someone** tener un buen concepto de uno; **he is well thought of** aquí se le estima mucho; **we don't — much of X** tenemos un concepto más bien bajo de X; **I don't — much of that cheese** no me gusta nada ese queso; **I told him what I thought of him** le dije la opinión que tenía de él; le dije un par de cosas; *see* **nothing (d)** *etc.*

(i) (*devote thought to, bear in mind, remember*) **to — of** pensar en; **I — of you always, I am always —ing of you** pienso constantemente en ti; **— of me tomorrow in the exam** ayúdame mañana en el examen con tus pensamientos; **one can't — of everything** es imposible atender a todo, es imposible preverlo todo; **I couldn't — of the right word** no pude recordar la palabra exacta; **what can you have been —ing of?** ¿qué demonios pensabas hacer?; ¿cómo se te ocurrió hacer (*etc*) eso?; **his style makes me — of Baroja** su estilo me hace pensar en Baroja, su estilo me recuerda el de Baroja; **that is worth —ing about** eso vale la pena de pensarlo un poco; **there is so much to — about** hay tantas cosas que tener en cuenta; **you've given us a lot to — about** nos ha dado Vd muchas cosas en que pensar; **— what you have done** recapacite lo que ha hecho.

(j) (*be sympathetic to, take into account*) considerar, tener en cuenta; **to — of other people's feelings** tener en cuenta los sentimientos de los demás; **one has to — of the expense** hay que considerar lo que se gasta; **he —s of nobody but himself** no piensa más que en sí mismo.

3 *n:* **I'll have a — about it** lo pensaré; **to have a good — about something** meditar algo, pensar mucho acerca de algo; **you'd better have another —** conviene volver a pensarlo, conviene reconsiderarlo; **I was having a quiet —** meditaba tranquilamente.

thinkable ['θiŋkəbl] *adj* concebible; **is it — that . . .?** ¿es concebible que + *subj*?, ¿se concibe que + *subj*?

thinker ['θiŋkə*] *n* pensador *m.*

thinking ['θiŋkiŋ] **1** *adj* pensante, que piensa; inteligente, racional; serio; **to any — person** para cualquier persona seria.

2 *n* pensamiento *m*; (*thoughts collectively*) pensamientos *mpl*; **wishful —** espejismo *m*, ilusionismo *m*; **his way of —** su modo de pensar; **to my way of —** a mi juicio, en mi opinión.

thin-lipped ['θin'lipt] *adj* de labios apretados.

thinly ['θinli] *adv:* **— disguised as . . .** ligeramente disfrazado de . . .; **with — spread butter** con una capa delgada de mantequilla.

thinness ['θinnis] *n* delgadez *f*; flaqueza *f*; tenuidad *f.*

thin-skinned ['θin'skind] *adj* de piel fina; (*fig*) sensible, demasiado sensible.

third [θə:d] **1** *adj* tercero.

2 *n* tercio *m*, tercera parte *f*; (Mus) tercera *f*; **two-thirds of the votes** dos tercios de los votos; **two-thirds of those present** las dos terceras partes de los asistentes.

3 *adv:* **to travel —** viajar en tercera clase.

third-class ['θə:d'kla:s] **1** *adj* de tercera clase; (*pej*) de tercera clase, de baja categoría. **2** *adv:* **to travel —** viajar en tercera.

thirdly ['θə:dli] *adv* en tercer lugar.

third-party ['θə:d'pɑːti] *attr:* **— insurance** seguro *m* contra tercera persona.

third-rate ['θə:d'reit] *adj* de baja categoría.

thirst [θə:st] **1** *n* sed *f*; **the — for** (*fig*) la sed de, el ansia de, el afán de; **to quench one's —** apagar la sed. **2** *vi:* **to — for** (*fig*) tener sed de.

thirsty ['θə:sti] *adj* sediento; *land* árido, que necesita regarse mucho; **to be —** tener sed; **how — I am!** ¡qué sed tengo!; **it's — work** es un trabajo que hace sudar.

thirteen ['θə:'ti:n] *adj* trece.

thirteenth ['θə:'ti:nθ] *adj* decimotercio, decimotercero.

thirtieth ['θə:tiiθ] *adj* trigésimo.

thirty ['θə:ti] *adj* treinta; **the thirties** (*eg* 1930s) los años treinta; **to be in one's thirties** tener más de treinta años.

this [ðis] (*pl* **these**) **1** *dem adj m:* este; *f:* esta; **— evening** esta tarde; **this coming week** esta semana que viene; **— day last year** hoy hace un año; **— day fortnight** hoy a quince días.

2 *dem pron m:* éste; *f:* ésta; "*neuter*": esto; **— is new** esto es nuevo; **like —** así, de este modo; **it was like —** le contaré la cosa como pasó; le diré lo que pasó; **what's all —?** ¿qué pasa?; **who's —?** ¿quién es?; **— is Joe** (*on telephone etc*) soy

Pepe; — **is Joe Soap** (*introduction*) quiero presentarle al señor Joe Soap; — **is Tuesday** hoy es martes; **but** — **is May** pero estamos en mayo.

3 *adv*: — **far** tan lejos; — **high** tan alto, así de alto (*and see* **that 4**).

thistle ['θisl] *n* cardo *m*.

thistledown ['θisldaun] *n* borrilla *f* de cardo.

thistly ['θisli] *adj* (*prickly*) espinoso; (*full of thistles*) lleno de cardos; **problem etc** espinoso, erizado de dificultades.

thither ['ðiðə*] *adv* (*arch*) allá.

thole [θəul] *n* escálamo *m*.

Thomas ['tɔməs] *m* Tomás; **Saint** — Santo Tomás; — **More** Tomás Moro.

Thomism ['tɔmizəm] *n* tomismo *m*.

Thomist 1 ['tɔmist] *adj* tomista. **2** *n* tomista *mf*.

thong [θɔŋ] *n* correa *f*.

thoracic [θɔː'ræsik] *adj* torácico.

thorax ['θɔːræks] *n* tórax *m*.

thorium ['θɔːriəm] *n* torio *m*.

thorn [θɔːn] *n* espina *f* (*also fig*); **to be a** — **in the flesh of someone** ser una espina en el costado de uno.

thorn bush ['θɔːnbuʃ] *n* espino *m*.

thornless ['θɔːnlis] *adj* sin espinas.

thorn tree ['θɔːntriː] *n* espino *m*.

thorny ['θɔːni] *adj* espinoso; (*fig*) espinoso, erizado de dificultades.

thorough ['θʌrə] *adj* (*complete*) completo, cabal; acabado; (*not superficial*) minucioso, concienzudo, meticuloso; **he's very** — es muy cuidadoso, es muy concienzudo; **to have a** — **knowledge of a region** conocer una región a fondo; **we made a** — **search** lo registramos minuciosamente; **there will be a** — **investigation into the charges** las acusaciones serán investigadas a fondo.

thoroughbred ['θʌrəbred] **1** *adj* de pura sangre. **2** *n* pura sangre *mf*.

thoroughfare ['θʌrəfɛə*] *n* vía *f* pública; carretera *f*, calle *f*; **"no** —**"** "prohibido el paso".

thoroughgoing ['θʌrəˌgəuiŋ] *adj* **person** cien por cien, totalista, de cuerpo entero; **examination etc** minucioso, a fondo.

thoroughly ['θʌrəli] *adv*: **to know something** — conocer algo a fondo; **to investigate something** — investigar algo a fondo; **he works** — trabaja cuidadosamente, trabaja concienzudamente; **a** — **bad influence** una influencia totalmente mala; **a** — **stupid thing to do** una acción completamente estúpida.

thoroughness ['θʌrənis] *n* minuciosidad *f*, meticulosidad *f*; perfección *f*; **with great** — con el mayor cuidado, con todo cuidado.

those [ðəuz] (*pl of* **that**) **1** *dem adj* m: esos, (*more remote*) aquellos; *f*: esas, (*more remote*) aquellas.

2 *dem pron* m: ésos, (*more remote*) aquéllos; *f*: ésas, (*more remote*) aquéllas; — **of** los de, las de; — **which** los que, las que; — **who** los que, las que, quienes; *see also* **that**.

thou [ðau] *pron* (*arch*) tú.

though [ðəu] **1** *conj* aunque; si bien; — **it was raining at the time** aunque llovía entonces; (**even**) — **he doesn't want to** aunque no quiera; **as** — como si + *subj*; — **small it's good** aunque es pequeño es bueno; **strange** — **it may appear** aunque parezca extraño, por extraño que parezca; **what** — **there is no money?** ¿qué importa que no hay dinero?

2 *adv* sin embargo; **it's not so easy,** — sin embargo no es tán fácil; **did he** —? ¿de veras?

thought [θɔːt] **1** *pret and ptp of* **think**.

2 *n* (**a**) pensamiento *m*; idea *f*, concepto *m*; reflexión *f*, meditación *f*; consideración *f*; (*thoughtfulness*) solicitud *f*; **the** — **of Sartre** el pensamiento de Sartre; **happy** — idea *f* luminosa; **that's a** —! eso hay que tenerlo en cuenta; **after much** —, **on second** —s después de pensarlo bien, después de mucho pensar; **my** —s **were elsewhere** pensaba en otra cosa; **his one** — **is to** + *infin* su único propósito es de + *infin*; **the very** — **frightens me** sólo pensar en ello me da miedo; **to collect one's** —s orientarse, concentrarse; **let me collect my** —s déjame pensar; **to give** — **to something** pensar algo, meditar algo; **consider algo detenidamente; we must give some** — **to the others** hay que tener en cuenta a los demás, conviene tener presentes a los demás; **I didn't give it another** — no volví a pensar en ello; **I had no** — **of offending you** no tenía la intención de ofenderle; **then I had second** —s luego tuve otra idea, mudé luego de parecer; **to be lost in** — estar absorto en meditación; **perish the** —! ¡ni por pensamiento!; **to read somebody's** —s adivinar el pensamiento de uno; **to**

take — **how to do something** pensar cómo hacer algo; **to take no** — **for the morrow** no pensar en mañana.

(**b**) (*fig*) pizca *f*, poquito *m*; **it's a** — **too bright** es un poquito claro.

thoughtful ['θɔːtful] *adj* (*pensive*) pensativo, meditabundo; (*in character*) serio; (*kind*) atento, solícito, considerado; (*far-sighted*) clarividente, previsor; **how** — **of you!**, **that's very** — **of you!** ¡qué detalle!, ¡es Vd muy amable!; **he's a** — **boy** es un chico serio.

thoughtfully ['θɔːtfəli] *adv* pensativamente; seriamente; atentamente, solícitamente, con consideración; con clarividencia, con previsión; **"Yes", he said** — "Sí", dijo pensativo; **someone had** — **provided a cup** alguien había puesto amablemente una taza.

thoughtfulness ['θɔːtfulnis] *n* seriedad *f*; carácter *m* reflexivo; atención *f*, solicitud *f*, consideración *f*; clarividencia *f*, previsión *f*.

thoughtless ['θɔːtlis] *adj* act irreflexivo, descuidado; **person** inconsiderado, desconsiderado, inconsciente.

thoughtlessly ['θɔːtlisli] *adv* sin pensar, irreflexivamente; inconscientemente; **to act** — obrar con poca consideración, obrar sin pensar.

thoughtlessness ['θɔːtlisnis] *n* irreflexión *f*, descuido *m*; inconsideración *f*, inconsciencia *f*.

thought reading ['θɔːtˌriːdiŋ] *n* adivinación *f* de pensamientos.

thousand ['θauzənd] **1** *adj* mil; **a** —, **one** — mil; **4** — **specimens** cuatro mil ejemplares.

2 *n* mil *m*; (*more loosely*) millar *m*; **they sell them by the** — los venden a millares; **they were there in** —**s** los había a millares.

thousandfold ['θauzəndfəuld] **1** *adj* multiplicado por mil; de mil veces. **2** *adv* mil veces.

thousandth ['θauzəntθ] **1** *adj* milésimo. **2** milésimo *m*.

thraldom ['θrɔːldəm] *n* esclavitud *f*.

thrall [θrɔːl] *n* (*person*) esclavo *m*, a *f*; (*state*) esclavitud *f*; **to be in** — ser esclavo de; **to hold someone in** — retener a uno en la esclavitud.

thrash [θræʃ] **1** *vt* golpear; **person** apalear, (*as punishment*) azotar, zurrar; (*Sport etc*) derrotar, cascar; **to** — **out** resolver mediante larga discusión, discutir largamente.

2 *vi*: **to** — **about** sacudirse, dar vueltas; revolcarse; debatirse; **he** —**ed about with his stick** daba golpes por todos lados con su bastón; **they were** —**ing about in the water** se estaban debatiendo en el agua; *see also* **thresh**.

thrashing ['θræʃiŋ] *n* zurra *f*, paliza *f*; **to give someone a** — zurrar a uno; **to give a team a** — dar una paliza a un equipo.

thread [θred] **1** *n* (*Sew etc*) hilo *m*; (*fibre*) hebra *f*, fibra *f*; (*of silkworm, spider etc*) hebra *f*; (*of screw*) filete *m*, rosca *f*; **to hang by a** — pender de un hilo; **to lose the** — (*of what one is saying*) perder el hilo (de su discurso); **to pick** (*or* **take**) **up the** — **again** coger el hilo, reanudar lo que uno estaba diciendo (*or* haciendo *etc*).

2 *vt* needle enhebrar; **beads etc** ensartar; **to** — **one's way through** colarse a través de, abrirse paso por, lograr pasar por.

threadbare ['θredbɛə*] *adj* raído, gastado; **tyre** poco cubierto; **excuse etc** flojo, poco convincente.

threat [θret] *n* amenaza *f*; **it is a grave** — **to . . .** constituye una grave amenaza para . . .

threaten ['θretn] *vt* amenazar; proferir amenazas contra; **to** — **violence** amenazar violencia, amenazar con ponerse violento; **to** — **someone with something** amenazar a uno con algo; **a species** — **ed with extinction** una especie amenazada de extinción; **to** — **to** + *infin* amenazar con + *infin*; **to** — **to kill someone** amenazar con matar a uno; **it is** —**ing to rain** amenaza llover.

threatening ['θretniŋ] *adj* amenazador, amenazante.

threateningly ['θretniŋli] *adv* de modo amenazador; **say etc** en tono amenazador.

three [θriː] **1** *adj* tres. **2** *n* tres *m*.

three-act ['θriːˌækt] *adj* play de tres actos, en tres actos.

three-colour(ed), (*US*) **-color(ed)** ['θriːˈkʌləd] *adj* attr de tres colores.

three-cornered ['θriːˈkɔːnəd] *adj* triangular; — **hat** tricornio *m*, sombrero *m* de tres picos.

three-decker ['θriːˈdekə*] *n* (*also* — **novel**) novelón *m*, novela *f* larga.

three-dimensional ['θriːdiˈmenʃənl] *adj* tridimensional.

threefold ['θriːfəuld] **1** *adj* triple. **2** *adv* tres veces.

three-legged ['θriːˈlegid] *adj* de tres piernas; **stool** de tres patas.

three-masted ['θriːˈmɑːstid] *adj* de tres palos.
threepence ['θrepəns] *n* 3 peniques *mpl*.
threepenny ['θrepəni] *adj* de 3 peniques; (*fig*) de poca monta, despreciable; — **bit,** — **piece** moneda *f* de 3 peniques.
three-phase ['θriːfeiz] *adj* (*Elec*) trifásico.
three-piece ['θriːpiːs] *adj*: — **suite** tresillo *m*.
three-ply ['θriːplai] *adj* *wood* de tres capas; *wool* triple.
three-quarter [ˌθriːˈkwɔːtə*] *adj*: — **length sleeves** mangas *fpl* tres cuartos.
threescore ['θriːskɔː*] *n* sesenta; — **years and ten** setenta años.
three-sided ['θriːˈsaidid] *adj* trilátero.
threesome ['θriːsəm] *n* grupo *m* de tres, conjunto *m* de tres.
three-wheeler ['θriːˈwiːlə*] *n* (*Aut*) coche-cabina *m* triciclo.
threnody ['θrenədi] *n* lamento *m*; canto *m* fúnebre.
thresh [θreʃ] *vt* (*Agr*) trillar; *see also* **thrash.**
thresher ['θreʃə*] *n* trilladora *f*.
threshing ['θreʃiŋ] *n* trilla *f*.
threshing floor ['θreʃiŋflɔː*] *n* era *f*.
threshing machine ['θreʃiŋməˌʃiːn] *n* trilladora *f*.
threshold ['θreʃhəʊld] *n* umbral *m*; **to be on the** — **of** (*fig*) estar en los umbrales de, estar en la antesala de, estar al borde de; **to cross someone's** — traspasar el umbral de uno.
threw [θruː] *pret of* **throw.**
thrice [θrais] *adv* (*arch*) tres veces.
thrift [θrift] *n*, **thriftiness** ['θriftinis] *n* economía *f*, frugalidad *f*.
thriftless ['θriftlis] *adj* malgastador, pródigo.
thriftlessness ['θriftlisnis] *n* prodigalidad *f*.
thrifty ['θrifti] *adj* económico, frugal, ahorrativo.
thrill [θril] **1** *n* emoción *f*; sensación *f*; estremecimiento *m*; **with a** — **of excitement, he . . .** estremecido de emoción, él . . .; **what a** —! ¡qué emoción!; **it's the** — **of the year** es la sensación del año; **he just does it for the** — lo hace simplemente porque ello le emociona; **to get a** — **out of something** emocionarse con algo; **it gives me a** — me emociona; me hace mucha ilusión.
2 *vt* emocionar, conmover, estremecer; hacer ilusión a; **the film** —**ed me** la película me emocionó; **I was** —**ed to get your letter** tu carta me hizo mucha ilusión; **we were** —**ed with** (*or* **about, at**) **your news** tu noticia nos emocionó muchísimo.
3 *vi* emocionarse, conmoverse, estremecerse; **to** — **to someone's touch** estremecerse al ser tocado por uno.
thriller ['θrilə*] *n* novela *f* (*or* obra *f*, película *f*) escalofriante, novela *f* de suspense, novela *f* de misterio.
thrilling ['θriliŋ] *adj* emocionante, conmovedor; apasionante; sensacional; **an absolutely** — **journey** un viaje de lo más interesante; **a** — **play** una obra muy emocionante; **how** —! ¡qué emoción!; **how** — **for you!** ¡qué bien!
thrillingly ['θriliŋli] *adv* de modo emocionante; de modo sensacional.
thrive [θraiv] (*irr*: *pret* **throve,** *ptp* **thriven**) *vi* (*do well*) prosperar, medrar; florecer; (*grow*) crecer mucho, desarrollarse bien; **he** —**s on hard work** le gusta estar muy ocupado, se encuentra perfectamente bien con un trabajo agotador; **the plant** —**s here** la planta crece muy bien aquí; **children** — **on milk** a los niños les aprovecha la leche.
thriven ['θrivn] *ptp of* **thrive.**
thriving ['θraiviŋ] *adj* próspero, floreciente.
throat [θrəʊt] *n* garganta *f*; (*from exterior*) cuello *m*; **to clear one's** — carraspear, aclarar la voz; **to cut one's** — cortarse la garganta; **to have a sore** — tener anginas; **to moisten one's** — remojar el gaznate; **to thrust something down someone's** — (*fig*) hacer que uno trague algo a la fuerza, imponer algo a uno.
throaty ['θrəʊti] *adj* gutural; ronco.
throb [θrɒb] **1** *n* (*of heart etc*) latido *m*, pulsación *f*; palpitación *f*; (*of engine*) vibración *f*; (*of emotion*) estremecimiento *m*.
2 *vi* latir; palpitar; vibrar; estremecerse; **the crowd** —**bed with excitement** la multitud se estremeció emocionada.
throbbing ['θrɒbiŋ] **1** *adj* palpitante; vibrante; *pain* pungente; *rhythm* marcado, fuerte.
2 *n* latido *m*, pulsación *f*; palpitación *f*; vibración *f*; estremecimiento *m*.
throes [θrəʊz] *npl* (*of death*) agonía *f*; (*of childbirth etc*) dolores *mpl*; (*fig*) angustia *f*, agonía *f*; **to be in the** — **of** estar en medio de; estar sufriendo todas las molestias de.

thrombosis [θrɒmˈbəʊsis] *n* trombosis *f*.
throne [θrəʊn] *n* trono *m*; (*fig freq*) corona *f*, poder *m* real; **to ascend the** —, **to come to the** — subir al trono.
throne room ['θrəʊnrum] *n* sala *f* del trono.
throng [θrɒŋ] **1** *n* multitud *f*, tropel *m*, muchedumbre *f*; **great** —**s of tourists** multitudes *fpl* de turistas; **to come in a** — venir en tropel.
2 *vt* atestar, llenar de bote en bote.
3 *vi*: **to come** —**ing** venir en tropel, venir en masa; **to** — **round someone** apiñarse en torno a uno; **to** — **to hear someone** venir en tropel a escuchar a uno; **to** — **together** reunirse en tropel.
thronged [θrɒŋd] *adj* atestado, lleno de bote en bote; **the streets are** — **with tourists** las calles están llenas de turistas; **everywhere is** — **with** todo está lleno, no queda espacio libre en ninguna parte.
thronging ['θrɒŋiŋ] *adj* *crowd etc* grande, apretado, nutrido.
throttle ['θrɒtl] **1** *n* (*Anat*) gaznate *m*; (*Mech*) regulador *m*, válvula *f* reguladora, estrangulador *m*; (*Aut, loosely*) acelerador *m*; **to give an engine full** — acelerar un motor al máximo.
2 *vt* ahogar, estrangular; (*Mech*) estrangular.
3 *vi*: **to** — **back,** **to** — **down** moderar la marcha.
through [θruː] **1** *adv* (**a**) (*of place*) de parte a parte, completamente; **the nail went right** — el clavo penetró de parte a parte; **the wood has rotted** — la madera se ha podrido completamente.
(**b**) (*of time, process*) desde el principio hasta el fin; hasta el fin; **did you stay right** —? ¿te quedaste hasta el final?; **we're staying** — **till Tuesday** nos quedamos hasta el martes; **to sleep the whole night** — dormir la noche entera; **he knew it right** — lo sabía todo, lo sabía de corrido.
(**c**) (*with to be*) **you're** —! (*Tel*) ¡puede hablar!, ¡hable!; **are you** —? ¿has terminado?; **we'll be** — **at 7** terminaremos a las 7; **when I'm** — **with him** cuando haya terminado con él; **I'm not** — **with you yet** todavía no he terminado de decir (*etc*) lo que tenía pensado; **I'm** — **with bridge** renuncio al bridge, ya no vuelvo a jugar al bridge; **I'm** — **with her** he roto con ella.
(**d**) **a Catalan** — **and** — catalán hasta los tuétanos, catalán por los cuatro costados; *see* **carry, fall** *etc*.
2 *prep* (**a**) (*of place*) por; a través de; de un lado a otro de; **to look** — **a telescope** mirar por un telescopio; **to walk** — **the woods** dar un paseo por el bosque; **the bullet went** — **3 layers** la bala penetró 3 capas; **it went right** — **the wall** atravesó la pared y salió al otro lado.
(**b**) (*of time*) (*US*) hasta, hasta e incluso; (**from**) **Monday** — **Friday** desde el lunes hasta el viernes, de lunes a viernes; **all** — **our stay** durante toda nuestra estancia; **right** — **the year** durante el año entero.
(**c**) **he's** — **the exam** ha aprobado el examen.
(**d**) (*of means*) mediante, por medio de; por, por causa de; debido a; gracias a; — **him I found out that . . .** por él supe que . . .; — **not knowing the way** por no saber el camino; **he got it** — **friends** lo consiguió gracias a los amigos; **it was** — **you that we were late** fue por vosotros por lo que llegamos tarde; **to act** — **fear** obrar movido por el miedo.
3 *adj* *carriage, traffic, train* directo.
throughout [θruːˈaʊt] **1** *adv* (**a**) (*of place*) en todas partes, por todas partes; **the hull is welded** — el casco esta totalmente soldado; **the room has been cleaned** — el cuarto ha sido limpiado completamente; **the house has electric light** — la casa tiene luz eléctrica en todos los cuartos.
(**b**) (*of time, process*) todo el tiempo, desde el principio hasta el fin; **the weather was good** — hizo buen tiempo todos los días; **it's a boring journey** — es un viaje pesado en todo el recorrido, todo el viaje es monótono.
2 *prep* (**a**) (*of place*) por todo, por todas partes de; — **the country** por todo el país, en todo el país.
(**b**) (*of time, process*) durante todo, en todo.
throughput ['θruːput] *n* cantidad *f* invertida, cantidad *f* de materias primas.
throve [θrəʊv] *pret of* **thrive.**
throw [θrəʊ] **1** *n* echada *f*, tirada *f*, tiro *m*; (*move, at games*) jugada *f*; (*in wrestling*) derribo *m*; (*at dice*) lance *m*; **within a stone's** — a tiro de piedra.
2 (*irr*: *pret* **threw,** *ptp* **thrown**) *vt* (**a**) (*general sense*) echar, tirar, lanzar, arrojar; *dice* echar; *glance* lanzar, dirigir; *kiss* echar, tirar; **to** — **a coat over someone** cubrir a uno con un abrigo, envolver a uno en un abrigo; **to** — **a ball 200 metres** lanzar

una pelota 200 metros; **to — a bridge over a river** tender (or construir) un puente sobre un río; **to — a door open** abrir una puerta de golpe, abrir una puerta de par en par; **to — two rooms into one** hacer un solo cuarto de dos que había; **to — the blame on someone** echar la culpa a uno; **to — temptation in someone's path** exponer a uno a la tentación; **to be —n on one's own resources** tener que depender de sí mismo, no tener más que los propios recursos.

(b) light, shadow, slides etc proyectar; **to — light on** (fig) aclarar, arrojar luz sobre.

(c) rider desmontar, desarzonar; opponent derribar; skin mudar, quitarse; **to be —n** (of rider) ser desarzonado.

(d) (disconcert) confundir, desconcertar, dejar perplejo; **this answer seemed to — him** esta respuesta parecía desconcertarle.

(e) (Tech) pot formar, dar forma a, hacer; silk torcer.

(f) (fam phrases) **to — a fight** perder deliberadamente un encuentro; **to — a fit** (Med) sufrir un ataque (epiléptico); sufrir una crisis nerviosa; desmayarse; (fig) subirse por las paredes (fam); **to — a party** ofrecer una fiesta, organizar una fiesta (for someone en honor de uno).

(g) (with adv or prep) **to — about** tirar por aquí y por allá, esparcir; **to — money about** derrochar dinero; **to — aside** tirar a un lado; apartar, desechar; **to — away** tirar, echar; desechar; money malgastar; derrochar; one's life sacrificar inútilmente; chance desperdiciar; **it's old and can be —n away** es viejo y se puede tirar; **to — back** ball devolver; enemy rechazar, arrollar; hair, head echar hacia atrás; offer rechazar (con desprecio); **to — down** ball etc echar a tierra; lanzar hacia abajo; building, defences derribar, echar abajo; arms, tools dejar, abandonar; challenge lanzar; glove (fig) arrojar; **it's —ing it down** (of rain) está lloviendo a cántaros; **to — in** ball (Sport) sacar; remark hacer, insertar, lanzar (de improviso); cards arrojar sobre la mesa (en señal de abandono); (as addition) añadir; dar de más; ofrecer de más; **with an extra meal —n in** con una comida de más, con una comida gratis; **to — off** burden, yoke sacudirse, deshacerse de, quitarse de encima; clothes quitarse (de prisa); disguise abandonar; habit renunciar a; idea, suggestion ofrecer (de improviso); composition hacer rápidamente; improvisar; (emit) emitir, despedir; arrojar; **to — the dogs off the scent** despistar los perros; **in order to — the police off the trail** para despistar a la policía; **to — on** clothes ponerse (de prisa); **to — out** rubbish tirar; defective articles desechar, tirar; person expulsar, echar; poner de patitas en la calle; (Parl) bill rechazar; (emit) emitir, despedir, arrojar; hint proferir; idea, suggestion hacer (de improviso); **to — out one's chest** sacar el pecho, abultar el pecho; **it has —n many men out of work** ha privado de trabajo a muchos hombres; **to — over** (abandon) dejar, abandonar; friend romper con, sweetheart dar calabazas a; **to — together** reunir de prisa; **they where —n together by chance** se conocieron por casualidad; **to — up** (cast upwards) lanzar al aire; lanzar hacia arriba; work, project abandonar; claim, post renunciar a; defences levantar rápidamente, construir de prisa; (vomit) devolver, vomitar; see sponge etc.

3 vi: **to — up** vomitar; **it makes me — up** me da asco, me repugna.

4 vr: **to — oneself about** agitar mucho el cuerpo; **to — oneself at someone's feet** echarse a los pies de uno; **to — oneself at someone** (or at someone's head) proponerse conquistar a uno (como novio); **to — oneself backwards** echarse hacia atrás; **to — oneself down from a building** arrojarse desde un edificio; **to — oneself into the fray** lanzarse a la batalla; **to — oneself on someone** lanzarse sobre uno, precipitarse sobre uno; **to — oneself to the ground** tirarse al suelo; see mercy etc.

throwaway ['θrəuəwei] adj: **— wrapping** envase m desechable, envase m a tirar.

throwback ['θrəubæk] n (Bio) reversión f (to a).

thrower ['θrəuə*] n lanzador m, ora f.

throw-in ['θrəuin] n (Sport) saque m (de banda).

thrown ['θrəun] ptp of **throw**.

throw-out ['θrəuaut] n cosa f desechada, cosa f inútil.

thru [θru:] (US) see **through**.

thrum [θrʌm] **1** vt piano teclear en; guitar rasguear, rasguear las cuerdas de. **2** vi teclear; rasguear las cuerdas.

thrush[1] [θrʌʃ] n (Orn) zorzal m.

thrush[2] [θrʌʃ] n (Med) ubrera f; (Vet) higo m.

thrust [θrʌst] **1** n (push) empuje m (also Mech etc); (Mil) avance m, ataque m; (of sword) estocada f; (of dagger) puñalada f; (of knife) cuchillada f; (thrustfulness) empuje m; **a shrewd —** un golpe certero, un golpe bien dado; **that was a — at you** eso lo dijo por ti, esa observación iba dirigida contra ti.

2 (irr: pret and ptp **thrust**) vt (push) empujar; (drive) impeler, impulsar; (insert) introducir, meter (into en); (insert piercingly) clavar, hincar (into en); **to — a dagger into someone's back** clavar un puñal en la espalda de uno; **to — a stick into the ground** hincar un palo en el suelo; **to — one's hands into one's pockets** meter las manos en los bolsillos; **to — someone through with a sword** atravesar a uno (de parte a parte) con una espada; **with an arrow — through his hat** con una flecha que le atravesaba el sombrero; **to — one's way to the front** abrirse paso (empujando) hasta la parte delantera; **to — aside** person apartar bruscamente, plan rechazar; **to — back** crowd hacer retroceder, enemy arrollar, rechazar, thought rechazar; **to — forward** empujar hacia adelante; **to — something on someone** imponer algo a uno; obligar a uno a aceptar algo; **Spain had greatness — upon her** España recibió su grandeza sin buscarla, se le impuso la grandeza a España sin quererlo ella; **to — out** sacar, sacar fuera; hand tender, (Aut etc) sacar; tongue sacar; head asomar; **to — someone out of a door** expulsar a uno por una puerta.

3 vi: **to — at someone** asestar un golpe a uno; **to — forward** seguir adelante, proseguir su marcha (etc), (Mil) avanzar; **to — past someone** cruzar (empujando) delante de uno; **to — through** abrirse paso por la fuerza.

4 vr: **to — oneself forward** (fig) ponerse delante de otros, darse importancia; ofrecerse para hacer algo (con poca modestia); **to — oneself in** introducirse a la fuerza; (fig) entrometerse.

thrustful ['θrʌstful] adj, **thrusting** ['θrʌstiŋ] adj emprendedor, vigoroso, enérgico; ambicioso; (pej) agresivo.

thrustfulness ['θrʌstfulnis] n empuje m, pujanza f, espíritu m emprendedor; ambición f; (pej) espíritu m agresivo.

thruway ['θru:wei] n (US) supercarretera f directa.

thud [θʌd] **1** n ruido m sordo, golpe m sordo.

2 vi hacer un ruido sordo, caer (etc) con un ruido sordo; **to — across the floor** andar con pasos pesados; **he was —ding about upstairs all night** pasó la noche andando con pasos pesados por el piso de arriba; **a shell —ded into the hillside** una granada estalló con ruido sordo en la ladera del monte.

thug [θʌg] n asesino m, ladrón m, criminal m (brutal); (fig, as term of abuse etc) bruto m, bestia f, desalmado m.

thumb [θʌm] **1** n pulgar m; **I'm all —s today** hoy no hago nada bien, hoy estoy terriblemente desmañado; **to be under someone's —** estar dominado por uno; **to twiddle one's —s** voltear los pulgares, (fig) no tener nada que hacer.

2 vt **(a)** manosear; **to — through a book** hojear un libro; **a well —ed book** un libro muy manoseado.

(b) to — a lift, to — a ride hacer autostop; **to — a lift to London** viajar gratis en coche (etc) ajeno a Londres.

thumb index ['θʌm'indeks] n índice m recortado.

thumbnail ['θʌmneil] n uña f del pulgar; **— sketch** dibujo m en miniatura.

thumbprint ['θʌmprint] n impresión f del pulgar.

thumbscrew ['θʌmskru:] n empulgueras fpl.

thumbtack ['θʌmtæk] n (US) chinche f.

thump [θʌmp] **1** n (blow) golpazo m, porrazo m; (noise of fall etc) ruido m sordo; **it came down with a —** cayó con un ruido sordo.

2 vt golpear, aporrear; **to — the table** golpear la mesa, dar golpes en la mesa; **to — out a tune on the piano** tocar una melodía al piano golpeando las teclas.

3 vi (of heart) latir con golpes pesados; (of machine) funcionar con ruido sordo, vibrar con violencia; **it came —ing down** cayó con un ruido sordo; **he —ed across the floor** anduvo con pasos pesados.

thumping ['θʌmpiŋ] adj (fam) enorme, enorme de grande; **a — great book** un enorme libro, un librote (fam).

thunder ['θʌndə*] **1** n trueno m; (loud report) tronido m; (of passing vehicle etc) rodar m pesado, estruendo m; (of applause) estruendo m; (of hooves) estampido m; **there is — about, there is — in the air** amenaza tronar; **to steal someone's —** adelantarse a uno robándole una idea (or un chiste, una observación etc).

2 vt: **to — threats against someone** fulminar amenazas contra uno; **to — out an order** dar una orden en tono muy fuerte; **"yes", he —ed "sí",** rugió.

3 vi tronar; **the guns —ed in the distance** los cañones retumbaban a lo lejos; **the train —ed past** el tren pasó con gran estruendo.

thunderbolt ['θʌndəbəult] n rayo m (also fig).

thunderclap ['θʌndəklæp] n tronido m.

thundercloud ['θʌndəklaud] n nubarrón m.

thunderer ['θʌndərə*] n: **the T—** el Fulminador; (Jupiter) Júpiter tonante.

thunderflash ['θʌndəflæʃ] n petardo m.

thundering ['θʌndəriŋ] adj (fam) enorme, imponente; **a — great row** un ruido de todos los demonios; **it's a — nuisance** es una tremenda lata (fam); **it was a — success** obtuvo un tremendo éxito.

thunderous ['θʌndərəs] adj applause etc atronador, ensordecedor.

thunderstorm ['θʌndəstɔ:m] n tronada f, tempestad f de truenos.

thunderstruck ['θʌndəstrʌk] adj (fig) pasmado, estupefacto.

thundery ['θʌndəri] adj weather tormentoso, bochornoso.

Thursday ['θə:zdi] n jueves m; **Holy T—** Jueves m Santo.

thus [ðʌs] adv así; de este modo; **— far** hasta aquí; **— it is that** . . . así es que . . .; **—, when he got home** . . . así que, cuando llegó a casa . . .

thwack [θwæk] see **whack**.

thwart [θwɔ:t] **1** n (Naut) bancada f. **2** vt frustrar; impedir, estorbar; plan etc frustrar, desbaratar; **to be —ed at every turn** verse frustrado en todo.

thy [ðai] poss adj (arch) tu(s).

thyme [taim] n tomillo m.

thyroid ['θairɔid] **1** adj tiroideo. **2** n (also **— gland**) tiroides m.

thyself [ðai'self] pron (arch) (subject) tú mismo, tú misma; (acc, dat) te; (after prep) ti (mismo, misma).

tiara [ti'ɑ:rə] n diadema f.

Tiber ['taibə*] Tíber m.

Tiberius [tai'biəriəs] m Tiberio.

Tibet [ti'bet] el Tíbet.

Tibetan [ti'betən] **1** adj tibetano. **2** n tibetano m, a f. **3** n (language) tibetano m.

tibia ['tibiə] n tibia f.

tic [tik] n (Med) tic m.

tick[1] [tik] **1** n (a) (of clock) tictac m.

(b) (moment) momento m, instante m; **at 6 o'clock on the —** a las 6 en punto; **to arrive at** (or on) **the —** llegar puntualmente; **half a —!,** **just a —!** ¡un momentito!; **I shan't be a —** tardo dos minutos nada más, termino en seguida; **he won't take two —s to do it** lo hará en menos de nada.

(c) (mark) señal f, marca f (de aprobación); palomita f; **to put a — against someone's name** poner una señal contra el nombre de uno.

2 vt (also **to — off**) poner una señal contra; **to — someone off** poner a uno como un trapo (fam), echar un rapapolvo a uno (fam).

3 vi hacer tictac; **to — over** (Aut, Mech) marchar en vacío.

tick[2] [tik] n (Zool) garrapata f.

tick[3] [tik] n (cover) funda f.

tick[4] [tik] n (fam): **to buy something on —** comprar algo de fiado; **to live on —** vivir de compras hechas de fiado.

ticker ['tikə*] n (fam) (watch) reloj m; (heart) corazón m.

ticker-tape ['tikəteip] n cinta f de cotizaciones.

ticket ['tikit] **1** n (bus —, Rail etc) billete m; boleto m (SAm); (Cine, Theat) entrada f; localidad f; (label) etiqueta f, rótulo m; (counterfoil) talón m; (Aut: fam) multa f (por infracción del código etc); (US Pol) lista f de candidatos, candidatura f; programa m político; **complimentary —** entrada f de favor; **return —, round-trip —** (US) billete m de ida y vuelta; **runabout —** billete m kilométrico; **single —** billete m sencillo; **that's the —!** ¡muy bien!, ¡eso es!; ¡así me gustas!; see **season —**.

2 vt rotular, poner etiqueta a.

ticket agency ['tikit,eidʒənsi] n (Rail etc) agencia f de viajes; (Theat) agencia f de teatros.

ticket collector ['tikitkə,lektə*] n, **ticket inspector** ['tikitin,spektə*] n revisor m.

ticket holder ['tikit,həuldə*] n tenedor m de billete; (season —) abonado m, a f.

ticket office ['tikit,ɔfis] n (Rail) despacho m de billetes; (Theat etc) taquilla f.

ticket-of-leave ['tikitəv'li:v] n cédula f de libertad condicional; **— man** hombre m bajo libertad condicional.

ticket window ['tikit,windəu] n (Rail) despacho m de billetes; (Theat etc) taquilla f.

ticking ['tikiŋ] n cutí m, terliz m.

ticking-off ['tikiŋ'ɔf] n bronca f; **to give someone a —** echar una bronca a uno.

tickle ['tikl] **1** n: **to have a — behind one's ear** sentir cosquillas detrás de la oreja; **to have a — in one's throat** tener picor de garganta, tener anginas; **he never got a — all day** (Fishing) no picó pez alguno en todo el día; **at £5 he never got a —** a 5 libras nadie le echó un tiento.

2 vt (a) cosquillear, hacer cosquillas a.

(b) (amuse) divertir; hacer gracia a; **it —d us no end** nos divirtió mucho, nos hizo mucha gracia; **we were —d to death about it, we were —d pink about it** nos moríamos de risa con eso; see **fancy**.

3 vi: **my ear —s** siento cosquillas en la oreja, siento hormiguillo en la oreja; **don't, it —s!** ¡por Dios, que me hace cosquillas!

tickling ['tikliŋ] n cosquillas fpl.

ticklish ['tikliʃ] adj (a) cosquilloso; **to be —** tener cosquillas, ser cosquilloso.

(b) (problem etc) peliagudo, espinoso; delicado; **it's a — business** es un asunto delicado.

tick tock ['tik'tɔk] n tictac m.

tidal ['taidl] adj de marea; **— wave** maremoto m, ola f de marea; (fig) ola f gigantesca; **— basin** dique m de marea; **the river is — up to here** la marea sube hasta aquí; **the Mediterranean is not —** en el Mediterráneo no hay mareas.

tidbit ['tidbit] (US) see **titbit**.

tiddler ['tidlə*] n (fam) espinoso m; pececillo m.

tiddly ['tidli] adj (fam) achispado (fam).

tiddlywinks ['tidliwiŋks] n juego m de la pulga.

tide [taid] **1** n marea f; (fig) corriente m; marcha f, progreso m; tendencia f; **high —** pleamar f, (fig) cumbre f, apogeo m; **low —** bajamar f, (fig) punto m más bajo; **slack —** repunte m de la marea; **the — of battle turned** cambió la suerte de la batalla; **the — of events** la marcha de los sucesos; **to go against the —** ir contra la corriente; **to go with the —** seguir la corriente.

2 vt: **to — someone over** ayudar a uno a salvar el bache, ayudar a uno a salir de un apuro.

tideland ['taidlænd] n terreno m inundado por la marea.

tideless ['taidlis] adj sin mareas.

tidemark ['taidmɑ:k] n lengua f del agua.

tiderace ['taidreis] n aguaje m, marejada f.

tidewater ['taid,wɔ:tə*] n agua f de marea.

tideway ['taidwei] n canal m de marea.

tidily ['taidili] adv bien, en orden; aseadamente, pulcramente; metódicamente; **to be — dressed** ir bien vestido; **to arrange things —** poner las cosas en orden.

tidiness ['taidinis] n buen orden m; limpieza f; aseo m, pulcritud f; carácter m metódico.

tidings ['taidiŋz] npl noticias fpl.

tidy ['taidi] **1** adj (a) objects etc en orden, ordenado; room, desk limpio; bien arreglado; appearance, dress aseado, pulcro; person metódico; **to get a — room** limpiar un cuarto, arreglar un cuarto; **he has a — mind** tiene una mentalidad lógica, tiene una inteligencia metódica.

(b) (fam) pace bastante rápido; sum considerable; **it cost a — bit** costó bastante; **he's a pretty — player** es un jugador bastante estimable.

2 vt (also **— up**) arreglar, poner en orden, limpiar; **to — one's hair** arreglarse el pelo; **to — books away** devolver los libros a su lugar; **to — the dishes away** quitar los platos.

3 vi: **to — up** arreglar las cosas, ponerlo todo en orden.

4 vr: **to — oneself up** asearse, arreglarse.

tie [tai] **1** n (a) (bond) lazo m, vínculo m; **the —s of friendship** los lazos de la amistad; **the —s of blood** los lazos del parentesco.

(b) (hindrance) estorbo m; **the children are a — in the evenings** los pequeños son un estorbo para poder salir por las tardes; **he has no —s here** no tiene nada que le retenga aquí, no tiene nada que le impida irse de aquí.

(c) (cord etc) atadura f, ligazón f; (neck—) corbata f; (Archit) tirante m; (US Rail) traviesa f; (Mus) ligado m; **black —** corbata f de lazo,

corbata *f* de smoking; **white —** corbatín *m* blanco.
  (**d**) (*Sport: match*) encuentro *m*, partido *m*.
  (**e**) (*draw*) empate *m*; **it ended in a — at 3-all** terminó en empate a 3; **there was a — in the voting** en la votación resultó un empate.
  2 *vt* (**a**) atar, liar; enlazar, unir; (*Mus*) ligar; *bow, knot, necktie* hacer; (*fig, with bond*) liar, ligar, vincular; **to — two things together** atar dos cosas; **to — a dog to a post** atar un perro a un poste; **to — someone's hands** atar las manos a uno (*also fig*); **his hands are —d** tiene las manos atadas (*also fig*); **to be —d hand and foot** (*fig*) verse atado de pies y manos.
  (**b**) (*hinder*) estorbar; (*limit*) limitar, restringir (*to* a); **we are very —d in the evenings** por las tardes nos vemos estorbados para salir; **are we —d to this plan?** ¿estamos restringidos a este plan?; **the house is —d to her husband's job** la casa está ligada al puesto que tiene su marido, la casa pertenece a la compañía en que trabaja su marido.
  (**c**) (*with adv or prep*) **to — down** atar; sujetar; afianzar (con cuerdas *etc*); inmovilizar; **to — someone down to a task** obligar a uno a hacer una tarea (sin pensar en otra cosa); **to — someone down to a contract** obligar a uno a cumplir (*or* respetar) un contrato; **we can't — him down to a date** no podemos conseguir que fije una fecha; **we're —d down for months to come** no podemos aceptar otro compromiso hasta que hayan pasado muchos meses; **I refuse to — down** me niego a aceptar compromisos molestos; **to — a label on** atar una etiqueta, pegar una etiqueta; **to — up** atar; envolver; (*Naut*) atracar (*to* a); *traffic etc* obstruir, bloquear; *deal, business* concluir, despachar, arreglar; *capital* invertir (sin poder retirarlo); **he's —d up with the manager at the moment** ahora está conferenciando con el gerente, de momento está ocupado en un asunto con el gerente; **he's —d up with a girl in Lima** tiene un lío con una chica en Lima; **the fog —d up all shipping** la niebla inmovilizó toda la navegación; **he has a fortune —d up in property** tiene una fortuna invertida en bienes raíces.
  3 *vi* (**a**) **to — up** (*Naut*) atracar; **to — up to a post** atracar a un poste; **to — up at a wharf** atracar en un muelle.
  (**b**) (*draw*) empatar; **we —d with them 4-all** empatamos con ellos a 4.
tie-in ['taiin] *n* (*fig*) unión *f*; relación *f* estrecha (*between entre*).
tieless ['tailis] *adj* sin corbata.
tiepin ['taipin] *n* alfiler *m* de corbata.
tier [tiə*] *n* grada *f*, fila *f*; piso *m*; nivel *m*; **to arrange in —s** disponer en gradas.
tiered ['tiəd] *adj* con gradas, en una serie de gradas; **steeply —** con gradas en pendiente; **a three-tiered cake** un pastel de tres pisos.
tie-up ['taiʌp] *n* (*link*) enlace *m*; (*by strike etc*) paralización *f*; (*of traffic*) bloqueo *m*; embotellamiento *m*.
tiff [tif] *n* disgusto *m*, fregado *m*.
tiffin ['tifin] *n* (*Indian*) almuerzo *m*.
tig [tig] *n*: **to play —** dar la despedida.
tiger ['taigə*] *n* tigre *mf*.
tigerish ['taigərif] *adj* (*fig*) salvaje, feroz.
tiger lily ['taigə,lili] *n* tigridia *f*.
tight [tait] **1** *adj* (**a**) (*not leaky*) impermeable; a prueba de . . .; *container* estanco; *joint* hermético.
  (**b**) (*taut*) tieso, tirante; (*stretched*) estirado; *nut etc* apretado; *clothing* ajustado, ceñido, (*too —*) apretado, estrecho; *embrace* estrecho; *box* bien cerrado; *curve* cerrado; **as — as a drum** muy tirante; **to be in a — corner** (*or* situation) estar en un aprieto; **to keep — hold of something** seguir fuertemente agarrado a algo.
  (**c**) *money* escaso; *credit* difícil.
  (**d**) (*close-fisted*) agarrado, tacaño.
  (**e**) (*drunk*) borracho; **to be —** estar borracho; **to get —** emborracharse (*on gin* bebiendo ginebra).
  2 *adv* herméticamente; de modo tirante; apretadamente, estrechamente; **the door was shut —** la puerta estaba bien cerrada; **shut the box —** cierra bien la caja; **screw the nut up —** aprieta la tuerca a fondo, apriete bien la tuerca; **to hold something — agarrar algo fuertemente; to hold someone —** abrazar a uno estrechamente; **hold —!** ¡agárrense bien!; **to sit —** estarse quieto, no moverse, seguir en su lugar; seguir sin hacer nada; **to squeeze someone's hand —** apretar mucho la mano a uno.
tighten ['taitn] **1** *vt* (*also* **to — up**; *tauten*) atiesar, estirar; estrechar; *nut etc* apretar; *regulations etc* hacer más severo; hacer observar, velar por la

observancia de; *restrictions* reforzar, aplicar en forma más rigurosa; *see* belt.
  2 *vi* atiesarse, estirarse; estrecharse; apretarse; **to — up on** *see* vt.
tight-fisted ['tait'fistid] *adj* agarrado, tacaño.
tight-fitting ['tait'fitiŋ] *adj* muy ajustado, muy ceñido.
tightknit ['tait'nit] *adj* estrechamente unidos entre sí; *family etc* muy unido.
tight-lipped ['tait'lipt] *adj* (*fig*) callado; hermético; **to maintain a — silence** mantener un silencio absoluto; **he's being very — about it** sobre eso no dice nada en absoluto.
tightly ['taitli] *adv see* tight 2.
tightness ['taitnis] *n* impermeabilidad *f*; lo estanco; lo hermético; tensión *f*, tirantez *f*; lo apretado; estrechez *f*; escasez *f*; tacañería *f*; **to have a — in the chest** sentir opresión en el pecho.
tightrope ['taitrəup] *n* alambre *m* (de circo *etc*).
tightrope walker ['taitrəup,wɔ:kə*] *n* funámbulo *m*, a *f*, volatinero *m*, a *f*.
tights [taits] *npl* pantalón *m* ajustado; (*Theat etc*) traje *m* de malla.
tightwad ['taitwɔd] *n* (*US fam*) cicatero *m* (*fam*).
tigress ['taigris] *n* tigresa *f*.
Tigris ['taigris] Tigris *m*.
tilde ['tildi] *n* tilde *f*.
tile [tail] **1** *n* (*roof —*) teja *f*; (*floor —*) baldosa *f*; (*wall —, coloured, glazed*) azulejo *m*; (*sl*) sombrero *m*; **he's got a — loose** le falta un tornillo; **to spend a night on the —s** estar fuera toda la noche, pasar la noche de juerga.
  2 *vt roof* tejar; cubrir de tejas; *floor* embaldosar; *wall* adornar con azulejos.
tiler ['tailə*] *n* tejero *m*.
tiling ['tailiŋ] *n* tejas *fpl*, tejado *m*; baldosas *fpl*, embaldosado *m*; azulejos *mpl*.
till¹ [til] *vt* (*Agr*) cultivar, labrar.
till² [til] **1** *prep* hasta. **2** *conj* hasta que; (*for usage, see* until).
till³ [til] *n* (*drawer*) cajón *m*; (*machine*) caja *f* registradora.
tillage ['tilidʒ] *n* cultivo *m*, labranza *f*.
tiller¹ ['tilə*] *n* (*Agr*) labrador *m*.
tiller² ['tilə*] *n* (*Naut*) caña *f* del timón.
tilt [tilt] **1** *n* (*sloping*) inclinación *f*; ladeo *m*; **it is on the —, it has a — to it** está ladeado; **to give something a —** inclinar algo, ladear algo.
  (**b**) (*Hist*) torneo *m*, justa *f*; (**at**) **full — a** toda velocidad; **to run full — into a wall** dar de lleno contra una pared; **to have a — at** arremeter contra.
  2 *vt* inclinar, ladear; **— it this way** inclínelo hacia este lado; **— it back** inclínelo hacia atrás; **to — something out of a container** verter algo de un recipiente (inclinando éste); **to — over a table** volcar una mesa.
  3 *vi* (**a**) inclinarse, ladearse; **to — over** (*lean*) inclinarse, (*fall*) volcarse, caer; **lorry that —s up** camión *m* que bascula, camión *m* basculante; **seat that —s up** asiento m abatible.
  (**b**) (*Hist*) justar; **to — against** arremeter contra.
tilth [tilθ] *n* cultivo *m*, labranza *f*; condición *f* (cultivable) de la tierra.
Tim [tim] *nombre cariñoso de* **Timothy**.
timber ['timbə*] **1** *n* (*material*) madera *f* (de construcción); (*growing trees*) árboles *mpl*, árboles *mpl* de monte; bosque *m*; (*beam*) madero *m*, viga *f*, (*Naut*) cuaderna *f*; **—!** ¡ojo, que cae!, ¡agua va!
  2 *vt* enmaderar.
timbered ['timbəd] *adj house etc* enmaderado; *land* arbolado; **the land is well —** el terreno tiene mucho bosque.
timbering ['timbəriŋ] *n* maderamen *m*.
timberland ['timbəlænd] *n* (*US*) tierras *fpl* maderables.
timber line ['timbəlain] *n* límite *m* forestal.
timber merchant ['timbə,mə:tʃənt] *n* maderero *m*.
timberyard ['timbəja:d] *n* almacén *m* de madera.
timbre [tɛ:mbr] *n* timbre *m*.
time [taim] **1** *n* (**a**) (*general sense*) tiempo *m*; (**Father**) **T—** el Tiempo; **— flies** el tiempo vuela; **— presses** el tiempo apremia; **— will show, — will tell** el tiempo lo dirá; **race against —** carrera *f* contra reloj; **in (good) —, in process of —, as — goes on** andando el tiempo, con el tiempo; **all in good —** todo a su tiempo; **all in good —!** ¡despacio!; **— and motion study** estudios *mpl* de tiempo y movimiento; **—!** ¡es la hora!, ¡la hora!; **— gentlemen please!** ¡se cierra!; **my — is my own** dispongo libremente de mi tiempo; **to find — for** tener tiempo para; **to gain —** ganar tiempo; **we have —, we have plenty of —** tenemos tiempo de

sobra; **to have no — to read** no tener tiempo para leer; **I've no — for him** (fig) no le estimo, tengo un concepto más bien bajo de él; **I've no — for sport** (fig) desprecio los deportes, no apruebo los deportes; **to have — on one's hands** estar ocioso; no saber cómo ocuparse; tener tiempo libre; **to kill** — entretener el tiempo, pasar el rato; **to lose** — atrasarse; **to lose no — in** + ger no tardar en + infin; **to make up for lost** — recuperar el tiempo perdido; **to play for** — tratar de ganar tiempo; **to be pressed for** — tener poco tiempo; **it takes** — es una cosa lenta, en esto se tarda bastante; **it takes — to** + infin se tarda bastante en + infin; **it took him all his — to find it** sólo encontrarlo le ocupó bastante tiempo; **to take one's** — hacer las cosas con calma; ir despacio, no darse prisa; **he's certainly taking his** — es cierto que tarda bastante ya; **take your** —! ¡hágalo con calma!, ¡no hay prisa!; **to take — by the forelock** aprovechar la ocasión.

(b) (period) período m, tiempo m; plazo m; **extra** — (Sport) prórroga f; **spare** — ratos mpl libres, horas fpl libres; ratos mpl de ocio; **a long —** mucho tiempo; **a long — ago** hace mucho tiempo; **a short** — poco tiempo, un rato; **a short — ago** hace poco; **a short — after** poco tiempo después, al poco tiempo; **for a** — durante un rato, durante una temporada; **for a long — to come** hasta que haya transcurrido mucho tiempo; **for some — past** de algún tiempo a esta parte; **for the — being** por ahora; **he hasn't been seen for a long —** hace mucho tiempo que no se le ve; **in (good) — (early)** a tiempo, con tiempo; **to arrive in good —** llegar con bastante anticipación; **let me know in good —** avíseme con anticipación; **he'll come in his own good** — vendrá cuando le parezca conveniente; **in a short** — en breve; con la mayor brevedad; **in a short —** they were all gone muy pronto habían desaparecido todos; **in 2 weeks'** — en 2 semanas; al cabo de 2 semanas; **in no — at all** en muy poco tiempo; **within the agreed** — antes del plazo convenido; dentro del límite de tiempo que se había fijado; **to do** — (fam) cumplir una condena; **it will last our** — durará lo que nosotros; **to serve one's** — hacer su aprendizaje; servir; **to take a long — to** + infin tardar mucho en + infin.

(c) (at work) horas fpl de trabajo; jornada f; **he did the draft in his own** — preparó el borrador fuera de las horas normales de trabajo; **to be on (or to work) short** — trabajar en jornadas reducidas; see also **full—**, **short—** etc.

(d) (epoch, period; often **—s**) época f, tiempos mpl; **a sign of the —s** un indicio de cómo cambian los tiempos; **the good old —s** los buenos tiempos pasados; **the —s we live in** los tiempos en que vivimos; **these naughty —s** estos tiempos tan escandalosos; **in my —(s)** en mis tiempos; **in Victoria's —(s)** en los tiempos de Victoria, en la época victoriana, bajo el reinado de Victoria; **in our —** en nuestra época; **in —s past, in former (or olden, older) —s** en otro tiempo, antiguamente; **in —s to come** en los siglos venideros; **—s are somewhat hard** atravesamos un período bastante difícil; **those were tough —s** fue un período de grandes dificultades; **what —s they were!, what —s we had!** ¡qué tiempos aquellos!; **the —s are out of joint** los tiempos actuales estan revueltos; **— was when . . .** hubo un tiempo en que . . .; **to be behind the —s** (person) ser un atrasado; estar atrasado de noticias; (thing) estar fuera de moda, haber quedado anticuado; **to fall on hard —s** estar en el tiempo de las vacas flacas; **to keep abreast of (or up with) the —s** ir con los tiempos, mantenerse al día.

(e) (moment, point of —) momento m; **any —** en cualquier momento; **come (at) any — (you like)** ven cuando quieras; **it might happen (at) any —** podría ocurrir de un momento a otro; **at the —, at that** — por entonces; en aquella época, en aquel entonces; a la sazón; **at this particular —** en este preciso momento; **at the present** — en la actualidad, actualmente; **at one** — en cierto momento, en cierta época; había momentos en que . . ., **at one — . . ., at another — . . .** ora . . ., ora . . .; **Rodriguez, at one — minister of . . .** Rodríguez, ministro que fue de . . .; **at no** — jamás, nunca; **at a given** — en un momento convenido; **at a convenient** — en un momento oportuno; **at the proper** — en el momento oportuno; **at the same** — al mismo tiempo; a la vez; **at —s** a veces; **at all —s** en todo momento, siempre; **at odd —s** de vez en cuando; **at various —s in the past** en

determinados momentos del pasado; **between —s** en los intervalos; **by this** — ya, antes de esto; **(by) this — next year** para estas fechas del año que viene; **by the** — we got there antes de que llegásemos, antes de nuestra llegada, antes de llegar nosotros; cuando llegamos; **from — to —** de vez en cuando; **from that** — (on) a partir de entonces; **until such** — as he agrees hasta que consienta; **now is the — to do it** éste es el momento en que conviene hacerlo; **now is the — to plant roses** ésta es la época para plantar las rosas; **the proper — to do it . . .** el momento más indicado para hacerlo es . . .; **when the — comes** cuando llegue el momento; **the — has come to** + infin ha llegado el momento de + infin; **to choose one's — carefully** elegir con cuidado el momento más propicio; **this is no — for superstition** éste no es el momento para mostrarse supersticioso, tal momento no es para tomar en serio las supersticiones.

(f) (as marked on clock) hora f; **closing —** hora f de cerrar; **opening** — hora f de abrir; **Greenwich mean** — hora f media de Greenwich; **standard** — hora f normal; **summer** — hora f de verano; **what's the —?** ¿qué hora es?; **what — do you make it?, what do you make the —?** ¿qué hora tienes?; **have you the right —?** ¿tiene Vd la hora exacta?; **the — is 2.30** son las 2 y media; **a watch that keeps good** — un reloj muy exacto; **to look at the** — mirar su reloj.

(g) (as marked on clock: phrases with prep etc) **(and) about — too!** ¡ya era hora!; **it is about —** he was there ya era hora que estuviera allí; **to be 23 minutes ahead of** — llevar 23 minutos de adelanto; **to arrive ahead of** — llegar temprano; **to die before one's** — morir temprano; **to be behind** — atrasarse, retrasarse; **the train is 8 minutes behind** — el tren lleva 8 minutos de retraso; **to come in (good) — for lunch** venir con bastante anticipación a comer; **we were just in — to see it** llegamos justo a tiempo para verlo; **to start in good** — partir temprano, partir pronto; **to be on —** ser puntual, llegar (etc) puntualmente; **to be up to** — llegar con retraso; **at any — of the day or night** en cualquier momento del día o de la noche; **at this — of day** a esta hora; **to pass the — of day with someone** detenerse a charlar un rato con uno; **it's — for tea** es la hora del té; **ha llegado la hora de servir el té; it's coffee —** es la hora del café; **it's — to go** ya es hora de marcharse; **it's high** — ya era hora; **there's a — and a place for everything** todo tiene su hora y su lugar debidos; **éste no es ni el momento ni el lugar indicado.**

(h) (as marked by calendar) época f; temporada f; estación f; **at my — of life** a mi edad, con los años que yo tengo; **at this — of year** en esta época del año; **it's a lovely — of year** es una estación encantadora; **my favourite — is autumn** mi estación predilecta es el otoño.

(i) (good etc) **to have a good — (of it)** pasarlo bien; **have a good —!** ¡que lo pases bien!; **to give someone a good** — hacer que uno lo pase bien; **she's out for a good** — se propone divertirse; **all they want to do is have a good** — no quieren más que divertirse; **we have a lovely** — lo pasamos la mar de bien; **I hope you have a lovely —!** ¡que os divertáis!; **to have a rough (or bad, thin etc) — of it** pasarlo mal, pasarlas negras; **what a — we'll have with the girls!** ¡vaya juergazo que nos vamos a correr con las chicas!

(j) (occasion) vez f; **3 —s** 3 veces; **this —** esta vez; **last** — la última vez; **next** — la próxima vez; **the first — I did it** la primera vez que lo hice; **for the first** — por primera vez; **for the last —** por última vez; **after —, — and again** repetidas veces; **each —, every** — cada vez; **each — that . . .** cada vez que . . .; **he won every** — ganó todas las veces; **it's the best, every —!** ¡es el mejor, no hay duda!; **many —s** muchas veces; **many a — I saw him act, many's the — I saw him act** muchas veces le vi representar; **several —s** varias veces; **third — lucky!** ¡a la tercera va la vencida!; **I remember the — when . . .** me acuerdo de cuando . . .; **to bide one's** — esperar la hora propicia; **for weeks at a** — durante semanas enteras, durante varias semanas seguidas; **to do 2 things at a** — hacer 2 cosas a la vez; hacer 2 cosas al mismo tiempo; **to eat biscuits 4 at a** — comer 4 galletas a la vez; **he ran upstairs 3 at a** — subió la escalera de 3 en 3 escalones.

(k) (*Math*) **4 —s 3 4 por 3; it's 4 —s as fast as yours** es 4 veces más rápido que el tuyo.

(l) (*adv phrase*) **at the same — you must remember that . . .** de todas formas conviene recordar que . . .; **at the same — as** (*fig*) al mismo tiempo que, al igual que, a la par que.

(m) (*Mus*) tiempo *m*; compás *m*; **in 3/4 —** al compás de 3 por 4; **in — to the music** al compás de la música; **to beat** (*or* **keep**) **—** llevar el compás; **to get out of —** perder el ritmo, dejar de llevar el compás; **to mark —** (*Mil*) llevar el paso; (*fig*) esperar, hacer tiempo.

(n) (*Mech*) **the ignition is out of —** el encendido está fuera de fase, el encendido funciona mal.

2 *vt* **(a)** (*reckon — of*) medir el tiempo de, calcular la duración de; *race* cronometrar.

(b) (*regulate*) *watch* regular, poner en hora; **it is —d to go off at midnight** la espoleta está graduada para que haga explosión a medianoche; **the train is —d for 6** el tren debe llegar a las 6.

(c) (*do at right —*) hacer en el momento oportuno; **you —d that perfectly** elegiste a la perfección el momento para hacerlo (*etc*).

time bomb ['taimbɔm] *n* bomba *f* de relojería.

time clock ['taimklɔk] *n* reloj *m* registrador.

time-consuming ['taimkən,sju:miŋ] *adj* que exige mucho tiempo.

time exposure ['taimik,spəuʒə*] *n* (*Phot*) pose *f*.

time fuse ['taimfju:z] *n* espoleta *f* de tiempo, espoleta *f* graduada.

time-honoured, (*US*) **time-honored** ['taim,ɔnəd] *adj* sacramental, consagrado, clásico.

timekeeper ['taim,ki:pə*] *n* (*watch*) reloj *m*, cronómetro *m*; (*person*) cronometrador *m*, apuntador *m* del tiempo.

time-lag ['taimlæg] *n* intervalo *m*; retraso *m*, pérdida *f* de tiempo.

timeless ['taimlis] *adj* eterno; *race etc* sin limitación de tiempo.

time limit ['taim,limit] *n* limitación *f* de tiempo; (*esp Comm*) plazo *m*; (*closing date*) fecha *f* tope; **without a —** sin limitación de tiempo; **to fix a — for something** fijar un plazo para algo, señalar un plazo a algo.

timeliness ['taimlinis] *n* oportunidad *f*.

timely ['taimli] *adj* oportuno.

timepiece ['taimpi:s] *n* reloj *m*.

timer ['taimə*] *n* (*egg — etc*) reloj *m* de arena; (*Mech*) reloj *m* automático; (*Aut etc*) distribuidor *m* de encendido.

time-saving ['taim,seiviŋ] *adj* que ahorra tiempo.

timeserver ['taim,sə:və*] *n* contemporizador *m*.

time signature ['taim'signitʃə*] *n* (*Mus*) signatura *f*.

time sheet ['taimʃi:t] *n* tarjeta *f* registradora (de horas trabajadas), hoja *f* de presencia.

time signal ['taim,signl] *n* (*Radio*) señal *f* horaria.

time switch ['taimswitʃ] *n* interruptor *m* horario.

timetable ['taim,teibl] *n* horario *m*; (*programme of classes etc*) programa *m*.

timework ['taimwə:k] *n* trabajo *m* a jornal; trabajo *m* por horas.

timeworn ['taimwɔ:n] *adj* deteriorado por el tiempo.

timid ['timid] *adj* tímido.

timidity [ti'miditi] *n* timidez *f*.

timidness ['timidnis] *n* timidez *f*.

timing ['taimiŋ] **1** *n* (*reckoning of time*) medida *f* del tiempo, medida *f* de la duración; (*Sport etc*) cronometraje *m*; **the — of this is important** importa hacer esto en el momento exacto, importa elegir el momento más propicio para hacer esto.

2 *attr* (*Mech*) de distribución, de encendido; **— gear** engranaje *m* de distribución; **it has a — mechanism** tiene un dispositivo para medir el tiempo.

timorous ['timərəs] *adj* temeroso, tímido; *animal* huraño, asustadizo.

Timothy ['timəθi] *m* Timoteo.

timpani ['timpəni] *npl* (*Mus*) tímpanos *mpl*, atabales *mpl*.

tin [tin] **1** *n* **(a)** (*element, metal*) estaño *m*; (*—plate*) hojalata *f*.

(b) (*container*) lata *f*; **meat in —s** carne *f* en lata, carne *f* enlatada.

(c) (*sl*) parné *m* (*sl*).

2 *adj, attr* de estaño; de hojalata; *hat* de acero; *soldier* de plomo; (*fam, pej*) inferior, de poco valor, de pacotilla.

3 *vt* **(a)** (*cover with —*) estañar.

(b) (*can*) envasar en lata, conservar en lata, enlatar; *see also* **tinned.**

tin can ['tin'kæn] *n* lata *f*.

tincture ['tiŋktʃə*] **1** *n* tintura *f* (*also fig*); (*Pharm*) tintura *f*. **2** *vt* tinturar, teñir (*with* de).

tinder ['tində*] *n* yesca *f* (*also fig*); **to burn like —** arder como la yesca.

tinderbox ['tindəbɔks] *n* yescas *fpl*.

tine [tain] *n* púa *f*.

tinfoil ['tinfɔil] *n* papel *m* de estaño.

ting [tiŋ] *see* **tinkle.**

ting-a-ling ['tiŋə'liŋ] *n* tilín *m*; **to go —** hacer tilín.

tinge [tindʒ] **1** *n* tinte *m*; (*fig*) dejo *m*; matiz *m*; **not without a — of regret** no sin cierto sentimiento.

2 *vt* teñir (*with* de); (*fig*) matizar (*with* de); **pleasure —d with sadness** placer *m* matizado de tristeza, placer *m* no exento de tristeza.

tingle ['tiŋgl] **1** *n* comezón *f*; hormigueo *m* (de la piel); (*thrill*) estremecimiento *m*.

2 *vi* sentir comezón, sentir hormigueo; (*ears*) zumbar; (*thrill*) estremecerse (*with* de).

tingly ['tiŋgli] *adj*: — **feeling** sensación *f* de hormigueo; **my arm feels —** siento hormigueo en el brazo; **I feel — all over** se me estremece todo el cuerpo.

tin hat ['tin'hæt] *n* casco *m* de acero.

tinker ['tiŋkə*] **1** *n* calderero *m* hojalatero; (*gipsy*) gitano *m*; (*fam: child*) pícaro *m*, tunante *m*; **you —!** ¡tunante!

2 *vt* (*also* **to — up**) remendar; (*pej*) remendar mal, remendar chapuceramente.

3 *vi*: **to — with** (*mend*) tratar de reparar; (*play*) jugar con, manosear; (*and damage*) estropear; **they're only —ing with the problem** no se esfuerzan seriamente por resolver el problema; **he's been —ing with the car all day** ha pasado todo el día tratando de reparar el coche.

tinkle ['tiŋkl] **1** *n* tilín *m*, retintín *m*; campanilleo *m*, cencerreo *m*; **"A resounding —"** "Un sonoro retintín".

2 *vt* hacer retiñir; hacer tintinar; hacer campillear.

3 *vi* retiñir, tintinar; campanillear.

tinkling ['tiŋkliŋ] **1** *adj* que hace tilín (*etc*); **a — sound** un tilín (*etc*); **a — stream** un arroyo cantarín.

2 *n* tilín *m*, retintín *m*; campanilleo *m*, cencerreo *m*; **the — of the telephone** el campanilleo del teléfono.

tin mine ['tinmain] *n* mina *f* de estaño.

tin miner ['tin,mainə*] *n* minero *m* de estaño.

tinned [tind] *adj* en lata, de lata.

tinny ['tini] *adj* *taste* que sabe a lata; *sound* cascado, que suena a lata; (*fam*) inferior, de poco valor, de pacotilla; desvencijado.

tin opener ['tin,əupnə*] *n* abrelatas *m*.

tinplate ['tinpleit] *n* hojalata *f*.

tinsel ['tinsəl] **1** *n* oropel *m* (*also fig*); (*cloth*) lama *f* de oro (*or* de plata).

2 *adj* de oropel; (*fig*) de oropel, de relumbrón.

3 *vt* oropelar.

tinsmith ['tinsmiθ] *n* hojalatero *m*.

tin soldier ['tin'səuldʒə*] *n* soldado *m* de plomo.

tint [tint] **1** *n* tinte *m*, matiz *m*, color *m*; media tinta *f*.

2 *vt* teñir, matizar (*blue* de azul); **it's yellow —ed with red** es amarillo matizado de rojo; **to — one's hair** teñirse el pelo.

tintack ['tintæk] *n* tachuela *f*.

tintinnabulation ['tinti,næbju'leiʃən] *n* campanilleo *m*.

tintype ['tintaip] *n* (*Phot*) ferrotipo *m*.

tiny ['taini] *adj* pequeñito, chiquitín, diminuto, minúsculo.

tip¹ [tip] **1** *n* (*end*) punta *f*, cabo *m*, extremidad *f*; (*of stick etc*) regatón *m*, casquillo *m*; (*of cigarette*) boquilla *f*, embocadura *f*; **from — to toe** de pies a cabeza; **I had it on the — of my tongue** lo tenía en la punta de la lengua.

2 *vt* poner regatón a; **—ped with steel** con punta de acero.

tip² [tip] **1** *n* **(a)** (*tap*) golpecito *m*.

(b) (*gratuity*) propina *f*; **to give** (*or* **leave**) **someone a —** dar una propina a uno.

(c) (*hint*) aviso *m*, advertencia *f*; consejo *m*, indicación *f*; (*to police etc*) soplo *m*; (*Racing*) confidencia *f*; pronóstico *m* confidencial; **let me give you a —** permítame darle un consejo; **if you take my —** si sigues mi consejo; **the horse is a hot — for the 2.30** se pronostica con seguridad que el caballo ganará la carrera de las 2 y media.

(d) (*rubbish —*) vertedero *m*, basurero *m*; escombrera *f*.

2 *vt* **(a)** (*tap, strike*) golpear ligeramente, tocar ligeramente (al pasar), chocar ligeramente con; **to — one's hat to someone** tocarse el sombrero para saludar a uno.

(b) (*incline*) inclinar, ladear; *drinking vessel* empinar; *seat* abatir, levantar; **to — away** *liquid* vaciar, verter, echar; **to — forward** inclinar hacia adelante; **to — someone off his seat** hacer que uno caiga de su asiento; **to — out the contents of a box** verter el contenido de una caja; **all the passengers were —ped out** todos los pasajeros cayeron fuera; **to — over** volcar; **to — up** (*incline*) inclinar, ladear; *container* volcar; *person* hacer perder el equilibrio; *hacer caer, volcar; derribar*; **to — someone into the water** hacer caer a uno al agua (empujándole); **he —s the scales at 100 kg** pesa 100 kg justos.

(c) (*reward*) dar una propina a, dejar una propina para; **to — someone a pound** dar a uno una libra de propina; **to — someone generously** dar a uno una propina generosa.

(d) to — someone off advertir a uno clandestinamente; **the police had been —ped off** la policía había recibido una confidencia.

(e) *winner* pronosticar, recomendar, elegir; **I — that horse to win** pronostico que ganará ese caballo; **he is being freely —ped for the job** muchos creen que le darán el puesto; **he is strongly —ped as prime minister** se pronostica con confianza que será primer ministro.

3 *vi* (*incline*) inclinarse, ladearse; (*topple*) tambalearse; **he —ped off into the sea** perdió el equilibrio y cayó al mar; **to — over** volcarse; caer; **to — up** volcarse; (*seat*) abatirse, levantarse; (*lorry etc*) bascular.

tip-cart ['tipkɑ:t] *n* volquete *m*.

tip-off ['tipɔf] *n* advertencia *f* (clandestina), aviso *m*; soplo *m*, confidencia *f*.

tipped [tipt] *adj* cigarette emboquillado.

tipple ['tipl] **1** *n* bebida *f* (alcohólica); **his — is Cointreau** él bebe Cointreau; **what's your —?** ¿qué quieres tomar?
2 *vi* beber más de la cuenta; envasar, empinar el codo.

tippler ['tiplə*] *n* bebedor *m*, borracho *m*.

tipsily ['tipsili] *adv* como borracho; **to walk —** andar con pasos de borracho.

tipsiness ['tipsinis] *n* borrachera *f*.

tipster ['tipstə*] *n* pronosticador *m*.

tipsy ['tipsi] *adj* achispado, algo borracho.

tiptoe ['tiptəu] **1** *n:* **to walk on —** caminar de puntillas; **to stand on —** ponerse de puntillas.
2 *vi:* **to — across the floor** atravesar el suelo de puntillas; **to — to the window** ir de puntillas a la ventana.

tiptop ['tip'tɔp] *adj* de primera, excelente; **in — condition** en excelentes condiciones; **a — show** un espectáculo de primerísima calidad.

tip-up ['tipʌp] *attr lorry* basculante; *seat* abatible.

tirade [tai'reid] *n* invectiva *f*, diatriba *f*.

tire[1] ['taiə*] **1** *vt* cansar, fatigar; (*bore*) aburrir; **to — someone out** cansar a uno, rendir a uno de cansancio, agotar las fuerzas de uno.
2 *vi* cansarse, fatigarse; aburrirse; **to — of** cansarse de; aburrirse con; **she —s easily** se cansa pronto.

tire[2] ['taiə*] *n* (*US*) *see* **tyre.**

tired ['taiəd] *adj* **(a)** cansado; **in a — voice** con voz cansada; **the — old clichés** los lugares comunes de siempre, los tópicos trillados.
(b) *person* cansado, fatigado; **to be — estar** cansado; **to be — out** estar rendido, estar agotado; **I'm — of all that** estoy harto de todo eso; **to get** (*or* **grow**) **— of doing something** cansarse de hacer algo; **I get — of telling you** estoy harto de decírtelo; **you make me —** me fastidias terriblemente.

tiredly ['taiədli] *adv walk etc* como cansado; *say* con voz cansada.

tiredness ['taiədnis] *n* cansancio *m*, fatiga *f*.

tireless ['taiəlis] *adj* infatigable, incansable.

tirelessly ['taiəlisli] *adv* infatigablemente, incansablemente.

tiresome ['taiəsəm] *adj* molesto, fastidioso; *person* pesado; **how very —!** ¡qué lata!; **he's a — sort** es un pesado; **he can be —** a veces es un pesado.

tiresomeness ['taiəsəmnis] *n* molestia *f*, fastidio *m*, lo fastidioso; pesadez *f*.

tiring ['taiəriŋ] *adj* molesto, fatigoso, que cansa, agotador; **after a — journey** después de un viaje cansado; **it's — work** es un trabajo agotador.

tiro ['taiərəu] *n* novicio *m*, principiante *m*.

tisane [ti'zæn] *n* tisana *f*.

tissue ['tiʃu:] *n* (*cloth*) tisú *m*, lama *f*; (*Anat etc*) tejido *m*; **a — of lies** una sarta de mentiras.

tissue paper ['tiʃu:,peipə*] *n* papel *m* de seda.

tit[1] [tit] *n* (*blue—*) herrerillo *m* común; (*coal—*) carbonero *m* garrapinos; (*long-tailed —*) mito *m*.

tit[2] [tit] *n:* **— for tat!** ¡donde las dan las toman!; **so that was — for tat** así que ajustamos cuentas, así que le pagué en la misma moneda.

tit[3] [tit] *n* (*fam*) pecho *m*, seno *m*.

Titan [tai'tæn] *n* titán *m*.

titanic [tai'tænik] *adj* titánico; inmenso, gigantesco.

titanium [ti'teiniəm] *n* titanio *m*.

titbit ['titbit] *n*, (*US*) **tidbit** *n* golosina *f* (*also fig*).

tithe [taið] *n* (*Eccl*) diezmo *m*.

Titian ['tiʃən] *m* Ticiano.

titillate ['titileit] *vt* estimular, excitar.

titillation [,titi'leiʃən] *n* estimulación *f*, excitación *f*.

titivate ['titiveit] **1** *vt* emperejilar, ataviar, adornar.
2 *vi* emperejilarse, ataviarse; arreglarse.

title ['taitl] **1** *n* **(a)** (*appellation, heading*) título *m*; (*Sport*) título *m*, campeonato *m*; **noble —, — of nobility** título *m* de nobleza; **what — are you giving the book?** ¿qué título vas a dar al libro?, ¿cómo vas a titular el libro?; **what — should I give him?** ¿qué tratamiento debo darle?; **George V gave him a —** Jorge V le ennobleció.
(b) (*Law*) título *m*, derecho *m*; **his — to the property** su derecho a la propiedad.
2 *vt* titular, intitular.

titled ['taitld] *adj* con título de nobleza, noble.

title deed ['taitldi:d] *n* título *m* de propiedad.

title holder ['taitl,həuldə*] *n* (*Sport*) titular *mf*, campeón *m*, ona *f*.

title page ['taitlpeidʒ] *n* portada *f*.

title rôle ['taitl'rəul] *n* papel *m* principal.

titmouse ['titmaus] *n*, *pl* **—mice** [mais] *see* **tit**[1].

titrate ['taitreit] *vt* valorar.

titration [tai'treiʃən] *n* valoración *f*.

titter ['titə*] **1** *n* risa *f* disimulada. **2** *vi* reírse disimuladamente.

tittle ['titl] *n* pizca *f*, ápice *m*; **there's not a — of truth in it** eso no tiene ni pizca de verdad.

tittle-tattle ['titl,tætl] **1** *n* chismes *m*, chismografía *f*. **2** *vi* chismear.

titular ['titjulə*] *adj* titular; nominal.

tizzy ['tizi] *n* (*fam*): **to get into a —** ponerse nervioso, aturdirse, armarse un lío.

to [tu:, tə] **1** *prep* **(a)** (*dat*) a; **to give something — someone** dar algo a uno; **I gave it — my friend** se lo di a mi amigo; **the person I sold it — la** persona a quien lo vendí; **it belongs — me** me pertenece a mí, es mío; **it's new — me** es nuevo para mí; **I said — myself** dije para mí; **what is that — me?** y eso ¿qué me importa?; **they were kind — me** fueron amables conmigo.
(b) (*of movement, direction*) a; hacia; **to go — the town** ir a la ciudad; **to go — school** ir a la escuela; **to go — Italy** ir a Italia; **to go — Rome** ir a Roma; **to go — Peru** ir al Perú; **to go — the doctor** ir a ver al médico; **let's go — John's** vamos a casa de Juan; **she went back — her husband** volvió a estar con su marido, volvió a vivir con su marido; **from door — door** de puerta en puerta; **the road — Zaragoza** la carretera de Zaragoza; **it's 90 kilometres — Lima** de aquí a Lima hay 90 kilómetros; **— the left** a la izquierda; **— the west** al oeste, hacia el oeste.
(c) (*as far as, right up to*) hasta; **to count up — 20** contar hasta 20; **— this day** hasta hoy, hasta el día de hoy; **I'll see you — the door** te acompaño hasta la puerta; **funds — the value of . . .** fondos *mpl* por valor de . . .; **— some degree** hasta cierto punto; **it's accurate — a millimetre** es exacto hasta el milímetro; **to be wet — the skin** estar mojado hasta los huesos; **they perished — a man** perecieron todos (sin excepción); **everybody down — the youngest** todos hasta el más joven.
(d) (*against*) a, contra; **to stand back — back** estar espalda con espalda; **to talk to someone man — man** hablar con uno de hombre a hombre; **to turn a picture — the wall** volver un cuadro contra la pared; **to clasp someone — one's breast** estrechar a uno contra su pecho.
(e) (*of time*) a, hasta; **from morning — night** de la mañana a la noche, desde la mañana hasta la noche; **8 years ago — the day** hoy hace exactamente 8 años; **at 8 minutes — 10** a las 10 menos 8; **a quarter — 5** las 5 menos cuarto.
(f) (*of*) de; **wife — Mr Milton** mujer *f* del Sr Milton; **secretary — the manager** secretaria *f* del gerente; **ambassador — King Cole** embajador *m* cerca del rey Cole; **he is heir — the duke** es heredero del duque; **he was heir — a million** heredó un millón de libras; **he has been a good friend — us** ha sido buen amigo nuestro.

(g) (*of dedications*) a; **greetings — all our friends!** ¡saludos a todos los amigos!; **welcome — you all!** ¡bienvenida a todos!, ¡bienvenidos todos!; **to build a monument — someone** erigir un monumento en honor de uno; **here's — you!** ¡vaya por Vd!, ¡por Vd!; **to drink — someone** brindar por uno, beber a la salud de uno.

(h) (*in comparisons*) a; **inferior —** inferior a; **that's nothing — what is — come** eso no es nada en comparación con lo que está todavía por venir.

(i) (*of proportion*) a; **A is — B as C is — D** A es a B como C es a D; **by a majority of 12 — 10** por una mayoría de 12 a 10; **Slobodia won by 4 goals — 2** ganó Eslobodia por 4 goles a 2; **the odds are 8 — 1** los puntos de ventaja son de 8 a 1; **200 people — the square mile** 200 personas por milla cuadrada.

(j) (*concerning*) a; **what do you say — this?** ¿qué contestación me das a esto?, ¿cómo contestas a esta pregunta?; **that's all there is — it** no hay nada más; no hay ningún misterio; todo queda tan sencillo como ves; **"— repairing pipes: ..."** (*bill*) "Reparación de los tubos: ..."; **"— services rendered: ..."** "Por los servicios que se han prestado: ..."

(k) (*according to*) según; **— all appearances** al parecer, según todos los indicios; **— my way of thinking** según mi modo de pensar; **it is not — my taste** no me gusta; **to write — someone's dictation** escribir al dictado de uno; **— the best of my recollection** que yo recuerde; **it is sung — the tune of "Tipperary"** se canta con la melodía de "Tipperary"; **they came out — the strains of the national anthem** salieron a los compases del himno nacional.

(l) (*of purpose, result*) **— this end** con este propósito; **to come — someone's aid** acudir en ayuda de uno; **to sentence someone — death** condenar a uno a muerte; **— my great surprise** con gran sorpresa mía; **— my lasting shame I did nothing — me** avergüenzo siempre de no haber hecho nada; **to put an army — flight** poner en fuga a un ejército; **to go — ruin** arruinarse, echarse a perder; **to run — seed** granar, dar en grana (*and see* seed).

2 *prep* (*before infin*) **(a)** (*with simple infin, not translated*) — know saber, conocer; **"— be or not — be"** "ser o no ser"; (*following another verb a variety of constructions appears, for which see the verb in each case, eg*) **to forbid someone — do something** prohibir a uno hacer algo; **to begin — do something** comenzar a hacer algo, empezar a hacer algo; **to try — do something** tratar de hacer algo, procurar hacer algo; **I want you — do it** quiero que tú lo hagas; **I wanted you — do it** quería que tú lo hicieras; **they asked me — do it** me rogaron hacerlo.

(b) (*purpose*) para; **I did it — help you** lo hice para ayudarte.

(c) (*purpose, with verbs of motion*) a, para; **I came — see you** vine a verte; **I came specially — see you** vine expresamente para verte.

(d) (*result*) **I have done nothing — deserve** this no he hecho nada que mereciera esto.

(e) (*equivalent to on* + *ger*) **— see him now** one would never think that ... al verle (*or* viéndole) ahora no creería nadie que ...

(f) (*expressing subsequent fact*) para; **I arrived — find she had gone** llegué para descubrir que ella se había ido; **it disappeared never — be found again** desapareció para no volver a encontrarse jamás.

(g) (*with ellipsis of verb*) **I don't want —** no quiero; **you ought —** debieras hacerlo (*etc*); **I should love —!** ¡ojalá!, ¡cuánto me gustaría hacerlo (*etc*)!; **we didn't want to sell it but we had to** no queríamos venderlo pero tuvimos que hacerlo, no queríamos venderlo pero no había más remedio.

(h) I have things — do tengo cosas que hacer; **there is much — be done** hay mucho que hacer; **that book is still — be written** ese libro está todavía por escribir; **there was no-one for me — consult** no había nadie a quien yo pudiese consultar; **he is not — be trusted** no hay que fiarse de él; **he's not the sort — do** that no es capaz de hacer eso, tal cosa no cabe en él; **this is the time — do it** éste es el momento de hacerlo; **and who is the Academy — protest?** ¿y quién es la Academia para protestar?

(i) (*construction after adjs etc*) **to be ready — go** estar listo para partir; **it's hard — get hold of** es difícil de obtener; **he's slow — learn** es lento en aprender, aprende lentamente; **you are foolish —**

try it eres un tonto si lo emprendes; **is it good — eat?** ¿es bueno de comer?, ¿se puede comer?; **to be the first — do something** ser el primero en hacer algo; **who was the last — see her?** ¿quién la vio por última vez?; **he's a big boy — be still in short trousers** es mayorcito ya para llevar todavía pantalón corto; **it's too heavy — lift** es demasiado pesado para poder levantarlo; **it's too hot — touch** no se puede tocar por el mucho calor; **he's too old — manage it** es demasiado viejo para poder hacerlo.

3 *adv*: **to come —** (*Naut*) fachear; (*Med*) volver en sí; **to lie —** (*Naut*) ponerse a la capa; *see* **fro**.

toad [təud] *n* sapo *m*.

toadflax ['təudflæks] *n* linaria *f*, pajarita *f*.

toadstool ['təudstu:l] *n* hongo *m* (venenoso).

toady ['təudi] **1** *n* pelotillero *m*, lameculos *m*. **2** *vi*: **to — to someone** hacer la pelotilla a uno, adular servilmente a uno.

toadying ['təudiiŋ] *n*, **toadyism** ['təudiizəm] *n* adulación *f* servil.

toast [təust] **1** *n* **(a)** (*Cook*) pan *m* tostado, tostada *f*; **a piece of —** un trozo de pan tostado.

(b) (*drink*) brindis *m* (*to* por); **to drink a — to someone** brindar por uno; **here's a — to all who ...** brindemos por todos los que ...; **A will propose a — to B** A pronunciará algunas palabras al brindar por B.

(c) she was the — of the town la celebraron mucho en toda la ciudad, en todas partes de la ciudad se brindó por ella.

2 *vt* **(a)** (*Cook*) tostar.

(b) (*drink to*) brindar por, beber a la salud de; **we —ed the victory in champagne** celebramos la victoria bebiendo champán.

toaster ['təustə*] *n* tostador *m*, tostadora *f*.

toasting fork ['təustiŋfɔ:k] *n* tostadera *f*.

toast list ['təustlist] *n* lista *f* de brindis.

toastmaster ['təust‚mɑːstə*] *n* oficial *m* que anuncia a los oradores en un banquete.

toast rack ['təustræk] *n* portatostadas *m*.

tobacco [tə'bækəu] *n* tabaco *m*; **cut —** picadura *f* (de tabaco); **leaf —** tabaco *m* en rama; **pipe — tabaco** *m* de pipa; **Turkish —** tabaco *m* turco; **Virginian —** tabaco *m* rubio.

tobacco jar [tə'bækəudʒɑ:*] *n* tabaquera *f*.

tobacconist [tə'bækənist] *n* estanquero *m*, tabaquero *m*; **—'s (shop)** estanco *m*, tabaquería *f*.

tobacco plantation [tə'bækəuplæn‚teiʃən] *n* tabacal *m*, plantación *f* de tabaco.

tobacco pouch [tə'bækəupautʃ] *n* petaca *f*.

toboggan [tə'bɔgən] **1** *n* tobogán *m*. **2** *vi* ir en tobogán, deslizarse en tobogán; (*fig*) deslizarse, correr.

toboggan run [tə'bɔgənrʌn] *n* pista *f* de tobogán.

tocsin ['tɔksin] *n* campana *f* de alarma; campanada *f* de alarma; (*fig*) voz *f* de alarma; **to sound the —** (*fig*) dar la voz de alarma.

today [tə'dei] *adv* hoy; (*at the present time*) hoy día, hoy en día; **— week, a week —** de hoy en ocho días; **a fortnight —** de hoy en quince (días); **what day is it —?** ¿qué día es hoy?; ¿a cuántos estamos?; **— is the 4th** estamos a 4; **a year ago —** hoy hace un año; **from —** desde hoy, a partir de hoy.

toddle ['tɔdl] *vi* (*begin to walk*) empezar a andar, dar los primeros pasos; (*walk unsteadily*) caminar sin seguridad; (*fam: go*) ir; (*stroll*) dar un paseo; (*depart*) irse, marcharse (*also* **— off**); **we must be toddling** es hora de irnos; **so I —d round to see him** así que fui a visitarle.

toddler ['tɔdlə*] *n* pequeñito *m*, a *f* (que aprende a andar, que da sus primeros pasos).

toddy ['tɔdi] *n* ponche *m*.

to-do [tə'du:] *n* (*fam*) lío *m* (*fam*), follón *m* (*fam*); **there was a great —** hubo un tremendo follón; **what's all the — about?** ¿qué pasa?; **she made a great —** armó un lío imponente.

toe [təu] **1** *n* (*Anat*) dedo *m* del pie; punta *f* del pie; (*of sock*) punta *f*; (*of shoe*) puntera *f*; **big — dedo** *m* gordo del pie, dedo *m* grande del pie; **little —** dedo *m* pequeño del pie; **he put the cigarette out with his —** apagó el cigarrillo con la punta del pie; **to keep someone on his —s** mantener a uno en estado de vigilancia, hacer que uno siga estando alerta; **you have to keep on your —s** hay que estar alerta, hay que mantenerse bien despierto; **to turn up one's —s** (*fam*) estirar la pata (*fam*).

2 *vt* tocar con la punta del pie; **to — the line** conformarse, someterse.

toecap ['təukæp] *n* puntera *f*.

-toed [təud] *adj* de ... dedos del pie, *eg* **four-toed** de cuatros dedos del pie.

toenail ['təuneil] n uña f del dedo del pie; **ingrowing** — uñero m (del pie).

toff [tɔf] n (fam) currutaco m, chuleta m (fam).

toffee ['tɔfi] n caramelo m; **he can't do it for** — (fam) no tiene la menor idea de cómo hay que hacerlo.

toffee apple ['tɔfi,æpl] n pirulí m.

toffee-nosed ['tɔfi'nəuzd] adj presumido, engreído.

tog [tɔg] **1** vt: **to** — **someone up** ataviar a uno (in de), vestir a uno (in de) de modo impresionante (or ridículo etc); **to get** — **ged up** ataviarse, vestirse.
2 vr: **to** — **oneself up** ataviarse, vestirse (in de), emperejilarse.

toga ['təugə] n toga f.

together [tə'geðə*] adv (a) (in company) junto, juntos, juntamente; (in concert) juntos, a la vez, a un tiempo; (uninterruptedly) sin interrupción; (consecutively) seguido; **all** — **now** ! (pulling) ¡todos a la vez!; ¡bien, ahora!; **for weeks** — durante varias semanas seguidas; **now we're** — ahora estamos juntos; **they were all** — **in the bar** todos estaban reunidos en el bar; **we're in this** — en esto tenemos igual responsabilidad los dos; nos une la misma suerte; **they were both in it** — resultó que los dos se habían confabulado, los dos estaban metidos en el asunto; **you can't all get in** — no podéis entrar todos a la vez; **we'll do parts A and B** — haremos juntamente las partes A y B; — **they managed it** entre los dos lo lograron; **they belong** — están bien juntos, forman una pareja; **they work** — trabajan juntos; see **bring, call** etc.
(b) — **with** junto con; conjuntamente con; — **with A, B is important** junto con A es importante B.

togetherness [tə'geðənis] n sentimiento m de estar todos estrechamente unidos; compañerismo m; espíritu m de familia (or de grupo etc).

toggle ['tɔgl] n cazonete m de aparejo; fiador m.

Togoland ['təugəulænd] Togolandia f.

togs [tɔgz] npl (fam) ropa f.

toil [tɔil] **1** n labor f, trabajo m; fatiga f; afán m, esfuerzo m; **after months of** — después de varios meses de trabajo (agotador).
2 vi (a) trabajar; fatigarse; apurarse, afanarse; **to** — **to do something** esforzarse por hacer algo, afanarse por hacer algo; **we** — **ed at it for hours** trabajamos en ello durante muchas horas (sin éxito); **they** — **ed on into the night** siguieron trabajando hasta muy entrada la noche.
(b) **to** — **along** caminar con dificultad, avanzar penosamente; **to** — **up a hill** subir penosamente una colina; **the engine is beginning to** — el motor empieza a funcionar con dificultad.

toilet ['tɔilit] **1** n (process of dressing) tocado m; atavío m; (dress) vestido m; (euph: lavatory) inodoro m, lavabo m, wáter m; (dressing table) tocador m.
2 attr de tocador; — **requisites** artículos mpl de limpieza; — **set** juego m de tocador.

toilet bag ['tɔilitbæg] n, **toilet case** ['tɔilitkeis] n neceser m, estuche m de aseo.

toilet paper ['tɔilit,peipə*] n papel m higiénico.

toiletries ['tɔilitriz] npl artículos mpl de tocador, artículos mpl de limpieza.

toilet roll ['tɔilit,rəul] n rollo m de papel higiénico.

toilet soap ['tɔilit,səup] n jabón m de tocador.

toilet water ['tɔilit'wɔːtə*] n agua f de tocador.

toilette [twaː'let] n = **toilet**.

toils [tɔilz] npl red f, lazo m.

toilsome ['tɔilsəm] adj penoso, fatigoso.

toilworn ['tɔilwɔːn] adj completamente cansado, rendido.

token ['təukən] **1** n (a) (sign, symbol) señal f, muestra f, indicio m; (remembrance) prenda f, recuerdo m; (of one's appreciation etc) detalle m, señal f de agradecimiento; **as a** — **of, in** — **of** en señal de; como recuerdo de; **by the same** — igualmente (bien), del mismo modo; **love** — prenda f de amor.
(b) (disc etc) ficha f, disco m (metálico).
2 adj, attr simbólico; — **payment** pago m nominal, pago m simbólico; **to put up a** — **resistance** oponer una resistencia simbólica, resistirse por pura fórmula.

told [təuld] pret and ptp of **tell**.

tolerable ['tɔlərəbl] adj (bearable) tolerable, soportable; (fair) regular, pasable.

tolerably ['tɔlərəbli] adv bastante; pasablemente; **a** — **good player** un jugador bastante bueno, un jugador pasable; **it is** — **certain that** ... es casi seguro que ...

tolerance ['tɔlərəns] n tolerancia f; paciencia f, indulgencia f.

tolerant ['tɔlərənt] adj tolerante; indulgente.

tolerantly ['tɔlərəntli] adv con tolerancia; con indulgencia.

tolerate ['tɔləreit] vt tolerar, soportar, aguantar; **are we to** — **this**? ¿hemos de soportar esto sin protestar?; **I can't** — **any more** no aguanto más; **it is not to be** — **d** es intolerable, es insoportable.

toleration [,tɔlə'reiʃən] n tolerancia f; **religious** — tolerancia f religiosa; libertad f de cultos.

toll¹ [təul] n (a) (on road) peaje m, portazgo m; (on bridge) pontazgo m; **to pay** — pagar el peaje.
(b) (losses, casualties) mortalidad f, número m de víctimas, número m de pérdidas; **the** — **on the roads** el número de víctimas en accidentes de circulación; **there is a heavy** — hay muchas víctimas, son muchos los muertos; **the disease takes a heavy** — **each year** cada año la enfermedad se lleva a muchas víctimas, cada año la enfermedad causa gran número de muertes; **to take** — **of** causar bajas en, tener su efecto en.

toll² [təul] **1** vt bell tañer, tocar, doblar (a muerto); **to** — **the hour** dar la hora.
2 vi doblar (a muerto); **the bells were** — **ing in mourning for** ... doblaron las campanas en señal de duelo por ...

tollbar ['təulbɑː*] n barrera f de peaje.

tollbridge ['təulbridʒ] n puente m de peaje.

toll call ['təulkɔːl] n (US Tel) conferencia f interurbana.

tollgate ['təulgeit] n barrera f de peaje.

tolling ['təuliŋ] n tañido m, doblar m.

tollkeeper ['təul,kiːpə*] n peajero m, portazguero m.

tollway ['təulwei] n (Aut) autopista f de peaje.

Tom [tɔm] nombre cariñoso de **Thomas**; — **Dick and Harry** el hombre medio, el hombre de la calle; **you shan't marry any** — **Dick or Harry** no te casarás con un cualquiera; — **Thumb** Pulgarcito; **peeping** — curioso m.

tom [tɔm] n gato m (macho).

tomahawk ['tɔməhɔːk] n tomahawk m.

tomato [tə'mɑːtəu, US tə'meitəu] n, pl **tomatoes** [tə'mɑːtəuz] (fruit) tomate m; (plant) tomatera f.

tomato plant [tə'mɑːtəuplɑːnt] n tomatera f.

tomb [tuːm] n tumba f, sepulcro m.

tombola [tɔm'bəulə] n tómbola f.

tomboy ['tɔmbɔi] n muchacha f hombruna, muchachota f, chica f poco femenina.

tombstone ['tuːmstəun] n lápida f sepulcral.

tomcat ['tɔmkæt] n gato m (macho).

tome [təum] n (hum) librote m.

tomfool ['tɔm'fuːl] **1** adj tonto, estúpido. **2** n tonto m, imbécil m.

tomfoolery [tɔm'fuːləri] n pataratas fpl, payasadas fpl.

Tommy ['tɔmi] nombre cariñoso de **Thomas**; — **Atkins** el soldado raso inglés.

tommy gun ['tɔmigʌn] n metralleta f, pistola f ametralladora.

tommyrot ['tɔmirɔt] n tonterías fpl.

tomorrow [tə'mɔrəu] **1** adv mañana; **a week** — de mañana en ocho días; — **morning** mañana por la mañana; — **evening** mañana por la tarde.
2 n mañana f; **the day after** — pasado mañana; — **is Sunday** mañana es domingo; — **is another day** mañana es otro día; **will** — **do**? ¿lo puedo dejar para mañana?, ¿le conviene mañana?

tomtit ['tɔmtit] n carbonero m común.

tomtom ['tɔmtɔm] n tantán m.

ton [tʌn] n (a) tonelada f; **metric** — tonelada f métrica; **register** — tonelada f de registro; **a ship of 60,000 gross register** —**s** un buque de 60.000 toneladas de registro bruto.
(b) —**s** (fam) montones mpl; **we have** —**s of it at home** tenemos montones de eso en casa; **we have** —**s of time** nos sobra tiempo, tenemos tiempo de sobra.
(c) (sl) velocidad f de 100 millas por hora; **to do a** — ir a 100 millas por hora (en moto).

tonal ['təunl] adj tonal.

tonality [təu'næliti] n tonalidad f.

tone [təun] **1** n (a) (in most senses) tono m; (of colour) tono m, tonalidad f; matiz m; **in low** —**s** en tono bajo; **in an angry** — en tono de enojo.
(b) (class) distinción f, buen tono m, elegancia f; **the place has** — el sitio tiene buen tono, es un sitio elegante; **the clientèle gives the restaurant** — la clientela da distinción al restaurante.
(c) (tendency) tendencia f; **the prevailing** — la tendencia actual, la tendencia predominante; **the** — **of the market** la tendencia general del mercado.

2 *vt* (*Mus*) entonar; (*Phot*) virar; **to — down** amortiguar, suavizar el tono de; (*fig*) suavizar, modificar; **to — up** (*Med*) tonificar, entonar; (*fig*) elevar el tono de.

3 *vi* armonizar, ir bien juntos; **to — down** moderarse, hablar (*etc*) con más calma; **to — in with** armonizar con, ir bien con, ir bien con.

tone control ['təunkən,trəul] *n* (*Radio etc*) control *m* de tonalidad.

tone-deaf ['təun'def] *adj* falto de sentido musical.

toneless ['təunlis] *adj* soso, flojo; *voice* monótono.

tonelessly ['təunlisli] *adv* monótonamente.

tone poem ['təun,pəuim] *n* poema *m* sinfónico.

tongs [tɔŋz] *npl* (*for coal etc*) tenazas *fpl*; (*for sweets, sugar etc*) tenacillas *fpl*; **a pair of —** unas tenazas, unas tenacillas.

tongue [tʌŋ] *n* (*Anat*) lengua *f*; (*language*) lengua *f*. idioma *m*; (*of shoe etc*) lengüeta *f*; (*of bell*) badajo *m*; (*of flame, land*) lengua *f*; **mother —, native —** lengua *f* materna; **in the vulgar —** en la lengua vulgar, en la lengua vernácula; **with one's — in one's cheek** irónicamente, burla burlando; **to give —** empezar a ladrar; **to give a ready —** no morderse la lengua; **to hold one's —** callarse; **hold your —!** ¡a callarse!; **to loosen someone's —** hacer hablar a uno; **wine loosens the —** el vino hace soltar la lengua.

tongue-lashing ['tʌŋ'læʃiŋ] *n* latigazo *m*, reprensión *f*; **to give someone a —** poner a uno como un trapo.

tongue-tied ['tʌŋtaid] *adj* que tiene dificultad al hablar, que tiene defecto del habla; (*fig*) tímido, premioso, confuso.

tongue twister ['tʌŋ,twistə*] *n* trabalenguas *m*.

tonic ['tɔnik] **1** *adj* tónico.

2 *n* (a) (*Mus*) tónica *f*.

(b) (*Med*) tónico *m*; (*as drink, with gin etc*) tónica *f*; (*fig*) tónico *m*; **this news will be a — for the market** esta noticia será un tónico para la bolsa.

tonicity [tɔ'nisiti] *n* tonicidad *f*.

tonight [tə'nait] *adv* esta noche.

toning solution ['təuninsə'lu:ʃən] *n* solución *f* entonadora.

tonnage ['tʌnidʒ] *n* tonelaje *m*; **gross register —** toneladas *fpl* de registro bruto; **the — lost in 1942** la cantidad de buques hundidos en 1942 (expresada en toneladas).

-tonner ['tʌnə*] *n* de . . . toneladas, *eg* **a 1,000—** un barco de 1.000 toneladas.

tonsil ['tɔnsl] *n* amígdala *f*.

tonsillectomy [,tɔnsi'lektəmi] *n* amigdalotomía *f*.

tonsillitis [,tɔnsi'laitis] *n* amigdalitis *f*.

tonsorial [tɔn'sɔːriəl] *adj* (*esp hum*) barberil; relativo a la barba.

tonsure ['tɔnʃə*] **1** *n* tonsura *f*. **2** *vt* tonsurar.

tonsured ['tɔnʃəd] *adj* tonsurado.

Tony ['təuni] *nombre cariñoso de* **Anthony**.

too [tu:] *adv* (a) (*excessively*) demasiado; muy; **it's — hard** es demasiado duro, es muy duro; **it's — easy** es muy fácil, es muy sencillo; **it's — heavy for me to lift** es demasiado pesado para que yo lo levante; **— often** con demasiada frecuencia, muy a menudo; **it's — early for that** es (muy) temprano para eso; *see* **many, much, well**.

(b) (*also*) también; además, por otra parte; **I went —** yo fui también; **and it's broken —** y además está roto.

took [tuk] *pret of* **take**.

tool [tu:l] **1** *n* (a) herramienta *f*; utensilio *m*; (*set of*) **—s** útiles *mpl*, utillaje *m*; **garden —s** útiles *mpl* de jardinería; **plumber's —s** útiles *mpl* de fontanero; **to down —s** suspender el trabajo; (*strike*) declararse en huelga; **give us the —s and we will finish the job** dadnos las herramientas y nosotros terminaremos la obra.

(b) (*fig: person, book etc*) instrumento *m*; **the book is an essential —** el libro es indispensable, el libro es instrumento imprescindible; **he was an unwilling — of the gang** sin quererlo fue un instrumento de la pandilla; **he is just the — of the minister** es la criatura del ministro nada más.

2 *vt* labrar con herramienta; *book* estampar en seco; filetear.

toolbag ['tu:lbæg] *n* bolsa *f* de herramientas.

toolbox ['tu:lbɔks] *n*, **tool chest** ['tu:ltʃest] *n* caja *f* de herramientas.

tooling ['tu:liŋ] *n* estampación *f* en seco; fileteado *m*.

toolkit ['tu:lkit] *n* juego *m* de herramientas.

toolshed ['tu:lʃed] *n* cobertizo *m* para herramientas.

toot [tu:t] **1** *n* sonido *m* breve (de claxon *etc*); **he went off with a — on the horn** partió con un breve toque de bocina.

2 *vt* sonar, tocar.

3 *vi* sonar (la bocina *etc*); (*of person, Aut*) tocar la bocina, dar un bocinazo.

tooth [tu:θ] *n*, *pl* **teeth** [ti:θ] (a) (*Anat*) diente *m*; (*esp molar*) muela *f*; **back —** muela *f*; **false teeth** dentadura *f* postiza; **front —** incisivo *m*; **wisdom —** muela *f* del juicio; **in the teeth of the wind** contra un viento violento; **in the teeth of great opposition** contra una resistencia de lo más terco; **to be armed to the teeth** estar armado hasta los dientes; **to cast something in someone's teeth** echar algo en cara a uno; **to cut one's teeth** endentecer, echar los dientes; **to be fed up to the (back) teeth with** estar hasta la coronilla de; **to fight — and nail** luchar encarnizadamente; **to get one's teeth into** hincar el diente a (*also fig*); **to be getting long in the —** ser bastante viejo ya; **to have a — out** hacerse sacar una muela; **she has a sweet —** le gustan las cosas dulces; es golosa; **to show one's teeth** enseñar los dientes.

(b) (*of saw, wheel*) diente *m*; (*of comb*) púa *f*.

toothache ['tu:θeik] *n* dolor *m* de muelas.

toothbrush ['tu:θbrʌʃ] *n* cepillo *m* de dientes; **— moustache** bigote *m* de cepillo.

toothcomb ['tu:θkəum] *n*: **to go through something with a fine —** registrar algo minuciosamente.

toothed ['tu:θt] *adj wheel etc* dentado; **de dientes . . .**, *eg* **big-toothed** de dientes grandes.

toothing ['tu:θiŋ] *n* (*Archit*) adaraja *f*.

toothless ['tu:θlis] *adj* desdentado.

toothpaste ['tu:θpeist] *n* pasta *f* dentífrica, pasta *f* de dientes, crema *f* dental.

toothpick ['tu:θpik] *n* palillo *m* mondadientes.

tooth powder ['tu:θ,paudə*] *n* polvos *mpl* dentífricos.

toothsome ['tu:θsəm] *adj* sabroso.

toothy ['tu:θi] *adj* dentón; **to give someone a — smile** sonreír a uno mostrando mucho los dientes.

tootle ['tu:tl] **1** *n* sonido *m* breve (de flauta, trompeta *etc*); serie *f* de notas breves; **give us a — on your trumpet** tócanos algo a la trompeta; *see also* **toot**.

2 *vt flute etc* tocar.

3 *vi* (a) tocar la flauta (*etc*); *see also* **toot**.

(b) (*Aut: fam*) **we —d down to Brighton** hicimos una escapada a Brighton, fuimos de excursión a Brighton; **we were tootling along at 60** íbamos a 60 millas por hora.

too-too ['tu:'tu:] *adj* (*fam*): **she's terribly —** es la mar de afectada (*fam*), es una persona muy exagerada; **isn't it just —?** ¡qué monada! (*fam*), ¡qué precioso!

toots(y) ['tu:ts(i)] *n* (*US fam*) chica *f*, gachí *f* (*sl*); **hey —!** ¡oye, guapa!

top¹ [tɔp] **1** *n* (a) (*topmost point*) cumbre *f*, cima *f*; ápice *m*; (*of tree*) copa *f*; (*of head*) coronilla *f*; (*of building*) remate *m*; (*of wall*) coronamiento *m*; (*of wave*) cresta *f*; (*of stairs etc*) lo alto, parte *f* alta; (*of list, page, table, classification*) cabeza *f*; primer puesto *m*, primera posición *f*; (*of plant*) hojas *fpl*, parte *f* superior; **at the — of the hill** en la cumbre de la colina; **at the — of the tree** en lo alto del árbol; **at the — of the list** a la cabeza de la lista, en la primera posición de la lista; **executives who are at the — of their companies** ejecutivos que están en la cumbre de sus empresas; **Toboso is at the — of the league** Toboso encabeza la liga, Toboso va en posición primera de la liga; **he lives at the — of the house** ocupa el piso más alto de la casa; **from — to bottom** de arriba abajo, de cabo a rabo; **the system is rotten from — to bottom** el sistema entero está podrido; **from — to toe** de pies a cabeza; **on —** encima; **to be on —** estar encima; estar en la parte superior; (*fig*) llevar ventaja, estar ganando; **to come out on —** salir ganando, salir ganancioso; **it's just one thing on — of another** es una cosa tras otra; **and then on — of all that . . .** y luego por añadidura . . .; y luego para colmo de desgracias; **to go over the —** lanzarse al ataque (saliendo de las trincheras).

(b) (*surface*) superficie *f*; **on — of** sobre, encima de; **it floats on — of the water** flota sobre el agua; **oil comes to the —** el aceite sale a la superficie; **the table — is damaged** la superficie de la mesa está deteriorada.

(c) (*further part*) otro extremo *m*, parte *f* más lejana; **I saw him at the — of the street** le vi al otro extremo de la calle; **he sits at the — of the table** se sienta a la cabecera de la mesa.

(d) (*Naut*) cofa *f*.

(e) (*cap of bottle*) cápsula *f*, tapa *f*; (*of pen*) capuchón *m*; (*lid*) tapa *f*, tapadera *f*; (*of carriage*) baca *f*; (*of bus*) piso *m* superior, imperial *f*; (*Aut, US*) capota *f*; **with a sliding —, with a sunshine —**

descapotable, con techo corredizo; **to blow one's —** (*fam*) subirse por las paredes (*fam*).

(f) (*best*) lo mejor; **the — of the flood** (*or* tide) la pleamar; **the — of the morning to you!** ¡buenos días!; **to be at the — of one's form** estar en plena forma; **to shout at the — of one's voice** llamar a voz en grito; **it's the —s** (*fam*) es tremendo (*fam*), es fabuloso (*fam*), es la flor de la canela.

2 *adj* (*highest*) más alto, el más alto; cimero; *part* superior, más alto; *floor, stair etc* más alto, último; (*first*) primero; (*greatest*) máximo; (*highest in rank*) principal, primero; *price* máximo, tope; **at — speed** a máxima velocidad; **the — 20** (*records*) los primeros 20 discos en la clasificación nacional; **the — men in the party** los líderes del partido, los jerarcas del partido; **he was — boy** se clasificó primero (entre los muchachos); **to come —** ganar, ganar el primer puesto, clasificarse primero; **he came — in maths** tuvo la mejor nota en matemáticas; *see* **dog, people** etc.

3 *vt* **(a)** *tree* desmochar; *plant* descabezar; *fruit etc* quitar las hojas (*etc*) de; *person* (*hang: sl*) colgar, (*murder: sl*) apiolar (*fam*), cargarse a (*fam*).

(b) (*complete upper part of*) coronar, rematar; **the wall is —ped with stone** el muro tiene un coronamiento de piedras; **and to — it all . . .** y por añadidura . . .; y para colmo de desgracias; **he —ped this off by saying that . . .** esto lo remató diciendo que . . .; **he —ped off the 8th course with a cup of coffee** para completar el octavo plato se bebió una taza de café; **to — up someone's glass** acabar de llenar (*or* volver a llenar) el vaso de uno; **to — up a battery** llenar una pila hasta el nivel indicado.

(c) (*exceed*) exceder, aventajar; salir por encima de; **to — someone in height** ser más alto que uno; **to — someone by a head** sacar a uno una cabeza; **this —s everything** esto supera a todo lo demás; **we have —ped last year's takings by £20** hemos recaudado 20 libras más que el año pasado, los ingresos exceden a los del año pasado en 20 libras.

(d) (*reach summit of*) llegar a la cumbre de; *class, list* encabezar, estar a la cabeza de; llegar a ocupar la primera posición de; **the team —ped the league all season** el equipo iba en cabeza de la liga toda la temporada.

top² [tɔp] *n* (*spinning —*) peonza *f*, peón *m*; (*humming—, musical —*) trompa *f*.

topaz ['təupæz] *n* topacio *m*.

top boots ['tɔpbuːts] *npl* botas *fpl* de campaña.

topcoat ['tɔpkəut] *n* sobretodo *m*.

tope [təup] *vi* beber (más de la cuenta), emborracharse.

topee ['təupiː] *n* casco *m* colonial.

toper ['təupə*] *n* borrachín *m*.

topflight ['tɔpflait] *adj* sobresaliente, de primera clase.

topgallant [tɔp'gælənt, *Naut* tə'gælənt] *n* (*also — sail*) juanete *m*.

top hat ['tɔp'hæt] *n* chistera *f*, sombrero *m* de copa.

top-hatted ['tɔp'hætid] *adj* en chistera, enchisterado.

top-heavy ['tɔp'hevi] *adj* demasiado pesado por arriba; (*fig*) falto de equilibrio, mal equilibrado.

top-hole ['tɔp'həul] *adj* (*sl*) de primera; **—!** ¡estupendo!, ¡pipudo! (*sl*).

topic ['tɔpik] *n* asunto *m*, tema *m*.

topical ['tɔpikəl] *adj* actual, de interés actual, corriente; **— talk** charla *f* sobre cuestiones del día, charla *f* sobre actualidades; **a highly — question** una cuestión de palpitante actualidad.

topicality [ˌtɔpi'kæliti] *n* actualidad *f*; importancia *f* actual, interés *m* actual.

topknot ['tɔpnɔt] *n* moño *m* (*also Orn*); (*fam*) cabeza *f*.

topless ['tɔplis] *adj dress* que deja el pecho al descubierto, que no cubre el pecho.

top-level ['tɔp'levl] *adj*: **— conference** conferencia *f* al más alto nivel.

topmast ['tɔpmɑːst] *n* mastelero *m*.

topmost ['tɔpməust] *adj* más alto, el más alto.

topnotch ['tɔp'nɔtʃ] *adj* (*fam*) de rango muy alto; de primera, estupendo.

topographer [tə'pɔgrəfə*] *n* topógrafo *m*.

topographic(al) [ˌtɔpə'græfik] *adj* topográfico.

topography [tə'pɔgrəfi] *n* topografía *f*.

topper ['tɔpə*] *n* (*fam*) chistera *f*, sombrero *m* de copa.

topping ['tɔpiŋ] *adj* (*fam*) bárbaro (*fam*), pistonudo (*fam*).

topple ['tɔpl] **1** *vt* (*also* **to — over**) derribar, derrocar; hacer caer; volcar.

2 *vi* (*also* **to — down**) caerse, venirse abajo; (*also*

to — over) ₊olcarse; (*lose balance*) perder el equilibrio; (*totter*) tambalearse; **he —d over a cliff** cayó por un precipicio; **after the crash the bus —d over** después del choque el autobús se volcó.

top-rank ['tɔp'ræŋk] *adj* de primera categoría; *officer* de alta graduación.

topsail ['tɔpsl] *n* gavia *f*.

top-secret ['tɔp'siːkrit] *adj* de lo más secreto, de reserva absoluta.

topsoil ['tɔpsɔil] *n* capa *f* superficial del suelo.

topsy-turvy ['tɔpsi'təːvi] **1** *adv* en desorden, patas arriba; **everything is —** todo está patas arriba. **2** *adj* confuso, desordenado.

toque [təuk] *n* toca *f*.

tor [tɔː*] *n* colina *f* abrupta y rocosa, pico *m* pequeño (*en el suroeste de Inglaterra*).

torch [tɔːtʃ] *n* (*flaming*) antorcha *f*, tea *f*, hacha *f*; (*electric*) linterna *f* eléctrica, lámpara *f* de bolsillo; **Olympic — antorcha** *f* olímpica; **to carry a — for someone** (*fig*) seguir enamorado de uno a pesar de no ser correspondido por él.

torchbearer ['tɔːtʃˌbɛərə*] *n* portahachón *m*.

torchlight ['tɔːtʃlait] *n* luz *f* de antorcha; **— procession** desfile *m* de portahachones.

tore ['tɔː*] *pret of* **tear**.

toreador ['tɔriədɔː*] *n* torero *m*.

torment ['tɔːment] *n* tormento *m*; angustia *f*; suplicio *m*; **the —s of jealousy** los tormentos de los celos; **to be in —** estar sufriendo, sufrir mucho.

torment [tɔː'ment] *vt* atormentar, martirizar; (*torture*) torturar; **we were —ed by thirst** sufrimos los tormentos de la sed; **she was —ed by doubts** la atormentaron las dudas; **don't — the cat** no le des guerra al gato.

tormentor [tɔː'mentə*] *n* atormentador *m*, ora *f*.

torn [tɔːn] *pt ptp of* **tear**.

tornado [tɔː'neidəu] *n, pl* **tornadoes** [tɔː'neidəuz] tornado *m*.

torpedo [tɔː'piːdəu] **1** *n, pl* **torpedoes** [tɔː'piːdəuz] torpedo *m*. **2** *vt* torpedear (*also fig*).

torpedo boat [tɔː'piːdəubəut] *n* torpedero *m*, lancha *f* torpedera.

torpedo tube [tɔː'piːdəutjuːb] *n* tubo *m* lanzatorpedos.

torpid ['tɔːpid] *adj* aletargado, inactivo; (*fig*) torpe, apático; aburrido.

torpidity [tɔː'piditi] *n*, **torpor** ['tɔːpə*] *n* letargo *m*, inactividad *f*; (*fig*) torpeza *f*, apatía *f*; aburrimiento *m*.

torque [tɔːk] *n* par *m* de torsión.

torrent ['tɔrənt] *n* torrente *m* (*also fig*); **to rain in —s** llover a cántaros, diluviar.

torrential [tɔ'renʃəl] *adj* torrencial.

torrid ['tɔrid] *adj* tórrido.

torsion ['tɔːʃən] *n* torsión *f*.

torsional ['tɔːʃənl] *adj* torsional.

torso ['tɔːsəu] *n, pl* **torsos** ['tɔːsəuz] torso *m*.

tort [tɔːt] *n* agravio *m*, tuerto *m*.

tortoise ['tɔːtəs] *n* tortuga *f*.

tortoiseshell ['tɔːtəʃel] *n* carey *m*; **— glasses** gafas *fpl* de carey.

tortuous ['tɔːtjuəs] *adj* tortuoso.

torture ['tɔːtʃə*] **1** *n* tortura *f*; (*fig*) tormento *m*; **it was —!** ¡lo que sufrí!; **to put someone to the —** torturar a uno.

2 *vt* torturar; (*fig*) atormentar; *sense etc* torcer, violentar; **to be —d by doubts** ser atormentado por las dudas.

torturer ['tɔːtʃərə*] *n* verdugo *m*.

torturing ['tɔːtʃəriŋ] *adj* torturador, atormentador.

Tory ['tɔːri] **1** *adj* conservador; **the T— Party** el Partido Conservador. **2** *n* conservador *m*, ora *f*.

Toryism ['tɔːriizəm] *n* conservatismo *m*, conservadurismo *m*.

tosh [tɔʃ] *n* (*fam*) música *f* celestial; **—!** ¡tonterías!

toss [tɔs] **1** *n* **(a)** (*movement: of head etc*) movimiento *m* brusco; sacudida *f*, meneo *m*; (*throw*) echada *f*, tirada *f*; (*by bull*) cogida *f*; (*fall from horse*) caída *f*; **the ball came to him full —** la pelota llegó a sus manos sin tocar la tierra; **he took a bad —** sufrió una violenta caída.

(b) (*of coin*) echada *f*; sorteo *m* (*para la elección de lado etc*); **to argue the —** andar en dimes y diretes, discutir; **to win the —** ganar el sorteo; **it's a — up** puede ser lo uno tanto como lo otro; **it's a — up whether I go or stay** no decido si irme o quedarme.

2 *vt head etc* mover bruscamente, hacer un movimiento brusco de; sacudir, menear; (*throw*) echar, tirar; (*of bull*) coger (y lanzar al aire); *coin* echar a cara o cruz; **to — someone in a blanket** mantear a uno; **the currents —ed the boat about**

las corrientes zarandeaban la embarcación; **the horse —ed its head** el caballo levantó airosamente la cabeza; **to — aside** echar a un lado, apartar bruscamente, abandonar; **to — off a drink** beberse algo de un trago, beberse algo rápidamente; **to — a book over to someone** tirar un libro a uno; **— it over!** ¡dámelo!; **to — up** coin echar a cara o cruz.

3 vi **(a)** agitarse, sacudirse; (of plumes etc) ondear; (in a boat: gently) balancearse sobre las ondas, (violently) ser sacudido por las ondas; **to — (in one's sleep), to — and turn** revolverse (en la cama).

(b) (also **to — up**) jugar a cara o cruz (for something algo); (Sport) sortear (for something algo); **we'll — up to see who does it** jugaremos a cara o cruz para decidir quién lo hará.

tot¹ [tɔt] n **(a)** (drink) trago m, copita f; **just a —** unas gotitas nada más; **let's go in here for a —** entremos aquí a tomar algo. **(b)** (child) nene m, a f.

tot² [tɔt] **1** vt: **to — up** sumar. **2** vi: **it —s up to £5** suma 5 libras, viene a ser 5 libras; **what does it — up to?** ¿cuánto suma?

total ['təutl] **1** adj (Math etc) total; (complete, utter) total, completo, entero; **the — losses amount to . . .** las pérdidas suman un total de . . .; **what is the — amount?** ¿cuánto es el importe total?; **— failure** fracaso m completo, fracaso m rotundo; **— war** guerra f total; **we were in — ignorance** lo ignorábamos por completo; **the disagreement is —** el desacuerdo es total.

2 n total m; suma f; cantidad f global; **grand —** importe m total; **it comes to a — of . . .** suma en total . . ., asciende a . . .; **the sum — of people** la colectividad de las personas.

3 vt sumar (also **to — up**).

4 vi ascender a, sumar, totalizar.

totalitarian [ˌtəutælɪ'tɛəriən] adj totalitario.

totalitarianism [ˌtəutælɪ'tɛəriənɪzəm] n totalitarismo m.

totality [təu'tælɪti] n totalidad f.

totalizator ['təutəlaizeitə*] n totalizador m.

totalize ['təutəlaiz] vt totalizar.

totally ['təutəli] adv totalmente, completamente.

tote¹ [təut] n (fam) totalizador m.

tote² [təut] vt (fam) acarrear, llevar (con dificultad); **I —d it around all day** lo llevé de acá para allá todo el día.

totem ['təutəm] n tótem m.

totemic [təu'temik] adj totémico.

totem pole ['təutəmpəul] n poste m totémico.

totter ['tɔtə*] vi (stagger) bambolearse, tambalearse; (be about to fall) tambalearse, estar para desplomarse.

tottering ['tɔtəriŋ] adj, **tottery** ['tɔtəri] adj tambaleante; nada seguro; ruinoso; **he's getting tottery** empieza a andar con poca seguridad; **with tottering steps** con pasos inseguros, con pasos vacilantes.

toucan ['tu:kən] n tucán m.

touch [tʌtʃ] **1** n **(a)** (sense of —) tacto m; **it feels rough to the —** es áspero al tacto.

(b) (act of —ing, contact) toque m; contacto m; (light brushing) roce m; (Mus, of typist) pulsación f; (Art) pincelada f, toque m; **final —, finishing —** última mano f, último toque m; **to give something a finishing —, to put the finishing — to something** dar el último toque a algo; **human —, personal —** (in person's character) don m de gentes, (in contacts etc) nota f personal, nota f humana; **the master's —** la mano del maestro; **it has the — of genius** lleva el sello de la genialidad; **it's the Nelson —** es el genio de Nelson; **the cold — of a dead fish** el contacto glacial con un pez muerto; **at a — of her hand, I . . .** al tocarme la mano de ella, yo . . .; **with the barest — of a finger** con una ligerísima presión del dedo; **by —** a tiento, tentándolo; **I felt a — on my neck** sentí que alguien me tocaba el cuello; **to give someone a — on the arm** tocar el brazo de uno.

(c) (contact, fit) contacto m; **to be in — with someone** estar en contacto (or comunicación) con uno; **to be in — with new inventions** estar al tanto de los inventos, mantenerse al corriente de los inventos; **to be out of — with someone** haber perdido contacto con uno; **he's completely out of —** sus ideas están completamente postergadas, está quedando anticuado; **we're very much out of — here** aquí casi ni recibimos noticias de lo que pasa; **to get into — with someone** ponerse en contacto con uno; **you can get into — with me at No. 7** si me quiere para algo llame al número 7; **you ought to get into — with the police** conviene informar a la policía; **to keep in — with someone** mantener relaciones con uno; **well, keep in —!** ¡bueno, téngame al corriente!; **to lose — with someone**

perder contacto con uno; **to put someone into — with another person** ayudar a uno a establecer contacto con otra persona.

(d) (sl) **he's good for a —** seguramente nos dará (or prestará) algo; **to make a —** lograr sacar dinero de uno, lograr dar un sablazo a uno.

(e) (small quantity) pizca f; poquito m; (Med) ataque m leve; **a — of the sun** una insolación; **with a — of irony** con un dejo de ironía, con un punto de ironía; **add a — of salt** agregue un poquitín de sal; **to have a — of 'flu** tener un ataque leve de gripe.

(f) (Sport) touché f, parte f fuera de juego; **to be in —** estar fuera de juego; **to kick for —, to kick the ball into —** poner el balón fuera de juego.

2 vt **(a)** (come into contact with) tocar; (and explore) palpar; (brush against) rozar; (reach) alcanzar; **to — something with one's finger** tocar algo con el dedo; **someone —ed me on the arm** alguien me tocó el brazo; **don't —!** ¡no tocar!, ¡fuera las manos!; **his property —es ours** su propiedad linda con la nuestra, su finca es contigua a la nuestra; **and the police can't — him** y la policía no tiene motivo para detenerle, la policía no tiene autoridad para detenerle; **I never —ed her!** ¡no la toqué siquiera!; **I wouldn't — it (with a barge pole)** no lo quiero ver ni de lejos; **to — ground** (Aer) tocar tierra, tomar tierra; see **bottom, wood.**

(b) (eat, drink) tomar, probar; **I haven't —ed a mouthful** no he probado un solo bocado; **I never — onion** no pruebo la cebolla; **I never — gin** no bebo nunca ginebra.

(c) (equal) compararse con, igualar; **there's no violinist to — him, no one can — him as a violinist** no hay violinista que se le iguale, no hay violinista que pueda compararse con él.

(d) (make an impression on) hacer efecto en, hacer mella en; **this saw won't — it** esta sierra no le hace mella, esta sierra es inútil para esto; **I couldn't — the third question** quedé muy lejos de poder contestar la tercera pregunta.

(e) (move) conmover, enternecer; **I was deeply —ed** me conmoví mucho, me emocioné profundamente; **it —ed our hearts** enterneció nuestros corazones; **no one can see it without being —ed** nadie lo ve sin conmoverse.

(f) (concern) afectar, tocar; **it —es us all closely** nos toca de cerca a todos; **if it —es the national interest** si afecta al interés nacional.

(g) (sl) **to — someone for a loan** dar un sablazo a uno, lograr sacar dinero de uno; **to — someone for £5** lograr que uno preste 5 libras.

(h) **to — down** (Sport) poner en tierra; **to — off explosion** hacer estallar; revolt hacer estallar, provocar; **it —ed off a series of ideas** dio origen a una serie de ideas; **it —ed off a fierce argument** causó una violenta discusión; **to — up** retocar (also Art, Phot).

3 vi **(a)** (come into contact) tocarse; encontrarse; tocar al pasar, pasar rozando; (collide) chocar ligeramente; (be adjacent) lindar, estar contiguo; **our hands —ed** se encontraron nuestras manos; **the subjects — at several points** los temas tienen varios aspectos en común.

(b) **to — at** (Naut) tocar en, hacer escala en; **to — down** (Aer) tocar tierra, aterrizar; (of space capsule) amerizar; (Sport) tocar en tierra; **to — on, to — upon** tocar, aludir (brevemente) a.

touch-and-go ['tʌtʃən'gəu] **1** adj decision difícil, dudoso. **2** n: **it's — whether . . .** está en vilo si . . ., es difícil decidir si . . .

touchdown ['tʌtʃdaun] n (Aer) aterrizaje m; (of space capsule) amerizaje m; (Sport) tocado m en tierra.

touched [tʌtʃt] adj (fam) chiflado, tocado.

touchiness ['tʌtʃinis] n susceptibilidad f.

touching ['tʌtʃiŋ] **1** adj conmovedor, patético. **2** prep tocante a.

touchingly ['tʌtʃiŋli] adv de modo conmovedor, patéticamente.

touchline ['tʌtʃlain] n línea f de banda, línea f de toque, línea f lateral.

touchstone ['tʌtʃstəun] n piedra f de toque (also fig).

touch-typing ['tʌtʃˌtaipiŋ] n mecanografía f al tacto.

touchy ['tʌtʃi] adj susceptible, quisquilloso; **to be —** ofenderse por poca cosa, tener prontos enojos; **he's — about his weight** no le hacen gracia las referencias a su gordura, no le gusta que se le tome el pelo con motivo de su gordura.

tough [tʌf] **1** adj **(a)** (of materials) duro, fuerte, resistente; meat duro, estropajoso; (leathery) correoso.

(b) (*hardy*) resistente, fuerte, vigoroso; **the — sports** los deportes violentos; **he's pretty —** tiene mucha resistencia.

(c) (*unyielding, stubborn*) tenaz, terco; *person* (*pej*) duro, malvado; **we can expect — resistance** hemos de contar con una resistencia tensa.

(d) (*difficult*) difícil, penoso; *problem* espinoso; *journey, work* arduo; **there's a — road ahead** el camino a recorrer es arduo; **to have a — time of it** pasar las de Caín.

(e) (*of luck etc*) malo; **— luck!** ¡mala suerte!; **that's pretty —** eso me parece muy injusto; **but it was — on the others** pero perjudicó a los demás, pero fue muy desagradable para los demás.

2 *n* (*fam*) machote *m*; (*pej*) gorila *m*, forzudo *m*; caradura *m*; **a gang of —s** una pandilla de forzudos.

toughen ['tʌfn] **1** *vt* endurecer. **2** *vi* endurecerse.

toughly ['tʌfli] *adv* vigorosamente; tenazmente, tercamente.

toughness ['tʌfnis] *n* dureza *f*, resistencia *f*; lo correoso; vigor *m*; tenacidad *f*, terquedad *f*; lo difícil, lo penoso; lo arduo; **the job needs a certain —** el trabajo exige cierta resistencia.

Toulon ['tu:'lɔ̃:ŋ] Tolón *f*.

Toulouse ['tu:'lu:z] Tolosa (de Francia).

toupée ['tu:pei] *n* casquete *m*, peluca *f*.

tour ['tuə*] **1** *n* (*journey*) viaje *m* (largo), excursión *f* (larga); (*by team, actors, musicians etc*) gira *f*; (*of building, exhibition*) visita *f*; inspección *f*; **— of duty** período *m* de servicio; **— of inspection** visita *f*; recorrido *m* de inspección; **circular —** viaje *m* redondo; **conducted —** excursión *f* con guía; visita *f* en grupo, visita *f* de inspección; **package —** viaje *m* (de turismo) con todo incluido; **walking —** excursión *f* (larga) a pie; **the Australian — of 1972** la gira australiana de 1972; **the — includes a week in Venice** el programa del viaje incluye una semana en Venecia; **to be on —** estar de viaje; (*of team etc*) estar gira; **to go on —** partir de viaje, (*of team etc*) partir de gira; **to take a company on —** (*Theat*) llevar a una compañía de gira; **to take a play on —** llevar una obra a una serie de teatros (*de provincia etc*).

2 *vt country etc* viajar por, recorrer (como turista); *building, exhibition* visitar, recorrer.

3 *vi* viajar; estar de viaje, hacer viaje de turista; **we're just —ing around** hacemos viajes de turismo aquí y allá.

Touraine [tu'rein] Turena *f*.

tour de force ['tuədə'fɔːs] *n* juego *m* de destreza; demostración *f* de genialidad.

tourer ['tuərə*] *n* (coche *m* de) turismo *m*.

touring ['tuəriŋ] **1** *n* turismo *m*; viajes *mpl* turísticos.

2 *attr company* (*Theat*) que hace una gira; ambulante.

touring car ['tuəriŋkɑ:*] *n* (coche *m* de) turismo *m*.

tourism ['tuərizəm] *n* turismo *m*.

tourist ['tuərist] **1** *n* turista *mf*.

2 *attr* turista, turístico; para turistas; de viajes; **of — interest** de interés turístico; **the — trade** la industria del turismo; *see* **agency, class** *etc*.

tournament ['tuənəmənt] *n* torneo *m*; concurso *m*, certamen *m*; **chess —** torneo *m* de ajedrez; **tennis —** torneo *m* de tenis.

tourney ['tuəni] *n* (*Hist*) torneo *m*.

tourniquet ['tuənikei] *n* torniquete *m*.

touse [tauz] *vt* dar una paliza a (*also fig*).

tousing ['tauziŋ] *n* paliza *f* (*also fig*).

tousle ['tauzl] *vt* ajar, desarreglar; *hair* despeinar.

tousled ['tauzld] *adj* ajado, desarreglado, en desorden; *hair* despeinado.

tout [taut] **1** *n* (*seller*) pregonero *m*; (*agent*) gancho *m*; (*ticket—*) revendedor *m*; (*Racing*) pronosticador *m*.

2 *vt wares* ofrecer, pregonar; *tickets* revender.

3 *vi*: **to — for custom** solicitar clientes; tratar de hacer un negocio.

tout court ['tu:'kuə*] *adv*: **his name is Rodríguez —** se llama Rodríguez a secas.

tow¹ [təu] **1** (*act*) remolque *m*; (*rope*) remolque *m*, cable *m* de remolque; (*thing towed*) vehículo *m* (*etc*) remolcado; **to be on —** ser remolcado, ser llevado a remolque; **to have a car in —** dar remolque a un coche; **he had 3 girls in —** iba acompañado de 3 chicas, (*fig*) andaba en relaciones con 3 chicas, tenía 3 chicas al retortero; **to take in —** dar remolque a.

2 *vt* remolcar, llevar a remolque; **to — something about** (*fig*) llevar algo consigo.

tow² [təu] *n* estopa *f*.

towage ['təuidʒ] *n* (*act*) remolque *m*; (*fee*) derechos *mpl* de remolque.

toward(s) [tə'wɔːd(z)] *prep* (*of direction*) hacia; (*of time*) hacia, cerca de; (*of attitude*) con, para con; **his feelings — the church** sus sentimientos para con la iglesia; **— noon** hacia mediodía; **— 6 o'clock** hacia las 6, a eso de las 6; **we're saving — our holiday** ahorramos dinero para nuestras vacaciones; **it helps — a solution** contribuye a la solución, ayuda en el esfuerzo por encontrar una solución.

towboat ['təubəut] *n* remolcador *m*.

tow car ['təukɑ:*] *n* (US) coche *m* que remolca otro.

towel ['tauəl] **1** *n* toalla *f*. **2** *vt* secar con toalla; frotar con toalla.

towel rail ['tauəlreil] *n* toallero *m*.

tower ['tauə*] **1** *n* torre *f*; (*bell—*) campanario *m*; **ivory —** (*fig*) torre *f* de marfil; **to be a — of strength to someone** ayudar muchísimo a uno.

2 *vi* elevarse; encumbrarse; **to — above, to — over** dominar, destacarse sobre, (*fig*) descollar entre; **it —s to over 300 metres** se eleva a más de 300 metros; **he —s above his contemporaries** descuella fuertemente entre sus coetáneos.

towering ['tauəriŋ] *adj mountain* encumbrado; elevado, elevadísimo; *building* muy alto, imponente por su altura; *figure* destacado, dominante; *rage* muy violento.

towline ['təulain] *n* sirga *f*.

town [taun] **1** *n* ciudad *f*; (*smaller, country —*) pueblo *m*, población *f*; **— and gown** ciudadanos *mpl* y universitarios, ciudad *f* y universidad; **model —** ciudad *f* modelo; **new —** poblado *m* de absorción; **satellite —** ciudad *f* satélite; **to be on the —** estar en plan de juerga; **to go on the —** salir de juerga; **to live in —** vivir en la capital (*esp* Londres); **to go up to —** ir a la capital (*esp* Londres); **to go to —** ir a la ciudad; **to go to — on** (*fam*) dedicarse con entusiasmo a, entregarse de lleno a; **he certainly went to — on that mistake** cierto que aprovechó todas las posibilidades de ese error; **he's out of —** está fuera, está de viaje; **to paint the — red** echar una cana al aire.

2 *attr* urbano; urbanístico; de (la) ciudad, municipal; **— house** casa *f* de ciudad; **— life** vida *f* urbana; *see* **clerk, crier** *etc*.

town plan ['taun'plæn] *n* plan *m* de desarrollo urbano.

town planner ['taun'plænə*] *n* urbanista *mf*.

town planning ['taun'plæniŋ] *n* urbanismo *m*.

townsfolk ['taunzfəuk] *npl* ciudadanos *mpl*.

township ['taunʃip] *n* municipio *m*, término *m* municipal; pueblo *m*.

townsman ['taunzmən] *n*, *pl* **—men** [mən] ciudadano *m*; (*as opposed to countryman*) hombre *m* de la ciudad, habitante *m* de la ciudad.

townspeople ['taunz,pi:pl] *npl* ciudadanos *mpl*.

towpath ['təupɑ:θ] *n* camino *m* de sirga.

towrope ['təurəup] *n* remolque *m*, cable *m* de remolque; (*on canal*) sirga *f*.

toxic ['tɔksik] *adj* tóxico.

toxicological [,tɔksikə'lɔdʒikəl] *adj* toxicológico.

toxicology [,tɔksi'kɔlədʒi] *n* toxicología *f*.

toxin ['tɔksin] *n* toxina *f*.

toy [tɔi] **1** *n* juguete *m*; (*pej, iro*) juguete *m*, chuchería *f*.

2 *adj, attr railway etc* de juguete, de jugar; *dog etc* de raza muy pequeña, miniatura; **— car** coche *m* de juguete; **— soldier** soldadito *m* de plomo; **— theatre** teatro *m* de títeres.

3 *vi*: **to — with** *object* jugar con, divertirse jugando con; *food* comer melindrosamente; *idea* acariciar; *someone's affections* divertirse con.

toybox ['tɔibɔks] *n* caja *f* de juguetes.

toy maker ['tɔi,meikə*] *n* fabricante *m* de juguetes.

toyshop ['tɔiʃɔp] *n* juguetería *f*.

trace¹ [treis] **1** *n* rastro *m*, huella *f*; vestigio *m*; señal *f*, indicio *m*; (*small amount*) pequeñísima cantidad *f*, pizca *f*; (*remaining taste etc*) dejo *m*; **without a — of ill feeling** sin asomo de rencor; **sunk without —** desaparecido sin dejar el menor indicio; **to vanish without —** desaparecer sin dejar rastro; **there is no — of it now** no queda vestigio alguno de ello ahora; **we looked all over but couldn't find a single —** buscamos por todas partes pero sin encontrar el menor indicio.

2 *vt curve, line etc* trazar; (*with tracing paper*) calcar; (*follow trail of*) seguir, seguir la pista de; *rastrear*; (*find, locate*) encontrar; averiguar el paradero de; **I cannot — any reference to it** no he logrado encontrar ninguna referencia a ello; **she was finally —d to a house in Soho** por fin la encontraron en una casa del Soho; **to — an idea for someone** exponer una idea a uno; **to — one's ancestry back to Ferdinand III** hacer remontar su ascendencia hasta Fernando III; **to — a rumour back to its source** averiguar dónde se originó un rumor, seguir la pista de un rumor hasta llegar a su punto de partida.

trace[2] [treis] *n* tirante *m*, correa *f*; **to kick over the —s** (*fig*) sacar los pies del plato, mostrar las herraduras.

traceable ['treisǝbl] *adj*: **a person not now —** una persona cuyo paradero actual es imposible de encontrar; **an easily — reference** una referencia fácil de encontrar.

tracer ['treisǝ*] *n*, **tracer bullet** ['treisǝˌbulit] *n* bala *f* trazadora.

tracer element ['treisǝrˌelimǝnt] *n* (*Phys*) elemento *m* trazador.

tracery ['treisǝri] *n* tracería *f*.

trachea [trǝ'kiǝ] *n* tráquea *f*.

trachoma [træ'kǝumǝ] *n* tracoma *m*.

tracing ['treisiŋ] *n* calco *m*.

tracing paper ['treisiŋˌpeipǝ*] *n* papel *m* de calco, papel *m* transparente.

track [træk] **1** *n* (**a**) (*mark: of animal*) huella *f*; pista *f*, rastro *m*; (*of person*) pista *f*; (*of vehicle*) huella *f*; (*of wheel*) rodada *f*; (*of boat*) estela *f*; (*of hurricane*) rastro *m*, marcha *f*; (*of bullet, rocket etc*) trayectoria *f*; **to be on someone's —(s)** seguir la pista de uno, andar a los alcances de uno; **he had the police on his —** le buscaba la policía, le estaba cazando la policía; **they got on to his — very quickly** se pusieron sobre la pista sin pérdida de tiempo; **to cover up one's —s** borrar sus huellas, procurar no dejar rastro de sí; **to follow in someone's —** seguir el camino que ha marcado uno; **to keep — of someone** no perder de vista a uno; seguir la suerte a uno; **to keep — of new inventions** mantenerse al tanto de los nuevos inventos; **to lose — of someone** perder a uno de vista; **to lose — of what someone is saying** perder el hilo de lo que está diciendo uno; **to make —s** (*fam*) irse, largarse; **we must be making —s** tenemos que marcharnos; **to throw someone off the —** despistar a uno.

(**b**) (*path*) senda *f*, camino *m*; **beaten —** camino *m* trillado (*also fig*); **a village off the beaten —** un pueblo poco conocido, un pueblo apartado de las carreteras principales; **to get off the beaten —** apartarse del camino trillado, explorar un terreno menos conocido; **forest —** camino *m* forestal; **mule —** camino *m* carretero; **sheep —** cañada *f*; **to be on the right —** ir por buen camino; **to be on the wrong —** (*fig*) haberse equivocado, estar equivocado; **to be way off the —** estar totalmente despistado; **to put someone on the right —** mostrar a uno el camino que le conviene seguir.

(**c**) (*Sport*) pista *f*; **dog-racing —** canódromo *m*; **motor-racing —** pista *f* de automovilismo.

(**d**) (*Rail*) vía *f*; **double —** vía *f* doble; **single —** vía *f* única; **he has a one-— mind** no tiene más que un solo pensamiento; **to cross the —s** cruzar la vía; **to run off the —s** descarrilar.

(**e**) (*Mech: also* **caterpillar —s**) llanta *f* de oruga.

2 *attr*: **— athletics** atletismo *m* en pista; **— events** pruebas *fpl* en pista; **— maintenance** (*Rail*) conservación *f* de la vía.

3 *vt animal* rastrear, seguir la pista de; *satellite etc* rastrear, seguir la trayectoria de; **to — down** averiguar el paradero (*or* origen) de, buscar y encontrar; **finally we —ed it down in the library** por fin lo encontramos en la biblioteca.

4 *vi*: **to — along** avanzar por, ir por, seguir.

tracker ['trækǝ*] *n* rastreador *m*.

tracker dog ['trækǝdɔg] *n* perro *m* rastreador.

tracking ['trækiŋ] *n* rastreo *m*.

tracking station ['trækiŋˌsteiʃǝn] *n* centro *m* de rastreo, estación *f* de rastreo.

trackless ['træklis] *adj* sin caminos, impenetrable.

track meet ['træk'miːt] *n* (*US*) concurso *m* de carreras y saltos.

track race ['trækreis] *n* carrera *f* en pista.

track racing ['trækˌreisiŋ] *n* carreras *fpl* en pista, ciclismo *m* (*etc*) en pista.

tract[1] [trækt] *n* región *f*, zona *f*; extensión *f*; (*Anat*) región *f*; **digestive —** canal *m* digestivo; **respiratory —** vías *fpl* respiratorias, sistema *m* respiratorio.

tract[2] [trækt] *n* (*pamphlet*) folleto *m*; (*treatise*) tratado *m*.

tractable ['træktǝbl] *adj person* tratable, dócil; *problem* soluble; *material* dúctil, maleable.

traction ['trækʃǝn] *n* tracción *f*.

traction engine ['trækʃǝnˌendʒin] *n* locomóvil *f*, máquina *f* de tracción.

tractive ['træktiv] *adj* tractivo.

tractor ['træktǝ*] *n* tractor *m*; **agricultural —, farm —** tractor *m* agrícola.

tractor-drawn ['træktǝdrɔːn] *adj* arrastrado por tractor.

tractor driver ['træktǝˌdraivǝ*] *n* tractorista *mf*.

trade [treid] **1** *n* (**a**) (*commerce*) comercio *m*; negocio *m*; tráfico *m* (*in* en); industria *f*; **the wool —** la industria de la lana; **the — in drugs, the drug —** el tráfico en narcóticos, el comercio de narcóticos; **Board of T—** Ministerio *m* de Comercio; **coasting —** cabotaje *m*; **foreign —** comercio *m* exterior; **to be in —** ser comerciante, tener un negocio, (*esp*) tener una tienda; **to do a good** (*or* **brisk, roaring**) **—** hacer un buen negocio (*in* con); *see* **fair, retail** *etc*.

(**b**) (*calling*) oficio *m*, profesión *f*; empleo *m*; oficio *m* manual; **a butcher by —** de oficio carnicero; **a lawyer by —** (*hum*) de profesión abogado; **to carry on a —** ejercer un oficio; **to put someone to a —** hacer que uno aprenda un oficio; **known in the — as ...** conocido por los que son del oficio como ...

(**c**) (*persons collectively*) comerciantes *mpl*.

(**d**) **—s** (*Geog*) vientos *mpl* alisios.

2 *attr* (**a**) de comercio, comercial; **— discount** descuento *m* comercial; **— secret** secreto *m* comercial; **the — returns for March** las estadísticas del balance del comercio (exterior) de marzo.

(**b**) **— allowance** descuento *m*, rebaja *f* (del precio al por menor); **— price** precio *m* al comerciante, precio *m* al por mayor.

3 *vt* (*fig*) vender; **to — A for B** cambiar A por B, trocar A por B; **to — a car** in ofrecer un coche como parte del pago, devolver un coche usado al comprar otro nuevo.

4 *vi* comerciar (*in* en, *with* con); **we do not — with Ruritania** no tenemos relaciones comerciales con Ruritania; **to — on an advantage** aprovecharse de una ventaja, explotar una ventaja.

trade-in ['treidin] *attr*: **— arrangements** sistema *m* de devolver un artículo usado al comprar otro nuevo; **— price,** valor *m* de un artículo usado que se descuenta del precio de otro nuevo.

trademark ['treidmɑːk] *n* marca *f* registrada, marca *f* de fábrica; (*fig*) marca *f*, sello *m*.

trade name ['treidneim] *n* nombre *m* comercial, nombre *m* de fábrica.

trader ['treidǝ*] *n* comerciante *m*; traficante *m*; (*street —*) vendedor *m* ambulante; (*Hist*) mercader *m*.

trade school ['treidskuːl] *n* universidad *f* laboral, escuela *f* de artes y oficios.

tradesman ['treidzmǝn] *n, pl* **—men** [mǝn] (*shopkeeper*) tendero *m*; (*roundsman*) repartidor *m*, proveedor *m*; (*artisan*) artesano *m*; **—'s entrance** puerta *f* de servicio.

tradespeople ['treidzˌpiːpl] *npl* tenderos *mpl*.

trade union ['treid'juːnjǝn] **1** *n* sindicato *m*, gremio *m* (obrero); **to form a —** formar un sindicato, agremiarse.

2 trade-union *attr* sindical, gremial; **— labour** mano *f* de obra agremiada; **— shop** taller *m* donde todos los obreros son miembros de un sindicato.

trade unionism ['treid'juːnjǝnizǝm] *n* sindicalismo *m*, sistema *m* de sindicatos.

trade unionist ['treid'juːnjǝnist] *n* sindicalista *mf*, miembro *m* de un sindicato.

trade winds ['treidwindz] *npl* vientos *mpl* alisios.

trading ['treidiŋ] **1** *adj, attr* comercial, mercantil; **— nation** nación *f* con importante comercio exterior; **— profits for 1975** beneficios *mpl* obtenidos en el ejercicio de 1975.

2 *n* comercio *m*; tráfico *m*.

trading estate ['treidiŋisˌteit] *n* zona *f* industrial.

trading post ['treidiŋpǝust] *n* factoría *f*.

trading stamp ['treidiŋstæmp] *n* cupón *m*.

tradition [trǝ'diʃǝn] *n* tradición *f*.

traditional [trǝ'diʃǝnl] *adj* tradicional; clásico, consagrado.

traditionalism [trǝ'diʃǝnǝlizǝm] *n* tradicionalismo *m*.

traditionalist [trǝ'diʃǝnǝlist] **1** *adj* tradicionalista. **2** *n* tradicionalista *mf*.

traditionally [trǝ'diʃǝnǝli] *adv* tradicionalmente; según tradición, de acuerdo con la tradición.

traduce [trǝ'djuːs] *vt* calumniar, denigrar.

traffic ['træfik] **1** *n* (**a**) (*Aut etc*) circulación *f*, tráfico *m*; movimiento *m*; **holiday —** (*Aut*) movimiento *m* de coches que llevan a las familias a veranear, (*Aer etc*) tránsito *m* de pasajeros que van de vacaciones; **peak —** movimiento *m* máximo; **rail —** tráfico *m* por ferrocarril; **road —** circulación *f* por carretera; **tourist —** tránsito *m* de turistas, movimiento *m* de turistas; turismo *m*; **vehicular —** circulación *f* rodada; **the — is heavy this morning**

esta mañana hay muchos coches; — **was quite light** había poco movimiento de coches, circulaban poco los coches; — **was blocked for some hours** la circulación quedó interrumpida durante varias horas.

(b) (*trade*) tráfico *m*, comercio *m* (*in* en); (*pej*) trata *f* (*in* de); **the drug** — el tráfico en narcóticos.

2 *attr* de la circulación, del tráfico; — **problems in Buenos Aires** los problemas de la circulación en Buenos Aires.

3 *vi* traficar, comerciar (*in* en); (*pej*) tratar (*in* en).

trafficator ['træfikeitə*] *n* indicador *m* de dirección, flecha *f* de dirección.

traffic circle ['træfik'sə:kl] *n* (*US*) cruce *m* giratorio, glorieta *f*, redondel *m*.

traffic island ['træfik'ailənd] *n* (*Aut*) refugio *m*.

traffic jam ['træfikdʒæm] *n* embotellamiento *m*, aglomeración *f*; **a 5-mile** — una cola de coches que se extiende hasta 5 millas; **there are always** —**s here** aquí siempre se embotella el tráfico.

trafficker ['træfikə*] *n* traficante *m* (*in* en), tratante *m* (*in* en).

traffic lights ['træfiklaits] *npl* luces *fpl* de tráfico, señales *fpl* luminosas, semáforo *m*.

traffic police ['træfikpə,li:s] *n* policía *f* de tráfico.

traffic sign ['træfiksain] *n* señal *f* de tráfico.

tragedian [trə'dʒi:diən] *n* trágico *m*.

tragedienne [trədʒi:di'en] *n* trágica *f*, actriz *f* trágica.

tragedy ['trædʒidi] *n* tragedia *f*; **it is a — that . . .** es trágico que . . .; **what a —!** ¡qué trágico!; **the — of it is that . . .** lo trágico es que . . .

tragic ['trədʒik] *adj* trágico.

tragically ['trædʒikəli] *adv* trágicamente; **don't take it too —** no seas tan pesimista.

tragicomedy ['trædʒi'kɔmidi] *n* tragicomedia *f*.

tragicomic ['trædʒi'kɔmik] *adj* tragicómico.

trail [treil] **1** *n* **(a)** (*wake*) estela *f*; (*of comet, rocket*) cola *f*; — **of fire** estela *f* de fuego; **vapour** — estela *f* de humo; **the speech left a long — of comments** el discurso ha dejado larga estela de comentarios; **the hurricane left a — of destruction** el huracán dejó una estela de estragos.

(b) (*track of animal*) rastro *m*, pista *f*; **false —** pista *f* falsa; **to be on the — of, to follow the —** of seguir la pista de; **to pick up the —** encontrar la pista.

(c) (*path*) camino *m*, sendero *m*; **forest —** camino *m* forestal.

2 *vt* **(a)** (*drag*) arrastrar; **arms** bajar.

(b) (*track*) rastrear, seguir la pista de; seguir de cerca; (*of detective etc*) vigilar; **have that man —ed** que vigilen a ese hombre.

3 *vi* **(a)** (*be drawn along*) arrastrarse; **he walked with his coat —ing on the ground** andaba arrastrando su abrigo por los suelos; **with a small boat —ing behind** con un bote remolcado.

(b) (*of person*) **to — along** arrastrarse; caminar penosamente, ir con aire desanimado; **to — far behind** quedar muy a la zaga, rezagarse mucho; **El Toboso is —ing at the foot of the league** El Toboso va en última posición de la liga; **the children —ed home in the rain** los niños se fueron muy tristes a su casa bajo la lluvia.

(c) (*of plant*) arrastrarse; trepar.

(d) to — away, to — off ir desapareciendo (hasta perderse completamente), desvanecerse poco a poco.

trailer ['treilə*] *n* (*Aut etc*) remolque *m*; (*Cine*) trailer *m*, avance *m* (*Acad*).

trailing ['treiliŋ] *adj* colgado; *plant* rastrero, trepador; *edge* posterior.

train [trein] **1** *n* **(a)** (*Rail*) tren *m*; **accommodation —** (*US*) tren *m* ómnibus; **down —** tren *m* descendente; **excursion —** tren *m* de excursión, tren *m* de recreo; **express —** rápido *m*; **freight —**, **goods —** tren *m* de) mercancias *m*; **passenger —** tren *m* de pasajeros; **relief —** tren *m* suplementario; **slow —**, **stopping —** tren *m* correo, tren *m* ómnibus; **through —** tren *m* directo; **up —** tren *m* ascendente; **by —** (*go*) en tren, (*send*) por ferrocarril; **to catch a —** coger un tren, tomar un tren; **to change —s** cambiar de tren, hacer transbordo.

(b) (*Mech*) tren *m*; — **of gears** tren *m* de engranajes.

(c) (*series*) serie *f*, sucesión *f*; **a — of cars** una serie de coches; — **of powder** reguero *m* de pólvora; — **of events** serie *f* de sucesos; — **of thought** hilo *m* del pensamiento; **he began another — of thought** dejó de discurrir el pensamiento en otra cosa, dirigió el pensamiento a otra cosa; **in an unbroken —** en una serie ininterrumpida; **sin solución de**

continuidad; **it is in —** está en preparación; **to set something in —** poner algo en movimiento, empezar a poner algo en obra.

(d) (*of dress*) cola *f*; **to carry someone's —** llevar la cola del vestido de una.

(e) (*entourage*) séquito *m*, comitiva *f*; (*of mules*) recua *f*, reata *f*; **baggage —** tren *m* de equipajes; **it brought ruin in its —** acarreó la ruina, trajo consigo la ruina.

2 *vt* **(a)** (*instruct etc*) adiestrar; preparar, formar; (*Mil*) adiestrar, ejercitar; disciplinar; *child* enseñar; (*Sport*) entrenar, preparar; *animal* amaestrar; *voice* educar; **they — boys for the Navy** preparan a los muchachos para la Marina; **to — someone in firearms** enseñar a uno el manejo de las armas de fuego; **where were you —ed?** ¿donde cursó Vd sus estudios?; **he was —ed at Salamanca** tuvo su formación profesional en Salamanca; **to — someone to do something** enseñar a uno a hacer algo, enseñar a uno el arte (*or* la técnica *etc*) de hacer algo; habituar a uno a hacer algo, acostumbrar a uno a hacer algo; **to — someone up** preparar a uno, formar a uno.

(b) (*direct*) *gun* apuntar (*on* a); *camera, telescope* enfocar (*on* a); *plant* guiar (*up, along* por).

3 *vi* **(a)** (*instruct oneself*) adiestrarse; prepararse, formarse; educarse; (*Mil*) adiestrarse, ejercitarse; (*Sport etc*) entrenarse; **I — for 6 hours a day** me entreno 6 horas diarias, hago prácticas durante 6 horas cada día; **to — as a teacher, to — to become a teacher** seguir un curso de formación pedagógica; **we're —ing for the cup game** nos entrenamos para el partido de copa; **where did you —?** ¿dónde cursó Vd sus estudios?, ¿dónde se formó Vd?

(b) (*Rail*) ir en tren; **then we —ed to Seville** luego fuimos en tren a Sevilla.

4 *vr*: **to — oneself in a craft** enseñarse un arte, adiestrarse en un arte; **to — oneself to do something** enseñarse a hacer algo; habituarse a hacer algo, formarse la costumbre de hacer algo.

trained [treind] *adj teacher etc* graduado, diplomado; *worker* cualificado, capacitado, especializado; *animal* amaestrado; **a well-— child** un niño (bien) educado, un niño bien enseñado; **a well-— horse** un caballo bien preparado; **a well-— army** un ejército disciplinado; **a fully-— nurse** una enfermera diplomada.

trainee [trei'ni:] *n* aprendiz *m* (profesional), aprendiza *f* (profesional); **business —** aprendiz *m* de comercio, joven *m* que sigue un curso de formación comercial; **management —** aspirante *m* a un puesto en la dirección (de una compañía).

trainer ['treinə*] *n* **(a)** (*Sport: person*) entrenador *m*, preparador *m* físico; (*of horses*) preparador *m*, cuidador *m*; (*of circus animals*) domador *m*.

(b) (*plane*) entrenador *m*.

training ['treiniŋ] **1** *n* adiestramiento *m*; preparación *f*, formación *f* (profesional); orientación *f*; instrucción *f*; (*Mil*) instrucción *f*, ejercicios *mpl*; (*Sport*) entrenamiento *m*, preparación *f* (física); (*of staff for new job*) capacitación *f*; **military —** instrucción *f* militar, (*loosely*) servicio *m* militar; **physical —** gimnasia *f*, cultura *f* física; **to be in —** estar entrenado, estar en forma; **to be out of —** estar desentrenado.

2 *adj, attr*: — **camp** campamento *m* de instrucción; — **centre** centro *m* de instrucción; centro *m* de formación laboral; — **manual** manual *m* de instrucción; — **plane** entrenador *m*.

training college ['treiniŋ,kɔlidʒ] *n* escuela *f* normal.

training ship ['treiniŋʃip] *n* buque-escuela *m*.

trainman ['treinmæn] *n*, *pl* —**men** [men] ferroviario *m*; guardafrenos *m*.

train oil ['treinɔil] *n* aceite *m* de ballena.

traipse [treips] *vi see* **trapes.**

trait [treit] *n* rasgo *m*.

traitor ['treitə*] *n* traidor *m*; **to be a — to one's country** traicionar a la patria; **to turn —** volverse traidor, volver la casaca.

traitorous ['treitərəs] *adj* traidor; traicionero.

traitorously ['treitərəsli] *adv* traidoramente, con traición.

traitress ['treitris] *n* traidora *f*.

Trajan ['treidʒən] *m* Trajano.

trajectory [trə'dʒektəri] *n* trayectoria *f*.

tram [træm] *n*, **tramcar** ['træmka:*] *n* tranvía *m*.

tramlines ['træmlainz] *npl* carriles *mpl* de tranvía.

trammel ['træməl] *vt* poner trabas a, trabar, impedir.

trammels ['træməlz] *npl* trabas *fpl*.

tramp [træmp] **1** *n* **(a)** (*sound of feet*) marcha *f* pesada, pasos *mpl* pesados.

(b) (*hike*) paseo m largo, caminata f, excursión f a pie; **to go for a — in the hills** hacer una excursión a pie por la montaña; **after a — of many miles** después de recorrer muchos kilómetros a pie; **it's a long —** es mucho camino.

(c) (*person: man*) vago m, vagabundo m; (*woman*) puta f, fulana f; **you (little) —!** ¡lagarta!

(d) (*Naut*) vapor m volandero, mercante m (*also* **— steamer**).

2 vt (*stamp on*) pisar con fuerza; (*walk across*) recorrer a pie, hacer una excursión por; **to — the streets** andar (penosamente) por las calles, recorrer (de muy mala gana) las calles; **they had to — it** tuvieron que ir a pie.

3 vi marchar pesadamente, andar con pasos pesados; ir a pie; **someone —ed up to the door** alguien se acercó con pasos pesados a la puerta.

trample ['træmpl] 1 vt pisar, pisotear, hollar (*also* **to — underfoot**).

2 vi pisar fuerte, andar con pasos pesados (*also* **to — about, to — along**); **to — on something** pisar algo, pisotear algo, hollar algo; **to — on someone** (*fig*) tratar a uno sin miramientos; **to — on someone's feelings** herir los sentimientos de uno.

trampoline ['træmpəlin] n trampolín m.

tramway ['træmwei] n tranvía m.

trance [trɑːns] n rapto m, arrobamiento m, éxtasis m; (*Med*) catalepsia f; (*spiritualistic*) trance m; estado m hipnótico; **to go into a —** entrar en un estado hipnótico, (*fig*) extasiarse.

tranquil ['træŋkwil] adj tranquilo.

tranquility [træŋ'kwiliti] n tranquilidad f.

tranquillize, (US) tranquilize ['træŋkwilaiz] vt tranquilizar.

tranquilliser, (US) tranquilizer ['træŋkwilaizə*] n (*Med*) tranquilizante m.

trans . . . [trænz] trans . . .

transact [træn'zækt] vt hacer, despachar; tramitar.

transaction [træn'zækʃən] n (*deal*) negocio m, transacción f, operación f; (*act*) negociación f, tramitación f; **—s** (*of society*) actas fpl, memorias fpl.

transatlantic ['trænzət'læntik] adj transatlántico.

transcend [træn'send] vt exceder, superar, rebasar.

transcendence [træn'sendəns] n, **transcendency** [træn'sendənsi] n superioridad f; lo sobresaliente; (*Philos*) trascendencia f.

transcendent [træn'sendənt] adj superior; sobresaliente.

transcendental [,trænsen'dentl] adj (*Philos*) trascendental.

transcontinental ['trænz,kɔnti'nentl] adj transcontinental.

transcribe [træn'skraib] vt transcribir, copiar.

transcript ['trænskript] n trasunto m, copia f.

transcription [træn'skripʃən] n (*act*) transcripción f; (*copy*) transcripción f, trasunto m, copia f; **phonetic —** pronunciación f figurada.

transept ['trænsept] n (*Archit*) crucero m.

transfer ['trænsfə*] n (a) (*act*) transferencia f, traspaso m; (*Law*) transferencia f, cesión f; enajenación f; transbordo m; (*Sport*) traspaso m; traslado m; **— of ownership** cesión f de propiedad.

(b) (*picture*) cromo m, calcomanía f.

transfer [træns'fə:*] 1 vt property etc transferir, traspasar, pasar (*to* a); (*Law*) transferir, ceder; enajenar; passenger etc transbordar; (*Sport*) traspasar; (*to new post, place etc*) trasladar; (*in banking, accounting etc*) transferir; **to — one's affections to another** dar su amor a otro.

2 vi (*to a post etc*) trasladarse (*to* a); (*Rail etc*) cambiar, hacer transbordo (*to* a); **to — to a new course** (*Univ*) cambiar a otra asignatura; **the firm is —ring to Quito** la compañía se traslada a Quito.

transferable [træns'fə:rəbl] adj transferible; **not — inalienable.**

transference ['trænsfərəns] n transferencia f; traspaso m; traslado m.

transfiguration [,trænsfigə'reiʃən] n transfiguración f.

transfigure [træns'figə*] vt transfigurar, transformar (*into* en).

transfix [træns'fiks] vt traspasar, pasar de parte a parte; **to be —ed, to stand —ed** (*fig*) estar totalmente pasmado (*with* de), estar completamente paralizado (*with* de).

transform [træns'fɔ:m] vt transformar (*into* en), convertir; metamorfosear (*into* en).

transformation [,trænsfə'meiʃən] n transformación f, conversión f; metamorfosis f.

transformer [træns'fɔ:mə*] n (*Elec*) transformador m.

transformer station [træns'fɔ:mə,steiʃən] n estación f transformadora.

transfuse [træns'fju:z] vt transfundir; blood hacer una transfusión de.

transfusion [træns'fju:ʒən] n transfusión f; **to give someone a blood —** hacer a uno una transfusión de sangre.

transgress [træns'gres] 1 vt (*go beyond*) traspasar, exceder, ir más allá de; (*violate*) violar, infringir; (*sin against*) pecar contra.

2 vi pecar, cometer una transgresión.

transgression [træns'greʃən] n pecado m, transgresión f; infracción f.

transgressor [træns'gresə*] n transgresor m, ora f; pecador m, ora f; infractor m, ora f.

tranship [træn'ʃip] vt transbordar.

transhipment [træn'ʃipmənt] n transbordo m.

transience ['trænziəns] n lo pasajero, transitoriedad f.

transient ['trænziənt] 1 adj pasajero, transitorio, fugaz. 2 n (*US*) transeúnte mf.

transistor [træn'zistə*] n transistor m.

transistorized [træn'zistəraizd] adj transistorizado.

transit ['trænzit] n tránsito m, paso m; **in —** de tránsito, de paso; **— visa** visado m de tránsito.

transition [træn'ziʃən] n transición f, paso m (*from* de, *to* a); transformación f, evolución f (*to* en).

transitional [træn'ziʃənəl] adj transicional, de transición.

transitive ['trænzitiv] adj transitivo.

transitively ['trænzitivli] adv transitivamente.

transitory ['trænzitəri] adj transitorio.

translatable [trænz'leitəbl] adj traducible.

translate [trænz'leit] vt (a) traducir (*from* de, *into* a); (*fig*) interpretar; **to — words into deeds** dar efecto a palabras, poner por obra lo que sólo son palabras; **how do you — "posh"?** ¿cómo se traduce "posh"?

(b) (*change place or post of*) trasladar (*from* de, *to* a).

translation [trænz'leiʃən] n (a) traducción f; versión f. (b) traslado m.

translator [trænz'leitə*] n traductor m, ora f.

transliterate [trænz'litəreit] vt transcribir.

translucence [trænz'lu:sns] n translucidez f.

translucent [trænz'lu:snt] adj translúcido.

transmigrate ['trænzmai'greit] vi transmigrar.

transmigration [,trænzmai'greiʃən] n transmigración f.

transmissible [trænz'misəbl] adj transmisible.

transmission [trænz'miʃən] n (*all senses*) transmisión f.

transmit [trænz'mit] vt (*all senses*) transmitir (*to* a).

transmitter [trænz'mitə*] n (*apparatus*) transmisor m; (*station*) estación f transmisora, emisora f.

transmitting station [trænz'mitiŋ,steiʃən] n estación f transmisora, emisora f.

transmogrify [trænz'mɔgrifai] vt transformar (como por encanto; *into* en), metamorfosear (extrañamente; *into* en).

transmutable [trænz'mju:təbl] adj transmutable.

transmutation [,trænzmju:'teiʃən] n transmutación f; (*Bio*) transformismo m.

transmute [trænz'mju:t] vt transmutar (*into* en).

transom ['trænsəm] n travesaño m.

transparency [træns'pɛərənsi] n (*quality*) transparencia f; (*Phot*) diapositiva f, proyección f.

transparent [træns'pɛərənt] adj transparente, diáfano; (*fig*) claro, limpio; excuse etc transparente, clarísimo.

transpiration [,trænspi'reiʃən] n transpiración f.

transpire [træns'paiə*] 1 vt transpirar.

2 vi (a) (*of fluid, odour*) transpirar.

(b) (*become known*) revelarse, divulgarse, saberse; **finally it —d that . . .** por fin se supo que . . ., por fin se desprendió que . . .

(c) (*happen*) tener lugar, pasar, ocurrir; **his report on what —d** su informe acerca de lo que pasó.

transplant [træns'plɑ:nt] vt trasplantar (*also Med*).

transplantation [,trænsplɑ:n'teiʃən] n trasplante m (*also Med*).

transport ['trænspɔ:t] 1 n (a) (*general sense*) transporte m; acarreo m; road **—** transportes mpl por carretera; rail **—** transportes mpl por ferrocarril; **Ministry of T—** Ministerio m de Transportes.

(b) (*ship*) navío m de transporte; (*Aer*) avión m de transporte.

(c) (*fig*) transporte m, éxtasis m; **to be in a — of delight** estar extasiado, extasiarse; **to be in a — of rage** estar fuera de sí (de rabia).

2 attr: **— costs** gastos mpl de transporte, gastos mpl de acarreo.

transport [træns'pɔːt] *vt* **(a)** transportar; llevar, acarrear; (*Hist*) *convict* deportar.
(b) (*fig*) transportar, embelesar; **to be —ed with joy** estar extasiado, extasiarse.
transportable [træns'pɔːtəbl] *adj* transportable.
transportation [ˌtrænspɔː'teiʃən] *n* transporte *m*, transportación *f*; transportes *mpl*; (*Hist: Law*) deportación *f*; **the — system** el sistema de transportes.
transpose [træns'pəuz] *vt* transponer, cambiar (*into* a); (*Mus*) transportar.
transposition [ˌtrænspə'ziʃən] *n* transposición *f* (*also Mus*), cambio *m*.
transship [træns'ʃip] *vt* transbordar.
transshipment [træns'ʃipmənt] *n* transbordo *m*.
trans-Siberian [trænzsai'biəriən] *adj* transiberiano.
transubstantiate [ˌtrænsəb'stænʃieit] *vt* transustanciar.
transubstantiation [ˈtrænsəbˌstænʃi'eiʃən] *n* transustanciación *f*.
transversal [trænz'vəːsəl] *adj* transversal.
transverse ['trænzvəːs] *adj* transverso, trasversal.
transversely [trænz'vəːsli] *adv* transversalmente.
transvestism ['trænzˌvestizəm] *n* transvestismo *m*.
transvestite [trænz'vestait] **1** *adj* transvestido. **2** *n* transvestido *m*, a *f*.
trap [træp] **1** *n* **(a)** (*general sense*) trampa *f*; (*fig*) trampa *f*, lazo *m*; **it's a —** aquí hay trampa; **to catch an animal in a —** capturar un animal con una trampa; **he was caught in his own —** cayó en su misma trampa; **we were caught like rats in a —** estábamos como ratas en ratonera; **to lure someone into a —** hacer que uno caiga en una trampa; **to set a — for someone** tender un lazo a uno.
(b) (*sl*) boca *f*; **to keep one's — shut** callarse; **you keep your — shut about this** de esto no digas ni pío; **shut your —!** ¡callarse!
(c) (*Tech*) sifón *m*; bombillo *m*.
(d) (*—door*) escotilla *f*, trampa *f*; (*Theat*) escotillón *m*.
(e) (*carriage*) coche *m* ligero de dos ruedas.
2 *vt* **(a)** *animal* coger en una trampa, entrampar, atrapar; coger con trampas.
(b) *person* atrapar, aprisionar; *vehicle, ship etc* aprisionar, bloquear; **the miners are —ped** los mineros están aprisionados, los mineros están sepultados; **we were —ped in the snow** estábamos aprisionados por la nieve; **the climbers were —ped** los escaladores estaban atrapados, los escaladores no podían moverse en ninguna dirección.
(c) to — a ball (*Sport*) parar el balón (con los pies); **to — one's foot in the door** cogerse el pie en la puerta.
(d) (*fig*) hacer caer en el lazo, entrampar; **to — someone into an admission** lograr mediante un ardid que uno haga una confesión; **she —ped him into marriage** logró mañosamente que él se casara con ella; **to — someone into saying something** lograr mañosamente que uno diga algo.
trap door ['træpdɔː*] *n* escotilla *f*, trampa *f*; (*Theat*) escotillón *m*.
trapes [treips] *vi* (*fam*) ir (a desgana), andar (penosamente); andar sin propósito fijo; **I had to — over to see him** tuve que tomarme la molestia de ir a verle; **we —ed about all morning** pasamos la mañana yendo de acá para allá.
trapeze [trə'piːz] *n* trapecio *m* (de circo, de gimnasia).
trapeze artist [trə'piːzˌɑːtist] *n* trapecista *mf*.
trapezium [trə'piːziəm] *n* (*Math*) trapecio *m*.
trapezoid ['træpizɔid] *n* trapezoide *m*.
trapper ['træpə*] *n* cazador *m* (*esp* de animales de piel), trampero *m*.
trappings ['træpiŋz] *npl* arreos *mpl*; jaeces *mpl*; (*fig*) adornos *mpl*, galas *fpl*; **shorn of all its —** sin ninguno de sus adornos, desprovisto de adorno; **that statement, shorn of its — ...** esa declaración, en términos sencillos ...; **with all the — of kingship** con todo el boato de la monarquía.
trappist ['træpist] **1** *adj* trapense. **2** *n* trapense *m*.
traps [træps] *npl* (*fam*) cosas *fpl*, chismes *mpl*, cachivaches *mpl*; **to pack up one's —s** hacer las maletas, (*fig*) liar el petate (*fam*).
trash [træʃ] *n* pacotilla *f*, hojarasca *f*; trastos *mpl* viejos; **the book is —** el libro es una basura, el libro no vale para nada; **he talks a lot of —** no dice más que tonterías; **human —** gente *f* inútil, personas *fpl* inútiles; **—!** ¡tonterías!
trash can ['træʃ'kæn] *n* (*US*) cubo *m* de la basura.
trashy ['træʃi] *adj* inútil, baladí.
trauma ['trɔːmə] *n* trauma *m*.
traumatic [trɔː'mætik] *adj* traumático.
traumatism ['trɔːmætizəm] *n* traumatismo *m*.
travail ['træveil] *n* (*arch or hum: Med*) dolores *mpl*

del parto; **to be in —** afanarse, azacanarse; (*Med*) estar de parto.
travel ['trævl] **1** *n* **(a)** viajes *mpl*, el viajar; **—s** viajes *mpl*; **to be on one's —s** estar de viaje.
(b) (*Mech*) recorrido *m*.
2 *attr* *agency etc* de viajes, de turismo.
3 *vt* **(a)** *country etc* viajar por (todas partes de), recorrer.
(b) *distance* recorrer, hacer, cubrir; **we —led 50 miles that day** ese día cubrimos 50 millas.
4 *vi* **(a)** (*make a journey*) viajar; **to — by car** viajar en coche, ir en coche; **he —s into the centre to work** se desplaza al centro a trabajar; **they have —led a lot** han viajado mucho, han visto mucho mundo; **to — round the world** dar la vuelta al mundo; **to — over** viajar por, recorrer; **we've —led a lot since then** (*fig*) hemos recorrido mucho terreno desde entonces, mucho ha llovido desde entonces.
(b) (*go at a speed etc*) ir; **it —s at 600 mph** tiene una velocidad de 600 mph; **we were —ling at 30 mph** íbamos a 30 mph; **you were —ling too fast** Vd iba a una velocidad excesiva, Vd iba demasiado de prisa; **he was certainly —ling** es cierto que iba a buen tren; **light —s at a speed of ...** la luz viaja a una velocidad de . . .; **news —s fast** las noticias se propagan con una rapidez extraordinaria.
(c) (*move, pass*) correr; moverse, desplazarse; **it —s along this wire** corre por este hilo; **it doesn't — freely on its rod** no corre lisamente por la varilla; **it —s 3 centimetres** (*Mech*) tiene un recorrido de 3 centímetros; **his eye —led slowly over the scene** examinó detenidamente la escena.
(d) (*reach*) llegar, extenderse; **will it — that far?** ¿llega hasta allí?, ¿se puede estirar hasta allí?
(e) (*of wine etc*) poderse transportar; **it's a nice wine but it won't —** es un buen vino pero pierde calidad cuando se le transporta.
(f) (*Comm*) ser viajante; **he —s for Pérez** es viajante de la compañía Pérez; **he —s in underwear** es viajante de una compañía que fabrica ropa interior; **he —s in soap** es viajante en jabones.
travelled, (*US*) **traveled** ['trævld] *adj* que ha viajado; **much —, widely —** que ha viajado mucho, que ha visto mucho mundo.
traveller, (*US*) **traveler** ['trævlə*] *n* viajero *m*, a *f*; (*Comm*) viajante *m* (*also* **commercial —**); **a — in soap** un viajante en jabones.
traveller's joy, (*US*) **traveler's joy** ['trævləz'dʒɔi] *n* (*Bot*) clemátide *f*.
travelling, (*US*) **traveling** ['trævliŋ] **1** *adj*, *attr* *salesman, exhibition etc* ambulante; *expenses* de viaje; *crane etc* corredero, corredizo; *bag, rug* de viaje.
2 *n* el viajar, viajes *mpl*.
travelogue ['trævələg] *n* película *f* de viajes; documental *m* de interés turístico.
travel sickness ['trævlˌsiknis] *n* propensión *f* a marearse en un coche (*or* avión *etc*).
travel-worn ['trævlwɔːn] *adj* fatigado por el viaje, rendido después de tanto viajar.
traverse ['trævəs] **1** *n* (*Tech*) travesaño *m*; (*Mil*) través *m*; (*Mountaineering*) escalada *f* oblicua, camino *m* oblicuo.
2 *vt* atravesar, cruzar; recorrer; pasar por; **we are traversing a difficult period** atravesamos un momento difícil.
3 *vi* (*Mountaineering*) hacer una escalada oblicua.
travesty ['trævisti] **1** *n* parodia *f* (*also fig*). **2** *vt* parodiar.
trawl [trɔːl] **1** *n* red *f* barredera.
2 *vt* rastrear; dragar; **to — up** pescar, sacar a la superficie.
3 *vi* pescar al arrastre, rastrear.
trawler ['trɔːlə*] *n* barco *m* rastreador, barco *m* de pesca a la rastra.
trawling ['trɔːliŋ] *n* pesca *f* a la rastra.
tray [trei] *n* bandeja *f*; (*of balance*) platillo *m*; (*drawer*) cajón *m*, batea *f*; (*Phot, Tech*) cubeta *f*.
traycloth ['treiklɔθ] *n* cubrebandeja *m*.
treacherous ['tretʃərəs] *adj* traidor, traicionero; falso; (*fig*) engañoso, incierto, nada seguro; *memory* infiel; *ground* movedizo; *ice etc* peligroso, poco firme.
treacherously ['tretʃərəsli] *adv* traidoramente, a traición; falsamente; engañosamente; peligrosamente.
treachery ['tretʃəri] *n* traición *f*, perfidia *f*; falsedad *f*; **an act of —** una traición.
treacle ['triːkl] *n* melado *m*, melaza *f*.

treacly ['tri:kli] *adj* parecido a melado; cubierto de melado.

tread [tred] **1** *n* (a) (*step*) paso *m*, pisada *f*; (*gait*) andar *m*, modo *m* de andar; **with heavy —** con pasos pesados, pisando fuertemente; **with measured —** con pasos rítmicos.

(b) (*of stair*) huella *f*; (*of shoe*) suela *f*; (*of tyre*) huella *f*, (banda *f* de) rodamiento *m*.

2 (*irr*: *pret* **trod**, *ptp* **trodden**) *vt* (*also* **to — down**, **to — underfoot**) pisar, pisotear, hollar; *path* batir, (*fig*) abrir; *grapes* pisar; *dance* bailar; **to — water** pedalear en agua; **a place never trodden by human feet** un sitio no hollado por pie humano; **he trod his cigarette end into the mud** apagó la colilla pisándola en el lodo.

3 *vi* pisar; poner el pie; **to — on** pisar; **to — on someone's heels** pisar los talones a uno; **careful you don't — on it!** ¡ojo, que lo vas a pisar!; **to — carefully, to — warily** (*fig*) andar con pies de plomo; **we must — very carefully in this matter** en este asunto conviene andar con pies de plomo; **to — softly** pisar dulcemente, no hacer ruido al andar.

treadle ['tredl] **1** *n* pedal *m*. **2** *vi* pedalear.

treadmill ['tredmil] *n* rueda *f* de andar; (*fig*) rutina *f*, monotonía *f*; tráfago *m*; **back to the —!** ¡volvamos al trabajo!

treason ['tri:zn] *n* traición *f*; **high —** alta traición *f*.

treasonable ['tri:zənəbl] *adj* traidor, desleal.

treasure ['treʒə*] **1** *n* tesoro *m*; (*fig*) tesoro *m*; joya *f*, preciosidad *f*; **yes, my —** sí, mi tesoro; **— s of Spanish art** joyas *fpl* del arte español; **our charlady is a real —** nuestra asistenta es una verdadera joya.

2 *vt* (a) **to — up** atesorar; guardar, acumular.

(b) (*fig*) guardar como un tesoro; apreciar muchísimo; *memory etc* guardar.

treasure-house ['treʒəhaus] *n*, *pl* **—houses** [,hauziz] tesoro *m* (*also fig*).

treasure hunt ['treʒəhʌnt] *n* (*game*) caza *f* al tesoro.

treasurer ['treʒərə*] *n* tesorero *m*.

treasure-trove ['treʒətrəuv] *n* tesoro *m* hallado; (*fig*) tesoro *m*.

treasury ['treʒəri] **1** *n* (a) tesoro *m*, tesorería *f*, erario *m*, hacienda *f*; **T—** (*Brit*), **T— Department** (*US*) Ministerio *m* de Hacienda.

(b) (*anthology*) tesoro *m*, antología *f*, florilegio *m*.

2 *attr*: **T— Bench** (*Brit Pol*) banco *m* azul, banco *m* del gobierno; **— bill** vale *m* de la Hacienda.

treat [tri:t] **1** *n* (a) (*entertainment*) convite *m*, extraordinario *m*; (*present*) regalo *m*; (*outing*) visita *f*; **it's my —** invito yo; **to have a Dutch —** pagar cada uno su cuota, ir a escote; **to stand someone a —** invitar a uno a un extraordinario.

(b) (*pleasure*) placer *m*, gusto *m*; recompensa *f* (especial); **a — in store** un placer futuro, un placer guardado para el futuro; **it is a — to hear you** da gusto escucharte, es un placer escucharte; **it's no sort of — for me** para mí no es ningún placer; **just to give them all a —** sólo para darles placer a todos; **to give oneself a —** permitirse un lujo, permitirse hacer algo no acostumbrado.

2 *vt* (a) (*behave towards*) tratar; **to — someone well** tratar bien a uno; **to — someone as if he were a child** tratar a uno como a un niño; **to — something as a joke** tomar algo en broma, tomar algo en chunga.

(b) (*invite*) invitar, convidar (*to* a); **I'm —ing you** invito yo; **they —ed him to a dinner** le obsequiaron con un banquete; **let me — you to a drink** permítame invitarle a tomar algo.

(c) (*Med*) tratar, curar; atender, asistir; **to — someone for a broken leg** curar la pierna rota de uno; **to — someone with X-rays** dar a uno un tratamiento de rayos X; **which doctor is —ing you?** ¿qué médico le atiende?

(d) (*Tech*) tratar; **to — a substance with acid** tratar una sustancia con ácido.

(e) *subject, theme* tratar, discutir; **he —s the subject objectively** trata el asunto con objetividad.

3 *vi* (a) (*negotiate*) **to — for peace** pedir la paz; **to — with someone** tratar con uno, negociar con uno.

(b) (*discuss*) **to — of** tratar de, discutir; versar sobre.

4 *vr*: **to — oneself to something** permitirse el lujo, permitirse hacer algo no acostumbrado.

treatise ['tri:tiz] *n* tratado *m*.

treatment ['tri:tmənt] *n* tratamiento *m*; (*Med*) tratamiento *m*, cura *f*, medicación *f*; **good —** buen tratamiento *m*, buenos tratos *mpl*; **medical —** tratamiento *m* médico; asistencia *f* médica; **preferential —** (*Comm*) trato *m* preferente; **his —**

of his parents su conducta con sus padres; **our — of foreigners** el trato que damos a los extranjeros; **to give someone the —** (*fam*) hacer sufrir a uno; **to respond to —** responder al tratamiento.

treaty ['tri:ti] *n* tratado *m*.

treble ['trebl] **1** *adj* triple; (*Mus*) de tiple; **— clef** clave *f* de sol.

2 *n* (*Mus*) tiple *mf*; voz *f* de tiple.

3 *vt* triplicar.

4 *vi* triplicarse.

trebly ['trebli] *adv* tres veces; **it is — dangerous to ...** es tres veces más peligroso ...

tree [tri:] **1** *n* árbol *m*; (*for shoes*) horma *f*; (*of saddle*) arzón *m*; **family —** árbol *m* genealógico; **— of knowledge** árbol *m* de la ciencia; **to be at the top of the —** estar en la cumbre de su profesión; **to be up a —** (*fam*) estar en un aprieto; **to be barking up the wrong —** tomar el rábano por las hojas.

2 *vt* *animal etc* ahuyentar por un árbol, hacer refugiarse en un árbol.

tree-covered ['tri:,kʌvəd] *adj* arbolado.

tree creeper ['tri:,kri:pə*] *n* agateador *m*.

tree frog ['tri:frɔg] *n* rana *f* de San Antonio, rana *f* arbórea.

treeless ['tri:lis] *adj* pelado, sin árboles.

tree-lined ['tri:laind] *adj*: **— street** calle *f* con árboles en las aceras, alameda *f*.

treetop ['tri:tɔp] *n* copa *f*, cima *f* de árbol.

tree trunk ['tri:trʌŋk] *n* tronco *m* de árbol.

trefoil ['trefɔil] *n* trébol *m*.

trek [trek] **1** *n* migración *f*; (*day's march*) jornada *f*; (*fam*) viaje *m* largo y aburrido; caminata *f*; excursión *f*.

2 *vi* emigrar; viajar; (*fam*) ir (de mala gana), caminar (penosamente); **we —ked for days on end** caminamos día tras día; **I had to — up to the top floor** tuve que darme la molestia de subir al último piso.

trellis ['trelis] *n* enrejado *m*; (*Bot*) espaldera *f*, espaldar *m*.

trelliswork ['treliswə:k] *n* enrejado *m*.

tremble ['trembl] **1** *n* temblor *m*, estremecimiento *m*; **to be all of a —** estar todo tembloroso; **she said with a —** dijo temblando.

2 *vi* temblar, estremecerse (*at* ante, *with* de); vibrar; agitarse; **to — all over** estar todo tembloroso.

trembling ['tremblinŋ] **1** *adj* tembloroso. **2** *n* temblar *m*, temblor *m*, estremecimiento *m*; vibración *f*; agitación *f*.

tremendous [trə'mendəs] *adj* tremendo, inmenso, formidable; (*fam*) tremendo, estupendo; **that's —!** ¡qué estupendo!; **there was a — crowd** habia una inmensa multitud.

tremendously [trə'mendəsli] *adv* tremendamente; **— good** tremendamente bueno.

tremor ['tremə*] *n* temblor *m*; estremecimiento *m*; vibración *f*; **earth —** temblor *m* de tierra; **he said without a —** dijo sin inmutarse.

tremulous ['tremjuləs] *adj* trémulo, tembloroso; tímido.

tremulously ['tremjuləsli] *adv* trémulamente; tímidamente.

trench [trentʃ] **1** *n* zanja *f*, foso *m*; (*Mil*) trinchera *f*; (*shelter*) refugio *m* antiaéreo.

2 *vt* hacer zanjas (*or* fosos) en; (*Mil*) hacer trincheras en, atrincherar; (*Agr*) excavar, remover.

trenchant ['trentʃənt] *adj* mordaz, incisivo.

trenchantly ['trentʃəntli] *adv* mordazmente.

trench coat ['trentʃkəut] *n* trinchera *f*.

trencher ['trentʃə*] *n* tajadero *m*.

trencherman ['trentʃəmæn] *n*, *pl* **—men** [mən]: **to be a good —** comer bien, tener siempre buen apetito.

trend [trend] **1** *n* tendencia *f*; curso *m*, dirección *f*, marcha *f*; (*fashion*) boga *f*, moda *f*; **now there is a — towards ...** ahora hay tendencia hacia ...; **—s in popular music** tendencias *fpl* de la música popular.

2 *vi* tender.

trendy ['trendi] *adj* (*sl*) según la última moda, elegante; de acuerdo con las tendencias actuales, modernísimo.

Trent [trent] Trento.

trepan [tri'pæn] *vt* trepanar.

trephine [tre'fi:n] *vt* trefinar.

trepidation [,trepi'deiʃən] *n* turbación *f*, agitación *f*; **in some —** algo turbado, agitado.

trespass ['trespas] **1** *n* (*illegal entry*) intrusión *f*, entrada *f* ilegal; entrada *f* sin derecho, penetración *f* en finca ajena; (*transgression*) infracción *f*, violación *f*, ofensa *f*; (*Eccl*) pecado *m*; **forgive us our —es** perdónanos nuestras deudas.

2 *vi* entrar sin derecho (*on* en), entrar ilegalmente (*on* en); penetración *f* en finca ajena; **to — against** infringir, violar, (*Eccl*) pecar contra; **to — upon** (*fig*) abusar de; **to — upon someone's privacy** invadir la vida íntima de uno; **may I — upon your kindness to ask that...** permítame molestarle pidiendo que...; perdone Vd que le moleste pidiendo que...

trespasser ['trespəsə*] *n* intruso *m*, a *f*; **"T—s will be prosecuted"** "Se procesará a los intrusos", (*loosely*) "Prohibida la entrada".

tress [tres] *n* trenza *f*; **—es** cabellera *f*, pelo *m*.

trestle ['tresl] *n* caballete *m*.

trestle bridge ['tresl'bridʒ] *n* puente *m* de caballetes.

trestle table ['tresl'teibl] *n* mesa *f* de caballete.

trews [tru:z] *npl* (*Scot*) pantalón *m*.

tri... [trai] tri...

triad ['traiəd] *n* tríada *f*.

trial ['traiəl] **1** *n* (a) (*Law*) proceso *m*, juicio *m*, vista *f* de una causa; **— by jury** juicio *m* por jurado; **new —** revisión *f*; **to be on —** estar en juicio; **to be on — for one's part in a crime** ser procesado por su complicidad en un crimen; **to be on — for one's life** ser acusado de un crimen que pudiera castigarse con pena de muerte; **to bring someone to —** procesar a uno; **to commit someone for —** remitir a uno al tribunal; **to go on —, to stand one's —** ser procesado.

(b) (*test*) prueba *f*, ensayo *m*; tentativa *f*; (*of sheepdogs etc*) concurso *m*; **—s** (*Sport, Tech*) pruebas *fpl*; **— of strength** lucha *f*; **by a system of — and error** por un sistema de prueba y desacierto, por un método de tanteos; **to be on —** estar a prueba; **to give someone a —** poner a uno a prueba.

(c) (*hardship*) aflicción *f*, adversidad *f*; desgracia *f*; (*nuisance*) molestia *f*; **the —s of old age** las aflicciones de la vejez; **the child is a great — to them** el niño les amarga la vida, el niño es terrible.

2 *attr* (a) (*Law*) procesal; relativo al proceso.

(b) de prueba, de ensayo; **— flight** vuelo *m* de prueba; **— run, — trip** viaje *m* de ensayo.

triangle ['traiæŋgl] *n* triángulo *m* (*also Mus*).

triangular [trai'æŋgjulə*] *adj* triangular.

triangulate [trai'æŋgjuleit] *vt* triangular.

triangulation [trai,æŋgju'leiʃən] *n* triangulación *f*.

tribal ['traibəl] *adj* tribal, tribual.

tribalism ['traibəlizəm] *n* organización *f* en tribus; sistema *m* de tribus; mentalidad *f* de la tribu.

tribe [traib] *n* tribu *f* (*also Zool*); (*fig*) tropel *f*, masa *f*; ralea *f*.

tribesman ['traibzmən] *n*, *pl* **—men** [mən] miembro *m* de una tribu; **to stir up the tribesmen** sublevar las tribus; **the tribesmen are friendly** las tribus no son peligrosas.

tribulation [,tribju'leiʃən] *n* tribulación *f*; **—s** aflicciones *fpl*, dificultades *fpl*, sufrimientos *mpl*.

tribunal [trai'bju:nl] *n* tribunal *m*.

tribune ['tribju:n] *n* (*stand*) tribuna *f*; (*person*) tribuno *m*.

tributary ['tribjutəri] **1** *adj* tributario. **2** *n* (*person*) tributario *m*; (*Geog*) afluente *m*.

tribute ['tribju:t] *n* (*payment, tax*) tributo *m*; (*fig*) homenaje *m*; elogio *m*; **floral —** ofrenda *f* floral; **that is a — to his loyalty** eso acredita su lealtad, eso hace honor a su lealtad; **to pay —** to rendir homenaje a, elogiar, pronunciar elogios de.

trice [trais] *n*: **in a —** en un santiamén.

trichina [tri'kainə] *n* triquina *f*.

trichinosis [,triki'nəusis] *n* triquinosis *f*.

trick [trik] **1** *n* (a) (*deceit*) engaño *m*, truco *m*; (*swindle*) estafa *f*; (*ruse*) trampa *f*, ardid *f*, estratagema *f*; (*harmless deception*) travesura *f*; (*hoax*) trastada *f*, primada *f*, burla *f*; **dirty —, low —, shabby —** mala pasada *f*, faena *f*; **—s of the trade** trucos *mpl* del oficio, triquiñuelas *fpl* del oficio; **there must be a — in it** aquí debe haber trampa; **he's up to all the —s, he knows a — or two** se lo sabe todo; **he's up to his old —s again** ha vuelto a hacer de las suyas; **I know a — worth two of that** yo me sé algo mucho mejor; **to play a — on someone** hacer una mala pasada a uno, hacer una faena a uno; (*practical joke*) gastar una broma a uno; **his memory played him a —** le falló la memoria; **unless my eyes are playing me —s** a menos que me engañen mis ojos.

(b) (*peculiarity*) peculiaridad *f* (personal); (*custom*) hábito *m*, manía *f*; **certain —s of style** ciertas peculiaridades estilísticas, ciertos rasgos del estilo; **it's just a — he has** es una manía suya; **it's a — of the light** es una ilusión de la luz; **history has a — of repeating itself** la historia tiene tendencia a repetirse.

(c) (*card —*) juego *m* de naipes, truco *m* de naipes; (*conjuring —*) juego *m* de manos; **the whole bag of —s** todo el negocio; todo ello; **that should do the —** eso seguramente será satisfactorio, eso habrá de bastar.

(d) (*Cards*) baza *f*; **to take all the —s** ganar (*or* hacer) todas las bazas; **he doesn't miss a —** (*fig*) es la mar de listo; no pierde detalle por pequeño que sea.

(e) (*knack*) tino *m*, truco *m*; **to get the — of it** coger el tino, aprender el modo de hacer algo.

2 *attr*: **— photography** trucaje *m*; **— question** pregunta *f* de pega; **— riding** acrobacia *f* ecuestre.

3 *vt* (a) (*deceive*) engañar; trampear; burlar; (*swindle*) estafar, timar; **we were —d** nos engañaron, nos dejamos engañar; **to — someone into doing something** lograr mañosamente que uno haga algo, inducir fraudulentamente a uno a hacer algo; **to — someone out of something** quitar mañosamente algo a uno, estafar algo a uno.

(b) **to — out** (*decorate*) ataviar, adornar (*with* de).

trickery ['trikəri] *n* astucia *f*, superchería *f*, mañas *fpl*; (*Law*) fraude *m*; **to obtain something by —** obtener algo fraudulentamente.

trickle ['trikl] **1** *n* hilo *m*, chorro *m* delgado, goteo *m*; (*fig*) pequeña cantidad *f*; **a — of people** unas pocas personas; **we received a — of news** nos llegaba alguna noticia de vez en cuando; **what was a — is now a flood** lo que era un goteo es ya un torrente.

2 *vt* dejar caer gota a gota, dejar salir en un chorro delgado; **you're trickling blood** estás sangrando un poquito.

3 *vi* (a) gotear, salir gota a gota, salir en un chorro delgado; (*fig*) salir poco a poco; **blood —d down his cheek** la sangre le corría gota a gota por la mejilla; **our money is trickling away** nuestro dinero se consume poco a poco.

(b) (*of persons*) salir (*etc*) poco a poco; **people kept trickling in** iban llegando unas cuantas personas; **shall we — over to the café?** (*fam*) ¿nos trasladamos al café?

trickster ['trikstə*] *n* estafador *m*, embustero *m*.

tricky ['triki] *adj person* astuto; mañoso, tramposo; *situation etc* delicado, difícil; *problem* espinoso; **it's all rather —** es un poco complicado, es un tanto difícil.

tricolour ['trikələ*] *n* tricolor *f*, bandera *f* tricolor.

tricot ['trikəu] *n* tejido *m* de punto.

tricycle ['traisikl] *n* triciclo *m*.

trident ['traidənt] *n* tridente *m*.

tried [traid] *adj* probado, de toda garantía.

triennial [trai'eniəl] *adj* trienal.

triennially [trai'eniəli] *adv* trienalmente, cada tres años.

trier ['traiə*] *n* persona *f* que se esfuerza mucho.

trifle ['traifl] **1** *n* (a) (*unimportant thing*) friolera *f*, bagatela *f*, fruslería *f*; **£5 is a mere —** 5 libras son una bagatela; **he worries about —s** se preocupa por pequeñeces; **any — can distract her** le distrae cualquier tontería; **you could have bought it for a —** hubieras podido comprarlo por muy poco dinero.

(b) **a —** (*as adv*) un poquito, un poquitín; **it's a — difficult** es un tantico difícil; **it's a — too much** es un poquito demasiado; **we were a — put out** quedamos un poquito desconcertados.

(c) (*Cook*) dulce *m* de bizcocho borracho.

2 *vt*: **to — away** malgastar, desperdiciar; *money* despilfarrar.

3 *vi*: **to — with one's food** comer melindrosamente, hacer melindres al comer; **to — with someone** jugar con uno, tratar a uno con poca seriedad; **he's not a person to be —d with** es persona que hay que tratar con la mayor seriedad; **to — with a girl's affections** divertirse fingiendo querer a una joven.

trifler ['traiflə*] *n* persona *f* frívola, persona *f* informal.

trifling ['traifliŋ] *adj* insignificante, sin importancia, de poca monta.

triforium [trai'fɔ:riəm] *n* triforio *m*.

trigger ['trigə*] **1** *n* (*Mil*) gatillo *m*; (*Tech*) disparador *m*, tirador *m*.

2 *vt*: **to — off** hacer estallar; (*fig*) provocar, hacer estallar, desencadenar.

trigger finger ['trigə,fiŋgə*] *n* índice *m* de la mano derecha (empleado para apretar el gatillo).

trigger-happy ['trigə,hæpi] *adj* que está dispuesto a apretar el gatillo por cualquier motivo.

trigonometric(al) ['trigənə'metrik(əl)] adj trigonométrico.

trigonometry [,trigə'nɔmitri] n trigonometría f.

trike [traik] n (fam) triciclo m.

trilateral ['trai'lætərəl] adj trilátero.

trilby ['trilbi] n sombrero m flexible.

trilingual ['trai'liŋgwəl] adj trilingüe.

trill [tril] **1** n (of bird) trino m, gorjeo m; (Mus) trino m, quiebro m; (of R) vibración f. **2** vt pronunciar con vibración. **3** vi trinar, gorjear.

trillion ['triliən] n (Brit) trillón m; (US) billón m.

trilogy ['trilədʒi] n trilogía f.

trim [trim] **1** adj aseado, arreglado; elegante; en buen estado; **she has a — figure** tiene buen tipo.
  2 n (a) (condition) estado m, condición f; buen estado m; (of boat) asiento m; (of sails) orientación f; **in good —** en buen estado, en buenas condiciones; person en forma; **in fighting —** listo para el combate, listo para entrar en acción; **to get things into —** arreglar las cosas; hacer sus preparativos.
  (b) (cut) recorte m; **to give one's hair a —** recortarse el pelo.
  3 vt (a) (tidy) arreglar, ordenar; disponer; ajustar; componer; boat equilibrar; sails orientar; **to — up** arreglar, componer.
  (b) (Sewing) dress adornar, guarnecer (with de); sleeves **—med with lace** mangas fpl guarnecidas de encaje.
  (c) (cut) cortar; hair, hedge recortar; bush etc podar; lamp, wick despabilar; wood desbastar, alisar.
  4 vr: **to — oneself up** arreglarse.

trimming ['trimiŋ] n adorno m, guarnición f; orla f; **—s** (cuttings) recortes mpl; (adornments) adornos mpl; accesorios mpl; (pej) arrequives mpl; **without all the —s** sin todos aquellos adornos.

trimness ['trimnis] n aseo m; elegancia f; buen estado m.

Trinidad ['trinidæd] Trinidad f.

trinitrotoluene [trai'naitrəu'tɔljuːin] n trinitrotolueno m.

Trinity ['triniti] n Trinidad f.

trinket ['triŋkit] n dije m, chuchería f; (pej) baratijas fpl, chucherías fpl.

trinomial [trai'nəumiəl] **1** adj trinomio. **2** n trinomio m.

trio ['triəu] n trío m.

trip [trip] **1** n (a) (journey) viaje m; (excursion) excursión f; business — viaje m de negocios; **cheap —s to Majorca** viajes mpl en plan económico a Mallorca; **pleasure —** viaje m de recreo; excursión f; **round —** viaje m de ida y vuelta; tourist — viaje m turístico; excursión f turística; **he's away on a —** está de viaje; **to take a —** hacer un viaje; **salir de excursión; I must take a — into town** tengo que ir a la ciudad.
  (b) (stumble) tropiezo m, traspié m; (in wrestling etc) zancadilla f; (fig) desliz m, tropiezo m.
  (c) (Mech) trinquete m, disparo m.
  2 vt (also **to — up**) hacer tropezar, hacer caer, (deliberately) echar la zancadilla a; **to — someone up** (fig) coger a uno en una falta; **the fourth question —ped him up** la cuarta pregunta le confundió, la cuarta pregunta le desconcertó.
  3 vi (a) **to — along, to go —ing along** andar (or ir, correr etc) con paso ligero, andar airosamente.
  (b) (also **to — up**) tropezar (against, on, over en), caer, dar un tropezón; (fig) tropezar, equivocarse.

tripartite ['trai'pɑːtait] adj tripartito.

tripe [traip] n (a) (Cook) callos mpl; (Anat, hum) tripas fpl.
  (b) (fam) tonterías fpl, bobadas fpl; **what utter —!** ¡tonterías!; **he talks a lot of —** no habla más que bobadas.

triphase ['traifeiz] adj (Elec) trifásico.

triphthong ['trifθɔŋ] n triptongo m.

triple ['tripl] **1** adj triple; **— the sum** el triple; **T— Alliance** Triple Alianza f.
  2 n triple m.
  3 vt triplicar.
  4 vi triplicarse.

triplet ['triplit] n (Mus) tresillo m; (Poet) terceto m; **—s** (persons) trillizos mpl, as fpl.

triplicate ['triplikit] **1** adj triplicado. **2** n: **in —** por triplicado.

triplicate ['triplikeit] vt triplicar.

triply ['tripli] adv tres veces; **— dangerous** tres veces más peligroso.

tripod ['traipɔd] n trípode m.

tripper ['tripə*] n excursionista mf; turista mf (que hace una visita de un día).

tripping ['tripiŋ] adj ligero, airoso.

trippingly ['tripiŋli] adv ligeramente, airosamente.

triptych ['triptik] n tríptico m.

trireme ['trairiːm] n trirreme m.

trisect [trai'sekt] vt trisecar.

Tristram ['tristrəm] m Tristán.

trisyllabic ['traisi'læbik] adj trisilábico.

trisyllable ['trai'siləbl] n trisílabo m.

trite [trait] adj vulgar, trivial; gastado, trillado y llevado.

triteness ['traitnis] n vulgaridad f, trivialidad f; lo gastado.

Triton ['traitn] m Tritón.

triturate ['tritʃəreit] vt triturar.

trituration [,tritʃə'reiʃən] n trituración f.

triumph ['traiʌmf] **1** n triunfo m; éxito m; **a new — for Slobodian industry** nuevo éxito de la industria eslobodia; **to achieve a great —** obtener un gran éxito; **it is a — of man over nature** en esto el hombre triunfa de la naturaleza; **to come home in —** volver a casa triunfalmente.
  2 vi triunfar; **to — over** triunfar de, vencer.

triumphal [trai'ʌmfəl] adj triunfal.

triumphant [trai'ʌmfənt] adj triunfante; victorioso; **he was —** estaba jubiloso, estaba lleno de júbilo.

triumphantly [trai'ʌmfəntli] adv triunfalmente, de modo triunfal; **he said —** dijo en tono triunfal.

triumvirate [trai'ʌmvirit] n triunvirato m.

trivia ['triviə] npl trivialidades fpl.

trivial ['triviəl] adj trivial, insignificante; banal; superficial; excuse, pretext etc frívolo, poco serio.

triviality [,trivi'æliti] n trivialidad f, insignificancia f; banalidad f; superficialidad f; frivolidad f, falta f de seriedad; trivialidades fpl.

triweekly ['trai'wiːkli] **1** adj trisemanal. **2** adv trisemanalmente, tres veces por semana.

trochaic [trɔ'keiik] adj trocaico.

trochee ['trɔki] n troqueo m.

trod [trɔd] pret of tread.

trodden ['trɔdn] ptp of tread.

troglodyte ['trɔglədait] n troglodita m.

troika ['trɔikə] n troica f.

Trojan ['trəudʒən] **1** adj troyano; **— horse** caballo m de Troya; **— War** Guerra f de Troya. **2** n troyano m, a f.

troll [trəul] n gnomo m, duende m.

trolley ['trɔli] n (hand —) carretilla f; (tea —) mesita f de ruedas; (child's) carretón m; (Tech) corredera f elevada; (Elec) trole m, arco m de trole; (US) tranvía m.

trolley bus ['trɔlibʌs] n trolebús m.

trolley car ['trɔlikɑ:*] n (US) tranvía m.

trolley pole ['trɔlipəul] n trole m.

trollop ['trɔləp] n marrana f; puta f.

trombone [trɔm'bəun] n trombón m.

trombonist [trɔm'bəunist] n trombón m.

troop [truːp] **1** n (a) banda f, grupo m, compañía f; (Mil) tropa f, (of cavalry) escuadrón m; (Theat) see **troupe; —s** (Mil) tropas fpl; **to come in a —** venir en tropel, venir en masa.
  (b) **the steady — of feet** el ruido rítmico de pasos.
  2 vt: **to — the colour** presentar la bandera, desfilar con la bandera.
  3 vi: **to — along** marchar (todos juntos); **to — away, to — off** marcharse en tropel; **to — out** salir todos juntos, salir en masa; **to — past** desfilar (ante); **to — together** reunirse en masa.

troop carrier ['truːp,kæriə*] n (Naut) transporte m; (Aut) camión m blindado.

trooper ['truːpə*] n soldado m de caballería; **state —** (US) soldado m de reserva.

troopship ['truːpʃip] n transporte m.

troop train ['truːptrein] n tren m militar.

trope [trəup] n tropo m.

trophy ['trəufi] n trofeo m.

tropic ['trɔpik] n trópico m; **—s** trópicos mpl, zona f tropical; **T— of Cancer** trópico m de Cáncer; **T— of Capricorn** trópico m de Capricornio.

tropic(al) ['trɔpik(əl)] adj tropical.

trot¹ [trɔt] **1** n trote m; **at an easy —**, **at a slow —** a trote corto; **to break into a —** empezar a trotar; **for 5 days on the —** durante 5 días seguidos; **to be always on the —** estar ocupado siempre; tener una vida ajetreada; **to keep someone on the —** no dejar a uno descansar.
  2 vt (a) horse hacer trotar.
  (b) **to — out** excuses etc ensartar; arguments sacar a relucir, presentar otra vez; erudition hacer alarde de.
  3 vi (a) trotar, ir al trote.

(b) (*fam: of person*) ir; irse, marcharse; **he —s round to the shop** va a la tienda; **we must be —ting** es hora de marcharnos.

trot² [trɔt] *n* (*US sl*) chuleta *f*.

troth [trəʊθ] *n* (*arch or hum*) see **plight**.

trotter ['trɔtə*] *n* (*horse*) trotón *m*, caballo *m* trotón; (*Cook*) pie *m* de cerdo, manita *f* de cerdo.

troubadour ['truːbədɔː*] *n* trovador *m*.

trouble ['trʌbl] **1** *n* **(a)** (*grief, affliction*) aflicción *f*; pena *f*, angustia *f*; (*misfortune*) desgracia *f*, desventura *f*; (*worry*) inquietud *f*, preocupación *f*; (*jam*) apuro *m*, aprieto *m*; **to be in** — estar en un apuro; **to be in great** — estar muy apurado; **now your —s are over** ya no tendrás de que preocuparte, se acabaron las preocupaciones; **life is full of —s** la vida está llena de aflicciones; **then this — came upon them** luego sufrieron esta aflicción; **to drown one's —s** beber para olvidar sus aflicciones; **to lay up — for oneself** hacer algo que causará pena en el futuro; **to tell someone one's —s** contar sus desventuras a uno.

(b) (*difficulty*) dificultad *f*; disgusto *m*; (*hindrance*) estorbo *m*, inconveniente *m*; **family —s** dificultades *fpl* con la familia; **money —s** dificultades *fpl* económicas; **the — is that . . .** la dificultad es que . . ., lo malo es que . . ., el inconveniente es que . . .; **what's the —?**, **what seems to be the —?** ¿pasa algo?; **their aunt is a great — to them** su tía constituye un gran estorbo para ellos; **it's just asking for —** eso es buscar tres pies al gato; **to get into —** meterse en un lío; **Peter got into — for saying that** Pedro se mereció una bronca diciendo eso; **he got into — with the police** tuvo una dificultad con la policía; **to get someone into —** comprometer a uno, crear un lío a uno; **to get a girl into —** (*euph*) dejar encinta a una joven; **to get out of —** salir del apuro; **to get someone out of —** ayudar a uno a salir del apuro; echar un cable a uno; **you'll have — with it** tendrás dificultades con eso; **did you have any —?** ¿tuviste alguna dificultad?; **to make — for someone** crear un lío a uno; amargar la vida a uno.

(c) (*bother*) molestia *f*; dificultad *f*; (*effort*) esfuerzo *m*; **with no little —** con bastante dificultad, con no poca dificultad; **it's no —** no es molestia; **it's no — to do it properly** no cuesta nada hacerlo bien; **it's not worth the —** no vale la pena; **nothing is too much — for her** pone el máximo cuidado en todo lo que hace, se presta a todo sin reparar en las molestias que pudiera suponer para ella; **to give someone —** causar molestia a uno; **to go to the — of** + *ger* darse la molestia de + *infin*; **we had — getting here in time** nos costó trabajo llegar aquí a tiempo; **we had all our — for nothing** todo aquello fue trabajo perdido; **to put someone to the — of doing something** molestar a uno pidiéndole que haga algo; **I fear I am putting you to a lot of —** me temo que esto le vaya a molestar bastante; **to save oneself the —** ahorrarse el trabajo; **to spare no — in order to** + *infin* no regatear medio para + *infin*; **to take the —** to + *infin* tomarse la molestia de + *infin*; **he didn't even take the — to say thank you** ni se dignó siquiera darme las gracias; **to take a lot of —** esmerarse, trabajar (*etc*) con el mayor cuidado.

(d) (*upset: Med*) enfermedad *f*, mal *m*; **chest —** enfermedad *f* del pecho; **heart —** enfermedad *f* cardíaca.

(e) (*upset: Mech*) avería *f*; fallo *m*; **engine —** avería *f* del motor; **a mechanic put the — right** un mecánico reparó las piezas averiadas; **we drove 5,000 miles without — of any kind** cubrimos 5.000 millas sin la menor avería.

(f) (*upset: between persons*) disgusto *m*, desavenencia *f*, sinsabor *m*; **the Parnell —** el caso Parnell; **there is constant — between them** riñen constantemente; **X caused — between Y and Z** X provocó un disgusto entre Y y Z.

(g) (*unrest, Pol etc*) conflicto *m*; trastorno *m*, disturbio *m*; **the Irish —s** los conflictos de los irlandeses, la guerra civil irlandesa; **labour —s** conflictos *mpl* laborales; **there's — at t'mill** hay un disturbio en la fábrica, hay huelga en la fábrica; **there's — brewing** soplan vientos de fronda; **to stir up —** meter cizaña, revolver el ajo.

2 *vt* **(a)** (*afflict, grieve*) afligir; (*worry*) inquietar, preocupar; (*disturb*) agitar, turbar; **the thought —d him** el pensamiento le afligió; **the heat —d us** nos molestó el calor; **his eyes — him** le duelen los ojos; **I am deeply —d** estoy sumamente inquieto; **it's not that that —s me** no me inquieto por eso, eso me trae sin cuidado.

(b) (*bother*) molestar, incomodar; (*badger*) importunar; **I'm sorry to — you** lamento tener que molestarle; **may I — you for a match?** ¿tiene fuego por favor?, ¿me hace el favor de darme fuego?; **may I — you to hold this?** ¿le molestaría tener esto?; **does it — you if I smoke?** ¿le molesta que fume?; **I shan't — you with all the details** no les molesto citando todos los detalles; **maths never —d me at all** las matemáticas no me costaron trabajo en absoluto.

3 *vi* preocuparse, molestarse; **please don't —!** ¡no se moleste!, ¡no se preocupe!; **don't — to write** no se moleste en escribir; **he didn't — to shut the door** no se tomó la molestia de cerrar la puerta; **if you had —d to find out** si se hubiera tomado la molestia de averiguarlo.

4 *vr:* **to — oneself about something** preocuparse por algo; **to — oneself to do something** tomarse la molestia de hacer algo; **don't — yourself!** ¡no se moleste!, ¡no se preocupe!

troubled ['trʌbld] *adj person* inquieto, preocupado; *expression* preocupado; *period* turbulento, agitado; *life, story* accidentado; *waters* revueltos, turbio; **to look —** parecer estar preocupado.

trouble-free ['trʌblfriː] *adj* libre de inquietudes, totalmente tranquilo; (*Pol etc*) libre de disturbios; (*Aut, Mech*) exento de averías; **a thousand — miles** mil millas sin avería alguna.

troublemaker ['trʌbl,meikə*] *n* alborotador *m*, buscarruidos *m*, elemento *m* perturbador.

troubleshooter ['trʌbl,ʃuːtə*] *n* investigador *m* de conflictos laborales, árbitro *m* de conflictos laborales.

troublesome ['trʌblsəm] *adj* molesto, fastidioso; importuno; dificultoso; **it's very —** es terriblemente molesto; **now don't be —** no seas difícil, no te pongas así.

trouble spot ['trʌblspɔt] *n* (*Pol*) centro *m* de fricción, lugar *m* turbulento.

troublous ['trʌbləs] *adj times* turbulento, agitado, revuelto.

trough [trɔf] *n* **(a)** (*depression*) depresión *f*, hoyo *m*; (*between waves*) seno *m*; (*channel*) canal *m*; (*Meteorol*) mínimo *m* de presión; (*fig*) parte *f* baja, punto *m* más bajo.

(b) (*drinking —*) abrevadero *m*; (*feeding —*) comedero *m*; (*kneading —*) artesa *f*; (*of stone*) pila *f*.

trounce [trauns] *vt* (*thrash*) pegar, zurrar, dar una paliza a; (*defeat*) derrotar, cascar; (*castigate*) fustigar.

troupe [truːp] *n* (*Theat etc*) compañía *f*, grupo *m*, conjunto *m*.

trouper ['truːpə*] *n* (*Theat*) miembro *m* de una compañía de actores; **old —** actor *m* veterano, actriz *f* veterana.

trouser press ['trauzəpres] *n* prensa *f* para pantalones.

trousers ['trauzəz] *npl* pantalones *mpl*, pantalón *m*; **a pair of —** un pantalón, unos pantalones; **to wear the —s** (*fig*) llevar los pantalones.

trousseau ['truːsəu] *n* ajuar *m*, equipo *m* (de novia).

trout [traut] *n* trucha *f*.

trout fisherman ['traut,fiʃəmən] *n*, *pl* **—men** [mən] pescador *m* de truchas.

trout fishing ['traut,fiʃiŋ] *n* pesca *f* de truchas.

trowel ['trauəl] *n* (*Agr*) desplantador *m*, transplantador *m*; (*builder's*) paleta *f*, llana *f*.

Troy [trɔi] Troya *f*.

troy (weight) ['trɔi('weit)] *n* peso *m* troy.

truancy ['truənsi] *n* ausencia *f* sin permiso.

truant ['truənt] **1** *adj* (*slack*) gandul, haragán, vago; (*absent*) ausente, desaparecido.

2 *n* (*slacker*) gandul *m*, vago *m*; (*absentee*) novillero *m*; **to play —** ausentarse, (*School*) hacer novillos.

truce [truːs] *n* (*Mil*) tregua *f*; (*fig*) suspensión *f*, cesación *f*; **to call a — to something** suspender algo.

truck¹ [trʌk] **1** *n:* **to have no — with someone** tratar con uno, no tener relaciones con uno; **we want no — with that** no queremos tener nada que ver con eso.

2 *attr:* **— system** pago *m* de salarios en especie.

truck² [trʌk] *n* (*waggon*) carro *m*; (*hand—*) carretilla *f*; (*Rail*) vagón *m* (de mercancías); (*lorry*) camión *m*.

truckage ['trʌkidʒ] *n* (*US*) acarreo *m*.

truckdriver ['trʌk,draivə*] *n* camionero *m*, camionista *m*, conductor *m* de camión.

trucker ['trʌkə*] *n* (*US*) camionero *m*, camionista *m*.

truck farm ['trʌk'faːm] *n* (*US*), **truck garden** ['trʌk'gaːdn] *n* (*US*) huerto *m* de hortalizas.

trucking ['trʌkiŋ] *n* acarreo *m*, transporte *m*.

truckle ['trʌkl] *vi:* **to — to someone** someterse servilmente a uno.

truckle bed ['trʌkl'bed] *n* carriola *f*.

truckload ['trʌkləud] n carretada f; vagón m (lleno); **—s of soldiers** camiones mpl llenos de soldados; **by the —** (fig) a carretadas, a montones.

truckman ['trʌkmən] n, pl **—men** [mən] (US) camionero m, camionista m.

truculence ['trʌkjuləns] n agresividad f; mal humor m, aspereza f.

truculent ['trʌkjulənt] adj agresivo; malhumorado, áspero.

truculently ['trʌkjuləntli] adv behave de modo agresivo; answer malhumorado, ásperamente.

trudge [trʌdʒ] **1** n caminata f (difícil, larga, penosa).
2 vt recorrer a pie (penosamente); **we —d the streets looking for him** nos cansamos buscándole por las calles.
3 vi (also **to — along**) caminar penosamente, andar con dificultad.

true [tru:] **1** adj **(a)** (not false) verdadero; **—!, too —!** ¡es verdad!; **it is — that . . .** es verdad que . . .; **can this be —?** ¿es cierto esto?; **so — is this that . . .** tan es así que . . .; **to come —** realizarse, cumplirse, verificarse; **to hold something to be —** creer que algo es verdad; **it holds — of . . .** también es cierto por lo que se refiere a . . .
(b) (genuine) auténtico, verdadero, genuino; account verídico; copy fiel, exacto; **what is the — situation?** ¿cuál es la verdadera situación?; **it is not a — account of what happened** no es un informe verdadero de lo que pasó; **in a — spirit of service** en un auténtico espíritu de servicio; **like a — Englishman** como un inglés auténtico.
(c) (of measures etc) exacto; surface, join uniforme, a nivel; upright a plomo; **the walls are not —** las paredes no están a plomo.
(d) (faithful) fiel, leal; **a — friend** un fiel amigo; **all good men and —** todos los buenos y leales; **to be — to someone** ser fiel a uno; **to be — to one's word** cumplir su promesa, cumplir lo prometido.
(e) voice etc puro.
(f) (Bio etc) **— to life** conforme con la realidad; **— to type** conforme con el tipo.
2 adv: **to aim —** apuntar bien, acertar en la puntería; **to breed —** reproducirse conforme con el tipo; **to run — to type** estar conforme con el tipo; **now tell me —** dime la verdad.
3 n: **to be out of —** (of things joining) no estar a nivel, estar mal alineado, estar desalineado; (of things vertical) no estar a plomo; (of wheel) estar descentrado.

true-blue ['tru:'blu:] **1** adj de lo más leal, acérrimo. **2** n partidario m de lo más leal, partidario m acérrimo.

true-born ['tru:'bɔːn] adj auténtico, verdadero.

true-bred ['tru:'bred] adj de casta legítima, de pura sangre.

true-hearted ['tru:'hɑːtid] adj fiel, leal; sincero.

true-life ['tru:laif] adj verdadero, conforme con la realidad.

truelove ['tru:lʌv] n novio m, a f, fiel amante mf.

truffle ['trʌfl] n trufa f.

truism ['tru:izəm] n perogrullada f, tópico m; **it is a — to say that . . .** es un tópico decir que . . .

truly ['tru:li] adv verdaderamente; auténticamente; exactamente; fielmente; **and — it was tough** y efectivamente fue difícil; **a — great painting** un cuadro verdaderamente grande; **really and —?** ¿de veras?; **yours —** le saluda atentamente; **nobody knows it better than yours —** nadie lo sabe mejor que este pobre hombre.

trump [trʌmp] **1** n triunfo m; **hearts are —s** triunfan corazones, pintan corazones; **what's —s?** ¿a qué pinta?; **he always turns up —s** no nos falla nunca, es persona de la mayor confianza.
2 vt **(a)** (Cards) fallar.
(b) to — up charge forjar, falsificar, inventar.
3 vi triunfar, poner un triunfo.

trumped-up ['trʌmpt'ʌp] adj accusation etc forjado, inventado.

trumpery ['trʌmpəri] **1** adj frívolo; (valueless) inútil, sin valor; (insignificant) sin importancia; (trashy) de relumbrón. **2** n oropel m.

trumpet ['trʌmpit] **1** n trompeta f. **2** vt trompetear; (fig: also **— forth**) pregonar, anunciar (a son de trompeta). **3** vi (elephant) barritar.

trumpet blast ['trʌmpitblɑːst] n, **trumpet call** ['trʌmpitkɔːl] n trompetazo m; (fig) clarinazo m.

trumpeter ['trʌmpitə*] n trompetero m, trompeta m.

truncate [trʌŋ'keit] vt truncar.

truncated [trʌŋ'keitid] adj truncado, trunco.

truncation [trʌŋ'keiʃən] n truncamiento m.

truncheon ['trʌntʃən] n porra f.

trundle ['trʌndl] **1** vt hacer rodar, hacer correr (sobre ruedas); (fig) llevar, arrastrar (con dificultad).

2 vi rodar (con mucho ruido, pesadamente).

trunk [trʌŋk] **1** n (Anat, Bot) tronco m; (case) baúl m; (US Aut) portaequipaje m; (elephant's) trompa f.
2 attr: **— line** (Rail) línea f troncal; (Tel) línea f principal; see **call, road.**

trunks [trʌŋks] npl taparrabo m.

trunnion ['trʌniən] n muñón m.

truss [trʌs] **1** n (bundle) lío m, paquete m; (of hay etc) haz m, lío m; (of fruit) racimo m; (Archit) entramado m; (Med) braguero m.
2 vt (tie) liar, atar; fowl espetar; (Archit) apuntalar, apoyar con entramado; **to — someone up** atar a uno con cuerdas (etc).

trust [trʌst] **1** n **(a)** (belief, faith) confianza f (in en); **breach of —** abuso m de confianza; **to put one's — in** confiar en; **to take something on —** aceptar algo a ojos cerrados, creer algo sin tener (or pedir) pruebas de ello.
(b) (Comm) **to supply goods on —** suministrar artículos al fiado, proveer artículos a crédito.
(c) (charge) cargo m, deber m, obligación f; responsabilidad f; **our sacred —** nuestra sagrada obligación; **position of —** puesto m de responsabili-dad, puesto m de confianza; **to commit something to someone's —** hacer que uno se encargue de algo; **to desert one's —** faltar a su deber.
(d) (Law) fideicomiso m; **to hold money in — for someone** tener dinero en administración a nombre de uno.
(e) (Comm, Fin) trust m; (pej) monopolio m, cartel m; **investment —** compañía f inversionista.
2 attr: **— company** banco m fideicomisario.
3 vt **(a)** (believe in, rely on) confiar en, fiarse de; tener confianza en; creer; **don't you — me?** ¿no te fías de mí?; **she is not to be —ed** ella no es de fiar; **you can't — a word he says** es imposible creer ninguna palabra suya; **to — someone with something** confiar algo a uno; **to — someone with a task** confiar un cometido a uno; **will you — me with your bike?** ¿me permites usar tu bicicleta?; **to — someone to do something** confiar en que uno haga algo; **— you!** ¡siempre igual!, ¡lo mismo que siempre!; **— him to make a mess of it** no es sorprendente que lo haya hecho mal; **mother wouldn't — us out of her sight** mamá no permitía que nos alejásemos de ella, mamá nos tenía cosidos a sus faldas.
(b) (Comm) dar al fiado.
(c) (hope) esperar; **I — not** espero que no; **I — that all will go well** espero que todo vaya bien.
3 vi confiar; esperar; **to — in God** confiar en Dios; **to — to chance, to — to luck** confiar en tener suerte; hacer algo a la ventura.

trusted ['trʌstid] adj leal, de confianza.

trustee [trʌs'tiː] n (in bankruptcy) síndico m; (holder of property for another) fideicomisario m, depositario m; administrador m; (of college) regente m.

trusteeship [trʌs'tiːʃip] n cargo m de síndico, cargo m de fideicomisario (etc); administración f fiduciaria.

trustful ['trʌstful] adj, **trusting** ['trʌstiŋ] adj confiado.

trustingly ['trʌstiŋli] adv confiadamente.

trustworthiness ['trʌst,wəːðinis] n formalidad f, honradez f, confiabilidad f; carácter m fidedigno; exactitud f.

trustworthy ['trʌst,wəːði] adj person formal, honrado, confiable, de confianza; news, source etc fidedigno; statistics etc exacto.

trusty ['trʌsti] **1** adj servant etc fiel, leal; weapon seguro, bueno. **2** n (fam) preso m que ha dado pruebas de buena conducta.

truth [truːθ] n, pl **truths** [truːðz] verdad f; realidad f; verosimilitud f; **the plain —** la pura verdad, la verdad lisa y llana; **the whole —** toda la verdad; **the — of the matter is that . . ., — to tell . . .** la verdad del caso es que . . ., a decir verdad . . .; **there is some — in this** hay una parte de verdad en esto; **— will out** no hay mentira que no salga; **to tell the —** decir la verdad; **to tell someone a few home —s** decir a uno cuatro verdades; **in —** en verdad.

truthful ['truːθful] adj account verídico, exacto; person veraz; **are you being —?** ¿es esto la verdad?

truthfully ['truːθfəli] adv con verdad; **now tell me —** ahora bien, dime la verdad.

truthfulness ['truːθfulnis] n veracidad f; verdad f, exactitud f.

try [trai] **1** n **(a)** (attempt) tentativa f; **to have a —** hacer una tentativa, probar suerte; **to have a — for a job** presentarse como candidato a un puesto,

solicitar un puesto; **have another —!** ¡a probar otra vez!; **it's worth a —** vale la pena probarlo.
 (b) (*Rugby*) ensayo *m*; **to score a —** marcar un ensayo.
 2 *vt* **(a)** (*attempt*) intentar, probar; **shall we — it?** ¿lo probamos?; **you tried only 3 questions** Vd intentó 3 preguntas nada más.
 (b) (*test*) probar, poner a prueba, ensayar; **to — one's strength** ensayar sus fuerzas; **to — one's strength against someone** ensayarse para determinar cuál de los dos es más fuerte; **he was tried and found wanting** fue sometido a prueba y resultó ser deficiente.
 (c) (*expose to suffering*) hacer sufrir; afligir; **his much-tried relations** sus familiares que tanto habían sufrido; **they have been sorely tried** han sufrido mucho.
 (d) (*tire*) *eyes* cansar; *person* irritar; **to — one's eyes by reading too much** cansarse los ojos leyendo demasiado; **you — my patience** me haces perder la paciencia.
 (e) (*taste, sample*) probar; **have you tried these olives?** ¿has probado estas aceitunas?
 (f) (*Law*) *case* ver; *person* procesar (*for* por), juzgar; **to be tried for murder** ser procesado por asesino; **to be tried by one's peers** ser juzgado por sus iguales.
 (g) (*with adv or prep*) **to — on** *clothes* probarse; **to — it on with someone** (*fam*) tratar de embaucar a uno; **he's just —ing it on** lo hace nada más para ver si tragamos el anzuelo; **to — out** probar, poner a prueba, someter a prueba, ensayar; **— it out on the dog first** dáselo primero al perro para ver qué pasa, pruébalo dándoselo de comer al perro; **to — over** (*Mus etc*) ensayar, ensayar a tocar (*etc*).
 3 *vi* probar; esforzarse; **to — one's best, to — one's hardest** esforzarse mucho, poner todo su esfuerzo; **— as he would . . .** por más que se esforzase . . .; **to — again** volver a probar; **you had better not —** más vale no probarlo; le aconsejo no hacerlo; **to — for something** tratar de obtener algo; **to — for a post** presentarse como candidato a un puesto, solicitar un puesto; **to — to do something, to — and do something** tratar de hacer algo, intentar hacer algo; procurar hacer algo; querer hacer algo; **it's —ing to rain** empieza a llover, quiere llover; **not to cough** procura no toser, procura contener la tos; **do — to understand** trata de comprender; **it's no use —ing to persuade him** no vale la pena tratar de convencerle.
trying ['traiiŋ] *adj* molesto; cansado; difícil.
try-on ['traiɒn] (*fam*) trampa *f*, tentativa *f* de engañar.
tryout ['traiaut] *n* prueba *f*; **to give a car a —** someter un coche a prueba.
tryst [trist] *n* (*lit, hum*) cita *f*; lugar *m* de una cita.
tsar [zɑ:*] *n* zar *m*.
tsarina [zɑ:'ri:nə] *n* zarina *f*.
tsetse fly ['tsetsiflai] *n* mosca *f* tsetsé.
T-shirt ['ti:ʃə:t] *n* camiseta *f*.
T-square ['ti:skweə*] *n* regla *f* T, té *f*.
tub [tʌb] **1** *n* tina *f*; cubo *m*, cuba *f*; artesón *m*; (*bath—*) baño *m*, bañera *f*; (*Naut*) carcamán *m*; **to have a —** (*bath*) tomar un baño.
 2 *vi* tomar un baño.
tuba ['tju:bə] *n* tuba *f*, bombardón *m*.
tubby ['tʌbi] *adj* rechoncho.
tube [tju:b] *n* tubo *m*; (*TV*) tubo *m*; (*US Radio*) lámpara *f*; (*Aut*) cámara *f* de aire; (*Rail*) metro *m*; **Eustachian —** trompa *f* de Eustaquio; **Fallopian —** trompa *f* de Falopio; **inner —** cámara *f* de aire; **to go by —** ir en el metro, viajar por metro.
tubeless ['tju:blis] *adj* *tyre* sin cámara.
tuber ['tju:bə*] *n* tubérculo *m*.
tubercle ['tju:bə:kl] *n* (*all senses*) tubérculo *m*.
tubercular [tju'bə:kjulə*] *adj* tubercular; (*Med*) tuberculoso.
tuberculosis [tju,bə:kju'ləusis] *n* tuberculosis *f*.
tuberculous [tju'bə:kjuləs] *adj* tuberculoso.
tube station ['tju:b,steiʃən] *n* estación *f* de metro.
tubing ['tju:biŋ] *n* tubería *f*; tubos *mpl*; **a piece of —** un trozo de tubo.
tub-thumper ['tʌb,θʌmpə*] *n* orador *m* demagógico.
tub-thumping ['tʌb,θʌmpiŋ] **1** *adj* demagógico.
 2 *n* oratoria *f* demagógica.
tubular ['tju:bjulə*] *adj* tubular, en forma de tubo; *furniture* de tubo.
tuck [tʌk] **1** *n* **(a)** (*Sew*) alforza *f*; pliegue *m*; **to take a — in a dress** hacer una alforza en un vestido.
 (b) (*fam: food*) provisiones *fpl*, comestibles *mpl*, (*sweets*) dulces *fpl*, golosinas *fpl*.
 2 *vt* (*Sew*) alforzar; plegar; **to — away** (*hide*) ocultar, esconder; *food* (*fam*) devorar, zampar; **he**

can certainly — **it away** ése sí sabe comer; **I can't think where he —s it all away** no llego a comprender dónde lo almacena; **— it away out of sight** ocúltalo para que no se vea; **the village is —ed away among the woods** la aldea se esconde en el bosque; **he —ed it away in his pocket** lo guardó en el bolsillo; **to — in a flap** meter una solapa para dentro; **to — bedclothes in** guarnecer una cama con su ropa; **to — A under B** poner A debajo de B; esconder A debajo de B; **to — up** *skirt, sleeves* arremangar; **to — someone up in bed** arropar a uno en la cama; (*fig*) acostar a uno; **you'll soon be nicely —ed up** pronto te verás instalado cómodamente en la cama.
 3 *vi*: **to — in** (*fam*) comer con apetito, comer vorazmente; **— in!** ¡a comer!, ¡a ello!; **to — into something** comer algo vorazmente, zamparse algo.
tucker ['tʌkə*] *vt* (*US fam*) cansar, agotar (*also* **to — out**).
tuck-in ['tʌk'in] *n* (*fam*) banquetazo *m*, comilona *f*; **to have a good —** darse un atracón.
tuck-shop ['tʌkʃɒp] *n* (*School*) bombonería *f*, confitería *f*.
Tuesday ['tju:zdi] *n* martes *m*.
tufa ['tju:fə] *n* toba *f*.
tuft [tʌft] *n* (*of hair*) copete *m*; (*of hairs, wool*) mechón *m*; (*of feathers*) cresta *f*, copete *m*; (*on helmet etc*) penacho *m*; (*of grass etc*) manojo *m*.
tufted ['tʌftid] *adj* copetudo.
tug [tʌg] **1** *n* **(a)** (*action*) tirón *m*; estirón *m*; **to give something a —** tirar de algo, dar un estirón a algo.
 (b) (*Naut*) remolcador *m*; **ocean-going —** remolcador *m* de alta mar.
 2 *vt* **(a)** tirar de; dar un estirón a; **to — something along** arrastrar algo, llevar algo arrastrándolo.
 (b) (*Naut*) remolcar; **eventually they —ged the boat clear** por fin sacaron el barco a flote.
 3 *vi*: **to — at something** tirar de algo; **someone was —ging at my sleeve** alguien me tiraba de la manga; **they —ged their hardest** se esforzaron muchísimo tirando de él.
tugboat ['tʌgbəut] *n* remolcador *m*.
tug-of-war ['tʌgə(v)'wɔ:*] *n* lucha *f* de la cuerda; (*fig*) lucha *f*, tira *m* y afloja; **the — between rival interests** el tira y afloja de intereses opuestos; **then comes the —** luego es el momento crítico, luego se inicia la lucha decisiva.
tuition [tju'iʃən] *n* enseñanza *f*, instrucción *f*; **private —** clases *fpl* particulares (*in* de).
tulip ['tju:lip] *n* tulipán *m*.
tulip tree ['tju:liptri:] *n* tulipanero *m*, tulipero *m*.
tulle [tju:l] *n* tul *m*.
tumble ['tʌmbl] **1** *n* caída *f*; (*somersault*) voltereta *f*; **to have a —, to take a —** caerse; **to have a — in the hay** retozar, hacer el amor (en el pajar); **to take a —** (*fig*) bajar de golpe, dar un bajón.
 2 *vt* (*knock down*) derribar, abatir, tumbar; (*fig*) derrocar; (*upset: also* **to — over**) derramar, hacer caer; (*disarrange*) desarreglar; **to — someone in the hay** tumbar a uno (en el pajar); **to — out** echar en desorden.
 3 *vi* (*fall*) caer; (*stumble*) tropezar; **to toss and —** (*in bed*) agitarse, revolverse mucho; **to — down** caer; desplomarse, hundirse, venirse abajo; **to — in, to — into bed** acostarse; acostarse del modo que sea; **to — out** salir en desorden; **to — out of a car** caerse de un coche; **to — out of bed** levantarse de prisa; **to go tumbling over and over** ir rodando, ir dando tumbos; **to — to something** caer en la cuenta de algo, comprender algo.
tumbledown ['tʌmbldaun] *adj* destartalado, ruinoso.
tumbler ['tʌmblə*] *n* (*glass*) vaso *m*; (*of lock*) seguro *m*, fiador *m*; (*person*) volteador *m*, ora *f*; (*Orn*) pichón *m* volteador.
tumbrel ['tʌmbrəl], **tumbril** ['tʌmbril] *n* chirrión *m*, carreta *f*.
tumefaction [,tju:mi'fækʃən] *n* tumefacción *f*.
tumescent [tju:'mesnt] *adj* tumescente.
tumid ['tju:mid] *adj* túmido.
tummy ['tʌmi] *n* (*fam*) estómago *m*, vientre *m*.
tumour ['tju:mə*] *n* tumor *m*.
tumult ['tju:mʌlt] *n* tumulto *m*.
tumultuous [tju:'mʌltjuəs] *adj* tumultuoso.
tumultuously [tju:'mʌltjuəsli] *adv* tumultuosamente.
tumulus ['tju:mjuləs] *n*, *pl* **tumuli** ['tju:mjulai] túmulo *m*.
tun [tʌn] *n* tonel *m*.
tuna ['tju:nə] *n* atún *m*.
tundra ['tʌndrə] *n* tundra *f*.
tune [tju:n] **1** *n* aire *m*, melodía *f*, tonada *f*; (*fig*) tono *m*; **to be in —** (*Mus*) estar templado, estar afinado; **to sing in —** cantar afinadamente, cantar

bien; **to be in — with** (*fig*) armonizar con, concordar con; **to be out of —** (*Mus*) estar destemplado, estar desafinado; **to sing out of —** cantar desafinadamente, cantar mal; **to be out of — with** (*fig*) desentonar con, estar en desacuerdo con; **to go out of —** desafinar; **to change one's —, to sing another —** mudar de tono; **to the — of** (*fig*) por la suma de, por la cantidad de.

2 *vti* afinar, acordar, templar (*also* **to — up**); **to — up** (*in practice*) tocar algunas notas (para afinar los instrumentos); **to — up** (*fig*) prepararse, ejercitarse; (*Aut*) poner a punto, reglar.

3 *vi*: **to — in** (*Radio*) sintonizar; (*loosely*) escuchar, escuchar un programa; **to — in to a station** sintonizar una emisora.

tuneful ['tjuːnful] *adj* melodioso, armonioso.

tunefully ['tjuːnfəli] *adv* melodiosamente, armoniosamente.

tunefulness ['tjuːnfulnis] *n* lo melodioso, lo armonioso.

tuneless ['tjuːnlis] *adj* disonante, discordante.

tunelessly ['tjuːnlisli] *adv* de modo disonante.

tuner ['tjuːnə*] *n* (*person*) afinador *m*; (*Radio*: knob) botón *m* sintonizador.

tune-up ['tjuːnʌp] *n* (*Mus*) afinación *f*; (*Aut*) puesta *f* a punto, reglaje *m*.

tungsten ['tʌŋstən] *n* tungsteno *m*.

tunic ['tjuːnik] *n* túnica *f*.

tuning ['tjuːniŋ] *n* (*Mus*) afinación *f*; (*Radio*) sintonización *f*.

tuning coil ['tjuːniŋkɔil] *n* bobina *f* sintonizadora.

tuning fork ['tjuːniŋfɔːk] *n* diapasón *m*.

tuning knob ['tjuːniŋnɔb] *n* botón *m* sintonizador.

Tunis ['tjuːnis] Túnez (*ciudad*).

Tunisia [tjuːˈniziə] Túnez *m* (*país*).

Tunisian [tjuːˈniziən] **1** *adj* tunecino. **2** *n* tunecino *m*, a *f*.

tunnel ['tʌnl] **1** *n* túnel *m*; (*Min*) galería *f*.

2 *vt* construir un túnel bajo, construir un túnel a través de; **a mound —led by rabbits** un montículo lleno de madrigueras de conejo; **wood —led by beetles** madera *f* carcomida, madera *f* agujereada por coleópteros; **shelters —led out in the hillsides** refugios *mpl* horadados en las colinas.

3 *vi* construir un túnel (*or* galería); (*of animal*) excavar una madriguera; **they — into the hill** construyen un túnel bajo la colina; **to — down into the earth** perforar un túnel en la tierra; **the rabbits — under the fence** los conejos hacen madrigueras que pasan debajo de la valla.

tunny ['tʌni] *n* atún *m*; **striped —** bonito *m*.

tunny fishery ['tʌni,fiʃəri] *n* almadraba *f*.

tuppence ['tʌpəns] *n see* **twopence.**

tuppenny ['tʌpəni] *adj see* **twopenny.**

turban ['təːbən] *n* turbante *m*.

turbid ['təːbid] *adj* turbio.

turbine ['təːbain] *n* turbina *f*; **gas —** turbina *f* de gas.

turbojet ['təːbəuˈdʒet] **1** *n* turborreactor *m*. **2** *adj*, *attr* turborreactor.

turboprop ['təːbəuˈprɔp] **1** *n* turbohélice *m*. **2** *adj*, *attr* turbohélice.

turbot ['təːbət] *n* rodaballo *m*.

turbulence ['təːbjuləns] *n* turbulencia *f*; desorden *m*, disturbios *mpl*; (*Meteorol*) turbulencia *f*.

turbulent ['təːbjulənt] *adj* turbulento; revoltoso.

tureen [təˈriːn] *n* sopera *f*.

turf [təːf] **1** *n* (*sward*) césped *m*; (*clod*) tepe *m*, césped *m*; (*peat*) turba *f*; **the T— (Sport*) el turf, las carreras de caballos.

2 *vt* encespedar, cubrir con céspedes (*also* **to — over**); **to — someone out** (*fam*) echar a uno, expulsar a uno.

turgid ['təːdʒid] *adj* turgente; (*fig*) hinchado; pesado, indigesto.

turgidity [təːˈdʒiditi] *n* turgencia *f*; (*fig*) hinchazón *f*; pesadez *f*.

Turk [təːk] *n* turco *m*, a *f*; **little —, young — tunante *m*.**

Turkey ['təːki] Turquía *f*.

turkey ['təːki] *n* pavo *m*, a *f*; **to talk — (fam)** no tener pelos en la lengua.

turkey cock ['təːkikɔk] *n* pavo *m* (*also fig*).

Turkish ['təːkiʃ] **1** *adj* turco. **2** *n* turco *m*.

turmeric ['təːmərik] *n* (*Bot*) cúrcuma *f*.

turmoil ['təːmɔil] *n* confusión *f*, desorden *m*; alboroto *m*; tumulto *m*; **everything is in a —** todo está en confusión, todo está revuelto; **we had complete — for a week** durante una semana reinó la confusión.

turn [təːn] **1** *n* (a) (*revolution*) vuelta *f*, revolución *f*; (*of spiral*) espira *f*; **with a quick — of the hand** con un movimiento rápido de la mano; **he never does a hand's —** no da golpe; **the meat is done to**

a **—** la carne está en su punto; **to give a screw another —** apretar un tornillo una vuelta más.

(b) (*change of direction*) cambio *m* de dirección; (*Aut*) giro *m*, vuelta *f*; (*Naut*) viraje *m*; **reverse —** vuelta *f* al revés; **"no left —"** (*Aut*) "prohibido girar a la izquierda"; **— of the tide** cambio *m* de la marea, vuelta *f* de la marea (*also fig*); **at every —** a cada paso, a cada momento; **the tide is on the —** la marea está cambiando; **the milk is on the —** la leche está cortándose; **to make a — to the left** girar a la izquierda; **to make a — to port** virar a babor; **things took a new —** las cosas cambiaron de aspecto; **events took a tragic —** los acontecimientos tomaron un cariz trágico; **events are taking a sensational —** los acontecimientos vienen tomando un rumbo sensacional; **then things took a — for the better** luego las cosas empezaron a mejorar.

(c) (*Med: fainting fit etc*) vahido *m*, desmayo *m*; (*crisis*) crisis *f*, ataque *m*; (*fright*) susto *m*; **it gave me quite a —** me dio un susto; **he had another —** last night anoche le dio otro ataque.

(d) (*short walk*) vuelta *f*; **to take a — in the park** dar una vuelta por el parque.

(e) (*successive opportunity*) turno *m*, vez *f*; oportunidad *f*; **— and — about** cada uno por turno; ahora esto y luego aquello; **by —s, in —** por turnos, sucesivamente; **I felt hot and cold by —s** tuve calor y luego frío en momentos sucesivos; **it's my —** me toca a mí; **then it was my — to protest** luego protesté a mi vez; **it's her — next** le toca a ella después, ella es la primera en turno; **your — will come** Vd tendrá su oportunidad; **to give up one's —** ceder la vez; **to go out of —** jugar (*etc*) fuera de orden; **to miss one's —** perder la vez; perder la ocasión; **the player shall miss two —s** el jugador deberá perder dos jugadas; **to take one's —** esperar su turno; turnar, alternar; **to take —s at the controls** alternar a los mandos; **to take a — at the wheel** conducir por su turno; **to take —s at doing something, to take it in —s to do something** turnar para hacer algo.

(f) (*Theat etc*) número *m*; **the star — of the evening** la atracción principal del programa; **she was the star —** ella fue la atracción principal; **he came on and did a funny —** salió a escena y presentó un número cómico.

(g) (*service*) **bad —** mala jugada *f*, mala pasada *f*; **good —** favor *m*, servicio *m*; **to do someone a bad —** hacer una mala pasada a uno; **a scout does a good —** each day el explorador presta un servicio cada día; **one good — deserves another** una buena acción merece recompensa; **it will serve my —** servirá para lo que yo quiero.

(h) (*inclination*) propensión *f* (*to* a); (*of mind*) disposición *f*, sesgo *m*; (*talent*) talento *m*, aptitud *f*; **to have a — for business** tener aptitud para los negocios; **it showed an odd — of mind** demostró una disposición de ánimo algo rara.

(i) (*form*) forma *f*; **the — of her arm** la configuración de su brazo, el contorno de su brazo; **— of phrase** giro *m*, expresión *f*; **that's a French —** of style eso es un modismo francés; **the car has a good — of speed** el coche tiene buena capacidad para acelerar.

(j) (*bend*) curva *f*, recodo *m*; **sharp —, sudden —** curva *f* cerrada, curva *f* brusca; **the road is full of twists and —s** la carretera tiene muchísimas curvas.

2 *vt* (a) (*revolve*) girar, hacer girar; *handle* dar vueltas a, torcer; *key* dar vuelta a; *screw* atornillar, destornillar; **the belt —s the wheel** la correa hace girar la rueda; **— it to the left** dale una vuelta hacia la izquierda; **you can — it through 90°** se puede girarlo hasta 90 grados.

(b) (**— to the other side**) volver; *ankle* torcer; *brain* trastornar; *stomach, soil etc* revolver; hay *etc* volver al revés; **to — a page** volver una hoja; **to — a dress inside out** volver un vestido del revés; **the plough —s the soil** el arado revuelve la tierra.

(c) (*direct*) volver; dirigir; *blow* desviar; **to — one's head** volver la cabeza; **to — one's steps homeward** dirigirse a casa, volver los pasos hacia casa; **to — one's eyes in someone's direction** volver la mirada hacia donde está uno; **to — a gun on someone** apuntar un revólver a uno; **to — someone's argument against himself** volver el arma contra el que la empleó; **to — A against B** predisponer a A en contra de B; **they —ed him against his parents** le enemistaron con sus padres; **to — someone from doing something** disuadir a uno de hacer algo; **we must — our thoughts to . . .** hemos de concentrar nuestro pensamiento en . . .; **if you will — your**

attention to . . . tengan la bondad de fijar la atención en . . .

(d) (*pass*) *corner* doblar; **he has —ed 50** ha cumplido los 50, ya tiene lo menos 50 años; **it's —ed 11 o'clock** son las 11 ya, ya dieron las 11.

(e) (*transform*) cambiar, mudar (*into*, *to* en); convertir, transformar (*into*, *to* en); *milk* agriar, volver agrio; **to — iron into gold** transformar el hierro en oro; **his admiration was —ed to scorn** su admiración se transformó en desprecio; **to — verse into prose** hacer una versión en prosa de un poema; **to — a play into a film** hacer una versión cinematográfica de una obra dramática; **to — English into Spanish** traducir el inglés al español, verter el inglés en español; **to — colour** cambiar de color; **the heat —ed the walls black** el calor volvió negras las paredes, el calor ennegreció las paredes.

(f) (*Tech*) tornear; **to — wood on a lathe** labrar la madera en un torno; **a well —ed leg** una pierna bien formada, una pierna bien torneada; **a well —ed sentence** una frase elegante.

(g) (*with adv or prep*) **to — about** see **to — round**; **to — aside** desviar, apartar; **to — away** desviar, apartar; *head* volver; *person* despedir; *business*, *offer etc* rechazar, desechar; **to — back** (*fold*) doblar; *clock* retrasar; *person* hacer retroceder; hacer volver; **they were —ed back at the frontier** en la frontera les hicieron volver; **to — down** (*bend*, *fold*) doblar (hacia abajo); *glass etc* poner boca abajo; *thumb* volver hacia abajo; *gas*, *radio etc* bajar; *offer* rechazar; *suitor*, *candidate* no aceptar; **to — in** doblar hacia adentro; *wanted man etc* entregar (a la policía); **to — off** *light* apagar; (*Elec*) desconectar, quitar; *engine* parar; *tap* cerrar; *gas* cortar, cerrar la llave de; **to — on** (*Elec*) encender, conectar; poner; *tap* abrir; *gas* abrir la llave de; **to leave the radio —ed on** dejar encendida la radio; **to — out** *light* apagar; *gas* cortar, cerrar la llave de; *person* echar, expulsar; poner en la calle; *pocket* vaciar; *product* producir, fabricar; **to — out the guard** (*Mil*) formar la guardia; **to be well —ed out** ir bien trajeado, ir bien vestido; **the college —s out good secretaries** la escuela produce secretarias con buena formación profesional; **to — over** *page etc* volver; *container*, *vehicle etc* volcar; (**— upside down**) volver, poner al revés; *engine* hacer girar; *matter in mind* revolver, meditar; (*hand over*) entregar; ceder, traspasar (*to* a); **to — round** volver, poner al revés; **to — up** (*bend*) doblar hacia arriba; *gas* abrir, abrir más; *radio etc* poner más fuerte; *earth* revolver; *buried object* desenterrar, hacer salir a la superficie; (*fig*) encontrar; tropezar con; *reference* buscar, consultar; see **upside**.

3 *vi* **(a)** (*revolve*) girar, dar vueltas; (*of person*) volverse; girar sobre los talones; **my head is —ing** mi cabeza está dando vueltas; **to toss and — in bed** revolverse en la cama; **everything —s on whether . . .** todo depende de si . . .; **the conversation —ed on newts** la conversación versaba sobre los tritones, el tema de la conversación era los tritones.

(b) (*change direction*) volver, volverse; (*Aer*, *Naut*) virar; (*Aut*) girar, torcer; (*of tide*) repuntar; (*of weather etc*) cambiar; **to — left** torcer a la izquierda; **right —!** (*Mil*) ¡media vuelta a la derecha!; **to — to port** virar a babor; **to — for home** ir hacia casa; **the wind has —ed** el viento ha cambiado de dirección; **to wait for the weather to —** esperar a que cambie el tiempo; **then our luck —ed** luego mejoraron de suerte; **he —ed to me and smiled** se volvió hacia mí y sonrió; **to — to someone for help** acudir a uno a pedir ayuda; **he —ed to politics** se dedicó a la política; **he —ed to mysticism** recurrió al misticismo; empezó a estudiar el misticismo; **our thoughts — to those who . . .** concentramos el pensamiento en los que . . .; pensamos ahora en los que . . .; **I don't know which way to —** estoy para volverme loco; **I don't know where to — for money** no sé en qué parte ir a buscar dinero; **to — against someone**, **to — on someone** volverse contra uno; **to — against something** coger aversión a algo.

(c) (*change*) cambiar, cambiarse; convertirse, transformarse (*into*, *to* en); (*+ adj*) ponerse, volverse; (*+ n*) hacerse; (*of leaves*) descolorarse; dorarse; (*of milk*) agriarse, cortarse; **it —s red** se pone colorado; **matters are —ing serious** las cosas se ponen graves; **then he began to — awkward** luego empezó a ponerse difícil; **the princess —ed into a toad** la princesa se transformó en sapo, la princesa quedó transformada en sapo; **it —ed to stone** se convirtió en piedra; **to — soldier**

hacerse soldado; **to — communist** hacerse comunista.

(d) (*with adv or prep*) **to — about** dar una vuelta completa; (*Pol etc*) cambiar completamente de política; **about —!** (*Mil*) media vuelta — ¡ar!; **to — aside** desviarse (*from* de); apartarse del camino; **I —ed aside in disgust** me aparté lleno de asco; **to — away** volver la cara, volver la cabeza; (*coldly*) volver la espalda; **to — away from** apartarse de; renunciar a; **to — back** volverse (atrás); retroceder; volverse sobre sus pasos; **to — from** apartarse de; **to — in** doblarse hacia adentro; (*go to bed*) acostarse; **to — off** desviarse; **to — off the path** desviarse del camino; **to — out** (*from bed*) levantarse, abandonar la cama; (*from house*) salir de casa, salir a la calle; (*of guard etc*) formarse, presentarse para servicio; **how are things —ing out?** ¿cómo van tus cosas?; **it all —ed out well** todo salió bien; **it —s out to be harder than we thought** resulta ser más difícil de lo que pensábamos; **it —s out that he's a vegetarian** resulta que él es vegetariano; **as it —ed out nobody went** resultó que no fue nadie; **that depends how it —s out** eso depende del éxito que tenga, eso depende de los resultados; **he has feet that — out** sus pies están vueltos hacia fuera; **to — over** revolverse; (*Aut etc*) capotar, dar una vuelta de campana; **it —ed over and over** fue dando tumbos; **my stomach —ed over** se me revolvió el estómago; **it's enough to make your stomach — over** es para revolver a uno el estómago; **to — round** (*revolve*) girar; dar vueltas; (*person*) volverse; girar sobre los talones; **I could hardly — round** apenas pude revolverme; **as soon as I —ed round they were quarrelling again** en cuanto les volví la espalda se pusieron otra vez a reñir; **the government has —ed right round** el gobierno ha cambiado completamente de política; **to — round and round** seguir dando vueltas; **to — to** (*adv*) empezar; empezar a trabajar (en serio); **to — up** (*point upwards*) doblarse hacia arriba, apuntar hacia arriba; (*appear*) aparecer, surgir; (*of card etc*) salir; (*arrive*, *show up*) llegar, acudir; presentarse; asomar la cara; (*be found again*) volver a aparecer, reaparecer; **we'll see if anyone —s up** veremos si se viene alguien; **he —ed up 2 hours late** llegó con 2 horas de retraso; **he never —s up at class** no asiste nunca a la clase; **something is sure to — up** es seguro que surgirá alguna solución.

turnabout [ˈtəːnəbaut] *n* (*US*), **turnaround** [ˈtəːnəraund] *n* (*US*) = **turn-round**.

turncoat [ˈtəːnkəut] *n* renegado *m*, a *f*; **to become a —** volver la chaqueta.

turned-down [ˈtəːndˈdaun] *adj* doblado hacia abajo.

turned-up [ˈtəːndˈʌp] *adj* doblado hacia arriba; **— nose** respingona.

turner [ˈtəːnə*] *n* tornero *m*.

turnery [ˈtəːnəri] *n* tornería *f*.

turning [ˈtəːniŋ] *n* vuelta *f*; ángulo *m*; recodo *m*; **the first — on the left** la primera bocacalle a la izquierda; **we parked in a side —** aparcamos el coche en una calle que salía de la carretera.

turning lathe [ˈtəːniŋleið] *n* torno *m* (de tornero).

turning point [ˈtəːniŋpɔint] *n* (*fig*) punto *m* decisivo, coyuntura *f* crítica; **that was the —** eso fue la vuelta de la marea, eso marcó el cambio decisivo.

turning radius [ˈtəːniŋˌreidiəs] *n* (*Aut*) diámetro *m* de giro.

turnip [ˈtəːnip] *n* nabo *m*.

turnkey [ˈtəːnkiː] *n* (*Hist*) llavero *m* (de una cárcel), carcelero *m*.

turnout [ˈtəːnaut] *n* (*attendance*) concurrencia *f*; número *m* de asistentes; (*paying spectators*) entrada *f*, público *m*; (*production*) producción *f*; (*dress*) atuendo *m*; **there was a poor —** había poca gente, asistieron pocos; **we hope for a good — at the dance** esperamos que el baile sea muy concurrido.

turnover [ˈtəːnˌəuvə*] *n* **(a)** (*Comm*) volumen *m* de negocios, volumen *m* de ventas; número *m* de transacciones; movimiento *m* de mercancías; rotación *f* de existencias; **there is a rapid — in staff** hay mucho movimiento de personal; **our difficulty is labour —** tenemos problema con la rotación de la mano de obra.

(b) (*Cook*) pastel *m* con repulgo.

turnpike [ˈtəːnpaik] *n* (*Hist*) barrera *f* de portazgo; (*US Aut*) autopista *f* de peaje.

turn-round [ˈtəːnraund] *n* (*Naut*) período *m* de descarga y carga (de un buque).

turnspit [ˈtəːnspit] *n* mecanismo *m* que da vueltas al asador.

turnstile [ˈtəːnstail] *n* torniquete *m*.

turntable ['tə:n,teibl] n (Rail) placa f giratoria; (of gramophone) plato m giratorio.

turn-up ['tə:nʌp] n (of trousers) vuelta f; (fam: quarrel) riña f, trifulca f; **that was a — for him** (fam) en eso tuvo mucha suerte.

turpentine ['tə:pəntain] n trementina f.

turpitude ['tə:pitju:d] n (lit) infamia f, vileza f; **to be dismissed for gross moral** — ser despedido por su inmoralidad manifiesta, ser expulsado por su conducta infame.

turps [tə:ps] n (fam) see turpentine.

turquoise ['tə:kwɔiz] n turquesa f.

turret ['tʌrit] n (Archit) torreón m; (Mil, Hist) torre f, torrecilla f; (of tank, warship, aircraft) torreta f; (US, Tech) cabrestante m.

turreted ['tʌritid] adj con torres, con torretas.

turret lathe ['tʌritleiθ] n torno m revolvedor.

turtle ['tə:tl] n tortuga f marina; **to turn** — volverse patas arriba, (Naut) zozobrar, (Aut etc) volcarse, dar una vuelta de campana.

turtledove ['tə:tldʌv] n tórtola f.

Tuscan ['tʌskən] 1 adj toscano. 2 n toscano m, a f. 3 n (dialect) toscano m.

Tuscany ['tʌskəni] la Toscana.

tush [tʌʃ] n = **tosh**.

tusk [tʌsk] n colmillo m.

tussle ['tʌsl] 1 n (struggle) lucha f (for por); (scuffle) pelea f, agarrada f.

2 vi luchar (with con); pelearse, reñir (about, over por causa de); **they —d with the police** se pelearon con la policía.

tussock ['tʌsək] n montecillo m de hierbas.

tut [tʌt] (also **tut-tut**) 1 interj ¡vamos!, ¡eso no!, ¡qué horror! 2 vi hacer un gesto de desaprobación, hacer un gesto de horror.

tutelage ['tju:tilidʒ] n tutela f; **under the — of** bajo la tutela de.

tutelary ['tju:tiləri] adj tutelar.

tutor ['tju:tə*] 1 n (Hist) ayo m; (private teacher) preceptor m; profesor m particular; (Univ, approx) profesor m que tiene a su cargo un pequeño grupo de estudiantes; (moral —) profesor m consejero moral; (Law) tutor m.

2 vt enseñar, instruir; dar clase particular a; **to — a boy in French** dar a un muchacho clases particulares de francés.

tutorial [tju:'tɔ:riəl] 1 adj preceptoral; (Law) tutelar. 2 n (Univ) clase f particular, clase f que consiste en un grupo pequeño de estudiantes.

tutu ['tu:tu:] n tutú m.

tuxedo [tʌk'si:dəu] n (US) smoking m, esmoquin m (Acad).

twaddle ['twɔdl] n tonterías fpl, bobadas fpl.

twain [twein] (arch) n: **the** — los dos; **to split something in** — partir algo en dos; **and ne'er the — shall meet** sin que el uno se acerque al otro jamás; sin que tengan nada en común.

twang [twæŋ] 1 n (Mus etc) tañido m, punteado m; (of bow etc) ruido m, sonido m (de cuerda que se estira y se suelta); **nasal** — gangueo m, timbre m nasal; **with an American** — con voz gangosa americana.

2 vt (Mus) puntear; bowstring estirar y soltar repentinamente.

twangy ['twæŋi] adj string etc elástico, muy estirado; accent nasal, gangoso.

'twas [twɔz] (arch) = **it was**.

tweak [twi:k] 1 n pellizco m; **to give someone a** — dar un pellizco a uno. 2 vt pellizcar (retorciendo); **to** — something off quitar algo pellizcándolo.

tweed [twi:d] n tweed m, mezcla f de lana; **—s** (suit) traje m de tweed.

'tween [twi:n] prep = **between**.

tweeter ['twi:tə*] n altavoz m para altas audio-frecuencias.

tweezers ['twi:zəz] npl bruselas fpl, pinzas fpl; **a pair of** — unas bruselas, unas pinzas.

twelfth [twelfθ] 1 adj duodécimo. 2 n duodécimo m; dozavo m, duodécima parte f.

Twelfth Night ['twelfθ'nait] n Día m de Reyes, Epifanía f.

twelve [twelv] 1 adj doce. 2 n doce m.

twelvemonth ['twelvmʌnθ] n año m; **this day** — de hoy en un año; **we've not seen him for a** — hace un año que no le vemos.

twentieth ['twentiiθ] 1 adj vigésimo. 2 n vigésimo m, vigésima parte f.

twenty ['twenti] adj veinte; **the twenties** (eg 1920s) los años veinte; **to be in one's twenties** tener más de veinte años.

twentyfold ['twentifəuld] 1 adv veinte veces. 2 adj veinte veces mayor.

twerp [twə:p] n (sl) tío m (fam); **you** —! ¡imbécil!

twice [twais] adv dos veces; — **as much** dos veces más; **A is** — **as big as B** A es dos veces más grande que B; **I am** — **as old as you are** tengo dos veces la edad de Vd, tengo el doble de la edad de Vd; — **the sum**, — **the quantity** el doble; **at a speed** — **that of sound** a una velocidad dos veces superior a la del sonido; **to do something** — over hacer algo dos veces, volver a hacer algo; **to go to a meeting** — **weekly** ir a una reunión dos veces cada semana; **he didn't have to be asked** — no se hizo de rogar; see think 2 (a).

twiddle ['twidl] 1 n vuelta f (ligera); **to give a knob a** — girar un botón.

2 vt girar, hacer girar; jugar con; revolver ociosamente; **to** — **one's thumbs** voltear los pulgares, (fig) no tener nada que hacer.

twig[1] [twig] n ramita f; **—s** (for fire) leña f menuda.

twig[2] [twig] (fam) 1 vt comprender, caer en la cuenta de. 2 vi comprender, caer en la cuenta.

twilight ['twailait] 1 n crepúsculo m; (fig) crepúsculo m, ocaso m; **at** — al anochecer; **in the** — en el crepúsculo; **in the** — **of his room** en la media luz de su habitación.

2 adj crepuscular; — **sleep** (Med) sueño m crepuscular.

twill [twil] n tela f cruzada.

'twill[twil] = **it will**.

twin [twin] 1 adj gemelo; — **brother** hermano m gemelo; — **sister** hermana f gemela; — **beds** camas fpl gemelas; — **town** ciudad f gemela.

2 n gemelo m, a f; **John and his** — Juan y su hermano gemelo; **identical** —**s** gemelos mpl idénticos; **Siamese** —**s** hermanos mpl siameses.

3 vt: **the town with which Wigan is** —**ned** la ciudad que tiene a Wigan como gemela.

twin-cylinder ['twin'silində*] adj de dos cilindros.

twine [twain] 1 n guita f, hilo m, bramante m.

2 vt (weave) tejer; (encircle) ceñir, rodear; (roll up) enrollar; **she** —**d the string round her finger** enrolló la cuerda sobre el dedo; **she** —**d her arms about his neck** le rodeó el cuello con los brazos.

3 vi (of spiral movement) enroscarse; (of plant) trepar, entrelazarse; (of road) serpentear.

twin-engined ['twin'endʒind] adj bimotor.

twinge [twindʒ] n punzada f, dolor m agudo; (fig) remordimiento m; **I've been having** —**s of conscience** me ha estado remordiendo la conciencia.

twining ['twainiŋ] adj plant sarmentoso, trepador.

twin-jet ['twin'dʒet] 1 adj birreactor. 2 n birreactor m.

twinkle ['twiŋkl] 1 n centelleo m, parpadeo m; **in a** — en un instante; **"No"**, **he said with a** — **"No"**, dijo maliciosamente, **"No"** dijo medio riendo; **he had a** — **in his eye** tenía los ojos risueños.

2 vi (of light) centellear, parpadear, titilar; (of eyes) brillar; (of feet) moverse rápidamente.

twinkling ['twiŋkliŋ] 1 adj light centelleante, titilante; eye brillante, risueño; feet rápido, ligero.

2 n centelleo m, parpadeo m; **in the** — **of an eye** en un abrir y cerrar de ojos.

twinset ['twinset] n (Sew) conjunto m.

twirl [twə:l] 1 n vuelta f (rápida), giro m; (of pen etc) rasgo m; (of body) pirueta f.

2 vt girar rápidamente, dar vueltas rápidas a; voltear; (twist) torcer.

3 vi girar rápidamente, dar vueltas rápidas; piruetear.

twist [twist] 1 n (a) (of yarn) torzal m; (of hair) mecha f; trenza f; (of tobacco) rollo m; (of paper) barquillo m.

(b) (twisting action) torsión f, torcimiento m; (Med) torcedura f; (on ball) efecto m; **to give one's ankle a** — torcerse el tobillo; **to give a knob a** — girar un botón; **with a quick** — **of the hand** torciendo rápidamente la mano.

(c) (of mind) rasgo m peculiar, sesgo m, peculiaridad f.

(d) (coil) vuelta f; (spiral shape) enroscadura f; (in road etc) vuelta f, recodo m; —**s and turns** vueltas fpl; **to take a** — **round a post with a rope** atar una cuerda alrededor de un poste; **the plot has an unexpected** — la trama tiene un esguince inesperado, la trama tiene un giro imprevisto.

(e) (Mus) twist m.

(f) (fam) trampa f; **it's a** —! ¡aquí hay trampa!; ¡me han robado!

2 vt (wrench out of shape) torcer, retorcer; ball dar efecto a, lanzar con efecto; (turn) dar vueltas a, girar; (give spiral form to) enroscar, formar en espiral; (interweave) trenzar, entrelazar; (fam) estafar; (fig) sense, words, argument forzar, retorcer,

torcer; **to — someone's arm** torcer el brazo a uno; **to — one's arm** torcerse el brazo; **to — a piece off** separar un trozo torciéndolo; **to — something out of shape** deformar algo torciéndolo; **to — paper up into a ball** retorcer un papel en forma de pelota; **I've been —ed!** *(fam)* ¡me han robado!

3 *vi* torcerse, retorcerse; *(coil up)* enroscarse, ensortijarse; *(of road etc)* serpentear, dar vueltas; *(writhe)* retorcerse, revolcarse; *(dance)* bailar el twist.

twister ['twistə*] *n (fam)* tramposo *m*, estafador *m*.

twit[1] [twit] *n (fam)* imbécil *m*, tonto *m*.

twit[2] [twit] *vt* embromar, tomar el pelo a, guasearse con; **to — someone about something** tomar el pelo a uno con motivo de algo.

twitch [twitʃ] **1** *n* sacudida *f* repentina, tirón *m*; *(nervous)* tic *m*, contracción *f* nerviosa; movimiento *m* espasmódico.

2 *vt* tirar bruscamente de, tirar ligeramente de; *hands* crispar, retorcer; *ears, nose etc* mover nerviosamente; **to — something away from someone** quitar algo a uno con un movimiento rápido.

3 *vi* crisparse; moverse nerviosamente.

twitter ['twitə*] **1** *n (of bird)* gorjeo *m*; *(fig)* agitación *f*, inquietud *f*, nerviosismo *m*; **to be all of a —, to be in a —** *(fam)* estar nerviosísimo, estar muy agitado.

2 *vi* gorjear; *(fig)* agitarse, estar inquieto, estar nervioso.

'twixt [twikst] *prep* = **betwixt**, *see* **between**.

two [tuː] **1** *adj* dos.

2 *n* dos *m*; **— by —, in —s** de dos en dos; **to break something in —** romper algo en dos, partir algo por la mitad; **they're — of a kind** son idénticos, son dos ejemplares del mismo fenómeno; **to put — and — together** atar cabos.

two-chamber ['tuː'tʃeimbə*] *adj parliament* bicamaral, de dos cámaras.

two-decker ['tuː'dekə*] *n* autobús *m* de dos pisos.

two-door ['tuː'dɔ:*] *adj car* de dos puertas.

two-edged ['tuː'edʒd] *adj* de doble filo.

two-engined ['tuː'endʒind] *adj* bimotor.

two-faced ['tuː'feist] *adj (fig)* doble, falso.

twofold ['tuːfəuld] **1** *adv* dos veces. **2** *adj* doble.

two-handed ['tuː'hændid] *adj* de dos manos; *tool etc* para dos manos.

two-legged ['tuː'legid] *adj* de dos piernas, bípedo.

two-masted ['tuː'mɑːstid] *adj* de dos palos.

two-party ['tuː'pɑːti] *adj state etc* de dos partidos.

twopence ['tʌpəns] *npl* 2 peniques *mpl*; *see* **care**.

twopenny ['tʌpəni] *adj* de 2 peniques, que vale 2 peniques; *(fig)* insignificante, miserable, despreciable.

two-phase ['tuː'feiz] *adj (Elec)* bifásico.

two-piece ['tuː'piːs] **1** *adj* de dos piezas. **2** *n* dos piezas *m*.

two-ply ['tuː'plai] *adj wood* de dos capas; *wool* doble.

two-seater ['tuː'siːtə*] **1** *attr* biplaza, de dos plazas. **2** *n* coche *m (or* avión *m etc)* biplaza.

twosome ['tuːsəm] *n* pareja *f*; grupo *m* de dos, partido *m* de dos.

two-step ['tuːstep] *n* paso *m* doble.

two-storey ['tuː'stɔːri] *adj house* de dos pisos.

two-stroke ['tuː'strəuk] *adj engine* de dos tiempos.

two-time ['tuː'taim] *vt (US fam)* engañar; hacer una mala jugada a; traicionar.

two-tone ['tuː'təun] *adj car* bicolor.

two-way ['tuː'wei] *adj:* **— switch** conmutador *m* de dos direcciones; **— traffic** circulación *f* en ambas direcciones.

'twould [twud] = **it would**.

tycoon [tai'kuːn] *n* magnate *m*.

tyke [taik] *n* **(a)** *(fam: dog)* perro *m* de la calle; *(child)* chiquillo *m*; **you little —!** ¡tunante! **(b)** *(prov)* hombre *m* de Yorkshire.

tympanum ['timpənəm] *n (Anat, Archit)* tímpano *m*.

type [taip] **1** *n* **(a)** *(characteristic specimen)* tipo *m*; **to deviate from the —** apartarse del tipo; **to revert to**

— saltar atrás en la cadena natural; **she was the very — of Spanish beauty** era el tipo exacto de la belleza española.

(b) *(person: fam)* tipo *m*, sujeto *m*; **he's an odd —** es un tipo raro; **a — I know** un tío que yo conozco.

(c) *(class)* tipo *m*, género *m*; **people of that —** la gente de ese tipo; **he's not my —** ese tipo de hombre no me gusta, no me gustan los hombres así; **what — of car is it?** ¿qué modelo de coche es?

(d) *(Typ)* tipo *m*, letra *f*, carácter *m*; *(collectively)* tipos *mpl*; **Gothic —** letras *fpl* góticas; **bold —, heavy —** negrita *f*; **in heavy —** en negrita.

2 *vt* escribir a máquina, hacer a máquina, mecanografiar.

3 *vi* escribir a máquina; **"secretary ... must be able to —"** "secretaria ... sabiendo mecanografía".

type-cast ['taipkɑːst] *(irr: see* **cast**) **1** *vt:* **to — an actor** dar a un actor papeles de la misma clase siempre. **2** *ptp, adj actor* encasillado.

typeface ['taipfeis] *n* = **type 1 (d)**; área *f* de texto impreso, *(loosely)* tipografía *f*.

typescript ['taipskript] **1** *adj* mecanografiado. **2** *n* mecanografiado *m*.

typesetter ['taip,setə*] *n (person)* cajista *m*; *(machine)* máquina *f* de componer.

typesetting ['taip,setiŋ] *n* composición *f* (tipográfica).

typewrite ['taiprait] *(irr: see* **write**) *vt see* **type 2.**

typewriter ['taip,raitə*] *n* máquina *f* de escribir.

typewriting ['taip,raitiŋ] *n* mecanografía *f*.

typewritten ['taip,ritn] *adj* mecanografiado, hecho a máquina.

typhoid ['taifɔid] *n* tifoidea *f*, fiebre *f* tifoidea.

typhoon [tai'fuːn] *n* tifón *m*.

typhus ['taifəs] *n* tifus *m*.

typical ['tipikəl] *adj* típico; característico; clásico; **the — Spaniard** el español típico; **wearing the — beret** con la clásica boina; **it is — of him that ...** es característico de él que ...; **isn't that just —!** ¡eso es muy de él!

typically ['tipikəli] *adv* típicamente; **all that is — Spanish** todo lo que es típico de España; **a — smug person** una persona típicamente satisfecha.

typify ['tipifai] *vt* tipificar; simbolizar; representar, ser ejemplo de.

typing ['taipiŋ] *n* mecanografía *f*.

typing paper ['taipiŋ,peipə*] *n* papel *m* para máquina de escribir.

typist ['taipist] *n* mecanógrafo *m*, a *f*.

typographer [tai'pɒgrəfə*] *n* tipógrafo *m*.

typographic(al) [,taipə'græfik(əl)] *adj* tipográfico.

typography [tai'pɒgrəfi] *n* tipografía *f*.

tyrannic(al) [ti'rænik(əl)] *adj* tiránico.

tyrannically [ti'rænikəli] *adv* tiránicamente.

tyrannicide [ti'rænisaid] *n (act)* tiranicidio *m*; *(person)* tiranicida *mf*.

tyrannize ['tirənaiz] **1** *vt* tiranizar. **2** *vi:* **to — over a people** tiranizar un pueblo.

tyranny ['tirəni] *n* tiranía *f*.

tyrant ['taiərənt] *n* tirano *m*, a *f*.

Tyre ['taiə*] Tiro.

tyre ['taiə*] *n (Aut etc)* neumático *m*, llanta *f (S Am)*; *(outer cover)* cubierta *f*; *(inner tube)* cámara *f* (de aire); *(of cart)* llanta *f*, calce *m*; *(of pram etc)* rueda *f* de goma; **non-skid —** neumático *m* antideslizante; **pneumatic —** neumático *m*; **solid —** neumático *m* macizo; **spare —** neumático *m* de recambio.

tyre-burst ['taiəbɜːst] *n* pinchazo *m*, reventón *m*.

tyre valve ['taiəvælv] *n* válvula *m* de neumático.

tyro ['taiərəu] *n see* **tiro.**

Tyrol [ti'rəul] el Tirol.

Tyrolean [,tirə'li(ː)ən], **Tyrolese** ['tirə'liːz] **1** *adj* tirolés. **2** *n* tirolés *m*, esa *f*.

tzar [zɑ:*] *n* zar *m*.

tzarina [zɑ:'riːnə] *n* zarina *f*.

U

ubiquitous [juː'bikwitəs] *adj* ubicuo, omnipresente, que se encuentra en todas partes: **it is — in Spain** se encuentra en toda España; **the secretary has to be —** el secretario tiene que estar constantemente en todas partes.

ubiquity [juː'bikwiti] *n* ubicuidad *f*, omnipresencia *f*.

U-boat ['juːbəut] *n* submarino *m* alemán.

udder ['ʌdə*] *n* ubre *f*.

ugh [əːh] *interj* ¡puf!

uglify ['ʌglifai] *vt* (*fam*) afear.

ugliness ['ʌglinis] *n* fealdad *f*, lo feo; lo peligroso; lo repugnante.

ugly ['ʌgli] *adj appearance, person* feo; *custom, vice etc* feo, repugnante, asqueroso; *situation, wound* peligroso; *rumour etc* nada grato, inquietante; *mood* peligroso, violento; **to be as — as sin** ser feísimo; **to cut up —, to turn —** (*fam*) ponerse violento, amenazar violencia.

Ukraine [juː'krein] Ucrania *f*.

Ukrainian [juː'kreiniən] **1** *adj* ucraniano. **2** *n* ucraniano *m*, a *f*.

ukulele [ˌjuːkə'leili] *n* guitarra *f* hawaiana.

ulcer ['ʌlsə*] *n* úlcera *f*; (*fig*) llaga *f*.

ulcerate ['ʌlsəreit] **1** *vt* ulcerar. **2** *vi* ulcerarse.

ulceration [ˌʌlsə'reiʃən] *n* ulceración *f*.

ulcerous ['ʌlsərəs] *adj* ulceroso.

ulna ['ʌlnə] *n*, *pl* **ulnae** ['ʌlniː] cúbito *m*.

ulster ['ʌlstə*] *n* úlster *m*.

ulterior [ʌl'tiəriə*] *adj* ulterior; (*motive*) oculto.

ultimate ['ʌltimit] *adj* (*furthest*) más remoto, extremo; (*final*) último, final; *destination etc* definitivo; *purpose, reason, truth etc* fundamental, esencial.

ultimately ['ʌltimitli] *adv* (*in the end*) por último, al final; (*in the long run*) a la larga; (*fundamentally*) en el fondo, fundamentalmente.

ultimatum [ˌʌlti'meitəm] *n*, *pl* **ultimata** [ˌʌlti'meitə] ultimátum *m*.

ultimo ['ʌltiməu] *adv* (Comm): **the 5th —** el 5 del mes pasado.

ultra ... ['ʌltrə] ultra ...

ultra-fashionable ['ʌltrə'fæʃnəbl] *adj* muy de moda, elegantísimo.

ultramarine [ˌʌltrəmə'riːn] **1** *adj* ultramarino. **2** *n* azul *m* de ultramar.

ultramodern ['ʌltrə'mɔdən] *adj* ultramoderno.

ultramontane [ˌʌltrə'mɔntein] **1** *adj* ultramontano. **2** *n* ultramontano *m*.

ultramontanism [ˌʌltrə'mɔntinizəm] *n* ultramontanismo *m*.

ultra-red [ˌʌltrə'red] *adj* infrarrojo.

ultra-short wave ['ʌltrə'ʃɔːt'weiv] **1** *n* onda *f* extracorta. **2** *attr* de onda extracorta.

ultrasonic ['ʌltrə'sɔnik] *adj* ultrasónico.

ultraviolet ['ʌltrə'vaiəlit] *adj* ultravioleta; **— rays** rayos *mpl* ultravioleta; **— treatment** tratamiento *m* de onda ultravioleta.

ululate ['juːljuleit] *vi* ulular.

ululation [ˌjuːlju'leiʃən] *n* ululato *m*.

Ulysses [juː'lisiːz] *m* Ulises.

umber ['ʌmbə*] **1** *n* tierra *f* de sombra. **2** *adj* color ocre oscuro, pardo oscuro.

umbilical [ˌʌmbi'laikəl] *adj* umbilical.

umbilicus [ˌʌmbi'laikəs] *n* ombligo *m*.

umbrage ['ʌmbridʒ] *n* resentimiento *m*; **to take —** ofenderse (*at* por), resentirse (*at* de).

umbrella [ʌm'brelə] *n* paraguas *m*; (Mil: *of fire*) cortina *f* de fuego antiaéreo; (*of aircraft*) sombrilla *f* protectora.

umbrella stand [ʌm'breləstænd] *n* paragüero *m*.

umpire ['ʌmpaiə*] **1** *n* árbitro *m*. **2** *vti* arbitrar.

umpteen ['ʌmptiːn] *adj* (*fam*) tantísimos, muchísimos.

umpteenth ['ʌmptiːnθ] *adj* (*fam*) enésimo; **for the — time** por enésima vez.

un ... [ʌn] in ...; des ...; no ...; nada ...; poco ...; sin ...; anti ...

unabashed ['ʌnə'bæʃt] *adj* descarado, desvergonzado; desenfadado; **"Yes", he said quite —** "Sí", dijo sin alterarse.

unabated ['ʌnə'beitid] *adj* sin disminución, no disminuido.

unable ['ʌn'eibl] *adj*: **to be — to do something** no poder hacer algo; ser incapaz de hacer algo; verse imposibilitado de hacer algo; **I am — to see why** no veo por qué, no comprendo cómo; **those — to go** los que no pueden ir.

unabridged ['ʌnə'bridʒd] *adj* íntegro; **the — text** la versión íntegra.

unaccented ['ʌnæk'sentid] *adj* inacentuado, átono.

unacceptable ['ʌnək'septəbl] *adj* inaceptable.

unaccommodating ['ʌnə'kɔmədeitiŋ] *adj* poco amable, poco servicial.

unaccompanied ['ʌnə'kʌmpənid] *adj* (Mus) sin acompañamiento, no acompañado; **to go somewhere —** ir a un sitio sin compañía, ir solo a un sitio.

unaccountable ['ʌnə'kauntəbl] *adj* inexplicable.

unaccountably ['ʌnə'kauntəbl] *adv* inexplicablemente; **— annoyed** extrañamente enfadado, enfadado sin motivo.

unaccounted ['ʌnə'kauntid] *adj*: **two passengers are — for** no hay noticias de dos de los pasajeros, se ignora la suerte de dos de los pasajeros.

unaccustomed ['ʌnə'kʌstəmd] *adj* (a) **to be — to something** no estar acostumbrado a algo; **to be — to doing something** no acostumbrar hacer algo, no tener la costumbre de hacer algo.
(b) **with — zeal** con un entusiasmo insólito.

unacknowledged ['ʌnək'nɔlidʒd] *adj* no reconocido; (*letter etc*) no contestado, sin contestar.

unacquainted ['ʌnə'kweintid] *adj*: **to be — with something** desconocer algo, ignorar algo.

unadaptable ['ʌnə'dæptəbl] *adj* inadaptable.

unaddressed ['ʌnə'drest] *adj letter* sin señas.

unadorned ['ʌnə'dɔːnd] *adj* sin adorno, sencillo; **beauty —** la hermosura sin adorno.

unadulterated ['ʌnə'dʌltəreitid] *adj* sin mezcla, puro.

unadvisable ['ʌnəd'vaizəbl] *adj* poco aconsejable; **it is — to +** *infin* es poco aconsejable + *infin*.

unaesthetic [ˌʌniːs'θetik] *adj* antiestético.

unaffected ['ʌnə'fektid] *adj* (a) *person etc* sin afectación. (b) **to be — by** no ser afectado por.

unaffectedly ['ʌnə'fektidli] *adv* sin afectación; sinceramente, hondamente.

unafraid ['ʌnə'freid] *adj* sin temor, impertérrito.

unaided ['ʌn'eidid] **1** *adv* sin ayuda, por sí solo. **2** *adj*: **by his own — efforts** por sí solo, sin ayuda de nadie.

unalloyed ['ʌnə'lɔid] *adj* sin mezcla, puro.

unalterable [ʌn'ɔltərəbl] *adj* inalterable.

unalterably [ʌn'ɔltərəbli] *adv* de modo inalterable; **we are — opposed to it** nos oponemos rotundamente a ello.

unaltered ['ʌn'ɔltəd] *adj* inalterado, sin cambiar, sin alteración.

unambiguous ['ʌnæm'bigjuəs] *adj* inequívoco.

unambiguously ['ʌnæm'bigjuəsli] *adv* de modo inequívoco.

unambitious ['ʌnæm'biʃəs] *adj* poco ambicioso, poco emprendedor.

un-American ['ʌnə'merikən] *adj* antiamericano.

unamiable ['ʌn'eimiəbl] *adj* poco simpático.

unanimity [ˌjuːnə'nimiti] *n* unanimidad *f*.

unanimous [juː'næniməs] *adj* unánime.

unanimously [juː'næniməsli] *adv* unánimemente; por unanimidad; **the motion was passed —** la moción fue aprobada por unanimidad.

unanswerable [ʌn'ɑːnsərəbl] *adj* (*question*) incontestable; (*attack etc*) irrebatible, irrefutable.

unanswered ['ʌn'ɑːnsəd] *adj question* incontestado, sin contestar; *letter* no contestado, sin contestar.

unappealable ['ʌnə'piːləbl] *adj* inapelable.

unappetizing ['ʌn'æpitaiziŋ] *adj* poco apetitoso; *(fig)* repugnante, nada atractivo.

unappreciative ['ʌnə'priːʃiətiv] *adj* desagradecido; **to be — of something** no agradecer algo debidamente.

unapproachable ['ʌnə'prəutʃəbl] *adj* inaccesible; *person* intratable, inabordable.

unappropriated ['ʌnə'prəuprieitid] *adj* no asignado.

unarmed ['ʌn'ɑːmd] *adj* que no lleva armas, desarmado; *(defenceless)* inerme.

unascertained ['ʌnæsə'teind] *adj* no averiguado, que queda por averiguar.

unashamed ['ʌnə'ʃeimd] *adj* desvergonzado, descarado; **he was quite — about it** no tuvo remordimiento alguno por esto, no sintió el menor remordimiento.

unashamedly ['ʌnə'ʃeimidli] *adv* desvergonzadamente; **to be — proud of something** enorgullecerse sin remordimiento de algo.

unasked ['ʌn'ɑːskt] *adj*: **to do something —** hacer algo sin ser rogado; **they came to the party —** vinieron al guateque sin ser invitados.

unassailable [,ʌnə'seiləbl] *adj fortress* inexpugnable; *position* inatacable; *argument* irrebatible; **he is quite — on that score** ne se le puede atacar por ese lado.

unassisted ['ʌnə'sistid] *adj* sin ayuda, por sí solo.

unassuming ['ʌnə'sjuːmiŋ] *adj* modesto, sin pretensiones.

unassumingly ['ʌnə'sjuːmiŋli] *adv* modestamente.

unattached ['ʌnə'tætʃt] *adj part etc* suelto, separable; *person* libre, no prometido, que no tiene novio (*or* novia); *(Mil)* de reemplazo; *(Law)* no embargado.

unattainable ['ʌnə'teinəbl] *adj* inasequible; *record etc* inalcanzable.

unattended ['ʌnə'tendid] *adj* sin guardia, sin personal; **to leave something —** dejar algo sin personal.

unattractive ['ʌnə'træktiv] *adj* poco atractivo.

unattractiveness ['ʌnə'træktivnis] *n* falta *f* de atractivo.

unauthorized ['ʌn'ɔːθəraizd] *adj* desautorizado.

unavailable ['ʌnə'veiləbl] *adj* indisponible, inasequible; *person* que no puede atender a uno, que no está libre.

unavailing ['ʌnə'veiliŋ] *adj* inútil, vano, infructuoso.

unavailingly ['ʌnə'veiliŋli] *adv* inútilmente, en vano.

unavoidable [,ʌnə'vɔidəbl] *adj* inevitable, ineludible; **it is — that . . .** es inevitable que . . .

unavoidably [,ʌnə'vɔidəbli] *adv* inevitablemente; **he is — detained** tiene un retraso inevitable.

unaware ['ʌnə'wɛə*] *adj*: **to be — that** ignorar que; **I am not — that** no ignoro que; **to be — of something** ignorar algo, no darse cuenta de algo.

unawares ['ʌnə'wɛəz] *adv* de improviso, inopinadamente; **to catch someone —** coger a uno desprevenido.

unbacked ['ʌn'bækt] *adj (Fin)* a descubierto.

unbalance ['ʌn'bæləns] *n* desequilibrio *m*.

unbalanced ['ʌn'bælənst] *adj* desequilibrado; *(mentally)* trastornado, desequilibrado.

unbandage ['ʌn'bændidʒ] *vt* desvendar, quitar las vendas a.

unbaptized ['ʌnbæp'taizd] *adj* sin bautizar.

unbar ['ʌn'bɑː*] *vt door etc* desatrancar; *(fig)* abrir, franquear.

unbearable [ʌn'bɛərəbl] *adj* inaguantable, insufrible, intolerable.

unbearably [ʌn'bɛərəbli] *adv* insoportablemente; **it is — hot** hace un calor inaguantable; **she is — vain** es vanidosa en un grado inaguantable.

unbeatable ['ʌn'biːtəbl] *adj team etc* imbatible; *price, offer* inmejorable.

unbeaten ['ʌn'biːtn] *adj team* imbatido; *army* invicto; *price* no mejorado.

unbecoming ['ʌnbi'kʌmiŋ] *adj* indecoroso, impropio; *dress etc* que sienta mal a uno; **it is — to + infin** no es elegante + *infin*.

unbeknown ['ʌnbi'nəun] *adj*: **— to me** sin saberlo yo.

unbelief ['ʌnbi'liːf] *n (Rel: in general)* descreimiento *m*, *(of person)* falta *f* de fe; *(astonishment)* incredulidad *f*.

unbelievable [,ʌnbi'liːvəbl] *adj* increíble; **it is — that . . .** es increíble que + *subj*.

unbelievably [,ʌnbi'liːvəbli] *adv* increíblemente.

unbeliever ['ʌnbi'liːvə*] *n* no creyente *mf*, descreído *m*, a *f*.

unbelieving ['ʌnbi'liːviŋ] *adj* incrédulo.

unbend ['ʌn'bend] *(irr: see* **bend***)* **1** *vt* desencorvar, enderezar. **2** *vi (fig)* suavizarse; *(person)* hacerse más afable.

unbending ['ʌn'bendiŋ] *adj* inflexible, rígido; *(person)* inflexible; poco afable.

unbias(s)ed ['ʌn'baiəst] *adj* imparcial.

unbidden ['ʌn'bidn] *adj*: **to do something —** hacer algo sin ser rogado; **they came to the party —** vinieron al guateque sin ser invitados.

unbind ['ʌn'baind] *(irr: see* **bind***)* *vt* desatar; *(unbandage)* desvendar.

unbleached ['ʌn'bliːtʃt] *adj* sin blanquear.

unblemished ['ʌn'blemiʃt] *adj* sin tacha, intachable.

unblinking ['ʌn'bliŋkiŋ] *adj* imperturbable; *(pej)* desvergonzado.

unblock ['ʌn'blɔk] *vt pipe etc* desatascar, desobstruir; *road etc* abrir, franquear.

unblushing [ʌn'blʌʃiŋ] *adj* desvergonzado, fresco.

unblushingly [ʌn'blʌʃiŋli] *adv* desvergonzadamente; **he said —** dijo tan fresco.

unbolt ['ʌn'bəult] *vt* desatrancar.

unborn ['ʌn'bɔːn] *adj* no nacido aún, nonato; **generations yet —** generaciones *fpl* que están todavía por nacer.

unbosom [ʌn'buzəm] *vr*: **to — oneself of something** desahogarse de algo, confesar algo abiertamente; **to — oneself to someone** abrir su pecho a uno.

unbound ['ʌn'baund] *adj* en hojas sueltas, sin encuadernar.

unbounded [ʌn'baundid] *adj* ilimitado, infinito.

unbowed ['ʌn'baud] *adj*: **with head —** con la cabeza erguida; orgullosamente.

unbreakable ['ʌn'breikəbl] *adj* irrompible.

unbribable ['ʌn'braibəbl] *adj* insobornable.

unbridled [ʌn'braidld] *adj (fig)* desenfrenado.

unbroken ['ʌn'brəukən] *adj crockery etc* entero, intacto; *seal* intacto; *time, silence* no interrumpido; *series* continuo, sin solución de continuidad; *sheet of ice etc* continuo; *record* imbatido; *horse* no domado; *spirit* indómito.

unbuckle ['ʌn'bʌkl] *vt* deshebillar.

unburden [ʌn'bəːdn] **1** *vt person* aliviar; **to — someone of a load** aliviar a uno quitándole un peso; **to — one's heart** abrir su pecho.
2 *vr*: **to — oneself** abrir su pecho (*to someone* a uno); **to — oneself of something** desahogarse de algo, confesar algo abiertamente.

unburied ['ʌn'berid] *adj* insepulto.

unbusinesslike [ʌn'biznislaik] *adj* poco práctico, poco metódico; *informal*; que carece de instinto comercial.

unbutton ['ʌn'bʌtn] **1** *vt* desabotonar, desabrochar. **2** *vi (fam)* hacerse más afable.

uncalled-for [ʌn'kɔːldfɔ:*] *adj* gratuito, inmerecido; impertinente.

uncannily [ʌn'kænili] *adv* misteriosamente; **it is — like the other one** tiene un extraño parecido con el otro, se parece extraordinariamente al otro.

uncanny [ʌn'kæni] *adj* misterioso, extraño, extraordinario; **it's quite —** es extraordinario; **it's — how he does it** no llego a comprender cómo lo hace.

uncap ['ʌn'kæp] *vt* destapar.

uncared-for ['ʌn'kɛədfɔ:*] *adj person* abandonado, desamparado; *appearance* desaseado, de abandono; *building etc* abandonado.

unceasing [ʌn'siːsiŋ] *adj* incesante.

unceasingly [ʌn'siːsiŋli] *adv* incesantemente, sin cesar.

uncensored ['ʌn'sensəd] *adj* no censurado.

unceremonious ['ʌn,seri'məuniəs] *adj* descortés, brusco, poco formal.

unceremoniously ['ʌn,seri'məuniəsli] *adv* sin miramientos.

uncertain [ʌn'səːtn] *adj* incierto, dudoso; *person (of character)* indeciso, vacilante; *temper* vivo; **to be — of** no estar seguro de; **I am — whether . . .** no estoy seguro si . . .

uncertainly [ʌn'səːtnli] *adv* inciertamente; **he said —** dijo indeciso.

uncertainty [ʌn'səːtnti] *n* incertidumbre *f*, duda *f*; indecisión *f*, irresolución *f*; **in view of this — . . .** teniendo en cuenta estas dudas . . .; **in order to remove any —** para disipar estas dudas.

uncertificated ['ʌnsə'tifikeitid] *adj teacher etc* sin título.

unchain [ʌn'tʃein] *vt* desencadenar.

unchallengeable ['ʌn'tʃælindʒəbl] *adj* incontestable, incuestionable.

unchallenged ['ʌn'tʃælindʒd] *adj* incontestado; **we cannot let that go —** eso no lo podemos dejar pasar sin protesta.

unchangeable [ʌn'tʃeindʒəbl] *adj* inalterable, inmutable.
unchanged ['ʌn'tʃeindʒd] *adj* sin alterar.
unchanging [ʌn'tʃeindʒiŋ] *adj* inalterable, inmutable.
uncharitable [ʌn'tʃæritəbl] *adj* poco caritativo, duro.
uncharted ['ʌn'tʃɑːtid] *adj* inexplorado, desconocido.
unchaste ['ʌn'tʃeist] *adj* impúdico; *wife* infiel.
unchecked ['ʌn'tʃekt] **1** *adv* libremente, sin estorbo, sin restricción. **2** *adj abuse etc* desenfrenado; *fact etc* no comprobado.
unchivalrous ['ʌn'ʃivəlrəs] *adj* poco caballeroso.
unchristian ['ʌn'kristiən] *adj* poco cristiano, indigno de un cristiano.
uncial ['ʌnsiəl] **1** *adj* uncial. **2** *n* uncial *f*.
uncircumcised ['ʌn'sə:kəmsaizd] *adj* incircunciso.
uncivil ['ʌn'sivil] *adj* descortés, grosero, incivil; **to be — to someone** ser grosero con uno.
uncivilized ['ʌn'sivilaizd] *adj* incivilizado, inculto.
unclad ['ʌn'klæd] *adj* desnudo.
unclaimed ['ʌn'kleimd] *adj* sin reclamar, sin dueño.
unclasp ['ʌn'klɑːsp] *vt dress etc* desabrochar; *hands* soltar, separar.
unclassified ['ʌn'klæsifaid] *adj* sin clasificar.
uncle ['ʌŋkl] *n* tío *m*; (*sl*) prestamista *m*; prendero *m*; **my — and aunt** mis tíos; **to talk to someone like a Dutch —** decir a uno cuatro verdades; **U— Sam** el tío Sam (*personificación de EE.UU.*).
unclean ['ʌn'kliːn] *adj* sucio,⸴inmundo; (*fig*) deshonesto; (*ritually*) poluto.
uncleanliness ['ʌn'klenlinis] *n* suciedad *f*; (*fig*) deshonestidad *f*.
unclench ['ʌn'klentʃ] *vt* desapretar, soltar.
uncloak ['ʌn'kləuk] *vt* desencapotar.
unclog ['ʌn'klɔg] *vt* desobstruir, desatrancar.
unclothe ['ʌn'kləuð] *vt* desnudar.
unclothed ['ʌn'kləuðd] *adj* desnudo.
unclouded ['ʌn'klaudid] *adj* despejado.
uncoil ['ʌn'kɔil] **1** *vt* desenrollar. **2** *vi* desenrollarse; desovillarse; (*snake*) desanillarse.
uncollected ['ʌnkə'lektid] *adj fare etc* sin cobrar.
uncoloured ['ʌn'kʌləd] *adj* en blanco; *account etc* objetivo.
uncombed ['ʌn'kəumd] *adj* despeinado, sin peinar.
uncomely ['ʌn'kʌmli] *adj* desgarbado.
uncomfortable [ʌn'kʌmfətəbl] *adj* (*physically*) incómodo; *feeling* molesto; **to be —** (*chair etc*) ser incómodo; *person* (*ill at ease*) estar inquieto, sentirse molesto; **to feel — about something** preocuparse por algo, inquietarse por algo, no estar del todo satisfecho acerca de algo; remorderle a uno la conciencia por algo; **we had an — few minutes** pasamos un mal rato; **to make life — for someone** amargar la vida a uno, crear dificultades a uno.
uncomfortably [ʌn'kʌmfətəbli] *adv* incómodamente; **he thought —** pensaba con cierto remordimiento, pensaba algo inquieto; **the shell fell — close** cayó el proyectil inquietantemente cerca.
uncommitted ['ʌnkə'mitid] *adj nation* no comprometido, no alineado.
uncommon [ʌn'kɔmən] **1** *adj* poco común, nada frecuente; extraño, insólito. **2** *adv* (*fam*) sumamente, extraordinariamente.
uncommonly [ʌn'kɔmənli] *adv* raramente, rara vez; extraordinariamente; **that's — kind of you** ha sido Vd amabilísimo; **not —** con cierta frecuencia.
uncommunicative ['ʌnkə'mjuːnikətiv] *adj* poco comunicativo, reservado.
uncomplaining ['ʌnkəm'pleiniŋ] *adj* resignado, sumiso.
uncomplainingly ['ʌnkəm'pleiniŋli] *adv* con resignación, sumisamente.
uncomplicated [ʌn'kɔmplikeitid] *adj person etc* sin complicaciones, sencillo.
uncomplimentary ['ʌn,kɔmpli'mentəri] *adj* nada lisonjero, poco halagüeño.
uncompromising [ʌn'kɔmprəmaiziŋ] *adj* intransigente.
unconcealed ['ʌnkən'siːld] *adj* abierto, no disimulado; **with — glee** con abierta satisfacción.
unconcern ['ʌnkən'sə:n] *n* (*calm*) calma *f*, tranquilidad *f*, (*in face of danger*) sangre *f* fría; (*lack of interest*) indiferencia *f*, despreocupación *f*.
unconcerned ['ʌnkən'sə:nd] *adj* tranquilo; indiferente; despreocupado; **he went on speaking —** siguió hablando sin inmutarse; **to be — about something** no inquietarse por algo.
unconcernedly ['ʌnkən'sə:nidli] *adv* con calma, tranquilamente; con sangre fría; con indiferencia; sin preocuparse, sin inquietarse.
unconditional ['ʌnkən'diʃənl] *adj* incondicional, sin condiciones.

unconditionally ['ʌnkən'diʃnəli] *adv* incondicionalmente.
unconfessed ['ʌnkən'fest] *adj* inconfeso.
unconfined ['ʌnkən'faind] *adj* ilimitado, no restringido, libre; **let joy be —** que se regocijen todos.
unconfirmed ['ʌnkən'fə:md] *adj* no confirmado, inconfirmado.
uncongenial ['ʌnkən'dʒiːniəl] *adj* antipático; desagradable.
unconnected ['ʌnkə'nektid] *adj* inconexo; **— with** no relacionado con.
unconquerable [ʌn'kɔŋkərəbl] *adj* inconquistable, invencible.
unconquered [ʌn'kɔŋkəd] *adj* invicto.
unconscionable [ʌn'kɔnʃnəbl] *adj* desmedido, desrazonable.
unconscious [ʌn'kɔnʃəs] **1** *adj* (a) inconsciente, no intencional; **to be — of** estar inconsciente de, ignorar, no darse cuenta de; **to remain blissfully — of the danger** continuar tranquilamente sin darse cuenta del peligro.
  (b) (*Med*) sin sentido, desmayado, inconsciente; **to be —** estar sin sentido, estar desmayado; **to be — for 3 hours** pasar 3 horas antes de volver en sí; **to become —** perder el sentido, perder el conocimiento, desmayarse; **to fall —** caer sin sentido; **they found him —** le encontraron inconsciente. **2** *n*: **the —** lo inconsciente.
unconsciously [ʌn'kɔnʃəsli] *adv* inconscientemente; **an — funny remark** una observación que no quería ser humorística, una observación hecha sin intención humorística.
unconsciousness [ʌn'kɔnʃəsnis] *n* (*Med*) insensibilidad *f*, pérdida *f* de conocimiento, falta *f* de sentido.
unconsidered ['ʌnkən'sidəd] *adj* desatendido; **— trifles** pequeñeces *fpl* a las que nadie ha prestado atención.
unconstitutional ['ʌn,kɔnsti'tjuːʃənl] *adj* inconstitucional.
unconstitutionally [ʌn,kɔnsti'tjuːʃnəli] *adv* inconstitucionalmente.
unconstrained ['ʌnkən'streind] *adj* libre, no franco.
uncontested ['ʌnkən'testid] *adj* incontestado; (*Parl*) *seat* ganado sin oposición.
uncontrollable ['ʌnkən'trəuləbl] *adj* incontrolable; *temper* ingobernable; *laughter* incontenible; *terror etc* irrefrenable.
uncontrolled ['ʌnkən'trəuld] *adj* incontrolado, libre, desenfrenado.
unconventional ['ʌnkən'venʃənl] *adj* poco convencional; *person* poco formalista, extravagante, original, despreocupado.
unconversant ['ʌnkən'və:sənt] *adj*: **to be — with** estar poco versado en.
unconverted ['ʌnkən'və:tid] *adj* no convertido (*also Fin*).
unconvinced ['ʌnkən'vinst] *adj*: **to remain —** seguir sin convencerse.
unconvincing ['ʌnkən'vinsiŋ] *adj* poco convincente.
unconvincingly ['ʌnkən'vinsiŋli] *adv* (*argue etc*) sin convencer a nadie.
uncooked ['ʌn'kukt] *adj* sin cocer, crudo.
uncork ['ʌn'kɔːk] *vt* descorchar, destapar.
uncorrected ['ʌnkə'rektid] *adj* sin corregir.
uncorroborated ['ʌnkə'rɔbəreitid] *adj* no confirmado.
uncorrupted ['ʌnkə'rʌptid] *adj* incorrupto; **— by** no corrompido por.
uncountable ['ʌn'kauntəbl] *adj* incontable.
uncounted ['ʌn'kauntid] *adj* sin cuenta.
uncouple ['ʌn'kʌpl] *vt* desacoplar, desenganchar.
uncouth [ʌn'kuːθ] *adj* grosero, ineducado, inculto.
uncover [ʌn'kʌvə*] *vt* descubrir; (*remove lid of*) destapar; (*remove coverings of*) dejar al descubierto; (*disclose*) descubrir, dejar al descubierto, dejar patente.
uncovered [ʌn'kʌvəd] *adj* descubierto, sin cubierta.
uncritical ['ʌn'kritikəl] *adj* falto de sentido crítico.
uncrossed ['ʌn'krɔst] *adj cheque* sin cruzar.
uncrowned ['ʌn'kraund] *adj* sin corona; **the — king of Slobodia** el rey sin corona de Eslobodia.
unction ['ʌŋkʃən] *n* (*unguent*) unción *f*, ungüento *m*; (*fig*) unción *f*; celo *m*, fervor *m*; (*pej*) efusión *f*, celo *m* fingido, fervor *m* afectado; zalamería *f*; **extreme —** (*Eccl*) extremaunción *f*; **he said with —** dijo efusivo.
unctuous ['ʌŋktjuəs] *adj* (*fig*) afectadamente fervoroso; sobón, zalamero; **in an — voice** en tono efusivo, en tono meloso.
unctuousness ['ʌŋktjuəsnis] *n* (*fig*) efusión *f*, celo *m* fingido, fervor *m* afectado; zalamería *f*.
uncultivable ['ʌn'kʌltivəbl] *adj* incultivable.
uncultivated ['ʌn'kʌltiveitid] *adj* inculto (*also fig*).

uncultured ['ʌn'kʌltʃəd] *adj* inculto, iletrado.
uncurl ['ʌn'kə:l] **1** *vt* desrizar, desenrollar, abrir. **2** *vi* desrizarse, desenrollarse, abrirse; desovillarse.
uncut ['ʌn'kʌt] *adj* sin cortar; *stone* sin labrar; *diamond* en bruto, sin tallar; *book* intonso.
undamaged [ʌn'dæmidʒd] *adj* indemne, intacto; sin sufrir desperfectos.
undamped ['ʌn'dæmpt] *adj* (*fig*) no disminuido.
undated ['ʌn'deitid] *adj* sin fecha.
undaunted ['ʌn'dɔ:ntid] *adj* impávido, impertérrito; **he carried on quite —** siguió sin inmutarse; **with — bravery** con valor intrépido; **to be — by** no dejarse desanimar por.
undeceive ['ʌndi'si:v] *vt* desengañar, desilusionar.
undecided ['ʌndi'saidid] *adj question* pendiente, no resuelto; *person's character* indeciso; **we are still — whether to** + *infin* no hemos decidido todavía si + *infin*; **that is still —** eso queda por resolver.
undecipherable ['ʌndi'saifərəbl] *adj* indescifrable.
undeclinable ['ʌndi'klainəbl] *adj* (*Gram*) indeclinable.
undefeated ['ʌndi'fi:tid] *adj* invicto, imbatido; **he was — at the end** siguió invicto al final.
undefended ['ʌndi'fendid] *adj* indefenso; (*Law*) *suit* ganado por incomparecencia del demandado.
undefiled ['ʌndi'faild] *adj* puro, inmaculado; **— by any contact with ...** no corrompido por contacto alguno con ...
undefined [,ʌndi'faind] *adj* indefinido.
undemonstrative ['ʌndi'mɔnstrətiv] *adj* reservado, cohibido, poco expresivo.
undeniable [,ʌndi'naiəbl] *adj* innegable; **it is — that ...** es innegable que ...
undeniably [,ʌndi'naiəbli] *adv* indudablemente; **it is — true that ...** es innegable que . . .; **an — successful trip** un viaje de éxito innegable.
undenominational ['ʌndi,nɔmi'neiʃənl] *adj* no sectario.
undependable ['ʌndi'pendəbl] *adj* poco formal, poco confiable.
under ['ʌndə*] **1** *adv* debajo; abajo; *see* **down** *etc*.
2 *prep* **(a)** (*place: precise*) debajo de, eg **— the table** debajo de la mesa; (*less precise*) bajo, *eg* **— the sky** bajo el cielo, **— the water** bajo el agua.
(b) (*place, fig*) **— the Romans** bajo los romanos; **— Ferdinand VII** bajo Fernando VII, bajo el reinado de Fernando VII; **— the command of** bajo el mando de; **— lock and key** bajo llave; **— oath** bajo juramento; **— full sail** a todo trapo, a vela llena; **— a toda vela**; **the field is — wheat** el campo está sembrado de trigo.
(c) (*number etc*) **— 50** menos de 50; **any number — 90** cualquier número inferior a 90; **in — 2 hours** en menos de 2 horas; **aged — 21** que tiene menos de 21 años; **it sells at — £5** se vende a menos de 5 libras.
(d) (*according to, by*) con arreglo a, de acuerdo con, conforme a, según; **— Article 25 of the Code** conforme al Artículo 25 del Código; **his rights — the contract** sus derechos según el contrato.
under- ['ʌndə*] *in compounds:* **(a)** *adv* insuficientemente, *eg* **under-prepared** insuficientemente preparado.
(b) *prep:* **an under-15** un menor de 15 años, una persona que tiene menos de 15 años.
(c) *adj part* eg bajo, inferior; *clothing* inferior; (*in rank*) subalterno, segundo, eg **the under-cook** la cocinera segunda; **the under-gardener** el mozo de huerto.
underact ['ʌndər'ækt] *vi* no dar de sí, hacer un papel sin el debido brío.
underarm ['ʌndərɑ:m] **1** *adj* (*Anat*) sobacal, del sobaco; *service etc* hecho con la mano debajo del hombro.
2 *adv:* **to serve —** sacar con la mano debajo del hombro.
underbelly ['ʌndə,beli] *n* (*fig*) parte *f* indefensa, parte *f* más expuesta al ataque.
underbid ['ʌndə'bid] (*irr: see* **bid**) **1** *vt* ofrecer precio más bajo que. **2** *vi* (*Bridge*) declarar menos de lo que tiene uno.
underbrush ['ʌndəbrʌʃ] *n* maleza *f*, monte *m* bajo.
undercarriage ['ʌndə,kæridʒ] *n*, **undercart** ['ʌndəkɑ:t] *n* (*fam*) tren *m* de aterrizaje.
undercharge ['ʌndə'tʃɑ:dʒ] *vt* cobrar menos del precio justo a.
underclothes ['ʌndəkləuðz] *npl*, **underclothing** ['ʌndə,kləuðiŋ] *n* ropa *f* interior.
undercoat ['ʌndəkəut] *n* (*of paint*) primera capa *f*.
undercover ['ʌndə,kʌvə*] *adj* secreto, clandestino.
undercurrent ['ʌndə,kʌrənt] *n* corriente *f* submarina, contracorriente *f*; (*fig*) nota *f* callada; tendencia *f*

oculta; **an — of criticism** una serie de críticas calladas.
undercut ['ʌndəkʌt] (*irr: see* **cut**) *vt competitor* rebajar los precios para competir con.
underdeveloped ['ʌndədi'veləpt] *adj* subdesarrollado.
underdevelopment ['ʌndədi'veləpmənt] *n* subdesarrollo *m*.
underdog ['ʌndədɔg] *n* (*socially*) desvalido *m*; (*in game*) perdidoso *m*, el que está perdiendo; **the —s** los de abajo, los débiles, los desamparados.
underdone ['ʌndə'dʌn] *adj* poco hecho, medio asado.
underdrawers ['ʌndə'drɔːəz] *npl* (US) calzoncillos *mpl*.
underdress ['ʌndə'dres] *vi* vestirse sin la debida elegancia.
underemployed ['ʌndərim'plɔid] *adj:* **— person** persona *f* a la que no se exige todo el trabajo de que es capaz, persona *f* de una capacidad que no se utiliza debidamente; **the factory is —** la fábrica tiene capacidad no utilizada, la fábrica tiene menos trabajo del que quisiera.
underestimate ['ʌndər'estimit] *n* estimación *f* demasiado baja.
underestimate ['ʌndər'estimeit] *vt* subestimar; *person etc* tener en menos de lo que merece; **to — one's opponent** menospreciar a su adversario.
underexpose ['ʌndəriks'pəuz] *vt* (*Phot*) exponer insuficientemente.
underexposed ['ʌndəriks'pəuzd] *adj* (*Phot*) subexpuesto.
underexposure ['ʌndəriks'pəuʒə*] *n* (*Phot*) exposición *f* insuficiente.
underfed ['ʌndə'fed] *adj* subalimentado.
underfeed ['ʌndə'fi:d] (*irr: see* **feed**) *vt* alimentar insuficientemente.
underfeeding ['ʌndə'fi:diŋ] *n* subalimentación *f*.
underfoot ['ʌndə'fut] *adv* debajo de los pies; **it's very wet —** el suelo está muy mojado.
undergarment ['ʌndə,gɑ:mənt] *n* prenda *f* de ropa interior; **—s** ropa *f* interior.
undergo ['ʌndə'gəu] (*irr: see* **go**) *vt* sufrir, experimentar; *operation* someterse a; *treatment* recibir; **to — repairs** ser reparado.
undergraduate ['ʌndə'grædjuit] **1** *n* estudiante *mf* (*no graduado*).
2 *adj, attr student* no graduado; *study* de licenciatura, para estudiantes no graduados; **70 — rooms** 70 habitaciones para estudiantes.
underground ['ʌndəgraund] **1** *adj* subterráneo; (*fig*) clandestino, secreto.
2 *adv* bajo tierra; **it's 6 feet —** está a 6 pies bajo tierra.
3 *n* (*Rail*) metro *m*; (*Mil, Pol*) resistencia *f*; movimiento *m* clandestino.
undergrowth ['ʌndəgrəuθ] *n* maleza *f*, monte *m* bajo.
underhand ['ʌndəhænd] **1** *adj service etc* hecho con la mano debajo del hombro; (*fig*) *method* turbio, poco limpio; *trick* malo; *attack* solapado.
2 *adv:* **to serve —** sacar con la mano debajo del hombro.
underlie [,ʌndə'lai] (*irr: see* **lie**) *vt* estar debajo de, extenderse debajo de; servir de base a; (*fig*) estar a la base de, ser la razón fundamental de.
underline [,ʌndə'lain] *vt* subrayar (*also fig*).
underling ['ʌndəliŋ] *n* subordinado *m*, inferior *m*; (*follower*) secuaz *m*.
underlining ['ʌndə'lainiŋ] *n* subrayado *m*.
underlying ['ʌndə'laiiŋ] *adj* subyacente; (*fig*) fundamental, esencial.
undermanned ['ʌndə'mænd] *adj:* **to be —** estar sin la debida tripulación, no tener el debido personal.
undermentioned ['ʌndə'menʃənd] *adj* abajo citado.
undermine ['ʌndə'main] *vt* socavar, minar (*also fig*); **his health is being —d by ...** su salud está siendo arruinada por ...
undermost ['ʌndəməust] *adj* (el) más bajo.
underneath ['ʌndə'ni:θ] **1** *adv* debajo. **2** *prep* bajo, debajo de. **3** *adj* inferior, de abajo; **the — one** el de abajo. **4** *n* superficie *f* inferior.
undernourished ['ʌndə'nʌriʃt] *adj* desnutrido.
undernourishment ['ʌndə'nʌriʃmənt] *n* desnutrición *f*.
underpaid ['ʌndə'peid] *adj* insuficientemente retribuido, mal pagado.
underpants ['ʌndəpænts] *npl* calzoncillos *mpl*.
underpass ['ʌndəpɑ:s] *n* paso *m* inferior.
underpay ['ʌndə'pei] (*irr: see* **pay**) *vt* pagar mal, pagar un sueldo insuficiente a.
underpin [,ʌndə'pin] *vt* apuntalar.
underpinning [,ʌndə'piniŋ] *n* apuntalamiento *m*.

underplay ['ʌndə'plei] **1** *vt* (a) to — a card poner una carta de menos valor que otra.
(b) (*Theat*) to — a part hacer flojamente un papel.
2 *vi* (*Theat*) hacer flojamente su papel, estar muy flojo en su papel.

underpopulated ['ʌndə'pɔpjuleitid] *adj* poco poblado, con baja densidad de poblacion.

underpraise ['ʌndə'preiz] *vt* no alabar debidamente, no tributar el debido elogio a.

underprice ['ʌndə'prais] *vt* señalar un precio demasiado bajo a; **at 5 dollars it is —d** el precio de 5 dólares es más bien bajo.

underprivileged ['ʌndə'privilidʒd] *adj* desvalido, desamparado.

underproduction ['ʌndəprə'dʌkʃən] *n* producción *f* deficiente.

underrate [,ʌndə'reit] *vt opponent etc* menospreciar, tener en menos de lo que merece; *danger etc* subestimar, juzgar mal.

underripe ['ʌndə'raip] *adj* poco maduro, verde.

underscore [,ʌndə'skɔ:*] *vt* subrayar.

undersea ['ʌndəsi:] **1** *adj* submarino. **2** *adv* bajo la superficie del mar.

undersecretary ['ʌndə'sekrətəri] *n* subsecretario *m*, a *f*.

undersecretaryship ['ʌndə'sekrətəriʃip] *n* subsecretaría *f*.

undersell ['ʌndə'sel] (*irr: see* **sell**) *vt person* vender a precio más bajo que; *article* malvender; **Burnley has been undersold as a tourist centre** no se ha hecho la debida publicidad de Burnley como centro turístico.

undershirt ['ʌndəʃə:t] *n* (*US*) camiseta *f*.

undershorts ['ʌndə,ʃɔ:ts] *npl* (*US*) calzoncillos *mpl*.

underside ['ʌndəsaid] *n* superficie *f* inferior; (*of small object*) envés *m*, cara *f* inferior.

undersigned ['ʌndəsaind] *adj:* **the —** el abajo firmante, (*pl*) los abajo firmantes.

undersized ['ʌndə'saizd] *adj* pequeño, no bastante grande, de tamaño insuficiente; *person* (*pej*) sietemesino.

underskirt ['ʌndəskə:t] *n* enaguas *fpl*.

underslung ['ʌndəslʌŋ] *adj* con bajo centro de gravedad; colocado debajo del eje.

understaffed ['ʌndə'stɑ:ft] *adj:* **to be —** no tener el debido personal.

understand [,ʌndə'stænd] (*irr: see* **stand**) *vti* (a) comprender, entender; **I —** lo comprendo; **I quite —** lo comprendo perfectamente; **do you —?** ¿me entiende?, ¿comprende?; **I don't — Arabic** no entiendo el árabe; **I don't —** you no te entiendo; **I don't — why** no entiendo por qué; **we — each other** nos entendemos, nos comprendemos; **to give someone to —** that . . . dar a uno a entender que . . .; **I was given to —** that . . . me dieron a entender que . . ., me hicieron creer que . . .; **I — you have been absent** tengo entendido que Vd ha estado ausente.
(b) (*assume*) sobreentender; **one has to — 3 words here** aquí se sobreentienden 3 palabras; *see also* **understood.**

understandable [,ʌndə'stændəbl] *adj* comprensible; **it is — that** . . . se comprende que . . .; **it is very — that** . . . se comprende perfectamente que . . .

understanding [,ʌndə'stændiŋ] **1** *adj* comprensivo, compasivo; **they were very — about it** se mostraron muy comprensivos; **he gave me an — look** me miró compasivo.
2 *n* (a) (*intelligence*) entendimiento *m*, inteligencia *f*; (*grasp*) comprensión *f*; **he has good —** tiene una inteligencia fina; **his — of these problems** su comprensión de estos problemas, su capacidad para comprender estos problemas; **she has reached the age of —** ha llegado a la edad de discreción.
(b) (*agreement*) acuerdo *m*, arreglo *m*; **to come to an — with someone** ponerse de acuerdo con uno, llegar a un acuerdo con uno; **to have an — with someone** tener un acuerdo (*esp* verbal) con uno; **I have an — with the milkman** tengo un arreglo con el lechero, nos entendemos el lechero y yo.
(c) (*sympathy*) comprensión *f* mutua, inteligencia *f*; **this will encourage good — between peoples** esto ha de fomentar la buena inteligencia entre los pueblos.
(d) **on the — that . . .** con tal que + *subj*, bien entendido que + *subj*.

understandingly [,ʌndə'stændiŋli] *adv* con comprensión, compasivamente; **he looked at me —** me miró compasivamente.

understate ['ʌndə'steit] *vt situation* exponer incompletamente, describir sin el debido énfasis; *needs* subestimar; (*Gram*) atenuar.

understatement [,ʌndə,steitmənt] *n* exposición *f* incompleta, descripción *f* insuficiente; (*Gram*) atenuación *f*; (*quality*) moderación *f*, modestia *f* excesiva; **the — of the year** la declaración más modesta del año.

understood [,ʌndə'stud] *adj and ptp* (a) **it is — that** (*believed*) se cree que, tenemos entendido que; (*understandable*) se comprende que; **that is —** eso se entiende; **it being —** that . . . con tal que + *subj*; **I wish it to be — that . . .** entiéndase que . . ., quiero decir bien claro que . . .; **to make oneself —** hacerse entender.
(b) **with 3 words —** con 3 palabras que se sobreentienden.
(c) **it is an — thing that . . .** se entiende que . . ., se acepta el que . . .

understudy ['ʌndə,stʌdi] **1** *n* suplente *mf*, sobresaliente *mf*. **2** *vt* doblar a, aprender un papel para poder suplir a.

undertake [,ʌndə'teik] (*irr: see* **take**) *vt task etc* emprender; acometer; *duty etc* encargarse de; **to — to do something** comprometerse a hacer algo, prometer hacer algo; **to — that . . .** comprometerse a que . . ., prometer que . . .

undertaker ['ʌndə,teikə*] *n* director *m* de pompas fúnebres; **—'s** funeraria *f*.

undertaking [,ʌndə'teikiŋ] *n* (*Comm*) empresa *f*; (*task*) empresa *f*, tarea *f*; (*pledge*) garantía *f*, compromiso *m*, promesa *f*; **it's quite an —** es una tarea bastante grande; **to give an — that . . .** prometer que . . ., asegurar que . . .; **I can give no such —** no puedo comprometerme a eso, no puedo dar esa promesa.

undertone ['ʌndətəun] *n* (*sound*) voz *f* baja, sonido *m* suave; (*Art*) matiz *m* suave; (*of criticism etc*) nota *f* callada, trasfondo *m*; **in an —** en voz baja; **there are —s of protest here** aquí hay notas calladas de protesta.

undertow ['ʌndətəu] *n* resaca *f*.

undervalue ['ʌndə'vælju:] *vt* valorizar incompletamente, apreciar en menos de su justo valor; (*fig*) subestimar; menospreciar; **he has been —d as a writer** como escritor no se le ha apreciado debidamente.

underwater ['ʌndə'wɔ:tə*] *adj* submarino; **— fisherman** submarinista *mf*; **— fishing** pesca *f* submarina.

underwear ['ʌndəwɛə*] *n* ropa *f* interior.

underweight [,ʌndə'weit] *adj* de peso insuficiente; **to be —** (*person*) no pesar bastante.

underworld ['ʌndəwə:ld] *n* (*hell*) infierno *m*; (*criminal*) hampa *f*, inframundo *m*; bajos fondos *mpl*.

underwrite ['ʌndərait] (*irr: see* **write**) *vt* asegurar, asegurar contra riesgos; (*on 2nd insurance*) reasegurar; (*fig*) apoyar, respaldar, aprobar, garantizar.

underwriter ['ʌndə,raitə*] *n* asegurador *m*, reasegurador *m*.

undeserved ['ʌndi'zə:vd] *adj* inmerecido.

undeservedly ['ʌndi'zə:vidli] *adv* inmerecidamente.

undeserving ['ʌndi'zə:viŋ] *adj* indigno.

undesirable ['ʌndi'zaiərəbl] **1** *adj* indeseable; **it is — that . . .** no es recomendable que + *subj*, es poco aconsejable que + *subj*. **2** *n* indeseable *mf*.

undetected ['ʌndi'tektid] *adj* no descubierto; **to go — pasar inadvertido.**

undeterred ['ʌndi'tə:d] *adj:* **he was — by . . .** no se dejó intimidar por . . .; **he carried on —** siguió sin inmutarse.

undeveloped ['ʌndi'veləpt] *adj* subdesarrollado; *fruit etc* verde, inmaturo; *film* sin revelar; *land* sin cultivar; *resources* sin explotar.

undeviating ['ʌn'di:vieitiŋ] *adj* directo, constante; **to follow an — path** seguir un curso recto.

undeviatingly ['ʌn'di:vieitiŋli] *adv* directamente, constantemente; **to hold — to one's course** seguir su curso sin apartarse para nada de él.

undies ['ʌndiz] *npl* (*fam*) paños *mpl* menores.

undigested ['ʌndai'dʒestid] *adj* indigesto.

undignified ['ʌn'dignifaid] *adj act, position etc* indecoroso; *person* sin dignidad, informal, poco serio.

undiluted ['ʌndai'lu:tid] *adj* sin diluir, puro; (*fig*) puro.

undiminished ['ʌndi'miniʃt] *adj* no disminuido.

undimmed ['ʌn'dimd] *adj* tan brillante como antes.

undiplomatic ['ʌn,diplə'mætik] *adj* impolítico, indiscreto.

undiscernible ['ʌndi'sə:nəbl] *adj* imperceptible.

undiscerning ['ʌndi'sə:niŋ] *adj* sin discernimiento, poco discernidor.

undischarged ['ʌndis'tʃɑ:dʒd] *adj debt* impagado, por pagar; *promise* no cumplido; **— bankrupt** persona *f* que sigue en estado de quiebra.

undisciplined [ʌn'disiplind] *adj* indisciplinado.

undisclosed ['ʌndis'kləuzd] *adj* no revelado.

undiscovered ['ʌndis'kʌvəd] *adj* no descubierto; **he remained — for 3 days** siguió durante 3 dias sin que averiguasen su paradero.

undiscriminating ['ʌndis'krimineitiŋ] *adj* sin discernimiento, poco discernidor.

undisguised ['ʌndis'gaizd] *adj* sin disfraz; (*fig*) franco, abierto; **with — satisfaction** con abierta satisfacción.

undismayed ['ʌndis'meid] *adj* impávido; **he was — by this** no se dejó desanimar por esto; **he said —** dijo sin inmutarse.

undisposed-of ['ʌndis'pəuzdɔv] *adj* (*Comm*) no vendido.

undisputed ['ʌndis'pju:tid] *adj* incontestable.

undistinguished ['ʌndis'tiŋwiʃt] *adj* más bien mediocre.

undisturbed ['ʌndis'tə:bd] *adj*: **to leave things —** dejar las cosas como están, dejar las cosas sin tocar; **he was — by this** no se perturbó con esto; **to go on with one's work —** continuar su trabajo en paz; **he likes to be left —** no quiere que le interrumpan las visitas (*or* llamadas *etc*).

undivided ['ʌndi'vaidid] *adj* indiviso, íntegro, entero; **I want your — attention** quiero que me presten toda su atención.

undo ['ʌn'du:] (*irr: see* **do**) *vt arrangement etc* anular; *work* deshacer; *knot* desatar; *clasp* desabrochar; *box* abrir; *mischief* reparar; *see also* **undone**.

undoing ['ʌn'du:iŋ] *n* ruina *f*, perdición *f*; **that was his —** aquello fue su ruina.

undomesticated ['ʌndə'mestikeitid] *adj* indomado, no domesticado.

undone ['ʌn'dʌn] *adj*: **I am —!** ¡estoy perdido!, ¡es mi ruina!; **to come —** desatarse; **to leave something —** dejar algo sin hacer.

undoubted [ʌn'dautid] *adj* indudable.

undoubtedly [ʌn'dautidli] *adv* indudablemente, sin duda.

undreamt-of [ʌn'dremtɔv] *adj* no soñado, nunca pensado.

undress ['ʌn'dres] **1** *n* traje *m* de casa, desabillé *m*; (*Mil*) traje *m* de cuartel; **in a state of —** desnudo. **2** *vt* desnudar. **3** *vi* desnudarse.

undrinkable ['ʌn'driŋkəbl] *adj* no potable, que no se puede beber.

undue ['ʌn'dju:] *adj* indebido, excesivo.

undulate ['ʌndjuleit] *vi* ondular, ondear.

undulating ['ʌndjuleitiŋ] *adj* ondulante, ondeante; *land* ondulado.

undulation [,ʌndju'leiʃən] *n* ondulación *f*.

undulatory ['ʌndjulətəri] *adj* ondulatorio.

unduly ['ʌn'dju:li] *adv* indebidamente, excesivamente, con exceso; **we are not — worried** no estamos demasiado preocupados.

undying [ʌn'daiiŋ] *adj* (*fig*) imperecedero, inmarcesible.

unearned ['ʌn'ə:nd] *adj* no ganado.

unearth ['ʌn'ə:θ] *vt* desenterrar; (*fig*) desenterrar, descubrir.

unearthly [ʌn'ə:θli] *adj* sobrenatural; *light etc* misterioso, fantástico; *hour etc* inverosímil.

uneasily [ʌn'i:zili] *adv* inquietamente, con inquietud; **I noted — that . . .** me inquieté al observar que . . .

uneasiness [ʌn'i:zinis] *n* inquietud *f*; desasosiego *m*, intranquilidad *f*.

uneasy [ʌn'i:zi] *adj* calm, peace, *etc* inseguro; *sleep* poco tranquilo; *conscience* desasosegado, intranquilo; **to be —** estar inquieto (*about* por), sentirse mal a gusto; **to become —** empezar a inquietarse (*about* por); **I have an — feeling that . . .** me inquieta la posibilidad de que + *subj*; **to make someone —** intranquilizar a uno, turbar a uno.

uneatable ['ʌn'i:təbl] *adj* incomible, que no se puede comer.

uneaten ['ʌn'i:tn] *adj* no comido, sin comer.

uneconomic(al) ['ʌn,i:kə'nɔmik(əl)] *adj* antieconómico.

unedifying ['ʌn'edifaiiŋ] *adj* indecoroso, poco edificante.

uneducated ['ʌn'edjukeitid] *adj* ineducado, ignorante.

unemotional ['ʌni'məuʃənl] *adj* character impasible, reservado; *person* que no se deja emocionar; *account etc* objetivo.

unemotionally ['ʌni'məuʃnəli] *adv*: **to look on —** mirar impasible, mirar sin dejarse emocionar.

unemployable ['ʌnim'plɔiəbl] *adj* inútil para el trabajo.

unemployed ['ʌnim'plɔid] **1** *adj* parado, sin empleo, desempleado. **2** *n*: **the —** los parados, los sin trabajo, los desempleados.

unemployment ['ʌnim'plɔimənt] *n* paro *m* (forzoso), desempleo *m*, desocupación *f*; **seasonal —** paro estacional.

unencumbered ['ʌnin'kʌmbəd] *adj* suelto, sin trabas; (*estate etc*) libre de gravamen; **— by** no impedido por, sin el estorbo de.

unending [ʌn'endiŋ] *adj* interminable, sin fin.

unendurable ['ʌnin'djuərəbl] *adj* inaguantable, insufrible.

unengaged ['ʌnin'geidʒd] *adj* libre; sin compromiso.

un-English ['ʌn'iŋgliʃ] *adj* (*unworthy*) indigno de un inglés; (*unlike*) nada típico de un inglés.

unenlightened ['ʌnin'laitnd] *adj person*, *age* ignorante, poco instruido; *policy etc* estúpido.

unenterprising ['ʌn'entəpraiziŋ] *adj person* falto de iniciativa, poco emprendedor; *policy etc* tímido.

unenthusiastic ['ʌnin,θu:zi'æstik] *adj* poco entusiasta; **everybody seemed rather — about it** nadie mostró gran entusiasmo por la idea.

unenviable ['ʌn'enviəbl] *adj* poco envidiable.

unequal ['ʌn'i:kwəl] *adj* desigual, desproporcionado; **to be — to a task** no estar a la altura de una tarea, no tener fuerzas para una tarea.

unequalled ['ʌn'i:kwəld] *adj* inigualado, sin par; **a record — by anybody** un historial mejor que el de nadie.

unequally ['ʌn'i:kwəli] *adv* desigualmente; desproporcionadamente.

unequivocal ['ʌni'kwivəkəl] *adj* inequívoco.

unequivocally ['ʌni'kwivəkəli] *adv* de modo inequívoco, sin dejar lugar a dudas.

unerring ['ʌn'ə:riŋ] *adj* infalible.

unerringly ['ʌn'ə:riŋli] *adv* infaliblemente.

unessential ['ʌni'senʃəl] *adj* no esencial.

unesthetic ['ʌni:s'θetik] *adj* antiestético.

unethical ['ʌn'eθikəl] *adj* inmoral; injusto.

uneven ['ʌn'i:vən] *adj* desigual; *road etc* escabroso, quebrado, ondulado.

unevenly ['ʌn'i:vənli] *adv* desigualmente.

unevenness ['ʌn'i:vənnis] *n* desigualdad *f*; escabrosidad *f*.

uneventful ['ʌni'ventful] *adj* sin incidentes notables, sin accidentes, tranquilo.

unexampled ['ʌnig'zɑ:mpld] *adj* sin igual.

unexceptionable [,ʌnik'sepʃnəbl] *adj* intachable, impecable.

unexceptional [,ʌnik'sepʃənl] *adj* usual, corriente, normal.

unexciting ['ʌnik'saitiŋ] *adj* poco emocionante, de poco interés.

unexpected ['ʌniks'pektid] *adj* inesperado, inopinado.

unexpectedly ['ʌniks'pektidli] *adv* inesperadamente, inopinadamente.

unexpendable ['ʌniks'pendəbl] *adj* que no se puede gastar.

unexpended ['ʌniks'pendid] *adj* no gastado.

unexpired ['ʌniks'paiəd] *adj bill* no vencido; *lease, ticket* no caducado.

unexplained ['ʌniks'pleind] *adj* inexplicado.

unexploded ['ʌniks'pləudid] *adj* sin explotar.

unexploited ['ʌniks'plɔitid] *adj* inexplotado, sin explotar.

unexplored ['ʌniks'plɔ:d] *adj* inexplorado.

unexposed ['ʌniks'pəuzd] *adj* (*Phot*) inexpuesto.

unexpressed ['ʌniks'prest] *adj* no expresado; tácito.

unexpressive ['ʌniks'presiv] *adj* inexpresivo.

unexpurgated ['ʌn'ekspə:geitid] *adj* sin expurgar, íntegro.

unfading [ʌn'feidiŋ] *adj* (*fig*) inmarcesible.

unfailing [ʌn'feiliŋ] *adj* indefectible; *zeal* infalible; *supply* inagotable.

unfailingly [ʌn'feiliŋli] *adv* indefectiblemente; infaliblemente; inagotablemente; **to be — courteous** ser siempre cortés, no faltar en ningún momento a la cortesía.

unfair ['ʌn'fɛə*] *adj comment etc* injusto; *practice* sin equidad; *competition* desleal; *play* sucio; *tactics* no aprobado, no permitido por las reglas; **that's very —** eso es muy injusto; **how —!** ¡no hay derecho!; **it was — of him to** + *infin* era injusto que él + *subj*.

unfairly ['ʌn'fɛəli] *adv* injustamente; deslealmente; de modo contrario a las reglas; **he was — condemned** se le condenó injustamente.

unfairness ['ʌn'fɛənis] *n* injusticia *f*; deslealtad *f*; suciedad *f*.

unfaithful ['ʌn'feiθful] *adj* infiel; **to be — to someone** ser infiel a uno.

unfaithfulness ['ʌn'feiθfulnis] *n* infidelidad *f*.

unfaltering [ʌn'fɔ:ltəriŋ] *adj* resuelto, firme.

unfamiliar ['ʌnfə'miliə*] *adj subject etc* desconocido, nuevo; **to be — with** desconocer, ignorar.

unfashionable [ʌn'fæʃnəbl] *adj* pasado de moda, fuera de moda; poco elegante; **it is now — to talk of** . . . no está de moda ahora hablar de . . .

unfasten [ʌn'fɑːsn] *vt* (*untie*) desatar; *dress* desabrochar; *door* abrir; (*get free*) soltar; (*loosen*) aflojar.

unfathomable [ʌn'fæðəməbl] *adj* insondable.

unfathomed [ʌn'fæðəmd] *adj* no sondado.

unfavourable, (US) **unfavorable** [ʌn'feivərəbl] *adj* desfavorable, adverso; *outlook etc* poco propicio; *weather* malo.

unfavourably, (US) **unfavorably** [ʌn'feivərəbli] *adv* desfavorablemente; **to be — impressed** formarse una impresión desfavorable.

unfeeling [ʌn'fiːliŋ] *adj* insensible.

unfeelingly [ʌn'fiːliŋli] *adv* insensiblemente.

unfeigned [ʌn'feind] *adj* no fingido, verdadero.

unfeignedly [ʌn'feinidli] *adv* sin fingimiento, verdaderamente.

unfermented [ʌnfə'mentid] *adj* no fermentado.

unfettered [ʌn'fetəd] *adj* sin trabas.

unfinished [ʌn'finiʃt] *adj* incompleto, inacabado, sin terminar; **I have 3 — letters** tengo 3 cartas por terminar; **we have — business** tenemos asuntos pendientes.

unfit [ʌn'fit] *adj* (*incompetent*) incapaz, incompetente; (*unsuitable*) no apto (*for* para); (*useless*) inservible, inadecuado (*for* para); (*unworthy*) indigno (*to* de); (*ill*) enfermo, indispuesto; (*injured*) lesionado; **— to eat** impropio para el consumo humano; **— for publication** indigno de publicarse; **— for military service** no apto para el servicio militar; **he is quite — to hold office** es totalmente incapaz de ocupar ningún cargo; **the road is — for lorries** el camino es intransitable para los camiones.

unfit [ʌn'fit] *vt:* **to — someone for something** inhabilitar a uno para algo, incapacitar a uno para algo; **he is —ted for such a career** no es apto para tal carrera.

unfitness [ʌn'fitnis] *n* incapacidad *f*, incompetencia *f*; falta *f* de aptitud; inadecuación *f*; (*Med*) mala salud *f*, falta *f* de salud.

unflagging [ʌn'flægiŋ] *adj* incansable.

unflaggingly [ʌn'flægiŋli] *adv* incansablemente.

unflappable [ʌn'flæpəbl] *adj* imperturbable.

unflattering [ʌn'flætəriŋ] *adj* poco lisonjero, poco grato.

unflatteringly [ʌn'flætəriŋli] *adv* de modo poco lisonjero.

unfledged [ʌn'fledʒd] *adj* implume.

unflinching [ʌn'flintʃiŋ] *adj* impávido, resuelto.

unflinchingly [ʌn'flintʃiŋli] *adv* impávidamente, resueltamente.

unflyable [ʌn'flaiəbl] *adj:* **— weather** tiempo *m* que imposibilita el despegue de aviones.

unfold [ʌn'fəuld] **1** *vt* desplegar, desdoblar, abrir; *idea, plan* exponer; *secret* revelar; **to — a map on a table** extender un mapa sobre una mesa.

   2 *vi* desplegarse, desdoblarse, abrirse; (*view etc*) revelarse, extenderse.

unforeseeable [ʌnfɔː'siːəbl] *adj* imprevisible.

unforeseen [ʌnfɔː'siːn] *adj* imprevisto.

unforgettable [ʌnfə'getəbl] *adj* inolvidable.

unforgivable [ʌnfə'givəbl] *adj* imperdonable, indisculpable.

unforgiving [ʌnfə'giviŋ] *adj* implacable.

unformed [ʌn'fɔːmd] *adj* informe, sin formar aún.

unfortified [ʌn'fɔːtifaid] *adj* no fortificado; *town* abierto.

unfortunate [ʌn'fɔːtʃnit] **1** *adj person* desgraciado, desdichado, desventurado; (*lately dead*) malogrado; *event* funesto, desgraciado; *manner, remark* infeliz, inoportuno; **how very —!** ¡qué mala suerte!, ¡qué desgracia!; **it is most — that** . . . es muy de lamentar que + *subj*; **you have been most —** ha tenido muy mala suerte.

   2 *n* desgraciado *m*, a *f*.

unfortunately [ʌn'fɔːtʃnitli] *adv* por desgracia, desgraciadamente, desafortunadamente; **it is — true that** . . . desgraciadamente es verdad que . . .; **an — phrased statement** una declaración expresada en términos infelices.

unfounded [ʌn'faundid] *adj* infundado, que carece de fundamento.

unframed [ʌn'freimd] *adj* sin marco.

unfrequented [ʌnfri'kwentid] *adj* poco frecuentado.

unfriendliness [ʌn'frendlinis] *n* hostilidad *f*.

unfriendly [ʌn'frendli] *adj* poco amistoso.

unfrock [ʌn'frɔk] *vt* degradar, expulsar; **an —ed priest** un sacerdote a quien han quitado las órdenes.

unfruitful [ʌn'fruːtful] *adj* infructuoso.

unfulfilled [ʌnful'fild] *adj* incumplido.

unfurl [ʌn'fɔːl] *vt* desplegar.

unfurnished [ʌn'fɔːniʃt] *adj* desamueblado, sin muebles.

ungainliness [ʌn'geinlinis] *n* desgarbo *m*, torpeza *f*.

ungainly [ʌn'geinli] *adj* desgarbado, torpe.

ungallant [ʌn'gælənt] *adj* falto de cortesía, descortés.

ungenerous [ʌn'dʒenərəs] *adj* poco generoso.

ungentlemanly [ʌn'dʒentlmənli] *adj* poco caballeroso, indigno de un caballero.

un-get-at-able [ʌnget'ætəbl] *adj* inaccesible.

ungird [ʌn'gɔːd] (*irr: see* **gird**) *vt* desceñir.

unglazed [ʌn'gleizd] *adj* no vidriado.

ungodliness [ʌn'gɔdlinis] *n* impiedad *f*.

ungodly [ʌn'gɔdli] *adj* impío, irreligioso; (*fam*) atroz; **at this — hour** a hora tan inverosímil.

ungovernable [ʌn'gʌvənəbl] *adj* ingobernable; *temper* incontrolable, irrefrenable.

ungracious [ʌn'greiʃəs] *adj* descortés, grosero; **it would be — to refuse** sería descortés no aceptarlo.

ungrammatical [ʌngrə'mætikəl] *adj* incorrecto.

ungrammatically [ʌngrə'mætikəli] *adv* incorrectamente; **to talk Spanish —** hablar español con poca corrección.

ungrateful [ʌn'greitful] *adj* desagradecido, ingrato.

ungratefully [ʌn'greitfəli] *adv* desagradecidamente.

ungrudging [ʌn'grʌdʒiŋ] *adj* liberal, generoso; *support etc* incondicional.

ungrudgingly [ʌn'grʌdʒiŋli] *adv* liberalmente, generosamente, de buena gana, incondicionalmente.

unguarded [ʌn'gɑːdid] *adj* (*Mil*) indefenso, no defendido, sin protección; *remark etc* imprudente; **in an — moment** en un momento de descuido.

unguent [ʌngwənt] *n* ungüento *m*.

ungulate [ʌngjuleit] **1** *adj* ungulado. **2** *n* ungulado *m*.

unhallowed [ʌn'hæləud] *adj* no consagrado; (*fig*) profano.

unhampered [ʌn'hæmpəd] *adj* libre, sin estorbos; **— by** no estorbado por.

unhand [ʌn'hænd] *vt* soltar; **— me, sir!** ¡suélteme, señor!

unhandsome [ʌn'hænsəm] *adj* feo, nada atractivo.

unhandy [ʌn'hændi] *adj person* desmañado; *thing* incómodo; **to be — with something** ser desmañado en el manejo de algo.

unhappily [ʌn'hæpili] *adv* (*miserably*) infelizmente; (*unfortunately*) desgraciadamente.

unhappiness [ʌn'hæpinis] *n* desdicha *f*, tristeza *f*; desgracia *f*.

unhappy [ʌn'hæpi] *adj person* infeliz, desdichado; *childhood etc* desgraciado; (*ill-fated*) malhadado; *remark etc* inoportuno; **that — time** aquella triste época; **to be — about something** inquietarse por algo, no aceptar algo de buena gana; **we are — about the decision** no nos gusta la decisión; **to make someone —** poner triste a uno, amargar la vida a uno; **she was — in her marriage** era desgraciada en su matrimonio.

unharmed [ʌn'hɑːmd] *adj person* ileso, incólume; *thing* indemne; **to escape —** salir ileso.

unharness [ʌn'hɑːnis] *vt* desguarnecer.

unhealthy [ʌn'helθi] *adj person* enfermizo; *place* malsano, insalubre; *complexion* de aspecto poco sano; *curiosity* morboso.

unheard [ʌn'hɔːd] *adj:* **to condemn someone —** condenar a uno sin escuchar su defensa.

unheard-of [ʌn'hɔːdɔv] *adj* inaudito; **it's quite —** es totalmente inaudito.

unheeded [ʌn'hiːdid] *adj* desatendido; **the warning went —** nadie prestó atención a la advertencia, nadie hizo caso de la advertencia.

unheeding [ʌn'hiːdiŋ] *adj* desatento, sordo; **they passed by —** pasaron sin prestar atención.

unhelpful [ʌn'helpful] *adj person* poco servicial; *advice etc* inútil.

unhesitating [ʌn'heziteitiŋ] *adj person etc* resuelto; *reply etc* pronto.

unhesitatingly [ʌn'heziteitiŋli] *adv:* **he said —** dijo sin vacilar, dijo decidido.

unhindered [ʌn'hindəd] *adj* libre, sin estorbos; **— by** no estorbado por.

unhinge [ʌn'hindʒ] *vt* desquiciar; (*fig*) *mind* trastornar; *person* trastornar el juicio de.

unhistorical [ʌnhis'tɔrikəl] *adj* antihistórico, que no tiene nada de histórico.

unhitch [ʌn'hitʃ] *vt* desenganchar.

unholy [ʌn'həuli] *adj* impío; (*fam*) atroz.

unhook [ʌn'huk] *vt* desenganchar; (*from wall etc*) descolgar; *dress* desabrochar.

unhoped-for [ʌn'həuptfɔː*] *adj* inesperado.

unhopeful [ʌn'həupful] *adj* *prospect* poco prometedor; *person* pesimista.

unhorse [ʌn'hɔːs] *vt* desarzonar.

unhurried ['ʌn'hʌrid] *adj* lento, pausado, parsimonioso.

unhurriedly ['ʌn'hʌridli] *adv* lentamente, pausadamente, con parsimonia.

unhurt ['ʌn'həːt] *adj* ileso, incólume; **to escape —** salir ileso.

unhygienic ['ʌnhai'dʒiːnik] *adj* antihigiénico.

unicameral ['juːni'kæmərəl] *adj* unicameral.

unicellular ['juːni'seljulə*] *adj* unicelular.

unicorn ['juːnikɔːn] *n* unicornio *m*.

unidentified ['ʌnai'dentifaid] *adj* sin identificar, no identificado aún.

unification [ˌjuːnifi'keiʃən] *n* unificación *f*.

uniform ['juːnifɔːm] **1** *adj* uniforme; igual, constante; **to make something —** hacer algo uniforme, uniformar algo.
   2 *n* uniforme *m*; **in full —** de gran uniforme.

uniformed ['juːnifɔːmd] *adj* uniformado.

uniformity [ˌjuːni'fɔːmiti] *n* uniformidad *f*.

uniformly ['juːnifɔːmli] *adv* uniformemente, de modo uniforme.

unify ['juːnifai] *vt* unificar, unir.

unilateral ['juːni'lætərəl] *adj* unilateral.

unilaterally ['juːni'lætərəli] *adv* unilateralmente.

unimaginable [ˌʌni'mædʒinəbl] *adj* inimaginable.

unimaginative ['ʌni'mædʒinətiv] *adj* poco imaginativo.

unimpaired ['ʌnim'pɛəd] *adj* no disminuido; no afectado; intacto, entero.

unimpeachable [ˌʌnim'piːtʃəbl] *adj* irrecusable, intachable; **from an — source** de fuente fidedigna.

unimpeded ['ʌnim'piːdid] *adj* sin estorbo.

unimportant [ʌnim'pɔːtənt] *adj* sin importancia, insignificante.

unimposing ['ʌnim'pəuziŋ] *adj* poco impresionante.

unimpressed ['ʌnim'prest] *adj*: **he remained —** no se convenció; **I remain — by the new building** el nuevo edificio no me hace buena impresión.

unimpressive ['ʌnim'presiv] *adj* poco impresionante, poco convincente; *person* soso, insignificante.

unimproved ['ʌnim'pruːvd] *adj* no mejorado, sin mejora; tan malo (*or* defectuoso *etc*) como antes.

unincorporated [ˌʌnin'kɔːpəreitid] *adj* no incorporado.

uninfluenced ['ʌn'influənst] *adj*: **— by. any argument** no afectado por ningún argumento; **a style — by any other** un estilo no influido por ningún otro.

uninformed ['ʌnin'fɔːmd] *adj* *character* poco instruido, ignorante; **to be — about something** no estar enterado de algo, desconocer algo.

uninhabitable ['ʌnin'hæbitəbl] *adj* inhabitable.

uninhabited ['ʌnin'hæbitid] *adj* deshabitado, inhabitado; desierto.

uninhibited ['ʌnin'hibitid] *adj* nada cohibido, totalmente libre.

uninitiated [ʌni'niʃieitid] **1** *adj* no iniciado. **2** *n*: **the —** los no iniciados.

uninjured ['ʌn'indʒəd] *adj* ileso; **to escape —** salir ileso.

uninspired ['ʌnin'spaiəd] *adj* sin inspiración, soso, mediocre.

uninsured ['ʌnin'ʃuəd] *adj* no asegurado.

unintelligent ['ʌnin'telidʒənt] *adj* ininteligente.

unintelligibility ['ʌnin,telidʒə'biliti] *n* ininteligibilidad *f*, incomprensibilidad *f*.

unintelligible ['ʌnin'telidʒəbl] *adj* ininteligible, incomprensible.

unintelligibly ['ʌnin'telidʒəbli] *adv* de modo ininteligible, de modo incomprensible.

unintended ['ʌnin'tendid] *adj*, **unintentional** ['ʌnin'tenʃənl] *adj* involuntario, no intencional; **it was —** fue sin querer.

unintentionally ['ʌnin'tenʃnəli] *adv* sin querer.

uninterested [ʌn'intristid] *adj* sin interés; **to be — in a subject** no tener interés alguno en un asunto.

uninteresting ['ʌn'intristiŋ] *adj* poco interesante, falto de interés.

uninterrupted ['ʌn,intə'rʌptid] *adj* ininterrumpido.

uninterruptedly ['ʌn,intə'rʌptidli] *adv* ininterrumpidamente.

uninvited ['ʌnin'vaitid] *adj* *guest* no invitado; *comment* gratuito; **to do something —** hacer algo sin ser rogado; **they came to the party —** vinieron al guateque sin ser invitados.

uninviting ['ʌnin'vaitiŋ] *adj* poco atractivo.

union ['juːnjən] **1** *n* unión *f*; (*marriage*) enlace *m*; (*Pol*) sindicato *m*, gremio *m* obrero; (*Mech*) unión *f*, manguito *m* de unión; **customs —** unión *f* aduanera; **Universal Postal U—** Unión *f* Postal Universal; **the U—** (*USA*) la Unión.
   2 *attr* sindical, de los sindicatos, gremial; **— shop** taller *m* de obreros agremiados.

unionism ['juːnjənizəm] *n* *see* **trade unionism**; **U—** (*British Pol*) conservatismo *m*, Partido *m* Conservador.

unionist ['juːnjənist] *n* *see* **trade unionist**; **U—** (*British Pol*) conservador *m*, ora *f*.

unionize ['juːnjənaiz] **1** *vt* agremiar. **2** *vi* agremiarse.

Union Jack ['juːnjən'dʒæk] *n* bandera *del Reino Unido*.

Union of South Africa ['juːnjənəv,sauθ'æfrikə] Unión *f* Sudafricana.

Union of Soviet Socialist Republics ['juːnjənəv'səuviət'səuʃəlistri'pʌbliks] Unión *f* de Repúblicas Socialistas Soviéticas.

union suit ['juːnjənsuːt] *n* (*US*) traje *m* interior de una sola pieza.

unique [juː'niːk] *adj* único.

uniquely [juː'niːkli] *adv* especialmente.

uniqueness [juː'niːknis] *n* unicidad *f*; lo singular, lo incomparable; **because of its —** por su carácter incomparable.

unison ['juːnizn] *n* armonía *f*; (*Mus*) unisonancia *f*; **to sing in —** cantar al unísono; **to act in — with someone** obrar de acuerdo con uno.

unit ['juːnit] **1** *n* unidad *f* (*also* Math, Mil); (*Elec: measurement*) unidad *f*; (*Mech*, *Elec*) grupo *m*; **compressor —** grupo *m* compresor; **generating —** grupo *m* electrógeno; **mobile —** (*TV*) unidad *f* móvil; **monetary —** unidad *f* monetaria.
   2 *attr*: **— furniture** muebles *mpl* de elementos adicionales, muebles *mpl* combinados.

Unitarian [ˌjuːni'tɛəriən] **1** *adj* unitario. **2** *n* unitario *m*, a *f*.

Unitarianism [ˌjuːni'tɛəriənizəm] *n* unitarismo *m*.

unitary ['juːnitəri] *adj* unitario.

unite [juː'nait] **1** *vt* unir, juntar; (*marry*) casar; *parts of country* unificar.
   2 *vi* unirse, juntarse; **to — against someone** unirse para hacer frente a uno; **to — in doing something** unirse para hacer algo, concertarse para hacer algo.

united [juː'naitid] *adj* unido.

United Arab Republic [juː'naitid'ærəbri'pʌblik] República *f* Árabe Unida.

United Kingdom [juː'naitid'kiŋdəm] Reino *m* Unido (*Inglaterra, Gales, Escocia, Irlanda del Norte*).

United Nations [juː'naitid'neiʃənz] *pl* Naciones *fpl* Unidas.

United States (of America) [juː'naitid'steits-(əvə'merikə)] *pl* (Los) Estados *mpl* Unidos (de América).

unity ['juːniti] *n* unidad *f*; unión *f*; armonía *f*; **— is strength** la unión hace la fuerza; **— of place** unidad *f* de lugar; **— of time** unidad *f* de tiempo.

univalent ['juːni'veilənt] *adj* univalente.

univalve ['juːnivælv] **1** *adj* univalvo. **2** *n* molusco *m* univalvo.

universal [ˌjuːni'vəːsəl] *adj* universal; *joint, suffrage, union etc* universal; **a — favourite** una cosa querida de todos; **its use has been — since 1900** desde 1900 tiene un empleo general; **soap is now —** el jabón se emplea ahora en todas partes; **to become —** universalizarse, generalizarse; **to make — univer-**salizar, generalizar.

universality [ˌjuːnivəː'sæliti] *n* universalidad *f*.

universalize [ˌjuːni'vəːsəlaiz] *vt* universalizar.

universally [ˌjuːni'vəːsəli] *adj* universalmente; generalmente, comúnmente; **— known** mundialmente conocido.

universe ['juːnivəːs] *n* universo *m*.

university [ˌjuːni'vəːsiti] **1** *n* universidad *f*; **to be at —** estar en la universidad; **to go to —** ir a la universidad.
   2 *adj*, *attr degree, year etc* universitario; *professor, student* de universidad.

unjust ['ʌn'dʒʌst] *adj* injusto.

unjustifiable [ʌn'dʒʌstifaiəbl] *adj* injustificable.

unjustifiably [ʌn'dʒʌstifaiəbli] *adv* injustificadamente.

unjustified ['ʌn'dʒʌstifaid] *adj* injustificado.

unjustly ['ʌn'dʒʌstli] *adv* injustamente.

unkempt ['ʌn'kempt] *adj* *appearance* desaseado, descuidado; *hair* despeinado.

unkind [ʌn'kaind] *adj* (*of person etc*) poco amable, nada amistoso; poco compasivo; cruel, despiadado; *remark, word, blow* cruel; *climate* riguroso; **that was very — of him** en eso no se mostró nada amable; **he was — enough to + infin** fue lo bastante cruel como para + *infin*.

unkindly [ʌn'kaindli] *adv* cruelmente; **don't take it
— if . . .** no lo tome a mal si . . .
unkindness [ʌn'kaindnis] *n* falta *f* de amabilidad;
crueldad *f*, rigor *m*, severidad *f*; (*act*) acto *m* de
crueldad.
unknowable ['ʌn'nəuəbl] *adj* inconocible; insondable,
impenetrable; **the —** lo inconocible.
unknowingly ['ʌn'nəuiŋli] *adv* sin querer; sin
saberlo; **he did it all —** lo hizo sin darse cuenta en
absoluto de ello.
unknown ['ʌn'nəun] **1** *adj* desconocido, ignorado;
ignoto; incógnito; **the — soldier** el soldado desconocido; **towards — regions** hacia regiones
desconocidas; **a substance — to science** una sustancia
ignorada por la ciencia.
2 *adv*: **— to me** sin saberlo yo.
3 *n* (*person*) desconocido *m*, a *f*; (*Math, also fig*)
incógnita *f*; **the —** lo desconocido; **to go out into
the —** salir a explorar tierras incógnitas.
unlace ['ʌn'leis] *vt* desenlazar.
unladen ['ʌn'leidn] *adj* vacío, sin cargamento.
unladylike ['ʌn'leidilaik] *adj* vulgar, ordinario,
impropio de una señora.
unlamented ['ʌnlə'mentid] *adj* no llorado, no
lamentado.
unlatch ['ʌn'lætʃ] *vt* alzar el pestillo de, abrir
levantando el picaporte de.
unlawful ['ʌn'lɔ:ful] *adj* ilegal, ilícito.
unlawfully ['ʌn'lɔ:fəli] *adv* ilegalmente, ilícitamente.
unlearn ['ʌn'lə:n] *vt* desaprender, olvidar.
unlearned ['ʌn'lə:nid] *adj* indocto, ignorante.
unleash ['ʌn'li:ʃ] *vt dog* destraillar, soltar; (*fig*)
desencadenar, desatar.
unleavened ['ʌn'levnd] *adj* ázimo, sin levadura.
unless [ən'les] *conj* a menos que + *subj*; a no ser que
+ *subj*; **— you can find another one** a menos que
pueda encontrar otro; **— I am mistaken** si no me
equivoco; **— I hear to the contrary** a menos que
me digan lo contrario.
unlettered ['ʌn'letəd] *adj* indocto.
unlicensed ['ʌn'laisənst] *adj* sin permiso, sin licencia,
no autorizado.
unlike ['ʌn'laik] **1** *adj* desemejante, distinto; (*Math*)
de signo contrario; **they are quite —** son muy
distintos, no se parecen en nada.
2 *prep* a diferencia de; **it's quite — him** no es nada
característico de él; **the photo is quite — him** la
foto no le representa en absoluto; **I, — others, . . .**
yo, a diferencia de otros . . .
unlikelihood [ʌn'laiklihud] *n*, **unlikeliness** [ʌn-
'laiklinis] *n* improbabilidad *f*.
unlikely [ʌn'laikli] *adj* improbable, poco probable;
(*odd*) inverosímil; **it is most —** no es nada probable;
it is — that he will come, he is — to come no es
probable que venga; **wearing a most — hat** con un
sombrero inverosímil.
unlimited [ʌn'limitid] *adj* ilimitado, sin límite.
unlined ['ʌn'laind] *adj coat* sin forro; *face* sin arrugas;
paper sin rayar.
unlisted ['ʌn'listid] *adj* que no figura en una lista.
unlit ['ʌn'lit] *adj* oscuro, sin luz; *street* sin alumbrado,
sin faroles.
unload ['ʌn'ləud] **1** *vt* descargar; (*get rid of*) deshacerse. **2** *vi* descargar.
unlock ['ʌn'lɔk] *vt* abrir (con llave); *mystery etc*
resolver.
unlooked-for [ʌn'luktfɔ:*] *adj* inesperado, inopinado.
unloose ['ʌn'lu:s], **unloosen** [ʌn'lu:sn] *vt* aflojar,
soltar.
unlovable ['ʌn'lʌvəbl] *adj* poco apetecible, repugnante; *person* antipático.
unlovely ['ʌn'lʌvli] *adj* feo, desgarbado.
unloving ['ʌn'lʌviŋ] *adj* nada cariñoso.
unluckily [ʌn'lʌkili] *adv*: **— I couldn't go** desgraciadamente no pude ir; **it was — left at the
station** por desgracia quedó olvidado en la estación.
unluckiness [ʌn'lʌkinis] *n* mala suerte *f*; lo
nefasto.
unlucky [ʌn'lʌki] *adj person, stroke etc* desgraciado;
(*ill-omened*) funesto, nefasto; **a very — day** un día
de los menos propicios; **to be — (person)** tener mala
suerte; **I've been — all my life** toda la vida he sido
desgraciado; **how very —!** ¡qué mala suerte!;
it's — to go under ladders pasar por debajo de las
escaleras trae mala suerte.
unmake ['ʌn'meik] (*irr: see* **make**) *vt* deshacer.
unman ['ʌn'mæn] *vt* acobardar.
unmanageable [ʌn'mænidʒəbl] *adj* (*unwieldy*)
inmanejable, difícil de manejar; *person* indócil,
ingobernable.
unmanly ['ʌn'mænli] *adj* afeminado; cobarde.
unmannerly [ʌn'mænəli] *adj* descortés, mal educado.

unmarked ['ʌn'mɑːkt] *adj* sin marcar; (*uninjured*)
ileso; (*Sport*) desmarcado.
unmarketable ['ʌn'mɑːkitəbl] *adj* invendible.
unmarriageable ['ʌn'mæridʒəbl] *adj* incasable.
unmarried ['ʌn'mærid] *adj* soltero; **the — state** el
estado de soltero.
unmask ['ʌn'mɑːsk] **1** *vt* desenmascarar (*also fig*).
2 *vi* quitarse la máscara, descubrirse.
unmast ['ʌn'mɑːst] *vt* desarbolar.
unmatched ['ʌn'mætʃt] *adj* incomparable, sin par.
unmentionable [ʌn'menʃnəbl] **1** *adj* que no se puede
mencionar; indescriptible, indecible. **2 —s** *npl* (*hum*)
prendas *fpl* íntimas, pantalones *mpl*.
unmerciful [ʌn'mə:siful] *adj* despiadado.
unmercifully [ʌn'mə:sifəli] *adv* despiadadamente.
unmerited [ʌn'meritid] *adj* inmerecido.
unmethodical ['ʌnmi'θɔdikəl] *adj* poco metódico,
desordenado.
unmindful [ʌn'maindful] *adj*: **to be — of** no pensar
en; **he, — of the danger** él, sin pensar en el peligro.
unmistakable ['ʌnmis'teikəbl] *adj* inconfundible,
inequívoco.
unmistakably ['ʌnmis'teikəbli] *adv* de modo
inconfundible; **it is — mine** sin duda alguna es
mío.
unmitigated [ʌn'mitigeitid] *adj* no mitigado,
absoluto; *rogue etc* redomado.
unmixed ['ʌn'mikst] *adj* sin mezcla, puro.
unmolested ['ʌnmə'lestid] *adj* indemne.
unmortgaged ['ʌn'mɔ:gidʒd] *adj* libre de hipoteca.
unmotivated ['ʌn'məutiveitid] *adj* inmotivado, sin
motivo.
unmounted ['ʌn'mauntid] *adj rider* desmontado;
stone sin engastar; *photo, stamp* sin pegar.
unmourned ['ʌn'mɔ:nd] *adj* no llorado.
unmoved ['ʌn'mu:vd] *adj* impasible; **to remain —
by** no dejarse conmover por, seguir siendo insensible
a; **it leaves me —** me trae sin cuidado.
unmoving ['ʌn'mu:viŋ] *adj* inmóvil.
unmusical ['ʌn'mju:zikəl] *adj* (*Mus*) inarmónico;
person sin instinto musical, sin oído para la música.
unnamed ['ʌn'neimd] *adj* sin nombre.
unnatural [ʌn'nætʃrəl] *adj* antinatural, no natural,
contrario a la naturaleza; *anormal*; *habit, vice*
perverso; *person's manner* afectado.
unnavigable ['ʌn'nævigəbl] *adj* innavegable.
unnecessarily [ʌn'nesisərili] *adv* innecesariamente,
sin necesidad.
unnecessary [ʌn'nesisəri] *adj* innecesario, inútil;
it is — to add that . . . apenas hace falta añadir
que . . .
unneighbourly, (US) unneighborly ['ʌn'neibəli]
adj poco amistoso, impropio de un buen vecino.
unnerve ['ʌn'nə:v] *vt* acobardar.
unnoticed ['ʌn'nəutist] *adj* inadvertido, desapercibido; **to go —, to pass —** pasar inadvertido.
unnumbered ['ʌn'nʌmbəd] *adj* sin numerar;
(*countless*) innumerable.
unobjectionable ['ʌnəb'dʒekʃnəbl] *adj* intachable,
impecable; *person* aceptable; *person etc* inofensivo; **it
seems perfectly — to me** me parece perfectamente
aceptable.
unobservant ['ʌnəb'zə:vənt] *adj* distraído, que no
se fija.
unobserved ['ʌnəb'zə:vd] *adj* desapercibido; **to get
away —** lograr escapar inadvertido.
unobstructed ['ʌnəb'strʌktid] *adj* libre, sin obstáculos, despejado.
unobtainable ['ʌnəb'teinəbl] *adj* inasequible.
unobtrusive ['ʌnəb'tru:siv] *adj* discreto, modesto,
no demasiado visible.
unobtrusively ['ʌnəb'tru:sivli] *adv* discretamente,
modestamente.
unoccupied ['ʌn'ɔkjupaid] *adj house* deshabitado;
territory despoblado, sin habitantes, (*Pol*) sin
colonizar; *seat, place* libre; *post* vacante; *person*
desocupado, ocioso.
unofficial ['ʌnə'fiʃəl] *adj* extraoficial, no oficial.
unofficially ['ʌnə'fiʃəli] *adv* de modo extraoficial.
unopened ['ʌn'əupənd] *adj* sin abrir.
unopposed ['ʌnə'pəuzd] *adj* sin oposición; (*Mil*) sin
encontrar resistencia; **to be returned — (Parl)**
ganar un escaño por ser el único candidato que
se presenta.
unorganized ['ʌn'ɔ:gənaizd] *adj* no organizado.
unoriginal ['ʌnə'ridʒinəl] *adj* poco original.
unorthodox ['ʌn'ɔ:θədɔks] *adj* poco ortodoxo, nada
convencional; (*Eccl*) heterodoxo.
unostentatious ['ʌn,ɔsten'teiʃəs] *adj* modesto, sin
ostentación.
unpack ['ʌn'pæk] **1** *vt* desembalar, desempaquetar;
suitcase vaciar, deshacer. **2** *vi* deshacer las maletas.

unpaid ['ʌn'peid] *adj* bill por pagar, no pagado; *debt* no liquidado; *work, person* no retribuido.

unpalatable [ʌn'pælitəbl] *adj* food incomible, de mal sabor; (fig) desagradable, intragable, nada grato; **the — truth** la verdad lisa y llana.

unparalleled [ʌn'pærəleld] *adj* incomparable, sin par; sin precedentes; **this is — in our history** esto no tiene precedentes en nuestra historia.

unpardonable [ʌn'pɑːdnəbl] *adj* imperdonable, indisculpable.

unparliamentary ['ʌn,pɑːlə'mentəri] *adj* antiparlamentario.

unpatented ['ʌn'peitntid] *adj* sin patentar.

unpatriotic ['ʌn,pætri'ɔtik] *adj* antipatriótico.

unpatriotically ['ʌn,pætri'ɔtikəli] *adv* de modo antipatriótico.

unpaved ['ʌn'peivd] *adj* sin pavimentar.

unperceived ['ʌnpə'siːvd] *adj* inadvertido, desapercibido.

unperturbed ['ʌnpə'təːbd] *adj* impertérrito; **he carried on** — continuó sin alterarse, siguió sin inmutarse; **— by this disaster ...** sin dejarse desanimar por esta catástrofe ...

unpick ['ʌn'pik] *vt* seam descoser.

unpin ['ʌn'pin] *vt* desprender; quitar los alfileres de.

unplaced ['ʌn'pleist] *adj* (Sport) no colocado.

unpleasant [ʌn'plezht] *adj* desagradable; repugnante; person (by character) antipático, (in words etc) grosero, mal educado; **he was — to her** se portó groseramente con ella; **he had some very — things to say** hizo unas observaciones de las más desagradables; **it was a most — hour** fue una hora muy desagradable.

unpleasantly [ʌn'plezntli] *adv* desagradablemente; **"No", he said —** "No", dijo en tono más amistoso; **the bomb fell — close** cayó la bomba lo bastante cerca como para inquietarnos.

unpleasantness [ʌn'plezntnis] *n* lo desagradable; lo repugnante; antipatía *f*; (quarrel) desavenencia *f*, disgusto *m*; **that — with the conductor** aquel disgusto con el cobrador; **there has been a lot of —** ha habido muchos disgustos.

unpleasing [ʌn'pliːzin] *adj* poco atractivo, antiestético.

unplug ['ʌn'plʌg] *vt* desenchufar, desconectar.

unplumbed ['ʌn'plʌmd] *adj* no sondado.

unpoetic(al) ['ʌnpəu'etik(əl)] *adj* poco poético.

unpolished ['ʌn'pɔliʃt] *adj* sin pulir; diamond en bruto; (fig) grosero, tosco, inculto.

unpolluted ['ʌnpə'luːtid] *adj* impoluto.

unpopular ['ʌn'pɔpjulə*] *adj* impopular, poco popular; **it is — with the miners** los mineros no lo quieren; **the decision is —** la decisión resulta inaceptable; **to make oneself —** hacerse detestar; **you will be very — with me** no se lo agradeceré.

unpopularity ['ʌn,pɔpju'læriti] *n* impopularidad *f*.

unpractical ['ʌn'præktikəl] *adj* falto de sentido práctico, poco práctico, desmañado.

unpractised, (US) unpracticed [ʌn'præktist] *adj* inexperto.

unprecedented [ʌn'presidəntid] *adj* sin precedentes, inaudito.

unpredictable ['ʌnpri'diktəbl] *adj* thing impredictible, incierto; person imprevisible, voluble, de reacciones imprevisibles, desconcertante.

unprejudiced [ʌn'predʒudist] *adj* imparcial.

unpremeditated ['ʌnpri'mediteitid] *adj* impremeditado.

unprepared ['ʌnpri'pɛəd] *adj* no preparado; speech etc improvisado; **to be — for something** no contar con algo, no esperar algo; **to catch someone —** coger a uno desprevenido.

unpreparedness ['ʌnpri'pɛəridnis] *n* desapercibimiento *m*, desprevención *f*.

unprepossessing ['ʌn,priːpə'zesin] *adj* poco atractivo.

unpresentable ['ʌnpri'zentəbl] *adj* mal apersonado.

unpretentious ['ʌnpri'tenʃəs] *adj* modesto, sin pretensiones.

unprincipled [ʌn'prinsipld] *adj* poco escrupuloso, cínico, sin conciencia.

unprintable ['ʌn'printəbl] *adj* intranscribible.

unproductive ['ʌnprə'dʌktiv] *adj* soil etc improductivo; meeting etc infructuoso.

unprofessional ['ʌnprə'feʃənl] *adj* (ethically) indigno de su profesión; contrario a la ética profesional; (unskilled) inexperto.

unprofitable [ʌn'prɔfitəbl] *adj* enterprise improductivo; meeting etc infructuoso; (useless) inútil; (financially) poco provechoso, nada lucrativo.

unpromising ['ʌn'prɔmisin] *adj* poco prometedor; **it looks —** no promete mucho.

unpronounceable ['ʌnprə'naunsəbl] *adj* impronunciable.

unpropitious ['ʌnprə'piʃəs] *adj* impropicio, poco propicio.

unprotected ['ʌnprə'tektid] *adj* sin protección, indefenso.

unproved ['ʌn'pruːvd] *adj* no probado.

unprovided ['ʌnprə'vaidid] *adj*: **— for** (unforeseen) imprevisto; (person) desamparado, desvalido; **— with** desprovisto de.

unprovoked ['ʌnprə'vəukt] *adj* no provocado, sin provocación.

unpublished ['ʌn'pʌbliʃt] *adj* inédito.

unpunctual ['ʌn'pʌŋktjuəl] *adj* impuntual, poco puntual; **this train is always —** este tren siempre llega con retraso.

unpunctuality ['ʌn,pʌŋktju'æliti] *n* impuntualidad *f*.

unpunished ['ʌn'pʌniʃt] *adj* impune; **to go —** (crime) quedar sin castigo; (person) escapar sin castigo, salir impune.

unqualified ['ʌn'kwɔlifaid] *adj* person incompetente; teacher sin título; workman no cualificado; success, assertion incondicional; praise grande; **to be — to do something** no reunir las condiciones para hacer algo.

unquenchable [ʌn'kwentʃəbl] *adj* (fig) inextinguible; thirst inapagable; desire etc insaciable.

unquestionable [ʌn'kwestʃənəbl] *adj* incuestionable, indiscutible.

unquestionably [ʌn'kwestʃənəbli] *adv* indudablemente.

unquestioned [ʌn'kwestʃənd] *adj* incontestable.

unquestioning [ʌn'kwestʃənin] *adj* incondicional; faith etc ciego.

unquiet [ʌn'kwaiət] *adj* inquieto.

unquote ['ʌn'kwəut] *n*: **"—"** "fin *m* de la cita".

unquoted ['ʌn'kwəutid] *adj* (Fin) no cotizado.

unravel [ʌn'rævəl] *vt* desenmarañar (also fig).

unread ['ʌn'red] *adj* no leído; **to leave something —** dejar algo sin leer.

unreadable ['ʌn'riːdəbl] *adj* ilegible; (fig) imposible de leer, de lectura muy pesada; **I found the book —** el libro me resultó pesadísimo.

unreadiness ['ʌn'redinis] *n* desapercibimiento *m*; desprevención *f*.

unready ['ʌn'redi] *adj* desapercibido, desprevenido.

unreal ['ʌn'riəl] *adj* irreal; imaginario, ilusorio.

unrealistic ['ʌnriə'listik] *adj* ilusorio, fantástico; estimate etc no basado en los hechos, que no tiene que ver con la realidad; scheme impracticable; person poco realista.

unreality ['ʌnri'æliti] *n* irrealidad *f*.

unrealizable ['ʌnriə'laizəbl] *adj* irrealizable.

unrealized ['ʌn'riːəlaizd] *adj* no realizado, que ha quedado sin realizar; objective no logrado.

unreason ['ʌn'riːzn] *n* insensatez *f*.

unreasonable [ʌn'riːznəbl] *adj* irrazonable, poco razonable; demand etc excesivo; **he was most — about it** se negó a considerarlo razonablemente; **don't be so —!** ¡no seas tan porfiado!; ¡no te pongas así!

unreasonableness [ʌn'riːznəblnis] *n* irracionalidad *f*; exorbitancia *f*, lo excesivo; (of person) porfía *f*.

unreasonably [ʌn'riːznəbli] *adv*: **to be — difficult about something** porfiar estúpidamente en algo.

unreclaimed ['ʌnri'kleimd] *adj* land no rescatado, no utilizado.

unrecognizable ['ʌn'rekəgnaizəbl] *adj* irreconocible.

unrecognized ['ʌn'rekəgnaizd] *adj* no reconocido; **he went — through the market** atravesó el mercado sin que nadie le conociese.

unrecorded ['ʌnri'kɔːdid] *adj* no registrado, de que no hay constancia.

unredeemed ['ʌnri'diːmd] *adj* no redimido; promise sin cumplir, incumplido; pledge no desempeñado; **— by** no mitigado por.

unreel [ʌn'riəl] *vt* desenrollar.

unrefined ['ʌnri'faind] *adj* material no refinado; (fig) inculto.

unreflecting ['ʌnri'flektin] *adj* irreflexivo.

unreformed ['ʌnri'fɔːmd] *adj* no reformado.

unregarded ['ʌnri'gɑːdid] *adj* desatendido, no estimado; **those — aspects** aquellos aspectos de los que nadie hace caso.

unregenerate ['ʌnri'dʒenərit] *adj* empedernido.

unregistered ['ʌn'redʒistəd] *adj* no registrado; letter sin certificar.

unregretted ['ʌnri'gretid] *adj* no llorado, no lamentado.

unrehearsed ['ʌnri'həːst] *adj* speech etc improvisado; incident imprevisto.

unrelated [ˌʌnri'leitid] *adj* inconexo.
unrelenting [ˌʌnri'lentiŋ] *adj* inexorable, implacable.
unreliable [ˌʌnri'laiəbl] *adj person* informal, de poca confianza; *news* nada fidedigno; *machine, service etc* en lo que no se puede confiar del todo.
unrelieved [ˌʌnri'liːvd] *adj* absoluto, monótono, total; — **by** no aliviado por, no mitigado por; **3 hours of** — **boredom** 3 horas de aburrimiento total.
unremitting [ˌʌnri'mitiŋ] *adj* infatigable, incansable.
unremittingly [ˌʌnri'mitiŋli] *adv* incansablemente.
unremunerative [ˌʌnri'mjuːnərətiv] *adj* poco provechoso, infructuoso; *(financially)* poco lucrativo.
unrepealed [ˌʌnri'piːld] *adj* no revocado.
unrepeatable [ˌʌnri'piːtəbl] *adj* que no puede repetirse; **what he said is quite** — no me atrevo a repetir lo que me dijo.
unrepentant [ˌʌnri'pentənt] *adj* impenitente.
unrepresentative [ˌʌnˌrepri'zentətiv] *adj assembly etc* poco representativo; *(untypical)* poco típico, nada característico.
unrepresented [ˌʌnˌrepri'zentid] *adj* sin representación; **they are** — **in the House** no tienen representación en la Cámara.
unrequited [ˌʌnri'kwaitid] *adj* no correspondido.
unreserved [ˌʌnri'zɔːvd] *adj* no reservado, libre.
unreservedly [ˌʌnri'zɔːvidli] *adv* sin reserva, incondicionalmente.
unresisting [ˌʌnri'zistiŋ] *adj* sumiso.
unresolved [ˌʌnri'zɔlvd] *adj problem* no resuelto, pendiente.
unresponsive [ˌʌnris'pɔnsiv] *adj* insensible, sordo *(to a)*.
unrest [ʌn'rest] *n* malestar *m*, inquietud *f*; *(Pol)* desasosiego *m*, *(active)* desorden *m*; **the** — **in the Congo** los disturbios del Congo.
unrestrained [ˌʌnri'streind] *adj* desenfrenado, desembarazado (de trabas); *language, remarks* libre.
unrestricted [ˌʌnri'striktid] *adj* sin restricción, libre.
unrevealed [ˌʌnri'viːld] *adj* no revelado.
unrewarded [ˌʌnri'wɔːdid] *adj* sin recompensa, sin premio; **his work went** — su labor quedó sin recompensa.
unrewarding [ˌʌnri'wɔːdiŋ] *adj* sin provecho, infructuoso, inútil.
unrighteous [ʌn'raitʃəs] *adj* malo, perverso.
unripe [ʌn'raip] *adj* verde, inmaturo.
unrivalled [ʌn'raivəld] *adj* sin par, incomparable; **Bilbao is** — **for food** la cocina bilbaína es incomparable.
unroll [ʌn'rəul] **1** *vt* desenrollar. **2** *vi* desenrollarse.
unromantic [ˌʌnrə'mæntik] *adj* poco romántico.
unroof [ʌn'ruːf] *vt* destechar, quitar el techo de.
unrope [ʌn'rəup] **1** *vt* desatar. **2** *vi* desatarse.
unruffled [ʌn'rʌfld] *adj person* imperturbable, ecuánime; *hair, surface* liso; **he carried on quite** — siguió sin inmutarse.
unruled [ʌn'ruːld] *adj paper* sin rayar.
unruly [ʌn'ruːli] *adj* revoltoso, ingobernable; *hair* despeinado.
unsaddle [ʌn'sædl] *vt rider* desarzonar; *horse* desensillar, quitar la silla a.
unsafe [ʌn'seif] *adj machine, car etc* inseguro; *policy, journey* peligroso, arriesgado; — **to eat** malo para comer; — **to drink** malo para beber; **it is** — **to rely on it** no se puede contar con eso; **it is** — **to let him have a gun** es peligroso permitirle llevar escopeta.
unsaid [ʌn'sed] *adj* sin decir, sin expresar; **to leave something** — callar algo, dejar de decir algo; **much was left** — se dejaron de decir muchas cosas.
unsalaried [ʌn'sælərid] *adj* sin sueldo, no remunerado.
unsal(e)able [ʌn'seiləbl] *adj* invendible.
unsatisfactory [ˌʌnˌsætis'fæktəri] *adj* insatisfactorio.
unsatisfied [ʌn'sætisfaid] *adj* insatisfecho.
unsatisfying [ʌn'sætisfaiiŋ] *adj* que no satisface, insuficiente.
unsavoury, *(US)* **unsavory** [ʌn'seivəri] *adj* desagradable, repugnante; *person* indeseable.
unsay [ʌn'sei] *(irr: see* **say***) vt* desdecirse de.
unscathed [ʌn'skeiðd] *adj* ileso; **to get out** — salir ileso.
unscholarly [ʌn'skɔləli] *adj person* nada erudito; poco metódico; *work* indigno de un erudito.
unschooled [ʌn'skuːld] *adj* indocto; no instruido, sin instrucción; **to be** — **in a technique** no haber aprendido nada de una técnica.
unscientific [ˌʌnˌsaiən'tifik] *adj* poco científico.
unscramble [ʌn'skræmbl] *vt message* descifrar.
unscrew [ʌn'skruː] *vt* destornillar.

unscrupulous [ʌn'skruːpjuləs] *adj* poco escrupuloso, sin escrúpulos, desaprensivo.
unscrupulously [ʌn'skruːpjuləsli] *adv* de modo poco escrupuloso.
unscrupulousness [ʌn'skruːpjuləsnis] *n* falta *f* de escrúpulos, desaprensión *f*.
unseal [ʌn'siːl] *vt* desellar, abrir.
unseaworthy [ʌn'siːˌwəːði] *adj* innavegable.
unseemliness [ʌn'siːmlinis] *n* lo indecoroso, falta *f* de decoro.
unseemly [ʌn'siːmli] *adj* indecoroso.
unseen [ʌn'siːn] **1** *adj* invisible; secreto, oculto; inadvertido; *translation* hecho a primera vista; **he managed to get through** — logró pasar inadvertido.
   2 *n* traducción *f* hecha a primera vista; **the** — lo invisible, lo oculto.
unselfish [ʌn'selfiʃ] *adj* desinteresado; abnegado; altruista.
unselfishly [ʌn'selfiʃli] *adv* desinteresadamente; abnegadamente; de modo altruista, con altruismo.
unselfishness [ʌn'selfiʃnis] *n* desinterés *m*; abnegación *f*; altruismo *m*.
unserviceable [ʌn'sɔːvisəbl] *adj* inservible, inútil.
unsettle [ʌn'setl] *vt* perturbar, agitar, inquietar.
unsettled [ʌn'setld] *adj person* inquieto, intranquilo; *weather* variable; *state, market* inestable; *land* inhabitado, despoblado, no colonizado; *question* pendiente; *account* no pagar; **he's feeling** — **in his job** no está del todo contento en su puesto, se siente algo molesto en su puesto.
unsettling [ʌn'setliŋ] *adj influence etc* perturbador.
unsex [ʌn'seks] *vt* privar de la sexualidad, suprimir el instinto sexual de.
unshackle [ʌn'ʃækl] *vt* desencadenar, quitar los grillos a.
unshakeable [ʌn'ʃeikəbl] *adj resolve* inquebrantable; **he was** — **in his resolve** se mostró totalmente resuelto; **after 3 hours he was still** — después de 3 horas siguió tan resuelto como antes.
unshaken [ʌn'ʃeikən] *adj* impertérrito; **he was** — **by what had happened** no se dejó amedrentar por lo que había pasado.
unshaven [ʌn'ʃeivn] *adj* sin afeitar.
unsheathe [ʌn'ʃiːð] *vt* desenvainar.
unship [ʌn'ʃip] *vt goods* desembarcar; *rudder, mast etc* desmontar.
unshod [ʌn'ʃɔd] *adj* descalzo; *horse* desherrado.
unshrinkable [ʌn'ʃriŋkəbl] *adj* inencogible.
unshrinking [ʌn'ʃriŋkiŋ] *adj* impávido.
unsighted [ʌn'saitid] *adj*: **I was** — **for a moment** por un momento no pude ver, por un momento tuve la vista impedida.
unsightly [ʌn'saitli] *adj* feo, repugnante.
unsigned [ʌn'saind] *adj* sin firmar.
unsinkable [ʌn'siŋkəbl] *adj* insumergible.
unskilled [ʌn'skild] *adj worker* no cualificado.
unskil(l)ful [ʌn'skilful] *adj* inexperto, desmañado.
unskimmed [ʌn'skimd] *adj* sin desnatar.
unsociability [ˌʌnˌsəuʃə'biliti] *n* insociabilidad *f*.
unsociable [ʌn'səuʃəbl] *adj* insociable.
unsold [ʌn'səuld] *adj* sin vender; **to remain** — quedar sin vender.
unsoldierly [ʌn'səuldʒəli] *adj* indigno de un militar.
unsolicited [ˌʌnsə'lisitid] *adj* no solicitado.
unsolvable [ʌn'sɔlvəbl] *adj* irresoluble.
unsolved [ʌn'sɔlvd] *adj* no resuelto.
unsophisticated [ˌʌnsə'fistikeitid] *adj* sencillo, cándido.
unsought [ʌn'sɔːt] *adj* no solicitado; no buscado; **the offer came quite** — se hizo la oferta sin que se hubiera pedido nada.
unsound [ʌn'saund] *adj* *(in construction)* defectuoso; *fruit* podrido; *argument, opinion* falso, erróneo; **of** — **mind** mentalmente incapacitado; **the book is** — **on some points** no hay que fiarse del libro en ciertos aspectos, el libro tiene algunas cosas erróneas.
unsoundness [ʌn'saundnis] *n* lo defectuoso; falsedad *f*, lo erróneo.
unsparing [ʌn'spɛəriŋ] *adj* *(generous)* generoso, pródigo; *effort* incansable; *(cruel)* despiadado; **to be** — **of praises** no escatimar las alabanzas; **to be** — **in one's efforts to** + *infin* no regatear ningún esfuerzo por + *infin*.
unsparingly [ʌn'spɛəriŋli] *adv* generosamente, pródigamente; incansablemente.
unspeakable [ʌn'spiːkəbl] *adj* indecible; *(very bad)* horrible.
unspeakably [ʌn'spiːkəbli] *adv*: **to suffer** — sufrir lo indecible; **it was** — **bad** fue horroroso.
unspecified [ʌn'spesifaid] *adj* no especificado.

unspent ['ʌn'spent] *adj* no gastado.

unsplinterable ['ʌn'splintərəbl] *adj* inastillable.

unspoiled, unspoilt ['ʌn'spɔilt] *adj* intacto; no estropeado; *child* natural, no mimado; *countryside* que conserva sus encantos, que sigue en su estado natural.

unspoken ['ʌn'spəukən] *adj* no expresado, tácito.

unsporting ['ʌn'spɔːtiŋ] *adj*, **unsportsmanlike** ['ʌn'spɔːtsmənlaik] *adj* antideportivo.

unspotted ['ʌn'spɔtid] *adj* sin manchas, inmaculado.

unstable ['ʌn'steibl] *adj* inestable.

unstamped ['ʌn'stæmpt] *adj* sin sello, sin franquear.

unstatesmanlike ['ʌn'steitsmənlaik] *adj* indigno de un estadista.

unsteadiness ['ʌn'stedinis] *n* inestabilidad *f*, inseguridad *f*; inconstancia *f*; lo movedizo, falta *f* de firmeza.

unsteady ['ʌn'stedi] *adj* inestable, inseguro; inconstante; (*shaky*) movedizo, poco firme; **to be — on one's feet** no poder estar de pie sin tambalearse.

unstick ['ʌn'stik] *vt* despegar.

unstinted [ʌn'stintid] *adj praise etc* generoso; *effort* incansable.

unstinting [ʌn'stintiŋ] *adj*: **to be — in one's praise** no escatimar sus alabanzas; **to be — in one's efforts to** + *infin* no regatear ningún esfuerzo por + *infin*.

unstitch ['ʌn'stitʃ] *vt* descoser; **to come —ed** descoserse.

unstop ['ʌn'stɔp] *vt* desobstruir, desatascar.

unstoppable ['ʌn'stɔpəbl] *adj* incontenible, irrefrenable; (*Sport*) *shot etc* imparable.

unstressed ['ʌn'strest] *adj* átono, inacentuado.

unstring ['ʌn'striŋ] (*irr: see* **string**) *vt* (*Mus*) desencordar; *nerves* trastornar; *pearls* desensartar.

unstuck ['ʌn'stʌk] *adj*: **to come —** despegarse, desprenderse, soltarse; (*fig*) fracasar; sufrir un revés.

unstudied ['ʌn'stʌdid] *adj* natural, sin afectación.

unsubdued ['ʌnsəb'djuːd] *adj* indomado.

unsubmissive ['ʌnsəb'misiv] *adj* insumiso.

unsubstantial ['ʌnsəb'stænʃəl] *adj* insustancial.

unsuccessful ['ʌnsək'sesful] *adj person, negotiation etc* fracasado; *effort etc* infructuoso, inútil, ineficaz; **to be —** fracasar, malograrse, no tener éxito; **to be — in doing something** no lograr hacer algo, fracasar en sus esfuerzos por hacer algo.

unsuccessfully ['ʌnsək'sesfəli] *adv* en vano, sin éxito, inútilmente.

unsuitability ['ʌn,suːtə'biliti] *n* impropiedad *f*; inconveniencia *f*; lo inadecuado; lo inoportuno; incompetencia *f*; **his — for the post** su incompetencia para el puesto.

unsuitable ['ʌn'suːtəbl] *adj* inapropiado; inconveniente; inadecuado; inoportuno; (*in a post etc*) incompetente; **a most — word** una palabra sumamente impropia; **he married a most — girl** se casó con una chica nada conveniente; **the film is — for children** la película no es apta para menores.

unsuited ['ʌn'suːtid] *adj*: **— for** inapto para; **— to do something** inapto para hacer algo; **they are — to each other** no están hechos el uno para el otro.

unsullied ['ʌn'sʌlid] *adj* inmaculado, no corrompido; **— by** no corrompido por.

unsung ['ʌn'sʌŋ] *adj* desconocido, que no recibe los elogios que merece.

unsupported ['ʌnsə'pɔːtid] *adj statement etc* que carece de base firme, no apoyado por datos; *candidate* sin apoyo, no respaldado por nadie.

unsure ['ʌn'ʃuə*] *adj* poco seguro; **he seemed very — about it** no parecía estar muy seguro de ello.

unsurmountable ['ʌnsə'mauntəbl] *adj* insuperable.

unsurpassable ['ʌnsə'pɑːsəbl] *adj* inmejorable, insuperable.

unsurpassed ['ʌnsə'pɑːst] *adj* insuperado, sin par; **— in quality** de calidad inmejorable; **— by anybody** no superado por nadie.

unsuspected ['ʌnsəs'pektid] *adj* insospechado.

unsuspecting ['ʌnsəs'pektiŋ] *adj* nada suspicaz, sin recelo, confiado, inocente.

unsweetened ['ʌn'swiːtnd] *adj* sin azucarar.

unswerving [ʌn'swəːviŋ] *adv resolve* inquebrantable; *loyalty* inquebrantable, firme; *course* sin vacilar.

unswervingly [ʌn'swəːviŋli] *adv*: **to be — loyal to someone** seguir totalmente leal a uno; **to hold — to one's course** seguir sin vacilar.

unsympathetic ['ʌn,simpə'θetik] *adj* incompasivo, poco compasivo; falto de comprensión; **he was totally —** no mostró la más mínima comprensión; **they were — to my plea** no hicieron caso de mi ruego; **I am not — to your request** no veo con malos ojos su petición.

unsystematic ['ʌn,sisti'mætik] *adj* poco metódico.

unsystematically ['ʌn,sisti'mætikəli] *adv* de modo poco metódico.

untainted ['ʌn'teintid] *adj* inmaculado, no corrompido; **— by** no corrompido por.

untam(e)able ['ʌn'teiməbl] *adj* indomable.

untamed ['ʌn'teimd] *adj* indomado.

untangle ['ʌn'tæŋgl] *vt* desenmarañar.

untanned ['ʌn'tænd] *adj* sin curtir.

untapped ['ʌn'tæpt] *adj resources* sin explotar.

untarnished ['ʌn'tɑːniʃt] *adj reputation etc* sin tacha.

untasted ['ʌn'teistid] *adj* sin probar.

untaught ['ʌn'tɔːt] *adj* no enseñado.

untaxed ['ʌn'tækst] *adj* libre de impuestos, no sujeto a contribuciones.

unteachable ['ʌn'tiːtʃəbl] *adj* demasiado estúpido para aprender nada.

untempered ['ʌn'tempəd] *adj steel etc* sin templar.

untenable ['ʌn'tenəbl] *adj* insostenible.

untenanted ['ʌn'tenəntid] *adj* desocupado.

untested ['ʌn'testid] *adj* no probado.

unthinkable [ʌn'θiŋkəbl] *adj* inconcebible, impensable; **it is — that . . .** es inconcebible que + *subj*.

unthinking ['ʌn'θiŋkiŋ] *adj* irreflexivo.

unthinkingly ['ʌn'θiŋkiŋli] *adv* irreflexivamente, sin pensar.

unthread ['ʌn'θred] *vt cloth* deshebrar, descoser; *needle* desenhebrar; *pearls* desensartar.

unthrifty ['ʌn'θrifti] *adj* manirroto, derrochador.

untidily [ʌn'taidili] *adv* desaliñadamente; sin método; en desorden; **she does everything —** todo lo hace de cualquier modo.

untidiness [ʌn'taidinis] *n* desaliño *m*; falta *f* de método; desorden *m*.

untidy [ʌn'taidi] *adj* (*in dress, appearance*) desaliñado, desaseado; *work* poco metódico; *room* en desorden; **she's a very — person** es una persona que vive sin método, es una persona que hace las cosas (*or* deja sus cosas) de cualquier modo, es una persona desordenada.

untie ['ʌn'tai] *vt* desatar.

until [ən'til] **1** *prep* hasta; **— 10** hasta las 10; **— his arrival** hasta su llegada.
   2 *conj* (**a**) (*of future time*) hasta que + *subj*, eg **wait — I get back** espera hasta que yo vuelva.
   (**b**) (*of past time*) hasta que + *indic*, eg **he did nothing — I told him** no hizo nada hasta que yo se lo dije.

untilled ['ʌn'tild] *adj* sin cultivar.

untimely [ʌn'taimli] *adj* intempestivo, inoportuno; prematuro.

untiring [ʌn'taiəriŋ] *adj* incansable.

untiringly [ʌn'taiəriŋli] *adv* incansablemente.

unto ['ʌntu] *prep* (*arch*) *see* **to**; **towards**.

untold ['ʌn'təuld] *adj story* nunca contado, inédito; *secret* nunca revelado; *loss, wealth etc* incalculable; *suffering* indecible.

untouchable [ʌn'tʌtʃəbl] (*India*) **1** *adj* intocable. **2** *n* intocable *mf*.

untouched ['ʌn'tʌtʃt] *adj* intacto; (*safe*) incólume, indemne; **a product — by human hand** un producto que ninguna mano humana ha tocado; **he is — by any plea** es insensible a todas las súplicas; **to leave one's food —** dejar su comida sin probar; **those peoples — by civilization** esos pueblos no influidos por la civilización.

untoward [,ʌntə'wɔːd] *adj* desfavorable; adverso; *event etc* fatal, funesto.

untrained ['ʌn'treind] *adj person* inexperto; (*unskilled*) no cualificado; *teacher etc* sin título, que no tiene título; (*Sport*) no entrenado; *animal* sin amaestrar, no adiestrado.

untransferable ['ʌntræns'fəːrəbl] *adj* intransferible.

untranslatable ['ʌntræns'leitəbl] *adj* intraducible.

untravelled ['ʌn'trævld] *adj place* inexplorado; *road etc* no trillado, poco frecuentado; *person* que no ha viajado.

untried ['ʌn'traid] *adj* (**a**) *method etc* no probado; *person* novicio, no puesto a prueba; *soldier* bisoño. (**b**) (*Law*) *person* no procesado, *case* no visto.

untrodden ['ʌn'trɔdn] *adj* no trillado.

untroubled ['ʌn'trʌbld] *adj* tranquilo; **— by thoughts of her** sin pensar en ella para nada, no afectado por ningún recuerdo de ella.

untrue ['ʌn'truː] *adj statement etc* falso; *world etc* ficticio, imaginario; *person* infiel, desleal; **that is wholly —** eso es completamente falso.

untrustworthy ['ʌn'trʌst,wəːði] *adj person* informal, indigno de confianza; *source etc* no fidedigno; *book etc* de dudosa autoridad; *machine, car* inseguro.

untruth ['ʌn'truːθ] *n*, *pl* **—truths** [truːðz] mentira *f*.

untruthful [ʌn'truːθful] *adj* mentiroso, falso.
untruthfully [ʌn'truːθfəli] *adv* falsamente.
untruthfulness [ʌn'truːθfulnis] *n* falsedad *f*.
untutored [ʌn'tjuːtəd] *adj* indocto, poco instruido.
untwine [ʌn'twain] *vt*, **untwist** [ʌn'twist] *vt* destorcer.
unusable [ʌn'juːzəbl] *adj* inservible, inútil.
unused [ʌn'juːzd] *adj* *stamp etc* nuevo, sin usar; sin estrenar.
unused [ʌn'juːst] *adj*: **to be —** to no estar acostumbrado a.
unusual [ʌn'juːʒuəl] *adj* insólito, poco común, extraordinario.
unusually [ʌn'juːʒuəli] *adv*: **an — awkward matter** un asunto extraordinariamente difícil; **an — gifted man** un hombre de talentos poco comunes.
unutterable [ʌn'ʌtərəbl] *adj* indecible.
unutterably [ʌn'ʌtərəbli] *adv* indeciblemente.
unvaried [ʌn'veərid] *adj* sin variación, constante; *(pej)* monótono.
unvarnished [ʌn'vɑːniʃt] *adj* sin barnizar; *(fig)* sencillo, llano, sin adornos; **the — truth** la verdad lisa y llana.
unvarying [ʌn'veəriiŋ] *adj* invariable, constante.
unveil [ʌn'veil] *vt* quitar el velo a; *statue etc* descubrir.
unventilated [ʌn'ventileitid] *adj* sin ventilación, sin aire.
unverifiable [ʌn'verifaiəbl] *adj* que no puede verificarse.
unverified [ʌn'verifaid] *adj* sin verificar.
unversed [ʌn'vɜːst] *adj*: **—** in poco ducho en.
unvisited [ʌn'vizitid] *adj* no visitado, no frecuentado.
unvoiced [ʌn'vɔist] *adj* no expresado; *(Gram)* sordo.
unvouched-for [ʌn'vautʃfɔː*] *adj* no garantizado.
unwanted [ʌn'wɔntid] *adj* superfluo; *child* no deseado.
unwarily [ʌn'weərili] *adv* imprudentemente, incautamente.
unwariness [ʌn'weərinis] *n* imprudencia *f*.
unwarlike [ʌn'wɔːlaik] *adj* pacífico, poco belicoso.
unwarranted [ʌn'wɔrəntid] *adj* injustificado.
unwary [ʌn'weəri] *adj* imprudente, incauto.
unwashed [ʌn'wɔʃt] *adj* sin lavar, sucio; **the Great U—** la plebe.
unwavering [ʌn'weivəriŋ] *adj loyalty, resolve* inquebrantable, firme; *course* constante; *gaze* fijo.
unwaveringly [ʌn'weivəriŋli] *adv* firmemente; constantemente; **to hold — to one's course** seguir su curso sin apartarse para nada de él.
unwearying [ʌn'wiəriiŋ] *adj* incansable.
unwelcome [ʌn'welkəm] *adj* importuno, molesto, inoportuno; desagradable; **a most — piece of news** una noticia nada grata *(to* para); **the change is not —** el cambio no es del todo molesto para nosotros.
unwell [ʌn'wel] *adj*: **to be —** estar indispuesto; **to feel —** sentirse mal; **I felt — on the ship** me mareé en el barco.
unwholesome [ʌn'həulsəm] *adj* insalubre, nocivo; *(morally)* indeseable.
unwieldy [ʌn'wiːldi] *adj* pesado, abultado, difícil de manejar.
unwilling [ʌn'wiliŋ] *adj* desinclinado; **to be — to do something** estar poco dispuesto a hacer algo; **to be — for someone to do something** estar poco dispuesto a permitir que uno haga algo.
unwillingly [ʌn'wiliŋli] *adv* de mala gana.
unwillingness [ʌn'wiliŋnis] *n* falta *f* de inclinación, desgana *f*; **his — to help us** su desgana para ayudarnos, el que no esté dispuesto a ayudarnos.
unwind [ʌn'waind] *(irr: see* **wind)** 1 *vt* desenvolver; *thread* desovillar. 2 *vi* desenvolverse; desovillarse; *(fig: relax)* esparcirse, calmar los nervios.
unwisdom [ʌn'wizdəm] *n* imprudencia *f*.
unwise [ʌn'waiz] *adj* imprudente; poco aconsejable; **it would be —** to + *infin* sería poco aconsejable + *infin;* **that was most —** of you en eso has sido muy imprudente.
unwisely [ʌn'waizli] *adv* imprudentemente.
unwitting [ʌn'witiŋ] *adj* inconsciente.
unwittingly [ʌn'witiŋli] *adv* inconscientemente; sin saber, sin darse cuenta.
unwomanly [ʌn'wumənli] *adj* poco femenino.
unwonted [ʌn'wəuntid] *adj* insólito, inusitado.
unworkable [ʌn'wɜːkəbl] *adj* impracticable.
unwordly [ʌn'wɜːldli] *adj* poco mundano, poco realista.
unworn [ʌn'wɔːn] *adj* nuevo, sin estrenar.
unworthiness [ʌn'wɜːðinis] *n* indignidad *f*.
unworthy [ʌn'wɜːði] *adj* indigno *(of* de); **to be — to do something** ser indigno de hacer algo; **it is —**

of attention no merece que se la preste atención.
unwounded [ʌn'wuːndid] *adj* ileso.
unwrap [ʌn'ræp] *vt* desenvolver; *parcel* deshacer.
unwritten [ʌn'ritn] *adj* no escrito.
unyielding [ʌn'jiːldiŋ] *adj* inflexible.
unyoke [ʌn'jəuk] *vt* desuncir.
unzip [ʌn'zip] *vt* abrir la cremallera de.
up [ʌp] **1** *adv* **(a)** *(general sense)* hacia arriba; arriba, para arriba; en el aire, en lo alto; **—!** ¡arriba!, *(from bed)* ¡levántate!; **all the way —** durante toda la subida, en todo el recorrido; en toda su extensión; **halfway —** a mitad de camino; **"this side —"** "este lado hacia arriba"; **"road —"** "cerrado por obras"; **— above** allí arriba; **to be — above something** estar por encima de algo; **— in London** allá en Londres; **my office is 5 floors —** mi oficina está en el quinto piso; **we're — for the day** hemos venido a pasar el día; **when I was —** *(Univ)* cuando yo estaba en la universidad, cuando yo era estudiante; **to throw something — (in the air)** lanzar algo al aire, lanzar algo por alto; **to walk — and down** pasearse, andar de un lado para otro, andar de acá para allá.
(b) to be — *(out of bed)* estar levantado; **we were — at 7** nos levantamos a las 7; **to be — and about again** estar levantado y salir *(después de una enfermedad),* estar mucho mejor; **to be — and doing** ser activo; **to be — all night** no acostarse en toda la noche; **we were still — at midnight** a medianoche seguíamos sin acostarnos.
(c) when the sun is — después de la salida del sol; cuando brilla el sol; **the river is —** el río ha subido; **the tide is —** la marea está alta.
(d) *(of price, quantity etc)* **potatoes are —** han subido las patatas; **the thermometer is — 2 degrees** ha subido el termómetro 2 grados; **Ceuta was 3 goals —** Ceuta tenía 3 goles de ventaja; **we were 20 points — on them** nos llevábamos una ventaja de 20 puntos.
(e) *(and upwards)* **from £2 —** de 2 libras para arriba; **from the age of 13 —** desde los 13 años para arriba; a partir de los 13 años.
(f) *(on a level)* **put it — beside the other one** ponlo junto al otro; **to be — with someone** estar a la altura de uno, haber alcanzado el nivel de uno; **is he — to advanced work?** ¿tiene capacidad para estudios superiores?; **to be — to a task** estar a la altura de un cometido; **I don't feel — to it** no me siento con fuerzas para ello; **it's not — to much** no vale gran cosa; **to be well — in maths** estar fuerte en matemáticas.
(g) to be — against difficulties tener dificultades, haber tropezado con dificultades; **to be — against it** estar en un aprieto; **now we're really — against it!** ¡con la iglesia hemos topado!; **to be — against someone** tener que habérselas con uno; *see* **hard** *etc.*
(h) what's —? ¿qué pasa?; **what's — with John?** ¿qué le pasa a Juan?; **there's something —** pasa algo malo, *(of a plot)* están tramando algo.
(i) *(finished)* **time is —** se ha terminado el tiempo permitido, es la hora; **when the period is —** cuando termine el plazo; **his holiday is —** han terminado ya sus vacaciones; **our time here is —** no podemos estar más tiempo aquí, se ha acabado nuestra estancia aquí; *see* **all.**
(j) — to hasta; **— to now** hasta ahora; **— to here** hasta aquí; **— to this week** hasta esta semana; **— to £10** hasta 10 libras; **to count — to 100** contar hasta 100; **they advanced — to the wood** avanzaron hasta el bosque.
(k) they're — to something están tramando algo; **what are you — to?** ¿qué haces ahí?; **what are you — to with that knife?** ¿qué haces con ese cuchillo?; **what does he think he's — to?** ¿qué diablos piensa hacer?
(l) it is — to you to decide le toca a Vd decidir; **I feel it is — to me to tell him** creo que me incumbe a mí decírselo; **if it was — to me** si yo tuviera que decidirlo.
2 *prep* en lo alto de; encima de; **— a tree** en lo alto de un árbol; **halfway — the stairs** a mitad de la escalera; **halfway — the mountain** a mitad de la subida del monte; **they live further — the road** viven en esta calle pero más arriba; **he went off — the road** se fue calle arriba; **— (the) river** río arriba.
3 *adj*: **the — train** el tren ascendente.
4 *n* **(a) — s and downs** vicisitudes *fpl*, alternativas *fpl*, altibajos *mpl*, peripecias *fpl*; **after many —s and downs** después de mil peripecias; **the —s and downs that every politician has** las alternativas a que está sometido todo político.

(b) to be on the — and — ir cada vez mejor.

5 vi (fam): **to — and +** inf ponerse de repente a + infin; **he —ped and hit her** sin más la pegó.

up-and-coming ['ʌpənd'kʌmiŋ] adj joven y prometedor, nuevo y emprendedor.

up-and-down ['ʌpən'daun] adj movement vertical, perpendicular; business, progress etc poco uniforme, variable; eventful accidentado.

upbraid [ʌp'breid] vt reprender, censurar; **to — someone with something** censurar algo a uno.

upbringing ['ʌp,briŋiŋ] n educación f, crianza f.

upcast ['ʌpkɑːst] n (Min; also — **shaft**) pozo m de ventilación.

upcountry ['ʌp'kʌntri] **1** adv: **to be —** estar tierra adentro, estar en el interior; **to go —** ir hacia el interior, penetrar en el interior.
2 adj del interior.

up-current ['ʌp'kʌrənt] n (Aer) viento m ascendente.

update [ʌp'deit] vt modernizar, actualizar; **to — someone on a matter** poner a uno al tanto de un asunto, dar a uno los últimos detalles de un asunto.

upend [ʌp'end] vt volver de arriba abajo, poner al revés; person volcar.

upgrade ['ʌpgreid] n cuesta f, pendiente f; **to be on the —** ir cuesta arriba, prosperar, estar en auge; (Med) estar mejor, estar reponiéndose.

upgrade [ʌp'greid] vt person ascender; job asignar a un grado más alto; valorar en más.

upheaval [ʌp'hiːvəl] n (Geol) solevantamiento m; (fig) cataclismo m, sacudida f, trastorno m.

uphill ['ʌp'hil] **1** adv cuesta arriba; **to go —** ir cuesta arriba; **the road goes — for 2 miles** la carretera sube durante 2 millas.
2 adj task arduo, penoso.

uphold [ʌp'həuld] (irr: see **hold**) vt (hold up) sostener, apoyar; (maintain) sostener, defender; (Law) confirmar.

upholder [ʌp'həuldə*] n defensor m, ora f.

upholster [ʌp'həulstə*] vt tapizar, entapizar (with de).

upholsterer [ʌp'həulstərə*] n tapicero m.

upholstery [ʌp'həulstəri] n tapicería f, tapizado m; (cushioning etc) almohadillado m.

upkeep ['ʌpkiːp] n conservación f; (of car, house etc) mantenimiento m; (cost) gastos mpl de mantenimiento.

upland ['ʌplənd] **1** n tierra f alta, meseta f; **—s** tierras fpl altas. **2** adj de la meseta.

uplift ['ʌplift] n sustentación f; (fig) inspiración f, edificación f; moral — edificación f.

uplift [ʌp'lift] vt (fig) inspirar, edificar.

upon [ə'pɔn] prep see **on**.

upper ['ʌpə*] adj superior, más alto; de arriba; class, house (Pol) alto; (in Geog names) alto, eg **U— Egypt** Alto Egipto m; deck, floor etc superior, de arriba.

upper-class ['ʌpə'klɑːs] adj de la clase alta.

upper-crust ['ʌpə'krʌst] adj de categoría (social) superior, de buen tono.

uppercut ['ʌpəkʌt] n (Boxing) golpe m de abajo arriba.

uppermost ['ʌpəməust] adj (a) (el) más alto; **to put something face —** poner algo con la cara hacia arriba.
(b) (fig) principal, predominante; **what is — in someone's mind** lo que ocupa el primer lugar en el pensamiento de uno; **it was — in my mind** pensé en eso antes que en otra cosa.

uppers ['ʌpəz] npl (of shoe) pala f; **to be on one's —** no tener un céntimo.

uppish ['ʌpiʃ] adj, **uppity** ['ʌpiti] adj (fam) engreído; fresco; **to get —** engreírse.

upraise [ʌp'reiz] vt levantar.

upright ['ʌprait] **1** adj vertical; derecho; piano vertical, recto; (fig) honrado, recto, probo.
2 adv: **to hold oneself —** mantenerse erguido; **to sit bolt —** ponerse derecho en su silla.
3 n montante m; (of goalpost) poste m.

uprightly ['ʌp,raitli] adv (fig) honradamente, rectamente.

uprightness ['ʌp,raitnis] n (fig) honradez f, rectitud f.

uprising [ʌp'raiziŋ] n alzamiento m, sublevación f.

up-river ['ʌp'rivə*] adv = **upstream**.

uproar ['ʌprɔː*] n alboroto m, tumulto m; escándalo m; **at this there was —** en esto estallaron ruidosas las protestas, en esto se armó un escándalo; **the whole place was in —** la sala estaba alborotada.

uproarious [ʌp'rɔːriəs] adj tumultuoso, estrepitoso; laughter tumultuoso, escandaloso; joke etc divertidísimo; success clamoroso.

uproariously [ʌp'rɔːriəsli] adv tumultuosamente, con estrépito; **to laugh —** estar para morirse de risa.

uproot [ʌp'ruːt] vt desarraigar, arrancar; (destroy) extirpar; **whole families have been —ed** se han desplazado familias enteras.

upset ['ʌpset] n (accident) vuelco m; (in plans etc) revés m, contratiempo m; (Med) trastorno m, desarreglo m; **to have a stomach —** tener un trastorno estomacal, tener el estómago trastornado.

upset [ʌp'set] **1** (irr: see **set**) vt (overturn) volcar, trastornar; (spill) derramar; stomach trastornar, hacer daño a; plans etc dar al traste con; person (emotionally) desconcertar, alterar, perturbar; **garlic —s me** el ajo no me sienta bien; **the news — her** a lot la noticia le causó gran pesar; **I didn't intend to — her** no tenía la intención de alterarla.
2 vr: **to — oneself** acongojarse, apurarse; **don't — yourself!** ¡no te acongojes!
3 adj: **to be —** estar perturbado, estar acongojado, estar preocupado; sentirse molesto; **to get —** alterarse, perturbarse; **she looked terribly —** parecía estar apuradísima; **she is easily —** se apura por cualquier cosa; **what are you so — about?** ¿qué motivo tienes para emocionarte tanto?, ¿a qué se debe tanto sentimiento?; **I have an — stomach** tengo el estómago trastornado.
4 attr: **— price** precio m mínimo.

upsetting [ʌp'setiŋ] adj inquietante, desconcertante; **it's very —** es para volverse loco.

upshot ['ʌpʃɔt] n resultado m; **in the —** al fin y al cabo; **the — of it all was . . .** resultó por fin que . . .

upside ['ʌpsaid] n: **to be — down** estar al revés, tener lo de arriba abajo; **to turn a box — down** volver una caja al revés, invertir una caja; **the room was — down** reinaba la mayor confusión en el cuarto, en el cuarto todo estaba patas arriba; **to turn a room — down** introducir el desorden en un cuarto; **we turned everything — down looking for it** al buscarlo lo revolvimos todo, en la búsqueda lo registramos todo de arriba abajo.

upstage ['ʌp'steidʒ] **1** adv: **to be —** estar en el fondo de la escena; **to go —** ir hacia el fondo de la escena.
2 adj (fam) engreído.
3 vt: **to — someone** lograr captar la atención del público a costa de otro.

upstairs ['ʌp'stɛəz] **1** adv arriba; **to go —** ir arriba, subir al piso superior; **to walk slowly —** subir lentamente la escalera.
2 adj de arriba; **we looked out of an — window** nos asomamos a una ventana del piso superior.

upstanding [ʌp'stændiŋ] adj **(a)** a fine — young man un buen mozo gallardo. **(b) to be —** levantarse, ponerse de pie.

upstart ['ʌpstɑːt] **1** adj arribista; advenedizo; **some — youth** algún joven presuntuoso. **2** n arribista mf; advenedizo m, a f; insolente mf.

upstate ['ʌp'steit] adj (US, esp of New York) interior, septentrional.

upstream ['ʌp'striːm] adv aguas arriba, río arriba (from de); **to go —** ir río arriba; **to swim —** nadar contra la corriente; **a town — from Windsor** una ciudad más arriba de Windsor; **about 3 miles — from Seville** unas 3 millas más arriba de Sevilla.

upstretched ['ʌpstretʃt] adj extendido hacia arriba.

upstroke ['ʌpstrəuk] n (with pen) plumada f ascendente; (Mech) carrera f ascendente.

upsurge ['ʌpsɜːdʒ] n acceso m, aumento m grande; **a great — of interest in Góngora** un gran renacimiento del interés por Góngora; **there has been an — of feeling about this question** ha aumentado de pronto la preocupación por esta cuestión.

upswept ['ʌpswept] adj wing elevado, inclinado hacia arriba; **with — hair** con peinado alto.

upswing ['ʌpswiŋ] n movimiento m hacia arriba; (fig) curva f ascensional, mejora f notable (in, of de).

uptake ['ʌpteik] n: **to be quick on the —** ser muy listo; **to be a bit slow on the —** ser algo torpe.

upthrust ['ʌp'θrʌst] **1** adj empujado hacia arriba, dirigido hacia arriba; (Geol) solevantado. **2** n empuje m hacia arriba; (Geol) solevantamiento m.

up-to-date ['ʌptə'deit] adj moderno, actual; see also **date**.

uptown ['ʌp'taun] **1** adv go hacia la parte alta de la ciudad; be en la parte alta de la ciudad. **2** adj de la parte alta de la ciudad.

upturn ['ʌptɜːn] n mejora f, aumento m (in de).

upturn [ʌp'tɜːn] vt volver hacia arriba; (overturn) volcar.

upturned ['ʌptɜːnd] adj vuelto hacia arriba; nose respingona.

upward ['ʌpwəd] adj curve, movement etc ascendente, ascensional; slope en pendiente; tendency al alza.

upward(s) ['ʌpwəd(z)] *adv* hacia arriba; **to lay something face** — poner algo con la cara hacia arriba; **to look** — mirar hacia arriba; £50 **and** — de 50 libras para arriba; **from the age of 13** — desde los 13 años para arriba; a partir de los 13 años; — **of 200** más de 200.

upwind ['ʌp'wind] *adv*: **to stay** — quedarse en la parte de donde sopla el viento.

Urals ['juərəlz] *pl* Urales *mpl*, Montes *mpl* Urales.

uranium [juə'reiniəm] *n* uranio *m*.

Uranus [juə'reinəs] Urano *m*.

urban ['əːbən] *adj* urbano.

urbane [əː'bein] *adj* urbano, cortés, fino.

urbanity [əː'bæniti] *n* urbanidad *f*, cortesía *f*, fineza *f*.

urbanization [‚əːbənai'zeiʃən] *n* urbanización *f*.

urbanize ['əːbənaiz] *vt* urbanizar.

urchin ['əːtʃin] *n* galopín *m*, pilluelo *m*, golfillo *m*.

Urdu ['uəduː] *n* urdu *m*.

urea ['juəriə] *n* urea *f*.

ureter [juə'riːtə*] *n* uréter *m*.

urethra [juə'riːθrə] *n* uretra *f*.

urge [əːdʒ] **1** *n* impulso *m*; instinto *m*, deseo *m*; ambición *f*; **the** — **to win** el afán de victoria; **the** — **to write** el deseo apremiante de escribir algo, la ambición de hacerse escritor; **to feel an** — **to do something** sentir un deseo apremiante de hacer algo, sentirse impulsado a hacer algo; **to get the** —, **to have the** — desear algo con vehemencia.

2 *vt* (a) **to** — **someone on** animar a uno, instar a uno a ir adelante; **to** — **someone to do something** instar a uno a hacer algo, incitar a uno a hacer algo, recomendar a uno encarecidamente que haga algo; **to** — **that something should be done** recomendar encarecidamente que se haga algo.

(b) **to** — **something on someone** incitar a uno a algo, recomendar encarecidamente algo a uno; **to** — **a policy on the government** hacer presión en el gobierno para que adopte una política.

urgency ['əːdʒənsi] *n* urgencia *f*; **with a note of** — **in his voice** en tono algo perentorio, con una nota de perentoriedad; **is there much** — **about this?** ¿corre prisa esto?; **it is a matter of** — es un asunto urgente.

urgent ['əːdʒənt] *adj* urgente; *tone etc* apremiante, perentorio; *entreaty etc* insistente, apremiante; **it is** — **that . . .** urge que + *subj*; **is this** —? ¿corre prisa esto?

urgently ['əːdʒəntli] *adv* urgentemente; de modo apremiante, con insistencia.

uric ['juərik] *adj* úrico; — **acid** ácido *m* úrico.

urinal ['juərinl] *n* (*building*) urinario *m*; (*vessel*) orinal *m*.

urinary ['juərinəri] *adj* urinario.

urinate ['juərineit] **1** *vt* orinar. **2** *vi* orinar(se).

urine ['juərin] *n* orina *f*, orines *mpl*.

urn [əːn] *n* urna *f*; (*for tea*) tetera *f*.

urogenital [‚juərəu'dʒenitl] *adj* urogenital.

urologist [juə'rɔlədʒist] *n* urólogo *m*.

urology [juə'rɔlədʒi] *n* urología *f*.

Ursa Major ['əːsə'meidʒə*] Osa *f* Mayor.

Ursa Minor ['əːsə'mainə*] Osa *f* Menor.

Uruguay ['juərəgwai] el Uruguay.

Uruguayan [‚juərə'gwaiən] **1** *adj* uruguayo. **2** *n* uruguayo *m*, a *f*.

us [ʌs] *pron* nos; (*after prep*) nosotros, nosotras.

usable ['juːzəbl] *adj* utilizable, aprovechable; **it is no longer** — ya no sirve.

usage ['juːzidʒ] *n* (a) (*custom*) uso *m*, costumbre *f*; **in the** — **of railwaymen** en el lenguaje de los ferroviarios, en el uso ferroviario; **an ancient** — **of the Celts** una antigua costumbre de los celtas.

(b) (*treatment*) tratamiento *m*; (*handling*) manejo *m*; **kind** — buenos tratos *mpl*, buen tratamiento *m*; **it's had some rough** — ha sido manejado con bastante dureza.

use [juːs] *n* (a) uso *m*, empleo *m*; manejo *m*; **a new** — **for old tyres** nuevo método *m* para utilizar los neumáticos viejos; **"directions for** —**"** "modo *m* de empleo"; **for the** — **of the blind** para uso de los ciegos, para los ciegos; **fit for** — servible, en buen estado; **ready for** — listo para ser usado; **care in the** — **of guns** cuidado *m* en el manejo de las armas de fuego; **word in** — palabra *f* en uso, palabra *f* que se usa; **it is not now in** — ya no se usa; **it has not been in** — **for 5 years** hace 5 años que no se usa; **an article of everyday** — un artículo de uso corriente; **it is now out of** — ya no se usa; eso ha quedado anticuado, eso está fuera de moda ya; **to find a** — **for something** utilizar algo, aprovechar algo; **it improves with** — parece mejor a medida que se va usando; **to make** — **of** servirse de; utilizar, aprovechar; explotar; (*right etc*) valerse

de, ejercer; **to make good** — **of** aprovecharse debidamente de; **to put something to good** — servirse de algo, sacar partido de algo; hacer que algo trabaje (*or* rinda *etc*); **to put something into** — poner algo en servicio.

(b) **to have the** — **of a garage** poder usar un garaje; **I have the** — **of it on Sundays** me permiten usarlo los domingos; **I should like to have the** — **of it** quisiera poderlo usar; **he lost the** — **of his arm** se le quedó inútil el brazo.

(c) (*usefulness*) utilidad *f*; **to be of** — servir (*for* para); **to be of no** — no servir; **can I be of any** —? ¿puedo ayudar?; **it's (of) no** — es inútil; **it's no** — **your protesting** de nada sirve quejarse, es inútil quejarse; **it's no** — **discussing it further** no vale la pena discutirlo más; **he's no** — no vale para nada; **he's no** — **as a goalkeeper** no vale para portero; **what's the** — **of all this?** ¿de qué sirve todo esto?, ¿qué utilidad tiene todo esto?, ¿qué finalidad tiene todo esto?; **to have no** — **for something** no necesitar algo; **to have no** — **for someone** despreciar a uno; **I've no** — **for those who . . .** detesto a los que . . .; **to have no further** — **for something** no poder usar algo más.

(d) (*custom*) uso *m*, costumbre *f*.

use [juːz] *vt* (a) usar, emplear; servirse de, utilizar; *tool etc* manejar; **he** —**d a knife** empleó un cuchillo; **are you using this book?** ¿te hace falta este libro?, ¿estás trabajando con este libro?; **which book did you** —? ¿qué libro consultaste?; **I could** — **a drink!** (*fam*) ¡qué sed tengo!; **this room could** — **some paint** (*fam*) no le vendría mal a este cuarto una mano de pintura; **careful how you** — **that razor!** ¡cuidado con la navaja esa!; **have you** —**d a gun before?** ¿has manejado alguna vez una escopeta?; **the money is** —**d for the poor** el dinero se dedica a los pobres, el dinero se emplea en los pobres; **the word is no longer** —**d** la palabra ya no se usa; **may I** — **your name?** ¿puedo dar su nombre?; **to** — **something as a hammer** emplear algo como martillo; **to** — **something for a purpose** servirse de algo con un propósito.

(b) (*of abstract things*) emplear; **to** — **force** emplear la fuerza; **to** — **every means** emplear todos los medios; **to** — **no** — no perdonar esfuerzo (*to* + *infin* por + *infin*); **to** — **one's influence** valerse de su influencia.

(c) (*treat*) tratar; **to** — **someone well** tratar bien a uno; **to** — **someone roughly** tratar a uno brutalmente; **she had been cruelly** —**d by . . .** había sido tratada con crueldad por . . .

(d) **to** — **something (up)** consumir algo, agotar algo; **it's all** —**d up** todo está agotado; **when we've** —**d up all our money** cuando hayamos gastado todo nuestro dinero; **please** — **up all the coffee** que no quede café sin beber.

(e) (*v/aux*) [juːst] **I** —**d to go** iba, solía ir, acostumbraba ir, tenía la costumbre de ir; **but I** —**d not to** pero antes no; **things aren't what they** —**d to be** las cosas ya no son lo que eran.

used [juːzd] *adj* usado; gastado, viejo; *stamp* usado.

used [juːst] *ptp of* **use**: **to be** — **to** estar acostumbrado a; **to be** — **to** + *gen* estar acostumbrado a + *infin*; **to get** — **to** acostumbrarse a; **I still haven't got** — **to the lifts** todavía no me he acostumbrado a los ascensores.

useful ['juːsful] *adj* útil; provechoso; **a** — **player** un buen jugador, un jugador que vale; **it is very** — **to be able to . . .** es muy útil poder . . .; **he's** — **with his fists** sabe defenderse con los puños; **he's** — **with a gun** sabe manejar un fusil; **to come in** — servir, ser útil; venir a propósito; **to make oneself** — ayudar, trabajar (*etc*); **come on, make yourself** —! ¡vamos, a trabajar!; **we had a** — **time in Spain** nuestra estancia en España fue muy provechosa.

usefully ['juːsfəli] *adv* útilmente; provechosamente, con provecho.

usefulness ['juːsfulnis] *n* utilidad *f*; valor *m*; provecho *m*; **it has outlived its** — ha dejado de tener utilidad.

useless ['juːslis] *adj* inútil; inservible; *person* inepto, incompetente; **he's** — no vale para nada; **he's** — **as a forward** no vale para delantero; **it is** — **to shout** de nada sirve gritar, es inútil gritar; **to make** (*or* **render**) **something** — inutilizar algo.

uselessly ['juːslisli] *adv* inútilmente, en vano.

uselessness ['juːslisnis] *n* inutilidad *f*.

user ['juːzə*] *n* usuario *m*, a *f*.

U-shaped ['juːʃeipt] *adj* en forma de U.

usher ['ʌʃə*] **1** *n* ujier *m*, portero *m*; (*Theat*) acomodador *m*; (*at public meeting etc*) guardia *m* de sala, encargado *m* del orden.

2 *vt* (a) **to** — **someone in** (*Theat etc*) acomodar a uno; **to** — **someone into a room** hacer pasar a uno a un cuarto, hacer entrar a uno en un cuarto; **I was —ed in by the butler** el mayordomo me hizo pasar, el mayordomo acudió a la puerta para recibirme; **to — someone out** acompañar a uno a la puerta.

(b) it —ed in a new reign anunció un nuevo reinado, marcó el comienzo del reinado nuevo; **summer was —ed in by storms** el verano empezó con tormentas.

usherette [ˌʌʃəˈret] *n* acomodadora *f*.

usual [ˈjuːʒuəl] *adj* usual; acostumbrado, habitual; corriente; normal; **as — como** de costumbre, como siempre; **as per —!** (*fam*) ¡lo de siempre!; **more than —** más que de costumbre, más que lo normal; **his — restaurant** su restaurante habitual; **to come earlier than —** venir antes de la hora (*or* fecha *etc*) acostumbrada; **it's not — no** es normal; **it's not — for people to leave so soon** no es normal que la gente se marche tan pronto.

usually [ˈjuːʒuəli] *adv* por lo general, por regla general; **we — wash it ourselves** acostumbramos a lavarlo nosotros mismos; **what do you do —?** ¿qué hacen Vds normalmente?

usufruct [ˈjuːzjufrʌkt] *n* usufructo *m*.

usufructuary [ˌjuːzjuˈfrʌktəri] *n* usufructuario *m*.

usurer [ˈjuːʒərə*] *n* usurero *m*.

usurious [juːˈzjuəriəs] *adj* usurario.

usurp [juːˈzəːp] *vt* usurpar.

usurpation [ˌjuːzəːˈpeiʃən] *n* usurpación *f*.

usurper [juːˈzəːpə*] *n* usurpador *m*, ora *f*.

usurping [juːˈzəːpiŋ] *adj* usurpador.

usury [ˈjuːʒuri] *n* usura *f*.

utensil [juːˈtensl] *n* utensilio *m*; **kitchen —s** batería *f* de cocina.

uterine [ˈjuːtərain] *adj* uterino.

uterus [ˈjuːtərəs] *n* útero *m*.

utilitarian [ˌjuːtiliˈtɛəriən] **1** *adj* utilitario. **2** *n* utilitarista *mf*.

utilitarianism [ˌjuːtiliˈtɛəriənizəm] *n* utilitarismo *m*

utility [juːˈtiliti] **1** *n* utilidad *f*; **public —** empresa *f* de servicio público. **2** *attr car, clothing etc* utilitario.

utility room [ˈjuːtilitiˌrum] *n* trascocina *f*.

utilization [ˌjuːtilaiˈzeiʃən] *n* utilización *f*.

utilize [ˈjuːtilaiz] *vt* utilizar.

utmost [ˈʌtməust] **1** *adj* mayor; supremo; **of the — importance** de primerísima importancia; **with the — ease** con suma facilidad.

2 *n*: **the — that one can do** todo lo que puede hacer uno; **to do one's —** hacer todo lo posible (*to + infin* por + *infin*); **200 at the —** 200 a lo más, 200 a lo sumo; **to the — al** máximo, hasta más no poder; **to the — of one's ability** lo mejor que sepa uno.

Utopia [juːˈtəupiə] *n* Utopía *f*.

Utopian [juːˈtəupiən] **1** *adj dream etc* utópico; *person* utopista. **2** *n* utopista *mf*.

utricle [ˈjuːtrikl] *n* utrículo *m*.

utter[1] [ˈʌtə*] *adj* completo, total, absoluto; *fool, madness etc* puro; **— nonsense!** ¡tonterías!; **it was an — disaster** fue un desastre total; **he was in a state of — depression** estaba completamente abatido.

utter[2] [ˈʌtə*] *vt* (a) *words* pronunciar; *cry etc* dar; *threat, insult etc* proferir; *libel* publicar; **she never —ed a word** no dijo nada, no dijo ni pío; **don't — a word about it** de esto no digas ni pío.

(b) *counterfeit money* poner en circulación, expender.

utterance [ˈʌtərəns] *n* pronunciación *f*; palabras *fpl*; declaración *f*; **to give — to** manifestar, declarar.

utterly [ˈʌtəli] *adv* completamente, totalmente, del todo.

uttermost [ˈʌtəməust] *adj* más remoto, más lejano; extremo; *see* **utmost**.

U-turn [ˈjuːˈtəːn] *n* viraje *m* en U.

uvula [ˈjuːvjələ] *n* úvula *f*.

uvular [ˈjuːvjələ*] *adj* uvular.

uxorious [ʌkˈsɔːriəs] *adj* gurrumino.

V

vac [væk] *n* (*fam*) = **vacation.**

vacancy ['veikənsi] *n* (**a**) (*emptiness*) lo vacío; (*of mind etc*) vaciedad *f*, vacuidad *f*.
(**b**) (*in boarding house etc*) cuarto *m* vacante; **have you any vacancies?** ¿hay algún cuarto libre?, ¿tiene algo disponible?; **we have no vacancies for August** para agosto no hay nada disponible, en agosto todo está lleno.
(**c**) (*in post*) vacante *f*; **"vacancies"** "se ofrece trabajo", "se necesita mano de obra"; **"vacancy for keen young man"** "búscase joven enérgico"; **to fill a** — proveer una vacante.

vacant ['veikənt] *adj* (**a**) *seat, room etc* libre, desocupado; disponible; *space* vacío, desocupado; **is this seat** —? ¿está libre este asiento?; **have you a room** —? ¿tienen algo disponible?; **to become** —, **to fall** — vaciar.
(**b**) *look etc* distraído, vago, (*stupid*) de bobo.

vacantly ['veikəntli] *adv look etc* distraídamente, vagamente, (*stupidly*) sin comprender, boquiabierto.

vacate [və'keit] *vt house* desocupar; *post* dejar, dejar vacante, salir de; *throne etc* renunciar a.

vacation [və'keiʃən] **1** *n* vacación *f*, vacaciones *fpl*; **long** — (*Univ*) vacación *f* de verano; **to be on** — estar de vacaciones.
2 *attr:* — **course** curso *m* de vacaciones, (*esp*) curso *m* de verano.
3 *vi* (*US*) estar de vacaciones; tomarse unas vacaciones; pasar las vacaciones; *see also* **holiday.**

vacationist [və'keiʃənist] *n* (*US*) vacacionista *mf*.

vaccinate ['væksineit] *vt* vacunar.

vaccination [ˌvæksi'neiʃən] *n* vacunación *f*.

vaccine ['væksiːn] *n* vacuna *f*.

vacillate ['væsileit] *vi* (*sway, vary*) oscilar (*between* entre); (*hesitate*) vacilar, dudar; **to** — **about a course of action** no resolverse a seguir una política determinada.

vacillating ['væsileitiŋ] *adj* vacilante, irresoluto.

vacillation [ˌvæsi'leiʃən] *n* vacilación *f*.

vacuity [væ'kjuːiti] *n* vacuidad *f*.

vacuous ['vækjuəs] *adj* bobo, necio.

vacuum ['vækjum] **1** *n* vacío *m*. **2** *attr* de vacío; **al vacío.**

vacuum bottle ['vækjum,bɔtl] *n* (*US*) termo(s) *m*.

vacuum brake ['vækjum'breik] *n* freno *m* de vacío.

vacuum cleaner ['vækjum,kliːnə*] *n* aspirador *m*.

vacuum flask ['vækjumflɑːsk] *n* termo(s) *m*.

vacuum pump ['vækjum'pʌmp] *n* bomba *f* al vacío.

vacuum tube ['vækjumtjuːb] *n* tubo *m* al vacío.

vade mecum ['vɑːdi'meikum] *n* vademécum *m*.

vagabond ['vægəbɔnd] **1** *adj* vagabundo. **2** *n* vagabundo *m*, a *f*.

vagary ['veigəri] *n* (*whim*) capricho *m*, extravagancia *f*; (*of thermometer etc*) irregularidad *f*, variación *f*; (*of the mind*) divagación *f*; **the vagaries of taste** lo caprichoso del gusto, la inconstancia de la moda.

vagina [və'dʒainə] *n* vagina *f*.

vaginal [və'dʒainəl] *adj* vaginal.

vagrancy ['veigrənsi] *n* vagancia *f*, vagabundaje *m*; — **in 16th century Spain** los vagabundos (*or* el vagabundeo) en España en el siglo XVI.

vagrant ['veigrənt] **1** *adj* vagabundo, vagante; (*fig*) errante. **2** *n* vagabundo *m*, a *f*.

vague [veig] *n* (**a**) vago; indistinto, borroso; incierto; impreciso; **the** — **outline of a ship** el perfil indistinto de un buque; **the outlook is somewhat** — la perspectiva es algo incierta; **it is a** — **concept** es un concepto impreciso; **he made some** — **promises** hizo varias promesas imprecisas; **I haven't the** —**st** no tengo la más remota idea.
(**b**) (*of person: in giving details etc*) impreciso, equívoco; (*absent-minded*) despistado, distraído: **he was** — **about the date** no quiso precisar la fecha, no dijo concretamente cuál era la fecha; **he's**

terribly — tiene un tremendo despiste, es un despistado; **you mustn't be so** — hay que decir las cosas con claridad, hay que concretar; **I am** — **on the subject of ants** sé muy poca cosa en concreto de las hormigas.

vaguely ['veigli] *adv* vagamente; indistintamente; imprecisamente; distraídamente; **a picture** — **resembling another** un cuadro que tiene cierto parecido vago con otro; **he talks very** — habla en términos muy vagos; **she looked at me** — me miró distraída, me miró sin comprender.

vagueness ['veignis] *n* vaguedad *f*; lo indistinto, lo borroso; incertidumbre *f*, imprecisión *f*; despiste *m*, distracción *f*.

vain [vein] *adj* (**a**) (*useless*) vano, inútil; **in** — en vano; **it is** — **to try** es inútil intentarlo; **all our efforts were in** — todos nuestros esfuerzos resultaron ser infructuosos; **to take someone's name in** — hablar con poco respeto de uno.
(**b**) (*conceited*) vanidoso; presumido, engreído; **she is very** — **about her hair** es muy orgullosa de su cabello, se enorgullece de su cabello.

vainglorious [vein'glɔːriəs] *adj* vanaglorioso.

vainglory [vein'glɔːri] *n* vanagloria *f*.

vainly ['veinli] *adv* (**a**) vanamente, inútilmente; infructuosamente; sin éxito. (**b**) vanidosamente.

valance ['væləns] *n* cenefa *f*, doselera *f*.

vale [veil] *n* valle *m*; — **of tears** valle *m* de lágrimas.

valediction [ˌvæli'dikʃən] *n* despedida *f*.

valedictory [ˌvæli'diktəri] *adj address etc* de despedida.

valence ['veiləns] *n* valencia *f*.

Valencian [və'lensiən] **1** *adj* valenciano. **2** *n* valenciano *m*, a *f*. **3** *n* (*dialect*) valenciano *m*.

valency ['veilənsi] *n* valencia *f*.

valentine ['væləntain] *n* tarjeta *f* del día de San Valentín (*enviada por jóvenes, sin firmar, de tono amoroso o jocoso*); (*person*) novio *m*, a *f* (*escogido el día de San Valentín*).

valerian [və'liəriən] *n* valeriana *f*.

valet ['vælei] *n* ayuda *m* de cámara.

valetudinarian ['væli,tjuːdi'nɛəriən] **1** *adj* valetudinario. **2** *n* valetudinario *m*, a *f*.

Valhalla [væl'hælə] Valhala *m*.

valiant ['væliənt] *adj* (*lit*) esforzado, denodado.

valiantly ['væliəntli] *adv* esforzadamente, denodadamente, con denuedo.

valid ['vælid] *adj válido; ticket etc* valedero; *law* vigente; **a ticket** — **for 3 months** un billete valedero para 3 meses; **that ticket is no longer** — ese billete ya no vale, ese billete ha caducado ya; **that argument is not** — ese argumento no vale, ese argumento no es válido.

validate ['vælideit] *vt* validar.

validation [ˌvæli'deiʃən] *n* validación *f*.

validity [və'liditi] *n* validez *f*; vigencia *f*.

valise [və'liːz] *n* portamantas *m*.

Valkyrie ['vælkiri] *n* Valquiria *f*.

valley ['væli] *n* valle *m*.

valorous ['vælərəs] *adj* (*lit*) esforzado, denodado.

valour, (*US*) **valor** ['vælə*] *n* valor *m*, valentía *f*.

valuable ['væljuəbl] **1** *adj* valioso; estimable; costoso; **a** — **contribution** una valiosa aportación; **is it** —? ¿vale mucho?
2 —**s** *npl* objetos *mpl* de valor.

valuation [ˌvælju'eiʃən] *n* valuación *f*, valorización *f*; tasación *f*; **to take someone at his own** — aceptar todo lo que dice uno acerca de sí mismo.

value ['væljuː] **1** *n* (**a**) (*general sense*) valor *m*; estimación *f*; importancia *f*; (*Gram, Mus etc*) valor *m*; **aggregate** — valor *m* total, valor *m* global; **sentimental** — valor *m* sentimental; **things of** — cosas *fpl* de valor; **of great** — de gran valor, muy valioso (*to* para); **of no** — sin valor; **to be of** —

to someone ser de valor para uno, ser útil a uno; **to be of little — to someone** ser de poco valor para uno, servir poco a uno; **of what — is Greek nowadays?** ¿qué valor tiene el griego hoy?, ¿qué utilidad tiene el griego hoy?; **to the — of** por valor de; **this dress is good —** este vestido bien vale lo que pagué por él; **to get good — for one's money** estar satisfecho de una compra; **to set a — of £20 on something** tasar algo en 20 libras; **to set a high — on someone** estimar a uno en mucho, tener un concepto muy bueno de uno; **to attach no — to** no conceder importancia a.

(b) *(moral)* **—s** valores *mpl* morales, principios *mpl*; **sense of —s** sentido m de los valores morales; **— judgement** juicio m de valor.

2 *vt (financially)* valorar, valorizar, tasar *(at* en); *(morally etc)* estimar, apreciar; *(— highly)* tener un mucho, tener un buen concepto de, apreciar; **it is —d at £8** está valorado en 8 libras; **I — my leisure** para mí son muy importantes mis ratos de ocio; **he doesn't — his life** desprecia su vida, no hace estimación de su vida; **she sent her rings to be —d** envió sus joyas para que se las tasaran.

valued ['væljuːd] *adj* estimado, apreciado; **my — colleague** mi estimado colega.

valueless ['væljulis] *adj* sin valor.

valuer ['valjuə*] n tasador m.

valve [vælv] n *(Anat, Mech)* válvula f; *(Radio)* lámpara f, válvula f; *(Bot, Zool)* valva f; **inlet —** válvula f de admisión.

valve tester ['vælv,testə*] n comprobador m de válvulas.

vamoose [və'muːs] *vi (sl)* largarse; desaparecer.

vamp[1] [væmp] 1 n *(of shoe)* empella f; *(patch)* remiendo m.

2 *vt shoe* poner empella a; remendar; *(Mus)* improvisar, improvisar un acompañamiento para; **to — up an engine** *(repair)* componer un motor, *(supercharge)* sobrealimentar un motor.

3 *vi* improvisar.

vamp[2] [væmp] 1 n vampiresa f.

2 *vt* coquetear con, flirtear con; **to — someone into doing something** engatusar a uno para que haga algo, fascinar a uno lo bastante para que consienta en hacer algo.

vampire ['væmpaiə*] n (a) *(also Zool)* vampiro m. (b) *(fig: extortioner)* desollador m; *(woman)* vampiresa f.

van[1] [væn] n *(Mil, fig)* vanguardia f; **to be in the —** ir a la vanguardia; **to be in the — of progress** estar en la vanguardia del progreso.

van[2] [væn] n *(Aut)* camioneta f, furgoneta f; *(for removals)* camión m de mudanzas; *(Rail)* furgón m de equipajes.

Vandal ['vændəl] 1 *adj* vándalo, vandálico. 2 n vándalo m, a f.

Vandalic [væn'dælik] *adj* vándalo, vandálico.

vandalism ['vændəlizəm] n vandalismo m; **piece of —** acto m de vandalismo.

vandalize ['vændəlaiz] *vt* destruir, estropear, arruinar.

vane [vein] n *(weathercock)* veleta f; *(of mill)* aspa f; *(of propeller)* paleta f; *(of feather)* barba f.

vanguard ['vængɑːd] n vanguardia f; **to be in the —** ir a la vanguardia; **to be in the — of progress** estar en la vanguardia del progreso.

vanilla [və'nilə] n vainilla f.

vanillin ['vænilin] n vainillina f.

vanish ['væniʃ] *vi* desaparecer, desvanecerse; **to — without trace** desaparecer sin dejar rastro.

vanishing cream ['væniʃiŋ,kriːm] n crema f de belleza.

vanishing point ['væniʃiŋ,pɔint] n punto m de fuga.

vanity ['væniti] n vanidad f; **all is —** todo es vanidad; **to do something out of —** hacer algo por vanidad.

vanity case ['væniti,keis] n neceser m de belleza, polvera f (de bolsillo).

vanquish ['væŋkwiʃ] *vt (lit)* vencer, derrotar.

vantage ['vɑːntidʒ] n *(Tennis)* ventaja f.

vantage point ['vɑːntidʒ,pɔint] n posición f ventajosa, lugar m estratégico; *(for views)* punto m panorámico; **from our modern — we can see that . . .** desde nuestra atalaya moderna vemos que . . .

vapid ['væpid] *adj* insípido, soso.

vapidity [væ'piditi] n insipidez f, sosería f.

vapour, (US) vapor ['veipə*] 1 n vapor m; vaho m, exhalación f; **the —s** *(Med)* los vapores.

2 *vi (boast)* fanfarronear; **to — about** decir disparates acerca de.

vapourization, (US) vaporization [,veipərai'zeiʃən] n vaporización f.

vapourize, (US) vaporize ['veipəraiz] 1 *vt* vaporizar, volatilizar. 2 *vi* vaporizarse, volatilizarse.

vapourizer, (US) vaporizer ['veipəraizə*] n vaporizador m.

vaporous ['veipərəs] *adj* vaporoso.

variability [,vɛəriə'biliti] n variabilidad f.

variable ['vɛəriəbl] 1 *adj* variable. 2 n variable f.

variance ['vɛəriəns] n: **to be at —** estar en desacuerdo *(with* con), desentonar *(with* con), estar reñidos *(with* con).

variant ['vɛəriənt] 1 *adj* variante. 2 n variante f.

variation [,vɛəri'eiʃən] n variación f *(also Mus)*; *(variant form)* variedad f.

varicoloured *adj*, *(US)* **varicolored** ['vɛəri'kʌləd] *adj* abigarrado, multicolor.

varicose ['værikəus] *adj* varicoso; **— veins** varices *fpl*.

varied ['vɛərid] *adj* variado.

variegated ['vɛərigeitid] *adj* abigarrado; jaspeado.

variegation [,vɛəri'geiʃən] n abigarramiento m.

variety [və'raiəti] n variedad f *(also Bio)*; diversidad f; *(Comm: of stock)* surtido m; **in a — of colours** en muchos colores, de diversos colores, *(Comm)* en gran surtido de colores; **in a — of ways** de diversas maneras; **a — of opinions was expressed** se expresaron diversas opiniones; **for —** por variar; **to lend — to something** servir para variar algo, dar diversidad a algo; *see* **artist** etc.

variety store [və'raiəti'stɔː*] n *(US)* tienda f barata que vende de todo.

variola [və'raiələ] n viruela f.

various ['vɛəriəs] *adj* vario, diverso; **for — reasons** por diversas razones; **in — ways** de diversos modos; **at — times in the past** en determinados momentos del pasado.

variously ['vɛəriəsli] *adv* diversamente, de diversos modos; **she stated her age —** declaraba su edad de diversos modos.

varmint ['vɑːmint] n *(Hunting)* bicho m; *(fam)* golfo m, bribón m.

varnish ['vɑːniʃ] 1 n barniz m; *(for nails)* esmalte m para las uñas, laca f para las uñas; *(fig)* barniz m, capa f, apariencia f.

2 *vt* barnizar; *nails* laquear, esmaltar; *(fig: also* **to — over**) dar apariencia respetable a, disimular, paliar.

varsity ['vɑːsiti] n *(fam)* universidad f.

vary ['vɛəri] 1 *vt* variar; *decision etc* cambiar, modificar.

2 *vi* variar; *(disagree)* estar en desacuerdo; discrepar *(from* de); *(deviate)* desviarse *(from* de); **it varies** depende; **it varies from 2 to 10** varía de 2 a 10; **it varies a lot from the norm** se desvía mucho de la norma; **authors — about the date** los autores discrepan acerca de la fecha; **it varies in price** varía de precio; **they — in price** los hay de diversos precios; **it varies inversely with . . .** varía en razón inversa según . . .

varying ['vɛəriiŋ] *adj* cambiante; diverso; **with — results** con resultados diversos.

vascular ['væskjulə*] *adj* vascular.

vase [vɑːz] n florero m, jarrón m.

Vaseline ['væsiliːn] *(Protected Trade Name)* n vaselina f.

vassal ['væsəl] n vasallo m.

vassalage ['væsəlidʒ] n vasallaje m.

vast [vɑːst] *adj* vasto; inmenso, enorme; *majority* abrumador.

vastly ['vɑːstli] *adv* enormemente; **— improved** muy mejorado; **— superior to** con mucho superior a; **we were — amused** nos reímos muchísimo con eso; **— different** muy distinto.

vastness ['vɑːstnis] n inmensidad f.

vat [væt] n tina f, tinaja f.

Vatican ['vætikən] 1 n Vaticano m. 2 *adj* vaticano, del Vaticano.

vaudeville ['vəudəvil] n vaudeville m.

vault[1] [vɔːlt] 1 n *(Archit)* bóveda f; *(for wine)* bodega f; *(of bank)* sótano m, cámara f acorazada; *(tomb)* tumba f; *(of church)* cripta f; **barrel —** bóveda f de cañón; **family —** panteón m familiar; **— of heaven** bóveda f celeste.

2 *vt* abovedar.

vault[2] [vɔːlt] 1 n salto m; **at one —, with one —** de un salto.

2 *vti* saltar; **to — into the saddle** colocarse de un salto en la silla; **to — over a stream** cruzar un arroyo de un salto.

vaulted ['vɔːltid] *adj* abovedado.

vaulting ['vɔːltiŋ] n abovedado m.

vaulting horse ['vɔːltiŋ,hɔːs] n potro m de madera, caballo m de aros.

vaunt [vɔːnt] 1 *vt* jactarse de, hacer alarde de; lucir, ostentar. 2 *vi* jactarse.

vaunted ['vɔːntid] *adj* cacareado, alardeado; **much — tan cacareado.**

vaunting ['vɔːntiŋ] **1** *adj* jactancioso. **2** *n* jactancia *f*.

V-Day ['viːdei] *n* día *m* de la victoria (*esp de los aliados en Europa*, 8 mayo de 1945).

veal [viːl] *n* ternera *f*.

vector ['vektə*] *n* vector *m*.

Veda ['veidə] Veda *m*.

Vedic ['veidik] *adj* védico.

veep [viːp] *n* (*US fam*) vicepresidente *m*.

veer [viə*] *vi* (*also to — round*) (*ship, also fig*) virar; (*wind*) girar, cambiar; **the country has —ed to the left** el país ha virado hacia la izquierda; **it —s from one extreme to the other** oscila- desde un extremo al otro; **people are —ing round to our point of view** la gente está empezando a aceptar nuestro criterio.

vegetable ['vedʒitəbl] **1** *adj* vegetal; **— kingdom** reino *m* vegetal.
   2 *n* (*Bot*) vegetal *f*; (*edible plant*) legumbre *f*, hortaliza *f*; **—s** (*on sale as food, as item of diet*) legumbres *fpl*, hortalizas *fpl*, (*cooked, greens*) verduras *fpl*.

vegetable dish ['vedʒitəbldiʃ] *n* fuente *f* de legumbres.

vegetable garden ['vedʒitəbl,gɑːdn] *n* huerto *m*.

vegetarian [,vedʒi'teəriən] **1** *adj* vegetariano. **2** *n* vegetariano *m*, a *f*.

vegetarianism [,vedʒi'teəriənizəm] *n* vegetarianismo *m*.

vegetate ['vedʒiteit] *vi* vegetar (*also fig*).

vegetation [,vedʒi'teiʃən] *n* vegetación *f*.

vegetative ['vedʒitətiv] *adj* vegetativo.

vehemence ['viːiməns] *n* vehemencia *f*; violencia *f*, pasión *f*.

vehement ['viːimənt] *adj* vehemente; violento, aspasionado; **a — speech** un discurso apasionado; **there was — opposition** hubo una resistencia violenta.

vehemently ['viːiməntli] *adv* con vehemencia; violentamente, apasionadamente; **we are — opposed to it** nos oponemos totalmente a ello, estamos cien por cien en contra.

vehicle ['viːikl] *n* vehículo *m*; (*means*) vehículo *m*, medio *m*, instrumento *m* (*for* de).

vehicular [vi'hikjulə*] *adj* road etc de vehículos, para coches; *traffic* rodado.

veil [veil] **1** *n* velo *m* (*also Phot and fig*); **under a — of secrecy** en el mayor secreto; **to draw a — over something** correr un velo sobre algo, encubrir algo; **we had better draw a — over that** es mejor no hablar de eso; **to take the —** tomar el hábito, meterse monja.
   2 *vt* velar (*also fig*); **eyes —ed by tears** ojos *mpl* velados por lágrimas; **the town was —ed by mist** la ciudad estaba cubierta por un velo de niebla.

veiled [veild] *adj* velado; **with — irony** con velada ironía; **that was a — reference to the bishop** fue una referencia velada al obispo.

veiling ['veiliŋ] *n* (*Phot*) velo *m*.

vein [vein] *n* (*Anat, Bot*) vena *f*; (*Min: of ore etc*) filón *m*, veta *f*; (*in stone*) vena *f*; (*in wood*) fibra *f*; hebra *f*, veta *f*; (*fig*) vena *f*, rasgo *m*; **a — of madness** una vena de loco, un rasgo de locura; **to be in the —** estar en vena; **to be in the — for** estar de humor para.

veined [veind] *adj* veteado.

velar ['viːlə*] *adj* velar.

Velasquez [vi'læskwiz] *m* Velázquez.

vellum ['veləm] *n* vitela *f*.

velocipede [və'lɔsipiːd] *n* velocípedo *m*.

velocity [vi'lɔsiti] *n* velocidad *f*.

velour [və'luə*] *n* terciopelo *m*.

velum ['viːləm] *n* (*Anat*) velo *m* del paladar.

velvet ['velvit] **1** *n* terciopelo *m*; (*Anat*) piel *f* velluda, vello *m*; **to be on —** (*fam*) estar en situación muy ventajosa; **a skin like —** una piel aterciopelada.
   2 *adj, attr* (*velvety*) aterciopelado; (*of —*) de terciopelo.

velveteen ['velvitiːn] *n* pana *f*.

velvety ['velviti] *adj* aterciopelado.

venal ['viːnl] *adj* venal.

venality [viː'næliti] *n* venalidad *f*.

vend [vend] *n* (*Comm*) vender.

vendetta [ven'detə] *n* enemistad *f*; odio *m* de sangre; disputa *f*; **to carry on a — against someone** hacer una campaña contra uno; hostigar a uno, perseguir a uno.

vending ['vendiŋ] *n* (*Comm*) venta *f*, distribución *f*.

vending machine ['vendiŋmə,ʃiːn] *n* distribuidor *m* automático.

vendor ['vendɔ*] *n* vendedor *m*, ora *f*; (*pedlar*) buhonero *m*.

veneer [və'niə*] **1** *n* chapa *f*, enchapado *m*; (*fig*) barniz *m*, apariencia *f*; **with a — of culture** con un barniz de cultura; **it's just a — es** un barniz superficial nada más.
   2 *vt* chapear.

venerable ['venərəbl] *adj* venerable.

venerate ['venəreit] *vt* venerar, reverenciar.

veneration [,venə'reiʃən] *n* veneración *f*; **his — for ... la** veneración que sentía por . . .; **to hold someone in — reverenciar** a uno.

venereal [vi'niəriəl] *adj* venéreo.

Venetian [vi'niːʃən] **1** *adj* veneciano. **2** *n* veneciano *m*, a *f*.

Venezuela [,vene'zweilə] Venezuela *f*.

Venezuelan [,vene'zweilən] **1** *adj* venezolano. **2** *n* venezolano *m*, a *f*.

vengeance ['vendʒəns] *n* venganza *f*; **with a — con creces**; de verdad; **it's raining with a — está** lloviendo de verdad; **to take — on someone** tomar venganza en uno.

vengeful ['vendʒful] *adj* (*lit*) vengativo.

venial ['viːniəl] *adj* venial.

veniality [,viːni'æliti] *n* venialidad *f*.

Venice ['venis] Venecia *f*.

venison ['venizn] *n* carne *f* de venado.

venom ['venəm] *n* veneno *m*; (*fig*) virulencia *f*, malignidad *f*; **he spoke with real — in his voice** habló en tono de verdadero odio.

venomous ['venəməs] *adj* venenoso; (*fig*) virulento, maligno.

venomously ['venəməsli] *adv* (*fig*) con malignidad, con odio.

venous ['viːnəs] *adj* venoso.

vent [vent] **1** *n* (*opening*) abertura *f*; válvula *f*; (*Mech*) válvula *f* de purga, orificio *m*, lumbrera *f*; (*airhole*) respiradero *m*; (*in pipe*) ventosa *f*; (*Orn*) cloaca *f*; **to give — to** dar salida a, desahogar, expresar; **to give — to one's feelings** desahogarse; **to give — to a sigh** exhalar un suspiro.
   2 *vt* (*Mech*) purgar; (*discharge*) descargar, emitir, dejar escapar; (*pierce*) agujerear; *feelings etc* desahogar, descargar; **to — one's anger** desahogar su cólera, desahogarse; **to — one's spleen** descargar la bilis (*on* contra).

ventilate ['ventileit] *vt* ventilar (*also fig*).

ventilation [,venti'leiʃən] *n* ventilación *f*.

ventilator ['ventileitə*] *n* ventilador *m*.

ventral ['ventrəl] *adj* ventral.

ventricle ['ventrikl] *n* ventrículo *m*.

ventriloquism [ven'triləkwizəm] *n* ventriloquia *f*.

ventriloquist [ven'triləkwist] *n* ventrílocuo *m*, a *f*.

venture ['ventʃə*] **1** *n* aventura *f*, empresa *f* (*arriesgada*); **at a — a** la ventura; **his — into business** su aventura en el mundo de los negocios; **it seemed a stupid — at the time** en aquel momento parecía ser una empresa descabellada; **a new — in publishing** un nuevo rumbo en la edición de libros, una nueva empresa editorial.
   2 *vt* aventurar; (*stake*) jugar; *opinion etc* osar expresar; **they —d everything** lo jugaron todo; **if I may — an opinion** si se me permite expresar mi opinión; **may I — a guess?** ¿puedo hacer una conjetura? **he —d to remark that . . .** se permitió observar que . . .; **nothing — nothing gain** quien no se arriesga no pasa la mar.
   3 *vi* (a) **to — on something** arriesgarse en algo, osar emprender algo, lanzarse a algo; **when we —d on this** cuando emprendimos esto; **to — into a wood** (osar) penetrar en un bosque; **to — out of doors** osar salir fuera, arriesgarse fuera.
   (b) **to — to + infin** osar + *infin*, atreverse a + *infin*; permitirse + *infin*; **I — to add that . . .** me permito agregar que . . .; **I — to write to you** me tomo la libertad de dirigirme a Vd; **but he did not — to speak** pero no osó hablar.

venturesome ['ventʃəsəm] *adj* person atrevido, audaz; *enterprise* arriesgado, azaroso.

venue ['venjuː] *n* punto *m* de reunión, lugar *m* en que se han de reunir dos (*etc*) personas; **the — for the next match** el campo para el próximo partido; **the — has been changed** se ha cambiado de lugar.

Venus ['viːnəs] (*Myth*) Venus *f*; (*Astron*) Venus *m*.

Venusian [və'nuːziən] **1** *adj* venusiano. **2** *n* venusiano *m*, a *f*.

veracious [və'reiʃəs] *adj* veraz.

veracity [və'ræsiti] *n* veracidad *f*.

veranda(h) [və'rændə] *n* veranda *f*, terraza *f*, galería *f*.

verb [vəːb] *n* verbo *m*; **auxiliary — verbo** *m* auxiliar; **defective — verbo** *m* defectivo; **deponent — verbo**

m deponente; **finite** — verbo *m* finito; **intransitive** — verbo *m* intransitivo, verbo *m* neutro; **reflexive** — verbo *m* reflexivo; **transitive** — verbo *m* transitivo.

verbal ['vɜːbəl] *adj* verbal.

verbalize ['vɜːbəlaiz] **1** *vt* expresar en palabras; exteriorizar hablando. **2** *vi* expresarse en palabras; **he does not** — **easily** no se expresa con facilidad.

verbally ['vɜːbəli] *adv* verbalmente; de palabra, por boca.

verbatim [vɜː'beitim] *adv, adj* palabra por palabra.

verbena [vɜː'biːnə] *n* verbena *f*.

verbiage ['vɜːbiidʒ] *n* verbosidad *f*, palabrería *f*.

verbose [vɜː'bəus] *adj* verboso, prolijo.

verbosely [vɜː'bəusli] *adv* prolijamente.

verbosity [vɜː'bɒsiti] *n* verbosidad *f*.

verdant ['vɜːdənt] *adj* verde.

verdict ['vɜːdikt] *n* (*Law*) veredicto *m*, fallo *m*, sentencia *f*, juicio *m*; (*fig*) opinión *f*, juicio *m*; **a** — **of guilty** una sentencia de culpabilidad; **open** — juicio *m* en el que se determina el crimen sin designar el culpable; **what's your** —? ¿qué opinas de esto?, ¿qué juicio te has formado sobre esto?; **his** — **on the wine was unfavourable** hizo un juicio desfavorable acerca del vino; **to bring in a** —, **to return a** — pronunciar una sentencia, dar un fallo; **to bring in a** — **of guilty** pronunciar una sentencia de culpabilidad.

verdigris ['vɜːdigriːs] *n* verdete *m*, cardenillo *m*.

verdure ['vɜːdjuə*] *n* verdura *f*.

verge [vɜːdʒ] **1** *n* borde *m*, margen *m*; **to be on the** — **of disaster** estar a dos dedos del desastre, estar en el mismo borde de la catástrofe; **to be on the** — **of a nervous breakdown** estar al borde de una crisis nerviosa; **to be on the** — **of a great discovery** estar en la antesala de un gran descubrimiento; **we are on the** — **of war** estamos al borde de la guerra; **she was on the** — **of tears** estaba para deshacerse en lágrimas; **to be on the** — **of** + *ger* estar a punto de + *infin*.

2 *vi*: **to** — **on** acercarse a, rayar en; estar a un paso mínimo de; **a state verging on madness** un estado que raya en la locura.

verger ['vɜːdʒə*] *n* sacristán *m*.

Vergil ['vɜːdʒil] *m* Virgilio.

Vergilian [vɜː'dʒiliən] *adj* virgiliano.

verifiable ['verifaiəbl] *adj* comprobable, verificable.

verification [,verifi'keiʃən] *n* comprobación *f*, verificación *f*.

verify ['verifai] *vt* comprobar, verificar.

verisimilitude [,verisi'militjuːd] *n* verosimilitud *f*.

veritable ['veritəbl] *adj* verdadero; **a** — **monster** un verdadero monstruo.

veritably ['veritəbli] *adv* verdaderamente.

verity ['veriti] *n* verdad *f*; **the eternal verities** las verdades eternas.

vermicelli [,vɜːmi'seli] *n* fideos *mpl*.

vermicide ['vɜːmisaid] *n* vermicida *m*.

vermifuge ['vɜːmifjuːdʒ] *n* vermífugo *m*.

vermilion [vɜː'miliən] **1** *n* bermellón *m*. **2** *adj* bermejo.

vermin ['vɜːmin] *n* bichos *mpl*, sabandijas *fpl*; parásitos *mpl*; (*fig*) sabandijas *pl*.

verminous ['vɜːminəs] *adj* verminoso, piojoso; (*fig*) vil.

vermouth ['vɜːməθ] *n* vermut *m*.

vernacular [vɜː'nækjulə*] **1** *adj* vernáculo, vulgar; **in** — **Persian** en persa vulgar, en la lengua vernácula de Persia.

2 *n* lengua *f* vernácula; (*fig*) lenguaje *m* corriente, lenguaje *m* vulgar.

veronica [vɜː'rɒnikə] *n* (*Bot*) verónica *f*.

Veronica [vɜː'rɒnikə] *f* Verónica.

Versailles [veə'sai] Versalles.

versatile ['vɜːsətail] *adj* person versátil, hábil para muchas cosas, de talentos variados, polifacético, de genio multiforme; *mind* adaptable, flexible; universal; *writer etc* que domina varios géneros.

versatility [,vɜːsə'tiliti] *n* versatilidad *f*; talentos *mpl* variados, aptitudes *fpl* diversas; adaptabilidad *f*, flexibilidad *f*; universalidad *f*.

verse [vɜːs] *n* (*stanza*) estrofa *f*; (*of Bible*) versículo *m*; (*genre*) verso *m*; (*poetry*) poesías *fpl*, versos *mpl*; **comic** —, **light** — poesías *fpl* jocosas; **is it in** —? ¿está en verso?; — **drama** teatro *m* en verso, drama *m* poético; **a** — **version of the "Celestina"** una versión en verso de la "Celestina".

versed [vɜːst] *adj*: **to be well** — **in** estar versado en, conocer, ser conocedor de.

versification [,vɜːsifi'keiʃən] *n* versificación *f*.

versifier ['vɜːsifaiə*] *n* versificador *m*, ora *f*.

versify ['vɜːsifai] **1** *vt* versificar. **2** *vi* versificar, escribir versos.

version ['vɜːʃən] *n* versión *f*; **in Lope's** — **of the story** en la versión que hizo Lope de la historia;

my — **of events is as follows . . .** yo veo los sucesos del siguiente modo . . .; **according to his** — según su interpretación; **that's a different** — **again** ése es otro modo distinto de contarlo.

versus ['vɜːsəs] *prep* contra; **Ceuta** — **Alcoy** Ceuta contra Alcoy.

vertebra ['vɜːtibrə] *n, pl* **vertebrae** ['vɜːtibriː] vértebra *f*.

vertebral ['vɜːtibrəl] *adj* vertebral.

vertebrate ['vɜːtibrit] **1** *adj* vertebrado. **2** *n* vertebrado *m*.

vertex ['vɜːteks] *n, pl* **vertices** [vɜːtisiːz] vértice *m*.

vertical ['vɜːtikəl] **1** *adj* vertical. **2** *n* vertical *f*.

vertically ['vɜːtikəli] *adv* verticalmente.

vertiginous [vɜː'tidʒinəs] *adj* vertiginoso.

vertigo ['vɜːtigəu] *n* vértigo *m*.

verve [vɜːv] *n* energía *f*, empuje *m*; brío *m*; entusiasmo *m*.

very ['veri] **1** *adv* (a) muy; — **good** muy bueno, — **well** muy bien; — **much** mucho, muchísimo; **she felt** — **much better** se encontró muchísimo mejor; **I was** — (**much**) **surprised** me sorprendió mucho, para mí era una gran sorpresa; **it's not so** — **difficult** no es tan difícil, la dificultad no es tan grande; **that's** — **kind of you** es Vd muy amable; **you're not being** — **helpful** realmente no nos ayudas nada.

(b) **it is** — **cold** (*object*) está muy frío, (*weather*) hace mucho frío.

(c) **the** — **first** el primero, el primero de todos; **the** — **best** el mejor, el mejor que haya; **we did our** — **best** hicimos todo lo que pudimos; **try your** — **hardest** esfuércese al máximo; **at the** — **most** a lo más, a lo sumo, todo lo más; **the** — **most we can offer** el límite de lo que podemos ofrecer; **the** — **next day** precisamente el día siguiente; **the** — **same hat** el idéntico sombrero.

(d) (*alone, in reply to question*) mucho; **are you tired?** . . . — ¿estás cansado? . . . mucho.

(e) (*emotional use*) **they are so** — **poor** son pobrísimos; **it is a** — **good wine** es un vino rebueno, es un vino requetebueno.

2 *adj* (a) mismo; **in this** — **house** en esta misma casa; **at that** — **moment** en ese mismo momento; **to the** — **bone** hasta el mismo hueso; **he's the** — **man we want** es precisamente el hombre que buscamos; **it's the** — **thing!** ¡es exactamente lo que necesitamos!; **at the** — **beginning** ya en los comienzos; **the** — **bishop himself was there** el mismísimo obispo estaba allí, hasta el propio obispo estaba allí; **the** — **idea!** ¡ni hablar!, ¡qué cosas dices!; **the** — **thought frightens me** sólo pensar en ello me da miedo.

(b) **the veriest rascal** el mayor bribón.

vesicle ['vesikl] *n* vesícula *f*.

vespers ['vespəz] *npl* vísperas *fpl*.

vessel ['vesl] *n* (a) (*Anat, Bot*) vaso *m*; (*receptacle*) vasija *f*, recipiente *m*; **he's a weak** — es una persona sin carácter.

(b) (*Naut*) buque *m*, barco *m*.

vest[1] [vest] *n* camiseta *f*; (US) chaleco *m*.

vest[2] [vest] *vt* (a) **to** — **someone with something** investir a uno de algo.

(b) **to** — **rights in someone** conferir derechos a uno, conceder derechos a uno, revestir a uno de derechos; **by the authority** —**ed in me** en virtud de la autoridad que se me ha concedido; **to** — **property in someone** ceder una propiedad a uno, hacer a uno titular de una propiedad.

vesta ['vestə] *n* cerilla *f*.

vestal ['vestl] **1** *adj* vestal. **2** *n* vestal *f*.

vested ['vestid] *adj* right inalienable; *interest* creado.

vestibule ['vestibjuːl] *n* vestíbulo *m*; (*hall of house*) zaguán *m*; (*anteroom*) antecámara *f*.

vestige ['vestidʒ] *n* vestigio *m*, rastro *m*; (*Bio*) rudimento *m*; **not a** — **of it remains** no queda rastro de ello, de ello no queda ni el menor vestigio; **without a** — **of decency** sin la menor decencia; **if there is a** — **of doubt** si hay una sombra de duda.

vestigial [ves'tidʒiəl] *adj* vestigial; rudimentario.

vestment ['vestmənt] *n* vestidura *f*.

vest-pocket ['vest'pɒkit] *adj* (US) en miniatura.

vestry ['vestri] *n* sacristía *f*.

vesture ['vestʃə*] *n* (*lit*) vestidura *f*.

Vesuvius [vi'suːviəs] Vesubio.

vet [vet] (*fam*) **1** *n* veterinario *m*.

2 *vt* repasar, revisar; examinar, investigar; aprobar; **he's** —**ting the proofs** está corrigiendo las pruebas; **we'll have it** —**ted by the boss** haremos que el jefe lo repase; **he was** —**ted by Security** fue sometido a investigación por la Seguridad.

vetch [vetʃ] *n* arveja *f*.

veteran ['vetərən] **1** adj veterano. **2** n veterano m; ex combatiente m.

veterinarian [,vetəri'neəriən] n (US) veterinario m.

veterinary ['vetərinəri] adj veterinario; — **medicine**, — **science** medicina f veterinaria, veterinaria f; — **surgeon** veterinario m.

veto ['viːtəu] **1** n, pl **vetoes** ['viːtəuz] veto m; **to have a** — tener veto; **to put a** — **on something** poner su veto a algo.
2 vt vedar, vetar, prohibir; **he** —ed **it** él lo prohibió, él lo vedó; **the president** —ed **it** el presidente le puso su veto.

vex [veks] vt (anger) fastidiar, irritar, contrariar; (make impatient) impacientar, sacar de quicio; (afflict) afligir; **the problems that are** —ing **the country** los problemas que afligen el país, los problemas que alteran el país.

vexation [vek'seiʃən] n irritación f, contrariedad f; impaciencia f; aflicción f; **he had to put up with numerous** —s tuvo que soportar muchos disgustos.

vexatious [vek'seiʃəs] adj fastidioso, molesto, engorroso.

vexed [vekst] adj (a) **to be** — **about something** estar enfadado de algo, estar enfadado por algo; **to be** — **with someone** estar enfadado con uno; **to be very** — estar muy enfadado; **to get** — enfadarse, impacientarse.
(b) **in a** — **tone** en tono ofendido, en tono de enojo.
(c) **question** batallón.

vexing ['veksiŋ] adj fastidioso, molesto, engorroso; **it's very** — es una lata.

via ['vaiə] prep por, por vía de; **we came to** — **London** pasamos por Londres.

viability [,vaiə'biliti] n viabilidad f.

viable ['vaiəbl] adj viable.

viaduct ['vaiədʌkt] n viaducto m.

vial ['vaiəl] n see **phial**.

viands ['vaiəndz] npl (lit) manjares mpl (exquisitos).

viaticum [vai'ætikəm] n viático m.

vibrant ['vaibrənt] **1** n vibrante (also fig; with de). **2** n vibrante f.

vibrate [vai'breit] vti vibrar.

vibration [vai'breiʃən] n vibración f.

vibrator [vai'breitə*] n vibrador m.

vibratory ['vaibrətəri] adj vibratorio.

viburnum [vai'bəːnəm] n viburno m.

vicar ['vikə*] n vicario m; (parish priest) párroco m, cura m.

vicarage ['vikəridʒ] n casa f del párroco.

vicar-general ['vikə'dʒenərəl] n vicario m general.

vicarious [vi'keəriəs] adj experimentado por otro; **to get** — **pleasure out of something** sentir placer por lo que está haciendo otro; **I got a** — **thrill** me emocioné mucho sin tener nada que ver con lo que pasaba.

vicariously [vi'keəriəsli] adv: **to feel excitement** — emocionarse por lo que está haciendo otro, emocionarse a través de la emoción de otro.

vice[1] [vais] n vicio m.

vice[2] [vais] n (Mech) torno m de banco, tornillo m de banco.

vice[3] ['vaisi] prep en lugar de, sustituyendo a.

vice . . . [vais] in compounds: vice . . .

vice-admiral ['vais'ædmərəl] n vicealmirante m.

vice-chairman ['vais'tʃeəmən] n, pl —**men** [mən] vicepresidente m.

vice-chairmanship ['vais,tʃeəmənʃip] n vicepresidencia f.

vice-chancellor ['vais'tʃɑːnsələ*] n (Univ, approx) rector m.

vice-consul ['vais'kɔnsəl] n vicecónsul m.

vice-presidency ['vais'prezidənsi] n vicepresidencia f.

vice-president ['vais'prezidənt] n vicepresidente m.

viceroy ['vaisrɔi] n virrey m.

viceroyalty ['vais'rɔiəlti] n virreinato m.

vice squad ['vaisskwɔd] n brigada f contra el vicio.

vice versa ['vaisi'vəːsə] adv viceversa, a la inversa; **and** — y a la inversa.

vicinity [vi'siniti] n (area) vecindad f, región f; (nearness) proximidad f (to de); **and other towns in the** — y otras ciudades de la región, y otras ciudades cercanas; **we are in the** — **of Wigan** estamos en la región de Wigan, estamos cerca de Wigan; **in the** — **of 90** unos 90, alrededor de 90.

vicious ['viʃəs] adj (related to vice) vicioso; person depravado, perverso; cruel; dog bravo; horse resabiado, arisco; blow cruel, sañudo; crime atroz; criticism virulento, cruel, rencoroso; **with** — **intent** con mala intención, con intención criminal.

viciously ['viʃəsli] adv viciosamente; perversamente; cruelmente; con virulencia, con rencor, rencorosamente.

viciousness ['viʃəsnis] n viciosidad f; perversidad f, crueldad f; bravura f, resabios mpl; atrocidad f; virulencia f, rencor m.

vicissitudes [vi'sisitjuːdz] npl vicisitudes fpl; altibajos mpl, peripecias fpl.

vicissitudinous [vi,sisi'tjuːdinəs] adj accidentado.

victim ['viktim] n víctima f; **to be the** — **of an accident** ser víctima de un accidente, morir (etc) en un accidente; **to be the** — **of a swindle** ser víctima de una estafa; **to fall a** — **to flu** enfermar con la gripe; **to fall a** — **to someone's charms** rendirse (or sucumbir) a los encantos de uno.

victimization [,viktimai'zeiʃən] n sacrificio m; persecución f; (of striker etc) castigo m, represalias fpl.

victimize ['viktimaiz] vt hacer víctima de; escoger y castigar, tomar represalias contra; **the strikers should not be** —d no hay por qué castigar a los huelguistas; **she feels she has been** —d ella cree que ha sido escogida como víctima.

victor ['viktə*] n vencedor m, ora f.

Victoria [vik'tɔːriə] f Victoria.

Victoria Falls [vik'tɔːriə'fɔːlz] pl Cataratas fpl de Victoria.

Victorian [vik'tɔːriən] **1** adj victoriano. **2** n victoriano m, a f.

victorious [vik'tɔːriəs] adj victorioso; **the** — **team** el equipo vencedor, los vencedores; **to be** — triunfar (over sobre), salir victorioso, vencer.

victoriously [vik'tɔːriəsli] adv victoriosamente, triunfalmente.

victory ['viktəri] n victoria f; triunfo m; **moral** — victoria f moral; **Pyrrhic** — victoria f pírrica; **to win a famous** — obtener un triunfo señalado.

victual ['vitl] **1** vt abastecer, avituallar. **2** vi abastecerse, avituallarse, tomar provisiones.

victualler ['vitlə*] n: **licensed** — vendedor m de bebidas alcohólicas.

victuals ['vitlz] npl víveres mpl, provisiones fpl, vitualla f.

vicuna [vi'kjuːnə] n vicuña f.

vide ['videi] (vt) vea, véase.

videlicet [vi'diːliset] adv a saber.

video ['videiəu] **1** n vídeo m. **2** attr de vídeo.

vie [vai] vi competir, ser rivales; **to** — **for something** disputarse algo; **to** — **with someone for something** disputar algo a alguien, luchar contra uno para conseguir algo; **to** — **with someone** competir con uno, rivalizar con uno.

Vienna [vi'enə] Viena.

Viennese [,viə'niːz] **1** adj vienés. **2** n vienés m, esa f.

Vietnam ['vjet'næm] Vietnam m.

Vietnamese [,vjetnə'miːz] **1** adj vietnamita. **2** n vietnamita mf. **3** n (language) vietnamita m.

vieux jeu ['viəː'ʒəː] adj anticuado, fuera de moda.

view [vjuː] **1** n (a) (general sense) vista f; panorama m; perspectiva f; (Art, Phot) panorama m; (landscape) paisaje m; private — inauguración f privada; **it's a beautiful** — es un bello panorama; **there is a fine** — **from the top** desde la cumbre se ofrece un magnífico panorama; **50** —**s of Venice** 50 vistas de Venecia; **a** — **of Toledo from the north** Toledo en su aspecto norte, Toledo visto desde el norte; **to be in** — ser visible; **to be in full** — ser totalmente visible; **he did it in full** — **of hundreds of people** lo hizo estando delante centenares de personas, lo hizo a plena vista de centenares de personas; **to have (or keep) someone in** — no perder a uno de vista; **to be on** — estar expuesto; **the house will be on** — **to the public on Saturdays** la casa estará abierta al público los sábados.
(b) (opinion etc) opinión f, parecer m; criterio m; actitud f; **in my** — en mi opinión; **in** — **of this** en vista de esto; **with a** — **to doing something** con miras a hacer algo, con el propósito de hacer algo; **our** — **of the problem** nuestro modo de enfocar el problema; **what is the government's** —? ¿cuál es la actitud del gobierno?; **it is not easy to form a** — no es fácil llegar a una conclusión; **to have (or keep) something in** — tener algo en cuenta, tener algo presente; **I do not share that** — no comparto ese criterio; **to take the** — **that** . . . opinar que . . .; **we take a different** — nosotros pensamos de otro modo; **to take a dim (or poor)** — **of someone** tener un concepto desfavorable de uno, tener a uno en poco; **I should take a dim** — **if** . . . no me agradaría que + subj.
2 vt mirar; ver, contemplar; examinar, inspeccionar; considerar; **we went to** — **the house** fuimos a ver la casa; **Cadiz** —ed **from the sea** Cádiz visto desde el mar; **we** — **it with some alarm** para nosotros se motivo de cierta alarma; **how does the government** — **it?** ¿cuál es la actitud del gobierno?

viewer ['vjuːə*] n (onlooker) espectador m, ora f; (TV) televidente mf, telespectador m, ora f.

viewfinder ['vjuːˌfaində*] n (Phot) visor m de imagen.

viewpoint ['vjuːpɔint] n (a) (Geog) mirador m, punto m panorámico.
(b) (fig) punto m de vista; criterio m; from the — of the economy desde el punto de vista de la economía.

vigil ['vidʒil] n vigilia f; to keep — velar.

vigilance ['vidʒiləns] n vigilancia f; to escape someone's —;burlar la vigilancia de uno.

vigilant ['vidʒilənt] adj vigilante; desvelado, alerta.

vigilante [ˌvidʒi'lænti] n vigilante m.

vigilantly ['vidʒiləntli] adv vigilantemente.

vignette [vi'njet] n (Phot, Typ) viñeta f.

vigorous ['vigərəs] adj vigoroso, enérgico.

vigorously ['vigərəsli] adv vigorosamente, con vigor, enérgicamente.

vigour, (US) **vigor** ['vigə*] n vigor m, energía f; in the full — of manhood en la flor de la edad viril.

Viking ['vaikiŋ] n vikingo m.

vile [vail] adj vil; infame, detestable; (very bad) horrible, asqueroso; the weather was — el tiempo fue horrible; it's a — play es una obra malísima; he has a — temper tiene un genio muy vivo, es un hombre de malas pulgas; that was a — thing to say eso fue infame.

vilely ['vailli] adv vilmente; de modo infame, de modo detestable; malísimamente, horriblemente; he treated her — la trató de modo infame.

vileness ['vailnis] n vileza f; infamia f; lo horrible, lo asqueroso; the — of the weather el tiempo tan horrible que hace.

vilification [ˌvilifi'keiʃən] n vilipendio m.

vilify ['vilifai] vt vilipendiar.

villa ['vilə] n (Roman etc) villa f; (seaside) chalet m; (country house) casa f de campo, quinta f.

village ['vilidʒ] 1 n (small) aldea f, pueblecito m; lugar m; (large) pueblo m. 2 attr aldeano; pueblerino; de aldea, de la aldea.

villager ['vilidʒə*] n aldeano m, a f.

villain ['vilən] n malvado m; (Lit) malo m, traidor m; (criminal) ladrón m, criminal m; (hum) tunante m, bribón m; you —! ¡ladrón!; the — of the piece es X el que debiera cargar con la culpa de esto es X, el verdadero responsable es X.

villainous ['vilənəs] adj malvado, vil, infame; (very bad) malísimo, horrible; and other — characters y otros personajes infames.

villainously ['vilənəsli] adv vilmente; — ugly feísimo.

villainy ['viləni] n maldad f, vileza f; they must be up to some — estarán tramando algo malo.

villein ['vilin] n (Hist) villano m, a f.

vim [vim] n energía f, empuje m, vigor m.

Vincent ['vinsənt] m Vicente.

vindicate ['vindikeit] 1 vt vindicar, justificar. 2 vr: to — oneself justificarse.

vindication [ˌvindi'keiʃən] n vindicación f, justificación f.

vindictive [vin'diktiv] adj vengativo; rencoroso; to feel — about something guardar rencor por motivo de algo; to feel — towards someone guardar rencor a uno.

vindictively [vin'diktivli] adv rencorosamente, con rencor.

vindictiveness [vin'diktivnis] n deseo m de venganza, espíritu m de venganza; rencor m.

vine [vain] n vid f; (climbing, trained) parra f.

vine arbour, (US) **— arbor** ['vain,ɑːbə*] n emparrado m.

vinedresser ['vain,dresə*] n viñador m.

vinegar ['vinigə*] n vinagre m.

vinegary ['vinigəri] adj vinagroso.

vine grower ['vain,grəuə*] n viticultor m, viñador m.

vine growing ['vain,grəuiŋ] n viticultura f.

vine leaf ['vainliːf] n, pl — **leaves** [liːvz] hoja f de parra, hoja f de vid, pámpana f.

vineyard ['vinjəd] n viña f, viñedo m.

vinous ['vainəs] adj vinoso.

vintage ['vintidʒ] 1 n (season, harvest) vendimia f; (with reference to quality or year) cosecha f; the 1970 — la cosecha de 1970; it will be a good — la cosecha promete ser buena.
2 adj: — wine vino m añejo, vino m de calidad; — car coche m de época, coche m antiguo, coche m clásico; it was a — year fue un año famoso, fue un año clásico; it has been a — year for plays en el teatro ha sido una temporada excelente.

vintner ['vintnə*] n vinatero m.

vinyl ['vainl] n vinilo m.

viol ['vaiəl] n viola f.

viola ['vaiələ] n (Bot) viola f.

viola [vi'əulə] n (Mus) viola f.

violate ['vaiəleit] vt (all senses) violar.

violation [ˌvaiə'leiʃən] n violación f; in — of a law violando así una ley; in — of someone's privacy invadiendo la vida privada de uno.

violator ['vaiəleitə*] n violador m, ora f.

violence ['vaiələns] n violencia f; there was — se recurrió a la fuerza; there has been — on the streets ha estallado la violencia en las calles; to die by — morir violentamente; to do someone a — agredir a uno, herir a uno; to do — to a theory torcer una teoría; to offer — mostrarse violento; to resort to — recurrir a la fuerza, venirse a las manos; tomar medidas violentas; to rob someone with — robar algo a uno a mano airada.

violent ['vaiələnt] adj violento; feeling etc intenso, acerbo; colour chillón; to become — mostrarse violento; apelar a la fuerza; to lay — hands on someone agredir a uno; to take a — dislike to someone tomar un odio intenso a uno.

violently ['vaiələntli] adv violentamente, con violencia; to die — morir violentamente; to fall — in love with someone enamorarse perdidamente de uno; he expresses himself rather — se expresa en términos algo violentos.

violet ['vaiəlit] 1 n (Bot) violeta f; (colour) violado m. 2 adj violado.

violin [ˌvaiə'lin] n violín m; first — (person) primer violín m.

violinist [ˌvaiə'linist] n violinista mf.

violoncellist [ˌvaiələn'tʃelist] n violoncelista mf.

violoncello [ˌvaiələn'tʃeləu] n violoncelo m.

viper ['vaipə*] n víbora f.

viperish ['vaipəriʃ] adj (fig) viperino.

virago [vi'rɑːgəu] n fiera f, arpía f.

Virgil ['vəːdʒil] m Virgilio.

Virgilian [vəː'dʒiliən] adj virgiliano.

virgin ['vəːdʒin] 1 adj virgen; cork, forest, soil etc virgen. 2 n virgen f; the V— la Virgen; the Blessed V— la Santísima Virgen.

virginal ['vəːdʒinl] adj virginal.

Virginian [və'dʒiniən] n (also — tobacco) tabaco m rubio.

Virgin Isles ['vəːdʒin,ailz] pl Islas fpl Vírgenes.

virginity [və'dʒiniti] n virginidad f.

virile ['virail] adj viril.

virility [vi'riliti] n virilidad f.

virologist [ˌvaiə'rɒlədʒist] n virólogo m.

virology [ˌvaiə'rɒlədʒi] n virología f.

virtual ['vəːtjuəl] adj virtual; the — dictator of the country el que es en efecto el dictador del país; it was a — defeat era casi una derrota; he made a — admission of guilt en efecto se confesó culpable.

virtually ['vəːtjuəli] adv virtualmente; it is — impossible to do anything es prácticamente imposible hacer nada, es casi imposible hacer nada; it — destroyed the building destruyó virtualmente el edificio.

virtue ['vəːtjuː] n virtud f; a woman of easy — una mujer de vida alegre, una mujer de moralidad laxa; by — of, in — of en virtud de; to make a — of necessity poner a mal tiempo buena cara, lograr sacar provecho de lo inevitable; I see no — in that no encuentro ninguna ventaja en eso; I see no —s in trams no comprendo el porqué de los tranvías.

virtuosity [ˌvəːtju'ɒsiti] n virtuosismo m.

virtuoso [ˌvəːtju'əuzəu] n virtuoso m.

virtuous ['vəːtjuəs] adj virtuoso.

virtuously ['vəːtjuəsli] adv virtuosamente.

virulence ['viruləns] n virulencia f.

virulent ['virulənt] adj virulento.

virulently ['viruləntli] adv con virulencia.

virus ['vaiərəs] n virus m.

visa ['viːzə] 1 n visado m. 2 vt visar.

visage ['vizidʒ] n (lit) semblante m.

vis-à-vis ['viːzɑːviː] prep respecto de, con relación a.

viscera ['visərə] npl vísceras fpl.

viscid ['visid] adj viscoso.

viscose ['viskəus] 1 adj viscoso. 2 n viscosa f.

viscosity [vis'kɒsiti] n viscosidad f.

viscount ['vaikaunt] n vizconde m.

viscountcy ['vaikauntsi] n vizcondado m.

viscountess ['vaikauntis] n vizcondesa f.

viscous ['viskəs] adj viscoso.

vise [vais] n (US) = **vice²**.

visé ['viːzei] see **visa**.

visibility [,vizi'biliti] *n* visibilidad *f* (*also Aer etc*); **in good** — en buenas condiciones de visibilidad; **there was a** — **of 500 metres** la visibilidad era de 500 metros; — **is down to nil** la visibilidad queda reducida a cero.

visible ['vizəbl] *adj* visible.

visibly ['vizəbli] *adv* visiblemente; **he had got** — **thinner** había adelgazado visiblemente; **she was** — **moved** patentizó su emoción, acusó una fuerte conmoción.

Visigoth ['vizigɔθ] *n* visigodo *m*, a *f*.

Visigothic [,vizi'gɔθik] **1** *adj* visigodo, visigótico. **2** *n* lengua *f* visigótica.

vision ['viʒən] **(a)** visión *f* (*also Eccl*); (*eyesight*) vista *f*; **to have normal** — tener la vista normal.
(b) (*farsightedness*) clarividencia *f*; **a man of** — un hombre clarividente; **he had the** — **to see that** . . . era lo bastante clarividente como para ver que . . .
(c) (*dream*) sueño *m*; **my** — **of the future** mi sueño del porvenir, mi manera de imaginar el futuro; **to have** —**s of wealth** soñar con ser rico; **I had** —**s of having to walk home** me estaba viendo en el caso de tener que llegar a casa andando.

visionary ['viʒənəri] **1** *adj* visionario. **2** *n* visionario *m*, a *f*.

visit ['vizit] **1** *n* visita *f*; **to be on a** — **to** . . . estar de visita en . . .; **to pay someone a** — hacer una visita a uno; **to return a** — devolver una visita.
2 *vt* **(a)** visitar, hacer una visita a; ir a; conocer; **when we first** —**ed the town** cuando conocimos la ciudad por primera vez; **to** — **the sick** visitar a los enfermos.
(b) to — **a punishment on someone** castigar a uno con algo, mandar un castigo a uno; **they were** —**ed with the plague** sufrieron el azote de la peste.
3 *vi* hacer visitas (*also* **to go** —**ing**); (*US fam*) visitarse.

visitation [,vizi'teiʃən] *n* (*Eccl*) visitación *f*; (*inspection*) inspección *f*; (*fam*) visita *f* larga y molesta; (*punishment*) castigo *m*.

visiting ['vizitiŋ] *adj* **card** *etc* de visita; **team** visitante, de fuera; **to be on** — **terms with someone** conocerse bastante para visitarse.

visiting card ['vizitiŋka:d] *n* tarjeta *f* de visita.

visitor ['vizitə*] *n* visitante *mf*; (*to one's home*) visita *f*; (*tourist*) turista *mf*, visitante *mf*; (*tripper*) excursionista *mf*; (*stranger*) forastero *m*, a *f*; **the museum had 900** —**s** el museo recibió a 900 visitantes; **we can't invite you because we have** —**s** no podemos invitarte pues tenemos visita; **sorry, we're just** —**s here** lo siento, estamos aquí de visita nada más; **the summer** —**s bring a lot of money** los veraneantes aportan mucho dinero.

visitors' book ['vizitəzbuk] *n* libro *m* de visitas, libro *m* de honor.

visor ['vaizə*] *n* visera *f*.

vista ['vistə] *n* vista *f*, panorama *m*; (*fig*) perspectiva *f*; **there are new** —**s** hay perspectivas nuevas; **it opened up** —**s of wealth** ofreció perspectivas de riqueza.

visual ['vizjuəl] *adj* visual.

visualize ['vizjuəlaiz] *vt* **(a)** (*form a picture of*) representarse (en la mente), imaginarse.
(b) (*foresee*) prever; **the government** —**s that** . . . el gobierno prevé que . . .; **we do not** — **any great change** no prevemos ningún cambio de importancia; **that is not how we** —**d it** eso no corresponde a lo que nosotros preveíamos.

visually ['vizjuəli] *adv* visualmente.

vital ['vaitl] **1** *adj* **(a)** (*essential*) esencial; imprescindible; de suma importancia, trascendental; **of** — **importance** de primerísima importancia, de importancia primordial (*to para*); **the book is** — el libro es esencial; **it is** — **that** . . . es esencial que + *subj*, importa muchísimo que + *subj*.
(b) (*critical*) decisivo, crítico; **at the** — **moment** en el momento decisivo.
(c) *person* (*of character*) enérgico, vivo, lleno de vida; **she's a very** — **person** es una persona que rebosa de energía.
(d) (*relating to life*) vital; — **parts** partes *fpl* vitales; *see* **statistics**.
2 —**s** *npl* partes *fpl* vitales.

vitality [vai'tæliti] *n* vitalidad *f*, energía *f*.

vitalize ['vaitəlaiz] *vt* vitalizar, vivificar, infundir nueva vida a.

vitally ['vaitəli] *adv:* — **important** de primerísima importancia; **it is** — **important that** . . . es esencial que + *subj*.

vitamin ['vitəmin] **1** *n* vitamina *f*. **2** *attr* **content** *etc* vitamínico.

vitaminize ['vitəminaiz] *vt* vitaminar.

vitaminized ['vitəminaizd] *adj* vitaminado, reforzado con vitaminas.

vitiate ['viʃieit] *vt* viciar (*also Law*); estropear, destruir; quitar valor a.

viticulture ['vitikʌltʃə*] *n* viticultura *f*.

vitreous ['vitriəs] *adj* vítreo.

vitrifaction [,vitri'fækʃən] *n* vitrificación *f*.

vitrify ['vitrifai] **1** *vt* vitrificar. **2** *vi* vitrificarse.

vitriol ['vitriəl] *n* vitriolo *m*.

vitriolic [,vitri'ɔlik] *adj* (*fig*) mordaz.

vituperate [vi'tju:pəreit] *vt* vituperar, llenar de injurias.

vituperation [vi,tju:pə'reiʃən] *n* vituperio *m*, injurias *fpl*.

vituperative [vi'tju:pərətiv] *adj* vituperioso, injurioso.

viva ['vaivə] *see* **viva voce**.

vivacious [vi'veiʃəs] *adj* animado, vivaz, alegre, lleno de vida.

vivaciously [vi'veiʃəsli] *adv* animadamente, alegremente.

vivacity [vi'væsiti] *n* animación *f*, vivacidad *f*, vida *f*, alegría *f*.

vivarium [vi'vɛəriəm] *n* vivero *m*.

viva voce ['vaivə'vəusi] **1** *adv* de viva voz. **2** *adj* **exam** oral. **3** *n* examen *m* oral.

vivid ['vivid] *adj* **colour, light** intenso; **flash** súbito; **impression, memory** *etc* vivo; **description** gráfico, enérgico, pintoresco

vividly ['vividli] *adv* intensamente; súbitamente; vivamente; enérgicamente, con rasgos enérgicos, de modo pintoresco.

vividness ['vividnis] *n* intensidad *f*; vivacidad *f*; energía *f*.

vivify ['vivifai] *vt* vivificar.

viviparous [vi'vipərəs] *adj* vivíparo.

vivisection [,vivi'sekʃən] *n* vivisección *f*.

vixen ['viksn] *n* zorra *f*, raposa *f*; (*fig*) arpía *f*.

vizier [vi'ziə*] *n* visir *m*; **grand** — gran visir *m*.

vocable ['vəukəbl] *n* vocablo *m*.

vocabulary [vəu'kæbjuləri] *n* vocabulario *m*, léxico *m*.

vocal ['vəukəl] *adj* vocal (*also Mus*); (*noisy*) ruidoso, chillón, gritón; **they're getting rather** — **about it** están empezando a protestar; **there was some** — **opposition** algunos manifestaron su disconformidad con protestas ruidosas.

vocalic [vəu'kælik] *adj* vocálico.

vocalist ['vəukəlist] *n* cantante *mf*; (*in cabaret etc*) vocalista *mf*.

vocalize ['vəukəlaiz] **1** *vt* vocalizar. **2** *vi* vocalizarse.

vocally ['vəukəli] *adv* vocalmente; ruidosamente.

vocation [vəu'keiʃən] *n* vocación *f*; **to have a** — **for art** tener vocación por el arte; **he has missed his** — se ha equivocado de carrera.

vocational [vəu'keiʃənl] *adj* vocacional, profesional.

vocative ['vɔkətiv] *n* vocativo *m*.

vociferate [vəu'sifəreit] *vti* vociferar, gritar.

vociferation [vəu,sifə'reiʃən] *n* vociferación *f*.

vociferous [vəu'sifərəs] *adj* vinglero, clamoroso; (*noisy*) ruidoso; **there were** — **protests** hubo protestas ruidosas, se protestó ruidosamente.

vociferously [vəu'sifərəsli] *adv* a gritos, clamorosamente; ruidosamente.

vodka ['vɔdkə] *n* vodka *f*.

vogue [vəug] *n* boga *f*, moda *f*; **the** — **for short skirts** la moda de la falda corta; **to be in** — estar de moda, estar en boga.

voice [vɔis] **1** *n* voz *f*; **active** — voz *f* activa; **passive** — voz *f* pasiva; **in a gentle** — en tono dulce; **in a loud** — en voz alta; **in a low** — en voz baja; **with one** — a una voz, al unísono; **to be in (good)** — estar en voz; **to give** — **to** expresar, hacerse eco de; **to have no** — **in a matter** no tener voz en capítulo; **to raise one's** — levantar el tono, (*protest*) protestar; *see* **top** *etc*.
2 *vt* expresar, hacerse eco de; (*Gram*) sonorizar.
3 *vi* sonorizarse.

voiced [vɔist] *adj* (*Gram*) sonoro.

voiceless ['vɔislis] *adj* (*Gram*) sordo.

void [vɔid] **1** *adj* (*empty*) vacío; desocupado; *post* vacante; (*Law*) nulo, inválido; **to be** — **of** estar falto de, estar desprovisto de; **to make a contract** — anular un contrato, invalidar un contrato; **to make someone's efforts** — hacer inútiles los esfuerzos de uno; *see* **null**.
2 *n* **(a)** vacío *m*; hueco *m*, espacio *m*; **the** — la nada; **to fill the** — llenar el hueco; **to have an aching** — tener mucha hambre.
(b) (*Cards*) fallo *m*; **to have a** — **in hearts** tener fallo a corazones.
3 *vt* evacuar, vaciar; (*Law*) anular, invalidar.

volatile ['vɔlətail] *adj* volátil (*also* fig).
volatility [,vɔlə'tiliti] *n* volatilidad *f* (*also* fig).
volatilize [vɔ'lætəlaiz] **1** *vt* volatilizar. **2** *vi* volatilizarse.
volcanic [vɔl'kænik] *adj* volcánico.
volcano [vɔl'keinəu] *n*, *pl* **volcanoes** [vɔl'keinəuz] volcán *m*.
vole [vəul] *n* campañol *m*.
volition [və'liʃən] *n* volición *f*; **of one's own** — por voluntad propia.
volley ['vɔli] **1** *n* (*of shots*) descarga *f*, descarga *f* cerrada; (*of stones etc*) lluvia *f*; (*of applause*) salva *f*; (*of abuse etc*) torrente *m*, retahíla *f*; (*Tennis*) voleo *m*.
2 *vt* (*Tennis*) volear; *abuse etc* dirigir (*at* a).
3 *vi* (*Mil*) lanzar una descarga.
volleyball ['vɔlibɔːl] *n* balón *m* volea.
volt [vəult] *n* voltio *m*.
voltage ['vəultidʒ] *n* voltaje *m*.
voltaic [vɔl'teiik] *adj* voltaico.
volte-face ['vɔlt'fɑːs] *n* viraje *m*, cambio *m* súbito de opinión, tergiversación *f*.
voltmeter ['vəult,miːtə*] *n* voltímetro *m*.
volubility [,vɔlju'biliti] *n* locuacidad *f*.
voluble ['vɔljubl] *adj person* locuaz, hablador; **in** — **French** en francés elocuente y rápido; **a** — **protest** una protesta larga y enérgica.
volubly ['vɔljubli] *adv* de modo locuaz, con locuacidad; con soltura, rápidamente; larga y enérgicamente.
volume ['vɔljuːm] *n* volumen *m*; (*book, number in series*) tomo *m*; (*total*) cantidad *f*, masa *f*; (*of sound*) volumen *m* sonoro; (*of water*) cantidad *f* de agua; caudal *m* (de río *etc*); **in the third** — en el tercer tomo; **an edition in 4** —**s** una edición en 4 tomos; **it speaks** —**s** es sumamente significativo; **it speaks** —**s for it** lo evidencia de modo inconfundible; **it speaks** —**s for him** es un testimonio muy significativo acerca de él.
volume control ['vɔljuːmkən,trəul] *n* (*Radio etc*) control *m* del volumen sonoro.
volumetric [,vɔlju'metrik] *adj* volumétrico.
voluminous [və'luːminəs] *adj* voluminoso.
voluntarily ['vɔləntərili] *adv* voluntariamente, sin ser forzado, libremente.
voluntary ['vɔləntəri] **1** *adj* voluntario; espontáneo; libre. **2** *n* solo *m* de órgano; **trumpet** — solo *m* de trompeta.
volunteer [,vɔlən'tiə*] **1** *n* voluntario *m*.
2 *adj*, *attr force etc* de voluntarios.
3 *vt services* ofrecer; *remark* hacer.
4 *vi* ofrecerse; (*Mil*) alistarse como voluntario; **to** — **for service overseas** ofrecerse para servir en ultramar; **to** — **to do a job** ofrecerse a hacer un trabajo; **he wasn't forced to, he** —**ed** nadie le obligó a ello, se ofreció libremente.
voluptuary [və'lʌptjuəri] *n* voluptuoso *m*, a *f*.
voluptuous [və'lʌptjuəs] *adj* voluptuoso.
voluptuously [və'lʌptjuəsli] *adv* voluptuosamente.
voluptuousness [və'lʌptjuəsnis] *n* voluptuosidad *f*.
volute [və'luːt] *n* voluta *f*.
vomit ['vɔmit] **1** *n* vómito *m*. **2** *vt* vomitar, arrojar. **3** *vi* vomitar, tener vómitos.
voodoo ['vuːduː] *n* vudú *m*.
voracious [və'reiʃəs] *adj* voraz.
voraciously [və'reiʃəsli] *adv* vorazmente.
voracity [vɔ'ræsiti] *n* voracidad *f*.
vortex ['vɔːteks] *n*, *pl* **vortices** ['vɔːtisiːz] vórtice *m*.
Vosges [vəuʒ] *pl* Vosgos *mpl*.
votary ['vəutəri] *n* (*Rel*) devoto *m*, a *f*; (*fig*) partidario *m*, a *f*.
vote [vəut] **1** *n* (a) voto *m*; sufragio *m*; **casting** — voto *m* de calidad, voto *m* decisivo; **in the case of a tie the chairman shall have a casting** — el voto del presidente será dirimente en caso de empate; **by a majority** — por la mayoría de los votos; **to cast one's** —, **to give one's** — dar su voto (*for*, to a); **how many** —**s did he get?** ¿cuántos votos obtuvo?; **he won by 89** —**s** ganó por 89 votos.
(b) (*voting*) votación *f*; (*election*) elección *f*, elecciones *fpl*; — **of censure** voto *m* de censura; — **of confidence** voto *m* de confianza; — **of thanks** voto *m* de gracia; **by popular** — por votación popular, (*fig*) en la opinión de muchos; **by secret** — por votación secreta; **as the 1931** — **showed** según demostraron las elecciones de 1931; **to put a motion to the** —, **to take a** — **on a motion** someter una moción a votación; **let's take a** — **on it** (*fig*) veamos qué opiniones hay sobre esto.
(c) (*right to* —) derecho *m* de votar; **when women got the** — cuando se concedió a las mujeres

el derecho de votar; **to have the** — tener el derecho de votar.
2 *vt*: **to** — **a sum for defence** votar una cantidad para la defensa, aprobar por votación el presupuesto de la defensa; **she was** —**d Miss Granada 1970** fue elegida como Miss Granada 1970; **we** —**d it a failure** opinamos que fue un fracaso; **the team** —**d it a hit** el equipo pronosticó que tendría éxito; **to** — **a proposal down** rechazar una propuesta por votación; **we** —**d that idea down** (*fig*) rechazamos esa idea; **to** — **a government in** elegir un gobierno; **to** — **someone into office** elegir a uno para ocupar un puesto.
3 *vi* votar; (*go to polls*) ir a votar, acudir a las urnas; **to** — **for someone** votar por uno; **to** — **that...** resolver por votación que...; **I** — **that...** (*fam*) yo propongo que..., yo sugiero que...
voter ['vəutə*] *n* votante *mf*.
voting ['vəutiŋ] *n* votación *f*.
voting booth ['vəutiŋ,buːð] *n* caseta *f* de votar, cabina *f* de votación.
voting machine ['vəutiŋmə,ʃiːn] *n* (*US*) máquina *f* de votar.
voting paper ['vəutiŋ,peipə*] *n* papeleta *f* (de votación).
voting power ['vəutiŋ,pauə*] *n* potencia *f* electoral.
votive ['vəutiv] *adj* votivo.
vouch [vautʃ] **1** *vt* garantizar, atestiguar; confirmar; **to** — **that...** afirmar que..., asegurar que...
2 *vi*: **to** — **for something** garantizar algo; confirmar algo; responder de algo; **I cannot** — **for its authenticity** no puedo responder de su autenticidad; **to** — **for someone** responder por uno.
voucher ['vautʃə*] *n* documento *m* justificativo; (*Comm*) comprobante *m*; **cash** — vale *m* que representa una cantidad en metálico; **luncheon** — vale *m* de comida.
vouchsafe [vautʃ'seif] *vt* conceder, otorgar; *reply etc* servirse hacer, dignarse hacer; **to** — **to** + *infin* dignarse + *infin*.
vow [vau] **1** *n* voto *m* (*also Eccl*); promesa *f* solemne; **lovers'** —**s** promesas *fpl* solemnes de los amantes; **monastic** —**s** votos *mpl* monásticos; **the** — **of poverty** el voto de pobreza; **to be under a** — **to do something** haber hecho voto de hacer algo, haber prometido solemnemente hacer algo; **to take a** — **to** + *infin* hacer voto de *infin*, jurar + *infin*.
2 *vt*: **to** — **vengeance against someone** jurar vengarse (de uno); **to** — **that...** jurar que..., prometer solemnemente que...
3 *vi*: **to** — **to** + *infin* hacer voto de + *infin*, jurar + *infin*.
vowel [vauəl] **1** *n* vocal *f*. **2** *adj*, *attr* vocálico; — **sound** sonido *m* vocálico; — **system** sistema *m* vocálico.
voyage ['vɔiidʒ] **1** *n* viaje *m* (por mar, en barco); (*crossing*) travesía *f*; **the** — **out** el viaje de ida; **the** — **home** el viaje de regreso.
2 *vi* viajar (por mar); navegar; **to** — **across unknown seas** viajar por mares desconocidos.
voyager ['vɔiədʒə*] *n* viajero *m*, a *f* (por mar).
Vulcan ['vʌlkən] *m* Vulcano.
vulcanite ['vʌlkənait] *n* vulcanita *f*, ebonita *f*.
vulcanization [,vʌlkənai'zeiʃən] *n* vulcanización *f*.
vulcanize ['vʌlkənaiz] *vt* vulcanizar.
vulgar ['vʌlgə*] **1** *adj* (a) (*of the people*) vulgar; **in the** — **tongue** en la lengua vulgar, en la lengua vernácula; **that is a** — **error** eso es un error vulgar.
(b) (*indecent*) ordinario, grosero; (*in bad taste*) de mal gusto, cursi; *joke, song* verde; *person* ordinario.
2 *n*: **the** — el vulgo.
vulgarian [vʌl'gɛəriən] *n* persona *f* ordinaria; (*wealthy*) ricacho *m*.
vulgarism ['vʌlgərizəm] *n* vulgarismo *m*.
vulgarity [vʌl'gæriti] *n* vulgaridad *f*; ordinariez *f*, grosería *f*; mal gusto *m*, cursilería *f*; lo verde, indecencia *f*.
vulgarize ['vʌlgəraiz] *vt* vulgarizar.
vulgarly ['vʌlgəli] *adv* vulgarmente; de modo ordinario; groseramente; con mal gusto, de modo cursi; indecentemente; **X**, — **known as Y** X, vulgarmente llamado Y.
Vulgate ['vʌlgit] *n* Vulgata *f*.
vulnerability [,vʌlnərə'biliti] *n* vulnerabilidad *f*.
vulnerable ['vʌlnərəbl] *adj* vulnerable (*to* a).
vulpine ['vʌlpain] *adj* vulpino.
vulture ['vʌltʃə*] *n* buitre *m*.
vulva ['vʌlvə] *n* vulva *f*.
vying ['vaiiŋ] *ger of* **vie**.

W

wacky ['wæki] *adj* (*US sl*) *person* chiflado; *thing* absurdo.

wad [wɔd] **1** *n* (*used to stuff something*) taco *m*, tapón *m*; (*in gun, cartridge*) taco *m*; (*of cotton wool etc*) bolita *f* de algodón; (*of papers*) lío *m*; (*of notes: US*) fajo *m*; (*sl: cake*) pastel *m*.
2 *vt* (*stuff*) rellenar; (*Sew*) acolchar.

wadding ['wɔdiŋ] *n* taco *m*, tapón *m*; relleno *m*; (*lining*) entretela *f*, forro *m*; (*Med*) algodón *m* absorbente.

waddle ['wɔdl] **1** *n* anadeo *m*; **to walk with a —** anadear. **2** *vi* anadear; **she —d over to the window** fue anadeando a la ventana.

wade [weid] **1** *vt* vadear.
2 *vi* (*also* **to — along**) caminar por el agua (*or* nieve, lodo *etc*), caminar con el agua hasta la cintura (*etc*); **we shall have to —** tendremos que meternos en el agua; **to — ashore** llegar a tierra vadeando; **to — in** entrar en el agua; **to — into someone** (*fig*) emprenderla con uno, arremeter contra uno; **to — through a book** leer un libro a pesar de lo aburrido (*or* lo difícil *etc*); **it took me an hour to — through your essay** tardé una hora en leer su ensayo tan largo.

wader ['weidə*] *n* (*Orn*) ave *f* zancuda; **—s** botas *fpl* altas.

wafer ['weifə*] *n* (*biscuit*) galleta *f*; (*with ice cream*) barquillo *m*; (*for sealing*) oblea *f*; (*Eccl*) hostia *f*.

wafer-thin ['weifə'θin] *adj* delgadísimo, finísimo.

wafery ['weifəri] *adj* delgado, ligero.

waffle ['wɔfl] **1** *n* (*approx*) buñuelo *m*; (*fam*) palabras *fpl* inútiles, palabrería *f*; (*in essay etc*) paja *f*.
2 *vi* (*fam*) hablar mucho sin decir gran cosa, ser muy charlatán; (*in essay etc*) poner mucha paja.

waft [wɑːft] **1** *n* soplo *m*, ráfaga *f* de olor.
2 *vt* llevar por el aire; hacer flotar; (*stir*) mecer, mover.
3 *vi* moverse (de un sitio a otro); ser llevado por el aire; flotar.

wag[1] [wæg] **1** *n* meneo *m*, movimiento *m*; (*of tail*) coleada *f*.
2 *vt* mover, menear, agitar; **the dog —ged its tail** el perro meneó la cola.
3 *vi* moverse, menearse, agitarse.

wag[2] [wæg] *n* (*joker*) bromista *m*, zumbón *m*.

wage [weidʒ] **1** *n* (*also* **—s**) salario *m*; (*esp day* **—**) jornal *m*; (*fig*) pago *m*, premio *m*; **living —** jornal *m* suficiente para vivir; **minimum —** salario *m* mínimo.
2 *vt war* hacer; *battle* librar, dar; *campaign* proseguir.

wage earner ['weidʒ,əːnə*] *n* asalariado *m*, a *f*.

wage freeze ['weidʒfriːz] *n* congelación *f* de los salarios.

wager ['weidʒə*] **1** *n* apuesta *f*; **to lay a —** hacer una apuesta; **to lay a — on a horse** apostar dinero a un caballo.
2 *vti* apostar; **to — £2 on a horse** apostar 2 libras a un caballo; **to — that...** apostar a que...; **he won't do it, I —!** ¡a que no lo hace!

wages ['weidʒiz] *npl see* **wage.**

wages clerk ['weidʒizklɑːk] *n* pagador *m*, ora *f*.

waggish ['wægiʃ] *adj* zumbón *m*.

waggishly ['wægiʃli] *adv*: **he said —** dijo zumbón.

waggle ['wægl] = **wag**[1].

wag(g)on ['wægən] *n* carro *m*; (*Rail*) vagón *m*; **to be on the —** (*fam*) no beber; **to go on the —** (*fam*) resolverse a no beber.

wag(g)onette [,wægə'net] *n* break *m*.

wag(g)onload ['wægənləud] *n* carretada *f*, carga *f* de un carro (*etc*); **50 —s of coal** 50 vagones de carbón.

Wagnerian [vɑːg'niəriən] *adj* wagneriano.

wagtail ['wægteil] *n* lavandera *f*.

waif [weif] *n* niño *m* abandonado, niña *f* abandonada; **—s and strays** niños *mpl* desamparados.

wail [weil] **1** *n* lamento *m*, gemido *m*; (*baby's*) vagido *m*; (*complaint*) queja *f*, protesta *f*; **a great — went up** pusieron el grito en el cielo.
2 *vi* lamentarse, gemir; (*child*) gimotear; llorar; (*complain*) quejarse, protestar.

wailing ['weiliŋ] *n* lamentación *f*, lamentaciones *fpl*, gemidos *mpl*; vagidos *mpl*; quejas *fpl*, protestas *fpl*.

wain [wein] *n* carro *m*; **the W—** (*Astron*) el Carro.

wainscot ['weinskət] *n* friso *m*; entablado *m*, revestimiento *m* (de la pared).

waist [weist] *n* (*Anat etc*) cintura *f*, talle *m*; (*fig, narrow part*) cuello *m*; (*Naut*) combés *m*.

waistband ['weistbænd] *n* pretina *f*, cinturilla *f*.

waistcoat ['weiskəut] *n* chaleco *m*.

waist-deep ['weist'diːp] *adv* hasta la cintura.

-waisted ['weistid] *adj* de cintura..., de talle..., *eg* **slim-waisted** de cintura delgada.

waist-high ['weist'hai] **1** *adv* hasta la cintura; al nivel de la cintura. **2** *adj*: **— vegetation** vegetación *f* que crece hasta la altura de la cintura.

waistline ['weistlain] *n* talle *m*.

wait [weit] **1** *n* (**a**) espera *f*; (*pause*) pausa *f*, intervalo *m*; **there was a — of 10 minutes** tuvimos que esperar 10 minutos; **to have a long —** tener que esperar mucho tiempo; **to be** (*or* **lie**) **in —** acechar (*for someone* a uno).
(**b**) **—s** murga *f* (de Nochebuena).
2 *vt* esperar; aplazar; guardar para después; **to — one's chance** esperar su ocasión; **we'll — dinner for you** no empezaremos a cenar hasta que vengas.
3 *vi* (**a**) esperar; aguardar; **— a moment!** ¡un momento!, (*fig, querying*) ¡oiga!; **— and see!** espera y verás; **"repairs while you —"** "reparaciones en el acto", "reparaciones instantáneas"; **— till you're asked** espera hasta que te inviten; **— till you're older** eso es para cuando seas algo mayor; **to keep someone —ing** hacer que uno espere, hacer esperar a uno; **to — about** esperar, perder el tiempo; **to — for someone** esperar a uno, (*in ambush*) acechar a uno; **to — for someone to do something** esperar hasta que uno haga algo; **we are —ing for you to decide** estamos pendientes de la decisión de Vd; **to — up** velar, no acostarse, seguir sin acostarse; **don't — up for me!** ¡idos a la cama sin esperar hasta que yo vuelva!
(**b**) (*as servant etc*) servir; **to — at table** servir a la mesa; **to — on someone** servir a uno; **to — on someone hand and foot** atender a los menores gustos de uno, mimar a uno; **to — upon someone** cumplimentar a uno, presentar sus respetos a uno.

waiter ['weitə*] *n* camarero *m*.

waiting ['weitiŋ] *n* (**a**) espera *f*; **all this —!** ¡tanto esperar! (**b**) servicio *m*.

waiting list ['weitiŋ'list] *n* lista *f* de solicitudes no atendidas, lista *f* de aspirantes; **there is a long — for housing** hay muchas solicitudes de vivienda (que no hemos podido atender).

waiting room ['weitiŋrum] *n* sala *f* de espera.

waitress ['weitris] *n* camarera *f*; **—!** ¡señorita!

waive [weiv] *vt* renunciar a.

waiver ['weivə*] *n* renuncia *f*.

wake[1] [weik] *n* (*Naut*) estela *f*; **in the — of** (*fig*) como consecuencia de, tras, a raíz de; **wars bring misery in their —** las guerras acarrean la miseria; **they came in the — of the invaders** siguieron a los invasores.

wake[2] [weik] **1** *n* (*over corpse*) vela *f*, velatorio *m*.
2 (*irr: pret* **woke**, *ptp* **woken, waked**) *vt* despertar (*also* **to — up**); *corpse* velar; **a noise which would — the dead** un ruido que despertaría a un muerto.

3 *vi* despertar, despertarse (*also to* — up); — up!
¡despierta!; **she woke up with a start** despertó
sobresaltada; **he woke up** (*to find himself*) **in
prison** amaneció en la cárcel; **he woke up to find
himself rich** a la mañana siguiente encontró que
era rico; **to** — **up to reality** despertar a la realidad;
to — **up to the truth** darse cuenta de la verdad.
wakeful ['weikful] *adj* (*awake*) despierto; (*alert*)
vigilante; desvelado; (*unable to sleep*) insomne; **to
have a** — **night** pasar la noche sin dormir.
wakefulness ['weikfulnis] *n* vigilancia *f*, desvelo *m*;
insomnia *f*.
waken ['weikən] **1** *vt* despertar. **2** *vi* despertar,
despertarse.
waker ['weikə*] *n*: **to be an early** — despertar
temprano por costumbre.
waking ['weikiŋ] **1** *adj*: **in one's** — **hours** en las
horas en que uno está despierto. **2** *n* despertar *m*;
on — al despertar.
Wales [weilz] Gales *f*; **South** — Gales *f* del Sur.
walk [wɔːk] **1** *n* (a) (*spell of* —*ing: stroll*) paseo *m*;
(*hike*) caminata *f*, excursión *f* a pie; **it's only a
10-minute** — **from here** ir desde aquí a pie es solo
cosa de 10 minutos; **from there you have a short** —
to his house desde allí a su casa se va a pie en muy
poco tiempo; **to go for** (*or have, take*) **a** — dar un
paseo, dar una vuelta; **to take someone for a** —
llevar a uno de paseo.
(b) (*gait*) andar *m*, paso *m*; **he has an odd sort
of** — tiene un modo de andar algo raro; **to know
someone by** (*or from*) **his** — conocer a uno por su
modo de andar; **he went at a quick** — caminó a un
paso rápido.
(c) (*route*) **there's a nice** — **by the river** se
pasea muy bien a lo largo del río, es encantador
pasearse a lo largo del río; **this is my favourite** —
ésta es mi ruta favorita para dar un paseo.
(d) — **of life** profesión *f*; esfera *f*; clase *f* social;
people from every — **of life** gente *f* de toda
condición.
(e) (*avenue*) paseo *m*, alameda *f*.
2 *vt* (a) *person* llevar a paseo, pasear; **to** —
someone off his legs dejar a uno rendido tras una
larguísima caminata.
(b) **to** — **a horse** llevar un caballo al paso.
(c) (*distance*) cubrir, recorrer a pie, andar; **we
—ed 40 kilometres yesterday** ayer recorrimos 40
kilómetros a pie.
(d) **to** — **the streets** andar por las calles,
(*aimlessly*) vagar por las calles; **to** — **the boards**
(*Theat*) salir a escena; **to** — **the wards** (*Med*) hacer
prácticas de clínica.
(e) **to** — **off a headache** quitarse de un dolor de
cabeza a fuerza de andar; dar una vuelta para
quitarse de un dolor de cabeza; **to** — **off one's lunch**
bajar la comida dando un paseo.
3 *vi* (a) (*general sense*) andar; **can the boy** — **yet?**
¿sabe andar el niño ya?; — **a little with me** ven a
acompañarme un poco; **to** — **in one's sleep** ser
sonámbulo, pasearse dormido; **to** — **slowly** andar
despacio.
(b) (*not ride*) andar, ir a pie; (*stroll*) pasearse;
we had to — tuvimos que ir andando; **to** — **home**
ir andando hasta casa; **you can** — **there in 5 minutes**
en 5 minutos se va allá andando; **we were out** —**ing**
nos estábamos paseando.
(c) (*of ghost*) andar, aparecer.
(d) (*with adv or prep*) **to** — **about** pasearse; ir y
venir; **to** — **away** irse, alejarse; **to** — **away from
someone** alejarse de uno; **to** — **back** volverse;
volver a pie, regresar a pie; **to** — **down** bajar (a
pie); **to** — **downstairs** bajar la escalera; **to** — **in**
entrar; **"please** — **in"** "entren sin llamar"; **to** —
into food (*fam*) devorar la comida, zampar la
comida; **to** — **into a room** entrar en un cuarto; **to**
— **into someone** (*fam*) atacar a uno, arremeter
contra uno; **who should** — **in but John!** y fíjate,
¡aparece Juan!; **to** — **off** irse; **to** —**ed off angrily** se
fue enfadado; **to** — **off with something** llevarse
algo; **they** —**ed off with the first three prizes**
coparon los tres primeros premios; **to** — **on** (*step on*)
pisar; **to** — **out** (*from conference*) salir, retirarse (*of*
de); (*on strike*) declararse en huelga; **you can't** —
out now! ¡no podéis abandonar ahora!; **to** — **out on
a girl** dejar plantada a una chica, plantar a una
chica; **to** — **out with a boy** salir con un chico; **to** —
over (*Sport*) ganar la carrera por ser el único caballo
(*etc*) que participa; **to** — **all over someone** (*fig*)
tratar a uno con el mayor desprecio; **she lets him** —
all over her permite que él la trate malísimamente
sin protestar; **to** — **up** subir (a pie); **to** — **upstairs**
subir la escalera; **to** — **up to someone** acercarse a

uno, abordar a uno; **to** — **up and down** pasearse de
acá para allá.
walker ['wɔːkə*] *n* (*stroller*) paseante *mf*; (*not rider*)
peatón *m*; (*Sport*) andarín *m*; (*baby* —) pollera *f*;
to be a great — ser gran andarín; ser aficionado a
las excursiones a pie.
walker-on ['wɔːkər'ɔn] *n* (*Theat*) figurante *m*, a *f*.
walkie-talkie ['wɔːki'tɔːki] *n* transmisor-receptor *m*
portátil.
walking ['wɔːkiŋ] **1** *adj* ambulante; *race* pedestre;
at a — **pace** a paso de andadura; — **tour** viaje *m* a
pie, excursión *f* a pie; **it's within** — **distance** se
puede ir allí andando; **he's a** — **encyclopaedia** es
una enciclopedia ambulante.
walking stick ['wɔːkiŋstik] *n* bastón *m*.
walk-on ['wɔːkɔn] *adj* (*Theat etc*): — **part** papel *m*
de figurante.
walkout ['wɔːkaut] *n* (*from conference*) salida *f*,
retirada *f*; (*strike*) huelga *f*.
walkover ['wɔːk‚əuvə*] *n* (*Sport*) walkover *m*; (*fig*)
triunfo *m* fácil.
walk-ups ['wɔːkʌps] *npl* pisos *mpl* sin ascensor.
wall [wɔːl] **1** *n* muro *m*; (*interior*, *Anat etc*) pared *f*;
(*city* —) muralla *f*; (*garden* —) tapia *f*; **containing** —
muro *m* de contención; **partition** — tabique *m*;
party — pared *f* medianera; **a high tariff** — una
alta barrera arancelaria; **the Great W** — **of China** la
Gran Muralla China; **the north** — **of the Eiger** la
pared norte del Eiger; **to come up against a blank**
— (*fig*) tener por delante una barrera infranqueable;
it drives me up the — (*fam*) me vuelve loco, me
hace subir por las paredes; **to go to the** — ser
desechado por inútil; —**s have ears** las paredes oyen.
2 *attr map etc* de pared, mural.
3 *vt* murar; cerrar con muro (*also to* — **in**); *city*
amurallar; *garden* tapiar, cercar con tapia; **to** — **up**
person emparedar; *opening* cerrar con muro, tabicar.
wallaby ['wɔləbi] *n* ualabí *m*.
wallah ['wɔlə] *n* (*fam*) hombre *m*; (*pej*) tío *m*, sujeto
m; **the ice-cream** — el hombre de los helados; **the** —
with the beard él de la barba.
wallboard ['wɔːlbɔːd] *n* (*US*) cartón *m* de yeso.
wall clock ['wɔːlklɔk] *n* reloj *m* de pared.
walled [wɔːld] *adj* *city* amurallado; *garden* con tapia.
wallet ['wɔlit] *n* cartera *f*.
wall-eyed ['wɔːl'aid] *adj* de ojos incoloros; de ojos
desviados hacia fuera.
wallflower ['wɔːl‚flauə*] *n* alhelí *m*; **to be a** — (*fig*)
comer pavo.
wall fruit ['wɔːlfruːt] *n* fruta *f* de espalera.
wall map ['wɔːlmæp] *n* mapa *m* mural.
Walloon [wɔ'luːn] **1** *adj* valón. **2** *n* valón *m*, ona *f*.
wallop ['wɔləp] **1** *n* (a) (*blow: fam*) golpe *m*, golpazo
m; —! ¡zas!; **to give someone a** — pegar a uno.
(b) (*speed: fam*) velocidad *f*; **to go at a fair** —
correr rápidamente.
(c) (*beer: sl*) cerveza *f*.
2 *vt* (*fam*) golpear fuertemente; (*punish*) zurrar.
walloping ['wɔləpiŋ] **1** *adj* (*fam*) colosal, grandote. **2**
n zurra *f*, paliza *f*; **to give someone a** — dar una
paliza a uno (*also fig*).
wallow ['wɔləu] *vi* revolcarse (*in* en); **to** — **in
money** nadar en la opulencia; **to** — **in vices**
revolcarse en los vicios.
wall painting ['wɔːl‚peintiŋ] *n* pintura *f* mural.
wallpaper ['wɔːl‚peipə*] *n* papel *m* pintado, papel *m*
de paredes.
wall socket ['wɔːl‚sɔkit] *n* enchufe *m* de pared.
walnut ['wɔːlnʌt] *n* (*nut*) nuez *f*; (*tree*, *wood*) nogal *m*.
walnut tree ['wɔːlnʌttriː] *n* nogal *m*.
walrus ['wɔːlrəs] *n* morsa *f*.
Walter ['wɔːltə*] *m* Gualterio.
waltz [wɔːlts] **1** *n* vals *m*. **2** *vi* valsar.
wan [wɔn] *adj* pálido, maciento; (*sad*) triste.
wand [wɔnd] *n* (*of office*) vara *f*; **magic** — varilla *f* de
virtudes.
wander ['wɔndə*] **1** *vt* vagar por, recorrer; **to** — **the
streets** vagar por las calles, pasearse por las calles;
to — **the world** ir por el mundo.
2 *vi* vagar, errar; pasearse sin propósito fijo; (*get
lost*) extraviarse; **to** — **about**, **to** — **aimlessly**
deambular; **to** — (*in one's mind*) divagar, delirar;
to — **from the path** desviarse (sin darse cuenta) del
camino; **to** — **from the point** salirse del tema; **to** —
off irse (distraído); **the children** —**ed off into the
woods** los niños se alejaron y entraron casi sin
darse cuenta en el bosque; **his speech** —**ed on and
on** continuó incansable su discurso tan confuso; **to**
— **round a shop** curiosear en una tienda; **to let
one's mind** — dejar que la imaginación fantasee.
wanderer ['wɔndərə*] *n* hombre *m* errante, mujer *f*
errante; (*traveller*) viajero *m*, a *f*; (*pej*) vagabundo

m, a *f*; (*tribesman etc*) nómada *mf*; **I've always been a —** nunca he querido establecerme de fijo en un sitio.

wandering ['wɔndəriŋ] *adj* errante, errabundo; *salesman etc* ambulante; *tribesman* nómada; *mind, thoughts* distraído.

wanderings ['wɔndəriŋz] *npl* viajes *mpl*; errabundeo *m*; (*pej*) vagabundeo *m*; (*Med*) delirio *m*.

wanderlust ['wɔndəlʌst] *n* pasión *f* de viajar, ansia *f* de ver mundo.

wane [wein] **1** *n*: **to be on the —** menguar, estar menguando; (*fig*) decaer, menguar, disminuir; declinar, estar en decadencia. **2** *vi* = **to be on the —**.

wangle ['wæŋgl] (*fam*) **1** *n* chanchullo *m*, trampa *f*, truco *m*; **it's a —** aquí hay trampa; **he got in by a —** fue admitido gracias a un truco.

2 *vt job etc* mamarse, agenciarse; **he —d his way in** logró entrar gracias a un truco; **he'll — it for you** él te lo procurará por el sistema que él se sabe; **can you — me a free ticket?** ¿puedes procurarme una entrada de favor?

wangler ['wæŋglə*] *n* (*fam*) chanchullero *m*, trapisondista *m*.

wangling ['wæŋgliŋ] *n* chanchullos *mpl*, trampas *fpl*; **there's a lot of —** goes on hay muchas trampas.

waning ['weiniŋ] **1** *adj moon* {menguante; (*fig*) decadente. **2** *n* (*of moon*) menguante *f*; (*fig*) mengua *f*; disminución *f*; decadencia *f*.

wanly ['wɔnli] *adv* pálidamente; (*sadly*) tristemente.

wanness ['wɔnnis] *n* palidez *f*.

want [wɔnt] **1** *n* (a) (*lack*) falta *f*; ausencia *f*; (*shortage*) carencia *f*, escasez *f*; **— of judgement** falta *f* de juicio; **for — of** por falta de; **for — of anything better** por falta de algo mejor; **for — of something to do** por no tener nada que hacer; **to feel the — of** sentir la falta de.

(b) (*poverty*) miseria *f*, pobreza *f*, indigencia *f*; **to be in —** estar necesitado.

(c) (*need*) necesidad *f*; **my —s are few** necesito poco; **to be in — of** necesitar; **to attend to someone's —s** atender a las necesidades de uno; **it fills a long-felt —** viene a llenar un vacío hace tiempo sentido; **— ad** (*US fam*) anuncio *m* clasificado.

2 *vt* (a) (*need: of person*) necesitar; **all I — is sleep** lo único que necesito es dormirme; **children — lots of sleep** es necesario que los niños duerman mucho tiempo; **we have all we —** tenemos todo lo que necesitamos; **you — to be careful** (*fam*) hay que tener cuidado, conviene proceder con cuidado; **what you — is a good hiding** (*fam*) no te vendría mal una paliza de las buenas; **those —ing a job** los que buscan trabajo; **"—ed"** (*police notice*) "se busca"; **the —ed man** el hombre buscado; **"—ed: general maid"** (*advert*) "necesítase criada para todo"; **he is —ed for murder** se le busca por asesino.

(b) (*need: of thing*) exigir, requerir; **it —s some doing** exige mucho esfuerzo (*etc*) hacerlo; **that work —s a lot of time** ese trabajo exige mucho tiempo; **does my hair — cutting?** ¿me hace falta cortar el pelo?; **the house will — painting next year** el año que viene será necesario pintar la casa.

(c) (*wish*) querer, desear; **she knows what she —s** sabe lo que quiere; **I — to see the manager!** ¡quiero ver al gerente!; **to — someone to do something** querer que uno haga algo; **I — him sent away at once** quiero que se le despida en seguida; **I was —ing to leave** estaba deseando marcharme; **what does he — with me?** ¿qué quiere decirme?, ¿qué tiene que ver conmigo?; **he —s £20 for the picture** pide 20 libras por el cuadro; **you don't — much** (*iro*) ¡eso no es mucho pedir!; **you're —ed on the 'phone** le llaman al teléfono.

(d) (*lack*) carecer de; **he —s talent** carece de talento; **he —s enterprise** le falta iniciativa; **it —s 2 for a complete set** faltan 2 para hacer una serie completa.

3 *vi*: **to — for** necesitar, carecer de; **they — for nothing** no carecen de nada, lo tienen todo; **it —ed only this last step to +** *infin* sólo hacía falta que se diese este último paso para + *infin*.

wanting ['wɔntiŋ] *adj* defectuoso; deficiente (*in* en), falto (*in* de); **charity is — in the novel** a la novela le falta caridad, la novela es deficiente en caridad; **there is something —** falta algo; **he is —ing in enterprise** le falta iniciativa, está falto de iniciativa; **he was tried and found —** se le sometió a la prueba y resultó que le faltaban las cualidades indispensables.

wanton ['wɔntən] **1** *adj* (a) (*playful*) juguetón; (*wayward*) travieso; (*capricious*) caprichoso; (*unrestrained*) desenfrenado; (*licentious*) lascivo.

(b) (*motiveless*) sin motivo, inmotivado; *destruction* sin propósito, sin sentido; *cruelty* gratuito.

2 *n* libertino *m*, a *f*.

3 *vi* jugar, retozar.

wantonly ['wɔntənli] *adv* (a) caprichosamente; desenfrenadamente; lascivamente. (b) sin motivo; sin propósito; gratuitamente.

wantonness ['wɔntənnis] *n* (a) lo caprichoso; desenfreno *m*; lascivia *f*. (b) falta *f* de motivo; lo gratuito.

war [wɔ:*] **1** *n* guerra *f*; **cold —** guerra *f* fría; **hot —**, **shooting —** guerra *f* a tiros; **— of nerves** guerra *f* de nervios; **— of words** guerra *f* de propaganda; **— to the knife** guerra *f* a muerte; **Great W—** (1914-18) Primera Guerra *f* Mundial; **Second World W—** (1939-45) Segunda Guerra *f* Mundial; **the period between the —s** (1918-39) el período de entreguerras; **to be at —** estar en guerra (*with* con); **to declare —** declarar la guerra (*on* a); **to go to —** emprender la guerra; hacer la guerra; **we shall not go to — over the Slobodian question** no emprenderemos la guerra por la cuestión de Eslobodia; **they went to — singing** fueron a la guerra cantando; **to make —** hacer la guerra (*on* a).

2 *attr* (*in most senses*) de guerra; *effort, material* bélico; *memorial* a los caídos; **W— Office** (*Brit*), **W— Department** (*US*) Ministerio *m* de Guerra.

3 *vi* (*lit*) guerrear (*on* con).

warble ['wɔ:bl] **1** *n* trino *m*, gorjeo *m*. **2** *vt song etc* cantar en voz atiplada. **3** *vi* trinar, gorjear.

warbler ['wɔ:blə*] *n* mosquitero *m*, curruca *f*.

war correspondent ['wɔ:,kɔris'pɔndənt] *n* corresponsal *m* de guerra.

war crime ['wɔ:kraim] *n* crimen *m* de guerra.

war cry ['wɔ:krai] *n* grito *m* de guerra.

ward ['wɔ:d] **1** *n* (a) (*—ship*) tutela *f*, custodia *f*; **in —** bajo tutela.

(b) (*person*) pupilo *m*, a *f*; **— of court** persona *f* bajo la protección del tribunal.

(c) (*Pol*) distrito *m* electoral.

(d) (*of hospital*) sala *f*, crujía *f*; **"W— 7"** "Sala 7"; **to walk the —s** hacer práctica de clínica; **casual —** asilo *m* para pobres, asilo *m* para vagabundos.

(e) (*of key*) guarda *f*.

2 *vt*: **to — off** *blow* desviar, parar; *danger* evitar; *attack* rechazar, defenderse contra.

-ward(s) [wəd(z)] *in compounds* hacia, *eg* **townward(s)** hacia la ciudad; **pubward(s)** hacia la taberna.

war dance ['wɔ:dɑ:ns] *n* danza *f* guerrera.

war debt ['wɔ:det] *n* deuda *f* de guerra.

warden ['wɔ:dn] *n* guardián *m*; (*Univ etc*) director *m*; (*of castle etc*) alcaide *m*.

warder ['wɔ:də*] *n* guardián *m*, vigilante *m*, carcelero *m*.

ward heeler ['wɔ:d'hi:lə*] *n* (*US Pol*) muñidor *m*.

wardress ['wɔ:dris] *n* guardiana *f*.

wardrobe ['wɔ:drəub] *n* (*clothes*) vestidos *mpl*, trajes *mpl*; (*Theat*) vestuario *m*; (*cupboard*) guardarropa *m*, armario *m* (ropero).

wardrobe dealer ['wɔ:drəub,di:lə*] *n* ropavejero *m*.

wardrobe mistress ['wɔ:drəub,mistris] *n* encargada *f* de vestuario.

wardrobe trunk ['wɔ:drəubtrʌŋk] *n* baúl *m* ropero.

wardroom ['wɔ:drum] *n* (*Naut*) cuarto *m* de oficiales.

wardship ['wɔ:dʃip] *n* tutela *f*.

-ware [wɛə*] *n* loza *f*; *eg* **kitchenware** batería *f* de cocina.

warehouse ['wɛəhaus] *n*, *pl* **—houses** [,hauziz] almacén *m*, depósito *m*.

warehouse ['wɛəhauz] *vt* almacenar.

warehouseman ['wɛəhausmən] *n*, *pl* **—men** [mən] almacenista *m*.

wares [wɛəz] *npl* mercancías *fpl*; **to cry one's —** pregonar sus mercancías.

warfare ['wɔ:fɛə*] *n* guerra *f*; (*as study*) arte *m* militar, arte *m* de la guerra; **chemical —** guerra *f* química; **naval —** guerra *f* naval; **siege —** guerra *f* de sitio; **trench —** guerra *f* de trincheras.

war fever ['wɔ:,fi:və*] *n* psicosis *f* de guerra.

war game ['wɔ:geim] *n* simulacro *m* de guerra; juego *m* en que se simula la guerra, juego *m* de carácter militar.

war guilt ['wɔ:gilt] *n* responsabilidad *f* de la guerra.

warhead ['wɔ:hed] *n* (*of torpedo*) punta *f* de combate; (*of rocket*) cabeza *f* de guerra; **atomic —** cabeza *f* atómica.

warhorse ['wɔ:hɔ:s] *n* caballo *m* de guerra; (*fig*) veterano *m*.

warily ['wɛərili] *adv* con cautela, cautelosamente; **to tread —** andar con pies de plomo (*also fig*).

wariness ['wɛərinis] n cautela f, precaución f; recelo m.

warlike ['wɔ:laik] adj guerrero, belicoso.

war loan ['wɔ:ləun] n empréstito m de guerra.

war lord ['wɔ:lɔ:d] n jefe m militar.

warm [wɔ:m] **1** adj **(a)** caliente (pero no con exceso); *climate* cálido; *day, summer* caluroso, de calor; *blanket, clothing etc* cálido; **to be —** (*person*) tener calor, (*thing*) estar caliente, (*weather*) hacer calor; **to be very —** (*person*) tener mucho calor, (*thing*) estar muy caliente, (*weather*) hacer mucho calor; **to get —** (*thing*) calentarse, (*weather*) empezar a hacer calor; **to get —** (*person*) entrar en calor; **I still haven't got —** todavía no he entrado en calor; **you're getting —!** (*in games*) ¡te quemas!; **to keep oneself —** mantener el calor del cuerpo; **to keep something —** tener algo caliente, mantener el calor de algo; **to be as — as toast** disfrutar de un calor agradable.

(b) (*fig*) *scent* fresco; *tint* cálido; *thanks* efusivo; *heart, temperament* afectuoso; *dispute* acalorado; *greeting, welcome* caluroso; *applause* cálido, entusiasta; *supporter* entusiasta; **it's — work** es un trabajo que hace sudar; **the book is rather —** (*fam*) el libro es algo verde.

2 vt calentar; *heart etc* alegrar, regocijar; (*fam*) zurrar (*fam*); **to — up** *food* recalentar; *atmosphere etc* avivar, reanimar.

3 vi **(a)** **to — up** calentarse; (*Sport*) hacer ejercicios (para entrar en calor); (*argument*) acalorarse; **things are —ing up** hay más actividad, hay más animación; **the game is —ing up** el partido se está animando.

(b) **I (or my heart) —ed to him** le fui cobrando afición; **to — to one's subject** entusiasmarse con su tema.

2 vr: **to — oneself at the fire** calentarse junto a la lumbre.

warm-blooded ['wɔ:m'blʌdid] adj de sangre caliente; (*fig*) ardiente, apasionado.

warmed-up ['wɔ:md'ʌp] adj recalentado.

warm-hearted ['wɔ:m'hɑ:tid] adj bondadoso, afectuoso.

warming ['wɔ:miŋ] n (*fam*) zurra f (*fam*).

warming pan ['wɔ:miŋpæn] n calentador m (de cama).

warmly ['wɔ:mli] adv **(a) the sun shone —** brillaba el sol y hacía calor.

(b) (*fig*) efusivamente, con efusión; afectuosamente; calurosamente; con entusiasmo; **he thanked me most —** me dio las gracias con efusión; **we — welcome it** nosotros lo acogemos con entusiasmo.

warmonger ['wɔ:ˌmʌŋgə*] n belicista m, incendiario m de la guerra.

warmongering ['wɔ:ˌmʌŋgəriŋ] **1** adj belicista. **2** n belicismo m.

warmth [wɔ:mθ] n **(a)** calor m; lo cálido, lo caluroso.

(b) (*fig*) efusión f; afecto m; lo caluroso; entusiasmo m; **the — of their greeting** su acogida calurosa; **he replied with some —** contestó bastante indignado.

warm-up ['wɔ:mʌp] n (*Sport*) ejercicios mpl (para entrar en calor); actividad f preliminar, preparativos mpl.

warn [wɔ:n] vt avisar, advertir; amonestar; prevenir; **to — the police** avisar a la policía; **the bell is to — the workmen** el timbre es para dar aviso a los obreros; **— me before you blow it up** avíseme antes de volarlo; **you have been —ed!** Vd no podrá decir que no se le haya avisado; **to — someone not to do something** advertir a uno que no haga algo; **to — someone about something** amonestar a uno acerca de algo; **to — someone against someone else** prevenir a uno contra otra persona; **to — someone of a danger** prevenir a uno contra un peligro; **to — someone off** expulsar a uno; **to — someone off a subject** advertir a uno que no se meta en un asunto; **I —ed him off Espronceda** le dije que no le convenía estudiar a Espronceda.

warning ['wɔ:niŋ] **1** n aviso m, advertencia f; **without — sin dar aviso, sin previo aviso; it fell without —** cayó de repente, cayó inesperadamente; **they came without —** vinieron sin avisarnos; **let this be a — to you** que esto le sirva de escarmiento; **thank you for the —** gracias por la advertencia; **the bell gives —** el timbre da la alarma; **to give someone a week's —** avisar a uno con ocho días de anticipación; **to give someone due —** avisar a uno con mucha antelación; **you were given due —** le avisamos a Vd debidamente; **I give you due — that . . .** le advierto en serio que . . .; **to send a — to the police** avisar a la policía; **to take — from** aprender la lección de, escarmentar en.

2 adj: **— device** dispositivo m de alarma; **— light** luz f de advertencia; **— notice** aviso m; **— shot** disparo m de aviso; **— sign** señal f admonitoria; **in a — tone** en tono amonestador; **— voices** voces fpl admonitorias.

warp [wɔ:p] **1** n (*in weaving*) urdimbre f; (*of wood*) deformación f, alabeo m, comba f; (*fig*) sesgo m. **2** vt *wood* deformar, alabear, torcer; *mind* pervertir, torcer, afectar. **3** vi deformarse, alabearse, torcerse.

war paint ['wɔ:peint] n pintura f de guerra.

warpath ['wɔ:pɑ:θ] n: **to be on the —** estar en pie de guerra, estar preparado para la guerra; (*fig*) estar dispuesto a armar un lío; estar buscando pendencia.

warped [wɔ:pt] adj *wood* deformado, torcido; *character, sense of humour etc* pervertido.

warping ['wɔ:piŋ] n (*of wood*) deformación f, alabeo m; (*Aer*) torsión f.

warplane ['wɔ:plein] n avión m militar.

warrant ['wɔrənt] **1** n autorización f, justificación f; (*certificate*) cédula f, certificado m; (*Comm*) garantía f; (*Law*) mandamiento m judicial; mandato m, orden f; **— of arrest** orden f de prisión; **there is a — out for his arrest** se ha ordenado su detención. **2** vt autorizar, justificar; (*Comm etc*) garantizar; **I —, I — you** se lo aseguro; **nothing —s such an assumption** no hay nada que autorice tal suposición; **the facts do not —** it los hechos no lo justifican.

warrantable ['wɔrəntəbl] adj justificable.

warranted ['wɔrəntid] adj justificado; (*Comm*) garantizado.

warrant officer ['wɔrəntˌɔfisə*] n (*Mil*) suboficial m; (*Naut*) contramaestre m.

warranty ['wɔrənti] n (*Comm*) garantía f.

warren ['wɔrən] n madriguera f (de conejos); (*fig*) (*house etc*) conejera f, casa f con muchísimos inquilinos; casa f laberíntica; (*area of town*) barrio m densamente poblado; **it is a — of little streets** el barrio tiene muchas callejuelas estrechas, el barrio consiste en callejuelas sin ningún plano lógico.

warring ['wɔriŋ] adj *interests, nations etc* opuesto, en lucha abierta entre sí.

warrior ['wɔriə*] n guerrero m; **the Unknown W—** el Soldado Desconocido.

Warsaw ['wɔ:sɔ:] Varsovia.

warship ['wɔ:ʃip] n buque m de guerra, barco m de guerra.

wart [wɔ:t] n (*Med, Bot*) verruga f.

wart hog ['wɔ:thɔg] n jabalí m de verrugas.

wartime ['wɔ:taim] **1** n tiempo m de guerra; **in — en tiempos de guerra, en la guerra. 2** attr de tiempos de guerra, de guerra.

warty ['wɔ:ti] adj verrugoso.

war-weary ['wɔ:ˌwiəri] adj cansado de la guerra.

wary ['wɛəri] adj cauteloso, cauto; **it's best to be — here** aquí conviene andar con pies de plomo; **I was — about it** tuve mis dudas acerca de ello, me recelé, desconfié de ello; **to keep a — eye on someone** vigilar a uno con recelo, observar a uno con recelo.

war zone ['wɔ:zəun] n zona f de guerra.

was [wɔz, wəz] *see* **be**.

wash [wɔʃ] **1** n **(a)** (*act of —ing*) lavado m; baño m; **to give something a —** lavar algo; **to have a —** lavarse; **to have a — and brush-up** lavarse y arreglarse; **my shirt is at the —** mi camisa está siendo lavada, mi camisa está en la lavandería; **to send sheets to the —** mandar sábanas a la lavandería; **it will all come out in the —** todo se arreglará, no será un estorbo permanente.

(b) (*clothes: dirty*) ropa f sucia, ropa f para lavar; (*hung to dry*) tendido m, colada f; **the Monday —** la ropa para lavar el lunes.

(c) (*of ship*) estela f, remolinos mpl; (*Aer*) disturbio m aerodinámico; **the — of the water** (*sound*) el movimiento del agua, el chapoteo del agua.

(d) (*liquid: hair—*) champú m; (*mouth—*) enjuague m; (*of distemper, paint*) capa f; pintura f; (*of insecticide etc*) baño m; (*liquid remains*) lavazas fpl, despojos mpl líquidos; (*pej*) aguachirle f; **a coat of blue —** una capa de pintura azul.

2 vt **(a)** (*clean with water etc*) lavar; *dishes* fregar; *clothes* lavar; **to — one's hair** lavarse el pelo; **to — one's hands** lavarse las manos; **to — something clean** limpiar algo lavándolo, lavar algo hasta dejarlo limpio; **the sea —ed it clean of oil** el mar quitó todo el aceite y lo dejó limpio.

(b) **to — the walls with distemper** dar una capa de pintura (al temple) a las paredes; **to —**

a metal with gold dar una capa de oro a un metal, bañar un metal en oro.

(c) an island —ed by a blue sea una isla bañada por el mar azul.

(d) (of river, sea; carry) llevar, llevarse; the house was —ed downstream la casa fue llevada aguas abajo; the sea —ed it ashore el mar lo echó a la playa; he was —ed overboard fue arrastrado por las olas.

(e) (with adv or prep) to — dirt away quitar la suciedad lavando; the boat was —ed away el bote fue arrastrado por la corriente; the river —ed away part of the bank el río se llevó una parte de la orilla; to — a car down limpiar un coche lavándolo; to — one's dinner down with wine regar la cena con vino; to — off quitar lavando, hacer desaparecer lavando; to — out a saucepan limpiar una cacerola lavándola; to — out an insult lavar un insulto; to feel —ed out no estar bien de salud; to look —ed out estar ojeroso; the game was —ed out el partido tuvo que ser cancelado por la lluvia; let's — it all out abandonémoslo todo, renunciemos a la empresa; you can — that out for a start conviene renunciar a esa idea desde el principio; to — up the dishes fregar los platos; it was —ed up on the shore apareció echado en la playa; that's all —ed up eso es un fracaso total, eso ya se acabó.

3 vi (a) (have a —) lavarse; (do the —ing) lavar la ropa.

(b) a cloth that —es well una tela que puede lavarse; it's nice but it won't — es atractivo pero no se puede lavar; that excuse won't — ! ¡esa razón es inaceptable!

(c) (of sea etc) moverse; chapotear; the river was —ing against the top of the bridge el río estaba a la altura de la parte alta del puente; the sea —ed over the promenade el mar inundó el paseo marítimo.

(d) (with adv or prep) it —es off (or out) easily es fácil quitarlo lavando; the colour —es out el color se destiñe; to — up fregar los platos.

washable ['wɔʃəbl] adj lavable.

wash-and-wear ['wɔʃən'wɛə*] adj clothing de lava y pon.

washbasin ['wɔʃ,beisn] n, **washbowl** n ['wɔʃbəul] palangana f, jofaina f.

washboard ['wɔʃbɔːd] n tabla f de lavar.

washcloth ['wɔʃklɔθ] n, pl —cloths [klɔθs, klɔθz] (US) paño m para lavarse, manopla f.

washday ['wɔʃdei] n día m de colada.

washer ['wɔʃə*] n (a) (Tech) arandela f, (on tap) arandela f, zapatilla f. (b) (washing machine) lavadora f.

washerwoman ['wɔʃə,wumən] n, pl —women [,wimin] lavandera f.

wash house ['wɔʃhaus] n, pl — houses [,hauziz] lavadero m.

washing ['wɔʃiŋ] n (act) lavado m, el lavar; (clothes: dirty) ropa f sucia, ropa f para lavar; (hung to dry) tendido m, colada f; —s lavazas fpl, lavadura f; to take in — ser lavandera.

washing day ['wɔʃiŋdei] n día m de colada.

washing machine ['wɔʃiŋmə,ʃiːn] n lavadora f.

washing powder ['wɔʃiŋ,paudə*] n jabón m en polvo.

washing soda ['wɔʃiŋ,səudə] n carbonato m sódico.

washing-up ['wɔʃiŋ'ʌp] n (act) fregado m, el fregar (los platos); (dishes) platos mpl para lavar; platos mpl lavados; he did all the — fregó todos los platos.

wash leather ['wɔʃ,leðə*] n gamuza f.

wash-out ['wɔʃaut] n (fam): it was a — fue un fracaso total; he's a — es una calamidad (fam).

washrag ['wɔʃræg] n (US) paño m de cocina; = washcloth.

washroom ['wɔʃrum] n (euph) aseos mpl; urinario m público.

washstand ['wɔʃstænd] n lavabo m, lavamanos m.

washtub ['wɔʃtʌb] n tina f de lavar; (bath) bañera f.

washy ['wɔʃi] adj aguado, diluido; débil; (fig) flojo, soso.

wasn't ['wɔznt] = was not.

wasp [wɔsp] n avispa f.

waspish ['wɔspiʃ] adj character irascible; person de prontos enojos, fácil de enojar; comment mordaz, punzante.

waspishly ['wɔspiʃli] adv mordazmente.

wasp's nest ['wɔspsnest] n avispero m.

wasp waist ['wɔsp'weist] n (fig) talle m de avispa.

wasp-waisted ['wɔsp'weistid] adj (fig) con talle de avispa.

wastage ['weistidʒ] n desgaste m, desperdicio m; pérdida f; (from container) merma f; the — of our resources el desperdicio de nuestros recursos; the — rate among students la proporción de estudiantes que no obtienen su licenciatura (etc); the — rate among entrants to the profession el porcentaje de los que abandonan la profesión poco tiempo después de ingresar en ella.

waste [weist] 1 adj (rejected) desechado, de desecho; (left over) sobrante, superfluo; (useless) inútil; land baldío; yermo; paper viejo, usado; "The W— Land" "Tierra f baldía"; to lay — asolar, devastar; to lie — quedar sin cultivar; quedar sin utilizar; see product etc.

2 n (a) (act) despilfarro m, derroche m; (of time etc) pérdida f; (wastage) desgaste m, desperdicio m; merma f; it's a — of time es tiempo perdido; it's a — of effort es un esfuerzo inútil; there's a lot of — here hay mucho desperdicio aquí, aquí despilfarran todo; to go to —, to run to — echarse a perder, perderse.

(b) (— material) desperdicios mpl, desechos mpl; (rubbish) basura f; cotton — borra f; metal — metales mpl de desecho.

(c) (land) yermo m, tierra f baldía; desierto m; lost in the —s of Siberia perdido en la inmensidad de Siberia; to plough the —s of Siberia cultivar la tierra baldía de Siberia.

3 vt (squander) despilfarrar, derrochar; malgastar; time etc perder; (not use) desperdiciar; opportunity etc desaprovechar, desperdiciar; (use up) agotar, consumir; a —d life una vida desperdiciada; nothing is —d no queda nada sin aprovechar; we —d 3 litres of petrol usamos inútilmente 3 litros de gasolina; you're wasting your time talking to him es tiempo perdido hablar con él; don't — your efforts on him no te canses tratando de hacer cosas por él.

4 vi gastarse, perderse; to — away consumirse, mermar; (person) consumirse; you're not exactly wasting away (iro) no pareces haber enflaquecido de modo peligroso, que digamos.

wastebasket ['weist,baskit] n (US) cesto m de los papeles, papelera f.

wasteful ['weistful] adj person etc pródigo, despilfarrado, derrochador; process antieconómico; expenditure pródigo, excesivo; it is — of effort no utiliza debidamente el esfuerzo.

wastefully ['weistfəli] adv pródigamente; antieconómicamente; excesivamente.

wastefulness ['weistfulnis] n prodigalidad f, despilfarro m; falta f de economía, lo antieconómico; lo excesivo.

wasteland ['weistlænd] n tierra f baldía, yermo m.

wastepaper basket [weist'peipə,ba:skit] n cesto m de los papeles, papelera f.

waste pipe ['weistpaip] n tubo m de desagüe.

waster ['weistə*] n artículo m defectuoso, desecho m; (person) derrochador m, perdido m.

wastrel ['weistrəl] n derrochador m, perdido m.

watch [wɔtʃ] 1 n (a) (vigilance) vigilancia f; (act of —ing) vigilia f, vela f; to be on the — estar a la mira (for de), velar, vigilar; they're on the — for smugglers están a la mira de contrabandistas; to keep — estar de guardia; to keep — all night velar toda la noche; to keep a close — on something vigilar algo con mucho cuidado; to keep — over person velar, vigilar; thing vigilar por; to set a — on someone ordenar que se vigile a uno.

(b) (period of duty) guardia f; middle —, dog — media guardia f; to have a 4-hour — estar de guardia durante 4 horas.

(c) (persons: Hist) ronda f; (Mil: persons) guardia f, (1 man) guardia m, centinela m; (Naut: persons) guardia f, vigía f, (1 man) vigía m; officer of the — oficial m de guardia.

(d) (timepiece) reloj m (de bolsillo, de pulsera); what does your — say? ¿qué hora tienes?

2 vt (a) (guard) guardar, vigilar; proteger.

(b) (observe) observar, mirar; (at length) contemplar; (spy on) espiar, acechar; TV etc ver; did you — the programme? ¿viste el programa?; to — someone doing something mirar a uno hacer algo, observar a uno hacer algo; now — this closely ahora observa esto con mucho cuidado; we are being —ed nos están observando; have you ever —ed an operation? ¿ha visto Vd alguna vez una operación?

(c) (be careful with) ser cuidadoso con, prestar atención a, tener ojo a; — it! ¡ojo!, ¡cuidado!; you'd better — it conviene tener más cuidado; we shall have to — the expenses tendremos que estudiar cuidadosamente los gastos, convendrá tener ojo a los gastos; — **how you go!** ¡anda con cuidado!; *see* **step** *etc.*

(d) *chance etc* esperar, aguardar; **he —ed his chance and slipped out** esperó el momento propicio y se escabulló.

3 *vi* ver, mirar; observar; (*watchfully*) vigilar; **to — for someone** esperar a uno, aguardar a uno; **to — for something to happen** esperar a que pase algo; **to — out** tener ojo, tener cuidado; **— out!** ¡ojo!; **— out for thieves** cuidado con los ladrones; **to — out for trouble** estar dispuesto a aguantar cualquier disturbio; **then you'd better — out!** ¡pues aténgase a las consecuencias!; **to — over someone** velar a uno; **to — over the safety of the country** velar por la seguridad de la patria; **to — over a property** vigilar una propiedad.

watchband ['wɔtʃbænd] *n* (*US*) pulsera *f* de reloj.
watchcase ['wɔtʃkeis] *n* caja *f* de reloj.
watchdog ['wɔtʃdɔg] *n* perro *m* guardián.
watcher ['wɔtʃə*] *n* observador *m*, ora *f*; espectador *m*, ora *f*; (*pej*) mirón *m*, ona *f*.
watchful ['wɔtʃful] *adj* vigilante; observador; (*esp fig*) desvelado.
watchfully ['wɔtʃfəli] *adv* vigilantemente.
watchfulness ['wɔtʃfulnis] *n* vigilancia *f*; desvelo *m*.
watch glass ['wɔtʃglɑ:s] *n* cristal *m* de reloj.
watchmaker ['wɔtʃ,meikə*] *n* relojero *m*; **—'s (shop)** relojería *f*.
watchman ['wɔtʃmən] *n*, *pl* **—men** [mən] guardián *m*; (*night* —: *in street, flats*) sereno *m*, (*in factory etc*) vigilante *m*, nocturno.
watch strap ['wɔtʃstræp] *n* pulsera *f* de reloj.
watchtower ['wɔtʃ,tauə*] *n* atalaya *f*, vigía *f*.
watchword ['wɔtʃwə:d] *n* (*Mil etc*) santo *m* y seña; (*motto*) lema *m*, consigna *f*.
water ['wɔ:tə*] **1** *n* **(a)** agua *f*; **boiling —** agua *f* hirviendo; **cold —** agua *f* fría; **distilled —** agua *f* destilada; **fresh —** agua *f* dulce; **hard —** agua *f* dura; **heavy —** agua *f* pesada; **holy —** agua *f* bendita; **hot —** agua *f* caliente; **running —** agua *f* corriente; **salt —** agua *f* salada; **soft —** agua *f* blanda; **like —** (*fig*) como agua, pródigamente, en abundancia; **the square is under —** la plaza está inundada; **much — has flowed under the bridges** ya ha llovido desde entonces; **to get into hot —** cargársela (*for, over* en el asunto de); **to hold —** retener el agua, (*fig*) estar bien fundado, ser lógico; **that excuse won't hold —** esa excusa no vale; **to pour cold — on an idea** echar un jarro de agua fría a una idea; **to take on —** (*Rail*) tomar agua; **to turn on the —** hacer correr el agua; (*from tap*) abrir el grifo; **still —s run deep** la procesión va por dentro.

(b) (*urine*) orina *f*, orines *mpl*; **to make —** hacer aguas, mear.

(c) —s (*Med*) aguas *fpl*; **to drink** (*or* **take**) **the —s at Harrogate** tomar las aguas en Harrogate.

(d) (*of sea etc*) agua *f*; **the —s of the Ebro** las aguas del Ebro; **high —** pleamar *f*, marea *f* alta; **low —** bajamar *f*, marea *f* baja; **slack —** repunte *m* de la marea; **home —s** aguas *fpl* cerca de la patria; **territorial —s** aguas *fpl* jurisdiccionales, aguas *fpl* territoriales; **by —** por mar; **on land and — por** tierra y por mar; **to back —** (*Naut*) ciar; **to fish in troubled —s** pescar en río revuelto; **to get into deep —(s)** meterse en honduras; **to tread —** mantenerse a flote pataleando en el agua.

(e) (*Med*) **— on the brain** hidrocefalia *f*; **— on the knee** derrame *m* sinovial.

(f) of the first — de lo mejor, de primerísima calidad.

2 *adj, attr* acuático; de agua; para agua; **— supply** abastecimiento *m* de agua; **— plants** plantas *fpl* acuáticas.

3 *vt garden, plant* regar; *horses* abrevar; *wine* aguar; diluir; (*moisten*) mojar, humedecer; **to — a plant with an insecticide** regar (*or* rociar) una planta con insecticida; **the river —s the provinces of . . .** el río riega las provincias de . . .; **to — capital** (*Fin*) emitir un número excesivo de acciones; **to — down** aguar; diluir; (*fig*) mitigar; suavizar; **I should — the abuse down a bit** conviene suavizar un poco las injurias.

4 *vi* (*of eyes*) hacerse agua, lagrimear, llorar; **my mouth —ed** se me hizo la boca agua; **it's enough to make your mouth —** se hace la boca agua.

water bird ['wɔ:təbə:d] *n* ave *f* acuática.
waterborne ['wɔ:təbɔ:n] *adj* llevado por barco (*etc*).
water bottle ['wɔ:tə,bɔtl] *n* cantimplora *f*.
water carrier ['wɔ:tə,kæriə*] *n* aguador *m*.
water cart ['wɔ:təkɑ:t] *n* cuba *f* de riego, carro *m* aljibe; (*motorized*) camión *m* de agua.

water closet ['wɔ:tə,klɔzit] *n* (*freq abbreviated* WC) wáter *m*, inodoro *m*.
watercolour, (US) watercolor ['wɔ:tə,kʌlə*] *n* acuarela *f*.
watercolourist, (US) —colorist ['wɔ:tə,kʌlərist] *n* acuarelista *mf*.
water-cooled ['wɔ:təku:ld] *adj* refrigerado por agua.
water-cooling ['wɔ:təku:liŋ] *n* refrigeración *f* por agua.
watercourse ['wɔ:təkɔ:s] *n* (*stream*) arroyo *m*; (*bed*) lecho *m*, cauce *m*; (*dried*) torrentera *f*.
watercress ['wɔ:təkres] *n* berro *m*, mastuerzo *m*.
water diviner ['wɔ:tədi,vainə*] *n* zahorí *m*.
water divining ['wɔ:tədi,vainiŋ] *n* arte *m* del zahorí.
waterfall ['wɔ:təfɔ:l] *n* cascada *f*, salto *m* de agua.
water fountain ['wɔ:tə'fauntin] *n* (*US*) surtidor *m* de agua, fuente *f*.
waterfowl ['wɔ:təfaul] *npl* aves *fpl* acuáticas.
waterfront ['wɔ:təfrʌnt] *n* (*esp US*) terreno *m* ribereño; (*harbour area*) puerto *m*, muelles *mpl*, dársenas *fpl*.
water hole ['wɔ:təhəul] *n* charco *m*.
water ice ['wɔ:tərais] *n* sorbete *m*, helado *m*.
watering ['wɔ:təriŋ] *n* riego *m*; **frequent — is needed** hay que regar con frecuencia.
watering can ['wɔ:təriŋkæn] *n* regadera *f*.
watering place ['wɔ:təriŋpleis] *n* (*spa*) balneario *m*; (*seaside resort*) playa *f*, ciudad *f* marítima de veraneo; (*Agr*) abrevadero *m*.
water jacket ['wɔ:tə,dʒækit] *n* camisa *f* de agua.
waterless ['wɔ:təlis] *adj* sin agua, árido.
water level ['wɔ:tə,levl] *n* nivel *m* del agua; (*Naut*) línea *f* de agua.
water lily ['wɔ:tə,lili] *n* nenúfar *m*.
waterline ['wɔ:təlain] *n* línea *f* de flotación.
waterlogged ['wɔ:təlɔgd] *adj ground etc* anegado, inundado; *wood etc* empapado; **to get —** anegarse; empaparse.
Waterloo [,wɔ:tə'lu:] Waterloo (1815); **to meet one's —** llegar hasta el desastre.
waterman ['wɔ:təmən] *n*, *pl* **—men** [mən] barquero *m*.
watermark ['wɔ:təmɑ:k] *n* filigrana *f*.
water meadow ['wɔ:tə,medəu] *n* vega *f*.
watermelon ['wɔ:tə,melən] *n* sandía *f*.
water mill ['wɔ:təmil] *n* molino *m* de agua.
water pipe ['wɔ:təpaip] *n* caño *m* de agua.
water polo ['wɔ:tə'pəuləu] *n* polo *m* acuático, water-polo *m*.
water power ['wɔ:tə,pauə*] *n* fuerza *f* hidráulica.
waterproof ['wɔ:təpru:f] **1** *adj* impermeable. **2** *n* impermeable *m*. **3** *vt* impermeabilizar.
water pump ['wɔ:təpʌmp] *n* bomba *f* de agua.
water rat ['wɔ:təræt] *n* rata *f* de agua.
water rate ['wɔ:təreit] *n* tarifa *f* de agua.
watershed ['wɔ:təʃed] *n* (*Geog*) línea *f* divisoria de las aguas; cuenca *f*; (*fig*) división *f*, línea *f* divisoria; **the — of the Duero** la cuenca del Duero.
waterside ['wɔ:təsaid] **1** *n* orilla *f* del agua, ribera *f*. **2** *attr* ribereño; situado en la orilla.
water-ski ['wɔ:təski:] *vi* practicar el esquí acuático.
water-skiing ['wɔ:tə,ski:iŋ] *n* esquí *m* acuático.
waterspout ['wɔ:təspaut] *n* tromba *f* marina.
water table ['wɔ:tə,teibl] *n* nivel *m* del subsuelo acuífero.
water tank ['wɔ:tətæŋk] *n* cisterna *f*, depósito *m* de agua; aljibe *m*.
watertight ['wɔ:tətait] *adj compartment etc* estanco; hermético; (*fig*) irrecusable, completamente lógico.
water tower ['wɔ:tə,tauə*] *n* arca *f* de agua, alcubilla *f*.
water vapour ['wɔ:tə,veipə*] *n* vapor *m* de agua.
waterway ['wɔ:təwei] *n* vía *f* fluvial; (*inland —*) canal *m*, canal *m* navegable.
waterwheel ['wɔ:təwi:l] *n* rueda *f* hidráulica; (*Agr*) noria *f*.
water wings ['wɔ:təwiŋz] *npl* nadaderas *fpl*, flotadores *mpl*.
waterworks ['wɔ:təwə:ks] *n* central *f* depuradora.
watery ['wɔ:təri] *adj substance* acuoso; (*wet*) húmedo, mojado; *eye* lagrimoso; *sky* que amenaza lluvia, lluvioso; *soup, wine* débil, flojo.
watt [wɔt] *n* vatio *m*.
wattage ['wɔtidʒ] *n* vatiaje *m*.
wattle[1] ['wɔtl] *n* zarzo *m*.
wattle[2] ['wɔtl] *n* (*Orn*) barba *f*.
wave [weiv] **1** *n* **(a)** (*of water*) ola *f*.
(b) (*Phys, Radio*) onda *f*; **long — onda** *f* larga; **medium — onda** *f* media; **short — onda** *f* corta.
(c) (*in hair, on surface*) ondulación *f*; **permanent — ondulación** *f* permanente.
(d) (*fig*) oleada *f*; **— of enthusiasm** oleada *f* de entusiasmo; **— of panic** oleada *f* de pánico; **— of**

strikes oleada f de huelgas; **cold** — oleada f de frío; **the first — of the attack** la primera oleada de asalto; **the attackers came in —s** las tropas atacaron en oleadas.

(e) (movement of hand) movimiento m, ademán m (de la mano), señal f (hecha con la mano); **with a — of his hand** con un movimiento de la mano, haciendo una señal con la mano; **with a — he was gone** hizo una señal con la mano y desapareció.

2 vt (a) (brandish) agitar, (threateningly) blandir; flag etc ondear, agitar; **don't — it about!** ¡no lo agites!; **he —d the ticket under my nose** agitó el billete en mis narices; **to — one's hand to someone** hacer una señal a uno con la mano; **to — one's arms about** agitar mucho los brazos; **to — someone goodbye** decir adiós a uno con la mano; **to — a handkerchief to someone** agitar el pañuelo para dar una señal a uno; **he —ed a greeting to the crowd** saludó a la multitud con un movimiento de la mano; **to — an offer aside** rechazar una oferta; **to — someone aside** hacer una señal a uno para que se aparte; **he —d my help aside** indicó con un movimiento de la mano que no necesitaba mi ayuda; **to — a car down** hacer señales a un coche para que se detenga; **to — someone on** hacer señales a uno para que avance.

(b) hair etc ondular; **to have one's hair —d** hacerse ondular el pelo, hacerse una permanente.

3 vi (a) (person) hacer señales con la mano, agitar el brazo; **to — to someone** hacer señales con la mano a uno; **we —d as the train drew out** cuando partió el tren nos dijimos adiós con la mano.

(b) (of flag etc) ondear; flotar; (of arm etc) agitarse.

waveband ['weivbænd] n banda f de ondas; **long —** banda f de onda larga.

wavelength ['weivleŋθ] n longitud f de onda.

wavelet ['weivlit] n pequeña ola f, rizo m.

waver ['weivə*] vi (oscillate) oscilar (between entre); (hesitate) vacilar; (weaken) flaquear; **I —ed for some days** durante varios días no me resolví; **he's beginning to —** está empezando a vacilar.

wave range ['weivreindʒ] n (Radio) gama f de ondas.

waverer ['weivərə*] n irresoluto m, a f.

wavering ['weivəriŋ] **1** adj irresoluto, vacilante. **2** n oscilación f, vacilación f, irresolución f.

wavy ['weivi] adj hair, surface ondulado; motion ondulante.

wax¹ [wæks] **1** n cera f; (in ear) cerilla f. **2** adj de cera. **3** vt encerar.

wax² [wæks] vi (moon) crecer; (with adj) ponerse, hacerse; **to — enthusiastic** entusiasmarse; **to — talkative** empezar a hablar mucho.

waxed [wækst] adj paper etc encerado.

wax(ed) paper ['wæks(t)'peipə*] n papel m encerado.

waxen ['wæksən] adj (of wax) de cera; (like wax) ceroso, parecido a cera; como cera; de color de cera.

waxing ['wæksiŋ] **1** adj moon creciente. **2** n crecimiento m.

waxwork ['wækswə:k] n figura f de cera; **—s** museo m de (figuras de) cera.

waxy ['wæksi] adj = **waxen**.

way [wei] **1** n (a) (road) camino m, vía f; carretera f; calle f; **W— of the Cross** Vía f Crucis; **permanent —** (Rail) vía f; **the public —** la vía pública; **across the —, over the —** enfrente (from de); **by — of** vía, por vía de; pasando por.

(b) (route) camino m, ruta f (to de); **the — to the station** el camino de la estación; **which is the — to the town hall, please?** por favor, ¿qué camino tomo para ir al Ayuntamiento?; **this isn't the — to Lugo!** ¡por aquí no se va a Lugo!; **the — is hard** el camino es duro; **the — of virtue** el camino de la virtud; **to go the shortest —** ir por el camino más corto; **to go the — of all things** padecer la suerte de todas las cosas; **to lead the —** ir primero, (fig) dar el ejemplo, mostrar el camino; **to prepare the —** preparar el terreno (for a, para); **on the —** en el camino; durante el viaje; **on the — here** mientras veníamos aquí; **on the — to Aranjuez** camino de Aranjuez; **it's on the — to Murcia** está en la carretera de Murcia; **you pass it on your — home** al ir a casa pasas delante de él; **an out-of-the— place** un lugar apartado, un lugar remoto; **an out-of-the— subject** un tema insólito, un tema poco conocido, un tema original; **her painting is nothing out of the —** su pintura no tiene nada de particular; **to go out of one's —** desviarse del camino; **to go out of one's — to + infin** (fig) tomarse la molestia de + infin; desvivirse por + infin.

(c) (route, with adv) — **down** ruta f para bajar; — **in** entrada f; **"— in"** "entrada"; **Spain's — into the United Nations** el camino que siguió España para ingresar en las Naciones Unidas; **to find a — in** encontrar un modo de entrar; — **out** salida f; **"— out"** "salida"; **you'll find it on the — out** lo encontrarás cerca de la salida; **it's on its — out** está en camino de desaparecer, ya está pasando de moda; **there's no — out** (fig) no hay solución, esto no tiene solución; **there's no other — out** (fig) no hay más remedio; — **through** paso m; **"no — through"** "cerrado el paso"; — **up** ruta f para subir.

(d) (route, with personal associations) **to ask one's —** preguntar por el camino; **to feel one's —** andar a tientas, (fig) proceder con tiento; **to find one's — into a building** encontrar un modo de entrar en un edificio; **the cat found the — into the pantry** el gato logró introducirse en la despensa; **can you find your — home?** ¿sabes por dónde ir a tu casa?; **to go the wrong —** equivocarse de camino; **to go one's own —** (fig) ir a la suya; hacer rancho aparte; **I know my — about town** conozco el plano de la ciudad; **she knows her — about** (fig) tiene bastante experiencia; no es que sea una inocente; **to lose one's —** extraviarse, errar el camino; **to make one's — to** dirigirse a; **to make one's — home** ir a casa, volver a casa; **to make one's — through a crowd** abrirse camino entre una multitud; **to make one's — in the world** hacer progresos en su profesión, hacerse una carrera; valerse por sí mismo; **he had to make his own — in the art world** tuvo que introducirse por sus propios medios en el mundo del arte; **to pay one's —** (as fare) pagar su billete; (in restaurant) pagar su parte; (Fin) ser solvente; **the company isn't paying its —** la compañía tiene un saldo negativo; **Britain must pay her —** Gran Bretaña ha de lograr la solvencia; **to see one's — to + ger or infin** ver la forma de + infin; **could you possibly see your — to + infin?** ¿sería Vd tan amable como para + infin?; **to start on one's —** ponerse en camino; **to work one's — up a rock** escalar a duras penas una roca, escalar poco a poco una roca; **to work one's — to the front** abrirse camino hacia la primera fila (etc); **he worked his — up in the company** a fuerza de trabajar llegó a ocupar un alto puesto en la sociedad; logró ser ascendido en la sociedad gracias a sus esfuerzos personales; **he worked his — up from nothing** empezó sin nada y fue muy lejos por sus méritos personales.

(e) (path) camino m, vía f; **the middle —** el camino de en medio; **to be in someone's —** estorbar a uno; **am I in the —?** ¿estorbo?; **to get in the —** estorbar; **to get in one another's —** estorbarse uno a otro; **to put difficulties in someone's —** crear dificultades a uno; **to stand in someone's —** estorbar; **now nothing stands in our —** ahora no hay obstáculo alguno; **his age stands in his —** su edad es una desventaja para él; **to stand in the — of progress** estorbar el progreso, ser un estorbo para el progreso; **out of my —!** ¡quítese allá!; **it's out of the — of the wind** está al abrigo del viento; **to get out of the —** quitarse de en medio; **to get something out of the —** quitar algo de en medio; **to get someone out of the —** (fig) quitar a uno de en medio; **as soon as I've got my exams out of the —** en cuanto esté libre de exámenes; **one should keep matches out of the — of children** conviene no poner las cerillas al alcance de los niños; **I kept well out of the —** me mantuve muy lejos; **I try to keep out of his —** procuro evitar cualquier contacto con él; **he wants his wife out of the —** quiere deshacerse de su mujer; **to bar the —, to block the —** cerrar el paso; **to clear a — for** abrir camino para; **to clear the —** despejar el camino; **to fight one's — out** lograr salir luchando; **to fight one's — to the sea** abrirse paso luchando hacia el mar; **to force one's — through** abrirse paso luchando; **to force one's — in** introducirse a la fuerza; **to hack one's — through something** abrirse paso por algo a fuerza de tajos; **to leave the — open for further talks** dejar la vía libre para otra conferencia; **to leave the — open to abuse** dejar vía libre al desafuero; **make —!** ¡calle!; **to make —** hacer lugar (for para).

(f) (distance) distancia f; trayecto m, recorrido m; **there are flowers all the —** por todo el recorrido hay flores; **it rained all the —** there durante todo el viaje llovió; **I was sick part of the —** me mareé durante una parte del viaje; **a little — away, a little — off** no muy lejos, a poca distancia; **a long**

— away, a long — off muy lejos, a gran distancia; a lo lejos; it's a long (or good) — es mucho camino; it's a long — from here está muy lejos de aquí; you're a long — out Vd se ha extraviado bastante, (fig) Vd está muy lejos de acertar; to go the long — round ir por rodeos; he'll go a long — irá lejos; we have a long — to go tenemos mucho camino por delante; it should go a long — towards + ger ha de contribuir mucho a + infin; a little help goes a long — un poco de ayuda puede ser muy valioso; better by a long — mejor con mucho; not by a long — ni con mucho; a short — off no muy lejos, a poca distancia.

(g) (direction) dirección f, sentido m; this — por aquí; "this — for the lions" "a los leones"; this — and that por aquí y por allá, en todas direcciones; down our — en nuestro barrio; en nuestra región; it's out Vd de vivimos nosotros; it's out Windsor — está en la región de Windsor, está cerca de Windsor; está en la carretera de Windsor; which — are you going? ¿adónde vas?; which — did it go? ¿hacia dónde fue?; which — do we go from here? ¿en qué dirección continuamos desde aquí?; which — is the wind blowing? ¿de dónde sopla el viento?; she didn't know which — to look no sabía adónde poner los ojos; to look the other — (fig) hacer la vista gorda; no darse por aludido; it doesn't matter to me one — or the other me es igual, no me importa que sea lo uno o lo otro; it doesn't often come my — para mí es una oportunidad poco frecuente; if the chance comes your — si tienes la oportunidad, si la suerte te favorece; are you going my —? ¿vas por donde voy yo?

(h) (of position) it's the wrong — up está al revés, lo de abajo está arriba; put it right — up póngalo en su posición correcta; to rub an animal up the wrong — frotar a un animal a contrapelo; to rub someone up the wrong — irritar a uno, sacar a uno de quicio; they seem to rub each other up the wrong — parecen irritarse mutuamente; we'll split it 3 —s lo dividiremos en 3 partes iguales.

(i) (means) medio m; —s and means medios mpl; that's not the right — no es ése el método correcto; we'll find a — of doing it buscaremos el método de hacerlo; love will find a — el amor lo arreglará, el amor triunfará a la larga.

(j) (manner) manera f, modo m; forma f; método m, sistema m; — of life estilo m de vida; each — (Racing) ganador y colocado; this —, in this — de este modo; an odd — of talking un extraño modo de hablar; the only — of doing it la única forma de hacerlo; there are many —s of ... hay muchas maneras de ...; her — of looking at things su modo de ver las cosas; my — is to + infin mi sistema consiste en + infin; he has his own — of doing it tiene su sistema particular para hacerlo; that's the —! ¡así!; ¡eso es!; that's the — money goes así se gasta el dinero; the — things are tal como están las cosas; to leave things the — they are dejar las cosas donde están; the — things are going we shall have nothing left si esto continúa así nos vamos a quedar sin nada; it was this — ... lo que pasó fue esto ...; that's always the — with him siempre le pasa igual; there are no two —s about it no cabe otra posibilidad, no le encuentro otra posibilidad; yo lo veo perfectamente claro.

(k) (manner: phrases with in) in this — de este modo; in one — or another de algún que otro modo; in a general — this is true en general esto es verdad; without in any — wishing to + infin sin querer en lo más mínimo + infin, sin tener intención alguna de + infin; I'll do it in my own — lo haré según mi método particular; he's a good sort in his — tiene sus rarezas pero es buena persona; a pesar de todo es buena persona; they interpret it each in his own — lo interpretan cada uno a su modo; he said in his rough — dijo en ese tono suyo un poco brusco; to go on in the same old — continuar como siempre, seguir empleando los viejos métodos; to be in a small — of business tener un negocio modesto; to be in the family — estar en estado de buena esperanza; to get someone in the family — dejar a una encinta; to get oneself in the family — empreñar, hacerse una criatura.

(l) (custom) costumbre f; the —s of the Spaniards las costumbres de los españoles; the —s of good society los modales de la buena sociedad; la etiqueta de la buena sociedad; that is our — with traitors así tratamos a los traidores; he has a — with him tiene atractivo personal, es simpático; tiene mucha persuasiva; he has his little —s

tiene sus manías, tiene sus rarezas; he has a — with children maneja bien los niños, los niños le creen muy simpático; he has a — with people tiene don de gentes; the child has some pretty —s el niño hace las cosas de un modo que encanta; to mend one's —s enmendarse, reformarse; to be out of the — of + ger haber perdido la costumbre de + infin; to get out of the — of + ger perder la costumbre de + infin; to get into the — of + ger (by habit) adquirir la costumbre de + infin, (by learning) aprender el modo de + infin.

(m) (of will) to get one's (own) — salirse con la suya; hacer aceptar su opinión; they had it all their own — in the second half en el segundo tiempo hicieron lo que les dio la gana; they didn't have things all their own — no dominaron el partido (etc) completamente, su dominio no fue completo; he wants his own — all the time todo el tiempo insiste en su punto de vista, todo el tiempo insiste en hacer únicamente lo que él mismo quiere.

(n) (respect) respecto m; in a — en cierto modo, hasta cierto punto; in no — de ningún modo; in every possible — en todos los respectos; desde todos los puntos de vista; I will help in every possible — ayudaré por todos los medios a mi disposición; in many —s en muchos respectos, por muchas cosas; in some —s en ciertos modos; in a big —s en grande, en gran escala; we lost in a really big — perdimos de modo realmente espectacular; in a small — en pequeña escala; we help in a small — ayudamos un poco, prestamos una modesta ayuda; he's not a plumber in the ordinary — no es de esos fontaneros corrientes; no es un fontanero de profesión; in the ordinary — we go out once a week en general salimos una vez por semana.

(o) (Naut etc) to be under — estar en marcha, (fig) estar en curso; to gather — empezar a moverse; acelerar, ir más rápidamente; to get under — (Naut) zarpar, hacerse a la vela; (Aut etc) ponerse en marcha; (of person) partir, ponerse en camino; things are getting under — at last por fin las cosas están haciendo progresos; to get a ship under — hacer navegar un barco; to give — (break) romperse; (Aut etc) ceder el paso; "give —" "ceda el paso"; to give — to the left ceder el paso a los coches que vienen de la izquierda; the radio gave — to a television set la radio cedió el paso a un televisor; you gave — too easily abandonaste demasiado pronto, te dejaste vencer demasiado fácilmente; she gave — to tears se deshizo en lágrimas; he never gives — to despair no se deja ganar en ningún momento por la desesperación.

(p) (state) estado m; things are in a bad — las cosas van mal; the car is in a bad — el coche está en mal estado; he's in a very bad — (Med) está grave, está de cuidado; he's in a fair — to succeed tiene buenas posibilidades de lograrlo.

(q) (with by) by the — a propósito; entre paréntesis, de paso; by the —! ¡eh!; ¡oiga!; oh, and by the — ... hay otra cosa ..., antes que se me olvide ...; all this is by the — todo esto está un poco al margen, todo esto está entre paréntesis; by — of an answer a título de respuesta; by — of a warning a modo de advertencia; he's by — of being a painter es algo a modo de pintor, tiene sus ribetes de pintor.

2 adv (fam): — back in 1900 allá en 1900; that was — back eso fue hace mucho tiempo ya.

waybill ['weibil] n hoja f de ruta.

wayfarer ['wei.fεərə*] n caminante mf; viajero m, a f.

wayfaring tree ['weifεəriŋ.triː] n viburno m.

waylay [wei'lei] (irr: see lay) vt acechar; salir al paso a; detener; they were waylaid by thieves les atacaron unos ladrones; I was waylaid by the manager me detuvo el gerente.

way-out ['wei'aut] 1 adv: it's — in Nevada está muy lejos en Nevada, está en una región remota de Nevada. 2 adj (fam) ultramoderno, revolucionario, nueva ola.

wayside ['weisaid] 1 n borde m del camino, borde m de la carretera; by the — al borde de la carretera. 2 attr del borde del camino; inn etc de camino, de carretera; flower silvestre.

wayward ['weiwəd] adj (self-willed) voluntarioso; (naughty) travieso; rebelde; (capricious) caprichoso; (freakish) caprichoso, variable, inexplicable.

waywardness ['weiwədnis] n voluntariedad f; travesura f; rebeldía f; lo caprichoso; variabilidad f.

we [wiː] pron nosotros, nosotras.

weak [wiːk] adj débil; flojo; argument etc flojo, poco convincente; market etc flojo; sound débil, tenue;

character débil; _tea etc_ claro, no muy cargado; **to grow** — debilitarse; **to have** — **eyes** ser corto de vista; **to have a** — **stomach** tener el estómago débil; **her maths is** —, **she is** — **at maths** es floja en matemáticas.

weaken ['wiːkən] **1** _vt_ debilitar; _(lessen)_ disminuir, reducir; _(mitigate)_ atenuar, mitigar; **this fact** —**s your case** este dato quita fuerza a su argumento; **his resignation** —**ed the party** su dimisión debilitó el partido.

2 _vi_ debilitarse; flaquear, desfallecer; _(give way)_ ceder, abandonar; **his influence is** —**ing** su influencia flaquea; **we must not** — **now** ahora tenemos que ser más firmes que nunca; **prices have** —**ed** las cotizaciones han aflojado.

weak-kneed ['wiːk'niːd] _adj_ _(fig)_ sin voluntad, débil.

weakling ['wiːklɪŋ] _n_ ser _m_ delicado, persona _f_ débil; cobarde _m_; _(of litter etc)_ redrojo _m_; _(in health)_ persona _f_ enfermiza; **he's no** — no es ningún alfeñique.

weakly ['wiːklɪ] **1** _adj_ enclenque, achacoso, enfermizo. **2** _adv_ débilmente; flojamente; tenuemente.

weak-minded ['wiːk'maɪndɪd] _adj_ vacilante, sin voluntad, sin carácter; _(Med)_ imbécil.

weakness ['wiːknɪs] _n_ _(quality)_ debilidad _f_; flojedad _f_; tenuidad _f_; _(weak point)_ flaco _m_, lado _m_ débil; desventaja _f_; _(of character)_ falta _f_ de voluntad, falta _f_ de carácter; **to have a** — **for** tener gusto por, ser muy aficionado a; **to make allowances for human** — tener en cuenta la flaqueza humana.

weak-willed ['wiːk'wɪld] _adj_ de voluntad débil, indeciso.

weal[1] [wiːl] _n_ _(arch)_ bienestar _m_; **the common** — el bien público.

weal[2] [wiːl] _n_ _(Med)_ verdugón _m_.

wealth [welθ] _n_ riqueza _f_; abundancia _f_; "**The W— of Nations**" "La riqueza de las naciones"; **for all his** — a pesar de su riqueza; **por rico que sea**; **with a** — **of details** con abundantes detalles, con acopio de datos.

wealthy ['welθɪ] _adj_ rico; acaudalado, pudiente; **the** — los ricos.

wean [wiːn] _vt_ destetar; **to** — **someone from something** _(fig)_ apartar a uno gradualmente de algo, hacer que uno abandone algo poco a poco.

weaning ['wiːnɪŋ] _n_ destete _m_, ablactación _f_.

weapon ['wepən] _n_ arma _f_; **nuclear** — arma _f_ nuclear.

weaponry ['wepənrɪ] _n_ armas _fpl_.

wear [wɛə*] **1** _n_ **(a)** _(use)_ uso _m_; **for evening** — para la noche, para llevar de noche; **for everyday** — para todos los días, para todo trote _(fam)_; **for hard** — resistente, duradero; **he got 4 years'** — **out of it** la prenda le duró 4 años; **you will get plenty of** — **out of this** esto te ha de durar muchos años, esto tiene gran durabilidad.

(b) _(— and tear)_ deterioro _m_, desgaste _m_, uso _m_; **the** — **on the engine** el desgaste del motor; **one has to allow for** — **and tear** hay que tener en cuenta el desgaste natural; **to look the worse for** —, **to show signs of** — mostrarse deteriorado, dar indicios de deterioro; **she looks the worse for** — parece algo desmejorada.

(c) _(clothing)_ ropa _f_; prenda _f_; **children's** — ropa _f_ para niños; **summer** — ropa _f_ para verano; **light** — **for hot countries** ropa _f_ ligera para países cálidos; **it is compulsory** — **for schoolboys** la prenda es obligatoria para los colegiales.

2 _(irr: pret_ **wore**, _ptp_ **worn**) _vt_ **(a)** _objects in general_ llevar, usar, gastar; _clothing_ llevar; traer, traer puesto; vestir; _shoes etc_ calzar; _look, smile etc_ tener; _(put on)_ ponerse; **she wore her blue dress** llevaba el vestido azul; **she wore blue** se vestía de azul, vestía un vestido azul; **what shall I** —? ¿qué vestido me pongo?; **I have nothing to** — **to the dinner** no tengo qué ponerme para ir a la cena; **I haven't worn that for ages** hace mucho tiempo que no me pongo eso; **were you** —**ing a watch?** ¿llevabas el reloj?; **my uncle wore a beard** mi tío gastaba barba; **Eskimos don't** — **bikinis** los esquimales no usan bikini; **what size do you** —? ¿qué número usa Vd?; **to** — **one's hair long** llevar el pelo largo, dejarse el pelo largo; **he wore a big smile** sonreía alegremente; **he wore a serious look** parecía grave, tenía el gesto grave.

(b) _(— out)_ desgastar, deteriorar; **to** — **something into holes, to** — **holes in something** hacer agujeros en algo (rayéndolo _etc_); **to** — **something to a threadbare state** dejar algo raído.

(c) _(tolerate: fam)_ aguantar, consentir, permitir; **he won't** — **that** eso no lo permitirá; **we'll see if he'll** — **it** veremos si consiente en ello.

(d) _(with adv or prep)_ **to** — **away** gastar, desgastar; raer; consumir; **he's worn away to a shadow** está hecho una sombra; **the water has worn away the rock** el agua ha desgastado la roca; **to** — **down** gastar, desgastar; _resistance_ agotar; rendir; _patience_ agotar, cansar; _enemy_ cansar hasta rendir; **the heels are very worn down** los tacones están muy desgastados; **to** — **out** _clothes_ usar, desgastar; romper con el uso; _(exhaust, tire)_ agotar, rendir; **children** — **shoes out so quickly** los niños rompen tan pronto los zapatos; **you can** — **them out next winter** el invierno que viene te los volverás a poner hasta que se rompan, los acabarás el invierno que viene.

3 _vi_ **(a)** _(last)_ durar; **they will** — **for years** le durarán muchos años; **that dress has worn well** ese vestido ha sido muy duradero; **she's worn well** se ha conservado muy bien, no representa su edad; **the theory has worn well** la teoría ha resistido muy bien, la teoría ha sido muy duradera.

(b) **the cloth has worn into holes** al paño le han salido agujeros con el uso; **the rock has worn smooth** la roca se ha alisado.

(c) _(of time)_ pasar, transcurrir; **the year is** —**ing on** pasan los meses; **as the evening wore on** a medida que pasaban las horas de la tarde.

(d) _(with adv or prep)_ **to** — **away** gastarse, desgastarse; consumirse; **the metal has almost worn away** el metal se ha desgastado casi completamente; **to** — **off** quitarse; pasar, desaparecer; **the pain is** —**ing off** está desapareciendo el dolor, ya duele menos; **it soon wore off** pronto desapareció; **to** — **out** usarse, romperse con el uso, quedar inservible; consumirse.

4 _vr:_ **to** — **oneself to death** matarse (trabajando _etc_); **to** — **oneself out** agotarse, matarse.

wearable ['wɛərəbl] _adj_ que se puede llevar; **it's still** — todavía se puede llevar.

wearer ['wɛərə*] _n_ el _(or_ la_)_ que lleva puesto algo; —**s of bowler hats** los que llevan hongo; **straight from maker to** — directamente del fabricante al cliente.

wearily ['wɪərɪlɪ] _adv_ cansadamente, fatigadamente; **he said** — dijo cansado, dijo en tono de hastío.

weariness ['wɪərɪnɪs] _n_ cansancio _m_, fatiga _f_; abatimiento _m_, hastío _m_; aburrimiento _m_.

wearing ['wɛərɪŋ] _adj_ cansado, pesado, molesto.

wearisome ['wɪərɪsəm] _adj_ cansado, pesado; fatigoso, agotador.

weary ['wɪərɪ] **1** _adj_ _(tired)_ cansado, fatigado; _(dispirited)_ abatido, hastiado; _(tiring)_ aburrido, pesado; _(annoying)_ fastidioso; **to be** — **of** estar cansado de, estar harto de; **to grow** — **of** cansarse de; **three** — **hours** tres horas aburridas; **five** — **miles** cinco millas pesadas.

2 _vt_ cansar, fatigar; aburrir.

3 _vi_ cansarse, fatigarse; **to** — **of** cansarse de; aburrirse de; **to** — **of** + _ger_ cansarse de + _infin_.

weasel ['wiːzl] _n_ comadreja _f_.

weather ['weðə*] **1** _n_ tiempo _m_; _(harsh —)_ intemperie _f_; — **permitting** si el tiempo no lo impide; **in the hot** — en tiempo de calor, cuando el calor; **in this** — con el tiempo que hace; **it is fine** — hace buen tiempo, el tiempo es bueno; **what's the** — **like?** ¿qué tiempo hace?; **he has to go out in all** —**s** tiene que salir en todo tiempo; **it gets left outside in all** —**s** está fuera a la intemperie; **to be under the** — _(Med)_ estar mal, estar indispuesto, _(with drink)_ estar con la turca _(fam)_; **to make heavy** — **of something** encontrar algo difícil; crearse dificultades al tratar de hacer algo.

2 _adj, attr_ meteorológico, del tiempo; _(Naut)_ de barlovento; — **report** boletín _m_ meteorológico; — **side** costado _m_ de barlovento.

3 _vt_ **(a)** _storm etc (also to_ — **out**) aguantar, hacer frente a; **the government has** —**ed many storms** el gobierno ha aguantado muchas tempestades.

(b) _(Naut)_ _cape_ doblar; pasar a barlovento.

(c) _(Geol etc)_ desgastar; _wood_ curar; _skin_ curtir.

4 _vi_ _(Geol)_ desgastarse; _(skin etc)_ curtirse a la intemperie.

weather-beaten ['weðə,biːtn] _adj_ curtido por la intemperie.

weatherboard ['weðəbɔːd] _n_ tabla _f_ de chilla.

weather-bound ['weðəbaund] _adj_ bloqueado por el mal tiempo.

weather bureau ['weðə,bjuərəu] _n_ oficina _f_ meteorológica, servicio _m_ meteorológico.

weather chart ['weðətʃɑːt] _n_ mapa _m_ meteorológico.

weather cock ['weðəkɔk] _n_ veleta _f_.

weathered ['weðəd] _adj_ _oak etc_ maduro, curado.

weather forecast ['weðə'fɔːkɑːst] n parte m (or boletín m, pronóstico m) meteorológico.
weatherman ['weðəmæn] n, pl —**men** [men] hombre m del tiempo, meteorólogo m.
weather map ['weðəmæp] n mapa m meteorológico.
weatherproof ['weðəpruːf] adj a prueba de la intemperie.
weather ship ['weðəʃip] n barco m del servicio meteorológico.
weather station ['weðə‚steiʃən] n estación f meteorológica.
weather strip ['weðəstrip] n burlete m.
weather vane ['weðəvein] n veleta f.
weave [wiːv] **1** n tejido m; textura f.
2 (irr: pret **wove**, ptp **woven**) vt tejer; trenzar; entretejer, entrelazar; (fig) plot urdir, tramar; **to** — **details into a story** insertar detalles en un cuento; **to** — **episodes into a plot** ir entretejiendo episodios para formar un argumento.
3 vi tejer; **to** — **in and out** (boxer etc) evadirse torciendo rápidamente a derecha e izquierda; **the plane was weaving in and out among the clouds** el avión cambiaba constantemente de dirección entre las nubes; **to** — **in and out among traffic** aprovecharse de cualquier espacio entre los vehículos para adelantarse a toda prisa; **the road** —**s about a lot** el camino serpentea mucho.
weaver ['wiːvə*] n tejedor m, ora f.
weaving ['wiːviŋ] **1** n tejeduría f. **2** attr de tejer, para tejer; de tejidos.
weaving machine ['wiːviŋmə‚ʃiːn] n telar m.
weaving mill ['wiːviŋmil] n tejeduría f.
web [web] n (fabric) tela f, tejido m; (spider's) telaraña f; (membrane) membrana f; (fig) red f.
webbed [webd] adj palmeado.
webbing ['webiŋ] n cincha f, (Tech) pretina f de reps.
webfooted ['web'futid] adj palmipedo.
wed [wed] **1** vt casarse con; (of priest etc, also fig) casar. **2** vi casarse.
we'd [wiːd] = **we would; we had.**
wedded ['wedid] adj (a) (person) casado; bliss, life etc conyugal; **his** — **wife** su legítima esposa.
(b) to be — **to** estar casado con; (fig: connected) estar relacionado con, estar unido a; **to be** — **to an opinion** aferrarse a una opinión, estar aferrado a una opinión; **to be** — **to a pursuit** ser aficionado a una actividad, ser entusiasta de un pasatiempo.
wedding ['wediŋ] **1** n boda f; casamiento m; boda fpl; (fig) unión f, enlace m; **diamond** — bodas fpl de diamante; **golden** — bodas fpl de oro; **silver** — bodas fpl de plata; **civil** — matrimonio m civil; **to have a civil** — casarse por lo civil; **to have a church** — casarse por la iglesia; **to have a quiet** — casarse en la intimidad, casarse en privado.
2 attr de boda, de bodas; nupcial.
wedding breakfast ['wediŋ'brekfəst] n banquete m de boda.
wedding cake ['wediŋkeik] n tarta f de boda, pastel m de boda.
wedding day ['wediŋdei] n día m de boda.
wedding dress ['wediŋdres] n traje m de novia.
wedding march ['wediŋmɑːtʃ] n marcha f nupcial.
wedding night ['wediŋnait] n noche f de boda.
wedding present ['wediŋ‚preznt] n regalo m de boda.
wedding ring ['wediŋriŋ] n anillo m de boda.
wedge [wedʒ] **1** n cuña f; calce m, calza f; (Typ) cuña f de fijación; (of cake etc) porción f, pedazo m (grande); **it's the thin end of the** — éste es el primer paso hacia el desastre, esto puede ser el principio de muchos males; **to drive a** — **between two people** romper el vínculo que une a dos personas, enemistar a dos personas, separar a dos personas.
2 vt acuñar, calzar; **to** — **a door open** hacer que una puerta quede abierta introduciendo una calza debajo de ella; **it's** —**d** está sin poderse mover, se ha agarrado; **I was** —**d between two bishops** me encontré apretado entre dos obispos, estuve entre dos obispos sin poderme mover; **can we** — **a few more in?** ¿podemos introducir algunos más? (por apretados que estén).
3 vr: **to** — **oneself in** introducirse con dificultad.
wedge-shaped ['wedʒʃeipt] adj de forma de cuña.
wedlock ['wedlɔk] n matrimonio m; **to be born out of** — nacer fuera del matrimonio.
Wednesday ['wenzdei] n miércoles.
wee [wiː] adj (Scot, fam) pequeñito, diminuto; **a** — **bit** un poquitín; **I'm a** — **bit worried** estoy un poco inquieto.
weed [wiːd] **1** n mala hierba f; (person, fam) madeja f (fam); **the** — (hum) el tabaco.
2 vt ground escardar, desherbar, sachar; **to** — **out** plant arrancar; (fig) suprimir, quitar, eliminar.

weeding ['wiːdiŋ] n desherbaje m.
weed-killer ['wiːd‚kilə*] n herbicida m; **selective** — herbicida m selectivo.
weeds [wiːdz] npl: **widow's** — ropa f de luto.
weedy ['wiːdi] adj ground lleno de malas hierbas; person (fam) flaco, desmirriado; — **youth** mozalbete m.
week [wiːk] n semana f; **Holy W**— Semana f Santa; **working** — semana f laborable; —, **in**, — **out** semana tras semana; **twice a** — dos veces a la semana; **this day** —, **a**] — today de hoy en ocho días; **tomorrow** — de mañana en ocho días; **Tuesday** — del martes en ocho días; **in a** — or so en una semana o poco más; **in the middle of the** — a mitad de semana; **to knock someone into the middle of next** — (fam) dar una tremenda paliza a uno.
weekday ['wiːkdei] n día m laborable.
weekend ['wiːk'end] **1** n fin m de semana, weekend m; **a** — **trip** una excursión de fin de semana; — **case** neceser m de fin de semana; **to stay over the** — pasar el fin de semana; **to take a long** — hacer puente.
2 vi pasar el fin de semana.
weekender ['wiːk'endə*] n persona f que va a pasar solamente el fin de semana (en una casa de campo etc).
weekly ['wiːkli] **1** adj semanal; de cada semana. **2** adv semanalmente, cada semana; £15 — 15 libras por semana. **3** n semanario m.
weep [wiːp] (irr: pret and ptp **wept**) **1** vt tears llorar, derramar; **to** — **one's eyes out** llorar a mares.
2 vi llorar; **I could have wept** era para desesperarse; **to** — **for someone** llorar a uno; **to** — **for joy** llorar de alegría; **to** — **for what has happened** llorar por lo que ha pasado; **to** — **to see something** llorar al ver algo.
3 n: **to have a good** — llorar a mares; aliviarse llorando.
weeping ['wiːpiŋ] **1** adj lloroso. **2** n llanto m, lágrimas fpl.
weepy ['wiːpi] adj lloroso; que llora por poca cosa.
weevil ['wiːvl] n gorgojo m.
weewee ['wiːwiː] (fam) **1** n pipí m (fam). **2** vi hacer pipí (fam).
weft [weft] n trama f; (fig) red f.
weigh [wei] **1** vt (a) pesar; **to** — **something in one's hand** pesar algo en la mano.
(b) (fig) pesar, ponderar; **to** — **something in one's mind** ponderar algo, meditar algo; **to** — **A against B** contraponer A y B, considerar A con relación a B; **to** — **the pros and cons** pesar las ventajas y las desventajas.
(c) to — **anchor** levar anclas.
(d) to — **down** sobrecargar; (fig) abrumar, agobiar (with de); **she was** —**ed down with parcels** iba muy cargada de paquetes; **a branch** —**ed down with fruit** una rama doblada bajo el peso del fruto; **to be** —**ed down with sorrow** estar agobiado de dolor; **to** — **out**, **to** — **up** pesar.
2 vi (a) pesar; **it** —**s 4 kilos** pesa 4 kilos; **how much does it** —? ¿cuánto pesa?; **it** —**s heavy** pesa mucho.
(b) it —**s on his mind** pesa sobre su mente, le preocupa, le inquieta; **these factors do not** — **with him** estos factores no tienen importancia para él, estos factores no influyen en él.
(c) to — **in** (jockey) pesarse; **to** — **in with an argument** intervenir afirmando que . . .
weighbridge ['weibridʒ] n báscula-puente f, báscula f de puente.
weighing machine ['weiiŋmə‚ʃiːn] n báscula f.
weight [weit] **1** n (a) peso m; (heaviness) peso m, pesadez f; **atomic** — peso m atómico; **gross** — peso m bruto; **live** — peso m en vivo; **net** — peso m neto; **specific** — peso m específico; **3 kilos in** — que pesa 3 kilos, de 3 kilos; **it is worth its** — **in gold** vale su peso en oro; **to feel the** — **of**, **to test** (or **try**) **the** — **of something** sopesar algo; **to gain** —, **to put on** — engordar, hacerse más gordo; **to lose** — adelgazar.
(b) (of clock; disc etc used on scales) pesa f; **system of** —**s and measures** sistema m de pesos y medidas; **to put the** — lanzar el peso; **putting the** — lanzamiento m del peso.
(c) (fig: of worries etc) peso, m, carga f; (of blow) fuerza f; (importance) peso m, autoridad f, importancia f; **the** — **of the years** la carga de los años; **a blow without much** — **behind it** un golpe de poca fuerza; **a person of no** — una persona de poca monta, una persona de escasa importancia; **these are arguments of some** — son argumentos de

cierto peso; **that's a — off my mind** es un gran alivio para mí; **he carries no —** no tiene autoridad; **those arguments carry great — with the minister** esos argumentos influyen poderosamente en el ministro; **to chuck** (*or* **throw**) **one's — about** darse importancia; hablar (*etc*) en tono autoritario; **to give due — to an argument** conceder la debida importancia a un argumento; **he doesn't pull his — in the section** no trabaja en la sección tanto como debiera.

2 *vt* cargar (*with* de), añadir peso a; (*hold down*) sujetar con un peso; (*statistically*) ponderar; **this is —ed in your favour** esto se inclina del lado de Vd, esto le favorece a Vd.

weightiness ['weitinis] *n* peso *m*; (*fig*) peso *m*, importancia *f*; influencia *f*.

weightless ['weitlis] *adj* ingrávido.

weightlessness ['weitlisnis] *n* ingravidez *f*.

weight lifter ['weit,liftə*] *n* levantador *m* de pesos.

weight lifting ['weit,liftiŋ] *n* levantamiento *m* de pesos.

weighty ['weiti] *adj* pesado; (*fig*) importante, de peso, influyente.

weir [wiə*] *n* vertedero *m*, vertedor *m*; (*fish trap*) presa *f*, pesquera *f*.

weird [wiəd] *adj* misterioso, fantástico, sobrenatural; (*odd*) raro, extraño; **how —!** ¡qué raro!

weirdly ['wiədli] *adv* misteriosamente, fantásticamente; extrañamente; **— dressed** vestido de un modo raro.

weirdness ['wiədnis] *n* misterio *m*, lo fantástico, lo sobrenatural; rareza *f*.

weirdy ['wiədi] *n* (*fam*) persona *f* rara.

welch [welʃ] *vi* (*fam*) dejar de cumplir una obligación (*on someone* contraída con uno); (*in gambling*) dejar de pagar una apuesta (*on someone* a uno).

welcome ['welkəm] **1** *adj* (a) bienvenido; **—!** ¡bienvenido!; **— on board!** (Aer) ¡bienvenidos a bordo!; **— to Spain!** ¡bienvenido a España!; **to make someone —** recibir a uno afectuosamente, dar una buena acogida a uno; **I didn't feel very — there** no creía que mi presencia allí les fuera muy grata.

(b) (*pleasing*) grato, agradable; **that is — news** es una noticia grata; **it's a — change** es un cambio beneficioso; **a glass of sherry is always —** siempre se agradece una copita de jerez, una copita de jerez siempre viene bien.

(c) **you're —!** (*answer to thanks*) ¡de nada!, ¡no hay de qué!; (*iro*) ¡buen provecho le haga!; **you are — to it** está a su disposición; **you are — to try** Vd es muy dueño de probarlo, Vd tiene permiso para probarlo; **you will always be — here** está Vd en su casa.

2 *n* bienvenida *f*; (buena) acogida *f*, recepción *f*; **to bid someone —** dar la bienvenida a uno; **to give someone a hearty —** acoger a uno con entusiasmo; **the crowd gave him an enthusiastic —** el público le dispensó una calurosa acogida; **to meet with a cold —** ser recibido fríamente; **what sort of a — will this product get?** ¿qué aceptación tendrá este artículo?; *see* **outstay**.

3 *vt* dar la bienvenida a; acoger, recibir; aprobar; **they went to the airport to — him** fueron a recibirle al aeropuerto; **we should — this tendency** deberíamos dar la bienvenida a esta tendencia; **we — this step** aprobamos esta medida.

welcoming ['welkəmiŋ] *adj* acogedor, cordial.

weld [weld] **1** *vt* (a) (Tech) soldar; **to — parts together** soldar unas piezas; **the hull is —ed throughout** el casco es totalmente soldado.

(b) (*fig*) **to — together** soldar, unir, unificar; **we must — them together into a new body** hemos de soldarlos para formar un nuevo organismo.

2 *vi* soldarse.

welder ['weldə*] *n* soldador *m*.

welding ['weldiŋ] **1** *n* soldadura *f*. **2** *attr* de soldar, de soldadura, soldador; **— torch** soplete *m* soldador.

welfare ['welfeə*] **1** *n* (a) bienestar *m*, bien *m*; prosperidad *f*; **child —** bienestar *m* de los niños; **to work for the nation's —** trabajar en bien de la nación.

(b) (*social aid etc*) asistencia *f* social; **to live on —** vivir a cargo de la asistencia social.

2 *attr*: **— centre** centro *m* de asistencia social; **— state** estado *m* benefactor; **— work** trabajos *mpl* de asistencia social; **— worker** empleado *m* de asistencia social.

well¹ [wel] **1** *n* pozo *m*; (*fig*) fuente *f*, manantial *m*; (*of stairs*) hueco *m*, caja *f*; **to sink a —** perforar un pozo.

2 *vi* (*also* **to — out**, **to — up**) brotar, manar.

well² [wel] **1** *adv* (a) bien; **the child speaks —** el niño habla bien; **it's — painted** está bien pintado.

(b) (*intensive*) **— and good** bien está; **we got — and truly wet** nos mojamos de verdad; **— over a thousand** mucho más de mil; **it was — worth the trouble** realmente valió la pena; **we were — beaten** nos derrotaron fácilmente.

(c) (*with qualifying adv*) **very —** muy bien; **very —, I'll do it** bueno, lo haré; **that's all very —, but . . .** todo eso está muy bien, pero . . .; **all too —, only too —** de sobra, sobradamente.

(d) **as —** también; **she cried, as — she might** lloró, y con razón; **it is as — to remember that . . .** conviene recordar que . . .; **in cars as —** en coches así como en bicicletas; **she swims as — as she walks** nada tan bien como anda; **A as — as B** A además de B, tanto A como B.

(e) (*concessive*) pues; **— now** ahora bien; **—, it was like this** bueno, se lo diré; bueno, pasó lo siguiente; **—? ¿**y entonces?; **— then** pues bien; **— then?** ¿y qué?

(f) (*exclamatory*) **—!** ¡vaya!, ¡caramba!; **—, —!** ¡vaya, vaya!; **—, that's that!** ¡bueno, asunto concluido!

2 *adj* bien, bien de salud; **are you —?** ¿qué tal estás?; **I'm very —, thanks** estoy muy bien, gracias; **I'm fairly —** estoy regular; **she's not been — lately** recientemente ha estado algo indispuesta; **I don't feel at all —** no me siento bien del todo; **to get —** reponerse (*after* de); **to make someone —** curar a uno, devolver la salud a uno.

well- [wel] *adv in compounds*: bien . . ., *eg* **well-preserved** bien conservado.

we'll [wi:l] = **we will**, **we shall**.

well-aimed ['wel'eimd] *adj* certero.

well-appointed ['welə'pɔintid] *adj* bien amueblado, bien equipado.

well-attended ['welə'tendid] *adj* muy concurrido.

well-balanced ['wel'bælənsd] *adj* bien equilibrado.

well-behaved ['welbi'heivd] *adj* bien educado, formal; *animal* manso.

well-being ['wel,bi:iŋ] *n* bienestar *m*.

wellborn ['wel'bɔːn] *adj* bien nacido.

well-bred ['wel'bred] *adj* bien educado, culto, cortés; *accent etc* culto; *animal* de pura raza.

well-built ['wel'bilt] *adj* sólidamente construido, de construcción sólida; *person* fornido.

well-chosen ['wel'tʃəuzn] *adj* elegido con cuidado; *remarks, words etc* acertado.

well-defined ['weldi'faind] *adj* bien definido.

well-deserved ['weldi'zəːvd] *adj* merecido.

well-developed ['weldi'veləpt] *adj* *arm, muscle etc* bien desarrollado; *sense* agudo, fino.

well-disposed ['weldis'pəuzd] *adj* favorable, benévolo; **to be — towards something** estar bien dispuesto hacia algo.

well-dressed ['wel'drest] *adj* bien vestido, elegantemente vestido.

well-earned ['wel'əːnd] *adj* merecido.

well-educated ['wel'edjukeitid] *adj* instruido, culto.

well-equipped ['weli'kwipt] *adj* bien equipado.

well-favoured ['wel'feivəd] *adj* bien parecido.

well-fed ['wel'fed] *adj* bien alimentado, que come bien; (*in appearance*) regordete.

well-founded ['wel'faundid] *adj* bien fundado.

well-grown ['wel'grəun] *adj* grande, maduro, adulto.

wellhead ['welhed] *n* fuente *f*, manantial *m*.

well-informed ['welin'fɔːmd] *adj* (*in general*) enterado, instruido; **to be — about something** estar enterado de algo, estar al corriente de algo.

wellingtons ['weliŋtənz] *npl* botas *fpl* de goma.

well-intentioned ['welin'tenʃnd] *adj* bienintencionado; *lie* piadoso.

well-judged ['wel'dʒʌdʒd] *adj* bien calculado.

well-kept ['wel'kept] *adj* bien cuidado, bien conservado, en buen orden; **a — secret** un secreto bien guardado.

well-knit ['wel'nit] *adj* bien ensamblado; (*fig*) *body* robusto, fornido; *scheme etc* lógico, bien razonado; *speech etc* bien pensado, de estructura lógica.

well-known ['wel'nəun] *adj* conocido.

well-made ['wel'meid] *adj* bien hecho, fuerte.

well-mannered ['wel'mænəd] *adj* educado, culto, cortés.

well-marked ['wel'mɑːkt] *adj* bien marcado.

well-meaning ['wel'miːniŋ] *adj* bienintencionado.

well-meant ['wel'ment] *adj* bienintencionado.

well-nigh ['welnai] *adv* casi; poco menos que; **it's — finished** está casi terminado; **this is — impossible** esto es punto menos que imposible.

well-off ['wel'ɔf] *adj* acomodado; pudiente; (*with pej sense*) adinerado; **the less —** las gentes menos pudientes; **he spoke with a — accent** habló con acento culto, (*pej*) habló con acento afectado.

well-oiled ['wel'ɔild] *adj* bien lubricado.

well-preserved ['welpri'zɜːvd] *adj* = **well-kept**; *person* de buen aspecto (a pesar de su edad).

well-proportioned ['welprə'pɔːʃnd] *adj* bien proporcionado, de forma elegante; *person* de talle elegante.

well-read ['wel'red] *adj* leído, instruido; culto; **to be — in history** haber leído mucha historia, estar muy documentado en historia.

well-rounded ['wel'raundid] *adj* redondeado, acabado.

well-spent ['wel'spent] *adj* bien empleado, fructuoso.

well-spoken ['wel'spəukən] *adj* bienhablado, con acento culto.

well-stocked ['wel'stɔkt] *adj* bien provisto, bien surtido; **— shelves** estantes *mpl* llenos.

well-timed ['wel'taimd] *adj* oportuno.

well-to-do ['weltə'duː] *adj* acomodado, pudiente; **the —** la gente pudiente, (*pej*) la gente bien.

well-trodden ['wel'trɔdn] *adj* trillado.

well-turned ['wel'tɜːnd] *adj* elegante.

well-wisher ['wel,wiʃə*] *n* amigo *m*, a *f*.

well-worn ['wel'wɔːn] *adj* *garment* raído; *path* trillado; *cliché* trillado y llevado, trillado, manoseado.

Welsh [welʃ] **1** *adj* galés, de Gales; **the —** los galeses. **2** *n* (*language*) galés *m*.

welsh [welʃ] *vi* see **welch**.

Welshman ['welʃmən] *n*, *pl* **—men** [mən] galés *m*.

Welshwoman ['welʃ,wumən] *n*, *pl* **—women** [,wimin] galesa *f*.

welt [welt] **1** *n* (*of shoe*) vira *f*; (*weal*) verdugón *m*. **2** *vt* poner vira a; pegar, zurrar, hacer verdugones a.

welter ['weltə*] **1** *n* confusión *f*, mezcla *f* confusa; **in a — of blood** en un mar de sangre. **2** *vi* revolcarse; **to — in** estar bañado en, bañarse en.

welterweight ['weltəweit] *n* wélter *m*.

wen [wen] *n* lobanillo *m*, quiste *m* sebáceo; **the Great W—** el gran basurero (*Londres*).

wench [wentʃ] **1** *n* mozuela *f*, muchacha *f*; (*pej*) moza *f*; (*whore*) puta *f*. **2** *vi* (*also* **to go —ing**) putañear.

wend [wend] *vt*: **to — one's way** to dirigirse a.

went [went] *pret of* **go**.

wept [wept] *pret and ptp of* **weep**.

were [wɜː*] *pret of* **be**.

we're [wiə*] = **we are**.

weren't [wɜːnt] = **were not**.

werewolf ['wiəwulf] *n*, *pl* **—wolves** [wulvz] ser *m* humano transformado en lobo.

wert [wɜːt] (*arch*) see **be**.

Wesleyan ['wezliən] **1** *adj* metodista. **2** *n* metodista *mf*.

Wesleyanism ['wezliənizəm] *n* metodismo *m*.

west [west] **1** *n* oeste *m*, occidente *m*; **the W—** el Oeste, el Occidente; **tales of the American W—** cuentos *mpl* del Oeste americano. **2** *adj* del oeste, occidental; *wind* del oeste; **to go —** (*fam*: *object*, *machine*) romperse, estropearse; (*plan etc*) fracasar; (*person*) estirar la pata (*fam*).

westerly ['westəli] *adj* *point, direction* oeste; *wind* del oeste.

western ['westən] **1** *adj* occidental, del oeste. **2** *n* película *f* de cowboys, película *f* que se desarrolla en el Oeste de EE.UU.

westerner ['westənə*] *n* habitante *mf* del Oeste (*Pol etc*) occidental *mf*.

westernization ['westənai'zeiʃən] *n* occidentalización *f*.

westernize ['westənaiz] *vt* occidentalizar, convertir al estilo de vida del Occidente.

westernized ['westənaizd] *adj* occidentalizado, influido por el Occidente; **to become —** occidentalizarse, adoptar el estilo de vida del Occidente.

westernmost ['westənməust] *adj* (el) más occidental, situado más al oeste.

West Indian ['west'indiən] **1** *adj* antillano. **2** *n* antillano *m*, a *f*.

West Indies ['west'indiːz] *pl* Antillas *fpl*.

westward(s) ['westwəd(z)] *adv* hacia el oeste.

wet [wet] **1** *adj* (a) (*naturally*) húmedo; (*accidentally*, *temporarily*) mojado; (*US fam*) no prohibicionista; *paint etc* fresco; **in — clothes** en ropa mojada; **to be — through, to be — to the skin, to be — wringing —** estar mojado hasta los huesos; **the ink is still —** la tinta no se ha secado todavía; **to get —** mojarse; **to get one's feet —** mojarse los pies; **it grows in — places** se encuentra en lugares húmedos.

(b) (*of weather*) lluvioso; **a — day** un día de lluvia; **a — climate** un clima lluvioso; **the — season**

la estación de las lluvias; **in — weather** cuando llueve; **it was — in the night** llovió durante la noche; **it was too — for us to go out** llovió tanto que no pudimos salir.

(c) (*fam*) soso, bobo; **don't be so —** ¡no seas bobo!

2 *n* humedad *f*; (*rain*) lluvia *f*; **it's out in the —** está fuera a la intemperie.

3 *vt* mojar, humedecer; *tea* hacer; echar agua hirviente a; *bargain* (*fam*) cerrar con un brindis; **to — the baby's head** (*fam*) celebrar un nacimiento bebiendo a la salud del niño; **to — the bed** orinarse en la cama; **to — one's pants** orinarse en las bragas.

wether ['weðə*] *n* carnero *m* castrado.

wetness ['wetnis] *n* humedad *f*; (*raininess*) lo lluvioso.

wet-nurse ['wetnɜːs] *n* nodriza *f*, ama *f* de cría.

wetting ['wetiŋ] *n* mojada *f*; **to get a —** mojarse; **to give someone a —** mojar a uno.

we've [wiːv] = **we have**.

whack [wæk] *n* (a) (*blow*) golpe *m* grande, golpe *m* ruidoso; **to give something a —** golpear algo ruidosamente.

(b) (*fam*: *attempt*) tentativa *f*; **to have a — at something** intentar algo, probar algo; **let's have a — probemos.**

(c) (*fam*: *share*) parte *f*, porción *f*; **you should get your —** seguramente recibirás lo que te corresponde.

whacking ['wækiŋ] **1** (*fam*) *adj* grandote, enorme, imponente.

2 (*fam*) *adv*: **a — big book** un libro enorme de grande.

3 *n* zurra *f*; **to give someone a —** zurrar a uno, pegar a uno.

whale [weil] *n* ballena *f*; **a — of a difference** una enorme diferencia; **to have a — of a time** divertirse en grande, pasarlo bomba (*fam*).

whalebone ['weilbəun] *n* ballena *f* (*lámina, material*).

whale oil ['weilɔil] *n* aceite *m* de ballena.

whaler ['weilə*] *n* (*person, ship*) ballenero *m*.

whaling ['weiliŋ] *n* pesca *f* de ballenas.

whaling ship ['weiliŋʃip] *n* ballenero *m*.

whaling station ['weiliŋ,steiʃən] *n* estación *f* ballenera.

wham [wæm] = **whang**; *interj* = ¡zas!

whang [wæŋ] **1** *n* golpe *m* resonante.

2 *vt* golpear de modo resonante.

3 *vi*: **to — against something, to — into something** chocar ruidosamente con algo.

wharf [wɔːf] *n*, *pl* **wharfs** *or* **wharves** [wɔːvz] muelle *m*.

wharfage ['wɔːfidʒ] *n* muellaje *m*.

what [wɔt] **1** *adj* (a) (*rel*) que; **— little I had** lo poco que tenía; **with — money I have** con el dinero que tengo; **buy — food you like** compra la comida que quieras.

(b) (*interrog*) qué? cuál de . . .; **— book do you want?** ¿qué libro quieres?, ¿cuál de los libros quieres?; **— news did he bring?** ¿qué noticias trajo?

(c) (*interj*) qué —; **— a man!** ¡qué hombre!; **— luck!** ¡qué suerte!; **— a fool I've been!** ¡qué tonto he sido!; **— an ugly dog!** ¡qué perro más (*or* tan) feo!

(d) (*interj, iro*) lindo, valiente, bueno; **— a general!** ¡valiente general!; **— an excuse!** ¡buen pretexto!

2 *pron* (a) (*rel*, = **that which**) el que, la que, lo que (*etc*); **— I like is tea** lo que me gusta de verdad es el té; **that is not — I asked for** eso no es lo que pedí; **— is done is done** lo que está hecho no se puede cambiar; **and — not** y qué sé yo qué más; **and — is more . . .** y además . . .; **— with the weather and the crisis** entre el mal tiempo y la crisis; **— with one thing and another** entre una cosa y otra; **come what may** venga lo que viniere; **say — he will** diga lo que quiere; **not a day but — it rains** no hay día que no llueva; **to give someone — for** cargarse a uno.

(b) (*interrog*) ¿qué?; (*please repeat*) ¿cómo?; **— is it?** ¿qué es?; **—'s that?** ¿y eso qué es?; **— is that to you?** y eso ¿qué te importa?; **— is the reason?** ¿cuál es la razón?; **— is the formula for . . .?** ¿cuál es la fórmula de . . .?; **— is this called?** ¿cómo se llama esto?; **— can we do?** ¿qué podemos hacer?; **— do 4 and 3 make?** ¿cuánto suman 4 y 3?; **so . . .?** ¿y qué?; **— if . . .?** ¿y si . . .?, ¿qué será si . . .?; **— of it?, — of that?** y eso ¿qué importa?; **I know — you're after** yo sé lo que buscas; **I don't know — to do** no sé qué hacer; **I'll tell you —** se me ocurre una idea, tengo una idea; **he knows —'s —** sabe cuántas son cinco; ¿qué **about, for** *etc*.

(c) (*interj*) ¡cómo!; **—! you sold it!** ¡cómo! ¡lo has vendido!; **—! a man in your room?** ¡qué horror! ¿un hombre en tu cuarto?; **shameful, —?** vergonzoso, ¿no?

what-d'ye-call-him ['wɔtdʒu,kɔːlim] *pron* fulano; **old — with the red nose** ése que tiene la nariz tan coloradota.

what-d'ye-call-it ['wɔtdʒu,kɔːlit] *pron* cosa *f*, chisme *m*; **he does it with the —** lo hace con el chisme ese; **that green — on the front** esa cosa verde en la parte delantera.

whatever [wɔt'evə*] **1** *pron* lo que; todo lo que; **— you like** lo que quieras; **— you find** cualquier cosa que encuentres; **— I have is yours** todo lo que tengo es tuyo; **— it may be** sea lo que sea; **— he says** diga lo que diga; **— happens** pase lo que pase; **or — they're called** o como quiera que se llamen; **— do you mean?** ¿qué quiere Vd decir?; **or —** o lo que sea.

　2 *adj* **(a) — book you choose** cualquier libro que elija Vd; **— books you choose** cualesquier libros que elija Vd; **every book of — size** todo libro de no importa qué tamaño.

　(b) no man — ningún hombre sea quien sea; **nothing —** nada en absoluto; **he said nothing — of interest** no dijo nada en absoluto que tuviera interés; **it's of no use —** no sirve para nada en absoluto.

what-ho ['wɔt'həu] *interj* (*surprise*) ¡caramba!, ¡vaya!; (*greeting*) ¡hola!, ¡oye!

whatnot ['wɔtnɔt] *n* estantería *f*, mueble *m* de estantes.

whatsoever [,wɔtsəu'evə*] *pron, adj* = **whatever.**

wheat [wiːt] **1** *n* trigo *m*. **2** *attr* de trigo, triguero; **— loaf** pan *m* de trigo.

wheatear ['wiːtiə*] *n* (*Orn*) collalba *f*.

wheaten ['wiːtn] *adj* de trigo; de color de trigo.

wheat field ['wiːtfiːld] *n* trigal *m*.

wheat sheaf ['wiːtʃiːf] *n* haz *f* de trigo.

wheedle ['wiːdl] *vt* engatusar; **to — someone into doing something** engatusar a uno para que haga algo, conseguir por medio de halagos que uno haga algo; **to — something out of someone** sonsacar algo a alguien.

wheedling ['wiːdliŋ] **1** *adj* mimoso. **2** *n* mimos *mpl*, halagos *mpl*.

wheel [wiːl] **1** *n* **(a)** rueda *f*; (*steering —*) volante *m*; (*Naut*) timón *m*; **— of fortune** rueda *f* de fortuna; **the —s of government** el mecanismo del gobierno; **back —** rueda *f* trasera; **big —** (*at fair*) noria *f*, (*person: fam*) personaje *m*, pez *m* gordo (*fam*); **fixed —** rueda *f* fija; **front —** rueda *f* delantera; **potter's —** torno *m* de alfarero; **there are —s within —s** esto es más complicado de lo que parece, esto tiene su miga.

　(b) (*Mil*) vuelta *f*, conversión *f*; **a — to the right** una vuelta hacia la derecha.

　2 *vt* (*turn*) hacer girar; hacer rodar; *bicycle, pram* empujar; *child* pasear en cochecito; **we —ed it over to the window** lo empujamos hasta la ventana; **when it broke down I had to — it** cuando se averió tuve que empujarlo.

　3 *vi* (*turn*) girar; rodar; dar vueltas; (*of birds*) revolotear; (*Mil*) dar un vuelta, cambiar de frente; **to — left** dar una vuelta hacia la izquierda; **to — round** (*person*) girar sobre los talones; (*fig*) cambiar de rumbo, cambiar de opinión.

wheelbarrow ['wiːl,bærəu] *n* carretilla *f*.

wheelbase ['wiːlbeis] *n* batalla *f*, distancia *f* entre ejes.

wheelchair ['wiːltʃɛə*] *n* silla *f* de ruedas.

wheeled [wiːld] *adj*: **— traffic** tránsito *m* rodado; **— transport** transporte *m* rodado.

-wheeled [wiːld] *adj eg* **four-wheeled** de cuatro ruedas.

wheelhouse ['wiːlhaus] *n, pl* **—houses** [,hauziz] timonera *f*, cámara *f* del timonel.

wheel spider ['wiːl,spaidə*] *n* estrella *f* de rueda.

wheelwright ['wiːlrait] *n* ruedero *m*, carretero *m*.

wheeze [wiːz] **1** *n* **(a)** resuelto *m* (ruidoso), respiración *f* sibilante.

　(b) (*fam*) truco *m*, treta *f*; idea *f*; **that's a good —** es buena idea; **to think up a —** idear una treta.

　2 *vti* resollar (con ruido), jadear; ser asmático; **"Yes," he —ed** "Sí", dijo resollando con ruido (*or* respirando con dificultad).

wheezing ['wiːziŋ] *adj*, **wheezy** ['wiːzi] *adv breath* ruidoso, difícil; *pronunciation* sibilante.

whelk [welk] *n* buccino *m*.

whelp [welp] **1** *n* cachorro *m*. **2** *vi* parir (*la perra etc*).

when [wen] **1** *adv* cuándo; **— did it happen?** ¿cuándo ocurrió?; **I know — it happened** yo sé cuándo

ocurrió; **— is the interview?** ¿cuándo es la interviú?; **since —?** ¿desde cuándo?; **since — do you have a car?** ¿de cuándo acá tienes tú coche?

　2 *conj* **(a)** cuando; **— I came in** cuando yo entré; **al entrar (yo); — I was young** cuando era joven; en mi juventud; **you can go — I have finished** puedes irte en cuanto yo termine; **— the bridge is built** cuando se construya el puente; **he's only happy — drunk** es feliz únicamente cuando está borracho; **he did it — a child** lo hizo de niño, lo hizo siendo niño.

　(b) (*rel*) cuando; **this is — it always rains** esto es cuando llueve siempre; **at the very moment — . . .** en el mismo momento cuando . . .; **one day — the tide is out** un día cuando la marea esté baja.

whence [wens] *adv* (*lit*) **(a)** (*of place*) ¿de dónde?; **— comes it that . . .?** ¿cómo es que . . .?

　(b) (*fig*) por lo cual, y por consiguiente; **— I conclude that . . .** por lo cual concluyo que . . .

whenever [wen'evə*] *adv* **(a)** (*rel*) siempre que, cuando quiera que; cuando, todas las veces que; **come — you like** ven cuando quieras; **I go — I can** voy todas las veces que puedo; **— you see one of those, stop** cuando quiera que vea uno de ésos, pare.

　(b) (*interrog*) **— can he have done it?** ¿cuándo demonios ha podido hacerlo?; **— do I have the time for such things?** ¿cuándo cree Vd que tengo tiempo para estas cosas?

where [wɛə*] *adv* **(a)** (*interrog*) ¿dónde?; **— am I?** ¿dónde estoy?; **I know — he is** yo sé dónde está; **— are you going?** ¿adónde vas?; **— are you from?** ¿de dónde eres?; **— should we be if . . .?** ¿dónde estaríamos nosotros si . . .?; **— is the sense of it?** ¿qué sentido tiene esto?

　(b) (*rel*) donde; **go — you like** ve donde quieras; **this is — we got to** éste es el punto al que habíamos llegado; **this is — we got out** nos apeamos aquí; **the house — I was born** la casa donde nací, la casa en la que nací; **from — I'm sitting** desde aquí; **that's just — you're wrong** en eso se equivoca Vd.

whereabouts ['wɛərə'bauts] *adv* ¿dónde?

whereabouts ['wɛərəbauts] *n* paradero *m*; **nobody knows his —** se desconoce su paradero actual.

whereas [wɛər'æz] *conj* visto que, por cuanto, mientras; (*in legal parlance*) considerando que.

whereat [wɛər'æt] *adv* con lo cual.

whereby [wɛə'bai] *adv* por lo cual, por donde; **the rule — it is not allowed to +** *infin* la regla según la cual no se permite + *infin*.

wherefore ['wɛəfɔː*] **1** *adv* (*why*) por qué; (*and for this reason*) y por tanto, por lo cual.

　2 *n*: **the whys and —s** las razones, el por qué; los detalles, la explicación detallada.

wherein [wɛər'in] *adv* en donde.

whereof [wɛər'ɔv] *adv* de que.

whereon [wɛər'ɔn] *adv* en que.

wheresoever [,wɛəsəu'evə*] *adv* dondequiera que.

whereupon ['wɛərəpɔn] *adv* con lo cual, después de lo cual.

wherever [wɛər'evə*] *adv* **(a)** (*rel*) dondequiera que; **— you go I'll go too** dondequiera que vayas yo te acompañaré; **— they went they were cheered** por dondequiera que fueron se les aplaudió; **sit — you like** siéntate donde te parezca bien; **I'll buy them — they come from** los compraré no importa su procedencia.

　(b) (*interrog*) **— did you put it?** ¿dónde demonios lo pusiste?; **— can they have got to?** ¿dónde demonios se habrán metido?

wherewith [wɛə'wiθ] *adv* con lo cual.

wherewithal ['wɛəwiðɔːl] *n* medios *mpl*, recursos *mpl*, cónquibus *m*; **they haven't got the —** no tienen los medios.

wherry ['weri] *n* chalana *f*.

whet [wet] *vt tool* afilar, amolar; *appetite, curiosity* estimular, despertar, aguzar.

whether ['weðə*] *conj* si; **I am not certain — . . .** no sé si . . .; **I doubt — . . .** dudo que + *subj*; **— he is here or in Madrid** que esté aquí o en Madrid; **— she sings or dances** que cante o que baile; **— they come or not** vengan o no (vengan).

whetstone ['wetstəun] *n* piedra *f* de amolar, afiladera *f*.

whew [hwjuː] *interj* ¡vaya!

whey [wei] *n* suero *m*.

which [witʃ] **1** *adj* **(a)** (*interrog*) ¿qué?; ¿cuál?; **— picture do you prefer?** ¿qué cuadro prefieres?, ¿cuál de los cuadros prefieres?; **I don't know — tie he wants** yo no sé qué corbata quiere; **— way**

did she go? ¿por dónde se fue?; — one? ¿cuál?;
— one of us? ¿cuál de nosotros?; — house do you
live in? ¿cuál es la casa en que vive Vd?

(b) (rel) he used "peradventure", — word is
now archaic dijo "peradventure", palabra que ha
quedado anticuada; look — way you will . . . miren
por donde quieran . . .

2 pron (a) (interrog) ¿cuál?; — do you want?
¿cuál quieres?; — of you did it? ¿cuál de vosotros
lo hizo?; I don't mind — no me importa cuál;
I can't tell — is — no sé cuál es cuál.

(b) (rel) que; lo que; the bear — I saw el oso
que vi; two forms — are to be filled in dos formu-
larios que han de llenarse; the meeting — we
attended la reunión a que asistimos; it rained hard
— upset her llovió mucho, lo que la desconcertó;
. . . — God forbid . . . lo que Dios no quiera.

(c) (rel governed by prep) el que (etc), el cual
(etc); lo cual; the hotel at — we stayed el hotel en el
que nos hospedamos; the cities to — we are going
las ciudades a las que vamos; the bull — I'm
talking about el toro del que hablo; at — con lo
cual, sobre lo cual; from — we deduce that . . .
de lo cual deducimos que . . .; after — we went
to bed después de lo cual nos acostamos.

whichever [witʃ'evə*] 1 adj cualquier; — possibility
you choose cualquier posibilidad que elija Vd;
you can choose — system you want Vd puede
elegir el sistema que quiera; — system you have
there are difficulties hay dificultades no importa
el sistema que tenga Vd.

2 pron cualquiera; el que, la que; — of the methods
you choose cualquiera de los métodos que elija
Vd, no importa el método que elija Vd; — can he
mean? ¿cuál quiere decir?

whiff [wif] 1 n soplo m, soplo m fugaz; vaharada f;
bocanada f; (smell) olorcillo m; a — of grapeshot
un poco de metralla; not a — of wind ni el menor
soplo de viento; to catch a — of something percibir
un olorcillo de algo, oler algo brevemente; to go
out for a — of air salir a tomar el fresco.

2 vt soplar.

3 vi (fam) oler (mal); to — of oler a.

while [wail] 1 n (a) rato m, tiempo m; after a — poco
tiempo después, al poco tiempo; for a — durante
algún tiempo; a good —, a great —, a long —
largo rato, mucho tiempo; a long — ago hace mucho;
it will be a good — before he gets here tardará
bastante en llegar; it will be a good — before they
finish tardarán bastante en terminarlo; a little —
ago hace poco; it takes quite a — es cosa de
bastante tiempo, exige mucho tiempo; in a short —
dentro de poco; stay a — with us quédate un rato
con nosotros.

(b) the — entretanto, mientras tanto; he looked
at me the — mientras tanto me estaba mirando.

(c) it is worth — to ask whether . . . vale la
pena preguntar si . . .; it's not worth my — desde
mi punto de vista no vale la pena; we'll make it
worth your — le pagaremos bien, le compensaremos
generosamente.

2 conj (a) (time) mientras; — this was happening
mientras pasaba esto; — you are away mientras
estés fuera; she fell asleep — reading mientras
leía quedó dormida, se durmió mientras leía;
to drink — on duty beber estando de servicio.

(b) (concessive) aunque, bien que; — I admit
it is awkward aunque confieso que es difícil.

(c) (whereas) mientras; I have a blue car —
you have a red one yo tengo un coche azul mientras
Vd tiene uno rojo.

3 vt: to — away the time pasar el rato, entretener
los ocios.

whilst [wailst] conj = while.

whim [wim] n capricho m, antojo m; manía f;
a passing — un capricho; her every — todos sus
antojos y fantasías; it's just a — of hers es un
capricho suyo; as the — takes me según se me
antoja.

whimper ['wimpə*] 1 n quejido m, gemido m;
without a — sin quejarse. 2 vi lloriquear; quejarse,
gemir; "Yes", she —ed "Sí", dijo lloriqueando.

whimpering ['wimpəriŋ] 1 adj que lloriquea. 2 n
lloriqueo m, gimoteo m.

whimsical ['wimzikəl] adj person caprichoso; idea
caprichoso, fantástico; to be in a — mood estar de
humor para dejar volar la fantasía.

whimsicality [wimzi'kæliti] n capricho m; fantasía
f; a novel of a pleasing — una novela de agradable
fantasía.

whimsically ['wimzikəli] adv caprichosamente; fantásticamente.

whimsy ['wimzi] n (whim) capricho m, antojo m;
(whimsicality) fantasía f, extravagancia f.

whin [win] n tojo m.

whine [wain] 1 n (complaining cry) quejido m,
gimoteo m; (of dog) gañido m; (of bullet) silbido
m.

2 vi quejarse, gimotear; gañir; silbar; "Yes", he
—d "Sí", dijo gimoteando; don't come whining
to me about it no venga a mí a quejarse; the dog
was whining to be let in el perro estaba gañendo
para que le abrieran.

whining ['wainiŋ] 1 adj quejumbroso; que gimotea.
2 n quejidos mpl, gimoteo m; el silbar.

whinny ['wini] 1 n relincho m. 2 vi relinchar.

whip [wip] 1 n (a) (riding —) látigo m; (used in
punishment) azote m, zurriago m.

(b) (Parl: call) llamada f; three-line — llamada
f apremiante (para que un diputado acuda a votar
en un debate importante).

(c) (Parl: person) oficial m disciplinario de
partido.

2 vt (a) azotar; dar con un látigo; (Cook) batir;
(defeat) batir, cascar; (criticize etc) fustigar; (Sew)
sobrecoser; rope ligar, envolver con cuerda.

(b) to — something away from someone
arrebatar algo a uno; to — in (Parl) member llamar
(para que vote); (Parl) electors hacer que acudan
a las urnas; the conductor was —ping the orchestra
into a frenzy el director exigía el máximo esfuerzo
a los músicos; to — off lid quitar con un movimiento brusco; dress quitarse con toda rapidez;
to — someone off to a meeting llevar a uno con
toda prisa a una reunión; to — on lid poner con un
movimiento brusco; dress ponerse con toda rapidez;
to — out sacar de repente; to — up (pick up) coger de
repente; feeling etc avivar, estimular; support
procurar, obtener.

3 vi moverse rápidamente; ir con toda prisa;
the car —ped past el coche pasó como un rayo;
to — round (person) volverse de repente; I'll
— round to the shop voy corriendo a la tienda;
the car —ped round the corner el coche dobló la
esquina a gran velocidad; to — round for someone
(fam) hacer una colecta a beneficio de uno.

whipcord ['wipkɔ:d] n tralla f.

whip hand ['wip'hænd] n: to have the — llevar la
ventaja (over someone a uno); mandar.

whiplash ['wiplæʃ] n tralla f.

whipped [wipt] adj cream etc batido.

whipper-in ['wipər'in] n (Hunting) piqueur m,
montero m que cuida los perros de caza.

whippersnapper ['wipə,snæpə*] n (also young —)
mequetrefe m.

whippet ['wipit] n perro m lebrel.

whipping ['wipiŋ] n azotamiento m; flagelación f;
(defeat) derrota f; (criticism etc) paliza f; to give
someone a — azotar a uno, (fig) dar una paliza a
uno.

whipping boy ['wipiŋbɔi] n cabeza f de turco.

whipping top ['wipiŋtɔp] n peonza f, trompo m.

whip-round ['wipraund] n (fam) colecta f; to have a
— for someone hacer una colecta a beneficio de uno.

whipsaw ['wipsɔ:] n sierra f cabrilla.

whirl [wə:l] 1 n (turn) giro m, vuelta f; (turning)
rotación f; el girar; (of dust, water etc) remolino m;
a — of pleasures una serie vertiginosa de placeres;
my head is in a — mi cabeza está dando vueltas;
he disappeared in a — of dust desapareció en una
nube de polvo.

2 vt (make turn) hacer girar, hacer dar vueltas;
(wave, shake) agitar; (transport) llevar con toda
rapidez; he —ed his hat round his head agitaba el
sombrero alrededor de la cabeza; he —ed her off
to the dance la llevó con toda rapidez al baile; the
train —ed us up to Paris el tren nos llevó muy
rápidamente a París.

3 vi (spin: also to — round) girar rápidamente,
dar vueltas; (of dust, water) arremolinarse; my
head —s mi cabeza está dando vueltas; they —ed
past us in the dance pasaron delante de nosotros
girando alegremente en el baile.

whirligig ['wə:ligig] n (toy) molinete m; (roundabout)
tiovivo m; (Ent) girino m; (fig) vicisitudes fpl;
movimiento m confuso.

whirlpool ['wə:lpu:l] n torbellino m, remolino m;
(fig) vorágine f.

whirlwind ['wə:lwind] n torbellino m, manga f
de viento; like a — como un torbellino, como una
tromba; to reap the — segar lo que se ha sembrado.

whirlybird ['wə:libə:d] n (US fam) helicóptero m.

whirr [wə:*] 1 n (of bird's wings) ruido m, batir
m, (of insect's wings) zumbido m; (of machine:

quiet) zumbido *m*, runrún *m*, *(louder)* rechino *m*.

2 *vi* hacer ruido, batir; zumbar, runrunear; rechinar; **the cameras —ed** runruneaban las cámaras.

whisk [wisk] **1** *n* **(a)** *(brush)* escobilla *f*; *(fly—)* mosqueador *m*; *(Cook)* batidor *m*, *(electric etc)* batidora *f*.

(b) *(movement)* movimiento *m* brusco; movimiento *m* rápido.

2 *vt* *(Cook)* batir; **to — away, to — off** *dust etc* quitar con un movimiento brusco; **the horse —ed the flies away with its tail** el caballo ahuyentó las moscas con un movimiento brusco de la cola; **she —ed it away from me** me lo arrebató; me lo quitó de repente; **the waiter —ed the dishes away** el camarero se llevó de repente los platos; **they —ed him off to a meeting** le llevaron con toda prisa a una reunión; **we were —ed up in the lift to the 9th floor** el ascensor nos llevó con toda rapidez al piso 9.

3 *vi* moverse rápidamente; **to — away** desaparecer de repente.

whisker ['wiskə*] *n* pelo *m* (de la barba); **—s** barbas *fpl*; *(moustache)* bigotes *mpl*; *(side —s)* patillas *fpl*; *(Zool)* bigotes *mpl*.

whiskered ['wiskəd] *adj* bigotudo.

whisk(e)y ['wiski] *n* whisk(e)y *m*; **— and soda** whisky *m* con sifón.

whisper ['wispə*] **1** *n* **(a)** *(low tone)* cuchicheo *m*; *(of leaves)* susurro *m*; **at the least — of scandal** al menor indicio del escándalo; **to say something in a —** decir algo en tono muy bajo; **to speak in a —** hablar muy bajo; **her voice scarcely rose above a —** apenas pudo hablar sino en tono muy bajo.

(b) *(rumour)* rumor *m*, voz *f*; **there is a — that ...** corre la voz de que ..., se rumorea que ...

2 *vt* **(a)** decir en tono muy bajo; **to — something to someone, to — a word in someone's ear** decir algo al oído de uno.

(b) **it is —ed that ...** corre la voz de que ..., se rumorea que ...

3 *vi* cuchichear, hablar muy bajo; *(of leaves)* susurrar; **to — to someone** cuchichear a uno, decir algo al oído de uno; **just — to me** dímelo al oído; **stop —ing!** ¡silencio!; **it's rude to — in company** es de mala educación hablar entre sí en tono bajo estando otras personas delante.

whispering ['wispəriŋ] *n* cuchicheo *m*; *(of leaves)* susurro *m*; *(gossip)* chismes *mpl*, chismografía *f*; *(rumours)* rumores *mpl*; **— campaign** campaña *f* de rumores; campaña *f* de difamación; **— gallery** galería *f* de los murmullos.

whist [wist] *n* whist *m*.

whist drive ['wistdraiv] *n* certamen *m* de whist.

whistle ['wisl] **1** *n* *(sound)* silbido *m*, silbo *m*; *(instrument)* silbato *m*, pito *m*; **blast on the —** pitido *m*; **the referee blew his —** el árbitro pitó; **to wet one's —** *(fam)* remojar el gaznate, beber un trago.

2 *vt* silbar; **to — a tune** silbar una melodía; **to — up one's dog** llamar a su perro con un silbido.

3 *vi* silbar; *(Sport etc)* pitar; **it —d past my ear** pasó (silbando) muy cerca de mi oreja, me rozó casi la oreja al pasar; **the car —d past us** el coche pasó como una bala; **the boys — at the girls** los chicos silban a las chicas; **the crowd —d at the referee** el público silbó al árbitro; **he —d for a taxi** llamó un taxi con un silbido; **the referee —d for a foul** el arbitró pitó para señalar una falta; **he can — for it** lo pedirá en vano, que siga esperando hasta siempre.

whistle stop ['wislstɔp] *n* *(US)* población *f* pequeña.

Whit [wit] **1** *n* Pentecostés *m*. **2** *attr* de Pentecostés.

whit [wit] *n*: **never a —, not a —** ni pizca; **without a —** of sin pizca de; **every — as good as** de ningún modo inferior a.

white [wait] **1** *adj* blanco; *bread, hair, meat, wine etc* blanco; *face (of complexion)* blanco, *(with fear)* pálido; *(fig)* honorable, decente; *lie* piadoso; **a — man** un blanco, **a — woman** una blanca; **to be as — as a sheet** estar pálido como la muerte; **to go —, to turn —** *(thing)* blanquear, *(person)* palidecer, ponerse pálido.

2 *n* *(colour)* blanco *m*, color *m* blanco; *(whiteness)* blancura *f*; *(person)* blanco *m*, a *f*; *(of egg)* clara *f* del huevo; **the — of the eye** el blanco del ojo.

whitebait ['waitbeit] *n* salmonetes *mpl*.

whitebeam ['waitbi:m] *n* mojera *f*.

white-collar ['wait͵kɔlə*] *adj worker* profesional, de oficina; *work* oficinesco.

whitefish ['waitfiʃ] *n* *(species)* corégono *m*; *(col·*

lectively) peces *mpl* de mar *(excepto el arenque y el salmón)*.

white-haired ['wait'hɛəd] *adj*, **white-headed** ['wait'hedid] *adj* de cabeza blanca, de pelo blanco; *(fam)* favorito, protegido.

white-hot ['wait'hɔt] *adj* candente, calentado al blanco.

White House ['waithaus] *n*: **the —** la Casa Blanca.

whiten ['waitn] **1** *vt* blanquear. **2** *vi* blanquear; *(person)* palidecer, ponerse pálido.

whiteness ['waitnis] *n* blancura *f*.

whitening ['waitniŋ] *n* tiza *f*; blanco *m* para zapatos; *(whitewash)* jalbegue *m*.

White Paper ['wait'peipə*] *n* Libro *m* Rojo.

whitesmith ['waitsmiθ] *n* hojalatero *m*.

whitethorn ['waitθɔ:n] *n* espino *m*.

whitethroat ['waitθrəut] *n* curruca *f* zarcera.

whitewash ['waitwɔʃ] **1** *n* jalbegue *m*; *(fig)* excusas *fpl*, argumentos *mpl* con que se intenta encubrir una falta.

2 *vt* enjalbegar, encalar, blanquear; *(fig) fault* encubrir, intentar justificar; *person* disculpar, absolver (injustamente).

whither ['wiðə*] *adv (lit)* ¿adónde?

whiting[1] ['waitiŋ] *n* *(colouring)* tiza *f*; blanco *m* para zapatos.

whiting[2] ['waitiŋ] *n* *(Fish)* pescadilla *f*.

whitish ['waitiʃ] *adj* blanquecino.

whitlow ['witləu] *n* panadizo *m*.

Whitsun ['witsn] **1** *n* Pentecostés *m*. **2** *attr* de Pentecostés.

Whitsunday ['wit'sʌndei] *n* domingo *m* de Pentecostés.

Whitsuntide ['witsntaid] **1** *n* Pentecostés *m*. **2** *attr* de Pentecostés.

whittle ['witl] *vt* cortar pedazos a (con un cuchillo); **to — away, to — down** *(fig)* reducir poco a poco, rebajar gradualmente.

whizz [wiz] **1** *n* silbido *m*, zumbido *m*.

2 *vi* silbar, zumbar; *(arrow)* rehilar; **to — along, to go —ing along** ir como una bala; **it —ed past my head** pasó (silbando) muy cerca de mi cabeza; **me rozó casi la cabeza al pasar; the sledge —ed down the slope** el trineo bajó la cuesta a gran velocidad.

whizz kid ['wizkid] *n* *(sl)* joven *m* prometedor, promesa *f*; persona *f* muy activa, persona *f* emprendedora.

who [hu:] *pron* **(a)** *(interrog)* quién; **— is it?** ¿quién es?; **— are they?** ¿quiénes son?; **I know — it was** yo sé quién fue; **— do you think you are?** ¿quién le mete a Vd en esto?; **— does she think she is?** ¿qué derecho se cree tener para hacer *(etc)* eso?; **"W—'s W—"** "Quién es Quién"; **you'll soon get to know —'s — in the office** pronto aprenderás los nombres y los cargos del personal de la oficina.

(b) *(=whom)* **— are you looking for?** ¿a quién buscas?; **— should it be but Jaimito?** y henos aquí a Jaimito, y como por milagro aparece Jaimito.

(c) *(rel)* que; el *(etc)* que, quien; **my cousin — plays the accordion** mi primo que toca el acordeón; **he — wishes to ...** el que quiera ...; **those — swim** los que nadan; **deny it — may** aunque habrá quien lo niegue.

whoa [wəu] *interj* ¡so!

whodunit [hu:'dʌnit] *n* *(sl)* novela *f* policíaca.

whoever [hu:'evə*] *pron* **(a)** *(rel)* quienquiera que, cualquiera que; **— finds it can keep it** quienquiera que lo encuentre puede quedarse con él; **— said that was an idiot** el que dijo eso fue un imbécil; **ask — you like** pregúntaselo a cualquiera, pregúntaselo a quien te parezca bien.

(b) *(interrog)* ¿quién?; **— can have told you that?** ¿quién diablos te dijo eso?

whole [həul] **1** *adj* **(a)** *(entire)* todo, entero; total; íntegro; **the — world** el mundo entero; **she swallowed it —** se lo tragó entero; **a pig roasted —** un cerdo asado entero; **along its — length** por todo el largo; **is that the — truth?** ¿me has contado toda la verdad?; **but the — man eludes us** pero el hombre en su totalidad se nos escapa; **but the — purpose was to ...** pero la única finalidad era de ...; **a — lot of people will be glad** muchísimas personas se alegrarán.

(b) *(unbroken)* sano; ileso, intacto; **not a cup was left — after the party** después de la fiesta no quedó copa sana; **to our surprise he came back —** nos asombramos al verle volver ileso.

2 *n* todo *m*; total *m*; conjunto *m*, totalidad *f*; **nearly the —** **of our production** casi toda nuestra producción; **the — of Madrid** todo Madrid; **the**

— **of his works** todas sus obras, la totalidad de sus obras; **the — and its parts** el todo y sus partes; **as a —** en su totalidad, en conjunto; **on the —** en general, por regla general.

wholehearted ['həul'hɑːtid] *adj* entusiasta, incondicional, cien por cien.

wholeheartedly ['həul'hɑːtidli] *adv* con entusiasmo, incondicionalmente, cien por cien.

wholeheartedness ['həul'hɑːtidnis] *n* entusiasmo *m*.

wholemeal ['həulmiːl] **1** *adj* íntegro, de harina integral. **2** *n* harina *f* integral.

wholesale ['həulseil] **1** *n* venta *f* al por mayor.

2 *attr, adj* (a) **— dealer, — trader** comerciante *mf* al por mayor, mayorista *mf*; **— price** precio *m* al por mayor; **— trade** comercio *m* al por mayor.

(b) (*fig*) en masa; general; **— destruction** destrucción *f* general.

3 *adv* (a) **to sell something —** vender algo al por mayor.

(b) (*fig*) en masa; sin hacer distinción de personas (*etc*); **the books were burnt —** los libros fueron quemados en masa.

wholesaler ['həul,seilə*] *n* comerciante *mf* al por mayor, mayorista *mf*.

wholesome ['həulsəm] *adj* sano, saludable.

wholesomeness ['həulsəmnis] *n* lo sano, lo saludable.

whole-wheat ['həulwiːt] *adj* de trigo integral, hecho con trigo entero.

wholly ['həuli] *adv* enteramente, completamente.

whom [huːm] *pron* (a) (*interrog*) **— did you see?** ¿a quién viste?; **of — are you talking?** ¿de quién hablas?; **I know of — you are talking** yo sé de quién hablas; **from — did you receive it?** ¿de quién lo recibiste?

(b) (*rel*) que, a quien; **the lady — I saw** la señora a quien vi; **the lady with — I was talking** la señora con quien hablaba; **three policemen, all of — were drunk** tres policías, todos ellos borrachos; **three policemen, none of — wore a helmet** tres policías, ninguno de los cuales llevaba casco.

whomever [huːm'evə*] *pron see* **whoever**.

whoop [huːp] **1** *n* alarido *m*, grito *m*; **with a — of joy** con un grito de alegría.

2 *vt*: **to — it up** (*fam*) divertirse ruidosamente; echar una cana al aire.

3 *vi* gritar, dar alaridos.

whoopee [wu'piː] *n*: **to make —** (*fam*) divertirse una barbaridad (*fam*).

whooping cough ['huːpiŋ,kɔf] *n* tos *f* ferina, coqueluche *f*.

whoosh [wu(ː)ʃ] *n* ruido del agua *etc* que sale bajo presión, o del viento fuerte; **it came out with a —** salió con mucho ruido.

whop [wɔp] *vt* (*sl*) pegar.

whopper ['wɔpə*] *n* (*sl: big thing*) cosa *f* muy grande; (*lie*) mentirón *m*; **that fish is a —** ese pez es enorme; **what a —!** ¡qué grande es!

whopping ['wɔpiŋ] *adj* (*sl*) enorme, muy grande, grandísimo.

whore ['hɔː*] **1** *n* puta *f*. **2** *vi* (*also* **to go whoring**) putañear, putear.

whorehouse ['hɔːhaus] *n, pl* **—houses** [,hauziz] (*US*) casa *f* de putas.

whorl [wəːl] *n* (*of shell*) espira *f*; (*Bot*) verticilo *m*; (*Tech*) espiral *f*.

whortleberry ['wəːtl,bəri] *n* arándano *m*.

whose [huːz] *pron* (a) (*interrog*) ¿de quién?; **— is this?** ¿de quién es esto?, ¿a quién pertenece esto?; **— car did you go in?** ¿en qué coche fuiste?; **— fault was it?** ¿quién tuvo la culpa?; **— umbrella did you take?** ¿qué paraguas tomaste?; **I know — it was** yo sé de quién era.

(b) (*rel*) cuyo; **the man — hat I took** el hombre cuyo sombrero tomé; **the man — seat I sat in** el hombre en cuya silla me senté; **those — passports I have** aquellas personas cuyos pasaportes tengo.

whosoever [,huːsəu'evə*] *see* **whoever**.

why [wai] **1** *adv* ¿por qué?, ¿para qué?; ¿por qué razón?, ¿con qué objeto?; **— not?** ¿por qué no?, ¿cómo no?; **— did you do it?** ¿por qué lo hiciste?; **— on earth didn't you tell me?** ¿por qué demonios no me lo dijiste?; **I know — you did it** yo sé por qué lo hiciste; **— he did it we shall never know** no sabremos nunca por qué razón lo hizo; **that's — I couldn't come** por eso no pude venir, ésa es la razón por la que no pude venir.

2 *interj* ¡cómo!, ¡toma!; **—, what's the matter?** bueno, ¿qué pasa?; **—, it's you!** ¡toma, eres tú!; **—, there are 8 of us!** ¡sí somos 8!

3 *n* por qué *m*; causa *f*, razón *f*; **I don't know — or wherefore** no sé por qué ni cómo; *see* **wherefore**.

wick [wik] *n* mecha *f*.

wicked ['wikid] *adj* (a) (*iniquitous*) malo, malvado; perverso; inicuo; **you're a — man** eres muy malo; **that was a — thing to do** eso fue inicuo.

(b) (*fig*) *satire etc* muy mordaz, cruel; *temper* muy vivo; (*fam*) horroroso, horrible, malísimo.

wickedly ['wikidli] *adv* mal; perversamente; inicuamente; cruelmente; (*fam*) horriblemente.

wickedness ['wikidnis] *n* maldad *f*; perversidad *f*; iniquidad *f*; crueldad *f*; **all manner of —** toda clase de maldades.

wicker ['wikə*] **1** *n* mimbre *m or f*. **2** *adj, attr* de mimbre.

wickerwork ['wikəwəːk] **1** *n* artículos *mpl* de mimbre; cestería *f*; (*of chair etc*) rejilla *f*. **2** *adj, attr* de mimbre.

wicket ['wikit] *n* (*gate*) postigo *m*, portillo *m*; (*Cricket: stumps*) rastrillo *m*, palos *mpl*, (*pitch*) terreno *m*; **to be on a sticky —** estar en una situación difícil.

wide [waid] **1** *adj* ancho; extenso, vasto; *gap* grande, muy abierto; *difference* grande, considerable; *understanding etc* amplio; **it is 3 metres —** tiene 3 metros de ancho; **how — is it?** ¿cuánto tiene de ancho?; **the — plains of Castile** las extensas llanuras de Castilla; **his — knowledge of the subject** sus amplios conocimientos del tema.

2 *adv* lejos; extensamente; **far and — por todas partes; to be — open** estar muy abierto, (*door etc*) estar abierto de par en par; **to be — open to criticism** estar expuesto a ser criticado desde muchos puntos de vista; **to fling the door — abrir** la puerta de par en par; **they are set — apart** están puestos muy lejos uno de otro, están muy apartados.

-wide [waid] *eg* **nation-wide** por toda la nación, a escala nacional; de toda la nación; **a country-wide inquiry** una investigación a escala nacional.

wide-angle ['waid,æŋgl] *adj lens etc* granangular, de ángulo ancho, de gran diámetro.

wide-awake ['waidə'weik] *adj* muy despierto; (*fig*) despabilado; vigilante, alerta.

wide-eyed ['waid'aid] *adj* con los ojos desorbitados, con los ojos desmesuradamente abiertos.

widely ['waidli] *adv* extensamente; generalmente; **to travel —** viajar extensamente; viajar por muchos países (*etc*); **it is — believed that . . .** existe una creencia general de que . . .; **the opinion is — held** es una creencia general; **a —-known author** un autor generalmente conocido; **a —-read student** un estudiante que ha leído mucho.

widen ['waidn] **1** *vt* ensanchar. **2** *vi* (*also* **to — out**) ensancharse; **the passage —s out into a cave** el pasillo se ensancha para formar una caverna.

wideness ['waidnis] *n* anchura *f*; extensión *f*, amplitud *f*.

wide-ranging ['waid,reindʒiŋ] *adj survey etc* de gran alcance, de amplia extensión; *interests* múltiples, muy diversos.

wide-screen ['waidskriːn] *adj film* para pantalla ancha.

widespread ['waidspred] *adj* (a) extendido; **with — arms** con los brazos extendidos, con los brazos abiertos.

(b) (*fig*) extenso, amplio; muy difundido, general; **to become —** extenderse, generalizarse; **there is — fear that . . .** muchos temen que . . .; **knowledge of this is now —** el conocimiento de esto está muy difundido ahora.

widow ['widəu] **1** *n* viuda *f*; **W— Twankey** la viuda de Twankey; **I'm a golf —** paso mucho tiempo sola mientras mi marido juega al golf; **all the cricket —s got together for tea** las mujeres cuyos maridos estaban jugando al críquet se reunieron para tomar el té; **to be left a —** enviudar, quedar viuda; *see* **grass**.

2 *vt* dejar viuda; **she was twice —ed** quedó viuda dos veces.

widowed ['widəud] *adj* viudo.

widower ['widəuə*] *n* viudo *m*.

widowhood ['widəuhud] *n* viudez *f*.

width [widθ] *n* anchura *f*; extensión *f*, amplitud *f*; (*of cloth*) ancho *m*; **to be 6 centimetres in —** tener 6 centímetros de ancho.

wield [wiːld] *vt pen, sword etc* manejar; *sceptre* empuñar; *power* ejercer, poseer; **to — a pen in the service of . . .** menear cálamo al servicio de . . .

wife [waif] *n, pl* **wives** [waivz] mujer *f*, esposa *f*; **the —** (*fam*) la parienta (*fam*); **"The Merry Wives**

of Windsor" "Las alegres comadres de Windsor"; **this is my** — ésta es mi mujer; **my boss and his** — mi jefe y su esposa; **to take a** — casarse; **to take someone to** — casarse con una, contraer matrimonio con una.

wifely ['waifli] *adj* de esposa, de mujer casada.

wig [wig] *n* peluca *f*.

wigeon ['widʒən] *n* ánade *m* silbón.

wigging ['wigiŋ] *n* (*fam*) peluca *f* (*fam*); **to give someone a** — echar una peluca a uno.

wiggle ['wigl] **1** *n* meneo *m* rápido, movimiento *m* rápido.

2 *vt* menear rápidamente; *hips etc* mover rítmicamente, mover mucho.

3 *vi* menearse rápidamente; moverse rítmicamente, moverse mucho.

wiggly ['wigli] *adj* que se menea rápidamente, que se mueve mucho.

wight [wait] *n* (*arch or hum*) criatura *f*, pobre hombre *m*.

wigmaker ['wig,meikə*] *n* peluquero *m*.

wigwam ['wigwæm] *n* tienda *f* de pieles rojas, tipi *m*.

wild [waild] **1** *adj* (a) (*not domesticated*) *animal, man* salvaje; *plant* silvestre; campestre, de los campos; *country* agreste, difícil, bravo; **to grow** — crecer libre, crecer sin cultivo; **to run** — (*plant*) volver al estado silvestre.

(b) (*of cruel disposition*) feroz, fiero, bravo; *horse* sin domar, arisco.

(c) (*rough*) *wind etc* furioso, violento; *weather* tormentoso; *sea* bravo; **it was a** — **night** fue una noche de tormenta.

(d) (*unrestrained, disordered*) *child* desmandado, desgobernado; **he was** — **in his youth, he had a** — **youth** tuvo una juventud desordenada; **to lead a** — **life** vivir desenfrenadamente; **the room was in** — **disorder** el cuarto estaba en el mayor desorden; **they were** — **times** fue un período turbulento, fueron años alborotados; **to run** — (*children*) vivir como salvajes.

(e) (*of person*) loco, insensato, frenético; **to be** — **about someone** andar loco por uno; **to be** — **with joy** estar loco de alegría; **to be** — **with someone** estar furioso contra uno; **it drives me** —, **it makes me** — me saca de quicio, me hace rabiar; **to get** — ponerse furioso, ponerse negro; **he has** — **eyes** tiene ojos de loco; **there were moments of** — **enthusiasm** hubo momentos de loco entusiasmo.

(f) (*rash, ill-judged*) extravagante, estrafalario; disparatado, descabellado; fantástico; **there was some** — **talk** se propusieron unas ideas estrafalarias, se dijeron cosas insensatas; **it's a** — **exaggeration** es una enorme exageración; **to make a** — **guess** hacer una conjetura poco lógica; **he had some** — **scheme for** . . . tuvo algún proyecto disparatado de . . .

2 *n* tierra *f* virgen, tierra *f* poco poblada (*or* poco conocida); soledad *f*, yermo *m*; **the call of the** — la atracción de la soledad, el encanto de las tierras vírgenes; **to go out into the** —**s** ir a vivir en tierras poco conocidas; **they live out in the** —**s of Berkshire** viven en las soledades de Berkshire.

wildcat ['waild,kæt] **1** *n* gato *m* montés.

2 *adj*: — **strike** huelga *f* espontánea, huelga *f* no sancionada por el sindicato; — **scheme** proyecto *m* descabellado, proyecto *m* arriesgado.

wildebeest ['wildibi:st] *n* ñu *m*.

wilderness ['wildənis] *n* desierto *m*, yermo *m*, soledad *f*; **a** — **of ruins** un desierto de ruinas, una infinidad de ruinas.

wildfire ['waild,faiə*] *n*: **to spread like** — propagarse como la pólvora.

wildfowl ['waildfaul] *n* ánades *mpl*.

wildfowler ['waild,faulə*] *n* cazador *m* de ánades.

wildfowling ['waild,fauliŋ] *n* caza *f* de ánades.

wild-goose chase [,waild'gu:stʃeis] *n* empresa *f* desatinada, búsqueda *f* inútil.

wildlife ['waildlaif] *n* fauna *f*.

wildly ['waildli] *adv blow etc* (*of wind*) furiosamente, violentamente; *live* desordenadamente, de modo alborotado; *behave* de modo indisciplinado; (*madly*) locamente, insensatamente, frenéticamente; *act* sin reflexión; **to be** — **happy** estar loco de contento; **to shoot** — disparar sin apuntar; **to hit out** — repartir golpes a tontas y a locas; **to talk** — (*loosely*) hablar sin ton ni son, hablar incoherentemente, (*extravagantly*) hablar como un loco; **she looked** — **from one to another** miró con ojos espantados a uno y a otro; **you're guessing** — haces conjeturas sin pensar lógicamente; **to clap** — aplaudir con el

mayor entusiasmo; **to dash about** — correr de un lado para otro sin mirar dónde.

wildness ['waildnis] *n* (a) lo salvaje; selvatiquez *f*, estado *m* silvestre; lo agreste, lo difícil; braveza *f*.

(b) ferocidad *f*, fiereza *f*.

(c) furia *f*, violencia *f*.

(d) desgobierno *m*, desenfreno *m*; turbulencia *f*, lo alborotado.

(e) locura *f*, insensatez *f*; frenesí *m*.

(f) extravagancia *f*, lo estrafalario; lo disparatado; lo fantástico.

wiles [wailz] *npl* engaños *mpl*, tretas *fpl*, ardides *mpl*.

wilful ['wilful] *adj person* voluntarioso; testarudo; *child* travieso; *act* intencionado, deliberado; *murder etc* premeditado; **you have been** — **about it** has sido testarudo en esto.

wilfully ['wilfəli] *adv* voluntariosamente; intencionadamente; deliberadamente; con premeditación; **you have** — **ignored** . . . te has obstinado en no hacer caso de . . .

wilfulness ['wilfulnis] *n* voluntariedad *f*; testarudez *f*; lo travieso; lo intencionado; lo premeditado.

wiliness ['wailinis] *n* astucia *f*.

Will [wil] *nombre cariñoso de* **William**.

will¹ [wil] *v aux* **1** (*forming fut tense*) **he** — **come** vendrá; **no, he won't** no, no quiere; **you won't lose it,** — **you?** ¿no lo vas a perder, eh?; **you** — **come to see us, won't you?** ¿vendrás a vernos, no?

(b) (*fut emphatic*) **I** — **do it!** ¡sí lo haré!; **no he won't!** ¡no lo hará!; **I** — (*marriage service*) sí quiero.

2 (a) (*wish*) querer; **come when you** — venga cuando quiera; **do as you** — haga lo que quiera, haga lo que le parezca bien; **look where you** — mire dondequiera que sea; dondequiera que mire . . .

(b) (*consent*) **the engine won't start** el motor no arranca, el motor no quiere arrancar; **wait a moment,** — **you?** espera un momento, ¿quieres?; **won't you sit down?** ¿quiere sentarse?, siéntese, por favor; **I** — **not have it!** ¡no lo permito!; **he** — **have none of it** no lo aprueba de ningún modo, no quiere siquiera pensarlo; **I** — **not have it that** . . . no permito que se diga que + *subj*; *see also* have 1 (i).

(c) (*habit, potentiality*) **the car** — **do up to 120 kph** el coche hará hasta 120 kph; **accidents** — **happen** ocurren inevitablemente accidentes; **boys** — **be boys** eso es muy de chicos.

will² [wil] **1** *n* (a) (*faculty*) voluntad *f*; (*free* —) albedrío *m*; (*wish*) voluntad *f*, placer *m*, deseo *m*; **iron** —, — **of iron** voluntad *f* de hierro; **the** — **to win** el afán de triunfar; **the** — **of God** la voluntad de Dios; **against one's** — contra su voluntad; a pesar suyo, a desgana; **at** — a voluntad; **of one's own free** — por voluntad propia; **what is your** —? ¿qué manda?; **it is my** — **that you should do it** quiero que lo hagas; **where there's a** — **there's a way** querer es poder; **to do someone's** — cumplir la voluntad de uno; **Thy W** — **be done** hágase tu voluntad; **she has a** — **of her own** tiene voluntad propia; **to set to work with a** — empezar a trabajar con ilusión (*or* con entusiasmo), emprender resueltamente una tarea.

(b) *see* **good**—, **ill** —.

(c) (*testament*) testamento *m*; **the last** — **and testament of** . . . la última disposición de . . . ; **to make one's** — hacer su testamento, otorgar testamento.

2 *vt* (a) (*dispose*) querer; ordenar, disponer; **God has so** —**ed it** Dios lo ha ordenado así; **if God** —**s** si lo quiere Dios.

(b) (*urge by willpower*) lograr por fuerza de voluntad; sugestionar; **to** — **someone to do something** sugestionar a uno para que haga algo; **having** —**ed the end we must** — **the means** habiendo creado el fin a fuerza de voluntad también hemos de crear los medios por la misma; **I was** —**ing you to win** estaba deseando tanto que ganaras, te estaba ayudando a ganar con la fuerza de mi voluntad.

(c) (*by testament*) legar, dejar en testamento; **he** —**ed his pictures to the nation** legó sus cuadros a la nación.

William ['wiljəm] *m* Guillermo; — **the Conqueror** Guillermo el Conquistador.

willies ['wiliz] *npl* (*sl*): **to get the** — pegarse un susto (*fam*), pasar horrores (*fam*); **I get the** — **whenever I think about it** me horroriza pensar en ello; **it gives me the** — me da horror.

willing ['wiliŋ] (a) (*helpful*) servicial; complaciente; de buena voluntad, de buen corazón; **a** — **boy** un chico de buen corazón, un chico que trabaja *(etc)* de buena gana; **we need — helpers** necesitamos personas dispuestas a ayudarnos; **there were plenty of — hands** hubo muchos que nos ayudaron espontáneamente.

(b) to be — querer, querer hacerlo *(etc)*; **are you —?** ¿quieres?; **God —** si Dios quiere; **I asked her and she was —** se lo pedí y ella asintió gustosa; **to be — to do something** estar dispuesto a hacer algo, hacer algo de buena gana; **he was — for me to take it** me permitió llevarlo, consintió en que yo me lo llevase; **to be — that . . .** consentir en que + *subj*, permitir que + *subj*.

willingly ['wiliŋli] *adv* de buena gana, con gusto; **they — helped us** nos ayudaron de buena gana; **did he come — or by force?** ¿vino libremente o a la fuerza?; **yes, —** sí, con mucho gusto.

willingness ['wiliŋnis] *n* buena voluntad *f*, complacencia *f*; deseo *m* de servir *(or* ayudar *etc)*; consentimiento *m*; **in spite of his — to buy it** a pesar de que estaba dispuesto a comprarlo.

will-o'-the-wisp ['wiləðə'wisp] *n* fuego *m* fatuo; *(fig)* quimera *f*, ilusión *f*, sueño *m* imposible.

willow ['wiləu] *n* sauce *m (also* **willow tree**); **weeping —** sauce *m* llorón.

willowherb ['wiləuhə:b] *n* adelfa *f*.

willow pattern ['wiləu,pætən] *adj*: **— plate** plato *m* de estilo chino.

willow warbler ['wiləu,wɔ:blə*] *n* mosquitero *m* musical.

willowy ['wiləui] *adj (fig)* esbelto, cimbreño.

willy-nilly ['wili'nili] *adv* de grado o por fuerza, quiera o no quiera.

wilt¹ [wilt] *(arch) see* **will 1.**

wilt² [wilt] **1** *vt* marchitar; *(fig)* debilitar, hacer decaer.

2 *vi* marchitarse; *(fig)* debilitarse, decaer; *(lose courage)* perder el ánimo; *(of effort etc)* languidecer.

wily ['waili] *adj* astuto, mañoso.

wimple ['wimpl] *n (arch)* griñón *m*.

win [win] **1** *n* victoria *f*, triunfo *m*; éxito *m*; **another — for Real Madrid** nueva victoria del Real Madrid; **their fifth — in a row** su quinta victoria consecutiva; **to back a horse for a —** apostar dinero a un caballo para el primer puesto; **to have a —** ganar, vencer; **to play for a —** jugar para ganar.

2 *(irr: pret and ptp* **won)** *vt race, cup, prize etc* ganar; *victory* llevarse; *(obtain)* lograr, conseguir, *(Mil sl)* agenciarse *(fam); sympathy, support* atraerse, captar; *metal* arrancar *(from* a); **how to — friends and influence people** cómo hacer amistades y ejercer influencia sobre las personas; **to — someone's esteem** llegar a ser estimado por uno; **to — someone's favour** alcanzar el favor de uno; **to — someone's love** enamorar a uno; **to — glory** laurearse; **to — a reputation for honesty** hacerse una reputación de honrado; **it won him the first prize** le valió el primer premio; **to — back** *land* volver a conquistar; *gaming loss etc* recobrar; **to — over, to — round** *support, supporters* atraerse, conquistar; **we won him round eventually** por fin le convencimos; **we won him round to our point of view** le persuadimos a adoptar nuestro punto de vista.

3 *vi* ganar; triunfar; tener éxito; **to — by a head** ganar por una cabeza; **to — out** ganar, tener éxito; **to — through** triunfar por fin, tener al fin el éxito deseado; **to — through to a place** alcanzar un sitio, llegar por fin a un sitio.

wince [wins] **1** *n* mueca *f* de dolor; **he said with a —** dijo con una mueca de dolor.

2 *vi* hacer una mueca de dolor, estremecerse; *(flinch)* retroceder, asustarse; **without wincing** sin quejarse.

winch [wintʃ] **1** *n* cabrestante *m*, torno *m*. **2** *vt*: **to — up** levantar con un torno *(etc)*.

wind [wind] **1** *n* **(a)** *(in general)* viento *m*; **high —** viento *m* fuerte; **west —** viento *m* del oeste; **—s of change** aires *mpl* de cambio; **where is the —?, which way is the —?** ¿de dónde sopla el viento?; **it's an ill — that blows nobody any good** no hay mal que por bien no venga; a río revuelto, ganancia de pescadores; **to be in the —** *(fig)* estar en el aire, estar en preparación; **there's something in the —** están tramando algo; **to get — of something** llegar a saber algo, husmear algo; **to get *(or* have) the — up** encogérsele a uno el ombligo; **to put the — up someone** meter a uno el ombligo para dentro; **it properly put the — up me** me asustó de verdad; **to raise the —** dar un sablazo; **to see which way the — blows** esperar antes de resolverse, ver qué pasa antes de tomar partido.

(b) *(Naut)* viento *m*; **following —** viento *m* en popa; **between — and water** cerca de la línea de flotación; **in the teeth of the —** contra el viento; **to run before the —** navegar viento en popa; **to sail close to the —** *(fig)* decir *(etc)* cosas algo peligrosas, correr riesgo de provocar un escándalo; **to take the — out of someone's sails** bajar los humos a uno.

(c) *(Med)* flatulencia *f; (from bowel)* pedo *m, (from stomach)* eructo *m*; **to break —** ventosear, soltar un pedo; **to bring up —** eructar.

(d) *(breath)* aliento *m*, resuello *m*; **to be short of —** respirar con dificultad, estar corto de aliento; **to get one's second —** volver a respirar normalmente, cobrar el aliento.

(e) *(Mus)* **the —** los instrumentos de viento.

2 *vt*: **to — someone** dejar a uno sin aliento; **to be —ed by a ball** quedar sin aliento después de ser golpeado por un balón; **to be —ed after a race** quedar sin aliento después de una carrera.

wind [waind] *(irr: pret and ptp* **wound) 1** *vt* **(a)** *(wrap etc)* enrollar, envolver; *wool etc* devanar, ovillar; **to — one's arms round someone** rodear a uno con los brazos, abrazar a uno estrechamente; **to — in a fishing line** ir cobrando sedal; **to — wool into a ball** ovillar lana, hacer un ovillo de lana; **to — off** devanar; desenrollar; **— this round your head** envuélvete la cabeza con esto, líate esto a la cabeza; **with a rope wound tightly round his waist** con una cuerda que le ceñía estrechamente la cintura; **to — something up with a winch** levantar algo con cabrestante.

(b) *handle (also* **to — round, to —** up) dar vueltas a, girar; *clock, watch, clockwork toy etc* dar cuerda a remontar.

(c) the road —s its way through the valley la carretera serpentea por el valle.

(d) to — up *(end)* terminar, concluir; *(Comm)* liquidar; **he wound up his speech by saying that . . .** terminó su discurso diciendo que . . .; **the company was ordered to be wound up** se ordenó la liquidación de la sociedad.

(e) to — up *(nervously)* agitar, emocionar con exceso; **she's dreadfully wound up** está nerviosísima; **it gets me all wound up** *(inside)* con esto me pongo nervioso, esto me emociona terriblemente.

2 *vi* **(a)** *(also* **to — along, to — round** *(of road etc)* serpentear; **the road —s up the valley** el camino serpentea por el valle; **to — round** *(of snakes etc)* enroscarse; **the procession wound round the town** el desfile serpenteaba por la ciudad; **the car wound slowly up the hill** el coche subió lentamente la colina (torciéndose a la izquierda y a la derecha).

(b) to — up terminar, acabar; **how does the play — up?** ¿cómo termina la obra?; **we wound up in Santander** fuimos a parar a Santander; **he —s up for the government** cierra el debate hablando como representante del gobierno.

windbag ['windbæg] *n* saco *m* de aire; *(person)* charlatán *m*.

windblown ['windbləun] *adj leaf etc* llevado por el viento, arrancado por el viento; *hair* despeinado por el viento.

windbreak ['windbreik] *n* abrigada *f*, mampara *f*; protección *f* contra el viento.

windcheater ['wind,tʃi:tə*] *n* chaqueta *f* forrada.

wind cone ['windkəun] *n (Aer)* manga *f*, indicador *m* cónico de la dirección del viento.

winder ['waində*] *n* devanadera *f*; carrete *m*, bobina *f*.

windfall ['windfɔ:l] *n* fruta *f* caída; *(fig)* ganancia *f* inesperada, golpe *m* de suerte inesperado, cosa *f* llovida del cielo.

wind gauge ['windgeidʒ] *n (Aer)* anemómetro *m*, manga *f*.

winding ['waindiŋ] **1** *adj* tortuoso, sinuoso, serpentino; *staircase* de caracol.

2 *n (of watch)* cuerda *f; (of road)* tortuosidad *f; (Elec)* bobinado *m*, devanado *m*; **the —s of a river** las vueltas de un río, los meandros de un río.

winding gear ['waindiŋgiə*] *n* manubrio *m*, cabrestante *m*.

winding sheet ['waindiŋʃi:t] *n* mortaja *f*.

winding-up ['waindiŋ'ʌp] *n* conclusión *f; (Comm)* liquidación *f*.

wind instrument ['wind,instrumənt] *n* instrumento *m* de viento.

windjammer ['wind,dʒæmə*] *n* buque *m* de vela (grande y veloz).

windlass ['windləs] *n* torno *m*, maquinilla *f*; cabrestante *m*.

windless ['windlis] *adj* sin viento.

windmill ['windmil] *n* molino *m* (de viento); *(toy)* molinete *m*.

window ['windəu] *n* ventana *f*; *(shop* —*)* escaparate *m*; *(of vehicle, of booking office etc, of envelope)* ventanilla *f*; **French** — puerta *f* ventana; **stained-glass** — vidriera *f*; **to lean out of the** — asomarse a la ventana; **to look out of the** — mirar por la ventana.

window box ['windəubɔks] *n* jardinera *f* de ventana.

window cleaner ['windəu,kli:nə*] *n* limpiacristales *m*.

window dresser ['windəu,dresə*] *n* escaparatista *mf*.

window dressing ['windəu,dresiŋ] *n* decoración *f* de escaparates; *(fig)* camuflaje *m*; *(esfuerzo m* por salvar las) apariencias *fpl*.

window frame ['windəufreim] *n* marco *m* de ventana.

window ledge ['windəuledʒ] *n* antepecho *m*, alféizar *m*.

window pane ['windəupein] *n* cristal *m*.

window seat ['windəusi:t] *n* asiento *m* junto a una ventana, *(Rail etc)* asiento *m* junto a una ventanilla.

window-shop ['windəuʃɔp] *vi* mirar los escaparates de las tiendas (sin tener intención de comprar), curiosear por las tiendas.

windowsill ['windəusil] *n* alféizar *m*.

windpipe ['windpaip] *n* tráquea *f*.

windproof ['windpru:f] *adj* a prueba de viento.

windscreen ['windskri:n] *n*, *(US)* **windshield** ['windʃi:ld] *n* parabrisas *m*.

windscreen wiper ['windskri:n,waipə*] *n*, *(US)* **windshield** —['windʃi:ld] *n* limpiaparabrisas *m*.

windsleeve ['windsli:v] *n*, **windsock** ['windsɔk] *n* *(Aer)* manga *f*.

windstorm ['windstɔ:m] *n* ventarrón *m*, huracán *m*.

windswept ['windswept] *adj* azotado por el viento, barrido por el viento; *person* despeinado.

wind tunnel ['wind,tʌnl] *n* túnel *m* aerodinámico, túnel *m* de pruebas aerodinámicas.

windward ['windwəd] **1** *adj* de barlovento. **2** *n* barlovento *m*; **to** — a barlovento.

Windward Isles ['windwəd,ailz] *pl* Islas *fpl* de Barlovento.

windy ['windi] *adj* **(a)** *day* de mucho viento; *place* expuesto al viento; **it is** — **today** hoy hace viento; **it's** — **out here** aquí fuera el viento sopla fuerte.

(b) *speech, style etc* pomposo, hinchado.

(c) *(sl)* **to be** — pasar miedo; **to get** — encogérsele a uno el ombligo; **are you** —**?** ¿tienes miedo?

wine [wain] **1** *n* vino *m*; **heavy** — vino *m* fuerte; **light** — vino *m* ligero; **local** — vino *m* del país; **red** — vino *m* tinto; **sparkling** — vino *m* espumoso; **white** — vino *m* blanco; **good** — **needs no bush** el buen paño en el arca se vende.

2 *vt*: **to** — **and dine someone** dar a uno muy bien de comer y de beber, hacer grandes agasajos a uno.

winebibber ['wain,bibə*] *n* bebedor *m* de vino.

wine bottle ['wain,bɔtl] *n* botella *f* para vino.

wine cask ['wainkɑ:sk] *n* tonel *m* para vino, barril *m* para vino.

wine cellar ['wain,selə*] *n* bodega *f*.

wineglass ['waingla:s] *n* copa *f* para vino, vaso *m* para vino.

wine grower ['wain,grəuə*] *n* viñador *m*, vinicultor *m*.

wine growing ['wain,grəuiŋ] **1** *adj* vinícola. **2** *n* vinicultura *f*.

wine list ['wainlist] *n* lista *f* de vinos.

wine merchant ['wain,mə:tʃənt] *n* vinatero *m*.

wine press ['wainpres] *n* prensa *f* de uvas, lagar *m*.

winery ['wainəri] *n* lagar *m*.

wineskin ['wainskin] *n* pellejo *m*, odre *m*.

wine taster ['wain,teistə*] *n* probador *m* de vinos, catador *m* de vinos.

wine waiter ['wain,weitə*] *n* escanciador *m*.

wing [wiŋ] *n* ala *f*; *(Archit)* ala *f*; *(Aut)* aleta *f*, guardabarros *m*; *(of chair)* cabecera *f*, oreja *f*; *(Sport: position)* ala *f*, exterior *m*, *(player)* extremo *m*; *(Aer: section)* escuadrilla *f*; —**s** *(Theat)* bastidores *mpl*; **left** — *(Pol)* ala *f* izquierda; **right** — *(Pol)* ala *f* derecha; **on the** —**s of fantasy** en alas de la fantasía; **to be on the** — estar volando; **to be on the left** —, **to belong to the left** — *(Pol)* ser de izquierdas; **to clip someone's** —**s** cortar las alas a uno; **to shoot a bird on the** — matar un pájaro mientras está volando; **to take** — irse volando, alzar el vuelo; **to take someone under one's** — tomar a uno bajo su protección.

2 *vt bird* tocar, herir en el ala; *person* herir en el brazo; **to** — **one's way** volar, ir volando.

3 *vi* volar.

wing case ['wiŋkeis] *n* *(Zool)* élitro *m*.

wing chair ['wiŋtʃeə*] *n* butaca *f* de orejas.

wing commander ['wiŋkə,ma:ndə*] *n* teniente *m* coronel de aviación.

winged [wiŋd] *adj* *(Zool)* alado; *seed* con alas; **de alas** . . ., *eg* **brown-winged** de alas pardas; **four-winged** de cuatro alas.

winger ['wiŋə*] *n* *(Sport)* extremo *m*.

wingless ['wiŋlis] *adj* sin alas.

wing nut ['wiŋnʌt] *n* tuerca *f* mariposa.

wingspan ['wiŋspæn] *n*, **wingspread** ['wiŋspred] *n* envergadura *f* (de alas).

wing tip ['wiŋtip] *n* punta *f* del ala.

wink [wiŋk] **1** *n* *(blink)* pestañeo *m*; *(meaningful)* guiño *m*; **I didn't get a** — **of sleep** no pegué los ojos; **to give someone a** — guiñar el ojo a uno; **to have 40** —**s** descabezar un sueño, echarse una siestecita; **he said with a** — dijo guiñándome el ojo; **I didn't sleep a** — no pegué los ojos; **to tip someone the** — *(fam)* avisar a uno clandestinamente.

2 *vt eye* guiñar.

3 *vi* *(blink)* pestañear; *(meaningfully)* guiñar el ojo; *(of light, star etc)* titilar, parpadear; **to** — **at someone** guiñar el ojo a uno; **to** — **at something** *(fig)* hacer la vista gorda a algo.

winkle ['wiŋkl] **1** *n* bigarro *m*.

2 *vt*: **to** — **someone out** hacer salir a uno; **to** — **a secret out of someone** hacer que uno revele un secreto; **to** — **something out of a crevice** sacar algo con dificultad de una grieta.

winner ['winə*] *n* *(person, horse etc)* ganador *m*, ora *f*, vencedor *m*, ora *f*; *(book, entry etc)* obra *f* premiada; *(Tennis: ball)* pelota *f* imposible de restar; **this disc is a** —**!** *(fam)* ¡este disco es fabuloso! *(fam)*; **the tune is bound to be a** — *(fam)* la melodía obtendrá seguramente un éxito.

winning ['winiŋ] **1** *adj* *person, horse, team etc* vencedor, victorioso; *book, entry etc* premiado; *hit, shot* decisivo; *smile, ways etc* atractivo, encantador.

2 —**s** *npl* ganancias *fpl*.

winning post ['winiŋpəust] *n* poste *m* de llegada, meta *f*.

winnow ['winəu] *vt* aventar.

winnower ['winəuə*] *n*, **winnowing machine** ['winəuiŋmə,ʃi:n] *n* aventadora *f*.

winsome ['winsəm] *adj* atractivo, encantador.

winter ['wintə*] **1** *n* invierno *m*; **"W**—**'s Tale"** "Cuento *m* de invierno".

2 *adj, attr* de invierno, invernal; — **quarters** cuarteles *mpl* de invierno; — **solstice** solsticio *m* invernal; — **sports** deportes *mpl* de invierno.

3 *vi* invernar.

wintergreen ['wintəgri:n] *n* aceite *m* de gualteria.

winterize ['wintəraiz] *vt* *(US)* adaptar para el invierno, proteger contra el rigor del invierno.

wintertime ['wintətaim] *n* *(season)* invierno *m*; *(hour)* hora *f* de invierno.

wintry ['wintri] *adj* frío, glacial; *(fig)* glacial.

wipe [waip] **1** *n* limpión *m*, limpiadura *f*; *(sl)* cate *m* *(sl)*, lapo *m* *(sl)*; **to give something a** — **(down** etc*)* limpiar algo, pasar un trapo *(etc)* sobre algo.

2 *vt* limpiar; enjugar; **to** — **a table dry** secar una mesa con un trapo, enjugar una mesa; **to** — **one's brow** enjugarse la frente; **to** — **one's eyes** enjugarse las lágrimas; **to** — **a child's eyes** enjugar las lágrimas a un niño; **to** — **one's nose** sonarse (las narices); **to** — **away, to** — **off** quitar con un trapo, quitar frotando; **to** — **out** *(erase)* borrar; *(suppress)* borrar, cancelar; suprimir; *debt* liquidar; *memory* borrar; *(destroy)* destruir, extirpar; *(kill off completely)* aniquilar.

wiper ['waipə*] *n* paño *m*, trapo *m*.

wire ['waiə*] **1** *n* alambre *m*; *(Tel)* telegrama *m*; **live** — alambre *m* cargado, alambre *m* con corriente, *(fig)* polvorilla *m*; **to pull** —**s** tocar resortes; **he can pull** —**s** tiene muchos enchufes, tiene buenas agarraderas; **to send someone a** — poner un telegrama a uno.

2 *vt* **(a)** *house* instalar el alambrado de; *fence* alambrar; **to** — **up** instalar el alambrado de, completar la instalación eléctrica de; **it's all** —**d up for television** se ha completado la instalación eléctrica para la televisión.

(b) **to** — **someone** poner un telegrama a uno; **to** — **information to someone** enviar información a uno por telegrama.

3 *vi* poner un telegrama *(for something* pidiendo algo, *to someone* a uno).

wire cutters ['waiə,kʌtəz] *npl* cizalla *f*, cortaalambres *m*; **a pair of** — una cizalla, un cortaalambres.

wire gauge ['waiəgeidʒ] *n* calibre *m* para alambres.

wire gauze ['waiə'gɔːz] n tela f metálica.

wire-haired ['waiəhɛəd] adj de pelo áspero.

wireless ['waiəlis] **1** n (as science etc) radio f, radiofonía f; (set) radio f, receptor m de radio, radiorreceptor m; **by —, on the —, over the —** por radio; **to talk on the —** hablar por radio.

2 attr de radio, radiofónica; **— message** radiograma m.

3 vt radiar, transmitir por radio.

4 vi: **to — to someone** enviar un mensaje a uno por radio.

wireless cabin ['waiəlis,kæbin] n cabina f de radio.

wireless operator ['waiəlis,ɔpəreitə*] n radiotelegrafista mf.

wireless set ['waiəlisset] n radio f, receptor m de radio, radiorreceptor m.

wireless station ['waiəlis,steiʃən] n emisora f.

wire netting ['waiə'netiŋ] n red f de alambre, alambrada f de tela metálica.

wirepuller ['waiə,pulə*] n (fam) enchufista mf (fam).

wirepulling ['waiə,puliŋ] n (fam) empleo m de resortes (fam), uso m de enchufes (fam).

wiretap ['waiətæp] vi intervenir las conexiones telefónicas.

wiretapper ['waiə,tæpə*] n persona f que interviene las conexiones telefónicas.

wiretapping ['waiə,tæpiŋ] n intervención f de las conexiones telefónicas.

wireworm ['waiəwəːm] n gusano m de elatérido.

wiring ['waiəriŋ] n alambrado m, instalación f de alambres; **— diagram** esquema m del alambrado.

wiry ['waiəri] adj person, build delgado pero fuerte; hand nervudo, nervioso.

wisdom ['wizdəm] n sabiduría f; saber m; prudencia f, juicio m; lo acertado, acierto m.

wise¹ [waiz] adj (a) (learned) sabio; (prudent) prudente, juicioso; move, step etc acertado; **a — man** un sabio; **the (Three) Wise Men (of the East)** los Reyes Magos; **it does not seem — to + infin** no parece aconsejable + infin; **the —st thing to do is . . .** lo más prudente es . . .; **I'm none the —r** sigo sin entenderlo, ahora lo entiendo menos que antes; **nobody will be any the —r** nadie sabrá de esto, nadie se dará cuenta.

(b) (fam) **to be — to someone** conocer el juego de uno, calar a uno (fam); **to get — to something** caer en la cuenta de algo; **to put someone — to something** poner a uno al tanto de algo, informar a uno acerca de algo.

wise² [waiz] (arch) guisa f, modo m; **in this —** de esta guisa; **in no —** de ningún modo.

-wise [waiz] suffix con respecto a, en cuanto a, relativo a, por lo que se refiere a, eg **profitwise** en cuanto a las ganancias; **how are you off money-wise?** ¿cómo te va el dinero?

wiseacre ['waiz,eikə*] n sabihondo m.

wisecrack ['waizkræk] **1** n cuchufleta f, chiste m.

2 vi cuchufletear; **"—", he —ed "—"** dijo bromeando.

wisely ['waizli] adv sabiamente; prudentemente, con prudencia; acertadamente.

wish [wiʃ] **1** n (a) deseo m (for de); ruego m; **according to one's —es** según los deseos de uno; **her — to do it** su deseo de hacerlo; **your — is my command** sus deseos son órdenes para mí; **it has long been my — to + infin** desde hace mucho tiempo vengo deseando + infin, desde hace mucho tengo la intención de + infin; **to go against someone's —es** oponerse a los deseos de uno; **the fairy granted her 3 —es** el hada le concedió 3 deseos; **you shall have your —** se hará lo que Vd pide, se cumplirá tu deseo; **I have no great — to go** me apetece poco ir, realmente no tengo ganas de ir; **to make a —** pensar en algo que uno quiere.

(b) **with best —es** (in letter) saludos de tu amigo . . ., un abrazo de . . .; **with best —es for the future** con mis augurios para el porvenir; **I went to give him my best —es** fui a darle la enhorabuena; **please give him my best —es** por favor dale recuerdos míos, salúdale de mi parte; **we sent a message of good —es on Slobodia independence day** enviamos un mensaje de buenos augurios el día de la independencia de Eslobodia.

2 vt (a) desear, querer; **I do not —it** no lo quiero, no quiero que se haga; **to — something on someone** lograr que uno acepte algo que no desea; **it was —ed on me** apareció sin que yo lo pidiera; **the job was —ed on to me** me dieron el cometido sin quererlo yo.

(b) **to — someone good luck, to — someone well** desear a uno mucha suerte; **I — you all**

possible happiness os deseo muchísima felicidad; **I don't — her ill, I don't — her any harm** no le deseo ningún mal; **to — someone good morning** dar los buenos días a uno; **to — someone goodbye** despedirse de uno; **to — someone a happy Christmas** desear a uno unas Pascuas muy felices.

(c) (with verb complement) **to — to do something** querer hacer algo, desear hacer algo; **to — someone to do something** querer que uno haga algo; **what do you — me to do?** ¿qué quieres que haga yo?; **I do — you'd let me help** me gustaría muchísimo que me dejaras ayudar; **I — she'd come** estoy deseando que venga ella; **I —ed after that I had stayed till the end** después de eso sentí no haberme quedado hasta el fin; **I — I could!** ¡ojalá!, ¡ojalá pudiera!; **I — it were not so** ojalá no fuera así; **I — I could be there!** ¡ojalá estuviera allí!

3 vi: **to — for something** desear algo, anhelar algo; **what more could you — for?** ¿qué más pudieras desear?; **she has everything she could — for** tiene todo cuanto pudiera desear.

wishbone ['wiʃbəun] n espoleta f.

wishful ['wiʃful] adj deseoso (to + infin de + infin); ilusionado; see thinking.

wishing bone ['wiʃiŋbəun] n espoleta f.

wish-wash ['wiʃwɔʃ] n (fam) aguachirle f.

wishy-washy ['wiʃi,wɔʃi] adj (fam) soso, flojo, insípido.

wisp [wisp] n (fragment) trozo m ligero, pedazo m menudo; (trace) vestigio m; (of grass) manojito m; brizna f; (of hair) mechón m; (of cloud) jirón m; **— of smoke** columna f delgada, espiral f ligera.

wispy ['wispi] adj delgado, sutil, tenue.

wistaria [wis'tɛəriə] n vistaria f.

wistful ['wistful] adj triste, melancólico; pensativo; ansioso.

wistfully ['wistfəli] adv tristemente, con melancolía; pensativamente; con ansia; **she looked at me —** me miró pensativa.

wistfulness ['wistfulnis] n tristeza f, melancolía f; lo pensativo; ansia f.

wit¹ [wit] n: **to — a** saber, esto es.

wit² [wit] n (a) (understanding) inteligencia f, entendimiento m, juicio m; talento m; **mother —, native —** sentido m común; **a battle of —s** una contienda entre dos inteligencias; **to be at one's—'s end** estar para volverse loco (wondering what to do pensando qué hacer); **to be out of one's —s** estar fuera de sí; **to collect one's —s** reconcentrarse; **to frighten someone out of his —s** dar a uno un susto mortal; **to have (or keep) one's —s about one** tener mucho ojo; conservar su presencia de ánimo; **he hadn't the — to see that . . .** no tenía bastante inteligencia para comprender que . . .; **to live by one's —s** vivir del cuento, ser caballero de industria; **to sharpen one's —s** despabilarse; **to use one's —s** usar su sentido común; valerse de su ingenio.

(b) (humour, wittiness) ingenio m, agudeza f; sal f; gracia f; **to have a ready (or pretty) —** ser ingenioso, tener chispa; **there's a lot of — in the book** el libro tiene mucha sal; **a story told without —** un cuento narrado sin gracia; **in a flash of — he said . . .** con un rasgo de ingenio dijo . . .

(c) (person) chistoso m, a f, persona f de mucha sal; (Hist) ingenio m; **an Elizabethan —** un ingenio de la época isabelina.

witch [witʃ] n bruja f, hechicera f.

witchcraft ['witʃkrɑːft] n brujería f.

witch doctor ['witʃ,dɔktə*] n hechicero m.

witchery ['witʃəri] n brujería f; (fig) encanto m, magia f.

witch hunt ['witʃhʌnt] n lucha f contra la subversión; (pej) persecución f de personas subversivas, persecución f (política).

with [wið, wiθ] prep (a) (general sense) con; en compañía de; **I was — him** yo estaba con él; **she stayed with friends** se hospedó con unos amigos; **I'll be — you in a moment** un momento y estoy con vosotros; **to leave something — someone** dejar algo en manos de uno; **to leave a child — someone** dejar a un niño al cuidado de uno; **that problem is always — us** ese problema sigue afectándonos, ese problema no se resuelve; **the fashion ended — the century** la moda terminó al terminar el siglo, la moda terminó cuando el siglo; **— the Alcántara it is the biggest ship of its class** junto con el Alcántara es el mayor buque de su tipo; **she's good — children** sabe manejar a los niños, se adapta perfectamente al mundo infantil; **I am — you there** en eso estoy de acuerdo con Vd; **he took**

it away — him se lo llevó consigo; — no sin, *eg* — no trouble at all sin dificultad alguna.

(b) (*descriptive*) de, con; **a house — big windows** una casa con grandes ventanas; **the fellow — the big beard** él de la barba grande; **you can't speak to the queen — your hat on** no se puede hablar con la reina llevando puesto el sombrero.

(c) (*in spite of*) con; **— all his faults** con todos sus defectos.

(d) (*according to*) según, de acuerdo con; **it varies — the season** varía según la estación.

(e) (*manner*) con; **— all his might** con todas sus fuerzas; **— all speed** a toda prisa; **— one blow** de un solo golpe; **to cut wood — a knife** cortar madera con un cuchillo; **to welcome someone — open arms** recibir a uno con los brazos abiertos; **to walk — a stick** andar apoyándose en un bastón.

(f) (*cause*) de; **to jump — joy** saltar de alegría; **to shake — fear** temblar de miedo; **to shiver — cold** tiritar de frío; **the hills are white — snow** las colinas están cubiertas de nieve; **to be ill — measles** tener sarampión; **it's pouring — rain** está lloviendo a cántaros; **to fill a glass — wine** llenar un vaso de vino.

(g) (*construction with certain verbs*) **the trouble — Harry** la dificultad con Enrique; **el disgusto que hubo con Enrique; it's a habit — him** es una costumbre que él tiene, es cosa de él; **be honest — me** cuéntamelo con toda franqueza; **be honest — yourself** no te forjes ilusiones; **you must be patient — her** hay que tener paciencia con ella; **we agree — you** estamos de acuerdo con Vd; **to fill someone — fear** infundir miedo a uno; llenar a uno de miedo.

(h) — it (*fam: also* with-it); **to be — it** estar al tanto, estar al día; tener ideas modernas; comprender el mundo actual, estar de acuerdo con las tendencias actuales; (*of dress etc*) estar de moda; **to get — it** ponerse al día, (*in dress etc*) ponerse a la moda; **a with-it dress** un vestido a la moda.

withal [wi'ɔːl] *adv* (*arch*) además, también; por añadidura.

withdraw [wiθ'drɔː] (*irr: see* **draw**) **1** *vt object* retirar, sacar, quitar (*from* de); *troops, money, stamps, ambassador etc* retirar (*from* de); *words* retractar; *charge* (*Law*) apartar.

2 *vi* (*Mil etc*) retirarse (*from* de, *to* a), replegarse; (*Sport*) abandonar; (*move away*) apartarse, alejarse, irse; **he withdrew a few paces** se retiró unos pasos, se apartó un poco; **then they all withdrew** luego se retiraron todos; **to — from business** retirarse de los negocios; **to — from a contest** abandonar, renunciar a tomar parte en una contienda; **to — in favour of someone else** renunciar en favor de otro; **to — into oneself** ensimismarse; **you can't — now** Vd no puede abandonar ahora.

withdrawal [wiθ'drɔːəl] *n* retirada *f*; retiro *m*; abandono *m*; retractación *f*; renuncia *f*; **to make a — of funds from a bank** efectuar una retirada de fondos de un banco; **they made a rapid —** se retiraron rápidamente.

withdrawn [wiθ'drɔːn] **1** *ptp of* **withdraw**. **2** *adj* reservado, encerrado en sí mismo, introvertido.

withe [wiθ] *n* mimbre *m or f*.

wither ['wiðə*] **1** *vt* marchitar, secar; (*fig*) aplastar; **to — someone with a look** aplastar a uno con una mirada, hacer callar a uno mirándole severo.

2 *vi* marchitarse, secarse.

withered ['wiðəd] *adj* marchito, seco.

withering ['wiðəriŋ] *adj heat* abrasador; *gunfire etc* arrollador; *look, tone* lleno de desprecio, desdeñoso; *criticism* mordaz.

withers ['wiðəz] *npl* cruz *f*.

withhold [wiθ'həuld] (*irr: see* **hold**) *vt* (*keep back*) retener; (*refuse*) negar; (*refuse to reveal*) ocultar; no revelar; **to — a pound of someone's pay** retener una libra del pago a uno; **to — one's help** negarse a ayudar a uno; **to — the truth from someone** no revelar la verdad a uno.

withholding tax [wiθ'həuldiŋˌtæks] *n* (*US*) descuento *m* anticipado de las contribuciones.

within [wið'in] **1** *adv* dentro; **from —** desde dentro, desde el interior.

2 *prep* (*inside*) dentro de; (**— range of**) al alcance de; **here —** aquí dentro de la ciudad; **— a radius of 10 kilometres** en un radio de 10 kilómetros; **we were — 100 metres of the summit** estábamos a 100 metros nada más de la cumbre, nos faltaron sólo 100 metros para llegar a la cumbre; **the village is — a mile of the river** el pueblo dista poco menos de una milla del pueblo; **to be — an inch of** estar a dos dedos de; **to be — call** estar al

alcance de la voz; **— the week** antes de terminar la semana; **— a year of her death** menos de un año después de su muerte; **— the stipulated time** dentro del plazo señalado; **to keep — the law** obrar dentro de los límites que impone la ley; **to live — one's income** vivir con arreglo a los ingresos; **a voice — me said . . .** una voz interior me dijo . . .

without [wið'aut] **1** *adv* (*lit*) fuera; por fuera; **from —** desde fuera.

2 *prep* sin; a falta de, en ausencia de; **— a tie** sin corbata; **3 days — food** 3 días sin comer; **— speaking** sin hablar, sin decir nada; **— my noticing it** sin verlo yo, sin que yo lo notase; **not — some difficulty** no sin alguna dificultad.

withstand [wiθ'stænd] (*irr: see* **stand**) *vt* resistir a; oponerse a; aguantar.

withy ['wiði] *n* mimbre *m or f*.

witless ['witlis] *adj* estúpido, tonto.

witness ['witnis] **1** *n* **(a)** (*evidence*) testimonio *m*; **in — of** en fe de; **in — whereof** en fe de lo cual; **to bear — to** dar fe de, atestiguar; **to bear false —** perjurarse.

(b) (*person*) testigo *mf*; espectador *m*, ora *f*; **— for the defence** testigo *mf* de descargo; **— for the prosecution** testigo *mf* de cargo; **there were no —es** no hubo testigos; **we want no —es to this** no queremos que nadie vea esto, que nadie sepa de esto; **to call someone as —** citar a uno como testigo.

2 *vt* **(a)** (*see*) asistir a, presenciar, ser espectador de; ver; **the accident was —ed by two people** hay dos testigos del accidente, dos personas vieron el accidente; **I have never —ed such scenes before** no he visto nunca tales escenas; **to — someone doing something** ver a uno que hace algo, ver como uno hace algo.

(b) — what happened when . . . ved lo que pasó cuando . . ., consideren lo que pasó cuando . . .; **— the case of X** según quedó demostrado en el caso de X; **— my hand** en fe de lo cual firmo.

(c) to — a document firmar un documento como testigo.

witness box ['witnisbɔks] *n*, (*US*) **witness stand** ['witnisstænd] *n* barra *f* de los testigos, puesto *m* de los testigos, tribuna *f* de los testigos.

witticism ['witisizəm] *n* agudeza *f*, chiste *m*, dicho *m* gracioso.

wittily ['witili] *adv* ingeniosamente; con gracia, de modo divertido.

wittiness ['witinis] *n* agudeza *f*, viveza *f* de ingenio; gracia *f*, lo divertido.

wittingly ['witiŋli] *adv* a sabiendas.

witty ['witi] *adj person* ingenioso, chistoso, salado; *remark, speech etc* gracioso, divertido; **he's very —** tiene mucha gracia, es un tipo muy salado.

wives [waivz] *npl of* **wife**.

wizard ['wizəd] **1** *n* hechicero *m*, brujo *m*; (*fam*) as *m* (*fam*), genio *m*; experto *m*. **2** *adj* (*sl*) estupendo, maravilloso.

wizardry ['wizədri] *n* hechicería *f*, brujería *f*.

wizened ['wiznd] *adj* seco, marchito; *person, skin etc* arrugado, apergaminado.

wo [wəu] *interj*, **woa** [wəu] *interj* ¡so!

woad [wəud] *n* hierba *f* pastel.

wobble ['wɔbl] **1** *n* bamboleo *m*, tambaleo *m*; **to walk with a —** tambalearse al andar, andar tambaleándose; **this chair has a —** esta silla no es nada firme, esta silla baila.

2 *vi* bambolear, tambalearse; vacilar, oscilar; (*rock*) balancearse; (*of chair etc*) bailar, ser poco firme; (*be indecisive*) vacilar.

wobbly ['wɔbli] *adj* inseguro, poco firme.

woe [wəu] *n* (*lit*) aflicción *f*, dolor *m*; mal *m*, infortunio *m*; **— is me!** ¡ay de mí!; **— betide him who . . .!** ¡ay del que . . .!; **to tell someone one's —s** contar a uno sus males; **it was such a tale of —** fue una historia tan triste, fue una historia tan llena de desgracias.

woebegone ['wəubiˌgɔn] *adj* desconsolado, angustiado.

woeful ['wəuful] *adj person etc* triste, afligido, desconsolado; *sight, story etc* triste, lamentable.

woefully ['wəufəli] *adv* tristemente; lamentablemente.

woke [wəuk] *pret and ptp of* **wake**.

wold [wəuld] *n* (*approx*) rasa *f* ondulada.

wolf [wulf] **1** *n, pl* **wolves** [wulvz] lobo *m*, a *f*; (*fam*) tenorio *m*; **lone —** (*fig*) caballero *m* solitario; **— in sheep's clothing** lobo *m* en piel de cordero; **to cry —** gritar el lobo; **to keep the — from the door** guardarse del hambre, evitar caer en la miseria;

to throw someone to the wolves arrojar a uno a los lobos.
2 vt food zampar, comer vorazmente.
wolf cub ['wulfkʌb] n lobezno m.
wolfhound ['wulfhaund] n perro m lobo.
wolfish ['wulfiʃ] adj lobuno.
wolf pack ['wulfpæk] n manada f de lobos.
wolfram ['wulfrəm] n wolfram m, volframio m.
wolverine ['wulvəriːn] n carcayú m, glotón m de América.
wolves [wulvz] npl of **wolf.**
woman ['wumən] **1** n, pl **women** ['wimin] mujer f; (servant) criada f; **young** — joven f; **old** — vieja f; **my old** — (fam) la parienta (fam); **he's rather an old** — es una persona bastante sosa; se queja por poca cosa; se inquieta sin motivo; — **of the town** prostituta f; — **of the world** mujer f mundana; **X and all his women** X y todas sus queridas; **Z and his kept** — Z y su querida; **to make an honest** — **of someone** casarse con una (a causa de haberla dejado encinta); **he runs after women** se dedica a la caza de mujeres.
2 as adj: — **doctor** médica f; — **pilot** mujer f piloto; — **writer** escritora f.
woman-hater ['wumən,heitə*] n misógino m.
womanhood ['wumənhud] n (women in general) mujeres fpl, sexo m femenino; (age) edad f adulta (de mujer); (womanliness) feminidad f; **to reach** — llegar a la edad adulta (de mujer).
womanish ['wuməniʃ] adj mujeril, propio de mujer; **man** afeminado.
womankind ['wumən'kaind] n mujeres fpl, sexo m femenino.
womanlike ['wumənlaik] adj mujeril.
womanliness ['wumənlinis] n feminidad f.
womanly ['wumənli] adj femenino.
womb [wuːm] n matriz f, útero m; (fig) seno m.
women ['wimin] npl of **woman;** —**'s rights** derechos mpl de la mujer; —**'s page** sección f para la mujer; —**'s team** equipo m femenino.
womenfolk ['wiminfəuk] npl las mujeres.
won [wʌn] pret and ptp of **win.**
wonder ['wʌndə*] **1** n (a) (object) maravilla f; prodigio m; portento m, milagro m; **the** — **of electricity** el milagro de la electricidad; —**s of science** maravillas fpl de la ciencia; **the 7** —**s of the world** las 7 maravillas del mundo; **a nine-days'** — un prodigio que deja pronto de serlo; **and no** — y con razón, como era lógico, como era de esperar; **he paid cash, for a** — pagó al contado, lo cual asombró a todos; **the** — **of it was that** . . . lo asombroso fue que . . .; **it is a** — **that** . . . es un milagro que . . .; **it is no** (or **little, small**) — **that** . . . no es sorprendente que + subj, no es mucho que + subj; **to do** —**s with something** hacer maravillas con algo; **to work** —**s** hacer milagros.
(b) (sense of —) admiración f, asombro m; **to be lost in** — quedar asombrado.
2 as adj: — **drug** fármaco m milagroso.
3 vti (a) desear saber, preguntarse; **I** —! ¡quizá!, ¡quién sabe!; **I** — **what he'll do now** me pregunto qué hará ahora; **I** — **if she'll come** me pregunto si viene, ¿si vendrá?; **I** — **who first said that** ¿quién habrá dicho eso por primera vez?; **I** — **if you really love me** a veces me pregunto si me quieres de verdad.
(b) admirarse, asombrarse, maravillarse (at de); **I** — **at your rashness** me admiro de su temeridad, me asombra su temeridad; **that's hardly to be** —**ed at** eso no tiene nada de extraño, no hay que asombrarse de eso; **it set me** —**ing** me hizo pensar; **she's married by now, I shouldn't** — se habrá casado ya cómo sería lógico, cabe presumir que está casada ya.
wonderful ['wʌndəful] adj maravilloso; estupendo; —! ¡estupendo!
wonderfully ['wʌndəfəli] adv maravillosamente.
wondering ['wʌndəriŋ] adj tone, look etc perplejo, sorprendido.
wonderingly ['wʌndəriŋli] adv: **to look** — **at someone** mirar a uno perplejo, mirar a uno sorprendido.
wonderland ['wʌndəlænd] n admiración f, asombro m.
wonderment ['wʌndəmənt] n = **wonder 1 (b).**
wonderstruck ['wʌndəstrʌk] adj asombrado, pasmado.
wonder-worker ['wʌndə,wəːkə*] n (Med etc) droga f (etc) que efectúa curas al parecer milagrosas.
wondrous ['wʌndrəs] adj maravilloso.
wondrously ['wʌndrəsli] adv maravillosamente;

— **beautiful** extraordinariamente hermoso, hermoso en extremo.
wonky ['wɔŋki] adj (fam) poco firme, poco seguro; flojo; **to put something on** — poner algo mal, colocar algo incorrectamente.
won't [wəunt] = **will not.**
wont [wəunt] **1** adj: **to be** — **to** + infin soler + infin, acostumbrar + infin; **as he was** — (to) como solía (hacer).
2 n costumbre f; **it is his** — **to** + infin suele + infin, acostumbra + infin.
wonted ['wəuntid] adj acostumbrado.
woo [wuː] vt (lit) pretender, cortejar; (fig) procurar ganarse la amistad de, solicitar el apoyo de.
wood [wud] **1** n (a) (forest) bosque m; —**s** bosque m, bosques mpl, monte m; **we're not out of the** — yet no estamos todavía a salvo, todavía queda algún peligro (or dificultad etc); **he can't see the** — **for the trees** se anda por las ramas, está obsesionado por los detalles sin ver el problema en conjunto; **to take to the** —**s** echarse al monte.
(b) (material) madera f; (fire—) leña f; **dead** — ramas fpl muertas; leña f seca; (fig) material m inútil, personas fpl inútiles; **to knock on** —, **to touch** — tocar madera; **touch** —! ¡toca madera!; **we shall manage it, touch** — lo lograremos si Dios quiere (or Dios mediante).
(c) (in winemaking etc) barril m; **drawn from the** — de barril.
(d) (Mus) instrumento m de viento de madera.
(e) (Bowls) bola f.
2 adj, attr (a) de los bosques, selvático.
(b) de madera.
wood alcohol ['wud'ælkəhɔl] n alcohol m metálico.
wood anemone ['wudən'eməni] n nemorosa f, anémona f de los bosques.
woodbine ['wudbain] n madreselva f.
wood block ['wudblɔk] n bloque m de madera; (in paving) adoquín m de madera.
wood carving ['wud,kaːviŋ] n escultura f en madera.
woodchuck ['wudtʃʌk] n marmota f de América.
woodcock ['wudkɔk] n chocha f perdiz.
woodcraft ['wudkraːft] n conocimiento m de la vida del bosque; destreza f en la montería.
woodcut ['wudkʌt] n grabado m en madera.
woodcutter ['wud,kʌtə*] n leñador m.
wooded ['wudid] adj arbolado, enselvado.
wooden ['wudn] adj (a) de madera; de palo.
(b) (fig) face etc sin expresión, inexpresivo; personality soso, poco imaginativo, sin animación; response etc inflexible.
wood engraving ['wudin'greiviŋ] n grabado m en madera.
woodland ['wudlənd] **1** n bosque m, monte m, arbolado m. **2** adj, attr de los bosques, selvático.
woodlark ['wudlaːk] n totovía f.
woodlouse ['wudlaus] n, pl —**lice** [lais] cochinilla f.
woodman ['wudmən] n, pl —**men** [mən] leñador m; trabajador m forestal.
woodpecker ['wud,pekə*] n pito m, pico m; **green** — pito m real; **lesser spotted** — pico m menor.
woodpigeon ['wud,pidʒən] n paloma f torcaz.
woodpile ['wudpail] n montón m de leña.
wood pulp ['wudpʌlp] n pulpa f de madera, ligno-celulosa f, pasta f celulosa.
wood shavings ['wud,ʃeivinz] npl virutas fpl.
woodshed ['wudʃed] n leñera f.
woodsy ['wudzi] adj (US) densamente poblado de árboles, cubierto (or rodeado etc) de bosques; selvático.
woodwind ['wudwind] n (also — **instruments**) instrumentos mpl de viento de madera.
woodwork ['wudwəːk] n (wood) maderaje m; molduras fpl; (craft) carpintería f, ebanistería f.
woodworm ['wudwəːm] n carcoma f.
woody ['wudi] adj tissue etc leñoso.
wooer ['wuːə*] n pretendiente m.
woof [wuːf] n trama f.
wooing ['wuːiŋ] n galanteo m.
wool [wul] **1** n lana f; (fam) pelo m; **a dyed in the** — **supporter** un partidario fanático, un partidario acérrimo; **to pull the** — **over someone's eyes** dar a uno gato por liebre.
2 adj, attr de lana; lanar; — **trade** comercio m de lana.
wool gathering ['wul,gæðəriŋ] n: **to go** — estar en la luna de Valencia, estar en Babia.
woollen, (US) woolen ['wulən] **1** adj de lana; lanar, lanero; — **industry** industria f de la lana.
2 n npl ropa f (esp interior) de lana; (Comm) géneros mpl de lana.

woollies, (US) **woolies** ['wuliz] *npl* ropa *f* (*esp* interior) de lana.

woolliness, (US) **wooliness** ['wulinis] *n* lanosidad *f*; (*fig*) lo borroso; confusión *f*.

woolly, (US) **wooly** ['wuli] *adj* lanudo, lanoso; de lana; *outline etc* borroso; *idea* confuso.

woolman ['wulmæn] *n, pl* **—men** [men] comerciante *m* en lanas; dueño *m* de una fábrica textil, lanero *m*.

wool merchant ['wul,mə:tʃənt] *n* comerciante *m* en lanas, lanero *m*.

woolsack ['wulsæk] *n* saco *m* de lana (*silla del Gran Canciller en la Cámara de los Lores*).

woozy ['wu:zi] *adj* (*fam*) aturdido, confuso; (*Med*) ligeramente indispuesto.

wop [wɔp] *n* (*sl*) italiano *m*.

word [wə:d] **1** *n* (a) (*general sense*) palabra *f*; vocablo *m*; voz *f*, término *m*; **—s** (*of song*) letra *f*; **— for —** palabra por palabra; **— of honour** palabra *f*, palabra *f* de honor; **high —s** palabras *fpl* airadas, palabras *fpl* mayores; **fine —s** palabras *fpl* elocuentes (pero quizá poco sinceras); **a man of few —s** un hombre nada locuaz; **never a —** ni una palabra; **by — of mouth** de palabra; **too funny for —s** tremendamente divertido; **too stupid for —s** de lo más estúpido; **in a —** en una palabra; **in other —s** en otros términos; es decir . . ., esto es; **in the —s of** Calderón con palabras de Calderón, como dice Calderón; **with these —s he finished** diciendo esto terminó; **without a —** sin decir palabra; **a — to the wise is sufficient** al buen entendedor pocas palabras le bastan; **that's not the —** I would have chosen yo no me hubiera expresado así; **his — is law** su palabra es ley; **it's his — against mine** se trata de contraponer su testimonio al mío; **it's the last — in luxury** es la última palabra en lujo; **rough isn't the — for it** no hay que llamarlo brutal sino algo más fuerte; **—s fail me** no encuentro palabras para expresarme; **—s passed between them** cambiaron algunas palabras injuriosas; **not to breathe a —** no decir palabra, no decir ni pío; **to eat one's —s** desdecirse, retractarse; **I can't get a — out of him** no logro sacarle una palabra; **not to let someone get a — in edgeways** no dejar a uno meter baza; **to have a — with someone** cambiar unas palabras con uno; **I'll have a — with him about it** hablaré con él, lo discutiré con él, se lo mencionaré; **could I have a — with you?** ¿me hace el favor de escucharme un momento?; **to have —s with someone** reñir con uno; **to have the last — in an argument** salir victorioso de una discusión; **I won't hear a — against him** no permito que se le critique; **not to mince one's —s** no tener pelos en la lengua, no morderse la lengua; **to put in a — for someone** defender a uno, hablar por uno; **she didn't say so in so many —s** no lo dijo exactamente así, no lo dijo así concretamente; **he never said a —** no dijo una sola palabra; **don't say a — about this** de esto no digas ni pío; **nobody had a good — to say for him** nadie quería defenderle, nadie habló en su favor; **I now call on Mr X to say a few —s** ahora le cedo la palabra al Señor X; **you took the —s right out of my mouth** me quitaste la palabra de la boca.

(b) (*message*) aviso *m*, recado *m*; noticia *f*; **— came that . . .** llegó noticia de que . . ., se supo que . . .; **to bring — of something to someone** llevar a uno la noticia de algo; **to leave —** dejar recado; **to leave — that . . .** dejar dicho que . . .; **to send —** mandar recado; **to send someone — of something** avisar a uno de algo.

(c) (*promise*) palabra *f*; (**upon**) **my —!** ¡caramba!; **he is a man of his —** es hombre de entera confianza; **his — is as good as his bond** su palabra merece entera confianza; **to be as good as one's —** cumplir lo prometido; **to break one's —** faltar a la palabra; **to give someone one's — that . . .** prometer que . . .; **to go back on one's —** faltar a la palabra; **to keep one's —** cumplir su promesa, cumplir lo prometido; **take my — for it** te lo aseguro; **I take your — for it** acepto lo que Vd me dice, lo creo; **to take someone at his —** coger a uno la palabra.

(d) (*order*) orden *f*; (*pass—*) santo *m* y seña; **— of command** voz *f* de mando; **the — has gone round that . . .** se ha transmitido la orden de que . . .; **to give the —** dar la orden; **you have only to say the —** solamente hace falta que Vd dé la orden.

(e) (*Rel*) Verbo *m*; **the W— of God** el Verbo de Dios.

2 *vt* redactar; expresar; **a well—ed declaration** una declaración bien expresada; **how shall we — it?** ¿cómo lo expresamos?

wordbook ['wə:dbuk] *n* vocabulario *m*.

word count ['wə:dkaunt] *n* recuento *m* de vocabulario.

word game ['wə:dgeim] *n* juego *m* de formación (*or* adivinación *etc*) de palabras.

wordiness ['wə:dinis] *n* verbosidad *f*, prolijidad *f*.

wording ['wə:diŋ] *n* fraseología *f*, estilo *m*; términos *mpl*.

word list ['wə:dlist] *n* lista *f* de palabras, vocabulario *m*.

word-of-mouth ['wə:dəv'mauθ] *adj* verbal, oral; *see also* word 1 (a).

word perfect ['wə:d'pə:fikt] *adj*: **to be —** saber perfectamente su papel.

wordplay ['wə:dplei] *n* juego *m* de palabras.

wordy ['wə:di] *adj* verboso, prolijo.

wore [wɔ:*] *pret of* **wear.**

work [wə:k] **1** *n* (a) (*in general*) trabajo *m*; empleo *m*, ocupación *f*; **to be at —** estar trabajando; estar en la fábrica, estar en la oficina (*etc*); tener trabajo; **there are forces at —** hay fuerzas en movimiento; **to be in —** tener trabajo, tener un empleo; **to be out of —** estar desempleado; estar parado, no tener trabajo; *see* off 3 (d); **to put** (*or* throw) **someone out of —** privar a uno de trabajo; **to make short — of something** concluir algo con toda rapidez, (*fig*) comerse algo rápidamente; **to go the right way to —** empezar correctamente; **to set to —** ponerse a trabajar, (*fig*) poner manos a la obra; **to set someone to —** poner a uno a trabajar.

(b) (*task, — to be done*) trabajo *m*; labor *f*; **a piece of —** un trabajo, una labor; **domestic —** trabajo *m* de casa, labor *f* doméstica; **social —** asistencia *f* social; **day's —** jornal *m*; **it's all in a day's —** estamos acostumbrados a eso; **it's thirsty —**, **it's warm —** es un trabajo que hace sudar; **it was grim —** (*fig*) fue una cosa repugnante; **there's been dirty — (at the crossroads)** en esto no se ha jugado limpio, han pasado cosas asquerosas; **it's nice — if you can get it** (*fig*) es muy agradable para los que tienen esa suerte; **— has been begun on the new dam** se han comenzado las obras del nuevo embalse; **it's closed for — on the steeple** está cerrado debido a las obras del campanario; **I have my — cut out as it is** ya tengo trabajo hasta por encima de las cejas; **I had my — cut out to stop it** tuve que hacer grandes esfuerzos para detenerlo; **you'll have your — cut out trying to stop him** le costará muchísimo trabajo impedirle; **to do one's —** hacer su trabajo; **the medicine had done its —** la medicina había tenido efecto; **to do someone's dirty — for him** sacar a uno las castañas del fuego.

(c) (*product: Art, Lit etc*) obra *f*; **the —s of God** las obras de Dios; **good —s** buenas obras *fpl*; **a literary —** una obra literaria; **— of art** obra *f* de arte; **the —s of Cervantes** las obras de Cervantes; **collected —s, complete —s** obras *fpl* completas; **— of reference** libro *m* de consulta; **standard —** obra *f* clásica.

(d) **—s** (*Mil*) obras *fpl*, fortificaciones *fpl*; **defensive —s** fortificaciones *fpl*; **public —s** obras *fpl* públicas; **road —s** obras *fpl* de carretera; **Ministry of W—s** Ministerio *m* de Obras Públicas.

(e) **—s** (*Mech*) mecanismo *m*; motor *m*.

(f) **—s** (*factory*) fábrica *f*; taller *m*; *eg* **gasworks** fábrica *f* de gas.

2 *vt* (a) (*cause to —*) **men** hacer trabajar; **they —ed us from 8 till 6** nos hicieron trabajar de 8 a 6.

(b) (*Mech etc*) *machine* hacer funcionar; manejar, operar; *brake* accionar; *moving part* mover; **it is —ed by electricity** funciona con electricidad, es accionado por electricidad; **can you — it?** ¿sabes manejarlo?; **can we — that scheme again?** ¿podemos volver a emplear ese sistema?; **he —ed the lever up and down** movió la palanca hacia arriba y hacia abajo.

(c) (*bring out*) *change* producir, motivar; *miracle, cure etc* hacer, efectuar, operar; *mischief* hacer; **to — it** lograrlo, conseguirlo, manejar las cosas; **they —ed it so that she could come** se las arreglaron para que ella pudiese venir; **they —ed his promotion** agenciaron su ascenso, hicieron diligencias para asegurar su ascenso.

(d) (*Sew*) bordar; **—ed with blue thread** bordado de hilo azul.

(e) *wood etc* tallar; *metal* trabajar.

(f) *mine* explotar; *land* cultivar; **he —s the eastern part of the province** él trabaja en la parte este de la provincia; él se dedica a cubrir la parte este de la provincia; **we —ed the river bank looking for the plant** recorrimos la orilla del río buscando la planta; **this land has not been —ed for many years** estas tierras hace mucho tiempo que no se cultivan.

(g) **to — one's passage on a boat** pagar el precio del viaje en un barco haciendo trabajos de marinero (etc), viajar gratis en un barco a cambio de trabajar como marinero.

(h) (manoeuvre etc) ship maniobrar; **to — an incident into a book** introducir un episodio en un libro; **we'll try to — in a reference somewhere** trataremos de insinuar una referencia en alguna parte; **can't you — me into your plans?** ¿no sería posible dejarme entrar a formar parte de tus proyectos?; **to — one's hands free** lograr soltar las manos; **to — one's way to the top of the company** llegar a ocupar un alto puesto en la sociedad a fuerza de trabajar; **to — one's way up a cliff** escalar a duras penas un precipicio, escalar poco a poco un precipicio (and see way (d)).

(i) (with adv or prep) **to — something in** introducir algo poco a poco; **to — off one's feelings** desahogarse, aliviarse; **to — off one's surplus fat** quitarse sus grasas excesivas trabajando; **don't — your bad temper off on me!** ¡no desahogue Vd su mal humor en mí!; **to — out** problem resolver; sum calcular, hacer; idea desarrollar; plan trazar, elaborar; mine etc agotar; **to — out one's salvation** determinar su suerte; **to — out one's time** servir el plazo de su aprendizaje; **who —ed all this out?** ¿quién ideó todo esto?; **the mine is —ed out** la mina está agotada; **to — up** business desarrollar, fomentar; theme desarrollar, elaborar; feelings excitar; **the speaker was —ing them up into a frenzy** el orador excitaba los ánimos hasta el frenesí; **it gets me properly —ed up** me emociona mucho, con esto me emociono mucho; **to get —ed up** exaltarse, sofocarse; **now don't get —ed up!** ¡no te exaltes!; ¡cálmate!; **together they —ed the business up from nothing** entre los dos crearon el negocio de la nada.

3 vi (a) (general sense) trabajar (at, on en); (be in a job) tener trabajo, tener un empleo; **to — hard** trabajar mucho; **to — like a maniac** (or a Trojan etc) trabajar como un negro, trabajar como un demonio; **what are you —ing at now?** ¿en qué trabajas ahora?, (more generally) ¿a qué te dedicas ahora?

(b) (Mech etc) funcionar, marchar; **it won't —** no funciona; **"not —ing"** (lift etc) "no funciona"; **to get something —ing** hacer funcionar algo; reparar algo para que funcione; **it —s off the mains** funciona con electricidad de la red, se conecta con la red; **the motor —s with gas** el motor funciona con gas.

(c) (of medicine etc) ser eficaz, surtir efecto, obrar; **how long does it take to —?** ¿cuánto tiempo hace falta para que empiece a surtir efecto?; **this can — both ways** esto puede ser un arma de dos filos, esto puede ser contraproducente; **the scheme won't —** el proyecto no es práctico, esto no será factible, el proyecto no tendrá resultados útiles; **it won't —, I tell you!** ¡te digo que no se puede (hacer)!

(d) (of yeast) fermentar.

(e) (of mouth, face) torcerse, moverse.

(f) **to — loose** see loose.

(g) (with adv or prep) **to — in** penetrar poco a poco, calarse; **to — off** separarse, soltarse (con el uso); **to — on** (adv) seguir trabajando; **what are you —ing on?** ¿a qué se dedica Vd?, ¿qué trae Vd entre manos?; **they —ed on the car for 2 days** durante 2 días trabajaron en la reparación del coche; **they will get —ing on it at once** empezarán la reparación (etc) en seguida; **the police are —ing on it** la policía lo está investigando; **have you any clue to — on?** ¿tienen alguna pista que seguir?; **there are few facts to — on** apenas hay datos en que basarse; **we — on the principle that...** nos atenemos al principio de que...; **they —ed on him for 3 hours** durante 3 horas se esforzaron por persuadirle; **to — out** resultar; resolverse; **it doesn't — out** (of sum) parece que no hay solución; **it —s out at £8** llega a 8 libras, asciende a 8 libras, viene a sumar 8 libras; **how much does it — out at?** ¿cuánto suma?; **everything —ed out extremely well** todo resultó ser perfecto, la cosa salió perfectamente; **how did it — out?** ¿qué tal salió?, ¿qué resultados tuvo?; **what are you —ing up to?** ¿qué propósito tiene todo esto?; **I thought he was —ing up to a proposal** creía que estaba preparando el terreno para hacerme una declaración.

4 vr: **to — oneself to death** matarse trabajando, matarse con exceso de trabajo; **to — oneself into a frenzy** excitarse hasta el frenesí, exaltarse en grado extremo; **to — oneself up** exaltarse, sofocarse.

workable ['wəːkəbl] adj práctico, factible.

workaday ['wəːkədei] adj de cada día; (fig) rutinario, prosaico.

workbasket ['wəːk,bɑːskit] n (Sew) neceser m de costura.

workbench ['wəːkbentʃ] n obrador m, banco m de trabajo.

workbook ['wəːkbuk] n libro m de trabajo; (School) cuaderno m.

workbox ['wəːkbɔks] n neceser m de costura.

workday ['wəːkdei] n día m laborable.

worker ['wəːkə*] n trabajador m, ora f; obrero m, a f (also Pol); operario m, a f; (ant) obrera f; **research —** investigador m, ora f; **skilled —** obrero m cualificado, obrera f cualificada; **all the —s in the industry** todos los trabajadores de la industria; **what about the —s?** ¿y los obreros?, ¡justicia para los obreros!; **he's a fast —** trabaja con toda prisa; (fig) obra con mucha prontitud.

worker ant ['wəːkərænt] n hormiga f obrera.

worker bee ['wəːkəbiː] n abeja f obrera.

worker priest ['wəːkəpriːst] n sacerdote m obrero.

workhouse ['wəːkhaus] n, pl **—houses** [,hauziz] asilo m de pobres; asilo m de ancianos; asilo m para desamparados.

working ['wəːkiŋ] 1 adj, attr model que funciona; capital, expenses de explotación; day laborable; class obrero; face etc (Min) de trabajo; population, partner etc activo; majority suficiente; hypothesis de guía; see day, order etc.

2 n trabajo m, el trabajar; funcionamiento m; explotación f; manejo m, operación f; labra f, laboreo m; **—s** (Min etc) labores fpl.

working-class ['wəːkiŋklɑːs] adj de la clase obrera.

working clothes ['wəːkiŋkləuðz] npl ropa f de trabajo.

working man ['wəːkiŋmæn] n, pl **— men** [men] obrero m.

working party ['wəːkiŋ,pɑːti] n comisión f de investigación.

workman ['wəːkmən] n, pl **—men** [mən] obrero m; trabajador m; **to be a good —** ser buen trabajador, trabajar bien.

workmanlike ['wəːkmənlaik] adj competente, hábil (pero no brillante).

workmanship ['wəːkmənʃip] n hechura f; arte m, artificio m; destreza f, habilidad f; **of fine —** esmerado, exquisito.

workout ['wəːkaut] n (Sport) (período m de) entrenamiento m, ejercicios mpl.

workpeople ['wəːk,piːpl] n obreros mpl; personal m, mano f de obra.

workroom ['wəːkrum] n taller m, sala f de trabajo.

work sharing ['wəːk,ʃeəriŋ] n repartimiento m del trabajo (entre los obreros de una fábrica, para evitar el desempleo).

workshop ['wəːkʃɔp] n taller m.

workshy ['wəːkʃai] adj gandul, holgazán.

world [wəːld] 1 n (a) (general sense, Geog) mundo m, tierra f; **all the — over** en todas partes del mundo; **are there — s other than ours?** ¿existen otros mundos aparte de éste nuestro?; **it's a small —** el mundo es un pañuelo; **to feel on top of the —** estar como un reloj; **to go round the —** dar la vuelta al mundo; **to have the best of both —s** salir ganando cualquiera que sea el resultado; **to knock about the —**, to see the — ver mundo; **he lives in a — of his own** habita un pequeño mundo suyo, queda absorto en sus cosas sin prestar atención a otros.

(b) **New W—** Nuevo Mundo m; **Old W—** Viejo Mundo m.

(c) (realm) mundo m; **the — of sport**, **the sporting —** el mundo deportivo, el mundo de los deportes; **the business —** el mundo comercial, los negocios; **the animal —** el reino animal; **the Roman —** el mundo romano; **the — of dreams** el mundo de la fantasía, el mundo de los sueños.

(d) **man of the —** hombre m de mundo; **to come down in the —** venir a menos; **to go up in the —** ir adelante; hacer progresos en su carrera, ser ascendido; **to have the —** at one's feet triunfar, estar en la cumbre de la fama (etc); **to take the — as it is** adaptarse a la realidad, aceptar la vida como es; see lead, rise etc.

(e) (this life, Rel etc) mundo m; siglo m; **the other —**, **the next —**, **the — to come** el otro mundo; **— without end** por los siglos de los siglos; **in the —** (Eccl) en el siglo; **in this —** en esta vida; **it's out of** this — es tremendo, es increíble; **he's not long for this** — le queda poco tiempo de vida; **to bring into the** — echar al mundo; **to come into the** — nacer; **to go to a better** — pasar a mejor vida.

(f) *(emphatic idioms etc)* **not for all the** — por nada del mundo; **nothing in the** — would make me do it, I wouldn't do it for the — no lo haría por nada del mundo; **what in the** — can I do about it? ¿qué demonios puedo hacer?; **it's what she most wants in the** — es lo que ella más desea sobre todas las cosas; **to be alone in the** — estar totalmente solo, estar completamente desamparado; **it was for all the** — **as if** ... fue exactamente como si + subj; **I'm the** —**'s worst cook** yo soy el peor cocinero del mundo; **she's all the** — te mare para mí ella importa más que cualquier otra persona; **since the** — **began** desde que el mundo es mundo; **to be dead to the** — *(asleep)* estar profundamente dormido, *(drunk)* estar completamente borracho; **to think the** — **of someone** tener un altísimo concepto de uno.

2 *attr* mundial; universal; — **champion** campeón *m* mundial; — **fair** feria *f* mundial; — **language** lengua *f* universal; **on a** — **scale** a escala mundial.

World Bank ['wə:ld'bæŋk] *n* Banco *m* Mundial.

world-famous ['wə:ld'feiməs] *adj* mundialmente conocido, famosísimo.

worldliness ['wə:ldlinis] *n* mundanería *f*.

worldly ['wə:ldli] *adj* mundano.

worldly-wisdom ['wə:ldli'wizdəm] *n* mundología *f*; astucia *f*.

worldly-wise ['wə:ldli'waiz] *adj* que tiene mucho mundo; astuto.

world-weariness ['wə:ld'wiərinis] *n* hastío *m*.

world-weary ['wə:ld'wiəri] *adj* hastiado, cansado de la vida.

world-wide ['wə:ld'waid] *adj* mundial, universal.

worm [wə:m] **1** *n* **(a)** *(grub)* gusano *m*; *(earth-)* lombriz *f*; *(person)* canalla *m*, persona *f* de lo más vil; —**s** *(Med)* lombrices *fpl*; **the** — **will turn** un día se acabará la paciencia del más sufrido.

(b) *(Mech)* tornillo *m* sin fin.

2 *vt*: **to** — **one's way along** arrastrarse como un gusano; **to** — **one's way into a group** insinuarse en un grupo, introducirse astutamente en un grupo; **to** — **a secret out of someone** arrancar *(or* sonsacar*)* un secreto a uno.

3 *vr*: **to** — **oneself along** arrastrarse como un gusano; **to** — **oneself through something** atravesar algo serpenteando.

worm drive ['wə:mdraiv] *n* *(Mech)* transmisión *f* por tornillo sin fin.

worm-eaten ['wə:m,i:tn] *adj* *wood* carcomido; *cloth* apolillado.

worm gear ['wə:mgiə*] *n* engranaje *m* de tornillo sin fin.

wormhole ['wə:mhəul] *n* agujero *m* de gusano; picadura *f* de polilla.

wormwood ['wə:mwud] *n* ajenjo *m*; *(fig)* hiel *f*, amargura *f*.

wormy ['wə:mi] *adj* gusanoso, agusanado, lleno de gusanos; carcomido: apolillado.

worn [wɔ:n] *ptp* of **wear**.

worn-out ['wɔ:n'aut] *adj* gastado; estropeado; inservible; inútil; anticuado; **to be** — *(person)* estar rendido.

worried ['wʌrid] *adj* *tone, look etc* inquieto, preocupado; **to be** — **about something** inquietarse por algo, estar preocupado por algo; **to look** — tener aire preocupado, parecer estar inquieto.

worrier ['wʌriə*] *n* aprensivo *m*, a *f*; **he's a terrible** — es muy aprensivo, se inquieta por cualquier cosa.

worrisome ['wʌrisəm] *adj* inquietante; aprensivo.

worry ['wʌri] **1** *n* inquietud *f*, preocupación *f*; cuidado *m*; problema *m*; **financial worries** preocupaciones *fpl* de tipo financiero; **he had business worries** tenía problemas con sus negocios: **it's a great** — **to us** all nos trae a todos muy preocupados; **what's your** —? ¿qué mosca te ha picado?, ¿qué problema es éste?; **the** — **of having to** + *infin* el problema de tener que + *infin*; **to settle someone's** —**s** resolver los problemas de uno.

2 *vt* **(a)** inquietar, intranquilizar, preocupar; molestar; **that photo worries me** esa foto me inquieta; no estoy satisfecho con esa foto; **what worries me is not that at all** no es eso lo que me preocupa; **it worries me terribly** me tiene preocupadísimo; **that doesn't** — **me in the least** eso me tiene absolutamente sin cuidado.

(b) *(of dog etc)* *prey* pillar, sacudir y morder, morder sacudiendo; **that dog worries sheep** el

perro ese ataca las ovejas; **is this man worrying you, madam?** ¿le molesta este hombre, señora?

(c) to — **out a problem** esforzarse por resolver un problema, devanarse los sesos para resolver un problema; **finally we worried it out** por fin lo resolvimos a costa de mucho trabajo.

3 *vi* inquietarse, preocuparse *(about, over* por*)*; apurarse; molestarse; **he worries a lot** se apura por cualquier cosa; **don't** —! ¡no se preocupe!; ¡descuida!; **it's all right, don't** — está bien, no se moleste; **don't** — **about me** no te preocupes por mí; **I should** —! y a mí ¿qué?

worrying ['wʌriiŋ] *adj* inquietante.

worse [wə:s] **1** *adj comp of* **bad**; peor; inferior; **A is** — **than B** A es peor que B, A es inferior a B; **— and** —! ¡peor todavía!; **it gets** — **and** — va de mal en peor; **it's** — **than ever** es peor que nunca; **it could have been** —! ¡menos mal!; **it would have been** — **if** ... hubiera sido más grave si ... ; **it will be the** — **for you** será peor para Vd; **so much the** — **for him** tanto peor para él; **to be the** — **for drink** estar algo borracho; **to be the** — **for wear** estar deteriorado *(and see* wear*)*; **he is none the** — **for it** no se ha hecho daño; la experiencia no le ha hecho mal *(and see* none*)*; **to get** —, **to grow** — empeorar, hacerse peor, *(Med)* ponerse peor; **to make a situation** — hacer una situación más difícil; **to make matters** — para colmo de desgracias; **I don't think any the** — **of you** esto no afecta la opinión que tengo de Vd.

2 *adv comp of* **badly**; **it hurts** — me duele más; **she behaves** — **than ever** se comporta peor que nunca; **you might do** — hay cosas peores; **you might do** — **than to** + *infin* sería quizá posible + *infin*, quizá sea aconsejable + *infin*; **he is now** — **off than before** ahora está en peores circunstancias que antes, ahora está en una situación más apurada que antes; **we are** — **off than them for books** en cuanto a libros nosotros estamos peores que ellos.

3 *n* el peor, lo peor; **there is** — **to come** hay más, todavía no te he dicho *(etc)* lo peor; **it's changed for the** — ha cambiado y está peor; *see* **bad**.

worsen ['wə:sn] **1** *vt* agravar, hacer peor; hacer más difícil.

2 *vi* empeorar, hacerse peor; agravarse; hacerse más difícil; *(Med)* ponerse peor.

worship ['wə:ʃip] **1** *n* **(a)** *(adoration)* adoración *f*, veneración *f*; *(organized* —*)* culto *m* *(of* a*)*; *(church service)* culto *m*, oficio *m*; **with a look of** — con una mirada llena de adoración; **place of** — edificio *m* de culto. **(b)** *(in titles)* **His W—** the Mayor of X el señor alcalde de X; **Your W—** *(to judge)* señor juez, *(to mayor)* señor alcalde; **if your w—** **wishes** *(iro)* si el caballero lo desea. 2 *vt* adorar *(also fig)*, venerar.

worshipful ['wə:ʃipful] *adj* *(in titles)* excelentísimo.

worshipper ['wə:ʃipə*] *n* adorador *m*, ora *f*, devoto *m*, a *f*; —**s** *(collectively)* fieles *mpl*.

worst [wə:st] **1** *adj superl of* **bad**; (el) peor; **the** — **film of the three** la peor película de las tres.

2 *adv superl of* **badly**; peor; **I did it** — yo lo hice peor.

3 *n* lo peor; **in the** — **of the winter** en lo más recio del invierno; **in the** — **of the storm** en el peor momento de la tormenta; **when the crisis was at its** — en el momento más grave de la crisis; **at (the)** — en el peor de los casos; **that's the** — **of it** ésa es la peor parte; **the** — **of it is that** ... lo peor del caso es que ... ; **if the** — **comes to the** — si pasa lo peor; **do your** —! ¡haga todo lo que quiera!; **to get the** — **of it** salir perdiendo, llevar la peor parte, sufrir más que su contrincante; **to give someone the** — **of it** derrotar a uno; **we're over** *(or* **past***)* **the** — **of it now** hemos vencido la cuesta ya; **once you get the** — **over** en cuanto salves el bache.

worsted ['wustid] *n* estambre *m*.

worth [wə:θ] **1** *adj* **(a)** *(in monetary senses)* equivalente a, que vale, del valor de; **it's** — £5 vale 5 libras; **what's this** —? ¿cuánto vale esto?; **it's not** — **much** no vale mucho; apenas tiene valor; **he was** — **a million when he died** murió millonario, murió dejando una fortuna de un millón; **one Ruritanian is** — **3 Slobodians** un ruritano vale por *(or* equivale a*)* 3 eslobodios; **I tell you this for what it's** — te digo esto sin poder afirmar que sea cierto, te digo esto por si acaso el dato te interesa; **to run for all one is** — correr a todo correr; **to sing for all one is** — cantar con toda el alma.

(b) *(deserving)* digno de, que merece; **it's not** — **it, it's not** — **the trouble** no vale la pena; **a thing** — **having** una cosa digna de ser poseída, una cosa que vale la pena adquirir; **is the book — buying?** ¿me vale la pena comprar el libro?; **it's — thinking about** merece que se considere, merece consideración; *see* while.

2 *n* (*monetary*) valor *m*; (*fig*) valía *f*, mérito *m*; **£10's — of books** libros *mpl* por valor de 10 libras; **5 pesetas' — of sweets** 5 pesetas de bombones; **he had no chance to show his true —** no tuvo ocasión de demostrar su verdadera valía; **his moral — is not in question** no se trata de su valor moral; **what's the — of this table?** ¿cuánto vale esta mesa?; *see* **money's-worth**.

worthily ['wəːðili] *adv* dignamente; **to respond — to an occasion** estar a la altura de las circunstancias.

worthiness ['wəːðinis] *n* mérito *m*, merecimiento *m*.

worthless ['wəːθlis] *adj* sin valor; inútil, que no vale para nada; **a — individual** una persona despreciable, una persona sin carácter; **he's not completely —** no es que carezca absolutamente de buenas cualidades.

worthlessness ['wəːθlisnis] *n* falta *f* de valor; inutilidad *f*; lo despreciable, falta *f* de carácter.

worthwhile ['wəːθ'wail] *adj* valioso, útil; digno de consideración; que vale la pena; **a — film** una película seria, una película que merece atención; *see also* **while**.

worthy ['wəːði] **1** *adj* (a) meritorio; benemérito; respetable; loable, plausible; *motive etc* honesto, honrado; **a — person** una persona respetable; **your — newspaper** (*letter to editor*) su estimado periódico.

(b) **— of** digno de; **— of remark** notable, digno de notar; **— of respect** digno de respeto, respetable; **to be — of something** digno de algo, merecer algo; **it is — of note that . . .** vale observar que . . . ; es notable que . . . ; **that comment was not — of you** esa observación fue indigna de Vd; **the car is — of a better driver** el coche merece tener mejor conductor.

2 *n* personaje *m*; dignatario *m*.

would [wud] *v aux* **1** (a) (*used to form conditional tense*) **she — come** vendría; **if you asked him he — do it** si se lo pidieras lo haría; **if you had asked him he — have done it** si se lo hubieras pedido lo habría hecho (*or* lo hubiera hecho); **I thought you — want to know** se me figuraba que desearías enterarte.

(b) (*conditional, emphatic*) **you — be the one to forget** desde luego eres tú el que se olvida.

(c) (*conditional, probability*) **it — seem so** así parece ser; **it — be about 8 o'clock** serían las 8.

(d) (*conjecture*) **what — this be?** ¿esto qué será?

2 (a) (*wish*) querer; **what — you have me do?** ¿qué quieres que haga?; **try as he —** por mucho que se esforzara, por más que intentase; **the place where I — be** el lugar donde me gustaría estar; **— (that) it were not so!** ¡ojalá no fuera así!; **— to God!, — to heaven!** ¡ojalá!

(b) (*consent*) querer; **— you care for some tea?** ¿quieres una taza de té?; **— you tell me your name?** ¿me hace el favor de darme su nombre?; **he — not do it** no quería hacerlo, se negó a hacerlo.

(c) (*habit*) **he — paint it each year** solía pintarlo cada año, lo pintaba cada año.

would-be ['wudbiː] *adj*: **a — poet** un aspirante a poeta, uno que presume de poeta, uno que quiere ser poeta.

wouldn't ['wudnt] = **would not**.

wound [wuːnd] **1** *n* herida *f*; **deep —** herida *f* profunda; **skin —** herida *f* superficial; **to lick one's —s** lamer sus heridas.

2 *vt* herir (*also fig*); **the —ed** los heridos; **to — someone's feelings** herir los sentimientos de uno.

wound [waund] *pret and ptp of* **wind**.

wounding ['wuːndiŋ] *adj remark, tone* hiriente, mordaz.

wove [wəuv] *pret of* **weave**.

woven ['wəuvən] *ptp of* **weave**.

wow [wau] *n* (*sl*): **it's a —!** ¡es tremendo!

wrack[1] [ræk] *n* (*Bot*) fuco *m*.

wrack[2] [ræk] *see* **rack**[1] *and* **rack**[2].

wraith [reiθ] *n* fantasma *m*.

wrangle ['ræŋgl] **1** *n* altercado *m*, riña *f* (indecorosa).

2 *vi* reñir (indecorosamente) (*about, over* a causa de, *with* con); (*in bargaining*) regatear.

wrap [ræp] **1** *n* (*indoor*) bata *f*, (*outdoor*) abrigo *m*.

2 *vt* (*also to — up*) envolver; (*for warmth*) arropar; (*cover*) cubrir; **shall I — it up for you?** ¿quiere que se lo envuelva?; **he does so — it up** (*fig*) lo dice con tal exceso de palabras, lo expone de manera tan enmarañada; **to be —ped up in** estar envuelto en; (*fig*) estar absorto en, estar completamente dedicado a; **he is —ped up in her** no quiere pensar en nada

sino en ella, le dedica todas sus atenciones a ella; **they are —ped up in each other** están absortos el uno en el otro.

3 *vi*: **to — up** arroparse, arrebujarse; **— up!** (*sl*) ¡cállate!; **see that you — up warm** cuida de arroparte bien.

wrapper ['ræpə*] *n* envoltura *f*, envase *m*; (*of book*) sobrecubierta *f*, camisa *f*; (*postal*) faja *f*.

wrapping ['ræpiŋ] *n* envoltura *f*.

wrapping paper ['ræpiŋˌpeipə*] *n* papel *m* de envolver.

wrath [rɔθ] *n* (*lit*) cólera *f*, ira *f*; (*fig*) ira *f*.

wrathful ['rɔθful] *adj* (*lit*) colérico, airado.

wrathfully ['rɔθfəli] *adv* coléricamente, airadamente.

wreak [riːk] *vt* (*lit*) ejecutar; *destruction etc* hacer, causar; *vengeance* tomar (*on* en); *anger* descargar (*on* en); *punishment* infligir (*on* en); **to — havoc** hacer estragos.

wreath [riːθ] *n*, *pl* **wreaths** [riːðz] (*of flowers etc*) guirnalda *f*, (*funeral* —) corona *f*; (*of smoke*) espiral *f*; **laurel —** corona *f* de laurel.

wreathe [riːð] **1** *vt* (*encircle*) ceñir, rodear (*with* de); (*plait*) trenzar; entrelazar; (*garland*) enguirnaldar (*with* con); **to — flowers into one's hair** ponerse flores en el pelo; **a face —d in smiles** una cara muy sonriente, una cara muy risueña; **trees —d in mist** árboles *mpl* envueltos en niebla.

2 *vi* (*of smoke etc*; *also* **to — upwards**) enroscarse, formar espirales, elevarse en espirales.

wreck [rek] **1** *n* (a) (*Naut act*) naufragio *m*; (*ship*) buque *m* naufragado, buque *m* hundido; **the ship was a total —** el buque se consideró como totalmente perdido, fue imposible salvar el buque.

(b) (*Rail etc*) colisión *f*, accidente *m*.

(c) (*fig*) ruina *f*, destrucción *f*; **the — of one's hopes** la ruina de las esperanzas de uno; **he's a —** es un carcamal; **I'm a —, I feel a —** estoy hecho polvo; **she's a nervous —** tiene una tremenda tensión nerviosa; **I'm a nervous —** tengo los nervios de punta; **if this goes on I shall be a nervous —** si las cosas siguen así acabaré con los nervios destrozados; **she looks a —** está hecha una pena.

2 *vt* (a) (*ship*) hacer naufragar, hundir, destruir; *train* descarrilar; *car, plane, mechanism etc* estropear, destrozar; **you've —ed my gears** Vd ha estropeado la caja de cambios; **to be —ed** (*Naut*) naufragar, irse a pique, ser hundido; **the ship was —ed on those rocks** el buque naufragó en aquellas rocas.

(b) (*fig*) *hopes etc* arruinar, destruir, acabar con.

wreckage ['rekidʒ] *n* (a) (*act*) naufragio *m*; (*fig*) naufragio *m*, ruina *f*, destrucción *f*.

(b) (*remains: Naut*) pecios *mpl*, restos *mpl* de un buque naufragado; (*of car etc*) restos *mpl*; (*of house etc*) escombros *mpl*, ruinas *fpl*.

wrecked [rekt] *adj ship* naufragado, hundido; *car etc* estropeado, averiado.

wrecker ['rekə*] *n* (*Naut*) raquero *m*; (*Rail*) descarrilador *m*; (*fig*) destructor *m*, ora *f*.

wrecking service ['rekiŋˌsəːvis] *n* (*Aut*) servicio *m* de auxilio (para coches averiados).

wren [ren] *n* chochín *m*.

wrench [rentʃ] **1** *n* (*tug*) arranque *m*, tirón *m*; (*Med*) torcedura *f*; **to give something a —** tirar violentamente de algo, torcer algo violentamente; **to give one's arm a —** torcerse el brazo.

(b) (*tool*) llave *f* inglesa.

(c) (*fig*) dolor *m*; sacudida *f*; choque *m*; **the — of parting** el dolor de la separación, la angustia de la separación; **it was a — to have to leave** me causó pena tener que partir.

2 *vt* arrancar, tirar violentamente de; **to — one's arm** torcerse el brazo, dislocarse el brazo; **to — something (away) from someone** arrebatar algo violentamente a uno; **to — something off** quitar algo torciéndolo violentamente; **to — a door open** abrir una puerta tirando violentamente de ella; **to — a bulb out** sacar una bombilla torciéndola violentamente.

wrest [rest] **1** *vt*: **to — something from someone** arrebatar algo a uno, arrancar algo a uno; **to — gold from the rocks** extraer a duras penas oro de las rocas; **to — a living from the soil** ganarse la vida cultivando con mucha dificultad el suelo.

2 *vr*: **to — oneself free** (lograr) libertarse tras grandes esfuerzos; **try to — yourself free** procura soltarte haciendo un esfuerzo.

wrestle ['resl] **1** *n* lucha *f*; partido *m* de lucha; **to have a — with someone** luchar con uno.

2 *vt* luchar con, luchar contra.

3 *vi* luchar (*with* con, *contra*); **to — with** (*fig*) luchar con; **we are wrestling with the problem** estamos luchando con el problema, nos esforzamos por resolver el problema; **the pilot —d with the controls** el piloto luchaba con los mandos.

wrestler ['reslə*] n luchador m (de lucha libre).

wrestling ['resliŋ] n lucha f libre.

wrestling match ['resliŋmætʃ] n partido m de lucha.

wretch [retʃ] n desgraciado m, a f, infeliz mf; **little —** (often hum) tunante m, pícaro m, a f; **some poor —** algún desgraciado, algún pobre diablo; **you —!** (hum) ¡canalla!

wretched ['retʃid] adj (unfortunate) desgraciado, desdichado; (contemptible) miserable, despreciable; pobre, lamentable; (very bad) horrible; (ill) malo, enfermo; **that — dog** ese maldito perro; **where's that — stick?** ¿dónde está el condenado bastón ese?; **it's — weather** hace un tiempo horrible; **what — luck!** ¡qué mala suerte!; **I'm a — player** juego malísimamente; **to feel —** (Med) sentirse muy mal; (depressed) estar deprimido, estar abatido; **I felt — about it** me daba grandes remordimientos.

wretchedly ['retʃidli] adv lamentablemente; horriblemente; muy mal; **to be — unlucky** tener malísima suerte; **she plays —** toca horriblemente mal; **they treated her —** la trataron de modo infame.

wretchedness ['retʃidnis] n desgracia f, desdicha f; lo despreciable; lo lamentable; lo horrible; infamia f; depresión f, abatimiento m.

wrick [rik] **1** n torcedura f. **2** vt torcer; **to — one's neck** darse un torticolis.

wriggle ['rigl] **1** n meneo m; serpenteo m, culebreo m. **2** vt menear; ears, hips etc mover; **to — one's way into** deslizarse en, introducirse (con dificultad) en; **to — one's way through** lograr pasar (con dificultad) por. **3** vi menearse; (also **to — along**) culebrear, moverse culebreando, avanzar serpenteando; **to — away** escaparse culebreando; **to — out of a difficulty** escapar mañosamente de un apuro; **to — through a hole** pasar (culebreando, con dificultad) por un agujero; **to — with pain** retorcerse de dolor.

wriggly ['rigli] adj sinuoso, tortuoso.

wring [riŋ] (irr: pret and ptp **wrung**) **1** vt (a) torcer, retorcer; clothes exprimir el agua de, escurrir; hands retorcer; animal's neck torcer; **to — clothes out** escurrir la ropa; **to — water out of clothes** exprimir el agua de la ropa.

(b) (fig) heart etc acongojar, apenar; **to — money out of someone** sacar dinero por la fuerza a uno; **to — a concession out of someone** persuadir a uno (tras muchos esfuerzos) a hacer una concesión, lograr (con dificultad) que uno haga una concesión; **eventually we wrung the truth out of them** por fin logramos que nos dijeran la verdad.

2 n: **to give clothes a —** exprimir el agua de la ropa.

wringer ['riŋə*] n escurridor m, máquina f de exprimir.

wringing ['riŋiŋ] adj: **to be — (wet)** estar completamente mojado, (person) estar mojado hasta los huesos.

wrinkle[1] ['riŋkl] **1** n arruga f; pliegue m. **2** vt arrugar; brow fruncir. **3** vi arrugarse; plegarse, ajarse.

wrinkle[2] ['riŋkl] n (fam) idea f, noción f; (tip) sugerencia f, indicación f; (dodge) truco m, estratagema f.

wrinkled ['riŋkld] adj, **wrinkly** ['riŋkli] adj arrugado, lleno de arrugas.

wrist [rist] n muñeca f.

wristband ['ristbænd] n puño m (de camisa).

wristlet ['ristlit] n pulsera f, muñequera f, brazalete m.

wrist watch ['ristwɔtʃ] n reloj m de pulsera.

writ [rit] n escritura f; (Law) orden f, mandato m, decreto m judicial; (fig) autoridad f; **Holy W—** Sagrada Escritura f; **— for an election** autorización f para celebrar elecciones; **— of attachment** orden f de detención; **— of execution** auto m de ejecución; **— of restraint** inhibitoria f; **to issue a —** dar orden, hacer un decreto judicial; **to issue a — against someone** demandar a uno en juicio; **to issue a — for slander against someone** demandar a uno por calumnia; **to serve a — on someone** entregar una orden (etc) a uno; **his — does not run here** aquí él no tiene autoridad, su autoridad no se extiende hasta aquí.

write [rait] (irr: pret **wrote**, ptp **written**) **1** vt (a) (general sense) escribir; redactar; poner por escrito; **did I — that?** ¿lo escribí yo así?; ¿fui capaz de escribir eso?; **how is that written?** ¿cómo se escribe eso?; **she —s a good hand** tiene buena letra.

(b) (compose) escribir; componer.

(c) (fig) **his guilt was written all over him** tenía aspecto de culpable, todo en él daba indicios

de su culpabilidad; **he had "policeman" written all over him** su aspecto entero revelaba que era policía, daba indicios inconfundibles de ser policía.

(d) (+ adv or prep) **to — down** (note) apuntar, anotar; (put in writing) poner por escrito; (record) hacer constar; (Comm) rebajar, bajar el precio de; reducir el valor nominal de; **we wrote him down as useless** decidimos que era inútil; **to — in** escribir, insertar; name of candidate (US) añadir a la lista oficial; **to — off** (quickly) escribir rápidamente, (at once) escribir en seguida; (Comm) debt borrar (como incobrable), (fig) cancelar, anular; **to — something off as a total loss** considerar algo como totalmente perdido; **to — £100 off for depreciation** quitar 100 libras al valor nominal de algo debido a la depreciación; **to — out** cheque escribir, extender; (transcribe) copiar, transcribir; (in full) escribir su forma completa, escribir sin abreviar; **to — up** report etc escribir; event escribir una crónica de, hacer un reportaje de; diary, ledger poner al día; **to — someone up (in a big way)** dar bombo a uno (en un artículo etc), describir a uno en términos elogiosos; **to — something up (in a big way)** describir algo exageradamente.

2 vi (a) escribir; **as I —** mientras escribo estas líneas; **we — to each other** nos escribimos, nos carteamos; **will you — to me?** ¿me escribirás?; **I wrote to him to come** le escribí diciéndole que viniera; **that's nothing to — home about** eso no tiene nada de particular; **I'll — for it at once** lo pediré por escrito en seguida, escribiré para pedirlo en seguida.

(b) (as profession) escribir, ser escritor; **he —s for a living** se gana la vida escribiendo, es escritor de profesión; **he —s as a hobby** escribe como distracción; **to — for a paper** colaborar en un periódico, escribir en un periódico.

(c) (with adv) **to — back** contestar; **to — in** escribir (for something pidiendo algo); **to — off** escribir (con prontitud; for something pidiendo algo).

write-off ['raitɔf] n (Comm) depreciación f; (fig) pérdida f total.

writer ['raitə*] n escritor m, ora f; autor m, ora f; **the (present) —** el que esto escribe; **— to the signet** (Scot) notario m; **a — of detective stories** un autor de novelas policíacas; **to be a poor —** (in handwriting) tener mala letra.

write-up ['raitʌp] n (report) crónica f, reportaje m; (pej) bombo m, descripción f exagerada, descripción f muy elogiosa.

writhe [raið] vi retorcerse, contorcerse; debatirse; **to — with pain, to — in pain** retorcerse de dolor; **to make someone —** (painfully) hacer sufrir a uno, atormentar a uno, (with disgust) dar asco a uno; **it made me — with embarrassment** con eso me sentí terriblemente molesto.

writing ['raitiŋ] **1** n (a) (art in general) el escribir, escritura f; **in —** por escrito; **evidence in —** declaración f escrita, testimonio m por escrito; **at the time of —** en el momento de escribir esto; **to commit something to —, to put something in —** poner algo por escrito.

(b) (hand-) escritura f, letra f; **in one's own —** de su propia letra; **in Góngora's own —** de puño y letra de Góngora; **the — on the wall** advertencias fpl graves, profecías fpl terribles; **the — is on the wall for them** es una advertencia muy clara para ellos; **he had seen the — on the wall** se había dado cuenta de lo grave de su situación.

(c) (thing written) escrito m; obra f; **the —s of Cela** las obras de Cela.

(d) (profession) profesión f de autor; trabajo m literario; **he earns a bit from his —** gana algo con su trabajo literario.

2 attr de escribir.

writing case ['raitiŋkeis] n cartera f (or cartapacio m) para papeles de escribir.

writing desk ['raitiŋdesk] n escritorio m.

writing pad ['raitiŋpæd] n taco m de papel, bloc m.

writing paper ['raitiŋ.peipə*] n papel m de escribir.

written ['ritn] **1** ptp of **write**. **2** adj escrito.

wrong [rɔŋ] **1** adj (a) (morally: wicked) malo, inicuo; (unfair) injusto; **it's — to steal** robar es un crimen; **that was very — of you** en eso has hecho muy mal; **you were — to + infin** hiciste mal en + infin; **what's — with a drink now and again?** ¿será pecado tomar algo de vez en cuando?; **what's — in cuddling?** ¿por qué no nos podemos abrazar?, ¿es que es un pecado abrazarse?

(b) (incorrect) erróneo, incorrecto, inexacto, equivocado; **the — use of drugs** el uso impropio de las drogas; **to be —** (*person*) no tener razón; equivocarse, estar equivocado; **that is —** eso no es exacto, eso no es cierto; **the answer is —** la respuesta es inexacta; **is that still —?** ¿eso está mal todavía?; **that clock is —** ese reloj anda mal, ese reloj no marcha bien.

(**c**) (*improper, not sought, not wanted*) impropio, inoportuno; **it's the — one** no es el que buscaba (*or* quería), no es el que hacía falta; **on the — side of the road** en el lado contrario de la carretera, (*Brit*) en el lado derecho de la carretera, (*US*) en el lado izquierdo de la carretera; **at the — time** inoportunamente; **it's in the — place** está mal situado, está mal colocado; **I'm in the — job** tengo un puesto que no me conviene, soy miembro de una profesión que no me conviene; **me he** equivocado de profesión; **we were on the — train** nos habíamos equivocado de tren; **is this the — road?** ¿nos habremos equivocado de camino?; **to play a — note** equivocarse al tocar una nota; **to say the — thing** decir algo inoportuno; **you have the — number** (*Tel*) Vd se ha confundido de número; *see* **way** etc.

(**d**) (*amiss*) **something is —** hay algo que no está bien; **is anything —?, is something— ?** ¿pasa algo?; **what's — with you?** ¿qué te pasa?; **I hope there's nothing — at home** espero que no pasa nada malo en casa; **something's — with my watch** le pasa algo a mi reloj, mi reloj no anda bien; **there is something — with my lights** los faros tienen una avería, los faros están averiados.

2 *adv* mal; sin razón; injustamente; incorrectamente, equivocadamente; al revés; **to answer —** contestar mal, contestar incorrectamente; **you did — hiciste mal; you're doing it all —** no se hace así, no comprendes el modo de hacerlo; **to get it —** (*misunderstand*) comprender mal; no acertar; (*Math etc*) calcular mal, equivocarse en el cálculo; **to go —** (*on route*) equivocarse de camino; extraviarse; (*in calculation*) equivocarse; (*morally*) extraviarse, caer en el vicio; (*of affair*) ir mal, salir mal; (*Mech*) fallar; estropearse, averiarse; dejar de funcionar; **something went — with the gears** se averió la caja de cambios; **something went — with their plans** algo falló en sus planes, fracasaron sus planes; **something is seriously —** pasa algo grave; **you can't go —!** ¡es imposible perder!

3 *n* (**a**) (*the* **—**) mal *m*; **to know right from —** saber distinguir el bien del mal; **two —s do not make a right** no se subsana un error cometiendo otro.

(**b**) (*injustice*) injusticia *f*; agravio *m*, entuerto *m*; **to do someone a great —** ser muy injusto con uno, agraviar gravemente a uno; **to labour under a sense of —** sentirse agraviado, creer que uno ha sido tratado injustamente; **to right a —** deshacer un agravio, acabar con un abuso.

(**c**) **to be in the —** no tener razón, estar equivocado; tener la culpa; **to put someone in the —** quitar la razón a uno; hacer que otro cargue con la culpa.

4 *vt* agraviar; ser injusto con; **you — me** eso no es justo; **to feel that one has been —ed** sentirse agraviado, creer que uno ha sido tratado injustamente.

wrongdoer ['rɔŋˌduːə*] *n* malhechor *m*, ora *f*; pecador *m*, ora *f*.

wrongdoing ['rɔŋˌduːiŋ] *n* maldad *f*; pecados *mpl*; perversidad *f*; crímenes *mpl*.

wrongful ['rɔŋful] *adj* injusto; ilegal.

wrongfully ['rɔŋfəli] *adv* injustamente; ilegalmente.

wrong-headed ['rɔŋ'hedid] *adj* obstinado, terco, perversamente equivocado; **to be — about something** obstinarse perversamente en sostener (*etc*) algo.

wrong-headedly ['rɔŋ'hedidli] *adv* obstinadamente, perversamente.

wrong-headedness ['rɔŋ'hedidnis] *n* obstinación *f*, terquedad *f*; error *m* perverso.

wrongly ['rɔŋli] *adv* mal; injustamente; incorrectamente; equivocadamente; al revés; **he — maintains that . . .** él sostiene equivocadamente que . . .; **to put a screw in —** poner un tornillo mal; **she had been very — treated** la habían tratado muy injustamente.

wrongness ['rɔŋnis] *n* iniquidad *f*; injusticia *f*; inexactitud *f*, error *m*, falsedad *f*; impropiedad *f*, inoportunidad *f*.

wrote [rəut] *pret of* **write.**

wrought [rɔːt] **1** (*arch*) *pret and ptp of* **work; he — valiantly** luchó denodadamente, trabajó con esfuerzo; **great changes have been —** se han efectuado grandes cambios.

2 *adj* (**a**) *iron etc* forjado; *silver etc* labrado.

(**b**) **to be — (up)** (*person*) estar muy agitado, estar muy nervioso.

wrought-up ['rɔːt'ʌp] *adj* agitado, nervioso.

wrung [rʌŋ] *pret and ptp of* **wring.**

wry [rai] *adj* torcido; *sense of humour, joke etc* pervertido, raro; *speech etc* irónico, lleno de ironía; **to make a — face** hacer una mueca, torcer el gesto.

wryly ['raili] *adv* irónicamente, con ironía.

wryneck ['rainek] *n* (*Orn*) torcecuello *m*.

wych-elm ['witʃ'elm] *n* olmo *m* escocés.

X

x [eks] *n* (*Math*, *fig*) x *f*; incógnita *f*; — **marks the spot** el sitio está señalado con una X; **if you have —** **pesetas a year** si se tiene equis pesetas al año.
Xavier ['zeiviə*] *m* Javier.
xenon ['zenɔn] *n* xeno *m*, xenón *m*.
xenophobe ['zenəfəub] *n* xenófobo *m*.
xenophobia [ˌzenəˈfəubiə] *n* xenofobia *f*.
Xenophon ['zenəfən] *m* Jenofonte.
Xmas ['eksməs] *n* (*fam*) *abbr of* **Christmas**.

X-ray ['eks'rei] **1** *n* radiografía *f*; —**s** rayos *mpl* X.
2 *adj*, *attr* radiográfico; — **examination** examen *m* con rayos X; — **photograph** radiografía *f*.
3 *vt* radiografiar.
xylograph ['zailəgrɑːf] *n* xilografía *f*, grabado *m* en madera.
xylographic [zailəˈgræfik] *adj* xilográfico.
xylography [zaiˈlɔgrəfi] *n* xilografía *f*.
xylophone ['zailəfəun] *n* xilófono *m*.

Y

yacht [jɔt] **1** n (esp large, seagoing) yate m; (small, model) balandro m.
    2 vi pasear en yate, navegar en yate; tomar parte en regatas de balandros; dedicarse al balandrismo.
yacht club ['jɔtklʌb] n club m náutico.
yachting ['jɔtiŋ] **1** n deporte m de la vela, balandrismo m; pasear m en yate, navegar m en yate; regatas fpl de balandros.
    2 attr de yates, de balandros; de balandristas; **in — circles** entre los aficionados al deporte de la vela, entre balandristas; **it's not a — coast** en esa costa no se practica el deporte de la vela.
yacht race ['jɔtreis] n regata f de yates, regata f de balandros.
yachtsman ['jɔtsmən] n, pl **—men** [mən] deportista m náutico; balandrista m.
yachtsmanship ['jɔtsmənʃip] n arte m de navegar en yate (or balandro).
yackety-yak ['jækiti'jæk] n (chatter) palabreo m, cháchara f; (argument) dimes mpl y diretes; (insistence) machaqueo m.
yah [jɑ] interj ¡bah!
yahoo [jɑ:'hu:] n patán m.
yak [jæk] n yac m, yak m.
yam [jæm] n batata f, ñame m.
yank [jæŋk] **1** n tirón m; **to give a rope a —** tirar de una cuerda. **2** vt tirar de; **to — a nail out** sacar un clavo de un tirón.
Yank [jæŋk] n (fam) yanqui mf (fam).
Yankee ['jæŋki] (fam) **1** adj yanqui (fam). **2** n yanqui mf (fam).
yap [jæp] **1** n ladrido m agudo. **2** vi dar ladridos agudos; (fam: chat) charlar; (protest) quejarse, protestar (sin razón).
yapping ['jæpiŋ] n ladridos mpl agudos.
yard¹ [jɑ:d] n (a) yarda f (= 91,44 cm); **an essay —s long** un ensayo larguísimo; **he pulled out —s of handkerchief** sacó un enorme pañuelo; **with a face a — long** muy cariacontecido, tristísimo; **a few —s off** a varios metros, a poca distancia.
    (b) (Naut) verga f.
yard² [jɑ:d] n (of house) patio m; (of farm etc) corral m; (School) patio m de recreo; **the Y—**, **Scotland Y—** oficina central de la policía de Londres.
yardarm ['jɑ:dɑ:m] n verga f, penol m.
yardstick ['jɑ:dstik] n (fig) criterio m, norma f.
yarn [jɑ:n] **1** n (a) hilo m, hilaza f.
    (b) (tale) cuento m, historia f; **to spin a —** contar una historia; contar cosas inverosímiles; **to spin someone a —** disculparse con un pretexto inverosímil.
    2 vi contar historias; contar cosas inverosímiles; contar chistes.
yarrow ['jærəu] n milenrama f.
yashmak ['jæʃmæk] n velo m (de musulmana).
yaw [jɔ:] (Naut) **1** n guiñada f. **2** vi guiñar, hacer una guiñada.
yawl [jɔ:l] n yol m, yola f.
yawn [jɔ:n] **1** n bostezo m; **it was a — from start to finish** fue aburridísimo; **to say something with a —** decir algo bostezando.
    2 vt decir bostezando (also **to — out**); **to — one's head off** bostezar mucho; bostezar abriendo muchísimo la boca.
    3 vi bostezar.
yawning ['jɔ:niŋ] adj (fig) muy abierto, grande.
yaws [jɔ:z] n (Med) frambesia f.
ye [ji:] pron (arch) vosotros, vosotras.
yea [jei] (arch) **1** adv (yes) sí; (indeed) sin duda, ciertamente; (moreover) además. **2** n sí m; **the —s and the nays** los votos afirmativos y los negativos.
yeah [jeə] adv (fam) = **yes**.
year [jiə*] n (a) año m; **— of grace** año m de gracia; **in the — of our Lord** ... en el año del Señor ...; **all the — round** durante todo el año; **— in, — out**

año tras año; todos los años sin falta; **3 times a —** 3 veces al año; **100 dollars a —** 100 dólares al año; **to reckon by the —** calcular por años; **in after —s** en los años siguientes, años después; **in my early —s** en mi infancia, en mi tierna edad, en mi juventud; **in his later —s** en sus últimos años; **of late —s** en estos últimos años; **last —** el año pasado; **the — before last** el año antepasado; **next —** (looking to future) el año que viene, (in past time) el año siguiente; **he looks old for his —s** parece más viejo de lo que es en realidad; **he's getting on in —s** es bastante viejo, va para viejo; **he got 10 —s** le condenaron a 10 años de prisión; **it takes —s** es cosa de años y años, se tarda años y años; **we waited —s** esperamos una eternidad.
    (b) calendar **—** año m civil; financial **—** año m económico; school **—** año m escolar; New Y— Año m Nuevo; New Y—'s Day día m de Año Nuevo; New Y—'s Eve noche f vieja; **happy new —!** ¡feliz año nuevo!; **to see the old — out** festejar el año nuevo.
    (c) (school, Univ) curso m; **he's in (the) second —** está en el segundo curso; **the fellows in my —** los chicos de mi curso; **he's in fourth — Law** estudia cuarto de Derecho.
yearbook ['jiəbuk] n anuario m.
yearling ['jiəliŋ] **1** adj primal. **2** n primal m, ala f.
yearlong ['jiə'lɔŋ] adj que dura un año (entero).
yearly ['jiəli] **1** adj anual. **2** adv anualmente, cada año; (once) una vez al año.
yearn [jɔ:n] vi suspirar; **to — for** anhelar, añorar, ansiar, suspirar por; **person** suspirar por; **to — to +** infin anhelar + infin, suspirar por + infin.
yearning ['jɔ:niŋ] **1** adj ansioso, anhelante; look, tone etc tierno, amoroso. **2** n ansia f, anhelo m, añoranza f (for de).
yearningly ['jɔ:niŋli] adv ansiosamente, con ansia; tiernamente, amorosamente.
yeast [ji:st] n levadura f.
yeasty ['ji:sti] adj (fig) frívolo, superficial.
yell [jel] **1** n grito m, alarido m, chillido m; **to give a —**, **to let out a —** dar un alarido. **2** vt gritar, decir a gritos, vociferar. **3** vi gritar, dar un alarido.
yelling ['jeliŋ] n gritos mpl, alaridos mpl, chillidos mpl.
yellow ['jeləu] **1** adj amarillo; hair rubio; (cowardly) cobarde; paper, press sensacionalista; **— novel** novelucha f; **to go —**, **to turn —** amarillear, amarillecer.
    2 n amarillo m.
    3 vt volver amarillo.
    4 vi amarillecer, amarillear, ponerse amarillo.
yellowback ['jeləubæk] n novelucha f.
yellowhammer ['jeləu‚hæmə*] n escribano m cerillo.
yellowish ['jeləuiʃ] adj amarillento.
yellowness ['jeləunis] n amarillez f.
yellowy ['jeləui] adj amarillento, que tira a amarillo.
yelp [jelp] **1** n gañido m. **2** vi gañir; (of person) gritar, dar un grito.
yelping ['jelpiŋ] n gañidos mpl.
yen [jen] n (fam) deseo m vivo; **to have a — to +** infin desear vivamente + infin, anhelar + infin.
yeoman ['jəumən] n, pl **—men** [mən] (Brit) **(a)** labrador m rico, pequeño propietario m rural, pequeño terrateniente m.
    (b) (Mil) soldado m (voluntario) de caballería; **— of the guard** alabardero m de la Casa Real.
yeomanry ['jəumənri] n **(a)** clase f de los labradores ricos, pequeños propietarios mpl rurales. **(b)** (Mil) caballería f voluntaria.
yep [jep] adv (fam, esp US) sí.
yes [jes] **1** adv sí; **—?** (doubtfully) ¿es cierto eso?, ¿ah sí?; **—?** (awaiting further reply) ¿y qué más?; **—?** (answering knock at door) ¿quién es?, ¡adelante!;

to say — decir que sí, (*to marriage proposal*) dar el sí; **he says** — **to everything** se allana a todo, se conforma con cualquier cosa.

2 *n* sí *m*; **he gave a reluctant** — asintió pero de mala gana.

yes man ['jesmæn] *n, pl* — **men** [men] (*sl*) pelotillero *m*.

yesterday ['jestədei] **1** *adv* ayer; — **afternoon** ayer por la tarde; — **morning** ayer por la mañana; **late** — ayer a última hora; **no later than** — no más lejos que ayer.

2 *n* ayer *m*; **the day before** — anteayer; — **was Monday** ayer era lunes; **all our** —**s** todos nuestros recuerdos de antaño.

yesteryear ['jestə'jiə*] *adv* (*poet*) antaño.

yet [jet] **1** *adv* (**a**) (*time*) todavía, aún; **as** — hasta ahora, todavía; **not** —, **not just** — todavía no; **I hear it** — lo oigo todavía; **need you go** — ? ¿no te puedes quedar un poco más?; **I don't have to go** — me puedo quedar todavía un poco; **it is** — **to be settled** eso queda por resolver; **half is** — **to be built** la mitad queda todavía por construir; **it hasn't happened** — todavía no ha ocurrido; no ha ocurrido aún; **it's not time** — todavía no ha llegado la hora.

(**b**) (*emphatic*) todavía; — **again** otra vez (más); — **more** todavía más, más todavía, más aun.

2 *conj* con todo, a pesar de todo; **and** — y sin embargo, pero con todo; **we'll do it** — a pesar de todo lo lograremos.

yeti ['jeti] *n* yeti *m*.

yew [ju:] *n* tejo *m* (*also* **yew tree**).

Yid [jid] *n* (*fam, pej*) judío *m, a f*.

Yiddish ['jidiʃ] **1** *adj* judío. **2** *n* lengua *f* (*alemán-hebreo*) que emplean varios sectores de los judíos.

yield [ji:ld] **1** *n* producción *f*; (*Agr*) cosecha *f*; (*Fin, Comm*) rendimiento *m*, (*on capital*) rédito *m*; **net** — rédito *m* neto; **a** — **of 5%** un rédito de 5 por cien; **what is the** — **on the shares?** ¿cuánto rinden las acciones?

2 *vt crop, result* producir, dar; *profit* rendir; *opportunity etc* ofrecer, dar, deparar; (*give up*) entregar, ceder (*also* **to** — **up**); **the shares** — **5%** las acciones rinden el 5 por cien, las acciones dan un rédito de 5 por cien.

3 *vi* (*submit*) rendirse, someterse; (*give way*) ceder; (*US Aut*) ceder el paso; **to** — **to a plea** ceder a un ruego; **to** — **to temptation** ceder a la tentación; **I** — **to nobody in my admiration for . . .** yo admiro como todos a . . . , no me quedo corto en mi admiración por . . . ; **finally the door** —**ed** por fin cedió la puerta; **the ice began to** — el hielo empezó a ceder; el hielo empezó a romperse; **we shall never** — no nos rendiremos nunca.

yielding ['ji:ldiŋ] *adj* flexible, blando; (*fig*) dócil, complaciente; tierno, amoroso.

yippee [ji'pi:] *interj* (*fam*) ¡estupendo!

yod [jɔd] *n* yod *f*.

yodel, yodle ['jəudl] **1** *n* canto *m* a la tirolesa. **2** *vti* cantar a la tirolesa.

yoga ['jəugə] *n* yoga *f*.

yogi ['jəugi] *n* yogui *m*.

yogourt ['jəugət] *n* yogur *m*.

yo-heave-ho ['jəu'hi:v'həu] *interj see* **heave-ho**.

yoke [jəuk] **1** *n* (*of oxen*) yunta *f*; (*carried on shoulder*) balancín *m*, percha *f*; (*Mech*) horquilla *f*; (*Sew*) canesú *m*; (*fig*) yugo *m*; **under the** — **of the Nazis** bajo el yugo de los nazis, bajo la férula de los nazis; **to throw off the** — sacudir el yugo.

2 *vt* (*also* **to** — **together**) uncir, acoplar; (*fig*) unir.

yokel ['jəukəl] *n* palurdo *m*, patán *m*.

yolk [jəuk] *n* yema *f* (de huevo).

yon [jɔn] *adv* (*arch, prov*) aquel.

yonder ['jɔndə*] (*arch*) **1** *adj* aquel. **2** *adv* allá, a lo lejos.

yore [jɔ:*] *n* (*arch*): **of** — (*lit*) de antaño, de otro tiempo, de hace siglos.

you [ju:] *pron* **1** *in familiar use, with second person verb*: (*subject*: *sing*) tú, (*pl*) vosotros, vosotras; (*acc, dat*: *sing*) te, (*pl*) os; (*after prep*: *sing*) ti, (*pl*) vosotros, vosotras; **with** — (*sing, reflexive*) contigo, (*pl, reflexive*) con vosotros, con vosotras.

2 *in formal use, with third person verb*: (*subject*: *sing*) usted, (*pl*) ustedes; (*acc, dat*: *sing*) le, la, (*pl*) les; (*after prep*: *sing*) usted, (*pl*) ustedes; **with** — (*sing and pl, reflexive*) consigo.

I.S.D.—40

3 *when impersonal or general, often translated by* (**a**) *reflexive*: — **can't do that** eso no se hace, eso no se permite; — **can't smoke here** no se puede fumar aquí, no se permite fumar aquí, se prohíbe fumar aquí; **when** — **need one it's not here** cuando se necesita uno, no está aquí.

(**b**) uno: — **never know whether . . .** uno nunca sabe si . . .

(**c**) *impersonal constructions*: — **need to check it every day** hay que comprobarlo cada día, conviene comprobarlo cada día; — **must paint it** hace falta pintarlo.

4 *phrases and special uses*: — **rogue!** ¡canalla!; — **there!** ¡eh! ¡usted!; — **doctors** vosotros los médicos; — **Spaniards** vosotros los españoles; **poor** —!, **poor old** —!, — **poor old thing!** ¡pobrecito!; **away with** —! ¡vete!, ¡fuera de aquí!; **between** — **and me** entre tú y yo; **if I were** — yo que tú, yo en tu lugar; **there's a pretty girl for** —! ¡mira que chica más guapa!

you'd [ju:d] = **you would**; **you had**.

you'll [ju:l] = **you will, you shall**.

young [jʌŋ] **1** *adj* joven; nuevo, reciente; *brother etc* menor; **a** — **man** un joven; **a** — **woman** una joven; **the** — los jóvenes, la juventud; **old and** — grandes y pequeños; **the** —**er son** el hijo menor; **Pitt the Y**—**er** Pitt el Joven, Pitt hijo; **the** — **idea, Y**—**England** las nuevas generaciones, la juventud de hoy; **in my** — **days** en mi juventud; **if I were 10 years** —**er** si tuviera 10 años menos; **you're only** — **once** no se es joven más que una vez en la vida, hay que aprovechar la juventud mientras dure; **I'm not so** — **as I was** empiezo a notar los efectos de la edad, ya no soy lo que fui en mis veinte; **the night is** — la noche es joven; **the pile is like a** — **mountain** el montón se parece a una montaña menor de edad; **to marry** — casarse joven.

2 *npl* (*Zool*) cría *f*, hijuelos *mpl*.

youngish ['jʌŋiʃ] *adj* bastante joven, más bien joven.

young-looking ['jʌŋ,lukiŋ] *adj* de aspecto joven.

youngster ['jʌŋstə*] *n* joven *mf*, jovencito *m*, a *f*.

your ['juə*] *poss adj* **1** *in familiar use, second person*: tu(s); vuestro(s), vuestra(s).

2 *in formal use, third person*: su(s).

you're ['juə*] = **you are**.

yours ['juəz] *poss pron* **1** *in familiar use, second person*: (el) tuyo, (la) tuya *etc*; (el) vuestro, (la) vuestra *etc*.

2 *in formal use, third person*: (el) suyo, (la) suya *etc*; **you and** — Vd y los suyos.

3 *in ending letters*: — **faithfully** le saluda atentamente; *see* **sincerely** *etc*.

yourself [jə'self] *pron* **1** *in familiar use, second person*: (*subject*) tú mismo, tú misma; (*acc, dat*) te; (*after prep*) ti (mismo, misma).

2 *in formal use, third person*: (*subject*) usted mismo, usted misma; (*acc, dat*) se; (*after prep*) sí (mismo, misma); *see* **oneself**.

yourselves [jə'selvz] *pron pl* **1** *in familiar use, second person*: (*subject*) vosotros mismos, vosotras mismas; (*acc, dat*) os; (*after prep*) vosotros (mismos), vosotras (mismas).

2 *in formal use, third person*: (*subject*) ustedes mismos, ustedes mismas; (*acc, dat*) se; (*after prep*) sí (mismos, mismas); *see* **oneself**.

youth [ju:θ] *n, pl* **youths** [ju:ðz] (*in general*) juventud *f*; (*person*) joven *m*; (*persons collectively*) jóvenes *mpl*, juventud *f*; **present-day British** — la juventud actual inglesa; **Hitler Y**— Juventudes *fpl* Hitlerianas.

youthful ['ju:θful] *adj* juvenil; joven; **to look** — tener aspecto joven, parecer joven.

youthfulness ['ju:θfulnis] *n* juventud *f*.

youth hostel ['ju:θ,hɔstl] *n* albergue *m* para jóvenes.

you've [ju:v] = **you have**.

yowl [jaul] **1** *n* aullido *m*, alarido *m*. **2** *vi* aullar, dar alaridos.

yucca ['jʌkə] *n* yuca *f*.

Yugoslav ['ju:gəu'sla:v] **1** *adj* yugo(e)slavo. **2** *n* yugo(e)slavo *m*, yugo(e)slava *f*.

Yugoslavia ['ju:gəu'sla:viə] *n* Yugo(e)slavia *f*.

Yule(tide) ['ju:l(taid)] *n* (*lit*) Navidad; **at** — por Navidades; — **log** leño *m* de Navidad.

yummy ['jʌmi] *adj* (*fam*) de rechupete.

Z

Zambesi [zæm'biːzi] Zambeze *m.*
Zambia ['zæmbiə] Zambia *f.*
zany ['zeini] **1** *adj* tonto; *humour etc* estrafalario, surrealista. **2** *n* bufón *m*, tonto *m.*
Zanzibar ['zænzibɑː*] Zanzíbar *m.*
zeal [ziːl] *n* celo *m*, estusiasmo *m* (*for* por), ardor *m.*
zealot ['zelət] *n* fanático *m.*
zealotry ['zelətri] *n* fanatismo *m.*
zealous ['zeləs] *adj* celoso (*for* de), entusiasta (*for* de); apasionado (*for* por).
zealously ['zeləsli] *adv* con entusiasmo.
zebra ['ziːbrə] *n* cebra *f.*
zebra crossing ['ziːbrə'krɔsiŋ] *n* paso *m* de peatones.
zebu ['ziːbuː] *n* cebú *m.*
zenana [ze'nɑːnə] *n* harén *m* indio.
zenith ['zeniθ] *n* cenit *m*; (*fig*) cenit *m*, apogeo *m*, punto *m* culminante; **to be at the — of one's power** estar en el apogeo de su poder.
Zeno ['ziːnəu] *m* Zenón.
zephyr ['zefə*] *n* céfiro *m.*
zeppelin ['zeplin] *n* zepelín *m.*
zero ['ziərəu] **1** *adj* cero, nulo. **2** *n* cero *m*; **absolute — cero** *m* absoluto; **it is 5° below —** hace cinco grados bajo cero.
zero hour ['ziərəu,auə*] *n* (*Mil*) hora *f* de ataque; (*fig*) momento *m* decisivo, momento *m* crítico.
zest [zest] *n* gusto *m*, entusiasmo *m*; **to do something with —** hacer algo con entusiasmo; **to eat with —** comer con gusto.
zestful ['zestful] *adj* entusiasta.
zestfully ['zestfəli] *adv* con entusiasmo.
zigzag ['zigzæg] **1** *n* zigzag *m.* **2** *adj* en zigzag. **3** *vi* zigzaguear, moverse en zigzag; (*person*) hacer eses.
zinc [ziŋk] *n* cinc *m.*
zinnia ['ziniə] *n* (*Bot*) rascamoño *m.*
Zion ['zaiən] Sión *m.*

Zionism ['zaiənizəm] *n* sionismo *m.*
Zionist ['zaiənist] **1** *adj* sionista. **2** *n* sionista *mf.*
zip [zip] **1** *n* (a) (*sound*) silbido *m*, zumbido *m.*
  (b) (**— fastener**) cremallera *f*, cierre *m* de cremallera.
  (c) (*fig*) energía *f*, vigor *m.*
2 *vt*: **to — up** cerrar (la cremallera de).
3 *vi*: **to — past** pasar silbando; (*fig*) pasar como un rayo.
zip code ['zipkəud] *n* (*US Post*) *número cifrado para facilitar la distribución del correo.*
zip fastener ['zip,fɑːsnə*] *n*, **zipper** ['zipə*] *n* cremallera *f*, cierre *m* de cremallera.
zippy ['zipi] *adj* enérgico, vigoroso; pronto, rápido.
zircon ['zɜːkən] *n* circón *m.*
zither ['ziðə*] *n* cítara *f.*
zodiac ['zəudiæk] *n* zodíaco *m.*
zombie ['zɔmbi] *n* cadáver *m* resucitado por arte mágico.
zonal ['zəunl] *adj* zonal.
zone [zəun] *n* zona *f.*
zoo [zuː] *n* zoo *m*, jardín *m* zoológico, parque *m* zoológico; (*small, private*) colección *f* de fieras.
zoological [,zəuə'lɔdʒikəl] *adj* zoológico; **— gardens** *see* **zoo.**
zoologist [zəu'ɔlədʒist] *n* zoólogo *m.*
zoology [zəu'ɔlədʒi] *n* zoología *f.*
zoom [zuːm] **1** *n* (*sound*) zumbido *m*; (*Aer*) empinadura *f.* **2** *vi* zumbar; (*Aer*) empinarse; **it —ed past my ear** pasó zumbando cerca de mi oído.
zoomorphic [,zəuəu'mɔːfik] *adj* zoomórfico.
Zoroaster [,zɔrəu'æstə*] *m* Zoroastro.
Zulu ['zuːluː] **1** *adj* zulú. **2** *n* zulú *mf.*
Zululand ['zuːlulænd] Zululandia *f.*
zygote ['zaigəut] *n* cigoto *m.*

Abbreviations commonly used in Spanish and English

Abreviaturas más usadas en español e inglés

Spanish Abbreviations
Abreviaturas españolas

A

A	bomba A: bomba *f* atómica.
a.	área*.
AA	Aerolíneas *fpl* Argentinas.
ab.¹, abr.	abril *m* (*Ap., Apr.:* April).
A.C.	**1** año *m* de Cristo (*A.D.: Anno Domini, in the year of our Lord*). **2** (*Rel*) Acción *f* Católica.
a.c.	año *m* corriente (*current year*).
a/c	**1** al cuidado de (*c/o: care of*). **2** (*Fin*) a cuenta (*on account*).
acr.	acreedor *m* (*Cr.: creditor*).
A. de C.	= A.C. 1.
a. de C.	antes de Cristo (*A.C.: ante Christum, before Christ*).
a. de J.C.	antes de Jesucristo (*B.C.: before Christ*).
a D.g.	a Dios gracias (*thanks be to God*).
adj.	adjunto (*encl.: enclosure(s); enclosed*).
admón.	administración *f* (*admin.: administration*).
A.E.C.E.	Asociación *f* Española de Cooperación Europea.

a/f.	a favor (*in favour*)
afma., afmo., affma, affmo.	afectísima, afectísimo*.
ag., ag.º	agosto *m* (*Aug.: August*).
A.H.N.	Archivo *m* Histórico Nacional.
A.L.A.L.C.	Asociación *f* Latinoamericana de Libre Comercio.
a L.R.P.	a los reales pies (*courtesy formula*).
a.m.	(*SAm*) ante meridiem.
A.P.D.	Asistencia *f* Pública Domiciliara (*social welfare organization*).
apdo.	apartado *m* (de correos) (*P.O.B.: post-office box*).
A.P.E.	Asociaciones *fpl* Profesionales de Estudiantes.
A.P.R.A.	Alianza *f* Popular Revolucionaria Americana.
A.R.	Alteza *f* Real (*R.H.: Royal Highness*).
Arz.	Arzobispo *m* (*Abp: Archbishop*).
A.T.	Antiguo Testamento *m* (*O.T.: Old Testament*).
atta., atto.	atenta, atento* (*used in courtesy formulae in letters, with* servidor *etc*).
Av., Avda.	Avenida *f* (*Av., Ave: Avenue*).
a /v.	a vista (*at sight*).
AVIANCA	Aerovías *fpl* Nacionales de Colombia.

A.Y.C.	Aviación *f* y Comercio (*Spanish airline*).

B

B.	**1** Barcelona. **2** (*Eccl*) Beata, Beato (*B.: Beatus, Blessed*).
B.A.E.	Biblioteca *f* de Autores Españoles.
Barna.	Barcelona.
Bib.	Biblioteca *f* (*Lib.: Library*).
B.I.C.	Brigada *f* de Investigación Criminal (*equivalent to CID, (US) FBI*).
B.I.D.	Banco *m* Interamericano de Desarrollo.
b.l.m	besa las manos (*courtesy formula*).
b.l.p.	besa los pies (*courtesy formula*).
B.N.	Biblioteca *f* Nacional (*Madrid*).
B.O.	Boletín *m* Oficial.
B.º	banco *m* (*bk: bank*).
B.O.E.	Boletín *m* Oficial del Estado.
Bol.	Boletín *m* (*bulletin, journal*).
Bs.As.	Buenos Aires (*B.A.*).
Bta., Bto.	Beata, Beato (*B.: Beatus, Blessed*).

C

C.	(*Comm, Fin*) compañía *f* (*Co.: company*).

C/ Calle *f* (*Rd*: *Road*; *St*: *Street*).

c. = cap.

c³ centímetro(s) *m*(*pl*) cúbico(s) (*c.c.*: *cubic centimetre(s)*).

c / cuenta *f* (*a* /*c*: *account*).

C.A. 1 (*Elec*) corriente *f* alterna (*A.C.*: *alternating current*). 2 (*Sport*) Club *m* Atlético (*A.C.*: *Athletic Club*).

C.A.E. cóbrese al entregar (*C.O.D.*: *cash on delivery*).

CAMPSA Compañía *f* Arrendataria del Monopolio de Petróleos, Sociedad Anónima.

cap., cap.º capítulo *m* (*cap.*, *ch.*: *chapter*).

C.A.T. Comisaría *f* de Abastecimientos y Transportes.

c /c cuenta *f* corriente (*C/A*: *current account*).

C.D. 1 (*Pol*) Cuerpo *m* Diplomático (*C.D.*: *Corps Diplomatique*). 2 (*Elec*) corriente *f* directa (*D.C.*: *direct current*). 3 (*Sport*) Club *m* Deportivo (*S.C.*: *Sports Club*).

c /d 1 en casa de (*c /o*: *care of*). 2 (*Comm*, *Fin*) con descuento (*with discount*).

C. de J. Compañía de Jesús (*S.J.*: *Society of Jesus*).

CECA Comunidad *f* Europea del Carbón y del Acero (*ECSC*: *European Coal and Steel Community*).

C.E.D.A. Confederación *f* Española de Derechas Autónomas.

CEE Comunidad *f* Económica Europea (*EEC*: *European Economic Community*).

cént(s). céntimo(s) *m*(*pl*) (*c.*: *centime(s)*).

CEPSA Compañía *f* Española de Petróleos, Sociedad Anónima.

C.F. Club *m* de Fútbol.

c.f. caballo *m* de fuerza, caballos *mpl* de fuerza (*H.P.*: *horsepower*).

cfr. confróntese, compárese (*cf.*: *confer*, *compare*).

Cía. Compañía *f* (*Co.*: *Company*).

C.I.D. Centro *m* Internacional para el Desarrollo.

cje. corretaje *m* (*brokerage*).

cm² centímetro(s) *m*(*pl*) cuadrado(s) (*sq. cm.*: *square centimetre(s)*).

cm³ centímetro *m* cúbico, centímetros *mpl* cúbicos (*c.c.*: *cubic centimetre(s)*).

c.m.b. cuya mano beso (*courtesy formula*).

C.N.S. Confederación *f* Nacional de Sindicatos.

C.N.T. Confederación *f* Nacional del Trabajo.

col., col.ª columna *f* (*col.*: *column*).

comp. compárese (*cp.*: *compare*).

CONDESA Consorcio *m* de Diarios Españoles, Sociedad Anónima(*press agency*).

C.P. contestación *f* pagada (*R.P.*: *reply paid*).

c.p.b. cuyos pies beso (*courtesy formula*).

cs. 1 centavos *mpl* (*c.*: *cents*). 2 céntimos *mpl* (*c.*: *cents*).

c.s.f. coste, seguro y flete (*c.i.f.*: *cost, insurance and freight*).

cta., c.ta cuenta *f* (*a* /*c*: *account*).

cte. corriente, de los corrientes (*inst.*: *instant, of the present month*).

c /u cada uno (*ea.*: *each*).

C.V. caballos *mpl* de vapor (*H.P.*: *horsepower*).

CH

ch. cheque *m* (*ch.*: *cheque*).

D

D. 1 debe (*debit side*). 2 Don* (*Esq.*: *Esquire*).

Da., D.ª Doña*.

D.A. duración *f* ampliada (*E.P.*: *extended play*).

dcha. derecha (*r.h.*: *right hand*).

d. de J.C. después de Jesucristo (*A.D.*: *Anno Domini, in the year of our Lord*).

der., der.º derecho (*r.*: *right*).

D.F. (*Mex*) Distrito *m* Federal (*Federal District*).

D.G.T. Dirección *f* General de Turismo.

dha., dho. dicha, dicho (*aforesaid*).

dic., dic.e diciembre *m* (*Dec.*: *December*).

D.m. Dios mediante (*D.V.*: *Deo volente*).

D.n Don* (*Esq.*: *Esquire*).

D.N.D. Delegación *f* Nacional de Deportes.

D.N.S. Delegación *f* Nacional de Sindicatos.

do. descuento *m* (*discount*).

doc. 1 docena *f* (*doz.*: *dozen*). 2 documento *m* (*doc.*: *document*).

dom.º domingo *m* (*Sun.*: *Sunday*).

D.R.A.E. Diccionario *m* de la Real Academia Española.

D.R.C. Departamento *m* de Relaciones Culturales.

d.to descuento *m* (*discount*).

dup., dup.do duplicado (*duplicated*).

E

E. este *m*, *adj* (*E.*: *east*).

e / envío *m* (*consignment*).

EE.UU. Estados *mpl* Unidos (*US*, *USA*: *United States (of America)*).

ej. ejemplo *m* (*ex.*: *example*).

E.M. Estado *m* Mayor (*G.S.*: *General Staff*).

Em.ª Eminencia (*Eminence*).

ENE. estenordeste (*E.N.E.*: *east-north-east*).

ene., en.º enero *m* (*Jan.*: *January*).

ENESA Empresa *f* Nacional de Electricidad, Sociedad Anónima.

ENSIDESA Empresa *f* Nacional Siderúrgica, Sociedad Anónima.

entlo. entresuelo*.

E.P.D. en paz descanse (*R.I.P.*: *requiescat in pace*).

ESE. estesudeste (*E.S.E.*: *east-south-east*).

esp. español *m* (*also adj*) (*Sp.*, *Span.*: *Spanish*).

Exc.ª Excelencia (*Excellency*).

Excmo. Excelentísimo (*courtesy title*).

F

f.ª factura *f* (*bill*, *account*).

f.a.b. franco a bordo (*f.o.b.*: *free on board*).

F.C., f.c. ferrocarril *m* (*Rly*: *Railway*).

feb.º febrero *m* (*Feb.*: *February*).

F.E.C.I.T. Federación *f* Española de Centros de Iniciativas y Turismo.

F.E.F. Federación *f* Española de Fútbol.

F.E.T. Falange *f* Española Tradicionalista.

fha. fecha *f* (*d.*: *date*).

F.M.I. Fondo *m* Monetario Internacional (*IMF*: *International Monetary Fund*).

F.N.A.S. Fondo *m* Nacional de Asistencia Social.

F.N.P.T. Fondo *m* Nacional de Protección del Trabajo.

f.º, fol. folio *m* (*Fo.*, *fol.*: *folio*).

F.P.A. Formación *f* Profesional Acelerada.

Fr. Fray *m* (*Fr*: *Friar*).

fr(s). franco(s) *m*(*pl*) (*fr.*: *franc(s)*).

fra. factura *f* (*bill*, *account*).

G

g / giro *m* (*draft*, *money order*).

gob.no gobierno *m* (*govt*: *government*).

g.p. giro *m* postal (*money order*).

gr. gramo(s) *m*(*pl*) (*g.*, *gm.*: *gram(s)*, *gramme(s)*).

Gral. General *m* (*Gen.*: *General*).

H

H. 1 (*Fin*) haber *m* (*Cr.*: *credit*). 2 bomba H: bomba *f* de hidrógeno. 3 hectárea(s) *f*(*pl*) (*hectare(s)*). 4 (*Eccl*) Hermano *m* (*Br.*: *Brother*).

h. 1 hacia (*c.*: *circa*). 2 hora(s) *f*(*pl*) (*h.*, *hr*: *hour(s)*). 3 habitantes *mpl* (*pop.*: *population*).

Ha(s). = H. 3.

hect. = H. 3.

Hg. hectogramo(s) *m*(*pl*) (*hg.*: *hectogram(s)*, *hectogramme(s)*).

Hm. hectómetro *m*, hectómetros *mpl* (*hm.*: *hectometre(s)*).

Hnos. Hermanos *mpl* (*Bros*: *Brothers*).

I

I.C.H. Instituto *m* de Cultura Hispánica.

íd. ídem, lo mismo (*do.*: *ditto*).

I.L.A.R.I. Instituto *m* Latinoamericano de Relaciones Internacionales.

Ilmo. Ilustrísimo (*courtesy title*).

Imp. Imprenta *f* (*printers*, *printing works*).

I.N.C. Instituto *m* Nacional de Colonización (*land settlement institute*).

I.N.E. Instituto *m* Nacional de Estadística.

I.N.E.F. Instituto *m* Nacional de Educación Física.

I.N.I. Instituto *m* Nacional de Industria.

I.N.L.E. Instituto *m* Nacional del Libro Español.

I.N.P. Instituto *m* Nacional de Previsión.

I.N.T.A. Instituto *m* Nacional de Técnicas Aéreas.

izq., izq.ª izquierda *f* (*l.h.: left hand*).

izq., izq.º izquierdo (*l.: left*).

J

J.C. Jesucristo (*J.C.: Jesus Christ*).

J.E.N. Junta *f* de Energía Nuclear.

J.O.C.I. Juventud *f* Obrera Católica Internacional.

J.O.N.S. Juntas *fpl* de Ofensiva Nacional-Sindicalista.

jul. julio *m* (*July*).

jun. junio *m* (*June*).

K

k/c. kilociclos *mpl* (*k/c.: kilocycles*).

km/h. kilómetros *mpl* por hora (*in Britain and US reckoned in m.p.h.: miles per hour*).

kv. kilovatio *m*, kilovatios *mpl* (*kw.: kilowatt(s)*).

kv/h. kilovatios-hora *mpl* (*kw/h.: kilowatt-hours*).

L

l. **1** libro *m* (*bk: book*). **2** (*Law*) ley *f* (*law*). **3** litro *m*, litros *mpl* (*l.: litre(s)*).

L/ letra *f* (*letter*).

Lda., Ldo. = Lic.

lib. libro *m* (*bk: book*).

Lic. Licenciado *m*, Licenciada *f*; Lic. en Fil. y Let. = Licenciado *m* en Filosofía y Letras (*B.A.: Bachelor of Arts*).

M

M. Madrid.

m. **1** metro(s) *m(pl)* (*m.: metre(s)*). **2** minuto(s) *m(pl)* (*m., min.: minute(s)*).

m² metro(s) *m(pl)* cuadrado(s) (*sq. m.: square metre(s)*).

m³ metro(s) *m(pl)* cúbicos (*cu. m.: cubic metre(s)*).

mar. marzo *m* (*Mar.: March*).

M.C. Mercado *m* Común (*C.M.: Common Market*).

m/c **1** mi cuenta (*my account*). **2** mi casa (*my firm*).

M.F. modulación *f* de frecuencia (*FM: frequency modulation*).

miérc. miércoles *m* (*Wed., Weds.: Wednesday*).

M.I.J.A.R.C. Movimiento *m* Internacional de la Juventad Agrícola y Rural Católica.

M.I.T. Ministerio *m* de Información y Turismo.

M.º **1** Ministerio *m* (*Ministry*). **2** Maestro *m* (*Master*).

m/n. moneda *f* nacional (*national currency*).

m/o. mi orden (*my order*).

Mons. Monseñor *m* (*Mgr, Mons.: Monsignor*).

N

N. norte *m, adj* (*N.: north*).

n. nacido (*b.: born*).

n/ nuestro (*our*).

N.ª S.ʳᵃ Nuestra Señora (*Our Lady, The Virgin*).

N.B.A.E. Nueva Biblioteca de Autores Españoles.

n/cta. nuestra cuenta (*our account*).

N. de la R. nota *f* de la redacción (*editor's note*).

NE. nor(d)este *m, adj* (*N.E.: north-east*).

n/f. nuestro favor (*our favour*).

n/g. nuestro giro (*our money order*).

n/L. nuestra letra (*our letter*).

NNE. nornordeste (*N.N.E.: north-north-east*).

NNO. nornoroeste (*N.N.W.: north-north-west*).

NN.UU. Naciones *fpl* Unidas (*UN: United Nations*).

NO. noroeste *m, adj* (*N.W.: north-west*).

n.º número *m* (*No.: number*).

n/o. nuestra orden (*our order*).

NODO Noticiario *m* y Documentales Cinematográficos (*Spanish newsreel and documentary films*).

nov. noviembre *m* (*Nov.: November*).

nra., nro. nuestra, nuestro (*our*).

N.R.F.H. Nueva Revista *f* de Filología Hispánica.

N.S. Nuestro Señor (*Our Lord*).

N.T. Nuevo Testamento *m* (*N.T.: New Testament*).

N.U. Naciones *fpl* Unidas (*UN: United Nations*).

núm. número *m* (*No.: number*).

O

O. oeste *m, adj* (*W.: west*).

o/ orden *m* (*order*).

OACI Organización *f* de Aviación Civil Internacional (*ICAO: International Civil Aviation Organization*).

Ob.ᵖᵒ Obispo *m* (*Bp: Bishop*).

obr. cit. obra *f* citada (*op. cit.: opere citato*).

O.C.A.S.E.I. Obra *f* Católica de Asistencia a Estudiantes Iberoamericanos.

O.C.A.S.H.A. Obra *f* de Cooperación Apostólica Seglar Hispanoamericana.

O.C.A.U. Obra *f* Católica de Asistencia Universitaria.

O.C.E.D. Organización *f* de Cooperación Económica y Desarrollo (*OECD: Organization for European Cooperation and Development*).

O.C.I.C. Oficina *f* Católica Internacional del Cine.

oct. octubre *m* (*Oct.: October*).

O.E.A. Organización *f* de Estados Americanos (*OAS: Organization of American States*).

O.E.C.E. Organización *f* Europea de Cooperación Económica (*OEEC: Organization for European Economic Cooperation*).

O.E.I. Oficina *f* de Educación Iberoamericana.

O.I.S.S. Organización *f* Iberoamericana de Seguridad Social.

O.I.T. Organización *f* (*or* Oficina *f*) Internacional del Trabajo (*ILO: International Labour Organization*).

O.J.E. Organización *f* Juvenil Española.

O.M. **1** Orden *f* Ministerial (*ministry order*). **2** Orden *f* de la Merced.

O.M.S. Organización *f* Mundial de la Salud (*WHO: World Health Organization*).

ONO. oesnoroeste (*W.N.W.: west-north-west*).

ONU Organización *f* de las Naciones Unidas (*UNO: United Nations Organization*).

O.P. **1** Obras *fpl* Públicas. **2** (*Eccl*) Orden *f* de Predicadores (*O.S.D.: Order of St Dominic*).

Op.D. Opus *m* Dei (*Catholic lay order*).

OSO. oessudoeste (*W.S.W.: west-south-west*).

OTAN Organización *f* del Tratado del Atlántico Norte (*NATO: North Atlantic Treaty Organization*).

OTASE Organización *f* del Tratado del Sudeste Asiático (*SEATO: South-East Asia Treaty Organization*).

OVNI objeto *m* volante no identificado (*UFO: unidentified flying object*).

P

P. **1** Padre *m* (*F., Fr: Father*). **2** Papa *m* (*Pope*).

p.ª para*.

p.a. **1** por autorización (*as authorized, by authority*). **2** por ausencia (*owing to absence*).

pág(s). página(s) *f(pl)* (*p(b).: page(s)*).

pat. patente *f* (*pat.: patent*).

P.C. Partido *m* Comunista (*C.P.: Communist Party*).

p.c. por cien, por ciento (*p.c., %: per cent*).

P.D. posdata *f* (*P.S.: postscript*).

pdo. pasado (*ult.: ultimo*).

P.ᵉ = P.P.

p.ej. por ejemplo (*e.g.: exempli gratia, for example*).

p.m. (*SAm*) post meridiem (*p.m.: post meridiem*).

pmo. próximo (*prox.: proximo*).

P.N.A. Patronato *m* Nacional Antituberculoso.

P.º Paseo *m* (*Av., Ave: Avenue*).

p.o. por orden = p.p.

p.º n.º peso *m* neto (*nt wt: net weight*).

port. portugués *m* (*Port.: Portuguese*).

PP. Padres *mpl* (*Frs: Fathers*).

P.P. porte *m* pagado (*C.P.: carriage paid*).

p.p. por poder (*p.p.: per procurationem, by proxy*).

p.pdo. próximo pasado (*ult.*: *ultimo*).

P.P.M. Patronato *m* de Protección a la Mujer.

P.R. Puerto *m* Rico (*P.R.*: *Puerto Rico*).

pr.fr. próximo futuro (*proximo*).

prom. promedio *m* (*av.*: *average*).

Pta. (*Geog*) Punta *f* (*Point*).

pta., ptas. peseta *f*, pesetas *fpl* (*peseta(s)*).

P.V.P. precio *m* de venta al público (*sale price to the public*).

PYRESA Prensa y Radio Españolas, Sociedad Anónima (*press agency*).

Q

q.b.s.m. que besa sus manos (*courtesy formula*).

q.b.s.p. que besa sus pies (*courtesy formula*).

q.D.g. que Dios guarde (*whom God protect*).

q.e.g.e. que en gloria esté (*equivalent to R.I.P.*).

q.e.p.d. que en paz descanse (*R.I.P.*).

q.e.s.m. que estrecha su mano (*courtesy formula*).

quil., qts. quilates *mpl* (*carats*).

qm. quintale(s)* *m(pl)* métrico(s).

q.s.g.h. que santa gloria haya (*equivalent to R.I.P.*).

R

R. 1 Real (*royal*). 2 (*Eccl*) Reverendo (*Rev.*: *Reverend*).

R.A.C.E. Real Automóvil Club *m* de España.

R.A.E. Real Academia *f* Española.

R.A.H. Real Academia *f* de la Historia.

R.A.U. República *f* Árabe Unida (*U.A.R.*: *United Arab Republic*).

Rdo. Reverendo (*Rev.*: *Reverend*).

RENFE Red Nacional de los Ferrocarriles Españoles.

R.F.E. Revista *f* de Filología Española.

R.M. Reverenda Madre *f* (*Reverend Mother*).

Rmo. Reverendísimo (*Rt Rev.*: *Right Reverend*).

R.N.E. Radio *f* Nacional de España.

R.O. real orden *f* (*royal decree*).

R.P. Reverendo Padre *m* (*Reverend Father*).

rte. remite, remitente *mf* (*sender*).

S

S. 1 sur *m*, *adj* (*S.*: *south*). 2 (*Rel*) San, Santa (*St*: *Saint*).

s. 1 siglo *m* (*c.*: *century*). 2 siguiente (*foll.*: *following*).

s / su, sus (*your*).

S.ª Sierra *f* (*Mts*: *Mountains*).

S.A. 1 (*Comm, Fin*) Sociedad *f* Anónima (*Ltd*: *Limited*; *Corp.*: *Corporation*; *Inc.*: *Incorporated*). 2 Su Alteza (*H.H.*: *His Highness, Her Highness*).

sáb. sábado *m* (*Sat.*: *Saturday*).

S.A.R. Su Alteza Real (*H.R.H.*: *His Royal Highness, Her Royal Highness*).

s /c. 1 su casa (*your firm*). 2 su cuenta (*your account*).

SE. sudeste *m*, *adj* (*S.E.*: *south-east*).

S.E. Su Excelencia (*H.E.*: *His Excellency*).

S.Em.ª Su Eminencia (*H.E.*: *His Eminence*).

sep., sept. se(p)tiembre *m* (*Sept.*: *September*).

SEU Sindicato *m* Español Universitario.

s.e.u.o. salvo error u omisión (*E. & O.E.*: *errors and omissions excepted*.)

s.f. sin fecha (*n.d.*: *no date*).

s /f. su favor (*your favour*).

sgte(s). siguiente(s) (*f.*, *ff.*, *foll.*: *following*).

S.M. Su Majestad (*H.M.*: *His (Her) Majesty*).

S.M.N. Servicio *m* Meteorológico Nacional.

SO. suroeste *m*, *adj* (*S.W.*: *south-west*).

s /o. su orden (*your order*).

S.O.E. Seguro *m* Obligatorio de Enfermedad.

Sr. Señor *m* (*Mr*: *Mister*).

Sra. Señora *f* (*Mrs*: *Mistress*).

S.R.C. se ruega contestación (*RSVP*).

Sres., Srs. Señores *mpl* (*Messrs*: *Messieurs*).

Srta. Señorita *f* (*Miss*).

S.S. Su Santidad (*H.H.*: *His Holiness*).

SS Santos, Santas (*SS*: *Saints*).

s.s. seguro servidor (*courtesy formula*).

SSE. sudsudeste (*S.S.E.*: *south-south-east*).

SSO. sudsudoeste (*S.S.W.*: *south-south-west*).

s.s.s. su seguro servidor (*courtesy formula*).

Sta. Santa (*St*: *Saint*).

Sto. San (*St*: *Saint*).

T

t. tomo(s) *m(pl)* (*vol(s)*: *volume(s)*).

T /año toneladas *fpl* por año.

tel., teléf. teléfono *m* (*Tel.*: *telephone*).

tít. título *m* (*title*).

Tm. tonelada *f* métrica, toneladas *fpl* métricas (*metric ton(s)*).

trad. traducido (*trans.*: *translated*).

T.R.B. toneladas *fpl* de registro bruto (*G.R.T.*: *gross register tons*).

TVE Televisión *f* Española.

U

Ud. usted (*you*).

Uds. ustedes (*you*).

U.E.P. Unión *f* Europea de Pagos (*EPU*: *European Payments Union*).

U.G.T. Unión *f* General de Trabajadores.

U.P.A. Unión *f* Panamericana (*PAU*: *Pan-American Union*).

U.P.A.E. Unión *f* Postal de las Américas y de España.

U.R.S.S. Unión *f* de Repúblicas Socialistas Soviéticas (*USSR*: *Union of Socialist Soviet Republics*).

V

V. usted (*you*)

v. 1 (*Elec*) voltio(s) *m(pl)* (*v.*: *volt(s)*). 2 véase (*v.*: *vide, see*).

V.A. Vuestra Alteza (*Your Highness*).

Vd. usted (*you*).

Vda. de viuda *f* de (*widow of*).

Vds. ustedes (*you*).

vers.º, (*Bib*) versículo *m* (*v.*: *verse*).

v.g., v.gr. verbigracia (*viz.*: *videlicet, namely*).

vier. viernes *m* (*Fri.*: *Friday*).

V.M. Vuestra Majestad (*Your Majesty*).

V.º B.º visto bueno*.

vra., vro. vuestra, vuestro (*your*).

VV. ustedes (*you*).

English Abbreviations
Abreviaturas inglesas

A

A 1 answer (*respuesta f*). 2 (*Cine: Brit*) adults (*película f apta para mayores*).

AA 1 (*Aut*) Automobile Association. 2 Alcoholics Anonymous (*sociedad de los alcohólicos reformados*). 3 (*Cine: Brit*) Restricted (*película f más apta para mayores*).

AAA 1 (*Sport*) Amateur Athletic Association. 2 (*US*) American Automobile Association.

AAU (*US*) Amateur Athletic Union.

A.A.U.P. American Association of University Professors.

AB 1 (*Naut*) able-bodied seaman (*marinero m de primera*). 2 (*US: Univ*) = **B.A.**

ABA Amateur Boxing Association.

A-bomb atomic bomb (*bomba A. bomba f atómica*).

Abp Archbishop (*Arz.: arzobispo m*).

abr. abridged (*abreviado, resumido*).

abs., absol. absolutely (*absolutamente*).

abs., abstr. abstract (*abstracto*).

A/C account current (*c/c: cuenta f corriente*).

a/c account (*c.ta: cuenta f*).

AC 1 (*Elec*) alternating current. 2 (*Aer*) aircraftman (*soldado raso de las fuerzas aéreas*).

acc. (*Fin*) account (*c.ta: cuenta f*).

ACGB Arts Council of Great Britain (*organización para el fomento de las artes*).

A.D. Anno Domini, in the year of our Lord (*A. C.: año m de Cristo*).

ad advertisement (*anuncio m*).

ADC aide-de-camp (*edecán m*).

Adjt adjutant (*ayudante m*).

ad lib.* ad libitum, at pleasure.

admin. administration (*admón.*).

advt advertisement (*anuncio m*).

AEC (*US*) Atomic Energy Commission.

AEF 1 Amalgamated Union of Engineering and Foundry Workers. 2 (*US*) American Expeditionary Forces.

AEU Amalgamated Engineering Union (*sindicato de ingenieros*).

A.F.C. (*US*) Air Force Cross (*condecoración*).

AFL-CIO American Federation of Labor and Congress of Industrial Organizations.

A.F.M. (*US*) Air Force Medal (*condecoración*).

AFN (*US*) American Forces Network (*Red f de Radiodifusión de las Fuerzas Armadas de EE. UU.*).

AGM Annual General Meeting (*Junta f Anual*).

A 1* first class.

A.I.D. artificial insemination by donor.

Ala. (*US*) Alabama.

Alas. (*US*) Alaska.

A-level Advanced level (*grado superior del General Certificate of Education (a los 17–18 años); = bachillerato m superior*).

Alta. Alberta (*provincia canadiense*).

Am. 1 America (*América f*). 2 American (*americano*).

A.M. (*US: Univ*) = **M.A.**

a.m. ante meridiem, before noon (*antes del mediodía, de la mañana*).

A.M.A. American Medical Association.

anon. anonymous (*anónimo*).

AOB Any Other Business (*ruegos mpl y preguntas*).

AP Associated Press.

Ap., Apr. April (*abr.: abril m*).

A.P.O. (*US*) Army Post Office.

app. appendix (*apéndice m*).

appro.* approval.

apt. (*US*) apartment (*apartamento m*).

A.R.A.M. Associate of the Royal Academy of Music.

A.R.C.M. Associate of the Royal College of Music.

A.R.I.B.A. Associate of the Royal Institute of British Architects.

Ariz. (*US*) Arizona.

Ark. (*US*) Arkansas.

ARP air-raid precautions (*servicios de defensa civil contra los bombardeos aéreos*).

arr. arrives (*llega*).

A/S account sales (*cuenta f de ventas*).

A.S.P.C.A. American Society for the Prevention of Cruelty to Animals (*sociedad f protectora de animales*).

assn association (*asociación f*).

asst assistant (*ayudante mf*).

ASTMS Association of Scientific, Technical and Managerial Staffs.

ATS Auxiliary Territorial Service (*reserva de la sección femenina del ejército*).

Att., Atty Attorney (*abogado m*).

Atty. Gen. Attorney-General.

Aug. August (*ag.: agosto m*).

AUT Association of University Teachers.

A.V. Authorized Version (of the Bible) (*versión oficial de la Biblia en lengua inglesa*).

av. average (*prom.: promedio m*).

Av., Ave Avenue (*Av., Avda.: avenida f*).

avdp. avoirdupois*.

a.w. atomic weight (*peso m atómico*).

AWOL (*Mil*) absent without leave (*ausente sin permiso*).

B

B black (*negro: mina del lápiz*).

b. born (*n.: nacido*).

b. & b. bed and breakfast (*cama f con desayuno,*

en los hoteles, pensiones etc).

B.A. 1 (*Univ*) Bachelor of Arts (*Lic. en Fil. y Let.*). 2 British Academy (*academia literaria*). 3 British Association (for the Advancement of Science). 4 (*Geog*) Buenos Aires (*Bs. As.*).

BAOR British Army of the Rhine (*ejército británico en Alemania*).

Bart Baronet (*título de la nobleza británica*).

Battn battalion (*Bón.: batallón m*).

BB Boy's Brigade.

BBC British Broadcasting Corporation (*Radio Nacional de Gran Bretaña*).

B.C. 1 before Christ (*a. de J.C.: antes de Jesucristo*). 2 British Columbia.

BCG Bacillus Calmette-Guérin (*bacilo antituberculosis*).

B.D. Bachelor of Divinity (*Licenciado m en Teología*).

b.e. bill of exchange (*letra f de cambio*).

BEA British European Airways.

Beds. Bedfordshire (*condado inglés*).

BEF British Expeditionary Force.

B.E.M. British Empire Medal (*condecoración británica*).

Benelux Belgium, Netherlands, Luxembourg.

Berks. Berkshire (*condado inglés*).

B.F. (*euph*) bloody fool (*idiota m*).

b/f brought forward (*suma f del anterior*).

BFI British Film Institute.

B.F.P.O. British Forces Post Office.

b/fwd brought forward (*suma f del anterior*).

B'ham Birmingham.

b.h.p. brake horsepower (*potencia f al freno*).

BIF British Industries Fair (*Feria f de Muestras de la Industria Británica*).

biog. 1 biography (*biografía f*). 2 biographical (*biográfico*).

bk 1 book (*l.: libro m*). 2 (*Fin*) bank (*B.º: banco m*).

B.L. Bachelor of Law.

B/L bill of lading (*conocimiento m de embarque*).

bldg building (*edificio m*).

B. Litt. Bachelor of Letters.

Blvd Boulevard (*bulevar m*).

B.M. 1 Bachelor of Medicine. 2 British Museum.

BMA British Medical Association.

B.Mus. Bachelor of Music.

B.O. (*euph*) body odour (*olor m a sudor*).

BOAC British Overseas Airways Corporation.

B. of E. Bank of England.

bor. borough (*municipio m*).

bot. bought (*comprado*).

BOT Board of Trade (*Ministerio m de Comercio*).

Bp Bishop (*ob.ᵛᵒ: obispo m*).

BP British Petroleum (*compañía de petróleo*).

Br Brother (*hermano m*).

BR British Rail (*ferrocarriles británicos*).

B/R bills receivable (*obligaciones fpl por cobrar*).

Brecon. Breconshire (*condado galés*).

Brig. Brigadier (*general de brigada*).

Brit. 1 Britain (*Gran Bretaña f*). 2 British (*británico*).

Bro. Brother (*hermano m*).

Bros Brothers (*Hnos.: Hermanos*).

B/S bill of sale (*hipoteca f de bienes*).

B.Sc. Bachelor of Science.

B.Sc.Econ. Bachelor of Economic Science.

BSI British Standards Institution (*instituto de normas británico*).

BST 1 British Summer Time (*hora de verano*). 2 British Standard Time.

Bucks. Buckinghamshire (*condado inglés*).

BUP British United Press (*agencia de noticias*).

B.V.M. Blessed Virgin Mary (*B.M.V.*).

B.W.I. British West Indies (*Antillas fpl Británicas*).

C

C. 1 (*Lit*) chapter (*c., cap., cap.ᵒ: capítulo m*). 2 (*Geog*) Cape (*Cabo m*). 3 central (*central*). 4 centigrade (*termómetro m centigrado*). 5 Conservative (*conservador m: also adj*).

c. 1 (*Fin: US*) cent (*centavo m*). 2 (*Fin: France*) centime (*céntimo m*). 3 century (*s.: siglo m*). 4 (*Hist*) circa, about (*h.: hacia; eg c. 1490 = hacia 1490*). 5 (*Math*) cubic (*cúbico*).

C.A. Chartered Accountant (*contable m diplomado*).

C/A current account (*c/c: cuenta f corriente*).

Caer. Caernarvonshire (*condado galés*).

Cal., Calif. (*US*) California.

Cambs. Cambridgeshire (*condado inglés*).

Can. 1 Canada (*El Canadá*). 2 Canadian (*canadiense*).

Cantab. Cantabrigiensis, of Cambridge (*de la Universidad de Cambridge*).

cap. (*Typ*) capital letter (*mayúscula f*).

Capt. Captain (*capitán m*).

Card. Cardiganshire (*condado galés*).

Carm. Carmarthenshire (*condado galés*).

carr. carriage (*porte m*).

cat. catalogue (*catálogo m*).

CAT College of Advanced Technology (*equivalent to universidad laboral*).

C.B. 1 Companion of the Bath (*título honorífico británico*). 2 (*Mil*) confined to barracks ((*men*) *arresto m menor en ᵌ cuartel*, (*officers*) *arresto m en banderas*). 3 cash book (*libro m de caja*).

CBC Canadian Broadcasting Corporation (*radio nacional del Canadá*).

C.B.E. Commander of the Order of the British Empire (*título honorífico británico*).

CBI Confederation of British Industries (*organización patronal*).

CC 1 Chamber of Commerce (*cámara f de comercio*). 2 County Council (*concejo m del condado*). 3 Cricket Club; Cycling Club.

Cent. centigrade (*termómetro m centigrado*).

CENTO Central Treaty Organization.

cert. certificate (*certificado m*).

CEWC Council for Education in World Citizenship.

cf. confer, compare (*cfr.: confróntese, compárese*).

c/f, c/fwd carried forward (*suma y sigue*).

ch. 1 (*Lit*) chapter (*c., cap., cap.ᵒ: capítulo m*). 2 (*Fin*) cheque (*ch.: cheque m*).

Ch.B Chirurgiae Baccalaureus, Bachelor of Surgery.

Ches. Cheshire (*condado inglés*).

chq. cheque (*ch.: cheque m*).

C.I. Channel Islands (*Islas fpl Normandas*).

c/i certificate of insurance (*certificado m de seguro*).

CIA (*US*) Central Intelligence Agency (*servicio secreto y de contraespionaje*).

CID Criminal Investigation Department (*equivalent to Brigada f de Investigación Criminal*).

c.i.f. cost, insurance and freight (*c.i.f., c.s.f.: coste, seguro y flete*).

C.(I.)G.S. Chief of (Imperial) General Staff.

C.-in-C. Commander-in-Chief.

CIO (*US*) Congress of Industrial Organizations.

C.M. Common Market (*M.C.: Mercado m Común*).

C.M.S. Church Missionary Society (*sociedad misionera de la Iglesia Anglicana*).

CND Campaign for Nuclear Disarmament.

Co. 1 (*Comm*) company (*C., Cía.: compañía f*). 2 county (*condado m*).

C.O. 1 (*Mil*) Commanding Officer. 2 conscientious objector (*objetor m de conciencia*).

c/o care of (*c/d: en casa de; a/c: al cuidado de*).

C.O.D. 1 (*Comm*) cash on delivery (*pagar contra recepción, cóbrese a la entrega*). 2 Concise Oxford Dictionary.

C. of E. Church of England.

COI Central Office of Information.

Col. (*Mil*) Colonel (*Cnel.: coronel m*).

col. column (*col.: columna f*).

coll. college (*colegio m*).

Colo. (*US*) Colorado.

Com. Communist (*comunista mf: also adj*).

conj. conjugation (*conjugación f*).

Conn. (*US*) Connecticut.

Cons. Conservative (*conservador m: also adj*).

cont., cont'd continued (*continuación f*).

Co-op Co-operative (Society).

Corn. Cornwall (*Cornualles, condado inglés*).

Corp. 1 (*Comm, Fin*) Corporation (*S.A.: sociedad f anónima*). 2 (*Pol*) Corporation (*ayuntamiento m; municipio m*). 3 (*Mil*) Corporal (*cabo m*).

Coy company (*C., Cía.: compañía f*).

C.P. 1 (*Pol*) Communist Party (*P.C.: Partido m Comunista*). 2 (*Comm*) carriage paid (*P.P.: porte m pagado*).

cp. compare (*comp.: compárese*).

c.p. candlepower (*potencia f lumínica*).

C.P.A. (*US*) Certified Public Accountant (*contable m diplomado*).

Cpl Corporal (*cabo m*).

Cr. 1 (*Comm*) credit (*haber m*). 2 (*Comm*) creditor (*acreedor m*). 3 (*Pol*) councillor (*concejal m*).

C.R.T. cathode-ray tube (*tubo m de rayos catódicos*).

C.S.M. Company Sergeant-Major (*approx: brigada m de compañía*).

C.U. Cambridge University.

cu. cubic (*cúbico*).

cu. ft. cubic foot, cubic feet (*pie m cúbico, pies mpl cúbicos*).

cu. in. cubic inch(es) (*pulgada f cúbica, pulgadas fpl cúbicas*).

Cumb. Cumberland (*condado inglés*).

CUP Cambridge University Press.

c.w.o. cash with order (*pago m al contado*).

CWS Cooperative Wholesale Society (*cooperativo de consumidores*).

cwt hundredweight(s)*.

C.Z. Canal Zone (*Zona f del Canal de Panamá*).

D

d. 1 date (*fecha f*). 2 daughter (*hija f*). 3 died (*m.: murió*). 4 (*Rail etc*) departs (*sale*). 5 (*Fin*) denarius, penny (*penique m*).

D.A. 1 (*Fin*) deposit account (*approx: cuenta f de ahorros*). 2 (*US*) District Attorney (*fiscal m de distrito*).

DAB (*US*) Dictionary of American Biography.

dag. decagram(s), decagramme(s) (*Dg.: decagramo m, decagramos mpl*).

dal. decalitre(s) (*Dl.: decalitro m, decalitros mpl*).

dam. decametre(s) (*Dm.: decámetro m, decámetros mpl*).

D.B.E. Dame Commander of the Order of the British Empire (*título honorífico británico*).

D.C. 1 (*Elec*) direct current. 2 (*US*) District of Columbia (*Washington, capital de Estados Unidos, y sus alrededores*).

D.C.M. Distinguished Conduct Medal (*condecoración británica*).

D.D. Doctor of Divinity (*Doctor m en Teología*).

D.D.S. Doctor of Dental Surgery.

Dec. December (*dic.: diciembre m*).

dec. deceased (*m.: murió; fallecido*).

Del. (*US*) Delaware.

del. delete (*táchese, a suprimir*).

Dem. Democrat (*demócrata mf; also adj*).

Denb. Denbighshire (*condado galés*).

dep. departs (*sale*).

dept department (*departamento m*).

Derbys. Derbyshire (*condado inglés*).

DES Department of Education and Science.

D.F.C. Distinguished Flying Cross (*condecoración británica*).

D.F.M. Distinguished Flying Medal (*condecoración británica*).

diam. diameter (*diámetro m*).

Dip. Diploma (*diploma m*).

dist. district (*distrito m*).

div. dividend (*dividendo m*).

DJ 1 dinner jacket (*smoking m*). 2 (*Radio*) disc jockey (*presentador m de discos*).

D.Lit. Doctor of Letters.

DM Deutschmark (*marco m alemán*).

D.M. Doctor of Medicine.

D.N.B. Dictionary of National Biography.

do. ditto (*íd.: ídem, lo mismo*).

D.O.A. (*US*) dead on arrival (*e.g. at hospital*).

dol. dollar(s) (*dólar m, dólares mpl*).

doz. dozen (*d.ⁿᵃ: docena f*).

D.P. displaced person (*desplazado m, desplazada f*).

D.Phil. Doctor of Philosophy.

D.P.P. Director of Public Prosecutions.

dpt department (*departamento m*).

Dr 1 Doctor (*Dr.: doctor m*). 2 (*Comm*) debtor (*deudor m*).

dr. drachm, dram (*US*) (*dracma f*).

d/s. days after sight (*d/v: a . . . días vista*).

D.S.C. Distinguished Service Cross (*condecoración británica*).

D.Sc. Doctor of Science.

D.S.M. Distinguished Service Medal (*condecoración británica*).

D.S.O. Distinguished Service Order (*condecoración británica*).

DTs delirium tremens*.

D.V. Deo volente, God willing (*D.m.: Dios mediante*).

E

E. east (*E.: este m, adj*).

E. & O.E. errors and omissions excepted (*s.e.u.o.: salvo error u omisión*).

ea. each (*c/u: cada uno*).

ECG electrocardiogram*.

ECOSOC Economic and Social Council (*Consejo m Económico y Social (de las Naciones Unidas)*).

ECSC European Coal and Steel Community (*CECA: Comunidad f Europea del Carbón y del Acero*).

ed. 1 edition (*ed.: edición f*). 2 editor*. 3 edited*.

E/E. errors excepted (*salvo error*).

EEC European Economic Community (*CEE: Comunidad f Económica Europea*).

EFTA European Free Trade Association (*EFTA: Asociación f Europea de Libre Comercio*).

e.g. exempli gratia, for example (*p.ej.: por ejemplo*).

encl. enclosure(s) (*adjunto*).

E.N.E. east-north-east (*ENE.: estenordeste*).

Eng. 1 England (*Inglaterra f*). 2 English (*inglés m; also adj*).

E.P. 1 electroplate*. 2 (*Mus*) extended play (*duración f ampliada*).

EPU European Payments Union (*Unión f Europea de Pagos*).

E.R. Elizabeth Regina, Queen Elizabeth.

ERNIE Electronic Random Number Indicator Equipment (*máquina electrónica que elige los números premiados entre los Premium Bonds (bonos de la Caja de Ahorros británica)*).

E.S.E. east-south-east (*ESE.: estesudeste*).

E.S.N. (*euph*) educationally subnormal (*de inteligencia inferior a la normal*).

E.S.P. extrasensory perception (*percepción f extrasensorial*).

Esq. Esquire*.

est. established (*eg est. 1899 = se fundó en 1899*).

et al. et alii, and others (*y otros*).

et seq. et sequentia, and the following (*y sigs.: y siguientes*).

ETU Electrical Trades Union.

Eur. 1 Europe (*Europa f*). 2 European (*europeo*).

ex. example (*ej.: ejemplo m*).

ex div. ex dividend, without dividend (*sin dividendo*).

ex int. ex interest, without interest (*sin interés*).

ext. (*Tel*) extension*.

F

F. 1 Fahrenheit (*termómetro m Fahrenheit*).

2 (*Eccl*) Father (*P., P.ᵉ: padre m*). 3 French (*fr.: francés m*).

f. 1 (*Naut*) fathom (*braza f*). 2 (*Math*) foot, feet (*pie m, pies mpl*). 3 following (*sig.: siguiente*). 4 female (*hembra f*).

FA Football Association.

FAA (*US*) Federal Aviation Agency.

fac(s). facsimile (*facsímil m*).

FAO Food and Agriculture Organization (*FAO: Organización f para la Alimentación y la Agricultura*).

FBI (*US*) Federal Bureau of Investigation (*equivalent to Brigada f de Investigación Criminal*).

F.C. Football Club (*C.F.: club m de fútbol*).

FCC (*US*) Federal Communications Commission.

F.D. Fidei Defensor, Defender of the Faith (*uno de los títulos del monarca británico*).

FDA (*US*) Food and Drug Administration.

Feb. February (*feb.º: febrero m*).

ff. following (*sigs.: siguientes*).

FHA (*US*) Federal Housing Administration.

F'hold freehold*.

Fla. (*US*) Florida.

Flint. Flintshire (*condado galés*).

F/Lt Flight Lieutenant (*teniente m de aviación*).

F.M. 1 (*Mil*) Field Marshal*. 2 (*Radio*) frequency modulation.

fm fathom (*braza f*).

F.O. 1 (*Brit Pol*) Foreign Office (*Ministerio m de Asuntos Exteriores*). 2 (*Aer*) Flying Officer (*subteniente m de aviación*).

Fo., fol. folio (*fol.: folio m*).

f.o.b. free on board (*f.a.b.: franco a bordo*).

foll. following (*sig., sigs.: siguiente, siguientes*).

f.o.r. free on rail (*el precio de la mercancía incluye el transporte por ferrocarril*).

F.P. 1 fire plug (*boca f de agua*). 2 freezing point (*punto m de congelación*).

Fr 1 Father (*P., P.ᵉ: padre m*). 2 Friar (*Fr.: fray m*).

fr. 1 (*Fin*) franc(s) (*fr., frs.: franco m, francos mpl*). 2 from (*de; de parte de*).

Fri. Friday (*vier.: viernes m*).

F.R.I.B.A. Fellow of the Royal Institute of British Architects.

F.R.S. Fellow of the Royal Society.

ft foot, feet (*pie m, pies mpl*).

FTC (*US*) Federal Trade Commission.

G

G (*Cine: US*) General (*película apta para todos los públicos*).

g. 1 (*Fin*) guinea(s)*. 2 gram(s), gramme(s) (*gr.: gramo m, gramos mpl*).

Ga. (*US*) Georgia.

gal. gallon(s)*.

GATT General Agreement on Tariffs and Trade (*GATT: Acuerdo m General Sobre Aranceles Aduaneros y Comercio*).

G.B. Great Britain (*Gran Bretaña f*).

G.C. George Cross (*condecoración británica*).

G.C.E. General Certificate of Education (equivalent to *bachillerato elemental y superior*).

G.C.F. greatest common factor (*máximo común divisor m*).

Gdns Gardens (*jardines mpl*).

Gen. General (*Genl.: general m*).

gen. genitive (*gen.: genitivo*).

Ger. 1 Germany (*Alemania f*). 2 German (*alemán m; also adj*).

GHQ General Headquarters (*cuartel m general*).

G.I. (*US*) government issue (*propiedad f del Estado; por extensión, se le llama así al soldado raso norteamericano*).

Gib. Gibraltar.

Gk Greek (*griego m; also adj*).

Glam. Glamorgan (*condado galés*).

GLC Greater London Council (*ayuntamiento de Londres*).

Glos. Gloucestershire (*condado inglés*).

G.M. George Medal (*condecoración británica*).

gm, gms gram(s), gramme(s) (*gr.: gramo m, gramos mpl*).

GMC General Medical Council (*consejo regidor de la medicina*).

GMT Greenwich Mean Time.

GMWU General and Municipal Workers' Union.

gn., gns. guinea(s)*.

GNP gross national product (*producto m nacional bruto*).

G.O.C. General Officer Commanding (*general m, jefe m*).

G.O.M. grand old man (*viejo m distinguido, antiguo jefe m (del partido etc) muy respetado*).

G.O.P. (*US*) Grand Old Party (*Partido m Republicano*).

Gov. Governor (*gobernador m*).

Govt Government (*gob.no: gobierno m*).

G.P. general practitioner (*médico m general, médica f general*).

GP (*Cine: US*) for mature audiences (*película f más apta para los mayores*).

GPO General Post Office (*Administración f General de Correos*).

G.R. Georgius Rex, King George.

gr. 1 gross (*bruto*). 2 gross (*gruesa f; = 12 docenas, = 144*).

G.R.T. gross register tons (*T.R.B.: toneladas fpl de registro bruto*).

G.S. General Staff (*E.M.: estado m mayor*).

Gt Br. Great Britain (*Gran Bretaña f*).

guar. guaranteed (*garantizado*).

H hard (*duro: mina del lápiz*).

h. hour(s) (*h:. hora f, horas fpl*).

h. & c. hot and cold (water) (*con agua corriente caliente y fría*).

Hants. Hampshire (*condado inglés*).

HB hard black (*negro duro: mina del lápiz*).

H-bomb hydrogen bomb (*bomba H: bomba f de hidrógeno*).

H.C. House of Commons (*Cámara f de los Comunes*).

H.C.F. highest common factor (*máximo común divisor m*).

H.E. 1 high explosive*. 2 His Excellency (*S.E.: Su Excelencia*). 3 (*Eccl*) His Eminence (*S.Em.ª: Su Eminencia*).

Herts. Hertfordshire (*condado inglés*).

HEW (*US*) Department of Health, Education and Welfare.

H.F. high frequency ((*de*) *alta frecuencia*).

H.G. Home Guard (*cuerpo de voluntarios para la defensa de la patria (1940)*).

hg. hectogram(s), hectogramme(s) (*Hg.: hectogramo m, hectogramos mpl*).

H.H. 1 His Highness, Her Highness (*S.A.: Su Alteza*). 2 (*Eccl*) His Holiness (*S.S.: Su Santidad*).

hl. hectolitre(s) (*H.: hectolitro m, hectolitros mpl*).

hm. hectometre(s) (*Hm.: hectómetro m, hectómetros mpl*).

H.M. His (Her) Majesty (*S.M.: Su Majestad*).

H.M.I. His (Her) Majesty's Inspector.

HMS His (Her) Majesty's Ship (*buque de guerra británico*).

ho. house (*casa f*).

Hon. 1 Honorary*. 2 Honourable (*título de la nobleza británica*).

H.P., h.p. 1 (*Comm*) hire purchase (*compra f a plazos*). 2 (*Mech*) horsepower (*caballos mpl de vapor*). 3 (*Tech*) high-pressure (*de alta presión*).

HQ Headquarters (*cuartel m general*).

hr(s) hour(s) (*h.: hora f, horas fpl*).

H.R.H. His (Her) Royal Highness (*S.A.R.: Su Alteza Real*).

ht height (*alt.: altura f*).

HT high-tension (*de alta tensión*).

Hunts. Huntingdonshire (*condado inglés*).

HV high-voltage (*de alto voltaje*).

I

I. (*Geog*) Island, Isle (*isla f*).

Ia. (*US*) Iowa.

IAAF International Amateur Athletic Federation.

I.B. 1 (*Comm*) invoice book (*libro m de facturas*). 2 (*Pol*) International Brigade (*Brigadas fpl Internacionales*).

I.C. Intelligence Corps (equivalent to *S.I.M.: Servicio m de Información Militar*).

i/c in charge (of) (*encargado de*).

I.C.A. 1 Institute of Chartered Accountants. 2 Institute of Contemporary Arts.

ICAO International Civil Aviation Organization (*OACI: Organización f de Aviación Civil Internacional*).

ICBM intercontinental ballistic missile*.

ICFTU International Confederation of Free Trade Unions (*Confederación f Internacional de Sindicatos Libres*).

Ida. (*US*) Idaho.

i.e. id est, that is, namely (*esto es, a saber*).

I.L.G.W.U. (*US*) International Ladies' Garment Workers' Union.

Ill. (*US*) Illinois.

ill. 1 illustrated (*con grabados, con láminas*). 2 illustration (*grabado m, lámina f*).

ILO International Labour Organization (*O.I.T.: Organización f Internacional del Trabajo*).

ILP Independent Labour Party (*partido laborista independiente*).

IMF International Monetary Fund (*F.M.I.: Fondo m Monetario Internacional*).

in., ins inch(es) (*pulgada f, pulgadas fpl*).

Inc. (*US*) Incorporated (*S.A.: sociedad f anónima*).

incl. 1 including (*incluso*). 2 inclusive*.

incog. incognito*.

Ind. 1 (*US*) Indiana. 2 (*Pol*) Independent (*independiente m; also adj*).

I.N.S. International News Service (*agencia de noticias*).

ins. insurance (*seguro m*).

Inst. Institute (*instituto m*).

inst. instant, of the present month (*cte.: corriente, de los corrientes*).

intro. introduction (*introducción f*).

I.O.M. Isle of Man.

IOU I owe you (*pagaré m*).

I.O.W. Isle of Wight.

IPA 1 International Phonetic Association. 2 International Phonetic Alphabet.

IQ intelligence quotient (*cociente m intelectual*).

I.R.A. Irish Republican Army.

IRS (US) Internal Revenue Service.

Is. Isle(s), Island(s) (*isla(s) f(pl)*).

It. 1 Italy (*Italia f*). 2 Italian (*italiano m; also adj*).

ITA Independent Television Authority (*comisión regidora de la TV independiente*).

ital. italics*.

ITN Independent Television Network (*red transmisora de la TV independiente*).

ITV Independent Television (*televisión independiente*).

IUS International Union of Students.

J

Jan. January (*ene., en.º: enero m*).

J.C. Jesus Christ (*J.C.: Jesucristo*).

Jn junction (*estación f de empalme*).

J.P. Justice of the Peace (*juez m de paz*).

Jr, Jun., Junr junior*.

Jul. July (*jul.: julio m*).

Jun. June (*jun.: junio m*).

K

Kan. (US) Kansas.

K.B.E. Knight of the British Empire (*título honorífico británico*).

K.C. King's Counsel (*abogado m de categoría superior*).

Ken. (US) Kentucky.

K.G. Knight of the Garter (*título honorífico británico*).

KKK (US) Ku Klux Klan (*organización secreta del Sur de Estados Unidos*).

K.O. knock-out*.

Kt Knight (*título de la nobleza británica*).

kw. kilowatt(s) (*kv.: kilovatio m, kilovatios mpl*).

kw/h. kilowatt-hours (*kv/h.: kilovatios-hora mpl*).

Ky. (US) Kentucky.

L

L. 1 (*Ling*) Latin (*latín m*). 2 (*Pol*) Liberal (*liberal m; also adj*). 3 (*Aut*) learner (*aprendiz m de conductor, aprendiza f de conductora*). 4 Lake (*lago m*).

l. 1 left (*izq., izq.º: izquierdo*). 2 litre(s) (*l.: litro m, litros mpl*).

La. (US) Louisiana.

Lab. 1 (*Pol*) Labour (*laborista m; also adj*). 2 (*Canada*) Labrador.

Lancs. Lancashire (*condado inglés*).

Lat. Latin (*latín m*).

lat. latitude (*latitud f*).

lb. libra, pound* (*libra f*).

L.C. 1 Lord Chancellor (*presidente de la Cámara de los Lores etc*). 2 (*Comm*) letter of credit (*carta f de crédito*).

l.c. lower case (*minúscula f*).

LCC London County Council.

L.C.D. lowest common denominator (*mínimo común denominador m*).

L.C.F. lowest common factor (*mínimo común factor m*).

L.C.M. lowest common multiple (*mínimo común múltiplo m*).

L-Cpl Lance-Corporal (*soldado m primera*).

Ld Lord (*título de la nobleza británica*).

LEA Local Education Authority (*comisión municipal etc de educación*).

Leics. Leicestershire (*condado inglés*).

l.h. left hand (*izq., izq.ª: izquierda f*).

L.I. Long Island (*Estados Unidos*).

Lib. 1 Library (*Bib.: biblioteca f*). 2 (*Pol*) Liberal (*liberal m; also adj*).

Lieut. Lieutenant (*ten.te: teniente m*).

Lieut.-Col. Lieutenant-Colonel (*teniente coronel m*).

Lincs. Lincolnshire (*condado inglés*).

Litt.D. Litterarum Doctor, Doctor of Letters.

ll. lines (*líneas fpl*).

Ll.B. Legum Baccalaureus, Bachelor of Laws.

Ll.D. Legum Doctor, Doctor of Laws.

Lon. London (*Londres*).

long. longitude (*longitud f*).

L.P. 1 (*Pol*) Labour Party (*Partido m Laborista*). 2 (*Mus etc*) long-playing (*microsurco, de larga duración*).

L.P., l.p. low-pressure (*de baja presión*).

L'pl, L'pool Liverpool.

L.R.A.M. Licenciate of the Royal Academy of Music.

L.s.d. Librae, solidi, denarii; pounds, shillings and pence (*libras, chelines y peniques: (fam) pasta f (sl), dinero m*).

LSD (*Chem*) lysergic acid diethylomide (*droga*).

LSE London School of Economics (*colegio de la Universidad de Londres*).

Lt Lieutenant (*ten.te: teniente m*).

LT 1 low-tension (*de baja tensión*). 2 London Transport.

Lt-Col. Lieutenant-Colonel (*teniente coronel m*).

Ltd Limited (*S.A.: sociedad f anónima*).

Lt-Gen. Lieutenant-General (*teniente general m*).

LV luncheon voucher (*vale para la comida de mediodía, entregado al empleado como plus de sueldo*).

M

M (*Cine: US: old*) = GP

m. 1 married (*se casó con*). 2 metre(s) (*m.: metro m, metros mpl*). 3 mile(s) (*milla f, millas fpl*). 4 male (*macho m*). 5 minute(s) (*m.: minuto m, minutos mpl*). 6 (*Math*) million (*millón m, millones mpl*).

M.A. Master of Arts.

Maj. Major (*comandante m*).

Maj.-Gen. Major-General (*general m de división*).

Man., Manit. Manitoba (*provincia canadiense*).

Mar. March (*mar.: marzo m*).

Mass. (US) Massachusetts.

max. maximum (*máximo m, máximum m*).

M.B. Medicinae Baccalaureus, Bachelor of Medicine.

M.B.E. Member of the Order of the British Empire (*título honorífico británico*).

M.C. 1 Master of Ceremonies. 2 (US) Member of Congress. 3 (*Mil*) Military Cross (*condecoración británica*).

MCC Marylebone Cricket Club.

M.D. 1 Medicinae Doctor, Doctor of Medicine. 2 (*euph*) mentally deficient (*de inteligencia inferior a la normal*).

Md. (US) Maryland.

Mddx Middlesex (*condado inglés*).

Me. (US) Maine.

Med. 1 medieval (*medieval*). 2 (*Med*) medical (*médico*).

Medit. Mediterranean (*Mediterráneo m*).

memo. memorandum*.

Mer. Merionethshire (*condado galés*).

Messrs Messieurs (*Sres.: Señores mpl*).

Met. Metropolitan (*metropolitano*).

met. meterological (*meteorológico*).

mfd manufactured (*fabricado adj*).

mfg manufacturing (*fabricación f, manufacturero adj*).

mfr manufacturer (*fabricante m*).

mfs manufacturers (*fabricante m*).

Mgr Monsignor (*Mons.: Monseñor m*).

M.I.5 Military Intelligence (5) (*servicio secreto y de contraespionaje*).

Mich. (US) Michigan.

Min. 1 Minister (*ministro m*). 2 Ministry (*ministerio m*).

min. 1 minute(s) (*m.: minuto m, minutos mpl*). 2 minimum (*mínimo m, mínimum m*).

Minn. (US) Minnesota.

misc. miscellaneous (*vario, diverso*).

Miss. (US) Mississippi.

M.I.T. Massachusetts Institute of Technology.

MLA Modern Language Association.

M.M. Military Medal (*condecoración británica*).

MM Messieurs (*Sres.: Señores mpl*).

M.N. Merchant Navy (*marina f mercante*).

Mo. (US) Missouri.

M.O. 1 (*Fin*) money order (*giro m postal*). 2 medical officer (*médico m*).

M.O.H. 1 Medical Officer of Health (*jefe de los servicios de sanidad (de* *una ciudad etc)).* **2** Ministry of Health (*Ministerio* m *de Sanidad,* equivalent to (Spain) *Dirección* f *General de Sanidad).*

mol. wt molecular weight (*peso* m *molecular).*

Mon. **1** Monday (*lunes* m). **2** Monmouthshire (*condado anglo-galés).*

Mont. **1** Montgomeryshire (*condado galés).* **2** (*US*) Montana.

MOT Ministry of Transport.

M.P. **1** (*Pol*) Member of Parliament. **2** (*Mil*) Military Police. **3** Metropolitan Police (*policía de Londres).*

M.P.B.W. Ministry of Public Building and Works (*Ministerio* m *de Obras Públicas).*

m.p.g. miles per gallon (in Spain reckoned in *kilómetros por litro).*

m.p.h. miles per hour (in Spain reckoned in *km./h.: kilómetros por hora).*

M.P.S. Member of the Pharmaceutical Society.

Mr Mister*.

MRC Medical Research Council.

Mrs Mistress*.

M.S. motorship (*motonave* f).

M.Sc. Master of Science.

M.S.L. mean sea-level (*nivel* m *medio del mar).*

Mt Mount (*monte* m, *montaña* f).

MTB motor torpedo-boat (*torpedero* m).

Mus.B. Musicae Baccalaureus, Bachelor of Music.

Mus.D. Musicae Doctor, Doctor of Music.

Mx Middlesex (*condado inglés).*

N

N. north (*N.: norte* m, adj).

n. **1** neuter (*neutro*). **2** name (*nombre* m). **3** natus, born (*n.:nacido).*

NAACP (*US*) National Association for the Advancement of Colored People (*asociación para el fomento del progreso de la gente de color).*

NAAFI Navy, Army and Air Force Institutes (*servicio de cantinas etc para las fuerzas armadas).*

NALGO National Association of Local Government Officers.

NAS **1** National Association of Schoolmasters. **2** (*US*) National Academy of Science.

NASA (*US*) National Astronautics and Space Administration.

Nat. **1** National (*nacional).* **2** (*Pol*) Nationalist (*nacionalista* m).

Nat. Hist. Natural History (*historia* f *natural).*

NATO North Atlantic Treaty Organization (*NATO, OTAN: Organización* f *del Tratado del Atlántico Norte).*

N.B. **1** nota bene, note well (*N.B.: nótese bien).* **2** New Brunswick (*provincia canadiense).*

N.C. (*US*) North Carolina.

NCB National Coal Board (*junta nacional del carbón).*

N.C.O. non-commissioned officer*.

N.D., N.Dak. (*US*) North Dakota.

n.d. no date (*s.f.: sin fecha).*

N.E. **1** (*US*) New England (*región de EE.UU.).* **2** north-east (*NE.: nor(d)este* m, adj).

N.E.B. New English Bible.

Neb., Nebr. (*US*) Nebraska.

N.E.D. New English Dictionary.

NEDC (*fam:* Neddy) National Economic Development Council.

Neth. Netherlands (*Países* mpl *Bajos).*

Nev. (*US*) Nevada.

N.F. Newfoundland (*Terranova* f).

NFS National Fire Service (*servicio de bomberos).*

NFU National Farmers' Union (*asociación de agricultores).*

N.H. (*US*) New Hampshire.

N.H.(I.) National Health (Insurance) (*Seguro* m *Social Nacional,* equivalent to (Spain) *Seguro* m *de Enfermedad).*

N.H.S. National Health Service (*Servicio* m *Nacional de Sanidad).*

NIBMAR no independence before majority rule (*fórmula que resume la política del gobierno del Reino Unido en el asunto de Rodesia (1965 etc)).*

N.J. (*US*) New Jersey.

NLI National Lifeboat Institution (*servicio de lanchas de socorro).*

N.M., N.Mex. (*US*) New Mexico (*Nuevo Méjico).*

N.N.E. north - north - east (*NNE.: nornordeste).*

N.N.W. north - north - west (*NNO.: nornoroeste).*

No. **1** numero, number (*n.º, núm.: número* m). **2 = N.**

non seq. non sequitur, it does not follow (*no sigue).*

Northants. Northamptonshire (*condado inglés).*

Northumb. Northumberland (*condado inglés).*

Nos. numbers (*n.º, núm.: números* mpl).

Notts. Nottinghamshire (*condado inglés).*

Nov. November (*nov.: noviembre* m).

n.p. new paragraph ((*punto* y) *aparte).*

n.p. or d. no place or date (*s.l. ni f.: sin lugar ni fecha).*

nr near (*cerca de).*

N.S. Nova Scotia (*Nueva Escocia, provincia canadiense).*

NSPCC National Society for the Prevention of Cruelty to Children (*sociedad protectora de los niños).*

N.S.W. New South Wales (*Nueva Gales* f *del Sur, estado australiano).*

nt wt net weight (*p.º n.º: peso* m *neto).*

N.U.I. National University of Ireland.

NUJ National Union of Journalists.

NUM National Union of Mineworkers.

NUR National Union of Railwaymen.

NUS National Union of Students.

NUT National Union of Teachers.

N.W. north-west (*NO.: noroeste* m, adj).

N.W.T. North West Territory (*parte del Canadá).*

N.Y. New York (*Nueva York, estado norteamericano).*

N.Y.C. New York City (*Ciudad de Nueva York).*

N.Z. New Zealand (*Nueva Zelanda* f).

O

O. **1** (*US*) Ohio. **2** (*Canada*) Ontario (*provincia canadiense).*

O. & M. Organization and Methods (*estudio de la organización y de los métodos (en las empresas comerciales etc)).*

OAS Organization of American States (*O.E.A.: Organización* f *de Estados Americanos).*

ob. obiit, died (*m.: murió).*

O.B.E. Officer of the Order of the British Empire (*título honorífico británico).*

O.C. Officer Commanding (*jefe* m).

Oct. October (*oct.: octubre* m).

OECD Organization for European Cooperation and Development (*O.C.E.D.).*

O.E.D. Oxford English Dictionary.

OEEC Organization for European Economic Cooperation (*O.E.C.E.).*

O.H.M.S. On His (Her) Majesty's Service.

O.K.* O.K.

Oklá. (*US*) Oklahoma.

O-level Ordinary level (*grado inferior del General Certificate of Education (a los 15–16 años);* = *bachillerato* m *elemental).*

O.M. Order of Merit (*título honorífico británico).*

o.n.o. or near offer (*en los anuncios: se admitirán ofertas un poco más bajas que el precio mencionado).*

Ont. Ontario (*provincia canadiense).*

op. cit. opere citato, in the work cited (*obr. cit.: obra* f *citada).*

opp. opposite (*en frente de).*

O.R. operational research (*estudio de las operaciones de las compañías y organizaciones)).*

o.r. (at) owner's risk (*bajo la responsabilidad del cliente (or usuario)).*

ord. ordinary (*corriente, común, normal).*

Ore. (*US*) Oregon.

O.S. **1** (*Naut*) ordinary seaman (*marinero* m). **2**

O.T. (Geog) Ordnance Survey (servicio oficial de topografía). 3 (Sew) outsize (de tamaño extraordinario). 4 (Hist) old style (según el calendario juliano).

O.T. Old Testament (A.T.: Antiguo Testamento m).

OUP Oxford University Press.

Oxon. 1 Oxfordshire (condado inglés). 2 (Univ) Oxoniensis, of Oxford (de la Universidad de Oxford).

oz. ounce(s)* (onza f, onzas fpl).

P

p. page (pág: página f).

p (Fin) penny, pence pl (nuevo penique m británico).

P.A. Press Association (agencia de noticias).

Pa. (US) Pennsylvania (Pensilvania).

p.a. per annum, yearly (por año, al año).

par., para. paragraph (párrafo m).

pat. patent (pat.: patente f).

PAU Pan-American Union (U.P.A.).

P.A.Y.E. Pay as you earn (sistema de calcular el impuesto sobre la renta).

P.C. 1 police constable (policía m). 2 Privy Council (Consejo m Privado (de Su Majestad)). 3 Privy Councillor (miembro m del Consejo Privado). 4 Parish Council (consejo de parroquia).

p.c. 1 (Post) postcard (tarjeta f postal). 2 (Math) per cent (p.c.: por cien, por ciento).

p. & p. postage and packing (gastos mpl de embalaje y envío).

pd paid (pagado).

P.E. physical education (cultura f física).

P.E.I. Prince Edward Island (parte del Canadá).

Pemb. Pembrokeshire (condado galés).

P.E.N. Club (International Association of) Poets, Playwrights, Editors, Essayists and Novelists.

Penn. (US) Pennsylvania (Pensilvania).

per pro. per procurationem, by proxy (p.p.: por poder).

Pfc. (US: Mil) private first class (soldado m de primera).

Ph.D. Doctor of Philosophy.

PIB Price and Incomes Board (junta regidora de precios y rentas).

Pl. Place (plaza f).

P/L. profit and loss (ganancias fpl y pérdidas).

P.M. Prime Minister (primer ministro m).

p.m. post meridiem, after noon, in the afternoon (después del mediodía, de la tarde).

P.M.G. Postmaster General (Director m General de Correos).

P.O. 1 (Post) post office (oficina f de correos).

2 (Aer) Pilot Officer (oficial m piloto).

p.o. postal order (giro m postal).

P.O.B. post-office box (apartado m de correos).

pop. population (h.: habitantes mpl).

poss. 1 possible (posible). 2 possibly (posiblemente).

P.O.W. prisoner of war (prisionero m).

p.p. per procurationem, by proxy (p.p.: por poder).

pp. pages (págs.: páginas fpl).

PPE philosophy, politics and economics (grupo de asignaturas de la Universidad de Oxford).

PPS 1 (Pol) Parliamentary Private Secretary. 2 (Post) post-postscriptum (posdata f adicional).

P.R. 1 (Pol) proportional representation. 2 (Comm) public relations. 3 Puerto Rico (P.R.: Puerto m Rico).

pr pair (par m).

Pres. 1 president (presidente m). 2 (Eccl) Presbyterian (presbiteriano m).

P.R.O. 1 Public Record Office (archivo m nacional). 2 (Comm etc) public relations officer (encargado m de relaciones públicas).

prop. proprietor (propietario m).

Prot. Protestant (protestante m; also adj).

pro tem. pro tempore, for the time being (en el interin).

prox. proximo, in the next month (pr. fr.: próximo futuro).

P.S. postscript (P.D.: posdata f).

P.T. physical training (gimnasia f, cultura f física).

pt 1 part (parte f). 2 (Fin) payment (pago m). 3 pint(s)*. 4 point (punto m).

PTA Parent-Teacher Association (asociación de padres y profesores, en un colegio).

Pte Private (soldado m raso).

PTO please turn over (véase al dorso).

PVC polyvinyl chloride (sustancia plástica).

Pvt. (US: Mil) Private (soldado m raso).

PX (US) Post Exchange (organización de tiendas etc especiales para las fuerzas armadas).

Q

Q. 1 Queen (reina f). 2 (Canada) Quebec (provincia canadiense). 3 question (pregunta f).

q. 1 query (pregunta f; duda f). 2 quart(s)*.

Q.C. Queen's Counsel (abogado m (de categoría superior)).

Q.E.D. quod erat demonstrandum, which was to be proved (que es lo que había de probar).

Q.E.F. quod erat faciendum, which was to be done (que es lo que había de hacer).

Q.M. Quartermaster*.

qr 1 quarter(s)*. 2 quire(s)*.

qt quart(s)*.

qto quarto (in-4º: en cuarto).

Qu. Queen (reina f).

Que. Quebec (provincia canadiense).

quot. quotation (cotización f).

q.v. quod vide, which see (véase).

R

R. 1 Rex, King (rey m). 2 Regina, Queen (reina f). 3 (Geog) river (río m). 4 (Rail) railway (ferrocarril m). 5 Réaumur (termómetro m Réaumur).

R (Cine: US) Restricted (película f más apta para mayores).

r. right (der., der.º: derecho).

R.A. 1 (Art) Royal Academy (Real Academia f de Bellas Artes). 2 (Art) Royal Academician (miembro m de la Real Academia de Bellas Artes). 3 (Mil) Royal Artillery.

RAC 1 (Aut) Royal Automobile Club. 2 (Mil) Royal Armoured Corps.

Rad. Radnorshire (condado galés).

RADA Royal Academy of Dramatic Art (escuela de actores etc).

RAF Royal Air Force (fuerzas aéreas británicas).

R.C. Roman Catholic (católico m; also adj).

R.C.M. Royal College of Music.

R.C.P. Royal College of Physicians.

R.C.S. Royal College of Surgeons.

Rd Road (calle f).

R/D refer to drawer (protestar este cheque por falta de fondos).

RDC Rural District Council.

R.E. Royal Engineers.

recd received (recibido).

ref. 1 reference (referencia f). 2 (as prep) with reference to (en cuanto a, respecto de).

regd 1 (Comm etc) registered (registrado). 2 (Post) registered (certificado).

regt regiment (regimiento m).

REME Royal Electrical and Mechanical Engineers.

Rep. 1 Republic (república f). 2 (Pol) Republican (republicano m; also adj).

ret. retired (jubilado, (Mil) retirado).

Rev. Reverend (R., Rdo.: Reverendo).

Rgt regiment (regimiento m).

r.h. right hand (der., der.ª: derecha f).

R.H.S. 1 Royal Horticultural Society. 2 Royal Humane Society. 3 Royal Historical Society.

R.I. (US) Rhode Island.
R.I.B.A. Royal Institute of British Architects.
R.I.P. requiescat in pace, may he (etc) rest in peace (E.P.D.: en paz descanse).
Rly Railway (f.c.: ferrocarril m).
R.M. Royal Marines.
R.M.S. Royal Mail Steamer.
RN 1 Royal Navy. 2 (US) Registered Nurse (enfermera f diplomada).
RNIB Royal National Institute for the Blind.
RNLI Royal National Lifeboat Institution.
RNR Royal Naval Reserve.
RNVR Royal Naval Volunteer Reserve.
R.P. reply paid (C.P.: contestación f pagada).
R.P.M. resale price maintenance.
R.R. (US) Railroad (f.c.: ferrocarril m).
R.S. Royal Society.
R.S.A. 1 Royal Scottish Academy. 2 Royal Scottish Academician. 3 Royal Society of Arts. 4 Royal Society of Antiquaries.
R.S.M. Regimental Sergeant-Major (approx = brigada m de regimiento).
RSPCA Royal Society for the Prevention of Cruelty to Animals (sociedad protectora de animales).
RSVP répondez s'il vous plaît, please reply (S.R.C.: se ruega contestación).
Rt Hon. Right Honourable (título honorífico británico).
Rt Rev. Right Reverend (Rmo.: Reverendísimo).
RU Rugby Union.
Rutl. Rutland (condado inglés)
R.V. Revised Version (of the Bible).
r.v. rateable value*.
Ry Rail (f.c.: ferrocarril m).

S
S. 1 south (S.: sur m, adj). 2 (Rel) Saint (S.: San, Santa).
s. 1 second (segundo m). 2 son (hijo m). 3 (Fin) shilling(s) (chelín m, chelines mpl).
S.A. 1 South Africa (África f del Sur). 2 South America (América f del Sur, Sudamérica f). 3 South Australia (estado australiano). 4 Salvation Army (Ejército m de Salvación).
s.a.e. stamped addressed envelope (sobre m con las propias señas de uno y con sello).
Salop Shropshire (condado inglés).
Sask. Saskatchewan (provincia canadiense).
Sat. Saturday (sáb.: sábado m).
S.C. (US) South Carolina.
Sc.D. Scientiae Doctor, Doctor of Science.
S.C.E. Scottish Certificate of Education.
Sch. School (escuela f).

S.D., S.Dak. (US) South Dakota.
S.E. south-east (SE.: sudeste m, adj).
SEATO South-East Asia Treaty Organization (SEATO, OTASE: Organización f del Tratado de la Asia Sudeste).
sec. 1 secondary (segundo, secundario). 2 section (sección f). 3 second(s) (segundo m, segundos mpl).
Sec., Secy Secretary (Srio.: Secretario m).
S.E.D. Scottish Education Department.
Sen., Senr senior*.
Sept. September (sep.: septiembre m).
Serg., Sergt Sergeant (sargento m).
S.E.T. Selective Employment Tax (impuesto que paga el patrono por cada empleado).
SF science fiction (ciencia-ficción f).
s.g. specific gravity (peso m específico).
Sgt Sergeant (sargento m).
sh. shilling(s) (chelín m, chelines mpl).
SHAPE Supreme Headquarters Allied Powers in Europe.
S.M. Sergeant-Major (approx = brigado m).
So. = S. 1
Soc. 1 Society (sociedad f). 2 (Pol) Socialist (socialista mf; also adj).
S.O.E.D. Shorter Oxford English Dictionary.
Som. Somerset (condado inglés).
sov. sovereign (soberano m (moneda de oro de I libra)).
Sp., Span. Spanish (esp.: español m, adj).
S.P. starting price (en las carreras de caballos, puntos de ventaja ofrecidos a la salida).
sp. gr. specific gravity (peso m específico).
Sq. Square (plaza f).
sq. (Math) square (cuadrado).
sq. ft square foot, square feet (pie m cuadrado, pies mpl cuadrados).
Sr senior*.
S.R.N. state registered nurse (enfermera f diplomada).
SS Saints (SS: santos mpl, santas fpl).
S.S. steamship (vapor m).
S.S.E. south - south - east (SSE.: sudsudeste).
S.S.W. south - south - west (SSO.: sudsudoeste).
St 1 (Eccl) Saint (S.: San, Santa). 2 (Geog) Strait (estrecho m). 3 Street (calle f).
St. (Rail etc) Station (estación f).
st. stone(s)*.
Sta. = St.
Staffs. Staffordshire (condado inglés).
STD (Tel) subscriber trunk dialling.
stg sterling (moneda f esterlina, libras fpl esterlinas).
Stn Station (estación f).
Sun. Sunday (dom.º: domingo m).

supp. supplement (suplemento m).
Supt Superintendent (subjefe m de policía).
S.W. south-west (SO.: suroeste m, adj).
Sx Sussex (condado inglés).
syn. 1 synonym (sinónimo m). 2 synonymous (sinónimo).

T
t. ton(s) (tonelada f, toneladas fpl).
T.A. Territorial Army (reserva f del ejército).
TB tuberculosis (tuberculosis f).
TCD Trinity College, Dublin (universidad irlandesa).
T.D. 1 Territorial Decoration (condecoración británica). 2 (US) Treasury Department (Ministerio m de Hacienda).
Tel. telephone (tel.: teléfono m).
temp. temperature (temperatura f).
Tenn. (US) Tennessee.
Tex. (US) Texas (Tejas).
TGWU Transport and General Workers' Union.
Thurs. Thursday (jueves m).
T.O. Telegraph Office.
trans. 1 translation (traducción f). 2 translated (trad.: traducido). 3 transactions (actas fpl, memorias fpl).
Trs. Treasurer (tesorero m).
TT 1 teetotal, teetotaller*. 2 (Aut) Tourist Trophy. 3 (Agr) tuberculin-tested (a prueba de tuberculinas).
TU trade union.
TUC Trades Union Congress (confederación de los sindicatos (británicos)).
Tues. Tuesday (martes m).
TVA Tennessee Valley Authority (comisión para el fomento del desarrollo económico del Tennessee Valley, EE.UU.).

U
U (Cine) Universal (película f apta para todos los públicos).
U.A.R. United Arab Republic (R.A.U.: República f Árabe Unida).
UDC Urban District Council (ayuntamiento de distrito urbano).
UDI Unilateral Declaration of Independence (Rodesia: 1965).
UFO unidentified flying object (OVNI: objeto m volante no identificado).
UHF ultra-high frequency (frecuencia f extra alta).
U.K. United Kingdom (Reino m Unido (Inglaterra, Escocia, Gales e Irlanda del Norte)).
ult. ultimo, last month (p.pdo.: próximo pasado).
UMW (US) United Mineworkers.
UN United Nations (N.U., NN.UU.: Naciones fpl Unidas).
UNA United Nations Association.

UNESCO United Nations Educational, Scientific and Cultural Organization (*UNESCO: Organización f de las Naciones Unidas para la Educación, la Ciencia y la Cultura*).

UNICEF United Nations International Children's Emergency Fund (*UNICEF: Fondo m Internacional de las Naciones Unidas de Socorro a la Infancia*).

Univ. University (*universidad f*).

UNO United Nations Organization (*ONU: Organización f de las Naciones Unidas*).

U.P. United Press (*agencia de noticias*).

US United States (*EE.UU.: Estados mpl Unidos*).

USA 1 United States of America (*EE.UU.: Estados mpl Unidos*). 2 United States Army.

USAF United States Air Force.

U.S.C.G. United States Coast Guard.

USDA United States Department of Agriculture.

U.S.M. 1 (*Post*) United States Mail. 2 (*Mil*) United States Marines. 3 (*Fin*) United States Mint.

USN United States Navy.

USNG United States National Guard.

U.S.N.R. United States Naval Reserve.

USS 1 (*Pol*) United States Senate. 2 (*Naut*) United States Ship. 3 United States Service.

USSR Union of Soviet Socialist Republics (*U.R.S.S.: Unión f de Repúblicas Socialistas Soviéticas*).

U.S.T.C. United States Tariff Commission.

Ut. (*US*) Utah.

V

V 1 flying bomb (*bomba f volante (1944–45)*).

V 2 rocket bomb (*bomba f cohete (1944–45)*).

v. 1 (*Lit*) verse (*estrofa f*). 2 (*Bib*) verse (*vers.º: versículo m*). 3 (*Sport, Law etc*) versus, against (*contra*). 4 (*Elec*) volt(s) (*v.: voltio m, voltios mpl*). 5 vide, see (*v.: véase; vid.: vide*).

Va. (*US*) Virginia.

V.C. 1 (*Mil*) Victoria Cross (*condecoración británica*). 2 (*Univ*) Vice-Chancellor*. 3 Vice-Chairman (*vicepresidente m*).

V.D. venereal disease (*enfermedad f venérea*).

V.E. Day Victory in Europe Day (*día m de la victoria en Europa (8 mayo 1945)*).

Ven. Venerable (*venerable*).

v.g. very good (*muy bueno*).

VHF very high frequency (*frecuencia f muy alta*).

VIP very important person (*often hum*) (*persona f importante, personaje m*).

viz. videlicet, namely (*v.gr.: verbigracia*).

V.J. Day Victory over Japan Day (*día m de la victoria sobre el Japón (Brit: 15 agosto 1945; US: 2 setiembre 1945)*).

vol., vols volume(s) (*t.: tomo m, tomos mpl*).

V.P., V.Pres. Vice President (*vicepresidente m*).

V.R. Victoria Regina, Queen Victoria.

vs versus, against (*contra*).

VSO Voluntary Service Overseas.

Vt. (*US*) Vermont.

VTO(L) vertical takeoff (and landing) (*despegue m (y aterrizaje) vertical*).

vv. verses (see v. 1 and 2).

v.v. vice versa (*viceversa*).

W

W. west (*O.: oeste m, adj*).

w. watt(s) (*w.: vatio m, vatios mpl*).

WAAC Women's Auxiliary Army Corps.

WAAF Women's Auxiliary Air Force.

WAC (*US*) Women's Army Corps.

War., Warwicks. Warwickshire (*condado inglés*).

Wash. (*US*) Washington.

WAVES (*US*) Women's Appointed Volunteer Emergency Service.

W.C. water closet (*W.C.: váter m, inodoro m*).

W.D. War Department (*Ministerio m de Guerra*).

WEA Worker's Educational Association.

Wed(s). Wednesday (*miérc.: miércoles m*).

WFTU World Federation of Trade Unions (*Federación f Mundial de Sindicatos*).

WHO World Health Organization (*O.M.S.: Organización f Mundial de la Salud*).

W.I. 1 Women's Institute. 2 West Indies (*Antillas fpl*).

Wilts. Wiltshire (*condado inglés*).

Wis(c). (*US*) Wisconsin.

wk week (*semana f*).

W/L wavelength (*longitud f de onda*).

W.N.W. west - north - west (*ONO.: oesnoroeste*).

W.O. 1 (*Mil*) War Office (*Ministerio m de Guerra*). 2 (*Mil*) Warrant Officer (*suboficial m*). 3 (*Naut*) Warrant Officer (*contramaestre m*).

Worcs. Worcestershire (*condado inglés*).

W.P. weather permitting (*si lo permite el tiempo*).

WRAC Women's Royal Army Corps.

WRAF Women's Royal Air Force.

WRNS Women's Royal Naval Service.

W.S.W. west - south - west (*OSO.: oessudoeste*).

wt weight (*peso m*).

W/T wireless telegraphy (*radiotelegrafía f*).

WUS World University Service (*organización benéfica de las universidades del mundo*).

W.Va. (*US*) West Virginia.

W.V.S. Women's Voluntary Service.

Wyo. (*US*) Wyoming.

X

X (*Cine*) adults only (*película f únicamente para mayores*).

Xmas Christmas*.

X-ray*

Y

yd. yard(s)*.

YHA Youth Hostels Association.

YMCA Young Men's Christian Association.

YMHA Young Men's Hebrew Association.

Yorks. Yorkshire (*condado inglés*).

yr 1 year(s) (*año m, años pl*). 2 your (*su*).

yrs 1 years (*años mpl*). 2 yours (*suyo*).

YWCA Young Women's Christian Association.

YWHA Young Women's Hebrew Association.

The Spanish Verb   El verbo español

Each verb entry in the Spanish-English section of the Dictionary includes a reference by number and letter to the tables below, in which the simple tenses and parts of the three conjugations and of irregular verbs are set out. For verbs having only a slight irregularity the indication of it is given in the main text of the dictionary (*eg* escribir [3a; *ptp* escrito]) and is not repeated here. Certain other verbs have been marked in the main text as *defective* and in some cases indications of usage have been given there, but for further information it is best to consult a full grammar of the language.

Certain general points may be summarized here:

The **imperfect** is regular for all verbs except *ser* (*era* etc) and *ir* (*iba* etc).

The **conditional** is formed by adding to the stem of the future tense (in most cases the infinitive) the endings of the imperfect tense of *haber*: *contaría* etc. If the stem of the future tense is irregular, the conditional will have the same irregularity: *decir* — *diré*, *diría*; *poder* — *podré*, *podría*.

Compound tenses are formed with the auxiliary *haber* and the past participle:

perfect:	he cantado (*subj*: haya cantado)
pluperfect:	había cantado (*subj*: hubiera cantado, hubiese cantado)
future perfect:	habré cantado
conditional perfect:	habría cantado
perfect infinitive:	haber cantado
perfect gerund:	habiendo cantado

The **imperfect subjunctives** I and II can be seen as being formed from the 3rd person plural of the preterite, using as a stem what remains after removing the final *-ron* syllable and adding to it *-ra* (I) or *-se* (II), *eg*:

cantar: canta/ron — cantara, cantase
perder: perdie/ron — perdiera, perdiese
reducir: reduje/ron — redujera, redujese

The form of the **imperative** depends not only on number but also on whether the person(s) addressed are treated in familiar or in formal terms. The "true" imperative is used only in familiar address in the affirmative:

cantar: canta (tú), cantad (vosotros)
vender: vende (tú), vended (vosotros)
partir: parte (tú), partid (vosotros)

(There are a few irregular imperatives in the singular — *salir* — *sal*, *hacer* — *haz*, etc, but all the plurals are regular.) The imperative affirmative in formal address requires the subjunctive: *envíemelo*, *háganlo*, *conduzca Vd con más cuidado*, *¡oiga!* The imperative negative in both familiar and formal address also requires the subjunctive: *no me digas, no os preocupéis, no grite tanto Vd, no se desanimen Vds*.

Continuous tenses are formed with *estar* and the gerund: *está leyendo, estaba lloviendo, estábamos hablando de eso*. Other auxiliary verbs may occasionally replace *estar* in certain senses: *según voy viendo, va mejorando, iba cogiendo flores, lo venía estudiando desde hacía muchos años*. Usage of the continuous tenses does not exactly coincide with that of English.

The **passive** is formed with tenses of *ser* and the past participle, which agrees in number and gender with the subject: *las casas fueron construidas, será firmado mañana el tratado, después de haber sido vencido*. The passive is much less used in Spanish than in English, its function often being taken over by a reflexive construction, by *uno*, etc.

First Conjugation

[1a] cantar

INFINITIVE: cantar GERUND: cantando
PAST PARTICIPLE: cantado

INDICATIVE

PRESENT	IMPERFECT	FUTURE	CONDITIONAL	PRETERITE
canto	cantaba	cantaré	cantaría	canté
cantas	cantabas	cantarás	cantarías	cantaste
canta	cantaba	cantará	cantaría	cantó
cantamos	cantábamos	cantaremos	cantaríamos	cantamos
cantáis	cantabais	cantaréis	cantaríais	cantasteis
cantan	cantaban	cantarán	cantarían	cantaron

SUBJUNCTIVE

PRESENT	IMPERFECT I	IMPERFECT II
cante	cantara	cantase
cantes	cantaras	cantases
cante	cantara	cantase
cantemos	cantáramos	cantásemos
cantéis	cantarais	cantaseis
canten	cantaran	cantasen

IMPERATIVE

canta (tú) cantad (vosotros)

[1b] cambiar
The i of the stem is not stressed and the verb is regular

INFINITIVE	PRESENT INDICATIVE	PRESENT SUBJUNCTIVE	PRETERITE
cambiar	cambio	cambie	cambié
	cambias	cambies	cambiaste
	cambia	cambie	cambió
	cambiamos	cambiemos	cambiamos
	cambiáis	cambiéis	cambiasteis
	cambian	cambien	cambiaron

[1c] enviar
The i of the stem is stressed in parts of the present tenses

INFINITIVE	PRESENT INDICATIVE	PRESENT SUBJUNCTIVE	PRETERITE
enviar	envío	envíe	envié
	envías	envíes	enviaste
	envía	envíe	envió
	enviamos	enviemos	enviamos
	enviáis	enviéis	enviasteis
	envían	envíen	enviaron

[1d] evacuar
The u of the stem is not stressed and the verb is regular

INFINITIVE	PRESENT INDICATIVE	PRESENT SUBJUNCTIVE	PRETERITE
evacuar	evacuo	evacue	evacué
	evacuas	evacues	evacuaste
	evacua	evacue	evacuó
	evacuamos	evacuemos	evacuamos
	evacuáis	evacuéis	evacuasteis
	evacuan	evacuen	evacuaron

[1e] situar
The u of the stem is stressed in parts of the present tenses

INFINITIVE	PRESENT INDICATIVE	PRESENT SUBJUNCTIVE	PRETERITE
situar	sitúo	sitúe	situé
	sitúas	sitúes	situaste
	sitúa	sitúe	situó
	situamos	situemos	situamos
	situáis	situéis	situasteis
	sitúan	sitúen	situaron

[1f] cruzar
The stem consonant z is written c before e

INFINITIVE	PRESENT INDICATIVE	PRESENT SUBJUNCTIVE	PRETERITE
cruzar	cruzo	cruce	crucé
	cruzas	cruces	cruzaste
	cruza	cruce	cruzó
	cruzamos	crucemos	cruzamos
	cruzáis	crucéis	cruzasteis
	cruzan	crucen	cruzaron

[1g] picar
The stem consonant c is written qu before e

INFINITIVE	PRESENT INDICATIVE	PRESENT SUBJUNCTIVE	PRETERITE
picar	pico	pique	piqué
	picas	piques	picaste
	pica	pique	picó
	picamos	piquemos	picamos
	picáis	piquéis	picasteis
	pican	piquen	picaron

[1h] pagar
The stem consonant g is written gu (with u silent) before e

INFINITIVE	PRESENT INDICATIVE	PRESENT SUBJUNCTIVE	PRETERITE
pagar	pago	pague	pagué
	pagas	pagues	pagaste
	paga	pague	pagó
	pagamos	paguemos	pagamos
	pagáis	paguéis	pagasteis
	pagan	paguen	pagaron

[1i] averiguar
The u of the stem is written ü (so that it should be pronounced) before e

INFINITIVE	PRESENT INDICATIVE	PRESENT SUBJUNCTIVE	PRETERITE
averiguar	averiguo	averigüe	averigüé
	averiguas	averigües	averiguaste
	averigua	averigüe	averiguó
	averiguamos	averigüemos	averiguamos
	averiguáis	averigüéis	averiguasteis
	averiguan	averigüen	averiguaron

[1] Series

INFINITIVE	PRESENT INDICATIVE	PRESENT SUBJUNCTIVE	PRETERITE
[1k] cerrar The stem vowel **e** becomes **ie** when stressed	cierro cierras cierra cerramos cerráis cierran	cierre cierres cierre cerremos cerréis cierren	cerré cerraste cerró cerramos cerrasteis cerraron
[1l] errar As [1k], but the diphthong is written **ye-** at the start of the word	yerro yerras yerra erramos erráis yerran	yerre yerres yerre erremos erréis yerren	erré erraste erró erramos errasteis erraron
[1m] contar The stem vowel **o** becomes **ue** when stressed	cuento cuentas cuenta contamos contáis cuentan	cuente cuentes cuente contemos contéis cuenten	conté contaste contó contamos contasteis contaron
[1n] agorar As [1m], but the diphthong is written **üe** (so that the **u** should be pronounced)	agüero agüeras agüera agoramos agoráis agüeran	agüere agüeras agüere agoremos agoréis agüeren	agoré agoraste agoró agoramos agorasteis agoraron
[1o] jugar The stem vowel **u** becomes **ue** when stressed; the stem consonant **g** is written **gu** (with **u** silent) before **e**	juego juegas juega jugamos jugáis juegan	juegue juegues juegue juguemos juguéis jueguen	jugué jugaste jugó jugamos jugasteis jugaron
[1p] estar Irregular. Imperative: *está (tú)*	estoy estás está estamos estáis están	esté estés esté estemos estéis estén	estuve estuviste estuvo estuvimos estuvisteis estuvieron
[1q] andar Irregular	ando andas anda andamos andáis andan	ande andes ande andemos andéis anden	anduve anduviste anduvo anduvimos anduvisteis anduvieron

[2] Series

INFINITIVE	PRESENT INDICATIVE	PRESENT SUBJUNCTIVE	PRETERITE
[2b] vencer The stem consonant **c** is written **z** before **a** and **o**	venzo vences vence vencemos vencéis vencen	venza venzas venza venzamos venzáis venzan	vencí venciste venció vencimos vencisteis vencieron
[2c] coger The stem consonant **g** is written **j** before **a** and **o**	cojo coges coge cogemos cogéis cogen	coja cojas coja cojamos cojáis cojan	cogí cogiste cogió cogimos cogisteis cogieron
[2d] conocer The stem consonant **c** becomes **zc** before **a** and **o**	conozco conoces conoce conocemos conocéis conocen	conozca conozcas conozca conozcamos conozcáis conozcan	conocí conociste conoció conocimos conocisteis conocieron
[2e] leer Unstressed **i** between vowels is written **y**. Past Participle: *leído* Gerund: *leyendo*	leo lees lee leemos leéis leen	lea leas lea leamos leáis lean	leí leíste leyó leímos leísteis leyeron
[2f] tañer Unstressed **i** after **ñ** (and also after **ll**) is omitted	taño tañes tañe tañemos tañéis tañen	taña tañas taña tañamos tañáis taña	tañí tañiste tañó tañimos tañisteis tañeron
[2g] perder The stem vowel **e** becomes **ie** when stressed	pierdo pierdes pierde perdemos perdéis pierden	pierda pierdas pierda perdamos perdáis pierdan	perdí perdiste perdió perdimos perdisteis perdieron
[2h] mover The stem vowel **o** becomes **ue** when stressed	muevo mueves mueve movemos movéis mueven	mueva muevas mueva movamos mováis muevan	moví moviste movió movimos movisteis movieron

dar — Irregular

PRESENT	SUBJUNCTIVE	PRETERITE
doy	dé	di
das	des	diste
da	dé	dio
damos	demos	dimos
dais	deis	disteis
dan	den	dieron

Second Conjugation

[2a] temer

INFINITIVE: **temer**   GERUND: **temiendo**

PAST PARTICIPLE: **temido**

INDICATIVE

PRESENT	IMPERFECT	PRETERITE
temo	temía	temí
temes	temías	temiste
teme	temía	temió
tememos	temíamos	temimos
teméis	temíais	temisteis
temen	temían	temieron

FUTURE	CONDITIONAL
temeré	temería
temerás	temerías
temerá	temería
temeremos	temeríamos
temeréis	temeríais
temerán	temerían

SUBJUNCTIVE

PRESENT	IMPERFECT I	IMPERFECT II
tema	temiera	temiese
temas	temieras	temieses
tema	temiera	temiese
temamos	temiéramos	temiésemos
temáis	temierais	temieseis
teman	temieran	temiesen

IMPERATIVE

teme (tú)   temed (vosotros)

As [2h], but the diphthong is written **hue-** at the start of the word

PRESENT	SUBJUNCTIVE	PRETERITE
huele	huelas	oliste
olemos	huela	olió
oléis	olamos	olimos
huelen	oláis	olisteis
	huelan	olieron

[2k] haber
Irregular.
Future: *habré*

PRESENT	SUBJUNCTIVE	PRETERITE
he	haya	hube
has	hayas	hubiste
ha	haya	hubo
hemos	hayamos	hubimos
habéis	hayáis	hubisteis
han	hayan	hubieron

[2l] tener
Irregular.
Future: *tendré*
Imperative: *ten (tú)*

PRESENT	SUBJUNCTIVE	PRETERITE
tengo	tenga	tuve
tienes	tengas	tuviste
tiene	tenga	tuvo
tenemos	tengamos	tuvimos
tenéis	tengáis	tuvisteis
tienen	tengan	tuvieron

[2m] caber
Irregular.
Future: *cabré*

PRESENT	SUBJUNCTIVE	PRETERITE
quepo	quepa	cupe
cabes	quepas	cupiste
cabe	quepa	cupo
cabemos	quepamos	cupimos
cabéis	quepáis	cupisteis
caben	quepan	cupieron

[2n] saber
Irregular.
Future: *sabré*

PRESENT	SUBJUNCTIVE	PRETERITE
sé	sepa	supe
sabes	sepas	supiste
sabe	sepa	supo
sabemos	sepamos	supimos
sabéis	sepáis	supisteis
saben	sepan	supieron

[2o] caer
Irregular.
Unstressed i between vowels is written
y, as [2e].
Past Participle: *caído*
Gerund: *cayendo*

PRESENT	SUBJUNCTIVE	PRETERITE
caigo	caiga	caí
caes	caigas	caíste
cae	caiga	cayó
caemos	caigamos	caímos
caéis	caigáis	caísteis
caen	caigan	cayeron

[2p] traer
Irregular.
Past Participle: *traído*
Gerund: *trayendo*

PRESENT	SUBJUNCTIVE	PRETERITE
traigo	traiga	traje
traes	traigas	trajiste
trae	traiga	trajo
traemos	traigamos	trajimos
traéis	traigáis	trajisteis
traen	traigan	trajeron

[3b]–[3h]

INFINITIVE	PRESENT INDICATIVE	PRESENT SUBJUNCTIVE	PRETERITE
[3b] esparcir The stem consonant **c** is written **z** before **a** and **o**.	esparzo esparces esparce esparcimos esparcís esparcen	esparza esparzas esparza esparzamos esparzáis esparzan	esparcí esparciste esparció esparcimos esparcisteis esparcieron
[3c] dirigir The stem consonant **g** is written **j** before **a** and **o**.	dirijo diriges dirige dirigimos dirigís dirigen	dirija dirijas dirija dirijamos dirijáis dirijan	dirigí dirigiste dirigió dirigimos dirigisteis dirigieron
[3d] distinguir The **u** after the stem consonant **g** is omitted before **a** and **o**	distingo distingues distingue distinguimos distinguís distinguen	distinga distingas distinga distingamos distingáis distingan	distinguí distinguiste distinguió distinguimos distinguisteis distinguieron
[3e] delinquir The stem consonant **qu** is written **c** before **a** and **o**	delinco delinques delinque delinquimos delinquís delinquen	delinca delincas delinca delincamos delincáis delincan	delinquí delinquiste delinquió delinquimos delinquisteis delinquieron
[3f] lucir The stem consonant **c** becomes **zc** before **a** and **o**	luzco luces luce lucimos lucís lucen	luzca luzcas luzca luzcamos luzcáis luzcan	lucí luciste lució lucimos lucisteis lucieron
[3g] huir The **i** of **-ió** and **-ie** becomes **y**; a **y** is inserted before endings not beginning with **i**. Gerund: *huyendo*	huyo huyes huye huimos huis huyen	huya huyas huya huyamos huyáis huyan	huí huiste huyó huimos huisteis huyeron
[3h] gruñir Unstressed **i** after **ñ** (and also after **ch** and **ll**) is omitted	gruño gruñes gruñe gruñimos gruñís gruñen	gruña gruñas gruña gruñamos gruñáis gruñan	gruñí gruñiste gruñó gruñimos gruñisteis gruñeron

[2q]–[2w]

INFINITIVE	PRESENT INDICATIVE	PRESENT SUBJUNCTIVE	PRETERITE
[2q] valer Irregular. Future: *valdré*.	valgo vales vale valemos valéis valen	valga valgas valga valgamos valgáis valgan	valí valiste valió valimos valisteis valieron
[2r] poner Irregular. Future: *pondré*. Past Participle: *puesto* Imperative: *pon (tú)*	pongo pones pone ponemos ponéis ponen	ponga pongas ponga pongamos pongáis pongan	puse pusiste puso pusimos pusisteis pusieron
[2s] hacer Irregular. Future: *haré*. Past Participle: *hecho* Imperative: *haz (tú)*	hago haces hace hacemos hacéis hacen	haga hagas haga hagamos hagáis hagan	hice hiciste hizo hicimos hicisteis hicieron
[2t] poder Irregular. In present tenses like [2h]. Future: *podré*. Gerund: *pudiendo*	puedo puedes puede podemos podéis pueden	pueda puedas pueda podamos podáis puedan	pude pudiste pudo pudimos pudisteis pudieron
[2u] querer Irregular. In present tenses like [2g]. Future: *querré*.	quiero quieres quiere queremos queréis quieren	quiera quieras quiera queramos queráis quieran	quise quisiste quiso quisimos quisisteis quisieron
[2v] ver Irregular. Imperfect: *veía*. Past Participle: *visto*	veo ves ve vemos veis ven	vea veas vea veamos veáis vean	vi viste vio vimos visteis vieron
[2w] ser Irregular. Imperfect: *era*. Future: *seré*. Part Participle: *sido*. Gerund: *siendo*. Imperative: *sé (tú), sed (vosotros)*	soy eres es somos sois son	sea seas sea seamos seáis sean	fui fuiste fue fuimos fuisteis fueron

Irregular verb tables

	senti (sentir)		
	sienteo	sienta	sentiste
	sientes	sientas	sintió
	siente	sienta	sentimos
	sentimos	sintamos	sentisteis
	sentís	sintáis	sintieron
	sienten	sientan	

[3i] sentir
The stem vowel **e** becomes **ie** when stressed; unstressed **e** becomes **i** in 3rd persons of Preterite, 1st and 2nd persons pl. of Present Subjunctive. Gerund: *sintiendo*.
In *adquirir* the stem vowel **i** becomes **ie** when stressed

	dormir (Indic.)	(Subj.)	(Pret.)
	duermo	duerma	dormí
	duermes	duermas	dormiste
	duerme	duerma	durmió
	dormimos	durmamos	dormimos
	dormís	durmáis	dormisteis
	duermen	duerman	durmieron

[3k] dormir
The stem vowel **o** becomes **ue** when stressed; unstressed **o** becomes **u** in 3rd persons of Preterite, 1st and 2nd persons pl. of Present Subjunctive. Gerund: *durmiendo*.

	pedir (Indic.)	(Subj.)	(Pret.)
	pido	pida	pedí
	pides	pidas	pediste
	pide	pida	pidió
	pedimos	pidamos	pedimos
	pedís	pidáis	pedisteis
	piden	pidan	pidieron

[3l] pedir
The stem vowel **e** becomes **i** when stressed, and also when unstressed in 3rd persons of Preterite, 1st and 2nd persons pl. of Present Subjunctive. Gerund: *pidiendo*.

	reír (Indic.)	(Subj.)	(Pret.)
	río	ría	reí
	ríes	rías	reíste
	ríe	ría	rio
	reímos	riamos	reímos
	reís	riáis	reísteis
	ríen	rían	rieron

[3m] reír
Irregular.
Past Participle: *reído*.
Gerund: *riendo*.
Imperative: *ríe (tú)*

	erguir (Indic.)	(Subj.)	(Pret.)
	yergo	yerga	erguí
	yergues	yergas	erguiste
	yergue	yerga	irguió
	erguimos	yergamos	erguimos
	erguís	yergáis	erguisteis
	yerguen	yergan	irguieron

(also, less commonly)

	(Indic.)	(Subj.)
	irgo	irga
	irgues	irgas
	irgue	irga
	erguimos	irgamos
	erguís	irgáis
	irguen	irgan

[3n] erguir
Irregular.
Gerund: *irguiendo*.
Imperative: *yergue (tú)* and less commonly *irgue (tú)*

	reducir (Indic.)	(Subj.)	(Pret.)
	reduzco	reduzca	reduje
	reduces	reduzcas	redujiste
	reduce	reduzca	redujo
	reducimos	reduzcamos	redujimos
	reducís	reduzcáis	redujisteis
	reducen	reduzcan	redujeron

[3o] reducir
The stem consonant **c** becomes **zc** before **a** and **o** as [3f]; but there is an irregular preterite in **-uje**

[2x] placer. Now used exclusively in 3rd person singular. Irregular forms: Present subj. *plazca* (less commonly *plega* or *plegue*); Preterite *plugo* (less commonly *plació*); Imperfect subj. I *pluguiera*, II *pluguiese* (less commonly *placiera*, *placiese*).

[2y] yacer. Now rather archaic. Irregular forms: Present indic. *yazco* (less commonly *yazgo* or *yago*), *yaces* etc; Present subj. *yazca* (less commonly *yazga* or *yaga*), *yazcas* etc; Imperative *yace (tú)* (less commonly *yaz*).

[2z] raer. The Present indic. is usually *raigo*, *raes* etc (like *caer* [2o]), but *rayo* is occasionally found; Present subj. usually *raiga*, *raigas* etc (also like *caer*), but *raya*, *rayas* etc is occasionally found.

[2za] roer. Alternative forms in present tenses: Indicative, *roo*, *roigo* or *royo*; *roes*, *roe* etc. Subjunctive, *roa*, *roiga* or *roya*. The first persons are usually avoided because of the uncertainty. The gerund is *royendo*.

Third Conjugation

(3a) partir

INFINITIVE: partir GERUND: partiendo

PAST PARTICIPLE: partido

INDICATIVE

PRESENT	IMPERFECT	PRETERITE
parto	partía	partí
partes	partías	partiste
parte	partía	partió
partimos	partíamos	partimos
partís	partíais	partisteis
parten	partían	partieron

SUBJUNCTIVE

PRESENT	IMPERFECT I	IMPERFECT II
parta	partiera	partiese
partas	partieras	partieses
parta	partiera	partiese
partamos	partiéramos	partiésemos
partáis	partierais	partieseis
partan	partieran	partiesen

IMPERATIVE

parte (tú)   partid (vosotros)

INFINITIVE	PRESENT INDICATIVE	PRESENT SUBJUNCTIVE	PRETERITE
[3p] decir Irregular. Future: *diré* Past Participle: *dicho* Gerund: *diciendo* Imperative: *di (tú)*	digo dices dice decimos decís dicen	diga digas diga digamos digáis digan	dije dijiste dijo dijimos dijisteis dijeron
[3q] oír Irregular, Unstressed **i** between vowels becomes **y.** Part Participle: *oído* Gerund: *oyendo*	oigo oyes oye oímos oís oyen	oiga oigas oiga oigamos oigáis oigan	oí oíste oyó oímos oísteis oyeron
[3r] salir Irregular. Future: *saldré* Imperative: *sal (tú)*	salgo sales sale salimos salís salen	salga salgas salga salgamos salgáis salgan	salí saliste salió salimos salisteis salieron
[3s] venir Irregular. Future: *vendré* Gerund: *viniendo* Imperaitve: *ven (tú)*	vengo vienes viene venimos venís vienen	venga vengas venga vengamos vengáis vengan	vine viniste vino vinimos vinisteis vinieron
[3t] ir Irregular. Imperfect: *iba* Gerund: *yendo* Imperative: *ve (tú), id (vosotros)*	voy vas va vamos vais van	vaya vayas vaya vayamos vayáis vayan	fui fuiste fue fuimos fuisteis fueron

The English Verb　　　*El verbo inglés*

El verbo inglés es bastante más sencillo que el español, a lo menos en cuanto a su forma. Hay muchos verbos fuertes o irregulares (damos una lista de ellos a continuación) y varias clases de irregularidad ortográfica (véanse las notas al final); pero hay una sola conjugación, y dentro de cada tiempo no hay variación para las seis personas excepto en el presente (tercera persona de singular). Por tanto, no es necesario ofrecer para el verbo inglés los cuadros y paradigmas con que se suele explicar el verbo español; la estructura general y las formas del verbo inglés se resumen en las siguientes notas.

1 Indicativo

(a) Presente: tiene la misma forma que el infinitivo en todas las personas menos la tercera del singular; en ésta, se añade una *-s* al infinitivo, p.ej. *he sells*, o se añade *-es* si el infinitivo termina en sibilante (los sonidos [s], [z], [ʃ] y [tʃ]; en la escritura *-ss*, *-zz*, *-sh* y *-ch*, etc). Esta *-s* añadida tiene dos pronunciaciones: tras consonante sorda se pronuncia sorda [s], p.ej. *scoffs* [skɔfs], *likes* [laiks], *taps* [tæps], *waits* [weits], *baths* [bɑːθs]; tras consonante sonora se pronuncia sonora, p.ej. *robs* [rɔbz], *bends* [bendz], *seems* [siːmz], *gives* [givz], *bathes* ['beiðz]; *-es* se pronuncia también sonora tras sibilante o consonante sonora, *-es* o letra final del infinitivo, p.ej. *races* ['reisiz], *urges* ['ɜːdʒiz], *lashes* ['læʃiz], *passes* ['pɑːsiz].

Los verbos que terminan en *-y* la cambian en *-ies* en la tercera persona del singular, p.ej. *tries, pities, satisfies*; pero son regulares los verbos que en el infinitivo tienen una vocal delante de la *-y*, p.ej. *pray—he prays, annoy—she annoys*.

El verbo *be* es irregular en todas las personas:

I am	we are
you are	you are
he is	they are

Cuatro verbos más tienen forma irregular en la tercera persona del singular:

do—he does [dʌz]	go—he goes [gəuz]
have—he has [hæz]	say—he says [sez]

(b) Pretérito (o pasado simple) y participio de pasado: tienen la misma forma en inglés; se forman añadiendo *-ed* al infinitivo, p.ej. *paint—I painted—painted*, o bien añadiendo *-d* a los infinitivos terminados en *-e* muda, p.ej. *bare—I bared—bared, move—I moved—moved, revise—I revised—revised.* (Para los muchos verbos irregulares, véase la lista abajo.) Esta *-d* o *-ed* se pronuncia por lo general [t]: *raced* [reist], *passed* [pɑːst]; pero cuando se añade a un infinitivo terminado en consonante sonora o en *r*, se pronuncia [d], p.ej. *bared* [bɛəd], *moved* [muːvd], *seemed* [siːmd], *buzzed* [bʌzd]. Si el infinitivo termina en *-d* o *-t*, la desinencia *-ed* se pronuncia como una sílaba más, [id], p.ej. *raided* ['reidid], *dented* ['dentid]. Para los verbos cuyo infinitivo termina en *-y*, véase 7 (e) abajo.

(c) Tiempos compuestos del pasado: se forman como en español con el verbo auxiliar *to have* y el participio de pasado: perfecto *I have painted*, pluscuamperfecto *I had painted*.

(d) Futuro y condicional (o potencial): se forma el futuro con el auxiliar *will* o *shall* y el infinitivo, p.ej. *I will do it, they shall not pass*; se forma el condicional (o potencial) con el auxiliar *would* o *should* y el infinitivo, p.ej. *I would go, if she should come.* Como en español y de igual formación existen los tiempos compuestos llamados futuro perfecto, p.ej. *I shall have finished*, y potencial compuesto, p.ej. *I would have paid.*

(e) Para cada tiempo del indicativo existe una forma continua que se forma con el tiempo apropiado del verbo *to be* (equivalente en este caso al español *estar*) y el participio de presente (véase abajo): *I am waiting, we were hoping, they will be buying it, they would have been waiting still, I had been painting all day.* Conviene subrayar que el modo de emplear estas formas continuas no corresponde siempre al sistema español.

2 Subjuntivo

Este modo tiene muy poco uso en inglés. En el presente tiene la misma forma que el infinitivo en todas las personas, (*that*) *I go*, (*that*) *she go* etc. En el pasado simple el único verbo que tiene forma especial es *to be*, que es *were* en todas las personas, (*that*) *I were*, (*that*) *we were* etc. En los demás casos donde la lógica de los tiempos en español pudiera parecer exigir una forma de subjuntivo en pasado, el inglés emplea el presente, p.ej. *he had urged that we do it at once.* El subjuntivo se emplea obligatoriamente en inglés en *if I were you, if he were to do it, were I to attempt it* (el indicativo *was* es tenido por vulgar en estas frases y análogas); se encuentra también en la frase fosilizada *so be it*, y en el lenguaje oficial de las actas, etc, p.ej. *it is*

agreed that nothing be done, it was resolved that the pier be painted (pero son igualmente correctos *should be done, should be painted*).

3 Gerundio y participio de presente

Tienen la misma forma en inglés; se añade al infinitivo la desinencia *-ing*, p.ej. *washing, sending, passing*. Para las muchas irregularidades ortográficas de esta desinencia, véase la sección 7.

4 Voz pasiva

Se forma exactamente como en español, con el tiempo apropiado del verbo *to be* (equivalente en este caso a *ser*) y el participio de pasado: *we are forced to, he was killed, they had been injured, the company will be taken over, it ought to have been rebuilt, were it to be agreed.*

5 Imperativo

Hay solamente una forma, que es la del infinitivo: *tell me, come here, don't do that.*

6 Verbos fuertes (o irregulares)

Infinitivo	Pretérito	Participio de pasado	Infinitivo	Pretérito	Participio de pasado
abide	abode *or* abided	abode *or* abided	heave	heaved, (*Naut*) hove	heaved, (*Naut*) hove
arise	arose	arisen			
awake	awoke	awaked	hew	hewed	hewed *or* hewn
be	was, were	been	hide	hid	hidden
bear	bore	(*llevado*) borne, (*nacido*) born	hit	hit	hit
			hold	held	held
beat	beat	beaten	hurt	hurt	hurt
become	became	become	keep	kept	kept
beget	begot, (*arch*) begat	begotten	kneel	knelt	knelt
			know	know	known
begin	began	begun	lade	laded	laden
bend	bent	bent	lay	laid	laid
beseech	besought	besought	lead	led	led
bet	bet *or* betted	bet *or* betted	lean	leaned *or* leant	leaned *or* leant
bid (*ordenar*)	bade	bidden	leap	leaped *or* leapt	leaped *or* leapt
(*licitar etc*)	bid	bid	learn	learned *or* learnt	learned *or* learnt
bind	bound	bound	leave	left	left
bite	bit	bitten	lend	lent	lent
bleed	bled	bled	let	let	let
blow	blew	blown	lie	lay	lain
break	broke	broken	light	lit *or* lighted	lit *or* lighted
breed	bred	bred	lose	lost	lost
bring	brought	brought	make	made	made
build	built	built	may	might	—
burn	burned *or* burnt	burned *or* burnt	mean	meant	meant
burst	burst	burst	meet	met	met
buy	bought	bought	mow	mowed	mown *or* mowed
can	could	—	pay	paid	paid
cast	cast	cast	put	put	put
catch	caught	caught	quit	quit *or* quitted	quit *or* quitted
chide	chid	chidden *or* chid	read [ri:d]	read [red]	read [red]
choose	chose	chosen	rend	rent	rent
cleave¹ (*vt*)	clove *or* cleft	cloven *or* cleft	rid	rid	rid
cleave² (*vi*)	cleaved	cleaved	ride	rode	ridden
cling	clung	clung	ring²	rang	rung
come	came	come	rise	rose	risen
cost (*vt*)	costed	costed	run	ran	run
(*vi*)	cost	cost	saw	sawed	sawed *or* sawn
creep	crept	crept	say	said	said
cut	cut	cut	see	saw	seen
deal	dealt	dealt	seek	sought	sought
dig	dug	dug	sell	sold	sold
do	did	done	send	sent	sent
draw	drew	drawn	set	set	set
dream	dreamed *or* dreamt	dreamed *or* dreamt	sew	sewed	sewn
			shake	shook	shaken
drink	drank	drunk	shave	shaved	shaved *or* shaven
drive	drove	driven	shear	sheared	shorn
dwell	dwelt	dwelt	shed	shed	shed
eat	ate	eaten	shine	shone	shone
fall	fell	fallen	shoe	shod	shod
feed	fed	fed	shoot	shot	shot
feel	felt	felt	show	showed	shown
fight	fought	fought	shrink	shrank	shrunk
find	found	found	shut	shut	shut
flee	fled	fled	sing	sang	sung
fling	flung	flung	sink	sank	sunk
fly	flew	flown	sit	sat	sat
forbid	forbad(e)	forbidden	slay	slew	slain
forget	forgot	forgotten	sleep	slept	slept
forsake	forsook	forsaken	slide	slid	slid
freeze	froze	frozen	sling	slung	slung
get	got	got, (*US*) gotten	slink	slunk	slunk
gild	gilded	gilded *or* gilt	slit	slit	slit
gird	girded *or* girt	girded *or* girt	smell	smelled *or* smelt	smelled *or* smelt
give	gave	given	smite	smote	smitten
go	went	gone	sow	sowed	sown
grind	ground	ground	speak	spoke	spoken
grow	grew	grown	speed (*vt*)	speeded	speeded
hang	hung, (*Law*) hanged	hung, (*Law*) hanged	(*vi*)	sped	sped
			spell	spelled *or* spelt	spelled *or* spelt
have	had	had	spend	spent	spent
hear	heard	heard	spill	spilled *or* spilt	spilled *or* spilt

Infinitivo	Pretérito	Participio de pasado	Infinitivo	Pretérito	Participio de pasado
spin	spun *or* span	spun	swell	swelled	swollen
spit	spat	spat	swim	swam	swum
split	split	split	swing	swung	swung
spoil	spoiled *or* spoilt	spoiled *or* spoilt	take	took	taken
spread	spread	spread	teach	taught	taught
spring	sprang	sprung	tear	tore	torn
stand	stood	stood	tell	told	told
stave	stove *or* staved	stove *or* staved	think	thought	thought
steal	stole	stolen	thrive	throve	thriven
stick	stuck	stuck	throw	threw	thrown
sting	stung	stung	thrust	thrust	thrust
stink	stank	stunk	tread	trod	trodden
strew	strewed	strewed *or* strewn	wake	woke	woken *or* waked
			wear	wore	worn
stride	strode	stridden	weave	wove	woven
strike	struck	struck	weep	wept	wept
string	strung	strung	win	won	won
strive	strove	striven	wind	wound	wound
swear	swore	sworn	wring	wrung	wrung
sweep	swept	swept	write	wrote	written

N.B.—No constan en esta lista los verbos compuestos con prefijo etc; para ellos véase el verbo básico, p.ej. para *forbear* véase *bear*, para *understand* véase *stand*.

7 Verbos débiles con irregularidad ortográfica

(a) Hay muchos verbos cuya ortografía varía ligeramente en el participio de pasado y en el gerundio. Son los que terminan en consonante simple precedida de vocal simple acentuada; antes de añadirles la desinencia -*ed* o -*ing*, se dobla la consonante:

Infinitivo	Participio de pasado	Gerundio
sob	sobbed	sobbing
wed	wedded	wedding
lag	lagged	lagging
control	controlled	controlling
dim	dimmed	dimming
tan	tanned	tanning
tap	tapped	tapping
prefer	preferred	preferring
pat	patted	patting

(pero *cook-cooked-cooking, fear-feared-fearing, roar-roared-roaring*, donde la vocal no es simple y por tanto no se dobla la consonante).

(b) Los verbos que terminan en -*c* la cambian en -*ck* al añadirse las desinencias -*ed*, -*ing*:

frolic	frolicked	frolicking
traffic	trafficked	trafficking

(c) Los verbos terminados en -*l*, -*p*, aunque precedida de vocal átona, tienen doblada la

consonante en el participio de pasado y en el gerundio en el inglés británico, pero simple en el de Estados Unidos:

grovel	(*Brit*) grovelled	(*Brit*) grovelling
	(*US*) groveled	(*US*) groveling
travel	(*Brit*) travelled	(*Brit*) travelling
	(*US*) traveled	(*US*) traveling
worship	(*Brit*) worshipped	(*Brit*) worshipping
	(*US*) worshiped	(*US*) worshiping

Nota — existe la misma diferencia en los sustantivos formados sobre tales verbos: *Brit* traveller = *US* traveler, *Brit* worshipper = *US* worshiper.

(d) Si el verbo termina en -*e* muda, se suprime ésta al añadir las desinencias -*ed*, -*ing*:

rake	raked	raking
care	cared	caring
smile	smiled	smiling
move	moved	moving
invite	invited	inviting

(Pero se conserva esta -*e* muda delante de -*ing* en los verbos *dye, singe* y otros, y en los pocos que terminan en -*oe*: *dyeing, singeing, hoeing*.)

(e) Si el verbo termina en -*y* (con las dos pronunciaciones de [i] y [ai]) se cambia ésta en -*ied* (con las pronunciaciones respectivas de [id] y [aid]) para formar el pretérito y el participio de pasado: *worry-worried-worried; pity-pitied-pitied; falsify-falsified-falsified; try-tried-tried*. El gerundio de tales verbos es regular: *worrying, trying* etc. Pero el gerundio de los verbos monosílabos *die, lie, vie* se escribe *dying, lying, vying*.

Numerals, Weights and Measures

Los números, pesos y medidas

I NUMERALS — LOS NÚMEROS

1 Cardinal numbers—Números cardinales

nought	0	cero
one	1	(m) uno, (f) una
two	2	dos
three	3	tres
four	4	cuatro
five	5	cinco
six	6	seis
seven	7	siete
eight	8	ocho
nine	9	nueve
ten	10	diez
eleven	11	once
twelve	12	doce
thirteen	13	trece
fourteen	14	catorce
fifteen	15	quince
sixteen	16	dieciséis
seventeen	17	diecisiete
eighteen	18	dieciocho
nineteen	19	diecinueve
twenty	20	veinte
twenty-one	21	veintiuno (see note b)
twenty-two	22	veintidós
twenty-three	23	veintitrés
thirty	30	treinta
thirty-one	31	treinta y uno
thirty-two	32	treinta y dos
forty	40	cuarenta
fifty	50	cincuenta
sixty	60	sesenta
seventy	70	setenta
eighty	80	ochenta
ninety	90	noventa
ninety-nine	99	noventa y nueve
a (or one) hundred	100	cien, ciento (see note c)
a hundred and one	101	ciento uno
a hundred and two	102	ciento dos
a hundred and ten	110	ciento diez

a hundred and eighty-two	182	ciento ochenta y dos
two hundred	200	(m) doscientos, (f) —as
three hundred	300	(m) trescientos, (f) —as
four hundred	400	(m) cuatrocientos, (f) —as
five hundred	500	(m) quinientos, (f) —as
six hundred	600	(m) seiscientos, (f) —as
seven hundred	700	(m) setecientos, (f) —as
eight hundred	800	(m) ochocientos, (f) —as
nine hundred	900	(m) novecientos, (f) —as
a (or one) thousand	1000	mil
a thousand and two	1002	mil dos
two thousand	2000	dos mil
ten thousand	10000	diez mil
a (or one) hundred thousand	100000	cien mil
a (or one) million	1000000	un millón (see note d)
two million	2000000	dos millones (see note d)

Notes on usage of the cardinal numbers

(a) One, and the other numbers ending in one, agree in Spanish with the noun (stated or implied): *una casa, un coche, si se trata de pagar en libras ello viene a sumar treinta y una, había ciento una personas.*

(b) 21: In Spanish there is some uncertainty when the number is accompanied by a feminine noun. In the spoken language both *veintiuna peseta* and *veintiuna pesetas* are heard; in "correct" literary language only *veintiuna pesetas* is found. With a masculine noun the numeral is shortened in the usual way: *veintiún perros rabiosos.* These remarks apply also to 31, 41 *etc.*

(c) 100: When the number is spoken alone or in counting a series of numbers both *cien* and *ciento* are heard. When there is an accompanying noun the form is always *cien: cien hombres, cien chicas.* In the compound numbers note 101 = *ciento uno*, 110 = *ciento diez*, but 100000 = *cien mil.*

(d) 1000000: In Spanish the word *millón* is a noun, so the numeral takes *de* when there is a following noun: *un millón de fichas, tres millones de árboles quemados.*

(e) In Spanish the cardinal numbers may be used as nouns, as in English; they are always masculine: *jugó el siete de corazones, el once nacional de Ruritania, éste es el trece y nosotros buscamos el quince.*

(f) To divide the larger numbers clearly a point is used in Spanish where English places a comma: English 1,000 = Spanish 1.000, English 2,304,770 = Spanish 2.304.770. (This does not apply to dates: see below.)

2 Ordinal numbers—Números ordinales

first	1	primero (*see note* **b**)
second	2	segundo
third	3	tercero (*see note* **b**)
fourth	4	cuarto
fifth	5	quinto
sixth	6	sexto
seventh	7	séptimo
eighth	8	octavo
ninth	9	noveno, nono
tenth	10	décimo
eleventh	11	undécimo
twelfth	12	duodécimo
thirteenth	13	decimotercio, decimotercero
fourteenth	14	decimocuarto
fifteenth	15	decimoquinto
sixteenth	16	decimosexto
seventeenth	17	decimoséptimo
eighteenth	18	decimoctavo
nineteenth	19	decimonoveno, decimonono
twentieth	20	vigésimo
twenty-first	21	vigésimo primero, vigésimo primo
twenty-second	22	vigésimo segundo
thirtieth	30	trigésimo
thirty-first	31	trigésimo primero, trigésimo primo
fortieth	40	cuadragésimo

fiftieth	50	quincuagésimo
sixtieth	60	sexagésimo
seventieth	70	septuagésimo
eightieth	80	octogésimo
ninetieth	90	nonagésimo
hundredth	100	centésimo
hundred and first	101	centésimo primero
hundred and tenth	110	centésimo décimo
two hundredth	200	ducentésimo
three hundredth	300	trecentésimo
four hundredth	400	cuadringentésimo
five hundredth	500	quingentésimo
six hundredth	600	sexcentésimo
seven hundredth	700	septingentésimo
eight hundredth	800	octingentésimo
nine hundredth	900	noningentésimo
thousandth	1000	milésimo
two thousandth	2000	dos milésimo
millionth	1000000	millonésimo
two millionth	2000000	dos millonésimo

Notes on usage of the ordinal numbers

(a) All these numbers are adjectives in *-o*, and therefore agree with the noun in number and gender: *la quinta vez, en segundas nupcias, en octavo lugar.*

(b) *primero* and *tercero* are shortened to *primer, tercer* when they directly precede a masculine singular noun: *en el primer capítulo, el tercer hombre* (but *los primeros coches en llegar, el primero y más importante hecho*).

(c) In Spanish the ordinal numbers from 1 to 10 are commonly used; from 11 to 20 rather less; above 21 they are rarely written and almost never heard in speech (except for *milésimo*, which is frequent). The custom is to replace the forms for 21 and above by the cardinal number: *en el capítulo treinta y seis, celebran el setenta aniversario* (or *el aniversario setenta*), *en el poste ciento cinco contando desde la esquina.*

(d) Kings, popes and centuries. The ordinal numbers from 1 to 9 are employed for these in Spanish as in English: *en el siglo cuarto, Eduardo octavo, Pío nono, Enrique primero.* For 10 either the cardinal or the ordinal may be used: *siglo diez* or *siglo décimo, Alfonso diez* or *Alfonso décimo.* For 11 and above it is now customary to use only the cardinal number: *Alfonso once* (but *onceno* in the Middle Ages), *Juan veintitrés, en el siglo dieciocho.*

(e) Abbreviations. English 1st, 2nd, 3rd, 4th, 5th *etc* = Spanish 1º *or* 1ᵉʳ, 2º, 3º *or* 3ᵉʳ, 4º, 5º and so on (*f*: 1ᵉʳᵃ, 2ª).

(f) See also the notes on Dates, below.

3 Fractions—números quebrados

$\frac{1}{2}$: one half, a half/(m) *medio*, (f) *media*

$1\frac{1}{2}$: one and a half helpings/(*una*) *porción y media*

$2\frac{1}{2}$: two and a half kilos/*dos kilos y medio*

$\frac{1}{3}$: one third, a third/*un tercio, la tercera parte*

$\frac{2}{3}$: two thirds/*dos tercios, las dos terceras partes*

$\frac{1}{4}$: one quarter, a quarter/*un cuarto, la cuarta parte*

$\frac{3}{4}$: three quarters/*tres cuartos, las tres cuartas partes*

$\frac{1}{6}$: one sixth, a sixth/*un sexto, la sexta parte*

$5\frac{5}{6}$: five and five sixths/*cinco y cinco sextos*

$\frac{1}{12}$: one twelfth, a twelfth/*un duodécimo; un dozavo, la duodécima parte*

$\frac{7}{12}$: seven twelfths/*siete dozavos*

$\frac{1}{100}$: one hundredth, a hundredth/*un centésimo, una centésima parte*

$\frac{1}{1000}$: one thousandth, a thousandth/*un milésimo*

4 Decimals—las decimales

In Spanish a comma is written where English writes a point: English 3·56 (three point five six) = Spanish 3,56 (*tres coma cinco seis*); English ·07 (point nought seven) = Spanish ,07 (*coma cero siete*). The recurring decimal 3·3333 may be written in English as 3·3̇ and in Spanish as 3,3̄.

5 Nomenclature—nomenclatura

3,684 is a four-digit number/*3.684 es un número de cuatro dígitos* (or *guarismos*). It contains 4 units, 8 tens, 6 hundreds and 3 thousands/*Contiene 4 unidades, 8 decenas, 6 centenas y 3 unidades de millar.* The decimal ·234 contains 2 tenths, 3 hundredths and 4 thousandths/*la fracción decimal ,234 contiene 2 décimas, 3 centésimas y 4 milésimas.*

6 Percentages—los porcentajes

$2\frac{1}{2}\%$ two and a half per cent/*$2\frac{1}{2}$ por 100,* (less frequently) $2\frac{1}{2}\%$; *dos y medio por cien, dos y medio por ciento* (in spoken usage and among the authorities there is disagreement about *cien/ciento* here).

18% of the people here are over 65/*el dieciocho por cien de la gente aquí tienen más de 65 años.* Production has risen by 8%/*la producción ha aumentado en un 8 por 100.*
(*See also* per, hundred *in the main text.*)

7 Signs—los signos

English

+ addition sign

+ plus sign (*eg* + 7 = plus seven)

− subtraction sign

− minus sign (*eg* − 3 = minus three)

× multiplication sign

÷ division sign

√ square root sign

∞ infinity

≡ sign of identity, is exactly equal to

= sign of equality, equals

≏ is approximately equal to

≠ sign of inequality, is not equal to

> is greater than

< is less than

Spanish

+ signo de adición

+ signo de más (*p.ej.* + 7 = 7 de más)

− signo de sustracción

− signo de menos (*p.ej.* − 3 = 3 de menos)

× signo de multiplicación

: signo de división

√ signo de raíz cuadrada

∞ infinito

≡ signo de identidad, es exactamente igual a

= signo de igualdad, es igual a

≈ es aproximadamente igual a

≠ signo de no identidad, no es igual a

> es mayor que

< es menor que

8 Calculations—el cálculo

$8 + 6 = 14$ eight and (*or* plus) six are (*or* make) fourteen/*ocho y* (or *más*) *seis son catorce*

$15 − 3 = 12$ fifteen take away three are (*or* equals) twelve, three from fifteen leaves twelve/*quince menos tres resta doce, de tres a quince van doce*

$3 × 3 = 9$ three threes are nine, three times three is nine/*tres por tres son nueve*

$32 ÷ 8 = 4$ thirty-two divided by eight is (*or* equals) four/*32 : 8 = 4 treinta y dos dividido por ocho es cuatro*

$3^2 = 9$ three squared is nine/*tres al cuadrado son nueve*

$2^5 = 32$ two to the fifth (*or* to the power of five) is (*or* equals) thirty-two/*dos a la quinta potencia son treinta y dos*

$\sqrt{16} = 4$ the square root of sixteen is four/*la raíz cuadrada de dieciséis es cuatro.*

9 Time—la hora

2 hours 33 minutes and 14 seconds/*2 horas 33 minutos y 14 segundos*

half an hour/*media hora*

a quarter of an hour/*un cuarto de hora*

three quarters of an hour/*tres cuartos de hora*

what's the time?/*¿qué hora es?*

what do you make the time?/*¿qué hora tienes?*

have you the right time?/*¿tiene Vd la hora exacta?*

I make it 2.20/*yo tengo las dos veinte*

my watch says 3.37/*mi reloj marca las tres treinta y siete*

it's 1 o'clock/*es la una*

it's 2 o'clock/*son las dos*

it's 5 past 4/*son las cuatro y cinco*

it's 10 to 6/*son las seis menos diez*

it's half-past 8/*son las ocho y media*

it's a quarter past 9/*son las nueve y cuarto*

it's a quarter to 2/*son las dos menos cuarto*

at 10 a.m./*a las diez de la mañana*

at 4 p.m./*a las cuatro de la tarde*

at 11 p.m./*a las once de la noche*

at exactly 3 o'clock, at 3 sharp, at 3 on the dot/*a las tres en punto*

the train leaves at 19.32/*el tren sale a las diecinueve treinta y dos*

(at) what time does it start?/*¿a qué hora comienza?*

it is just after 3/*son un poco más de las tres*

it is nearly 9/*son casi las nueve*

about 8 o'clock/*cerca de las ocho, hacia las ocho, a eso de las ocho*

at (*or* by) 6 o'clock at the latest/*a las seis a más tardar*

have it ready for 5 o'clock/*téngalo listo para las cinco*

it is full each night from 7 to 9/*está lleno todas las noches de siete a nueve*

"closed from 1.30 to 4.30"/*"cerrado de 1.30 a 4.30"*

until 8 o'clock/*hasta las ocho*

it would be about 11/*serán las once*

it would have been about 10/*serían las diez*

at midnight/*a medianoche*

before midday, before noon/*antes del mediodía*

10 Dates—las fechas

N.B. The days of the week and the months are written with small letters in Spanish: *lunes, martes, febrero, mayo.*

the 1st of July, July 1st/*el 1º de julio, el primero de julio*

the 2nd of May, May 2nd/*el 2 de mayo, el dos de mayo* (the cardinal numbers are used in Spanish for dates from 2nd to 31st)

on the 21st (of) June/*el 21 de junio, el día veintiuno de junio*

on Monday/*el lunes*

he comes on Mondays/*viene los lunes*

"closed on Fridays"/*"cerrado los viernes"*

he lends it to me from Monday to Friday/*me lo presta de lunes a viernes*

from the 14th to the 18th/*desde el 14 hasta el 18, desde el catorce hasta el dieciocho*

what's the date?, what date is it today?/*¿qué día es hoy?*

today's the 12th/*hoy es el doce, estamos a doce*

one Thursday in October/*un jueves en octubre*

about the 4th of July/*hacia el cuatro de julio*

Heading of letters: 19th May 1984/*19 de mayo de 1984*

1975, nineteen (hundred and) seventy-five/*mil novecientos setenta y cinco*

4 B.C., B.C. 4/*4 a. de J.C.* (*see* Abbreviations)

70 A.D., A.D. 70/*70 d. de J.C.* (*see* Abbreviations)

in the 13th Century/*en el siglo XIII, en el siglo trece*

in (*or* during) the 1930s/*en el decenio de 1930 a 40, durante los años treinta*

in 1940 something/*en el año 1940 y tantos*

(*See* also in the main text of the dictionary week, year *etc.*)

II WEIGHTS AND MEASURES— PESOS Y MEDIDAS

1 Metric system—sistema métrico

(Measures formed with the following prefixes are mostly omitted/*se omiten la mayor parte de las medidas formadas con los siguientes prefijos:*

deca-	10 times,	10 veces
hecto-	100 times,	100 veces
kilo-	1000 times,	1000 veces
deci-	one tenth,	una décima
centi-	one hundredth,	une centésima
mil(l)i-	one thousandth,	una milésima)

Linear measures—medidas de longitud

1 millimetre (milímetro)	= 0·03937 inch (pulgada)
1 centimetre (centímetro)	= 0·3937 inch (pulgada)
1 metre (metro)	= 39·37 inches (pulgadas)
	= 1·094 yards (yardas)
1 kilometre (kilómetro)	= 0·6214 mile (milla) *or* almost exactly five-eighths of a mile

Square measures—medidas cuadradas o de superficie

1 square centimetre (centímetro cuadrado)	= 0·155 square inch (pulgada cuadrada)
1 square metre (metro cuadrado)	= 10·764 square feet (pies cuadrados)
	= 1·196 square yards (yardas cuadradas)
1 square kilometre (kilómetro cuadrado)	= 0·3861 square mile (milla cuadrada)
	= 247·1 acres (acres)
1 are = 100 square metres (área)	= 119·6 square yards (yardas cuadradas)
1 hectare = 100 ares (hectárea)	= 2·471 acres (acres)

Cubic measures—medidas cúbicas

1 cubic centimetre (centímetro cúbico)	= 0·061 cubic inch (pulgada cúbica)
1 cubic metre (metro cúbico)	= 35·315 cubic feet (pies cúbicos)
	= 1·308 cubic yards (yardas cúbicas)

Measure of capacity—medida de capacidad

1 litre (litro) = 1000 cubic centimetres	= 1·76 pints (pintas)
	= 0·22 gallon (galón)

Weights—pesos

1 gramme (gramo)	= 15·4 grains (granos)
1 kilogramme (kilogramo)	= 2·2046 pounds (libras)
1 quintal (quintal métrico) = 100 kilogrammes	= 220·46 pounds (libras)
1 metric ton (tonelada métrica) = 1000 kilogrammes	= 0·9842 ton (tonelada)

2 British system—sistema británico

Linear measures—medidas de longitud

1 inch (pulgada)	= 2,54 centímetros
1 foot (pie) = 12 inches	= 30,48 centímetros
1 yard (yarda) = 3 feet	= 91,44 centímetros
1 furlong (estadio) = 220 yards	= 201,17 metros
1 mile (milla) = 1760 yards	= 1609,33 metros = 1,609 kilómetros

Surveyors' measures—medidas de agrimensura

1 link = 7·92 inches	= 20,12 centímetros
1 rod (*or* pole, perch) = 25 links	= 5,029 metros
1 chain = 22 yards = 4 rods	= 20,12 metros

Square measures—medidas cuadradas o de superficie

1 square inch (pulgada cuadrada)	= 6,45 cm²
1 square foot (pie cuadrado) = 144 square inches	= 929,03 cm²
1 square yard (yarda cuadrada) = 9 square feet	= 0,836 m²
1 square rod = 30·25 square yards	= 25,29 m²
1 acre = 4840 square yards	= 40,47 áreas
1 square mile (milla cuadrada) = 640 acres	= 2,59 km²

Cubic measures—medidas cúbicas

1 cubic inch (pulgada cúbica)	= 16,387 cm³
1 cubic foot (pie cúbico) = 1728 cubic inches	= 0,028 m³
1 cubic yard (yarda cúbica) = 27 cubic feet	= 0,765 m³
1 register ton (tonelada de registro) = 100 cubic feet	= 2,832 m³

Measures of capacity—medidas de capacidad

(a) Liquid—para líquidos

1 gill	= 0,142 litro
1 pint (pinta) = 4 gills	= 0,57 litro
1 quart = 2 pints	= 1,136 litros
1 gallon (galón) = 4 quarts	= 4,546 litros

(b) Dry—para áridos

1 peck = 2 gallons	= 9,087 litros
1 bushel = 4 pecks	= 36,36 litros
1 quarter = 8 bushels	= 290,94 litros

Weights—pesos (Avoirdupois system—sistema avoirdupois)

1 grain (grano)	= 0,0648 gramo
1 drachm *or* dram	= 1,77 gramos
= 27,34 grains	
1 ounce (onza)	= 28,35 gramos
= 16 dra(ch)ms	
1 pound (libra)	= 453,6 gramos
= 16 ounces	= 0,453 kilogramo
1 stone = 14 pounds	= 6,348 kilogramos
1 quarter = 28 pounds	= 12,7 kilogramos
1 hundredweight	= 50,8 kilogramos
= 112 pounds	
1 ton (tonelada)	= 1,016 kilogramos
= 2240 pounds	
= 20 hundredweight	

3 US Measures—medidas norteamericanas

In the US the same system as that which applies in Great Britain is used for the most part; the main differences are mentioned below/*En EE.UU. se emplea en general el mismo sistema que en Gran Bretaña; las principales diferencias son las siguientes:*

Measures of capacity—medidas de capacidad

(a) Liquid—para líquidos

1 US liquid gill	= 0,118 litro
1 US liquid pint = 4 gills	= 0,473 litro
1 US liquid quart = 2 pints	= 0,946 litro
1 US gallon = 4 quarts	= 3,785 litros

(b) Dry—para áridos

1 US dry pint	= 0,550 litro
1 US dry quart = 2 dry pints	= 1,1 litros
1 US peck = 8 dry quarts	= 8,81 litros
1 US bushel = 4 pecks	= 35,24 litros

Weights—pesos

1 hundredweight	= 45,36 kilogramos
(*or* short hundredweight)	
= 100 pounds	
1 ton (*or* short ton)	= 907,18 kilogramos
= 2000 pounds = 20	
short hundredweights	

4 Traditional Spanish weights and measures—pesos y medidas españoles tradicionales

(These are the measures which were standard until the introduction of the metric system in Spain in 1871, and they are still in use in some provinces and in agriculture/*Son éstas las medidas que se emplearon hasta la introducción del sistema métrico en España en 1871. Se emplean todavía en algunas provincias y en la agricultura*)

Linear measures—medidas de longitud

1 vara	= 0·836 metre
1 braza	= 1·67 metres
1 milla	= 1·852 kilometres
1 legua	= 5·5727 kilometres

Square measure—medida cuadrada o de superficie

1 fanega = 6460 square metres = 1·59 acres

Measures of capacity—medidas de capacidad

(a) Liquid—para líquidos

1 cuartillo	= 0·504 litre
1 azumbre	= 2·016 litres
= 4 cuartillos	
1 cántara	= 16·128 litres
= 8 azumbres	

(b) Dry—para áridos

1 celemín	= 4·625 litres
1 fanega	= 55·5 litres = 1·58 bushels
= 12 celemines	

Weights—pesos

1 onza	= 28·7 grammes
1 libra	= 460 grammes
= 16 onzas	
1 arroba	= 11·502 kilogrammes
= 25 libras	= 25 pounds
1 quintal	= 46 kilogrammes
= 4 arrobas	

Abbreviations and Field labels

Abreviaturas e Indicaciones semánticas

abbreviated	abbr	abreviado
Academy	Acad	Academia
accusative	acc	acusativo
adjective	adj	adjetivo
adverb	adv	adverbio
Aeronautics	Aer	Aeronáutica
Agriculture	Agr	Agricultura
Anatomy	Anat	Anatomía
anglicism	angl	anglicismo
Antilles, West Indies	Ant	Antillas
approximately	approx	aproximadamente
archaic	arch	arcaico
Architecture	Archit	Arquitectura
Argentina	Arg	
article	art	artículo
	Art	Arte
Astronomy	Astron	Astronomía
attributive	attr	atributivo
Automobiles	Aut	Automóviles
Bible	Bib	Biblia
Biology	Bio	Biología
Bolivia	Bol	
Botany	Bot	Botánica
	Boxing	Boxeo
	Bridge	
British	Brit	británico
Central America	CAm	Centroamérica
	Cards	Naipes
	Carpentry	Carpintería
Chemistry	Chem	Química
	Chess	Ajedrez
Chile	Chi	
Cinematography	Cine	Cinematografía
Colombia	Col	
Commerce	Comm	Comercio
comparative	comp	comparativo
conjunction	conj	conjunción
Cooking	Cook	Cocina
Costa Rica	CR	
Cuba	Cu	
	Dancing	Baile
dative	dat	dativo
definite	def	definido
demonstrative	dem	demostrativo
direct	dir	directo
Ecuador	Ec	
Ecclesiastical	Eccl	eclesiástico
Economics	Econ	Economía
(exempli gratia) for example	eg	por ejemplo
Electricity	Elec	Electricidad
Entomology	Ent	Entomología
especially	esp	especialmente
et cetera	etc	etcétera
euphemism	euph	eufemismo
exclamation	excl	exclamación
feminine	f	femenino
familiar	fam	familiar
	Fencing	Esgrima
figurative	fig	figurado
Finance	Fin	Finanzas
	Fish	Peces
	Football	Fútbol
feminine plural	fpl	femenino plural
frequently	freq	frecuentemente
gallicism	gall	galicismo
generally	gen	generalmente
Geography	Geog	Geografía
Geology	Geol	Geología
gerund	ger	gerundio
	Golf	
Grammar	Gram	Gramática
Guatemala	Guat	
Heraldry	Her	Heráldica
History	Hist	Historia
Honduras	Hond	
Horticulture	Hort	Horticultura
humorous	hum	humorístico
	Hunting	Caza
(id est) that is	ie	esto es, es decir
impersonal	impers	impersonal
indefinite	indef	indefinido
indicative	indic	indicativo
infinitive	infin	infinitivo
interjection	interj	interjección